Statistics Sources

ISSN 0585-198X

Statistics Sources

32nd Edition

2009

A Subject Guide to Data on Industrial, Business, Social, Educational, Financial, and Other Topics for the United States and Internationally

Volume 1

A-K

GALE
CENGAGE Learning™

Detroit • New York • San Francisco • New Haven, Conn • Waterville, Maine • London

GALE
CENGAGE Learning

Statistics Sources, 32nd Edition

Project Editor: Tara Atterberry
Editorial Support Services: Wayne Fong
Composition and Electronic Prepress: Gary Oudersluys
Manufacturing: Rita Wimberley
Project Management: Michele LaMeau

For product information and technology assistance, contact us at
Gale Customer Support, 1-800-877-4253.
For permission to use material from this text or product,
submit all requests online at **www.cengage.com/permissions.**
Further permissions questions can be emailed to
permissionrequest@cengage.com

Gale
27500 Drake Rd.
Farmington Hills, MI, 48331-3535

ISBN-13: 978-0-7876-9953-6 (set)
ISBN-10: 0-7876-9953-5 (set)

ISBN-13: 978-0-7876-9954-3 (Vol. 1)
ISBN-10: 0-7876-9954-3 (Vol. 1)

ISBN-13: 978-0-7876-9955-0 (Vol. 2)
ISBN-10: 0-7876-9955-1 (Vol. 2)

ISSN 0585-198X

Printed in the United States of America
1 2 3 4 5 6 7 12 11 10 09 08

Table of Contents

As *Statistics Sources* continues into its thirty-second edition, the constant and painstaking effort to continue to bolster and add value to its content and the interest of its users continues unabated. The work continues to be an easy-to-use alphabetically-arranged dictionary and guide to current sources of factual qualitative information on well over 30,000 specific subjects, incorporating more than 152,000 citations and more than 1,700 sources, readily leading users to the widest possible range of print and non-print, published and unpublished, and electronic and other forms of U.S. and international statistical sources for economic, business, financial, industrial, cultural, social, educational, and other topics.

Preparation of This Edition

This edition of *Statistics Sources* fully and thoroughly updates, revises, and extends the scope and content of the thirtieth edition. Complete revisions incorporate a wider range of current data sources from the *Selected Bibliography of Key Statistical Sources* and *Federal Statistical Telephone Contacts* sections, through the main body, as well as the appendixes.

During the preparation of the edition, as in earlier editions, the editors thoroughly analyzed and indexed hundreds of American information sources, several years of Statistical Abstract of the United States, numerous basic statistical publications from many organizations, and special statistical issues of professional, technical and trade journals. Additional sources of international statistics are cited in this edition, increasing the range of access points within a user's reference shelves.

Arrangement and Content

The familiar and convenient arrangement of the basic work continues as a straight alphabetic list of subjects. Sources of statistical information are arranged alphabetically by issuing organization within each subject category. In addition to both print and machine-readable sources, a considerable number of organizations, government agencies, trade and professional groups, and international bodies are cited because they are important sources of statistical data, even if they do not ordinarily publish all of the statistics they compile. In such instances, specific inquiries may be addressed to the organization mentioned. As in earlier editions, the street address of the publisher of any work cited has been provided wherever possible, followed by the telephone number of the source, as well as email and web site information, where available.

Interfiled within the subject categories are geographic headings for states and individual countries. Listings for state data center agencies that make census information and data available to the public are included within the citations of sources for each state. These listings appear under the heading *State Data Center Agencies*, which immediately follows the citation for *Primary Statistics Source* under each state subheading.

Individual citations for each country are sub-arranged by an alphabetic list of specific subjects, enabling the user to pin-point sources of statistics on subjects such as agriculture, education, energy, imports, population and consumer prices. Two types of key statistical sources are cited in listings for countries (as applicable and available) and precede the alphabetical listing of specific subjects for the country. The first citation is the National Statistical Office, if the country has such an office. This is followed by a reference to the major printed sources for the country, termed the Primary Statistics Source of Sources. These sources should be consulted by users seeking more in-depth data, particularly for technical and commercial activities in countries other than the U.S. and Canada.

Introductory Materials Pinpoint Key Sources and Individuals

The *Selected Bibliography of Key Statistical Sources* and *Federal Statistical Telephone Contacts* sections precede the main section. The *Selected Bibliography* provides an annotated guide to a selected group of major, general statistical compendia and related works, and includes dictionaries of terms, almanacs, census publications, periodical sources, and guides to machine-readable and online data sources. Both governmental and non-governmental sources are cited. A source's availability in machine-readable form or as an online database is noted wherever possible. The *Telephone Contacts* section provides the names and telephone numbers of individuals and agencies within the U.S. federal government with expertise in identifying the most current sources of statistical data.

Appendixes Identify Published and Nonpublished Sources

The two appendixes identify the sources of information used to compile this directory. The *Source Publications Appendix* provides an alphabetic listing of the specific publication titles of every printed source mentioned in *Statistics Sources*, along with the issuing or publishing bodies, their addresses and phone numbers. The *Sources of Nonpublished Statistical Data Appendix* identifies the agencies, institutions, and other organizations which are cited as sources of nonpublished statistical information in this edition.

Selected Bibliography of Key Statistical Sources

This section describes a selected group of major, general statistical compendia and related works in the English language. Both governmental and non-governmental sources are included. For ease of reference, these sources are presented according to the categories listed below.

ENCYCLOPEDIAS, DICTIONARIES OF TERMS, AND OTHER GENERAL SOURCES
ALMANACS
U.S. STATISTICS
- Non-Government U.S. Publications
- Publications of the U.S. Bureau of the Census
- Publications and Other Materials from U.S. Government Agencies and Departments
- Guides to Machine-Readable U.S. Government Data Sources

INTERNATIONAL SOURCES
- General International Publications
- Publications of the Organisation for Economic Cooperation and Development (OECD)
- Publications of the United Nations and Affiliated Organizations

INTERNET AND WORLD WIDE WEB SITES
STATISTICAL DATABASES ONLINE
- Guides to Online Databases
- Selected Online Statistical Databases
- Selected Vendors of Online Statistical Databases

Many of the sources are available in machine-readable form, as online databases, or in CD-ROM form, and this has been noted wherever possible in the individual source citations.

ENCYCLOPEDIAS, DICTIONARIES OF TERMS, AND OTHER GENERAL SOURCES

Melvyn N. Freed and Virgil P. Diodato. *Business Information Desk Reference: Where to Find Answers to Business Questions.* New York, MacMillan Publishers, ((646) 307-5151), www.macmillan.com, 1991.

Directs users to appropriate business sources in a question-answer format. Section A offers Guidelines for Finding and Evaluating Business Information especially asking the right question. Section B, Linking the Research Question to the Business Information Source is a mini-guide listing types of questions and linking them to types of appropriate sources. Sections describe and characterize both print and online sources.

Alfred Garwood and Louise Hornor. *Dictionary of U.S. Government Statistical Terms.* Palo Alto, CA, Information Publications, ((877) 544-4636), www.informationpublications.com, 1991.

Provides U.S. government statistical terms with the government agency name appearing in each entry along with abbreviations where appropriate. An introduction, list of abbreviations, and bibliography round out the volume.

David R. Gerhan. *Bibliography of American Demographic History: The Literature From 1984 to 1994.* Westport, CT, Greenwood Press, ((203) 226-3571), www.greenwood.com, 1995.

A companion to the ALA-award-winning *Retrospective Bibliography of American Demographic History* (1989), this volume includes literature on American demographic history published from 1984 to 1994. It covers such topics as marriage and fertility; health, sickness, and mortality; immigration, settlement, and cultural patterns; and family and its structures, roles and values (including both gender and sexuality issues). It also cites works showing the broad intersections between population matters and such economic, political, and social phenomena as war, oppression, government policy, elections, labor stereotype, discrimination, and cross-cultural contact or relations.

Maurice G. Kendall and A.E. Doig. *Bibliography of Statistical Literature.* 3 vols. Edinburgh and London, Oliver and Boyd.

With a total of over 26,000 entries, this work covers the literature of statistics from the sixteenth century to 1958; vol. 1, 1950-1958; vol. 2, 1940-1949; and vol. 3, pre-1940. The material cited is that which the compilers believe will be most useful to historians and researchers. Arranged by author, this bibliography covers periodicals, international conferences, and national meetings. Twelve statistical journals are indexed almost completely and forty-three others analyzed for relevant articles. Coverage is worldwide, but the bulk of the citations are from American, British, and Russian publications.

Samuel Kotz, Campbell B. Read, N. Balakrishnan and Brani Vidakovic, eds. *Encyclopedia of Statistical Sciences.* New Jersey, John Wiley & Sons, ((800) 225-5945), www.wiley.com, 2005.

A sixteen-volume source of information on statistical theory, methods, and applications. This edition (available in both print and on-line versions) is designed to bring the encyclopedia in line with the latest topics and advances made in statistical science over the past decade--in areas such as computer-intensive statistical methodology, genetics, medicine, the environment, and other applications.

Joe Morehead. *Introduction to United States Government Information Sources.* Portsmouth, NH, Libraries Unlimited, ((800) 225-5800, http://lu.com, 1999.

After opening with a discussion of public access as a constitutional right, chapters in this book describe administrative machinery and information systems of the Government Printing Office; introduce general checklists, indexes, and guides to government information; and discuss prominent sources of federal government information. They also summarize numerous pertinent statistical sources; address components of the research activities commissioned by the government in partnership with the private sector; and portray the consequential role geographic information systems play in the creation and provision of maps, charts, and gazetteers.

Moss, Rita W. *Strauss's Handbook of Business Information: A Guide for Librarians, Students, and Researchers.* Portsmouth, NH, Libraries Unlimited, ((800) 225-5800, http://lu.com, 2003.

A long awaited update of the popular 1988 handbook by Diane Wheeler Strauss, this book is divided into two main parts. The first seven chapters cover business information according to the formats in which it is made available: BL Guides, BL Bibliographies and quick reference sources, BL Directories, BL Periodicals and newspapers, BL Looseleaf services, BL Government documents, BL Statistics, BL Examples of different types of electronic sources.

M. G. Mulhall. *The Dictionary of Statistics.* 4th ed. Farmington Hills, MI, Gale, ((248) 699-4253), www.gale.com, 1974.

Originally published in 1899, this reference book is useful for locating historical statistical information not available in other standard sources. Comparative tables on a wide variety of subjects from the time of the Emperor Diocletian to 1899. Supplemented by *The New Dictionary of Statistics,* covering the period 1899-1909. Martha A. Tucker and Nancy D. Anderson. *Guide to Information Sources in Mathematics and Statistics.* Portsmouth, NH, Libraries Unlimited, ((800) 225-5800, http://lu.com, 2004.

This book is a reference for librarians, mathematicians, and statisticians involved in college and research level mathematics and statistics in the 21st century. Part I is a historical survey of the past 15 years tracking this huge transition in scholarly communications in mathematics. Part II of the book is the bibliography of resources recommended to support the disciplines of mathematics and statistics.

W. Paul Vogt. *Dictionary of Statistics & Methodology: A Nontechnical Guide for the Social Sciences.* 3rd ed. Thousand Oaks, CA, SAGE Publications, ((800) 818-7243), www.sagepub.com, 2005.

First published in 1993, this is a sourcebook of simple definitions and explanations of statistical and statistics-related concepts. Since the publication of the bestselling Second Edition, author W. Paul Vogt has examined relevant literature in the social sciences to keep readers alert to the appearance of new methods, new language, and newly popular terms. The Third Edition has been thoroughly revised and expanded, with 400 additional definitions and illustrations compiled from readers' requests and suggestions.

Miriam Uhlan and Doris B. Katz, eds. *Guide to Special Issues and Indexes of Periodicals.* Alexandria, VA, Special Libraries Association, (703) 647-4900, www.sla.org, 1994.

Arranged alphabetically, 1,748 U.S. and Canadian periodicals that publish recurring special issues like yearbooks, buyers' guides, forecasts, statistical reports, marketing studies, and membership rosters are listed here. An update of the 1985 edition, this volume has greatly expanded its coverage of regional publications, which are often difficult to locate; a highlight of these regionals are Books of Lists, which rank companies, institutions, professionals, and executives in their areas. A listing of Online Producers/Vendors is an important new addition for researchers and librarians.

Jean Slemmons Stratford and Juri Stratford, eds. *Major U.S. Statistical Series: Definitions, Publications, Limitations.* Chicago, ALA Books, ((800) 545-2433), 1992.

The text provides the reader (both information specialist and patron) with a framework for understanding statistical data and locating the series which report such data on a regular basis. It describes the construction and publications of a number of basic statistical measures and provides an introduction to data producing agencies and their publication series.

Arthur S. Banks, Thomas C. Muller, William R. Overstreet, eds. *Political Handbook of the World 2008.* Washington, DC, CQ Press, ((202) 729-1900), www.cqpress.com, 2008.

With more than 200 entries on countries and territories throughout the world, this volume is renowned for its extensive coverage of major, minor, and anti-systemic political parties in each political system around the world. It also provides names of key ambassadors and international memberships of each country and profiles over 120 intergovernmental organizations.

Robert Sicignano and Doris Prichard, compilers. *Special Issues Index.* Westport, CT, Greenwood Publishing Group, ((203) 226-3571), 1982.

Includes more than 1,300 North American business, industrial and consumer journals, identifying which issue annually offers a special statistical number, buyer's guide or directory. Entries include journal title, address, frequency, subscription rate, individual issue price and presence of classified or product/service ads. This is supplemented by an index.

Taylor, Arlene G. *The Organization of Information.* 2nd edition. Portsmouth, NH, Libraries Unlimited, ((800) 225-5800, http://lu.com, 2003.

Examines many of the tools, standards, theories, and principles underlying the organization of information in different types of environments. Chapters are devoted to the organization and development of recorded information, retrieval tools, encoding standards, subject analysis, systems for vocabulary control and categorization, and arrangement and display. This edition offers readers a new chapter on metadata and new sections treating digital libraries, information architecture, knowledge management, pathfinders, search engines, and bibliographic classifications and taxonomies, among other topics.

ALMANACS

Laura Mars-Proietti, ed. *Canadian Almanac & Directory 2008.* Millerton, NY, Grey House Publishing, ((800) 562-2139), www.greyhouse.com, 2007.

This national directory and guide, updated every year, gives readers access to statistics, images and over 100,000 names and addresses for everything from Airlines to Zoos.

Sumner N. Levine, Caroline Levine, ed. *The Irwin Business and Investment Almanac.* Burr Ridge, IL, Irwin Professional Publishing, ((630) 789-4000), 1977-. (Annual).

Covers such topics as: Largest Corporations, Stock and Commodities Market, Price Data and World Population, and Gross National Product by Country. Prefixed by a day-to-day accounting of the Business Year in Review.

Manthi Nguyen, ed. *Almanac of the 50 States 2008.* Palo Alto, CA, Information Publications ((877) 544-4636), www.informationpublications.com, 2005.

An annual ready-reference source which contains eight statistical profile pages for every state. The main portion of the book is a collection of 52 basic data profiles; one for each of the 50 states; one for the District of Columbia; and one for the U.S. in summary. Supplementing the profiles is a group of 54 comparative tables, which list the states in rank order on 54 key characteristics selected from the individual profiles.

Time: Almanac 2008. Boston, Houghton Mifflin, ((617) 351-5000), 1947-. (Annual).

An almanac of miscellaneous information, with a general arrangement and a subject index. Offers statistical details covering many types of phenomena.

Whitaker's Almanac 2008. London, J. Whitaker and Sons, 1868-. (Annual). (Distributed in the U.S. by Farmington Hills, MI, Gale, ((248) 699-4253), www.gale.com.

Similar to American almanacs except for emphasis on Britain and the Commonwealth.

World Almanac and Book of Facts 2008. New York, World Almanac Books, ((646) 312-6800). (Annual).

The most comprehensive and frequently useful of the American almanacs of miscellaneous information. Contains statistics on social, industrial, political, financial, religious, educational and other subjects, political organizations, societies, historical lists of famous events, etc.; up-to-date and in general, reliable; sources for many of the statistics are given.

U.S. STATISTICS

NON-GOVERNMENT U.S. PUBLICATIONS

A Matter of Fact. Ann Arbor, MI, Pierian Press, ((800) 678-2435), www.pierianpress.com, 1984-present.

Contains abstracts which include statistics on current social, economic, environmental, and political issues. This publication comes out twice each year and covers policy issues such as health care, environment, technological growth and other issues with political implications. It is available online through OCLC EPIC and OCLC First Search Catalog. It is also available on CD-ROM from Silver Platter Information, Inc. Note: Print volumes were discontinued in 2002.

A to Z Guide to American Consumers: Quick Links to Free Demographics. Ithaca, NY, New Strategist, ((800) 848-0842), www.newstrategist.com, 2008.

Offers quick links to free information about topics ranging from Adoption to Zip Code Demographics, plus a contact list of 54 major surveys of data collection efforts.

Adolescent Health in the United States, 2007. Atlanta, GA, U.S. National Center for Health Statistics, Centers for Disease Control and Prevention, ((301) 458-4000), www.cdc.gov/nchs, 2007.

This publication describes the health of the population 10-19 years of age examining a variety of current measures of health status, risk behavior, and health care from national data sources.

Susan Mitchell, ed. *American Generations: Who They Are, How They Live, What They Think.* 6th edition. Ithaca, NY, New Strategist, www.newstrategist.com ((800) 848-0842), 2008.

Offers a wealth of information. Chapters include The Generations; Attitudes and Behavior; Education, Health, Housing, Income, Labor Force, Arrangements, Population, Spending, and Wealth.

American Health: Demographics and Spending of Health Care Consumers. 2nd edition. Ithaca, NY, New Strategist, www.newstrategist.com ((800) 848-0842), 2007.

Focuses on health care consumers rather than industry statistics and reveals future market and policy needs. The 14 chapters examine addictions, aging, alternative medicine, attitudes toward health care, births, deaths, disability, diseases and conditions, health care coverage and cost, health care visits, hospital care, mental health, sexual attitudes and behavior, weight and exercise.

American Incomes: Demographics of Who Has Money. 6th ed. Ithaca, NY, New Strategist, ((800) 848-0842), www.newstrategist.com, 2007.

Explores and explains the economic status of Americans by looking at household income trends by age, household type, race and Hispanic origin, education, region, and work status. It examines trends in the incomes of men and women by a variety of demographic characteristics, and includes an analysis of discretionary income.

The American Marketplace: Demographics and Spending Patterns. 8th edition. Ithaca, NY, New Strategist, ((800) 848-0842), www.newstrategist.com, 2007.

This comprehensive book is a great resource for demographic and spending data. Topics covered include: attitudes, education, health, income, labor force, living arrangements, population, spending, and wealth.

American Men: Who They Are and How They Live. 2nd edition. Ithaca, NY, New Strategist, ((800) 848-0842), 2005.

Offers demographic statistics in a variety of areas including attitudes, business, education, health, income, labor force, living arrangements, population, spending, and wealth.

American Religion Data Archive (ARDA), www.thearda.com, University Park, PA, ARDA, ((814) 865-6258).

Collects quantitative data sets for the study of American religion. Most files are from surveys but all forms of quantitative data collections on religion are available as well.

American Statistics Index: A Comprehensive Guide and Index to the Statistical Publications of the United States Government. Bethesda, MD, Congressional Information Service, ((800) 638-8380), 1973-.

Covers more than 500 active federal statistics-producers including major statistical agencies, analytic and research agencies, and administrative and regulatory agencies. Indexed by subjects and names, by categories (such as geographic, economic and demographic breakdown), by titles and by agency report number. The annual supplement includes a guide to selected standard classifications used by the various federal agencies to arrange and present data. The 1974 edition is the base edition. Monthly issues are cumulated into annual supplements. A retrospective edition covering from the early 1960's to 1974 is also available. American Statistics Index is accessible online (from Dialog Information Services, Inc.) and documents indexed are available on microfiche. ASI is also available on CD-ROM on *Statistical Masterfile* from Congressional Information Service.

The American Tally: Statistics & Comparative Rankings for U.S. Cities with Populations over 10,000: 2002-2003 Edition. Millerton, NY, Grey House Publishing ((800) 562-2139), www.greyhouse.com, 2004.

Presents comparative raw data for 27 variables for cities and towns with populations greater than 10,000. There are sections for ethnic and age distribution, educational attendance and achievement, language and nativity, income and employment, and housing.

American Wholesalers and Distributors Directory. Farmington Hills, MI, Gale, ((248) 699-4253), www.gale.com, 2008.

Readers may now easily identify new distribution channels or prime licensing opportunities using this directory. Discover more than 27,000 large and small wholesalers and distributors throughout the U.S and Puerto Rico. Readers will easily find the name and address of the organization, fax number, SIC code, principal product lines, total number of employees, estimated annual sales volume and principal officers.

American Women: Who They Are and How They Live. 3rd edition. Ithaca, NY, New Strategist, ((800) 848-0842), 2005.

Offers demographic statistics in a variety of areas including attitudes, business, education, health, income, labor force, living arrangements, population, spending, and wealth.

Joseph H. Astrachan, ed. *Family Business Review.* Malden, MA, Blackwell Publishing Inc., ((781) 388 8200), www.blackwellpublishing.com.

This journal offers information and statistics on family-owned business in a global economy. Covers such topics as succession planning, impact of family dynamics on managerial behaviors, estate and tax planning, liquidity issues, financial management, generation and gender issues, international family-owned business, organizational structures, and strategic planning and organizational changes in family firms.

Awards, Honors & Prizes. Farmington Hills, MI, Gale, ((248) 699-4253), www.gale.com, 2008.

This international directory describes awards given for achievements in virtually every field of endeavor. Awards are listed alphabetically by the name of the administering organization, followed by alphabetical listings and descriptions of each of the awards it offers.

David D. Baer, ed. *State Handbook of Economic, Demographic and Fiscal Indicators 2008*, Washington, DC, American Association of Retired Persons, Public Policy Institute, www.aarp.org, ((888) 687-2277), 2006.

This handbook provides data on state and local government revenues and spending programs, poverty rates, per capita state personal income, and state and local revenues, expenditures, tax rates, and property tax relief programs. State and national comparisons as well as 10-year comparisons may be found. Summaries for each state are followed by tables and maps for making state-by-state summary comparisons on a single item of information.

Linda Holman Bentley and Jennifer J. Kiesl. *Investment Statistics Locator.* Westport, CT, Oryx Press, ((800) 225-5800), www.greenwood.com/catalog.aspx, 1994.

A guide to data on investment and economic statistical sources. Contains 53 source listings, including CD-ROM titles for such data as statistics on the furnishings industry or orange juice futures. Building on Chapman's original guide this edition has more periodicals and electronic sources, in addition to selected government documents. A wider variety of subjects is covered, including mutual funds and variable annuity/life accounts, overseas investment data, and worldwide economic statistics.

Paula Berinstein, ed., *The Statistical Handbook on Technology.* Westport, CT, Oryx Press, ((800) 225-5800), www.greenwood.com, 1999.

Provides comprehensive information on such areas related to research and development, employment of scientists and engineers, funding and technological advances.

Book of the States. Lexington, KY, Council of State Governments, ((859) 244-8000), 1935-. (Annual).

Statistical coverage for state activities is grouped under major headings such as intergovernmental relations, legislatures, finances, services, etc.

Brands and Their Companies. Farmington Hills, MI, Gale, ((248) 699-4253), www.gale.com, 2007.

This source lists manufactures and distributors from small businesses to large corporations, from both the public and private sectors, offering complete coverage of more than 426,000 U.S. consumer brands; 115,000 manufacturers, importers or distributors; and companies that are out of business as well as brands that are no longer in production or are now considered generic. Includes an inter-edition supplement. *Companies and Their Brands* offers a convenient rearrangement, presenting an alphabetical list sorted by manufactures, distributors and importers.

Business Rankings Annual. Farmington Hills, MI, Gale, ((248) 699-4253), www.gale.com, 2008.

Helps librarians answer reference questions related to rankings information. Working from a bibliographic file built up over the years, Gale has culled thousands of items from periodicals, newspapers, financial services, directories, statistical annuals and other printed material.

CEDDS: The Complete Economic and Demographic Data Source. Washington, DC, Woods and Poole Economics, Inc., ((800) 786-1915), www.woodsandpoole.com, 2007.

Reliable forecasts and historic data for all counties and MSAs in the U.S. Contains more than 118 million statistics. This combination of economic and demographic data allows you to select sites and analyze regional economies. Data include income, employment, population changes, households, and retail sales potential. Forecast to 2025 make long-term planning possible. Also available on CD-ROM.

Census CD. East Brunswick, NJ, GeoLytics, Inc., ((732-651-2000), www.geolytics.com, on CD-ROM.

Census CD delivers all of the 2000 U.S. Census of Population and Housing long-form results on a single CD-ROM.

Bruce A. Chadwick and Tim B. Heaton, eds. *Statistical Handbook on Adolescents in America.* Westport, CT, Oryx Press, ((800) 225-5800), www.greenwood.com/catalog.aspx, 1996.

This handbook includes a wide variety of information about American adolescents, aged 12 to 21, who must deal with societal and cultural pressures unique to their generation. A comprehensive data analysis introduces each section and pulls the highlights from the tables and charts.

Bruce A. Chadwick and Tim B. Heaton, eds. *Statistical Handbook on the American Family.* Westport, CT, Oryx Press, ((800) 225-5800), www.greenwood.com/catalog.aspx, 1998.

Offers some 400 tables, charts and tabulations collected from federal and state agencies, polls, periodicals and other research sources. Topics treated include education, health, politics, employment, economic expenditures, social characteristics and other demographic and historical data.

CIS Statistical Periodicals. Bethesda, MD, Congressional Information Service, ((800) 638-8380), www.lexisnexis.com/academic/3cis/cisMnu.asp, 1975-.

Complete text of more than 200 U.S. federal statistical periodicals including both depository and non-depository items. Covers the period 1975 - present.

Commercial Atlas and Marketing Guide. Skokie, IL, Rand McNally, ((800) 333-0136), www.randmcnally.com, 1911-. (Annual).

Detailed listings and statistical material on more than 120,000 places in the United States, and indexes many additional thousands of foreign cities. In 1980 the 111th edition appeared (earlier editions were published more frequently than the current annual cycle). Most of the index and tabular material is available from the publisher on microfiche, computer tape, or online.

Commodity Yearbook. Chicago, IL, Commodity Research Bureau, Knight-Ridder Financial Publishing, ((800) 621-5271), www.crbtrader.com, 1939-. (Annual).

A reference volume covering the major raw and semi-finished products, arranged alphabetically by commodity. For each material listed there is complete statistical data, for the latest year and for earlier years, of production, distribution, sales, etc. This Yearbook is supplemented by the *Commodity Yearbook Statistical Abstract Service* which provides current information four times yearly, and the weekly *Commodity Chart Service.* In addition, this is now available from the same source, *CRB INFOTECH Commodity Data.* This CD-ROM service provides 50 years of data on some 100 commodities as well as historical prices on over 300 cash, future and option markets.

Consumer Market Guide. New York, The Conference Board ((212) 339-0345), www.conference-board.org, continuously updated.

A basic statistical profile of consumers and the consumer market, presented in tabular form. Statistics are organized into 12 chapters - population, marriages and births, households and families, education, labor force and occupation, employment and earnings, income, expenditures, housing, retailing and advertising, prices and production, and miscellaneous. The Conference Board's Consumer Research Center maintains an updated file of these statistics, and Guide users can secure such information by contacting Lynn Franco.

Consumer USA 2008. Chicago, Euromonitor International Inc. ((312) 922-1115), www.euromonitor.com, 2007.

Provides volume and value market size data in historical (2001-2006) and forecasted (2007-2011) time series for over 330 consumer markets. It also provides data and analysis on the US economy and market. Overview and marketing parameters sections outline demographic, socio-economic, lifestyle and purchasing trends of the US consumer.

Arsen J. Darnay, ed. *American Cost of Living Survey.* Farmington Hills, MI, Gale, ((248) 699-4253), www.gale.com, 2001.

American Cost of Living Survey collects cost and expense data covering more than 450 American cities and metropolitan statistical areas, providing a broad and deep picture of each area's cost of living. Data is compiled from a variety of public and private publications. Subjects covered include groceries, housing, transportation, food, clothing and other consumer goods, utilities, insurance, entertainment, taxes, education and many others. New to this 3rd edition is a section of U.S. averages covering such things as the costs of medical procedures, recreation at national parks and other information not reported at the city/metro level.

Arsen J. Darnay, ed. *Economic Indicators Handbook.* 6th ed. Farmington Hills, MI, Gale, ((248) 699-4253), www.gale.com, 2002.

Offers a unique source of aggregate national statistics on approximately 175 U.S. economic indicators including those covering economics and general business; government and personal finance; prices; and personal income, expenditures, and savings. *Economic Indicators Handbook* provides both historical and current perspectives on the U.S. economy by presenting original values for all statistics since their inception as well as recalculated and rebased figures reflecting current values. In addition, each statistical series includes methods of calculation, inclusions and exclusions, an historical overview, and changes in definition over time.

Arsen J. Darnay, ed. *Statistical Record of Health and Medicine.* Farmington Hills, MI, Gale, ((248) 699-4253), www.gale.com, 1998.

More than 900 statistical tables, graphs and charts combine hard-to-locate research in a single volume. Twelve convenient chapters provide comprehensive insight into virtually every aspect of health and medicine including lifestyles and health, politics, opinion and law, medical professions, and more.

Demographic Information Service. New York, The Conference Board ((212) 339-0345), www.conference-board.org, Four times each year.

A series of statistical reports showing distribution of households and income by major demographic characteristics based on special Census Bureau data developed for the Consumer Research Center. Characteristics include age, household, type, household size, children, earners, income, education, occupation, home ownership, and race.

Adam Dobrin, Brian Wiersema, Colin Loftin, David McDowall, eds. *Statistical Handbook on Violence in America.* Westport, CT, Oryx Press, ((800) 225-5800), www.greenwood.com/catalog.aspx, 1995.

Features nearly 400 tables, graphs, and charts that reveal the startling growth of violence in America and its impact on the home and the workplace, health care and the economy, individual attitudes, and public policy. The handbook presents researchers with national data on interpersonal violence, both fatal and nonfatal. Data on high-risk groups and situations and the measurable consequences of violence are also included.

Donald B. Dodd, ed. *Historical Statistics of the States of the United States: Two Centuries of the Census, 1790-1990.* Westport, CT, Greenwood Publishing Group, ((800) 225-5800), 1993.

A state-by-state presentation of 18 population items, 1790-1990, 27 agriculture items, 1850-1990, six manufacturing items 1850-1990, and 12 manufacturing items, 1899-1989. There are also population figures, 1790-1990, for the 200 cities that had 100,000 inhabitants or more in 1990. Many footnotes to the tables define the data items, and the data sources are cited in endnotes. A glossary explains historical variations in the definitions, noting the effects of such changes on the comparability of the figures.

Henry J. Dubester, ed. *Catalog of United States Census Publications, 1790-1945.* U.S. Library of Congress. Westport, CT, Greenwood Publishing Group, ((800) 225-5800), 1969.

This book lists all materials issued by the Bureau of the Census and its predecessor organizations starting with the first decennial census report of 1790 and ending with publications released to the close of 1945. The CATALOG is divided into two general sections: the first covers publications issued in concert with the successive decennial censuses, and the second includes Bureau of the Census publications released as a result of its other surveys. Its primary importance now is historical statistics. From 1946 to the present, refer to the Bureau of the Census *Catalog and Guide* or see Greenwood Press's *Catalog of United States Census Publications: 1946-72.*

Editor and Publisher Market Guide. New York, Editor and Publisher Company, Inc., ((800) 562-2706), http://www.editorandpublisher.com, 1901-. (Annual).

Organized by states and territories of the United States and Canada, with separate city entries listed thereunder. Each city entry includes such data as location, market area, economic features, transportation, population, housing, banks, auto registration, numbers of electric and gas meters and telephones of principal industries with number of wage earners and average weekly pay, colleges and universities, climate, water, agriculture, mining, retailing, with location of shopping centers, names of chief stores, and other data, retail sales figures, names of newspapers with circulations. Also available on CD-ROM.

Encyclopedia of American Religions. Farmington Hills, MI, Gale, ((248) 699-4253), www.gale.com.

This is a comprehensive and compelling resource, with coverage on more than 2,300 North American religious groups in the U.S. and Canada -- from Adventists to Zen Buddhists. Information on these groups is presented in two distinct sections. These sections contain essays and directory listings that describe the historical development of religious families and give factual information about each group within those families, including, when available, rubrics for membership figures, educational facilities and periodicals.

Encyclopedia of Drugs, Alcohol, and Addictive Behavior. Farmington Hills, MI, Gale, ((248) 699-4253), www.gale.com, 2001.

Provides a wide range of information about the diverse area of drug use and addiction. More than 700 articles intended for the student and layperson cover the social, medical and political issues related to drugs and alcohol, as well as types of addiction.

Helen S. Fisher, ed. *Gale City and Metro Rankings Reporter.* Farmington Hills, MI, Gale, ((248) 699-4253), www.gale.com, 1997.

This compilation of statistical rankings covers more than 1,500 cities and metropolitan statistical areas in the U.S. The approximately 3,000 tables cover topics such as crime, education, cost of living, employment, environment, government, health, housing, industry, income, population, poverty and occupations. The statistical sources are federal, state, and local governments, companies, associations and societies, newspapers and periodicals and directories.

Norman Frumkin. *Guide to Economic Indicators.* 4th ed. Armonk, NY, M. E. Sharpe, ((800) 541-6563), www.mesharpe.com, 2005.

Offers information about the main characteristics and sources of 50 key economic indicators, primarily developed by governmental agencies. Now revised and expanded, Fumkin has added distribution of wealth, bankruptcies, consumer credit delinquency, mortgage delinquency and foreclosure, housing affordability index, employment household survey, job quality index, non-manufacturing business activity index, business starts, and the Russell 2000 stock index.

Gale State Rankings Reporter, 2nd ed. Farmington Hills, MI, Gale, ((248) 699-4253), www.gale.com, 1996.

More than 3,000 ranked lists of states under 35 subject headings such as housing, education, income levels, the environment, arts and leisure, and more. Rankings are derived from diverse sources, like newspapers and popular magazines, books, journals and research institution publications, as well as federal and state government publications.

Susan B. Gall and Timothy L. Gall, eds. *Statistical Record of Asian Americans.* 1st ed. Farmington Hills, MI, Gale, ((248) 699-4253), www.gale.com, 1993.

This unique graphic reference is the only source of its kind to provide up-to-date U.S. and Canadian government census data as well as information culled from organization reports and journals and other widely scattered published and unpublished sources. More than 850 charts, graphs and tables give insight into the current and historical status of 19 Asian nationality groups in the U.S. and Canada.

John V. Ganly, ed. *Data Sources for Business and Market Analysis.* 4th ed. Lanham, MD, Scarecrow Press, ((800) 462-6420), www.scarecrowpress.com, 1994.

A guide to public and private sources of information available both in print and as computerized databases. Emphasis on data, both domestic and international, relating to economic conditions, business trends, and consumer and industrial markets.

Deirdre A. Gaquin and Katherine A. DeBrandt, eds. *County and City Extra.* Lanham, MD, Bernan Press, ((800) 274-4888), www.bernan.com. (Annual).

This comprehensive source augments the information found in the U.S. Census Bureau's *County and City Data Book.* Unlike the *County and City Data Book*, the *County and City Extra* is updated annually. Includes comprehensive statistics on every county, state, city, and metropolitan area within the U.S. gathered from government and private agencies. This is also available on CD-ROM under the title *County and City Plus.*

Deirdre A. Gaquin, ed. *Education Statistics.* 4th ed. Lanham, MD, Bernan Press, ((800) 274-4888), www.bernan.com, 2003.

Covers a broad range of geographic areas in one volume for anyone needing up-to-date statistics on American education. Using school district data from the National Center for Education Statistics the editors have developed both county and state totals on enrollment, student-teacher ratios, revenue, expenditure, and related information.

Deirdre A. Gaquin and Katherine A. DeBrandt, eds. 4th ed. *Places, Towns, and Townships.* Lanham, MD, Bernan Press, ((800) 274-4888), www.bernan.com, 2007.

This volume provides access to hard-to-find demographic data for U.S. cities, towns, townships, villages, and census-designated places with populations of 25,000 or less.

David Garoogian, ed. *America's Top-Rated Cities: A Statistical Handbook, 2008.* Millerton, NY, Grey House Publishing, ((800) 562-2139), 2008.

Provides current, comprehensive statistical information on 100 top-rated U.S. cities. Arranged by city, this Four Volume Set allows readers to see, at a glance, a concise social, business, economic, demographic and environmental profile of each city, including brief evaluative comments. Comparisons with MSA and US figures are shown in most tables. A special section with comparative statistics is also included.

Tim B. Heaton, Bruce A. Chadwick, and Cardell K. Jacobson, editors. *Statistical Handbook on Racial Groups in the United States.* Westport, CT, Oryx Press, ((800) 225-5800), www.greenwood.com/catalog.aspx, 2000.

Containing more than 400 charts and tables covering non-Hispanic whites, Native Americans, and African, Hispanic and Asian Americans, the *Handbook* presents a broad range of data on demographic context; education; economics and employment; health well being and lifestyles; family sex, fertility, and contraception; religion; crime and delinquency; and political participation. This comprehensive resource documents important differences among the racial groups and also points out some major similarities. The book also presents shifting trends and helps the reader to understand the importance of racial differences.

Homelessness in America. Westport, CT, Oryx Press, ((800) 225-5800), www.greenwood.com/catalog.aspx, 1996 (in conjunction with National Coalition for the Homeless).

The book features articles and approximately 400 statistical tables and charts on homelessness, covering its history, causes, demographics (and changes in demographics), shelters and shelter clients, legal issues, governmental attempts at solutions, public attitudes, and more.

Hospital Statistics: The Comprehensive Reference Source for Analysis and Comparison of Hospital Trends. Chicago, American Hospital Association, ((312) 422-3000), www.aha.org, 1971-. (Annual).

Aggregate trend data at the state and national level are presented for a 15-year period. Tables present aggregate utilization, personnel, and financial data by census divisions, individual states, territories, SMSAs, and the 100 largest central cities. Data for individual hospitals can be found in a companion volume, the *AHA Guide to the Health Care Field,* which is also available on diskette.

Kendra A. Hovey and Harold A. Hovey, ed. *CQ's State Fact Finder 2006: Rankings Across America.* Washington, DC, CQ Press, ((866) 427-7737, www.cqpress.com, 2006.

Covers the social, political, and economic currents and trends in the states. At the core of this resource is a Subject Ranking section that provides over 265 tables, each including data and rankings for all fifty states plus the District of Columbia. The tables are organized into thirteen topical chapters that cover topics including crime/law enforcement, economies, education, government, health, taxes, technology, welfare and many more.

Eva E. Jacobs. *Handbook of U.S. Labor Statistics: Employment, Earnings, Prices, Productivity, and Other Labor Data.* Lanham, MD, Bernan Press, ((800) 274-4888), www.bernan.com, 2008.

Based on the *Handbook of Labor Statistics*, formerly published by the Bureau of Labor Statistics, this work presents historical data on labor market trends. Topics covered include: population, labor force, and employment status; employment and unemployment; hourly and weekly earnings; consumer prices; producer prices; export and import prices; consumer expenditures; employment costs; and productivity.

Chandrika Kaul and Valerie Tomaselli-Maschovitis, eds. *Statistical Handbook on Consumption and Wealth in the United States.* Westport, CT, Oryx Press, ((800) 225-5800), www.greenwood.com, 1999.

Containing more than 300 tables, charts, and graphs, this handbook focuses on the latest statistical information available on our nation's spending habits by exploring a wide range of economic, demographic, and geographic variables. Statistical information, arranged by region, state, age level, race, and gender, offers a comprehensive picture of our nation's financial habits.

Chandrika Kaul and Valerie Tomaselli-Maschovitis, eds. *Statistical Handbook on Poverty in the Developing World.* Westport, CT, Oryx Press, ((800) 225-5800), www.greenwood.com/catalog.aspx, 1999.

The Handbook includes statistics on economic indicators, demographic patterns, income distribution, and other factors that paint an accurate picture of the poverty existing in the world today. Along with helpful introductions, important features of this resource includes its depth of coverage and diversity of sources. Two special sections focusing on women and children and on poverty in selected cities worldwide provide significant data not typically found in other statistical resources.

George Kurian, ed. *Datapedia of the United States: American History in Numbers.* 4th ed. Lanham, MD, Bernan Press, ((800) 274-4888), www.bernan.com, 2007.

Presenting data on several hundred indicators of social, economic, political, and cultural developments within the nation, the third edition of *Datapedia* boasts expanded coverage on a wide range of topics, including: health and healthcare; food and nutrition; education and learning; law enforcement, courts, and prisons; arts, entertainment, recreation, and travel; politics and elections; public finance; and national defense. Data series in Datapedia cover the history of the United States from 1790 to 2003 and include select data projections through 2050.

Michael R. Lavin, ed. *Understanding the Census: A Guide for Marketers, Planners, Grant-Writers and Other Data Users.* Westport, CT, Oryx Press, ((800) 225-5800), www.greenwood.com/catalog.aspx, 1996.

This book helps researchers explore the *Census of the Population and Housing.* Lavin combines in-depth explanations of important concepts with detailed descriptions of resources and discussions of research methods. In addition, a cumulative subject index and finding guide to all tables appearing in the 1990 printed reports are also included.

Law and Legal Information Directory. Farmington Hills, MI, Gale, ((248) 699-4253), www.gale.com, 2009.

This directory provides descriptions and contact information for more than 21,000 institutions, services and facilities in the law and legal information industry. Look for sections on bar review courses; national and international organizations; bar associations; federal court systems; law schools, scholarships and grants; legal periodicals; lawyer referral services; legal aid offices; public defender offices; small claims courts; and more. Features include URLs and e-mail addresses.

The Lifestyle Market Analyst. Des Plaines, IL, SRDS, www.srds.com, ((800) 851-7737).

Useful resource for demographic and lifestyle data compiled from more than 12 million households.

Market Share Reporter. Farmington Hills, MI, Gale, ((248) 699-4253), www.gale.com, 2008.

Presenting comparative business statistics in a clear, straightforward manner, *Market Share Reporter* affords an immediate overview of companies, products and services and cites original sources. A convenient arrangement by four-digit SIC code helps business decision-makers and researchers easily access needed data for more than 2,000 entries. Each entry features a descriptive title; data and market description; a list of producers/ products along with their market share; and more.

John Maxymuk, ed. *Government Online: One-Click Access to 3,400 Federal and State Web Sites,* New York, Neal-Schuman Publishers, Inc. ((212) 925-8650), www.neal-schuman.com, 2001. Book and CD-ROM.

In this sequel to his previous book, *Find Government Information on the Internet* (1995), Maxymuk focuses on the sweeping changes brought by the shift of federal, state, local, foreign, and international government information from print to electronic format. Compiled by subject area experts, each chapter begins with an overview of the most useful web sites. Entries include the URL, a brief description of the site, and highlights designed to answer most commonly asked questions. Agency web site maps and lists of state agencies are also provided.

Medical and Health Information Directory. Farmington Hills, MI, Gale, ((248) 699-4253), www.gale.com, 2008.

This comprehensive guide to organizations, agencies, institutions, services and information sources in medicine and health-related fields provides complete contact information and a description of the organization. Each edition includes more than 33,000 organizations; nearly 20,000 libraries, publications and electronic resources; and more than 40,500 health service providers.

Gordon Melton, ed. *Statistical Record of Religion in America.* 2nd ed. Farmington Hills, MI, Gale, ((248) 699-4253), www.gale.com, 1996.

Covers all religions and religious groups currently active in the U.S. Provides comprehensive information on such topics as: number of churches or other places of worship, numbers/ sizes of affiliated institutions, church membership, church attendance, charitable activities, attitudes and opinions on religious issues, and more.

Ellen Meltzer, ed. *The New Book of American Rankings.* New York, Facts on File, www.factsonfile.com, ((800) 322-8755), 1998.

Features over 300 tables with more than 20,000 facts. Illustrates how the 50 states stack up against each other in over 27 different areas, from geography to pollution, income to poverty, and education to health. A large number of the tables include statistics for a range of years.

Susan Mitchell, ed. *American Generations: Who They Are, How They Live, What They Think.* 6th edition. Ithaca, NY, New Strategist, www.newstrategist.com ((800) 848-0842), 2008.

Offers a wealth of information. Chapters include The Generations; Attitudes and Behavior; Education, Health, Housing, Income, Labor Force, Arrangements, Population, Spending, and Wealth.

MSA Profile: Metropolitan Area Forecasts to 2030. Washington, DC Woods and Poole Economics, Inc., ((800) 786-1915), www.woodsandpoole.com, 2004.

MSA Profile has data for all newly defined Metropolitan Areas in the U.S. and contains historical data from 1970 and projections to 2030 of population by age and race, employment by industry, earnings of employees by industry, personal income by source, households by income bracket and retail sales by kind of business. The data and projections are for all Metropolitan Statistical Areas (MSAs), states, and regions in the U.S. The 900-page volume has more than 450,000 statistics. Data tables, and a pdf file of the printed book, are also available on CD-ROM; the CD-ROM also has data for all the newly defined Micropolitan Statistical Areas.

Municipal Year Book. Washington, DC, ICMA-The Professional Local Government Management Association, ((800) 745-8780), www.icma.org, 1934-. (Annual).

Information on population and economic data is supplied on American cities. A number of statistical charts portray municipal activities, finances, and other areas. Government data in municipalities 25,000 and under is also available from ICMA.

The Native North American Almanac. 2nd ed. Farmington Hills, MI, Gale, ((248) 699-4253), 2001.

This updated source covers the civilization and culture of the indigenous peoples of the U.S. and Canada - both historic and contemporary. Included are signed essays, annotated directories, excerpts and biographies. Each chapter contains a subject-specific bibliography, photographs, maps and charts -- 400 illustrations in all. This 2nd edition also includes a new chapter, Women and Gender Relations.

Manthi Nguyen, ed. *Black Americans: A Statistical Sourcebook* Palo Alto, CA, Information Publications, ((877) 544-4636), www.informationpublications.com. (Annual).

This volume is a compilation of statistical information about the black American population of the United States. Tables included have been taken from previously published standard statistical sources produced by the government. Topics covered include: demographics and characteristics of the population; vital statistics and health; education; government; elections and public opinion; crime; law enforcement and corrections; labor force, employment and unemployment; earnings, income, poverty and wealth; and a section of special topics. A companion volume, *Hispanic Americans: A Statistical Sourcebook* is also available.

Manthi Nguyen, ed. *Hispanic Americans: A Statistical Sourcebook.* Palo Alto, CA, Information Publications ((877)544-4636, www.informationpublications.com, 2003.

Comprehensive annual statistical reference work. Provides detailed tables on demographics; social and economic characteristics; earnings, income, poverty and wealth; labor, employment and unemployment; crime and corrections; vital statistics and health; and education.

Richard G. Niemi and Harold W. Stanley, eds. *Vital Statistics on American Politics 2007-2008.* Washington, DC, CQ Press, www.cqpress.com. ((866) 427-7737.

Provided in over 200 tables and figures, chapters are devoted to key subjects areas such as elections and political parties, public opinion and voting, the media, the three branches of U.S. government, foreign, military, social and economic policy, and much more. The scholars consult hundreds of sources to calculate and locate the data, facts, and figures that offer a vivid and multifaceted portrait of the broad spectrum of United States politics and policies.

Frederick M. O'Hara, Jr., ed. *Handbook of United States Economic and Financial Indicators.* Westport, CT, Greenwood Publishing Group, ((800) 225-5800), 2000.

Designed to answer questions about the makeup, purpose, use, and availability of economic indicators in a broad sense of the term, this book includes entries on 284 indicators, 137 of which are new to this edition. In addition to identifying and describing indicators, the entries show how they are calculated, where they are published, how they are used, where their values are published, and where one can find further information about them. Arranged in dictionary format with extensive cross-references and indexing.

Marlita A. Reddy, ed. *Statistical Record of Hispanic Americans.* 2nd ed. Farmington Hills, MI, Gale, ((248) 699-4253), 1995.

This reference quantifies the current state of Hispanic American culture through a series of highly accessible charts, graphs and tables based on a wide variety of reliable published information. Offers wide-ranging facts that bear on political, economic and social aspects of Americans with ancestry or origins in Mexico, Puerto Rico, Cuba, Spanish-speaking Central and South America and Spain.

Robinson, Judith Schiek, *Tapping the Government Grapevine: The User-Friendly Guide to U.S. Government Information Sources.* 3rd edition. Westport, CT, Oryx Press, ((800) 225-5800), www.greenwood.com, 1998.

This highly readable text explains the intricacies of government information and how to find sources that meet specific research needs. New features in the third edition include detailed coverage of Internet resources, directories of World Wide Web addresses, and quick tips on which government Web sites to search for different types of information. Helpful guides to government abbreviations and citations are also included, as are numerous new tables, user guides, exercises, and illustrations.

Cheryl Russell, ed. *Demographics of the U.S.: Trends and Projections.* Ithaca, NY, New Strategist, ((800)848-0842), www.newstrategist.com, 2002.

A reference book of historical statistics covering the years 1950 to 2000 and an archive of the socioeconomic trends of the last half of the twentieth century. New to this edition of Demographics of the U.S. is more comprehensive coverage of historical statistics, including single-year data on many topics, such as school enrollment, SAT scores, hospital admissions, AIDS victims, employment status of men and women, living arrangements of children, marital status, and geographical mobility. Also new to this edition are exclusive New Strategist projections of the population by age, sex, race, and Hispanic origin to the year 2010 based on 2000 census counts-projections that are not yet available from the Census Bureau.

Cheryl Russell, ed. *Racial and Ethnic Diversity: Asians, Blacks, Hispanics, Native Americans, and Whites.* Ithaca, NY, New Strategist, ((800) 848-0842), www.newstrategist.com 2002.

Statistical reference on ethnic America. Topics covered include: education, health, households and living, arrangements, housing, income, labor force, population, wealth and spending, and attitudes.

Frank L. Schick and Renee Schick, eds. *Statistical Handbook on Aging Americans.* 2nd ed. Westport, CT, Oryx Press, ((800) 225-5800), www.greenwood.com/catalog.aspx, 1994.

Contains recent statistical data about older Americans, including information about the economic, social, health, employment, and financial status of the elderly. Contains more than 300 statistical tables and illustrative charts, accompanied by explanatory text. Also includes a bibliographic guide to statistical sources.

Frank L. Schick and Renee Schick, eds. *Statistical Handbook on U.S. Hispanics.* Westport, CT, Oryx Press, ((800) 225-5800), www.greenwood.com/catalog.aspx, 1991.

Provides access to over 300 statistical charts, graphs, and tables. Contains recent data on U.S. Hispanics, including demographics, immigration and naturalization, social characterization, education, health, politics, labor force, and economic conditions.

Jean L. Sears and Marilyn K. Moody. *Using Government Information Sources: Electronic and Print.* 2nd ed. Westport, CT, Oryx Press, ((800) 225-5800), www.greenwood.com/catalog.aspx, 2001.

Explains the uses and accessibility of government information sources within the context of actual research. Coverage has been expanded to include the wealth of information now available through electronic sources. Each section provides a checklist for quick identification of sources, suggests a series of steps for using the listed sources, and supplies a narrative analysis of each source. Also included are descriptions of related references to consult for additional information.

Patrick A. Simmons, eds. *Housing Statistics of the United States.* 2001 Ed. Lanham, MD, Bernan Press, ((800) 274-4888), www.bernan.com, 2000.

Source for current and historical information on households, housing, and housing finance. A wide variety of data including: household characteristics; housing stock characteristics; housing production and investment; prices, rents, and affordability; home mortgage lending; secondary mortgage markets; and federal housing programs.

Courtenay Slater, ed. *Foreign Trade of the United States: Including State and Metro Area Export Data.* Lanham, MD, Bernan Press, ((800) 274-4888), www.bernan.com, 1999.

This edition of Foreign Trade of the United States provides comprehensive statistical information about U.S. imports and exports of both goods and services; a complete accounting of U.S. international transactions from 1960 to 1999; U.S. exports of goods by destination, and imports by country or region of origin; U.S. exports and imports of agricultural and manufactured goods, and goods trade balances, with nearly 200 countries and country groups; and other related topics.

2008 Community Sourcebook of ZIP Code Demographics. Arlington, VA, ESRI, ((800) 292-2224), 2008.

Contains accurate demographic information for every U.S. ZIP Code, based on the release of ESRI's 2008/2013 projections of key population and income data. Updated variables for population, households, families, income, race, age, and consumer spending for a wide variety of products and services are included in this reference tool. The same consumer and business data is also available in a separate volume for each county in the *2008 Community Sourcebook of County Demographics.* Both titles are also available on CD-ROM.

Stat Fact. Quarterly or Annual Subscription, New Canaan, CT, NewsBank, ((800) 762-8182). On CD ROM.

A collection of more than a half million facts and statistics on each of the 50 states. Data covers such areas as labor, education, government and elections, and business. Can be used to search individual state data or comparative data.

State Profile. Washington, DC, Woods and Poole Economics, Inc., ((800) 786-1915), www.woodsandpoole.com.

Contains historical data for all counties and Metropolitan Areas in a particular state. State Profiles contain historical data from 1970 and projections to 2030 of population by age and race, employment by industry, earnings of employees by industry, personal income by source, households by income bracket and retail sales by kind of business. The data and projections are for every county, MSA, and DMA in a particular state (some volumes contain more than one state).

Statistical Handbook of Working America. Farmington Hills, MI, Gale, ((248) 699-4253), www.gale.com, 1997.

Contains a unique compilation of statistics, rankings, and forecasts on a variety of occupations, careers and the working environment. Entries offer statistical pictures of about 600 occupations, and include: demographic profile, industry statistics, educational enrollment within the field, employment patterns, accidents and injuries on the job, receipt of pensions and other benefits, legal and ethical issues, skills training and education, industrial relations, production and technology, and more.

Statistical Record of the Environment. 3rd ed. Farmington Hills, MI, Gale, ((248) 699-4253), www.gale.com, 1995.

Charity Anne Dorgan, ed. Provides approximately 851 graphs, charts and tables reporting information and analysis on today's hottest environmental topics. Information is presented in 10 subject chapters covering pollutants, costs, solutions, industry and government data, laws and regulations, politics, and opinions.

Statistical Reference Index. Bethesda, MD, Congressional Information Service, ((800) 638-8380), 1980-.

This publication is a selective guide to American statistic sources from sources other than the United States government. Covers information on business, industry, finance, economic and social conditions, government and politics, the environment, population, and other subjects. Although the sources are American, coverage includes data on foreign countries. Indexed by subjects, names and categories. Published in monthly index and monthly abstract issues with an annual accumulation. Most cited publications are available in microfiche from the publisher. SRI is also available on CD-ROM on *Statistical Masterfile* from Congressional Information Service.

Cornelia J. Strawser, ed. *Business Statistics of the United States.* Lanham, MD, Bernan Press, ((800) 274-4888), www.bernan.com, 2005.

Based on *Business Statistics,* formerly published by the U.S. Department of Commerce, this work presents annual and monthly time series data on business trends. Information on more than 2,000 data series, as well as industry profiles on: construction and housing; mining, oil and gas; manufacturing; transportation and utilities; retail and wholesale trade; services; and government. Also features extensive overview of historical economic trends, including data on: gross domestic product; consumer income and spending; industrial production; employment hours and earnings; business sales; and money and financial markets.

Paul Stuart. *Nations Within a Nation.* Westport, CT, Greenwood Publishing Group, ((800) 225-5800), 1987.

This historical abstract on native Americans draws on a variety of mostly federal government sources published during the past 100 years. Statistics are organized in chapters covering a wide range of topics such as population, health, employment, and economic development.

Cynthia M. Taeuber, ed. *Statistical Handbook on Women in America.* Westport, CT, Oryx Press, ((800) 225-5800), www.greenwood.com/catalog.aspx, 1996.

This compendium features over 400 tables and charts for specific and detailed reference. The contents present statistics covering population, births, marriage and divorce, voting and political involvement, labor force issues, economic issues, alcoholism and drug abuse, and many more topics.

Vital Statistics in Corrections. Lanham, MD, American Correctional Association, ((800) 222-5646), 1998.

This statistical compendium provides current information on correctional departments in the U.S. Covers information on jails and detention centers, inmate populations, state corrections budgets and operating expenditures, educational requirements, salaries, and unions.

Frieda O. Weise, Patricia G. Hinegardner, Barbara L. Kuchan, and Phyllis S. Lansinged, eds. *Health Statistics: An Annotated Bibliographic Guide to Information Resources.* Lanham, MD, Scarecrow Press, ((800) 462-6420), www.scarecrowpress.com, 1996.

The monograph is organized into eight chapters covering subjects such as vital statistics, morbidity, health services utilization, and health-care costs and expenditures. A short paragraph introduces each chapter and sometimes parts of chapters. Each entry includes standard bibliographic information with annotations provided.

Helmut F. Wendel, Katherine A. DeBrandt, Sohair Abu-Aish, eds. *State Profiles: The Population and Economy of Each U.S. State.* Lanham, MD, Bernan Press, ((800) 274-4888), www.bernan.com, 2006.

Economic and demographic data for each U.S. state are presented using charts, tables, and interpretive text. Each state is covered by a compact, standardized chapter that allows for easy data comparisons between states and with national and regional averages. A 10-page profile for each U.S. state plus the District of Columbia provides reliable, up-to-date information on a wide range of topics, including: population and labor force; income and poverty; government finances; economic structure; and education and health. Much of the information in this edition has been drawn from the 2000 Decennial Census and is often accompanied by data from the 1990 Census.

Who Knows What: A Guide to Experts. Washington, DC, MarketResearch.com, www.marketresearch.

com, ((202) 333-3499), (Annual).
United States government experts for a wide variety of topics are listed by subject area and department. More than 15,000 experts and 14,000 topics are covered. Useful as a supplement to printed sources of statistics.

James Woy, ed. *Encyclopedia of Business Information Sources*. Farmington Hills, MI, Gale, ((248) 699-4253), 2005.
This volume identifies live, print and electronic sources of information listed under alphabetically arranged subjects--industries and business concepts and practices. Listings are arranged by type of resource (directories, databases, newsletters, indexes, research centers, etc.) within each subject. Many entries also provide e-mail addresses and URLs covering online resources.

PUBLICATIONS OF THE U.S. BUREAU OF THE CENSUS

The U.S. Bureau of the Census is a prolific publisher of statistical data in print, computerized, CD-ROM, and online formats. The data are, for the most part, based on the following periodic censuses:

2000 Census of Housing
2000 Census of Population
2002 Census of Agriculture
2002 Economic Census
2002 Census of Construction Industries
2002 Census of Governments
2002 Census of Manufactures
2002 Census of Mineral Industries
2002 Census of Retail Trade
2002 Census of Service Industries
2002 Census of Transportation
2002 Census of Wholesale Trade

Many current and historical Bureau of the Census publications are available in PDF and HTML versions online, or in microfiche from Congressional Information Service, 4520 East-West Highway, Bethesda, MD, 20814, ((800) 638-8380). Available are all Decennial Censuses from 1790 to 2000, as well as Non-Decennial Census Publications.

The Census Bureau offers an Internet data stop that provides access to product descriptions and a wide cross section of information ranging from agriculture to industry to population. All Census Bureau publications released by the Government Printing Office since January 1996, as well as selected reports printed before January 1996, are presented in the Electronic Subscription Service section of the Census Internet site. The Census Bureau's Internet site can be accessed on the World Wide Web at www.census.gov

For more information on Census Bureau products and programs, contact U.S. Census Bureau, 4700 Silver Hill Road, Suitland, MD, 20746, www.census.gov, (301) 457-4100.

Descriptions of the Bureau's best known publication, the *Statistical Abstract of the United States*, and of other important Bureau publications follow.

Annual Survey of Manufactures. Washington, DC, U.S. Bureau of the Census, www.census.gov, ((301) 457-4100), 1949-. (Annual).
Provides data on manufacturing activity for industry groups; important individual industries; and for geographic divisions, States, large standard metropolitan district areas, and large industrial counties. Items include value added by manufacture; value of shipments; cost of materials, fuels, electric energy consumed, employment, man-hours, payrolls, and capital expenditures. Available in CD-ROM.

Census Product Update. Washington, DC, U.S. Bureau of the Census, www.census.gov, ((301) 457-4100). Biweekly.
A biweekly newsletter with timely information on recently released and key upcoming data products.

Congressional District Atlas, 109th Congress of the U.S. Washington, DC, U.S. Bureau of the Census, www.census.gov, ((301) 457-4100).
Presents maps showing boundaries of the congressional districts for the 109th Congress and includes maps for the District of Columbia, Puerto Rico, and the outlying areas.

Congressional Districts of the 109th Congress. Washington, DC, Bureau of the Census, www.census.gov, ((301) 457-4100), 1993-1995.
Based on 2000 data, this series of 51 state (and District of Columbia) reports, presents selected statistics for congressional districts of the 109th Congress. Each report includes district boundary maps. Data are also available on microfiche, computer tape, and CD-ROM.

County and City Data Book. (A Statistical Abstract Supplement). Washington, DC, U.S. Bureau of the Census, www.census.gov, ((301) 457-4100), issued every five years.
Covers U.S. regions, divisions, states, counties, incorporated cities of 25,000 or more, and places of 2,500 or more. Brings together a variety of social and economic data from Census Bureau and other sources. Subject coverage is broadest for the largest areas. The publications presents 220 data items for counties and larger areas, 194 items for cities of 25,000 or more, and 33 items for places of 2,500 or more. Available also on diskettes, magnetic tapes, and CD-ROM.

County Business Patterns. Washington, DC, U.S. Bureau of the Census, www.census.gov, ((301) 457-4100), 1946-. (Annual).
Data are presented on employment, number and employment size of reporting units, and taxable payrolls by industry groups for private nonfarm activities. Annual edition includes a separate paper bound report for each state, District of Columbia, and Puerto Rico and Outlying Areas. Also available on diskette, computer tape, and CD-ROM.

Digest of Education Statistics. Washington, DC, National Center for Education Statistics (NCES), ((877) 433-7827), nces.ed.gov, 1962-. (Annual).
Provides an abstract of statistical information covering the entire field of American education from prekindergarten through graduate school. Listed are figures pertaining to such topics as schools, enrollments, teachers, graduates, attainment, and expenditures. A companion volume published annually, *Projections of Education Statistics*, shows trends for the past 10 years and projects data for the next 10 years. A related publication, *The Condition of Education*, provides an overview of trends and current issues.

Economic Indicators. Washington, DC, U.S. President's Council of Economic Advisors, ((202) 456-1414), www.whitehouse.gov/cea, 1948-. (Monthly).
Available from April 1995 forward, this monthly compilation is prepared for the Joint Economic Committee by the Council of Economic Advisors and provides economic information on prices, wages, production, business activity, purchasing power, credit, money and Federal finance.

Economic Report of the President. Washington, DC, Executive Office of the President, ((202) 456-1414), www.whitehouse.gov/government/eop.html, 1947-. (Annual).
This publication includes the economic report of the President to Congress, the annual report of the Council of Economic Advisors and a series of statistical tables pertaining to national income, employment, productivity, government finances, international trade and finance, agriculture, and prices. Statistics are both current and retrospective.

EIA Publications Database. Washington, DC, Energy Information Administration, ((202) 586-8800), www.eia.doe.gov, 1980-. (Annual).
Presented is a guide to the data contained in publications of the Energy Information Administration of the U.S. Department of Energy. EIA publishes statistical information on actual and projected energy resource reserves, production, consumption, supply and demand, prices, and related economic information.

Factfinder for the Nation. Washington, DC, U.S. Bureau of the Census, www.census.gov, ((301) 457-4100), 1976-. (Irregular).
Originally published as a single volume, this publication now appears on an irregular basis as a series of brief, topical brochures which are sometimes revised and updated. Some of the subjects included in the series are statistics on minorities, agriculture, foreign trade, manufactures, and transportation. (Other brochures cover topics such as the history and organization of the Census Bureau). Computer tape availability is generally noted. For statistics users, one of the most important issues is the periodic *Reference Sources*, last published in 1988. It lists guides, directories, catalogs, and indexes to Census Bureau and related statistics. Selected reprints of the *Factfinders* are included as an appendix to the *Census Catalog and Guide*.

Global Population Profile. Washington, DC, U.S. Bureau of the Census, www.census.gov, ((301) 457-4100), 2002.
This report is the latest published compendium and analysis of data on population, fertility, mortality, contraceptive use and related demographic topics by the U.S. Census Bureau.

Guide to Foreign Trade Statistics. Washington, DC, U.S. Bureau of the Census, ((301) 457-3041), periodic.
This is a guide to the published and unpublished sources of foreign trade statistics prepared by the Bureau of the Census; it describes the content and arrangement of the data and tells where the statistics can be found. It lists the titles of the published reports and illustrates the tables included in them. Unpublished tabulations are also listed and the statistics in these are illustrated. The book also describes the coverage of the import and export statistics program, and discusses the methodology of the data, such as the procedure for estimating low-valued shipments. Special services available from the Census Bureau for those wishing to obtain additional statistics are also described.

Historical Statistics of the United States, Colonial Times to 1970. Washington, DC, U.S. Bureau of the Census, www.census.gov, ((301) 457-4100), 1976.
This periodically-revised supplement to the *Statistical Abstract of the United States* includes more than 12,500 statistical time series, largely annual, on American social and economic development covering the period 1610 to 1970. Definitions of terms and descriptive text are provided, as well as source notes guiding the reader to original published sources for further reference and additional data. Indexed by subject. Also available on CD-ROM.

International Data Base (IDB). Washington, DC, U.S. Bureau of the Census, www.census.gov, ((301) 457-4100).
A computerized data bank containing statistical tables of demographic and socio-economic data for 227 countries and areas of the world. The IDB was created in the Census Bureau's International Programs Center in response to the information requirements of IPC staff to meet the needs of organizations that sponsor IPC's research efforts. The IDB provides quick access to specialized information, with emphasis on demographic measures, for individual countries or selected groups of countries. Access IDB on the web at www.census.gov/ipc/www/idbnew.html.

Monthly Product Announcement. Washington, DC, U.S. Bureau of the Census, www.census.gov, ((301) 457-4100). (Monthly).
A free listing of all Census Bureau products becoming available each month with ordering information and descriptive details for data files, microfiche, printed maps, publications, and selected abstracts. Supplements the annual *Census Catalog and Guide*. This report is available on the Internet and by free e-mail subscription.

Population Profile of the United States. Washington, DC, Bureau of the Census, www.census.gov, ((301) 457-4100), Biennial.

Biennial report that contains current information on a wide range of topics including national and state population trends and projections; geographical mobility; school enrollment; educational attainment; postsecondary school finances; households and families; marital status and living arrangements; fertility; child care arrangements; child support; disability; program participation; health insurance; labor force and occupation; money, income poverty; and sections on the Black, Hispanic, Asian and Pacific Islander, American Indian, Eskimo and Aleut, and elderly populations.

Quarterly Financial Report for Manufacturing, Mining and Trade Corporations. Washington, DC, U.S. Bureau of the Census, www.census.gov, ((301) 457-4100), 1947-. (Quarterly).

The purpose of this publication is to present aggregate statistics on the financial results and position of United States corporations classified by both industry and asset size. Data are presented in financial statement and balance sheet form. Also available on diskette and online.

State and Metropolitan Area Data Book. 5th ed. Washington, DC, U.S. Bureau of the Census, www.census.gov, ((301) 457-4100), 1998.

Similar in presentation to the *County and City Data Book*, this volume covers the states, SMSA's and their component counties with both current and historical data. Available online in pdf format.

Statistical Abstract of the United States 2008. Washington, DC, U.S. Bureau of the Census, www.census.gov, ((301) 457-4100), 1878-. (Annual).

Provides tables and graphs of statistics on the social, political, and economic conditions of the United States. Each section has an introductory text. Each table and graph has a source note. Appendix 1 includes guides to sources of statistics, State statistical abstracts, and foreign statistical abstracts. Also contains over 1,000 additional charts and tables on every facet of American activity. Charts are arranged by variables such as age, state, and geographic area.

Statistical Briefs. Washington, DC, U.S. Bureau of the Census, www.census.gov, ((301) 457-4100), 1992, periodic.

Includes succinct reports issued occasionally and providing timely data on specific issues of public policy. Presented in narrative style with graphs, the reports summarize data from demographic surveys of the U.S. population.

Census Briefs. Washington, DC, U.S. Bureau of the Census, www.census.gov, ((301) 457-4100), periodic.

Short documents providing findings from Census 2000, current demographic surveys, and the 1997 Economic Census. They contain colorful charts to illustrate major points.

USA Counties. Washington, DC, U.S. Bureau of the Census, www.census.gov, ((301) 457-4100), database.

Features over 5,700 data items for the United States, States and counties from a variety of sources. Files include data published for 2004 estimates and many items from the 2000 Census of Population and Housing, the 1990 census, the 1980 census and the 2002, 1997, 1992, 1987, 1982 and 1977 economic censuses.

U.S. Merchandise Trade: Selected Highlights. Washington, DC, U.S. Bureau of the Census, www.census.gov, ((301) 457-4100). (Monthly).

Presents data on domestic and foreign exports, general imports, and imports for consumption. The report also includes data on U.S. customs districts and method of transportation, and world area by country of origin and country of destination.

PUBLICATIONS AND OTHER MATERIALS FROM U.S. GOVERNMENT AGENCIES AND DEPARTMENTS

Note: Approximately 200 Federal statistical publications are available on microfiche from: Congressional Information Service, 4520 East-West Highway, Bethesda, MD, 20814 (800) 638-8380.

Agricultural Outlook. Washington, DC, U.S. Department of Agriculture, Economic Research Service, ((800) 999-6779). (Monthly).

Contains data and analysis on U.S. food and fiber economy. Includes information on commodity supply and demand, prices and marketing, farm income, and world agriculture and trade.

Agricultural Statistics. Washington, DC, U.S. Department of Agriculture, National Agricultural Statistics Service, ((800) 999-6779), 1936-. (Annual).

Brings together the more important series of statistics compiled in this department and others whose work concerns agriculture. Prior to 1936, statistical data appeared in the Statistical Section of the *Yearbook of Agriculture*.

Agriculture Fact Book. Washington, DC, U.S. Department of Agriculture, ((800) 999-6779), www.usda.gov, 1979-. (Annual).

Describes major trends in U.S. agriculture. Includes information on production, operation, marketing, agricultural services, and rural social environment.

Annual Energy Review. Washington, DC, U.S. Energy Information Administration, ((202) 586-8800), 1984-. (Annual).

Provides statistics on U.S. energy supply, production, disposition, and consumption. Ten sections cover energy overview; energy indicators; energy exploration, resources, development and reserves; petroleum; natural gas; wood, waste, solar and geothermal energy; and international energy.

BLS News Releases On-line. Washington, DC, U.S. Bureau of Labor Statistics, ((202) 691-5200), www.bls.gov.

Economic Indicators from BLS are available at the time of their release. The information is available through a commercial contractor by paying only for actual computer time used. The data includes more then 100 releases a year on all the fields in which BLS collects information regularly.

Budget of the United States Government. Washington, DC, Office of Management and Budget, ((202) 395-3080), www.whitehouse.gov/omb, 1923-. (Annual).

Comprehensive details, contained in summary tables, on receipts, expenditures, etc. of the federal government. Accompanying the Budget Message is a detailed account by departments and agencies of proposed budget items, giving previous year's actual figures, present year's estimated, and coming year's proposed amounts.

Current Employment Statistics. Washington, DC, U.S. Bureau of Labor Statistics, ((202) 691-5200), www.bls.gov.

The Current Employment Statistics (CES) survey of payroll records covers over 390,000 businesses on a monthly basis and provide detailed industry data on employment, hours, and earnings of workers on nonfarm payrolls for all 50 States, the District of Columbia, Puerto Rico, the Virgin Islands, and over 270 metropolitan areas.

Farm Balance Sheet Data. Washington, DC, U.S. Department of Agriculture, Economic Research Service, ((800) 999-6779), www.ers.usda.gov, 1945-. (Annual).

Estimates of farm business balance sheets are presented for the United States and individual States. The balance sheet includes component accounts for assets, debt, and equity, where equity equals assets minus debt, 1960 to the present. The disaggregated balance sheets enable users to assess the status and trends of wealth within the farm sector.

Federal Reserve Bulletin. Washington, DC, Board of Governors of the Federal Reserve System, ((202) 452-3000), www.federalreserve.gov, 1915-. (Quarterly).

Articles on economic topics and news about the Federal Reserve System are included along with both national and international financial and business statistics.

Foreign Agricultural Trade of the United States (FATUS). Washington, DC, U.S. Department of Agriculture, Economic Research Service, ((800) 999-6779), www.ers.usda.gov, 1962-. (Updated periodically).

Contains tables showing value and quantity of agricultural commodities imported and exported, with annual supplements on trade by commodities and trade by countries.

Foreign Direct Investment in the United States. Washington, DC, U.S. Department of Commerce, Bureau of Economic Analysis, ((202) 606-9900), www.bea.gov, 1980-. (Annual).

Includes financial and operating data, and direct investment positions and balance of payment data for U.S. businesses which are owned 10 percent or more by a foreign entity.

Health, United States. Atlanta, GA, U.S. National Center for Health Statistics, Centers for Disease Control and Prevention, ((301) 458-4000), www.cdc.gov/nchs, 1976-. (Annual).

Health, United States is an annual report on trends in health statistics. The report consists of two main sections: A chartbook containing text and figures that illustrates major trends in the health of Americans; and a trend tables section that contains 153 detailed data tables. The two main components are supplemented by an executive summary, a highlights section, an extensive appendix and reference section, and an index.

Monthly Energy Review. Washington, DC, U.S. Energy Information Administration, ((202) 586-8800), www.eia.doe.gov, 1975-. (Monthly).

Current data for production, consumption, stocks, imports, exports, and prices for the major energy commodities in the U.S. Annual data is published in the *Annual Energy Review*. Data from *Monthly Energy Review* can also be obtained from ePUB.

Monthly Labor Review. Washington, DC, U.S. Bureau of Labor Statistics, ((202) 691-5200), www.bls.gov, 1915-. (Monthly).

Established in 1915, *Monthly Labor Review* is the principal journal of fact, analysis, and research from the Bureau of Labor Statistics, an agency within the U.S. Department of Labor. Each month, economists, statisticians, and experts from the Bureau join with private sector professionals and State and local government specialists to provide a wealth of research in a wide variety of fields - the labor force, the economy, employment, inflation, productivity, occupational injuries and illnesses, wages, prices, and many more.

National Transportation Statistics. Washington, DC, U.S. Department of Transportation, ((202) 366-4000), www.dot.gov, 1969-. (Annual).

Selected transportation statistics from government and private sources. Includes cost, inventory, and performance data for cargo and passenger operations for major transportation modes.

Producer Price Indexes. Washington, DC, U.S. Bureau of Labor Statistics, ((202) 691-5200), www.bls.gov, 1978-. (Monthly).

Covers producer price movements in both textual and tabular format with technical notes. Annual supplement contains monthly data for the calendar year, annual averages, and information on weights and changes in the sample. Available on computer tape. Also available online from Reuters Information Services, Canada, Ltd., and The WEFA Group.

Science Indicators. Arlington, VA, National Science Board, National Science Foundation, ((703) 292-

5111), search.nsf.gov, 1972-. (Biennial).

Data are presented on international research and development, resources for research and development, resources for basic research, industrial research and development and innovation, science and engineering personnel, and public attitudes toward science and technology. A combination of text, tables, and graphs is used.

Social Security Bulletin. Washington, DC, U.S. Social Security Administration, ((202) 358-6274), www.ssa.gov, 1938-. (Monthly).

Provides current data on social security program operations. Also contains data on recipients and payments under public assistance programs; unemployment insurance; and railroad, civil service, and veterans programs. An annual statistical supplement is also published.

Sourcebook of Criminal Justice Statistics. Rockville, MD, National Criminal Justice Reference Service (NCJRS), ((800) 851-3420), www.ncjrs.org, 1973-. (Annual).

This work compiles statistical information from all levels of government, public and private agencies, academic institutions, research organizations, and public opinion polling firms. It is divided into six sections: characteristics of the criminal justice system, public attitudes toward crime, nature and distribution of known offenses, characteristics and distribution of persons arrested, judicial processing of defendants, and persons under correctional supervision. Information is generally provided at the national or state level, with some information for large cities. Sources are listed at the end of each table, and an annotated list of references is also provided. Indexed.

State and Local Personal Income. Washington, DC, U.S. Bureau of Economic Analysis, ((202) 606-9900), www.bea.gov, (Quarterly and annual updates).

Quarterly and annual estimates of state and local area personal income, including news releases and interactive tables.

Statistics of Communications Common Carriers Washington, DC, Federal Communications Commission, ((202) 632-7000), www.fcc.gov, 1939-. (Annual).

Each year since 1939, the FCC has published the Statistics of Communications Common Carriers, a reference work widely used by academics, consultants, and other researchers in the field of telecommunications. This report includes a wealth of data on telecommunications costs, revenues, prices, and usage.

Statistics of Income (SOI) Bulletin. Washington, DC, U.S. Internal Revenue Service, ((800) 829-1040), www.irs.gov, 1916-. (Quarterly).

Gives summary tabulations on financial information obtained from the various tax returns. Individual reports have been issued for each type of return beginning with data from 1954. For 1953 and prior years, the information was released in two parts: Part 1 for individuals, and Part 2 for Corporations, with special studies for selected years included in Part 1.

Survey of Current Business. Washington, DC, U.S. Bureau of Economic Analysis, ((202) 606-9900), www.bea.gov, 1921-. (Monthly).

The major reporting publication for business statistics, including indexes for income payments, industrial production, commodity prices, statistics on construction and real estate, domestic trade, employment conditions and wages, finance, foreign trade, transportation and communication, products by kind, etc. Some reports on the business situation and conditions in specific industries are included.

Treasury Bulletin. Washington, DC, U.S. Department of the Treasury, ((202) 622-2000), www.treas.gov, 1939-. (Monthly).

This official organ of the Treasury Department consists entirely of statistical tables and charts on all phases of public finance. Major categories of tables and charts include: federal fiscal operations; federal obligations; account of the U.S. Treasury; monetary statistics; federal debt; public debt operations; U.S. Savings Bonds; U.S. Savings Notes; ownership of federal securities; Treasury survey of ownership; market quotations on federal securities; average yields of long term bonds; exchange stabilization fund; international financial statistics; capital movements; financial operations of government agencies and funds.

Uniform Crime Reports. Washington, DC, Federal Bureau of Investigation, ((202) 324-3000), www.fbi.gov, 1930-. (Annual).

Data for this publication are received by the FBI from over 15,000 law enforcement agencies that participate in the Uniform Crime Reporting Program. Information is provided for eight offenses: murder and nonnegligent manslaughter, aggravated assault, forcible rape, robbery, burglary, larceny-theft, motor vehicle theft, and arson. National, state, county, metropolitan area, and selected city data are provided. Not indexed.

U.S. Global Trade Outlook, 1995-2000 Washington, DC, U.S. Department of Commerce, International Trade Administration, ((202) 482-2185), www.first-gov.gov.

This reference replaces the *U.S. Industrial Outlook* and emphasizes the importance of foreign markets to U.S. businesses. It is also designed to focus attention on a longer trade horizon. Also available on CD-ROM as part of the National Trade Data Bank.

Vital Statistics of the United States (VSUS). Atlanta, GA, U.S. National Center for Health Statistics, Centers for Disease Control and Prevention, ((301) 458-4000), www.cdc.gov/nchs, 1937-. (Annual).

Covers matters of life, health and welfare. Reports on birth and death registrations, causes of death, incidence of specified diseases; marriage and divorce, etc. In three volumes: Volume 1, Natality; Volume 2, Mortality; Volume 3, Marriage and Divorce. Supplemented by the *Monthly Vital Statistics Report*.

GUIDES TO MACHINE-READABLE U.S. GOVERNMENT DATA SOURCES

In addition to the print sources described below, statistics users may want to contact the Federal Computer Products Center at the National Technical Information Service (NTIS) in Springfield, VA (703) 605-6000, www.ntis.gov/products/types. The Center currently sells more than 4,500 software packages and data files from over 100 Federal agencies.

National Archive of Criminal Justice Data (NACJD). Washington, DC, Sponsored by the Bureau of Justice Statistics, U.S. Department of Justice and operated by the Inter-University Consortium for Political and Social Research, ((800) 999-0960), www.icpsr.umich.edu/NACJD.

The National Archive of Criminal Justice Data (NACJD) preserves and distributes computerized crime and justice data from Federal agencies, state agencies, and investigator initiated research projects to users for secondary statistical analysis.

STAT-USA/Internet. Washington, DC, U.S. Department of Commerce, ((202) 482-1986), www.stat-usa.gov.

Online service for business and economic information produced by the federal government. It gathers the most crucial and timely business and economic information from over 50 federal agencies and distributes it from a central source. This World Wide Web site also provides quick and easy access to thousands of files, including trade statistics, overseas contacts, market research reports, daily economic releases, procurement information.

INTERNATIONAL SOURCES

GENERAL INTERNATIONAL PUBLICATIONS

Africa South of the Sahara 2008. New York, Routledge, ((212) 216-7800), http://www.routledge.com, 2007.

Over 1,400 pages of economic and demographic statistics, wide-ranging directory material and authoritative articles; contributions from over 50 leading experts on African affairs; and incisive analysis of the latest available information.

African Development Indicators. Washington, DC, The World Bank Group, ((800) 645-7247), www.worldbank.org, 2005.

Drawn from the World Bank Africa Database, this publication provides the most detailed collection of development data on Africa in one volume. It presents data from 53 African countries and 5 regional country groups, arranged in separate tables or matrices for more than 500 indicators of development. This volume provides data from 1980-2003 with a wealth of Indicators, grouped into 17 chapters: background data; national accounts; prices and exchange rates; money and banking; external sector; external debt and related flows; government finance; agriculture; power, communications, and transportation; doing business; labor force and employment; aid flows; social indicators; environmental indicators; HIPC debt initiative; Household Welfare Indicators and public enterprises.

Agriculture: Statistical Yearbook 1992-2001.) Newport, South Wales, EU Statistics UK, (+44) 1633 652699, www.eustatistics.gov.uk, 2003.

A summary of the most important information from Eurostat's publications on agriculture, forestry and fisheries, including: area and crop production, animal production, structure of agricultural holdings, prices and price indices, agricultural accounts, forestry, and fisheries.

Annual Abstract of Statistics. Norwich, United Kingdom, Her Majesty's Stationary Office (HMSO). (Annual).

This key statistics publication covers a wide range of topics for the whole United Kingdom. Among these are climate, social conditions, labor, production, balance of payments, etc. An index of sources and a subject index are included.

Annual Reports of the World's Central Banks. Alexandria, VA, Chadwyck-Healey Inc., ((800) 752-0515).

From the comprehensive collection in the Joint Library of the International Monetary Fund and the World Bank, financial, economic and statistical profiles of 128 countries available as a complete collection, by region and by country. Available on microfiche with MARC cataloguing and annual updates. Each report contains detailed statistical tables and graphs.

Annual Statistical Bulletin. Vienna, Organization of the Petroleum Exporting Countries (OPEC), ((+43) 1 21112), www.opec.org, 1966-. (Annual).

The Annual Statistical Bulletin (ASB) contains nearly 150 pages of tables, charts and graphs detailing the world's oil and gas reserves, crude oil and product output, exports, refining, tankers, plus economic and other data.

Balance of Payments Statistics Yearbook. Washington, DC, International Monetary Fund, ((202) 623-7000), www.imf.org, 1949-. (Annual).

Balance of payment statistics for over 140 countries are presented. Each edition covers the eight or nine most recent periods available. Analytical tables and commentaries on significant developments are included. Annual issue contains data for standard components and their aggregates. Monthly booklets are published to update the aggregated statements, and a supplement presenting series topically, rather than by country is also available. Available on magnetic tape. Data also available online from The WEFA Group.

Basic Petroleum Data Book, Washington, DC, American Petroleum Institute, ((202) 682-8000), www.api.org. (Biannual).

This compendium provides domestic and world statistical background information. Included are data on energy, reserves, exploration and drilling, production, finances, prices, demand, refining, imports, exports, offshore transportation, natural gas and the Organization of Petroleum Exporting Countries.

Bibliography on Income and Wealth. Ottawa, International Association for Research in Income and Wealth, ((613) 233-8891), www.iariw.org. (Vol. 1--, 1937/47).

The eighth volume of this annotated bibliography covers the four-year period 1957 to 1960 inclusive. This volume, like its predecessors, is the cooperative effort of national income scholars, from nearly forty countries and from numerous international organizations. The general subject covered is the measurement of income and wealth of nations, including distribution of income, labor force, and economic analysis related to income or wealth. This is an excellent source for locating data, both factual and theoretical, on countries outside of the United States. Still a useful source work. The Association's quarterly publication, *The Review of Income and Wealth*, provides a current treatment of the subject.

Judith Blake and Jerry J. Donovan. *Western European Censuses, 1960, An English Language Guide*. University of California, Institute of International Studies, Berkeley, 1971. (Reprinted by Greenwood Press, Westport, CT, 1976).

An annotated guide to Western European Censuses of Population. Entries are both in English and in the language of original publication for the most widely spoken language of publication. Includes detailed annotations, glossaries of technical terms, comparative analyses of concepts common to more than one country, and descriptive titles for statistical tables in census reports.

Bulletin of International Statistical Institute. Voorburg, The Netherlands, International Statistical Institute, ((+31) 70-3375737), www.cbs.nl/isi. (Biennial).

Statistics on economics, housing, building, public utilities, population, and transportation, as well as cultural, sports, and vital statistics are reported from major European cities. Non-European cities in Africa, India, Korea, Japan, Israel, Canada and South America are also represented.

By the Numbers. Farmington Hills, MI, Gale, ((248) 699-4253), www.gale.com, 1998.

Provides a one-step source for in-depth statistics and rankings in a series of industry specific volumes. Each title is divided into chapters that provide context to the tables, charts, and textual materials presented. The four volumes in this series include: Volume 1: Electronic and Online Publishing; Volume 2: Emerging Industries; Volume 3: Nonprofits; and Volume 4: Publishing.

Central and South-Eastern Europe 2008. New York, Routledge, ((212) 216-7800), http://www.routledge.com, 2007.

Offers detailed analyses by the world's foremost authorities; an accurate and impartial view of the region and individual chapters on each country containing in-depth articles on geography, history and economy, as well as economic and demographic statistics and contact details of key individuals.

Asian Marketing Data and Statistics 2007/2008. Chicago, Euromonitor International, ((312) 922-1115), www.euromonitor.com, 2007.

Asian Marketing Data & Statistics allows users to compile detailed demographic and economic profiles of 45 Asian countries, making it an extremely valuable reference and powerful marketing tool.

International Marketing Data and Statistics 2008. Chicago, Euromonitor International, ((312) 922-1115), www.euromonitor.com, 2007.

Presents hard-to-find demographic, economic and lifestyle data for 161 non-European countries including the USA, Asia-Pacific and Latin America.

Consumer Asia 2008. Chicago, Euromonitor, ((312) 922-1115), www.euromonitor.com, 2007.

This title presents statistical and analytical surveys of diverse Asian consumer markets, concentrating on Hong Kong, Taiwan, Singapore, South Korea, Indonesia, and Malaysia, with assessments and overviews of the region as a whole.

Consumer China 2008. Chicago, Euromonitor, ((312) 922-1115), www.euromonitor.com, 2007.

Provides comprehensive statistical coverage of China's consumer markets, together with a wealth of background data on business, economic and social conditions.

Consumer Eastern Europe 2007-2008. Chicago, Euromonitor, ((312) 922-1115), www.euromonitor.com, 2007.

This reference provides valuable data on the market for consumer goods and services in Eastern European countries. Subject chapters include demography, economic indicators, standard of living, household characteristics, advertising and media access, regional distribution, consumer expenditure, market demand, service industries, consumer markets, and more.

Consumer Western Europe 2007-2008. Chicago, Euromonitor, ((312) 922-1115), www.euromonitor.com, 2007.

This handbook covers over 330 consumer goods markets across 17 European countries. Topics covered for each country include, among others, productive capacity, import and export levels, annual consumption, brand share and manufacturers. General data are provided for basic market indicators.

Consumer International 2007-2008. Chicago, Euromonitor, ((312) 922-1115), www.euromonitor.com, 2007.

This updated edition provides you with valuable insight into 27 non-European consumer markets, with volume and value market size data for hundreds of consumer products, such as clothing and footwear, OTC healthcare, cosmetics and toiletries, disposable paper products, consumer electronics. Presented in fully comparable form, this volume allows readers to analyze market data and trends across countries, products and over six years (1999-2005). To add further value to the data and put market data in context, Consumer International provides readers with key socio-economic and lifestyle statistics for all countries covered.

Consumer Latin America 2008. Chicago, Euromonitor, ((312) 922-1115), www.euromonitor.com, 2007.

Consumer Latin America provides essential information for companies looking to sell products or services in the region. Providing volume and value statistics for over 330 product sectors (1999-2004) in 6 Latin American countries.

Consumer Middle East 2006. Chicago, Euromonitor, ((312) 922-1115), www.euromonitor.com, 2006.

An essential resource of clearly presented, comparable consumer market size data. It provides volume and value statistics for over 330 product sectors (1999-2004) in 10 countries of the Middle East.

Countries of the World and Their Leaders Yearbook. Farmington Hills, MI, Gale, ((248) 699-4253), www.gale.com, 19-. (Annual).

Covering nearly 200 countries, this yearbook is filled with reports from the U.S. Department of State. Entries typically cover politicians, geography, defense, agriculture and trade. Includes information on passport applications, regulations and duties, international health and disease, national holidays and more.

Country by Country New York, Economist Intelligence Unit, ((212) 554-0600), www.eiu.com. (Annual).

The 2008 edition of this annual report, formerly known as World Outlook,, provides clear and simple comparisons of one country with another, including key variables such as GDP growth, inflation, exchange rates and balance of payments.

Country Profiles. New York, Economist Intelligence Unit, ((212) 554-0600), www.eiu.com. (Annual).

Country Profiles outline a country's economic and political status and background. They put an annual perspective on the long-term political and social issues affecting each country, providing a complete introduction to all international markets. Reports on more than 200 countries present figures and analysis in an historical context; they map out the infrastructure and the major industrial sectors of the economy; and they also stand back from the process of change and evaluate longer-term developments. Revised annually, they organize data from a diverse range of national and international sources into a compact, coherent and standard format. The statistical tables give a five-year run of data on issues such as manufacturing, fiscal policy and unemployment which, together with the text, provide a detailed insight into the structure and functioning of each country.

Country Reports. New York, Economist Intelligence Unit, ((212) 554-0600), www.eiu.com. Quarterly.

Country Reports cover more than 200 countries producing consolidated analysis every three months in the form of main reports and for a wide range of key countries, and monthly updates which are available via electronic subscription. Coverage includes the political scene, economic policy, the economy, sectoral trends, and foreign trade and payments. An outlook section give 12-24 month forecasts, dissecting the issues currently affecting the economy and discussing what will happen next year. Clearly presented statistical tables and charts complement the expert commentary. Country Reports are researched by a global network of correspondents and editing by experienced economists and country analysts.

Current National Statistical Compendiums. Bethesda, MD, Congressional Information Service, ((800) 638-8380), 1970-. (Annual).

A microfiche collection of national statistical compendiums from more than 100 countries. Coverage begins in 1970 and is updated annually. Generally published in English or another western language, each compendium presents a wide range of social, economic, and demographic data.

The Developing Economies. Tokyo, Institute of Developing Economies (IDE), www.ide.go.jp/English. (Quarterly).

An international and interdisciplinary forum for studies on social sciences relating to the developing countries. Provides an opportunity for discussions and exchanges across a wide spectrum of scholarly opinions to promote empirical and comparative studies on the problems confronted by developing countries.

Direction of Trade Statistics Yearbook 2005. Washington, DC, International Monetary Fund, ((202) 623-7000), www.imf.org, 1958/62-. (Annual).

This publication presents statistics for value of trade (separated into exports and imports) between member countries and other countries, providing full year data for a number of years, and summary tables for various areas of the world and world aggregates. Also available on magnetic tape. For more information, contact Publications Section, IMF, Washington, DC 20431. Online database available from Reuters Information Services (Canada), Ltd. and Global Insight.

Eastern Europe, Russia and Central Asia 2008. New York, Routledge, ((212) 216-7800), http://www.routledge.com, 2007.
Offers detailed analyses by the world's foremost authorities; an accurate and impartial view of the region; and individual chapters on each country containing in-depth articles on geography, history and economy, as well as economic and demographic statistics and contact details of key individuals.

The Economist Book of Vital World Statistics. London, Economist Books, (Available in U.S. ((800) 456-6086), 1990.
Data is presented on 110 topics. Information is drawn from the Economist Intelligence Unit and treats some 146 countries on such subjects as population, land use, trade, labor force, consumer goods, and demographic information.

eStat Database. New York, NY ((800) 405-0844), www.emarketer.com.
eMarketer's research team monitors more than 1,700 sources daily, culling relevant e-business information and Internet statistics from research firms, consultancies and government reports around the world, making the eStat Database the most complete, up-to-the-minute source for Internet and e-business statistics.

The Europa World Year Book 2007. New York, Routledge, ((212) 216-7800), http://www.routledge.com, 2007.
This reference work on the political and economic life of countries throughout the world includes a statistical survey for each country. Published in two volumes. Topics covered include: area and population, agriculture, forestry, mining industry, finance, external trade, tourism, transport, communications media, and education.

European Marketing Data And Statistics 2008. Chicago, Euromonitor International, ((312) 922-1115), www.euromonitor.com, 2007.
Now in its 43rd edition, this highly acclaimed book presents hard-to-find demographic, economic and lifestyle data for 44 European countries.

EU Energy and Transport in Figures - Statistical Pocketbook 2005. Washington, DC, Transportation Research Board of the National Academies, ((202) 334-2934), www.trb.org.
The European Union (EU) has released the latest issue of its annual overview of energy and transport statistics for the EU and its member states. The report covers all modes of transportation and provides general statistics, as well as measurements on the performance of freight and passenger transport and a summary of infrastructure assets. The full report is available, as well as individual reports on general data, energy, and transport.

Far East and Australasia 2008. New York, Routledge, ((212) 216-7800), http://www.routledge.com, 2007.
Similar to other area publications by Europa, this volume reports on 30 countries and territories with an individual chapter devoted to each. Chapters include a statistical survey, as well as articles on such topics as geography, religion and economy. Some statistical data are also presented in the general survey section.

Michael C. Fleming and Joseph G. Nellis. *Instat: International Statistics Sources: Subject Guide to Sources of International Comparative Statistics*. New York, Routledge, ((212) 216-7800), www.routledge.com, 1994.
This source brings together nearly 400 published sources of statistical data produced by private and public entities. Editions indexed are those published from 1991 to mid-1994. *Instat* is divided into 46 main subject sections. Each entry notes territorial coverage.

Gale Country and World Rankings Reporter, 2nd ed. Farmington Hills, MI, Gale, ((248) 699-4253), www.gale.com, 1997.
More than 235 countries are represented and approximately 3,000 statistical charts and tables from a diverse range of sources, including the United Nations and national government publications. Users can easily compare the world's physical, social, business, cultural, economic, demographic, governmental, leisure, and other statistics.

Global Development Finance 2007, Washington, DC, The World Bank Group, ((800) 645-7247), www.worldbank.org, 2007.
This replaces the World Debt Tables. The two-volume publication includes a wealth of debt-related data from over 150 countries. CD-ROM and diskette versions are also available.

Government Finance Statistics Yearbook 2008. Washington, DC, International Monetary Fund, ((202) 623-7000), www.imf.org, 1977-. (Annual).
Data on revenues, grants, expenditures, leadings minus repayments, and financing are presented for more than 100 countries. For each country, statistical tables, institutional tables, and information sources are presented. World tables are also included. Also available in machine-readable form from Publications Section, IMF, Washington, DC 20431; available online from Global Insight.

Guide to Official Statistics. No. 6. London, Office for National Statistics, ((+44) (0) 845 601 3034), www.statistics.gov.uk, 2000.
Guide to Official Statistics is a comprehensive directory of all statistical censuses, surveys, administrative systems, publications and other services produced by government and a range of other organizations in the United Kingdom.

Handbook of International Economic Statistics. Washington, DC, Central Intelligence Agency, ((703) 482-0623), www.cia.gov, 1998.
Provides basic statistics for comparing worldwide economic performance. Topics include environmental issues, labor force and labor costs, energy, agriculture, minerals and metals, chemicals and manufactured goods, and foreign trade and aid. A subject index and conversion factors are provided.

Index to International Statistics. Bethesda, MD, Congressional Information Service, ((800) 638-8380), 1983-1999.
A guide to statistics from more than 90 international governmental organizations (IGOs) including various United Nations bodies. Abstracts describe publications and data, and entries are extensively indexed.

International Energy Annual 2005. Washington, DC, U.S. Energy Information Administration, ((202) 586-8800), www.eia.doe.gov, 1980-. (Annual).
This volume presents an overview of key international energy trends for production, consumption, imports, and exports of primary energy commodities in over 220 countries, dependencies, and areas of special sovereignty. Also included are population and gross domestic product data, as well as prices for crude oil and petroleum products in selected countries.

International Financial Statistics. Washington, DC, International Monetary Fund, ((202) 623-7000), www.imf.org, 1948-. (Monthly).
A journal which provides a continuing statistical record of the financial status of member nations. All indicators are listed in terms on the value of the United States dollar. Tables covering such factors as exchange rates, gold prices and production, world trade, and price levels are regularly featured. In addition, *International Financial Statistics; Supplement on Countries of the Former Soviet Union* is also available.

International Marketing Data and Statistics 2008. Chicago, Euromonitor, ((312) 922 1115), www.euromonitor.com, 2007.
A marketing handbook presenting hard-to-find demographic, economic and lifestyle data for 161 non-European countries including the USA, Asia-Pacific and Latin America. Deals with such topics as population, employment, labor costs, energy, ownership and consumption, tourism, and mass media. Includes an index and notes on sources. Also available are *European Marketing Data and Statistics* and *World Marketing Data and Statistics*.

George Kurian, ed. *Global Data Locator*. Lanham, MD, Bernan Press, ((800) 274-4888), www.bernan.com, 1997.
An update to the *Sourcebook of Global Statistics*, this guidebook contains the table of contents pages for 240 statistical publications, as well as a subject index to these tables. In addition, information is available on online databases, descriptions of major international and intergovernmental organizations, and a listing of statistical sources accessible via the Internet.

Middle East and North Africa 2008. New York, Routledge, ((212) 216-7800), http://www.routledge.com, 2007. 1948-. (Annual).
Countries are covered individually in chapters that include a statistical survey, as well as articles on such topics as geography, religion, and economy. Some statistical data are also presented in the general survey section.

B.R. Mitchell, ed. *International Historical Statistics Europe 1750-1988*. New York, Stockton Press, ((800) 221-2123), 1992.
This volume provides data, in easy-to-use tables, for all principal economic and social activity for European countries. The user will find statistics relating to agriculture, industry, trade, finance, labor, transportation, communication and education. *Volume Two: The Americas 1750-1988* and *Volume Three: Africa, Asia & Oceana 1750-1988* are also available.

David Mort, ed. *Sources of Non-Official UK Statistics*. 6th edition. Farnborough, England, Gower Publishing Company, ((802) 862-0095) in U.S., www.gowerpub.com, 2006.
Sources of Non-Official UK Statistics gives details of nearly 1000 publications and services (including electronic publications) produced by trade associations, professional bodies, banks, consultants, employers' federations, forecasting organizations and others, together with statistics appearing in trade journals and periodicals.

Ruth A. Pagell and Michael Halprin, eds. *International Business Information, How To Find It, How To Use It*. Westport, CT, Oryx Press, ((800) 225-5800), www.greenwood.com, 1997.
All major business environments outside the U.S. are covered in this comprehensive resource, including special coverage of the most recent sources on Eastern Europe, the former Soviet Union, and Asia. A wealth of electronic and print sources for information about companies, industries, markets, and finance.

Population Index. Princeton, NJ, Office of Population Research, Princeton University and the Population Association of America, popindex.princeton.edu, 1986-2000. (Quarterly).
This publication is an annotated bibliography of book and periodical literature on all phases of population problems. Arranged by class with annual cumulated indexes by author and country. Includes special articles and current items. Arrangement is by authors and geographic areas. Also available online from Johns Hopkins University, Center for Communication Programs (410) 659-6300, on POPLINE.

Annemarie Muth, ed. *Statistical Abstract of the World*. Farmington Hills, MI, Gale, ((248) 699-4253), www.gale.com, 1997.
Provides statistical facts on a wide array of subjects from nearly 200 countries. Subjects include labor, employment and occupations, income, expenditure and wealth, population, health and medical care, education, law enforcement, environment, energy, geography, politics and government, and more.

Renewables Information 2008. Paris, France. International Energy Agency, ((33-1) 40 57 66 90), www.iea.org, 2002-. (Annual).
This annual publication of comprehensive information on the use of renewables and waste in the OECD region addresses a need for development of reliable statistics on this energy

form. The report contains analysis of renewables and waste energy supply, electricity production and installed electricity generating capacity in OECD countries.

Retail Trade International 2007. Chicago, Euromonitor International, ((312) 922 1115), www.euromonitor.com, 2007.

This is a comprehensive study of the global retailing industry in which industry experts have analyzed key trends and developments in 52 countries, ranging from the impact of Internet shopping to the use of store and loyalty cards.

Curtis L. Richardson, ed. *Russia and Eurasia Facts and Figures Annual*. Gulf Breeze, Florida, Academic International Press, www.ai-press.com, 1977-. (Annual).

Presents an extensive range of social and economic data on topics such as government, party, armed forces, economy, foreign trade, and transportation. Contains both narrative and tabular information. Former name was *U.S.S.R. Facts and Figures Annual*.

Sources of European Economic and Business Information. Farnborough, England, Gower Publishing Company, ((802) 864-7626), www.gowerpub.com, 1995.

A guide to sources of economic and business data for Western European countries. More than 2,000 entries for statistical bulletins, yearbooks, general publications, directories, special supplements and reports. A title list, subject index, and addresses and telephone numbers of publishing bodies are included.

South America, Central America, and the Caribbean 2008. New York, Routledge, ((212) 216-7800), http://www.routledge.com, 2007.

Similar to other Europa regional guides, this volume provides detailed statistics and directories for major countries of the region.

Statesman's Yearbook 2008: The Politics, Cultures and Economies of the World. London, Macmillan, 1864-. ((212) 726-9200), www.macmillan.com. (Annual).

A primary statistical summary of the countries of the world. Separate sections for the international organizations, British Commonwealth, and the United States of America; other countries arranged alphabetically, with constitution and government (including national flag and anthem), area, population, religion, education, justice, social welfare, finance, defense, agriculture, post and telegraph, planning, transportation, industry, commerce, communications, money, diplomatic representatives, and valuable bibliography for each country (statistical, official, and unofficial publications).

Statistics Canada Catalogue. Ottawa, Statistics Canada, ((800) 267-6677), www.statcan.ca, 2001.

This publication lists and in many cases annotates statistical documents available from the Canadian government. Publications are presented in broad subject categories with a title, subject, and commodity index following. *Historical Statistics of Canada* is also available. An online database of socio-economic data from Statistics Canada programs, CANSIM, is also available.

Vienna Institute, ed. *COMECON Data*. Westport, CT, Greenwood Publishing Group, ((800) 225-5800), www.greenwood.com, 1990.

Provides a variety of economic data on Eastern European countries. Data are derived from more than 50 statistical yearbooks and similar publications.

Western Europe 2008. New York, Routledge, ((212) 216-7800), http://www.routledge.com, 2007.

More than 40 acknowledged experts provide insight into all countries of the region and offer scholarly examinations of the area's political, economic, and social background. Separate chapters for every country provide details of geography, recent history, and the economy.

Gloria Westfall, ed. *Guide to Official Publications of Foreign Countries*. Bethesda, MD, Congressional Information Service, ((800) 638-8380), 1997.

The second edition of this acclaimed guide gives librarians and researchers an authoritative list of major documents published by foreign governments, along with brief descriptions of content, acquisition information, and a title index.

James W. Wilkie, ed. *Statistical Abstract of Latin America (SALA)*. Los Angeles, U.C.L.A. Latin America Center Publications, ((310) 825-4571), www.isop.ucla.edu/lac, 1955-. (Annual).

Statistics are presented primarily in tabular form covering the following topic areas: Main indicators; geographical, social, socioeconomic, and economic data; international statistics; and political data. A subject index and list of sources are provided.

World Agricultural Supply and Demand Estimates. Washington, DC, U.S. Department of Agriculture, Economic Research Service, ((800) 999-6779), www.ers.usda.gov. (Monthly).

Provides the most current USDA information on global supply use balances of the major grains, soybeans and products, cotton and U.S. supply and use of livestock products.

World Bank Atlas. Washington, DC, The World Bank Group, ((800) 645-7247), www.worldbank.org, 1966-. (Annual).

Provides estimates of population, GNP, and average annual growth rates for 184 countries, and territories by continent. Material is presented by a combination of tables and maps.

World Development Indicators 2008. Washington, DC, The World Bank Group, ((800) 645-7247), www.worldbank.org. (Annual).

World Development Indicators 2006 is the World Bank's premier annual compilation of data about development. The 2008 WDI includes more than 800 indicators in over 80 tables organized in 6 sections: World View, People, Environment, Economy, States and Markets, and Global Links. Data are shown for 153 economies with populations of more than 1 million, and table 1.6 presents selected indicators for 56 other economies - small economies with populations between 30,000 and 1 million and smaller economies if they are members of the World Bank.

World Development Report 2007: Equity and Development. Washington, DC, The World Bank Group, ((800) 645-7247), www.worldbank.org, 1978-. (Annual).

Narrative, graphic, and tabular presentations are used to provide a review of world development trends and issues for 126 countries. Beginning with the 1984 edition, a new *Population Data Supplement* is included covering age composition, density and capacity, fertility, status of women, and policy indicators.

World Economic Factbook 2008. Chicago, Euromonitor International, ((312) 922-1115), www.euromonitor.com, 2007.

Provides international statistics on over 200 countries. Covers economic and demographic indicators including area, location, political structure, head of state, governing party, political risk, territorial disputes, currency, principal industries, energy requirements, balance of trade, economic situation, inflation, exchange rate, GDP, exports, imports, consumer expenditure, population, households, and tourism.

World Energy Outlook 2008. Paris, France. International Energy Agency, www.iea.org, 2008.

Presents projections until the year 2030 for supply and demand of oil, gas, coal, renewable energy sources, nuclear power and electricity. It covers the world and 18 major regions. It draws lessons for energy security, trade and investment. It also assesses energy-related carbon dioxide emissions and policies designed to reduce them.

The 2008 World Factbook. Washington, DC, Central Intelligence Agency, ((703) 482-0623), www.cia.gov/cia/publications/factbook, 1972-. (Annual).

Brief description of each country of the world. Includes statistics on the land, nationality, religion, language, literacy, political parties, economy, exports and imports. Available on tape and diskette.

World Military Expenditures and Arms Transfers. Washington, DC, U.S. Arms Control and Disarmament Agency (ACDA), ((800) 581-ACDA), dosfan.lib.uic.edu/acda, 1997.

Projections of world military expenditures, gross national product, central government expenditures, arms transfers, imports and exports. Also includes population by region, organization, and country.

Yearbook of Tourism Statistics 2007. Madrid, World Tourism Organization (WTO), ((+34) 91 567 81 00), www.world-tourism.org, 19-. (Annual).

Presents data on a variety of travel topics including: international tourist arrivals; international tourism receipts and expenditures; international fare payments and receipts. Tabular data on domestic tourism is presented for major countries.

PUBLICATIONS OF THE ORGANISATION FOR ECONOMIC COOPERATION AND DEVELOPMENT (OECD)

OECD was established in 1961 and now has 30 member countries. Countries of the OECD are Australia, Austria, Belgium, Canada, Czech Republic, Denmark, Finland, France, Germany, Greece, Hungary, Iceland, Ireland, Italy, Japan, Korea, Luxembourg, Mexico, Netherlands, New Zealand, Norway, Poland, Portugal, Slovak Republic, Spain, Sweden, Switzerland, Turkey, United Kingdom, and the United States. It is a prolific publisher of statistics as well as research and policy studies. Many OECD statistical publications are available in more than one medium (print, online PDF, fiche, and machine-readable). Several OECD databases are also available online from commercial database vendors (these are noted in the citations). For complete details on OECD statistical publications, consult OECD's annual catalog titled, *OECD Key Publications Catalogue*. OECD's main office is located at: 2, rue Andre-Pascal, F-75775 Paris Cedex 16, France. In the U.S., contact the OECD Publications and Information Center, 2001 L Street, NW, Suite 700, Washington, DC 20036-4095 (202) 785-6323. Visit OECD on the web at www.oecd.org. A selection of some of the more important OECD statistical resources follows.

Coal Information. Paris, Organisation for Economic Cooperation and Development ((202) 785-6323) in the U.S., www.oecd.org, 1983-. (Annual).

This volume is a reference book on current trends in the world coal market. Part I contains an analysis of the 2005 international coal market using IEA statistics that covers prices, demand, trade, supply and production. Part II contains over 300 pages of country-specific statistics on coal in 30 OECD Member countries and 8 OECD and IEA regional aggregates. Part III contains over 50 pages of statistics on coal markets in key non-OECD coal producing and consuming countries.

Education at a Glance 2007: OECD Indicators. Paris, Organisation for Economic Cooperation and Development, ((202) 785-6323), 2007. (Annual).

The 2007 edition of the publication *Education at a Glance* provides a rich, comparable and up-to-date array of indicators on the performance of education systems. The indicators look at who participates in education, operate and at the results achieved. The latter includes indicators on a wide range of outcomes, from comparisons of student's performance in key subject areas to the impact of education on earnings and on adults' chances of employment.

Energy Statistics of OECD Countries. Paris, Organisation for Economic Cooperation and Development, ((202) 785-6323), 1961-. (Annual).

The 2006 edition contains data on energy supply and consumption in original units for coal, oil, gas, electricity, heat, renewables and waste. Historical tables summarize data on production, trade and final consumption. The book also includes definitions of products and flows and explanatory notes on the individual country data. In *Energy Balances of OECD Countries 2003-2004*, the sister volume of this publication, the data are presented as comprehensive energy balances expressed in million tons of oil equivalent. (Bilingual edition: English-French).

Energy Statistics of Non-OECD Countries. Paris, Organisation for Economic Cooperation and Development, ((202) 785-6323). (Annual).
The 2006 edition contains data on energy supply and consumption in original units for coal, oil, gas, electricity, heat, renewables and waste for over 100 non-OECD countries. Historical tables summarise data on production, trade and final consumption. The book includes definition of products and flows and explanatory notes on the individual country data. The companion volume, *Energy Balances of Non-OECD Countries 2003-2004*, contains data on the supply and demand of coal, oil, gas, electricity, heat, combustible renewables and waste in an energy balance format. (Bilingual edition: English-French).

International Direct Investment Statistics Yearbook 1992-2003: 2004 Edition. Paris, Organisation for Economic Cooperation and Development, ((202) 785-6323), 2005.
This Yearbook gathers detailed statistics on international direct investment to and from the OECD area. Comparative tables and charts complement the information included for individual countries by geographical and sectoral breakdowns for direct investment flows and stocks. For some countries this information may go as far back as 1980. The OECD has published international direct investment statistics since 1993.

International Trade by Commodity Statistics. Paris, Organisation for Economic Cooperation, ((202) 785-6323). (Annual).
This paper covers a wide range of international statistics on foreign trade of OECD countries and provides detailed data in value by commodity and by partner country. Each of the first four volumes of International Trade by Commodities contains the tables for seven countries that are published as they become available. The fifth volume includes the OECD main country groupings (OECD-Total, NAFTA, OECD-Asia and Pacific, OECD-Europe, EU-15, etc.). For each country, the tables show both imports and exports over the latest six-year period available by commodity with about one hundred partner countries or country groupings (e.g. NAFTA, etc.).

Labour Force Statistics 1986-2006: 2007 Edition. Paris, Organisation for Economic Cooperation and Development, (202) 785-6323), 1961-. (Annual).
This annual edition provides detailed statistics on population, labor force, employment and unemployment, broken down by gender, as well as unemployment duration, employment status, employment by sector of activity and part-time employment. It also contains participation and unemployment rates by gender and detailed age groups as well as comparative tables for the main components of the labor force. Data are available for each OECD Member country and for OECD-Total, Euro zone and EU15. The time series presented in the publication cover 20 years for most countries.

Main Economic Indicators. Paris, Organisation for Economic Cooperation and Development, ((202) 785-6323), 1965-. (Monthly).
The monthly *Main Economic Indicators* presents comparative statistics that provide an overview of recent international economic developments for OECD countries and selected non-member countries. The indicators cover national accounts, business surveys and consumer opinions, leading indicators, retail sales, production, construction, prices, employment, unemployment, wages, finance, foreign trade and balance of payments.

Monthly Statistics of International Trade. Paris, Organisation for Economic Cooperation and Development ((202) 785-6323). (Monthly).
Provides the most recent trends in trading patterns for OECD countries with the rest of world. Data are broken down by economic groupings, by country and by regions, and include seasonally adjusted series as well as indices. Tables contain statistics for imports and exports over a time period of 10 years.

National Accounts of OECD Countries. Paris, Organisation for Economic Cooperation and Development, ((202) 785-6323), 1966-. (Annual).
A two-volume compendium of statistics on such areas as production, income, and capital transactions for OECD member countries. Data are shown for 23 of the 30 OECD countries for the period from 1991 to 2002 in the paper version and from 1970 onwards in the electronic version, depending on data availability. Available in print, CD-ROM and online from SourceOECD.

OECD Agricultural Databases. 2008 edition on CD-ROM. Paris, Organisation for Economic Cooperation and Development, ((202) 785-6323), 2008.
This CD-ROM includes 4 databases: Agricultural Commodities Outlook Database 1970-2016; Economic Accounts for Agriculture 1995-2003; Fisheries Database 1995-2005; and Agricultural Support Estimates Database 1986-2005.

OECD Economic Outlook. Paris, Organisation for Economic Cooperation and Development, ((202) 785-6323), 1970-. (Biannual).
This edition of the OECD Economic Outlook analyses the major trends that will mark the years 2007 and 2008. It provides in-depth coverage of the main economic policy issues and the policy measures required to foster growth in each member country. Forthcoming developments in major non-OECD economies are also evaluated in detail. Each edition of this Outlook provides a unique tool to keep abreast of world economic developments.

OECD Economic Surveys. Paris, Organisation for Economic Cooperation and Development, ((202) 785-6323), 1953-. (Annual).
Separate annual surveys of economic developments in each of the 30 OECD countries. Coverage includes demand, production, employment, prices and wages, conditions in the money and capital markets, and balance of payments.

OECD Financial Statistics. Paris, Organisation for Economic Cooperation and Development, ((202) 785-6323), 1967-. (Annual).
Financial statistics published by the OECD cover a range of indicators including financial accounts, central government debt instruments, institutional saving and investment, financial statement of banks, external finance, balance of payments, monetary aggregates, interest rates, share prices, and exchange rates.

OECD Health Data 2007: Statistics and Indicators for 30 Countries. 2007.
Offers the most comprehensive source of comparable statistics on health and health systems across OECD countries. Available online and as a CD-ROM.

OECD Main Science and Technology Indicators 2008. Paris, Organisation for Economic Cooperation and Development, ((202) 785-6323), 1984-. (Biannual).
This biannual publication provides a set of indicators that reflect the level and structure of the efforts undertaken by OECD Member countries and nine non-member economies (Argentina, China, Israel, Romania, Russian Federation, Singapore, Slovenia, South Africa, Chinese Taipei) in the field of science and technology. These data include final or provisional results as well as forecasts established by government authorities.

Oil Information 2007. Paris, Organisation for Economic Cooperation and Development, ((202) 785-6323), 1976-. (Annual).
A comprehensive reference book on current developments in oil supply and demand. The first part of this publication contains key data on world production, trade, prices and consumption of major oil product groups, with time series back to the early 1970s. The second part gives a more detailed and comprehensive picture of oil supply, demand, trade, production and consumption by end-user for each OECD country individually and for the OECD regions. Trade data are reported extensively by origin and destination.

Revenue Statistics 1965-2006 - 2007 Edition. Paris, Organisation for Economic Cooperation and Development, ((202) 785-6323), 1965-. (Annual).
Data on government sector receipts, and on taxes in particular, are basic inputs to most structural economic descriptions and economic analyses and are increasingly used in international comparisons. This annual publication gives a conceptual framework to define which government receipts should be regarded as taxes and to classify different types of taxes. It presents a unique set of detailed and internationally comparable tax data in a common format for all OECD countries from 1965 onwards.

PUBLICATIONS OF THE UNITED NATIONS AND AFFILIATED ORGANIZATIONS

The United Nations publishes scores of yearbooks, specialized studies, bulletins, and other compilations of interest to statistics users. The annual *Catalogue of United Nations Publications* (United Nations Publications, Room DC2-0853, New York, NY 10017) provides a comprehensive guide to U.N. publications in print. Microfiche users should consult *United Nations Documentation in Microfiche. UNDOC: Current Index (United Nations Documentation Index)* provides monthly bibliographic coverage of U.N. documentation.

Many of the international statistics published by the United Nations are available in machine readable format. Databases are currently available for the following areas: demographics, energy, external trade, maritime transport, industry, national accounts, and women and youth. Tapes or diskettes of these data files are produced by the United Nations Statistical Office. For more information on the format and prices of these databases please write to: United Nations Publications, 2 United Nations Plaza, Room DC2-853, New York, NY 10017, USA or call (800) 253-9646.

Some U.N. databases are also available online from commercial vendors as noted in the individual citations below. In addition several publications are available online from United Nations Publications at https://unp.un.org.

The following section covers many of the more important U.N. statistical publications.

African Statistical Yearbook 2006. New York, United Nations, Economic Commission for Africa, ((800) 253-9646). (Biennial), 2008.
Published in different volumes and parts covering the following regions: Central Africa and other African countries, East and Southern Africa, North Africa, and West Africa. Data are arranged on a country basis for 52 countries and cover statistics on population and employment, national accounts, agriculture, forestry and fishing, industry, transport and communications, foreign trade, prices, finance, and social statistics.

2007 AIDS Epidemic Update. Geneva, Switzerland, UNAIDS, (+41-22-791-3666), www.unaids.org. 2008.
Reports on the latest developments in the global AIDS epidemic. The 2007 edition provides the most recent estimates of the AIDS epidemic and explores new findings and trends in the epidemic's evolution.

Arab Human Development Report 2008: Towards Freedom in the Arab World. New York, United Nations Development Programme (UNDP) ((800) 253-9649), 2008.
The *Arab Human Development Report Series* aims at building human development in the Arab world. The 2004 Report describes free societ-

ies, in their normative dimension, as fundamental contrasts with present-day Arab countries.

Commodity Atlas. New York, United Nations, United Nations Conference on Trade and Development, ((800) 253-9646), 2004.

This publication presents some basic facts on commodity production and trade in an easily accessible form to governments, industry, the media, and the public at large. Prepared jointly by the United Nations Conference on Trade and Development (UNCTAD) and the Common Fund for Commodities (CFC), this publication is intended to complement the detailed statistical information produced by both organizations and to serve as a useful analytical tool.

Compendium of Social Statistics and Indicators: Toward Achieving the Millennium Development Goals. New York, United Nations, Economic and Social Commission for Western Asia, ((800) 253-9646), 2004.

This bulletin presents social statistics illustrating some of the key socio-economic indicators for countries of Western Asia. The data contains information on education, death rates, maternal health, HIV prevalence, poverty and hunger, employment, literacy rates, mortality and gender. It is a useful resource for researchers and planners studying socio-economic changes in Western Asia. This bilingual publication contains information in English and Arabic.

Compendium of Social Statistics and Indicators: Social Indicators of the Commission of Sustainable Development. New York, United Nations, Economic and Social Commission for Western Asia, ((800) 253-9646), 2008.

This issue of the Compendium reflects on the social development in the countries of Western Asia through tabulation of time series statistics and indicators covering areas such as population, education, household and family, human settlements, health, work and economic activity, income and expenditure, and others. This bilingual publication contains information in English and Arabic.

Compendium of Social Statistics and Indicators: A Special Issue on Youth. New York, United Nations, Economic and Social Commission for Western Asia, ((800) 253-9646), 2006.

This issue of the bulletin is dedicated to youth, exploring issues of education employment and health.

Demographic Yearbook. New York, United Nations, (Available from Bernan (800) 274-4888), www.bernan.com, 1948-. (Annual).

The Demographic Yearbook provides official national population statistics for over 230 countries and areas of the world. Published annually, since 1948, the Demographic Yearbook meets the needs of demographers, economists, public-health workers, sociologists, and other specialists. It presents general tables giving a world summary of basic demographic statistics and includes tables on the size, distribution, and trends of population, fertility, mortality, marriage and divorce, international migration and population census data. The information is provided in English and French.

Disability Statistics Compendium. New York, United Nations, ((800) 253-9646), 1990.

Based on national statistics available in DISTAT, United Nations Disability Statistics Data Base, this first international compendium of disability statistics provides detailed national data from 55 countries. The 12 major topics covering disabled persons include age, sex, residence, educational attainment, economic activity, marital status, household characteristics, causes of impairment, and special aids used.

Economic and Social Survey of Asia and the Pacific 2004: Asia Pacific Economies - Sustaining Growth and Tackling Poverty. Bangkok, United Nations, Economic and Social Commission for Asia and the Pacific (ESCAP), ((800) 253-9646), 2004.

Despite the war in Iraq and the SARS crisis, the Economic and Social Commission for Asia and the Pacific (ESCAP) region continued to show robust economic growth in 2003. This completely updated edition of the Economic and Social Survey of Asia and the Pacific analyzes regional economic developments, macroeconomic performance and poverty reduction strategies.

Economic and Social Survey of Asia and the Pacific 2005: Dealing with Shocks. Bangkok, United Nations, Economic and Social Commission for Asia and the Pacific (ESCAP), ((800) 253-9646), 2005.

This edition of the Survey covers present and future possible shocks and gives Governments remedies for recovery and long-term strategies. The oil price spiral, tsunami fallout, the aging population and poverty reduction are some of the major subjects discussed.

Economic and Social Survey of Asia and the Pacific 2006: Energizing the Global Economy. Bangkok, United Nations, Economic and Social Commission for Asia and the Pacific (ESCAP), ((800) 253-9646), 2006.

The principal policy issues and challenges facing the region are addressed, such as the course of oil prices, the threat of global external payment imbalances unwinding precipitously, the impact of higher interest rates and the potential for the avian influenza to develop into a human pandemic. Longer-term issues relate to the ongoing challenge of poverty reduction, utilizing the benefits of home remittances to simultaneously improve social indicators and macroeconomic fundamentals, and re-energizing the trade liberalization agenda following the Sixth World Trade Organization Ministerial Conference, held in Hong Kong, China in December 2005.

Economic and Social Survey of Asia and the Pacific 2007: Surging Ahead in Uncertain Times. Bangkok, United Nations, Economic and Social Commission for Asia and the Pacific (ESCAP), ((800) 253-9646), 2007.

The region's oldest and most comprehensive annual review of economic and social developments forecasts the external environment in Asia-Pacific to be less favourable in 2007, mainly due to the slowing of the US economy and a moderate decline in global electronics demand, but sees continued dynamism despite risks of further oil price shocks, and a sharp depreciation of the US dollar.

Economic and Social Survey of Asia and the Pacific 2008: Sustaining Growth and Sharing Prosperity. Bangkok, United Nations, Economic and Social Commission for Asia and the Pacific (ESCAP), ((800) 253-9646), 2008.

This year's Survey says 218 million - a third of the region's poor, largely living in rural areas - could be lifted out of poverty by raising agricultural productivity if governments address decades of policy neglect and failure in the agricultural sector. The Survey also calls for a comprehensive liberalization of global trade in agriculture, as this would take a further 48 million people out of poverty in the region.

Economic Survey of Europe. New York, United Nations, (Available from Bernan (800) 274-4888, www.bernan.com). (Annual).

The Economic and Social Survey of Europe provides statistics and a review of macroeconomic developments in Europe, the CIS and North America. Each issue contains statistics for a large array of variables and an extensive statistical appendix with long time series.

Economic Report on Africa 2004: Unlocking Africa's Trade Potential. New York, United Nations, Economic Commission for Africa, ((800) 253-9646), 2005. (Annual).

The *Economic Report on Africa* is an annual series that reviews the continent's economic performance and near-term prospects. Statistical data providing details for overall trade, trade between nations, regional trade and specific product information are presented.

Economic Report on Africa 2005: Meeting the Challenges of Unemployment and Poverty in Africa. New York, United Nations, Economic Commission for Africa, ((800) 253-9646), 2005. (Annual).

Economic Report on Africa 2006: Capital Flows and Development Financing in Africa. New York, United Nations, Economic Commission for Africa, ((800) 253-9646), 2006. (Annual).

Economic Report on Africa 2007: Accelerating Africa's Development through Diversification. New York, United Nations, Economic Commission for Africa, ((800) 253-9646), 2007. (Annual).

Energy Statistics Yearbook 2004. New York, United Nations, Department of Economic and Social Affairs, (Available from Bernan (800) 274-4888), www.bernan.com, 1952-. (Annual).

This publication supplies detailed and aggregated information on production, trade and consumption of different fuel types, which could support a wide spectrum of users from within the energy sector as well as policy makers and academia. 48th in a series of annual publications, it provides internationally comparable series of commercial energy statistics summarizing world level and regional energy trends. Annual data for 215 countries and areas for the period 2001 to 2004 are presented on production, trade and consumption of energy: solids, liquids, gaseous, traditional fuels and electricity in a series of 38 comprehensive tables. In addition, per capita consumption series are also provided for all energy products.

Family Indicators. New York, United Nations, Department of Economic and Social Affairs, 2003.

To develop family policies effectively, the ability to rely on a system of elaborate family indicators is necessary. This study analyzes statistical and sociological approaches available to define the term family and looks for appropriate family indicators to characterize the concept of family.

FAO Production Yearbook. Rome, United Nations Food and Agriculture Organization, (Available from Bernan (800) 274-4888), www.bernan.com, 1947-. (Annual).

The Yearbook is a compendium of statistical data on basic agricultural products and related information for all countries and territories of the world. Data series give details on area, yield, and production for a wide variety of crops, including fiber crops and natural rubber. Information on livestock numbers and products, population, land use, irrigation, and farm machinery are included as well. Useful features of this trilingual (English, French, Spanish) text include explanatory notes, notes on the tables, country notes, and a classification of countries. Index numbers highlight trends in food and agricultural production across all countries and continents.

FAO Trade Yearbook. Rome, United Nations Food and Agriculture Organization, (Available from Bernan (800) 274-4888), www.bernan.com, 1947-. (Annual).

The *FAO Trade Yearbook* presents a compilation of statistical data on basic food and agricultural products for all countries and territories of the world. The Yearbook includes commodity trade tables (imports and exports, quantity and value) for the years 2001-2003. Statistical information is based on data provided by countries through electronic media, questionnaires of the FAO Statistics Division or official statistics publications. The data will serve the needs of scholars, economists, policy-makers, decision-makers as well as industry professionals. This is a multilingual publication in English, French, Spanish, Arabic and Chinese.

Foreign Trade Statistics of Asia and the Pacific. New York, United Nations, Economic and Social Commission for Asia and the Pacific, ((800) 253-9646), 2003.

This publication contains statistics on import/export trade in the Asian/Oceanic region. Tables give data for overall trade, trade between countries, intra-regional trade and major products.

Global Report on Human Settlements 2003: The Challenge of Slums. New York, United Nations Human Settlements Programme (HABITAT), ((800) 253-9646), 2003.

The *Challenge of Slums* presents the first global assessment of slums, highlighting their main problems and prospects. Using a newly formulated operational definition of slums, it presents estimates of the numbers of urban slum dwellers and points out the key factors that have led to the formation of these settlements. It explains their social, spatial and economic characteristics, and evaluates the principal policy responses to the slum challenges in the last few decades.

Global Report on Human Settlements 2005: Financing Urban Shelter. New York, United Nations Human Settlements Programme (HABITAT), ((800) 253-9646), 2005.

This Report examines the challenges of financing urban shelter development, focusing on the shelter needs of the poor and within the overall context of the United Nations Millennium Development target on slums.

Global Report on Human Settlements 2007: Enhancing Urban Safety and Security. New York, United Nations Human Settlements Programme (HABITAT), ((800) 253-9646), 2007.

This publication addresses three major threats to the safety and security of cities: crime and violence; insecurity of tenure and forced evictions; and natural and human-made disasters. It analyses worldwide trends with respect to each of these threats, paying particular attention to their underlying causes and impacts, as well as to the good policies and best practices that have been adopted at the city, national and international levels in order to address these threats.

Human Development Report 2007/2008 - Fighting Climate Change: Human Solidarity in a Divided World. New York, United Nations Development Programme (UNDP), ((800) 253-9646), 2007.

Offers statistical information on demographic, social, economic and environmental issues of human development.

Industrial Commodity Statistics Yearbook. New York, United Nations, Department of Economic and Social Affairs, (Available from Bernan (800) 274-4888), www.bernan.com, 1950-. (Annual).

The *Industrial Commodity Statistics Yearbook* provides statistics on the production of about 530 industrial commodities by country, geographical region, economic grouping and for the world. The Yearbook includes data for the ten-year period 1993-2002 for about 200 countries and areas. The information is provided in English and French.

International Trade Statistics Yearbook. New York, United Nations, Department of Economic and Social Affairs, (Available from Bernan (800) 274-4888), www.bernan.com, 1950-. (Annual).

Volume I provides historical information on the external trade performance of individual countries in terms of current values. Information showing important commodities traded by an individual country (latest 4 years) and the country's trade with its major trading partners and regions (latest 5 years) are also shown. Summary tables for each country show imports by broad economic categories, exports by industrial origin and the percentage share of the country's trading partners and regions in relation to its total trade. This volume contains data for 184 countries or reporting customs areas. Volume II contains selected commodity tables showing total world trade of those commodities analyzed by regions and countries, as well as various specialized tables.

Monthly Bulletin of Statistics. New York, United Nations, ((800) 253-9646), 1947-. (Monthly).

The purpose of this publication is to present current monthly economic statistics for most of the countries and areas of the world. In addition, each month a different selection of special tables is presented showing annual and/or quarterly data on a variety of subjects illustrating important economic long-term trends and developments. Many of these special tables are also reproduced in the *United Nations Statistical Yearbook*. Also available online.

National Accounts Statistics. New York, United Nations, Department of Economic and Social Affairs, (Available from Bernan (800) 274-4888, www.bernan.com), 1957-. (Annual).

This publication presents, in the form of analytical tables, a summary of the principal national accounting aggregates based on official detailed national accounts data for more than 200 countries and areas of the world. Where official data is not available estimates are provided by the Statistics Division of the United Nations. The analysis covers the level of total and per capita gross domestic product, economic structures, economic development and price development.

Population and HIV/AIDS 2007 (Wall Chart). New York, United Nations, Department of Economic and Social Affairs, ((800) 253-9646), 2008.

This wall chart presents the latest available data and information on HIV/AIDS for all countries and regions of the world, with emphasis on government measures implemented in response to the HIV/AIDS epidemic.

Population and Vital Statistics Report, July 2007. New York, United Nations, Department of Economic and Social Affairs, ((800) 253-9646), 2008.

Population and vital statistics for over 200 countries and areas of the world are covered. Provides latest census data plus worldwide demographic statistics on birth and mortality.

State of Agriculture Commodity Markets 2006. Rome, United Nations Food and Agriculture Organization, (Available from Bernan (800) 274-4888, www.bernan.com), 2008.

The aim of this publication is to present commodity market issues in an objective and accessible way to policy-makers, commodity market observers and all those interested in agricultural commodity market developments and their impacts on developing countries. It is intended to raise awareness of the impacts of international commodity price movements on the livelihoods and food security of people in the developing world as well as the economies of developing countries that depend on commodity exports for a substantial part of their export earnings or on food imports for a substantial share of their available food supplies.

The State of Food and Agriculture. Rome, United Nations Food and Agriculture Organization, (Available from Bernan, (800) 274-4888, www.bernan.com), 1947-. (Annual).

The potential of agricultural biotechnology, especially transgenic crops, to meet the needs of the poor, is explored in this report. An analysis of the socio-economic impacts of technological change in agriculture is discussed, and the safety of transgenic crops for human health and the environment is examined.

The State of the World's Children 2008: Child Survival. New York, United Nations International Children's Emergency Fund (UNICEF), ((800) 253-9649), 2008.

The 2008 edition of this publication assesses the state of child survival and primary health care for mothers, newborns and children today. These issues serve as sensitive barometers of a country's development and wellbeing and as evidence of its priorities and values. Investing in the health of children and their mothers is a human rights imperative and one of the surest ways for a country to set its course towards a better future.

State of the World's Cities 2006-2007. New York, United Nations Human Settlements Programme (HABITAT), ((800) 253-9646), 2006.

It is generally assumed that urban populations are healthier, more literate and more prosperous than rural populations. However, UN-HABITAT's State of the World's Cities Report 2006/7 has broken new ground by showing that the urban poor suffer from an urban penalty: Slum dwellers in developing countries are as badly off if not worse off than their rural relatives.

Statistical Yearbook. New York, United Nations, Department of Economic and Social Affairs, ((800) 253-9646), 1949-. (Annual).

The *Statistical Yearbook* is a comprehensive compendium of vital internationally comparable data for the analysis of socio-economic developments at the world, regional and national levels. The Yearbook provides data on the world economy, its structure, major trends and current performance, as well as on issues such as population and social statistics, economic activity and international economic relations. The information is available in English and French.

Statistical Yearbook for Asia and the Pacific. Bangkok, United Nations, Economic and Social Commission for Asia and the Pacific (ESCAP), ((800) 253-9646), 1973-. (Annual).

The Yearbook provides a comprehensive compilation of statistical tables relating to ESCAP region. It provides each country's data in a single section: population, manpower, national accounts, agriculture, forestry and fishing, industry, energy, transport and communications, external trade, wages, prices, consumption, finance and social statistics, covering 10 years of annual figures. Regional tables offer consolidated data of the world, of ESCAP region and of the developing countries within ESCAP. This is a bilingual publication, in English and French.

Statistical Yearbook for Latin America and the Caribbean. New York, United Nations, Economic Commission for Latin America and the Caribbean, ((800) 253-9646), 1975-. (Annual).

Provides statistical series for the overall region as well as subregions in the area. In addition, statistical series are presented for each country covering population, national accounts, agriculture, industry, transport, external trade, prices, balance of payments, and social statistics.

Timber Bulletin: Forest Products Annual Market Review 2006-2007. Rome, United Nations Food and Agriculture Organization, (Available from Bernan (800) 274-4888, www.bernan.com), 1947-. (Annual).

This bulletin provides comprehensive statistics and analysis on forest products markets with an emphasis on policy implications. It also reveals the most recent trends and developments in the forestry industry. This is a bilingual publication, in English and French.

UNCTAD Handbook of Statistics. New York, United Nations Conference on Trade and Development (UNCTAD), ((800) 253-9646), 1984-. (Annual).

The *UNCTAD Handbook of Statistics* provides a comprehensive collection of statistical data relevant to the analysis of world trade, investment and development. Its presentation of data is unique in the following respect: data is presented in an analytical way, through the use of rank-orderings, growth rates, shares and other special calculations so as to facilitate their interpretation, time series of basic trade data cover periods that the UNCTAD secretariat considers as particularly relevant to statistical and other applicable analysis, and, efforts have been made to take account of all available information in order to provide as complete coverage as possible for individual countries.

WIPO Industrial Property Statistics. Geneva, Switzerland, World Intellectual Property Organization (WIPO), www.wipo.int, 2008.

WIPO collects and publishes annual statistics on industrial property, by country and in accordance with the relevant international industrial property classification systems administered by WIPO. The statistics relate to patents, utility models, marks, industrial designs, plant varieties and microorganisms and are published in a unique collection of statistical tables which bring together data supplied by Industrial Property Offices in respect of filings under national, regional and international legislations.

WISTAT: Women's Indicators and Statistics Database (CD-ROM), New York, United Nations, Department of Economic and Social Affairs, ((800) 253-9646), 2000.

This is a global database of statistics and indicators available up to mid-1999, on gender, population and social development. It contains detailed statistics and indicators for 206 countries or areas of the world on a wide range of topics, including: population composition and distribution, education, economic activity, households, marital status and fertility, reproductive health, public affairs and political participation, and violence.

World Economic and Social Survey 2007: Development in an Ageing World. New York, United Nations, Department of Economic and Social Affairs, (Available from Bernan (800) 274-4888, www.bernan.com), 1948-. (Annual).

This publication is an annual analysis of the state of the world economy and emerging policy issues. The *Survey* provides authoritative and reliable information and data on the state of the world's economic and social situation, including developed, developing, and transition economies. The *Survey* also contains data on output, inflation, employment, macroeconomic policies and developments, international trade and finance, statistical tables, and major trends in international trade and financial flows.

World Health Statistics 2008. Geneva, World Health Organization, www.who.int, 1969-. (Telephone Number in U.S. (518) 436-9686), 2005.

World Health Statistics 2008 presents the most recent health statistics for WHO's 193 Member States. This fourth edition includes 10 highlights in health statistics, as well as an expanded set of over 70 key health indicators. It includes, for the first time, trend data where the statistics are available and of acceptable quality.

World Statistics Pocketbook 2007. New York, United Nations, ((800) 253-9646). (Biennial), 2008.

This pocketbook provides an international compilation of basic economic, social and environmental indicators for 208 countries and areas worldwide. It covers 57 key indicators in the areas of population, economic activity, agriculture, industry, energy, international trade, transport, communications, gender, education and environment, drawn from over 20 international statistical sources. The layout provides a comprehensive statistical profile of each country or area.

The World's Women 2005: Progress in Statistics. New York, United Nations, ((800) 253-9646).

This report uniquely focuses on national reporting of sex disaggregated statistics in such areas as demographics, health, education, work, violence against women, poverty, human rights and decision-making. This is the fourth World's Women report since 1990. The previous three focused on statistical trends in the situation of women.

Yearbook of Fishery Statistics 2003: Capture Production. United Nations Food and Agriculture Organization, (Available from Bernan, (800) 274-4888, www.bernan.com), 1947-. (Annual).

This volume of The FAO Yearbook presents the annual statistics for a varying series of recent years ending in 2002 on a worldwide basis on nominal catches of fish, crustaceans, mollusks, other aquatic animals, residues, and plants, taken for all purposes (commercial, industrial, recreational, and subsistence) by all types and classes of fishing units (fishermen, vessels, gear, etc.) operating both in inland, fresh, and brackish water areas, and in inshore, offshore, and high-seas fishing areas, with the exclusion of aquaculture production. The statistics are presented by country or territory, species, major fishing area, and year.

Yearbook of Labour Statistics. Geneva, International Labour Office, (Available from Bernan, (800) 274-4888), 1950-. (Annual).

Statistical data from more than 180 countries and territories are provided on such subjects as population, employment, hours of work, wages, consumer prices, household budgets, industrial accidents, industrial disputes and exchange rates. An index of countries, territories, and areas is provided. The *Yearbook* is supplemented by the *Bulletin of Labour Statistics*, published quarterly with eight supplements. A technical guide, *Statistical Sources and Methods*, is also available. All information is given in English, French and Spanish.

INTERNET AND WORLD WIDE WEB SITES

This listing of World Wide Web and Internet sites consists of national statistical offices and related government and non-government organizations, international statistical organizations, and United States government agencies which produce statistical information for the public. Entries are arranged alphabetically by country and organization name and include Internet and World Wide Web addresses (URLs). Sites listed are for the English version where available.

NATIONAL STATISTICAL OFFICES AND RELATED ORGANIZATIONS

AFGHANISTAN

Central Statistics Office (CSO)
http://www.aims.org.af

ALBANIA

Institute of Statistics (INSTAT)
http://www.instat.gov.al

ALGERIA

National Office of Statistics (Office National des Statistiques)
http://www.ons.dz/English/indexag.htm

AMERICAN SAMOA

Statistics Division, Department of Commerce
http://www.spc.int/prism/country/as/stats/

ANDORRA

Servei d'Estudis, Ministeri de Finances
http://www.estadistica.ad/

ANGOLA

Instituto Nacional de Estatistica (INE) (National Institute of Statistics)
http://www.angola.org

ANGUILLA

Anguilla Statistics Department
http://www.gov.ai/statistics/

ARGENTINA

National Institute of Statistics and Censuses (Instituto Nacional de Estadistica y Censos (INDEC))
http://www.indec.mecon.ar

ARMENIA

National Statistical Service of the Republic of Armenia
http://www.armstat.am

ARUBA

Central Bureau of Statistics (CBS)
http://www.aruba.com/extlinks/govs/cbstats.php

AUSTRALIA

Australian Bureau of Statistics (ABS)
http://www.abs.gov.au

OTHER STATISTICAL ORGANIZATIONS:

Australian Institute of Health and Welfare
http://www.aihw.gov.au

AUSTRIA

Statistik Osterreich (Statistics Austria)
http://www.statistik.at/

AZERBAIJAN

State Statistical Committee of Azerbaijan Republic
http://www.azstat.org/indexen.php

BAHAMAS, THE

Department of Statistics
http://www.bahamas.gov.bs/

BAHRAIN

Central Statistics Organisation
http://www.e.gov.bh/wps/portal

BANGLADESH

Bangladesh Bureau of Statistics (BBS)
http://www.bbs.gov.bd/

BARBADOS

Barbados Statistical Service, Barbados Government Information Service (BGIS)
http://www.barbados.gov.bb/

BELARUS

Ministry of Statistics and Analysis of the Republic of Belarus
http://www.belstat.gov.by/homep/en/main.html

BELGIUM

Statistics Belgium
http://www.statbel.fgov.be/home_en.asp

BELIZE

Central Statistical Office (CSO)
http://www.cso.gov.bz/

BENIN

Institut National de la Statistique et de l'Analyse Economique (INSAE)
http://www.insae-bj.org/

BERMUDA

Department of Statistics, Cabinet Office, Bermuda Government
http://www.gov.bm

BHUTAN

National Statistical Bureau
http://www.bhutan.gov.bt/government/reports-AndStatistics.php

BOLIVIA

Instituto Nacional de Estadistica (INE)
http://www.ine.gov.bo

BOSNIA AND HERZEGOVINA

Agency for Statistics of Bosnia and Herzegovina
http://www.bhas.ba/Engleski/en_main.html

BOTSWANA

Central Statistics Office (CSO), Ministry of Finance and Development Planning
http://www.cso.gov.bw

BRAZIL

Brazilian Statistical and Geographic Institute (Instituto Brasileiro de Geografia e Estatistica (IBGE))
http://www.ibge.gov.br/english/default.php

BRUNEI

Department of Economic Planning and Development
http://www.brunei.gov.bn/

BULGARIA

National Statistical Insitute (NSI)
http://www.nsi.bg/Index_e.htm

CAMBODIA

National Institute of Statistics (NIS), Ministry of Planning
http://www.nis.gov.kh

CAMEROON

Ministere de l'Economie et des Finances
http://www.statistics-cameroon.org/

CANADA

Statistics Canada
http://www.statcan.ca/menu-en.htm

PROVINCIAL STATISTICAL OFFICES:

Alberta
http://www.alberta-canada.com/statpub/

British Columbia
http://www.vs.gov.bc.ca

Manitoba
http://web2.gov.mb.ca/cca/vital/

New Brunswick
http://www.gnb.ca/0024/

Newfoundland and Labrador
http://www.stats.gov.nl.ca/Statistics/

Northwest Territories
http://www.fin.gov.nt.ca

Nova Scotia
http://www.gov.ns.ca/finance/statistics/agency/

Nunavut
http://www.gov.nu.ca/Nunavut/

Ontario
http://www.gov.on.ca/

Prince Edward Island
http://www.gov.pe.ca/pt/

Quebec
http://www.stat.gouv.qc.ca/default_an.htm

Saskatchewan
http://www.stats.gov.sk.ca/

Yukon
http://www.eco.gov.yk.ca/stats/

OTHER STATISTICAL ORGANIZATIONS:

Statistical Society of Canada
http://www.mast.queensu.ca

Industry Canada, Strategis
http://strategis.ic.gc.ca/engdoc/main.html

CAPE VERDE

Instituto Nacional de Estatistica (INE)
http://www.ine.cv/

CAYMAN ISLANDS

Economics & Statistics Office
http://www.eso.ky

CENTRAL AFRICAN REPUBLIC

Division des Statistiques, des Etudes Economiques et Sociales
http://www.stat-centrafrique.com

CHAD

Institut National de la Statistique, des Etudes Economiques et Demographiques
http://www.inseed-tchad.org

CHILE

Instituto Nacional de Estadisticas (INE)
http://www.ine.cl

CHINA

National Bureau of Statistics of China (NBS)
http://www.stats.gov.cn/english/

COLOMBIA

Departamento Administrativo Nacional de Estadisticas (DANE)
http://www.dane.gov.co

CONGO, REPUBLIC OF THE

Centre National de la Statistique et des Etudes Economiques (CNSEE)
http://www.cnsee.org

COOK ISLANDS

Statistics Office
http://www.stats.gov.ck

COSTA RICA

Instituto Nacional de Estadistica y Censos (INEC)
http://www.inec.go.cr

COTE D'IVOIRE

Institut National de la Statistique
http://www.ins.ci

CROATIA

Croatian Bureau of Statistics
http://www.dzs.hr/

CUBA

La Oficina Nacional de Estadisticas
http://www.cubagob.cu/ingles/default.htm

CYPRUS

Statistical Service of Cyprus (CYSTAT), Ministry of Finance
http://www.mof.gov.cy/mof/mof.nsf/

CZECH REPUBLIC

Czech Statistical Office (CSU)
http://www.czso.cz

DENMARK

Statistics Denmark (Danmarks Statistik)
http://www.dst.dk/HomeUK.aspx

DJIBOUTI

Direction Nationale de la Statistique, Ministere de l'Economie, des Finances et de la Planification Charge de la Privatisation
http://www.ministere-finances.dj/

DOMINICAN REPUBLIC

Oficina Nacional de Estadistica
http://www.one.gov.do

EAST TIMOR

Directorate of National Statistics
http://dne.mopf.gov.tp

ECUADOR

Instituto Nacional de Estadistica y Censos (INEC)
http://www.inec.gov.ec

EGYPT

Central Agency for Public Mobilization and Statistics (CAPMAS)
http://www.capmas.gov.eg/eng_ver/homeE.htm

EL SALVADOR

Direccion General de Estadisticas y Censos (DIGESTYC)
http://www.minec.gob.sv

EQUATORIAL GUINEA

Direccion General de Estadistica (DGE), Ministerio de Planificacion, Desarrollo Economico e Inversiones Publicas
http://www.dgecnstat-ge.org

ESTONIA

Statistical Office of Estonia (Statistikaamet)
http://www.stat.ee

FIJI

Fiji Islands Bureau of Statistics (FIBOS)
http://www.statsfiji.gov.fj

FINLAND

Statistics Finland
http://www.stat.fi/

OTHER STATISTICAL ORGANIZATIONS:

Bank of Finland
http://www.bof.fi/en/

Geological Survey of Finland
http://en.gtk.fi/

Ministry of Education
http://www.minedu.fi/OPM/?lang=en

National Research and Development Centre for Welfare and Health
http://www.stakes.fi/EN/index.htm

FRANCE

National Institute for Statistics and Economic Studies (Institut National de la Statistique et des Etudes Economiques (INSEE))
http://www.insee.fr/en/home/home_page.asp

OTHER STATISTICAL ORGANIZATIONS:

Banque de France
http://www.banque-france.fr/home.htm

Centre de Renseignements Statistiques
http://www.douane.gouv.fr

Institut National de la Statistique et des Etudes Economiques (INSEE), Service Regional de la Martinique
http://www.insee.fr/fr/insee_regions/martinique/

Ministry of Economics, Finance and Industry
http://www.minefi.gouv.fr

FRENCH POLYNESIA

Institut Statistique de Polynesie Francaise (ISPF)
http://www.ispf.pf

GABON

Direction Generale de la Statistique et des Etudes Economiques (DGSEE)
http://www.legabon.ga/uk/home.php

GEORGIA

State Department for Statistics (SDS) of Georgia
http://www.mfa.gov.ge/

GERMANY

Federal Statistical Office, Statistical Information Service
http://www.destatis.de/

OTHER STATISTICAL ORGANIZATIONS:

Cologne Institute for Business Research
http://www.iwkoeln.de

Landesamt fur Datenverarbeitung und Statistik Nordrheim-Westfalen
http://www.lds.nrw.de/statistik/

GIBRALTAR

Statistics Office
http://www.gibraltar.gov.gi

GREECE

National Statistical Service of Greece (NSSG)
http://www.statistics.gr

GREENLAND

Statistics Greenland
http://www.statgreen.gl/english/

GUAM

Department of Labor, Economic Research Center
http://www.spc.int/prism/country/gu/stats/

GUATEMALA

Instituto Nacional de Estadistica (INE)
http://www.ine.gob.gt/

GUERNSEY

Policy and Research Unit
http://www.gov.gg/ccm/navigation/government/

GUINEA

Direction Nationale de la Statistique, Ministere du Plan
http://www.stat-guinee.org

GUINEA-BISSAU

Instituto Nacional de Estatistica e Censos (INEC)
http://www.stat-guinebissau.com/

GUYANA

Government Information Agency (GINA)
http://www.gina.gov.gy

HONDURAS

Instituto Nacional de Estadistica (INE)
http://www.ine-hn.org

HONG KONG

Census and Statistics Department (C& SD)
http://www.censtatd.gov.hk/home/index.jsp

HUNGARY

Hungarian Central Statistical Office (HCSO) (Kozponti Statisztikai Hivatal (KSH))
http://www.ksh.hu

INDIA

Ministry of Statistics and Programme Implementation
http://www.mospi.nic.in

OTHER STATISTICAL ORGANIZATIONS:

Reserve Bank of India
http://www.censusindia.net

INDONESIA

Statistics Indonesia (Badan Pusat Statistik (BPS))
http://www.bps.go.id

IRELAND

Central Statistics Office (CSO) Ireland
http://www.cso.ie

ISRAEL

Central Bureau of Statistics (CBS) Israel
http://www1.cbs.gov.il/reader

Ministry of Finance
http://www.mof.gov.il/mainpage_eng.asp

ITALY

Istat - National Institute of Statistics (Instituto Nazionale di Statistica)
http://www.istat.it/english/

JAMAICA

Statistical Institute of Jamaica (STATIN)
http://www.statinja.com

JAPAN

Statistics Bureau, Ministry of Internal Affairs and Communication
http://www.stat.go.jp/english/

OTHER STATISTICAL ORGANIZATIONS:

Japan External Trade Organization
http://www.jetro.go.jp

Japan Ministry of Economic Affairs
http://www.mofa.go.jp/policy/economy/index.html

Ministry of Finance
http://www.mof.go.jp/english/files.htm

JORDAN

Department of Statistics (DOS)
http://www.dos.gov.jo/dos_home_e/main/index.htm

KAZAKHSTAN

Agency of Statistics of the Republic of Kazakhstan
http://www.stat.kz/index.php?lang=eng

KENYA

Central Bureau of Statistics (CBS), Ministry of Economic Planning and Development
http://www.cbs.go.ke

Government of Kenya, Ministry of Finance
http://www.treasury.go.ke

KIRIBATI

Kiribati Statistics Office, Ministry of Finance and Economic Planning
http://www.spc.int/prism/country/ki/stats/

KOREA, SOUTH

Korea National Statistical Office (KNSO)
http://www.nso.go.kr/eng2006/emain/index.html

KUWAIT

Statistics and Census Sector, Ministry of Planning
http://www.mop.gov.kw/MopWebSite/english/default.asp

KYRGYZSTAN

National Statistical Committee (NSC) of the Kyrgyz Republic
http://www.gov.kg/

LAOS

National Statistics Centre (NSC)
http://www.nsc.gov.la

LEBANON

Central Administration for Statistics (CAS)
http://www.cas.gov.lb/Index_en.asp

LESOTHO

Lesotho Bureau of Statistics
http://www.bos.gov.ls

LIBYA

Libyan Jamahiriya Broadcasting Corporation
http://en.ljbc.net/

LIECHTENSTEIN

Amt fur Volkswirtschaft/Statistik
http://www.llv.li/amtsstellen/llv-avw-statistik.htm

LITHUANIA

Lithuanian Department of Statistics (Statistics Lithuania)
http://www.stat.gov.lt/en/

LUXEMBOURG

Central Service for Statistics and Economic Studies (Statec) (Service central de la statistique et des etudes economiques)
http://www.statec.public.lu/en/

MACAU

Direccao de Servicos de Estatistica e Censos
http://www.dsec.gov.mo/e_index.html

MACEDONIA, THE REPUBLIC OF

State Statistical Office of Macedonia (SSOM)
http://www.stat.gov.mk/english/glavna_eng.asp

MADAGASCAR

Institut National de la Statistique
http://www.cite.mg/instat/

MALAWI

National Statistical Office of Malawi
http://www.nso.malawi.net

MALAYSIA

Department of Statistics Malaysia
http://www.statistics.gov.my

MALDIVES

Ministry of Planning and National Development
http://www.planning.gov.mv/en/

MALI

Direction Nationale de la Statistique et de l'Informatique (DNSI)
http://www.dnsi.gov.ml/index.htm

MALTA

National Statistics Office (NSO)
http://www.nso.gov.mt

MAN, ISLE OF

Isle of Man Government
http://www.gov.im/infocentre/

MARSHALL ISLANDS

Economic Policy, Planning and Statistics Office (EPPSO)
http://www.spc.int/prism/country/mh/stats/

MAURITANIA

Office National de la Statistique (National Office of of Statistics)
http://www.ons.mr

MAURITIUS

Central Statistical Office, Ministry of Economic Planning and Development
http://www.gov.mu/portal/sites/ncb/cso/index.htm

MEXICO

Instituto Nacional de Estadistica Geografia e Informatica (INEGI)
http://www.inegi.gob.mx/inegi/default.aspx

MICRONESIA, FEDERATED STATES OF

Department of Economic Affairs
http://www.fsminvest.fm

MOLDOVA

Department of Statistics and Sociology of the Republic of Moldova
http://www.statistica.md/?lang=en

MONACO

Divison des Statistiques et des Etudes Economiques
http://www.monaco.gouv.mc

MONGOLIA

National Statistical Office (NSO)
http://www.nso.mn/eng/

MONTSERRAT

Economic Development Unit, Government of Montserrat
http://www.devunit.gov.ms

MOROCCO

Direction de la Statistique
http://www.statistic-hcp.ma

MOZAMBIQUE

Instituto Nacional de Estatistica (INE)
http://www.ine.gov.mz

NAMIBIA

National Planning Commission (NPC), Central Statistics Bureau (CSB)
http://www.npc.gov.na

NAURU

Nauru Bureau of Statistics, Department of Finance
http://www.spc.int/prism/country/nr/stats/

NEPAL

Central Bureau of Statistics, National Planning Commission Secretariat
http://www.cbs.gov.np

NETHERLANDS

Statistics Netherlands
http://www.cbs.nl/en-GB/default.htm

NETHERLANDS ANTILLES

Central Bureau of Statistics (CBS)
http://www.cbs.an

NEW CALEDONIA

Institute de la Statistique et des Etudes Economiques (ISEE)
http://www.isee.nc

NEW ZEALAND

Statistics New Zealand
http://www.stats.govt.nz

NICARAGUA

Instituto Nacional de Estadisdicas y Censos (INEC)
http://www.inec.gob.ni

NIGER

Institut National de la Statistique (INS), Ministere de l'Economie et des Finances
http://www.stat-niger.org

NIGERIA

National Data Bank (NDB)
http://www.nigeriandatabank.org

NIUE

Economic, Planning, Development & Statistics Unit, Premiers Department
http://www.gov.nu/

NORTHERN MARIANA ISLANDS

Department of Commerce, Central Statistics Division
http://www.commerce.gov.mp

NORWAY

Statistics Norway
http://www.ssb.no/vis/english/

OMAN

Information and Publication Center, Ministry of National Economy
http://www.moneoman.gov.om/index.asp

PAKISTAN

Federal Bureau of Statistics (FBS)
http://www.statpak.gov.pk/depts/index.html

PALAU

Office of Planning and Statistics
http://www.palaugov.net/stats/

PANAMA

Direccion de Estadistica y Censo
http://www.contraloria.gob.pa/dec/

PAPUA NEW GUINEA

National Statistics Office (NSO)
http://www.spc.int/prism/country/pg/stats/

PARAGUAY

Direccion General de Estadistica, Encuestas y Censos (DGEEC)
http://www.dgeec.gov.py

PERU

Instituto Nacional de Estadistica e Informatica (INEI)
http://www.inei.gob.pe

PHILIPPINES

National Statistics Office (NSO)
http://www.census.gov.ph

OTHER STATISTICAL ORGANIZATIONS:

National Statistical Coordination Board
http://www.nscb.gov.ph

POLAND

Central Statistical Office (CSO)
http://www.stat.gov.pl/gus/index_ENG_HTML.htm

PORTUGAL

National Statistical Institute (Instituto Nacional de Estatistica (INE))
http://www.ine.pt/portal/page/portal/PORTAL_INE

PUERTO RICO

Departamento de Educacion
http://www.de.gobierno.pr/

Oficina del Censo, Programa de Planificacion Economica y Social, Junta de Planificacion
http://www.censo.gobierno.pr

Recinto Universitario de Mayaguez, Universidad de Puerto Rico
http://www.uprm.edu

QATAR

Planning Council, Statistics Department
http://www.planning.gov.qa

ROMANIA

National Institute of Statistics (NIS) Romania
http://www.insse.ro/

RUSSIA

Federal State Statistics Service (FSSS)
http://www.gks.ru/wps/portal/english

RWANDA

Department of Statistics, Ministry of Finance and Economic Planning
http://www.minecofin.gov.rw

SAINT HELENA

Saint Helena Development & Economic Planning Department
http://www.sainthelena.gov.sh

SAINT LUCIA

Saint Lucia Government Statistics Department
http://www.stats.gov.lc

SAMOA

Statistical Services Division, Ministry of Finance
http://www.spc.int/prism/Country/WS/stats/

SAO TOME AND PRINCIPE

Instituto Nacional de Estatistica (INE)
http://www.ine.st/

SAUDI ARABIA

Central Department of Statistics (CDS), Ministry of Finance
http://www.planning.gov.sa/

SENEGAL

Direction de la Prevision et de la Statistique, Ministere de l'Economie et des Finances
http://www.ansd.org

SERBIA AND MONTENEGRO

Statistical Office of the Republic of Serbia
http://webrzs.statserb.sr.gov.yu/axd/en/index.php

SEYCHELLES

National Statistics Bureau
http://www.seychelles.net/misdstat/

SIERRA LEONE

Statistics Sierra Leone
http://www.sierra-leone.org/govt.html

SINGAPORE

Singapore Department of Statistics
http://www.singstat.gov.sg

SLOVENIA

Statistical Office of the Republic of Slovenia
http://www.stat.si/eng/

SOLOMON ISLANDS

Solomon Islands National Statistics Office (SINSO)
http://www.spc.int/prism/country/sb/stats/

SOUTH AFRICA

Statistics South Africa
http://www.statssa.gov.za

SPAIN

Ministerio de Economia y Hacienda
http://www.meh.es/portal/

National Statistics Institute (Instituto Nacional de Estadistica (INE))
http://www.ine.es/en/welcome_en.htm

SRI LANKA

Department of Census and Statistics
http://www.statistics.gov.lk/

SUDAN

Central Bureau of Statistics (CBS), Ministry of Council of Ministers
http://www.sudanmfa.com/

SURINAME

General Bureau of Statistics (GBS)
http://www.statistics-suriname.org

SWAZILAND

Central Statistical Office, Ministry of Economic Planning And Development
http://www.gov.sz/

SWEDEN

Statistics Sweden (Statistiska Centralbyran (SCB))
http://www.scb.se/default____2154.asp

OTHER STATISTICAL ORGANIZATIONS:

Swedish National Agency for Higher Education
http://www.hsv.se/2.539a949110f3d5914ec800056285.html

Swedish Environmental Protection Agency
http://www.internat.naturvardsverket.se

Swedish National Board for Industrial and Technical Development
http://www.nutek.se/sb/d/113

Swedish National Board of Student Aid
http://www.csn.se/english/default.asp

SWITZERLAND

Office Federale de la Statistique (Swiss Federal Statistical Office)
http://www.bfs.admin.ch/bfs/portal/en/index.html

SYRIA

Office of the Prime Minister, Central Bureau of Statistics
http://www.cbssyr.org/estart.htm

TAIWAN

Ministry of Economic Affairs
http://www.moea.gov.tw/

Ministry of Education, Department of Statistics
http://english.moe.gov.tw/mp.asp?mp=1

TANZANIA

National Bureau of Statistics (NBS)
http://www.nbs.go.tz

THAILAND

National Statistical Office (NSO)
http://web.nso.go.th/eng/index.htm

OTHER STATISTICAL ORGANIZATIONS:

Bank of Thailand (BOT)
http://www.bot.or.th

TOGO

Direction Generale de la Statistique et de la Comptabilite Nationale (DGSCN)
http://www.stat-togo.org

TONGA

Tonga Statistics Department
http://www.spc.int/prism/country/to/stats/

TRINIDAD AND TOBAGO

Central Statistical Office (CSO)
http://www.cso.gov.tt

TUNISIA

Institut National de la Statistique (INS)
http://www.ins.nat.tn

TURKEY

State Institute of Statistics (SIS), Prime Ministry
http://www.die.gov.tr/ENGLISH

TUVALU

Central Statistics Division, Ministry of Finance, Economic Planning and Industry
http://www.spc.int/prism/country/tv/stats/

UGANDA

Uganda Bureau of Statistics (UBOS)
http://www.ubos.org/

UNITED ARAB EMIRATES

Central Statistical Organisation, Ministry of Economy & Planning
http://www.government.ae/gov/en/gov/federal/moec.jsp

UNITED KINGDOM

Office for National Statistics (ONS)
http://www.statistics.gov.uk/

OTHER STATISTICAL ORGANIZATIONS:

Confederation of British Industry
http://www.cbi.org.uk/

Department of Trade and Industry
http://www.dti.gov.uk

Financial Statistics Division, Bank of England
http://www.bankofengland.co.uk/

Her Majesty's Treasury
http://www.hm-treasury.gov.uk/

Directgov
http://www.direct.gov.uk/

URUGUAY

Cenci Uruguay S.R.L.
http://www.cenci.com.uy/

UZBEKISTAN

State Statistics Committee of the Republic of Uzbekistan (SCS)
http://www.gov.uz/en/section.scm?sectionId=2513

VANUATU

Vanuatu Statistics Office (VSO)
http://www.vanuatustatistics.gov.vu/

VENEZUELA

Instituto Nacional de Estadistica (INE)
http://www.ine.gov.ve/

VIETNAM

General Statistics Office (GSO)
http://www.gso.gov.vn/default_en.aspx?tabid=491

VIRGIN ISLANDS

University of the Virgin Islands Conservation Data Center (CDC), Eastern Caribbean Center
http://www.uvi.edu/pub-relations/uvi/home.html

VIRGIN ISLANDS

Virgin Islands Economic Development Commission (EDC)
http://www.usvieda.org/

ZAMBIA

Central Statistical Office of Zambia
http://www.zamstats.gov.zm/

UNITED STATES GOVERNMENT AGENCIES

DEPARTMENT OF AGRICULTURE

Department of Agriculture (Home Page)
http://www.usda.gov

Economics and Statistics System
http://usda.mannlib.cornell.edu

Economic Research Service
http://www.ers.usda.gov

National Agricultural Library
http://www.nal.usda.gov

National Agriculture Statistics Service
http://www.nass.usda.gov

DEPARTMENT OF COMMERCE

Department of Commerce (Home Page)
http://www.doc.gov

Bureau of Economic Analysis
http://www.bea.doc.gov

Bureau of the Census
http://www.census.gov

Economics and Statistics Administration
https://www.esa.doc.gov

International Trade Administration
http://www.ita.doc.gov

National Marine Fisheries Service
http://www.nmfs.noaa.gov

National Marine Fisheries Statistics Division
http://www.st.nmfs.gov/st1/

National Oceanic and Atmospheric Administration
http://www.noaa.gov

National Oceanographic Data Center
http://www.nodc.noaa.gov

National Weather Service
http://nws.noaa.gov

Patent and Trademark Office
http://www.uspto.gov

STAT-USA
http://www.stat-usa.gov

DEPARTMENT OF DEFENSE

Department of Defense (Home Page)
http://www.defenselink.mil

DEPARTMENT OF EDUCATION

National Center for Education Statistics
http://nces.ed.gov

DEPARTMENT OF ENERGY

Department of Energy (Home Page)
http://www.energy.gov

Energy Information Administration
http://www.eia.doe.gov

Federal Energy Regulatory Commission
http://www.ferc.gov

DEPARTMENT OF HEALTH AND HUMAN SERVICES

Department of Health and Human Services (Home Page)
http://www.os.dhhs.gov

Centers for Disease Control
http://www.cdc.gov

National Cancer Institute (NCI) Cancer Statistics
http://www.nci.nih.gov/statistics

National Center for Health Statistics
http://www.cdc.gov/nchs/

National Institutes of Health
http://www.nih.gov

DEPARTMENT OF HOMELAND SECURITY

Department of Homeland Security (Home Page)
http://www.dhs.gov

National Counterterrorism Center
http://www.nctc.gov/

U.S. Coast Guard
http://www.uscg.mil

U.S. Customs & Border Protection
http://www.cbp.gov

DEPARTMENT OF HOUSING AND URBAN DEVELOPMENT

Department of Housing and Urban Development (Home Page)
http://www.hud.gov

DEPARTMENT OF JUSTICE

Department of Justice (Home Page)
http://www.usdoj.gov

Bureau of Justice Statistics
http://www.ojp.usdoj.gov/bjs/

Civil Rights Division
http://www.usdoj.gov/crt/

Drug Enforcement Administration
http://www.dea.gov

Federal Bureau of Investigation
http://www.fbi.gov

Immigration and Naturalization Service
http://www.uscis.gov/portal/site/uscis

National Criminal Justice Reference Service
http://www.ncjrs.org

National Institute of Justice
http://www.ojp.usdoj.gov/nij/

Office of Juvenile Justice and Delinquency Prevention
http://ojjdp.ncjrs.org

DEPARTMENT OF LABOR

Employment Standards Administration
http://www.dol.gov/esa/

U.S. Bureau of Labor Statistics
http://www.bls.gov

Occupational Safety and Health Administration
http://www.osha.gov

DEPARTMENT OF THE INTERIOR

Department of the Interior (Home Page)
http://www.doi.gov

Bureau of Reclamation
http://www.usbr.gov

Minerals Management Service
http://www.mms.gov

U.S. Geological Survey
http://www.usgs.gov

DEPARTMENT OF THE TREASURY

Department of the Treasury (Home Page)
http://www.ustreas.gov

Alcohol and Tobacco Tax and Trade Bureau
http://www.ttb.gov

Internal Revenue Service
http://www.irs.gov/

Office of Thrift Supervision
http://www.ots.treas.gov

DEPARTMENT OF TRANSPORTATION

Department of Transportation (Home Page)
http://www.dot.gov

Bureau of Transportation Statistics
http://www.bts.gov

Federal Aviation Administration
http://www.faa.gov

Federal Highway Administration
http://www.fhwa.dot.gov

Federal Railroad Administration
http://www.fra.dot.gov

Federal Transit Administration
http://www.fta.dot.gov

Maritime Administration
http://www.marad.dot.gov

National Highway Traffic Safety Administration
http://www.nhtsa.dot.gov

DEPARTMENT OF VETERANS AFFAIRS

Department of Veterans Affairs (Home Page)
http://www.va.gov

OTHER U.S. GOVERNMENT DEPARTMENTS AND AGENCIES

Federal Geographic Data Committee
http://www.fgdc.gov

Foreign Agriculture Service
http://www.fas.usda.gov

Library of Congress
http://www.loc.gov

National Archives and Records Administration
http://www.archives.gov

National Biological Service
http://biology.usgs.gov

National Endowment for the Humanities
http://www.neh.gov/

National Geophysical Data Center
http://www.ngdc.noaa.gov

National Institute of Standards and Technology
http://www.nist.gov

National Science Foundation
http://www.nsf.gov

National Science Foundation - Division of Science Resource Statistics
http://www.nsf.gov/statistics/

Social Security Administration
http://www.ssa.gov

INTERNATIONAL STATISTICAL ORGANIZATIONS

EUROSTAT (Statistical Office of the European Communities)
http://epp.eurostat.cec.eu.int

International Atomic Energy Agency (IAEA)
http://www.iaea.org

International Civil Aviation Organization (ICAO)
http://www.icao.int

International Fund for Agricultural Development (IFAD)
http://www.ifad.org

International Labor Organization (ILO)
http://www.ilo.org

International Maritime Organization (IMO)
http://www.imo.org

International Monetary Fund
http://www.imf.org

International Monetary Fund (Dissemination Standards Bulletin Board)
http://dsbb.imf.org

International Statistical Institute (ISI)
http://www.cbs.nl/isi/

International Telecommunications Union (ITU)
http://www.itu.int

OECD Statistics (Organization for Economic Co-operation and Development)
http://www.oecd.org

Oxford Economic Forecasting Ltd.
http://www.oef.com

United Nations
http://www.un.org

United Nations Children's Fund (UNICEF)
http://www.unicef.org

United Nations Conference on Trade and Development (UNCTAD)
http://www.unctad.org

United Nations Industrial Development Organization (UNIDO)
http://www.unido.org

Universal Postal Union (UPU)
http://www.upu.int

UN Development Programme
http://www.undp.org

UN Economic Commission for Europe (UN/ECE)
http://www.unece.org

UN Economic Commission for Latin America and the Caribbean (UN/ECLAC)
http://www.eclac.org

UN Economic Commission for Africa (ECA)
http://www.uneca.org

UN Economic and Social Commission for Asia and the Pacific (ESCAP)
http://www.unescap.org

UN Economic and Social Commission for Western Asia (ESCWA)
http://www.escwa.org.lb

UN Educational, Scientific and Cultural Organization (UNESCO)
http://www.unesco.org

UN Food and Agriculture Organization (FAO)
http://www.fao.org

UN Population Fund (UNFPA)
http://www.unfpa.org

UN Population Information Network (POPIN)
http://www.un.org/popin/

UN Statistics Division
http://unstats.un.org/unsd/

World Bank Group
http://www.worldbank.org

World Food Programme (WFP)
http://www.wfp.org

World Health Organization (WHO)
http://www.who.int

World Intellectual Property Organization (WIPO)
http://www.wipo.int

World Meteorological Organization (WMO)
http://www.wmo.ch

World Tourism Organization
http://www.world-tourism.org

World Trade Organization (WTO)
http://www.wto.org

STATISTICAL DATABASES ONLINE

There are literally hundreds of commercially available online databases of interest to statistics users. These are described, along with thousands of other databases, in the sources listed below under Guides to Online Databases. Because excellent coverage of online databases is readily available in these guides, we have limited our specific database coverage in Selected Online Statistical Databases to capsule descriptions of a small, representative sampling of key statistical files featuring either U.S. or international statistics. However, because the list of currently available online databases is constantly changing, it is perhaps even more important to be aware of the major commercial vendors of online statistical databases. These are described in the

Selected Vendors of Online Statistical Databases part of this section.

GUIDES TO ONLINE DATABASES

Laurie Andriot, ed. *Internet Blue Pages: The Guide to Federal Government Web Sites*. Medford, NJ, Information Today, Inc., 2002.

The *Internet Blue Pages*, provides listings for over 900 Federal Government web sites. Entries are arranged by agency in the manner of the U.S. Government Manual. Listings include agency name, URL, purpose of the agency, and information found at the home page. There is also an extensive index to help locate sites by subject.

Paula Berinstein and Susanne Bjrner, eds. *Finding Statistics Online: How to Locate the Elusive Numbers You Need*. San Diego, CA, Independent Publishing Group, 1998.

Explains how to find statistics through professional systems and services on the Internet, and includes information on the nature of statistics and how to evaluate their validity.

Sonya D. Hill, ed. *Information Industry Directory*. 31st edition. Farmington Hills, MI, Gale, ((248) 699-4253), www.gale.com, 2007.

Information Industry Directory tracks the companies that produce and provide electronic systems, services and products. Each entry includes contact information complete with e-mail address, thorough descriptions of organization systems, services and products, data sources, computer-based products and services and much more. The Supplement includes approximately 800 new entries.

Fedstats: One Stop Shopping for Federal Statistics, www.fedstats.gov.

Developed by the Clinton administration's Interagency Council on Statistical Policy, it is a subject guide to web sites of more than 100 statistics-producing agencies of the U.S. Government. An A to Z directory provides alphabetically arranged links to statistics found in federal agency web sites.

Peggy Garvin, ed. *The United States Government Internet Manual 2008*. Lanham, MD, Bernan Press, ((800) 274-4888), www.bernan.com, 2008.

An indispensable guidebook for anyone who is looking for official U.S. government resources on the Web. The Manual contains more than 2,000 site records that provide descriptions and URLs for each site. Evaluations are given for the most important and frequently sought sites.

Peter Hernon, John A. Shuller, and Robert E. Dugan, eds. Third edition. *U.S. Government on the Web: Getting the Information You Need*. Portsmouth, NH, Libraries Unlimited, ((800) 225-5800, http://lu.com, 2003.

Aids researchers in finding government and other Internet sites.

Lisa Kumar, ed. *Gale Directory of Online, Portable, and Internet Databases*. Farmington Hills, MI, Gale, ((248) 699-4253), www.gale.com, 2002.

Provides detailed information on publicly available databases and database products accessible through an online vendor, Internet, or batch processor, or available for direct lease, license, or purchase as a CD-ROM, diskette, magnetic tape, or handheld product. Covers more than 15,600 databases and database products of all types in all subject areas produced worldwide in English and other languages by more than 4,000 database producers.

SELECTED ONLINE STATISTICAL DATABASES

American Statistics Index (ASI)

Systematically canvassing major statistical and research agencies, *American Statistics Index (ASI)* covers every type of statistical publication (periodicals, series, special reports, annuals and biennials, etc.) regardless of whether issued by the Government Printing Office or an individual agency, whether in print or online, or whether offered to libraries through the government's depository library program. Available from LexisNexis.

CANSIM

A computerized information system for socioeconomic time series and multidimensional data acquired from Statistics Canada and other governmental and private sources. Produced by Statistics Canada and available from Global Insight, Haver Analytics, Nomura Research Institute, Thomson Financial Investment Management Group, as well as Statistics Canada.

COMPUSTAT

Contains financial and statistical information on thousands of New York Stock Exchange, American Stock Exchange, and over-the-counter companies. Produced by Standard & Poor's on a subscription basis.

Datafinder. Washington, DC, Population Reference Bureau, ((800) 877-9881).

On the web at www.prb.org/Datafinder.aspx, this is a database with hundreds of variables for the U.S. and the world.

Dun's Financial Records Plus

Provides up to three years of comprehensive financial statements for over 2.9 million private and public companies. Depending on the company, information provided may include balance sheet, income statement, and fourteen of the most widely used business ratios for measuring solvency, efficiency, and profitability. Also contains company identification data, such as company name, address, primary and secondary SIC codes, DUNS number, and number of employees. Textual paragraphs cover the history and operation background of a firm. Available from The Dialog Corporation.

InfoNation

InfoNation is an easy-to-use, two-step database that allows you to view and compare the most up-to-date statistical data for the member states of the United Nations. To access this web site go to: http://cyberschoolbus.un.org/infonation3/menu/advanced.asp.

International Financial Statistics (IFS)

Produced by the International Monetary Fund (IMF) and corresponding to the print publication of the same name, *IFS* is a basic source of economic and financial statistics on more than 200 countries. Data are provided on such topics as exchange rates, banking, production, and prices. Coverage dates back as far as 1948. Available online at http://ifs.apdi.net/imf/.

LABSTAT

This computer readable system comprises more than 230,000 data series gathered by the U.S. Bureau of Labor Statistics. Its range of coverage treats every aspect of labor including employment, unemployment, economic growth, prices, occupational safety and health. Available from the Bureau of Labor Statistics, Two Massachusetts Avenue, NE, Washington, DC 20212 (202) 606-5900. Available at http://stats.bls.gov.

Millennium Development Goals Indicators

This site presents the official data, definitions, methodologies and sources for the 48 indicators to measure progress towards the Millennium Development Goals. The data and analysis are the product of the work of the Inter-agency and Expert Group (IAEG) on MDG Indicators, coordinated by the United Nations Statistics Division. Also included are official progress reports and documents produced by IAEG. Links to related sites and documents and constantly updated news will keep users up to date with ongoing activities on MDG monitoring. Available at http://mdgs.un.org/unsd/mdg.

National Accounts Main Aggregates Database

The Economic Statistics Branch of the United Nations Statistics Division maintains this database of main national accounts aggregates. It is the product of a global cooperation effort between the United Nations Statistics Division, international statistical agencies and the national statistical services of more than 200 countries and is in accordance with the request of the Statistical Commission that the most recent available data on national accounts of as many countries and areas as possible be published and disseminated regularly. In addition, to the values of national accounts statistics, it contains analytical indicators and ratios derived from the main national accounts aggregates related to economic structure and development. Available at http://unstats.un.org/unsd/snaama/selectionbasicFast.asp.

OECD Main Economic Indicators

The OECD collects an extensive range of statistics from both the 29 member, and 10 non-member countries within the program of activities of the Centre for Co-operation with Non-Members (CCNM).The primary purpose for collecting such information is to provide a statistical base for use by various directorates within the organization, in country surveys, economic analyses and the formulation of policy recommendations to member governments in current areas of OECD activity. Available online at SourceOECD at http://caliban.sourceoecd.org/.

LexisNexis Statistical

LexisNexis Statistical enables easy access to statistics produced by the U.S. government, major international intergovernmental organizations, professional and trade organizations, commercial publishers, independent research organizations, state government agencies, and universities. Available online from LexisNexis at www.lexisnexis.com/academic/1univ/stat.

Dialog TradStat

With comprehensive data on the shipment of thousands of individual products around the world, TradStat offers authoritative reports covering more than 90

of world trade. Use TradStat standard or custom reports to explore business opportunities, track shifting demand, and identify developing markets. Produced by Data-Star and available online from Thomson Dialog at www.tradstatweb.com.

UNCDB Database

The United Nations Common Database is a wide-ranging statistical database which contains numerous selected statistical series, drawn from more than 30 specialized international data sources for all available countries and areas. Subjects include merchandise trade, national accounts, demography and population, energy, status of women, industrial commodities production, and statistics from the Population Division, the Project Link of the UN Department of Economic and Social Affairs, FAO, ILO, IMF, ITU, OECD, UNESCO, WHO, WIPO, World Bank and World Tourism among others. Available at http://unstats.un.org/unsd/cdb.

United Nations Commodity Trade Statistics Database (UN Comtrade)

Every year over 130 countries provide the United Nations Statistics Division with their annual international trade statistics, detailed by commodity and partner country. These data are processed into a standard format with consistent coding and valuation. All values are converted into US dollars using exchange rates supplied by the countries, or derived from monthly market rates and volume of trade. The data are then stored in a computerized data base system. For many countries the data coverage starts as far back as 1962 and goes up to the most recent completed year. Available at http://unstats.un.org/unsd/comtrade.

UNIDO Industrial Statistics Database

Provides industrial data on over 200 countries. The main emphasis in on employment, wages and salaries, value added, gross output and index numbers of industrial production. Statistics are compiled by the United Nations Industrial Development Organization in Vienna. Available online at http://www.unido.org/doc/3474.

SELECTED VENDORS OF ONLINE STATISTICAL DATABASES

Dialog Corporation
11000 Regency Parkway, Suite 10
Cary, NC 27511
(800) 3-DIALOG
http://www.dialog.com

Dialog is a worldwide leader in providing online-based information services to organizations seeking competitive advantages in such fields as business, science, engineering, finance and law. Products and services, including Dialog, Dialog Profound, Dialog DataStar, Dialog NewsEdge and Dialog Intelliscope, offer organizations the ability to precisely retrieve data from more than 1.4 billion unique records of key information, accessible via the Internet or through delivery to enterprise intranets.

Dow Jones & Company
1 World Financial Center
200 Liberty Street
New York, NY 10281
(212) 416-2000
http://www.dowjones.com

Dow Jones offers a variety of textual and statistical files, primarily in economics and finance. Representative databases of interest to statistics users include: *Dow Jones Futures and Index Quotes*; and *Media General Financial Services.*

Enerdata
2 Avenue de Vignate
38610 Gieres, France
(+33) 476422546
http://www.enerdata.fr

Enerdata is an independent consulting and information services company specializing in the energy sector and its interactions with the environment. Experts have experience in the downstream energy sector, particularly in energy demand prospective and energy efficiency. Products include: *GlobalStat*; *OilStat*; *Key Energy Stat*; and *EuropaStat.*

Factiva
30 Wall Street, 5th Floor
New York, NY 10005
(800) 369-0166
http://www.factiva.com

Factiva, a Dow Jones & Reuters Company, provides essential business news and information together with the content delivery tools and services that enable access to data from an unrivaled collection of more than 9,000 authoritative sources. Products include: *Factiva.com*; *Factiva Companies & Executives*; *Factiva iWorks*; and *Factiva SalesWorks.*

Global Insight
1000 Winter Street
Waltham, MA 02451-1241
(781) 487-2100
(781) 890-6187 (Fax)
http://www.globalinsight.com

Global Insight offers more than 90 databases, most providing economic, financial, and industrial sector data. U.S., foreign country, and worldwide statistics are all covered. Professional analysts, researchers and economists on a staff of over 450 bring expertise spanning 120 industries and over 200 countries.

Haver Analytics
60 East 42nd Street, Suite 3310
New York, NY 10165-3310
(212) 986-9300
http://www.haver.com

Specializes in databases and software products for economic analysis and business decision making. Approximately 150 statistical databases are available from Haver Analytics. New databases of interest to statistics users include: *U.S. Bond Indexes (BONDINDX)*; and *Country Surveys (INTSRVYS).*

Reuters Information Services Canada Ltd.
Exchange Tower, Suite 1900
2 First Canadian Place
Toronto, Ontario M5X 1E3, Canada
(416) 364-5361
(800) 387-1588
http://www.reuters.com

Reuters is a global information company providing information tailored for professionals in the financial services, media and corporate markets. Products include *Reuters 3000 Xtra*; *Dealing 3000 Direct*; *Reuters Trader*; *Reuters Markets Monitor.*

SunGard Data Management Solutions
888 7th Avenue, 12th Floor
New York, NY 10106
(212) 506-0300
http://www.data.sungard.com

SunGard Data Management Solutions provides a wide array of solutions to the financial, energy and public sector markets, providing mission-critical data, delivery, management and decision-support solutions that serve a wide range of investment applications. Products include the FAME Energy Data Service; PowerData End-of-Day Service; PowerData Fundamental; and PowerData Stream.

Federal Statistical Telephone Contacts

The federal government is the most important collector, disseminator, and repository of statistical information available, covering virtually every subject in today's society. Its highly-informed cadre of subject specialists is of great potential assistance to information-seekers. In a time when those seekers are becoming more inclined to go beyond traditional published sources in their search for the most current data, federal government specialists represent a unique, but often untapped, source of information.

An inventory of the federal government's statistical information sources is listed below. First arranged under broader subject categories, the inventory is then broken down further to name precise government units or individual specialists who can be called upon for help in a specific topic area. The specialists are experienced at answering questions, and do not charge for their time or assistance. When they cannot provide the specific data sought, the specialists can often make referrals to other expert contacts with the most current statistical information available.

AGRICULTURE

The National Agricultural Statistics Service collects data on crops, livestock, poultry, dairy, chemical use, prices, and labor. Its 45 field offices can provide information about agricultural production, stocks, prices and other data on an individual county and/or state basis. The agricultural experts are listed below. For a current listing see www.nass.usda.gov. Also phone the Agricultural Statistics Hotline at (800) 727-9540.

Almonds
Marousek, Doug
(202) 720-4215
doug_marousek@nass.usda.gov

Apples
O'Connor, Terry
(202) 720-4288
terry_oconnor@nass.usda.gov

Apricots
O'Connor, Terry
(202) 720-4288
terry_oconnor@nass.usda.gov

Aquaculture
Jantzi, Darin
(202) 720-0585
darin_jantzi@nass.usda.gov

Artichokes
Flippin, Debbie
(202) 720-2157
debbie_flippin@nass.usda.gov

Asparagus
Flippin, Debbie
(202) 720-2157
darin_jantzi@nass.usda.gov

Avocados
Holcomb, Rich
(202) 720-5412
rich_holcomb@nass.usda.gov

Bananas
Holcomb, Rich
(202) 720-5412
rich_holcomb@nass.usda.gov

Barley
Young, Brian
(202) 720-7621
brian_young@nass.usda.gov

Beans, Dry Edible
Scherrer, Cathy
(202) 720-4285
cathryn_scherrer@nass.usda.gov

Beans, Snap
Flippin, Debbie
(202) 720-2157
debbie_flippin@nass.usda.gov

Beans, Lima
Flippin, Debbie
(202) 720-2157
debbie_flippin@nass.usda.gov

Berries
Colburn, Leslie
(202) 720-7235
leslie_colburn@nass.usda.gov

Bison Slaughter
Clark, Shawn
(202) 690-3236
shawn_clark@nass.usda.gov

Broccoli
Flippin, Debbie
(202) 720-2157
debbie_flippin@nass.usda.gov

Broilers
Lavender, Sharyn
(202) 720-3244
sharyn_lavender@nass.usda.gov

Butter
Clark, Shawn
(202) 690-3236
shawn_clark@nass.usda.gov

Cabbage
Flippin, Debbie
(202) 720-2157
debbie_flippin@nass.usda.gov

Canola
Lamprecht, Jason
(202) 720-7369
jason_lamprecht@nass.usda.gov

Cantaloupe Melons
Flippin, Debbie
(202) 720-2157
debbie_flippin@nass.usda.gov

Carrots
Flippin, Debbie
(202) 720-2157
debbie_flippin@nass.usda.gov

Catfish
Gibson, Fleming
(202) 690-3237
fleming_gibson@nass.usda.gov

Cattle, All
Miller, Mike
(202) 720-3040
mike_miller@nass.usda.gov

Cattle on Feed
Miller, Mike
(202) 720-3040
mike_miller@nass.usda.gov

Cattle Slaughter
Paulsen, Katy
(515) 284-4340
katy_paulsen@nass.usda.gov

Cauliflower
Flippin, Debbie
(202) 720-2157
debbie_flippin@nass.usda.gov

Celery
Flippin, Debbie
(202) 720-2157
debbie_flippin@nass.usda.gov

Cheese, All
Clark, Shawn
(202) 690-3236
shawn_clark@nass.usda.gov

Cherries (Sweet, Tart)
O'Connor, Terry
(202) 720-4288
terry_oconnor@nass.usda.gov

Chickens
Lavender, Sharyn
(202) 720-3244
sharyn_lavender@nass.usda.gov

Citrus Fruits
Holcomb, Rich
(202) 720-5412
rich_holcomb@nass.usda.gov

Coffee
Holcomb, Rich
(202) 720-5412
rich_holcomb@nass.usda.gov

Cold Storage
Colwell, David
(202) 720-8784
david_colwell@nass.usda.gov

Corn, Field
Kalaus, Ty
(202) 720-9526
ty_kalaus@nass.usda.gov

Corn, Sweet
Flippin, Debbie
(202) 720-2157
debbie_flippin@nass.usda.gov

Cost of Inputs
Brown, Jennifer
(202) 720-5446
jennifer_brown@nass.usda.gov

Cotton
Corley, Shiela
(202) 720-5944
shiela_corley@nass.usda.gov

Cotton Ginnings
Corley, Shiela
(202) 720-5944
shiela_corley@nass.usda.gov

Cottonseed
Corley, Shiela
(202) 720-5944
shiela_corley@nass.usda.gov

Cranberries
O'Connor, Terry
(202) 720-4288
terry_oconnor@nass.usda.gov

Crop Progress
Young, Brian
(202) 720-7621
brian_young@nass.usda.gov

Crop Values

Young, Brian
(202) 720-7621
brian_young@nass.usda.gov

Crop Weather
Young, Brian
(202) 720-7621
brian_young@nass.usda.gov

Cucumbers
Flippin, Debbie
(202) 720-2157
debbie_flippin@nass.usda.gov

Dairy Product Prices
Clark, Shawn
(202) 690-3236
shawn_clark@nass.usda.gov

Dairy Products, Frozen
Clark, Shawn
(202) 690-3236
shawn_clark@nass.usda.gov

Dates
Holcomb, Rich
(202) 720-5412
rich_holcomb@nass.usda.gov

Eggs
Gibson, Fleming
(202) 690-3237
fleming_gibson@nass.usda.gov

Equine Slaughter
Paulsen, Katy
(515) 284-4340
katy_paulsen@nass.usda.gov

Farm and Land
Miller, Julie
(202) 690-3231
julie_miller@nass.usda.gov

Farm Production Expenditures
Barton, Rich
(202) 690-1052
rich_barton@nass.usda.gov

Figs
Holcomb, Rich
(202) 720-5412
rich_holcomb@nass.usda.gov

Flaxseed
Kalaus, Ty
(202) 720-9526
ty_kalaus@nass.usda.gov

Floriculture
Marousek, Doug
(202) 720-4215
doug_marousek@nass.usda.gov

Garlic
Flippin, Debbie
(202) 720-2157
debbie_flippin@nass.usda.gov

Genetic Modified Organisms
Kalaus, Ty
(202) 720-9526
ty_kalaus@nass.usda.gov

Ginger Root
Holcomb, Rich
(202) 720-5412
rich_holcomb@nass.usda.gov

Goats
Hollis, Scott
(202) 720-4751
scott_hollis@nass.usda.gov

Goats Slaughter
Paulsen, Katy
(515) 284-4340
katy_paulsen@nass.usda.gov

Grain Stocks
Kalaus, Ty
(202) 720-9526
ty_kalaus@nass.usda.gov

Grapefruit
Holcomb, Rich
(202) 720-5412
rich_holcomb@nass.usda.gov

Grapes
Colburn, Leslie
(202) 720-7235
leslie_colburn@nass.usda.gov

Grazing Fees, Private
Barnes, Eric
(202) 690-4752
eric_barnes@nass.usda.gov

Guava
Holcomb, Rich
(202) 720-5412
rich_holcomb@nass.usda.gov

Hay
Thorson, Travis
(202) 690-3234
travis_thorson@nass.usda.gov

Hazelnuts
Marousek, Doug
(202) 720-4215
doug_marousek@nass.usda.gov

Hogs and Pigs
Boess, Bruce
(202) 720-3106
bruce_boess@nass.usda.gov

Hog Slaughter
Paulsen, Katy
(515) 284-4340
katy_paulsen@nass.usda.gov

Honey
Lavender, Sharyn
(202) 720-3244
sharyn_lavender@nass.usda.gov

Honeydew Melons
Flippin, Debbie
(202) 720-2157
debbie_flippin@nass.usda.gov

Hops
Ritchie, Kim
(360) 902-1962
dara_kim_ritchie@nass.usda.gov

Horticulture Specialties
Marousek, Doug
(202) 720-4215
doug_marousek@nass.usda.gov

Input Costs
Williams, Jim
(202) 690-3225
jim_williams@nass.usda.gov

Kiwifruit
Holcomb, Rich
(202) 720-5412
rich_holcomb@nass.usda.gov

Labor, Farm
Aitken, Mark
(202) 720-9525
mark_aitken@nass.usda.gov

Land Values
Williams, Jim
(202) 690-3225
jim_williams@nass.usda.gov

Lemons
Holcomb, Rich
(202) 720-5412
rich_holcomb@nass.usda.gov

Lentils
Norris, Dan
(202) 720-3250
dan_norris@nass.usda.gov

Lettuce
Flippin, Debbie
(202) 720-2157
debbie_flippin@nass.usda.gov

Limes
Holcomb, Rich
(202) 720-5412
rich_holcomb@nass.usda.gov

Macadamia Nuts
Marousek, Doug
(202) 720-4215
doug_marousek@nass.usda.gov

Maple Syrup
Colburn, Leslie
(202) 720-7235
leslie_colburn@nass.usda.gov

Milk
Summa, Ann
(202) 720-3278
ann_summa@nass.usda.gov

Milk Used in Manufacturing Products
Clark, Shawn
(202) 690-3236
shawn_clark@nass.usda.gov

Millet (Proso)
Kalaus, Ty
(202) 720-9526
ty_kalaus@nass.usda.gov

Mink
Gibson, Fleming
(202) 690-3237
fleming_gibson@nass.usda.gov

Mohair
Hollis, Scott
(202) 720-4751
scott_hollis@nass.usda.gov

Mushrooms
Norris, Dan
(202) 720-3250
dan_norris@nass.usda.gov

Mustard Seed
Lamprecht, Jason
(202) 720-7369
jason_lamprecht@nass.usda.gov

Nectarines
Holcomb, Rich
(202) 720-5412
rich_holcomb@nass.usda.gov

Nursery Crops
Marousek, Doug
(202) 720-4215
doug_marousek@nass.usda.gov

Nuts
Marousek, Doug
(202) 720-4215
doug_marousek@nass.usda.gov

Oats
Thorson, Travis
(202) 690-3234
travis_thorson@nass.usda.gov

Olives
Holcomb, Rich
(202) 720-5412
rich_holcomb@nass.usda.gov

Onions
Flippin, Debbie
(202) 720-2157
debbie_flippin@nass.usda.gov

Oranges
Holcomb, Rich
(202) 720-5412
rich_holcomb@nass.usda.gov

Papayas
Holcomb, Rich
(202) 720-5412
rich_holcomb@nass.usda.gov

Peaches
Norris, Dan
(202) 720-3250
dan_norris@nass.usda.gov

Peanuts
Koong, Dennis
(202) 720-7688
dennis_koong@nass.usda.gov

Pears
Norris, Dan
(202) 720-3250
dan_norris@nass.usda.gov

Peas, Dry Edible
Norris, Dan

(202) 720-3250
dan_norris@nass.usda.gov

Peas, Wrinkled Seed
Norris, Dan
(202) 720-3250
dan_norris@nass.usda.gov

Peas, Green
Flippin, Debbie
(202) 720-2157
debbie_flippin@nass.usda.gov

Pecans
Marousek, Doug
(202) 720-4215
doug_marousek@nass.usda.gov

Peppermint Oil
Norris, Dan
(202) 720-3250
dan_norris@nass.usda.gov

Peppers (Bell, Chile)
Flippin, Debbie
(202) 720-2157
debbie_flippin@nass.usda.gov

Pickle Stocks
Flippin, Debbie
(202) 720-2157
debbie_flippin@nass.usda.gov

Pineapples
Holcomb, Rich
(202) 720-5412
rich_holcomb@nass.usda.gov

Pistachios
Marousek, Doug
(202) 720-4215
doug_marousek@nass.usda.gov

Plums
O'Connor, Terry
(202) 720-4288
terry_oconnor@nass.usda.gov

Potatoes
Scherrer, Cathy
(202) 720-4285
cathryn_scherrer@nass.usda.gov

Poultry Slaughter
Gibson, Fleming
(202) 690-3237
fleming_gibson@nass.usda.gov

Prices Paid by Farmers
Williams, James
(202) 690-3225
james_williams@nass.usda.gov

Prices Paid Indexes
Williams, James
(202) 690-3225
james_williams@nass.usda.gov

Prunes
O'Connor, Terry
(202) 720-4288
terry_oconnor@nass.usda.gov

Pumpkins
Flippin, Debbie
(202) 720-2157
debbie_flippin@nass.usda.gov

Rapeseed
Lamprecht, Jason
(202) 720-7369
jason_lamprecht@nass.usda.gov

Rice
Koong, Dennis
(202) 720-7688
dennis_koong@nass.usda.gov

Rye
Cox, Scott
(202) 720-8068
lance_honig@nass.usda.gov

Safflower
Lamprecht, Jason
(202) 720-7369
jason_lamprecht@nass.usda.gov

Sheep and Lambs
Hollis, Scott
(202) 720-4751
scott_hollis@nass.usda.gov

Sheep and Lamb Slaughter
Paulsen, Katy
(515) 284-4340
katy_paulsen@nass.usda.gov

Slaughter (Plants)
Paulsen, Katy
(515) 284-4340
katy_paulsen@nass.usda.gov

Sorghum
Thorson, Travis
(202) 690-3234
travis_thorson@nass.usda.gov

Soybeans
Lamprecht, Jason
(202) 720-7369
jason_lamprecht@nass.usda.gov

Spearmint Oil
Norris, Dan
(202) 720-3250
dan_norris@nass.usda.gov

Spinach
Flippin, Debbie
(202) 720-2157
debbie_flippin@nass.usda.gov

Strawberries
Flippin, Debbie
(202) 720-2157
debbie_flippin@nass.usda.gov

Sugarbeets
Young, Brian
(202) 720-7621
brian_young@nass.usda.gov

Sugarcane
Young, Brian
(202) 720-7621
brian_young@nass.usda.gov

Sunflower
Lamprecht, Jason
(202) 720-7369
jason_lamprecht@nass.usda.gov

Sweetpotatoes
Scherrer, Cathy
(202) 720-4285
cathryn_scherrer@nass.usda.gov

Tangelos
Holcomb, Rich
(202) 720-5412
rich_holcomb@nass.usda.gov

Tangerines
Holcomb, Rich
(202) 720-5412
rich_holcomb@nass.usda.gov

Taro
Holcomb, Rich
(202) 720-5412
rich_holcomb@nass.usda.gov

Temples
Holcomb, Rich
(202) 720-5412
rich_holcomb@nass.usda.gov

Tobacco
Colburn, Leslie
(202) 720-7235
leslie_colburn@nass.usda.gov

Tomatoes
Flippin, Debbie
(202) 720-2157
debbie_flippin@nass.usda.gov

Trout
Jantzi, Darin
(202) 720-0585
darin_jantzi@nass.usda.gov

Turkeys, Hatchery
Jantzi, Darin
(202) 720-0585
darin_jantzi@nass.usda.gov

Turkeys, Raised
Jantzi, Darin
(202) 720-0585
darin_jantzi@nass.usda.gov

Walnuts
Marousek, Doug
(202) 720-4215
doug_marousek@nass.usda.gov

Wage Rates
Aitken, Mark
(202) 720-9525
mark_aitken@nass.usda.gov

Watermelon
Flippin, Debbie
(202) 720-2157
debbie_flippin@nass.usda.gov

Wheat
Cox, Scott
(202) 720-8068
scott_cox@nass.usda.gov

Whey Products
Clark, Shawn
(202) 690-3236
shawn_clark@nass.usda.gov

Wool
Hollis, Scott
(202) 720-4751
scott_hollis@nass.usda.gov

State Statistical Offices

The following people can provide information about agricultural production, stocks, prices and other data for individual States and, in many cases, for counties in those States. For an updated list, go to Internet site http://www.usda.gov/nass/offices.htm.

ALABAMA - Montgomery
H.L. Vanderberry
(334) 279-3555
(800) 832-4181
Fax: (334) 279-3590
nass-al@nass.usda.gov

ALASKA - Palmer
S. Benz
(907) 745-4272
(800) 478-6079
Fax: (907) 746-4654
nass-ak@nass.usda.gov

ARIZONA - Phoenix
S.A. Manheimer
(602) 280-8850
(800) 645-7286
Fax: (602) 280-8897
nass-az@nass.usda.gov

ARKANSAS - Little Rock
B.F. Klugh
(501) 228-9926
(800) 327-2970
Fax: (501) 296-9960
nass-ar@nass.usda.gov

CALIFORNIA - Sacramento
V. Tolomeo
(916) 498-5161
(800) 851-1127
Fax: (916) 498-5186
nass-ca@nass.usda.gov

COLORADO - Lakewood
R.R. Picanso
(303) 236-2300
(800) 392-3202
Fax: (303) 236-2299
nass-co@nass.usda.gov

CONNECTICUT - See NEW ENGLAND

DELAWARE - Dover
C.L. Cadwallader
(302) 698-4537
(800) 282-8685
Fax: (302) 697-4450
nass-de@nass.usda.gov

FLORIDA - Orlando
J.D. Witzig

(407) 648-6013
(800) 344-6277
Fax: (407) 648-6029
nass-fl@nass.usda.gov

GEORGIA - Athens
D.S. Abbe
(706) 546-2236
(800) 253-4419
Fax: (706) 546-2416
nass-ga@nass.usda.gov

HAWAII - Honolulu
D.A. Martin
(808) 973-2907
(800) 804-9514
Fax: (808) 973-2909
nass-hi@nass.usda.gov

IDAHO - Boise
D.G. Gerhardt
(208) 334-1507
(800) 691-9987
Fax: (208) 334-1114
nass-id@nass.usda.gov

ILLINOIS - Springfield
B.E. Schwab
(217) 492-4295
(800) 622-9865
Fax: (217) 492-4291
nass-il@nass.usda.gov

INDIANA - West Lafayette
G. Preston
(765) 494-8371
(800) 363-0469
Fax: (765) 494-4315
nass-in@nass.usda.gov

IOWA - Des Moines
J.K. Sands
(515) 284-4340
(800) 772-0825
Fax: (515) 284-4342
nass-ia@nass.usda.gov

KANSAS - Topeka
E.J. Thiessen
(785) 233-2230
(800) 258-4564
Fax: (785) 233-2518
nass-ks@nass.usda.gov

KENTUCKY - Louisville
L.E. Brown
(502) 582-5293
(800) 928-5277
Fax: (502) 582-5114
nass-ky@nass.usda.gov

LOUISIANA - Baton Rouge
A.D. Frank
(504) 922-1362
(800) 256-4485
Fax: (504) 922-0744
nass-la@nass.usda.gov

MAINE - See NEW ENGLAND

MARYLAND - Annapolis
N. Bennett
(410) 841-5740
(800) 675-0295
Fax: (410) 841-5755
nass-md@nass.usda.gov

MASSACHUSETTS - See NEW ENGLAND

MICHIGAN - Lansing
D.D. Kleweno
(517) 324-5300
(800) 453-7501
Fax: (517) 324-5299
nass-mi@nass.usda.gov

MINNESOTA - St. Paul
D.A. Hartwig
(651) 296-2230
(800) 453-7502
Fax: (651) 296-3192
nass-mn@nass.usda.gov

MISSISSIPPI - Jackson
T.L. Gregory
(601) 965-4575
(800) 535-9609
Fax: (601) 965-5622
nass-ms@nass.usda.gov

MISSOURI - Columbia
G. Danekas
(573) 876-0950
(800) 551-1014
Fax: (573) 876-0973
nass-mo@nass.usda.gov

MONTANA - Helena
P. Stringer
(406) 441-1240
(800) 835-2612
Fax: (406) 441-1250
nass-mt@nass.usda.gov

NEBRASKA - Lincoln
J.M. Harris
(402) 437-5541
(800) 582-6443
Fax: (402) 437-5547
nass-ne@nass.usda.gov

NEVADA - Reno
M.J. Owens
(702) 784-5584
(888) 456-7211
Fax: (702) 784-5766
nass-nv@nass.usda.gov

NEW ENGLAND - Concord, NH
A.R. Davis
(603) 224-9639
(800) 642-9571
Fax: (603) 225-1434
nass-nh@nass.usda.gov

NEW HAMPSHIRE - See NEW ENGLAND

NEW JERSEY - Trenton
B.L. Cross
(609) 292-6385
(800) 328-0179
Fax: (609) 633-9231
nass-nj@nass.usda.gov

NEW MEXICO - Las Cruces
D.C. Nelson
(505) 522-6023
(800) 530-8810
Fax: (505) 522-7646
nass-nm@nass.usda.gov

NEW YORK - Albany
S.C. Ropel
(518) 457-5570
(800) 821-1276
Fax: (518) 453-6564
nass-ny@nass.usda.gov

NORTH CAROLINA - Raleigh
R.M. Murphy
(919) 856-4394
(800) 437-8451
Fax: (919) 856-4139
nass-nc@nass.usda.gov

NORTH DAKOTA - Fargo
D.P. Knopf
(701) 239-5306
(800) 626-3134
Fax: (701) 239-5613
nass-nd@nass.usda.gov

OHIO - Reynoldsburg
J.E. Ramey
(614) 728-2100
(800) 858-8144
Fax: (614) 728-2206
nass-oh@nass.usda.gov

OKLAHOMA - Oklahoma City
B.L. Bloyd
(405) 522-6190
(888) 525-9226
Fax: (405) 528-2296
nass-ok@nass.usda.gov

OREGON - Portland
J.A. Goodwin
(503) 326-2131
(800) 338-2157
Fax: (503) 326-2549
nass-or@nass.usda.gov

PENNSYLVANIA - Harrisburg
M. Tosiano
(717) 787-3904
(800) 498-1518
Fax: (717) 782-4011
nass-pa@nass.usda.gov

PUERTO RICO - Santurce
A.M. Cruz
(787)723-3773
Fax: (787) 721-8355
nass-pr@nass.usda.gov

RHODE ISLAND - See NEW ENGLAND

SOUTH CAROLINA - Columbia
R.A. Graham
(803) 765-5333
(800) 424-9406
Fax: (803) 765-5310
nass-sc@nass.usda.gov

SOUTH DAKOTA - Sioux Falls
C.D. Anderson
(605) 323-4235
(800) 338-2557
Fax: (605) 330-6500
nass-sd@nass.usda.gov

TENNESSEE - Nashville
D.K. Kenerson
(615) 781-5300
(800) 626-0987
Fax: (615) 781-5303
nass-tn@nass.usda.gov

TEXAS - Austin
R.O. Roark
(512) 916-5581
(800) 626-3142
Fax: (512) 916-5956
nass-tx@nass.usda.gov

UTAH - Salt Lake City
R. Kestle
(801) 524-5003
(800) 747-8522
Fax: (801) 524-3090
nass-ut@nass.usda.gov

VERMONT - See NEW ENGLAND

VIRGINIA - Richmond
K.L. Barnes
(804) 771-2493
(800) 772-0670
Fax: (804) 771-2651
nass-va@nass.usda.gov

WASHINGTON - Olympia
R. Garibay
(360) 902-1940
(800) 435-5883
Fax: (360) 902-2091
nass-wa@nass.usda.gov

WEST VIRGINIA - Charleston
D. King
(304) 345-5958
(800) 535-7088
Fax: (304) 558-0297
nass-wv@nass.usda.gov

WISCONSIN - Madison
R.G. Battaglia
(608) 224-4848
(800) 789-9277
Fax: (608) 224-4855
nass-wi@nass.usda.gov

WYOMING - Cheyenne
D.W. Coulter
(307) 432-5600
(800) 892-1660
Fax: (307) 432-5598
nass-wy@nass.usda.gov

BANKING AND FINANCIAL DATA

The Federal Reserve Board's Division of Research and Statistics is responsible for developing and presenting economic and financial data and analysis for the use of the Board, the Federal Open Market

Committee, and other Federal Reserve System officials. This information serves as background for the formulation and conduct of monetary, regulatory, and supervisory policies. In addition, the division fosters a broader understanding of issues relating to economic policy by providing leadership in economic and statistical research and by supplying data and analyses for public release.

Capital Markets
Paul Harrison
Economist, Capital Markets Section
(202) 452-3637
paul.harrison@frb.gov
Gene Amromin
Economist, Capital Markets Section
(202) 452-2995
gene.amromin@frb.gov
Daniel M. Covitz
Senior Economist, Capital Markets Section
(202) 452-5267
daniel.m.covitz@frb.gov
Song Han
Economist, Capital Markets Section
(202) 736-1971
song.han@frb.gov
Greg Nini
Economist, International Banking and Finance Section
Division of International Finance
(202) 452-2626
gregory.p.nini@frb.gov
Steven A. Sharpe
Senior Economist, Capital Markets Section
steve.a.sharpe@frb.gov

Financial Structure
Robin Prager
Chief, Financial Structure Section
(202) 452-3643
robin.prager@frb.gov
Robert M. Adams
Economist, Financial Structure Section
robert.m.adams@frb.gov
Ron Borzekowski
Economist, Financial Structure Section
(202) 452-3080
ron.borzekowski@frb.gov
Andrew M. Cohen
Economist, Financial Structure Section
(202) 452-2612
andrew.m.cohen@frb.gov
Timothy H. Hannan
Senior Economist, Financial Structure Section
(202) 452-2919
timothy.h.hannan@frb.gov
Elizabeth K. Kiser
Economist, Financial Structure Section
(202) 452-2584
elizabeth.k.kiser@frb.gov
Steven J. Pilloff
Economist, Financial Structure Section
(202) 736-5622
steven.j.pilloff@frb.gov

Fiscal Analysis
Wolfhard Ramm
Chief, Fiscal Analysis Section
(202) 452-2381
wolf.ramm@frb.gov
Darrel S. Cohen
Senior Economist, Fiscal Analysis Section
(202) 452-2376
darrel.s.cohen@frb.gov
Glenn R. Follette
Senior Economist, Fiscal Analysis Section
(202) 452-2940
glenn.r.follette@frb.gov
Louise M. Sheiner
Senior Economist, Fiscal Analysis Section
(202) 452-2761
louise.m.sheiner@frb.gov

Flow of Funds
Michael G. Palumbo
Chief, Flow of Funds Section
michael.g.palumbo@frb.gov
Morris A. Davis
Economist, Flow of Funds Section
(202) 452-3628
morris.a.davis@frb.gov
Susan Hume McIntosh
Senior Economist, Flow of Funds Section
(202) 452-3484
susanhume.mcintosh@frb.gov
Ellen A. Merry
Economist, Flow of Funds Section
ellen.a.merry@frb.gov
Maria G. Perozek
Economist, Flow of Funds Section
maria.g.perozek@frb.gov
Paul A. Smith
Economist, Flow of Funds Section
paul.a.smith@frb.gov

Household and Real Estate Finance
Karen Dynan
Chief, Household and Real Estate Finance Section
(202) 452-2553
karen.dynan@frb.gov
Kathleen W. Johnson
Economist, Household and Real Estate Finance Section
(202) 452-3644
kathleen.w.johnson@frb.gov
Andreas Lehnert
Economist, Household and Real Estate Finance Section
(202) 452-3325
andreas.lehnert@frb.gov
Karen M. Pence
Economist, Household and Real Estate Finance Section
(202) 452-2342
karen.pence@frb.gov
Shane M. Sherlund
Economist, Household and Real Estate Finance Section
(202) 452-3589
shane.m.sherlund@frb.gov

Industrial Output
Carol A. Corrado, Chief
Industrial Output Section
(202) 452-3521
carol.a.corrado@frb.gov
Kimberly N. Bayard
Economist, Industrial Output Section
(202) 452-2570
kimberly.n.bayard@frb.gov
David M. Byrne
Economist, Industrial Output Section
(202) 452-3587
david.m.byrne@frb.gov
William P. Cleveland
Senior Statistician, Industrial Output Section
(202) 452-2436
william.p.cleveland@frb.gov
Adam M. Copeland
Economist, Industrial Output Section
(202) 452-2980
adam.m.copeland@frb.gov
Wendy E. Dunn
Economist, Industrial Output Section
(202) 452-2939
wendy.e.dunn@frb.gov
Paul Lengermann
Economist, Industrial Output Section
(202) 452-3928
paul.a.lengermann@frb.gov
Norman J. Morin
Senior Economist, Industrial Output Section
(202) 452-2476
norman.j.morin@frb.gov
John J. Stevens
Economist, Industrial Output Section
(202) 452-2206
john.j.stevens@frb.gov
Daniel J. Vine
Economist, Industrial Output Section
(202) 452-3468
daniel.j.vine@frb.gov

Macroeconomic Analysis
Douglas W. Elmendorf, Assistant Director
Chief, Macroeconomic Analysis Section
(202) 452-3623
douglas.w.elmendorf@frb.gov
Stephanie R. Aaronson
Economist, Macroeconomic Analysis Section
stephanie.r.aaronson@frb.gov
Wendy M. Edelberg
Economist, Macroeconomic Analysis Section
(202) 452-2715
wendy.m.edelberg@frb.gov
Bruce Fallick
Senior Economist, Macroeconomic Analysis Section
(202) 452-3722
bruce.fallick@frb.gov
Michael Feroli
Economist, Macroeconomic Analysis Section
(202) 452-3792
michael.feroli@frb.gov
Andrew Figura
Economist, Macroeconomic Analysis Section
(202) 452-2583
andrew.figura@frb.gov
Charles A. Fleischman
Economist, Macroeconomic Analysis Section
(202) 452-6473
charles.a.fleischman@frb.gov
Mark W. French
Economist, Macroeconomic Analysis Section
(202) 452-3801
mark.w.french@frb.gov
Joshua Gallin
Senior Economist, Macroeconomic Analysis Section
(202) 452-2788
joshua.h.gallin@frb.gov
Pierre M. Lafourcade
Economist, Macroeconomic Analysis Section
(202) 452-3408
pierre.m.lafourcade@frb.gov
David E. Lebow
Senior Economist, Macroeconomic Analysis Section
(202) 452-3057
david.e.lebow@frb.gov
Deb Lindner
Senior Economist, Macroeconomic Analysis Section
(202) 452-2363
deb.lindner@frb.gov
Joseph P. Lupton
Economist, Macroeconomic Analysis Section
joseph.p.lupton@frb.gov
Jonathan N. Millar
Economist, Macroeconomic Analysis Section
(202) 452-2868
jonathan.n.millar@frb.gov
Jonathan F. Pingle
Economist, Macroeconomic Analysis Section
(202) 452-3816
jonathan.f.pingle@frb.gov
Jeremy Rudd
Senior Economist, Macroeconomic Analysis Section
(202) 452-3780
jeremy.rudd@frb.gov
Stacey Tevlin
Senior Economist, Macroeconomic Analysis Section
(202) 452-2322
stacey.m.tevlin@frb.gov

Macroeconomic and Quantitative Studies
Michael T. Kiley
Chief, Macroeconomic and Quantitative Studies Section
(202) 452-2448
michael.t.kiley@frb.gov
David M. Arseneau
Economist, Macroeconomic and Quantitative Studies Section
(202) 452-2534
david.m.arseneau@frb.gov
Flint Brayton
Senior Economist, Macroeconomic and Quantitative Studies Section
(202) 452-2670
flint.brayton@frb.gov
Rochelle M. Edge
Economist, Macroeconomic and Quantitative Studies Section
(202) 452-2339
rochelle.m.edge@frb.gov
Thomas Laubach
Economist, Macroeconomic and Quantitative Studies Section

(202) 452-2715
thomas.laubach@frb.gov
John M. Roberts
Senior Economist, Macroeconomic and Quantitative Studies Section
(202) 452-2946
john.m.roberts@frb.gov
Thomas D. Tallarini, Jr.
Economist, Macroeconomic and Quantitative Studies Section
(202) 452-3970
thomas.d.tallarini@frb.gov
Robert J. Tetlow
Senior Economist, Macroeconomic and Quantitative Studies Section
(202) 452-2437
robert.j.tetlow@frb.gov

Micro Statistics
Darrel W. Parke
Chief, Micro Statistics Section
(202) 452-2470
darrel.w.parke@frb.gov
May X. Liu
Statistician, Micro Statistics Section
(202) 452-3592
may.x.liu@frb.gov

Monetary and Financial Studies
Diana Hancock
Chief, Monetary and Financial Studies Section
(202) 452-3019
diana.hancock@frb.gov
Robert B. Avery
Senior Economist, Monetary and Financial Studies Section
(202) 452-2906
robert.b.avery@frb.gov
Allen N. Berger
Senior Economist, Monetary and Financial Studies Section
(202) 452-2903
allen.n.berger@frb.gov
Brian Bucks
Economist, Monetary and Financial Studies Section
(202) 736-5625
brian.k.bucks@frb.gov
Michael Gordy
Senior Economist, Monetary and Financial Studies Section
(202) 452-3705
michael.gordy@frb.gov
Erik A. Heitfield
Economist, Monetary and Financial Studies Section
(202) 452-2613
erik.a.heitfield@frb.gov
Arthur Kennickell
Senior Economist, Monetary and Financial Studies Section
(202) 452-2247
arthur.kennickell@frb.gov
Kevin B. Moore
Economist, Monetary and Financial Studies Section
(202) 452-3887
kevin.b.moore@frb.gov
Frank Xiaoling Zhang
Economist, Monetary and Financial Studies Section
(202) 452-2581
xiaoling.zhang@frb.gov

Trading Risk Analysis
Michael S. Gibson
Assistant Director
Chief, Trading Risk Analysis Section
(202) 452-2495
michael.s.gibson@frb.gov
Sean D. Campbell
Economist, Trading Risk Analysis Section
sean.d.campbell@frb.gov
James M. O'Brien
Senior Economist, Trading Risk Analysis Section
(202) 452-2384
james.m.o'brien@frb.gov
Matthew Pritsker
Senior Economist, Trading Risk Analysis Section
(202) 452-3534
matthew.pritsker@frb.gov
Hao Zhou
Economist, Trading Risk Analysis Section
(202) 452-3360
hao.zhou@frb.gov

Program Direction
David J. Stockton
Director, Division of Research and Statistics
(202) 452-3068
dave.stockton@frb.gov
Glenn B. Canner
Senior Adviser, Division of Research and Statistics
(202) 452-2910
glenn.b.canner@frb.gov
Myron L. Kwast
Associate Director, Division of Research and Statistics
(202) 452-2909
myron.l.kwast@frb.gov
Nellie Liang
Assistant Director, Division of Research and Statistics
Chief, Capital Markets Section
(202) 452-2918
jnellie.liang@frb.gov
Stephen D. Oliner
Associate Director, Division of Research and Statistics
(202) 452-3134
stephen.d.oliner@frb.gov
David Reifschneider
Deputy Associate Director, Division of Research and Statistics
(202) 452-2941
david.l.reifschneider@frb.gov
Janice Shack-Marquez
Assistant Director, Division of Research and Statistics
(202) 452-2672
janice.shack-marquez@frb.gov
Daniel E. Sichel
Assistant Director, Division of Research and Statistics
dan.sichel@frb.gov
Larry Slifman
Associate Director, Division of Research and Statistics
(202) 452-2543
larry.slifman@frb.gov
William L. Wascher
Deputy Associate Director, Division of Research and Statistics
(202) 452-2812
william.l.wascher@frb.gov
David W. Wilcox
Deputy Director, Division of Research and Statistics
(202) 452-2991
david.w.wilcox@frb.gov

CENSUS DATA

These specialists can tell precisely what statistical data is available in their subject areas. The information is arranged by program and subject area. To contact any of the specialists by mail, use their name, division and address: U.S. Census Bureau, Washington, D.C. 20233. E-mail comments or other requests to the editor, Mary G. Thomas, at mary.g.thomas@census.gov or call (301) 763-2800/3030.

AMERICAN FACTFINDER

American FactFinderAmerican FactFinder Staff (MSO)
(301) 763-INFO (4636)
factfinder@census.gov

CENSUS ADVISORY COMMITTEES OFFICE

Census Advisory Committees
Jeri Green (CACO)
(301) 763-2070

Census Advisory Committee of Professional Association
Sue Knight (CACO)
(301) 763-2095

Decennial Census Advisory Committee
Sue Knight (CACO)
(301) 763-2095

Race and Ethnic Advisory Committees
Edwina Jaramillo (CACO)
(301) 763-4047

CENSUS INFORMATION CENTERS

The Census Information Centers (CICs) are national, regional, and local nonprofit organizations in partnership with the Census Bureau to make census data available to underserved communities. The CICs provide access to and understanding of the value and uses of census data to communities and neighborhoods across the country.

Arab American Institute, Washington, DC
Sabeen Altaf
(202) 429-9210
saltaf@aaiusa.org

Asian American Federation of New York, New York, NY
Parag Khandhar
(212) 344-5878
parag@aafny.org

Asian and Pacific Islander American Health Forum, Inc., Washington, DC
Gem Daus
(202) 466-7772
gdaus@apiahf.org

ASIAN, Inc., San Francisco, CA
David Moulton
(415) 928-5910
dmoulton@asianinc.org

Barber-Scotia College, Concord, NC
Alexander Erwin
(704) 789-2948
aerwin@b-sc.edu

Bayamon Central University, Bayamon, PR
Jose R. Jorge
(787) 786-3030 ext. 2142
jorgejose97@hotmail.com

California Indian Manpower Consortium, Inc., Sacramento, CA
Lorenda Sanchez
(916) 920-0285
lorendas@cimcinc.com

Center on Pacific Studies, San Diego State University, San Diego, CA
Kehaulani L. Galeai
(619) 594-0139
kehau@interwork.sdsu.edu

Child Welfare League of America, Inc., Washington, DC
Noel Kinder
(202) 639-4957
nkinder@cwla.org

Children's Defense Fund, Washington, DC
Deborah Cutterortiz
(202) 662-3537
dortiz@childrensdefense.org

Chinese American Voters Education Committee, San Francisco, CA
David Lee
(415) 397-8133
cavec1@aol.com

Dillard University, New Orleans, LA
Dr. Robert A. Collins
(504) 816-4092
rcollins@dillard.edu

First Nations Development Institute, Fredericksburg, VA
Kammi Johannsen
(540) 371-5615 ext. 47
kjohannsen@firstnations.org

Florida Agricultural and Mechanical University, Tallahassee, FL
Dr. Juanita Gaston
(850) 412-7545
juanita.gaston@famu.edu

Goodwill Industries International, Inc., Bethesda, MD
Lisa Bowers
(301) 530-6500
lisa.bowers@goodwill.org

Howard University, Center for Urban Progress, Washington, DC
Lorenzo Morris
(202) 806-6720
Lmorris@howard.edu

Indian and Native American Employment and Training Coalition, Anchorage, AK
Norman DeWeaver
(907) 265-5975
norm_deweaver@rocketmail.com

Jackson State University, Jackson, MS
Sam Mozee, Jr.
(601) 979-4100
smozee@murc.org

Joint Center for Political and Economic Studies, Washington, DC
Dr. Roderick Harrison
(202) 789-3514
rharrison@jointcenter.org

Korean American Coalition, Los Angeles, CA
Steven Lee
(213) 265-5999
steve@kacla.org

Langston University, Langston, OK
Lawrence Grear
(405) 466-3344
ldgrear@lunet.edu

Latin American Chamber of Commerce, Chicago, IL
Lorenzo Padron
(773) 252-5211
dlpadron@lacc1.com

Leadership Conference on Civil Rights, Washington, DC
Theora Sumler
(202) 466-5672
sumler@civilrights.org

LeMoyne-Owen College, Memphis, TN
Austin Emeagwai
(901) 942-7372
austin_emeagwai@nile.lemoyne-owen.edu

Louisiana State University, Center for Business and Economic Research, Shreveport, LA
Susan Beal
(318) 797-5187
sbeal@pilot.lsus.edu

Medgar Evers College of the City University of NY, Dubois Bunche, Center for Public Policy, Brooklyn, NY
John Flateau
(718) 270-5110
jflat@mec.cuny.edu

Meharry Medical College, Nashville, TN
Green A. Ekadi
(615) 327-5516
gekadi@mmc.edu

NAACP, Baltimore, MD
Zakia Richburg
(410) 580-5756
zrichburg@naacpnet.org

National Asian Pacific Center on Aging, Seattle, WA
Kenneth Bostock
(206) 624-1221
kjb@napca.org

National Council of La Raza, Washington, DC
Eric Rodriguez
(202) 785-1670
erodriguez@nclr.org

National Urban League, Washington, DC
Cheryl Hill-Lee
(202) 898-1604
clee@nul.org

The Navajo Nation, Window Rock, AZ
Trib Choudhary
(928) 871-6810
tribthar@cia-g.com

Norfolk State University, Norfolk, VA
Rudolph Wilson
(757) 823-9575
rwilson@nsu.edu

Northeast Council of Governments, Aberdeen, SD
Eric Senger
(605) 626-2595
eric.necog@midconetwork.com

Organization of Chinese Americans, Washington, DC
Christine Chen
(202) 223-5500
cchen@ocanatl.org

Papa Ola Lokahi, Honolulu, HI
Momi Lovell
(808) 597-6550 ext. 804
mlovell@papaolalokahi.org

Puerto Rican Legal Defense and Education Fund, New York, NY
Jose Garcia
(212) 739-7501
jose_garcia@prldef.org

Rural Community Assistance Program, Washington, DC
Stephen Gasteyer
(202) 408-1273
sgasteyer@rcap.org

SER-Jobs for Progress National, Inc., Irving, TX
Raul Santa
(972) 506-7815
rsanta@ser-national.org

Siete del Norte, Embudo, NM
Dr. Alvin O. Korte
(505) 579-4217
alvinkorte@mail.cybermesa.com

Sitting Bull College, Ft. Yates, ND
Mark Holman
(701) 854-3861
markh@sbci.edu

Special Service for Groups, Los Angeles, CA
Takuya Maruyama
(213) 553-1800
accisla@ssgmain.org

Spelman College, Atlanta, GA
Bruce H. Wade
(404) 270-5629
censusinfocenter@spelman.edu

United States Hispanic Leadership Institute, Chicago, IL
Rudy Lopez
(312) 427-8683
rlopez@ushli.com

University of California, Los Angeles, CA
Melany de la Cruz
(310) 825-2974
melanyd@ucla.edu

University of Notre Dame, Notre Dame, IN
Sung-Chang Chun
(574) 631-8146
sung-chang.chun.1@nd.edu
Dr. Tim Ready
(574) 631-8146
tready@nd.edu

University of Puerto Rico, Cayey, PR
Jaime Cruz Candelavia
(787) 738-5651
cruzje@caribe.net
Isar Godreau
(787) 738-5651
igodreau@caribe.net

University of Texas-Pan American, Edinburg, TX
Jorge R. Manzano
(956) 381-2301
jmanzano@panam-edu

The Urban Coalition, Saint Paul, MN
Amy Maheswaian Lopez
(612) 348-8550
amymaheswaianlopez@urbancoalition.org

Vanderbilt University, Peabody Library, Nashville, TN
Cyndi Taylor
(615) 343-7542
cynthia.j.taylor@vanderbilt.edu

William C. Velasquez Institute, Los Angeles, CA
Zachary Gonzalez
(323) 222-2217
zgonzalez@wcvi.org

COMMUNICATIONS AND UTILITIES

Current Programs
Ruth Bramblett (SSSD)
(301) 763-2787
svsd@census.gov

Economic Census
James Barron (SSSD)
(301) 763-2786
ucb@census.gov

COMMUNICATIONS OFFICE

CONGRESSIONAL AFFAIRS OFFICE
Paul Pisano (CAO)
(301) 763-2171

PUBLIC INFORMATION OFFICE

Chief
Kenneth Meyer (PIO)
(301) 763-3100

Deputy Chief
Mark Tolbert, III (PIO)
(301) 763-8237

American Community Survey
Stephen Buckner (PIO)
(301) 763-3586

Broadcast and Photo Zone
Victor Romero (PIO)
(301) 763-3011

Census CounterParts (employee newsletter)
Tom Edwards (PIO)
(301) 763-2184

Census in Schools
Kim Crews (PIO)
(301) 763-8565

Decennial Census
Kim Crews (PIO)
(301) 763-8565

Demographic Programs
Robert Bernstein
(301) 763-2603

Economic Statistics
Mike Bergman (PIO)
(301) 763-3046

Minority Media Outreach
Dwight Johnson (PIO)
(301) 763-3013

News Media Inquiries
Staff (PIO)
(301) 763-3030

Special Events
Stephen Buckner (PIO)
(301) 763-3586

CONSTRUCTION

Building Permits
Staff (MCD)
(301) 763-5160

Economic Census
Susan Bucci (MCD)
(301) 763-4680

Housing Starts and Completions
Staff (MCD)
(301) 763-5160

Manufactured Housing
Mike Davis (MCD)
(301) 763-4590

Residential Characteristics, Price Index and Sales
Staff (MCD)
(301) 763-5160

Residential Improvements and Repairs

Joe Huesman (MCD)
(301) 763-1605

Value of Construction Put in Place
Mike Davis (MCD)
(301) 763-1605

CORRESPONDENCE QUALITY ASSURANCE OFFICE

Correspondence
Jackie Yates (DIR)
(301) 763-2501

Broadcast
Bobbie Glencer (DIR)
(301) 763-2501

CUSTOMER LIAISON OFFICE

Customer Liaison Office
Stan Rolark (CLO)
(301) 763-1305

Governors' Liaison Program
Frank Ambrose (CLO)
(301) 763-1305

Non-governmental Programs (Including Census Information Centers)
Barbara Harris (CLO)
(301) 763-1305

State and Governmental Programs (Includes State Data Centers, Business and Industry Data Centers, Census Depository Libraries and National Governmental Partners)
Renee Jefferson-Copeland (CLO)
(301) 763-1305

DEMOGRAPHIC PROGRAMS

Africa, Asia, Latin America, North America and Oceania
Staff (POP)
(301) 763-1358

Aging Population (Domestic)
Staff (POP)
(301) 763-2378

Aging Population (International)
Staff (POP)
(301) 763-1371

American Community Survey
Cheryl Chambers (DSD)
(301) 763-3572

American Housing Survey
Jane Kneessi/Barbara Williams
(301) 763-3235

American Housing Survey - Data
Paul Harple/Susin Scott (HHES)
(301) 763-3235

American Housing Survey - Methodology
LaTerri Bynum (DSD)
(301) 763-3858

Ancestry
Staff (POP)
(301) 763-2403

Apportionment
Ed Byerly (POP)
(301) 763-2381

Apportionment and Redistricting
Cathy McCully (DIR)
(301) 763-4039

Census - Housing
Staff (HHES)
(301) 763-3237

Census - Population
Staff (POP)
(301) 763-2422

Census 2010
Edison Gore (DMD)
(301) 763-3998

Child Care
Martin O'Connell/Julia Overturf (POP)
(301) 763-2416

Children
Rose Kreider (POP)
(301) 763-2416

China, People's Republic
Staff (POP)
(301) 763-1360

Citizenship Status
Staff (POP)
(301) 763-2411

Commuting, Means of Transportation and Place of Work
Clara Reschovsky/Celia Boertlein (POP)
(301) 763-2454

Consumer Expenditure Survey
Janice Sebold (DSD)
(301) 763-3916

County Population
Staff (POP
(301) 763-2422

Crime
Marilyn Monahan (DSD)
(301) 763-5315

Current Population Survey - General Information
Staff (DSD)
(301) 763-3806

Current Population Survey - Questionnaire Content
Staff (DSD)
(301) 763-3806

Current Population Survey - Sampling Methods
Harland Shoemaker (DSMD)
(301) 763-4275

Demographic Surveys - Demographic Statistics
Staff (POP)
(301) 763-2422TTY: 301-457-2435

Demographic Surveys - General Information
Staff (POP)
(301) 763-2422

Disability
Staff (HHES)
(301) 763-3242

Educational Attainment
Staff (POP)
(301) 763-2464

Education Surveys
Steve Tourkin (DSD)
(301) 763-3791

Employment and Unemployment
Staff (HHES)
(301) 763-3242

Equal Employment Opportunity Data
Katie Earle (HHES)
(301) 763-3239

Europe/Former Soviet Union
Staff (POP)
(301) 763-1360

Fertility
Jane Dye (POP)
(301) 763-2416

Foreign-Born Population - General Information
Staff (POP)
(301) 763-2422

Foreign-Born Population - Concepts and Analysis
Staff (POP)
(301) 763-2411

Group Quarters Population
Denise Smith (POP)
(301) 763-2378

Health Insurance Statistics
Staff (HHES)
(301) 763-3242

Health Surveys
Andrea Piani (DSD)
(301) 763-5379

Hispanic Population - General Information
Staff (POP)
(301) 763-2422

Hispanic Population - Concepts and Analysis
Staff (POP)
(301) 763-2403

Hispanic Statistics
Staff (POP)
(301) 763-2403

Homeless
Karen Humes (POP)
(301) 763-2448

Homeownership and Vacancy Data
Linda Cavanaugh/ Robert Callis (HHES)
(301) 763-3199

Household Wealth
Staff (HHES)
(301) 763-3242

Households and Families
Terry Lugaila (POP)
(301) 763-2416

Housing Affordability
Howard Savage (HHES)
(301) 763-3199

Immigration and Emigration - General Information
Staff (POP)
(301) 763-2422

Immigration and Emigration - Concepts and Analysis
Staff (POP)
(301) 763-2411

Income Statistics
Staff (HHES)
(301) 763-3243

International Data Base
Pat Dickerson
(301) 763-1351
Peter Johnson (POP)
(301) 763-1410

International HIV/AIDS
Staff (POP)
(301) 763-1433

Journey to Work
Phil Salopek/Celia Boertlein (POP)
(301) 763-2454

Language
Staff (POP)
(301) 763-2464

Market Absorption
Alan Friedman/Venus Anderson (HHES)
(301) 763-3199

Metropolitan and Micropolitan Statistical Areas
Staff (POP)
(301) 763-2422

Metropolitan and Micropolitan Statistical Areas - Standards
Paul Mackun (POP)
(301) 763-2419

Migration - General Information
Staff (POP)
(301) 763-2422

Migration - Domestic/Internal
Staff (POP)
(301) 763-2454

Migration - International
Staff (POP)
(301) 763-2411

National Longitudinal Surveys
Ron Dopkowski (DSD)
(301) 763-3801

New York City Housing and Vacancy Survey
Alan Friedman/ Robert Callis (HHES)
(301) 763-3199

Occupational and Industrial Statistics
Staff (HHES)
(301) 763-3239

Outlying Areas
Michael Levin (POP)
(301) 763-1444

Place of Birth - General Information
Staff (POP)

(301) 763-2422

Place of Birth - U.S. Puerto Rico and U.S. Island Areas
Carol Faber (POP)
(301) 763-2454

Place of Birth - Other Places of Birth
Staff (POP)
(301) 763-2411

Population Estimates and Projections
Staff (POP)
(301) 763-2422

Population Information
Staff (POP)
(301) 763-2422TTY: 301-457-2435

Poverty Statistics
Staff (HHES)
(301) 763-3242

Prisoner Surveys
Marilyn Monahan (DSD)
(301) 763-5315

Puerto Rico
Idabelle Hovland (DMD)
(301) 763-8443

Race Statistics
Staff (POP)
(301) 763-2422

Race Statistics - Concepts and Interpretation
Staff (POP)
(301) 763-2402

Residential Finance
Howard Savage (HHES)
(301) 763-3199

School Enrollment
Staff (POP)
(301) 763-2464

Small Area Income and Poverty Estimates
Staff (HHES)
(301) 763-3193

Special Censuses
Mike Stump (FLD)
(301) 763-1429

Special Surveys
Ron Dopkowski (DSD)
(301) 763-3801

Special Tabulations
Linda Showalter (POP)
(301) 763-2429

State Population Estimates
Staff (POP)
(301) 763-2422

Survey of Income and Program Participation (SIPP)
Staff (HHES)
(301) 763-3242

Survey of Income and Program Participation (SIPP) - Microdata Files
Carole Popoff (HHES)
(301) 763-3222

Survey of Income and Program Participation (SIPP) - Statistical Methods
Tracy Mattingly (DSMD)
(301) 763-6445

Survey-Related Information
Judith Eargle (DSD)
(301) 763-5263

Technical Assistance and Training
Staff (POP)
(301) 763-1444

Undercount, Demographic Analysis
Gregg Robinson (POP)
(301) 763-6133

Veterans Status
Staff (HHES)
(301) 763-3230

Voters, Characteristics
Staff (POP)
(301) 763-2464

Voting-Age Population
Staff (POP)
(301) 763-2464

Women
Renee Spraggins (POP)
(301) 763-2378

Women in Development
Victoria Velkoff (POP)
(301) 763-1371

ECONOMIC CENSUS

General Information
Paul Zeisset
(301) 763-4151
Robert Marske (EPCD)
(301) 763-6718

E-Commerce
Tom Mesenbourg (DIR)
(301) 763-2932

ECONOMIC CENSUS: 2002

Accommodation and Food Services
Fay Dorsett (SSSD)
(301) 763-2687

Construction
Staff (MCD)
(301) 763-4680

Finance and Insurance
Faye Jacobs (SSSD)
(301) 763-2824

General Information
Robert Marske (EPCD)
(301) 763-6718

Internet Dissemination
Paul Zeisset (EPCD)
(301) 763-4151

Manufacturing - Consumer Goods Industries
Robert Reinard (MCD)
(301) 763-4810

Manufacturing - Investment Goods Industries
Kenneth Hansen (MCD)
(301) 763-4755

Manufacturing - Primary Goods Industries
Nat Shelton (MCD)
(301) 763-6614

Mining
Susan Bucci (MCD)
(301) 763-4680

Minority/Women-Owned Businesses
Valerie Strang (CSD)
(301) 763-3316

North American Industry Classification System (NAICS)
Wanda Dougherty (SSSD)
(301) 763-2790

Puerto Rico and the Island Areas
Lillyana Najafzadeh (CSD)
(301) 763-6544

Real Estate and Rental/Leasing
Pam Palmer (SSSD)
(301) 763-2824

Retail Trade
Fay Dorsett (SSSD)
(301) 763-2687

Services - Administrative and Support, Waste Management and Remediation Services
Dan Wellwood (SSSD)
(301) 763-5181

Services - Arts, Entertainment and Recreation
Tara Dryden (SSSD)
(301) 763-5181

Services - Educational Services
Kim Casey (SSSD)
(301) 763-5181

Services - Health Care and Social Assistance
Laurie Davis (SSSD)
(301) 763-5181

Services - Information
Joyce Kiessling/Joy Pierson/ Steve Cornell (SSSD)
(301) 763-5181

Services - Management of Companies and Enterprises
Julie Ishman (SSSD)
(301) 763-5181

Services - Other Services (except Public Administration)
Patrice Norman (SSSD)
(301) 763-5181

Services - Professional, Scientific and Technical Services
Karen Dennison/John Goodenough (SSSD)
(301) 763-5181

Transportation and Utilities - Commodity Flow Survey
John Fowler (SSSD)
(301) 763-2108

Transportation and Utilities - Establishments
James Barron (SSSD)
(301) 763-2786

Transportation and Utilities - Vehicle Inventory and Use Survey
Thomas Zabelsky (SSSD)
(301) 763-5175

Transportation and Utilities - Wholesale Trade
Donna Hambric (SSSD)
(301) 763-2725

ZIP Codes - Accommodation and Food Services
Fay Dorsett (SSSD)
(301) 763-5180

ZIP Codes - Retail Trade
Fay Dorsett (SSSD)
(301) 763-5180

EXECUTIVE STAFF

Director
Charles Louis Kincannon
(301) 763-2135

Executive Assistant
Betty Ann Saucier
(301) 763-2135

Depufy Director and Chief Operating Officer
Hermann Habermann
(301) 763-2138

Chief Privacy Officer
Gerald W. Gates
(301) 763-2515

Chief of International Relations
Jay K. Keller
(301) 763-2883

Assistant Director for American Community Survey and Decennial Census
Teresa Angueira
(301) 763-1764

Associate Director for Communications
Jefferson Taylor
(301) 763-2164

Assistant to the Associate Director
Vacant
(301) 763-8469

Associate Director for Decennial Census
Preston J. Waite
(301) 763-3968

Assistant Director for Decennial Information Technology and Geographic Systems
Arnold A. Jackson
(301) 763-8626

Associate Director for Demographic Programs
Nancy M. Gordon
(301) 763-2126

Associate Director for Economic Programs
Thomas L. Mesenbourg (Acting)
(301) 763-2112

Associate Director for Field Operations
Marvin D. Raines
(301) 763-2072

Associate Director for Administration and Chief Financial Officer
Theodore A. Johnson
(301) 763-3464

Comptroller
Andrew H. Moxam
(301) 763-9575

Associate Director for Information Technology and Chief Information Officer
Richard W. Swartz
(301) 763-2117

Assistant to the Associate Director for Information Technology
Douglas Clift
(301) 763-5499

Associate Director for Methodology and Standards
Vacant
(301) 763-2160

Assistant Director for Marketing and Customer Liaison
Theodore A. Johnson (Acting)
(301) 763-3464

FIELD DIVISION

Administration
Sneha Desai (FLD)
(301) 763-2011

Decennial Managament, Analysis, and Special Censuses
Janet Cummings (FLD)
(301) 763-7879

Evaluation
Richard Blass (FLD)
(301) 763-7879

Geography
Gail Leithauser (FLD)
(301) 763-7879

Partnership and Data Services
Brenda August (FLD)
(301) 763-2032

Surveys
Richard Bitzer (FLD)
(301) 763-2011

FINANCE, INSURANCE AND REAL ESTATE

Economic Census
Faye Jacobs (SSSD)
(301) 763-2824

FOREIGN TRADE

Data Dissemination Branch
Vanessa Ware (FTD)
(301) 763-3041

Regulations, Outreach, and Education Branch
Jerry Greenwell (FTD)
(301) 763-2238

Trade Data Inquiries and Controls
Reba Higbee (FTD)
(301) 763-2227

GEOGRAPHIC CONCEPTS

1990 Census Map Orders
Jerry Watson (NPC)
(812) 218-3622

2000 Census Maps
Staff (MSO)
(301) 763-INFO (4636)

American Indian and Alaska Native Areas
Barbara Saville (GEO)
(301) 763-1099

Annexations and Boundary Changes
Laura Waggoner (GEO)
(301) 763-1099

Area Measurement - Land
Jim Davis (GEO)
(301) 763-1099

Area Measurement - Water
Staff (GEO)
(301) 763-1099

Census Blocks
Joe Marinucci (GEO)
(301) 763-1099

Census County Divisions
Eric Joe (GEO)
(301) 763-3056

Census Designated Places
Noemi Mendez (GEO)
(301) 763-3056

Census Geographic Concepts
Staff (GEO)
(301) 763-3056

Census Tracts
Noemi Mendez (GEO)
(301) 763-3056

Centers of Population
Staff (GEO)
(301) 763-1128

Combined Statistical Areas
Paul Mackun (POP)
(301) 763-2419

Congressional and State Legislative Districts - Address Allocations
Staff (GEO)
(301) 763-1050

Congressional and State Legislative Districts - Boundaries
John Byle (GEO)
(301) 763-1099

Core Based Statistical Areas
Paul Mackun (POP)
(301) 763-2419

Federal Geographic Data Committee and Geographic Standards
Randy Fusaro (GEO)
(301) 763-1056

Federal Information Processing System (FIPS) Codes
Mike Fournier (GEO)
(301) 763-1099

Geographic Products and Services (including TIGER)
Staff (GEO)
(301) 763-1128

Governmental Unit Boundaries
Laura Waggoner (GEO)
(301) 763-1099

Internal Points
Staff (GEO)
(301) 763-1128

Island Areas
Jim Davis (GEO)
(301) 763-1099

LandView
Staff (GEO)
(301) 763-1128

Local Update of Census Addresses
Al Pfeiffer (GEO)
(301) 763-8630

Master Address File
Joel Sobel (GEO)
(301) 763-1106

Metropolitan and Micropolitan Statistical Areas
Paul Mackun (POP)
(301) 763-2419

Native Hawaiian Areas
Barbara Saville (GEO)
(301) 763-1099

Place Concepts
Noemi Mendez/Eric Joe (GEO)
(301) 763-3056

Population Circles (Radii)
Staff (GEO)
(301) 763-1128

Postal Geography
Dan Sweeney (GEO)
(301) 763-1106

School District
Pat Ream/Ian Millet (GEO)
(301) 763-1099

Spatial Data Quality and Geographic Standards
Leslie Godwin (GEO)
(301) 763-1056

Thematic Mapping and Boundary Files
Staff (GEO)
(301) 763-1101

TIGER System
Staff (GEO)
(301) 763-1100

TIGER Update Partnerships
Staff (GEO)
(301) 763-1100

Traffic Analysis Zones
Staff (GEO)
(301) 763-1099

Urban/Rural Concepts
Mei-Ling Freeman/Mike Ratcliffe (GEO)
(301) 763-3056

Urbanized Areas
Mei-Ling Freeman/Mike Ratcliffe (GEO)
(301) 763-3056

Voting Districts
John Byle (GEO)
(301) 763-1099

ZIP Code Tabulation Areas (ZCTAs)
Andy Flora (GEO)
(301) 763-1100

ZIP Codes - Demographic Data
Staff (MSO)
(301) 763-INFO (4636)

ZIP Codes - Economic Data
Andy Hait (EPCD)
(301) 763-6747

ZIP Codes - Geography
Andy Flora (GEO)
(301) 763-1100

GOVERNMENTS

Census of Governments
Donna Hirsch (GOVS)
(301) 763-5154

Criminal and Juvenile Justice
Charlene Sebold (GOVS)
(301) 763-1591

Education - Elementary-Secondary (fiscal)
Staff (GOVS)
(301) 763-1563

Education - Elementary-Secondary (nonfiscal)
Johnny Monaco (GOVS)
(301) 763-2584

Education - Library Statistics
Johnny Monaco (GOVS)
(301) 763-2584

Employment
Ellen Thompson (GOVS)
(301) 763-1531

Federal Expenditure Data
Gerard Keffer (GOVS)
(301) 763-1522

Government Finance
Stephen Poyta
(301) 763-1580
David Kellerman (GOVS)
(301) 763-7242

Government Organization
Stephen Owens (GOVS)
(301) 763-5149

Medical Expenditure Panel Survey
Sheryl Jones (GOVS)
(301) 763-3099

Public Retirement Systems
Ellen Thompson (GOVS)

(301) 763-1531

MANUFACTURING AND MINING

Concentration
Patrick Duck (MCD)
(301) 763-4699

Exports From Manufacturing Establishments
John Gates (MCD)
(301) 763-4589

Financial Statistics (Quarterly Financial Report)
Yolando St George (CSD)
(301) 763-3343

Foreign Direct Investment
Julius Smith (MCD)
(301) 763-4683

Fuels and Electric Energy Consumed and Production Index
Susan Bucci (MCD)
(301) 763-4680

General Information and Data Requests
Nishea Quash (MCD)
(301) 763-4673

Industries - Electrical and Transp. Equip., Instruments and Machinery
Kenneth Hansen (MCD)
(301) 763-4755

Industries - Food, Textiles and Apparel
Robert Reinard (MCD)
(301) 763-4810

Industries - Furniture, Printing and Miscellaneous
Robert Reinard (MCD)
(301) 763-4810

Industries - Metals
Nat Shelton (MCD)
(301) 763-6614

Industries - Wood, Paper, Chemicals, Petroleum Products, Rubber and Plastics
Nat Shelton (MCD)
(301) 763-6614

Industries - Mining
Susan Bucci (MCD)
(301) 763-4680

Monthly Shipments, Inventories and Orders
Dan Sansbury (MCD)
(301) 763-4832

Plant Capacity Utilization
Julius Smith (MCD)
(301) 763-4683

Research and Development
Julius Smith (MCD)
(301) 763-4683

MARKETING SERVICES OFFICE

American Community Survey/C2SS Results
Staff (MSO)
(301) 763-INFO (4636)

Census Customer Services
Staff (MSO)
(301) 763-INFO (4636)
Fax: (301) 457-4714 (general information)
Fax: (888) 249-7295 (orders only)

Census Product Update
Greg Pewett
(301) 763-5114
Belva Kirk (MSO)
(301) 763-4502

Exhibits
Noel Velez
(301) 763-1717
Charles Pennington (MSO)
(301) 763-1766

Geographic Updated Population Certification Program (Fee-Based)
Staff (MSO)
(301) 763-4636

MISCELLANEOUS SUBJECTS

Census Job Information (Recording)
(301) 763-4748

Census Personnel Locator
Staff (HRD)
(301) 763-4748

Census Records (Age search)
Staff (NPC)
(812) 218-3046

Conferences
Staff (ACSD)
(301) 763-2308

Confidentiality and Privacy
Jerry Gates (POL)
(301) 763-2515

County and City, State and Metropolitan Area Data Books
Wanda Cevis (ACSD)
(301) 763-1166

Freedom of Information Act (FOIA)
Jerry Gates (POL)
(301) 763-2515

History Staff
Staff (POL)
(301) 763-1167

Internet Site(general information)
Stephanie Pinkney (ACSD)
(301) 763-1326

Legal Office
Phil Freije (POL)
(301) 763-2918

Legislation
Thomas Jones (POL)
(301) 763-2512

Library
Staff (POL)
(301) 763-2511

Microdata Files
Anne Ross (ACSD)
(301) 763-2429

Statistical Abstract
Glenn King (ACSD)
(301) 763-1171

Statistical Research
Tommy Wright (SRD)
(301) 763-1030

Technical Support (CD-ROM Products)
Staff
(301) 763-1324

U.S. Government Printing Office (GPO)
Staff
(202) 512-1800

POPULATION AND HOUSING STATISTICS

Aging Population, U.S.
Staff (POP)
(301) 763-2378

American Community Survey
Cheryl Chambers (DSD)
(301) 763-3572

American FactFinder
Staff (MSO)
(301) 763-INFO (4636)

Annexations/Boundary Changes
Laura Waggoner (GEO)
(301) 763-1099

Apportionment
Edwin Byerly (POP)
(301) 763-2381

Census 2010
Ed Gore (DMD)
(301) 763-3998

Census History
Dave Pemberton (DIR)
(301) 763-1167

Census in Schools
Kim Crews (PIO)
(301) 763-3626

Citizenship
Staff (POP)
(301) 763-2411

Commuting, Means of Transportation and Place of Work
Clara Reschovsky/Celia Boertlein (POP)
(301) 763-2454

Confidentiality and Privacy
Jerry Gates (POL)
(301) 763-2515

Count Review
Paul Campbell (POP)
(301) 763-2381

Data Dissemination
Staff (MSO)
(301) 763-INFO (4636)

Disability
Staff (HHES)
(301) 763-3242

Education
Staff (POP)
(301) 763-2464

Employment/Unemployment (General Information)
Staff (HHES)
(301) 763-3230

Foreign-born
Staff (POP)
(301) 763-2411

Geographic Entities
Staff (GEO)
(301) 763-3056

Grandparents as Caregivers
Tavia Simmons (POP)
(301) 763-2416

Group Quarters Population
Denise Smith (POP)
(301) 763-2378

Hispanic Origin/Ethnicity/Ancestry
Staff (POP)
(301) 763-2403

Homeless
Karen Humes (POP)
(301) 763-2448

Housing (General Information)
Staff (HHES)
(301) 763-3237

Immigration/Emigration
Staff (POP)
(301) 763-2411

Income
Staff (HHES)
(301) 763-3243

Island Areas (Puerto Rico, U.S. Virgin Islands, Pacific Islands)
Idabelle Hovland (DMD)
(301) 763-8443

Labor Force Status/Work Experience (General Information)
Staff (HHES)
(301) 763-3230

Language Spoken at Home
Staff (POP)
(301) 763-2464

Living Arrangements
Staff (POP)
(301) 763-2416

Maps
Customer Services (MSO)
(301) 763-INFO (4636)

Marital Status
Rose Kreider (POP)
(301) 763-2416

Metropolitan and Micropolitan Statistical Areas Standards
Paul Mackun (POP)
(301) 763-2419

Microdata Files
Carole Popoff (HHES)

(301) 763-3222

Migration
Staff (POP)
(301) 763-2454

News Media Inquiries
Staff (PIO)
(301) 763-3030

Occupation/Industry
Staff (HHES)
(301) 763-3239

Partnership and Data Services
Brenda August (FLD)
(301) 763-2032

Place of Birth/Native Born
Carol Faber (POP)
(301) 763-2454

Population (General Information)
Staff (POP)
(301) 763-2422TTY: 301-457-2435

Poverty
Alemayehu Bishaw (HHES)
(301) 763-3213

Redistricting
Cathy McCully (DIR)
(301) 763-4039

Residence Rules
Karen Mills (POP)
(301) 763-2381

Race
Staff (POP)
(301) 763-2402

Small Area Income and Poverty Estimates
David Waddington (HHES)
(301) 763-3193

Special Censuses
Mike Stump (FLD)
(301) 763-1429

Special Population
Staff (POP)
(301) 763-2378

Special Tabulations
Linda Showalter (POP)
(301) 763-2429

TIGER/Line files
Staff (GEO)
(301) 763-1128

Undercount
Phil Gbur (DSSD)
(301) 763-4206

Undercount - Demographic Analysis
Greg Robinson (POP)
(301) 763-2110

Unmarried Partners
Tavia Simmons (POP)
(301) 763-2416

Urban/Rural
Mei-Ling Freeman/Mike Ratcliffe (GEO)
(301) 763-3056

U.S. Citizens Abroad
Staff (POP)
(301) 763-2422

Veteran Status
Staff (HHES)
(301) 763-3230

Voting Districts
John Byle (GEO)
(301) 763-1099

Women
Renee Spraggins (POP)
(301) 763-2378

ZIP Codes
Staff (POP)
(301) 763-2422

REGIONAL OFFICES

Atlanta (AL, FL, GA)
101 Marietta Street, NW, Suite 3200
Atlanta, GA 30303-2700
(404) 730-3833TDD: (404) 730-3964http://www.census.gov/atlanta

Boston, MA (CT, MA, ME, NH, NY, RI, VT, Puerto Rico)
4 Copley Place, Suite 301
PO Box 9108
Boston, MA 02117-9108
(617) 424-4510TDD: (617) 424-0565http://www.census.gov/boston

Charlotte (KY, NC, SC, TN, VA)
901 Center Park Drive, Suite 106
Charlotte, NC 28217-2935
(704) 424-6430TDD: (704) 344-6114http://www.census.gov/charlotte

Chicago (IL, IN, WI)
2255 Enterprise Drive, Suite 5501
Westchester, IL 60154
(708) 562-1350TDD: (708) 562-1791http://www.census.gov/chicago

Dallas (LA, MS, TX)
8585 N. Stemmons Fwy, Suite 800 S
Dallas, TX 75247-3836
(214) 253-4481TDD: (214) 655-5363http://www.census.gov/dallas

Denver (AZ, CO, MT, NE, ND, NM, NV, SD, UT, WY)
6900 W. Jefferson Avenue, Suite 100
Lakewood, CO 80235-2032
(303) 264-0220TDD: (303) 969-6767http://www.census.gov/denver

Detroit (MI, OH, WV)
1395 Brewery Park Blvd.
Detroit, MI 48207
(313) 259-1875TDD: (313) 259-5169http://www.census.gov/detroit

Kansas City (AR, IA, KS, MN, MO, OK)
1211 North 8th Street
Kansas City, KS 66101-2129
(913) 551-6711TDD: (913) 551-5839http://www.census.gov/kansascity

Los Angeles (southern CA, HI)
15350 Sherman Way, Suite 300
Van Nuys, CA 91406-4224
(818) 904-6339TDD: (818) 904-6249http://www.census.gov/losangeles

New York (NY, NJ, selected counties)
395 Hudson Street, Suite 800
New York, NY 10014
(212) 584-3440TDD: (212) 478-4793http://www.census.gov/newyork

Philadelphia (DE, DC, MD, NJ, selected counties, PA)
833 Chestnut Street, 5th Floor, Suite 504
Philadelphia, PA 19107-4405
(215) 717-1820TDD: (215) 717-0894http://www.census.gov/philadelphia

Seattle (northern CA, AK, ID, OR, WA)
700 Fifth Avenue, Suite 5100
Seattle, WA 98104-5018
(206) 553-5835TDD: (206) 553-5859http://www.census.gov/seattle

RETAIL TRADE

Advance Monthly
Scott Scheleur (SSSD)
(301) 763-2713
svsd@census.gov

Annual Retail
Nancy Piesto (SSSD)
(301) 763-2747
sssd.wholesale.trade@census.gov

Economic Census
Fay Dorsett (SSSD)
(301) 763-5180
rcb@census.gov

Monthly Sales and Inventory
Scott Scheleur (SSSD)
(301) 763-2713
retail.trade@census.gov

Quarterly Financial Report
Yolando St George (CSD)
(301) 763-3343
csd@census.gov

SERVICES

Current Reports
Ruth Bramblett (SSSD)
(301) 763-2787
svsd@census.gov

Economic Census
Jack Moody (SSSD)
(301) 763-5181
scb@census.gov

General Information
Staff (SSSD)
(800) 541-8345
scb@census.gov

Service Indicators Staff
David Lassman (SSSD)
(301) 763-2797
svsd@census.gov

SPECIAL TOPICS

Business Expenditures
Sheldon Ziman (CSD)
(301) 763-3315

Business Investment
Charles Funk (CSD)
(301) 763-3324

County Business Patterns
Philip Thompson (EPCD)
(301) 763-2580

Economic Studies
Arnold Reznek (CES)
(301) 763-1856

Enterprise Statistics
Melvin Cole (CSD)
(301) 763-3321

Industry and Commodity Classification
Wanda Dougherty
(301) 763-7106
Scott Handmaker(SSSD)
(301) 763-7107

Mineral Industries
Susan Bucci (MCD)
(301) 763-4680

Minority/Women-Owned Businesses
Valerie Strang (CSD)
(301) 763-3316

Nonemployer Statistics
Philip Thompson (EPCD)
(301) 763-2580

North American Industry Classification System (NAICS)
Wanda Dougherty (SSSD)
(301) 763-2790

Pollution Abatement Costs and Expenditures
Julius Smith (MCD)
(301) 763-4683

Puerto Rico and Island Areas
Lillyana Najafzadeh (CSD)
(301) 763-6544

Quarterly Financial Report
Yolando St George (CSD)
(301) 763-3343

Statistics of U.S. Businesses
Melvin Cole (CSD)
(301) 763-3321

STATE DATA CENTERS (SDCS) AND BUSINESS AND INDUSTRY DATA CENTERS (BIDCS)

Lead data centers are usually state government agencies, universities or libraries that head a network of affiliate centers. Below are listed the SDC and BIDC lead agency contacts only. All states have

SDCs, but not all states have BIDCs. In some states, one agency serves as the lead for both the SDC and the BIDC. BIDCs are listed separately where there is a separate agency serving as the lead. For more information, direct e-mail comments and questions to your local affiliate, or for general inquiries, contact: renee.jeffersoncopeland@census.gov.

Alabama (SDC)
Annette Watters, University of Alabama
(205) 348-6191
awatters@cba.ua.edu

Alaska (SDC)
Kathryn Lizik, Department of Labor
(907) 465-2437
kathryn_lizik@labor.state.ak.us

American Samoa (SDC)
Vaitoelau Filiga, Department of Commerce
(684) 633-5155
vfiliga@doc.asg.us

Arizona (SDC and BIDC)
Betty Jeffries, Department of Economic Security
(602) 542-5984
bjeffries@azdes.gov

Arkansas (SDC)
Sarah Breshears, University of Arkansas at Little Rock
(501) 569-8530
sgbreshears@ualr.edu

California (SDC)
Julie Hoang, Department of Finance
(916) 323-4086
fijhoang@dof.ca.gov

Colorado (SDC)
Rebecca Picaso, Department of Local Affairs
(303) 866-3120
rebecca.picaso@state.co.us

Connecticut (SDC)
Vacant

Delaware (SDC and BIDC)
Elaine Tull, Economic Development Office
(302) 672-6845
elaine.tull@state.de.us

District of Columbia (SDC)
Joy Phillips, Mayor's Office of Planning
(202) 442-7614
joy.phillips@dc.gov

Florida (SDC and BIDC)
Pam Schenker, Florida Agency for Workforce Innovation
(850) 488-1048
pamela.schenker@awi.state.fl.us

Georgia (SDC)
Robert Giacomini, Office of Planning and Budget
(404) 656-6505
robert.giacomini@mail.opb.state.ga.us

Guam (SDC)
Monica Jesus Guerrero, Bureau of Statistics and Plans
(671) 472-4201/2/3
mjguerrero@mail.gov.gu

Hawaii (SDC)
Jan Nakamoto, Department of Business, Economic Development, and Tourism
(808) 586-2493
jnakamot@dbedt.hawaii.gov

Idaho (SDC)
Alan Porter, Idaho Commerce and Labor
(208) 334-2470
alan.porter@business.idaho.gov

Illinois (SDC)
Suzanne Ebetsch, Department of Commerce and Community Affairs
(217) 782-1381
sebetsch@ildceo.net

Illinois (BIDC)
Ed Taft, Department of Commerce and Community Affairs
(217) 785-6117
etaft@ildceo.net

Indiana (SDC)
Frank Wilmot, State Library
(317) 232-3732
fwilmot@statelib.lib.in.us

Indiana (BIDC)
Carol Rogers, Business Research Center
(317) 274-2205
rogersc@indiana.edu

Iowa (SDC)
Beth Henning, State Library
(515) 281-4350
beth.henning@lib.state.ia.us

Kansas (SDC)
Marc Galbraith, State Library
(785) 296-3296
marcg@kslib.info

Kentucky (SDC and BIDC)
Ron Crouch, University of Louisville
(502) 852-7990
rtcrou01@gwise.louisville.edu

Louisiana (SDC)
Karen Paterson, Office of Planning and Budget
(225) 219-5987
kpaters@doa.state.la.us

Maine (SDC and BIDC)
Michael Montagna, Maine State Planning Office
(207) 287-1475
michael.montagna@maine.gov

Maryland (SDC and BIDC)
Jane Traynham, Office of Planning
(410) 767-4450
jtraynham@mdp.state.md.us

Massachusetts (SDC and BIDC)
John Gaviglio, UMass Donahue Institute
(413) 545-0176
msdc-info@donahue.umass.edu

Michigan (SDC)
Darren Warner, Library of Michigan
(517) 373-2548
warnerd@michigan.gov

Minnesota (SDC and BIDC)
Barbara Ronningen, State Demographer's Office
(651) 296-4886
barbara.ronningen@state.mn.us

Mississippi (SDC)
Rachel McNeely, University of Mississippi
(662) 915-7288
rmcneely@olemiss.edu

Mississippi (BIDC)
Deloise Tate, Department of Economic and Community Development
(601) 359-3593
dtate@mississippi.org

Missouri (SDC)
Nathaniel Albers, James C. Kirkpatrick State Information Center
(573) 526-6734
nathaniel.albers@sos.mo.gov

Missouri (BIDC)
Cathy Frank, Small Business Research Information Center
(573) 341-6484
cfrank@umr.edu

Montana (SDC and BIDC)
Pam Harris, Department of Commerce
(406) 841-2739
paharris@mt.gov

Nebraska (SDC)
Jerome Deichert, University of Nebraska at Omaha
(402) 554-2134
jerome_deichert@unomaha.edu

Nevada (SDC)
Ramona Reno, State Library and Archives
(775) 684-3326
rlreno@clan.lib.nv.us

New Hampshire (SDC)
Thomas Duffy, Office of State Planning
(603) 271-2155
tom.duffy@nh.gov

New Jersey (SDC and BIDC)
Leonard Preston, Department of Labor
(609) 984-2595
leonard.preston@dol.state.nj.us

New Mexico (SDC)
Beth Davis, Economic Development Department
(505) 827-0264
edavis@edd.state.nm.us

New Mexico (BIDC)
Karma Shore, University of New Mexico
(505) 277-6626
kshore@unm.edu

New York (SDC and BIDC)
Staff, Department of Economic Development
(518) 292-5300
rscardamalia@empire.state.ny.us

North Carolina (SDC and BIDC)
Francine Stephenson, State Library
(919) 733-7061
francine.stephenson@ncmail.net

North Dakota (SDC)
Richard Rathge, North Dakota State University
(701) 231-8621
richard.rathge@ndsu.nodak.edu

Northern Mariana Islands (SDC)
Justin Andrew, Department of Commerce
(670) 664-3033
csd@itecnmi.com

Ohio (SDC and BIDC)
Steve Kelley, Department of Development
(614) 466-2116
skelley@odod.state.oh.us

Oklahoma (SDC and BIDC)
Jeff Wallace, Department of Commerce
(405) 815-5184
jeff_wallace@odoc.state.ok.us

Oregon (SDC)
George Hough, Portland State University
(503) 725-5159
houghg@pdx.edu

Pennsylvania (SDC and BIDC)
Sue Copella, Pennsylvania State University at Harrisburg
(717) 948-6336
sdc3@psu.edu

Puerto Rico (SDC)
Lillian Torres Aguirre, Planning Board
(787) 728-4430
torres_l@jp.gobierno.pr

Rhode Island (SDC)
Mark Brown, Department of Administration
(401) 222-6183
mbrown@planning.state.ri.us

South Carolina (SDC)
Mike MacFarlane, Budget and Control Board
(803) 734-3780
mmacfarl@drss.state.sc.us

South Dakota (SDC)
Nancy Nelson, University of South Dakota
(605) 677-5287
nnelson@usd.edu

Tennessee (SDC)
Joan Snoderly, University of Tennessee-Knoxville
(865) 974-5441
jsnoderly@utk.edu

Texas (SDC and BIDC)
Steve Murdock, University of Texas at San Antonio
(210) 458-6536
steve.murdock@utsa.edu

Utah (SDC and BIDC)
Morgan Lyon, Governor's Office of Planning and Budget
(801) 538-1038
mlyon@utah.gov

Vermont (SDC)

William Sawyer, Center for Rural Studies
(802) 656-3021
william.sawyer@uvm.edu

Virgin Islands (SDC)
Frank Mills, University of the Virgin Islands
(340) 693-1027
fmills@uvi.edu

Virginia (SDC and BIDC)
Don Lillywhite, Virginia Employment Commission
(804) 786-7496
dlillywhite@vec.state.va.us

Washington (SDC and BIDC)
Yi Zhao, Office of Financial Management
(360) 902-0592
yi.zhao@ofm.wa.gov

West Virginia (SDC)
Delphine Coffey, West Virginia Development Office
(304) 558-4010
dcoffey@wvdo.org

West Virginia (BIDC)
Randy Childs, Bureau of Business and Economic Research
(304) 293-7832
randy.childs@mail.wvu.edu

Wisconsin (SDC)
Robert Naylor, Demographic Services Center
(608) 266-1927
bob.naylor@doa.state.wi.us

Wisconsin (BIDC)
Dan Veroff, University of Wisconsin
(608) 265-9545
dlveroff@facstaff.wisc.edu

Wyoming (SDC)
Wenlin Liu, Department of Administration and Information
(307) 777-7504
wliu@missc.state.wy.us

TRANSPORTATION

Commodity Flow Survey
John Fowler (SSSD)
(301) 763-2108
svsd@census.gov

Economic Census
James Barron (SSSD)
(301) 763-2786
ucb@census.gov

Vehicle Inventory and Use
Tom Zabelsky (SSSD)
(301) 763-5175
vius@census.gov

Warehousing and Trucking
Ruth Bramblett (SSSD)
(301) 763-2787
svsd@census.gov

WHOLESALE TRADE

Annual Wholesale
John Trimble (SSSD)
(301) 763-7223
svsd@census.gov

Current Sales and Inventories
Nancy Piesto (SSSD)
(301) 763-2747
sssd.wholesale.trade@census.gov

Economic Census
Donna Hambric (SSSD)
(301) 763-2725
wcb@census.gov

Quarterly Financial Report
Yolando St George (CSD)
(301) 763-3343
csd@census.gov

DIVISION ABBREVIATIONS WITH ADMIN PHONE NUMBER

ACSD
Administrative and Customer Services Division
(301) 763-2495

CACO
Census Advisory Committee Office
(301) 763-2495

CAO
Congressional Affairs Office
(301) 763-2495

CLO
Customer Liaison Office
(301) 763-2495

CSD
Company Statistics Division
(301) 763-2203

DADSO
Data Access and Dissemination Office
(301) 763-2495

DMD
Decennial Management Division
(301) 763-3999

DSD
Demographic Surveys Division
(301) 763-3788

DSMD
Demographic Statistical Methods Division
(301) 763-4224

DSSD
Decennial Statistical Studies Division
(301) 763-3999

EPCD
Economic Planning and Coordination Division
(301) 763-2709

ESMPD
Economic Statistical Methods and Programming Division
(301) 763-4596

FLD
Field Division
(301) 763-2864

FTD
Foreign Trade Division
(301) 763-2203

GEO
Geography Division
(301) 763-1133

GOVS
Governments Division
(301) 763-1500

HHES
Housing and Household Economic Statistics Division
(301) 763-3211

MCD
Manufacturing and Construction Division
(301) 763-4596

MSO
Marketing Services Office
(301) 763-2495

NPC
National Processing Center (Jeffersonville, IN)
(812) 218-3344

PIO
Public Information Office
(301) 763-2495

POL
Policy Office
(301) 763-2495

POP
Population Division
(301) 763-2430

SRD
Statistical Research Division
(301) 763-4849

SSSD
Service Sector Statistics Division
(301) 763-2709

TMO
Technologies Management Office
(301) 763-2864

PROCUREMENT/ACQUISITION

Further questions about information acquisition may be directed to:

Chief, Acquisition Division
Mike Palensky
(301) 763-3342

CHILDREN

Listed below is contact information for staff from federal agencies who have expertise with National data sets in the following areas: Population and Family Characteristics; Economic Security; Health; Behavior and Social Environment; Education. For more information visit http://www.childstats.gov/ or contact a staff member directly.

POPULATION AND FAMILY CHARACTERISTICS

Adoptions (NCHS)
Anjani Chandra
ayc3@cdc.gov
Rose Kreider

Adoptions (CENSUS)
rose.kreider@census.gov

Birth Certificate Data (NCHS)
Joyce Martin
jmartin@cdc.gov
Stephanie Ventura
sjv1@cdc.gov

Childhood Living Arrangements (CENSUS)
Rose Kreider
rose.kreider@census.gov

Childlessness (CENSUS)
Jane Dye
jane.l.dye@census.gov

Family Structure (NCHS)
Debbie Blackwell
dblackwell@cdc.gov

Fertility and Family Statistics (NICHD)
Christine Bachrach
bachracc@hd01.nichd.nih

Fertility and Family Statistics (NCHS)
Stephanie Ventura
sjv1@cdc.gov

Fertility and Family Statistics (CENSUS)
Jane Dye
jane.l.dye@census.gov

Immigrant Children (CENSUS)
Rose Kreider
rose.kreider@census.gov

Life Tables (NCHS)
Robert Anderson
rca7@cdc.gov

Marriage/Cohabitation (NCHS)
Anjani Chandra
ayc3@cdc.gov

Marriage/Cohabitation (CENSUS)
Rose Kreider
rose.kreider@census.gov
Tavia Simmons
tavia.simmons@census.gov

Migration (INS)
Staff
(202) 305-1613

Migration (NICHD)
Rebecca Clark
rclark@mail.nih.gov

Mothers Race/Ethnic Composition (NCHS)
Stephanie Ventura
sjv1@cdc.gov

Nonmarital Childbearing (NCHS)
Stephanie Ventura
sjv1@cdc.gov

ECONOMIC SECURITY

Family and Fertility Statistics (BLS)
Howard Hayghe
hayghe_h@bls.gov

Food Security (CSFII) (FNS)
Dawn Aldridge
dawn.aldridge@fns.usda.gov

Health Insurance Statistics (NCHS)
Robin Cohen
rzc6@cdc.gov

Housing Problems (OPDR)
Kathy Nelson
kathryn_p._nelson@hud.gov

Maternity Leave (BLS)
Tallese Johnson
tallese.d.johnson@census.gov

Maternity Leave (CENSUS)
David Johnson
johnson_david_scott@bls.gov

Parental Employment (BLS)
Howard Hayghe
hayghe_h@bls.gov

Poverty and Health (NCHS)
John Pleis
jpleis@cdc.gov

Poverty, WIC Program (ARS)
Mary Hama
mhama@rbhnrc.usda.gov

HEALTH

Acute and Chronic Conditions (NCHS)
Lara Akinbami
lakinbami@dhs.ca.gov

Birth Certificate Data (NCHS)
Joyce Martin
jmartin@cdc.gov

Birth/Death Records (NCHS)
Marian Mac Dorman
mfm1@cdc.gov

Child Mortality (NCHS)
John Kiely
jlk2@cdc.gov
Kenneth Schoendorf
kxs2@cdc.gov

Children's Health (NCHS)
Susan Lukacs
srl2@cdc.gov

Contraception (NCHS)
Joyce Abma
jabma@cdc.gov

Disability (NIH)
Louis Quatrano
lq2n@nih.gov

Family Planning Services (NCHS)
Gladys Martinez
gmartinez@cdc.gov

Fetal Mortality (NCHS)
Joyce Martin
jmartin@cdc.gov

Growth and Nutrition (NCHS)
Cynthia Ogden
cao9@cdc.gov

Health Care Access (NCHS)
Robin Cohen
rzc6@cdc.gov

Healthy People 2010 (NCHS)
Richard Klein
rjk6@cdc.gov

Infant and Child Health (CDHS)
Susan Lukacs
srl2@cdc.gov

Infants (NCHS)
Amy Branum
zvl5@cdc.gov

Infertility and Surgical Sterilization (NCHS)
Anjani Chandra
ayc3@cdc.gov

Injuries (NCHS)
Pat Barnes
plb8@cdc.gov
Lois Fingerhut
laf4@cdc.gov

Life Tables (NCHS)
Robert Anderson
rca7@cdc.gov

Low Birthweight Infants (NCHS)
Amy Branum
zvl5@cdc.gov

Mental Health (NCHS)
Gloria Simpson
gas4@cdc.gov

Perinatal Outcome/Maternal Nutrition and Weight Gain (NCHS)
Joyce Martin
jmartin@cdc.gov

Pregnancy and Health (NCHS)
Anjani Chandra
ayc3@cdc.gov

Pregnancy/Family Planning Services/Contraception (NICHD)
Susan Newcomer
newcomes@hd01.nichd.nih

Prenatal Care and Delivery Payment (NCHS)
Anjani Chandra
ayc3@cdc.gov

Preterm Births (NCHS)
Joyce Martin
jmartin@cdc.gov

Sexual Activity (NCHS)
Joyce Abma
jabma@cdc.gov

Teen Pregnancy (NCHS)
Stephanie Ventura
sjv1@cdc.gov

Teen Sex/Teen Pregnancy (NCHS)
Joyce Abma
jabma@cdc.gov

BEHAVIOR AND SOCIAL ENVIRONMENT

Alcohol Use (NIDA)
Douglas Rugh
drugh@mail.nih.gov

Illicit Drug Use (NIDA)
Douglas Rugh
drugh@mail.nih.gov

Maternal Smoking (NCHS)
John Kiely
jlk2@cdc.gov

Smoking (NIDA)
Douglas Rugh
drugh@mail.nih.gov

Violence (OJJDP)
Barbara Allen-Hagen
barbara@ojp.usdoj.gov
Janet Chiancone
chiancoj@ojp.usdoj.gov

Violence (BJS)
Michael Rand
randm@ojp.usdoj.gov

EDUCATION

Achievement (NCES)
Arnold Goldstein
arnold.goldstein@ed.gov
Tom Snyder
tom.snyder@ed.gov

Coursetaking/Transcripts, Postsecondary (NCES)
Paula Knepper
paula.knepper@ed.gov

Disabled Students (NCES)
Arnold Goldstein
arnold.goldstein@ed.gov

Dropouts (NCES)
Chris Chapman
chris.chapman@ed.gov

Early Childhood Education & Child Care (NCES)
Chris Chapman
chris.chapman@ed.gov

Education and Health (NCHS)
Debbie Blackwell
dblackwell@cdc.gov

High School Completion (NCES)
Chris Chapman
chris.chapman@ed.gov

Language/Racial & Ethnic Minorities (NCES)
Edie McArthur
edith.mcarthur@ed.gov

Related Behavior and Characteristics (NCES)
Tom Snyder
tom.snyder@ed.gov

School Crime (NCES)
Kathryn Chandler
kathryn.chandler@ed.gov
Tom Snyder
tom.snyder@ed.gov

School Finances (NCES)
Bill Fowler
william.fowler@ed.gov

Vocational Education (NCES)
Lisa Hudson
lisa.hudson@ed.gov

Youth Indicators (NCES)
Tom Snyder
tom.snyder@ed.gov

CRIME

The National Criminal Justice Reference Service (NCJRS) of the U.S. Justice Department's Office of Justice Programs operates a valuable fact finding service and can be a highly useful source of data on crime statistics and juvenile justice statistics in the United States. Reference assistance is available at http://askncjrs.ncjrs.org, or by calling 800-851-3420.

STATISTICAL ANALYSIS CENTERS

Statistical Analysis Centers (SACs) are state agencies that collect, analyze, and disseminate justice data. They contribute to effective state policies through statistical services, research, evaluation, and policy analysis. For more information about SAC activities and publications, visit http://www.jrsa.org/ or one of the state offices listed below.

ALABAMA
Becki Goggins
Uniform Crime Reporting Division/Statistical Analysis Center
Alabama Criminal Justice Information Center
770 Washington Avenue, Suite 350
PO Box 300660 Montgomery, AL 36130-0660
(334) 242-4937
Fax: (334) 242-0577
bgoggins@acjic.state.al.ushttp://acjic.state.al.us/

ALASKA
Alan McKelvie
Director, Statistical Analysis Center
University of Alaska Anchorage Justice Center
3211 Providence Drive
Anchorage, AK 99508
(907) 786-1810
Fax: (907) 786-7777
anarm@uaa.alaska.eduhttp://webserver.cts.uaa.alaska.edu/just/research/akjsau.html

ARIZONA
Phillip Stevenson, SAC Director
Arizona Criminal Justice Commission
1110 West Washington, Suite 230
Phoenix, AZ 85007
(602) 364-1157
Fax: (602) 364-1175

pstevenson@azcjc.govhttp://acjc.state.az.us/sac/index.asp

ARKANSAS
Gwen Ervin-McLarty
Management Project Analyst
Arkansas Crime Information Center
One Capitol Mall, 4D-200
Little Rock, AR 72201
(501) 682-7421
Fax: (501) 682-2530
gmclarty@acic.state.ar.ushttp://www.acic.org/

CALIFORNIA
Georgia Fong, Assistant Bureau Chief
California Department of Justice
Division of California Justice Information Services
Bureau of Criminal Information and Analysis
Criminal Justice Statistics Center
4949 Broadway, G-243
Sacramento, CA 95820
(916) 227-2372
Fax: (916) 227-0427
georgia.fong@doj.ca.govhttp://ag.ca.gov/cjsc/

COLORADO
Kim English, Research Director
Division of Criminal Justice
Colorado Department of Public Safety
700 Kipling Street, Suite 3000
Denver, CO 80215
(303) 239-4453
Fax: (303) 239-4491
kim.english@cdps.state.co.ushttp://dcj.state.co.us/ors

CONNECTICUT
Stephen M. Cox, Ph.D., SAC Director
Associate Professor
Department of Criminology and Criminal Justice
Central Connecticut State University
1615 Stanley Street
New Britain, CT 06050
(860) 832-3138
Fax: (860) 832-3014
coxs@mail.ccsu.eduhttp://www.opm.state.ct.us/pdpd1/justice/sac.htm

DELAWARE
John O'Connell, Director
Delaware Statistical Analysis Center
60 The Plaza
Dover, DE 19901
(302) 739-4626
Fax: (302) 739-4630
john.o'connell@state.de.ushttp://www.state.de.us/budget/sac/default.shtml

DISTRICT OF COLUMBIA
Nancy Ware, Executive Director
Criminal Justice Coordinating Council
One Judiciary Center
441 4th Street, NW, Room 727N
Washington, DC 20001
(202) 442-9283
Fax: (202) 442-4922
nancy.ware@dc.gov

FLORIDA
Susan Burton, Administator
Statistical Analysis Center
Florida Department of Law Enforcement
2331 Phillips Road
Tallahassee, FL 32302
(850) 410-7140
Fax: (850) 410-7150
sueburton@fdle.state.fl.ushttp://www.fdle.state.fl.us/FSAC/index.asp

GEORGIA
LaSonja Fillingame, Director
Statistical Analysis Center
Criminal Justice Coordinating Council
503 Oak Place, Suite 540
Atlanta, GA 30349
(404) 559-4949
Fax: (404) 559-4960
lfilling@cjcc.state.ga.ushttp://www.ganet.org/cjcc/sac.html

HAWAII
Paul Perrone, Chief of Research and Statistics
Crime Prevention & Justice Assistance Division
235 South Beretania Street, Suite 401
Honolulu, HI 96813
(808) 586-1150
Fax: (808) 586-1373
paul.a.perrone@hawaii.govhttp://www.cpja.ag.state.hi.us/rs/index.shtml

IDAHO
Janeena J. Wing, SAC Director
Idaho State Police
Planning, Grants, and Research
PO Box 700
Meridian, ID 83680-0700
(208) 884-7044
Fax: (208) 884-7094
janeena.wing@isp.idaho.govhttp://www.isp.state.id.us/pgr/Research/sac.html

ILLINOIS
Robert Bauer, Acting SAC Associate Director
Illinois Criminal Justice Information Authority
120 South Riverside Plaza, Suite 1016
Chicago, IL 60606-3997
(312) 793-8512
Fax: (312) 793-8422
bob.bauer@illinois.govhttp://www.icjia.org/public/index.cfm

INDIANA
Amanda Thornton , SAC Director
Director of Research & Planning
Indiana Criminal Justice Institute
One North Capitol Ave, Suite 1000
Indianapolis, IN 46204
(317) 233-0387
Fax: (317) 232-4979
athornton@cji.in.govhttp://www.in.gov/cji/

IOWA
Paul Stageberg, Ph.D., Acting Administrator
Statistical Analysis Center
Iowa Division of Criminal & Juvenile Justice Planning
Lucas State Office Building
321 East 12th Street
Des Moines, IA 50319
(515) 242-6122
Fax: (515) 242-6119
paul.stageberg@iowa.govhttp://www.state.ia.us/government/dhr/cjjp/index.html

KANSAS
Jan Brasher, SAC Director
Kansas Sentencing Commission
Kansas Criminal Justice Coordinating Council
700 Southwest Jackson Street
Jayhawk Tower, Suite 501
Topeka, KS 66603
(785) 296-0923
Fax: (785) 296-0927
janb@sentencing.ks.govwww.accesskansas.org/ksc

KENTUCKY
Tanya Dickinson, SAC Contact
Kentucky Justice Cabinet
Kentucky Criminal Justice Council
403 Wapping Street
Frankfort, KY 40601
(502) 564-3251
Fax: (502) 564-5244
tanya.dickinson@ky.govhttp://www.sac.state.ky.us/index.html

LOUISIANA
Fredia Dunn, State Policy Planning Administrator
Louisiana Commission on Law Enforcement
1885 Woodale Boulevard, Suite 1230
Baton Rouge, LA 70806
(225) 925-7465
Fax: (225) 925-3889
frediad@cole.state.la.ushttp://www.cole.state.la.us/louisiana_statistical_analysis_c.htm

MAINE
Carmen Dorsey, Director
Maine Statistical Analysis Center
Edmund S. Muskie School of Public Service
PO Box 9300
15 Baxter Boulevard
Portland, ME 04104-9300
(207) 228-8342
Fax: (207) 228-8460
cdorsey@usm.maine.eduhttp://muskie.usm.maine.edu/justiceresearch/

MARYLAND
Charles Wellford, Ph.D., Director
Maryland Justice Analysis Center
University of Maryland
2220 LeFrak Hall
College Park, MD 20742
(301) 405-4701
Fax: (301) 314-0179
cwellford@crim.umd.eduhttp://mjac.umd.edu

MASSACHUSETTS
Sarah Lawrence, Acting SAC Director
Programs Division
Massachusetts Executive Office of Public Safety
1 Ashburton Place, Room 611
Boston, MA 02108
(617) 727-7775, ext. 25572
Fax: (617) 727-5356
sarah.lawrence@state.ma.ushttp://www.mass.gov/portal/

MICHIGAN
Timothy Bynum, Ph.D., Director/Professor
Michigan Justice Statistics Center
Michigan State University School of Criminal Justice
560 Baker Hall
East Lansing, MI 48824
(517) 353-4515
Fax: (517) 432-1787
bynum@msu.eduhttp://www.cj.msu.edu/7Epeople/stats.html

MINNESOTA
Danette Buskovick, SAC Director
Minnesota Office of Justice Programs
444 Cedar Street, Suite 100
St. Paul, MN 55101-5100
(651) 201-7309
Fax: (651) 284-3317
danette.buskovick@state.mn.ushttp://www.ojp.state.mn.us/cj

MISSISSIPPI
Lisa Nored, Ph.D., SAC Director
Mississippi Statistical Analysis Center
University of Southern Mississippi
POBox 5127
Hattiesburg, MS 39406
(601) 266-4509
Fax: (601) 266-4391
lisa.nored@usm.eduhttp://www.usm.edu/mssac/

MISSOURI
Ronald Beck, Director
Statistical Analysis Center
Missouri State Highway Patrol
1510 East Elm Street
PO Box 568
Jefferson City, MO 65102
(573) 751-9000, ext. 2991
Fax: (573) 526-6274
ron.beck@mshp.dps.mo.govhttp://www.mshp.dps.missouri.gov/MSHPWeb/SAC/index.html

MONTANA
Scott Furois, Director
Statistical Analysis Center
Montana Board of Crime Control
3075 North Montana Avenue
PO Box 201408
Helena, MT 59620
(406) 444-4298
Fax: (406) 444-4722
sfurois@mt.govhttp://bccdoj.doj.state.mt.us/sac/

NEBRASKA
Michael Overton, Director
Statistical Analysis Center
Nebraska Crime Commission
PO Box 94946
Lincoln, NE 68509
(402) 471-3992
Fax: (402) 471-2837
michael.overton@ncc.ne.govhttp://www.nol.org/home/crimecom/

NEVADA
Timothy Hart, Ph.D., Director
Center for Analysis of Crime Statistics

Department of Criminal Justice
University of Nevada Las Vegas
4505 Maryland Parkway
Box 5009
Las Vegas, NV 89154-5009
(702) 895-0236
Fax: (702) 895-0252
timothy.hart@unlv.eduhttp://www.unlv.edu/centers/crimestats/index.htm

NEW HAMPSHIRE
Valerie Hall, SAC Director
New Hampshire Office of the Attorney General
33 Capitol Street
Concord, NH 03301
(603) 271-1234
Fax: (603) 271-2110
valerie.hall@doj.nh.govwww.doj.nh.gov/index.html

NEW JERSEY
Jean Petherbridge, SAC Contact
Acting Chief, Research and Evaluation
Department of Law and Public Safety
25 Market Street, CN-085
Trenton, NJ 08625
(609) 984-5693
Fax: (609) 984-4473
petherbridgej@njdcj.orghttp://www.state.nj.us/lps/

NEW MEXICO
Lisa Broidy, Ph.D., Director
Statistical Analysis Center
University of New Mexico
Institute for Social Research
MSC05 - 3080
Albuquerque, NM 87106
(505) 277-2002
Fax: (505) 277-2501
lbroidy@unm.eduhttp://www.unm.edu/[]isrnet

NEW YORK
Donna Hall, Director
Bureau of Justice Research and Innovation
New York State Division of Criminal Justice Services
4 Tower Place
Albany, NY 12203-3764
(518) 457-7301
Fax: (518) 457-9700
donna.hall@dcjs.state.ny.ushttp://criminaljustice.state.ny.us

NORTH CAROLINA
Doug Yearwood, SAC Director
Governor's Crime Commission
1201 Front Street, Suite 200
Raleigh, NC 27609
(919) 733-4564
Fax: (919) 733-4625
dyearwood@ncgccd.orghttp://www.gcc.state.nc.us/cjac.htm

NORTH DAKOTA
Judith Volk, Information Services Manager
North Dakota Bureau of Criminal Investigation
PO Box 1054
Bismarck, ND 58502
(701) 328-5500
Fax: (701) 328-5510
jvolk@state.nd.ushttp://www.ag.state.nd.us/

NORTHERN MARIANA ISLANDS
Doris S. Chong, Executive Director
Criminal Justice Planning Agency
CNMI Criminal Justice Statistical Analysis Center
PO Box 501133 - Chalan Kanoa
Saipan, MP 96950
(670) 664-4550, ext. 7
Fax: (670) 664-4560
doris.chong@cjpa.gov.mphttp://www.saipan.com/gov/branches/cjpa

OHIO
Lisa Shoaf, Ph.D., Director
Ohio Statistical Analysis Center
1970 West Broad Street
Columbus, OH 43218-2632
(614) 466-5997
Fax: (614) 466-0308
lshoaf@dps.state.oh.ushttp://www.ocjs.oh.gov

OKLAHOMA
Christopher M. Hill, Ph.D., SAC Director
Oklahoma Statistical Analysis Center
Oklahoma Criminal Justice Resource Center
3812 N. Santa Fe, Suite 290
Oklahoma City, OK 73118-8500
(405) 524-2059, ext. 115
Fax: (405) 524-2792
christopher.hill@ocjrc.nethttp://www.ocjrc.net

OREGON
Michael Wilson, SAC Director
Statistical Analysis Center
Oregon Criminal Justice Commission
885 Summer Street, NE
Salem, OR 97301
(503) 378-4850
Fax: (503) 986-4574
michael.k.wilson@das.state.or.uswww.oregon.gov/CJC/index.shtml

PENNSYLVANIA
Douglas E. Hoffman, Director
Center for Research, Evaluation, and Statistical Analysis
Pennsylvania Commission on Crime and Delinquency
PO Box 1167
Harrisburg, PA 17108-1167
(717) 787-5152, ext. 3046
Fax: (717) 705-0891
douhoffman@state.pa.ushttp://www.pccd.state.pa.us/pccd/site/default.asp
Julio Rosa, Director

PUERTO RICO
Statistical Analysis Center
Criminal Justice Information System
PO Box 9020192
San Juan, PR 00902
(787) 729-2657
Fax: (787) 729-2261
jrosa@justicia.gobierno.pr

RHODE ISLAND
Thomas H. Mongeau, SAC Director
Rhode Island Justice Commission
One Capitol Hill, 4th Floor
Providence, RI 02908
(401) 222-4499
Fax: (401) 277-1294
tmongeau@gw.doa.state.ri.ushttp://www.rijustice.state.ri.us/sac/sac.htm

SOUTH CAROLINA
Robert McManus, SAC Director
Planning and Research Division
South Carolina Department of Public Safety
PO Box 1993
Blythewood, SC 29016
(803) 896-8717
Fax: (803) 896-8717
robertmcmanus@scdps.nethttp://www.scdps.org/ojp/statistics.asp

SOUTH DAKOTA
Trevor Jones
South Dakota Division of Criminal Investigation
Criminal Justice Training Center
500 East Capitol Avenue
Pierre, SD 57501-5070
(605) 773-3331
Fax: (605) 773-4629
trevor.jones@state.sd.ushttp://dci.sd.gov/administration/sac/

TENNESSEE
Jackie Vandercook, Director
Statistical Analysis Center
Tennessee Bureau of Investigation
Crime Statistics Unit
901 R.S. Gass Blvd.
Nashville, TN 37216-2639
(615) 744-4014
Fax: (615) 744-4662
jackie.vandercook@state.tn.ushttp://www.tbi.state.tn.us/divisions/isd_csu_sac.htm

TEXAS
Janna Burleson (interim contact)
Criminal Justice Budget and Policy Director
Office of the Governor
(512) 463-1958
jburleson@governor.state.tx.us.

UTAH
Michael Haddon, SAC Director
Utah Commission on Criminal and Juvenile Justice
Utah State Capitol Complex
East Office Building, Suite E330
Salt Lake City, UT 84114
(801) 538-1047
Fax: (801) 538-1024
mhaddon@utah.govhttp://www.justice.state.ut.us/

VERMONT
William Clements, Ph.D., Executive Director
Vermont Center for Justice Research
PO Box 396
Northfield, VT 05663
(802) 485-2368
Fax: (802) 485-2533
bclements@norwich.eduwww.vcjr.org

VIRGINIA
James McDonough Ph.D., Director
Oklahoma Criminal Justice Research Center
Department of Criminal Justice Services
805 East Broad Street, Tenth Floor
Richmond, VA 23219
(804) 371-0532
Fax: (804) 225-3853
jim.mcdonough@dcjs.virginia.govhttp://www.dcjs.org/research/

WASHINGTON
Harold Nelson, Ph.D., SAC Director
Office of Financial Management
PO Box 43113
Olympia, WA 98504-3113
(360) 902-0603
Fax: (360) 664-8941
harold.nelson@ofm.wa.govwww.ofm.wa.gov/criminaljustice

WEST VIRGINIA
Stephen Haas, Ph.D., SAC Director
Statistical Analysis Center
1204 Kanawha Boulevard, East
Charleston, WV 25301
(304) 558-8814
Fax: (304) 558-0391
shaas@wvdcjs.orghttp://www.wvdcjs.com/statsanalysis/index.html

WISCONSIN
Dean Ziemke, Ph.D., SAC Director
Office of Justice Assistance
131 West Wilson Street, Suite 202
Madison, WI 53702
(608) 261-2437
Fax: (608) 266-6676
dean.ziemke@wisconsin.govoja.wi.gov/sac

WYOMING
Burke Grandjean, Ph.D., Executive Director
Rodney Wambeam, Ph.D., SAC Manager
Wyoming Survey & Analysis Center
710 Garfield Street, Suite 320
Laramie WY 82071
(307) 742-2223
Fax: (307) 742-3058
wysac@uwyo.eduhttp://www.uwyo.edu/wysac/

DRUGS

The Drug Enforcement Administration of the U.S. Justice Department is a source of data on facts, figures and trends of the illicit use of drugs. The information includes statistics on drug-related deaths and hospital admission due to drug abuse.

Telephone inquiries can be made to the Drug Enforcement Administration (202) 307-7977. Internet site http://www.usdoj.gov/dea.

ECONOMICS

A list of the experts within the Bureau of Economic Analysis follows: Internet site: http://www.bea.doc.gov

NATIONAL ECONOMICS

Associate Director
Brent R. Moulton
(202) 606-9606

Auto Output
Everette P. Johnson
(202) 606-9725

Capital Consumption
David B. Wasshausen
(202) 606-9752

Capital Expenditures - By Industry
Michael D. Glenn
(202) 606-9718

Capital Expenditures - By Type
Paul R. Lally
(202) 606-9743

Capital Flows
Douglas S. Meade
(202) 606-5585

Capital Stocks
David B. Wasshausen
(202) 606-9752

Computer Price Index
Todd P. Siebeneck
(202) 606-9705

Construction
Velma P. Henry
(202) 606-9760

Consumption (personal)
Clinton P. McCully
(202) 606-9735

Corporate Profits and Taxes
M. Gregory Key
(202) 606-9727

Depreciation
David B. Wasshausen
(202) 606-9752

Disposable Personal Income
James E. Rankin
(202) 606-9741

Dividends
M. Gregory Key
(202) 606-9727

Employee Benefit Plans
Kurt Kunze
(202) 606-9748

Employee Compensation
Kurt Kunze
(202) 606-9748

Equipment and Software
Linden L. Webber
(202) 606-9765

Farm Output, Product, and Income
Nicole M. Mayerhauser
(202) 606-9742

Fixed Investment
Paul R. Lally
(202) 606-9743

Government, Federal
Pamela A. Kelly
(202) 606-9781

Government, Federal: Consumption Expenditures and Gross Investment
Michelle D. Robinson
(202) 606-9783

Government, Federal: Consumption Expenditures and Gross Investment - National Defense
Michelle D. Robinson
(202) 606-9783

Government, Federal: Consumption Expenditures and Gross Investment - Nondefense
Andrea L. Cook
(202) 606-9777

Government, Federal: Contributions
Benyam M. Tsehaye
(202) 606-9791

Government, Federal: Other taxes and current expenditures
William R. Armstrong
(202) 606-9799

Government, Federal: Other taxes and current expenditures - Capital Stocks
Steven Payson
(202) 606-9788

Government, Federal: Other taxes and current expenditures - Functions
Benjamin A. Mandel
(202) 606-9296

Government, Federal: Social Benefit Payments
Michelle D. Robinson
(202) 606-9783

Government, Federal: Social Benefit Payments - Personal Taxes
Mary L. Roy
(202) 606-9664

Government, Special Studies
Steven Payson
(202) 606-9788

Government, State and Local (Note: National estimates only)
Bruce E. Baker
(202) 606-9663

Government, State and Local: Consumption Expenditures and Investment
Benjamin D. Cowan
(202) 606-9693

Government, State and Local: Contributions and Social Benefit Payments
Alyssa E. Holdren
(202) 606-9789

Government, State and Local: Taxes and Other Current Expenditures
Benjamin D. Cowan
(202) 606-9693

Government, State and Local: Taxes and Other Current Expenditures - Capital Stocks
Steven Payson
(202) 606-9788

Government, State and Local: Taxes and Other Current Expenditures - Functions
Steven J. Andrews
(202) 606-9770

Gross Domestic Product (Gross National Product): Current Estimates
Virginia H. Mannering
(202) 606-9732

Gross Private Domestic Investment
Paul R. Lally
(202) 606-9743

Interest Income and Payments
Shaunda M. Villones
(202) 606-9632

Inventories
Soo J. Kim
(202) 606-9757

Inventory/Sales Ratios
Tony Troy
(202) 606-9726

Investment
Paul R. Lally
(202) 606-9743

Motor Vehicle Output
Everette P. Johnson
(202) 606-9725

National Income
Virginia H. Mannering
(202) 606-9732

Net Exports
Andrew K. Hummel
(202) 606-9674

Output Measures (Chain-type)
Brian C. Moyer
(202) 606-9734

Personal Consumption Expenditures
Clinton P. McCully
(202) 606-9735

Personal Consumption Expenditures - Autos
Everette P. Johnson
(202) 606-9725

Personal Consumption Expenditures - Motor Vehicles
Everette P. Johnson
(202) 606-9725

Personal Consumption Expenditures - Other Goods
Harvey Lee Davis, Jr.
(202) 606-9719

Personal Consumption Expenditures - Prices
Clinton P. McCully
(202) 606-9735

Personal Consumption Expenditures - Services
Michael Armah
(202) 606-9721

Personal Income
Toui Chen Pomsouvan
(202) 606-9739

Price Measures (Chain-type)
Brian C. Moyer
(202) 606-9734

Proprietors Income, Nonfarm
Charles S. Robinson
(202) 606-9794

Rental Income
Denise A. McBride
(202) 606-9733

Residential Construction
Bonnie A. Retus
(202) 606-9740

Saving
Kurt Kunze
(202) 606-9748

Structures
Jennifer A. Ribarsky
(202) 606-9759

Transportation Satellite Accounts
Jiemin Guo
(202) 606-5587

Travel and Tourism Satellite Accounts
Peter D. Kuhbach
(202) 606-5587

Truck Output
Everette P. Johnson
(202) 606-9725

United Nations and OECD System of National Accounts
Karin E. Moses
(202) 606-9620

Wages and Salaries
Kurt Kunze
(202) 606-9748

Wealth Estimates
David B. Wasshausen
(202) 606-9752

INTERNATIONAL ECONOMICS

Associate Director
Ralph H. Kozlow
(202) 606-9604

Balance of Payments
Christopher L. Bach
(202) 606-9545

Balance of Payments - Current Account Transactions
Michael A. Mann
(202) 606-9573

Balance of Payments - Financial Account Transactions
Christopher A. Gohrband
(202) 606-9564

Balance of Payments - Foreign Military Sales
Michael A. Mann
(202) 606-9573

Balance of Payments - Government Transactions
Christopher L. Bach
(202) 606-9545

Balance of Payments - International Services
Michael A. Mann
(202) 606-9573

Balance of Payments - International Transportation
Edward F. Dozier, III
(202) 606-9559

Balance of Payments - International Travel
Joan E. Bolyard
(202) 606-9550

Balance of Payments - Merchandise Trade
Staff
(202) 606-3384

Balance of Payments - Private Remittances and Other Transfers
Michael A. Mann
(202) 606-9573

Balance of Payments - Special Studies
John W. Rutter
(202) 606-9587

Foreign Direct Investment in the U.S. - Annual and Benchmark Surveys
Charles R. Gravitz
(202) 606-9874

Foreign Direct Investment in the U.S. - Establishment-level (Linked) Data
Thomas W. Anderson
(202) 606-9879

Foreign Direct Investment in the U.S. - New Investment Analysis and Data
Thomas W. Anderson
(202) 606-9879

Foreign Direct Investment in the U.S. - New Investment Surveys
Dorrett E. Williams
(202) 606-9892

Foreign Direct Investment in the U.S. - Quarterly Balance of Payments Survey
Gregory G. Fouch
(202) 606-9831

Foreign Direct Investment in the U.S. - Quarterly Balance of Payments Survey Quarterly and Annual Data
Gregory G. Fouch
(202) 606-9831

Foreign Direct Investment in the U.S. - Quarterly Balance of Payments Transactions, Analysis
Maria Borga
(202) 606-9853

Foreign Direct Investment in the U.S. - U.S. Affiliates of Foreign Companies, Analysis and Data
William J. Zeile
(202) 606-9893

U.S. Direct Investment Abroad - Annual and Benchmark Surveys
Patricia C. Walker
(202) 606-9889

U.S. Direct Investment Abroad - Quarterly Balance of Payments Survey
Mark W. New
(202) 606-9875

U.S. Direct Investment Abroad - Quarterly Balance of Payments Survey Quarterly and Annual Data
Mark W. New
(202) 606-9875

U.S. Direct Investment Abroad - Quarterly Balance of Payments Transactions, Analysis
Daniel R. Yorgason
(202) 606-9804

U.S. Direct Investment Abroad - U.S. Multinational Companies, Analysis and Data
Raymond J. Mataloni, Jr.
(202) 606-9867

U.S. Services Transactions with Unaffiliated Foreigners - Annual and Benchmark Financial Services Surveys
Faith M. Brannam
(202) 606-9813

U.S. Services Transactions with Unaffiliated Foreigners - Construction and Engineering Services
Rafael I. Font
(202) 606-9830

U.S. Services Transactions with Unaffiliated Foreigners - Insurance Services
Rafael I. Font
(202) 606-9830

U.S. Services Transactions with Unaffiliated Foreigners - Royalties and License Fees and Intangible Rights
Rafael I. Font
(202) 606-9830

U.S. Services Transactions with Unaffiliated Foreigners - Sales by Affiliates -- Analysis and Data
Maria Borga
(202) 606-9853

U.S. Services Transactions with Unaffiliated Foreigners - Selected Services Surveys
Christopher J. Emond
(202) 606-9826

REGIONAL ECONOMICS

Associate Director
John W. Ruser
(202) 606-9605

Gross State Product Estimates
Staff
(202) 606-5340

Gross State Product Estimates - Banking and Services Industries
Sharon D. Panek
(202) 606-9228

Gross State Product Estimates - Compensation and Proprietors Income Estimates
Caitlin E. Wenum
(202) 606-9216

Gross State Product Estimates - Manufacturing Industries
Ndidi O. Obidoa
(202) 606-9229

Gross State Product Estimates - Methodology Questions
George K. Downey
(202) 606-9214

Gross State Product Estimates - Mining
Joseph A. Polka
(202) 606-9231

Gross State Product Estimates - Real Estate
Sharon D. Panek
(202) 606-9228

Gross State Product Estimates - Taxes on Production and Imports
Clifford H. Woodruff
(202) 606-9234

Gross State Product Estimates - Transportation and Government
Eric C. Erickson
(202) 606-9213

GSP Web Applications
Gerard P. Aman
(202) 606-9207

Personal Income and Employment
Staff
(202) 606-5360

Personal Income and Employment - Disposable Personal Income
Ann E. Dunbar
(202) 606-9215

Personal Income and Employment - Dividends, Interest, and Rental Income
Charles A. Jolley, III
(202) 606-9257

Personal Income and Employment - Farm Proprietors Income and Employment
Carrie L. Litkowski
(202) 606-9253

Personal Income and Employment - Methodology
Kathy A. Albetski
(202) 606-9240

Personal Income and Employment - Nonfarm Proprietors Income and Employment
Charles A. Jolley, III
(202) 606-9257

Personal Income and Employment - Residence Adjustment
Jeffrey L. Newman
(202) 606-9265

Personal Income and Employment - State Quarterly Personal Income
Matthew A. von Kerczek
(202) 606-9250

Personal Income and Employment - Transfer Payments
James P. Stehle
(202) 606-9279

Personal Income and Employment - Wage and Salary Income and Employment
Sharon C. Carnevale
(202) 606-9247

RIMS II, Regional Multipliers
Staff
(202) 606-5343

INDUSTRY ECONOMICS

Associate Director
Sumiye Okubo
(202) 606-9612

Benchmark Input-Output
Mary L. Streitwieser
(202) 606-5585

Capital Flow
Douglas S. Meade
(202) 606-5585

Gross Domestic Product by Industry
George M. Smith
(202) 606-5307

Input-Output Accounts
George M. Smith
(202) 606-5307

Transportation Satellite Accounts
Jiemin Guo
(202) 606-5587

Travel and Tourism Satellite Accounts
Peter D. Kuhbach
(202) 606-5587

EDUCATION

The National Center for Education Statistics (NCES) is the primary federal entity for collecting and analyzing data related to education in the U.S. and other nations. NCES is located within the U.S. Department of Education and the Institute of Education Sciences. NCES fulfills a Congressional mandate to collect, collate, analyze, and report complete statistics on the condition of American education; conduct and publish reports; and review and report on education activities internationally.

For more information, call the NCES at (202) 502-7300, or via the web at http://nces.ed.gov.

ENERGY

The National Energy Information Center of the U.S. Department of Energy provides statistical and analytical energy data, information, and referral assistance to the government and private sectors, academia, and the general public. For questions of a general nature about energy data call (202) 586-8800. Internet site http://www.eia.doe.gov/contacts/main.html. For specific topics, call information contacts listed below:

COAL
Main Fax: (202) 287-1946/44

Coke Plants

Mary Lilly
(202) 287-1742
mary.lilly@eia.doe.gov

Annual Distribution
Thomas Murphy
(202) 287-1739
thomas.murphy@eia.doe.gov

Manufacturing Plants: Consumption, Receipts
Mary Lilly
(202) 287-1742
mary.lilly@eia.doe.gov

Monthly Data: Production, Imports, Exports, Consumption, Stocks
Mary Lilly
(202) 287-1742
mary.lilly@eia.doe.gov

Annual Producer and Distributor Stocks
Thomas Murphy
(202) 287-1739
thomas.murphy@eia.doe.gov

Annual Production
Patty Chou
(202) 287-1977
patty.chou@eia.doe.gov

Quarterly Production
Mary Paull
(202) 287-1741
mary.paull@eia.doe.gov

Weekly Production
Mary Lilly
(202) 287-1742
mary.lilly@eia.doe.gov

Quarterly Data: Production, Imports, Exports, Receipts, Consumption, Stocks
Paulette Young
(202) 287-1738
paulette.young@eia.doe.gov

Reserves and Transportation
Richard Bonskowski
(202) 287-1725
richard.bonskowski@eia.doe.gov

Short-Term Projections
Fred Freme
(202) 287-1740
frederick.freme@eia.doe.gov

ELECTRIC POWER
Main Fax: (202) 287-1944

Capacity
Elsie Bess
(202) 287-1730
elsie.bess@eia.doe.gov

Demand-Side Management
Karen McDaniel
(202) 287-1799
karen.mcdaniel@eia.doe.gov

Electricity Imports/Exports
John Makens
(202) 287-1749
john.makens@eia.doe.gov

Emergency Alert Notice
John Makens
(202) 287-1749
john.makens@eia.doe.gov

Emissions
Natalie Ko
(202) 287-1957
natalie.ko@eia.doe.gov

Finance (Investor- and Publicly Owned)
Karen McDaniel
(202) 287-1799
karen.mcdaniel@eia.doe.gov

Fuel Receipts, Cost, and Quality (Utility)
Stephen Scott
(202) 287-1737
stephen.scott@eia.doe.gov

Fuel Receipts, Cost, and Quality (Nonutility)
Rebecca McNerney
(202) 287-1913
rebecca.mcnerney@eia.doe.gov

Generation, Consumption, and Stocks (Utility)
Melvin Johnson
(202) 287-1754
melvin.johnson@eia.doe.gov

Generation, Consumption, and Stocks (Nonutility)
Ron Hankey
(202) 287-1762
rhankey@eia.doe.gov

Publications
Robert Schnapp
(202) 287-1787
robert.schnapp@eia.doe.gov

Reliability Data
John Makens
(202) 287-1749
john.makens@eia.doe.gov

Sales, Revenue, Customers, and Price (Monthly)
Rick Farace
(202) 287-1727
rick.farace@eia.doe.gov

Sales, Revenue, Customers, and Price (Annual)
Karen McDaniel
(202) 287-1799
karen.mcdaniel@eia.doe.gov

Transmission Data
John Makens
(202) 287-1749
john.makens@eia.doe.gov

Wholesale Data
Karen McDaniel
(202) 287-1799
karen.mcdaniel@eia.doe.gov

RENEWABLE ENERGY FORECAST EXPERTS
Main Fax: (202) 287-1933

Alternative-Fueled Vehicles; Alternative Transportation Fuels
Mary Joyce
(202) 287-1752
mary.joyce@eia.doe.gov

Alternative-Fueled Vehicle Suppliers & Users, Survey Manager (EIA-886)
Cynthia Sirk
(202) 287-1925
Cynthia.sirk@eia.doe.gov

Alternative-Fueled Inventory Estimates
Fred Mayes
(202) 287-1750
fred.mayes@eia.doe.gov

Alternative-Fueled Vehicles; Alternative Transportation Fuels and Renewable Energy
Chris V. Buckner
(202) 287-1751
chris.buckner@eia.doe.gov

Biomass/Biofuels
Fred Mayes
(202) 287-1750
fred.mayes@eia.doe.gov

Geothermal Heat Pump (EIA-902), Survey Manager
Susan Henry
(202) 287-1792
susan.henry@eia.doe.gov

Municipal Solid Waste
Fred Mayes
(202) 287-1750
fred.mayes@eia.doe.gov

Solar Thermal and Photovoltaic Cells/Modules (EIA-63A & EIA-63B), Survey Manager
Peter Wong
(202) 287-1986
peter.wong@eia.doe.gov

Renewable Resources, Hydro and Geothermal
Mark Gielecki
(202) 287-1729
mark.gielecki@eia.doe.gov

Renewable Resources, Solar Collector, Photovoltaic; Solar Collector Cells/Modules
Fred Mayes
(202) 287-1750
fred.mayes@eia.doe.gov

Renewable Resources, Wind
Louise Guey-Lee
(202) 287-1731
louise.guey-lee@eia.doe.gov

Renewable Resources
Chris Buckner
(202) 287-1751
chris.buckner@eia.doe.gov

NATURAL GAS
Main Fax: (202) 586-4420

Coalbed Methane/Tight Gas
Bob King
(202) 586-4787
robert.king@eia.doe.gov

Consumption (by sector)
Roy Kass
(202) 586-4790
nathaniel.kass@eia.doe.gov

Drilling
Bob King
(202) 586-4787
robert.king@eia.doe.gov

Exploration
Dave Morehouse
(202) 586-4853
david.morehouse@eia.doe.gov

Spot Market
Jose Villar
(202) 586-9613
jose.villar@eia.doe.gov

Imports/Exports
Damien Gaul
(202) 586-2073
damien.gaul@eia.doe.gov

Liquefied Natural Gas
Damien Gaul
(202) 586-2073
damien.gaul@eia.doe.gov

Natural Gas Liquids
David Hinton
(202) 586-2990
david.hinton@eia.doe.gov

Pipelines
James Tobin
(202) 586-4835
james.tobin@eia.doe.gov

Prices - Consumer and City Gate
Roy Kass
(202) 586-4790
nathaniel.kass@eia.doe.gov

Prices - Wellhead
William Trapmann
(202) 586-6408
william.trapmann@eia.doe.gov

Productive Capacity
John Wood
(214) 720-6160
john.wood@eia.doe.gov

Regulatory Issues
Barbara Mariner-Volpe
(202) 586-5878
barbara.marinervolpe@eia.doe.gov

Reserves
John Wood
(214) 720-6160
john.wood@eia.doe.gov

Resources
Dave Morehouse
(202) 586-4853
david.morehouse@eia.doe.gov

Retail Restructuring
Barbara Mariner-Volpe
(202) 586-5878
Barbara.marinervolpe@eia.doe.gov

Rigs Count
Bob King
(202) 586-4787
robert.king@eia.doe.gov

Underground Storage

Roy Kass
(202) 586-4790
nathaniel.kass@eia.doe.gov

PETROLEUM
Main Fax: (202) 586-5846

Refiner Crude Oil; Acquisition Cost
Elizabeth Scott
(202) 586-1258
elizabeth.scott@eia.doe.gov

Crude Oil/Wellhead Value; Domestic Crude Oil First Purchase Report
Dave Gatton
(202) 586-5995
david.gatton@eia.doe.gov

Crude Oil Production
Mir Yousufuddin
(214) 720-6186
mir.yousufuddin@eia.doe.gov

Crude Oil Reserves
John Wood
(214) 720-6160
john.wood@eia.doe.gov

Product Prices
Tammy Heppner
(202) 586-4748
tammy.heppner@eia.doe.gov

Retail Gasoline/Diesel Prices
Michael Burdette
(202) 586-6649
michael.burdette@eia.doe.gov

Supply and Disposition
Mike Conner
(202) 586-1795
michael.conner@eia.doe.gov

Exports
Jennifer Fama
(202) 586-6254
jennifer.fama@eia.doe.gov

Imports
Matt Breslin
(202) 586-2992
matt.breslin@eia.doe.gov

Refinery Operations; Stocks; Transportation
Mike Conner
(202) 586-1795
michael.conner@eia.doe.gov

Natural Gas Liquids; Propane Data
David Hinton
(202) 586-2990
david.hinton@eia.doe.gov

Fuel Oil Sales
Dan Walzer
(202) 586-3511
daniel.walzer@eia.doe.gov

Product Consumption
Tammy Heppner
(202) 586-4748
tammy.heppner@eia.doe.gov

Resources
Dave Morehouse
(202) 586-4853
david.morehouse@eia.doe.gov

Petroleum Demand Analysis
Mike Conner
(202) 586-1795
michael.conner@eia.doe.gov

Weekly Petroleum Status Report
John Duff
(202) 586-9612
john.duff@eia.doe.gov

NUCLEAR and URANIUM
Main Fax: (202) 287-1933

Analysis - Potential market growth, US and World
Ron Hagen
(202) 287-1917
ronald.hagen@eia.doe.gov

Capacity, US and World
John Moens
(202) 287-1976
john.moens@eia.doe.gov

Capacity Factor, U.S.
John Moens
(202) 287-1976
john.moens@eia.doe.gov

Environment - Greenhouse Gases
Dan Nikodem
(202) 287-1759
zdenek.nikodem@eia.doe.gov

Environment - Nuclear Waste
Jim Finucane
(202) 287-1966
jim.finucane@eia.doe.gov

Forecasts - International Nuclear Fuel Cycle Model: US Enrichment svc.; US Spent Fuel; US/World Uranium requirements
Dan Nikodem
(202) 287-1759
zdenek.nikodem@eia.doe.gov

Generation, Electric; U.S. nuclear output, current and historical
John Moens
(202) 287-1976
john.moens@eia.doe.gov

Nuclear Waste, Characteristics, Waste Fund Fees
Jim Finucane
(202) 287-1966
jim.finucane@eia.doe.gov

Uprates, US Reactors
Ron Hagen
(202) 287-1917
ronald.hagen@eia.doe.gov

Uranium; EIA Form-858, Uranium Industry Annual Survey; EIA Form-851, Domestic Uranium Production Report
Doug Bonnar
(202) 287-1911
douglas.bonnar@eia.doe.gov

Uranium Publications *Uranium Industry Annual, Domestic Uranium Production Report*
Doug Bonnar
(202) 287-1911
douglas.bonnar@eia.doe.gov

ECONOMIC AND FINANCIAL ANALYSIS
Main Fax: (202) 586-9753

Alternate Energy Financial Analysis
Robert Schmitt
(202) 586-8644
robert.schmitt@eia.doe.gov

Coal Industry Financial Analysis
Neal Davis
(202) 586-6581
neal.davis@eia.doe.gov

Corporate Finance
Robert Schmitt
(202) 586-8644
robert.schmitt@eia.doe.gov

Domestic Refining and Worldwide Gasoline Marketing Financial Analysis
Neal Davis
(202) 586-6581
neal.davis@eia.doe.gov

Energy Taxation
Robert Schmitt
(202) 586-8644
robert.schmitt@eia.doe.gov

Foreign Investment
Larry Spancake
(202) 586-8597
larry.spancake@eia.doe.gov

Foreign Refining and Worldwide Transportation Financial Analysis
Neal Davis
(202) 586-6581
neal.davis@eia.doe.gov

Worldwide Oil and Gas Exploration, Development, and Production Financial Analysis
Larry Spancake
(202) 586-8597
larry.spancake@eia.doe.gov

MULTIFUEL CONSUMPTION
Main Fax: (202) 586-0018

Alternative Fuels
Dwight French
(202) 586-1126
dwight.french@eia.doe.gov

Commercial Buildings
Joelle Michaels
(202) 586-8952
joelle.michaels@eia.doe.gov

Energy Efficiency
Behjat Hojjati
(202) 586-1068
behjat.hojjati@eia.doe.gov

Energy Maps
Barbara T. Fichman
(202) 586-5737
barbara.fichman@eia.doe.gov

Manufacturing Establishments
Robert Adler
(202) 586-1134
robert.adler@eia.doe.gov

Manufacturing Sector Characteristics/Analysis
Mark Schipper
(202) 586-1136
mark.schipper@eia.doe.gov

Regional Energy Profiles
Barbara T. Fichman
(202) 586-5737
barbara.fichman@eia.doe.gov

Residential Households
Eileen M. O'Brien
(202) 586-1122
eileen.obrien@eia.doe.gov

Residential Characteristics/Analysis
Michael Laurence
(202) 586-2453
michael.laurence@eia.doe.gov

Residential Transportation
Mark Schipper
(202) 586-1136
mark.schipper@eia.doe.gov

State-Level Consumption, Prices, Expenditures
Julia F. Hutchins
(202) 586-5138
julia.hutchins@eia.doe.gov

ENVIRONMENTAL CONTACTS
Main Fax: (202) 586-3045

Biodiesel/Ethanol
Anthony Radich
(202) 586-0504
anthony.radich@eia.doe.gov

Electric Power Emissions
Natalie Ko
(202) 287-1957
natalie.ko@eia.doe.gov

Electric Power Sector Pollutant Emissions - Modeling and Projections
Robert Smith
(202) 586-9413
robert.smith@eia.doe.gov

Carbon Dioxide - Modeling and Projections
Daniel Skelly
(202) 586-1722
daniel.skelly@eia.doe.gov

Greenhouse Gases
Paul McArdle, GHG Program Manager
(202) 586-4445
paul.mcardle@eia.doe.gov

Greenhouse Gases and International Carbon Dioxide Emissions - Modeling and Projections
Perry Lindstrom
(202) 586-0934
perry.lindstrom@eia.doe.gov

International Carbon Dioxide Emissions - Current Data
Karen Griffin
(202) 586-1357
karen.griffin@eia.doe.gov

MBE, Oxygenated Gasoline, and Reformulated Gasoline
Tancred Lidderdale
(202) 586-7321
tlidderd@eia.doe.gov

Tier 2 Gasoline and Ultra Low Sulfur Diesel
William Brown
(202) 586-8181
william.brown@eia.doe.gov

Voluntary Reporting of Greenhouse Gas Emissions
Stephen Calopedis, Project Leader
(202) 586-1156
stephen.calopedis@eia.doe.gov

FORECASTING & ANALYSIS
Main Fax: (202) 586-3045

Annual Energy Outlook
John J. Conti
(202) 586-2222
john.conti@eia.doe.gov
Paul Holtberg
(202) 586-1284
paul.holtberg@eia.doe.gov
Andy S. Kydes
(202) 586-2222
andy.kydes@eia.doe.gov

Coal Production/Minemouth Prices
Michael Mellish
(202) 586-2136
michael.mellish@eia.doe.gov

Coal Distribution/End-Use Prices
Diane Kearney
(202) 586-2415
diane.kearney@eia.doe.gov

Coal Exports
Michael Mellish
(202) 586-2136
michael.mellish@eia.doe.gov

Commercial Demand
Erin Boedecker
(202) 586-4791
erin.boedecker@eia.doe.gov

Crude Oil Supply
Ted McCallister
(202) 586-4820
ted.mccallister@eia.doe.gov

Electricity Generation and Cost
Laura Martin
(202) 586-1494
laura.martin@eia.doe.gov

Ethanol and Biodiesel
Anthony Radich
(202) 586-0504
anthony.radich@eia.doe.gov

Industrial Demand
Crawford Honeycutt
(202) 586-1420
crawford.honeycutt@eia.doe.gov

Liquefied Natural Gas Markets
Phyllis Martin
(202) 586-9592
phyllis.martin@eia.doe.gov

Macroeconomic Analysis
Ronald F. Earley
(202) 586-1398
ronald.earley@eia.doe.gov

National Energy Modeling System
Andy Kydes
(202) 586-2222
andy.kydes@eia.doe.gov
Daniel Skelly
(202) 586-1722
daniel.skelly@eia.doe.gov

Natural Gas Supply
Ted McCallister
(202) 586-4820
ted.mccallister@eia.doe.gov

Natural Gas Markets
Joseph Benneche
(202) 586-6132
joseph.benneche@eia.doe.gov

Nuclear Energy
Robert T. Eynon
(202) 586-2392
robert.eynon@eia.doe.gov
James Hewlett
(202) 586-9536
james.hewlett@eia.doe.gov

Petroleum Product Markets
William Brown
(202) 586-8181
william.brown@eia.doe.gov

Renewable Energy
Chris Namovicz
(202) 586-7120
christopher.namovicz@eia.doe.gov

Residential Demand
John Cymbalsky
(202) 586-4815
john.cymbalsky@eia.doe.gov

Technology Learning
Andy Kydes
(202) 586-2222
andy.kydes@eia.doe.gov
James Hewlett
(202) 586-9536
james.hewlett@eia.doe.gov

Transportation Demand
John Maples
(202) 586-1757
john.maples@eia.doe.gov

World Oil Prices
John Staub
(202) 586-6344
john.staub@eia.doe.gov

INTERNATIONAL FORECASTING
Main Fax: (202) 586-3045

International Energy Outlook
Glen Sweetnam
(202) 586-2188
glen.sweetnam@eia.doe.gov
Linda Doman
(202) 586-1041
linda.doman@eia.doe.gov

Carbon Dioxide
Perry Lindstrom
(202) 586-0934
perry.lindstrom@eia.doe.gov

Coal
Michael Mellish
(202) 586-2136
michael.mellish@eia.doe.gov

Commercial Energy Use
Erin Boedecker
(202) 586-4791
erin.boedecker@eia.doe.gov

Electricity
Linda Doman
(202) 586-1041
linda.doman@eia.doe.gov
John Staub
(202) 586-6344
john.staub@eia.doe.gov

Industrial Energy Use
Crawford Honeycutt
(202) 586-1420
crawford.honeycutt@eia.doe.gov

Macroeconomic Assumptions
Nasir Khilji
(202) 586-1294
nasir.khilji@eia.doe.gov

Natural Gas
Phyllis Martin
(202) 586-9592
phyllis.martin@eia.doe.gov
Justine Barden
(202) 586-3508
justine.barden@eia.doe.gov

Residential Energy Use
John Cymbalsky
(202) 586-4815
john.cymbalsky@eia.doe.gov

Sage Model
Randal Cook
(202) 586-1395
randal.cook@eia.doe.gov
Barry Kapilow-Cohen
(202) 586-5359
barry.kapilow-cohen@eia.doe.gov

Transportation Energy Use
John Maples
(202) 586-1757
john.maples@eia.doe.gov

World Oil Markets
John Staub
(202) 586-6344
john.staub@eia.doe.gov

RENEWABLE ENERGY - FORECASTING

Alternative-Fueled Vehicles
John Maples
(202) 586-1757
john.maples@eia.doe.gov

BioFuels Demand
Anthony Radich
(202) 586-0504
anthony.radich@eia.doe.gov

Biomass
Zia Haq
(202) 586-2869
zia.haq@eia.doe.gov

Conventional Hydroelectric
Chris Namovicz
(202) 586-7120
christopher.namovicz@eia.doe.gov

Geothermal
Chris Namovicz
(202) 586-7120
christopher.namovicz@eia.doe.gov

International
Linda Doman
(202) 586-1041
linda.doman@eia.doe.gov

Municipal Solid Waste/Landfill Gas
Zia Haq
(202) 586-2869
zia.haq@eia.doe.gov

Renewable Resources Assessment
Chris Namovicz
(202) 586-7120
christopher.namovicz@eia.doe.gov

Solar - Central Station
Chris Namovicz
(202) 586-7120
christopher.namovicz@eia.doe.gov

Solar - Distributed
Erin Boedecker
(202) 586-4791
erin.boedecker@eia.doe.gov

Wind
Chris Namovicz
(202) 586-7120
christopher.namovicz@eia.doe.gov

SHORT TERM ANALYSIS & FORECASTING
Main Fax: (202) 586-9753

Short Term Energy Outlook
Dave Costello
(202) 586-1468
dave.costello@eia.doe.gov

World Oil Price
Erik Kreil
(202) 586-6573
erik.kreil@eia.doe.gov

Energy Fuel Price
Neil Gamson
(202) 586-2418
neil.gamson@eia.doe.gov

Petroleum Markets
Michael Morris
(202) 586-1199
michael.morris@eia.doe.gov

Petroleum Supply

Tancred Lidderdale
(202) 586-7321
tancred.lidderdale@eia.doe.gov

Natural Gas Markets
Khadija El-Amin
(202) 586-8760
khadija.el-amin@eia.doe.gov

Coal Markets
Elias Johnson
(202) 586-7277
elias.johnson@eia.doe.gov

Electricity
Khadija El-Amin
(202) 586-8760
khadija.el-amin@eia.doe.gov

Renewables
Dave Costello
(202) 586-1468
dave.costello@eia.doe.gov

Macroeconomic Projections
Yvonne Taylor
(202) 586-1455
yvonne.taylor@eia.doe.gov

Domestic Crude Oil Production
John H. Wood
(214) 720-6160
john.wood.@eia.doe.gov

Coal Production, Imports & Exports
Frederick Freme
(202) 287-1740
frederick.freme.@eia.doe.gov

Hydrolectric Generation and Electricity Imports
Mark Gielecki
(202) 287-1729
mark.gielecki@eia.doe.gov

Nuclear Energy
Jim Finucane
(202) 287-1966
jim.finucane@eia.doe.gov

INTERNATIONAL ENERGY ANALYSIS
Main Fax: (202) 586-9753

Country Analysis Briefs
Charles Esser
(202) 586-6120
charles.esser@eia.doe.gov

Midterm Energy Projections
Linda Doman
(202) 586-1041
Fax: (202) 586-3045
linda.doman@eia.doe.gov

Petroleum Market Short-Term Projections
Erik Kreil
(202) 586-6573
erik.kreil@eia.doe.gov

Petroleum Supplies
Charles Esser
(202) 586-6120
charles.esser@eia.doe.gov

Former Soviet Union
Michael Cohen
(202) 586-7057
michael.cohen@eia.doe.gov

World Oil Market Disruption Analysis
Erik Kreil
(202) 586-6573
erik.kreil@eia.doe.gov

Contingency Analysis/Regional Issues
Charles Esser
(202) 586-6120
charles.esser@eia.doe.gov

INTERNATIONAL ENERGY STATISTICS
Main Fax: (202) 586-9753

Carbon Dioxide Emissions
Karen Griffin
(202) 586-1357
karen.griffin@eia.doe.gov

Coal
Joel Lou
(202) 586-1457
joel.lou@eia.doe.gov

Crude Oil and Natural Gas Plant Liquids Production; Crude Oil Reserves
Patricia Smith
(202) 586-6925
patricia.smith@eia.doe.gov

Electricity
Patricia Smith
(202) 586-6925
patricia.smith@eia.doe.gov

Natural Gas
Karen Griffin
(202) 586-1357
karen.griffin@eia.doe.gov

Oil Consumption, Imports, Exports, Refinery Capacity and Production
Joel Lou
(202) 586-1457
joel.lou@eia.doe.gov

Population and Gross Domestic Product
Joel Lou
(202) 586-1457
joel.lou@eia.doe.gov

Total Energy
Mike Grillot
(202) 586-6577
michael.grillot@eia.doe.gov

STATISTICAL METHODS CONTACTS
Main Fax: (202) 287-1705

Data Quality
Renee Miller
(202) 287-1718
renee.miller@eia.doe.gov

Economic Analysis
Doug Hale
(202) 287-1801
douglas.hale@eia.doe.gov

EIA Forms Clearance
Jay Casselberry
(202) 586-8616
jay.casselberry@eia.doe.gov

EIA Privacy and Confidentiality Policy
Jay Casselberry
(202) 586-8616
jay.casselberry@eia.doe.gov

EIA Standards Program
Jay Casselberry
(202) 586-8616
jay.casselberry@eia.doe.gov

Information Quality Guidelines
Jay Casselberry
(202) 586-8616
jay.casselberry@eia.doe.gov

Statistical Issues
Nancy Kirkendall
(202) 287-1706
nancy.kirkendall@eia.doe.gov

FOREIGN COUNTRIES STATISTICS OR INTERNATIONAL STATISTICS ON SPECIFIC COUNTRIES

The Census Bureau's International Programs Center (IPC) maintains the International Data Base (IDB). The IDB is a computerized source of demographic and socioeconomic statistics for 227 countries and areas of the world. The IDB provides quick access to specialized information, with emphasis on demographic measures, for individual countries or selected groups of countries of the world. For more information about the IDB contact Pat Dickerson or Peter Johnson at (301) 763-1351 or e-mail: idb@census.gov. To access via the web go to http://www.census.gov/ipc/www/idbnew.html.

HEALTH

The National Center for Health Statistics (NCHS) of the U.S. Department of Health and Human Services (HHS) collects and disseminates data on every aspect of health and health care in the United States. To identify specific agency programs which provide inquiry assistance, callers may contact (866) 441-NCHS. Internet site http://www.cdc.gov/nchs.

HOUSING

The U.S. Department of Housing and Urban Development (HUD) is the principal federal agency responsible for programs concerned with the Nation's housing needs, fair housing opportunities, and improvement and development of the Nation's communities. Inquiries on housing statistics can be made to (800) 245-2691. Internet site http://www.hud.gov.

INTERNATIONAL TRADE

The U.S. Department of Commerce (DOC), Manufacturing & Services (MAS) office will provide a statistical expert for a specific industry by contacting them toll free at (800) USA-TRADE. The internet site is: http://www.ita.doc.gov/td/td_home/tdhome.html.

The U.S. Department of Commerce (DOC), International Trade Administration (ITA) will provide a statistical expert from a specific country desk by contacting them toll free at (800) USA-TRADE. The internet site is: http://www.ita.doc.gov/tradestats.

LABOR

EMPLOYMENT AND UNEMPLOYMENT STATISTICS

The following experts are drawn from the Department of Labor Statistics. Internet site http://www.bls.gov/help/hlpcont.htm.

Absences from Work
Staff
(202) 691-6378

Contingent Workers
Staff
(202) 691-6378

Discouraged Workers
Staff
(202) 691-6378

Displaced Workers
Staff
(202) 691-6378

Educational Attainment
Staff
(202) 691-6378

Employment and Earnings Periodical
John Stinson
(202) 691-6373

Employment and Unemployment Trends
Staff
(202) 691-6378

Flexitime and Shift Work
Staff
(202) 691-6378

Home-Based Work
Staff
(202) 691-6378

Job Tenure
Staff
(202) 691-6378

Labor Force Concepts
Staff
(202) 691-6378

Longitudinal Data/Gross Flows
Staff
(202) 691-6345

Marital and Family Characteristics
Staff
(202) 691-6378

Microdata Tapes and CD-ROM's
Rowena Johnson
(202) 691-6345

Minimum Wage Data
Steven Haugen
(202) 691-6378

Minority Workers
Staff
(202) 691-6378

Multiple Jobholders
Staff
(202) 691-6373

Occupational Data
Staff
(202) 691-6378

Older Workers
Staff
(202) 691-6378

Part-Time Workers
Staff
(202) 691-6378

Seasonal Adjustment Methodology
Richard Tiller
(202) 691-6370
Thomas Evans
(202) 691-6354

Union membership
Staff
(202) 691-6378

Veterans
Staff
(202) 691-6378

Weekly Earnings
Staff
(202) 691-6378

Women in the Labor Force
Staff
(202) 691-6378

Work Experience
Staff
(202) 691-6378

Working Poor
Staff
(202) 691-6378

Youth, Students, and Dropouts
Staff
(202) 691-6378

EMPLOYMENT PROJECTIONS

INDUSTRY EMPLOYMENT PROJECTIONS TELEPHONE CONTACTS TOPIC

Aggregate economy, GDP
Betty Su
(202) 691-5729

Demographics
Mitra Toosi
(202) 691-5721

Employment impact studies
Norman Saunders
(202) 691-5707

Employment requirements table
Carl Chentrens
(202) 691-5697

FINAL DEMAND

Personal consumption expenditures
Eric Figueroa
(202) 691-6869

Foreign trade
Mirko Novakovic
(202) 691-5008

Investment
Katy Laurence
(202) 691-5691

Government
Jeffrey Gruenert
(202) 691-5725

Industry classification issues (NAICS)
Jay Berman
(202) 691-5733

Industry output and employment
Jay Berman
(202) 691-5733

Industry projections coordination
James Franklin
(202) 691-5709

Input-output tables
Carl Chentrens
(202) 691-5697

Input-output theory and practice
Charles Bowman
(202) 691-5702

Labor force
Mitra Toosi
(202) 691-5721

National income and product accounts
Norman Saunders
(202) 691-5707
Betty Su
(202) 691-5729

Population
Mitra Toosi
(202) 691-5721

Productivity
James Franklin
(202) 691-5709

Value added
Charles Bowman
(202) 691-5702

OCCUPATIONAL OUTLOOK

College Graduate Job Outlook
Arlene Dohm
(202) 691-5727
Jill Lacey
(202) 691-5806

Education and training categories and statistics
Chet Levine
(202) 691-5715
Jon Sargent
(202) 691-5722

Occupational Outlook Quarterly
Kathleen Green
(202) 691-5717
Olivia Crosby
(202) 691-5716
Elka Jones
(202) 691-5719

Replacement and separation rates
Lynn Shniper
(202) 691-5732
Alan Lacey
(202) 691-5731

Occupational information, general
Chet Levine
(202) 691-5715
Jon Sargent
(202) 691-5722

OCCUPATIONAL PROJECTIONS

Computer
Doug Braddock
(202) 691-5695
Roger Moncarz
(202) 691-5694

Construction
Arlene Dohm
(202) 691-5727
William Lawhorn
(202) 691-5093

Education
Arlene Dohm
(202) 691-5727
Michael Wolf
(202) 691-5714

Engineering
Doug Braddock
(202) 691-5695
Nick Terrell
(202) 691-5711

Food and lodging
Theresa Cosca
(202) 691-5712
Jon Kelinson
(202) 691-5688

Health
Jill Lacey
(202) 691-5806
Terry Schau
(202) 691-5720

Legal
Tamara Dillon
(202) 691-5733
Terry Schau
(202) 691-5720

Mechanics and repairers
Arlene Dohm
(202) 691-5727
Doug Braddock
(202) 691-5695
Terry Schau
(202) 691-5720

Sales
Doug Braddock
(202) 691-5695
Tamara Dillon
(202) 691-5733

Scientific
Henry Kasper
(202) 691-5696
Doug Braddock
(202) 691-5695

FOREIGN LABOR STATISTICS

Productivity & Unit Labor Costs: Analysis & Methodology
Wolodar Lysko
(202) 691-5026

Gross Domestic Product Per Capita & Per Employed Person
Wolodar Lysko
(202) 691-5026

Hourly Compensation Costs: Analysis & Methodology Data
Chris Sparks
(202) 691-5034

Hourly Compensation Costs: Data
Vladimir Kats
(202) 691-5024

Labor Force & Unemployment Analysis and Methodology
Susan Fleck
(202) 691-5014

Labor Force & Unemployment Data
Joyanna Moy
(202) 691-5030

Consumer Prices
Christine Valenti
(202) 691-5020

MULTIFACTOR PRODUCTIVITY

Multifactor Productivity for Major Sectors (Annual Measures), Analysis and methodology
Larry Rosenblum
(202) 691-5605
Rosenblum.Larry@bls.gov

Multifactor Productivity for Major Sectors (Annual Measures), Data
Steve Rosenthal
(202) 691-5609
Rosenthal.Steve@bls.gov

Multifactor Productivity for Manufacturing and 2-digit SIC Industries (KLEMS Annual Measures)
Steve Rosenthal
(202) 691-5608
Rosenthal.Steve@bls.gov

Multifactor Productivity for 3 and 4-digit Industries, Analysis and Methodology

Lisa Usher
(202) 691-5641
Usher.Lisa@bls.gov

Multifactor Productivity for 3 and 4-digit Industries, Data
Staff
(202) 691-5618
dipsweb@bls.gov

Multifactor Productivity for Gas and Electric Utilities, SIC 4900
John Glaser
(202) 691-5607
Glaser.John@bls.gov

Multifactor Productivity for Foreign Countries
Wolodar Lysko
(202) 691-5026
Lysko.Wolodar@bls.gov

Capital Measurement for Major Sector and 2-digit SIC Industries, Analysis and Methodology
Mike Harper
(202) 691-5606
Harper.Mike@bls.gov

Capital Measurement for Major Sector and 2-digit SIC Industries, Data
Steve Rosenthal
(202) 691-5609
Rosenthal.Steve@bls.gov

Labor Composition, Analysis and Methodology
Larry Rosenblum
(202) 691-5605
Rosenblum.Larry@bls.gov

Labor Composition, Data
Steve Rosenthal
(202) 691-5609
Rosenblum.Larry@bls.gov

Hours at Work Survey
Aklilu Zegeye
(202) 691-5611
Zegeye.Aklilu@bls.gov

Research and Development
Leo Sveikauskas
(202) 691-5677
Sveikauskas.Leo@bls.gov

PRODUCTIVITY AND COSTS

Manufacturing Industries
John Duke
(202) 691-5624
duke.john@bls.gov
Lisa Usher
(202) 691-5641
Usher.Lisa@bls.gov

Service-Sector Industries and Mining Industries
Brian Friedman
(202) 691-5638

E-Mail Requests
Staff
dipsweb@bls.gov

News Release: Div. of Major Sector Productivity
Staff
(202) 691-5606

Division Chief
Larry Rosenblum
(202) 691-5605
Rosenblum.Larry@bls.gov

Labor Prod. and Related Data: Analysis and Methodology
Phyllis Otto
(202) 691-5604
Otto.Phyllis@bls.gov

Labor Prod. and Related Data: Data
John Glaser
(202) 691-5607
Glaser.John@bls.gov

Hours at Work Survey
Aklilu Zegeye
(202) 691-5611
Zegeye.Aklilu@bls.gov

PRODUCER PRICE INDEXES

For industry specific contacts, see internet site: http://www.bls.gov/ppi/ppicon.htm

MEDICARE AND MEDICAID

Data on Medicare and Medicaid, as well as hospitals, nursing homes, doctors, and recipients, are amassed and made available from the Department of Health and Human Services (HHS), Centers for Medicare & Medicaid Services (CMS). Inquiries can be made to (877) 267-2323.

MINES AND MINERALS

The following experts are drawn from U.S. Geological Survey (USGS). Internet site: http://minerals.usgs.gov

COMMODITY SPECIALISTS

Abrasives, Manufactured
Donald W. Olson
(703) 648-7721
Fax: (703) 648-7975
dolson@usgs.gov

Alumina
Patricia Plunkert
(703) 648-4979
Fax: (703) 648-7757
pplunker@usgs.gov

Aluminum (Al)
Patricia Plunkert
(703) 648-4979
Fax: (703) 648-7757
pplunker@usgs.gov

Aluminum Oxide, Fused
Donald W. Olson
(703) 648-7721
Fax: (703) 648-7975
dolson@usgs.gov

Antimony (Sb)
James F. Carlin, Jr.
(703) 648-4985
Fax: (703) 648-7757
jcarlin@usgs.gov

Arsenic (As)
William Brooks
(703) 648-7791
Fax: (703) 648-7757
wbrooks@usgs.gov

Asbestos
Robert Virta
(703) 648-7726
Fax: (703) 648-7975
rvirta@usgs.gov

Asphalt, Natural
Hendrik van Oss
(703) 648-7712
Fax: (703) 648-7757
hvanoss@usgs.gov

Barite
M. Michael Miller (acting)
(703) 648-7716
Fax: (703) 648-7757
mmiller1@usgs.gov

Bauxite
Patricia Plunkert
(703) 648-4979
Fax: (703) 648-7757
pplunker@usgs.gov

Beryllium (Be)
Kim B. Shedd (acting)
(703) 648-4974
Fax: (703) 648-7757
kshedd@usgs.gov

Bismuth (Bi)
Peter Gabby
(703) 648-4957
Fax: (703) 648-7757
pgabby@usgs.gov

Boron (B)
Phyllis A. Lyday
(703) 648-7713
Fax: (703) 648-7757
plyday@usgs.gov

Bromine (Br)
Phyllis A. Lyday
(703) 648-7713
Fax: (703) 648-7757
plyday@usgs.gov

Calcium
M. Michael Miller
(703) 648-7716
Fax: (703) 648-7757
mmiller1@usgs.gov

Calcium Carbonate
Valentin V. Tepordei
(703) 648-7728
Fax: (703) 648-7975
vteporde@usgs.gov

Cadmium (Cd)
Edward Klimasauskas
(703) 648-4975
Fax: (703) 648-7757
eklimasauskas@usgs.gov

Cement
Hendrik van Oss
(703) 648-7712
Fax: (703) 648-7757
hvanoss@usgs.gov

Cesium (Cs)
William Brooks
(703) 648-7791
Fax: (703) 648-7757
wbrooks@usgs.gov

Chromium (Cr)
John F. Papp
(703) 648-4963
Fax: (703) 648-7757
jpapp@usgs.gov

Clays
Robert Virta
(703) 648-7726
Fax: (703) 648-7975
rvirta@usgs.gov

Coal Combustion Products
Hendrik van Oss
(703) 648-7712
Fax: (703) 648-7757
hvanoss@usgs.gov

Cobalt (Co)
Kim B. Shedd
(703) 648-4974
Fax: (703) 648-7757
kshedd@usgs.gov

Columbium (Nb)
Michael J. Magyar (acting)
(703) 648-4964
Fax: (703) 648-7757
mmagyar@usgs.gov

Copper (Cu)
Daniel L. Edelstein
(703) 648-4978
Fax: (703) 648-7757
dedelste@usgs.gov

Corundum
Donald W. Olson
(703) 648-7721
Fax: (703) 648-7975
dolson@usgs.gov

Diamond
Donald W. Olson
(703) 648-7721
Fax: (703) 648-7975
dolson@usgs.gov

Diatomite
Alan Founie
(703) 648-7720
Fax: (703) 648-7975
alfounie@usgs.gov

Explosives
Deborah A. Kramer

(703) 648-7719
Fax: (703) 648-7975
dkramer@usgs.gov

Feldspar
Michael J. Potter
(703) 648-7723
Fax: (703) 648-7975
mpotter@usgs.gov

Ferroalloys
John D. Jorgenson
(703) 648-4912
Fax: (703) 648-7757
jjorgenson@usgs.gov

Fluorspar
M. Michael Miller
(703) 648-7716
Fax: (703) 648-7757
mmiller1@usgs.gov

Gallium (Ga)
Deborah A. Kramer
(703) 648-7719
Fax: (703) 648-7975
dkramer@usgs.gov

Garnet
Donald W. Olson
(703) 648-7721
Fax: (703) 648-7975
dolson@usgs.gov

Gemstones
Donald W. Olson
(703) 648-7721
Fax: (703) 648-7975
dolson@usgs.gov

Germanium (Ge)
Edward P. Klimasauskas
(703) 648-4975
Fax: (703) 648-7757
eklimasauskas@usgs.gov

Gold (Au)
Micheal George
(703) 648-4962
Fax: (703) 648-7757
mgeorge@usgs.gov

Graphite
Donald W. Olson
(703) 648-7721
Fax: (703) 648-7975
dolson@usgs.gov

Greensand
James P. Searls
(703) 648-7724
Fax: (703) 648-7975
jsearls@usgs.gov

Gypsum
Alan Founie
(703) 648-7720
Fax: (703) 648-7975
alfounie@usgs.gov

Hafnium (Hf)
James B. Hedrick
(703) 648-7725
Fax: (703) 648-7757
jhedrick@usgs.gov

Indium (In)
Edward P. Klimasauskas
(703) 648-4975
Fax: (703) 648-7757
eklimasauskas@usgs.gov

Iodine (I)
Phyllis A. Lyday
(703) 648-7713
Fax: (703) 648-7757
plyday@usgs.gov

Iron
Michael Fenton
(703) 648-4972
Fax: (703) 648-7757
mfenton@usgs.gov

Iron Ore
John D. Jorgenson
(703) 648-4912
Fax: (703) 648-7757
jjorgenson@usgs.gov

Iron Oxide Pigments
Michael J. Potter
(703) 648-7723
Fax: (703) 648-7975
mpotter@usgs.gov

Iron and Steel Scrap
Michael Fenton
(703) 648-4972
Fax: (703) 648-7757
mfenton@usgs.gov

Iron and Steel Slag
Hendrik van Oss
(703) 648-7712
Fax: (703) 648-7757
hvanoss@usgs.gov

Kyanite
Michael J. Potter
(703) 648-7723
Fax: (703) 648-7975
mpotter@usgs.gov

Lead (Pb)
Peter Gabby
(703) 648-4957
Fax: (703) 648-7757
pgabby@usgs.gov

Lime
M. Michael Miller
(703) 648-7716
Fax: (703) 648-7757
mmiller1@usgs.gov

Lithium (Li)
Joyce A. Ober
(703) 648-7717
Fax: (703) 648-7757
jober@usgs.gov

Magnesium (Mg)
Deborah A. Kramer
(703) 648-7719
Fax: (703) 648-7975
dkramer@usgs.gov

Manganese (Mn)
Lisa A. Corathers
(703) 648-4973
Fax: (703) 648-7757
lcorathers@usgs.gov

Mercury (Hg)
William Brooks
(703) 648-7791
Fax: (703) 648-7757
wbrooks@usgs.gov

Mica
James B. Hedrick
(703) 648-7725
Fax: (703) 648-7757
jhedrick@usgs.gov

Molybdenum (Mo)
Michael J. Magyar
(703) 648-4964
Fax: (703) 648-7757
mmagyar@usgs.gov

Mullite
Michael J. Potter
(703) 648-7723
Fax: (703) 648-7975
mpotter@usgs.gov

Nepheline Syenite
Michael J. Potter
(703) 648-7723
Fax: (703) 648-7975
mpotter@usgs.gov

Nickel (Ni)
Peter H. Kuck
(703) 648-4965
Fax: (703) 648-7757
pkuck@usgs.gov

Niobium (Nb)
Larry D. Cunningham
(703) 648-4977
Fax: (703) 648-7757
lcunning@usgs.gov

Nitrogen (N)
Deborah A. Kramer
(703) 648-7719
Fax: (703) 648-7975
dkramer@usgs.gov

Peat
Stephen Jasinski
(703) 648-7711
Fax: (703) 648-7975
sjasinsk@usgs.gov

Perlite
Wallace P. Bolen
(703) 648-7727
Fax: (703) 648-7975
wbolen@usgs.gov

Phosphate Rock
Stephen Jasinski
(703) 648-7711
Fax: (703) 648-7975
sjasinsk@usgs.gov

Platinum-Group Metals
Micheal George (acting)
(703) 648-4962
Fax: (703) 648-7757
mgeorge@usgs.gov

Potash
Dennis S. Kostick (acting)
(703) 648-7715
Fax: (703) 648-7757
dkostick@usgs.gov

Pumice
Alan Founie
(703) 648-7720
Fax: (703) 648-7975
alfounie@usgs.gov

Pyrophyllite
Robert Virta
(703) 648-7726
Fax: (703) 648-7975
rvirta@usgs.gov

Quartz Crystal
Wallace P. Bolen
(703) 648-7727
Fax: (703) 648-7975
wbolen@usgs.gov

Rare Earths
James B. Hedrick
(703) 648-7725
Fax: (703) 648-7757
jhedrick@usgs.gov

Rhenium (Re)
Michael J. Magyar
(703) 648-4964
Fax: (703) 648-7757
mmagyar@usgs.gov

Rubidium (Rb)
William Brooks
(703) 648-7791
Fax: (703) 648-7757
wbrooks@usgs.gov

Salt
Dennis S. Kostick
(703) 648-7715
Fax: (703) 648-7757
dkostick@usgs.gov

Sand and Gravel, Construction
Wallace P. Bolen
(703) 648-7727
Fax: (703) 648-7975
wbolen@usgs.gov

Sand and Gravel, Industrial
Wallace P. Bolen
(703) 648-7727
Fax: (703) 648-7975
wbolen@usgs.gov

Scandium (Sc)
James B. Hedrick
(703) 648-7725
Fax: (703) 648-7757
jhedrick@usgs.gov

Selenium (Se)
Micheal George
(703) 648-4962
Fax: (703) 648-7757
mgeorge@usgs.gov

Silicon (Si)
Lisa A. Corathers
(703) 648-4973
Fax: (703) 648-7757
lcorathers@usgs.gov

Silicon carbide
Donald W. Olson
(703) 648-7721
Fax: (703) 648-7975
dolson@usgs.gov

Silver (Ag)
Micheal George (acting)
(703) 648-4962
Fax: (703) 648-7757
mgeorge@usgs.gov

Soda Ash
Dennis S. Kostick
(703) 648-7715
Fax: (703) 648-7757
dkostick@usgs.gov

Sodium Carbonate
Dennis S. Kostick
(703) 648-7715
Fax: (703) 648-7757
dkostick@usgs.gov

Sodium Sulfate
Dennis S. Kostick
(703) 648-7715
Fax: (703) 648-7757
dkostick@usgs.gov

Staurolite
Donald W. Olson
(703) 648-7721
Fax: (703) 648-7975
dolson@usgs.gov

Steel
Michael Fenton
(703) 648-4972
Fax: (703) 648-7757
mfenton@usgs.gov

Stone, Crushed
Valentin V. Tepordei
(703) 648-7728
Fax: (703) 648-7975
vteporde@usgs.gov

Stone, Dimension
Thomas Dolley
(703) 648-7710
Fax: (703) 648-7975
tdolley@usgs.gov

Strontium (Sr)
Joyce A. Ober
(703) 648-7717
Fax: (703) 648-7757
jober@usgs.gov

Sulfur (S)
Joyce A. Ober
(703) 648-7717
Fax: (703) 648-7757
jober@usgs.gov

Talc
Robert Virta
(703) 648-7726
Fax: (703) 648-7975
rvirta@usgs.gov

Tantalum (Ta)
Michael J. Magyar (acting)
(703) 648-4964
Fax: (703) 648-7757
mmagyar@usgs.gov

Tellurium (Te)
Micheal George
(703) 648-4962
Fax: (703) 648-7757
mgeorge@usgs.gov

Thallium (Tl)
Peter Gabby
(703) 648-4957
Fax: (703) 648-7757
pgabby@usgs.gov

Thorium (Th)
James B. Hedrick
(703) 648-7725
Fax: (703) 648-7757
jhedrick@usgs.gov

Tin (Sn)
James F. Carlin, Jr.
(703) 648-4985
Fax: (703) 648-7757
jcarlin@usgs.gov

Titanium (Ti)
Joseph Gambogi
(703) 648-7718
Fax: (703) 648-7975
jgambogi@usgs.gov

Tripoli
Wallace P. Bolen
(703) 648-7727
Fax: (703) 648-7975
wbolen@usgs.gov

Tungsten (W)
Kim B. Shedd
(703) 648-4974
Fax: (703) 648-7757
kshedd@usgs.gov

Vanadium (V)
Michael J. Magyar
(703) 648-4964
Fax: (703) 648-7757
mmagyar@usgs.gov

Vermiculite
Michael J. Potter
(703) 648-7723
Fax: (703) 648-7975
mpotter@usgs.gov

Wollastonite
Robert Virta
(703) 648-7726
Fax: (703) 648-7975
rvirta@usgs.gov

Yttrium (Y)
James B. Hedrick
(703) 648-7725
Fax: (703) 648-7757
jhedrick@usgs.gov

Zeolites
Robert Virta
(703) 648-7726
Fax: (703) 648-7975
rvirta@usgs.gov

Zinc (Zn)
Edward Klimasauskas
(703) 648-4975
Fax: (703) 648-7757
eklimasauskas@usgs.gov

Zirconium (Zr)
James B. Hedrick
(703) 648-7725
Fax: (703) 648-7757
jhedrick@usgs.gov

COUNTRY SPECIALISTS

Afghanistan
Chin Kuo
(703) 648-7748
Fax: (703) 648-7737
ckuo@usgs.gov

Albania
Walter Steblez
(703) 648-7743
Fax: (703) 648-7737
wsteblez@usgs.gov

Algeria
Philip Mobbs
(703) 648-7740
Fax: (703) 648-7737
pmobbs@usgs.gov

Angola
Omayra Bermudez-Lugo
(703) 648-4946
Fax: (703) 648-7737
obermude@usgs.gov

Antigua and Barbuda
Omayra Bermudez-Lugo
(703) 648-4946
Fax: (703) 648-7737
obermude@usgs.gov

Argentina
Ivette Torres
(703) 648-7746
Fax: (703) 648-7737
itorres@usgs.gov

Armenia
Richard Levine
(703) 648-7741
Fax: (703) 648-7737
rlevine@usgs.gov

Aruba
Omayra Bermudez-Lugo
(703) 648-4946
Fax: (703) 648-7737
obermude@usgs.gov

Australia
Pui-Kwan Tse
(703) 648-7750
Fax: (703) 648-7737
ptse@usgs.gov

Austria
Harold Newman
(703) 648-7742
Fax: (703) 648-7737
hnewman@usgs.gov

Azerbaijan
Richard Levine
(703) 648-7741
Fax: (703) 648-7737
rlevine@usgs.gov

Bahamas
Omayra Bermudez-Lugo
(703) 648-4946
Fax: (703) 648-7737
obermude@usgs.gov

Bahrain
Philip Mobbs
(703) 648-7740
Fax: (703) 648-7737
pmobbs@usgs.gov

Bangladesh
Chin Kuo
(703) 648-7748
Fax: (703) 648-7737
ckuo@usgs.gov

Barbados
Omayra Bermudez-Lugo
(703) 648-4946
Fax: (703) 648-7737
obermude@usgs.gov

Belarus
Richard Levine
(703) 648-7741
Fax: (703) 648-7737
rlevine@usgs.gov

Belgium
Harold Newman
(703) 648-7742
Fax: (703) 648-7737
hnewman@usgs.gov

Belize
Steven T. Anderson
(703) 648-7744
Fax: (703) 648-7737
sanderson@usgs.gov

Benin
Omayra Bermudez-Lugo
(703) 648-4946
Fax: (703) 648-7737
obermude@usgs.gov

Bermuda

Omayra Bermudez-Lugo
(703) 648-4946
Fax: (703) 648-7737
obermude@usgs.gov

Bhutan
Chin Kuo
(703) 648-7748
Fax: (703) 648-7737
ckuo@usgs.gov

Bolivia
Steven T. Anderson
(703) 648-7744
Fax: (703) 648-7737
sanderson@usgs.gov

Bosnia and Herzegovina
Walter Steblez
(703) 648-7743
Fax: (703) 648-7737
wsteblez@usgs.gov

Botswana
Harold Newman
(703) 648-7742
Fax: (703) 648-7737
hnewman@usgs.gov

Brazil
Alfredo Gurmendi
(703) 648-7745
Fax: (703) 648-7737
agurmend@usgs.gov

Brunei
Pui-Kwan Tse
(703) 648-7750
Fax: (703) 648-7737
ptse@usgs.gov

Bulgaria
Walter Steblez
(703) 648-7743
Fax: (703) 648-7737
wsteblez@usgs.gov

Burkina Faso
Omayra Bermudez-Lugo
(703) 648-4946
Fax: (703) 648-7737
obermude@usgs.gov

Burma (Myanmar)
Yolanda Fong-Sam
(703) 648-7756
Fax: (703) 648-7737
yfong-sam@usgs.gov

Burundi
Thomas Yager
(703) 648-7739
Fax: (703) 648-7737
tyager@usgs.gov

Cambodia
John C. Wu
(703) 648-7751
Fax: (703) 648-7737
jwu@usgs.gov

Cameroon
Harold Newman
(703) 648-7742
Fax: (703) 648-7737
hnewman@usgs.gov

Canada
Alfredo Gurmendi
(703) 648-7745
Fax: (703) 648-7737
agurmend@usgs.gov

Cape Verde
Harold Newman
(703) 648-7742
Fax: (703) 648-7737
hnewman@usgs.gov

Central African Republic
Omayra Bermudez-Lugo
(703) 648-4946
Fax: (703) 648-7737
obermude@usgs.gov

Chad
Philip Mobbs
(703) 648-7740
Fax: (703) 648-7737
pmobbs@usgs.gov

Chile
Steven T. Anderson
(703) 648-7744
Fax: (703) 648-7737
sanderson@usgs.gov

China
Pui-Kwan Tse
(703) 648-7750
Fax: (703) 648-7737
ptse@usgs.gov

Christmas Island
Pui-Kwan Tse
(703) 648-7750
Fax: (703) 648-7737
ptse@usgs.gov

Colombia
Ivette Torres
(703) 648-7746
Fax: (703) 648-7737
itorres@usgs.gov

Comoros
Thomas Yager
(703) 648-7739
Fax: (703) 648-7737
tyager@usgs.gov

Congo (Brazzaville)
George Coakley
(703) 648-7738
Fax: (703) 648-7737
gcoakley@usgs.gov

Congo (Kinshasa)
George Coakley
(703) 648-7738
Fax: (703) 648-7737
gcoakley@usgs.gov

Costa Rica
Steven T. Anderson
(703) 648-7744
Fax: (703) 648-7737
sanderson@usgs.gov

Cote d'Ivoire
Omayra Bermudez-Lugo
(703) 648-4946
Fax: (703) 648-7737
obermude@usgs.gov

Croatia
Walter Steblez
(703) 648-7743
Fax: (703) 648-7737
wsteblez@usgs.gov

Cuba
uyt

Cyprus
Philip Mobbs
(703) 648-7740
Fax: (703) 648-7737
pmobbs@usgs.gov

Czech Republic
Walter Steblez
(703) 648-7743
Fax: (703) 648-7737
wsteblez@usgs.gov

Denmark
Chin Kuo
(703) 648-7748
Fax: (703) 648-7737
ckuo@usgs.gov

Djibouti
Thomas Yager
(703) 648-7739
Fax: (703) 648-7737
tyager@usgs.gov

Dominica
Ivette Torres
(703) 648-7746
Fax: (703) 648-7737
itorres@usgs.gov

Dominican Republic
Ivette Torres
(703) 648-7746
Fax: (703) 648-7737
itorres@usgs.gov

East Timor
Pui-Kwan Tse
(703) 648-7750
Fax: (703) 648-7737
ptse@usgs.gov

Ecuador
Steven T. Anderson
(703) 648-7744
Fax: (703) 648-7737
sanderson@usgs.gov

Egypt
Harold Newman
(703) 648-7742
Fax: (703) 648-7737
hnewman@usgs.gov

El Salvador
Steven T. Anderson
(703) 648-7744
Fax: (703) 648-7737
sanderson@usgs.gov

Equatorial Guinea
Philip Mobbs
(703) 648-7740
Fax: (703) 648-7737
pmobbs@usgs.gov

Eritrea
Thomas Yager
(703) 648-7739
Fax: (703) 648-7737
tyager@usgs.gov

Estonia
Chin Kuo
(703) 648-7748
Fax: (703) 648-7737
ckuo@usgs.gov

Ethiopia
Thomas Yager
(703) 648-7739
Fax: (703) 648-7737
tyager@usgs.gov

Fiji
Travis Lyday
(703) 648-7749
Fax: (703) 648-7737
tlyday@usgs.gov

Finland
Chin Kuo
(703) 648-7748
Fax: (703) 648-7737
ckuo@usgs.gov

France
Harold Newman
(703) 648-7742
Fax: (703) 648-7737
hnewman@usgs.gov

French Guiana
Yolanda Fong-Sam
(703) 648-7756
Fax: (703) 648-7737
yfong-sam@usgs.gov

Gabon
Omayra Bermudez-Lugo
(703) 648-4946
Fax: (703) 648-7737
obermude@usgs.gov

Gambia
Omayra Bermudez-Lugo
(703) 648-4946
Fax: (703) 648-7737
obermude@usgs.gov

Georgia
Richard Levine
(703) 648-7741
Fax: (703) 648-7737
rlevine@usgs.gov

Germany

Steven T. Anderson
(703) 648-7744
Fax: (703) 648-7737
sanderson@usgs.gov

Ghana
George Coakley
(703) 648-7738
Fax: (703) 648-7737
gcoakley@usgs.gov

Greece
Harold Newman
(703) 648-7742
Fax: (703) 648-7737
hnewman@usgs.gov

Greenland
Chin Kuo
(703) 648-7748
Fax: (703) 648-7737
ckuo@usgs.gov

Grenada
Ivette Torres
(703) 648-7746
Fax: (703) 648-7737
itorres@usgs.gov

Guadeloupe
Ivette Torres
(703) 648-7746
Fax: (703) 648-7737
itorres@usgs.gov

Guatemala
Steven T. Anderson
(703) 648-7744
Fax: (703) 648-7737
sanderson@usgs.gov

Guinea
Omayra Bermudez-Lugo
(703) 648-4946
Fax: (703) 648-7737
obermude@usgs.gov

Guinea-Bissau
Omayra Bermudez-Lugo
(703) 648-4946
Fax: (703) 648-7737
obermude@usgs.gov

Guyana
Yolanda Fong-Sam
(703) 648-7756
Fax: (703) 648-7737
yfong-sam@usgs.gov

Haiti
Ivette Torres
(703) 648-7746
Fax: (703) 648-7737
itorres@usgs.gov

Honduras
Steven T. Anderson
(703) 648-7744
Fax: (703) 648-7737
sanderson@usgs.gov

Hong Kong
Pui-Kwan Tse
(703) 648-7750
Fax: (703) 648-7737
ptse@usgs.gov

Hungary
Walter Steblez
(703) 648-7743
Fax: (703) 648-7737
wsteblez@usgs.gov

Iceland
Chin Kuo
(703) 648-7748
Fax: (703) 648-7737
ckuo@usgs.gov

India
Chin Kuo
(703) 648-7748
Fax: (703) 648-7737
ckuo@usgs.gov

Indonesia
Pui-Kwan Tse
(703) 648-7750
Fax: (703) 648-7737
ptse@usgs.gov

Iran
Philip Mobbs
(703) 648-7740
Fax: (703) 648-7737
pmobbs@usgs.gov

Iraq
Philip Mobbs
(703) 648-7740
Fax: (703) 648-7737
pmobbs@usgs.gov

Ireland
Harold Newman
(703) 648-7742
Fax: (703) 648-7737
hnewman@usgs.gov

Israel
Thomas Yager
(703) 648-7739
Fax: (703) 648-7737
tyager@usgs.gov

Italy
Harold Newman
(703) 648-7742
Fax: (703) 648-7737
hnewman@usgs.gov

Jamaica
Ivette Torres
(703) 648-7746
Fax: (703) 648-7737
itorres@usgs.gov

Japan
John C. Wu
(703) 648-7751
Fax: (703) 648-7737
jwu@usgs.gov

Jordan
Thomas Yager
(703) 648-7739
Fax: (703) 648-7737
tyager@usgs.gov

Kazakstan
Richard Levine
(703) 648-7741
Fax: (703) 648-7737
rlevine@usgs.gov

Kenya
Thomas Yager
(703) 648-7739
Fax: (703) 648-7737
tyager@usgs.gov

Kiribati
Travis Lyday
(703) 648-7749
Fax: (703) 648-7737
tlyday@usgs.gov

Korea, North
John C. Wu
(703) 648-7751
Fax: (703) 648-7737
jwu@usgs.gov

Korea, Republic of
John C. Wu
(703) 648-7751
Fax: (703) 648-7737
jwu@usgs.gov

Kuwait
Philip Mobbs
(703) 648-7740
Fax: (703) 648-7737
pmobbs@usgs.gov

Kyrgyzstan
Richard Levine
(703) 648-7741
Fax: (703) 648-7737
rlevine@usgs.gov

Laos
John C. Wu
(703) 648-7751
Fax: (703) 648-7737
jwu@usgs.gov

Latvia
Chin Kuo
(703) 648-7748
Fax: (703) 648-7737
ckuo@usgs.gov

Lebanon
Thomas Yager
(703) 648-7739
Fax: (703) 648-7737
tyager@usgs.gov

Lesotho
George Coakley
(703) 648-7738
Fax: (703) 648-7737
gcoakley@usgs.gov

Liberia
Omayra Bermudez-Lugo
(703) 648-4946
Fax: (703) 648-7737
obermude@usgs.gov

Libya
Philip Mobbs
(703) 648-7740
Fax: (703) 648-7737
pmobbs@usgs.gov

Lithuania
Chin Kuo
(703) 648-7748
Fax: (703) 648-7737
ckuo@usgs.gov

Luxembourg
Harold Newman
(703) 648-7742
Fax: (703) 648-7737
hnewman@usgs.gov

Macedonia
Walter Steblez
(703) 648-7743
Fax: (703) 648-7737
wsteblez@usgs.gov

Madagascar
Thomas Yager
(703) 648-7739
Fax: (703) 648-7737
tyager@usgs.gov

Malawi
Thomas Yager
(703) 648-7739
Fax: (703) 648-7737
tyager@usgs.gov

Malaysia
Pui-Kwan Tse
(703) 648-7750
Fax: (703) 648-7737
ptse@usgs.gov

Mali
Omayra Bermudez-Lugo
(703) 648-4946
Fax: (703) 648-7737
obermude@usgs.gov

Malta
Harold Newman
(703) 648-7742
Fax: (703) 648-7737
hnewman@usgs.gov

Martinique
Ivette Torres
(703) 648-7746
Fax: (703) 648-7737
itorres@usgs.gov

Mauritania
Omayra Bermudez-Lugo
(703) 648-4946
Fax: (703) 648-7737
obermude@usgs.gov

Mauritius
Thomas Yager
(703) 648-7739
Fax: (703) 648-7737

tyager@usgs.gov

Mexico
Ivette Torres
(703) 648-7746
Fax: (703) 648-7737
itorres@usgs.gov

Moldova
Richard Levine
(703) 648-7741
Fax: (703) 648-7737
rlevine@usgs.gov

Mongolia
Pui-Kwan Tse
(703) 648-7750
Fax: (703) 648-7737
ptse@usgs.gov

Monserrat
Ivette Torres
(703) 648-7746
Fax: (703) 648-7737
itorres@usgs.gov

Morocco & Western Sahara
Omayra Bermudez-Lugo
(703) 648-4946
Fax: (703) 648-7737
obermude@usgs.gov

Mozambique
Thomas Yager
(703) 648-7739
Fax: (703) 648-7737
tyager@usgs.gov

Namibia
George Coakley
(703) 648-7738
Fax: (703) 648-7737
gcoakley@usgs.gov

Nauru
Travis Lyday
(703) 648-7749
Fax: (703) 648-7737
tlyday@usgs.gov

Nepal
Chin Kuo
(703) 648-7748
Fax: (703) 648-7737
ckuo@usgs.gov

Netherlands
Harold Newman
(703) 648-7742
Fax: (703) 648-7737
hnewman@usgs.gov

Netherlands Antilles
Harold Newman
(703) 648-7742
Fax: (703) 648-7737
hnewman@usgs.gov

New Caledonia
Travis Lyday
(703) 648-7749
Fax: (703) 648-7737
tlyday@usgs.gov

New Zealand
Travis Lyday
(703) 648-7749
Fax: (703) 648-7737
tlyday@usgs.gov

Nicaragua
Steven T. Anderson
(703) 648-7744
Fax: (703) 648-7737
sanderson@usgs.gov

Niger
Omayra Bermudez-Lugo
(703) 648-4946
Fax: (703) 648-7737
obermude@usgs.gov

Nigeria
Philip Mobbs
(703) 648-7740
Fax: (703) 648-7737
pmobbs@usgs.gov

Norway
Chin Kuo
(703) 648-7748
Fax: (703) 648-7737
ckuo@usgs.gov

Oman
Philip Mobbs
(703) 648-7740
Fax: (703) 648-7737
pmobbs@usgs.gov

Pakistan
Travis Lyday
(703) 648-7749
Fax: (703) 648-7737
tlyday@usgs.gov

Palau
Travis Lyday
(703) 648-7749
Fax: (703) 648-7737
tlyday@usgs.gov

Panama
Steven T. Anderson
(703) 648-7744
Fax: (703) 648-7737
sanderson@usgs.gov

Papua New Guinea
Travis Lyday
(703) 648-7749
Fax: (703) 648-7737
tlyday@usgs.gov

Paraguay
Yolanda Fong-Sam
(703) 648-7756
Fax: (703) 648-7737
yfong-sam@usgs.gov

Peru
Alfredo Gurmendi
(703) 648-7745
Fax: (703) 648-7737
agurmend@usgs.gov

Philippines
Travis Lyday
(703) 648-7749
Fax: (703) 648-7737
tlyday@usgs.gov

Poland
Walter Steblez
(703) 648-7743
Fax: (703) 648-7737
wsteblez@usgs.gov

Portugal
Harold Newman
(703) 648-7742
Fax: (703) 648-7737
hnewman@usgs.gov

Qatar
Philip Mobbs
(703) 648-7740
Fax: (703) 648-7737
pmobbs@usgs.gov

Reunion
Thomas Yager
(703) 648-7739
Fax: (703) 648-7737
tyager@usgs.gov

Romania
Walter Steblez
(703) 648-7743
Fax: (703) 648-7737
wsteblez@usgs.gov

Russia
Richard Levine
(703) 648-7741
Fax: (703) 648-7737
rlevine@usgs.gov

Rwanda
Thomas Yager
(703) 648-7739
Fax: (703) 648-7737
tyager@usgs.gov

Saint Kitts and Nevis
Ivette Torres
(703) 648-7746
Fax: (703) 648-7737
itorres@usgs.gov

Saint Lucia
Ivette Torres
(703) 648-7746
Fax: (703) 648-7737
itorres@usgs.gov

Saint Vincent and the Grenadines
Ivette Torres
(703) 648-7746
Fax: (703) 648-7737
itorres@usgs.gov

Sao Tome and Principe
Omayra Bermudez-Lugo
(703) 648-4946
Fax: (703) 648-7737
obermude@usgs.gov

Saudi Arabia
Philip Mobbs
(703) 648-7740
Fax: (703) 648-7737
pmobbs@usgs.gov

Senegal
Omayra Bermudez-Lugo
(703) 648-4946
Fax: (703) 648-7737
obermude@usgs.gov

Serbia and Montenegro
Walter Steblez
(703) 648-7743
Fax: (703) 648-7737
wsteblez@usgs.gov

Seychelles
Thomas Yager
(703) 648-7739
Fax: (703) 648-7737
tyager@usgs.gov

Sierra Leone
Omayra Bermudez-Lugo
(703) 648-4946
Fax: (703) 648-7737
obermude@usgs.gov

Singapore
Pui-Kwan Tse
(703) 648-7750
Fax: (703) 648-7737
ptse@usgs.gov

Slovakia
Walter Steblez
(703) 648-7743
Fax: (703) 648-7737
wsteblez@usgs.gov

Slovenia
Walter Steblez
(703) 648-7743
Fax: (703) 648-7737
wsteblez@usgs.gov

Solomon Islands
Travis Lyday
(703) 648-7749
Fax: (703) 648-7737
tlyday@usgs.gov

Somalia
Thomas Yager
(703) 648-7739
Fax: (703) 648-7737
tyager@usgs.gov

South Africa
George Coakley
(703) 648-7738
Fax: (703) 648-7737
gcoakley@usgs.gov

Spain
Harold Newman
(703) 648-7742
Fax: (703) 648-7737
hnewman@usgs.gov

Sri Lanka
Chin Kuo

(703) 648-7748
Fax: (703) 648-7737
ckuo@usgs.gov

Sudan
Thomas Yager
(703) 648-7739
Fax: (703) 648-7737
tyager@usgs.gov

Suriname
Yolanda Fong-Sam
(703) 648-7756
Fax: (703) 648-7737
yfong-sam@usgs.gov

Swaziland
George Coakley
(703) 648-7738
Fax: (703) 648-7737
gcoakley@usgs.gov

Sweden
Chin Kuo
(703) 648-7748
Fax: (703) 648-7737
ckuo@usgs.gov

Switzerland
Harold Newman
(703) 648-7742
Fax: (703) 648-7737
hnewman@usgs.gov

Syria
Thomas Yager
(703) 648-7739
Fax: (703) 648-7737
tyager@usgs.gov

Taiwan
Pui-Kwan Tse
(703) 648-7750
Fax: (703) 648-7737
ptse@usgs.gov

Tajikistan
Richard Levine
(703) 648-7741
Fax: (703) 648-7737
rlevine@usgs.gov

Tanzania
Thomas Yager
(703) 648-7739
Fax: (703) 648-7737
tyager@usgs.gov

Thailand
John C. Wu
(703) 648-7751
Fax: (703) 648-7737
jwu@usgs.gov

Togo
Omayra Bermudez-Lugo
(703) 648-4946
Fax: (703) 648-7737
obermude@usgs.gov

Tonga
Travis Lyday
(703) 648-7749
Fax: (703) 648-7737
tlyday@usgs.gov

Trinidad and Tobago
Ivette Torres
(703) 648-7746
Fax: (703) 648-7737
itorres@usgs.gov

Tunisia
Philip Mobbs
(703) 648-7740
Fax: (703) 648-7737
pmobbs@usgs.gov

Turkey
Philip Mobbs
(703) 648-7740
Fax: (703) 648-7737
pmobbs@usgs.gov

Turkmenistan
Richard Levine
(703) 648-7741
Fax: (703) 648-7737
rlevine@usgs.gov

Uganda
Thomas Yager
(703) 648-7739
Fax: (703) 648-7737
tyager@usgs.gov

Ukraine
Richard Levine
(703) 648-7741
Fax: (703) 648-7737
rlevine@usgs.gov

United Arab Emirates
Philip Mobbs
(703) 648-7740
Fax: (703) 648-7737
pmobbs@usgs.gov

United Kingdom
Harold Newman
(703) 648-7742
Fax: (703) 648-7737
hnewman@usgs.gov

Uruguay
Yolanda Fong-Sam
(703) 648-7756
Fax: (703) 648-7737
yfong-sam@usgs.gov

Uzbekistan
Richard Levine
(703) 648-7741
Fax: (703) 648-7737
rlevine@usgs.gov

Vanuatu
Travis Lyday
(703) 648-7749
Fax: (703) 648-7737
tlyday@usgs.gov

Venezuela
Ivette Torres
(703) 648-7746
Fax: (703) 648-7737
itorres@usgs.gov

Vietnam
John C. Wu
(703) 648-7751
Fax: (703) 648-7737
jwu@usgs.gov

Western Sahara
Philip Mobbs
(703) 648-7740
Fax: (703) 648-7737
pmobbs@usgs.gov

Yemen
Philip Mobbs
(703) 648-7740
Fax: (703) 648-7737
pmobbs@usgs.gov

Zaire (See Congo Kinshasa)

Zambia
George Coakley
(703) 648-7738
Fax: (703) 648-7737
gcoakley@usgs.gov

Zimbabwe
George Coakley
(703) 648-7738
Fax: (703) 648-7737
gcoakley@usgs.gov

RURAL DEVELOPMENT

The U.S. Department of Agriculture's Rural Development office administers rural business, cooperative, housing, utilities and community development programs. Its financial programs support such essential public facilities and services as water and sewer systems, housing, health clinics, emergency service facilities and electric and telephone service. The office promotes economic development by supporting loans to businesses through banks and community-managed lending pools. Valuable statistical data is collected in this process. For more information please visit http://www.rurdev.usda.gov/ or telephone (202) 720-4323.

SOCIAL SECURITY

The Social Security Administration (SSA) collects a great deal of data on the composition of the population in relation to demographic information such as age and income levels, and the years of population concentration. The statistics deal with historic, current and projected trends. The main office can direct callers to staff specialists who are knowledgeable on specific subjects; the general information number is (800) 772-1213. Internet site: http://www.ssa.gov.

TRANSPORTATION

The U.S. Department of Transportation (DOT) establishes the nation's overall transportation policy. There are ten separate administrations within the DOT whose main offices can direct callers to specialists who are knowledgeable on specific subjects. The internet site is: http://www.dot.gov.

Bureau of Transportation Statistics
(202) 366-DATA

Federal Aviation Administration
(202) 367-3484

Federal Highway Administration
(202) 366-0660

Federal Railroad Administration
(202) 493-6395

Federal Transit Administration
(202) 366-4043

Maritime Administration
(202) 366-5807

National Highway Traffic Safety Administration
(202) 366-9550

Research and Special Programs Administration
(202) 366-4433

Saint Lawrence Seaway Development Corporation
(202) 366-0091

U.S. Coast Guard
(202) 267-1587

ABORTION

Alan Guttmacher Institute, 125 Maiden Lane, 7th Floor, New York, NY 10038, (212) 248-1111, Fax: (212) 248-1951, www.agi-usa.org; *Estimates of U.S. Abortion Incidence, 2001-2003; Public Funding for Contraceptive, Sterilization and Abortion Services, FY 1980-2001; State Facts About Abortion; Three Decades of Legal Abortion: New Research and Analysis;* and unpublished data.

National Center for Health Statistics (NCHS), Centers for Disease Control and Prevention (CDC), U.S. Department of Health and Human Services (HHS), 3311 Toledo Road, Hyattsville, MD 20782, (866) 232-4636, www.cdc.gov/nchs; *Pregnancy, Birth, and Abortion Rates for Teenagers Aged 15-17 Years: United States, 1976-2003.*

ABRASIVES - STONE

U.S. Department of the Interior (DOI), U.S. Geological Survey (USGS), Office of Minerals Information, 12201 Sunrise Valley Drive, Reston, VA 20192, Mr. Kenneth A. Beckman, (703) 648-4916, Fax: (703) 648-4995, http://minerals.usgs.gov/minerals; *Mineral Commodity Summaries.*

ACCIDENTS

Association of American Railroads (AAR), 50 F Street, NW, Washington, DC 20001-1564, (202) 639-2100, www.aar.org; *Analysis of Class I Railroads* and *Railroad Facts.*

Health and Consumer Protection Directorate-General, European Commission, B-1049 Brussels, Belgium, http://ec.europa.eu/dgs/health_consumer/index_en.htm; *Injuries in the European Union: Statistics Summary 2002-2004.*

National Center for Health Statistics (NCHS), Centers for Disease Control and Prevention (CDC), U.S. Department of Health and Human Services (HHS), 3311 Toledo Road, Hyattsville, MD 20782, (866) 232-4636, www.cdc.gov/nchs; *Faststats A to Z* and unpublished data.

National Center for Statistics and Analysis (NCSA) of the National Highway Traffic Safety Administration, West Building, 1200 New Jersey Avenue, S.E., Washington, DC 20590, (202) 366-1503, Fax: (202) 366-7078, www.nhtsa.gov; *Alcohol Involvement in Fatal Motor Vehicle Traffic Crashes, 2003; Analysis of Crashes Involving 15-Passenger Vans; Analysis of Speeding-Related Fatal Motor Vehicle Traffic Crashes; An Assessment of the Crash-Reducing Effectiveness of Passenger Vehicle Daytime Running Lamps (DRLs); Cell Phone Use on the Roads in 2002; Child Passenger Fatalities and Injuries, Based on Restraint Use, Vehicle Type, Seat Position, and Number of Vehicles in the Crash; Fatal Motor Vehicle Crashes on Indian Reservations 1975-2002; Impaired Motorcycle Operators Involved in Fatal Crashes; Individual State Data from the State Alcohol Related Fatality Report; Large-Truck Crash Causation Study: An Initial Overview; Most Fatalities in Young (15- to 20-Year-Old) Driver Crashes Are Young Drivers and Their Young Passengers; Motor Vehicle Traffic Crashes as a Leading Cause of Death in the U.S., 2002 - A Demographic Perspective; Motorcycle Helmet Effectiveness Revisited; New England Low Fatality Rates versus Low Safety Belt Use; Pedestrian Roadway Fatalities; Race and Ethnicity in Fatal Motor Vehicle Traffic Crashes 1999-2004; Recent Trends in Fatal Motorcycle Crashes: An Update; Rollover Crash Mechanisms and Injury Outcomes for Restrained Occupants; The Rollover Propensity of Fifteen-Passenger Vans; Safety Belt Use in 2003: Demographic Characteristics; Safety Belt Use in 2003: Use Rates in the States and Territories; State Alcohol-Related Fatality Rates 2003; Total and Alcohol-Related Fatality Rates by State, 2003-2004; Traffic Safety Fact Sheets, 2005 Data - State Alcohol Estimates; Traffic Safety Fact Sheets, 2006 Data - Alcohol-Impaired Driving; Traffic Safety Fact Sheets, 2006 Data - Bicyclists and Other Cyclists; Traffic Safety Fact Sheets, 2006 Data - Children; Traffic Safety Fact Sheets, 2006 Data - Motorcycles; Traffic Safety Fact Sheets, 2006 Data - Occupant Protection; Traffic Safety Fact Sheets, 2006 Data - Pedestrians; Traffic Safety Fact Sheets, 2006 Data - Rural/Urban Comparison; Traffic Safety Fact Sheets, 2006 Data - School Transportation-Related Crashes; Traffic Safety Fact Sheets, 2006 Data - Young Drivers; Traffic Safety Facts Annual Report: 2005;* and *Trend and Pattern Analysis of Highway Crash Fatality by Month and Day.*

National Safety Council (NSC), 1121 Spring Lake Drive, Itasca, IL 60143-3201, (630) 285-1121, www.nsc.org; *Injury Facts.*

National Transportation Safety Board (NTSB), 490 L'Enfant Plaza, SW, Washington, DC 20594, (202) 314-6000, www.ntsb.gov; *Transportation Safety Databases* and *Vehicle- and Infrastructure-based Technology for the Prevention of Rear-end Collisions.*

U.S. Department of Transportation (DOT), Research and Innovative Technology Administration (RITA), Bureau of Transportation Statistics (BTS), 1200 New Jersey Avenue, SE, Washington, DC 20590, (800) 853-1351, www.bts.gov; *TranStats.*

ACCIDENTS - AGE OF DRIVER

National Center for Statistics and Analysis (NCSA) of the National Highway Traffic Safety Administration, West Building, 1200 New Jersey Avenue, S.E., Washington, DC 20590, (202) 366-1503, Fax: (202) 366-7078, www.nhtsa.gov; *Most Fatalities in Young (15- to 20-Year-Old) Driver Crashes Are Young Drivers and Their Young Passengers; Traffic Safety Fact Sheets, 2006 Data - Young Drivers;* and *Traffic Safety Facts Annual Report: 2005.*

National Safety Council (NSC), 1121 Spring Lake Drive, Itasca, IL 60143-3201, (630) 285-1121, www.nsc.org; *Injury Facts.*

ACCIDENTS - AIRCRAFT

Federal Aviation Administration (FAA) Office of Aviation Safety, Aviation Safety Information Analysis and Sharing (ASIAS) System, 800 Independence Avenue, SW, Room 1006, Washington, DC 20591, (866) 835-5322, www.asias.faa.gov; Near Midair Collision System (NMACS).

International Civil Aviation Organization (ICAO), External Relations and Public Information Office (EPO), 999 University Street, Montreal, Quebec H3C 5H7, Canada, (Dial from U.S. (514) 954-8219), (Fax from U.S. (514) 954-6077), www.icao.int; *Civil Aviation Statistics of the World.*

National Transportation Safety Board (NTSB), 490 L'Enfant Plaza, SW, Washington, DC 20594, (202) 314-6000, www.ntsb.gov; *The Annual Review of Aircraft Accident Data* and *Transportation Safety Databases.*

U.S. Department of Transportation (DOT), Research and Innovative Technology Administration (RITA), Bureau of Transportation Statistics (BTS), 1200 New Jersey Avenue, SE, Washington, DC 20590, (800) 853-1351, www.bts.gov; *TranStats.*

ACCIDENTS - ALCOHOL INVOLVEMENT

National Center for Statistics and Analysis (NCSA) of the National Highway Traffic Safety Administration, West Building, 1200 New Jersey Avenue, S.E., Washington, DC 20590, (202) 366-1503, Fax: (202) 366-7078, www.nhtsa.gov; *Alcohol Involvement in Fatal Motor Vehicle Traffic Crashes, 2003; Impaired Motorcycle Operators Involved in Fatal Crashes; Individual State Data from the State Alcohol Related Fatality Report; State Alcohol-Related Fatality Rates 2003; Total and Alcohol-Related Fatality Rates by State, 2003-2004; Traffic Safety Fact Sheets, 2005 Data - State Alcohol Estimates; Traffic Safety Fact Sheets, 2006 Data - Alcohol-Impaired Driving;* and *Traffic Safety Facts Annual Report: 2005.*

National Criminal Justice Reference Service (NCJRS), PO Box 6000, Rockville, MD 20849-6000, (800) 851-3420, Fax: (301) 519-5212, www.ncjrs.org; *Driving Under the Influence in the City and County of Honolulu.*

National Safety Council (NSC), 1121 Spring Lake Drive, Itasca, IL 60143-3201, (630) 285-1121, www.nsc.org; unpublished data.

U.S. Department of Justice (DOJ), National Institute of Justice (NIJ), 810 Seventh Street, NW, Washington, DC 20531, (202) 307-2942, Fax: (202) 616-0275, www.ojp.usdoj.gov/nij/; *Risky Mix: Drinking, Drug Use, and Homicide.*

ACCIDENTS - COSTS

National Center for Statistics and Analysis (NCSA) of the National Highway Traffic Safety Administration, West Building, 1200 New Jersey Avenue, S.E., Washington, DC 20590, (202) 366-1503, Fax: (202) 366-7078, www.nhtsa.gov; *Traffic Safety Facts Annual Report: 2005.*

National Safety Council (NSC), 1121 Spring Lake Drive, Itasca, IL 60143-3201, (630) 285-1121, www.nsc.org; *Injury Facts.*

ACCIDENTS - DEATHS AND DEATH RATES

Association of American Railroads (AAR), 50 F Street, NW, Washington, DC 20001-1564, (202) 639-2100, www.aar.org; *Analysis of Class I Railroads* and *Railroad Facts.*

Australian Institute of Health and Welfare (AIHW), GPO Box 570, Canberra ACT 2601, Australia, www.aihw.gov.au; *Deaths and Hospitalisations Due to Drowning, Australia 1999-00 to 2003-04.*

Bernan Essential Government Publications, 4611-F Assembly Drive, Lanham MD, 20706-4391, (301) 459-2255, Fax: (800) 865-3450, www.bernan.com; *Vital Statistics of the United States: Births, Life Expectancy, Deaths, and Selected Health Data.*

Kids and Cars, 2913 West 113th Street, Leawood, KS 66211, (913) 327-0013, www.kidsandcars.org; www.kidsandcars.org.

National Center for Health Statistics (NCHS), Centers for Disease Control and Prevention (CDC), U.S. Department of Health and Human Services (HHS), 3311 Toledo Road, Hyattsville, MD 20782, (866) 232-4636, www.cdc.gov/nchs; *National Vital Statistics Reports (NVSR); Vital Statistics of the United States (VSUS);* and unpublished data.

National Center for Statistics and Analysis (NCSA) of the National Highway Traffic Safety Administration, West Building, 1200 New Jersey Avenue, S.E., Washington, DC 20590, (202) 366-1503, Fax: (202) 366-7078, www.nhtsa.gov; *Alcohol Involvement in Fatal Motor Vehicle Traffic Crashes, 2003; Analysis of Crashes Involving 15-Passenger Vans; Analysis of Speeding-Related Fatal Motor Vehicle Traffic Crashes; An Assessment of the Crash-Reducing Effectiveness of Passenger Vehicle Daytime Running Lamps (DRLs); Cell Phone Use on the Roads in 2002; Child Passenger Fatalities and Injuries, Based on Restraint Use, Vehicle Type, Seat Position, and Number of Vehicles in the Crash; Fatal Motor Vehicle Crashes on Indian Reservations 1975-2002; Impaired Motorcycle Operators Involved in Fatal Crashes; Individual State Data from the State Alcohol Related Fatality Report; Most Fatalities in Young (15- to 20-Year-Old) Driver Crashes Are Young Drivers and Their Young Passengers; Motor Vehicle Traffic Crashes as a Leading Cause of Death in the U.S., 2002 - A Demographic Perspective; Motorcycle Helmet Effectiveness Revisited; New England Low Fatality Rates versus Low Safety Belt Use; Pedestrian Roadway Fatalities; Race and Ethnicity in Fatal Motor Vehicle Traffic Crashes 1999-2004; Recent Trends in Fatal Motorcycle Crashes: An Update; The Relationship between Occupant Compartment Deformation and Occupant Injury; Rollover Crash Mechanisms and Injury Outcomes for Restrained Occupants; Safety Belt Use in 2003: Demographic Characteristics; Safety Belt Use in 2003: Use Rates in the States and Territories; State Alcohol-Related Fatality Rates 2003; States With Primary Enforcement Laws Have Lower Fatality Rates; Total and Alcohol-Related Fatality Rates by State, 2003-2004; Traffic Safety Fact Sheets, 2005 Data - State Alcohol Estimates; Traffic Safety Fact Sheets, 2006 Data - Alcohol-Impaired Driving; Traffic Safety Fact Sheets, 2006 Data - Bicyclists and Other Cyclists; Traffic Safety Fact Sheets, 2006 Data - Children; Traffic Safety Fact Sheets, 2006 Data - Large Trucks; Traffic Safety Fact Sheets, 2006 Data - Motorcycles; Traffic Safety Fact Sheets, 2006 Data - Older Population; Traffic Safety Fact Sheets, 2006 Data - Pedestrians; Traffic Safety Fact Sheets, 2006 Data - Rural/Urban Comparison; Traffic Safety Fact Sheets, 2006 Data - School Transportation-Related Crashes; Traffic Safety Fact Sheets, 2006 Data - Young Drivers; Traffic Safety Facts Annual Report: 2005; Trend and Pattern Analysis of Highway Crash Fatality by Month and Day;* and *Vehicle Survivability and Travel Mileage Schedules.*

National Safety Council (NSC), 1121 Spring Lake Drive, Itasca, IL 60143-3201, (630) 285-1121, www.nsc.org; *Injury Facts.*

National Transportation Safety Board (NTSB), 490 L'Enfant Plaza, SW, Washington, DC 20594, (202) 314-6000, www.ntsb.gov; *Transportation Safety Databases.*

ACCIDENTS - DEATHS AND DEATH RATES - INFANTS

Bernan Essential Government Publications, 4611-F Assembly Drive, Lanham MD, 20706-4391, (301) 459-2255, Fax: (800) 865-3450, www.bernan.com; *Vital Statistics of the United States: Births, Life Expectancy, Deaths, and Selected Health Data.*

National Center for Health Statistics (NCHS), Centers for Disease Control and Prevention (CDC), U.S. Department of Health and Human Services (HHS), 3311 Toledo Road, Hyattsville, MD 20782, (866) 232-4636, www.cdc.gov/nchs; *National Vital Statistics Reports (NVSR); Vital Statistics of the United States (VSUS);* and unpublished data.

ACCIDENTS - FIRES

National Fire Protection Association (NFPA), One Batterymarch Park, Quincy, MA 02169-7471, (617) 770-3000, Fax: (617) 770-0700, www.nfpa.org; *Fire statistics.*

ACCIDENTS - INDUSTRIAL

National Agricultural Statistics Service (NASS), U.S. Department of Agriculture (USDA), 1400 Independence Avenue, SW, Washington, DC 20250, (800) 727-9540, Fax: (202) 690-2090, www.nass.usda.gov; *Adult Agricultural Related Injuries 2004.*

National Safety Council (NSC), 1121 Spring Lake Drive, Itasca, IL 60143-3201, (630) 285-1121, www.nsc.org; *Injury Facts.*

U.S. Bureau of Labor Statistics (BLS), Postal Square Building, 2 Massachusetts Avenue, NE, Washington, DC 20212-0001, (202) 691-5200, Fax: (202) 691-6325, www.bls.gov; *Injuries, Illnesses, and Fatalities (IIF).*

U.S. Department of Labor (DOL), Bureau of Labor Statistics (BLS), Postal Square Building, 2 Massachusetts Avenue, NE, Washington, DC 20212-0001, (202) 691-5200, Fax: (202) 691-6325, www.bls.gov; *Injuries, Illnesses, and Fatalities (IIF).*

ACCIDENTS - INJURIES

Australian Institute of Health and Welfare (AIHW), GPO Box 570, Canberra ACT 2601, Australia, www.aihw.gov.au; *Deaths and Hospitalisations Due to Drowning, Australia 1999-00 to 2003-04.*

Indian Health Service (IHS), U.S. Department of Health and Human Services, The Reyes Building, 801 Thompson Avenue, Suite 400, Rockville, MD 20852-1627, (301) 443-1180, www.ihs.gov; *Indian Health Focus - Injuries.*

Kids and Cars, 2913 West 113th Street, Leawood, KS 66211, (913) 327-0013, www.kidsandcars.org; www.kidsandcars.org.

National Agricultural Statistics Service (NASS), U.S. Department of Agriculture (USDA), 1400 Independence Avenue, SW, Washington, DC 20250, (800) 727-9540, Fax: (202) 690-2090, www.nass.usda.gov; *Adult Agricultural Related Injuries 2004.*

National Center for Health Statistics (NCHS), Centers for Disease Control and Prevention (CDC), U.S. Department of Health and Human Services (HHS), 3311 Toledo Road, Hyattsville, MD 20782, (866) 232-4636, www.cdc.gov/nchs; unpublished data.

National Center for Statistics and Analysis (NCSA) of the National Highway Traffic Safety Administration, West Building, 1200 New Jersey Avenue, S.E., Washington, DC 20590, (202) 366-1503, Fax: (202) 366-7078, www.nhtsa.gov; *Alcohol Involvement in Fatal Motor Vehicle Traffic Crashes, 2003; Analysis of Crashes Involving 15-Passenger Vans; Analysis of Speeding-Related Fatal Motor Vehicle Traffic Crashes; An Assessment of the Crash-Reducing Effectiveness of Passenger Vehicle Daytime Running Lamps (DRLs); Cell Phone Use on the Roads in 2002; Child Passenger Fatalities and Injuries, Based on Restraint Use, Vehicle Type, Seat Position, and Number of Vehicles in the Crash; Fatal Motor Vehicle Crashes on Indian Reservations 1975-2002; Motor Vehicle Traffic Crashes as a Leading Cause of Death in the U.S., 2002 - A Demographic Perspective; New England Low Fatality Rates versus Low Safety Belt Use; Pedestrian Roadway Fatalities; The Relationship between Occupant Compartment Deformation and Occupant Injury; Rollover Crash Mechanisms and Injury Outcomes for Restrained Occupants; Safety Belt Use in 2003: Demographic Characteristics; Safety Belt Use in 2003: Use Rates in the States and Territories; State Alcohol-Related Fatality Rates 2003; Traffic Safety Fact Sheets, 2006 Data - Alcohol-Impaired Driving; Traffic Safety Fact Sheets, 2006 Data - Bicyclists and Other Cyclists; Traffic Safety Fact Sheets, 2006 Data - Children; Traffic Safety Fact Sheets, 2006 Data - Large Trucks; Traffic Safety Fact Sheets, 2006 Data - Motorcycles; Traffic Safety Fact Sheets, 2006 Data - Older Population; Traffic Safety Fact Sheets, 2006 Data - Pedestrians; Traffic Safety Fact Sheets, 2006 Data - Young Drivers; Traffic Safety Facts Annual Report: 2005;* and *Trend and Pattern Analysis of Highway Crash Fatality by Month and Day.*

National Council on Compensation Insurance, Inc. (NCCI), 901 Peninsula Corporate Circle, Boca Raton, FL 33487, (800) NCCI-123, www.ncci.com; *Age as a Driver of Frequency and Severity* and *Traffic Accidents - A Growing Contributor to Workers Compensation Losses - Winter 2006.*

National Safety Council (NSC), 1121 Spring Lake Drive, Itasca, IL 60143-3201, (630) 285-1121, www.nsc.org; *Injury Facts.*

National Transportation Safety Board (NTSB), 490 L'Enfant Plaza, SW, Washington, DC 20594, (202) 314-6000, www.ntsb.gov; *Transportation Safety Databases.*

Robert Wood Johnson Foundation, PO Box 2316, College Road East and Route 1, Princeton, NJ 08543, (877) 843-7953, www.rwjf.org; *Medical Errors Involving Trainees: A Study of Closed Malpractice Claims From 5 Insurers.*

U.S. Bureau of Labor Statistics (BLS), Postal Square Building, 2 Massachusetts Avenue, NE, Washington, DC 20212-0001, (202) 691-5200, Fax: (202) 691-6325, www.bls.gov; *Fatal Occupational Injuries to Members of the Resident Military, 1992-2003.*

U.S. Department of Labor (DOL), Bureau of Labor Statistics (BLS), Postal Square Building, 2 Massachusetts Avenue, NE, Washington, DC 20212-0001, (202) 691-5200, Fax: (202) 691-6325, www.bls.gov; *Injuries, Illnesses, and Fatalities (IIF).*

ACCIDENTS - MOTOR VEHICLES

Bernan Essential Government Publications, 4611-F Assembly Drive, Lanham MD, 20706-4391, (301) 459-2255, Fax: (800) 865-3450, www.bernan.com; *Vital Statistics of the United States: Births, Life Expectancy, Deaths, and Selected Health Data.*

Kids and Cars, 2913 West 113th Street, Leawood, KS 66211, (913) 327-0013, www.kidsandcars.org; www.kidsandcars.org.

National Center for Health Statistics (NCHS), Centers for Disease Control and Prevention (CDC), U.S. Department of Health and Human Services (HHS), 3311 Toledo Road, Hyattsville, MD 20782, (866) 232-4636, www.cdc.gov/nchs; *National Vital Statistics Reports (NVSR); Vital Statistics of the United States (VSUS);* and unpublished data.

National Center for Statistics and Analysis (NCSA) of the National Highway Traffic Safety Administration, West Building, 1200 New Jersey Avenue, S.E., Washington, DC 20590, (202) 366-1503, Fax: (202) 366-7078, www.nhtsa.gov; *Alcohol Involvement in Fatal Motor Vehicle Traffic Crashes, 2003; Analysis of Crashes Involving 15-Passenger Vans; Analysis of Speeding-Related Fatal Motor Vehicle Traffic Crashes; An Assessment of the Crash-Reducing Effectiveness of Passenger Vehicle Daytime Running Lamps (DRLs); Cell Phone Use on the Roads in 2002; Fatal Motor Vehicle Crashes on Indian Reservations 1975-2002; Fatality Analysis Report-*

ing System (FARS); Impaired Motorcycle Operators Involved in Fatal Crashes; Individual State Data from the State Alcohol Related Fatality Report; Large-Truck Crash Causation Study: An Initial Overview; Most Fatalities in Young (15- to 20-Year-Old) Driver Crashes Are Young Drivers and Their Young Passengers; Motor Vehicle Traffic Crashes as a Leading Cause of Death in the U.S., 2002 - A Demographic Perspective; Motorcycle Helmet Effectiveness Revisited; New England Low Fatality Rates versus Low Safety Belt Use; Pedestrian Roadway Fatalities; Race and Ethnicity in Fatal Motor Vehicle Traffic Crashes 1999-2004; Recent Trends in Fatal Motorcycle Crashes: An Update; The Relationship between Occupant Compartment Deformation and Occupant Injury; Rollover Crash Mechanisms and Injury Outcomes for Restrained Occupants; The Rollover Propensity of Fifteen-Passenger Vans; Safety Belt Use in 2003: Demographic Characteristics; Safety Belt Use in 2003: Use Rates in the States and Territories; State Alcohol-Related Fatality Rates 2003; States With Primary Enforcement Laws Have Lower Fatality Rates; Total and Alcohol-Related Fatality Rates by State, 2003-2004; Total and Alcohol-Related Fatality Rates by State, 2003-2004; Traffic Safety Fact Sheets, 2005 Data - State Alcohol Estimates; Traffic Safety Fact Sheets, 2006 Data - Alcohol-Impaired Driving; Traffic Safety Fact Sheets, 2006 Data - Bicyclists and Other Cyclists; Traffic Safety Fact Sheets, 2006 Data - Children; Traffic Safety Fact Sheets, 2006 Data - Large Trucks; Traffic Safety Fact Sheets, 2006 Data - Motorcycles; Traffic Safety Fact Sheets, 2006 Data - Occupant Protection; Traffic Safety Fact Sheets, 2006 Data - Older Population; Traffic Safety Fact Sheets, 2006 Data - Pedestrians; Traffic Safety Fact Sheets, 2006 Data - Rural/Urban Comparison; Traffic Safety Fact Sheets, 2006 Data - School Transportation-Related Crashes; Traffic Safety Fact Sheets, 2006 Data - Speeding; Traffic Safety Fact Sheets, 2006 Data - Young Drivers; Traffic Safety Facts Annual Report: 2005; Trend and Pattern Analysis of Highway Crash Fatality by Month and Day; and *Vehicle Survivability and Travel Mileage Schedules.*

National Safety Council (NSC), 1121 Spring Lake Drive, Itasca, IL 60143-3201, (630) 285-1121, www.nsc.org; *Injury Facts.*

National Transportation Safety Board (NTSB), 490 L'Enfant Plaza, SW, Washington, DC 20594, (202) 314-6000, www.ntsb.gov; *Transportation Safety Databases* and *Vehicle- and Infrastructure-based Technology for the Prevention of Rear-end Collisions.*

U.S. Department of Transportation (DOT), Federal Highway Administration (FHA), 1200 New Jersey Avenue, SE, Washington, DC 20590, (202) 366-0660, www.fhwa.dot.gov; *Highway Statistics 2006.*

U.S. Department of Transportation (DOT), Research and Innovative Technology Administration (RITA), Bureau of Transportation Statistics (BTS), 1200 New Jersey Avenue, SE, Washington, DC 20590, (800) 853-1351, www.bts.gov; *TranStats.*

ACCIDENTS - MOTORCYCLE

National Center for Statistics and Analysis (NCSA) of the National Highway Traffic Safety Administration, West Building, 1200 New Jersey Avenue, S.E., Washington, DC 20590, (202) 366-1503, Fax: (202) 366-7078, www.nhtsa.gov; *Impaired Motorcycle Operators Involved in Fatal Crashes; Motorcycle Helmet Effectiveness Revisited; Motorcycle Helmet Use in 2006 - Overall Results; Recent Trends in Fatal Motorcycle Crashes: An Update;* and *Traffic Safety Fact Sheets, 2006 Data - Motorcycles.*

National Safety Council (NSC), 1121 Spring Lake Drive, Itasca, IL 60143-3201, (630) 285-1121, www.nsc.org; *Injury Facts.*

National Transportation Safety Board (NTSB), 490 L'Enfant Plaza, SW, Washington, DC 20594, (202) 314-6000, www.ntsb.gov; *Transportation Safety Databases.*

ACCIDENTS - POLICE OFFICERS ASSAULTED, KILLED

Federal Bureau of Investigation (FBI), J. Edgar Hoover Building, 935 Pennsylvania Avenue, NW, Washington, DC 20535-0001, (202) 324-3000, www.fbi.gov; *Law Enforcement Officers Killed and Assaulted (LEOKA) 2007 (Preliminary).*

ACCIDENTS - RAILROAD

Association of American Railroads (AAR), 50 F Street, NW, Washington, DC 20001-1564, (202) 639-2100, www.aar.org; *Analysis of Class I Railroads* and *Railroad Facts.*

National Transportation Safety Board (NTSB), 490 L'Enfant Plaza, SW, Washington, DC 20594, (202) 314-6000, www.ntsb.gov; *Transportation Safety Databases.*

U.S. Department of Transportation (DOT), Federal Railroad Administration (FRA), 1200 New Jersey Avenue, SE, Washington, DC 20590, (202) 366-4000, www.fra.dot.gov; FRA Office of Safety Analysis Web Site.

ACCIDENTS - TRANSPORTATION

National Transportation Safety Board (NTSB), 490 L'Enfant Plaza, SW, Washington, DC 20594, (202) 314-6000, www.ntsb.gov; *Transportation Safety Databases.*

RAND Corporation, 1776 Main Street, PO Box 2138, Santa Monica, CA 90407-2138, (310) 393-0411, www.rand.org; *Effect of Improved Helicopter Crashworthiness Design on Helicopter Accident Statistics.*

U.S. Department of Transportation (DOT), Research and Innovative Technology Administration (RITA), Bureau of Transportation Statistics (BTS), 1200 New Jersey Avenue, SE, Washington, DC 20590, (800) 853-1351, www.bts.gov; *TranStats.*

ACCIDENTS - WORK FATALITIES

U.S. Bureau of Labor Statistics (BLS), Postal Square Building, 2 Massachusetts Avenue, NE, Washington, DC 20212-0001, (202) 691-5200, Fax: (202) 691-6325, www.bls.gov; *Fatal Occupational Injuries to Members of the Resident Military, 1992-2003; Monthly Labor Review (MLR);* and unpublished data.

U.S. Department of Labor (DOL), Bureau of Labor Statistics (BLS), Postal Square Building, 2 Massachusetts Avenue, NE, Washington, DC 20212-0001, (202) 691-5200, Fax: (202) 691-6325, www.bls.gov; *Injuries, Illnesses, and Fatalities (IIF).*

ACCIDENTS - WORK TIME LOST

National Safety Council (NSC), 1121 Spring Lake Drive, Itasca, IL 60143-3201, (630) 285-1121, www.nsc.org; *Injury Facts.*

ACCOUNTANTS AND AUDITORS

U.S. Bureau of Labor Statistics (BLS), Postal Square Building, 2 Massachusetts Avenue, NE, Washington, DC 20212-0001, (202) 691-5200, Fax: (202) 691-6325, www.bls.gov; *Employment and Earnings (EE)* and unpublished data.

ACCOUNTING, TAX PREPARATION, BOOKKEEPING, AND PAYROLL SERVICES

U.S. Census Bureau, Company Statistics Division, 4700 Silver Hill Road, Washington DC 20233-0001, (301) 763-3030, www.census.gov/csd/; *County Business Patterns 2004.*

U.S. Census Bureau, Service Sector Statistics Division, 4700 Silver Hill Road, Washington DC 20233-0001, (301) 763-3030, www.census.gov/svsd/www/economic.html; *2004 Service Annual Survey: Professional, Scientific and Technical Services.*

ACCOUNTING, TAX PREPARATION, BOOKKEEPING, AND PAYROLL SERVICES - EARNINGS

U.S. Census Bureau, Company Statistics Division, 4700 Silver Hill Road, Washington DC 20233-0001, (301) 763-3030, www.census.gov/csd/; *County Business Patterns 2004.*

U.S. Census Bureau, Service Sector Statistics Division, 4700 Silver Hill Road, Washington DC 20233-0001, (301) 763-3030, www.census.gov/svsd/www/economic.html; *2004 Service Annual Survey: Professional, Scientific and Technical Services.*

ACCOUNTING, TAX PREPARATION, BOOKKEEPING, AND PAYROLL SERVICES - EMPLOYEES

U.S. Census Bureau, Company Statistics Division, 4700 Silver Hill Road, Washington DC 20233-0001, (301) 763-3030, www.census.gov/csd/; *County Business Patterns 2004.*

U.S. Census Bureau, Service Sector Statistics Division, 4700 Silver Hill Road, Washington DC 20233-0001, (301) 763-3030, www.census.gov/svsd/www/economic.html; *2004 Service Annual Survey: Professional, Scientific and Technical Services.*

ACCOUNTING, TAX PREPARATION, BOOKKEEPING, AND PAYROLL SERVICES - FINANCES

U.S. Department of the Treasury (DOT), Internal Revenue Service (IRS), Statistics of Income Division (SIS), PO Box 2608, Washington, DC, 20013-2608, (202) 874-0410, Fax: (202) 874-0964, www.irs.ustreas.gov; *Statistics of Income Bulletin* and various fact sheets.

ACCOUNTING, TAX PREPARATION, BOOKKEEPING, AND PAYROLL SERVICES - RECEIPTS

U.S. Census Bureau, Company Statistics Division, 4700 Silver Hill Road, Washington DC 20233-0001, (301) 763-3030, www.census.gov/csd/; *County Business Patterns 2004.*

U.S. Census Bureau, Service Sector Statistics Division, 4700 Silver Hill Road, Washington DC 20233-0001, (301) 763-3030, www.census.gov/svsd/www/economic.html; *2004 Service Annual Survey: Professional, Scientific and Technical Services.*

U.S. Department of the Treasury (DOT), Internal Revenue Service (IRS), Statistics of Income Division (SIS), PO Box 2608, Washington, DC, 20013-2608, (202) 874-0410, Fax: (202) 874-0964, www.irs.ustreas.gov; *Statistics of Income Bulletin* and various fact sheets.

ACQUISITION OF TERRITORY BY THE UNITED STATES

General Services Administration (GSA), 1800 F Street, NW, Washington, DC 20405, (202) 708-5082, www.gsa.gov; *Federal Real Property Profile 2004 (FRPP).*

ACTIVITIES OF DAILY LIVING (ADLs)

National Center for Health Statistics (NCHS), Centers for Disease Control and Prevention (CDC), U.S. Department of Health and Human Services (HHS), 3311 Toledo Road, Hyattsville, MD 20782, (866) 232-4636, www.cdc.gov/nchs; *Health, United States, 2006, with Chartbook on Trends in the Health of Americans with Special Feature on Pain.*

ACTIVITY LIMITATION CAUSED BY CHRONIC CONDITIONS

National Center for Chronic Disease Prevention and Health Promotion (NCCDPHP), Centers for Disease Control and Prevention (CDC), 4770 Buford Hwy, NE, MS K-40, Atlanta, GA 30341-3717, (404) 639-3311, www.cdc.gov/nccdphp; *The Burden of Chronic Disease and the Future of Public Health* and *The Burden of Chronic Diseases and Their Risk Factors: National and State Perspectives 2004.*

National Center for Health Statistics (NCHS), Centers for Disease Control and Prevention (CDC), U.S. Department of Health and Human Services (HHS), 3311 Toledo Road, Hyattsville, MD 20782, (866) 232-4636, www.cdc.gov/nchs; *Health, United States, 2006, with Chartbook on Trends in the Health of Americans with Special Feature on Pain.*

ACTORS

U.S. Bureau of Labor Statistics (BLS), Postal Square Building, 2 Massachusetts Avenue, NE,

Washington, DC 20212-0001, (202) 691-5200, Fax: (202) 691-6325, www.bls.gov; *Employment and Earnings (EE)* and unpublished data.

ADOPTION

Australian Institute of Health and Welfare (AIHW), GPO Box 570, Canberra ACT 2601, Australia, www.aihw.gov.au; *Adoptions Australia 2006-07.*

National Council For Adoption (NCFA), 225 N. Washington Street, Alexandria, VA 22314-2561, (703) 299-6633, Fax: (703) 299-6004, www.ncfa-usa.org; *Adoption Factbook III* and unpublished data.

ADULT EDUCATION

The Annie E. Casey Foundation, 701 Saint Paul Street, Baltimore, MD 21202, (410) 547-6600, Fax: (410) 547-3610, www.aecf.org; *Of, By, And For the Community: The Story of PUENTE Learning Center.*

National Center for Education Statistics (NCES), 1990 K Street, NW, Washington, DC 20006, (202) 502-7300, http://nces.ed.gov; *The National Household Education Surveys Program (NHES).*

Turkish Statistical Institute (Turkstat), Prime Ministry State Institute of Statistics (SIS), Information Dissemination Division, Necatibey Caddesi No. 114, 06100 Bakanliklar, Ankara, Turkey, www.die.gov.tr/ENGLISH; *National Education Statistics; Adult Education, 2002-2003.*

ADVERTISING AND RELATED SERVICES

Mediamark Research, Inc., 75 Ninth Avenue, 5th Floor, New York, NY 10011, (212) 884-9200, Fax: (212) 884-9339, www.mediamark.com; *The American Kids Study.*

Television Bureau of Advertising, Inc., 3 East 54th Street, New York, NY 10022-3108, (212) 486-1111, Fax: (212) 935-5631, www.tvb.org; *Trends in Media.*

ADVERTISING AND RELATED SERVICES - EARNINGS

U.S. Bureau of Labor Statistics (BLS), Postal Square Building, 2 Massachusetts Avenue, NE, Washington, DC 20212-0001, (202) 691-5200, Fax: (202) 691-6325, www.bls.gov; *Current Employment Statistics Survey (CES)* and *Employment and Earnings (EE).*

U.S. Census Bureau, Center for Economic Studies, 4600 Silver Hill Road, Washington DC 20233, (301) 457-1235, www.ces.census.gov; *2002 Economic Census, Professional, Scientific and Technical Services.*

U.S. Census Bureau, Company Statistics Division, 4700 Silver Hill Road, Washington DC 20233-0001, (301) 763-3030, www.census.gov/csd/; *County Business Patterns 2004.*

ADVERTISING AND RELATED SERVICES - EMPLOYEES

U.S. Bureau of Labor Statistics (BLS), Postal Square Building, 2 Massachusetts Avenue, NE, Washington, DC 20212-0001, (202) 691-5200, Fax: (202) 691-6325, www.bls.gov; *Current Employment Statistics Survey (CES)* and *Employment and Earnings (EE).*

U.S. Census Bureau, Center for Economic Studies, 4600 Silver Hill Road, Washington DC 20233, (301) 457-1235, www.ces.census.gov; *2002 Economic Census, Professional, Scientific and Technical Services.*

U.S. Census Bureau, Company Statistics Division, 4700 Silver Hill Road, Washington DC 20233-0001, (301) 763-3030, www.census.gov/csd/; *County Business Patterns 2004.*

ADVERTISING AND RELATED SERVICES - ESTABLISHMENTS

Arbitron, Inc., 142 West 57th Street, New York, NY 10019-3300, (212) 887-1300, www.arbitron.com; *Arbitron Ratings Data* and unpublished data.

U.S. Census Bureau, Company Statistics Division, 4700 Silver Hill Road, Washington DC 20233-0001, (301) 763-3030, www.census.gov/csd/; *County Business Patterns 2004.*

U.S. Census Bureau, Service Sector Statistics Division, 4700 Silver Hill Road, Washington DC 20233-0001, (301) 763-3030, www.census.gov/svsd/www/economic.html; *2004 Service Annual Survey: Professional, Scientific and Technical Services.*

ADVERTISING AND RELATED SERVICES - FINANCES

McCann Erickson Worldwide, 622 Third Avenue, New York, NY 10017, (646) 865-2000, www.mccann.com; unpublished data.

ADVERTISING AND RELATED SERVICES - MERGERS AND ACQUISITIONS

Thomson Financial, 195 Broadway, New York, NY 10007, (646) 822-2000, www.thomson.com; Thomson Research.

ADVERTISING AND RELATED SERVICES - RECEIPTS

U.S. Census Bureau, Service Sector Statistics Division, 4700 Silver Hill Road, Washington DC 20233-0001, (301) 763-3030, www.census.gov/svsd/www/economic.html; *2004 Service Annual Survey: Professional, Scientific and Technical Services.*

AEROBICS

National Sporting Goods Association (NSGA), 1601 Feehanville Drive, Suite 300, Mount Prospect, IL 60056, (847) 296-6742, Fax: (847) 391-9827, www.nsga.org; *2006 Sports Participation* and *Ten-Year History of Selected Sports Participation, 1996-2006.*

AERONAUTICS, CIVIL

See AERONAUTICS, COMMERCIAL

AERONAUTICS, COMMERCIAL

Air Transport Association of America, 1301 Pennsylvania Avenue, NW, Suite 1100, Washington, DC 20004-7017, (202) 626-4000, Fax: (202) 626-6584, www.air-transport.org; *Air Transportation and the Economy: A State-by-State Review* and *2007 Economic Report.*

Jane's Information Group, 110 North Royal Street, Suite 200, Alexandria, VA 22314, (703) 683-3700, Fax: (800) 836-0297, www.janes.com; *Jane's World Airlines.*

National Transportation Safety Board (NTSB), 490 L'Enfant Plaza, SW, Washington, DC 20594, (202) 314-6000, www.ntsb.gov; *Transportation Safety Databases.*

State of Connecticut, Department of Economic and Community Development (DECD), 505 Hudson Street, Hartford, CT 06106-7107, (860) 270-8000, www.ct.gov/ecd/; *The Contribution of Bradley International Airport to Connecticut's Economy.*

U.S. Census Bureau, Center for Economic Studies, 4600 Silver Hill Road, Washington DC 20233, (301) 457-1235, www.ces.census.gov; *2002 Economic Census, Transportation and Warehousing.*

U.S. Census Bureau, Company Statistics Division, 4700 Silver Hill Road, Washington DC 20233-0001, (301) 763-3030, www.census.gov/csd/; *County Business Patterns 2004.*

U.S. Department of Transportation (DOT), Research and Innovative Technology Administration (RITA), Bureau of Transportation Statistics (BTS), 1200 New Jersey Avenue, SE, Washington, DC 20590, (800) 853-1351, www.bts.gov; unpublished data.

AERONAUTICS, COMMERCIAL - ACCIDENTS

Federal Aviation Administration (FAA), 800 Independence Avenue, SW, Washington, DC 20591, (866) 835-5322, www.faa.gov; Aviation Safety Information Analysis and Sharing (ASIAS) System and *Preliminary Accident and Incident Data.*

Federal Aviation Administration (FAA) Office of Aviation Safety, Aviation Safety Information Analysis and Sharing (ASIAS) System, 800 Independence Avenue, SW, Room 1006, Washington, DC 20591, (866) 835-5322, www.asias.faa.gov; Near Midair Collision System (NMACS).

International Civil Aviation Organization (ICAO), External Relations and Public Information Office (EPO), 999 University Street, Montreal, Quebec H3C 5H7, Canada, (Dial from U.S. (514) 954-8219), (Fax from U.S. (514) 954-6077), www.icao.int; *Civil Aviation Statistics of the World.*

National Transportation Safety Board (NTSB), 490 L'Enfant Plaza, SW, Washington, DC 20594, (202) 314-6000, www.ntsb.gov; *The Annual Review of Aircraft Accident Data.*

U.S. Department of Transportation (DOT), Research and Innovative Technology Administration (RITA), Bureau of Transportation Statistics (BTS), 1200 New Jersey Avenue, SE, Washington, DC 20590, (800) 853-1351, www.bts.gov; *TranStats.*

AERONAUTICS, COMMERCIAL - AIRLINE MARKETS

Air Transport Association of America, 1301 Pennsylvania Avenue, NW, Suite 1100, Washington, DC 20004-7017, (202) 626-4000, Fax: (202) 626-6584, www.air-transport.org; *2007 Economic Report.*

AERONAUTICS, COMMERCIAL - AIRPORT SUMMARY

Regional Airline Association (RAA), 2025 M Street, NW, Suite 800, Washington, DC 20036-3309, (202) 367-1170, Fax: (202) 367-2170, www.raa.org; *2007 Industry Traffic Statistics* and *Top 50 Individual Regional Airlines (as of December 2006).*

U.S. Department of Transportation (DOT), Office of Aviation Enforcement and Proceedings (OAEP), 1200 New Jersey Ave, SE, Washington, DC 20590, (202) 366-4000, http://airconsumer.ost.dot.gov; *Air Travel Consumer Report 2008.*

AERONAUTICS, COMMERCIAL - AIRPORT SUMMARY - FLIGHT ON-TIME PERFORMANCE

U.S. Department of Transportation (DOT), Office of Aviation Enforcement and Proceedings (OAEP), 1200 New Jersey Ave, SE, Washington, DC 20590, (202) 366-4000, http://airconsumer.ost.dot.gov; *Air Travel Consumer Report 2008.*

U.S. Department of Transportation (DOT), Research and Innovative Technology Administration (RITA), Bureau of Transportation Statistics (BTS), 1200 New Jersey Avenue, SE, Washington, DC 20590, (800) 853-1351, www.bts.gov; Airline On-Time Statistics and Delay Causes (web app).

AERONAUTICS, COMMERCIAL - BOMB THREATS

U.S. Department of Transportation (DOT), Research and Innovative Technology Administration (RITA), Bureau of Transportation Statistics (BTS), 1200 New Jersey Avenue, SE, Washington, DC 20590, (800) 853-1351, www.bts.gov; *TranStats.*

AERONAUTICS, COMMERCIAL - CIVIL AVIATION

U.S. Department of Transportation (DOT), Office of Aviation Enforcement and Proceedings (OAEP), 1200 New Jersey Ave, SE, Washington, DC 20590, (202) 366-4000, http://airconsumer.ost.dot.gov; *Air Travel Consumer Report 2008.*

U.S. Department of Transportation (DOT), Research and Innovative Technology Administration (RITA), Bureau of Transportation Statistics (BTS), 1200 New Jersey Avenue, SE, Washington, DC 20590, (800) 853-1351, www.bts.gov; *TranStats.*

AERONAUTICS, COMMERCIAL - COST INDEXES

Air Transport Association of America, 1301 Pennsylvania Avenue, NW, Suite 1100, Washington, DC 20004-7017, (202) 626-4000, Fax: (202) 626-6584, www.air-transport.org; *2007 Economic Report* and unpublished data.

AMSTAT, 44 Apple Street, Tinton Falls, NJ 07724, (732) 530-6400, www.amstatcorp.com; *AMSTAT Premier* and *AMSTAT StatPak.*

AERONAUTICS, COMMERCIAL - EARNINGS

U.S. Bureau of Labor Statistics (BLS), Postal Square Building, 2 Massachusetts Avenue, NE, Washington, DC 20212-0001, (202) 691-5200, Fax: (202) 691-6325, www.bls.gov; *Current Employment Statistics Survey (CES)* and *Employment and Earnings (EE).*

U.S. Census Bureau, Center for Economic Studies, 4600 Silver Hill Road, Washington DC 20233, (301) 457-1235, www.ces.census.gov; *2002 Economic Census, Transportation and Warehousing.*

U.S. Census Bureau, Company Statistics Division, 4700 Silver Hill Road, Washington DC 20233-0001, (301) 763-3030, www.census.gov/csd/; *County Business Patterns 2004.*

AERONAUTICS, COMMERCIAL - EMPLOYEES

Air Transport Association of America, 1301 Pennsylvania Avenue, NW, Suite 1100, Washington, DC 20004-7017, (202) 626-4000, Fax: (202) 626-6584, www.air-transport.org; *Air Transportation and the Economy: A State-by-State Review* and *2007 Economic Report.*

U.S. Bureau of Labor Statistics (BLS), Postal Square Building, 2 Massachusetts Avenue, NE, Washington, DC 20212-0001, (202) 691-5200, Fax: (202) 691-6325, www.bls.gov; *Current Employment Statistics Survey (CES)* and *Employment and Earnings (EE).*

U.S. Census Bureau, Center for Economic Studies, 4600 Silver Hill Road, Washington DC 20233, (301) 457-1235, www.ces.census.gov; *2002 Economic Census, Transportation and Warehousing.*

U.S. Census Bureau, Company Statistics Division, 4700 Silver Hill Road, Washington DC 20233-0001, (301) 763-3030, www.census.gov/csd/; *County Business Patterns 2004.*

AERONAUTICS, COMMERCIAL - FEDERAL OUTLAYS

The Office of Management and Budget (OMB), 725 17th Street, NW, Washington, DC 20503, (202) 395-3080, Fax: (202) 395-3888, www.whitehouse.gov/omb; *Budget of the United States Government, Federal Year 2009* and *Historical Tables.*

AERONAUTICS, COMMERCIAL - FINANCES

Air Transport Association of America, 1301 Pennsylvania Avenue, NW, Suite 1100, Washington, DC 20004-7017, (202) 626-4000, Fax: (202) 626-6584, www.air-transport.org; *Air Transportation and the Economy: A State-by-State Review; 2007 Economic Report;* and unpublished data.

AMSTAT, 44 Apple Street, Tinton Falls, NJ 07724, (732) 530-6400, www.amstatcorp.com; *AMSTAT Premier* and *AMSTAT StatPak.*

AERONAUTICS, COMMERCIAL - FREIGHT

Air Transport Association of America, 1301 Pennsylvania Avenue, NW, Suite 1100, Washington, DC 20004-7017, (202) 626-4000, Fax: (202) 626-6584, www.air-transport.org; *Air Transportation and the Economy: A State-by-State Review; 2007 Economic Report;* and unpublished data.

Directorate General of Commercial Intelligence and Statistics (DGCIS), Ministry of Commerce and Industry, 1, Council House Street, Calcutta-700 001, India, www.dgciskol.nic.in; *Inter-State Movements/ Flows of Goods by Rail, River and Air.*

AERONAUTICS, COMMERCIAL - INDUSTRIAL SAFETY

Federal Aviation Administration (FAA) Office of Aviation Safety, Aviation Safety Information Analysis and Sharing (ASIAS) System, 800 Independence Avenue, SW, Room 1006, Washington, DC 20591, (866) 835-5322, www.asias.faa.gov; Near Midair Collision System (NMACS).

National Aeronautics and Space Administration (NASA), Public Communications Office, NASA Headquarters, Suite 5K39, Washington, DC 20546-0001, (202) 358-0000, Fax: (202) 358-3469, www.nasa.gov; Aviation Safety Reporting System (ASRS).

Regional Airline Association (RAA), 2025 M Street, NW, Suite 800, Washington, DC 20036-3309, (202) 367-1170, Fax: (202) 367-2170, www.raa.org; *Regional Airline Industry Safety Statistics.*

U.S. Bureau of Labor Statistics (BLS), Postal Square Building, 2 Massachusetts Avenue, NE, Washington, DC 20212-0001, (202) 691-5200, Fax: (202) 691-6325, www.bls.gov; *Injuries, Illnesses, and Fatalities (IIF).*

AERONAUTICS, COMMERCIAL - ORDERS BOOKED/ANNOUNCED

Aerospace Industries Association (AIA), 1000 Wilson Boulevard, Suite 1700, Arlington, VA 22209-3928, (703) 358-1000, www.aia-aerospace.org; *Aerospace Facts and Figures 2007; Aerospace Statistics;* and *AIA's Year-End Review and Forecast.*

Federal Aviation Administration (FAA), 800 Independence Avenue, SW, Washington, DC 20591, (866) 835-5322, www.faa.gov; *FAA Aerospace Forecasts - Fiscal Years 2007-2020.*

U.S. Census Bureau, Manufacturing and Construction Division, 4600 Silver Hill Road, Washington DC 20233, (301) 763-4673, www.census.gov/mcd; *Aerospace Industry.*

AERONAUTICS, COMMERCIAL - PASSENGER OUTLAYS

Eno Transportation Foundation, 1634 I Street, NW, Suite 500, Washington, DC 20006, (202) 879-4700, Fax: (202) 879-4719, www.enotrans.com; *Transportation in America.*

AERONAUTICS, COMMERCIAL - PASSENGER SCREENING

U.S. Department of Transportation (DOT), Research and Innovative Technology Administration (RITA), Bureau of Transportation Statistics (BTS), 1200 New Jersey Avenue, SE, Washington, DC 20590, (800) 853-1351, www.bts.gov; *TranStats.*

AERONAUTICS, COMMERCIAL - PRICE INDEXES

U.S. Bureau of Labor Statistics (BLS), Postal Square Building, 2 Massachusetts Avenue, NE, Washington, DC 20212-0001, (202) 691-5200, Fax: (202) 691-6325, www.bls.gov; *Consumer Price Index Detailed Report* and *Monthly Labor Review (MLR).*

AERONAUTICS, COMMERCIAL - PRODUCTIVITY

U.S. Bureau of Labor Statistics (BLS), Postal Square Building, 2 Massachusetts Avenue, NE, Washington, DC 20212-0001, (202) 691-5200, Fax: (202) 691-6325, www.bls.gov; *Industry Productivity and Costs.*

AERONAUTICS, COMMERCIAL - PROFITS

Air Transport Association of America, 1301 Pennsylvania Avenue, NW, Suite 1100, Washington, DC 20004-7017, (202) 626-4000, Fax: (202) 626-6584, www.air-transport.org; *Air Transportation and the Economy: A State-by-State Review* and *2007 Economic Report.*

AERONAUTICS, COMMERCIAL - REGIONAL AIRLINES

Regional Airline Association (RAA), 2025 M Street, NW, Suite 800, Washington, DC 20036-3309, (202) 367-1170, Fax: (202) 367-2170, www.raa.org; *2007 Regional Airline Industry Annual Report.*

AERONAUTICS, COMMERCIAL - TRAFFIC CARRIED

Air Transport Association of America, 1301 Pennsylvania Avenue, NW, Suite 1100, Washington, DC 20004-7017, (202) 626-4000, Fax: (202) 626-6584, www.air-transport.org; *Air Transportation and the Economy: A State-by-State Review* and *2007 Economic Report.*

Eno Transportation Foundation, 1634 I Street, NW, Suite 500, Washington, DC 20006, (202) 879-4700, Fax: (202) 879-4719, www.enotrans.com; *Transportation in America.*

International Civil Aviation Organization (ICAO), External Relations and Public Information Office (EPO), 999 University Street, Montreal, Quebec H3C 5H7, Canada, (Dial from U.S. (514) 954-8219), (Fax from U.S. (514) 954-6077), www.icao.int; *Traffic - Commercial Air Carriers.*

Regional Airline Association (RAA), 2025 M Street, NW, Suite 800, Washington, DC 20036-3309, (202) 367-1170, Fax: (202) 367-2170, www.raa.org; *2007 Industry Traffic Statistics* and *2007 Regional Airline Industry Annual Report.*

AEROSPACE INDUSTRY

U.S. Census Bureau, Manufacturing and Construction Division, 4600 Silver Hill Road, Washington DC 20233, (301) 763-4673, www.census.gov/mcd; *Annual Survey of Manufactures, Statistics for Industry Groups and Industries.*

AEROSPACE INDUSTRY - EMPLOYEES

U.S. Census Bureau, Manufacturing and Construction Division, 4600 Silver Hill Road, Washington DC 20233, (301) 763-4673, www.census.gov/mcd; *Annual Survey of Manufactures, Statistics for Industry Groups and Industries.*

U.S. Department of Transportation (DOT), Research and Innovative Technology Administration (RITA), Bureau of Transportation Statistics (BTS), 1200 New Jersey Avenue, SE, Washington, DC 20590, (800) 853-1351, www.bts.gov; *TranStats.*

AEROSPACE INDUSTRY - INTERNATIONAL TRADE

Aerospace Industries Association (AIA), 1000 Wilson Boulevard, Suite 1700, Arlington, VA 22209-3928, (703) 358-1000, www.aia-aerospace.org; *Aerospace Facts and Figures 2007; Aerospace Statistics;* and *AIA's Year-End Review and Forecast.*

Federal Aviation Administration (FAA), 800 Independence Avenue, SW, Washington, DC 20591, (866) 835-5322, www.faa.gov; *FAA Aerospace Forecasts - Fiscal Years 2007-2020.*

U.S. Census Bureau, Manufacturing and Construction Division, 4600 Silver Hill Road, Washington DC 20233, (301) 763-4673, www.census.gov/mcd; *Aerospace Industry.*

AEROSPACE INDUSTRY - NEW ORDERS - BACKLOG

U.S. Census Bureau, Manufacturing and Construction Division, 4600 Silver Hill Road, Washington DC 20233, (301) 763-4673, www.census.gov/mcd; *Current Industrial Reports.*

AEROSPACE INDUSTRY - RESEARCH AND DEVELOPMENT

National Science Foundation, Division of Science Resources Statistics (SRS), 4201 Wilson Boulevard, Arlington, VA 22230, (703) 292-8780, Fax: (703) 292-9092, www.nsf.gov; *Research and Development in Industry: 2003.*

AEROSPACE INDUSTRY - SALES

AMSTAT, 44 Apple Street, Tinton Falls, NJ 07724, (732) 530-6400, www.amstatcorp.com; *AMSTAT Premier* and *AMSTAT StatPak.*

U.S. Census Bureau, Manufacturing and Construction Division, 4600 Silver Hill Road, Washington DC 20233, (301) 763-4673, www.census.gov/mcd; *Current Industrial Reports.*

AEROSPACE INDUSTRY - SHIPMENTS

Aerospace Industries Association (AIA), 1000 Wilson Boulevard, Suite 1700, Arlington, VA 22209-

3928, (703) 358-1000, www.aia-aerospace.org; *Aerospace Facts and Figures 2007; Aerospace Statistics;* and *AIA's Year-End Review and Forecast.*

Federal Aviation Administration (FAA), 800 Independence Avenue, SW, Washington, DC 20591, (866) 835-5322, www.faa.gov; *FAA Aerospace Forecasts - Fiscal Years 2007-2020.*

U.S. Census Bureau, Manufacturing and Construction Division, 4600 Silver Hill Road, Washington DC 20233, (301) 763-4673, www.census.gov/mcd; *Aerospace Industry; Annual Survey of Manufactures, Statistics for Industry Groups and Industries;* and *Current Industrial Reports.*

AFGHANISTAN - NATIONAL STATISTICAL OFFICE

Central Statistics Office (CSO), Ansar-i-Watt, Kabul, Afghanistan, www.cso.gov.af; National Data Center.

AFGHANISTAN - PRIMARY STATISTICS SOURCES

Central Statistics Office (CSO), Ansar-i-Watt, Kabul, Afghanistan, www.cso.gov.af; *Population by Province, 2003.*

AFGHANISTAN - AGRICULTURE

Asian Development Bank (ADB), PO Box 789, 0980 Manila, Philippines, www.adb.org; *Key Indicators of Developing Asian and Pacific Countries 2006.*

Central Statistics Office (CSO), Ansar-i-Watt, Kabul, Afghanistan, www.cso.gov.af; *Agriculture Sector Comparison.*

Economist Intelligence Unit, 111 West 57th Street, New York, NY 10019, (212) 554-0600, Fax: (212) 586-1181, www.eiu.com; *Afghanistan Country Report.*

Euromonitor International, Inc., 224 S. Michigan Avenue, Suite 1500, Chicago, IL 60604, (312) 922-1115, Fax: (312) 922-1157, www.euromonitor.com; *International Marketing Data and Statistics 2008* and *World Marketing Data and Statistics.*

M.E. Sharpe, 80 Business Park Drive, Armonk, NY 10504, (800) 541-6563, Fax: (914) 273-2106, www.mesharpe.com; *The Illustrated Book of World Rankings.*

Palgrave Macmillan Ltd., Houndmills, Basingstoke, Hampshire, RG21 6XS, England, (Telephone in U.S. (888) 330-8477), (Fax in U.S. (800) 672-2054), www.palgrave.com; *The Statesman's Yearbook 2008.*

Taylor and Francis Group, An Informa Business, 2 Park Square, Milton Park, Abingdon, Oxford OX14 4RN, United Kingdom, (Dial from U.S. (212) 216-7800), (Fax from U.S. (212) 564-7854), www.tandf.co.uk; *The Europa World Year Book.*

United Nations Conference on Trade and Development (UNCTAD), DC2-1120, United Nations, New York, NY 10017, (212) 963-0027, www.unctad.org; *UNCTAD Commodity Yearbook.*

United Nations Food and Agricultural Organization (FAO), Viale delle Terme di Caracalla, 00100 Rome, Italy, (Dial from U.S. (202) 653-2400), (Fax from U.S. (202) 653 5760), www.fao.org; AQUASTAT; *FAO Production Yearbook 2002; FAO Trade Yearbook;* and *The State of Food and Agriculture (SOFA) 2006.*

United Nations Statistics Division, New York, NY 10017, (800) 253-9646, Fax: (212) 963-4116, http://unstats.un.org; *Asia-Pacific in Figures 2004; Statistical Yearbook;* and *Statistical Yearbook for Asia and the Pacific 2004.*

The World Bank, 1818 H Street, NW, Washington, DC 20433, (202) 473-1000, Fax: (202) 477-6391, www.worldbank.org; *Afghanistan.*

AFGHANISTAN - AIRLINES

Economist Intelligence Unit, 111 West 57th Street, New York, NY 10019, (212) 554-0600, Fax: (212) 586-1181, www.eiu.com; *Business Asia.*

International Civil Aviation Organization (ICAO), External Relations and Public Information Office (EPO), 999 University Street, Montreal, Quebec H3C 5H7, Canada, (Dial from U.S. (514) 954-8219), (Fax from U.S. (514) 954-6077), www.icao.int; *Civil Aviation Statistics of the World.*

M.E. Sharpe, 80 Business Park Drive, Armonk, NY 10504, (800) 541-6563, Fax: (914) 273-2106, www.mesharpe.com; *The Illustrated Book of World Rankings.*

Palgrave Macmillan Ltd., Houndmills, Basingstoke, Hampshire, RG21 6XS, England, (Telephone in U.S. (888) 330-8477), (Fax in U.S. (800) 672-2054), www.palgrave.com; *The Statesman's Yearbook 2008.*

Taylor and Francis Group, An Informa Business, 2 Park Square, Milton Park, Abingdon, Oxford OX14 4RN, United Kingdom, (Dial from U.S. (212) 216-7800), (Fax from U.S. (212) 564-7854), www.tandf.co.uk; *The Europa World Year Book.*

United Nations Statistics Division, New York, NY 10017, (800) 253-9646, Fax: (212) 963-4116, http://unstats.un.org; *Statistical Yearbook.*

AFGHANISTAN - AIRPORTS

Central Intelligence Agency, Office of Public Affairs, Washington, DC 20505, (703) 482-0623, Fax: (703) 482-1739, www.cia.gov; *The World Factbook.*

AFGHANISTAN - ALUMINUM PRODUCTION

See AFGHANISTAN - MINERAL INDUSTRIES

AFGHANISTAN - ARMED FORCES

Central Intelligence Agency, Office of Public Affairs, Washington, DC 20505, (703) 482-0623, Fax: (703) 482-1739, www.cia.gov; *The World Factbook.*

Economist Intelligence Unit, 111 West 57th Street, New York, NY 10019, (212) 554-0600, Fax: (212) 586-1181, www.eiu.com; *Business Asia.*

Euromonitor International, Inc., 224 S. Michigan Avenue, Suite 1500, Chicago, IL 60604, (312) 922-1115, Fax: (312) 922-1157, www.euromonitor.com; *World Marketing Data and Statistics.*

International Institute for Strategic Studies (IISS), Arundel House, 13-15 Arundel Street, Temple Place, London WC2R 3DX, England, www.iiss.org; *The Military Balance 2007.*

Palgrave Macmillan Ltd., Houndmills, Basingstoke, Hampshire, RG21 6XS, England, (Telephone in U.S. (888) 330-8477), (Fax in U.S. (800) 672-2054), www.palgrave.com; *The Statesman's Yearbook 2008.*

U.S. Department of State (DOS), 2201 C Street NW, Washington, DC 20520, (202) 647-4000, www.state.gov; *World Military Expenditures and Arms Transfers (WMEAT).*

AFGHANISTAN - BALANCE OF PAYMENTS

International Monetary Fund (IMF), 700 Nineteenth Street, NW, Washington, DC 20431, (202) 623-7000, Fax: (202) 623-4661, www.imf.org; *International Financial Statistics Yearbook 2007.*

Taylor and Francis Group, An Informa Business, 2 Park Square, Milton Park, Abingdon, Oxford OX14 4RN, United Kingdom, (Dial from U.S. (212) 216-7800), (Fax from U.S. (212) 564-7854), www.tandf.co.uk; *The Europa World Year Book.*

United Nations Conference on Trade and Development (UNCTAD), DC2-1120, United Nations, New York, NY 10017, (212) 963-0027, www.unctad.org; *Handbook of Statistics 2005.*

The World Bank, 1818 H Street, NW, Washington, DC 20433, (202) 473-1000, Fax: (202) 477-6391, www.worldbank.org; *Afghanistan.*

AFGHANISTAN - BANKS AND BANKING

Asian Development Bank (ADB), PO Box 789, 0980 Manila, Philippines, www.adb.org; *Key Indicators of Developing Asian and Pacific Countries 2006.*

Euromonitor International, Inc., 224 S. Michigan Avenue, Suite 1500, Chicago, IL 60604, (312) 922-1115, Fax: (312) 922-1157, www.euromonitor.com; *World Marketing Data and Statistics.*

International Monetary Fund (IMF), 700 Nineteenth Street, NW, Washington, DC 20431, (202) 623-7000, Fax: (202) 623-4661, www.imf.org; *International Financial Statistics Yearbook 2007.*

M.E. Sharpe, 80 Business Park Drive, Armonk, NY 10504, (800) 541-6563, Fax: (914) 273-2106, www.mesharpe.com; *The Illustrated Book of World Rankings.*

Palgrave Macmillan Ltd., Houndmills, Basingstoke, Hampshire, RG21 6XS, England, (Telephone in U.S. (888) 330-8477), (Fax in U.S. (800) 672-2054), www.palgrave.com; *The Statesman's Yearbook 2008.*

Taylor and Francis Group, An Informa Business, 2 Park Square, Milton Park, Abingdon, Oxford OX14 4RN, United Kingdom, (Dial from U.S. (212) 216-7800), (Fax from U.S. (212) 564-7854), www.tandf.co.uk; *The Europa World Year Book.*

AFGHANISTAN - BARLEY PRODUCTION

See AFGHANISTAN - CROPS

AFGHANISTAN - BEVERAGE INDUSTRY

M.E. Sharpe, 80 Business Park Drive, Armonk, NY 10504, (800) 541-6563, Fax: (914) 273-2106, www.mesharpe.com; *The Illustrated Book of World Rankings.*

AFGHANISTAN - BROADCASTING

Central Intelligence Agency, Office of Public Affairs, Washington, DC 20505, (703) 482-0623, Fax: (703) 482-1739, www.cia.gov; *The World Factbook.*

Economist Intelligence Unit, 111 West 57th Street, New York, NY 10019, (212) 554-0600, Fax: (212) 586-1181, www.eiu.com; *Business Asia.*

Euromonitor International, Inc., 224 S. Michigan Avenue, Suite 1500, Chicago, IL 60604, (312) 922-1115, Fax: (312) 922-1157, www.euromonitor.com; *World Marketing Data and Statistics.*

Palgrave Macmillan Ltd., Houndmills, Basingstoke, Hampshire, RG21 6XS, England, (Telephone in U.S. (888) 330-8477), (Fax in U.S. (800) 672-2054), www.palgrave.com; *The Statesman's Yearbook 2008.*

UNESCO Institute for Statistics, C.P. 6128 Succursale Centre-Ville, Montreal, Quebec, H3C 3J7 Canada, (Dial from U.S. (514) 343-6880), (Fax from U.S. (514) 343 6882), www.uis.unesco.org; *Statistical Tables.*

WRTH Publications Limited, PO Box 290, Oxford OX2 7FT, UK, www.wrth.com; *World Radio TV Handbook 2007.*

AFGHANISTAN - BUDGET

Central Intelligence Agency, Office of Public Affairs, Washington, DC 20505, (703) 482-0623, Fax: (703) 482-1739, www.cia.gov; *The World Factbook.*

AFGHANISTAN - BUSINESS

United Nations Statistics Division, New York, NY 10017, (800) 253-9646, Fax: (212) 963-4116, http://unstats.un.org; *Statistical Yearbook for Asia and the Pacific 2004.*

AFGHANISTAN - CAPITAL INVESTMENTS

Asian Development Bank (ADB), PO Box 789, 0980 Manila, Philippines, www.adb.org; *Key Indicators of Developing Asian and Pacific Countries 2006.*

AFGHANISTAN - CAPITAL LEVY

Asian Development Bank (ADB), PO Box 789, 0980 Manila, Philippines, www.adb.org; *Key Indicators of Developing Asian and Pacific Countries 2006.*

AFGHANISTAN - CATTLE

See AFGHANISTAN - LIVESTOCK

AFGHANISTAN - CHICKENS

See AFGHANISTAN - LIVESTOCK

AFGHANISTAN - CHILDBIRTH - STATISTICS

Central Intelligence Agency, Office of Public Affairs, Washington, DC 20505, (703) 482-0623, Fax: (703) 482-1739, www.cia.gov; *The World Factbook.*

Economist Intelligence Unit, 111 West 57th Street, New York, NY 10019, (212) 554-0600, Fax: (212) 586-1181, www.eiu.com; *Business Asia.*

Euromonitor International, Inc., 224 S. Michigan Avenue, Suite 1500, Chicago, IL 60604, (312) 922-1115, Fax: (312) 922-1157, www.euromonitor.com; *International Marketing Data and Statistics 2008* and *The World Economic Factbook 2008.*

M.E. Sharpe, 80 Business Park Drive, Armonk, NY 10504, (800) 541-6563, Fax: (914) 273-2106, www.mesharpe.com; *The Illustrated Book of World Rankings.*

Palgrave Macmillan Ltd., Houndmills, Basingstoke, Hampshire, RG21 6XS, England, (Telephone in U.S. (888) 330-8477), (Fax in U.S. (800) 672-2054), www.palgrave.com; *The Statesman's Yearbook 2008.*

Taylor and Francis Group, An Informa Business, 2 Park Square, Milton Park, Abingdon, Oxford OX14 4RN, United Kingdom, (Dial from U.S. (212) 216-7800), (Fax from U.S. (212) 564-7854), www.tandf.co.uk; *The Europa World Year Book.*

United Nations Statistics Division, New York, NY 10017, (800) 253-9646, Fax: (212) 963-4116, http://unstats.un.org; *Asia-Pacific in Figures 2004* and *Demographic Yearbook.*

AFGHANISTAN - CLIMATE

M.E. Sharpe, 80 Business Park Drive, Armonk, NY 10504, (800) 541-6563, Fax: (914) 273-2106, www.mesharpe.com; *The Illustrated Book of World Rankings.*

Palgrave Macmillan Ltd., Houndmills, Basingstoke, Hampshire, RG21 6XS, England, (Telephone in U.S. (888) 330-8477), (Fax in U.S. (800) 672-2054), www.palgrave.com; *The Statesman's Yearbook 2008.*

AFGHANISTAN - COAL PRODUCTION

See AFGHANISTAN - MINERAL INDUSTRIES

AFGHANISTAN - COFFEE

See AFGHANISTAN - CROPS

AFGHANISTAN - COMMERCE

Palgrave Macmillan Ltd., Houndmills, Basingstoke, Hampshire, RG21 6XS, England, (Telephone in U.S. (888) 330-8477), (Fax in U.S. (800) 672-2054), www.palgrave.com; *The Statesman's Yearbook 2008.*

AFGHANISTAN - COMMODITY EXCHANGES

Commodity Research Bureau, 330 South Wells Street, Suite 612, Chicago, IL 60606-7110, (800) 621-5271, Fax: (312) 939-4135, www.crbtrader.com; *2006 CRB Commodity Yearbook and CD.*

International Monetary Fund (IMF), 700 Nineteenth Street, NW, Washington, DC 20431, (202) 623-7000, Fax: (202) 623-4661, www.imf.org; *IMF Primary Commodity Prices.*

United Nations Food and Agricultural Organization (FAO), Viale delle Terme di Caracalla, 00100 Rome, Italy, (Dial from U.S. (202) 653-2400), (Fax from U.S. (202) 653 5760), www.fao.org; *The State of Food and Agriculture (SOFA) 2006.*

AFGHANISTAN - COMMUNICATION AND TRAFFIC

United Nations Statistics Division, New York, NY 10017, (800) 253-9646, Fax: (212) 963-4116, http://unstats.un.org; *Statistical Yearbook.*

AFGHANISTAN - CONSTRUCTION INDUSTRY

M.E. Sharpe, 80 Business Park Drive, Armonk, NY 10504, (800) 541-6563, Fax: (914) 273-2106, www.mesharpe.com; *The Illustrated Book of World Rankings.*

AFGHANISTAN - CONSUMER PRICE INDEXES

Asian Development Bank (ADB), PO Box 789, 0980 Manila, Philippines, www.adb.org; *Key Indicators of Developing Asian and Pacific Countries 2006.*

Taylor and Francis Group, An Informa Business, 2 Park Square, Milton Park, Abingdon, Oxford OX14 4RN, United Kingdom, (Dial from U.S. (212) 216-7800), (Fax from U.S. (212) 564-7854), www.tandf.co.uk; *The Europa World Year Book.*

United Nations Statistics Division, New York, NY 10017, (800) 253-9646, Fax: (212) 963-4116, http://unstats.un.org; *Statistical Yearbook.*

The World Bank, 1818 H Street, NW, Washington, DC 20433, (202) 473-1000, Fax: (202) 477-6391, www.worldbank.org; *Afghanistan.*

AFGHANISTAN - COPPER INDUSTRY AND TRADE

See AFGHANISTAN - MINERAL INDUSTRIES

AFGHANISTAN - CORN INDUSTRY

See AFGHANISTAN - CROPS

AFGHANISTAN - COTTON

See AFGHANISTAN - CROPS

AFGHANISTAN - CROPS

Asian Development Bank (ADB), PO Box 789, 0980 Manila, Philippines, www.adb.org; *Key Indicators of Developing Asian and Pacific Countries 2006.*

International Monetary Fund (IMF), 700 Nineteenth Street, NW, Washington, DC 20431, (202) 623-7000, Fax: (202) 623-4661, www.imf.org; *International Financial Statistics Yearbook 2007.*

M.E. Sharpe, 80 Business Park Drive, Armonk, NY 10504, (800) 541-6563, Fax: (914) 273-2106, www.mesharpe.com; *The Illustrated Book of World Rankings.*

Palgrave Macmillan Ltd., Houndmills, Basingstoke, Hampshire, RG21 6XS, England, (Telephone in U.S. (888) 330-8477), (Fax in U.S. (800) 672-2054), www.palgrave.com; *The Statesman's Yearbook 2008.*

Taylor and Francis Group, An Informa Business, 2 Park Square, Milton Park, Abingdon, Oxford OX14 4RN, United Kingdom, (Dial from U.S. (212) 216-7800), (Fax from U.S. (212) 564-7854), www.tandf.co.uk; *The Europa World Year Book.*

United Nations Conference on Trade and Development (UNCTAD), DC2-1120, United Nations, New York, NY 10017, (212) 963-0027, www.unctad.org; *UNCTAD Commodity Yearbook.*

United Nations Food and Agricultural Organization (FAO), Viale delle Terme di Caracalla, 00100 Rome, Italy, (Dial from U.S. (202) 653-2400), (Fax from U.S. (202) 653 5760), www.fao.org; *The State of Food and Agriculture (SOFA) 2006.*

United Nations Statistics Division, New York, NY 10017, (800) 253-9646, Fax: (212) 963-4116, http://unstats.un.org; *Statistical Yearbook.*

AFGHANISTAN - CUSTOMS ADMINISTRATION

Palgrave Macmillan Ltd., Houndmills, Basingstoke, Hampshire, RG21 6XS, England, (Telephone in U.S. (888) 330-8477), (Fax in U.S. (800) 672-2054), www.palgrave.com; *The Statesman's Yearbook 2008.*

AFGHANISTAN - DAIRY PROCESSING

M.E. Sharpe, 80 Business Park Drive, Armonk, NY 10504, (800) 541-6563, Fax: (914) 273-2106, www.mesharpe.com; *The Illustrated Book of World Rankings.*

Taylor and Francis Group, An Informa Business, 2 Park Square, Milton Park, Abingdon, Oxford OX14 4RN, United Kingdom, (Dial from U.S. (212) 216-7800), (Fax from U.S. (212) 564-7854), www.tandf.co.uk; *The Europa World Year Book.*

United Nations Food and Agricultural Organization (FAO), Viale delle Terme di Caracalla, 00100 Rome, Italy, (Dial from U.S. (202) 653-2400), (Fax from U.S. (202) 653 5760), www.fao.org; *The State of Food and Agriculture (SOFA) 2006.*

United Nations Statistics Division, New York, NY 10017, (800) 253-9646, Fax: (212) 963-4116, http://unstats.un.org; *Statistical Yearbook.*

AFGHANISTAN - DEATH RATES

See AFGHANISTAN - MORTALITY

AFGHANISTAN - DEBTS, EXTERNAL

Asian Development Bank (ADB), PO Box 789, 0980 Manila, Philippines, www.adb.org; *Key Indicators of Developing Asian and Pacific Countries 2006.*

Palgrave Macmillan Ltd., Houndmills, Basingstoke, Hampshire, RG21 6XS, England, (Telephone in U.S. (888) 330-8477), (Fax in U.S. (800) 672-2054), www.palgrave.com; *The Statesman's Yearbook 2008.*

The World Bank, 1818 H Street, NW, Washington, DC 20433, (202) 473-1000, Fax: (202) 477-6391, www.worldbank.org; *Global Development Finance 2007.*

Worldinformation.com, 2 Market Street, Saffron Walden, Essex CB10 1HZ, United Kingdom, www.worldinformation.com; The World of Information (www.worldinformation.com).

AFGHANISTAN - DEFENSE EXPENDITURES

See AFGHANISTAN - ARMED FORCES

AFGHANISTAN - DEMOGRAPHY

Economist Intelligence Unit, 111 West 57th Street, New York, NY 10019, (212) 554-0600, Fax: (212) 586-1181, www.eiu.com; *Business Asia.*

Euromonitor International, Inc., 224 S. Michigan Avenue, Suite 1500, Chicago, IL 60604, (312) 922-1115, Fax: (312) 922-1157, www.euromonitor.com; *International Marketing Data and Statistics 2008; The World Economic Factbook 2008;* and *World Marketing Data and Statistics.*

M.E. Sharpe, 80 Business Park Drive, Armonk, NY 10504, (800) 541-6563, Fax: (914) 273-2106, www.mesharpe.com; *The Illustrated Book of World Rankings.*

United Nations Statistics Division, New York, NY 10017, (800) 253-9646, Fax: (212) 963-4116, http://unstats.un.org; *Asia-Pacific in Figures 2004.*

The World Bank, 1818 H Street, NW, Washington, DC 20433, (202) 473-1000, Fax: (202) 477-6391, www.worldbank.org; *Afghanistan.*

AFGHANISTAN - DIAMONDS

See AFGHANISTAN - MINERAL INDUSTRIES

AFGHANISTAN - DISPOSABLE INCOME

M.E. Sharpe, 80 Business Park Drive, Armonk, NY 10504, (800) 541-6563, Fax: (914) 273-2106, www.mesharpe.com; *The Illustrated Book of World Rankings.*

United Nations Statistics Division, New York, NY 10017, (800) 253-9646, Fax: (212) 963-4116, http://unstats.un.org; *National Accounts Statistics: Compendium of Income Distribution Statistics* and *Statistical Yearbook.*

AFGHANISTAN - DIVORCE

M.E. Sharpe, 80 Business Park Drive, Armonk, NY 10504, (800) 541-6563, Fax: (914) 273-2106, www.mesharpe.com; *The Illustrated Book of World Rankings.*

United Nations Statistics Division, New York, NY 10017, (800) 253-9646, Fax: (212) 963-4116, http://unstats.un.org; *Demographic Yearbook.*

AFGHANISTAN - ECONOMIC ASSISTANCE

Asian Development Bank (ADB), PO Box 789, 0980 Manila, Philippines, www.adb.org; *Key Indicators of Developing Asian and Pacific Countries 2006.*

United Nations Statistics Division, New York, NY 10017, (800) 253-9646, Fax: (212) 963-4116, http://unstats.un.org; *Statistical Yearbook.*

AFGHANISTAN - ECONOMIC CONDITIONS

Asian Development Bank (ADB), PO Box 789, 0980 Manila, Philippines, www.adb.org; *Key Indicators of Developing Asian and Pacific Countries 2006.*

Center for International Business Education Research (CIBER), Columbia Business School and School of International and Public Affairs, Uris Hall, Room 212, 3022 Broadway, New York, NY 10027-6902, Mr. Joshua Safier, (212) 854-4750, Fax: (212) 222-9821, www.columbia.edu/cu/ciber/; Datastream International.

Central Intelligence Agency, Office of Public Affairs, Washington, DC 20505, (703) 482-0623, Fax: (703) 482-1739, www.cia.gov; *The World Factbook.*

DSI Data Service Information, Xantener Strasse 51a, D-47495 Rheinberg, Germany, www.dsidata.com; *Campus Solution.*

Dun and Bradstreet (DB) Corporation, 103 JFK Parkway, Short Hills, NJ 07078, (973) 921-5500, www.dnb.com; *Country Report.*

Economist Intelligence Unit, 111 West 57th Street, New York, NY 10019, (212) 554-0600, Fax: (212) 586-1181, www.eiu.com; *Afghanistan Country Report.*

Euromonitor International, Inc., 224 S. Michigan Avenue, Suite 1500, Chicago, IL 60604, (312) 922-1115, Fax: (312) 922-1157, www.euromonitor.com; *International Marketing Data and Statistics 2008; The World Economic Factbook 2008;* and *World Marketing Data and Statistics.*

International Monetary Fund (IMF), 700 Nineteenth Street, NW, Washington, DC 20431, (202) 623-7000, Fax: (202) 623-4661, www.imf.org; *World Economic Outlook Reports.*

M.E. Sharpe, 80 Business Park Drive, Armonk, NY 10504, (800) 541-6563, Fax: (914) 273-2106, www.mesharpe.com; *The Illustrated Book of World Rankings.*

Nomura Research Institute (NRI), 2 World Financial Center, Building B, 19th Fl., New York, NY 10281-1198, (212) 667-1670, www.nri.co.jp/english; *Asian Economic Outlook 2003-2004.*

Palgrave Macmillan Ltd., Houndmills, Basingstoke, Hampshire, RG21 6XS, England, (Telephone in U.S. (888) 330-8477), (Fax in U.S. (800) 672-2054), www.palgrave.com; *The Statesman's Yearbook 2008.*

Taylor and Francis Group, An Informa Business, 2 Park Square, Milton Park, Abingdon, Oxford OX14 4RN, United Kingdom, (Dial from U.S. (212) 216-7800), (Fax from U.S. (212) 564-7854), www.tandf.co.uk; *The Europa World Year Book.*

United Nations Statistics Division, New York, NY 10017, (800) 253-9646, Fax: (212) 963-4116, http://unstats.un.org; *World Statistics Pocketbook.*

The World Bank, 1818 H Street, NW, Washington, DC 20433, (202) 473-1000, Fax: (202) 477-6391, www.worldbank.org; *Afghanistan; Global Economic Monitor (GEM); Global Economic Prospects 2008;* and *The World Bank Atlas 2003-2004.*

AFGHANISTAN - EDUCATION

Economist Intelligence Unit, 111 West 57th Street, New York, NY 10019, (212) 554-0600, Fax: (212) 586-1181, www.eiu.com; *Business Asia.*

Euromonitor International, Inc., 224 S. Michigan Avenue, Suite 1500, Chicago, IL 60604, (312) 922-1115, Fax: (312) 922-1157, www.euromonitor.com; *International Marketing Data and Statistics 2008* and *World Marketing Data and Statistics.*

M.E. Sharpe, 80 Business Park Drive, Armonk, NY 10504, (800) 541-6563, Fax: (914) 273-2106, www.mesharpe.com; *The Illustrated Book of World Rankings.*

Palgrave Macmillan Ltd., Houndmills, Basingstoke, Hampshire, RG21 6XS, England, (Telephone in U.S. (888) 330-8477), (Fax in U.S. (800) 672-2054), www.palgrave.com; *The Statesman's Yearbook 2008.*

Taylor and Francis Group, An Informa Business, 2 Park Square, Milton Park, Abingdon, Oxford OX14 4RN, United Kingdom, (Dial from U.S. (212) 216-7800), (Fax from U.S. (212) 564-7854), www.tandf.co.uk; *The Europa World Year Book.*

UNESCO Institute for Statistics, C.P. 6128 Succursale Centre-Ville, Montreal, Quebec, H3C 3J7 Canada, (Dial from U.S. (514) 343-6880), (Fax from U.S. (514) 343 6882), www.uis.unesco.org; *Statistical Tables.*

United Nations Statistics Division, New York, NY 10017, (800) 253-9646, Fax: (212) 963-4116, http://unstats.un.org; *Asia-Pacific in Figures 2004* and *Statistical Yearbook for Asia and the Pacific 2004.*

The World Bank, 1818 H Street, NW, Washington, DC 20433, (202) 473-1000, Fax: (202) 477-6391, www.worldbank.org; *Afghanistan.*

AFGHANISTAN - ELECTRICITY

Asian Development Bank (ADB), PO Box 789, 0980 Manila, Philippines, www.adb.org; *Key Indicators of Developing Asian and Pacific Countries 2006.*

M.E. Sharpe, 80 Business Park Drive, Armonk, NY 10504, (800) 541-6563, Fax: (914) 273-2106, www.mesharpe.com; *The Illustrated Book of World Rankings.*

Palgrave Macmillan Ltd., Houndmills, Basingstoke, Hampshire, RG21 6XS, England, (Telephone in U.S. (888) 330-8477), (Fax in U.S. (800) 672-2054), www.palgrave.com; *The Statesman's Yearbook 2008.*

United Nations Statistics Division, New York, NY 10017, (800) 253-9646, Fax: (212) 963-4116, http://unstats.un.org; *Electric Power in Asia and the Pacific 2001 and 2002* and *Statistical Yearbook.*

AFGHANISTAN - EMPLOYMENT

Euromonitor International, Inc., 224 S. Michigan Avenue, Suite 1500, Chicago, IL 60604, (312) 922-1115, Fax: (312) 922-1157, www.euromonitor.com; *International Marketing Data and Statistics 2008.*

International Labour Office, I.L.O. Publications, 4 route des Morillons, CH-1211 Geneva 22, Switzerland, (Telephone in U.S. (202) 653-7652), (Fax in U.S. (202) 653-7687), www.ilo.org; *Yearbook of Labour Statistics 2006.*

M.E. Sharpe, 80 Business Park Drive, Armonk, NY 10504, (800) 541-6563, Fax: (914) 273-2106, www.mesharpe.com; *The Illustrated Book of World Rankings.*

United Nations Statistics Division, New York, NY 10017, (800) 253-9646, Fax: (212) 963-4116, http://unstats.un.org; *Asia-Pacific in Figures 2004.*

The World Bank, 1818 H Street, NW, Washington, DC 20433, (202) 473-1000, Fax: (202) 477-6391, www.worldbank.org; *Afghanistan.*

AFGHANISTAN - ENERGY INDUSTRIES

Enerdata, 10 Rue Royale, 75008 Paris, France, www.enerdata.fr; *Global Energy Market Data.*

United Nations Statistics Division, New York, NY 10017, (800) 253-9646, Fax: (212) 963-4116, http://unstats.un.org; *Electric Power in Asia and the Pacific 2001 and 2002.*

AFGHANISTAN - ENVIRONMENTAL CONDITIONS

DSI Data Service Information, Xantener Strasse 51a, D-47495 Rheinberg, Germany, www.dsidata.com; *Campus Solution* and *DSI's Global Environmental Database.*

Economist Intelligence Unit, 111 West 57th Street, New York, NY 10019, (212) 554-0600, Fax: (212) 586-1181, www.eiu.com; *Afghanistan Country Report.*

United Nations Statistics Division, New York, NY 10017, (800) 253-9646, Fax: (212) 963-4116, http://unstats.un.org; *World Statistics Pocketbook.*

AFGHANISTAN - EXPORTS

Asian Development Bank (ADB), PO Box 789, 0980 Manila, Philippines, www.adb.org; *Key Indicators of Developing Asian and Pacific Countries 2006.*

Central Intelligence Agency, Office of Public Affairs, Washington, DC 20505, (703) 482-0623, Fax: (703) 482-1739, www.cia.gov; *The World Factbook.*

Economist Intelligence Unit, 111 West 57th Street, New York, NY 10019, (212) 554-0600, Fax: (212) 586-1181, www.eiu.com; *Afghanistan Country Report.*

Euromonitor International, Inc., 224 S. Michigan Avenue, Suite 1500, Chicago, IL 60604, (312) 922-1115, Fax: (312) 922-1157, www.euromonitor.com; *International Marketing Data and Statistics 2008* and *The World Economic Factbook 2008.*

International Monetary Fund (IMF), 700 Nineteenth Street, NW, Washington, DC 20431, (202) 623-7000, Fax: (202) 623-4661, www.imf.org; *Direction of Trade Statistics Yearbook 2007* and *International Financial Statistics Yearbook 2007.*

Palgrave Macmillan Ltd., Houndmills, Basingstoke, Hampshire, RG21 6XS, England, (Telephone in U.S. (888) 330-8477), (Fax in U.S. (800) 672-2054), www.palgrave.com; *The Statesman's Yearbook 2008.*

Taylor and Francis Group, An Informa Business, 2 Park Square, Milton Park, Abingdon, Oxford OX14 4RN, United Kingdom, (Dial from U.S. (212) 216-7800), (Fax from U.S. (212) 564-7854), www.tandf.co.uk; *The Europa World Year Book.*

United Nations Conference on Trade and Development (UNCTAD), DC2-1120, United Nations, New York, NY 10017, (212) 963-0027, www.unctad.org; *Handbook of Statistics 2005.*

United Nations Food and Agricultural Organization (FAO), Viale delle Terme di Caracalla, 00100 Rome, Italy, (Dial from U.S. (202) 653-2400), (Fax from U.S. (202) 653 5760), www.fao.org; *The State of Food and Agriculture (SOFA) 2006.*

United Nations Statistics Division, New York, NY 10017, (800) 253-9646, Fax: (212) 963-4116, http://unstats.un.org; *Statistical Yearbook.*

Worldinformation.com, 2 Market Street, Saffron Walden, Essex CB10 1HZ, United Kingdom, www.worldinformation.com; The World of Information (www.worldinformation.com).

AFGHANISTAN - FEMALE WORKING POPULATION

See AFGHANISTAN - EMPLOYMENT

AFGHANISTAN - FERTILITY, HUMAN

M.E. Sharpe, 80 Business Park Drive, Armonk, NY 10504, (800) 541-6563, Fax: (914) 273-2106, www.mesharpe.com; *The Illustrated Book of World Rankings.*

United Nations Statistics Division, New York, NY 10017, (800) 253-9646, Fax: (212) 963-4116, http://unstats.un.org; *Demographic Yearbook.*

The World Bank, 1818 H Street, NW, Washington, DC 20433, (202) 473-1000, Fax: (202) 477-6391, www.worldbank.org; *The World Bank Atlas 2003-2004.*

AFGHANISTAN - FERTILIZER INDUSTRY

United Nations Food and Agricultural Organization (FAO), Viale delle Terme di Caracalla, 00100 Rome, Italy, (Dial from U.S. (202) 653-2400), (Fax from U.S. (202) 653 5760), www.fao.org; *FAO Fertilizer Yearbook* and *The State of Food and Agriculture (SOFA) 2006.*

United Nations Statistics Division, New York, NY 10017, (800) 253-9646, Fax: (212) 963-4116, http://unstats.un.org; *Statistical Yearbook.*

AFGHANISTAN - FETAL MORTALITY

See AFGHANISTAN - MORTALITY

AFGHANISTAN - FILM

See AFGHANISTAN - MOTION PICTURES

AFGHANISTAN - FINANCE

International Monetary Fund (IMF), 700 Nineteenth Street, NW, Washington, DC 20431, (202) 623-7000, Fax: (202) 623-4661, www.imf.org; *International Financial Statistics Yearbook 2007.*

Taylor and Francis Group, An Informa Business, 2 Park Square, Milton Park, Abingdon, Oxford OX14 4RN, United Kingdom, (Dial from U.S. (212) 216-7800), (Fax from U.S. (212) 564-7854), www.tandf.co.uk; *The Europa World Year Book.*

United Nations Statistics Division, New York, NY 10017, (800) 253-9646, Fax: (212) 963-4116, http://unstats.un.org; *Asia-Pacific in Figures 2004; National Accounts Statistics: Compendium of Income Distribution Statistics; Statistical Yearbook;* and *Statistical Yearbook for Asia and the Pacific 2004.*

The World Bank, 1818 H Street, NW, Washington, DC 20433, (202) 473-1000, Fax: (202) 477-6391, www.worldbank.org; *Afghanistan.*

AFGHANISTAN - FINANCE, PUBLIC

Asian Development Bank (ADB), PO Box 789, 0980 Manila, Philippines, www.adb.org; *Key Indicators of Developing Asian and Pacific Countries 2006.*

Bernan Essential Government Publications, 4611-F Assembly Drive, Lanham MD, 20706-4391, (301) 459-2255, Fax: (800) 865-3450, www.bernan.com; *National Accounts Statistics.*

Economist Intelligence Unit, 111 West 57th Street, New York, NY 10019, (212) 554-0600, Fax: (212) 586-1181, www.eiu.com; *Afghanistan Country Report.*

International Monetary Fund (IMF), 700 Nineteenth Street, NW, Washington, DC 20431, (202) 623-7000, Fax: (202) 623-4661, www.imf.org; *International Financial Statistics; International Financial Statistics Online Service;* and *International Financial Statistics Yearbook 2007.*

M.E. Sharpe, 80 Business Park Drive, Armonk, NY 10504, (800) 541-6563, Fax: (914) 273-2106, www.mesharpe.com; *The Illustrated Book of World Rankings.*

Palgrave Macmillan Ltd., Houndmills, Basingstoke, Hampshire, RG21 6XS, England, (Telephone in U.S. (888) 330-8477), (Fax in U.S. (800) 672-2054), www.palgrave.com; *The Statesman's Yearbook 2008.*

Taylor and Francis Group, An Informa Business, 2 Park Square, Milton Park, Abingdon, Oxford OX14 4RN, United Kingdom, (Dial from U.S. (212) 216-7800), (Fax from U.S. (212) 564-7854), www.tandf.co.uk; *The Europa World Year Book.*

United Nations Statistics Division, New York, NY 10017, (800) 253-9646, Fax: (212) 963-4116, http://unstats.un.org; *Statistical Yearbook for Asia and the Pacific 2004.*

The World Bank, 1818 H Street, NW, Washington, DC 20433, (202) 473-1000, Fax: (202) 477-6391, www.worldbank.org; *Afghanistan.*

AFGHANISTAN - FISHERIES

M.E. Sharpe, 80 Business Park Drive, Armonk, NY 10504, (800) 541-6563, Fax: (914) 273-2106, www.mesharpe.com; *The Illustrated Book of World Rankings.*

Taylor and Francis Group, An Informa Business, 2 Park Square, Milton Park, Abingdon, Oxford OX14 4RN, United Kingdom, (Dial from U.S. (212) 216-7800), (Fax from U.S. (212) 564-7854), www.tandf.co.uk; *The Europa World Year Book.*

United Nations Conference on Trade and Development (UNCTAD), DC2-1120, United Nations, New York, NY 10017, (212) 963-0027, www.unctad.org; *UNCTAD Commodity Yearbook.*

United Nations Food and Agricultural Organization (FAO), Viale delle Terme di Caracalla, 00100 Rome, Italy, (Dial from U.S. (202) 653-2400), (Fax from U.S. (202) 653 5760), www.fao.org; *FAO Yearbook of Fishery Statistics;* Fishery Databases; FISHSTAT Database. Subjects covered include: Aquaculture production, capture production, fishery commodities; and *The State of Food and Agriculture (SOFA) 2006.*

United Nations Statistics Division, New York, NY 10017, (800) 253-9646, Fax: (212) 963-4116, http://unstats.un.org; *Statistical Yearbook.*

The World Bank, 1818 H Street, NW, Washington, DC 20433, (202) 473-1000, Fax: (202) 477-6391, www.worldbank.org; *Afghanistan.*

AFGHANISTAN - FOOD

United Nations Conference on Trade and Development (UNCTAD), DC2-1120, United Nations, New York, NY 10017, (212) 963-0027, www.unctad.org; *UNCTAD Commodity Yearbook.*

United Nations Food and Agricultural Organization (FAO), Viale delle Terme di Caracalla, 00100 Rome, Italy, (Dial from U.S. (202) 653-2400), (Fax from U.S. (202) 653 5760), www.fao.org; *FAO Production Yearbook 2002* and *The State of Food and Agriculture (SOFA) 2006.*

United Nations Statistics Division, New York, NY 10017, (800) 253-9646, Fax: (212) 963-4116, http://unstats.un.org; *Statistical Yearbook for Asia and the Pacific 2004.*

AFGHANISTAN - FOREIGN EXCHANGE RATES

Asian Development Bank (ADB), PO Box 789, 0980 Manila, Philippines, www.adb.org; *Key Indicators of Developing Asian and Pacific Countries 2006.*

Central Intelligence Agency, Office of Public Affairs, Washington, DC 20505, (703) 482-0623, Fax: (703) 482-1739, www.cia.gov; *The World Factbook.*

Economist Intelligence Unit, 111 West 57th Street, New York, NY 10019, (212) 554-0600, Fax: (212) 586-1181, www.eiu.com; *Business Asia.*

Euromonitor International, Inc., 224 S. Michigan Avenue, Suite 1500, Chicago, IL 60604, (312) 922-1115, Fax: (312) 922-1157, www.euromonitor.com; *International Marketing Data and Statistics 2008* and *The World Economic Factbook 2008.*

International Civil Aviation Organization (ICAO), External Relations and Public Information Office (EPO), 999 University Street, Montreal, Quebec H3C 5H7, Canada, (Dial from U.S. (514) 954-8219), (Fax from U.S. (514) 954-6077), www.icao.int; *Civil Aviation Statistics of the World.*

International Monetary Fund (IMF), 700 Nineteenth Street, NW, Washington, DC 20431, (202) 623-7000, Fax: (202) 623-4661, www.imf.org; *International Financial Statistics Yearbook 2007.*

Taylor and Francis Group, An Informa Business, 2 Park Square, Milton Park, Abingdon, Oxford OX14 4RN, United Kingdom, (Dial from U.S. (212) 216-7800), (Fax from U.S. (212) 564-7854), www.tandf.co.uk; *The Europa World Year Book.*

United Nations Statistics Division, New York, NY 10017, (800) 253-9646, Fax: (212) 963-4116, http://unstats.un.org; *Statistical Yearbook* and *World Statistics Pocketbook.*

Worldinformation.com, 2 Market Street, Saffron Walden, Essex CB10 1HZ, United Kingdom, www.worldinformation.com; The World of Information (www.worldinformation.com).

AFGHANISTAN - FORESTS AND FORESTRY

Economist Intelligence Unit, 111 West 57th Street, New York, NY 10019, (212) 554-0600, Fax: (212) 586-1181, www.eiu.com; *Business Asia.*

M.E. Sharpe, 80 Business Park Drive, Armonk, NY 10504, (800) 541-6563, Fax: (914) 273-2106, www.mesharpe.com; *The Illustrated Book of World Rankings.*

Palgrave Macmillan Ltd., Houndmills, Basingstoke, Hampshire, RG21 6XS, England, (Telephone in U.S. (888) 330-8477), (Fax in U.S. (800) 672-2054), www.palgrave.com; *The Statesman's Yearbook 2008.*

Taylor and Francis Group, An Informa Business, 2 Park Square, Milton Park, Abingdon, Oxford OX14 4RN, United Kingdom, (Dial from U.S. (212) 216-7800), (Fax from U.S. (212) 564-7854), www.tandf.co.uk; *The Europa World Year Book.*

UNESCO Institute for Statistics, C.P. 6128 Succursale Centre-Ville, Montreal, Quebec, H3C 3J7 Canada, (Dial from U.S. (514) 343-6880), (Fax from U.S. (514) 343 6882), www.uis.unesco.org; *Statistical Tables.*

United Nations Conference on Trade and Development (UNCTAD), DC2-1120, United Nations, New York, NY 10017, (212) 963-0027, www.unctad.org; *UNCTAD Commodity Yearbook.*

United Nations Food and Agricultural Organization (FAO), Viale delle Terme di Caracalla, 00100 Rome, Italy, (Dial from U.S. (202) 653-2400), (Fax from U.S. (202) 653 5760), www.fao.org; *FAO Yearbook of Forest Products* and *The State of Food and Agriculture (SOFA) 2006.*

United Nations Statistics Division, New York, NY 10017, (800) 253-9646, Fax: (212) 963-4116, http://unstats.un.org; *Statistical Yearbook.*

The World Bank, 1818 H Street, NW, Washington, DC 20433, (202) 473-1000, Fax: (202) 477-6391, www.worldbank.org; *Afghanistan.*

AFGHANISTAN - FRUIT PRODUCTION

See AFGHANISTAN - CROPS

AFGHANISTAN - GAS PRODUCTION

See AFGHANISTAN - MINERAL INDUSTRIES

AFGHANISTAN - GEOGRAPHIC INFORMATION SYSTEMS

M.E. Sharpe, 80 Business Park Drive, Armonk, NY 10504, (800) 541-6563, Fax: (914) 273-2106, www.mesharpe.com; *The Illustrated Book of World Rankings.*

The World Bank, 1818 H Street, NW, Washington, DC 20433, (202) 473-1000, Fax: (202) 477-6391, www.worldbank.org; *Afghanistan.*

AFGHANISTAN - GOLD INDUSTRY

International Monetary Fund (IMF), 700 Nineteenth Street, NW, Washington, DC 20431, (202) 623-7000, Fax: (202) 623-4661, www.imf.org; *International Financial Statistics Yearbook 2007.*

United Nations Statistics Division, New York, NY 10017, (800) 253-9646, Fax: (212) 963-4116, http://unstats.un.org; *Statistical Yearbook.*

AFGHANISTAN - GOLD PRODUCTION

See AFGHANISTAN - MINERAL INDUSTRIES

AFGHANISTAN - GROSS DOMESTIC PRODUCT

Asian Development Bank (ADB), PO Box 789, 0980 Manila, Philippines, www.adb.org; *Key Indicators of Developing Asian and Pacific Countries 2006.*

Economist Intelligence Unit, 111 West 57th Street, New York, NY 10019, (212) 554-0600, Fax: (212) 586-1181, www.eiu.com; *Afghanistan Country Report* and *Business Asia.*

Euromonitor International, Inc., 224 S. Michigan Avenue, Suite 1500, Chicago, IL 60604, (312) 922-1115, Fax: (312) 922-1157, www.euromonitor.com; *International Marketing Data and Statistics 2008* and *The World Economic Factbook 2008.*

M.E. Sharpe, 80 Business Park Drive, Armonk, NY 10504, (800) 541-6563, Fax: (914) 273-2106, www.mesharpe.com; *The Illustrated Book of World Rankings.*

United Nations Statistics Division, New York, NY 10017, (800) 253-9646, Fax: (212) 963-4116, http://unstats.un.org; *National Accounts Statistics: Compendium of Income Distribution Statistics* and *Statistical Yearbook.*

AFGHANISTAN - GROSS NATIONAL PRODUCT

Asian Development Bank (ADB), PO Box 789, 0980 Manila, Philippines, www.adb.org; *Key Indicators of Developing Asian and Pacific Countries 2006.*

Euromonitor International, Inc., 224 S. Michigan Avenue, Suite 1500, Chicago, IL 60604, (312) 922-1115, Fax: (312) 922-1157, www.euromonitor.com; *International Marketing Data and Statistics 2008.*

M.E. Sharpe, 80 Business Park Drive, Armonk, NY 10504, (800) 541-6563, Fax: (914) 273-2106, www.mesharpe.com; *The Illustrated Book of World Rankings.*

Palgrave Macmillan Ltd., Houndmills, Basingstoke, Hampshire, RG21 6XS, England, (Telephone in U.S. (888) 330-8477), (Fax in U.S. (800) 672-2054), www.palgrave.com; *The Statesman's Yearbook 2008.*

U.S. Department of State (DOS), 2201 C Street NW, Washington, DC 20520, (202) 647-4000, www.state.gov; *World Military Expenditures and Arms Transfers (WMEAT).*

United Nations Statistics Division, New York, NY 10017, (800) 253-9646, Fax: (212) 963-4116, http://unstats.un.org; *Statistical Yearbook.*

The World Bank, 1818 H Street, NW, Washington, DC 20433, (202) 473-1000, Fax: (202) 477-6391, www.worldbank.org; *The World Bank Atlas 2003-2004.*

Worldinformation.com, 2 Market Street, Saffron Walden, Essex CB10 1HZ, United Kingdom, www.worldinformation.com; The World of Information (www.worldinformation.com).

AFGHANISTAN - HIDES AND SKINS INDUSTRY

International Monetary Fund (IMF), 700 Nineteenth Street, NW, Washington, DC 20431, (202) 623-7000, Fax: (202) 623-4661, www.imf.org; *International Financial Statistics Yearbook 2007.*

United Nations Food and Agricultural Organization (FAO), Viale delle Terme di Caracalla, 00100 Rome, Italy, (Dial from U.S. (202) 653-2400), (Fax from U.S. (202) 653 5760), www.fao.org; *FAO Production Yearbook 2002.*

AFGHANISTAN - HOUSING

Euromonitor International, Inc., 224 S. Michigan Avenue, Suite 1500, Chicago, IL 60604, (312) 922-1115, Fax: (312) 922-1157, www.euromonitor.com; *World Marketing Data and Statistics.*

M.E. Sharpe, 80 Business Park Drive, Armonk, NY 10504, (800) 541-6563, Fax: (914) 273-2106, www.mesharpe.com; *The Illustrated Book of World Rankings.*

AFGHANISTAN - ILLITERATE PERSONS

Euromonitor International, Inc., 224 S. Michigan Avenue, Suite 1500, Chicago, IL 60604, (312) 922-1115, Fax: (312) 922-1157, www.euromonitor.com; *The World Economic Factbook 2008.*

Palgrave Macmillan Ltd., Houndmills, Basingstoke, Hampshire, RG21 6XS, England, (Telephone in U.S. (888) 330-8477), (Fax in U.S. (800) 672-2054), www.palgrave.com; *The Statesman's Yearbook 2008.*

UNESCO Institute for Statistics, C.P. 6128 Succursale Centre-Ville, Montreal, Quebec, H3C 3J7 Canada, (Dial from U.S. (514) 343-6880), (Fax from U.S. (514) 343 6882), www.uis.unesco.org; *Statistical Tables.*

United Nations Statistics Division, New York, NY 10017, (800) 253-9646, Fax: (212) 963-4116, http://unstats.un.org; *Asia-Pacific in Figures 2004.*

AFGHANISTAN - IMPORTS

Asian Development Bank (ADB), PO Box 789, 0980 Manila, Philippines, www.adb.org; *Key Indicators of Developing Asian and Pacific Countries 2006.*

Central Intelligence Agency, Office of Public Affairs, Washington, DC 20505, (703) 482-0623, Fax: (703) 482-1739, www.cia.gov; *The World Factbook.*

Economist Intelligence Unit, 111 West 57th Street, New York, NY 10019, (212) 554-0600, Fax: (212) 586-1181, www.eiu.com; *Afghanistan Country Report.*

Euromonitor International, Inc., 224 S. Michigan Avenue, Suite 1500, Chicago, IL 60604, (312) 922-1115, Fax: (312) 922-1157, www.euromonitor.com; *International Marketing Data and Statistics 2008* and *The World Economic Factbook 2008.*

International Monetary Fund (IMF), 700 Nineteenth Street, NW, Washington, DC 20431, (202) 623-7000, Fax: (202) 623-4661, www.imf.org; *Direction of Trade Statistics Yearbook 2007* and *International Financial Statistics Yearbook 2007.*

Palgrave Macmillan Ltd., Houndmills, Basingstoke, Hampshire, RG21 6XS, England, (Telephone in U.S. (888) 330-8477), (Fax in U.S. (800) 672-2054), www.palgrave.com; *The Statesman's Yearbook 2008.*

Taylor and Francis Group, An Informa Business, 2 Park Square, Milton Park, Abingdon, Oxford OX14 4RN, United Kingdom, (Dial from U.S. (212) 216-7800), (Fax from U.S. (212) 564-7854), www.tandf.co.uk; *The Europa World Year Book.*

United Nations Conference on Trade and Development (UNCTAD), DC2-1120, United Nations, New York, NY 10017, (212) 963-0027, www.unctad.org; *Handbook of Statistics 2005.*

United Nations Food and Agricultural Organization (FAO), Viale delle Terme di Caracalla, 00100 Rome, Italy, (Dial from U.S. (202) 653-2400), (Fax from U.S. (202) 653 5760), www.fao.org; *The State of Food and Agriculture (SOFA) 2006.*

Worldinformation.com, 2 Market Street, Saffron Walden, Essex CB10 1HZ, United Kingdom, www.worldinformation.com; The World of Information (www.worldinformation.com).

AFGHANISTAN - INDUSTRIAL PRODUCTIVITY

Euromonitor International, Inc., 224 S. Michigan Avenue, Suite 1500, Chicago, IL 60604, (312) 922-1115, Fax: (312) 922-1157, www.euromonitor.com; *International Marketing Data and Statistics 2008.*

M.E. Sharpe, 80 Business Park Drive, Armonk, NY 10504, (800) 541-6563, Fax: (914) 273-2106, www.mesharpe.com; *The Illustrated Book of World Rankings.*

AFGHANISTAN - INDUSTRIES

Central Intelligence Agency, Office of Public Affairs, Washington, DC 20505, (703) 482-0623, Fax: (703) 482-1739, www.cia.gov; *The World Factbook.*

Economist Intelligence Unit, 111 West 57th Street, New York, NY 10019, (212) 554-0600, Fax: (212) 586-1181, www.eiu.com; *Afghanistan Country Report.*

Euromonitor International, Inc., 224 S. Michigan Avenue, Suite 1500, Chicago, IL 60604, (312) 922-1115, Fax: (312) 922-1157, www.euromonitor.com; *International Marketing Data and Statistics 2008; The World Economic Factbook 2008;* and *World Marketing Data and Statistics.*

International Labour Office, I.L.O. Publications, 4 route des Morillons, CH-1211 Geneva 22, Switzerland, (Telephone in U.S. (202) 653-7652), (Fax in U.S. (202) 653-7687), www.ilo.org; *Yearbook of Labour Statistics 2006.*

M.E. Sharpe, 80 Business Park Drive, Armonk, NY 10504, (800) 541-6563, Fax: (914) 273-2106, www.mesharpe.com; *The Illustrated Book of World Rankings.*

Palgrave Macmillan Ltd., Houndmills, Basingstoke, Hampshire, RG21 6XS, England, (Telephone in U.S. (888) 330-8477), (Fax in U.S. (800) 672-2054), www.palgrave.com; *The Statesman's Yearbook 2008.*

Taylor and Francis Group, An Informa Business, 2 Park Square, Milton Park, Abingdon, Oxford OX14 4RN, United Kingdom, (Dial from U.S. (212) 216-7800), (Fax from U.S. (212) 564-7854), www.tandf.co.uk; *The Europa World Year Book.*

United Nations Industrial Development Organization (UNIDO), 1 United Nations Plaza, New York, NY 10017, (212) 963 6890, Fax: (212) 963-7904, http://unido.org; Industrial Statistics Database 2008 (INDSTAT) and *The International Yearbook of Industrial Statistics 2008.*

United Nations Statistics Division, New York, NY 10017, (800) 253-9646, Fax: (212) 963-4116, http://unstats.un.org; *Asia-Pacific in Figures 2004; 2004 Industrial Commodity Statistics Yearbook;* and *Statistical Yearbook for Asia and the Pacific 2004.*

AFGHANISTAN - INFANT AND MATERNAL MORTALITY

See AFGHANISTAN - MORTALITY

AFGHANISTAN - INTERNATIONAL FINANCE

Asian Development Bank (ADB), PO Box 789, 0980 Manila, Philippines, www.adb.org; *Key Indicators of Developing Asian and Pacific Countries 2006.*

AFGHANISTAN - INTERNATIONAL LIQUIDITY

International Monetary Fund (IMF), 700 Nineteenth Street, NW, Washington, DC 20431, (202) 623-7000, Fax: (202) 623-4661, www.imf.org; *International Financial Statistics Yearbook 2007.*

AFGHANISTAN - INTERNATIONAL STATISTICS

Asian Development Bank (ADB), PO Box 789, 0980 Manila, Philippines, www.adb.org; *Key Indicators of Developing Asian and Pacific Countries 2006.*

AFGHANISTAN - INTERNATIONAL TRADE

Asian Development Bank (ADB), PO Box 789, 0980 Manila, Philippines, www.adb.org; *Key Indicators of Developing Asian and Pacific Countries 2006.*

Central Statistics Office (CSO), Ansar-i-Watt, Kabul, Afghanistan, www.cso.gov.af; *Exports and Imports by Country, 1995-2002.*

Economist Intelligence Unit, 111 West 57th Street, New York, NY 10019, (212) 554-0600, Fax: (212) 586-1181, www.eiu.com; *Afghanistan Country Report* and *Business Asia.*

Euromonitor International, Inc., 224 S. Michigan Avenue, Suite 1500, Chicago, IL 60604, (312) 922-1115, Fax: (312) 922-1157, www.euromonitor.com; *International Marketing Data and Statistics 2008; The World Economic Factbook 2008;* and *World Marketing Data and Statistics.*

M.E. Sharpe, 80 Business Park Drive, Armonk, NY 10504, (800) 541-6563, Fax: (914) 273-2106, www.mesharpe.com; *The Illustrated Book of World Rankings.*

Organisation for Economic Cooperation and Development (OECD), 2 rue Andre Pascal, F-75775 Paris Cedex 16, France, (Telephone in U.S. (202) 785-6323), (Fax in U.S. (202) 785-0350), www.oecd.org; *International Trade by Commodity Statistics (ITCS).*

Palgrave Macmillan Ltd., Houndmills, Basingstoke, Hampshire, RG21 6XS, England, (Telephone in U.S. (888) 330-8477), (Fax in U.S. (800) 672-2054), www.palgrave.com; *The Statesman's Yearbook 2008.*

Taylor and Francis Group, An Informa Business, 2 Park Square, Milton Park, Abingdon, Oxford OX14 4RN, United Kingdom, (Dial from U.S. (212) 216-7800), (Fax from U.S. (212) 564-7854), www.tandf.co.uk; *The Europa World Year Book.*

United Nations Conference on Trade and Development (UNCTAD), DC2-1120, United Nations, New York, NY 10017, (212) 963-0027, www.unctad.org; *UNCTAD Commodity Yearbook.*

United Nations Food and Agricultural Organization (FAO), Viale delle Terme di Caracalla, 00100 Rome, Italy, (Dial from U.S. (202) 653-2400), (Fax from U.S. (202) 653 5760), www.fao.org; *FAO Trade Yearbook* and *The State of Food and Agriculture (SOFA) 2006.*

United Nations Statistics Division, New York, NY 10017, (800) 253-9646, Fax: (212) 963-4116, http://

unstats.un.org; *Asia-Pacific in Figures 2004; International Trade Statistics Yearbook; Statistical Yearbook;* and *Statistical Yearbook for Asia and the Pacific 2004.*

The World Bank, 1818 H Street, NW, Washington, DC 20433, (202) 473-1000, Fax: (202) 477-6391, www.worldbank.org; *Afghanistan.*

World Trade Organization (WTO), Centre William Rappard, Rue de Lausanne 154, CH-1211 Geneva 21, Switzerland, www.wto.org; *International Trade Statistics 2006.*

AFGHANISTAN - INTERNET USERS

International Telecommunication Union (ITU), Place des Nations, 1211 Geneva 20, Switzerland, www.itu.int; *World Telecommunication/ICT Indicators Database on CD-ROM; World Telecommunication/ICT Indicators Database Online;* and *Yearbook of Statistics - Telecommunication Services (Chronological Time Series 1997-2006).*

The World Bank, 1818 H Street, NW, Washington, DC 20433, (202) 473-1000, Fax: (202) 477-6391, www.worldbank.org; *Afghanistan.*

AFGHANISTAN - INVESTMENTS

International Monetary Fund (IMF), 700 Nineteenth Street, NW, Washington, DC 20431, (202) 623-7000, Fax: (202) 623-4661, www.imf.org; *International Financial Statistics Yearbook 2007.*

AFGHANISTAN - IRON AND IRON ORE PRODUCTION

See AFGHANISTAN - MINERAL INDUSTRIES

AFGHANISTAN - IRRIGATION

Euromonitor International, Inc., 224 S. Michigan Avenue, Suite 1500, Chicago, IL 60604, (312) 922-1115, Fax: (312) 922-1157, www.euromonitor.com; *International Marketing Data and Statistics 2008.*

AFGHANISTAN - LABOR

Central Intelligence Agency, Office of Public Affairs, Washington, DC 20505, (703) 482-0623, Fax: (703) 482-1739, www.cia.gov; *The World Factbook.*

Economist Intelligence Unit, 111 West 57th Street, New York, NY 10019, (212) 554-0600, Fax: (212) 586-1181, www.eiu.com; *Business Asia.*

Euromonitor International, Inc., 224 S. Michigan Avenue, Suite 1500, Chicago, IL 60604, (312) 922-1115, Fax: (312) 922-1157, www.euromonitor.com; *International Marketing Data and Statistics 2008* and *World Marketing Data and Statistics.*

International Labour Office, I.L.O. Publications, 4 route des Morillons, CH-1211 Geneva 22, Switzerland, (Telephone in U.S. (202) 653-7652), (Fax in U.S. (202) 653-7687), www.ilo.org; *Yearbook of Labour Statistics 2006.*

M.E. Sharpe, 80 Business Park Drive, Armonk, NY 10504, (800) 541-6563, Fax: (914) 273-2106, www.mesharpe.com; *The Illustrated Book of World Rankings.*

Palgrave Macmillan Ltd., Houndmills, Basingstoke, Hampshire, RG21 6XS, England, (Telephone in U.S. (888) 330-8477), (Fax in U.S. (800) 672-2054), www.palgrave.com; *The Statesman's Yearbook 2008.*

Taylor and Francis Group, An Informa Business, 2 Park Square, Milton Park, Abingdon, Oxford OX14 4RN, United Kingdom, (Dial from U.S. (212) 216-7800), (Fax from U.S. (212) 564-7854), www.tandf.co.uk; *The Europa World Year Book.*

United Nations Food and Agricultural Organization (FAO), Viale delle Terme di Caracalla, 00100 Rome, Italy, (Dial from U.S. (202) 653-2400), (Fax from U.S. (202) 653 5760), www.fao.org; *The State of Food and Agriculture (SOFA) 2006.*

The World Bank, 1818 H Street, NW, Washington, DC 20433, (202) 473-1000, Fax: (202) 477-6391, www.worldbank.org; *The World Bank Atlas 2003-2004.*

AFGHANISTAN - LAND USE

Central Intelligence Agency, Office of Public Affairs, Washington, DC 20505, (703) 482-0623, Fax: (703) 482-1739, www.cia.gov; *The World Factbook.*

Euromonitor International, Inc., 224 S. Michigan Avenue, Suite 1500, Chicago, IL 60604, (312) 922-1115, Fax: (312) 922-1157, www.euromonitor.com; *International Marketing Data and Statistics 2008.*

United Nations Food and Agricultural Organization (FAO), Viale delle Terme di Caracalla, 00100 Rome, Italy, (Dial from U.S. (202) 653-2400), (Fax from U.S. (202) 653 5760), www.fao.org; *FAO Production Yearbook 2002.*

AFGHANISTAN - LIBRARIES

M.E. Sharpe, 80 Business Park Drive, Armonk, NY 10504, (800) 541-6563, Fax: (914) 273-2106, www.mesharpe.com; *The Illustrated Book of World Rankings.*

AFGHANISTAN - LIFE EXPECTANCY

Economist Intelligence Unit, 111 West 57th Street, New York, NY 10019, (212) 554-0600, Fax: (212) 586-1181, www.eiu.com; *Business Asia.*

Euromonitor International, Inc., 224 S. Michigan Avenue, Suite 1500, Chicago, IL 60604, (312) 922-1115, Fax: (312) 922-1157, www.euromonitor.com; *The World Economic Factbook 2008.*

Palgrave Macmillan Ltd., Houndmills, Basingstoke, Hampshire, RG21 6XS, England, (Telephone in U.S. (888) 330-8477), (Fax in U.S. (800) 672-2054), www.palgrave.com; *The Statesman's Yearbook 2008.*

United Nations Statistics Division, New York, NY 10017, (800) 253-9646, Fax: (212) 963-4116, http://unstats.un.org; *Asia-Pacific in Figures 2004* and *World Statistics Pocketbook.*

The World Bank, 1818 H Street, NW, Washington, DC 20433, (202) 473-1000, Fax: (202) 477-6391, www.worldbank.org; *The World Bank Atlas 2003-2004.*

AFGHANISTAN - LITERACY

Euromonitor International, Inc., 224 S. Michigan Avenue, Suite 1500, Chicago, IL 60604, (312) 922-1115, Fax: (312) 922-1157, www.euromonitor.com; *World Marketing Data and Statistics.*

AFGHANISTAN - LIVESTOCK

Euromonitor International, Inc., 224 S. Michigan Avenue, Suite 1500, Chicago, IL 60604, (312) 922-1115, Fax: (312) 922-1157, www.euromonitor.com; *International Marketing Data and Statistics 2008.*

M.E. Sharpe, 80 Business Park Drive, Armonk, NY 10504, (800) 541-6563, Fax: (914) 273-2106, www.mesharpe.com; *The Illustrated Book of World Rankings.*

Palgrave Macmillan Ltd., Houndmills, Basingstoke, Hampshire, RG21 6XS, England, (Telephone in U.S. (888) 330-8477), (Fax in U.S. (800) 672-2054), www.palgrave.com; *The Statesman's Yearbook 2008.*

Taylor and Francis Group, An Informa Business, 2 Park Square, Milton Park, Abingdon, Oxford OX14 4RN, United Kingdom, (Dial from U.S. (212) 216-7800), (Fax from U.S. (212) 564-7854), www.tandf.co.uk; *The Europa World Year Book.*

United Nations Conference on Trade and Development (UNCTAD), DC2-1120, United Nations, New York, NY 10017, (212) 963-0027, www.unctad.org; *UNCTAD Commodity Yearbook.*

United Nations Food and Agricultural Organization (FAO), Viale delle Terme di Caracalla, 00100 Rome, Italy, (Dial from U.S. (202) 653-2400), (Fax from U.S. (202) 653 5760), www.fao.org; *FAO Production Yearbook 2002* and *The State of Food and Agriculture (SOFA) 2006.*

United Nations Statistics Division, New York, NY 10017, (800) 253-9646, Fax: (212) 963-4116, http://unstats.un.org; *Statistical Yearbook.*

AFGHANISTAN - LOCAL TAXATION

Euromonitor International, Inc., 224 S. Michigan Avenue, Suite 1500, Chicago, IL 60604, (312) 922-1115, Fax: (312) 922-1157, www.euromonitor.com; *International Marketing Data and Statistics 2008.*

AFGHANISTAN - MANPOWER

United Nations Statistics Division, New York, NY 10017, (800) 253-9646, Fax: (212) 963-4116, http://unstats.un.org; *Statistical Yearbook for Asia and the Pacific 2004.*

AFGHANISTAN - MANUFACTURES

Asian Development Bank (ADB), PO Box 789, 0980 Manila, Philippines, www.adb.org; *Key Indicators of Developing Asian and Pacific Countries 2006.*

M.E. Sharpe, 80 Business Park Drive, Armonk, NY 10504, (800) 541-6563, Fax: (914) 273-2106, www.mesharpe.com; *The Illustrated Book of World Rankings.*

United Nations Statistics Division, New York, NY 10017, (800) 253-9646, Fax: (212) 963-4116, http://unstats.un.org; *Statistical Yearbook.*

AFGHANISTAN - MARRIAGE

M.E. Sharpe, 80 Business Park Drive, Armonk, NY 10504, (800) 541-6563, Fax: (914) 273-2106, www.mesharpe.com; *The Illustrated Book of World Rankings.*

United Nations Statistics Division, New York, NY 10017, (800) 253-9646, Fax: (212) 963-4116, http://unstats.un.org; *Demographic Yearbook.*

AFGHANISTAN - MEAT PRODUCTION

See AFGHANISTAN - LIVESTOCK

AFGHANISTAN - MILK PRODUCTION

See AFGHANISTAN - DAIRY PROCESSING

AFGHANISTAN - MINERAL INDUSTRIES

Asian Development Bank (ADB), PO Box 789, 0980 Manila, Philippines, www.adb.org; *Key Indicators of Developing Asian and Pacific Countries 2006.*

International Monetary Fund (IMF), 700 Nineteenth Street, NW, Washington, DC 20431, (202) 623-7000, Fax: (202) 623-4661, www.imf.org; *International Financial Statistics Yearbook 2007.*

M.E. Sharpe, 80 Business Park Drive, Armonk, NY 10504, (800) 541-6563, Fax: (914) 273-2106, www.mesharpe.com; *The Illustrated Book of World Rankings.*

Palgrave Macmillan Ltd., Houndmills, Basingstoke, Hampshire, RG21 6XS, England, (Telephone in U.S. (888) 330-8477), (Fax in U.S. (800) 672-2054), www.palgrave.com; *The Statesman's Yearbook 2008.*

Taylor and Francis Group, An Informa Business, 2 Park Square, Milton Park, Abingdon, Oxford OX14 4RN, United Kingdom, (Dial from U.S. (212) 216-7800), (Fax from U.S. (212) 564-7854), www.tandf.co.uk; *The Europa World Year Book.*

United Nations Conference on Trade and Development (UNCTAD), DC2-1120, United Nations, New York, NY 10017, (212) 963-0027, www.unctad.org; *UNCTAD Commodity Yearbook.*

United Nations Statistics Division, New York, NY 10017, (800) 253-9646, Fax: (212) 963-4116, http://unstats.un.org; *Statistical Yearbook.*

AFGHANISTAN - MONEY EXCHANGE RATES

See AFGHANISTAN - FOREIGN EXCHANGE RATES

AFGHANISTAN - MONEY SUPPLY

Asian Development Bank (ADB), PO Box 789, 0980 Manila, Philippines, www.adb.org; *Key Indicators of Developing Asian and Pacific Countries 2006.*

Economist Intelligence Unit, 111 West 57th Street, New York, NY 10019, (212) 554-0600, Fax: (212) 586-1181, www.eiu.com; *Afghanistan Country Report.*

Euromonitor International, Inc., 224 S. Michigan Avenue, Suite 1500, Chicago, IL 60604, (312) 922-1115, Fax: (312) 922-1157, www.euromonitor.com; *International Marketing Data and Statistics 2008.*

International Monetary Fund (IMF), 700 Nineteenth Street, NW, Washington, DC 20431, (202) 623-7000, Fax: (202) 623-4661, www.imf.org; *International Financial Statistics Yearbook 2007.*

Taylor and Francis Group, An Informa Business, 2 Park Square, Milton Park, Abingdon, Oxford OX14 4RN, United Kingdom, (Dial from U.S. (212) 216-7800), (Fax from U.S. (212) 564-7854), www.tandf.co.uk; *The Europa World Year Book.*

United Nations Statistics Division, New York, NY 10017, (800) 253-9646, Fax: (212) 963-4116, http://unstats.un.org; *Statistical Yearbook.*

The World Bank, 1818 H Street, NW, Washington, DC 20433, (202) 473-1000, Fax: (202) 477-6391, www.worldbank.org; *Afghanistan.*

AFGHANISTAN - MORTALITY

Central Intelligence Agency, Office of Public Affairs, Washington, DC 20505, (703) 482-0623, Fax: (703) 482-1739, www.cia.gov; *The World Factbook.*

Euromonitor International, Inc., 224 S. Michigan Avenue, Suite 1500, Chicago, IL 60604, (312) 922-1115, Fax: (312) 922-1157, www.euromonitor.com; *The World Economic Factbook 2008.*

Palgrave Macmillan Ltd., Houndmills, Basingstoke, Hampshire, RG21 6XS, England, (Telephone in U.S. (888) 330-8477), (Fax in U.S. (800) 672-2054), www.palgrave.com; *The Statesman's Yearbook 2008.*

Taylor and Francis Group, An Informa Business, 2 Park Square, Milton Park, Abingdon, Oxford OX14 4RN, United Kingdom, (Dial from U.S. (212) 216-7800), (Fax from U.S. (212) 564-7854), www.tandf.co.uk; *The Europa World Year Book.*

UNICEF, 3 United Nations Plaza, New York, NY 10017, (800) 253-9646, Fax: (212) 887-7465, www.unicef.org; *The State of the World's Children 2008.*

United Nations Statistics Division, New York, NY 10017, (800) 253-9646, Fax: (212) 963-4116, http://unstats.un.org; *Asia-Pacific in Figures 2004; Demographic Yearbook;* and *World Statistics Pocketbook.*

The World Bank, 1818 H Street, NW, Washington, DC 20433, (202) 473-1000, Fax: (202) 477-6391, www.worldbank.org; *The World Bank Atlas 2003-2004.*

World Health Organization (WHO), Avenue Appia 20, 1211 Geneve 27, Switzerland, (Telephone in U.S. (212) 331-9081), www.who.int; The WHO Global Atlas of Infectious Diseases and *World Health Report 2006.*

AFGHANISTAN - MOTION PICTURES

UNESCO Institute for Statistics, C.P. 6128 Succursale Centre-Ville, Montreal, Quebec, H3C 3J7 Canada, (Dial from U.S. (514) 343-6880), (Fax from U.S. (514) 343 6882), www.uis.unesco.org; *Statistical Tables.*

United Nations Statistics Division, New York, NY 10017, (800) 253-9646, Fax: (212) 963-4116, http://unstats.un.org; *Statistical Yearbook.*

AFGHANISTAN - MOTOR VEHICLES

International Road Federation (IFR), Madison Place, 500 Montgomery Street, 5th Floor, Alexandria, VA 22314, (703) 535-1001, Fax: (703) 535-1007, www.irfnet.org; *World Road Statistics 2006.*

Taylor and Francis Group, An Informa Business, 2 Park Square, Milton Park, Abingdon, Oxford OX14 4RN, United Kingdom, (Dial from U.S. (212) 216-7800), (Fax from U.S. (212) 564-7854), www.tandf.co.uk; *The Europa World Year Book.*

United Nations Statistics Division, New York, NY 10017, (800) 253-9646, Fax: (212) 963-4116, http://unstats.un.org; *Statistical Yearbook.*

AFGHANISTAN - MUSEUMS

M.E. Sharpe, 80 Business Park Drive, Armonk, NY 10504, (800) 541-6563, Fax: (914) 273-2106, www.mesharpe.com; *The Illustrated Book of World Rankings.*

UNESCO Institute for Statistics, C.P. 6128 Succursale Centre-Ville, Montreal, Quebec, H3C 3J7 Canada, (Dial from U.S. (514) 343-6880), (Fax from U.S. (514) 343 6882), www.uis.unesco.org; *Statistical Tables.*

AFGHANISTAN - NATIONAL INCOME

United Nations Statistics Division, New York, NY 10017, (800) 253-9646, Fax: (212) 963-4116, http://unstats.un.org; *Statistical Yearbook.*

AFGHANISTAN - NATURAL GAS PRODUCTION

See AFGHANISTAN - MINERAL INDUSTRIES

AFGHANISTAN - NUPTIALITY

See AFGHANISTAN - MARRIAGE

AFGHANISTAN - NUTRITION

Asian Development Bank (ADB), PO Box 789, 0980 Manila, Philippines, www.adb.org; *Key Indicators of Developing Asian and Pacific Countries 2006.*

United Nations Food and Agricultural Organization (FAO), Viale delle Terme di Caracalla, 00100 Rome, Italy, (Dial from U.S. (202) 653-2400), (Fax from U.S. (202) 653 5760), www.fao.org; *The State of Food and Agriculture (SOFA) 2006.*

AFGHANISTAN - OLDER PEOPLE

M.E. Sharpe, 80 Business Park Drive, Armonk, NY 10504, (800) 541-6563, Fax: (914) 273-2106, www.mesharpe.com; *The Illustrated Book of World Rankings.*

AFGHANISTAN - PAPER

See AFGHANISTAN - FORESTS AND FORESTRY

AFGHANISTAN - PEANUT PRODUCTION

See AFGHANISTAN - CROPS

AFGHANISTAN - PERIODICALS

UNESCO Institute for Statistics, C.P. 6128 Succursale Centre-Ville, Montreal, Quebec, H3C 3J7 Canada, (Dial from U.S. (514) 343-6880), (Fax from U.S. (514) 343 6882), www.uis.unesco.org; *Statistical Tables.*

AFGHANISTAN - PESTICIDES

United Nations Food and Agricultural Organization (FAO), Viale delle Terme di Caracalla, 00100 Rome, Italy, (Dial from U.S. (202) 653-2400), (Fax from U.S. (202) 653 5760), www.fao.org; *The State of Food and Agriculture (SOFA) 2006.*

AFGHANISTAN - PETROLEUM INDUSTRY AND TRADE

Asian Development Bank (ADB), PO Box 789, 0980 Manila, Philippines, www.adb.org; *Key Indicators of Developing Asian and Pacific Countries 2006.*

M.E. Sharpe, 80 Business Park Drive, Armonk, NY 10504, (800) 541-6563, Fax: (914) 273-2106, www.mesharpe.com; *The Illustrated Book of World Rankings.*

PennWell Corporation, 1421 South Sheridan Road, Tulsa, OK 74112, (918) 835-3161, www.pennwell.com; *International Petroleum Encyclopedia 2007.*

United Nations Conference on Trade and Development (UNCTAD), DC2-1120, United Nations, New York, NY 10017, (212) 963-0027, www.unctad.org; *UNCTAD Commodity Yearbook.*

AFGHANISTAN - POLITICAL SCIENCE

Asian Development Bank (ADB), PO Box 789, 0980 Manila, Philippines, www.adb.org; *Key Indicators of Developing Asian and Pacific Countries 2006.*

Central Intelligence Agency, Office of Public Affairs, Washington, DC 20505, (703) 482-0623, Fax: (703) 482-1739, www.cia.gov; *The World Factbook.*

Palgrave Macmillan Ltd., Houndmills, Basingstoke, Hampshire, RG21 6XS, England, (Telephone in U.S. (888) 330-8477), (Fax in U.S. (800) 672-2054), www.palgrave.com; *The Statesman's Yearbook 2008.*

Taylor and Francis Group, An Informa Business, 2 Park Square, Milton Park, Abingdon, Oxford OX14 4RN, United Kingdom, (Dial from U.S. (212) 216-7800), (Fax from U.S. (212) 564-7854), www.tandf.co.uk; *The Europa World Year Book.*

United Nations Statistics Division, New York, NY 10017, (800) 253-9646, Fax: (212) 963-4116, http://unstats.un.org; *Asia-Pacific in Figures 2004* and *National Accounts Statistics: Compendium of Income Distribution Statistics.*

AFGHANISTAN - POPULATION

Asian Development Bank (ADB), PO Box 789, 0980 Manila, Philippines, www.adb.org; *Key Indicators of Developing Asian and Pacific Countries 2006.*

Central Intelligence Agency, Office of Public Affairs, Washington, DC 20505, (703) 482-0623, Fax: (703) 482-1739, www.cia.gov; *The World Factbook.*

Economist Intelligence Unit, 111 West 57th Street, New York, NY 10019, (212) 554-0600, Fax: (212) 586-1181, www.eiu.com; *Afghanistan Country Report* and *Business Asia.*

Euromonitor International, Inc., 224 S. Michigan Avenue, Suite 1500, Chicago, IL 60604, (312) 922-1115, Fax: (312) 922-1157, www.euromonitor.com; *International Marketing Data and Statistics 2008.*

International Labour Office, I.L.O. Publications, 4 route des Morillons, CH-1211 Geneva 22, Switzerland, (Telephone in U.S. (202) 653-7652), (Fax in U.S. (202) 653-7687), www.ilo.org; *Yearbook of Labour Statistics 2006.*

M.E. Sharpe, 80 Business Park Drive, Armonk, NY 10504, (800) 541-6563, Fax: (914) 273-2106, www.mesharpe.com; *The Illustrated Book of World Rankings.*

Palgrave Macmillan Ltd., Houndmills, Basingstoke, Hampshire, RG21 6XS, England, (Telephone in U.S. (888) 330-8477), (Fax in U.S. (800) 672-2054), www.palgrave.com; *The Statesman's Yearbook 2008.*

Taylor and Francis Group, An Informa Business, 2 Park Square, Milton Park, Abingdon, Oxford OX14 4RN, United Kingdom, (Dial from U.S. (212) 216-7800), (Fax from U.S. (212) 564-7854), www.tandf.co.uk; *The Europa World Year Book.*

U.S. Department of State (DOS), 2201 C Street NW, Washington, DC 20520, (202) 647-4000, www.state.gov; *World Military Expenditures and Arms Transfers (WMEAT).*

United Nations Food and Agricultural Organization (FAO), Viale delle Terme di Caracalla, 00100 Rome, Italy, (Dial from U.S. (202) 653-2400), (Fax from U.S. (202) 653 5760), www.fao.org; *FAO Production Yearbook 2002.*

United Nations Statistics Division, New York, NY 10017, (800) 253-9646, Fax: (212) 963-4116, http://unstats.un.org; *Asia-Pacific in Figures 2004; Demographic Yearbook; Statistical Yearbook; Statistical Yearbook for Asia and the Pacific 2004;* and *World Statistics Pocketbook.*

The World Bank, 1818 H Street, NW, Washington, DC 20433, (202) 473-1000, Fax: (202) 477-6391, www.worldbank.org; *Afghanistan* and *The World Bank Atlas 2003-2004.*

World Health Organization (WHO), Avenue Appia 20, 1211 Geneve 27, Switzerland, (Telephone in U.S. (212) 331-9081), www.who.int; *World Health Report 2006.*

Worldinformation.com, 2 Market Street, Saffron Walden, Essex CB10 1HZ, United Kingdom, www.worldinformation.com; The World of Information (www.worldinformation.com).

AFGHANISTAN - POPULATION DENSITY

Central Intelligence Agency, Office of Public Affairs, Washington, DC 20505, (703) 482-0623, Fax: (703) 482-1739, www.cia.gov; *The World Factbook.*

Euromonitor International, Inc., 224 S. Michigan Avenue, Suite 1500, Chicago, IL 60604, (312) 922-1115, Fax: (312) 922-1157, www.euromonitor.com; *International Marketing Data and Statistics 2008* and *The World Economic Factbook 2008.*

M.E. Sharpe, 80 Business Park Drive, Armonk, NY 10504, (800) 541-6563, Fax: (914) 273-2106, www.mesharpe.com; *The Illustrated Book of World Rankings.*

Palgrave Macmillan Ltd., Houndmills, Basingstoke, Hampshire, RG21 6XS, England, (Telephone in U.S. (888) 330-8477), (Fax in U.S. (800) 672-2054), www.palgrave.com; *The Statesman's Yearbook 2008.*

Taylor and Francis Group, An Informa Business, 2 Park Square, Milton Park, Abingdon, Oxford OX14 4RN, United Kingdom, (Dial from U.S. (212) 216-7800), (Fax from U.S. (212) 564-7854), www.tandf.co.uk; *The Europa World Year Book.*

United Nations Food and Agricultural Organization (FAO), Viale delle Terme di Caracalla, 00100 Rome, Italy, (Dial from U.S. (202) 653-2400), (Fax from U.S. (202) 653 5760), www.fao.org; *The State of Food and Agriculture (SOFA) 2006.*

United Nations Statistics Division, New York, NY 10017, (800) 253-9646, Fax: (212) 963-4116, http://unstats.un.org; *Statistical Yearbook.*

The World Bank, 1818 H Street, NW, Washington, DC 20433, (202) 473-1000, Fax: (202) 477-6391, www.worldbank.org; *Afghanistan.*

AFGHANISTAN - POSTAL SERVICE

M.E. Sharpe, 80 Business Park Drive, Armonk, NY 10504, (800) 541-6563, Fax: (914) 273-2106, www.mesharpe.com; *The Illustrated Book of World Rankings.*

United Nations Statistics Division, New York, NY 10017, (800) 253-9646, Fax: (212) 963-4116, http://unstats.un.org; *Statistical Yearbook.*

AFGHANISTAN - POWER RESOURCES

Euromonitor International, Inc., 224 S. Michigan Avenue, Suite 1500, Chicago, IL 60604, (312) 922-1115, Fax: (312) 922-1157, www.euromonitor.com; *International Marketing Data and Statistics 2008; The World Economic Factbook 2008;* and *World Marketing Data and Statistics.*

M.E. Sharpe, 80 Business Park Drive, Armonk, NY 10504, (800) 541-6563, Fax: (914) 273-2106, www.mesharpe.com; *The Illustrated Book of World Rankings.*

Palgrave Macmillan Ltd., Houndmills, Basingstoke, Hampshire, RG21 6XS, England, (Telephone in U.S. (888) 330-8477), (Fax in U.S. (800) 672-2054), www.palgrave.com; *The Statesman's Yearbook 2008.*

Platts, 2 Penn Plaza, 25th Floor, New York, NY 10121-2298, (212) 904-3070, www.platts.com; *Energy Economist.*

United Nations Food and Agricultural Organization (FAO), Viale delle Terme di Caracalla, 00100 Rome, Italy, (Dial from U.S. (202) 653-2400), (Fax from U.S. (202) 653 5760), www.fao.org; *The State of Food and Agriculture (SOFA) 2006.*

United Nations Statistics Division, New York, NY 10017, (800) 253-9646, Fax: (212) 963-4116, http://unstats.un.org; *Asia-Pacific in Figures 2004; Energy Statistics Yearbook 2003; Statistical Yearbook;* and *World Statistics Pocketbook.*

The World Bank, 1818 H Street, NW, Washington, DC 20433, (202) 473-1000, Fax: (202) 477-6391, www.worldbank.org; *The World Bank Atlas 2003-2004.*

AFGHANISTAN - PRICES

Asian Development Bank (ADB), PO Box 789, 0980 Manila, Philippines, www.adb.org; *Key Indicators of Developing Asian and Pacific Countries 2006.*

Euromonitor International, Inc., 224 S. Michigan Avenue, Suite 1500, Chicago, IL 60604, (312) 922-1115, Fax: (312) 922-1157, www.euromonitor.com; *World Marketing Data and Statistics.*

International Labour Office, I.L.O. Publications, 4 route des Morillons, CH-1211 Geneva 22, Switzerland, (Telephone in U.S. (202) 653-7652), (Fax in U.S. (202) 653-7687), www.ilo.org; *Yearbook of Labour Statistics 2006.*

M.E. Sharpe, 80 Business Park Drive, Armonk, NY 10504, (800) 541-6563, Fax: (914) 273-2106, www.mesharpe.com; *The Illustrated Book of World Rankings.*

United Nations Food and Agricultural Organization (FAO), Viale delle Terme di Caracalla, 00100 Rome, Italy, (Dial from U.S. (202) 653-2400), (Fax from U.S. (202) 653 5760), www.fao.org; *FAO Production Yearbook 2002* and *The State of Food and Agriculture (SOFA) 2006.*

The World Bank, 1818 H Street, NW, Washington, DC 20433, (202) 473-1000, Fax: (202) 477-6391, www.worldbank.org; *Afghanistan.*

AFGHANISTAN - PUBLIC HEALTH

Economist Intelligence Unit, 111 West 57th Street, New York, NY 10019, (212) 554-0600, Fax: (212) 586-1181, www.eiu.com; *Business Asia.*

Euromonitor International, Inc., 224 S. Michigan Avenue, Suite 1500, Chicago, IL 60604, (312) 922-1115, Fax: (312) 922-1157, www.euromonitor.com; *World Marketing Data and Statistics.*

M.E. Sharpe, 80 Business Park Drive, Armonk, NY 10504, (800) 541-6563, Fax: (914) 273-2106, www.mesharpe.com; *The Illustrated Book of World Rankings.*

Palgrave Macmillan Ltd., Houndmills, Basingstoke, Hampshire, RG21 6XS, England, (Telephone in U.S. (888) 330-8477), (Fax in U.S. (800) 672-2054), www.palgrave.com; *The Statesman's Yearbook 2008.*

UNICEF, 3 United Nations Plaza, New York, NY 10017, (800) 253-9646, Fax: (212) 887-7465, www.unicef.org; *The State of the World's Children 2008.*

United Nations Statistics Division, New York, NY 10017, (800) 253-9646, Fax: (212) 963-4116, http://unstats.un.org; *Asia-Pacific in Figures 2004* and *Statistical Yearbook.*

The World Bank, 1818 H Street, NW, Washington, DC 20433, (202) 473-1000, Fax: (202) 477-6391, www.worldbank.org; *Afghanistan.*

World Health Organization (WHO), Avenue Appia 20, 1211 Geneve 27, Switzerland, (Telephone in U.S. (212) 331-9081), www.who.int; The WHO Global Atlas of Infectious Diseases and *World Health Report 2006.*

AFGHANISTAN - PUBLIC UTILITIES

United Nations Statistics Division, New York, NY 10017, (800) 253-9646, Fax: (212) 963-4116, http://unstats.un.org; *Electric Power in Asia and the Pacific 2001 and 2002.*

AFGHANISTAN - PUBLISHERS AND PUBLISHING

UNESCO Institute for Statistics, C.P. 6128 Succursale Centre-Ville, Montreal, Quebec, H3C 3J7 Canada, (Dial from U.S. (514) 343-6880), (Fax from U.S. (514) 343 6882), www.uis.unesco.org; *Statistical Tables.*

AFGHANISTAN - RADIO BROADCASTING

Palgrave Macmillan Ltd., Houndmills, Basingstoke, Hampshire, RG21 6XS, England, (Telephone in U.S. (888) 330-8477), (Fax in U.S. (800) 672-2054), www.palgrave.com; *The Statesman's Yearbook 2008.*

AFGHANISTAN - RAILROADS

Jane's Information Group, 110 North Royal Street, Suite 200, Alexandria, VA 22314, (703) 683-3700, Fax: (800) 836-0297, www.janes.com; *Jane's World Railways.*

AFGHANISTAN - RELIGION

Central Intelligence Agency, Office of Public Affairs, Washington, DC 20505, (703) 482-0623, Fax: (703) 482-1739, www.cia.gov; *The World Factbook.*

M.E. Sharpe, 80 Business Park Drive, Armonk, NY 10504, (800) 541-6563, Fax: (914) 273-2106, www.mesharpe.com; *The Illustrated Book of World Rankings.*

Palgrave Macmillan Ltd., Houndmills, Basingstoke, Hampshire, RG21 6XS, England, (Telephone in U.S. (888) 330-8477), (Fax in U.S. (800) 672-2054), www.palgrave.com; *The Statesman's Yearbook 2008.*

AFGHANISTAN - RENT CHARGES

International Labour Office, I.L.O. Publications, 4 route des Morillons, CH-1211 Geneva 22, Switzerland, (Telephone in U.S. (202) 653-7652), (Fax in U.S. (202) 653-7687), www.ilo.org; *Yearbook of Labour Statistics 2006.*

AFGHANISTAN - RESERVES (ACCOUNTING)

Asian Development Bank (ADB), PO Box 789, 0980 Manila, Philippines, www.adb.org; *Key Indicators of Developing Asian and Pacific Countries 2006.*

Euromonitor International, Inc., 224 S. Michigan Avenue, Suite 1500, Chicago, IL 60604, (312) 922-1115, Fax: (312) 922-1157, www.euromonitor.com; *International Marketing Data and Statistics 2008.*

AFGHANISTAN - RETAIL TRADE

Euromonitor International, Inc., 224 S. Michigan Avenue, Suite 1500, Chicago, IL 60604, (312) 922-1115, Fax: (312) 922-1157, www.euromonitor.com; *World Marketing Data and Statistics.*

AFGHANISTAN - RICE PRODUCTION

See AFGHANISTAN - CROPS

AFGHANISTAN - ROADS

Central Intelligence Agency, Office of Public Affairs, Washington, DC 20505, (703) 482-0623, Fax: (703) 482-1739, www.cia.gov; *The World Factbook.*

Economist Intelligence Unit, 111 West 57th Street, New York, NY 10019, (212) 554-0600, Fax: (212) 586-1181, www.eiu.com; *Business Asia.*

International Road Federation (IFR), Madison Place, 500 Montgomery Street, 5th Floor, Alexandria, VA 22314, (703) 535-1001, Fax: (703) 535-1007, www.irfnet.org; *World Road Statistics 2006.*

Palgrave Macmillan Ltd., Houndmills, Basingstoke, Hampshire, RG21 6XS, England, (Telephone in U.S. (888) 330-8477), (Fax in U.S. (800) 672-2054), www.palgrave.com; *The Statesman's Yearbook 2008.*

AFGHANISTAN - RUBBER INDUSTRY AND TRADE

International Rubber Study Group (IRSG), 1st Floor, Heron House, 109/115 Wembley Hill Road, Wembley, Middlesex HA9 8DA, United Kingdom, www.rubberstudy.com; *Rubber Statistical Bulletin; Summary of World Rubber Statistics 2005; World Rubber Statistics Handbook (Volume 6, 1975-2001);* and *World Rubber Statistics Historic Handbook.*

M.E. Sharpe, 80 Business Park Drive, Armonk, NY 10504, (800) 541-6563, Fax: (914) 273-2106, www.mesharpe.com; *The Illustrated Book of World Rankings.*

AFGHANISTAN - RUG AND CARPET INDUSTRY

International Monetary Fund (IMF), 700 Nineteenth Street, NW, Washington, DC 20431, (202) 623-7000, Fax: (202) 623-4661, www.imf.org; *International Financial Statistics Yearbook 2007.*

AFGHANISTAN - SALT PRODUCTION

See AFGHANISTAN - MINERAL INDUSTRIES

AFGHANISTAN - SHEEP

See AFGHANISTAN - LIVESTOCK

AFGHANISTAN - SHIPPING

Palgrave Macmillan Ltd., Houndmills, Basingstoke, Hampshire, RG21 6XS, England, (Telephone in U.S. (888) 330-8477), (Fax in U.S. (800) 672-2054), www.palgrave.com; *The Statesman's Yearbook 2008.*

AFGHANISTAN - SILVER PRODUCTION

See AFGHANISTAN - MINERAL INDUSTRIES

AFGHANISTAN - SOCIAL ECOLOGY

Asian Development Bank (ADB), PO Box 789, 0980 Manila, Philippines, www.adb.org; *Key Indicators of Developing Asian and Pacific Countries 2006.*

M.E. Sharpe, 80 Business Park Drive, Armonk, NY 10504, (800) 541-6563, Fax: (914) 273-2106, www.mesharpe.com; *The Illustrated Book of World Rankings.*

United Nations Statistics Division, New York, NY 10017, (800) 253-9646, Fax: (212) 963-4116, http://unstats.un.org; *World Statistics Pocketbook.*

AFGHANISTAN - SOCIAL SECURITY

United Nations Statistics Division, New York, NY 10017, (800) 253-9646, Fax: (212) 963-4116, http://unstats.un.org; *National Accounts Statistics: Compendium of Income Distribution Statistics.*

AFGHANISTAN - STEEL PRODUCTION

See AFGHANISTAN - MINERAL INDUSTRIES

AFGHANISTAN - SUGAR PRODUCTION

See AFGHANISTAN - CROPS

AFGHANISTAN - TAXATION

International Road Federation (IFR), Madison Place, 500 Montgomery Street, 5th Floor, Alexandria, VA 22314, (703) 535-1001, Fax: (703) 535-1007, www.irfnet.org; *World Road Statistics 2006.*

Taylor and Francis Group, An Informa Business, 2 Park Square, Milton Park, Abingdon, Oxford OX14 4RN, United Kingdom, (Dial from U.S. (212) 216-7800), (Fax from U.S. (212) 564-7854), www.tandf.co.uk; *The Europa World Year Book.*

AFGHANISTAN - TEA PRODUCTION

See AFGHANISTAN - CROPS

AFGHANISTAN - TELEPHONE

Economist Intelligence Unit, 111 West 57th Street, New York, NY 10019, (212) 554-0600, Fax: (212) 586-1181, www.eiu.com; *Business Asia.*

International Telecommunication Union (ITU), Place des Nations, 1211 Geneva 20, Switzerland, www.itu.int; World Telecommunication Indicators Database.

Palgrave Macmillan Ltd., Houndmills, Basingstoke, Hampshire, RG21 6XS, England, (Telephone in U.S. (888) 330-8477), (Fax in U.S. (800) 672-2054), www.palgrave.com; *The Statesman's Yearbook 2008.*

Taylor and Francis Group, An Informa Business, 2 Park Square, Milton Park, Abingdon, Oxford OX14 4RN, United Kingdom, (Dial from U.S. (212) 216-7800), (Fax from U.S. (212) 564-7854), www.tandf.co.uk; *The Europa World Year Book.*

United Nations Statistics Division, New York, NY 10017, (800) 253-9646, Fax: (212) 963-4116, http://unstats.un.org; *Statistical Yearbook* and *World Statistics Pocketbook.*

AFGHANISTAN - TEXTILE INDUSTRY

International Monetary Fund (IMF), 700 Nineteenth Street, NW, Washington, DC 20431, (202) 623-7000, Fax: (202) 623-4661, www.imf.org; *International Financial Statistics Yearbook 2007.*

M.E. Sharpe, 80 Business Park Drive, Armonk, NY 10504, (800) 541-6563, Fax: (914) 273-2106, www.mesharpe.com; *The Illustrated Book of World Rankings.*

Palgrave Macmillan Ltd., Houndmills, Basingstoke, Hampshire, RG21 6XS, England, (Telephone in U.S. (888) 330-8477), (Fax in U.S. (800) 672-2054), www.palgrave.com; *The Statesman's Yearbook 2008.*

United Nations Conference on Trade and Development (UNCTAD), DC2-1120, United Nations, New York, NY 10017, (212) 963-0027, www.unctad.org; *UNCTAD Commodity Yearbook.*

United Nations Statistics Division, New York, NY 10017, (800) 253-9646, Fax: (212) 963-4116, http://unstats.un.org; *Statistical Yearbook.*

AFGHANISTAN - TOBACCO INDUSTRY

Foreign Agricultural Service (FAS), U.S. Department of Agriculture (USDA), 1400 Independence Avenue, SW, Washington, DC 20250, (202) 720-3935, www.fas.usda.gov; *Tobacco: World Markets and Trade.*

M.E. Sharpe, 80 Business Park Drive, Armonk, NY 10504, (800) 541-6563, Fax: (914) 273-2106, www.mesharpe.com; *The Illustrated Book of World Rankings.*

AFGHANISTAN - TOURISM

Euromonitor International, Inc., 224 S. Michigan Avenue, Suite 1500, Chicago, IL 60604, (312) 922-1115, Fax: (312) 922-1157, www.euromonitor.com; *The World Economic Factbook 2008* and *World Marketing Data and Statistics.*

M.E. Sharpe, 80 Business Park Drive, Armonk, NY 10504, (800) 541-6563, Fax: (914) 273-2106, www.mesharpe.com; *The Illustrated Book of World Rankings.*

Taylor and Francis Group, An Informa Business, 2 Park Square, Milton Park, Abingdon, Oxford OX14 4RN, United Kingdom, (Dial from U.S. (212) 216-7800), (Fax from U.S. (212) 564-7854), www.tandf.co.uk; *The Europa World Year Book.*

United Nations Statistics Division, New York, NY 10017, (800) 253-9646, Fax: (212) 963-4116, http://unstats.un.org; *Statistical Yearbook.*

The World Bank, 1818 H Street, NW, Washington, DC 20433, (202) 473-1000, Fax: (202) 477-6391, www.worldbank.org; *Afghanistan* and *Afghanistan.*

AFGHANISTAN - TRADE

See AFGHANISTAN - INTERNATIONAL TRADE

AFGHANISTAN - TRANSPORTATION

Central Intelligence Agency, Office of Public Affairs, Washington, DC 20505, (703) 482-0623, Fax: (703) 482-1739, www.cia.gov; *The World Factbook.*

Economist Intelligence Unit, 111 West 57th Street, New York, NY 10019, (212) 554-0600, Fax: (212) 586-1181, www.eiu.com; *Business Asia.*

Euromonitor International, Inc., 224 S. Michigan Avenue, Suite 1500, Chicago, IL 60604, (312) 922-1115, Fax: (312) 922-1157, www.euromonitor.com; *International Marketing Data and Statistics 2008* and *World Marketing Data and Statistics.*

M.E. Sharpe, 80 Business Park Drive, Armonk, NY 10504, (800) 541-6563, Fax: (914) 273-2106, www.mesharpe.com; *The Illustrated Book of World Rankings.*

Palgrave Macmillan Ltd., Houndmills, Basingstoke, Hampshire, RG21 6XS, England, (Telephone in U.S. (888) 330-8477), (Fax in U.S. (800) 672-2054), www.palgrave.com; *The Statesman's Yearbook 2008.*

Taylor and Francis Group, An Informa Business, 2 Park Square, Milton Park, Abingdon, Oxford OX14 4RN, United Kingdom, (Dial from U.S. (212) 216-7800), (Fax from U.S. (212) 564-7854), www.tandf.co.uk; *The Europa World Year Book.*

United Nations Statistics Division, New York, NY 10017, (800) 253-9646, Fax: (212) 963-4116, http://unstats.un.org; *Statistical Yearbook for Asia and the Pacific 2004.*

The World Bank, 1818 H Street, NW, Washington, DC 20433, (202) 473-1000, Fax: (202) 477-6391, www.worldbank.org; *Afghanistan.*

AFGHANISTAN - UNEMPLOYMENT

Central Intelligence Agency, Office of Public Affairs, Washington, DC 20505, (703) 482-0623, Fax: (703) 482-1739, www.cia.gov; *The World Factbook.*

Euromonitor International, Inc., 224 S. Michigan Avenue, Suite 1500, Chicago, IL 60604, (312) 922-1115, Fax: (312) 922-1157, www.euromonitor.com; *International Marketing Data and Statistics 2008.*

International Labour Office, I.L.O. Publications, 4 route des Morillons, CH-1211 Geneva 22, Switzerland, (Telephone in U.S. (202) 653-7652), (Fax in U.S. (202) 653-7687), www.ilo.org; *Yearbook of Labour Statistics 2006.*

AFGHANISTAN - VITAL STATISTICS

Euromonitor International, Inc., 224 S. Michigan Avenue, Suite 1500, Chicago, IL 60604, (312) 922-1115, Fax: (312) 922-1157, www.euromonitor.com; *International Marketing Data and Statistics 2008.*

Palgrave Macmillan Ltd., Houndmills, Basingstoke, Hampshire, RG21 6XS, England, (Telephone in U.S. (888) 330-8477), (Fax in U.S. (800) 672-2054), www.palgrave.com; *The Statesman's Yearbook 2008.*

World Health Organization (WHO), Avenue Appia 20, 1211 Geneve 27, Switzerland, (Telephone in U.S. (212) 331-9081), www.who.int; *World Health Report 2006.*

AFGHANISTAN - WAGES

International Labour Office, I.L.O. Publications, 4 route des Morillons, CH-1211 Geneva 22, Switzerland, (Telephone in U.S. (202) 653-7652), (Fax in U.S. (202) 653-7687), www.ilo.org; *Yearbook of Labour Statistics 2006.*

United Nations Statistics Division, New York, NY 10017, (800) 253-9646, Fax: (212) 963-4116, http://unstats.un.org; *Statistical Yearbook* and *Statistical Yearbook for Asia and the Pacific 2004.*

The World Bank, 1818 H Street, NW, Washington, DC 20433, (202) 473-1000, Fax: (202) 477-6391, www.worldbank.org; *Afghanistan.*

AFGHANISTAN - WEATHER

See AFGHANISTAN - CLIMATE

AFGHANISTAN - WHEAT PRODUCTION

See AFGHANISTAN - CROPS

AFGHANISTAN - WHOLESALE PRICE INDEXES

Asian Development Bank (ADB), PO Box 789, 0980 Manila, Philippines, www.adb.org; *Key Indicators of Developing Asian and Pacific Countries 2006.*

AFGHANISTAN - WINE PRODUCTION

See AFGHANISTAN - BEVERAGE INDUSTRY

AFGHANISTAN - WOOL PRODUCTION

See AFGHANISTAN - TEXTILE INDUSTRY

AFGHANISTAN - YARN PRODUCTION

See AFGHANISTAN - TEXTILE INDUSTRY

AFRICA

See also Individual countries

Economist Intelligence Unit, 111 West 57th Street, New York, NY 10019, (212) 554-0600, Fax: (212) 586-1181, www.eiu.com; *Business Africa.*

International Institute for Environment and Development (IIED), 3 Endsleigh Street, London, England, WC1H 0DD, United Kingdom, www.iied.org; *Environment Urbanization; Environment Urbanization;* and *Haramata - Bulletin of the Drylands.*

International Telecommunication Union (ITU), Place des Nations, 1211 Geneva 20, Switzerland, www.itu.int; *African Telecommunication/ICT Indicators 2008: At a Crossroads.*

United Nations Economic Commission for Africa (ECA), PO Box 3001, Addis Ababa, Ethiopia, (Telephone in U.S. (212) 963-4957), www.uneca.org; *Economic Report on Africa 2007.*

United Nations Environment Programme (UNEP), PO Box 30552, Nairobi, Kenya, www.unep.org; *Africa's Lakes: Atlas of Our Changing Environment* and *Eastern African Atlas of Coastal Resources.*

United Nations World Tourism Organization (UNWTO), Capitan Haya 42, 28020 Madrid, Spain, www.world-tourism.org; *Tourism Market Trends 2004 - Africa.*

The World Bank, 1818 H Street, NW, Washington, DC 20433, (202) 473-1000, Fax: (202) 477-6391, www.worldbank.org; *Africa Household Survey Databank.*

World Food Programme, Via C.G.Viola 68, Parco dei Medici, 00148 Rome, Italy, www.wfp.org; *WFP in Africa: 2006 Facts, Figures and Partners.*

AGE OF POPULATION

See POPULATION

AGGRAVATED ASSAULT

Federal Bureau of Investigation (FBI), J. Edgar Hoover Building, 935 Pennsylvania Avenue, NW, Washington, DC 20535-0001, (202) 324-3000, www.fbi.gov; *Crime in the United States (CIUS) 2007 (Preliminary).*

Justice Research and Statistics Association (JRSA), 777 N. Capitol Street, NE, Suite 801, Washington, DC 20002, (202) 842-9330, Fax: (202) 842-9329, www.jrsa.org; *Crime and Justice Atlas 2001.*

U.S. Department of Justice (DOJ), Bureau of Justice Statistics, 810 Seventh Street, NW, Washington, DC 20531, (202) 307-0765, www.ojp.usdoj.gov/bjs/; *Hispanic Victims of Violent Crime, 1993-2000.*

AGRICULTURAL LOANS

See FARM MORTGAGE LOANS

AGRICULTURAL PRODUCTS

See FARMS

AGRICULTURAL SCIENCES - DEGREES CONFERRED

National Center for Education Statistics (NCES), 1990 K Street, NW, Washington, DC 20006, (202) 502-7300, http://nces.ed.gov; *Digest of Education Statistics 2007.*

National Science Foundation, Division of Science Resources Statistics (SRS), 4201 Wilson Boulevard, Arlington, VA 22230, (703) 292-8780, Fax: (703) 292-9092, www.nsf.gov; *Selected Data on Science and Engineering Doctorate Awards* and *Survey of Earned Doctorates 2006.*

AGRICULTURE

See also FARMS

Department of Statistics (DOS), PO Box 2015, Amman 11181, Jordan, www.dos.gov.jo; *Agricultural Statistics 2006.*

Economist Intelligence Unit, 111 West 57th Street, New York, NY 10019, (212) 554-0600, Fax: (212) 586-1181, www.eiu.com; *United States of America Country Report.*

International Food Policy Research Institute (IFPRI), 2033 K Street, NW, Washington, D.C., 2006, (202) 862-5600, www.ifpri.org; *Food Prices, Biofuels, and Climate Change* and *Kenya: The Influence of Social Capital on Sustainable Agriculture in Marginal Areas, 2003.*

Lithuanian Department of Statistics (Statistics Lithuania), Gedimino av. 29, LT-01500 Vilnius, Lithuania, www.stat.gov.lt/en; *Agriculture in Lithuania 2008.*

National Agricultural Statistics Service (NASS), U.S. Department of Agriculture (USDA), 1400 Independence Avenue, SW, Washington, DC 20250, (800) 727-9540, Fax: (202) 690-2090, www.nass.usda.gov; *2006 Agricultural Statistics* and *Cold Storage.*

U.S. Department of Agriculture (USDA), 1400 Independence Ave, SW, Washington, DC 20250, (202) 264-8600, www.usda.gov; *The Agricultural Fact Book 2001-2002.*

United Nations Food and Agricultural Organization (FAO), Viale delle Terme di Caracalla, 00100 Rome, Italy, (Dial from U.S. (202) 653-2400), (Fax from U.S. (202) 653 5760), www.fao.org; *FAO Statistical Yearbook 2004* and FAOSTAT Database. Subjects covered include: Agriculture, nutrition, fisheries, forestry, food aid, land use and population.

AGRICULTURE - EMPLOYEES

National Agricultural Statistics Service (NASS), U.S. Department of Agriculture (USDA), 1400 Independence Avenue, SW, Washington, DC 20250, (800) 727-9540, Fax: (202) 690-2090, www.nass.usda.gov; *Adult Agricultural Related Injuries 2004* and *Farm Labor.*

U.S. Bureau of Labor Statistics (BLS), Postal Square Building, 2 Massachusetts Avenue, NE, Washington, DC 20212-0001, (202) 691-5200, Fax: (202) 691-6325, www.bls.gov; *Employment and Earnings (EE)* and unpublished data.

AGRICULTURE - FEDERAL AID TO STATE AND LOCAL GOVERNMENTS

The Office of Management and Budget (OMB), 725 17th Street, NW, Washington, DC 20503, (202) 395-3080, Fax: (202) 395-3888, www.whitehouse.gov/omb; *Budget of the United States Government, Federal Year 2009* and *Historical Tables.*

AGRICULTURE - INTERNATIONAL TRADE

Economic Research Service (ERS), U.S. Department of Agriculture (USDA), 1800 M Street, NW, Washington, DC 20036-5831, (202) 694-5050, Fax: (202) 694-5689, www.ers.usda.gov; *Agricultural Statistics; Foreign Agricultural Trade of the United States (FATUS);* and *U.S. Agricultural Trade Update: 2006.*

National Agricultural Statistics Service (NASS), U.S. Department of Agriculture (USDA), 1400 Independence Avenue, SW, Washington, DC 20250, (800) 727-9540, Fax: (202) 690-2090, www.nass.usda.gov; *2006 Agricultural Statistics.*

Organisation for Economic Cooperation and Development (OECD), 2 rue Andre Pascal, F-75775 Paris Cedex 16, France, (Telephone in U.S. (202) 785-6323), (Fax in U.S. (202) 785-0350), www.oecd.org; *OECD Agricultural Outlook: 2007-2016.*

AGRICULTURE - VALUE ADDED

Economic Research Service (ERS), U.S. Department of Agriculture (USDA), 1800 M Street, NW, Washington, DC 20036-5831, (202) 694-5050, Fax: (202) 694-5689, www.ers.usda.gov; *Farm Income: Data Files.*

AGRICULTURE, FORESTRY, AND FISHING INDUSTRY - CAPITAL

U.S. Census Bureau, Company Statistics Division, 4700 Silver Hill Road, Washington DC 20233-0001, (301) 763-3030, www.census.gov/csd/; *Annual Capital Expenditures Survey (ACES).*

AGRICULTURE, FORESTRY, AND FISHING INDUSTRY - EARNINGS

Bureau of Economic Analysis (BEA), U.S. Department of Commerce (DOC), 1441 L Street NW, Washington, DC 20230, (202) 606-9900, www.bea.gov; *2007 Annual Revision of the National Income and Product Accounts (NIPA)* and *Survey of Current Business (SCB).*

U.S. Census Bureau, Company Statistics Division, 4700 Silver Hill Road, Washington DC 20233-0001, (301) 763-3030, www.census.gov/csd/; *County Business Patterns 2004* and *Survey of Women-Owned Businesses.*

AGRICULTURE, FORESTRY, AND FISHING INDUSTRY - EMPLOYEES

National Agricultural Statistics Service (NASS), U.S. Department of Agriculture (USDA), 1400 Independence Avenue, SW, Washington, DC 20250, (800) 727-9540, Fax: (202) 690-2090, www.nass.usda.gov; *Farm Labor.*

U.S. Census Bureau, 4700 Silver Hill Road, Washington DC 20233-0001, (301) 763-3030, www.census.gov; unpublished data.

U.S. Census Bureau, Company Statistics Division, 4700 Silver Hill Road, Washington DC 20233-0001, (301) 763-3030, www.census.gov/csd/; *County Business Patterns 2004; Statistics of U.S. Businesses (SUSB);* and *Survey of Women-Owned Businesses.*

U.S. Census Bureau, Demographic Surveys Division, 4700 Silver Hill Road, Washington DC 20233-0001, (301) 763-3030, www.census.gov; *Demographic Profiles: 100-percent and Sample Data.*

AGRICULTURE, FORESTRY, AND FISHING INDUSTRY - ESTABLISHMENTS

U.S. Census Bureau, Company Statistics Division, 4700 Silver Hill Road, Washington DC 20233-0001, (301) 763-3030, www.census.gov/csd/; *County Business Patterns 2004* and *Statistics of U.S. Businesses (SUSB).*

AGRICULTURE, FORESTRY, AND FISHING INDUSTRY - FINANCES

National Marine Fisheries Service (NMFS), National Oceanic and Atmospheric Administration (NOAA), Office of Constituent Services, 1315 East West Highway, 9th Floor, Silver Spring, MD 20910, (301) 713-2379, Fax: (301) 713-2385, www.nmfs.noaa.gov; *Our Living Oceans: The Economic Status of U.S. Fisheries.*

U.S. Census Bureau, Company Statistics Division, 4700 Silver Hill Road, Washington DC 20233-0001, (301) 763-3030, www.census.gov/csd/; *Statistics of U.S. Businesses (SUSB).*

U.S. Department of the Treasury (DOT), Internal Revenue Service (IRS), Statistics of Income Division (SIS), PO Box 2608, Washington, DC, 20013-2608, (202) 874-0410, Fax: (202) 874-0964, www.irs.ustreas.gov; *Statistics of Income Bulletin* and various fact sheets.

AGRICULTURE, FORESTRY, AND FISHING INDUSTRY - GROSS DOMESTIC PRODUCT

Bureau of Economic Analysis (BEA), U.S. Department of Commerce (DOC), 1441 L Street NW, Washington, DC 20230, (202) 606-9900, www.bea.gov; *Survey of Current Business (SCB).*

AGRICULTURE, FORESTRY, AND FISHING INDUSTRY - INDUSTRIAL SAFETY

National Agricultural Statistics Service (NASS), U.S. Department of Agriculture (USDA), 1400 Independence Avenue, SW, Washington, DC 20250, (800) 727-9540, Fax: (202) 690-2090, www.nass.usda.gov; *Adult Agricultural Related Injuries 2004.*

National Safety Council (NSC), 1121 Spring Lake Drive, Itasca, IL 60143-3201, (630) 285-1121, www.nsc.org; *Injury Facts.*

U.S. Bureau of Labor Statistics (BLS), Postal Square Building, 2 Massachusetts Avenue, NE, Washington, DC 20212-0001, (202) 691-5200, Fax: (202) 691-6325, www.bls.gov; *Injuries, Illnesses, and Fatalities (IIF); Monthly Labor Review (MLR);* and unpublished data.

AGRICULTURE, FORESTRY, AND FISHING INDUSTRY - MERGERS AND ACQUISITIONS

Thomson Financial, 195 Broadway, New York, NY 10007, (646) 822-2000, www.thomson.com; Thomson Research.

AGRICULTURE, FORESTRY, AND FISHING INDUSTRY - MINORITY-OWNED BUSINESSES

U.S. Census Bureau, Company Statistics Division, 4700 Silver Hill Road, Washington DC 20233-0001,

(301) 763-3030, www.census.gov/csd/; *Survey of Minority-Owned Business Enterprises.*

AGRICULTURE, FORESTRY, AND FISHING INDUSTRY - PROFITS

Bureau of Economic Analysis (BEA), U.S. Department of Commerce (DOC), 1441 L Street NW, Washington, DC 20230, (202) 606-9900, www.bea.gov; *2007 Annual Revision of the National Income and Product Accounts (NIPA)* and *Survey of Current Business (SCB).*

Statistics Canada, 100 Tunney's Pasture Driveway, Ottawa, Ontario K1A 0T6, (Dial from U.S. (800) 263-1136), (Fax from U.S. (877) 287-4369), www.statcan.ca; *Net Farm Income - Agriculture Economic Statistics.*

U.S. Department of the Treasury (DOT), Internal Revenue Service (IRS), Statistics of Income Division (SIS), PO Box 2608, Washington, DC, 20013-2608, (202) 874-0410, Fax: (202) 874-0964, www.irs.ustreas.gov; *Statistics of Income Bulletin* and various fact sheets.

AGRICULTURE, FORESTRY, AND FISHING INDUSTRY - SALES, SHIPMENTS AND RECEIPTS

Bureau of Economic Analysis (BEA), U.S. Department of Commerce (DOC), 1441 L Street NW, Washington, DC 20230, (202) 606-9900, www.bea.gov; *2007 Annual Revision of the National Income and Product Accounts (NIPA)* and *Survey of Current Business (SCB).*

Eurostat, Batiment Jean Monnet, Rue Alcide de Gasperi, L-2920 Luxembourg, http://epp.eurostat.ec.europa.eu; *EU Agricultural Prices in 2007.*

U.S. Department of the Treasury (DOT), Internal Revenue Service (IRS), Statistics of Income Division (SIS), PO Box 2608, Washington, DC, 20013-2608, (202) 874-0410, Fax: (202) 874-0964, www.irs.ustreas.gov; *Statistics of Income Bulletin* and various fact sheets.

AID TO FAMILIES WITH DEPENDENT CHILDREN

See TEMPORARY ASSISTANCE FOR NEEDY FAMILIES PROGRAM

AIDS (DISEASE)

Bernan Essential Government Publications, 4611-F Assembly Drive, Lanham MD, 20706-4391, (301) 459-2255, Fax: (800) 865-3450, www.bernan.com; *Vital Statistics of the United States: Births, Life Expectancy, Deaths, and Selected Health Data.*

Caribbean Epidemiology Centre (CAREC), 16-18 Jamaica Boulevard, Federation Park, PO Box 164, Port of Spain, Republic of Trinidad and Tobago, (Dial from U.S. (868) 622-4261), (Fax from U.S. (868) 622-2792), www.carec.org; *20 Years of the HIV/AIDS Epidemic in the Caribbean* and AIDS Statistics.

Centers for Disease Control and Prevention (CDC), U.S. Department of Health and Human Services (HHS), 1600 Clifton Road, Atlanta, GA 30333, (800) 311-3435, www.cdc.gov; *HIV/AIDS Surveillance Report; Morbidity and Mortality Weekly Report (MMWR); Summary of Notifiable Diseases, United States, 2006;* and unpublished data.

European Centre for Disease Prevention and Control (ECDC), 171 83 Stockholm, Sweden, www.ecdc.europa.eu; *HIV Infection in Europe: 25 Years into the Pandemic.*

National Center for Chronic Disease Prevention and Health Promotion (NCCDPHP), Centers for Disease Control and Prevention (CDC), 4770 Buford Hwy, NE, MS K-40, Atlanta, GA 30341-3717, (404) 639-3311, www.cdc.gov/nccdphp; *Racial and Ethnic Approaches to Community Health (REACH 2010): Addressing Disparities in Health.*

National Center for Health Statistics (NCHS), Centers for Disease Control and Prevention (CDC), U.S. Department of Health and Human Services (HHS), 3311 Toledo Road, Hyattsville, MD 20782, (866) 232-4636, www.cdc.gov/nchs; *Faststats A to Z; Health, United States, 2006, with Chartbook on Trends in the Health of Americans with Special Feature on Pain; National Vital Statistics Reports (NVSR); Vital Statistics of the United States (VSUS);* and unpublished data.

Tonga Statistics Department, PO Box 149, Nuku'alofa, Tonga, www.spc.int/prism/country/to/stats/; *Surveillance Surveys of HIV, Other STIs and Risk Behaviours in 6 Pacific Island Countries 2004-2005.*

U.S. Department of Justice (DOJ), Bureau of Justice Statistics, 810 Seventh Street, NW, Washington, DC 20531, (202) 307-0765, www.ojp.usdoj.gov/bjs/; *HIV in Prisons, 2004.*

UNAIDS, 20, Avenue Appia, CH-1211 Geneva 27, Switzerland, www.unaids.org; *2007 AIDS Epidemic Update.*

World Health Organization (WHO), Avenue Appia 20, 1211 Geneve 27, Switzerland, (Telephone in U.S. (212) 331-9081), www.who.int; The WHO Global Atlas of Infectious Diseases.

AIR CONDITIONING - HOMES WITH

U.S. Census Bureau, Housing and Household Economics Statistics Division, 4700 Silver Hill Road, Washington DC 20233-0001, (301) 763-3030, www.census.gov/hhes/www; *2006 American Community Survey (ACS)* and *American Housing Survey (AHS).*

AIR CONDITIONING - SHIPMENTS

U.S. Census Bureau, Manufacturing and Construction Division, 4600 Silver Hill Road, Washington DC 20233, (301) 763-4673, www.census.gov/mcd; *Current Industrial Reports.*

AIR FORCE - DEPARTMENT OF - PERSONNEL

U.S. Department of Defense (DOD), Statistical Information Analysis Division (SIAD), The Pentagon, Washington, DC 20301, (703) 545-6700, http://siadapp.dior.whs.mil/; *Selected Manpower Statistics, Fiscal Year 2005.*

AIR POLLUTION - AIR POLLUTION CONTROL EQUIPMENT

Environmental Business International, Inc., 4452 Park Boulevard, Suite 306, San Diego, CA 92116, (619) 295-7685, Fax: (619) 295-5743, www.ebiusa.com; *Environmental Business Journal (EBJ) 2006; Environmental Market Reports;* and *U.S. and Global Environmental Market Data.*

AIR POLLUTION - EMISSIONS

Environmental Defense Fund, 257 Park Avenue South, New York, NY 10010, (800) 684-3322, www.edf.org; *All Choked Up: Heavy Traffic, Dirty Air and the Risk to New Yorkers; Cars and Climate Change: How Automakers Stack Up;* and *Smokestacks on Rails: Locomotive Pollution Impacts Public Health.*

Organisation for Economic Cooperation and Development (OECD), 2 rue Andre Pascal, F-75775 Paris Cedex 16, France, (Telephone in U.S. (202) 785-6323), (Fax in U.S. (202) 785-0350), www.oecd.org; *Key Environmental Indicators 2004.*

Platts, 2 Penn Plaza, 25th Floor, New York, NY 10121-2298, (212) 904-3070, www.platts.com; *Emissions Daily.*

U.S. Environmental Protection Agency (EPA), Ariel Rios Building, 1200 Pennsylvania Avenue, NW, Washington, DC 20460, (202) 272-0167, www.epa.gov; Air Quality System (AQS) Database; *National Emission Inventory (NEI) Database;* and Toxics Release Inventory (TRI) Database.

World Resources Institute (WRI), 10 G Street, NE, Suite 800 Washington, DC 20002, (202) 729-7600, www.wri.org; *Charting the Midwest: An Inventory and Analysis of Greenhouse Gas Emissions in America's Heartland.*

AIR POLLUTION - GREENHOUSE GASES

Intergovernmental Panel on Climate Change (IPCC), www.ipcc.ch; *Carbon Dioxide Capture and Storage; Climate Change 2007: Working Group II Report - Impacts, Adaptation and Vulnerability; The Regional Impacts of Climate Change: An Assessment of Vulnerability;* and *Safeguarding the Ozone Layer and the Global Climate System: Issues Related to Hydrofluorocarbons and Perfluorocarbons.*

U.S. Department of Energy (DOE), Energy Information Administration (EIA), 1000 Independence Avenue, SW, Washington, DC 20585, (202) 586-8800, www.eia.doe.gov; *Emissions of Greenhouse Gases in the United States 2005.*

World Resources Institute (WRI), 10 G Street, NE, Suite 800 Washington DC 20002, (202) 729-7600, www.wri.org; *Charting the Midwest: An Inventory and Analysis of Greenhouse Gas Emissions in America's Heartland.*

AIR POLLUTION - INDUSTRY

Environmental Business International, Inc., 4452 Park Boulevard, Suite 306, San Diego, CA 92116, (619) 295-7685, Fax: (619) 295-5743, www.ebiusa.com; *Environmental Business Journal (EBJ) 2006; Environmental Market Reports;* and *U.S. and Global Environmental Market Data.*

AIRCRAFT AND PARTS INDUSTRY

AMSTAT, 44 Apple Street, Tinton Falls, NJ 07724, (732) 530-6400, www.amstatcorp.com; *AMSTAT Premier* and *AMSTAT StatPak.*

The World Bank, 1818 H Street, NW, Washington, DC 20433, (202) 473-1000, Fax: (202) 477-6391, www.worldbank.org; *The World Bank Atlas 2003-2004* and *The World Bank Atlas 2003-2004.*

AIRCRAFT AND PARTS INDUSTRY - MANUFACTURING - EARNINGS

U.S. Census Bureau, Center for Economic Studies, 4600 Silver Hill Road, Washington DC 20233, (301) 457-1235, www.ces.census.gov; *2002 Economic Census, Transportation and Warehousing.*

AIRCRAFT MANUFACTURING

See AEROSPACE INDUSTRY

AIRLINE OPERATIONS

See AERONAUTICS, COMMERCIAL

AIRMAIL SERVICE

U.S. Postal Service (USPS), 475 L'Enfant Plaza West, SW, Washington, DC 20260, (202) 268-2500, Fax: (202) 268-4860, www.usps.gov; *Quarterly Statistics Report (QSR)* and unpublished data.

AIRPLANES

AMSTAT, 44 Apple Street, Tinton Falls, NJ 07724, (732) 530-6400, www.amstatcorp.com; *AMSTAT Premier* and *AMSTAT StatPak.*

Eurostat, Batiment Jean Monnet, Rue Alcide de Gasperi, L-2920 Luxembourg, http://epp.eurostat.ec.europa.eu; *Regional Passenger and Freight Air Transport in Europe in 2006.*

U.S. Census Bureau, Foreign Trade Division, 4700 Silver Hill Road, Washington DC 20233-0001, (301) 763-3030, www.census.gov/foreign-trade/www/; *U.S. International Trade in Goods and Services.*

AIRPORTS

Eurostat, Batiment Jean Monnet, Rue Alcide de Gasperi, L-2920 Luxembourg, http://epp.eurostat.ec.europa.eu; *Regional Passenger and Freight Air Transport in Europe in 2006.*

Regional Airline Association (RAA), 2025 M Street, NW, Suite 800, Washington, DC 20036-3309, (202) 367-1170, Fax: (202) 367-2170, www.raa.org; *Top 50 US Airports with Regional Service (for the Calendar Year 2007).*

State of Connecticut, Department of Economic and Community Development (DECD), 505 Hudson Street, Hartford, CT 06106-7107, (860) 270-8000, www.ct.gov/ecd/; *The Contribution of Bradley International Airport to Connecticut's Economy.*

U.S. Department of Transportation (DOT), Research and Innovative Technology Administration (RITA), Bureau of Transportation Statistics (BTS), 1200 New Jersey Avenue, SE, Washington, DC 20590, (800) 853-1351, www.bts.gov; *TranStats*.

AIRPORTS - FEDERAL AID TO STATE AND LOCAL GOVERNMENTS

The Office of Management and Budget (OMB), 725 17th Street, NW, Washington, DC 20503, (202) 395-3080, Fax: (202) 395-3888, www.whitehouse.gov/omb; *Budget of the United States Government, Federal Year 2009* and *Historical Tables*.

AIRPORTS - SERVING REGIONAL AIRLINES

Regional Airline Association (RAA), 2025 M Street, NW, Suite 800, Washington, DC 20036-3309, (202) 367-1170, Fax: (202) 367-2170, www.raa.org; *2007 Regional Airline Industry Annual Report* and *Top 50 US Airports with Regional Service (for the Calendar Year 2007)*.

AIRPORTS - TRAFFIC

International Civil Aviation Organization (ICAO), External Relations and Public Information Office (EPO), 999 University Street, Montreal, Quebec H3C 5H7, Canada, (Dial from U.S. (514) 954-8219), (Fax from U.S. (514) 954-6077), www.icao.int; *Traffic - Commercial Air Carriers*.

Regional Airline Association (RAA), 2025 M Street, NW, Suite 800, Washington, DC 20036-3309, (202) 367-1170, Fax: (202) 367-2170, www.raa.org; *2007 Industry Traffic Statistics* and *Top 50 Individual Regional Airlines (as of December 2006)*.

U.S. Department of Transportation (DOT), Office of Aviation Enforcement and Proceedings (OAEP), 1200 New Jersey Ave, SE, Washington, DC 20590, (202) 366-4000, http://airconsumer.ost.dot.gov; *Air Travel Consumer Report 2008*.

U.S. Department of Transportation (DOT), Research and Innovative Technology Administration (RITA), Bureau of Transportation Statistics (BTS), 1200 New Jersey Avenue, SE, Washington, DC 20590, (800) 853-1351, www.bts.gov; Airline On-Time Statistics and Delay Causes (web app).

AIRPORTS OR AIRFIELDS - AIRPORT AND AIRWAY TRUST FUND

The Office of Management and Budget (OMB), 725 17th Street, NW, Washington, DC 20503, (202) 395-3080, Fax: (202) 395-3888, www.whitehouse.gov/omb; *Budget of the United States Government, Federal Year 2009*.

ALABAMA

See also - STATE DATA (FOR INDIVIDUAL STATES)

ALABAMA - STATE DATA CENTERS

Alabama Department of Economic and Community Affairs (ADECA), PO Box 5690, Montgomery, AL 36103-5690, (334) 242-5100, Fax: (334) 242-5099, www.adeca.state.al.us; State Data Center.

Alabama Public Library Service (APLS), 6030 Monticello Drive, Montgomery, AL 36130, (334) 213-3900, Fax: (334) 213-3993, http://statelibrary.alabama.gov; State Data Center.

Center for Business and Economic Research, University of Alabama, Box 870221, Tuscaloosa, AL 35487-0221, Annette Watters, Project Manager, (205) 348-6191, Fax: (205) 348-2951, http://cber.cba.ua.edu; State Data Center.

ALABAMA - PRIMARY STATISTICS SOURCES

Center for Business and Economic Research, University of Alabama, Box 870221, Tuscaloosa, AL 35487-0221, Annette Watters, Project Manager, (205) 348-6191, Fax: (205) 348-2951, http://cber.cba.ua.edu; *Alabama Business; Alabama Economic Outlook;* and *Alabama Population Projections, 2000-2025*.

ALASKA

See also - STATE DATA (FOR INDIVIDUAL STATES)

ALASKA - STATE DATA CENTERS

Alaska Department of Commerce, Community Economic Development, 4300 B Street, Suite 101, Anchorage, Alaska 99503, Mr. Pat Ladner, Executive Director, (907) 561-3338, Fax: (907) 561-3339, www.dced.state.ak.us; State Data Center.

Alaska State Library, Alaska State Publications Program, PO Box 110571, Juneau, AK 99811-0571, (907) 465-2927, Fax: (907) 465-2665, www.library.state.ak.us; State Data Center.

State of Alaska Department of Labor and Workforce Development, 1111 W Eighth Street, Juneau, AK 99801, (907) 465-4500, Fax: (907) 465-4506, http://almis.labor.state.ak.us; State Data Center.

University of Alaska-Anchorage, Institute of Social and Economic Research, 3211 Providence Drive, Anchorage, AK 99508, Ms. Stephanie Martin, (907) 786-5430, Fax: (907) 786-7739, www.iser.uaa.alaska.edu; State Data Center.

ALASKA - PRIMARY STATISTICS SOURCES

Alaska Department of Commerce, Community Economic Development, 4300 B Street, Suite 101, Anchorage, Alaska 99503, Mr. Pat Ladner, Executive Director, (907) 561-3338, Fax: (907) 561-3339, www.dced.state.ak.us; *The Alaska Economic Performance Report 2006* and unpublished data.

ALBANIA - NATIONAL STATISTICAL OFFICE

Institute of Statistics (INSTAT), Rr. Gjergj Fishta, Number 3, Tirana, Albania, www.instat.gov.al; National Data Center.

ALBANIA - PRIMARY STATISTICS SOURCES

Institute of Statistics (INSTAT), Rr. Gjergj Fishta, Number 3, Tirana, Albania, www.instat.gov.al; *Albania in Figures 2007* and *Social Indicators Yearbook 2006*.

ALBANIA - ABORTION

United Nations Statistics Division, New York, NY 10017, (800) 253-9646, Fax: (212) 963-4116, http://unstats.un.org; *Trends in Europe and North America: The Statistical Yearbook of the ECE 2005*.

ALBANIA - AGRICULTURE

Economist Intelligence Unit, 111 West 57th Street, New York, NY 10019, (212) 554-0600, Fax: (212) 586-1181, www.eiu.com; *Albania Country Report*.

Euromonitor International, Inc., 224 S. Michigan Avenue, Suite 1500, Chicago, IL 60604, (312) 922-1115, Fax: (312) 922-1157, www.euromonitor.com; *World Marketing Data and Statistics*.

M.E. Sharpe, 80 Business Park Drive, Armonk, NY 10504, (800) 541-6563, Fax: (914) 273-2106, www.mesharpe.com; *The Illustrated Book of World Rankings*.

Palgrave Macmillan Ltd., Houndmills, Basingstoke, Hampshire, RG21 6XS, England, (Telephone in U.S. (888) 330-8477), (Fax in U.S. (800) 672-2054), www.palgrave.com; *The Statesman's Yearbook 2008*.

Taylor and Francis Group, An Informa Business, 2 Park Square, Milton Park, Abingdon, Oxford OX14 4RN, United Kingdom, (Dial from U.S. (212) 216-7800), (Fax from U.S. (212) 564-7854), www.tandf.co.uk; *The Europa World Year Book*.

United Nations Conference on Trade and Development (UNCTAD), DC2-1120, United Nations, New York, NY 10017, (212) 963-0027, www.unctad.org; *UNCTAD Commodity Yearbook*.

United Nations Food and Agricultural Organization (FAO), Viale delle Terme di Caracalla, 00100 Rome, Italy, (Dial from U.S. (202) 653-2400), (Fax from U.S. (202) 653 5760), www.fao.org; AQUASTAT; *FAO Production Yearbook 2002; FAO Trade Yearbook;* and *The State of Food and Agriculture (SOFA) 2006*.

United Nations Statistics Division, New York, NY 10017, (800) 253-9646, Fax: (212) 963-4116, http://unstats.un.org; *Statistical Yearbook*.

The World Bank, 1818 H Street, NW, Washington, DC 20433, (202) 473-1000, Fax: (202) 477-6391, www.worldbank.org; *Albania*.

ALBANIA - AIRLINES

M.E. Sharpe, 80 Business Park Drive, Armonk, NY 10504, (800) 541-6563, Fax: (914) 273-2106, www.mesharpe.com; *The Illustrated Book of World Rankings*.

Palgrave Macmillan Ltd., Houndmills, Basingstoke, Hampshire, RG21 6XS, England, (Telephone in U.S. (888) 330-8477), (Fax in U.S. (800) 672-2054), www.palgrave.com; *The Statesman's Yearbook 2008*.

ALBANIA - AIRPORTS

Central Intelligence Agency, Office of Public Affairs, Washington, DC 20505, (703) 482-0623, Fax: (703) 482-1739, www.cia.gov; *The World Factbook*.

ALBANIA - ALUMINUM PRODUCTION

See ALBANIA - MINERAL INDUSTRIES

ALBANIA - ARMED FORCES

Central Intelligence Agency, Office of Public Affairs, Washington, DC 20505, (703) 482-0623, Fax: (703) 482-1739, www.cia.gov; *The World Factbook*.

Euromonitor International, Inc., 224 S. Michigan Avenue, Suite 1500, Chicago, IL 60604, (312) 922-1115, Fax: (312) 922-1157, www.euromonitor.com; *World Marketing Data and Statistics*.

International Institute for Strategic Studies (IISS), Arundel House, 13-15 Arundel Street, Temple Place, London WC2R 3DX, England, www.iiss.org; *The Military Balance 2007*.

Palgrave Macmillan Ltd., Houndmills, Basingstoke, Hampshire, RG21 6XS, England, (Telephone in U.S. (888) 330-8477), (Fax in U.S. (800) 672-2054), www.palgrave.com; *The Statesman's Yearbook 2008*.

U.S. Department of State (DOS), 2201 C Street NW, Washington, DC 20520, (202) 647-4000, www.state.gov; *World Military Expenditures and Arms Transfers (WMEAT)*.

United Nations Statistics Division, New York, NY 10017, (800) 253-9646, Fax: (212) 963-4116, http://unstats.un.org; *Human Development Report 2006*.

ALBANIA - BALANCE OF PAYMENTS

United Nations Conference on Trade and Development (UNCTAD), DC2-1120, United Nations, New York, NY 10017, (212) 963-0027, www.unctad.org; *Handbook of Statistics 2005*.

The World Bank, 1818 H Street, NW, Washington, DC 20433, (202) 473-1000, Fax: (202) 477-6391, www.worldbank.org; *Albania* and *World Development Report 2008*.

ALBANIA - BANKS AND BANKING

Euromonitor International, Inc., 224 S. Michigan Avenue, Suite 1500, Chicago, IL 60604, (312) 922-

1115, Fax: (312) 922-1157, www.euromonitor.com; *World Marketing Data and Statistics.*

M.E. Sharpe, 80 Business Park Drive, Armonk, NY 10504, (800) 541-6563, Fax: (914) 273-2106, www.mesharpe.com; *The Illustrated Book of World Rankings.*

Palgrave Macmillan Ltd., Houndmills, Basingstoke, Hampshire, RG21 6XS, England, (Telephone in U.S. (888) 330-8477), (Fax in U.S. (800) 672-2054), www.palgrave.com; *The Statesman's Yearbook 2008.*

ALBANIA - BARLEY PRODUCTION

See ALBANIA - CROPS

ALBANIA - BEVERAGE INDUSTRY

M.E. Sharpe, 80 Business Park Drive, Armonk, NY 10504, (800) 541-6563, Fax: (914) 273-2106, www.mesharpe.com; *The Illustrated Book of World Rankings.*

United Nations Statistics Division, New York, NY 10017, (800) 253-9646, Fax: (212) 963-4116, http://unstats.un.org; *Statistical Yearbook.*

ALBANIA - BROADCASTING

Central Intelligence Agency, Office of Public Affairs, Washington, DC 20505, (703) 482-0623, Fax: (703) 482-1739, www.cia.gov; *The World Factbook.*

Euromonitor International, Inc., 224 S. Michigan Avenue, Suite 1500, Chicago, IL 60604, (312) 922-1115, Fax: (312) 922-1157, www.euromonitor.com; *World Marketing Data and Statistics.*

M.E. Sharpe, 80 Business Park Drive, Armonk, NY 10504, (800) 541-6563, Fax: (914) 273-2106, www.mesharpe.com; *The Illustrated Book of World Rankings.*

Palgrave Macmillan Ltd., Houndmills, Basingstoke, Hampshire, RG21 6XS, England, (Telephone in U.S. (888) 330-8477), (Fax in U.S. (800) 672-2054), www.palgrave.com; *The Statesman's Yearbook 2008.*

United Nations Statistics Division, New York, NY 10017, (800) 253-9646, Fax: (212) 963-4116, http://unstats.un.org; *Trends in Europe and North America: The Statistical Yearbook of the ECE 2005.*

WRTH Publications Limited, PO Box 290, Oxford OX2 7FT, UK, www.wrth.com; *World Radio TV Handbook 2007.*

ALBANIA - BUDGET

Central Intelligence Agency, Office of Public Affairs, Washington, DC 20505, (703) 482-0623, Fax: (703) 482-1739, www.cia.gov; *The World Factbook.*

ALBANIA - BUSINESS

Economist Intelligence Unit, 111 West 57th Street, New York, NY 10019, (212) 554-0600, Fax: (212) 586-1181, www.eiu.com; *Business Eastern Europe.*

ALBANIA - CATTLE

See ALBANIA - LIVESTOCK

ALBANIA - CHILDBIRTH - STATISTICS

Central Intelligence Agency, Office of Public Affairs, Washington, DC 20505, (703) 482-0623, Fax: (703) 482-1739, www.cia.gov; *The World Factbook.*

M.E. Sharpe, 80 Business Park Drive, Armonk, NY 10504, (800) 541-6563, Fax: (914) 273-2106, www.mesharpe.com; *The Illustrated Book of World Rankings.*

Palgrave Macmillan Ltd., Houndmills, Basingstoke, Hampshire, RG21 6XS, England, (Telephone in U.S. (888) 330-8477), (Fax in U.S. (800) 672-2054), www.palgrave.com; *The Statesman's Yearbook 2008.*

Taylor and Francis Group, An Informa Business, 2 Park Square, Milton Park, Abingdon, Oxford OX14 4RN, United Kingdom, (Dial from U.S. (212) 216-7800), (Fax from U.S. (212) 564-7854), www.tandf.co.uk; *The Europa World Year Book.*

United Nations Statistics Division, New York, NY 10017, (800) 253-9646, Fax: (212) 963-4116, http://unstats.un.org; *Demographic Yearbook* and *Statistical Yearbook.*

ALBANIA - CLIMATE

M.E. Sharpe, 80 Business Park Drive, Armonk, NY 10504, (800) 541-6563, Fax: (914) 273-2106, www.mesharpe.com; *The Illustrated Book of World Rankings.*

Palgrave Macmillan Ltd., Houndmills, Basingstoke, Hampshire, RG21 6XS, England, (Telephone in U.S. (888) 330-8477), (Fax in U.S. (800) 672-2054), www.palgrave.com; *The Statesman's Yearbook 2008.*

ALBANIA - COAL PRODUCTION

See ALBANIA - MINERAL INDUSTRIES

ALBANIA - COFFEE

See ALBANIA - CROPS

ALBANIA - COMMERCE

Palgrave Macmillan Ltd., Houndmills, Basingstoke, Hampshire, RG21 6XS, England, (Telephone in U.S. (888) 330-8477), (Fax in U.S. (800) 672-2054), www.palgrave.com; *The Statesman's Yearbook 2008.*

ALBANIA - COMMODITY EXCHANGES

Commodity Research Bureau, 330 South Wells Street, Suite 612, Chicago, IL 60606-7110, (800) 621-5271, Fax: (312) 939-4135, www.crbtrader.com; *2006 CRB Commodity Yearbook and CD.*

International Monetary Fund (IMF), 700 Nineteenth Street, NW, Washington, DC 20431, (202) 623-7000, Fax: (202) 623-4661, www.imf.org; *IMF Primary Commodity Prices.*

United Nations Food and Agricultural Organization (FAO), Viale delle Terme di Caracalla, 00100 Rome, Italy, (Dial from U.S. (202) 653-2400), (Fax from U.S. (202) 653 5760), www.fao.org; *The State of Food and Agriculture (SOFA) 2006.*

ALBANIA - CONSTRUCTION INDUSTRY

M.E. Sharpe, 80 Business Park Drive, Armonk, NY 10504, (800) 541-6563, Fax: (914) 273-2106, www.mesharpe.com; *The Illustrated Book of World Rankings.*

Palgrave Macmillan Ltd., Houndmills, Basingstoke, Hampshire, RG21 6XS, England, (Telephone in U.S. (888) 330-8477), (Fax in U.S. (800) 672-2054), www.palgrave.com; *The Statesman's Yearbook 2008.*

ALBANIA - CONSUMER PRICE INDEXES

United Nations Statistics Division, New York, NY 10017, (800) 253-9646, Fax: (212) 963-4116, http://unstats.un.org; *Trends in Europe and North America: The Statistical Yearbook of the ECE 2005.*

The World Bank, 1818 H Street, NW, Washington, DC 20433, (202) 473-1000, Fax: (202) 477-6391, www.worldbank.org; *Albania.*

ALBANIA - CONSUMPTION (ECONOMICS)

The World Bank, 1818 H Street, NW, Washington, DC 20433, (202) 473-1000, Fax: (202) 477-6391, www.worldbank.org; *World Development Report 2008.*

ALBANIA - COPPER INDUSTRY AND TRADE

See ALBANIA - MINERAL INDUSTRIES

ALBANIA - CORN INDUSTRY

See ALBANIA - CROPS

ALBANIA - COTTON

See ALBANIA - CROPS

ALBANIA - CRIME

United Nations Statistics Division, New York, NY 10017, (800) 253-9646, Fax: (212) 963-4116, http://unstats.un.org; *Trends in Europe and North America: The Statistical Yearbook of the ECE 2005.*

ALBANIA - CROPS

Euromonitor International, Inc., 224 S. Michigan Avenue, Suite 1500, Chicago, IL 60604, (312) 922-1115, Fax: (312) 922-1157, www.euromonitor.com; *European Marketing Data and Statistics 2008.*

M.E. Sharpe, 80 Business Park Drive, Armonk, NY 10504, (800) 541-6563, Fax: (914) 273-2106, www.mesharpe.com; *The Illustrated Book of World Rankings.*

Palgrave Macmillan Ltd., Houndmills, Basingstoke, Hampshire, RG21 6XS, England, (Telephone in U.S. (888) 330-8477), (Fax in U.S. (800) 672-2054), www.palgrave.com; *The Statesman's Yearbook 2008.*

Taylor and Francis Group, An Informa Business, 2 Park Square, Milton Park, Abingdon, Oxford OX14 4RN, United Kingdom, (Dial from U.S. (212) 216-7800), (Fax from U.S. (212) 564-7854), www.tandf.co.uk; *The Europa World Year Book.*

United Nations Conference on Trade and Development (UNCTAD), DC2-1120, United Nations, New York, NY 10017, (212) 963-0027, www.unctad.org; *UNCTAD Commodity Yearbook.*

United Nations Food and Agricultural Organization (FAO), Viale delle Terme di Caracalla, 00100 Rome, Italy, (Dial from U.S. (202) 653-2400), (Fax from U.S. (202) 653 5760), www.fao.org; *FAO Production Yearbook 2002* and *The State of Food and Agriculture (SOFA) 2006.*

United Nations Statistics Division, New York, NY 10017, (800) 253-9646, Fax: (212) 963-4116, http://unstats.un.org; *Statistical Yearbook.*

ALBANIA - CUSTOMS ADMINISTRATION

Palgrave Macmillan Ltd., Houndmills, Basingstoke, Hampshire, RG21 6XS, England, (Telephone in U.S. (888) 330-8477), (Fax in U.S. (800) 672-2054), www.palgrave.com; *The Statesman's Yearbook 2008.*

ALBANIA - DAIRY PROCESSING

M.E. Sharpe, 80 Business Park Drive, Armonk, NY 10504, (800) 541-6563, Fax: (914) 273-2106, www.mesharpe.com; *The Illustrated Book of World Rankings.*

Palgrave Macmillan Ltd., Houndmills, Basingstoke, Hampshire, RG21 6XS, England, (Telephone in U.S. (888) 330-8477), (Fax in U.S. (800) 672-2054), www.palgrave.com; *The Statesman's Yearbook 2008.*

Taylor and Francis Group, An Informa Business, 2 Park Square, Milton Park, Abingdon, Oxford OX14 4RN, United Kingdom, (Dial from U.S. (212) 216-7800), (Fax from U.S. (212) 564-7854), www.tandf.co.uk; *The Europa World Year Book.*

United Nations Food and Agricultural Organization (FAO), Viale delle Terme di Caracalla, 00100 Rome, Italy, (Dial from U.S. (202) 653-2400), (Fax from U.S. (202) 653 5760), www.fao.org; *The State of Food and Agriculture (SOFA) 2006.*

United Nations Statistics Division, New York, NY 10017, (800) 253-9646, Fax: (212) 963-4116, http://unstats.un.org; *Statistical Yearbook.*

ALBANIA - DEATH RATES

See ALBANIA - MORTALITY

ALBANIA - DEBTS, EXTERNAL

Palgrave Macmillan Ltd., Houndmills, Basingstoke, Hampshire, RG21 6XS, England, (Telephone in U.S. (888) 330-8477), (Fax in U.S. (800) 672-2054), www.palgrave.com; *The Statesman's Yearbook 2008.*

The World Bank, 1818 H Street, NW, Washington, DC 20433, (202) 473-1000, Fax: (202) 477-6391, www.worldbank.org; *Global Development Finance 2007* and *World Development Report 2008.*

ALBANIA - DEFENSE EXPENDITURES

See ALBANIA - ARMED FORCES

ALBANIA - DEMOGRAPHY

Euromonitor International, Inc., 224 S. Michigan Avenue, Suite 1500, Chicago, IL 60604, (312) 922-

1115, Fax: (312) 922-1157, www.euromonitor.com; *World Marketing Data and Statistics.*

M.E. Sharpe, 80 Business Park Drive, Armonk, NY 10504, (800) 541-6563, Fax: (914) 273-2106, www.mesharpe.com; *The Illustrated Book of World Rankings.*

United Nations Statistics Division, New York, NY 10017, (800) 253-9646, Fax: (212) 963-4116, http://unstats.un.org; *Human Development Report 2006.*

The World Bank, 1818 H Street, NW, Washington, DC 20433, (202) 473-1000, Fax: (202) 477-6391, www.worldbank.org; *Albania.*

ALBANIA - DIAMONDS

See ALBANIA - MINERAL INDUSTRIES

ALBANIA - DISPOSABLE INCOME

M.E. Sharpe, 80 Business Park Drive, Armonk, NY 10504, (800) 541-6563, Fax: (914) 273-2106, www.mesharpe.com; *The Illustrated Book of World Rankings.*

United Nations Statistics Division, New York, NY 10017, (800) 253-9646, Fax: (212) 963-4116, http://unstats.un.org; *National Accounts Statistics: Compendium of Income Distribution Statistics.*

ALBANIA - DIVORCE

M.E. Sharpe, 80 Business Park Drive, Armonk, NY 10504, (800) 541-6563, Fax: (914) 273-2106, www.mesharpe.com; *The Illustrated Book of World Rankings.*

United Nations Statistics Division, New York, NY 10017, (800) 253-9646, Fax: (212) 963-4116, http://unstats.un.org; *Demographic Yearbook; Statistical Yearbook;* and *Trends in Europe and North America: The Statistical Yearbook of the ECE 2005.*

ALBANIA - ECONOMIC CONDITIONS

Center for International Business Education Research (CIBER), Columbia Business School and School of International and Public Affairs, Uris Hall, Room 212, 3022 Broadway, New York, NY 10027-6902, Mr. Joshua Safier, (212) 854-4750, Fax: (212) 222-9821, www.columbia.edu/cu/ciber/; Datastream International.

Central Intelligence Agency, Office of Public Affairs, Washington, DC 20505, (703) 482-0623, Fax: (703) 482-1739, www.cia.gov; *The World Factbook.*

DSI Data Service Information, Xantener Strasse 51a, D-47495 Rheinberg, Germany, www.dsidata.com; *Campus Solution.*

Dun and Bradstreet (DB) Corporation, 103 JFK Parkway, Short Hills, NJ 07078, (973) 921-5500, www.dnb.com; *Country Report.*

Economist Intelligence Unit, 111 West 57th Street, New York, NY 10019, (212) 554-0600, Fax: (212) 586-1181, www.eiu.com; *Albania Country Report.*

Euromonitor International, Inc., 224 S. Michigan Avenue, Suite 1500, Chicago, IL 60604, (312) 922-1115, Fax: (312) 922-1157, www.euromonitor.com; *European Marketing Data and Statistics 2008* and *World Marketing Data and Statistics.*

International Monetary Fund (IMF), 700 Nineteenth Street, NW, Washington, DC 20431, (202) 623-7000, Fax: (202) 623-4661, www.imf.org; *World Economic Outlook Reports.*

M.E. Sharpe, 80 Business Park Drive, Armonk, NY 10504, (800) 541-6563, Fax: (914) 273-2106, www.mesharpe.com; *The Illustrated Book of World Rankings.*

Palgrave Macmillan Ltd., Houndmills, Basingstoke, Hampshire, RG21 6XS, England, (Telephone in U.S. (888) 330-8477), (Fax in U.S. (800) 672-2054), www.palgrave.com; *The Statesman's Yearbook 2008.*

Taylor and Francis Group, An Informa Business, 2 Park Square, Milton Park, Abingdon, Oxford OX14 4RN, United Kingdom, (Dial from U.S. (212) 216-7800), (Fax from U.S. (212) 564-7854), www.tandf.co.uk; *The Europa World Year Book.*

United Nations Statistics Division, New York, NY 10017, (800) 253-9646, Fax: (212) 963-4116, http://unstats.un.org; *World Statistics Pocketbook.*

The World Bank, 1818 H Street, NW, Washington, DC 20433, (202) 473-1000, Fax: (202) 477-6391, www.worldbank.org; *Albania; Global Economic Monitor (GEM); Global Economic Prospects 2008; The World Bank Atlas 2003-2004;* and *World Development Report 2008.*

ALBANIA - EDUCATION

Euromonitor International, Inc., 224 S. Michigan Avenue, Suite 1500, Chicago, IL 60604, (312) 922-1115, Fax: (312) 922-1157, www.euromonitor.com; *European Marketing Data and Statistics 2008* and *World Marketing Data and Statistics.*

European Union, Delegation of the European Commission to the United States, 2300 M Street, NW, Washington, DC 20037, (202) 862-9500, Fax: (202) 429-1766, www.eurunion.org; *Education across Europe 2003.*

M.E. Sharpe, 80 Business Park Drive, Armonk, NY 10504, (800) 541-6563, Fax: (914) 273-2106, www.mesharpe.com; *The Illustrated Book of World Rankings.*

Palgrave Macmillan Ltd., Houndmills, Basingstoke, Hampshire, RG21 6XS, England, (Telephone in U.S. (888) 330-8477), (Fax in U.S. (800) 672-2054), www.palgrave.com; *The Statesman's Yearbook 2008.*

Taylor and Francis Group, An Informa Business, 2 Park Square, Milton Park, Abingdon, Oxford OX14 4RN, United Kingdom, (Dial from U.S. (212) 216-7800), (Fax from U.S. (212) 564-7854), www.tandf.co.uk; *The Europa World Year Book.*

UNESCO Institute for Statistics, C.P. 6128 Succursale Centre-Ville, Montreal, Quebec, H3C 3J7 Canada, (Dial from U.S. (514) 343-6880), (Fax from U.S. (514) 343 6882), www.uis.unesco.org; *Statistical Tables.*

United Nations Statistics Division, New York, NY 10017, (800) 253-9646, Fax: (212) 963-4116, http://unstats.un.org; *Human Development Report 2006* and *Trends in Europe and North America: The Statistical Yearbook of the ECE 2005.*

The World Bank, 1818 H Street, NW, Washington, DC 20433, (202) 473-1000, Fax: (202) 477-6391, www.worldbank.org; *Albania* and *World Development Report 2008.*

ALBANIA - ELECTRICITY

M.E. Sharpe, 80 Business Park Drive, Armonk, NY 10504, (800) 541-6563, Fax: (914) 273-2106, www.mesharpe.com; *The Illustrated Book of World Rankings.*

Organisation for Economic Cooperation and Development (OECD), 2 rue Andre Pascal, F-75775 Paris Cedex 16, France, (Telephone in U.S. (202) 785-6323), (Fax in U.S. (202) 785-0350), www.oecd.org; *World Energy Outlook 2007.*

Palgrave Macmillan Ltd., Houndmills, Basingstoke, Hampshire, RG21 6XS, England, (Telephone in U.S. (888) 330-8477), (Fax in U.S. (800) 672-2054), www.palgrave.com; *The Statesman's Yearbook 2008.*

Platts, 2 Penn Plaza, 25th Floor, New York, NY 10121-2298, (212) 904-3070, www.platts.com; *European Electricity Review 2004.*

U.S. Department of Energy (DOE), Energy Information Administration (EIA), 1000 Independence Avenue, SW, Washington, DC 20585, (202) 586-8800, www.eia.doe.gov; *International Energy Annual 2004* and *International Energy Outlook 2006.*

United Nations Statistics Division, New York, NY 10017, (800) 253-9646, Fax: (212) 963-4116, http://unstats.un.org; *Human Development Report 2006; Statistical Yearbook;* and *Trends in Europe and North America: The Statistical Yearbook of the ECE 2005.*

ALBANIA - EMPLOYMENT

Euromonitor International, Inc., 224 S. Michigan Avenue, Suite 1500, Chicago, IL 60604, (312) 922-1115, Fax: (312) 922-1157, www.euromonitor.com; *European Marketing Data and Statistics 2008.*

M.E. Sharpe, 80 Business Park Drive, Armonk, NY 10504, (800) 541-6563, Fax: (914) 273-2106, www.mesharpe.com; *The Illustrated Book of World Rankings.*

United Nations Statistics Division, New York, NY 10017, (800) 253-9646, Fax: (212) 963-4116, http://unstats.un.org; *Trends in Europe and North America: The Statistical Yearbook of the ECE 2005.*

The World Bank, 1818 H Street, NW, Washington, DC 20433, (202) 473-1000, Fax: (202) 477-6391, www.worldbank.org; *Albania.*

ALBANIA - ENERGY INDUSTRIES

Platts, 2 Penn Plaza, 25th Floor, New York, NY 10121-2298, (212) 904-3070, www.platts.com; *Energy in East Europe.*

ALBANIA - ENVIRONMENTAL CONDITIONS

Center for Research on the Epidemiology of Disasters (CRED), Universite Catholique de Louvain, Ecole de Sante Publique, 30.94 Clos Chapelle-aux-Champs, 1200 Brussels, Belgium, www.cred.be; *Three Decades of Floods in Europe: A Preliminary Analysis of EMDAT Data.*

DSI Data Service Information, Xantener Strasse 51a, D-47495 Rheinberg, Germany, www.dsidata.com; *Campus Solution* and *DSI's Global Environmental Database.*

Economist Intelligence Unit, 111 West 57th Street, New York, NY 10019, (212) 554-0600, Fax: (212) 586-1181, www.eiu.com; *Albania Country Report.*

Eurostat, Batiment Jean Monnet, Rue Alcide de Gasperi, L-2920 Luxembourg, http://epp.eurostat.ec.europa.eu; *Environmental Protection Expenditure in Europe.*

United Nations Statistics Division, New York, NY 10017, (800) 253-9646, Fax: (212) 963-4116, http://unstats.un.org; *Trends in Europe and North America: The Statistical Yearbook of the ECE 2005* and *World Statistics Pocketbook.*

ALBANIA - EXPORTS

Central Intelligence Agency, Office of Public Affairs, Washington, DC 20505, (703) 482-0623, Fax: (703) 482-1739, www.cia.gov; *The World Factbook.*

Economist Intelligence Unit, 111 West 57th Street, New York, NY 10019, (212) 554-0600, Fax: (212) 586-1181, www.eiu.com; *Albania Country Report.*

International Monetary Fund (IMF), 700 Nineteenth Street, NW, Washington, DC 20431, (202) 623-7000, Fax: (202) 623-4661, www.imf.org; *Direction of Trade Statistics Yearbook 2007.*

Palgrave Macmillan Ltd., Houndmills, Basingstoke, Hampshire, RG21 6XS, England, (Telephone in U.S. (888) 330-8477), (Fax in U.S. (800) 672-2054), www.palgrave.com; *The Statesman's Yearbook 2008.*

Taylor and Francis Group, An Informa Business, 2 Park Square, Milton Park, Abingdon, Oxford OX14 4RN, United Kingdom, (Dial from U.S. (212) 216-7800), (Fax from U.S. (212) 564-7854), www.tandf.co.uk; *The Europa World Year Book.*

United Nations Conference on Trade and Development (UNCTAD), DC2-1120, United Nations, New York, NY 10017, (212) 963-0027, www.unctad.org; *Handbook of Statistics 2005.*

United Nations Food and Agricultural Organization (FAO), Viale delle Terme di Caracalla, 00100 Rome, Italy, (Dial from U.S. (202) 653-2400), (Fax from U.S. (202) 653 5760), www.fao.org; *The State of Food and Agriculture (SOFA) 2006.*

United Nations Statistics Division, New York, NY 10017, (800) 253-9646, Fax: (212) 963-4116, http://unstats.un.org; *Trends in Europe and North America: The Statistical Yearbook of the ECE 2005.*

The World Bank, 1818 H Street, NW, Washington, DC 20433, (202) 473-1000, Fax: (202) 477-6391, www.worldbank.org; *World Development Report 2008.*

ALBANIA - FERTILITY, HUMAN

M.E. Sharpe, 80 Business Park Drive, Armonk, NY 10504, (800) 541-6563, Fax: (914) 273-2106, www.mesharpe.com; *The Illustrated Book of World Rankings.*

United Nations Statistics Division, New York, NY 10017, (800) 253-9646, Fax: (212) 963-4116, http://unstats.un.org; *Demographic Yearbook; Human Development Report 2006;* and *Trends in Europe and North America: The Statistical Yearbook of the ECE 2005.*

The World Bank, 1818 H Street, NW, Washington, DC 20433, (202) 473-1000, Fax: (202) 477-6391, www.worldbank.org; *The World Bank Atlas 2003-2004* and *World Development Report 2008.*

ALBANIA - FERTILIZER INDUSTRY

United Nations Food and Agricultural Organization (FAO), Viale delle Terme di Caracalla, 00100 Rome, Italy, (Dial from U.S. (202) 653-2400), (Fax from U.S. (202) 653 5760), www.fao.org; *FAO Fertilizer Yearbook* and *The State of Food and Agriculture (SOFA) 2006.*

United Nations Statistics Division, New York, NY 10017, (800) 253-9646, Fax: (212) 963-4116, http://unstats.un.org; *Statistical Yearbook.*

ALBANIA - FETAL MORTALITY

See ALBANIA - MORTALITY

ALBANIA - FINANCE

Taylor and Francis Group, An Informa Business, 2 Park Square, Milton Park, Abingdon, Oxford OX14 4RN, United Kingdom, (Dial from U.S. (212) 216-7800), (Fax from U.S. (212) 564-7854), www.tandf.co.uk; *The Europa World Year Book.*

United Nations Statistics Division, New York, NY 10017, (800) 253-9646, Fax: (212) 963-4116, http://unstats.un.org; *Statistical Yearbook.*

The World Bank, 1818 H Street, NW, Washington, DC 20433, (202) 473-1000, Fax: (202) 477-6391, www.worldbank.org; *Albania.*

ALBANIA - FINANCE, PUBLIC

Bernan Essential Government Publications, 4611-F Assembly Drive, Lanham MD, 20706-4391, (301) 459-2255, Fax: (800) 865-3450, www.bernan.com; *National Accounts Statistics.*

Economist Intelligence Unit, 111 West 57th Street, New York, NY 10019, (212) 554-0600, Fax: (212) 586-1181, www.eiu.com; *Albania Country Report.*

International Monetary Fund (IMF), 700 Nineteenth Street, NW, Washington, DC 20431, (202) 623-7000, Fax: (202) 623-4661, www.imf.org; *International Financial Statistics; International Financial Statistics Online Service;* and *International Financial Statistics Yearbook 2007.*

M.E. Sharpe, 80 Business Park Drive, Armonk, NY 10504, (800) 541-6563, Fax: (914) 273-2106, www.mesharpe.com; *The Illustrated Book of World Rankings.*

Palgrave Macmillan Ltd., Houndmills, Basingstoke, Hampshire, RG21 6XS, England, (Telephone in U.S. (888) 330-8477), (Fax in U.S. (800) 672-2054), www.palgrave.com; *The Statesman's Yearbook 2008.*

Taylor and Francis Group, An Informa Business, 2 Park Square, Milton Park, Abingdon, Oxford OX14 4RN, United Kingdom, (Dial from U.S. (212) 216-7800), (Fax from U.S. (212) 564-7854), www.tandf.co.uk; *The Europa World Year Book.*

The World Bank, 1818 H Street, NW, Washington, DC 20433, (202) 473-1000, Fax: (202) 477-6391, www.worldbank.org; *Albania.*

ALBANIA - FISHERIES

Euromonitor International, Inc., 224 S. Michigan Avenue, Suite 1500, Chicago, IL 60604, (312) 922-1115, Fax: (312) 922-1157, www.euromonitor.com; *European Marketing Data and Statistics 2008.*

M.E. Sharpe, 80 Business Park Drive, Armonk, NY 10504, (800) 541-6563, Fax: (914) 273-2106, www.mesharpe.com; *The Illustrated Book of World Rankings.*

Palgrave Macmillan Ltd., Houndmills, Basingstoke, Hampshire, RG21 6XS, England, (Telephone in U.S. (888) 330-8477), (Fax in U.S. (800) 672-2054), www.palgrave.com; *The Statesman's Yearbook 2008.*

Taylor and Francis Group, An Informa Business, 2 Park Square, Milton Park, Abingdon, Oxford OX14 4RN, United Kingdom, (Dial from U.S. (212) 216-7800), (Fax from U.S. (212) 564-7854), www.tandf.co.uk; *The Europa World Year Book.*

United Nations Conference on Trade and Development (UNCTAD), DC2-1120, United Nations, New York, NY 10017, (212) 963-0027, www.unctad.org; *UNCTAD Commodity Yearbook.*

United Nations Food and Agricultural Organization (FAO), Viale delle Terme di Caracalla, 00100 Rome, Italy, (Dial from U.S. (202) 653-2400), (Fax from U.S. (202) 653 5760), www.fao.org; *FAO Yearbook of Fishery Statistics;* Fishery Databases; FISHSTAT Database. Subjects covered include: Aquaculture production, capture production, fishery commodities; and *The State of Food and Agriculture (SOFA) 2006.*

United Nations Statistics Division, New York, NY 10017, (800) 253-9646, Fax: (212) 963-4116, http://unstats.un.org; *Statistical Yearbook.*

The World Bank, 1818 H Street, NW, Washington, DC 20433, (202) 473-1000, Fax: (202) 477-6391, www.worldbank.org; *Albania.*

ALBANIA - FOOD

United Nations Conference on Trade and Development (UNCTAD), DC2-1120, United Nations, New York, NY 10017, (212) 963-0027, www.unctad.org; *UNCTAD Commodity Yearbook.*

United Nations Food and Agricultural Organization (FAO), Viale delle Terme di Caracalla, 00100 Rome, Italy, (Dial from U.S. (202) 653-2400), (Fax from U.S. (202) 653 5760), www.fao.org; *FAO Production Yearbook 2002* and *The State of Food and Agriculture (SOFA) 2006.*

United Nations Statistics Division, New York, NY 10017, (800) 253-9646, Fax: (212) 963-4116, http://unstats.un.org; *Human Development Report 2006.*

ALBANIA - FOREIGN EXCHANGE RATES

Central Intelligence Agency, Office of Public Affairs, Washington, DC 20505, (703) 482-0623, Fax: (703) 482-1739, www.cia.gov; *The World Factbook.*

Taylor and Francis Group, An Informa Business, 2 Park Square, Milton Park, Abingdon, Oxford OX14 4RN, United Kingdom, (Dial from U.S. (212) 216-7800), (Fax from U.S. (212) 564-7854), www.tandf.co.uk; *The Europa World Year Book.*

United Nations Statistics Division, New York, NY 10017, (800) 253-9646, Fax: (212) 963-4116, http://unstats.un.org; *Statistical Yearbook; Trends in Europe and North America: The Statistical Yearbook of the ECE 2005;* and *World Statistics Pocketbook.*

ALBANIA - FORESTS AND FORESTRY

Euromonitor International, Inc., 224 S. Michigan Avenue, Suite 1500, Chicago, IL 60604, (312) 922-1115, Fax: (312) 922-1157, www.euromonitor.com; *European Marketing Data and Statistics 2008.*

M.E. Sharpe, 80 Business Park Drive, Armonk, NY 10504, (800) 541-6563, Fax: (914) 273-2106, www.mesharpe.com; *The Illustrated Book of World Rankings.*

Palgrave Macmillan Ltd., Houndmills, Basingstoke, Hampshire, RG21 6XS, England, (Telephone in U.S. (888) 330-8477), (Fax in U.S. (800) 672-2054), www.palgrave.com; *The Statesman's Yearbook 2008.*

Taylor and Francis Group, An Informa Business, 2 Park Square, Milton Park, Abingdon, Oxford OX14 4RN, United Kingdom, (Dial from U.S. (212) 216-7800), (Fax from U.S. (212) 564-7854), www.tandf.co.uk; *The Europa World Year Book.*

UNESCO Institute for Statistics, C.P. 6128 Succursale Centre-Ville, Montreal, Quebec, H3C 3J7 Canada, (Dial from U.S. (514) 343-6880), (Fax from U.S. (514) 343 6882), www.uis.unesco.org; *Statistical Tables.*

United Nations Conference on Trade and Development (UNCTAD), DC2-1120, United Nations, New York, NY 10017, (212) 963-0027, www.unctad.org; *UNCTAD Commodity Yearbook.*

United Nations Food and Agricultural Organization (FAO), Viale delle Terme di Caracalla, 00100 Rome, Italy, (Dial from U.S. (202) 653-2400), (Fax from U.S. (202) 653 5760), www.fao.org; *FAO Yearbook of Forest Products* and *The State of Food and Agriculture (SOFA) 2006.*

United Nations Statistics Division, New York, NY 10017, (800) 253-9646, Fax: (212) 963-4116, http://unstats.un.org; *Statistical Yearbook* and *Trends in Europe and North America: The Statistical Yearbook of the ECE 2005.*

The World Bank, 1818 H Street, NW, Washington, DC 20433, (202) 473-1000, Fax: (202) 477-6391, www.worldbank.org; *Albania* and *World Development Report 2008.*

ALBANIA - GAS PRODUCTION

See ALBANIA - MINERAL INDUSTRIES

ALBANIA - GEOGRAPHIC INFORMATION SYSTEMS

M.E. Sharpe, 80 Business Park Drive, Armonk, NY 10504, (800) 541-6563, Fax: (914) 273-2106, www.mesharpe.com; *The Illustrated Book of World Rankings.*

The World Bank, 1818 H Street, NW, Washington, DC 20433, (202) 473-1000, Fax: (202) 477-6391, www.worldbank.org; *Albania.*

ALBANIA - GOLD PRODUCTION

See ALBANIA - MINERAL INDUSTRIES

ALBANIA - GROSS DOMESTIC PRODUCT

Economist Intelligence Unit, 111 West 57th Street, New York, NY 10019, (212) 554-0600, Fax: (212) 586-1181, www.eiu.com; *Albania Country Report.*

M.E. Sharpe, 80 Business Park Drive, Armonk, NY 10504, (800) 541-6563, Fax: (914) 273-2106, www.mesharpe.com; *The Illustrated Book of World Rankings.*

United Nations Statistics Division, New York, NY 10017, (800) 253-9646, Fax: (212) 963-4116, http://unstats.un.org; *Human Development Report 2006; National Accounts Statistics: Compendium of Income Distribution Statistics;* and *Trends in Europe and North America: The Statistical Yearbook of the ECE 2005.*

The World Bank, 1818 H Street, NW, Washington, DC 20433, (202) 473-1000, Fax: (202) 477-6391, www.worldbank.org; *World Development Report 2008.*

ALBANIA - GROSS NATIONAL PRODUCT

M.E. Sharpe, 80 Business Park Drive, Armonk, NY 10504, (800) 541-6563, Fax: (914) 273-2106, www.mesharpe.com; *The Illustrated Book of World Rankings.*

Palgrave Macmillan Ltd., Houndmills, Basingstoke, Hampshire, RG21 6XS, England, (Telephone in U.S. (888) 330-8477), (Fax in U.S. (800) 672-2054), www.palgrave.com; *The Statesman's Yearbook 2008.*

U.S. Department of State (DOS), 2201 C Street NW, Washington, DC 20520, (202) 647-4000, www.state.gov; *World Military Expenditures and Arms Transfers (WMEAT).*

United Nations Statistics Division, New York, NY 10017, (800) 253-9646, Fax: (212) 963-4116, http://unstats.un.org; *Statistical Yearbook.*

The World Bank, 1818 H Street, NW, Washington, DC 20433, (202) 473-1000, Fax: (202) 477-6391,

www.worldbank.org; *The World Bank Atlas 2003-2004* and *World Development Report 2008.*

ALBANIA - HIDES AND SKINS INDUSTRY

United Nations Food and Agricultural Organization (FAO), Viale delle Terme di Caracalla, 00100 Rome, Italy, (Dial from U.S. (202) 653-2400), (Fax from U.S. (202) 653 5760), www.fao.org; *FAO Production Yearbook 2002.*

ALBANIA - HOUSING

Euromonitor International, Inc., 224 S. Michigan Avenue, Suite 1500, Chicago, IL 60604, (312) 922-1115, Fax: (312) 922-1157, www.euromonitor.com; *World Marketing Data and Statistics.*

M.E. Sharpe, 80 Business Park Drive, Armonk, NY 10504, (800) 541-6563, Fax: (914) 273-2106, www.mesharpe.com; *The Illustrated Book of World Rankings.*

United Nations Statistics Division, New York, NY 10017, (800) 253-9646, Fax: (212) 963-4116, http://unstats.un.org; *Trends in Europe and North America: The Statistical Yearbook of the ECE 2005.*

ALBANIA - ILLITERATE PERSONS

UNESCO Institute for Statistics, C.P. 6128 Succursale Centre-Ville, Montreal, Quebec, H3C 3J7 Canada, (Dial from U.S. (514) 343-6880), (Fax from U.S. (514) 343 6882), www.uis.unesco.org; *Statistical Tables.*

United Nations Statistics Division, New York, NY 10017, (800) 253-9646, Fax: (212) 963-4116, http://unstats.un.org; *Human Development Report 2006.*

ALBANIA - IMPORTS

Central Intelligence Agency, Office of Public Affairs, Washington, DC 20505, (703) 482-0623, Fax: (703) 482-1739, www.cia.gov; *The World Factbook.*

Economist Intelligence Unit, 111 West 57th Street, New York, NY 10019, (212) 554-0600, Fax: (212) 586-1181, www.eiu.com; *Albania Country Report.*

International Monetary Fund (IMF), 700 Nineteenth Street, NW, Washington, DC 20431, (202) 623-7000, Fax: (202) 623-4661, www.imf.org; *Direction of Trade Statistics Yearbook 2007.*

Palgrave Macmillan Ltd., Houndmills, Basingstoke, Hampshire, RG21 6XS, England, (Telephone in U.S. (888) 330-8477), (Fax in U.S. (800) 672-2054), www.palgrave.com; *The Statesman's Yearbook 2008.*

Taylor and Francis Group, An Informa Business, 2 Park Square, Milton Park, Abingdon, Oxford OX14 4RN, United Kingdom, (Dial from U.S. (212) 216-7800), (Fax from U.S. (212) 564-7854), www.tandf.co.uk; *The Europa World Year Book.*

United Nations Conference on Trade and Development (UNCTAD), DC2-1120, United Nations, New York, NY 10017, (212) 963-0027, www.unctad.org; *Handbook of Statistics 2005.*

United Nations Food and Agricultural Organization (FAO), Viale delle Terme di Caracalla, 00100 Rome, Italy, (Dial from U.S. (202) 653-2400), (Fax from U.S. (202) 653 5760), www.fao.org; *The State of Food and Agriculture (SOFA) 2006.*

United Nations Statistics Division, New York, NY 10017, (800) 253-9646, Fax: (212) 963-4116, http://unstats.un.org; *Trends in Europe and North America: The Statistical Yearbook of the ECE 2005.*

The World Bank, 1818 H Street, NW, Washington, DC 20433, (202) 473-1000, Fax: (202) 477-6391, www.worldbank.org; *World Development Report 2008.*

ALBANIA - INDUSTRIAL PRODUCTIVITY

M.E. Sharpe, 80 Business Park Drive, Armonk, NY 10504, (800) 541-6563, Fax: (914) 273-2106, www.mesharpe.com; *The Illustrated Book of World Rankings.*

ALBANIA - INDUSTRIES

Central Intelligence Agency, Office of Public Affairs, Washington, DC 20505, (703) 482-0623, Fax: (703) 482-1739, www.cia.gov; *The World Factbook.*

Economist Intelligence Unit, 111 West 57th Street, New York, NY 10019, (212) 554-0600, Fax: (212) 586-1181, www.eiu.com; *Albania Country Report.*

Euromonitor International, Inc., 224 S. Michigan Avenue, Suite 1500, Chicago, IL 60604, (312) 922-1115, Fax: (312) 922-1157, www.euromonitor.com; *World Marketing Data and Statistics.*

M.E. Sharpe, 80 Business Park Drive, Armonk, NY 10504, (800) 541-6563, Fax: (914) 273-2106, www.mesharpe.com; *The Illustrated Book of World Rankings.*

Palgrave Macmillan Ltd., Houndmills, Basingstoke, Hampshire, RG21 6XS, England, (Telephone in U.S. (888) 330-8477), (Fax in U.S. (800) 672-2054), www.palgrave.com; *The Statesman's Yearbook 2008.*

Taylor and Francis Group, An Informa Business, 2 Park Square, Milton Park, Abingdon, Oxford OX14 4RN, United Kingdom, (Dial from U.S. (212) 216-7800), (Fax from U.S. (212) 564-7854), www.tandf.co.uk; *The Europa World Year Book.*

United Nations Industrial Development Organization (UNIDO), 1 United Nations Plaza, New York, NY 10017, (212) 963 6890, Fax: (212) 963-7904, http://unido.org; Industrial Statistics Database 2008 (INDSTAT) and *The International Yearbook of Industrial Statistics 2008.*

United Nations Statistics Division, New York, NY 10017, (800) 253-9646, Fax: (212) 963-4116, http://unstats.un.org; *Trends in Europe and North America: The Statistical Yearbook of the ECE 2005.*

The World Bank, 1818 H Street, NW, Washington, DC 20433, (202) 473-1000, Fax: (202) 477-6391, www.worldbank.org; *Albania.*

ALBANIA - INFANT AND MATERNAL MORTALITY

See ALBANIA - MORTALITY

ALBANIA - INTERNATIONAL TRADE

Economist Intelligence Unit, 111 West 57th Street, New York, NY 10019, (212) 554-0600, Fax: (212) 586-1181, www.eiu.com; *Albania Country Report.*

Euromonitor International, Inc., 224 S. Michigan Avenue, Suite 1500, Chicago, IL 60604, (312) 922-1115, Fax: (312) 922-1157, www.euromonitor.com; *European Marketing Data and Statistics 2008* and *World Marketing Data and Statistics.*

M.E. Sharpe, 80 Business Park Drive, Armonk, NY 10504, (800) 541-6563, Fax: (914) 273-2106, www.mesharpe.com; *The Illustrated Book of World Rankings.*

Organisation for Economic Cooperation and Development (OECD), 2 rue Andre Pascal, F-75775 Paris Cedex 16, France, (Telephone in U.S. (202) 785-6323), (Fax in U.S. (202) 785-0350), www.oecd.org; *International Trade by Commodity Statistics (ITCS).*

Palgrave Macmillan Ltd., Houndmills, Basingstoke, Hampshire, RG21 6XS, England, (Telephone in U.S. (888) 330-8477), (Fax in U.S. (800) 672-2054), www.palgrave.com; *The Statesman's Yearbook 2008.*

Taylor and Francis Group, An Informa Business, 2 Park Square, Milton Park, Abingdon, Oxford OX14 4RN, United Kingdom, (Dial from U.S. (212) 216-7800), (Fax from U.S. (212) 564-7854), www.tandf.co.uk; *The Europa World Year Book.*

United Nations Conference on Trade and Development (UNCTAD), DC2-1120, United Nations, New York, NY 10017, (212) 963-0027, www.unctad.org; *UNCTAD Commodity Yearbook.*

United Nations Food and Agricultural Organization (FAO), Viale delle Terme di Caracalla, 00100 Rome, Italy, (Dial from U.S. (202) 653-2400), (Fax from U.S. (202) 653 5760), www.fao.org; *FAO Trade Yearbook* and *The State of Food and Agriculture (SOFA) 2006.*

United Nations Statistics Division, New York, NY 10017, (800) 253-9646, Fax: (212) 963-4116, http://unstats.un.org; *Statistical Yearbook.*

The World Bank, 1818 H Street, NW, Washington, DC 20433, (202) 473-1000, Fax: (202) 477-6391, www.worldbank.org; *Albania* and *World Development Report 2008.*

World Trade Organization (WTO), Centre William Rappard, Rue de Lausanne 154, CH-1211 Geneva 21, Switzerland, www.wto.org; *International Trade Statistics 2006.*

ALBANIA - INTERNET USERS

International Telecommunication Union (ITU), Place des Nations, 1211 Geneva 20, Switzerland, www.itu.int; *World Telecommunication/ICT Indicators Database on CD-ROM; World Telecommunication/ICT Indicators Database Online;* and *Yearbook of Statistics - Telecommunication Services (Chronological Time Series 1997-2006).*

The World Bank, 1818 H Street, NW, Washington, DC 20433, (202) 473-1000, Fax: (202) 477-6391, www.worldbank.org; *Albania.*

ALBANIA - IRON AND IRON ORE PRODUCTION

See ALBANIA - MINERAL INDUSTRIES

ALBANIA - LABOR

Central Intelligence Agency, Office of Public Affairs, Washington, DC 20505, (703) 482-0623, Fax: (703) 482-1739, www.cia.gov; *The World Factbook.*

Euromonitor International, Inc., 224 S. Michigan Avenue, Suite 1500, Chicago, IL 60604, (312) 922-1115, Fax: (312) 922-1157, www.euromonitor.com; *World Marketing Data and Statistics.*

M.E. Sharpe, 80 Business Park Drive, Armonk, NY 10504, (800) 541-6563, Fax: (914) 273-2106, www.mesharpe.com; *The Illustrated Book of World Rankings.*

Palgrave Macmillan Ltd., Houndmills, Basingstoke, Hampshire, RG21 6XS, England, (Telephone in U.S. (888) 330-8477), (Fax in U.S. (800) 672-2054), www.palgrave.com; *The Statesman's Yearbook 2008.*

Taylor and Francis Group, An Informa Business, 2 Park Square, Milton Park, Abingdon, Oxford OX14 4RN, United Kingdom, (Dial from U.S. (212) 216-7800), (Fax from U.S. (212) 564-7854), www.tandf.co.uk; *The Europa World Year Book.*

United Nations Food and Agricultural Organization (FAO), Viale delle Terme di Caracalla, 00100 Rome, Italy, (Dial from U.S. (202) 653-2400), (Fax from U.S. (202) 653 5760), www.fao.org; *The State of Food and Agriculture (SOFA) 2006.*

United Nations Statistics Division, New York, NY 10017, (800) 253-9646, Fax: (212) 963-4116, http://unstats.un.org; *Human Development Report 2006.*

The World Bank, 1818 H Street, NW, Washington, DC 20433, (202) 473-1000, Fax: (202) 477-6391, www.worldbank.org; *The World Bank Atlas 2003-2004* and *World Development Report 2008.*

ALBANIA - LAND USE

Central Intelligence Agency, Office of Public Affairs, Washington, DC 20505, (703) 482-0623, Fax: (703) 482-1739, www.cia.gov; *The World Factbook.*

Euromonitor International, Inc., 224 S. Michigan Avenue, Suite 1500, Chicago, IL 60604, (312) 922-1115, Fax: (312) 922-1157, www.euromonitor.com; *European Marketing Data and Statistics 2008.*

United Nations Food and Agricultural Organization (FAO), Viale delle Terme di Caracalla, 00100 Rome, Italy, (Dial from U.S. (202) 653-2400), (Fax from U.S. (202) 653 5760), www.fao.org; *FAO Production Yearbook 2002.*

The World Bank, 1818 H Street, NW, Washington, DC 20433, (202) 473-1000, Fax: (202) 477-6391, www.worldbank.org; *World Development Report 2008.*

ALBANIA - LIBRARIES

Euromonitor International, Inc., 224 S. Michigan Avenue, Suite 1500, Chicago, IL 60604, (312) 922-

1115, Fax: (312) 922-1157, www.euromonitor.com; *European Marketing Data and Statistics 2008.*

M.E. Sharpe, 80 Business Park Drive, Armonk, NY 10504, (800) 541-6563, Fax: (914) 273-2106, www.mesharpe.com; *The Illustrated Book of World Rankings.*

United Nations Statistics Division, New York, NY 10017, (800) 253-9646, Fax: (212) 963-4116, http://unstats.un.org; *Trends in Europe and North America: The Statistical Yearbook of the ECE 2005.*

ALBANIA - LIFE EXPECTANCY

Palgrave Macmillan Ltd., Houndmills, Basingstoke, Hampshire, RG21 6XS, England, (Telephone in U.S. (888) 330-8477), (Fax in U.S. (800) 672-2054), www.palgrave.com; *The Statesman's Yearbook 2008.*

United Nations Statistics Division, New York, NY 10017, (800) 253-9646, Fax: (212) 963-4116, http://unstats.un.org; *Human Development Report 2006; Trends in Europe and North America: The Statistical Yearbook of the ECE 2005;* and *World Statistics Pocketbook.*

The World Bank, 1818 H Street, NW, Washington, DC 20433, (202) 473-1000, Fax: (202) 477-6391, www.worldbank.org; *The World Bank Atlas 2003-2004* and *World Development Report 2008.*

ALBANIA - LITERACY

Euromonitor International, Inc., 224 S. Michigan Avenue, Suite 1500, Chicago, IL 60604, (312) 922-1115, Fax: (312) 922-1157, www.euromonitor.com; *World Marketing Data and Statistics.*

ALBANIA - LIVESTOCK

Euromonitor International, Inc., 224 S. Michigan Avenue, Suite 1500, Chicago, IL 60604, (312) 922-1115, Fax: (312) 922-1157, www.euromonitor.com; *European Marketing Data and Statistics 2008.*

M.E. Sharpe, 80 Business Park Drive, Armonk, NY 10504, (800) 541-6563, Fax: (914) 273-2106, www.mesharpe.com; *The Illustrated Book of World Rankings.*

Palgrave Macmillan Ltd., Houndmills, Basingstoke, Hampshire, RG21 6XS, England, (Telephone in U.S. (888) 330-8477), (Fax in U.S. (800) 672-2054), www.palgrave.com; *The Statesman's Yearbook 2008.*

Taylor and Francis Group, An Informa Business, 2 Park Square, Milton Park, Abingdon, Oxford OX14 4RN, United Kingdom, (Dial from U.S. (212) 216-7800), (Fax from U.S. (212) 564-7854), www.tandf.co.uk; *The Europa World Year Book.*

United Nations Conference on Trade and Development (UNCTAD), DC2-1120, United Nations, New York, NY 10017, (212) 963-0027, www.unctad.org; *UNCTAD Commodity Yearbook.*

United Nations Food and Agricultural Organization (FAO), Viale delle Terme di Caracalla, 00100 Rome, Italy, (Dial from U.S. (202) 653-2400), (Fax from U.S. (202) 653 5760), www.fao.org; *FAO Production Yearbook 2002* and *The State of Food and Agriculture (SOFA) 2006.*

United Nations Statistics Division, New York, NY 10017, (800) 253-9646, Fax: (212) 963-4116, http://unstats.un.org; *Statistical Yearbook.*

ALBANIA - MANUFACTURES

M.E. Sharpe, 80 Business Park Drive, Armonk, NY 10504, (800) 541-6563, Fax: (914) 273-2106, www.mesharpe.com; *The Illustrated Book of World Rankings.*

ALBANIA - MARRIAGE

M.E. Sharpe, 80 Business Park Drive, Armonk, NY 10504, (800) 541-6563, Fax: (914) 273-2106, www.mesharpe.com; *The Illustrated Book of World Rankings.*

Taylor and Francis Group, An Informa Business, 2 Park Square, Milton Park, Abingdon, Oxford OX14 4RN, United Kingdom, (Dial from U.S. (212) 216-7800), (Fax from U.S. (212) 564-7854), www.tandf.co.uk; *The Europa World Year Book.*

United Nations Statistics Division, New York, NY 10017, (800) 253-9646, Fax: (212) 963-4116, http://unstats.un.org; *Demographic Yearbook; Statistical Yearbook;* and *Trends in Europe and North America: The Statistical Yearbook of the ECE 2005.*

ALBANIA - MEAT PRODUCTION

See ALBANIA - LIVESTOCK

ALBANIA - MERCHANT SHIPS

See ALBANIA - SHIPPING

ALBANIA - MILK PRODUCTION

See ALBANIA - DAIRY PROCESSING

ALBANIA - MINERAL INDUSTRIES

Asian Development Bank (ADB), PO Box 789, 0980 Manila, Philippines, www.adb.org; *Key Indicators of Developing Asian and Pacific Countries 2006.*

Commodity Research Bureau, 330 South Wells Street, Suite 612, Chicago, IL 60606-7110, (800) 621-5271, Fax: (312) 939-4135, www.crbtrader.com; *2006 CRB Commodity Yearbook and CD.*

M.E. Sharpe, 80 Business Park Drive, Armonk, NY 10504, (800) 541-6563, Fax: (914) 273-2106, www.mesharpe.com; *The Illustrated Book of World Rankings.*

Organisation for Economic Cooperation and Development (OECD), 2 rue Andre Pascal, F-75775 Paris Cedex 16, France, (Telephone in U.S. (202) 785-6323), (Fax in U.S. (202) 785-0350), www.oecd.org; *World Energy Outlook 2007.*

Palgrave Macmillan Ltd., Houndmills, Basingstoke, Hampshire, RG21 6XS, England, (Telephone in U.S. (888) 330-8477), (Fax in U.S. (800) 672-2054), www.palgrave.com; *The Statesman's Yearbook 2008.*

Platts, 2 Penn Plaza, 25th Floor, New York, NY 10121-2298, (212) 904-3070, www.platts.com; *Energy in East Europe.*

Taylor and Francis Group, An Informa Business, 2 Park Square, Milton Park, Abingdon, Oxford OX14 4RN, United Kingdom, (Dial from U.S. (212) 216-7800), (Fax from U.S. (212) 564-7854), www.tandf.co.uk; *The Europa World Year Book.*

United Nations Conference on Trade and Development (UNCTAD), DC2-1120, United Nations, New York, NY 10017, (212) 963-0027, www.unctad.org; *UNCTAD Commodity Yearbook.*

United Nations Statistics Division, New York, NY 10017, (800) 253-9646, Fax: (212) 963-4116, http://unstats.un.org; *Statistical Yearbook.*

ALBANIA - MONEY EXCHANGE RATES

See ALBANIA - FOREIGN EXCHANGE RATES

ALBANIA - MONEY SUPPLY

Economist Intelligence Unit, 111 West 57th Street, New York, NY 10019, (212) 554-0600, Fax: (212) 586-1181, www.eiu.com; *Albania Country Report.*

The World Bank, 1818 H Street, NW, Washington, DC 20433, (202) 473-1000, Fax: (202) 477-6391, www.worldbank.org; *Albania.*

ALBANIA - MORTALITY

Central Intelligence Agency, Office of Public Affairs, Washington, DC 20505, (703) 482-0623, Fax: (703) 482-1739, www.cia.gov; *The World Factbook.*

Palgrave Macmillan Ltd., Houndmills, Basingstoke, Hampshire, RG21 6XS, England, (Telephone in U.S. (888) 330-8477), (Fax in U.S. (800) 672-2054), www.palgrave.com; *The Statesman's Yearbook 2008.*

Taylor and Francis Group, An Informa Business, 2 Park Square, Milton Park, Abingdon, Oxford OX14 4RN, United Kingdom, (Dial from U.S. (212) 216-7800), (Fax from U.S. (212) 564-7854), www.tandf.co.uk; *The Europa World Year Book.*

UNICEF, 3 United Nations Plaza, New York, NY 10017, (800) 253-9646, Fax: (212) 887-7465, www.unicef.org; *The State of the World's Children 2008.*

United Nations Statistics Division, New York, NY 10017, (800) 253-9646, Fax: (212) 963-4116, http://unstats.un.org; *Demographic Yearbook; Human Development Report 2006; Statistical Yearbook; Trends in Europe and North America: The Statistical Yearbook of the ECE 2005;* and *World Statistics Pocketbook.*

The World Bank, 1818 H Street, NW, Washington, DC 20433, (202) 473-1000, Fax: (202) 477-6391, www.worldbank.org; *The World Bank Atlas 2003-2004* and *World Development Report 2008.*

World Health Organization (WHO), Avenue Appia 20, 1211 Geneve 27, Switzerland, (Telephone in U.S. (212) 331-9081), www.who.int; The WHO Global Atlas of Infectious Diseases.

ALBANIA - MOTION PICTURES

Palgrave Macmillan Ltd., Houndmills, Basingstoke, Hampshire, RG21 6XS, England, (Telephone in U.S. (888) 330-8477), (Fax in U.S. (800) 672-2054), www.palgrave.com; *The Statesman's Yearbook 2008.*

ALBANIA - MOTOR VEHICLES

Taylor and Francis Group, An Informa Business, 2 Park Square, Milton Park, Abingdon, Oxford OX14 4RN, United Kingdom, (Dial from U.S. (212) 216-7800), (Fax from U.S. (212) 564-7854), www.tandf.co.uk; *The Europa World Year Book.*

ALBANIA - MUSEUMS

M.E. Sharpe, 80 Business Park Drive, Armonk, NY 10504, (800) 541-6563, Fax: (914) 273-2106, www.mesharpe.com; *The Illustrated Book of World Rankings.*

ALBANIA - NATURAL GAS PRODUCTION

See ALBANIA - MINERAL INDUSTRIES

ALBANIA - NICKEL AND NICKEL ORE

See ALBANIA - MINERAL INDUSTRIES

ALBANIA - NUPTIALITY

See ALBANIA - MARRIAGE

ALBANIA - NUTRITION

United Nations Food and Agricultural Organization (FAO), Viale delle Terme di Caracalla, 00100 Rome, Italy, (Dial from U.S. (202) 653-2400), (Fax from U.S. (202) 653 5760), www.fao.org; *The State of Food and Agriculture (SOFA) 2006.*

ALBANIA - OATS PRODUCTION

See ALBANIA - CROPS

ALBANIA - OLDER PEOPLE

M.E. Sharpe, 80 Business Park Drive, Armonk, NY 10504, (800) 541-6563, Fax: (914) 273-2106, www.mesharpe.com; *The Illustrated Book of World Rankings.*

ALBANIA - PEANUT PRODUCTION

See ALBANIA - CROPS

ALBANIA - PESTICIDES

United Nations Food and Agricultural Organization (FAO), Viale delle Terme di Caracalla, 00100 Rome, Italy, (Dial from U.S. (202) 653-2400), (Fax from U.S. (202) 653 5760), www.fao.org; *The State of Food and Agriculture (SOFA) 2006.*

ALBANIA - PETROLEUM INDUSTRY AND TRADE

Euromonitor International, Inc., 224 S. Michigan Avenue, Suite 1500, Chicago, IL 60604, (312) 922-1115, Fax: (312) 922-1157, www.euromonitor.com; *European Marketing Data and Statistics 2008.*

M.E. Sharpe, 80 Business Park Drive, Armonk, NY 10504, (800) 541-6563, Fax: (914) 273-2106, www.mesharpe.com; *The Illustrated Book of World Rankings.*

Organisation for Economic Cooperation and Development (OECD), 2 rue Andre Pascal, F-75775 Paris Cedex 16, France, (Telephone in U.S. (202) 785-6323), (Fax in U.S. (202) 785-0350), www.oecd.org; *World Energy Outlook 2007.*

Palgrave Macmillan Ltd., Houndmills, Basingstoke, Hampshire, RG21 6XS, England, (Telephone in U.S. (888) 330-8477), (Fax in U.S. (800) 672-2054), www.palgrave.com; *The Statesman's Yearbook 2008.*

PennWell Corporation, 1421 South Sheridan Road, Tulsa, OK 74112, (918) 835-3161, www.pennwell.com; *International Petroleum Encyclopedia 2007.*

U.S. Department of Energy (DOE), Energy Information Administration (EIA), 1000 Independence Avenue, SW, Washington, DC 20585, (202) 586-8800, www.eia.doe.gov; *International Energy Annual 2004* and *International Energy Outlook 2006.*

United Nations Conference on Trade and Development (UNCTAD), DC2-1120, United Nations, New York, NY 10017, (212) 963-0027, www.unctad.org; *UNCTAD Commodity Yearbook.*

United Nations Food and Agricultural Organization (FAO), Viale delle Terme di Caracalla, 00100 Rome, Italy, (Dial from U.S. (202) 653-2400), (Fax from U.S. (202) 653 5760), www.fao.org; *The State of Food and Agriculture (SOFA) 2006.*

United Nations Statistics Division, New York, NY 10017, (800) 253-9646, Fax: (212) 963-4116, http://unstats.un.org; *Statistical Yearbook* and *Trends in Europe and North America: The Statistical Yearbook of the ECE 2005.*

ALBANIA - POLITICAL SCIENCE

Central Intelligence Agency, Office of Public Affairs, Washington, DC 20505, (703) 482-0623, Fax: (703) 482-1739, www.cia.gov; *The World Factbook.*

Taylor and Francis Group, An Informa Business, 2 Park Square, Milton Park, Abingdon, Oxford OX14 4RN, United Kingdom, (Dial from U.S. (212) 216-7800), (Fax from U.S. (212) 564-7854), www.tandf.co.uk; *The Europa World Year Book.*

United Nations Statistics Division, New York, NY 10017, (800) 253-9646, Fax: (212) 963-4116, http://unstats.un.org; *Human Development Report 2006* and *National Accounts Statistics: Compendium of Income Distribution Statistics.*

The World Bank, 1818 H Street, NW, Washington, DC 20433, (202) 473-1000, Fax: (202) 477-6391, www.worldbank.org; *World Development Report 2008.*

ALBANIA - POPULATION

Central Intelligence Agency, Office of Public Affairs, Washington, DC 20505, (703) 482-0623, Fax: (703) 482-1739, www.cia.gov; *The World Factbook.*

Economist Intelligence Unit, 111 West 57th Street, New York, NY 10019, (212) 554-0600, Fax: (212) 586-1181, www.eiu.com; *Albania Country Report.*

Euromonitor International, Inc., 224 S. Michigan Avenue, Suite 1500, Chicago, IL 60604, (312) 922-1115, Fax: (312) 922-1157, www.euromonitor.com; *European Marketing Data and Statistics 2008.*

M.E. Sharpe, 80 Business Park Drive, Armonk, NY 10504, (800) 541-6563, Fax: (914) 273-2106, www.mesharpe.com; *The Illustrated Book of World Rankings.*

Palgrave Macmillan Ltd., Houndmills, Basingstoke, Hampshire, RG21 6XS, England, (Telephone in U.S. (888) 330-8477), (Fax in U.S. (800) 672-2054), www.palgrave.com; *The Statesman's Yearbook 2008.*

Taylor and Francis Group, An Informa Business, 2 Park Square, Milton Park, Abingdon, Oxford OX14 4RN, United Kingdom, (Dial from U.S. (212) 216-7800), (Fax from U.S. (212) 564-7854), www.tandf.co.uk; *The Europa World Year Book.*

U.S. Department of State (DOS), 2201 C Street NW, Washington, DC 20520, (202) 647-4000, www.state.gov; *World Military Expenditures and Arms Transfers (WMEAT).*

United Nations Food and Agricultural Organization (FAO), Viale delle Terme di Caracalla, 00100 Rome, Italy, (Dial from U.S. (202) 653-2400), (Fax from U.S. (202) 653 5760), www.fao.org; *FAO Production Yearbook 2002.*

United Nations Statistics Division, New York, NY 10017, (800) 253-9646, Fax: (212) 963-4116, http://unstats.un.org; *Demographic Yearbook; Human Development Report 2006; Statistical Yearbook;* and *Trends in Europe and North America: The Statistical Yearbook of the ECE 2005.*

The World Bank, 1818 H Street, NW, Washington, DC 20433, (202) 473-1000, Fax: (202) 477-6391, www.worldbank.org; *Albania; The World Bank Atlas 2003-2004;* and *World Development Report 2008.*

World Health Organization (WHO), Avenue Appia 20, 1211 Geneve 27, Switzerland, (Telephone in U.S. (212) 331-9081), www.who.int; *World Health Report 2006.*

ALBANIA - POPULATION DENSITY

Central Intelligence Agency, Office of Public Affairs, Washington, DC 20505, (703) 482-0623, Fax: (703) 482-1739, www.cia.gov; *The World Factbook.*

M.E. Sharpe, 80 Business Park Drive, Armonk, NY 10504, (800) 541-6563, Fax: (914) 273-2106, www.mesharpe.com; *The Illustrated Book of World Rankings.*

Palgrave Macmillan Ltd., Houndmills, Basingstoke, Hampshire, RG21 6XS, England, (Telephone in U.S. (888) 330-8477), (Fax in U.S. (800) 672-2054), www.palgrave.com; *The Statesman's Yearbook 2008.*

Taylor and Francis Group, An Informa Business, 2 Park Square, Milton Park, Abingdon, Oxford OX14 4RN, United Kingdom, (Dial from U.S. (212) 216-7800), (Fax from U.S. (212) 564-7854), www.tandf.co.uk; *The Europa World Year Book.*

United Nations Food and Agricultural Organization (FAO), Viale delle Terme di Caracalla, 00100 Rome, Italy, (Dial from U.S. (202) 653-2400), (Fax from U.S. (202) 653 5760), www.fao.org; *The State of Food and Agriculture (SOFA) 2006.*

United Nations Statistics Division, New York, NY 10017, (800) 253-9646, Fax: (212) 963-4116, http://unstats.un.org; *Statistical Yearbook* and *Trends in Europe and North America: The Statistical Yearbook of the ECE 2005.*

The World Bank, 1818 H Street, NW, Washington, DC 20433, (202) 473-1000, Fax: (202) 477-6391, www.worldbank.org; *Albania* and *World Development Report 2008.*

ALBANIA - POSTAL SERVICE

M.E. Sharpe, 80 Business Park Drive, Armonk, NY 10504, (800) 541-6563, Fax: (914) 273-2106, www.mesharpe.com; *The Illustrated Book of World Rankings.*

Palgrave Macmillan Ltd., Houndmills, Basingstoke, Hampshire, RG21 6XS, England, (Telephone in U.S. (888) 330-8477), (Fax in U.S. (800) 672-2054), www.palgrave.com; *The Statesman's Yearbook 2008.*

United Nations Statistics Division, New York, NY 10017, (800) 253-9646, Fax: (212) 963-4116, http://unstats.un.org; *Trends in Europe and North America: The Statistical Yearbook of the ECE 2005.*

ALBANIA - POULTRY

See ALBANIA - LIVESTOCK

ALBANIA - POWER RESOURCES

Euromonitor International, Inc., 224 S. Michigan Avenue, Suite 1500, Chicago, IL 60604, (312) 922-1115, Fax: (312) 922-1157, www.euromonitor.com; *European Marketing Data and Statistics 2008* and *World Marketing Data and Statistics.*

M.E. Sharpe, 80 Business Park Drive, Armonk, NY 10504, (800) 541-6563, Fax: (914) 273-2106, www.mesharpe.com; *The Illustrated Book of World Rankings.*

Organisation for Economic Cooperation and Development (OECD), 2 rue Andre Pascal, F-75775 Paris Cedex 16, France, (Telephone in U.S. (202) 785-6323), (Fax in U.S. (202) 785-0350), www.oecd.org; *World Energy Outlook 2007.*

Palgrave Macmillan Ltd., Houndmills, Basingstoke, Hampshire, RG21 6XS, England, (Telephone in U.S. (888) 330-8477), (Fax in U.S. (800) 672-2054), www.palgrave.com; *The Statesman's Yearbook 2008.*

Platts, 2 Penn Plaza, 25th Floor, New York, NY 10121-2298, (212) 904-3070, www.platts.com; *Energy Economist* and *European Power Daily.*

U.S. Department of Energy (DOE), Energy Information Administration (EIA), 1000 Independence Avenue, SW, Washington, DC 20585, (202) 586-8800, www.eia.doe.gov; *International Energy Annual 2004* and *International Energy Outlook 2006.*

United Nations Food and Agricultural Organization (FAO), Viale delle Terme di Caracalla, 00100 Rome, Italy, (Dial from U.S. (202) 653-2400), (Fax from U.S. (202) 653 5760), www.fao.org; *The State of Food and Agriculture (SOFA) 2006.*

United Nations Statistics Division, New York, NY 10017, (800) 253-9646, Fax: (212) 963-4116, http://unstats.un.org; *Energy Statistics Yearbook 2003; Human Development Report 2006; Statistical Yearbook; Trends in Europe and North America: The Statistical Yearbook of the ECE 2005;* and *World Statistics Pocketbook.*

The World Bank, 1818 H Street, NW, Washington, DC 20433, (202) 473-1000, Fax: (202) 477-6391, www.worldbank.org; *The World Bank Atlas 2003-2004* and *World Development Report 2008.*

ALBANIA - PRICES

Euromonitor International, Inc., 224 S. Michigan Avenue, Suite 1500, Chicago, IL 60604, (312) 922-1115, Fax: (312) 922-1157, www.euromonitor.com; *European Marketing Data and Statistics 2008* and *World Marketing Data and Statistics.*

M.E. Sharpe, 80 Business Park Drive, Armonk, NY 10504, (800) 541-6563, Fax: (914) 273-2106, www.mesharpe.com; *The Illustrated Book of World Rankings.*

United Nations Food and Agricultural Organization (FAO), Viale delle Terme di Caracalla, 00100 Rome, Italy, (Dial from U.S. (202) 653-2400), (Fax from U.S. (202) 653 5760), www.fao.org; *FAO Production Yearbook 2002* and *The State of Food and Agriculture (SOFA) 2006.*

The World Bank, 1818 H Street, NW, Washington, DC 20433, (202) 473-1000, Fax: (202) 477-6391, www.worldbank.org; *Albania.*

ALBANIA - PUBLIC HEALTH

M.E. Sharpe, 80 Business Park Drive, Armonk, NY 10504, (800) 541-6563, Fax: (914) 273-2106, www.mesharpe.com; *The Illustrated Book of World Rankings.*

Palgrave Macmillan Ltd., Houndmills, Basingstoke, Hampshire, RG21 6XS, England, (Telephone in U.S. (888) 330-8477), (Fax in U.S. (800) 672-2054), www.palgrave.com; *The Statesman's Yearbook 2008.*

UNICEF, 3 United Nations Plaza, New York, NY 10017, (800) 253-9646, Fax: (212) 887-7465, www.unicef.org; *The State of the World's Children 2008.*

United Nations Statistics Division, New York, NY 10017, (800) 253-9646, Fax: (212) 963-4116, http://unstats.un.org; *Human Development Report 2006; Statistical Yearbook;* and *Trends in Europe and North America: The Statistical Yearbook of the ECE 2005.*

The World Bank, 1818 H Street, NW, Washington, DC 20433, (202) 473-1000, Fax: (202) 477-6391; www.worldbank.org; *Albania* and *World Development Report 2008.*

World Health Organization (WHO), Avenue Appia 20, 1211 Geneve 27, Switzerland, (Telephone in U.S. (212) 331-9081), www.who.int; The WHO Global Atlas of Infectious Diseases.

ALBANIA - PUBLISHERS AND PUBLISHING

Palgrave Macmillan Ltd., Houndmills, Basingstoke, Hampshire, RG21 6XS, England, (Telephone in U.S.

(888) 330-8477), (Fax in U.S. (800) 672-2054), www.palgrave.com; *The Statesman's Yearbook 2008.*

Taylor and Francis Group, An Informa Business, 2 Park Square, Milton Park, Abingdon, Oxford OX14 4RN, United Kingdom, (Dial from U.S. (212) 216-7800), (Fax from U.S. (212) 564-7854), www.tandf.co.uk; *The Europa World Year Book.*

United Nations Statistics Division, New York, NY 10017, (800) 253-9646, Fax: (212) 963-4116, http://unstats.un.org; *Trends in Europe and North America: The Statistical Yearbook of the ECE 2005.*

ALBANIA - RADIO BROADCASTING

Palgrave Macmillan Ltd., Houndmills, Basingstoke, Hampshire, RG21 6XS, England, (Telephone in U.S. (888) 330-8477), (Fax in U.S. (800) 672-2054), www.palgrave.com; *The Statesman's Yearbook 2008.*

ALBANIA - RAILROADS

Euromonitor International, Inc., 224 S. Michigan Avenue, Suite 1500, Chicago, IL 60604, (312) 922-1115, Fax: (312) 922-1157, www.euromonitor.com; *European Marketing Data and Statistics 2008.*

Jane's Information Group, 110 North Royal Street, Suite 200, Alexandria, VA 22314, (703) 683-3700, Fax: (800) 836-0297, www.janes.com; *Jane's World Railways.*

Palgrave Macmillan Ltd., Houndmills, Basingstoke, Hampshire, RG21 6XS, England, (Telephone in U.S. (888) 330-8477), (Fax in U.S. (800) 672-2054), www.palgrave.com; *The Statesman's Yearbook 2008.*

Taylor and Francis Group, An Informa Business, 2 Park Square, Milton Park, Abingdon, Oxford OX14 4RN, United Kingdom, (Dial from U.S. (212) 216-7800), (Fax from U.S. (212) 564-7854), www.tandf.co.uk; *The Europa World Year Book.*

United Nations Statistics Division, New York, NY 10017, (800) 253-9646, Fax: (212) 963-4116, http://unstats.un.org; *Trends in Europe and North America: The Statistical Yearbook of the ECE 2005.*

ALBANIA - RELIGION

Central Intelligence Agency, Office of Public Affairs, Washington, DC 20505, (703) 482-0623, Fax: (703) 482-1739, www.cia.gov; *The World Factbook.*

M.E. Sharpe, 80 Business Park Drive, Armonk, NY 10504, (800) 541-6563, Fax: (914) 273-2106, www.mesharpe.com; *The Illustrated Book of World Rankings.*

Palgrave Macmillan Ltd., Houndmills, Basingstoke, Hampshire, RG21 6XS, England, (Telephone in U.S. (888) 330-8477), (Fax in U.S. (800) 672-2054), www.palgrave.com; *The Statesman's Yearbook 2008.*

ALBANIA - RETAIL TRADE

Euromonitor International, Inc., 224 S. Michigan Avenue, Suite 1500, Chicago, IL 60604, (312) 922-1115, Fax: (312) 922-1157, www.euromonitor.com; *World Marketing Data and Statistics.*

ALBANIA - RICE PRODUCTION

See ALBANIA - CROPS

ALBANIA - ROADS

Central Intelligence Agency, Office of Public Affairs, Washington, DC 20505, (703) 482-0623, Fax: (703) 482-1739, www.cia.gov; *The World Factbook.*

Palgrave Macmillan Ltd., Houndmills, Basingstoke, Hampshire, RG21 6XS, England, (Telephone in U.S. (888) 330-8477), (Fax in U.S. (800) 672-2054), www.palgrave.com; *The Statesman's Yearbook 2008.*

United Nations Statistics Division, New York, NY 10017, (800) 253-9646, Fax: (212) 963-4116, http://unstats.un.org; *Trends in Europe and North America: The Statistical Yearbook of the ECE 2005.*

ALBANIA - RUBBER INDUSTRY AND TRADE

International Rubber Study Group (IRSG), 1st Floor, Heron House, 109/115 Wembley Hill Road, Wembley, Middlesex HA9 8DA, United Kingdom, www.rubberstudy.com; *Rubber Statistical Bulletin; Summary of World Rubber Statistics 2005; World Rubber Statistics Handbook (Volume 6, 1975-2001);* and *World Rubber Statistics Historic Handbook.*

M.E. Sharpe, 80 Business Park Drive, Armonk, NY 10504, (800) 541-6563, Fax: (914) 273-2106, www.mesharpe.com; *The Illustrated Book of World Rankings.*

ALBANIA - SHEEP

See ALBANIA - LIVESTOCK

ALBANIA - SHIPPING

Palgrave Macmillan Ltd., Houndmills, Basingstoke, Hampshire, RG21 6XS, England, (Telephone in U.S. (888) 330-8477), (Fax in U.S. (800) 672-2054), www.palgrave.com; *The Statesman's Yearbook 2008.*

Taylor and Francis Group, An Informa Business, 2 Park Square, Milton Park, Abingdon, Oxford OX14 4RN, United Kingdom, (Dial from U.S. (212) 216-7800), (Fax from U.S. (212) 564-7854), www.tandf.co.uk; *The Europa World Year Book.*

U.S. Department of Transportation (DOT), Maritime Administration (MARAD), West Building, Southeast Federal Center, 1200 New Jersey Avenue, SE, Washington, DC 20590, (800) 99-MARAD, www.marad.dot.gov; *World Merchant Fleet 2005.*

United Nations Statistics Division, New York, NY 10017, (800) 253-9646, Fax: (212) 963-4116, http://unstats.un.org; *Statistical Yearbook.*

ALBANIA - SILVER PRODUCTION

See ALBANIA - MINERAL INDUSTRIES

ALBANIA - SOCIAL ECOLOGY

M.E. Sharpe, 80 Business Park Drive, Armonk, NY 10504, (800) 541-6563, Fax: (914) 273-2106, www.mesharpe.com; *The Illustrated Book of World Rankings.*

United Nations Statistics Division, New York, NY 10017, (800) 253-9646, Fax: (212) 963-4116, http://unstats.un.org; *World Statistics Pocketbook.*

ALBANIA - SOCIAL SECURITY

United Nations Statistics Division, New York, NY 10017, (800) 253-9646, Fax: (212) 963-4116, http://unstats.un.org; *National Accounts Statistics: Compendium of Income Distribution Statistics.*

ALBANIA - STEEL PRODUCTION

See ALBANIA - MINERAL INDUSTRIES

ALBANIA - SUGAR PRODUCTION

See ALBANIA - CROPS

ALBANIA - TELEPHONE

Central Intelligence Agency, Office of Public Affairs, Washington, DC 20505, (703) 482-0623, Fax: (703) 482-1739, www.cia.gov; *The World Factbook.*

International Telecommunication Union (ITU), Place des Nations, 1211 Geneva 20, Switzerland, www.itu.int; World Telecommunication Indicators Database.

Palgrave Macmillan Ltd., Houndmills, Basingstoke, Hampshire, RG21 6XS, England, (Telephone in U.S. (888) 330-8477), (Fax in U.S. (800) 672-2054), www.palgrave.com; *The Statesman's Yearbook 2008.*

United Nations Statistics Division, New York, NY 10017, (800) 253-9646, Fax: (212) 963-4116, http://unstats.un.org; *Trends in Europe and North America: The Statistical Yearbook of the ECE 2005* and *World Statistics Pocketbook.*

ALBANIA - TEXTILE INDUSTRY

M.E. Sharpe, 80 Business Park Drive, Armonk, NY 10504, (800) 541-6563, Fax: (914) 273-2106, www.mesharpe.com; *The Illustrated Book of World Rankings.*

Palgrave Macmillan Ltd., Houndmills, Basingstoke, Hampshire, RG21 6XS, England, (Telephone in U.S. (888) 330-8477), (Fax in U.S. (800) 672-2054), www.palgrave.com; *The Statesman's Yearbook 2008.*

United Nations Conference on Trade and Development (UNCTAD), DC2-1120, United Nations, New York, NY 10017, (212) 963-0027, www.unctad.org; *UNCTAD Commodity Yearbook.*

ALBANIA - TOBACCO INDUSTRY

Euromonitor International, Inc., 224 S. Michigan Avenue, Suite 1500, Chicago, IL 60604, (312) 922-1115, Fax: (312) 922-1157, www.euromonitor.com; *European Marketing Data and Statistics 2008.*

Foreign Agricultural Service (FAS), U.S. Department of Agriculture (USDA), 1400 Independence Avenue, SW, Washington, DC 20250, (202) 720-3935, www.fas.usda.gov; *Tobacco: World Markets and Trade.*

M.E. Sharpe, 80 Business Park Drive, Armonk, NY 10504, (800) 541-6563, Fax: (914) 273-2106, www.mesharpe.com; *The Illustrated Book of World Rankings.*

United Nations Statistics Division, New York, NY 10017, (800) 253-9646, Fax: (212) 963-4116, http://unstats.un.org; *Statistical Yearbook.*

ALBANIA - TOURISM

Euromonitor International, Inc., 224 S. Michigan Avenue, Suite 1500, Chicago, IL 60604, (312) 922-1115, Fax: (312) 922-1157, www.euromonitor.com; *European Marketing Data and Statistics 2008* and *World Marketing Data and Statistics.*

M.E. Sharpe, 80 Business Park Drive, Armonk, NY 10504, (800) 541-6563, Fax: (914) 273-2106, www.mesharpe.com; *The Illustrated Book of World Rankings.*

Palgrave Macmillan Ltd., Houndmills, Basingstoke, Hampshire, RG21 6XS, England, (Telephone in U.S. (888) 330-8477), (Fax in U.S. (800) 672-2054), www.palgrave.com; *The Statesman's Yearbook 2008.*

United Nations Statistics Division, New York, NY 10017, (800) 253-9646, Fax: (212) 963-4116, http://unstats.un.org; *Trends in Europe and North America: The Statistical Yearbook of the ECE 2005.*

The World Bank, 1818 H Street, NW, Washington, DC 20433, (202) 473-1000, Fax: (202) 477-6391, www.worldbank.org; *Albania.*

ALBANIA - TRADE

See ALBANIA - INTERNATIONAL TRADE

ALBANIA - TRANSPORTATION

Central Intelligence Agency, Office of Public Affairs, Washington, DC 20505, (703) 482-0623, Fax: (703) 482-1739, www.cia.gov; *The World Factbook.*

Euromonitor International, Inc., 224 S. Michigan Avenue, Suite 1500, Chicago, IL 60604, (312) 922-1115, Fax: (312) 922-1157, www.euromonitor.com; *World Marketing Data and Statistics.*

M.E. Sharpe, 80 Business Park Drive, Armonk, NY 10504, (800) 541-6563, Fax: (914) 273-2106, www.mesharpe.com; *The Illustrated Book of World Rankings.*

Palgrave Macmillan Ltd., Houndmills, Basingstoke, Hampshire, RG21 6XS, England, (Telephone in U.S. (888) 330-8477), (Fax in U.S. (800) 672-2054), www.palgrave.com; *The Statesman's Yearbook 2008.*

Taylor and Francis Group, An Informa Business, 2 Park Square, Milton Park, Abingdon, Oxford OX14 4RN, United Kingdom, (Dial from U.S. (212) 216-7800), (Fax from U.S. (212) 564-7854), www.tandf.co.uk; *The Europa World Year Book.*

United Nations Statistics Division, New York, NY 10017, (800) 253-9646, Fax: (212) 963-4116, http://unstats.un.org; *Human Development Report 2006* and *Trends in Europe and North America: The Statistical Yearbook of the ECE 2005.*

The World Bank, 1818 H Street, NW, Washington, DC 20433, (202) 473-1000, Fax: (202) 477-6391, www.worldbank.org; *Albania.*

ALBANIA - UNEMPLOYMENT

Central Intelligence Agency, Office of Public Affairs, Washington, DC 20505, (703) 482-0623, Fax: (703) 482-1739, www.cia.gov; *The World Factbook.*

Euromonitor International, Inc., 224 S. Michigan Avenue, Suite 1500, Chicago, IL 60604, (312) 922-1115, Fax: (312) 922-1157, www.euromonitor.com; *European Marketing Data and Statistics 2008.*

Palgrave Macmillan Ltd., Houndmills, Basingstoke, Hampshire, RG21 6XS, England, (Telephone in U.S. (888) 330-8477), (Fax in U.S. (800) 672-2054), www.palgrave.com; *The Statesman's Yearbook 2008.*

United Nations Statistics Division, New York, NY 10017, (800) 253-9646, Fax: (212) 963-4116, http://unstats.un.org; *Trends in Europe and North America: The Statistical Yearbook of the ECE 2005.*

ALBANIA - VITAL STATISTICS

Palgrave Macmillan Ltd., Houndmills, Basingstoke, Hampshire, RG21 6XS, England, (Telephone in U.S. (888) 330-8477), (Fax in U.S. (800) 672-2054), www.palgrave.com; *The Statesman's Yearbook 2008.*

United Nations Statistics Division, New York, NY 10017, (800) 253-9646, Fax: (212) 963-4116, http://unstats.un.org; *Statistical Yearbook.*

World Health Organization (WHO), Avenue Appia 20, 1211 Geneve 27, Switzerland, (Telephone in U.S. (212) 331-9081), www.who.int; *World Health Report 2006.*

ALBANIA - WAGES

Euromonitor International, Inc., 224 S. Michigan Avenue, Suite 1500, Chicago, IL 60604, (312) 922-1115, Fax: (312) 922-1157, www.euromonitor.com; *European Marketing Data and Statistics 2008.*

The World Bank, 1818 H Street, NW, Washington, DC 20433, (202) 473-1000, Fax: (202) 477-6391, www.worldbank.org; *Albania.*

ALBANIA - WEATHER

See ALBANIA - CLIMATE

ALBANIA - WHEAT PRODUCTION

See ALBANIA - CROPS

ALBANIA - WINE PRODUCTION

See ALBANIA - BEVERAGE INDUSTRY

ALBANIA - WOOL PRODUCTION

See ALBANIA - TEXTILE INDUSTRYAlberta

Alberta Economic Development (AED), 6th Floor, Commerce Place, 10155 - 102 Street, Edmonton, AB T5J 4L6, Canada, (Dial from U.S. (780) 415-1319), www.alberta-canada.com/statpub/; *Facts on Alberta.*

ALCOHOL INVOLVEMENT FOR DRIVERS IN FATAL CRASHES

National Center for Statistics and Analysis (NCSA) of the National Highway Traffic Safety Administration, West Building, 1200 New Jersey Avenue, S.E., Washington, DC 20590, (202) 366-1503, Fax: (202) 366-7078, www.nhtsa.gov; *Alcohol Involvement in Fatal Motor Vehicle Traffic Crashes, 2003; Impaired Motorcycle Operators Involved in Fatal Crashes; Individual State Data from the State Alcohol Related Fatality Report; Large-Truck Crash Causation Study: An Initial Overview; Recent Trends in Fatal Motorcycle Crashes: An Update; State Alcohol-Related Fatality Rates 2003; Total and Alcohol-Related Fatality Rates by State, 2003-2004; Traffic Safety Fact Sheets, 2005 Data - State Alcohol Estimates; Traffic Safety Fact Sheets, 2006 Data - Alcohol-Impaired Driving;* and *Traffic Safety Facts Annual Report: 2005.*

National Criminal Justice Reference Service (NCJRS), PO Box 6000, Rockville, MD 20849-6000, (800) 851-3420, Fax: (301) 519-5212, www.ncjrs.org; *Driving Under the Influence in the City and County of Honolulu.*

ALCOHOLIC BEVERAGES

See also LIQUORS AND BEVERAGES

U.S. Department of Justice (DOJ), National Institute of Justice (NIJ), 810 Seventh Street, NW, Washington, DC 20531, (202) 307-2942, Fax: (202) 616-0275, www.ojp.usdoj.gov/nij/; *Risky Mix: Drinking, Drug Use, and Homicide.*

ALCOHOLIC BEVERAGES - CONSUMER EXPENDITURES

Economic Research Service (ERS), U.S. Department of Agriculture (USDA), 1800 M Street, NW, Washington, DC 20036-5831, (202) 694-5050, Fax: (202) 694-5689, www.ers.usda.gov; *Food CPI, Prices, and Expenditures.*

U.S. Bureau of Labor Statistics (BLS), Postal Square Building, 2 Massachusetts Avenue, NE, Washington, DC 20212-0001, (202) 691-5200, Fax: (202) 691-6325, www.bls.gov; *Consumer Expenditures in 2006.*

ALCOHOLIC BEVERAGES - CONSUMPTION

Alcohol and Tobacco Tax and Trade Bureau (TTB), U.S. Department of the Treasury (DOT), Public Information Officer, 1310 G Street, NW, Suite 300, Washington, D.C. 20220, (202) 927-5000, Fax: (202) 927-5611, www.ttb.gov; *Wine Statistics.*

Economic Research Service (ERS), U.S. Department of Agriculture (USDA), 1800 M Street, NW, Washington, DC 20036-5831, (202) 694-5050, Fax: (202) 694-5689, www.ers.usda.gov; *Agricultural Outlook* and *Food CPI, Prices, and Expenditures.*

National Center for Health Statistics (NCHS), Centers for Disease Control and Prevention (CDC), U.S. Department of Health and Human Services (HHS), 3311 Toledo Road, Hyattsville, MD 20782, (866) 232-4636, www.cdc.gov/nchs; *Faststats A to Z.*

Robert Wood Johnson Foundation, PO Box 2316, College Road East and Route 1, Princeton, NJ 08543, (877) 843-7953, www.rwjf.org; *Community-Based Substance Abuse Reduction and the Gap Between Treatment Need and Treatment Utilization: Analysis of Data From the "Fighting Back" General Population Survey; Neighborhood Crime Victimization, Drug Use and Drug Sales: Results from the "Fighting Back" Evaluation;* and *Varieties of Substance Use and Visible Drug Problems: Individual and Neighborhood Factors.*

Substance Abuse and Mental Health Services Administration (SAMHSA), 1 Choke Cherry Road, Rockville, MD 20857, (240) 777-1311, www.oas.samhsa.gov; *Alcohol and Drug Services Study (ADSS)* and *National Survey on Drug Use Health (NSDUH).*

U.S. Department of Justice (DOJ), National Institute of Justice (NIJ), 810 Seventh Street, NW, Washington, DC 20531, (202) 307-2942, Fax: (202) 616-0275, www.ojp.usdoj.gov/nij/; *Risky Mix: Drinking, Drug Use, and Homicide.*

ALCOHOLIC BEVERAGES - CONSUMPTION - BINGE USE

Substance Abuse and Mental Health Services Administration (SAMHSA), 1 Choke Cherry Road, Rockville, MD 20857, (240) 777-1311, www.oas.samhsa.gov; *National Survey on Drug Use Health (NSDUH).*

ALCOHOLIC BEVERAGES - INTERNATIONAL TRADE

U.S. Census Bureau, Foreign Trade Division, 4700 Silver Hill Road, Washington DC 20233-0001, (301) 763-3030, www.census.gov/foreign-trade/www/; *U.S. International Trade in Goods and Services.*

ALCOHOLIC BEVERAGES - PRICE INDEXES

U.S. Bureau of Labor Statistics (BLS), Postal Square Building, 2 Massachusetts Avenue, NE, Washington, DC 20212-0001, (202) 691-5200, Fax: (202) 691-6325, www.bls.gov; *Consumer Price Index Detailed Report* and *Monthly Labor Review (MLR).*

ALCOHOLIC BEVERAGES - SALES

Office of Trade and Industry Information (OTII), Manufacturing and Services, International Trade Administration, U.S. Department of Commerce, 1401 Constitution Ave, NW, Washington, DC 20230, (800) USA TRAD(E), http://trade.gov/index.asp; *TradeStats Express.*

U.S. Census Bureau, Center for Economic Studies, 4600 Silver Hill Road, Washington DC 20233, (301) 457-1235, www.ces.census.gov; *2002 Economic Census, Retail Trade* and *2002 Economic Census, Wholesale Trade.*

ALCOHOLISM

U.S. Department of Justice (DOJ), National Institute of Justice (NIJ), 810 Seventh Street, NW, Washington, DC 20531, (202) 307-2942, Fax: (202) 616-0275, www.ojp.usdoj.gov/nij/; *Risky Mix: Drinking, Drug Use, and Homicide.*

ALCOHOLISM - TREATMENT

National Center for Health Statistics (NCHS), Centers for Disease Control and Prevention (CDC), U.S. Department of Health and Human Services (HHS), 3311 Toledo Road, Hyattsville, MD 20782, (866) 232-4636, www.cdc.gov/nchs; *Health, United States, 2006, with Chartbook on Trends in the Health of Americans with Special Feature on Pain.*

Robert Wood Johnson Foundation, PO Box 2316, College Road East and Route 1, Princeton, NJ 08543, (877) 843-7953, www.rwjf.org; *Changes in the Number of Methadone Maintenance Slots as Measures of "Fighting Back" Program Effectiveness; Community-Based Substance Abuse Reduction and the Gap Between Treatment Need and Treatment Utilization: Analysis of Data From the "Fighting Back" General Population Survey; Neighborhood Crime Victimization, Drug Use and Drug Sales: Results from the "Fighting Back" Evaluation;* and *Varieties of Substance Use and Visible Drug Problems: Individual and Neighborhood Factors.*

Substance Abuse and Mental Health Services Administration (SAMHSA), 1 Choke Cherry Road, Rockville, MD 20857, (240) 777-1311, www.oas.samhsa.gov; *Health Services Utilization by Individuals with Substance Abuse and Mental Disorders* and *National Survey of Substance Abuse Treatment Services (N-SSATS).*

U.S. Department of Justice (DOJ), Bureau of Justice Statistics, 810 Seventh Street, NW, Washington, DC 20531, (202) 307-0765, www.ojp.usdoj.gov/bjs/; *Substance Dependence, Abuse, and Treatment of Jail Inmates, 2002.*

ALEUT POPULATION

U.S. Census Bureau, Population Division, 4700 Silver Hill Road, Washington DC 20233-0001, (301) 763-3030, www.census.gov/population/www/; *The American Indian, Eskimo, and Aleut Population.*

ALFALFA - ORGANIC ACREAGE

Economic Research Service (ERS), U.S. Department of Agriculture (USDA), 1800 M Street, NW, Washington, DC 20036-5831, (202) 694-5050, Fax: (202) 694-5689, www.ers.usda.gov; *Organic Production.*

ALGERIA - NATIONAL STATISTICAL OFFICE

National Office of Statistics (Office National des Statistiques), 8/10 Rue des moussebilines, BP 202 Ferhat Boussad Alger, Algeria, www.ons.dz; National Data Center.

ALGERIA - PRIMARY STATISTICS SOURCES

National Office of Statistics (Office National des Statistiques), 8/10 Rue des moussebilines, BP 202 Ferhat Boussad Alger, Algeria, www.ons.dz; *Statistical Yearbook of Algeria.*

ALGERIA - AGRICULTURE

Economist Intelligence Unit, 111 West 57th Street, New York, NY 10019, (212) 554-0600, Fax: (212) 586-1181, www.eiu.com; *Algeria Country Report.*

Euromonitor International, Inc., 224 S. Michigan Avenue, Suite 1500, Chicago, IL 60604, (312) 922-1115, Fax: (312) 922-1157, www.euromonitor.com; *International Marketing Data and Statistics 2008* and *World Marketing Data and Statistics.*

M.E. Sharpe, 80 Business Park Drive, Armonk, NY 10504, (800) 541-6563, Fax: (914) 273-2106, www.mesharpe.com; *The Illustrated Book of World Rankings.*

Palgrave Macmillan Ltd., Houndmills, Basingstoke, Hampshire, RG21 6XS, England, (Telephone in U.S. (888) 330-8477), (Fax in U.S. (800) 672-2054), www.palgrave.com; *The Statesman's Yearbook 2008.*

Taylor and Francis Group, An Informa Business, 2 Park Square, Milton Park, Abingdon, Oxford OX14 4RN, United Kingdom, (Dial from U.S. (212) 216-7800), (Fax from U.S. (212) 564-7854), www.tandf.co.uk; *The Europa World Year Book.*

United Nations Conference on Trade and Development (UNCTAD), DC2-1120, United Nations, New York, NY 10017, (212) 963-0027, www.unctad.org; *UNCTAD Commodity Yearbook.*

United Nations Economic Commission for Africa (ECA), PO Box 3001, Addis Ababa, Ethiopia, (Telephone in U.S. (212) 963-4957), www.uneca.org; *African Statistical Yearbook 2006.*

United Nations Food and Agricultural Organization (FAO), Viale delle Terme di Caracalla, 00100 Rome, Italy, (Dial from U.S. (202) 653-2400), (Fax from U.S. (202) 653 5760), www.fao.org; AQUASTAT; *FAO Production Yearbook 2002; FAO Trade Yearbook;* and *The State of Food and Agriculture (SOFA) 2006.*

United Nations Statistics Division, New York, NY 10017, (800) 253-9646, Fax: (212) 963-4116, http://unstats.un.org; *Statistical Yearbook* and *Survey of Economic and Social Conditions in Africa 2005.*

The World Bank, 1818 H Street, NW, Washington, DC 20433, (202) 473-1000, Fax: (202) 477-6391, www.worldbank.org; *Africa Live Database (LDB); African Development Indicators (ADI) 2007; Algeria;* and *World Development Indicators (WDI) 2008.*

ALGERIA - AIRLINES

International Civil Aviation Organization (ICAO), External Relations and Public Information Office (EPO), 999 University Street, Montreal, Quebec H3C 5H7, Canada, (Dial from U.S. (514) 954-8219), (Fax from U.S. (514) 954-6077), www.icao.int; *Civil Aviation Statistics of the World.*

M.E. Sharpe, 80 Business Park Drive, Armonk, NY 10504, (800) 541-6563, Fax: (914) 273-2106, www.mesharpe.com; *The Illustrated Book of World Rankings.*

Palgrave Macmillan Ltd., Houndmills, Basingstoke, Hampshire, RG21 6XS, England, (Telephone in U.S. (888) 330-8477), (Fax in U.S. (800) 672-2054), www.palgrave.com; *The Statesman's Yearbook 2008.*

Taylor and Francis Group, An Informa Business, 2 Park Square, Milton Park, Abingdon, Oxford OX14 4RN, United Kingdom, (Dial from U.S. (212) 216-7800), (Fax from U.S. (212) 564-7854), www.tandf.co.uk; *The Europa World Year Book.*

United Nations Economic Commission for Africa (ECA), PO Box 3001, Addis Ababa, Ethiopia, (Telephone in U.S. (212) 963-4957), www.uneca.org; *African Statistical Yearbook 2006.*

United Nations Statistics Division, New York, NY 10017, (800) 253-9646, Fax: (212) 963-4116, http://unstats.un.org; *Statistical Yearbook.*

ALGERIA - AIRPORTS

Central Intelligence Agency, Office of Public Affairs, Washington, DC 20505, (703) 482-0623, Fax: (703) 482-1739, www.cia.gov; *The World Factbook.*

ALGERIA - ALMOND PRODUCTION

See ALGERIA - CROPS

ALGERIA - ALUMINUM PRODUCTION

See ALGERIA - MINERAL INDUSTRIES

ALGERIA - ARMED FORCES

Central Intelligence Agency, Office of Public Affairs, Washington, DC 20505, (703) 482-0623, Fax: (703) 482-1739, www.cia.gov; *The World Factbook.*

Euromonitor International, Inc., 224 S. Michigan Avenue, Suite 1500, Chicago, IL 60604, (312) 922-1115, Fax: (312) 922-1157, www.euromonitor.com; *World Marketing Data and Statistics.*

International Institute for Strategic Studies (IISS), Arundel House, 13-15 Arundel Street, Temple Place, London WC2R 3DX, England, www.iiss.org; *The Military Balance 2007.*

Palgrave Macmillan Ltd., Houndmills, Basingstoke, Hampshire, RG21 6XS, England, (Telephone in U.S. (888) 330-8477), (Fax in U.S. (800) 672-2054), www.palgrave.com; *The Statesman's Yearbook 2008.*

U.S. Department of State (DOS), 2201 C Street NW, Washington, DC 20520, (202) 647-4000, www.state.gov; *World Military Expenditures and Arms Transfers (WMEAT).*

United Nations Statistics Division, New York, NY 10017, (800) 253-9646, Fax: (212) 963-4116, http://unstats.un.org; *Human Development Report 2006.*

ALGERIA - ARTICHOKE PRODUCTION

See ALGERIA - CROPS

ALGERIA - AUTOMOBILE INDUSTRY AND TRADE

United Nations Statistics Division, New York, NY 10017, (800) 253-9646, Fax: (212) 963-4116, http://unstats.un.org; *Statistical Yearbook.*

ALGERIA - BALANCE OF PAYMENTS

African Development Bank Group, Rue Joseph Anoma, 01 BP 1387 Abidjan 01, Cote d'Ivoire, www.afdb.org; *Statistics Pocketbook 2008.*

International Monetary Fund (IMF), 700 Nineteenth Street, NW, Washington, DC 20431, (202) 623-7000, Fax: (202) 623-4661, www.imf.org; *Balance of Payments Statistics Newsletter; Balance of Payments Statistics Yearbook 2007;* and *International Financial Statistics Yearbook 2007.*

Taylor and Francis Group, An Informa Business, 2 Park Square, Milton Park, Abingdon, Oxford OX14 4RN, United Kingdom, (Dial from U.S. (212) 216-7800), (Fax from U.S. (212) 564-7854), www.tandf.co.uk; *The Europa World Year Book.*

United Nations Conference on Trade and Development (UNCTAD), DC2-1120, United Nations, New York, NY 10017, (212) 963-0027, www.unctad.org; *Handbook of Statistics 2005.*

United Nations Economic Commission for Africa (ECA), PO Box 3001, Addis Ababa, Ethiopia, (Telephone in U.S. (212) 963-4957), www.uneca.org; *African Statistical Yearbook 2006.*

The World Bank, 1818 H Street, NW, Washington, DC 20433, (202) 473-1000, Fax: (202) 477-6391, www.worldbank.org; *Algeria; World Development Indicators (WDI) 2008;* and *World Development Report 2008.*

ALGERIA - BANKS AND BANKING

Euromonitor International, Inc., 224 S. Michigan Avenue, Suite 1500, Chicago, IL 60604, (312) 922-1115, Fax: (312) 922-1157, www.euromonitor.com; *World Marketing Data and Statistics.*

International Monetary Fund (IMF), 700 Nineteenth Street, NW, Washington, DC 20431, (202) 623-7000, Fax: (202) 623-4661, www.imf.org; *International Financial Statistics Yearbook 2007.*

M.E. Sharpe, 80 Business Park Drive, Armonk, NY 10504, (800) 541-6563, Fax: (914) 273-2106, www.mesharpe.com; *The Illustrated Book of World Rankings.*

Palgrave Macmillan Ltd., Houndmills, Basingstoke, Hampshire, RG21 6XS, England, (Telephone in U.S. (888) 330-8477), (Fax in U.S. (800) 672-2054), www.palgrave.com; *The Statesman's Yearbook 2008.*

Taylor and Francis Group, An Informa Business, 2 Park Square, Milton Park, Abingdon, Oxford OX14 4RN, United Kingdom, (Dial from U.S. (212) 216-7800), (Fax from U.S. (212) 564-7854), www.tandf.co.uk; *The Europa World Year Book.*

United Nations Economic Commission for Africa (ECA), PO Box 3001, Addis Ababa, Ethiopia, (Telephone in U.S. (212) 963-4957), www.uneca.org; *African Statistical Yearbook 2006.*

ALGERIA - BARLEY PRODUCTION

See ALGERIA - CROPS

ALGERIA - BEVERAGE INDUSTRY

M.E. Sharpe, 80 Business Park Drive, Armonk, NY 10504, (800) 541-6563, Fax: (914) 273-2106, www.mesharpe.com; *The Illustrated Book of World Rankings.*

United Nations Statistics Division, New York, NY 10017, (800) 253-9646, Fax: (212) 963-4116, http://unstats.un.org; *Statistical Yearbook.*

ALGERIA - BROADCASTING

Central Intelligence Agency, Office of Public Affairs, Washington, DC 20505, (703) 482-0623, Fax: (703) 482-1739, www.cia.gov; *The World Factbook.*

Euromonitor International, Inc., 224 S. Michigan Avenue, Suite 1500, Chicago, IL 60604, (312) 922-1115, Fax: (312) 922-1157, www.euromonitor.com; *World Marketing Data and Statistics.*

M.E. Sharpe, 80 Business Park Drive, Armonk, NY 10504, (800) 541-6563, Fax: (914) 273-2106, www.mesharpe.com; *The Illustrated Book of World Rankings.*

Palgrave Macmillan Ltd., Houndmills, Basingstoke, Hampshire, RG21 6XS, England, (Telephone in U.S. (888) 330-8477), (Fax in U.S. (800) 672-2054), www.palgrave.com; *The Statesman's Yearbook 2008.*

WRTH Publications Limited, PO Box 290, Oxford OX2 7FT, UK, www.wrth.com; *World Radio TV Handbook 2007.*

ALGERIA - BUDGET

Central Intelligence Agency, Office of Public Affairs, Washington, DC 20505, (703) 482-0623, Fax: (703) 482-1739, www.cia.gov; *The World Factbook.*

ALGERIA - CATTLE

See ALGERIA - LIVESTOCK

ALGERIA - CHICK PEA PRODUCTION

See ALGERIA - CROPS

ALGERIA - CHICKENS

See ALGERIA - LIVESTOCK

ALGERIA - CHILDBIRTH - STATISTICS

Central Intelligence Agency, Office of Public Affairs, Washington, DC 20505, (703) 482-0623, Fax: (703) 482-1739, www.cia.gov; *The World Factbook.*

Euromonitor International, Inc., 224 S. Michigan Avenue, Suite 1500, Chicago, IL 60604, (312) 922-1115, Fax: (312) 922-1157, www.euromonitor.com; *International Marketing Data and Statistics 2008* and *The World Economic Factbook 2008.*

M.E. Sharpe, 80 Business Park Drive, Armonk, NY 10504, (800) 541-6563, Fax: (914) 273-2106, www.mesharpe.com; *The Illustrated Book of World Rankings.*

Palgrave Macmillan Ltd., Houndmills, Basingstoke, Hampshire, RG21 6XS, England, (Telephone in U.S. (888) 330-8477), (Fax in U.S. (800) 672-2054), www.palgrave.com; *The Statesman's Yearbook 2008.*

Taylor and Francis Group, An Informa Business, 2 Park Square, Milton Park, Abingdon, Oxford OX14

4RN, United Kingdom, (Dial from U.S. (212) 216-7800), (Fax from U.S. (212) 564-7854), www.tandf.co.uk; *The Europa World Year Book.*

United Nations Statistics Division, New York, NY 10017, (800) 253-9646, Fax: (212) 963-4116, http://unstats.un.org; *Demographic Yearbook* and *Survey of Economic and Social Conditions in Africa 2005.*

The World Bank, 1818 H Street, NW, Washington, DC 20433, (202) 473-1000, Fax: (202) 477-6391, www.worldbank.org; *World Development Indicators (WDI) 2008.*

ALGERIA - CLIMATE

International Institute for Environment and Development (IIED), 3 Endsleigh Street, London, England, WC1H 0DD, United Kingdom, www.iied.org; *Environment Urbanization* and *Haramata - Bulletin of the Drylands.*

M.E. Sharpe, 80 Business Park Drive, Armonk, NY 10504, (800) 541-6563, Fax: (914) 273-2106, www.mesharpe.com; *The Illustrated Book of World Rankings.*

Palgrave Macmillan Ltd., Houndmills, Basingstoke, Hampshire, RG21 6XS, England, (Telephone in U.S. (888) 330-8477), (Fax in U.S. (800) 672-2054), www.palgrave.com; *The Statesman's Yearbook 2008.*

ALGERIA - CLOTHING EXPORTS AND IMPORTS

See ALGERIA - TEXTILE INDUSTRY

ALGERIA - COAL PRODUCTION

See ALGERIA - MINERAL INDUSTRIES

ALGERIA - COFFEE

See ALGERIA - CROPS

ALGERIA - COMMERCE

Palgrave Macmillan Ltd., Houndmills, Basingstoke, Hampshire, RG21 6XS, England, (Telephone in U.S. (888) 330-8477), (Fax in U.S. (800) 672-2054), www.palgrave.com; *The Statesman's Yearbook 2008.*

ALGERIA - COMMODITY EXCHANGES

Commodity Research Bureau, 330 South Wells Street, Suite 612, Chicago, IL 60606-7110, (800) 621-5271, Fax: (312) 939-4135, www.crbtrader.com; *2006 CRB Commodity Yearbook and CD.*

International Lead and Zinc Study Group (ILZSG), Rua Almirante Barroso 38, 5th Floor, Lisbon 1000 - 013, Portugal, www.ilzsg.org; Interactive Statistical Database.

International Monetary Fund (IMF), 700 Nineteenth Street, NW, Washington, DC 20431, (202) 623-7000, Fax: (202) 623-4661, www.imf.org; *IMF Primary Commodity Prices.*

United Nations Food and Agricultural Organization (FAO), Viale delle Terme di Caracalla, 00100 Rome, Italy, (Dial from U.S. (202) 653-2400), (Fax from U.S. (202) 653 5760), www.fao.org; *The State of Food and Agriculture (SOFA) 2006.*

ALGERIA - COMMUNICATION AND TRAFFIC

United Nations Statistics Division, New York, NY 10017, (800) 253-9646, Fax: (212) 963-4116, http://unstats.un.org; *Statistical Yearbook.*

ALGERIA - CONSTRUCTION INDUSTRY

M.E. Sharpe, 80 Business Park Drive, Armonk, NY 10504, (800) 541-6563, Fax: (914) 273-2106, www.mesharpe.com; *The Illustrated Book of World Rankings.*

Palgrave Macmillan Ltd., Houndmills, Basingstoke, Hampshire, RG21 6XS, England, (Telephone in U.S. (888) 330-8477), (Fax in U.S. (800) 672-2054), www.palgrave.com; *The Statesman's Yearbook 2008.*

United Nations Economic Commission for Africa (ECA), PO Box 3001, Addis Ababa, Ethiopia, (Telephone in U.S. (212) 963-4957), www.uneca.org; *African Statistical Yearbook 2006.*

United Nations Statistics Division, New York, NY 10017, (800) 253-9646, Fax: (212) 963-4116, http://unstats.un.org; *Statistical Yearbook.*

ALGERIA - CONSUMER PRICE INDEXES

Taylor and Francis Group, An Informa Business, 2 Park Square, Milton Park, Abingdon, Oxford OX14 4RN, United Kingdom, (Dial from U.S. (212) 216-7800), (Fax from U.S. (212) 564-7854), www.tandf.co.uk; *The Europa World Year Book.*

United Nations Economic Commission for Africa (ECA), PO Box 3001, Addis Ababa, Ethiopia, (Telephone in U.S. (212) 963-4957), www.uneca.org; *African Statistical Yearbook 2006.*

United Nations Statistics Division, New York, NY 10017, (800) 253-9646, Fax: (212) 963-4116, http://unstats.un.org; *Statistical Yearbook* and *Survey of Economic and Social Conditions in Africa 2005.*

The World Bank, 1818 H Street, NW, Washington, DC 20433, (202) 473-1000, Fax: (202) 477-6391, www.worldbank.org; *Algeria.*

ALGERIA - CONSUMPTION (ECONOMICS)

African Development Bank Group, Rue Joseph Anoma, 01 BP 1387 Abidjan 01, Cote d'Ivoire, www.afdb.org; *Statistics Pocketbook 2008.*

International Lead and Zinc Study Group (ILZSG), Rua Almirante Barroso 38, 5th Floor, Lisbon 1000 - 013, Portugal, www.ilzsg.org; Interactive Statistical Database.

United Nations Statistics Division, New York, NY 10017, (800) 253-9646, Fax: (212) 963-4116, http://unstats.un.org; *Survey of Economic and Social Conditions in Africa 2005.*

The World Bank, 1818 H Street, NW, Washington, DC 20433, (202) 473-1000, Fax: (202) 477-6391, www.worldbank.org; *World Development Report 2008.*

ALGERIA - COPPER INDUSTRY AND TRADE

See ALGERIA - MINERAL INDUSTRIES

ALGERIA - CORN INDUSTRY

See ALGERIA - CROPS

ALGERIA - COTTON

See ALGERIA - CROPS

ALGERIA - CROPS

M.E. Sharpe, 80 Business Park Drive, Armonk, NY 10504, (800) 541-6563, Fax: (914) 273-2106, www.mesharpe.com; *The Illustrated Book of World Rankings.*

Palgrave Macmillan Ltd., Houndmills, Basingstoke, Hampshire, RG21 6XS, England, (Telephone in U.S. (888) 330-8477), (Fax in U.S. (800) 672-2054), www.palgrave.com; *The Statesman's Yearbook 2008.*

Taylor and Francis Group, An Informa Business, 2 Park Square, Milton Park, Abingdon, Oxford OX14 4RN, United Kingdom, (Dial from U.S. (212) 216-7800), (Fax from U.S. (212) 564-7854), www.tandf.co.uk; *The Europa World Year Book.*

United Nations Conference on Trade and Development (UNCTAD), DC2-1120, United Nations, New York, NY 10017, (212) 963-0027, www.unctad.org; *UNCTAD Commodity Yearbook.*

United Nations Economic Commission for Africa (ECA), PO Box 3001, Addis Ababa, Ethiopia, (Telephone in U.S. (212) 963-4957), www.uneca.org; *African Statistical Yearbook 2006.*

United Nations Food and Agricultural Organization (FAO), Viale delle Terme di Caracalla, 00100 Rome, Italy, (Dial from U.S. (202) 653-2400), (Fax from U.S. (202) 653 5760), www.fao.org; *FAO Production Yearbook 2002* and *The State of Food and Agriculture (SOFA) 2006.*

United Nations Statistics Division, New York, NY 10017, (800) 253-9646, Fax: (212) 963-4116, http://unstats.un.org; *Statistical Yearbook.*

ALGERIA - CUSTOMS ADMINISTRATION

Palgrave Macmillan Ltd., Houndmills, Basingstoke, Hampshire, RG21 6XS, England, (Telephone in U.S. (888) 330-8477), (Fax in U.S. (800) 672-2054), www.palgrave.com; *The Statesman's Yearbook 2008.*

ALGERIA - DAIRY PROCESSING

M.E. Sharpe, 80 Business Park Drive, Armonk, NY 10504, (800) 541-6563, Fax: (914) 273-2106, www.mesharpe.com; *The Illustrated Book of World Rankings.*

Palgrave Macmillan Ltd., Houndmills, Basingstoke, Hampshire, RG21 6XS, England, (Telephone in U.S. (888) 330-8477), (Fax in U.S. (800) 672-2054), www.palgrave.com; *The Statesman's Yearbook 2008.*

Taylor and Francis Group, An Informa Business, 2 Park Square, Milton Park, Abingdon, Oxford OX14 4RN, United Kingdom, (Dial from U.S. (212) 216-7800), (Fax from U.S. (212) 564-7854), www.tandf.co.uk; *The Europa World Year Book.*

United Nations Food and Agricultural Organization (FAO), Viale delle Terme di Caracalla, 00100 Rome, Italy, (Dial from U.S. (202) 653-2400), (Fax from U.S. (202) 653 5760), www.fao.org; *The State of Food and Agriculture (SOFA) 2006.*

United Nations Statistics Division, New York, NY 10017, (800) 253-9646, Fax: (212) 963-4116, http://unstats.un.org; *Statistical Yearbook.*

ALGERIA - DEATH RATES

See ALGERIA - MORTALITY

ALGERIA - DEBTS, EXTERNAL

African Development Bank Group, Rue Joseph Anoma, 01 BP 1387 Abidjan 01, Cote d'Ivoire, www.afdb.org; *Statistics Pocketbook 2008.*

Palgrave Macmillan Ltd., Houndmills, Basingstoke, Hampshire, RG21 6XS, England, (Telephone in U.S. (888) 330-8477), (Fax in U.S. (800) 672-2054), www.palgrave.com; *The Statesman's Yearbook 2008.*

United Nations Statistics Division, New York, NY 10017, (800) 253-9646, Fax: (212) 963-4116, http://unstats.un.org; *Human Development Report 2006* and *Survey of Economic and Social Conditions in Africa 2005.*

The World Bank, 1818 H Street, NW, Washington, DC 20433, (202) 473-1000, Fax: (202) 477-6391, www.worldbank.org; *Africa Live Database (LDB); African Development Indicators (ADI) 2007; Global Development Finance 2007;* and *World Development Indicators (WDI) 2008.*

ALGERIA - DEFENSE EXPENDITURES

See ALGERIA - ARMED FORCES

ALGERIA - DEMOGRAPHY

Euromonitor International, Inc., 224 S. Michigan Avenue, Suite 1500, Chicago, IL 60604, (312) 922-1115, Fax: (312) 922-1157, www.euromonitor.com; *International Marketing Data and Statistics 2008; The World Economic Factbook 2008;* and *World Marketing Data and Statistics.*

M.E. Sharpe, 80 Business Park Drive, Armonk, NY 10504, (800) 541-6563, Fax: (914) 273-2106, www.mesharpe.com; *The Illustrated Book of World Rankings.*

United Nations Statistics Division, New York, NY 10017, (800) 253-9646, Fax: (212) 963-4116, http://unstats.un.org; *Human Development Report 2006* and *Survey of Economic and Social Conditions in Africa 2005.*

The World Bank, 1818 H Street, NW, Washington, DC 20433, (202) 473-1000, Fax: (202) 477-6391, www.worldbank.org; *Algeria.*

ALGERIA - DIAMONDS

See ALGERIA - MINERAL INDUSTRIES

ALGERIA - DISPOSABLE INCOME

M.E. Sharpe, 80 Business Park Drive, Armonk, NY 10504, (800) 541-6563, Fax: (914) 273-2106, www.mesharpe.com; *The Illustrated Book of World Rankings.*

United Nations Statistics Division, New York, NY 10017, (800) 253-9646, Fax: (212) 963-4116, http://unstats.un.org; *National Accounts Statistics: Compendium of Income Distribution Statistics* and *Statistical Yearbook.*

ALGERIA - DIVORCE

M.E. Sharpe, 80 Business Park Drive, Armonk, NY 10504, (800) 541-6563, Fax: (914) 273-2106, www.mesharpe.com; *The Illustrated Book of World Rankings.*

United Nations Statistics Division, New York, NY 10017, (800) 253-9646, Fax: (212) 963-4116, http://unstats.un.org; *Demographic Yearbook* and *Statistical Yearbook.*

ALGERIA - ECONOMIC ASSISTANCE

United Nations Statistics Division, New York, NY 10017, (800) 253-9646, Fax: (212) 963-4116, http://unstats.un.org; *Statistical Yearbook.*

ALGERIA - ECONOMIC CONDITIONS

African Development Bank Group, Rue Joseph Anoma, 01 BP 1387 Abidjan 01, Cote d'Ivoire, www.afdb.org; *The African Statistical Journal; Gender, Poverty and Environmental Indicators on African Countries 2007; Selected Statistics on African Countries 2007;* and *Statistics Pocketbook 2008.*

Center for International Business Education Research (CIBER), Columbia Business School and School of International and Public Affairs, Uris Hall, Room 212, 3022 Broadway, New York, NY 10027-6902, Mr. Joshua Safier, (212) 854-4750, Fax: (212) 222-9821, www.columbia.edu/cu/ciber/; Datastream International.

Central Intelligence Agency, Office of Public Affairs, Washington, DC 20505, (703) 482-0623, Fax: (703) 482-1739, www.cia.gov; *The World Factbook.*

DSI Data Service Information, Xantener Strasse 51a, D-47495 Rheinberg, Germany, www.dsidata.com; *Campus Solution.*

Dun and Bradstreet (DB) Corporation, 103 JFK Parkway, Short Hills, NJ 07078, (973) 921-5500, www.dnb.com; *Country Report.*

Economist Intelligence Unit, 111 West 57th Street, New York, NY 10019, (212) 554-0600, Fax: (212) 586-1181, www.eiu.com; *Algeria Country Report* and *Business Africa.*

Euromonitor International, Inc., 224 S. Michigan Avenue, Suite 1500, Chicago, IL 60604, (312) 922-1115, Fax: (312) 922-1157, www.euromonitor.com; *International Marketing Data and Statistics 2008; The World Economic Factbook 2008;* and *World Marketing Data and Statistics.*

International Monetary Fund (IMF), 700 Nineteenth Street, NW, Washington, DC 20431, (202) 623-7000, Fax: (202) 623-4661, www.imf.org; *World Economic Outlook Reports.*

M.E. Sharpe, 80 Business Park Drive, Armonk, NY 10504, (800) 541-6563, Fax: (914) 273-2106, www.mesharpe.com; *The Illustrated Book of World Rankings.*

Palgrave Macmillan Ltd., Houndmills, Basingstoke, Hampshire, RG21 6XS, England, (Telephone in U.S. (888) 330-8477), (Fax in U.S. (800) 672-2054), www.palgrave.com; *The Statesman's Yearbook 2008.*

Taylor and Francis Group, An Informa Business, 2 Park Square, Milton Park, Abingdon, Oxford OX14 4RN, United Kingdom, (Dial from U.S. (212) 216-7800), (Fax from U.S. (212) 564-7854), www.tandf.co.uk; *The Europa World Year Book.*

United Nations Statistics Division, New York, NY 10017, (800) 253-9646, Fax: (212) 963-4116, http://unstats.un.org; *Compendium of Intra-African and Related Foreign Trade Statistics 2003* and *World Statistics Pocketbook.*

The World Bank, 1818 H Street, NW, Washington, DC 20433, (202) 473-1000, Fax: (202) 477-6391, www.worldbank.org; *Africa Household Survey Databank; Africa Live Database (LDB); Africa Standardized Files and Indicators; African Development Indicators (ADI) 2007; Algeria; Global Economic Monitor (GEM); Global Economic Prospects 2008; The World Bank Atlas 2003-2004;* and *World Development Report 2008.*

ALGERIA - EDUCATION

African Development Bank Group, Rue Joseph Anoma, 01 BP 1387 Abidjan 01, Cote d'Ivoire, www.afdb.org; *Statistics Pocketbook 2008.*

Euromonitor International, Inc., 224 S. Michigan Avenue, Suite 1500, Chicago, IL 60604, (312) 922-1115, Fax: (312) 922-1157, www.euromonitor.com; *International Marketing Data and Statistics 2008* and *World Marketing Data and Statistics.*

M.E. Sharpe, 80 Business Park Drive, Armonk, NY 10504, (800) 541-6563, Fax: (914) 273-2106, www.mesharpe.com; *The Illustrated Book of World Rankings.*

Palgrave Macmillan Ltd., Houndmills, Basingstoke, Hampshire, RG21 6XS, England, (Telephone in U.S. (888) 330-8477), (Fax in U.S. (800) 672-2054), www.palgrave.com; *The Statesman's Yearbook 2008.*

Taylor and Francis Group, An Informa Business, 2 Park Square, Milton Park, Abingdon, Oxford OX14 4RN, United Kingdom, (Dial from U.S. (212) 216-7800), (Fax from U.S. (212) 564-7854), www.tandf.co.uk; *The Europa World Year Book.*

UNESCO Institute for Statistics, C.P. 6128 Succursale Centre-Ville, Montreal, Quebec, H3C 3J7 Canada, (Dial from U.S. (514) 343-6880), (Fax from U.S. (514) 343 6882), www.uis.unesco.org; *Statistical Tables.*

United Nations Economic Commission for Africa (ECA), PO Box 3001, Addis Ababa, Ethiopia, (Telephone in U.S. (212) 963-4957), www.uneca.org; *African Statistical Yearbook 2006.*

United Nations Statistics Division, New York, NY 10017, (800) 253-9646, Fax: (212) 963-4116, http://unstats.un.org; *Human Development Report 2006* and *Survey of Economic and Social Conditions in Africa 2005.*

The World Bank, 1818 H Street, NW, Washington, DC 20433, (202) 473-1000, Fax: (202) 477-6391, www.worldbank.org; *Algeria; World Development Indicators (WDI) 2008;* and *World Development Report 2008.*

ALGERIA - ELECTRICITY

M.E. Sharpe, 80 Business Park Drive, Armonk, NY 10504, (800) 541-6563, Fax: (914) 273-2106, www.mesharpe.com; *The Illustrated Book of World Rankings.*

Organisation for Economic Cooperation and Development (OECD), 2 rue Andre Pascal, F-75775 Paris Cedex 16, France, (Telephone in U.S. (202) 785-6323), (Fax in U.S. (202) 785-0350), www.oecd.org; *World Energy Outlook 2007.*

Palgrave Macmillan Ltd., Houndmills, Basingstoke, Hampshire, RG21 6XS, England, (Telephone in U.S. (888) 330-8477), (Fax in U.S. (800) 672-2054), www.palgrave.com; *The Statesman's Yearbook 2008.*

U.S. Department of Energy (DOE), Energy Information Administration (EIA), 1000 Independence Avenue, SW, Washington, DC 20585, (202) 586-8800, www.eia.doe.gov; *International Energy Annual 2004* and *International Energy Outlook 2006.*

United Nations Economic Commission for Africa (ECA), PO Box 3001, Addis Ababa, Ethiopia, (Telephone in U.S. (212) 963-4957), www.uneca.org; *African Statistical Yearbook 2006.*

United Nations Statistics Division, New York, NY 10017, (800) 253-9646, Fax: (212) 963-4116, http://unstats.un.org; *Human Development Report 2006; Statistical Yearbook;* and *Survey of Economic and Social Conditions in Africa 2005.*

ALGERIA - EMPLOYMENT

Euromonitor International, Inc., 224 S. Michigan Avenue, Suite 1500, Chicago, IL 60604, (312) 922-1115, Fax: (312) 922-1157, www.euromonitor.com; *International Marketing Data and Statistics 2008.*

International Labour Office, I.L.O. Publications, 4 route des Morillons, CH-1211 Geneva 22, Switzerland, (Telephone in U.S. (202) 653-7652), (Fax in U.S. (202) 653-7687), www.ilo.org; *Yearbook of Labour Statistics 2006.*

M.E. Sharpe, 80 Business Park Drive, Armonk, NY 10504, (800) 541-6563, Fax: (914) 273-2106, www.mesharpe.com; *The Illustrated Book of World Rankings.*

United Nations Economic Commission for Africa (ECA), PO Box 3001, Addis Ababa, Ethiopia, (Telephone in U.S. (212) 963-4957), www.uneca.org; *African Statistical Yearbook 2006.*

United Nations Statistics Division, New York, NY 10017, (800) 253-9646, Fax: (212) 963-4116, http://unstats.un.org; *Bulletin of Industrial Statistics for the Arab Countries* and *Survey of Economic and Social Conditions in Africa 2005.*

The World Bank, 1818 H Street, NW, Washington, DC 20433, (202) 473-1000, Fax: (202) 477-6391, www.worldbank.org; *Algeria.*

ALGERIA - ENVIRONMENTAL CONDITIONS

DSI Data Service Information, Xantener Strasse 51a, D-47495 Rheinberg, Germany, www.dsidata.com; *Campus Solution* and *DSI's Global Environmental Database.*

Economist Intelligence Unit, 111 West 57th Street, New York, NY 10019, (212) 554-0600, Fax: (212) 586-1181, www.eiu.com; *Algeria Country Report.*

International Institute for Environment and Development (IIED), 3 Endsleigh Street, London, England, WC1H 0DD, United Kingdom, www.iied.org; *Environment Urbanization* and *Haramata - Bulletin of the Drylands.*

United Nations Statistics Division, New York, NY 10017, (800) 253-9646, Fax: (212) 963-4116, http://unstats.un.org; *World Statistics Pocketbook.*

ALGERIA - EXPORTS

African Development Bank Group, Rue Joseph Anoma, 01 BP 1387 Abidjan 01, Cote d'Ivoire, www.afdb.org; *Statistics Pocketbook 2008.*

Central Intelligence Agency, Office of Public Affairs, Washington, DC 20505, (703) 482-0623, Fax: (703) 482-1739, www.cia.gov; *The World Factbook.*

Economist Intelligence Unit, 111 West 57th Street, New York, NY 10019, (212) 554-0600, Fax: (212) 586-1181, www.eiu.com; *Algeria Country Report.*

Euromonitor International, Inc., 224 S. Michigan Avenue, Suite 1500, Chicago, IL 60604, (312) 922-1115, Fax: (312) 922-1157, www.euromonitor.com; *International Marketing Data and Statistics 2008* and *The World Economic Factbook 2008.*

International Lead and Zinc Study Group (ILZSG), Rua Almirante Barroso 38, 5th Floor, Lisbon 1000 - 013, Portugal, www.ilzsg.org; Interactive Statistical Database.

International Monetary Fund (IMF), 700 Nineteenth Street, NW, Washington, DC 20431, (202) 623-7000, Fax: (202) 623-4661, www.imf.org; *Direction of Trade Statistics Yearbook 2007* and *International Financial Statistics Yearbook 2007.*

Organization of Petroleum Exporting Countries (OPEC), Obere Donaustrasse 93, A-1020, Vienna, Austria, www.opec.org; *Annual Statistical Bulletin 2006.*

Palgrave Macmillan Ltd., Houndmills, Basingstoke, Hampshire, RG21 6XS, England, (Telephone in U.S. (888) 330-8477), (Fax in U.S. (800) 672-2054), www.palgrave.com; *The Statesman's Yearbook 2008.*

Taylor and Francis Group, An Informa Business, 2 Park Square, Milton Park, Abingdon, Oxford OX14

4RN, United Kingdom, (Dial from U.S. (212) 216-7800), (Fax from U.S. (212) 564-7854), www.tandf.co.uk; *The Europa World Year Book.*

United Nations Conference on Trade and Development (UNCTAD), DC2-1120, United Nations, New York, NY 10017, (212) 963-0027, www.unctad.org; *Handbook of Statistics 2005.*

United Nations Economic Commission for Africa (ECA), PO Box 3001, Addis Ababa, Ethiopia, (Telephone in U.S. (212) 963-4957), www.uneca.org; *African Statistical Yearbook 2006.*

United Nations Food and Agricultural Organization (FAO), Viale delle Terme di Caracalla, 00100 Rome, Italy, (Dial from U.S. (202) 653-2400), (Fax from U.S. (202) 653 5760), www.fao.org; *The State of Food and Agriculture (SOFA) 2006.*

United Nations Statistics Division, New York, NY 10017, (800) 253-9646, Fax: (212) 963-4116, http://unstats.un.org; *Bulletin of Industrial Statistics for the Arab Countries; Compendium of Intra-African and Related Foreign Trade Statistics 2003; Statistical Yearbook;* and *Survey of Economic and Social Conditions in Africa 2005.*

The World Bank, 1818 H Street, NW, Washington, DC 20433, (202) 473-1000, Fax: (202) 477-6391, www.worldbank.org; *World Development Indicators (WDI) 2008* and *World Development Report 2008.*

ALGERIA - FEMALE WORKING POPULATION

See ALGERIA - EMPLOYMENT

ALGERIA - FERTILITY, HUMAN

M.E. Sharpe, 80 Business Park Drive, Armonk, NY 10504, (800) 541-6563, Fax: (914) 273-2106, www.mesharpe.com; *The Illustrated Book of World Rankings.*

United Nations Statistics Division, New York, NY 10017, (800) 253-9646, Fax: (212) 963-4116, http://unstats.un.org; *Demographic Yearbook; Human Development Report 2006;* and *Survey of Economic and Social Conditions in Africa 2005.*

The World Bank, 1818 H Street, NW, Washington, DC 20433, (202) 473-1000, Fax: (202) 477-6391, www.worldbank.org; *The World Bank Atlas 2003-2004; World Development Indicators (WDI) 2008;* and *World Development Report 2008.*

World Health Organization (WHO), Avenue Appia 20, 1211 Geneve 27, Switzerland, (Telephone in U.S. (212) 331-9081), www.who.int; *World Health Report 2006.*

ALGERIA - FERTILIZER INDUSTRY

United Nations Food and Agricultural Organization (FAO), Viale delle Terme di Caracalla, 00100 Rome, Italy, (Dial from U.S. (202) 653-2400), (Fax from U.S. (202) 653 5760), www.fao.org; *FAO Fertilizer Yearbook* and *The State of Food and Agriculture (SOFA) 2006.*

United Nations Statistics Division, New York, NY 10017, (800) 253-9646, Fax: (212) 963-4116, http://unstats.un.org; *Statistical Yearbook.*

ALGERIA - FETAL MORTALITY

See ALGERIA - MORTALITY

ALGERIA - FILM

See ALGERIA - MOTION PICTURES

ALGERIA - FINANCE

International Monetary Fund (IMF), 700 Nineteenth Street, NW, Washington, DC 20431, (202) 623-7000, Fax: (202) 623-4661, www.imf.org; *International Financial Statistics Yearbook 2007.*

Taylor and Francis Group, An Informa Business, 2 Park Square, Milton Park, Abingdon, Oxford OX14 4RN, United Kingdom, (Dial from U.S. (212) 216-7800), (Fax from U.S. (212) 564-7854), www.tandf.co.uk; *The Europa World Year Book.*

United Nations Economic Commission for Africa (ECA), PO Box 3001, Addis Ababa, Ethiopia, (Telephone in U.S. (212) 963-4957), www.uneca.org; *African Statistical Yearbook 2006.*

United Nations Statistics Division, New York, NY 10017, (800) 253-9646, Fax: (212) 963-4116, http://unstats.un.org; *National Accounts Statistics: Compendium of Income Distribution Statistics.*

The World Bank, 1818 H Street, NW, Washington, DC 20433, (202) 473-1000, Fax: (202) 477-6391, www.worldbank.org; *Algeria.*

ALGERIA - FINANCE, PUBLIC

African Development Bank Group, Rue Joseph Anoma, 01 BP 1387 Abidjan 01, Cote d'Ivoire, www.afdb.org; *Statistics Pocketbook 2008.*

Bernan Essential Government Publications, 4611-F Assembly Drive, Lanham MD, 20706-4391, (301) 459-2255, Fax: (800) 865-3450, www.bernan.com; *National Accounts Statistics.*

Economist Intelligence Unit, 111 West 57th Street, New York, NY 10019, (212) 554-0600, Fax: (212) 586-1181, www.eiu.com; *Algeria Country Report.*

International Monetary Fund (IMF), 700 Nineteenth Street, NW, Washington, DC 20431, (202) 623-7000, Fax: (202) 623-4661, www.imf.org; *International Financial Statistics; International Financial Statistics Online Service;* and *International Financial Statistics Yearbook 2007.*

M.E. Sharpe, 80 Business Park Drive, Armonk, NY 10504, (800) 541-6563, Fax: (914) 273-2106, www.mesharpe.com; *The Illustrated Book of World Rankings.*

Palgrave Macmillan Ltd., Houndmills, Basingstoke, Hampshire, RG21 6XS, England, (Telephone in U.S. (888) 330-8477), (Fax in U.S. (800) 672-2054), www.palgrave.com; *The Statesman's Yearbook 2008.*

Taylor and Francis Group, An Informa Business, 2 Park Square, Milton Park, Abingdon, Oxford OX14 4RN, United Kingdom, (Dial from U.S. (212) 216-7800), (Fax from U.S. (212) 564-7854), www.tandf.co.uk; *The Europa World Year Book.*

United Nations Economic Commission for Africa (ECA), PO Box 3001, Addis Ababa, Ethiopia, (Telephone in U.S. (212) 963-4957), www.uneca.org; *African Statistical Yearbook 2006.*

The World Bank, 1818 H Street, NW, Washington, DC 20433, (202) 473-1000, Fax: (202) 477-6391, www.worldbank.org; *Algeria.*

ALGERIA - FISHERIES

M.E. Sharpe, 80 Business Park Drive, Armonk, NY 10504, (800) 541-6563, Fax: (914) 273-2106, www.mesharpe.com; *The Illustrated Book of World Rankings.*

Palgrave Macmillan Ltd., Houndmills, Basingstoke, Hampshire, RG21 6XS, England, (Telephone in U.S. (888) 330-8477), (Fax in U.S. (800) 672-2054), www.palgrave.com; *The Statesman's Yearbook 2008.*

Taylor and Francis Group, An Informa Business, 2 Park Square, Milton Park, Abingdon, Oxford OX14 4RN, United Kingdom, (Dial from U.S. (212) 216-7800), (Fax from U.S. (212) 564-7854), www.tandf.co.uk; *The Europa World Year Book.*

United Nations Conference on Trade and Development (UNCTAD), DC2-1120, United Nations, New York, NY 10017, (212) 963-0027, www.unctad.org; *UNCTAD Commodity Yearbook.*

United Nations Economic Commission for Africa (ECA), PO Box 3001, Addis Ababa, Ethiopia, (Telephone in U.S. (212) 963-4957), www.uneca.org; *African Statistical Yearbook 2006.*

United Nations Food and Agricultural Organization (FAO), Viale delle Terme di Caracalla, 00100 Rome, Italy, (Dial from U.S. (202) 653-2400), (Fax from U.S. (202) 653 5760), www.fao.org; *FAO Yearbook of Fishery Statistics;* Fishery Databases; FISHSTAT Database. Subjects covered include: Aquaculture production, capture production, fishery commodities; and *The State of Food and Agriculture (SOFA) 2006.*

United Nations Statistics Division, New York, NY 10017, (800) 253-9646, Fax: (212) 963-4116, http://unstats.un.org; *Statistical Yearbook* and *Survey of Economic and Social Conditions in Africa 2005.*

The World Bank, 1818 H Street, NW, Washington, DC 20433, (202) 473-1000, Fax: (202) 477-6391, www.worldbank.org; *Algeria.*

ALGERIA - FLOUR INDUSTRY

United Nations Statistics Division, New York, NY 10017, (800) 253-9646, Fax: (212) 963-4116, http://unstats.un.org; *Statistical Yearbook.*

ALGERIA - FOOD

African Development Bank Group, Rue Joseph Anoma, 01 BP 1387 Abidjan 01, Cote d'Ivoire, www.afdb.org; *Statistics Pocketbook 2008.*

United Nations Conference on Trade and Development (UNCTAD), DC2-1120, United Nations, New York, NY 10017, (212) 963-0027, www.unctad.org; *UNCTAD Commodity Yearbook.*

United Nations Food and Agricultural Organization (FAO), Viale delle Terme di Caracalla, 00100 Rome, Italy, (Dial from U.S. (202) 653-2400), (Fax from U.S. (202) 653 5760), www.fao.org; *FAO Production Yearbook 2002* and *The State of Food and Agriculture (SOFA) 2006.*

United Nations Statistics Division, New York, NY 10017, (800) 253-9646, Fax: (212) 963-4116, http://unstats.un.org; *Human Development Report 2006.*

ALGERIA - FOREIGN EXCHANGE RATES

African Development Bank Group, Rue Joseph Anoma, 01 BP 1387 Abidjan 01, Cote d'Ivoire, www.afdb.org; *Statistics Pocketbook 2008.*

Central Intelligence Agency, Office of Public Affairs, Washington, DC 20505, (703) 482-0623, Fax: (703) 482-1739, www.cia.gov; *The World Factbook.*

Euromonitor International, Inc., 224 S. Michigan Avenue, Suite 1500, Chicago, IL 60604, (312) 922-1115, Fax: (312) 922-1157, www.euromonitor.com; *International Marketing Data and Statistics 2008* and *The World Economic Factbook 2008.*

International Civil Aviation Organization (ICAO), External Relations and Public Information Office (EPO), 999 University Street, Montreal, Quebec H3C 5H7, Canada, (Dial from U.S. (514) 954-8219), (Fax from U.S. (514) 954-6077), www.icao.int; *Civil Aviation Statistics of the World.*

International Monetary Fund (IMF), 700 Nineteenth Street, NW, Washington, DC 20431, (202) 623-7000, Fax: (202) 623-4661, www.imf.org; *International Financial Statistics Yearbook 2007.*

Organization of Petroleum Exporting Countries (OPEC), Obere Donaustrasse 93, A-1020, Vienna, Austria, www.opec.org; *Annual Statistical Bulletin 2006.*

Taylor and Francis Group, An Informa Business, 2 Park Square, Milton Park, Abingdon, Oxford OX14 4RN, United Kingdom, (Dial from U.S. (212) 216-7800), (Fax from U.S. (212) 564-7854), www.tandf.co.uk; *The Europa World Year Book.*

United Nations Statistics Division, New York, NY 10017, (800) 253-9646, Fax: (212) 963-4116, http://unstats.un.org; *Compendium of Intra-African and Related Foreign Trade Statistics 2003; Statistical Yearbook;* and *World Statistics Pocketbook.*

ALGERIA - FORESTS AND FORESTRY

M.E. Sharpe, 80 Business Park Drive, Armonk, NY 10504, (800) 541-6563, Fax: (914) 273-2106, www.mesharpe.com; *The Illustrated Book of World Rankings.*

Palgrave Macmillan Ltd., Houndmills, Basingstoke, Hampshire, RG21 6XS, England, (Telephone in U.S. (888) 330-8477), (Fax in U.S. (800) 672-2054), www.palgrave.com; *The Statesman's Yearbook 2008.*

Taylor and Francis Group, An Informa Business, 2 Park Square, Milton Park, Abingdon, Oxford OX14 4RN, United Kingdom, (Dial from U.S. (212) 216-7800), (Fax from U.S. (212) 564-7854), www.tandf.co.uk; *The Europa World Year Book.*

UNESCO Institute for Statistics, C.P. 6128 Succursale Centre-Ville, Montreal, Quebec, H3C 3J7 Canada, (Dial from U.S. (514) 343-6880), (Fax from U.S. (514) 343 6882), www.uis.unesco.org; *Statistical Tables.*

United Nations Conference on Trade and Development (UNCTAD), DC2-1120, United Nations, New York, NY 10017, (212) 963-0027, www.unctad.org; *UNCTAD Commodity Yearbook.*

United Nations Economic Commission for Africa (ECA), PO Box 3001, Addis Ababa, Ethiopia, (Telephone in U.S. (212) 963-4957), www.uneca.org; *African Statistical Yearbook 2006.*

United Nations Food and Agricultural Organization (FAO), Viale delle Terme di Caracalla, 00100 Rome, Italy, (Dial from U.S. (202) 653-2400), (Fax from U.S. (202) 653 5760), www.fao.org; *FAO Yearbook of Forest Products* and *The State of Food and Agriculture (SOFA) 2006.*

United Nations Statistics Division, New York, NY 10017, (800) 253-9646, Fax: (212) 963-4116, http://unstats.un.org; *Statistical Yearbook.*

The World Bank, 1818 H Street, NW, Washington, DC 20433, (202) 473-1000, Fax: (202) 477-6391, www.worldbank.org; *Algeria* and *World Development Report 2008.*

ALGERIA - GAS PRODUCTION

See ALGERIA - MINERAL INDUSTRIES

ALGERIA - GEOGRAPHIC INFORMATION SYSTEMS

M.E. Sharpe, 80 Business Park Drive, Armonk, NY 10504, (800) 541-6563, Fax: (914) 273-2106, www.mesharpe.com; *The Illustrated Book of World Rankings.*

The World Bank, 1818 H Street, NW, Washington, DC 20433, (202) 473-1000, Fax: (202) 477-6391, www.worldbank.org; *Algeria.*

ALGERIA - GOLD PRODUCTION

See ALGERIA - MINERAL INDUSTRIES

ALGERIA - GROSS DOMESTIC PRODUCT

African Development Bank Group, Rue Joseph Anoma, 01 BP 1387 Abidjan 01, Cote d'Ivoire, www.afdb.org; *Statistics Pocketbook 2008.*

Economist Intelligence Unit, 111 West 57th Street, New York, NY 10019, (212) 554-0600, Fax: (212) 586-1181, www.eiu.com; *Algeria Country Report.*

Euromonitor International, Inc., 224 S. Michigan Avenue, Suite 1500, Chicago, IL 60604, (312) 922-1115, Fax: (312) 922-1157, www.euromonitor.com; *International Marketing Data and Statistics 2008* and *The World Economic Factbook 2008.*

International Monetary Fund (IMF), 700 Nineteenth Street, NW, Washington, DC 20431, (202) 623-7000, Fax: (202) 623-4661, www.imf.org; *International Financial Statistics Yearbook 2007.*

M.E. Sharpe, 80 Business Park Drive, Armonk, NY 10504, (800) 541-6563, Fax: (914) 273-2106, www.mesharpe.com; *The Illustrated Book of World Rankings.*

Taylor and Francis Group, An Informa Business, 2 Park Square, Milton Park, Abingdon, Oxford OX14 4RN, United Kingdom, (Dial from U.S. (212) 216-7800), (Fax from U.S. (212) 564-7854), www.tandf.co.uk; *The Europa World Year Book.*

United Nations Economic Commission for Africa (ECA), PO Box 3001, Addis Ababa, Ethiopia, (Telephone in U.S. (212) 963-4957), www.uneca.org; *African Statistical Yearbook 2006.*

United Nations Statistics Division, New York, NY 10017, (800) 253-9646, Fax: (212) 963-4116, http://unstats.un.org; *Bulletin of Industrial Statistics for the Arab Countries; Human Development Report 2006; National Accounts Statistics: Compendium of Income Distribution Statistics; Statistical Yearbook;* and *Survey of Economic and Social Conditions in Africa 2005.*

The World Bank, 1818 H Street, NW, Washington, DC 20433, (202) 473-1000, Fax: (202) 477-6391, www.worldbank.org; *World Development Indicators (WDI) 2008* and *World Development Report 2008.*

ALGERIA - GROSS NATIONAL PRODUCT

Euromonitor International, Inc., 224 S. Michigan Avenue, Suite 1500, Chicago, IL 60604, (312) 922-1115, Fax: (312) 922-1157, www.euromonitor.com; *International Marketing Data and Statistics 2008.*

M.E. Sharpe, 80 Business Park Drive, Armonk, NY 10504, (800) 541-6563, Fax: (914) 273-2106, www.mesharpe.com; *The Illustrated Book of World Rankings.*

Organization of Petroleum Exporting Countries (OPEC), Obere Donaustrasse 93, A-1020, Vienna, Austria, www.opec.org; *Annual Statistical Bulletin 2006.*

Palgrave Macmillan Ltd., Houndmills, Basingstoke, Hampshire, RG21 6XS, England, (Telephone in U.S. (888) 330-8477), (Fax in U.S. (800) 672-2054), www.palgrave.com; *The Statesman's Yearbook 2008.*

Taylor and Francis Group, An Informa Business, 2 Park Square, Milton Park, Abingdon, Oxford OX14 4RN, United Kingdom, (Dial from U.S. (212) 216-7800), (Fax from U.S. (212) 564-7854), www.tandf.co.uk; *The Europa World Year Book.*

U.S. Department of State (DOS), 2201 C Street NW, Washington, DC 20520, (202) 647-4000, www.state.gov; *World Military Expenditures and Arms Transfers (WMEAT).*

The World Bank, 1818 H Street, NW, Washington, DC 20433, (202) 473-1000, Fax: (202) 477-6391, www.worldbank.org; *The World Bank Atlas 2003-2004; World Development Indicators (WDI) 2008;* and *World Development Report 2008.*

ALGERIA - HEALTH

See ALGERIA - PUBLIC HEALTH

ALGERIA - HIDES AND SKINS INDUSTRY

United Nations Food and Agricultural Organization (FAO), Viale delle Terme di Caracalla, 00100 Rome, Italy, (Dial from U.S. (202) 653-2400), (Fax from U.S. (202) 653 5760), www.fao.org; *FAO Production Yearbook 2002.*

ALGERIA - HOUSING

Euromonitor International, Inc., 224 S. Michigan Avenue, Suite 1500, Chicago, IL 60604, (312) 922-1115, Fax: (312) 922-1157, www.euromonitor.com; *World Marketing Data and Statistics.*

M.E. Sharpe, 80 Business Park Drive, Armonk, NY 10504, (800) 541-6563, Fax: (914) 273-2106, www.mesharpe.com; *The Illustrated Book of World Rankings.*

ALGERIA - ILLITERATE PERSONS

Euromonitor International, Inc., 224 S. Michigan Avenue, Suite 1500, Chicago, IL 60604, (312) 922-1115, Fax: (312) 922-1157, www.euromonitor.com; *The World Economic Factbook 2008.*

Palgrave Macmillan Ltd., Houndmills, Basingstoke, Hampshire, RG21 6XS, England, (Telephone in U.S. (888) 330-8477), (Fax in U.S. (800) 672-2054), www.palgrave.com; *The Statesman's Yearbook 2008.*

UNESCO Institute for Statistics, C.P. 6128 Succursale Centre-Ville, Montreal, Quebec, H3C 3J7 Canada, (Dial from U.S. (514) 343-6880), (Fax from U.S. (514) 343 6882), www.uis.unesco.org; *Statistical Tables.*

United Nations Statistics Division, New York, NY 10017, (800) 253-9646, Fax: (212) 963-4116, http://unstats.un.org; *Human Development Report 2006.*

ALGERIA - IMPORTS

Central Intelligence Agency, Office of Public Affairs, Washington, DC 20505, (703) 482-0623, Fax: (703) 482-1739, www.cia.gov; *The World Factbook.*

Economist Intelligence Unit, 111 West 57th Street, New York, NY 10019, (212) 554-0600, Fax: (212) 586-1181, www.eiu.com; *Algeria Country Report.*

Euromonitor International, Inc., 224 S. Michigan Avenue, Suite 1500, Chicago, IL 60604, (312) 922-1115, Fax: (312) 922-1157, www.euromonitor.com; *International Marketing Data and Statistics 2008* and *The World Economic Factbook 2008.*

International Lead and Zinc Study Group (ILZSG), Rua Almirante Barroso 38, 5th Floor, Lisbon 1000 - 013, Portugal, www.ilzsg.org; Interactive Statistical Database.

International Monetary Fund (IMF), 700 Nineteenth Street, NW, Washington, DC 20431, (202) 623-7000, Fax: (202) 623-4661, www.imf.org; *Direction of Trade Statistics Yearbook 2007* and *International Financial Statistics Yearbook 2007.*

Palgrave Macmillan Ltd., Houndmills, Basingstoke, Hampshire, RG21 6XS, England, (Telephone in U.S. (888) 330-8477), (Fax in U.S. (800) 672-2054), www.palgrave.com; *The Statesman's Yearbook 2008.*

Taylor and Francis Group, An Informa Business, 2 Park Square, Milton Park, Abingdon, Oxford OX14 4RN, United Kingdom, (Dial from U.S. (212) 216-7800), (Fax from U.S. (212) 564-7854), www.tandf.co.uk; *The Europa World Year Book.*

United Nations Conference on Trade and Development (UNCTAD), DC2-1120, United Nations, New York, NY 10017, (212) 963-0027, www.unctad.org; *Handbook of Statistics 2005.*

United Nations Economic Commission for Africa (ECA), PO Box 3001, Addis Ababa, Ethiopia, (Telephone in U.S. (212) 963-4957), www.uneca.org; *African Statistical Yearbook 2006.*

United Nations Food and Agricultural Organization (FAO), Viale delle Terme di Caracalla, 00100 Rome, Italy, (Dial from U.S. (202) 653-2400), (Fax from U.S. (202) 653 5760), www.fao.org; *The State of Food and Agriculture (SOFA) 2006.*

United Nations Statistics Division, New York, NY 10017, (800) 253-9646, Fax: (212) 963-4116, http://unstats.un.org; *Bulletin of Industrial Statistics for the Arab Countries; Compendium of Intra-African and Related Foreign Trade Statistics 2003; Statistical Yearbook;* and *Survey of Economic and Social Conditions in Africa 2005.*

The World Bank, 1818 H Street, NW, Washington, DC 20433, (202) 473-1000, Fax: (202) 477-6391, www.worldbank.org; *World Development Indicators (WDI) 2008* and *World Development Report 2008.*

ALGERIA - INDUSTRIAL PRODUCTIVITY

Euromonitor International, Inc., 224 S. Michigan Avenue, Suite 1500, Chicago, IL 60604, (312) 922-1115, Fax: (312) 922-1157, www.euromonitor.com; *International Marketing Data and Statistics 2008.*

International Lead and Zinc Study Group (ILZSG), Rua Almirante Barroso 38, 5th Floor, Lisbon 1000 - 013, Portugal, www.ilzsg.org; Interactive Statistical Database.

M.E. Sharpe, 80 Business Park Drive, Armonk, NY 10504, (800) 541-6563, Fax: (914) 273-2106, www.mesharpe.com; *The Illustrated Book of World Rankings.*

ALGERIA - INDUSTRIAL PROPERTY

United Nations Statistics Division, New York, NY 10017, (800) 253-9646, Fax: (212) 963-4116, http://unstats.un.org; *Statistical Yearbook.*

World Intellectual Property Organization (WIPO), PO Box 18, CH-1211 Geneva 20, Switzerland, www.wipo.int; *Industrial Property Statistics* and *Industrial Property Statistics Online Directory.*

ALGERIA - INDUSTRIES

Central Intelligence Agency, Office of Public Affairs, Washington, DC 20505, (703) 482-0623, Fax: (703) 482-1739, www.cia.gov; *The World Factbook.*

Economist Intelligence Unit, 111 West 57th Street, New York, NY 10019, (212) 554-0600, Fax: (212) 586-1181, www.eiu.com; *Algeria Country Report.*

Euromonitor International, Inc., 224 S. Michigan Avenue, Suite 1500, Chicago, IL 60604, (312) 922-

1115, Fax: (312) 922-1157, www.euromonitor.com; *International Marketing Data and Statistics 2008; The World Economic Factbook 2008;* and *World Marketing Data and Statistics.*

International Labour Office, I.L.O. Publications, 4 route des Morillons, CH-1211 Geneva 22, Switzerland, (Telephone in U.S. (202) 653-7652), (Fax in U.S. (202) 653-7687), www.ilo.org; *Yearbook of Labour Statistics 2006.*

M.E. Sharpe, 80 Business Park Drive, Armonk, NY 10504, (800) 541-6563, Fax: (914) 273-2106, www.mesharpe.com; *The Illustrated Book of World Rankings.*

Palgrave Macmillan Ltd., Houndmills, Basingstoke, Hampshire, RG21 6XS, England, (Telephone in U.S. (888) 330-8477), (Fax in U.S. (800) 672-2054), www.palgrave.com; *The Statesman's Yearbook 2008.*

Taylor and Francis Group, An Informa Business, 2 Park Square, Milton Park, Abingdon, Oxford OX14 4RN, United Kingdom, (Dial from U.S. (212) 216-7800), (Fax from U.S. (212) 564-7854), www.tandf.co.uk; *The Europa World Year Book.*

United Nations Economic Commission for Africa (ECA), PO Box 3001, Addis Ababa, Ethiopia, (Telephone in U.S. (212) 963-4957), www.uneca.org; *African Statistical Yearbook 2006.*

United Nations Industrial Development Organization (UNIDO), 1 United Nations Plaza, New York, NY 10017, (212) 963 6890, Fax: (212) 963-7904, http://unido.org; Industrial Statistics Database 2008 (INDSTAT) and *The International Yearbook of Industrial Statistics 2008.*

United Nations Statistics Division, New York, NY 10017, (800) 253-9646, Fax: (212) 963-4116, http://unstats.un.org; *Bulletin of Industrial Statistics for the Arab Countries* and *Statistical Yearbook.*

The World Bank, 1818 H Street, NW, Washington, DC 20433, (202) 473-1000, Fax: (202) 477-6391, www.worldbank.org; *Algeria* and *World Development Indicators (WDI) 2008.*

World Intellectual Property Organization (WIPO), PO Box 18, CH-1211 Geneva 20, Switzerland, www.wipo.int; *Industrial Property Statistics* and *Industrial Property Statistics Online Directory.*

ALGERIA - INFANT AND MATERNAL MORTALITY

See ALGERIA - MORTALITY

ALGERIA - INTERNATIONAL LIQUIDITY

International Monetary Fund (IMF), 700 Nineteenth Street, NW, Washington, DC 20431, (202) 623-7000, Fax: (202) 623-4661, www.imf.org; *International Financial Statistics Yearbook 2007.*

ALGERIA - INTERNATIONAL TRADE

African Development Bank Group, Rue Joseph Anoma, 01 BP 1387 Abidjan 01, Cote d'Ivoire, www.afdb.org; *Statistics Pocketbook 2008.*

Economist Intelligence Unit, 111 West 57th Street, New York, NY 10019, (212) 554-0600, Fax: (212) 586-1181, www.eiu.com; *Algeria Country Report.*

Euromonitor International, Inc., 224 S. Michigan Avenue, Suite 1500, Chicago, IL 60604, (312) 922-1115, Fax: (312) 922-1157, www.euromonitor.com; *International Marketing Data and Statistics 2008; The World Economic Factbook 2008;* and *World Marketing Data and Statistics.*

M.E. Sharpe, 80 Business Park Drive, Armonk, NY 10504, (800) 541-6563, Fax: (914) 273-2106, www.mesharpe.com; *The Illustrated Book of World Rankings.*

Organisation for Economic Cooperation and Development (OECD), 2 rue Andre Pascal, F-75775 Paris Cedex 16, France, (Telephone in U.S. (202) 785-6323), (Fax in U.S. (202) 785-0350), www.oecd.org; *International Trade by Commodity Statistics (ITCS).*

Palgrave Macmillan Ltd., Houndmills, Basingstoke, Hampshire, RG21 6XS, England, (Telephone in U.S. (888) 330-8477), (Fax in U.S. (800) 672-2054), www.palgrave.com; *The Statesman's Yearbook 2008.*

Taylor and Francis Group, An Informa Business, 2 Park Square, Milton Park, Abingdon, Oxford OX14 4RN, United Kingdom, (Dial from U.S. (212) 216-7800), (Fax from U.S. (212) 564-7854), www.tandf.co.uk; *The Europa World Year Book.*

United Nations Conference on Trade and Development (UNCTAD), DC2-1120, United Nations, New York, NY 10017, (212) 963-0027, www.unctad.org; *UNCTAD Commodity Yearbook.*

United Nations Economic Commission for Africa (ECA), PO Box 3001, Addis Ababa, Ethiopia, (Telephone in U.S. (212) 963-4957), www.uneca.org; *African Statistical Yearbook 2006.*

United Nations Food and Agricultural Organization (FAO), Viale delle Terme di Caracalla, 00100 Rome, Italy, (Dial from U.S. (202) 653-2400), (Fax from U.S. (202) 653 5760), www.fao.org; *FAO Trade Yearbook* and *The State of Food and Agriculture (SOFA) 2006.*

United Nations Statistics Division, New York, NY 10017, (800) 253-9646, Fax: (212) 963-4116, http://unstats.un.org; *Bulletin of Industrial Statistics for the Arab Countries; Compendium of Intra-African and Related Foreign Trade Statistics 2003; International Trade Statistics Yearbook;* and *Statistical Yearbook.*

The World Bank, 1818 H Street, NW, Washington, DC 20433, (202) 473-1000, Fax: (202) 477-6391, www.worldbank.org; *Algeria; World Development Indicators (WDI) 2008;* and *World Development Report 2008.*

World Trade Organization (WTO), Centre William Rappard, Rue de Lausanne 154, CH-1211 Geneva 21, Switzerland, www.wto.org; *International Trade Statistics 2006.*

ALGERIA - INTERNET USERS

International Telecommunication Union (ITU), Place des Nations, 1211 Geneva 20, Switzerland, www.itu.int; *World Telecommunication/ICT Indicators Database on CD-ROM; World Telecommunication/ICT Indicators Database Online;* and *Yearbook of Statistics - Telecommunication Services (Chronological Time Series 1997-2006).*

The World Bank, 1818 H Street, NW, Washington, DC 20433, (202) 473-1000, Fax: (202) 477-6391, www.worldbank.org; *Algeria.*

ALGERIA - INVESTMENTS

International Monetary Fund (IMF), 700 Nineteenth Street, NW, Washington, DC 20431, (202) 623-7000, Fax: (202) 623-4661, www.imf.org; *International Financial Statistics Yearbook 2007.*

ALGERIA - IRON AND IRON ORE PRODUCTION

See ALGERIA - MINERAL INDUSTRIES

ALGERIA - IRRIGATION

Euromonitor International, Inc., 224 S. Michigan Avenue, Suite 1500, Chicago, IL 60604, (312) 922-1115, Fax: (312) 922-1157, www.euromonitor.com; *International Marketing Data and Statistics 2008.*

ALGERIA - LABOR

African Development Bank Group, Rue Joseph Anoma, 01 BP 1387 Abidjan 01, Cote d'Ivoire, www.afdb.org; *Statistics Pocketbook 2008.*

Central Intelligence Agency, Office of Public Affairs, Washington, DC 20505, (703) 482-0623, Fax: (703) 482-1739, www.cia.gov; *The World Factbook.*

Euromonitor International, Inc., 224 S. Michigan Avenue, Suite 1500, Chicago, IL 60604, (312) 922-1115, Fax: (312) 922-1157, www.euromonitor.com; *International Marketing Data and Statistics 2008* and *World Marketing Data and Statistics.*

International Labour Office, I.L.O. Publications, 4 route des Morillons, CH-1211 Geneva 22, Switzerland, (Telephone in U.S. (202) 653-7652), (Fax in U.S. (202) 653-7687), www.ilo.org; *Yearbook of Labour Statistics 2006.*

M.E. Sharpe, 80 Business Park Drive, Armonk, NY 10504, (800) 541-6563, Fax: (914) 273-2106, www.mesharpe.com; *The Illustrated Book of World Rankings.*

Palgrave Macmillan Ltd., Houndmills, Basingstoke, Hampshire, RG21 6XS, England, (Telephone in U.S. (888) 330-8477), (Fax in U.S. (800) 672-2054), www.palgrave.com; *The Statesman's Yearbook 2008.*

United Nations Food and Agricultural Organization (FAO), Viale delle Terme di Caracalla, 00100 Rome, Italy, (Dial from U.S. (202) 653-2400), (Fax from U.S. (202) 653 5760), www.fao.org; *The State of Food and Agriculture (SOFA) 2006.*

United Nations Statistics Division, New York, NY 10017, (800) 253-9646, Fax: (212) 963-4116, http://unstats.un.org; *Human Development Report 2006.*

The World Bank, 1818 H Street, NW, Washington, DC 20433, (202) 473-1000, Fax: (202) 477-6391, www.worldbank.org; *The World Bank Atlas 2003-2004; World Development Indicators (WDI) 2008;* and *World Development Report 2008.*

ALGERIA - LAND USE

Central Intelligence Agency, Office of Public Affairs, Washington, DC 20505, (703) 482-0623, Fax: (703) 482-1739, www.cia.gov; *The World Factbook.*

Euromonitor International, Inc., 224 S. Michigan Avenue, Suite 1500, Chicago, IL 60604, (312) 922-1115, Fax: (312) 922-1157, www.euromonitor.com; *International Marketing Data and Statistics 2008.*

United Nations Food and Agricultural Organization (FAO), Viale delle Terme di Caracalla, 00100 Rome, Italy, (Dial from U.S. (202) 653-2400), (Fax from U.S. (202) 653 5760), www.fao.org; *FAO Production Yearbook 2002.*

The World Bank, 1818 H Street, NW, Washington, DC 20433, (202) 473-1000, Fax: (202) 477-6391, www.worldbank.org; *World Development Report 2008.*

ALGERIA - LIBRARIES

M.E. Sharpe, 80 Business Park Drive, Armonk, NY 10504, (800) 541-6563, Fax: (914) 273-2106, www.mesharpe.com; *The Illustrated Book of World Rankings.*

UNESCO Institute for Statistics, C.P. 6128 Succursale Centre-Ville, Montreal, Quebec, H3C 3J7 Canada, (Dial from U.S. (514) 343-6880), (Fax from U.S. (514) 343 6882), www.uis.unesco.org; *Statistical Tables.*

ALGERIA - LIFE EXPECTANCY

African Development Bank Group, Rue Joseph Anoma, 01 BP 1387 Abidjan 01, Cote d'Ivoire, www.afdb.org; *Statistics Pocketbook 2008.*

Euromonitor International, Inc., 224 S. Michigan Avenue, Suite 1500, Chicago, IL 60604, (312) 922-1115, Fax: (312) 922-1157, www.euromonitor.com; *The World Economic Factbook 2008.*

Palgrave Macmillan Ltd., Houndmills, Basingstoke, Hampshire, RG21 6XS, England, (Telephone in U.S. (888) 330-8477), (Fax in U.S. (800) 672-2054), www.palgrave.com; *The Statesman's Yearbook 2008.*

United Nations Statistics Division, New York, NY 10017, (800) 253-9646, Fax: (212) 963-4116, http://unstats.un.org; *Human Development Report 2006* and *World Statistics Pocketbook.*

The World Bank, 1818 H Street, NW, Washington, DC 20433, (202) 473-1000, Fax: (202) 477-6391, www.worldbank.org; *The World Bank Atlas 2003-2004* and *World Development Report 2008.*

ALGERIA - LITERACY

Euromonitor International, Inc., 224 S. Michigan Avenue, Suite 1500, Chicago, IL 60604, (312) 922-1115, Fax: (312) 922-1157, www.euromonitor.com; *World Marketing Data and Statistics.*

United Nations Statistics Division, New York, NY 10017, (800) 253-9646, Fax: (212) 963-4116, http://unstats.un.org; *Survey of Economic and Social Conditions in Africa 2005.*

ALGERIA - LIVESTOCK

Euromonitor International, Inc., 224 S. Michigan Avenue, Suite 1500, Chicago, IL 60604, (312) 922-1115, Fax: (312) 922-1157, www.euromonitor.com; *International Marketing Data and Statistics 2008.*

M.E. Sharpe, 80 Business Park Drive, Armonk, NY 10504, (800) 541-6563, Fax: (914) 273-2106, www.mesharpe.com; *The Illustrated Book of World Rankings.*

Palgrave Macmillan Ltd., Houndmills, Basingstoke, Hampshire, RG21 6XS, England, (Telephone in U.S. (888) 330-8477), (Fax in U.S. (800) 672-2054), www.palgrave.com; *The Statesman's Yearbook 2008.*

Taylor and Francis Group, An Informa Business, 2 Park Square, Milton Park, Abingdon, Oxford OX14 4RN, United Kingdom, (Dial from U.S. (212) 216-7800), (Fax from U.S. (212) 564-7854), www.tandf.co.uk; *The Europa World Year Book.*

United Nations Conference on Trade and Development (UNCTAD), DC2-1120, United Nations, New York, NY 10017, (212) 963-0027, www.unctad.org; *UNCTAD Commodity Yearbook.*

United Nations Economic Commission for Africa (ECA), PO Box 3001, Addis Ababa, Ethiopia, (Telephone in U.S. (212) 963-4957), www.uneca.org; *African Statistical Yearbook 2006.*

United Nations Food and Agricultural Organization (FAO), Viale delle Terme di Caracalla, 00100 Rome, Italy, (Dial from U.S. (202) 653-2400), (Fax from U.S. (202) 653 5760), www.fao.org; *FAO Production Yearbook 2002* and *The State of Food and Agriculture (SOFA) 2006.*

United Nations Statistics Division, New York, NY 10017, (800) 253-9646, Fax: (212) 963-4116, http://unstats.un.org; *Statistical Yearbook* and *Survey of Economic and Social Conditions in Africa 2005.*

ALGERIA - LOCAL TAXATION

Euromonitor International, Inc., 224 S. Michigan Avenue, Suite 1500, Chicago, IL 60604, (312) 922-1115, Fax: (312) 922-1157, www.euromonitor.com; *International Marketing Data and Statistics 2008.*

ALGERIA - MANUFACTURES

M.E. Sharpe, 80 Business Park Drive, Armonk, NY 10504, (800) 541-6563, Fax: (914) 273-2106, www.mesharpe.com; *The Illustrated Book of World Rankings.*

United Nations Economic Commission for Africa (ECA), PO Box 3001, Addis Ababa, Ethiopia, (Telephone in U.S. (212) 963-4957), www.uneca.org; *African Statistical Yearbook 2006.*

United Nations Statistics Division, New York, NY 10017, (800) 253-9646, Fax: (212) 963-4116, http://unstats.un.org; *Bulletin of Industrial Statistics for the Arab Countries; Statistical Yearbook;* and *Survey of Economic and Social Conditions in Africa 2005.*

The World Bank, 1818 H Street, NW, Washington, DC 20433, (202) 473-1000, Fax: (202) 477-6391, www.worldbank.org; *World Development Indicators (WDI) 2008.*

ALGERIA - MARRIAGE

M.E. Sharpe, 80 Business Park Drive, Armonk, NY 10504, (800) 541-6563, Fax: (914) 273-2106, www.mesharpe.com; *The Illustrated Book of World Rankings.*

United Nations Statistics Division, New York, NY 10017, (800) 253-9646, Fax: (212) 963-4116, http://unstats.un.org; *Demographic Yearbook* and *Statistical Yearbook.*

ALGERIA - MEAT PRODUCTION

See ALGERIA - LIVESTOCK

ALGERIA - MERCHANT SHIPS

See ALGERIA - SHIPPING

ALGERIA - MERCURY PRODUCTION

See ALGERIA - MINERAL INDUSTRIES

ALGERIA - MILK PRODUCTION

See ALGERIA - DAIRY PROCESSING

ALGERIA - MINERAL INDUSTRIES

Commodity Research Bureau, 330 South Wells Street, Suite 612, Chicago, IL 60606-7110, (800) 621-5271, Fax: (312) 939-4135, www.crbtrader.com; *2006 CRB Commodity Yearbook and CD.*

International Lead and Zinc Study Group (ILZSG), Rua Almirante Barroso 38, 5th Floor, Lisbon 1000 - 013, Portugal, www.ilzsg.org; Interactive Statistical Database.

International Monetary Fund (IMF), 700 Nineteenth Street, NW, Washington, DC 20431, (202) 623-7000, Fax: (202) 623-4661, www.imf.org; *International Financial Statistics Yearbook 2007.*

Organisation for Economic Cooperation and Development (OECD), 2 rue Andre Pascal, F-75775 Paris Cedex 16, France, (Telephone in U.S. (202) 785-6323), (Fax in U.S. (202) 785-0350), www.oecd.org; *World Energy Outlook 2007.*

Organization of Petroleum Exporting Countries (OPEC), Obere Donaustrasse 93, A-1020, Vienna, Austria, www.opec.org; *Annual Statistical Bulletin 2006.*

Palgrave Macmillan Ltd., Houndmills, Basingstoke, Hampshire, RG21 6XS, England, (Telephone in U.S. (888) 330-8477), (Fax in U.S. (800) 672-2054), www.palgrave.com; *The Statesman's Yearbook 2008.*

Taylor and Francis Group, An Informa Business, 2 Park Square, Milton Park, Abingdon, Oxford OX14 4RN, United Kingdom, (Dial from U.S. (212) 216-7800), (Fax from U.S. (212) 564-7854), www.tandf.co.uk; *The Europa World Year Book.*

United Nations Conference on Trade and Development (UNCTAD), DC2-1120, United Nations, New York, NY 10017, (212) 963-0027, www.unctad.org; *UNCTAD Commodity Yearbook.*

United Nations Economic Commission for Africa (ECA), PO Box 3001, Addis Ababa, Ethiopia, (Telephone in U.S. (212) 963-4957), www.uneca.org; *African Statistical Yearbook 2006.*

United Nations Statistics Division, New York, NY 10017, (800) 253-9646, Fax: (212) 963-4116, http://unstats.un.org; *Bulletin of Industrial Statistics for the Arab Countries* and *Statistical Yearbook.*

The World Bank, 1818 H Street, NW, Washington, DC 20433, (202) 473-1000, Fax: (202) 477-6391, www.worldbank.org; *World Development Indicators (WDI) 2008.*

ALGERIA - MONEY EXCHANGE RATES

See ALGERIA - FOREIGN EXCHANGE RATES

ALGERIA - MONEY SUPPLY

African Development Bank Group, Rue Joseph Anoma, 01 BP 1387 Abidjan 01, Cote d'Ivoire, www.afdb.org; *Statistics Pocketbook 2008.*

Economist Intelligence Unit, 111 West 57th Street, New York, NY 10019, (212) 554-0600, Fax: (212) 586-1181, www.eiu.com; *Algeria Country Report.*

Euromonitor International, Inc., 224 S. Michigan Avenue, Suite 1500, Chicago, IL 60604, (312) 922-1115, Fax: (312) 922-1157, www.euromonitor.com; *International Marketing Data and Statistics 2008.*

International Monetary Fund (IMF), 700 Nineteenth Street, NW, Washington, DC 20431, (202) 623-7000, Fax: (202) 623-4661, www.imf.org; *International Financial Statistics Yearbook 2007.*

Taylor and Francis Group, An Informa Business, 2 Park Square, Milton Park, Abingdon, Oxford OX14 4RN, United Kingdom, (Dial from U.S. (212) 216-7800), (Fax from U.S. (212) 564-7854), www.tandf.co.uk; *The Europa World Year Book.*

United Nations Statistics Division, New York, NY 10017, (800) 253-9646, Fax: (212) 963-4116, http://unstats.un.org; *Statistical Yearbook.*

The World Bank, 1818 H Street, NW, Washington, DC 20433, (202) 473-1000, Fax: (202) 477-6391, www.worldbank.org; *Algeria* and *World Development Indicators (WDI) 2008.*

ALGERIA - MORTALITY

Central Intelligence Agency, Office of Public Affairs, Washington, DC 20505, (703) 482-0623, Fax: (703) 482-1739, www.cia.gov; *The World Factbook.*

Euromonitor International, Inc., 224 S. Michigan Avenue, Suite 1500, Chicago, IL 60604, (312) 922-1115, Fax: (312) 922-1157, www.euromonitor.com; *International Marketing Data and Statistics 2008* and *The World Economic Factbook 2008.*

Palgrave Macmillan Ltd., Houndmills, Basingstoke, Hampshire, RG21 6XS, England, (Telephone in U.S. (888) 330-8477), (Fax in U.S. (800) 672-2054), www.palgrave.com; *The Statesman's Yearbook 2008.*

Taylor and Francis Group, An Informa Business, 2 Park Square, Milton Park, Abingdon, Oxford OX14 4RN, United Kingdom, (Dial from U.S. (212) 216-7800), (Fax from U.S. (212) 564-7854), www.tandf.co.uk; *The Europa World Year Book.*

UNICEF, 3 United Nations Plaza, New York, NY 10017, (800) 253-9646, Fax: (212) 887-7465, www.unicef.org; *The State of the World's Children 2008.*

United Nations Statistics Division, New York, NY 10017, (800) 253-9646, Fax: (212) 963-4116, http://unstats.un.org; *Demographic Yearbook; Human Development Report 2006; Statistical Yearbook; Survey of Economic and Social Conditions in Africa 2005;* and *World Statistics Pocketbook.*

The World Bank, 1818 H Street, NW, Washington, DC 20433, (202) 473-1000, Fax: (202) 477-6391, www.worldbank.org; *The World Bank Atlas 2003-2004; World Development Indicators (WDI) 2008;* and *World Development Report 2008.*

World Health Organization (WHO), Avenue Appia 20, 1211 Geneve 27, Switzerland, (Telephone in U.S. (212) 331-9081), www.who.int; The WHO Global Atlas of Infectious Diseases and *World Health Report 2006.*

ALGERIA - MOTION PICTURES

Palgrave Macmillan Ltd., Houndmills, Basingstoke, Hampshire, RG21 6XS, England, (Telephone in U.S. (888) 330-8477), (Fax in U.S. (800) 672-2054), www.palgrave.com; *The Statesman's Yearbook 2008.*

UNESCO Institute for Statistics, C.P. 6128 Succursale Centre-Ville, Montreal, Quebec, H3C 3J7 Canada, (Dial from U.S. (514) 343-6880), (Fax from U.S. (514) 343 6882), www.uis.unesco.org; *Statistical Tables.*

United Nations Statistics Division, New York, NY 10017, (800) 253-9646, Fax: (212) 963-4116, http://unstats.un.org; *Statistical Yearbook.*

ALGERIA - MOTOR VEHICLES

International Road Federation (IFR), Madison Place, 500 Montgomery Street, 5th Floor, Alexandria, VA 22314, (703) 535-1001, Fax: (703) 535-1007, www.irfnet.org; *World Road Statistics 2006.*

Taylor and Francis Group, An Informa Business, 2 Park Square, Milton Park, Abingdon, Oxford OX14 4RN, United Kingdom, (Dial from U.S. (212) 216-7800), (Fax from U.S. (212) 564-7854), www.tandf.co.uk; *The Europa World Year Book.*

United Nations Statistics Division, New York, NY 10017, (800) 253-9646, Fax: (212) 963-4116, http://unstats.un.org; *Statistical Yearbook* and *Survey of Economic and Social Conditions in Africa 2005.*

ALGERIA - MUSEUMS

M.E. Sharpe, 80 Business Park Drive, Armonk, NY 10504, (800) 541-6563, Fax: (914) 273-2106, www.mesharpe.com; *The Illustrated Book of World Rankings.*

UNESCO Institute for Statistics, C.P. 6128 Succursale Centre-Ville, Montreal, Quebec, H3C 3J7 Canada, (Dial from U.S. (514) 343-6880), (Fax from U.S. (514) 343 6882), www.uis.unesco.org; *Statistical Tables.*

ALGERIA - NATIONAL INCOME

United Nations Statistics Division, New York, NY 10017, (800) 253-9646, Fax: (212) 963-4116, http://unstats.un.org; *Statistical Yearbook.*

ALGERIA - NATURAL GAS PRODUCTION

See ALGERIA - MINERAL INDUSTRIES

ALGERIA - NUPTIALITY

See ALGERIA - MARRIAGE

ALGERIA - NUTRITION

African Development Bank Group, Rue Joseph Anoma, 01 BP 1387 Abidjan 01, Cote d'Ivoire, www.afdb.org; *Statistics Pocketbook 2008.*

United Nations Food and Agricultural Organization (FAO), Viale delle Terme di Caracalla, 00100 Rome, Italy, (Dial from U.S. (202) 653-2400), (Fax from U.S. (202) 653 5760), www.fao.org; *The State of Food and Agriculture (SOFA) 2006.*

ALGERIA - OATS PRODUCTION

See ALGERIA - CROPS

ALGERIA - OLDER PEOPLE

M.E. Sharpe, 80 Business Park Drive, Armonk, NY 10504, (800) 541-6563, Fax: (914) 273-2106, www.mesharpe.com; *The Illustrated Book of World Rankings.*

ALGERIA - ORANGES PRODUCTION

See ALGERIA - CROPS

ALGERIA - PAPER

See ALGERIA - FORESTS AND FORESTRY

ALGERIA - PEANUT PRODUCTION

See ALGERIA - CROPS

ALGERIA - PERIODICALS

UNESCO Institute for Statistics, C.P. 6128 Succursale Centre-Ville, Montreal, Quebec, H3C 3J7 Canada, (Dial from U.S. (514) 343-6880), (Fax from U.S. (514) 343 6882), www.uis.unesco.org; *Statistical Tables.*

ALGERIA - PESTICIDES

United Nations Food and Agricultural Organization (FAO), Viale delle Terme di Caracalla, 00100 Rome, Italy, (Dial from U.S. (202) 653-2400), (Fax from U.S. (202) 653 5760), www.fao.org; *The State of Food and Agriculture (SOFA) 2006.*

ALGERIA - PETROLEUM INDUSTRY AND TRADE

International Monetary Fund (IMF), 700 Nineteenth Street, NW, Washington, DC 20431, (202) 623-7000, Fax: (202) 623-4661, www.imf.org; *International Financial Statistics Yearbook 2007.*

M.E. Sharpe, 80 Business Park Drive, Armonk, NY 10504, (800) 541-6563, Fax: (914) 273-2106, www.mesharpe.com; *The Illustrated Book of World Rankings.*

Organisation for Economic Cooperation and Development (OECD), 2 rue Andre Pascal, F-75775 Paris Cedex 16, France, (Telephone in U.S. (202) 785-6323), (Fax in U.S. (202) 785-0350), www.oecd.org; *World Energy Outlook 2007.*

Organization of Petroleum Exporting Countries (OPEC), Obere Donaustrasse 93, A-1020, Vienna, Austria, www.opec.org; *Annual Statistical Bulletin 2006.*

Palgrave Macmillan Ltd., Houndmills, Basingstoke, Hampshire, RG21 6XS, England, (Telephone in U.S. (888) 330-8477), (Fax in U.S. (800) 672-2054), www.palgrave.com; *The Statesman's Yearbook 2008.*

PennWell Corporation, 1421 South Sheridan Road, Tulsa, OK 74112, (918) 835-3161, www.pennwell.com; *International Petroleum Encyclopedia 2007.*

U.S. Department of Energy (DOE), Energy Information Administration (EIA), 1000 Independence Avenue, SW, Washington, DC 20585, (202) 586-8800, www.eia.doe.gov; *International Energy Annual 2004* and *International Energy Outlook 2006.*

United Nations Conference on Trade and Development (UNCTAD), DC2-1120, United Nations, New York, NY 10017, (212) 963-0027, www.unctad.org; *UNCTAD Commodity Yearbook.*

United Nations Food and Agricultural Organization (FAO), Viale delle Terme di Caracalla, 00100 Rome, Italy, (Dial from U.S. (202) 653-2400), (Fax from U.S. (202) 653 5760), www.fao.org; *The State of Food and Agriculture (SOFA) 2006.*

United Nations Statistics Division, New York, NY 10017, (800) 253-9646, Fax: (212) 963-4116, http://unstats.un.org; *Statistical Yearbook.*

ALGERIA - PHOSPHATES PRODUCTION

See ALGERIA - MINERAL INDUSTRIES

ALGERIA - PIPELINES

Organization of Petroleum Exporting Countries (OPEC), Obere Donaustrasse 93, A-1020, Vienna, Austria, www.opec.org; *Annual Statistical Bulletin 2006.*

ALGERIA - POLITICAL SCIENCE

Central Intelligence Agency, Office of Public Affairs, Washington, DC 20505, (703) 482-0623, Fax: (703) 482-1739, www.cia.gov; *The World Factbook.*

International Monetary Fund (IMF), 700 Nineteenth Street, NW, Washington, DC 20431, (202) 623-7000, Fax: (202) 623-4661, www.imf.org; *International Financial Statistics Yearbook 2007.*

Palgrave Macmillan Ltd., Houndmills, Basingstoke, Hampshire, RG21 6XS, England, (Telephone in U.S. (888) 330-8477), (Fax in U.S. (800) 672-2054), www.palgrave.com; *The Statesman's Yearbook 2008.*

Taylor and Francis Group, An Informa Business, 2 Park Square, Milton Park, Abingdon, Oxford OX14 4RN, United Kingdom, (Dial from U.S. (212) 216-7800), (Fax from U.S. (212) 564-7854), www.tandf.co.uk; *The Europa World Year Book.*

United Nations Statistics Division, New York, NY 10017, (800) 253-9646, Fax: (212) 963-4116, http://unstats.un.org; *National Accounts Statistics: Compendium of Income Distribution Statistics* and *Survey of Economic and Social Conditions in Africa 2005.*

The World Bank, 1818 H Street, NW, Washington, DC 20433, (202) 473-1000, Fax: (202) 477-6391, www.worldbank.org; *World Development Indicators (WDI) 2008* and *World Development Report 2008.*

ALGERIA - POPULATION

African Development Bank Group, Rue Joseph Anoma, 01 BP 1387 Abidjan 01, Cote d'Ivoire, www.afdb.org; *The African Statistical Journal; Gender, Poverty and Environmental Indicators on African Countries 2007; Selected Statistics on African Countries 2007;* and *Statistics Pocketbook 2008.*

Central Intelligence Agency, Office of Public Affairs, Washington, DC 20505, (703) 482-0623, Fax: (703) 482-1739, www.cia.gov; *The World Factbook.*

Economist Intelligence Unit, 111 West 57th Street, New York, NY 10019, (212) 554-0600, Fax: (212) 586-1181, www.eiu.com; *Algeria Country Report.*

Euromonitor International, Inc., 224 S. Michigan Avenue, Suite 1500, Chicago, IL 60604, (312) 922-1115, Fax: (312) 922-1157, www.euromonitor.com; *International Marketing Data and Statistics 2008* and *The World Economic Factbook 2008.*

Eurostat, Batiment Jean Monnet, Rue Alcide de Gasperi, L-2920 Luxembourg, http://epp.eurostat.ec.europa.eu; *Demographic Indicators - Population by Age-Classes.*

International Labour Office, I.L.O. Publications, 4 route des Morillons, CH-1211 Geneva 22, Switzerland, (Telephone in U.S. (202) 653-7652), (Fax in U.S. (202) 653-7687), www.ilo.org; *Yearbook of Labour Statistics 2006.*

M.E. Sharpe, 80 Business Park Drive, Armonk, NY 10504, (800) 541-6563, Fax: (914) 273-2106, www.mesharpe.com; *The Illustrated Book of World Rankings.*

Palgrave Macmillan Ltd., Houndmills, Basingstoke, Hampshire, RG21 6XS, England, (Telephone in U.S. (888) 330-8477), (Fax in U.S. (800) 672-2054), www.palgrave.com; *The Statesman's Yearbook 2008.*

Taylor and Francis Group, An Informa Business, 2 Park Square, Milton Park, Abingdon, Oxford OX14 4RN, United Kingdom, (Dial from U.S. (212) 216-7800), (Fax from U.S. (212) 564-7854), www.tandf.co.uk; *The Europa World Year Book.*

U.S. Department of State (DOS), 2201 C Street NW, Washington, DC 20520, (202) 647-4000, www.state.gov; *World Military Expenditures and Arms Transfers (WMEAT).*

United Nations Food and Agricultural Organization (FAO), Viale delle Terme di Caracalla, 00100 Rome, Italy, (Dial from U.S. (202) 653-2400), (Fax from U.S. (202) 653 5760), www.fao.org; *FAO Production Yearbook 2002.*

United Nations Statistics Division, New York, NY 10017, (800) 253-9646, Fax: (212) 963-4116, http://unstats.un.org; *Demographic Yearbook; Human Development Report 2006; Statistical Yearbook; Survey of Economic and Social Conditions in Africa 2005;* and *World Statistics Pocketbook.*

The World Bank, 1818 H Street, NW, Washington, DC 20433, (202) 473-1000, Fax: (202) 477-6391, www.worldbank.org; *Algeria; The World Bank Atlas 2003-2004;* and *World Development Report 2008.*

World Health Organization (WHO), Avenue Appia 20, 1211 Geneve 27, Switzerland, (Telephone in U.S. (212) 331-9081), www.who.int; *World Health Report 2006.*

ALGERIA - POPULATION DENSITY

African Development Bank Group, Rue Joseph Anoma, 01 BP 1387 Abidjan 01, Cote d'Ivoire, www.afdb.org; *Statistics Pocketbook 2008.*

Central Intelligence Agency, Office of Public Affairs, Washington, DC 20505, (703) 482-0623, Fax: (703) 482-1739, www.cia.gov; *The World Factbook.*

Euromonitor International, Inc., 224 S. Michigan Avenue, Suite 1500, Chicago, IL 60604, (312) 922-1115, Fax: (312) 922-1157, www.euromonitor.com; *International Marketing Data and Statistics 2008* and *The World Economic Factbook 2008.*

M.E. Sharpe, 80 Business Park Drive, Armonk, NY 10504, (800) 541-6563, Fax: (914) 273-2106, www.mesharpe.com; *The Illustrated Book of World Rankings.*

Palgrave Macmillan Ltd., Houndmills, Basingstoke, Hampshire, RG21 6XS, England, (Telephone in U.S. (888) 330-8477), (Fax in U.S. (800) 672-2054), www.palgrave.com; *The Statesman's Yearbook 2008.*

Taylor and Francis Group, An Informa Business, 2 Park Square, Milton Park, Abingdon, Oxford OX14 4RN, United Kingdom, (Dial from U.S. (212) 216-7800), (Fax from U.S. (212) 564-7854), www.tandf.co.uk; *The Europa World Year Book.*

United Nations Food and Agricultural Organization (FAO), Viale delle Terme di Caracalla, 00100 Rome, Italy, (Dial from U.S. (202) 653-2400), (Fax from U.S. (202) 653 5760), www.fao.org; *The State of Food and Agriculture (SOFA) 2006.*

United Nations Statistics Division, New York, NY 10017, (800) 253-9646, Fax: (212) 963-4116, http://unstats.un.org; *Statistical Yearbook* and *Survey of Economic and Social Conditions in Africa 2005.*

The World Bank, 1818 H Street, NW, Washington, DC 20433, (202) 473-1000, Fax: (202) 477-6391, www.worldbank.org; *Algeria* and *World Development Report 2008.*

ALGERIA - POSTAL SERVICE

M.E. Sharpe, 80 Business Park Drive, Armonk, NY 10504, (800) 541-6563, Fax: (914) 273-2106, www.mesharpe.com; *The Illustrated Book of World Rankings.*

United Nations Statistics Division, New York, NY 10017, (800) 253-9646, Fax: (212) 963-4116, http://unstats.un.org; *Statistical Yearbook.*

ALGERIA - POULTRY

See ALGERIA - LIVESTOCK

ALGERIA - POWER RESOURCES

Euromonitor International, Inc., 224 S. Michigan Avenue, Suite 1500, Chicago, IL 60604, (312) 922-1115, Fax: (312) 922-1157, www.euromonitor.com; *International Marketing Data and Statistics 2008; The World Economic Factbook 2008;* and *World Marketing Data and Statistics.*

M.E. Sharpe, 80 Business Park Drive, Armonk, NY 10504, (800) 541-6563, Fax: (914) 273-2106, www.mesharpe.com; *The Illustrated Book of World Rankings.*

Organisation for Economic Cooperation and Development (OECD), 2 rue Andre Pascal, F-75775 Paris Cedex 16, France, (Telephone in U.S. (202) 785-6323), (Fax in U.S. (202) 785-0350), www.oecd.org; *World Energy Outlook 2007.*

Palgrave Macmillan Ltd., Houndmills, Basingstoke, Hampshire, RG21 6XS, England, (Telephone in U.S. (888) 330-8477), (Fax in U.S. (800) 672-2054), www.palgrave.com; *The Statesman's Yearbook 2008.*

Platts, 2 Penn Plaza, 25th Floor, New York, NY 10121-2298, (212) 904-3070, www.platts.com; *Energy Economist.*

U.S. Department of Energy (DOE), Energy Information Administration (EIA), 1000 Independence Avenue, SW, Washington, DC 20585, (202) 586-8800, www.eia.doe.gov; *International Energy Annual 2004* and *International Energy Outlook 2006.*

United Nations Economic Commission for Africa (ECA), PO Box 3001, Addis Ababa, Ethiopia, (Telephone in U.S. (212) 963-4957), www.uneca.org; *African Statistical Yearbook 2006.*

United Nations Food and Agricultural Organization (FAO), Viale delle Terme di Caracalla, 00100 Rome, Italy, (Dial from U.S. (202) 653-2400), (Fax from U.S. (202) 653 5760), www.fao.org; *The State of Food and Agriculture (SOFA) 2006.*

United Nations Statistics Division, New York, NY 10017, (800) 253-9646, Fax: (212) 963-4116, http://unstats.un.org; *Bulletin of Industrial Statistics for the Arab Countries; Energy Statistics Yearbook 2003; Human Development Report 2006; Statistical Yearbook;* and *World Statistics Pocketbook.*

The World Bank, 1818 H Street, NW, Washington, DC 20433, (202) 473-1000, Fax: (202) 477-6391, www.worldbank.org; *The World Bank Atlas 2003-2004* and *World Development Report 2008.*

ALGERIA - PRICES

Euromonitor International, Inc., 224 S. Michigan Avenue, Suite 1500, Chicago, IL 60604, (312) 922-1115, Fax: (312) 922-1157, www.euromonitor.com; *World Marketing Data and Statistics.*

International Labour Office, I.L.O. Publications, 4 route des Morillons, CH-1211 Geneva 22, Switzerland, (Telephone in U.S. (202) 653-7652), (Fax in U.S. (202) 653-7687), www.ilo.org; *Yearbook of Labour Statistics 2006.*

International Lead and Zinc Study Group (ILZSG), Rua Almirante Barroso 38, 5th Floor, Lisbon 1000 - 013, Portugal, www.ilzsg.org; Interactive Statistical Database.

International Monetary Fund (IMF), 700 Nineteenth Street, NW, Washington, DC 20431, (202) 623-7000, Fax: (202) 623-4661, www.imf.org; *International Financial Statistics Yearbook 2007.*

M.E. Sharpe, 80 Business Park Drive, Armonk, NY 10504, (800) 541-6563, Fax: (914) 273-2106, www.mesharpe.com; *The Illustrated Book of World Rankings.*

United Nations Economic Commission for Africa (ECA), PO Box 3001, Addis Ababa, Ethiopia, (Telephone in U.S. (212) 963-4957), www.uneca.org; *African Statistical Yearbook 2006.*

United Nations Food and Agricultural Organization (FAO), Viale delle Terme di Caracalla, 00100 Rome, Italy, (Dial from U.S. (202) 653-2400), (Fax from U.S. (202) 653 5760), www.fao.org; *FAO Production Yearbook 2002* and *The State of Food and Agriculture (SOFA) 2006.*

The World Bank, 1818 H Street, NW, Washington, DC 20433, (202) 473-1000, Fax: (202) 477-6391, www.worldbank.org; *Algeria.*

ALGERIA - PROFESSIONS

UNESCO Institute for Statistics, C.P. 6128 Succursale Centre-Ville, Montreal, Quebec, H3C 3J7 Canada, (Dial from U.S. (514) 343-6880), (Fax from U.S. (514) 343 6882), www.uis.unesco.org; *Statistical Tables.*

United Nations Statistics Division, New York, NY 10017, (800) 253-9646, Fax: (212) 963-4116, http://unstats.un.org; *Statistical Yearbook.*

ALGERIA - PUBLIC HEALTH

African Development Bank Group, Rue Joseph Anoma, 01 BP 1387 Abidjan 01, Cote d'Ivoire, www.afdb.org; *Statistics Pocketbook 2008.*

Euromonitor International, Inc., 224 S. Michigan Avenue, Suite 1500, Chicago, IL 60604, (312) 922-1115, Fax: (312) 922-1157, www.euromonitor.com; *World Health Databook 2007/2008* and *World Marketing Data and Statistics.*

M.E. Sharpe, 80 Business Park Drive, Armonk, NY 10504, (800) 541-6563, Fax: (914) 273-2106, www.mesharpe.com; *The Illustrated Book of World Rankings.*

Palgrave Macmillan Ltd., Houndmills, Basingstoke, Hampshire, RG21 6XS, England, (Telephone in U.S. (888) 330-8477), (Fax in U.S. (800) 672-2054), www.palgrave.com; *The Statesman's Yearbook 2008.*

UNICEF, 3 United Nations Plaza, New York, NY 10017, (800) 253-9646, Fax: (212) 887-7465, www.unicef.org; *The State of the World's Children 2008.*

United Nations Economic Commission for Africa (ECA), PO Box 3001, Addis Ababa, Ethiopia, (Telephone in U.S. (212) 963-4957), www.uneca.org; *African Statistical Yearbook 2006.*

United Nations Statistics Division, New York, NY 10017, (800) 253-9646, Fax: (212) 963-4116, http://unstats.un.org; *Human Development Report 2006* and *Statistical Yearbook.*

The World Bank, 1818 H Street, NW, Washington, DC 20433, (202) 473-1000, Fax: (202) 477-6391, www.worldbank.org; *Algeria* and *World Development Report 2008.*

World Health Organization (WHO), Avenue Appia 20, 1211 Geneve 27, Switzerland, (Telephone in U.S. (212) 331-9081), www.who.int; The WHO Global Atlas of Infectious Diseases and *World Health Report 2006.*

ALGERIA - RADIO - RECEIVERS AND RECEPTION

Palgrave Macmillan Ltd., Houndmills, Basingstoke, Hampshire, RG21 6XS, England, (Telephone in U.S. (888) 330-8477), (Fax in U.S. (800) 672-2054), www.palgrave.com; *The Statesman's Yearbook 2008.*

United Nations Statistics Division, New York, NY 10017, (800) 253-9646, Fax: (212) 963-4116, http://unstats.un.org; *Statistical Yearbook.*

ALGERIA - RAILROADS

Jane's Information Group, 110 North Royal Street, Suite 200, Alexandria, VA 22314, (703) 683-3700, Fax: (800) 836-0297, www.janes.com; *Jane's World Railways.*

Palgrave Macmillan Ltd., Houndmills, Basingstoke, Hampshire, RG21 6XS, England, (Telephone in U.S. (888) 330-8477), (Fax in U.S. (800) 672-2054), www.palgrave.com; *The Statesman's Yearbook 2008.*

Taylor and Francis Group, An Informa Business, 2 Park Square, Milton Park, Abingdon, Oxford OX14 4RN, United Kingdom, (Dial from U.S. (212) 216-7800), (Fax from U.S. (212) 564-7854), www.tandf.co.uk; *The Europa World Year Book.*

United Nations Economic Commission for Africa (ECA), PO Box 3001, Addis Ababa, Ethiopia, (Telephone in U.S. (212) 963-4957), www.uneca.org; *African Statistical Yearbook 2006.*

United Nations Statistics Division, New York, NY 10017, (800) 253-9646, Fax: (212) 963-4116, http://unstats.un.org; *Statistical Yearbook* and *Survey of Economic and Social Conditions in Africa 2005.*

ALGERIA - RELIGION

Central Intelligence Agency, Office of Public Affairs, Washington, DC 20505, (703) 482-0623, Fax: (703) 482-1739, www.cia.gov; *The World Factbook.*

M.E. Sharpe, 80 Business Park Drive, Armonk, NY 10504, (800) 541-6563, Fax: (914) 273-2106, www.mesharpe.com; *The Illustrated Book of World Rankings.*

Palgrave Macmillan Ltd., Houndmills, Basingstoke, Hampshire, RG21 6XS, England, (Telephone in U.S. (888) 330-8477), (Fax in U.S. (800) 672-2054), www.palgrave.com; *The Statesman's Yearbook 2008.*

ALGERIA - RENT CHARGES

International Labour Office, I.L.O. Publications, 4 route des Morillons, CH-1211 Geneva 22, Switzerland, (Telephone in U.S. (202) 653-7652), (Fax in U.S. (202) 653-7687), www.ilo.org; *Yearbook of Labour Statistics 2006.*

ALGERIA - RESERVES (ACCOUNTING)

African Development Bank Group, Rue Joseph Anoma, 01 BP 1387 Abidjan 01, Cote d'Ivoire, www.afdb.org; *Statistics Pocketbook 2008.*

The World Bank, 1818 H Street, NW, Washington, DC 20433, (202) 473-1000, Fax: (202) 477-6391, www.worldbank.org; *World Development Indicators (WDI) 2008.*

ALGERIA - RETAIL TRADE

Euromonitor International, Inc., 224 S. Michigan Avenue, Suite 1500, Chicago, IL 60604, (312) 922-1115, Fax: (312) 922-1157, www.euromonitor.com; *Retail Trade International 2007* and *World Marketing Data and Statistics.*

ALGERIA - RICE PRODUCTION

See ALGERIA - CROPS

ALGERIA - ROADS

Central Intelligence Agency, Office of Public Affairs, Washington, DC 20505, (703) 482-0623, Fax: (703) 482-1739, www.cia.gov; *The World Factbook.*

International Road Federation (IFR), Madison Place, 500 Montgomery Street, 5th Floor, Alexandria, VA 22314, (703) 535-1001, Fax: (703) 535-1007, www.irfnet.org; *World Road Statistics 2006.*

Palgrave Macmillan Ltd., Houndmills, Basingstoke, Hampshire, RG21 6XS, England, (Telephone in U.S. (888) 330-8477), (Fax in U.S. (800) 672-2054), www.palgrave.com; *The Statesman's Yearbook 2008.*

United Nations Economic Commission for Africa (ECA), PO Box 3001, Addis Ababa, Ethiopia, (Telephone in U.S. (212) 963-4957), www.uneca.org; *African Statistical Yearbook 2006.*

United Nations Statistics Division, New York, NY 10017, (800) 253-9646, Fax: (212) 963-4116, http://unstats.un.org; *Survey of Economic and Social Conditions in Africa 2005.*

ALGERIA - RUBBER INDUSTRY AND TRADE

International Rubber Study Group (IRSG), 1st Floor, Heron House, 109/115 Wembley Hill Road, Wembley, Middlesex HA9 8DA, United Kingdom, www.rubberstudy.com; *Rubber Statistical Bulletin; Summary of World Rubber Statistics 2005; World Rubber Statistics Handbook (Volume 6, 1975-2001);* and *World Rubber Statistics Historic Handbook.*

M.E. Sharpe, 80 Business Park Drive, Armonk, NY 10504, (800) 541-6563, Fax: (914) 273-2106, www.mesharpe.com; *The Illustrated Book of World Rankings.*

ALGERIA - SALT PRODUCTION

See ALGERIA - MINERAL INDUSTRIES

ALGERIA - SHEEP

See ALGERIA - LIVESTOCK

ALGERIA - SHIPPING

Organization of Petroleum Exporting Countries (OPEC), Obere Donaustrasse 93, A-1020, Vienna, Austria, www.opec.org; *Annual Statistical Bulletin 2006.*

Palgrave Macmillan Ltd., Houndmills, Basingstoke, Hampshire, RG21 6XS, England, (Telephone in U.S. (888) 330-8477), (Fax in U.S. (800) 672-2054), www.palgrave.com; *The Statesman's Yearbook 2008.*

Taylor and Francis Group, An Informa Business, 2 Park Square, Milton Park, Abingdon, Oxford OX14 4RN, United Kingdom, (Dial from U.S. (212) 216-7800), (Fax from U.S. (212) 564-7854), www.tandf.co.uk; *The Europa World Year Book.*

U.S. Department of Transportation (DOT), Maritime Administration (MARAD), West Building, Southeast Federal Center, 1200 New Jersey Avenue, SE, Washington, DC 20590, (800) 99-MARAD, www.marad.dot.gov; *World Merchant Fleet 2005.*

United Nations Economic Commission for Africa (ECA), PO Box 3001, Addis Ababa, Ethiopia, (Telephone in U.S. (212) 963-4957), www.uneca.org; *African Statistical Yearbook 2006.*

United Nations Statistics Division, New York, NY 10017, (800) 253-9646, Fax: (212) 963-4116, http://unstats.un.org; *Statistical Yearbook.*

ALGERIA - SILVER PRODUCTION

See ALGERIA - MINERAL INDUSTRIES

ALGERIA - SOCIAL ECOLOGY

M.E. Sharpe, 80 Business Park Drive, Armonk, NY 10504, (800) 541-6563, Fax: (914) 273-2106, www.mesharpe.com; *The Illustrated Book of World Rankings.*

United Nations Statistics Division, New York, NY 10017, (800) 253-9646, Fax: (212) 963-4116, http://unstats.un.org; *World Statistics Pocketbook.*

ALGERIA - SOCIAL SECURITY

United Nations Statistics Division, New York, NY 10017, (800) 253-9646, Fax: (212) 963-4116, http://unstats.un.org; *National Accounts Statistics: Compendium of Income Distribution Statistics.*

ALGERIA - STEEL PRODUCTION

See ALGERIA - MINERAL INDUSTRIES

ALGERIA - SUGAR PRODUCTION

See ALGERIA - CROPS

ALGERIA - SULPHUR PRODUCTION

See ALGERIA - MINERAL INDUSTRIES

ALGERIA - TAXATION

International Road Federation (IFR), Madison Place, 500 Montgomery Street, 5th Floor, Alexandria, VA 22314, (703) 535-1001, Fax: (703) 535-1007, www.irfnet.org; *World Road Statistics 2006.*

The World Bank, 1818 H Street, NW, Washington, DC 20433, (202) 473-1000, Fax: (202) 477-6391, www.worldbank.org; *World Development Indicators (WDI) 2008.*

ALGERIA - TEA PRODUCTION

See ALGERIA - CROPS

ALGERIA - TELEPHONE

Central Intelligence Agency, Office of Public Affairs, Washington, DC 20505, (703) 482-0623, Fax: (703) 482-1739, www.cia.gov; *The World Factbook.*

International Telecommunication Union (ITU), Place des Nations, 1211 Geneva 20, Switzerland, www.itu.int; World Telecommunication Indicators Database.

Palgrave Macmillan Ltd., Houndmills, Basingstoke, Hampshire, RG21 6XS, England, (Telephone in U.S. (888) 330-8477), (Fax in U.S. (800) 672-2054), www.palgrave.com; *The Statesman's Yearbook 2008.*

Taylor and Francis Group, An Informa Business, 2 Park Square, Milton Park, Abingdon, Oxford OX14 4RN, United Kingdom, (Dial from U.S. (212) 216-7800), (Fax from U.S. (212) 564-7854), www.tandf.co.uk; *The Europa World Year Book.*

United Nations Statistics Division, New York, NY 10017, (800) 253-9646, Fax: (212) 963-4116, http://unstats.un.org; *Statistical Yearbook* and *World Statistics Pocketbook.*

ALGERIA - TELEVISION - RECEIVERS AND RECEPTION

United Nations Statistics Division, New York, NY 10017, (800) 253-9646, Fax: (212) 963-4116, http://unstats.un.org; *Statistical Yearbook.*

ALGERIA - TEXTILE INDUSTRY

M.E. Sharpe, 80 Business Park Drive, Armonk, NY 10504, (800) 541-6563, Fax: (914) 273-2106, www.mesharpe.com; *The Illustrated Book of World Rankings.*

United Nations Conference on Trade and Development (UNCTAD), DC2-1120, United Nations, New York, NY 10017, (212) 963-0027, www.unctad.org; *UNCTAD Commodity Yearbook.*

United Nations Statistics Division, New York, NY 10017, (800) 253-9646, Fax: (212) 963-4116, http://unstats.un.org; *Statistical Yearbook.*

ALGERIA - TIRE INDUSTRY

United Nations Statistics Division, New York, NY 10017, (800) 253-9646, Fax: (212) 963-4116, http://unstats.un.org; *Statistical Yearbook.*

ALGERIA - TOBACCO INDUSTRY

Foreign Agricultural Service (FAS), U.S. Department of Agriculture (USDA), 1400 Independence Avenue, SW, Washington, DC 20250, (202) 720-3935, www.fas.usda.gov; *Tobacco: World Markets and Trade.*

M.E. Sharpe, 80 Business Park Drive, Armonk, NY 10504, (800) 541-6563, Fax: (914) 273-2106, www.mesharpe.com; *The Illustrated Book of World Rankings.*

United Nations Statistics Division, New York, NY 10017, (800) 253-9646, Fax: (212) 963-4116, http://unstats.un.org; *Statistical Yearbook.*

ALGERIA - TOURISM

Euromonitor International, Inc., 224 S. Michigan Avenue, Suite 1500, Chicago, IL 60604, (312) 922-1115, Fax: (312) 922-1157, www.euromonitor.com; *The World Economic Factbook 2008* and *World Marketing Data and Statistics.*

M.E. Sharpe, 80 Business Park Drive, Armonk, NY 10504, (800) 541-6563, Fax: (914) 273-2106, www.mesharpe.com; *The Illustrated Book of World Rankings.*

Palgrave Macmillan Ltd., Houndmills, Basingstoke, Hampshire, RG21 6XS, England, (Telephone in U.S. (888) 330-8477), (Fax in U.S. (800) 672-2054), www.palgrave.com; *The Statesman's Yearbook 2008.*

Taylor and Francis Group, An Informa Business, 2 Park Square, Milton Park, Abingdon, Oxford OX14 4RN, United Kingdom, (Dial from U.S. (212) 216-7800), (Fax from U.S. (212) 564-7854), www.tandf.co.uk; *The Europa World Year Book.*

United Nations Economic Commission for Africa (ECA), PO Box 3001, Addis Ababa, Ethiopia, (Telephone in U.S. (212) 963-4957), www.uneca.org; *African Statistical Yearbook 2006.*

The World Bank, 1818 H Street, NW, Washington, DC 20433, (202) 473-1000, Fax: (202) 477-6391, www.worldbank.org; *Algeria.*

ALGERIA - TRADE

See ALGERIA - INTERNATIONAL TRADE

ALGERIA - TRANSPORTATION

Central Intelligence Agency, Office of Public Affairs, Washington, DC 20505, (703) 482-0623, Fax: (703) 482-1739, www.cia.gov; *The World Factbook.*

Euromonitor International, Inc., 224 S. Michigan Avenue, Suite 1500, Chicago, IL 60604, (312) 922-1115, Fax: (312) 922-1157, www.euromonitor.com; *International Marketing Data and Statistics 2008* and *World Marketing Data and Statistics.*

M.E. Sharpe, 80 Business Park Drive, Armonk, NY 10504, (800) 541-6563, Fax: (914) 273-2106, www.mesharpe.com; *The Illustrated Book of World Rankings.*

Palgrave Macmillan Ltd., Houndmills, Basingstoke, Hampshire, RG21 6XS, England, (Telephone in U.S. (888) 330-8477), (Fax in U.S. (800) 672-2054), www.palgrave.com; *The Statesman's Yearbook 2008.*

Taylor and Francis Group, An Informa Business, 2 Park Square, Milton Park, Abingdon, Oxford OX14 4RN, United Kingdom, (Dial from U.S. (212) 216-7800), (Fax from U.S. (212) 564-7854), www.tandf.co.uk; *The Europa World Year Book.*

United Nations Economic Commission for Africa (ECA), PO Box 3001, Addis Ababa, Ethiopia, (Telephone in U.S. (212) 963-4957), www.uneca.org; *African Statistical Yearbook 2006.*

United Nations Statistics Division, New York, NY 10017, (800) 253-9646, Fax: (212) 963-4116, http://unstats.un.org; *Human Development Report 2006.*

The World Bank, 1818 H Street, NW, Washington, DC 20433, (202) 473-1000, Fax: (202) 477-6391, www.worldbank.org; *Africa Live Database (LDB)* and *Algeria.*

ALGERIA - TURKEYS

See ALGERIA - LIVESTOCK

ALGERIA - UNEMPLOYMENT

Central Intelligence Agency, Office of Public Affairs, Washington, DC 20505, (703) 482-0623, Fax: (703) 482-1739, www.cia.gov; *The World Factbook.*

Euromonitor International, Inc., 224 S. Michigan Avenue, Suite 1500, Chicago, IL 60604, (312) 922-1115, Fax: (312) 922-1157, www.euromonitor.com; *International Marketing Data and Statistics 2008.*

International Labour Office, I.L.O. Publications, 4 route des Morillons, CH-1211 Geneva 22, Switzerland, (Telephone in U.S. (202) 653-7652), (Fax in U.S. (202) 653-7687), www.ilo.org; *Yearbook of Labour Statistics 2006.*

ALGERIA - URANIUM PRODUCTION AND CONSUMPTION

See ALGERIA - MINERAL INDUSTRIES

ALGERIA - VITAL STATISTICS

Euromonitor International, Inc., 224 S. Michigan Avenue, Suite 1500, Chicago, IL 60604, (312) 922-1115, Fax: (312) 922-1157, www.euromonitor.com; *International Marketing Data and Statistics 2008.*

Palgrave Macmillan Ltd., Houndmills, Basingstoke, Hampshire, RG21 6XS, England, (Telephone in U.S. (888) 330-8477), (Fax in U.S. (800) 672-2054), www.palgrave.com; *The Statesman's Yearbook 2008.*

United Nations Statistics Division, New York, NY 10017, (800) 253-9646, Fax: (212) 963-4116, http://unstats.un.org; *Statistical Yearbook.*

World Health Organization (WHO), Avenue Appia 20, 1211 Geneve 27, Switzerland, (Telephone in U.S. (212) 331-9081), www.who.int; *World Health Report 2006.*

ALGERIA - WAGES

International Labour Office, I.L.O. Publications, 4 route des Morillons, CH-1211 Geneva 22, Switzerland, (Telephone in U.S. (202) 653-7652), (Fax in U.S. (202) 653-7687), www.ilo.org; *Yearbook of Labour Statistics 2006.*

United Nations Statistics Division, New York, NY 10017, (800) 253-9646, Fax: (212) 963-4116, http://unstats.un.org; *Statistical Yearbook.*

The World Bank, 1818 H Street, NW, Washington, DC 20433, (202) 473-1000, Fax: (202) 477-6391, www.worldbank.org; *Algeria.*

ALGERIA - WEATHER

See ALGERIA - CLIMATE

ALGERIA - WELFARE STATE

Palgrave Macmillan Ltd., Houndmills, Basingstoke, Hampshire, RG21 6XS, England, (Telephone in U.S. (888) 330-8477), (Fax in U.S. (800) 672-2054), www.palgrave.com; *The Statesman's Yearbook 2008.*

ALGERIA - WHEAT PRODUCTION

See ALGERIA - CROPS

ALGERIA - WINE PRODUCTION

See ALGERIA - BEVERAGE INDUSTRY

ALGERIA - WOOD AND WOOD PULP

See ALGERIA - FORESTS AND FORESTRY

ALGERIA - WOOL PRODUCTION

See ALGERIA - TEXTILE INDUSTRY

ALGERIA - YARN PRODUCTION

See ALGERIA - TEXTILE INDUSTRY

ALGERIA - ZINC AND ZINC ORE

See ALGERIA - MINERAL INDUSTRIES

ALIENS - DEPORTED

U.S. Citizenship and Immigration Services (USCIS), Washington District Office, 2675 Prosperity Avenue, Fairfax, VA 22031, (800) 375-5283, http://uscis.gov; *2005 Yearbook of Immigration Statistics.*

U.S. Library of Congress (LOC), Congressional Research Service (CRS), The Library of Congress, 101 Independence Avenue, SE, Washington, DC 20540-7500, (202) 707-5700, www.loc.gov/crsinfo; *Border Security: The Role of the U.S. Border Patrol.*

ALLERGIES

National Center for Health Statistics (NCHS), Centers for Disease Control and Prevention (CDC), U.S. Department of Health and Human Services (HHS), 3311 Toledo Road, Hyattsville, MD 20782, (866) 232-4636, www.cdc.gov/nchs; *Faststats A to Z.*

ALMONDS

Economic Research Service (ERS), U.S. Department of Agriculture (USDA), 1800 M Street, NW, Washington, DC 20036-5831, (202) 694-5050, Fax: (202) 694-5689, www.ers.usda.gov; *Agricultural Income and Finance Outlook.*

ALTITUDES - GEOGRAPHICAL

U.S. Department of the Interior (DOI), U.S. Geological Survey (USGS), 12201 Sunrise Valley Drive, Reston, VA 20192, USA, (888) 275-8747, www.usgs.gov; *Elevations and Distances in the United States.*

ALUMINUM - CONSUMPTION

U.S. Department of the Interior (DOI), U.S. Geological Survey (USGS), Office of Minerals Information, 12201 Sunrise Valley Drive, Reston, VA 20192, Mr. Kenneth A. Beckman, (703) 648-4916, Fax: (703) 648-4995, http://minerals.usgs.gov/minerals; *Mineral Commodity Summaries.*

ALUMINUM - EMPLOYMENT

U.S. Department of the Interior (DOI), U.S. Geological Survey (USGS), Office of Minerals Information, 12201 Sunrise Valley Drive, Reston, VA 20192, Mr. Kenneth A. Beckman, (703) 648-4916, Fax: (703) 648-4995, http://minerals.usgs.gov/minerals; *Mineral Commodity Summaries.*

ALUMINUM - INTERNATIONAL TRADE

U.S. Census Bureau, Foreign Trade Division, 4700 Silver Hill Road, Washington DC 20233-0001, (301) 763-3030, www.census.gov/foreign-trade/www/; *U.S. International Trade in Goods and Services.*

U.S. Department of the Interior (DOI), U.S. Geological Survey (USGS), Office of Minerals Information, 12201 Sunrise Valley Drive, Reston, VA 20192, Mr. Kenneth A. Beckman, (703) 648-4916, Fax: (703) 648-4995, http://minerals.usgs.gov/minerals; *Mineral Commodity Summaries.*

ALUMINUM - PRICES

U.S. Department of the Interior (DOI), U.S. Geological Survey (USGS), Office of Minerals Information, 12201 Sunrise Valley Drive, Reston, VA 20192, Mr. Kenneth A. Beckman, (703) 648-4916, Fax: (703) 648-4995, http://minerals.usgs.gov/minerals; *Metal Industry Indicators (MII)* and *Mineral Commodity Summaries.*

ALUMINUM - PRODUCTION

The Aluminum Association, Inc., 1525 Wilson Boulevard, Arlington, VA 22209-2411, (703) 358-2960, Fax: (703) 358-2961, www.aluminum.org; *Aluminum Situation* and *Facts at a Glance.*

ALUMINUM - RECYCLING

U.S. Environmental Protection Agency (EPA), Ariel Rios Building, 1200 Pennsylvania Avenue, NW, Washington, DC 20460, (202) 272-0167, www.epa.gov; *Municipal Solid Waste.*

ALUMINUM - WORLD PRODUCTION

U.S. Department of the Interior (DOI), U.S. Geological Survey (USGS), Office of Minerals Information, 12201 Sunrise Valley Drive, Reston, VA 20192, Mr. Kenneth A. Beckman, (703) 648-4916, Fax: (703) 648-4995, http://minerals.usgs.gov/minerals; *Mineral Commodity Summaries.*

ALZHEIMER'S DISEASE

National Center for Health Statistics (NCHS), Centers for Disease Control and Prevention (CDC), U.S. Department of Health and Human Services (HHS), 3311 Toledo Road, Hyattsville, MD 20782, (866) 232-4636, www.cdc.gov/nchs; *Faststats A to Z.*

AMBULATORY HEALTH CARE SERVICES INDUSTRY

National Center for Health Statistics (NCHS), Centers for Disease Control and Prevention (CDC), U.S. Department of Health and Human Services (HHS), 3311 Toledo Road, Hyattsville, MD 20782, (866) 232-4636, www.cdc.gov/nchs; *Faststats A to Z.*

AMBULATORY HEALTH CARE SERVICES INDUSTRY - EARNINGS

U.S. Census Bureau, Service Sector Statistics Division, 4700 Silver Hill Road, Washington DC 20233-0001, (301) 763-3030, www.census.gov/svsd/www/economic.html; *2004 Service Annual Survey: Health Care and Social Assistance.*

AMBULATORY HEALTH CARE SERVICES INDUSTRY - EMPLOYERS

U.S. Census Bureau, 4700 Silver Hill Road, Washington DC 20233-0001, (301) 763-3030, www.census.gov; *2002 Economic Census, Nonemployer Statistics.*

U.S. Census Bureau, Service Sector Statistics Division, 4700 Silver Hill Road, Washington DC 20233-0001, (301) 763-3030, www.census.gov/svsd/www/economic.html; *2004 Service Annual Survey: Health Care and Social Assistance.*

AMBULATORY HEALTH CARE SERVICES INDUSTRY - ESTABLISHMENTS

U.S. Census Bureau, 4700 Silver Hill Road, Washington DC 20233-0001, (301) 763-3030, www.census.gov; *2002 Economic Census, Nonemployer Statistics.*

U.S. Census Bureau, Service Sector Statistics Division, 4700 Silver Hill Road, Washington DC 20233-0001, (301) 763-3030, www.census.gov/svsd/www/economic.html; *2004 Service Annual Survey: Health Care and Social Assistance.*

AMBULATORY HEALTH CARE SERVICES INDUSTRY - FINANCES

U.S. Department of the Treasury (DOT), Internal Revenue Service (IRS), Statistics of Income Division (SIS), PO Box 2608, Washington, DC, 20013-2608, (202) 874-0410, Fax: (202) 874-0964, www.irs.ustreas.gov; *Statistics of Income Bulletin* and various fact sheets.

AMBULATORY HEALTH CARE SERVICES INDUSTRY - SALES - RECEIPTS

U.S. Department of the Treasury (DOT), Internal Revenue Service (IRS), Statistics of Income Division (SIS), PO Box 2608, Washington, DC, 20013-2608, (202) 874-0410, Fax: (202) 874-0964, www.irs.ustreas.gov; *Statistics of Income Bulletin* and various fact sheets.

AMERICAN COLLEGE TESTING (ACT) PROGRAM

ACT, 500 ACT Drive, Box 168, Iowa City, IA 52243-0168, (319) 337-1000, Fax: (319) 339-3020, www.act.org; *ACT National and State Scores.*

AMERICAN INDIAN, ESKIMO, ALEUT POPULATION

The Annie E. Casey Foundation, 701 Saint Paul Street, Baltimore, MD 21202, (410) 547-6600, Fax: (410) 547-3610, www.aecf.org; *Faith Matters: Race/Ethnicity, Religion, and Substance Abuse.*

Indian Health Service (IHS), U.S. Department of Health and Human Services, The Reyes Building, 801 Thompson Avenue, Suite 400, Rockville, MD 20852-1627, (301) 443-1180, www.ihs.gov; *Annual Federal Year 2001 IHS and Tribal Hospital Inpatient Statistics and Comparison with Federal Year 2000; Indian Health Focus - Elders; Indian Health Focus - Injuries; Indian Health Focus - Women; Indian Health Focus - Youth; Regional Differences in Indian Health 2000-2001;* and *Trends in Indian Health 2000-2001.*

National Agricultural Statistics Service (NASS), U.S. Department of Agriculture (USDA), 1400 Independence Avenue, SW, Washington, DC 20250, (800) 727-9540, Fax: (202) 690-2090, www.nass.usda.gov; *2007 Census of Agriculture.*

National Center for Health Statistics (NCHS), Centers for Disease Control and Prevention (CDC), U.S. Department of Health and Human Services (HHS), 3311 Toledo Road, Hyattsville, MD 20782, (866) 232-4636, www.cdc.gov/nchs; *Indicators of Social and Economic Well-Being by Race and Hispanic Origin.*

National Center for Statistics and Analysis (NCSA) of the National Highway Traffic Safety Administration, West Building, 1200 New Jersey Avenue, S.E., Washington, DC 20590, (202) 366-1503, Fax: (202) 366-7078, www.nhtsa.gov; *Fatal Motor Vehicle Crashes on Indian Reservations 1975-2002* and *Race and Ethnicity in Fatal Motor Vehicle Traffic Crashes 1999-2004.*

U.S. Census Bureau, Population Division, 4700 Silver Hill Road, Washington DC 20233-0001, (301) 763-3030, www.census.gov/population/www/; *The American Indian, Eskimo, and Aleut Population;*

2000 Census of Population and Housing: Characteristics of American Indians and Alaska Natives by Tribe and Language; and *National Population Projections.*

AMERICAN INDIAN, ESKIMO, ALEUT POPULATION - AGE AND/OR SEX

U.S. Census Bureau, 4700 Silver Hill Road, Washington DC 20233-0001, (301) 763-3030, www.census.gov; unpublished data.

U.S. Census Bureau, Population Division, 4700 Silver Hill Road, Washington DC 20233-0001, (301) 763-3030, www.census.gov/population/www/; *The American Indian, Eskimo, and Aleut Population* and *2000 Census of Population and Housing: Characteristics of American Indians and Alaska Natives by Tribe and Language.*

AMERICAN INDIAN, ESKIMO, ALEUT POPULATION - BUSINESS OWNERS

U.S. Census Bureau, Company Statistics Division, 4700 Silver Hill Road, Washington DC 20233-0001, (301) 763-3030, www.census.gov/csd/; *2002 Survey of Business Owners (SBO)* and *Survey of Women-Owned Businesses.*

U.S. Census Bureau, Population Division, 4700 Silver Hill Road, Washington DC 20233-0001, (301) 763-3030, www.census.gov/population/www/; *The American Indian, Eskimo, and Aleut Population.*

AMERICAN INDIAN, ESKIMO, ALEUT POPULATION - CANCER

National Cancer Institute (NCI), National Institutes of Health (NIH), Public Inquiries Office, 6116 Executive Boulevard, Room 3036A, Bethesda, MD 20892-8322, (800) 422-6237, www.cancer.gov; *2006-2007 Annual Report to the Nation; Assessing Progress, Advancing Change: 2005-2006 Annual President's Cancer Panel; Fighting Cancer in Indian Country: The Yakama Nation and Pacific Northwest Tribes President's Cancer Panel Annual Report 2002;* and *SEER Cancer Statistics Review, 1975-2005.*

AMERICAN INDIAN, ESKIMO, ALEUT POPULATION - CHILDREN UNDER EIGHTEEN YEARS OLD

Federal Interagency Forum on Child and Family Statistics, 2070 Chain Bridge Road, Suite 450, Vienna, VA 22182-2536, (888) ASK-HRSA, www.childstats.gov; *America's Children: Key National Indicators of Well-Being 2006.*

AMERICAN INDIAN, ESKIMO, ALEUT POPULATION - CHILDREN UNDER EIGHTEEN YEARS OLD - POVERTY

National Center for Children in Poverty (NCCP), 215 W. 125th Street, 3rd Floor, New York, NY 10027, (646) 284-9600, Fax: (646) 284-9623, www.nccp.org; *Basic Facts About Low-Income Children; Child Poverty in 21st Century America; Low-Income Children in the United States: National and State Trend Data, 1996-2006;* and *Predictors of Child Care Subsidy Use.*

Population Reference Bureau, 1875 Connecticut Avenue, NW, Suite 520, Washington, DC, 20009-5728, (800) 877-9881, Fax: (202) 328-3937, www.prb.org; *Child Poverty in Rural America* and *Strengthening Rural Families: America's Rural Children.*

AMERICAN INDIAN, ESKIMO, ALEUT POPULATION - CITIES

Population Reference Bureau, 1875 Connecticut Avenue, NW, Suite 520, Washington, DC, 20009-5728, (800) 877-9881, Fax: (202) 328-3937, www.prb.org; *The American People Series.*

U.S. Census Bureau, 4700 Silver Hill Road, Washington DC 20233-0001, (301) 763-3030, www.census.gov; American FactFinder (web app); *County and City Data Book 2007;* and *State and County QuickFacts.*

U.S. Census Bureau, Population Division, 4700 Silver Hill Road, Washington DC 20233-0001, (301) 763-3030, www.census.gov/population/www/; *Census 2000 Profiles of General Demographic Characteristics* and Population Estimates Program (web app).

AMERICAN INDIAN, ESKIMO, ALEUT POPULATION - COLLEGE ENROLLMENT

National Center for Education Statistics (NCES), 1990 K Street, NW, Washington, DC 20006, (202) 502-7300, http://nces.ed.gov; *Digest of Education Statistics 2007.*

AMERICAN INDIAN, ESKIMO, ALEUT POPULATION - COLLEGE ENROLLMENT - CREDIT CARD USE

National Center for Education Statistics (NCES), 1990 K Street, NW, Washington, DC 20006, (202) 502-7300, http://nces.ed.gov; *Profile of Undergraduates in U.S. Postsecondary Education Institutions: 2003-04, With a Special Analysis of Community College Students.*

AMERICAN INDIAN, ESKIMO, ALEUT POPULATION - COLLEGE ENROLLMENT - DISABILITY

National Center for Education Statistics (NCES), 1990 K Street, NW, Washington, DC 20006, (202) 502-7300, http://nces.ed.gov; *Profile of Undergraduates in U.S. Postsecondary Education Institutions: 2003-04, With a Special Analysis of Community College Students.*

AMERICAN INDIAN, ESKIMO, ALEUT POPULATION - COLLEGE ENROLLMENT - DISTANCE EDUCATION

National Center for Education Statistics (NCES), 1990 K Street, NW, Washington, DC 20006, (202) 502-7300, http://nces.ed.gov; *Profile of Undergraduates in U.S. Postsecondary Education Institutions: 2003-04, With a Special Analysis of Community College Students.*

AMERICAN INDIAN, ESKIMO, ALEUT POPULATION - CONSUMER EXPENDITURES

Selig Center for Economic Growth, Terry College of Business, University of Georgia, Athens, GA 30602-6269, Mr. Jeffrey M. Humphreys, Director, (706) 425-2962, www.selig.uga.edu; *The Multicultural Economy: Minority Buying Power in 2006.*

AMERICAN INDIAN, ESKIMO, ALEUT POPULATION - CRIMINAL STATISTICS

Federal Bureau of Investigation (FBI), J. Edgar Hoover Building, 935 Pennsylvania Avenue, NW, Washington, DC 20535-0001, (202) 324-3000, www.fbi.gov; *Crime in the United States (CIUS) 2007 (Preliminary).*

Justice Research and Statistics Association (JRSA), 777 N. Capitol Street, NE, Suite 801, Washington, DC 20002, (202) 842-9330, Fax: (202) 842-9329, www.jrsa.org; *Crime and Justice Atlas 2001.*

U.S. Department of Justice (DOJ), Bureau of Justice Statistics, 810 Seventh Street, NW, Washington, DC 20531, (202) 307-0765, www.ojp.usdoj.gov/bjs/; *American Indians and Crime: A BJS Statistical Profile, 1992-2002; Census of Jails; Census of Tribal Justice Agencies in Indian Country, 2002; Crime and the Nation's Households, 2004; Jails in Indian Country, 2003; State Court Sentencing of Convicted Felons; Substance Dependence, Abuse, and Treatment of Jail Inmates, 2002; Tribal Law Enforcement, 2000;* and *Violent Felons in Large Urban Counties.*

AMERICAN INDIAN, ESKIMO, ALEUT POPULATION - CRIMINAL VICTIMIZATION

U.S. Department of Justice (DOJ), Bureau of Justice Statistics, 810 Seventh Street, NW, Washington, DC 20531, (202) 307-0765, www.ojp.usdoj.gov/bjs/; *Tribal Law Enforcement, 2000* and *Weapon Use and Violent Crime, 1993-2001.*

AMERICAN INDIAN, ESKIMO, ALEUT POPULATION - DEATHS AND DEATH RATES

National Cancer Institute (NCI), National Institutes of Health (NIH), Public Inquiries Office, 6116 Executive Boulevard, Room 3036A, Bethesda, MD 20892-8322, (800) 422-6237, www.cancer.gov; *Fighting Cancer in Indian Country: The Yakama Nation and Pacific Northwest Tribes President's Cancer Panel Annual Report 2002.*

National Center for Statistics and Analysis (NCSA) of the National Highway Traffic Safety Administration, West Building, 1200 New Jersey Avenue, S.E., Washington, DC 20590, (202) 366-1503, Fax: (202) 366-7078, www.nhtsa.gov; *Fatal Motor Vehicle Crashes on Indian Reservations 1975-2002; Motor Vehicle Traffic Crashes as a Leading Cause of Death in the U.S., 2002 - A Demographic Perspective;* and *Race and Ethnicity in Fatal Motor Vehicle Traffic Crashes 1999-2004.*

AMERICAN INDIAN, ESKIMO, ALEUT POPULATION - DEGREES CONFERRED

National Center for Education Statistics (NCES), 1990 K Street, NW, Washington, DC 20006, (202) 502-7300, http://nces.ed.gov; *Digest of Education Statistics 2007.*

AMERICAN INDIAN, ESKIMO, ALEUT POPULATION - FARM OPERATORS AND WORKERS

National Agricultural Statistics Service (NASS), U.S. Department of Agriculture (USDA), 1400 Independence Avenue, SW, Washington, DC 20250, (800) 727-9540, Fax: (202) 690-2090, www.nass.usda.gov; *2007 Census of Agriculture.*

AMERICAN INDIAN, ESKIMO, ALEUT POPULATION - FOOD STAMP PARTICIPANTS

Food and Nutrition Service (FNS), U.S. Department of Agriculture (USDA), 3101 Park Center Drive, Alexandria, VA 22302, (703) 305-2062, www.fns.usda.gov/fns; *Characteristics of Food Stamp Households: Fiscal Year 2005.*

AMERICAN INDIAN, ESKIMO, ALEUT POPULATION - HEALTH CARE VISITS TO PROFESSIONALS

Indian Health Service (IHS), U.S. Department of Health and Human Services, The Reyes Building, 801 Thompson Avenue, Suite 400, Rockville, MD 20852-1627, (301) 443-1180, www.ihs.gov; *Annual Federal Year 2001 IHS and Tribal Hospital Inpatient Statistics and Comparison with Federal Year 2000; Indian Health Focus - Elders; Indian Health Focus - Injuries; Indian Health Focus - Women; Indian Health Focus - Youth; Regional Differences in Indian Health 2000-2001;* and *Trends in Indian Health 2000-2001.*

National Center for Health Statistics (NCHS), Centers for Disease Control and Prevention (CDC), U.S. Department of Health and Human Services (HHS), 3311 Toledo Road, Hyattsville, MD 20782, (866) 232-4636, www.cdc.gov/nchs; *Health, United States, 2006, with Chartbook on Trends in the Health of Americans with Special Feature on Pain.*

AMERICAN INDIAN, ESKIMO, ALEUT POPULATION - HEALTH INSURANCE COVERAGE

Indian Health Service (IHS), U.S. Department of Health and Human Services, The Reyes Building, 801 Thompson Avenue, Suite 400, Rockville, MD 20852-1627, (301) 443-1180, www.ihs.gov; *Indian Health Focus - Elders; Indian Health Focus - Women; Indian Health Focus - Youth; Regional Differences in Indian Health 2000-2001;* and *Trends in Indian Health 2000-2001.*

National Center for Health Statistics (NCHS), Centers for Disease Control and Prevention (CDC), U.S. Department of Health and Human Services (HHS), 3311 Toledo Road, Hyattsville, MD 20782, (866) 232-4636, www.cdc.gov/nchs; *Faststats A to Z.*

AMERICAN INDIAN, ESKIMO, ALEUT POPULATION - HOSPITAL UTILIZATION

Indian Health Service (IHS), U.S. Department of Health and Human Services, The Reyes Building,

801 Thompson Avenue, Suite 400, Rockville, MD 20852-1627, (301) 443-1180, www.ihs.gov; *Annual Federal Year 2001 IHS and Tribal Hospital Inpatient Statistics and Comparison with Federal Year 2000; Indian Health Focus - Elders; Indian Health Focus - Injuries; Indian Health Focus - Women; Indian Health Focus - Youth; Regional Differences in Indian Health 2000-2001;* and *Trends in Indian Health 2000-2001.*

National Center for Health Statistics (NCHS), Centers for Disease Control and Prevention (CDC), U.S. Department of Health and Human Services (HHS), 3311 Toledo Road, Hyattsville, MD 20782, (866) 232-4636, www.cdc.gov/nchs; unpublished data.

AMERICAN INDIAN, ESKIMO, ALEUT POPULATION - HOUSEHOLDS

U.S. Census Bureau, Population Division, 4700 Silver Hill Road, Washington DC 20233-0001, (301) 763-3030, www.census.gov/population/www/; *The American Indian, Eskimo, and Aleut Population* and *2000 Census of Population and Housing: Characteristics of American Indians and Alaska Natives by Tribe and Language.*

AMERICAN INDIAN, ESKIMO, ALEUT POPULATION - IMMUNIZATION OF CHILDREN

Centers for Disease Control and Prevention (CDC), U.S. Department of Health and Human Services (HHS), 1600 Clifton Road, Atlanta, GA 30333, (800) 311-3435, www.cdc.gov; *Immunization Coverage in the U.S.* and *Morbidity and Mortality Weekly Report (MMWR).*

Indian Health Service (IHS), U.S. Department of Health and Human Services, The Reyes Building, 801 Thompson Avenue, Suite 400, Rockville, MD 20852-1627, (301) 443-1180, www.ihs.gov; *Indian Health Focus - Youth; Regional Differences in Indian Health 2000-2001;* and *Trends in Indian Health 2000-2001.*

National Center for Health Statistics (NCHS), Centers for Disease Control and Prevention (CDC), U.S. Department of Health and Human Services (HHS), 3311 Toledo Road, Hyattsville, MD 20782, (866) 232-4636, www.cdc.gov/nchs; *2005 National Immunization Survey (NIS).*

AMERICAN INDIAN, ESKIMO, ALEUT POPULATION - INCOME

Selig Center for Economic Growth, Terry College of Business, University of Georgia, Athens, GA 30602-6269, Mr. Jeffrey M. Humphreys, Director, (706) 425-2962, www.selig.uga.edu; *The Multicultural Economy: Minority Buying Power in 2006.*

AMERICAN INDIAN, ESKIMO, ALEUT POPULATION - LAW ENFORCEMENT

U.S. Department of Justice (DOJ), Bureau of Justice Statistics, 810 Seventh Street, NW, Washington, DC 20531, (202) 307-0765, www.ojp.usdoj.gov/bjs/; *Census of Tribal Justice Agencies in Indian Country, 2002* and *Tribal Law Enforcement, 2000.*

AMERICAN INDIAN, ESKIMO, ALEUT POPULATION - MEDICAL CARE

Indian Health Service (IHS), U.S. Department of Health and Human Services, The Reyes Building, 801 Thompson Avenue, Suite 400, Rockville, MD 20852-1627, (301) 443-1180, www.ihs.gov; *Annual Federal Year 2001 IHS and Tribal Hospital Inpatient Statistics and Comparison with Federal Year 2000; Indian Health Focus - Elders; Indian Health Focus - Injuries; Indian Health Focus - Women; Indian Health Focus - Youth; Regional Differences in Indian Health 2000-2001;* and *Trends in Indian Health 2000-2001.*

National Cancer Institute (NCI), National Institutes of Health (NIH), Public Inquiries Office, 6116 Executive Boulevard, Room 3036A, Bethesda, MD 20892-8322, (800) 422-6237, www.cancer.gov; *Fighting Cancer in Indian Country: The Yakama Nation and Pacific Northwest Tribes President's Cancer Panel Annual Report 2002.*

National Center for Health Statistics (NCHS), Centers for Disease Control and Prevention (CDC), U.S. Department of Health and Human Services (HHS), 3311 Toledo Road, Hyattsville, MD 20782, (866) 232-4636, www.cdc.gov/nchs; *Faststats A to Z* and *Women's Health and Mortality Chartbook (2004 Edition).*

U.S. Department of Health and Human Services, 200 Independence Avenue, S.W., Washington, D.C. 20201, (202) 619-0257, www.hhs.gov; *Eliminating Health Disparities: Strengthening Data on Race, Ethnicity, and Primary Language in the United States.*

AMERICAN INDIAN, ESKIMO, ALEUT POPULATION - NURSES

Health Resources and Services Administration (HRSA), National Center for Health Workforce Analysis (NCHWA), 5600 Fishers Lane, Rockville, MD 20857, (301) 443-2216, www.hrsa.gov; Registered Nurse Population: Findings from the 2004 National Sample Survey of Registered Nurses.

AMERICAN INDIAN, ESKIMO, ALEUT POPULATION - PROJECTIONS

U.S. Census Bureau, Population Division, 4700 Silver Hill Road, Washington DC 20233-0001, (301) 763-3030, www.census.gov/population/www/; *The American Indian, Eskimo, and Aleut Population.*

AMERICAN SAMOA - NATIONAL STATISTICAL OFFICE

Statistics Division, Department of Commerce, Government of American Samoa, Pago Pago 96799, American Samoa, www.asdoc.info; Data Center.

AMERICAN SAMOA - PRIMARY STATISTICS SOURCES

Statistics Division, Department of Commerce, Government of American Samoa, Pago Pago 96799, American Samoa, www.asdoc.info; *2005 Statistical Yearbook of American Samoa.*

AMERICAN SAMOA - AGRICULTURE

Euromonitor International, Inc., 224 S. Michigan Avenue, Suite 1500, Chicago, IL 60604, (312) 922-1115, Fax: (312) 922-1157, www.euromonitor.com; *World Marketing Data and Statistics.*

Palgrave Macmillan Ltd., Houndmills, Basingstoke, Hampshire, RG21 6XS, England, (Telephone in U.S. (888) 330-8477), (Fax in U.S. (800) 672-2054), www.palgrave.com; *The Statesman's Yearbook 2008.*

Taylor and Francis Group, An Informa Business, 2 Park Square, Milton Park, Abingdon, Oxford OX14 4RN, United Kingdom, (Dial from U.S. (212) 216-7800), (Fax from U.S. (212) 564-7854), www.tandf.co.uk; *The Europa World Year Book.*

United Nations Conference on Trade and Development (UNCTAD), DC2-1120, United Nations, New York, NY 10017, (212) 963-0027, www.unctad.org; *UNCTAD Commodity Yearbook.*

United Nations Food and Agricultural Organization (FAO), Viale delle Terme di Caracalla, 00100 Rome, Italy, (Dial from U.S. (202) 653-2400), (Fax from U.S. (202) 653 5760), www.fao.org; AQUASTAT; *FAO Production Yearbook 2002; FAO Trade Yearbook;* and *The State of Food and Agriculture (SOFA) 2006.*

United Nations Statistics Division, New York, NY 10017, (800) 253-9646, Fax: (212) 963-4116, http://unstats.un.org; *Statistical Yearbook.*

The World Bank, 1818 H Street, NW, Washington, DC 20433, (202) 473-1000, Fax: (202) 477-6391, www.worldbank.org; *American Samoa.*

AMERICAN SAMOA - AIRLINES

Palgrave Macmillan Ltd., Houndmills, Basingstoke, Hampshire, RG21 6XS, England, (Telephone in U.S. (888) 330-8477), (Fax in U.S. (800) 672-2054), www.palgrave.com; *The Statesman's Yearbook 2008.*

Taylor and Francis Group, An Informa Business, 2 Park Square, Milton Park, Abingdon, Oxford OX14 4RN, United Kingdom, (Dial from U.S. (212) 216-7800), (Fax from U.S. (212) 564-7854), www.tandf.co.uk; *The Europa World Year Book.*

AMERICAN SAMOA - AIRPORTS

Central Intelligence Agency, Office of Public Affairs, Washington, DC 20505, (703) 482-0623, Fax: (703) 482-1739, www.cia.gov; *The World Factbook.*

AMERICAN SAMOA - ARMED FORCES

Central Intelligence Agency, Office of Public Affairs, Washington, DC 20505, (703) 482-0623, Fax: (703) 482-1739, www.cia.gov; *The World Factbook.*

Euromonitor International, Inc., 224 S. Michigan Avenue, Suite 1500, Chicago, IL 60604, (312) 922-1115, Fax: (312) 922-1157, www.euromonitor.com; *World Marketing Data and Statistics.*

AMERICAN SAMOA - BANKS AND BANKING

Euromonitor International, Inc., 224 S. Michigan Avenue, Suite 1500, Chicago, IL 60604, (312) 922-1115, Fax: (312) 922-1157, www.euromonitor.com; *World Marketing Data and Statistics.*

Palgrave Macmillan Ltd., Houndmills, Basingstoke, Hampshire, RG21 6XS, England, (Telephone in U.S. (888) 330-8477), (Fax in U.S. (800) 672-2054), www.palgrave.com; *The Statesman's Yearbook 2008.*

AMERICAN SAMOA - BROADCASTING

Central Intelligence Agency, Office of Public Affairs, Washington, DC 20505, (703) 482-0623, Fax: (703) 482-1739, www.cia.gov; *The World Factbook.*

Euromonitor International, Inc., 224 S. Michigan Avenue, Suite 1500, Chicago, IL 60604, (312) 922-1115, Fax: (312) 922-1157, www.euromonitor.com; *World Marketing Data and Statistics.*

Palgrave Macmillan Ltd., Houndmills, Basingstoke, Hampshire, RG21 6XS, England, (Telephone in U.S. (888) 330-8477), (Fax in U.S. (800) 672-2054), www.palgrave.com; *The Statesman's Yearbook 2008.*

WRTH Publications Limited, PO Box 290, Oxford OX2 7FT, UK, www.wrth.com; *World Radio TV Handbook 2007.*

AMERICAN SAMOA - BUDGET

Central Intelligence Agency, Office of Public Affairs, Washington, DC 20505, (703) 482-0623, Fax: (703) 482-1739, www.cia.gov; *The World Factbook.*

AMERICAN SAMOA - CHILDBIRTH - STATISTICS

Central Intelligence Agency, Office of Public Affairs, Washington, DC 20505, (703) 482-0623, Fax: (703) 482-1739, www.cia.gov; *The World Factbook.*

Euromonitor International, Inc., 224 S. Michigan Avenue, Suite 1500, Chicago, IL 60604, (312) 922-1115, Fax: (312) 922-1157, www.euromonitor.com; *International Marketing Data and Statistics 2008* and *The World Economic Factbook 2008.*

Taylor and Francis Group, An Informa Business, 2 Park Square, Milton Park, Abingdon, Oxford OX14 4RN, United Kingdom, (Dial from U.S. (212) 216-7800), (Fax from U.S. (212) 564-7854), www.tandf.co.uk; *The Europa World Year Book.*

United Nations Statistics Division, New York, NY 10017, (800) 253-9646, Fax: (212) 963-4116, http://unstats.un.org; *Demographic Yearbook.*

World Health Organization (WHO), Avenue Appia 20, 1211 Geneve 27, Switzerland, (Telephone in U.S. (212) 331-9081), www.who.int; *World Health Report 2006.*

AMERICAN SAMOA - CLIMATE

Palgrave Macmillan Ltd., Houndmills, Basingstoke, Hampshire, RG21 6XS, England, (Telephone in U.S.

(888) 330-8477), (Fax in U.S. (800) 672-2054), www.palgrave.com; *The Statesman's Yearbook 2008.*

AMERICAN SAMOA - CLOTHING EXPORTS AND IMPORTS

See AMERICAN SAMOA - TEXTILE INDUSTRY

AMERICAN SAMOA - COMMERCE

Palgrave Macmillan Ltd., Houndmills, Basingstoke, Hampshire, RG21 6XS, England, (Telephone in U.S. (888) 330-8477), (Fax in U.S. (800) 672-2054), www.palgrave.com; *The Statesman's Yearbook 2008.*

AMERICAN SAMOA - COMMODITY EXCHANGES

Commodity Research Bureau, 330 South Wells Street, Suite 612, Chicago, IL 60606-7110, (800) 621-5271, Fax: (312) 939-4135, www.crbtrader.com; *2006 CRB Commodity Yearbook and CD.*

International Monetary Fund (IMF), 700 Nineteenth Street, NW, Washington, DC 20431, (202) 623-7000, Fax: (202) 623-4661, www.imf.org; *IMF Primary Commodity Prices.*

United Nations Food and Agricultural Organization (FAO), Viale delle Terme di Caracalla, 00100 Rome, Italy, (Dial from U.S. (202) 653-2400), (Fax from U.S. (202) 653 5760), www.fao.org; *The State of Food and Agriculture (SOFA) 2006.*

AMERICAN SAMOA - CONSTRUCTION INDUSTRY

United Nations Statistics Division, New York, NY 10017, (800) 253-9646, Fax: (212) 963-4116, http://unstats.un.org; *Statistical Yearbook.*

AMERICAN SAMOA - CONSUMER PRICE INDEXES

International Labour Office, I.L.O. Publications, 4 route des Morillons, CH-1211 Geneva 22, Switzerland, (Telephone in U.S. (202) 653-7652), (Fax in U.S. (202) 653-7687), www.ilo.org; *Yearbook of Labour Statistics 2006.*

Taylor and Francis Group, An Informa Business, 2 Park Square, Milton Park, Abingdon, Oxford OX14 4RN, United Kingdom, (Dial from U.S. (212) 216-7800), (Fax from U.S. (212) 564-7854), www.tandf.co.uk; *The Europa World Year Book.*

The World Bank, 1818 H Street, NW, Washington, DC 20433, (202) 473-1000, Fax: (202) 477-6391, www.worldbank.org; *American Samoa.*

AMERICAN SAMOA - CONSUMPTION (ECONOMICS)

Secretariat of the Pacific Community (SPC), BP D5, 98848 Noumea Cedex, New Caledonia, www.spc.int/corp; *Selected Pacific Economies - a Statistical Summary (SPESS).*

AMERICAN SAMOA - CORN INDUSTRY

See AMERICAN SAMOA - CROPS

AMERICAN SAMOA - COST AND STANDARD OF LIVING

Secretariat of the Pacific Community (SPC), BP D5, 98848 Noumea Cedex, New Caledonia, www.spc.int/corp; *Selected Pacific Economies - a Statistical Summary (SPESS).*

AMERICAN SAMOA - CROPS

Palgrave Macmillan Ltd., Houndmills, Basingstoke, Hampshire, RG21 6XS, England, (Telephone in U.S. (888) 330-8477), (Fax in U.S. (800) 672-2054), www.palgrave.com; *The Statesman's Yearbook 2008.*

Taylor and Francis Group, An Informa Business, 2 Park Square, Milton Park, Abingdon, Oxford OX14 4RN, United Kingdom, (Dial from U.S. (212) 216-7800), (Fax from U.S. (212) 564-7854), www.tandf.co.uk; *The Europa World Year Book.*

United Nations Conference on Trade and Development (UNCTAD), DC2-1120, United Nations, New York, NY 10017, (212) 963-0027, www.unctad.org; *UNCTAD Commodity Yearbook.*

United Nations Food and Agricultural Organization (FAO), Viale delle Terme di Caracalla, 00100 Rome, Italy, (Dial from U.S. (202) 653-2400), (Fax from U.S. (202) 653 5760), www.fao.org; *The State of Food and Agriculture (SOFA) 2006.*

AMERICAN SAMOA - DAIRY PROCESSING

Palgrave Macmillan Ltd., Houndmills, Basingstoke, Hampshire, RG21 6XS, England, (Telephone in U.S. (888) 330-8477), (Fax in U.S. (800) 672-2054), www.palgrave.com; *The Statesman's Yearbook 2008.*

United Nations Food and Agricultural Organization (FAO), Viale delle Terme di Caracalla, 00100 Rome, Italy, (Dial from U.S. (202) 653-2400), (Fax from U.S. (202) 653 5760), www.fao.org; *The State of Food and Agriculture (SOFA) 2006.*

AMERICAN SAMOA - DEATH RATES

See AMERICAN SAMOA - MORTALITY

AMERICAN SAMOA - DEBTS, EXTERNAL

The World Bank, 1818 H Street, NW, Washington, DC 20433, (202) 473-1000, Fax: (202) 477-6391, www.worldbank.org; *Global Development Finance 2007.*

Worldinformation.com, 2 Market Street, Saffron Walden, Essex CB10 1HZ, United Kingdom, www.worldinformation.com; The World of Information (www.worldinformation.com).

AMERICAN SAMOA - DEMOGRAPHY

Euromonitor International, Inc., 224 S. Michigan Avenue, Suite 1500, Chicago, IL 60604, (312) 922-1115, Fax: (312) 922-1157, www.euromonitor.com; *International Marketing Data and Statistics 2008; The World Economic Factbook 2008;* and *World Marketing Data and Statistics.*

The World Bank, 1818 H Street, NW, Washington, DC 20433, (202) 473-1000, Fax: (202) 477-6391, www.worldbank.org; *American Samoa.*

AMERICAN SAMOA - DIVORCE

United Nations Statistics Division, New York, NY 10017, (800) 253-9646, Fax: (212) 963-4116, http://unstats.un.org; *Demographic Yearbook* and *Statistical Yearbook.*

AMERICAN SAMOA - ECONOMIC CONDITIONS

Center for International Business Education Research (CIBER), Columbia Business School and School of International and Public Affairs, Uris Hall, Room 212, 3022 Broadway, New York, NY 10027-6902, Mr. Joshua Safier, (212) 854-4750, Fax: (212) 222-9821, www.columbia.edu/cu/ciber/; Datastream International.

Central Intelligence Agency, Office of Public Affairs, Washington, DC 20505, (703) 482-0623, Fax: (703) 482-1739, www.cia.gov; *The World Factbook.*

DSI Data Service Information, Xantener Strasse 51a, D-47495 Rheinberg, Germany, www.dsidata.com; *Campus Solution.*

Dun and Bradstreet (DB) Corporation, 103 JFK Parkway, Short Hills, NJ 07078, (973) 921-5500, www.dnb.com; *Country Report.*

Euromonitor International, Inc., 224 S. Michigan Avenue, Suite 1500, Chicago, IL 60604, (312) 922-1115, Fax: (312) 922-1157, www.euromonitor.com; *The World Economic Factbook 2008* and *World Marketing Data and Statistics.*

International Monetary Fund (IMF), 700 Nineteenth Street, NW, Washington, DC 20431, (202) 623-7000, Fax: (202) 623-4661, www.imf.org; *World Economic Outlook Reports.*

Palgrave Macmillan Ltd., Houndmills, Basingstoke, Hampshire, RG21 6XS, England, (Telephone in U.S. (888) 330-8477), (Fax in U.S. (800) 672-2054), www.palgrave.com; *The Statesman's Yearbook 2008.*

Secretariat of the Pacific Community (SPC), BP D5, 98848 Noumea Cedex, New Caledonia, www.spc.int/corp; PRISM (Pacific Regional Information System).

Taylor and Francis Group, An Informa Business, 2 Park Square, Milton Park, Abingdon, Oxford OX14 4RN, United Kingdom, (Dial from U.S. (212) 216-7800), (Fax from U.S. (212) 564-7854), www.tandf.co.uk; *The Europa World Year Book.*

United Nations Statistics Division, New York, NY 10017, (800) 253-9646, Fax: (212) 963-4116, http://unstats.un.org; *World Statistics Pocketbook.*

The World Bank, 1818 H Street, NW, Washington, DC 20433, (202) 473-1000, Fax: (202) 477-6391, www.worldbank.org; *American Samoa; Global Economic Monitor (GEM); Global Economic Prospects 2008;* and *The World Bank Atlas 2003-2004.*

AMERICAN SAMOA - EDUCATION

Euromonitor International, Inc., 224 S. Michigan Avenue, Suite 1500, Chicago, IL 60604, (312) 922-1115, Fax: (312) 922-1157, www.euromonitor.com; *International Marketing Data and Statistics 2008* and *World Marketing Data and Statistics.*

Palgrave Macmillan Ltd., Houndmills, Basingstoke, Hampshire, RG21 6XS, England, (Telephone in U.S. (888) 330-8477), (Fax in U.S. (800) 672-2054), www.palgrave.com; *The Statesman's Yearbook 2008.*

Taylor and Francis Group, An Informa Business, 2 Park Square, Milton Park, Abingdon, Oxford OX14 4RN, United Kingdom, (Dial from U.S. (212) 216-7800), (Fax from U.S. (212) 564-7854), www.tandf.co.uk; *The Europa World Year Book.*

UNESCO Institute for Statistics, C.P. 6128 Succursale Centre-Ville, Montreal, Quebec, H3C 3J7 Canada, (Dial from U.S. (514) 343-6880), (Fax from U.S. (514) 343 6882), www.uis.unesco.org; *Statistical Tables.*

The World Bank, 1818 H Street, NW, Washington, DC 20433, (202) 473-1000, Fax: (202) 477-6391, www.worldbank.org; *American Samoa.*

AMERICAN SAMOA - ELECTRICITY

Palgrave Macmillan Ltd., Houndmills, Basingstoke, Hampshire, RG21 6XS, England, (Telephone in U.S. (888) 330-8477), (Fax in U.S. (800) 672-2054), www.palgrave.com; *The Statesman's Yearbook 2008.*

United Nations Statistics Division, New York, NY 10017, (800) 253-9646, Fax: (212) 963-4116, http://unstats.un.org; *Statistical Yearbook.*

AMERICAN SAMOA - EMPLOYMENT

Euromonitor International, Inc., 224 S. Michigan Avenue, Suite 1500, Chicago, IL 60604, (312) 922-1115, Fax: (312) 922-1157, www.euromonitor.com; *International Marketing Data and Statistics 2008.*

International Labour Office, I.L.O. Publications, 4 route des Morillons, CH-1211 Geneva 22, Switzerland, (Telephone in U.S. (202) 653-7652), (Fax in U.S. (202) 653-7687), www.ilo.org; *Yearbook of Labour Statistics 2006.*

The World Bank, 1818 H Street, NW, Washington, DC 20433, (202) 473-1000, Fax: (202) 477-6391, www.worldbank.org; *American Samoa.*

AMERICAN SAMOA - ENVIRONMENTAL CONDITIONS

DSI Data Service Information, Xantener Strasse 51a, D-47495 Rheinberg, Germany, www.dsidata.com; *Campus Solution* and *DSI's Global Environmental Database.*

United Nations Statistics Division, New York, NY 10017, (800) 253-9646, Fax: (212) 963-4116, http://unstats.un.org; *World Statistics Pocketbook.*

AMERICAN SAMOA - EXPORTS

Central Intelligence Agency, Office of Public Affairs, Washington, DC 20505, (703) 482-0623, Fax: (703) 482-1739, www.cia.gov; *The World Factbook.*

Euromonitor International, Inc., 224 S. Michigan Avenue, Suite 1500, Chicago, IL 60604, (312) 922-

1115, Fax: (312) 922-1157, www.euromonitor.com; *International Marketing Data and Statistics 2008* and *The World Economic Factbook 2008.*

Secretariat of the Pacific Community (SPC), BP D5, 98848 Noumea Cedex, New Caledonia, www.spc.int/corp; *Selected Pacific Economies - a Statistical Summary (SPESS).*

Taylor and Francis Group, An Informa Business, 2 Park Square, Milton Park, Abingdon, Oxford OX14 4RN, United Kingdom, (Dial from U.S. (212) 216-7800), (Fax from U.S. (212) 564-7854), www.tandf.co.uk; *The Europa World Year Book.*

United Nations Food and Agricultural Organization (FAO), Viale delle Terme di Caracalla, 00100 Rome, Italy, (Dial from U.S. (202) 653-2400), (Fax from U.S. (202) 653 5760), www.fao.org; *The State of Food and Agriculture (SOFA) 2006.*

Worldinformation.com, 2 Market Street, Saffron Walden, Essex CB10 1HZ, United Kingdom, www.worldinformation.com; The World of Information (www.worldinformation.com).

AMERICAN SAMOA - FERTILITY, HUMAN

The World Bank, 1818 H Street, NW, Washington, DC 20433, (202) 473-1000, Fax: (202) 477-6391, www.worldbank.org; *The World Bank Atlas 2003-2004.*

AMERICAN SAMOA - FERTILIZER INDUSTRY

United Nations Food and Agricultural Organization (FAO), Viale delle Terme di Caracalla, 00100 Rome, Italy, (Dial from U.S. (202) 653-2400), (Fax from U.S. (202) 653 5760), www.fao.org; *The State of Food and Agriculture (SOFA) 2006.*

AMERICAN SAMOA - FETAL MORTALITY

See AMERICAN SAMOA - MORTALITY

AMERICAN SAMOA - FINANCE, PUBLIC

Bernan Essential Government Publications, 4611-F Assembly Drive, Lanham MD, 20706-4391, (301) 459-2255, Fax: (800) 865-3450, www.bernan.com; *National Accounts Statistics.*

International Monetary Fund (IMF), 700 Nineteenth Street, NW, Washington, DC 20431, (202) 623-7000, Fax: (202) 623-4661, www.imf.org; *International Financial Statistics; International Financial Statistics Online Service;* and *International Financial Statistics Yearbook 2007.*

Taylor and Francis Group, An Informa Business, 2 Park Square, Milton Park, Abingdon, Oxford OX14 4RN, United Kingdom, (Dial from U.S. (212) 216-7800), (Fax from U.S. (212) 564-7854), www.tandf.co.uk; *The Europa World Year Book.*

The World Bank, 1818 H Street, NW, Washington, DC 20433, (202) 473-1000, Fax: (202) 477-6391, www.worldbank.org; *American Samoa* and *American Samoa.*

AMERICAN SAMOA - FISHERIES

Palgrave Macmillan Ltd., Houndmills, Basingstoke, Hampshire, RG21 6XS, England, (Telephone in U.S. (888) 330-8477), (Fax in U.S. (800) 672-2054), www.palgrave.com; *The Statesman's Yearbook 2008.*

Taylor and Francis Group, An Informa Business, 2 Park Square, Milton Park, Abingdon, Oxford OX14 4RN, United Kingdom, (Dial from U.S. (212) 216-7800), (Fax from U.S. (212) 564-7854), www.tandf.co.uk; *The Europa World Year Book.*

United Nations Conference on Trade and Development (UNCTAD), DC2-1120, United Nations, New York, NY 10017, (212) 963-0027, www.unctad.org; *UNCTAD Commodity Yearbook.*

United Nations Food and Agricultural Organization (FAO), Viale delle Terme di Caracalla, 00100 Rome, Italy, (Dial from U.S. (202) 653-2400), (Fax from U.S. (202) 653 5760), www.fao.org; *FAO Yearbook of Fishery Statistics;* Fishery Databases; FISHSTAT Database. Subjects covered include: Aquaculture production, capture production, fishery commodities; and *The State of Food and Agriculture (SOFA) 2006.*

The World Bank, 1818 H Street, NW, Washington, DC 20433, (202) 473-1000, Fax: (202) 477-6391, www.worldbank.org; *American Samoa.*

AMERICAN SAMOA - FOOD

Secretariat of the Pacific Community (SPC), BP D5, 98848 Noumea Cedex, New Caledonia, www.spc.int/corp; *Selected Pacific Economies - a Statistical Summary (SPESS).*

United Nations Conference on Trade and Development (UNCTAD), DC2-1120, United Nations, New York, NY 10017, (212) 963-0027, www.unctad.org; *UNCTAD Commodity Yearbook.*

United Nations Food and Agricultural Organization (FAO), Viale delle Terme di Caracalla, 00100 Rome, Italy, (Dial from U.S. (202) 653-2400), (Fax from U.S. (202) 653 5760), www.fao.org; *FAO Production Yearbook 2002* and *The State of Food and Agriculture (SOFA) 2006.*

AMERICAN SAMOA - FOREIGN EXCHANGE RATES

Central Intelligence Agency, Office of Public Affairs, Washington, DC 20505, (703) 482-0623, Fax: (703) 482-1739, www.cia.gov; *The World Factbook.*

Euromonitor International, Inc., 224 S. Michigan Avenue, Suite 1500, Chicago, IL 60604, (312) 922-1115, Fax: (312) 922-1157, www.euromonitor.com; *International Marketing Data and Statistics 2008* and *The World Economic Factbook 2008.*

Taylor and Francis Group, An Informa Business, 2 Park Square, Milton Park, Abingdon, Oxford OX14 4RN, United Kingdom, (Dial from U.S. (212) 216-7800), (Fax from U.S. (212) 564-7854), www.tandf.co.uk; *The Europa World Year Book.*

United Nations Statistics Division, New York, NY 10017, (800) 253-9646, Fax: (212) 963-4116, http://unstats.un.org; *World Statistics Pocketbook.*

Worldinformation.com, 2 Market Street, Saffron Walden, Essex CB10 1HZ, United Kingdom, www.worldinformation.com; The World of Information (www.worldinformation.com).

AMERICAN SAMOA - FORESTS AND FORESTRY

UNESCO Institute for Statistics, C.P. 6128 Succursale Centre-Ville, Montreal, Quebec, H3C 3J7 Canada, (Dial from U.S. (514) 343-6880), (Fax from U.S. (514) 343 6882), www.uis.unesco.org; *Statistical Tables.*

United Nations Conference on Trade and Development (UNCTAD), DC2-1120, United Nations, New York, NY 10017, (212) 963-0027, www.unctad.org; *UNCTAD Commodity Yearbook.*

United Nations Food and Agricultural Organization (FAO), Viale delle Terme di Caracalla, 00100 Rome, Italy, (Dial from U.S. (202) 653-2400), (Fax from U.S. (202) 653 5760), www.fao.org; *The State of Food and Agriculture (SOFA) 2006.*

United Nations Statistics Division, New York, NY 10017, (800) 253-9646, Fax: (212) 963-4116, http://unstats.un.org; *Statistical Yearbook.*

The World Bank, 1818 H Street, NW, Washington, DC 20433, (202) 473-1000, Fax: (202) 477-6391, www.worldbank.org; *American Samoa* and *American Samoa.*

AMERICAN SAMOA - GROSS DOMESTIC PRODUCT

Euromonitor International, Inc., 224 S. Michigan Avenue, Suite 1500, Chicago, IL 60604, (312) 922-1115, Fax: (312) 922-1157, www.euromonitor.com; *International Marketing Data and Statistics 2008* and *The World Economic Factbook 2008.*

AMERICAN SAMOA - GROSS NATIONAL PRODUCT

The World Bank, 1818 H Street, NW, Washington, DC 20433, (202) 473-1000, Fax: (202) 477-6391, www.worldbank.org; *The World Bank Atlas 2003-2004.*

Worldinformation.com, 2 Market Street, Saffron Walden, Essex CB10 1HZ, United Kingdom, www.worldinformation.com; The World of Information (www.worldinformation.com).

AMERICAN SAMOA - HIDES AND SKINS INDUSTRY

United Nations Food and Agricultural Organization (FAO), Viale delle Terme di Caracalla, 00100 Rome, Italy, (Dial from U.S. (202) 653-2400), (Fax from U.S. (202) 653 5760), www.fao.org; *FAO Production Yearbook 2002.*

AMERICAN SAMOA - HOUSING

Euromonitor International, Inc., 224 S. Michigan Avenue, Suite 1500, Chicago, IL 60604, (312) 922-1115, Fax: (312) 922-1157, www.euromonitor.com; *World Marketing Data and Statistics.*

Secretariat of the Pacific Community (SPC), BP D5, 98848 Noumea Cedex, New Caledonia, www.spc.int/corp; *Selected Pacific Economies - a Statistical Summary (SPESS).*

AMERICAN SAMOA - ILLITERATE PERSONS

Euromonitor International, Inc., 224 S. Michigan Avenue, Suite 1500, Chicago, IL 60604, (312) 922-1115, Fax: (312) 922-1157, www.euromonitor.com; *The World Economic Factbook 2008.*

AMERICAN SAMOA - IMPORTS

Central Intelligence Agency, Office of Public Affairs, Washington, DC 20505, (703) 482-0623, Fax: (703) 482-1739, www.cia.gov; *The World Factbook.*

Euromonitor International, Inc., 224 S. Michigan Avenue, Suite 1500, Chicago, IL 60604, (312) 922-1115, Fax: (312) 922-1157, www.euromonitor.com; *International Marketing Data and Statistics 2008* and *The World Economic Factbook 2008.*

Secretariat of the Pacific Community (SPC), BP D5, 98848 Noumea Cedex, New Caledonia, www.spc.int/corp; *Selected Pacific Economies - a Statistical Summary (SPESS).*

Taylor and Francis Group, An Informa Business, 2 Park Square, Milton Park, Abingdon, Oxford OX14 4RN, United Kingdom, (Dial from U.S. (212) 216-7800), (Fax from U.S. (212) 564-7854), www.tandf.co.uk; *The Europa World Year Book.*

United Nations Food and Agricultural Organization (FAO), Viale delle Terme di Caracalla, 00100 Rome, Italy, (Dial from U.S. (202) 653-2400), (Fax from U.S. (202) 653 5760), www.fao.org; *The State of Food and Agriculture (SOFA) 2006.*

Worldinformation.com, 2 Market Street, Saffron Walden, Essex CB10 1HZ, United Kingdom, www.worldinformation.com; The World of Information (www.worldinformation.com).

AMERICAN SAMOA - INDUSTRIES

Central Intelligence Agency, Office of Public Affairs, Washington, DC 20505, (703) 482-0623, Fax: (703) 482-1739, www.cia.gov; *The World Factbook.*

Euromonitor International, Inc., 224 S. Michigan Avenue, Suite 1500, Chicago, IL 60604, (312) 922-1115, Fax: (312) 922-1157, www.euromonitor.com; *The World Economic Factbook 2008* and *World Marketing Data and Statistics.*

International Labour Office, I.L.O. Publications, 4 route des Morillons, CH-1211 Geneva 22, Switzerland, (Telephone in U.S. (202) 653-7652), (Fax in U.S. (202) 653-7687), www.ilo.org; *Yearbook of Labour Statistics 2006.*

Palgrave Macmillan Ltd., Houndmills, Basingstoke, Hampshire, RG21 6XS, England, (Telephone in U.S. (888) 330-8477), (Fax in U.S. (800) 672-2054), www.palgrave.com; *The Statesman's Yearbook 2008.*

Taylor and Francis Group, An Informa Business, 2 Park Square, Milton Park, Abingdon, Oxford OX14 4RN, United Kingdom, (Dial from U.S. (212) 216-7800), (Fax from U.S. (212) 564-7854), www.tandf.co.uk; *The Europa World Year Book.*

United Nations Industrial Development Organization (UNIDO), 1 United Nations Plaza, New York, NY 10017, (212) 963 6890, Fax: (212) 963-7904, http://unido.org; Industrial Statistics Database 2008 (INDSTAT) and *The International Yearbook of Industrial Statistics 2008.*

The World Bank, 1818 H Street, NW, Washington, DC 20433, (202) 473-1000, Fax: (202) 477-6391, www.worldbank.org; *American Samoa.*

AMERICAN SAMOA - INFANT AND MATERNAL MORTALITY

See AMERICAN SAMOA - MORTALITY

AMERICAN SAMOA - INTERNATIONAL TRADE

Euromonitor International, Inc., 224 S. Michigan Avenue, Suite 1500, Chicago, IL 60604, (312) 922-1115, Fax: (312) 922-1157, www.euromonitor.com; *The World Economic Factbook 2008* and *World Marketing Data and Statistics.*

Organisation for Economic Cooperation and Development (OECD), 2 rue Andre Pascal, F-75775 Paris Cedex 16, France, (Telephone in U.S. (202) 785-6323), (Fax in U.S. (202) 785-0350), www.oecd.org; *International Trade by Commodity Statistics (ITCS).*

Palgrave Macmillan Ltd., Houndmills, Basingstoke, Hampshire, RG21 6XS, England, (Telephone in U.S. (888) 330-8477), (Fax in U.S. (800) 672-2054), www.palgrave.com; *The Statesman's Yearbook 2008.*

Secretariat of the Pacific Community (SPC), BP D5, 98848 Noumea Cedex, New Caledonia, www.spc.int/corp; *Selected Pacific Economies - a Statistical Summary (SPESS).*

Taylor and Francis Group, An Informa Business, 2 Park Square, Milton Park, Abingdon, Oxford OX14 4RN, United Kingdom, (Dial from U.S. (212) 216-7800), (Fax from U.S. (212) 564-7854), www.tandf.co.uk; *The Europa World Year Book.*

United Nations Conference on Trade and Development (UNCTAD), DC2-1120, United Nations, New York, NY 10017, (212) 963-0027, www.unctad.org; *UNCTAD Commodity Yearbook.*

United Nations Food and Agricultural Organization (FAO), Viale delle Terme di Caracalla, 00100 Rome, Italy, (Dial from U.S. (202) 653-2400), (Fax from U.S. (202) 653 5760), www.fao.org; *FAO Trade Yearbook* and *The State of Food and Agriculture (SOFA) 2006.*

United Nations Statistics Division, New York, NY 10017, (800) 253-9646, Fax: (212) 963-4116, http://unstats.un.org; *Statistical Yearbook.*

The World Bank, 1818 H Street, NW, Washington, DC 20433, (202) 473-1000, Fax: (202) 477-6391, www.worldbank.org; *American Samoa.*

World Trade Organization (WTO), Centre William Rappard, Rue de Lausanne 154, CH-1211 Geneva 21, Switzerland, www.wto.org; *International Trade Statistics 2006.*

AMERICAN SAMOA - INTERNET USERS

International Telecommunication Union (ITU), Place des Nations, 1211 Geneva 20, Switzerland, www.itu.int; *World Telecommunication/ICT Indicators Database on CD-ROM; World Telecommunication/ICT Indicators Database Online;* and *Yearbook of Statistics - Telecommunication Services (Chronological Time Series 1997-2006).*

The World Bank, 1818 H Street, NW, Washington, DC 20433, (202) 473-1000, Fax: (202) 477-6391, www.worldbank.org; *American Samoa.*

AMERICAN SAMOA - LABOR

Central Intelligence Agency, Office of Public Affairs, Washington, DC 20505, (703) 482-0623, Fax: (703) 482-1739, www.cia.gov; *The World Factbook.*

Euromonitor International, Inc., 224 S. Michigan Avenue, Suite 1500, Chicago, IL 60604, (312) 922-1115, Fax: (312) 922-1157, www.euromonitor.com; *International Marketing Data and Statistics 2008* and *World Marketing Data and Statistics.*

International Labour Office, I.L.O. Publications, 4 route des Morillons, CH-1211 Geneva 22, Switzerland, (Telephone in U.S. (202) 653-7652), (Fax in U.S. (202) 653-7687), www.ilo.org; *Yearbook of Labour Statistics 2006.*

Palgrave Macmillan Ltd., Houndmills, Basingstoke, Hampshire, RG21 6XS, England, (Telephone in U.S. (888) 330-8477), (Fax in U.S. (800) 672-2054), www.palgrave.com; *The Statesman's Yearbook 2008.*

Taylor and Francis Group, An Informa Business, 2 Park Square, Milton Park, Abingdon, Oxford OX14 4RN, United Kingdom, (Dial from U.S. (212) 216-7800), (Fax from U.S. (212) 564-7854), www.tandf.co.uk; *The Europa World Year Book.*

United Nations Food and Agricultural Organization (FAO), Viale delle Terme di Caracalla, 00100 Rome, Italy, (Dial from U.S. (202) 653-2400), (Fax from U.S. (202) 653 5760), www.fao.org; *The State of Food and Agriculture (SOFA) 2006.*

The World Bank, 1818 H Street, NW, Washington, DC 20433, (202) 473-1000, Fax: (202) 477-6391, www.worldbank.org; *The World Bank Atlas 2003-2004.*

AMERICAN SAMOA - LAND USE

Central Intelligence Agency, Office of Public Affairs, Washington, DC 20505, (703) 482-0623, Fax: (703) 482-1739, www.cia.gov; *The World Factbook.*

Euromonitor International, Inc., 224 S. Michigan Avenue, Suite 1500, Chicago, IL 60604, (312) 922-1115, Fax: (312) 922-1157, www.euromonitor.com; *International Marketing Data and Statistics 2008.*

United Nations Food and Agricultural Organization (FAO), Viale delle Terme di Caracalla, 00100 Rome, Italy, (Dial from U.S. (202) 653-2400), (Fax from U.S. (202) 653 5760), www.fao.org; *FAO Production Yearbook 2002.*

AMERICAN SAMOA - LIBRARIES

UNESCO Institute for Statistics, C.P. 6128 Succursale Centre-Ville, Montreal, Quebec, H3C 3J7 Canada, (Dial from U.S. (514) 343-6880), (Fax from U.S. (514) 343 6882), www.uis.unesco.org; *Statistical Tables.*

AMERICAN SAMOA - LIFE EXPECTANCY

Euromonitor International, Inc., 224 S. Michigan Avenue, Suite 1500, Chicago, IL 60604, (312) 922-1115, Fax: (312) 922-1157, www.euromonitor.com; *The World Economic Factbook 2008.*

United Nations Statistics Division, New York, NY 10017, (800) 253-9646, Fax: (212) 963-4116, http://unstats.un.org; *World Statistics Pocketbook.*

The World Bank, 1818 H Street, NW, Washington, DC 20433, (202) 473-1000, Fax: (202) 477-6391, www.worldbank.org; *The World Bank Atlas 2003-2004.*

AMERICAN SAMOA - LITERACY

Euromonitor International, Inc., 224 S. Michigan Avenue, Suite 1500, Chicago, IL 60604, (312) 922-1115, Fax: (312) 922-1157, www.euromonitor.com; *World Marketing Data and Statistics.*

AMERICAN SAMOA - LIVESTOCK

Palgrave Macmillan Ltd., Houndmills, Basingstoke, Hampshire, RG21 6XS, England, (Telephone in U.S. (888) 330-8477), (Fax in U.S. (800) 672-2054), www.palgrave.com; *The Statesman's Yearbook 2008.*

Taylor and Francis Group, An Informa Business, 2 Park Square, Milton Park, Abingdon, Oxford OX14 4RN, United Kingdom, (Dial from U.S. (212) 216-7800), (Fax from U.S. (212) 564-7854), www.tandf.co.uk; *The Europa World Year Book.*

United Nations Conference on Trade and Development (UNCTAD), DC2-1120, United Nations, New York, NY 10017, (212) 963-0027, www.unctad.org; *UNCTAD Commodity Yearbook.*

United Nations Food and Agricultural Organization (FAO), Viale delle Terme di Caracalla, 00100 Rome, Italy, (Dial from U.S. (202) 653-2400), (Fax from U.S. (202) 653 5760), www.fao.org; *FAO Production Yearbook 2002* and *The State of Food and Agriculture (SOFA) 2006.*

AMERICAN SAMOA - MARRIAGE

Taylor and Francis Group, An Informa Business, 2 Park Square, Milton Park, Abingdon, Oxford OX14 4RN, United Kingdom, (Dial from U.S. (212) 216-7800), (Fax from U.S. (212) 564-7854), www.tandf.co.uk; *The Europa World Year Book.*

United Nations Statistics Division, New York, NY 10017, (800) 253-9646, Fax: (212) 963-4116, http://unstats.un.org; *Demographic Yearbook* and *Statistical Yearbook.*

AMERICAN SAMOA - MEAT PRODUCTION

See AMERICAN SAMOA - LIVESTOCK

AMERICAN SAMOA - MINERAL INDUSTRIES

Taylor and Francis Group, An Informa Business, 2 Park Square, Milton Park, Abingdon, Oxford OX14 4RN, United Kingdom, (Dial from U.S. (212) 216-7800), (Fax from U.S. (212) 564-7854), www.tandf.co.uk; *The Europa World Year Book.*

United Nations Conference on Trade and Development (UNCTAD), DC2-1120, United Nations, New York, NY 10017, (212) 963-0027, www.unctad.org; *UNCTAD Commodity Yearbook.*

AMERICAN SAMOA - MONEY SUPPLY

The World Bank, 1818 H Street, NW, Washington, DC 20433, (202) 473-1000, Fax: (202) 477-6391, www.worldbank.org; *American Samoa.*

AMERICAN SAMOA - MORTALITY

Central Intelligence Agency, Office of Public Affairs, Washington, DC 20505, (703) 482-0623, Fax: (703) 482-1739, www.cia.gov; *The World Factbook.*

Euromonitor International, Inc., 224 S. Michigan Avenue, Suite 1500, Chicago, IL 60604, (312) 922-1115, Fax: (312) 922-1157, www.euromonitor.com; *International Marketing Data and Statistics 2008* and *The World Economic Factbook 2008.*

Taylor and Francis Group, An Informa Business, 2 Park Square, Milton Park, Abingdon, Oxford OX14 4RN, United Kingdom, (Dial from U.S. (212) 216-7800), (Fax from U.S. (212) 564-7854), www.tandf.co.uk; *The Europa World Year Book.*

United Nations Statistics Division, New York, NY 10017, (800) 253-9646, Fax: (212) 963-4116, http://unstats.un.org; *Statistical Yearbook* and *World Statistics Pocketbook.*

The World Bank, 1818 H Street, NW, Washington, DC 20433, (202) 473-1000, Fax: (202) 477-6391, www.worldbank.org; *The World Bank Atlas 2003-2004.*

World Health Organization (WHO), Avenue Appia 20, 1211 Geneve 27, Switzerland, (Telephone in U.S. (212) 331-9081), www.who.int; *The WHO Global Atlas of Infectious Diseases* and *World Health Report 2006.*

AMERICAN SAMOA - MOTION PICTURES

United Nations Statistics Division, New York, NY 10017, (800) 253-9646, Fax: (212) 963-4116, http://unstats.un.org; *Statistical Yearbook.*

AMERICAN SAMOA - MOTOR VEHICLES

Taylor and Francis Group, An Informa Business, 2 Park Square, Milton Park, Abingdon, Oxford OX14 4RN, United Kingdom, (Dial from U.S. (212) 216-7800), (Fax from U.S. (212) 564-7854), www.tandf.co.uk; *The Europa World Year Book.*

United Nations Statistics Division, New York, NY 10017, (800) 253-9646, Fax: (212) 963-4116, http://unstats.un.org; *Statistical Yearbook.*

AMERICAN SAMOA - MUSEUMS

UNESCO Institute for Statistics, C.P. 6128 Succursale Centre-Ville, Montreal, Quebec, H3C 3J7

Canada, (Dial from U.S. (514) 343-6880), (Fax from U.S. (514) 343 6882), www.uis.unesco.org; *Statistical Tables.*

AMERICAN SAMOA - NUTRITION

United Nations Food and Agricultural Organization (FAO), Viale delle Terme di Caracalla, 00100 Rome, Italy, (Dial from U.S. (202) 653-2400), (Fax from U.S. (202) 653 5760), www.fao.org; *The State of Food and Agriculture (SOFA) 2006.*

AMERICAN SAMOA - PERIODICALS

UNESCO Institute for Statistics, C.P. 6128 Succursale Centre-Ville, Montreal, Quebec, H3C 3J7 Canada, (Dial from U.S. (514) 343-6880), (Fax from U.S. (514) 343 6882), www.uis.unesco.org; *Statistical Tables.*

AMERICAN SAMOA - PESTICIDES

United Nations Food and Agricultural Organization (FAO), Viale delle Terme di Caracalla, 00100 Rome, Italy, (Dial from U.S. (202) 653-2400), (Fax from U.S. (202) 653 5760), www.fao.org; *The State of Food and Agriculture (SOFA) 2006.*

AMERICAN SAMOA - PETROLEUM INDUSTRY AND TRADE

PennWell Corporation, 1421 South Sheridan Road, Tulsa, OK 74112, (918) 835-3161, www.pennwell.com; *International Petroleum Encyclopedia 2007.*

United Nations Conference on Trade and Development (UNCTAD), DC2-1120, United Nations, New York, NY 10017, (212) 963-0027, www.unctad.org; *UNCTAD Commodity Yearbook.*

United Nations Food and Agricultural Organization (FAO), Viale delle Terme di Caracalla, 00100 Rome, Italy, (Dial from U.S. (202) 653-2400), (Fax from U.S. (202) 653 5760), www.fao.org; *The State of Food and Agriculture (SOFA) 2006.*

AMERICAN SAMOA - POLITICAL SCIENCE

Central Intelligence Agency, Office of Public Affairs, Washington, DC 20505, (703) 482-0623, Fax: (703) 482-1739, www.cia.gov; *The World Factbook.*

Palgrave Macmillan Ltd., Houndmills, Basingstoke, Hampshire, RG21 6XS, England, (Telephone in U.S. (888) 330-8477), (Fax in U.S. (800) 672-2054), www.palgrave.com; *The Statesman's Yearbook 2008.*

Taylor and Francis Group, An Informa Business, 2 Park Square, Milton Park, Abingdon, Oxford OX14 4RN, United Kingdom, (Dial from U.S. (212) 216-7800), (Fax from U.S. (212) 564-7854), www.tandf.co.uk; *The Europa World Year Book.*

AMERICAN SAMOA - POPULATION

Central Intelligence Agency, Office of Public Affairs, Washington, DC 20505, (703) 482-0623, Fax: (703) 482-1739, www.cia.gov; *The World Factbook.*

Euromonitor International, Inc., 224 S. Michigan Avenue, Suite 1500, Chicago, IL 60604, (312) 922-1115, Fax: (312) 922-1157, www.euromonitor.com; *International Marketing Data and Statistics 2008* and *The World Economic Factbook 2008.*

International Labour Office, I.L.O. Publications, 4 route des Morillons, CH-1211 Geneva 22, Switzerland, (Telephone in U.S. (202) 653-7652), (Fax in U.S. (202) 653-7687), www.ilo.org; *Yearbook of Labour Statistics 2006.*

Palgrave Macmillan Ltd., Houndmills, Basingstoke, Hampshire, RG21 6XS, England, (Telephone in U.S. (888) 330-8477), (Fax in U.S. (800) 672-2054), www.palgrave.com; *The Statesman's Yearbook 2008.*

Taylor and Francis Group, An Informa Business, 2 Park Square, Milton Park, Abingdon, Oxford OX14 4RN, United Kingdom, (Dial from U.S. (212) 216-7800), (Fax from U.S. (212) 564-7854), www.tandf.co.uk; *The Europa World Year Book.*

United Nations Food and Agricultural Organization (FAO), Viale delle Terme di Caracalla, 00100 Rome, Italy, (Dial from U.S. (202) 653-2400), (Fax from U.S. (202) 653 5760), www.fao.org; *FAO Production Yearbook 2002.*

United Nations Statistics Division, New York, NY 10017, (800) 253-9646, Fax: (212) 963-4116, http://unstats.un.org; *Demographic Yearbook; Statistical Yearbook;* and *World Statistics Pocketbook.*

The World Bank, 1818 H Street, NW, Washington, DC 20433, (202) 473-1000, Fax: (202) 477-6391, www.worldbank.org; *American Samoa* and *The World Bank Atlas 2003-2004.*

World Health Organization (WHO), Avenue Appia 20, 1211 Geneve 27, Switzerland, (Telephone in U.S. (212) 331-9081), www.who.int; *World Health Report 2006.*

Worldinformation.com, 2 Market Street, Saffron Walden, Essex CB10 1HZ, United Kingdom, www.worldinformation.com; The World of Information (www.worldinformation.com).

AMERICAN SAMOA - POPULATION DENSITY

Central Intelligence Agency, Office of Public Affairs, Washington, DC 20505, (703) 482-0623, Fax: (703) 482-1739, www.cia.gov; *The World Factbook.*

Euromonitor International, Inc., 224 S. Michigan Avenue, Suite 1500, Chicago, IL 60604, (312) 922-1115, Fax: (312) 922-1157, www.euromonitor.com; *The World Economic Factbook 2008.*

Palgrave Macmillan Ltd., Houndmills, Basingstoke, Hampshire, RG21 6XS, England, (Telephone in U.S. (888) 330-8477), (Fax in U.S. (800) 672-2054), www.palgrave.com; *The Statesman's Yearbook 2008.*

Taylor and Francis Group, An Informa Business, 2 Park Square, Milton Park, Abingdon, Oxford OX14 4RN, United Kingdom, (Dial from U.S. (212) 216-7800), (Fax from U.S. (212) 564-7854), www.tandf.co.uk; *The Europa World Year Book.*

United Nations Food and Agricultural Organization (FAO), Viale delle Terme di Caracalla, 00100 Rome, Italy, (Dial from U.S. (202) 653-2400), (Fax from U.S. (202) 653 5760), www.fao.org; *The State of Food and Agriculture (SOFA) 2006.*

United Nations Statistics Division, New York, NY 10017, (800) 253-9646, Fax: (212) 963-4116, http://unstats.un.org; *Statistical Yearbook.*

The World Bank, 1818 H Street, NW, Washington, DC 20433, (202) 473-1000, Fax: (202) 477-6391, www.worldbank.org; *American Samoa.*

AMERICAN SAMOA - POWER RESOURCES

Euromonitor International, Inc., 224 S. Michigan Avenue, Suite 1500, Chicago, IL 60604, (312) 922-1115, Fax: (312) 922-1157, www.euromonitor.com; *International Marketing Data and Statistics 2008; The World Economic Factbook 2008;* and *World Marketing Data and Statistics.*

Palgrave Macmillan Ltd., Houndmills, Basingstoke, Hampshire, RG21 6XS, England, (Telephone in U.S. (888) 330-8477), (Fax in U.S. (800) 672-2054), www.palgrave.com; *The Statesman's Yearbook 2008.*

Platts, 2 Penn Plaza, 25th Floor, New York, NY 10121-2298, (212) 904-3070, www.platts.com; *Energy Economist.*

United Nations Food and Agricultural Organization (FAO), Viale delle Terme di Caracalla, 00100 Rome, Italy, (Dial from U.S. (202) 653-2400), (Fax from U.S. (202) 653 5760), www.fao.org; *The State of Food and Agriculture (SOFA) 2006.*

United Nations Statistics Division, New York, NY 10017, (800) 253-9646, Fax: (212) 963-4116, http://unstats.un.org; *Energy Statistics Yearbook 2003; Statistical Yearbook;* and *World Statistics Pocketbook.*

The World Bank, 1818 H Street, NW, Washington, DC 20433, (202) 473-1000, Fax: (202) 477-6391, www.worldbank.org; *The World Bank Atlas 2003-2004.*

AMERICAN SAMOA - PRICES

Euromonitor International, Inc., 224 S. Michigan Avenue, Suite 1500, Chicago, IL 60604, (312) 922-1115, Fax: (312) 922-1157, www.euromonitor.com; *World Marketing Data and Statistics.*

International Labour Office, I.L.O. Publications, 4 route des Morillons, CH-1211 Geneva 22, Switzerland, (Telephone in U.S. (202) 653-7652), (Fax in U.S. (202) 653-7687), www.ilo.org; *Yearbook of Labour Statistics 2006.*

Secretariat of the Pacific Community (SPC), BP D5, 98848 Noumea Cedex, New Caledonia, www.spc.int/corp; *Selected Pacific Economies - a Statistical Summary (SPESS).*

United Nations Food and Agricultural Organization (FAO), Viale delle Terme di Caracalla, 00100 Rome, Italy, (Dial from U.S. (202) 653-2400), (Fax from U.S. (202) 653 5760), www.fao.org; *FAO Production Yearbook 2002* and *The State of Food and Agriculture (SOFA) 2006.*

The World Bank, 1818 H Street, NW, Washington, DC 20433, (202) 473-1000, Fax: (202) 477-6391, www.worldbank.org; *American Samoa.*

AMERICAN SAMOA - PROFESSIONS

United Nations Statistics Division, New York, NY 10017, (800) 253-9646, Fax: (212) 963-4116, http://unstats.un.org; *Statistical Yearbook.*

AMERICAN SAMOA - PUBLIC HEALTH

Euromonitor International, Inc., 224 S. Michigan Avenue, Suite 1500, Chicago, IL 60604, (312) 922-1115, Fax: (312) 922-1157, www.euromonitor.com; *World Marketing Data and Statistics.*

Secretariat of the Pacific Community (SPC), BP D5, 98848 Noumea Cedex, New Caledonia, www.spc.int/corp; *Selected Pacific Economies - a Statistical Summary (SPESS).*

United Nations Statistics Division, New York, NY 10017, (800) 253-9646, Fax: (212) 963-4116, http://unstats.un.org; *Statistical Yearbook.*

The World Bank, 1818 H Street, NW, Washington, DC 20433, (202) 473-1000, Fax: (202) 477-6391, www.worldbank.org; *American Samoa.*

World Health Organization (WHO), Avenue Appia 20, 1211 Geneve 27, Switzerland, (Telephone in U.S. (212) 331-9081), www.who.int; The WHO Global Atlas of Infectious Diseases and *World Health Report 2006.*

AMERICAN SAMOA - PUBLISHERS AND PUBLISHING

UNESCO Institute for Statistics, C.P. 6128 Succursale Centre-Ville, Montreal, Quebec, H3C 3J7 Canada, (Dial from U.S. (514) 343-6880), (Fax from U.S. (514) 343 6882), www.uis.unesco.org; *Statistical Tables.*

AMERICAN SAMOA - RADIO BROADCASTING

Palgrave Macmillan Ltd., Houndmills, Basingstoke, Hampshire, RG21 6XS, England, (Telephone in U.S. (888) 330-8477), (Fax in U.S. (800) 672-2054), www.palgrave.com; *The Statesman's Yearbook 2008.*

AMERICAN SAMOA - RELIGION

Central Intelligence Agency, Office of Public Affairs, Washington, DC 20505, (703) 482-0623, Fax: (703) 482-1739, www.cia.gov; *The World Factbook.*

Palgrave Macmillan Ltd., Houndmills, Basingstoke, Hampshire, RG21 6XS, England, (Telephone in U.S. (888) 330-8477), (Fax in U.S. (800) 672-2054), www.palgrave.com; *The Statesman's Yearbook 2008.*

AMERICAN SAMOA - RENT CHARGES

International Labour Office, I.L.O. Publications, 4 route des Morillons, CH-1211 Geneva 22, Switzerland, (Telephone in U.S. (202) 653-7652), (Fax in U.S. (202) 653-7687), www.ilo.org; *Yearbook of Labour Statistics 2006.*

AMERICAN SAMOA - RETAIL TRADE

Euromonitor International, Inc., 224 S. Michigan Avenue, Suite 1500, Chicago, IL 60604, (312) 922-1115, Fax: (312) 922-1157, www.euromonitor.com; *World Marketing Data and Statistics.*

AMERICAN SAMOA - ROADS

Central Intelligence Agency, Office of Public Affairs, Washington, DC 20505, (703) 482-0623, Fax: (703) 482-1739, www.cia.gov; *The World Factbook.*

Palgrave Macmillan Ltd., Houndmills, Basingstoke, Hampshire, RG21 6XS, England, (Telephone in U.S. (888) 330-8477), (Fax in U.S. (800) 672-2054), www.palgrave.com; *The Statesman's Yearbook 2008.*

AMERICAN SAMOA - SHIPPING

Palgrave Macmillan Ltd., Houndmills, Basingstoke, Hampshire, RG21 6XS, England, (Telephone in U.S. (888) 330-8477), (Fax in U.S. (800) 672-2054), www.palgrave.com; *The Statesman's Yearbook 2008.*

Taylor and Francis Group, An Informa Business, 2 Park Square, Milton Park, Abingdon, Oxford OX14 4RN, United Kingdom, (Dial from U.S. (212) 216-7800), (Fax from U.S. (212) 564-7854), www.tandf.co.uk; *The Europa World Year Book.*

United Nations Statistics Division, New York, NY 10017, (800) 253-9646, Fax: (212) 963-4116, http://unstats.un.org; *Statistical Yearbook.*

AMERICAN SAMOA - SOCIAL ECOLOGY

United Nations Statistics Division, New York, NY 10017, (800) 253-9646, Fax: (212) 963-4116, http://unstats.un.org; *World Statistics Pocketbook.*

AMERICAN SAMOA - TAXATION

Taylor and Francis Group, An Informa Business, 2 Park Square, Milton Park, Abingdon, Oxford OX14 4RN, United Kingdom, (Dial from U.S. (212) 216-7800), (Fax from U.S. (212) 564-7854), www.tandf.co.uk; *The Europa World Year Book.*

AMERICAN SAMOA - TELEPHONE

International Telecommunication Union (ITU), Place des Nations, 1211 Geneva 20, Switzerland, www.itu.int; World Telecommunication Indicators Database.

Taylor and Francis Group, An Informa Business, 2 Park Square, Milton Park, Abingdon, Oxford OX14 4RN, United Kingdom, (Dial from U.S. (212) 216-7800), (Fax from U.S. (212) 564-7854), www.tandf.co.uk; *The Europa World Year Book.*

United Nations Statistics Division, New York, NY 10017, (800) 253-9646, Fax: (212) 963-4116, http://unstats.un.org; *Statistical Yearbook* and *World Statistics Pocketbook.*

AMERICAN SAMOA - TEXTILE INDUSTRY

Secretariat of the Pacific Community (SPC), BP D5, 98848 Noumea Cedex, New Caledonia, www.spc.int/corp; *Selected Pacific Economies - a Statistical Summary (SPESS).*

United Nations Conference on Trade and Development (UNCTAD), DC2-1120, United Nations, New York, NY 10017, (212) 963-0027, www.unctad.org; *UNCTAD Commodity Yearbook.*

AMERICAN SAMOA - TOBACCO INDUSTRY

Foreign Agricultural Service (FAS), U.S. Department of Agriculture (USDA), 1400 Independence Avenue, SW, Washington, DC 20250, (202) 720-3935, www.fas.usda.gov; *Tobacco: World Markets and Trade.*

Secretariat of the Pacific Community (SPC), BP D5, 98848 Noumea Cedex, New Caledonia, www.spc.int/corp; *Selected Pacific Economies - a Statistical Summary (SPESS).*

AMERICAN SAMOA - TOURISM

Euromonitor International, Inc., 224 S. Michigan Avenue, Suite 1500, Chicago, IL 60604, (312) 922-1115, Fax: (312) 922-1157, www.euromonitor.com; *The World Economic Factbook 2008* and *World Marketing Data and Statistics.*

Taylor and Francis Group, An Informa Business, 2 Park Square, Milton Park, Abingdon, Oxford OX14 4RN, United Kingdom, (Dial from U.S. (212) 216-7800), (Fax from U.S. (212) 564-7854), www.tandf.co.uk; *The Europa World Year Book.*

United Nations World Tourism Organization (UNWTO), Capitan Haya 42, 28020 Madrid, Spain, www.world-tourism.org; *Yearbook of Tourism Statistics.*

The World Bank, 1818 H Street, NW, Washington, DC 20433, (202) 473-1000, Fax: (202) 477-6391, www.worldbank.org; *American Samoa.*

AMERICAN SAMOA - TRADE

See AMERICAN SAMOA - INTERNATIONAL TRADE

AMERICAN SAMOA - TRANSPORTATION

Central Intelligence Agency, Office of Public Affairs, Washington, DC 20505, (703) 482-0623, Fax: (703) 482-1739, www.cia.gov; *The World Factbook.*

Euromonitor International, Inc., 224 S. Michigan Avenue, Suite 1500, Chicago, IL 60604, (312) 922-1115, Fax: (312) 922-1157, www.euromonitor.com; *International Marketing Data and Statistics 2008* and *World Marketing Data and Statistics.*

Palgrave Macmillan Ltd., Houndmills, Basingstoke, Hampshire, RG21 6XS, England, (Telephone in U.S. (888) 330-8477), (Fax in U.S. (800) 672-2054), www.palgrave.com; *The Statesman's Yearbook 2008.*

Secretariat of the Pacific Community (SPC), BP D5, 98848 Noumea Cedex, New Caledonia, www.spc.int/corp; *Selected Pacific Economies - a Statistical Summary (SPESS).*

Taylor and Francis Group, An Informa Business, 2 Park Square, Milton Park, Abingdon, Oxford OX14 4RN, United Kingdom, (Dial from U.S. (212) 216-7800), (Fax from U.S. (212) 564-7854), www.tandf.co.uk; *The Europa World Year Book.*

The World Bank, 1818 H Street, NW, Washington, DC 20433, (202) 473-1000, Fax: (202) 477-6391, www.worldbank.org; *American Samoa.*

AMERICAN SAMOA - UNEMPLOYMENT

Central Intelligence Agency, Office of Public Affairs, Washington, DC 20505, (703) 482-0623, Fax: (703) 482-1739, www.cia.gov; *The World Factbook.*

International Labour Office, I.L.O. Publications, 4 route des Morillons, CH-1211 Geneva 22, Switzerland, (Telephone in U.S. (202) 653-7652), (Fax in U.S. (202) 653-7687), www.ilo.org; *Yearbook of Labour Statistics 2006.*

Palgrave Macmillan Ltd., Houndmills, Basingstoke, Hampshire, RG21 6XS, England, (Telephone in U.S. (888) 330-8477), (Fax in U.S. (800) 672-2054), www.palgrave.com; *The Statesman's Yearbook 2008.*

United Nations Statistics Division, New York, NY 10017, (800) 253-9646, Fax: (212) 963-4116, http://unstats.un.org; *Statistical Yearbook.*

AMERICAN SAMOA - VITAL STATISTICS

United Nations Statistics Division, New York, NY 10017, (800) 253-9646, Fax: (212) 963-4116, http://unstats.un.org; *Statistical Yearbook.*

World Health Organization (WHO), Avenue Appia 20, 1211 Geneve 27, Switzerland, (Telephone in U.S. (212) 331-9081), www.who.int; *World Health Report 2006.*

AMERICAN SAMOA - WAGES

International Labour Office, I.L.O. Publications, 4 route des Morillons, CH-1211 Geneva 22, Switzerland, (Telephone in U.S. (202) 653-7652), (Fax in U.S. (202) 653-7687), www.ilo.org; *Yearbook of Labour Statistics 2006.*

The World Bank, 1818 H Street, NW, Washington, DC 20433, (202) 473-1000, Fax: (202) 477-6391, www.worldbank.org; *American Samoa.*

AMERICAN SAMOA - WELFARE STATE

Palgrave Macmillan Ltd., Houndmills, Basingstoke, Hampshire, RG21 6XS, England, (Telephone in U.S. (888) 330-8477), (Fax in U.S. (800) 672-2054), www.palgrave.com; *The Statesman's Yearbook 2008.*

AMERICAN SIGN LANGUAGE

Association of Departments of Foreign Languages (ADFL), 26 Broadway, 3rd Floor, New York, NY 10004-1789, (646) 576-5140, www.adfl.org; *ADFL Bulletin.*

AMERICAN STOCK EXCHANGE

Securities and Exchange Commission (SEC), 100 F Street, NE, Washington, DC 20549, (202) 942-8088, www.sec.gov; *2007 Annual Report.*

AMERICAN STOCK EXCHANGE - COMPOSITE INDEX

Global Financial Data, Inc., 784 Fremont Villas, Los Angeles, CA 90042, (323) 924-1016, www.globalfindata.com; *Global Stock Market Indices.*

AMTRAK

Association of American Railroads (AAR), 50 F Street, NW, Washington, DC 20001-1564, (202) 639-2100, www.aar.org; *Analysis of Class I Railroads* and *Railroad Facts.*

AMUSEMENT PARKS

National Endowment for the Arts (NEA), 1100 Pennsylvania Avenue, NW, Washington, DC 20506-0001, (202) 682-5400, www.arts.gov; *2002 Survey of Public Participation in the Arts.*

U.S. Census Bureau, Center for Economic Studies, 4600 Silver Hill Road, Washington DC 20233, (301) 457-1235, www.ces.census.gov; *2002 Economic Census, Arts, Entertainment and Recreation.*

AMUSEMENT, GAMBLING, AND RECREATION INDUSTRY

U.S. Census Bureau, Company Statistics Division, 4700 Silver Hill Road, Washington DC 20233-0001, (301) 763-3030, www.census.gov/csd/; *County Business Patterns 2004.*

U.S. Census Bureau, Service Sector Statistics Division, 4700 Silver Hill Road, Washington DC 20233-0001, (301) 763-3030, www.census.gov/svsd/www/economic.html; *2004 Service Annual Survey: Arts, Entertainment, and Recreation.*

AMUSEMENT, GAMBLING, AND RECREATION INDUSTRY - EARNINGS

U.S. Census Bureau, Company Statistics Division, 4700 Silver Hill Road, Washington DC 20233-0001, (301) 763-3030, www.census.gov/csd/; *County Business Patterns 2004.*

U.S. Census Bureau, Service Sector Statistics Division, 4700 Silver Hill Road, Washington DC 20233-0001, (301) 763-3030, www.census.gov/svsd/www/economic.html; *2004 Service Annual Survey: Arts, Entertainment, and Recreation.*

AMUSEMENT, GAMBLING, AND RECREATION INDUSTRY - EMPLOYEES

U.S. Census Bureau, Company Statistics Division, 4700 Silver Hill Road, Washington DC 20233-0001, (301) 763-3030, www.census.gov/csd/; *County Business Patterns 2004.*

U.S. Census Bureau, Service Sector Statistics Division, 4700 Silver Hill Road, Washington DC 20233-0001, (301) 763-3030, www.census.gov/svsd/www/economic.html; *2004 Service Annual Survey: Arts, Entertainment, and Recreation.*

AMUSEMENT, GAMBLING, AND RECREATION INDUSTRY - NONEMPLOYER ESTABLISHMENTS

U.S. Census Bureau, 4700 Silver Hill Road, Washington DC 20233-0001, (301) 763-3030, www.census.gov; *2002 Economic Census, Nonemployer Statistics.*

AMUSEMENT, GAMBLING, AND RECREATION INDUSTRY - RECEIPTS AND REVENUE

U.S. Census Bureau, Center for Economic Studies, 4600 Silver Hill Road, Washington DC 20233, (301) 457-1235, www.ces.census.gov; *2002 Economic Census, Information.*

U.S. Census Bureau, Company Statistics Division, 4700 Silver Hill Road, Washington DC 20233-0001, (301) 763-3030, www.census.gov/csd/; *County Business Patterns 2004.*

U.S. Census Bureau, Service Sector Statistics Division, 4700 Silver Hill Road, Washington DC 20233-0001, (301) 763-3030, www.census.gov/svsd/www/economic.html; *2004 Service Annual Survey: Arts, Entertainment, and Recreation.*

ANALGESICS

Substance Abuse and Mental Health Services Administration (SAMHSA), 1 Choke Cherry Road, Rockville, MD 20857, (240) 777-1311, www.oas.samhsa.gov; *National Survey on Drug Use Health (NSDUH).*

ANCESTRY

Population Reference Bureau, 1875 Connecticut Avenue, NW, Suite 520, Washington, DC, 20009-5728, (800) 877-9881, Fax: (202) 328-3937, www.prb.org; *The American People Series.*

U.S. Census Bureau, 4700 Silver Hill Road, Washington DC 20233-0001, (301) 763-3030, www.census.gov; American FactFinder (web app); *County and City Data Book 2007;* and *State and County QuickFacts.*

U.S. Census Bureau, Demographic Surveys Division, 4700 Silver Hill Road, Washington DC 20233-0001, (301) 763-3030, www.census.gov; *Demographic Profiles: 100-percent and Sample Data.*

U.S. Census Bureau, Population Division, 4700 Silver Hill Road, Washington DC 20233-0001, (301) 763-3030, www.census.gov/population/www/; *Census 2000 Profiles of General Demographic Characteristics.*

ANCHOVIES

National Marine Fisheries Service (NMFS), National Oceanic and Atmospheric Administration (NOAA), Office of Constituent Services, 1315 East West Highway, 9th Floor, Silver Spring, MD 20910, (301) 713-2379, Fax: (301) 713-2385, www.nmfs.noaa.gov; *Fisheries of the United States - 2006.*

ANDORRA - NATIONAL STATISTICAL OFFICE

Servei d'Estudis, Ministeri de Finances, C/ Prat de la Creu, num. 62-64, Andorra la Vella, Andorra, www.estadistica.ad; National Data Center.

ANDORRA - ABORTION

United Nations Statistics Division, New York, NY 10017, (800) 253-9646, Fax: (212) 963-4116, http://unstats.un.org; *Trends in Europe and North America: The Statistical Yearbook of the ECE 2005.*

ANDORRA - AGRICULTURE

Palgrave Macmillan Ltd., Houndmills, Basingstoke, Hampshire, RG21 6XS, England, (Telephone in U.S. (888) 330-8477), (Fax in U.S. (800) 672-2054), www.palgrave.com; *The Statesman's Yearbook 2008.*

Taylor and Francis Group, An Informa Business, 2 Park Square, Milton Park, Abingdon, Oxford OX14 4RN, United Kingdom, (Dial from U.S. (212) 216-7800), (Fax from U.S. (212) 564-7854), www.tandf.co.uk; *The Europa World Year Book.*

United Nations Conference on Trade and Development (UNCTAD), DC2-1120, United Nations, New York, NY 10017, (212) 963-0027, www.unctad.org; *UNCTAD Commodity Yearbook.*

United Nations Food and Agricultural Organization (FAO), Viale delle Terme di Caracalla, 00100 Rome, Italy, (Dial from U.S. (202) 653-2400), (Fax from U.S. (202) 653 5760), www.fao.org; AQUASTAT; *FAO Production Yearbook 2002; FAO Trade Yearbook;* and *The State of Food and Agriculture (SOFA) 2006.*

The World Bank, 1818 H Street, NW, Washington, DC 20433, (202) 473-1000, Fax: (202) 477-6391, www.worldbank.org; *Andorra.*

ANDORRA - AIRLINES

Palgrave Macmillan Ltd., Houndmills, Basingstoke, Hampshire, RG21 6XS, England, (Telephone in U.S. (888) 330-8477), (Fax in U.S. (800) 672-2054), www.palgrave.com; *The Statesman's Yearbook 2008.*

ANDORRA - AIRPORTS

Central Intelligence Agency, Office of Public Affairs, Washington, DC 20505, (703) 482-0623, Fax: (703) 482-1739, www.cia.gov; *The World Factbook.*

ANDORRA - ARMED FORCES

Central Intelligence Agency, Office of Public Affairs, Washington, DC 20505, (703) 482-0623, Fax: (703) 482-1739, www.cia.gov; *The World Factbook.*

ANDORRA - BROADCASTING

Central Intelligence Agency, Office of Public Affairs, Washington, DC 20505, (703) 482-0623, Fax: (703) 482-1739, www.cia.gov; *The World Factbook.*

Palgrave Macmillan Ltd., Houndmills, Basingstoke, Hampshire, RG21 6XS, England, (Telephone in U.S. (888) 330-8477), (Fax in U.S. (800) 672-2054), www.palgrave.com; *The Statesman's Yearbook 2008.*

United Nations Statistics Division, New York, NY 10017, (800) 253-9646, Fax: (212) 963-4116, http://unstats.un.org; *Trends in Europe and North America: The Statistical Yearbook of the ECE 2005.*

WRTH Publications Limited, PO Box 290, Oxford OX2 7FT, UK, www.wrth.com; *World Radio TV Handbook 2007.*

ANDORRA - BUDGET

Central Intelligence Agency, Office of Public Affairs, Washington, DC 20505, (703) 482-0623, Fax: (703) 482-1739, www.cia.gov; *The World Factbook.*

ANDORRA - CHILDBIRTH - STATISTICS

Central Intelligence Agency, Office of Public Affairs, Washington, DC 20505, (703) 482-0623, Fax: (703) 482-1739, www.cia.gov; *The World Factbook.*

Euromonitor International, Inc., 224 S. Michigan Avenue, Suite 1500, Chicago, IL 60604, (312) 922-1115, Fax: (312) 922-1157, www.euromonitor.com; *The World Economic Factbook 2008.*

Taylor and Francis Group, An Informa Business, 2 Park Square, Milton Park, Abingdon, Oxford OX14 4RN, United Kingdom, (Dial from U.S. (212) 216-7800), (Fax from U.S. (212) 564-7854), www.tandf.co.uk; *The Europa World Year Book.*

United Nations Statistics Division, New York, NY 10017, (800) 253-9646, Fax: (212) 963-4116, http://unstats.un.org; *Demographic Yearbook.*

World Health Organization (WHO), Avenue Appia 20, 1211 Geneve 27, Switzerland, (Telephone in U.S. (212) 331-9081), www.who.int; *World Health Report 2006.*

ANDORRA - CLIMATE

Palgrave Macmillan Ltd., Houndmills, Basingstoke, Hampshire, RG21 6XS, England, (Telephone in U.S. (888) 330-8477), (Fax in U.S. (800) 672-2054), www.palgrave.com; *The Statesman's Yearbook 2008.*

ANDORRA - COMMERCE

Palgrave Macmillan Ltd., Houndmills, Basingstoke, Hampshire, RG21 6XS, England, (Telephone in U.S. (888) 330-8477), (Fax in U.S. (800) 672-2054), www.palgrave.com; *The Statesman's Yearbook 2008.*

ANDORRA - COMMODITY EXCHANGES

United Nations Food and Agricultural Organization (FAO), Viale delle Terme di Caracalla, 00100 Rome, Italy, (Dial from U.S. (202) 653-2400), (Fax from U.S. (202) 653 5760), www.fao.org; *The State of Food and Agriculture (SOFA) 2006.*

ANDORRA - CONSUMER PRICE INDEXES

United Nations Statistics Division, New York, NY 10017, (800) 253-9646, Fax: (212) 963-4116, http://unstats.un.org; *Trends in Europe and North America: The Statistical Yearbook of the ECE 2005.*

The World Bank, 1818 H Street, NW, Washington, DC 20433, (202) 473-1000, Fax: (202) 477-6391, www.worldbank.org; *Andorra.*

ANDORRA - CORN INDUSTRY

See ANDORRA - CROPS

ANDORRA - CRIME

United Nations Statistics Division, New York, NY 10017, (800) 253-9646, Fax: (212) 963-4116, http://unstats.un.org; *Trends in Europe and North America: The Statistical Yearbook of the ECE 2005.*

ANDORRA - CROPS

Palgrave Macmillan Ltd., Houndmills, Basingstoke, Hampshire, RG21 6XS, England, (Telephone in U.S. (888) 330-8477), (Fax in U.S. (800) 672-2054), www.palgrave.com; *The Statesman's Yearbook 2008.*

Taylor and Francis Group, An Informa Business, 2 Park Square, Milton Park, Abingdon, Oxford OX14 4RN, United Kingdom, (Dial from U.S. (212) 216-7800), (Fax from U.S. (212) 564-7854), www.tandf.co.uk; *The Europa World Year Book.*

United Nations Conference on Trade and Development (UNCTAD), DC2-1120, United Nations, New York, NY 10017, (212) 963-0027, www.unctad.org; *UNCTAD Commodity Yearbook.*

United Nations Food and Agricultural Organization (FAO), Viale delle Terme di Caracalla, 00100 Rome, Italy, (Dial from U.S. (202) 653-2400), (Fax from U.S. (202) 653 5760), www.fao.org; *The State of Food and Agriculture (SOFA) 2006.*

ANDORRA - CUSTOMS ADMINISTRATION

Palgrave Macmillan Ltd., Houndmills, Basingstoke, Hampshire, RG21 6XS, England, (Telephone in U.S. (888) 330-8477), (Fax in U.S. (800) 672-2054), www.palgrave.com; *The Statesman's Yearbook 2008.*

ANDORRA - DEATH RATES

See ANDORRA - MORTALITY

ANDORRA - DEMOGRAPHY

Euromonitor International, Inc., 224 S. Michigan Avenue, Suite 1500, Chicago, IL 60604, (312) 922-1115, Fax: (312) 922-1157, www.euromonitor.com; *The World Economic Factbook 2008.*

The World Bank, 1818 H Street, NW, Washington, DC 20433, (202) 473-1000, Fax: (202) 477-6391, www.worldbank.org; *Andorra.*

ANDORRA - DIVORCE

United Nations Statistics Division, New York, NY 10017, (800) 253-9646, Fax: (212) 963-4116, http://unstats.un.org; *Demographic Yearbook* and *Trends in Europe and North America: The Statistical Yearbook of the ECE 2005.*

ANDORRA - ECONOMIC CONDITIONS

Central Intelligence Agency, Office of Public Affairs, Washington, DC 20505, (703) 482-0623, Fax: (703) 482-1739, www.cia.gov; *The World Factbook.*

Euromonitor International, Inc., 224 S. Michigan Avenue, Suite 1500, Chicago, IL 60604, (312) 922-1115, Fax: (312) 922-1157, www.euromonitor.com; *The World Economic Factbook 2008.*

Palgrave Macmillan Ltd., Houndmills, Basingstoke, Hampshire, RG21 6XS, England, (Telephone in U.S. (888) 330-8477), (Fax in U.S. (800) 672-2054), www.palgrave.com; *The Statesman's Yearbook 2008.*

Taylor and Francis Group, An Informa Business, 2 Park Square, Milton Park, Abingdon, Oxford OX14 4RN, United Kingdom, (Dial from U.S. (212) 216-7800), (Fax from U.S. (212) 564-7854), www.tandf.co.uk; *The Europa World Year Book.*

United Nations Statistics Division, New York, NY 10017, (800) 253-9646, Fax: (212) 963-4116, http://unstats.un.org; *World Statistics Pocketbook.*

The World Bank, 1818 H Street, NW, Washington, DC 20433, (202) 473-1000, Fax: (202) 477-6391, www.worldbank.org; *Andorra* and *The World Bank Atlas 2003-2004.*

ANDORRA - EDUCATION

European Union, Delegation of the European Commission to the United States, 2300 M Street, NW, Washington, DC 20037, (202) 862-9500, Fax: (202) 429-1766, www.eurunion.org; *Education across Europe 2003.*

Palgrave Macmillan Ltd., Houndmills, Basingstoke, Hampshire, RG21 6XS, England, (Telephone in U.S. (888) 330-8477), (Fax in U.S. (800) 672-2054), www.palgrave.com; *The Statesman's Yearbook 2008.*

Taylor and Francis Group, An Informa Business, 2 Park Square, Milton Park, Abingdon, Oxford OX14 4RN, United Kingdom, (Dial from U.S. (212) 216-7800), (Fax from U.S. (212) 564-7854), www.tandf.co.uk; *The Europa World Year Book.*

United Nations Statistics Division, New York, NY 10017, (800) 253-9646, Fax: (212) 963-4116, http://unstats.un.org; *Trends in Europe and North America: The Statistical Yearbook of the ECE 2005.*

The World Bank, 1818 H Street, NW, Washington, DC 20433, (202) 473-1000, Fax: (202) 477-6391, www.worldbank.org; *Andorra.*

ANDORRA - EGG TRADE

United Nations Food and Agricultural Organization (FAO), Viale delle Terme di Caracalla, 00100 Rome, Italy, (Dial from U.S. (202) 653-2400), (Fax from U.S. (202) 653 5760), www.fao.org; *The State of Food and Agriculture (SOFA) 2006.*

ANDORRA - ELECTRICITY

Palgrave Macmillan Ltd., Houndmills, Basingstoke, Hampshire, RG21 6XS, England, (Telephone in U.S. (888) 330-8477), (Fax in U.S. (800) 672-2054), www.palgrave.com; *The Statesman's Yearbook 2008.*

United Nations Statistics Division, New York, NY 10017, (800) 253-9646, Fax: (212) 963-4116, http://unstats.un.org; *Trends in Europe and North America: The Statistical Yearbook of the ECE 2005.*

ANDORRA - EMPLOYMENT

United Nations Statistics Division, New York, NY 10017, (800) 253-9646, Fax: (212) 963-4116, http://unstats.un.org; *Trends in Europe and North America: The Statistical Yearbook of the ECE 2005.*

The World Bank, 1818 H Street, NW, Washington, DC 20433, (202) 473-1000, Fax: (202) 477-6391, www.worldbank.org; *Andorra.*

ANDORRA - ENVIRONMENTAL CONDITIONS

Center for Research on the Epidemiology of Disasters (CRED), Universite Catholique de Louvain, Ecole de Sante Publique, 30.94 Clos Chapelle-aux-Champs, 1200 Brussels, Belgium, www.cred.be; *Three Decades of Floods in Europe: A Preliminary Analysis of EMDAT Data.*

DSI Data Service Information, Xantener Strasse 51a, D-47495 Rheinberg, Germany, www.dsidata.com; *Campus Solution.*

Eurostat, Batiment Jean Monnet, Rue Alcide de Gasperi, L-2920 Luxembourg, http://epp.eurostat.ec.europa.eu; *Environmental Protection Expenditure in Europe.*

United Nations Statistics Division, New York, NY 10017, (800) 253-9646, Fax: (212) 963-4116, http://unstats.un.org; *Trends in Europe and North America: The Statistical Yearbook of the ECE 2005* and *World Statistics Pocketbook.*

ANDORRA - EXPORTS

Central Intelligence Agency, Office of Public Affairs, Washington, DC 20505, (703) 482-0623, Fax: (703) 482-1739, www.cia.gov; *The World Factbook.*

Euromonitor International, Inc., 224 S. Michigan Avenue, Suite 1500, Chicago, IL 60604, (312) 922-1115, Fax: (312) 922-1157, www.euromonitor.com; *The World Economic Factbook 2008.*

Palgrave Macmillan Ltd., Houndmills, Basingstoke, Hampshire, RG21 6XS, England, (Telephone in U.S. (888) 330-8477), (Fax in U.S. (800) 672-2054), www.palgrave.com; *The Statesman's Yearbook 2008.*

Taylor and Francis Group, An Informa Business, 2 Park Square, Milton Park, Abingdon, Oxford OX14 4RN, United Kingdom, (Dial from U.S. (212) 216-7800), (Fax from U.S. (212) 564-7854), www.tandf.co.uk; *The Europa World Year Book.*

United Nations Food and Agricultural Organization (FAO), Viale delle Terme di Caracalla, 00100 Rome, Italy, (Dial from U.S. (202) 653-2400), (Fax from U.S. (202) 653 5760), www.fao.org; *The State of Food and Agriculture (SOFA) 2006.*

United Nations Statistics Division, New York, NY 10017, (800) 253-9646, Fax: (212) 963-4116, http://unstats.un.org; *Trends in Europe and North America: The Statistical Yearbook of the ECE 2005.*

ANDORRA - FERTILITY, HUMAN

United Nations Statistics Division, New York, NY 10017, (800) 253-9646, Fax: (212) 963-4116, http://unstats.un.org; *Trends in Europe and North America: The Statistical Yearbook of the ECE 2005.*

The World Bank, 1818 H Street, NW, Washington, DC 20433, (202) 473-1000, Fax: (202) 477-6391, www.worldbank.org; *The World Bank Atlas 2003-2004.*

ANDORRA - FERTILIZER INDUSTRY

United Nations Food and Agricultural Organization (FAO), Viale delle Terme di Caracalla, 00100 Rome, Italy, (Dial from U.S. (202) 653-2400), (Fax from U.S. (202) 653 5760), www.fao.org; *The State of Food and Agriculture (SOFA) 2006.*

ANDORRA - FETAL MORTALITY

See ANDORRA - MORTALITY

ANDORRA - FINANCE, PUBLIC

Banque de France, 48 rue Croix des Petits champs, 75001 Paris, France, www.banque-france.fr/home.htm; *Public Finance.*

Palgrave Macmillan Ltd., Houndmills, Basingstoke, Hampshire, RG21 6XS, England, (Telephone in U.S. (888) 330-8477), (Fax in U.S. (800) 672-2054), www.palgrave.com; *The Statesman's Yearbook 2008.*

Taylor and Francis Group, An Informa Business, 2 Park Square, Milton Park, Abingdon, Oxford OX14 4RN, United Kingdom, (Dial from U.S. (212) 216-7800), (Fax from U.S. (212) 564-7854), www.tandf.co.uk; *The Europa World Year Book.*

The World Bank, 1818 H Street, NW, Washington, DC 20433, (202) 473-1000, Fax: (202) 477-6391, www.worldbank.org; *Andorra.*

ANDORRA - FISHERIES

United Nations Conference on Trade and Development (UNCTAD), DC2-1120, United Nations, New York, NY 10017, (212) 963-0027, www.unctad.org; *UNCTAD Commodity Yearbook.*

United Nations Food and Agricultural Organization (FAO), Viale delle Terme di Caracalla, 00100 Rome, Italy, (Dial from U.S. (202) 653-2400), (Fax from U.S. (202) 653 5760), www.fao.org; *FAO Yearbook of Fishery Statistics;* Fishery Databases; FISHSTAT Database. Subjects covered include: Aquaculture production, capture production, fishery commodities; and *The State of Food and Agriculture (SOFA) 2006.*

The World Bank, 1818 H Street, NW, Washington, DC 20433, (202) 473-1000, Fax: (202) 477-6391, www.worldbank.org; *Andorra.*

ANDORRA - FOOD

United Nations Conference on Trade and Development (UNCTAD), DC2-1120, United Nations, New York, NY 10017, (212) 963-0027, www.unctad.org; *UNCTAD Commodity Yearbook.*

United Nations Food and Agricultural Organization (FAO), Viale delle Terme di Caracalla, 00100 Rome, Italy, (Dial from U.S. (202) 653-2400), (Fax from U.S. (202) 653 5760), www.fao.org; *FAO Production Yearbook 2002* and *The State of Food and Agriculture (SOFA) 2006.*

ANDORRA - FOREIGN EXCHANGE RATES

Central Intelligence Agency, Office of Public Affairs, Washington, DC 20505, (703) 482-0623, Fax: (703) 482-1739, www.cia.gov; *The World Factbook.*

Euromonitor International, Inc., 224 S. Michigan Avenue, Suite 1500, Chicago, IL 60604, (312) 922-1115, Fax: (312) 922-1157, www.euromonitor.com; *The World Economic Factbook 2008.*

Taylor and Francis Group, An Informa Business, 2 Park Square, Milton Park, Abingdon, Oxford OX14 4RN, United Kingdom, (Dial from U.S. (212) 216-7800), (Fax from U.S. (212) 564-7854), www.tandf.co.uk; *The Europa World Year Book.*

United Nations Statistics Division, New York, NY 10017, (800) 253-9646, Fax: (212) 963-4116, http://unstats.un.org; *Trends in Europe and North America: The Statistical Yearbook of the ECE 2005* and *World Statistics Pocketbook.*

ANDORRA - FORESTS AND FORESTRY

Palgrave Macmillan Ltd., Houndmills, Basingstoke, Hampshire, RG21 6XS, England, (Telephone in U.S. (888) 330-8477), (Fax in U.S. (800) 672-2054), www.palgrave.com; *The Statesman's Yearbook 2008.*

UNESCO Institute for Statistics, C.P. 6128 Succursale Centre-Ville, Montreal, Quebec, H3C 3J7 Canada, (Dial from U.S. (514) 343-6880), (Fax from U.S. (514) 343 6882), www.uis.unesco.org; *Statistical Tables.*

United Nations Conference on Trade and Development (UNCTAD), DC2-1120, United Nations, New York, NY 10017, (212) 963-0027, www.unctad.org; *UNCTAD Commodity Yearbook.*

United Nations Food and Agricultural Organization (FAO), Viale delle Terme di Caracalla, 00100 Rome, Italy, (Dial from U.S. (202) 653-2400), (Fax from U.S. (202) 653 5760), www.fao.org; *The State of Food and Agriculture (SOFA) 2006.*

United Nations Statistics Division, New York, NY 10017, (800) 253-9646, Fax: (212) 963-4116, http://unstats.un.org; *Trends in Europe and North America: The Statistical Yearbook of the ECE 2005.*

The World Bank, 1818 H Street, NW, Washington, DC 20433, (202) 473-1000, Fax: (202) 477-6391, www.worldbank.org; *Andorra.*

ANDORRA - GROSS DOMESTIC PRODUCT

Euromonitor International, Inc., 224 S. Michigan Avenue, Suite 1500, Chicago, IL 60604, (312) 922-1115, Fax: (312) 922-1157, www.euromonitor.com; *The World Economic Factbook 2008.*

United Nations Statistics Division, New York, NY 10017, (800) 253-9646, Fax: (212) 963-4116, http://unstats.un.org; *Trends in Europe and North America: The Statistical Yearbook of the ECE 2005.*

The World Bank, 1818 H Street, NW, Washington, DC 20433, (202) 473-1000, Fax: (202) 477-6391, www.worldbank.org; *The World Bank Atlas 2003-2004.*

ANDORRA - HOUSING

United Nations Statistics Division, New York, NY 10017, (800) 253-9646, Fax: (212) 963-4116, http://unstats.un.org; *Trends in Europe and North America: The Statistical Yearbook of the ECE 2005.*

ANDORRA - ILLITERATE PERSONS

Euromonitor International, Inc., 224 S. Michigan Avenue, Suite 1500, Chicago, IL 60604, (312) 922-

1115, Fax: (312) 922-1157, www.euromonitor.com; *The World Economic Factbook 2008.*

ANDORRA - IMPORTS

Central Intelligence Agency, Office of Public Affairs, Washington, DC 20505, (703) 482-0623, Fax: (703) 482-1739, www.cia.gov; *The World Factbook.*

Euromonitor International, Inc., 224 S. Michigan Avenue, Suite 1500, Chicago, IL 60604, (312) 922-1115, Fax: (312) 922-1157, www.euromonitor.com; *The World Economic Factbook 2008.*

Palgrave Macmillan Ltd., Houndmills, Basingstoke, Hampshire, RG21 6XS, England, (Telephone in U.S. (888) 330-8477), (Fax in U.S. (800) 672-2054), www.palgrave.com; *The Statesman's Yearbook 2008.*

Taylor and Francis Group, An Informa Business, 2 Park Square, Milton Park, Abingdon, Oxford OX14 4RN, United Kingdom, (Dial from U.S. (212) 216-7800), (Fax from U.S. (212) 564-7854), www.tandf.co.uk; *The Europa World Year Book.*

United Nations Food and Agricultural Organization (FAO), Viale delle Terme di Caracalla, 00100 Rome, Italy, (Dial from U.S. (202) 653-2400), (Fax from U.S. (202) 653 5760), www.fao.org; *The State of Food and Agriculture (SOFA) 2006.*

United Nations Statistics Division, New York, NY 10017, (800) 253-9646, Fax: (212) 963-4116, http://unstats.un.org; *Trends in Europe and North America: The Statistical Yearbook of the ECE 2005.*

ANDORRA - INDUSTRIES

Central Intelligence Agency, Office of Public Affairs, Washington, DC 20505, (703) 482-0623, Fax: (703) 482-1739, www.cia.gov; *The World Factbook.*

Euromonitor International, Inc., 224 S. Michigan Avenue, Suite 1500, Chicago, IL 60604, (312) 922-1115, Fax: (312) 922-1157, www.euromonitor.com; *The World Economic Factbook 2008.*

Palgrave Macmillan Ltd., Houndmills, Basingstoke, Hampshire, RG21 6XS, England, (Telephone in U.S. (888) 330-8477), (Fax in U.S. (800) 672-2054), www.palgrave.com; *The Statesman's Yearbook 2008.*

United Nations Statistics Division, New York, NY 10017, (800) 253-9646, Fax: (212) 963-4116, http://unstats.un.org; *Trends in Europe and North America: The Statistical Yearbook of the ECE 2005.*

The World Bank, 1818 H Street, NW, Washington, DC 20433, (202) 473-1000, Fax: (202) 477-6391, www.worldbank.org; *Andorra.*

ANDORRA - INFANT AND MATERNAL MORTALITY

See ANDORRA - MORTALITY

ANDORRA - INTERNATIONAL TRADE

Banque de France, 48 rue Croix des Petits champs, 75001 Paris, France, www.banque-france.fr/home.htm; *Monthly Business Survey Overview.*

Euromonitor International, Inc., 224 S. Michigan Avenue, Suite 1500, Chicago, IL 60604, (312) 922-1115, Fax: (312) 922-1157, www.euromonitor.com; *The World Economic Factbook 2008.*

Palgrave Macmillan Ltd., Houndmills, Basingstoke, Hampshire, RG21 6XS, England, (Telephone in U.S. (888) 330-8477), (Fax in U.S. (800) 672-2054), www.palgrave.com; *The Statesman's Yearbook 2008.*

Taylor and Francis Group, An Informa Business, 2 Park Square, Milton Park, Abingdon, Oxford OX14 4RN, United Kingdom, (Dial from U.S. (212) 216-7800), (Fax from U.S. (212) 564-7854), www.tandf.co.uk; *The Europa World Year Book.*

United Nations Conference on Trade and Development (UNCTAD), DC2-1120, United Nations, New York, NY 10017, (212) 963-0027, www.unctad.org; *UNCTAD Commodity Yearbook.*

United Nations Food and Agricultural Organization (FAO), Viale delle Terme di Caracalla, 00100 Rome, Italy, (Dial from U.S. (202) 653-2400), (Fax from U.S. (202) 653 5760), www.fao.org; *FAO Trade Yearbook* and *The State of Food and Agriculture (SOFA) 2006.*

The World Bank, 1818 H Street, NW, Washington, DC 20433, (202) 473-1000, Fax: (202) 477-6391, www.worldbank.org; *Andorra.*

World Trade Organization (WTO), Centre William Rappard, Rue de Lausanne 154, CH-1211 Geneva 21, Switzerland, www.wto.org; *International Trade Statistics 2006.*

ANDORRA - LABOR

Central Intelligence Agency, Office of Public Affairs, Washington, DC 20505, (703) 482-0623, Fax: (703) 482-1739, www.cia.gov; *The World Factbook.*

Palgrave Macmillan Ltd., Houndmills, Basingstoke, Hampshire, RG21 6XS, England, (Telephone in U.S. (888) 330-8477), (Fax in U.S. (800) 672-2054), www.palgrave.com; *The Statesman's Yearbook 2008.*

United Nations Food and Agricultural Organization (FAO), Viale delle Terme di Caracalla, 00100 Rome, Italy, (Dial from U.S. (202) 653-2400), (Fax from U.S. (202) 653 5760), www.fao.org; *The State of Food and Agriculture (SOFA) 2006.*

The World Bank, 1818 H Street, NW, Washington, DC 20433, (202) 473-1000, Fax: (202) 477-6391, www.worldbank.org; *The World Bank Atlas 2003-2004.*

ANDORRA - LAND USE

Central Intelligence Agency, Office of Public Affairs, Washington, DC 20505, (703) 482-0623, Fax: (703) 482-1739, www.cia.gov; *The World Factbook.*

United Nations Food and Agricultural Organization (FAO), Viale delle Terme di Caracalla, 00100 Rome, Italy, (Dial from U.S. (202) 653-2400), (Fax from U.S. (202) 653 5760), www.fao.org; *FAO Production Yearbook 2002.*

ANDORRA - LIBRARIES

United Nations Statistics Division, New York, NY 10017, (800) 253-9646, Fax: (212) 963-4116, http://unstats.un.org; *Trends in Europe and North America: The Statistical Yearbook of the ECE 2005.*

ANDORRA - LIFE EXPECTANCY

Euromonitor International, Inc., 224 S. Michigan Avenue, Suite 1500, Chicago, IL 60604, (312) 922-1115, Fax: (312) 922-1157, www.euromonitor.com; *The World Economic Factbook 2008.*

United Nations Statistics Division, New York, NY 10017, (800) 253-9646, Fax: (212) 963-4116, http://unstats.un.org; *Trends in Europe and North America: The Statistical Yearbook of the ECE 2005* and *World Statistics Pocketbook.*

The World Bank, 1818 H Street, NW, Washington, DC 20433, (202) 473-1000, Fax: (202) 477-6391, www.worldbank.org; *The World Bank Atlas 2003-2004.*

ANDORRA - LIVESTOCK

Taylor and Francis Group, An Informa Business, 2 Park Square, Milton Park, Abingdon, Oxford OX14 4RN, United Kingdom, (Dial from U.S. (212) 216-7800), (Fax from U.S. (212) 564-7854), www.tandf.co.uk; *The Europa World Year Book.*

United Nations Conference on Trade and Development (UNCTAD), DC2-1120, United Nations, New York, NY 10017, (212) 963-0027, www.unctad.org; *UNCTAD Commodity Yearbook.*

United Nations Food and Agricultural Organization (FAO), Viale delle Terme di Caracalla, 00100 Rome, Italy, (Dial from U.S. (202) 653-2400), (Fax from U.S. (202) 653 5760), www.fao.org; *FAO Production Yearbook 2002* and *The State of Food and Agriculture (SOFA) 2006.*

ANDORRA - MARRIAGE

Taylor and Francis Group, An Informa Business, 2 Park Square, Milton Park, Abingdon, Oxford OX14 4RN, United Kingdom, (Dial from U.S. (212) 216-7800), (Fax from U.S. (212) 564-7854), www.tandf.co.uk; *The Europa World Year Book.*

United Nations Statistics Division, New York, NY 10017, (800) 253-9646, Fax: (212) 963-4116, http://unstats.un.org; *Demographic Yearbook* and *Trends in Europe and North America: The Statistical Yearbook of the ECE 2005.*

ANDORRA - MEAT PRODUCTION

See ANDORRA - LIVESTOCK

ANDORRA - MINERAL INDUSTRIES

United Nations Conference on Trade and Development (UNCTAD), DC2-1120, United Nations, New York, NY 10017, (212) 963-0027, www.unctad.org; *UNCTAD Commodity Yearbook.*

ANDORRA - MORTALITY

Central Intelligence Agency, Office of Public Affairs, Washington, DC 20505, (703) 482-0623, Fax: (703) 482-1739, www.cia.gov; *The World Factbook.*

Euromonitor International, Inc., 224 S. Michigan Avenue, Suite 1500, Chicago, IL 60604, (312) 922-1115, Fax: (312) 922-1157, www.euromonitor.com; *The World Economic Factbook 2008.*

Taylor and Francis Group, An Informa Business, 2 Park Square, Milton Park, Abingdon, Oxford OX14 4RN, United Kingdom, (Dial from U.S. (212) 216-7800), (Fax from U.S. (212) 564-7854), www.tandf.co.uk; *The Europa World Year Book.*

United Nations Statistics Division, New York, NY 10017, (800) 253-9646, Fax: (212) 963-4116, http://unstats.un.org; *Demographic Yearbook; Trends in Europe and North America: The Statistical Yearbook of the ECE 2005;* and *World Statistics Pocketbook.*

The World Bank, 1818 H Street, NW, Washington, DC 20433, (202) 473-1000, Fax: (202) 477-6391, www.worldbank.org; *The World Bank Atlas 2003-2004.*

World Health Organization (WHO), Avenue Appia 20, 1211 Geneve 27, Switzerland, (Telephone in U.S. (212) 331-9081), www.who.int; *World Health Report 2006.*

ANDORRA - MOTOR VEHICLES

Taylor and Francis Group, An Informa Business, 2 Park Square, Milton Park, Abingdon, Oxford OX14 4RN, United Kingdom, (Dial from U.S. (212) 216-7800), (Fax from U.S. (212) 564-7854), www.tandf.co.uk; *The Europa World Year Book.*

ANDORRA - MUSEUMS

UNESCO Institute for Statistics, C.P. 6128 Succursale Centre-Ville, Montreal, Quebec, H3C 3J7 Canada, (Dial from U.S. (514) 343-6880), (Fax from U.S. (514) 343 6882), www.uis.unesco.org; *Statistical Tables.*

ANDORRA - NUTRITION

United Nations Food and Agricultural Organization (FAO), Viale delle Terme di Caracalla, 00100 Rome, Italy, (Dial from U.S. (202) 653-2400), (Fax from U.S. (202) 653 5760), www.fao.org; *The State of Food and Agriculture (SOFA) 2006.*

ANDORRA - PESTICIDES

United Nations Food and Agricultural Organization (FAO), Viale delle Terme di Caracalla, 00100 Rome, Italy, (Dial from U.S. (202) 653-2400), (Fax from U.S. (202) 653 5760), www.fao.org; *The State of Food and Agriculture (SOFA) 2006.*

ANDORRA - PETROLEUM INDUSTRY AND TRADE

PennWell Corporation, 1421 South Sheridan Road, Tulsa, OK 74112, (918) 835-3161, www.pennwell.com; *International Petroleum Encyclopedia 2007.*

United Nations Conference on Trade and Development (UNCTAD), DC2-1120, United Nations, New York, NY 10017, (212) 963-0027, www.unctad.org; *UNCTAD Commodity Yearbook.*

United Nations Food and Agricultural Organization (FAO), Viale delle Terme di Caracalla, 00100 Rome,

Italy, (Dial from U.S. (202) 653-2400), (Fax from U.S. (202) 653 5760), www.fao.org; *The State of Food and Agriculture (SOFA) 2006.*

United Nations Statistics Division, New York, NY 10017, (800) 253-9646, Fax: (212) 963-4116, http://unstats.un.org; *Trends in Europe and North America: The Statistical Yearbook of the ECE 2005.*

ANDORRA - POLITICAL SCIENCE

Central Intelligence Agency, Office of Public Affairs, Washington, DC 20505, (703) 482-0623, Fax: (703) 482-1739, www.cia.gov; *The World Factbook.*

Palgrave Macmillan Ltd., Houndmills, Basingstoke, Hampshire, RG21 6XS, England, (Telephone in U.S. (888) 330-8477), (Fax in U.S. (800) 672-2054), www.palgrave.com; *The Statesman's Yearbook 2008.*

Taylor and Francis Group, An Informa Business, 2 Park Square, Milton Park, Abingdon, Oxford OX14 4RN, United Kingdom, (Dial from U.S. (212) 216-7800), (Fax from U.S. (212) 564-7854), www.tandf.co.uk; *The Europa World Year Book.*

ANDORRA - POPULATION

Central Intelligence Agency, Office of Public Affairs, Washington, DC 20505, (703) 482-0623, Fax: (703) 482-1739, www.cia.gov; *The World Factbook.*

Euromonitor International, Inc., 224 S. Michigan Avenue, Suite 1500, Chicago, IL 60604, (312) 922-1115, Fax: (312) 922-1157, www.euromonitor.com; *The World Economic Factbook 2008.*

Palgrave Macmillan Ltd., Houndmills, Basingstoke, Hampshire, RG21 6XS, England, (Telephone in U.S. (888) 330-8477), (Fax in U.S. (800) 672-2054), www.palgrave.com; *The Statesman's Yearbook 2008.*

Taylor and Francis Group, An Informa Business, 2 Park Square, Milton Park, Abingdon, Oxford OX14 4RN, United Kingdom, (Dial from U.S. (212) 216-7800), (Fax from U.S. (212) 564-7854), www.tandf.co.uk; *The Europa World Year Book.*

United Nations Food and Agricultural Organization (FAO), Viale delle Terme di Caracalla, 00100 Rome, Italy, (Dial from U.S. (202) 653-2400), (Fax from U.S. (202) 653 5760), www.fao.org; *FAO Production Yearbook 2002.*

United Nations Statistics Division, New York, NY 10017, (800) 253-9646, Fax: (212) 963-4116, http://unstats.un.org; *Demographic Yearbook; Statistical Yearbook; Trends in Europe and North America: The Statistical Yearbook of the ECE 2005;* and *World Statistics Pocketbook.*

The World Bank, 1818 H Street, NW, Washington, DC 20433, (202) 473-1000, Fax: (202) 477-6391, www.worldbank.org; *Andorra* and *The World Bank Atlas 2003-2004.*

World Health Organization (WHO), Avenue Appia 20, 1211 Geneve 27, Switzerland, (Telephone in U.S. (212) 331-9081), www.who.int; *World Health Report 2006.*

ANDORRA - POPULATION DENSITY

Central Intelligence Agency, Office of Public Affairs, Washington, DC 20505, (703) 482-0623, Fax: (703) 482-1739, www.cia.gov; *The World Factbook.*

Euromonitor International, Inc., 224 S. Michigan Avenue, Suite 1500, Chicago, IL 60604, (312) 922-1115, Fax: (312) 922-1157, www.euromonitor.com; *The World Economic Factbook 2008.*

Palgrave Macmillan Ltd., Houndmills, Basingstoke, Hampshire, RG21 6XS, England, (Telephone in U.S. (888) 330-8477), (Fax in U.S. (800) 672-2054), www.palgrave.com; *The Statesman's Yearbook 2008.*

Taylor and Francis Group, An Informa Business, 2 Park Square, Milton Park, Abingdon, Oxford OX14 4RN, United Kingdom, (Dial from U.S. (212) 216-7800), (Fax from U.S. (212) 564-7854), www.tandf.co.uk; *The Europa World Year Book.*

United Nations Food and Agricultural Organization (FAO), Viale delle Terme di Caracalla, 00100 Rome, Italy, (Dial from U.S. (202) 653-2400), (Fax from U.S. (202) 653 5760), www.fao.org; *The State of Food and Agriculture (SOFA) 2006.*

United Nations Statistics Division, New York, NY 10017, (800) 253-9646, Fax: (212) 963-4116, http://unstats.un.org; *Statistical Yearbook* and *Trends in Europe and North America: The Statistical Yearbook of the ECE 2005.*

The World Bank, 1818 H Street, NW, Washington, DC 20433, (202) 473-1000, Fax: (202) 477-6391, www.worldbank.org; *Andorra.*

ANDORRA - POSTAL SERVICE

United Nations Statistics Division, New York, NY 10017, (800) 253-9646, Fax: (212) 963-4116, http://unstats.un.org; *Trends in Europe and North America: The Statistical Yearbook of the ECE 2005.*

ANDORRA - POWER RESOURCES

Euromonitor International, Inc., 224 S. Michigan Avenue, Suite 1500, Chicago, IL 60604, (312) 922-1115, Fax: (312) 922-1157, www.euromonitor.com; *The World Economic Factbook 2008.*

Palgrave Macmillan Ltd., Houndmills, Basingstoke, Hampshire, RG21 6XS, England, (Telephone in U.S. (888) 330-8477), (Fax in U.S. (800) 672-2054), www.palgrave.com; *The Statesman's Yearbook 2008.*

United Nations Food and Agricultural Organization (FAO), Viale delle Terme di Caracalla, 00100 Rome, Italy, (Dial from U.S. (202) 653-2400), (Fax from U.S. (202) 653 5760), www.fao.org; *The State of Food and Agriculture (SOFA) 2006.*

United Nations Statistics Division, New York, NY 10017, (800) 253-9646, Fax: (212) 963-4116, http://unstats.un.org; *Trends in Europe and North America: The Statistical Yearbook of the ECE 2005* and *World Statistics Pocketbook.*

The World Bank, 1818 H Street, NW, Washington, DC 20433, (202) 473-1000, Fax: (202) 477-6391, www.worldbank.org; *The World Bank Atlas 2003-2004.*

ANDORRA - PRICES

United Nations Food and Agricultural Organization (FAO), Viale delle Terme di Caracalla, 00100 Rome, Italy, (Dial from U.S. (202) 653-2400), (Fax from U.S. (202) 653 5760), www.fao.org; *FAO Production Yearbook 2002* and *The State of Food and Agriculture (SOFA) 2006.*

The World Bank, 1818 H Street, NW, Washington, DC 20433, (202) 473-1000, Fax: (202) 477-6391, www.worldbank.org; *Andorra.*

ANDORRA - PUBLIC HEALTH

Palgrave Macmillan Ltd., Houndmills, Basingstoke, Hampshire, RG21 6XS, England, (Telephone in U.S. (888) 330-8477), (Fax in U.S. (800) 672-2054), www.palgrave.com; *The Statesman's Yearbook 2008.*

United Nations Statistics Division, New York, NY 10017, (800) 253-9646, Fax: (212) 963-4116, http://unstats.un.org; *Trends in Europe and North America: The Statistical Yearbook of the ECE 2005.*

The World Bank, 1818 H Street, NW, Washington, DC 20433, (202) 473-1000, Fax: (202) 477-6391, www.worldbank.org; *Andorra.*

ANDORRA - PUBLISHERS AND PUBLISHING

United Nations Statistics Division, New York, NY 10017, (800) 253-9646, Fax: (212) 963-4116, http://unstats.un.org; *Trends in Europe and North America: The Statistical Yearbook of the ECE 2005.*

ANDORRA - RADIO BROADCASTING

Palgrave Macmillan Ltd., Houndmills, Basingstoke, Hampshire, RG21 6XS, England, (Telephone in U.S. (888) 330-8477), (Fax in U.S. (800) 672-2054), www.palgrave.com; *The Statesman's Yearbook 2008.*

ANDORRA - RAILROADS

United Nations Statistics Division, New York, NY 10017, (800) 253-9646, Fax: (212) 963-4116, http://unstats.un.org; *Trends in Europe and North America: The Statistical Yearbook of the ECE 2005.*

ANDORRA - RELIGION

Central Intelligence Agency, Office of Public Affairs, Washington, DC 20505, (703) 482-0623, Fax: (703) 482-1739, www.cia.gov; *The World Factbook.*

Palgrave Macmillan Ltd., Houndmills, Basingstoke, Hampshire, RG21 6XS, England, (Telephone in U.S. (888) 330-8477), (Fax in U.S. (800) 672-2054), www.palgrave.com; *The Statesman's Yearbook 2008.*

ANDORRA - ROADS

Central Intelligence Agency, Office of Public Affairs, Washington, DC 20505, (703) 482-0623, Fax: (703) 482-1739, www.cia.gov; *The World Factbook.*

Palgrave Macmillan Ltd., Houndmills, Basingstoke, Hampshire, RG21 6XS, England, (Telephone in U.S. (888) 330-8477), (Fax in U.S. (800) 672-2054), www.palgrave.com; *The Statesman's Yearbook 2008.*

United Nations Statistics Division, New York, NY 10017, (800) 253-9646, Fax: (212) 963-4116, http://unstats.un.org; *Trends in Europe and North America: The Statistical Yearbook of the ECE 2005.*

ANDORRA - SOCIAL ECOLOGY

United Nations Statistics Division, New York, NY 10017, (800) 253-9646, Fax: (212) 963-4116, http://unstats.un.org; *World Statistics Pocketbook.*

ANDORRA - TELEPHONE

International Telecommunication Union (ITU), Place des Nations, 1211 Geneva 20, Switzerland, www.itu.int; World Telecommunication Indicators Database.

Palgrave Macmillan Ltd., Houndmills, Basingstoke, Hampshire, RG21 6XS, England, (Telephone in U.S. (888) 330-8477), (Fax in U.S. (800) 672-2054), www.palgrave.com; *The Statesman's Yearbook 2008.*

Taylor and Francis Group, An Informa Business, 2 Park Square, Milton Park, Abingdon, Oxford OX14 4RN, United Kingdom, (Dial from U.S. (212) 216-7800), (Fax from U.S. (212) 564-7854), www.tandf.co.uk; *The Europa World Year Book.*

United Nations Statistics Division, New York, NY 10017, (800) 253-9646, Fax: (212) 963-4116, http://unstats.un.org; *Trends in Europe and North America: The Statistical Yearbook of the ECE 2005* and *World Statistics Pocketbook.*

ANDORRA - TEXTILE INDUSTRY

United Nations Conference on Trade and Development (UNCTAD), DC2-1120, United Nations, New York, NY 10017, (212) 963-0027, www.unctad.org; *UNCTAD Commodity Yearbook.*

ANDORRA - THEATER

UNESCO Institute for Statistics, C.P. 6128 Succursale Centre-Ville, Montreal, Quebec, H3C 3J7 Canada, (Dial from U.S. (514) 343-6880), (Fax from U.S. (514) 343 6882), www.uis.unesco.org; *Statistical Tables.*

ANDORRA - TOURISM

Euromonitor International, Inc., 224 S. Michigan Avenue, Suite 1500, Chicago, IL 60604, (312) 922-1115, Fax: (312) 922-1157, www.euromonitor.com; *The World Economic Factbook 2008.*

Palgrave Macmillan Ltd., Houndmills, Basingstoke, Hampshire, RG21 6XS, England, (Telephone in U.S. (888) 330-8477), (Fax in U.S. (800) 672-2054), www.palgrave.com; *The Statesman's Yearbook 2008.*

Taylor and Francis Group, An Informa Business, 2 Park Square, Milton Park, Abingdon, Oxford OX14 4RN, United Kingdom, (Dial from U.S. (212) 216-7800), (Fax from U.S. (212) 564-7854), www.tandf.co.uk; *The Europa World Year Book.*

United Nations Statistics Division, New York, NY 10017, (800) 253-9646, Fax: (212) 963-4116, http://unstats.un.org; *Trends in Europe and North America: The Statistical Yearbook of the ECE 2005.*

The World Bank, 1818 H Street, NW, Washington, DC 20433, (202) 473-1000, Fax: (202) 477-6391, www.worldbank.org; *Andorra.*

ANDORRA - TRADE

See ANDORRA - INTERNATIONAL TRADE

ANDORRA - TRANSPORTATION

Central Intelligence Agency, Office of Public Affairs, Washington, DC 20505, (703) 482-0623, Fax: (703) 482-1739, www.cia.gov; *The World Factbook.*

Palgrave Macmillan Ltd., Houndmills, Basingstoke, Hampshire, RG21 6XS, England, (Telephone in U.S. (888) 330-8477), (Fax in U.S. (800) 672-2054), www.palgrave.com; *The Statesman's Yearbook 2008.*

Taylor and Francis Group, An Informa Business, 2 Park Square, Milton Park, Abingdon, Oxford OX14 4RN, United Kingdom, (Dial from U.S. (212) 216-7800), (Fax from U.S. (212) 564-7854), www.tandf.co.uk; *The Europa World Year Book.*

United Nations Statistics Division, New York, NY 10017, (800) 253-9646, Fax: (212) 963-4116, http://unstats.un.org; *Trends in Europe and North America: The Statistical Yearbook of the ECE 2005.*

The World Bank, 1818 H Street, NW, Washington, DC 20433, (202) 473-1000, Fax: (202) 477-6391, www.worldbank.org; *Andorra.*

ANDORRA - UNEMPLOYMENT

Central Intelligence Agency, Office of Public Affairs, Washington, DC 20505, (703) 482-0623, Fax: (703) 482-1739, www.cia.gov; *The World Factbook.*

United Nations Statistics Division, New York, NY 10017, (800) 253-9646, Fax: (212) 963-4116, http://unstats.un.org; *Trends in Europe and North America: The Statistical Yearbook of the ECE 2005.*

ANDORRA - VITAL STATISTICS

Palgrave Macmillan Ltd., Houndmills, Basingstoke, Hampshire, RG21 6XS, England, (Telephone in U.S. (888) 330-8477), (Fax in U.S. (800) 672-2054), www.palgrave.com; *The Statesman's Yearbook 2008.*

United Nations Statistics Division, New York, NY 10017, (800) 253-9646, Fax: (212) 963-4116, http://unstats.un.org; *Statistical Yearbook.*

World Health Organization (WHO), Avenue Appia 20, 1211 Geneve 27, Switzerland, (Telephone in U.S. (212) 331-9081), www.who.int; *World Health Report 2006.*

ANEMIA

National Center for Health Statistics (NCHS), Centers for Disease Control and Prevention (CDC), U.S. Department of Health and Human Services (HHS), 3311 Toledo Road, Hyattsville, MD 20782, (866) 232-4636, www.cdc.gov/nchs; *Faststats A to Z.*

ANEMIA - DEATHS

National Center for Health Statistics (NCHS), Centers for Disease Control and Prevention (CDC), U.S. Department of Health and Human Services (HHS), 3311 Toledo Road, Hyattsville, MD 20782, (866) 232-4636, www.cdc.gov/nchs; *Vital Statistics of the United States (VSUS).*

ANESTHESIOLOGISTS

American Medical Association, 515 North State Street, Chicago, IL 60610, (800) 621-8335, www.ama-assn.org; *Physician Characteristics and Distribution in the United States, 2008* and *Physician Compensation and Production Survey: 2007 Report Based on 2006 Data.*

ANGIOCARDIOGRAPHY

National Center for Health Statistics (NCHS), Centers for Disease Control and Prevention (CDC), U.S. Department of Health and Human Services (HHS), 3311 Toledo Road, Hyattsville, MD 20782, (866) 232-4636, www.cdc.gov/nchs; unpublished data.

ANGOLA - NATIONAL STATISTICAL OFFICE

Instituto Nacional de Estatistica (INE) (National Institute of Statistics), Unidade de Indice de Precos, CP 1215, Luanda, Angola, www.angola.org; National Data Center.

ANGOLA - AGRICULTURE

Economist Intelligence Unit, 111 West 57th Street, New York, NY 10019, (212) 554-0600, Fax: (212) 586-1181, www.eiu.com; *Angola Country Report.*

Euromonitor International, Inc., 224 S. Michigan Avenue, Suite 1500, Chicago, IL 60604, (312) 922-1115, Fax: (312) 922-1157, www.euromonitor.com; *International Marketing Data and Statistics 2008* and *World Marketing Data and Statistics.*

M.E. Sharpe, 80 Business Park Drive, Armonk, NY 10504, (800) 541-6563, Fax: (914) 273-2106, www.mesharpe.com; *The Illustrated Book of World Rankings.*

Palgrave Macmillan Ltd., Houndmills, Basingstoke, Hampshire, RG21 6XS, England, (Telephone in U.S. (888) 330-8477), (Fax in U.S. (800) 672-2054), www.palgrave.com; *The Statesman's Yearbook 2008.*

Taylor and Francis Group, An Informa Business, 2 Park Square, Milton Park, Abingdon, Oxford OX14 4RN, United Kingdom, (Dial from U.S. (212) 216-7800), (Fax from U.S. (212) 564-7854), www.tandf.co.uk; *The Europa World Year Book.*

United Nations Conference on Trade and Development (UNCTAD), DC2-1120, United Nations, New York, NY 10017, (212) 963-0027, www.unctad.org; *UNCTAD Commodity Yearbook.*

United Nations Economic Commission for Africa (ECA), PO Box 3001, Addis Ababa, Ethiopia, (Telephone in U.S. (212) 963-4957), www.uneca.org; *African Statistical Yearbook 2006.*

United Nations Food and Agricultural Organization (FAO), Viale delle Terme di Caracalla, 00100 Rome, Italy, (Dial from U.S. (202) 653-2400), (Fax from U.S. (202) 653 5760), www.fao.org; AQUASTAT; *FAO Production Yearbook 2002; FAO Trade Yearbook;* and *The State of Food and Agriculture (SOFA) 2006.*

United Nations Statistics Division, New York, NY 10017, (800) 253-9646, Fax: (212) 963-4116, http://unstats.un.org; *Statistical Yearbook* and *Survey of Economic and Social Conditions in Africa 2005.*

The World Bank, 1818 H Street, NW, Washington, DC 20433, (202) 473-1000, Fax: (202) 477-6391, www.worldbank.org; *Africa Live Database (LDB); African Development Indicators (ADI) 2007;* and *Angola.*

ANGOLA - AIRLINES

M.E. Sharpe, 80 Business Park Drive, Armonk, NY 10504, (800) 541-6563, Fax: (914) 273-2106, www.mesharpe.com; *The Illustrated Book of World Rankings.*

Palgrave Macmillan Ltd., Houndmills, Basingstoke, Hampshire, RG21 6XS, England, (Telephone in U.S. (888) 330-8477), (Fax in U.S. (800) 672-2054), www.palgrave.com; *The Statesman's Yearbook 2008.*

Taylor and Francis Group, An Informa Business, 2 Park Square, Milton Park, Abingdon, Oxford OX14 4RN, United Kingdom, (Dial from U.S. (212) 216-7800), (Fax from U.S. (212) 564-7854), www.tandf.co.uk; *The Europa World Year Book.*

United Nations Economic Commission for Africa (ECA), PO Box 3001, Addis Ababa, Ethiopia, (Telephone in U.S. (212) 963-4957), www.uneca.org; *African Statistical Yearbook 2006.*

ANGOLA - AIRPORTS

Central Intelligence Agency, Office of Public Affairs, Washington, DC 20505, (703) 482-0623, Fax: (703) 482-1739, www.cia.gov; *The World Factbook.*

ANGOLA - ALUMINUM PRODUCTION

See ANGOLA - MINERAL INDUSTRIES

ANGOLA - ANIMAL FEEDING

United Nations Statistics Division, New York, NY 10017, (800) 253-9646, Fax: (212) 963-4116, http://unstats.un.org; *Statistical Yearbook.*

ANGOLA - ARMED FORCES

Central Intelligence Agency, Office of Public Affairs, Washington, DC 20505, (703) 482-0623, Fax: (703) 482-1739, www.cia.gov; *The World Factbook.*

Euromonitor International, Inc., 224 S. Michigan Avenue, Suite 1500, Chicago, IL 60604, (312) 922-1115, Fax: (312) 922-1157, www.euromonitor.com; *World Marketing Data and Statistics.*

International Institute for Strategic Studies (IISS), Arundel House, 13-15 Arundel Street, Temple Place, London WC2R 3DX, England, www.iiss.org; *The Military Balance 2007.*

Palgrave Macmillan Ltd., Houndmills, Basingstoke, Hampshire, RG21 6XS, England, (Telephone in U.S. (888) 330-8477), (Fax in U.S. (800) 672-2054), www.palgrave.com; *The Statesman's Yearbook 2008.*

U.S. Department of State (DOS), 2201 C Street NW, Washington, DC 20520, (202) 647-4000, www.state.gov; *World Military Expenditures and Arms Transfers (WMEAT).*

United Nations Statistics Division, New York, NY 10017, (800) 253-9646, Fax: (212) 963-4116, http://unstats.un.org; *Human Development Report 2006.*

ANGOLA - AUTOMOBILE INDUSTRY AND TRADE

United Nations Statistics Division, New York, NY 10017, (800) 253-9646, Fax: (212) 963-4116, http://unstats.un.org; *Statistical Yearbook.*

ANGOLA - BALANCE OF PAYMENTS

African Development Bank Group, Rue Joseph Anoma, 01 BP 1387 Abidjan 01, Cote d'Ivoire, www.afdb.org; *Statistics Pocketbook 2008.*

Taylor and Francis Group, An Informa Business, 2 Park Square, Milton Park, Abingdon, Oxford OX14 4RN, United Kingdom, (Dial from U.S. (212) 216-7800), (Fax from U.S. (212) 564-7854), www.tandf.co.uk; *The Europa World Year Book.*

UNICEF, 3 United Nations Plaza, New York, NY 10017, (800) 253-9646, Fax: (212) 887-7465, www.unicef.org; *The State of the World's Children 2008.*

The World Bank, 1818 H Street, NW, Washington, DC 20433, (202) 473-1000, Fax: (202) 477-6391, www.worldbank.org; *Angola.*

ANGOLA - BANKS AND BANKING

Euromonitor International, Inc., 224 S. Michigan Avenue, Suite 1500, Chicago, IL 60604, (312) 922-1115, Fax: (312) 922-1157, www.euromonitor.com; *World Marketing Data and Statistics.*

M.E. Sharpe, 80 Business Park Drive, Armonk, NY 10504, (800) 541-6563, Fax: (914) 273-2106, www.mesharpe.com; *The Illustrated Book of World Rankings.*

Palgrave Macmillan Ltd., Houndmills, Basingstoke, Hampshire, RG21 6XS, England, (Telephone in U.S. (888) 330-8477), (Fax in U.S. (800) 672-2054), www.palgrave.com; *The Statesman's Yearbook 2008.*

ANGOLA - BARLEY PRODUCTION

See ANGOLA - CROPS

ANGOLA - BEVERAGE INDUSTRY

M.E. Sharpe, 80 Business Park Drive, Armonk, NY 10504, (800) 541-6563, Fax: (914) 273-2106, www.mesharpe.com; *The Illustrated Book of World Rankings.*

United Nations Statistics Division, New York, NY 10017, (800) 253-9646, Fax: (212) 963-4116, http://unstats.un.org; *Statistical Yearbook.*

ANGOLA - BROADCASTING

Central Intelligence Agency, Office of Public Affairs, Washington, DC 20505, (703) 482-0623, Fax: (703) 482-1739, www.cia.gov; *The World Factbook.*

Euromonitor International, Inc., 224 S. Michigan Avenue, Suite 1500, Chicago, IL 60604, (312) 922-1115, Fax: (312) 922-1157, www.euromonitor.com; *World Marketing Data and Statistics.*

M.E. Sharpe, 80 Business Park Drive, Armonk, NY 10504, (800) 541-6563, Fax: (914) 273-2106, www.mesharpe.com; *The Illustrated Book of World Rankings.*

Palgrave Macmillan Ltd., Houndmills, Basingstoke, Hampshire, RG21 6XS, England, (Telephone in U.S. (888) 330-8477), (Fax in U.S. (800) 672-2054), www.palgrave.com; *The Statesman's Yearbook 2008.*

WRTH Publications Limited, PO Box 290, Oxford OX2 7FT, UK, www.wrth.com; *World Radio TV Handbook 2007.*

ANGOLA - BUDGET

Central Intelligence Agency, Office of Public Affairs, Washington, DC 20505, (703) 482-0623, Fax: (703) 482-1739, www.cia.gov; *The World Factbook.*

ANGOLA - CATTLE

See ANGOLA - LIVESTOCK

ANGOLA - CHICKENS

See ANGOLA - LIVESTOCK

ANGOLA - CHILDBIRTH - STATISTICS

Central Intelligence Agency, Office of Public Affairs, Washington, DC 20505, (703) 482-0623, Fax: (703) 482-1739, www.cia.gov; *The World Factbook.*

Euromonitor International, Inc., 224 S. Michigan Avenue, Suite 1500, Chicago, IL 60604, (312) 922-1115, Fax: (312) 922-1157, www.euromonitor.com; *International Marketing Data and Statistics 2008* and *The World Economic Factbook 2008.*

M.E. Sharpe, 80 Business Park Drive, Armonk, NY 10504, (800) 541-6563, Fax: (914) 273-2106, www.mesharpe.com; *The Illustrated Book of World Rankings.*

Palgrave Macmillan Ltd., Houndmills, Basingstoke, Hampshire, RG21 6XS, England, (Telephone in U.S. (888) 330-8477), (Fax in U.S. (800) 672-2054), www.palgrave.com; *The Statesman's Yearbook 2008.*

Taylor and Francis Group, An Informa Business, 2 Park Square, Milton Park, Abingdon, Oxford OX14 4RN, United Kingdom, (Dial from U.S. (212) 216-7800), (Fax from U.S. (212) 564-7854), www.tandf.co.uk; *The Europa World Year Book.*

United Nations Statistics Division, New York, NY 10017, (800) 253-9646, Fax: (212) 963-4116, http://unstats.un.org; *Demographic Yearbook; Statistical Yearbook;* and *Survey of Economic and Social Conditions in Africa 2005.*

ANGOLA - CLIMATE

International Institute for Environment and Development (IIED), 3 Endsleigh Street, London, England, WC1H 0DD, United Kingdom, www.iied.org; *Environment Urbanization* and *Haramata - Bulletin of the Drylands.*

M.E. Sharpe, 80 Business Park Drive, Armonk, NY 10504, (800) 541-6563, Fax: (914) 273-2106, www.mesharpe.com; *The Illustrated Book of World Rankings.*

Palgrave Macmillan Ltd., Houndmills, Basingstoke, Hampshire, RG21 6XS, England, (Telephone in U.S. (888) 330-8477), (Fax in U.S. (800) 672-2054), www.palgrave.com; *The Statesman's Yearbook 2008.*

ANGOLA - COAL PRODUCTION

See ANGOLA - MINERAL INDUSTRIES

ANGOLA - COCOA PRODUCTION

See ANGOLA - CROPS

ANGOLA - COFFEE

See ANGOLA - CROPS

ANGOLA - COMMERCE

Palgrave Macmillan Ltd., Houndmills, Basingstoke, Hampshire, RG21 6XS, England, (Telephone in U.S. (888) 330-8477), (Fax in U.S. (800) 672-2054), www.palgrave.com; *The Statesman's Yearbook 2008.*

ANGOLA - COMMODITY EXCHANGES

Commodity Research Bureau, 330 South Wells Street, Suite 612, Chicago, IL 60606-7110, (800) 621-5271, Fax: (312) 939-4135, www.crbtrader.com; *2006 CRB Commodity Yearbook and CD.*

International Monetary Fund (IMF), 700 Nineteenth Street, NW, Washington, DC 20431, (202) 623-7000, Fax: (202) 623-4661, www.imf.org; *IMF Primary Commodity Prices.*

United Nations Food and Agricultural Organization (FAO), Viale delle Terme di Caracalla, 00100 Rome, Italy, (Dial from U.S. (202) 653-2400), (Fax from U.S. (202) 653 5760), www.fao.org; *The State of Food and Agriculture (SOFA) 2006.*

ANGOLA - COMMUNICATION AND TRAFFIC

United Nations Statistics Division, New York, NY 10017, (800) 253-9646, Fax: (212) 963-4116, http://unstats.un.org; *Statistical Yearbook.*

ANGOLA - CONSTRUCTION INDUSTRY

M.E. Sharpe, 80 Business Park Drive, Armonk, NY 10504, (800) 541-6563, Fax: (914) 273-2106, www.mesharpe.com; *The Illustrated Book of World Rankings.*

United Nations Economic Commission for Africa (ECA), PO Box 3001, Addis Ababa, Ethiopia, (Telephone in U.S. (212) 963-4957), www.uneca.org; *African Statistical Yearbook 2006.*

United Nations Statistics Division, New York, NY 10017, (800) 253-9646, Fax: (212) 963-4116, http://unstats.un.org; *Statistical Yearbook.*

ANGOLA - CONSUMER PRICE INDEXES

United Nations Statistics Division, New York, NY 10017, (800) 253-9646, Fax: (212) 963-4116, http://unstats.un.org; *Survey of Economic and Social Conditions in Africa 2005.*

The World Bank, 1818 H Street, NW, Washington, DC 20433, (202) 473-1000, Fax: (202) 477-6391, www.worldbank.org; *Angola.*

ANGOLA - CONSUMPTION (ECONOMICS)

African Development Bank Group, Rue Joseph Anoma, 01 BP 1387 Abidjan 01, Cote d'Ivoire, www.afdb.org; *Statistics Pocketbook 2008.*

United Nations Statistics Division, New York, NY 10017, (800) 253-9646, Fax: (212) 963-4116, http://unstats.un.org; *Survey of Economic and Social Conditions in Africa 2005.*

ANGOLA - COPPER INDUSTRY AND TRADE

See ANGOLA - MINERAL INDUSTRIES

ANGOLA - CORN INDUSTRY

See ANGOLA - CROPS

ANGOLA - COTTON

See ANGOLA - CROPS

ANGOLA - CROPS

M.E. Sharpe, 80 Business Park Drive, Armonk, NY 10504, (800) 541-6563, Fax: (914) 273-2106, www.mesharpe.com; *The Illustrated Book of World Rankings.*

Palgrave Macmillan Ltd., Houndmills, Basingstoke, Hampshire, RG21 6XS, England, (Telephone in U.S. (888) 330-8477), (Fax in U.S. (800) 672-2054), www.palgrave.com; *The Statesman's Yearbook 2008.*

Taylor and Francis Group, An Informa Business, 2 Park Square, Milton Park, Abingdon, Oxford OX14 4RN, United Kingdom, (Dial from U.S. (212) 216-7800), (Fax from U.S. (212) 564-7854), www.tandf.co.uk; *The Europa World Year Book.*

United Nations Conference on Trade and Development (UNCTAD), DC2-1120, United Nations, New York, NY 10017, (212) 963-0027, www.unctad.org; *UNCTAD Commodity Yearbook.*

United Nations Economic Commission for Africa (ECA), PO Box 3001, Addis Ababa, Ethiopia, (Telephone in U.S. (212) 963-4957), www.uneca.org; *African Statistical Yearbook 2006.*

United Nations Food and Agricultural Organization (FAO), Viale delle Terme di Caracalla, 00100 Rome, Italy, (Dial from U.S. (202) 653-2400), (Fax from U.S. (202) 653 5760), www.fao.org; *FAO Production Yearbook 2002* and *The State of Food and Agriculture (SOFA) 2006.*

United Nations Statistics Division, New York, NY 10017, (800) 253-9646, Fax: (212) 963-4116, http://unstats.un.org; *Statistical Yearbook.*

ANGOLA - CUSTOMS ADMINISTRATION

Palgrave Macmillan Ltd., Houndmills, Basingstoke, Hampshire, RG21 6XS, England, (Telephone in U.S. (888) 330-8477), (Fax in U.S. (800) 672-2054), www.palgrave.com; *The Statesman's Yearbook 2008.*

ANGOLA - DAIRY PROCESSING

M.E. Sharpe, 80 Business Park Drive, Armonk, NY 10504, (800) 541-6563, Fax: (914) 273-2106, www.mesharpe.com; *The Illustrated Book of World Rankings.*

Palgrave Macmillan Ltd., Houndmills, Basingstoke, Hampshire, RG21 6XS, England, (Telephone in U.S. (888) 330-8477), (Fax in U.S. (800) 672-2054), www.palgrave.com; *The Statesman's Yearbook 2008.*

Taylor and Francis Group, An Informa Business, 2 Park Square, Milton Park, Abingdon, Oxford OX14 4RN, United Kingdom, (Dial from U.S. (212) 216-7800), (Fax from U.S. (212) 564-7854), www.tandf.co.uk; *The Europa World Year Book.*

United Nations Food and Agricultural Organization (FAO), Viale delle Terme di Caracalla, 00100 Rome, Italy, (Dial from U.S. (202) 653-2400), (Fax from U.S. (202) 653 5760), www.fao.org; *The State of Food and Agriculture (SOFA) 2006.*

United Nations Statistics Division, New York, NY 10017, (800) 253-9646, Fax: (212) 963-4116, http://unstats.un.org; *Statistical Yearbook.*

ANGOLA - DEATH RATES

See ANGOLA - MORTALITY

ANGOLA - DEBTS, EXTERNAL

African Development Bank Group, Rue Joseph Anoma, 01 BP 1387 Abidjan 01, Cote d'Ivoire, www.afdb.org; *Statistics Pocketbook 2008.*

Palgrave Macmillan Ltd., Houndmills, Basingstoke, Hampshire, RG21 6XS, England, (Telephone in U.S. (888) 330-8477), (Fax in U.S. (800) 672-2054), www.palgrave.com; *The Statesman's Yearbook 2008.*

United Nations Statistics Division, New York, NY 10017, (800) 253-9646, Fax: (212) 963-4116, http://unstats.un.org; *Survey of Economic and Social Conditions in Africa 2005.*

The World Bank, 1818 H Street, NW, Washington, DC 20433, (202) 473-1000, Fax: (202) 477-6391, www.worldbank.org; *Africa Live Database (LDB); African Development Indicators (ADI) 2007;* and *Global Development Finance 2007.*

ANGOLA - DEFENSE EXPENDITURES

See ANGOLA - ARMED FORCES

ANGOLA - DEMOGRAPHY

Euromonitor International, Inc., 224 S. Michigan Avenue, Suite 1500, Chicago, IL 60604, (312) 922-

1115, Fax: (312) 922-1157, www.euromonitor.com; *International Marketing Data and Statistics 2008; The World Economic Factbook 2008;* and *World Marketing Data and Statistics.*

M.E. Sharpe, 80 Business Park Drive, Armonk, NY 10504, (800) 541-6563, Fax: (914) 273-2106, www.mesharpe.com; *The Illustrated Book of World Rankings.*

United Nations Statistics Division, New York, NY 10017, (800) 253-9646, Fax: (212) 963-4116, http://unstats.un.org; *Human Development Report 2006* and *Survey of Economic and Social Conditions in Africa 2005.*

The World Bank, 1818 H Street, NW, Washington, DC 20433, (202) 473-1000, Fax: (202) 477-6391, www.worldbank.org; *Angola.*

ANGOLA - DIAMONDS

See ANGOLA - MINERAL INDUSTRIES

ANGOLA - DISPOSABLE INCOME

M.E. Sharpe, 80 Business Park Drive, Armonk, NY 10504, (800) 541-6563, Fax: (914) 273-2106, www.mesharpe.com; *The Illustrated Book of World Rankings.*

United Nations Statistics Division, New York, NY 10017, (800) 253-9646, Fax: (212) 963-4116, http://unstats.un.org; *National Accounts Statistics: Compendium of Income Distribution Statistics* and *Statistical Yearbook.*

ANGOLA - DIVORCE

M.E. Sharpe, 80 Business Park Drive, Armonk, NY 10504, (800) 541-6563, Fax: (914) 273-2106, www.mesharpe.com; *The Illustrated Book of World Rankings.*

United Nations Statistics Division, New York, NY 10017, (800) 253-9646, Fax: (212) 963-4116, http://unstats.un.org; *Demographic Yearbook* and *Statistical Yearbook.*

ANGOLA - ECONOMIC ASSISTANCE

International Organization for Migration (IOM), 17, Route des Morillons, CH-1211 Geneva 19, Switzerland, www.iom.int; *Migration and Development: New Strategic Outlooks and Practical Ways Forward - The Cases of Angola and Zambia.*

United Nations Statistics Division, New York, NY 10017, (800) 253-9646, Fax: (212) 963-4116, http://unstats.un.org; *Statistical Yearbook.*

ANGOLA - ECONOMIC CONDITIONS

African Development Bank Group, Rue Joseph Anoma, 01 BP 1387 Abidjan 01, Cote d'Ivoire, www.afdb.org; *The African Statistical Journal; Gender, Poverty and Environmental Indicators on African Countries 2007; Selected Statistics on African Countries 2007;* and *Statistics Pocketbook 2008.*

Center for International Business Education Research (CIBER), Columbia Business School and School of International and Public Affairs, Uris Hall, Room 212, 3022 Broadway, New York, NY 10027-6902, Mr. Joshua Safier, (212) 854-4750, Fax: (212) 222-9821, www.columbia.edu/cu/ciber/; Datastream International.

Central Intelligence Agency, Office of Public Affairs, Washington, DC 20505, (703) 482-0623, Fax: (703) 482-1739, www.cia.gov; *The World Factbook.*

DSI Data Service Information, Xantener Strasse 51a, D-47495 Rheinberg, Germany, www.dsidata.com; *Campus Solution.*

Dun and Bradstreet (DB) Corporation, 103 JFK Parkway, Short Hills, NJ 07078, (973) 921-5500, www.dnb.com; *Country Report.*

Economist Intelligence Unit, 111 West 57th Street, New York, NY 10019, (212) 554-0600, Fax: (212) 586-1181, www.eiu.com; *Angola Country Report* and *Business Africa.*

Euromonitor International, Inc., 224 S. Michigan Avenue, Suite 1500, Chicago, IL 60604, (312) 922-1115, Fax: (312) 922-1157, www.euromonitor.com; *International Marketing Data and Statistics 2008; The World Economic Factbook 2008;* and *World Marketing Data and Statistics.*

International Monetary Fund (IMF), 700 Nineteenth Street, NW, Washington, DC 20431, (202) 623-7000, Fax: (202) 623-4661, www.imf.org; *World Economic Outlook Reports.*

M.E. Sharpe, 80 Business Park Drive, Armonk, NY 10504, (800) 541-6563, Fax: (914) 273-2106, www.mesharpe.com; *The Illustrated Book of World Rankings.*

Palgrave Macmillan Ltd., Houndmills, Basingstoke, Hampshire, RG21 6XS, England, (Telephone in U.S. (888) 330-8477), (Fax in U.S. (800) 672-2054), www.palgrave.com; *The Statesman's Yearbook 2008.*

Taylor and Francis Group, An Informa Business, 2 Park Square, Milton Park, Abingdon, Oxford OX14 4RN, United Kingdom, (Dial from U.S. (212) 216-7800), (Fax from U.S. (212) 564-7854), www.tandf.co.uk; *The Europa World Year Book.*

United Nations Statistics Division, New York, NY 10017, (800) 253-9646, Fax: (212) 963-4116, http://unstats.un.org; *Compendium of Intra-African and Related Foreign Trade Statistics 2003* and *World Statistics Pocketbook.*

The World Bank, 1818 H Street, NW, Washington, DC 20433, (202) 473-1000, Fax: (202) 477-6391, www.worldbank.org; *Africa Household Survey Databank; Africa Live Database (LDB); Africa Standardized Files and Indicators; African Development Indicators (ADI) 2007; Angola; Global Economic Monitor (GEM); Global Economic Prospects 2008;* and *The World Bank Atlas 2003-2004.*

ANGOLA - EDUCATION

African Development Bank Group, Rue Joseph Anoma, 01 BP 1387 Abidjan 01, Cote d'Ivoire, www.afdb.org; *Statistics Pocketbook 2008.*

Euromonitor International, Inc., 224 S. Michigan Avenue, Suite 1500, Chicago, IL 60604, (312) 922-1115, Fax: (312) 922-1157, www.euromonitor.com; *International Marketing Data and Statistics 2008* and *World Marketing Data and Statistics.*

M.E. Sharpe, 80 Business Park Drive, Armonk, NY 10504, (800) 541-6563, Fax: (914) 273-2106, www.mesharpe.com; *The Illustrated Book of World Rankings.*

Palgrave Macmillan Ltd., Houndmills, Basingstoke, Hampshire, RG21 6XS, England, (Telephone in U.S. (888) 330-8477), (Fax in U.S. (800) 672-2054), www.palgrave.com; *The Statesman's Yearbook 2008.*

Taylor and Francis Group, An Informa Business, 2 Park Square, Milton Park, Abingdon, Oxford OX14 4RN, United Kingdom, (Dial from U.S. (212) 216-7800), (Fax from U.S. (212) 564-7854), www.tandf.co.uk; *The Europa World Year Book.*

UNESCO Institute for Statistics, C.P. 6128 Succursale Centre-Ville, Montreal, Quebec, H3C 3J7 Canada, (Dial from U.S. (514) 343-6880), (Fax from U.S. (514) 343 6882), www.uis.unesco.org; *Statistical Tables.*

United Nations Economic Commission for Africa (ECA), PO Box 3001, Addis Ababa, Ethiopia, (Telephone in U.S. (212) 963-4957), www.uneca.org; *African Statistical Yearbook 2006.*

The World Bank, 1818 H Street, NW, Washington, DC 20433, (202) 473-1000, Fax: (202) 477-6391, www.worldbank.org; *Angola.*

ANGOLA - ELECTRICITY

M.E. Sharpe, 80 Business Park Drive, Armonk, NY 10504, (800) 541-6563, Fax: (914) 273-2106, www.mesharpe.com; *The Illustrated Book of World Rankings.*

Organisation for Economic Cooperation and Development (OECD), 2 rue Andre Pascal, F-75775 Paris Cedex 16, France, (Telephone in U.S. (202) 785-6323), (Fax in U.S. (202) 785-0350), www.oecd.org; *World Energy Outlook 2007.*

Palgrave Macmillan Ltd., Houndmills, Basingstoke, Hampshire, RG21 6XS, England, (Telephone in U.S. (888) 330-8477), (Fax in U.S. (800) 672-2054), www.palgrave.com; *The Statesman's Yearbook 2008.*

U.S. Department of Energy (DOE), Energy Information Administration (EIA), 1000 Independence Avenue, SW, Washington, DC 20585, (202) 586-8800, www.eia.doe.gov; *International Energy Annual 2004* and *International Energy Outlook 2006.*

United Nations Economic Commission for Africa (ECA), PO Box 3001, Addis Ababa, Ethiopia, (Telephone in U.S. (212) 963-4957), www.uneca.org; *African Statistical Yearbook 2006.*

United Nations Statistics Division, New York, NY 10017, (800) 253-9646, Fax: (212) 963-4116, http://unstats.un.org; *Human Development Report 2006; Statistical Yearbook;* and *Survey of Economic and Social Conditions in Africa 2005.*

ANGOLA - EMIGRATION AND IMMIGRATION

International Organization for Migration (IOM), 17, Route des Morillons, CH-1211 Geneva 19, Switzerland, www.iom.int; *Migration and Development: New Strategic Outlooks and Practical Ways Forward - The Cases of Angola and Zambia.*

ANGOLA - EMPLOYMENT

Euromonitor International, Inc., 224 S. Michigan Avenue, Suite 1500, Chicago, IL 60604, (312) 922-1115, Fax: (312) 922-1157, www.euromonitor.com; *International Marketing Data and Statistics 2008.*

M.E. Sharpe, 80 Business Park Drive, Armonk, NY 10504, (800) 541-6563, Fax: (914) 273-2106, www.mesharpe.com; *The Illustrated Book of World Rankings.*

United Nations Economic Commission for Africa (ECA), PO Box 3001, Addis Ababa, Ethiopia, (Telephone in U.S. (212) 963-4957), www.uneca.org; *African Statistical Yearbook 2006.*

United Nations Statistics Division, New York, NY 10017, (800) 253-9646, Fax: (212) 963-4116, http://unstats.un.org; *Statistical Yearbook* and *Survey of Economic and Social Conditions in Africa 2005.*

The World Bank, 1818 H Street, NW, Washington, DC 20433, (202) 473-1000, Fax: (202) 477-6391, www.worldbank.org; *Angola.*

ANGOLA - ENVIRONMENTAL CONDITIONS

DSI Data Service Information, Xantener Strasse 51a, D-47495 Rheinberg, Germany, www.dsidata.com; *Campus Solution* and *DSI's Global Environmental Database.*

Economist Intelligence Unit, 111 West 57th Street, New York, NY 10019, (212) 554-0600, Fax: (212) 586-1181, www.eiu.com; *Angola Country Report.*

International Institute for Environment and Development (IIED), 3 Endsleigh Street, London, England, WC1H 0DD, United Kingdom, www.iied.org; *Environment Urbanization* and *Haramata - Bulletin of the Drylands.*

United Nations Statistics Division, New York, NY 10017, (800) 253-9646, Fax: (212) 963-4116, http://unstats.un.org; *World Statistics Pocketbook.*

ANGOLA - EXPORTS

African Development Bank Group, Rue Joseph Anoma, 01 BP 1387 Abidjan 01, Cote d'Ivoire, www.afdb.org; *Statistics Pocketbook 2008.*

Central Intelligence Agency, Office of Public Affairs, Washington, DC 20505, (703) 482-0623, Fax: (703) 482-1739, www.cia.gov; *The World Factbook.*

Economist Intelligence Unit, 111 West 57th Street, New York, NY 10019, (212) 554-0600, Fax: (212) 586-1181, www.eiu.com; *Angola Country Report.*

Euromonitor International, Inc., 224 S. Michigan Avenue, Suite 1500, Chicago, IL 60604, (312) 922-1115, Fax: (312) 922-1157, www.euromonitor.com; *International Marketing Data and Statistics 2008* and *The World Economic Factbook 2008.*

International Monetary Fund (IMF), 700 Nineteenth Street, NW, Washington, DC 20431, (202) 623-7000, Fax: (202) 623-4661, www.imf.org; *Direction of Trade Statistics Yearbook 2007.*

Organization of Petroleum Exporting Countries (OPEC), Obere Donaustrasse 93, A-1020, Vienna, Austria, www.opec.org; *Annual Statistical Bulletin 2006.*

Palgrave Macmillan Ltd., Houndmills, Basingstoke, Hampshire, RG21 6XS, England, (Telephone in U.S. (888) 330-8477), (Fax in U.S. (800) 672-2054), www.palgrave.com; *The Statesman's Yearbook 2008.*

Secretariat of the Pacific Community (SPC), BP D5, 98848 Noumea Cedex, New Caledonia, www.spc.int/corp; *Selected Pacific Economies - a Statistical Summary (SPESS).*

Taylor and Francis Group, An Informa Business, 2 Park Square, Milton Park, Abingdon, Oxford OX14 4RN, United Kingdom, (Dial from U.S. (212) 216-7800), (Fax from U.S. (212) 564-7854), www.tandf.co.uk; *The Europa World Year Book.*

United Nations Economic Commission for Africa (ECA), PO Box 3001, Addis Ababa, Ethiopia, (Telephone in U.S. (212) 963-4957), www.uneca.org; *African Statistical Yearbook 2006.*

United Nations Food and Agricultural Organization (FAO), Viale delle Terme di Caracalla, 00100 Rome, Italy, (Dial from U.S. (202) 653-2400), (Fax from U.S. (202) 653 5760), www.fao.org; *The State of Food and Agriculture (SOFA) 2006.*

United Nations Statistics Division, New York, NY 10017, (800) 253-9646, Fax: (212) 963-4116, http://unstats.un.org; *Compendium of Intra-African and Related Foreign Trade Statistics 2003* and *Survey of Economic and Social Conditions in Africa 2005.*

ANGOLA - FEMALE WORKING POPULATION

See ANGOLA - EMPLOYMENT

ANGOLA - FERTILITY, HUMAN

M.E. Sharpe, 80 Business Park Drive, Armonk, NY 10504, (800) 541-6563, Fax: (914) 273-2106, www.mesharpe.com; *The Illustrated Book of World Rankings.*

United Nations Statistics Division, New York, NY 10017, (800) 253-9646, Fax: (212) 963-4116, http://unstats.un.org; *Human Development Report 2006* and *Survey of Economic and Social Conditions in Africa 2005.*

The World Bank, 1818 H Street, NW, Washington, DC 20433, (202) 473-1000, Fax: (202) 477-6391, www.worldbank.org; *The World Bank Atlas 2003-2004.*

ANGOLA - FERTILIZER INDUSTRY

United Nations Food and Agricultural Organization (FAO), Viale delle Terme di Caracalla, 00100 Rome, Italy, (Dial from U.S. (202) 653-2400), (Fax from U.S. (202) 653 5760), www.fao.org; *FAO Fertilizer Yearbook* and *The State of Food and Agriculture (SOFA) 2006.*

United Nations Statistics Division, New York, NY 10017, (800) 253-9646, Fax: (212) 963-4116, http://unstats.un.org; *Statistical Yearbook.*

ANGOLA - FETAL MORTALITY

See ANGOLA - MORTALITY

ANGOLA - FINANCE

Taylor and Francis Group, An Informa Business, 2 Park Square, Milton Park, Abingdon, Oxford OX14 4RN, United Kingdom, (Dial from U.S. (212) 216-7800), (Fax from U.S. (212) 564-7854), www.tandf.co.uk; *The Europa World Year Book.*

United Nations Economic Commission for Africa (ECA), PO Box 3001, Addis Ababa, Ethiopia, (Telephone in U.S. (212) 963-4957), www.uneca.org; *African Statistical Yearbook 2006.*

The World Bank, 1818 H Street, NW, Washington, DC 20433, (202) 473-1000, Fax: (202) 477-6391, www.worldbank.org; *Angola.*

ANGOLA - FINANCE, PUBLIC

African Development Bank Group, Rue Joseph Anoma, 01 BP 1387 Abidjan 01, Cote d'Ivoire, www.afdb.org; *Statistics Pocketbook 2008.*

Bernan Essential Government Publications, 4611-F Assembly Drive, Lanham MD, 20706-4391, (301) 459-2255, Fax: (800) 865-3450, www.bernan.com; *National Accounts Statistics.*

Economist Intelligence Unit, 111 West 57th Street, New York, NY 10019, (212) 554-0600, Fax: (212) 586-1181, www.eiu.com; *Angola Country Report.*

International Monetary Fund (IMF), 700 Nineteenth Street, NW, Washington, DC 20431, (202) 623-7000, Fax: (202) 623-4661, www.imf.org; *International Financial Statistics; International Financial Statistics Online Service;* and *International Financial Statistics Yearbook 2007.*

M.E. Sharpe, 80 Business Park Drive, Armonk, NY 10504, (800) 541-6563, Fax: (914) 273-2106, www.mesharpe.com; *The Illustrated Book of World Rankings.*

Palgrave Macmillan Ltd., Houndmills, Basingstoke, Hampshire, RG21 6XS, England, (Telephone in U.S. (888) 330-8477), (Fax in U.S. (800) 672-2054), www.palgrave.com; *The Statesman's Yearbook 2008.*

Taylor and Francis Group, An Informa Business, 2 Park Square, Milton Park, Abingdon, Oxford OX14 4RN, United Kingdom, (Dial from U.S. (212) 216-7800), (Fax from U.S. (212) 564-7854), www.tandf.co.uk; *The Europa World Year Book.*

The World Bank, 1818 H Street, NW, Washington, DC 20433, (202) 473-1000, Fax: (202) 477-6391, www.worldbank.org; *Angola.*

ANGOLA - FISHERIES

M.E. Sharpe, 80 Business Park Drive, Armonk, NY 10504, (800) 541-6563, Fax: (914) 273-2106, www.mesharpe.com; *The Illustrated Book of World Rankings.*

Palgrave Macmillan Ltd., Houndmills, Basingstoke, Hampshire, RG21 6XS, England, (Telephone in U.S. (888) 330-8477), (Fax in U.S. (800) 672-2054), www.palgrave.com; *The Statesman's Yearbook 2008.*

Taylor and Francis Group, An Informa Business, 2 Park Square, Milton Park, Abingdon, Oxford OX14 4RN, United Kingdom, (Dial from U.S. (212) 216-7800), (Fax from U.S. (212) 564-7854), www.tandf.co.uk; *The Europa World Year Book.*

United Nations Conference on Trade and Development (UNCTAD), DC2-1120, United Nations, New York, NY 10017, (212) 963-0027, www.unctad.org; *UNCTAD Commodity Yearbook.*

United Nations Economic Commission for Africa (ECA), PO Box 3001, Addis Ababa, Ethiopia, (Telephone in U.S. (212) 963-4957), www.uneca.org; *African Statistical Yearbook 2006.*

United Nations Food and Agricultural Organization (FAO), Viale delle Terme di Caracalla, 00100 Rome, Italy, (Dial from U.S. (202) 653-2400), (Fax from U.S. (202) 653 5760), www.fao.org; *FAO Yearbook of Fishery Statistics;* Fishery Databases; FISHSTAT Database. Subjects covered include: Aquaculture production, capture production, fishery commodities; and *The State of Food and Agriculture (SOFA) 2006.*

United Nations Statistics Division, New York, NY 10017, (800) 253-9646, Fax: (212) 963-4116, http://unstats.un.org; *Human Development Report 2006; Statistical Yearbook;* and *Survey of Economic and Social Conditions in Africa 2005.*

The World Bank, 1818 H Street, NW, Washington, DC 20433, (202) 473-1000, Fax: (202) 477-6391, www.worldbank.org; *Angola.*

ANGOLA - FLOUR INDUSTRY

United Nations Statistics Division, New York, NY 10017, (800) 253-9646, Fax: (212) 963-4116, http://unstats.un.org; *Statistical Yearbook.*

ANGOLA - FOOD

African Development Bank Group, Rue Joseph Anoma, 01 BP 1387 Abidjan 01, Cote d'Ivoire, www.afdb.org; *Statistics Pocketbook 2008.*

United Nations Conference on Trade and Development (UNCTAD), DC2-1120, United Nations, New York, NY 10017, (212) 963-0027, www.unctad.org; *UNCTAD Commodity Yearbook.*

United Nations Food and Agricultural Organization (FAO), Viale delle Terme di Caracalla, 00100 Rome, Italy, (Dial from U.S. (202) 653-2400), (Fax from U.S. (202) 653 5760), www.fao.org; *FAO Production Yearbook 2002* and *The State of Food and Agriculture (SOFA) 2006.*

ANGOLA - FOREIGN EXCHANGE RATES

African Development Bank Group, Rue Joseph Anoma, 01 BP 1387 Abidjan 01, Cote d'Ivoire, www.afdb.org; *Statistics Pocketbook 2008.*

Central Intelligence Agency, Office of Public Affairs, Washington, DC 20505, (703) 482-0623, Fax: (703) 482-1739, www.cia.gov; *The World Factbook.*

Euromonitor International, Inc., 224 S. Michigan Avenue, Suite 1500, Chicago, IL 60604, (312) 922-1115, Fax: (312) 922-1157, www.euromonitor.com; *International Marketing Data and Statistics 2008* and *The World Economic Factbook 2008.*

International Civil Aviation Organization (ICAO), External Relations and Public Information Office (EPO), 999 University Street, Montreal, Quebec H3C 5H7, Canada, (Dial from U.S. (514) 954-8219), (Fax from U.S. (514) 954-6077), www.icao.int; *Civil Aviation Statistics of the World.*

Organization of Petroleum Exporting Countries (OPEC), Obere Donaustrasse 93, A-1020, Vienna, Austria, www.opec.org; *Annual Statistical Bulletin 2006.*

Taylor and Francis Group, An Informa Business, 2 Park Square, Milton Park, Abingdon, Oxford OX14 4RN, United Kingdom, (Dial from U.S. (212) 216-7800), (Fax from U.S. (212) 564-7854), www.tandf.co.uk; *The Europa World Year Book.*

United Nations Statistics Division, New York, NY 10017, (800) 253-9646, Fax: (212) 963-4116, http://unstats.un.org; *Compendium of Intra-African and Related Foreign Trade Statistics 2003* and *World Statistics Pocketbook.*

ANGOLA - FORESTS AND FORESTRY

M.E. Sharpe, 80 Business Park Drive, Armonk, NY 10504, (800) 541-6563, Fax: (914) 273-2106, www.mesharpe.com; *The Illustrated Book of World Rankings.*

Palgrave Macmillan Ltd., Houndmills, Basingstoke, Hampshire, RG21 6XS, England, (Telephone in U.S. (888) 330-8477), (Fax in U.S. (800) 672-2054), www.palgrave.com; *The Statesman's Yearbook 2008.*

Taylor and Francis Group, An Informa Business, 2 Park Square, Milton Park, Abingdon, Oxford OX14 4RN, United Kingdom, (Dial from U.S. (212) 216-7800), (Fax from U.S. (212) 564-7854), www.tandf.co.uk; *The Europa World Year Book.*

UNESCO Institute for Statistics, C.P. 6128 Succursale Centre-Ville, Montreal, Quebec, H3C 3J7 Canada, (Dial from U.S. (514) 343-6880), (Fax from U.S. (514) 343 6882), www.uis.unesco.org; *Statistical Tables.*

United Nations Conference on Trade and Development (UNCTAD), DC2-1120, United Nations, New York, NY 10017, (212) 963-0027, www.unctad.org; *UNCTAD Commodity Yearbook.*

United Nations Economic Commission for Africa (ECA), PO Box 3001, Addis Ababa, Ethiopia, (Telephone in U.S. (212) 963-4957), www.uneca.org; *African Statistical Yearbook 2006.*

United Nations Food and Agricultural Organization (FAO), Viale delle Terme di Caracalla, 00100 Rome, Italy, (Dial from U.S. (202) 653-2400), (Fax from U.S. (202) 653 5760), www.fao.org; *FAO Yearbook of Forest Products* and *The State of Food and Agriculture (SOFA) 2006.*

United Nations Statistics Division, New York, NY 10017; (800) 253-9646, Fax: (212) 963-4116, http://unstats.un.org; *Statistical Yearbook.*

The World Bank, 1818 H Street, NW, Washington, DC 20433, (202) 473-1000, Fax: (202) 477-6391, www.worldbank.org; *Angola.*

ANGOLA - GAS PRODUCTION

See ANGOLA - MINERAL INDUSTRIES

ANGOLA - GEOGRAPHIC INFORMATION SYSTEMS

M.E. Sharpe, 80 Business Park Drive, Armonk, NY 10504, (800) 541-6563, Fax: (914) 273-2106, www.mesharpe.com; *The Illustrated Book of World Rankings.*

The World Bank, 1818 H Street, NW, Washington, DC 20433, (202) 473-1000, Fax: (202) 477-6391, www.worldbank.org; *Angola.*

ANGOLA - GOLD PRODUCTION

See ANGOLA - MINERAL INDUSTRIES

ANGOLA - GROSS DOMESTIC PRODUCT

African Development Bank Group, Rue Joseph Anoma, 01 BP 1387 Abidjan 01, Cote d'Ivoire, www.afdb.org; *Statistics Pocketbook 2008.*

Economist Intelligence Unit, 111 West 57th Street, New York, NY 10019, (212) 554-0600, Fax: (212) 586-1181, www.eiu.com; *Angola Country Report.*

Euromonitor International, Inc., 224 S. Michigan Avenue, Suite 1500, Chicago, IL 60604, (312) 922-1115, Fax: (312) 922-1157, www.euromonitor.com; *International Marketing Data and Statistics 2008* and *The World Economic Factbook 2008.*

M.E. Sharpe, 80 Business Park Drive, Armonk, NY 10504, (800) 541-6563, Fax: (914) 273-2106, www.mesharpe.com; *The Illustrated Book of World Rankings.*

Taylor and Francis Group, An Informa Business, 2 Park Square, Milton Park, Abingdon, Oxford OX14 4RN, United Kingdom, (Dial from U.S. (212) 216-7800), (Fax from U.S. (212) 564-7854), www.tandf.co.uk; *The Europa World Year Book.*

United Nations Economic Commission for Africa (ECA), PO Box 3001, Addis Ababa, Ethiopia, (Telephone in U.S. (212) 963-4957), www.uneca.org; *African Statistical Yearbook 2006.*

United Nations Statistics Division, New York, NY 10017, (800) 253-9646, Fax: (212) 963-4116, http://unstats.un.org; *Human Development Report 2006; National Accounts Statistics: Compendium of Income Distribution Statistics; Statistical Yearbook;* and *Survey of Economic and Social Conditions in Africa 2005.*

ANGOLA - GROSS NATIONAL PRODUCT

Euromonitor International, Inc., 224 S. Michigan Avenue, Suite 1500, Chicago, IL 60604, (312) 922-1115, Fax: (312) 922-1157, www.euromonitor.com; *International Marketing Data and Statistics 2008.*

M.E. Sharpe, 80 Business Park Drive, Armonk, NY 10504, (800) 541-6563, Fax: (914) 273-2106, www.mesharpe.com; *The Illustrated Book of World Rankings.*

Organization of Petroleum Exporting Countries (OPEC), Obere Donaustrasse 93, A-1020, Vienna, Austria, www.opec.org; *Annual Statistical Bulletin 2006.*

Palgrave Macmillan Ltd., Houndmills, Basingstoke, Hampshire, RG21 6XS, England, (Telephone in U.S. (888) 330-8477), (Fax in U.S. (800) 672-2054), www.palgrave.com; *The Statesman's Yearbook 2008.*

Taylor and Francis Group, An Informa Business, 2 Park Square, Milton Park, Abingdon, Oxford OX14 4RN, United Kingdom, (Dial from U.S. (212) 216-7800), (Fax from U.S. (212) 564-7854), www.tandf.co.uk; *The Europa World Year Book.*

U.S. Department of State (DOS), 2201 C Street NW, Washington, DC 20520, (202) 647-4000, www.state.gov; *World Military Expenditures and Arms Transfers (WMEAT).*

The World Bank, 1818 H Street, NW, Washington, DC 20433, (202) 473-1000, Fax: (202) 477-6391, www.worldbank.org; *The World Bank Atlas 2003-2004.*

ANGOLA - HIDES AND SKINS INDUSTRY

United Nations Food and Agricultural Organization (FAO), Viale delle Terme di Caracalla, 00100 Rome, Italy, (Dial from U.S. (202) 653-2400), (Fax from U.S. (202) 653 5760), www.fao.org; *FAO Production Yearbook 2002.*

ANGOLA - HOUSING

Euromonitor International, Inc., 224 S. Michigan Avenue, Suite 1500, Chicago, IL 60604, (312) 922-1115, Fax: (312) 922-1157, www.euromonitor.com; *World Marketing Data and Statistics.*

M.E. Sharpe, 80 Business Park Drive, Armonk, NY 10504, (800) 541-6563, Fax: (914) 273-2106, www.mesharpe.com; *The Illustrated Book of World Rankings.*

ANGOLA - ILLITERATE PERSONS

Euromonitor International, Inc., 224 S. Michigan Avenue, Suite 1500, Chicago, IL 60604, (312) 922-1115, Fax: (312) 922-1157, www.euromonitor.com; *The World Economic Factbook 2008.*

Palgrave Macmillan Ltd., Houndmills, Basingstoke, Hampshire, RG21 6XS, England, (Telephone in U.S. (888) 330-8477), (Fax in U.S. (800) 672-2054), www.palgrave.com; *The Statesman's Yearbook 2008.*

UNESCO Institute for Statistics, C.P. 6128 Succursale Centre-Ville, Montreal, Quebec, H3C 3J7 Canada, (Dial from U.S. (514) 343-6880), (Fax from U.S. (514) 343 6882), www.uis.unesco.org; *Statistical Tables.*

United Nations Statistics Division, New York, NY 10017, (800) 253-9646, Fax: (212) 963-4116, http://unstats.un.org; *Human Development Report 2006.*

ANGOLA - IMPORTS

Central Intelligence Agency, Office of Public Affairs, Washington, DC 20505, (703) 482-0623, Fax: (703) 482-1739, www.cia.gov; *The World Factbook.*

Economist Intelligence Unit, 111 West 57th Street, New York, NY 10019, (212) 554-0600, Fax: (212) 586-1181, www.eiu.com; *Angola Country Report.*

Euromonitor International, Inc., 224 S. Michigan Avenue, Suite 1500, Chicago, IL 60604, (312) 922-1115, Fax: (312) 922-1157, www.euromonitor.com; *International Marketing Data and Statistics 2008* and *The World Economic Factbook 2008.*

International Monetary Fund (IMF), 700 Nineteenth Street, NW, Washington, DC 20431, (202) 623-7000, Fax: (202) 623-4661, www.imf.org; *Direction of Trade Statistics Yearbook 2007.*

Palgrave Macmillan Ltd., Houndmills, Basingstoke, Hampshire, RG21 6XS, England, (Telephone in U.S. (888) 330-8477), (Fax in U.S. (800) 672-2054), www.palgrave.com; *The Statesman's Yearbook 2008.*

Taylor and Francis Group, An Informa Business, 2 Park Square, Milton Park, Abingdon, Oxford OX14 4RN, United Kingdom, (Dial from U.S. (212) 216-7800), (Fax from U.S. (212) 564-7854), www.tandf.co.uk; *The Europa World Year Book.*

UNICEF, 3 United Nations Plaza, New York, NY 10017, (800) 253-9646, Fax: (212) 887-7465, www.unicef.org; *The State of the World's Children 2008.*

United Nations Economic Commission for Africa (ECA), PO Box 3001, Addis Ababa, Ethiopia, (Telephone in U.S. (212) 963-4957), www.uneca.org; *African Statistical Yearbook 2006.*

United Nations Food and Agricultural Organization (FAO), Viale delle Terme di Caracalla, 00100 Rome, Italy, (Dial from U.S. (202) 653-2400), (Fax from U.S. (202) 653 5760), www.fao.org; *The State of Food and Agriculture (SOFA) 2006.*

United Nations Statistics Division, New York, NY 10017, (800) 253-9646, Fax: (212) 963-4116, http://unstats.un.org; *Compendium of Intra-African and Related Foreign Trade Statistics 2003* and *Survey of Economic and Social Conditions in Africa 2005.*

ANGOLA - INDUSTRIAL METALS PRODUCTION

See ANGOLA - MINERAL INDUSTRIES

ANGOLA - INDUSTRIAL PRODUCTIVITY

Euromonitor International, Inc., 224 S. Michigan Avenue, Suite 1500, Chicago, IL 60604, (312) 922-1115, Fax: (312) 922-1157, www.euromonitor.com; *International Marketing Data and Statistics 2008.*

M.E. Sharpe, 80 Business Park Drive, Armonk, NY 10504, (800) 541-6563, Fax: (914) 273-2106, www.mesharpe.com; *The Illustrated Book of World Rankings.*

ANGOLA - INDUSTRIES

Central Intelligence Agency, Office of Public Affairs, Washington, DC 20505, (703) 482-0623, Fax: (703) 482-1739, www.cia.gov; *The World Factbook.*

Economist Intelligence Unit, 111 West 57th Street, New York, NY 10019, (212) 554-0600, Fax: (212) 586-1181, www.eiu.com; *Angola Country Report.*

Euromonitor International, Inc., 224 S. Michigan Avenue, Suite 1500, Chicago, IL 60604, (312) 922-1115, Fax: (312) 922-1157, www.euromonitor.com; *International Marketing Data and Statistics 2008; The World Economic Factbook 2008;* and *World Marketing Data and Statistics.*

M.E. Sharpe, 80 Business Park Drive, Armonk, NY 10504, (800) 541-6563, Fax: (914) 273-2106, www.mesharpe.com; *The Illustrated Book of World Rankings.*

Palgrave Macmillan Ltd., Houndmills, Basingstoke, Hampshire, RG21 6XS, England, (Telephone in U.S. (888) 330-8477), (Fax in U.S. (800) 672-2054), www.palgrave.com; *The Statesman's Yearbook 2008.*

Taylor and Francis Group, An Informa Business, 2 Park Square, Milton Park, Abingdon, Oxford OX14 4RN, United Kingdom, (Dial from U.S. (212) 216-7800), (Fax from U.S. (212) 564-7854), www.tandf.co.uk; *The Europa World Year Book.*

United Nations Economic Commission for Africa (ECA), PO Box 3001, Addis Ababa, Ethiopia, (Telephone in U.S. (212) 963-4957), www.uneca.org; *African Statistical Yearbook 2006.*

United Nations Industrial Development Organization (UNIDO), 1 United Nations Plaza, New York, NY 10017, (212) 963 6890, Fax: (212) 963-7904, http://unido.org; Industrial Statistics Database 2008 (INDSTAT) and *The International Yearbook of Industrial Statistics 2008.*

United Nations Statistics Division, New York, NY 10017, (800) 253-9646, Fax: (212) 963-4116, http://unstats.un.org; *2004 Industrial Commodity Statistics Yearbook* and *Survey of Economic and Social Conditions in Africa 2005.*

The World Bank, 1818 H Street, NW, Washington, DC 20433, (202) 473-1000, Fax: (202) 477-6391, www.worldbank.org; *Angola.*

ANGOLA - INFANT AND MATERNAL MORTALITY

See ANGOLA - MORTALITY

ANGOLA - INTERNATIONAL TRADE

African Development Bank Group, Rue Joseph Anoma, 01 BP 1387 Abidjan 01, Cote d'Ivoire, www.afdb.org; *Statistics Pocketbook 2008.*

Economist Intelligence Unit, 111 West 57th Street, New York, NY 10019, (212) 554-0600, Fax: (212) 586-1181, www.eiu.com; *Angola Country Report.*

Euromonitor International, Inc., 224 S. Michigan Avenue, Suite 1500, Chicago, IL 60604, (312) 922-1115, Fax: (312) 922-1157, www.euromonitor.com; *International Marketing Data and Statistics 2008; The World Economic Factbook 2008;* and *World Marketing Data and Statistics.*

M.E. Sharpe, 80 Business Park Drive, Armonk, NY 10504, (800) 541-6563, Fax: (914) 273-2106, www.mesharpe.com; *The Illustrated Book of World Rankings.*

Organisation for Economic Cooperation and Development (OECD), 2 rue Andre Pascal, F-75775 Paris Cedex 16, France, (Telephone in U.S. (202) 785-6323), (Fax in U.S. (202) 785-0350), www.oecd.org; *International Trade by Commodity Statistics (ITCS).*

Palgrave Macmillan Ltd., Houndmills, Basingstoke, Hampshire, RG21 6XS, England, (Telephone in U.S. (888) 330-8477), (Fax in U.S. (800) 672-2054), www.palgrave.com; *The Statesman's Yearbook 2008.*

Taylor and Francis Group, An Informa Business, 2 Park Square, Milton Park, Abingdon, Oxford OX14 4RN, United Kingdom, (Dial from U.S. (212) 216-7800), (Fax from U.S. (212) 564-7854), www.tandf.co.uk; *The Europa World Year Book.*

United Nations Conference on Trade and Development (UNCTAD), DC2-1120, United Nations, New York, NY 10017, (212) 963-0027, www.unctad.org; *UNCTAD Commodity Yearbook.*

United Nations Economic Commission for Africa (ECA), PO Box 3001, Addis Ababa, Ethiopia, (Telephone in U.S. (212) 963-4957), www.uneca.org; *African Statistical Yearbook 2006.*

United Nations Food and Agricultural Organization (FAO), Viale delle Terme di Caracalla, 00100 Rome, Italy, (Dial from U.S. (202) 653-2400), (Fax from U.S. (202) 653 5760), www.fao.org; *FAO Trade Yearbook* and *The State of Food and Agriculture (SOFA) 2006.*

United Nations Statistics Division, New York, NY 10017, (800) 253-9646, Fax: (212) 963-4116, http://unstats.un.org; *Compendium of Intra-African and Related Foreign Trade Statistics 2003; International Trade Statistics Yearbook;* and *Statistical Yearbook.*

The World Bank, 1818 H Street, NW, Washington, DC 20433, (202) 473-1000, Fax: (202) 477-6391, www.worldbank.org; *Angola.*

World Trade Organization (WTO), Centre William Rappard, Rue de Lausanne 154, CH-1211 Geneva 21, Switzerland, www.wto.org; *International Trade Statistics 2006.*

ANGOLA - INTERNET USERS

International Telecommunication Union (ITU), Place des Nations, 1211 Geneva 20, Switzerland, www.itu.int; *World Telecommunication/ICT Indicators Database on CD-ROM; World Telecommunication/ICT Indicators Database Online;* and *Yearbook of Statistics - Telecommunication Services (Chronological Time Series 1997-2006).*

The World Bank, 1818 H Street, NW, Washington, DC 20433, (202) 473-1000, Fax: (202) 477-6391, www.worldbank.org; *Angola.*

ANGOLA - IRON AND IRON ORE PRODUCTION

See ANGOLA - MINERAL INDUSTRIES

ANGOLA - IRRIGATION

Euromonitor International, Inc., 224 S. Michigan Avenue, Suite 1500, Chicago, IL 60604, (312) 922-1115, Fax: (312) 922-1157, www.euromonitor.com; *International Marketing Data and Statistics 2008.*

ANGOLA - JUTE PRODUCTION

See ANGOLA - CROPS

ANGOLA - LABOR

African Development Bank Group, Rue Joseph Anoma, 01 BP 1387 Abidjan 01, Cote d'Ivoire, www.afdb.org; *Statistics Pocketbook 2008.*

Central Intelligence Agency, Office of Public Affairs, Washington, DC 20505, (703) 482-0623, Fax: (703) 482-1739, www.cia.gov; *The World Factbook.*

Euromonitor International, Inc., 224 S. Michigan Avenue, Suite 1500, Chicago, IL 60604, (312) 922-1115, Fax: (312) 922-1157, www.euromonitor.com; *International Marketing Data and Statistics 2008* and *World Marketing Data and Statistics.*

M.E. Sharpe, 80 Business Park Drive, Armonk, NY 10504, (800) 541-6563, Fax: (914) 273-2106, www.mesharpe.com; *The Illustrated Book of World Rankings.*

Palgrave Macmillan Ltd., Houndmills, Basingstoke, Hampshire, RG21 6XS, England, (Telephone in U.S. (888) 330-8477), (Fax in U.S. (800) 672-2054), www.palgrave.com; *The Statesman's Yearbook 2008.*

United Nations Food and Agricultural Organization (FAO), Viale delle Terme di Caracalla, 00100 Rome, Italy, (Dial from U.S. (202) 653-2400), (Fax from U.S. (202) 653 5760), www.fao.org; *The State of Food and Agriculture (SOFA) 2006.*

United Nations Statistics Division, New York, NY 10017, (800) 253-9646, Fax: (212) 963-4116, http://unstats.un.org; *Human Development Report 2006.*

The World Bank, 1818 H Street, NW, Washington, DC 20433, (202) 473-1000, Fax: (202) 477-6391, www.worldbank.org; *The World Bank Atlas 2003-2004.*

ANGOLA - LAND USE

Central Intelligence Agency, Office of Public Affairs, Washington, DC 20505, (703) 482-0623, Fax: (703) 482-1739, www.cia.gov; *The World Factbook.*

Euromonitor International, Inc., 224 S. Michigan Avenue, Suite 1500, Chicago, IL 60604, (312) 922-1115, Fax: (312) 922-1157, www.euromonitor.com; *International Marketing Data and Statistics 2008.*

United Nations Food and Agricultural Organization (FAO), Viale delle Terme di Caracalla, 00100 Rome, Italy, (Dial from U.S. (202) 653-2400), (Fax from U.S. (202) 653 5760), www.fao.org; *FAO Production Yearbook 2002.*

ANGOLA - LIBRARIES

M.E. Sharpe, 80 Business Park Drive, Armonk, NY 10504, (800) 541-6563, Fax: (914) 273-2106, www.mesharpe.com; *The Illustrated Book of World Rankings.*

ANGOLA - LIFE EXPECTANCY

African Development Bank Group, Rue Joseph Anoma, 01 BP 1387 Abidjan 01, Cote d'Ivoire, www.afdb.org; *Statistics Pocketbook 2008.*

Euromonitor International, Inc., 224 S. Michigan Avenue, Suite 1500, Chicago, IL 60604, (312) 922-1115, Fax: (312) 922-1157, www.euromonitor.com; *The World Economic Factbook 2008.*

Palgrave Macmillan Ltd., Houndmills, Basingstoke, Hampshire, RG21 6XS, England, (Telephone in U.S. (888) 330-8477), (Fax in U.S. (800) 672-2054), www.palgrave.com; *The Statesman's Yearbook 2008.*

United Nations Statistics Division, New York, NY 10017, (800) 253-9646, Fax: (212) 963-4116, http://unstats.un.org; *Human Development Report 2006* and *World Statistics Pocketbook.*

The World Bank, 1818 H Street, NW, Washington, DC 20433, (202) 473-1000, Fax: (202) 477-6391, www.worldbank.org; *The World Bank Atlas 2003-2004.*

ANGOLA - LITERACY

Euromonitor International, Inc., 224 S. Michigan Avenue, Suite 1500, Chicago, IL 60604, (312) 922-1115, Fax: (312) 922-1157, www.euromonitor.com; *International Marketing Data and Statistics 2008* and *World Marketing Data and Statistics.*

M.E. Sharpe, 80 Business Park Drive, Armonk, NY 10504, (800) 541-6563, Fax: (914) 273-2106, www.mesharpe.com; *The Illustrated Book of World Rankings.*

Palgrave Macmillan Ltd., Houndmills, Basingstoke, Hampshire, RG21 6XS, England, (Telephone in U.S. (888) 330-8477), (Fax in U.S. (800) 672-2054), www.palgrave.com; *The Statesman's Yearbook 2008.*

Taylor and Francis Group, An Informa Business, 2 Park Square, Milton Park, Abingdon, Oxford OX14 4RN, United Kingdom, (Dial from U.S. (212) 216-7800), (Fax from U.S. (212) 564-7854), www.tandf.co.uk; *The Europa World Year Book.*

United Nations Conference on Trade and Development (UNCTAD), DC2-1120, United Nations, New York, NY 10017, (212) 963-0027, www.unctad.org; *UNCTAD Commodity Yearbook.*

United Nations Economic Commission for Africa (ECA), PO Box 3001, Addis Ababa, Ethiopia, (Telephone in U.S. (212) 963-4957), www.uneca.org; *African Statistical Yearbook 2006.*

United Nations Food and Agricultural Organization (FAO), Viale delle Terme di Caracalla, 00100 Rome, Italy, (Dial from U.S. (202) 653-2400), (Fax from U.S. (202) 653 5760), www.fao.org; *FAO Production Yearbook 2002* and *The State of Food and Agriculture (SOFA) 2006.*

United Nations Statistics Division, New York, NY 10017, (800) 253-9646, Fax: (212) 963-4116, http://unstats.un.org; *Statistical Yearbook* and *Survey of Economic and Social Conditions in Africa 2005.*

ANGOLA - LIVESTOCK

United Nations Statistics Division, New York, NY 10017, (800) 253-9646, Fax: (212) 963-4116, http://unstats.un.org; *Survey of Economic and Social Conditions in Africa 2005.*

ANGOLA - LOCAL TAXATION

Euromonitor International, Inc., 224 S. Michigan Avenue, Suite 1500, Chicago, IL 60604, (312) 922-1115, Fax: (312) 922-1157, www.euromonitor.com; *International Marketing Data and Statistics 2008.*

ANGOLA - MANUFACTURES

M.E. Sharpe, 80 Business Park Drive, Armonk, NY 10504, (800) 541-6563, Fax: (914) 273-2106, www.mesharpe.com; *The Illustrated Book of World Rankings.*

United Nations Economic Commission for Africa (ECA), PO Box 3001, Addis Ababa, Ethiopia, (Telephone in U.S. (212) 963-4957), www.uneca.org; *African Statistical Yearbook 2006.*

United Nations Statistics Division, New York, NY 10017, (800) 253-9646, Fax: (212) 963-4116, http://unstats.un.org; *Statistical Yearbook* and *Survey of Economic and Social Conditions in Africa 2005.*

ANGOLA - MARRIAGE

M.E. Sharpe, 80 Business Park Drive, Armonk, NY 10504, (800) 541-6563, Fax: (914) 273-2106, www.mesharpe.com; *The Illustrated Book of World Rankings.*

United Nations Statistics Division, New York, NY 10017, (800) 253-9646, Fax: (212) 963-4116, http://unstats.un.org; *Demographic Yearbook* and *Statistical Yearbook.*

ANGOLA - MEAT PRODUCTION

See ANGOLA - LIVESTOCK

ANGOLA - MERCHANT SHIPS

See ANGOLA - SHIPPING

ANGOLA - MILK PRODUCTION

See ANGOLA - DAIRY PROCESSING

ANGOLA - MINERAL INDUSTRIES

M.E. Sharpe, 80 Business Park Drive, Armonk, NY 10504, (800) 541-6563, Fax: (914) 273-2106, www.mesharpe.com; *The Illustrated Book of World Rankings.*

Organisation for Economic Cooperation and Development (OECD), 2 rue Andre Pascal, F-75775 Paris Cedex 16, France, (Telephone in U.S. (202) 785-6323), (Fax in U.S. (202) 785-0350), www.oecd.org; *World Energy Outlook 2007.*

Palgrave Macmillan Ltd., Houndmills, Basingstoke, Hampshire, RG21 6XS, England, (Telephone in U.S.

(888) 330-8477), (Fax in U.S. (800) 672-2054), www.palgrave.com; *The Statesman's Yearbook 2008.*

Taylor and Francis Group, An Informa Business, 2 Park Square, Milton Park, Abingdon, Oxford OX14 4RN, United Kingdom, (Dial from U.S. (212) 216-7800), (Fax from U.S. (212) 564-7854), www.tandf.co.uk; *The Europa World Year Book.*

United Nations Conference on Trade and Development (UNCTAD), DC2-1120, United Nations, New York, NY 10017, (212) 963-0027, www.unctad.org; *UNCTAD Commodity Yearbook.*

United Nations Economic Commission for Africa (ECA), PO Box 3001, Addis Ababa, Ethiopia, (Telephone in U.S. (212) 963-4957), www.uneca.org; *African Statistical Yearbook 2006.*

United Nations Statistics Division, New York, NY 10017, (800) 253-9646, Fax: (212) 963-4116, http://unstats.un.org; *Statistical Yearbook.*

ANGOLA - MONEY EXCHANGE RATES

See ANGOLA - FOREIGN EXCHANGE RATES

ANGOLA - MONEY SUPPLY

African Development Bank Group, Rue Joseph Anoma, 01 BP 1387 Abidjan 01, Cote d'Ivoire, www.afdb.org; *Statistics Pocketbook 2008.*

Economist Intelligence Unit, 111 West 57th Street, New York, NY 10019, (212) 554-0600, Fax: (212) 586-1181, www.eiu.com; *Angola Country Report.*

Euromonitor International, Inc., 224 S. Michigan Avenue, Suite 1500, Chicago, IL 60604, (312) 922-1115, Fax: (312) 922-1157, www.euromonitor.com; *International Marketing Data and Statistics 2008.*

The World Bank, 1818 H Street, NW, Washington, DC 20433, (202) 473-1000, Fax: (202) 477-6391, www.worldbank.org; *Angola.*

ANGOLA - MORTALITY

Central Intelligence Agency, Office of Public Affairs, Washington, DC 20505, (703) 482-0623, Fax: (703) 482-1739, www.cia.gov; *The World Factbook.*

Euromonitor International, Inc., 224 S. Michigan Avenue, Suite 1500, Chicago, IL 60604, (312) 922-1115, Fax: (312) 922-1157, www.euromonitor.com; *International Marketing Data and Statistics 2008* and *The World Economic Factbook 2008.*

Palgrave Macmillan Ltd., Houndmills, Basingstoke, Hampshire, RG21 6XS, England, (Telephone in U.S. (888) 330-8477), (Fax in U.S. (800) 672-2054), www.palgrave.com; *The Statesman's Yearbook 2008.*

Taylor and Francis Group, An Informa Business, 2 Park Square, Milton Park, Abingdon, Oxford OX14 4RN, United Kingdom, (Dial from U.S. (212) 216-7800), (Fax from U.S. (212) 564-7854), www.tandf.co.uk; *The Europa World Year Book.*

UNICEF, 3 United Nations Plaza, New York, NY 10017, (800) 253-9646, Fax: (212) 887-7465, www.unicef.org; *The State of the World's Children 2008.*

United Nations Statistics Division, New York, NY 10017, (800) 253-9646, Fax: (212) 963-4116, http://unstats.un.org; *Demographic Yearbook; Human Development Report 2006; Statistical Yearbook; Survey of Economic and Social Conditions in Africa 2005;* and *World Statistics Pocketbook.*

The World Bank, 1818 H Street, NW, Washington, DC 20433, (202) 473-1000, Fax: (202) 477-6391, www.worldbank.org; *The World Bank Atlas 2003-2004.*

World Health Organization (WHO), Avenue Appia 20, 1211 Geneve 27, Switzerland, (Telephone in U.S. (212) 331-9081), www.who.int; The WHO Global Atlas of Infectious Diseases.

ANGOLA - MOTION PICTURES

Palgrave Macmillan Ltd., Houndmills, Basingstoke, Hampshire, RG21 6XS, England, (Telephone in U.S. (888) 330-8477), (Fax in U.S. (800) 672-2054), www.palgrave.com; *The Statesman's Yearbook 2008.*

United Nations Statistics Division, New York, NY 10017, (800) 253-9646, Fax: (212) 963-4116, http://unstats.un.org; *Statistical Yearbook.*

ANGOLA - MOTOR VEHICLES

International Road Federation (IFR), Madison Place, 500 Montgomery Street, 5th Floor, Alexandria, VA 22314, (703) 535-1001, Fax: (703) 535-1007, www.irfnet.org; *World Road Statistics 2006.*

United Nations Statistics Division, New York, NY 10017, (800) 253-9646, Fax: (212) 963-4116, http://unstats.un.org; *Statistical Yearbook* and *Survey of Economic and Social Conditions in Africa 2005.*

ANGOLA - MUSEUMS

M.E. Sharpe, 80 Business Park Drive, Armonk, NY 10504, (800) 541-6563, Fax: (914) 273-2106, www.mesharpe.com; *The Illustrated Book of World Rankings.*

ANGOLA - NATURAL GAS PRODUCTION

See ANGOLA - MINERAL INDUSTRIES

ANGOLA - NUTRITION

African Development Bank Group, Rue Joseph Anoma, 01 BP 1387 Abidjan 01, Cote d'Ivoire, www.afdb.org; *Statistics Pocketbook 2008.*

United Nations Food and Agricultural Organization (FAO), Viale delle Terme di Caracalla, 00100 Rome, Italy, (Dial from U.S. (202) 653-2400), (Fax from U.S. (202) 653 5760), www.fao.org; *The State of Food and Agriculture (SOFA) 2006.*

ANGOLA - OLDER PEOPLE

M.E. Sharpe, 80 Business Park Drive, Armonk, NY 10504, (800) 541-6563, Fax: (914) 273-2106, www.mesharpe.com; *The Illustrated Book of World Rankings.*

ANGOLA - PAPER

See ANGOLA - FORESTS AND FORESTRY

ANGOLA - PEANUT PRODUCTION

See ANGOLA - CROPS

ANGOLA - PESTICIDES

United Nations Food and Agricultural Organization (FAO), Viale delle Terme di Caracalla, 00100 Rome, Italy, (Dial from U.S. (202) 653-2400), (Fax from U.S. (202) 653 5760), www.fao.org; *The State of Food and Agriculture (SOFA) 2006.*

ANGOLA - PETROLEUM INDUSTRY AND TRADE

M.E. Sharpe, 80 Business Park Drive, Armonk, NY 10504, (800) 541-6563, Fax: (914) 273-2106, www.mesharpe.com; *The Illustrated Book of World Rankings.*

Organisation for Economic Cooperation and Development (OECD), 2 rue Andre Pascal, F-75775 Paris Cedex 16, France, (Telephone in U.S. (202) 785-6323), (Fax in U.S. (202) 785-0350), www.oecd.org; *World Energy Outlook 2007.*

Organization of Petroleum Exporting Countries (OPEC), Obere Donaustrasse 93, A-1020, Vienna, Austria, www.opec.org; *Annual Statistical Bulletin 2006.*

Palgrave Macmillan Ltd., Houndmills, Basingstoke, Hampshire, RG21 6XS, England, (Telephone in U.S. (888) 330-8477), (Fax in U.S. (800) 672-2054), www.palgrave.com; *The Statesman's Yearbook 2008.*

PennWell Corporation, 1421 South Sheridan Road, Tulsa, OK 74112, (918) 835-3161, www.pennwell.com; *International Petroleum Encyclopedia 2007.*

United Nations Conference on Trade and Development (UNCTAD), DC2-1120, United Nations, New York, NY 10017, (212) 963-0027, www.unctad.org; *UNCTAD Commodity Yearbook.*

United Nations Food and Agricultural Organization (FAO), Viale delle Terme di Caracalla, 00100 Rome, Italy, (Dial from U.S. (202) 653-2400), (Fax from U.S. (202) 653 5760), www.fao.org; *The State of Food and Agriculture (SOFA) 2006.*

United Nations Statistics Division, New York, NY 10017, (800) 253-9646, Fax: (212) 963-4116, http://unstats.un.org; *Statistical Yearbook.*

ANGOLA - PIPELINES

Organization of Petroleum Exporting Countries (OPEC), Obere Donaustrasse 93, A-1020, Vienna, Austria, www.opec.org; *Annual Statistical Bulletin 2006.*

ANGOLA - POLITICAL SCIENCE

Central Intelligence Agency, Office of Public Affairs, Washington, DC 20505, (703) 482-0623, Fax: (703) 482-1739, www.cia.gov; *The World Factbook.*

Palgrave Macmillan Ltd., Houndmills, Basingstoke, Hampshire, RG21 6XS, England, (Telephone in U.S. (888) 330-8477), (Fax in U.S. (800) 672-2054), www.palgrave.com; *The Statesman's Yearbook 2008.*

Taylor and Francis Group, An Informa Business, 2 Park Square, Milton Park, Abingdon, Oxford OX14 4RN, United Kingdom, (Dial from U.S. (212) 216-7800), (Fax from U.S. (212) 564-7854), www.tandf.co.uk; *The Europa World Year Book.*

United Nations Statistics Division, New York, NY 10017, (800) 253-9646, Fax: (212) 963-4116, http://unstats.un.org; *National Accounts Statistics: Compendium of Income Distribution Statistics* and *Survey of Economic and Social Conditions in Africa 2005.*

ANGOLA - POPULATION

African Development Bank Group, Rue Joseph Anoma, 01 BP 1387 Abidjan 01, Cote d'Ivoire, www.afdb.org; *The African Statistical Journal; Gender, Poverty and Environmental Indicators on African Countries 2007; Selected Statistics on African Countries 2007;* and *Statistics Pocketbook 2008.*

Central Intelligence Agency, Office of Public Affairs, Washington, DC 20505, (703) 482-0623, Fax: (703) 482-1739, www.cia.gov; *The World Factbook.*

Economist Intelligence Unit, 111 West 57th Street, New York, NY 10019, (212) 554-0600, Fax: (212) 586-1181, www.eiu.com; *Angola Country Report.*

Euromonitor International, Inc., 224 S. Michigan Avenue, Suite 1500, Chicago, IL 60604, (312) 922-1115, Fax: (312) 922-1157, www.euromonitor.com; *International Marketing Data and Statistics 2008* and *The World Economic Factbook 2008.*

Eurostat, Batiment Jean Monnet, Rue Alcide de Gasperi, L-2920 Luxembourg, http://epp.eurostat.ec.europa.eu; *Demographic Indicators - Population by Age-Classes.*

International Organization for Migration (IOM), 17, Route des Morillons, CH-1211 Geneva 19, Switzerland, www.iom.int; *Migration and Development: New Strategic Outlooks and Practical Ways Forward - The Cases of Angola and Zambia.*

M.E. Sharpe, 80 Business Park Drive, Armonk, NY 10504, (800) 541-6563, Fax: (914) 273-2106, www.mesharpe.com; *The Illustrated Book of World Rankings.*

Palgrave Macmillan Ltd., Houndmills, Basingstoke, Hampshire, RG21 6XS, England, (Telephone in U.S. (888) 330-8477), (Fax in U.S. (800) 672-2054), www.palgrave.com; *The Statesman's Yearbook 2008.*

Taylor and Francis Group, An Informa Business, 2 Park Square, Milton Park, Abingdon, Oxford OX14 4RN, United Kingdom, (Dial from U.S. (212) 216-7800), (Fax from U.S. (212) 564-7854), www.tandf.co.uk; *The Europa World Year Book.*

U.S. Department of State (DOS), 2201 C Street NW, Washington, DC 20520, (202) 647-4000, www.state.gov; *World Military Expenditures and Arms Transfers (WMEAT).*

United Nations Food and Agricultural Organization (FAO), Viale delle Terme di Caracalla, 00100 Rome, Italy, (Dial from U.S. (202) 653-2400), (Fax from U.S. (202) 653 5760), www.fao.org; *FAO Production Yearbook 2002.*

United Nations Statistics Division, New York, NY 10017, (800) 253-9646, Fax: (212) 963-4116, http://

unstats.un.org; *Demographic Yearbook; Human Development Report 2006; Statistical Yearbook; Survey of Economic and Social Conditions in Africa 2005;* and *World Statistics Pocketbook.*

The World Bank, 1818 H Street, NW, Washington, DC 20433, (202) 473-1000, Fax: (202) 477-6391, www.worldbank.org; *Angola* and *The World Bank Atlas 2003-2004.*

World Health Organization (WHO), Avenue Appia 20, 1211 Geneve 27, Switzerland, (Telephone in U.S. (212) 331-9081), www.who.int; *World Health Report 2006.*

ANGOLA - POPULATION DENSITY

African Development Bank Group, Rue Joseph Anoma, 01 BP 1387 Abidjan 01, Cote d'Ivoire, www.afdb.org; *Statistics Pocketbook 2008.*

Central Intelligence Agency, Office of Public Affairs, Washington, DC 20505, (703) 482-0623, Fax: (703) 482-1739, www.cia.gov; *The World Factbook.*

Euromonitor International, Inc., 224 S. Michigan Avenue, Suite 1500, Chicago, IL 60604, (312) 922-1115, Fax: (312) 922-1157, www.euromonitor.com; *International Marketing Data and Statistics 2008* and *The World Economic Factbook 2008.*

M.E. Sharpe, 80 Business Park Drive, Armonk, NY 10504, (800) 541-6563, Fax: (914) 273-2106, www.mesharpe.com; *The Illustrated Book of World Rankings.*

Palgrave Macmillan Ltd., Houndmills, Basingstoke, Hampshire, RG21 6XS, England, (Telephone in U.S. (888) 330-8477), (Fax in U.S. (800) 672-2054), www.palgrave.com; *The Statesman's Yearbook 2008.*

Taylor and Francis Group, An Informa Business, 2 Park Square, Milton Park, Abingdon, Oxford OX14 4RN, United Kingdom, (Dial from U.S. (212) 216-7800), (Fax from U.S. (212) 564-7854), www.tandf.co.uk; *The Europa World Year Book.*

United Nations Food and Agricultural Organization (FAO), Viale delle Terme di Caracalla, 00100 Rome, Italy, (Dial from U.S. (202) 653-2400), (Fax from U.S. (202) 653 5760), www.fao.org; *The State of Food and Agriculture (SOFA) 2006.*

United Nations Statistics Division, New York, NY 10017, (800) 253-9646, Fax: (212) 963-4116, http://unstats.un.org; *Survey of Economic and Social Conditions in Africa 2005.*

The World Bank, 1818 H Street, NW, Washington, DC 20433, (202) 473-1000, Fax: (202) 477-6391, www.worldbank.org; *Angola.*

ANGOLA - POSTAL SERVICE

M.E. Sharpe, 80 Business Park Drive, Armonk, NY 10504, (800) 541-6563, Fax: (914) 273-2106, www.mesharpe.com; *The Illustrated Book of World Rankings.*

United Nations Statistics Division, New York, NY 10017, (800) 253-9646, Fax: (212) 963-4116, http://unstats.un.org; *Statistical Yearbook.*

ANGOLA - POULTRY

See ANGOLA - LIVESTOCK

ANGOLA - POWER RESOURCES

Euromonitor International, Inc., 224 S. Michigan Avenue, Suite 1500, Chicago, IL 60604, (312) 922-1115, Fax: (312) 922-1157, www.euromonitor.com; *International Marketing Data and Statistics 2008; The World Economic Factbook 2008;* and *World Marketing Data and Statistics.*

M.E. Sharpe, 80 Business Park Drive, Armonk, NY 10504, (800) 541-6563, Fax: (914) 273-2106, www.mesharpe.com; *The Illustrated Book of World Rankings.*

Organisation for Economic Cooperation and Development (OECD), 2 rue Andre Pascal, F-75775 Paris Cedex 16, France, (Telephone in U.S. (202) 785-6323), (Fax in U.S. (202) 785-0350), www.oecd.org; *World Energy Outlook 2007.*

Palgrave Macmillan Ltd., Houndmills, Basingstoke, Hampshire, RG21 6XS, England, (Telephone in U.S. (888) 330-8477), (Fax in U.S. (800) 672-2054), www.palgrave.com; *The Statesman's Yearbook 2008.*

Platts, 2 Penn Plaza, 25th Floor, New York, NY 10121-2298, (212) 904-3070, www.platts.com; *Energy Economist.*

U.S. Department of Energy (DOE), Energy Information Administration (EIA), 1000 Independence Avenue, SW, Washington, DC 20585, (202) 586-8800, www.eia.doe.gov; *International Energy Annual 2004* and *International Energy Outlook 2006.*

United Nations Economic Commission for Africa (ECA), PO Box 3001, Addis Ababa, Ethiopia, (Telephone in U.S. (212) 963-4957), www.uneca.org; *African Statistical Yearbook 2006.*

United Nations Food and Agricultural Organization (FAO), Viale delle Terme di Caracalla, 00100 Rome, Italy, (Dial from U.S. (202) 653-2400), (Fax from U.S. (202) 653 5760), www.fao.org; *The State of Food and Agriculture (SOFA) 2006.*

United Nations Statistics Division, New York, NY 10017, (800) 253-9646, Fax: (212) 963-4116, http://unstats.un.org; *Energy Statistics Yearbook 2003; Human Development Report 2006; Statistical Yearbook;* and *World Statistics Pocketbook.*

The World Bank, 1818 H Street, NW, Washington, DC 20433, (202) 473-1000, Fax: (202) 477-6391, www.worldbank.org; *The World Bank Atlas 2003-2004.*

ANGOLA - PRICES

Euromonitor International, Inc., 224 S. Michigan Avenue, Suite 1500, Chicago, IL 60604, (312) 922-1115, Fax: (312) 922-1157, www.euromonitor.com; *World Marketing Data and Statistics.*

M.E. Sharpe, 80 Business Park Drive, Armonk, NY 10504, (800) 541-6563, Fax: (914) 273-2106, www.mesharpe.com; *The Illustrated Book of World Rankings.*

United Nations Food and Agricultural Organization (FAO), Viale delle Terme di Caracalla, 00100 Rome, Italy, (Dial from U.S. (202) 653-2400), (Fax from U.S. (202) 653 5760), www.fao.org; *FAO Production Yearbook 2002* and *The State of Food and Agriculture (SOFA) 2006.*

The World Bank, 1818 H Street, NW, Washington, DC 20433, (202) 473-1000, Fax: (202) 477-6391, www.worldbank.org; *Angola.*

ANGOLA - PUBLIC HEALTH

African Development Bank Group, Rue Joseph Anoma, 01 BP 1387 Abidjan 01, Cote d'Ivoire, www.afdb.org; *Statistics Pocketbook 2008.*

Euromonitor International, Inc., 224 S. Michigan Avenue, Suite 1500, Chicago, IL 60604, (312) 922-1115, Fax: (312) 922-1157, www.euromonitor.com; *World Marketing Data and Statistics.*

M.E. Sharpe, 80 Business Park Drive, Armonk, NY 10504, (800) 541-6563, Fax: (914) 273-2106, www.mesharpe.com; *The Illustrated Book of World Rankings.*

Palgrave Macmillan Ltd., Houndmills, Basingstoke, Hampshire, RG21 6XS, England, (Telephone in U.S. (888) 330-8477), (Fax in U.S. (800) 672-2054), www.palgrave.com; *The Statesman's Yearbook 2008.*

UNICEF, 3 United Nations Plaza, New York, NY 10017, (800) 253-9646, Fax: (212) 887-7465, www.unicef.org; *The State of the World's Children 2008.*

United Nations Economic Commission for Africa (ECA), PO Box 3001, Addis Ababa, Ethiopia, (Telephone in U.S. (212) 963-4957), www.uneca.org; *African Statistical Yearbook 2006.*

United Nations Statistics Division, New York, NY 10017, (800) 253-9646, Fax: (212) 963-4116, http://unstats.un.org; *Human Development Report 2006* and *Statistical Yearbook.*

The World Bank, 1818 H Street, NW, Washington, DC 20433, (202) 473-1000, Fax: (202) 477-6391, www.worldbank.org; *Angola.*

World Health Organization (WHO), Avenue Appia 20, 1211 Geneve 27, Switzerland, (Telephone in U.S. (212) 331-9081), www.who.int; The WHO Global Atlas of Infectious Diseases.

ANGOLA - PUBLISHERS AND PUBLISHING

Taylor and Francis Group, An Informa Business, 2 Park Square, Milton Park, Abingdon, Oxford OX14 4RN, United Kingdom, (Dial from U.S. (212) 216-7800), (Fax from U.S. (212) 564-7854), www.tandf.co.uk; *The Europa World Year Book.*

UNESCO Institute for Statistics, C.P. 6128 Succursale Centre-Ville, Montreal, Quebec, H3C 3J7 Canada, (Dial from U.S. (514) 343-6880), (Fax from U.S. (514) 343 6882), www.uis.unesco.org; *Statistical Tables.*

ANGOLA - RADIO - RECEIVERS AND RECEPTION

Palgrave Macmillan Ltd., Houndmills, Basingstoke, Hampshire, RG21 6XS, England, (Telephone in U.S. (888) 330-8477), (Fax in U.S. (800) 672-2054), www.palgrave.com; *The Statesman's Yearbook 2008.*

United Nations Statistics Division, New York, NY 10017, (800) 253-9646, Fax: (212) 963-4116, http://unstats.un.org; *Statistical Yearbook.*

ANGOLA - RAILROADS

Jane's Information Group, 110 North Royal Street, Suite 200, Alexandria, VA 22314, (703) 683-3700, Fax: (800) 836-0297, www.janes.com; *Jane's World Railways.*

Palgrave Macmillan Ltd., Houndmills, Basingstoke, Hampshire, RG21 6XS, England, (Telephone in U.S. (888) 330-8477), (Fax in U.S. (800) 672-2054), www.palgrave.com; *The Statesman's Yearbook 2008.*

United Nations Economic Commission for Africa (ECA), PO Box 3001, Addis Ababa, Ethiopia, (Telephone in U.S. (212) 963-4957), www.uneca.org; *African Statistical Yearbook 2006.*

United Nations Statistics Division, New York, NY 10017, (800) 253-9646, Fax: (212) 963-4116, http://unstats.un.org; *Statistical Yearbook* and *Survey of Economic and Social Conditions in Africa 2005.*

ANGOLA - RELIGION

Central Intelligence Agency, Office of Public Affairs, Washington, DC 20505, (703) 482-0623, Fax: (703) 482-1739, www.cia.gov; *The World Factbook.*

M.E. Sharpe, 80 Business Park Drive, Armonk, NY 10504, (800) 541-6563, Fax: (914) 273-2106, www.mesharpe.com; *The Illustrated Book of World Rankings.*

Palgrave Macmillan Ltd., Houndmills, Basingstoke, Hampshire, RG21 6XS, England, (Telephone in U.S. (888) 330-8477), (Fax in U.S. (800) 672-2054), www.palgrave.com; *The Statesman's Yearbook 2008.*

ANGOLA - RESERVES (ACCOUNTING)

African Development Bank Group, Rue Joseph Anoma, 01 BP 1387 Abidjan 01, Cote d'Ivoire, www.afdb.org; *Statistics Pocketbook 2008.*

Euromonitor International, Inc., 224 S. Michigan Avenue, Suite 1500, Chicago, IL 60604, (312) 922-1115, Fax: (312) 922-1157, www.euromonitor.com; *International Marketing Data and Statistics 2008.*

ANGOLA - RETAIL TRADE

Euromonitor International, Inc., 224 S. Michigan Avenue, Suite 1500, Chicago, IL 60604, (312) 922-1115, Fax: (312) 922-1157, www.euromonitor.com; *World Marketing Data and Statistics.*

ANGOLA - RICE PRODUCTION

See ANGOLA - CROPS

ANGOLA - ROADS

Central Intelligence Agency, Office of Public Affairs, Washington, DC 20505, (703) 482-0623, Fax: (703) 482-1739, www.cia.gov; *The World Factbook.*

International Road Federation (IFR), Madison Place, 500 Montgomery Street, 5th Floor, Alexandria, VA 22314, (703) 535-1001, Fax: (703) 535-1007, www.irfnet.org; *World Road Statistics 2006.*

Palgrave Macmillan Ltd., Houndmills, Basingstoke, Hampshire, RG21 6XS, England, (Telephone in U.S. (888) 330-8477), (Fax in U.S. (800) 672-2054), www.palgrave.com; *The Statesman's Yearbook 2008.*

United Nations Economic Commission for Africa (ECA), PO Box 3001, Addis Ababa, Ethiopia, (Telephone in U.S. (212) 963-4957), www.uneca.org; *African Statistical Yearbook 2006.*

United Nations Statistics Division, New York, NY 10017, (800) 253-9646, Fax: (212) 963-4116, http://unstats.un.org; *Survey of Economic and Social Conditions in Africa 2005.*

ANGOLA - RUBBER INDUSTRY AND TRADE

International Rubber Study Group (IRSG), 1st Floor, Heron House, 109/115 Wembley Hill Road, Wembley, Middlesex HA9 8DA, United Kingdom, www.rubberstudy.com; *Rubber Statistical Bulletin; Summary of World Rubber Statistics 2005; World Rubber Statistics Handbook (Volume 6, 1975-2001);* and *World Rubber Statistics Historic Handbook.*

M.E. Sharpe, 80 Business Park Drive, Armonk, NY 10504, (800) 541-6563, Fax: (914) 273-2106, www.mesharpe.com; *The Illustrated Book of World Rankings.*

ANGOLA - SALT PRODUCTION

See ANGOLA - MINERAL INDUSTRIES

ANGOLA - SHEEP

See ANGOLA - LIVESTOCK

ANGOLA - SHIPPING

Lloyd's Register - Fairplay, 8410 N.W. 53rd Terrace, Suite 207, Miami FL 33166, (305) 718-9929, Fax: (305) 718-9663, www.lrfairplay.com; *Register of Ships 2007-2008; World Casualty Statistics 2007; World Fleet Statistics 2006; World Marine Propulsion Report 2006-2010; World Shipbuilding Statistics 2007;* and The World Shipping Encyclopaedia.

Organization of Petroleum Exporting Countries (OPEC), Obere Donaustrasse 93, A-1020, Vienna, Austria, www.opec.org; *Annual Statistical Bulletin 2006.*

Palgrave Macmillan Ltd., Houndmills, Basingstoke, Hampshire, RG21 6XS, England, (Telephone in U.S. (888) 330-8477), (Fax in U.S. (800) 672-2054), www.palgrave.com; *The Statesman's Yearbook 2008.*

Taylor and Francis Group, An Informa Business, 2 Park Square, Milton Park, Abingdon, Oxford OX14 4RN, United Kingdom, (Dial from U.S. (212) 216-7800), (Fax from U.S. (212) 564-7854), www.tandf.co.uk; *The Europa World Year Book.*

U.S. Department of Transportation (DOT), Maritime Administration (MARAD), West Building, Southeast Federal Center, 1200 New Jersey Avenue, SE, Washington, DC 20590, (800) 99-MARAD, www.marad.dot.gov; *World Merchant Fleet 2005.*

United Nations Economic Commission for Africa (ECA), PO Box 3001, Addis Ababa, Ethiopia, (Telephone in U.S. (212) 963-4957), www.uneca.org; *African Statistical Yearbook 2006.*

United Nations Statistics Division, New York, NY 10017, (800) 253-9646, Fax: (212) 963-4116, http://unstats.un.org; *Statistical Yearbook.*

ANGOLA - SILVER PRODUCTION

See ANGOLA - MINERAL INDUSTRIES

ANGOLA - SOCIAL ECOLOGY

M.E. Sharpe, 80 Business Park Drive, Armonk, NY 10504, (800) 541-6563, Fax: (914) 273-2106, www.mesharpe.com; *The Illustrated Book of World Rankings.*

United Nations Statistics Division, New York, NY 10017, (800) 253-9646, Fax: (212) 963-4116, http://unstats.un.org; *World Statistics Pocketbook.*

ANGOLA - SOCIAL SECURITY

United Nations Statistics Division, New York, NY 10017, (800) 253-9646, Fax: (212) 963-4116, http://unstats.un.org; *National Accounts Statistics: Compendium of Income Distribution Statistics.*

ANGOLA - STEEL PRODUCTION

See ANGOLA - MINERAL INDUSTRIES

ANGOLA - SUGAR PRODUCTION

See ANGOLA - CROPS

ANGOLA - TAXATION

International Road Federation (IFR), Madison Place, 500 Montgomery Street, 5th Floor, Alexandria, VA 22314, (703) 535-1001, Fax: (703) 535-1007, www.irfnet.org; *World Road Statistics 2006.*

ANGOLA - TELEPHONE

International Telecommunication Union (ITU), Place des Nations, 1211 Geneva 20, Switzerland, www.itu.int; World Telecommunication Indicators Database.

Palgrave Macmillan Ltd., Houndmills, Basingstoke, Hampshire, RG21 6XS, England, (Telephone in U.S. (888) 330-8477), (Fax in U.S. (800) 672-2054), www.palgrave.com; *The Statesman's Yearbook 2008.*

United Nations Statistics Division, New York, NY 10017, (800) 253-9646, Fax: (212) 963-4116, http://unstats.un.org; *Statistical Yearbook* and *World Statistics Pocketbook.*

ANGOLA - TEXTILE INDUSTRY

M.E. Sharpe, 80 Business Park Drive, Armonk, NY 10504, (800) 541-6563, Fax: (914) 273-2106, www.mesharpe.com; *The Illustrated Book of World Rankings.*

Palgrave Macmillan Ltd., Houndmills, Basingstoke, Hampshire, RG21 6XS, England, (Telephone in U.S. (888) 330-8477), (Fax in U.S. (800) 672-2054), www.palgrave.com; *The Statesman's Yearbook 2008.*

United Nations Conference on Trade and Development (UNCTAD), DC2-1120, United Nations, New York, NY 10017, (212) 963-0027, www.unctad.org; *UNCTAD Commodity Yearbook.*

United Nations Statistics Division, New York, NY 10017, (800) 253-9646, Fax: (212) 963-4116, http://unstats.un.org; *Statistical Yearbook.*

ANGOLA - TIRE INDUSTRY

United Nations Statistics Division, New York, NY 10017, (800) 253-9646, Fax: (212) 963-4116, http://unstats.un.org; *Statistical Yearbook.*

ANGOLA - TOBACCO INDUSTRY

Foreign Agricultural Service (FAS), U.S. Department of Agriculture (USDA), 1400 Independence Avenue, SW, Washington, DC 20250, (202) 720-3935, www.fas.usda.gov; *Tobacco: World Markets and Trade.*

M.E. Sharpe, 80 Business Park Drive, Armonk, NY 10504, (800) 541-6563, Fax: (914) 273-2106, www.mesharpe.com; *The Illustrated Book of World Rankings.*

United Nations Statistics Division, New York, NY 10017, (800) 253-9646, Fax: (212) 963-4116, http://unstats.un.org; *Statistical Yearbook.*

ANGOLA - TOURISM

Euromonitor International, Inc., 224 S. Michigan Avenue, Suite 1500, Chicago, IL 60604, (312) 922-1115, Fax: (312) 922-1157, www.euromonitor.com; *The World Economic Factbook 2008* and *World Marketing Data and Statistics.*

M.E. Sharpe, 80 Business Park Drive, Armonk, NY 10504, (800) 541-6563, Fax: (914) 273-2106, www.mesharpe.com; *The Illustrated Book of World Rankings.*

United Nations Economic Commission for Africa (ECA), PO Box 3001, Addis Ababa, Ethiopia, (Telephone in U.S. (212) 963-4957), www.uneca.org; *African Statistical Yearbook 2006.*

The World Bank, 1818 H Street, NW, Washington, DC 20433, (202) 473-1000, Fax: (202) 477-6391, www.worldbank.org; *Angola.*

ANGOLA - TRADE

See ANGOLA - INTERNATIONAL TRADE

ANGOLA - TRANSPORTATION

Central Intelligence Agency, Office of Public Affairs, Washington, DC 20505, (703) 482-0623, Fax: (703) 482-1739, www.cia.gov; *The World Factbook.*

Euromonitor International, Inc., 224 S. Michigan Avenue, Suite 1500, Chicago, IL 60604, (312) 922-1115, Fax: (312) 922-1157, www.euromonitor.com; *International Marketing Data and Statistics 2008* and *World Marketing Data and Statistics.*

M.E. Sharpe, 80 Business Park Drive, Armonk, NY 10504, (800) 541-6563, Fax: (914) 273-2106, www.mesharpe.com; *The Illustrated Book of World Rankings.*

Palgrave Macmillan Ltd., Houndmills, Basingstoke, Hampshire, RG21 6XS, England, (Telephone in U.S. (888) 330-8477), (Fax in U.S. (800) 672-2054), www.palgrave.com; *The Statesman's Yearbook 2008.*

Taylor and Francis Group, An Informa Business, 2 Park Square, Milton Park, Abingdon, Oxford OX14 4RN, United Kingdom, (Dial from U.S. (212) 216-7800), (Fax from U.S. (212) 564-7854), www.tandf.co.uk; *The Europa World Year Book.*

United Nations Economic Commission for Africa (ECA), PO Box 3001, Addis Ababa, Ethiopia, (Telephone in U.S. (212) 963-4957), www.uneca.org; *African Statistical Yearbook 2006.*

United Nations Statistics Division, New York, NY 10017, (800) 253-9646, Fax: (212) 963-4116, http://unstats.un.org; *Human Development Report 2006.*

The World Bank, 1818 H Street, NW, Washington, DC 20433, (202) 473-1000, Fax: (202) 477-6391, www.worldbank.org; *Africa Live Database (LDB)* and *Angola.*

ANGOLA - UNEMPLOYMENT

Central Intelligence Agency, Office of Public Affairs, Washington, DC 20505, (703) 482-0623, Fax: (703) 482-1739, www.cia.gov; *The World Factbook.*

Euromonitor International, Inc., 224 S. Michigan Avenue, Suite 1500, Chicago, IL 60604, (312) 922-1115, Fax: (312) 922-1157, www.euromonitor.com; *International Marketing Data and Statistics 2008.*

ANGOLA - VITAL STATISTICS

Euromonitor International, Inc., 224 S. Michigan Avenue, Suite 1500, Chicago, IL 60604, (312) 922-1115, Fax: (312) 922-1157, www.euromonitor.com; *International Marketing Data and Statistics 2008.*

International Organization for Migration (IOM), 17, Route des Morillons, CH-1211 Geneva 19, Switzerland, www.iom.int; *Migration and Development: New Strategic Outlooks and Practical Ways Forward - The Cases of Angola and Zambia.*

Palgrave Macmillan Ltd., Houndmills, Basingstoke, Hampshire, RG21 6XS, England, (Telephone in U.S. (888) 330-8477), (Fax in U.S. (800) 672-2054), www.palgrave.com; *The Statesman's Yearbook 2008.*

United Nations Statistics Division, New York, NY 10017, (800) 253-9646, Fax: (212) 963-4116, http://unstats.un.org; *Statistical Yearbook.*

World Health Organization (WHO), Avenue Appia 20, 1211 Geneve 27, Switzerland, (Telephone in U.S. (212) 331-9081), www.who.int; *World Health Report 2006.*

ANGOLA - WAGES

The World Bank, 1818 H Street, NW, Washington, DC 20433, (202) 473-1000, Fax: (202) 477-6391, www.worldbank.org; *Angola.*

ANGOLA - WEATHER

See ANGOLA - CLIMATE

ANGOLA - WHEAT PRODUCTION

See ANGOLA - CROPS

ANGOLA - WINE PRODUCTION

See ANGOLA - BEVERAGE INDUSTRY

ANGOLA - WOOD AND WOOD PULP

See ANGOLA - FORESTS AND FORESTRY

ANGOLA - WOOL PRODUCTION

See ANGOLA - TEXTILE INDUSTRY

ANGOLA - YARN PRODUCTION

See ANGOLA - TEXTILE INDUSTRY

ANGUILLA - NATIONAL STATISTICAL OFFICE

Anguilla Statistics Department, Old Court House, PO Box 60, The Valley, Anguilla, (Dial from U.S. (264) 497-5731), (Fax from U.S. (264) 497-3986), www.gov.ai/statistics/; National Data Center.

ANGUILLA - AGRICULTURE

Economist Intelligence Unit, 111 West 57th Street, New York, NY 10019, (212) 554-0600, Fax: (212) 586-1181, www.eiu.com; *Organisation of Eastern Caribbean States.*

Euromonitor International, Inc., 224 S. Michigan Avenue, Suite 1500, Chicago, IL 60604, (312) 922-1115, Fax: (312) 922-1157, www.euromonitor.com; *World Marketing Data and Statistics.*

Palgrave Macmillan Ltd., Houndmills, Basingstoke, Hampshire, RG21 6XS, England, (Telephone in U.S. (888) 330-8477), (Fax in U.S. (800) 672-2054), www.palgrave.com; *The Statesman's Yearbook 2008.*

Taylor and Francis Group, An Informa Business, 2 Park Square, Milton Park, Abingdon, Oxford OX14 4RN, United Kingdom, (Dial from U.S. (212) 216-7800), (Fax from U.S. (212) 564-7854), www.tandf.co.uk; *The Europa World Year Book.*

United Nations Food and Agricultural Organization (FAO), Viale delle Terme di Caracalla, 00100 Rome, Italy, (Dial from U.S. (202) 653-2400), (Fax from U.S. (202) 653 5760), www.fao.org; AQUASTAT.

ANGUILLA - AIRLINES

Palgrave Macmillan Ltd., Houndmills, Basingstoke, Hampshire, RG21 6XS, England, (Telephone in U.S. (888) 330-8477), (Fax in U.S. (800) 672-2054), www.palgrave.com; *The Statesman's Yearbook 2008.*

ANGUILLA - AIRPORTS

Central Intelligence Agency, Office of Public Affairs, Washington, DC 20505, (703) 482-0623, Fax: (703) 482-1739, www.cia.gov; *The World Factbook.*

ANGUILLA - ARMED FORCES

Central Intelligence Agency, Office of Public Affairs, Washington, DC 20505, (703) 482-0623, Fax: (703) 482-1739, www.cia.gov; *The World Factbook.*

Euromonitor International, Inc., 224 S. Michigan Avenue, Suite 1500, Chicago, IL 60604, (312) 922-1115, Fax: (312) 922-1157, www.euromonitor.com; *World Marketing Data and Statistics.*

ANGUILLA - BALANCE OF PAYMENTS

Taylor and Francis Group, An Informa Business, 2 Park Square, Milton Park, Abingdon, Oxford OX14 4RN, United Kingdom, (Dial from U.S. (212) 216-7800), (Fax from U.S. (212) 564-7854), www.tandf.co.uk; *The Europa World Year Book.*

ANGUILLA - BANKS AND BANKING

Euromonitor International, Inc., 224 S. Michigan Avenue, Suite 1500, Chicago, IL 60604, (312) 922-1115, Fax: (312) 922-1157, www.euromonitor.com; *World Marketing Data and Statistics.*

ANGUILLA - BROADCASTING

Central Intelligence Agency, Office of Public Affairs, Washington, DC 20505, (703) 482-0623, Fax: (703) 482-1739, www.cia.gov; *The World Factbook.*

Euromonitor International, Inc., 224 S. Michigan Avenue, Suite 1500, Chicago, IL 60604, (312) 922-1115, Fax: (312) 922-1157, www.euromonitor.com; *World Marketing Data and Statistics.*

WRTH Publications Limited, PO Box 290, Oxford OX2 7FT, UK, www.wrth.com; *World Radio TV Handbook 2007.*

ANGUILLA - BUDGET

Central Intelligence Agency, Office of Public Affairs, Washington, DC 20505, (703) 482-0623, Fax: (703) 482-1739, www.cia.gov; *The World Factbook.*

ANGUILLA - CHILDBIRTH - STATISTICS

Central Intelligence Agency, Office of Public Affairs, Washington, DC 20505, (703) 482-0623, Fax: (703) 482-1739, www.cia.gov; *The World Factbook.*

Euromonitor International, Inc., 224 S. Michigan Avenue, Suite 1500, Chicago, IL 60604, (312) 922-1115, Fax: (312) 922-1157, www.euromonitor.com; *International Marketing Data and Statistics 2008* and *The World Economic Factbook 2008.*

Taylor and Francis Group, An Informa Business, 2 Park Square, Milton Park, Abingdon, Oxford OX14 4RN, United Kingdom, (Dial from U.S. (212) 216-7800), (Fax from U.S. (212) 564-7854), www.tandf.co.uk; *The Europa World Year Book.*

ANGUILLA - CLIMATE

Palgrave Macmillan Ltd., Houndmills, Basingstoke, Hampshire, RG21 6XS, England, (Telephone in U.S. (888) 330-8477), (Fax in U.S. (800) 672-2054), www.palgrave.com; *The Statesman's Yearbook 2008.*

ANGUILLA - COMMERCE

Palgrave Macmillan Ltd., Houndmills, Basingstoke, Hampshire, RG21 6XS, England, (Telephone in U.S. (888) 330-8477), (Fax in U.S. (800) 672-2054), www.palgrave.com; *The Statesman's Yearbook 2008.*

ANGUILLA - CONSUMER PRICE INDEXES

Taylor and Francis Group, An Informa Business, 2 Park Square, Milton Park, Abingdon, Oxford OX14 4RN, United Kingdom, (Dial from U.S. (212) 216-7800), (Fax from U.S. (212) 564-7854), www.tandf.co.uk; *The Europa World Year Book.*

ANGUILLA - DAIRY PROCESSING

Palgrave Macmillan Ltd., Houndmills, Basingstoke, Hampshire, RG21 6XS, England, (Telephone in U.S. (888) 330-8477), (Fax in U.S. (800) 672-2054), www.palgrave.com; *The Statesman's Yearbook 2008.*

ANGUILLA - DEATH RATES

See ANGUILLA - MORTALITY

ANGUILLA - DEMOGRAPHY

Euromonitor International, Inc., 224 S. Michigan Avenue, Suite 1500, Chicago, IL 60604, (312) 922-1115, Fax: (312) 922-1157, www.euromonitor.com; *International Marketing Data and Statistics 2008; The World Economic Factbook 2008;* and *World Marketing Data and Statistics.*

ANGUILLA - DISPOSABLE INCOME

United Nations Statistics Division, New York, NY 10017, (800) 253-9646, Fax: (212) 963-4116, http://unstats.un.org; *National Accounts Statistics: Compendium of Income Distribution Statistics.*

ANGUILLA - ECONOMIC CONDITIONS

Center for International Business Education Research (CIBER), Columbia Business School and School of International and Public Affairs, Uris Hall, Room 212, 3022 Broadway, New York, NY 10027-6902, Mr. Joshua Safier, (212) 854-4750, Fax: (212) 222-9821, www.columbia.edu/cu/ciber/; Datastream International.

Central Intelligence Agency, Office of Public Affairs, Washington, DC 20505, (703) 482-0623, Fax: (703) 482-1739, www.cia.gov; *The World Factbook.*

DSI Data Service Information, Xantener Strasse 51a, D-47495 Rheinberg, Germany, www.dsidata.com; *Campus Solution.*

Dun and Bradstreet (DB) Corporation, 103 JFK Parkway, Short Hills, NJ 07078, (973) 921-5500, www.dnb.com; *Country Report.*

Economist Intelligence Unit, 111 West 57th Street, New York, NY 10019, (212) 554-0600, Fax: (212) 586-1181, www.eiu.com; *Organisation of Eastern Caribbean States.*

Euromonitor International, Inc., 224 S. Michigan Avenue, Suite 1500, Chicago, IL 60604, (312) 922-1115, Fax: (312) 922-1157, www.euromonitor.com; *The World Economic Factbook 2008* and *World Marketing Data and Statistics.*

International Monetary Fund (IMF), 700 Nineteenth Street, NW, Washington, DC 20431, (202) 623-7000, Fax: (202) 623-4661, www.imf.org; *World Economic Outlook Reports.*

Palgrave Macmillan Ltd., Houndmills, Basingstoke, Hampshire, RG21 6XS, England, (Telephone in U.S. (888) 330-8477), (Fax in U.S. (800) 672-2054), www.palgrave.com; *The Statesman's Yearbook 2008.*

The World Bank, 1818 H Street, NW, Washington, DC 20433, (202) 473-1000, Fax: (202) 477-6391, www.worldbank.org; *Global Economic Monitor (GEM)* and *Global Economic Prospects 2008.*

ANGUILLA - EDUCATION

Euromonitor International, Inc., 224 S. Michigan Avenue, Suite 1500, Chicago, IL 60604, (312) 922-1115, Fax: (312) 922-1157, www.euromonitor.com; *International Marketing Data and Statistics 2008* and *World Marketing Data and Statistics.*

Palgrave Macmillan Ltd., Houndmills, Basingstoke, Hampshire, RG21 6XS, England, (Telephone in U.S. (888) 330-8477), (Fax in U.S. (800) 672-2054), www.palgrave.com; *The Statesman's Yearbook 2008.*

Taylor and Francis Group, An Informa Business, 2 Park Square, Milton Park, Abingdon, Oxford OX14 4RN, United Kingdom, (Dial from U.S. (212) 216-7800), (Fax from U.S. (212) 564-7854), www.tandf.co.uk; *The Europa World Year Book.*

ANGUILLA - ELECTRICITY

Palgrave Macmillan Ltd., Houndmills, Basingstoke, Hampshire, RG21 6XS, England, (Telephone in U.S. (888) 330-8477), (Fax in U.S. (800) 672-2054), www.palgrave.com; *The Statesman's Yearbook 2008.*

ANGUILLA - EMPLOYMENT

Euromonitor International, Inc., 224 S. Michigan Avenue, Suite 1500, Chicago, IL 60604, (312) 922-1115, Fax: (312) 922-1157, www.euromonitor.com; *International Marketing Data and Statistics 2008.*

ANGUILLA - ENVIRONMENTAL CONDITIONS

DSI Data Service Information, Xantener Strasse 51a, D-47495 Rheinberg, Germany, www.dsidata.com; *Campus Solution.*

Economist Intelligence Unit, 111 West 57th Street, New York, NY 10019, (212) 554-0600, Fax: (212) 586-1181, www.eiu.com; *Organisation of Eastern Caribbean States.*

ANGUILLA - EXPORTS

Central Intelligence Agency, Office of Public Affairs, Washington, DC 20505, (703) 482-0623, Fax: (703) 482-1739, www.cia.gov; *The World Factbook.*

Economist Intelligence Unit, 111 West 57th Street, New York, NY 10019, (212) 554-0600, Fax: (212) 586-1181, www.eiu.com; *Organisation of Eastern Caribbean States.*

Euromonitor International, Inc., 224 S. Michigan Avenue, Suite 1500, Chicago, IL 60604, (312) 922-1115, Fax: (312) 922-1157, www.euromonitor.com; *International Marketing Data and Statistics 2008* and *The World Economic Factbook 2008.*

Palgrave Macmillan Ltd., Houndmills, Basingstoke, Hampshire, RG21 6XS, England, (Telephone in U.S. (888) 330-8477), (Fax in U.S. (800) 672-2054), www.palgrave.com; *The Statesman's Yearbook 2008.*

Taylor and Francis Group, An Informa Business, 2 Park Square, Milton Park, Abingdon, Oxford OX14 4RN, United Kingdom, (Dial from U.S. (212) 216-7800), (Fax from U.S. (212) 564-7854), www.tandf.co.uk; *The Europa World Year Book.*

ANGUILLA - FINANCE, PUBLIC

Bernan Essential Government Publications, 4611-F Assembly Drive, Lanham MD, 20706-4391, (301) 459-2255, Fax: (800) 865-3450, www.bernan.com; *National Accounts Statistics.*

Economist Intelligence Unit, 111 West 57th Street, New York, NY 10019, (212) 554-0600, Fax: (212) 586-1181, www.eiu.com; *Organisation of Eastern Caribbean States.*

International Monetary Fund (IMF), 700 Nineteenth Street, NW, Washington, DC 20431, (202) 623-7000, Fax: (202) 623-4661, www.imf.org; *International Financial Statistics* and *International Financial Statistics Online Service.*

Taylor and Francis Group, An Informa Business, 2 Park Square, Milton Park, Abingdon, Oxford OX14 4RN, United Kingdom, (Dial from U.S. (212) 216-7800), (Fax from U.S. (212) 564-7854), www.tandf.co.uk; *The Europa World Year Book.*

ANGUILLA - FISHERIES

Palgrave Macmillan Ltd., Houndmills, Basingstoke, Hampshire, RG21 6XS, England, (Telephone in U.S. (888) 330-8477), (Fax in U.S. (800) 672-2054), www.palgrave.com; *The Statesman's Yearbook 2008.*

Taylor and Francis Group, An Informa Business, 2 Park Square, Milton Park, Abingdon, Oxford OX14 4RN, United Kingdom, (Dial from U.S. (212) 216-7800), (Fax from U.S. (212) 564-7854), www.tandf.co.uk; *The Europa World Year Book.*

ANGUILLA - FOREIGN EXCHANGE RATES

Central Intelligence Agency, Office of Public Affairs, Washington, DC 20505, (703) 482-0623, Fax: (703) 482-1739, www.cia.gov; *The World Factbook.*

Euromonitor International, Inc., 224 S. Michigan Avenue, Suite 1500, Chicago, IL 60604, (312) 922-1115, Fax: (312) 922-1157, www.euromonitor.com; *International Marketing Data and Statistics 2008* and *The World Economic Factbook 2008.*

Taylor and Francis Group, An Informa Business, 2 Park Square, Milton Park, Abingdon, Oxford OX14 4RN, United Kingdom, (Dial from U.S. (212) 216-7800), (Fax from U.S. (212) 564-7854), www.tandf.co.uk; *The Europa World Year Book.*

ANGUILLA - GROSS DOMESTIC PRODUCT

Economist Intelligence Unit, 111 West 57th Street, New York, NY 10019, (212) 554-0600, Fax: (212) 586-1181, www.eiu.com; *Organisation of Eastern Caribbean States.*

Euromonitor International, Inc., 224 S. Michigan Avenue, Suite 1500, Chicago, IL 60604, (312) 922-1115, Fax: (312) 922-1157, www.euromonitor.com; *International Marketing Data and Statistics 2008* and *The World Economic Factbook 2008.*

Taylor and Francis Group, An Informa Business, 2 Park Square, Milton Park, Abingdon, Oxford OX14 4RN, United Kingdom, (Dial from U.S. (212) 216-7800), (Fax from U.S. (212) 564-7854), www.tandf.co.uk; *The Europa World Year Book.*

United Nations Statistics Division, New York, NY 10017, (800) 253-9646, Fax: (212) 963-4116, http://unstats.un.org; *National Accounts Statistics: Compendium of Income Distribution Statistics.*

ANGUILLA - HOUSING

Euromonitor International, Inc., 224 S. Michigan Avenue, Suite 1500, Chicago, IL 60604, (312) 922-1115, Fax: (312) 922-1157, www.euromonitor.com; *World Marketing Data and Statistics.*

ANGUILLA - ILLITERATE PERSONS

Euromonitor International, Inc., 224 S. Michigan Avenue, Suite 1500, Chicago, IL 60604, (312) 922-1115, Fax: (312) 922-1157, www.euromonitor.com; *The World Economic Factbook 2008.*

ANGUILLA - IMPORTS

Central Intelligence Agency, Office of Public Affairs, Washington, DC 20505, (703) 482-0623, Fax: (703) 482-1739, www.cia.gov; *The World Factbook.*

Economist Intelligence Unit, 111 West 57th Street, New York, NY 10019, (212) 554-0600, Fax: (212) 586-1181, www.eiu.com; *Organisation of Eastern Caribbean States.*

Euromonitor International, Inc., 224 S. Michigan Avenue, Suite 1500, Chicago, IL 60604, (312) 922-1115, Fax: (312) 922-1157, www.euromonitor.com; *International Marketing Data and Statistics 2008* and *The World Economic Factbook 2008.*

Palgrave Macmillan Ltd., Houndmills, Basingstoke, Hampshire, RG21 6XS, England, (Telephone in U.S. (888) 330-8477), (Fax in U.S. (800) 672-2054), www.palgrave.com; *The Statesman's Yearbook 2008.*

ANGUILLA - INDUSTRIES

Central Intelligence Agency, Office of Public Affairs, Washington, DC 20505, (703) 482-0623, Fax: (703) 482-1739, www.cia.gov; *The World Factbook.*

Economist Intelligence Unit, 111 West 57th Street, New York, NY 10019, (212) 554-0600, Fax: (212) 586-1181, www.eiu.com; *Organisation of Eastern Caribbean States.*

Euromonitor International, Inc., 224 S. Michigan Avenue, Suite 1500, Chicago, IL 60604, (312) 922-1115, Fax: (312) 922-1157, www.euromonitor.com; *The World Economic Factbook 2008* and *World Marketing Data and Statistics.*

Palgrave Macmillan Ltd., Houndmills, Basingstoke, Hampshire, RG21 6XS, England, (Telephone in U.S. (888) 330-8477), (Fax in U.S. (800) 672-2054), www.palgrave.com; *The Statesman's Yearbook 2008.*

United Nations Industrial Development Organization (UNIDO), 1 United Nations Plaza, New York, NY 10017, (212) 963 6890, Fax: (212) 963-7904, http://unido.org; Industrial Statistics Database 2008 (INDSTAT) and *The International Yearbook of Industrial Statistics 2008.*

ANGUILLA - INTERNATIONAL TRADE

Economist Intelligence Unit, 111 West 57th Street, New York, NY 10019, (212) 554-0600, Fax: (212) 586-1181, www.eiu.com; *Organisation of Eastern Caribbean States.*

Euromonitor International, Inc., 224 S. Michigan Avenue, Suite 1500, Chicago, IL 60604, (312) 922-1115, Fax: (312) 922-1157, www.euromonitor.com; *The World Economic Factbook 2008* and *World Marketing Data and Statistics.*

World Trade Organization (WTO), Centre William Rappard, Rue de Lausanne 154, CH-1211 Geneva 21, Switzerland, www.wto.org; *International Trade Statistics 2006.*

ANGUILLA - INTERNET USERS

International Telecommunication Union (ITU), Place des Nations, 1211 Geneva 20, Switzerland, www.itu.int; *World Telecommunication/ICT Indicators Database on CD-ROM; World Telecommunication/ICT Indicators Database Online;* and *Yearbook of Statistics - Telecommunication Services (Chronological Time Series 1997-2006).*

ANGUILLA - LABOR

Central Intelligence Agency, Office of Public Affairs, Washington, DC 20505, (703) 482-0623, Fax: (703) 482-1739, www.cia.gov; *The World Factbook.*

Euromonitor International, Inc., 224 S. Michigan Avenue, Suite 1500, Chicago, IL 60604, (312) 922-1115, Fax: (312) 922-1157, www.euromonitor.com; *International Marketing Data and Statistics 2008* and *World Marketing Data and Statistics.*

Taylor and Francis Group, An Informa Business, 2 Park Square, Milton Park, Abingdon, Oxford OX14 4RN, United Kingdom, (Dial from U.S. (212) 216-7800), (Fax from U.S. (212) 564-7854), www.tandf.co.uk; *The Europa World Year Book.*

ANGUILLA - LAND USE

Central Intelligence Agency, Office of Public Affairs, Washington, DC 20505, (703) 482-0623, Fax: (703) 482-1739, www.cia.gov; *The World Factbook.*

Euromonitor International, Inc., 224 S. Michigan Avenue, Suite 1500, Chicago, IL 60604, (312) 922-1115, Fax: (312) 922-1157, www.euromonitor.com; *International Marketing Data and Statistics 2008.*

ANGUILLA - LIFE EXPECTANCY

Euromonitor International, Inc., 224 S. Michigan Avenue, Suite 1500, Chicago, IL 60604, (312) 922-1115, Fax: (312) 922-1157, www.euromonitor.com; *The World Economic Factbook 2008.*

ANGUILLA - LITERACY

Euromonitor International, Inc., 224 S. Michigan Avenue, Suite 1500, Chicago, IL 60604, (312) 922-1115, Fax: (312) 922-1157, www.euromonitor.com; *World Marketing Data and Statistics.*

ANGUILLA - LIVESTOCK

Palgrave Macmillan Ltd., Houndmills, Basingstoke, Hampshire, RG21 6XS, England, (Telephone in U.S. (888) 330-8477), (Fax in U.S. (800) 672-2054), www.palgrave.com; *The Statesman's Yearbook 2008.*

Taylor and Francis Group, An Informa Business, 2 Park Square, Milton Park, Abingdon, Oxford OX14 4RN, United Kingdom, (Dial from U.S. (212) 216-7800), (Fax from U.S. (212) 564-7854), www.tandf.co.uk; *The Europa World Year Book.*

ANGUILLA - MARRIAGE

Taylor and Francis Group, An Informa Business, 2 Park Square, Milton Park, Abingdon, Oxford OX14 4RN, United Kingdom, (Dial from U.S. (212) 216-7800), (Fax from U.S. (212) 564-7854), www.tandf.co.uk; *The Europa World Year Book.*

ANGUILLA - MINERAL INDUSTRIES

Taylor and Francis Group, An Informa Business, 2 Park Square, Milton Park, Abingdon, Oxford OX14 4RN, United Kingdom, (Dial from U.S. (212) 216-7800), (Fax from U.S. (212) 564-7854), www.tandf.co.uk; *The Europa World Year Book.*

ANGUILLA - MONEY SUPPLY

Economist Intelligence Unit, 111 West 57th Street, New York, NY 10019, (212) 554-0600, Fax: (212) 586-1181, www.eiu.com; *Organisation of Eastern Caribbean States.*

ANGUILLA - MORTALITY

Central Intelligence Agency, Office of Public Affairs, Washington, DC 20505, (703) 482-0623, Fax: (703) 482-1739, www.cia.gov; *The World Factbook.*

Euromonitor International, Inc., 224 S. Michigan Avenue, Suite 1500, Chicago, IL 60604, (312) 922-1115, Fax: (312) 922-1157, www.euromonitor.com; *International Marketing Data and Statistics 2008* and *The World Economic Factbook 2008.*

Taylor and Francis Group, An Informa Business, 2 Park Square, Milton Park, Abingdon, Oxford OX14 4RN, United Kingdom, (Dial from U.S. (212) 216-7800), (Fax from U.S. (212) 564-7854), www.tandf.co.uk; *The Europa World Year Book.*

World Health Organization (WHO), Avenue Appia 20, 1211 Geneve 27, Switzerland, (Telephone in U.S. (212) 331-9081), www.who.int; The WHO Global Atlas of Infectious Diseases.

ANGUILLA - MOTOR VEHICLES

Taylor and Francis Group, An Informa Business, 2 Park Square, Milton Park, Abingdon, Oxford OX14 4RN, United Kingdom, (Dial from U.S. (212) 216-7800), (Fax from U.S. (212) 564-7854), www.tandf.co.uk; *The Europa World Year Book.*

ANGUILLA - POLITICAL SCIENCE

Central Intelligence Agency, Office of Public Affairs, Washington, DC 20505, (703) 482-0623, Fax: (703) 482-1739, www.cia.gov; *The World Factbook.*

Palgrave Macmillan Ltd., Houndmills, Basingstoke, Hampshire, RG21 6XS, England, (Telephone in U.S. (888) 330-8477), (Fax in U.S. (800) 672-2054), www.palgrave.com; *The Statesman's Yearbook 2008.*

Taylor and Francis Group, An Informa Business, 2 Park Square, Milton Park, Abingdon, Oxford OX14 4RN, United Kingdom, (Dial from U.S. (212) 216-7800), (Fax from U.S. (212) 564-7854), www.tandf.co.uk; *The Europa World Year Book.*

United Nations Statistics Division, New York, NY 10017, (800) 253-9646, Fax: (212) 963-4116, http://unstats.un.org; *National Accounts Statistics: Compendium of Income Distribution Statistics.*

ANGUILLA - POPULATION

Caribbean Epidemiology Centre (CAREC), 16-18 Jamaica Boulevard, Federation Park, PO Box 164, Port of Spain, Republic of Trinidad and Tobago, (Dial from U.S. (868) 622-4261), (Fax from U.S. (868) 622-2792), www.carec.org; *Population Data.*

Central Intelligence Agency, Office of Public Affairs, Washington, DC 20505, (703) 482-0623, Fax: (703) 482-1739, www.cia.gov; *The World Factbook.*

Economist Intelligence Unit, 111 West 57th Street, New York, NY 10019, (212) 554-0600, Fax: (212) 586-1181, www.eiu.com; *Organisation of Eastern Caribbean States.*

Euromonitor International, Inc., 224 S. Michigan Avenue, Suite 1500, Chicago, IL 60604, (312) 922-1115, Fax: (312) 922-1157, www.euromonitor.com; *International Marketing Data and Statistics 2008* and *The World Economic Factbook 2008.*

Palgrave Macmillan Ltd., Houndmills, Basingstoke, Hampshire, RG21 6XS, England, (Telephone in U.S. (888) 330-8477), (Fax in U.S. (800) 672-2054), www.palgrave.com; *The Statesman's Yearbook 2008.*

Taylor and Francis Group, An Informa Business, 2 Park Square, Milton Park, Abingdon, Oxford OX14 4RN, United Kingdom, (Dial from U.S. (212) 216-7800), (Fax from U.S. (212) 564-7854), www.tandf.co.uk; *The Europa World Year Book.*

ANGUILLA - POPULATION DENSITY

Central Intelligence Agency, Office of Public Affairs, Washington, DC 20505, (703) 482-0623, Fax: (703) 482-1739, www.cia.gov; *The World Factbook.*

Euromonitor International, Inc., 224 S. Michigan Avenue, Suite 1500, Chicago, IL 60604, (312) 922-1115, Fax: (312) 922-1157, www.euromonitor.com; *The World Economic Factbook 2008.*

Palgrave Macmillan Ltd., Houndmills, Basingstoke, Hampshire, RG21 6XS, England, (Telephone in U.S. (888) 330-8477), (Fax in U.S. (800) 672-2054), www.palgrave.com; *The Statesman's Yearbook 2008.*

Taylor and Francis Group, An Informa Business, 2 Park Square, Milton Park, Abingdon, Oxford OX14 4RN, United Kingdom, (Dial from U.S. (212) 216-7800), (Fax from U.S. (212) 564-7854), www.tandf.co.uk; *The Europa World Year Book.*

ANGUILLA - POWER RESOURCES

Euromonitor International, Inc., 224 S. Michigan Avenue, Suite 1500, Chicago, IL 60604, (312) 922-1115, Fax: (312) 922-1157, www.euromonitor.com; *International Marketing Data and Statistics 2008; The World Economic Factbook 2008;* and *World Marketing Data and Statistics.*

ANGUILLA - PRICES

Euromonitor International, Inc., 224 S. Michigan Avenue, Suite 1500, Chicago, IL 60604, (312) 922-1115, Fax: (312) 922-1157, www.euromonitor.com; *World Marketing Data and Statistics.*

ANGUILLA - PUBLIC HEALTH

Euromonitor International, Inc., 224 S. Michigan Avenue, Suite 1500, Chicago, IL 60604, (312) 922-1115, Fax: (312) 922-1157, www.euromonitor.com; *World Marketing Data and Statistics.*

Palgrave Macmillan Ltd., Houndmills, Basingstoke, Hampshire, RG21 6XS, England, (Telephone in U.S. (888) 330-8477), (Fax in U.S. (800) 672-2054), www.palgrave.com; *The Statesman's Yearbook 2008.*

World Health Organization (WHO), Avenue Appia 20, 1211 Geneve 27, Switzerland, (Telephone in U.S. (212) 331-9081), www.who.int; The WHO Global Atlas of Infectious Diseases.

ANGUILLA - RELIGION

Central Intelligence Agency, Office of Public Affairs, Washington, DC 20505, (703) 482-0623, Fax: (703) 482-1739, www.cia.gov; *The World Factbook.*

Palgrave Macmillan Ltd., Houndmills, Basingstoke, Hampshire, RG21 6XS, England, (Telephone in U.S. (888) 330-8477), (Fax in U.S. (800) 672-2054), www.palgrave.com; *The Statesman's Yearbook 2008.*

ANGUILLA - RETAIL TRADE

Euromonitor International, Inc., 224 S. Michigan Avenue, Suite 1500, Chicago, IL 60604, (312) 922-1115, Fax: (312) 922-1157, www.euromonitor.com; *World Marketing Data and Statistics.*

ANGUILLA - ROADS

Central Intelligence Agency, Office of Public Affairs, Washington, DC 20505, (703) 482-0623, Fax: (703) 482-1739, www.cia.gov; *The World Factbook.*

Palgrave Macmillan Ltd., Houndmills, Basingstoke, Hampshire, RG21 6XS, England, (Telephone in U.S. (888) 330-8477), (Fax in U.S. (800) 672-2054), www.palgrave.com; *The Statesman's Yearbook 2008.*

ANGUILLA - SOCIAL SECURITY

United Nations Statistics Division, New York, NY 10017, (800) 253-9646, Fax: (212) 963-4116, http://unstats.un.org; *National Accounts Statistics: Compendium of Income Distribution Statistics.*

ANGUILLA - TAXATION

Taylor and Francis Group, An Informa Business, 2 Park Square, Milton Park, Abingdon, Oxford OX14 4RN, United Kingdom, (Dial from U.S. (212) 216-7800), (Fax from U.S. (212) 564-7854), www.tandf.co.uk; *The Europa World Year Book.*

ANGUILLA - TELEPHONE

Palgrave Macmillan Ltd., Houndmills, Basingstoke, Hampshire, RG21 6XS, England, (Telephone in U.S. (888) 330-8477), (Fax in U.S. (800) 672-2054), www.palgrave.com; *The Statesman's Yearbook 2008.*

Taylor and Francis Group, An Informa Business, 2 Park Square, Milton Park, Abingdon, Oxford OX14 4RN, United Kingdom, (Dial from U.S. (212) 216-7800), (Fax from U.S. (212) 564-7854), www.tandf.co.uk; *The Europa World Year Book.*

ANGUILLA - TOURISM

Euromonitor International, Inc., 224 S. Michigan Avenue, Suite 1500, Chicago, IL 60604, (312) 922-1115, Fax: (312) 922-1157, www.euromonitor.com; *The World Economic Factbook 2008* and *World Marketing Data and Statistics.*

Palgrave Macmillan Ltd., Houndmills, Basingstoke, Hampshire, RG21 6XS, England, (Telephone in U.S. (888) 330-8477), (Fax in U.S. (800) 672-2054), www.palgrave.com; *The Statesman's Yearbook 2008.*

Taylor and Francis Group, An Informa Business, 2 Park Square, Milton Park, Abingdon, Oxford OX14 4RN, United Kingdom, (Dial from U.S. (212) 216-7800), (Fax from U.S. (212) 564-7854), www.tandf.co.uk; *The Europa World Year Book.*

United Nations World Tourism Organization (UNWTO), Capitan Haya 42, 28020 Madrid, Spain, www.world-tourism.org; *Yearbook of Tourism Statistics.*

ANGUILLA - TRANSPORTATION

Central Intelligence Agency, Office of Public Affairs, Washington, DC 20505, (703) 482-0623, Fax: (703) 482-1739, www.cia.gov; *The World Factbook.*

Euromonitor International, Inc., 224 S. Michigan Avenue, Suite 1500, Chicago, IL 60604, (312) 922-1115, Fax: (312) 922-1157, www.euromonitor.com; *International Marketing Data and Statistics 2008* and *World Marketing Data and Statistics.*

Palgrave Macmillan Ltd., Houndmills, Basingstoke, Hampshire, RG21 6XS, England, (Telephone in U.S. (888) 330-8477), (Fax in U.S. (800) 672-2054), www.palgrave.com; *The Statesman's Yearbook 2008.*

Taylor and Francis Group, An Informa Business, 2 Park Square, Milton Park, Abingdon, Oxford OX14 4RN, United Kingdom, (Dial from U.S. (212) 216-7800), (Fax from U.S. (212) 564-7854), www.tandf.co.uk; *The Europa World Year Book.*

ANGUILLA - UNEMPLOYMENT

Central Intelligence Agency, Office of Public Affairs, Washington, DC 20505, (703) 482-0623, Fax: (703) 482-1739, www.cia.gov; *The World Factbook.*

ANIMAL OILS AND FATS

See OILS - ANIMAL

ANIMALS, DOMESTIC - GRAZING - NATIONAL FORESTS

Economic Research Service (ERS), U.S. Department of Agriculture (USDA), 1800 M Street, NW, Washington, DC 20036-5831, (202) 694-5050, Fax: (202) 694-5689, www.ers.usda.gov; *Agricultural Statistics.*

USDA Forest Service, 1400 Independence Ave, SW, Washington, DC 20250-0003, (202) 205-8333, www.fs.fed.us; *Timber Products Supply and Demand.*

ANIMALS, DOMESTIC - INVENTORY AND PRODUCTION

Economic Research Service (ERS), U.S. Department of Agriculture (USDA), 1800 M Street, NW, Washington, DC 20036-5831, (202) 694-5050, Fax: (202) 694-5689, www.ers.usda.gov; *Agricultural Statistics.*

Foreign Agricultural Service (FAS), U.S. Department of Agriculture (USDA), 1400 Independence Avenue, SW, Washington, DC 20250, (202) 720-3935, www.fas.usda.gov; *Livestock and Poultry: World Markets and Trade.*

National Agricultural Statistics Service (NASS), U.S. Department of Agriculture (USDA), 1400 Independence Avenue, SW, Washington, DC 20250, (800) 727-9540, Fax: (202) 690-2090, www.nass.usda.gov; *2006 Agricultural Statistics; Hogs and Pigs;* and *Meat Animals Production, Disposition, and Income.*

ANNUITIES

See PENSIONS AND RETIREMENT BENEFITS

ANTIGUA AND BARBUDA - NATIONAL STATISTICAL OFFICE

Statistics Division, Ministry of Finance and Economy, 1st Floor, A.C.T. Building, Market and Church Streets, St. John's, Antigua and Barbuda, (Dial from U.S. (268) 462-4775), (Fax from U.S. (268) 562-2542); National Data Center.

ANTIGUA AND BARBUDA - AGRICULTURE

Economist Intelligence Unit, 111 West 57th Street, New York, NY 10019, (212) 554-0600, Fax: (212) 586-1181, www.eiu.com; *Organisation of Eastern Caribbean States.*

Euromonitor International, Inc., 224 S. Michigan Avenue, Suite 1500, Chicago, IL 60604, (312) 922-1115, Fax: (312) 922-1157, www.euromonitor.com; *World Marketing Data and Statistics.*

Palgrave Macmillan Ltd., Houndmills, Basingstoke, Hampshire, RG21 6XS, England, (Telephone in U.S. (888) 330-8477), (Fax in U.S. (800) 672-2054), www.palgrave.com; *The Statesman's Yearbook 2008.*

Taylor and Francis Group, An Informa Business, 2 Park Square, Milton Park, Abingdon, Oxford OX14 4RN, United Kingdom, (Dial from U.S. (212) 216-7800), (Fax from U.S. (212) 564-7854), www.tandf.co.uk; *The Europa World Year Book.*

United Nations Conference on Trade and Development (UNCTAD), DC2-1120, United Nations, New York, NY 10017, (212) 963-0027, www.unctad.org; *UNCTAD Commodity Yearbook.*

United Nations Food and Agricultural Organization (FAO), Viale delle Terme di Caracalla, 00100 Rome, Italy, (Dial from U.S. (202) 653-2400), (Fax from U.S. (202) 653 5760), www.fao.org; AQUASTAT; *FAO Production Yearbook 2002; FAO Trade Yearbook;* and *The State of Food and Agriculture (SOFA) 2006.*

United Nations Statistics Division, New York, NY 10017, (800) 253-9646, Fax: (212) 963-4116, http://unstats.un.org; *Statistical Yearbook.*

The World Bank, 1818 H Street, NW, Washington, DC 20433, (202) 473-1000, Fax: (202) 477-6391, www.worldbank.org; *Antigua and Barbuda* and *World Development Indicators (WDI) 2008.*

ANTIGUA AND BARBUDA - AIRLINES

International Civil Aviation Organization (ICAO), External Relations and Public Information Office (EPO), 999 University Street, Montreal, Quebec H3C 5H7, Canada, (Dial from U.S. (514) 954-8219), (Fax from U.S. (514) 954-6077), www.icao.int; *Civil Aviation Statistics of the World.*

Palgrave Macmillan Ltd., Houndmills, Basingstoke, Hampshire, RG21 6XS, England, (Telephone in U.S. (888) 330-8477), (Fax in U.S. (800) 672-2054), www.palgrave.com; *The Statesman's Yearbook 2008.*

Taylor and Francis Group, An Informa Business, 2 Park Square, Milton Park, Abingdon, Oxford OX14 4RN, United Kingdom, (Dial from U.S. (212) 216-7800), (Fax from U.S. (212) 564-7854), www.tandf.co.uk; *The Europa World Year Book.*

ANTIGUA AND BARBUDA - AIRPORTS

Central Intelligence Agency, Office of Public Affairs, Washington, DC 20505, (703) 482-0623, Fax: (703) 482-1739, www.cia.gov; *The World Factbook.*

ANTIGUA AND BARBUDA - ARMED FORCES

Central Intelligence Agency, Office of Public Affairs, Washington, DC 20505, (703) 482-0623, Fax: (703) 482-1739, www.cia.gov; *The World Factbook.*

Euromonitor International, Inc., 224 S. Michigan Avenue, Suite 1500, Chicago, IL 60604, (312) 922-1115, Fax: (312) 922-1157, www.euromonitor.com; *World Marketing Data and Statistics.*

Palgrave Macmillan Ltd., Houndmills, Basingstoke, Hampshire, RG21 6XS, England, (Telephone in U.S. (888) 330-8477), (Fax in U.S. (800) 672-2054), www.palgrave.com; *The Statesman's Yearbook 2008.*

United Nations Statistics Division, New York, NY 10017, (800) 253-9646, Fax: (212) 963-4116, http://unstats.un.org; *Human Development Report 2006.*

ANTIGUA AND BARBUDA - BALANCE OF PAYMENTS

International Monetary Fund (IMF), 700 Nineteenth Street, NW, Washington, DC 20431, (202) 623-7000, Fax: (202) 623-4661, www.imf.org; *Balance of Payments Statistics Newsletter* and *Balance of Payments Statistics Yearbook 2007.*

Taylor and Francis Group, An Informa Business, 2 Park Square, Milton Park, Abingdon, Oxford OX14 4RN, United Kingdom, (Dial from U.S. (212) 216-7800), (Fax from U.S. (212) 564-7854), www.tandf.co.uk; *The Europa World Year Book.*

United Nations Statistics Division, New York, NY 10017, (800) 253-9646, Fax: (212) 963-4116, http://unstats.un.org; *Economic Survey of Latin America and the Caribbean 2004-2005.*

The World Bank, 1818 H Street, NW, Washington, DC 20433, (202) 473-1000, Fax: (202) 477-6391, www.worldbank.org; *Antigua and Barbuda* and *World Development Indicators (WDI) 2008.*

ANTIGUA AND BARBUDA - BANKS AND BANKING

Euromonitor International, Inc., 224 S. Michigan Avenue, Suite 1500, Chicago, IL 60604, (312) 922-1115, Fax: (312) 922-1157, www.euromonitor.com; *World Marketing Data and Statistics.*

Palgrave Macmillan Ltd., Houndmills, Basingstoke, Hampshire, RG21 6XS, England, (Telephone in U.S. (888) 330-8477), (Fax in U.S. (800) 672-2054), www.palgrave.com; *The Statesman's Yearbook 2008.*

Taylor and Francis Group, An Informa Business, 2 Park Square, Milton Park, Abingdon, Oxford OX14 4RN, United Kingdom, (Dial from U.S. (212) 216-7800), (Fax from U.S. (212) 564-7854), www.tandf.co.uk; *The Europa World Year Book.*

ANTIGUA AND BARBUDA - BROADCASTING

Central Intelligence Agency, Office of Public Affairs, Washington, DC 20505, (703) 482-0623, Fax: (703) 482-1739, www.cia.gov; *The World Factbook.*

Euromonitor International, Inc., 224 S. Michigan Avenue, Suite 1500, Chicago, IL 60604, (312) 922-1115, Fax: (312) 922-1157, www.euromonitor.com; *World Marketing Data and Statistics.*

Palgrave Macmillan Ltd., Houndmills, Basingstoke, Hampshire, RG21 6XS, England, (Telephone in U.S. (888) 330-8477), (Fax in U.S. (800) 672-2054), www.palgrave.com; *The Statesman's Yearbook 2008.*

WRTH Publications Limited, PO Box 290, Oxford OX2 7FT, UK, www.wrth.com; *World Radio TV Handbook 2007.*

ANTIGUA AND BARBUDA - BUDGET

Central Intelligence Agency, Office of Public Affairs, Washington, DC 20505, (703) 482-0623, Fax: (703) 482-1739, www.cia.gov; *The World Factbook.*

ANTIGUA AND BARBUDA - CATTLE

See ANTIGUA AND BARBUDA - LIVESTOCK

ANTIGUA AND BARBUDA - CHILDBIRTH - STATISTICS

Central Intelligence Agency, Office of Public Affairs, Washington, DC 20505, (703) 482-0623, Fax: (703) 482-1739, www.cia.gov; *The World Factbook.*

Euromonitor International, Inc., 224 S. Michigan Avenue, Suite 1500, Chicago, IL 60604, (312) 922-1115, Fax: (312) 922-1157, www.euromonitor.com; *International Marketing Data and Statistics 2008* and *The World Economic Factbook 2008.*

Taylor and Francis Group, An Informa Business, 2 Park Square, Milton Park, Abingdon, Oxford OX14 4RN, United Kingdom, (Dial from U.S. (212) 216-7800), (Fax from U.S. (212) 564-7854), www.tandf.co.uk; *The Europa World Year Book.*

United Nations Statistics Division, New York, NY 10017, (800) 253-9646, Fax: (212) 963-4116, http://unstats.un.org; *Demographic Yearbook* and *Statistical Yearbook.*

World Health Organization (WHO), Avenue Appia 20, 1211 Geneve 27, Switzerland, (Telephone in U.S. (212) 331-9081), www.who.int; *World Health Report 2006.*

ANTIGUA AND BARBUDA - CLIMATE

Palgrave Macmillan Ltd., Houndmills, Basingstoke, Hampshire, RG21 6XS, England, (Telephone in U.S. (888) 330-8477), (Fax in U.S. (800) 672-2054), www.palgrave.com; *The Statesman's Yearbook 2008.*

ANTIGUA AND BARBUDA - COMMERCE

Palgrave Macmillan Ltd., Houndmills, Basingstoke, Hampshire, RG21 6XS, England, (Telephone in U.S. (888) 330-8477), (Fax in U.S. (800) 672-2054), www.palgrave.com; *The Statesman's Yearbook 2008.*

ANTIGUA AND BARBUDA - COMMODITY EXCHANGES

United Nations Food and Agricultural Organization (FAO), Viale delle Terme di Caracalla, 00100 Rome, Italy, (Dial from U.S. (202) 653-2400), (Fax from U.S. (202) 653 5760), www.fao.org; *The State of Food and Agriculture (SOFA) 2006.*

ANTIGUA AND BARBUDA - CONSUMER PRICE INDEXES

United Nations Statistics Division, New York, NY 10017, (800) 253-9646, Fax: (212) 963-4116, http://unstats.un.org; *Statistical Yearbook.*

The World Bank, 1818 H Street, NW, Washington, DC 20433, (202) 473-1000, Fax: (202) 477-6391, www.worldbank.org; *Antigua and Barbuda.*

ANTIGUA AND BARBUDA - CORN INDUSTRY

See ANTIGUA AND BARBUDA - CROPS

ANTIGUA AND BARBUDA - CROPS

Palgrave Macmillan Ltd., Houndmills, Basingstoke, Hampshire, RG21 6XS, England, (Telephone in U.S. (888) 330-8477), (Fax in U.S. (800) 672-2054), www.palgrave.com; *The Statesman's Yearbook 2008.*

Taylor and Francis Group, An Informa Business, 2 Park Square, Milton Park, Abingdon, Oxford OX14 4RN, United Kingdom, (Dial from U.S. (212) 216-7800), (Fax from U.S. (212) 564-7854), www.tandf.co.uk; *The Europa World Year Book.*

United Nations Conference on Trade and Development (UNCTAD), DC2-1120, United Nations, New York, NY 10017, (212) 963-0027, www.unctad.org; *UNCTAD Commodity Yearbook.*

United Nations Food and Agricultural Organization (FAO), Viale delle Terme di Caracalla, 00100 Rome, Italy, (Dial from U.S. (202) 653-2400), (Fax from U.S. (202) 653 5760), www.fao.org; *The State of Food and Agriculture (SOFA) 2006.*

United Nations Statistics Division, New York, NY 10017, (800) 253-9646, Fax: (212) 963-4116, http://unstats.un.org; *Statistical Yearbook.*

ANTIGUA AND BARBUDA - DAIRY PROCESSING

Palgrave Macmillan Ltd., Houndmills, Basingstoke, Hampshire, RG21 6XS, England, (Telephone in U.S. (888) 330-8477), (Fax in U.S. (800) 672-2054), www.palgrave.com; *The Statesman's Yearbook 2008.*

United Nations Food and Agricultural Organization (FAO), Viale delle Terme di Caracalla, 00100 Rome, Italy, (Dial from U.S. (202) 653-2400), (Fax from U.S. (202) 653 5760), www.fao.org; *The State of Food and Agriculture (SOFA) 2006.*

ANTIGUA AND BARBUDA - DEATH RATES

See ANTIGUA AND BARBUDA - MORTALITY

ANTIGUA AND BARBUDA - DEBTS, EXTERNAL

United Nations Statistics Division, New York, NY 10017, (800) 253-9646, Fax: (212) 963-4116, http://unstats.un.org; *Economic Survey of Latin America and the Caribbean 2004-2005.*

The World Bank, 1818 H Street, NW, Washington, DC 20433, (202) 473-1000, Fax: (202) 477-6391, www.worldbank.org; *World Development Indicators (WDI) 2008.*

ANTIGUA AND BARBUDA - DEMOGRAPHY

Euromonitor International, Inc., 224 S. Michigan Avenue, Suite 1500, Chicago, IL 60604, (312) 922-

1115, Fax: (312) 922-1157, www.euromonitor.com; *International Marketing Data and Statistics 2008; The World Economic Factbook 2008;* and *World Marketing Data and Statistics.*

United Nations Statistics Division, New York, NY 10017, (800) 253-9646, Fax: (212) 963-4116, http://unstats.un.org; *Human Development Report 2006.*

The World Bank, 1818 H Street, NW, Washington, DC 20433, (202) 473-1000, Fax: (202) 477-6391, www.worldbank.org; *Antigua and Barbuda.*

ANTIGUA AND BARBUDA - DISPOSABLE INCOME

United Nations Statistics Division, New York, NY 10017, (800) 253-9646, Fax: (212) 963-4116, http://unstats.un.org; *National Accounts Statistics: Compendium of Income Distribution Statistics* and *Statistical Yearbook.*

ANTIGUA AND BARBUDA - DIVORCE

United Nations Statistics Division, New York, NY 10017, (800) 253-9646, Fax: (212) 963-4116, http://unstats.un.org; *Demographic Yearbook* and *Statistical Yearbook.*

ANTIGUA AND BARBUDA - ECONOMIC CONDITIONS

Central Intelligence Agency, Office of Public Affairs, Washington, DC 20505, (703) 482-0623, Fax: (703) 482-1739, www.cia.gov; *The World Factbook.*

Economist Intelligence Unit, 111 West 57th Street, New York, NY 10019, (212) 554-0600, Fax: (212) 586-1181, www.eiu.com; *Organisation of Eastern Caribbean States.*

Euromonitor International, Inc., 224 S. Michigan Avenue, Suite 1500, Chicago, IL 60604, (312) 922-1115, Fax: (312) 922-1157, www.euromonitor.com; *International Marketing Data and Statistics 2008; The World Economic Factbook 2008;* and *World Marketing Data and Statistics.*

Palgrave Macmillan Ltd., Houndmills, Basingstoke, Hampshire, RG21 6XS, England, (Telephone in U.S. (888) 330-8477), (Fax in U.S. (800) 672-2054), www.palgrave.com; *The Statesman's Yearbook 2008.*

Taylor and Francis Group, An Informa Business, 2 Park Square, Milton Park, Abingdon, Oxford OX14 4RN, United Kingdom, (Dial from U.S. (212) 216-7800), (Fax from U.S. (212) 564-7854), www.tandf.co.uk; *The Europa World Year Book.*

UNESCO Institute for Statistics, C.P. 6128 Succursale Centre-Ville, Montreal, Quebec, H3C 3J7 Canada, (Dial from U.S. (514) 343-6880), (Fax from U.S. (514) 343 6882), www.uis.unesco.org; *Statistical Tables.*

United Nations Statistics Division, New York, NY 10017, (800) 253-9646, Fax: (212) 963-4116, http://unstats.un.org; *Economic Survey of Latin America and the Caribbean 2004-2005; Human Development Report 2006;* and *World Statistics Pocketbook.*

The World Bank, 1818 H Street, NW, Washington, DC 20433, (202) 473-1000, Fax: (202) 477-6391, www.worldbank.org; *Antigua and Barbuda; The World Bank Atlas 2003-2004;* and *World Development Indicators (WDI) 2008.*

ANTIGUA AND BARBUDA - EDUCATION

The World Bank, 1818 H Street, NW, Washington, DC 20433, (202) 473-1000, Fax: (202) 477-6391, www.worldbank.org; *Antigua and Barbuda* and *The World Bank Atlas 2003-2004.*

ANTIGUA AND BARBUDA - ELECTRICITY

United Nations Statistics Division, New York, NY 10017, (800) 253-9646, Fax: (212) 963-4116, http://unstats.un.org; *Human Development Report 2006* and *Statistical Yearbook.*

ANTIGUA AND BARBUDA - EMPLOYMENT

Euromonitor International, Inc., 224 S. Michigan Avenue, Suite 1500, Chicago, IL 60604, (312) 922-1115, Fax: (312) 922-1157, www.euromonitor.com; *International Marketing Data and Statistics 2008.*

International Labour Office, I.L.O. Publications, 4 route des Morillons, CH-1211 Geneva 22, Switzerland, (Telephone in U.S. (202) 653-7652), (Fax in U.S. (202) 653-7687), www.ilo.org; *Yearbook of Labour Statistics 2006.*

The World Bank, 1818 H Street, NW, Washington, DC 20433, (202) 473-1000, Fax: (202) 477-6391, www.worldbank.org; *Antigua and Barbuda.*

ANTIGUA AND BARBUDA - ENVIRONMENTAL CONDITIONS

DSI Data Service Information, Xantener Strasse 51a, D-47495 Rheinberg, Germany, www.dsidata.com; *Campus Solution.*

Economist Intelligence Unit, 111 West 57th Street, New York, NY 10019, (212) 554-0600, Fax: (212) 586-1181, www.eiu.com; *Organisation of Eastern Caribbean States.*

United Nations Statistics Division, New York, NY 10017, (800) 253-9646, Fax: (212) 963-4116, http://unstats.un.org; *World Statistics Pocketbook.*

ANTIGUA AND BARBUDA - EXPORTS

Central Intelligence Agency, Office of Public Affairs, Washington, DC 20505, (703) 482-0623, Fax: (703) 482-1739, www.cia.gov; *The World Factbook.*

Economist Intelligence Unit, 111 West 57th Street, New York, NY 10019, (212) 554-0600, Fax: (212) 586-1181, www.eiu.com; *Organisation of Eastern Caribbean States.*

Euromonitor International, Inc., 224 S. Michigan Avenue, Suite 1500, Chicago, IL 60604, (312) 922-1115, Fax: (312) 922-1157, www.euromonitor.com; *International Marketing Data and Statistics 2008* and *The World Economic Factbook 2008.*

Palgrave Macmillan Ltd., Houndmills, Basingstoke, Hampshire, RG21 6XS, England, (Telephone in U.S. (888) 330-8477), (Fax in U.S. (800) 672-2054), www.palgrave.com; *The Statesman's Yearbook 2008.*

Taylor and Francis Group, An Informa Business, 2 Park Square, Milton Park, Abingdon, Oxford OX14 4RN, United Kingdom, (Dial from U.S. (212) 216-7800), (Fax from U.S. (212) 564-7854), www.tandf.co.uk; *The Europa World Year Book.*

United Nations Food and Agricultural Organization (FAO), Viale delle Terme di Caracalla, 00100 Rome, Italy, (Dial from U.S. (202) 653-2400), (Fax from U.S. (202) 653 5760), www.fao.org; *The State of Food and Agriculture (SOFA) 2006.*

The World Bank, 1818 H Street, NW, Washington, DC 20433, (202) 473-1000, Fax: (202) 477-6391, www.worldbank.org; *World Development Indicators (WDI) 2008.*

ANTIGUA AND BARBUDA - FERTILITY, HUMAN

United Nations Statistics Division, New York, NY 10017, (800) 253-9646, Fax: (212) 963-4116, http://unstats.un.org; *Human Development Report 2006.*

The World Bank, 1818 H Street, NW, Washington, DC 20433, (202) 473-1000, Fax: (202) 477-6391, www.worldbank.org; *The World Bank Atlas 2003-2004* and *World Development Indicators (WDI) 2008.*

ANTIGUA AND BARBUDA - FERTILIZER INDUSTRY

United Nations Food and Agricultural Organization (FAO), Viale delle Terme di Caracalla, 00100 Rome, Italy, (Dial from U.S. (202) 653-2400), (Fax from U.S. (202) 653 5760), www.fao.org; *The State of Food and Agriculture (SOFA) 2006.*

ANTIGUA AND BARBUDA - FETAL MORTALITY

See ANTIGUA AND BARBUDA - MORTALITY

ANTIGUA AND BARBUDA - FINANCE

United Nations Statistics Division, New York, NY 10017, (800) 253-9646, Fax: (212) 963-4116, http://unstats.un.org; *National Accounts Statistics: Compendium of Income Distribution Statistics.*

The World Bank, 1818 H Street, NW, Washington, DC 20433, (202) 473-1000, Fax: (202) 477-6391, www.worldbank.org; *Antigua and Barbuda.*

ANTIGUA AND BARBUDA - FINANCE, PUBLIC

Economist Intelligence Unit, 111 West 57th Street, New York, NY 10019, (212) 554-0600, Fax: (212) 586-1181, www.eiu.com; *Organisation of Eastern Caribbean States.*

International Monetary Fund (IMF), 700 Nineteenth Street, NW, Washington, DC 20431, (202) 623-7000, Fax: (202) 623-4661, www.imf.org; *International Financial Statistics Yearbook 2007.*

Palgrave Macmillan Ltd., Houndmills, Basingstoke, Hampshire, RG21 6XS, England, (Telephone in U.S. (888) 330-8477), (Fax in U.S. (800) 672-2054), www.palgrave.com; *The Statesman's Yearbook 2008.*

Taylor and Francis Group, An Informa Business, 2 Park Square, Milton Park, Abingdon, Oxford OX14 4RN, United Kingdom, (Dial from U.S. (212) 216-7800), (Fax from U.S. (212) 564-7854), www.tandf.co.uk; *The Europa World Year Book.*

The World Bank, 1818 H Street, NW, Washington, DC 20433, (202) 473-1000, Fax: (202) 477-6391, www.worldbank.org; *Antigua and Barbuda.*

ANTIGUA AND BARBUDA - FISHERIES

Taylor and Francis Group, An Informa Business, 2 Park Square, Milton Park, Abingdon, Oxford OX14 4RN, United Kingdom, (Dial from U.S. (212) 216-7800), (Fax from U.S. (212) 564-7854), www.tandf.co.uk; *The Europa World Year Book.*

United Nations Conference on Trade and Development (UNCTAD), DC2-1120, United Nations, New York, NY 10017, (212) 963-0027, www.unctad.org; *UNCTAD Commodity Yearbook.*

United Nations Food and Agricultural Organization (FAO), Viale delle Terme di Caracalla, 00100 Rome, Italy, (Dial from U.S. (202) 653-2400), (Fax from U.S. (202) 653 5760), www.fao.org; *FAO Yearbook of Fishery Statistics;* Fishery Databases; FISHSTAT Database. Subjects covered include: Aquaculture production, capture production, fishery commodities; and *The State of Food and Agriculture (SOFA) 2006.*

The World Bank, 1818 H Street, NW, Washington, DC 20433, (202) 473-1000, Fax: (202) 477-6391, www.worldbank.org; *Antigua and Barbuda.*

ANTIGUA AND BARBUDA - FOOD

United Nations Conference on Trade and Development (UNCTAD), DC2-1120, United Nations, New York, NY 10017, (212) 963-0027, www.unctad.org; *UNCTAD Commodity Yearbook.*

United Nations Food and Agricultural Organization (FAO), Viale delle Terme di Caracalla, 00100 Rome, Italy, (Dial from U.S. (202) 653-2400), (Fax from U.S. (202) 653 5760), www.fao.org; *FAO Production Yearbook 2002* and *The State of Food and Agriculture (SOFA) 2006.*

United Nations Statistics Division, New York, NY 10017, (800) 253-9646, Fax: (212) 963-4116, http://unstats.un.org; *Human Development Report 2006.*

ANTIGUA AND BARBUDA - FOREIGN EXCHANGE RATES

Central Intelligence Agency, Office of Public Affairs, Washington, DC 20505, (703) 482-0623, Fax: (703) 482-1739, www.cia.gov; *The World Factbook.*

Euromonitor International, Inc., 224 S. Michigan Avenue, Suite 1500, Chicago, IL 60604, (312) 922-1115, Fax: (312) 922-1157, www.euromonitor.com; *International Marketing Data and Statistics 2008* and *The World Economic Factbook 2008.*

International Civil Aviation Organization (ICAO), External Relations and Public Information Office (EPO), 999 University Street, Montreal, Quebec

H3C 5H7, Canada, (Dial from U.S. (514) 954-8219), (Fax from U.S. (514) 954-6077), www.icao.int; *Civil Aviation Statistics of the World.*

Taylor and Francis Group, An Informa Business, 2 Park Square, Milton Park, Abingdon, Oxford OX14 4RN, United Kingdom, (Dial from U.S. (212) 216-7800), (Fax from U.S. (212) 564-7854), www.tandf.co.uk; *The Europa World Year Book.*

United Nations Statistics Division, New York, NY 10017, (800) 253-9646, Fax: (212) 963-4116, http://unstats.un.org; *World Statistics Pocketbook.*

ANTIGUA AND BARBUDA - FORESTS AND FORESTRY

UNESCO Institute for Statistics, C.P. 6128 Succursale Centre-Ville, Montreal, Quebec, H3C 3J7 Canada, (Dial from U.S. (514) 343-6880), (Fax from U.S. (514) 343 6882), www.uis.unesco.org; *Statistical Tables.*

United Nations Conference on Trade and Development (UNCTAD), DC2-1120, United Nations, New York, NY 10017, (212) 963-0027, www.unctad.org; *UNCTAD Commodity Yearbook.*

United Nations Food and Agricultural Organization (FAO), Viale delle Terme di Caracalla, 00100 Rome, Italy, (Dial from U.S. (202) 653-2400), (Fax from U.S. (202) 653 5760), www.fao.org; *The State of Food and Agriculture (SOFA) 2006.*

United Nations Statistics Division, New York, NY 10017, (800) 253-9646, Fax: (212) 963-4116, http://unstats.un.org; *Statistical Yearbook.*

The World Bank, 1818 H Street, NW, Washington, DC 20433, (202) 473-1000, Fax: (202) 477-6391, www.worldbank.org; *Antigua and Barbuda.*

ANTIGUA AND BARBUDA - GOLD INDUSTRY

The World Bank, 1818 H Street, NW, Washington, DC 20433, (202) 473-1000, Fax: (202) 477-6391, www.worldbank.org; *World Development Indicators (WDI) 2008.*

ANTIGUA AND BARBUDA - GROSS DOMESTIC PRODUCT

Economist Intelligence Unit, 111 West 57th Street, New York, NY 10019, (212) 554-0600, Fax: (212) 586-1181, www.eiu.com; *Organisation of Eastern Caribbean States.*

Euromonitor International, Inc., 224 S. Michigan Avenue, Suite 1500, Chicago, IL 60604, (312) 922-1115, Fax: (312) 922-1157, www.euromonitor.com; *International Marketing Data and Statistics 2008* and *The World Economic Factbook 2008.*

Taylor and Francis Group, An Informa Business, 2 Park Square, Milton Park, Abingdon, Oxford OX14 4RN, United Kingdom, (Dial from U.S. (212) 216-7800), (Fax from U.S. (212) 564-7854), www.tandf.co.uk; *The Europa World Year Book.*

United Nations Statistics Division, New York, NY 10017, (800) 253-9646, Fax: (212) 963-4116, http://unstats.un.org; *Human Development Report 2006; National Accounts Statistics: Compendium of Income Distribution Statistics;* and *Statistical Yearbook.*

The World Bank, 1818 H Street, NW, Washington, DC 20433, (202) 473-1000, Fax: (202) 477-6391, www.worldbank.org; *World Development Indicators (WDI) 2008.*

ANTIGUA AND BARBUDA - GROSS NATIONAL PRODUCT

Palgrave Macmillan Ltd., Houndmills, Basingstoke, Hampshire, RG21 6XS, England, (Telephone in U.S. (888) 330-8477), (Fax in U.S. (800) 672-2054), www.palgrave.com; *The Statesman's Yearbook 2008.*

The World Bank, 1818 H Street, NW, Washington, DC 20433, (202) 473-1000, Fax: (202) 477-6391, www.worldbank.org; *The World Bank Atlas 2003-2004* and *World Development Indicators (WDI) 2008.*

ANTIGUA AND BARBUDA - HIDES AND SKINS INDUSTRY

United Nations Food and Agricultural Organization (FAO), Viale delle Terme di Caracalla, 00100 Rome, Italy, (Dial from U.S. (202) 653-2400), (Fax from U.S. (202) 653 5760), www.fao.org; *FAO Production Yearbook 2002.*

ANTIGUA AND BARBUDA - HOUSING

Euromonitor International, Inc., 224 S. Michigan Avenue, Suite 1500, Chicago, IL 60604, (312) 922-1115, Fax: (312) 922-1157, www.euromonitor.com; *World Marketing Data and Statistics.*

ANTIGUA AND BARBUDA - ILLITERATE PERSONS

Euromonitor International, Inc., 224 S. Michigan Avenue, Suite 1500, Chicago, IL 60604, (312) 922-1115, Fax: (312) 922-1157, www.euromonitor.com; *The World Economic Factbook 2008.*

UNESCO Institute for Statistics, C.P. 6128 Succursale Centre-Ville, Montreal, Quebec, H3C 3J7 Canada, (Dial from U.S. (514) 343-6880), (Fax from U.S. (514) 343 6882), www.uis.unesco.org; *Statistical Tables.*

United Nations Statistics Division, New York, NY 10017, (800) 253-9646, Fax: (212) 963-4116, http://unstats.un.org; *Human Development Report 2006.*

ANTIGUA AND BARBUDA - IMPORTS

Central Intelligence Agency, Office of Public Affairs, Washington, DC 20505, (703) 482-0623, Fax: (703) 482-1739, www.cia.gov; *The World Factbook.*

Economist Intelligence Unit, 111 West 57th Street, New York, NY 10019, (212) 554-0600, Fax: (212) 586-1181, www.eiu.com; *Organisation of Eastern Caribbean States.*

Euromonitor International, Inc., 224 S. Michigan Avenue, Suite 1500, Chicago, IL 60604, (312) 922-1115, Fax: (312) 922-1157, www.euromonitor.com; *International Marketing Data and Statistics 2008* and *The World Economic Factbook 2008.*

Palgrave Macmillan Ltd., Houndmills, Basingstoke, Hampshire, RG21 6XS, England, (Telephone in U.S. (888) 330-8477), (Fax in U.S. (800) 672-2054), www.palgrave.com; *The Statesman's Yearbook 2008.*

Taylor and Francis Group, An Informa Business, 2 Park Square, Milton Park, Abingdon, Oxford OX14 4RN, United Kingdom, (Dial from U.S. (212) 216-7800), (Fax from U.S. (212) 564-7854), www.tandf.co.uk; *The Europa World Year Book.*

United Nations Food and Agricultural Organization (FAO), Viale delle Terme di Caracalla, 00100 Rome, Italy, (Dial from U.S. (202) 653-2400), (Fax from U.S. (202) 653 5760), www.fao.org; *The State of Food and Agriculture (SOFA) 2006.*

The World Bank, 1818 H Street, NW, Washington, DC 20433, (202) 473-1000, Fax: (202) 477-6391, www.worldbank.org; *World Development Indicators (WDI) 2008.*

ANTIGUA AND BARBUDA - INDUSTRIES

Central Intelligence Agency, Office of Public Affairs, Washington, DC 20505, (703) 482-0623, Fax: (703) 482-1739, www.cia.gov; *The World Factbook.*

Economist Intelligence Unit, 111 West 57th Street, New York, NY 10019, (212) 554-0600, Fax: (212) 586-1181, www.eiu.com; *Organisation of Eastern Caribbean States.*

Euromonitor International, Inc., 224 S. Michigan Avenue, Suite 1500, Chicago, IL 60604, (312) 922-1115, Fax: (312) 922-1157, www.euromonitor.com; *The World Economic Factbook 2008.*

International Labour Office, I.L.O. Publications, 4 route des Morillons, CH-1211 Geneva 22, Switzerland, (Telephone in U.S. (202) 653-7652), (Fax in U.S. (202) 653-7687), www.ilo.org; *Yearbook of Labour Statistics 2006.*

Palgrave Macmillan Ltd., Houndmills, Basingstoke, Hampshire, RG21 6XS, England, (Telephone in U.S. (888) 330-8477), (Fax in U.S. (800) 672-2054), www.palgrave.com; *The Statesman's Yearbook 2008.*

Taylor and Francis Group, An Informa Business, 2 Park Square, Milton Park, Abingdon, Oxford OX14 4RN, United Kingdom, (Dial from U.S. (212) 216-7800), (Fax from U.S. (212) 564-7854), www.tandf.co.uk; *The Europa World Year Book.*

United Nations Statistics Division, New York, NY 10017, (800) 253-9646, Fax: (212) 963-4116, http://unstats.un.org; *Economic Survey of Latin America and the Caribbean 2004-2005.*

The World Bank, 1818 H Street, NW, Washington, DC 20433, (202) 473-1000, Fax: (202) 477-6391, www.worldbank.org; *Antigua and Barbuda* and *World Development Indicators (WDI) 2008.*

ANTIGUA AND BARBUDA - INFANT AND MATERNAL MORTALITY

See ANTIGUA AND BARBUDA - MORTALITY

ANTIGUA AND BARBUDA - INFLATION (FINANCE)

United Nations Statistics Division, New York, NY 10017, (800) 253-9646, Fax: (212) 963-4116, http://unstats.un.org; *Economic Survey of Latin America and the Caribbean 2004-2005.*

ANTIGUA AND BARBUDA - INTERNATIONAL TRADE

Economist Intelligence Unit, 111 West 57th Street, New York, NY 10019, (212) 554-0600, Fax: (212) 586-1181, www.eiu.com; *Organisation of Eastern Caribbean States.*

Euromonitor International, Inc., 224 S. Michigan Avenue, Suite 1500, Chicago, IL 60604, (312) 922-1115, Fax: (312) 922-1157, www.euromonitor.com; *The World Economic Factbook 2008* and *World Marketing Data and Statistics.*

Organisation for Economic Cooperation and Development (OECD), 2 rue Andre Pascal, F-75775 Paris Cedex 16, France, (Telephone in U.S. (202) 785-6323), (Fax in U.S. (202) 785-0350), www.oecd.org; *International Trade by Commodity Statistics (ITCS).*

Palgrave Macmillan Ltd., Houndmills, Basingstoke, Hampshire, RG21 6XS, England, (Telephone in U.S. (888) 330-8477), (Fax in U.S. (800) 672-2054), www.palgrave.com; *The Statesman's Yearbook 2008.*

Taylor and Francis Group, An Informa Business, 2 Park Square, Milton Park, Abingdon, Oxford OX14 4RN, United Kingdom, (Dial from U.S. (212) 216-7800), (Fax from U.S. (212) 564-7854), www.tandf.co.uk; *The Europa World Year Book.*

United Nations Conference on Trade and Development (UNCTAD), DC2-1120, United Nations, New York, NY 10017, (212) 963-0027, www.unctad.org; *UNCTAD Commodity Yearbook.*

United Nations Food and Agricultural Organization (FAO), Viale delle Terme di Caracalla, 00100 Rome, Italy, (Dial from U.S. (202) 653-2400), (Fax from U.S. (202) 653 5760), www.fao.org; *FAO Production Yearbook 2002* and *The State of Food and Agriculture (SOFA) 2006.*

United Nations Statistics Division, New York, NY 10017, (800) 253-9646, Fax: (212) 963-4116, http://unstats.un.org; *Economic Survey of Latin America and the Caribbean 2004-2005* and *International Trade Statistics Yearbook.*

The World Bank, 1818 H Street, NW, Washington, DC 20433, (202) 473-1000, Fax: (202) 477-6391, www.worldbank.org; *Antigua and Barbuda* and *World Development Indicators (WDI) 2008.*

World Trade Organization (WTO), Centre William Rappard, Rue de Lausanne 154, CH-1211 Geneva 21, Switzerland, www.wto.org; *International Trade Statistics 2006.*

ANTIGUA AND BARBUDA - LABOR

Central Intelligence Agency, Office of Public Affairs, Washington, DC 20505, (703) 482-0623, Fax: (703) 482-1739, www.cia.gov; *The World Factbook.*

Euromonitor International, Inc., 224 S. Michigan Avenue, Suite 1500, Chicago, IL 60604, (312) 922-1115, Fax: (312) 922-1157, www.euromonitor.com; *International Marketing Data and Statistics 2008* and *World Marketing Data and Statistics.*

International Labour Office, I.L.O. Publications, 4 route des Morillons, CH-1211 Geneva 22, Switzerland, (Telephone in U.S. (202) 653-7652), (Fax in U.S. (202) 653-7687), www.ilo.org; *Yearbook of Labour Statistics 2006.*

Palgrave Macmillan Ltd., Houndmills, Basingstoke, Hampshire, RG21 6XS, England, (Telephone in U.S. (888) 330-8477), (Fax in U.S. (800) 672-2054), www.palgrave.com; *The Statesman's Yearbook 2008.*

Taylor and Francis Group, An Informa Business, 2 Park Square, Milton Park, Abingdon, Oxford OX14 4RN, United Kingdom, (Dial from U.S. (212) 216-7800), (Fax from U.S. (212) 564-7854), www.tandf.co.uk; *The Europa World Year Book.*

United Nations Food and Agricultural Organization (FAO), Viale delle Terme di Caracalla, 00100 Rome, Italy, (Dial from U.S. (202) 653-2400), (Fax from U.S. (202) 653 5760), www.fao.org; *The State of Food and Agriculture (SOFA) 2006.*

United Nations Statistics Division, New York, NY 10017, (800) 253-9646, Fax: (212) 963-4116, http://unstats.un.org; *Human Development Report 2006.*

The World Bank, 1818 H Street, NW, Washington, DC 20433, (202) 473-1000, Fax: (202) 477-6391, www.worldbank.org; *The World Bank Atlas 2003-2004* and *World Development Indicators (WDI) 2008.*

ANTIGUA AND BARBUDA - LAND USE

Central Intelligence Agency, Office of Public Affairs, Washington, DC 20505, (703) 482-0623, Fax: (703) 482-1739, www.cia.gov; *The World Factbook.*

Euromonitor International, Inc., 224 S. Michigan Avenue, Suite 1500, Chicago, IL 60604, (312) 922-1115, Fax: (312) 922-1157, www.euromonitor.com; *International Marketing Data and Statistics 2008.*

United Nations Food and Agricultural Organization (FAO), Viale delle Terme di Caracalla, 00100 Rome, Italy, (Dial from U.S. (202) 653-2400), (Fax from U.S. (202) 653 5760), www.fao.org; *FAO Production Yearbook 2002.*

ANTIGUA AND BARBUDA - LIFE EXPECTANCY

Euromonitor International, Inc., 224 S. Michigan Avenue, Suite 1500, Chicago, IL 60604, (312) 922-1115, Fax: (312) 922-1157, www.euromonitor.com; *The World Economic Factbook 2008.*

United Nations Statistics Division, New York, NY 10017, (800) 253-9646, Fax: (212) 963-4116, http://unstats.un.org; *Human Development Report 2006* and *World Statistics Pocketbook.*

ANTIGUA AND BARBUDA - LITERACY

Euromonitor International, Inc., 224 S. Michigan Avenue, Suite 1500, Chicago, IL 60604, (312) 922-1115, Fax: (312) 922-1157, www.euromonitor.com; *World Marketing Data and Statistics.*

The World Bank, 1818 H Street, NW, Washington, DC 20433, (202) 473-1000, Fax: (202) 477-6391, www.worldbank.org; *The World Bank Atlas 2003-2004.*

ANTIGUA AND BARBUDA - LIVESTOCK

Palgrave Macmillan Ltd., Houndmills, Basingstoke, Hampshire, RG21 6XS, England, (Telephone in U.S. (888) 330-8477), (Fax in U.S. (800) 672-2054), www.palgrave.com; *The Statesman's Yearbook 2008.*

Taylor and Francis Group, An Informa Business, 2 Park Square, Milton Park, Abingdon, Oxford OX14 4RN, United Kingdom, (Dial from U.S. (212) 216-7800), (Fax from U.S. (212) 564-7854), www.tandf.co.uk; *The Europa World Year Book.*

United Nations Conference on Trade and Development (UNCTAD), DC2-1120, United Nations, New York, NY 10017, (212) 963-0027, www.unctad.org; *UNCTAD Commodity Yearbook.*

United Nations Food and Agricultural Organization (FAO), Viale delle Terme di Caracalla, 00100 Rome, Italy, (Dial from U.S. (202) 653-2400), (Fax from U.S. (202) 653 5760), www.fao.org; *FAO Production Yearbook 2002* and *The State of Food and Agriculture (SOFA) 2006.*

United Nations Statistics Division, New York, NY 10017, (800) 253-9646, Fax: (212) 963-4116, http://unstats.un.org; *Statistical Yearbook.*

ANTIGUA AND BARBUDA - MANUFACTURES

The World Bank, 1818 H Street, NW, Washington, DC 20433, (202) 473-1000, Fax: (202) 477-6391, www.worldbank.org; *World Development Indicators (WDI) 2008.*

ANTIGUA AND BARBUDA - MARRIAGE

Taylor and Francis Group, An Informa Business, 2 Park Square, Milton Park, Abingdon, Oxford OX14 4RN, United Kingdom, (Dial from U.S. (212) 216-7800), (Fax from U.S. (212) 564-7854), www.tandf.co.uk; *The Europa World Year Book.*

United Nations Statistics Division, New York, NY 10017, (800) 253-9646, Fax: (212) 963-4116, http://unstats.un.org; *Demographic Yearbook* and *Statistical Yearbook.*

ANTIGUA AND BARBUDA - MEAT PRODUCTION

See ANTIGUA AND BARBUDA - LIVESTOCK

ANTIGUA AND BARBUDA - MINERAL INDUSTRIES

United Nations Conference on Trade and Development (UNCTAD), DC2-1120, United Nations, New York, NY 10017, (212) 963-0027, www.unctad.org; *UNCTAD Commodity Yearbook.*

ANTIGUA AND BARBUDA - MONEY SUPPLY

Economist Intelligence Unit, 111 West 57th Street, New York, NY 10019, (212) 554-0600, Fax: (212) 586-1181, www.eiu.com; *Organisation of Eastern Caribbean States.*

Taylor and Francis Group, An Informa Business, 2 Park Square, Milton Park, Abingdon, Oxford OX14 4RN, United Kingdom, (Dial from U.S. (212) 216-7800), (Fax from U.S. (212) 564-7854), www.tandf.co.uk; *The Europa World Year Book.*

The World Bank, 1818 H Street, NW, Washington, DC 20433, (202) 473-1000, Fax: (202) 477-6391, www.worldbank.org; *Antigua and Barbuda* and *World Development Indicators (WDI) 2008.*

ANTIGUA AND BARBUDA - MORTALITY

Central Intelligence Agency, Office of Public Affairs, Washington, DC 20505, (703) 482-0623, Fax: (703) 482-1739, www.cia.gov; *The World Factbook.*

Euromonitor International, Inc., 224 S. Michigan Avenue, Suite 1500, Chicago, IL 60604, (312) 922-1115, Fax: (312) 922-1157, www.euromonitor.com; *International Marketing Data and Statistics 2008* and *The World Economic Factbook 2008.*

Taylor and Francis Group, An Informa Business, 2 Park Square, Milton Park, Abingdon, Oxford OX14 4RN, United Kingdom, (Dial from U.S. (212) 216-7800), (Fax from U.S. (212) 564-7854), www.tandf.co.uk; *The Europa World Year Book.*

United Nations Statistics Division, New York, NY 10017, (800) 253-9646, Fax: (212) 963-4116, http://unstats.un.org; *Demographic Yearbook; Human Development Report 2006; Statistical Yearbook;* and *World Statistics Pocketbook.*

The World Bank, 1818 H Street, NW, Washington, DC 20433, (202) 473-1000, Fax: (202) 477-6391, www.worldbank.org; *The World Bank Atlas 2003-2004* and *World Development Indicators (WDI) 2008.*

World Health Organization (WHO), Avenue Appia 20, 1211 Geneve 27, Switzerland, (Telephone in U.S. (212) 331-9081), www.who.int; *World Health Report 2006.*

ANTIGUA AND BARBUDA - MOTOR VEHICLES

Taylor and Francis Group, An Informa Business, 2 Park Square, Milton Park, Abingdon, Oxford OX14 4RN, United Kingdom, (Dial from U.S. (212) 216-7800), (Fax from U.S. (212) 564-7854), www.tandf.co.uk; *The Europa World Year Book.*

ANTIGUA AND BARBUDA - MUSEUMS

UNESCO Institute for Statistics, C.P. 6128 Succursale Centre-Ville, Montreal, Quebec, H3C 3J7 Canada, (Dial from U.S. (514) 343-6880), (Fax from U.S. (514) 343 6882), www.uis.unesco.org; *Statistical Tables.*

ANTIGUA AND BARBUDA - NUTRITION

United Nations Food and Agricultural Organization (FAO), Viale delle Terme di Caracalla, 00100 Rome, Italy, (Dial from U.S. (202) 653-2400), (Fax from U.S. (202) 653 5760), www.fao.org; *The State of Food and Agriculture (SOFA) 2006.*

ANTIGUA AND BARBUDA - PESTICIDES

United Nations Food and Agricultural Organization (FAO), Viale delle Terme di Caracalla, 00100 Rome, Italy, (Dial from U.S. (202) 653-2400), (Fax from U.S. (202) 653 5760), www.fao.org; *The State of Food and Agriculture (SOFA) 2006.*

ANTIGUA AND BARBUDA - PETROLEUM INDUSTRY AND TRADE

PennWell Corporation, 1421 South Sheridan Road, Tulsa, OK 74112, (918) 835-3161, www.pennwell.com; *International Petroleum Encyclopedia 2007.*

United Nations Conference on Trade and Development (UNCTAD), DC2-1120, United Nations, New York, NY 10017, (212) 963-0027, www.unctad.org; *UNCTAD Commodity Yearbook.*

United Nations Food and Agricultural Organization (FAO), Viale delle Terme di Caracalla, 00100 Rome, Italy, (Dial from U.S. (202) 653-2400), (Fax from U.S. (202) 653 5760), www.fao.org; *The State of Food and Agriculture (SOFA) 2006.*

United Nations Statistics Division, New York, NY 10017, (800) 253-9646, Fax: (212) 963-4116, http://unstats.un.org; *Statistical Yearbook.*

ANTIGUA AND BARBUDA - POLITICAL SCIENCE

Central Intelligence Agency, Office of Public Affairs, Washington, DC 20505, (703) 482-0623, Fax: (703) 482-1739, www.cia.gov; *The World Factbook.*

Palgrave Macmillan Ltd., Houndmills, Basingstoke, Hampshire, RG21 6XS, England, (Telephone in U.S. (888) 330-8477), (Fax in U.S. (800) 672-2054), www.palgrave.com; *The Statesman's Yearbook 2008.*

Taylor and Francis Group, An Informa Business, 2 Park Square, Milton Park, Abingdon, Oxford OX14 4RN, United Kingdom, (Dial from U.S. (212) 216-7800), (Fax from U.S. (212) 564-7854), www.tandf.co.uk; *The Europa World Year Book.*

United Nations Statistics Division, New York, NY 10017, (800) 253-9646, Fax: (212) 963-4116, http://unstats.un.org; *National Accounts Statistics: Compendium of Income Distribution Statistics.*

The World Bank, 1818 H Street, NW, Washington, DC 20433, (202) 473-1000, Fax: (202) 477-6391, www.worldbank.org; *World Development Indicators (WDI) 2008.*

ANTIGUA AND BARBUDA - POPULATION

Caribbean Epidemiology Centre (CAREC), 16-18 Jamaica Boulevard, Federation Park, PO Box 164, Port of Spain, Republic of Trinidad and Tobago, (Dial from U.S. (868) 622-4261), (Fax from U.S. (868) 622-2792), www.carec.org; *Population Data.*

Central Intelligence Agency, Office of Public Affairs, Washington, DC 20505, (703) 482-0623, Fax: (703) 482-1739, www.cia.gov; *The World Factbook.*

Economist Intelligence Unit, 111 West 57th Street, New York, NY 10019, (212) 554-0600, Fax: (212) 586-1181, www.eiu.com; *Organisation of Eastern Caribbean States.*

Euromonitor International, Inc., 224 S. Michigan Avenue, Suite 1500, Chicago, IL 60604, (312) 922-1115, Fax: (312) 922-1157, www.euromonitor.com; *International Marketing Data and Statistics 2008* and *The World Economic Factbook 2008.*

Eurostat, Batiment Jean Monnet, Rue Alcide de Gasperi, L-2920 Luxembourg, http://epp.eurostat.ec.europa.eu; *Demographic Indicators - Population by Age-Classes.*

International Labour Office, I.L.O. Publications, 4 route des Morillons, CH-1211 Geneva 22, Switzerland, (Telephone in U.S. (202) 653-7652), (Fax in U.S. (202) 653-7687), www.ilo.org; *Yearbook of Labour Statistics 2006.*

Palgrave Macmillan Ltd., Houndmills, Basingstoke, Hampshire, RG21 6XS, England, (Telephone in U.S. (888) 330-8477), (Fax in U.S. (800) 672-2054), www.palgrave.com; *The Statesman's Yearbook 2008.*

Taylor and Francis Group, An Informa Business, 2 Park Square, Milton Park, Abingdon, Oxford OX14 4RN, United Kingdom, (Dial from U.S. (212) 216-7800), (Fax from U.S. (212) 564-7854), www.tandf.co.uk; *The Europa World Year Book.*

United Nations Food and Agricultural Organization (FAO), Viale delle Terme di Caracalla, 00100 Rome, Italy, (Dial from U.S. (202) 653-2400), (Fax from U.S. (202) 653 5760), www.fao.org; *FAO Production Yearbook 2002.*

United Nations Statistics Division, New York, NY 10017, (800) 253-9646, Fax: (212) 963-4116, http://unstats.un.org; *Demographic Yearbook; Human Development Report 2006; Statistical Yearbook;* and *World Statistics Pocketbook.*

The World Bank, 1818 H Street, NW, Washington, DC 20433, (202) 473-1000, Fax: (202) 477-6391, www.worldbank.org; *Antigua and Barbuda* and *The World Bank Atlas 2003-2004.*

World Health Organization (WHO), Avenue Appia 20, 1211 Geneve 27, Switzerland, (Telephone in U.S. (212) 331-9081), www.who.int; *World Health Report 2006.*

ANTIGUA AND BARBUDA - POPULATION DENSITY

Central Intelligence Agency, Office of Public Affairs, Washington, DC 20505, (703) 482-0623, Fax: (703) 482-1739, www.cia.gov; *The World Factbook.*

Euromonitor International, Inc., 224 S. Michigan Avenue, Suite 1500, Chicago, IL 60604, (312) 922-1115, Fax: (312) 922-1157, www.euromonitor.com; *The World Economic Factbook 2008.*

Palgrave Macmillan Ltd., Houndmills, Basingstoke, Hampshire, RG21 6XS, England, (Telephone in U.S. (888) 330-8477), (Fax in U.S. (800) 672-2054), www.palgrave.com; *The Statesman's Yearbook 2008.*

Taylor and Francis Group, An Informa Business, 2 Park Square, Milton Park, Abingdon, Oxford OX14 4RN, United Kingdom, (Dial from U.S. (212) 216-7800), (Fax from U.S. (212) 564-7854), www.tandf.co.uk; *The Europa World Year Book.*

United Nations Food and Agricultural Organization (FAO), Viale delle Terme di Caracalla, 00100 Rome, Italy, (Dial from U.S. (202) 653-2400), (Fax from U.S. (202) 653 5760), www.fao.org; *The State of Food and Agriculture (SOFA) 2006.*

United Nations Statistics Division, New York, NY 10017, (800) 253-9646, Fax: (212) 963-4116, http://unstats.un.org; *Statistical Yearbook.*

The World Bank, 1818 H Street, NW, Washington, DC 20433, (202) 473-1000, Fax: (202) 477-6391, www.worldbank.org; *Antigua and Barbuda.*

ANTIGUA AND BARBUDA - POSTAL SERVICE

United Nations Statistics Division, New York, NY 10017, (800) 253-9646, Fax: (212) 963-4116, http://unstats.un.org; *Statistical Yearbook.*

ANTIGUA AND BARBUDA - POWER RESOURCES

Euromonitor International, Inc., 224 S. Michigan Avenue, Suite 1500, Chicago, IL 60604, (312) 922-1115, Fax: (312) 922-1157, www.euromonitor.com; *International Marketing Data and Statistics 2008; The World Economic Factbook 2008;* and *World Marketing Data and Statistics.*

Platts, 2 Penn Plaza, 25th Floor, New York, NY 10121-2298, (212) 904-3070, www.platts.com; *Energy Economist.*

United Nations Food and Agricultural Organization (FAO), Viale delle Terme di Caracalla, 00100 Rome, Italy, (Dial from U.S. (202) 653-2400), (Fax from U.S. (202) 653 5760), www.fao.org; *The State of Food and Agriculture (SOFA) 2006.*

United Nations Statistics Division, New York, NY 10017, (800) 253-9646, Fax: (212) 963-4116, http://unstats.un.org; *Energy Statistics Yearbook 2003; Human Development Report 2006; Statistical Yearbook;* and *World Statistics Pocketbook.*

The World Bank, 1818 H Street, NW, Washington, DC 20433, (202) 473-1000, Fax: (202) 477-6391, www.worldbank.org; *The World Bank Atlas 2003-2004.*

ANTIGUA AND BARBUDA - PRICES

Euromonitor International, Inc., 224 S. Michigan Avenue, Suite 1500, Chicago, IL 60604, (312) 922-1115, Fax: (312) 922-1157, www.euromonitor.com; *World Marketing Data and Statistics.*

International Labour Office, I.L.O. Publications, 4 route des Morillons, CH-1211 Geneva 22, Switzerland, (Telephone in U.S. (202) 653-7652), (Fax in U.S. (202) 653-7687), www.ilo.org; *Yearbook of Labour Statistics 2006.*

United Nations Food and Agricultural Organization (FAO), Viale delle Terme di Caracalla, 00100 Rome, Italy, (Dial from U.S. (202) 653-2400), (Fax from U.S. (202) 653 5760), www.fao.org; *FAO Production Yearbook 2002* and *The State of Food and Agriculture (SOFA) 2006.*

United Nations Statistics Division, New York, NY 10017, (800) 253-9646, Fax: (212) 963-4116, http://unstats.un.org; *Economic Survey of Latin America and the Caribbean 2004-2005.*

The World Bank, 1818 H Street, NW, Washington, DC 20433, (202) 473-1000, Fax: (202) 477-6391, www.worldbank.org; *Antigua and Barbuda.*

ANTIGUA AND BARBUDA - PROFESSIONS

United Nations Statistics Division, New York, NY 10017, (800) 253-9646, Fax: (212) 963-4116, http://unstats.un.org; *Statistical Yearbook.*

ANTIGUA AND BARBUDA - PUBLIC HEALTH

Euromonitor International, Inc., 224 S. Michigan Avenue, Suite 1500, Chicago, IL 60604, (312) 922-1115, Fax: (312) 922-1157, www.euromonitor.com; *World Marketing Data and Statistics.*

Palgrave Macmillan Ltd., Houndmills, Basingstoke, Hampshire, RG21 6XS, England, (Telephone in U.S. (888) 330-8477), (Fax in U.S. (800) 672-2054), www.palgrave.com; *The Statesman's Yearbook 2008.*

United Nations Statistics Division, New York, NY 10017, (800) 253-9646, Fax: (212) 963-4116, http://unstats.un.org; *Human Development Report 2006* and *Statistical Yearbook.*

The World Bank, 1818 H Street, NW, Washington, DC 20433, (202) 473-1000, Fax: (202) 477-6391, www.worldbank.org; *Antigua and Barbuda.*

World Health Organization (WHO), Avenue Appia 20, 1211 Geneve 27, Switzerland, (Telephone in U.S. (212) 331-9081), www.who.int; *World Health Report 2006.*

ANTIGUA AND BARBUDA - RADIO BROADCASTING

Palgrave Macmillan Ltd., Houndmills, Basingstoke, Hampshire, RG21 6XS, England, (Telephone in U.S. (888) 330-8477), (Fax in U.S. (800) 672-2054), www.palgrave.com; *The Statesman's Yearbook 2008.*

ANTIGUA AND BARBUDA - RELIGION

Central Intelligence Agency, Office of Public Affairs, Washington, DC 20505, (703) 482-0623, Fax: (703) 482-1739, www.cia.gov; *The World Factbook.*

Palgrave Macmillan Ltd., Houndmills, Basingstoke, Hampshire, RG21 6XS, England, (Telephone in U.S. (888) 330-8477), (Fax in U.S. (800) 672-2054), www.palgrave.com; *The Statesman's Yearbook 2008.*

ANTIGUA AND BARBUDA - RENT CHARGES

International Labour Office, I.L.O. Publications, 4 route des Morillons, CH-1211 Geneva 22, Switzerland, (Telephone in U.S. (202) 653-7652), (Fax in U.S. (202) 653-7687), www.ilo.org; *Yearbook of Labour Statistics 2006.*

ANTIGUA AND BARBUDA - RESERVES (ACCOUNTING)

The World Bank, 1818 H Street, NW, Washington, DC 20433, (202) 473-1000, Fax: (202) 477-6391, www.worldbank.org; *World Development Indicators (WDI) 2008.*

ANTIGUA AND BARBUDA - RETAIL TRADE

Euromonitor International, Inc., 224 S. Michigan Avenue, Suite 1500, Chicago, IL 60604, (312) 922-1115, Fax: (312) 922-1157, www.euromonitor.com; *World Marketing Data and Statistics.*

ANTIGUA AND BARBUDA - ROADS

Central Intelligence Agency, Office of Public Affairs, Washington, DC 20505, (703) 482-0623, Fax: (703) 482-1739, www.cia.gov; *The World Factbook.*

Palgrave Macmillan Ltd., Houndmills, Basingstoke, Hampshire, RG21 6XS, England, (Telephone in U.S. (888) 330-8477), (Fax in U.S. (800) 672-2054), www.palgrave.com; *The Statesman's Yearbook 2008.*

ANTIGUA AND BARBUDA - SHEEP

See ANTIGUA AND BARBUDA - LIVESTOCK

ANTIGUA AND BARBUDA - SHIPPING

Taylor and Francis Group, An Informa Business, 2 Park Square, Milton Park, Abingdon, Oxford OX14 4RN, United Kingdom, (Dial from U.S. (212) 216-7800), (Fax from U.S. (212) 564-7854), www.tandf.co.uk; *The Europa World Year Book.*

United Nations Statistics Division, New York, NY 10017, (800) 253-9646, Fax: (212) 963-4116, http://unstats.un.org; *Statistical Yearbook.*

ANTIGUA AND BARBUDA - SOCIAL ECOLOGY

United Nations Statistics Division, New York, NY 10017, (800) 253-9646, Fax: (212) 963-4116, http://unstats.un.org; *World Statistics Pocketbook.*

ANTIGUA AND BARBUDA - SOCIAL SECURITY

United Nations Statistics Division, New York, NY 10017, (800) 253-9646, Fax: (212) 963-4116, http://unstats.un.org; *National Accounts Statistics: Compendium of Income Distribution Statistics.*

ANTIGUA AND BARBUDA - SUGAR PRODUCTION

See ANTIGUA AND BARBUDA - CROPS

ANTIGUA AND BARBUDA - TAXATION

The World Bank, 1818 H Street, NW, Washington, DC 20433, (202) 473-1000, Fax: (202) 477-6391, www.worldbank.org; *World Development Indicators (WDI) 2008.*

ANTIGUA AND BARBUDA - TELEPHONE

International Telecommunication Union (ITU), Place des Nations, 1211 Geneva 20, Switzerland, www.itu.int; World Telecommunication Indicators Database.

Palgrave Macmillan Ltd., Houndmills, Basingstoke, Hampshire, RG21 6XS, England, (Telephone in U.S. (888) 330-8477), (Fax in U.S. (800) 672-2054), www.palgrave.com; *The Statesman's Yearbook 2008.*

Taylor and Francis Group, An Informa Business, 2 Park Square, Milton Park, Abingdon, Oxford OX14 4RN, United Kingdom, (Dial from U.S. (212) 216-7800), (Fax from U.S. (212) 564-7854), www.tandf.co.uk; *The Europa World Year Book.*

United Nations Statistics Division, New York, NY 10017, (800) 253-9646, Fax: (212) 963-4116, http://unstats.un.org; *Statistical Yearbook* and *World Statistics Pocketbook.*

ANTIGUA AND BARBUDA - TEXTILE INDUSTRY

Palgrave Macmillan Ltd., Houndmills, Basingstoke, Hampshire, RG21 6XS, England, (Telephone in U.S. (888) 330-8477), (Fax in U.S. (800) 672-2054), www.palgrave.com; *The Statesman's Yearbook 2008.*

United Nations Conference on Trade and Development (UNCTAD), DC2-1120, United Nations, New York, NY 10017, (212) 963-0027, www.unctad.org; *UNCTAD Commodity Yearbook.*

ANTIGUA AND BARBUDA - TOURISM

Euromonitor International, Inc., 224 S. Michigan Avenue, Suite 1500, Chicago, IL 60604, (312) 922-1115, Fax: (312) 922-1157, www.euromonitor.com; *The World Economic Factbook 2008* and *World Marketing Data and Statistics.*

Palgrave Macmillan Ltd., Houndmills, Basingstoke, Hampshire, RG21 6XS, England, (Telephone in U.S. (888) 330-8477), (Fax in U.S. (800) 672-2054), www.palgrave.com; *The Statesman's Yearbook 2008.*

Taylor and Francis Group, An Informa Business, 2 Park Square, Milton Park, Abingdon, Oxford OX14 4RN, United Kingdom, (Dial from U.S. (212) 216-7800), (Fax from U.S. (212) 564-7854), www.tandf.co.uk; *The Europa World Year Book.*

United Nations World Tourism Organization (UNWTO), Capitan Haya 42, 28020 Madrid, Spain, www.world-tourism.org; *Yearbook of Tourism Statistics.*

The World Bank, 1818 H Street, NW, Washington, DC 20433, (202) 473-1000, Fax: (202) 477-6391, www.worldbank.org; *Antigua and Barbuda.*

ANTIGUA AND BARBUDA - TRADE

See ANTIGUA AND BARBUDA - INTERNATIONAL TRADE

ANTIGUA AND BARBUDA - TRANSPORTATION

Central Intelligence Agency, Office of Public Affairs, Washington, DC 20505, (703) 482-0623, Fax: (703) 482-1739, www.cia.gov; *The World Factbook.*

Euromonitor International, Inc., 224 S. Michigan Avenue, Suite 1500, Chicago, IL 60604, (312) 922-1115, Fax: (312) 922-1157, www.euromonitor.com; *International Marketing Data and Statistics 2008* and *World Marketing Data and Statistics.*

Palgrave Macmillan Ltd., Houndmills, Basingstoke, Hampshire, RG21 6XS, England, (Telephone in U.S. (888) 330-8477), (Fax in U.S. (800) 672-2054), www.palgrave.com; *The Statesman's Yearbook 2008.*

Taylor and Francis Group, An Informa Business, 2 Park Square, Milton Park, Abingdon, Oxford OX14 4RN, United Kingdom, (Dial from U.S. (212) 216-7800), (Fax from U.S. (212) 564-7854), www.tandf.co.uk; *The Europa World Year Book.*

United Nations Statistics Division, New York, NY 10017, (800) 253-9646, Fax: (212) 963-4116, http://unstats.un.org; *Human Development Report 2006.*

The World Bank, 1818 H Street, NW, Washington, DC 20433, (202) 473-1000, Fax: (202) 477-6391, www.worldbank.org; *Antigua and Barbuda.*

ANTIGUA AND BARBUDA - UNEMPLOYMENT

Central Intelligence Agency, Office of Public Affairs, Washington, DC 20505, (703) 482-0623, Fax: (703) 482-1739, www.cia.gov; *The World Factbook.*

International Labour Office, I.L.O. Publications, 4 route des Morillons, CH-1211 Geneva 22, Switzerland, (Telephone in U.S. (202) 653-7652), (Fax in U.S. (202) 653-7687), www.ilo.org; *Yearbook of Labour Statistics 2006.*

Palgrave Macmillan Ltd., Houndmills, Basingstoke, Hampshire, RG21 6XS, England, (Telephone in U.S. (888) 330-8477), (Fax in U.S. (800) 672-2054), www.palgrave.com; *The Statesman's Yearbook 2008.*

United Nations Statistics Division, New York, NY 10017, (800) 253-9646, Fax: (212) 963-4116, http://unstats.un.org; *Statistical Yearbook.*

ANTIGUA AND BARBUDA - VITAL STATISTICS

Palgrave Macmillan Ltd., Houndmills, Basingstoke, Hampshire, RG21 6XS, England, (Telephone in U.S. (888) 330-8477), (Fax in U.S. (800) 672-2054), www.palgrave.com; *The Statesman's Yearbook 2008.*

United Nations Statistics Division, New York, NY 10017, (800) 253-9646, Fax: (212) 963-4116, http://unstats.un.org; *Statistical Yearbook.*

World Health Organization (WHO), Avenue Appia 20, 1211 Geneve 27, Switzerland, (Telephone in U.S. (212) 331-9081), www.who.int; *World Health Report 2006.*

ANTIGUA AND BARBUDA - WAGES

International Labour Office, I.L.O. Publications, 4 route des Morillons, CH-1211 Geneva 22, Switzerland, (Telephone in U.S. (202) 653-7652), (Fax in U.S. (202) 653-7687), www.ilo.org; *Yearbook of Labour Statistics 2006.*

The World Bank, 1818 H Street, NW, Washington, DC 20433, (202) 473-1000, Fax: (202) 477-6391, www.worldbank.org; *Antigua and Barbuda.*

ANTIMONY

U.S. Department of the Interior (DOI), U.S. Geological Survey (USGS), Office of Minerals Information, 12201 Sunrise Valley Drive, Reston, VA 20192, Mr. Kenneth A. Beckman, (703) 648-4916, Fax: (703) 648-4995, http://minerals.usgs.gov/minerals; *Mineral Commodity Summaries.*

APPAREL GOODS - ADVERTISING

The NPD Group, Port Washington, 900 West Shore Road, Port Washington, NY 11050, (866) 444-1411, www.npd.com; *Market Research for the Apparel and Footwear Industries.*

APPAREL GOODS - CONSUMER EXPENDITURES

The NPD Group, Port Washington, 900 West Shore Road, Port Washington, NY 11050, (866) 444-1411, www.npd.com; *Market Research for the Apparel and Footwear Industries.*

U.S. Bureau of Labor Statistics (BLS), Postal Square Building, 2 Massachusetts Avenue, NE, Washington, DC 20212-0001, (202) 691-5200, Fax: (202) 691-6325, www.bls.gov; *Consumer Expenditures in 2006.*

APPAREL GOODS - INTERNATIONAL TRADE

The NPD Group, Port Washington, 900 West Shore Road, Port Washington, NY 11050, (866) 444-1411, www.npd.com; *Market Research for the Apparel and Footwear Industries.*

U.S. Census Bureau, Foreign Trade Division, 4700 Silver Hill Road, Washington DC 20233-0001, (301) 763-3030, www.census.gov/foreign-trade/www/; *U.S. International Trade in Goods and Services.*

APPAREL GOODS - PRICES

Bureau of Economic Analysis (BEA), U.S. Department of Commerce (DOC), 1441 L Street NW, Washington, DC 20230, (202) 606-9900, www.bea.gov; *2007 Annual Revision of the National Income and Product Accounts (NIPA)* and *Survey of Current Business (SCB).*

The NPD Group, Port Washington, 900 West Shore Road, Port Washington, NY 11050, (866) 444-1411, www.npd.com; *Market Research for the Apparel and Footwear Industries.*

U.S. Bureau of Labor Statistics (BLS), Postal Square Building, 2 Massachusetts Avenue, NE, Washington, DC 20212-0001, (202) 691-5200, Fax: (202) 691-6325, www.bls.gov; *Monthly Labor Review (MLR).*

U.S. Department of Labor (DOL), Bureau of Labor Statistics (BLS), Postal Square Building, 2 Massachusetts Avenue, NE, Washington, DC 20212-0001, (202) 691-5200, Fax: (202) 691-6325, www.bls.gov; *Consumer Price Indexes (CPI).*

APPAREL MANUFACTURING - EARNINGS

The NPD Group, Port Washington, 900 West Shore Road, Port Washington, NY 11050, (866) 444-1411, www.npd.com; *Market Research for the Apparel and Footwear Industries.*

U.S. Bureau of Labor Statistics (BLS), Postal Square Building, 2 Massachusetts Avenue, NE, Washington, DC 20212-0001, (202) 691-5200, Fax: (202) 691-6325, www.bls.gov; *Current Employment Statistics Survey (CES)* and *Employment and Earnings (EE).*

U.S. Census Bureau, Company Statistics Division, 4700 Silver Hill Road, Washington DC 20233-0001, (301) 763-3030, www.census.gov/csd/; *County Business Patterns 2004.*

APPAREL MANUFACTURING - ELECTRONIC COMMERCE

U.S. Census Bureau, 4700 Silver Hill Road, Washington DC 20233-0001, (301) 763-3030, www.census.gov; *E-Stats - Measuring the Electronic Economy.*

APPAREL MANUFACTURING - EMPLOYEES

Bureau of Economic Analysis (BEA), U.S. Department of Commerce (DOC), 1441 L Street NW, Washington, DC 20230, (202) 606-9900, www.bea.gov; *Survey of Current Business (SCB).*

U.S. Bureau of Labor Statistics (BLS), Postal Square Building, 2 Massachusetts Avenue, NE, Washington, DC 20212-0001, (202) 691-5200, Fax: (202) 691-6325, www.bls.gov; *Current Employment Statistics Survey (CES); Employment and Earnings (EE);* and *Monthly Labor Review (MLR).*

U.S. Census Bureau, Company Statistics Division, 4700 Silver Hill Road, Washington DC 20233-0001, (301) 763-3030, www.census.gov/csd/; *County Business Patterns 2004.*

U.S. Census Bureau, Manufacturing and Construction Division, 4600 Silver Hill Road, Washington DC 20233, (301) 763-4673, www.census.gov/mcd; *Annual Survey of Manufactures, Statistics for Industry Groups and Industries.*

APPAREL MANUFACTURING - ENERGY CONSUMPTION

U.S. Department of Energy (DOE), Energy Information Administration (EIA), 1000 Independence Avenue, SW, Washington, DC 20585, (202) 586-8800, www.eia.doe.gov; *Manufacturing Energy Consumption Survey (MECS) 2002.*

APPAREL MANUFACTURING - ESTABLISHMENTS

U.S. Census Bureau, Company Statistics Division, 4700 Silver Hill Road, Washington DC 20233-0001, (301) 763-3030, www.census.gov/csd/; *County Business Patterns 2004.*

U.S. Census Bureau, Manufacturing and Construction Division, 4600 Silver Hill Road, Washington DC 20233, (301) 763-4673, www.census.gov/mcd; *Annual Survey of Manufactures, Statistics for Industry Groups and Industries.*

APPAREL MANUFACTURING - GROSS DOMESTIC PRODUCT

Bureau of Economic Analysis (BEA), U.S. Department of Commerce (DOC), 1441 L Street NW, Washington, DC 20230, (202) 606-9900, www.bea.gov; *2007 Annual Revision of the National Income and Product Accounts (NIPA)* and *Survey of Current Business (SCB).*

The NPD Group, Port Washington, 900 West Shore Road, Port Washington, NY 11050, (866) 444-1411, www.npd.com; *Market Research for the Apparel and Footwear Industries.*

APPAREL MANUFACTURING - INDUSTRIAL SAFETY

U.S. Bureau of Labor Statistics (BLS), Postal Square Building, 2 Massachusetts Avenue, NE, Washington, DC 20212-0001, (202) 691-5200, Fax: (202) 691-6325, www.bls.gov; *Injuries, Illnesses, and Fatalities (IIF).*

APPAREL MANUFACTURING - INTERNATIONAL TRADE

The NPD Group, Port Washington, 900 West Shore Road, Port Washington, NY 11050, (866) 444-1411, www.npd.com; *Market Research for the Apparel and Footwear Industries.*

U.S. Census Bureau, 4700 Silver Hill Road, Washington DC 20233-0001, (301) 763-3030, www.census.gov; unpublished data.

U.S. Census Bureau, Foreign Trade Division, 4700 Silver Hill Road, Washington DC 20233-0001, (301) 763-3030, www.census.gov/foreign-trade/www/; *U.S. International Trade in Goods and Services.*

APPAREL MANUFACTURING - MERGERS AND ACQUISITIONS

Thomson Financial, 195 Broadway, New York, NY 10007, (646) 822-2000, www.thomson.com; Thomson Research.

APPAREL MANUFACTURING - PRODUCTIVITY

The NPD Group, Port Washington, 900 West Shore Road, Port Washington, NY 11050, (866) 444-1411, www.npd.com; *Market Research for the Apparel and Footwear Industries.*

U.S. Bureau of Labor Statistics (BLS), Postal Square Building, 2 Massachusetts Avenue, NE, Washington, DC 20212-0001, (202) 691-5200, Fax: (202) 691-6325, www.bls.gov; *Industry Productivity and Costs.*

APPAREL MANUFACTURING - SHIPMENTS

U.S. Census Bureau, Manufacturing and Construction Division, 4600 Silver Hill Road, Washington DC 20233, (301) 763-4673, www.census.gov/mcd; *Annual Survey of Manufactures, Statistics for Industry Groups and Industries.*

APPAREL MANUFACTURING - TOXIC CHEMICAL RELEASES

U.S. Environmental Protection Agency (EPA), Ariel Rios Building, 1200 Pennsylvania Avenue, NW, Washington, DC 20460, (202) 272-0167, www.epa.gov; Toxics Release Inventory (TRI) Database.

APPLES

Economic Research Service (ERS), U.S. Department of Agriculture (USDA), 1800 M Street, NW, Washington, DC 20036-5831, (202) 694-5050, Fax: (202) 694-5689, www.ers.usda.gov; *Agricultural Income and Finance Outlook; Agricultural Outlook;* and *Food CPI, Prices, and Expenditures.*

National Agricultural Statistics Service (NASS), U.S. Department of Agriculture (USDA), 1400 Independence Avenue, SW, Washington, DC 20250, (800) 727-9540, Fax: (202) 690-2090, www.nass.usda.gov; *Noncitrus Fruits and Nuts: Final Estimates 1998-2003.*

U.S. Bureau of Labor Statistics (BLS), Postal Square Building, 2 Massachusetts Avenue, NE, Washington, DC 20212-0001, (202) 691-5200, Fax: (202) 691-6325, www.bls.gov; *Consumer Price Index Detailed Report* and *Monthly Labor Review (MLR).*

APPLIANCES (HOUSEHOLD) INDUSTRY - MANUFACTURING - EARNINGS

The NPD Group, Port Washington, 900 West Shore Road, Port Washington, NY 11050, (866) 444-1411, www.npd.com; *Market Research for the Appliances, Home Improvement, Home Textiles, and Housewares Industries.*

U.S. Bureau of Labor Statistics (BLS), Postal Square Building, 2 Massachusetts Avenue, NE, Washington, DC 20212-0001, (202) 691-5200, Fax: (202) 691-6325, www.bls.gov; *Current Employment Statistics Survey (CES)* and *Employment and Earnings (EE).*

APPLIANCES (HOUSEHOLD) INDUSTRY - MANUFACTURING - EMPLOYEES

U.S. Bureau of Labor Statistics (BLS), Postal Square Building, 2 Massachusetts Avenue, NE, Washington, DC 20212-0001, (202) 691-5200, Fax: (202) 691-6325, www.bls.gov; *Current Employment Statistics Survey (CES); Employment and Earnings (EE);* and *Monthly Labor Review (MLR).*

APPLIANCES (HOUSEHOLD) INDUSTRY - MANUFACTURING - INVENTORIES

U.S. Census Bureau, Manufacturing and Construction Division, 4600 Silver Hill Road, Washington DC 20233, (301) 763-4673, www.census.gov/mcd; *Current Industrial Reports.*

APPLIANCES (HOUSEHOLD) INDUSTRY - MANUFACTURING - PRODUCTIVITY

The NPD Group, Port Washington, 900 West Shore Road, Port Washington, NY 11050, (866) 444-1411, www.npd.com; *Market Research for the Appliances, Home Improvement, Home Textiles, and Housewares Industries.*

U.S. Bureau of Labor Statistics (BLS), Postal Square Building, 2 Massachusetts Avenue, NE, Washington, DC 20212-0001, (202) 691-5200, Fax: (202) 691-6325, www.bls.gov; *Industry Productivity and Costs.*

APPLIANCES (HOUSEHOLD) INDUSTRY - MANUFACTURING - SHIPMENTS

U.S. Census Bureau, Manufacturing and Construction Division, 4600 Silver Hill Road, Washington DC 20233, (301) 763-4673, www.census.gov/mcd; *Current Industrial Reports.*

APPLIANCES, HOUSEHOLD - CONSUMER EXPENDITURES

The NPD Group, Port Washington, 900 West Shore Road, Port Washington, NY 11050, (866) 444-1411, www.npd.com; *Market Research for the Appliances, Home Improvement, Home Textiles, and Housewares Industries.*

U.S. Bureau of Labor Statistics (BLS), Postal Square Building, 2 Massachusetts Avenue, NE, Washington, DC 20212-0001, (202) 691-5200, Fax: (202) 691-6325, www.bls.gov; *Consumer Expenditures in 2006.*

APPLIANCES, HOUSEHOLD - PRICE INDEXES

U.S. Bureau of Labor Statistics (BLS), Postal Square Building, 2 Massachusetts Avenue, NE, Washington, DC 20212-0001, (202) 691-5200, Fax: (202) 691-6325, www.bls.gov; *Consumer Price Index Detailed Report* and *Monthly Labor Review (MLR).*

APPLIANCES, HOUSEHOLD - SALES, SHIPMENTS AND RECEIPTS

The NPD Group, Port Washington, 900 West Shore Road, Port Washington, NY 11050, (866) 444-1411, www.npd.com; *Market Research for the Appliances, Home Improvement, Home Textiles, and Housewares Industries.*

U.S. Census Bureau, Manufacturing and Construction Division, 4600 Silver Hill Road, Washington DC 20233, (301) 763-4673, www.census.gov/mcd; *Annual Survey of Manufactures, Statistics for Industry Groups and Industries* and *Current Industrial Reports.*

APRICOTS

National Agricultural Statistics Service (NASS), U.S. Department of Agriculture (USDA), 1400 Independence Avenue, SW, Washington, DC 20250, (800) 727-9540, Fax: (202) 690-2090, www.nass.usda.gov; *Noncitrus Fruits and Nuts: Final Estimates 1998-2003.*

AQUACULTURE

National Agricultural Statistics Service (NASS), U.S. Department of Agriculture (USDA), 1400 Independence Avenue, SW, Washington, DC 20250, (800) 727-9540, Fax: (202) 690-2090, www.nass.usda.gov; *Catfish Processing; Catfish Production;* and *Trout Production.*

ARCHERY

National Sporting Goods Association (NSGA), 1601 Feehanville Drive, Suite 300, Mount Prospect, IL 60056, (847) 296-6742, Fax: (847) 391-9827, www.nsga.org; *2006 Sports Participation* and *Ten-Year History of Selected Sports Participation, 1996-2006.*

ARCHITECTURAL SERVICES

See ENGINEERING AND ARCHITECTURAL SERVICES

ARCHIVAL RESOURCES

LISU, Holywell Park, Loughborough University, Leicestershire, LE11 3TU, United Kingdom, www.lboro.ac.uk/departments/dis/lisu; *Digest of Statistics.*

U.S. National Archives and Records Administration, 8601 Adelphi Road, College Park, MD 20740-6001, (866) 272-6272, Fax: (301) 837-0483, www.archives.gov; unpublished data.

ARCTIC REGIONS

National Oceanographic Data Center (NOCD), National Oceanic and Atmospheric Administration (NOAA), SSMC3, 4th Floor, 1315 East-West Highway, Silver Spring, MD 20910-3282, (301) 713-3277, Fax: (301) 713-3302, www.nodc.noaa.gov; *Climatic Atlas of the Arctic Seas 2004.*

AREA OF - FOREIGN COUNTRIES

U.S. Census Bureau, Population Division, 4700 Silver Hill Road, Washington DC 20233-0001, (301) 763-3030, www.census.gov/population/www/; International Data Base (IDB).

AREA OF - FOREST LAND

USDA Forest Service, 1400 Independence Ave, SW, Washington, DC 20250-0003, (202) 205-8333, www.fs.fed.us; *Forest Resources of the United States, 2002; Land Areas of the National Forest System 2006;* and *Timber Products Supply and Demand.*

AREA OF - PARKS

National Association of State Park Directors (NASPD), 8829 Woodyhill Road, Raleigh, NC 27613, (919) 676-8365, Fax: (919) 676-8365, www.naspd.org; *Trends in State Park Operations.*

National Park Service (NPS), U.S. Department of the Interior (DOI), Park Headquarters, PO Box 128, West Glacier, MT 59936, (406) 888-7800, Fax: (406) 888-7808, www.nps.gov; unpublished data.

AREA OF - UNITED STATES

U.S. Census Bureau, Population Division, 4700 Silver Hill Road, Washington DC 20233-0001, (301) 763-3030, www.census.gov/population/www/; *Current Population Reports* and International Data Base (IDB).

AREA OF - UNITED STATES - CITIES

Population Reference Bureau, 1875 Connecticut Avenue, NW, Suite 520, Washington, DC, 20009-5728, (800) 877-9881, Fax: (202) 328-3937, www.prb.org; *The American People Series.*

U.S. Census Bureau, Population Division, 4700 Silver Hill Road, Washington DC 20233-0001, (301) 763-3030, www.census.gov/population/www/; *Census 2000 Profiles of General Demographic Characteristics.*

AREA OF - UNITED STATES - WATER

U.S. Census Bureau, Population Division, 4700 Silver Hill Road, Washington DC 20233-0001, (301) 763-3030, www.census.gov/population/www/; *Current Population Reports.*

AREA OF - WORLD

U.S. Census Bureau, Population Division, 4700 Silver Hill Road, Washington DC 20233-0001, (301) 763-3030, www.census.gov/population/www/; International Data Base (IDB).

ARGENTINA - NATIONAL STATISTICAL OFFICE

National Institute of Statistics and Censuses (Instituto Nacional de Estadistica y Censos (INDEC)), Av. Julio A. Roca 615, PB (1067) Ciudad de Buenos Aires, Argentina, www.indec.mecon.ar; National Data Center.

ARGENTINA - PRIMARY STATISTICS SOURCES

National Institute of Statistics and Censuses (Instituto Nacional de Estadistica y Censos (INDEC)), Av. Julio A. Roca 615, PB (1067) Ciudad de Buenos Aires, Argentina, www.indec.mecon.ar; *Statistical Yearbook of the Argentine Republic.*

ARGENTINA - AGRICULTURAL MACHINERY

Economist Intelligence Unit, 111 West 57th Street, New York, NY 10019, (212) 554-0600, Fax: (212) 586-1181, www.eiu.com; *Business Latin America.*

ARGENTINA - AGRICULTURE

Economist Intelligence Unit, 111 West 57th Street, New York, NY 10019, (212) 554-0600, Fax: (212) 586-1181, www.eiu.com; *Argentina Country Report* and *Business Latin America.*

Euromonitor International, Inc., 224 S. Michigan Avenue, Suite 1500, Chicago, IL 60604, (312) 922-1115, Fax: (312) 922-1157, www.euromonitor.com; *International Marketing Data and Statistics 2008* and *World Marketing Data and Statistics.*

Inter-American Development Bank (IDB), 1300 New York Avenue, NW, Washington, DC 20577, (202) 623-1000, Fax: (202) 623-3096, www.iadb.org; *The Politics of Policies: Economic and Social Progress in Latin America - 2006 Report.*

M.E. Sharpe, 80 Business Park Drive, Armonk, NY 10504, (800) 541-6563, Fax: (914) 273-2106, www.mesharpe.com; *The Illustrated Book of World Rankings.*

Palgrave Macmillan Ltd., Houndmills, Basingstoke, Hampshire, RG21 6XS, England, (Telephone in U.S. (888) 330-8477), (Fax in U.S. (800) 672-2054), www.palgrave.com; *The Statesman's Yearbook 2008.*

Taylor and Francis Group, An Informa Business, 2 Park Square, Milton Park, Abingdon, Oxford OX14 4RN, United Kingdom, (Dial from U.S. (212) 216-7800), (Fax from U.S. (212) 564-7854), www.tandf.co.uk; *The Europa World Year Book.*

UCLA Latin American Institute, 10343 Bunche Hall, Box 951447, Los Angeles, CA 90095-1447, (310) 825-4571, Fax: (310) 206-6859, www.international.ucla.edu/lac; *Statistical Abstract of Latin America.*

United Nations Conference on Trade and Development (UNCTAD), DC2-1120, United Nations, New York, NY 10017, (212) 963-0027, www.unctad.org; *UNCTAD Commodity Yearbook.*

United Nations Food and Agricultural Organization (FAO), Viale delle Terme di Caracalla, 00100 Rome, Italy, (Dial from U.S. (202) 653-2400), (Fax from U.S. (202) 653 5760), www.fao.org; AQUASTAT; *FAO Production Yearbook 2002; FAO Trade Yearbook;* and *The State of Food and Agriculture (SOFA) 2006.*

United Nations Statistics Division, New York, NY 10017, (800) 253-9646, Fax: (212) 963-4116, http://unstats.un.org; *Statistical Yearbook* and *Statistical Yearbook for Latin America and the Caribbean 2004.*

The World Bank, 1818 H Street, NW, Washington, DC 20433, (202) 473-1000, Fax: (202) 477-6391, www.worldbank.org; *Argentina* and *World Development Indicators (WDI) 2008.*

ARGENTINA - AIRLINES

Economist Intelligence Unit, 111 West 57th Street, New York, NY 10019, (212) 554-0600, Fax: (212) 586-1181, www.eiu.com; *Business Latin America.*

International Civil Aviation Organization (ICAO), External Relations and Public Information Office (EPO), 999 University Street, Montreal, Quebec H3C 5H7, Canada, (Dial from U.S. (514) 954-8219), (Fax from U.S. (514) 954-6077), www.icao.int; *Civil Aviation Statistics of the World.*

M.E. Sharpe, 80 Business Park Drive, Armonk, NY 10504, (800) 541-6563, Fax: (914) 273-2106, www.mesharpe.com; *The Illustrated Book of World Rankings.*

Palgrave Macmillan Ltd., Houndmills, Basingstoke, Hampshire, RG21 6XS, England, (Telephone in U.S. (888) 330-8477), (Fax in U.S. (800) 672-2054), www.palgrave.com; *The Statesman's Yearbook 2008.*

Taylor and Francis Group, An Informa Business, 2 Park Square, Milton Park, Abingdon, Oxford OX14 4RN, United Kingdom, (Dial from U.S. (212) 216-7800), (Fax from U.S. (212) 564-7854), www.tandf.co.uk; *The Europa World Year Book.*

United Nations Statistics Division, New York, NY 10017, (800) 253-9646, Fax: (212) 963-4116, http://unstats.un.org; *Statistical Yearbook.*

ARGENTINA - AIRPORTS

Central Intelligence Agency, Office of Public Affairs, Washington, DC 20505, (703) 482-0623, Fax: (703) 482-1739, www.cia.gov; *The World Factbook.*

ARGENTINA - ALMOND PRODUCTION

See ARGENTINA - CROPS

ARGENTINA - ALUMINUM PRODUCTION

See ARGENTINA - MINERAL INDUSTRIES

ARGENTINA - APPLE PRODUCTION

See ARGENTINA - CROPS

ARGENTINA - AREA

Economist Intelligence Unit, 111 West 57th Street, New York, NY 10019, (212) 554-0600, Fax: (212) 586-1181, www.eiu.com; *Business Latin America.*

ARGENTINA - ARMED FORCES

Central Intelligence Agency, Office of Public Affairs, Washington, DC 20505, (703) 482-0623, Fax: (703) 482-1739, www.cia.gov; *The World Factbook.*

Economist Intelligence Unit, 111 West 57th Street, New York, NY 10019, (212) 554-0600, Fax: (212) 586-1181, www.eiu.com; *Business Latin America.*

Euromonitor International, Inc., 224 S. Michigan Avenue, Suite 1500, Chicago, IL 60604, (312) 922-1115, Fax: (312) 922-1157, www.euromonitor.com; *World Marketing Data and Statistics.*

International Institute for Strategic Studies (IISS), Arundel House, 13-15 Arundel Street, Temple Place, London WC2R 3DX, England, www.iiss.org; *The Military Balance 2007.*

International Monetary Fund (IMF), 700 Nineteenth Street, NW, Washington, DC 20431, (202) 623-7000, Fax: (202) 623-4661, www.imf.org; *Government Finance Statistics Yearbook (2008 Edition).*

Palgrave Macmillan Ltd., Houndmills, Basingstoke, Hampshire, RG21 6XS, England, (Telephone in U.S. (888) 330-8477), (Fax in U.S. (800) 672-2054), www.palgrave.com; *The Statesman's Yearbook 2008.*

U.S. Department of State (DOS), 2201 C Street NW, Washington, DC 20520, (202) 647-4000, www.state.gov; *World Military Expenditures and Arms Transfers (WMEAT).*

UCLA Latin American Institute, 10343 Bunche Hall, Box 951447, Los Angeles, CA 90095-1447, (310) 825-4571, Fax: (310) 206-6859, www.international.ucla.edu/lac; *Statistical Abstract of Latin America.*

United Nations Statistics Division, New York, NY 10017, (800) 253-9646, Fax: (212) 963-4116, http://unstats.un.org; *Human Development Report 2006.*

ARGENTINA - ARTICHOKE PRODUCTION

See ARGENTINA - CROPS

ARGENTINA - AUTOMOBILE INDUSTRY AND TRADE

United Nations Statistics Division, New York, NY 10017, (800) 253-9646, Fax: (212) 963-4116, http://unstats.un.org; *Statistical Yearbook.*

ARGENTINA - BALANCE OF PAYMENTS

Economist Intelligence Unit, 111 West 57th Street, New York, NY 10019, (212) 554-0600, Fax: (212) 586-1181, www.eiu.com; *Business Latin America.*

Inter-American Development Bank (IDB), 1300 New York Avenue, NW, Washington, DC 20577, (202) 623-1000, Fax: (202) 623-3096, www.iadb.org; *The Politics of Policies: Economic and Social Progress in Latin America - 2006 Report.*

International Monetary Fund (IMF), 700 Nineteenth Street, NW, Washington, DC 20431, (202) 623-7000, Fax: (202) 623-4661, www.imf.org; *Balance of Payments Statistics Newsletter; Balance of Payments Statistics Yearbook 2007;* and *International Financial Statistics Yearbook 2007.*

Organization of American States (OAS), 17th Street Constitution Avenue NW, Washington, DC 20006, (202) 458-3000, www.oas.org; *The OAS in Transition: 1994-2004.*

Taylor and Francis Group, An Informa Business, 2 Park Square, Milton Park, Abingdon, Oxford OX14 4RN, United Kingdom, (Dial from U.S. (212) 216-7800), (Fax from U.S. (212) 564-7854), www.tandf.co.uk; *The Europa World Year Book.*

United Nations Conference on Trade and Development (UNCTAD), DC2-1120, United Nations, New York, NY 10017, (212) 963-0027, www.unctad.org; *Handbook of Statistics 2005.*

United Nations Statistics Division, New York, NY 10017, (800) 253-9646, Fax: (212) 963-4116, http://unstats.un.org; *Economic Survey of Latin America and the Caribbean 2004-2005* and *Statistical Yearbook for Latin America and the Caribbean 2004.*

The World Bank, 1818 H Street, NW, Washington, DC 20433, (202) 473-1000, Fax: (202) 477-6391, www.worldbank.org; *Argentina; World Development Indicators (WDI) 2008;* and *World Development Report 2008.*

ARGENTINA - BANKS AND BANKING

Euromonitor International, Inc., 224 S. Michigan Avenue, Suite 1500, Chicago, IL 60604, (312) 922-

1115, Fax: (312) 922-1157, www.euromonitor.com; *World Marketing Data and Statistics.*

Inter-American Development Bank (IDB), 1300 New York Avenue, NW, Washington, DC 20577, (202) 623-1000, Fax: (202) 623-3096, www.iadb.org; *The Politics of Policies: Economic and Social Progress in Latin America - 2006 Report.*

International Monetary Fund (IMF), 700 Nineteenth Street, NW, Washington, DC 20431, (202) 623-7000, Fax: (202) 623-4661, www.imf.org; *Government Finance Statistics Yearbook (2008 Edition)* and *International Financial Statistics Yearbook 2007.*

M.E. Sharpe, 80 Business Park Drive, Armonk, NY 10504, (800) 541-6563, Fax: (914) 273-2106, www.mesharpe.com; *The Illustrated Book of World Rankings.*

Palgrave Macmillan Ltd., Houndmills, Basingstoke, Hampshire, RG21 6XS, England, (Telephone in U.S. (888) 330-8477), (Fax in U.S. (800) 672-2054), www.palgrave.com; *The Statesman's Yearbook 2008.*

Taylor and Francis Group, An Informa Business, 2 Park Square, Milton Park, Abingdon, Oxford OX14 4RN, United Kingdom, (Dial from U.S. (212) 216-7800), (Fax from U.S. (212) 564-7854), www.tandf.co.uk; *The Europa World Year Book.*

United Nations Statistics Division, New York, NY 10017, (800) 253-9646, Fax: (212) 963-4116, http://unstats.un.org; *Statistical Yearbook for Latin America and the Caribbean 2004.*

ARGENTINA - BARLEY PRODUCTION

See ARGENTINA - CROPS

ARGENTINA - BEVERAGE INDUSTRY

M.E. Sharpe, 80 Business Park Drive, Armonk, NY 10504, (800) 541-6563, Fax: (914) 273-2106, www.mesharpe.com; *The Illustrated Book of World Rankings.*

United Nations Statistics Division, New York, NY 10017, (800) 253-9646, Fax: (212) 963-4116, http://unstats.un.org; *Statistical Yearbook.*

ARGENTINA - BIRTH CONTROL

UCLA Latin American Institute, 10343 Bunche Hall, Box 951447, Los Angeles, CA 90095-1447, (310) 825-4571, Fax: (310) 206-6859, www.international.ucla.edu/lac; *Statistical Abstract of Latin America.*

ARGENTINA - BONDS

Inter-American Development Bank (IDB), 1300 New York Avenue, NW, Washington, DC 20577, (202) 623-1000, Fax: (202) 623-3096, www.iadb.org; *The Politics of Policies: Economic and Social Progress in Latin America - 2006 Report.*

International Monetary Fund (IMF), 700 Nineteenth Street, NW, Washington, DC 20431, (202) 623-7000, Fax: (202) 623-4661, www.imf.org; *Government Finance Statistics Yearbook (2008 Edition).*

ARGENTINA - BROADCASTING

Central Intelligence Agency, Office of Public Affairs, Washington, DC 20505, (703) 482-0623, Fax: (703) 482-1739, www.cia.gov; *The World Factbook.*

Euromonitor International, Inc., 224 S. Michigan Avenue, Suite 1500, Chicago, IL 60604, (312) 922-1115, Fax: (312) 922-1157, www.euromonitor.com; *World Marketing Data and Statistics.*

M.E. Sharpe, 80 Business Park Drive, Armonk, NY 10504, (800) 541-6563, Fax: (914) 273-2106, www.mesharpe.com; *The Illustrated Book of World Rankings.*

Palgrave Macmillan Ltd., Houndmills, Basingstoke, Hampshire, RG21 6XS, England, (Telephone in U.S. (888) 330-8477), (Fax in U.S. (800) 672-2054), www.palgrave.com; *The Statesman's Yearbook 2008.*

WRTH Publications Limited, PO Box 290, Oxford OX2 7FT, UK, www.wrth.com; *World Radio TV Handbook 2007.*

ARGENTINA - BUDGET

Central Intelligence Agency, Office of Public Affairs, Washington, DC 20505, (703) 482-0623, Fax: (703) 482-1739, www.cia.gov; *The World Factbook.*

ARGENTINA - BUSINESS

Inter-American Development Bank (IDB), 1300 New York Avenue, NW, Washington, DC 20577, (202) 623-1000, Fax: (202) 623-3096, www.iadb.org; *The Politics of Policies: Economic and Social Progress in Latin America - 2006 Report.*

ARGENTINA - CAPITAL INVESTMENTS

Inter-American Development Bank (IDB), 1300 New York Avenue, NW, Washington, DC 20577, (202) 623-1000, Fax: (202) 623-3096, www.iadb.org; *The Politics of Policies: Economic and Social Progress in Latin America - 2006 Report.*

ARGENTINA - CAPITAL LEVY

Inter-American Development Bank (IDB), 1300 New York Avenue, NW, Washington, DC 20577, (202) 623-1000, Fax: (202) 623-3096, www.iadb.org; *The Politics of Policies: Economic and Social Progress in Latin America - 2006 Report.*

International Monetary Fund (IMF), 700 Nineteenth Street, NW, Washington, DC 20431, (202) 623-7000, Fax: (202) 623-4661, www.imf.org; *Government Finance Statistics Yearbook (2008 Edition).*

ARGENTINA - CATTLE

See ARGENTINA - LIVESTOCK

ARGENTINA - CHICK PEA PRODUCTION

See ARGENTINA - CROPS

ARGENTINA - CHICKENS

See ARGENTINA - LIVESTOCK

ARGENTINA - CHILDBIRTH - STATISTICS

Central Intelligence Agency, Office of Public Affairs, Washington, DC 20505, (703) 482-0623, Fax: (703) 482-1739, www.cia.gov; *The World Factbook.*

Euromonitor International, Inc., 224 S. Michigan Avenue, Suite 1500, Chicago, IL 60604, (312) 922-1115, Fax: (312) 922-1157, www.euromonitor.com; *International Marketing Data and Statistics 2008* and *The World Economic Factbook 2008.*

M.E. Sharpe, 80 Business Park Drive, Armonk, NY 10504, (800) 541-6563, Fax: (914) 273-2106, www.mesharpe.com; *The Illustrated Book of World Rankings.*

Palgrave Macmillan Ltd., Houndmills, Basingstoke, Hampshire, RG21 6XS, England, (Telephone in U.S. (888) 330-8477), (Fax in U.S. (800) 672-2054), www.palgrave.com; *The Statesman's Yearbook 2008.*

Taylor and Francis Group, An Informa Business, 2 Park Square, Milton Park, Abingdon, Oxford OX14 4RN, United Kingdom, (Dial from U.S. (212) 216-7800), (Fax from U.S. (212) 564-7854), www.tandf.co.uk; *The Europa World Year Book.*

United Nations Statistics Division, New York, NY 10017, (800) 253-9646, Fax: (212) 963-4116, http://unstats.un.org; *Demographic Yearbook; Statistical Yearbook;* and *Statistical Yearbook for Latin America and the Caribbean 2004.*

The World Bank, 1818 H Street, NW, Washington, DC 20433, (202) 473-1000, Fax: (202) 477-6391, www.worldbank.org; *World Development Indicators (WDI) 2008.*

World Health Organization (WHO), Avenue Appia 20, 1211 Geneve 27, Switzerland, (Telephone in U.S. (212) 331-9081), www.who.int; *World Health Report 2006.*

ARGENTINA - CLIMATE

M.E. Sharpe, 80 Business Park Drive, Armonk, NY 10504, (800) 541-6563, Fax: (914) 273-2106, www.mesharpe.com; *The Illustrated Book of World Rankings.*

Palgrave Macmillan Ltd., Houndmills, Basingstoke, Hampshire, RG21 6XS, England, (Telephone in U.S. (888) 330-8477), (Fax in U.S. (800) 672-2054), www.palgrave.com; *The Statesman's Yearbook 2008.*

ARGENTINA - CLOTHING EXPORTS AND IMPORTS

See ARGENTINA - TEXTILE INDUSTRY

ARGENTINA - COAL PRODUCTION

See ARGENTINA - MINERAL INDUSTRIES

ARGENTINA - COFFEE

See ARGENTINA - CROPS

ARGENTINA - COMMERCE

Palgrave Macmillan Ltd., Houndmills, Basingstoke, Hampshire, RG21 6XS, England, (Telephone in U.S. (888) 330-8477), (Fax in U.S. (800) 672-2054), www.palgrave.com; *The Statesman's Yearbook 2008.*

ARGENTINA - COMMODITY EXCHANGES

Commodity Research Bureau, 330 South Wells Street, Suite 612, Chicago, IL 60606-7110, (800) 621-5271, Fax: (312) 939-4135, www.crbtrader.com; *2006 CRB Commodity Yearbook and CD.*

International Lead and Zinc Study Group (ILZSG), Rua Almirante Barroso 38, 5th Floor, Lisbon 1000 - 013, Portugal, www.ilzsg.org; Interactive Statistical Database.

International Monetary Fund (IMF), 700 Nineteenth Street, NW, Washington, DC 20431, (202) 623-7000, Fax: (202) 623-4661, www.imf.org; *IMF Primary Commodity Prices.*

United Nations Food and Agricultural Organization (FAO), Viale delle Terme di Caracalla, 00100 Rome, Italy, (Dial from U.S. (202) 653-2400), (Fax from U.S. (202) 653 5760), www.fao.org; *The State of Food and Agriculture (SOFA) 2006.*

ARGENTINA - COMMUNICATION AND TRAFFIC

United Nations Statistics Division, New York, NY 10017, (800) 253-9646, Fax: (212) 963-4116, http://unstats.un.org; *Statistical Yearbook.*

ARGENTINA - CONSTRUCTION INDUSTRY

Economist Intelligence Unit, 111 West 57th Street, New York, NY 10019, (212) 554-0600, Fax: (212) 586-1181, www.eiu.com; *Business Latin America.*

Inter-American Development Bank (IDB), 1300 New York Avenue, NW, Washington, DC 20577, (202) 623-1000, Fax: (202) 623-3096, www.iadb.org; *The Politics of Policies: Economic and Social Progress in Latin America - 2006 Report.*

M.E. Sharpe, 80 Business Park Drive, Armonk, NY 10504, (800) 541-6563, Fax: (914) 273-2106, www.mesharpe.com; *The Illustrated Book of World Rankings.*

UCLA Latin American Institute, 10343 Bunche Hall, Box 951447, Los Angeles, CA 90095-1447, (310) 825-4571, Fax: (310) 206-6859, www.international.ucla.edu/lac; *Statistical Abstract of Latin America.*

United Nations Statistics Division, New York, NY 10017, (800) 253-9646, Fax: (212) 963-4116, http://unstats.un.org; *Statistical Yearbook.*

ARGENTINA - CONSUMER COOPERATIVES

UCLA Latin American Institute, 10343 Bunche Hall, Box 951447, Los Angeles, CA 90095-1447, (310) 825-4571, Fax: (310) 206-6859, www.international.ucla.edu/lac; *Statistical Abstract of Latin America.*

ARGENTINA - CONSUMER PRICE INDEXES

Taylor and Francis Group, An Informa Business, 2 Park Square, Milton Park, Abingdon, Oxford OX14 4RN, United Kingdom, (Dial from U.S. (212) 216-7800), (Fax from U.S. (212) 564-7854), www.tandf.co.uk; *The Europa World Year Book.*

UCLA Latin American Institute, 10343 Bunche Hall, Box 951447, Los Angeles, CA 90095-1447, (310)

825-4571, Fax: (310) 206-6859, www.international.ucla.edu/lac; *Statistical Abstract of Latin America.*

United Nations Statistics Division, New York, NY 10017, (800) 253-9646, Fax: (212) 963-4116, http://unstats.un.org; *Statistical Yearbook.*

The World Bank, 1818 H Street, NW, Washington, DC 20433, (202) 473-1000, Fax: (202) 477-6391, www.worldbank.org; *Argentina.*

ARGENTINA - CONSUMPTION (ECONOMICS)

Economist Intelligence Unit, 111 West 57th Street, New York, NY 10019, (212) 554-0600, Fax: (212) 586-1181, www.eiu.com; *Business Latin America.*

Inter-American Development Bank (IDB), 1300 New York Avenue, NW, Washington, DC 20577, (202) 623-1000, Fax: (202) 623-3096, www.iadb.org; *The Politics of Policies: Economic and Social Progress in Latin America - 2006 Report.*

International Lead and Zinc Study Group (ILZSG), Rua Almirante Barroso 38, 5th Floor, Lisbon 1000 - 013, Portugal, www.ilzsg.org; Interactive Statistical Database.

United Nations Statistics Division, New York, NY 10017, (800) 253-9646, Fax: (212) 963-4116, http://unstats.un.org; *Statistical Yearbook for Latin America and the Caribbean 2004.*

The World Bank, 1818 H Street, NW, Washington, DC 20433, (202) 473-1000, Fax: (202) 477-6391, www.worldbank.org; *World Development Report 2008.*

ARGENTINA - COPPER INDUSTRY AND TRADE

See ARGENTINA - MINERAL INDUSTRIES

ARGENTINA - CORN INDUSTRY

See ARGENTINA - CROPS

ARGENTINA - COST AND STANDARD OF LIVING

International Monetary Fund (IMF), 700 Nineteenth Street, NW, Washington, DC 20431, (202) 623-7000, Fax: (202) 623-4661, www.imf.org; *Government Finance Statistics Yearbook (2008 Edition).*

ARGENTINA - COTTON

See ARGENTINA - CROPS

ARGENTINA - CRIME

Yale University Press, PO Box 209040, New Haven, CT 06520-9040, (203) 432-0960, Fax: (203) 432-0948, http://yalepress.yale.edu/yupbooks; *Violence and Crime in Cross-National Perspective.*

ARGENTINA - CROPS

Economist Intelligence Unit, 111 West 57th Street, New York, NY 10019, (212) 554-0600, Fax: (212) 586-1181, www.eiu.com; *Business Latin America.*

International Monetary Fund (IMF), 700 Nineteenth Street, NW, Washington, DC 20431, (202) 623-7000, Fax: (202) 623-4661, www.imf.org; *International Financial Statistics Yearbook 2007.*

M.E. Sharpe, 80 Business Park Drive, Armonk, NY 10504, (800) 541-6563, Fax: (914) 273-2106, www.mesharpe.com; *The Illustrated Book of World Rankings.*

Palgrave Macmillan Ltd., Houndmills, Basingstoke, Hampshire, RG21 6XS, England, (Telephone in U.S. (888) 330-8477), (Fax in U.S. (800) 672-2054), www.palgrave.com; *The Statesman's Yearbook 2008.*

Taylor and Francis Group, An Informa Business, 2 Park Square, Milton Park, Abingdon, Oxford OX14 4RN, United Kingdom, (Dial from U.S. (212) 216-7800), (Fax from U.S. (212) 564-7854), www.tandf.co.uk; *The Europa World Year Book.*

United Nations Conference on Trade and Development (UNCTAD), DC2-1120, United Nations, New York, NY 10017, (212) 963-0027, www.unctad.org; *UNCTAD Commodity Yearbook.*

United Nations Food and Agricultural Organization (FAO), Viale delle Terme di Caracalla, 00100 Rome, Italy, (Dial from U.S. (202) 653-2400), (Fax from U.S. (202) 653 5760), www.fao.org; *FAO Production Yearbook 2002* and *The State of Food and Agriculture (SOFA) 2006.*

United Nations Statistics Division, New York, NY 10017, (800) 253-9646, Fax: (212) 963-4116, http://unstats.un.org; *Statistical Yearbook.*

ARGENTINA - CUSTOMS ADMINISTRATION

Inter-American Development Bank (IDB), 1300 New York Avenue, NW, Washington, DC 20577, (202) 623-1000, Fax: (202) 623-3096, www.iadb.org; *The Politics of Policies: Economic and Social Progress in Latin America - 2006 Report.*

International Monetary Fund (IMF), 700 Nineteenth Street, NW, Washington, DC 20431, (202) 623-7000, Fax: (202) 623-4661, www.imf.org; *Government Finance Statistics Yearbook (2008 Edition).*

Palgrave Macmillan Ltd., Houndmills, Basingstoke, Hampshire, RG21 6XS, England, (Telephone in U.S. (888) 330-8477), (Fax in U.S. (800) 672-2054), www.palgrave.com; *The Statesman's Yearbook 2008.*

ARGENTINA - DAIRY PROCESSING

M.E. Sharpe, 80 Business Park Drive, Armonk, NY 10504, (800) 541-6563, Fax: (914) 273-2106, www.mesharpe.com; *The Illustrated Book of World Rankings.*

Palgrave Macmillan Ltd., Houndmills, Basingstoke, Hampshire, RG21 6XS, England, (Telephone in U.S. (888) 330-8477), (Fax in U.S. (800) 672-2054), www.palgrave.com; *The Statesman's Yearbook 2008.*

Taylor and Francis Group, An Informa Business, 2 Park Square, Milton Park, Abingdon, Oxford OX14 4RN, United Kingdom, (Dial from U.S. (212) 216-7800), (Fax from U.S. (212) 564-7854), www.tandf.co.uk; *The Europa World Year Book.*

United Nations Food and Agricultural Organization (FAO), Viale delle Terme di Caracalla, 00100 Rome, Italy, (Dial from U.S. (202) 653-2400), (Fax from U.S. (202) 653 5760), www.fao.org; *The State of Food and Agriculture (SOFA) 2006.*

United Nations Statistics Division, New York, NY 10017, (800) 253-9646, Fax: (212) 963-4116, http://unstats.un.org; *Statistical Yearbook.*

ARGENTINA - DEATH RATES

See ARGENTINA - MORTALITY

ARGENTINA - DEBT

Economist Intelligence Unit, 111 West 57th Street, New York, NY 10019, (212) 554-0600, Fax: (212) 586-1181, www.eiu.com; *Business Latin America.*

ARGENTINA - DEBTS, EXTERNAL

Economist Intelligence Unit, 111 West 57th Street, New York, NY 10019, (212) 554-0600, Fax: (212) 586-1181, www.eiu.com; *Business Latin America.*

Inter-American Development Bank (IDB), 1300 New York Avenue, NW, Washington, DC 20577, (202) 623-1000, Fax: (202) 623-3096, www.iadb.org; *The Politics of Policies: Economic and Social Progress in Latin America - 2006 Report.*

International Monetary Fund (IMF), 700 Nineteenth Street, NW, Washington, DC 20431, (202) 623-7000, Fax: (202) 623-4661, www.imf.org; *Government Finance Statistics Yearbook (2008 Edition).*

Palgrave Macmillan Ltd., Houndmills, Basingstoke, Hampshire, RG21 6XS, England, (Telephone in U.S. (888) 330-8477), (Fax in U.S. (800) 672-2054), www.palgrave.com; *The Statesman's Yearbook 2008.*

United Nations Statistics Division, New York, NY 10017, (800) 253-9646, Fax: (212) 963-4116, http://unstats.un.org; *Economic Survey of Latin America and the Caribbean 2004-2005* and *Statistical Yearbook for Latin America and the Caribbean 2004.*

The World Bank, 1818 H Street, NW, Washington, DC 20433, (202) 473-1000, Fax: (202) 477-6391, www.worldbank.org; *Global Development Finance 2007; World Development Indicators (WDI) 2008;* and *World Development Report 2008.*

ARGENTINA - DEFENSE EXPENDITURES

See ARGENTINA - ARMED FORCES

ARGENTINA - DEMOGRAPHY

Euromonitor International, Inc., 224 S. Michigan Avenue, Suite 1500, Chicago, IL 60604, (312) 922-1115, Fax: (312) 922-1157, www.euromonitor.com; *International Marketing Data and Statistics 2008; The World Economic Factbook 2008;* and *World Marketing Data and Statistics.*

M.E. Sharpe, 80 Business Park Drive, Armonk, NY 10504, (800) 541-6563, Fax: (914) 273-2106, www.mesharpe.com; *The Illustrated Book of World Rankings.*

UCLA Latin American Institute, 10343 Bunche Hall, Box 951447, Los Angeles, CA 90095-1447, (310) 825-4571, Fax: (310) 206-6859, www.international.ucla.edu/lac; *Statistical Abstract of Latin America.*

United Nations Statistics Division, New York, NY 10017, (800) 253-9646, Fax: (212) 963-4116, http://unstats.un.org; *Human Development Report 2006.*

The World Bank, 1818 H Street, NW, Washington, DC 20433, (202) 473-1000, Fax: (202) 477-6391, www.worldbank.org; *Argentina.*

ARGENTINA - DIAMONDS

See ARGENTINA - MINERAL INDUSTRIES

ARGENTINA - DISPOSABLE INCOME

Inter-American Development Bank (IDB), 1300 New York Avenue, NW, Washington, DC 20577, (202) 623-1000, Fax: (202) 623-3096, www.iadb.org; *The Politics of Policies: Economic and Social Progress in Latin America - 2006 Report.*

M.E. Sharpe, 80 Business Park Drive, Armonk, NY 10504, (800) 541-6563, Fax: (914) 273-2106, www.mesharpe.com; *The Illustrated Book of World Rankings.*

United Nations Statistics Division, New York, NY 10017, (800) 253-9646, Fax: (212) 963-4116, http://unstats.un.org; *National Accounts Statistics: Compendium of Income Distribution Statistics; Statistical Yearbook;* and *Statistical Yearbook for Latin America and the Caribbean 2004.*

ARGENTINA - DIVORCE

M.E. Sharpe, 80 Business Park Drive, Armonk, NY 10504, (800) 541-6563, Fax: (914) 273-2106, www.mesharpe.com; *The Illustrated Book of World Rankings.*

United Nations Statistics Division, New York, NY 10017, (800) 253-9646, Fax: (212) 963-4116, http://unstats.un.org; *Demographic Yearbook.*

ARGENTINA - ECONOMIC ASSISTANCE

Inter-American Development Bank (IDB), 1300 New York Avenue, NW, Washington, DC 20577, (202) 623-1000, Fax: (202) 623-3096, www.iadb.org; *The Politics of Policies: Economic and Social Progress in Latin America - 2006 Report.*

United Nations Statistics Division, New York, NY 10017, (800) 253-9646, Fax: (212) 963-4116, http://unstats.un.org; *Statistical Yearbook.*

ARGENTINA - ECONOMIC CONDITIONS

Center for International Business Education Research (CIBER), Columbia Business School and School of International and Public Affairs, Uris Hall, Room 212, 3022 Broadway, New York, NY 10027-6902, Mr. Joshua Safier, (212) 854-4750, Fax: (212) 222-9821, www.columbia.edu/cu/ciber/; Datastream International.

Central Intelligence Agency, Office of Public Affairs, Washington, DC 20505, (703) 482-0623, Fax: (703) 482-1739, www.cia.gov; *The World Factbook.*

DSI Data Service Information, Xantener Strasse 51a, D-47495 Rheinberg, Germany, www.dsidata.com; *Campus Solution.*

Dun and Bradstreet (DB) Corporation, 103 JFK Parkway, Short Hills, NJ 07078, (973) 921-5500, www.dnb.com; *Country Report.*

Economist Intelligence Unit, 111 West 57th Street, New York, NY 10019, (212) 554-0600, Fax: (212) 586-1181, www.eiu.com; *Argentina Country Report.*

Euromonitor International, Inc., 224 S. Michigan Avenue, Suite 1500, Chicago, IL 60604, (312) 922-1115, Fax: (312) 922-1157, www.euromonitor.com; *International Marketing Data and Statistics 2008; The World Economic Factbook 2008;* and *World Marketing Data and Statistics.*

Inter-American Development Bank (IDB), 1300 New York Avenue, NW, Washington, DC 20577, (202) 623-1000, Fax: (202) 623-3096, www.iadb.org; *The Politics of Policies: Economic and Social Progress in Latin America - 2006 Report.*

International Monetary Fund (IMF), 700 Nineteenth Street, NW, Washington, DC 20431, (202) 623-7000, Fax: (202) 623-4661, www.imf.org; *World Economic Outlook Reports.*

M.E. Sharpe, 80 Business Park Drive, Armonk, NY 10504, (800) 541-6563, Fax: (914) 273-2106, www.mesharpe.com; *The Illustrated Book of World Rankings.*

Palgrave Macmillan Ltd., Houndmills, Basingstoke, Hampshire, RG21 6XS, England, (Telephone in U.S. (888) 330-8477), (Fax in U.S. (800) 672-2054), www.palgrave.com; *The Statesman's Yearbook 2008.*

Taylor and Francis Group, An Informa Business, 2 Park Square, Milton Park, Abingdon, Oxford OX14 4RN, United Kingdom, (Dial from U.S. (212) 216-7800), (Fax from U.S. (212) 564-7854), www.tandf.co.uk; *The Europa World Year Book.*

UCLA Latin American Institute, 10343 Bunche Hall, Box 951447, Los Angeles, CA 90095-1447, (310) 825-4571, Fax: (310) 206-6859, www.international.ucla.edu/lac; *Statistical Abstract of Latin America.*

United Nations Statistics Division, New York, NY 10017, (800) 253-9646, Fax: (212) 963-4116, http://unstats.un.org; *Economic Survey of Latin America and the Caribbean 2004-2005* and *World Statistics Pocketbook.*

The World Bank, 1818 H Street, NW, Washington, DC 20433, (202) 473-1000, Fax: (202) 477-6391, www.worldbank.org; *Argentina; Global Economic Monitor (GEM); Global Economic Prospects 2008; The World Bank Atlas 2003-2004;* and *World Development Report 2008.*

ARGENTINA - ECONOMICS - SOCIOLOGICAL ASPECTS

Inter-American Development Bank (IDB), 1300 New York Avenue, NW, Washington, DC 20577, (202) 623-1000, Fax: (202) 623-3096, www.iadb.org; *The Politics of Policies: Economic and Social Progress in Latin America - 2006 Report.*

UCLA Latin American Institute, 10343 Bunche Hall, Box 951447, Los Angeles, CA 90095-1447, (310) 825-4571, Fax: (310) 206-6859, www.international.ucla.edu/lac; *Statistical Abstract of Latin America.*

ARGENTINA - EDUCATION

Economist Intelligence Unit, 111 West 57th Street, New York, NY 10019, (212) 554-0600, Fax: (212) 586-1181, www.eiu.com; *Business Latin America.*

Euromonitor International, Inc., 224 S. Michigan Avenue, Suite 1500, Chicago, IL 60604, (312) 922-1115, Fax: (312) 922-1157, www.euromonitor.com; *International Marketing Data and Statistics 2008* and *World Marketing Data and Statistics.*

International Monetary Fund (IMF), 700 Nineteenth Street, NW, Washington, DC 20431, (202) 623-7000, Fax: (202) 623-4661, www.imf.org; *Government Finance Statistics Yearbook (2008 Edition).*

M.E. Sharpe, 80 Business Park Drive, Armonk, NY 10504, (800) 541-6563, Fax: (914) 273-2106, www.mesharpe.com; *The Illustrated Book of World Rankings.*

Palgrave Macmillan Ltd., Houndmills, Basingstoke, Hampshire, RG21 6XS, England, (Telephone in U.S. (888) 330-8477), (Fax in U.S. (800) 672-2054), www.palgrave.com; *The Statesman's Yearbook 2008.*

Taylor and Francis Group, An Informa Business, 2 Park Square, Milton Park, Abingdon, Oxford OX14 4RN, United Kingdom, (Dial from U.S. (212) 216-7800), (Fax from U.S. (212) 564-7854), www.tandf.co.uk; *The Europa World Year Book.*

UCLA Latin American Institute, 10343 Bunche Hall, Box 951447, Los Angeles, CA 90095-1447, (310) 825-4571, Fax: (310) 206-6859, www.international.ucla.edu/lac; *Statistical Abstract of Latin America.*

UNESCO Institute for Statistics, C.P. 6128 Succursale Centre-Ville, Montreal, Quebec, H3C 3J7 Canada, (Dial from U.S. (514) 343-6880), (Fax from U.S. (514) 343 6882), www.uis.unesco.org; *Statistical Tables.*

United Nations Statistics Division, New York, NY 10017, (800) 253-9646, Fax: (212) 963-4116, http://unstats.un.org; *Human Development Report 2006* and *Statistical Yearbook for Latin America and the Caribbean 2004.*

The World Bank, 1818 H Street, NW, Washington, DC 20433, (202) 473-1000, Fax: (202) 477-6391, www.worldbank.org; *Argentina; World Development Indicators (WDI) 2008;* and *World Development Report 2008.*

ARGENTINA - ELECTRICITY

Economist Intelligence Unit, 111 West 57th Street, New York, NY 10019, (212) 554-0600, Fax: (212) 586-1181, www.eiu.com; *Business Latin America.*

Inter-American Development Bank (IDB), 1300 New York Avenue, NW, Washington, DC 20577, (202) 623-1000, Fax: (202) 623-3096, www.iadb.org; *The Politics of Policies: Economic and Social Progress in Latin America - 2006 Report.*

M.E. Sharpe, 80 Business Park Drive, Armonk, NY 10504, (800) 541-6563, Fax: (914) 273-2106, www.mesharpe.com; *The Illustrated Book of World Rankings.*

Organisation for Economic Cooperation and Development (OECD), 2 rue Andre Pascal, F-75775 Paris Cedex 16, France, (Telephone in U.S. (202) 785-6323), (Fax in U.S. (202) 785-0350), www.oecd.org; *World Energy Outlook 2007.*

Palgrave Macmillan Ltd., Houndmills, Basingstoke, Hampshire, RG21 6XS, England, (Telephone in U.S. (888) 330-8477), (Fax in U.S. (800) 672-2054), www.palgrave.com; *The Statesman's Yearbook 2008.*

U.S. Department of Energy (DOE), Energy Information Administration (EIA), 1000 Independence Avenue, SW, Washington, DC 20585, (202) 586-8800, www.eia.doe.gov; *International Energy Annual 2004* and *International Energy Outlook 2006.*

United Nations Statistics Division, New York, NY 10017, (800) 253-9646, Fax: (212) 963-4116, http://unstats.un.org; *Human Development Report 2006* and *Statistical Yearbook.*

ARGENTINA - EMIGRATION AND IMMIGRATION

UCLA Latin American Institute, 10343 Bunche Hall, Box 951447, Los Angeles, CA 90095-1447, (310) 825-4571, Fax: (310) 206-6859, www.international.ucla.edu/lac; *Statistical Abstract of Latin America.*

ARGENTINA - EMPLOYMENT

Euromonitor International, Inc., 224 S. Michigan Avenue, Suite 1500, Chicago, IL 60604, (312) 922-1115, Fax: (312) 922-1157, www.euromonitor.com; *International Marketing Data and Statistics 2008.*

International Labour Office, I.L.O. Publications, 4 route des Morillons, CH-1211 Geneva 22, Switzerland, (Telephone in U.S. (202) 653-7652), (Fax in U.S. (202) 653-7687), www.ilo.org; *Yearbook of Labour Statistics 2006.*

M.E. Sharpe, 80 Business Park Drive, Armonk, NY 10504, (800) 541-6563, Fax: (914) 273-2106, www.mesharpe.com; *The Illustrated Book of World Rankings.*

UCLA Latin American Institute, 10343 Bunche Hall, Box 951447, Los Angeles, CA 90095-1447, (310) 825-4571, Fax: (310) 206-6859, www.international.ucla.edu/lac; *Statistical Abstract of Latin America.*

United Nations Statistics Division, New York, NY 10017, (800) 253-9646, Fax: (212) 963-4116, http://unstats.un.org; *Statistical Yearbook for Latin America and the Caribbean 2004.*

The World Bank, 1818 H Street, NW, Washington, DC 20433, (202) 473-1000, Fax: (202) 477-6391, www.worldbank.org; *Argentina.*

ARGENTINA - ENVIRONMENTAL CONDITIONS

DSI Data Service Information, Xantener Strasse 51a, D-47495 Rheinberg, Germany, www.dsidata.com; *Campus Solution* and *DSI's Global Environmental Database.*

Economist Intelligence Unit, 111 West 57th Street, New York, NY 10019, (212) 554-0600, Fax: (212) 586-1181, www.eiu.com; *Argentina Country Report.*

United Nations Statistics Division, New York, NY 10017, (800) 253-9646, Fax: (212) 963-4116, http://unstats.un.org; *World Statistics Pocketbook.*

ARGENTINA - EXCISE TAX

International Monetary Fund (IMF), 700 Nineteenth Street, NW, Washington, DC 20431, (202) 623-7000, Fax: (202) 623-4661, www.imf.org; *Government Finance Statistics Yearbook (2008 Edition).*

Organization of American States (OAS), 17th Street Constitution Avenue NW, Washington, DC 20006, (202) 458-3000, www.oas.org; *The OAS in Transition: 1994-2004.*

United Nations Statistics Division, New York, NY 10017, (800) 253-9646, Fax: (212) 963-4116, http://unstats.un.org; *World Statistics Pocketbook.*

ARGENTINA - EXPENDITURES, PUBLIC

Inter-American Development Bank (IDB), 1300 New York Avenue, NW, Washington, DC 20577, (202) 623-1000, Fax: (202) 623-3096, www.iadb.org; *The Politics of Policies: Economic and Social Progress in Latin America - 2006 Report.*

Organization of American States (OAS), 17th Street Constitution Avenue NW, Washington, DC 20006, (202) 458-3000, www.oas.org; *The OAS in Transition: 1994-2004.*

United Nations Statistics Division, New York, NY 10017, (800) 253-9646, Fax: (212) 963-4116, http://unstats.un.org; *Statistical Yearbook for Latin America and the Caribbean 2004.*

ARGENTINA - EXPORTS

Central Intelligence Agency, Office of Public Affairs, Washington, DC 20505, (703) 482-0623, Fax: (703) 482-1739, www.cia.gov; *The World Factbook.*

Economist Intelligence Unit, 111 West 57th Street, New York, NY 10019, (212) 554-0600, Fax: (212) 586-1181, www.eiu.com; *Argentina Country Report* and *Business Latin America.*

Euromonitor International, Inc., 224 S. Michigan Avenue, Suite 1500, Chicago, IL 60604, (312) 922-1115, Fax: (312) 922-1157, www.euromonitor.com; *International Marketing Data and Statistics 2008* and *The World Economic Factbook 2008.*

Inter-American Development Bank (IDB), 1300 New York Avenue, NW, Washington, DC 20577, (202) 623-1000, Fax: (202) 623-3096, www.iadb.org; *The Politics of Policies: Economic and Social Progress in Latin America - 2006 Report.*

International Lead and Zinc Study Group (ILZSG), Rua Almirante Barroso 38, 5th Floor, Lisbon 1000 - 013, Portugal, www.ilzsg.org; Interactive Statistical Database.

International Monetary Fund (IMF), 700 Nineteenth Street, NW, Washington, DC 20431, (202) 623-

7000, Fax: (202) 623-4661, www.imf.org; *Direction of Trade Statistics Yearbook 2007; Government Finance Statistics Yearbook (2008 Edition);* and *International Financial Statistics Yearbook 2007.*

Organization of American States (OAS), 17th Street Constitution Avenue NW, Washington, DC 20006, (202) 458-3000, www.oas.org; *The OAS in Transition: 1994-2004.*

Palgrave Macmillan Ltd., Houndmills, Basingstoke, Hampshire, RG21 6XS, England, (Telephone in U.S. (888) 330-8477), (Fax in U.S. (800) 672-2054), www.palgrave.com; *The Statesman's Yearbook 2008.*

Taylor and Francis Group, An Informa Business, 2 Park Square, Milton Park, Abingdon, Oxford OX14 4RN, United Kingdom, (Dial from U.S. (212) 216-7800), (Fax from U.S. (212) 564-7854), www.tandf.co.uk; *The Europa World Year Book.*

United Nations Conference on Trade and Development (UNCTAD), DC2-1120, United Nations, New York, NY 10017, (212) 963-0027, www.unctad.org; *Handbook of Statistics 2005.*

United Nations Food and Agricultural Organization (FAO), Viale delle Terme di Caracalla, 00100 Rome, Italy, (Dial from U.S. (202) 653-2400), (Fax from U.S. (202) 653 5760), www.fao.org; *The State of Food and Agriculture (SOFA) 2006.*

United Nations Statistics Division, New York, NY 10017, (800) 253-9646, Fax: (212) 963-4116, http://unstats.un.org; Commodity Trade Statistics Database (COMTRADE) and *Statistical Yearbook for Latin America and the Caribbean 2004.*

The World Bank, 1818 H Street, NW, Washington, DC 20433, (202) 473-1000, Fax: (202) 477-6391, www.worldbank.org; *World Development Indicators (WDI) 2008* and *World Development Report 2008.*

ARGENTINA - FEMALE WORKING POPULATION

See ARGENTINA - EMPLOYMENT

ARGENTINA - FERTILITY, HUMAN

M.E. Sharpe, 80 Business Park Drive, Armonk, NY 10504, (800) 541-6563, Fax: (914) 273-2106, www.mesharpe.com; *The Illustrated Book of World Rankings.*

United Nations Statistics Division, New York, NY 10017, (800) 253-9646, Fax: (212) 963-4116, http://unstats.un.org; *Human Development Report 2006.*

The World Bank, 1818 H Street, NW, Washington, DC 20433, (202) 473-1000, Fax: (202) 477-6391, www.worldbank.org; *The World Bank Atlas 2003-2004; World Development Indicators (WDI) 2008;* and *World Development Report 2008.*

ARGENTINA - FERTILIZER INDUSTRY

Economist Intelligence Unit, 111 West 57th Street, New York, NY 10019, (212) 554-0600, Fax: (212) 586-1181, www.eiu.com; *Business Latin America.*

United Nations Food and Agricultural Organization (FAO), Viale delle Terme di Caracalla, 00100 Rome, Italy, (Dial from U.S. (202) 653-2400), (Fax from U.S. (202) 653 5760), www.fao.org; *FAO Fertilizer Yearbook* and *The State of Food and Agriculture (SOFA) 2006.*

United Nations Statistics Division, New York, NY 10017, (800) 253-9646, Fax: (212) 963-4116, http://unstats.un.org; *Statistical Yearbook.*

ARGENTINA - FETAL MORTALITY

See ARGENTINA - MORTALITY

ARGENTINA - FILM

See ARGENTINA - MOTION PICTURES

ARGENTINA - FINANCE

Inter-American Development Bank (IDB), 1300 New York Avenue, NW, Washington, DC 20577, (202) 623-1000, Fax: (202) 623-3096, www.iadb.org; *The Politics of Policies: Economic and Social Progress in Latin America - 2006 Report.*

International Monetary Fund (IMF), 700 Nineteenth Street, NW, Washington, DC 20431, (202) 623-7000, Fax: (202) 623-4661, www.imf.org; *International Financial Statistics Yearbook 2007.*

Organization of American States (OAS), 17th Street Constitution Avenue NW, Washington, DC 20006, (202) 458-3000, www.oas.org; *The OAS in Transition: 1994-2004.*

Taylor and Francis Group, An Informa Business, 2 Park Square, Milton Park, Abingdon, Oxford OX14 4RN, United Kingdom, (Dial from U.S. (212) 216-7800), (Fax from U.S. (212) 564-7854), www.tandf.co.uk; *The Europa World Year Book.*

UCLA Latin American Institute, 10343 Bunche Hall, Box 951447, Los Angeles, CA 90095-1447, (310) 825-4571, Fax: (310) 206-6859, www.international.ucla.edu/lac; *Statistical Abstract of Latin America.*

United Nations Statistics Division, New York, NY 10017, (800) 253-9646, Fax: (212) 963-4116, http://unstats.un.org; *National Accounts Statistics: Compendium of Income Distribution Statistics.*

The World Bank, 1818 H Street, NW, Washington, DC 20433, (202) 473-1000, Fax: (202) 477-6391, www.worldbank.org; *Argentina.*

ARGENTINA - FINANCE, PUBLIC

Bernan Essential Government Publications, 4611-F Assembly Drive, Lanham MD, 20706-4391, (301) 459-2255, Fax: (800) 865-3450, www.bernan.com; *National Accounts Statistics.*

Economist Intelligence Unit, 111 West 57th Street, New York, NY 10019, (212) 554-0600, Fax: (212) 586-1181, www.eiu.com; *Argentina Country Report.*

Inter-American Development Bank (IDB), 1300 New York Avenue, NW, Washington, DC 20577, (202) 623-1000, Fax: (202) 623-3096, www.iadb.org; *The Politics of Policies: Economic and Social Progress in Latin America - 2006 Report.*

International Monetary Fund (IMF), 700 Nineteenth Street, NW, Washington, DC 20431, (202) 623-7000, Fax: (202) 623-4661, www.imf.org; *Government Finance Statistics Yearbook (2008 Edition); International Financial Statistics; International Financial Statistics Online Service;* and *International Financial Statistics Yearbook 2007.*

M.E. Sharpe, 80 Business Park Drive, Armonk, NY 10504, (800) 541-6563, Fax: (914) 273-2106, www.mesharpe.com; *The Illustrated Book of World Rankings.*

Organization of American States (OAS), 17th Street Constitution Avenue NW, Washington, DC 20006, (202) 458-3000, www.oas.org; *The OAS in Transition: 1994-2004.*

Palgrave Macmillan Ltd., Houndmills, Basingstoke, Hampshire, RG21 6XS, England, (Telephone in U.S. (888) 330-8477), (Fax in U.S. (800) 672-2054), www.palgrave.com; *The Statesman's Yearbook 2008.*

Taylor and Francis Group, An Informa Business, 2 Park Square, Milton Park, Abingdon, Oxford OX14 4RN, United Kingdom, (Dial from U.S. (212) 216-7800), (Fax from U.S. (212) 564-7854), www.tandf.co.uk; *The Europa World Year Book.*

UCLA Latin American Institute, 10343 Bunche Hall, Box 951447, Los Angeles, CA 90095-1447, (310) 825-4571, Fax: (310) 206-6859, www.international.ucla.edu/lac; *Statistical Abstract of Latin America.*

United Nations Statistics Division, New York, NY 10017, (800) 253-9646, Fax: (212) 963-4116, http://unstats.un.org; *Statistical Yearbook for Latin America and the Caribbean 2004.*

The World Bank, 1818 H Street, NW, Washington, DC 20433, (202) 473-1000, Fax: (202) 477-6391, www.worldbank.org; *Argentina.*

ARGENTINA - FISHERIES

Inter-American Development Bank (IDB), 1300 New York Avenue, NW, Washington, DC 20577, (202) 623-1000, Fax: (202) 623-3096, www.iadb.org; *The Politics of Policies: Economic and Social Progress in Latin America - 2006 Report.*

M.E. Sharpe, 80 Business Park Drive, Armonk, NY 10504, (800) 541-6563, Fax: (914) 273-2106, www.mesharpe.com; *The Illustrated Book of World Rankings.*

Palgrave Macmillan Ltd., Houndmills, Basingstoke, Hampshire, RG21 6XS, England, (Telephone in U.S. (888) 330-8477), (Fax in U.S. (800) 672-2054), www.palgrave.com; *The Statesman's Yearbook 2008.*

Taylor and Francis Group, An Informa Business, 2 Park Square, Milton Park, Abingdon, Oxford OX14 4RN, United Kingdom, (Dial from U.S. (212) 216-7800), (Fax from U.S. (212) 564-7854), www.tandf.co.uk; *The Europa World Year Book.*

UCLA Latin American Institute, 10343 Bunche Hall, Box 951447, Los Angeles, CA 90095-1447, (310) 825-4571, Fax: (310) 206-6859, www.international.ucla.edu/lac; *Statistical Abstract of Latin America.*

United Nations Conference on Trade and Development (UNCTAD), DC2-1120, United Nations, New York, NY 10017, (212) 963-0027, www.unctad.org; *UNCTAD Commodity Yearbook.*

United Nations Food and Agricultural Organization (FAO), Viale delle Terme di Caracalla, 00100 Rome, Italy, (Dial from U.S. (202) 653-2400), (Fax from U.S. (202) 653 5760), www.fao.org; *FAO Yearbook of Fishery Statistics;* Fishery Databases; FISHSTAT Database. Subjects covered include: Aquaculture production, capture production, fishery commodities; and *The State of Food and Agriculture (SOFA) 2006.*

United Nations Statistics Division, New York, NY 10017, (800) 253-9646, Fax: (212) 963-4116, http://unstats.un.org; *Statistical Yearbook.*

The World Bank, 1818 H Street, NW, Washington, DC 20433, (202) 473-1000, Fax: (202) 477-6391, www.worldbank.org; *Argentina.*

ARGENTINA - FLOUR INDUSTRY

United Nations Statistics Division, New York, NY 10017, (800) 253-9646, Fax: (212) 963-4116, http://unstats.un.org; *Statistical Yearbook.*

ARGENTINA - FOOD

Euromonitor International, Inc., 224 S. Michigan Avenue, Suite 1500, Chicago, IL 60604, (312) 922-1115, Fax: (312) 922-1157, www.euromonitor.com; *Retail Trade International 2007.*

United Nations Conference on Trade and Development (UNCTAD), DC2-1120, United Nations, New York, NY 10017, (212) 963-0027, www.unctad.org; *UNCTAD Commodity Yearbook.*

United Nations Food and Agricultural Organization (FAO), Viale delle Terme di Caracalla, 00100 Rome, Italy, (Dial from U.S. (202) 653-2400), (Fax from U.S. (202) 653 5760), www.fao.org; *FAO Production Yearbook 2002* and *The State of Food and Agriculture (SOFA) 2006.*

United Nations Statistics Division, New York, NY 10017, (800) 253-9646, Fax: (212) 963-4116, http://unstats.un.org; Commodity Trade Statistics Database (COMTRADE) and *Human Development Report 2006.*

ARGENTINA - FOREIGN EXCHANGE RATES

Central Intelligence Agency, Office of Public Affairs, Washington, DC 20505, (703) 482-0623, Fax: (703) 482-1739, www.cia.gov; *The World Factbook.*

Euromonitor International, Inc., 224 S. Michigan Avenue, Suite 1500, Chicago, IL 60604, (312) 922-1115, Fax: (312) 922-1157, www.euromonitor.com; *International Marketing Data and Statistics 2008* and *The World Economic Factbook 2008.*

Inter-American Development Bank (IDB), 1300 New York Avenue, NW, Washington, DC 20577, (202) 623-1000, Fax: (202) 623-3096, www.iadb.org; *The Politics of Policies: Economic and Social Progress in Latin America - 2006 Report.*

International Civil Aviation Organization (ICAO), External Relations and Public Information Office (EPO), 999 University Street, Montreal, Quebec

H3C 5H7, Canada, (Dial from U.S. (514) 954-8219), (Fax from U.S. (514) 954-6077), www.icao.int; *Civil Aviation Statistics of the World.*

International Monetary Fund (IMF), 700 Nineteenth Street, NW, Washington, DC 20431, (202) 623-7000, Fax: (202) 623-4661, www.imf.org; *International Financial Statistics Yearbook 2007.*

Taylor and Francis Group, An Informa Business, 2 Park Square, Milton Park, Abingdon, Oxford OX14 4RN, United Kingdom, (Dial from U.S. (212) 216-7800), (Fax from U.S. (212) 564-7854), www.tandf.co.uk; *The Europa World Year Book.*

UCLA Latin American Institute, 10343 Bunche Hall, Box 951447, Los Angeles, CA 90095-1447, (310) 825-4571, Fax: (310) 206-6859, www.international.ucla.edu/lac; *Statistical Abstract of Latin America.*

United Nations Statistics Division, New York, NY 10017, (800) 253-9646, Fax: (212) 963-4116, http://unstats.un.org; *World Statistics Pocketbook.*

ARGENTINA - FORESTS AND FORESTRY

American Forest Paper Association (AFPA), 1111 Nineteenth Street, NW, Suite 800, Washington, DC 20036, (800) 878-8878, www.afandpa.org; *2007 Annual Statistics of Paper, Paperboard, and Wood Pulp.*

Economist Intelligence Unit, 111 West 57th Street, New York, NY 10019, (212) 554-0600, Fax: (212) 586-1181, www.eiu.com; *Business Latin America.*

Inter-American Development Bank (IDB), 1300 New York Avenue, NW, Washington, DC 20577, (202) 623-1000, Fax: (202) 623-3096, www.iadb.org; *The Politics of Policies: Economic and Social Progress in Latin America - 2006 Report.*

M.E. Sharpe, 80 Business Park Drive, Armonk, NY 10504, (800) 541-6563, Fax: (914) 273-2106, www.mesharpe.com; *The Illustrated Book of World Rankings.*

Palgrave Macmillan Ltd., Houndmills, Basingstoke, Hampshire, RG21 6XS, England, (Telephone in U.S. (888) 330-8477), (Fax in U.S. (800) 672-2054), www.palgrave.com; *The Statesman's Yearbook 2008.*

Taylor and Francis Group, An Informa Business, 2 Park Square, Milton Park, Abingdon, Oxford OX14 4RN, United Kingdom, (Dial from U.S. (212) 216-7800), (Fax from U.S. (212) 564-7854), www.tandf.co.uk; *The Europa World Year Book.*

UCLA Latin American Institute, 10343 Bunche Hall, Box 951447, Los Angeles, CA 90095-1447, (310) 825-4571, Fax: (310) 206-6859, www.international.ucla.edu/lac; *Statistical Abstract of Latin America.*

UNESCO Institute for Statistics, C.P. 6128 Succursale Centre-Ville, Montreal, Quebec, H3C 3J7 Canada, (Dial from U.S. (514) 343-6880), (Fax from U.S. (514) 343 6882), www.uis.unesco.org; *Statistical Tables.*

United Nations Conference on Trade and Development (UNCTAD), DC2-1120, United Nations, New York, NY 10017, (212) 963-0027, www.unctad.org; *UNCTAD Commodity Yearbook.*

United Nations Food and Agricultural Organization (FAO), Viale delle Terme di Caracalla, 00100 Rome, Italy, (Dial from U.S. (202) 653-2400), (Fax from U.S. (202) 653 5760), www.fao.org; *FAO Yearbook of Forest Products* and *The State of Food and Agriculture (SOFA) 2006.*

United Nations Statistics Division, New York, NY 10017, (800) 253-9646, Fax: (212) 963-4116, http://unstats.un.org; *Statistical Yearbook.*

The World Bank, 1818 H Street, NW, Washington, DC 20433, (202) 473-1000, Fax: (202) 477-6391, www.worldbank.org; *Argentina* and *World Development Report 2008.*

ARGENTINA - GAS PRODUCTION

See ARGENTINA - MINERAL INDUSTRIES

ARGENTINA - GEOGRAPHIC INFORMATION SYSTEMS

M.E. Sharpe, 80 Business Park Drive, Armonk, NY 10504, (800) 541-6563, Fax: (914) 273-2106, www.mesharpe.com; *The Illustrated Book of World Rankings.*

UCLA Latin American Institute, 10343 Bunche Hall, Box 951447, Los Angeles, CA 90095-1447, (310) 825-4571, Fax: (310) 206-6859, www.international.ucla.edu/lac; *Statistical Abstract of Latin America.*

The World Bank, 1818 H Street, NW, Washington, DC 20433, (202) 473-1000, Fax: (202) 477-6391, www.worldbank.org; *Argentina.*

ARGENTINA - GOLD INDUSTRY

Economist Intelligence Unit, 111 West 57th Street, New York, NY 10019, (212) 554-0600, Fax: (212) 586-1181, www.eiu.com; *Business Latin America.*

International Monetary Fund (IMF), 700 Nineteenth Street, NW, Washington, DC 20431, (202) 623-7000, Fax: (202) 623-4661, www.imf.org; *International Financial Statistics Yearbook 2007.*

United Nations Statistics Division, New York, NY 10017, (800) 253-9646, Fax: (212) 963-4116, http://unstats.un.org; *Statistical Yearbook.*

The World Bank, 1818 H Street, NW, Washington, DC 20433, (202) 473-1000, Fax: (202) 477-6391, www.worldbank.org; *World Development Indicators (WDI) 2008.*

ARGENTINA - GOLD PRODUCTION

See ARGENTINA - MINERAL INDUSTRIES

ARGENTINA - GRANTS-IN-AID

International Monetary Fund (IMF), 700 Nineteenth Street, NW, Washington, DC 20431, (202) 623-7000, Fax: (202) 623-4661, www.imf.org; *Government Finance Statistics Yearbook (2008 Edition).*

ARGENTINA - GREEN PEPPER AND CHILIE PRODUCTION

See ARGENTINA - CROPS

ARGENTINA - GROSS DOMESTIC PRODUCT

Economist Intelligence Unit, 111 West 57th Street, New York, NY 10019, (212) 554-0600, Fax: (212) 586-1181, www.eiu.com; *Argentina Country Report* and *Business Latin America.*

Euromonitor International, Inc., 224 S. Michigan Avenue, Suite 1500, Chicago, IL 60604, (312) 922-1115, Fax: (312) 922-1157, www.euromonitor.com; *International Marketing Data and Statistics 2008* and *The World Economic Factbook 2008.*

Inter-American Development Bank (IDB), 1300 New York Avenue, NW, Washington, DC 20577, (202) 623-1000, Fax: (202) 623-3096, www.iadb.org; *The Politics of Policies: Economic and Social Progress in Latin America - 2006 Report.*

International Monetary Fund (IMF), 700 Nineteenth Street, NW, Washington, DC 20431, (202) 623-7000, Fax: (202) 623-4661, www.imf.org; *International Financial Statistics Yearbook 2007.*

M.E. Sharpe, 80 Business Park Drive, Armonk, NY 10504, (800) 541-6563, Fax: (914) 273-2106, www.mesharpe.com; *The Illustrated Book of World Rankings.*

Organization of American States (OAS), 17th Street Constitution Avenue NW, Washington, DC 20006, (202) 458-3000, www.oas.org; *The OAS in Transition: 1994-2004.*

Taylor and Francis Group, An Informa Business, 2 Park Square, Milton Park, Abingdon, Oxford OX14 4RN, United Kingdom, (Dial from U.S. (212) 216-7800), (Fax from U.S. (212) 564-7854), www.tandf.co.uk; *The Europa World Year Book.*

UCLA Latin American Institute, 10343 Bunche Hall, Box 951447, Los Angeles, CA 90095-1447, (310) 825-4571, Fax: (310) 206-6859, www.international.ucla.edu/lac; *Statistical Abstract of Latin America.*

United Nations Statistics Division, New York, NY 10017, (800) 253-9646, Fax: (212) 963-4116, http://unstats.un.org; *Human Development Report 2006; National Accounts Statistics: Compendium of Income Distribution Statistics; Statistical Yearbook;* and *Statistical Yearbook for Latin America and the Caribbean 2004.*

The World Bank, 1818 H Street, NW, Washington, DC 20433, (202) 473-1000, Fax: (202) 477-6391, www.worldbank.org; *World Development Indicators (WDI) 2008* and *World Development Report 2008.*

ARGENTINA - GROSS NATIONAL PRODUCT

Euromonitor International, Inc., 224 S. Michigan Avenue, Suite 1500, Chicago, IL 60604, (312) 922-1115, Fax: (312) 922-1157, www.euromonitor.com; *International Marketing Data and Statistics 2008.*

Inter-American Development Bank (IDB), 1300 New York Avenue, NW, Washington, DC 20577, (202) 623-1000, Fax: (202) 623-3096, www.iadb.org; *The Politics of Policies: Economic and Social Progress in Latin America - 2006 Report.*

M.E. Sharpe, 80 Business Park Drive, Armonk, NY 10504, (800) 541-6563, Fax: (914) 273-2106, www.mesharpe.com; *The Illustrated Book of World Rankings.*

Palgrave Macmillan Ltd., Houndmills, Basingstoke, Hampshire, RG21 6XS, England, (Telephone in U.S. (888) 330-8477), (Fax in U.S. (800) 672-2054), www.palgrave.com; *The Statesman's Yearbook 2008.*

U.S. Department of State (DOS), 2201 C Street NW, Washington, DC 20520, (202) 647-4000, www.state.gov; *World Military Expenditures and Arms Transfers (WMEAT).*

United Nations Statistics Division, New York, NY 10017, (800) 253-9646, Fax: (212) 963-4116, http://unstats.un.org; *Statistical Yearbook.*

The World Bank, 1818 H Street, NW, Washington, DC 20433, (202) 473-1000, Fax: (202) 477-6391, www.worldbank.org; *The World Bank Atlas 2003-2004; World Development Indicators (WDI) 2008;* and *World Development Report 2008.*

ARGENTINA - HIDES AND SKINS INDUSTRY

International Monetary Fund (IMF), 700 Nineteenth Street, NW, Washington, DC 20431, (202) 623-7000, Fax: (202) 623-4661, www.imf.org; *International Financial Statistics Yearbook 2007.*

United Nations Food and Agricultural Organization (FAO), Viale delle Terme di Caracalla, 00100 Rome, Italy, (Dial from U.S. (202) 653-2400), (Fax from U.S. (202) 653 5760), www.fao.org; *FAO Production Yearbook 2002.*

ARGENTINA - HOUSING

Euromonitor International, Inc., 224 S. Michigan Avenue, Suite 1500, Chicago, IL 60604, (312) 922-1115, Fax: (312) 922-1157, www.euromonitor.com; *World Marketing Data and Statistics.*

M.E. Sharpe, 80 Business Park Drive, Armonk, NY 10504, (800) 541-6563, Fax: (914) 273-2106, www.mesharpe.com; *The Illustrated Book of World Rankings.*

UCLA Latin American Institute, 10343 Bunche Hall, Box 951447, Los Angeles, CA 90095-1447, (310) 825-4571, Fax: (310) 206-6859, www.international.ucla.edu/lac; *Statistical Abstract of Latin America.*

United Nations Statistics Division, New York, NY 10017, (800) 253-9646, Fax: (212) 963-4116, http://unstats.un.org; *Statistical Yearbook for Latin America and the Caribbean 2004.*

ARGENTINA - ILLITERATE PERSONS

Euromonitor International, Inc., 224 S. Michigan Avenue, Suite 1500, Chicago, IL 60604, (312) 922-1115, Fax: (312) 922-1157, www.euromonitor.com; *The World Economic Factbook 2008.*

UNESCO Institute for Statistics, C.P. 6128 Succursale Centre-Ville, Montreal, Quebec, H3C 3J7

Canada, (Dial from U.S. (514) 343-6880), (Fax from U.S. (514) 343 6882), www.uis.unesco.org; *Statistical Tables.*

United Nations Statistics Division, New York, NY 10017, (800) 253-9646, Fax: (212) 963-4116, http://unstats.un.org; *Human Development Report 2006* and *Statistical Yearbook for Latin America and the Caribbean 2004.*

ARGENTINA - IMPORTS

Central Intelligence Agency, Office of Public Affairs, Washington, DC 20505, (703) 482-0623, Fax: (703) 482-1739, www.cia.gov; *The World Factbook.*

Economist Intelligence Unit, 111 West 57th Street, New York, NY 10019, (212) 554-0600, Fax: (212) 586-1181, www.eiu.com; *Argentina Country Report* and *Business Latin America.*

Euromonitor International, Inc., 224 S. Michigan Avenue, Suite 1500, Chicago, IL 60604, (312) 922-1115, Fax: (312) 922-1157, www.euromonitor.com; *International Marketing Data and Statistics 2008* and *The World Economic Factbook 2008.*

Inter-American Development Bank (IDB), 1300 New York Avenue, NW, Washington, DC 20577, (202) 623-1000, Fax: (202) 623-3096, www.iadb.org; *The Politics of Policies: Economic and Social Progress in Latin America - 2006 Report.*

International Lead and Zinc Study Group (ILZSG), Rua Almirante Barroso 38, 5th Floor, Lisbon 1000 - 013, Portugal, www.ilzsg.org; Interactive Statistical Database.

International Monetary Fund (IMF), 700 Nineteenth Street, NW, Washington, DC 20431, (202) 623-7000, Fax: (202) 623-4661, www.imf.org; *Direction of Trade Statistics Yearbook 2007; Government Finance Statistics Yearbook (2008 Edition);* and *International Financial Statistics Yearbook 2007.*

Organization of American States (OAS), 17th Street Constitution Avenue NW, Washington, DC 20006, (202) 458-3000, www.oas.org; *The OAS in Transition: 1994-2004.*

Palgrave Macmillan Ltd., Houndmills, Basingstoke, Hampshire, RG21 6XS, England, (Telephone in U.S. (888) 330-8477), (Fax in U.S. (800) 672-2054), www.palgrave.com; *The Statesman's Yearbook 2008.*

Taylor and Francis Group, An Informa Business, 2 Park Square, Milton Park, Abingdon, Oxford OX14 4RN, United Kingdom, (Dial from U.S. (212) 216-7800), (Fax from U.S. (212) 564-7854), www.tandf.co.uk; *The Europa World Year Book.*

United Nations Conference on Trade and Development (UNCTAD), DC2-1120, United Nations, New York, NY 10017, (212) 963-0027, www.unctad.org; *Handbook of Statistics 2005.*

United Nations Food and Agricultural Organization (FAO), Viale delle Terme di Caracalla, 00100 Rome, Italy, (Dial from U.S. (202) 653-2400), (Fax from U.S. (202) 653 5760), www.fao.org; *The State of Food and Agriculture (SOFA) 2006.*

United Nations Statistics Division, New York, NY 10017, (800) 253-9646, Fax: (212) 963-4116, http://unstats.un.org; Commodity Trade Statistics Database (COMTRADE) and *Statistical Yearbook for Latin America and the Caribbean 2004.*

The World Bank, 1818 H Street, NW, Washington, DC 20433, (202) 473-1000, Fax: (202) 477-6391, www.worldbank.org; *World Development Indicators (WDI) 2008* and *World Development Report 2008.*

ARGENTINA - INCOME DISTRIBUTION

UCLA Latin American Institute, 10343 Bunche Hall, Box 951447, Los Angeles, CA 90095-1447, (310) 825-4571, Fax: (310) 206-6859, www.international.ucla.edu/lac; *Statistical Abstract of Latin America.*

United Nations Statistics Division, New York, NY 10017, (800) 253-9646, Fax: (212) 963-4116, http://unstats.un.org; *Statistical Yearbook for Latin America and the Caribbean 2004.*

ARGENTINA - INCOME TAXES

See ARGENTINA - TAXATION

ARGENTINA - INDUSTRIAL METALS PRODUCTION

See ARGENTINA - MINERAL INDUSTRIES

ARGENTINA - INDUSTRIAL PRODUCTIVITY

Euromonitor International, Inc., 224 S. Michigan Avenue, Suite 1500, Chicago, IL 60604, (312) 922-1115, Fax: (312) 922-1157, www.euromonitor.com; *International Marketing Data and Statistics 2008.*

International Lead and Zinc Study Group (ILZSG), Rua Almirante Barroso 38, 5th Floor, Lisbon 1000 - 013, Portugal, www.ilzsg.org; Interactive Statistical Database.

M.E. Sharpe, 80 Business Park Drive, Armonk, NY 10504, (800) 541-6563, Fax: (914) 273-2106, www.mesharpe.com; *The Illustrated Book of World Rankings.*

ARGENTINA - INDUSTRIAL PROPERTY

United Nations Statistics Division, New York, NY 10017, (800) 253-9646, Fax: (212) 963-4116, http://unstats.un.org; *Statistical Yearbook.*

ARGENTINA - INDUSTRIES

Central Intelligence Agency, Office of Public Affairs, Washington, DC 20505, (703) 482-0623, Fax: (703) 482-1739, www.cia.gov; *The World Factbook.*

Economist Intelligence Unit, 111 West 57th Street, New York, NY 10019, (212) 554-0600, Fax: (212) 586-1181, www.eiu.com; *Argentina Country Report.*

Euromonitor International, Inc., 224 S. Michigan Avenue, Suite 1500, Chicago, IL 60604, (312) 922-1115, Fax: (312) 922-1157, www.euromonitor.com; *International Marketing Data and Statistics 2008; The World Economic Factbook 2008;* and *World Marketing Data and Statistics.*

International Labour Office, I.L.O. Publications, 4 route des Morillons, CH-1211 Geneva 22, Switzerland, (Telephone in U.S. (202) 653-7652), (Fax in U.S. (202) 653-7687), www.ilo.org; *Yearbook of Labour Statistics 2006.*

M.E. Sharpe, 80 Business Park Drive, Armonk, NY 10504, (800) 541-6563, Fax: (914) 273-2106, www.mesharpe.com; *The Illustrated Book of World Rankings.*

Palgrave Macmillan Ltd., Houndmills, Basingstoke, Hampshire, RG21 6XS, England, (Telephone in U.S. (888) 330-8477), (Fax in U.S. (800) 672-2054), www.palgrave.com; *The Statesman's Yearbook 2008.*

Taylor and Francis Group, An Informa Business, 2 Park Square, Milton Park, Abingdon, Oxford OX14 4RN, United Kingdom, (Dial from U.S. (212) 216-7800), (Fax from U.S. (212) 564-7854), www.tandf.co.uk; *The Europa World Year Book.*

UCLA Latin American Institute, 10343 Bunche Hall, Box 951447, Los Angeles, CA 90095-1447, (310) 825-4571, Fax: (310) 206-6859, www.international.ucla.edu/lac; *Statistical Abstract of Latin America.*

United Nations Industrial Development Organization (UNIDO), 1 United Nations Plaza, New York, NY 10017, (212) 963 6890, Fax: (212) 963-7904, http://unido.org; Industrial Statistics Database 2008 (INDSTAT) and *The International Yearbook of Industrial Statistics 2008.*

United Nations Statistics Division, New York, NY 10017, (800) 253-9646, Fax: (212) 963-4116, http://unstats.un.org; *Economic Survey of Latin America and the Caribbean 2004-2005; 2004 Industrial Commodity Statistics Yearbook;* and *Statistical Yearbook.*

The World Bank, 1818 H Street, NW, Washington, DC 20433, (202) 473-1000, Fax: (202) 477-6391, www.worldbank.org; *Argentina* and *World Development Indicators (WDI) 2008.*

ARGENTINA - INFANT AND MATERNAL MORTALITY

See ARGENTINA - MORTALITY

ARGENTINA - INFLATION (FINANCE)

United Nations Statistics Division, New York, NY 10017, (800) 253-9646, Fax: (212) 963-4116, http://unstats.un.org; *Economic Survey of Latin America and the Caribbean 2004-2005.*

ARGENTINA - INTEREST RATES

Inter-American Development Bank (IDB), 1300 New York Avenue, NW, Washington, DC 20577, (202) 623-1000, Fax: (202) 623-3096, www.iadb.org; *The Politics of Policies: Economic and Social Progress in Latin America - 2006 Report.*

ARGENTINA - INTERNAL REVENUE

Inter-American Development Bank (IDB), 1300 New York Avenue, NW, Washington, DC 20577, (202) 623-1000, Fax: (202) 623-3096, www.iadb.org; *The Politics of Policies: Economic and Social Progress in Latin America - 2006 Report.*

Organization of American States (OAS), 17th Street Constitution Avenue NW, Washington, DC 20006, (202) 458-3000, www.oas.org; *The OAS in Transition: 1994-2004.*

ARGENTINA - INTERNATIONAL FINANCE

Inter-American Development Bank (IDB), 1300 New York Avenue, NW, Washington, DC 20577, (202) 623-1000, Fax: (202) 623-3096, www.iadb.org; *The Politics of Policies: Economic and Social Progress in Latin America - 2006 Report.*

UCLA Latin American Institute, 10343 Bunche Hall, Box 951447, Los Angeles, CA 90095-1447, (310) 825-4571, Fax: (310) 206-6859, www.international.ucla.edu/lac; *Statistical Abstract of Latin America.*

ARGENTINA - INTERNATIONAL LIQUIDITY

Inter-American Development Bank (IDB), 1300 New York Avenue, NW, Washington, DC 20577, (202) 623-1000, Fax: (202) 623-3096, www.iadb.org; *The Politics of Policies: Economic and Social Progress in Latin America - 2006 Report.*

International Monetary Fund (IMF), 700 Nineteenth Street, NW, Washington, DC 20431, (202) 623-7000, Fax: (202) 623-4661, www.imf.org; *International Financial Statistics Yearbook 2007.*

ARGENTINA - INTERNATIONAL STATISTICS

Inter-American Development Bank (IDB), 1300 New York Avenue, NW, Washington, DC 20577, (202) 623-1000, Fax: (202) 623-3096, www.iadb.org; *The Politics of Policies: Economic and Social Progress in Latin America - 2006 Report.*

UCLA Latin American Institute, 10343 Bunche Hall, Box 951447, Los Angeles, CA 90095-1447, (310) 825-4571, Fax: (310) 206-6859, www.international.ucla.edu/lac; *Statistical Abstract of Latin America.*

ARGENTINA - INTERNATIONAL TRADE

Economist Intelligence Unit, 111 West 57th Street, New York, NY 10019, (212) 554-0600, Fax: (212) 586-1181, www.eiu.com; *Argentina Country Report* and *Business Latin America.*

Euromonitor International, Inc., 224 S. Michigan Avenue, Suite 1500, Chicago, IL 60604, (312) 922-1115, Fax: (312) 922-1157, www.euromonitor.com; *The World Economic Factbook 2008* and *World Marketing Data and Statistics.*

Inter-American Development Bank (IDB), 1300 New York Avenue, NW, Washington, DC 20577, (202) 623-1000, Fax: (202) 623-3096, www.iadb.org; *The Politics of Policies: Economic and Social Progress in Latin America - 2006 Report.*

M.E. Sharpe, 80 Business Park Drive, Armonk, NY 10504, (800) 541-6563, Fax: (914) 273-2106, www.mesharpe.com; *The Illustrated Book of World Rankings.*

Organisation for Economic Cooperation and Development (OECD), 2 rue Andre Pascal, F-75775 Paris Cedex 16, France, (Telephone in U.S. (202) 785-6323), (Fax in U.S. (202) 785-0350), www.oecd.org; *International Trade by Commodity Statistics (ITCS).*

Palgrave Macmillan Ltd., Houndmills, Basingstoke, Hampshire, RG21 6XS, England, (Telephone in U.S.

(888) 330-8477), (Fax in U.S. (800) 672-2054), www.palgrave.com; *The Statesman's Yearbook 2008.*

Taylor and Francis Group, An Informa Business, 2 Park Square, Milton Park, Abingdon, Oxford OX14 4RN, United Kingdom, (Dial from U.S. (212) 216-7800), (Fax from U.S. (212) 564-7854), www.tandf.co.uk; *The Europa World Year Book.*

UCLA Latin American Institute, 10343 Bunche Hall, Box 951447, Los Angeles, CA 90095-1447, (310) 825-4571, Fax: (310) 206-6859, www.international.ucla.edu/lac; *Statistical Abstract of Latin America.*

United Nations Conference on Trade and Development (UNCTAD), DC2-1120, United Nations, New York, NY 10017, (212) 963-0027, www.unctad.org; *UNCTAD Commodity Yearbook.*

United Nations Food and Agricultural Organization (FAO), Viale delle Terme di Caracalla, 00100 Rome, Italy, (Dial from U.S. (202) 653-2400), (Fax from U.S. (202) 653 5760), www.fao.org; *FAO Trade Yearbook* and *The State of Food and Agriculture (SOFA) 2006.*

United Nations Statistics Division, New York, NY 10017, (800) 253-9646, Fax: (212) 963-4116, http://unstats.un.org; *Economic Survey of Latin America and the Caribbean 2004-2005; International Trade Statistics Yearbook; Statistical Yearbook;* and *Statistical Yearbook for Latin America and the Caribbean 2004.*

The World Bank, 1818 H Street, NW, Washington, DC 20433, (202) 473-1000, Fax: (202) 477-6391, www.worldbank.org; *Argentina; World Development Indicators (WDI) 2008;* and *World Development Report 2008.*

World Trade Organization (WTO), Centre William Rappard, Rue de Lausanne 154, CH-1211 Geneva 21, Switzerland, www.wto.org; *International Trade Statistics 2006.*

ARGENTINA - INTERNET USERS

International Telecommunication Union (ITU), Place des Nations, 1211 Geneva 20, Switzerland, www.itu.int; *World Telecommunication/ICT Indicators Database on CD-ROM; World Telecommunication/ICT Indicators Database Online;* and *Yearbook of Statistics - Telecommunication Services (Chronological Time Series 1997-2006).*

The World Bank, 1818 H Street, NW, Washington, DC 20433, (202) 473-1000, Fax: (202) 477-6391, www.worldbank.org; *Argentina.*

ARGENTINA - INVESTMENTS

Inter-American Development Bank (IDB), 1300 New York Avenue, NW, Washington, DC 20577, (202) 623-1000, Fax: (202) 623-3096, www.iadb.org; *The Politics of Policies: Economic and Social Progress in Latin America - 2006 Report.*

International Monetary Fund (IMF), 700 Nineteenth Street, NW, Washington, DC 20431, (202) 623-7000, Fax: (202) 623-4661, www.imf.org; *International Financial Statistics Yearbook 2007.*

United Nations Statistics Division, New York, NY 10017, (800) 253-9646, Fax: (212) 963-4116, http://unstats.un.org; *Statistical Yearbook for Latin America and the Caribbean 2004.*

ARGENTINA - INVESTMENTS, FOREIGN

Economist Intelligence Unit, 111 West 57th Street, New York, NY 10019, (212) 554-0600, Fax: (212) 586-1181, www.eiu.com; *Business Latin America.*

ARGENTINA - IRON AND IRON ORE PRODUCTION

See ARGENTINA - MINERAL INDUSTRIES

ARGENTINA - IRRIGATION

Euromonitor International, Inc., 224 S. Michigan Avenue, Suite 1500, Chicago, IL 60604, (312) 922-1115, Fax: (312) 922-1157, www.euromonitor.com; *International Marketing Data and Statistics 2008.*

Inter-American Development Bank (IDB), 1300 New York Avenue, NW, Washington, DC 20577, (202) 623-1000, Fax: (202) 623-3096, www.iadb.org; *The Politics of Policies: Economic and Social Progress in Latin America - 2006 Report.*

ARGENTINA - LABOR

Central Intelligence Agency, Office of Public Affairs, Washington, DC 20505, (703) 482-0623, Fax: (703) 482-1739, www.cia.gov; *The World Factbook.*

Economist Intelligence Unit, 111 West 57th Street, New York, NY 10019, (212) 554-0600, Fax: (212) 586-1181, www.eiu.com; *Business Latin America.*

Euromonitor International, Inc., 224 S. Michigan Avenue, Suite 1500, Chicago, IL 60604, (312) 922-1115, Fax: (312) 922-1157, www.euromonitor.com; *International Marketing Data and Statistics 2008* and *World Marketing Data and Statistics.*

International Labour Office, I.L.O. Publications, 4 route des Morillons, CH-1211 Geneva 22, Switzerland, (Telephone in U.S. (202) 653-7652), (Fax in U.S. (202) 653-7687), www.ilo.org; *Yearbook of Labour Statistics 2006.*

M.E. Sharpe, 80 Business Park Drive, Armonk, NY 10504, (800) 541-6563, Fax: (914) 273-2106, www.mesharpe.com; *The Illustrated Book of World Rankings.*

Palgrave Macmillan Ltd., Houndmills, Basingstoke, Hampshire, RG21 6XS, England, (Telephone in U.S. (888) 330-8477), (Fax in U.S. (800) 672-2054), www.palgrave.com; *The Statesman's Yearbook 2008.*

Taylor and Francis Group, An Informa Business, 2 Park Square, Milton Park, Abingdon, Oxford OX14 4RN, United Kingdom, (Dial from U.S. (212) 216-7800), (Fax from U.S. (212) 564-7854), www.tandf.co.uk; *The Europa World Year Book.*

United Nations Food and Agricultural Organization (FAO), Viale delle Terme di Caracalla, 00100 Rome, Italy, (Dial from U.S. (202) 653-2400), (Fax from U.S. (202) 653 5760), www.fao.org; *The State of Food and Agriculture (SOFA) 2006.*

United Nations Statistics Division, New York, NY 10017, (800) 253-9646, Fax: (212) 963-4116, http://unstats.un.org; *Human Development Report 2006.*

The World Bank, 1818 H Street, NW, Washington, DC 20433, (202) 473-1000, Fax: (202) 477-6391, www.worldbank.org; *The World Bank Atlas 2003-2004; World Development Indicators (WDI) 2008;* and *World Development Report 2008.*

ARGENTINA - LAND USE

Central Intelligence Agency, Office of Public Affairs, Washington, DC 20505, (703) 482-0623, Fax: (703) 482-1739, www.cia.gov; *The World Factbook.*

Euromonitor International, Inc., 224 S. Michigan Avenue, Suite 1500, Chicago, IL 60604, (312) 922-1115, Fax: (312) 922-1157, www.euromonitor.com; *International Marketing Data and Statistics 2008.*

Inter-American Development Bank (IDB), 1300 New York Avenue, NW, Washington, DC 20577, (202) 623-1000, Fax: (202) 623-3096, www.iadb.org; *The Politics of Policies: Economic and Social Progress in Latin America - 2006 Report.*

United Nations Food and Agricultural Organization (FAO), Viale delle Terme di Caracalla, 00100 Rome, Italy, (Dial from U.S. (202) 653-2400), (Fax from U.S. (202) 653 5760), www.fao.org; *FAO Production Yearbook 2002.*

The World Bank, 1818 H Street, NW, Washington, DC 20433, (202) 473-1000, Fax: (202) 477-6391, www.worldbank.org; *World Development Report 2008.*

ARGENTINA - LEATHER INDUSTRY AND TRADE

United Nations Statistics Division, New York, NY 10017, (800) 253-9646, Fax: (212) 963-4116, http://unstats.un.org; Commodity Trade Statistics Database (COMTRADE).

ARGENTINA - LIBRARIES

M.E. Sharpe, 80 Business Park Drive, Armonk, NY 10504, (800) 541-6563, Fax: (914) 273-2106, www.mesharpe.com; *The Illustrated Book of World Rankings.*

UNESCO Institute for Statistics, C.P. 6128 Succursale Centre-Ville, Montreal, Quebec, H3C 3J7 Canada, (Dial from U.S. (514) 343-6880), (Fax from U.S. (514) 343 6882), www.uis.unesco.org; *Statistical Tables.*

ARGENTINA - LICENSES

International Monetary Fund (IMF), 700 Nineteenth Street, NW, Washington, DC 20431, (202) 623-7000, Fax: (202) 623-4661, www.imf.org; *Government Finance Statistics Yearbook (2008 Edition).*

ARGENTINA - LIFE EXPECTANCY

Economist Intelligence Unit, 111 West 57th Street, New York, NY 10019, (212) 554-0600, Fax: (212) 586-1181, www.eiu.com; *Business Latin America.*

Euromonitor International, Inc., 224 S. Michigan Avenue, Suite 1500, Chicago, IL 60604, (312) 922-1115, Fax: (312) 922-1157, www.euromonitor.com; *The World Economic Factbook 2008.*

Palgrave Macmillan Ltd., Houndmills, Basingstoke, Hampshire, RG21 6XS, England, (Telephone in U.S. (888) 330-8477), (Fax in U.S. (800) 672-2054), www.palgrave.com; *The Statesman's Yearbook 2008.*

United Nations Statistics Division, New York, NY 10017, (800) 253-9646, Fax: (212) 963-4116, http://unstats.un.org; *Human Development Report 2006; Statistical Yearbook for Latin America and the Caribbean 2004;* and *World Statistics Pocketbook.*

The World Bank, 1818 H Street, NW, Washington, DC 20433, (202) 473-1000, Fax: (202) 477-6391, www.worldbank.org; *The World Bank Atlas 2003-2004* and *World Development Report 2008.*

ARGENTINA - LITERACY

Economist Intelligence Unit, 111 West 57th Street, New York, NY 10019, (212) 554-0600, Fax: (212) 586-1181, www.eiu.com; *Business Latin America.*

Euromonitor International, Inc., 224 S. Michigan Avenue, Suite 1500, Chicago, IL 60604, (312) 922-1115, Fax: (312) 922-1157, www.euromonitor.com; *World Marketing Data and Statistics.*

ARGENTINA - LIVESTOCK

Euromonitor International, Inc., 224 S. Michigan Avenue, Suite 1500, Chicago, IL 60604, (312) 922-1115, Fax: (312) 922-1157, www.euromonitor.com; *International Marketing Data and Statistics 2008.*

M.E. Sharpe, 80 Business Park Drive, Armonk, NY 10504, (800) 541-6563, Fax: (914) 273-2106, www.mesharpe.com; *The Illustrated Book of World Rankings.*

Palgrave Macmillan Ltd., Houndmills, Basingstoke, Hampshire, RG21 6XS, England, (Telephone in U.S. (888) 330-8477), (Fax in U.S. (800) 672-2054), www.palgrave.com; *The Statesman's Yearbook 2008.*

Taylor and Francis Group, An Informa Business, 2 Park Square, Milton Park, Abingdon, Oxford OX14 4RN, United Kingdom, (Dial from U.S. (212) 216-7800), (Fax from U.S. (212) 564-7854), www.tandf.co.uk; *The Europa World Year Book.*

United Nations Conference on Trade and Development (UNCTAD), DC2-1120, United Nations, New York, NY 10017, (212) 963-0027, www.unctad.org; *UNCTAD Commodity Yearbook.*

United Nations Food and Agricultural Organization (FAO), Viale delle Terme di Caracalla, 00100 Rome, Italy, (Dial from U.S. (202) 653-2400), (Fax from U.S. (202) 653 5760), www.fao.org; *FAO Production Yearbook 2002* and *The State of Food and Agriculture (SOFA) 2006.*

United Nations Statistics Division, New York, NY 10017, (800) 253-9646, Fax: (212) 963-4116, http://unstats.un.org; *Statistical Yearbook.*

ARGENTINA - LOCAL TAXATION

Euromonitor International, Inc., 224 S. Michigan Avenue, Suite 1500, Chicago, IL 60604, (312) 922-1115, Fax: (312) 922-1157, www.euromonitor.com; *International Marketing Data and Statistics 2008.*

Inter-American Development Bank (IDB), 1300 New York Avenue, NW, Washington, DC 20577, (202) 623-1000, Fax: (202) 623-3096, www.iadb.org; *The Politics of Policies: Economic and Social Progress in Latin America - 2006 Report.*

ARGENTINA - MANUFACTURES

Economist Intelligence Unit, 111 West 57th Street, New York, NY 10019, (212) 554-0600, Fax: (212) 586-1181, www.eiu.com; *Business Latin America.*

Inter-American Development Bank (IDB), 1300 New York Avenue, NW, Washington, DC 20577, (202) 623-1000, Fax: (202) 623-3096, www.iadb.org; *The Politics of Policies: Economic and Social Progress in Latin America - 2006 Report.*

International Monetary Fund (IMF), 700 Nineteenth Street, NW, Washington, DC 20431, (202) 623-7000, Fax: (202) 623-4661, www.imf.org; *International Financial Statistics Yearbook 2007.*

M.E. Sharpe, 80 Business Park Drive, Armonk, NY 10504, (800) 541-6563, Fax: (914) 273-2106, www.mesharpe.com; *The Illustrated Book of World Rankings.*

Organization of American States (OAS), 17th Street Constitution Avenue NW, Washington, DC 20006, (202) 458-3000, www.oas.org; *The OAS in Transition: 1994-2004.*

United Nations Statistics Division, New York, NY 10017, (800) 253-9646, Fax: (212) 963-4116, http://unstats.un.org; *Statistical Yearbook* and *Statistical Yearbook for Latin America and the Caribbean 2004.*

The World Bank, 1818 H Street, NW, Washington, DC 20433, (202) 473-1000, Fax: (202) 477-6391, www.worldbank.org; *World Development Indicators (WDI) 2008.*

ARGENTINA - MARRIAGE

M.E. Sharpe, 80 Business Park Drive, Armonk, NY 10504, (800) 541-6563, Fax: (914) 273-2106, www.mesharpe.com; *The Illustrated Book of World Rankings.*

United Nations Statistics Division, New York, NY 10017, (800) 253-9646, Fax: (212) 963-4116, http://unstats.un.org; *Demographic Yearbook* and *Statistical Yearbook.*

ARGENTINA - MEAT INDUSTRY AND TRADE

International Monetary Fund (IMF), 700 Nineteenth Street, NW, Washington, DC 20431, (202) 623-7000, Fax: (202) 623-4661, www.imf.org; *International Financial Statistics Yearbook 2007.*

Organization of American States (OAS), 17th Street Constitution Avenue NW, Washington, DC 20006, (202) 458-3000, www.oas.org; *The OAS in Transition: 1994-2004.*

ARGENTINA - MEAT PRODUCTION

See ARGENTINA - LIVESTOCK

ARGENTINA - MEDICAL CARE, COST OF

International Monetary Fund (IMF), 700 Nineteenth Street, NW, Washington, DC 20431, (202) 623-7000, Fax: (202) 623-4661, www.imf.org; *Government Finance Statistics Yearbook (2008 Edition).*

United Nations Statistics Division, New York, NY 10017, (800) 253-9646, Fax: (212) 963-4116, http://unstats.un.org; *Statistical Yearbook for Latin America and the Caribbean 2004.*

ARGENTINA - MEDICAL PERSONNEL

UCLA Latin American Institute, 10343 Bunche Hall, Box 951447, Los Angeles, CA 90095-1447, (310) 825-4571, Fax: (310) 206-6859, www.international.ucla.edu/lac; *Statistical Abstract of Latin America.*

ARGENTINA - MERCHANT SHIPS

See ARGENTINA - SHIPPING

ARGENTINA - METAL PRODUCTS

United Nations Statistics Division, New York, NY 10017, (800) 253-9646, Fax: (212) 963-4116, http://unstats.un.org; Commodity Trade Statistics Database (COMTRADE).

ARGENTINA - MILK PRODUCTION

See ARGENTINA - DAIRY PROCESSING

ARGENTINA - MINERAL INDUSTRIES

Commodity Research Bureau, 330 South Wells Street, Suite 612, Chicago, IL 60606-7110, (800) 621-5271, Fax: (312) 939-4135, www.crbtrader.com; *2006 CRB Commodity Yearbook and CD.*

Economist Intelligence Unit, 111 West 57th Street, New York, NY 10019, (212) 554-0600, Fax: (212) 586-1181, www.eiu.com; *Business Latin America.*

Inter-American Development Bank (IDB), 1300 New York Avenue, NW, Washington, DC 20577, (202) 623-1000, Fax: (202) 623-3096, www.iadb.org; *The Politics of Policies: Economic and Social Progress in Latin America - 2006 Report.*

International Lead and Zinc Study Group (ILZSG), Rua Almirante Barroso 38, 5th Floor, Lisbon 1000 - 013, Portugal, www.ilzsg.org; Interactive Statistical Database.

M.E. Sharpe, 80 Business Park Drive, Armonk, NY 10504, (800) 541-6563, Fax: (914) 273-2106, www.mesharpe.com; *The Illustrated Book of World Rankings.*

Organisation for Economic Cooperation and Development (OECD), 2 rue Andre Pascal, F-75775 Paris Cedex 16, France, (Telephone in U.S. (202) 785-6323), (Fax in U.S. (202) 785-0350), www.oecd.org; *World Energy Outlook 2007.*

Palgrave Macmillan Ltd., Houndmills, Basingstoke, Hampshire, RG21 6XS, England, (Telephone in U.S. (888) 330-8477), (Fax in U.S. (800) 672-2054), www.palgrave.com; *The Statesman's Yearbook 2008.*

PennWell Corporation, 1421 South Sheridan Road, Tulsa, OK 74112, (918) 835-3161, www.pennwell.com; *Oil Gas Journal Latinoamericana.*

Taylor and Francis Group, An Informa Business, 2 Park Square, Milton Park, Abingdon, Oxford OX14 4RN, United Kingdom, (Dial from U.S. (212) 216-7800), (Fax from U.S. (212) 564-7854), www.tandf.co.uk; *The Europa World Year Book.*

UCLA Latin American Institute, 10343 Bunche Hall, Box 951447, Los Angeles, CA 90095-1447, (310) 825-4571, Fax: (310) 206-6859, www.international.ucla.edu/lac; *Statistical Abstract of Latin America.*

United Nations Conference on Trade and Development (UNCTAD), DC2-1120, United Nations, New York, NY 10017, (212) 963-0027, www.unctad.org; *UNCTAD Commodity Yearbook.*

United Nations Statistics Division, New York, NY 10017, (800) 253-9646, Fax: (212) 963-4116, http://unstats.un.org; *Statistical Yearbook* and *Statistical Yearbook for Latin America and the Caribbean 2004.*

ARGENTINA - MOLASSES PRODUCTION

See ARGENTINA - CROPS

ARGENTINA - MONEY EXCHANGE RATES

See ARGENTINA - FOREIGN EXCHANGE RATES

ARGENTINA - MONEY SUPPLY

Economist Intelligence Unit, 111 West 57th Street, New York, NY 10019, (212) 554-0600, Fax: (212) 586-1181, www.eiu.com; *Argentina Country Report.*

Euromonitor International, Inc., 224 S. Michigan Avenue, Suite 1500, Chicago, IL 60604, (312) 922-1115, Fax: (312) 922-1157, www.euromonitor.com; *International Marketing Data and Statistics 2008.*

Inter-American Development Bank (IDB), 1300 New York Avenue, NW, Washington, DC 20577, (202) 623-1000, Fax: (202) 623-3096, www.iadb.org; *The Politics of Policies: Economic and Social Progress in Latin America - 2006 Report.*

International Monetary Fund (IMF), 700 Nineteenth Street, NW, Washington, DC 20431, (202) 623-7000, Fax: (202) 623-4661, www.imf.org; *International Financial Statistics Yearbook 2007.*

Taylor and Francis Group, An Informa Business, 2 Park Square, Milton Park, Abingdon, Oxford OX14 4RN, United Kingdom, (Dial from U.S. (212) 216-7800), (Fax from U.S. (212) 564-7854), www.tandf.co.uk; *The Europa World Year Book.*

UCLA Latin American Institute, 10343 Bunche Hall, Box 951447, Los Angeles, CA 90095-1447, (310) 825-4571, Fax: (310) 206-6859, www.international.ucla.edu/lac; *Statistical Abstract of Latin America.*

United Nations Statistics Division, New York, NY 10017, (800) 253-9646, Fax: (212) 963-4116, http://unstats.un.org; *Statistical Yearbook.*

The World Bank, 1818 H Street, NW, Washington, DC 20433, (202) 473-1000, Fax: (202) 477-6391, www.worldbank.org; *Argentina* and *World Development Indicators (WDI) 2008.*

ARGENTINA - MORTALITY

Central Intelligence Agency, Office of Public Affairs, Washington, DC 20505, (703) 482-0623, Fax: (703) 482-1739, www.cia.gov; *The World Factbook.*

Economist Intelligence Unit, 111 West 57th Street, New York, NY 10019, (212) 554-0600, Fax: (212) 586-1181, www.eiu.com; *Business Latin America.*

Euromonitor International, Inc., 224 S. Michigan Avenue, Suite 1500, Chicago, IL 60604, (312) 922-1115, Fax: (312) 922-1157, www.euromonitor.com; *International Marketing Data and Statistics 2008* and *The World Economic Factbook 2008.*

Taylor and Francis Group, An Informa Business, 2 Park Square, Milton Park, Abingdon, Oxford OX14 4RN, United Kingdom, (Dial from U.S. (212) 216-7800), (Fax from U.S. (212) 564-7854), www.tandf.co.uk; *The Europa World Year Book.*

UNICEF, 3 United Nations Plaza, New York, NY 10017, (800) 253-9646, Fax: (212) 887-7465, www.unicef.org; *The State of the World's Children 2008.*

United Nations Statistics Division, New York, NY 10017, (800) 253-9646, Fax: (212) 963-4116, http://unstats.un.org; *Demographic Yearbook; Human Development Report 2006; Statistical Yearbook; Statistical Yearbook for Latin America and the Caribbean 2004;* and *World Statistics Pocketbook.*

The World Bank, 1818 H Street, NW, Washington, DC 20433, (202) 473-1000, Fax: (202) 477-6391, www.worldbank.org; *The World Bank Atlas 2003-2004; World Development Indicators (WDI) 2008;* and *World Development Report 2008.*

World Health Organization (WHO), Avenue Appia 20, 1211 Geneve 27, Switzerland, (Telephone in U.S. (212) 331-9081), www.who.int; The WHO Global Atlas of Infectious Diseases and *World Health Report 2006.*

ARGENTINA - MOTION PICTURES

Palgrave Macmillan Ltd., Houndmills, Basingstoke, Hampshire, RG21 6XS, England, (Telephone in U.S. (888) 330-8477), (Fax in U.S. (800) 672-2054), www.palgrave.com; *The Statesman's Yearbook 2008.*

UNESCO Institute for Statistics, C.P. 6128 Succursale Centre-Ville, Montreal, Quebec, H3C 3J7 Canada, (Dial from U.S. (514) 343-6880), (Fax from U.S. (514) 343 6882), www.uis.unesco.org; *Statistical Tables.*

United Nations Statistics Division, New York, NY 10017, (800) 253-9646, Fax: (212) 963-4116, http://unstats.un.org; *Statistical Yearbook.*

ARGENTINA - MOTOR VEHICLES

Economist Intelligence Unit, 111 West 57th Street, New York, NY 10019, (212) 554-0600, Fax: (212) 586-1181, www.eiu.com; *Business Latin America.*

International Road Federation (IFR), Madison Place, 500 Montgomery Street, 5th Floor, Alexandria, VA 22314, (703) 535-1001, Fax: (703) 535-1007, www.irfnet.org; *World Road Statistics 2006.*

Taylor and Francis Group, An Informa Business, 2 Park Square, Milton Park, Abingdon, Oxford OX14 4RN, United Kingdom, (Dial from U.S. (212) 216-7800), (Fax from U.S. (212) 564-7854), www.tandf.co.uk; *The Europa World Year Book.*

United Nations Statistics Division, New York, NY 10017, (800) 253-9646, Fax: (212) 963-4116, http://unstats.un.org; *Statistical Yearbook.*

ARGENTINA - MUSEUMS

M.E. Sharpe, 80 Business Park Drive, Armonk, NY 10504, (800) 541-6563, Fax: (914) 273-2106, www.mesharpe.com; *The Illustrated Book of World Rankings.*

UNESCO Institute for Statistics, C.P. 6128 Succursale Centre-Ville, Montreal, Quebec, H3C 3J7 Canada, (Dial from U.S. (514) 343-6880), (Fax from U.S. (514) 343 6882), www.uis.unesco.org; *Statistical Tables.*

ARGENTINA - NATURAL GAS PRODUCTION

See ARGENTINA - MINERAL INDUSTRIES

ARGENTINA - NUTRITION

United Nations Food and Agricultural Organization (FAO), Viale delle Terme di Caracalla, 00100 Rome, Italy, (Dial from U.S. (202) 653-2400), (Fax from U.S. (202) 653 5760), www.fao.org; *The State of Food and Agriculture (SOFA) 2006.*

United Nations Statistics Division, New York, NY 10017, (800) 253-9646, Fax: (212) 963-4116, http://unstats.un.org; *Statistical Yearbook for Latin America and the Caribbean 2004.*

ARGENTINA - OATS PRODUCTION

See ARGENTINA - CROPS

ARGENTINA - OLDER PEOPLE

M.E. Sharpe, 80 Business Park Drive, Armonk, NY 10504, (800) 541-6563, Fax: (914) 273-2106, www.mesharpe.com; *The Illustrated Book of World Rankings.*

ARGENTINA - ORANGES PRODUCTION

See ARGENTINA - CROPS

ARGENTINA - PAPER

See ARGENTINA - FORESTS AND FORESTRY

ARGENTINA - PEANUT PRODUCTION

See ARGENTINA - CROPS

ARGENTINA - PESTICIDES

United Nations Food and Agricultural Organization (FAO), Viale delle Terme di Caracalla, 00100 Rome, Italy, (Dial from U.S. (202) 653-2400), (Fax from U.S. (202) 653 5760), www.fao.org; *The State of Food and Agriculture (SOFA) 2006.*

ARGENTINA - PETROLEUM INDUSTRY AND TRADE

Economist Intelligence Unit, 111 West 57th Street, New York, NY 10019, (212) 554-0600, Fax: (212) 586-1181, www.eiu.com; *Business Latin America.*

Inter-American Development Bank (IDB), 1300 New York Avenue, NW, Washington, DC 20577, (202) 623-1000, Fax: (202) 623-3096, www.iadb.org; *The Politics of Policies: Economic and Social Progress in Latin America - 2006 Report.*

International Monetary Fund (IMF), 700 Nineteenth Street, NW, Washington, DC 20431, (202) 623-7000, Fax: (202) 623-4661, www.imf.org; *International Financial Statistics Yearbook 2007.*

M.E. Sharpe, 80 Business Park Drive, Armonk, NY 10504, (800) 541-6563, Fax: (914) 273-2106, www.mesharpe.com; *The Illustrated Book of World Rankings.*

Organisation for Economic Cooperation and Development (OECD), 2 rue Andre Pascal, F-75775 Paris Cedex 16, France, (Telephone in U.S. (202) 785-6323), (Fax in U.S. (202) 785-0350), www.oecd.org; *World Energy Outlook 2007.*

Organization of American States (OAS), 17th Street Constitution Avenue NW, Washington, DC 20006, (202) 458-3000, www.oas.org; *The OAS in Transition: 1994-2004.*

Palgrave Macmillan Ltd., Houndmills, Basingstoke, Hampshire, RG21 6XS, England, (Telephone in U.S. (888) 330-8477), (Fax in U.S. (800) 672-2054), www.palgrave.com; *The Statesman's Yearbook 2008.*

PennWell Corporation, 1421 South Sheridan Road, Tulsa, OK 74112, (918) 835-3161, www.pennwell.com; *International Petroleum Encyclopedia 2007* and *Oil Gas Journal Latinoamericana.*

U.S. Department of Energy (DOE), Energy Information Administration (EIA), 1000 Independence Avenue, SW, Washington, DC 20585, (202) 586-8800, www.eia.doe.gov; *International Energy Annual 2004* and *International Energy Outlook 2006.*

United Nations Conference on Trade and Development (UNCTAD), DC2-1120, United Nations, New York, NY 10017, (212) 963-0027, www.unctad.org; *UNCTAD Commodity Yearbook.*

United Nations Food and Agricultural Organization (FAO), Viale delle Terme di Caracalla, 00100 Rome, Italy, (Dial from U.S. (202) 653-2400), (Fax from U.S. (202) 653 5760), www.fao.org; *The State of Food and Agriculture (SOFA) 2006.*

United Nations Statistics Division, New York, NY 10017, (800) 253-9646, Fax: (212) 963-4116, http://unstats.un.org; *Statistical Yearbook.*

ARGENTINA - PLASTICS INDUSTRY AND TRADE

United Nations Statistics Division, New York, NY 10017, (800) 253-9646, Fax: (212) 963-4116, http://unstats.un.org; *Statistical Yearbook.*

ARGENTINA - POLITICAL SCIENCE

Central Intelligence Agency, Office of Public Affairs, Washington, DC 20505, (703) 482-0623, Fax: (703) 482-1739, www.cia.gov; *The World Factbook.*

Inter-American Development Bank (IDB), 1300 New York Avenue, NW, Washington, DC 20577, (202) 623-1000, Fax: (202) 623-3096, www.iadb.org; *The Politics of Policies: Economic and Social Progress in Latin America - 2006 Report.*

International Monetary Fund (IMF), 700 Nineteenth Street, NW, Washington, DC 20431, (202) 623-7000, Fax: (202) 623-4661, www.imf.org; *Government Finance Statistics Yearbook (2008 Edition)* and *International Financial Statistics Yearbook 2007.*

Palgrave Macmillan Ltd., Houndmills, Basingstoke, Hampshire, RG21 6XS, England, (Telephone in U.S. (888) 330-8477), (Fax in U.S. (800) 672-2054), www.palgrave.com; *The Statesman's Yearbook 2008.*

Taylor and Francis Group, An Informa Business, 2 Park Square, Milton Park, Abingdon, Oxford OX14 4RN, United Kingdom, (Dial from U.S. (212) 216-7800), (Fax from U.S. (212) 564-7854), www.tandf.co.uk; *The Europa World Year Book.*

UCLA Latin American Institute, 10343 Bunche Hall, Box 951447, Los Angeles, CA 90095-1447, (310) 825-4571, Fax: (310) 206-6859, www.international.ucla.edu/lac; *Statistical Abstract of Latin America.*

United Nations Statistics Division, New York, NY 10017, (800) 253-9646, Fax: (212) 963-4116, http://unstats.un.org; *National Accounts Statistics: Compendium of Income Distribution Statistics.*

The World Bank, 1818 H Street, NW, Washington, DC 20433, (202) 473-1000, Fax: (202) 477-6391, www.worldbank.org; *World Development Indicators (WDI) 2008* and *World Development Report 2008.*

ARGENTINA - POPULATION

Central Intelligence Agency, Office of Public Affairs, Washington, DC 20505, (703) 482-0623, Fax: (703) 482-1739, www.cia.gov; *The World Factbook.*

Economist Intelligence Unit, 111 West 57th Street, New York, NY 10019, (212) 554-0600, Fax: (212) 586-1181, www.eiu.com; *Argentina Country Report* and *Business Latin America.*

Euromonitor International, Inc., 224 S. Michigan Avenue, Suite 1500, Chicago, IL 60604, (312) 922-1115, Fax: (312) 922-1157, www.euromonitor.com; *International Marketing Data and Statistics 2008* and *The World Economic Factbook 2008.*

Inter-American Development Bank (IDB), 1300 New York Avenue, NW, Washington, DC 20577, (202) 623-1000, Fax: (202) 623-3096, www.iadb.org; *The Politics of Policies: Economic and Social Progress in Latin America - 2006 Report.*

International Labour Office, I.L.O. Publications, 4 route des Morillons, CH-1211 Geneva 22, Switzerland, (Telephone in U.S. (202) 653-7652), (Fax in U.S. (202) 653-7687), www.ilo.org; *Yearbook of Labour Statistics 2006.*

M.E. Sharpe, 80 Business Park Drive, Armonk, NY 10504, (800) 541-6563, Fax: (914) 273-2106, www.mesharpe.com; *The Illustrated Book of World Rankings.*

Organization of American States (OAS), 17th Street Constitution Avenue NW, Washington, DC 20006, (202) 458-3000, www.oas.org; *The OAS in Transition: 1994-2004.*

Palgrave Macmillan Ltd., Houndmills, Basingstoke, Hampshire, RG21 6XS, England, (Telephone in U.S. (888) 330-8477), (Fax in U.S. (800) 672-2054), www.palgrave.com; *The Statesman's Yearbook 2008.*

Taylor and Francis Group, An Informa Business, 2 Park Square, Milton Park, Abingdon, Oxford OX14 4RN, United Kingdom, (Dial from U.S. (212) 216-7800), (Fax from U.S. (212) 564-7854), www.tandf.co.uk; *The Europa World Year Book.*

U.S. Department of State (DOS), 2201 C Street NW, Washington, DC 20520, (202) 647-4000, www.state.gov; *World Military Expenditures and Arms Transfers (WMEAT).*

UCLA Latin American Institute, 10343 Bunche Hall, Box 951447, Los Angeles, CA 90095-1447, (310) 825-4571, Fax: (310) 206-6859, www.international.ucla.edu/lac; *Statistical Abstract of Latin America.*

United Nations Statistics Division, New York, NY 10017, (800) 253-9646, Fax: (212) 963-4116, http://unstats.un.org; *Demographic Yearbook; Human Development Report 2006; Statistical Yearbook; Statistical Yearbook for Latin America and the Caribbean 2004;* and *World Statistics Pocketbook.*

The World Bank, 1818 H Street, NW, Washington, DC 20433, (202) 473-1000, Fax: (202) 477-6391, www.worldbank.org; *Argentina; The World Bank Atlas 2003-2004;* and *World Development Report 2008.*

World Health Organization (WHO), Avenue Appia 20, 1211 Geneve 27, Switzerland, (Telephone in U.S. (212) 331-9081), www.who.int; *World Health Report 2006.*

ARGENTINA - POPULATION DENSITY

Central Intelligence Agency, Office of Public Affairs, Washington, DC 20505, (703) 482-0623, Fax: (703) 482-1739, www.cia.gov; *The World Factbook.*

Euromonitor International, Inc., 224 S. Michigan Avenue, Suite 1500, Chicago, IL 60604, (312) 922-1115, Fax: (312) 922-1157, www.euromonitor.com; *International Marketing Data and Statistics 2008* and *The World Economic Factbook 2008.*

Inter-American Development Bank (IDB), 1300 New York Avenue, NW, Washington, DC 20577, (202) 623-1000, Fax: (202) 623-3096, www.iadb.org; *The Politics of Policies: Economic and Social Progress in Latin America - 2006 Report.*

M.E. Sharpe, 80 Business Park Drive, Armonk, NY 10504, (800) 541-6563, Fax: (914) 273-2106, www.mesharpe.com; *The Illustrated Book of World Rankings.*

Palgrave Macmillan Ltd., Houndmills, Basingstoke, Hampshire, RG21 6XS, England, (Telephone in U.S. (888) 330-8477), (Fax in U.S. (800) 672-2054), www.palgrave.com; *The Statesman's Yearbook 2008.*

Taylor and Francis Group, An Informa Business, 2 Park Square, Milton Park, Abingdon, Oxford OX14 4RN, United Kingdom, (Dial from U.S. (212) 216-7800), (Fax from U.S. (212) 564-7854), www.tandf.co.uk; *The Europa World Year Book.*

United Nations Food and Agricultural Organization (FAO), Viale delle Terme di Caracalla, 00100 Rome, Italy, (Dial from U.S. (202) 653-2400), (Fax from U.S. (202) 653 5760), www.fao.org; *The State of Food and Agriculture (SOFA) 2006.*

United Nations Statistics Division, New York, NY 10017, (800) 253-9646, Fax: (212) 963-4116, http://unstats.un.org; *Statistical Yearbook.*

The World Bank, 1818 H Street, NW, Washington, DC 20433, (202) 473-1000, Fax: (202) 477-6391, www.worldbank.org; *Argentina* and *World Development Report 2008.*

ARGENTINA - POSTAL SERVICE

M.E. Sharpe, 80 Business Park Drive, Armonk, NY 10504, (800) 541-6563, Fax: (914) 273-2106, www.mesharpe.com; *The Illustrated Book of World Rankings.*

United Nations Statistics Division, New York, NY 10017, (800) 253-9646, Fax: (212) 963-4116, http://unstats.un.org; *Statistical Yearbook.*

ARGENTINA - POWER RESOURCES

Economist Intelligence Unit, 111 West 57th Street, New York, NY 10019, (212) 554-0600, Fax: (212) 586-1181, www.eiu.com; *Business Latin America.*

Euromonitor International, Inc., 224 S. Michigan Avenue, Suite 1500, Chicago, IL 60604, (312) 922-1115, Fax: (312) 922-1157, www.euromonitor.com; *International Marketing Data and Statistics 2008; The World Economic Factbook 2008;* and *World Marketing Data and Statistics.*

M.E. Sharpe, 80 Business Park Drive, Armonk, NY 10504, (800) 541-6563, Fax: (914) 273-2106, www.mesharpe.com; *The Illustrated Book of World Rankings.*

Organisation for Economic Cooperation and Development (OECD), 2 rue Andre Pascal, F-75775 Paris Cedex 16, France, (Telephone in U.S. (202) 785-6323), (Fax in U.S. (202) 785-0350), www.oecd.org; *World Energy Outlook 2007.*

Palgrave Macmillan Ltd., Houndmills, Basingstoke, Hampshire, RG21 6XS, England, (Telephone in U.S. (888) 330-8477), (Fax in U.S. (800) 672-2054), www.palgrave.com; *The Statesman's Yearbook 2008.*

Platts, 2 Penn Plaza, 25th Floor, New York, NY 10121-2298, (212) 904-3070, www.platts.com; *Energy Economist.*

U.S. Department of Energy (DOE), Energy Information Administration (EIA), 1000 Independence Avenue, SW, Washington, DC 20585, (202) 586-8800, www.eia.doe.gov; *International Energy Annual 2004* and *International Energy Outlook 2006.*

UCLA Latin American Institute, 10343 Bunche Hall, Box 951447, Los Angeles, CA 90095-1447, (310) 825-4571, Fax: (310) 206-6859, www.international.ucla.edu/lac; *Statistical Abstract of Latin America.*

United Nations Food and Agricultural Organization (FAO), Viale delle Terme di Caracalla, 00100 Rome, Italy, (Dial from U.S. (202) 653-2400), (Fax from U.S. (202) 653 5760), www.fao.org; *The State of Food and Agriculture (SOFA) 2006.*

United Nations Statistics Division, New York, NY 10017, (800) 253-9646, Fax: (212) 963-4116, http://unstats.un.org; *Energy Statistics Yearbook 2003; Human Development Report 2006; Statistical Yearbook; Statistical Yearbook for Latin America and the Caribbean 2004;* and *World Statistics Pocketbook.*

The World Bank, 1818 H Street, NW, Washington, DC 20433, (202) 473-1000, Fax: (202) 477-6391, www.worldbank.org; *The World Bank Atlas 2003-2004* and *World Development Report 2008.*

ARGENTINA - PRICES

Economist Intelligence Unit, 111 West 57th Street, New York, NY 10019, (212) 554-0600, Fax: (212) 586-1181, www.eiu.com; *Business Latin America.*

Euromonitor International, Inc., 224 S. Michigan Avenue, Suite 1500, Chicago, IL 60604, (312) 922-1115, Fax: (312) 922-1157, www.euromonitor.com; *World Marketing Data and Statistics.*

International Labour Office, I.L.O. Publications, 4 route des Morillons, CH-1211 Geneva 22, Switzerland, (Telephone in U.S. (202) 653-7652), (Fax in U.S. (202) 653-7687), www.ilo.org; *Yearbook of Labour Statistics 2006.*

International Lead and Zinc Study Group (ILZSG), Rua Almirante Barroso 38, 5th Floor, Lisbon 1000 - 013, Portugal, www.ilzsg.org; Interactive Statistical Database.

International Monetary Fund (IMF), 700 Nineteenth Street, NW, Washington, DC 20431, (202) 623-7000, Fax: (202) 623-4661, www.imf.org; *International Financial Statistics Yearbook 2007.*

M.E. Sharpe, 80 Business Park Drive, Armonk, NY 10504, (800) 541-6563, Fax: (914) 273-2106, www.mesharpe.com; *The Illustrated Book of World Rankings.*

Organization of American States (OAS), 17th Street Constitution Avenue NW, Washington, DC 20006, (202) 458-3000, www.oas.org; *The OAS in Transition: 1994-2004.*

United Nations Food and Agricultural Organization (FAO), Viale delle Terme di Caracalla, 00100 Rome, Italy, (Dial from U.S. (202) 653-2400), (Fax from U.S. (202) 653 5760), www.fao.org; *FAO Production Yearbook 2002* and *The State of Food and Agriculture (SOFA) 2006.*

United Nations Statistics Division, New York, NY 10017, (800) 253-9646, Fax: (212) 963-4116, http://unstats.un.org; *Statistical Yearbook for Latin America and the Caribbean 2004.*

The World Bank, 1818 H Street, NW, Washington, DC 20433, (202) 473-1000, Fax: (202) 477-6391, www.worldbank.org; *Argentina.*

ARGENTINA - PROFESSIONS

UCLA Latin American Institute, 10343 Bunche Hall, Box 951447, Los Angeles, CA 90095-1447, (310) 825-4571, Fax: (310) 206-6859, www.international.ucla.edu/lac; *Statistical Abstract of Latin America.*

United Nations Statistics Division, New York, NY 10017, (800) 253-9646, Fax: (212) 963-4116, http://unstats.un.org; *Statistical Yearbook.*

ARGENTINA - PUBLIC HEALTH

Economist Intelligence Unit, 111 West 57th Street, New York, NY 10019, (212) 554-0600, Fax: (212) 586-1181, www.eiu.com; *Business Latin America.*

Euromonitor International, Inc., 224 S. Michigan Avenue, Suite 1500, Chicago, IL 60604, (312) 922-1115, Fax: (312) 922-1157, www.euromonitor.com; *World Health Databook 2007/2008* and *World Marketing Data and Statistics.*

M.E. Sharpe, 80 Business Park Drive, Armonk, NY 10504, (800) 541-6563, Fax: (914) 273-2106, www.mesharpe.com; *The Illustrated Book of World Rankings.*

Palgrave Macmillan Ltd., Houndmills, Basingstoke, Hampshire, RG21 6XS, England, (Telephone in U.S. (888) 330-8477), (Fax in U.S. (800) 672-2054), www.palgrave.com; *The Statesman's Yearbook 2008.*

UCLA Latin American Institute, 10343 Bunche Hall, Box 951447, Los Angeles, CA 90095-1447, (310) 825-4571, Fax: (310) 206-6859, www.international.ucla.edu/lac; *Statistical Abstract of Latin America.*

UNICEF, 3 United Nations Plaza, New York, NY 10017, (800) 253-9646, Fax: (212) 887-7465, www.unicef.org; *The State of the World's Children 2008.*

United Nations Statistics Division, New York, NY 10017, (800) 253-9646, Fax: (212) 963-4116, http://unstats.un.org; *Human Development Report 2006* and *Statistical Yearbook.*

The World Bank, 1818 H Street, NW, Washington, DC 20433, (202) 473-1000, Fax: (202) 477-6391, www.worldbank.org; *Argentina* and *World Development Report 2008.*

World Health Organization (WHO), Avenue Appia 20, 1211 Geneve 27, Switzerland, (Telephone in U.S. (212) 331-9081), www.who.int; The WHO Global Atlas of Infectious Diseases and *World Health Report 2006.*

ARGENTINA - PUBLIC UTILITIES

UCLA Latin American Institute, 10343 Bunche Hall, Box 951447, Los Angeles, CA 90095-1447, (310) 825-4571, Fax: (310) 206-6859, www.international.ucla.edu/lac; *Statistical Abstract of Latin America.*

ARGENTINA - PUBLISHERS AND PUBLISHING

Palgrave Macmillan Ltd., Houndmills, Basingstoke, Hampshire, RG21 6XS, England, (Telephone in U.S. (888) 330-8477), (Fax in U.S. (800) 672-2054), www.palgrave.com; *The Statesman's Yearbook 2008.*

Taylor and Francis Group, An Informa Business, 2 Park Square, Milton Park, Abingdon, Oxford OX14 4RN, United Kingdom, (Dial from U.S. (212) 216-7800), (Fax from U.S. (212) 564-7854), www.tandf.co.uk; *The Europa World Year Book.*

UNESCO Institute for Statistics, C.P. 6128 Succursale Centre-Ville, Montreal, Quebec, H3C 3J7 Canada, (Dial from U.S. (514) 343-6880), (Fax from U.S. (514) 343 6882), www.uis.unesco.org; *Statistical Tables.*

ARGENTINA - RADIO BROADCASTING

Palgrave Macmillan Ltd., Houndmills, Basingstoke, Hampshire, RG21 6XS, England, (Telephone in U.S. (888) 330-8477), (Fax in U.S. (800) 672-2054), www.palgrave.com; *The Statesman's Yearbook 2008.*

ARGENTINA - RAILROADS

Economist Intelligence Unit, 111 West 57th Street, New York, NY 10019, (212) 554-0600, Fax: (212) 586-1181, www.eiu.com; *Business Latin America.*

Jane's Information Group, 110 North Royal Street, Suite 200, Alexandria, VA 22314, (703) 683-3700, Fax: (800) 836-0297, www.janes.com; *Jane's World Railways.*

Palgrave Macmillan Ltd., Houndmills, Basingstoke, Hampshire, RG21 6XS, England, (Telephone in U.S. (888) 330-8477), (Fax in U.S. (800) 672-2054), www.palgrave.com; *The Statesman's Yearbook 2008.*

Taylor and Francis Group, An Informa Business, 2 Park Square, Milton Park, Abingdon, Oxford OX14 4RN, United Kingdom, (Dial from U.S. (212) 216-7800), (Fax from U.S. (212) 564-7854), www.tandf.co.uk; *The Europa World Year Book.*

United Nations Statistics Division, New York, NY 10017, (800) 253-9646, Fax: (212) 963-4116, http://unstats.un.org; *Statistical Yearbook.*

ARGENTINA - RELIGION

Central Intelligence Agency, Office of Public Affairs, Washington, DC 20505, (703) 482-0623, Fax: (703) 482-1739, www.cia.gov; *The World Factbook.*

M.E. Sharpe, 80 Business Park Drive, Armonk, NY 10504, (800) 541-6563, Fax: (914) 273-2106, www.mesharpe.com; *The Illustrated Book of World Rankings.*

Palgrave Macmillan Ltd., Houndmills, Basingstoke, Hampshire, RG21 6XS, England, (Telephone in U.S. (888) 330-8477), (Fax in U.S. (800) 672-2054), www.palgrave.com; *The Statesman's Yearbook 2008.*

UCLA Latin American Institute, 10343 Bunche Hall, Box 951447, Los Angeles, CA 90095-1447, (310) 825-4571, Fax: (310) 206-6859, www.international.ucla.edu/lac; *Statistical Abstract of Latin America.*

ARGENTINA - RENT CHARGES

International Labour Office, I.L.O. Publications, 4 route des Morillons, CH-1211 Geneva 22, Switzerland, (Telephone in U.S. (202) 653-7652), (Fax in U.S. (202) 653-7687), www.ilo.org; *Yearbook of Labour Statistics 2006.*

ARGENTINA - RESERVES (ACCOUNTING)

Economist Intelligence Unit, 111 West 57th Street, New York, NY 10019, (212) 554-0600, Fax: (212) 586-1181, www.eiu.com; *Business Latin America.*

Euromonitor International, Inc., 224 S. Michigan Avenue, Suite 1500, Chicago, IL 60604, (312) 922-1115, Fax: (312) 922-1157, www.euromonitor.com; *International Marketing Data and Statistics 2008.*

Inter-American Development Bank (IDB), 1300 New York Avenue, NW, Washington, DC 20577, (202) 623-1000, Fax: (202) 623-3096, www.iadb.org; *The Politics of Policies: Economic and Social Progress in Latin America - 2006 Report.*

Organization of American States (OAS), 17th Street Constitution Avenue NW, Washington, DC 20006, (202) 458-3000, www.oas.org; *The OAS in Transition: 1994-2004.*

The World Bank, 1818 H Street, NW, Washington, DC 20433, (202) 473-1000, Fax: (202) 477-6391, www.worldbank.org; *World Development Indicators (WDI) 2008.*

ARGENTINA - RETAIL TRADE

Euromonitor International, Inc., 224 S. Michigan Avenue, Suite 1500, Chicago, IL 60604, (312) 922-1115, Fax: (312) 922-1157, www.euromonitor.com; *Retail Trade International 2007* and *World Marketing Data and Statistics.*

Inter-American Development Bank (IDB), 1300 New York Avenue, NW, Washington, DC 20577, (202) 623-1000, Fax: (202) 623-3096, www.iadb.org; *The Politics of Policies: Economic and Social Progress in Latin America - 2006 Report.*

ARGENTINA - RICE PRODUCTION

See ARGENTINA - CROPS

ARGENTINA - ROADS

Central Intelligence Agency, Office of Public Affairs, Washington, DC 20505, (703) 482-0623, Fax: (703) 482-1739, www.cia.gov; *The World Factbook.*

Economist Intelligence Unit, 111 West 57th Street, New York, NY 10019, (212) 554-0600, Fax: (212) 586-1181, www.eiu.com; *Business Latin America.*

International Road Federation (IFR), Madison Place, 500 Montgomery Street, 5th Floor, Alexandria, VA 22314, (703) 535-1001, Fax: (703) 535-1007, www.irfnet.org; *World Road Statistics 2006.*

Palgrave Macmillan Ltd., Houndmills, Basingstoke, Hampshire, RG21 6XS, England, (Telephone in U.S. (888) 330-8477), (Fax in U.S. (800) 672-2054), www.palgrave.com; *The Statesman's Yearbook 2008.*

ARGENTINA - RUBBER INDUSTRY AND TRADE

International Rubber Study Group (IRSG), 1st Floor, Heron House, 109/115 Wembley Hill Road, Wembley, Middlesex HA9 8DA, United Kingdom, www.rubberstudy.com; *Rubber Statistical Bulletin; Summary of World Rubber Statistics 2005; World Rubber Statistics Handbook (Volume 6, 1975-2001);* and *World Rubber Statistics Historic Handbook.*

M.E. Sharpe, 80 Business Park Drive, Armonk, NY 10504, (800) 541-6563, Fax: (914) 273-2106, www.mesharpe.com; *The Illustrated Book of World Rankings.*

United Nations Statistics Division, New York, NY 10017, (800) 253-9646, Fax: (212) 963-4116, http://unstats.un.org; *Statistical Yearbook.*

ARGENTINA - RYE PRODUCTION

See ARGENTINA - CROPS

ARGENTINA - SAFFLOWER SEED PRODUCTION

See ARGENTINA - CROPS

ARGENTINA - SALT PRODUCTION

See ARGENTINA - MINERAL INDUSTRIES

ARGENTINA - SHEEP

See ARGENTINA - LIVESTOCK

ARGENTINA - SHIPPING

Inter-American Development Bank (IDB), 1300 New York Avenue, NW, Washington, DC 20577, (202) 623-1000, Fax: (202) 623-3096, www.iadb.org; *The Politics of Policies: Economic and Social Progress in Latin America - 2006 Report.*

Lloyd's Register - Fairplay, 8410 N.W. 53rd Terrace, Suite 207, Miami FL 33166, (305) 718-9929, Fax: (305) 718-9663, www.lrfairplay.com; *Register of Ships 2007-2008; World Casualty Statistics 2007; World Fleet Statistics 2006; World Marine Propulsion Report 2006-2010; World Shipbuilding Statistics 2007;* and The World Shipping Encyclopaedia.

Palgrave Macmillan Ltd., Houndmills, Basingstoke, Hampshire, RG21 6XS, England, (Telephone in U.S. (888) 330-8477), (Fax in U.S. (800) 672-2054), www.palgrave.com; *The Statesman's Yearbook 2008.*

Taylor and Francis Group, An Informa Business, 2 Park Square, Milton Park, Abingdon, Oxford OX14 4RN, United Kingdom, (Dial from U.S. (212) 216-7800), (Fax from U.S. (212) 564-7854), www.tandf.co.uk; *The Europa World Year Book.*

U.S. Department of Transportation (DOT), Maritime Administration (MARAD), West Building, Southeast Federal Center, 1200 New Jersey Avenue, SE, Washington, DC 20590, (800) 99-MARAD, www.marad.dot.gov; *World Merchant Fleet 2005.*

United Nations Statistics Division, New York, NY 10017, (800) 253-9646, Fax: (212) 963-4116, http://unstats.un.org; *Statistical Yearbook.*

ARGENTINA - SILVER PRODUCTION

See ARGENTINA - MINERAL INDUSTRIES

ARGENTINA - SOCIAL ECOLOGY

M.E. Sharpe, 80 Business Park Drive, Armonk, NY 10504, (800) 541-6563, Fax: (914) 273-2106, www.mesharpe.com; *The Illustrated Book of World Rankings.*

UCLA Latin American Institute, 10343 Bunche Hall, Box 951447, Los Angeles, CA 90095-1447, (310) 825-4571, Fax: (310) 206-6859, www.international.ucla.edu/lac; *Statistical Abstract of Latin America.*

United Nations Statistics Division, New York, NY 10017, (800) 253-9646, Fax: (212) 963-4116, http://unstats.un.org; *World Statistics Pocketbook.*

ARGENTINA - SOCIAL SECURITY

Inter-American Development Bank (IDB), 1300 New York Avenue, NW, Washington, DC 20577, (202) 623-1000, Fax: (202) 623-3096, www.iadb.org; *The Politics of Policies: Economic and Social Progress in Latin America - 2006 Report.*

International Monetary Fund (IMF), 700 Nineteenth Street, NW, Washington, DC 20431, (202) 623-7000, Fax: (202) 623-4661, www.imf.org; *Government Finance Statistics Yearbook (2008 Edition).*

United Nations Statistics Division, New York, NY 10017, (800) 253-9646, Fax: (212) 963-4116, http://unstats.un.org; *National Accounts Statistics: Compendium of Income Distribution Statistics.*

ARGENTINA - SOYBEAN PRODUCTION

See ARGENTINA - CROPS

ARGENTINA - STEEL PRODUCTION

See ARGENTINA - MINERAL INDUSTRIES

ARGENTINA - SUGAR PRODUCTION

See ARGENTINA - CROPS

ARGENTINA - SULPHUR PRODUCTION

See ARGENTINA - MINERAL INDUSTRIES

ARGENTINA - TAXATION

Inter-American Development Bank (IDB), 1300 New York Avenue, NW, Washington, DC 20577, (202) 623-1000, Fax: (202) 623-3096, www.iadb.org; *The Politics of Policies: Economic and Social Progress in Latin America - 2006 Report.*

International Monetary Fund (IMF), 700 Nineteenth Street, NW, Washington, DC 20431, (202) 623-7000, Fax: (202) 623-4661, www.imf.org; *Government Finance Statistics Yearbook (2008 Edition).*

Taylor and Francis Group, An Informa Business, 2 Park Square, Milton Park, Abingdon, Oxford OX14 4RN, United Kingdom, (Dial from U.S. (212) 216-7800), (Fax from U.S. (212) 564-7854), www.tandf.co.uk; *The Europa World Year Book.*

United Nations Statistics Division, New York, NY 10017, (800) 253-9646, Fax: (212) 963-4116, http://unstats.un.org; *Statistical Yearbook for Latin America and the Caribbean 2004.*

The World Bank, 1818 H Street, NW, Washington, DC 20433, (202) 473-1000, Fax: (202) 477-6391, www.worldbank.org; *World Development Indicators (WDI) 2008.*

ARGENTINA - TEA PRODUCTION

See ARGENTINA - CROPS

ARGENTINA - TELEPHONE

Economist Intelligence Unit, 111 West 57th Street, New York, NY 10019, (212) 554-0600, Fax: (212) 586-1181, www.eiu.com; *Business Latin America.*

International Telecommunication Union (ITU), Place des Nations, 1211 Geneva 20, Switzerland, www.itu.int; World Telecommunication Indicators Database.

Palgrave Macmillan Ltd., Houndmills, Basingstoke, Hampshire, RG21 6XS, England, (Telephone in U.S. (888) 330-8477), (Fax in U.S. (800) 672-2054), www.palgrave.com; *The Statesman's Yearbook 2008.*

Taylor and Francis Group, An Informa Business, 2 Park Square, Milton Park, Abingdon, Oxford OX14 4RN, United Kingdom, (Dial from U.S. (212) 216-7800), (Fax from U.S. (212) 564-7854), www.tandf.co.uk; *The Europa World Year Book.*

United Nations Statistics Division, New York, NY 10017, (800) 253-9646, Fax: (212) 963-4116, http://unstats.un.org; *Statistical Yearbook* and *World Statistics Pocketbook.*

ARGENTINA - TELEVISION - RECEIVERS AND RECEPTION

Euromonitor International, Inc., 224 S. Michigan Avenue, Suite 1500, Chicago, IL 60604, (312) 922-1115, Fax: (312) 922-1157, www.euromonitor.com; *Retail Trade International 2007.*

International Monetary Fund (IMF), 700 Nineteenth Street, NW, Washington, DC 20431, (202) 623-7000, Fax: (202) 623-4661, www.imf.org; *International Financial Statistics Yearbook 2007.*

M.E. Sharpe, 80 Business Park Drive, Armonk, NY 10504, (800) 541-6563, Fax: (914) 273-2106, www.mesharpe.com; *The Illustrated Book of World Rankings.*

Palgrave Macmillan Ltd., Houndmills, Basingstoke, Hampshire, RG21 6XS, England, (Telephone in U.S. (888) 330-8477), (Fax in U.S. (800) 672-2054), www.palgrave.com; *The Statesman's Yearbook 2008.*

United Nations Conference on Trade and Development (UNCTAD), DC2-1120, United Nations, New York, NY 10017, (212) 963-0027, www.unctad.org; *UNCTAD Commodity Yearbook.*

United Nations Statistics Division, New York, NY 10017, (800) 253-9646, Fax: (212) 963-4116, http://unstats.un.org; *Statistical Yearbook.*

ARGENTINA - TEXTILE INDUSTRY

United Nations Statistics Division, New York, NY 10017, (800) 253-9646, Fax: (212) 963-4116, http://unstats.un.org; *Statistical Yearbook.*

ARGENTINA - TIN PRODUCTION

See ARGENTINA - MINERAL INDUSTRIES

ARGENTINA - TIRE INDUSTRY

United Nations Statistics Division, New York, NY 10017, (800) 253-9646, Fax: (212) 963-4116, http://unstats.un.org; *Statistical Yearbook.*

ARGENTINA - TOBACCO INDUSTRY

Foreign Agricultural Service (FAS), U.S. Department of Agriculture (USDA), 1400 Independence Avenue, SW, Washington, DC 20250, (202) 720-3935, www.fas.usda.gov; *Tobacco: World Markets and Trade.*

M.E. Sharpe, 80 Business Park Drive, Armonk, NY 10504, (800) 541-6563, Fax: (914) 273-2106, www.mesharpe.com; *The Illustrated Book of World Rankings.*

United Nations Statistics Division, New York, NY 10017, (800) 253-9646, Fax: (212) 963-4116, http://unstats.un.org; *Statistical Yearbook.*

ARGENTINA - TOURISM

Economist Intelligence Unit, 111 West 57th Street, New York, NY 10019, (212) 554-0600, Fax: (212) 586-1181, www.eiu.com; *Business Latin America.*

Euromonitor International, Inc., 224 S. Michigan Avenue, Suite 1500, Chicago, IL 60604, (312) 922-1115, Fax: (312) 922-1157, www.euromonitor.com; *The World Economic Factbook 2008* and *World Marketing Data and Statistics.*

M.E. Sharpe, 80 Business Park Drive, Armonk, NY 10504, (800) 541-6563, Fax: (914) 273-2106, www.mesharpe.com; *The Illustrated Book of World Rankings.*

Palgrave Macmillan Ltd., Houndmills, Basingstoke, Hampshire, RG21 6XS, England, (Telephone in U.S. (888) 330-8477), (Fax in U.S. (800) 672-2054), www.palgrave.com; *The Statesman's Yearbook 2008.*

Taylor and Francis Group, An Informa Business, 2 Park Square, Milton Park, Abingdon, Oxford OX14 4RN, United Kingdom, (Dial from U.S. (212) 216-7800), (Fax from U.S. (212) 564-7854), www.tandf.co.uk; *The Europa World Year Book.*

UCLA Latin American Institute, 10343 Bunche Hall, Box 951447, Los Angeles, CA 90095-1447, (310) 825-4571, Fax: (310) 206-6859, www.international.ucla.edu/lac; *Statistical Abstract of Latin America.*

United Nations Statistics Division, New York, NY 10017, (800) 253-9646, Fax: (212) 963-4116, http://unstats.un.org; *Statistical Yearbook* and *Statistical Yearbook for Latin America and the Caribbean 2004.*

United Nations World Tourism Organization (UNWTO), Capitan Haya 42, 28020 Madrid, Spain, www.world-tourism.org; *Yearbook of Tourism Statistics.*

The World Bank, 1818 H Street, NW, Washington, DC 20433, (202) 473-1000, Fax: (202) 477-6391, www.worldbank.org; *Argentina.*

ARGENTINA - TRADE

See ARGENTINA - INTERNATIONAL TRADE

ARGENTINA - TRANSPORTATION

Central Intelligence Agency, Office of Public Affairs, Washington, DC 20505, (703) 482-0623, Fax: (703) 482-1739, www.cia.gov; *The World Factbook.*

Economist Intelligence Unit, 111 West 57th Street, New York, NY 10019, (212) 554-0600, Fax: (212) 586-1181, www.eiu.com; *Business Latin America.*

Euromonitor International, Inc., 224 S. Michigan Avenue, Suite 1500, Chicago, IL 60604, (312) 922-1115, Fax: (312) 922-1157, www.euromonitor.com; *International Marketing Data and Statistics 2008* and *World Marketing Data and Statistics.*

Inter-American Development Bank (IDB), 1300 New York Avenue, NW, Washington, DC 20577, (202) 623-1000, Fax: (202) 623-3096, www.iadb.org; *The Politics of Policies: Economic and Social Progress in Latin America - 2006 Report.*

M.E. Sharpe, 80 Business Park Drive, Armonk, NY 10504, (800) 541-6563, Fax: (914) 273-2106, www.mesharpe.com; *The Illustrated Book of World Rankings.*

Palgrave Macmillan Ltd., Houndmills, Basingstoke, Hampshire, RG21 6XS, England, (Telephone in U.S. (888) 330-8477), (Fax in U.S. (800) 672-2054), www.palgrave.com; *The Statesman's Yearbook 2008.*

Taylor and Francis Group, An Informa Business, 2 Park Square, Milton Park, Abingdon, Oxford OX14 4RN, United Kingdom, (Dial from U.S. (212) 216-7800), (Fax from U.S. (212) 564-7854), www.tandf.co.uk; *The Europa World Year Book.*

UCLA Latin American Institute, 10343 Bunche Hall, Box 951447, Los Angeles, CA 90095-1447, (310) 825-4571, Fax: (310) 206-6859, www.international.ucla.edu/lac; *Statistical Abstract of Latin America.*

United Nations Statistics Division, New York, NY 10017, (800) 253-9646, Fax: (212) 963-4116, http://unstats.un.org; *Human Development Report 2006* and *Statistical Yearbook for Latin America and the Caribbean 2004.*

The World Bank, 1818 H Street, NW, Washington, DC 20433, (202) 473-1000, Fax: (202) 477-6391, www.worldbank.org; *Argentina.*

ARGENTINA - TRAVEL COSTS

International Monetary Fund (IMF), 700 Nineteenth Street, NW, Washington, DC 20431, (202) 623-7000, Fax: (202) 623-4661, www.imf.org; *Government Finance Statistics Yearbook (2008 Edition).*

ARGENTINA - TURKEYS

See ARGENTINA - LIVESTOCK

ARGENTINA - UNEMPLOYMENT

Central Intelligence Agency, Office of Public Affairs, Washington, DC 20505, (703) 482-0623, Fax: (703) 482-1739, www.cia.gov; *The World Factbook.*

Economist Intelligence Unit, 111 West 57th Street, New York, NY 10019, (212) 554-0600, Fax: (212) 586-1181, www.eiu.com; *Business Latin America.*

Euromonitor International, Inc., 224 S. Michigan Avenue, Suite 1500, Chicago, IL 60604, (312) 922-1115, Fax: (312) 922-1157, www.euromonitor.com; *International Marketing Data and Statistics 2008.*

International Labour Office, I.L.O. Publications, 4 route des Morillons, CH-1211 Geneva 22, Switzerland, (Telephone in U.S. (202) 653-7652), (Fax in U.S. (202) 653-7687), www.ilo.org; *Yearbook of Labour Statistics 2006.*

Organization of American States (OAS), 17th Street Constitution Avenue NW, Washington, DC 20006, (202) 458-3000, www.oas.org; *The OAS in Transition: 1994-2004.*

UCLA Latin American Institute, 10343 Bunche Hall, Box 951447, Los Angeles, CA 90095-1447, (310) 825-4571, Fax: (310) 206-6859, www.international.ucla.edu/lac; *Statistical Abstract of Latin America.*

United Nations Statistics Division, New York, NY 10017, (800) 253-9646, Fax: (212) 963-4116, http://unstats.un.org; *Statistical Yearbook.*

ARGENTINA - URANIUM PRODUCTION AND CONSUMPTION

See ARGENTINA - MINERAL INDUSTRIES

ARGENTINA - VITAL STATISTICS

Euromonitor International, Inc., 224 S. Michigan Avenue, Suite 1500, Chicago, IL 60604, (312) 922-1115, Fax: (312) 922-1157, www.euromonitor.com; *International Marketing Data and Statistics 2008.*

Palgrave Macmillan Ltd., Houndmills, Basingstoke, Hampshire, RG21 6XS, England, (Telephone in U.S. (888) 330-8477), (Fax in U.S. (800) 672-2054), www.palgrave.com; *The Statesman's Yearbook 2008.*

United Nations Statistics Division, New York, NY 10017, (800) 253-9646, Fax: (212) 963-4116, http://unstats.un.org; *Statistical Yearbook.*

World Health Organization (WHO), Avenue Appia 20, 1211 Geneve 27, Switzerland, (Telephone in U.S. (212) 331-9081), www.who.int; *World Health Report 2006.*

ARGENTINA - WAGES

International Labour Office, I.L.O. Publications, 4 route des Morillons, CH-1211 Geneva 22, Switzerland, (Telephone in U.S. (202) 653-7652), (Fax in U.S. (202) 653-7687), www.ilo.org; *Yearbook of Labour Statistics 2006.*

UCLA Latin American Institute, 10343 Bunche Hall, Box 951447, Los Angeles, CA 90095-1447, (310) 825-4571, Fax: (310) 206-6859, www.international.ucla.edu/lac; *Statistical Abstract of Latin America.*

United Nations Statistics Division, New York, NY 10017, (800) 253-9646, Fax: (212) 963-4116, http://unstats.un.org; *Statistical Yearbook.*

The World Bank, 1818 H Street, NW, Washington, DC 20433, (202) 473-1000, Fax: (202) 477-6391, www.worldbank.org; *Argentina.*

ARGENTINA - WALNUT PRODUCTION

See ARGENTINA - CROPS

ARGENTINA - WEATHER

See ARGENTINA - CLIMATE

ARGENTINA - WELFARE STATE

Inter-American Development Bank (IDB), 1300 New York Avenue, NW, Washington, DC 20577, (202) 623-1000, Fax: (202) 623-3096, www.iadb.org; *The Politics of Policies: Economic and Social Progress in Latin America - 2006 Report.*

International Monetary Fund (IMF), 700 Nineteenth Street, NW, Washington, DC 20431, (202) 623-7000, Fax: (202) 623-4661, www.imf.org; *Government Finance Statistics Yearbook (2008 Edition).*

Palgrave Macmillan Ltd., Houndmills, Basingstoke, Hampshire, RG21 6XS, England, (Telephone in U.S. (888) 330-8477), (Fax in U.S. (800) 672-2054), www.palgrave.com; *The Statesman's Yearbook 2008.*

ARGENTINA - WHEAT PRODUCTION

See ARGENTINA - CROPS

ARGENTINA - WHOLESALE PRICE INDEXES

Inter-American Development Bank (IDB), 1300 New York Avenue, NW, Washington, DC 20577, (202) 623-1000, Fax: (202) 623-3096, www.iadb.org; *The Politics of Policies: Economic and Social Progress in Latin America - 2006 Report.*

International Monetary Fund (IMF), 700 Nineteenth Street, NW, Washington, DC 20431, (202) 623-7000, Fax: (202) 623-4661, www.imf.org; *International Financial Statistics Yearbook 2007.*

Organization of American States (OAS), 17th Street Constitution Avenue NW, Washington, DC 20006, (202) 458-3000, www.oas.org; *The OAS in Transition: 1994-2004.*

ARGENTINA - WHOLESALE TRADE

Inter-American Development Bank (IDB), 1300 New York Avenue, NW, Washington, DC 20577, (202) 623-1000, Fax: (202) 623-3096, www.iadb.org; *The Politics of Policies: Economic and Social Progress in Latin America - 2006 Report.*

United Nations Statistics Division, New York, NY 10017, (800) 253-9646, Fax: (212) 963-4116, http://unstats.un.org; *Statistical Yearbook.*

ARGENTINA - WINE PRODUCTION

See ARGENTINA - BEVERAGE INDUSTRY

ARGENTINA - WOOD AND WOOD PULP

See ARGENTINA - FORESTS AND FORESTRY

ARGENTINA - WOOL PRODUCTION

See ARGENTINA - TEXTILE INDUSTRY

ARGENTINA - YARN PRODUCTION

See ARGENTINA - TEXTILE INDUSTRY

ARGENTINA - ZINC AND ZINC ORE

See ARGENTINA - MINERAL INDUSTRIES

ARGENTINA - ZOOS

UNESCO Institute for Statistics, C.P. 6128 Succursale Centre-Ville, Montreal, Quebec, H3C 3J7 Canada, (Dial from U.S. (514) 343-6880), (Fax from U.S. (514) 343 6882), www.uis.unesco.org; *Statistical Tables.*

ARIZONA

See also - STATE DATA (FOR INDIVIDUAL STATES)

ARIZONA - STATE DATA CENTERS

Arizona Department of Commerce, PO Box 6029, 1789 W. Jefferson Phoenix, Arizona 85005-6029, (602) 542-3871, Fax: (602) 542-6474, www.workforce.az.gov; State Data Center.

Arizona Rural Policy Institute, The W. A. Franke College of Business, Northern Arizona University, Box 15066, Flagstaff, AZ 86011-5066, Mr. Michael Lainoff, (928) 523-7373, Fax: (928) 523-5990, http://bber.cba.nau.edu; State Data Center.

Arizona State Library, Archives and Public Records, 1700 West Washington, Suite 200, Phoenix, AZ 85007, (602) 926-4035, Fax: (602) 256-7983, www.lib.az.us; State Data Center.

Center for Competitiveness and Prosperity Research, W. P. Carey School of Business, Box 874011, Tempe, AZ 85287-4011, Mr. Dennis Hoffman, (480) 965-3961, Fax: (480) 965-5458, www.cob.asu.edu/seid/cbr; State Data Center.

Economic and Business Research Center, University of Arizona, PO Box 210108, Tucson, AZ 85721-0108, (520) 621-2155, Fax: (520) 621-2150, http://ebr.eller.arizona.edu; State Data Center.

Economic and Business Research, Eller College of Management, The University of Arizona, PO Box 210108, Tucson, AZ 85721-0108, (520) 621-2155, Fax: (520) 621-2150, http://ebr.eller.arizona.edu/; State Data Center.

ARIZONA - PRIMARY STATISTICS SOURCES

Economic and Business Research, Eller College of Management, The University of Arizona, PO Box 210108, Tucson, AZ 85721-0108, (520) 621-2155, Fax: (520) 621-2150, http://ebr.eller.arizona.edu/; *Arizona Economic Indicators Databook; Arizona Statistical Abstract 2003;* and *Arizona's Economy.*

ARKANSAS

See also - STATE DATA (FOR INDIVIDUAL STATES)

Robert Wood Johnson Foundation, PO Box 2316, College Road East and Route 1, Princeton, NJ 08543, (877) 843-7953, www.rwjf.org; *Tracking Progress: The Third Annual Arkansas Assessment.*

ARKANSAS - STATE DATA CENTERS

Arkansas State Library, One Capitol Mall, Little Rock, AR 72201, (501) 682-2550, Fax: (501) 682-1529, www.asl.lib.ar.us; State Data Center.

Institute for Economic Advancement (IEA), University of Arkansas at Little Rock, 2801 South University Avenue, Little Rock, AR 72204-1099, Ms. Sarah Breshears, Senior Research Specialist (501) 569-8531, Fax: (501) 569-8538, www.aiea.ualr.edu/census; State Data Center.

Labor Market Information and Analysis, Department of Workforce Services, PO Box 2981, Little Rock, AR 72203-2981, Mr. Herman Sanders, (501) 682-3197, www.discoverarkansas.net/; State Data Center.

ARKANSAS - PRIMARY STATISTICS SOURCES

Institute for Economic Advancement (IEA), University of Arkansas at Little Rock, 2801 South University Avenue, Little Rock, AR 72204-1099, Ms. Sarah Breshears, Senior Research Specialist (501) 569-8531, Fax: (501) 569-8538, www.aiea.ualr.edu/census; *Arkansas Statistical Abstract 2006* and *Population and Social/Economic Characteristics by County.*

ARMED FORCES

U.S. Department of Defense (DOD), Statistical Information Analysis Division (SIAD), The Pentagon, Washington, DC 20301, (703) 545-6700, http://siadapp.dior.whs.mil/; *Selected Manpower Statistics, Fiscal Year 2005* and unpublished data.

U.S. Department of Transportation (DOT), Maritime Administration (MARAD), West Building, Southeast Federal Center, 1200 New Jersey Avenue, SE, Washington, DC 20590, (800) 99-MARAD, www.marad.dot.gov; *MARAD Annual Report 2006.*

U.S. Library of Congress (LOC), Congressional Research Service (CRS), The Library of Congress, 101 Independence Avenue, SE, Washington, DC 20540-7500, (202) 707-5700, www.loc.gov/crsinfo; *Homeland Security: Coast Guard Operations - Background and Issues for Congress* and *Port and Maritime Security: Background and Issues for Congress.*

U.S. National Guard Bureau, 1411 Jefferson Davis Highway, Arlington, VA 22202-3231, (703) 607-3162, www.ngb.army.mil; *Air National Guard Fact Sheet; Army National Guard Fact Sheet; National Guard and Militias Fact Sheet;* and unpublished data.

ARMED FORCES - FOREIGN COUNTRIES

Central Intelligence Agency, Office of Public Affairs, Washington, DC 20505, (703) 482-0623, Fax: (703) 482-1739, www.cia.gov; *The World Factbook.*

U.S. Department of Defense (DOD), Statistical Information Analysis Division (SIAD), The Pentagon, Washington, DC 20301, (703) 545-6700, http://siadapp.dior.whs.mil/; *Selected Manpower Statistics, Fiscal Year 2005.*

ARMED FORCES - PERSONNEL

U.S. Department of Defense (DOD), Statistical Information Analysis Division (SIAD), The Pentagon, Washington, DC 20301, (703) 545-6700, http://siadapp.dior.whs.mil/; *Selected Manpower Statistics, Fiscal Year 2005.*

U.S. Library of Congress (LOC), Congressional Research Service (CRS), The Library of Congress, 101 Independence Avenue, SE, Washington, DC 20540-7500, (202) 707-5700, www.loc.gov/crsinfo; *American War and Military Operations Casualties: Lists and Statistics* and *United States Military Casualty Statistics: Operation Iraqi Freedom and Operation Enduring Freedom.*

ARMENIA - NATIONAL STATISTICAL OFFICE

National Statistical Service of the Republic of Armenia, Republic Square, 3 Government House, Yerevan 375010, Republic of Armenia, www.armstat.am; National Data Center.

ARMENIA - PRIMARY STATISTICS SOURCES

National Statistical Service of the Republic of Armenia, Republic Square, 3 Government House, Yerevan 375010, Republic of Armenia, www.armstat.am; *Statistical Yearbook of Armenia 2007.*

ARMENIA - ABORTION

United Nations Statistics Division, New York, NY 10017, (800) 253-9646, Fax: (212) 963-4116, http://unstats.un.org; *Trends in Europe and North America: The Statistical Yearbook of the ECE 2005.*

ARMENIA - AGRICULTURE

Academic International Press, PO Box 1111, Gulf Breeze, FL 32562-1111, Fax: (850) 934-0953, www.ai-press.com; *Russia and Eurasia Facts and Figures Annual.*

Economist Intelligence Unit, 111 West 57th Street, New York, NY 10019, (212) 554-0600, Fax: (212) 586-1181, www.eiu.com; *Armenia Country Report.*

Euromonitor International, Inc., 224 S. Michigan Avenue, Suite 1500, Chicago, IL 60604, (312) 922-1115, Fax: (312) 922-1157, www.euromonitor.com; *World Marketing Data and Statistics.*

Palgrave Macmillan Ltd., Houndmills, Basingstoke, Hampshire, RG21 6XS, England, (Telephone in U.S. (888) 330-8477), (Fax in U.S. (800) 672-2054), www.palgrave.com; *The Statesman's Yearbook 2008.*

Taylor and Francis Group, An Informa Business, 2 Park Square, Milton Park, Abingdon, Oxford OX14 4RN, United Kingdom, (Dial from U.S. (212) 216-7800), (Fax from U.S. (212) 564-7854), www.tandf.co.uk; *The Europa World Year Book.*

United Nations Food and Agricultural Organization (FAO), Viale delle Terme di Caracalla, 00100 Rome, Italy, (Dial from U.S. (202) 653-2400), (Fax from U.S. (202) 653 5760), www.fao.org; AQUASTAT; *FAO Production Yearbook 2002; FAO Trade Yearbook;* and *The State of Food and Agriculture (SOFA) 2006.*

United Nations Statistics Division, New York, NY 10017, (800) 253-9646, Fax: (212) 963-4116, http://unstats.un.org; *2004 Industrial Commodity Statistics Yearbook* and *Statistical Yearbook.*

The World Bank, 1818 H Street, NW, Washington, DC 20433, (202) 473-1000, Fax: (202) 477-6391, www.worldbank.org; *Armenia; Statistical Handbook: States of the Former USSR;* and *World Development Indicators (WDI) 2008.*

ARMENIA - AIRLINES

International Civil Aviation Organization (ICAO), External Relations and Public Information Office (EPO), 999 University Street, Montreal, Quebec H3C 5H7, Canada, (Dial from U.S. (514) 954-8219), (Fax from U.S. (514) 954-6077), www.icao.int; *Civil Aviation Statistics of the World.*

Palgrave Macmillan Ltd., Houndmills, Basingstoke, Hampshire, RG21 6XS, England, (Telephone in U.S. (888) 330-8477), (Fax in U.S. (800) 672-2054), www.palgrave.com; *The Statesman's Yearbook 2008.*

United Nations Statistics Division, New York, NY 10017, (800) 253-9646, Fax: (212) 963-4116, http://unstats.un.org; *Statistical Yearbook.*

ARMENIA - AIRPORTS

Central Intelligence Agency, Office of Public Affairs, Washington, DC 20505, (703) 482-0623, Fax: (703) 482-1739, www.cia.gov; *The World Factbook.*

ARMENIA - ARMED FORCES

Academic International Press, PO Box 1111, Gulf Breeze, FL 32562-1111, Fax: (850) 934-0953, www.ai-press.com; *Russia and Eurasia Facts and Figures Annual.*

Central Intelligence Agency, Office of Public Affairs, Washington, DC 20505, (703) 482-0623, Fax: (703) 482-1739, www.cia.gov; *The World Factbook.*

Euromonitor International, Inc., 224 S. Michigan Avenue, Suite 1500, Chicago, IL 60604, (312) 922-1115, Fax: (312) 922-1157, www.euromonitor.com; *World Marketing Data and Statistics.*

International Institute for Strategic Studies (IISS), Arundel House, 13-15 Arundel Street, Temple Place, London WC2R 3DX, England, www.iiss.org; *The Military Balance 2007.*

Palgrave Macmillan Ltd., Houndmills, Basingstoke, Hampshire, RG21 6XS, England, (Telephone in U.S. (888) 330-8477), (Fax in U.S. (800) 672-2054), www.palgrave.com; *The Statesman's Yearbook 2008.*

United Nations Statistics Division, New York, NY 10017, (800) 253-9646, Fax: (212) 963-4116, http://unstats.un.org; *Human Development Report 2006.*

ARMENIA - BALANCE OF PAYMENTS

Taylor and Francis Group, An Informa Business, 2 Park Square, Milton Park, Abingdon, Oxford OX14 4RN, United Kingdom, (Dial from U.S. (212) 216-7800), (Fax from U.S. (212) 564-7854), www.tandf.co.uk; *The Europa World Year Book.*

United Nations Conference on Trade and Development (UNCTAD), DC2-1120, United Nations, New York, NY 10017, (212) 963-0027, www.unctad.org; *Handbook of Statistics 2005.*

The World Bank, 1818 H Street, NW, Washington, DC 20433, (202) 473-1000, Fax: (202) 477-6391, www.worldbank.org; *Armenia; World Development Indicators (WDI) 2008;* and *World Development Report 2008.*

ARMENIA - BANKS AND BANKING

Euromonitor International, Inc., 224 S. Michigan Avenue, Suite 1500, Chicago, IL 60604, (312) 922-1115, Fax: (312) 922-1157, www.euromonitor.com; *World Marketing Data and Statistics.*

ARMENIA - BEVERAGE INDUSTRY

United Nations Statistics Division, New York, NY 10017, (800) 253-9646, Fax: (212) 963-4116, http://unstats.un.org; *Statistical Yearbook.*

ARMENIA - BROADCASTING

Central Intelligence Agency, Office of Public Affairs, Washington, DC 20505, (703) 482-0623, Fax: (703) 482-1739, www.cia.gov; *The World Factbook.*

Euromonitor International, Inc., 224 S. Michigan Avenue, Suite 1500, Chicago, IL 60604, (312) 922-1115, Fax: (312) 922-1157, www.euromonitor.com; *World Marketing Data and Statistics.*

Palgrave Macmillan Ltd., Houndmills, Basingstoke, Hampshire, RG21 6XS, England, (Telephone in U.S. (888) 330-8477), (Fax in U.S. (800) 672-2054), www.palgrave.com; *The Statesman's Yearbook 2008.*

UNESCO Institute for Statistics, C.P. 6128 Succursale Centre-Ville, Montreal, Quebec, H3C 3J7 Canada, (Dial from U.S. (514) 343-6880), (Fax from U.S. (514) 343 6882), www.uis.unesco.org; *Statistical Tables.*

United Nations Statistics Division, New York, NY 10017, (800) 253-9646, Fax: (212) 963-4116, http://unstats.un.org; *Trends in Europe and North America: The Statistical Yearbook of the ECE 2005.*

ARMENIA - BUDGET

Central Intelligence Agency, Office of Public Affairs, Washington, DC 20505, (703) 482-0623, Fax: (703) 482-1739, www.cia.gov; *The World Factbook.*

ARMENIA - BUSINESS

United Nations Statistics Division, New York, NY 10017, (800) 253-9646, Fax: (212) 963-4116, http://unstats.un.org; *Statistical Yearbook.*

ARMENIA - CATTLE

See ARMENIA - LIVESTOCK

ARMENIA - CHILDBIRTH - STATISTICS

Central Intelligence Agency, Office of Public Affairs, Washington, DC 20505, (703) 482-0623, Fax: (703) 482-1739, www.cia.gov; *The World Factbook.*

Euromonitor International, Inc., 224 S. Michigan Avenue, Suite 1500, Chicago, IL 60604, (312) 922-1115, Fax: (312) 922-1157, www.euromonitor.com; *International Marketing Data and Statistics 2008* and *The World Economic Factbook 2008.*

Palgrave Macmillan Ltd., Houndmills, Basingstoke, Hampshire, RG21 6XS, England, (Telephone in U.S. (888) 330-8477), (Fax in U.S. (800) 672-2054), www.palgrave.com; *The Statesman's Yearbook 2008.*

Taylor and Francis Group, An Informa Business, 2 Park Square, Milton Park, Abingdon, Oxford OX14 4RN, United Kingdom, (Dial from U.S. (212) 216-7800), (Fax from U.S. (212) 564-7854), www.tandf.co.uk; *The Europa World Year Book.*

United Nations Statistics Division, New York, NY 10017, (800) 253-9646, Fax: (212) 963-4116, http://unstats.un.org; *Statistical Yearbook.*

World Health Organization (WHO), Avenue Appia 20, 1211 Geneve 27, Switzerland, (Telephone in U.S. (212) 331-9081), www.who.int; *World Health Report 2006.*

ARMENIA - COAL PRODUCTION

See ARMENIA - MINERAL INDUSTRIES

ARMENIA - COMMERCE

Palgrave Macmillan Ltd., Houndmills, Basingstoke, Hampshire, RG21 6XS, England, (Telephone in U.S. (888) 330-8477), (Fax in U.S. (800) 672-2054), www.palgrave.com; *The Statesman's Yearbook 2008.*

ARMENIA - CONSTRUCTION INDUSTRY

Academic International Press, PO Box 1111, Gulf Breeze, FL 32562-1111, Fax: (850) 934-0953, www.ai-press.com; *Russia and Eurasia Facts and Figures Annual.*

United Nations Statistics Division, New York, NY 10017, (800) 253-9646, Fax: (212) 963-4116, http://unstats.un.org; *Statistical Yearbook.*

ARMENIA - CONSUMER PRICE INDEXES

United Nations Statistics Division, New York, NY 10017, (800) 253-9646, Fax: (212) 963-4116, http://unstats.un.org; *Statistical Yearbook* and *Trends in Europe and North America: The Statistical Yearbook of the ECE 2005.*

The World Bank, 1818 H Street, NW, Washington, DC 20433, (202) 473-1000, Fax: (202) 477-6391, www.worldbank.org; *Armenia.*

ARMENIA - CONSUMPTION (ECONOMICS)

The World Bank, 1818 H Street, NW, Washington, DC 20433, (202) 473-1000, Fax: (202) 477-6391, www.worldbank.org; *World Development Report 2008.*

ARMENIA - COTTON

See ARMENIA - CROPS

ARMENIA - CRIME

Academic International Press, PO Box 1111, Gulf Breeze, FL 32562-1111, Fax: (850) 934-0953, www.ai-press.com; *Russia and Eurasia Facts and Figures Annual.*

United Nations Statistics Division, New York, NY 10017, (800) 253-9646, Fax: (212) 963-4116, http://unstats.un.org; *Trends in Europe and North America: The Statistical Yearbook of the ECE 2005.*

ARMENIA - CROPS

Palgrave Macmillan Ltd., Houndmills, Basingstoke, Hampshire, RG21 6XS, England, (Telephone in U.S. (888) 330-8477), (Fax in U.S. (800) 672-2054), www.palgrave.com; *The Statesman's Yearbook 2008.*

Taylor and Francis Group, An Informa Business, 2 Park Square, Milton Park, Abingdon, Oxford OX14 4RN, United Kingdom, (Dial from U.S. (212) 216-7800), (Fax from U.S. (212) 564-7854), www.tandf.co.uk; *The Europa World Year Book.*

United Nations Food and Agricultural Organization (FAO), Viale delle Terme di Caracalla, 00100 Rome, Italy, (Dial from U.S. (202) 653-2400), (Fax from U.S. (202) 653 5760), www.fao.org; *FAO Production Yearbook 2002* and *The State of Food and Agriculture (SOFA) 2006.*

United Nations Statistics Division, New York, NY 10017, (800) 253-9646, Fax: (212) 963-4116, http://unstats.un.org; *2004 Industrial Commodity Statistics Yearbook* and *Statistical Yearbook.*

ARMENIA - DAIRY PROCESSING

Palgrave Macmillan Ltd., Houndmills, Basingstoke, Hampshire, RG21 6XS, England, (Telephone in U.S. (888) 330-8477), (Fax in U.S. (800) 672-2054), www.palgrave.com; *The Statesman's Yearbook 2008.*

Taylor and Francis Group, An Informa Business, 2 Park Square, Milton Park, Abingdon, Oxford OX14 4RN, United Kingdom, (Dial from U.S. (212) 216-7800), (Fax from U.S. (212) 564-7854), www.tandf.co.uk; *The Europa World Year Book.*

United Nations Food and Agricultural Organization (FAO), Viale delle Terme di Caracalla, 00100 Rome, Italy, (Dial from U.S. (202) 653-2400), (Fax from U.S. (202) 653 5760), www.fao.org; *FAO Production Yearbook 2002* and *The State of Food and Agriculture (SOFA) 2006.*

United Nations Statistics Division, New York, NY 10017, (800) 253-9646, Fax: (212) 963-4116, http://unstats.un.org; *2004 Industrial Commodity Statistics Yearbook* and *Statistical Yearbook.*

ARMENIA - DEATH RATES

See ARMENIA - MORTALITY

ARMENIA - DEBTS, EXTERNAL

The World Bank, 1818 H Street, NW, Washington, DC 20433, (202) 473-1000, Fax: (202) 477-6391, www.worldbank.org; *Global Development Finance 2007; World Development Indicators (WDI) 2008;* and *World Development Report 2008.*

ARMENIA - DEMOGRAPHY

Euromonitor International, Inc., 224 S. Michigan Avenue, Suite 1500, Chicago, IL 60604, (312) 922-1115, Fax: (312) 922-1157, www.euromonitor.com; *International Marketing Data and Statistics 2008; The World Economic Factbook 2008;* and *World Marketing Data and Statistics.*

United Nations Statistics Division, New York, NY 10017, (800) 253-9646, Fax: (212) 963-4116, http://unstats.un.org; *Demographic Yearbook* and *Human Development Report 2006.*

The World Bank, 1818 H Street, NW, Washington, DC 20433, (202) 473-1000, Fax: (202) 477-6391, www.worldbank.org; *Armenia.*

ARMENIA - DISPOSABLE INCOME

United Nations Statistics Division, New York, NY 10017, (800) 253-9646, Fax: (212) 963-4116, http://unstats.un.org; *National Accounts Statistics: Compendium of Income Distribution Statistics* and *Statistical Yearbook.*

ARMENIA - DIVORCE

United Nations Statistics Division, New York, NY 10017, (800) 253-9646, Fax: (212) 963-4116, http://unstats.un.org; *Demographic Yearbook; Statistical Yearbook;* and *Trends in Europe and North America: The Statistical Yearbook of the ECE 2005.*

ARMENIA - ECONOMIC CONDITIONS

Center for International Business Education Research (CIBER), Columbia Business School and School of International and Public Affairs, Uris Hall, Room 212, 3022 Broadway, New York, NY 10027-6902, Mr. Joshua Safier, (212) 854-4750, Fax: (212) 222-9821, www.columbia.edu/cu/ciber/; Datastream International.

Central Intelligence Agency, Office of Public Affairs, Washington, DC 20505, (703) 482-0623, Fax: (703) 482-1739, www.cia.gov; *The World Factbook.*

DSI Data Service Information, Xantener Strasse 51a, D-47495 Rheinberg, Germany, www.dsidata.com; *Campus Solution.*

Dun and Bradstreet (DB) Corporation, 103 JFK Parkway, Short Hills, NJ 07078, (973) 921-5500, www.dnb.com; *Country Report.*

Economist Intelligence Unit, 111 West 57th Street, New York, NY 10019, (212) 554-0600, Fax: (212) 586-1181, www.eiu.com; *Armenia Country Report.*

Euromonitor International, Inc., 224 S. Michigan Avenue, Suite 1500, Chicago, IL 60604, (312) 922-1115, Fax: (312) 922-1157, www.euromonitor.com; *The World Economic Factbook 2008* and *World Marketing Data and Statistics.*

International Monetary Fund (IMF), 700 Nineteenth Street, NW, Washington, DC 20431, (202) 623-7000, Fax: (202) 623-4661, www.imf.org; *World Economic Outlook Reports.*

Nomura Research Institute (NRI), 2 World Financial Center, Building B, 19th Fl., New York, NY 10281-1198, (212) 667-1670, www.nri.co.jp/english; *Asian Economic Outlook 2003-2004.*

Palgrave Macmillan Ltd., Houndmills, Basingstoke, Hampshire, RG21 6XS, England, (Telephone in U.S. (888) 330-8477), (Fax in U.S. (800) 672-2054), www.palgrave.com; *The Statesman's Yearbook 2008.*

Taylor and Francis Group, An Informa Business, 2 Park Square, Milton Park, Abingdon, Oxford OX14 4RN, United Kingdom, (Dial from U.S. (212) 216-7800), (Fax from U.S. (212) 564-7854), www.tandf.co.uk; *The Europa World Year Book.*

United Nations Economic and Social Commission for Western Asia (ESCWA), PO Box 11-8575, Riad el-Solh Square, Beirut, Lebanon, www.escwa.un.org; *Annual Report 2006; Bulletin on Population and Vital Statistics in the ESCWA Region;* and *Survey of Economic and Social Developments in the ESCWA Region 2006-2007.*

United Nations Statistics Division, New York, NY 10017, (800) 253-9646, Fax: (212) 963-4116, http://unstats.un.org; *World Statistics Pocketbook.*

The World Bank, 1818 H Street, NW, Washington, DC 20433, (202) 473-1000, Fax: (202) 477-6391, www.worldbank.org; *Armenia; Global Economic Monitor (GEM); Global Economic Prospects 2008; The World Bank Atlas 2003-2004;* and *World Development Report 2008.*

ARMENIA - EDUCATION

Academic International Press, PO Box 1111, Gulf Breeze, FL 32562-1111, Fax: (850) 934-0953, www.ai-press.com; *Russia and Eurasia Facts and Figures Annual.*

Euromonitor International, Inc., 224 S. Michigan Avenue, Suite 1500, Chicago, IL 60604, (312) 922-1115, Fax: (312) 922-1157, www.euromonitor.com; *International Marketing Data and Statistics 2008* and *World Marketing Data and Statistics.*

European Union, Delegation of the European Commission to the United States, 2300 M Street, NW, Washington, DC 20037, (202) 862-9500, Fax: (202) 429-1766, www.eurunion.org; *Education across Europe 2003.*

Palgrave Macmillan Ltd., Houndmills, Basingstoke, Hampshire, RG21 6XS, England, (Telephone in U.S. (888) 330-8477), (Fax in U.S. (800) 672-2054), www.palgrave.com; *The Statesman's Yearbook 2008.*

Taylor and Francis Group, An Informa Business, 2 Park Square, Milton Park, Abingdon, Oxford OX14 4RN, United Kingdom, (Dial from U.S. (212) 216-7800), (Fax from U.S. (212) 564-7854), www.tandf.co.uk; *The Europa World Year Book.*

UNESCO Institute for Statistics, C.P. 6128 Succursale Centre-Ville, Montreal, Quebec, H3C 3J7 Canada, (Dial from U.S. (514) 343-6880), (Fax from U.S. (514) 343 6882), www.uis.unesco.org; *Statistical Tables.*

United Nations Statistics Division, New York, NY 10017, (800) 253-9646, Fax: (212) 963-4116, http://unstats.un.org; *Human Development Report 2006* and *Trends in Europe and North America: The Statistical Yearbook of the ECE 2005.*

The World Bank, 1818 H Street, NW, Washington, DC 20433, (202) 473-1000, Fax: (202) 477-6391, www.worldbank.org; *Armenia* and *World Development Report 2008.*

ARMENIA - ELECTRICITY

Palgrave Macmillan Ltd., Houndmills, Basingstoke, Hampshire, RG21 6XS, England, (Telephone in U.S. (888) 330-8477), (Fax in U.S. (800) 672-2054), www.palgrave.com; *The Statesman's Yearbook 2008.*

Platts, 2 Penn Plaza, 25th Floor, New York, NY 10121-2298, (212) 904-3070, www.platts.com; *Energy Economist.*

U.S. Department of Energy (DOE), Energy Information Administration (EIA), 1000 Independence Avenue, SW, Washington, DC 20585, (202) 586-8800, www.eia.doe.gov; *International Energy Annual 2004* and *International Energy Outlook 2006.*

United Nations Statistics Division, New York, NY 10017, (800) 253-9646, Fax: (212) 963-4116, http://unstats.un.org; *Energy Statistics Yearbook 2003; Human Development Report 2006; Statistical Yearbook;* and *Trends in Europe and North America: The Statistical Yearbook of the ECE 2005.*

ARMENIA - EMPLOYMENT

Euromonitor International, Inc., 224 S. Michigan Avenue, Suite 1500, Chicago, IL 60604, (312) 922-1115, Fax: (312) 922-1157, www.euromonitor.com; *International Marketing Data and Statistics 2008.*

United Nations Statistics Division, New York, NY 10017, (800) 253-9646, Fax: (212) 963-4116, http://unstats.un.org; *Statistical Yearbook* and *Trends in Europe and North America: The Statistical Yearbook of the ECE 2005.*

The World Bank, 1818 H Street, NW, Washington, DC 20433, (202) 473-1000, Fax: (202) 477-6391, www.worldbank.org; *Armenia.*

ARMENIA - ENVIRONMENTAL CONDITIONS

DSI Data Service Information, Xantener Strasse 51a, D-47495 Rheinberg, Germany, www.dsidata.com; *Campus Solution* and *DSI's Global Environmental Database.*

Economist Intelligence Unit, 111 West 57th Street, New York, NY 10019, (212) 554-0600, Fax: (212) 586-1181, www.eiu.com; *Armenia Country Report.*

United Nations Statistics Division, New York, NY 10017, (800) 253-9646, Fax: (212) 963-4116, http://unstats.un.org; *Statistical Yearbook; Trends in Europe and North America: The Statistical Yearbook of the ECE 2005;* and *World Statistics Pocketbook.*

ARMENIA - EXPORTS

Central Intelligence Agency, Office of Public Affairs, Washington, DC 20505, (703) 482-0623, Fax: (703) 482-1739, www.cia.gov; *The World Factbook.*

Economist Intelligence Unit, 111 West 57th Street, New York, NY 10019, (212) 554-0600, Fax: (212) 586-1181, www.eiu.com; *Armenia Country Report.*

Euromonitor International, Inc., 224 S. Michigan Avenue, Suite 1500, Chicago, IL 60604, (312) 922-1115, Fax: (312) 922-1157, www.euromonitor.com; *International Marketing Data and Statistics 2008* and *The World Economic Factbook 2008.*

International Monetary Fund (IMF), 700 Nineteenth Street, NW, Washington, DC 20431, (202) 623-7000, Fax: (202) 623-4661, www.imf.org; *Direction of Trade Statistics Yearbook 2007.*

Palgrave Macmillan Ltd., Houndmills, Basingstoke, Hampshire, RG21 6XS, England, (Telephone in U.S. (888) 330-8477), (Fax in U.S. (800) 672-2054), www.palgrave.com; *The Statesman's Yearbook 2008.*

Taylor and Francis Group, An Informa Business, 2 Park Square, Milton Park, Abingdon, Oxford OX14 4RN, United Kingdom, (Dial from U.S. (212) 216-7800), (Fax from U.S. (212) 564-7854), www.tandf.co.uk; *The Europa World Year Book.*

United Nations Conference on Trade and Development (UNCTAD), DC2-1120, United Nations, New York, NY 10017, (212) 963-0027, www.unctad.org; *Handbook of Statistics 2005.*

United Nations Statistics Division, New York, NY 10017, (800) 253-9646, Fax: (212) 963-4116, http://unstats.un.org; *International Trade Statistics Yearbook* and *Trends in Europe and North America: The Statistical Yearbook of the ECE 2005.*

The World Bank, 1818 H Street, NW, Washington, DC 20433, (202) 473-1000, Fax: (202) 477-6391, www.worldbank.org; *World Development Indicators (WDI) 2008* and *World Development Report 2008.*

ARMENIA - FERTILITY, HUMAN

United Nations Statistics Division, New York, NY 10017, (800) 253-9646, Fax: (212) 963-4116, http://unstats.un.org; *Human Development Report 2006* and *Trends in Europe and North America: The Statistical Yearbook of the ECE 2005.*

The World Bank, 1818 H Street, NW, Washington, DC 20433, (202) 473-1000, Fax: (202) 477-6391, www.worldbank.org; *The World Bank Atlas 2003-2004; World Development Indicators (WDI) 2008;* and *World Development Report 2008.*

World Health Organization (WHO), Avenue Appia 20, 1211 Geneve 27, Switzerland, (Telephone in U.S. (212) 331-9081), www.who.int; *World Health Report 2006.*

ARMENIA - FERTILIZER INDUSTRY

United Nations Food and Agricultural Organization (FAO), Viale delle Terme di Caracalla, 00100 Rome, Italy, (Dial from U.S. (202) 653-2400), (Fax from U.S. (202) 653 5760), www.fao.org; *FAO Fertilizer Yearbook.*

United Nations Statistics Division, New York, NY 10017, (800) 253-9646, Fax: (212) 963-4116, http://unstats.un.org; *2004 Industrial Commodity Statistics Yearbook* and *Statistical Yearbook.*

ARMENIA - FINANCE

Taylor and Francis Group, An Informa Business, 2 Park Square, Milton Park, Abingdon, Oxford OX14 4RN, United Kingdom, (Dial from U.S. (212) 216-7800), (Fax from U.S. (212) 564-7854), www.tandf.co.uk; *The Europa World Year Book.*

United Nations Statistics Division, New York, NY 10017, (800) 253-9646, Fax: (212) 963-4116, http://unstats.un.org; *National Accounts Statistics: Compendium of Income Distribution Statistics* and *Statistical Yearbook.*

The World Bank, 1818 H Street, NW, Washington, DC 20433, (202) 473-1000, Fax: (202) 477-6391, www.worldbank.org; *Armenia.*

ARMENIA - FINANCE, PUBLIC

Bernan Essential Government Publications, 4611-F Assembly Drive, Lanham MD, 20706-4391, (301) 459-2255, Fax: (800) 865-3450, www.bernan.com; *National Accounts Statistics.*

Economist Intelligence Unit, 111 West 57th Street, New York, NY 10019, (212) 554-0600, Fax: (212) 586-1181, www.eiu.com; *Armenia Country Report.*

International Monetary Fund (IMF), 700 Nineteenth Street, NW, Washington, DC 20431, (202) 623-7000, Fax: (202) 623-4661, www.imf.org; *International Financial Statistics* and *International Financial Statistics Online Service.*

Palgrave Macmillan Ltd., Houndmills, Basingstoke, Hampshire, RG21 6XS, England, (Telephone in U.S. (888) 330-8477), (Fax in U.S. (800) 672-2054), www.palgrave.com; *The Statesman's Yearbook 2008.*

Taylor and Francis Group, An Informa Business, 2 Park Square, Milton Park, Abingdon, Oxford OX14 4RN, United Kingdom, (Dial from U.S. (212) 216-7800), (Fax from U.S. (212) 564-7854), www.tandf.co.uk; *The Europa World Year Book.*

The World Bank, 1818 H Street, NW, Washington, DC 20433, (202) 473-1000, Fax: (202) 477-6391, www.worldbank.org; *Armenia.*

ARMENIA - FISHERIES

United Nations Food and Agricultural Organization (FAO), Viale delle Terme di Caracalla, 00100 Rome, Italy, (Dial from U.S. (202) 653-2400), (Fax from

U.S. (202) 653 5760), www.fao.org; *FAO Yearbook of Fishery Statistics;* Fishery Databases; FISHSTAT Database. Subjects covered include: Aquaculture production, capture production, fishery commodities; and *The State of Food and Agriculture (SOFA) 2006.*

United Nations Statistics Division, New York, NY 10017, (800) 253-9646, Fax: (212) 963-4116, http://unstats.un.org; *2004 Industrial Commodity Statistics Yearbook* and *Statistical Yearbook.*

The World Bank, 1818 H Street, NW, Washington, DC 20433, (202) 473-1000, Fax: (202) 477-6391, www.worldbank.org; *Armenia.*

ARMENIA - FOOD

United Nations Food and Agricultural Organization (FAO), Viale delle Terme di Caracalla, 00100 Rome, Italy, (Dial from U.S. (202) 653-2400), (Fax from U.S. (202) 653 5760), www.fao.org; *FAO Production Yearbook 2002* and *The State of Food and Agriculture (SOFA) 2006.*

United Nations Statistics Division, New York, NY 10017, (800) 253-9646, Fax: (212) 963-4116, http://unstats.un.org; *Human Development Report 2006* and *2004 Industrial Commodity Statistics Yearbook.*

ARMENIA - FOREIGN EXCHANGE RATES

Central Intelligence Agency, Office of Public Affairs, Washington, DC 20505, (703) 482-0623, Fax: (703) 482-1739, www.cia.gov; *The World Factbook.*

Euromonitor International, Inc., 224 S. Michigan Avenue, Suite 1500, Chicago, IL 60604, (312) 922-1115, Fax: (312) 922-1157, www.euromonitor.com; *International Marketing Data and Statistics 2008* and *The World Economic Factbook 2008.*

Taylor and Francis Group, An Informa Business, 2 Park Square, Milton Park, Abingdon, Oxford OX14 4RN, United Kingdom, (Dial from U.S. (212) 216-7800), (Fax from U.S. (212) 564-7854), www.tandf.co.uk; *The Europa World Year Book.*

United Nations Statistics Division, New York, NY 10017, (800) 253-9646, Fax: (212) 963-4116, http://unstats.un.org; *Statistical Yearbook; Trends in Europe and North America: The Statistical Yearbook of the ECE 2005;* and *World Statistics Pocketbook.*

ARMENIA - FORESTS AND FORESTRY

Academic International Press, PO Box 1111, Gulf Breeze, FL 32562-1111, Fax: (850) 934-0953, www.ai-press.com; *Russia and Eurasia Facts and Figures Annual.*

United Nations Food and Agricultural Organization (FAO), Viale delle Terme di Caracalla, 00100 Rome, Italy, (Dial from U.S. (202) 653-2400), (Fax from U.S. (202) 653 5760), www.fao.org; *FAO Yearbook of Forest Products* and *The State of Food and Agriculture (SOFA) 2006.*

United Nations Statistics Division, New York, NY 10017, (800) 253-9646, Fax: (212) 963-4116, http://unstats.un.org; *2004 Industrial Commodity Statistics Yearbook; Statistical Yearbook;* and *Trends in Europe and North America: The Statistical Yearbook of the ECE 2005.*

The World Bank, 1818 H Street, NW, Washington, DC 20433, (202) 473-1000, Fax: (202) 477-6391, www.worldbank.org; *Armenia* and *World Development Report 2008.*

ARMENIA - GROSS DOMESTIC PRODUCT

Academic International Press, PO Box 1111, Gulf Breeze, FL 32562-1111, Fax: (850) 934-0953, www.ai-press.com; *Russia and Eurasia Facts and Figures Annual.*

Economist Intelligence Unit, 111 West 57th Street, New York, NY 10019, (212) 554-0600, Fax: (212) 586-1181, www.eiu.com; *Armenia Country Report.*

Euromonitor International, Inc., 224 S. Michigan Avenue, Suite 1500, Chicago, IL 60604, (312) 922-1115, Fax: (312) 922-1157, www.euromonitor.com; *International Marketing Data and Statistics 2008* and *The World Economic Factbook 2008.*

United Nations Statistics Division, New York, NY 10017, (800) 253-9646, Fax: (212) 963-4116, http://unstats.un.org; *Human Development Report 2006; National Accounts Statistics: Compendium of Income Distribution Statistics; Statistical Yearbook;* and *Trends in Europe and North America: The Statistical Yearbook of the ECE 2005.*

The World Bank, 1818 H Street, NW, Washington, DC 20433, (202) 473-1000, Fax: (202) 477-6391, www.worldbank.org; *World Development Indicators (WDI) 2008* and *World Development Report 2008.*

ARMENIA - GROSS NATIONAL PRODUCT

Palgrave Macmillan Ltd., Houndmills, Basingstoke, Hampshire, RG21 6XS, England, (Telephone in U.S. (888) 330-8477), (Fax in U.S. (800) 672-2054), www.palgrave.com; *The Statesman's Yearbook 2008.*

United Nations Statistics Division, New York, NY 10017, (800) 253-9646, Fax: (212) 963-4116, http://unstats.un.org; *Statistical Yearbook.*

The World Bank, 1818 H Street, NW, Washington, DC 20433, (202) 473-1000, Fax: (202) 477-6391, www.worldbank.org; *The World Bank Atlas 2003-2004; World Development Indicators (WDI) 2008;* and *World Development Report 2008.*

ARMENIA - HOUSING

Euromonitor International, Inc., 224 S. Michigan Avenue, Suite 1500, Chicago, IL 60604, (312) 922-1115, Fax: (312) 922-1157, www.euromonitor.com; *World Marketing Data and Statistics.*

United Nations Statistics Division, New York, NY 10017, (800) 253-9646, Fax: (212) 963-4116, http://unstats.un.org; *Trends in Europe and North America: The Statistical Yearbook of the ECE 2005.*

ARMENIA - ILLITERATE PERSONS

Central Intelligence Agency, Office of Public Affairs, Washington, DC 20505, (703) 482-0623, Fax: (703) 482-1739, www.cia.gov; *The World Factbook.*

Euromonitor International, Inc., 224 S. Michigan Avenue, Suite 1500, Chicago, IL 60604, (312) 922-1115, Fax: (312) 922-1157, www.euromonitor.com; *The World Economic Factbook 2008.*

UNESCO Institute for Statistics, C.P. 6128 Succursale Centre-Ville, Montreal, Quebec, H3C 3J7 Canada, (Dial from U.S. (514) 343-6880), (Fax from U.S. (514) 343 6882), www.uis.unesco.org; *Statistical Tables.*

United Nations Statistics Division, New York, NY 10017, (800) 253-9646, Fax: (212) 963-4116, http://unstats.un.org; *Human Development Report 2006.*

ARMENIA - IMPORTS

Academic International Press, PO Box 1111, Gulf Breeze, FL 32562-1111, Fax: (850) 934-0953, www.ai-press.com; *Russia and Eurasia Facts and Figures Annual.*

Central Intelligence Agency, Office of Public Affairs, Washington, DC 20505, (703) 482-0623, Fax: (703) 482-1739, www.cia.gov; *The World Factbook.*

Economist Intelligence Unit, 111 West 57th Street, New York, NY 10019, (212) 554-0600, Fax: (212) 586-1181, www.eiu.com; *Armenia Country Report.*

Euromonitor International, Inc., 224 S. Michigan Avenue, Suite 1500, Chicago, IL 60604, (312) 922-1115, Fax: (312) 922-1157, www.euromonitor.com; *International Marketing Data and Statistics 2008* and *The World Economic Factbook 2008.*

International Monetary Fund (IMF), 700 Nineteenth Street, NW, Washington, DC 20431, (202) 623-7000, Fax: (202) 623-4661, www.imf.org; *Direction of Trade Statistics Yearbook 2007.*

Palgrave Macmillan Ltd., Houndmills, Basingstoke, Hampshire, RG21 6XS, England, (Telephone in U.S. (888) 330-8477), (Fax in U.S. (800) 672-2054), www.palgrave.com; *The Statesman's Yearbook 2008.*

Taylor and Francis Group, An Informa Business, 2 Park Square, Milton Park, Abingdon, Oxford OX14 4RN, United Kingdom, (Dial from U.S. (212) 216-7800), (Fax from U.S. (212) 564-7854), www.tandf.co.uk; *The Europa World Year Book.*

United Nations Conference on Trade and Development (UNCTAD), DC2-1120, United Nations, New York, NY 10017, (212) 963-0027, www.unctad.org; *Handbook of Statistics 2005.*

United Nations Statistics Division, New York, NY 10017, (800) 253-9646, Fax: (212) 963-4116, http://unstats.un.org; *International Trade Statistics Yearbook* and *Trends in Europe and North America: The Statistical Yearbook of the ECE 2005.*

The World Bank, 1818 H Street, NW, Washington, DC 20433, (202) 473-1000, Fax: (202) 477-6391, www.worldbank.org; *World Development Indicators (WDI) 2008* and *World Development Report 2008.*

ARMENIA - INDUSTRIAL PROPERTY

United Nations Statistics Division, New York, NY 10017, (800) 253-9646, Fax: (212) 963-4116, http://unstats.un.org; *Statistical Yearbook.*

ARMENIA - INDUSTRIES

Academic International Press, PO Box 1111, Gulf Breeze, FL 32562-1111, Fax: (850) 934-0953, www.ai-press.com; *Russia and Eurasia Facts and Figures Annual.*

Economist Intelligence Unit, 111 West 57th Street, New York, NY 10019, (212) 554-0600, Fax: (212) 586-1181, www.eiu.com; *Armenia Country Report.*

Euromonitor International, Inc., 224 S. Michigan Avenue, Suite 1500, Chicago, IL 60604, (312) 922-1115, Fax: (312) 922-1157, www.euromonitor.com; *The World Economic Factbook 2008* and *World Marketing Data and Statistics.*

Taylor and Francis Group, An Informa Business, 2 Park Square, Milton Park, Abingdon, Oxford OX14 4RN, United Kingdom, (Dial from U.S. (212) 216-7800), (Fax from U.S. (212) 564-7854), www.tandf.co.uk; *The Europa World Year Book.*

United Nations Industrial Development Organization (UNIDO), 1 United Nations Plaza, New York, NY 10017, (212) 963 6890, Fax: (212) 963-7904, http://unido.org; Industrial Statistics Database 2008 (INDSTAT) and *The International Yearbook of Industrial Statistics 2008.*

United Nations Statistics Division, New York, NY 10017, (800) 253-9646, Fax: (212) 963-4116, http://unstats.un.org; *2004 Industrial Commodity Statistics Yearbook; Statistical Yearbook;* and *Trends in Europe and North America: The Statistical Yearbook of the ECE 2005.*

The World Bank, 1818 H Street, NW, Washington, DC 20433, (202) 473-1000, Fax: (202) 477-6391, www.worldbank.org; *Armenia* and *World Development Indicators (WDI) 2008.*

ARMENIA - INFANT AND MATERNAL MORTALITY

See ARMENIA - MORTALITY

ARMENIA - INTERNATIONAL TRADE

Academic International Press, PO Box 1111, Gulf Breeze, FL 32562-1111, Fax: (850) 934-0953, www.ai-press.com; *Russia and Eurasia Facts and Figures Annual.*

Economist Intelligence Unit, 111 West 57th Street, New York, NY 10019, (212) 554-0600, Fax: (212) 586-1181, www.eiu.com; *Armenia Country Report.*

Euromonitor International, Inc., 224 S. Michigan Avenue, Suite 1500, Chicago, IL 60604, (312) 922-1115, Fax: (312) 922-1157, www.euromonitor.com; *The World Economic Factbook 2008* and *World Marketing Data and Statistics.*

International Monetary Fund (IMF), 700 Nineteenth Street, NW, Washington, DC 20431, (202) 623-7000, Fax: (202) 623-4661, www.imf.org; *Direction of Trade Statistics Yearbook 2007.*

United Nations Food and Agricultural Organization (FAO), Viale delle Terme di Caracalla, 00100 Rome, Italy, (Dial from U.S. (202) 653-2400), (Fax from U.S. (202) 653 5760), www.fao.org; *FAO Trade Yearbook.*

United Nations Statistics Division, New York, NY 10017, (800) 253-9646, Fax: (212) 963-4116, http://unstats.un.org; *International Trade Statistics Yearbook* and *Statistical Yearbook.*

The World Bank, 1818 H Street, NW, Washington, DC 20433, (202) 473-1000, Fax: (202) 477-6391, www.worldbank.org; *Armenia; World Development Indicators (WDI) 2008;* and *World Development Report 2008.*

World Trade Organization (WTO), Centre William Rappard, Rue de Lausanne 154, CH-1211 Geneva 21, Switzerland, www.wto.org; *International Trade Statistics 2006.*

ARMENIA - INTERNET USERS

International Telecommunication Union (ITU), Place des Nations, 1211 Geneva 20, Switzerland, www.itu.int; *World Telecommunication/ICT Indicators Database on CD-ROM; World Telecommunication/ICT Indicators Database Online;* and *Yearbook of Statistics - Telecommunication Services (Chronological Time Series 1997-2006).*

The World Bank, 1818 H Street, NW, Washington, DC 20433, (202) 473-1000, Fax: (202) 477-6391, www.worldbank.org; *Armenia.*

ARMENIA - LABOR

Academic International Press, PO Box 1111, Gulf Breeze, FL 32562-1111, Fax: (850) 934-0953, www.ai-press.com; *Russia and Eurasia Facts and Figures Annual.*

Central Intelligence Agency, Office of Public Affairs, Washington, DC 20505, (703) 482-0623, Fax: (703) 482-1739, www.cia.gov; *The World Factbook.*

Euromonitor International, Inc., 224 S. Michigan Avenue, Suite 1500, Chicago, IL 60604, (312) 922-1115, Fax: (312) 922-1157, www.euromonitor.com; *International Marketing Data and Statistics 2008* and *World Marketing Data and Statistics.*

Palgrave Macmillan Ltd., Houndmills, Basingstoke, Hampshire, RG21 6XS, England, (Telephone in U.S. (888) 330-8477), (Fax in U.S. (800) 672-2054), www.palgrave.com; *The Statesman's Yearbook 2008.*

United Nations Food and Agricultural Organization (FAO), Viale delle Terme di Caracalla, 00100 Rome, Italy, (Dial from U.S. (202) 653-2400), (Fax from U.S. (202) 653 5760), www.fao.org; *FAO Production Yearbook 2002.*

United Nations Statistics Division, New York, NY 10017, (800) 253-9646, Fax: (212) 963-4116, http://unstats.un.org; *Human Development Report 2006* and *Statistical Yearbook.*

The World Bank, 1818 H Street, NW, Washington, DC 20433, (202) 473-1000, Fax: (202) 477-6391, www.worldbank.org; *The World Bank Atlas 2003-2004; World Development Indicators (WDI) 2008;* and *World Development Report 2008.*

ARMENIA - LAND USE

Central Intelligence Agency, Office of Public Affairs, Washington, DC 20505, (703) 482-0623, Fax: (703) 482-1739, www.cia.gov; *The World Factbook.*

Euromonitor International, Inc., 224 S. Michigan Avenue, Suite 1500, Chicago, IL 60604, (312) 922-1115, Fax: (312) 922-1157, www.euromonitor.com; *International Marketing Data and Statistics 2008.*

The World Bank, 1818 H Street, NW, Washington, DC 20433, (202) 473-1000, Fax: (202) 477-6391, www.worldbank.org; *World Development Report 2008.*

ARMENIA - LIBRARIES

UNESCO Institute for Statistics, C.P. 6128 Succursale Centre-Ville, Montreal, Quebec, H3C 3J7 Canada, (Dial from U.S. (514) 343-6880), (Fax from U.S. (514) 343 6882), www.uis.unesco.org; *Statistical Tables.*

United Nations Statistics Division, New York, NY 10017, (800) 253-9646, Fax: (212) 963-4116, http://unstats.un.org; *Trends in Europe and North America: The Statistical Yearbook of the ECE 2005.*

ARMENIA - LIFE EXPECTANCY

Euromonitor International, Inc., 224 S. Michigan Avenue, Suite 1500, Chicago, IL 60604, (312) 922-1115, Fax: (312) 922-1157, www.euromonitor.com; *The World Economic Factbook 2008.*

United Nations Statistics Division, New York, NY 10017, (800) 253-9646, Fax: (212) 963-4116, http://unstats.un.org; *Demographic Yearbook; Human Development Report 2006; Trends in Europe and North America: The Statistical Yearbook of the ECE 2005;* and *World Statistics Pocketbook.*

The World Bank, 1818 H Street, NW, Washington, DC 20433, (202) 473-1000, Fax: (202) 477-6391, www.worldbank.org; *The World Bank Atlas 2003-2004; World Development Indicators (WDI) 2008;* and *World Development Report 2008.*

World Health Organization (WHO), Avenue Appia 20, 1211 Geneve 27, Switzerland, (Telephone in U.S. (212) 331-9081), www.who.int; *World Health Report 2006.*

ARMENIA - LITERACY

Euromonitor International, Inc., 224 S. Michigan Avenue, Suite 1500, Chicago, IL 60604, (312) 922-1115, Fax: (312) 922-1157, www.euromonitor.com; *World Marketing Data and Statistics.*

ARMENIA - LIVESTOCK

Academic International Press, PO Box 1111, Gulf Breeze, FL 32562-1111, Fax: (850) 934-0953, www.ai-press.com; *Russia and Eurasia Facts and Figures Annual.*

Palgrave Macmillan Ltd., Houndmills, Basingstoke, Hampshire, RG21 6XS, England, (Telephone in U.S. (888) 330-8477), (Fax in U.S. (800) 672-2054), www.palgrave.com; *The Statesman's Yearbook 2008.*

Taylor and Francis Group, An Informa Business, 2 Park Square, Milton Park, Abingdon, Oxford OX14 4RN, United Kingdom, (Dial from U.S. (212) 216-7800), (Fax from U.S. (212) 564-7854), www.tandf.co.uk; *The Europa World Year Book.*

United Nations Food and Agricultural Organization (FAO), Viale delle Terme di Caracalla, 00100 Rome, Italy, (Dial from U.S. (202) 653-2400), (Fax from U.S. (202) 653 5760), www.fao.org; *FAO Production Yearbook 2002* and *The State of Food and Agriculture (SOFA) 2006.*

United Nations Statistics Division, New York, NY 10017, (800) 253-9646, Fax: (212) 963-4116, http://unstats.un.org; *Statistical Yearbook.*

ARMENIA - MANUFACTURES

United Nations Statistics Division, New York, NY 10017, (800) 253-9646, Fax: (212) 963-4116, http://unstats.un.org; *Statistical Yearbook.*

The World Bank, 1818 H Street, NW, Washington, DC 20433, (202) 473-1000, Fax: (202) 477-6391, www.worldbank.org; *World Development Indicators (WDI) 2008.*

ARMENIA - MARRIAGE

Taylor and Francis Group, An Informa Business, 2 Park Square, Milton Park, Abingdon, Oxford OX14 4RN, United Kingdom, (Dial from U.S. (212) 216-7800), (Fax from U.S. (212) 564-7854), www.tandf.co.uk; *The Europa World Year Book.*

United Nations Statistics Division, New York, NY 10017, (800) 253-9646, Fax: (212) 963-4116, http://unstats.un.org; *Demographic Yearbook; Statistical Yearbook;* and *Trends in Europe and North America: The Statistical Yearbook of the ECE 2005.*

ARMENIA - MEAT PRODUCTION

See ARMENIA - LIVESTOCK

ARMENIA - MINERAL INDUSTRIES

Academic International Press, PO Box 1111, Gulf Breeze, FL 32562-1111, Fax: (850) 934-0953, www.ai-press.com; *Russia and Eurasia Facts and Figures Annual.*

Palgrave Macmillan Ltd., Houndmills, Basingstoke, Hampshire, RG21 6XS, England, (Telephone in U.S. (888) 330-8477), (Fax in U.S. (800) 672-2054), www.palgrave.com; *The Statesman's Yearbook 2008.*

Platts, 2 Penn Plaza, 25th Floor, New York, NY 10121-2298, (212) 904-3070, www.platts.com; *Energy Economist.*

United Nations Statistics Division, New York, NY 10017, (800) 253-9646, Fax: (212) 963-4116, http://unstats.un.org; *Energy Statistics Yearbook 2003* and *Statistical Yearbook.*

The World Bank, 1818 H Street, NW, Washington, DC 20433, (202) 473-1000, Fax: (202) 477-6391, www.worldbank.org; *Armenia.*

ARMENIA - MONEY SUPPLY

Economist Intelligence Unit, 111 West 57th Street, New York, NY 10019, (212) 554-0600, Fax: (212) 586-1181, www.eiu.com; *Armenia Country Report.*

The World Bank, 1818 H Street, NW, Washington, DC 20433, (202) 473-1000, Fax: (202) 477-6391, www.worldbank.org; *Armenia.*

ARMENIA - MONUMENTS AND HISTORIC SITES

UNESCO Institute for Statistics, C.P. 6128 Succursale Centre-Ville, Montreal, Quebec, H3C 3J7 Canada, (Dial from U.S. (514) 343-6880), (Fax from U.S. (514) 343 6882), www.uis.unesco.org; *Statistical Tables.*

ARMENIA - MORTALITY

Central Intelligence Agency, Office of Public Affairs, Washington, DC 20505, (703) 482-0623, Fax: (703) 482-1739, www.cia.gov; *The World Factbook.*

Euromonitor International, Inc., 224 S. Michigan Avenue, Suite 1500, Chicago, IL 60604, (312) 922-1115, Fax: (312) 922-1157, www.euromonitor.com; *International Marketing Data and Statistics 2008* and *The World Economic Factbook 2008.*

Palgrave Macmillan Ltd., Houndmills, Basingstoke, Hampshire, RG21 6XS, England, (Telephone in U.S. (888) 330-8477), (Fax in U.S. (800) 672-2054), www.palgrave.com; *The Statesman's Yearbook 2008.*

Taylor and Francis Group, An Informa Business, 2 Park Square, Milton Park, Abingdon, Oxford OX14 4RN, United Kingdom, (Dial from U.S. (212) 216-7800), (Fax from U.S. (212) 564-7854), www.tandf.co.uk; *The Europa World Year Book.*

United Nations Statistics Division, New York, NY 10017, (800) 253-9646, Fax: (212) 963-4116, http://unstats.un.org; *Demographic Yearbook; Human Development Report 2006; Statistical Yearbook; Trends in Europe and North America: The Statistical Yearbook of the ECE 2005;* and *World Statistics Pocketbook.*

The World Bank, 1818 H Street, NW, Washington, DC 20433, (202) 473-1000, Fax: (202) 477-6391, www.worldbank.org; *The World Bank Atlas 2003-2004; World Development Indicators (WDI) 2008;* and *World Development Report 2008.*

World Health Organization (WHO), Avenue Appia 20, 1211 Geneve 27, Switzerland, (Telephone in U.S. (212) 331-9081), www.who.int; The WHO Global Atlas of Infectious Diseases and *World Health Report 2006.*

ARMENIA - MOTION PICTURES

UNESCO Institute for Statistics, C.P. 6128 Succursale Centre-Ville, Montreal, Quebec, H3C 3J7 Canada, (Dial from U.S. (514) 343-6880), (Fax from U.S. (514) 343 6882), www.uis.unesco.org; *Statistical Tables.*

United Nations Statistics Division, New York, NY 10017, (800) 253-9646, Fax: (212) 963-4116, http://unstats.un.org; *Statistical Yearbook.*

ARMENIA - MOTOR VEHICLES

United Nations Statistics Division, New York, NY 10017, (800) 253-9646, Fax: (212) 963-4116, http://unstats.un.org; *Statistical Yearbook.*

ARMENIA - MUSEUMS

UNESCO Institute for Statistics, C.P. 6128 Succursale Centre-Ville, Montreal, Quebec, H3C 3J7 Canada, (Dial from U.S. (514) 343-6880), (Fax from U.S. (514) 343 6882), www.uis.unesco.org; *Statistical Tables.*

ARMENIA - PERIODICALS

UNESCO Institute for Statistics, C.P. 6128 Succursale Centre-Ville, Montreal, Quebec, H3C 3J7 Canada, (Dial from U.S. (514) 343-6880), (Fax from U.S. (514) 343 6882), www.uis.unesco.org; *Statistical Tables.*

ARMENIA - PETROLEUM INDUSTRY AND TRADE

PennWell Corporation, 1421 South Sheridan Road, Tulsa, OK 74112, (918) 835-3161, www.pennwell.com; *International Petroleum Encyclopedia 2007.*

Platts, 2 Penn Plaza, 25th Floor, New York, NY 10121-2298, (212) 904-3070, www.platts.com; *Energy Economist.*

U.S. Department of Energy (DOE), Energy Information Administration (EIA), 1000 Independence Avenue, SW, Washington, DC 20585, (202) 586-8800, www.eia.doe.gov; *International Energy Annual 2004* and *International Energy Outlook 2006.*

United Nations Food and Agricultural Organization (FAO), Viale delle Terme di Caracalla, 00100 Rome, Italy, (Dial from U.S. (202) 653-2400), (Fax from U.S. (202) 653 5760), www.fao.org; *The State of Food and Agriculture (SOFA) 2006.*

United Nations Statistics Division, New York, NY 10017, (800) 253-9646, Fax: (212) 963-4116, http://unstats.un.org; *Energy Statistics Yearbook 2003; Statistical Yearbook;* and *Trends in Europe and North America: The Statistical Yearbook of the ECE 2005.*

ARMENIA - POLITICAL SCIENCE

Central Intelligence Agency, Office of Public Affairs, Washington, DC 20505, (703) 482-0623, Fax: (703) 482-1739, www.cia.gov; *The World Factbook.*

Palgrave Macmillan Ltd., Houndmills, Basingstoke, Hampshire, RG21 6XS, England, (Telephone in U.S. (888) 330-8477), (Fax in U.S. (800) 672-2054), www.palgrave.com; *The Statesman's Yearbook 2008.*

Taylor and Francis Group, An Informa Business, 2 Park Square, Milton Park, Abingdon, Oxford OX14 4RN, United Kingdom, (Dial from U.S. (212) 216-7800), (Fax from U.S. (212) 564-7854), www.tandf.co.uk; *The Europa World Year Book.*

United Nations Statistics Division, New York, NY 10017, (800) 253-9646, Fax: (212) 963-4116, http://unstats.un.org; *National Accounts Statistics: Compendium of Income Distribution Statistics* and *Statistical Yearbook.*

The World Bank, 1818 H Street, NW, Washington, DC 20433, (202) 473-1000, Fax: (202) 477-6391, www.worldbank.org; *World Development Report 2008.*

ARMENIA - POPULATION

Academic International Press, PO Box 1111, Gulf Breeze, FL 32562-1111, Fax: (850) 934-0953, www.ai-press.com; *Russia and Eurasia Facts and Figures Annual.*

Central Intelligence Agency, Office of Public Affairs, Washington, DC 20505, (703) 482-0623, Fax: (703) 482-1739, www.cia.gov; *The World Factbook.*

Economist Intelligence Unit, 111 West 57th Street, New York, NY 10019, (212) 554-0600, Fax: (212) 586-1181, www.eiu.com; *Armenia Country Report.*

Euromonitor International, Inc., 224 S. Michigan Avenue, Suite 1500, Chicago, IL 60604, (312) 922-1115, Fax: (312) 922-1157, www.euromonitor.com; *International Marketing Data and Statistics 2008* and *The World Economic Factbook 2008.*

Palgrave Macmillan Ltd., Houndmills, Basingstoke, Hampshire, RG21 6XS, England, (Telephone in U.S. (888) 330-8477), (Fax in U.S. (800) 672-2054), www.palgrave.com; *The Statesman's Yearbook 2008.*

Taylor and Francis Group, An Informa Business, 2 Park Square, Milton Park, Abingdon, Oxford OX14 4RN, United Kingdom, (Dial from U.S. (212) 216-7800), (Fax from U.S. (212) 564-7854), www.tandf.co.uk; *The Europa World Year Book.*

UNESCO Institute for Statistics, C.P. 6128 Succursale Centre-Ville, Montreal, Quebec, H3C 3J7 Canada, (Dial from U.S. (514) 343-6880), (Fax from U.S. (514) 343 6882), www.uis.unesco.org; *Statistical Tables.*

United Nations Food and Agricultural Organization (FAO), Viale delle Terme di Caracalla, 00100 Rome, Italy, (Dial from U.S. (202) 653-2400), (Fax from U.S. (202) 653 5760), www.fao.org; *FAO Production Yearbook 2002.*

United Nations Statistics Division, New York, NY 10017, (800) 253-9646, Fax: (212) 963-4116, http://unstats.un.org; *Demographic Yearbook; Human Development Report 2006; Statistical Yearbook; Trends in Europe and North America: The Statistical Yearbook of the ECE 2005;* and *World Statistics Pocketbook.*

The World Bank, 1818 H Street, NW, Washington, DC 20433, (202) 473-1000, Fax: (202) 477-6391, www.worldbank.org; *Armenia; The World Bank Atlas 2003-2004; World Development Indicators (WDI) 2008;* and *World Development Report 2008.*

World Health Organization (WHO), Avenue Appia 20, 1211 Geneve 27, Switzerland, (Telephone in U.S. (212) 331-9081), www.who.int; *World Health Report 2006.*

ARMENIA - POPULATION DENSITY

Central Intelligence Agency, Office of Public Affairs, Washington, DC 20505, (703) 482-0623, Fax: (703) 482-1739, www.cia.gov; *The World Factbook.*

Euromonitor International, Inc., 224 S. Michigan Avenue, Suite 1500, Chicago, IL 60604, (312) 922-1115, Fax: (312) 922-1157, www.euromonitor.com; *The World Economic Factbook 2008.*

Palgrave Macmillan Ltd., Houndmills, Basingstoke, Hampshire, RG21 6XS, England, (Telephone in U.S. (888) 330-8477), (Fax in U.S. (800) 672-2054), www.palgrave.com; *The Statesman's Yearbook 2008.*

Taylor and Francis Group, An Informa Business, 2 Park Square, Milton Park, Abingdon, Oxford OX14 4RN, United Kingdom, (Dial from U.S. (212) 216-7800), (Fax from U.S. (212) 564-7854), www.tandf.co.uk; *The Europa World Year Book.*

UNESCO Institute for Statistics, C.P. 6128 Succursale Centre-Ville, Montreal, Quebec, H3C 3J7 Canada, (Dial from U.S. (514) 343-6880), (Fax from U.S. (514) 343 6882), www.uis.unesco.org; *Statistical Tables.*

United Nations Statistics Division, New York, NY 10017, (800) 253-9646, Fax: (212) 963-4116, http://unstats.un.org; *Statistical Yearbook* and *Trends in Europe and North America: The Statistical Yearbook of the ECE 2005.*

The World Bank, 1818 H Street, NW, Washington, DC 20433, (202) 473-1000, Fax: (202) 477-6391, www.worldbank.org; *Armenia* and *World Development Report 2008.*

ARMENIA - POSTAL SERVICE

United Nations Statistics Division, New York, NY 10017, (800) 253-9646, Fax: (212) 963-4116, http://unstats.un.org; *Statistical Yearbook* and *Trends in Europe and North America: The Statistical Yearbook of the ECE 2005.*

ARMENIA - POULTRY

See ARMENIA - LIVESTOCK

ARMENIA - POWER RESOURCES

Academic International Press, PO Box 1111, Gulf Breeze, FL 32562-1111, Fax: (850) 934-0953, www.ai-press.com; *Russia and Eurasia Facts and Figures Annual.*

Euromonitor International, Inc., 224 S. Michigan Avenue, Suite 1500, Chicago, IL 60604, (312) 922-1115, Fax: (312) 922-1157, www.euromonitor.com; *International Marketing Data and Statistics 2008; The World Economic Factbook 2008;* and *World Marketing Data and Statistics.*

Palgrave Macmillan Ltd., Houndmills, Basingstoke, Hampshire, RG21 6XS, England, (Telephone in U.S. (888) 330-8477), (Fax in U.S. (800) 672-2054), www.palgrave.com; *The Statesman's Yearbook 2008.*

Platts, 2 Penn Plaza, 25th Floor, New York, NY 10121-2298, (212) 904-3070, www.platts.com; *Energy Economist.*

U.S. Department of Energy (DOE), Energy Information Administration (EIA), 1000 Independence Avenue, SW, Washington, DC 20585, (202) 586-8800, www.eia.doe.gov; *International Energy Annual 2004* and *International Energy Outlook 2006.*

United Nations Statistics Division, New York, NY 10017, (800) 253-9646, Fax: (212) 963-4116, http://unstats.un.org; *Energy Statistics Yearbook 2003; Human Development Report 2006; Statistical Yearbook; Trends in Europe and North America: The Statistical Yearbook of the ECE 2005;* and *World Statistics Pocketbook.*

The World Bank, 1818 H Street, NW, Washington, DC 20433, (202) 473-1000, Fax: (202) 477-6391, www.worldbank.org; *The World Bank Atlas 2003-2004* and *World Development Report 2008.*

ARMENIA - PRICES

Euromonitor International, Inc., 224 S. Michigan Avenue, Suite 1500, Chicago, IL 60604, (312) 922-1115, Fax: (312) 922-1157, www.euromonitor.com; *World Marketing Data and Statistics.*

United Nations Food and Agricultural Organization (FAO), Viale delle Terme di Caracalla, 00100 Rome, Italy, (Dial from U.S. (202) 653-2400), (Fax from U.S. (202) 653 5760), www.fao.org; *FAO Production Yearbook 2002.*

The World Bank, 1818 H Street, NW, Washington, DC 20433, (202) 473-1000, Fax: (202) 477-6391, www.worldbank.org; *Armenia.*

ARMENIA - PROFESSIONS

United Nations Statistics Division, New York, NY 10017, (800) 253-9646, Fax: (212) 963-4116, http://unstats.un.org; *Statistical Yearbook.*

ARMENIA - PUBLIC HEALTH

Academic International Press, PO Box 1111, Gulf Breeze, FL 32562-1111, Fax: (850) 934-0953, www.ai-press.com; *Russia and Eurasia Facts and Figures Annual.*

Euromonitor International, Inc., 224 S. Michigan Avenue, Suite 1500, Chicago, IL 60604, (312) 922-1115, Fax: (312) 922-1157, www.euromonitor.com; *World Marketing Data and Statistics.*

Palgrave Macmillan Ltd., Houndmills, Basingstoke, Hampshire, RG21 6XS, England, (Telephone in U.S. (888) 330-8477), (Fax in U.S. (800) 672-2054), www.palgrave.com; *The Statesman's Yearbook 2008.*

United Nations Statistics Division, New York, NY 10017, (800) 253-9646, Fax: (212) 963-4116, http://unstats.un.org; *Human Development Report 2006; Statistical Yearbook;* and *Trends in Europe and North America: The Statistical Yearbook of the ECE 2005.*

The World Bank, 1818 H Street, NW, Washington, DC 20433, (202) 473-1000, Fax: (202) 477-6391, www.worldbank.org; *Armenia* and *World Development Report 2008.*

World Health Organization (WHO), Avenue Appia 20, 1211 Geneve 27, Switzerland, (Telephone in U.S. (212) 331-9081), www.who.int; The WHO Global Atlas of Infectious Diseases and *World Health Report 2006.*

ARMENIA - PUBLISHERS AND PUBLISHING

UNESCO Institute for Statistics, C.P. 6128 Succursale Centre-Ville, Montreal, Quebec, H3C 3J7

Canada, (Dial from U.S. (514) 343-6880), (Fax from U.S. (514) 343 6882), www.uis.unesco.org; *Statistical Tables.*

United Nations Statistics Division, New York, NY 10017, (800) 253-9646, Fax: (212) 963-4116, http://unstats.un.org; *Trends in Europe and North America: The Statistical Yearbook of the ECE 2005.*

ARMENIA - RADIO - RECEIVERS AND RECEPTION

Palgrave Macmillan Ltd., Houndmills, Basingstoke, Hampshire, RG21 6XS, England, (Telephone in U.S. (888) 330-8477), (Fax in U.S. (800) 672-2054), www.palgrave.com; *The Statesman's Yearbook 2008.*

United Nations Statistics Division, New York, NY 10017, (800) 253-9646, Fax: (212) 963-4116, http://unstats.un.org; *Statistical Yearbook.*

ARMENIA - RAILROADS

Palgrave Macmillan Ltd., Houndmills, Basingstoke, Hampshire, RG21 6XS, England, (Telephone in U.S. (888) 330-8477), (Fax in U.S. (800) 672-2054), www.palgrave.com; *The Statesman's Yearbook 2008.*

United Nations Statistics Division, New York, NY 10017, (800) 253-9646, Fax: (212) 963-4116, http://unstats.un.org; *Statistical Yearbook* and *Trends in Europe and North America: The Statistical Yearbook of the ECE 2005.*

ARMENIA - RELIGION

Academic International Press, PO Box 1111, Gulf Breeze, FL 32562-1111, Fax: (850) 934-0953, www.ai-press.com; *Russia and Eurasia Facts and Figures Annual.*

Central Intelligence Agency, Office of Public Affairs, Washington, DC 20505, (703) 482-0623, Fax: (703) 482-1739, www.cia.gov; *The World Factbook.*

Palgrave Macmillan Ltd., Houndmills, Basingstoke, Hampshire, RG21 6XS, England, (Telephone in U.S. (888) 330-8477), (Fax in U.S. (800) 672-2054), www.palgrave.com; *The Statesman's Yearbook 2008.*

ARMENIA - RETAIL TRADE

Euromonitor International, Inc., 224 S. Michigan Avenue, Suite 1500, Chicago, IL 60604, (312) 922-1115, Fax: (312) 922-1157, www.euromonitor.com; *World Marketing Data and Statistics.*

United Nations Statistics Division, New York, NY 10017, (800) 253-9646, Fax: (212) 963-4116, http://unstats.un.org; *Statistical Yearbook.*

ARMENIA - ROADS

Central Intelligence Agency, Office of Public Affairs, Washington, DC 20505, (703) 482-0623, Fax: (703) 482-1739, www.cia.gov; *The World Factbook.*

Palgrave Macmillan Ltd., Houndmills, Basingstoke, Hampshire, RG21 6XS, England, (Telephone in U.S. (888) 330-8477), (Fax in U.S. (800) 672-2054), www.palgrave.com; *The Statesman's Yearbook 2008.*

United Nations Statistics Division, New York, NY 10017, (800) 253-9646, Fax: (212) 963-4116, http://unstats.un.org; *Trends in Europe and North America: The Statistical Yearbook of the ECE 2005.*

ARMENIA - RUBBER INDUSTRY AND TRADE

International Rubber Study Group (IRSG), 1st Floor, Heron House, 109/115 Wembley Hill Road, Wembley, Middlesex HA9 8DA, United Kingdom, www.rubberstudy.com; *Rubber Statistical Bulletin; Summary of World Rubber Statistics 2005; World Rubber Statistics Handbook (Volume 6, 1975-2001);* and *World Rubber Statistics Historic Handbook.*

United Nations Statistics Division, New York, NY 10017, (800) 253-9646, Fax: (212) 963-4116, http://unstats.un.org; *Statistical Yearbook.*

ARMENIA - SHEEP

See ARMENIA - LIVESTOCK

ARMENIA - SHIPPING

United Nations Statistics Division, New York, NY 10017, (800) 253-9646, Fax: (212) 963-4116, http://unstats.un.org; *Statistical Yearbook.*

ARMENIA - SOCIAL ECOLOGY

United Nations Statistics Division, New York, NY 10017, (800) 253-9646, Fax: (212) 963-4116, http://unstats.un.org; *World Statistics Pocketbook.*

ARMENIA - SOCIAL SECURITY

United Nations Statistics Division, New York, NY 10017, (800) 253-9646, Fax: (212) 963-4116, http://unstats.un.org; *National Accounts Statistics: Compendium of Income Distribution Statistics.*

ARMENIA - STEEL PRODUCTION

See ARMENIA - MINERAL INDUSTRIES

ARMENIA - TAXATION

Taylor and Francis Group, An Informa Business, 2 Park Square, Milton Park, Abingdon, Oxford OX14 4RN, United Kingdom, (Dial from U.S. (212) 216-7800), (Fax from U.S. (212) 564-7854), www.tandf.co.uk; *The Europa World Year Book.*

ARMENIA - TELEPHONE

United Nations Statistics Division, New York, NY 10017, (800) 253-9646, Fax: (212) 963-4116, http://unstats.un.org; *Statistical Yearbook; Trends in Europe and North America: The Statistical Yearbook of the ECE 2005;* and *World Statistics Pocketbook.*

ARMENIA - TEXTILE INDUSTRY

Palgrave Macmillan Ltd., Houndmills, Basingstoke, Hampshire, RG21 6XS, England, (Telephone in U.S. (888) 330-8477), (Fax in U.S. (800) 672-2054), www.palgrave.com; *The Statesman's Yearbook 2008.*

United Nations Statistics Division, New York, NY 10017, (800) 253-9646, Fax: (212) 963-4116, http://unstats.un.org; *Statistical Yearbook.*

ARMENIA - THEATER

UNESCO Institute for Statistics, C.P. 6128 Succursale Centre-Ville, Montreal, Quebec, H3C 3J7 Canada, (Dial from U.S. (514) 343-6880), (Fax from U.S. (514) 343 6882), www.uis.unesco.org; *Statistical Tables.*

ARMENIA - TIRE INDUSTRY

United Nations Statistics Division, New York, NY 10017, (800) 253-9646, Fax: (212) 963-4116, http://unstats.un.org; *Statistical Yearbook.*

ARMENIA - TOBACCO INDUSTRY

Foreign Agricultural Service (FAS), U.S. Department of Agriculture (USDA), 1400 Independence Avenue, SW, Washington, DC 20250, (202) 720-3935, www.fas.usda.gov; *Tobacco: World Markets and Trade.*

United Nations Statistics Division, New York, NY 10017, (800) 253-9646, Fax: (212) 963-4116, http://unstats.un.org; *Statistical Yearbook.*

ARMENIA - TOURISM

Euromonitor International, Inc., 224 S. Michigan Avenue, Suite 1500, Chicago, IL 60604, (312) 922-1115, Fax: (312) 922-1157, www.euromonitor.com; *The World Economic Factbook 2008* and *World Marketing Data and Statistics.*

United Nations Statistics Division, New York, NY 10017, (800) 253-9646, Fax: (212) 963-4116, http://unstats.un.org; *Statistical Yearbook* and *Trends in Europe and North America: The Statistical Yearbook of the ECE 2005.*

The World Bank, 1818 H Street, NW, Washington, DC 20433, (202) 473-1000, Fax: (202) 477-6391, www.worldbank.org; *Armenia.*

ARMENIA - TRANSPORTATION

Academic International Press, PO Box 1111, Gulf Breeze, FL 32562-1111, Fax: (850) 934-0953, www.ai-press.com; *Russia and Eurasia Facts and Figures Annual.*

Central Intelligence Agency, Office of Public Affairs, Washington, DC 20505, (703) 482-0623, Fax: (703) 482-1739, www.cia.gov; *The World Factbook.*

Euromonitor International, Inc., 224 S. Michigan Avenue, Suite 1500, Chicago, IL 60604, (312) 922-1115, Fax: (312) 922-1157, www.euromonitor.com; *International Marketing Data and Statistics 2008* and *World Marketing Data and Statistics.*

Palgrave Macmillan Ltd., Houndmills, Basingstoke, Hampshire, RG21 6XS, England, (Telephone in U.S. (888) 330-8477), (Fax in U.S. (800) 672-2054), www.palgrave.com; *The Statesman's Yearbook 2008.*

United Nations Statistics Division, New York, NY 10017, (800) 253-9646, Fax: (212) 963-4116, http://unstats.un.org; *Human Development Report 2006* and *Trends in Europe and North America: The Statistical Yearbook of the ECE 2005.*

The World Bank, 1818 H Street, NW, Washington, DC 20433, (202) 473-1000, Fax: (202) 477-6391, www.worldbank.org; *Armenia.*

ARMENIA - UNEMPLOYMENT

Central Intelligence Agency, Office of Public Affairs, Washington, DC 20505, (703) 482-0623, Fax: (703) 482-1739, www.cia.gov; *The World Factbook.*

Palgrave Macmillan Ltd., Houndmills, Basingstoke, Hampshire, RG21 6XS, England, (Telephone in U.S. (888) 330-8477), (Fax in U.S. (800) 672-2054), www.palgrave.com; *The Statesman's Yearbook 2008.*

United Nations Statistics Division, New York, NY 10017, (800) 253-9646, Fax: (212) 963-4116, http://unstats.un.org; *Statistical Yearbook* and *Trends in Europe and North America: The Statistical Yearbook of the ECE 2005.*

The World Bank, 1818 H Street, NW, Washington, DC 20433, (202) 473-1000, Fax: (202) 477-6391, www.worldbank.org; *Armenia.*

ARMENIA - VITAL STATISTICS

Palgrave Macmillan Ltd., Houndmills, Basingstoke, Hampshire, RG21 6XS, England, (Telephone in U.S. (888) 330-8477), (Fax in U.S. (800) 672-2054), www.palgrave.com; *The Statesman's Yearbook 2008.*

United Nations Economic and Social Commission for Western Asia (ESCWA), PO Box 11-8575, Riad el-Solh Square, Beirut, Lebanon, www.escwa.un.org; *Annual Report 2006; Bulletin on Population and Vital Statistics in the ESCWA Region;* and *Survey of Economic and Social Developments in the ESCWA Region 2006-2007.*

United Nations Statistics Division, New York, NY 10017, (800) 253-9646, Fax: (212) 963-4116, http://unstats.un.org; *Statistical Yearbook.*

World Health Organization (WHO), Avenue Appia 20, 1211 Geneve 27, Switzerland, (Telephone in U.S. (212) 331-9081), www.who.int; *World Health Report 2006.*

ARMENIA - WAGES

United Nations Statistics Division, New York, NY 10017, (800) 253-9646, Fax: (212) 963-4116, http://unstats.un.org; *Statistical Yearbook.*

The World Bank, 1818 H Street, NW, Washington, DC 20433, (202) 473-1000, Fax: (202) 477-6391, www.worldbank.org; *Armenia.*

ARMENIA - WELFARE STATE

Palgrave Macmillan Ltd., Houndmills, Basingstoke, Hampshire, RG21 6XS, England, (Telephone in U.S. (888) 330-8477), (Fax in U.S. (800) 672-2054), www.palgrave.com; *The Statesman's Yearbook 2008.*

ARMENIA - WHOLESALE PRICE INDEXES

United Nations Statistics Division, New York, NY 10017, (800) 253-9646, Fax: (212) 963-4116, http://unstats.un.org; *Statistical Yearbook.*

ARMENIA - WHOLESALE TRADE

United Nations Statistics Division, New York, NY 10017, (800) 253-9646, Fax: (212) 963-4116, http://unstats.un.org; *Statistical Yearbook.*

ARMENIA - WOOL PRODUCTION

See ARMENIA - TEXTILE INDUSTRY

ARRESTS

See also LAW ENFORCEMENT

Federal Bureau of Investigation (FBI), J. Edgar Hoover Building, 935 Pennsylvania Avenue, NW, Washington, DC 20535-0001, (202) 324-3000, www.fbi.gov; *Crime in the United States (CIUS) 2007 (Preliminary).*

Justice Research and Statistics Association (JRSA), 777 N. Capitol Street, NE, Suite 801, Washington, DC 20002, (202) 842-9330, Fax: (202) 842-9329, www.jrsa.org; *Crime and Justice Atlas 2001.*

National Center for Juvenile Justice (NCJJ), 3700 South Water Street, Suite 200, Pittsburgh, PA 15203, (412) 227-6950, Fax: (412) 227-6955, http://ncjj.servehttp.com/NCJJWebsite/main.htm; *Detention and Delinquency Cases 1990-1999 (2003); Juvenile Arrests 2003 (2005);* and *Juveniles in Corrections (2004).*

U.S. Department of Homeland Security (DHS), Office of Immigration Statistics, Washington, DC 20528, (202) 282-8000, www.dhs.gov; *Immigration Enforcement Actions: 2005.*

U.S. Department of Justice (DOJ), Bureau of Justice Statistics, 810 Seventh Street, NW, Washington, DC 20531, (202) 307-0765, www.ojp.usdoj.gov/bjs/; *Contacts between Police and the Public: Findings from the 2002 National Survey; Federal Criminal Justice Trends, 2003;* and *The Sourcebook of Criminal Justice Statistics, 2003.*

U.S. Department of Justice (DOJ), National Institute of Justice (NIJ), 810 Seventh Street, NW, Washington, DC 20531, (202) 307-2942, Fax: (202) 616-0275, www.ojp.usdoj.gov/nij/; *Annual Report.*

ARSENIC

U.S. Department of the Interior (DOI), U.S. Geological Survey (USGS), Office of Minerals Information, 12201 Sunrise Valley Drive, Reston, VA 20192, Mr. Kenneth A. Beckman, (703) 648-4916, Fax: (703) 648-4995, http://minerals.usgs.gov/minerals; *Mineral Commodity Summaries.*

ARSON

Bureau of Alcohol, Tobacco, Firearms and Explosives (ATF), Office of Public and Governmental Affairs, 99 New York Avenue, NE, Mail Stop 5S144, Washington, DC 20226, (202) 927-7890, www.atf.gov; Bomb Arson Tracking System (BATS).

Federal Bureau of Investigation (FBI), J. Edgar Hoover Building, 935 Pennsylvania Avenue, NW, Washington, DC 20535-0001, (202) 324-3000, www.fbi.gov; *Crime in the United States (CIUS) 2007 (Preliminary).*

Justice Research and Statistics Association (JRSA), 777 N. Capitol Street, NE, Suite 801, Washington, DC 20002, (202) 842-9330, Fax: (202) 842-9329, www.jrsa.org; *Crime and Justice Atlas 2001.*

National Fire Protection Association (NFPA), One Batterymarch Park, Quincy, MA 02169-7471, (617) 770-3000, Fax: (617) 770-0700, www.nfpa.org; *Fire statistics.*

ARTERIOGRAPHY

National Center for Health Statistics (NCHS), Centers for Disease Control and Prevention (CDC), U.S. Department of Health and Human Services (HHS), 3311 Toledo Road, Hyattsville, MD 20782, (866) 232-4636, www.cdc.gov/nchs; unpublished data.

ARTERIOSCLEROSIS - DEATHS

Bernan Essential Government Publications, 4611-F Assembly Drive, Lanham MD, 20706-4391, (301) 459-2255, Fax: (800) 865-3450, www.bernan.com; *Vital Statistics of the United States: Births, Life Expectancy, Deaths, and Selected Health Data.*

National Center for Health Statistics (NCHS), Centers for Disease Control and Prevention (CDC), U.S. Department of Health and Human Services (HHS), 3311 Toledo Road, Hyattsville, MD 20782, (866) 232-4636, www.cdc.gov/nchs; *National Vital Statistics Reports (NVSR); Vital Statistics of the United States (VSUS);* and unpublished data.

ARTHRITIS

National Center for Health Statistics (NCHS), Centers for Disease Control and Prevention (CDC), U.S. Department of Health and Human Services (HHS), 3311 Toledo Road, Hyattsville, MD 20782, (866) 232-4636, www.cdc.gov/nchs; *Faststats A to Z.*

ARTISTS

National Endowment for the Arts (NEA), 1100 Pennsylvania Avenue, NW, Washington, DC 20506-0001, (202) 682-5400, www.arts.gov; *Artists in the Workforce: Employment and Earnings, 1970-1990* and *More Than Once in A Blue Moon: Multiple Jobholdings by American Artists.*

Statistics Iceland, Borgartuni 21a, 150 Reykjavik, Iceland, www.statice.is; *Associations of Media People, Graphic Designers and Artists 1980-2005.*

ARTS AND HUMANITIES

National Endowment for the Arts (NEA), 1100 Pennsylvania Avenue, NW, Washington, DC 20506-0001, (202) 682-5400, www.arts.gov; *The Changing Faces of Tradition: A Report on the Folk and Traditional Arts in the United States* and *Raising the Barre: The Geographic, Financial, and Economic Trends of Nonprofit Dance Companies.*

Statistics Iceland, Borgartuni 21a, 150 Reykjavik, Iceland, www.statice.is; *Associations of Media People, Graphic Designers and Artists 1980-2005.*

The Wallace Foundation, 5 Penn Plaza, 7th Floor, New York, NY 10001, (212) 251-9700, www.wallacefoundation.org; *Knowledge Center.*

ARTS AND HUMANITIES - AID TO

National Assembly of State Arts Agencies (NASAA), 1029 Vermont Avenue, NW, 2nd Floor, Washington, DC 20005, (202) 347-6352, Fax: (202) 737-0526, www.nasaa-arts.org; *Legislative Appropriations Annual Survey: Federal Year 2008.*

National Endowment for the Arts (NEA), 1100 Pennsylvania Avenue, NW, Washington, DC 20506-0001, (202) 682-5400, www.arts.gov; *2007 Annual Report.*

National Endowment for the Humanities (NEH), 1100 Pennsylvania Avenue, NW, Washington, DC 20506, (800) NEH-1121, www.neh.gov; *Annual Report.*

ARTS AND HUMANITIES - ARTS EDUCATION IN SCHOOLS

National Assembly of State Arts Agencies (NASAA), 1029 Vermont Avenue, NW, 2nd Floor, Washington, DC 20005, (202) 347-6352, Fax: (202) 737-0526, www.nasaa-arts.org; *Critical Evidence: How the Arts Benefit Student Achievement* and unpublished data.

National Center for Education Statistics (NCES), 1990 K Street, NW, Washington, DC 20006, (202) 502-7300, http://nces.ed.gov; *Arts Education in Public Elementary and Secondary Schools.*

National Endowment for the Arts (NEA), 1100 Pennsylvania Avenue, NW, Washington, DC 20506-0001, (202) 682-5400, www.arts.gov; *Effects of Arts Education on Participation in the Arts.*

ARTS AND HUMANITIES - ATTENDANCE

American Symphony Orchestra League, 33 West 60th Street, 5th Floor, New York, NY 10023-7905, (212) 262-5161, Fax: (212) 262-5198, www.symphony.org; *2005-2006 Orchestra Repertoire Report.*

The League of American Theatres and Producers, Inc., 226 West 47th Street, New York, NY 10036, (212) 764-1122, Fax: (212) 944-2136, www.livebroadway.com; *The Demographics of the Broadway Audience 2005-2006.*

National Endowment for the Arts (NEA), 1100 Pennsylvania Avenue, NW, Washington, DC 20506-0001, (202) 682-5400, www.arts.gov; *Age and Arts Participation: 1982-1997; American Participation in Theater; The Geography of Participation in the Arts and Culture;* and *2002 Survey of Public Participation in the Arts.*

OPERA America, 330 Seventh Avenue, 16th Floor, New York, NY 10001, (212) 796-8620, Fax: (212) 796-8631, www.operaamerica.org; *Annual Field Report 2005.*

Theatre Communications Group (TCG), 520 Eighth Avenue, 24th Floor, New York, NY 10018-4156, (212) 609-5900, Fax: (212) 609-5901, www.tcg.org; unpublished data.

ARTS AND HUMANITIES - CHARITABLE CONTRIBUTIONS

Independent Sector, 1200 Eighteenth Street, NW, Suite 200, Washington, DC 20036, (202) 467-6100, Fax: (202) 467-6101, www.independentsector.org; *Giving and Volunteering in the United States 2001.*

ARTS AND HUMANITIES - FEDERAL AID

National Assembly of State Arts Agencies (NASAA), 1029 Vermont Avenue, NW, 2nd Floor, Washington, DC 20005, (202) 347-6352, Fax: (202) 737-0526, www.nasaa-arts.org; *Legislative Appropriations Annual Survey: Federal Year 2008.*

National Endowment for the Arts (NEA), 1100 Pennsylvania Avenue, NW, Washington, DC 20506-0001, (202) 682-5400, www.arts.gov; *2007 Annual Report.*

National Endowment for the Humanities (NEH), 1100 Pennsylvania Avenue, NW, Washington, DC 20506, (800) NEH-1121, www.neh.gov; *Annual Report.*

ARTS AND HUMANITIES - GRANTS, FOUNDATIONS

The Foundation Center, 79 Fifth Avenue, New York, NY 10003-3076, (212) 620-4230, Fax: (212) 807-3677, www.fdncenter.org; *FC Stats - Grantmaker; FC Stats - Grants; Foundation Giving Trends (2008 Edition);* and *Top Funders: Top 100 U.S. Foundations by Asset Size.*

ARTS AND HUMANITIES - PARTICIPATION

National Endowment for the Arts (NEA), 1100 Pennsylvania Avenue, NW, Washington, DC 20506-0001, (202) 682-5400, www.arts.gov; *Age and Arts Participation: 1982-1997; American Participation in Theater; Effects of Arts Education on Participation in the Arts;* and *The Geography of Participation in the Arts and Culture.*

ARTS AND HUMANITIES - PHILANTHROPY

The Giving Institute, 4700 W. Lake Ave, Glenview, IL 60025, (800) 462-2372, Fax: (866) 607-0913, www.aafrc.org; *Giving USA 2006.*

ARTS AND HUMANITIES - PUBLIC CONFIDENCE

Independent Sector, 1200 Eighteenth Street, NW, Suite 200, Washington, DC 20036, (202) 467-6100, Fax: (202) 467-6101, www.independentsector.org; *Giving and Volunteering in the United States 2001.*

ARTS AND HUMANITIES - VOLUNTEER WORK

Independent Sector, 1200 Eighteenth Street, NW, Suite 200, Washington, DC 20036, (202) 467-6100, Fax: (202) 467-6101, www.independentsector.org; *Giving and Volunteering in the United States 2001.*

ARTS EDUCATION

National Center for Education Statistics (NCES), 1990 K Street, NW, Washington, DC 20006, (202) 502-7300, http://nces.ed.gov; *Arts Education in Public Elementary and Secondary Schools.*

National Endowment for the Arts (NEA), 1100 Pennsylvania Avenue, NW, Washington, DC 20506-0001, (202) 682-5400, www.arts.gov; *Effects of Arts Education on Participation in the Arts.*

ARTS, ENTERTAINMENT AND RECREATION

National Assembly of State Arts Agencies (NASAA), 1029 Vermont Avenue, NW, 2nd Floor, Washington, DC 20005, (202) 347-6352, Fax: (202) 737-0526, www.nasaa-arts.org; unpublished data.

National Endowment for the Arts (NEA), 1100 Pennsylvania Avenue, NW, Washington, DC 20506-0001, (202) 682-5400, www.arts.gov; *Age and Arts Participation: 1982-1997; American Participation in Theater;* and *The Geography of Participation in the Arts and Culture.*

U.S. Bureau of Labor Statistics (BLS), Postal Square Building, 2 Massachusetts Avenue, NE, Washington, DC 20212-0001, (202) 691-5200, Fax: (202) 691-6325, www.bls.gov; *Industries at a Glance.*

U.S. Census Bureau, Center for Economic Studies, 4600 Silver Hill Road, Washington DC 20233, (301) 457-1235, www.ces.census.gov; Economic Census (web app).

U.S. Census Bureau, Service Sector Statistics Division, 4700 Silver Hill Road, Washington DC 20233-0001, (301) 763-3030, www.census.gov/svsd/www/economic.html; *2004 Service Annual Survey: Arts, Entertainment, and Recreation.*

ARTS, ENTERTAINMENT AND RECREATION - CAPITAL

U.S. Census Bureau, Center for Economic Studies, 4600 Silver Hill Road, Washington DC 20233, (301) 457-1235, www.ces.census.gov; *2002 Economic Census, Arts, Entertainment and Recreation.*

U.S. Census Bureau, Company Statistics Division, 4700 Silver Hill Road, Washington DC 20233-0001, (301) 763-3030, www.census.gov/csd/; *Annual Capital Expenditures Survey (ACES).*

ARTS, ENTERTAINMENT AND RECREATION - EARNINGS

U.S. Census Bureau, 4700 Silver Hill Road, Washington DC 20233-0001, (301) 763-3030, www.census.gov; *2002 Economic Census, Nonemployer Statistics.*

U.S. Census Bureau, Center for Economic Studies, 4600 Silver Hill Road, Washington DC 20233, (301) 457-1235, www.ces.census.gov; *2002 Economic Census, Arts, Entertainment and Recreation; 2002 Economic Census, Geographic Area Series;* and *2002 Economic Census, Information.*

U.S. Census Bureau, Service Sector Statistics Division, 4700 Silver Hill Road, Washington DC 20233-0001, (301) 763-3030, www.census.gov/svsd/www/economic.html; *2004 Service Annual Survey: Arts, Entertainment, and Recreation.*

ARTS, ENTERTAINMENT AND RECREATION - EMPLOYEES

U.S. Census Bureau, Service Sector Statistics Division, 4700 Silver Hill Road, Washington DC 20233-0001, (301) 763-3030, www.census.gov/svsd/www/economic.html; *2004 Service Annual Survey: Arts, Entertainment, and Recreation.*

ARTS, ENTERTAINMENT AND RECREATION - FINANCES

U.S. Census Bureau, 4700 Silver Hill Road, Washington DC 20233-0001, (301) 763-3030, www.census.gov; *Survey of Income and Program Participation (SIPP).*

U.S. Census Bureau, Center for Economic Studies, 4600 Silver Hill Road, Washington DC 20233, (301) 457-1235, www.ces.census.gov; *2002 Economic Census, Arts, Entertainment and Recreation* and *2002 Economic Census, Information.*

U.S. Census Bureau, Company Statistics Division, 4700 Silver Hill Road, Washington DC 20233-0001, (301) 763-3030, www.census.gov/csd/; *County Business Patterns 2004.*

U.S. Census Bureau, Service Sector Statistics Division, 4700 Silver Hill Road, Washington DC 20233-0001, (301) 763-3030, www.census.gov/svsd/www/economic.html; *2004 Service Annual Survey: Arts, Entertainment, and Recreation.*

ARTS, ENTERTAINMENT AND RECREATION - INDUSTRIAL SAFETY

U.S. Bureau of Labor Statistics (BLS), Postal Square Building, 2 Massachusetts Avenue, NE, Washington, DC 20212-0001, (202) 691-5200, Fax: (202) 691-6325, www.bls.gov; *Injuries, Illnesses, and Fatalities (IIF).*

ARTS, ENTERTAINMENT AND RECREATION - MERGERS AND ACQUISITIONS

Thomson Financial, 195 Broadway, New York, NY 10007, (646) 822-2000, www.thomson.com; Thomson Research.

ARTS, ENTERTAINMENT AND RECREATION - NONEMPLOYER ESTABLISHMENTS

U.S. Census Bureau, 4700 Silver Hill Road, Washington DC 20233-0001, (301) 763-3030, www.census.gov; *2002 Economic Census, Nonemployer Statistics.*

U.S. Census Bureau, Center for Economic Studies, 4600 Silver Hill Road, Washington DC 20233, (301) 457-1235, www.ces.census.gov; *2002 Economic Census, Geographic Area Series.*

ARTS, ENTERTAINMENT AND RECREATION - REVENUE, RECEIPTS

U.S. Census Bureau, Center for Economic Studies, 4600 Silver Hill Road, Washington DC 20233, (301) 457-1235, www.ces.census.gov; *2002 Economic Census, Arts, Entertainment and Recreation.*

U.S. Census Bureau, Service Sector Statistics Division, 4700 Silver Hill Road, Washington DC 20233-0001, (301) 763-3030, www.census.gov/svsd/www/economic.html; *2004 Service Annual Survey: Arts, Entertainment, and Recreation.*

U.S. Department of the Treasury (DOT), Internal Revenue Service (IRS), Statistics of Income Division (SIS), PO Box 2608, Washington, DC, 20013-2608, (202) 874-0410, Fax: (202) 874-0964, www.irs.ustreas.gov; *Statistics of Income Bulletin* and various fact sheets.

ARTWORK

National Endowment for the Arts (NEA), 1100 Pennsylvania Avenue, NW, Washington, DC 20506-0001, (202) 682-5400, www.arts.gov; *2002 Survey of Public Participation in the Arts.*

ARUBA - NATIONAL STATISTICAL OFFICE

Central Bureau of Statistics (CBS), Sun Plaza Mall, L. G. Smith Boulevard 160, Aruba, www.aruba.com/extlinks/govs/cbstats.html; National Data Center.

ARUBA - AGRICULTURE

Economist Intelligence Unit, 111 West 57th Street, New York, NY 10019, (212) 554-0600, Fax: (212) 586-1181, www.eiu.com; *Aruba Country Report.*

Euromonitor International, Inc., 224 S. Michigan Avenue, Suite 1500, Chicago, IL 60604, (312) 922-1115, Fax: (312) 922-1157, www.euromonitor.com; *World Marketing Data and Statistics.*

United Nations Food and Agricultural Organization (FAO), Viale delle Terme di Caracalla, 00100 Rome, Italy, (Dial from U.S. (202) 653-2400), (Fax from U.S. (202) 653 5760), www.fao.org; AQUASTAT.

The World Bank, 1818 H Street, NW, Washington, DC 20433, (202) 473-1000, Fax: (202) 477-6391, www.worldbank.org; *Aruba.*

ARUBA - AIRLINES

Palgrave Macmillan Ltd., Houndmills, Basingstoke, Hampshire, RG21 6XS, England, (Telephone in U.S. (888) 330-8477), (Fax in U.S. (800) 672-2054), www.palgrave.com; *The Statesman's Yearbook 2008.*

ARUBA - AIRPORTS

Central Intelligence Agency, Office of Public Affairs, Washington, DC 20505, (703) 482-0623, Fax: (703) 482-1739, www.cia.gov; *The World Factbook.*

ARUBA - ARMED FORCES

Central Intelligence Agency, Office of Public Affairs, Washington, DC 20505, (703) 482-0623, Fax: (703) 482-1739, www.cia.gov; *The World Factbook.*

Euromonitor International, Inc., 224 S. Michigan Avenue, Suite 1500, Chicago, IL 60604, (312) 922-1115, Fax: (312) 922-1157, www.euromonitor.com; *World Marketing Data and Statistics.*

ARUBA - BALANCE OF PAYMENTS

Taylor and Francis Group, An Informa Business, 2 Park Square, Milton Park, Abingdon, Oxford OX14 4RN, United Kingdom, (Dial from U.S. (212) 216-7800), (Fax from U.S. (212) 564-7854), www.tandf.co.uk; *The Europa World Year Book.*

The World Bank, 1818 H Street, NW, Washington, DC 20433, (202) 473-1000, Fax: (202) 477-6391, www.worldbank.org; *Aruba.*

ARUBA - BANKS AND BANKING

Euromonitor International, Inc., 224 S. Michigan Avenue, Suite 1500, Chicago, IL 60604, (312) 922-1115, Fax: (312) 922-1157, www.euromonitor.com; *World Marketing Data and Statistics.*

Taylor and Francis Group, An Informa Business, 2 Park Square, Milton Park, Abingdon, Oxford OX14 4RN, United Kingdom, (Dial from U.S. (212) 216-7800), (Fax from U.S. (212) 564-7854), www.tandf.co.uk; *The Europa World Year Book.*

ARUBA - BROADCASTING

Central Intelligence Agency, Office of Public Affairs, Washington, DC 20505, (703) 482-0623, Fax: (703) 482-1739, www.cia.gov; *The World Factbook.*

Euromonitor International, Inc., 224 S. Michigan Avenue, Suite 1500, Chicago, IL 60604, (312) 922-1115, Fax: (312) 922-1157, www.euromonitor.com; *World Marketing Data and Statistics.*

Palgrave Macmillan Ltd., Houndmills, Basingstoke, Hampshire, RG21 6XS, England, (Telephone in U.S. (888) 330-8477), (Fax in U.S. (800) 672-2054), www.palgrave.com; *The Statesman's Yearbook 2008.*

WRTH Publications Limited, PO Box 290, Oxford OX2 7FT, UK, www.wrth.com; *World Radio TV Handbook 2007.*

ARUBA - BUDGET

Central Intelligence Agency, Office of Public Affairs, Washington, DC 20505, (703) 482-0623, Fax: (703) 482-1739, www.cia.gov; *The World Factbook.*

ARUBA - CHILDBIRTH - STATISTICS

Central Intelligence Agency, Office of Public Affairs, Washington, DC 20505, (703) 482-0623, Fax: (703) 482-1739, www.cia.gov; *The World Factbook.*

Euromonitor International, Inc., 224 S. Michigan Avenue, Suite 1500, Chicago, IL 60604, (312) 922-1115, Fax: (312) 922-1157, www.euromonitor.com; *International Marketing Data and Statistics 2008* and *The World Economic Factbook 2008.*

Taylor and Francis Group, An Informa Business, 2 Park Square, Milton Park, Abingdon, Oxford OX14 4RN, United Kingdom, (Dial from U.S. (212) 216-7800), (Fax from U.S. (212) 564-7854), www.tandf.co.uk; *The Europa World Year Book.*

ARUBA - CLIMATE

Palgrave Macmillan Ltd., Houndmills, Basingstoke, Hampshire, RG21 6XS, England, (Telephone in U.S. (888) 330-8477), (Fax in U.S. (800) 672-2054), www.palgrave.com; *The Statesman's Yearbook 2008.*

ARUBA - COMMERCE

Palgrave Macmillan Ltd., Houndmills, Basingstoke, Hampshire, RG21 6XS, England, (Telephone in U.S. (888) 330-8477), (Fax in U.S. (800) 672-2054), www.palgrave.com; *The Statesman's Yearbook 2008.*

ARUBA - CONSUMER PRICE INDEXES

Taylor and Francis Group, An Informa Business, 2 Park Square, Milton Park, Abingdon, Oxford OX14 4RN, United Kingdom, (Dial from U.S. (212) 216-7800), (Fax from U.S. (212) 564-7854), www.tandf.co.uk; *The Europa World Year Book.*

The World Bank, 1818 H Street, NW, Washington, DC 20433, (202) 473-1000, Fax: (202) 477-6391, www.worldbank.org; *Aruba.*

ARUBA - DEATH RATES

See ARUBA - MORTALITY

ARUBA - DEMOGRAPHY

Euromonitor International, Inc., 224 S. Michigan Avenue, Suite 1500, Chicago, IL 60604, (312) 922-1115, Fax: (312) 922-1157, www.euromonitor.com; *International Marketing Data and Statistics 2008; The World Economic Factbook 2008;* and *World Marketing Data and Statistics.*

The World Bank, 1818 H Street, NW, Washington, DC 20433, (202) 473-1000, Fax: (202) 477-6391, www.worldbank.org; *Aruba.*

ARUBA - ECONOMIC CONDITIONS

Center for International Business Education Research (CIBER), Columbia Business School and School of International and Public Affairs, Uris Hall, Room 212, 3022 Broadway, New York, NY 10027-6902, Mr. Joshua Safier, (212) 854-4750, Fax: (212) 222-9821, www.columbia.edu/cu/ciber/; Datastream International.

Central Intelligence Agency, Office of Public Affairs, Washington, DC 20505, (703) 482-0623, Fax: (703) 482-1739, www.cia.gov; *The World Factbook.*

DSI Data Service Information, Xantener Strasse 51a, D-47495 Rheinberg, Germany, www.dsidata.com; *Campus Solution.*

Dun and Bradstreet (DB) Corporation, 103 JFK Parkway, Short Hills, NJ 07078, (973) 921-5500, www.dnb.com; *Country Report.*

Economist Intelligence Unit, 111 West 57th Street, New York, NY 10019, (212) 554-0600, Fax: (212) 586-1181, www.eiu.com; *Aruba Country Report.*

Euromonitor International, Inc., 224 S. Michigan Avenue, Suite 1500, Chicago, IL 60604, (312) 922-1115, Fax: (312) 922-1157, www.euromonitor.com; *The World Economic Factbook 2008.*

International Monetary Fund (IMF), 700 Nineteenth Street, NW, Washington, DC 20431, (202) 623-7000, Fax: (202) 623-4661, www.imf.org; *World Economic Outlook Reports.*

United Nations Statistics Division, New York, NY 10017, (800) 253-9646, Fax: (212) 963-4116, http://unstats.un.org; *World Statistics Pocketbook.*

The World Bank, 1818 H Street, NW, Washington, DC 20433, (202) 473-1000, Fax: (202) 477-6391, www.worldbank.org; *Aruba; Global Economic Monitor (GEM); Global Economic Prospects 2008;* and *The World Bank Atlas 2003-2004.*

ARUBA - EDUCATION

Euromonitor International, Inc., 224 S. Michigan Avenue, Suite 1500, Chicago, IL 60604, (312) 922-1115, Fax: (312) 922-1157, www.euromonitor.com; *International Marketing Data and Statistics 2008* and *World Marketing Data and Statistics.*

Palgrave Macmillan Ltd., Houndmills, Basingstoke, Hampshire, RG21 6XS, England, (Telephone in U.S. (888) 330-8477), (Fax in U.S. (800) 672-2054), www.palgrave.com; *The Statesman's Yearbook 2008.*

Taylor and Francis Group, An Informa Business, 2 Park Square, Milton Park, Abingdon, Oxford OX14 4RN, United Kingdom, (Dial from U.S. (212) 216-7800), (Fax from U.S. (212) 564-7854), www.tandf.co.uk; *The Europa World Year Book.*

The World Bank, 1818 H Street, NW, Washington, DC 20433, (202) 473-1000, Fax: (202) 477-6391, www.worldbank.org; *Aruba.*

ARUBA - ELECTRICITY

Palgrave Macmillan Ltd., Houndmills, Basingstoke, Hampshire, RG21 6XS, England, (Telephone in U.S. (888) 330-8477), (Fax in U.S. (800) 672-2054), www.palgrave.com; *The Statesman's Yearbook 2008.*

ARUBA - EMPLOYMENT

Euromonitor International, Inc., 224 S. Michigan Avenue, Suite 1500, Chicago, IL 60604, (312) 922-1115, Fax: (312) 922-1157, www.euromonitor.com; *International Marketing Data and Statistics 2008.*

The World Bank, 1818 H Street, NW, Washington, DC 20433, (202) 473-1000, Fax: (202) 477-6391, www.worldbank.org; *Aruba.*

ARUBA - ENVIRONMENTAL CONDITIONS

DSI Data Service Information, Xantener Strasse 51a, D-47495 Rheinberg, Germany, www.dsidata.com; *Campus Solution* and *DSI's Global Environmental Database.*

Economist Intelligence Unit, 111 West 57th Street, New York, NY 10019, (212) 554-0600, Fax: (212) 586-1181, www.eiu.com; *Aruba Country Report.*

United Nations Statistics Division, New York, NY 10017, (800) 253-9646, Fax: (212) 963-4116, http://unstats.un.org; *World Statistics Pocketbook.*

ARUBA - EXPORTS

Central Intelligence Agency, Office of Public Affairs, Washington, DC 20505, (703) 482-0623, Fax: (703) 482-1739, www.cia.gov; *The World Factbook.*

Economist Intelligence Unit, 111 West 57th Street, New York, NY 10019, (212) 554-0600, Fax: (212) 586-1181, www.eiu.com; *Aruba Country Report.*

Euromonitor International, Inc., 224 S. Michigan Avenue, Suite 1500, Chicago, IL 60604, (312) 922-1115, Fax: (312) 922-1157, www.euromonitor.com; *International Marketing Data and Statistics 2008* and *The World Economic Factbook 2008.*

Palgrave Macmillan Ltd., Houndmills, Basingstoke, Hampshire, RG21 6XS, England, (Telephone in U.S. (888) 330-8477), (Fax in U.S. (800) 672-2054), www.palgrave.com; *The Statesman's Yearbook 2008.*

Taylor and Francis Group, An Informa Business, 2 Park Square, Milton Park, Abingdon, Oxford OX14 4RN, United Kingdom, (Dial from U.S. (212) 216-7800), (Fax from U.S. (212) 564-7854), www.tandf.co.uk; *The Europa World Year Book.*

ARUBA - FERTILITY, HUMAN

The World Bank, 1818 H Street, NW, Washington, DC 20433, (202) 473-1000, Fax: (202) 477-6391, www.worldbank.org; *The World Bank Atlas 2003-2004.*

ARUBA - FINANCE, PUBLIC

Bernan Essential Government Publications, 4611-F Assembly Drive, Lanham MD, 20706-4391, (301) 459-2255, Fax: (800) 865-3450, www.bernan.com; *National Accounts Statistics.*

Economist Intelligence Unit, 111 West 57th Street, New York, NY 10019, (212) 554-0600, Fax: (212) 586-1181, www.eiu.com; *Aruba Country Report.*

International Monetary Fund (IMF), 700 Nineteenth Street, NW, Washington, DC 20431, (202) 623-7000, Fax: (202) 623-4661, www.imf.org; *International Financial Statistics* and *International Financial Statistics Online Service.*

Palgrave Macmillan Ltd., Houndmills, Basingstoke, Hampshire, RG21 6XS, England, (Telephone in U.S. (888) 330-8477), (Fax in U.S. (800) 672-2054), www.palgrave.com; *The Statesman's Yearbook 2008.*

Taylor and Francis Group, An Informa Business, 2 Park Square, Milton Park, Abingdon, Oxford OX14 4RN, United Kingdom, (Dial from U.S. (212) 216-7800), (Fax from U.S. (212) 564-7854), www.tandf.co.uk; *The Europa World Year Book.*

The World Bank, 1818 H Street, NW, Washington, DC 20433, (202) 473-1000, Fax: (202) 477-6391, www.worldbank.org; *Aruba.*

ARUBA - FISHERIES

Taylor and Francis Group, An Informa Business, 2 Park Square, Milton Park, Abingdon, Oxford OX14 4RN, United Kingdom, (Dial from U.S. (212) 216-7800), (Fax from U.S. (212) 564-7854), www.tandf.co.uk; *The Europa World Year Book.*

The World Bank, 1818 H Street, NW, Washington, DC 20433, (202) 473-1000, Fax: (202) 477-6391, www.worldbank.org; *Aruba.*

ARUBA - FOREIGN EXCHANGE RATES

Central Intelligence Agency, Office of Public Affairs, Washington, DC 20505, (703) 482-0623, Fax: (703) 482-1739, www.cia.gov; *The World Factbook.*

Euromonitor International, Inc., 224 S. Michigan Avenue, Suite 1500, Chicago, IL 60604, (312) 922-1115, Fax: (312) 922-1157, www.euromonitor.com; *International Marketing Data and Statistics 2008* and *The World Economic Factbook 2008.*

Taylor and Francis Group, An Informa Business, 2 Park Square, Milton Park, Abingdon, Oxford OX14 4RN, United Kingdom, (Dial from U.S. (212) 216-7800), (Fax from U.S. (212) 564-7854), www.tandf.co.uk; *The Europa World Year Book.*

United Nations Statistics Division, New York, NY 10017, (800) 253-9646, Fax: (212) 963-4116, http://unstats.un.org; *World Statistics Pocketbook.*

ARUBA - GROSS DOMESTIC PRODUCT

Economist Intelligence Unit, 111 West 57th Street, New York, NY 10019, (212) 554-0600, Fax: (212) 586-1181, www.eiu.com; *Aruba Country Report.*

Euromonitor International, Inc., 224 S. Michigan Avenue, Suite 1500, Chicago, IL 60604, (312) 922-1115, Fax: (312) 922-1157, www.euromonitor.com; *International Marketing Data and Statistics 2008* and *The World Economic Factbook 2008.*

Taylor and Francis Group, An Informa Business, 2 Park Square, Milton Park, Abingdon, Oxford OX14 4RN, United Kingdom, (Dial from U.S. (212) 216-7800), (Fax from U.S. (212) 564-7854), www.tandf.co.uk; *The Europa World Year Book.*

ARUBA - GROSS NATIONAL PRODUCT

The World Bank, 1818 H Street, NW, Washington, DC 20433, (202) 473-1000, Fax: (202) 477-6391, www.worldbank.org; *The World Bank Atlas 2003-2004.*

ARUBA - HOUSING

Euromonitor International, Inc., 224 S. Michigan Avenue, Suite 1500, Chicago, IL 60604, (312) 922-1115, Fax: (312) 922-1157, www.euromonitor.com; *World Marketing Data and Statistics.*

ARUBA - ILLITERATE PERSONS

Central Intelligence Agency, Office of Public Affairs, Washington, DC 20505, (703) 482-0623, Fax: (703) 482-1739, www.cia.gov; *The World Factbook.*

Euromonitor International, Inc., 224 S. Michigan Avenue, Suite 1500, Chicago, IL 60604, (312) 922-1115, Fax: (312) 922-1157, www.euromonitor.com; *The World Economic Factbook 2008.*

ARUBA - IMPORTS

Central Intelligence Agency, Office of Public Affairs, Washington, DC 20505, (703) 482-0623, Fax: (703) 482-1739, www.cia.gov; *The World Factbook.*

Economist Intelligence Unit, 111 West 57th Street, New York, NY 10019, (212) 554-0600, Fax: (212) 586-1181, www.eiu.com; *Aruba Country Report.*

Euromonitor International, Inc., 224 S. Michigan Avenue, Suite 1500, Chicago, IL 60604, (312) 922-1115, Fax: (312) 922-1157, www.euromonitor.com; *The World Economic Factbook 2008.*

Palgrave Macmillan Ltd., Houndmills, Basingstoke, Hampshire, RG21 6XS, England, (Telephone in U.S. (888) 330-8477), (Fax in U.S. (800) 672-2054), www.palgrave.com; *The Statesman's Yearbook 2008.*

Taylor and Francis Group, An Informa Business, 2 Park Square, Milton Park, Abingdon, Oxford OX14 4RN, United Kingdom, (Dial from U.S. (212) 216-7800), (Fax from U.S. (212) 564-7854), www.tandf.co.uk; *The Europa World Year Book.*

ARUBA - INDUSTRIES

Central Intelligence Agency, Office of Public Affairs, Washington, DC 20505, (703) 482-0623, Fax: (703) 482-1739, www.cia.gov; *The World Factbook.*

Economist Intelligence Unit, 111 West 57th Street, New York, NY 10019, (212) 554-0600, Fax: (212) 586-1181, www.eiu.com; *Aruba Country Report.*

Euromonitor International, Inc., 224 S. Michigan Avenue, Suite 1500, Chicago, IL 60604, (312) 922-1115, Fax: (312) 922-1157, www.euromonitor.com; *The World Economic Factbook 2008* and *World Marketing Data and Statistics.*

Taylor and Francis Group, An Informa Business, 2 Park Square, Milton Park, Abingdon, Oxford OX14 4RN, United Kingdom, (Dial from U.S. (212) 216-7800), (Fax from U.S. (212) 564-7854), www.tandf.co.uk; *The Europa World Year Book.*

United Nations Industrial Development Organization (UNIDO), 1 United Nations Plaza, New York, NY 10017, (212) 963 6890, Fax: (212) 963-7904, http://unido.org; Industrial Statistics Database 2008 (INDSTAT) and *The International Yearbook of Industrial Statistics 2008.*

The World Bank, 1818 H Street, NW, Washington, DC 20433, (202) 473-1000, Fax: (202) 477-6391, www.worldbank.org; *Aruba.*

ARUBA - INTERNATIONAL TRADE

Economist Intelligence Unit, 111 West 57th Street, New York, NY 10019, (212) 554-0600, Fax: (212) 586-1181, www.eiu.com; *Aruba Country Report.*

Euromonitor International, Inc., 224 S. Michigan Avenue, Suite 1500, Chicago, IL 60604, (312) 922-1115, Fax: (312) 922-1157, www.euromonitor.com; *The World Economic Factbook 2008* and *World Marketing Data and Statistics.*

Palgrave Macmillan Ltd., Houndmills, Basingstoke, Hampshire, RG21 6XS, England, (Telephone in U.S. (888) 330-8477), (Fax in U.S. (800) 672-2054), www.palgrave.com; *The Statesman's Yearbook 2008.*

Taylor and Francis Group, An Informa Business, 2 Park Square, Milton Park, Abingdon, Oxford OX14 4RN, United Kingdom, (Dial from U.S. (212) 216-7800), (Fax from U.S. (212) 564-7854), www.tandf.co.uk; *The Europa World Year Book.*

The World Bank, 1818 H Street, NW, Washington, DC 20433, (202) 473-1000, Fax: (202) 477-6391, www.worldbank.org; *Aruba.*

World Trade Organization (WTO), Centre William Rappard, Rue de Lausanne 154, CH-1211 Geneva 21, Switzerland, www.wto.org; *International Trade Statistics 2006.*

ARUBA - INTERNET USERS

International Telecommunication Union (ITU), Place des Nations, 1211 Geneva 20, Switzerland, www.itu.int; *World Telecommunication/ICT Indicators Database on CD-ROM; World Telecommunication/ICT Indicators Database Online;* and *Yearbook of Statistics - Telecommunication Services (Chronological Time Series 1997-2006).*

The World Bank, 1818 H Street, NW, Washington, DC 20433, (202) 473-1000, Fax: (202) 477-6391, www.worldbank.org; *Aruba.*

ARUBA - LABOR

Central Intelligence Agency, Office of Public Affairs, Washington, DC 20505, (703) 482-0623, Fax: (703) 482-1739, www.cia.gov; *The World Factbook.*

Euromonitor International, Inc., 224 S. Michigan Avenue, Suite 1500, Chicago, IL 60604, (312) 922-1115, Fax: (312) 922-1157, www.euromonitor.com; *International Marketing Data and Statistics 2008* and *World Marketing Data and Statistics.*

The World Bank, 1818 H Street, NW, Washington, DC 20433, (202) 473-1000, Fax: (202) 477-6391, www.worldbank.org; *The World Bank Atlas 2003-2004.*

ARUBA - LAND USE

Central Intelligence Agency, Office of Public Affairs, Washington, DC 20505, (703) 482-0623, Fax: (703) 482-1739, www.cia.gov; *The World Factbook.*

Euromonitor International, Inc., 224 S. Michigan Avenue, Suite 1500, Chicago, IL 60604, (312) 922-1115, Fax: (312) 922-1157, www.euromonitor.com; *International Marketing Data and Statistics 2008.*

ARUBA - LIFE EXPECTANCY

Euromonitor International, Inc., 224 S. Michigan Avenue, Suite 1500, Chicago, IL 60604, (312) 922-1115, Fax: (312) 922-1157, www.euromonitor.com; *The World Economic Factbook 2008.*

United Nations Statistics Division, New York, NY 10017, (800) 253-9646, Fax: (212) 963-4116, http://unstats.un.org; *World Statistics Pocketbook.*

The World Bank, 1818 H Street, NW, Washington, DC 20433, (202) 473-1000, Fax: (202) 477-6391, www.worldbank.org; *The World Bank Atlas 2003-2004.*

ARUBA - LITERACY

Euromonitor International, Inc., 224 S. Michigan Avenue, Suite 1500, Chicago, IL 60604, (312) 922-1115, Fax: (312) 922-1157, www.euromonitor.com; *World Marketing Data and Statistics.*

ARUBA - MINERAL INDUSTRIES

Palgrave Macmillan Ltd., Houndmills, Basingstoke, Hampshire, RG21 6XS, England, (Telephone in U.S. (888) 330-8477), (Fax in U.S. (800) 672-2054), www.palgrave.com; *The Statesman's Yearbook 2008.*

ARUBA - MONEY SUPPLY

Economist Intelligence Unit, 111 West 57th Street, New York, NY 10019, (212) 554-0600, Fax: (212) 586-1181, www.eiu.com; *Aruba Country Report.*

Taylor and Francis Group, An Informa Business, 2 Park Square, Milton Park, Abingdon, Oxford OX14 4RN, United Kingdom, (Dial from U.S. (212) 216-7800), (Fax from U.S. (212) 564-7854), www.tandf.co.uk; *The Europa World Year Book.*

The World Bank, 1818 H Street, NW, Washington, DC 20433, (202) 473-1000, Fax: (202) 477-6391, www.worldbank.org; *Aruba.*

ARUBA - MORTALITY

Central Intelligence Agency, Office of Public Affairs, Washington, DC 20505, (703) 482-0623, Fax: (703) 482-1739, www.cia.gov; *The World Factbook.*

Euromonitor International, Inc., 224 S. Michigan Avenue, Suite 1500, Chicago, IL 60604, (312) 922-1115, Fax: (312) 922-1157, www.euromonitor.com; *International Marketing Data and Statistics 2008* and *The World Economic Factbook 2008.*

Taylor and Francis Group, An Informa Business, 2 Park Square, Milton Park, Abingdon, Oxford OX14 4RN, United Kingdom, (Dial from U.S. (212) 216-7800), (Fax from U.S. (212) 564-7854), www.tandf.co.uk; *The Europa World Year Book.*

United Nations Statistics Division, New York, NY 10017, (800) 253-9646, Fax: (212) 963-4116, http://unstats.un.org; *World Statistics Pocketbook.*

The World Bank, 1818 H Street, NW, Washington, DC 20433, (202) 473-1000, Fax: (202) 477-6391, www.worldbank.org; *The World Bank Atlas 2003-2004.*

World Health Organization (WHO), Avenue Appia 20, 1211 Geneve 27, Switzerland, (Telephone in U.S. (212) 331-9081), www.who.int; The WHO Global Atlas of Infectious Diseases.

ARUBA - MOTOR VEHICLES

Taylor and Francis Group, An Informa Business, 2 Park Square, Milton Park, Abingdon, Oxford OX14 4RN, United Kingdom, (Dial from U.S. (212) 216-7800), (Fax from U.S. (212) 564-7854), www.tandf.co.uk; *The Europa World Year Book.*

ARUBA - POLITICAL SCIENCE

Central Intelligence Agency, Office of Public Affairs, Washington, DC 20505, (703) 482-0623, Fax: (703) 482-1739, www.cia.gov; *The World Factbook.*

Palgrave Macmillan Ltd., Houndmills, Basingstoke, Hampshire, RG21 6XS, England, (Telephone in U.S. (888) 330-8477), (Fax in U.S. (800) 672-2054), www.palgrave.com; *The Statesman's Yearbook 2008.*

ARUBA - POPULATION

Caribbean Epidemiology Centre (CAREC), 16-18 Jamaica Boulevard, Federation Park, PO Box 164, Port of Spain, Republic of Trinidad and Tobago, (Dial from U.S. (868) 622-4261), (Fax from U.S. (868) 622-2792), www.carec.org; *Population Data.*

Central Intelligence Agency, Office of Public Affairs, Washington, DC 20505, (703) 482-0623, Fax: (703) 482-1739, www.cia.gov; *The World Factbook.*

Economist Intelligence Unit, 111 West 57th Street, New York, NY 10019, (212) 554-0600, Fax: (212) 586-1181, www.eiu.com; *Aruba Country Report.*

Euromonitor International, Inc., 224 S. Michigan Avenue, Suite 1500, Chicago, IL 60604, (312) 922-1115, Fax: (312) 922-1157, www.euromonitor.com; *International Marketing Data and Statistics 2008* and *The World Economic Factbook 2008.*

Eurostat, Batiment Jean Monnet, Rue Alcide de Gasperi, L-2920 Luxembourg, http://epp.eurostat.ec.europa.eu; *Demographic Indicators - Population by Age-Classes.*

Palgrave Macmillan Ltd., Houndmills, Basingstoke, Hampshire, RG21 6XS, England, (Telephone in U.S. (888) 330-8477), (Fax in U.S. (800) 672-2054), www.palgrave.com; *The Statesman's Yearbook 2008.*

Taylor and Francis Group, An Informa Business, 2 Park Square, Milton Park, Abingdon, Oxford OX14 4RN, United Kingdom, (Dial from U.S. (212) 216-7800), (Fax from U.S. (212) 564-7854), www.tandf.co.uk; *The Europa World Year Book.*

United Nations Statistics Division, New York, NY 10017, (800) 253-9646, Fax: (212) 963-4116, http://unstats.un.org; *World Statistics Pocketbook.*

The World Bank, 1818 H Street, NW, Washington, DC 20433, (202) 473-1000, Fax: (202) 477-6391, www.worldbank.org; *Aruba* and *The World Bank Atlas 2003-2004.*

ARUBA - POPULATION DENSITY

Central Intelligence Agency, Office of Public Affairs, Washington, DC 20505, (703) 482-0623, Fax: (703) 482-1739, www.cia.gov; *The World Factbook.*

Euromonitor International, Inc., 224 S. Michigan Avenue, Suite 1500, Chicago, IL 60604, (312) 922-1115, Fax: (312) 922-1157, www.euromonitor.com; *The World Economic Factbook 2008.*

Palgrave Macmillan Ltd., Houndmills, Basingstoke, Hampshire, RG21 6XS, England, (Telephone in U.S. (888) 330-8477), (Fax in U.S. (800) 672-2054), www.palgrave.com; *The Statesman's Yearbook 2008.*

Taylor and Francis Group, An Informa Business, 2 Park Square, Milton Park, Abingdon, Oxford OX14 4RN, United Kingdom, (Dial from U.S. (212) 216-7800), (Fax from U.S. (212) 564-7854), www.tandf.co.uk; *The Europa World Year Book.*

The World Bank, 1818 H Street, NW, Washington, DC 20433, (202) 473-1000, Fax: (202) 477-6391, www.worldbank.org; *Aruba.*

ARUBA - POWER RESOURCES

Euromonitor International, Inc., 224 S. Michigan Avenue, Suite 1500, Chicago, IL 60604, (312) 922-1115, Fax: (312) 922-1157, www.euromonitor.com; *International Marketing Data and Statistics 2008; The World Economic Factbook 2008;* and *World Marketing Data and Statistics.*

Palgrave Macmillan Ltd., Houndmills, Basingstoke, Hampshire, RG21 6XS, England, (Telephone in U.S. (888) 330-8477), (Fax in U.S. (800) 672-2054), www.palgrave.com; *The Statesman's Yearbook 2008.*

United Nations Statistics Division, New York, NY 10017, (800) 253-9646, Fax: (212) 963-4116, http://unstats.un.org; *World Statistics Pocketbook.*

The World Bank, 1818 H Street, NW, Washington, DC 20433, (202) 473-1000, Fax: (202) 477-6391, www.worldbank.org; *The World Bank Atlas 2003-2004.*

ARUBA - PRICES

Euromonitor International, Inc., 224 S. Michigan Avenue, Suite 1500, Chicago, IL 60604, (312) 922-1115, Fax: (312) 922-1157, www.euromonitor.com; *World Marketing Data and Statistics.*

The World Bank, 1818 H Street, NW, Washington, DC 20433, (202) 473-1000, Fax: (202) 477-6391, www.worldbank.org; *Aruba.*

ARUBA - PUBLIC HEALTH

Euromonitor International, Inc., 224 S. Michigan Avenue, Suite 1500, Chicago, IL 60604, (312) 922-1115, Fax: (312) 922-1157, www.euromonitor.com; *World Marketing Data and Statistics.*

Palgrave Macmillan Ltd., Houndmills, Basingstoke, Hampshire, RG21 6XS, England, (Telephone in U.S. (888) 330-8477), (Fax in U.S. (800) 672-2054), www.palgrave.com; *The Statesman's Yearbook 2008.*

The World Bank, 1818 H Street, NW, Washington, DC 20433, (202) 473-1000, Fax: (202) 477-6391, www.worldbank.org; *Aruba.*

World Health Organization (WHO), Avenue Appia 20, 1211 Geneve 27, Switzerland, (Telephone in U.S. (212) 331-9081), www.who.int; The WHO Global Atlas of Infectious Diseases.

ARUBA - RADIO BROADCASTING

Palgrave Macmillan Ltd., Houndmills, Basingstoke, Hampshire, RG21 6XS, England, (Telephone in U.S. (888) 330-8477), (Fax in U.S. (800) 672-2054), www.palgrave.com; *The Statesman's Yearbook 2008.*

ARUBA - RELIGION

Central Intelligence Agency, Office of Public Affairs, Washington, DC 20505, (703) 482-0623, Fax: (703) 482-1739, www.cia.gov; *The World Factbook.*

Palgrave Macmillan Ltd., Houndmills, Basingstoke, Hampshire, RG21 6XS, England, (Telephone in U.S. (888) 330-8477), (Fax in U.S. (800) 672-2054), www.palgrave.com; *The Statesman's Yearbook 2008.*

ARUBA - RETAIL TRADE

Euromonitor International, Inc., 224 S. Michigan Avenue, Suite 1500, Chicago, IL 60604, (312) 922-1115, Fax: (312) 922-1157, www.euromonitor.com; *World Marketing Data and Statistics.*

ARUBA - ROADS

Central Intelligence Agency, Office of Public Affairs, Washington, DC 20505, (703) 482-0623, Fax: (703) 482-1739, www.cia.gov; *The World Factbook.*

Palgrave Macmillan Ltd., Houndmills, Basingstoke, Hampshire, RG21 6XS, England, (Telephone in U.S. (888) 330-8477), (Fax in U.S. (800) 672-2054), www.palgrave.com; *The Statesman's Yearbook 2008.*

ARUBA - SOCIAL ECOLOGY

United Nations Statistics Division, New York, NY 10017, (800) 253-9646, Fax: (212) 963-4116, http://unstats.un.org; *World Statistics Pocketbook.*

ARUBA - TELEPHONE

Palgrave Macmillan Ltd., Houndmills, Basingstoke, Hampshire, RG21 6XS, England, (Telephone in U.S. (888) 330-8477), (Fax in U.S. (800) 672-2054), www.palgrave.com; *The Statesman's Yearbook 2008.*

Taylor and Francis Group, An Informa Business, 2 Park Square, Milton Park, Abingdon, Oxford OX14 4RN, United Kingdom, (Dial from U.S. (212) 216-7800), (Fax from U.S. (212) 564-7854), www.tandf.co.uk; *The Europa World Year Book.*

United Nations Statistics Division, New York, NY 10017, (800) 253-9646, Fax: (212) 963-4116, http://unstats.un.org; *World Statistics Pocketbook.*

ARUBA - TOURISM

Euromonitor International, Inc., 224 S. Michigan Avenue, Suite 1500, Chicago, IL 60604, (312) 922-1115, Fax: (312) 922-1157, www.euromonitor.com; *The World Economic Factbook 2008* and *World Marketing Data and Statistics.*

Palgrave Macmillan Ltd., Houndmills, Basingstoke, Hampshire, RG21 6XS, England, (Telephone in U.S. (888) 330-8477), (Fax in U.S. (800) 672-2054), www.palgrave.com; *The Statesman's Yearbook 2008.*

Taylor and Francis Group, An Informa Business, 2 Park Square, Milton Park, Abingdon, Oxford OX14 4RN, United Kingdom, (Dial from U.S. (212) 216-7800), (Fax from U.S. (212) 564-7854), www.tandf.co.uk; *The Europa World Year Book.*

United Nations World Tourism Organization (UNWTO), Capitan Haya 42, 28020 Madrid, Spain, www.world-tourism.org; *Yearbook of Tourism Statistics.*

The World Bank, 1818 H Street, NW, Washington, DC 20433, (202) 473-1000, Fax: (202) 477-6391, www.worldbank.org; *Aruba.*

ARUBA - TRANSPORTATION

Central Intelligence Agency, Office of Public Affairs, Washington, DC 20505, (703) 482-0623, Fax: (703) 482-1739, www.cia.gov; *The World Factbook.*

Euromonitor International, Inc., 224 S. Michigan Avenue, Suite 1500, Chicago, IL 60604, (312) 922-1115, Fax: (312) 922-1157, www.euromonitor.com; *International Marketing Data and Statistics 2008* and *World Marketing Data and Statistics.*

Palgrave Macmillan Ltd., Houndmills, Basingstoke, Hampshire, RG21 6XS, England, (Telephone in U.S. (888) 330-8477), (Fax in U.S. (800) 672-2054), www.palgrave.com; *The Statesman's Yearbook 2008.*

Taylor and Francis Group, An Informa Business, 2 Park Square, Milton Park, Abingdon, Oxford OX14 4RN, United Kingdom, (Dial from U.S. (212) 216-7800), (Fax from U.S. (212) 564-7854), www.tandf.co.uk; *The Europa World Year Book.*

The World Bank, 1818 H Street, NW, Washington, DC 20433, (202) 473-1000, Fax: (202) 477-6391, www.worldbank.org; *Aruba.*

ARUBA - UNEMPLOYMENT

Central Intelligence Agency, Office of Public Affairs, Washington, DC 20505, (703) 482-0623, Fax: (703) 482-1739, www.cia.gov; *The World Factbook.*

ASBESTOS

Environmental Business International, Inc., 4452 Park Boulevard, Suite 306, San Diego, CA 92116, (619) 295-7685, Fax: (619) 295-5743, www.ebiusa.com; *Environmental Business Journal (EBJ) 2006; Environmental Market Reports;* and *U.S. and Global Environmental Market Data.*

U.S. Department of Justice (DOJ), Bureau of Justice Statistics, 810 Seventh Street, NW, Washington, DC 20531, (202) 307-0765, www.ojp.usdoj.gov/bjs/; *Federal Tort Trials and Verdicts, 2002-03.*

U.S. Department of the Interior (DOI), U.S. Geological Survey (USGS), Office of Minerals Information, 12201 Sunrise Valley Drive, Reston, VA 20192, Mr. Kenneth A. Beckman, (703) 648-4916, Fax: (703) 648-4995, http://minerals.usgs.gov/minerals; *Mineral Commodity Summaries.*

ASIA

See also Individual countries

Eurostat, Batiment Jean Monnet, Rue Alcide de Gasperi, L-2920 Luxembourg, http://epp.eurostat.ec.europa.eu; *Demographic Indicators - Population by Age-Classes.*

International Institute for Environment and Development (IIED), 3 Endsleigh Street, London, England, WC1H 0DD, United Kingdom, www.iied.org; *Environment Urbanization* and *Up in Smoke? Asia and the Pacific.*

Nomura Research Institute (NRI), 2 World Financial Center, Building B, 19th Fl., New York, NY 10281-1198, (212) 667-1670, www.nri.co.jp/english; *Asian Economic Outlook 2003-2004* and unpublished data.

Platts, 2 Penn Plaza, 25th Floor, New York, NY 10121-2298, (212) 904-3070, www.platts.com; *Asian Electricity Outlook 2006* and *Emissions Daily.*

United Nations Economic and Social Commission for Western Asia (ESCWA), PO Box 11-8575, Riad el-Solh Square, Beirut, Lebanon, www.escwa.un.org; *Annual Report 2006* and *Survey of Economic and Social Developments in the ESCWA Region 2006-2007.*

United Nations World Tourism Organization (UNWTO), Capitan Haya 42, 28020 Madrid, Spain, www.world-tourism.org; *Tourism Market Trends 2004 - Asia.*

ASIAN AND PACIFIC ISLANDER POPULATION

The Annie E. Casey Foundation, 701 Saint Paul Street, Baltimore, MD 21202, (410) 547-6600, Fax: (410) 547-3610, www.aecf.org; *Faith Matters: Race/Ethnicity, Religion, and Substance Abuse.*

Bernan Essential Government Publications, 4611-F Assembly Drive, Lanham MD, 20706-4391, (301) 459-2255, Fax: (800) 865-3450, www.bernan.com; *Vital Statistics of the United States: Births, Life Expectancy, Deaths, and Selected Health Data.*

Eurostat, Batiment Jean Monnet, Rue Alcide de Gasperi, L-2920 Luxembourg, http://epp.eurostat.ec.europa.eu; *Demographic Indicators - Population by Age-Classes.*

International Institute for Environment and Development (IIED), 3 Endsleigh Street, London, England, WC1H 0DD, United Kingdom, www.iied.org; *Up in Smoke? Asia and the Pacific.*

National Center for Health Statistics (NCHS), Centers for Disease Control and Prevention (CDC), U.S. Department of Health and Human Services (HHS), 3311 Toledo Road, Hyattsville, MD 20782, (866) 232-4636, www.cdc.gov/nchs; *Indicators of Social and Economic Well-Being by Race and Hispanic Origin; National Vital Statistics Reports (NVSR); Vital Statistics of the United States (VSUS);* and unpublished data.

National Center for Statistics and Analysis (NCSA) of the National Highway Traffic Safety Administration, West Building, 1200 New Jersey Avenue, S.E., Washington, DC 20590, (202) 366-1503, Fax: (202) 366-7078, www.nhtsa.gov; *Race and Ethnicity in Fatal Motor Vehicle Traffic Crashes 1999-2004.*

National Science Foundation, Division of Science Resources Statistics (SRS), 4201 Wilson Boulevard, Arlington, VA 22230, (703) 292-8780, Fax: (703) 292-9092, www.nsf.gov; *Selected Data on Science and Engineering Doctorate Awards* and *Survey of Earned Doctorates 2006.*

Population Reference Bureau, 1875 Connecticut Avenue, NW, Suite 520, Washington, DC, 20009-5728, (800) 877-9881, Fax: (202) 328-3937, www.prb.org; *The American People Series.*

U.S. Census Bureau, 4700 Silver Hill Road, Washington DC 20233-0001, (301) 763-3030, www.census.gov; American FactFinder (web app); *County and City Data Book 2007;* and *State and County QuickFacts.*

U.S. Census Bureau, Demographic Surveys Division, 4700 Silver Hill Road, Washington DC 20233-

0001, (301) 763-3030, www.census.gov; *Census 2000: Demographic Profiles.*

U.S. Census Bureau, Population Division, 4700 Silver Hill Road, Washington DC 20233-0001, (301) 763-3030, www.census.gov/population/www/; *The Asian and Pacific Islander Population in the United States* and *Census 2000 Profiles of General Demographic Characteristics.*

United Nations Economic and Social Commission for Western Asia (ESCWA), PO Box 11-8575, Riad el-Solh Square, Beirut, Lebanon, www.escwa.un.org; *Bulletin on Population and Vital Statistics in the ESCWA Region.*

ASIAN AND PACIFIC ISLANDER POPULATION - BUSINESS OWNERS

U.S. Census Bureau, Company Statistics Division, 4700 Silver Hill Road, Washington DC 20233-0001, (301) 763-3030, www.census.gov/csd/; *2002 Survey of Business Owners (SBO)* and *Survey of Minority-Owned Business Enterprises.*

ASIAN AND PACIFIC ISLANDER POPULATION - CHILDBIRTH - STATISTICS

Alan Guttmacher Institute, 125 Maiden Lane, 7th Floor, New York, NY 10038, (212) 248-1111, Fax: (212) 248-1951, www.agi-usa.org; *U.S. Teenage Pregnancy Statistics: Overall Trends, Trends by Race and Ethnicity and State-by-State Information* and *U.S. Teenage Pregnancy Statistics: Overall Trends, Trends by Race and Ethnicity and State-by-State Information.*

Bernan Essential Government Publications, 4611-F Assembly Drive, Lanham MD, 20706-4391, (301) 459-2255, Fax: (800) 865-3450, www.bernan.com; *Vital Statistics of the United States: Births, Life Expectancy, Deaths, and Selected Health Data.*

National Center for Health Statistics (NCHS), Centers for Disease Control and Prevention (CDC), U.S. Department of Health and Human Services (HHS), 3311 Toledo Road, Hyattsville, MD 20782, (866) 232-4636, www.cdc.gov/nchs; *National Vital Statistics Reports (NVSR); Vital Statistics of the United States (VSUS);* and unpublished data.

ASIAN AND PACIFIC ISLANDER POPULATION - CHILDREN UNDER EIGHTEEN YEARS OLD - POVERTY

National Center for Children in Poverty (NCCP), 215 W. 125th Street, 3rd Floor, New York, NY 10027, (646) 284-9600, Fax: (646) 284-9623, www.nccp.org; *Basic Facts About Low-Income Children; Child Poverty in 21st Century America; Low-Income Children in the United States: National and State Trend Data, 1996-2006;* and *Predictors of Child Care Subsidy Use.*

Population Reference Bureau, 1875 Connecticut Avenue, NW, Suite 520, Washington, DC, 20009-5728, (800) 877-9881, Fax: (202) 328-3937, www.prb.org; *Child Poverty in Rural America* and *Strengthening Rural Families: America's Rural Children.*

U.S. Census Bureau, Housing and Household Economics Statistics Division, 4700 Silver Hill Road, Washington DC 20233-0001, (301) 763-3030, www.census.gov/hhes/www; *Historical Poverty Tables.*

ASIAN AND PACIFIC ISLANDER POPULATION - CITIES

Population Reference Bureau, 1875 Connecticut Avenue, NW, Suite 520, Washington, DC, 20009-5728, (800) 877-9881, Fax: (202) 328-3937, www.prb.org; *The American People Series.*

U.S. Census Bureau, 4700 Silver Hill Road, Washington DC 20233-0001, (301) 763-3030, www.census.gov; American FactFinder (web app); *County and City Data Book 2007;* and *State and County QuickFacts.*

U.S. Census Bureau, Population Division, 4700 Silver Hill Road, Washington DC 20233-0001, (301) 763-3030, www.census.gov/population/www/; *Census 2000 Profiles of General Demographic Characteristics.*

ASIAN AND PACIFIC ISLANDER POPULATION - COLLEGE ENROLLMENT

National Center for Education Statistics (NCES), 1990 K Street, NW, Washington, DC 20006, (202) 502-7300, http://nces.ed.gov; *Digest of Education Statistics 2007.*

ASIAN AND PACIFIC ISLANDER POPULATION - COLLEGE ENROLLMENT - CREDIT CARD USE

National Center for Education Statistics (NCES), 1990 K Street, NW, Washington, DC 20006, (202) 502-7300, http://nces.ed.gov; *Profile of Undergraduates in U.S. Postsecondary Education Institutions: 2003-04, With a Special Analysis of Community College Students.*

ASIAN AND PACIFIC ISLANDER POPULATION - COLLEGE ENROLLMENT - DISABILITY

National Center for Education Statistics (NCES), 1990 K Street, NW, Washington, DC 20006, (202) 502-7300, http://nces.ed.gov; *Profile of Undergraduates in U.S. Postsecondary Education Institutions: 2003-04, With a Special Analysis of Community College Students.*

ASIAN AND PACIFIC ISLANDER POPULATION - COLLEGE ENROLLMENT - DISTANCE EDUCATION

National Center for Education Statistics (NCES), 1990 K Street, NW, Washington, DC 20006, (202) 502-7300, http://nces.ed.gov; *Profile of Undergraduates in U.S. Postsecondary Education Institutions: 2003-04, With a Special Analysis of Community College Students.*

ASIAN AND PACIFIC ISLANDER POPULATION - COMPUTER USE

National Telecommunications and Information Administration (NTIA), U.S. Department of Commerce (DOC), 1401 Constitution Avenue, NW, Washington, DC 20230, (202) 482-7002, www.ntia.doc.gov; *A Nation Online: Entering the Broadband Age.*

U.S. Census Bureau, Population Division, 4700 Silver Hill Road, Washington DC 20233-0001, (301) 763-3030, www.census.gov/population/www/; *The Asian and Pacific Islander Population in the United States.*

ASIAN AND PACIFIC ISLANDER POPULATION - CONGRESS, MEMBERS OF

U.S. Government Printing Office (GPO), Office of Congressional Publishing Services (OCPS), 732 North Capitol Street NW, Washington, DC 20401, (202) 512-0224, www.gpo.gov/customerservices/cps.htm; *Congressional Directory.*

ASIAN AND PACIFIC ISLANDER POPULATION - CONSUMER EXPENDITURES

Selig Center for Economic Growth, Terry College of Business, University of Georgia, Athens, GA 30602-6269, Mr. Jeffrey M. Humphreys, Director, (706) 425-2962, www.selig.uga.edu; *The Multicultural Economy: Minority Buying Power in 2006.*

ASIAN AND PACIFIC ISLANDER POPULATION - CRIMINAL STATISTICS

Federal Bureau of Investigation (FBI), J. Edgar Hoover Building, 935 Pennsylvania Avenue, NW, Washington, DC 20535-0001, (202) 324-3000, www.fbi.gov; *Crime in the United States (CIUS) 2007 (Preliminary).*

Justice Research and Statistics Association (JRSA), 777 N. Capitol Street, NE, Suite 801, Washington, DC 20002, (202) 842-9330, Fax: (202) 842-9329, www.jrsa.org; *Crime and Justice Atlas 2001.*

U.S. Department of Justice (DOJ), Bureau of Justice Statistics, 810 Seventh Street, NW, Washington, DC 20531, (202) 307-0765, www.ojp.usdoj.gov/bjs/; *Census of Jails; Crime and the Nation's Households, 2004; Mental Health Problems of Prison and Jail Inmates; State Court Sentencing of Convicted Felons; Substance Dependence, Abuse, and Treatment of Jail Inmates, 2002; Violence by Gang Members, 1993-2003;* and *Violent Felons in Large Urban Counties.*

ASIAN AND PACIFIC ISLANDER POPULATION - CRIMINAL VICTIMIZATION

U.S. Department of Justice (DOJ), Bureau of Justice Statistics, 810 Seventh Street, NW, Washington, DC 20531, (202) 307-0765, www.ojp.usdoj.gov/bjs/; *Weapon Use and Violent Crime, 1993-2001.*

ASIAN AND PACIFIC ISLANDER POPULATION - DEATHS AND DEATH RATES

National Center for Statistics and Analysis (NCSA) of the National Highway Traffic Safety Administration, West Building, 1200 New Jersey Avenue, S.E., Washington, DC 20590, (202) 366-1503, Fax: (202) 366-7078, www.nhtsa.gov; *Motor Vehicle Traffic Crashes as a Leading Cause of Death in the U.S., 2002 - A Demographic Perspective* and *Race and Ethnicity in Fatal Motor Vehicle Traffic Crashes 1999-2004.*

ASIAN AND PACIFIC ISLANDER POPULATION - EDUCATIONAL ATTAINMENT

Robert Wood Johnson Foundation, PO Box 2316, College Road East and Route 1, Princeton, NJ 08543, (877) 843-7953, www.rwjf.org; *Race Ethnicity, and the Education Gradient in Health.*

U.S. Census Bureau, 4700 Silver Hill Road, Washington DC 20233-0001, (301) 763-3030, www.census.gov; unpublished data.

U.S. Census Bureau, Population Division, 4700 Silver Hill Road, Washington DC 20233-0001, (301) 763-3030, www.census.gov/population/www/; *The Asian and Pacific Islander Population in the United States.*

ASIAN AND PACIFIC ISLANDER POPULATION - ELECTIONS, VOTER REGISTRATION AND TURNOUT

The Eagleton Institute of Politics, Rutgers, The State University of New Jersey, 191 Ryders Lane, New Brunswick, NJ 08901-8557, (732) 932-9384, Fax: (732) 932-6778, www.eagleton.rutgers.edu; *America's Newest Voters: Understanding Immigrant and Minority Voting Behavior.*

ASIAN AND PACIFIC ISLANDER POPULATION - FAMILIES

U.S. Census Bureau, Population Division, 4700 Silver Hill Road, Washington DC 20233-0001, (301) 763-3030, www.census.gov/population/www/; *The Asian and Pacific Islander Population in the United States.*

ASIAN AND PACIFIC ISLANDER POPULATION - FOOD STAMP PARTICIPANTS

Food and Nutrition Service (FNS), U.S. Department of Agriculture (USDA), 3101 Park Center Drive, Alexandria, VA 22302, (703) 305-2062, www.fns.usda.gov/fns; *Characteristics of Food Stamp Households: Fiscal Year 2005.*

ASIAN AND PACIFIC ISLANDER POPULATION - FOREIGN BORN POPULATION

Migration Information Source, Migration Policy Institute (MPI), 1400 16th Street NW, Suite 300, Washington, DC 20036-2257, (202) 266-1940, Fax: (202) 266-1900, www.migrationinformation.org; *Maps of the Foreign Born in the United States; US Census Data on the Foreign Born; US Historical Trends;* and *Who's Where in the United States?*

U.S. Census Bureau, Population Division, 4700 Silver Hill Road, Washington DC 20233-0001, (301) 763-3030, www.census.gov/population/www/; *The Asian and Pacific Islander Population in the United States* and *Foreign-Born Population in the U.S. 2003.*

ASIAN AND PACIFIC ISLANDER POPULATION - HEALTH INSURANCE COVERAGE

National Center for Health Statistics (NCHS), Centers for Disease Control and Prevention (CDC),

U.S. Department of Health and Human Services (HHS), 3311 Toledo Road, Hyattsville, MD 20782, (866) 232-4636, www.cdc.gov/nchs; *Faststats A to Z.*

ASIAN AND PACIFIC ISLANDER POPULATION - HOUSING TENURE

U.S. Census Bureau, Housing and Household Economics Statistics Division, 4700 Silver Hill Road, Washington DC 20233-0001, (301) 763-3030, www.census.gov/hhes/www; *Housing Characteristics: 2000.*

U.S. Census Bureau, Population Division, 4700 Silver Hill Road, Washington DC 20233-0001, (301) 763-3030, www.census.gov/population/www/; *The Asian and Pacific Islander Population in the United States.*

ASIAN AND PACIFIC ISLANDER POPULATION - IMMUNIZATION OF CHILDREN

Centers for Disease Control and Prevention (CDC), U.S. Department of Health and Human Services (HHS), 1600 Clifton Road, Atlanta, GA 30333, (800) 311-3435, www.cdc.gov; *Immunization Coverage in the U.S.; Morbidity and Mortality Weekly Report (MMWR);* and unpublished data.

National Center for Health Statistics (NCHS), Centers for Disease Control and Prevention (CDC), U.S. Department of Health and Human Services (HHS), 3311 Toledo Road, Hyattsville, MD 20782, (866) 232-4636, www.cdc.gov/nchs; *2005 National Immunization Survey (NIS).*

ASIAN AND PACIFIC ISLANDER POPULATION - INCOME

Selig Center for Economic Growth, Terry College of Business, University of Georgia, Athens, GA 30602-6269, Mr. Jeffrey M. Humphreys, Director, (706) 425-2962, www.selig.uga.edu; *The Multicultural Economy: Minority Buying Power in 2006.*

U.S. Census Bureau, Population Division, 4700 Silver Hill Road, Washington DC 20233-0001, (301) 763-3030, www.census.gov/population/www/; *The Asian and Pacific Islander Population in the United States.*

ASIAN AND PACIFIC ISLANDER POPULATION - LIVING ARRANGEMENTS

U.S. Census Bureau, Housing and Household Economics Statistics Division, 4700 Silver Hill Road, Washington DC 20233-0001, (301) 763-3030, www.census.gov/hhes/www; *Families and Living Arrangements.*

ASIAN AND PACIFIC ISLANDER POPULATION - MEDICAL CARE

National Center for Chronic Disease Prevention and Health Promotion (NCCDPHP), Centers for Disease Control and Prevention (CDC), 4770 Buford Hwy, NE, MS K-40, Atlanta, GA 30341-3717, (404) 639-3311, www.cdc.gov/nccdphp; *Racial and Ethnic Approaches to Community Health (REACH 2010): Addressing Disparities in Health.*

National Center for Health Statistics (NCHS), Centers for Disease Control and Prevention (CDC), U.S. Department of Health and Human Services (HHS), 3311 Toledo Road, Hyattsville, MD 20782, (866) 232-4636, www.cdc.gov/nchs; *Faststats A to Z* and *Health, United States, 2006, with Chartbook on Trends in the Health of Americans with Special Feature on Pain.*

Robert Wood Johnson Foundation, PO Box 2316, College Road East and Route 1, Princeton, NJ 08543, (877) 843-7953, www.rwjf.org; *Race Ethnicity, and the Education Gradient in Health* and *Reducing Racial and Ethnic Disparities and Improving Quality of Health Care.*

U.S. Department of Health and Human Services, 200 Independence Avenue, S.W., Washington, D.C. 20201, (202) 619-0257, www.hhs.gov; *Eliminating Health Disparities: Strengthening Data on Race, Ethnicity, and Primary Language in the United States.*

U.S. Department of Justice (DOJ), Bureau of Justice Statistics, 810 Seventh Street, NW, Washington, DC 20531, (202) 307-0765, www.ojp.usdoj.gov/bjs/; *Mental Health Problems of Prison and Jail Inmates.*

ASIAN AND PACIFIC ISLANDER POPULATION - NURSES

Health Resources and Services Administration (HRSA), National Center for Health Workforce Analysis (NCHWA), 5600 Fishers Lane, Rockville, MD 20857, (301) 443-2216, www.hrsa.gov; Registered Nurse Population: Findings from the 2004 National Sample Survey of Registered Nurses.

ASIAN AND PACIFIC ISLANDER POPULATION - OVERWEIGHT

National Center for Health Statistics (NCHS), Centers for Disease Control and Prevention (CDC), U.S. Department of Health and Human Services (HHS), 3311 Toledo Road, Hyattsville, MD 20782, (866) 232-4636, www.cdc.gov/nchs; unpublished data.

ASIAN AND PACIFIC ISLANDER POPULATION - POVERTY

U.S. Census Bureau, Housing and Household Economics Statistics Division, 4700 Silver Hill Road, Washington DC 20233-0001, (301) 763-3030, www.census.gov/hhes/www; *Historical Poverty Tables.*

U.S. Census Bureau, Population Division, 4700 Silver Hill Road, Washington DC 20233-0001, (301) 763-3030, www.census.gov/population/www/; *The Asian and Pacific Islander Population in the United States.*

ASIAN AND PACIFIC ISLANDER POPULATION - PRISONERS

U.S. Department of Justice (DOJ), Bureau of Justice Statistics, 810 Seventh Street, NW, Washington, DC 20531, (202) 307-0765, www.ojp.usdoj.gov/bjs/; *Mental Health Problems of Prison and Jail Inmates; National Corrections Reporting Program; Probation and Parole in the United States, 2004;* and *Veterans in Prison or Jail.*

ASIAN AND PACIFIC ISLANDER POPULATION - PROJECTIONS

U.S. Census Bureau, Population Division, 4700 Silver Hill Road, Washington DC 20233-0001, (301) 763-3030, www.census.gov/population/www/; *National Population Projections* and *Projected State Populations, by Sex, Race, and Hispanic Origin: 1995-2025.*

ASIAN AND PACIFIC ISLANDER POPULATION - SCHOOL ENROLLMENT

National Center for Education Statistics (NCES), 1990 K Street, NW, Washington, DC 20006, (202) 502-7300, http://nces.ed.gov; *Profile of Undergraduates in U.S. Postsecondary Education Institutions: 2003-04, With a Special Analysis of Community College Students.*

U.S. Census Bureau, Population Division, 4700 Silver Hill Road, Washington DC 20233-0001, (301) 763-3030, www.census.gov/population/www/; *The Asian and Pacific Islander Population in the United States.*

ASIAN AND PACIFIC ISLANDER POPULATION - STATES

U.S. Census Bureau, Demographic Surveys Division, 4700 Silver Hill Road, Washington DC 20233-0001, (301) 763-3030, www.census.gov; *Census 2000: Demographic Profiles.*

ASIAN AND PACIFIC ISLANDER POPULATION - VOTER REGISTRATION AND TURNOUT

The Eagleton Institute of Politics, Rutgers, The State University of New Jersey, 191 Ryders Lane, New Brunswick, NJ 08901-8557, (732) 932-9384, Fax: (732) 932-6778, www.eagleton.rutgers.edu; *America's Newest Voters: Understanding Immigrant and Minority Voting Behavior.*

ASIAN INDIAN POPULATION

National Telecommunications and Information Administration (NTIA), U.S. Department of Commerce (DOC), 1401 Constitution Avenue, NW, Washington, DC 20230, (202) 482-7002, www.ntia.doc.gov; *A Nation Online: Entering the Broadband Age.*

U.S. Census Bureau, Demographic Surveys Division, 4700 Silver Hill Road, Washington DC 20233-0001, (301) 763-3030, www.census.gov; *Census 2000: Demographic Profiles.*

ASPARAGUS

Economic Research Service (ERS), U.S. Department of Agriculture (USDA), 1800 M Street, NW, Washington, DC 20036-5831, (202) 694-5050, Fax: (202) 694-5689, www.ers.usda.gov; *Agricultural Outlook; Agricultural Statistics;* and *Food CPI, Prices, and Expenditures.*

National Agricultural Statistics Service (NASS), U.S. Department of Agriculture (USDA), 1400 Independence Avenue, SW, Washington, DC 20250, (800) 727-9540, Fax: (202) 690-2090, www.nass.usda.gov; *Vegetables: 2004 Annual Summary.*

ASPHALT

U.S. Bureau of Labor Statistics (BLS), Postal Square Building, 2 Massachusetts Avenue, NE, Washington, DC 20212-0001, (202) 691-5200, Fax: (202) 691-6325, www.bls.gov; *Producer Price Indexes (PPI).*

U.S. Department of the Interior (DOI), U.S. Geological Survey (USGS), Office of Minerals Information, 12201 Sunrise Valley Drive, Reston, VA 20192, Mr. Kenneth A. Beckman, (703) 648-4916, Fax: (703) 648-4995, http://minerals.usgs.gov/minerals; *Mineral Commodity Summaries* and *Minerals Yearbook.*

ASSAULT

Federal Bureau of Investigation (FBI), J. Edgar Hoover Building, 935 Pennsylvania Avenue, NW, Washington, DC 20535-0001, (202) 324-3000, www.fbi.gov; *Crime in the United States (CIUS) 2007 (Preliminary).*

Justice Research and Statistics Association (JRSA), 777 N. Capitol Street, NE, Suite 801, Washington, DC 20002, (202) 842-9330, Fax: (202) 842-9329, www.jrsa.org; *Crime and Justice Atlas 2001.*

U.S. Department of Justice (DOJ), Bureau of Justice Statistics, 810 Seventh Street, NW, Washington, DC 20531, (202) 307-0765, www.ojp.usdoj.gov/bjs/; *Criminal Victimization, 2005; Hispanic Victims of Violent Crime, 1993-2000;* and *Weapon Use and Violent Crime, 1993-2001.*

ASSET-BACKED SECURITIES

Board of Governors of the Federal Reserve System, Constitution Avenue, NW, Washington, DC 20551, (202) 452-3000, www.federalreserve.gov; *Federal Reserve Board Statistical Release* and *Flow of Funds Accounts of the United States.*

ASSETS - PERSONAL

Board of Governors of the Federal Reserve System, Constitution Avenue, NW, Washington, DC 20551, (202) 452-3000, www.federalreserve.gov; *Federal Reserve Bulletin; Flow of Funds Accounts of the United States;* and unpublished data.

ASSOCIATIONS - NATIONAL - NONPROFIT

National Endowment for the Arts (NEA), 1100 Pennsylvania Avenue, NW, Washington, DC 20506-0001, (202) 682-5400, www.arts.gov; *Raising the Barre: The Geographic, Financial, and Economic Trends of Nonprofit Dance Companies.*

Thomson Gale, 27500 Drake Road, Farmington Hills, MI 48331, (248) 699-4253, www.galegroup.com; *Encyclopedia of Associations.*

ASTHMA

Bernan Essential Government Publications, 4611-F Assembly Drive, Lanham MD, 20706-4391, (301)

459-2255, Fax: (800) 865-3450, www.bernan.com; *Vital Statistics of the United States: Births, Life Expectancy, Deaths, and Selected Health Data.*

National Center for Health Statistics (NCHS), Centers for Disease Control and Prevention (CDC), U.S. Department of Health and Human Services (HHS), 3311 Toledo Road, Hyattsville, MD 20782, (866) 232-4636, www.cdc.gov/nchs; *Faststats A to Z; National Vital Statistics Reports (NVSR); Vital Statistics of the United States (VSUS);* and unpublished data.

RAND Corporation, 1776 Main Street, PO Box 2138, Santa Monica, CA 90407-2138, (310) 393-0411, www.rand.org; *Asthma Mortality in U.S. Hispanics of Mexican, Puerto Rican, and Cuban Heritage, 1990-1995.*

ASYLUM SEEKERS

U.S. Department of Homeland Security (DHS), Office of Immigration Statistics, Washington, DC 20528, (202) 282-8000, www.dhs.gov; *Refugees and Asylees: 2005.*

United Nations High Commissioner for Refugees (UNHCR), Case Postale 2500, CH-1211 Geneve 2 Depot, Switzerland, www.unhcr.org; *Measuring Protection by Numbers; The State of the World's Refugees 2006; Unaccompanied and Separated Children Seeking Asylum, 2001-2003;* and *UNHCR Statistical Yearbook 2006.*

ATHEROSCLEROSIS - DEATHS

Bernan Essential Government Publications, 4611-F Assembly Drive, Lanham MD, 20706-4391, (301) 459-2255, Fax: (800) 865-3450, www.bernan.com; *Vital Statistics of the United States: Births, Life Expectancy, Deaths, and Selected Health Data.*

National Center for Health Statistics (NCHS), Centers for Disease Control and Prevention (CDC), U.S. Department of Health and Human Services (HHS), 3311 Toledo Road, Hyattsville, MD 20782, (866) 232-4636, www.cdc.gov/nchs; *National Vital Statistics Reports (NVSR); Vital Statistics of the United States (VSUS);* and unpublished data.

ATHLETES

Elias Sports Bureau, Inc., 500 Fifth Avenue, Number 2140, New York, NY 10110, (212) 869-1530, www.esb.com; *The Elias Book of Baseball Records 2006.*

U.S. Bureau of Labor Statistics (BLS), Postal Square Building, 2 Massachusetts Avenue, NE, Washington, DC 20212-0001, (202) 691-5200, Fax: (202) 691-6325, www.bls.gov; *Employment and Earnings (EE)* and unpublished data.

ATHLETIC ASSOCIATIONS

Thomson Gale, 27500 Drake Road, Farmington Hills, MI 48331, (248) 699-4253, www.galegroup.com; *Encyclopedia of Associations.*

ATHLETIC GOODS

See SPORTING AND ATHLETIC GOODS

ATM'S (AUTOMATED TELLER MACHINES)

Board of Governors of the Federal Reserve System, Constitution Avenue, NW, Washington, DC 20551, (202) 452-3000, www.federalreserve.gov; *Annual Report to the Congress on Retail Fees and Services of Depository Institutions.*

ATOMIC ENERGY DEFENSE ACTIVITIES - EXPENDITURES

The Office of Management and Budget (OMB), 725 17th Street, NW, Washington, DC 20503, (202) 395-3080, Fax: (202) 395-3888, www.whitehouse.gov/omb; *Historical Tables.*

ATTENTION DEFICIT DISORDER

National Center for Health Statistics (NCHS), Centers for Disease Control and Prevention (CDC), U.S. Department of Health and Human Services (HHS), 3311 Toledo Road, Hyattsville, MD 20782, (866) 232-4636, www.cdc.gov/nchs; *Faststats A to Z.*

AUDIO EQUIPMENT

Electronic Industries Alliance (EIA), 2500 Wilson Boulevard, Arlington, VA 22201, (703) 907-7500, www.eia.org; unpublished data.

Office of Trade and Industry Information (OTII), Manufacturing and Services, International Trade Administration, U.S. Department of Commerce, 1401 Constitution Ave, NW, Washington, DC 20230, (800) USA TRAD(E), http://trade.gov/index.asp; *TradeStats Express.*

U.S. Census Bureau, Center for Economic Studies, 4600 Silver Hill Road, Washington DC 20233, (301) 457-1235, www.ces.census.gov; *2002 Economic Census, Retail Trade* and *2002 Economic Census, Wholesale Trade.*

AUDITING

See ACCOUNTING, TAX PREPARATION, BOOKKEEPING, AND PAYROLL SERVICES

AUSTRALIA - NATIONAL STATISTICAL OFFICE

Australian Bureau of Statistics (ABS), Locked Bag 10, Belconnen ACT 2616, Australia, www.abs.gov.au; National Data Center.

AUSTRALIA - PRIMARY STATISTICS SOURCES

Australian Bureau of Statistics (ABS), Locked Bag 10, Belconnen ACT 2616, Australia, www.abs.gov.au; *Australia at a Glance, 2008; Monthly Summary of Statistics; Pocket Year Book Australia;* and *Year Book Australia, 2008.*

AUSTRALIA - DATABASES

Australian Bureau of Statistics (ABS), Locked Bag 10, Belconnen ACT 2616, Australia, www.abs.gov.au; AusStats. Subject coverage: Economy, Demography, Education, Crime, Agriculture and OECD Data.

Australian National University (ANU), Research School of Social Sciences (RSSS), Canberra ACT 0200, Australia, http://rsss.anu.edu.au; Australian Demographic Data Bank. Subject coverage: Demographic data.

Department of Agriculture, Fisheries and Forestry, GPO Box 858, Canberra ACT 2601, Australia, www.dpie.gov.au/index.cfm; Databases. Subject coverage: Agriculture, fisheries and forestry.

Reserve Bank of Australia (RBA), The Secretary, GPO Box 3947, Sydney NSW 2001, Australia, www.rba.gov.au; *Reserve Bank of Australia Bulletin.*

AUSTRALIA - ABORTION

United Nations Statistics Division, New York, NY 10017, (800) 253-9646, Fax: (212) 963-4116, http://unstats.un.org; *Demographic Yearbook.*

AUSTRALIA - AGRICULTURE

Australian Bureau of Statistics (ABS), Locked Bag 10, Belconnen ACT 2616, Australia, www.abs.gov.au; *Australia at a Glance, 2008* and *Year Book Australia, 2008.*

Economist Intelligence Unit, 111 West 57th Street, New York, NY 10019, (212) 554-0600, Fax: (212) 586-1181, www.eiu.com; *Australia Country Report.*

Euromonitor International, Inc., 224 S. Michigan Avenue, Suite 1500, Chicago, IL 60604, (312) 922-1115, Fax: (312) 922-1157, www.euromonitor.com; *International Marketing Data and Statistics 2008* and *World Marketing Data and Statistics.*

M.E. Sharpe, 80 Business Park Drive, Armonk, NY 10504, (800) 541-6563, Fax: (914) 273-2106, www.mesharpe.com; *The Illustrated Book of World Rankings.*

Organisation for Economic Cooperation and Development (OECD), 2 rue Andre Pascal, F-75775 Paris Cedex 16, France, (Telephone in U.S. (202) 785-6323), (Fax in U.S. (202) 785-0350), www.oecd.org; *Indicators of Industrial Activity; 2005 OECD Agricultural Outlook Tables, 1970-2014; OECD Agricultural Outlook: 2007-2016; OECD Economic Survey - Australia 2006;* and STructural ANalysis (STAN) database.

Palgrave Macmillan Ltd., Houndmills, Basingstoke, Hampshire, RG21 6XS, England, (Telephone in U.S. (888) 330-8477), (Fax in U.S. (800) 672-2054), www.palgrave.com; *The Statesman's Yearbook 2008.*

Taylor and Francis Group, An Informa Business, 2 Park Square, Milton Park, Abingdon, Oxford OX14 4RN, United Kingdom, (Dial from U.S. (212) 216-7800), (Fax from U.S. (212) 564-7854), www.tandf.co.uk; *The Europa World Year Book.*

United Nations Conference on Trade and Development (UNCTAD), DC2-1120, United Nations, New York, NY 10017, (212) 963-0027, www.unctad.org; *UNCTAD Commodity Yearbook.*

United Nations Food and Agricultural Organization (FAO), Viale delle Terme di Caracalla, 00100 Rome, Italy, (Dial from U.S. (202) 653-2400), (Fax from U.S. (202) 653 5760), www.fao.org; AQUASTAT; *FAO Production Yearbook 2002; FAO Trade Yearbook;* and *The State of Food and Agriculture (SOFA) 2006.*

United Nations Statistics Division, New York, NY 10017, (800) 253-9646, Fax: (212) 963-4116, http://unstats.un.org; *Asia-Pacific in Figures 2004; Statistical Yearbook;* and *Statistical Yearbook for Asia and the Pacific 2004.*

The World Bank, 1818 H Street, NW, Washington, DC 20433, (202) 473-1000, Fax: (202) 477-6391, www.worldbank.org; *Australia* and *World Development Indicators (WDI) 2008.*

AUSTRALIA - AIRLINES

Economist Intelligence Unit, 111 West 57th Street, New York, NY 10019, (212) 554-0600, Fax: (212) 586-1181, www.eiu.com; *Business Asia.*

International Civil Aviation Organization (ICAO), External Relations and Public Information Office (EPO), 999 University Street, Montreal, Quebec H3C 5H7, Canada, (Dial from U.S. (514) 954-8219), (Fax from U.S. (514) 954-6077), www.icao.int; *Civil Aviation Statistics of the World.*

M.E. Sharpe, 80 Business Park Drive, Armonk, NY 10504, (800) 541-6563, Fax: (914) 273-2106, www.mesharpe.com; *The Illustrated Book of World Rankings.*

Organisation for Economic Cooperation and Development (OECD), 2 rue Andre Pascal, F-75775 Paris Cedex 16, France, (Telephone in U.S. (202) 785-6323), (Fax in U.S. (202) 785-0350), www.oecd.org; *Household, Tourism, Travel: Trends, Environmental Impacts and Policy Responses.*

Palgrave Macmillan Ltd., Houndmills, Basingstoke, Hampshire, RG21 6XS, England, (Telephone in U.S. (888) 330-8477), (Fax in U.S. (800) 672-2054), www.palgrave.com; *The Statesman's Yearbook 2008.*

Taylor and Francis Group, An Informa Business, 2 Park Square, Milton Park, Abingdon, Oxford OX14 4RN, United Kingdom, (Dial from U.S. (212) 216-7800), (Fax from U.S. (212) 564-7854), www.tandf.co.uk; *The Europa World Year Book.*

United Nations Statistics Division, New York, NY 10017, (800) 253-9646, Fax: (212) 963-4116, http://unstats.un.org; *Statistical Yearbook.*

AUSTRALIA - AIRPORTS

Central Intelligence Agency, Office of Public Affairs, Washington, DC 20505, (703) 482-0623, Fax: (703) 482-1739, www.cia.gov; *The World Factbook.*

AUSTRALIA - ALMOND PRODUCTION

See AUSTRALIA - CROPS

AUSTRALIA - ALUMINUM PRODUCTION

See AUSTRALIA - MINERAL INDUSTRIES

AUSTRALIA - ANIMAL FEEDING

Organisation for Economic Cooperation and Development (OECD), 2 rue Andre Pascal, F-75775 Paris Cedex 16, France, (Telephone in U.S. (202) 785-6323), (Fax in U.S. (202) 785-0350), www.oecd.org; *International Trade by Commodity Statistics (ITCS).*

United Nations Statistics Division, New York, NY 10017, (800) 253-9646, Fax: (212) 963-4116, http://unstats.un.org; *Statistical Yearbook.*

AUSTRALIA - APPLE PRODUCTION

See AUSTRALIA - CROPS

AUSTRALIA - ARMED FORCES

Australian Bureau of Statistics (ABS), Locked Bag 10, Belconnen ACT 2616, Australia, www.abs.gov.au; *Australia at a Glance, 2008* and *Year Book Australia, 2008.*

Central Intelligence Agency, Office of Public Affairs, Washington, DC 20505, (703) 482-0623, Fax: (703) 482-1739, www.cia.gov; *The World Factbook.*

Economist Intelligence Unit, 111 West 57th Street, New York, NY 10019, (212) 554-0600, Fax: (212) 586-1181, www.eiu.com; *Business Asia.*

Euromonitor International, Inc., 224 S. Michigan Avenue, Suite 1500, Chicago, IL 60604, (312) 922-1115, Fax: (312) 922-1157, www.euromonitor.com; *World Marketing Data and Statistics.*

International Institute for Strategic Studies (IISS), Arundel House, 13-15 Arundel Street, Temple Place, London WC2R 3DX, England, www.iiss.org; *The Military Balance 2007.*

International Monetary Fund (IMF), 700 Nineteenth Street, NW, Washington, DC 20431, (202) 623-7000, Fax: (202) 623-4661, www.imf.org; *Government Finance Statistics Yearbook (2008 Edition).*

Palgrave Macmillan Ltd., Houndmills, Basingstoke, Hampshire, RG21 6XS, England, (Telephone in U.S. (888) 330-8477), (Fax in U.S. (800) 672-2054), www.palgrave.com; *The Statesman's Yearbook 2008.*

U.S. Department of State (DOS), 2201 C Street NW, Washington, DC 20520, (202) 647-4000, www.state.gov; *World Military Expenditures and Arms Transfers (WMEAT).*

United Nations Statistics Division, New York, NY 10017, (800) 253-9646, Fax: (212) 963-4116, http://unstats.un.org; *Human Development Report 2006.*

AUSTRALIA - AUTOMOBILE INDUSTRY AND TRADE

Australian Bureau of Statistics (ABS), Locked Bag 10, Belconnen ACT 2616, Australia, www.abs.gov.au; *Australia at a Glance, 2008* and *Year Book Australia, 2008.*

Organisation for Economic Cooperation and Development (OECD), 2 rue Andre Pascal, F-75775 Paris Cedex 16, France, (Telephone in U.S. (202) 785-6323), (Fax in U.S. (202) 785-0350), www.oecd.org; *Indicators of Industrial Activity* and *International Trade by Commodity Statistics (ITCS).*

United Nations Statistics Division, New York, NY 10017, (800) 253-9646, Fax: (212) 963-4116, http://unstats.un.org; *Statistical Yearbook.*

AUSTRALIA - BALANCE OF PAYMENTS

Australian Bureau of Statistics (ABS), Locked Bag 10, Belconnen ACT 2616, Australia, www.abs.gov.au; *Australia at a Glance, 2008* and *Year Book Australia, 2008.*

International Monetary Fund (IMF), 700 Nineteenth Street, NW, Washington, DC 20431, (202) 623-7000, Fax: (202) 623-4661, www.imf.org; *Balance of Payments Statistics Newsletter; Balance of Payments Statistics Yearbook 2007;* and *International Financial Statistics Yearbook 2007.*

Organisation for Economic Cooperation and Development (OECD), 2 rue Andre Pascal, F-75775 Paris Cedex 16, France, (Telephone in U.S. (202) 785-6323), (Fax in U.S. (202) 785-0350), www.oecd.org; *Geographical Distribution of Financial Flows to Aid Recipients 2002-2006; OECD Economic Outlook 2008; OECD Economic Survey - Australia 2006;* and *OECD Main Economic Indicators (MEI).*

Taylor and Francis Group, An Informa Business, 2 Park Square, Milton Park, Abingdon, Oxford OX14 4RN, United Kingdom, (Dial from U.S. (212) 216-7800), (Fax from U.S. (212) 564-7854), www.tandf.co.uk; *The Europa World Year Book.*

United Nations Conference on Trade and Development (UNCTAD), DC2-1120, United Nations, New York, NY 10017, (212) 963-0027, www.unctad.org; *Handbook of Statistics 2005.*

The World Bank, 1818 H Street, NW, Washington, DC 20433, (202) 473-1000, Fax: (202) 477-6391, www.worldbank.org; *Australia; World Development Indicators (WDI) 2008;* and *World Development Report 2008.*

AUSTRALIA - BANKS AND BANKING

Euromonitor International, Inc., 224 S. Michigan Avenue, Suite 1500, Chicago, IL 60604, (312) 922-1115, Fax: (312) 922-1157, www.euromonitor.com; *World Marketing Data and Statistics.*

International Monetary Fund (IMF), 700 Nineteenth Street, NW, Washington, DC 20431, (202) 623-7000, Fax: (202) 623-4661, www.imf.org; *Government Finance Statistics Yearbook (2008 Edition)* and *International Financial Statistics Yearbook 2007.*

M.E. Sharpe, 80 Business Park Drive, Armonk, NY 10504, (800) 541-6563, Fax: (914) 273-2106, www.mesharpe.com; *The Illustrated Book of World Rankings.*

Organisation for Economic Cooperation and Development (OECD), 2 rue Andre Pascal, F-75775 Paris Cedex 16, France, (Telephone in U.S. (202) 785-6323), (Fax in U.S. (202) 785-0350), www.oecd.org; *Financial Market Trends: OECD Periodical; OECD Economic Outlook 2008;* and *OECD Economic Survey - Australia 2006.*

Palgrave Macmillan Ltd., Houndmills, Basingstoke, Hampshire, RG21 6XS, England, (Telephone in U.S. (888) 330-8477), (Fax in U.S. (800) 672-2054), www.palgrave.com; *The Statesman's Yearbook 2008.*

Reserve Bank of Australia (RBA), The Secretary, GPO Box 3947, Sydney NSW 2001, Australia, www.rba.gov.au; *Financial Stability Review; Reserve Bank of Australia Annual Report 2007;* and *Statement on Monetary Policy.*

Taylor and Francis Group, An Informa Business, 2 Park Square, Milton Park, Abingdon, Oxford OX14 4RN, United Kingdom, (Dial from U.S. (212) 216-7800), (Fax from U.S. (212) 564-7854), www.tandf.co.uk; *The Europa World Year Book.*

AUSTRALIA - BARLEY PRODUCTION

See AUSTRALIA - CROPS

AUSTRALIA - BEVERAGE INDUSTRY

M.E. Sharpe, 80 Business Park Drive, Armonk, NY 10504, (800) 541-6563, Fax: (914) 273-2106, www.mesharpe.com; *The Illustrated Book of World Rankings.*

Organisation for Economic Cooperation and Development (OECD), 2 rue Andre Pascal, F-75775 Paris Cedex 16, France, (Telephone in U.S. (202) 785-6323), (Fax in U.S. (202) 785-0350), www.oecd.org; *Indicators of Industrial Activity.*

United Nations Statistics Division, New York, NY 10017, (800) 253-9646, Fax: (212) 963-4116, http://unstats.un.org; *Statistical Yearbook.*

AUSTRALIA - BONDS

International Monetary Fund (IMF), 700 Nineteenth Street, NW, Washington, DC 20431, (202) 623-7000, Fax: (202) 623-4661, www.imf.org; *Government Finance Statistics Yearbook (2008 Edition).*

Organisation for Economic Cooperation and Development (OECD), 2 rue Andre Pascal, F-75775 Paris Cedex 16, France, (Telephone in U.S. (202) 785-6323), (Fax in U.S. (202) 785-0350), www.oecd.org; *Financial Market Trends: OECD Periodical.*

United Nations Statistics Division, New York, NY 10017, (800) 253-9646, Fax: (212) 963-4116, http://unstats.un.org; *Statistical Yearbook.*

AUSTRALIA - BROADCASTING

Central Intelligence Agency, Office of Public Affairs, Washington, DC 20505, (703) 482-0623, Fax: (703) 482-1739, www.cia.gov; *The World Factbook.*

Economist Intelligence Unit, 111 West 57th Street, New York, NY 10019, (212) 554-0600, Fax: (212) 586-1181, www.eiu.com; *Business Asia.*

Euromonitor International, Inc., 224 S. Michigan Avenue, Suite 1500, Chicago, IL 60604, (312) 922-1115, Fax: (312) 922-1157, www.euromonitor.com; *World Marketing Data and Statistics.*

M.E. Sharpe, 80 Business Park Drive, Armonk, NY 10504, (800) 541-6563, Fax: (914) 273-2106, www.mesharpe.com; *The Illustrated Book of World Rankings.*

Palgrave Macmillan Ltd., Houndmills, Basingstoke, Hampshire, RG21 6XS, England, (Telephone in U.S. (888) 330-8477), (Fax in U.S. (800) 672-2054), www.palgrave.com; *The Statesman's Yearbook 2008.*

UNESCO Institute for Statistics, C.P. 6128 Succursale Centre-Ville, Montreal, Quebec, H3C 3J7 Canada, (Dial from U.S. (514) 343-6880), (Fax from U.S. (514) 343 6882), www.uis.unesco.org; *Statistical Tables.*

WRTH Publications Limited, PO Box 290, Oxford OX2 7FT, UK, www.wrth.com; *World Radio TV Handbook 2007.*

AUSTRALIA - BUDGET

Central Intelligence Agency, Office of Public Affairs, Washington, DC 20505, (703) 482-0623, Fax: (703) 482-1739, www.cia.gov; *The World Factbook.*

AUSTRALIA - BUSINESS

Australian Bureau of Statistics (ABS), Locked Bag 10, Belconnen ACT 2616, Australia, www.abs.gov.au; *Australia at a Glance, 2008* and *Year Book Australia, 2008.*

Organisation for Economic Cooperation and Development (OECD), 2 rue Andre Pascal, F-75775 Paris Cedex 16, France, (Telephone in U.S. (202) 785-6323), (Fax in U.S. (202) 785-0350), www.oecd.org; *OECD Main Economic Indicators (MEI).*

United Nations Statistics Division, New York, NY 10017, (800) 253-9646, Fax: (212) 963-4116, http://unstats.un.org; *Statistical Yearbook for Asia and the Pacific 2004.*

AUSTRALIA - CADMIUM PRODUCTION

See AUSTRALIA - MINERAL INDUSTRIES

AUSTRALIA - CAPITAL INVESTMENTS

Organisation for Economic Cooperation and Development (OECD), 2 rue Andre Pascal, F-75775 Paris Cedex 16, France, (Telephone in U.S. (202) 785-6323), (Fax in U.S. (202) 785-0350), www.oecd.org; *Financial Market Trends: OECD Periodical* and *OECD Economic Outlook 2008.*

AUSTRALIA - CAPITAL LEVY

International Monetary Fund (IMF), 700 Nineteenth Street, NW, Washington, DC 20431, (202) 623-7000, Fax: (202) 623-4661, www.imf.org; *Government Finance Statistics Yearbook (2008 Edition).*

Organisation for Economic Cooperation and Development (OECD), 2 rue Andre Pascal, F-75775 Paris Cedex 16, France, (Telephone in U.S. (202) 785-6323), (Fax in U.S. (202) 785-0350), www.oecd.org;

Financial Market Trends: OECD Periodical and *OECD Economic Outlook 2008.*

AUSTRALIA - CATTLE

See AUSTRALIA - LIVESTOCK

AUSTRALIA - CHILDBIRTH - STATISTICS

Australian Bureau of Statistics (ABS), Locked Bag 10, Belconnen ACT 2616, Australia, www.abs.gov.au; *Australia at a Glance, 2008* and *Year Book Australia, 2008.*

Central Intelligence Agency, Office of Public Affairs, Washington, DC 20505, (703) 482-0623, Fax: (703) 482-1739, www.cia.gov; *The World Factbook.*

Economist Intelligence Unit, 111 West 57th Street, New York, NY 10019, (212) 554-0600, Fax: (212) 586-1181, www.eiu.com; *Business Asia.*

Euromonitor International, Inc., 224 S. Michigan Avenue, Suite 1500, Chicago, IL 60604, (312) 922-1115, Fax: (312) 922-1157, www.euromonitor.com; *International Marketing Data and Statistics 2008* and *The World Economic Factbook 2008.*

M.E. Sharpe, 80 Business Park Drive, Armonk, NY 10504, (800) 541-6563, Fax: (914) 273-2106, www.mesharpe.com; *The Illustrated Book of World Rankings.*

Palgrave Macmillan Ltd., Houndmills, Basingstoke, Hampshire, RG21 6XS, England, (Telephone in U.S. (888) 330-8477), (Fax in U.S. (800) 672-2054), www.palgrave.com; *The Statesman's Yearbook 2008.*

Taylor and Francis Group, An Informa Business, 2 Park Square, Milton Park, Abingdon, Oxford OX14 4RN, United Kingdom, (Dial from U.S. (212) 216-7800), (Fax from U.S. (212) 564-7854), www.tandf.co.uk; *The Europa World Year Book.*

United Nations Statistics Division, New York, NY 10017, (800) 253-9646, Fax: (212) 963-4116, http://unstats.un.org; *Asia-Pacific in Figures 2004; Demographic Yearbook;* and *Statistical Yearbook.*

The World Bank, 1818 H Street, NW, Washington, DC 20433, (202) 473-1000, Fax: (202) 477-6391, www.worldbank.org; *World Development Indicators (WDI) 2008.*

AUSTRALIA - CLIMATE

M.E. Sharpe, 80 Business Park Drive, Armonk, NY 10504, (800) 541-6563, Fax: (914) 273-2106, www.mesharpe.com; *The Illustrated Book of World Rankings.*

Palgrave Macmillan Ltd., Houndmills, Basingstoke, Hampshire, RG21 6XS, England, (Telephone in U.S. (888) 330-8477), (Fax in U.S. (800) 672-2054), www.palgrave.com; *The Statesman's Yearbook 2008.*

AUSTRALIA - CLOTHING EXPORTS AND IMPORTS

See AUSTRALIA - TEXTILE INDUSTRY

AUSTRALIA - COAL PRODUCTION

See AUSTRALIA - MINERAL INDUSTRIES

AUSTRALIA - COBALT PRODUCTION

See AUSTRALIA - MINERAL INDUSTRIES

AUSTRALIA - COFFEE

See AUSTRALIA - CROPS

AUSTRALIA - COMMERCE

Palgrave Macmillan Ltd., Houndmills, Basingstoke, Hampshire, RG21 6XS, England, (Telephone in U.S. (888) 330-8477), (Fax in U.S. (800) 672-2054), www.palgrave.com; *The Statesman's Yearbook 2008.*

AUSTRALIA - COMMODITY EXCHANGES

Commodity Research Bureau, 330 South Wells Street, Suite 612, Chicago, IL 60606-7110, (800) 621-5271, Fax: (312) 939-4135, www.crbtrader.com; *2006 CRB Commodity Yearbook and CD.*

International Lead and Zinc Study Group (ILZSG), Rua Almirante Barroso 38, 5th Floor, Lisbon 1000 - 013, Portugal, www.ilzsg.org; Interactive Statistical Database.

International Monetary Fund (IMF), 700 Nineteenth Street, NW, Washington, DC 20431, (202) 623-7000, Fax: (202) 623-4661, www.imf.org; *IMF Primary Commodity Prices.*

Organisation for Economic Cooperation and Development (OECD), 2 rue Andre Pascal, F-75775 Paris Cedex 16, France, (Telephone in U.S. (202) 785-6323), (Fax in U.S. (202) 785-0350), www.oecd.org; *OECD Main Economic Indicators (MEI).*

United Nations Food and Agricultural Organization (FAO), Viale delle Terme di Caracalla, 00100 Rome, Italy, (Dial from U.S. (202) 653-2400), (Fax from U.S. (202) 653 5760), www.fao.org; *The State of Food and Agriculture (SOFA) 2006.*

United Nations Statistics Division, New York, NY 10017, (800) 253-9646, Fax: (212) 963-4116, http://unstats.un.org; *Statistical Yearbook.*

World Bureau of Metal Statistics (WBMS), 27a High Street, Ware, Hertfordshire, SG12 9BA, United Kingdom, www.world-bureau.com; *Annual Stainless Steel Statistics; World Flow Charts; World Metal Statistics; World Nickel Statistics;* and *World Tin Statistics.*

AUSTRALIA - COMMUNICATION AND TRAFFIC

United Nations Statistics Division, New York, NY 10017, (800) 253-9646, Fax: (212) 963-4116, http://unstats.un.org; *Statistical Yearbook.*

AUSTRALIA - CONSTRUCTION INDUSTRY

Australian Bureau of Statistics (ABS), Locked Bag 10, Belconnen ACT 2616, Australia, www.abs.gov.au; *Australia at a Glance, 2008* and *Year Book Australia, 2008.*

Australian Institute of Health and Welfare (AIHW), GPO Box 570, Canberra ACT 2601, Australia, www.aihw.gov.au; *Housing Assistance in Australia 2008.*

M.E. Sharpe, 80 Business Park Drive, Armonk, NY 10504, (800) 541-6563, Fax: (914) 273-2106, www.mesharpe.com; *The Illustrated Book of World Rankings.*

Organisation for Economic Cooperation and Development (OECD), 2 rue Andre Pascal, F-75775 Paris Cedex 16, France, (Telephone in U.S. (202) 785-6323), (Fax in U.S. (202) 785-0350), www.oecd.org; *Iron and Steel Industry in 2004 (2006 Edition); OECD Economic Survey - Australia 2006; OECD Main Economic Indicators (MEI);* and STructural ANalysis (STAN) database.

Palgrave Macmillan Ltd., Houndmills, Basingstoke, Hampshire, RG21 6XS, England, (Telephone in U.S. (888) 330-8477), (Fax in U.S. (800) 672-2054), www.palgrave.com; *The Statesman's Yearbook 2008.*

United Nations Statistics Division, New York, NY 10017, (800) 253-9646, Fax: (212) 963-4116, http://unstats.un.org; *Statistical Yearbook.*

AUSTRALIA - CONSUMER PRICE INDEXES

Australian Bureau of Statistics (ABS), Locked Bag 10, Belconnen ACT 2616, Australia, www.abs.gov.au; *Australia at a Glance, 2008* and *Year Book Australia, 2008.*

Organisation for Economic Cooperation and Development (OECD), 2 rue Andre Pascal, F-75775 Paris Cedex 16, France, (Telephone in U.S. (202) 785-6323), (Fax in U.S. (202) 785-0350), www.oecd.org; *OECD Economic Outlook 2008.*

Taylor and Francis Group, An Informa Business, 2 Park Square, Milton Park, Abingdon, Oxford OX14 4RN, United Kingdom, (Dial from U.S. (212) 216-7800), (Fax from U.S. (212) 564-7854), www.tandf.co.uk; *The Europa World Year Book.*

United Nations Statistics Division, New York, NY 10017, (800) 253-9646, Fax: (212) 963-4116, http://unstats.un.org; *Statistical Yearbook.*

The World Bank, 1818 H Street, NW, Washington, DC 20433, (202) 473-1000, Fax: (202) 477-6391, www.worldbank.org; *Australia.*

AUSTRALIA - CONSUMPTION (ECONOMICS)

International Iron and Steel Institute (IISI), Rue Colonel Bourg 120, B-1140 Brussels, Belgium, www.worldsteel.org; *Steel Statistical Yearbook 2006.*

International Lead and Zinc Study Group (ILZSG), Rua Almirante Barroso 38, 5th Floor, Lisbon 1000 - 013, Portugal, www.ilzsg.org; Interactive Statistical Database.

International Monetary Fund (IMF), 700 Nineteenth Street, NW, Washington, DC 20431, (202) 623-7000, Fax: (202) 623-4661, www.imf.org; *International Financial Statistics Yearbook 2007.*

Organisation for Economic Cooperation and Development (OECD), 2 rue Andre Pascal, F-75775 Paris Cedex 16, France, (Telephone in U.S. (202) 785-6323), (Fax in U.S. (202) 785-0350), www.oecd.org; *Environmental Impacts of Foreign Direct Investment in the Mining Sector in the Newly Independent States (NIS); Iron and Steel Industry in 2004 (2006 Edition); A New World Map in Textiles and Clothing: Adjusting to Change; 2005 OECD Agricultural Outlook Tables, 1970-2014; Revenue Statistics 1965-2006 - 2007 Edition;* and *Towards Sustainable Household Consumption?: Trends and Policies in OECD Countries.*

Technical Association of the Pulp and Paper Industry (TAPPI), 15 Technology Parkway South, Norcross, GA 30092, (770) 446-1400, Fax: (770) 446-6947, www.tappi.org; *TAPPI Annual Report.*

The World Bank, 1818 H Street, NW, Washington, DC 20433, (202) 473-1000, Fax: (202) 477-6391, www.worldbank.org; *World Development Report 2008.*

AUSTRALIA - COPPER INDUSTRY AND TRADE

See AUSTRALIA - MINERAL INDUSTRIES

AUSTRALIA - CORN INDUSTRY

See AUSTRALIA - CROPS

AUSTRALIA - COST AND STANDARD OF LIVING

International Monetary Fund (IMF), 700 Nineteenth Street, NW, Washington, DC 20431, (202) 623-7000, Fax: (202) 623-4661, www.imf.org; *Government Finance Statistics Yearbook (2008 Edition).*

United Nations Statistics Division, New York, NY 10017, (800) 253-9646, Fax: (212) 963-4116, http://unstats.un.org; *Statistical Yearbook for Asia and the Pacific 2004.*

AUSTRALIA - COTTON

See AUSTRALIA - CROPS

AUSTRALIA - CRIME

Australian Government Office for Women, Department of Families, Community Services and Indigenous Affairs, Box 7788, Canberra Mail Centre ACT 2610, Australia, http://ofw.facsia.gov.au; *Cost of Domestic Violence to the Australian Economy.*

Australian Institute of Criminology, 74 Leichhardt Street, Griffith ACT 2603 Australia, www.aic.gov.au/; *Deaths in Custody in Australia: National Deaths in Custody Program Annual Report 2004* and *Final report on the North Queensland Drug Court.*

International Criminal Police Organization (INTERPOL), General Secretariat, 200 quai Charles de Gaulle, 69006 Lyon, France, www.interpol.int; *International Crime Statistics.*

U.S. Department of Justice (DOJ), Bureau of Justice Statistics, 810 Seventh Street, NW, Washington, DC 20531, (202) 307-0765, www.ojp.usdoj.gov/bjs/; *Cross-National Studies in Crime and Justice* and *The World Factbook of Criminal Justice Systems.*

U.S. Department of Justice (DOJ), National Institute of Justice (NIJ), 810 Seventh Street, NW, Washington, DC 20531, (202) 307-2942, Fax: (202) 616-0275, www.ojp.usdoj.gov/nij/; *I-ADAM in Eight Countries: Approaches and Challenges.*

Yale University Press, PO Box 209040, New Haven, CT 06520-9040, (203) 432-0960, Fax: (203) 432-0948, http://yalepress.yale.edu/yupbooks; *Violence and Crime in Cross-National Perspective.*

AUSTRALIA - CROPS

International Monetary Fund (IMF), 700 Nineteenth Street, NW, Washington, DC 20431, (202) 623-7000, Fax: (202) 623-4661, www.imf.org; *International Financial Statistics Yearbook 2007.*

M.E. Sharpe, 80 Business Park Drive, Armonk, NY 10504, (800) 541-6563, Fax: (914) 273-2106, www.mesharpe.com; *The Illustrated Book of World Rankings.*

Organisation for Economic Cooperation and Development (OECD), 2 rue Andre Pascal, F-75775 Paris Cedex 16, France, (Telephone in U.S. (202) 785-6323), (Fax in U.S. (202) 785-0350), www.oecd.org; *International Trade by Commodity Statistics (ITCS)* and *2005 OECD Agricultural Outlook Tables, 1970-2014.*

Palgrave Macmillan Ltd., Houndmills, Basingstoke, Hampshire, RG21 6XS, England, (Telephone in U.S. (888) 330-8477), (Fax in U.S. (800) 672-2054), www.palgrave.com; *The Statesman's Yearbook 2008.*

Taylor and Francis Group, An Informa Business, 2 Park Square, Milton Park, Abingdon, Oxford OX14 4RN, United Kingdom, (Dial from U.S. (212) 216-7800), (Fax from U.S. (212) 564-7854), www.tandf.co.uk; *The Europa World Year Book.*

United Nations Conference on Trade and Development (UNCTAD), DC2-1120, United Nations, New York, NY 10017, (212) 963-0027, www.unctad.org; *UNCTAD Commodity Yearbook.*

United Nations Food and Agricultural Organization (FAO), Viale delle Terme di Caracalla, 00100 Rome, Italy, (Dial from U.S. (202) 653-2400), (Fax from U.S. (202) 653 5760), www.fao.org; *FAO Production Yearbook 2002* and *The State of Food and Agriculture (SOFA) 2006.*

United Nations Statistics Division, New York, NY 10017, (800) 253-9646, Fax: (212) 963-4116, http://unstats.un.org; *Statistical Yearbook.*

AUSTRALIA - CULTURE

Australian Bureau of Statistics (ABS), Locked Bag 10, Belconnen ACT 2616, Australia, www.abs.gov.au; *Australia at a Glance, 2008* and *Year Book Australia, 2008.*

AUSTRALIA - CUSTOMS ADMINISTRATION

International Monetary Fund (IMF), 700 Nineteenth Street, NW, Washington, DC 20431, (202) 623-7000, Fax: (202) 623-4661, www.imf.org; *Government Finance Statistics Yearbook (2008 Edition).*

Organisation for Economic Cooperation and Development (OECD), 2 rue Andre Pascal, F-75775 Paris Cedex 16, France, (Telephone in U.S. (202) 785-6323), (Fax in U.S. (202) 785-0350), www.oecd.org; *Environmental Impacts of Foreign Direct Investment in the Mining Sector in the Newly Independent States (NIS).*

Palgrave Macmillan Ltd., Houndmills, Basingstoke, Hampshire, RG21 6XS, England, (Telephone in U.S. (888) 330-8477), (Fax in U.S. (800) 672-2054), www.palgrave.com; *The Statesman's Yearbook 2008.*

AUSTRALIA - DAIRY PROCESSING

M.E. Sharpe, 80 Business Park Drive, Armonk, NY 10504, (800) 541-6563, Fax: (914) 273-2106, www.mesharpe.com; *The Illustrated Book of World Rankings.*

Organisation for Economic Cooperation and Development (OECD), 2 rue Andre Pascal, F-75775 Paris Cedex 16, France, (Telephone in U.S. (202) 785-6323), (Fax in U.S. (202) 785-0350), www.oecd.org; *2005 OECD Agricultural Outlook Tables, 1970-2014.*

Palgrave Macmillan Ltd., Houndmills, Basingstoke, Hampshire, RG21 6XS, England, (Telephone in U.S. (888) 330-8477), (Fax in U.S. (800) 672-2054), www.palgrave.com; *The Statesman's Yearbook 2008.*

Taylor and Francis Group, An Informa Business, 2 Park Square, Milton Park, Abingdon, Oxford OX14 4RN, United Kingdom, (Dial from U.S. (212) 216-7800), (Fax from U.S. (212) 564-7854), www.tandf.co.uk; *The Europa World Year Book.*

United Nations Food and Agricultural Organization (FAO), Viale delle Terme di Caracalla, 00100 Rome, Italy, (Dial from U.S. (202) 653-2400), (Fax from U.S. (202) 653 5760), www.fao.org; *FAO Production Yearbook 2002* and *The State of Food and Agriculture (SOFA) 2006.*

United Nations Statistics Division, New York, NY 10017, (800) 253-9646, Fax: (212) 963-4116, http://unstats.un.org; *Statistical Yearbook.*

AUSTRALIA - DEATH RATES

See AUSTRALIA - MORTALITY

AUSTRALIA - DEBTS, EXTERNAL

International Monetary Fund (IMF), 700 Nineteenth Street, NW, Washington, DC 20431, (202) 623-7000, Fax: (202) 623-4661, www.imf.org; *Government Finance Statistics Yearbook (2008 Edition).*

Organisation for Economic Cooperation and Development (OECD), 2 rue Andre Pascal, F-75775 Paris Cedex 16, France, (Telephone in U.S. (202) 785-6323), (Fax in U.S. (202) 785-0350), www.oecd.org; *Financial Market Trends: OECD Periodical; Geographical Distribution of Financial Flows to Aid Recipients 2002-2006;* and *OECD Economic Outlook 2008.*

Palgrave Macmillan Ltd., Houndmills, Basingstoke, Hampshire, RG21 6XS, England, (Telephone in U.S. (888) 330-8477), (Fax in U.S. (800) 672-2054), www.palgrave.com; *The Statesman's Yearbook 2008.*

The World Bank, 1818 H Street, NW, Washington, DC 20433, (202) 473-1000, Fax: (202) 477-6391, www.worldbank.org; *Global Development Finance 2007; World Development Indicators (WDI) 2008;* and *World Development Report 2008.*

Worldinformation.com, 2 Market Street, Saffron Walden, Essex CB10 1HZ, United Kingdom, www.worldinformation.com; The World of Information (www.worldinformation.com).

AUSTRALIA - DEFENSE EXPENDITURES

See AUSTRALIA - ARMED FORCES

AUSTRALIA - DEMOGRAPHY

Australian Bureau of Statistics (ABS), Locked Bag 10, Belconnen ACT 2616, Australia, www.abs.gov.au; *Australia at a Glance, 2008* and *Year Book Australia, 2008.*

Australian Government Office for Women, Department of Families, Community Services and Indigenous Affairs, Box 7788, Canberra Mail Centre ACT 2610, Australia, http://ofw.facsia.gov.au; *Time Use Survey; Window on Women: Women's Data Warehouse;* and *Women in Australia 2004.*

Economist Intelligence Unit, 111 West 57th Street, New York, NY 10019, (212) 554-0600, Fax: (212) 586-1181, www.eiu.com; *Business Asia.*

Euromonitor International, Inc., 224 S. Michigan Avenue, Suite 1500, Chicago, IL 60604, (312) 922-1115, Fax: (312) 922-1157, www.euromonitor.com; *International Marketing Data and Statistics 2008; The World Economic Factbook 2008;* and *World Marketing Data and Statistics.*

M.E. Sharpe, 80 Business Park Drive, Armonk, NY 10504, (800) 541-6563, Fax: (914) 273-2106, www.mesharpe.com; *The Illustrated Book of World Rankings.*

United Nations Statistics Division, New York, NY 10017, (800) 253-9646, Fax: (212) 963-4116, http://unstats.un.org; *Asia-Pacific in Figures 2004* and *Human Development Report 2006.*

The World Bank, 1818 H Street, NW, Washington, DC 20433, (202) 473-1000, Fax: (202) 477-6391, www.worldbank.org; *Australia.*

AUSTRALIA - DIAMONDS

See AUSTRALIA - MINERAL INDUSTRIES

AUSTRALIA - DISPOSABLE INCOME

Australian Bureau of Statistics (ABS), Locked Bag 10, Belconnen ACT 2616, Australia, www.abs.gov.au; *Australia at a Glance, 2008* and *Year Book Australia, 2008.*

M.E. Sharpe, 80 Business Park Drive, Armonk, NY 10504, (800) 541-6563, Fax: (914) 273-2106, www.mesharpe.com; *The Illustrated Book of World Rankings.*

Organisation for Economic Cooperation and Development (OECD), 2 rue Andre Pascal, F-75775 Paris Cedex 16, France, (Telephone in U.S. (202) 785-6323), (Fax in U.S. (202) 785-0350), www.oecd.org; *OECD Economic Outlook 2008.*

United Nations Statistics Division, New York, NY 10017, (800) 253-9646, Fax: (212) 963-4116, http://unstats.un.org; *National Accounts Statistics: Compendium of Income Distribution Statistics* and *Statistical Yearbook.*

AUSTRALIA - DIVORCE

M.E. Sharpe, 80 Business Park Drive, Armonk, NY 10504, (800) 541-6563, Fax: (914) 273-2106, www.mesharpe.com; *The Illustrated Book of World Rankings.*

United Nations Statistics Division, New York, NY 10017, (800) 253-9646, Fax: (212) 963-4116, http://unstats.un.org; *Demographic Yearbook* and *Statistical Yearbook.*

AUSTRALIA - ECONOMIC ASSISTANCE

Organisation for Economic Cooperation and Development (OECD), 2 rue Andre Pascal, F-75775 Paris Cedex 16, France, (Telephone in U.S. (202) 785-6323), (Fax in U.S. (202) 785-0350), www.oecd.org; *Geographical Distribution of Financial Flows to Aid Recipients 2002-2006.*

United Nations Statistics Division, New York, NY 10017, (800) 253-9646, Fax: (212) 963-4116, http://unstats.un.org; *Statistical Yearbook.*

AUSTRALIA - ECONOMIC CONDITIONS

Australian Government Office for Women, Department of Families, Community Services and Indigenous Affairs, Box 7788, Canberra Mail Centre ACT 2610, Australia, http://ofw.facsia.gov.au; *Cost of Domestic Violence to the Australian Economy.*

Center for International Business Education Research (CIBER), Columbia Business School and School of International and Public Affairs, Uris Hall, Room 212, 3022 Broadway, New York, NY 10027-6902, Mr. Joshua Safier, (212) 854-4750, Fax: (212) 222-9821, www.columbia.edu/cu/ciber/; Datastream International.

Central Intelligence Agency, Office of Public Affairs, Washington, DC 20505, (703) 482-0623, Fax: (703) 482-1739, www.cia.gov; *The World Factbook.*

DSI Data Service Information, Xantener Strasse 51a, D-47495 Rheinberg, Germany, www.dsidata.com; *Campus Solution.*

Dun and Bradstreet (DB) Corporation, 103 JFK Parkway, Short Hills, NJ 07078, (973) 921-5500, www.dnb.com; *Country Report.*

Economist Intelligence Unit, 111 West 57th Street, New York, NY 10019, (212) 554-0600, Fax: (212) 586-1181, www.eiu.com; *Australia Country Report.*

Euromonitor International, Inc., 224 S. Michigan Avenue, Suite 1500, Chicago, IL 60604, (312) 922-1115, Fax: (312) 922-1157, www.euromonitor.com; *International Marketing Data and Statistics 2008;*

The World Economic Factbook 2008; and *World Marketing Data and Statistics.*

Federal Statistical Office Germany, D-65180 Wiesbaden, Germany, www.destatis.de; *Australia 2006.*

International Monetary Fund (IMF), 700 Nineteenth Street, NW, Washington, DC 20431, (202) 623-7000, Fax: (202) 623-4661, www.imf.org; *World Economic Outlook Reports.*

M.E. Sharpe, 80 Business Park Drive, Armonk, NY 10504, (800) 541-6563, Fax: (914) 273-2106, www.mesharpe.com; *The Illustrated Book of World Rankings.*

Organisation for Economic Cooperation and Development (OECD), 2 rue Andre Pascal, F-75775 Paris Cedex 16, France, (Telephone in U.S. (202) 785-6323), (Fax in U.S. (202) 785-0350), www.oecd.org; *Geographical Distribution of Financial Flows to Aid Recipients 2002-2006; ICT Sector Data and Metadata by Country; Labour Force Statistics: 1986-2005, 2007 Edition; OECD Composite Leading Indicators (CLIs), Updated September 2007; OECD Economic Outlook 2008; OECD Economic Survey - Australia 2006; OECD Employment Outlook 2007; OECD in Figures 2007;* and *OECD Main Economic Indicators (MEI).*

Palgrave Macmillan Ltd., Houndmills, Basingstoke, Hampshire, RG21 6XS, England, (Telephone in U.S. (888) 330-8477), (Fax in U.S. (800) 672-2054), www.palgrave.com; *The Statesman's Yearbook 2008.*

Reserve Bank of Australia (RBA), The Secretary, GPO Box 3947, Sydney NSW 2001, Australia, www.rba.gov.au; *Financial Stability Review* and *Statement on Monetary Policy.*

Taylor and Francis Group, An Informa Business, 2 Park Square, Milton Park, Abingdon, Oxford OX14 4RN, United Kingdom, (Dial from U.S. (212) 216-7800), (Fax from U.S. (212) 564-7854), www.tandf.co.uk; *The Europa World Year Book.*

United Nations Statistics Division, New York, NY 10017, (800) 253-9646, Fax: (212) 963-4116, http://unstats.un.org; *World Statistics Pocketbook.*

The World Bank, 1818 H Street, NW, Washington, DC 20433, (202) 473-1000, Fax: (202) 477-6391, www.worldbank.org; *Australia; Global Economic Monitor (GEM); Global Economic Prospects 2008; The World Bank Atlas 2003-2004;* and *World Development Report 2008.*

AUSTRALIA - ECONOMICS - SOCIOLOGICAL ASPECTS

Organisation for Economic Cooperation and Development (OECD), 2 rue Andre Pascal, F-75775 Paris Cedex 16, France, (Telephone in U.S. (202) 785-6323), (Fax in U.S. (202) 785-0350), www.oecd.org; *OECD Economic Outlook 2008.*

AUSTRALIA - EDUCATION

Australian Bureau of Statistics (ABS), Locked Bag 10, Belconnen ACT 2616, Australia, www.abs.gov.au; *Australia at a Glance, 2008* and *Year Book Australia, 2008.*

Economist Intelligence Unit, 111 West 57th Street, New York, NY 10019, (212) 554-0600, Fax: (212) 586-1181, www.eiu.com; *Business Asia.*

Euromonitor International, Inc., 224 S. Michigan Avenue, Suite 1500, Chicago, IL 60604, (312) 922-1115, Fax: (312) 922-1157, www.euromonitor.com; *International Marketing Data and Statistics 2008* and *World Marketing Data and Statistics.*

International Monetary Fund (IMF), 700 Nineteenth Street, NW, Washington, DC 20431, (202) 623-7000, Fax: (202) 623-4661, www.imf.org; *Government Finance Statistics Yearbook (2008 Edition).*

M.E. Sharpe, 80 Business Park Drive, Armonk, NY 10504, (800) 541-6563, Fax: (914) 273-2106, www.mesharpe.com; *The Illustrated Book of World Rankings.*

Organisation for Economic Cooperation and Development (OECD), 2 rue Andre Pascal, F-75775 Paris Cedex 16, France, (Telephone in U.S. (202) 785-6323), (Fax in U.S. (202) 785-0350), www.oecd.org; *Education at a Glance* (2007 Edition).

Palgrave Macmillan Ltd., Houndmills, Basingstoke, Hampshire, RG21 6XS, England, (Telephone in U.S. (888) 330-8477), (Fax in U.S. (800) 672-2054), www.palgrave.com; *The Statesman's Yearbook 2008.*

Taylor and Francis Group, An Informa Business, 2 Park Square, Milton Park, Abingdon, Oxford OX14 4RN, United Kingdom, (Dial from U.S. (212) 216-7800), (Fax from U.S. (212) 564-7854), www.tandf.co.uk; *The Europa World Year Book.*

UNESCO Institute for Statistics, C.P. 6128 Succursale Centre-Ville, Montreal, Quebec, H3C 3J7 Canada, (Dial from U.S. (514) 343-6880), (Fax from U.S. (514) 343 6882), www.uis.unesco.org; *Statistical Tables.*

United Nations Statistics Division, New York, NY 10017, (800) 253-9646, Fax: (212) 963-4116, http://unstats.un.org; *Asia-Pacific in Figures 2004; Human Development Report 2006;* and *Statistical Yearbook for Asia and the Pacific 2004.*

The World Bank, 1818 H Street, NW, Washington, DC 20433, (202) 473-1000, Fax: (202) 477-6391, www.worldbank.org; *Australia; World Development Indicators (WDI) 2008;* and *World Development Report 2008.*

AUSTRALIA - ELECTRICITY

M.E. Sharpe, 80 Business Park Drive, Armonk, NY 10504, (800) 541-6563, Fax: (914) 273-2106, www.mesharpe.com; *The Illustrated Book of World Rankings.*

Organisation for Economic Cooperation and Development (OECD), 2 rue Andre Pascal, F-75775 Paris Cedex 16, France, (Telephone in U.S. (202) 785-6323), (Fax in U.S. (202) 785-0350), www.oecd.org; *Coal Information: 2007 Edition; Energy Statistics of OECD Countries* (2007 Edition); *Indicators of Industrial Activity;* STructural ANalysis (STAN) database; and *World Energy Outlook 2007.*

Palgrave Macmillan Ltd., Houndmills, Basingstoke, Hampshire, RG21 6XS, England, (Telephone in U.S. (888) 330-8477), (Fax in U.S. (800) 672-2054), www.palgrave.com; *The Statesman's Yearbook 2008.*

Platts, 2 Penn Plaza, 25th Floor, New York, NY 10121-2298, (212) 904-3070, www.platts.com; *Asian Electricity Outlook 2006* and *Emissions Daily.*

U.S. Department of Energy (DOE), Energy Information Administration (EIA), 1000 Independence Avenue, SW, Washington, DC 20585, (202) 586-8800, www.eia.doe.gov; *International Energy Annual 2004* and *International Energy Outlook 2006.*

United Nations Statistics Division, New York, NY 10017, (800) 253-9646, Fax: (212) 963-4116, http://unstats.un.org; *Electric Power in Asia and the Pacific 2001 and 2002; Human Development Report 2006;* and *Statistical Yearbook.*

AUSTRALIA - EMPLOYMENT

Australian Government Office for Women, Department of Families, Community Services and Indigenous Affairs, Box 7788, Canberra Mail Centre ACT 2610, Australia, http://ofw.facsia.gov.au; *Time Use Survey.*

Bernan Essential Government Publications, 4611-F Assembly Drive, Lanham MD, 20706-4391, (301) 459-2255, Fax: (800) 865-3450, www.bernan.com; *OECD Factbook 2006.*

Euromonitor International, Inc., 224 S. Michigan Avenue, Suite 1500, Chicago, IL 60604, (312) 922-1115, Fax: (312) 922-1157, www.euromonitor.com; *International Marketing Data and Statistics 2008.*

International Labour Office, I.L.O. Publications, 4 route des Morillons, CH-1211 Geneva 22, Switzerland, (Telephone in U.S. (202) 653-7652), (Fax in U.S. (202) 653-7687), www.ilo.org; *Yearbook of Labour Statistics 2006.*

M.E. Sharpe, 80 Business Park Drive, Armonk, NY 10504, (800) 541-6563, Fax: (914) 273-2106, www.mesharpe.com; *The Illustrated Book of World Rankings.*

Organisation for Economic Cooperation and Development (OECD), 2 rue Andre Pascal, F-75775 Paris Cedex 16, France, (Telephone in U.S. (202) 785-6323), (Fax in U.S. (202) 785-0350), www.oecd.org; *ICT Sector Data and Metadata by Country; Iron and Steel Industry in 2004 (2006 Edition); Labour Force Statistics: 1986-2005, 2007 Edition; A New World Map in Textiles and Clothing: Adjusting to Change; OECD Composite Leading Indicators (CLIs), Updated September 2007; OECD Economic Outlook 2008; OECD Economic Survey - Australia 2006; OECD Employment Outlook 2007;* and *OECD in Figures 2007.*

United Nations Statistics Division, New York, NY 10017, (800) 253-9646, Fax: (212) 963-4116, http://unstats.un.org; *Asia-Pacific in Figures 2004* and *Statistical Yearbook.*

The World Bank, 1818 H Street, NW, Washington, DC 20433, (202) 473-1000, Fax: (202) 477-6391, www.worldbank.org; *Australia.*

AUSTRALIA - ENERGY INDUSTRIES

Enerdata, 10 Rue Royale, 75008 Paris, France, www.enerdata.fr; *Global Energy Market Data.*

International Energy Agency (IEA), 9, rue de la Federation, 75739 Paris Cedex 15, France, www.iea.org; *Key World Energy Statistics 2007.*

Organisation for Economic Cooperation and Development (OECD), 2 rue Andre Pascal, F-75775 Paris Cedex 16, France, (Telephone in U.S. (202) 785-6323), (Fax in U.S. (202) 785-0350), www.oecd.org; *Towards Sustainable Household Consumption?: Trends and Policies in OECD Countries.*

Platts, 2 Penn Plaza, 25th Floor, New York, NY 10121-2298, (212) 904-3070, www.platts.com; *Asian Electricity Outlook 2006* and *Emissions Daily.*

United Nations Statistics Division, New York, NY 10017, (800) 253-9646, Fax: (212) 963-4116, http://unstats.un.org; *Electric Power in Asia and the Pacific 2001 and 2002* and *Statistical Yearbook.*

AUSTRALIA - ENVIRONMENTAL CONDITIONS

DSI Data Service Information, Xantener Strasse 51a, D-47495 Rheinberg, Germany, www.dsidata.com; *Campus Solution* and *DSI's Global Environmental Database.*

Economist Intelligence Unit, 111 West 57th Street, New York, NY 10019, (212) 554-0600, Fax: (212) 586-1181, www.eiu.com; *Australia Country Report.*

Federal Statistical Office Germany, D-65180 Wiesbaden, Germany, www.destatis.de; *Australia 2006.*

Organisation for Economic Cooperation and Development (OECD), 2 rue Andre Pascal, F-75775 Paris Cedex 16, France, (Telephone in U.S. (202) 785-6323), (Fax in U.S. (202) 785-0350), www.oecd.org; *Key Environmental Indicators 2004.*

Platts, 2 Penn Plaza, 25th Floor, New York, NY 10121-2298, (212) 904-3070, www.platts.com; *Emissions Daily.*

United Nations Statistics Division, New York, NY 10017, (800) 253-9646, Fax: (212) 963-4116, http://unstats.un.org; *World Statistics Pocketbook.*

AUSTRALIA - EXPENDITURES, PUBLIC

Australian Institute of Health and Welfare (AIHW), GPO Box 570, Canberra ACT 2601, Australia, www.aihw.gov.au; *National Public Health Expenditure Report 2005-06.*

Organisation for Economic Cooperation and Development (OECD), 2 rue Andre Pascal, F-75775 Paris Cedex 16, France, (Telephone in U.S. (202) 785-6323), (Fax in U.S. (202) 785-0350), www.oecd.org; *Revenue Statistics 1965-2006 - 2007 Edition.*

AUSTRALIA - EXPORTS

Central Intelligence Agency, Office of Public Affairs, Washington, DC 20505, (703) 482-0623, Fax: (703) 482-1739, www.cia.gov; *The World Factbook.*

Economist Intelligence Unit, 111 West 57th Street, New York, NY 10019, (212) 554-0600, Fax: (212) 586-1181, www.eiu.com; *Australia Country Report.*

Euromonitor International, Inc., 224 S. Michigan Avenue, Suite 1500, Chicago, IL 60604, (312) 922-1115, Fax: (312) 922-1157, www.euromonitor.com; *International Marketing Data and Statistics 2008* and *The World Economic Factbook 2008.*

International Iron and Steel Institute (IISI), Rue Colonel Bourg 120, B-1140 Brussels, Belgium, www.worldsteel.org; *Steel Statistical Yearbook 2006.*

International Lead and Zinc Study Group (ILZSG), Rua Almirante Barroso 38, 5th Floor, Lisbon 1000 - 013, Portugal, www.ilzsg.org; Interactive Statistical Database.

International Monetary Fund (IMF), 700 Nineteenth Street, NW, Washington, DC 20431, (202) 623-7000, Fax: (202) 623-4661, www.imf.org; *Direction of Trade Statistics Yearbook 2007; Government Finance Statistics Yearbook (2008 Edition);* and *International Financial Statistics Yearbook 2007.*

Organisation for Economic Cooperation and Development (OECD), 2 rue Andre Pascal, F-75775 Paris Cedex 16, France, (Telephone in U.S. (202) 785-6323), (Fax in U.S. (202) 785-0350), www.oecd.org; *Geographical Distribution of Financial Flows to Aid Recipients 2002-2006; International Trade by Commodity Statistics (ITCS); Iron and Steel Industry in 2004 (2006 Edition); 2005 OECD Agricultural Outlook Tables, 1970-2014; OECD Economic Outlook 2008; OECD Economic Survey - Australia 2006; Review of Fisheries in OECD Countries: Country Statistics 2001 to 2003 - 2005 Edition;* and STructural ANalysis (STAN) database.

Palgrave Macmillan Ltd., Houndmills, Basingstoke, Hampshire, RG21 6XS, England, (Telephone in U.S. (888) 330-8477), (Fax in U.S. (800) 672-2054), www.palgrave.com; *The Statesman's Yearbook 2008.*

Taylor and Francis Group, An Informa Business, 2 Park Square, Milton Park, Abingdon, Oxford OX14 4RN, United Kingdom, (Dial from U.S. (212) 216-7800), (Fax from U.S. (212) 564-7854), www.tandf.co.uk; *The Europa World Year Book.*

Technical Association of the Pulp and Paper Industry (TAPPI), 15 Technology Parkway South, Norcross, GA 30092, (770) 446-1400, Fax: (770) 446-6947, www.tappi.org; *TAPPI Annual Report.*

United Nations Conference on Trade and Development (UNCTAD), DC2-1120, United Nations, New York, NY 10017, (212) 963-0027, www.unctad.org; *Handbook of Statistics 2005.*

United Nations Food and Agricultural Organization (FAO), Viale delle Terme di Caracalla, 00100 Rome, Italy, (Dial from U.S. (202) 653-2400), (Fax from U.S. (202) 653 5760), www.fao.org; *The State of Food and Agriculture (SOFA) 2006.*

United Nations Statistics Division, New York, NY 10017, (800) 253-9646, Fax: (212) 963-4116, http://unstats.un.org; *Foreign Trade Statistics of Asia and the Pacific 1996-2000.*

The World Bank, 1818 H Street, NW, Washington, DC 20433, (202) 473-1000, Fax: (202) 477-6391, www.worldbank.org; *World Development Indicators (WDI) 2008* and *World Development Report 2008.*

Worldinformation.com, 2 Market Street, Saffron Walden, Essex CB10 1HZ, United Kingdom, www.worldinformation.com; The World of Information (www.worldinformation.com).

AUSTRALIA - FEMALE WORKING POPULATION

See AUSTRALIA - EMPLOYMENT

AUSTRALIA - FERTILITY, HUMAN

M.E. Sharpe, 80 Business Park Drive, Armonk, NY 10504, (800) 541-6563, Fax: (914) 273-2106, www.mesharpe.com; *The Illustrated Book of World Rankings.*

United Nations Statistics Division, New York, NY 10017, (800) 253-9646, Fax: (212) 963-4116, http://unstats.un.org; *Human Development Report 2006.*

The World Bank, 1818 H Street, NW, Washington, DC 20433, (202) 473-1000, Fax: (202) 477-6391, www.worldbank.org; *The World Bank Atlas 2003-2004; World Development Indicators (WDI) 2008;* and *World Development Report 2008.*

AUSTRALIA - FERTILIZER INDUSTRY

Organisation for Economic Cooperation and Development (OECD), 2 rue Andre Pascal, F-75775 Paris Cedex 16, France, (Telephone in U.S. (202) 785-6323), (Fax in U.S. (202) 785-0350), www.oecd.org; *International Trade by Commodity Statistics (ITCS)* and *2005 OECD Agricultural Outlook Tables, 1970-2014.*

United Nations Food and Agricultural Organization (FAO), Viale delle Terme di Caracalla, 00100 Rome, Italy, (Dial from U.S. (202) 653-2400), (Fax from U.S. (202) 653 5760), www.fao.org; *FAO Fertilizer Yearbook* and *The State of Food and Agriculture (SOFA) 2006.*

United Nations Statistics Division, New York, NY 10017, (800) 253-9646, Fax: (212) 963-4116, http://unstats.un.org; *Statistical Yearbook.*

AUSTRALIA - FETAL MORTALITY

See AUSTRALIA - MORTALITY

AUSTRALIA - FILM

See AUSTRALIA - MOTION PICTURES

AUSTRALIA - FINANCE

Australian Bureau of Statistics (ABS), Locked Bag 10, Belconnen ACT 2616, Australia, www.abs.gov.au; *Australia at a Glance, 2008* and *Year Book Australia, 2008.*

International Monetary Fund (IMF), 700 Nineteenth Street, NW, Washington, DC 20431, (202) 623-7000, Fax: (202) 623-4661, www.imf.org; *International Financial Statistics Yearbook 2007.*

Organisation for Economic Cooperation and Development (OECD), 2 rue Andre Pascal, F-75775 Paris Cedex 16, France, (Telephone in U.S. (202) 785-6323), (Fax in U.S. (202) 785-0350), www.oecd.org; *OECD Economic Outlook 2008.*

Reserve Bank of Australia (RBA), The Secretary, GPO Box 3947, Sydney NSW 2001, Australia, www.rba.gov.au; *Financial Stability Review.*

Taylor and Francis Group, An Informa Business, 2 Park Square, Milton Park, Abingdon, Oxford OX14 4RN, United Kingdom, (Dial from U.S. (212) 216-7800), (Fax from U.S. (212) 564-7854), www.tandf.co.uk; *The Europa World Year Book.*

United Nations Statistics Division, New York, NY 10017, (800) 253-9646, Fax: (212) 963-4116, http://unstats.un.org; *Asia-Pacific in Figures 2004; National Accounts Statistics: Compendium of Income Distribution Statistics;* and *Statistical Yearbook for Asia and the Pacific 2004.*

The World Bank, 1818 H Street, NW, Washington, DC 20433, (202) 473-1000, Fax: (202) 477-6391, www.worldbank.org; *Australia.*

AUSTRALIA - FINANCE, PUBLIC

Bernan Essential Government Publications, 4611-F Assembly Drive, Lanham MD, 20706-4391, (301) 459-2255, Fax: (800) 865-3450, www.bernan.com; *National Accounts Statistics.*

Economist Intelligence Unit, 111 West 57th Street, New York, NY 10019, (212) 554-0600, Fax: (212) 586-1181, www.eiu.com; *Australia Country Report.*

International Monetary Fund (IMF), 700 Nineteenth Street, NW, Washington, DC 20431, (202) 623-7000, Fax: (202) 623-4661, www.imf.org; *Government Finance Statistics Yearbook (2008 Edition); International Financial Statistics; International Financial Statistics Online Service;* and *International Financial Statistics Yearbook 2007.*

M.E. Sharpe, 80 Business Park Drive, Armonk, NY 10504, (800) 541-6563, Fax: (914) 273-2106, www.mesharpe.com; *The Illustrated Book of World Rankings.*

Organisation for Economic Cooperation and Development (OECD), 2 rue Andre Pascal, F-75775 Paris Cedex 16, France, (Telephone in U.S. (202) 785-6323), (Fax in U.S. (202) 785-0350), www.oecd.org; *Financial Market Trends: OECD Periodical; Geographical Distribution of Financial Flows to Aid Recipients 2002-2006; OECD Economic Outlook 2008; OECD Main Economic Indicators (MEI);* and *Revenue Statistics 1965-2006 - 2007 Edition.*

Palgrave Macmillan Ltd., Houndmills, Basingstoke, Hampshire, RG21 6XS, England, (Telephone in U.S. (888) 330-8477), (Fax in U.S. (800) 672-2054), www.palgrave.com; *The Statesman's Yearbook 2008.*

Reserve Bank of Australia (RBA), The Secretary, GPO Box 3947, Sydney NSW 2001, Australia, www.rba.gov.au; *Financial Stability Review.*

Taylor and Francis Group, An Informa Business, 2 Park Square, Milton Park, Abingdon, Oxford OX14 4RN, United Kingdom, (Dial from U.S. (212) 216-7800), (Fax from U.S. (212) 564-7854), www.tandf.co.uk; *The Europa World Year Book.*

United Nations Statistics Division, New York, NY 10017, (800) 253-9646, Fax: (212) 963-4116, http://unstats.un.org; *Statistical Yearbook for Asia and the Pacific 2004.*

The World Bank, 1818 H Street, NW, Washington, DC 20433, (202) 473-1000, Fax: (202) 477-6391, www.worldbank.org; *Australia.*

AUSTRALIA - FISHERIES

Australian Bureau of Statistics (ABS), Locked Bag 10, Belconnen ACT 2616, Australia, www.abs.gov.au; *Australia at a Glance, 2008* and *Year Book Australia, 2008.*

M.E. Sharpe, 80 Business Park Drive, Armonk, NY 10504, (800) 541-6563, Fax: (914) 273-2106, www.mesharpe.com; *The Illustrated Book of World Rankings.*

Organisation for Economic Cooperation and Development (OECD), 2 rue Andre Pascal, F-75775 Paris Cedex 16, France, (Telephone in U.S. (202) 785-6323), (Fax in U.S. (202) 785-0350), www.oecd.org; *International Trade by Commodity Statistics (ITCS); Review of Fisheries in OECD Countries: Country Statistics 2001 to 2003 - 2005 Edition;* and STructural ANalysis (STAN) database.

Palgrave Macmillan Ltd., Houndmills, Basingstoke, Hampshire, RG21 6XS, England, (Telephone in U.S. (888) 330-8477), (Fax in U.S. (800) 672-2054), www.palgrave.com; *The Statesman's Yearbook 2008.*

Taylor and Francis Group, An Informa Business, 2 Park Square, Milton Park, Abingdon, Oxford OX14 4RN, United Kingdom, (Dial from U.S. (212) 216-7800), (Fax from U.S. (212) 564-7854), www.tandf.co.uk; *The Europa World Year Book.*

United Nations Conference on Trade and Development (UNCTAD), DC2-1120, United Nations, New York, NY 10017, (212) 963-0027, www.unctad.org; *UNCTAD Commodity Yearbook.*

United Nations Food and Agricultural Organization (FAO), Viale delle Terme di Caracalla, 00100 Rome, Italy, (Dial from U.S. (202) 653-2400), (Fax from U.S. (202) 653 5760), www.fao.org; *The State of Food and Agriculture (SOFA) 2006.*

United Nations Statistics Division, New York, NY 10017, (800) 253-9646, Fax: (212) 963-4116, http://unstats.un.org; *Statistical Yearbook.*

The World Bank, 1818 H Street, NW, Washington, DC 20433, (202) 473-1000, Fax: (202) 477-6391, www.worldbank.org; *Australia.*

AUSTRALIA - FLOUR INDUSTRY

United Nations Statistics Division, New York, NY 10017, (800) 253-9646, Fax: (212) 963-4116, http://unstats.un.org; *Statistical Yearbook.*

AUSTRALIA - FOOD

Euromonitor International, Inc., 224 S. Michigan Avenue, Suite 1500, Chicago, IL 60604, (312) 922-1115, Fax: (312) 922-1157, www.euromonitor.com; *Retail Trade International 2007.*

Organisation for Economic Cooperation and Development (OECD), 2 rue Andre Pascal, F-75775 Paris

Cedex 16, France, (Telephone in U.S. (202) 785-6323), (Fax in U.S. (202) 785-0350), www.oecd.org; *International Trade by Commodity Statistics (ITCS)* and *Towards Sustainable Household Consumption?: Trends and Policies in OECD Countries.*

United Nations Conference on Trade and Development (UNCTAD), DC2-1120, United Nations, New York, NY 10017, (212) 963-0027, www.unctad.org; *UNCTAD Commodity Yearbook.*

United Nations Food and Agricultural Organization (FAO), Viale delle Terme di Caracalla, 00100 Rome, Italy, (Dial from U.S. (202) 653-2400), (Fax from U.S. (202) 653 5760), www.fao.org; *FAO Production Yearbook 2002* and *The State of Food and Agriculture (SOFA) 2006.*

United Nations Statistics Division, New York, NY 10017, (800) 253-9646, Fax: (212) 963-4116, http://unstats.un.org; *Human Development Report 2006* and *Statistical Yearbook for Asia and the Pacific 2004.*

AUSTRALIA - FOOTWEAR

Organisation for Economic Cooperation and Development (OECD), 2 rue Andre Pascal, F-75775 Paris Cedex 16, France, (Telephone in U.S. (202) 785-6323), (Fax in U.S. (202) 785-0350), www.oecd.org; *Indicators of Industrial Activity.*

AUSTRALIA - FOREIGN EXCHANGE RATES

Central Intelligence Agency, Office of Public Affairs, Washington, DC 20505, (703) 482-0623, Fax: (703) 482-1739, www.cia.gov; *The World Factbook.*

Economist Intelligence Unit, 111 West 57th Street, New York, NY 10019, (212) 554-0600, Fax: (212) 586-1181, www.eiu.com; *Business Asia.*

Euromonitor International, Inc., 224 S. Michigan Avenue, Suite 1500, Chicago, IL 60604, (312) 922-1115, Fax: (312) 922-1157, www.euromonitor.com; *International Marketing Data and Statistics 2008* and *The World Economic Factbook 2008.*

International Civil Aviation Organization (ICAO), External Relations and Public Information Office (EPO), 999 University Street, Montreal, Quebec H3C 5H7, Canada, (Dial from U.S. (514) 954-8219), (Fax from U.S. (514) 954-6077), www.icao.int; *Civil Aviation Statistics of the World.*

International Monetary Fund (IMF), 700 Nineteenth Street, NW, Washington, DC 20431, (202) 623-7000, Fax: (202) 623-4661, www.imf.org; *International Financial Statistics Yearbook 2007.*

Organisation for Economic Cooperation and Development (OECD), 2 rue Andre Pascal, F-75775 Paris Cedex 16, France, (Telephone in U.S. (202) 785-6323), (Fax in U.S. (202) 785-0350), www.oecd.org; *Financial Market Trends: OECD Periodical; Household, Tourism, Travel: Trends, Environmental Impacts and Policy Responses; OECD Economic Outlook 2008;* and *Revenue Statistics 1965-2006 - 2007 Edition.*

Taylor and Francis Group, An Informa Business, 2 Park Square, Milton Park, Abingdon, Oxford OX14 4RN, United Kingdom, (Dial from U.S. (212) 216-7800), (Fax from U.S. (212) 564-7854), www.tandf.co.uk; *The Europa World Year Book.*

United Nations Statistics Division, New York, NY 10017, (800) 253-9646, Fax: (212) 963-4116, http://unstats.un.org; *Statistical Yearbook* and *World Statistics Pocketbook.*

Worldinformation.com, 2 Market Street, Saffron Walden, Essex CB10 1HZ, United Kingdom, www.worldinformation.com; The World of Information (www.worldinformation.com).

AUSTRALIA - FORESTS AND FORESTRY

American Forest Paper Association (AFPA), 1111 Nineteenth Street, NW, Suite 800, Washington, DC 20036, (800) 878-8878, www.afandpa.org; *2007 Annual Statistics of Paper, Paperboard, and Wood Pulp.*

Australian Bureau of Statistics (ABS), Locked Bag 10, Belconnen ACT 2616, Australia, www.abs.gov.au; *Australia at a Glance, 2008* and *Year Book Australia, 2008.*

M.E. Sharpe, 80 Business Park Drive, Armonk, NY 10504, (800) 541-6563, Fax: (914) 273-2106, www.mesharpe.com; *The Illustrated Book of World Rankings.*

Organisation for Economic Cooperation and Development (OECD), 2 rue Andre Pascal, F-75775 Paris Cedex 16, France, (Telephone in U.S. (202) 785-6323), (Fax in U.S. (202) 785-0350), www.oecd.org; *Indicators of Industrial Activity; International Trade by Commodity Statistics (ITCS);* and STructural ANalysis (STAN) database.

Palgrave Macmillan Ltd., Houndmills, Basingstoke, Hampshire, RG21 6XS, England, (Telephone in U.S. (888) 330-8477), (Fax in U.S. (800) 672-2054), www.palgrave.com; *The Statesman's Yearbook 2008.*

Taylor and Francis Group, An Informa Business, 2 Park Square, Milton Park, Abingdon, Oxford OX14 4RN, United Kingdom, (Dial from U.S. (212) 216-7800), (Fax from U.S. (212) 564-7854), www.tandf.co.uk; *The Europa World Year Book.*

Technical Association of the Pulp and Paper Industry (TAPPI), 15 Technology Parkway South, Norcross, GA 30092, (770) 446-1400, Fax: (770) 446-6947, www.tappi.org; *TAPPI Annual Report.*

UNESCO Institute for Statistics, C.P. 6128 Succursale Centre-Ville, Montreal, Quebec, H3C 3J7 Canada, (Dial from U.S. (514) 343-6880), (Fax from U.S. (514) 343 6882), www.uis.unesco.org; *Statistical Tables.*

United Nations Conference on Trade and Development (UNCTAD), DC2-1120, United Nations, New York, NY 10017, (212) 963-0027, www.unctad.org; *UNCTAD Commodity Yearbook.*

United Nations Food and Agricultural Organization (FAO), Viale delle Terme di Caracalla, 00100 Rome, Italy, (Dial from U.S. (202) 653-2400), (Fax from U.S. (202) 653 5760), www.fao.org; *FAO Yearbook of Forest Products* and *The State of Food and Agriculture (SOFA) 2006.*

United Nations Statistics Division, New York, NY 10017, (800) 253-9646, Fax: (212) 963-4116, http://unstats.un.org; *Statistical Yearbook.*

The World Bank, 1818 H Street, NW, Washington, DC 20433, (202) 473-1000, Fax: (202) 477-6391, www.worldbank.org; *Australia* and *World Development Report 2008.*

AUSTRALIA - FRUIT PRODUCTION

See AUSTRALIA - CROPS

AUSTRALIA - GAS PRODUCTION

See AUSTRALIA - MINERAL INDUSTRIES

AUSTRALIA - GEOGRAPHIC INFORMATION SYSTEMS

M.E. Sharpe, 80 Business Park Drive, Armonk, NY 10504, (800) 541-6563, Fax: (914) 273-2106, www.mesharpe.com; *The Illustrated Book of World Rankings.*

The World Bank, 1818 H Street, NW, Washington, DC 20433, (202) 473-1000, Fax: (202) 477-6391, www.worldbank.org; *Australia.*

AUSTRALIA - GLASS AND GLASS PRODUCTS

See AUSTRALIA - MINERAL INDUSTRIES

AUSTRALIA - GOLD PRODUCTION

See AUSTRALIA - MINERAL INDUSTRIES

AUSTRALIA - GRANTS-IN-AID

International Monetary Fund (IMF), 700 Nineteenth Street, NW, Washington, DC 20431, (202) 623-7000, Fax: (202) 623-4661, www.imf.org; *Government Finance Statistics Yearbook (2008 Edition).*

Organisation for Economic Cooperation and Development (OECD), 2 rue Andre Pascal, F-75775 Paris Cedex 16, France, (Telephone in U.S. (202) 785-6323), (Fax in U.S. (202) 785-0350), www.oecd.org; *Geographical Distribution of Financial Flows to Aid Recipients 2002-2006.*

AUSTRALIA - GROSS DOMESTIC PRODUCT

Australian Bureau of Statistics (ABS), Locked Bag 10, Belconnen ACT 2616, Australia, www.abs.gov.au; *Australia at a Glance, 2008* and *Year Book Australia, 2008.*

Economist Intelligence Unit, 111 West 57th Street, New York, NY 10019, (212) 554-0600, Fax: (212) 586-1181, www.eiu.com; *Australia Country Report* and *Business Asia.*

Euromonitor International, Inc., 224 S. Michigan Avenue, Suite 1500, Chicago, IL 60604, (312) 922-1115, Fax: (312) 922-1157, www.euromonitor.com; *International Marketing Data and Statistics 2008* and *The World Economic Factbook 2008.*

International Monetary Fund (IMF), 700 Nineteenth Street, NW, Washington, DC 20431, (202) 623-7000, Fax: (202) 623-4661, www.imf.org; *International Financial Statistics Yearbook 2007.*

M.E. Sharpe, 80 Business Park Drive, Armonk, NY 10504, (800) 541-6563, Fax: (914) 273-2106, www.mesharpe.com; *The Illustrated Book of World Rankings.*

Organisation for Economic Cooperation and Development (OECD), 2 rue Andre Pascal, F-75775 Paris Cedex 16, France, (Telephone in U.S. (202) 785-6323), (Fax in U.S. (202) 785-0350), www.oecd.org; *Comparison of Gross Domestic Product (GDP) for OECD Countries; Geographical Distribution of Financial Flows to Aid Recipients 2002-2006; OECD Economic Outlook 2008;* and *Revenue Statistics 1965-2006 - 2007 Edition.*

Taylor and Francis Group, An Informa Business, 2 Park Square, Milton Park, Abingdon, Oxford OX14 4RN, United Kingdom, (Dial from U.S. (212) 216-7800), (Fax from U.S. (212) 564-7854), www.tandf.co.uk; *The Europa World Year Book.*

United Nations Statistics Division, New York, NY 10017, (800) 253-9646, Fax: (212) 963-4116, http://unstats.un.org; *Human Development Report 2006; National Accounts Statistics: Compendium of Income Distribution Statistics;* and *Statistical Yearbook.*

The World Bank, 1818 H Street, NW, Washington, DC 20433, (202) 473-1000, Fax: (202) 477-6391, www.worldbank.org; *World Development Indicators (WDI) 2008* and *World Development Report 2008.*

AUSTRALIA - GROSS NATIONAL PRODUCT

Euromonitor International, Inc., 224 S. Michigan Avenue, Suite 1500, Chicago, IL 60604, (312) 922-1115, Fax: (312) 922-1157, www.euromonitor.com; *International Marketing Data and Statistics 2008.*

M.E. Sharpe, 80 Business Park Drive, Armonk, NY 10504, (800) 541-6563, Fax: (914) 273-2106, www.mesharpe.com; *The Illustrated Book of World Rankings.*

Organisation for Economic Cooperation and Development (OECD), 2 rue Andre Pascal, F-75775 Paris Cedex 16, France, (Telephone in U.S. (202) 785-6323), (Fax in U.S. (202) 785-0350), www.oecd.org; *Geographical Distribution of Financial Flows to Aid Recipients 2002-2006; OECD Composite Leading Indicators (CLIs), Updated September 2007; OECD Economic Outlook 2008;* and *OECD Main Economic Indicators (MEI).*

Palgrave Macmillan Ltd., Houndmills, Basingstoke, Hampshire, RG21 6XS, England, (Telephone in U.S. (888) 330-8477), (Fax in U.S. (800) 672-2054), www.palgrave.com; *The Statesman's Yearbook 2008.*

Taylor and Francis Group, An Informa Business, 2 Park Square, Milton Park, Abingdon, Oxford OX14 4RN, United Kingdom, (Dial from U.S. (212) 216-7800), (Fax from U.S. (212) 564-7854), www.tandf.co.uk; *The Europa World Year Book.*

U.S. Department of State (DOS), 2201 C Street NW, Washington, DC 20520, (202) 647-4000, www.state.gov; *World Military Expenditures and Arms Transfers (WMEAT).*

United Nations Statistics Division, New York, NY 10017, (800) 253-9646, Fax: (212) 963-4116, http://unstats.un.org; *Statistical Yearbook.*

The World Bank, 1818 H Street, NW, Washington, DC 20433, (202) 473-1000, Fax: (202) 477-6391, www.worldbank.org; *The World Bank Atlas 2003-2004; World Development Indicators (WDI) 2008;* and *World Development Report 2008.*

Worldinformation.com, 2 Market Street, Saffron Walden, Essex CB10 1HZ, United Kingdom, www.worldinformation.com; The World of Information (www.worldinformation.com).

AUSTRALIA - HIDES AND SKINS INDUSTRY

Organisation for Economic Cooperation and Development (OECD), 2 rue Andre Pascal, F-75775 Paris Cedex 16, France, (Telephone in U.S. (202) 785-6323), (Fax in U.S. (202) 785-0350), www.oecd.org; *Indicators of Industrial Activity* and *International Trade by Commodity Statistics (ITCS).*

United Nations Food and Agricultural Organization (FAO), Viale delle Terme di Caracalla, 00100 Rome, Italy, (Dial from U.S. (202) 653-2400), (Fax from U.S. (202) 653 5760), www.fao.org; *FAO Production Yearbook 2002.*

AUSTRALIA - HOPS PRODUCTION

See AUSTRALIA - CROPS

AUSTRALIA - HOUSING

Australian Bureau of Statistics (ABS), Locked Bag 10, Belconnen ACT 2616, Australia, www.abs.gov.au; *Australia at a Glance, 2008* and *Year Book Australia, 2008.*

Australian Institute of Health and Welfare (AIHW), GPO Box 570, Canberra ACT 2601, Australia, www.aihw.gov.au; *Housing Assistance in Australia 2008.*

Euromonitor International, Inc., 224 S. Michigan Avenue, Suite 1500, Chicago, IL 60604, (312) 922-1115, Fax: (312) 922-1157, www.euromonitor.com; *World Marketing Data and Statistics.*

M.E. Sharpe, 80 Business Park Drive, Armonk, NY 10504, (800) 541-6563, Fax: (914) 273-2106, www.mesharpe.com; *The Illustrated Book of World Rankings.*

AUSTRALIA - HOUSING - FINANCE

Organisation for Economic Cooperation and Development (OECD), 2 rue Andre Pascal, F-75775 Paris Cedex 16, France, (Telephone in U.S. (202) 785-6323), (Fax in U.S. (202) 785-0350), www.oecd.org; *OECD Main Economic Indicators (MEI).*

AUSTRALIA - HOUSING CONSTRUCTION

See AUSTRALIA - CONSTRUCTION INDUSTRY

AUSTRALIA - ILLITERATE PERSONS

Euromonitor International, Inc., 224 S. Michigan Avenue, Suite 1500, Chicago, IL 60604, (312) 922-1115, Fax: (312) 922-1157, www.euromonitor.com; *The World Economic Factbook 2008.*

Palgrave Macmillan Ltd., Houndmills, Basingstoke, Hampshire, RG21 6XS, England, (Telephone in U.S. (888) 330-8477), (Fax in U.S. (800) 672-2054), www.palgrave.com; *The Statesman's Yearbook 2008.*

United Nations Statistics Division, New York, NY 10017, (800) 253-9646, Fax: (212) 963-4116, http://unstats.un.org; *Asia-Pacific in Figures 2004* and *Human Development Report 2006.*

AUSTRALIA - IMPORTS

Central Intelligence Agency, Office of Public Affairs, Washington, DC 20505, (703) 482-0623, Fax: (703) 482-1739, www.cia.gov; *The World Factbook.*

Economist Intelligence Unit, 111 West 57th Street, New York, NY 10019, (212) 554-0600, Fax: (212) 586-1181, www.eiu.com; *Australia Country Report.*

Euromonitor International, Inc., 224 S. Michigan Avenue, Suite 1500, Chicago, IL 60604, (312) 922-1115, Fax: (312) 922-1157, www.euromonitor.com; *International Marketing Data and Statistics 2008* and *The World Economic Factbook 2008.*

International Iron and Steel Institute (IISI), Rue Colonel Bourg 120, B-1140 Brussels, Belgium, www.worldsteel.org; *Steel Statistical Yearbook 2006.*

International Lead and Zinc Study Group (ILZSG), Rua Almirante Barroso 38, 5th Floor, Lisbon 1000 - 013, Portugal, www.ilzsg.org; Interactive Statistical Database.

International Monetary Fund (IMF), 700 Nineteenth Street, NW, Washington, DC 20431, (202) 623-7000, Fax: (202) 623-4661, www.imf.org; *Direction of Trade Statistics Yearbook 2007* and *Government Finance Statistics Yearbook (2008 Edition).*

Organisation for Economic Cooperation and Development (OECD), 2 rue Andre Pascal, F-75775 Paris Cedex 16, France, (Telephone in U.S. (202) 785-6323), (Fax in U.S. (202) 785-0350), www.oecd.org; *Iron and Steel Industry in 2004 (2006 Edition); 2005 OECD Agricultural Outlook Tables, 1970-2014; OECD Economic Outlook 2008; OECD Economic Survey - Australia 2006; Review of Fisheries in OECD Countries: Country Statistics 2001 to 2003 - 2005 Edition;* and STructural ANalysis (STAN) database.

Palgrave Macmillan Ltd., Houndmills, Basingstoke, Hampshire, RG21 6XS, England, (Telephone in U.S. (888) 330-8477), (Fax in U.S. (800) 672-2054), www.palgrave.com; *The Statesman's Yearbook 2008.*

Taylor and Francis Group, An Informa Business, 2 Park Square, Milton Park, Abingdon, Oxford OX14 4RN, United Kingdom, (Dial from U.S. (212) 216-7800), (Fax from U.S. (212) 564-7854), www.tandf.co.uk; *The Europa World Year Book.*

Technical Association of the Pulp and Paper Industry (TAPPI), 15 Technology Parkway South, Norcross, GA 30092, (770) 446-1400, Fax: (770) 446-6947, www.tappi.org; *TAPPI Annual Report.*

United Nations Conference on Trade and Development (UNCTAD), DC2-1120, United Nations, New York, NY 10017, (212) 963-0027, www.unctad.org; *Handbook of Statistics 2005.*

United Nations Food and Agricultural Organization (FAO), Viale delle Terme di Caracalla, 00100 Rome, Italy, (Dial from U.S. (202) 653-2400), (Fax from U.S. (202) 653 5760), www.fao.org; *The State of Food and Agriculture (SOFA) 2006.*

United Nations Statistics Division, New York, NY 10017, (800) 253-9646, Fax: (212) 963-4116, http://unstats.un.org; *Foreign Trade Statistics of Asia and the Pacific 1996-2000.*

The World Bank, 1818 H Street, NW, Washington, DC 20433, (202) 473-1000, Fax: (202) 477-6391, www.worldbank.org; *World Development Indicators (WDI) 2008* and *World Development Report 2008.*

Worldinformation.com, 2 Market Street, Saffron Walden, Essex CB10 1HZ, United Kingdom, www.worldinformation.com; The World of Information (www.worldinformation.com).

AUSTRALIA - INCOME TAXES

See AUSTRALIA - TAXATION

AUSTRALIA - INDUSTRIAL METALS PRODUCTION

See AUSTRALIA - MINERAL INDUSTRIES

AUSTRALIA - INDUSTRIAL PRODUCTIVITY

Euromonitor International, Inc., 224 S. Michigan Avenue, Suite 1500, Chicago, IL 60604, (312) 922-1115, Fax: (312) 922-1157, www.euromonitor.com; *International Marketing Data and Statistics 2008.*

International Iron and Steel Institute (IISI), Rue Colonel Bourg 120, B-1140 Brussels, Belgium, www.worldsteel.org; *Steel Statistical Yearbook 2006.*

International Lead and Zinc Study Group (ILZSG), Rua Almirante Barroso 38, 5th Floor, Lisbon 1000 - 013, Portugal, www.ilzsg.org; Interactive Statistical Database.

M.E. Sharpe, 80 Business Park Drive, Armonk, NY 10504, (800) 541-6563, Fax: (914) 273-2106, www.mesharpe.com; *The Illustrated Book of World Rankings.*

Organisation for Economic Cooperation and Development (OECD), 2 rue Andre Pascal, F-75775 Paris Cedex 16, France, (Telephone in U.S. (202) 785-6323), (Fax in U.S. (202) 785-0350), www.oecd.org; *Environmental Impacts of Foreign Direct Investment in the Mining Sector in the Newly Independent States (NIS); Indicators of Industrial Activity; Iron and Steel Industry in 2004 (2006 Edition); A New World Map in Textiles and Clothing: Adjusting to Change; 2005 OECD Agricultural Outlook Tables, 1970-2014; OECD Economic Outlook 2008;* and STructural ANalysis (STAN) database.

Technical Association of the Pulp and Paper Industry (TAPPI), 15 Technology Parkway South, Norcross, GA 30092, (770) 446-1400, Fax: (770) 446-6947, www.tappi.org; *TAPPI Annual Report.*

AUSTRALIA - INDUSTRIAL PROPERTY

United Nations Statistics Division, New York, NY 10017, (800) 253-9646, Fax: (212) 963-4116, http://unstats.un.org; *Statistical Yearbook.*

World Intellectual Property Organization (WIPO), PO Box 18, CH-1211 Geneva 20, Switzerland, www.wipo.int; *Industrial Property Statistics* and *Industrial Property Statistics Online Directory.*

AUSTRALIA - INDUSTRIES

Central Intelligence Agency, Office of Public Affairs, Washington, DC 20505, (703) 482-0623, Fax: (703) 482-1739, www.cia.gov; *The World Factbook.*

Economist Intelligence Unit, 111 West 57th Street, New York, NY 10019, (212) 554-0600, Fax: (212) 586-1181, www.eiu.com; *Australia Country Report.*

Euromonitor International, Inc., 224 S. Michigan Avenue, Suite 1500, Chicago, IL 60604, (312) 922-1115, Fax: (312) 922-1157, www.euromonitor.com; *International Marketing Data and Statistics 2008; The World Economic Factbook 2008;* and *World Marketing Data and Statistics.*

International Labour Office, I.L.O. Publications, 4 route des Morillons, CH-1211 Geneva 22, Switzerland, (Telephone in U.S. (202) 653-7652), (Fax in U.S. (202) 653-7687), www.ilo.org; *Yearbook of Labour Statistics 2006.*

M.E. Sharpe, 80 Business Park Drive, Armonk, NY 10504, (800) 541-6563, Fax: (914) 273-2106, www.mesharpe.com; *The Illustrated Book of World Rankings.*

Organisation for Economic Cooperation and Development (OECD), 2 rue Andre Pascal, F-75775 Paris Cedex 16, France, (Telephone in U.S. (202) 785-6323), (Fax in U.S. (202) 785-0350), www.oecd.org; *Key Environmental Indicators 2004; OECD Economic Outlook 2008; OECD Main Economic Indicators (MEI);* and STructural ANalysis (STAN) database.

Palgrave Macmillan Ltd., Houndmills, Basingstoke, Hampshire, RG21 6XS, England, (Telephone in U.S. (888) 330-8477), (Fax in U.S. (800) 672-2054), www.palgrave.com; *The Statesman's Yearbook 2008.*

Taylor and Francis Group, An Informa Business, 2 Park Square, Milton Park, Abingdon, Oxford OX14 4RN, United Kingdom, (Dial from U.S. (212) 216-7800), (Fax from U.S. (212) 564-7854), www.tandf.co.uk; *The Europa World Year Book.*

United Nations Industrial Development Organization (UNIDO), 1 United Nations Plaza, New York, NY 10017, (212) 963 6890, Fax: (212) 963-7904, http://unido.org; Industrial Statistics Database 2008 (INDSTAT) and *The International Yearbook of Industrial Statistics 2008.*

United Nations Statistics Division, New York, NY 10017, (800) 253-9646, Fax: (212) 963-4116, http://unstats.un.org; *Asia-Pacific in Figures 2004; 2004*

Industrial Commodity Statistics Yearbook; Statistical Yearbook; and *Statistical Yearbook for Asia and the Pacific 2004.*

The World Bank, 1818 H Street, NW, Washington, DC 20433, (202) 473-1000, Fax: (202) 477-6391, www.worldbank.org; *Australia* and *World Development Indicators (WDI) 2008.*

World Intellectual Property Organization (WIPO), PO Box 18, CH-1211 Geneva 20, Switzerland, www.wipo.int; *Industrial Property Statistics* and *Industrial Property Statistics Online Directory.*

AUSTRALIA - INFANT AND MATERNAL MORTALITY

See AUSTRALIA - MORTALITY

AUSTRALIA - INORGANIC ACIDS

United Nations Statistics Division, New York, NY 10017, (800) 253-9646, Fax: (212) 963-4116, http://unstats.un.org; *Statistical Yearbook.*

AUSTRALIA - INTEREST RATES

Organisation for Economic Cooperation and Development (OECD), 2 rue Andre Pascal, F-75775 Paris Cedex 16, France, (Telephone in U.S. (202) 785-6323), (Fax in U.S. (202) 785-0350), www.oecd.org; *Financial Market Trends: OECD Periodical; OECD Economic Outlook 2008;* and *OECD Main Economic Indicators (MEI).*

AUSTRALIA - INTERNAL REVENUE

Organisation for Economic Cooperation and Development (OECD), 2 rue Andre Pascal, F-75775 Paris Cedex 16, France, (Telephone in U.S. (202) 785-6323), (Fax in U.S. (202) 785-0350), www.oecd.org; *Revenue Statistics 1965-2006 - 2007 Edition.*

AUSTRALIA - INTERNATIONAL FINANCE

International Finance Corporation (IFC), 2121 Pennsylvania Avenue, NW, Washington, DC 20433 USA, (202) 473-1000, Fax: (202) 974-4384, www.ifc.org; *Annual Report 2007.*

Organisation for Economic Cooperation and Development (OECD), 2 rue Andre Pascal, F-75775 Paris Cedex 16, France, (Telephone in U.S. (202) 785-6323), (Fax in U.S. (202) 785-0350), www.oecd.org; *Financial Market Trends: OECD Periodical* and *OECD Economic Outlook 2008.*

AUSTRALIA - INTERNATIONAL LIQUIDITY

International Monetary Fund (IMF), 700 Nineteenth Street, NW, Washington, DC 20431, (202) 623-7000, Fax: (202) 623-4661, www.imf.org; *International Financial Statistics Yearbook 2007.*

Organisation for Economic Cooperation and Development (OECD), 2 rue Andre Pascal, F-75775 Paris Cedex 16, France, (Telephone in U.S. (202) 785-6323), (Fax in U.S. (202) 785-0350), www.oecd.org; *Financial Market Trends: OECD Periodical* and *OECD Economic Outlook 2008.*

AUSTRALIA - INTERNATIONAL STATISTICS

Organisation for Economic Cooperation and Development (OECD), 2 rue Andre Pascal, F-75775 Paris Cedex 16, France, (Telephone in U.S. (202) 785-6323), (Fax in U.S. (202) 785-0350), www.oecd.org; *Financial Market Trends: OECD Periodical* and *Household, Tourism, Travel: Trends, Environmental Impacts and Policy Responses.*

AUSTRALIA - INTERNATIONAL TRADE

Bernan Essential Government Publications, 4611-F Assembly Drive, Lanham MD, 20706-4391, (301) 459-2255, Fax: (800) 865-3450, www.bernan.com; *OECD Factbook 2006.*

Economist Intelligence Unit, 111 West 57th Street, New York, NY 10019, (212) 554-0600, Fax: (212) 586-1181, www.eiu.com; *Australia Country Report* and *Business Asia.*

Euromonitor International, Inc., 224 S. Michigan Avenue, Suite 1500, Chicago, IL 60604, (312) 922-1115, Fax: (312) 922-1157, www.euromonitor.com; *International Marketing Data and Statistics 2008; The World Economic Factbook 2008;* and *World Marketing Data and Statistics.*

International Iron and Steel Institute (IISI), Rue Colonel Bourg 120, B-1140 Brussels, Belgium, www.worldsteel.org; *Steel Statistical Yearbook 2006.*

M.E. Sharpe, 80 Business Park Drive, Armonk, NY 10504, (800) 541-6563, Fax: (914) 273-2106, www.mesharpe.com; *The Illustrated Book of World Rankings.*

Organisation for Economic Cooperation and Development (OECD), 2 rue Andre Pascal, F-75775 Paris Cedex 16, France, (Telephone in U.S. (202) 785-6323), (Fax in U.S. (202) 785-0350), www.oecd.org; *International Trade by Commodity Statistics (ITCS); 2005 OECD Agricultural Outlook Tables, 1970-2014; OECD Economic Outlook 2008; OECD Economic Survey - Australia 2006; OECD in Figures 2007; OECD Main Economic Indicators (MEI);* and *Statistics on Ship Production, Exports and Orders in 2004.*

Palgrave Macmillan Ltd., Houndmills, Basingstoke, Hampshire, RG21 6XS, England, (Telephone in U.S. (888) 330-8477), (Fax in U.S. (800) 672-2054), www.palgrave.com; *The Statesman's Yearbook 2008.*

Taylor and Francis Group, An Informa Business, 2 Park Square, Milton Park, Abingdon, Oxford OX14 4RN, United Kingdom, (Dial from U.S. (212) 216-7800), (Fax from U.S. (212) 564-7854), www.tandf.co.uk; *The Europa World Year Book.*

United Nations Conference on Trade and Development (UNCTAD), DC2-1120, United Nations, New York, NY 10017, (212) 963-0027, www.unctad.org; *UNCTAD Commodity Yearbook.*

United Nations Food and Agricultural Organization (FAO), Viale delle Terme di Caracalla, 00100 Rome, Italy, (Dial from U.S. (202) 653-2400), (Fax from U.S. (202) 653 5760), www.fao.org; *FAO Production Yearbook 2002; FAO Trade Yearbook;* and *The State of Food and Agriculture (SOFA) 2006.*

United Nations Statistics Division, New York, NY 10017, (800) 253-9646, Fax: (212) 963-4116, http://unstats.un.org; *Asia-Pacific in Figures 2004;* Commodity Trade Statistics Database (COMTRADE); *International Trade Statistics Yearbook; Statistical Yearbook;* and *Statistical Yearbook for Asia and the Pacific 2004.*

The World Bank, 1818 H Street, NW, Washington, DC 20433, (202) 473-1000, Fax: (202) 477-6391, www.worldbank.org; *Australia; World Development Indicators (WDI) 2008;* and *World Development Report 2008.*

World Trade Organization (WTO), Centre William Rappard, Rue de Lausanne 154, CH-1211 Geneva 21, Switzerland, www.wto.org; *International Trade Statistics 2006.*

AUSTRALIA - INTERNET USERS

International Telecommunication Union (ITU), Place des Nations, 1211 Geneva 20, Switzerland, www.itu.int; *World Telecommunication/ICT Indicators Database on CD-ROM; World Telecommunication/ICT Indicators Database Online;* and *Yearbook of Statistics - Telecommunication Services (Chronological Time Series 1997-2006).*

The World Bank, 1818 H Street, NW, Washington, DC 20433, (202) 473-1000, Fax: (202) 477-6391, www.worldbank.org; *Australia.*

AUSTRALIA - INVESTMENTS

International Monetary Fund (IMF), 700 Nineteenth Street, NW, Washington, DC 20431, (202) 623-7000, Fax: (202) 623-4661, www.imf.org; *International Financial Statistics Yearbook 2007.*

Organisation for Economic Cooperation and Development (OECD), 2 rue Andre Pascal, F-75775 Paris Cedex 16, France, (Telephone in U.S. (202) 785-6323), (Fax in U.S. (202) 785-0350), www.oecd.org; *Financial Market Trends: OECD Periodical; Iron and Steel Industry in 2004 (2006 Edition); A New World Map in Textiles and Clothing: Adjusting to Change; OECD Economic Outlook 2008;* and STructural ANalysis (STAN) database.

AUSTRALIA - IRON AND IRON ORE PRODUCTION

See AUSTRALIA - MINERAL INDUSTRIES

AUSTRALIA - IRRIGATION

Euromonitor International, Inc., 224 S. Michigan Avenue, Suite 1500, Chicago, IL 60604, (312) 922-1115, Fax: (312) 922-1157, www.euromonitor.com; *International Marketing Data and Statistics 2008.*

AUSTRALIA - LABOR

Australian Bureau of Statistics (ABS), Locked Bag 10, Belconnen ACT 2616, Australia, www.abs.gov.au; *Australia at a Glance, 2008* and *Year Book Australia, 2008.*

Central Intelligence Agency, Office of Public Affairs, Washington, DC 20505, (703) 482-0623, Fax: (703) 482-1739, www.cia.gov; *The World Factbook.*

Economist Intelligence Unit, 111 West 57th Street, New York, NY 10019, (212) 554-0600, Fax: (212) 586-1181, www.eiu.com; *Business Asia.*

Euromonitor International, Inc., 224 S. Michigan Avenue, Suite 1500, Chicago, IL 60604, (312) 922-1115, Fax: (312) 922-1157, www.euromonitor.com; *International Marketing Data and Statistics 2008* and *World Marketing Data and Statistics.*

Federal Statistical Office Germany, D-65180 Wiesbaden, Germany, www.destatis.de; *Australia 2006.*

International Labour Office, I.L.O. Publications, 4 route des Morillons, CH-1211 Geneva 22, Switzerland, (Telephone in U.S. (202) 653-7652), (Fax in U.S. (202) 653-7687), www.ilo.org; *Yearbook of Labour Statistics 2006.*

M.E. Sharpe, 80 Business Park Drive, Armonk, NY 10504, (800) 541-6563, Fax: (914) 273-2106, www.mesharpe.com; *The Illustrated Book of World Rankings.*

Organisation for Economic Cooperation and Development (OECD), 2 rue Andre Pascal, F-75775 Paris Cedex 16, France, (Telephone in U.S. (202) 785-6323), (Fax in U.S. (202) 785-0350), www.oecd.org; *Iron and Steel Industry in 2004 (2006 Edition); A New World Map in Textiles and Clothing: Adjusting to Change; OECD Economic Outlook 2008; OECD Economic Survey - Australia 2006; OECD Employment Outlook 2007; OECD Main Economic Indicators (MEI);* and *Statistics on Ship Production, Exports and Orders in 2004.*

Palgrave Macmillan Ltd., Houndmills, Basingstoke, Hampshire, RG21 6XS, England, (Telephone in U.S. (888) 330-8477), (Fax in U.S. (800) 672-2054), www.palgrave.com; *The Statesman's Yearbook 2008.*

Taylor and Francis Group, An Informa Business, 2 Park Square, Milton Park, Abingdon, Oxford OX14 4RN, United Kingdom, (Dial from U.S. (212) 216-7800), (Fax from U.S. (212) 564-7854), www.tandf.co.uk; *The Europa World Year Book.*

U.S. Department of Labor (DOL), Bureau of International Labor Affairs (ILAB), Frances Perkins Building, Room C-4325, 200 Constitution Avenue, NW, Washington, DC 20210, (202) 693-4770, Fax: (202) 693-4780, www.dol.gov/ilab; *Labor Rights Report.*

United Nations Food and Agricultural Organization (FAO), Viale delle Terme di Caracalla, 00100 Rome, Italy, (Dial from U.S. (202) 653-2400), (Fax from U.S. (202) 653 5760), www.fao.org; *The State of Food and Agriculture (SOFA) 2006.*

United Nations Statistics Division, New York, NY 10017, (800) 253-9646, Fax: (212) 963-4116, http://unstats.un.org; *Human Development Report 2006.*

The World Bank, 1818 H Street, NW, Washington, DC 20433, (202) 473-1000, Fax: (202) 477-6391, www.worldbank.org; *The World Bank Atlas 2003-2004; World Development Indicators (WDI) 2008;* and *World Development Report 2008.*

AUSTRALIA - LAND USE

Central Intelligence Agency, Office of Public Affairs, Washington, DC 20505, (703) 482-0623, Fax: (703) 482-1739, www.cia.gov; *The World Factbook.*

Euromonitor International, Inc., 224 S. Michigan Avenue, Suite 1500, Chicago, IL 60604, (312) 922-1115, Fax: (312) 922-1157, www.euromonitor.com; *International Marketing Data and Statistics 2008.*

United Nations Food and Agricultural Organization (FAO), Viale delle Terme di Caracalla, 00100 Rome, Italy, (Dial from U.S. (202) 653-2400), (Fax from U.S. (202) 653 5760), www.fao.org; *FAO Production Yearbook 2002.*

The World Bank, 1818 H Street, NW, Washington, DC 20433, (202) 473-1000, Fax: (202) 477-6391, www.worldbank.org; *World Development Report 2008.*

AUSTRALIA - LEATHER INDUSTRY AND TRADE

Organisation for Economic Cooperation and Development (OECD), 2 rue Andre Pascal, F-75775 Paris Cedex 16, France, (Telephone in U.S. (202) 785-6323), (Fax in U.S. (202) 785-0350), www.oecd.org; *Indicators of Industrial Activity.*

AUSTRALIA - LIBRARIES

M.E. Sharpe, 80 Business Park Drive, Armonk, NY 10504, (800) 541-6563, Fax: (914) 273-2106, www.mesharpe.com; *The Illustrated Book of World Rankings.*

UNESCO Institute for Statistics, C.P. 6128 Succursale Centre-Ville, Montreal, Quebec, H3C 3J7 Canada, (Dial from U.S. (514) 343-6880), (Fax from U.S. (514) 343 6882), www.uis.unesco.org; *Statistical Tables.*

AUSTRALIA - LICENSES

International Monetary Fund (IMF), 700 Nineteenth Street, NW, Washington, DC 20431, (202) 623-7000, Fax: (202) 623-4661, www.imf.org; *Government Finance Statistics Yearbook (2008 Edition).*

AUSTRALIA - LIFE EXPECTANCY

Central Intelligence Agency, Office of Public Affairs, Washington, DC 20505, (703) 482-0623, Fax: (703) 482-1739, www.cia.gov; *The World Factbook.*

Economist Intelligence Unit, 111 West 57th Street, New York, NY 10019, (212) 554-0600, Fax: (212) 586-1181, www.eiu.com; *Business Asia.*

Euromonitor International, Inc., 224 S. Michigan Avenue, Suite 1500, Chicago, IL 60604, (312) 922-1115, Fax: (312) 922-1157, www.euromonitor.com; *The World Economic Factbook 2008.*

Organisation for Economic Cooperation and Development (OECD), 2 rue Andre Pascal, F-75775 Paris Cedex 16, France, (Telephone in U.S. (202) 785-6323), (Fax in U.S. (202) 785-0350), www.oecd.org; *OECD Economic Outlook 2008.*

Palgrave Macmillan Ltd., Houndmills, Basingstoke, Hampshire, RG21 6XS, England, (Telephone in U.S. (888) 330-8477), (Fax in U.S. (800) 672-2054), www.palgrave.com; *The Statesman's Yearbook 2008.*

United Nations Statistics Division, New York, NY 10017, (800) 253-9646, Fax: (212) 963-4116, http://unstats.un.org; *Asia-Pacific in Figures 2004; Human Development Report 2006;* and *World Statistics Pocketbook.*

The World Bank, 1818 H Street, NW, Washington, DC 20433, (202) 473-1000, Fax: (202) 477-6391, www.worldbank.org; *The World Bank Atlas 2003-2004* and *World Development Report 2008.*

AUSTRALIA - LITERACY

Euromonitor International, Inc., 224 S. Michigan Avenue, Suite 1500, Chicago, IL 60604, (312) 922-1115, Fax: (312) 922-1157, www.euromonitor.com; *World Marketing Data and Statistics.*

AUSTRALIA - LIVESTOCK

M.E. Sharpe, 80 Business Park Drive, Armonk, NY 10504, (800) 541-6563, Fax: (914) 273-2106, www.mesharpe.com; *The Illustrated Book of World Rankings.*

Organisation for Economic Cooperation and Development (OECD), 2 rue Andre Pascal, F-75775 Paris Cedex 16, France, (Telephone in U.S. (202) 785-6323), (Fax in U.S. (202) 785-0350), www.oecd.org; *2005 OECD Agricultural Outlook Tables, 1970-2014.*

Palgrave Macmillan Ltd., Houndmills, Basingstoke, Hampshire, RG21 6XS, England, (Telephone in U.S. (888) 330-8477), (Fax in U.S. (800) 672-2054), www.palgrave.com; *The Statesman's Yearbook 2008.*

Taylor and Francis Group, An Informa Business, 2 Park Square, Milton Park, Abingdon, Oxford OX14 4RN, United Kingdom, (Dial from U.S. (212) 216-7800), (Fax from U.S. (212) 564-7854), www.tandf.co.uk; *The Europa World Year Book.*

United Nations Conference on Trade and Development (UNCTAD), DC2-1120, United Nations, New York, NY 10017, (212) 963-0027, www.unctad.org; *UNCTAD Commodity Yearbook.*

United Nations Food and Agricultural Organization (FAO), Viale delle Terme di Caracalla, 00100 Rome, Italy, (Dial from U.S. (202) 653-2400), (Fax from U.S. (202) 653 5760), www.fao.org; *FAO Production Yearbook 2002* and *The State of Food and Agriculture (SOFA) 2006.*

United Nations Statistics Division, New York, NY 10017, (800) 253-9646, Fax: (212) 963-4116, http://unstats.un.org; *Statistical Yearbook.*

AUSTRALIA - LOCAL TAXATION

Euromonitor International, Inc., 224 S. Michigan Avenue, Suite 1500, Chicago, IL 60604, (312) 922-1115, Fax: (312) 922-1157, www.euromonitor.com; *International Marketing Data and Statistics 2008.*

AUSTRALIA - MACHINERY

Organisation for Economic Cooperation and Development (OECD), 2 rue Andre Pascal, F-75775 Paris Cedex 16, France, (Telephone in U.S. (202) 785-6323), (Fax in U.S. (202) 785-0350), www.oecd.org; *Indicators of Industrial Activity.*

AUSTRALIA - MAGNESIUM PRODUCTION AND CONSUMPTION

See AUSTRALIA - MINERAL INDUSTRIES

AUSTRALIA - MANPOWER

United Nations Statistics Division, New York, NY 10017, (800) 253-9646, Fax: (212) 963-4116, http://unstats.un.org; *Statistical Yearbook for Asia and the Pacific 2004.*

AUSTRALIA - MANUFACTURES

Australian Bureau of Statistics (ABS), Locked Bag 10, Belconnen ACT 2616, Australia, www.abs.gov.au; *Australia at a Glance, 2008* and *Year Book Australia, 2008.*

International Monetary Fund (IMF), 700 Nineteenth Street, NW, Washington, DC 20431, (202) 623-7000, Fax: (202) 623-4661, www.imf.org; *International Financial Statistics Yearbook 2007.*

M.E. Sharpe, 80 Business Park Drive, Armonk, NY 10504, (800) 541-6563, Fax: (914) 273-2106, www.mesharpe.com; *The Illustrated Book of World Rankings.*

Organisation for Economic Cooperation and Development (OECD), 2 rue Andre Pascal, F-75775 Paris Cedex 16, France, (Telephone in U.S. (202) 785-6323), (Fax in U.S. (202) 785-0350), www.oecd.org; *Indicators of Industrial Activity; International Trade by Commodity Statistics (ITCS);* and *OECD Economic Survey - Australia 2006.*

United Nations Statistics Division, New York, NY 10017, (800) 253-9646, Fax: (212) 963-4116, http://unstats.un.org; *Statistical Yearbook.*

The World Bank, 1818 H Street, NW, Washington, DC 20433, (202) 473-1000, Fax: (202) 477-6391, www.worldbank.org; *World Development Indicators (WDI) 2008.*

AUSTRALIA - MARRIAGE

M.E. Sharpe, 80 Business Park Drive, Armonk, NY 10504, (800) 541-6563, Fax: (914) 273-2106, www.mesharpe.com; *The Illustrated Book of World Rankings.*

Taylor and Francis Group, An Informa Business, 2 Park Square, Milton Park, Abingdon, Oxford OX14 4RN, United Kingdom, (Dial from U.S. (212) 216-7800), (Fax from U.S. (212) 564-7854), www.tandf.co.uk; *The Europa World Year Book.*

United Nations Statistics Division, New York, NY 10017, (800) 253-9646, Fax: (212) 963-4116, http://unstats.un.org; *Demographic Yearbook* and *Statistical Yearbook.*

AUSTRALIA - MEAT INDUSTRY AND TRADE

International Monetary Fund (IMF), 700 Nineteenth Street, NW, Washington, DC 20431, (202) 623-7000, Fax: (202) 623-4661, www.imf.org; *International Financial Statistics Yearbook 2007.*

AUSTRALIA - MEAT PRODUCTION

See AUSTRALIA - LIVESTOCK

AUSTRALIA - MEDICAL CARE, COST OF

Australian Institute of Health and Welfare (AIHW), GPO Box 570, Canberra ACT 2601, Australia, www.aihw.gov.au; *Australia's Health 2006; Expenditures on Health for Aboriginal and Torres Strait Islander Peoples 2004-05; National Public Health Expenditure Report 2005-06; Rural, Regional and Remote Health: Indicators of Health Status and Determinants of Health;* and *Veterans' Use of Health Services.*

International Monetary Fund (IMF), 700 Nineteenth Street, NW, Washington, DC 20431, (202) 623-7000, Fax: (202) 623-4661, www.imf.org; *Government Finance Statistics Yearbook (2008 Edition).*

AUSTRALIA - MERCURY PRODUCTION

See AUSTRALIA - MINERAL INDUSTRIES

AUSTRALIA - METAL PRODUCTS

United Nations Statistics Division, New York, NY 10017, (800) 253-9646, Fax: (212) 963-4116, http://unstats.un.org; Commodity Trade Statistics Database (COMTRADE).

AUSTRALIA - MILK PRODUCTION

See AUSTRALIA - DAIRY PROCESSING

AUSTRALIA - MINERAL INDUSTRIES

Australian Bureau of Statistics (ABS), Locked Bag 10, Belconnen ACT 2616, Australia, www.abs.gov.au; *Australia at a Glance, 2008* and *Year Book Australia, 2008.*

Commodity Research Bureau, 330 South Wells Street, Suite 612, Chicago, IL 60606-7110, (800) 621-5271, Fax: (312) 939-4135, www.crbtrader.com; *2006 CRB Commodity Yearbook and CD.*

International Energy Agency (IEA), 9, rue de la Federation, 75739 Paris Cedex 15, France, www.iea.org; *Key World Energy Statistics 2007.*

International Iron and Steel Institute (IISI), Rue Colonel Bourg 120, B-1140 Brussels, Belgium, www.worldsteel.org; *Steel Statistical Yearbook 2006.*

International Lead and Zinc Study Group (ILZSG), Rua Almirante Barroso 38, 5th Floor, Lisbon 1000 - 013, Portugal, www.ilzsg.org; Interactive Statistical Database.

International Monetary Fund (IMF), 700 Nineteenth Street, NW, Washington, DC 20431, (202) 623-7000, Fax: (202) 623-4661, www.imf.org; *International Financial Statistics Yearbook 2007.*

M.E. Sharpe, 80 Business Park Drive, Armonk, NY 10504, (800) 541-6563, Fax: (914) 273-2106, www.mesharpe.com; *The Illustrated Book of World Rankings.*

Organisation for Economic Cooperation and Development (OECD), 2 rue Andre Pascal, F-75775 Paris Cedex 16, France, (Telephone in U.S. (202) 785-6323), (Fax in U.S. (202) 785-0350), www.oecd.org; *Coal Information: 2007 Edition; Energy Statistics of OECD Countries* (2007 Edition); *Environmental Impacts of Foreign Direct Investment in the Mining*

Sector in the Newly Independent States (NIS); Indicators of Industrial Activity; International Trade by Commodity Statistics (ITCS); Iron and Steel Industry in 2004 (2006 Edition); OECD Economic Survey - Australia 2006; STructural ANalysis (STAN) database; and *World Energy Outlook 2007.*

Palgrave Macmillan Ltd., Houndmills, Basingstoke, Hampshire, RG21 6XS, England, (Telephone in U.S. (888) 330-8477), (Fax in U.S. (800) 672-2054), www.palgrave.com; *The Statesman's Yearbook 2008.*

Taylor and Francis Group, An Informa Business, 2 Park Square, Milton Park, Abingdon, Oxford OX14 4RN, United Kingdom, (Dial from U.S. (212) 216-7800), (Fax from U.S. (212) 564-7854), www.tandf.co.uk; *The Europa World Year Book.*

United Nations Conference on Trade and Development (UNCTAD), DC2-1120, United Nations, New York, NY 10017, (212) 963-0027, www.unctad.org; *UNCTAD Commodity Yearbook.*

United Nations Statistics Division, New York, NY 10017, (800) 253-9646, Fax: (212) 963-4116, http://unstats.un.org; *Statistical Yearbook.*

The World Bank, 1818 H Street, NW, Washington, DC 20433, (202) 473-1000, Fax: (202) 477-6391, www.worldbank.org; *World Development Indicators (WDI) 2008.*

World Bureau of Metal Statistics (WBMS), 27a High Street, Ware, Hertfordshire, SG12 9BA, United Kingdom, www.world-bureau.com; *Annual Stainless Steel Statistics; World Flow Charts; World Metal Statistics; World Nickel Statistics;* and *World Tin Statistics.*

AUSTRALIA - MOLASSES PRODUCTION

See AUSTRALIA - CROPS

AUSTRALIA - MONEY

European Central Bank (ECB), Postfach 160319, D-60066 Frankfurt am Main, Germany, www.ecb.int; *Monetary Developments in the Euro Area; Monthly Bulletin;* and *Statistics Pocket Book.*

Organisation for Economic Cooperation and Development (OECD), 2 rue Andre Pascal, F-75775 Paris Cedex 16, France, (Telephone in U.S. (202) 785-6323), (Fax in U.S. (202) 785-0350), www.oecd.org; *OECD Economic Survey - Australia 2006.*

AUSTRALIA - MONEY EXCHANGE RATES

See AUSTRALIA - FOREIGN EXCHANGE RATES

AUSTRALIA - MONEY SUPPLY

Economist Intelligence Unit, 111 West 57th Street, New York, NY 10019, (212) 554-0600, Fax: (212) 586-1181, www.eiu.com; *Australia Country Report.*

Euromonitor International, Inc., 224 S. Michigan Avenue, Suite 1500, Chicago, IL 60604, (312) 922-1115, Fax: (312) 922-1157, www.euromonitor.com; *International Marketing Data and Statistics 2008.*

International Monetary Fund (IMF), 700 Nineteenth Street, NW, Washington, DC 20431, (202) 623-7000, Fax: (202) 623-4661, www.imf.org; *International Financial Statistics Yearbook 2007.*

Organisation for Economic Cooperation and Development (OECD), 2 rue Andre Pascal, F-75775 Paris Cedex 16, France, (Telephone in U.S. (202) 785-6323), (Fax in U.S. (202) 785-0350), www.oecd.org; *OECD Economic Outlook 2008.*

Taylor and Francis Group, An Informa Business, 2 Park Square, Milton Park, Abingdon, Oxford OX14 4RN, United Kingdom, (Dial from U.S. (212) 216-7800), (Fax from U.S. (212) 564-7854), www.tandf.co.uk; *The Europa World Year Book.*

United Nations Statistics Division, New York, NY 10017, (800) 253-9646, Fax: (212) 963-4116, http://unstats.un.org; *Statistical Yearbook.*

The World Bank, 1818 H Street, NW, Washington, DC 20433, (202) 473-1000, Fax: (202) 477-6391, www.worldbank.org; *Australia* and *World Development Indicators (WDI) 2008.*

AUSTRALIA - MORTALITY

Australian Government Office for Women, Department of Families, Community Services and Indigenous Affairs, Box 7788, Canberra Mail Centre ACT 2610, Australia, http://ofw.facsia.gov.au; *Window on Women: Women's Data Warehouse* and *Women in Australia 2004.*

Australian Institute of Health and Welfare (AIHW), GPO Box 570, Canberra ACT 2601, Australia, www.aihw.gov.au; *Deaths and Hospitalisations Due to Drowning, Australia 1999-00 to 2003-04* and *Rural, Regional and Remote Health: a Study on Mortality (2nd Edition).*

Central Intelligence Agency, Office of Public Affairs, Washington, DC 20505, (703) 482-0623, Fax: (703) 482-1739, www.cia.gov; *The World Factbook.*

Economist Intelligence Unit, 111 West 57th Street, New York, NY 10019, (212) 554-0600, Fax: (212) 586-1181, www.eiu.com; *Business Asia.*

Euromonitor International, Inc., 224 S. Michigan Avenue, Suite 1500, Chicago, IL 60604, (312) 922-1115, Fax: (312) 922-1157, www.euromonitor.com; *International Marketing Data and Statistics 2008* and *The World Economic Factbook 2008.*

Palgrave Macmillan Ltd., Houndmills, Basingstoke, Hampshire, RG21 6XS, England, (Telephone in U.S. (888) 330-8477), (Fax in U.S. (800) 672-2054), www.palgrave.com; *The Statesman's Yearbook 2008.*

Taylor and Francis Group, An Informa Business, 2 Park Square, Milton Park, Abingdon, Oxford OX14 4RN, United Kingdom, (Dial from U.S. (212) 216-7800), (Fax from U.S. (212) 564-7854), www.tandf.co.uk; *The Europa World Year Book.*

UNICEF, 3 United Nations Plaza, New York, NY 10017, (800) 253-9646, Fax: (212) 887-7465, www.unicef.org; *The State of the World's Children 2008.*

United Nations Statistics Division, New York, NY 10017, (800) 253-9646, Fax: (212) 963-4116, http://unstats.un.org; *Asia-Pacific in Figures 2004; Demographic Yearbook; Human Development Report 2006; Statistical Yearbook;* and *World Statistics Pocketbook.*

The World Bank, 1818 H Street, NW, Washington, DC 20433, (202) 473-1000, Fax: (202) 477-6391, www.worldbank.org; *The World Bank Atlas 2003-2004; World Development Indicators (WDI) 2008;* and *World Development Report 2008.*

World Health Organization (WHO), Avenue Appia 20, 1211 Geneve 27, Switzerland, (Telephone in U.S. (212) 331-9081), www.who.int; The WHO Global Atlas of Infectious Diseases.

AUSTRALIA - MOTION PICTURES

Palgrave Macmillan Ltd., Houndmills, Basingstoke, Hampshire, RG21 6XS, England, (Telephone in U.S. (888) 330-8477), (Fax in U.S. (800) 672-2054), www.palgrave.com; *The Statesman's Yearbook 2008.*

UNESCO Institute for Statistics, C.P. 6128 Succursale Centre-Ville, Montreal, Quebec, H3C 3J7 Canada, (Dial from U.S. (514) 343-6880), (Fax from U.S. (514) 343 6882), www.uis.unesco.org; *Statistical Tables.*

United Nations Statistics Division, New York, NY 10017, (800) 253-9646, Fax: (212) 963-4116, http://unstats.un.org; *Statistical Yearbook.*

AUSTRALIA - MOTOR VEHICLES

International Road Federation (IFR), Madison Place, 500 Montgomery Street, 5th Floor, Alexandria, VA 22314, (703) 535-1001, Fax: (703) 535-1007, www.irfnet.org; *World Road Statistics 2006.*

Taylor and Francis Group, An Informa Business, 2 Park Square, Milton Park, Abingdon, Oxford OX14 4RN, United Kingdom, (Dial from U.S. (212) 216-7800), (Fax from U.S. (212) 564-7854), www.tandf.co.uk; *The Europa World Year Book.*

United Nations Statistics Division, New York, NY 10017, (800) 253-9646, Fax: (212) 963-4116, http://unstats.un.org; *Statistical Yearbook.*

AUSTRALIA - MUSEUMS

M.E. Sharpe, 80 Business Park Drive, Armonk, NY 10504, (800) 541-6563, Fax: (914) 273-2106, www.mesharpe.com; *The Illustrated Book of World Rankings.*

UNESCO Institute for Statistics, C.P. 6128 Succursale Centre-Ville, Montreal, Quebec, H3C 3J7 Canada, (Dial from U.S. (514) 343-6880), (Fax from U.S. (514) 343 6882), www.uis.unesco.org; *Statistical Tables.*

AUSTRALIA - NATIONAL INCOME

United Nations Statistics Division, New York, NY 10017, (800) 253-9646, Fax: (212) 963-4116, http://unstats.un.org; *Statistical Yearbook.*

AUSTRALIA - NATURAL GAS PRODUCTION

See AUSTRALIA - MINERAL INDUSTRIES

AUSTRALIA - NICKEL AND NICKEL ORE

See AUSTRALIA - MINERAL INDUSTRIES

AUSTRALIA - NUTRITION

United Nations Food and Agricultural Organization (FAO), Viale delle Terme di Caracalla, 00100 Rome, Italy, (Dial from U.S. (202) 653-2400), (Fax from U.S. (202) 653 5760), www.fao.org; *The State of Food and Agriculture (SOFA) 2006.*

AUSTRALIA - OATS PRODUCTION

See AUSTRALIA - CROPS

AUSTRALIA - OILSEED PLANTS

Organisation for Economic Cooperation and Development (OECD), 2 rue Andre Pascal, F-75775 Paris Cedex 16, France, (Telephone in U.S. (202) 785-6323), (Fax in U.S. (202) 785-0350), www.oecd.org; *International Trade by Commodity Statistics (ITCS).*

AUSTRALIA - OLDER PEOPLE

M.E. Sharpe, 80 Business Park Drive, Armonk, NY 10504, (800) 541-6563, Fax: (914) 273-2106, www.mesharpe.com; *The Illustrated Book of World Rankings.*

AUSTRALIA - ORANGES PRODUCTION

See AUSTRALIA - CROPS

AUSTRALIA - PAPER

See AUSTRALIA - FORESTS AND FORESTRY

AUSTRALIA - PEANUT PRODUCTION

See AUSTRALIA - CROPS

AUSTRALIA - PERIODICALS

UNESCO Institute for Statistics, C.P. 6128 Succursale Centre-Ville, Montreal, Quebec, H3C 3J7 Canada, (Dial from U.S. (514) 343-6880), (Fax from U.S. (514) 343 6882), www.uis.unesco.org; *Statistical Tables.*

AUSTRALIA - PESTICIDES

United Nations Food and Agricultural Organization (FAO), Viale delle Terme di Caracalla, 00100 Rome, Italy, (Dial from U.S. (202) 653-2400), (Fax from U.S. (202) 653 5760), www.fao.org; *The State of Food and Agriculture (SOFA) 2006.*

AUSTRALIA - PETROLEUM INDUSTRY AND TRADE

International Energy Agency (IEA), 9, rue de la Federation, 75739 Paris Cedex 15, France, www.iea.org; *Key World Energy Statistics 2007.*

M.E. Sharpe, 80 Business Park Drive, Armonk, NY 10504, (800) 541-6563, Fax: (914) 273-2106, www.mesharpe.com; *The Illustrated Book of World Rankings.*

Organisation for Economic Cooperation and Development (OECD), 2 rue Andre Pascal, F-75775 Paris Cedex 16, France, (Telephone in U.S. (202) 785-6323), (Fax in U.S. (202) 785-0350), www.oecd.org; *Energy Statistics of OECD Countries* (2007 Edition); *Indicators of Industrial Activity; International Trade by Commodity Statistics (ITCS); Oil Information 2006 Edition;* and *World Energy Outlook 2007.*

Palgrave Macmillan Ltd., Houndmills, Basingstoke, Hampshire, RG21 6XS, England, (Telephone in U.S. (888) 330-8477), (Fax in U.S. (800) 672-2054), www.palgrave.com; *The Statesman's Yearbook 2008.*

PennWell Corporation, 1421 South Sheridan Road, Tulsa, OK 74112, (918) 835-3161, www.pennwell.com; *International Petroleum Encyclopedia 2007.*

U.S. Department of Energy (DOE), Energy Information Administration (EIA), 1000 Independence Avenue, SW, Washington, DC 20585, (202) 586-8800, www.eia.doe.gov; *International Energy Annual 2004* and *International Energy Outlook 2006.*

United Nations Conference on Trade and Development (UNCTAD), DC2-1120, United Nations, New York, NY 10017, (212) 963-0027, www.unctad.org; *UNCTAD Commodity Yearbook.*

United Nations Food and Agricultural Organization (FAO), Viale delle Terme di Caracalla, 00100 Rome, Italy, (Dial from U.S. (202) 653-2400), (Fax from U.S. (202) 653 5760), www.fao.org; *The State of Food and Agriculture (SOFA) 2006.*

United Nations Statistics Division, New York, NY 10017, (800) 253-9646, Fax: (212) 963-4116, http://unstats.un.org; *Statistical Yearbook.*

AUSTRALIA - PHOSPHATES PRODUCTION

See AUSTRALIA - MINERAL INDUSTRIES

AUSTRALIA - PLASTICS INDUSTRY AND TRADE

Organisation for Economic Cooperation and Development (OECD), 2 rue Andre Pascal, F-75775 Paris Cedex 16, France, (Telephone in U.S. (202) 785-6323), (Fax in U.S. (202) 785-0350), www.oecd.org; *International Trade by Commodity Statistics (ITCS).*

United Nations Statistics Division, New York, NY 10017, (800) 253-9646, Fax: (212) 963-4116, http://unstats.un.org; *Statistical Yearbook.*

AUSTRALIA - PLATINUM PRODUCTION

See AUSTRALIA - MINERAL INDUSTRIES

AUSTRALIA - POLITICAL SCIENCE

Australian Bureau of Statistics (ABS), Locked Bag 10, Belconnen ACT 2616, Australia, www.abs.gov.au; *Australia at a Glance, 2008* and *Year Book Australia, 2008.*

Central Intelligence Agency, Office of Public Affairs, Washington, DC 20505, (703) 482-0623, Fax: (703) 482-1739, www.cia.gov; *The World Factbook.*

International Monetary Fund (IMF), 700 Nineteenth Street, NW, Washington, DC 20431, (202) 623-7000, Fax: (202) 623-4661, www.imf.org; *Government Finance Statistics Yearbook (2008 Edition)* and *International Financial Statistics Yearbook 2007.*

Organisation for Economic Cooperation and Development (OECD), 2 rue Andre Pascal, F-75775 Paris Cedex 16, France, (Telephone in U.S. (202) 785-6323), (Fax in U.S. (202) 785-0350), www.oecd.org; *OECD Economic Outlook 2008* and *Revenue Statistics 1965-2006 - 2007 Edition.*

Palgrave Macmillan Ltd., Houndmills, Basingstoke, Hampshire, RG21 6XS, England, (Telephone in U.S. (888) 330-8477), (Fax in U.S. (800) 672-2054), www.palgrave.com; *The Statesman's Yearbook 2008.*

Taylor and Francis Group, An Informa Business, 2 Park Square, Milton Park, Abingdon, Oxford OX14 4RN, United Kingdom, (Dial from U.S. (212) 216-7800), (Fax from U.S. (212) 564-7854), www.tandf.co.uk; *The Europa World Year Book.*

United Nations Statistics Division, New York, NY 10017, (800) 253-9646, Fax: (212) 963-4116, http://unstats.un.org; *Asia-Pacific in Figures 2004* and *National Accounts Statistics: Compendium of Income Distribution Statistics.*

The World Bank, 1818 H Street, NW, Washington, DC 20433, (202) 473-1000, Fax: (202) 477-6391, www.worldbank.org; *World Development Indicators (WDI) 2008* and *World Development Report 2008.*

AUSTRALIA - POPULATION

Australian Bureau of Statistics (ABS), Locked Bag 10, Belconnen ACT 2616, Australia, www.abs.gov.au; *Australia at a Glance, 2008* and *Year Book Australia, 2008.*

Australian Institute of Health and Welfare (AIHW), GPO Box 570, Canberra ACT 2601, Australia, www.aihw.gov.au; *Adoptions Australia 2006-07; Australia's Welfare 2007; Child Protection Australia 2006-07; Deaths and Hospitalisations Due to Drowning, Australia 1999-00 to 2003-04; Diabetes: Australian Facts 2008; The Effectiveness of the Illicit Drug Diversion Initiative in Rural and Remote Australia; Expenditures on Health for Aboriginal and Torres Strait Islander Peoples 2004-05; Housing Assistance in Australia 2008; Indicators for Chronic Diseases and Their Determinants 2008; Key National Indicators of Children's Health, Development and Wellbeing: Indicator Framework of 'A Picture of Australia's Children 2009'; National Public Health Expenditure Report 2005-06; Rural, Regional and Remote Health: a Study on Mortality (2nd Edition); Rural, Regional and Remote Health: Indicators of Health Status and Determinants of Health;* and *Veterans' Use of Health Services.*

Central Intelligence Agency, Office of Public Affairs, Washington, DC 20505, (703) 482-0623, Fax: (703) 482-1739, www.cia.gov; *The World Factbook.*

Economist Intelligence Unit, 111 West 57th Street, New York, NY 10019, (212) 554-0600, Fax: (212) 586-1181, www.eiu.com; *Australia Country Report* and *Business Asia.*

Euromonitor International, Inc., 224 S. Michigan Avenue, Suite 1500, Chicago, IL 60604, (312) 922-1115, Fax: (312) 922-1157, www.euromonitor.com; *International Marketing Data and Statistics 2008* and *The World Economic Factbook 2008.*

Federal Statistical Office Germany, D-65180 Wiesbaden, Germany, www.destatis.de; *Australia 2006.*

International Labour Office, I.L.O. Publications, 4 route des Morillons, CH-1211 Geneva 22, Switzerland, (Telephone in U.S. (202) 653-7652), (Fax in U.S. (202) 653-7687), www.ilo.org; *Yearbook of Labour Statistics 2006.*

M.E. Sharpe, 80 Business Park Drive, Armonk, NY 10504, (800) 541-6563, Fax: (914) 273-2106, www.mesharpe.com; *The Illustrated Book of World Rankings.*

Organisation for Economic Cooperation and Development (OECD), 2 rue Andre Pascal, F-75775 Paris Cedex 16, France, (Telephone in U.S. (202) 785-6323), (Fax in U.S. (202) 785-0350), www.oecd.org; *Labour Force Statistics: 1986-2005, 2007 Edition.*

Palgrave Macmillan Ltd., Houndmills, Basingstoke, Hampshire, RG21 6XS, England, (Telephone in U.S. (888) 330-8477), (Fax in U.S. (800) 672-2054), www.palgrave.com; *The Statesman's Yearbook 2008.*

Taylor and Francis Group, An Informa Business, 2 Park Square, Milton Park, Abingdon, Oxford OX14 4RN, United Kingdom, (Dial from U.S. (212) 216-7800), (Fax from U.S. (212) 564-7854), www.tandf.co.uk; *The Europa World Year Book.*

U.S. Department of State (DOS), 2201 C Street NW, Washington, DC 20520, (202) 647-4000, www.state.gov; *World Military Expenditures and Arms Transfers (WMEAT).*

United Nations Food and Agricultural Organization (FAO), Viale delle Terme di Caracalla, 00100 Rome, Italy, (Dial from U.S. (202) 653-2400), (Fax from U.S. (202) 653 5760), www.fao.org; *FAO Production Yearbook 2002.*

United Nations Statistics Division, New York, NY 10017, (800) 253-9646, Fax: (212) 963-4116, http://unstats.un.org; *Asia-Pacific in Figures 2004; Demographic Yearbook; Human Development Report 2006; Statistical Yearbook; Statistical Yearbook for Asia and the Pacific 2004;* and *World Statistics Pocketbook.*

The World Bank, 1818 H Street, NW, Washington, DC 20433, (202) 473-1000, Fax: (202) 477-6391, www.worldbank.org; *Australia; The World Bank Atlas 2003-2004;* and *World Development Report 2008.*

Worldinformation.com, 2 Market Street, Saffron Walden, Essex CB10 1HZ, United Kingdom, www.worldinformation.com; The World of Information (www.worldinformation.com).

AUSTRALIA - POPULATION DENSITY

Central Intelligence Agency, Office of Public Affairs, Washington, DC 20505, (703) 482-0623, Fax: (703) 482-1739, www.cia.gov; *The World Factbook.*

Euromonitor International, Inc., 224 S. Michigan Avenue, Suite 1500, Chicago, IL 60604, (312) 922-1115, Fax: (312) 922-1157, www.euromonitor.com; *International Marketing Data and Statistics 2008* and *The World Economic Factbook 2008.*

M.E. Sharpe, 80 Business Park Drive, Armonk, NY 10504, (800) 541-6563, Fax: (914) 273-2106, www.mesharpe.com; *The Illustrated Book of World Rankings.*

Palgrave Macmillan Ltd., Houndmills, Basingstoke, Hampshire, RG21 6XS, England, (Telephone in U.S. (888) 330-8477), (Fax in U.S. (800) 672-2054), www.palgrave.com; *The Statesman's Yearbook 2008.*

Taylor and Francis Group, An Informa Business, 2 Park Square, Milton Park, Abingdon, Oxford OX14 4RN, United Kingdom, (Dial from U.S. (212) 216-7800), (Fax from U.S. (212) 564-7854), www.tandf.co.uk; *The Europa World Year Book.*

United Nations Food and Agricultural Organization (FAO), Viale delle Terme di Caracalla, 00100 Rome, Italy, (Dial from U.S. (202) 653-2400), (Fax from U.S. (202) 653 5760), www.fao.org; *The State of Food and Agriculture (SOFA) 2006.*

United Nations Statistics Division, New York, NY 10017, (800) 253-9646, Fax: (212) 963-4116, http://unstats.un.org; *Statistical Yearbook.*

The World Bank, 1818 H Street, NW, Washington, DC 20433, (202) 473-1000, Fax: (202) 477-6391, www.worldbank.org; *Australia* and *World Development Report 2008.*

AUSTRALIA - POSTAL SERVICE

M.E. Sharpe, 80 Business Park Drive, Armonk, NY 10504, (800) 541-6563, Fax: (914) 273-2106, www.mesharpe.com; *The Illustrated Book of World Rankings.*

Palgrave Macmillan Ltd., Houndmills, Basingstoke, Hampshire, RG21 6XS, England, (Telephone in U.S. (888) 330-8477), (Fax in U.S. (800) 672-2054), www.palgrave.com; *The Statesman's Yearbook 2008.*

United Nations Statistics Division, New York, NY 10017, (800) 253-9646, Fax: (212) 963-4116, http://unstats.un.org; *Statistical Yearbook.*

AUSTRALIA - POULTRY

See AUSTRALIA - LIVESTOCK

AUSTRALIA - POWER RESOURCES

Australian Bureau of Statistics (ABS), Locked Bag 10, Belconnen ACT 2616, Australia, www.abs.gov.au; *Australia at a Glance, 2008* and *Year Book Australia, 2008.*

Euromonitor International, Inc., 224 S. Michigan Avenue, Suite 1500, Chicago, IL 60604, (312) 922-1115, Fax: (312) 922-1157, www.euromonitor.com; *International Marketing Data and Statistics 2008; The World Economic Factbook 2008;* and *World Marketing Data and Statistics.*

M.E. Sharpe, 80 Business Park Drive, Armonk, NY 10504, (800) 541-6563, Fax: (914) 273-2106, www.mesharpe.com; *The Illustrated Book of World Rankings.*

Organisation for Economic Cooperation and Development (OECD), 2 rue Andre Pascal, F-75775 Paris

Cedex 16, France, (Telephone in U.S. (202) 785-6323), (Fax in U.S. (202) 785-0350), www.oecd.org; *Coal Information: 2007 Edition; Energy Statistics of OECD Countries* (2007 Edition); *Key Environmental Indicators 2004; Oil Information 2006 Edition;* and *World Energy Outlook 2007.*

Palgrave Macmillan Ltd., Houndmills, Basingstoke, Hampshire, RG21 6XS, England, (Telephone in U.S. (888) 330-8477), (Fax in U.S. (800) 672-2054), www.palgrave.com; *The Statesman's Yearbook 2008.*

Platts, 2 Penn Plaza, 25th Floor, New York, NY 10121-2298, (212) 904-3070, www.platts.com; *Asian Electricity Outlook 2006; Emissions Daily;* and *Energy Economist.*

U.S. Department of Energy (DOE), Energy Information Administration (EIA), 1000 Independence Avenue, SW, Washington, DC 20585, (202) 586-8800, www.eia.doe.gov; *International Energy Annual 2004* and *International Energy Outlook 2006.*

United Nations Statistics Division, New York, NY 10017, (800) 253-9646, Fax: (212) 963-4116, http://unstats.un.org; *Asia-Pacific in Figures 2004; Energy Statistics Yearbook 2003; Human Development Report 2006; Statistical Yearbook;* and *World Statistics Pocketbook.*

The World Bank, 1818 H Street, NW, Washington, DC 20433, (202) 473-1000, Fax: (202) 477-6391, www.worldbank.org; *The World Bank Atlas 2003-2004* and *World Development Report 2008.*

AUSTRALIA - PRICES

Euromonitor International, Inc., 224 S. Michigan Avenue, Suite 1500, Chicago, IL 60604, (312) 922-1115, Fax: (312) 922-1157, www.euromonitor.com; *World Marketing Data and Statistics.*

International Labour Office, I.L.O. Publications, 4 route des Morillons, CH-1211 Geneva 22, Switzerland, (Telephone in U.S. (202) 653-7652), (Fax in U.S. (202) 653-7687), www.ilo.org; *Yearbook of Labour Statistics 2006.*

International Lead and Zinc Study Group (ILZSG), Rua Almirante Barroso 38, 5th Floor, Lisbon 1000 - 013, Portugal, www.ilzsg.org; Interactive Statistical Database.

International Monetary Fund (IMF), 700 Nineteenth Street, NW, Washington, DC 20431, (202) 623-7000, Fax: (202) 623-4661, www.imf.org; *International Financial Statistics Yearbook 2007.*

M.E. Sharpe, 80 Business Park Drive, Armonk, NY 10504, (800) 541-6563, Fax: (914) 273-2106, www.mesharpe.com; *The Illustrated Book of World Rankings.*

Organisation for Economic Cooperation and Development (OECD), 2 rue Andre Pascal, F-75775 Paris Cedex 16, France, (Telephone in U.S. (202) 785-6323), (Fax in U.S. (202) 785-0350), www.oecd.org; *Indicators of Industrial Activity; Iron and Steel Industry in 2004 (2006 Edition); OECD Economic Outlook 2008;* and *OECD Main Economic Indicators (MEI).*

Technical Association of the Pulp and Paper Industry (TAPPI), 15 Technology Parkway South, Norcross, GA 30092, (770) 446-1400, Fax: (770) 446-6947, www.tappi.org; *TAPPI Annual Report.*

United Nations Food and Agricultural Organization (FAO), Viale delle Terme di Caracalla, 00100 Rome, Italy, (Dial from U.S. (202) 653-2400), (Fax from U.S. (202) 653 5760), www.fao.org; *FAO Production Yearbook 2002* and *The State of Food and Agriculture (SOFA) 2006.*

The World Bank, 1818 H Street, NW, Washington, DC 20433, (202) 473-1000, Fax: (202) 477-6391, www.worldbank.org; *Australia.*

World Bureau of Metal Statistics (WBMS), 27a High Street, Ware, Hertfordshire, SG12 9BA, United Kingdom, www.world-bureau.com; *World Flow Charts* and *World Metal Statistics.*

AUSTRALIA - PROFESSIONS

United Nations Statistics Division, New York, NY 10017, (800) 253-9646, Fax: (212) 963-4116, http://unstats.un.org; *Statistical Yearbook.*

AUSTRALIA - PUBLIC HEALTH

Australian Bureau of Statistics (ABS), Locked Bag 10, Belconnen ACT 2616, Australia, www.abs.gov.au; *Australia at a Glance, 2008* and *Year Book Australia, 2008.*

Australian Government Department of Health and Ageing, GPO Box 9848, Canberra ACT 2601, Australia, www.health.gov.au; *Expenditure and Prescriptions: Twelve Months to 30 June 2007;* General Practice Statistics; and *Medicare Statistics - December Quarter 2007.*

Australian Institute of Health and Welfare (AIHW), GPO Box 570, Canberra ACT 2601, Australia, www.aihw.gov.au; *Australia's Health 2006; Child Protection Australia 2006-07; Deaths and Hospitalisations Due to Drowning, Australia 1999-00 to 2003-04; Diabetes: Australian Facts 2008; Expenditures on Health for Aboriginal and Torres Strait Islander Peoples 2004-05; Indicators for Chronic Diseases and Their Determinants 2008; Key National Indicators of Children's Health, Development and Wellbeing: Indicator Framework of 'A Picture of Australia's Children 2009';* and *National Public Health Expenditure Report 2005-06.*

Economist Intelligence Unit, 111 West 57th Street, New York, NY 10019, (212) 554-0600, Fax: (212) 586-1181, www.eiu.com; *Business Asia.*

Euromonitor International, Inc., 224 S. Michigan Avenue, Suite 1500, Chicago, IL 60604, (312) 922-1115, Fax: (312) 922-1157, www.euromonitor.com; *World Health Databook 2007/2008* and *World Marketing Data and Statistics.*

M.E. Sharpe, 80 Business Park Drive, Armonk, NY 10504, (800) 541-6563, Fax: (914) 273-2106, www.mesharpe.com; *The Illustrated Book of World Rankings.*

Organisation for Economic Cooperation and Development (OECD), 2 rue Andre Pascal, F-75775 Paris Cedex 16, France, (Telephone in U.S. (202) 785-6323), (Fax in U.S. (202) 785-0350), www.oecd.org; *Health at a Glance 2007 - OECD Indicators.*

Palgrave Macmillan Ltd., Houndmills, Basingstoke, Hampshire, RG21 6XS, England, (Telephone in U.S. (888) 330-8477), (Fax in U.S. (800) 672-2054), www.palgrave.com; *The Statesman's Yearbook 2008.*

UNICEF, 3 United Nations Plaza, New York, NY 10017, (800) 253-9646, Fax: (212) 887-7465, www.unicef.org; *The State of the World's Children 2008.*

United Nations Statistics Division, New York, NY 10017, (800) 253-9646, Fax: (212) 963-4116, http://unstats.un.org; *Asia-Pacific in Figures 2004; Human Development Report 2006;* and *Statistical Yearbook.*

The World Bank, 1818 H Street, NW, Washington, DC 20433, (202) 473-1000, Fax: (202) 477-6391, www.worldbank.org; *Australia* and *World Development Report 2008.*

World Health Organization (WHO), Avenue Appia 20, 1211 Geneve 27, Switzerland, (Telephone in U.S. (212) 331-9081), www.who.int; The WHO Global Atlas of Infectious Diseases and *World Health Report 2006.*

AUSTRALIA - PUBLIC UTILITIES

United Nations Statistics Division, New York, NY 10017, (800) 253-9646, Fax: (212) 963-4116, http://unstats.un.org; *Electric Power in Asia and the Pacific 2001 and 2002.*

AUSTRALIA - PUBLISHERS AND PUBLISHING

Organisation for Economic Cooperation and Development (OECD), 2 rue Andre Pascal, F-75775 Paris Cedex 16, France, (Telephone in U.S. (202) 785-6323), (Fax in U.S. (202) 785-0350), www.oecd.org; *Indicators of Industrial Activity.*

Palgrave Macmillan Ltd., Houndmills, Basingstoke, Hampshire, RG21 6XS, England, (Telephone in U.S. (888) 330-8477), (Fax in U.S. (800) 672-2054), www.palgrave.com; *The Statesman's Yearbook 2008.*

Taylor and Francis Group, An Informa Business, 2 Park Square, Milton Park, Abingdon, Oxford OX14 4RN, United Kingdom, (Dial from U.S. (212) 216-7800), (Fax from U.S. (212) 564-7854), www.tandf.co.uk; *The Europa World Year Book.*

UNESCO Institute for Statistics, C.P. 6128 Succursale Centre-Ville, Montreal, Quebec, H3C 3J7 Canada, (Dial from U.S. (514) 343-6880), (Fax from U.S. (514) 343 6882), www.uis.unesco.org; *Statistical Tables.*

AUSTRALIA - RADIO - RECEIVERS AND RECEPTION

Palgrave Macmillan Ltd., Houndmills, Basingstoke, Hampshire, RG21 6XS, England, (Telephone in U.S. (888) 330-8477), (Fax in U.S. (800) 672-2054), www.palgrave.com; *The Statesman's Yearbook 2008.*

United Nations Statistics Division, New York, NY 10017, (800) 253-9646, Fax: (212) 963-4116, http://unstats.un.org; *Statistical Yearbook.*

AUSTRALIA - RAILROADS

Jane's Information Group, 110 North Royal Street, Suite 200, Alexandria, VA 22314, (703) 683-3700, Fax: (800) 836-0297, www.janes.com; *Jane's World Railways.*

Palgrave Macmillan Ltd., Houndmills, Basingstoke, Hampshire, RG21 6XS, England, (Telephone in U.S. (888) 330-8477), (Fax in U.S. (800) 672-2054), www.palgrave.com; *The Statesman's Yearbook 2008.*

Taylor and Francis Group, An Informa Business, 2 Park Square, Milton Park, Abingdon, Oxford OX14 4RN, United Kingdom, (Dial from U.S. (212) 216-7800), (Fax from U.S. (212) 564-7854), www.tandf.co.uk; *The Europa World Year Book.*

United Nations Statistics Division, New York, NY 10017, (800) 253-9646, Fax: (212) 963-4116, http://unstats.un.org; *Statistical Yearbook.*

AUSTRALIA - RECREATION

Australian Bureau of Statistics (ABS), Locked Bag 10, Belconnen ACT 2616, Australia, www.abs.gov.au; *Australia at a Glance, 2008* and *Year Book Australia, 2008.*

AUSTRALIA - RELIGION

Central Intelligence Agency, Office of Public Affairs, Washington, DC 20505, (703) 482-0623, Fax: (703) 482-1739, www.cia.gov; *The World Factbook.*

M.E. Sharpe, 80 Business Park Drive, Armonk, NY 10504, (800) 541-6563, Fax: (914) 273-2106, www.mesharpe.com; *The Illustrated Book of World Rankings.*

Palgrave Macmillan Ltd., Houndmills, Basingstoke, Hampshire, RG21 6XS, England, (Telephone in U.S. (888) 330-8477), (Fax in U.S. (800) 672-2054), www.palgrave.com; *The Statesman's Yearbook 2008.*

AUSTRALIA - RENT CHARGES

International Labour Office, I.L.O. Publications, 4 route des Morillons, CH-1211 Geneva 22, Switzerland, (Telephone in U.S. (202) 653-7652), (Fax in U.S. (202) 653-7687), www.ilo.org; *Yearbook of Labour Statistics 2006.*

AUSTRALIA - RESERVES (ACCOUNTING)

Euromonitor International, Inc., 224 S. Michigan Avenue, Suite 1500, Chicago, IL 60604, (312) 922-1115, Fax: (312) 922-1157, www.euromonitor.com; *International Marketing Data and Statistics 2008.*

Organisation for Economic Cooperation and Development (OECD), 2 rue Andre Pascal, F-75775 Paris Cedex 16, France, (Telephone in U.S. (202) 785-6323), (Fax in U.S. (202) 785-0350), www.oecd.org; *Financial Market Trends: OECD Periodical* and *OECD Economic Outlook 2008.*

The World Bank, 1818 H Street, NW, Washington, DC 20433, (202) 473-1000, Fax: (202) 477-6391, www.worldbank.org; *World Development Indicators (WDI) 2008.*

AUSTRALIA - RETAIL TRADE

Australian Bureau of Statistics (ABS), Locked Bag 10, Belconnen ACT 2616, Australia, www.abs.gov.au; *Australia at a Glance, 2008* and *Year Book Australia, 2008.*

Euromonitor International, Inc., 224 S. Michigan Avenue, Suite 1500, Chicago, IL 60604, (312) 922-1115, Fax: (312) 922-1157, www.euromonitor.com; *Retail Trade International 2007* and *World Marketing Data and Statistics.*

United Nations Statistics Division, New York, NY 10017, (800) 253-9646, Fax: (212) 963-4116, http://unstats.un.org; *Statistical Yearbook.*

AUSTRALIA - RICE PRODUCTION

See AUSTRALIA - CROPS

AUSTRALIA - ROADS

Central Intelligence Agency, Office of Public Affairs, Washington, DC 20505, (703) 482-0623, Fax: (703) 482-1739, www.cia.gov; *The World Factbook.*

Economist Intelligence Unit, 111 West 57th Street, New York, NY 10019, (212) 554-0600, Fax: (212) 586-1181, www.eiu.com; *Business Asia.*

International Road Federation (IFR), Madison Place, 500 Montgomery Street, 5th Floor, Alexandria, VA 22314, (703) 535-1001, Fax: (703) 535-1007, www.irfnet.org; *World Road Statistics 2006.*

Palgrave Macmillan Ltd., Houndmills, Basingstoke, Hampshire, RG21 6XS, England, (Telephone in U.S. (888) 330-8477), (Fax in U.S. (800) 672-2054), www.palgrave.com; *The Statesman's Yearbook 2008.*

AUSTRALIA - RUBBER INDUSTRY AND TRADE

International Rubber Study Group (IRSG), 1st Floor, Heron House, 109/115 Wembley Hill Road, Wembley, Middlesex HA9 8DA, United Kingdom, www.rubberstudy.com; *Rubber Statistical Bulletin; Summary of World Rubber Statistics 2005; World Rubber Statistics Handbook (Volume 6, 1975-2001);* and *World Rubber Statistics Historic Handbook.*

M.E. Sharpe, 80 Business Park Drive, Armonk, NY 10504, (800) 541-6563, Fax: (914) 273-2106, www.mesharpe.com; *The Illustrated Book of World Rankings.*

Organisation for Economic Cooperation and Development (OECD), 2 rue Andre Pascal, F-75775 Paris Cedex 16, France, (Telephone in U.S. (202) 785-6323), (Fax in U.S. (202) 785-0350), www.oecd.org; *International Trade by Commodity Statistics (ITCS).*

United Nations Statistics Division, New York, NY 10017, (800) 253-9646, Fax: (212) 963-4116, http://unstats.un.org; *Statistical Yearbook.*

AUSTRALIA - SAFFLOWER SEED PRODUCTION

See AUSTRALIA - CROPS

AUSTRALIA - SALT PRODUCTION

See AUSTRALIA - MINERAL INDUSTRIES

AUSTRALIA - SHEEP

See AUSTRALIA - LIVESTOCK

AUSTRALIA - SHIPBUILDING

Organisation for Economic Cooperation and Development (OECD), 2 rue Andre Pascal, F-75775 Paris Cedex 16, France, (Telephone in U.S. (202) 785-6323), (Fax in U.S. (202) 785-0350), www.oecd.org; *Indicators of Industrial Activity.*

AUSTRALIA - SHIPPING

Lloyd's Register - Fairplay, 8410 N.W. 53rd Terrace, Suite 207, Miami FL 33166, (305) 718-9929, Fax: (305) 718-9663, www.lrfairplay.com; *Register of Ships 2007-2008; World Casualty Statistics 2007; World Fleet Statistics 2006; World Marine Propulsion Report 2006-2010; World Shipbuilding Statistics 2007;* and The World Shipping Encyclopaedia.

Organisation for Economic Cooperation and Development (OECD), 2 rue Andre Pascal, F-75775 Paris Cedex 16, France, (Telephone in U.S. (202) 785-6323), (Fax in U.S. (202) 785-0350), www.oecd.org; *Statistics on Ship Production, Exports and Orders in 2004.*

Palgrave Macmillan Ltd., Houndmills, Basingstoke, Hampshire, RG21 6XS, England, (Telephone in U.S. (888) 330-8477), (Fax in U.S. (800) 672-2054), www.palgrave.com; *The Statesman's Yearbook 2008.*

Taylor and Francis Group, An Informa Business, 2 Park Square, Milton Park, Abingdon, Oxford OX14 4RN, United Kingdom, (Dial from U.S. (212) 216-7800), (Fax from U.S. (212) 564-7854), www.tandf.co.uk; *The Europa World Year Book.*

U.S. Department of Transportation (DOT), Maritime Administration (MARAD), West Building, Southeast Federal Center, 1200 New Jersey Avenue, SE, Washington, DC 20590, (800) 99-MARAD, www.marad.dot.gov; *World Merchant Fleet 2005.*

United Nations Statistics Division, New York, NY 10017, (800) 253-9646, Fax: (212) 963-4116, http://unstats.un.org; *Statistical Yearbook.*

AUSTRALIA - SILVER PRODUCTION

See AUSTRALIA - MINERAL INDUSTRIES

AUSTRALIA - SOCIAL ECOLOGY

Australian Bureau of Statistics (ABS), Locked Bag 10, Belconnen ACT 2616, Australia, www.abs.gov.au; *Australia at a Glance, 2008* and *Year Book Australia, 2008.*

M.E. Sharpe, 80 Business Park Drive, Armonk, NY 10504, (800) 541-6563, Fax: (914) 273-2106, www.mesharpe.com; *The Illustrated Book of World Rankings.*

United Nations Statistics Division, New York, NY 10017, (800) 253-9646, Fax: (212) 963-4116, http://unstats.un.org; *World Statistics Pocketbook.*

AUSTRALIA - SOCIAL SECURITY

Australian Bureau of Statistics (ABS), Locked Bag 10, Belconnen ACT 2616, Australia, www.abs.gov.au; *Australia at a Glance, 2008* and *Year Book Australia, 2008.*

International Monetary Fund (IMF), 700 Nineteenth Street, NW, Washington, DC 20431, (202) 623-7000, Fax: (202) 623-4661, www.imf.org; *Government Finance Statistics Yearbook (2008 Edition).*

Organisation for Economic Cooperation and Development (OECD), 2 rue Andre Pascal, F-75775 Paris Cedex 16, France, (Telephone in U.S. (202) 785-6323), (Fax in U.S. (202) 785-0350), www.oecd.org; *Revenue Statistics 1965-2006 - 2007 Edition.*

Palgrave Macmillan Ltd., Houndmills, Basingstoke, Hampshire, RG21 6XS, England, (Telephone in U.S. (888) 330-8477), (Fax in U.S. (800) 672-2054), www.palgrave.com; *The Statesman's Yearbook 2008.*

United Nations Statistics Division, New York, NY 10017, (800) 253-9646, Fax: (212) 963-4116, http://unstats.un.org; *National Accounts Statistics: Compendium of Income Distribution Statistics.*

AUSTRALIA - SOYBEAN PRODUCTION

See AUSTRALIA - CROPS

AUSTRALIA - STEEL PRODUCTION

See AUSTRALIA - MINERAL INDUSTRIES

AUSTRALIA - SUGAR PRODUCTION

See AUSTRALIA - CROPS

AUSTRALIA - SULPHUR PRODUCTION

See AUSTRALIA - MINERAL INDUSTRIES

AUSTRALIA - TAXATION

International Monetary Fund (IMF), 700 Nineteenth Street, NW, Washington, DC 20431, (202) 623-7000, Fax: (202) 623-4661, www.imf.org; *Government Finance Statistics Yearbook (2008 Edition).*

International Road Federation (IFR), Madison Place, 500 Montgomery Street, 5th Floor, Alexandria, VA 22314, (703) 535-1001, Fax: (703) 535-1007, www.irfnet.org; *World Road Statistics 2006.*

Organisation for Economic Cooperation and Development (OECD), 2 rue Andre Pascal, F-75775 Paris Cedex 16, France, (Telephone in U.S. (202) 785-6323), (Fax in U.S. (202) 785-0350), www.oecd.org; *Revenue Statistics 1965-2006 - 2007 Edition.*

Palgrave Macmillan Ltd., Houndmills, Basingstoke, Hampshire, RG21 6XS, England, (Telephone in U.S. (888) 330-8477), (Fax in U.S. (800) 672-2054), www.palgrave.com; *The Statesman's Yearbook 2008.*

Taylor and Francis Group, An Informa Business, 2 Park Square, Milton Park, Abingdon, Oxford OX14 4RN, United Kingdom, (Dial from U.S. (212) 216-7800), (Fax from U.S. (212) 564-7854), www.tandf.co.uk; *The Europa World Year Book.*

The World Bank, 1818 H Street, NW, Washington, DC 20433, (202) 473-1000, Fax: (202) 477-6391, www.worldbank.org; *World Development Indicators (WDI) 2008.*

AUSTRALIA - TEA PRODUCTION

See AUSTRALIA - CROPS

AUSTRALIA - TELEPHONE

Economist Intelligence Unit, 111 West 57th Street, New York, NY 10019, (212) 554-0600, Fax: (212) 586-1181, www.eiu.com; *Business Asia.*

International Telecommunication Union (ITU), Place des Nations, 1211 Geneva 20, Switzerland, www.itu.int; World Telecommunication Indicators Database.

Palgrave Macmillan Ltd., Houndmills, Basingstoke, Hampshire, RG21 6XS, England, (Telephone in U.S. (888) 330-8477), (Fax in U.S. (800) 672-2054), www.palgrave.com; *The Statesman's Yearbook 2008.*

Taylor and Francis Group, An Informa Business, 2 Park Square, Milton Park, Abingdon, Oxford OX14 4RN, United Kingdom, (Dial from U.S. (212) 216-7800), (Fax from U.S. (212) 564-7854), www.tandf.co.uk; *The Europa World Year Book.*

United Nations Statistics Division, New York, NY 10017, (800) 253-9646, Fax: (212) 963-4116, http://unstats.un.org; *Statistical Yearbook* and *World Statistics Pocketbook.*

AUSTRALIA - TELEVISION - RECEIVERS AND RECEPTION

United Nations Statistics Division, New York, NY 10017, (800) 253-9646, Fax: (212) 963-4116, http://unstats.un.org; *Statistical Yearbook.*

AUSTRALIA - TEXTILE INDUSTRY

Euromonitor International, Inc., 224 S. Michigan Avenue, Suite 1500, Chicago, IL 60604, (312) 922-1115, Fax: (312) 922-1157, www.euromonitor.com; *Retail Trade International 2007.*

International Monetary Fund (IMF), 700 Nineteenth Street, NW, Washington, DC 20431, (202) 623-7000, Fax: (202) 623-4661, www.imf.org; *International Financial Statistics Yearbook 2007.*

M.E. Sharpe, 80 Business Park Drive, Armonk, NY 10504, (800) 541-6563, Fax: (914) 273-2106, www.mesharpe.com; *The Illustrated Book of World Rankings.*

Organisation for Economic Cooperation and Development (OECD), 2 rue Andre Pascal, F-75775 Paris Cedex 16, France, (Telephone in U.S. (202) 785-6323), (Fax in U.S. (202) 785-0350), www.oecd.org; *Indicators of Industrial Activity; International Trade by Commodity Statistics (ITCS); A New World Map in Textiles and Clothing: Adjusting to Change; 2005 OECD Agricultural Outlook Tables, 1970-2014;* and STructural ANalysis (STAN) database.

Palgrave Macmillan Ltd., Houndmills, Basingstoke, Hampshire, RG21 6XS, England, (Telephone in U.S. (888) 330-8477), (Fax in U.S. (800) 672-2054), www.palgrave.com; *The Statesman's Yearbook 2008.*

United Nations Conference on Trade and Development (UNCTAD), DC2-1120, United Nations, New York, NY 10017, (212) 963-0027, www.unctad.org; *UNCTAD Commodity Yearbook.*

United Nations Statistics Division, New York, NY 10017, (800) 253-9646, Fax: (212) 963-4116, http://unstats.un.org; Commodity Trade Statistics Database (COMTRADE) and *Statistical Yearbook.*

AUSTRALIA - TIN PRODUCTION

See AUSTRALIA - MINERAL INDUSTRIES

AUSTRALIA - TIRE INDUSTRY

United Nations Statistics Division, New York, NY 10017, (800) 253-9646, Fax: (212) 963-4116, http://unstats.un.org; *Statistical Yearbook.*

AUSTRALIA - TOBACCO INDUSTRY

Foreign Agricultural Service (FAS), U.S. Department of Agriculture (USDA), 1400 Independence Avenue, SW, Washington, DC 20250, (202) 720-3935, www.fas.usda.gov; *Tobacco: World Markets and Trade.*

M.E. Sharpe, 80 Business Park Drive, Armonk, NY 10504, (800) 541-6563, Fax: (914) 273-2106, www.mesharpe.com; *The Illustrated Book of World Rankings.*

Organisation for Economic Cooperation and Development (OECD), 2 rue Andre Pascal, F-75775 Paris Cedex 16, France, (Telephone in U.S. (202) 785-6323), (Fax in U.S. (202) 785-0350), www.oecd.org; *Indicators of Industrial Activity; International Trade by Commodity Statistics (ITCS);* and STructural ANalysis (STAN) database.

United Nations Statistics Division, New York, NY 10017, (800) 253-9646, Fax: (212) 963-4116, http://unstats.un.org; *Statistical Yearbook.*

AUSTRALIA - TOURISM

Euromonitor International, Inc., 224 S. Michigan Avenue, Suite 1500, Chicago, IL 60604, (312) 922-1115, Fax: (312) 922-1157, www.euromonitor.com; *The World Economic Factbook 2008* and *World Marketing Data and Statistics.*

M.E. Sharpe, 80 Business Park Drive, Armonk, NY 10504, (800) 541-6563, Fax: (914) 273-2106, www.mesharpe.com; *The Illustrated Book of World Rankings.*

Organisation for Economic Cooperation and Development (OECD), 2 rue Andre Pascal, F-75775 Paris Cedex 16, France, (Telephone in U.S. (202) 785-6323), (Fax in U.S. (202) 785-0350), www.oecd.org; *Household, Tourism, Travel: Trends, Environmental Impacts and Policy Responses.*

Palgrave Macmillan Ltd., Houndmills, Basingstoke, Hampshire, RG21 6XS, England, (Telephone in U.S. (888) 330-8477), (Fax in U.S. (800) 672-2054), www.palgrave.com; *The Statesman's Yearbook 2008.*

Taylor and Francis Group, An Informa Business, 2 Park Square, Milton Park, Abingdon, Oxford OX14 4RN, United Kingdom, (Dial from U.S. (212) 216-7800), (Fax from U.S. (212) 564-7854), www.tandf.co.uk; *The Europa World Year Book.*

United Nations Statistics Division, New York, NY 10017, (800) 253-9646, Fax: (212) 963-4116, http://unstats.un.org; *Statistical Yearbook.*

United Nations World Tourism Organization (UNWTO), Capitan Haya 42, 28020 Madrid, Spain, www.world-tourism.org; *Yearbook of Tourism Statistics.*

The World Bank, 1818 H Street, NW, Washington, DC 20433, (202) 473-1000, Fax: (202) 477-6391, www.worldbank.org; *Australia.*

AUSTRALIA - TRADE

See AUSTRALIA - INTERNATIONAL TRADE

AUSTRALIA - TRANSPORTATION

Australian Bureau of Statistics (ABS), Locked Bag 10, Belconnen ACT 2616, Australia, www.abs.gov.au; *Australia at a Glance, 2008* and *Year Book Australia, 2008.*

Central Intelligence Agency, Office of Public Affairs, Washington, DC 20505, (703) 482-0623, Fax: (703) 482-1739, www.cia.gov; *The World Factbook.*

Economist Intelligence Unit, 111 West 57th Street, New York, NY 10019, (212) 554-0600, Fax: (212) 586-1181, www.eiu.com; *Business Asia.*

Euromonitor International, Inc., 224 S. Michigan Avenue, Suite 1500, Chicago, IL 60604, (312) 922-1115, Fax: (312) 922-1157, www.euromonitor.com; *International Marketing Data and Statistics 2008* and *World Marketing Data and Statistics.*

M.E. Sharpe, 80 Business Park Drive, Armonk, NY 10504, (800) 541-6563, Fax: (914) 273-2106, www.mesharpe.com; *The Illustrated Book of World Rankings.*

Palgrave Macmillan Ltd., Houndmills, Basingstoke, Hampshire, RG21 6XS, England, (Telephone in U.S. (888) 330-8477), (Fax in U.S. (800) 672-2054), www.palgrave.com; *The Statesman's Yearbook 2008.*

Taylor and Francis Group, An Informa Business, 2 Park Square, Milton Park, Abingdon, Oxford OX14 4RN, United Kingdom, (Dial from U.S. (212) 216-7800), (Fax from U.S. (212) 564-7854), www.tandf.co.uk; *The Europa World Year Book.*

United Nations Statistics Division, New York, NY 10017, (800) 253-9646, Fax: (212) 963-4116, http://unstats.un.org; *Human Development Report 2006* and *Statistical Yearbook for Asia and the Pacific 2004.*

The World Bank, 1818 H Street, NW, Washington, DC 20433, (202) 473-1000, Fax: (202) 477-6391, www.worldbank.org; *Australia.*

AUSTRALIA - TRAVEL COSTS

Australian Bureau of Statistics (ABS), Locked Bag 10, Belconnen ACT 2616, Australia, www.abs.gov.au; *Australia at a Glance, 2008* and *Year Book Australia, 2008.*

AUSTRALIA - TURKEYS

See AUSTRALIA - LIVESTOCK

AUSTRALIA - UNEMPLOYMENT

Australian Bureau of Statistics (ABS), Locked Bag 10, Belconnen ACT 2616, Australia, www.abs.gov.au; *Australia at a Glance, 2008* and *Year Book Australia, 2008.*

Central Intelligence Agency, Office of Public Affairs, Washington, DC 20505, (703) 482-0623, Fax: (703) 482-1739, www.cia.gov; *The World Factbook.*

Euromonitor International, Inc., 224 S. Michigan Avenue, Suite 1500, Chicago, IL 60604, (312) 922-1115, Fax: (312) 922-1157, www.euromonitor.com; *International Marketing Data and Statistics 2008.*

International Labour Office, I.L.O. Publications, 4 route des Morillons, CH-1211 Geneva 22, Switzerland, (Telephone in U.S. (202) 653-7652), (Fax in U.S. (202) 653-7687), www.ilo.org; *Yearbook of Labour Statistics 2006.*

Organisation for Economic Cooperation and Development (OECD), 2 rue Andre Pascal, F-75775 Paris Cedex 16, France, (Telephone in U.S. (202) 785-6323), (Fax in U.S. (202) 785-0350), www.oecd.org; *Labour Force Statistics: 1986-2005, 2007 Edition; OECD Composite Leading Indicators (CLIs), Updated September 2007; OECD Economic Outlook 2008; OECD Economic Survey - Australia 2006;* and *OECD Employment Outlook 2007.*

Palgrave Macmillan Ltd., Houndmills, Basingstoke, Hampshire, RG21 6XS, England, (Telephone in U.S. (888) 330-8477), (Fax in U.S. (800) 672-2054), www.palgrave.com; *The Statesman's Yearbook 2008.*

United Nations Statistics Division, New York, NY 10017, (800) 253-9646, Fax: (212) 963-4116, http://unstats.un.org; *Statistical Yearbook.*

AUSTRALIA - URANIUM PRODUCTION AND CONSUMPTION

See AUSTRALIA - MINERAL INDUSTRIES

AUSTRALIA - VITAL STATISTICS

Australian Bureau of Statistics (ABS), Locked Bag 10, Belconnen ACT 2616, Australia, www.abs.gov.au; *Australia at a Glance, 2008* and *Year Book Australia, 2008.*

Australian Government Office for Women, Department of Families, Community Services and Indigenous Affairs, Box 7788, Canberra Mail Centre ACT 2610, Australia, http://ofw.facsia.gov.au; *Time Use Survey; Window on Women: Women's Data Warehouse;* and *Women in Australia 2004.*

Australian Institute of Health and Welfare (AIHW), GPO Box 570, Canberra ACT 2601, Australia, www.aihw.gov.au; *Adoptions Australia 2006-07; The Effectiveness of the Illicit Drug Diversion Initiative in Rural and Remote Australia; Rural, Regional and Remote Health: a Study on Mortality (2nd Edition); Rural, Regional and Remote Health: Indicators of Health Status and Determinants of Health;* and *Veterans' Use of Health Services.*

Euromonitor International, Inc., 224 S. Michigan Avenue, Suite 1500, Chicago, IL 60604, (312) 922-1115, Fax: (312) 922-1157, www.euromonitor.com; *International Marketing Data and Statistics 2008.*

Palgrave Macmillan Ltd., Houndmills, Basingstoke, Hampshire, RG21 6XS, England, (Telephone in U.S. (888) 330-8477), (Fax in U.S. (800) 672-2054), www.palgrave.com; *The Statesman's Yearbook 2008.*

United Nations Statistics Division, New York, NY 10017, (800) 253-9646, Fax: (212) 963-4116, http://unstats.un.org; *Statistical Yearbook.*

AUSTRALIA - WAGES

Australian Bureau of Statistics (ABS), Locked Bag 10, Belconnen ACT 2616, Australia, www.abs.gov.au; *Australia at a Glance, 2008* and *Year Book Australia, 2008.*

International Labour Office, I.L.O. Publications, 4 route des Morillons, CH-1211 Geneva 22, Switzerland, (Telephone in U.S. (202) 653-7652), (Fax in U.S. (202) 653-7687), www.ilo.org; *Yearbook of Labour Statistics 2006.*

Organisation for Economic Cooperation and Development (OECD), 2 rue Andre Pascal, F-75775 Paris Cedex 16, France, (Telephone in U.S. (202) 785-6323), (Fax in U.S. (202) 785-0350), www.oecd.org; *ICT Sector Data and Metadata by Country; OECD Economic Outlook 2008; OECD Main Economic Indicators (MEI);* and STructural ANalysis (STAN) database.

United Nations Statistics Division, New York, NY 10017, (800) 253-9646, Fax: (212) 963-4116, http://unstats.un.org; *Statistical Yearbook.*

The World Bank, 1818 H Street, NW, Washington, DC 20433, (202) 473-1000, Fax: (202) 477-6391, www.worldbank.org; *Australia.*

AUSTRALIA - WALNUT PRODUCTION

See AUSTRALIA - CROPS

AUSTRALIA - WEATHER

See AUSTRALIA - CLIMATE

AUSTRALIA - WELFARE STATE

Australian Bureau of Statistics (ABS), Locked Bag 10, Belconnen ACT 2616, Australia, www.abs.gov.au; *Australia at a Glance, 2008* and *Year Book Australia, 2008.*

Australian Institute of Health and Welfare (AIHW), GPO Box 570, Canberra ACT 2601, Australia, www.aihw.gov.au; *Australia's Welfare 2007; Housing Assistance in Australia 2008;* and *National Public Health Expenditure Report 2005-06.*

International Monetary Fund (IMF), 700 Nineteenth Street, NW, Washington, DC 20431, (202) 623-7000, Fax: (202) 623-4661, www.imf.org; *Government Finance Statistics Yearbook (2008 Edition).*

Palgrave Macmillan Ltd., Houndmills, Basingstoke, Hampshire, RG21 6XS, England, (Telephone in U.S. (888) 330-8477), (Fax in U.S. (800) 672-2054), www.palgrave.com; *The Statesman's Yearbook 2008.*

AUSTRALIA - WHALES

See AUSTRALIA - FISHERIES

AUSTRALIA - WHEAT PRODUCTION

See AUSTRALIA - CROPS

AUSTRALIA - WHOLESALE PRICE INDEXES

International Monetary Fund (IMF), 700 Nineteenth Street, NW, Washington, DC 20431, (202) 623-7000, Fax: (202) 623-4661, www.imf.org; *International Financial Statistics Yearbook 2007.*

AUSTRALIA - WHOLESALE TRADE

United Nations Statistics Division, New York, NY 10017, (800) 253-9646, Fax: (212) 963-4116, http://unstats.un.org; *Statistical Yearbook.*

AUSTRALIA - WINE PRODUCTION

See AUSTRALIA - BEVERAGE INDUSTRY

AUSTRALIA - WOOD AND WOOD PULP

See AUSTRALIA - FORESTS AND FORESTRY

AUSTRALIA - WOOD PRODUCTS

Organisation for Economic Cooperation and Development (OECD), 2 rue Andre Pascal, F-75775 Paris Cedex 16, France, (Telephone in U.S. (202) 785-6323), (Fax in U.S. (202) 785-0350), www.oecd.org; *International Trade by Commodity Statistics (ITCS)* and STructural ANalysis (STAN) database.

United Nations Statistics Division, New York, NY 10017, (800) 253-9646, Fax: (212) 963-4116, http://unstats.un.org; Commodity Trade Statistics Database (COMTRADE).

AUSTRALIA - WOOL PRODUCTION

See AUSTRALIA - TEXTILE INDUSTRY

AUSTRALIA - YARN PRODUCTION

See AUSTRALIA - TEXTILE INDUSTRY

AUSTRALIA - ZINC AND ZINC ORE

See AUSTRALIA - MINERAL INDUSTRIES

AUSTRIA - NATIONAL STATISTICAL OFFICE

Statistics Austria, Guglgasse 13, 1110 Vienna, Austria, www.statistik.at/index_englisch.shtml; National Data Center.

AUSTRIA - PRIMARY STATISTICS SOURCES

Eurostat, Batiment Jean Monnet, Rue Alcide de Gasperi, L-2920 Luxembourg, http://epp.eurostat.ec.europa.eu; *Pocketbook on Candidate and Potential Candidate Countries.*

Statistics Austria, Guglgasse 13, 1110 Vienna, Austria, www.statistik.at/index_englisch.shtml; *Statistical Yearbook 2006.*

AUSTRIA - DATABASES

Austrian Institute for Economic Research (WIFO) (Osterreichisches Institut fur Wirtschaftsforschung), PO Box 91, A-1103 Vienna, Austria, www.wifo.ac.at/(en)/index.html; Economic Databases. Subject coverage: Comprehensive statistical data on the Austrian economy (e.g., national income, production, foreign trade, the labor market, and the financial sector).

Computing Centre for Economics and Social Sciences (Wirtschafts- und Sozialwissenschaftliches Rechenzentrum), PO Box 63, A-1103 Vienna, Austria, www.wsr.ac.at; Databases offered: (1) The WIFO Economic Database (2) The WIIW Annual Database on Eastern Europe.

Statistics Austria, Guglgasse 13, 1110 Vienna, Austria, www.statistik.at/index_englisch.shtml; STATAS (Statistisches Tabellensystem) Database. Subject coverage: Official statistics, with special emphasis on economic data.

AUSTRIA - ABORTION

United Nations Statistics Division, New York, NY 10017, (800) 253-9646, Fax: (212) 963-4116, http://unstats.un.org; *Trends in Europe and North America: The Statistical Yearbook of the ECE 2005.*

AUSTRIA - AGRICULTURE

Economist Intelligence Unit, 111 West 57th Street, New York, NY 10019, (212) 554-0600, Fax: (212) 586-1181, www.eiu.com; *Austria Country Report.*

Euromonitor International, Inc., 224 S. Michigan Avenue, Suite 1500, Chicago, IL 60604, (312) 922-1115, Fax: (312) 922-1157, www.euromonitor.com; *World Marketing Data and Statistics.*

Eurostat, Batiment Jean Monnet, Rue Alcide de Gasperi, L-2920 Luxembourg, http://epp.eurostat.ec.europa.eu; *EU Agricultural Prices in 2007.*

M.E. Sharpe, 80 Business Park Drive, Armonk, NY 10504, (800) 541-6563, Fax: (914) 273-2106, www.mesharpe.com; *The Illustrated Book of World Rankings.*

Organisation for Economic Cooperation and Development (OECD), 2 rue Andre Pascal, F-75775 Paris Cedex 16, France, (Telephone in U.S. (202) 785-6323), (Fax in U.S. (202) 785-0350), www.oecd.org; *Indicators of Industrial Activity; 2005 OECD Agricultural Outlook Tables, 1970-2014; OECD Agricultural Outlook: 2007-2016; OECD Economic Survey - Austria 2007;* and STructural ANalysis (STAN) database.

Palgrave Macmillan Ltd., Houndmills, Basingstoke, Hampshire, RG21 6XS, England, (Telephone in U.S. (888) 330-8477), (Fax in U.S. (800) 672-2054), www.palgrave.com; *The Statesman's Yearbook 2008.*

Taylor and Francis Group, An Informa Business, 2 Park Square, Milton Park, Abingdon, Oxford OX14 4RN, United Kingdom, (Dial from U.S. (212) 216-7800), (Fax from U.S. (212) 564-7854), www.tandf.co.uk; *The Europa World Year Book.*

United Nations Conference on Trade and Development (UNCTAD), DC2-1120, United Nations, New York, NY 10017, (212) 963-0027, www.unctad.org; *UNCTAD Commodity Yearbook.*

United Nations Food and Agricultural Organization (FAO), Viale delle Terme di Caracalla, 00100 Rome, Italy, (Dial from U.S. (202) 653-2400), (Fax from U.S. (202) 653 5760), www.fao.org; AQUASTAT; *FAO Production Yearbook 2002; FAO Trade Yearbook;* and *The State of Food and Agriculture (SOFA) 2006.*

United Nations Statistics Division, New York, NY 10017, (800) 253-9646, Fax: (212) 963-4116, http://unstats.un.org; *Statistical Yearbook.*

The World Bank, 1818 H Street, NW, Washington, DC 20433, (202) 473-1000, Fax: (202) 477-6391, www.worldbank.org; *Austria* and *World Development Indicators (WDI) 2008.*

AUSTRIA - AIRLINES

Eurostat, Batiment Jean Monnet, Rue Alcide de Gasperi, L-2920 Luxembourg, http://epp.eurostat.ec.europa.eu; *Regional Passenger and Freight Air Transport in Europe in 2006.*

International Civil Aviation Organization (ICAO), External Relations and Public Information Office (EPO), 999 University Street, Montreal, Quebec H3C 5H7, Canada, (Dial from U.S. (514) 954-8219), (Fax from U.S. (514) 954-6077), www.icao.int; *Civil Aviation Statistics of the World.*

M.E. Sharpe, 80 Business Park Drive, Armonk, NY 10504, (800) 541-6563, Fax: (914) 273-2106, www.mesharpe.com; *The Illustrated Book of World Rankings.*

Organisation for Economic Cooperation and Development (OECD), 2 rue Andre Pascal, F-75775 Paris Cedex 16, France, (Telephone in U.S. (202) 785-6323), (Fax in U.S. (202) 785-0350), www.oecd.org; *Household, Tourism, Travel: Trends, Environmental Impacts and Policy Responses.*

Palgrave Macmillan Ltd., Houndmills, Basingstoke, Hampshire, RG21 6XS, England, (Telephone in U.S. (888) 330-8477), (Fax in U.S. (800) 672-2054), www.palgrave.com; *The Statesman's Yearbook 2008.*

Taylor and Francis Group, An Informa Business, 2 Park Square, Milton Park, Abingdon, Oxford OX14 4RN, United Kingdom, (Dial from U.S. (212) 216-7800), (Fax from U.S. (212) 564-7854), www.tandf.co.uk; *The Europa World Year Book.*

United Nations Statistics Division, New York, NY 10017, (800) 253-9646, Fax: (212) 963-4116, http://unstats.un.org; *Statistical Yearbook.*

AUSTRIA - AIRPORTS

Central Intelligence Agency, Office of Public Affairs, Washington, DC 20505, (703) 482-0623, Fax: (703) 482-1739, www.cia.gov; *The World Factbook.*

AUSTRIA - ALUMINUM PRODUCTION

See AUSTRIA - MINERAL INDUSTRIES

AUSTRIA - ANIMAL FEEDING

Organisation for Economic Cooperation and Development (OECD), 2 rue Andre Pascal, F-75775 Paris Cedex 16, France, (Telephone in U.S. (202) 785-6323), (Fax in U.S. (202) 785-0350), www.oecd.org; *International Trade by Commodity Statistics (ITCS).*

AUSTRIA - ARMED FORCES

Central Intelligence Agency, Office of Public Affairs, Washington, DC 20505, (703) 482-0623, Fax: (703) 482-1739, www.cia.gov; *The World Factbook.*

Euromonitor International, Inc., 224 S. Michigan Avenue, Suite 1500, Chicago, IL 60604, (312) 922-1115, Fax: (312) 922-1157, www.euromonitor.com; *World Marketing Data and Statistics.*

International Institute for Strategic Studies (IISS), Arundel House, 13-15 Arundel Street, Temple Place, London WC2R 3DX, England, www.iiss.org; *The Military Balance 2007.*

International Monetary Fund (IMF), 700 Nineteenth Street, NW, Washington, DC 20431, (202) 623-7000, Fax: (202) 623-4661, www.imf.org; *Government Finance Statistics Yearbook (2008 Edition).*

Palgrave Macmillan Ltd., Houndmills, Basingstoke, Hampshire, RG21 6XS, England, (Telephone in U.S. (888) 330-8477), (Fax in U.S. (800) 672-2054), www.palgrave.com; *The Statesman's Yearbook 2008.*

U.S. Department of State (DOS), 2201 C Street NW, Washington, DC 20520, (202) 647-4000, www.state.gov; *World Military Expenditures and Arms Transfers (WMEAT).*

United Nations Statistics Division, New York, NY 10017, (800) 253-9646, Fax: (212) 963-4116, http://unstats.un.org; *Human Development Report 2006.*

AUSTRIA - AUTOMOBILE INDUSTRY AND TRADE

Organisation for Economic Cooperation and Development (OECD), 2 rue Andre Pascal, F-75775 Paris Cedex 16, France, (Telephone in U.S. (202) 785-6323), (Fax in U.S. (202) 785-0350), www.oecd.org; *Indicators of Industrial Activity* and *International Trade by Commodity Statistics (ITCS).*

United Nations Statistics Division, New York, NY 10017, (800) 253-9646, Fax: (212) 963-4116, http://unstats.un.org; *Statistical Yearbook.*

AUSTRIA - BALANCE OF PAYMENTS

International Monetary Fund (IMF), 700 Nineteenth Street, NW, Washington, DC 20431, (202) 623-7000, Fax: (202) 623-4661, www.imf.org; *Balance of Payments Statistics Newsletter; Balance of Payments Statistics Yearbook 2007;* and *International Financial Statistics Yearbook 2007.*

Organisation for Economic Cooperation and Development (OECD), 2 rue Andre Pascal, F-75775 Paris Cedex 16, France, (Telephone in U.S. (202) 785-6323), (Fax in U.S. (202) 785-0350), www.oecd.org; *Geographical Distribution of Financial Flows to Aid Recipients 2002-2006; OECD Economic Outlook 2008; OECD Economic Survey - Austria 2007;* and *OECD Main Economic Indicators (MEI).*

Taylor and Francis Group, An Informa Business, 2 Park Square, Milton Park, Abingdon, Oxford OX14 4RN, United Kingdom, (Dial from U.S. (212) 216-7800), (Fax from U.S. (212) 564-7854), www.tandf.co.uk; *The Europa World Year Book.*

United Nations Conference on Trade and Development (UNCTAD), DC2-1120, United Nations, New York, NY 10017, (212) 963-0027, www.unctad.org; *Handbook of Statistics 2005.*

The World Bank, 1818 H Street, NW, Washington, DC 20433, (202) 473-1000, Fax: (202) 477-6391, www.worldbank.org; *Austria; World Development Indicators (WDI) 2008;* and *World Development Report 2008.*

AUSTRIA - BANKS AND BANKING

Euromonitor International, Inc., 224 S. Michigan Avenue, Suite 1500, Chicago, IL 60604, (312) 922-1115, Fax: (312) 922-1157, www.euromonitor.com; *World Marketing Data and Statistics.*

European Union, Delegation of the European Commission to the United States, 2300 M Street, NW, Washington, DC 20037, (202) 862-9500, Fax: (202) 429-1766, www.eurunion.org; *The EU Economy, 2007 Review: Moving Europe's Productivity Frontier.*

International Monetary Fund (IMF), 700 Nineteenth Street, NW, Washington, DC 20431, (202) 623-7000, Fax: (202) 623-4661, www.imf.org; *Government Finance Statistics Yearbook (2008 Edition)* and *International Financial Statistics Yearbook 2007.*

M.E. Sharpe, 80 Business Park Drive, Armonk, NY 10504, (800) 541-6563, Fax: (914) 273-2106, www.mesharpe.com; *The Illustrated Book of World Rankings.*

Organisation for Economic Cooperation and Development (OECD), 2 rue Andre Pascal, F-75775 Paris Cedex 16, France, (Telephone in U.S. (202) 785-6323), (Fax in U.S. (202) 785-0350), www.oecd.org; *Financial Market Trends: OECD Periodical; OECD Economic Outlook 2008; OECD Economic Survey - Austria 2007;* and *OECD Main Economic Indicators (MEI).*

Palgrave Macmillan Ltd., Houndmills, Basingstoke, Hampshire, RG21 6XS, England, (Telephone in U.S. (888) 330-8477), (Fax in U.S. (800) 672-2054), www.palgrave.com; *The Statesman's Yearbook 2008.*

Taylor and Francis Group, An Informa Business, 2 Park Square, Milton Park, Abingdon, Oxford OX14 4RN, United Kingdom, (Dial from U.S. (212) 216-7800), (Fax from U.S. (212) 564-7854), www.tandf.co.uk; *The Europa World Year Book.*

United Nations Statistics Division, New York, NY 10017, (800) 253-9646, Fax: (212) 963-4116, http://unstats.un.org; *Statistical Yearbook.*

AUSTRIA - BARLEY PRODUCTION

See AUSTRIA - CROPS

AUSTRIA - BEVERAGE INDUSTRY

M.E. Sharpe, 80 Business Park Drive, Armonk, NY 10504, (800) 541-6563, Fax: (914) 273-2106, www.mesharpe.com; *The Illustrated Book of World Rankings.*

Organisation for Economic Cooperation and Development (OECD), 2 rue Andre Pascal, F-75775 Paris Cedex 16, France, (Telephone in U.S. (202) 785-6323), (Fax in U.S. (202) 785-0350), www.oecd.org; *Indicators of Industrial Activity.*

United Nations Statistics Division, New York, NY 10017, (800) 253-9646, Fax: (212) 963-4116, http://unstats.un.org; *Statistical Yearbook.*

AUSTRIA - BONDS

International Monetary Fund (IMF), 700 Nineteenth Street, NW, Washington, DC 20431, (202) 623-7000, Fax: (202) 623-4661, www.imf.org; *Government Finance Statistics Yearbook (2008 Edition).*

Organisation for Economic Cooperation and Development (OECD), 2 rue Andre Pascal, F-75775 Paris Cedex 16, France, (Telephone in U.S. (202) 785-6323), (Fax in U.S. (202) 785-0350), www.oecd.org; *Financial Market Trends: OECD Periodical.*

United Nations Statistics Division, New York, NY 10017, (800) 253-9646, Fax: (212) 963-4116, http://unstats.un.org; *Statistical Yearbook.*

AUSTRIA - BROADCASTING

Central Intelligence Agency, Office of Public Affairs, Washington, DC 20505, (703) 482-0623, Fax: (703) 482-1739, www.cia.gov; *The World Factbook.*

Euromonitor International, Inc., 224 S. Michigan Avenue, Suite 1500, Chicago, IL 60604, (312) 922-1115, Fax: (312) 922-1157, www.euromonitor.com; *World Marketing Data and Statistics.*

M.E. Sharpe, 80 Business Park Drive, Armonk, NY 10504, (800) 541-6563, Fax: (914) 273-2106, www.mesharpe.com; *The Illustrated Book of World Rankings.*

Palgrave Macmillan Ltd., Houndmills, Basingstoke, Hampshire, RG21 6XS, England, (Telephone in U.S. (888) 330-8477), (Fax in U.S. (800) 672-2054), www.palgrave.com; *The Statesman's Yearbook 2008.*

UNESCO Institute for Statistics, C.P. 6128 Succursale Centre-Ville, Montreal, Quebec, H3C 3J7 Canada, (Dial from U.S. (514) 343-6880), (Fax from U.S. (514) 343 6882), www.uis.unesco.org; *Statistical Tables.*

United Nations Statistics Division, New York, NY 10017, (800) 253-9646, Fax: (212) 963-4116, http://unstats.un.org; *Trends in Europe and North America: The Statistical Yearbook of the ECE 2005.*

WRTH Publications Limited, PO Box 290, Oxford OX2 7FT, UK, www.wrth.com; *World Radio TV Handbook 2007.*

AUSTRIA - BUDGET

Central Intelligence Agency, Office of Public Affairs, Washington, DC 20505, (703) 482-0623, Fax: (703) 482-1739, www.cia.gov; *The World Factbook.*

Eurostat, Batiment Jean Monnet, Rue Alcide de Gasperi, L-2920 Luxembourg, http://epp.eurostat.ec.europa.eu; *Government Budgets.*

AUSTRIA - BUSINESS

Organisation for Economic Cooperation and Development (OECD), 2 rue Andre Pascal, F-75775 Paris Cedex 16, France, (Telephone in U.S. (202) 785-6323), (Fax in U.S. (202) 785-0350), www.oecd.org; *OECD Main Economic Indicators (MEI).*

AUSTRIA - CADMIUM PRODUCTION

See AUSTRIA - MINERAL INDUSTRIES

AUSTRIA - CAPITAL INVESTMENTS

Organisation for Economic Cooperation and Development (OECD), 2 rue Andre Pascal, F-75775 Paris Cedex 16, France, (Telephone in U.S. (202) 785-6323), (Fax in U.S. (202) 785-0350), www.oecd.org; *Financial Market Trends: OECD Periodical* and *OECD Economic Outlook 2008.*

AUSTRIA - CAPITAL LEVY

International Monetary Fund (IMF), 700 Nineteenth Street, NW, Washington, DC 20431, (202) 623-7000, Fax: (202) 623-4661, www.imf.org; *Government Finance Statistics Yearbook (2008 Edition).*

Organisation for Economic Cooperation and Development (OECD), 2 rue Andre Pascal, F-75775 Paris Cedex 16, France, (Telephone in U.S. (202) 785-6323), (Fax in U.S. (202) 785-0350), www.oecd.org; *Financial Market Trends: OECD Periodical* and *OECD Economic Outlook 2008.*

AUSTRIA - CATTLE

See AUSTRIA - LIVESTOCK

AUSTRIA - CHILDBIRTH - STATISTICS

Central Intelligence Agency, Office of Public Affairs, Washington, DC 20505, (703) 482-0623, Fax: (703) 482-1739, www.cia.gov; *The World Factbook.*

Euromonitor International, Inc., 224 S. Michigan Avenue, Suite 1500, Chicago, IL 60604, (312) 922-1115, Fax: (312) 922-1157, www.euromonitor.com; *The World Economic Factbook 2008.*

M.E. Sharpe, 80 Business Park Drive, Armonk, NY 10504, (800) 541-6563, Fax: (914) 273-2106, www.mesharpe.com; *The Illustrated Book of World Rankings.*

Palgrave Macmillan Ltd., Houndmills, Basingstoke, Hampshire, RG21 6XS, England, (Telephone in U.S. (888) 330-8477), (Fax in U.S. (800) 672-2054), www.palgrave.com; *The Statesman's Yearbook 2008.*

Taylor and Francis Group, An Informa Business, 2 Park Square, Milton Park, Abingdon, Oxford OX14 4RN, United Kingdom, (Dial from U.S. (212) 216-7800), (Fax from U.S. (212) 564-7854), www.tandf.co.uk; *The Europa World Year Book.*

United Nations Statistics Division, New York, NY 10017, (800) 253-9646, Fax: (212) 963-4116, http://unstats.un.org; *Demographic Yearbook* and *Statistical Yearbook.*

The World Bank, 1818 H Street, NW, Washington, DC 20433, (202) 473-1000, Fax: (202) 477-6391, www.worldbank.org; *World Development Indicators (WDI) 2008.*

World Health Organization (WHO), Avenue Appia 20, 1211 Geneve 27, Switzerland, (Telephone in U.S. (212) 331-9081), www.who.int; *World Health Report 2006.*

AUSTRIA - CLIMATE

M.E. Sharpe, 80 Business Park Drive, Armonk, NY 10504, (800) 541-6563, Fax: (914) 273-2106, www.mesharpe.com; *The Illustrated Book of World Rankings.*

Palgrave Macmillan Ltd., Houndmills, Basingstoke, Hampshire, RG21 6XS, England, (Telephone in U.S. (888) 330-8477), (Fax in U.S. (800) 672-2054), www.palgrave.com; *The Statesman's Yearbook 2008.*

AUSTRIA - CLOTHING EXPORTS AND IMPORTS

See AUSTRIA - TEXTILE INDUSTRY

AUSTRIA - COAL PRODUCTION

See AUSTRIA - MINERAL INDUSTRIES

AUSTRIA - COBALT PRODUCTION

See AUSTRIA - MINERAL INDUSTRIES

AUSTRIA - COFFEE

See AUSTRIA - CROPS

AUSTRIA - COMMERCE

Palgrave Macmillan Ltd., Houndmills, Basingstoke, Hampshire, RG21 6XS, England, (Telephone in U.S. (888) 330-8477), (Fax in U.S. (800) 672-2054), www.palgrave.com; *The Statesman's Yearbook 2008.*

AUSTRIA - COMMODITY EXCHANGES

Commodity Research Bureau, 330 South Wells Street, Suite 612, Chicago, IL 60606-7110, (800) 621-5271, Fax: (312) 939-4135, www.crbtrader.com; *2006 CRB Commodity Yearbook and CD.*

International Lead and Zinc Study Group (ILZSG), Rua Almirante Barroso 38, 5th Floor, Lisbon 1000 - 013, Portugal, www.ilzsg.org; Interactive Statistical Database.

International Monetary Fund (IMF), 700 Nineteenth Street, NW, Washington, DC 20431, (202) 623-7000, Fax: (202) 623-4661, www.imf.org; *IMF Primary Commodity Prices.*

United Nations Food and Agricultural Organization (FAO), Viale delle Terme di Caracalla, 00100 Rome, Italy, (Dial from U.S. (202) 653-2400), (Fax from U.S. (202) 653 5760), www.fao.org; *The State of Food and Agriculture (SOFA) 2006.*

United Nations Statistics Division, New York, NY 10017, (800) 253-9646, Fax: (212) 963-4116, http://unstats.un.org; *Statistical Yearbook.*

World Bureau of Metal Statistics (WBMS), 27a High Street, Ware, Hertfordshire, SG12 9BA, United Kingdom, www.world-bureau.com; *Annual Stainless Steel Statistics; World Flow Charts; World Metal Statistics; World Nickel Statistics;* and *World Tin Statistics.*

AUSTRIA - COMMUNICATION AND TRAFFIC

United Nations Statistics Division, New York, NY 10017, (800) 253-9646, Fax: (212) 963-4116, http://unstats.un.org; *Statistical Yearbook.*

AUSTRIA - CONSTRUCTION INDUSTRY

M.E. Sharpe, 80 Business Park Drive, Armonk, NY 10504, (800) 541-6563, Fax: (914) 273-2106, www.mesharpe.com; *The Illustrated Book of World Rankings.*

Organisation for Economic Cooperation and Development (OECD), 2 rue Andre Pascal, F-75775 Paris Cedex 16, France, (Telephone in U.S. (202) 785-6323), (Fax in U.S. (202) 785-0350), www.oecd.org; *Iron and Steel Industry in 2004 (2006 Edition); OECD Economic Survey - Austria 2007; OECD Main Economic Indicators (MEI);* and STructural ANalysis (STAN) database.

Palgrave Macmillan Ltd., Houndmills, Basingstoke, Hampshire, RG21 6XS, England, (Telephone in U.S. (888) 330-8477), (Fax in U.S. (800) 672-2054), www.palgrave.com; *The Statesman's Yearbook 2008.*

United Nations Statistics Division, New York, NY 10017, (800) 253-9646, Fax: (212) 963-4116, http://unstats.un.org; *Statistical Yearbook.*

AUSTRIA - CONSUMER PRICE INDEXES

Organisation for Economic Cooperation and Development (OECD), 2 rue Andre Pascal, F-75775 Paris Cedex 16, France, (Telephone in U.S. (202) 785-6323), (Fax in U.S. (202) 785-0350), www.oecd.org; *OECD Economic Outlook 2008.*

Taylor and Francis Group, An Informa Business, 2 Park Square, Milton Park, Abingdon, Oxford OX14 4RN, United Kingdom, (Dial from U.S. (212) 216-7800), (Fax from U.S. (212) 564-7854), www.tandf.co.uk; *The Europa World Year Book.*

United Nations Statistics Division, New York, NY 10017, (800) 253-9646, Fax: (212) 963-4116, http://unstats.un.org; *Statistical Yearbook* and *Trends in Europe and North America: The Statistical Yearbook of the ECE 2005.*

The World Bank, 1818 H Street, NW, Washington, DC 20433, (202) 473-1000, Fax: (202) 477-6391, www.worldbank.org; *Austria.*

AUSTRIA - CONSUMPTION (ECONOMICS)

International Iron and Steel Institute (IISI), Rue Colonel Bourg 120, B-1140 Brussels, Belgium, www.worldsteel.org; *Steel Statistical Yearbook 2006.*

International Lead and Zinc Study Group (ILZSG), Rua Almirante Barroso 38, 5th Floor, Lisbon 1000 - 013, Portugal, www.ilzsg.org; Interactive Statistical Database.

International Monetary Fund (IMF), 700 Nineteenth Street, NW, Washington, DC 20431, (202) 623-7000, Fax: (202) 623-4661, www.imf.org; *International Financial Statistics Yearbook 2007.*

Organisation for Economic Cooperation and Development (OECD), 2 rue Andre Pascal, F-75775 Paris Cedex 16, France, (Telephone in U.S. (202) 785-6323), (Fax in U.S. (202) 785-0350), www.oecd.org; *Environmental Impacts of Foreign Direct Investment in the Mining Sector in the Newly Independent States (NIS); Iron and Steel Industry in 2004 (2006 Edition); A New World Map in Textiles and Clothing: Adjusting to Change; 2005 OECD Agricultural Outlook Tables, 1970-2014; Revenue Statistics 1965-2006 - 2007 Edition;* and *Towards Sustainable Household Consumption?: Trends and Policies in OECD Countries.*

Technical Association of the Pulp and Paper Industry (TAPPI), 15 Technology Parkway South, Norcross, GA 30092, (770) 446-1400, Fax: (770) 446-6947, www.tappi.org; *TAPPI Annual Report.*

The World Bank, 1818 H Street, NW, Washington, DC 20433, (202) 473-1000, Fax: (202) 477-6391, www.worldbank.org; *World Development Report 2008.*

AUSTRIA - COPPER INDUSTRY AND TRADE

See AUSTRIA - MINERAL INDUSTRIES

AUSTRIA - CORN INDUSTRY

See AUSTRIA - CROPS

AUSTRIA - COST AND STANDARD OF LIVING

International Monetary Fund (IMF), 700 Nineteenth Street, NW, Washington, DC 20431, (202) 623-7000, Fax: (202) 623-4661, www.imf.org; *Government Finance Statistics Yearbook (2008 Edition).*

AUSTRIA - COTTON

See AUSTRIA - CROPS

AUSTRIA - CRIME

Eurostat, Batiment Jean Monnet, Rue Alcide de Gasperi, L-2920 Luxembourg, http://epp.eurostat.ec.europa.eu; *Crime and Criminal Justice; General Government Expenditure and Revenue in the EU, 2006;* and *Study on Crime Victimisation.*

International Criminal Police Organization (INTERPOL), General Secretariat, 200 quai Charles de Gaulle, 69006 Lyon, France, www.interpol.int; *International Crime Statistics.*

United Nations Statistics Division, New York, NY 10017, (800) 253-9646, Fax: (212) 963-4116, http://unstats.un.org; *Trends in Europe and North America: The Statistical Yearbook of the ECE 2005.*

Yale University Press, PO Box 209040, New Haven, CT 06520-9040, (203) 432-0960, Fax: (203) 432-0948, http://yalepress.yale.edu/yupbooks; *Violence and Crime in Cross-National Perspective.*

AUSTRIA - CROPS

Euromonitor International, Inc., 224 S. Michigan Avenue, Suite 1500, Chicago, IL 60604, (312) 922-1115, Fax: (312) 922-1157, www.euromonitor.com; *European Marketing Data and Statistics 2008.*

M.E. Sharpe, 80 Business Park Drive, Armonk, NY 10504, (800) 541-6563, Fax: (914) 273-2106, www.mesharpe.com; *The Illustrated Book of World Rankings.*

Organisation for Economic Cooperation and Development (OECD), 2 rue Andre Pascal, F-75775 Paris Cedex 16, France, (Telephone in U.S. (202) 785-6323), (Fax in U.S. (202) 785-0350), www.oecd.org; *International Trade by Commodity Statistics (ITCS)* and *2005 OECD Agricultural Outlook Tables, 1970-2014.*

Palgrave Macmillan Ltd., Houndmills, Basingstoke, Hampshire, RG21 6XS, England, (Telephone in U.S. (888) 330-8477), (Fax in U.S. (800) 672-2054), www.palgrave.com; *The Statesman's Yearbook 2008.*

Taylor and Francis Group, An Informa Business, 2 Park Square, Milton Park, Abingdon, Oxford OX14 4RN, United Kingdom, (Dial from U.S. (212) 216-7800), (Fax from U.S. (212) 564-7854), www.tandf.co.uk; *The Europa World Year Book.*

United Nations Conference on Trade and Development (UNCTAD), DC2-1120, United Nations, New York, NY 10017, (212) 963-0027, www.unctad.org; *UNCTAD Commodity Yearbook.*

United Nations Food and Agricultural Organization (FAO), Viale delle Terme di Caracalla, 00100 Rome, Italy, (Dial from U.S. (202) 653-2400), (Fax from U.S. (202) 653 5760), www.fao.org; *FAO Production Yearbook 2002* and *The State of Food and Agriculture (SOFA) 2006.*

United Nations Statistics Division, New York, NY 10017, (800) 253-9646, Fax: (212) 963-4116, http://unstats.un.org; *Statistical Yearbook.*

AUSTRIA - CUSTOMS ADMINISTRATION

International Monetary Fund (IMF), 700 Nineteenth Street, NW, Washington, DC 20431, (202) 623-7000, Fax: (202) 623-4661, www.imf.org; *Government Finance Statistics Yearbook (2008 Edition).*

Organisation for Economic Cooperation and Development (OECD), 2 rue Andre Pascal, F-75775 Paris Cedex 16, France, (Telephone in U.S. (202) 785-6323), (Fax in U.S. (202) 785-0350), www.oecd.org; *Environmental Impacts of Foreign Direct Investment in the Mining Sector in the Newly Independent States (NIS).*

Palgrave Macmillan Ltd., Houndmills, Basingstoke, Hampshire, RG21 6XS, England, (Telephone in U.S. (888) 330-8477), (Fax in U.S. (800) 672-2054), www.palgrave.com; *The Statesman's Yearbook 2008.*

AUSTRIA - DAIRY PROCESSING

Organisation for Economic Cooperation and Development (OECD), 2 rue Andre Pascal, F-75775 Paris Cedex 16, France, (Telephone in U.S. (202) 785-6323), (Fax in U.S. (202) 785-0350), www.oecd.org; *2005 OECD Agricultural Outlook Tables, 1970-2014.*

Palgrave Macmillan Ltd., Houndmills, Basingstoke, Hampshire, RG21 6XS, England, (Telephone in U.S. (888) 330-8477), (Fax in U.S. (800) 672-2054), www.palgrave.com; *The Statesman's Yearbook 2008.*

Taylor and Francis Group, An Informa Business, 2 Park Square, Milton Park, Abingdon, Oxford OX14 4RN, United Kingdom, (Dial from U.S. (212) 216-7800), (Fax from U.S. (212) 564-7854), www.tandf.co.uk; *The Europa World Year Book.*

United Nations Food and Agricultural Organization (FAO), Viale delle Terme di Caracalla, 00100 Rome, Italy, (Dial from U.S. (202) 653-2400), (Fax from U.S. (202) 653 5760), www.fao.org; *FAO Production Yearbook 2002* and *The State of Food and Agriculture (SOFA) 2006.*

United Nations Statistics Division, New York, NY 10017, (800) 253-9646, Fax: (212) 963-4116, http://unstats.un.org; *Statistical Yearbook.*

AUSTRIA - DEATH RATES

See AUSTRIA - MORTALITY

AUSTRIA - DEBTS, EXTERNAL

International Monetary Fund (IMF), 700 Nineteenth Street, NW, Washington, DC 20431, (202) 623-7000, Fax: (202) 623-4661, www.imf.org; *Government Finance Statistics Yearbook (2008 Edition).*

Organisation for Economic Cooperation and Development (OECD), 2 rue Andre Pascal, F-75775 Paris Cedex 16, France, (Telephone in U.S. (202) 785-6323), (Fax in U.S. (202) 785-0350), www.oecd.org; *Financial Market Trends: OECD Periodical; Geographical Distribution of Financial Flows to Aid Recipients 2002-2006;* and *OECD Economic Outlook 2008.*

Palgrave Macmillan Ltd., Houndmills, Basingstoke, Hampshire, RG21 6XS, England, (Telephone in U.S. (888) 330-8477), (Fax in U.S. (800) 672-2054), www.palgrave.com; *The Statesman's Yearbook 2008.*

The World Bank, 1818 H Street, NW, Washington, DC 20433, (202) 473-1000, Fax: (202) 477-6391, www.worldbank.org; *Global Development Finance 2007; World Development Indicators (WDI) 2008;* and *World Development Report 2008.*

AUSTRIA - DEFENSE EXPENDITURES

See AUSTRIA - ARMED FORCES

AUSTRIA - DEMOGRAPHY

Euromonitor International, Inc., 224 S. Michigan Avenue, Suite 1500, Chicago, IL 60604, (312) 922-1115, Fax: (312) 922-1157, www.euromonitor.com; *The World Economic Factbook 2008* and *World Marketing Data and Statistics.*

Eurostat, Batiment Jean Monnet, Rue Alcide de Gasperi, L-2920 Luxembourg, http://epp.eurostat.ec.europa.eu; *Demographic Outlook - National Reports on the Demographic Developments in 2006.*

M.E. Sharpe, 80 Business Park Drive, Armonk, NY 10504, (800) 541-6563, Fax: (914) 273-2106, www.mesharpe.com; *The Illustrated Book of World Rankings.*

United Nations Statistics Division, New York, NY 10017, (800) 253-9646, Fax: (212) 963-4116, http://unstats.un.org; *Human Development Report 2006.*

The World Bank, 1818 H Street, NW, Washington, DC 20433, (202) 473-1000, Fax: (202) 477-6391, www.worldbank.org; *Austria.*

AUSTRIA - DIAMONDS

See AUSTRIA - MINERAL INDUSTRIES

AUSTRIA - DISPOSABLE INCOME

M.E. Sharpe, 80 Business Park Drive, Armonk, NY 10504, (800) 541-6563, Fax: (914) 273-2106, www.mesharpe.com; *The Illustrated Book of World Rankings.*

Organisation for Economic Cooperation and Development (OECD), 2 rue Andre Pascal, F-75775 Paris Cedex 16, France, (Telephone in U.S. (202) 785-6323), (Fax in U.S. (202) 785-0350), www.oecd.org; *OECD Economic Outlook 2008.*

United Nations Statistics Division, New York, NY 10017, (800) 253-9646, Fax: (212) 963-4116, http://unstats.un.org; *National Accounts Statistics: Compendium of Income Distribution Statistics* and *Statistical Yearbook.*

AUSTRIA - DIVORCE

M.E. Sharpe, 80 Business Park Drive, Armonk, NY 10504, (800) 541-6563, Fax: (914) 273-2106, www.mesharpe.com; *The Illustrated Book of World Rankings.*

United Nations Statistics Division, New York, NY 10017, (800) 253-9646, Fax: (212) 963-4116, http://unstats.un.org; *Demographic Yearbook; Statistical Yearbook;* and *Trends in Europe and North America: The Statistical Yearbook of the ECE 2005.*

AUSTRIA - ECONOMIC ASSISTANCE

Organisation for Economic Cooperation and Development (OECD), 2 rue Andre Pascal, F-75775 Paris Cedex 16, France, (Telephone in U.S. (202) 785-6323), (Fax in U.S. (202) 785-0350), www.oecd.org; *Geographical Distribution of Financial Flows to Aid Recipients 2002-2006.*

United Nations Statistics Division, New York, NY 10017, (800) 253-9646, Fax: (212) 963-4116, http://unstats.un.org; *Statistical Yearbook.*

AUSTRIA - ECONOMIC CONDITIONS

Banque de France, 48 rue Croix des Petits champs, 75001 Paris, France, www.banque-france.fr/home.htm; *Key Data for the Euro Area.*

Center for International Business Education Research (CIBER), Columbia Business School and School of International and Public Affairs, Uris Hall, Room 212, 3022 Broadway, New York, NY 10027-6902, Mr. Joshua Safier, (212) 854-4750, Fax: (212) 222-9821, www.columbia.edu/cu/ciber/; Datastream International.

Central Intelligence Agency, Office of Public Affairs, Washington, DC 20505, (703) 482-0623, Fax: (703) 482-1739, www.cia.gov; *The World Factbook.*

DSI Data Service Information, Xantener Strasse 51a, D-47495 Rheinberg, Germany, www.dsidata.com; *Campus Solution.*

Dun and Bradstreet (DB) Corporation, 103 JFK Parkway, Short Hills, NJ 07078, (973) 921-5500, www.dnb.com; *Country Report.*

Economist Intelligence Unit, 111 West 57th Street, New York, NY 10019, (212) 554-0600, Fax: (212) 586-1181, www.eiu.com; *Austria Country Report.*

Euromonitor International, Inc., 224 S. Michigan Avenue, Suite 1500, Chicago, IL 60604, (312) 922-1115, Fax: (312) 922-1157, www.euromonitor.com; *European Marketing Data and Statistics 2008; The World Economic Factbook 2008;* and *World Marketing Data and Statistics.*

European Union, Delegation of the European Commission to the United States, 2300 M Street, NW, Washington DC 20037, (202) 862-9500, Fax: (202) 429-1766, www.eurunion.org; *The EU Economy, 2007 Review: Moving Europe's Productivity Frontier.*

Eurostat, Batiment Jean Monnet, Rue Alcide de Gasperi, L-2920 Luxembourg, http://epp.eurostat.ec.europa.eu; *EU Economic Data Pocketbook.*

International Monetary Fund (IMF), 700 Nineteenth Street, NW, Washington, DC 20431, (202) 623-7000, Fax: (202) 623-4661, www.imf.org; *World Economic Outlook Reports.*

M.E. Sharpe, 80 Business Park Drive, Armonk, NY 10504, (800) 541-6563, Fax: (914) 273-2106, www.mesharpe.com; *The Illustrated Book of World Rankings.*

Organisation for Economic Cooperation and Development (OECD), 2 rue Andre Pascal, F-75775 Paris Cedex 16, France, (Telephone in U.S. (202) 785-6323), (Fax in U.S. (202) 785-0350), www.oecd.org; *Geographical Distribution of Financial Flows to Aid Recipients 2002-2006; ICT Sector Data and Metadata by Country; Labour Force Statistics: 1986-2005, 2007 Edition; OECD Composite Leading Indicators (CLIs), Updated September 2007; OECD Economic Outlook 2008; OECD Economic Survey - Austria 2007; OECD Employment Outlook 2007; OECD in Figures 2007;* and *OECD Main Economic Indicators (MEI).*

Palgrave Macmillan Ltd., Houndmills, Basingstoke, Hampshire, RG21 6XS, England, (Telephone in U.S. (888) 330-8477), (Fax in U.S. (800) 672-2054), www.palgrave.com; *The Statesman's Yearbook 2008.*

Taylor and Francis Group, An Informa Business, 2 Park Square, Milton Park, Abingdon, Oxford OX14 4RN, United Kingdom, (Dial from U.S. (212) 216-7800), (Fax from U.S. (212) 564-7854), www.tandf.co.uk; *The Europa World Year Book.*

United Nations Statistics Division, New York, NY 10017, (800) 253-9646, Fax: (212) 963-4116, http://unstats.un.org; *World Statistics Pocketbook.*

The World Bank, 1818 H Street, NW, Washington, DC 20433, (202) 473-1000, Fax: (202) 477-6391, www.worldbank.org; *Austria; Global Economic Monitor (GEM); Global Economic Prospects 2008; The World Bank Atlas 2003-2004;* and *World Development Report 2008.*

AUSTRIA - ECONOMICS - SOCIOLOGICAL ASPECTS

Organisation for Economic Cooperation and Development (OECD), 2 rue Andre Pascal, F-75775 Paris Cedex 16, France, (Telephone in U.S. (202) 785-6323), (Fax in U.S. (202) 785-0350), www.oecd.org; *OECD Economic Outlook 2008.*

AUSTRIA - EDUCATION

Euromonitor International, Inc., 224 S. Michigan Avenue, Suite 1500, Chicago, IL 60604, (312) 922-1115, Fax: (312) 922-1157, www.euromonitor.com; *European Marketing Data and Statistics 2008* and *World Marketing Data and Statistics.*

European Union, Delegation of the European Commission to the United States, 2300 M Street, NW, Washington, DC 20037, (202) 862-9500, Fax: (202) 429-1766, www.eurunion.org; *Education across Europe 2003.*

Eurostat, Batiment Jean Monnet, Rue Alcide de Gasperi, L-2920 Luxembourg, http://epp.eurostat.ec.europa.eu; *Education, Science and Culture Statistics.*

International Monetary Fund (IMF), 700 Nineteenth Street, NW, Washington, DC 20431, (202) 623-7000, Fax: (202) 623-4661, www.imf.org; *Government Finance Statistics Yearbook (2008 Edition).*

M.E. Sharpe, 80 Business Park Drive, Armonk, NY 10504, (800) 541-6563, Fax: (914) 273-2106, www.mesharpe.com; *The Illustrated Book of World Rankings.*

Organisation for Economic Cooperation and Development (OECD), 2 rue Andre Pascal, F-75775 Paris Cedex 16, France, (Telephone in U.S. (202) 785-6323), (Fax in U.S. (202) 785-0350), www.oecd.org; *Education at a Glance* (2007 Edition).

Palgrave Macmillan Ltd., Houndmills, Basingstoke, Hampshire, RG21 6XS, England, (Telephone in U.S. (888) 330-8477), (Fax in U.S. (800) 672-2054), www.palgrave.com; *The Statesman's Yearbook 2008.*

Taylor and Francis Group, An Informa Business, 2 Park Square, Milton Park, Abingdon, Oxford OX14 4RN, United Kingdom, (Dial from U.S. (212) 216-7800), (Fax from U.S. (212) 564-7854), www.tandf.co.uk; *The Europa World Year Book.*

UNESCO Institute for Statistics, C.P. 6128 Succursale Centre-Ville, Montreal, Quebec, H3C 3J7 Canada, (Dial from U.S. (514) 343-6880), (Fax from U.S. (514) 343 6882), www.uis.unesco.org; *Statistical Tables.*

United Nations Statistics Division, New York, NY 10017, (800) 253-9646, Fax: (212) 963-4116, http://unstats.un.org; *Human Development Report 2006* and *Trends in Europe and North America: The Statistical Yearbook of the ECE 2005.*

The World Bank, 1818 H Street, NW, Washington, DC 20433, (202) 473-1000, Fax: (202) 477-6391, www.worldbank.org; *Austria; World Development Indicators (WDI) 2008;* and *World Development Report 2008.*

AUSTRIA - ELECTRICITY

Eurostat, Batiment Jean Monnet, Rue Alcide de Gasperi, L-2920 Luxembourg, http://epp.eurostat.ec.europa.eu; *Energy - Monthly Statistics* and *Panorama of Energy - 2007 Edition.*

M.E. Sharpe, 80 Business Park Drive, Armonk, NY 10504, (800) 541-6563, Fax: (914) 273-2106, www.mesharpe.com; *The Illustrated Book of World Rankings.*

Organisation for Economic Cooperation and Development (OECD), 2 rue Andre Pascal, F-75775 Paris Cedex 16, France, (Telephone in U.S. (202) 785-6323), (Fax in U.S. (202) 785-0350), www.oecd.org; *Coal Information: 2007 Edition; Energy Statistics of OECD Countries* (2007 Edition); *Indicators of Industrial Activity;* STructural ANalysis (STAN) database; and *World Energy Outlook 2007.*

Palgrave Macmillan Ltd., Houndmills, Basingstoke, Hampshire, RG21 6XS, England, (Telephone in U.S. (888) 330-8477), (Fax in U.S. (800) 672-2054), www.palgrave.com; *The Statesman's Yearbook 2008.*

Platts, 2 Penn Plaza, 25th Floor, New York, NY 10121-2298, (212) 904-3070, www.platts.com; *EU Energy* and *European Electricity Review 2004.*

U.S. Department of Energy (DOE), Energy Information Administration (EIA), 1000 Independence Avenue, SW, Washington, DC 20585, (202) 586-8800, www.eia.doe.gov; *International Energy Annual 2004* and *International Energy Outlook 2006.*

United Nations Statistics Division, New York, NY 10017, (800) 253-9646, Fax: (212) 963-4116, http://unstats.un.org; *Human Development Report 2006; Statistical Yearbook;* and *Trends in Europe and North America: The Statistical Yearbook of the ECE 2005.*

AUSTRIA - EMPLOYMENT

Bernan Essential Government Publications, 4611-F Assembly Drive, Lanham MD, 20706-4391, (301) 459-2255, Fax: (800) 865-3450, www.bernan.com; *OECD Factbook 2006.*

Euromonitor International, Inc., 224 S. Michigan Avenue, Suite 1500, Chicago, IL 60604, (312) 922-1115, Fax: (312) 922-1157, www.euromonitor.com; *European Marketing Data and Statistics 2008.*

International Labour Office, I.L.O. Publications, 4 route des Morillons, CH-1211 Geneva 22, Switzerland, (Telephone in U.S. (202) 653-7652), (Fax in U.S. (202) 653-7687), www.ilo.org; *Yearbook of Labour Statistics 2006.*

M.E. Sharpe, 80 Business Park Drive, Armonk, NY 10504, (800) 541-6563, Fax: (914) 273-2106, www.mesharpe.com; *The Illustrated Book of World Rankings.*

Organisation for Economic Cooperation and Development (OECD), 2 rue Andre Pascal, F-75775 Paris Cedex 16, France, (Telephone in U.S. (202) 785-6323), (Fax in U.S. (202) 785-0350), www.oecd.org; *ICT Sector Data and Metadata by Country; Iron and Steel Industry in 2004 (2006 Edition); Labour Force Statistics: 1986-2005, 2007 Edition; A New World Map in Textiles and Clothing: Adjusting to Change; OECD Composite Leading Indicators (CLIs), Updated September 2007; OECD Economic Outlook 2008; OECD Economic Survey - Austria 2007; OECD Employment Outlook 2007;* and *OECD in Figures 2007.*

United Nations Statistics Division, New York, NY 10017, (800) 253-9646, Fax: (212) 963-4116, http://unstats.un.org; *Statistical Yearbook* and *Trends in Europe and North America: The Statistical Yearbook of the ECE 2005.*

The World Bank, 1818 H Street, NW, Washington, DC 20433, (202) 473-1000, Fax: (202) 477-6391, www.worldbank.org; *Austria.*

AUSTRIA - ENERGY INDUSTRIES

Eurostat, Batiment Jean Monnet, Rue Alcide de Gasperi, L-2920 Luxembourg, http://epp.eurostat.ec.europa.eu; *Energy - Monthly Statistics* and *Panorama of Energy - 2007 Edition.*

International Energy Agency (IEA), 9, rue de la Federation, 75739 Paris Cedex 15, France, www.iea.org; *Key World Energy Statistics 2007.*

Platts, 2 Penn Plaza, 25th Floor, New York, NY 10121-2298, (212) 904-3070, www.platts.com; *EU Energy.*

AUSTRIA - ENVIRONMENTAL CONDITIONS

DSI Data Service Information, Xantener Strasse 51a, D-47495 Rheinberg, Germany, www.dsidata.com; *Campus Solution* and *DSI's Global Environmental Database.*

Economist Intelligence Unit, 111 West 57th Street, New York, NY 10019, (212) 554-0600, Fax: (212) 586-1181, www.eiu.com; *Austria Country Report.*

Platts, 2 Penn Plaza, 25th Floor, New York, NY 10121-2298, (212) 904-3070, www.platts.com; *Emissions Daily.*

United Nations Statistics Division, New York, NY 10017, (800) 253-9646, Fax: (212) 963-4116, http://unstats.un.org; *Trends in Europe and North America: The Statistical Yearbook of the ECE 2005* and *World Statistics Pocketbook.*

AUSTRIA - EXPENDITURES, PUBLIC

Eurostat, Batiment Jean Monnet, Rue Alcide de Gasperi, L-2920 Luxembourg, http://epp.eurostat.ec.europa.eu; *European Social Statistics - Social Protection Expenditure and Receipts - Data 1997-2005.*

Organisation for Economic Cooperation and Development (OECD), 2 rue Andre Pascal, F-75775 Paris Cedex 16, France, (Telephone in U.S. (202) 785-6323), (Fax in U.S. (202) 785-0350), www.oecd.org; *Revenue Statistics 1965-2006 - 2007 Edition.*

AUSTRIA - EXPORTS

Central Intelligence Agency, Office of Public Affairs, Washington, DC 20505, (703) 482-0623, Fax: (703) 482-1739, www.cia.gov; *The World Factbook.*

Economist Intelligence Unit, 111 West 57th Street, New York, NY 10019, (212) 554-0600, Fax: (212) 586-1181, www.eiu.com; *Austria Country Report.*

Euromonitor International, Inc., 224 S. Michigan Avenue, Suite 1500, Chicago, IL 60604, (312) 922-1115, Fax: (312) 922-1157, www.euromonitor.com; *The World Economic Factbook 2008.*

International Iron and Steel Institute (IISI), Rue Colonel Bourg 120, B-1140 Brussels, Belgium, www.worldsteel.org; *Steel Statistical Yearbook 2006.*

International Lead and Zinc Study Group (ILZSG), Rua Almirante Barroso 38, 5th Floor, Lisbon 1000 - 013, Portugal, www.ilzsg.org; Interactive Statistical Database.

International Monetary Fund (IMF), 700 Nineteenth Street, NW, Washington, DC 20431, (202) 623-7000, Fax: (202) 623-4661, www.imf.org; *Direction of Trade Statistics Yearbook 2007* and *International Financial Statistics Yearbook 2007.*

Organisation for Economic Cooperation and Development (OECD), 2 rue Andre Pascal, F-75775 Paris Cedex 16, France, (Telephone in U.S. (202) 785-6323), (Fax in U.S. (202) 785-0350), www.oecd.org; *Geographical Distribution of Financial Flows to Aid Recipients 2002-2006; International Trade by Commodity Statistics (ITCS); Iron and Steel Industry in 2004 (2006 Edition); 2005 OECD Agricultural Outlook Tables, 1970-2014; OECD Economic Outlook 2008; OECD Economic Survey - Austria 2007;* and STructural ANalysis (STAN) database.

Palgrave Macmillan Ltd., Houndmills, Basingstoke, Hampshire, RG21 6XS, England, (Telephone in U.S. (888) 330-8477), (Fax in U.S. (800) 672-2054), www.palgrave.com; *The Statesman's Yearbook 2008.*

Taylor and Francis Group, An Informa Business, 2 Park Square, Milton Park, Abingdon, Oxford OX14 4RN, United Kingdom, (Dial from U.S. (212) 216-7800), (Fax from U.S. (212) 564-7854), www.tandf.co.uk; *The Europa World Year Book.*

Technical Association of the Pulp and Paper Industry (TAPPI), 15 Technology Parkway South, Norcross, GA 30092, (770) 446-1400, Fax: (770) 446-6947, www.tappi.org; *TAPPI Annual Report.*

United Nations Conference on Trade and Development (UNCTAD), DC2-1120, United Nations, New York, NY 10017, (212) 963-0027, www.unctad.org; *Handbook of Statistics 2005.*

United Nations Food and Agricultural Organization (FAO), Viale delle Terme di Caracalla, 00100 Rome, Italy, (Dial from U.S. (202) 653-2400), (Fax from U.S. (202) 653 5760), www.fao.org; *The State of Food and Agriculture (SOFA) 2006.*

United Nations Statistics Division, New York, NY 10017, (800) 253-9646, Fax: (212) 963-4116, http://unstats.un.org; *Trends in Europe and North America: The Statistical Yearbook of the ECE 2005.*

The World Bank, 1818 H Street, NW, Washington, DC 20433, (202) 473-1000, Fax: (202) 477-6391, www.worldbank.org; *World Development Indicators (WDI) 2008* and *World Development Report 2008.*

AUSTRIA - FERTILITY, HUMAN

M.E. Sharpe, 80 Business Park Drive, Armonk, NY 10504, (800) 541-6563, Fax: (914) 273-2106, www.mesharpe.com; *The Illustrated Book of World Rankings.*

United Nations Statistics Division, New York, NY 10017, (800) 253-9646, Fax: (212) 963-4116, http://unstats.un.org; *Human Development Report 2006* and *Trends in Europe and North America: The Statistical Yearbook of the ECE 2005.*

The World Bank, 1818 H Street, NW, Washington, DC 20433, (202) 473-1000, Fax: (202) 477-6391, www.worldbank.org; *The World Bank Atlas 2003-2004; World Development Indicators (WDI) 2008;* and *World Development Report 2008.*

AUSTRIA - FERTILIZER INDUSTRY

Organisation for Economic Cooperation and Development (OECD), 2 rue Andre Pascal, F-75775 Paris Cedex 16, France, (Telephone in U.S. (202) 785-6323), (Fax in U.S. (202) 785-0350), www.oecd.org; *International Trade by Commodity Statistics (ITCS)* and *2005 OECD Agricultural Outlook Tables, 1970-2014.*

United Nations Food and Agricultural Organization (FAO), Viale delle Terme di Caracalla, 00100 Rome, Italy, (Dial from U.S. (202) 653-2400), (Fax from U.S. (202) 653 5760), www.fao.org; *FAO Fertilizer Yearbook* and *The State of Food and Agriculture (SOFA) 2006.*

United Nations Statistics Division, New York, NY 10017, (800) 253-9646, Fax: (212) 963-4116, http://unstats.un.org; *Statistical Yearbook.*

AUSTRIA - FETAL MORTALITY

See AUSTRIA - MORTALITY

AUSTRIA - FILM

See AUSTRIA - MOTION PICTURES

AUSTRIA - FINANCE

International Monetary Fund (IMF), 700 Nineteenth Street, NW, Washington, DC 20431, (202) 623-7000, Fax: (202) 623-4661, www.imf.org; *International Financial Statistics Yearbook 2007.*

Organisation for Economic Cooperation and Development (OECD), 2 rue Andre Pascal, F-75775 Paris Cedex 16, France, (Telephone in U.S. (202) 785-6323), (Fax in U.S. (202) 785-0350), www.oecd.org; *OECD Economic Outlook 2008.*

Taylor and Francis Group, An Informa Business, 2 Park Square, Milton Park, Abingdon, Oxford OX14 4RN, United Kingdom, (Dial from U.S. (212) 216-7800), (Fax from U.S. (212) 564-7854), www.tandf.co.uk; *The Europa World Year Book.*

United Nations Statistics Division, New York, NY 10017, (800) 253-9646, Fax: (212) 963-4116, http://unstats.un.org; *National Accounts Statistics: Compendium of Income Distribution Statistics.*

The World Bank, 1818 H Street, NW, Washington, DC 20433, (202) 473-1000, Fax: (202) 477-6391, www.worldbank.org; *Austria.*

AUSTRIA - FINANCE, PUBLIC

Banque de France, 48 rue Croix des Petits champs, 75001 Paris, France, www.banque-france.fr/home.htm; *Key Data for the Euro Area* and *Public Finance.*

Bernan Essential Government Publications, 4611-F Assembly Drive, Lanham MD, 20706-4391, (301) 459-2255, Fax: (800) 865-3450, www.bernan.com; *National Accounts Statistics.*

Economist Intelligence Unit, 111 West 57th Street, New York, NY 10019, (212) 554-0600, Fax: (212) 586-1181, www.eiu.com; *Austria Country Report.*

International Monetary Fund (IMF), 700 Nineteenth Street, NW, Washington, DC 20431, (202) 623-7000, Fax: (202) 623-4661, www.imf.org; *Government Finance Statistics Yearbook (2008 Edition); International Financial Statistics; International Financial Statistics Online Service;* and *International Financial Statistics Yearbook 2007.*

M.E. Sharpe, 80 Business Park Drive, Armonk, NY 10504, (800) 541-6563, Fax: (914) 273-2106, www.mesharpe.com; *The Illustrated Book of World Rankings.*

Organisation for Economic Cooperation and Development (OECD), 2 rue Andre Pascal, F-75775 Paris Cedex 16, France, (Telephone in U.S. (202) 785-6323), (Fax in U.S. (202) 785-0350), www.oecd.org; *Financial Market Trends: OECD Periodical; Geographical Distribution of Financial Flows to Aid Recipients 2002-2006; OECD Economic Outlook 2008;* and *Revenue Statistics 1965-2006 - 2007 Edition.*

Palgrave Macmillan Ltd., Houndmills, Basingstoke, Hampshire, RG21 6XS, England, (Telephone in U.S. (888) 330-8477), (Fax in U.S. (800) 672-2054), www.palgrave.com; *The Statesman's Yearbook 2008.*

Taylor and Francis Group, An Informa Business, 2 Park Square, Milton Park, Abingdon, Oxford OX14 4RN, United Kingdom, (Dial from U.S. (212) 216-7800), (Fax from U.S. (212) 564-7854), www.tandf.co.uk; *The Europa World Year Book.*

The World Bank, 1818 H Street, NW, Washington, DC 20433, (202) 473-1000, Fax: (202) 477-6391, www.worldbank.org; *Austria.*

AUSTRIA - FISHERIES

Euromonitor International, Inc., 224 S. Michigan Avenue, Suite 1500, Chicago, IL 60604, (312) 922-1115, Fax: (312) 922-1157, www.euromonitor.com; *European Marketing Data and Statistics 2008.*

M.E. Sharpe, 80 Business Park Drive, Armonk, NY 10504, (800) 541-6563, Fax: (914) 273-2106, www.mesharpe.com; *The Illustrated Book of World Rankings.*

Organisation for Economic Cooperation and Development (OECD), 2 rue Andre Pascal, F-75775 Paris

Cedex 16, France, (Telephone in U.S. (202) 785-6323), (Fax in U.S. (202) 785-0350), www.oecd.org; *International Trade by Commodity Statistics (ITCS)* and STructural ANalysis (STAN) database.

Palgrave Macmillan Ltd., Houndmills, Basingstoke, Hampshire, RG21 6XS, England, (Telephone in U.S. (888) 330-8477), (Fax in U.S. (800) 672-2054), www.palgrave.com; *The Statesman's Yearbook 2008.*

Taylor and Francis Group, An Informa Business, 2 Park Square, Milton Park, Abingdon, Oxford OX14 4RN, United Kingdom, (Dial from U.S. (212) 216-7800), (Fax from U.S. (212) 564-7854), www.tandf.co.uk; *The Europa World Year Book.*

United Nations Conference on Trade and Development (UNCTAD), DC2-1120, United Nations, New York, NY 10017, (212) 963-0027, www.unctad.org; *UNCTAD Commodity Yearbook.*

United Nations Food and Agricultural Organization (FAO), Viale delle Terme di Caracalla, 00100 Rome, Italy, (Dial from U.S. (202) 653-2400), (Fax from U.S. (202) 653 5760), www.fao.org; *FAO Yearbook of Fishery Statistics;* Fishery Databases; FISHSTAT Database. Subjects covered include: Aquaculture production, capture production, fishery commodities; and *The State of Food and Agriculture (SOFA) 2006.*

United Nations Statistics Division, New York, NY 10017, (800) 253-9646, Fax: (212) 963-4116, http://unstats.un.org; *Statistical Yearbook.*

The World Bank, 1818 H Street, NW, Washington, DC 20433, (202) 473-1000, Fax: (202) 477-6391, www.worldbank.org; *Austria.*

AUSTRIA - FLOUR INDUSTRY

United Nations Statistics Division, New York, NY 10017, (800) 253-9646, Fax: (212) 963-4116, http://unstats.un.org; *Statistical Yearbook.*

AUSTRIA - FOOD

Euromonitor International, Inc., 224 S. Michigan Avenue, Suite 1500, Chicago, IL 60604, (312) 922-1115, Fax: (312) 922-1157, www.euromonitor.com; *Retail Trade International 2007.*

Organisation for Economic Cooperation and Development (OECD), 2 rue Andre Pascal, F-75775 Paris Cedex 16, France, (Telephone in U.S. (202) 785-6323), (Fax in U.S. (202) 785-0350), www.oecd.org; *International Trade by Commodity Statistics (ITCS)* and *Towards Sustainable Household Consumption?: Trends and Policies in OECD Countries.*

United Nations Conference on Trade and Development (UNCTAD), DC2-1120, United Nations, New York, NY 10017, (212) 963-0027, www.unctad.org; *UNCTAD Commodity Yearbook.*

United Nations Food and Agricultural Organization (FAO), Viale delle Terme di Caracalla, 00100 Rome, Italy, (Dial from U.S. (202) 653-2400), (Fax from U.S. (202) 653 5760), www.fao.org; *FAO Production Yearbook 2002* and *The State of Food and Agriculture (SOFA) 2006.*

United Nations Statistics Division, New York, NY 10017, (800) 253-9646, Fax: (212) 963-4116, http://unstats.un.org; *Human Development Report 2006.*

AUSTRIA - FOOTWEAR

Organisation for Economic Cooperation and Development (OECD), 2 rue Andre Pascal, F-75775 Paris Cedex 16, France, (Telephone in U.S. (202) 785-6323), (Fax in U.S. (202) 785-0350), www.oecd.org; *Indicators of Industrial Activity.*

AUSTRIA - FOREIGN EXCHANGE RATES

Central Intelligence Agency, Office of Public Affairs, Washington, DC 20505, (703) 482-0623, Fax: (703) 482-1739, www.cia.gov; *The World Factbook.*

Euromonitor International, Inc., 224 S. Michigan Avenue, Suite 1500, Chicago, IL 60604, (312) 922-1115, Fax: (312) 922-1157, www.euromonitor.com; *The World Economic Factbook 2008.*

International Civil Aviation Organization (ICAO), External Relations and Public Information Office (EPO), 999 University Street, Montreal, Quebec H3C 5H7, Canada, (Dial from U.S. (514) 954-8219), (Fax from U.S. (514) 954-6077), www.icao.int; *Civil Aviation Statistics of the World.*

International Monetary Fund (IMF), 700 Nineteenth Street, NW, Washington, DC 20431, (202) 623-7000, Fax: (202) 623-4661, www.imf.org; *International Financial Statistics Yearbook 2007.*

Organisation for Economic Cooperation and Development (OECD), 2 rue Andre Pascal, F-75775 Paris Cedex 16, France, (Telephone in U.S. (202) 785-6323), (Fax in U.S. (202) 785-0350), www.oecd.org; *Financial Market Trends: OECD Periodical; Household, Tourism, Travel: Trends, Environmental Impacts and Policy Responses; OECD Economic Outlook 2008;* and *Revenue Statistics 1965-2006 - 2007 Edition.*

Taylor and Francis Group, An Informa Business, 2 Park Square, Milton Park, Abingdon, Oxford OX14 4RN, United Kingdom, (Dial from U.S. (212) 216-7800), (Fax from U.S. (212) 564-7854), www.tandf.co.uk; *The Europa World Year Book.*

United Nations Statistics Division, New York, NY 10017, (800) 253-9646, Fax: (212) 963-4116, http://unstats.un.org; *Statistical Yearbook; Trends in Europe and North America: The Statistical Yearbook of the ECE 2005;* and *World Statistics Pocketbook.*

AUSTRIA - FORESTS AND FORESTRY

American Forest Paper Association (AFPA), 1111 Nineteenth Street, NW, Suite 800, Washington, DC 20036, (800) 878-8878, www.afandpa.org; *2007 Annual Statistics of Paper, Paperboard, and Wood Pulp.*

Euromonitor International, Inc., 224 S. Michigan Avenue, Suite 1500, Chicago, IL 60604, (312) 922-1115, Fax: (312) 922-1157, www.euromonitor.com; *European Marketing Data and Statistics 2008.*

M.E. Sharpe, 80 Business Park Drive, Armonk, NY 10504, (800) 541-6563, Fax: (914) 273-2106, www.mesharpe.com; *The Illustrated Book of World Rankings.*

Organisation for Economic Cooperation and Development (OECD), 2 rue Andre Pascal, F-75775 Paris Cedex 16, France, (Telephone in U.S. (202) 785-6323), (Fax in U.S. (202) 785-0350), www.oecd.org; *Indicators of Industrial Activity; International Trade by Commodity Statistics (ITCS);* and STructural ANalysis (STAN) database.

Palgrave Macmillan Ltd., Houndmills, Basingstoke, Hampshire, RG21 6XS, England, (Telephone in U.S. (888) 330-8477), (Fax in U.S. (800) 672-2054), www.palgrave.com; *The Statesman's Yearbook 2008.*

Taylor and Francis Group, An Informa Business, 2 Park Square, Milton Park, Abingdon, Oxford OX14 4RN, United Kingdom, (Dial from U.S. (212) 216-7800), (Fax from U.S. (212) 564-7854), www.tandf.co.uk; *The Europa World Year Book.*

Technical Association of the Pulp and Paper Industry (TAPPI), 15 Technology Parkway South, Norcross, GA 30092, (770) 446-1400, Fax: (770) 446-6947, www.tappi.org; *TAPPI Annual Report.*

UNESCO Institute for Statistics, C.P. 6128 Succursale Centre-Ville, Montreal, Quebec, H3C 3J7 Canada, (Dial from U.S. (514) 343-6880), (Fax from U.S. (514) 343 6882), www.uis.unesco.org; *Statistical Tables.*

United Nations Conference on Trade and Development (UNCTAD), DC2-1120, United Nations, New York, NY 10017, (212) 963-0027, www.unctad.org; *UNCTAD Commodity Yearbook.*

United Nations Food and Agricultural Organization (FAO), Viale delle Terme di Caracalla, 00100 Rome, Italy, (Dial from U.S. (202) 653-2400), (Fax from U.S. (202) 653 5760), www.fao.org; *FAO Yearbook of Forest Products* and *The State of Food and Agriculture (SOFA) 2006.*

United Nations Statistics Division, New York, NY 10017, (800) 253-9646, Fax: (212) 963-4116, http://unstats.un.org; *Statistical Yearbook* and *Trends in Europe and North America: The Statistical Yearbook of the ECE 2005.*

The World Bank, 1818 H Street, NW, Washington, DC 20433, (202) 473-1000, Fax: (202) 477-6391, www.worldbank.org; *Austria* and *World Development Report 2008.*

AUSTRIA - FRUIT PRODUCTION

See AUSTRIA - CROPS

AUSTRIA - GAS PRODUCTION

See AUSTRIA - MINERAL INDUSTRIES

AUSTRIA - GEOGRAPHIC INFORMATION SYSTEMS

M.E. Sharpe, 80 Business Park Drive, Armonk, NY 10504, (800) 541-6563, Fax: (914) 273-2106, www.mesharpe.com; *The Illustrated Book of World Rankings.*

The World Bank, 1818 H Street, NW, Washington, DC 20433, (202) 473-1000, Fax: (202) 477-6391, www.worldbank.org; *Austria.*

AUSTRIA - GLASS AND GLASS PRODUCTS

See AUSTRIA - MINERAL INDUSTRIES

AUSTRIA - GOLD INDUSTRY

International Monetary Fund (IMF), 700 Nineteenth Street, NW, Washington, DC 20431, (202) 623-7000, Fax: (202) 623-4661, www.imf.org; *International Financial Statistics Yearbook 2007.*

United Nations Statistics Division, New York, NY 10017, (800) 253-9646, Fax: (212) 963-4116, http://unstats.un.org; *Statistical Yearbook.*

The World Bank, 1818 H Street, NW, Washington, DC 20433, (202) 473-1000, Fax: (202) 477-6391, www.worldbank.org; *World Development Indicators (WDI) 2008.*

AUSTRIA - GOLD PRODUCTION

See AUSTRIA - MINERAL INDUSTRIES

AUSTRIA - GRANTS-IN-AID

International Monetary Fund (IMF), 700 Nineteenth Street, NW, Washington, DC 20431, (202) 623-7000, Fax: (202) 623-4661, www.imf.org; *Government Finance Statistics Yearbook (2008 Edition).*

Organisation for Economic Cooperation and Development (OECD), 2 rue Andre Pascal, F-75775 Paris Cedex 16, France, (Telephone in U.S. (202) 785-6323), (Fax in U.S. (202) 785-0350), www.oecd.org; *Geographical Distribution of Financial Flows to Aid Recipients 2002-2006.*

AUSTRIA - GREEN PEPPER AND CHILIE PRODUCTION

See AUSTRIA - CROPS

AUSTRIA - GROSS DOMESTIC PRODUCT

Economist Intelligence Unit, 111 West 57th Street, New York, NY 10019, (212) 554-0600, Fax: (212) 586-1181, www.eiu.com; *Austria Country Report.*

Euromonitor International, Inc., 224 S. Michigan Avenue, Suite 1500, Chicago, IL 60604, (312) 922-1115, Fax: (312) 922-1157, www.euromonitor.com; *The World Economic Factbook 2008.*

International Monetary Fund (IMF), 700 Nineteenth Street, NW, Washington, DC 20431, (202) 623-7000, Fax: (202) 623-4661, www.imf.org; *International Financial Statistics Yearbook 2007.*

M.E. Sharpe, 80 Business Park Drive, Armonk, NY 10504, (800) 541-6563, Fax: (914) 273-2106, www.mesharpe.com; *The Illustrated Book of World Rankings.*

Organisation for Economic Cooperation and Development (OECD), 2 rue Andre Pascal, F-75775 Paris Cedex 16, France, (Telephone in U.S. (202) 785-6323), (Fax in U.S. (202) 785-0350), www.oecd.org; *Comparison of Gross Domestic Product (GDP) for OECD Countries; Geographical Distribution of Financial Flows to Aid Recipients 2002-2006; OECD*

Economic Outlook 2008; and *Revenue Statistics 1965-2006 - 2007 Edition.*

Taylor and Francis Group, An Informa Business, 2 Park Square, Milton Park, Abingdon, Oxford OX14 4RN, United Kingdom, (Dial from U.S. (212) 216-7800), (Fax from U.S. (212) 564-7854), www.tandf.co.uk; *The Europa World Year Book.*

United Nations Statistics Division, New York, NY 10017, (800) 253-9646, Fax: (212) 963-4116, http://unstats.un.org; *Human Development Report 2006; National Accounts Statistics: Compendium of Income Distribution Statistics; Statistical Yearbook;* and *Trends in Europe and North America: The Statistical Yearbook of the ECE 2005.*

The World Bank, 1818 H Street, NW, Washington, DC 20433, (202) 473-1000, Fax: (202) 477-6391, www.worldbank.org; *World Development Indicators (WDI) 2008* and *World Development Report 2008.*

AUSTRIA - GROSS NATIONAL PRODUCT

European Union, Delegation of the European Commission to the United States, 2300 M Street, NW, Washington, DC 20037, (202) 862-9500, Fax: (202) 429-1766, www.eurunion.org; *The EU Economy, 2007 Review: Moving Europe's Productivity Frontier.*

M.E. Sharpe, 80 Business Park Drive, Armonk, NY 10504, (800) 541-6563, Fax: (914) 273-2106, www.mesharpe.com; *The Illustrated Book of World Rankings.*

Organisation for Economic Cooperation and Development (OECD), 2 rue Andre Pascal, F-75775 Paris Cedex 16, France, (Telephone in U.S. (202) 785-6323), (Fax in U.S. (202) 785-0350), www.oecd.org; *Geographical Distribution of Financial Flows to Aid Recipients 2002-2006; OECD Composite Leading Indicators (CLIs), Updated September 2007;* and *OECD Economic Outlook 2008.*

Palgrave Macmillan Ltd., Houndmills, Basingstoke, Hampshire, RG21 6XS, England, (Telephone in U.S. (888) 330-8477), (Fax in U.S. (800) 672-2054), www.palgrave.com; *The Statesman's Yearbook 2008.*

Taylor and Francis Group, An Informa Business, 2 Park Square, Milton Park, Abingdon, Oxford OX14 4RN, United Kingdom, (Dial from U.S. (212) 216-7800), (Fax from U.S. (212) 564-7854), www.tandf.co.uk; *The Europa World Year Book.*

United Nations Economic Commission for Africa (ECA), PO Box 3001, Addis Ababa, Ethiopia, (Telephone in U.S. (212) 963-4957), www.uneca.org; *African Statistical Yearbook 2006.*

United Nations Statistics Division, New York, NY 10017, (800) 253-9646, Fax: (212) 963-4116, http://unstats.un.org; *Statistical Yearbook.*

The World Bank, 1818 H Street, NW, Washington, DC 20433, (202) 473-1000, Fax: (202) 477-6391, www.worldbank.org; *The World Bank Atlas 2003-2004; World Development Indicators (WDI) 2008;* and *World Development Report 2008.*

AUSTRIA - HIDES AND SKINS INDUSTRY

Organisation for Economic Cooperation and Development (OECD), 2 rue Andre Pascal, F-75775 Paris Cedex 16, France, (Telephone in U.S. (202) 785-6323), (Fax in U.S. (202) 785-0350), www.oecd.org; *Indicators of Industrial Activity* and *International Trade by Commodity Statistics (ITCS).*

United Nations Food and Agricultural Organization (FAO), Viale delle Terme di Caracalla, 00100 Rome, Italy, (Dial from U.S. (202) 653-2400), (Fax from U.S. (202) 653 5760), www.fao.org; *FAO Production Yearbook 2002.*

AUSTRIA - HOUSING

Euromonitor International, Inc., 224 S. Michigan Avenue, Suite 1500, Chicago, IL 60604, (312) 922-1115, Fax: (312) 922-1157, www.euromonitor.com; *World Marketing Data and Statistics.*

M.E. Sharpe, 80 Business Park Drive, Armonk, NY 10504, (800) 541-6563, Fax: (914) 273-2106, www.mesharpe.com; *The Illustrated Book of World Rankings.*

United Nations Statistics Division, New York, NY 10017, (800) 253-9646, Fax: (212) 963-4116, http://unstats.un.org; *Trends in Europe and North America: The Statistical Yearbook of the ECE 2005.*

AUSTRIA - HOUSING - FINANCE

Organisation for Economic Cooperation and Development (OECD), 2 rue Andre Pascal, F-75775 Paris Cedex 16, France, (Telephone in U.S. (202) 785-6323), (Fax in U.S. (202) 785-0350), www.oecd.org; *OECD Main Economic Indicators (MEI).*

AUSTRIA - HOUSING CONSTRUCTION

See AUSTRIA - CONSTRUCTION INDUSTRY

AUSTRIA - ILLITERATE PERSONS

Euromonitor International, Inc., 224 S. Michigan Avenue, Suite 1500, Chicago, IL 60604, (312) 922-1115, Fax: (312) 922-1157, www.euromonitor.com; *The World Economic Factbook 2008.*

Palgrave Macmillan Ltd., Houndmills, Basingstoke, Hampshire, RG21 6XS, England, (Telephone in U.S. (888) 330-8477), (Fax in U.S. (800) 672-2054), www.palgrave.com; *The Statesman's Yearbook 2008.*

United Nations Statistics Division, New York, NY 10017, (800) 253-9646, Fax: (212) 963-4116, http://unstats.un.org; *Human Development Report 2006.*

AUSTRIA - IMPORTS

Central Intelligence Agency, Office of Public Affairs, Washington, DC 20505, (703) 482-0623, Fax: (703) 482-1739, www.cia.gov; *The World Factbook.*

Economist Intelligence Unit, 111 West 57th Street, New York, NY 10019, (212) 554-0600, Fax: (212) 586-1181, www.eiu.com; *Austria Country Report.*

Euromonitor International, Inc., 224 S. Michigan Avenue, Suite 1500, Chicago, IL 60604, (312) 922-1115, Fax: (312) 922-1157, www.euromonitor.com; *The World Economic Factbook 2008* and *World Marketing Data and Statistics.*

International Iron and Steel Institute (IISI), Rue Colonel Bourg 120, B-1140 Brussels, Belgium, www.worldsteel.org; *Steel Statistical Yearbook 2006.*

International Lead and Zinc Study Group (ILZSG), Rua Almirante Barroso 38, 5th Floor, Lisbon 1000 - 013, Portugal, www.ilzsg.org; Interactive Statistical Database.

International Monetary Fund (IMF), 700 Nineteenth Street, NW, Washington, DC 20431, (202) 623-7000, Fax: (202) 623-4661, www.imf.org; *Direction of Trade Statistics Yearbook 2007* and *International Financial Statistics Yearbook 2007.*

Organisation for Economic Cooperation and Development (OECD), 2 rue Andre Pascal, F-75775 Paris Cedex 16, France, (Telephone in U.S. (202) 785-6323), (Fax in U.S. (202) 785-0350), www.oecd.org; *Iron and Steel Industry in 2004 (2006 Edition); 2005 OECD Agricultural Outlook Tables, 1970-2014; OECD Economic Outlook 2008; OECD Economic Survey - Austria 2007;* and STructural ANalysis (STAN) database.

Palgrave Macmillan Ltd., Houndmills, Basingstoke, Hampshire, RG21 6XS, England, (Telephone in U.S. (888) 330-8477), (Fax in U.S. (800) 672-2054), www.palgrave.com; *The Statesman's Yearbook 2008.*

Taylor and Francis Group, An Informa Business, 2 Park Square, Milton Park, Abingdon, Oxford OX14 4RN, United Kingdom, (Dial from U.S. (212) 216-7800), (Fax from U.S. (212) 564-7854), www.tandf.co.uk; *The Europa World Year Book.*

Technical Association of the Pulp and Paper Industry (TAPPI), 15 Technology Parkway South, Norcross, GA 30092, (770) 446-1400, Fax: (770) 446-6947, www.tappi.org; *TAPPI Annual Report.*

United Nations Conference on Trade and Development (UNCTAD), DC2-1120, United Nations, New York, NY 10017, (212) 963-0027, www.unctad.org; *Handbook of Statistics 2005.*

United Nations Food and Agricultural Organization (FAO), Viale delle Terme di Caracalla, 00100 Rome, Italy, (Dial from U.S. (202) 653-2400), (Fax from U.S. (202) 653 5760), www.fao.org; *The State of Food and Agriculture (SOFA) 2006.*

United Nations Statistics Division, New York, NY 10017, (800) 253-9646, Fax: (212) 963-4116, http://unstats.un.org; *Trends in Europe and North America: The Statistical Yearbook of the ECE 2005.*

The World Bank, 1818 H Street, NW, Washington, DC 20433, (202) 473-1000, Fax: (202) 477-6391, www.worldbank.org; *World Development Indicators (WDI) 2008* and *World Development Report 2008.*

AUSTRIA - INCOME TAXES

See AUSTRIA - TAXATION

AUSTRIA - INDUSTRIAL METALS PRODUCTION

See AUSTRIA - MINERAL INDUSTRIES

AUSTRIA - INDUSTRIAL PRODUCTIVITY

International Iron and Steel Institute (IISI), Rue Colonel Bourg 120, B-1140 Brussels, Belgium, www.worldsteel.org; *Steel Statistical Yearbook 2006.*

International Lead and Zinc Study Group (ILZSG), Rua Almirante Barroso 38, 5th Floor, Lisbon 1000 - 013, Portugal, www.ilzsg.org; Interactive Statistical Database.

M.E. Sharpe, 80 Business Park Drive, Armonk, NY 10504, (800) 541-6563, Fax: (914) 273-2106, www.mesharpe.com; *The Illustrated Book of World Rankings.*

Organisation for Economic Cooperation and Development (OECD), 2 rue Andre Pascal, F-75775 Paris Cedex 16, France, (Telephone in U.S. (202) 785-6323), (Fax in U.S. (202) 785-0350), www.oecd.org; *Environmental Impacts of Foreign Direct Investment in the Mining Sector in the Newly Independent States (NIS); Indicators of Industrial Activity; Iron and Steel Industry in 2004 (2006 Edition); A New World Map in Textiles and Clothing: Adjusting to Change; 2005 OECD Agricultural Outlook Tables, 1970-2014; OECD Economic Outlook 2008;* and STructural ANalysis (STAN) database.

Technical Association of the Pulp and Paper Industry (TAPPI), 15 Technology Parkway South, Norcross, GA 30092, (770) 446-1400, Fax: (770) 446-6947, www.tappi.org; *TAPPI Annual Report.*

AUSTRIA - INDUSTRIAL PROPERTY

Organisation for Economic Cooperation and Development (OECD), 2 rue Andre Pascal, F-75775 Paris Cedex 16, France, (Telephone in U.S. (202) 785-6323), (Fax in U.S. (202) 785-0350), www.oecd.org; *World Energy Outlook 2007.*

United Nations Statistics Division, New York, NY 10017, (800) 253-9646, Fax: (212) 963-4116, http://unstats.un.org; *Statistical Yearbook.*

AUSTRIA - INDUSTRIES

Central Intelligence Agency, Office of Public Affairs, Washington, DC 20505, (703) 482-0623, Fax: (703) 482-1739, www.cia.gov; *The World Factbook.*

Economist Intelligence Unit, 111 West 57th Street, New York, NY 10019, (212) 554-0600, Fax: (212) 586-1181, www.eiu.com; *Austria Country Report.*

Euromonitor International, Inc., 224 S. Michigan Avenue, Suite 1500, Chicago, IL 60604, (312) 922-1115, Fax: (312) 922-1157, www.euromonitor.com; *The World Economic Factbook 2008.*

International Labour Office, I.L.O. Publications, 4 route des Morillons, CH-1211 Geneva 22, Switzerland, (Telephone in U.S. (202) 653-7652), (Fax in U.S. (202) 653-7687), www.ilo.org; *Yearbook of Labour Statistics 2006.*

M.E. Sharpe, 80 Business Park Drive, Armonk, NY 10504, (800) 541-6563, Fax: (914) 273-2106, www.mesharpe.com; *The Illustrated Book of World Rankings.*

Organisation for Economic Cooperation and Development (OECD), 2 rue Andre Pascal, F-75775 Paris

Cedex 16, France, (Telephone in U.S. (202) 785-6323), (Fax in U.S. (202) 785-0350), www.oecd.org; *World Energy Outlook 2007.*

Palgrave Macmillan Ltd., Houndmills, Basingstoke, Hampshire, RG21 6XS, England, (Telephone in U.S. (888) 330-8477), (Fax in U.S. (800) 672-2054), www.palgrave.com; *The Statesman's Yearbook 2008.*

Taylor and Francis Group, An Informa Business, 2 Park Square, Milton Park, Abingdon, Oxford OX14 4RN, United Kingdom, (Dial from U.S. (212) 216-7800), (Fax from U.S. (212) 564-7854), www.tandf.co.uk; *The Europa World Year Book.*

United Nations Industrial Development Organization (UNIDO), 1 United Nations Plaza, New York, NY 10017, (212) 963 6890, Fax: (212) 963-7904, http://unido.org; Industrial Statistics Database 2008 (INDSTAT) and *The International Yearbook of Industrial Statistics 2008.*

United Nations Statistics Division, New York, NY 10017, (800) 253-9646, Fax: (212) 963-4116, http://unstats.un.org; *Demographic Yearbook; 2004 Industrial Commodity Statistics Yearbook; Statistical Yearbook;* and *Trends in Europe and North America: The Statistical Yearbook of the ECE 2005.*

The World Bank, 1818 H Street, NW, Washington, DC 20433, (202) 473-1000, Fax: (202) 477-6391, www.worldbank.org; *Austria* and *World Development Indicators (WDI) 2008.*

AUSTRIA - INFANT AND MATERNAL MORTALITY

See AUSTRIA - MORTALITY

AUSTRIA - INTEREST RATES

Organisation for Economic Cooperation and Development (OECD), 2 rue Andre Pascal, F-75775 Paris Cedex 16, France, (Telephone in U.S. (202) 785-6323), (Fax in U.S. (202) 785-0350), www.oecd.org; *Financial Market Trends: OECD Periodical* and *OECD Economic Outlook 2008.*

AUSTRIA - INTERNAL REVENUE

Organisation for Economic Cooperation and Development (OECD), 2 rue Andre Pascal, F-75775 Paris Cedex 16, France, (Telephone in U.S. (202) 785-6323), (Fax in U.S. (202) 785-0350), www.oecd.org; *Revenue Statistics 1965-2006 - 2007 Edition.*

AUSTRIA - INTERNATIONAL FINANCE

Organisation for Economic Cooperation and Development (OECD), 2 rue Andre Pascal, F-75775 Paris Cedex 16, France, (Telephone in U.S. (202) 785-6323), (Fax in U.S. (202) 785-0350), www.oecd.org; *Financial Market Trends: OECD Periodical; OECD Economic Outlook 2008;* and *OECD Main Economic Indicators (MEI).*

AUSTRIA - INTERNATIONAL LIQUIDITY

International Monetary Fund (IMF), 700 Nineteenth Street, NW, Washington, DC 20431, (202) 623-7000, Fax: (202) 623-4661, www.imf.org; *International Financial Statistics Yearbook 2007.*

Organisation for Economic Cooperation and Development (OECD), 2 rue Andre Pascal, F-75775 Paris Cedex 16, France, (Telephone in U.S. (202) 785-6323), (Fax in U.S. (202) 785-0350), www.oecd.org; *Financial Market Trends: OECD Periodical* and *OECD Economic Outlook 2008.*

AUSTRIA - INTERNATIONAL STATISTICS

Organisation for Economic Cooperation and Development (OECD), 2 rue Andre Pascal, F-75775 Paris Cedex 16, France, (Telephone in U.S. (202) 785-6323), (Fax in U.S. (202) 785-0350), www.oecd.org; *Financial Market Trends: OECD Periodical* and *Household, Tourism, Travel: Trends, Environmental Impacts and Policy Responses.*

AUSTRIA - INTERNATIONAL TRADE

Banque de France, 48 rue Croix des Petits champs, 75001 Paris, France, www.banque-france.fr/home.htm; *Monthly Business Survey Overview.*

Bernan Essential Government Publications, 4611-F Assembly Drive, Lanham MD, 20706-4391, (301) 459-2255, Fax: (800) 865-3450, www.bernan.com; *OECD Factbook 2006.*

Economist Intelligence Unit, 111 West 57th Street, New York, NY 10019, (212) 554-0600, Fax: (212) 586-1181, www.eiu.com; *Austria Country Report.*

Euromonitor International, Inc., 224 S. Michigan Avenue, Suite 1500, Chicago, IL 60604, (312) 922-1115, Fax: (312) 922-1157, www.euromonitor.com; *European Marketing Data and Statistics 2008; The World Economic Factbook 2008;* and *World Marketing Data and Statistics.*

Eurostat, Batiment Jean Monnet, Rue Alcide de Gasperi, L-2920 Luxembourg, http://epp.eurostat.ec.europa.eu; Intra- and Extra-EU Trade.

International Iron and Steel Institute (IISI), Rue Colonel Bourg 120, B-1140 Brussels, Belgium, www.worldsteel.org; *Steel Statistical Yearbook 2006.*

M.E. Sharpe, 80 Business Park Drive, Armonk, NY 10504, (800) 541-6563, Fax: (914) 273-2106, www.mesharpe.com; *The Illustrated Book of World Rankings.*

Organisation for Economic Cooperation and Development (OECD), 2 rue Andre Pascal, F-75775 Paris Cedex 16, France, (Telephone in U.S. (202) 785-6323), (Fax in U.S. (202) 785-0350), www.oecd.org; *International Trade by Commodity Statistics (ITCS); 2005 OECD Agricultural Outlook Tables, 1970-2014; OECD Economic Outlook 2008; OECD Economic Survey - Austria 2007; OECD in Figures 2007; OECD Main Economic Indicators (MEI);* and *Statistics on Ship Production, Exports and Orders in 2004.*

Palgrave Macmillan Ltd., Houndmills, Basingstoke, Hampshire, RG21 6XS, England, (Telephone in U.S. (888) 330-8477), (Fax in U.S. (800) 672-2054), www.palgrave.com; *The Statesman's Yearbook 2008.*

Taylor and Francis Group, An Informa Business, 2 Park Square, Milton Park, Abingdon, Oxford OX14 4RN, United Kingdom, (Dial from U.S. (212) 216-7800), (Fax from U.S. (212) 564-7854), www.tandf.co.uk; *The Europa World Year Book.*

United Nations Conference on Trade and Development (UNCTAD), DC2-1120, United Nations, New York, NY 10017, (212) 963-0027, www.unctad.org; *UNCTAD Commodity Yearbook.*

United Nations Food and Agricultural Organization (FAO), Viale delle Terme di Caracalla, 00100 Rome, Italy, (Dial from U.S. (202) 653-2400), (Fax from U.S. (202) 653 5760), www.fao.org; *FAO Trade Yearbook* and *The State of Food and Agriculture (SOFA) 2006.*

United Nations Statistics Division, New York, NY 10017, (800) 253-9646, Fax: (212) 963-4116, http://unstats.un.org; *International Trade Statistics Yearbook* and *Statistical Yearbook.*

The World Bank, 1818 H Street, NW, Washington, DC 20433, (202) 473-1000, Fax: (202) 477-6391, www.worldbank.org; *Austria; World Development Indicators (WDI) 2008;* and *World Development Report 2008.*

World Trade Organization (WTO), Centre William Rappard, Rue de Lausanne 154, CH-1211 Geneva 21, Switzerland, www.wto.org; *International Trade Statistics 2006.*

AUSTRIA - INTERNET USERS

International Telecommunication Union (ITU), Place des Nations, 1211 Geneva 20, Switzerland, www.itu.int; *World Telecommunication/ICT Indicators Database on CD-ROM; World Telecommunication/ICT Indicators Database Online;* and *Yearbook of Statistics - Telecommunication Services (Chronological Time Series 1997-2006).*

AUSTRIA - INVESTMENTS

International Monetary Fund (IMF), 700 Nineteenth Street, NW, Washington, DC 20431, (202) 623-7000, Fax: (202) 623-4661, www.imf.org; *International Financial Statistics Yearbook 2007.*

Organisation for Economic Cooperation and Development (OECD), 2 rue Andre Pascal, F-75775 Paris Cedex 16, France, (Telephone in U.S. (202) 785-6323), (Fax in U.S. (202) 785-0350), www.oecd.org; *Financial Market Trends: OECD Periodical; Iron and Steel Industry in 2004 (2006 Edition); A New World Map in Textiles and Clothing: Adjusting to Change; OECD Economic Outlook 2008;* and STructural ANalysis (STAN) database.

AUSTRIA - IRON AND IRON ORE PRODUCTION

See AUSTRIA - MINERAL INDUSTRIES

AUSTRIA - LABOR

Central Intelligence Agency, Office of Public Affairs, Washington, DC 20505, (703) 482-0623, Fax: (703) 482-1739, www.cia.gov; *The World Factbook.*

Euromonitor International, Inc., 224 S. Michigan Avenue, Suite 1500, Chicago, IL 60604, (312) 922-1115, Fax: (312) 922-1157, www.euromonitor.com; *World Marketing Data and Statistics.*

International Labour Office, I.L.O. Publications, 4 route des Morillons, CH-1211 Geneva 22, Switzerland, (Telephone in U.S. (202) 653-7652), (Fax in U.S. (202) 653-7687), www.ilo.org; *Yearbook of Labour Statistics 2006.*

M.E. Sharpe, 80 Business Park Drive, Armonk, NY 10504, (800) 541-6563, Fax: (914) 273-2106, www.mesharpe.com; *The Illustrated Book of World Rankings.*

Organisation for Economic Cooperation and Development (OECD), 2 rue Andre Pascal, F-75775 Paris Cedex 16, France, (Telephone in U.S. (202) 785-6323), (Fax in U.S. (202) 785-0350), www.oecd.org; *Iron and Steel Industry in 2004 (2006 Edition); A New World Map in Textiles and Clothing: Adjusting to Change; OECD Economic Outlook 2008; OECD Economic Survey - Austria 2007; OECD Employment Outlook 2007; OECD Main Economic Indicators (MEI);* and *Statistics on Ship Production, Exports and Orders in 2004.*

Palgrave Macmillan Ltd., Houndmills, Basingstoke, Hampshire, RG21 6XS, England, (Telephone in U.S. (888) 330-8477), (Fax in U.S. (800) 672-2054), www.palgrave.com; *The Statesman's Yearbook 2008.*

United Nations Food and Agricultural Organization (FAO), Viale delle Terme di Caracalla, 00100 Rome, Italy, (Dial from U.S. (202) 653-2400), (Fax from U.S. (202) 653 5760), www.fao.org; *The State of Food and Agriculture (SOFA) 2006.*

United Nations Statistics Division, New York, NY 10017, (800) 253-9646, Fax: (212) 963-4116, http://unstats.un.org; *Human Development Report 2006.*

The World Bank, 1818 H Street, NW, Washington, DC 20433, (202) 473-1000, Fax: (202) 477-6391, www.worldbank.org; *The World Bank Atlas 2003-2004; World Development Indicators (WDI) 2008;* and *World Development Report 2008.*

AUSTRIA - LAND USE

Central Intelligence Agency, Office of Public Affairs, Washington, DC 20505, (703) 482-0623, Fax: (703) 482-1739, www.cia.gov; *The World Factbook.*

Euromonitor International, Inc., 224 S. Michigan Avenue, Suite 1500, Chicago, IL 60604, (312) 922-1115, Fax: (312) 922-1157, www.euromonitor.com; *European Marketing Data and Statistics 2008.*

United Nations Food and Agricultural Organization (FAO), Viale delle Terme di Caracalla, 00100 Rome, Italy, (Dial from U.S. (202) 653-2400), (Fax from U.S. (202) 653 5760), www.fao.org; *FAO Production Yearbook 2002.*

The World Bank, 1818 H Street, NW, Washington, DC 20433, (202) 473-1000, Fax: (202) 477-6391, www.worldbank.org; *World Development Report 2008.*

AUSTRIA - LEATHER INDUSTRY AND TRADE

Organisation for Economic Cooperation and Development (OECD), 2 rue Andre Pascal, F-75775 Paris Cedex 16, France, (Telephone in U.S. (202) 785-

6323), (Fax in U.S. (202) 785-0350), www.oecd.org; *Indicators of Industrial Activity.*

AUSTRIA - LIBRARIES

Euromonitor International, Inc., 224 S. Michigan Avenue, Suite 1500, Chicago, IL 60604, (312) 922-1115, Fax: (312) 922-1157, www.euromonitor.com; *European Marketing Data and Statistics 2008.*

M.E. Sharpe, 80 Business Park Drive, Armonk, NY 10504, (800) 541-6563, Fax: (914) 273-2106, www.mesharpe.com; *The Illustrated Book of World Rankings.*

UNESCO Institute for Statistics, C.P. 6128 Succursale Centre-Ville, Montreal, Quebec, H3C 3J7 Canada, (Dial from U.S. (514) 343-6880), (Fax from U.S. (514) 343 6882), www.uis.unesco.org; *Statistical Tables.*

United Nations Statistics Division, New York, NY 10017, (800) 253-9646, Fax: (212) 963-4116, http://unstats.un.org; *Trends in Europe and North America: The Statistical Yearbook of the ECE 2005.*

AUSTRIA - LIFE EXPECTANCY

Central Intelligence Agency, Office of Public Affairs, Washington, DC 20505, (703) 482-0623, Fax: (703) 482-1739, www.cia.gov; *The World Factbook.*

Euromonitor International, Inc., 224 S. Michigan Avenue, Suite 1500, Chicago, IL 60604, (312) 922-1115, Fax: (312) 922-1157, www.euromonitor.com; *The World Economic Factbook 2008.*

Organisation for Economic Cooperation and Development (OECD), 2 rue Andre Pascal, F-75775 Paris Cedex 16, France, (Telephone in U.S. (202) 785-6323), (Fax in U.S. (202) 785-0350), www.oecd.org; *OECD Economic Outlook 2008.*

Palgrave Macmillan Ltd., Houndmills, Basingstoke, Hampshire, RG21 6XS, England, (Telephone in U.S. (888) 330-8477), (Fax in U.S. (800) 672-2054), www.palgrave.com; *The Statesman's Yearbook 2008.*

United Nations Statistics Division, New York, NY 10017, (800) 253-9646, Fax: (212) 963-4116, http://unstats.un.org; *Human Development Report 2006; Trends in Europe and North America: The Statistical Yearbook of the ECE 2005;* and *World Statistics Pocketbook.*

The World Bank, 1818 H Street, NW, Washington, DC 20433, (202) 473-1000, Fax: (202) 477-6391, www.worldbank.org; *The World Bank Atlas 2003-2004* and *World Development Report 2008.*

AUSTRIA - LITERACY

Euromonitor International, Inc., 224 S. Michigan Avenue, Suite 1500, Chicago, IL 60604, (312) 922-1115, Fax: (312) 922-1157, www.euromonitor.com; *World Marketing Data and Statistics.*

AUSTRIA - LIVESTOCK

Euromonitor International, Inc., 224 S. Michigan Avenue, Suite 1500, Chicago, IL 60604, (312) 922-1115, Fax: (312) 922-1157, www.euromonitor.com; *European Marketing Data and Statistics 2008.*

M.E. Sharpe, 80 Business Park Drive, Armonk, NY 10504, (800) 541-6563, Fax: (914) 273-2106, www.mesharpe.com; *The Illustrated Book of World Rankings.*

Organisation for Economic Cooperation and Development (OECD), 2 rue Andre Pascal, F-75775 Paris Cedex 16, France, (Telephone in U.S. (202) 785-6323), (Fax in U.S. (202) 785-0350), www.oecd.org; *2005 OECD Agricultural Outlook Tables, 1970-2014.*

Palgrave Macmillan Ltd., Houndmills, Basingstoke, Hampshire, RG21 6XS, England, (Telephone in U.S. (888) 330-8477), (Fax in U.S. (800) 672-2054), www.palgrave.com; *The Statesman's Yearbook 2008.*

Taylor and Francis Group, An Informa Business, 2 Park Square, Milton Park, Abingdon, Oxford OX14 4RN, United Kingdom, (Dial from U.S. (212) 216-7800), (Fax from U.S. (212) 564-7854), www.tandf.co.uk; *The Europa World Year Book.*

United Nations Conference on Trade and Development (UNCTAD), DC2-1120, United Nations, New York, NY 10017, (212) 963-0027, www.unctad.org; *UNCTAD Commodity Yearbook.*

United Nations Food and Agricultural Organization (FAO), Viale delle Terme di Caracalla, 00100 Rome, Italy, (Dial from U.S. (202) 653-2400), (Fax from U.S. (202) 653 5760), www.fao.org; *FAO Production Yearbook 2002* and *The State of Food and Agriculture (SOFA) 2006.*

United Nations Statistics Division, New York, NY 10017, (800) 253-9646, Fax: (212) 963-4116, http://unstats.un.org; *Statistical Yearbook.*

AUSTRIA - MACHINERY

Organisation for Economic Cooperation and Development (OECD), 2 rue Andre Pascal, F-75775 Paris Cedex 16, France, (Telephone in U.S. (202) 785-6323), (Fax in U.S. (202) 785-0350), www.oecd.org; *Indicators of Industrial Activity.*

AUSTRIA - MAGNESIUM PRODUCTION AND CONSUMPTION

See AUSTRIA - MINERAL INDUSTRIES

AUSTRIA - MANUFACTURES

M.E. Sharpe, 80 Business Park Drive, Armonk, NY 10504, (800) 541-6563, Fax: (914) 273-2106, www.mesharpe.com; *The Illustrated Book of World Rankings.*

Organisation for Economic Cooperation and Development (OECD), 2 rue Andre Pascal, F-75775 Paris Cedex 16, France, (Telephone in U.S. (202) 785-6323), (Fax in U.S. (202) 785-0350), www.oecd.org; *Indicators of Industrial Activity; International Trade by Commodity Statistics (ITCS); OECD Economic Survey - Austria 2007; OECD Main Economic Indicators (MEI);* and STructural ANalysis (STAN) database.

United Nations Statistics Division, New York, NY 10017, (800) 253-9646, Fax: (212) 963-4116, http://unstats.un.org; *Statistical Yearbook.*

The World Bank, 1818 H Street, NW, Washington, DC 20433, (202) 473-1000, Fax: (202) 477-6391, www.worldbank.org; *World Development Indicators (WDI) 2008.*

AUSTRIA - MARRIAGE

M.E. Sharpe, 80 Business Park Drive, Armonk, NY 10504, (800) 541-6563, Fax: (914) 273-2106, www.mesharpe.com; *The Illustrated Book of World Rankings.*

Taylor and Francis Group, An Informa Business, 2 Park Square, Milton Park, Abingdon, Oxford OX14 4RN, United Kingdom, (Dial from U.S. (212) 216-7800), (Fax from U.S. (212) 564-7854), www.tandf.co.uk; *The Europa World Year Book.*

United Nations Statistics Division, New York, NY 10017, (800) 253-9646, Fax: (212) 963-4116, http://unstats.un.org; *Demographic Yearbook; Statistical Yearbook;* and *Trends in Europe and North America: The Statistical Yearbook of the ECE 2005.*

AUSTRIA - MEAT PRODUCTION

See AUSTRIA - LIVESTOCK

AUSTRIA - MERCURY PRODUCTION

See AUSTRIA - MINERAL INDUSTRIES

AUSTRIA - MILK PRODUCTION

See AUSTRIA - DAIRY PROCESSING

AUSTRIA - MINERAL INDUSTRIES

Commodity Research Bureau, 330 South Wells Street, Suite 612, Chicago, IL 60606-7110, (800) 621-5271, Fax: (312) 939-4135, www.crbtrader.com; *2006 CRB Commodity Yearbook and CD.*

Eurostat, Batiment Jean Monnet, Rue Alcide de Gasperi, L-2920 Luxembourg, http://epp.eurostat.ec.europa.eu; *Energy - Monthly Statistics* and *Panorama of Energy - 2007 Edition.*

International Energy Agency (IEA), 9, rue de la Federation, 75739 Paris Cedex 15, France, www.iea.org; *Key World Energy Statistics 2007.*

International Iron and Steel Institute (IISI), Rue Colonel Bourg 120, B-1140 Brussels, Belgium, www.worldsteel.org; *Steel Statistical Yearbook 2006.*

International Lead and Zinc Study Group (ILZSG), Rua Almirante Barroso 38, 5th Floor, Lisbon 1000 - 013, Portugal, www.ilzsg.org; Interactive Statistical Database.

M.E. Sharpe, 80 Business Park Drive, Armonk, NY 10504, (800) 541-6563, Fax: (914) 273-2106, www.mesharpe.com; *The Illustrated Book of World Rankings.*

Organisation for Economic Cooperation and Development (OECD), 2 rue Andre Pascal, F-75775 Paris Cedex 16, France, (Telephone in U.S. (202) 785-6323), (Fax in U.S. (202) 785-0350), www.oecd.org; *Coal Information: 2007 Edition; Energy Statistics of OECD Countries* (2007 Edition); *Environmental Impacts of Foreign Direct Investment in the Mining Sector in the Newly Independent States (NIS); Indicators of Industrial Activity; International Trade by Commodity Statistics (ITCS); Iron and Steel Industry in 2004 (2006 Edition); OECD Economic Survey - Austria 2007; OECD Employment Outlook 2007; OECD Main Economic Indicators (MEI);* STructural ANalysis (STAN) database; and *World Energy Outlook 2007.*

Palgrave Macmillan Ltd., Houndmills, Basingstoke, Hampshire, RG21 6XS, England, (Telephone in U.S. (888) 330-8477), (Fax in U.S. (800) 672-2054), www.palgrave.com; *The Statesman's Yearbook 2008.*

Platts, 2 Penn Plaza, 25th Floor, New York, NY 10121-2298, (212) 904-3070, www.platts.com; *EU Energy.*

Taylor and Francis Group, An Informa Business, 2 Park Square, Milton Park, Abingdon, Oxford OX14 4RN, United Kingdom, (Dial from U.S. (212) 216-7800), (Fax from U.S. (212) 564-7854), www.tandf.co.uk; *The Europa World Year Book.*

United Nations Conference on Trade and Development (UNCTAD), DC2-1120, United Nations, New York, NY 10017, (212) 963-0027, www.unctad.org; *UNCTAD Commodity Yearbook.*

United Nations Statistics Division, New York, NY 10017, (800) 253-9646, Fax: (212) 963-4116, http://unstats.un.org; *Statistical Yearbook.*

The World Bank, 1818 H Street, NW, Washington, DC 20433, (202) 473-1000, Fax: (202) 477-6391, www.worldbank.org; *Austria.*

World Bureau of Metal Statistics (WBMS), 27a High Street, Ware, Hertfordshire, SG12 9BA, United Kingdom, www.world-bureau.com; *Annual Stainless Steel Statistics; World Flow Charts; World Metal Statistics; World Nickel Statistics;* and *World Tin Statistics.*

AUSTRIA - MONEY

European Central Bank (ECB), Postfach 160319, D-60066 Frankfurt am Main, Germany, www.ecb.int; *Monetary Developments in the Euro Area; Monthly Bulletin;* and *Statistics Pocket Book.*

Organisation for Economic Cooperation and Development (OECD), 2 rue Andre Pascal, F-75775 Paris Cedex 16, France, (Telephone in U.S. (202) 785-6323), (Fax in U.S. (202) 785-0350), www.oecd.org; *OECD Economic Survey - Austria 2007.*

AUSTRIA - MONEY EXCHANGE RATES

See AUSTRIA - FOREIGN EXCHANGE RATES

AUSTRIA - MONEY SUPPLY

Economist Intelligence Unit, 111 West 57th Street, New York, NY 10019, (212) 554-0600, Fax: (212) 586-1181, www.eiu.com; *Austria Country Report.*

International Monetary Fund (IMF), 700 Nineteenth Street, NW, Washington, DC 20431, (202) 623-7000, Fax: (202) 623-4661, www.imf.org; *International Financial Statistics Yearbook 2007.*

Organisation for Economic Cooperation and Development (OECD), 2 rue Andre Pascal, F-75775 Paris

Cedex 16, France, (Telephone in U.S. (202) 785-6323), (Fax in U.S. (202) 785-0350), www.oecd.org; *OECD Economic Outlook 2008.*

Taylor and Francis Group, An Informa Business, 2 Park Square, Milton Park, Abingdon, Oxford OX14 4RN, United Kingdom, (Dial from U.S. (212) 216-7800), (Fax from U.S. (212) 564-7854), www.tandf.co.uk; *The Europa World Year Book.*

United Nations Statistics Division, New York, NY 10017, (800) 253-9646, Fax: (212) 963-4116, http://unstats.un.org; *Statistical Yearbook.*

The World Bank, 1818 H Street, NW, Washington, DC 20433, (202) 473-1000, Fax: (202) 477-6391, www.worldbank.org; *Austria* and *World Development Indicators (WDI) 2008.*

AUSTRIA - MORTALITY

Central Intelligence Agency, Office of Public Affairs, Washington, DC 20505, (703) 482-0623, Fax: (703) 482-1739, www.cia.gov; *The World Factbook.*

Euromonitor International, Inc., 224 S. Michigan Avenue, Suite 1500, Chicago, IL 60604, (312) 922-1115, Fax: (312) 922-1157, www.euromonitor.com; *The World Economic Factbook 2008.*

Palgrave Macmillan Ltd., Houndmills, Basingstoke, Hampshire, RG21 6XS, England, (Telephone in U.S. (888) 330-8477), (Fax in U.S. (800) 672-2054), www.palgrave.com; *The Statesman's Yearbook 2008.*

Taylor and Francis Group, An Informa Business, 2 Park Square, Milton Park, Abingdon, Oxford OX14 4RN, United Kingdom, (Dial from U.S. (212) 216-7800), (Fax from U.S. (212) 564-7854), www.tandf.co.uk; *The Europa World Year Book.*

UNICEF, 3 United Nations Plaza, New York, NY 10017, (800) 253-9646, Fax: (212) 887-7465, www.unicef.org; *The State of the World's Children 2008.*

United Nations Statistics Division, New York, NY 10017, (800) 253-9646, Fax: (212) 963-4116, http://unstats.un.org; *Human Development Report 2006; Statistical Yearbook; Trends in Europe and North America: The Statistical Yearbook of the ECE 2005;* and *World Statistics Pocketbook.*

The World Bank, 1818 H Street, NW, Washington, DC 20433, (202) 473-1000, Fax: (202) 477-6391, www.worldbank.org; *The World Bank Atlas 2003-2004; World Development Indicators (WDI) 2008;* and *World Development Report 2008.*

World Health Organization (WHO), Avenue Appia 20, 1211 Geneve 27, Switzerland, (Telephone in U.S. (212) 331-9081), www.who.int; The WHO Global Atlas of Infectious Diseases and *World Health Report 2006.*

AUSTRIA - MOTION PICTURES

Palgrave Macmillan Ltd., Houndmills, Basingstoke, Hampshire, RG21 6XS, England, (Telephone in U.S. (888) 330-8477), (Fax in U.S. (800) 672-2054), www.palgrave.com; *The Statesman's Yearbook 2008.*

UNESCO Institute for Statistics, C.P. 6128 Succursale Centre-Ville, Montreal, Quebec, H3C 3J7 Canada, (Dial from U.S. (514) 343-6880), (Fax from U.S. (514) 343 6882), www.uis.unesco.org; *Statistical Tables.*

United Nations Statistics Division, New York, NY 10017, (800) 253-9646, Fax: (212) 963-4116, http://unstats.un.org; *Statistical Yearbook.*

AUSTRIA - MOTOR VEHICLES

International Labour Office, I.L.O. Publications, 4 route des Morillons, CH-1211 Geneva 22, Switzerland, (Telephone in U.S. (202) 653-7652), (Fax in U.S. (202) 653-7687), www.ilo.org; *Yearbook of Labour Statistics 2006.*

Taylor and Francis Group, An Informa Business, 2 Park Square, Milton Park, Abingdon, Oxford OX14 4RN, United Kingdom, (Dial from U.S. (212) 216-7800), (Fax from U.S. (212) 564-7854), www.tandf.co.uk; *The Europa World Year Book.*

United Nations Statistics Division, New York, NY 10017, (800) 253-9646, Fax: (212) 963-4116, http://unstats.un.org; *Statistical Yearbook.*

AUSTRIA - MUSEUMS

M.E. Sharpe, 80 Business Park Drive, Armonk, NY 10504, (800) 541-6563, Fax: (914) 273-2106, www.mesharpe.com; *The Illustrated Book of World Rankings.*

UNESCO Institute for Statistics, C.P. 6128 Succursale Centre-Ville, Montreal, Quebec, H3C 3J7 Canada, (Dial from U.S. (514) 343-6880), (Fax from U.S. (514) 343 6882), www.uis.unesco.org; *Statistical Tables.*

AUSTRIA - NATIONAL INCOME

United Nations Statistics Division, New York, NY 10017, (800) 253-9646, Fax: (212) 963-4116, http://unstats.un.org; *Statistical Yearbook.*

AUSTRIA - NATURAL GAS PRODUCTION

See AUSTRIA - MINERAL INDUSTRIES

AUSTRIA - NICKEL AND NICKEL ORE

See AUSTRIA - MINERAL INDUSTRIES

AUSTRIA - NUTRITION

United Nations Food and Agricultural Organization (FAO), Viale delle Terme di Caracalla, 00100 Rome, Italy, (Dial from U.S. (202) 653-2400), (Fax from U.S. (202) 653 5760), www.fao.org; *The State of Food and Agriculture (SOFA) 2006.*

AUSTRIA - OATS PRODUCTION

See AUSTRIA - CROPS

AUSTRIA - OILSEED PLANTS

Organisation for Economic Cooperation and Development (OECD), 2 rue Andre Pascal, F-75775 Paris Cedex 16, France, (Telephone in U.S. (202) 785-6323), (Fax in U.S. (202) 785-0350), www.oecd.org; *International Trade by Commodity Statistics (ITCS).*

AUSTRIA - OLDER PEOPLE

M.E. Sharpe, 80 Business Park Drive, Armonk, NY 10504, (800) 541-6563, Fax: (914) 273-2106, www.mesharpe.com; *The Illustrated Book of World Rankings.*

AUSTRIA - PAPER

See AUSTRIA - FORESTS AND FORESTRY

AUSTRIA - PEANUT PRODUCTION

See AUSTRIA - CROPS

AUSTRIA - PERIODICALS

UNESCO Institute for Statistics, C.P. 6128 Succursale Centre-Ville, Montreal, Quebec, H3C 3J7 Canada, (Dial from U.S. (514) 343-6880), (Fax from U.S. (514) 343 6882), www.uis.unesco.org; *Statistical Tables.*

AUSTRIA - PESTICIDES

United Nations Food and Agricultural Organization (FAO), Viale delle Terme di Caracalla, 00100 Rome, Italy, (Dial from U.S. (202) 653-2400), (Fax from U.S. (202) 653 5760), www.fao.org; *The State of Food and Agriculture (SOFA) 2006.*

AUSTRIA - PETROLEUM INDUSTRY AND TRADE

Euromonitor International, Inc., 224 S. Michigan Avenue, Suite 1500, Chicago, IL 60604, (312) 922-1115, Fax: (312) 922-1157, www.euromonitor.com; *European Marketing Data and Statistics 2008.*

International Energy Agency (IEA), 9, rue de la Federation, 75739 Paris Cedex 15, France, www.iea.org; *Key World Energy Statistics 2007.*

M.E. Sharpe, 80 Business Park Drive, Armonk, NY 10504, (800) 541-6563, Fax: (914) 273-2106, www.mesharpe.com; *The Illustrated Book of World Rankings.*

Organisation for Economic Cooperation and Development (OECD), 2 rue Andre Pascal, F-75775 Paris Cedex 16, France, (Telephone in U.S. (202) 785-6323), (Fax in U.S. (202) 785-0350), www.oecd.org; *Energy Statistics of OECD Countries* (2007 Edition); *Indicators of Industrial Activity; International Trade by Commodity Statistics (ITCS); Oil Information 2006 Edition;* and *World Energy Outlook 2007.*

Palgrave Macmillan Ltd., Houndmills, Basingstoke, Hampshire, RG21 6XS, England, (Telephone in U.S. (888) 330-8477), (Fax in U.S. (800) 672-2054), www.palgrave.com; *The Statesman's Yearbook 2008.*

PennWell Corporation, 1421 South Sheridan Road, Tulsa, OK 74112, (918) 835-3161, www.pennwell.com; *International Petroleum Encyclopedia 2007.*

U.S. Department of Energy (DOE), Energy Information Administration (EIA), 1000 Independence Avenue, SW, Washington, DC 20585, (202) 586-8800, www.eia.doe.gov; *International Energy Annual 2004* and *International Energy Outlook 2006.*

United Nations Conference on Trade and Development (UNCTAD), DC2-1120, United Nations, New York, NY 10017, (212) 963-0027, www.unctad.org; *UNCTAD Commodity Yearbook.*

United Nations Food and Agricultural Organization (FAO), Viale delle Terme di Caracalla, 00100 Rome, Italy, (Dial from U.S. (202) 653-2400), (Fax from U.S. (202) 653 5760), www.fao.org; *The State of Food and Agriculture (SOFA) 2006.*

United Nations Statistics Division, New York, NY 10017, (800) 253-9646, Fax: (212) 963-4116, http://unstats.un.org; *Statistical Yearbook* and *Trends in Europe and North America: The Statistical Yearbook of the ECE 2005.*

AUSTRIA - PHOSPHATES PRODUCTION

See AUSTRIA - MINERAL INDUSTRIES

AUSTRIA - PIPELINES

United Nations Statistics Division, New York, NY 10017, (800) 253-9646, Fax: (212) 963-4116, http://unstats.un.org; *Annual Bulletin of Transport Statistics for Europe and North America 2004.*

AUSTRIA - PLASTICS INDUSTRY AND TRADE

Organisation for Economic Cooperation and Development (OECD), 2 rue Andre Pascal, F-75775 Paris Cedex 16, France, (Telephone in U.S. (202) 785-6323), (Fax in U.S. (202) 785-0350), www.oecd.org; *International Trade by Commodity Statistics (ITCS).*

United Nations Statistics Division, New York, NY 10017, (800) 253-9646, Fax: (212) 963-4116, http://unstats.un.org; *Statistical Yearbook.*

AUSTRIA - PLATINUM PRODUCTION

See AUSTRIA - MINERAL INDUSTRIES

AUSTRIA - POLITICAL SCIENCE

Central Intelligence Agency, Office of Public Affairs, Washington, DC 20505, (703) 482-0623, Fax: (703) 482-1739, www.cia.gov; *The World Factbook.*

International Monetary Fund (IMF), 700 Nineteenth Street, NW, Washington, DC 20431, (202) 623-7000, Fax: (202) 623-4661, www.imf.org; *Government Finance Statistics Yearbook (2008 Edition)* and *International Financial Statistics Yearbook 2007.*

Organisation for Economic Cooperation and Development (OECD), 2 rue Andre Pascal, F-75775 Paris Cedex 16, France, (Telephone in U.S. (202) 785-6323), (Fax in U.S. (202) 785-0350), www.oecd.org; *OECD Economic Outlook 2008* and *Revenue Statistics 1965-2006 - 2007 Edition.*

Palgrave Macmillan Ltd., Houndmills, Basingstoke, Hampshire, RG21 6XS, England, (Telephone in U.S. (888) 330-8477), (Fax in U.S. (800) 672-2054), www.palgrave.com; *The Statesman's Yearbook 2008.*

Taylor and Francis Group, An Informa Business, 2 Park Square, Milton Park, Abingdon, Oxford OX14 4RN, United Kingdom, (Dial from U.S. (212) 216-

7800), (Fax from U.S. (212) 564-7854), www.tandf.co.uk; *The Europa World Year Book.*

United Nations Statistics Division, New York, NY 10017, (800) 253-9646, Fax: (212) 963-4116, http://unstats.un.org; *National Accounts Statistics: Compendium of Income Distribution Statistics.*

The World Bank, 1818 H Street, NW, Washington, DC 20433, (202) 473-1000, Fax: (202) 477-6391, www.worldbank.org; *World Development Indicators (WDI) 2008* and *World Development Report 2008.*

AUSTRIA - POPULATION

Banque de France, 48 rue Croix des Petits champs, 75001 Paris, France, www.banque-france.fr/home.htm; *Key Data for the Euro Area.*

Central Intelligence Agency, Office of Public Affairs, Washington, DC 20505, (703) 482-0623, Fax: (703) 482-1739, www.cia.gov; *The World Factbook.*

Economist Intelligence Unit, 111 West 57th Street, New York, NY 10019, (212) 554-0600, Fax: (212) 586-1181, www.eiu.com; *Austria Country Report.*

Euromonitor International, Inc., 224 S. Michigan Avenue, Suite 1500, Chicago, IL 60604, (312) 922-1115, Fax: (312) 922-1157, www.euromonitor.com; *European Marketing Data and Statistics 2008* and *The World Economic Factbook 2008.*

Eurostat, Batiment Jean Monnet, Rue Alcide de Gasperi, L-2920 Luxembourg, http://epp.eurostat.ec.europa.eu; *The Life of Women and Men in Europe - A Statistical Portrait.*

International Labour Office, I.L.O. Publications, 4 route des Morillons, CH-1211 Geneva 22, Switzerland, (Telephone in U.S. (202) 653-7652), (Fax in U.S. (202) 653-7687), www.ilo.org; *Yearbook of Labour Statistics 2006.*

M.E. Sharpe, 80 Business Park Drive, Armonk, NY 10504, (800) 541-6563, Fax: (914) 273-2106, www.mesharpe.com; *The Illustrated Book of World Rankings.*

Organisation for Economic Cooperation and Development (OECD), 2 rue Andre Pascal, F-75775 Paris Cedex 16, France, (Telephone in U.S. (202) 785-6323), (Fax in U.S. (202) 785-0350), www.oecd.org; *Labour Force Statistics: 1986-2005, 2007 Edition.*

Palgrave Macmillan Ltd., Houndmills, Basingstoke, Hampshire, RG21 6XS, England, (Telephone in U.S. (888) 330-8477), (Fax in U.S. (800) 672-2054), www.palgrave.com; *The Statesman's Yearbook 2008.*

Taylor and Francis Group, An Informa Business, 2 Park Square, Milton Park, Abingdon, Oxford OX14 4RN, United Kingdom, (Dial from U.S. (212) 216-7800), (Fax from U.S. (212) 564-7854), www.tandf.co.uk; *The Europa World Year Book.*

U.S. Department of State (DOS), 2201 C Street NW, Washington, DC 20520, (202) 647-4000, www.state.gov; *World Military Expenditures and Arms Transfers (WMEAT).*

United Nations Food and Agricultural Organization (FAO), Viale delle Terme di Caracalla, 00100 Rome, Italy, (Dial from U.S. (202) 653-2400), (Fax from U.S. (202) 653 5760), www.fao.org; *FAO Production Yearbook 2002.*

United Nations Statistics Division, New York, NY 10017, (800) 253-9646, Fax: (212) 963-4116, http://unstats.un.org; *Demographic Yearbook; Human Development Report 2006; Statistical Yearbook; Trends in Europe and North America: The Statistical Yearbook of the ECE 2005;* and *World Statistics Pocketbook.*

The World Bank, 1818 H Street, NW, Washington, DC 20433, (202) 473-1000, Fax: (202) 477-6391, www.worldbank.org; *Austria; The World Bank Atlas 2003-2004;* and *World Development Report 2008.*

World Health Organization (WHO), Avenue Appia 20, 1211 Geneve 27, Switzerland, (Telephone in U.S. (212) 331-9081), www.who.int; *World Health Report 2006.*

AUSTRIA - POPULATION DENSITY

Central Intelligence Agency, Office of Public Affairs, Washington, DC 20505, (703) 482-0623, Fax: (703) 482-1739, www.cia.gov; *The World Factbook.*

Euromonitor International, Inc., 224 S. Michigan Avenue, Suite 1500, Chicago, IL 60604, (312) 922-1115, Fax: (312) 922-1157, www.euromonitor.com; *The World Economic Factbook 2008.*

M.E. Sharpe, 80 Business Park Drive, Armonk, NY 10504, (800) 541-6563, Fax: (914) 273-2106, www.mesharpe.com; *The Illustrated Book of World Rankings.*

Palgrave Macmillan Ltd., Houndmills, Basingstoke, Hampshire, RG21 6XS, England, (Telephone in U.S. (888) 330-8477), (Fax in U.S. (800) 672-2054), www.palgrave.com; *The Statesman's Yearbook 2008.*

Taylor and Francis Group, An Informa Business, 2 Park Square, Milton Park, Abingdon, Oxford OX14 4RN, United Kingdom, (Dial from U.S. (212) 216-7800), (Fax from U.S. (212) 564-7854), www.tandf.co.uk; *The Europa World Year Book.*

United Nations Food and Agricultural Organization (FAO), Viale delle Terme di Caracalla, 00100 Rome, Italy, (Dial from U.S. (202) 653-2400), (Fax from U.S. (202) 653 5760), www.fao.org; *The State of Food and Agriculture (SOFA) 2006.*

United Nations Statistics Division, New York, NY 10017, (800) 253-9646, Fax: (212) 963-4116, http://unstats.un.org; *Statistical Yearbook* and *Trends in Europe and North America: The Statistical Yearbook of the ECE 2005.*

The World Bank, 1818 H Street, NW, Washington, DC 20433, (202) 473-1000, Fax: (202) 477-6391, www.worldbank.org; *Austria* and *World Development Report 2008.*

AUSTRIA - POSTAL SERVICE

M.E. Sharpe, 80 Business Park Drive, Armonk, NY 10504, (800) 541-6563, Fax: (914) 273-2106, www.mesharpe.com; *The Illustrated Book of World Rankings.*

Palgrave Macmillan Ltd., Houndmills, Basingstoke, Hampshire, RG21 6XS, England, (Telephone in U.S. (888) 330-8477), (Fax in U.S. (800) 672-2054), www.palgrave.com; *The Statesman's Yearbook 2008.*

United Nations Statistics Division, New York, NY 10017, (800) 253-9646, Fax: (212) 963-4116, http://unstats.un.org; *Statistical Yearbook* and *Trends in Europe and North America: The Statistical Yearbook of the ECE 2005.*

AUSTRIA - POULTRY

See AUSTRIA - LIVESTOCK

AUSTRIA - POWER RESOURCES

Euromonitor International, Inc., 224 S. Michigan Avenue, Suite 1500, Chicago, IL 60604, (312) 922-1115, Fax: (312) 922-1157, www.euromonitor.com; *European Marketing Data and Statistics 2008; The World Economic Factbook 2008;* and *World Marketing Data and Statistics.*

M.E. Sharpe, 80 Business Park Drive, Armonk, NY 10504, (800) 541-6563, Fax: (914) 273-2106, www.mesharpe.com; *The Illustrated Book of World Rankings.*

Organisation for Economic Cooperation and Development (OECD), 2 rue Andre Pascal, F-75775 Paris Cedex 16, France, (Telephone in U.S. (202) 785-6323), (Fax in U.S. (202) 785-0350), www.oecd.org; *Coal Information: 2007 Edition; Energy Statistics of OECD Countries* (2007 Edition); *Key Environmental Indicators 2004; Oil Information 2006 Edition;* and *World Energy Outlook 2007.*

Palgrave Macmillan Ltd., Houndmills, Basingstoke, Hampshire, RG21 6XS, England, (Telephone in U.S. (888) 330-8477), (Fax in U.S. (800) 672-2054), www.palgrave.com; *The Statesman's Yearbook 2008.*

Platts, 2 Penn Plaza, 25th Floor, New York, NY 10121-2298, (212) 904-3070, www.platts.com; *Energy Economist* and *European Power Daily.*

U.S. Department of Energy (DOE), Energy Information Administration (EIA), 1000 Independence Avenue, SW, Washington, DC 20585, (202) 586-8800, www.eia.doe.gov; *International Energy Annual 2004* and *International Energy Outlook 2006.*

United Nations Food and Agricultural Organization (FAO), Viale delle Terme di Caracalla, 00100 Rome, Italy, (Dial from U.S. (202) 653-2400), (Fax from U.S. (202) 653 5760), www.fao.org; *The State of Food and Agriculture (SOFA) 2006.*

United Nations Statistics Division, New York, NY 10017, (800) 253-9646, Fax: (212) 963-4116, http://unstats.un.org; *Energy Statistics Yearbook 2003; Human Development Report 2006; Trends in Europe and North America: The Statistical Yearbook of the ECE 2005;* and *World Statistics Pocketbook.*

The World Bank, 1818 H Street, NW, Washington, DC 20433, (202) 473-1000, Fax: (202) 477-6391, www.worldbank.org; *The World Bank Atlas 2003-2004* and *World Development Report 2008.*

AUSTRIA - PRICES

Euromonitor International, Inc., 224 S. Michigan Avenue, Suite 1500, Chicago, IL 60604, (312) 922-1115, Fax: (312) 922-1157, www.euromonitor.com; *European Marketing Data and Statistics 2008* and *World Marketing Data and Statistics.*

International Labour Office, I.L.O. Publications, 4 route des Morillons, CH-1211 Geneva 22, Switzerland, (Telephone in U.S. (202) 653-7652), (Fax in U.S. (202) 653-7687), www.ilo.org; *Yearbook of Labour Statistics 2006.*

International Lead and Zinc Study Group (ILZSG), Rua Almirante Barroso 38, 5th Floor, Lisbon 1000 - 013, Portugal, www.ilzsg.org; Interactive Statistical Database.

International Monetary Fund (IMF), 700 Nineteenth Street, NW, Washington, DC 20431, (202) 623-7000, Fax: (202) 623-4661, www.imf.org; *International Financial Statistics Yearbook 2007.*

M.E. Sharpe, 80 Business Park Drive, Armonk, NY 10504, (800) 541-6563, Fax: (914) 273-2106, www.mesharpe.com; *The Illustrated Book of World Rankings.*

Organisation for Economic Cooperation and Development (OECD), 2 rue Andre Pascal, F-75775 Paris Cedex 16, France, (Telephone in U.S. (202) 785-6323), (Fax in U.S. (202) 785-0350), www.oecd.org; *Indicators of Industrial Activity; Iron and Steel Industry in 2004 (2006 Edition); OECD Economic Outlook 2008;* and *OECD Main Economic Indicators (MEI).*

Technical Association of the Pulp and Paper Industry (TAPPI), 15 Technology Parkway South, Norcross, GA 30092, (770) 446-1400, Fax: (770) 446-6947, www.tappi.org; *TAPPI Annual Report.*

United Nations Food and Agricultural Organization (FAO), Viale delle Terme di Caracalla, 00100 Rome, Italy, (Dial from U.S. (202) 653-2400), (Fax from U.S. (202) 653 5760), www.fao.org; *FAO Production Yearbook 2002* and *The State of Food and Agriculture (SOFA) 2006.*

The World Bank, 1818 H Street, NW, Washington, DC 20433, (202) 473-1000, Fax: (202) 477-6391, www.worldbank.org; *Austria.*

World Bureau of Metal Statistics (WBMS), 27a High Street, Ware, Hertfordshire, SG12 9BA, United Kingdom, www.world-bureau.com; *World Flow Charts* and *World Metal Statistics.*

AUSTRIA - PROFESSIONS

United Nations Statistics Division, New York, NY 10017, (800) 253-9646, Fax: (212) 963-4116, http://unstats.un.org; *Statistical Yearbook.*

AUSTRIA - PUBLIC HEALTH

Euromonitor International, Inc., 224 S. Michigan Avenue, Suite 1500, Chicago, IL 60604, (312) 922-1115, Fax: (312) 922-1157, www.euromonitor.com; *World Health Databook 2007/2008* and *World Marketing Data and Statistics.*

Health and Consumer Protection Directorate-General, European Commission, B-1049 Brussels, Belgium, http://ec.europa.eu/dgs/health_consumer/index_en.htm; *Injuries in the European Union: Statistics Summary 2002-2004.*

M.E. Sharpe, 80 Business Park Drive, Armonk, NY 10504, (800) 541-6563, Fax: (914) 273-2106, www.mesharpe.com; *The Illustrated Book of World Rankings.*

Organisation for Economic Cooperation and Development (OECD), 2 rue Andre Pascal, F-75775 Paris Cedex 16, France, (Telephone in U.S. (202) 785-6323), (Fax in U.S. (202) 785-0350), www.oecd.org; *Health at a Glance 2007 - OECD Indicators.*

Palgrave Macmillan Ltd., Houndmills, Basingstoke, Hampshire, RG21 6XS, England, (Telephone in U.S. (888) 330-8477), (Fax in U.S. (800) 672-2054), www.palgrave.com; *The Statesman's Yearbook 2008.*

Robert Koch Institute, Nordufer 20, D 13353 Berlin, Germany, www.rki.de; *EUVAC-NET Report: Pertussis-Surveillance 1998-2002.*

UNICEF, 3 United Nations Plaza, New York, NY 10017, (800) 253-9646, Fax: (212) 887-7465, www.unicef.org; *The State of the World's Children 2008.*

United Nations Statistics Division, New York, NY 10017, (800) 253-9646, Fax: (212) 963-4116, http://unstats.un.org; *Human Development Report 2006; Statistical Yearbook;* and *Trends in Europe and North America: The Statistical Yearbook of the ECE 2005.*

The World Bank, 1818 H Street, NW, Washington, DC 20433, (202) 473-1000, Fax: (202) 477-6391, www.worldbank.org; *Austria* and *World Development Report 2008.*

World Health Organization (WHO), Avenue Appia 20, 1211 Geneve 27, Switzerland, (Telephone in U.S. (212) 331-9081), www.who.int; The WHO Global Atlas of Infectious Diseases and *World Health Report 2006.*

AUSTRIA - PUBLISHERS AND PUBLISHING

Organisation for Economic Cooperation and Development (OECD), 2 rue Andre Pascal, F-75775 Paris Cedex 16, France, (Telephone in U.S. (202) 785-6323), (Fax in U.S. (202) 785-0350), www.oecd.org; *Indicators of Industrial Activity.*

Taylor and Francis Group, An Informa Business, 2 Park Square, Milton Park, Abingdon, Oxford OX14 4RN, United Kingdom, (Dial from U.S. (212) 216-7800), (Fax from U.S. (212) 564-7854), www.tandf.co.uk; *The Europa World Year Book.*

UNESCO Institute for Statistics, C.P. 6128 Succursale Centre-Ville, Montreal, Quebec, H3C 3J7 Canada, (Dial from U.S. (514) 343-6880), (Fax from U.S. (514) 343 6882), www.uis.unesco.org; *Statistical Tables.*

United Nations Statistics Division, New York, NY 10017, (800) 253-9646, Fax: (212) 963-4116, http://unstats.un.org; *Trends in Europe and North America: The Statistical Yearbook of the ECE 2005.*

AUSTRIA - RADIO - RECEIVERS AND RECEPTION

Palgrave Macmillan Ltd., Houndmills, Basingstoke, Hampshire, RG21 6XS, England, (Telephone in U.S. (888) 330-8477), (Fax in U.S. (800) 672-2054), www.palgrave.com; *The Statesman's Yearbook 2008.*

United Nations Statistics Division, New York, NY 10017, (800) 253-9646, Fax: (212) 963-4116, http://unstats.un.org; *Statistical Yearbook.*

AUSTRIA - RAILROADS

Euromonitor International, Inc., 224 S. Michigan Avenue, Suite 1500, Chicago, IL 60604, (312) 922-1115, Fax: (312) 922-1157, www.euromonitor.com; *European Marketing Data and Statistics 2008.*

Jane's Information Group, 110 North Royal Street, Suite 200, Alexandria, VA 22314, (703) 683-3700, Fax: (800) 836-0297, www.janes.com; *Jane's World Railways.*

Palgrave Macmillan Ltd., Houndmills, Basingstoke, Hampshire, RG21 6XS, England, (Telephone in U.S. (888) 330-8477), (Fax in U.S. (800) 672-2054), www.palgrave.com; *The Statesman's Yearbook 2008.*

Taylor and Francis Group, An Informa Business, 2 Park Square, Milton Park, Abingdon, Oxford OX14 4RN, United Kingdom, (Dial from U.S. (212) 216-7800), (Fax from U.S. (212) 564-7854), www.tandf.co.uk; *The Europa World Year Book.*

United Nations Statistics Division, New York, NY 10017, (800) 253-9646, Fax: (212) 963-4116, http://unstats.un.org; *Annual Bulletin of Transport Statistics for Europe and North America 2004; Statistical Yearbook;* and *Trends in Europe and North America: The Statistical Yearbook of the ECE 2005.*

AUSTRIA - RELIGION

Central Intelligence Agency, Office of Public Affairs, Washington, DC 20505, (703) 482-0623, Fax: (703) 482-1739, www.cia.gov; *The World Factbook.*

M.E. Sharpe, 80 Business Park Drive, Armonk, NY 10504, (800) 541-6563, Fax: (914) 273-2106, www.mesharpe.com; *The Illustrated Book of World Rankings.*

Palgrave Macmillan Ltd., Houndmills, Basingstoke, Hampshire, RG21 6XS, England, (Telephone in U.S. (888) 330-8477), (Fax in U.S. (800) 672-2054), www.palgrave.com; *The Statesman's Yearbook 2008.*

AUSTRIA - RENT CHARGES

International Labour Office, I.L.O. Publications, 4 route des Morillons, CH-1211 Geneva 22, Switzerland, (Telephone in U.S. (202) 653-7652), (Fax in U.S. (202) 653-7687), www.ilo.org; *Yearbook of Labour Statistics 2006.*

AUSTRIA - RESERVES (ACCOUNTING)

Organisation for Economic Cooperation and Development (OECD), 2 rue Andre Pascal, F-75775 Paris Cedex 16, France, (Telephone in U.S. (202) 785-6323), (Fax in U.S. (202) 785-0350), www.oecd.org; *Financial Market Trends: OECD Periodical* and *OECD Economic Outlook 2008.*

The World Bank, 1818 H Street, NW, Washington, DC 20433, (202) 473-1000, Fax: (202) 477-6391, www.worldbank.org; *World Development Indicators (WDI) 2008.*

AUSTRIA - RETAIL TRADE

Banque de France, 48 rue Croix des Petits champs, 75001 Paris, France, www.banque-france.fr/home.htm; *Monthly Business Survey Overview.*

Euromonitor International, Inc., 224 S. Michigan Avenue, Suite 1500, Chicago, IL 60604, (312) 922-1115, Fax: (312) 922-1157, www.euromonitor.com; *Retail Trade International 2007* and *World Marketing Data and Statistics.*

United Nations Statistics Division, New York, NY 10017, (800) 253-9646, Fax: (212) 963-4116, http://unstats.un.org; *Statistical Yearbook.*

AUSTRIA - RICE PRODUCTION

See AUSTRIA - CROPS

AUSTRIA - ROADS

Central Intelligence Agency, Office of Public Affairs, Washington, DC 20505, (703) 482-0623, Fax: (703) 482-1739, www.cia.gov; *The World Factbook.*

International Road Federation (IFR), Madison Place, 500 Montgomery Street, 5th Floor, Alexandria, VA 22314, (703) 535-1001, Fax: (703) 535-1007, www.irfnet.org; *World Road Statistics 2006.*

Palgrave Macmillan Ltd., Houndmills, Basingstoke, Hampshire, RG21 6XS, England, (Telephone in U.S. (888) 330-8477), (Fax in U.S. (800) 672-2054), www.palgrave.com; *The Statesman's Yearbook 2008.*

United Nations Statistics Division, New York, NY 10017, (800) 253-9646, Fax: (212) 963-4116, http://unstats.un.org; *Annual Bulletin of Transport Statistics for Europe and North America 2004* and *Trends in Europe and North America: The Statistical Yearbook of the ECE 2005.*

AUSTRIA - RUBBER INDUSTRY AND TRADE

International Rubber Study Group (IRSG), 1st Floor, Heron House, 109/115 Wembley Hill Road, Wembley, Middlesex HA9 8DA, United Kingdom, www.rubberstudy.com; *Rubber Statistical Bulletin; Summary of World Rubber Statistics 2005; World Rubber Statistics Handbook (Volume 6, 1975-2001);* and *World Rubber Statistics Historic Handbook.*

M.E. Sharpe, 80 Business Park Drive, Armonk, NY 10504, (800) 541-6563, Fax: (914) 273-2106, www.mesharpe.com; *The Illustrated Book of World Rankings.*

Organisation for Economic Cooperation and Development (OECD), 2 rue Andre Pascal, F-75775 Paris Cedex 16, France, (Telephone in U.S. (202) 785-6323), (Fax in U.S. (202) 785-0350), www.oecd.org; *International Trade by Commodity Statistics (ITCS).*

AUSTRIA - RYE PRODUCTION

See AUSTRIA - CROPS

AUSTRIA - SALT PRODUCTION

See AUSTRIA - MINERAL INDUSTRIES

AUSTRIA - SHEEP

See AUSTRIA - LIVESTOCK

AUSTRIA - SHIPBUILDING

Organisation for Economic Cooperation and Development (OECD), 2 rue Andre Pascal, F-75775 Paris Cedex 16, France, (Telephone in U.S. (202) 785-6323), (Fax in U.S. (202) 785-0350), www.oecd.org; *Indicators of Industrial Activity.*

AUSTRIA - SHIPPING

Organisation for Economic Cooperation and Development (OECD), 2 rue Andre Pascal, F-75775 Paris Cedex 16, France, (Telephone in U.S. (202) 785-6323), (Fax in U.S. (202) 785-0350), www.oecd.org; *Statistics on Ship Production, Exports and Orders in 2004.*

Palgrave Macmillan Ltd., Houndmills, Basingstoke, Hampshire, RG21 6XS, England, (Telephone in U.S. (888) 330-8477), (Fax in U.S. (800) 672-2054), www.palgrave.com; *The Statesman's Yearbook 2008.*

Taylor and Francis Group, An Informa Business, 2 Park Square, Milton Park, Abingdon, Oxford OX14 4RN, United Kingdom, (Dial from U.S. (212) 216-7800), (Fax from U.S. (212) 564-7854), www.tandf.co.uk; *The Europa World Year Book.*

U.S. Department of Transportation (DOT), Maritime Administration (MARAD), West Building, Southeast Federal Center, 1200 New Jersey Avenue, SE, Washington, DC 20590, (800) 99-MARAD, www.marad.dot.gov; *World Merchant Fleet 2005.*

United Nations Statistics Division, New York, NY 10017, (800) 253-9646, Fax: (212) 963-4116, http://unstats.un.org; *Annual Bulletin of Transport Statistics for Europe and North America 2004.*

AUSTRIA - SILVER PRODUCTION

See AUSTRIA - MINERAL INDUSTRIES

AUSTRIA - SOCIAL ECOLOGY

M.E. Sharpe, 80 Business Park Drive, Armonk, NY 10504, (800) 541-6563, Fax: (914) 273-2106, www.mesharpe.com; *The Illustrated Book of World Rankings.*

United Nations Statistics Division, New York, NY 10017, (800) 253-9646, Fax: (212) 963-4116, http://unstats.un.org; *World Statistics Pocketbook.*

AUSTRIA - SOCIAL SECURITY

International Monetary Fund (IMF), 700 Nineteenth Street, NW, Washington, DC 20431, (202) 623-

7000, Fax: (202) 623-4661, www.imf.org; *Government Finance Statistics Yearbook (2008 Edition).*

Organisation for Economic Cooperation and Development (OECD), 2 rue Andre Pascal, F-75775 Paris Cedex 16, France, (Telephone in U.S. (202) 785-6323), (Fax in U.S. (202) 785-0350), www.oecd.org; *Revenue Statistics 1965-2006 - 2007 Edition.*

United Nations Statistics Division, New York, NY 10017, (800) 253-9646, Fax: (212) 963-4116, http://unstats.un.org; *National Accounts Statistics: Compendium of Income Distribution Statistics.*

AUSTRIA - STEEL PRODUCTION

See AUSTRIA - MINERAL INDUSTRIES

AUSTRIA - SUGAR PRODUCTION

See AUSTRIA - CROPS

AUSTRIA - SULPHUR PRODUCTION

See AUSTRIA - MINERAL INDUSTRIES

AUSTRIA - TAXATION

International Labour Office, I.L.O. Publications, 4 route des Morillons, CH-1211 Geneva 22, Switzerland, (Telephone in U.S. (202) 653-7652), (Fax in U.S. (202) 653-7687), www.ilo.org; *Yearbook of Labour Statistics 2006.*

International Monetary Fund (IMF), 700 Nineteenth Street, NW, Washington, DC 20431, (202) 623-7000, Fax: (202) 623-4661, www.imf.org; *Government Finance Statistics Yearbook (2008 Edition).*

Organisation for Economic Cooperation and Development (OECD), 2 rue Andre Pascal, F-75775 Paris Cedex 16, France, (Telephone in U.S. (202) 785-6323), (Fax in U.S. (202) 785-0350), www.oecd.org; *Revenue Statistics 1965-2006 - 2007 Edition.*

Taylor and Francis Group, An Informa Business, 2 Park Square, Milton Park, Abingdon, Oxford OX14 4RN, United Kingdom, (Dial from U.S. (212) 216-7800), (Fax from U.S. (212) 564-7854), www.tandf.co.uk; *The Europa World Year Book.*

The World Bank, 1818 H Street, NW, Washington, DC 20433, (202) 473-1000, Fax: (202) 477-6391, www.worldbank.org; *World Development Indicators (WDI) 2008.*

AUSTRIA - TELEPHONE

International Telecommunication Union (ITU), Place des Nations, 1211 Geneva 20, Switzerland, www.itu.int; World Telecommunication Indicators Database.

Palgrave Macmillan Ltd., Houndmills, Basingstoke, Hampshire, RG21 6XS, England, (Telephone in U.S. (888) 330-8477), (Fax in U.S. (800) 672-2054), www.palgrave.com; *The Statesman's Yearbook 2008.*

Taylor and Francis Group, An Informa Business, 2 Park Square, Milton Park, Abingdon, Oxford OX14 4RN, United Kingdom, (Dial from U.S. (212) 216-7800), (Fax from U.S. (212) 564-7854), www.tandf.co.uk; *The Europa World Year Book.*

United Nations Statistics Division, New York, NY 10017, (800) 253-9646, Fax: (212) 963-4116, http://unstats.un.org; *Statistical Yearbook; Trends in Europe and North America: The Statistical Yearbook of the ECE 2005;* and *World Statistics Pocketbook.*

AUSTRIA - TELEVISION - RECEIVERS AND RECEPTION

United Nations Statistics Division, New York, NY 10017, (800) 253-9646, Fax: (212) 963-4116, http://unstats.un.org; *Statistical Yearbook.*

AUSTRIA - TEXTILE INDUSTRY

Euromonitor International, Inc., 224 S. Michigan Avenue, Suite 1500, Chicago, IL 60604, (312) 922-1115, Fax: (312) 922-1157, www.euromonitor.com; *Retail Trade International 2007.*

M.E. Sharpe, 80 Business Park Drive, Armonk, NY 10504, (800) 541-6563, Fax: (914) 273-2106, www.mesharpe.com; *The Illustrated Book of World Rankings.*

Organisation for Economic Cooperation and Development (OECD), 2 rue Andre Pascal, F-75775 Paris Cedex 16, France, (Telephone in U.S. (202) 785-6323), (Fax in U.S. (202) 785-0350), www.oecd.org; *Indicators of Industrial Activity; International Trade by Commodity Statistics (ITCS); A New World Map in Textiles and Clothing: Adjusting to Change; 2005 OECD Agricultural Outlook Tables, 1970-2014;* and STructural ANalysis (STAN) database.

Palgrave Macmillan Ltd., Houndmills, Basingstoke, Hampshire, RG21 6XS, England, (Telephone in U.S. (888) 330-8477), (Fax in U.S. (800) 672-2054), www.palgrave.com; *The Statesman's Yearbook 2008.*

United Nations Conference on Trade and Development (UNCTAD), DC2-1120, United Nations, New York, NY 10017, (212) 963-0027, www.unctad.org; *UNCTAD Commodity Yearbook.*

United Nations Statistics Division, New York, NY 10017, (800) 253-9646, Fax: (212) 963-4116, http://unstats.un.org; *Statistical Yearbook.*

AUSTRIA - TIN PRODUCTION

See AUSTRIA - MINERAL INDUSTRIES

AUSTRIA - TOBACCO INDUSTRY

Euromonitor International, Inc., 224 S. Michigan Avenue, Suite 1500, Chicago, IL 60604, (312) 922-1115, Fax: (312) 922-1157, www.euromonitor.com; *European Marketing Data and Statistics 2008.*

Foreign Agricultural Service (FAS), U.S. Department of Agriculture (USDA), 1400 Independence Avenue, SW, Washington, DC 20250, (202) 720-3935, www.fas.usda.gov; *Tobacco: World Markets and Trade.*

M.E. Sharpe, 80 Business Park Drive, Armonk, NY 10504, (800) 541-6563, Fax: (914) 273-2106, www.mesharpe.com; *The Illustrated Book of World Rankings.*

Organisation for Economic Cooperation and Development (OECD), 2 rue Andre Pascal, F-75775 Paris Cedex 16, France, (Telephone in U.S. (202) 785-6323), (Fax in U.S. (202) 785-0350), www.oecd.org; *Indicators of Industrial Activity; International Trade by Commodity Statistics (ITCS);* and STructural ANalysis (STAN) database.

United Nations Statistics Division, New York, NY 10017, (800) 253-9646, Fax: (212) 963-4116, http://unstats.un.org; *Statistical Yearbook.*

AUSTRIA - TOURISM

Euromonitor International, Inc., 224 S. Michigan Avenue, Suite 1500, Chicago, IL 60604, (312) 922-1115, Fax: (312) 922-1157, www.euromonitor.com; *European Marketing Data and Statistics 2008; The World Economic Factbook 2008;* and *World Marketing Data and Statistics.*

Eurostat, Batiment Jean Monnet, Rue Alcide de Gasperi, L-2920 Luxembourg, http://epp.eurostat.ec.europa.eu; *Tourism in Europe: First Results for 2007.*

M.E. Sharpe, 80 Business Park Drive, Armonk, NY 10504, (800) 541-6563, Fax: (914) 273-2106, www.mesharpe.com; *The Illustrated Book of World Rankings.*

Organisation for Economic Cooperation and Development (OECD), 2 rue Andre Pascal, F-75775 Paris Cedex 16, France, (Telephone in U.S. (202) 785-6323), (Fax in U.S. (202) 785-0350), www.oecd.org; *Household, Tourism, Travel: Trends, Environmental Impacts and Policy Responses.*

Palgrave Macmillan Ltd., Houndmills, Basingstoke, Hampshire, RG21 6XS, England, (Telephone in U.S. (888) 330-8477), (Fax in U.S. (800) 672-2054), www.palgrave.com; *The Statesman's Yearbook 2008.*

Taylor and Francis Group, An Informa Business, 2 Park Square, Milton Park, Abingdon, Oxford OX14 4RN, United Kingdom, (Dial from U.S. (212) 216-7800), (Fax from U.S. (212) 564-7854), www.tandf.co.uk; *The Europa World Year Book.*

United Nations Statistics Division, New York, NY 10017, (800) 253-9646, Fax: (212) 963-4116, http://unstats.un.org; *Statistical Yearbook* and *Trends in Europe and North America: The Statistical Yearbook of the ECE 2005.*

United Nations World Tourism Organization (UNWTO), Capitan Haya 42, 28020 Madrid, Spain, www.world-tourism.org; *Tourism Market Trends 2004 - Europe* and *Yearbook of Tourism Statistics.*

The World Bank, 1818 H Street, NW, Washington, DC 20433, (202) 473-1000, Fax: (202) 477-6391, www.worldbank.org; *Austria.*

AUSTRIA - TRADE

See AUSTRIA - INTERNATIONAL TRADE

AUSTRIA - TRANSPORTATION

Central Intelligence Agency, Office of Public Affairs, Washington, DC 20505, (703) 482-0623, Fax: (703) 482-1739, www.cia.gov; *The World Factbook.*

Eurostat, Batiment Jean Monnet, Rue Alcide de Gasperi, L-2920 Luxembourg, http://epp.eurostat.ec.europa.eu; *Regional Passenger and Freight Air Transport in Europe in 2006* and *Regional Road and Rail Transport Networks.*

M.E. Sharpe, 80 Business Park Drive, Armonk, NY 10504, (800) 541-6563, Fax: (914) 273-2106, www.mesharpe.com; *The Illustrated Book of World Rankings.*

Palgrave Macmillan Ltd., Houndmills, Basingstoke, Hampshire, RG21 6XS, England, (Telephone in U.S. (888) 330-8477), (Fax in U.S. (800) 672-2054), www.palgrave.com; *The Statesman's Yearbook 2008.*

Taylor and Francis Group, An Informa Business, 2 Park Square, Milton Park, Abingdon, Oxford OX14 4RN, United Kingdom, (Dial from U.S. (212) 216-7800), (Fax from U.S. (212) 564-7854), www.tandf.co.uk; *The Europa World Year Book.*

United Nations Statistics Division, New York, NY 10017, (800) 253-9646, Fax: (212) 963-4116, http://unstats.un.org; *Human Development Report 2006* and *Trends in Europe and North America: The Statistical Yearbook of the ECE 2005.*

The World Bank, 1818 H Street, NW, Washington, DC 20433, (202) 473-1000, Fax: (202) 477-6391, www.worldbank.org; *Austria.*

AUSTRIA - TURKEYS

See AUSTRIA - LIVESTOCK

AUSTRIA - UNEMPLOYMENT

Central Intelligence Agency, Office of Public Affairs, Washington, DC 20505, (703) 482-0623, Fax: (703) 482-1739, www.cia.gov; *The World Factbook.*

Euromonitor International, Inc., 224 S. Michigan Avenue, Suite 1500, Chicago, IL 60604, (312) 922-1115, Fax: (312) 922-1157, www.euromonitor.com; *European Marketing Data and Statistics 2008.*

International Labour Office, I.L.O. Publications, 4 route des Morillons, CH-1211 Geneva 22, Switzerland, (Telephone in U.S. (202) 653-7652), (Fax in U.S. (202) 653-7687), www.ilo.org; *Yearbook of Labour Statistics 2006.*

Organisation for Economic Cooperation and Development (OECD), 2 rue Andre Pascal, F-75775 Paris Cedex 16, France, (Telephone in U.S. (202) 785-6323), (Fax in U.S. (202) 785-0350), www.oecd.org; *Labour Force Statistics: 1986-2005, 2007 Edition; OECD Composite Leading Indicators (CLIs), Updated September 2007; OECD Economic Outlook 2008; OECD Economic Survey - Austria 2007;* and *OECD Employment Outlook 2007.*

Palgrave Macmillan Ltd., Houndmills, Basingstoke, Hampshire, RG21 6XS, England, (Telephone in U.S. (888) 330-8477), (Fax in U.S. (800) 672-2054), www.palgrave.com; *The Statesman's Yearbook 2008.*

United Nations Statistics Division, New York, NY 10017, (800) 253-9646, Fax: (212) 963-4116, http://unstats.un.org; *Statistical Yearbook* and *Trends in Europe and North America: The Statistical Yearbook of the ECE 2005.*

AUSTRIA - URANIUM PRODUCTION AND CONSUMPTION

See AUSTRIA - MINERAL INDUSTRIES

AUSTRIA - VITAL STATISTICS

Palgrave Macmillan Ltd., Houndmills, Basingstoke, Hampshire, RG21 6XS, England, (Telephone in U.S. (888) 330-8477), (Fax in U.S. (800) 672-2054), www.palgrave.com; *The Statesman's Yearbook 2008.*

United Nations Statistics Division, New York, NY 10017, (800) 253-9646, Fax: (212) 963-4116, http://unstats.un.org; *Statistical Yearbook.*

World Health Organization (WHO), Avenue Appia 20, 1211 Geneve 27, Switzerland, (Telephone in U.S. (212) 331-9081), www.who.int; *World Health Report 2006.*

AUSTRIA - WAGES

Euromonitor International, Inc., 224 S. Michigan Avenue, Suite 1500, Chicago, IL 60604, (312) 922-1115, Fax: (312) 922-1157, www.euromonitor.com; *European Marketing Data and Statistics 2008.*

International Labour Office, I.L.O. Publications, 4 route des Morillons, CH-1211 Geneva 22, Switzerland, (Telephone in U.S. (202) 653-7652), (Fax in U.S. (202) 653-7687), www.ilo.org; *Yearbook of Labour Statistics 2006.*

Organisation for Economic Cooperation and Development (OECD), 2 rue Andre Pascal, F-75775 Paris Cedex 16, France, (Telephone in U.S. (202) 785-6323), (Fax in U.S. (202) 785-0350), www.oecd.org; *ICT Sector Data and Metadata by Country; OECD Economic Outlook 2008; OECD Main Economic Indicators (MEI);* and STructural ANalysis (STAN) database.

United Nations Statistics Division, New York, NY 10017, (800) 253-9646, Fax: (212) 963-4116, http://unstats.un.org; *Statistical Yearbook.*

The World Bank, 1818 H Street, NW, Washington, DC 20433, (202) 473-1000, Fax: (202) 477-6391, www.worldbank.org; *Austria.*

AUSTRIA - WALNUT PRODUCTION

See AUSTRIA - CROPS

AUSTRIA - WEATHER

See AUSTRIA - CLIMATE

AUSTRIA - WELFARE STATE

International Monetary Fund (IMF), 700 Nineteenth Street, NW, Washington, DC 20431, (202) 623-7000, Fax: (202) 623-4661, www.imf.org; *Government Finance Statistics Yearbook (2008 Edition).*

AUSTRIA - WHEAT PRODUCTION

See AUSTRIA - CROPS

AUSTRIA - WHOLESALE PRICE INDEXES

International Monetary Fund (IMF), 700 Nineteenth Street, NW, Washington, DC 20431, (202) 623-7000, Fax: (202) 623-4661, www.imf.org; *International Financial Statistics Yearbook 2007.*

AUSTRIA - WHOLESALE TRADE

United Nations Statistics Division, New York, NY 10017, (800) 253-9646, Fax: (212) 963-4116, http://unstats.un.org; *Statistical Yearbook.*

AUSTRIA - WINE PRODUCTION

See AUSTRIA - BEVERAGE INDUSTRY

AUSTRIA - WOOD AND WOOD PULP

See AUSTRIA - FORESTS AND FORESTRY

AUSTRIA - WOOD PRODUCTS

Organisation for Economic Cooperation and Development (OECD), 2 rue Andre Pascal, F-75775 Paris Cedex 16, France, (Telephone in U.S. (202) 785-6323), (Fax in U.S. (202) 785-0350), www.oecd.org; *International Trade by Commodity Statistics (ITCS)* and STructural ANalysis (STAN) database.

AUSTRIA - WOOL PRODUCTION

See AUSTRIA - TEXTILE INDUSTRY

AUSTRIA - YARN PRODUCTION

See AUSTRIA - TEXTILE INDUSTRY

AUSTRIA - ZINC AND ZINC ORE

See AUSTRIA - MINERAL INDUSTRIES

AUSTRIA - ZOOS

UNESCO Institute for Statistics, C.P. 6128 Succursale Centre-Ville, Montreal, Quebec, H3C 3J7 Canada, (Dial from U.S. (514) 343-6880), (Fax from U.S. (514) 343 6882), www.uis.unesco.org; *Statistical Tables.*

AUTHORS

U.S. Bureau of Labor Statistics (BLS), Postal Square Building, 2 Massachusetts Avenue, NE, Washington, DC 20212-0001, (202) 691-5200, Fax: (202) 691-6325, www.bls.gov; *Employment and Earnings (EE)* and unpublished data.

AUTOMOBILE LOANS

Board of Governors of the Federal Reserve System, Constitution Avenue, NW, Washington, DC 20551, (202) 452-3000, www.federalreserve.gov; *Federal Reserve Bulletin.*

AUTOMOBILES

See also MOTOR VEHICLES

Environmental Defense Fund, 257 Park Avenue South, New York, NY 10010, (800) 684-3322, www.edf.org; *Cars and Climate Change: How Automakers Stack Up.*

The NPD Group, Port Washington, 900 West Shore Road, Port Washington, NY 11050, (866) 444-1411, www.npd.com; *Market Research for the Automotive Aftermarket.*

Ward's Communications, 3000 Town Center, Suite 2750, Southfield, MI 48075, (248) 799-2645, Fax: (248) 357-0810, http://wardsauto.com; Ward's AutoInfoBank and unpublished data.

AUTOMOBILES - EXPENDITURE PER NEW CAR

Bureau of Economic Analysis (BEA), U.S. Department of Commerce (DOC), 1441 L Street NW, Washington, DC 20230, (202) 606-9900, www.bea.gov; *Survey of Current Business (SCB).*

AUTOMOBILES - FOREIGN COUNTRIES

R. L. Polk Co, 26955 Northwestern Hwy., Southfield, MI 48034, (800) Go-4-Polk, www.polk.com; unpublished data.

U.S. Department of Transportation (DOT), Federal Highway Administration (FHA), 1200 New Jersey Avenue, SE, Washington, DC 20590, (202) 366-0660, www.fhwa.dot.gov; *Highway Statistics 2006.*

AUTOMOBILES - IMPORTS

Bureau of Economic Analysis (BEA), U.S. Department of Commerce (DOC), 1441 L Street NW, Washington, DC 20230, (202) 606-9900, www.bea.gov; *Survey of Current Business (SCB).*

R. L. Polk Co, 26955 Northwestern Hwy., Southfield, MI 48034, (800) Go-4-Polk, www.polk.com; unpublished data.

Ward's Communications, 3000 Town Center, Suite 2750, Southfield, MI 48075, (248) 799-2645, Fax: (248) 357-0810, http://wardsauto.com; *Ward's Motor Vehicle Facts Figures.*

AUTOMOBILES - INSURANCE

National Association of Insurance Commissioners (NAIC), 2301 McGee Street, Suite 800, Kansas City, MO 64108-2662, (816) 842-3600, Fax: (816) 783-8175, www.naic.org; *2005 Insurance Department Resources Report.*

U.S. Department of Transportation (DOT), Research and Innovative Technology Administration (RITA), Bureau of Transportation Statistics (BTS), 1200 New Jersey Avenue, SE, Washington, DC 20590, (800) 853-1351, www.bts.gov; *TranStats.*

AUTOMOBILES - INTERNATIONAL TRADE

Alliance of Automobile Manufacturers (AAM), 1401 Eye Street, NW, Suite 900, Washington, DC 20005, (202) 326-5500, Fax: (202) 326-5598, www.autoalliance.org; various fact sheets.

R. L. Polk Co, 26955 Northwestern Hwy., Southfield, MI 48034, (800) Go-4-Polk, www.polk.com; unpublished data.

Ward's Communications, 3000 Town Center, Suite 2750, Southfield, MI 48075, (248) 799-2645, Fax: (248) 357-0810, http://wardsauto.com; *Ward's Automotive Reports.*

AUTOMOBILES - PRICE INDEXES

The NPD Group, Port Washington, 900 West Shore Road, Port Washington, NY 11050, (866) 444-1411, www.npd.com; *Market Research for the Automotive Aftermarket.*

U.S. Bureau of Labor Statistics (BLS), Postal Square Building, 2 Massachusetts Avenue, NE, Washington, DC 20212-0001, (202) 691-5200, Fax: (202) 691-6325, www.bls.gov; *Consumer Price Index Detailed Report* and *Monthly Labor Review (MLR).*

AUTOMOBILES - PRODUCTION

Alliance of Automobile Manufacturers (AAM), 1401 Eye Street, NW, Suite 900, Washington, DC 20005, (202) 326-5500, Fax: (202) 326-5598, www.autoalliance.org; various fact sheets.

Bureau of Economic Analysis (BEA), U.S. Department of Commerce (DOC), 1441 L Street NW, Washington, DC 20230, (202) 606-9900, www.bea.gov; *Survey of Current Business (SCB)* and unpublished data.

The NPD Group, Port Washington, 900 West Shore Road, Port Washington, NY 11050, (866) 444-1411, www.npd.com; *Market Research for the Automotive Aftermarket.*

Ward's Communications, 3000 Town Center, Suite 2750, Southfield, MI 48075, (248) 799-2645, Fax: (248) 357-0810, http://wardsauto.com; *Ward's Automotive Reports* and *Ward's Motor Vehicle Facts Figures.*

AUTOMOBILES - SALES

Alliance of Automobile Manufacturers (AAM), 1401 Eye Street, NW, Suite 900, Washington, DC 20005, (202) 326-5500, Fax: (202) 326-5598, www.autoalliance.org; various fact sheets.

Bureau of Economic Analysis (BEA), U.S. Department of Commerce (DOC), 1441 L Street NW, Washington, DC 20230, (202) 606-9900, www.bea.gov; *Survey of Current Business (SCB)* and unpublished data.

Manheim, 6205 Peachtree Dunwoody Road, Atlanta, GA 30328, (800) 777-2053, Fax: (404) 843-5378, www.manheim.com; *Manheim Market Report (MMR)* and Manheim Used Vehicle Value Index.

The NPD Group, Port Washington, 900 West Shore Road, Port Washington, NY 11050, (866) 444-1411, www.npd.com; *Market Research for the Automotive Aftermarket.*

R. L. Polk Co, 26955 Northwestern Hwy., Southfield, MI 48034, (800) Go-4-Polk, www.polk.com; unpublished data.

Ward's Communications, 3000 Town Center, Suite 2750, Southfield, MI 48075, (248) 799-2645, Fax: (248) 357-0810, http://wardsauto.com; *Ward's Automotive Reports.*

AUTOMOTIVE DEALERS - EARNINGS

The NPD Group, Port Washington, 900 West Shore Road, Port Washington, NY 11050, (866) 444-1411, www.npd.com; *Market Research for the Automotive Aftermarket.*

Office of Trade and Industry Information (OTII), Manufacturing and Services, International Trade Administration, U.S. Department of Commerce, 1401 Constitution Ave, NW, Washington, DC 20230, (800) USA TRAD(E), http://trade.gov/index.asp; *TradeStats Express.*

U.S. Census Bureau, Center for Economic Studies, 4600 Silver Hill Road, Washington DC 20233, (301) 457-1235, www.ces.census.gov; *2002 Economic Census, Retail Trade* and *2002 Economic Census, Wholesale Trade.*

U.S. Census Bureau, Company Statistics Division, 4700 Silver Hill Road, Washington DC 20233-0001, (301) 763-3030, www.census.gov/csd/; *County Business Patterns 2004.*

AUTOMOTIVE DEALERS - EMPLOYEES

U.S. Census Bureau, Center for Economic Studies, 4600 Silver Hill Road, Washington DC 20233, (301) 457-1235, www.ces.census.gov; *2002 Economic Census, Retail Trade* and *2002 Economic Census, Wholesale Trade.*

U.S. Census Bureau, Company Statistics Division, 4700 Silver Hill Road, Washington DC 20233-0001, (301) 763-3030, www.census.gov/csd/; *County Business Patterns 2004.*

AUTOMOTIVE DEALERS - ESTABLISHMENTS

Office of Trade and Industry Information (OTII), Manufacturing and Services, International Trade Administration, U.S. Department of Commerce, 1401 Constitution Ave, NW, Washington, DC 20230, (800) USA TRAD(E), http://trade.gov/index.asp; *TradeStats Express.*

U.S. Census Bureau, Center for Economic Studies, 4600 Silver Hill Road, Washington DC 20233, (301) 457-1235, www.ces.census.gov; *2002 Economic Census, Retail Trade* and *2002 Economic Census, Wholesale Trade.*

U.S. Census Bureau, Company Statistics Division, 4700 Silver Hill Road, Washington DC 20233-0001, (301) 763-3030, www.census.gov/csd/; *County Business Patterns 2004.*

AUTOMOTIVE DEALERS - INVENTORIES

Office of Trade and Industry Information (OTII), Manufacturing and Services, International Trade Administration, U.S. Department of Commerce, 1401 Constitution Ave, NW, Washington, DC 20230, (800) USA TRAD(E), http://trade.gov/index.asp; *TradeStats Express.*

U.S. Census Bureau, Center for Economic Studies, 4600 Silver Hill Road, Washington DC 20233, (301) 457-1235, www.ces.census.gov; *2002 Economic Census, Retail Trade* and *2002 Economic Census, Wholesale Trade.*

U.S. Census Bureau, Company Statistics Division, 4700 Silver Hill Road, Washington DC 20233-0001, (301) 763-3030, www.census.gov/csd/; *Current Business Reports.*

AUTOMOTIVE DEALERS - PRODUCTION

The NPD Group, Port Washington, 900 West Shore Road, Port Washington, NY 11050, (866) 444-1411, www.npd.com; *Market Research for the Automotive Aftermarket.*

U.S. Bureau of Labor Statistics (BLS), Postal Square Building, 2 Massachusetts Avenue, NE, Washington, DC 20212-0001, (202) 691-5200, Fax: (202) 691-6325, www.bls.gov; *Industry Productivity and Costs.*

AUTOMOTIVE DEALERS - SALES

The NPD Group, Port Washington, 900 West Shore Road, Port Washington, NY 11050, (866) 444-1411, www.npd.com; *Market Research for the Automotive Aftermarket.*

Office of Trade and Industry Information (OTII), Manufacturing and Services, International Trade Administration, U.S. Department of Commerce, 1401 Constitution Ave, NW, Washington, DC 20230, (800) USA TRAD(E), http://trade.gov/index.asp; *TradeStats Express.*

U.S. Census Bureau, 4700 Silver Hill Road, Washington DC 20233-0001, (301) 763-3030, www.census.gov; unpublished data.

U.S. Census Bureau, Center for Economic Studies, 4600 Silver Hill Road, Washington DC 20233, (301) 457-1235, www.ces.census.gov; *2002 Economic Census, Retail Trade* and *2002 Economic Census, Wholesale Trade.*

U.S. Census Bureau, Company Statistics Division, 4700 Silver Hill Road, Washington DC 20233-0001, (301) 763-3030, www.census.gov/csd/; *Current Business Reports.*

AUTOMOTIVE REPAIR AND MAINTENANCE SERVICE - EARNINGS

U.S. Bureau of Labor Statistics (BLS), Postal Square Building, 2 Massachusetts Avenue, NE, Washington, DC 20212-0001, (202) 691-5200, Fax: (202) 691-6325, www.bls.gov; *Employment and Earnings (EE).*

AUTOMOTIVE REPAIR AND MAINTENANCE SERVICE - EMPLOYEES

U.S. Bureau of Labor Statistics (BLS), Postal Square Building, 2 Massachusetts Avenue, NE, Washington, DC 20212-0001, (202) 691-5200, Fax: (202) 691-6325, www.bls.gov; *Employment and Earnings (EE)* and *Monthly Labor Review (MLR).*

AUTOMOTIVE REPAIR AND MAINTENANCE SERVICE - ESTABLISHMENTS

U.S. Census Bureau, 4700 Silver Hill Road, Washington DC 20233-0001, (301) 763-3030, www.census.gov; *2002 Economic Census, Nonemployer Statistics.*

U.S. Census Bureau, Company Statistics Division, 4700 Silver Hill Road, Washington DC 20233-0001, (301) 763-3030, www.census.gov/csd/; *County Business Patterns 2004.*

AUTOMOTIVE REPAIR AND MAINTENANCE SERVICE - MERGERS AND ACQUISITIONS

Thomson Financial, 195 Broadway, New York, NY 10007, (646) 822-2000, www.thomson.com; Thomson Research.

AUTOMOTIVE REPAIR AND MAINTENANCE SERVICE - PRODUCTIVITY

U.S. Bureau of Labor Statistics (BLS), Postal Square Building, 2 Massachusetts Avenue, NE, Washington, DC 20212-0001, (202) 691-5200, Fax: (202) 691-6325, www.bls.gov; *Industry Productivity and Costs.*

AUTOMOTIVE REPAIR AND MAINTENANCE SERVICE - RECEIPTS

U.S. Census Bureau, 4700 Silver Hill Road, Washington DC 20233-0001, (301) 763-3030, www.census.gov; *2002 Economic Census, Nonemployer Statistics.*

AVIAN FLU

European Centre for Disease Prevention and Control (ECDC), 171 83 Stockholm, Sweden, www.ecdc.europa.eu; *Avian Influenza A/H5N1 in Bathing and Potable (Drinking) Water and Risks to Human Health; The ECDC Avian Influenza Portofolio;* and *Technical Report of the Scientific Panel on Influenza in Reply to Eight Questions Concerning Avian Flu.*

AVOCADOS

Organisation for Economic Cooperation and Development (OECD), 2 rue Andre Pascal, F-75775 Paris Cedex 16, France, (Telephone in U.S. (202) 785-6323), (Fax in U.S. (202) 785-0350), www.oecd.org; *OECD Economic Outlook 2008.*

AZERBAIJAN - NATIONAL STATISTICAL OFFICE

State Statistical Committee of the Republic of Azerbaijan, Inshaatchilar Avenue, Baku, AZ1136, Azerbaijan, www.azstat.org; National Data Center.

AZERBAIJAN - PRIMARY STATISTICS SOURCES

State Statistical Committee of the Republic of Azerbaijan, Inshaatchilar Avenue, Baku, AZ1136, Azerbaijan, www.azstat.org; *Azerbaijan in Figures; Education, Science and Culture in Azerbaijan;* and *Statistical Yearbook of Azerbaijan 2007.*

AZERBAIJAN - ABORTION

United Nations Statistics Division, New York, NY 10017, (800) 253-9646, Fax: (212) 963-4116, http://unstats.un.org; *Trends in Europe and North America: The Statistical Yearbook of the ECE 2005.*

AZERBAIJAN - AGRICULTURE

Academic International Press, PO Box 1111, Gulf Breeze, FL 32562-1111, Fax: (850) 934-0953, www.ai-press.com; *Russia and Eurasia Facts and Figures Annual.*

Economist Intelligence Unit, 111 West 57th Street, New York, NY 10019, (212) 554-0600, Fax: (212) 586-1181, www.eiu.com; *Azerbaijan Country Report.*

Euromonitor International, Inc., 224 S. Michigan Avenue, Suite 1500, Chicago, IL 60604, (312) 922-1115, Fax: (312) 922-1157, www.euromonitor.com; *World Marketing Data and Statistics.*

Palgrave Macmillan Ltd., Houndmills, Basingstoke, Hampshire, RG21 6XS, England, (Telephone in U.S. (888) 330-8477), (Fax in U.S. (800) 672-2054), www.palgrave.com; *The Statesman's Yearbook 2008.*

Taylor and Francis Group, An Informa Business, 2 Park Square, Milton Park, Abingdon, Oxford OX14 4RN, United Kingdom, (Dial from U.S. (212) 216-7800), (Fax from U.S. (212) 564-7854), www.tandf.co.uk; *The Europa World Year Book.*

United Nations Food and Agricultural Organization (FAO), Viale delle Terme di Caracalla, 00100 Rome, Italy, (Dial from U.S. (202) 653-2400), (Fax from U.S. (202) 653 5760), www.fao.org; AQUASTAT; *FAO Production Yearbook 2002; FAO Trade Yearbook;* and *The State of Food and Agriculture (SOFA) 2006.*

United Nations Statistics Division, New York, NY 10017, (800) 253-9646, Fax: (212) 963-4116, http://unstats.un.org; *2004 Industrial Commodity Statistics Yearbook* and *Statistical Yearbook.*

The World Bank, 1818 H Street, NW, Washington, DC 20433, (202) 473-1000, Fax: (202) 477-6391, www.worldbank.org; *Azerbaijan; Statistical Handbook: States of the Former USSR;* and *World Development Indicators (WDI) 2008.*

AZERBAIJAN - AIRLINES

International Civil Aviation Organization (ICAO), External Relations and Public Information Office (EPO), 999 University Street, Montreal, Quebec H3C 5H7, Canada, (Dial from U.S. (514) 954-8219), (Fax from U.S. (514) 954-6077), www.icao.int; *Civil Aviation Statistics of the World.*

Palgrave Macmillan Ltd., Houndmills, Basingstoke, Hampshire, RG21 6XS, England, (Telephone in U.S. (888) 330-8477), (Fax in U.S. (800) 672-2054), www.palgrave.com; *The Statesman's Yearbook 2008.*

United Nations Statistics Division, New York, NY 10017, (800) 253-9646, Fax: (212) 963-4116, http://unstats.un.org; *Statistical Yearbook.*

AZERBAIJAN - AIRPORTS

Central Intelligence Agency, Office of Public Affairs, Washington, DC 20505, (703) 482-0623, Fax: (703) 482-1739, www.cia.gov; *The World Factbook.*

AZERBAIJAN - ARMED FORCES

Academic International Press, PO Box 1111, Gulf Breeze, FL 32562-1111, Fax: (850) 934-0953, www.ai-press.com; *Russia and Eurasia Facts and Figures Annual.*

Central Intelligence Agency, Office of Public Affairs, Washington, DC 20505, (703) 482-0623, Fax: (703) 482-1739, www.cia.gov; *The World Factbook.*

Euromonitor International, Inc., 224 S. Michigan Avenue, Suite 1500, Chicago, IL 60604, (312) 922-1115, Fax: (312) 922-1157, www.euromonitor.com; *World Marketing Data and Statistics.*

International Institute for Strategic Studies (IISS), Arundel House, 13-15 Arundel Street, Temple Place, London WC2R 3DX, England, www.iiss.org; *The Military Balance 2007.*

Palgrave Macmillan Ltd., Houndmills, Basingstoke, Hampshire, RG21 6XS, England, (Telephone in U.S. (888) 330-8477), (Fax in U.S. (800) 672-2054), www.palgrave.com; *The Statesman's Yearbook 2008.*

United Nations Statistics Division, New York, NY 10017, (800) 253-9646, Fax: (212) 963-4116, http://unstats.un.org; *Human Development Report 2006.*

AZERBAIJAN - BALANCE OF PAYMENTS

The World Bank, 1818 H Street, NW, Washington, DC 20433, (202) 473-1000, Fax: (202) 477-6391, www.worldbank.org; *Azerbaijan; World Development Indicators (WDI) 2008;* and *World Development Report 2008.*

AZERBAIJAN - BANKS AND BANKING

Euromonitor International, Inc., 224 S. Michigan Avenue, Suite 1500, Chicago, IL 60604, (312) 922-1115, Fax: (312) 922-1157, www.euromonitor.com; *World Marketing Data and Statistics.*

AZERBAIJAN - BEVERAGE INDUSTRY

United Nations Statistics Division, New York, NY 10017, (800) 253-9646, Fax: (212) 963-4116, http://unstats.un.org; *Statistical Yearbook.*

AZERBAIJAN - BROADCASTING

Central Intelligence Agency, Office of Public Affairs, Washington, DC 20505, (703) 482-0623, Fax: (703) 482-1739, www.cia.gov; *The World Factbook.*

Euromonitor International, Inc., 224 S. Michigan Avenue, Suite 1500, Chicago, IL 60604, (312) 922-1115, Fax: (312) 922-1157, www.euromonitor.com; *World Marketing Data and Statistics.*

Palgrave Macmillan Ltd., Houndmills, Basingstoke, Hampshire, RG21 6XS, England, (Telephone in U.S. (888) 330-8477), (Fax in U.S. (800) 672-2054), www.palgrave.com; *The Statesman's Yearbook 2008.*

UNESCO Institute for Statistics, C.P. 6128 Succursale Centre-Ville, Montreal, Quebec, H3C 3J7 Canada, (Dial from U.S. (514) 343-6880), (Fax from U.S. (514) 343 6882), www.uis.unesco.org; *Statistical Tables.*

United Nations Statistics Division, New York, NY 10017, (800) 253-9646, Fax: (212) 963-4116, http://unstats.un.org; *Trends in Europe and North America: The Statistical Yearbook of the ECE 2005.*

AZERBAIJAN - BUDGET

Central Intelligence Agency, Office of Public Affairs, Washington, DC 20505, (703) 482-0623, Fax: (703) 482-1739, www.cia.gov; *The World Factbook.*

AZERBAIJAN - BUSINESS

United Nations Statistics Division, New York, NY 10017, (800) 253-9646, Fax: (212) 963-4116, http://unstats.un.org; *Statistical Yearbook.*

AZERBAIJAN - CAPITAL INVESTMENTS

The World Bank, 1818 H Street, NW, Washington, DC 20433, (202) 473-1000, Fax: (202) 477-6391, www.worldbank.org; *Statistical Handbook: States of the Former USSR.*

AZERBAIJAN - CATTLE

See AZERBAIJAN - LIVESTOCK

AZERBAIJAN - CHILDBIRTH - STATISTICS

Central Intelligence Agency, Office of Public Affairs, Washington, DC 20505, (703) 482-0623, Fax: (703) 482-1739, www.cia.gov; *The World Factbook.*

Euromonitor International, Inc., 224 S. Michigan Avenue, Suite 1500, Chicago, IL 60604, (312) 922-1115, Fax: (312) 922-1157, www.euromonitor.com; *International Marketing Data and Statistics 2008* and *The World Economic Factbook 2008.*

Palgrave Macmillan Ltd., Houndmills, Basingstoke, Hampshire, RG21 6XS, England, (Telephone in U.S. (888) 330-8477), (Fax in U.S. (800) 672-2054), www.palgrave.com; *The Statesman's Yearbook 2008.*

Taylor and Francis Group, An Informa Business, 2 Park Square, Milton Park, Abingdon, Oxford OX14 4RN, United Kingdom, (Dial from U.S. (212) 216-7800), (Fax from U.S. (212) 564-7854), www.tandf.co.uk; *The Europa World Year Book.*

United Nations Statistics Division, New York, NY 10017, (800) 253-9646, Fax: (212) 963-4116, http://unstats.un.org; *Statistical Yearbook.*

World Health Organization (WHO), Avenue Appia 20, 1211 Geneve 27, Switzerland, (Telephone in U.S. (212) 331-9081), www.who.int; *World Health Report 2006.*

AZERBAIJAN - COAL PRODUCTION

See AZERBAIJAN - MINERAL INDUSTRIES

AZERBAIJAN - COMMERCE

Palgrave Macmillan Ltd., Houndmills, Basingstoke, Hampshire, RG21 6XS, England, (Telephone in U.S. (888) 330-8477), (Fax in U.S. (800) 672-2054), www.palgrave.com; *The Statesman's Yearbook 2008.*

AZERBAIJAN - CONSTRUCTION INDUSTRY

Academic International Press, PO Box 1111, Gulf Breeze, FL 32562-1111, Fax: (850) 934-0953, www.ai-press.com; *Russia and Eurasia Facts and Figures Annual.*

United Nations Statistics Division, New York, NY 10017, (800) 253-9646, Fax: (212) 963-4116, http://unstats.un.org; *Statistical Yearbook.*

AZERBAIJAN - CONSUMER GOODS

The World Bank, 1818 H Street, NW, Washington, DC 20433, (202) 473-1000, Fax: (202) 477-6391, www.worldbank.org; *Statistical Handbook: States of the Former USSR* and *World Development Report 2008.*

AZERBAIJAN - CONSUMER PRICE INDEXES

United Nations Statistics Division, New York, NY 10017, (800) 253-9646, Fax: (212) 963-4116, http://unstats.un.org; *Statistical Yearbook* and *Trends in Europe and North America: The Statistical Yearbook of the ECE 2005.*

The World Bank, 1818 H Street, NW, Washington, DC 20433, (202) 473-1000, Fax: (202) 477-6391, www.worldbank.org; *Azerbaijan.*

AZERBAIJAN - COTTON

See AZERBAIJAN - CROPS

AZERBAIJAN - CRIME

Academic International Press, PO Box 1111, Gulf Breeze, FL 32562-1111, Fax: (850) 934-0953, www.ai-press.com; *Russia and Eurasia Facts and Figures Annual.*

United Nations Statistics Division, New York, NY 10017, (800) 253-9646, Fax: (212) 963-4116, http://unstats.un.org; *Trends in Europe and North America: The Statistical Yearbook of the ECE 2005.*

AZERBAIJAN - CROPS

Palgrave Macmillan Ltd., Houndmills, Basingstoke, Hampshire, RG21 6XS, England, (Telephone in U.S. (888) 330-8477), (Fax in U.S. (800) 672-2054), www.palgrave.com; *The Statesman's Yearbook 2008.*

Taylor and Francis Group, An Informa Business, 2 Park Square, Milton Park, Abingdon, Oxford OX14 4RN, United Kingdom, (Dial from U.S. (212) 216-7800), (Fax from U.S. (212) 564-7854), www.tandf.co.uk; *The Europa World Year Book.*

United Nations Food and Agricultural Organization (FAO), Viale delle Terme di Caracalla, 00100 Rome, Italy, (Dial from U.S. (202) 653-2400), (Fax from U.S. (202) 653 5760), www.fao.org; *FAO Production Yearbook 2002* and *The State of Food and Agriculture (SOFA) 2006.*

United Nations Statistics Division, New York, NY 10017, (800) 253-9646, Fax: (212) 963-4116, http://unstats.un.org; *2004 Industrial Commodity Statistics Yearbook* and *Statistical Yearbook.*

The World Bank, 1818 H Street, NW, Washington, DC 20433, (202) 473-1000, Fax: (202) 477-6391, www.worldbank.org; *Statistical Handbook: States of the Former USSR.*

AZERBAIJAN - DAIRY PROCESSING

Palgrave Macmillan Ltd., Houndmills, Basingstoke, Hampshire, RG21 6XS, England, (Telephone in U.S. (888) 330-8477), (Fax in U.S. (800) 672-2054), www.palgrave.com; *The Statesman's Yearbook 2008.*

Taylor and Francis Group, An Informa Business, 2 Park Square, Milton Park, Abingdon, Oxford OX14 4RN, United Kingdom, (Dial from U.S. (212) 216-7800), (Fax from U.S. (212) 564-7854), www.tandf.co.uk; *The Europa World Year Book.*

United Nations Food and Agricultural Organization (FAO), Viale delle Terme di Caracalla, 00100 Rome, Italy, (Dial from U.S. (202) 653-2400), (Fax from U.S. (202) 653 5760), www.fao.org; *FAO Production Yearbook 2002* and *The State of Food and Agriculture (SOFA) 2006.*

United Nations Statistics Division, New York, NY 10017, (800) 253-9646, Fax: (212) 963-4116, http://unstats.un.org; *2004 Industrial Commodity Statistics Yearbook* and *Statistical Yearbook.*

AZERBAIJAN - DEATH RATES

See AZERBAIJAN - MORTALITY

AZERBAIJAN - DEBTS, EXTERNAL

The World Bank, 1818 H Street, NW, Washington, DC 20433, (202) 473-1000, Fax: (202) 477-6391, www.worldbank.org; *Global Development Finance 2007; World Development Indicators (WDI) 2008;* and *World Development Report 2008.*

AZERBAIJAN - DEMOGRAPHY

Euromonitor International, Inc., 224 S. Michigan Avenue, Suite 1500, Chicago, IL 60604, (312) 922-1115, Fax: (312) 922-1157, www.euromonitor.com; *International Marketing Data and Statistics 2008; The World Economic Factbook 2008;* and *World Marketing Data and Statistics.*

United Nations Statistics Division, New York, NY 10017, (800) 253-9646, Fax: (212) 963-4116, http://unstats.un.org; *Demographic Yearbook* and *Human Development Report 2006.*

The World Bank, 1818 H Street, NW, Washington, DC 20433, (202) 473-1000, Fax: (202) 477-6391, www.worldbank.org; *Azerbaijan* and *Statistical Handbook: States of the Former USSR.*

AZERBAIJAN - DISPOSABLE INCOME

United Nations Statistics Division, New York, NY 10017, (800) 253-9646, Fax: (212) 963-4116, http://unstats.un.org; *Statistical Yearbook.*

AZERBAIJAN - DIVORCE

United Nations Statistics Division, New York, NY 10017, (800) 253-9646, Fax: (212) 963-4116, http://

unstats.un.org; *Demographic Yearbook; Statistical Yearbook;* and *Trends in Europe and North America: The Statistical Yearbook of the ECE 2005.*

AZERBAIJAN - ECONOMIC CONDITIONS

Academic International Press, PO Box 1111, Gulf Breeze, FL 32562-1111, Fax: (850) 934-0953, www.ai-press.com; *Russia and Eurasia Facts and Figures Annual.*

Center for International Business Education Research (CIBER), Columbia Business School and School of International and Public Affairs, Uris Hall, Room 212, 3022 Broadway, New York, NY 10027-6902, Mr. Joshua Safier, (212) 854-4750, Fax: (212) 222-9821, www.columbia.edu/cu/ciber/; Datastream International.

Central Intelligence Agency, Office of Public Affairs, Washington, DC 20505, (703) 482-0623, Fax: (703) 482-1739, www.cia.gov; *The World Factbook.*

DSI Data Service Information, Xantener Strasse 51a, D-47495 Rheinberg, Germany, www.dsidata.com; *Campus Solution.*

Dun and Bradstreet (DB) Corporation, 103 JFK Parkway, Short Hills, NJ 07078, (973) 921-5500, www.dnb.com; *Country Report.*

Economist Intelligence Unit, 111 West 57th Street, New York, NY 10019, (212) 554-0600, Fax: (212) 586-1181, www.eiu.com; *Azerbaijan Country Report.*

Euromonitor International, Inc., 224 S. Michigan Avenue, Suite 1500, Chicago, IL 60604, (312) 922-1115, Fax: (312) 922-1157, www.euromonitor.com; *The World Economic Factbook 2008* and *World Marketing Data and Statistics.*

International Monetary Fund (IMF), 700 Nineteenth Street, NW, Washington, DC 20431, (202) 623-7000, Fax: (202) 623-4661, www.imf.org; *World Economic Outlook Reports.*

Nomura Research Institute (NRI), 2 World Financial Center, Building B, 19th Fl., New York, NY 10281-1198, (212) 667-1670, www.nri.co.jp/english; *Asian Economic Outlook 2003-2004.*

Palgrave Macmillan Ltd., Houndmills, Basingstoke, Hampshire, RG21 6XS, England, (Telephone in U.S. (888) 330-8477), (Fax in U.S. (800) 672-2054), www.palgrave.com; *The Statesman's Yearbook 2008.*

State Statistical Committee of the Republic of Azerbaijan, Inshaatchilar Avenue, Baku, AZ1136, Azerbaijan, www.azstat.org; *The Foreign Trade of Azerbaijan.*

Taylor and Francis Group, An Informa Business, 2 Park Square, Milton Park, Abingdon, Oxford OX14 4RN, United Kingdom, (Dial from U.S. (212) 216-7800), (Fax from U.S. (212) 564-7854), www.tandf.co.uk; *The Europa World Year Book.*

United Nations Economic and Social Commission for Western Asia (ESCWA), PO Box 11-8575, Riad el-Solh Square, Beirut, Lebanon, www.escwa.un.org; *Annual Report 2006; Bulletin on Population and Vital Statistics in the ESCWA Region;* and *Survey of Economic and Social Developments in the ESCWA Region 2006-2007.*

United Nations Statistics Division, New York, NY 10017, (800) 253-9646, Fax: (212) 963-4116, http://unstats.un.org; *World Statistics Pocketbook.*

The World Bank, 1818 H Street, NW, Washington, DC 20433, (202) 473-1000, Fax: (202) 477-6391, www.worldbank.org; *Azerbaijan; Global Economic Monitor (GEM); Global Economic Prospects 2008; The World Bank Atlas 2003-2004;* and *World Development Report 2008.*

AZERBAIJAN - EDUCATION

Academic International Press, PO Box 1111, Gulf Breeze, FL 32562-1111, Fax: (850) 934-0953, www.ai-press.com; *Russia and Eurasia Facts and Figures Annual.*

Euromonitor International, Inc., 224 S. Michigan Avenue, Suite 1500, Chicago, IL 60604, (312) 922-1115, Fax: (312) 922-1157, www.euromonitor.com; *International Marketing Data and Statistics 2008* and *World Marketing Data and Statistics.*

Palgrave Macmillan Ltd., Houndmills, Basingstoke, Hampshire, RG21 6XS, England, (Telephone in U.S. (888) 330-8477), (Fax in U.S. (800) 672-2054), www.palgrave.com; *The Statesman's Yearbook 2008.*

State Statistical Committee of the Republic of Azerbaijan, Inshaatchilar Avenue, Baku, AZ1136, Azerbaijan, www.azstat.org; *Education, Science and Culture in Azerbaijan.*

Taylor and Francis Group, An Informa Business, 2 Park Square, Milton Park, Abingdon, Oxford OX14 4RN, United Kingdom, (Dial from U.S. (212) 216-7800), (Fax from U.S. (212) 564-7854), www.tandf.co.uk; *The Europa World Year Book.*

UNESCO Institute for Statistics, C.P. 6128 Succursale Centre-Ville, Montreal, Quebec, H3C 3J7 Canada, (Dial from U.S. (514) 343-6880), (Fax from U.S. (514) 343 6882), www.uis.unesco.org; *Statistical Tables.*

United Nations Statistics Division, New York, NY 10017, (800) 253-9646, Fax: (212) 963-4116, http://unstats.un.org; *Human Development Report 2006* and *Trends in Europe and North America: The Statistical Yearbook of the ECE 2005.*

The World Bank, 1818 H Street, NW, Washington, DC 20433, (202) 473-1000, Fax: (202) 477-6391, www.worldbank.org; *Azerbaijan* and *World Development Report 2008.*

AZERBAIJAN - ELECTRICITY

Palgrave Macmillan Ltd., Houndmills, Basingstoke, Hampshire, RG21 6XS, England, (Telephone in U.S. (888) 330-8477), (Fax in U.S. (800) 672-2054), www.palgrave.com; *The Statesman's Yearbook 2008.*

Platts, 2 Penn Plaza, 25th Floor, New York, NY 10121-2298, (212) 904-3070, www.platts.com; *Energy Economist.*

U.S. Department of Energy (DOE), Energy Information Administration (EIA), 1000 Independence Avenue, SW, Washington, DC 20585, (202) 586-8800, www.eia.doe.gov; *International Energy Annual 2004* and *International Energy Outlook 2006.*

United Nations Statistics Division, New York, NY 10017, (800) 253-9646, Fax: (212) 963-4116, http://unstats.un.org; *Energy Statistics Yearbook 2003; Human Development Report 2006; Statistical Yearbook;* and *Trends in Europe and North America: The Statistical Yearbook of the ECE 2005.*

The World Bank, 1818 H Street, NW, Washington, DC 20433, (202) 473-1000, Fax: (202) 477-6391, www.worldbank.org; *Statistical Handbook: States of the Former USSR.*

AZERBAIJAN - EMPLOYMENT

Euromonitor International, Inc., 224 S. Michigan Avenue, Suite 1500, Chicago, IL 60604, (312) 922-1115, Fax: (312) 922-1157, www.euromonitor.com; *International Marketing Data and Statistics 2008.*

United Nations Statistics Division, New York, NY 10017, (800) 253-9646, Fax: (212) 963-4116, http://unstats.un.org; *Statistical Yearbook* and *Trends in Europe and North America: The Statistical Yearbook of the ECE 2005.*

The World Bank, 1818 H Street, NW, Washington, DC 20433, (202) 473-1000, Fax: (202) 477-6391, www.worldbank.org; *Azerbaijan* and *Statistical Handbook: States of the Former USSR.*

AZERBAIJAN - ENVIRONMENTAL CONDITIONS

DSI Data Service Information, Xantener Strasse 51a, D-47495 Rheinberg, Germany, www.dsidata.com; *Campus Solution* and *DSI's Global Environmental Database.*

Economist Intelligence Unit, 111 West 57th Street, New York, NY 10019, (212) 554-0600, Fax: (212) 586-1181, www.eiu.com; *Azerbaijan Country Report.*

United Nations Statistics Division, New York, NY 10017, (800) 253-9646, Fax: (212) 963-4116, http://unstats.un.org; *Statistical Yearbook; Trends in Europe and North America: The Statistical Yearbook of the ECE 2005;* and *World Statistics Pocketbook.*

AZERBAIJAN - EXPORTS

Academic International Press, PO Box 1111, Gulf Breeze, FL 32562-1111, Fax: (850) 934-0953, www.ai-press.com; *Russia and Eurasia Facts and Figures Annual.*

Central Intelligence Agency, Office of Public Affairs, Washington, DC 20505, (703) 482-0623, Fax: (703) 482-1739, www.cia.gov; *The World Factbook.*

Economist Intelligence Unit, 111 West 57th Street, New York, NY 10019, (212) 554-0600, Fax: (212) 586-1181, www.eiu.com; *Azerbaijan Country Report.*

Euromonitor International, Inc., 224 S. Michigan Avenue, Suite 1500, Chicago, IL 60604, (312) 922-1115, Fax: (312) 922-1157, www.euromonitor.com; *International Marketing Data and Statistics 2008* and *The World Economic Factbook 2008.*

International Monetary Fund (IMF), 700 Nineteenth Street, NW, Washington, DC 20431, (202) 623-7000, Fax: (202) 623-4661, www.imf.org; *Direction of Trade Statistics Yearbook 2007.*

Palgrave Macmillan Ltd., Houndmills, Basingstoke, Hampshire, RG21 6XS, England, (Telephone in U.S. (888) 330-8477), (Fax in U.S. (800) 672-2054), www.palgrave.com; *The Statesman's Yearbook 2008.*

State Statistical Committee of the Republic of Azerbaijan, Inshaatchilar Avenue, Baku, AZ1136, Azerbaijan, www.azstat.org; *The Foreign Trade of Azerbaijan.*

Taylor and Francis Group, An Informa Business, 2 Park Square, Milton Park, Abingdon, Oxford OX14 4RN, United Kingdom, (Dial from U.S. (212) 216-7800), (Fax from U.S. (212) 564-7854), www.tandf.co.uk; *The Europa World Year Book.*

United Nations Statistics Division, New York, NY 10017, (800) 253-9646, Fax: (212) 963-4116, http://unstats.un.org; *International Trade Statistics Yearbook* and *Trends in Europe and North America: The Statistical Yearbook of the ECE 2005.*

The World Bank, 1818 H Street, NW, Washington, DC 20433, (202) 473-1000, Fax: (202) 477-6391, www.worldbank.org; *Statistical Handbook: States of the Former USSR; World Development Indicators (WDI) 2008;* and *World Development Report 2008.*

AZERBAIJAN - FERTILITY, HUMAN

Central Intelligence Agency, Office of Public Affairs, Washington, DC 20505, (703) 482-0623, Fax: (703) 482-1739, www.cia.gov; *The World Factbook.*

United Nations Statistics Division, New York, NY 10017, (800) 253-9646, Fax: (212) 963-4116, http://unstats.un.org; *Human Development Report 2006* and *Trends in Europe and North America: The Statistical Yearbook of the ECE 2005.*

The World Bank, 1818 H Street, NW, Washington, DC 20433, (202) 473-1000, Fax: (202) 477-6391, www.worldbank.org; *Statistical Handbook: States of the Former USSR; The World Bank Atlas 2003-2004; World Development Indicators (WDI) 2008;* and *World Development Report 2008.*

World Health Organization (WHO), Avenue Appia 20, 1211 Geneve 27, Switzerland, (Telephone in U.S. (212) 331-9081), www.who.int; *World Health Report 2006.*

AZERBAIJAN - FERTILIZER INDUSTRY

United Nations Food and Agricultural Organization (FAO), Viale delle Terme di Caracalla, 00100 Rome, Italy, (Dial from U.S. (202) 653-2400), (Fax from U.S. (202) 653 5760), www.fao.org; *FAO Fertilizer Yearbook.*

United Nations Statistics Division, New York, NY 10017, (800) 253-9646, Fax: (212) 963-4116, http://unstats.un.org; *2004 Industrial Commodity Statistics Yearbook* and *Statistical Yearbook.*

AZERBAIJAN - FETAL MORTALITY

See AZERBAIJAN - MORTALITY

AZERBAIJAN - FINANCE

Taylor and Francis Group, An Informa Business, 2 Park Square, Milton Park, Abingdon, Oxford OX14

4RN, United Kingdom, (Dial from U.S. (212) 216-7800), (Fax from U.S. (212) 564-7854), www.tandf.co.uk; *The Europa World Year Book.*

United Nations Statistics Division, New York, NY 10017, (800) 253-9646, Fax: (212) 963-4116, http://unstats.un.org; *National Accounts Statistics: Compendium of Income Distribution Statistics* and *Statistical Yearbook.*

The World Bank, 1818 H Street, NW, Washington, DC 20433, (202) 473-1000, Fax: (202) 477-6391, www.worldbank.org; *Azerbaijan* and *Statistical Handbook: States of the Former USSR.*

AZERBAIJAN - FINANCE, PUBLIC

Bernan Essential Government Publications, 4611-F Assembly Drive, Lanham MD, 20706-4391, (301) 459-2255, Fax: (800) 865-3450, www.bernan.com; *National Accounts Statistics.*

Economist Intelligence Unit, 111 West 57th Street, New York, NY 10019, (212) 554-0600, Fax: (212) 586-1181, www.eiu.com; *Azerbaijan Country Report.*

International Monetary Fund (IMF), 700 Nineteenth Street, NW, Washington, DC 20431, (202) 623-7000, Fax: (202) 623-4661, www.imf.org; *International Financial Statistics* and *International Financial Statistics Online Service.*

Palgrave Macmillan Ltd., Houndmills, Basingstoke, Hampshire, RG21 6XS, England, (Telephone in U.S. (888) 330-8477), (Fax in U.S. (800) 672-2054), www.palgrave.com; *The Statesman's Yearbook 2008.*

Taylor and Francis Group, An Informa Business, 2 Park Square, Milton Park, Abingdon, Oxford OX14 4RN, United Kingdom, (Dial from U.S. (212) 216-7800), (Fax from U.S. (212) 564-7854), www.tandf.co.uk; *The Europa World Year Book.*

The World Bank, 1818 H Street, NW, Washington, DC 20433, (202) 473-1000, Fax: (202) 477-6391, www.worldbank.org; *Azerbaijan* and *Statistical Handbook: States of the Former USSR.*

AZERBAIJAN - FISHERIES

Palgrave Macmillan Ltd., Houndmills, Basingstoke, Hampshire, RG21 6XS, England, (Telephone in U.S. (888) 330-8477), (Fax in U.S. (800) 672-2054), www.palgrave.com; *The Statesman's Yearbook 2008.*

United Nations Food and Agricultural Organization (FAO), Viale delle Terme di Caracalla, 00100 Rome, Italy, (Dial from U.S. (202) 653-2400), (Fax from U.S. (202) 653 5760), www.fao.org; *FAO Yearbook of Fishery Statistics;* Fishery Databases; FISHSTAT Database. Subjects covered include: Aquaculture production, capture production, fishery commodities; and *The State of Food and Agriculture (SOFA) 2006.*

United Nations Statistics Division, New York, NY 10017, (800) 253-9646, Fax: (212) 963-4116, http://unstats.un.org; *2004 Industrial Commodity Statistics Yearbook* and *Statistical Yearbook.*

The World Bank, 1818 H Street, NW, Washington, DC 20433, (202) 473-1000, Fax: (202) 477-6391, www.worldbank.org; *Azerbaijan.*

AZERBAIJAN - FOOD

United Nations Food and Agricultural Organization (FAO), Viale delle Terme di Caracalla, 00100 Rome, Italy, (Dial from U.S. (202) 653-2400), (Fax from U.S. (202) 653 5760), www.fao.org; *FAO Production Yearbook 2002* and *The State of Food and Agriculture (SOFA) 2006.*

United Nations Statistics Division, New York, NY 10017, (800) 253-9646, Fax: (212) 963-4116, http://unstats.un.org; *Human Development Report 2006* and *2004 Industrial Commodity Statistics Yearbook.*

AZERBAIJAN - FOREIGN EXCHANGE RATES

Central Intelligence Agency, Office of Public Affairs, Washington, DC 20505, (703) 482-0623, Fax: (703) 482-1739, www.cia.gov; *The World Factbook.*

Euromonitor International, Inc., 224 S. Michigan Avenue, Suite 1500, Chicago, IL 60604, (312) 922-1115, Fax: (312) 922-1157, www.euromonitor.com; *International Marketing Data and Statistics 2008* and *The World Economic Factbook 2008.*

Taylor and Francis Group, An Informa Business, 2 Park Square, Milton Park, Abingdon, Oxford OX14 4RN, United Kingdom, (Dial from U.S. (212) 216-7800), (Fax from U.S. (212) 564-7854), www.tandf.co.uk; *The Europa World Year Book.*

United Nations Statistics Division, New York, NY 10017, (800) 253-9646, Fax: (212) 963-4116, http://unstats.un.org; *Statistical Yearbook; Trends in Europe and North America: The Statistical Yearbook of the ECE 2005;* and *World Statistics Pocketbook.*

AZERBAIJAN - FORESTS AND FORESTRY

Academic International Press, PO Box 1111, Gulf Breeze, FL 32562-1111, Fax: (850) 934-0953, www.ai-press.com; *Russia and Eurasia Facts and Figures Annual.*

Palgrave Macmillan Ltd., Houndmills, Basingstoke, Hampshire, RG21 6XS, England, (Telephone in U.S. (888) 330-8477), (Fax in U.S. (800) 672-2054), www.palgrave.com; *The Statesman's Yearbook 2008.*

UNESCO Institute for Statistics, C.P. 6128 Succursale Centre-Ville, Montreal, Quebec, H3C 3J7 Canada, (Dial from U.S. (514) 343-6880), (Fax from U.S. (514) 343 6882), www.uis.unesco.org; *Statistical Tables.*

United Nations Food and Agricultural Organization (FAO), Viale delle Terme di Caracalla, 00100 Rome, Italy, (Dial from U.S. (202) 653-2400), (Fax from U.S. (202) 653 5760), www.fao.org; *FAO Yearbook of Forest Products* and *The State of Food and Agriculture (SOFA) 2006.*

United Nations Statistics Division, New York, NY 10017, (800) 253-9646, Fax: (212) 963-4116, http://unstats.un.org; *2004 Industrial Commodity Statistics Yearbook; Statistical Yearbook;* and *Trends in Europe and North America: The Statistical Yearbook of the ECE 2005.*

The World Bank, 1818 H Street, NW, Washington, DC 20433, (202) 473-1000, Fax: (202) 477-6391, www.worldbank.org; *Azerbaijan* and *World Development Report 2008.*

AZERBAIJAN - GROSS DOMESTIC PRODUCT

Academic International Press, PO Box 1111, Gulf Breeze, FL 32562-1111, Fax: (850) 934-0953, www.ai-press.com; *Russia and Eurasia Facts and Figures Annual.*

Economist Intelligence Unit, 111 West 57th Street, New York, NY 10019, (212) 554-0600, Fax: (212) 586-1181, www.eiu.com; *Azerbaijan Country Report.*

Euromonitor International, Inc., 224 S. Michigan Avenue, Suite 1500, Chicago, IL 60604, (312) 922-1115, Fax: (312) 922-1157, www.euromonitor.com; *International Marketing Data and Statistics 2008* and *The World Economic Factbook 2008.*

United Nations Statistics Division, New York, NY 10017, (800) 253-9646, Fax: (212) 963-4116, http://unstats.un.org; *Human Development Report 2006; National Accounts Statistics: Compendium of Income Distribution Statistics; Statistical Yearbook;* and *Trends in Europe and North America: The Statistical Yearbook of the ECE 2005.*

The World Bank, 1818 H Street, NW, Washington, DC 20433, (202) 473-1000, Fax: (202) 477-6391, www.worldbank.org; *Statistical Handbook: States of the Former USSR; World Development Indicators (WDI) 2008;* and *World Development Report 2008.*

AZERBAIJAN - GROSS NATIONAL PRODUCT

Palgrave Macmillan Ltd., Houndmills, Basingstoke, Hampshire, RG21 6XS, England, (Telephone in U.S. (888) 330-8477), (Fax in U.S. (800) 672-2054), www.palgrave.com; *The Statesman's Yearbook 2008.*

United Nations Statistics Division, New York, NY 10017, (800) 253-9646, Fax: (212) 963-4116, http://unstats.un.org; *Statistical Yearbook.*

The World Bank, 1818 H Street, NW, Washington, DC 20433, (202) 473-1000, Fax: (202) 477-6391, www.worldbank.org; *The World Bank Atlas 2003-2004; World Development Indicators (WDI) 2008;* and *World Development Report 2008.*

AZERBAIJAN - HOUSING

Euromonitor International, Inc., 224 S. Michigan Avenue, Suite 1500, Chicago, IL 60604, (312) 922-1115, Fax: (312) 922-1157, www.euromonitor.com; *World Marketing Data and Statistics.*

United Nations Statistics Division, New York, NY 10017, (800) 253-9646, Fax: (212) 963-4116, http://unstats.un.org; *Human Development Report 2006; Statistical Yearbook;* and *Trends in Europe and North America: The Statistical Yearbook of the ECE 2005.*

AZERBAIJAN - ILLITERATE PERSONS

Euromonitor International, Inc., 224 S. Michigan Avenue, Suite 1500, Chicago, IL 60604, (312) 922-1115, Fax: (312) 922-1157, www.euromonitor.com; *The World Economic Factbook 2008.*

UNESCO Institute for Statistics, C.P. 6128 Succursale Centre-Ville, Montreal, Quebec, H3C 3J7 Canada, (Dial from U.S. (514) 343-6880), (Fax from U.S. (514) 343 6882), www.uis.unesco.org; *Statistical Tables.*

United Nations Statistics Division, New York, NY 10017, (800) 253-9646, Fax: (212) 963-4116, http://unstats.un.org; *Human Development Report 2006.*

AZERBAIJAN - IMPORTS

Academic International Press, PO Box 1111, Gulf Breeze, FL 32562-1111, Fax: (850) 934-0953, www.ai-press.com; *Russia and Eurasia Facts and Figures Annual.*

Central Intelligence Agency, Office of Public Affairs, Washington, DC 20505, (703) 482-0623, Fax: (703) 482-1739, www.cia.gov; *The World Factbook.*

Economist Intelligence Unit, 111 West 57th Street, New York, NY 10019, (212) 554-0600, Fax: (212) 586-1181, www.eiu.com; *Azerbaijan Country Report.*

Euromonitor International, Inc., 224 S. Michigan Avenue, Suite 1500, Chicago, IL 60604, (312) 922-1115, Fax: (312) 922-1157, www.euromonitor.com; *International Marketing Data and Statistics 2008* and *The World Economic Factbook 2008.*

International Monetary Fund (IMF), 700 Nineteenth Street, NW, Washington, DC 20431, (202) 623-7000, Fax: (202) 623-4661, www.imf.org; *Direction of Trade Statistics Yearbook 2007.*

Palgrave Macmillan Ltd., Houndmills, Basingstoke, Hampshire, RG21 6XS, England, (Telephone in U.S. (888) 330-8477), (Fax in U.S. (800) 672-2054), www.palgrave.com; *The Statesman's Yearbook 2008.*

State Statistical Committee of the Republic of Azerbaijan, Inshaatchilar Avenue, Baku, AZ1136, Azerbaijan, www.azstat.org; *The Foreign Trade of Azerbaijan.*

Taylor and Francis Group, An Informa Business, 2 Park Square, Milton Park, Abingdon, Oxford OX14 4RN, United Kingdom, (Dial from U.S. (212) 216-7800), (Fax from U.S. (212) 564-7854), www.tandf.co.uk; *The Europa World Year Book.*

United Nations Statistics Division, New York, NY 10017, (800) 253-9646, Fax: (212) 963-4116, http://unstats.un.org; *International Trade Statistics Yearbook* and *Trends in Europe and North America: The Statistical Yearbook of the ECE 2005.*

The World Bank, 1818 H Street, NW, Washington, DC 20433, (202) 473-1000, Fax: (202) 477-6391, www.worldbank.org; *Statistical Handbook: States of the Former USSR; World Development Indicators (WDI) 2008;* and *World Development Report 2008.*

AZERBAIJAN - INDUSTRIAL PRODUCTIVITY

The World Bank, 1818 H Street, NW, Washington, DC 20433, (202) 473-1000, Fax: (202) 477-6391, www.worldbank.org; *Statistical Handbook: States of the Former USSR.*

AZERBAIJAN - INDUSTRIAL PROPERTY

United Nations Statistics Division, New York, NY 10017, (800) 253-9646, Fax: (212) 963-4116, http://unstats.un.org; *Statistical Yearbook.*

AZERBAIJAN - INDUSTRIES

Academic International Press, PO Box 1111, Gulf Breeze, FL 32562-1111, Fax: (850) 934-0953, www.ai-press.com; *Russia and Eurasia Facts and Figures Annual.*

Central Intelligence Agency, Office of Public Affairs, Washington, DC 20505, (703) 482-0623, Fax: (703) 482-1739, www.cia.gov; *The World Factbook.*

Economist Intelligence Unit, 111 West 57th Street, New York, NY 10019, (212) 554-0600, Fax: (212) 586-1181, www.eiu.com; *Azerbaijan Country Report.*

Euromonitor International, Inc., 224 S. Michigan Avenue, Suite 1500, Chicago, IL 60604, (312) 922-1115, Fax: (312) 922-1157, www.euromonitor.com; *The World Economic Factbook 2008* and *World Marketing Data and Statistics.*

Palgrave Macmillan Ltd., Houndmills, Basingstoke, Hampshire, RG21 6XS, England, (Telephone in U.S. (888) 330-8477), (Fax in U.S. (800) 672-2054), www.palgrave.com; *The Statesman's Yearbook 2008.*

Taylor and Francis Group, An Informa Business, 2 Park Square, Milton Park, Abingdon, Oxford OX14 4RN, United Kingdom, (Dial from U.S. (212) 216-7800), (Fax from U.S. (212) 564-7854), www.tandf.co.uk; *The Europa World Year Book.*

United Nations Industrial Development Organization (UNIDO), 1 United Nations Plaza, New York, NY 10017, (212) 963 6890, Fax: (212) 963-7904, http://unido.org; Industrial Statistics Database 2008 (INDSTAT) and *The International Yearbook of Industrial Statistics 2008.*

United Nations Statistics Division, New York, NY 10017, (800) 253-9646, Fax: (212) 963-4116, http://unstats.un.org; *2004 Industrial Commodity Statistics Yearbook; Statistical Yearbook;* and *Trends in Europe and North America: The Statistical Yearbook of the ECE 2005.*

The World Bank, 1818 H Street, NW, Washington, DC 20433, (202) 473-1000, Fax: (202) 477-6391, www.worldbank.org; *Azerbaijan; Statistical Handbook: States of the Former USSR;* and *World Development Indicators (WDI) 2008.*

AZERBAIJAN - INFANT AND MATERNAL MORTALITY

See AZERBAIJAN - MORTALITY

AZERBAIJAN - INTERNATIONAL TRADE

Academic International Press, PO Box 1111, Gulf Breeze, FL 32562-1111, Fax: (850) 934-0953, www.ai-press.com; *Russia and Eurasia Facts and Figures Annual.*

Economist Intelligence Unit, 111 West 57th Street, New York, NY 10019, (212) 554-0600, Fax: (212) 586-1181, www.eiu.com; *Azerbaijan Country Report.*

Euromonitor International, Inc., 224 S. Michigan Avenue, Suite 1500, Chicago, IL 60604, (312) 922-1115, Fax: (312) 922-1157, www.euromonitor.com; *The World Economic Factbook 2008* and *World Marketing Data and Statistics.*

International Monetary Fund (IMF), 700 Nineteenth Street, NW, Washington, DC 20431, (202) 623-7000, Fax: (202) 623-4661, www.imf.org; *Direction of Trade Statistics Yearbook 2007.*

Palgrave Macmillan Ltd., Houndmills, Basingstoke, Hampshire, RG21 6XS, England, (Telephone in U.S. (888) 330-8477), (Fax in U.S. (800) 672-2054), www.palgrave.com; *The Statesman's Yearbook 2008.*

State Statistical Committee of the Republic of Azerbaijan, Inshaatchilar Avenue, Baku, AZ1136, Azerbaijan, www.azstat.org; *The Foreign Trade of Azerbaijan.*

Taylor and Francis Group, An Informa Business, 2 Park Square, Milton Park, Abingdon, Oxford OX14 4RN, United Kingdom, (Dial from U.S. (212) 216-7800), (Fax from U.S. (212) 564-7854), www.tandf.co.uk; *The Europa World Year Book.*

United Nations Food and Agricultural Organization (FAO), Viale delle Terme di Caracalla, 00100 Rome, Italy, (Dial from U.S. (202) 653-2400), (Fax from U.S. (202) 653 5760), www.fao.org; *FAO Trade Yearbook.*

United Nations Statistics Division, New York, NY 10017, (800) 253-9646, Fax: (212) 963-4116, http://unstats.un.org; *International Trade Statistics Yearbook* and *Statistical Yearbook.*

The World Bank, 1818 H Street, NW, Washington, DC 20433, (202) 473-1000, Fax: (202) 477-6391, www.worldbank.org; *Azerbaijan; Statistical Handbook: States of the Former USSR; World Development Indicators (WDI) 2008;* and *World Development Report 2008.*

World Trade Organization (WTO), Centre William Rappard, Rue de Lausanne 154, CH-1211 Geneva 21, Switzerland, www.wto.org; *International Trade Statistics 2006.*

AZERBAIJAN - INTERNET USERS

International Telecommunication Union (ITU), Place des Nations, 1211 Geneva 20, Switzerland, www.itu.int; *World Telecommunication/ICT Indicators Database on CD-ROM; World Telecommunication/ICT Indicators Database Online;* and *Yearbook of Statistics - Telecommunication Services (Chronological Time Series 1997-2006).*

The World Bank, 1818 H Street, NW, Washington, DC 20433, (202) 473-1000, Fax: (202) 477-6391, www.worldbank.org; *Azerbaijan.*

AZERBAIJAN - LABOR

Academic International Press, PO Box 1111, Gulf Breeze, FL 32562-1111, Fax: (850) 934-0953, www.ai-press.com; *Russia and Eurasia Facts and Figures Annual.*

Central Intelligence Agency, Office of Public Affairs, Washington, DC 20505, (703) 482-0623, Fax: (703) 482-1739, www.cia.gov; *The World Factbook.*

Euromonitor International, Inc., 224 S. Michigan Avenue, Suite 1500, Chicago, IL 60604, (312) 922-1115, Fax: (312) 922-1157, www.euromonitor.com; *International Marketing Data and Statistics 2008* and *World Marketing Data and Statistics.*

Palgrave Macmillan Ltd., Houndmills, Basingstoke, Hampshire, RG21 6XS, England, (Telephone in U.S. (888) 330-8477), (Fax in U.S. (800) 672-2054), www.palgrave.com; *The Statesman's Yearbook 2008.*

United Nations Statistics Division, New York, NY 10017, (800) 253-9646, Fax: (212) 963-4116, http://unstats.un.org; *Human Development Report 2006* and *Statistical Yearbook.*

The World Bank, 1818 H Street, NW, Washington, DC 20433, (202) 473-1000, Fax: (202) 477-6391, www.worldbank.org; *Statistical Handbook: States of the Former USSR; The World Bank Atlas 2003-2004; World Development Indicators (WDI) 2008;* and *World Development Report 2008.*

AZERBAIJAN - LAND USE

Central Intelligence Agency, Office of Public Affairs, Washington, DC 20505, (703) 482-0623, Fax: (703) 482-1739, www.cia.gov; *The World Factbook.*

Euromonitor International, Inc., 224 S. Michigan Avenue, Suite 1500, Chicago, IL 60604, (312) 922-1115, Fax: (312) 922-1157, www.euromonitor.com; *International Marketing Data and Statistics 2008.*

United Nations Food and Agricultural Organization (FAO), Viale delle Terme di Caracalla, 00100 Rome, Italy, (Dial from U.S. (202) 653-2400), (Fax from U.S. (202) 653 5760), www.fao.org; *FAO Production Yearbook 2002.*

The World Bank, 1818 H Street, NW, Washington, DC 20433, (202) 473-1000, Fax: (202) 477-6391, www.worldbank.org; *World Development Report 2008.*

AZERBAIJAN - LIBRARIES

UNESCO Institute for Statistics, C.P. 6128 Succursale Centre-Ville, Montreal, Quebec, H3C 3J7 Canada, (Dial from U.S. (514) 343-6880), (Fax from U.S. (514) 343 6882), www.uis.unesco.org; *Statistical Tables.*

United Nations Statistics Division, New York, NY 10017, (800) 253-9646, Fax: (212) 963-4116, http://unstats.un.org; *Human Development Report 2006; Statistical Yearbook;* and *Trends in Europe and North America: The Statistical Yearbook of the ECE 2005.*

AZERBAIJAN - LIFE EXPECTANCY

Central Intelligence Agency, Office of Public Affairs, Washington, DC 20505, (703) 482-0623, Fax: (703) 482-1739, www.cia.gov; *The World Factbook.*

Euromonitor International, Inc., 224 S. Michigan Avenue, Suite 1500, Chicago, IL 60604, (312) 922-1115, Fax: (312) 922-1157, www.euromonitor.com; *The World Economic Factbook 2008.*

United Nations Statistics Division, New York, NY 10017, (800) 253-9646, Fax: (212) 963-4116, http://unstats.un.org; *Demographic Yearbook; Human Development Report 2006; Trends in Europe and North America: The Statistical Yearbook of the ECE 2005;* and *World Statistics Pocketbook.*

The World Bank, 1818 H Street, NW, Washington, DC 20433, (202) 473-1000, Fax: (202) 477-6391, www.worldbank.org; *The World Bank Atlas 2003-2004; World Development Indicators (WDI) 2008;* and *World Development Report 2008.*

World Health Organization (WHO), Avenue Appia 20, 1211 Geneve 27, Switzerland, (Telephone in U.S. (212) 331-9081), www.who.int; *World Health Report 2006.*

AZERBAIJAN - LITERACY

Euromonitor International, Inc., 224 S. Michigan Avenue, Suite 1500, Chicago, IL 60604, (312) 922-1115, Fax: (312) 922-1157, www.euromonitor.com; *World Marketing Data and Statistics.*

AZERBAIJAN - LIVESTOCK

Academic International Press, PO Box 1111, Gulf Breeze, FL 32562-1111, Fax: (850) 934-0953, www.ai-press.com; *Russia and Eurasia Facts and Figures Annual.*

Palgrave Macmillan Ltd., Houndmills, Basingstoke, Hampshire, RG21 6XS, England, (Telephone in U.S. (888) 330-8477), (Fax in U.S. (800) 672-2054), www.palgrave.com; *The Statesman's Yearbook 2008.*

Taylor and Francis Group, An Informa Business, 2 Park Square, Milton Park, Abingdon, Oxford OX14 4RN, United Kingdom, (Dial from U.S. (212) 216-7800), (Fax from U.S. (212) 564-7854), www.tandf.co.uk; *The Europa World Year Book.*

United Nations Food and Agricultural Organization (FAO), Viale delle Terme di Caracalla, 00100 Rome, Italy, (Dial from U.S. (202) 653-2400), (Fax from U.S. (202) 653 5760), www.fao.org; *FAO Production Yearbook 2002* and *The State of Food and Agriculture (SOFA) 2006.*

United Nations Statistics Division, New York, NY 10017, (800) 253-9646, Fax: (212) 963-4116, http://unstats.un.org; *2004 Industrial Commodity Statistics Yearbook* and *Statistical Yearbook.*

AZERBAIJAN - MACHINERY

United Nations Statistics Division, New York, NY 10017, (800) 253-9646, Fax: (212) 963-4116, http://unstats.un.org; *2004 Industrial Commodity Statistics Yearbook.*

AZERBAIJAN - MANUFACTURES

United Nations Statistics Division, New York, NY 10017, (800) 253-9646, Fax: (212) 963-4116, http://unstats.un.org; *2004 Industrial Commodity Statistics Yearbook* and *Statistical Yearbook.*

The World Bank, 1818 H Street, NW, Washington, DC 20433, (202) 473-1000, Fax: (202) 477-6391, www.worldbank.org; *World Development Indicators (WDI) 2008.*

AZERBAIJAN - MARRIAGE

Taylor and Francis Group, An Informa Business, 2 Park Square, Milton Park, Abingdon, Oxford OX14 4RN, United Kingdom, (Dial from U.S. (212) 216-7800), (Fax from U.S. (212) 564-7854), www.tandf.co.uk; *The Europa World Year Book.*

United Nations Statistics Division, New York, NY 10017, (800) 253-9646, Fax: (212) 963-4116, http://unstats.un.org; *Demographic Yearbook; Statistical Yearbook;* and *Trends in Europe and North America: The Statistical Yearbook of the ECE 2005.*

AZERBAIJAN - MEAT PRODUCTION

See AZERBAIJAN - LIVESTOCK

AZERBAIJAN - MINERAL INDUSTRIES

Academic International Press, PO Box 1111, Gulf Breeze, FL 32562-1111, Fax: (850) 934-0953, www.ai-press.com; *Russia and Eurasia Facts and Figures Annual.*

Palgrave Macmillan Ltd., Houndmills, Basingstoke, Hampshire, RG21 6XS, England, (Telephone in U.S. (888) 330-8477), (Fax in U.S. (800) 672-2054), www.palgrave.com; *The Statesman's Yearbook 2008.*

Platts, 2 Penn Plaza, 25th Floor, New York, NY 10121-2298, (212) 904-3070, www.platts.com; *Energy Economist.*

Taylor and Francis Group, An Informa Business, 2 Park Square, Milton Park, Abingdon, Oxford OX14 4RN, United Kingdom, (Dial from U.S. (212) 216-7800), (Fax from U.S. (212) 564-7854), www.tandf.co.uk; *The Europa World Year Book.*

United Nations Statistics Division, New York, NY 10017, (800) 253-9646, Fax: (212) 963-4116, http://unstats.un.org; *Energy Statistics Yearbook 2003; 2004 Industrial Commodity Statistics Yearbook;* and *Statistical Yearbook.*

The World Bank, 1818 H Street, NW, Washington, DC 20433, (202) 473-1000, Fax: (202) 477-6391, www.worldbank.org; *Azerbaijan.*

AZERBAIJAN - MONEY SUPPLY

Economist Intelligence Unit, 111 West 57th Street, New York, NY 10019, (212) 554-0600, Fax: (212) 586-1181, www.eiu.com; *Azerbaijan Country Report.*

Taylor and Francis Group, An Informa Business, 2 Park Square, Milton Park, Abingdon, Oxford OX14 4RN, United Kingdom, (Dial from U.S. (212) 216-7800), (Fax from U.S. (212) 564-7854), www.tandf.co.uk; *The Europa World Year Book.*

The World Bank, 1818 H Street, NW, Washington, DC 20433, (202) 473-1000, Fax: (202) 477-6391, www.worldbank.org; *Azerbaijan.*

AZERBAIJAN - MONUMENTS AND HISTORIC SITES

UNESCO Institute for Statistics, C.P. 6128 Succursale Centre-Ville, Montreal, Quebec, H3C 3J7 Canada, (Dial from U.S. (514) 343-6880), (Fax from U.S. (514) 343 6882), www.uis.unesco.org; *Statistical Tables.*

AZERBAIJAN - MORTALITY

Central Intelligence Agency, Office of Public Affairs, Washington, DC 20505, (703) 482-0623, Fax: (703) 482-1739, www.cia.gov; *The World Factbook.*

Euromonitor International, Inc., 224 S. Michigan Avenue, Suite 1500, Chicago, IL 60604, (312) 922-1115, Fax: (312) 922-1157, www.euromonitor.com; *International Marketing Data and Statistics 2008* and *The World Economic Factbook 2008.*

Palgrave Macmillan Ltd., Houndmills, Basingstoke, Hampshire, RG21 6XS, England, (Telephone in U.S. (888) 330-8477), (Fax in U.S. (800) 672-2054), www.palgrave.com; *The Statesman's Yearbook 2008.*

Taylor and Francis Group, An Informa Business, 2 Park Square, Milton Park, Abingdon, Oxford OX14 4RN, United Kingdom, (Dial from U.S. (212) 216-7800), (Fax from U.S. (212) 564-7854), www.tandf.co.uk; *The Europa World Year Book.*

UNICEF, 3 United Nations Plaza, New York, NY 10017, (800) 253-9646, Fax: (212) 887-7465, www.unicef.org; *The State of the World's Children 2008.*

United Nations Statistics Division, New York, NY 10017, (800) 253-9646, Fax: (212) 963-4116, http://unstats.un.org; *Demographic Yearbook; Human Development Report 2006; Statistical Yearbook; Trends in Europe and North America: The Statistical Yearbook of the ECE 2005;* and *World Statistics Pocketbook.*

The World Bank, 1818 H Street, NW, Washington, DC 20433, (202) 473-1000, Fax: (202) 477-6391, www.worldbank.org; *The World Bank Atlas 2003-2004; World Development Indicators (WDI) 2008;* and *World Development Report 2008.*

World Health Organization (WHO), Avenue Appia 20, 1211 Geneve 27, Switzerland, (Telephone in U.S. (212) 331-9081), www.who.int; The WHO Global Atlas of Infectious Diseases and *World Health Report 2006.*

AZERBAIJAN - MOTION PICTURES

UNESCO Institute for Statistics, C.P. 6128 Succursale Centre-Ville, Montreal, Quebec, H3C 3J7 Canada, (Dial from U.S. (514) 343-6880), (Fax from U.S. (514) 343 6882), www.uis.unesco.org; *Statistical Tables.*

United Nations Statistics Division, New York, NY 10017, (800) 253-9646, Fax: (212) 963-4116, http://unstats.un.org; *Statistical Yearbook.*

AZERBAIJAN - MOTOR VEHICLES

United Nations Statistics Division, New York, NY 10017, (800) 253-9646, Fax: (212) 963-4116, http://unstats.un.org; *Statistical Yearbook.*

AZERBAIJAN - MUSEUMS

UNESCO Institute for Statistics, C.P. 6128 Succursale Centre-Ville, Montreal, Quebec, H3C 3J7 Canada, (Dial from U.S. (514) 343-6880), (Fax from U.S. (514) 343 6882), www.uis.unesco.org; *Statistical Tables.*

AZERBAIJAN - PERIODICALS

UNESCO Institute for Statistics, C.P. 6128 Succursale Centre-Ville, Montreal, Quebec, H3C 3J7 Canada, (Dial from U.S. (514) 343-6880), (Fax from U.S. (514) 343 6882), www.uis.unesco.org; *Statistical Tables.*

AZERBAIJAN - PETROLEUM INDUSTRY AND TRADE

Palgrave Macmillan Ltd., Houndmills, Basingstoke, Hampshire, RG21 6XS, England, (Telephone in U.S. (888) 330-8477), (Fax in U.S. (800) 672-2054), www.palgrave.com; *The Statesman's Yearbook 2008.*

PennWell Corporation, 1421 South Sheridan Road, Tulsa, OK 74112, (918) 835-3161, www.pennwell.com; *International Petroleum Encyclopedia 2007.*

Platts, 2 Penn Plaza, 25th Floor, New York, NY 10121-2298, (212) 904-3070, www.platts.com; *Energy Economist.*

U.S. Department of Energy (DOE), Energy Information Administration (EIA), 1000 Independence Avenue, SW, Washington, DC 20585, (202) 586-8800, www.eia.doe.gov; *International Energy Annual 2004* and *International Energy Outlook 2006.*

United Nations Food and Agricultural Organization (FAO), Viale delle Terme di Caracalla, 00100 Rome, Italy, (Dial from U.S. (202) 653-2400), (Fax from U.S. (202) 653 5760), www.fao.org; *The State of Food and Agriculture (SOFA) 2006.*

United Nations Statistics Division, New York, NY 10017, (800) 253-9646, Fax: (212) 963-4116, http://unstats.un.org; *Energy Statistics Yearbook 2003; 2004 Industrial Commodity Statistics Yearbook; Statistical Yearbook;* and *Trends in Europe and North America: The Statistical Yearbook of the ECE 2005.*

AZERBAIJAN - POLITICAL SCIENCE

Academic International Press, PO Box 1111, Gulf Breeze, FL 32562-1111, Fax: (850) 934-0953, www.ai-press.com; *Russia and Eurasia Facts and Figures Annual.*

Central Intelligence Agency, Office of Public Affairs, Washington, DC 20505, (703) 482-0623, Fax: (703) 482-1739, www.cia.gov; *The World Factbook.*

Palgrave Macmillan Ltd., Houndmills, Basingstoke, Hampshire, RG21 6XS, England, (Telephone in U.S. (888) 330-8477), (Fax in U.S. (800) 672-2054), www.palgrave.com; *The Statesman's Yearbook 2008.*

Taylor and Francis Group, An Informa Business, 2 Park Square, Milton Park, Abingdon, Oxford OX14 4RN, United Kingdom, (Dial from U.S. (212) 216-7800), (Fax from U.S. (212) 564-7854), www.tandf.co.uk; *The Europa World Year Book.*

United Nations Statistics Division, New York, NY 10017, (800) 253-9646, Fax: (212) 963-4116, http://unstats.un.org; *Statistical Yearbook.*

The World Bank, 1818 H Street, NW, Washington, DC 20433, (202) 473-1000, Fax: (202) 477-6391, www.worldbank.org; *Statistical Handbook: States of the Former USSR* and *World Development Report 2008.*

AZERBAIJAN - POPULATION

Academic International Press, PO Box 1111, Gulf Breeze, FL 32562-1111, Fax: (850) 934-0953, www.ai-press.com; *Russia and Eurasia Facts and Figures Annual.*

Central Intelligence Agency, Office of Public Affairs, Washington, DC 20505, (703) 482-0623, Fax: (703) 482-1739, www.cia.gov; *The World Factbook.*

Economist Intelligence Unit, 111 West 57th Street, New York, NY 10019, (212) 554-0600, Fax: (212) 586-1181, www.eiu.com; *Azerbaijan Country Report.*

Euromonitor International, Inc., 224 S. Michigan Avenue, Suite 1500, Chicago, IL 60604, (312) 922-1115, Fax: (312) 922-1157, www.euromonitor.com; *International Marketing Data and Statistics 2008* and *The World Economic Factbook 2008.*

Palgrave Macmillan Ltd., Houndmills, Basingstoke, Hampshire, RG21 6XS, England, (Telephone in U.S. (888) 330-8477), (Fax in U.S. (800) 672-2054), www.palgrave.com; *The Statesman's Yearbook 2008.*

State Statistical Committee of the Republic of Azerbaijan, Inshaatchilar Avenue, Baku, AZ1136, Azerbaijan, www.azstat.org; *Children in Azerbaijan* and *Women and Men in Azerbaijan.*

Taylor and Francis Group, An Informa Business, 2 Park Square, Milton Park, Abingdon, Oxford OX14 4RN, United Kingdom, (Dial from U.S. (212) 216-7800), (Fax from U.S. (212) 564-7854), www.tandf.co.uk; *The Europa World Year Book.*

UNESCO Institute for Statistics, C.P. 6128 Succursale Centre-Ville, Montreal, Quebec, H3C 3J7 Canada, (Dial from U.S. (514) 343-6880), (Fax from U.S. (514) 343 6882), www.uis.unesco.org; *Statistical Tables.*

United Nations Food and Agricultural Organization (FAO), Viale delle Terme di Caracalla, 00100 Rome, Italy, (Dial from U.S. (202) 653-2400), (Fax from U.S. (202) 653 5760), www.fao.org; *FAO Production Yearbook 2002.*

United Nations Statistics Division, New York, NY 10017, (800) 253-9646, Fax: (212) 963-4116, http://unstats.un.org; *Demographic Yearbook; Human Development Report 2006; Statistical Yearbook; Trends in Europe and North America: The Statistical Yearbook of the ECE 2005;* and *World Statistics Pocketbook.*

The World Bank, 1818 H Street, NW, Washington, DC 20433, (202) 473-1000, Fax: (202) 477-6391, www.worldbank.org; *Azerbaijan; Statistical Handbook: States of the Former USSR; The World Bank Atlas 2003-2004; World Development Indicators (WDI) 2008;* and *World Development Report 2008.*

World Health Organization (WHO), Avenue Appia 20, 1211 Geneve 27, Switzerland, (Telephone in U.S. (212) 331-9081), www.who.int; *World Health Report 2006.*

AZERBAIJAN - POPULATION DENSITY

Central Intelligence Agency, Office of Public Affairs, Washington, DC 20505, (703) 482-0623, Fax: (703) 482-1739, www.cia.gov; *The World Factbook.*

Euromonitor International, Inc., 224 S. Michigan Avenue, Suite 1500, Chicago, IL 60604, (312) 922-1115, Fax: (312) 922-1157, www.euromonitor.com; *The World Economic Factbook 2008.*

Palgrave Macmillan Ltd., Houndmills, Basingstoke, Hampshire, RG21 6XS, England, (Telephone in U.S. (888) 330-8477), (Fax in U.S. (800) 672-2054), www.palgrave.com; *The Statesman's Yearbook 2008.*

Taylor and Francis Group, An Informa Business, 2 Park Square, Milton Park, Abingdon, Oxford OX14 4RN, United Kingdom, (Dial from U.S. (212) 216-7800), (Fax from U.S. (212) 564-7854), www.tandf.co.uk; *The Europa World Year Book.*

UNESCO Institute for Statistics, C.P. 6128 Succursale Centre-Ville, Montreal, Quebec, H3C 3J7 Canada, (Dial from U.S. (514) 343-6880), (Fax from U.S. (514) 343 6882), www.uis.unesco.org; *Statistical Tables.*

United Nations Statistics Division, New York, NY 10017, (800) 253-9646, Fax: (212) 963-4116, http://unstats.un.org; *Statistical Yearbook* and *Trends in Europe and North America: The Statistical Yearbook of the ECE 2005.*

The World Bank, 1818 H Street, NW, Washington, DC 20433, (202) 473-1000, Fax: (202) 477-6391; www.worldbank.org; *Azerbaijan* and *World Development Report 2008.*

AZERBAIJAN - POSTAL SERVICE

United Nations Statistics Division, New York, NY 10017, (800) 253-9646, Fax: (212) 963-4116, http://unstats.un.org; *Statistical Yearbook* and *Trends in Europe and North America: The Statistical Yearbook of the ECE 2005.*

AZERBAIJAN - POULTRY

See AZERBAIJAN - LIVESTOCK

AZERBAIJAN - POWER RESOURCES

Academic International Press, PO Box 1111, Gulf Breeze, FL 32562-1111, Fax: (850) 934-0953, www.ai-press.com; *Russia and Eurasia Facts and Figures Annual.*

Euromonitor International, Inc., 224 S. Michigan Avenue, Suite 1500, Chicago, IL 60604, (312) 922-1115, Fax: (312) 922-1157, www.euromonitor.com; *International Marketing Data and Statistics 2008; The World Economic Factbook 2008;* and *World Marketing Data and Statistics.*

Palgrave Macmillan Ltd., Houndmills, Basingstoke, Hampshire, RG21 6XS, England, (Telephone in U.S. (888) 330-8477), (Fax in U.S. (800) 672-2054), www.palgrave.com; *The Statesman's Yearbook 2008.*

Platts, 2 Penn Plaza, 25th Floor, New York, NY 10121-2298, (212) 904-3070, www.platts.com; *Energy Economist.*

U.S. Department of Energy (DOE), Energy Information Administration (EIA), 1000 Independence Avenue, SW, Washington, DC 20585, (202) 586-8800, www.eia.doe.gov; *International Energy Annual 2004* and *International Energy Outlook 2006.*

United Nations Statistics Division, New York, NY 10017, (800) 253-9646, Fax: (212) 963-4116, http://unstats.un.org; *Energy Statistics Yearbook 2003; Human Development Report 2006; Statistical Yearbook; Trends in Europe and North America: The Statistical Yearbook of the ECE 2005;* and *World Statistics Pocketbook.*

The World Bank, 1818 H Street, NW, Washington, DC 20433, (202) 473-1000, Fax: (202) 477-6391, www.worldbank.org; *Statistical Handbook: States of the Former USSR; The World Bank Atlas 2003-2004;* and *World Development Report 2008.*

AZERBAIJAN - PRICES

Euromonitor International, Inc., 224 S. Michigan Avenue, Suite 1500, Chicago, IL 60604, (312) 922-1115, Fax: (312) 922-1157, www.euromonitor.com; *World Marketing Data and Statistics.*

United Nations Food and Agricultural Organization (FAO), Viale delle Terme di Caracalla, 00100 Rome, Italy, (Dial from U.S. (202) 653-2400), (Fax from U.S. (202) 653 5760), www.fao.org; *FAO Production Yearbook 2002.*

The World Bank, 1818 H Street, NW, Washington, DC 20433, (202) 473-1000, Fax: (202) 477-6391, www.worldbank.org; *Azerbaijan* and *Statistical Handbook: States of the Former USSR.*

AZERBAIJAN - PROFESSIONS

United Nations Statistics Division, New York, NY 10017, (800) 253-9646, Fax: (212) 963-4116, http://unstats.un.org; *Statistical Yearbook.*

AZERBAIJAN - PUBLIC HEALTH

Academic International Press, PO Box 1111, Gulf Breeze, FL 32562-1111, Fax: (850) 934-0953, www.ai-press.com; *Russia and Eurasia Facts and Figures Annual.*

Euromonitor International, Inc., 224 S. Michigan Avenue, Suite 1500, Chicago, IL 60604, (312) 922-1115, Fax: (312) 922-1157, www.euromonitor.com; *World Health Databook 2007/2008* and *World Marketing Data and Statistics.*

Palgrave Macmillan Ltd., Houndmills, Basingstoke, Hampshire, RG21 6XS, England, (Telephone in U.S. (888) 330-8477), (Fax in U.S. (800) 672-2054), www.palgrave.com; *The Statesman's Yearbook 2008.*

UNICEF, 3 United Nations Plaza, New York, NY 10017, (800) 253-9646, Fax: (212) 887-7465, www.unicef.org; *The State of the World's Children 2008.*

United Nations Statistics Division, New York, NY 10017, (800) 253-9646, Fax: (212) 963-4116, http://unstats.un.org; *Human Development Report 2006; Statistical Yearbook;* and *Trends in Europe and North America: The Statistical Yearbook of the ECE 2005.*

The World Bank, 1818 H Street, NW, Washington, DC 20433, (202) 473-1000, Fax: (202) 477-6391, www.worldbank.org; *Azerbaijan* and *World Development Report 2008.*

World Health Organization (WHO), Avenue Appia 20, 1211 Geneve 27, Switzerland, (Telephone in U.S. (212) 331-9081), www.who.int; The WHO Global Atlas of Infectious Diseases and *World Health Report 2006.*

AZERBAIJAN - PUBLISHERS AND PUBLISHING

UNESCO Institute for Statistics, C.P. 6128 Succursale Centre-Ville, Montreal, Quebec, H3C 3J7 Canada, (Dial from U.S. (514) 343-6880), (Fax from U.S. (514) 343 6882), www.uis.unesco.org; *Statistical Tables.*

United Nations Statistics Division, New York, NY 10017, (800) 253-9646, Fax: (212) 963-4116, http://unstats.un.org; *Trends in Europe and North America: The Statistical Yearbook of the ECE 2005.*

AZERBAIJAN - RADIO - RECEIVERS AND RECEPTION

Palgrave Macmillan Ltd., Houndmills, Basingstoke, Hampshire, RG21 6XS, England, (Telephone in U.S. (888) 330-8477), (Fax in U.S. (800) 672-2054), www.palgrave.com; *The Statesman's Yearbook 2008.*

United Nations Statistics Division, New York, NY 10017, (800) 253-9646, Fax: (212) 963-4116, http://unstats.un.org; *Statistical Yearbook.*

AZERBAIJAN - RAILROADS

Palgrave Macmillan Ltd., Houndmills, Basingstoke, Hampshire, RG21 6XS, England, (Telephone in U.S. (888) 330-8477), (Fax in U.S. (800) 672-2054), www.palgrave.com; *The Statesman's Yearbook 2008.*

United Nations Statistics Division, New York, NY 10017, (800) 253-9646, Fax: (212) 963-4116, http://unstats.un.org; *Statistical Yearbook* and *Trends in Europe and North America: The Statistical Yearbook of the ECE 2005.*

AZERBAIJAN - RELIGION

Academic International Press, PO Box 1111, Gulf Breeze, FL 32562-1111, Fax: (850) 934-0953, www.ai-press.com; *Russia and Eurasia Facts and Figures Annual.*

Central Intelligence Agency, Office of Public Affairs, Washington, DC 20505, (703) 482-0623, Fax: (703) 482-1739, www.cia.gov; *The World Factbook.*

Palgrave Macmillan Ltd., Houndmills, Basingstoke, Hampshire, RG21 6XS, England, (Telephone in U.S. (888) 330-8477), (Fax in U.S. (800) 672-2054), www.palgrave.com; *The Statesman's Yearbook 2008.*

AZERBAIJAN - RETAIL TRADE

Euromonitor International, Inc., 224 S. Michigan Avenue, Suite 1500, Chicago, IL 60604, (312) 922-1115, Fax: (312) 922-1157, www.euromonitor.com; *World Marketing Data and Statistics.*

United Nations Statistics Division, New York, NY 10017, (800) 253-9646, Fax: (212) 963-4116, http://unstats.un.org; *Statistical Yearbook.*

AZERBAIJAN - ROADS

Central Intelligence Agency, Office of Public Affairs, Washington, DC 20505, (703) 482-0623, Fax: (703) 482-1739, www.cia.gov; *The World Factbook.*

Palgrave Macmillan Ltd., Houndmills, Basingstoke, Hampshire, RG21 6XS, England, (Telephone in U.S. (888) 330-8477), (Fax in U.S. (800) 672-2054), www.palgrave.com; *The Statesman's Yearbook 2008.*

United Nations Statistics Division, New York, NY 10017, (800) 253-9646, Fax: (212) 963-4116, http://unstats.un.org; *Statistical Yearbook* and *Trends in Europe and North America: The Statistical Yearbook of the ECE 2005.*

AZERBAIJAN - RUBBER INDUSTRY AND TRADE

International Rubber Study Group (IRSG), 1st Floor, Heron House, 109/115 Wembley Hill Road, Wembley, Middlesex HA9 8DA, United Kingdom, www.rubberstudy.com; *Rubber Statistical Bulletin; Summary of World Rubber Statistics 2005; World Rubber Statistics Handbook (Volume 6, 1975-2001);* and *World Rubber Statistics Historic Handbook.*

United Nations Statistics Division, New York, NY 10017, (800) 253-9646, Fax: (212) 963-4116, http://unstats.un.org; *Statistical Yearbook.*

AZERBAIJAN - SHEEP

See AZERBAIJAN - LIVESTOCK

AZERBAIJAN - SHIPPING

United Nations Statistics Division, New York, NY 10017, (800) 253-9646, Fax: (212) 963-4116, http://unstats.un.org; *Statistical Yearbook.*

AZERBAIJAN - SOCIAL ECOLOGY

United Nations Statistics Division, New York, NY 10017, (800) 253-9646, Fax: (212) 963-4116, http://unstats.un.org; *World Statistics Pocketbook.*

AZERBAIJAN - STEEL PRODUCTION

See AZERBAIJAN - MINERAL INDUSTRIES

AZERBAIJAN - TAXATION

Taylor and Francis Group, An Informa Business, 2 Park Square, Milton Park, Abingdon, Oxford OX14 4RN, United Kingdom, (Dial from U.S. (212) 216-7800), (Fax from U.S. (212) 564-7854), www.tandf.co.uk; *The Europa World Year Book.*

AZERBAIJAN - TELEPHONE

United Nations Statistics Division, New York, NY 10017, (800) 253-9646, Fax: (212) 963-4116, http://unstats.un.org; *Statistical Yearbook; Trends in Europe and North America: The Statistical Yearbook of the ECE 2005;* and *World Statistics Pocketbook.*

AZERBAIJAN - TEXTILE INDUSTRY

Palgrave Macmillan Ltd., Houndmills, Basingstoke, Hampshire, RG21 6XS, England, (Telephone in U.S.

(888) 330-8477), (Fax in U.S. (800) 672-2054), www.palgrave.com; *The Statesman's Yearbook 2008.*

United Nations Statistics Division, New York, NY 10017, (800) 253-9646, Fax: (212) 963-4116, http://unstats.un.org; *2004 Industrial Commodity Statistics Yearbook* and *Statistical Yearbook.*

AZERBAIJAN - THEATER

UNESCO Institute for Statistics, C.P. 6128 Succursale Centre-Ville, Montreal, Quebec, H3C 3J7 Canada, (Dial from U.S. (514) 343-6880), (Fax from U.S. (514) 343 6882), www.uis.unesco.org; *Statistical Tables.*

AZERBAIJAN - TIRE INDUSTRY

United Nations Statistics Division, New York, NY 10017, (800) 253-9646, Fax: (212) 963-4116, http://unstats.un.org; *Statistical Yearbook.*

AZERBAIJAN - TOBACCO INDUSTRY

Foreign Agricultural Service (FAS), U.S. Department of Agriculture (USDA), 1400 Independence Avenue, SW, Washington, DC 20250, (202) 720-3935, www.fas.usda.gov; *Tobacco: World Markets and Trade.*

United Nations Statistics Division, New York, NY 10017, (800) 253-9646, Fax: (212) 963-4116, http://unstats.un.org; *Statistical Yearbook.*

AZERBAIJAN - TOURISM

Euromonitor International, Inc., 224 S. Michigan Avenue, Suite 1500, Chicago, IL 60604, (312) 922-1115, Fax: (312) 922-1157, www.euromonitor.com; *The World Economic Factbook 2008* and *World Marketing Data and Statistics.*

United Nations Statistics Division, New York, NY 10017, (800) 253-9646, Fax: (212) 963-4116, http://unstats.un.org; *Statistical Yearbook* and *Trends in Europe and North America: The Statistical Yearbook of the ECE 2005.*

The World Bank, 1818 H Street, NW, Washington, DC 20433, (202) 473-1000, Fax: (202) 477-6391, www.worldbank.org; *Azerbaijan.*

AZERBAIJAN - TRANSPORTATION

Academic International Press, PO Box 1111, Gulf Breeze, FL 32562-1111, Fax: (850) 934-0953, www.ai-press.com; *Russia and Eurasia Facts and Figures Annual.*

Central Intelligence Agency, Office of Public Affairs, Washington, DC 20505, (703) 482-0623, Fax: (703) 482-1739, www.cia.gov; *The World Factbook.*

Euromonitor International, Inc., 224 S. Michigan Avenue, Suite 1500, Chicago, IL 60604, (312) 922-1115, Fax: (312) 922-1157, www.euromonitor.com; *International Marketing Data and Statistics 2008* and *World Marketing Data and Statistics.*

Palgrave Macmillan Ltd., Houndmills, Basingstoke, Hampshire, RG21 6XS, England, (Telephone in U.S. (888) 330-8477), (Fax in U.S. (800) 672-2054), www.palgrave.com; *The Statesman's Yearbook 2008.*

United Nations Statistics Division, New York, NY 10017, (800) 253-9646, Fax: (212) 963-4116, http://unstats.un.org; *Trends in Europe and North America: The Statistical Yearbook of the ECE 2005.*

The World Bank, 1818 H Street, NW, Washington, DC 20433, (202) 473-1000, Fax: (202) 477-6391, www.worldbank.org; *Azerbaijan.*

AZERBAIJAN - UNEMPLOYMENT

Central Intelligence Agency, Office of Public Affairs, Washington, DC 20505, (703) 482-0623, Fax: (703) 482-1739, www.cia.gov; *The World Factbook.*

Palgrave Macmillan Ltd., Houndmills, Basingstoke, Hampshire, RG21 6XS, England, (Telephone in U.S. (888) 330-8477), (Fax in U.S. (800) 672-2054), www.palgrave.com; *The Statesman's Yearbook 2008.*

United Nations Statistics Division, New York, NY 10017, (800) 253-9646, Fax: (212) 963-4116, http://unstats.un.org; *Statistical Yearbook* and *Trends in Europe and North America: The Statistical Yearbook of the ECE 2005.*

The World Bank, 1818 H Street, NW, Washington, DC 20433, (202) 473-1000, Fax: (202) 477-6391, www.worldbank.org; *Azerbaijan.*

AZERBAIJAN - VITAL STATISTICS

Palgrave Macmillan Ltd., Houndmills, Basingstoke, Hampshire, RG21 6XS, England, (Telephone in U.S. (888) 330-8477), (Fax in U.S. (800) 672-2054), www.palgrave.com; *The Statesman's Yearbook 2008.*

State Statistical Committee of the Republic of Azerbaijan, Inshaatchilar Avenue, Baku, AZ1136, Azerbaijan, www.azstat.org; *Azerbaijan in Figures; Children in Azerbaijan;* and *Women and Men in Azerbaijan.*

United Nations Economic and Social Commission for Western Asia (ESCWA), PO Box 11-8575, Riad el-Solh Square, Beirut, Lebanon, www.escwa.un.org; *Annual Report 2006; Bulletin on Population and Vital Statistics in the ESCWA Region;* and *Survey of Economic and Social Developments in the ESCWA Region 2006-2007.*

United Nations Statistics Division, New York, NY 10017, (800) 253-9646, Fax: (212) 963-4116, http://unstats.un.org; *Statistical Yearbook.*

World Health Organization (WHO), Avenue Appia 20, 1211 Geneve 27, Switzerland, (Telephone in U.S. (212) 331-9081), www.who.int; *World Health Report 2006.*

AZERBAIJAN - WAGES

United Nations Statistics Division, New York, NY 10017, (800) 253-9646, Fax: (212) 963-4116, http://unstats.un.org; *Statistical Yearbook.*

The World Bank, 1818 H Street, NW, Washington, DC 20433, (202) 473-1000, Fax: (202) 477-6391, www.worldbank.org; *Azerbaijan* and *Statistical Handbook: States of the Former USSR.*

AZERBAIJAN - WELFARE STATE

Palgrave Macmillan Ltd., Houndmills, Basingstoke, Hampshire, RG21 6XS, England, (Telephone in U.S. (888) 330-8477), (Fax in U.S. (800) 672-2054), www.palgrave.com; *The Statesman's Yearbook 2008.*

AZERBAIJAN - WHOLESALE PRICE INDEXES

United Nations Statistics Division, New York, NY 10017, (800) 253-9646, Fax: (212) 963-4116, http://unstats.un.org; *Statistical Yearbook.*

AZERBAIJAN - WHOLESALE TRADE

United Nations Statistics Division, New York, NY 10017, (800) 253-9646, Fax: (212) 963-4116, http://unstats.un.org; *Statistical Yearbook.*STATISTICS SOURCES, Thirty-second Edition - 2009STATISTICS SOURCES, Thirty-second Edition - 2009

BACKPACKING

National Sporting Goods Association (NSGA), 1601 Feehanville Drive, Suite 300, Mount Prospect, IL 60056, (847) 296-6742, Fax: (847) 391-9827, www.nsga.org; *2006 Sports Participation.*

BACON

U.S. Bureau of Labor Statistics (BLS), Postal Square Building, 2 Massachusetts Avenue, NE, Washington, DC 20212-0001, (202) 691-5200, Fax: (202) 691-6325, www.bls.gov; *Consumer Price Index Detailed Report* and *Monthly Labor Review (MLR).*

BADMINTON

National Sporting Goods Association (NSGA), 1601 Feehanville Drive, Suite 300, Mount Prospect, IL 60056, (847) 296-6742, Fax: (847) 391-9827, www.nsga.org; *2006 Sports Participation.*

BAHAMAS, THE - NATIONAL STATISTICAL OFFICE

Department of Statistics, Ministry of Finance, Clarence Bain Building, Thompson Boulevard, N-3904, Nassau, Bahamas, (Dial from U.S. (242) 502-1000), (Fax from U.S. (242) 325-5149), www.bahamas.gov.bs/finance; National Data Center.

BAHAMAS, THE - PRIMARY STATISTICS SOURCES

Department of Statistics, Ministry of Finance, Clarence Bain Building, Thompson Boulevard, N-3904, Nassau, Bahamas, (Dial from U.S. (242) 502-1000), (Fax from U.S. (242) 325-5149), www.bahamas.gov.bs/finance; *The Bahamas in Figures* and *Statistical Abstract.*

BAHAMAS, THE - AGRICULTURE

Economist Intelligence Unit, 111 West 57th Street, New York, NY 10019, (212) 554-0600, Fax: (212) 586-1181, www.eiu.com; *Bahamas Country Report.*

Euromonitor International, Inc., 224 S. Michigan Avenue, Suite 1500, Chicago, IL 60604, (312) 922-1115, Fax: (312) 922-1157, www.euromonitor.com; *World Marketing Data and Statistics.*

Inter-American Development Bank (IDB), 1300 New York Avenue, NW, Washington, DC 20577, (202) 623-1000, Fax: (202) 623-3096, www.iadb.org; *The Politics of Policies: Economic and Social Progress in Latin America - 2006 Report.*

M.E. Sharpe, 80 Business Park Drive, Armonk, NY 10504, (800) 541-6563, Fax: (914) 273-2106, www.mesharpe.com; *The Illustrated Book of World Rankings.*

Palgrave Macmillan Ltd., Houndmills, Basingstoke, Hampshire, RG21 6XS, England, (Telephone in U.S. (888) 330-8477), (Fax in U.S. (800) 672-2054), www.palgrave.com; *The Statesman's Yearbook 2008.*

Taylor and Francis Group, An Informa Business, 2 Park Square, Milton Park, Abingdon, Oxford OX14 4RN, United Kingdom, (Dial from U.S. (212) 216-7800), (Fax from U.S. (212) 564-7854), www.tandf.co.uk; *The Europa World Year Book.*

United Nations Conference on Trade and Development (UNCTAD), DC2-1120, United Nations, New York, NY 10017, (212) 963-0027, www.unctad.org; *UNCTAD Commodity Yearbook.*

United Nations Food and Agricultural Organization (FAO), Viale delle Terme di Caracalla, 00100 Rome, Italy, (Dial from U.S. (202) 653-2400), (Fax from U.S. (202) 653 5760), www.fao.org; AQUASTAT; *FAO Production Yearbook 2002; FAO Trade Yearbook;* and *The State of Food and Agriculture (SOFA) 2006.*

United Nations Statistics Division, New York, NY 10017, (800) 253-9646, Fax: (212) 963-4116, http://unstats.un.org; *Statistical Yearbook.*

The World Bank, 1818 H Street, NW, Washington, DC 20433, (202) 473-1000, Fax: (202) 477-6391, www.worldbank.org; *Bahamas* and *World Development Indicators (WDI) 2008.*

BAHAMAS, THE - AIRLINES

M.E. Sharpe, 80 Business Park Drive, Armonk, NY 10504, (800) 541-6563, Fax: (914) 273-2106, www.mesharpe.com; *The Illustrated Book of World Rankings.*

Palgrave Macmillan Ltd., Houndmills, Basingstoke, Hampshire, RG21 6XS, England, (Telephone in U.S. (888) 330-8477), (Fax in U.S. (800) 672-2054), www.palgrave.com; *The Statesman's Yearbook 2008.*

Taylor and Francis Group, An Informa Business, 2 Park Square, Milton Park, Abingdon, Oxford OX14 4RN, United Kingdom, (Dial from U.S. (212) 216-7800), (Fax from U.S. (212) 564-7854), www.tandf.co.uk; *The Europa World Year Book.*

BAHAMAS, THE - AIRPORTS

Central Intelligence Agency, Office of Public Affairs, Washington, DC 20505, (703) 482-0623, Fax: (703) 482-1739, www.cia.gov; *The World Factbook.*

BAHAMAS, THE - ALUMINUM PRODUCTION

See BAHAMAS, THE - MINERAL INDUSTRIES

BAHAMAS, THE - ARMED FORCES

Central Intelligence Agency, Office of Public Affairs, Washington, DC 20505, (703) 482-0623, Fax: (703) 482-1739, www.cia.gov; *The World Factbook.*

Euromonitor International, Inc., 224 S. Michigan Avenue, Suite 1500, Chicago, IL 60604, (312) 922-1115, Fax: (312) 922-1157, www.euromonitor.com; *World Marketing Data and Statistics.*

International Institute for Strategic Studies (IISS), Arundel House, 13-15 Arundel Street, Temple Place, London WC2R 3DX, England, www.iiss.org; *The Military Balance 2007.*

International Monetary Fund (IMF), 700 Nineteenth Street, NW, Washington, DC 20431, (202) 623-7000, Fax: (202) 623-4661, www.imf.org; *Government Finance Statistics Yearbook (2008 Edition).*

Palgrave Macmillan Ltd., Houndmills, Basingstoke, Hampshire, RG21 6XS, England, (Telephone in U.S. (888) 330-8477), (Fax in U.S. (800) 672-2054), www.palgrave.com; *The Statesman's Yearbook 2008.*

United Nations Statistics Division, New York, NY 10017, (800) 253-9646, Fax: (212) 963-4116, http://unstats.un.org; *Human Development Report 2006.*

BAHAMAS, THE - BALANCE OF PAYMENTS

Inter-American Development Bank (IDB), 1300 New York Avenue, NW, Washington, DC 20577, (202) 623-1000, Fax: (202) 623-3096, www.iadb.org; *The Politics of Policies: Economic and Social Progress in Latin America - 2006 Report.*

International Monetary Fund (IMF), 700 Nineteenth Street, NW, Washington, DC 20431, (202) 623-7000, Fax: (202) 623-4661, www.imf.org; *Balance of Payments Statistics Newsletter* and *Balance of Payments Statistics Yearbook 2007.*

Taylor and Francis Group, An Informa Business, 2 Park Square, Milton Park, Abingdon, Oxford OX14 4RN, United Kingdom, (Dial from U.S. (212) 216-7800), (Fax from U.S. (212) 564-7854), www.tandf.co.uk; *The Europa World Year Book.*

United Nations Conference on Trade and Development (UNCTAD), DC2-1120, United Nations, New York, NY 10017, (212) 963-0027, www.unctad.org; *Handbook of Statistics 2005.*

United Nations Statistics Division, New York, NY 10017, (800) 253-9646, Fax: (212) 963-4116, http://unstats.un.org; *Economic Survey of Latin America and the Caribbean 2004-2005.*

The World Bank, 1818 H Street, NW, Washington, DC 20433, (202) 473-1000, Fax: (202) 477-6391, www.worldbank.org; *Bahamas* and *World Development Indicators (WDI) 2008.*

BAHAMAS, THE - BANKS AND BANKING

Euromonitor International, Inc., 224 S. Michigan Avenue, Suite 1500, Chicago, IL 60604, (312) 922-1115, Fax: (312) 922-1157, www.euromonitor.com; *World Marketing Data and Statistics.*

Inter-American Development Bank (IDB), 1300 New York Avenue, NW, Washington, DC 20577, (202) 623-1000, Fax: (202) 623-3096, www.iadb.org; *The Politics of Policies: Economic and Social Progress in Latin America - 2006 Report.*

International Monetary Fund (IMF), 700 Nineteenth Street, NW, Washington, DC 20431, (202) 623-7000, Fax: (202) 623-4661, www.imf.org; *Government Finance Statistics Yearbook (2008 Edition)* and *International Financial Statistics Yearbook 2007.*

M.E. Sharpe, 80 Business Park Drive, Armonk, NY 10504, (800) 541-6563, Fax: (914) 273-2106, www.mesharpe.com; *The Illustrated Book of World Rankings.*

Palgrave Macmillan Ltd., Houndmills, Basingstoke, Hampshire, RG21 6XS, England, (Telephone in U.S. (888) 330-8477), (Fax in U.S. (800) 672-2054), www.palgrave.com; *The Statesman's Yearbook 2008.*

Taylor and Francis Group, An Informa Business, 2 Park Square, Milton Park, Abingdon, Oxford OX14 4RN, United Kingdom, (Dial from U.S. (212) 216-7800), (Fax from U.S. (212) 564-7854), www.tandf.co.uk; *The Europa World Year Book.*

BAHAMAS, THE - BARLEY PRODUCTION

See BAHAMAS, THE - CROPS

BAHAMAS, THE - BEVERAGE INDUSTRY

M.E. Sharpe, 80 Business Park Drive, Armonk, NY 10504, (800) 541-6563, Fax: (914) 273-2106, www.mesharpe.com; *The Illustrated Book of World Rankings.*

BAHAMAS, THE - BONDS

Inter-American Development Bank (IDB), 1300 New York Avenue, NW, Washington, DC 20577, (202) 623-1000, Fax: (202) 623-3096, www.iadb.org; *The Politics of Policies: Economic and Social Progress in Latin America - 2006 Report.*

International Monetary Fund (IMF), 700 Nineteenth Street, NW, Washington, DC 20431, (202) 623-7000, Fax: (202) 623-4661, www.imf.org; *Government Finance Statistics Yearbook (2008 Edition).*

The World Bank, 1818 H Street, NW, Washington, DC 20433, (202) 473-1000, Fax: (202) 477-6391, www.worldbank.org; *World Development Indicators (WDI) 2008.*

BAHAMAS, THE - BROADCASTING

Central Intelligence Agency, Office of Public Affairs, Washington, DC 20505, (703) 482-0623, Fax: (703) 482-1739, www.cia.gov; *The World Factbook.*

Euromonitor International, Inc., 224 S. Michigan Avenue, Suite 1500, Chicago, IL 60604, (312) 922-1115, Fax: (312) 922-1157, www.euromonitor.com; *World Marketing Data and Statistics.*

M.E. Sharpe, 80 Business Park Drive, Armonk, NY 10504, (800) 541-6563, Fax: (914) 273-2106, www.mesharpe.com; *The Illustrated Book of World Rankings.*

Palgrave Macmillan Ltd., Houndmills, Basingstoke, Hampshire, RG21 6XS, England, (Telephone in U.S. (888) 330-8477), (Fax in U.S. (800) 672-2054), www.palgrave.com; *The Statesman's Yearbook 2008.*

WRTH Publications Limited, PO Box 290, Oxford OX2 7FT, UK, www.wrth.com; *World Radio TV Handbook 2007.*

BAHAMAS, THE - BUDGET

Central Intelligence Agency, Office of Public Affairs, Washington, DC 20505, (703) 482-0623, Fax: (703) 482-1739, www.cia.gov; *The World Factbook.*

BAHAMAS, THE - BUSINESS

Inter-American Development Bank (IDB), 1300 New York Avenue, NW, Washington, DC 20577, (202) 623-1000, Fax: (202) 623-3096, www.iadb.org; *The Politics of Policies: Economic and Social Progress in Latin America - 2006 Report.*

BAHAMAS, THE - CAPITAL INVESTMENTS

Inter-American Development Bank (IDB), 1300 New York Avenue, NW, Washington, DC 20577, (202) 623-1000, Fax: (202) 623-3096, www.iadb.org; *The Politics of Policies: Economic and Social Progress in Latin America - 2006 Report.*

BAHAMAS, THE - CAPITAL LEVY

Inter-American Development Bank (IDB), 1300 New York Avenue, NW, Washington, DC 20577, (202) 623-1000, Fax: (202) 623-3096, www.iadb.org; *The Politics of Policies: Economic and Social Progress in Latin America - 2006 Report.*

International Monetary Fund (IMF), 700 Nineteenth Street, NW, Washington, DC 20431, (202) 623-7000, Fax: (202) 623-4661, www.imf.org; *Government Finance Statistics Yearbook (2008 Edition).*

BAHAMAS, THE - CATTLE

See BAHAMAS, THE - LIVESTOCK

BAHAMAS, THE - CHILDBIRTH - STATISTICS

Central Intelligence Agency, Office of Public Affairs, Washington, DC 20505, (703) 482-0623, Fax: (703) 482-1739, www.cia.gov; *The World Factbook.*

Euromonitor International, Inc., 224 S. Michigan Avenue, Suite 1500, Chicago, IL 60604, (312) 922-1115, Fax: (312) 922-1157, www.euromonitor.com; *International Marketing Data and Statistics 2008* and *The World Economic Factbook 2008.*

M.E. Sharpe, 80 Business Park Drive, Armonk, NY 10504, (800) 541-6563, Fax: (914) 273-2106, www.mesharpe.com; *The Illustrated Book of World Rankings.*

Palgrave Macmillan Ltd., Houndmills, Basingstoke, Hampshire, RG21 6XS, England, (Telephone in U.S. (888) 330-8477), (Fax in U.S. (800) 672-2054), www.palgrave.com; *The Statesman's Yearbook 2008.*

Taylor and Francis Group, An Informa Business, 2 Park Square, Milton Park, Abingdon, Oxford OX14 4RN, United Kingdom, (Dial from U.S. (212) 216-7800), (Fax from U.S. (212) 564-7854), www.tandf.co.uk; *The Europa World Year Book.*

United Nations Statistics Division, New York, NY 10017, (800) 253-9646, Fax: (212) 963-4116, http://unstats.un.org; *Demographic Yearbook* and *Statistical Yearbook.*

The World Bank, 1818 H Street, NW, Washington, DC 20433, (202) 473-1000, Fax: (202) 477-6391, www.worldbank.org; *World Development Indicators (WDI) 2008.*

World Health Organization (WHO), Avenue Appia 20, 1211 Geneve 27, Switzerland, (Telephone in U.S. (212) 331-9081), www.who.int; *World Health Report 2006.*

BAHAMAS, THE - CLIMATE

M.E. Sharpe, 80 Business Park Drive, Armonk, NY 10504, (800) 541-6563, Fax: (914) 273-2106, www.mesharpe.com; *The Illustrated Book of World Rankings.*

Palgrave Macmillan Ltd., Houndmills, Basingstoke, Hampshire, RG21 6XS, England, (Telephone in U.S. (888) 330-8477), (Fax in U.S. (800) 672-2054), www.palgrave.com; *The Statesman's Yearbook 2008.*

BAHAMAS, THE - COAL PRODUCTION

See BAHAMAS, THE - MINERAL INDUSTRIES

BAHAMAS, THE - COFFEE

See BAHAMAS, THE - CROPS

BAHAMAS, THE - COMMERCE

Palgrave Macmillan Ltd., Houndmills, Basingstoke, Hampshire, RG21 6XS, England, (Telephone in U.S. (888) 330-8477), (Fax in U.S. (800) 672-2054), www.palgrave.com; *The Statesman's Yearbook 2008.*

BAHAMAS, THE - COMMODITY EXCHANGES

Commodity Research Bureau, 330 South Wells Street, Suite 612, Chicago, IL 60606-7110, (800) 621-5271, Fax: (312) 939-4135, www.crbtrader.com; *2006 CRB Commodity Yearbook and CD.*

International Monetary Fund (IMF), 700 Nineteenth Street, NW, Washington, DC 20431, (202) 623-7000, Fax: (202) 623-4661, www.imf.org; *IMF Primary Commodity Prices.*

United Nations Food and Agricultural Organization (FAO), Viale delle Terme di Caracalla, 00100 Rome, Italy, (Dial from U.S. (202) 653-2400), (Fax from U.S. (202) 653 5760), www.fao.org; *The State of Food and Agriculture (SOFA) 2006.*

BAHAMAS, THE - CONSTRUCTION INDUSTRY

Department of Statistics, Ministry of Finance, Clarence Bain Building, Thompson Boulevard, N-3904, Nassau, Bahamas, (Dial from U.S. (242) 502-1000), (Fax from U.S. (242) 325-5149), www.bahamas.gov.bs/finance; *Building Construction Statistics.*

Inter-American Development Bank (IDB), 1300 New York Avenue, NW, Washington, DC 20577, (202) 623-1000, Fax: (202) 623-3096, www.iadb.org; *The Politics of Policies: Economic and Social Progress in Latin America - 2006 Report.*

M.E. Sharpe, 80 Business Park Drive, Armonk, NY 10504, (800) 541-6563, Fax: (914) 273-2106, www.mesharpe.com; *The Illustrated Book of World Rankings.*

United Nations Statistics Division, New York, NY 10017, (800) 253-9646, Fax: (212) 963-4116, http://unstats.un.org; *Statistical Yearbook.*

BAHAMAS, THE - CONSUMER PRICE INDEXES

Taylor and Francis Group, An Informa Business, 2 Park Square, Milton Park, Abingdon, Oxford OX14 4RN, United Kingdom, (Dial from U.S. (212) 216-7800), (Fax from U.S. (212) 564-7854), www.tandf.co.uk; *The Europa World Year Book.*

United Nations Statistics Division, New York, NY 10017, (800) 253-9646, Fax: (212) 963-4116, http://unstats.un.org; *Statistical Yearbook.*

The World Bank, 1818 H Street, NW, Washington, DC 20433, (202) 473-1000, Fax: (202) 477-6391, www.worldbank.org; *Bahamas.*

BAHAMAS, THE - CONSUMPTION (ECONOMICS)

Inter-American Development Bank (IDB), 1300 New York Avenue, NW, Washington, DC 20577, (202) 623-1000, Fax: (202) 623-3096, www.iadb.org; *The Politics of Policies: Economic and Social Progress in Latin America - 2006 Report.*

BAHAMAS, THE - COPPER INDUSTRY AND TRADE

See BAHAMAS, THE - MINERAL INDUSTRIES

BAHAMAS, THE - CORN INDUSTRY

See BAHAMAS, THE - CROPS

BAHAMAS, THE - COST AND STANDARD OF LIVING

International Monetary Fund (IMF), 700 Nineteenth Street, NW, Washington, DC 20431, (202) 623-7000, Fax: (202) 623-4661, www.imf.org; *Government Finance Statistics Yearbook (2008 Edition).*

M.E. Sharpe, 80 Business Park Drive, Armonk, NY 10504, (800) 541-6563, Fax: (914) 273-2106, www.mesharpe.com; *The Illustrated Book of World Rankings.*

BAHAMAS, THE - COTTON

See BAHAMAS, THE - CROPS

BAHAMAS, THE - CRIME

International Criminal Police Organization (INTERPOL), General Secretariat, 200 quai Charles de Gaulle, 69006 Lyon, France, www.interpol.int; *International Crime Statistics.*

BAHAMAS, THE - CROPS

M.E. Sharpe, 80 Business Park Drive, Armonk, NY 10504, (800) 541-6563, Fax: (914) 273-2106, www.mesharpe.com; *The Illustrated Book of World Rankings.*

Palgrave Macmillan Ltd., Houndmills, Basingstoke, Hampshire, RG21 6XS, England, (Telephone in U.S. (888) 330-8477), (Fax in U.S. (800) 672-2054), www.palgrave.com; *The Statesman's Yearbook 2008.*

Taylor and Francis Group, An Informa Business, 2 Park Square, Milton Park, Abingdon, Oxford OX14 4RN, United Kingdom, (Dial from U.S. (212) 216-7800), (Fax from U.S. (212) 564-7854), www.tandf.co.uk; *The Europa World Year Book.*

United Nations Conference on Trade and Development (UNCTAD), DC2-1120, United Nations, New York, NY 10017, (212) 963-0027, www.unctad.org; *UNCTAD Commodity Yearbook.*

United Nations Food and Agricultural Organization (FAO), Viale delle Terme di Caracalla, 00100 Rome, Italy, (Dial from U.S. (202) 653-2400), (Fax from U.S. (202) 653 5760), www.fao.org; *The State of Food and Agriculture (SOFA) 2006.*

BAHAMAS, THE - CUSTOMS ADMINISTRATION

Inter-American Development Bank (IDB), 1300 New York Avenue, NW, Washington, DC 20577, (202) 623-1000, Fax: (202) 623-3096, www.iadb.org; *The Politics of Policies: Economic and Social Progress in Latin America - 2006 Report.*

International Monetary Fund (IMF), 700 Nineteenth Street, NW, Washington, DC 20431, (202) 623-7000, Fax: (202) 623-4661, www.imf.org; *Government Finance Statistics Yearbook (2008 Edition).*

Palgrave Macmillan Ltd., Houndmills, Basingstoke, Hampshire, RG21 6XS, England, (Telephone in U.S. (888) 330-8477), (Fax in U.S. (800) 672-2054), www.palgrave.com; *The Statesman's Yearbook 2008.*

BAHAMAS, THE - DAIRY PROCESSING

M.E. Sharpe, 80 Business Park Drive, Armonk, NY 10504, (800) 541-6563, Fax: (914) 273-2106, www.mesharpe.com; *The Illustrated Book of World Rankings.*

Palgrave Macmillan Ltd., Houndmills, Basingstoke, Hampshire, RG21 6XS, England, (Telephone in U.S. (888) 330-8477), (Fax in U.S. (800) 672-2054), www.palgrave.com; *The Statesman's Yearbook 2008.*

United Nations Food and Agricultural Organization (FAO), Viale delle Terme di Caracalla, 00100 Rome, Italy, (Dial from U.S. (202) 653-2400), (Fax from U.S. (202) 653 5760), www.fao.org; *FAO Production Yearbook 2002* and *The State of Food and Agriculture (SOFA) 2006.*

BAHAMAS, THE - DEATH RATES

See BAHAMAS, THE - MORTALITY

BAHAMAS, THE - DEBTS, EXTERNAL

Inter-American Development Bank (IDB), 1300 New York Avenue, NW, Washington, DC 20577, (202) 623-1000, Fax: (202) 623-3096, www.iadb.org; *The Politics of Policies: Economic and Social Progress in Latin America - 2006 Report.*

International Monetary Fund (IMF), 700 Nineteenth Street, NW, Washington, DC 20431, (202) 623-7000, Fax: (202) 623-4661, www.imf.org; *Government Finance Statistics Yearbook (2008 Edition).*

Palgrave Macmillan Ltd., Houndmills, Basingstoke, Hampshire, RG21 6XS, England, (Telephone in U.S. (888) 330-8477), (Fax in U.S. (800) 672-2054), www.palgrave.com; *The Statesman's Yearbook 2008.*

United Nations Statistics Division, New York, NY 10017, (800) 253-9646, Fax: (212) 963-4116, http://unstats.un.org; *Economic Survey of Latin America and the Caribbean 2004-2005.*

The World Bank, 1818 H Street, NW, Washington, DC 20433, (202) 473-1000, Fax: (202) 477-6391, www.worldbank.org; *Global Development Finance 2007* and *World Development Indicators (WDI) 2008.*

BAHAMAS, THE - DEFENSE EXPENDITURES

See BAHAMAS, THE - ARMED FORCES

BAHAMAS, THE - DEMOGRAPHY

Euromonitor International, Inc., 224 S. Michigan Avenue, Suite 1500, Chicago, IL 60604, (312) 922-1115, Fax: (312) 922-1157, www.euromonitor.com; *International Marketing Data and Statistics 2008; The World Economic Factbook 2008;* and *World Marketing Data and Statistics.*

M.E. Sharpe, 80 Business Park Drive, Armonk, NY 10504, (800) 541-6563, Fax: (914) 273-2106, www.mesharpe.com; *The Illustrated Book of World Rankings.*

United Nations Statistics Division, New York, NY 10017, (800) 253-9646, Fax: (212) 963-4116, http://unstats.un.org; *Human Development Report 2006.*

The World Bank, 1818 H Street, NW, Washington, DC 20433, (202) 473-1000, Fax: (202) 477-6391, www.worldbank.org; *Bahamas.*

BAHAMAS, THE - DIAMONDS

See BAHAMAS, THE - MINERAL INDUSTRIES

BAHAMAS, THE - DISPOSABLE INCOME

Inter-American Development Bank (IDB), 1300 New York Avenue, NW, Washington, DC 20577, (202) 623-1000, Fax: (202) 623-3096, www.iadb.org; *The Politics of Policies: Economic and Social Progress in Latin America - 2006 Report.*

M.E. Sharpe, 80 Business Park Drive, Armonk, NY 10504, (800) 541-6563, Fax: (914) 273-2106, www.mesharpe.com; *The Illustrated Book of World Rankings.*

United Nations Statistics Division, New York, NY 10017, (800) 253-9646, Fax: (212) 963-4116, http://unstats.un.org; *National Accounts Statistics: Compendium of Income Distribution Statistics.*

BAHAMAS, THE - DIVORCE

M.E. Sharpe, 80 Business Park Drive, Armonk, NY 10504, (800) 541-6563, Fax: (914) 273-2106, www.mesharpe.com; *The Illustrated Book of World Rankings.*

United Nations Statistics Division, New York, NY 10017, (800) 253-9646, Fax: (212) 963-4116, http://unstats.un.org; *Demographic Yearbook* and *Statistical Yearbook.*

BAHAMAS, THE - ECONOMIC ASSISTANCE

Inter-American Development Bank (IDB), 1300 New York Avenue, NW, Washington, DC 20577, (202) 623-1000, Fax: (202) 623-3096, www.iadb.org; *The Politics of Policies: Economic and Social Progress in Latin America - 2006 Report.*

United Nations Statistics Division, New York, NY 10017, (800) 253-9646, Fax: (212) 963-4116, http://unstats.un.org; *Statistical Yearbook.*

BAHAMAS, THE - ECONOMIC CONDITIONS

Center for International Business Education Research (CIBER), Columbia Business School and School of International and Public Affairs, Uris Hall, Room 212, 3022 Broadway, New York, NY 10027-6902, Mr. Joshua Safier, (212) 854-4750, Fax: (212) 222-9821, www.columbia.edu/cu/ciber/; Datastream International.

Central Intelligence Agency, Office of Public Affairs, Washington, DC 20505, (703) 482-0623, Fax: (703) 482-1739, www.cia.gov; *The World Factbook.*

Department of Statistics, Ministry of Finance, Clarence Bain Building, Thompson Boulevard, N-3904, Nassau, Bahamas, (Dial from U.S. (242) 502-1000), (Fax from U.S. (242) 325-5149), www.bahamas.gov.bs/finance; *Building Construction Statistics; External Trade Report;* and *Labour Force and Household Income.*

DSI Data Service Information, Xantener Strasse 51a, D-47495 Rheinberg, Germany, www.dsidata.com; *Campus Solution.*

Dun and Bradstreet (DB) Corporation, 103 JFK Parkway, Short Hills, NJ 07078, (973) 921-5500, www.dnb.com; *Country Report.*

Economist Intelligence Unit, 111 West 57th Street, New York, NY 10019, (212) 554-0600, Fax: (212) 586-1181, www.eiu.com; *Bahamas Country Report.*

Euromonitor International, Inc., 224 S. Michigan Avenue, Suite 1500, Chicago, IL 60604, (312) 922-1115, Fax: (312) 922-1157, www.euromonitor.com; *The World Economic Factbook 2008* and *World Marketing Data and Statistics.*

Inter-American Development Bank (IDB), 1300 New York Avenue, NW, Washington, DC 20577, (202) 623-1000, Fax: (202) 623-3096, www.iadb.org; *The Politics of Policies: Economic and Social Progress in Latin America - 2006 Report.*

International Monetary Fund (IMF), 700 Nineteenth Street, NW, Washington, DC 20431, (202) 623-7000, Fax: (202) 623-4661, www.imf.org; *World Economic Outlook Reports.*

M.E. Sharpe, 80 Business Park Drive, Armonk, NY 10504, (800) 541-6563, Fax: (914) 273-2106, www.mesharpe.com; *The Illustrated Book of World Rankings.*

Palgrave Macmillan Ltd., Houndmills, Basingstoke, Hampshire, RG21 6XS, England, (Telephone in U.S. (888) 330-8477), (Fax in U.S. (800) 672-2054), www.palgrave.com; *The Statesman's Yearbook 2008.*

Taylor and Francis Group, An Informa Business, 2 Park Square, Milton Park, Abingdon, Oxford OX14 4RN, United Kingdom, (Dial from U.S. (212) 216-7800), (Fax from U.S. (212) 564-7854), www.tandf.co.uk; *The Europa World Year Book.*

United Nations Statistics Division, New York, NY 10017, (800) 253-9646, Fax: (212) 963-4116, http://unstats.un.org; *Economic Survey of Latin America and the Caribbean 2004-2005* and *World Statistics Pocketbook.*

The World Bank, 1818 H Street, NW, Washington, DC 20433, (202) 473-1000, Fax: (202) 477-6391, www.worldbank.org; *Bahamas; Global Economic Monitor (GEM); Global Economic Prospects 2008;* and *The World Bank Atlas 2003-2004.*

BAHAMAS, THE - ECONOMICS - SOCIOLOGICAL ASPECTS

Inter-American Development Bank (IDB), 1300 New York Avenue, NW, Washington, DC 20577, (202) 623-1000, Fax: (202) 623-3096, www.iadb.org; *The Politics of Policies: Economic and Social Progress in Latin America - 2006 Report.*

BAHAMAS, THE - EDUCATION

Euromonitor International, Inc., 224 S. Michigan Avenue, Suite 1500, Chicago, IL 60604, (312) 922-1115, Fax: (312) 922-1157, www.euromonitor.com; *International Marketing Data and Statistics 2008* and *World Marketing Data and Statistics.*

International Monetary Fund (IMF), 700 Nineteenth Street, NW, Washington, DC 20431, (202) 623-7000, Fax: (202) 623-4661, www.imf.org; *Government Finance Statistics Yearbook (2008 Edition).*

M.E. Sharpe, 80 Business Park Drive, Armonk, NY 10504, (800) 541-6563, Fax: (914) 273-2106, www.mesharpe.com; *The Illustrated Book of World Rankings.*

Palgrave Macmillan Ltd., Houndmills, Basingstoke, Hampshire, RG21 6XS, England, (Telephone in U.S. (888) 330-8477), (Fax in U.S. (800) 672-2054), www.palgrave.com; *The Statesman's Yearbook 2008.*

Taylor and Francis Group, An Informa Business, 2 Park Square, Milton Park, Abingdon, Oxford OX14 4RN, United Kingdom, (Dial from U.S. (212) 216-7800), (Fax from U.S. (212) 564-7854), www.tandf.co.uk; *The Europa World Year Book.*

UNESCO Institute for Statistics, C.P. 6128 Succursale Centre-Ville, Montreal, Quebec, H3C 3J7 Canada, (Dial from U.S. (514) 343-6880), (Fax from U.S. (514) 343 6882), www.uis.unesco.org; *Statistical Tables.*

United Nations Statistics Division, New York, NY 10017, (800) 253-9646, Fax: (212) 963-4116, http://unstats.un.org; *Human Development Report 2006.*

The World Bank, 1818 H Street, NW, Washington, DC 20433, (202) 473-1000, Fax: (202) 477-6391, www.worldbank.org; *Bahamas* and *World Development Indicators (WDI) 2008.*

BAHAMAS, THE - ELECTRICITY

Inter-American Development Bank (IDB), 1300 New York Avenue, NW, Washington, DC 20577, (202) 623-1000, Fax: (202) 623-3096, www.iadb.org; *The Politics of Policies: Economic and Social Progress in Latin America - 2006 Report.*

M.E. Sharpe, 80 Business Park Drive, Armonk, NY 10504, (800) 541-6563, Fax: (914) 273-2106, www.mesharpe.com; *The Illustrated Book of World Rankings.*

Palgrave Macmillan Ltd., Houndmills, Basingstoke, Hampshire, RG21 6XS, England, (Telephone in U.S. (888) 330-8477), (Fax in U.S. (800) 672-2054), www.palgrave.com; *The Statesman's Yearbook 2008.*

United Nations Statistics Division, New York, NY 10017, (800) 253-9646, Fax: (212) 963-4116, http://unstats.un.org; *Human Development Report 2006* and *Statistical Yearbook.*

BAHAMAS, THE - EMPLOYMENT

Euromonitor International, Inc., 224 S. Michigan Avenue, Suite 1500, Chicago, IL 60604, (312) 922-1115, Fax: (312) 922-1157, www.euromonitor.com; *International Marketing Data and Statistics 2008.*

International Labour Office, I.L.O. Publications, 4 route des Morillons, CH-1211 Geneva 22, Switzerland, (Telephone in U.S. (202) 653-7652), (Fax in U.S. (202) 653-7687), www.ilo.org; *Yearbook of Labour Statistics 2006.*

M.E. Sharpe, 80 Business Park Drive, Armonk, NY 10504, (800) 541-6563, Fax: (914) 273-2106, www.mesharpe.com; *The Illustrated Book of World Rankings.*

The World Bank, 1818 H Street, NW, Washington, DC 20433, (202) 473-1000, Fax: (202) 477-6391, www.worldbank.org; *Bahamas.*

BAHAMAS, THE - ENVIRONMENTAL CONDITIONS

DSI Data Service Information, Xantener Strasse 51a, D-47495 Rheinberg, Germany, www.dsidata.com; *Campus Solution* and *DSI's Global Environmental Database.*

Economist Intelligence Unit, 111 West 57th Street, New York, NY 10019, (212) 554-0600, Fax: (212) 586-1181, www.eiu.com; *Bahamas Country Report.*

United Nations Statistics Division, New York, NY 10017, (800) 253-9646, Fax: (212) 963-4116, http://unstats.un.org; *World Statistics Pocketbook.*

BAHAMAS, THE - EXCISE TAX

International Monetary Fund (IMF), 700 Nineteenth Street, NW, Washington, DC 20431, (202) 623-7000, Fax: (202) 623-4661, www.imf.org; *Government Finance Statistics Yearbook (2008 Edition)* and *International Financial Statistics Yearbook 2007.*

BAHAMAS, THE - EXPENDITURES, PUBLIC

Inter-American Development Bank (IDB), 1300 New York Avenue, NW, Washington, DC 20577, (202) 623-1000, Fax: (202) 623-3096, www.iadb.org; *The Politics of Policies: Economic and Social Progress in Latin America - 2006 Report.*

BAHAMAS, THE - EXPORTS

Central Intelligence Agency, Office of Public Affairs, Washington, DC 20505, (703) 482-0623, Fax: (703) 482-1739, www.cia.gov; *The World Factbook.*

Economist Intelligence Unit, 111 West 57th Street, New York, NY 10019, (212) 554-0600, Fax: (212) 586-1181, www.eiu.com; *Bahamas Country Report.*

Euromonitor International, Inc., 224 S. Michigan Avenue, Suite 1500, Chicago, IL 60604, (312) 922-1115, Fax: (312) 922-1157, www.euromonitor.com; *International Marketing Data and Statistics 2008* and *The World Economic Factbook 2008.*

Inter-American Development Bank (IDB), 1300 New York Avenue, NW, Washington, DC 20577, (202) 623-1000, Fax: (202) 623-3096, www.iadb.org; *The Politics of Policies: Economic and Social Progress in Latin America - 2006 Report.*

International Monetary Fund (IMF), 700 Nineteenth Street, NW, Washington, DC 20431, (202) 623-7000, Fax: (202) 623-4661, www.imf.org; *Direction of Trade Statistics Yearbook 2007; Government Finance Statistics Yearbook (2008 Edition);* and *International Financial Statistics Yearbook 2007.*

Palgrave Macmillan Ltd., Houndmills, Basingstoke, Hampshire, RG21 6XS, England, (Telephone in U.S. (888) 330-8477), (Fax in U.S. (800) 672-2054), www.palgrave.com; *The Statesman's Yearbook 2008.*

Taylor and Francis Group, An Informa Business, 2 Park Square, Milton Park, Abingdon, Oxford OX14 4RN, United Kingdom, (Dial from U.S. (212) 216-7800), (Fax from U.S. (212) 564-7854), www.tandf.co.uk; *The Europa World Year Book.*

United Nations Conference on Trade and Development (UNCTAD), DC2-1120, United Nations, New York, NY 10017, (212) 963-0027, www.unctad.org; *Handbook of Statistics 2005.*

United Nations Food and Agricultural Organization (FAO), Viale delle Terme di Caracalla, 00100 Rome, Italy, (Dial from U.S. (202) 653-2400), (Fax from U.S. (202) 653 5760), www.fao.org; *The State of Food and Agriculture (SOFA) 2006.*

The World Bank, 1818 H Street, NW, Washington, DC 20433, (202) 473-1000, Fax: (202) 477-6391, www.worldbank.org; *World Development Indicators (WDI) 2008.*

BAHAMAS, THE - FERTILITY, HUMAN

M.E. Sharpe, 80 Business Park Drive, Armonk, NY 10504, (800) 541-6563, Fax: (914) 273-2106, www.mesharpe.com; *The Illustrated Book of World Rankings.*

United Nations Statistics Division, New York, NY 10017, (800) 253-9646, Fax: (212) 963-4116, http://unstats.un.org; *Human Development Report 2006.*

The World Bank, 1818 H Street, NW, Washington, DC 20433, (202) 473-1000, Fax: (202) 477-6391, www.worldbank.org; *The World Bank Atlas 2003-2004* and *World Development Indicators (WDI) 2008.*

BAHAMAS, THE - FERTILIZER INDUSTRY

United Nations Food and Agricultural Organization (FAO), Viale delle Terme di Caracalla, 00100 Rome, Italy, (Dial from U.S. (202) 653-2400), (Fax from U.S. (202) 653 5760), www.fao.org; *The State of Food and Agriculture (SOFA) 2006.*

BAHAMAS, THE - FETAL MORTALITY

See BAHAMAS, THE - MORTALITY

BAHAMAS, THE - FINANCE

Inter-American Development Bank (IDB), 1300 New York Avenue, NW, Washington, DC 20577, (202) 623-1000, Fax: (202) 623-3096, www.iadb.org; *The Politics of Policies: Economic and Social Progress in Latin America - 2006 Report.*

The World Bank, 1818 H Street, NW, Washington, DC 20433, (202) 473-1000, Fax: (202) 477-6391, www.worldbank.org; *Bahamas.*

BAHAMAS, THE - FINANCE, PUBLIC

Bernan Essential Government Publications, 4611-F Assembly Drive, Lanham MD, 20706-4391, (301) 459-2255, Fax: (800) 865-3450, www.bernan.com; *National Accounts Statistics.*

Economist Intelligence Unit, 111 West 57th Street, New York, NY 10019, (212) 554-0600, Fax: (212) 586-1181, www.eiu.com; *Bahamas Country Report.*

Inter-American Development Bank (IDB), 1300 New York Avenue, NW, Washington, DC 20577, (202) 623-1000, Fax: (202) 623-3096, www.iadb.org; *The Politics of Policies: Economic and Social Progress in Latin America - 2006 Report.*

International Monetary Fund (IMF), 700 Nineteenth Street, NW, Washington, DC 20431, (202) 623-7000, Fax: (202) 623-4661, www.imf.org; *Government Finance Statistics Yearbook (2008 Edition); International Financial Statistics;* and *International Financial Statistics Online Service.*

M.E. Sharpe, 80 Business Park Drive, Armonk, NY 10504, (800) 541-6563, Fax: (914) 273-2106, www.mesharpe.com; *The Illustrated Book of World Rankings.*

Palgrave Macmillan Ltd., Houndmills, Basingstoke, Hampshire, RG21 6XS, England, (Telephone in U.S. (888) 330-8477), (Fax in U.S. (800) 672-2054), www.palgrave.com; *The Statesman's Yearbook 2008.*

Taylor and Francis Group, An Informa Business, 2 Park Square, Milton Park, Abingdon, Oxford OX14 4RN, United Kingdom, (Dial from U.S. (212) 216-7800), (Fax from U.S. (212) 564-7854), www.tandf.co.uk; *The Europa World Year Book.*

The World Bank, 1818 H Street, NW, Washington, DC 20433, (202) 473-1000, Fax: (202) 477-6391, www.worldbank.org; *Bahamas.*

BAHAMAS, THE - FISHERIES

Inter-American Development Bank (IDB), 1300 New York Avenue, NW, Washington, DC 20577, (202) 623-1000, Fax: (202) 623-3096, www.iadb.org; *The Politics of Policies: Economic and Social Progress in Latin America - 2006 Report.*

M.E. Sharpe, 80 Business Park Drive, Armonk, NY 10504, (800) 541-6563, Fax: (914) 273-2106, www.mesharpe.com; *The Illustrated Book of World Rankings.*

Palgrave Macmillan Ltd., Houndmills, Basingstoke, Hampshire, RG21 6XS, England, (Telephone in U.S. (888) 330-8477), (Fax in U.S. (800) 672-2054), www.palgrave.com; *The Statesman's Yearbook 2008.*

Taylor and Francis Group, An Informa Business, 2 Park Square, Milton Park, Abingdon, Oxford OX14 4RN, United Kingdom, (Dial from U.S. (212) 216-7800), (Fax from U.S. (212) 564-7854), www.tandf.co.uk; *The Europa World Year Book.*

United Nations Conference on Trade and Development (UNCTAD), DC2-1120, United Nations, New York, NY 10017, (212) 963-0027, www.unctad.org; *UNCTAD Commodity Yearbook.*

United Nations Food and Agricultural Organization (FAO), Viale delle Terme di Caracalla, 00100 Rome, Italy, (Dial from U.S. (202) 653-2400), (Fax from U.S. (202) 653 5760), www.fao.org; *FAO Yearbook of Fishery Statistics;* Fishery Databases; FISHSTAT Database. Subjects covered include: Aquaculture production, capture production, fishery commodities; and *The State of Food and Agriculture (SOFA) 2006.*

United Nations Statistics Division, New York, NY 10017, (800) 253-9646, Fax: (212) 963-4116, http://unstats.un.org; *Statistical Yearbook.*

The World Bank, 1818 H Street, NW, Washington, DC 20433, (202) 473-1000, Fax: (202) 477-6391, www.worldbank.org; *Bahamas.*

BAHAMAS, THE - FOOD

United Nations Conference on Trade and Development (UNCTAD), DC2-1120, United Nations, New York, NY 10017, (212) 963-0027, www.unctad.org; *UNCTAD Commodity Yearbook.*

United Nations Food and Agricultural Organization (FAO), Viale delle Terme di Caracalla, 00100 Rome, Italy, (Dial from U.S. (202) 653-2400), (Fax from U.S. (202) 653 5760), www.fao.org; *FAO Production Yearbook 2002* and *The State of Food and Agriculture (SOFA) 2006.*

United Nations Statistics Division, New York, NY 10017, (800) 253-9646, Fax: (212) 963-4116, http://unstats.un.org; *Human Development Report 2006.*

BAHAMAS, THE - FOREIGN EXCHANGE RATES

Central Intelligence Agency, Office of Public Affairs, Washington, DC 20505, (703) 482-0623, Fax: (703) 482-1739, www.cia.gov; *The World Factbook.*

Euromonitor International, Inc., 224 S. Michigan Avenue, Suite 1500, Chicago, IL 60604, (312) 922-1115, Fax: (312) 922-1157, www.euromonitor.com; *International Marketing Data and Statistics 2008* and *The World Economic Factbook 2008.*

Inter-American Development Bank (IDB), 1300 New York Avenue, NW, Washington, DC 20577, (202) 623-1000, Fax: (202) 623-3096, www.iadb.org; *The Politics of Policies: Economic and Social Progress in Latin America - 2006 Report.*

International Monetary Fund (IMF), 700 Nineteenth Street, NW, Washington, DC 20431, (202) 623-7000, Fax: (202) 623-4661, www.imf.org; *International Financial Statistics Yearbook 2007.*

Taylor and Francis Group, An Informa Business, 2 Park Square, Milton Park, Abingdon, Oxford OX14 4RN, United Kingdom, (Dial from U.S. (212) 216-7800), (Fax from U.S. (212) 564-7854), www.tandf.co.uk; *The Europa World Year Book.*

United Nations Statistics Division, New York, NY 10017, (800) 253-9646, Fax: (212) 963-4116, http://unstats.un.org; *Statistical Yearbook* and *World Statistics Pocketbook.*

BAHAMAS, THE - FORESTS AND FORESTRY

Inter-American Development Bank (IDB), 1300 New York Avenue, NW, Washington, DC 20577, (202) 623-1000, Fax: (202) 623-3096, www.iadb.org; *The Politics of Policies: Economic and Social Progress in Latin America - 2006 Report.*

M.E. Sharpe, 80 Business Park Drive, Armonk, NY 10504, (800) 541-6563, Fax: (914) 273-2106, www.mesharpe.com; *The Illustrated Book of World Rankings.*

Taylor and Francis Group, An Informa Business, 2 Park Square, Milton Park, Abingdon, Oxford OX14 4RN, United Kingdom, (Dial from U.S. (212) 216-7800), (Fax from U.S. (212) 564-7854), www.tandf.co.uk; *The Europa World Year Book.*

UNESCO Institute for Statistics, C.P. 6128 Succursale Centre-Ville, Montreal, Quebec, H3C 3J7 Canada, (Dial from U.S. (514) 343-6880), (Fax from U.S. (514) 343 6882), www.uis.unesco.org; *Statistical Tables.*

United Nations Conference on Trade and Development (UNCTAD), DC2-1120, United Nations, New York, NY 10017, (212) 963-0027, www.unctad.org; *UNCTAD Commodity Yearbook.*

United Nations Food and Agricultural Organization (FAO), Viale delle Terme di Caracalla, 00100 Rome, Italy, (Dial from U.S. (202) 653-2400), (Fax from U.S. (202) 653 5760), www.fao.org; *FAO Yearbook of Forest Products* and *The State of Food and Agriculture (SOFA) 2006.*

United Nations Statistics Division, New York, NY 10017, (800) 253-9646, Fax: (212) 963-4116, http://unstats.un.org; *Statistical Yearbook.*

The World Bank, 1818 H Street, NW, Washington, DC 20433, (202) 473-1000, Fax: (202) 477-6391, www.worldbank.org; *Bahamas.*

BAHAMAS, THE - GAS PRODUCTION

See BAHAMAS, THE - MINERAL INDUSTRIES

BAHAMAS, THE - GEOGRAPHIC INFORMATION SYSTEMS

M.E. Sharpe, 80 Business Park Drive, Armonk, NY 10504, (800) 541-6563, Fax: (914) 273-2106, www.mesharpe.com; *The Illustrated Book of World Rankings.*

The World Bank, 1818 H Street, NW, Washington, DC 20433, (202) 473-1000, Fax: (202) 477-6391, www.worldbank.org; *Bahamas.*

BAHAMAS, THE - GOLD INDUSTRY

International Monetary Fund (IMF), 700 Nineteenth Street, NW, Washington, DC 20431, (202) 623-7000, Fax: (202) 623-4661, www.imf.org; *International Financial Statistics Yearbook 2007.*

United Nations Statistics Division, New York, NY 10017, (800) 253-9646, Fax: (212) 963-4116, http://unstats.un.org; *Statistical Yearbook.*

The World Bank, 1818 H Street, NW, Washington, DC 20433, (202) 473-1000, Fax: (202) 477-6391, www.worldbank.org; *World Development Indicators (WDI) 2008.*

BAHAMAS, THE - GOLD PRODUCTION

See BAHAMAS, THE - MINERAL INDUSTRIES

BAHAMAS, THE - GRANTS-IN-AID

International Monetary Fund (IMF), 700 Nineteenth Street, NW, Washington, DC 20431, (202) 623-7000, Fax: (202) 623-4661, www.imf.org; *Government Finance Statistics Yearbook (2008 Edition).*

BAHAMAS, THE - GROSS DOMESTIC PRODUCT

Economist Intelligence Unit, 111 West 57th Street, New York, NY 10019, (212) 554-0600, Fax: (212) 586-1181, www.eiu.com; *Bahamas Country Report.*

Euromonitor International, Inc., 224 S. Michigan Avenue, Suite 1500, Chicago, IL 60604, (312) 922-1115, Fax: (312) 922-1157, www.euromonitor.com; *International Marketing Data and Statistics 2008* and *The World Economic Factbook 2008.*

Inter-American Development Bank (IDB), 1300 New York Avenue, NW, Washington, DC 20577, (202) 623-1000, Fax: (202) 623-3096, www.iadb.org; *The Politics of Policies: Economic and Social Progress in Latin America - 2006 Report.*

M.E. Sharpe, 80 Business Park Drive, Armonk, NY 10504, (800) 541-6563, Fax: (914) 273-2106, www.mesharpe.com; *The Illustrated Book of World Rankings.*

Taylor and Francis Group, An Informa Business, 2 Park Square, Milton Park, Abingdon, Oxford OX14 4RN, United Kingdom, (Dial from U.S. (212) 216-7800), (Fax from U.S. (212) 564-7854), www.tandf.co.uk; *The Europa World Year Book.*

United Nations Statistics Division, New York, NY 10017, (800) 253-9646, Fax: (212) 963-4116, http://unstats.un.org; *Human Development Report 2006* and *National Accounts Statistics: Compendium of Income Distribution Statistics.*

The World Bank, 1818 H Street, NW, Washington, DC 20433, (202) 473-1000, Fax: (202) 477-6391, www.worldbank.org; *World Development Indicators (WDI) 2008.*

BAHAMAS, THE - GROSS NATIONAL PRODUCT

Inter-American Development Bank (IDB), 1300 New York Avenue, NW, Washington, DC 20577, (202) 623-1000, Fax: (202) 623-3096, www.iadb.org; *The Politics of Policies: Economic and Social Progress in Latin America - 2006 Report.*

M.E. Sharpe, 80 Business Park Drive, Armonk, NY 10504, (800) 541-6563, Fax: (914) 273-2106, www.mesharpe.com; *The Illustrated Book of World Rankings.*

Palgrave Macmillan Ltd., Houndmills, Basingstoke, Hampshire, RG21 6XS, England, (Telephone in U.S. (888) 330-8477), (Fax in U.S. (800) 672-2054), www.palgrave.com; *The Statesman's Yearbook 2008.*

The World Bank, 1818 H Street, NW, Washington, DC 20433, (202) 473-1000, Fax: (202) 477-6391, www.worldbank.org; *The World Bank Atlas 2003-2004* and *World Development Indicators (WDI) 2008.*

BAHAMAS, THE - HIDES AND SKINS INDUSTRY

United Nations Food and Agricultural Organization (FAO), Viale delle Terme di Caracalla, 00100 Rome, Italy, (Dial from U.S. (202) 653-2400), (Fax from U.S. (202) 653 5760), www.fao.org; *FAO Production Yearbook 2002.*

BAHAMAS, THE - HOUSING

Euromonitor International, Inc., 224 S. Michigan Avenue, Suite 1500, Chicago, IL 60604, (312) 922-1115, Fax: (312) 922-1157, www.euromonitor.com; *World Marketing Data and Statistics.*

BAHAMAS, THE - ILLITERATE PERSONS

Euromonitor International, Inc., 224 S. Michigan Avenue, Suite 1500, Chicago, IL 60604, (312) 922-1115, Fax: (312) 922-1157, www.euromonitor.com; *The World Economic Factbook 2008.*

UNESCO Institute for Statistics, C.P. 6128 Succursale Centre-Ville, Montreal, Quebec, H3C 3J7 Canada, (Dial from U.S. (514) 343-6880), (Fax from U.S. (514) 343 6882), www.uis.unesco.org; *Statistical Tables.*

United Nations Statistics Division, New York, NY 10017, (800) 253-9646, Fax: (212) 963-4116, http://unstats.un.org; *Human Development Report 2006.*

BAHAMAS, THE - IMPORTS

Central Intelligence Agency, Office of Public Affairs, Washington, DC 20505, (703) 482-0623, Fax: (703) 482-1739, www.cia.gov; *The World Factbook.*

Economist Intelligence Unit, 111 West 57th Street, New York, NY 10019, (212) 554-0600, Fax: (212) 586-1181, www.eiu.com; *Bahamas Country Report.*

Euromonitor International, Inc., 224 S. Michigan Avenue, Suite 1500, Chicago, IL 60604, (312) 922-1115, Fax: (312) 922-1157, www.euromonitor.com; *International Marketing Data and Statistics 2008* and *The World Economic Factbook 2008.*

Inter-American Development Bank (IDB), 1300 New York Avenue, NW, Washington, DC 20577, (202) 623-1000, Fax: (202) 623-3096, www.iadb.org; *The Politics of Policies: Economic and Social Progress in Latin America - 2006 Report.*

International Monetary Fund (IMF), 700 Nineteenth Street, NW, Washington, DC 20431, (202) 623-7000, Fax: (202) 623-4661, www.imf.org; *Direction of Trade Statistics Yearbook 2007* and *International Financial Statistics Yearbook 2007.*

Palgrave Macmillan Ltd., Houndmills, Basingstoke, Hampshire, RG21 6XS, England, (Telephone in U.S. (888) 330-8477), (Fax in U.S. (800) 672-2054), www.palgrave.com; *The Statesman's Yearbook 2008.*

Taylor and Francis Group, An Informa Business, 2 Park Square, Milton Park, Abingdon, Oxford OX14 4RN, United Kingdom, (Dial from U.S. (212) 216-7800), (Fax from U.S. (212) 564-7854), www.tandf.co.uk; *The Europa World Year Book.*

United Nations Conference on Trade and Development (UNCTAD), DC2-1120, United Nations, New York, NY 10017, (212) 963-0027, www.unctad.org; *Handbook of Statistics 2005.*

United Nations Food and Agricultural Organization (FAO), Viale delle Terme di Caracalla, 00100 Rome, Italy, (Dial from U.S. (202) 653-2400), (Fax from U.S. (202) 653 5760), www.fao.org; *The State of Food and Agriculture (SOFA) 2006.*

The World Bank, 1818 H Street, NW, Washington, DC 20433, (202) 473-1000, Fax: (202) 477-6391, www.worldbank.org; *World Development Indicators (WDI) 2008.*

BAHAMAS, THE - INCOME TAXES

See BAHAMAS, THE - TAXATION

BAHAMAS, THE - INDUSTRIAL PRODUCTIVITY

M.E. Sharpe, 80 Business Park Drive, Armonk, NY 10504, (800) 541-6563, Fax: (914) 273-2106, www.mesharpe.com; *The Illustrated Book of World Rankings.*

BAHAMAS, THE - INDUSTRIAL PROPERTY

United Nations Statistics Division, New York, NY 10017, (800) 253-9646, Fax: (212) 963-4116, http://unstats.un.org; *Statistical Yearbook.*

BAHAMAS, THE - INDUSTRIES

Central Intelligence Agency, Office of Public Affairs, Washington, DC 20505, (703) 482-0623, Fax: (703) 482-1739, www.cia.gov; *The World Factbook.*

Economist Intelligence Unit, 111 West 57th Street, New York, NY 10019, (212) 554-0600, Fax: (212) 586-1181, www.eiu.com; *Bahamas Country Report.*

Euromonitor International, Inc., 224 S. Michigan Avenue, Suite 1500, Chicago, IL 60604, (312) 922-1115, Fax: (312) 922-1157, www.euromonitor.com; *The World Economic Factbook 2008* and *World Marketing Data and Statistics.*

International Labour Office, I.L.O. Publications, 4 route des Morillons, CH-1211 Geneva 22, Switzerland, (Telephone in U.S. (202) 653-7652), (Fax in U.S. (202) 653-7687), www.ilo.org; *Yearbook of Labour Statistics 2006.*

M.E. Sharpe, 80 Business Park Drive, Armonk, NY 10504, (800) 541-6563, Fax: (914) 273-2106, www.mesharpe.com; *The Illustrated Book of World Rankings.*

Palgrave Macmillan Ltd., Houndmills, Basingstoke, Hampshire, RG21 6XS, England, (Telephone in U.S. (888) 330-8477), (Fax in U.S. (800) 672-2054), www.palgrave.com; *The Statesman's Yearbook 2008.*

Taylor and Francis Group, An Informa Business, 2 Park Square, Milton Park, Abingdon, Oxford OX14 4RN, United Kingdom, (Dial from U.S. (212) 216-7800), (Fax from U.S. (212) 564-7854), www.tandf.co.uk; *The Europa World Year Book.*

United Nations Industrial Development Organization (UNIDO), 1 United Nations Plaza, New York, NY 10017, (212) 963 6890, Fax: (212) 963-7904, http://unido.org; Industrial Statistics Database 2008 (INDSTAT) and *The International Yearbook of Industrial Statistics 2008.*

United Nations Statistics Division, New York, NY 10017, (800) 253-9646, Fax: (212) 963-4116, http://unstats.un.org; *Economic Survey of Latin America and the Caribbean 2004-2005.*

The World Bank, 1818 H Street, NW, Washington, DC 20433, (202) 473-1000, Fax: (202) 477-6391, www.worldbank.org; *Bahamas* and *World Development Indicators (WDI) 2008.*

BAHAMAS, THE - INFANT AND MATERNAL MORTALITY

See BAHAMAS, THE - MORTALITY

BAHAMAS, THE - INFLATION (FINANCE)

United Nations Statistics Division, New York, NY 10017, (800) 253-9646, Fax: (212) 963-4116, http://unstats.un.org; *Economic Survey of Latin America and the Caribbean 2004-2005.*

BAHAMAS, THE - INTEREST RATES

Inter-American Development Bank (IDB), 1300 New York Avenue, NW, Washington, DC 20577, (202) 623-1000, Fax: (202) 623-3096, www.iadb.org; *The Politics of Policies: Economic and Social Progress in Latin America - 2006 Report.*

United Nations Statistics Division, New York, NY 10017, (800) 253-9646, Fax: (212) 963-4116, http://unstats.un.org; *Statistical Yearbook.*

BAHAMAS, THE - INTERNAL REVENUE

Inter-American Development Bank (IDB), 1300 New York Avenue, NW, Washington, DC 20577, (202) 623-1000, Fax: (202) 623-3096, www.iadb.org; *The Politics of Policies: Economic and Social Progress in Latin America - 2006 Report.*

BAHAMAS, THE - INTERNATIONAL FINANCE

Inter-American Development Bank (IDB), 1300 New York Avenue, NW, Washington, DC 20577, (202) 623-1000, Fax: (202) 623-3096, www.iadb.org; *The Politics of Policies: Economic and Social Progress in Latin America - 2006 Report.*

BAHAMAS, THE - INTERNATIONAL LIQUIDITY

Inter-American Development Bank (IDB), 1300 New York Avenue, NW, Washington, DC 20577, (202) 623-1000, Fax: (202) 623-3096, www.iadb.org; *The Politics of Policies: Economic and Social Progress in Latin America - 2006 Report.*

International Monetary Fund (IMF), 700 Nineteenth Street, NW, Washington, DC 20431, (202) 623-7000, Fax: (202) 623-4661, www.imf.org; *International Financial Statistics Yearbook 2007.*

BAHAMAS, THE - INTERNATIONAL STATISTICS

Inter-American Development Bank (IDB), 1300 New York Avenue, NW, Washington, DC 20577, (202) 623-1000, Fax: (202) 623-3096, www.iadb.org; *The Politics of Policies: Economic and Social Progress in Latin America - 2006 Report.*

BAHAMAS, THE - INTERNATIONAL TRADE

Department of Statistics, Ministry of Finance, Clarence Bain Building, Thompson Boulevard, N-3904, Nassau, Bahamas, (Dial from U.S. (242) 502-1000), (Fax from U.S. (242) 325-5149), www.bahamas.gov.bs/finance; *External Trade Report.*

Economist Intelligence Unit, 111 West 57th Street, New York, NY 10019, (212) 554-0600, Fax: (212) 586-1181, www.eiu.com; *Bahamas Country Report.*

Euromonitor International, Inc., 224 S. Michigan Avenue, Suite 1500, Chicago, IL 60604, (312) 922-1115, Fax: (312) 922-1157, www.euromonitor.com; *The World Economic Factbook 2008* and *World Marketing Data and Statistics.*

Inter-American Development Bank (IDB), 1300 New York Avenue, NW, Washington, DC 20577, (202) 623-1000, Fax: (202) 623-3096, www.iadb.org; *The Politics of Policies: Economic and Social Progress in Latin America - 2006 Report.*

M.E. Sharpe, 80 Business Park Drive, Armonk, NY 10504, (800) 541-6563, Fax: (914) 273-2106, www.mesharpe.com; *The Illustrated Book of World Rankings.*

Organisation for Economic Cooperation and Development (OECD), 2 rue Andre Pascal, F-75775 Paris Cedex 16, France, (Telephone in U.S. (202) 785-6323), (Fax in U.S. (202) 785-0350), www.oecd.org; *International Trade by Commodity Statistics (ITCS).*

Palgrave Macmillan Ltd., Houndmills, Basingstoke, Hampshire, RG21 6XS, England, (Telephone in U.S. (888) 330-8477), (Fax in U.S. (800) 672-2054), www.palgrave.com; *The Statesman's Yearbook 2008.*

Taylor and Francis Group, An Informa Business, 2 Park Square, Milton Park, Abingdon, Oxford OX14 4RN, United Kingdom, (Dial from U.S. (212) 216-7800), (Fax from U.S. (212) 564-7854), www.tandf.co.uk; *The Europa World Year Book.*

United Nations Conference on Trade and Development (UNCTAD), DC2-1120, United Nations, New York, NY 10017, (212) 963-0027, www.unctad.org; *UNCTAD Commodity Yearbook.*

United Nations Food and Agricultural Organization (FAO), Viale delle Terme di Caracalla, 00100 Rome, Italy, (Dial from U.S. (202) 653-2400), (Fax from U.S. (202) 653 5760), www.fao.org; *FAO Trade Yearbook* and *The State of Food and Agriculture (SOFA) 2006.*

United Nations Statistics Division, New York, NY 10017, (800) 253-9646, Fax: (212) 963-4116, http://unstats.un.org; *Economic Survey of Latin America and the Caribbean 2004-2005; International Trade Statistics Yearbook;* and *Statistical Yearbook.*

The World Bank, 1818 H Street, NW, Washington, DC 20433, (202) 473-1000, Fax: (202) 477-6391, www.worldbank.org; *Bahamas* and *World Development Indicators (WDI) 2008.*

World Trade Organization (WTO), Centre William Rappard, Rue de Lausanne 154, CH-1211 Geneva 21, Switzerland, www.wto.org; *International Trade Statistics 2006.*

BAHAMAS, THE - INTERNET USERS

International Telecommunication Union (ITU), Place des Nations, 1211 Geneva 20, Switzerland, www.itu.int; *World Telecommunication/ICT Indicators Database on CD-ROM; World Telecommunication/ICT Indicators Database Online;* and *Yearbook of Statistics - Telecommunication Services (Chronological Time Series 1997-2006).*

The World Bank, 1818 H Street, NW, Washington, DC 20433, (202) 473-1000, Fax: (202) 477-6391, www.worldbank.org; *Bahamas.*

BAHAMAS, THE - INVESTMENTS

Inter-American Development Bank (IDB), 1300 New York Avenue, NW, Washington, DC 20577, (202) 623-1000, Fax: (202) 623-3096, www.iadb.org; *The Politics of Policies: Economic and Social Progress in Latin America - 2006 Report.*

BAHAMAS, THE - IRON AND IRON ORE PRODUCTION

See BAHAMAS, THE - MINERAL INDUSTRIES

BAHAMAS, THE - IRRIGATION

Inter-American Development Bank (IDB), 1300 New York Avenue, NW, Washington, DC 20577, (202) 623-1000, Fax: (202) 623-3096, www.iadb.org; *The Politics of Policies: Economic and Social Progress in Latin America - 2006 Report.*

BAHAMAS, THE - LABOR

Central Intelligence Agency, Office of Public Affairs, Washington, DC 20505, (703) 482-0623, Fax: (703) 482-1739, www.cia.gov; *The World Factbook.*

Department of Statistics, Ministry of Finance, Clarence Bain Building, Thompson Boulevard, N-3904, Nassau, Bahamas, (Dial from U.S. (242) 502-1000), (Fax from U.S. (242) 325-5149), www.bahamas.gov.bs/finance; *Labour Force and Household Income.*

Euromonitor International, Inc., 224 S. Michigan Avenue, Suite 1500, Chicago, IL 60604, (312) 922-1115, Fax: (312) 922-1157, www.euromonitor.com; *International Marketing Data and Statistics 2008* and *World Marketing Data and Statistics.*

International Labour Office, I.L.O. Publications, 4 route des Morillons, CH-1211 Geneva 22, Switzerland, (Telephone in U.S. (202) 653-7652), (Fax in U.S. (202) 653-7687), www.ilo.org; *Yearbook of Labour Statistics 2006.*

M.E. Sharpe, 80 Business Park Drive, Armonk, NY 10504, (800) 541-6563, Fax: (914) 273-2106, www.mesharpe.com; *The Illustrated Book of World Rankings.*

Palgrave Macmillan Ltd., Houndmills, Basingstoke, Hampshire, RG21 6XS, England, (Telephone in U.S. (888) 330-8477), (Fax in U.S. (800) 672-2054), www.palgrave.com; *The Statesman's Yearbook 2008.*

Taylor and Francis Group, An Informa Business, 2 Park Square, Milton Park, Abingdon, Oxford OX14 4RN, United Kingdom, (Dial from U.S. (212) 216-7800), (Fax from U.S. (212) 564-7854), www.tandf.co.uk; *The Europa World Year Book.*

United Nations Food and Agricultural Organization (FAO), Viale delle Terme di Caracalla, 00100 Rome, Italy, (Dial from U.S. (202) 653-2400), (Fax from U.S. (202) 653 5760), www.fao.org; *FAO Production Yearbook 2002* and *The State of Food and Agriculture (SOFA) 2006.*

United Nations Statistics Division, New York, NY 10017, (800) 253-9646, Fax: (212) 963-4116, http://unstats.un.org; *Human Development Report 2006.*

The World Bank, 1818 H Street, NW, Washington, DC 20433, (202) 473-1000, Fax: (202) 477-6391, www.worldbank.org; *The World Bank Atlas 2003-2004* and *World Development Indicators (WDI) 2008.*

BAHAMAS, THE - LAND USE

Central Intelligence Agency, Office of Public Affairs, Washington, DC 20505, (703) 482-0623, Fax: (703) 482-1739, www.cia.gov; *The World Factbook.*

Euromonitor International, Inc., 224 S. Michigan Avenue, Suite 1500, Chicago, IL 60604, (312) 922-1115, Fax: (312) 922-1157, www.euromonitor.com; *International Marketing Data and Statistics 2008.*

Inter-American Development Bank (IDB), 1300 New York Avenue, NW, Washington, DC 20577, (202) 623-1000, Fax: (202) 623-3096, www.iadb.org; *The Politics of Policies: Economic and Social Progress in Latin America - 2006 Report.*

BAHAMAS, THE - LIBRARIES

M.E. Sharpe, 80 Business Park Drive, Armonk, NY 10504, (800) 541-6563, Fax: (914) 273-2106, www.mesharpe.com; *The Illustrated Book of World Rankings.*

UNESCO Institute for Statistics, C.P. 6128 Succursale Centre-Ville, Montreal, Quebec, H3C 3J7 Canada, (Dial from U.S. (514) 343-6880), (Fax from U.S. (514) 343 6882), www.uis.unesco.org; *Statistical Tables.*

BAHAMAS, THE - LICENSES

International Monetary Fund (IMF), 700 Nineteenth Street, NW, Washington, DC 20431, (202) 623-7000, Fax: (202) 623-4661, www.imf.org; *Government Finance Statistics Yearbook (2008 Edition).*

BAHAMAS, THE - LIFE EXPECTANCY

Euromonitor International, Inc., 224 S. Michigan Avenue, Suite 1500, Chicago, IL 60604, (312) 922-1115, Fax: (312) 922-1157, www.euromonitor.com; *The World Economic Factbook 2008.*

Palgrave Macmillan Ltd., Houndmills, Basingstoke, Hampshire, RG21 6XS, England, (Telephone in U.S. (888) 330-8477), (Fax in U.S. (800) 672-2054), www.palgrave.com; *The Statesman's Yearbook 2008.*

United Nations Statistics Division, New York, NY 10017, (800) 253-9646, Fax: (212) 963-4116, http://unstats.un.org; *Human Development Report 2006* and *World Statistics Pocketbook.*

The World Bank, 1818 H Street, NW, Washington, DC 20433, (202) 473-1000, Fax: (202) 477-6391, www.worldbank.org; *The World Bank Atlas 2003-2004.*

BAHAMAS, THE - LITERACY

Euromonitor International, Inc., 224 S. Michigan Avenue, Suite 1500, Chicago, IL 60604, (312) 922-1115, Fax: (312) 922-1157, www.euromonitor.com; *World Marketing Data and Statistics.*

BAHAMAS, THE - LIVESTOCK

M.E. Sharpe, 80 Business Park Drive, Armonk, NY 10504, (800) 541-6563, Fax: (914) 273-2106, www.mesharpe.com; *The Illustrated Book of World Rankings.*

Palgrave Macmillan Ltd., Houndmills, Basingstoke, Hampshire, RG21 6XS, England, (Telephone in U.S. (888) 330-8477), (Fax in U.S. (800) 672-2054), www.palgrave.com; *The Statesman's Yearbook 2008.*

Taylor and Francis Group, An Informa Business, 2 Park Square, Milton Park, Abingdon, Oxford OX14 4RN, United Kingdom, (Dial from U.S. (212) 216-7800), (Fax from U.S. (212) 564-7854), www.tandf.co.uk; *The Europa World Year Book.*

United Nations Conference on Trade and Development (UNCTAD), DC2-1120, United Nations, New York, NY 10017, (212) 963-0027, www.unctad.org; *UNCTAD Commodity Yearbook.*

United Nations Food and Agricultural Organization (FAO), Viale delle Terme di Caracalla, 00100 Rome, Italy, (Dial from U.S. (202) 653-2400), (Fax from U.S. (202) 653 5760), www.fao.org; *FAO Production Yearbook 2002* and *The State of Food and Agriculture (SOFA) 2006.*

United Nations Statistics Division, New York, NY 10017, (800) 253-9646, Fax: (212) 963-4116, http://unstats.un.org; *Statistical Yearbook.*

BAHAMAS, THE - LOCAL TAXATION

Inter-American Development Bank (IDB), 1300 New York Avenue, NW, Washington, DC 20577, (202) 623-1000, Fax: (202) 623-3096, www.iadb.org; *The Politics of Policies: Economic and Social Progress in Latin America - 2006 Report.*

BAHAMAS, THE - MANUFACTURES

Inter-American Development Bank (IDB), 1300 New York Avenue, NW, Washington, DC 20577, (202) 623-1000, Fax: (202) 623-3096, www.iadb.org; *The Politics of Policies: Economic and Social Progress in Latin America - 2006 Report.*

M.E. Sharpe, 80 Business Park Drive, Armonk, NY 10504, (800) 541-6563, Fax: (914) 273-2106, www.mesharpe.com; *The Illustrated Book of World Rankings.*

United Nations Statistics Division, New York, NY 10017, (800) 253-9646, Fax: (212) 963-4116, http://unstats.un.org; *Statistical Yearbook.*

The World Bank, 1818 H Street, NW, Washington, DC 20433, (202) 473-1000, Fax: (202) 477-6391, www.worldbank.org; *World Development Indicators (WDI) 2008.*

BAHAMAS, THE - MARRIAGE

M.E. Sharpe, 80 Business Park Drive, Armonk, NY 10504, (800) 541-6563, Fax: (914) 273-2106, www.mesharpe.com; *The Illustrated Book of World Rankings.*

Taylor and Francis Group, An Informa Business, 2 Park Square, Milton Park, Abingdon, Oxford OX14 4RN, United Kingdom, (Dial from U.S. (212) 216-7800), (Fax from U.S. (212) 564-7854), www.tandf.co.uk; *The Europa World Year Book.*

United Nations Statistics Division, New York, NY 10017, (800) 253-9646, Fax: (212) 963-4116, http://unstats.un.org; *Demographic Yearbook* and *Statistical Yearbook.*

BAHAMAS, THE - MEAT PRODUCTION

See BAHAMAS, THE - LIVESTOCK

BAHAMAS, THE - MILK PRODUCTION

See BAHAMAS, THE - DAIRY PROCESSING

BAHAMAS, THE - MINERAL INDUSTRIES

Inter-American Development Bank (IDB), 1300 New York Avenue, NW, Washington, DC 20577, (202) 623-1000, Fax: (202) 623-3096, www.iadb.org; *The Politics of Policies: Economic and Social Progress in Latin America - 2006 Report.*

M.E. Sharpe, 80 Business Park Drive, Armonk, NY 10504, (800) 541-6563, Fax: (914) 273-2106, www.mesharpe.com; *The Illustrated Book of World Rankings.*

Palgrave Macmillan Ltd., Houndmills, Basingstoke, Hampshire, RG21 6XS, England, (Telephone in U.S. (888) 330-8477), (Fax in U.S. (800) 672-2054), www.palgrave.com; *The Statesman's Yearbook 2008.*

Taylor and Francis Group, An Informa Business, 2 Park Square, Milton Park, Abingdon, Oxford OX14 4RN, United Kingdom, (Dial from U.S. (212) 216-7800), (Fax from U.S. (212) 564-7854), www.tandf.co.uk; *The Europa World Year Book.*

United Nations Conference on Trade and Development (UNCTAD), DC2-1120, United Nations, New York, NY 10017, (212) 963-0027, www.unctad.org; *UNCTAD Commodity Yearbook.*

United Nations Statistics Division, New York, NY 10017, (800) 253-9646, Fax: (212) 963-4116, http://unstats.un.org; *Statistical Yearbook.*

BAHAMAS, THE - MONEY EXCHANGE RATES

See BAHAMAS, THE - FOREIGN EXCHANGE RATES

BAHAMAS, THE - MONEY SUPPLY

Economist Intelligence Unit, 111 West 57th Street, New York, NY 10019, (212) 554-0600, Fax: (212) 586-1181, www.eiu.com; *Bahamas Country Report.*

Inter-American Development Bank (IDB), 1300 New York Avenue, NW, Washington, DC 20577, (202) 623-1000, Fax: (202) 623-3096, www.iadb.org; *The Politics of Policies: Economic and Social Progress in Latin America - 2006 Report.*

International Monetary Fund (IMF), 700 Nineteenth Street, NW, Washington, DC 20431, (202) 623-7000, Fax: (202) 623-4661, www.imf.org; *International Financial Statistics Yearbook 2007.*

Taylor and Francis Group, An Informa Business, 2 Park Square, Milton Park, Abingdon, Oxford OX14 4RN, United Kingdom, (Dial from U.S. (212) 216-7800), (Fax from U.S. (212) 564-7854), www.tandf.co.uk; *The Europa World Year Book.*

United Nations Statistics Division, New York, NY 10017, (800) 253-9646, Fax: (212) 963-4116, http://unstats.un.org; *Statistical Yearbook.*

The World Bank, 1818 H Street, NW, Washington, DC 20433, (202) 473-1000, Fax: (202) 477-6391, www.worldbank.org; *Bahamas* and *World Development Indicators (WDI) 2008.*

BAHAMAS, THE - MORTALITY

Central Intelligence Agency, Office of Public Affairs, Washington, DC 20505, (703) 482-0623, Fax: (703) 482-1739, www.cia.gov; *The World Factbook.*

Euromonitor International, Inc., 224 S. Michigan Avenue, Suite 1500, Chicago, IL 60604, (312) 922-1115, Fax: (312) 922-1157, www.euromonitor.com; *International Marketing Data and Statistics 2008* and *The World Economic Factbook 2008.*

Palgrave Macmillan Ltd., Houndmills, Basingstoke, Hampshire, RG21 6XS, England, (Telephone in U.S. (888) 330-8477), (Fax in U.S. (800) 672-2054), www.palgrave.com; *The Statesman's Yearbook 2008.*

Taylor and Francis Group, An Informa Business, 2 Park Square, Milton Park, Abingdon, Oxford OX14 4RN, United Kingdom, (Dial from U.S. (212) 216-7800), (Fax from U.S. (212) 564-7854), www.tandf.co.uk; *The Europa World Year Book.*

United Nations Statistics Division, New York, NY 10017, (800) 253-9646, Fax: (212) 963-4116, http://unstats.un.org; *Demographic Yearbook; Human Development Report 2006; Statistical Yearbook;* and *World Statistics Pocketbook.*

The World Bank, 1818 H Street, NW, Washington, DC 20433, (202) 473-1000, Fax: (202) 477-6391, www.worldbank.org; *The World Bank Atlas 2003-2004* and *World Development Indicators (WDI) 2008.*

World Health Organization (WHO), Avenue Appia 20, 1211 Geneve 27, Switzerland, (Telephone in U.S. (212) 331-9081), www.who.int; The WHO Global Atlas of Infectious Diseases and *World Health Report 2006.*

BAHAMAS, THE - MOTION PICTURES

Palgrave Macmillan Ltd., Houndmills, Basingstoke, Hampshire, RG21 6XS, England, (Telephone in U.S. (888) 330-8477), (Fax in U.S. (800) 672-2054), www.palgrave.com; *The Statesman's Yearbook 2008.*

BAHAMAS, THE - MOTOR VEHICLES

Taylor and Francis Group, An Informa Business, 2 Park Square, Milton Park, Abingdon, Oxford OX14 4RN, United Kingdom, (Dial from U.S. (212) 216-7800), (Fax from U.S. (212) 564-7854), www.tandf.co.uk; *The Europa World Year Book.*

United Nations Statistics Division, New York, NY 10017, (800) 253-9646, Fax: (212) 963-4116, http://unstats.un.org; *Statistical Yearbook.*

BAHAMAS, THE - MUSEUMS

M.E. Sharpe, 80 Business Park Drive, Armonk, NY 10504, (800) 541-6563, Fax: (914) 273-2106, www.mesharpe.com; *The Illustrated Book of World Rankings.*

UNESCO Institute for Statistics, C.P. 6128 Succursale Centre-Ville, Montreal, Quebec, H3C 3J7 Canada, (Dial from U.S. (514) 343-6880), (Fax from U.S. (514) 343 6882), www.uis.unesco.org; *Statistical Tables.*

BAHAMAS, THE - NATURAL GAS PRODUCTION

See BAHAMAS, THE - MINERAL INDUSTRIES

BAHAMAS, THE - NUTRITION

United Nations Food and Agricultural Organization (FAO), Viale delle Terme di Caracalla, 00100 Rome, Italy, (Dial from U.S. (202) 653-2400), (Fax from U.S. (202) 653 5760), www.fao.org; *The State of Food and Agriculture (SOFA) 2006.*

BAHAMAS, THE - OLDER PEOPLE

M.E. Sharpe, 80 Business Park Drive, Armonk, NY 10504, (800) 541-6563, Fax: (914) 273-2106, www.mesharpe.com; *The Illustrated Book of World Rankings.*

BAHAMAS, THE - PAPER

See BAHAMAS, THE - FORESTS AND FORESTRY

BAHAMAS, THE - PEANUT PRODUCTION

See BAHAMAS, THE - CROPS

BAHAMAS, THE - PESTICIDES

United Nations Food and Agricultural Organization (FAO), Viale delle Terme di Caracalla, 00100 Rome, Italy, (Dial from U.S. (202) 653-2400), (Fax from U.S. (202) 653 5760), www.fao.org; *The State of Food and Agriculture (SOFA) 2006.*

BAHAMAS, THE - PETROLEUM INDUSTRY AND TRADE

Inter-American Development Bank (IDB), 1300 New York Avenue, NW, Washington, DC 20577, (202) 623-1000, Fax: (202) 623-3096, www.iadb.org; *The Politics of Policies: Economic and Social Progress in Latin America - 2006 Report.*

M.E. Sharpe, 80 Business Park Drive, Armonk, NY 10504, (800) 541-6563, Fax: (914) 273-2106, www.mesharpe.com; *The Illustrated Book of World Rankings.*

PennWell Corporation, 1421 South Sheridan Road, Tulsa, OK 74112, (918) 835-3161, www.pennwell.com; *International Petroleum Encyclopedia 2007.*

United Nations Conference on Trade and Development (UNCTAD), DC2-1120, United Nations, New York, NY 10017, (212) 963-0027, www.unctad.org; *UNCTAD Commodity Yearbook.*

United Nations Food and Agricultural Organization (FAO), Viale delle Terme di Caracalla, 00100 Rome, Italy, (Dial from U.S. (202) 653-2400), (Fax from U.S. (202) 653 5760), www.fao.org; *The State of Food and Agriculture (SOFA) 2006.*

United Nations Statistics Division, New York, NY 10017, (800) 253-9646, Fax: (212) 963-4116, http://unstats.un.org; *Statistical Yearbook.*

BAHAMAS, THE - POLITICAL SCIENCE

Central Intelligence Agency, Office of Public Affairs, Washington, DC 20505, (703) 482-0623, Fax: (703) 482-1739, www.cia.gov; *The World Factbook.*

Inter-American Development Bank (IDB), 1300 New York Avenue, NW, Washington, DC 20577, (202) 623-1000, Fax: (202) 623-3096, www.iadb.org; *The Politics of Policies: Economic and Social Progress in Latin America - 2006 Report.*

International Monetary Fund (IMF), 700 Nineteenth Street, NW, Washington, DC 20431, (202) 623-7000, Fax: (202) 623-4661, www.imf.org; *Government Finance Statistics Yearbook (2008 Edition).*

Palgrave Macmillan Ltd., Houndmills, Basingstoke, Hampshire, RG21 6XS, England, (Telephone in U.S. (888) 330-8477), (Fax in U.S. (800) 672-2054), www.palgrave.com; *The Statesman's Yearbook 2008.*

Taylor and Francis Group, An Informa Business, 2 Park Square, Milton Park, Abingdon, Oxford OX14 4RN, United Kingdom, (Dial from U.S. (212) 216-7800), (Fax from U.S. (212) 564-7854), www.tandf.co.uk; *The Europa World Year Book.*

United Nations Statistics Division, New York, NY 10017, (800) 253-9646, Fax: (212) 963-4116, http://unstats.un.org; *National Accounts Statistics: Compendium of Income Distribution Statistics.*

The World Bank, 1818 H Street, NW, Washington, DC 20433, (202) 473-1000, Fax: (202) 477-6391, www.worldbank.org; *World Development Indicators (WDI) 2008.*

BAHAMAS, THE - POPULATION

Caribbean Epidemiology Centre (CAREC), 16-18 Jamaica Boulevard, Federation Park, PO Box 164, Port of Spain, Republic of Trinidad and Tobago, (Dial from U.S. (868) 622-4261), (Fax from U.S. (868) 622-2792), www.carec.org; *Population Data.*

Central Intelligence Agency, Office of Public Affairs, Washington, DC 20505, (703) 482-0623, Fax: (703) 482-1739, www.cia.gov; *The World Factbook.*

Department of Statistics, Ministry of Finance, Clarence Bain Building, Thompson Boulevard, N-3904, Nassau, Bahamas, (Dial from U.S. (242) 502-1000), (Fax from U.S. (242) 325-5149), www.bahamas.gov.bs/finance; *Vital Statistics Report.*

Economist Intelligence Unit, 111 West 57th Street, New York, NY 10019, (212) 554-0600, Fax: (212) 586-1181, www.eiu.com; *Bahamas Country Report.*

Euromonitor International, Inc., 224 S. Michigan Avenue, Suite 1500, Chicago, IL 60604, (312) 922-1115, Fax: (312) 922-1157, www.euromonitor.com; *International Marketing Data and Statistics 2008* and *The World Economic Factbook 2008.*

Eurostat, Batiment Jean Monnet, Rue Alcide de Gasperi, L-2920 Luxembourg, http://epp.eurostat.ec.europa.eu; *Demographic Indicators - Population by Age-Classes.*

Inter-American Development Bank (IDB), 1300 New York Avenue, NW, Washington, DC 20577, (202) 623-1000, Fax: (202) 623-3096, www.iadb.org; *The Politics of Policies: Economic and Social Progress in Latin America - 2006 Report.*

International Labour Office, I.L.O. Publications, 4 route des Morillons, CH-1211 Geneva 22, Switzerland, (Telephone in U.S. (202) 653-7652), (Fax in U.S. (202) 653-7687), www.ilo.org; *Yearbook of Labour Statistics 2006.*

M.E. Sharpe, 80 Business Park Drive, Armonk, NY 10504, (800) 541-6563, Fax: (914) 273-2106, www.mesharpe.com; *The Illustrated Book of World Rankings.*

Palgrave Macmillan Ltd., Houndmills, Basingstoke, Hampshire, RG21 6XS, England, (Telephone in U.S. (888) 330-8477), (Fax in U.S. (800) 672-2054), www.palgrave.com; *The Statesman's Yearbook 2008.*

Taylor and Francis Group, An Informa Business, 2 Park Square, Milton Park, Abingdon, Oxford OX14 4RN, United Kingdom, (Dial from U.S. (212) 216-7800), (Fax from U.S. (212) 564-7854), www.tandf.co.uk; *The Europa World Year Book.*

UNESCO Institute for Statistics, C.P. 6128 Succursale Centre-Ville, Montreal, Quebec, H3C 3J7 Canada, (Dial from U.S. (514) 343-6880), (Fax from U.S. (514) 343 6882), www.uis.unesco.org; *Statistical Tables.*

United Nations Food and Agricultural Organization (FAO), Viale delle Terme di Caracalla, 00100 Rome, Italy, (Dial from U.S. (202) 653-2400), (Fax from U.S. (202) 653 5760), www.fao.org; *FAO Production Yearbook 2002.*

United Nations Statistics Division, New York, NY 10017, (800) 253-9646, Fax: (212) 963-4116, http://unstats.un.org; *Demographic Yearbook; Human Development Report 2006; Statistical Yearbook;* and *World Statistics Pocketbook.*

The World Bank, 1818 H Street, NW, Washington, DC 20433, (202) 473-1000, Fax: (202) 477-6391, www.worldbank.org; *Bahamas* and *The World Bank Atlas 2003-2004.*

World Health Organization (WHO), Avenue Appia 20, 1211 Geneve 27, Switzerland, (Telephone in U.S. (212) 331-9081), www.who.int; *World Health Report 2006.*

BAHAMAS, THE - POPULATION DENSITY

Central Intelligence Agency, Office of Public Affairs, Washington, DC 20505, (703) 482-0623, Fax: (703) 482-1739, www.cia.gov; *The World Factbook.*

Euromonitor International, Inc., 224 S. Michigan Avenue, Suite 1500, Chicago, IL 60604, (312) 922-1115, Fax: (312) 922-1157, www.euromonitor.com; *The World Economic Factbook 2008.*

Inter-American Development Bank (IDB), 1300 New York Avenue, NW, Washington, DC 20577, (202) 623-1000, Fax: (202) 623-3096, www.iadb.org; *The Politics of Policies: Economic and Social Progress in Latin America - 2006 Report.*

M.E. Sharpe, 80 Business Park Drive, Armonk, NY 10504, (800) 541-6563, Fax: (914) 273-2106, www.mesharpe.com; *The Illustrated Book of World Rankings.*

Palgrave Macmillan Ltd., Houndmills, Basingstoke, Hampshire, RG21 6XS, England, (Telephone in U.S. (888) 330-8477), (Fax in U.S. (800) 672-2054), www.palgrave.com; *The Statesman's Yearbook 2008.*

Taylor and Francis Group, An Informa Business, 2 Park Square, Milton Park, Abingdon, Oxford OX14 4RN, United Kingdom, (Dial from U.S. (212) 216-7800), (Fax from U.S. (212) 564-7854), www.tandf.co.uk; *The Europa World Year Book.*

United Nations Food and Agricultural Organization (FAO), Viale delle Terme di Caracalla, 00100 Rome, Italy, (Dial from U.S. (202) 653-2400), (Fax from U.S. (202) 653 5760), www.fao.org; *The State of Food and Agriculture (SOFA) 2006.*

United Nations Statistics Division, New York, NY 10017, (800) 253-9646, Fax: (212) 963-4116, http://unstats.un.org; *Statistical Yearbook.*

The World Bank, 1818 H Street, NW, Washington, DC 20433, (202) 473-1000, Fax: (202) 477-6391, www.worldbank.org; *Bahamas.*

BAHAMAS, THE - POSTAL SERVICE

M.E. Sharpe, 80 Business Park Drive, Armonk, NY 10504, (800) 541-6563, Fax: (914) 273-2106, www.mesharpe.com; *The Illustrated Book of World Rankings.*

Palgrave Macmillan Ltd., Houndmills, Basingstoke, Hampshire, RG21 6XS, England, (Telephone in U.S. (888) 330-8477), (Fax in U.S. (800) 672-2054), www.palgrave.com; *The Statesman's Yearbook 2008.*

United Nations Statistics Division, New York, NY 10017, (800) 253-9646, Fax: (212) 963-4116, http://unstats.un.org; *Statistical Yearbook.*

BAHAMAS, THE - POWER RESOURCES

Euromonitor International, Inc., 224 S. Michigan Avenue, Suite 1500, Chicago, IL 60604, (312) 922-1115, Fax: (312) 922-1157, www.euromonitor.com; *International Marketing Data and Statistics 2008; The World Economic Factbook 2008;* and *World Marketing Data and Statistics.*

M.E. Sharpe, 80 Business Park Drive, Armonk, NY 10504, (800) 541-6563, Fax: (914) 273-2106, www.mesharpe.com; *The Illustrated Book of World Rankings.*

Palgrave Macmillan Ltd., Houndmills, Basingstoke, Hampshire, RG21 6XS, England, (Telephone in U.S. (888) 330-8477), (Fax in U.S. (800) 672-2054), www.palgrave.com; *The Statesman's Yearbook 2008.*

Platts, 2 Penn Plaza, 25th Floor, New York, NY 10121-2298, (212) 904-3070, www.platts.com; *Energy Economist.*

United Nations Food and Agricultural Organization (FAO), Viale delle Terme di Caracalla, 00100 Rome, Italy, (Dial from U.S. (202) 653-2400), (Fax from U.S. (202) 653 5760), www.fao.org; *The State of Food and Agriculture (SOFA) 2006.*

United Nations Statistics Division, New York, NY 10017, (800) 253-9646, Fax: (212) 963-4116, http://unstats.un.org; *Energy Statistics Yearbook 2003; Human Development Report 2006; Statistical Yearbook;* and *World Statistics Pocketbook.*

The World Bank, 1818 H Street, NW, Washington, DC 20433, (202) 473-1000, Fax: (202) 477-6391, www.worldbank.org; *The World Bank Atlas 2003-2004.*

BAHAMAS, THE - PRICES

Euromonitor International, Inc., 224 S. Michigan Avenue, Suite 1500, Chicago, IL 60604, (312) 922-1115, Fax: (312) 922-1157, www.euromonitor.com; *World Marketing Data and Statistics.*

International Labour Office, I.L.O. Publications, 4 route des Morillons, CH-1211 Geneva 22, Switzerland, (Telephone in U.S. (202) 653-7652), (Fax in U.S. (202) 653-7687), www.ilo.org; *Yearbook of Labour Statistics 2006.*

International Monetary Fund (IMF), 700 Nineteenth Street, NW, Washington, DC 20431, (202) 623-7000, Fax: (202) 623-4661, www.imf.org; *International Financial Statistics Yearbook 2007.*

M.E. Sharpe, 80 Business Park Drive, Armonk, NY 10504, (800) 541-6563, Fax: (914) 273-2106, www.mesharpe.com; *The Illustrated Book of World Rankings.*

United Nations Food and Agricultural Organization (FAO), Viale delle Terme di Caracalla, 00100 Rome, Italy, (Dial from U.S. (202) 653-2400), (Fax from U.S. (202) 653 5760), www.fao.org; *FAO Production Yearbook 2002* and *The State of Food and Agriculture (SOFA) 2006.*

United Nations Statistics Division, New York, NY 10017, (800) 253-9646, Fax: (212) 963-4116, http://unstats.un.org; *Economic Survey of Latin America and the Caribbean 2004-2005.*

The World Bank, 1818 H Street, NW, Washington, DC 20433, (202) 473-1000, Fax: (202) 477-6391, www.worldbank.org; *Bahamas.*

BAHAMAS, THE - PROFESSIONS

UNESCO Institute for Statistics, C.P. 6128 Succursale Centre-Ville, Montreal, Quebec, H3C 3J7 Canada, (Dial from U.S. (514) 343-6880), (Fax from U.S. (514) 343 6882), www.uis.unesco.org; *Statistical Tables.*

United Nations Statistics Division, New York, NY 10017, (800) 253-9646, Fax: (212) 963-4116, http://unstats.un.org; *Statistical Yearbook.*

BAHAMAS, THE - PUBLIC HEALTH

Euromonitor International, Inc., 224 S. Michigan Avenue, Suite 1500, Chicago, IL 60604, (312) 922-1115, Fax: (312) 922-1157, www.euromonitor.com; *World Marketing Data and Statistics.*

International Monetary Fund (IMF), 700 Nineteenth Street, NW, Washington, DC 20431, (202) 623-7000, Fax: (202) 623-4661, www.imf.org; *Government Finance Statistics Yearbook (2008 Edition).*

M.E. Sharpe, 80 Business Park Drive, Armonk, NY 10504, (800) 541-6563, Fax: (914) 273-2106, www.mesharpe.com; *The Illustrated Book of World Rankings.*

Palgrave Macmillan Ltd., Houndmills, Basingstoke, Hampshire, RG21 6XS, England, (Telephone in U.S. (888) 330-8477), (Fax in U.S. (800) 672-2054), www.palgrave.com; *The Statesman's Yearbook 2008.*

United Nations Statistics Division, New York, NY 10017, (800) 253-9646, Fax: (212) 963-4116, http://unstats.un.org; *Human Development Report 2006* and *Statistical Yearbook.*

The World Bank, 1818 H Street, NW, Washington, DC 20433, (202) 473-1000, Fax: (202) 477-6391, www.worldbank.org; *Bahamas.*

World Health Organization (WHO), Avenue Appia 20, 1211 Geneve 27, Switzerland, (Telephone in U.S. (212) 331-9081), www.who.int; The WHO Global Atlas of Infectious Diseases and *World Health Report 2006.*

BAHAMAS, THE - RADIO BROADCASTING

Palgrave Macmillan Ltd., Houndmills, Basingstoke, Hampshire, RG21 6XS, England, (Telephone in U.S. (888) 330-8477), (Fax in U.S. (800) 672-2054), www.palgrave.com; *The Statesman's Yearbook 2008.*

BAHAMAS, THE - RELIGION

Central Intelligence Agency, Office of Public Affairs, Washington, DC 20505, (703) 482-0623, Fax: (703) 482-1739, www.cia.gov; *The World Factbook.*

M.E. Sharpe, 80 Business Park Drive, Armonk, NY 10504, (800) 541-6563, Fax: (914) 273-2106, www.mesharpe.com; *The Illustrated Book of World Rankings.*

Palgrave Macmillan Ltd., Houndmills, Basingstoke, Hampshire, RG21 6XS, England, (Telephone in U.S. (888) 330-8477), (Fax in U.S. (800) 672-2054), www.palgrave.com; *The Statesman's Yearbook 2008.*

BAHAMAS, THE - RENT CHARGES

International Labour Office, I.L.O. Publications, 4 route des Morillons, CH-1211 Geneva 22, Switzerland, (Telephone in U.S. (202) 653-7652), (Fax in U.S. (202) 653-7687), www.ilo.org; *Yearbook of Labour Statistics 2006.*

BAHAMAS, THE - RESERVES (ACCOUNTING)

Inter-American Development Bank (IDB), 1300 New York Avenue, NW, Washington, DC 20577, (202) 623-1000, Fax: (202) 623-3096, www.iadb.org; *The Politics of Policies: Economic and Social Progress in Latin America - 2006 Report.*

The World Bank, 1818 H Street, NW, Washington, DC 20433, (202) 473-1000, Fax: (202) 477-6391, www.worldbank.org; *World Development Indicators (WDI) 2008.*

BAHAMAS, THE - RETAIL TRADE

Euromonitor International, Inc., 224 S. Michigan Avenue, Suite 1500, Chicago, IL 60604, (312) 922-1115, Fax: (312) 922-1157, www.euromonitor.com; *World Marketing Data and Statistics.*

Inter-American Development Bank (IDB), 1300 New York Avenue, NW, Washington, DC 20577, (202) 623-1000, Fax: (202) 623-3096, www.iadb.org; *The Politics of Policies: Economic and Social Progress in Latin America - 2006 Report.*

BAHAMAS, THE - RICE PRODUCTION

See BAHAMAS, THE - CROPS

BAHAMAS, THE - ROADS

Central Intelligence Agency, Office of Public Affairs, Washington, DC 20505, (703) 482-0623, Fax: (703) 482-1739, www.cia.gov; *The World Factbook.*

Palgrave Macmillan Ltd., Houndmills, Basingstoke, Hampshire, RG21 6XS, England, (Telephone in U.S. (888) 330-8477), (Fax in U.S. (800) 672-2054), www.palgrave.com; *The Statesman's Yearbook 2008.*

BAHAMAS, THE - RUBBER INDUSTRY AND TRADE

International Rubber Study Group (IRSG), 1st Floor, Heron House, 109/115 Wembley Hill Road, Wembley, Middlesex HA9 8DA, United Kingdom, www.rubberstudy.com; *Rubber Statistical Bulletin; Summary of World Rubber Statistics 2005; World Rubber Statistics Handbook (Volume 6, 1975-2001);* and *World Rubber Statistics Historic Handbook.*

M.E. Sharpe, 80 Business Park Drive, Armonk, NY 10504, (800) 541-6563, Fax: (914) 273-2106, www.mesharpe.com; *The Illustrated Book of World Rankings.*

BAHAMAS, THE - SALT PRODUCTION

See BAHAMAS, THE - MINERAL INDUSTRIES

BAHAMAS, THE - SHEEP

See BAHAMAS, THE - LIVESTOCK

BAHAMAS, THE - SHIPPING

Lloyd's Register - Fairplay, 8410 N.W. 53rd Terrace, Suite 207, Miami FL 33166, (305) 718-9929, Fax: (305) 718-9663, www.lrfairplay.com; *Register of Ships 2007-2008; World Casualty Statistics 2007; World Fleet Statistics 2006; World Marine Propulsion Report 2006-2010; World Shipbuilding Statistics 2007;* and The World Shipping Encyclopaedia.

Palgrave Macmillan Ltd., Houndmills, Basingstoke, Hampshire, RG21 6XS, England, (Telephone in U.S. (888) 330-8477), (Fax in U.S. (800) 672-2054), www.palgrave.com; *The Statesman's Yearbook 2008.*

Taylor and Francis Group, An Informa Business, 2 Park Square, Milton Park, Abingdon, Oxford OX14 4RN, United Kingdom, (Dial from U.S. (212) 216-7800), (Fax from U.S. (212) 564-7854), www.tandf.co.uk; *The Europa World Year Book.*

United Nations Statistics Division, New York, NY 10017, (800) 253-9646, Fax: (212) 963-4116, http://unstats.un.org; *Statistical Yearbook.*

BAHAMAS, THE - SILVER PRODUCTION

See BAHAMAS, THE - MINERAL INDUSTRIES

BAHAMAS, THE - SOCIAL ECOLOGY

M.E. Sharpe, 80 Business Park Drive, Armonk, NY 10504, (800) 541-6563, Fax: (914) 273-2106, www.mesharpe.com; *The Illustrated Book of World Rankings.*

United Nations Statistics Division, New York, NY 10017, (800) 253-9646, Fax: (212) 963-4116, http://unstats.un.org; *World Statistics Pocketbook.*

BAHAMAS, THE - SOCIAL SECURITY

Inter-American Development Bank (IDB), 1300 New York Avenue, NW, Washington, DC 20577, (202) 623-1000, Fax: (202) 623-3096, www.iadb.org; *The Politics of Policies: Economic and Social Progress in Latin America - 2006 Report.*

International Monetary Fund (IMF), 700 Nineteenth Street, NW, Washington, DC 20431, (202) 623-7000, Fax: (202) 623-4661, www.imf.org; *Government Finance Statistics Yearbook (2008 Edition).*

United Nations Statistics Division, New York, NY 10017, (800) 253-9646, Fax: (212) 963-4116, http://unstats.un.org; *National Accounts Statistics: Compendium of Income Distribution Statistics.*

BAHAMAS, THE - STEEL PRODUCTION

See BAHAMAS, THE - MINERAL INDUSTRIES

BAHAMAS, THE - SUGAR PRODUCTION

See BAHAMAS, THE - CROPS

BAHAMAS, THE - TAXATION

Inter-American Development Bank (IDB), 1300 New York Avenue, NW, Washington, DC 20577, (202) 623-1000, Fax: (202) 623-3096, www.iadb.org; *The Politics of Policies: Economic and Social Progress in Latin America - 2006 Report.*

International Monetary Fund (IMF), 700 Nineteenth Street, NW, Washington, DC 20431, (202) 623-7000, Fax: (202) 623-4661, www.imf.org; *Government Finance Statistics Yearbook (2008 Edition).*

Taylor and Francis Group, An Informa Business, 2 Park Square, Milton Park, Abingdon, Oxford OX14 4RN, United Kingdom, (Dial from U.S. (212) 216-7800), (Fax from U.S. (212) 564-7854), www.tandf.co.uk; *The Europa World Year Book.*

The World Bank, 1818 H Street, NW, Washington, DC 20433, (202) 473-1000, Fax: (202) 477-6391, www.worldbank.org; *World Development Indicators (WDI) 2008.*

BAHAMAS, THE - TELEPHONE

International Telecommunication Union (ITU), Place des Nations, 1211 Geneva 20, Switzerland, www.itu.int; World Telecommunication Indicators Database.

Palgrave Macmillan Ltd., Houndmills, Basingstoke, Hampshire, RG21 6XS, England, (Telephone in U.S. (888) 330-8477), (Fax in U.S. (800) 672-2054), www.palgrave.com; *The Statesman's Yearbook 2008.*

Taylor and Francis Group, An Informa Business, 2 Park Square, Milton Park, Abingdon, Oxford OX14 4RN, United Kingdom, (Dial from U.S. (212) 216-7800), (Fax from U.S. (212) 564-7854), www.tandf.co.uk; *The Europa World Year Book.*

United Nations Statistics Division, New York, NY 10017, (800) 253-9646, Fax: (212) 963-4116, http://unstats.un.org; *Statistical Yearbook* and *World Statistics Pocketbook.*

BAHAMAS, THE - TEXTILE INDUSTRY

M.E. Sharpe, 80 Business Park Drive, Armonk, NY 10504, (800) 541-6563, Fax: (914) 273-2106, www.mesharpe.com; *The Illustrated Book of World Rankings.*

Palgrave Macmillan Ltd., Houndmills, Basingstoke, Hampshire, RG21 6XS, England, (Telephone in U.S. (888) 330-8477), (Fax in U.S. (800) 672-2054), www.palgrave.com; *The Statesman's Yearbook 2008.*

United Nations Conference on Trade and Development (UNCTAD), DC2-1120, United Nations, New York, NY 10017, (212) 963-0027, www.unctad.org; *UNCTAD Commodity Yearbook.*

BAHAMAS, THE - TOBACCO INDUSTRY

Foreign Agricultural Service (FAS), U.S. Department of Agriculture (USDA), 1400 Independence Avenue, SW, Washington, DC 20250, (202) 720-3935, www.fas.usda.gov; *Tobacco: World Markets and Trade.*

M.E. Sharpe, 80 Business Park Drive, Armonk, NY 10504, (800) 541-6563, Fax: (914) 273-2106, www.mesharpe.com; *The Illustrated Book of World Rankings.*

BAHAMAS, THE - TOURISM

Euromonitor International, Inc., 224 S. Michigan Avenue, Suite 1500, Chicago, IL 60604, (312) 922-1115, Fax: (312) 922-1157, www.euromonitor.com; *The World Economic Factbook 2008* and *World Marketing Data and Statistics.*

M.E. Sharpe, 80 Business Park Drive, Armonk, NY 10504, (800) 541-6563, Fax: (914) 273-2106, www.mesharpe.com; *The Illustrated Book of World Rankings.*

Palgrave Macmillan Ltd., Houndmills, Basingstoke, Hampshire, RG21 6XS, England, (Telephone in U.S. (888) 330-8477), (Fax in U.S. (800) 672-2054), www.palgrave.com; *The Statesman's Yearbook 2008.*

Taylor and Francis Group, An Informa Business, 2 Park Square, Milton Park, Abingdon, Oxford OX14 4RN, United Kingdom, (Dial from U.S. (212) 216-7800), (Fax from U.S. (212) 564-7854), www.tandf.co.uk; *The Europa World Year Book.*

United Nations Statistics Division, New York, NY 10017, (800) 253-9646, Fax: (212) 963-4116, http://unstats.un.org; *Statistical Yearbook.*

United Nations World Tourism Organization (UNWTO), Capitan Haya 42, 28020 Madrid, Spain, www.world-tourism.org; *Yearbook of Tourism Statistics.*

The World Bank, 1818 H Street, NW, Washington, DC 20433, (202) 473-1000, Fax: (202) 477-6391, www.worldbank.org; *Bahamas.*

BAHAMAS, THE - TRADE

See BAHAMAS, THE - INTERNATIONAL TRADE

BAHAMAS, THE - TRANSPORTATION

Central Intelligence Agency, Office of Public Affairs, Washington, DC 20505, (703) 482-0623, Fax: (703) 482-1739, www.cia.gov; *The World Factbook.*

Euromonitor International, Inc., 224 S. Michigan Avenue, Suite 1500, Chicago, IL 60604, (312) 922-1115, Fax: (312) 922-1157, www.euromonitor.com; *International Marketing Data and Statistics 2008* and *World Marketing Data and Statistics.*

Inter-American Development Bank (IDB), 1300 New York Avenue, NW, Washington, DC 20577, (202) 623-1000, Fax: (202) 623-3096, www.iadb.org; *The Politics of Policies: Economic and Social Progress in Latin America - 2006 Report.*

M.E. Sharpe, 80 Business Park Drive, Armonk, NY 10504, (800) 541-6563, Fax: (914) 273-2106, www.mesharpe.com; *The Illustrated Book of World Rankings.*

Palgrave Macmillan Ltd., Houndmills, Basingstoke, Hampshire, RG21 6XS, England, (Telephone in U.S. (888) 330-8477), (Fax in U.S. (800) 672-2054), www.palgrave.com; *The Statesman's Yearbook 2008.*

Taylor and Francis Group, An Informa Business, 2 Park Square, Milton Park, Abingdon, Oxford OX14 4RN, United Kingdom, (Dial from U.S. (212) 216-7800), (Fax from U.S. (212) 564-7854), www.tandf.co.uk; *The Europa World Year Book.*

United Nations Statistics Division, New York, NY 10017, (800) 253-9646, Fax: (212) 963-4116, http://unstats.un.org; *Human Development Report 2006.*

The World Bank, 1818 H Street, NW, Washington, DC 20433, (202) 473-1000, Fax: (202) 477-6391, www.worldbank.org; *Bahamas.*

BAHAMAS, THE - TRAVEL COSTS

International Monetary Fund (IMF), 700 Nineteenth Street, NW, Washington, DC 20431, (202) 623-7000, Fax: (202) 623-4661, www.imf.org; *Government Finance Statistics Yearbook (2008 Edition).*

BAHAMAS, THE - UNEMPLOYMENT

Central Intelligence Agency, Office of Public Affairs, Washington, DC 20505, (703) 482-0623, Fax: (703) 482-1739, www.cia.gov; *The World Factbook.*

International Labour Office, I.L.O. Publications, 4 route des Morillons, CH-1211 Geneva 22, Switzerland, (Telephone in U.S. (202) 653-7652), (Fax in U.S. (202) 653-7687), www.ilo.org; *Yearbook of Labour Statistics 2006.*

BAHAMAS, THE - VITAL STATISTICS

Department of Statistics, Ministry of Finance, Clarence Bain Building, Thompson Boulevard, N-3904, Nassau, Bahamas, (Dial from U.S. (242) 502-1000), (Fax from U.S. (242) 325-5149), www.bahamas.gov.bs/finance; *Vital Statistics Report.*

Palgrave Macmillan Ltd., Houndmills, Basingstoke, Hampshire, RG21 6XS, England, (Telephone in U.S. (888) 330-8477), (Fax in U.S. (800) 672-2054), www.palgrave.com; *The Statesman's Yearbook 2008.*

United Nations Statistics Division, New York, NY 10017, (800) 253-9646, Fax: (212) 963-4116, http://unstats.un.org; *Statistical Yearbook.*

World Health Organization (WHO), Avenue Appia 20, 1211 Geneve 27, Switzerland, (Telephone in U.S. (212) 331-9081), www.who.int; *World Health Report 2006.*

BAHAMAS, THE - WAGES

Department of Statistics, Ministry of Finance, Clarence Bain Building, Thompson Boulevard, N-3904, Nassau, Bahamas, (Dial from U.S. (242) 502-1000), (Fax from U.S. (242) 325-5149), www.bahamas.gov.bs/finance; *Labour Force and Household Income.*

International Labour Office, I.L.O. Publications, 4 route des Morillons, CH-1211 Geneva 22, Switzerland, (Telephone in U.S. (202) 653-7652), (Fax in U.S. (202) 653-7687), www.ilo.org; *Yearbook of Labour Statistics 2006.*

The World Bank, 1818 H Street, NW, Washington, DC 20433, (202) 473-1000, Fax: (202) 477-6391, www.worldbank.org; *Bahamas.*

BAHAMAS, THE - WEATHER

See BAHAMAS, THE - CLIMATE

BAHAMAS, THE - WELFARE STATE

Inter-American Development Bank (IDB), 1300 New York Avenue, NW, Washington, DC 20577, (202) 623-1000, Fax: (202) 623-3096, www.iadb.org; *The Politics of Policies: Economic and Social Progress in Latin America - 2006 Report.*

International Monetary Fund (IMF), 700 Nineteenth Street, NW, Washington, DC 20431, (202) 623-7000, Fax: (202) 623-4661, www.imf.org; *Government Finance Statistics Yearbook (2008 Edition).*

BAHAMAS, THE - WHALES

See BAHAMAS, THE - FISHERIES

BAHAMAS, THE - WHEAT PRODUCTION

See BAHAMAS, THE - CROPS

BAHAMAS, THE - WHOLESALE PRICE INDEXES

Inter-American Development Bank (IDB), 1300 New York Avenue, NW, Washington, DC 20577, (202) 623-1000, Fax: (202) 623-3096, www.iadb.org; *The Politics of Policies: Economic and Social Progress in Latin America - 2006 Report.*

BAHAMAS, THE - WHOLESALE TRADE

Inter-American Development Bank (IDB), 1300 New York Avenue, NW, Washington, DC 20577, (202) 623-1000, Fax: (202) 623-3096, www.iadb.org; *The Politics of Policies: Economic and Social Progress in Latin America - 2006 Report.*

BAHAMAS, THE - WINE PRODUCTION

See BAHAMAS, THE - BEVERAGE INDUSTRY

BAHAMAS, THE - WOOL PRODUCTION

See BAHAMAS, THE - TEXTILE INDUSTRY

BAHRAIN - NATIONAL STATISTICAL OFFICE

Central Statistics Organisation, PO Box 5835, Manama, Bahrain; National Data Center.

BAHRAIN - PRIMARY STATISTICS SOURCES

Central Statistics Organisation, PO Box 5835, Manama, Bahrain; *Statistical Abstract.*

BAHRAIN - AGRICULTURE

Economist Intelligence Unit, 111 West 57th Street, New York, NY 10019, (212) 554-0600, Fax: (212) 586-1181, www.eiu.com; *Bahrain Country Report.*

Euromonitor International, Inc., 224 S. Michigan Avenue, Suite 1500, Chicago, IL 60604, (312) 922-1115, Fax: (312) 922-1157, www.euromonitor.com; *International Marketing Data and Statistics 2008* and *World Marketing Data and Statistics.*

M.E. Sharpe, 80 Business Park Drive, Armonk, NY 10504, (800) 541-6563, Fax: (914) 273-2106, www.mesharpe.com; *The Illustrated Book of World Rankings.*

Palgrave Macmillan Ltd., Houndmills, Basingstoke, Hampshire, RG21 6XS, England, (Telephone in U.S. (888) 330-8477), (Fax in U.S. (800) 672-2054), www.palgrave.com; *The Statesman's Yearbook 2008.*

Taylor and Francis Group, An Informa Business, 2 Park Square, Milton Park, Abingdon, Oxford OX14 4RN, United Kingdom, (Dial from U.S. (212) 216-7800), (Fax from U.S. (212) 564-7854), www.tandf.co.uk; *The Europa World Year Book.*

United Nations Conference on Trade and Development (UNCTAD), DC2-1120, United Nations, New York, NY 10017, (212) 963-0027, www.unctad.org; *UNCTAD Commodity Yearbook.*

United Nations Economic and Social Commission for Western Asia (ESCWA), PO Box 11-8575, Riad el-Solh Square, Beirut, Lebanon, www.escwa.un.org; *Annual Report 2006* and *Statistical Abstract of the ESCWA Region 2007.*

United Nations Food and Agricultural Organization (FAO), Viale delle Terme di Caracalla, 00100 Rome, Italy, (Dial from U.S. (202) 653-2400), (Fax from

U.S. (202) 653 5760), www.fao.org; AQUASTAT; *FAO Production Yearbook 2002; FAO Trade Yearbook;* and *The State of Food and Agriculture (SOFA) 2006.*

The World Bank, 1818 H Street, NW, Washington, DC 20433, (202) 473-1000, Fax: (202) 477-6391, www.worldbank.org; *Bahrain* and *World Development Indicators (WDI) 2008.*

BAHRAIN - AIRLINES

M.E. Sharpe, 80 Business Park Drive, Armonk, NY 10504, (800) 541-6563, Fax: (914) 273-2106, www.mesharpe.com; *The Illustrated Book of World Rankings.*

Palgrave Macmillan Ltd., Houndmills, Basingstoke, Hampshire, RG21 6XS, England, (Telephone in U.S. (888) 330-8477), (Fax in U.S. (800) 672-2054), www.palgrave.com; *The Statesman's Yearbook 2008.*

Taylor and Francis Group, An Informa Business, 2 Park Square, Milton Park, Abingdon, Oxford OX14 4RN, United Kingdom, (Dial from U.S. (212) 216-7800), (Fax from U.S. (212) 564-7854), www.tandf.co.uk; *The Europa World Year Book.*

BAHRAIN - AIRPORTS

Central Intelligence Agency, Office of Public Affairs, Washington, DC 20505, (703) 482-0623, Fax: (703) 482-1739, www.cia.gov; *The World Factbook.*

BAHRAIN - ALUMINUM PRODUCTION

See BAHRAIN - MINERAL INDUSTRIES

BAHRAIN - ARMED FORCES

Central Intelligence Agency, Office of Public Affairs, Washington, DC 20505, (703) 482-0623, Fax: (703) 482-1739, www.cia.gov; *The World Factbook.*

Euromonitor International, Inc., 224 S. Michigan Avenue, Suite 1500, Chicago, IL 60604, (312) 922-1115, Fax: (312) 922-1157, www.euromonitor.com; *World Marketing Data and Statistics.*

International Institute for Strategic Studies (IISS), Arundel House, 13-15 Arundel Street, Temple Place, London WC2R 3DX, England, www.iiss.org; *The Military Balance 2007.*

International Monetary Fund (IMF), 700 Nineteenth Street, NW, Washington, DC 20431, (202) 623-7000, Fax: (202) 623-4661, www.imf.org; *Government Finance Statistics Yearbook (2008 Edition).*

Palgrave Macmillan Ltd., Houndmills, Basingstoke, Hampshire, RG21 6XS, England, (Telephone in U.S. (888) 330-8477), (Fax in U.S. (800) 672-2054), www.palgrave.com; *The Statesman's Yearbook 2008.*

U.S. Department of State (DOS), 2201 C Street NW, Washington, DC 20520, (202) 647-4000, www.state.gov; *World Military Expenditures and Arms Transfers (WMEAT).*

United Nations Statistics Division, New York, NY 10017, (800) 253-9646, Fax: (212) 963-4116, http://unstats.un.org; *Human Development Report 2006.*

BAHRAIN - BALANCE OF PAYMENTS

International Monetary Fund (IMF), 700 Nineteenth Street, NW, Washington, DC 20431, (202) 623-7000, Fax: (202) 623-4661, www.imf.org; *Balance of Payments Statistics Newsletter* and *Balance of Payments Statistics Yearbook 2007.*

Taylor and Francis Group, An Informa Business, 2 Park Square, Milton Park, Abingdon, Oxford OX14 4RN, United Kingdom, (Dial from U.S. (212) 216-7800), (Fax from U.S. (212) 564-7854), www.tandf.co.uk; *The Europa World Year Book.*

United Nations Conference on Trade and Development (UNCTAD), DC2-1120, United Nations, New York, NY 10017, (212) 963-0027, www.unctad.org; *Handbook of Statistics 2005.*

The World Bank, 1818 H Street, NW, Washington, DC 20433, (202) 473-1000, Fax: (202) 477-6391, www.worldbank.org; *Bahrain* and *World Development Indicators (WDI) 2008.*

BAHRAIN - BANKS AND BANKING

Euromonitor International, Inc., 224 S. Michigan Avenue, Suite 1500, Chicago, IL 60604, (312) 922-1115, Fax: (312) 922-1157, www.euromonitor.com; *World Marketing Data and Statistics.*

International Monetary Fund (IMF), 700 Nineteenth Street, NW, Washington, DC 20431, (202) 623-7000, Fax: (202) 623-4661, www.imf.org; *Government Finance Statistics Yearbook (2008 Edition)* and *International Financial Statistics Yearbook 2007.*

M.E. Sharpe, 80 Business Park Drive, Armonk, NY 10504, (800) 541-6563, Fax: (914) 273-2106, www.mesharpe.com; *The Illustrated Book of World Rankings.*

Palgrave Macmillan Ltd., Houndmills, Basingstoke, Hampshire, RG21 6XS, England, (Telephone in U.S. (888) 330-8477), (Fax in U.S. (800) 672-2054), www.palgrave.com; *The Statesman's Yearbook 2008.*

Taylor and Francis Group, An Informa Business, 2 Park Square, Milton Park, Abingdon, Oxford OX14 4RN, United Kingdom, (Dial from U.S. (212) 216-7800), (Fax from U.S. (212) 564-7854), www.tandf.co.uk; *The Europa World Year Book.*

United Nations Economic and Social Commission for Western Asia (ESCWA), PO Box 11-8575, Riad el-Solh Square, Beirut, Lebanon, www.escwa.un.org; *Annual Report 2006* and *Statistical Abstract of the ESCWA Region 2007.*

BAHRAIN - BARLEY PRODUCTION

See BAHRAIN - CROPS

BAHRAIN - BEVERAGE INDUSTRY

M.E. Sharpe, 80 Business Park Drive, Armonk, NY 10504, (800) 541-6563, Fax: (914) 273-2106, www.mesharpe.com; *The Illustrated Book of World Rankings.*

BAHRAIN - BROADCASTING

Central Intelligence Agency, Office of Public Affairs, Washington, DC 20505, (703) 482-0623, Fax: (703) 482-1739, www.cia.gov; *The World Factbook.*

Euromonitor International, Inc., 224 S. Michigan Avenue, Suite 1500, Chicago, IL 60604, (312) 922-1115, Fax: (312) 922-1157, www.euromonitor.com; *World Marketing Data and Statistics.*

M.E. Sharpe, 80 Business Park Drive, Armonk, NY 10504, (800) 541-6563, Fax: (914) 273-2106, www.mesharpe.com; *The Illustrated Book of World Rankings.*

Palgrave Macmillan Ltd., Houndmills, Basingstoke, Hampshire, RG21 6XS, England, (Telephone in U.S. (888) 330-8477), (Fax in U.S. (800) 672-2054), www.palgrave.com; *The Statesman's Yearbook 2008.*

UNESCO Institute for Statistics, C.P. 6128 Succursale Centre-Ville, Montreal, Quebec, H3C 3J7 Canada, (Dial from U.S. (514) 343-6880), (Fax from U.S. (514) 343 6882), www.uis.unesco.org; *Statistical Tables.*

WRTH Publications Limited, PO Box 290, Oxford OX2 7FT, UK, www.wrth.com; *World Radio TV Handbook 2007.*

BAHRAIN - BUDGET

Central Intelligence Agency, Office of Public Affairs, Washington, DC 20505, (703) 482-0623, Fax: (703) 482-1739, www.cia.gov; *The World Factbook.*

BAHRAIN - CAPITAL LEVY

International Monetary Fund (IMF), 700 Nineteenth Street, NW, Washington, DC 20431, (202) 623-7000, Fax: (202) 623-4661, www.imf.org; *Government Finance Statistics Yearbook (2008 Edition).*

BAHRAIN - CATTLE

See BAHRAIN - LIVESTOCK

BAHRAIN - CHILDBIRTH - STATISTICS

Central Intelligence Agency, Office of Public Affairs, Washington, DC 20505, (703) 482-0623, Fax: (703) 482-1739, www.cia.gov; *The World Factbook.*

Euromonitor International, Inc., 224 S. Michigan Avenue, Suite 1500, Chicago, IL 60604, (312) 922-1115, Fax: (312) 922-1157, www.euromonitor.com; *International Marketing Data and Statistics 2008* and *The World Economic Factbook 2008.*

M.E. Sharpe, 80 Business Park Drive, Armonk, NY 10504, (800) 541-6563, Fax: (914) 273-2106, www.mesharpe.com; *The Illustrated Book of World Rankings.*

Palgrave Macmillan Ltd., Houndmills, Basingstoke, Hampshire, RG21 6XS, England, (Telephone in U.S. (888) 330-8477), (Fax in U.S. (800) 672-2054), www.palgrave.com; *The Statesman's Yearbook 2008.*

Taylor and Francis Group, An Informa Business, 2 Park Square, Milton Park, Abingdon, Oxford OX14 4RN, United Kingdom, (Dial from U.S. (212) 216-7800), (Fax from U.S. (212) 564-7854), www.tandf.co.uk; *The Europa World Year Book.*

United Nations Statistics Division, New York, NY 10017, (800) 253-9646, Fax: (212) 963-4116, http://unstats.un.org; *Demographic Yearbook.*

The World Bank, 1818 H Street, NW, Washington, DC 20433, (202) 473-1000, Fax: (202) 477-6391, www.worldbank.org; *World Development Indicators (WDI) 2008.*

World Health Organization (WHO), Avenue Appia 20, 1211 Geneve 27, Switzerland, (Telephone in U.S. (212) 331-9081), www.who.int; *World Health Report 2006.*

BAHRAIN - CLIMATE

M.E. Sharpe, 80 Business Park Drive, Armonk, NY 10504, (800) 541-6563, Fax: (914) 273-2106, www.mesharpe.com; *The Illustrated Book of World Rankings.*

Palgrave Macmillan Ltd., Houndmills, Basingstoke, Hampshire, RG21 6XS, England, (Telephone in U.S. (888) 330-8477), (Fax in U.S. (800) 672-2054), www.palgrave.com; *The Statesman's Yearbook 2008.*

BAHRAIN - COAL PRODUCTION

See BAHRAIN - MINERAL INDUSTRIES

BAHRAIN - COFFEE

See BAHRAIN - CROPS

BAHRAIN - COMMERCE

Palgrave Macmillan Ltd., Houndmills, Basingstoke, Hampshire, RG21 6XS, England, (Telephone in U.S. (888) 330-8477), (Fax in U.S. (800) 672-2054), www.palgrave.com; *The Statesman's Yearbook 2008.*

BAHRAIN - COMMODITY EXCHANGES

Commodity Research Bureau, 330 South Wells Street, Suite 612, Chicago, IL 60606-7110, (800) 621-5271, Fax: (312) 939-4135, www.crbtrader.com; *2006 CRB Commodity Yearbook and CD.*

International Monetary Fund (IMF), 700 Nineteenth Street, NW, Washington, DC 20431, (202) 623-7000, Fax: (202) 623-4661, www.imf.org; *IMF Primary Commodity Prices.*

United Nations Food and Agricultural Organization (FAO), Viale delle Terme di Caracalla, 00100 Rome, Italy, (Dial from U.S. (202) 653-2400), (Fax from U.S. (202) 653 5760), www.fao.org; *The State of Food and Agriculture (SOFA) 2006.*

BAHRAIN - CONSTRUCTION INDUSTRY

M.E. Sharpe, 80 Business Park Drive, Armonk, NY 10504, (800) 541-6563, Fax: (914) 273-2106, www.mesharpe.com; *The Illustrated Book of World Rankings.*

Palgrave Macmillan Ltd., Houndmills, Basingstoke, Hampshire, RG21 6XS, England, (Telephone in U.S. (888) 330-8477), (Fax in U.S. (800) 672-2054), www.palgrave.com; *The Statesman's Yearbook 2008.*

BAHRAIN - CONSUMER PRICE INDEXES

Taylor and Francis Group, An Informa Business, 2 Park Square, Milton Park, Abingdon, Oxford OX14

4RN, United Kingdom, (Dial from U.S. (212) 216-7800), (Fax from U.S. (212) 564-7854), www.tandf.co.uk; *The Europa World Year Book.*

The World Bank, 1818 H Street, NW, Washington, DC 20433, (202) 473-1000, Fax: (202) 477-6391, www.worldbank.org; *Bahrain.*

BAHRAIN - COPPER INDUSTRY AND TRADE

See BAHRAIN - MINERAL INDUSTRIES

BAHRAIN - CORN INDUSTRY

See BAHRAIN - CROPS

BAHRAIN - COST AND STANDARD OF LIVING

International Monetary Fund (IMF), 700 Nineteenth Street, NW, Washington, DC 20431, (202) 623-7000, Fax: (202) 623-4661, www.imf.org; *Government Finance Statistics Yearbook (2008 Edition).*

BAHRAIN - COTTON

See BAHRAIN - CROPS

BAHRAIN - CRIME

Yale University Press, PO Box 209040, New Haven, CT 06520-9040, (203) 432-0960, Fax: (203) 432-0948, http://yalepress.yale.edu/yupbooks; *Violence and Crime in Cross-National Perspective.*

BAHRAIN - CROPS

M.E. Sharpe, 80 Business Park Drive, Armonk, NY 10504, (800) 541-6563, Fax: (914) 273-2106, www.mesharpe.com; *The Illustrated Book of World Rankings.*

Palgrave Macmillan Ltd., Houndmills, Basingstoke, Hampshire, RG21 6XS, England, (Telephone in U.S. (888) 330-8477), (Fax in U.S. (800) 672-2054), www.palgrave.com; *The Statesman's Yearbook 2008.*

Taylor and Francis Group, An Informa Business, 2 Park Square, Milton Park, Abingdon, Oxford OX14 4RN, United Kingdom, (Dial from U.S. (212) 216-7800), (Fax from U.S. (212) 564-7854), www.tandf.co.uk; *The Europa World Year Book.*

United Nations Conference on Trade and Development (UNCTAD), DC2-1120, United Nations, New York, NY 10017, (212) 963-0027, www.unctad.org; *UNCTAD Commodity Yearbook.*

United Nations Food and Agricultural Organization (FAO), Viale delle Terme di Caracalla, 00100 Rome, Italy, (Dial from U.S. (202) 653-2400), (Fax from U.S. (202) 653 5760), www.fao.org; *The State of Food and Agriculture (SOFA) 2006.*

BAHRAIN - CUSTOMS ADMINISTRATION

Palgrave Macmillan Ltd., Houndmills, Basingstoke, Hampshire, RG21 6XS, England, (Telephone in U.S. (888) 330-8477), (Fax in U.S. (800) 672-2054), www.palgrave.com; *The Statesman's Yearbook 2008.*

BAHRAIN - DAIRY PROCESSING

M.E. Sharpe, 80 Business Park Drive, Armonk, NY 10504, (800) 541-6563, Fax: (914) 273-2106, www.mesharpe.com; *The Illustrated Book of World Rankings.*

United Nations Food and Agricultural Organization (FAO), Viale delle Terme di Caracalla, 00100 Rome, Italy, (Dial from U.S. (202) 653-2400), (Fax from U.S. (202) 653 5760), www.fao.org; *The State of Food and Agriculture (SOFA) 2006.*

BAHRAIN - DEATH RATES

See BAHRAIN - MORTALITY

BAHRAIN - DEBTS, EXTERNAL

International Monetary Fund (IMF), 700 Nineteenth Street, NW, Washington, DC 20431, (202) 623-7000, Fax: (202) 623-4661, www.imf.org; *Government Finance Statistics Yearbook (2008 Edition).*

Palgrave Macmillan Ltd., Houndmills, Basingstoke, Hampshire, RG21 6XS, England, (Telephone in U.S. (888) 330-8477), (Fax in U.S. (800) 672-2054), www.palgrave.com; *The Statesman's Yearbook 2008.*

The World Bank, 1818 H Street, NW, Washington, DC 20433, (202) 473-1000, Fax: (202) 477-6391, www.worldbank.org; *Global Development Finance 2007* and *World Development Indicators (WDI) 2008.*

BAHRAIN - DEFENSE EXPENDITURES

See BAHRAIN - ARMED FORCES

BAHRAIN - DEMOGRAPHY

Euromonitor International, Inc., 224 S. Michigan Avenue, Suite 1500, Chicago, IL 60604, (312) 922-1115, Fax: (312) 922-1157, www.euromonitor.com; *International Marketing Data and Statistics 2008; The World Economic Factbook 2008;* and *World Marketing Data and Statistics.*

M.E. Sharpe, 80 Business Park Drive, Armonk, NY 10504, (800) 541-6563, Fax: (914) 273-2106, www.mesharpe.com; *The Illustrated Book of World Rankings.*

United Nations Statistics Division, New York, NY 10017, (800) 253-9646, Fax: (212) 963-4116, http://unstats.un.org; *Human Development Report 2006.*

The World Bank, 1818 H Street, NW, Washington, DC 20433, (202) 473-1000, Fax: (202) 477-6391, www.worldbank.org; *Bahrain.*

BAHRAIN - DIAMONDS

See BAHRAIN - MINERAL INDUSTRIES

BAHRAIN - DISPOSABLE INCOME

M.E. Sharpe, 80 Business Park Drive, Armonk, NY 10504, (800) 541-6563, Fax: (914) 273-2106, www.mesharpe.com; *The Illustrated Book of World Rankings.*

United Nations Statistics Division, New York, NY 10017, (800) 253-9646, Fax: (212) 963-4116, http://unstats.un.org; *National Accounts Statistics: Compendium of Income Distribution Statistics* and *Statistical Yearbook.*

BAHRAIN - DIVORCE

M.E. Sharpe, 80 Business Park Drive, Armonk, NY 10504, (800) 541-6563, Fax: (914) 273-2106, www.mesharpe.com; *The Illustrated Book of World Rankings.*

United Nations Statistics Division, New York, NY 10017, (800) 253-9646, Fax: (212) 963-4116, http://unstats.un.org; *Demographic Yearbook.*

BAHRAIN - ECONOMIC ASSISTANCE

United Nations Statistics Division, New York, NY 10017, (800) 253-9646, Fax: (212) 963-4116, http://unstats.un.org; *Statistical Yearbook.*

BAHRAIN - ECONOMIC CONDITIONS

Center for International Business Education Research (CIBER), Columbia Business School and School of International and Public Affairs, Uris Hall, Room 212, 3022 Broadway, New York, NY 10027-6902, Mr. Joshua Safier, (212) 854-4750, Fax: (212) 222-9821, www.columbia.edu/cu/ciber/; Datastream International.

Central Intelligence Agency, Office of Public Affairs, Washington, DC 20505, (703) 482-0623, Fax: (703) 482-1739, www.cia.gov; *The World Factbook.*

DSI Data Service Information, Xantener Strasse 51a, D-47495 Rheinberg, Germany, www.dsidata.com; *Campus Solution.*

Dun and Bradstreet (DB) Corporation, 103 JFK Parkway, Short Hills, NJ 07078, (973) 921-5500, www.dnb.com; *Country Report.*

Economist Intelligence Unit, 111 West 57th Street, New York, NY 10019, (212) 554-0600, Fax: (212) 586-1181, www.eiu.com; *Bahrain Country Report.*

Euromonitor International, Inc., 224 S. Michigan Avenue, Suite 1500, Chicago, IL 60604, (312) 922-1115, Fax: (312) 922-1157, www.euromonitor.com; *International Marketing Data and Statistics 2008; The World Economic Factbook 2008;* and *World Marketing Data and Statistics.*

International Monetary Fund (IMF), 700 Nineteenth Street, NW, Washington, DC 20431, (202) 623-7000, Fax: (202) 623-4661, www.imf.org; *World Economic Outlook Reports.*

M.E. Sharpe, 80 Business Park Drive, Armonk, NY 10504, (800) 541-6563, Fax: (914) 273-2106, www.mesharpe.com; *The Illustrated Book of World Rankings.*

Palgrave Macmillan Ltd., Houndmills, Basingstoke, Hampshire, RG21 6XS, England, (Telephone in U.S. (888) 330-8477), (Fax in U.S. (800) 672-2054), www.palgrave.com; *The Statesman's Yearbook 2008.*

Taylor and Francis Group, An Informa Business, 2 Park Square, Milton Park, Abingdon, Oxford OX14 4RN, United Kingdom, (Dial from U.S. (212) 216-7800), (Fax from U.S. (212) 564-7854), www.tandf.co.uk; *The Europa World Year Book.*

United Nations Economic and Social Commission for Western Asia (ESCWA), PO Box 11-8575, Riad el-Solh Square, Beirut, Lebanon, www.escwa.un.org; *Annual Report 2006; Bulletin on Population and Vital Statistics in the ESCWA Region;* and *Survey of Economic and Social Developments in the ESCWA Region 2006-2007.*

United Nations Statistics Division, New York, NY 10017, (800) 253-9646, Fax: (212) 963-4116, http://unstats.un.org; *World Statistics Pocketbook.*

The World Bank, 1818 H Street, NW, Washington, DC 20433, (202) 473-1000, Fax: (202) 477-6391, www.worldbank.org; *Bahrain; Global Economic Monitor (GEM); Global Economic Prospects 2008;* and *The World Bank Atlas 2003-2004.*

BAHRAIN - EDUCATION

Euromonitor International, Inc., 224 S. Michigan Avenue, Suite 1500, Chicago, IL 60604, (312) 922-1115, Fax: (312) 922-1157, www.euromonitor.com; *International Marketing Data and Statistics 2008* and *World Marketing Data and Statistics.*

International Monetary Fund (IMF), 700 Nineteenth Street, NW, Washington, DC 20431, (202) 623-7000, Fax: (202) 623-4661, www.imf.org; *Government Finance Statistics Yearbook (2008 Edition).*

M.E. Sharpe, 80 Business Park Drive, Armonk, NY 10504, (800) 541-6563, Fax: (914) 273-2106, www.mesharpe.com; *The Illustrated Book of World Rankings.*

Palgrave Macmillan Ltd., Houndmills, Basingstoke, Hampshire, RG21 6XS, England, (Telephone in U.S. (888) 330-8477), (Fax in U.S. (800) 672-2054), www.palgrave.com; *The Statesman's Yearbook 2008.*

Taylor and Francis Group, An Informa Business, 2 Park Square, Milton Park, Abingdon, Oxford OX14 4RN, United Kingdom, (Dial from U.S. (212) 216-7800), (Fax from U.S. (212) 564-7854), www.tandf.co.uk; *The Europa World Year Book.*

UNESCO Institute for Statistics, C.P. 6128 Succursale Centre-Ville, Montreal, Quebec, H3C 3J7 Canada, (Dial from U.S. (514) 343-6880), (Fax from U.S. (514) 343 6882), www.uis.unesco.org; *Statistical Tables.*

United Nations Economic and Social Commission for Western Asia (ESCWA), PO Box 11-8575, Riad el-Solh Square, Beirut, Lebanon, www.escwa.un.org; *Annual Report 2006* and *Statistical Abstract of the ESCWA Region 2007.*

United Nations Statistics Division, New York, NY 10017, (800) 253-9646, Fax: (212) 963-4116, http://unstats.un.org; *Human Development Report 2006.*

The World Bank, 1818 H Street, NW, Washington, DC 20433, (202) 473-1000, Fax: (202) 477-6391, www.worldbank.org; *Bahrain* and *World Development Indicators (WDI) 2008.*

BAHRAIN - ELECTRICITY

M.E. Sharpe, 80 Business Park Drive, Armonk, NY 10504, (800) 541-6563, Fax: (914) 273-2106, www.mesharpe.com; *The Illustrated Book of World Rankings.*

Organisation for Economic Cooperation and Development (OECD), 2 rue Andre Pascal, F-75775 Paris Cedex 16, France, (Telephone in U.S. (202) 785-6323), (Fax in U.S. (202) 785-0350), www.oecd.org; *World Energy Outlook 2007.*

Palgrave Macmillan Ltd., Houndmills, Basingstoke, Hampshire, RG21 6XS, England, (Telephone in U.S. (888) 330-8477), (Fax in U.S. (800) 672-2054), www.palgrave.com; *The Statesman's Yearbook 2008.*

U.S. Department of Energy (DOE), Energy Information Administration (EIA), 1000 Independence Avenue, SW, Washington, DC 20585, (202) 586-8800, www.eia.doe.gov; *International Energy Annual 2004* and *International Energy Outlook 2006.*

United Nations Statistics Division, New York, NY 10017, (800) 253-9646, Fax: (212) 963-4116, http://unstats.un.org; *Human Development Report 2006* and *Statistical Yearbook.*

BAHRAIN - EMPLOYMENT

Euromonitor International, Inc., 224 S. Michigan Avenue, Suite 1500, Chicago, IL 60604, (312) 922-1115, Fax: (312) 922-1157, www.euromonitor.com; *International Marketing Data and Statistics 2008.*

International Labour Office, I.L.O. Publications, 4 route des Morillons, CH-1211 Geneva 22, Switzerland, (Telephone in U.S. (202) 653-7652), (Fax in U.S. (202) 653-7687), www.ilo.org; *Yearbook of Labour Statistics 2006.*

M.E. Sharpe, 80 Business Park Drive, Armonk, NY 10504, (800) 541-6563, Fax: (914) 273-2106, www.mesharpe.com; *The Illustrated Book of World Rankings.*

United Nations Economic and Social Commission for Western Asia (ESCWA), PO Box 11-8575, Riad el-Solh Square, Beirut, Lebanon, www.escwa.un.org; *Annual Report 2006* and *Statistical Abstract of the ESCWA Region 2007.*

United Nations Statistics Division, New York, NY 10017, (800) 253-9646, Fax: (212) 963-4116, http://unstats.un.org; *Bulletin of Industrial Statistics for the Arab Countries.*

The World Bank, 1818 H Street, NW, Washington, DC 20433, (202) 473-1000, Fax: (202) 477-6391, www.worldbank.org; *Bahrain.*

BAHRAIN - ENVIRONMENTAL CONDITIONS

DSI Data Service Information, Xantener Strasse 51a, D-47495 Rheinberg, Germany, www.dsidata.com; *Campus Solution* and *DSI's Global Environmental Database.*

Economist Intelligence Unit, 111 West 57th Street, New York, NY 10019, (212) 554-0600, Fax: (212) 586-1181, www.eiu.com; *Bahrain Country Report.*

United Nations Statistics Division, New York, NY 10017, (800) 253-9646, Fax: (212) 963-4116, http://unstats.un.org; *World Statistics Pocketbook.*

BAHRAIN - EXPORTS

Central Intelligence Agency, Office of Public Affairs, Washington, DC 20505, (703) 482-0623, Fax: (703) 482-1739, www.cia.gov; *The World Factbook.*

Economist Intelligence Unit, 111 West 57th Street, New York, NY 10019, (212) 554-0600, Fax: (212) 586-1181, www.eiu.com; *Bahrain Country Report.*

Euromonitor International, Inc., 224 S. Michigan Avenue, Suite 1500, Chicago, IL 60604, (312) 922-1115, Fax: (312) 922-1157, www.euromonitor.com; *International Marketing Data and Statistics 2008* and *The World Economic Factbook 2008.*

International Monetary Fund (IMF), 700 Nineteenth Street, NW, Washington, DC 20431, (202) 623-7000, Fax: (202) 623-4661, www.imf.org; *Direction of Trade Statistics Yearbook 2007* and *International Financial Statistics Yearbook 2007.*

Palgrave Macmillan Ltd., Houndmills, Basingstoke, Hampshire, RG21 6XS, England, (Telephone in U.S. (888) 330-8477), (Fax in U.S. (800) 672-2054), www.palgrave.com; *The Statesman's Yearbook 2008.*

Taylor and Francis Group, An Informa Business, 2 Park Square, Milton Park, Abingdon, Oxford OX14 4RN, United Kingdom, (Dial from U.S. (212) 216-7800), (Fax from U.S. (212) 564-7854), www.tandf.co.uk; *The Europa World Year Book.*

United Nations Conference on Trade and Development (UNCTAD), DC2-1120, United Nations, New York, NY 10017, (212) 963-0027, www.unctad.org; *Handbook of Statistics 2005.*

United Nations Economic and Social Commission for Western Asia (ESCWA), PO Box 11-8575, Riad el-Solh Square, Beirut, Lebanon, www.escwa.un.org; *Annual Report 2006* and *Statistical Abstract of the ESCWA Region 2007.*

United Nations Food and Agricultural Organization (FAO), Viale delle Terme di Caracalla, 00100 Rome, Italy, (Dial from U.S. (202) 653-2400), (Fax from U.S. (202) 653 5760), www.fao.org; *The State of Food and Agriculture (SOFA) 2006.*

United Nations Statistics Division, New York, NY 10017, (800) 253-9646, Fax: (212) 963-4116, http://unstats.un.org; *Bulletin of Industrial Statistics for the Arab Countries.*

The World Bank, 1818 H Street, NW, Washington, DC 20433, (202) 473-1000, Fax: (202) 477-6391, www.worldbank.org; *World Development Indicators (WDI) 2008.*

BAHRAIN - FEMALE WORKING POPULATION

See BAHRAIN - EMPLOYMENT

BAHRAIN - FERTILITY, HUMAN

M.E. Sharpe, 80 Business Park Drive, Armonk, NY 10504, (800) 541-6563, Fax: (914) 273-2106, www.mesharpe.com; *The Illustrated Book of World Rankings.*

United Nations Statistics Division, New York, NY 10017, (800) 253-9646, Fax: (212) 963-4116, http://unstats.un.org; *Human Development Report 2006.*

The World Bank, 1818 H Street, NW, Washington, DC 20433, (202) 473-1000, Fax: (202) 477-6391, www.worldbank.org; *The World Bank Atlas 2003-2004* and *World Development Indicators (WDI) 2008.*

BAHRAIN - FERTILIZER INDUSTRY

United Nations Food and Agricultural Organization (FAO), Viale delle Terme di Caracalla, 00100 Rome, Italy, (Dial from U.S. (202) 653-2400), (Fax from U.S. (202) 653 5760), www.fao.org; *The State of Food and Agriculture (SOFA) 2006.*

BAHRAIN - FETAL MORTALITY

See BAHRAIN - MORTALITY

BAHRAIN - FINANCE

United Nations Economic and Social Commission for Western Asia (ESCWA), PO Box 11-8575, Riad el-Solh Square, Beirut, Lebanon, www.escwa.un.org; *Annual Report 2006* and *Statistical Abstract of the ESCWA Region 2007.*

United Nations Statistics Division, New York, NY 10017, (800) 253-9646, Fax: (212) 963-4116, http://unstats.un.org; *National Accounts Statistics: Compendium of Income Distribution Statistics* and *Statistical Yearbook.*

The World Bank, 1818 H Street, NW, Washington, DC 20433, (202) 473-1000, Fax: (202) 477-6391, www.worldbank.org; *Bahrain.*

BAHRAIN - FINANCE, PUBLIC

Bernan Essential Government Publications, 4611-F Assembly Drive, Lanham MD, 20706-4391, (301) 459-2255, Fax: (800) 865-3450, www.bernan.com; *National Accounts Statistics.*

Economist Intelligence Unit, 111 West 57th Street, New York, NY 10019, (212) 554-0600, Fax: (212) 586-1181, www.eiu.com; *Bahrain Country Report.*

International Monetary Fund (IMF), 700 Nineteenth Street, NW, Washington, DC 20431, (202) 623-7000, Fax: (202) 623-4661, www.imf.org; *Government Finance Statistics Yearbook (2008 Edition); International Financial Statistics;* and *International Financial Statistics Online Service.*

M.E. Sharpe, 80 Business Park Drive, Armonk, NY 10504, (800) 541-6563, Fax: (914) 273-2106, www.mesharpe.com; *The Illustrated Book of World Rankings.*

Palgrave Macmillan Ltd., Houndmills, Basingstoke, Hampshire, RG21 6XS, England, (Telephone in U.S. (888) 330-8477), (Fax in U.S. (800) 672-2054), www.palgrave.com; *The Statesman's Yearbook 2008.*

Taylor and Francis Group, An Informa Business, 2 Park Square, Milton Park, Abingdon, Oxford OX14 4RN, United Kingdom, (Dial from U.S. (212) 216-7800), (Fax from U.S. (212) 564-7854), www.tandf.co.uk; *The Europa World Year Book.*

United Nations Economic and Social Commission for Western Asia (ESCWA), PO Box 11-8575, Riad el-Solh Square, Beirut, Lebanon, www.escwa.un.org; *Annual Report 2006* and *Statistical Abstract of the ESCWA Region 2007.*

The World Bank, 1818 H Street, NW, Washington, DC 20433, (202) 473-1000, Fax: (202) 477-6391, www.worldbank.org; *Bahrain.*

BAHRAIN - FISHERIES

M.E. Sharpe, 80 Business Park Drive, Armonk, NY 10504, (800) 541-6563, Fax: (914) 273-2106, www.mesharpe.com; *The Illustrated Book of World Rankings.*

Palgrave Macmillan Ltd., Houndmills, Basingstoke, Hampshire, RG21 6XS, England, (Telephone in U.S. (888) 330-8477), (Fax in U.S. (800) 672-2054), www.palgrave.com; *The Statesman's Yearbook 2008.*

Taylor and Francis Group, An Informa Business, 2 Park Square, Milton Park, Abingdon, Oxford OX14 4RN, United Kingdom, (Dial from U.S. (212) 216-7800), (Fax from U.S. (212) 564-7854), www.tandf.co.uk; *The Europa World Year Book.*

United Nations Conference on Trade and Development (UNCTAD), DC2-1120, United Nations, New York, NY 10017, (212) 963-0027, www.unctad.org; *UNCTAD Commodity Yearbook.*

United Nations Economic and Social Commission for Western Asia (ESCWA), PO Box 11-8575, Riad el-Solh Square, Beirut, Lebanon, www.escwa.un.org; *Annual Report 2006* and *Statistical Abstract of the ESCWA Region 2007.*

United Nations Food and Agricultural Organization (FAO), Viale delle Terme di Caracalla, 00100 Rome, Italy, (Dial from U.S. (202) 653-2400), (Fax from U.S. (202) 653 5760), www.fao.org; *FAO Yearbook of Fishery Statistics;* Fishery Databases; FISHSTAT Database. Subjects covered include: Aquaculture production, capture production, fishery commodities; and *The State of Food and Agriculture (SOFA) 2006.*

United Nations Statistics Division, New York, NY 10017, (800) 253-9646, Fax: (212) 963-4116, http://unstats.un.org; *Statistical Yearbook.*

The World Bank, 1818 H Street, NW, Washington, DC 20433, (202) 473-1000, Fax: (202) 477-6391, www.worldbank.org; *Bahrain.*

BAHRAIN - FOOD

United Nations Conference on Trade and Development (UNCTAD), DC2-1120, United Nations, New York, NY 10017, (212) 963-0027, www.unctad.org; *UNCTAD Commodity Yearbook.*

United Nations Food and Agricultural Organization (FAO), Viale delle Terme di Caracalla, 00100 Rome, Italy, (Dial from U.S. (202) 653-2400), (Fax from U.S. (202) 653 5760), www.fao.org; *FAO Production Yearbook 2002* and *The State of Food and Agriculture (SOFA) 2006.*

United Nations Statistics Division, New York, NY 10017, (800) 253-9646, Fax: (212) 963-4116, http://unstats.un.org; *Human Development Report 2006.*

BAHRAIN - FOREIGN EXCHANGE RATES

Central Intelligence Agency, Office of Public Affairs, Washington, DC 20505, (703) 482-0623, Fax: (703) 482-1739, www.cia.gov; *The World Factbook.*

Euromonitor International, Inc., 224 S. Michigan Avenue, Suite 1500, Chicago, IL 60604, (312) 922-1115, Fax: (312) 922-1157, www.euromonitor.com; *International Marketing Data and Statistics 2008* and *The World Economic Factbook 2008.*

International Monetary Fund (IMF), 700 Nineteenth Street, NW, Washington, DC 20431, (202) 623-7000, Fax: (202) 623-4661, www.imf.org; *International Financial Statistics Yearbook 2007.*

Taylor and Francis Group, An Informa Business, 2 Park Square, Milton Park, Abingdon, Oxford OX14 4RN, United Kingdom, (Dial from U.S. (212) 216-7800), (Fax from U.S. (212) 564-7854), www.tandf.co.uk; *The Europa World Year Book.*

United Nations Statistics Division, New York, NY 10017, (800) 253-9646, Fax: (212) 963-4116, http://unstats.un.org; *Bulletin of Industrial Statistics for the Arab Countries; Statistical Yearbook;* and *World Statistics Pocketbook.*

BAHRAIN - FORESTS AND FORESTRY

M.E. Sharpe, 80 Business Park Drive, Armonk, NY 10504, (800) 541-6563, Fax: (914) 273-2106, www.mesharpe.com; *The Illustrated Book of World Rankings.*

UNESCO Institute for Statistics, C.P. 6128 Succursale Centre-Ville, Montreal, Quebec, H3C 3J7 Canada, (Dial from U.S. (514) 343-6880), (Fax from U.S. (514) 343 6882), www.uis.unesco.org; *Statistical Tables.*

United Nations Conference on Trade and Development (UNCTAD), DC2-1120, United Nations, New York, NY 10017, (212) 963-0027, www.unctad.org; *UNCTAD Commodity Yearbook.*

United Nations Food and Agricultural Organization (FAO), Viale delle Terme di Caracalla, 00100 Rome, Italy, (Dial from U.S. (202) 653-2400), (Fax from U.S. (202) 653 5760), www.fao.org; *FAO Yearbook of Forest Products* and *The State of Food and Agriculture (SOFA) 2006.*

United Nations Statistics Division, New York, NY 10017, (800) 253-9646, Fax: (212) 963-4116, http://unstats.un.org; *Statistical Yearbook.*

The World Bank, 1818 H Street, NW, Washington, DC 20433, (202) 473-1000, Fax: (202) 477-6391, www.worldbank.org; *Bahrain.*

BAHRAIN - GAS PRODUCTION

See BAHRAIN - MINERAL INDUSTRIES

BAHRAIN - GEOGRAPHIC INFORMATION SYSTEMS

M.E. Sharpe, 80 Business Park Drive, Armonk, NY 10504, (800) 541-6563, Fax: (914) 273-2106, www.mesharpe.com; *The Illustrated Book of World Rankings.*

The World Bank, 1818 H Street, NW, Washington, DC 20433, (202) 473-1000, Fax: (202) 477-6391, www.worldbank.org; *Bahrain.*

BAHRAIN - GOLD INDUSTRY

International Monetary Fund (IMF), 700 Nineteenth Street, NW, Washington, DC 20431, (202) 623-7000, Fax: (202) 623-4661, www.imf.org; *International Financial Statistics Yearbook 2007.*

United Nations Statistics Division, New York, NY 10017, (800) 253-9646, Fax: (212) 963-4116, http://unstats.un.org; *Statistical Yearbook.*

The World Bank, 1818 H Street, NW, Washington, DC 20433, (202) 473-1000, Fax: (202) 477-6391, www.worldbank.org; *World Development Indicators (WDI) 2008.*

BAHRAIN - GOLD PRODUCTION

See BAHRAIN - MINERAL INDUSTRIES

BAHRAIN - GRANTS-IN-AID

International Monetary Fund (IMF), 700 Nineteenth Street, NW, Washington, DC 20431, (202) 623-7000, Fax: (202) 623-4661, www.imf.org; *Government Finance Statistics Yearbook (2008 Edition).*

BAHRAIN - GROSS DOMESTIC PRODUCT

Economist Intelligence Unit, 111 West 57th Street, New York, NY 10019, (212) 554-0600, Fax: (212) 586-1181, www.eiu.com; *Bahrain Country Report.*

Euromonitor International, Inc., 224 S. Michigan Avenue, Suite 1500, Chicago, IL 60604, (312) 922-1115, Fax: (312) 922-1157, www.euromonitor.com; *International Marketing Data and Statistics 2008* and *The World Economic Factbook 2008.*

M.E. Sharpe, 80 Business Park Drive, Armonk, NY 10504, (800) 541-6563, Fax: (914) 273-2106, www.mesharpe.com; *The Illustrated Book of World Rankings.*

Taylor and Francis Group, An Informa Business, 2 Park Square, Milton Park, Abingdon, Oxford OX14 4RN, United Kingdom, (Dial from U.S. (212) 216-7800), (Fax from U.S. (212) 564-7854), www.tandf.co.uk; *The Europa World Year Book.*

United Nations Economic and Social Commission for Western Asia (ESCWA), PO Box 11-8575, Riad el-Solh Square, Beirut, Lebanon, www.escwa.un.org; *Annual Report 2006* and *Statistical Abstract of the ESCWA Region 2007.*

United Nations Statistics Division, New York, NY 10017, (800) 253-9646, Fax: (212) 963-4116, http://unstats.un.org; *Bulletin of Industrial Statistics for the Arab Countries; Human Development Report 2006; National Accounts Statistics: Compendium of Income Distribution Statistics;* and *Statistical Yearbook.*

The World Bank, 1818 H Street, NW, Washington, DC 20433, (202) 473-1000, Fax: (202) 477-6391, www.worldbank.org; *World Development Indicators (WDI) 2008.*

BAHRAIN - GROSS NATIONAL PRODUCT

Euromonitor International, Inc., 224 S. Michigan Avenue, Suite 1500, Chicago, IL 60604, (312) 922-1115, Fax: (312) 922-1157, www.euromonitor.com; *International Marketing Data and Statistics 2008.*

M.E. Sharpe, 80 Business Park Drive, Armonk, NY 10504, (800) 541-6563, Fax: (914) 273-2106, www.mesharpe.com; *The Illustrated Book of World Rankings.*

Palgrave Macmillan Ltd., Houndmills, Basingstoke, Hampshire, RG21 6XS, England, (Telephone in U.S. (888) 330-8477), (Fax in U.S. (800) 672-2054), www.palgrave.com; *The Statesman's Yearbook 2008.*

U.S. Department of State (DOS), 2201 C Street NW, Washington, DC 20520, (202) 647-4000, www.state.gov; *World Military Expenditures and Arms Transfers (WMEAT).*

The World Bank, 1818 H Street, NW, Washington, DC 20433, (202) 473-1000, Fax: (202) 477-6391, www.worldbank.org; *The World Bank Atlas 2003-2004* and *World Development Indicators (WDI) 2008.*

BAHRAIN - HIDES AND SKINS INDUSTRY

United Nations Food and Agricultural Organization (FAO), Viale delle Terme di Caracalla, 00100 Rome, Italy, (Dial from U.S. (202) 653-2400), (Fax from U.S. (202) 653 5760), www.fao.org; *FAO Production Yearbook 2002.*

BAHRAIN - HOUSING

Euromonitor International, Inc., 224 S. Michigan Avenue, Suite 1500, Chicago, IL 60604, (312) 922-1115, Fax: (312) 922-1157, www.euromonitor.com; *World Marketing Data and Statistics.*

M.E. Sharpe, 80 Business Park Drive, Armonk, NY 10504, (800) 541-6563, Fax: (914) 273-2106, www.mesharpe.com; *The Illustrated Book of World Rankings.*

United Nations Statistics Division, New York, NY 10017, (800) 253-9646, Fax: (212) 963-4116, http://unstats.un.org; *Statistical Yearbook.*

BAHRAIN - ILLITERATE PERSONS

Central Intelligence Agency, Office of Public Affairs, Washington, DC 20505, (703) 482-0623, Fax: (703) 482-1739, www.cia.gov; *The World Factbook.*

Euromonitor International, Inc., 224 S. Michigan Avenue, Suite 1500, Chicago, IL 60604, (312) 922-1115, Fax: (312) 922-1157, www.euromonitor.com; *The World Economic Factbook 2008.*

UNESCO Institute for Statistics, C.P. 6128 Succursale Centre-Ville, Montreal, Quebec, H3C 3J7 Canada, (Dial from U.S. (514) 343-6880), (Fax from U.S. (514) 343 6882), www.uis.unesco.org; *Statistical Tables.*

United Nations Statistics Division, New York, NY 10017, (800) 253-9646, Fax: (212) 963-4116, http://unstats.un.org; *Human Development Report 2006.*

BAHRAIN - IMPORTS

Central Intelligence Agency, Office of Public Affairs, Washington, DC 20505, (703) 482-0623, Fax: (703) 482-1739, www.cia.gov; *The World Factbook.*

Economist Intelligence Unit, 111 West 57th Street, New York, NY 10019, (212) 554-0600, Fax: (212) 586-1181, www.eiu.com; *Bahrain Country Report.*

Euromonitor International, Inc., 224 S. Michigan Avenue, Suite 1500, Chicago, IL 60604, (312) 922-1115, Fax: (312) 922-1157, www.euromonitor.com; *International Marketing Data and Statistics 2008* and *The World Economic Factbook 2008.*

International Monetary Fund (IMF), 700 Nineteenth Street, NW, Washington, DC 20431, (202) 623-7000, Fax: (202) 623-4661, www.imf.org; *Direction of Trade Statistics Yearbook 2007; Government Finance Statistics Yearbook (2008 Edition);* and *International Financial Statistics Yearbook 2007.*

Palgrave Macmillan Ltd., Houndmills, Basingstoke, Hampshire, RG21 6XS, England, (Telephone in U.S. (888) 330-8477), (Fax in U.S. (800) 672-2054), www.palgrave.com; *The Statesman's Yearbook 2008.*

Taylor and Francis Group, An Informa Business, 2 Park Square, Milton Park, Abingdon, Oxford OX14 4RN, United Kingdom, (Dial from U.S. (212) 216-7800), (Fax from U.S. (212) 564-7854), www.tandf.co.uk; *The Europa World Year Book.*

United Nations Conference on Trade and Development (UNCTAD), DC2-1120, United Nations, New York, NY 10017, (212) 963-0027, www.unctad.org; *Handbook of Statistics 2005.*

United Nations Economic and Social Commission for Western Asia (ESCWA), PO Box 11-8575, Riad el-Solh Square, Beirut, Lebanon, www.escwa.un.org; *Annual Report 2006* and *Statistical Abstract of the ESCWA Region 2007.*

United Nations Food and Agricultural Organization (FAO), Viale delle Terme di Caracalla, 00100 Rome, Italy, (Dial from U.S. (202) 653-2400), (Fax from U.S. (202) 653 5760), www.fao.org; *The State of Food and Agriculture (SOFA) 2006.*

United Nations Statistics Division, New York, NY 10017, (800) 253-9646, Fax: (212) 963-4116, http://unstats.un.org; *Bulletin of Industrial Statistics for the Arab Countries.*

The World Bank, 1818 H Street, NW, Washington, DC 20433, (202) 473-1000, Fax: (202) 477-6391, www.worldbank.org; *World Development Indicators (WDI) 2008.*

BAHRAIN - INCOME TAXES

See BAHRAIN - TAXATION

BAHRAIN - INDUSTRIAL PRODUCTIVITY

Euromonitor International, Inc., 224 S. Michigan Avenue, Suite 1500, Chicago, IL 60604, (312) 922-1115, Fax: (312) 922-1157, www.euromonitor.com; *International Marketing Data and Statistics 2008.*

M.E. Sharpe, 80 Business Park Drive, Armonk, NY 10504, (800) 541-6563, Fax: (914) 273-2106, www.mesharpe.com; *The Illustrated Book of World Rankings.*

BAHRAIN - INDUSTRIAL PROPERTY

United Nations Statistics Division, New York, NY 10017, (800) 253-9646, Fax: (212) 963-4116, http://unstats.un.org; *Statistical Yearbook.*

United Nations World Tourism Organization (UNWTO), Capitan Haya 42, 28020 Madrid, Spain, www.world-tourism.org; *Yearbook of Tourism Statistics.*

World Intellectual Property Organization (WIPO), PO Box 18, CH-1211 Geneva 20, Switzerland, www.wipo.int; *Industrial Property Statistics* and *Industrial Property Statistics Online Directory.*

BAHRAIN - INDUSTRIES

Central Intelligence Agency, Office of Public Affairs, Washington, DC 20505, (703) 482-0623, Fax: (703) 482-1739, www.cia.gov; *The World Factbook.*

Economist Intelligence Unit, 111 West 57th Street, New York, NY 10019, (212) 554-0600, Fax: (212) 586-1181, www.eiu.com; *Bahrain Country Report.*

Euromonitor International, Inc., 224 S. Michigan Avenue, Suite 1500, Chicago, IL 60604, (312) 922-1115, Fax: (312) 922-1157, www.euromonitor.com; *International Marketing Data and Statistics 2008; The World Economic Factbook 2008;* and *World Marketing Data and Statistics.*

International Labour Office, I.L.O. Publications, 4 route des Morillons, CH-1211 Geneva 22, Switzerland, (Telephone in U.S. (202) 653-7652), (Fax in U.S. (202) 653-7687), www.ilo.org; *Yearbook of Labour Statistics 2006.*

M.E. Sharpe, 80 Business Park Drive, Armonk, NY 10504, (800) 541-6563, Fax: (914) 273-2106, www.mesharpe.com; *The Illustrated Book of World Rankings.*

Palgrave Macmillan Ltd., Houndmills, Basingstoke, Hampshire, RG21 6XS, England, (Telephone in U.S. (888) 330-8477), (Fax in U.S. (800) 672-2054), www.palgrave.com; *The Statesman's Yearbook 2008.*

Taylor and Francis Group, An Informa Business, 2 Park Square, Milton Park, Abingdon, Oxford OX14 4RN, United Kingdom, (Dial from U.S. (212) 216-7800), (Fax from U.S. (212) 564-7854), www.tandf.co.uk; *The Europa World Year Book.*

United Nations Industrial Development Organization (UNIDO), 1 United Nations Plaza, New York, NY 10017, (212) 963 6890, Fax: (212) 963-7904, http://unido.org; Industrial Statistics Database 2008 (INDSTAT) and *The International Yearbook of Industrial Statistics 2008.*

United Nations Statistics Division, New York, NY 10017, (800) 253-9646, Fax: (212) 963-4116, http://unstats.un.org; *Bulletin of Industrial Statistics for the Arab Countries.*

The World Bank, 1818 H Street, NW, Washington, DC 20433, (202) 473-1000, Fax: (202) 477-6391, www.worldbank.org; *Bahrain* and *World Development Indicators (WDI) 2008.*

World Intellectual Property Organization (WIPO), PO Box 18, CH-1211 Geneva 20, Switzerland, www.wipo.int; *Industrial Property Statistics* and *Industrial Property Statistics Online Directory.*

BAHRAIN - INFANT AND MATERNAL MORTALITY

See BAHRAIN - MORTALITY

BAHRAIN - INTERNATIONAL LIQUIDITY

International Monetary Fund (IMF), 700 Nineteenth Street, NW, Washington, DC 20431, (202) 623-7000, Fax: (202) 623-4661, www.imf.org; *International Financial Statistics Yearbook 2007.*

BAHRAIN - INTERNATIONAL TRADE

Economist Intelligence Unit, 111 West 57th Street, New York, NY 10019, (212) 554-0600, Fax: (212) 586-1181, www.eiu.com; *Bahrain Country Report.*

Euromonitor International, Inc., 224 S. Michigan Avenue, Suite 1500, Chicago, IL 60604, (312) 922-1115, Fax: (312) 922-1157, www.euromonitor.com; *International Marketing Data and Statistics 2008; The World Economic Factbook 2008;* and *World Marketing Data and Statistics.*

M.E. Sharpe, 80 Business Park Drive, Armonk, NY 10504, (800) 541-6563, Fax: (914) 273-2106, www.mesharpe.com; *The Illustrated Book of World Rankings.*

Palgrave Macmillan Ltd., Houndmills, Basingstoke, Hampshire, RG21 6XS, England, (Telephone in U.S. (888) 330-8477), (Fax in U.S. (800) 672-2054), www.palgrave.com; *The Statesman's Yearbook 2008.*

Taylor and Francis Group, An Informa Business, 2 Park Square, Milton Park, Abingdon, Oxford OX14 4RN, United Kingdom, (Dial from U.S. (212) 216-7800), (Fax from U.S. (212) 564-7854), www.tandf.co.uk; *The Europa World Year Book.*

United Nations Conference on Trade and Development (UNCTAD), DC2-1120, United Nations, New York, NY 10017, (212) 963-0027, www.unctad.org; *UNCTAD Commodity Yearbook.*

United Nations Economic and Social Commission for Western Asia (ESCWA), PO Box 11-8575, Riad el-Solh Square, Beirut, Lebanon, www.escwa.un.org; *Annual Report 2006* and *Statistical Abstract of the ESCWA Region 2007.*

United Nations Food and Agricultural Organization (FAO), Viale delle Terme di Caracalla, 00100 Rome, Italy, (Dial from U.S. (202) 653-2400), (Fax from U.S. (202) 653 5760), www.fao.org; *FAO Trade Yearbook* and *The State of Food and Agriculture (SOFA) 2006.*

United Nations Statistics Division, New York, NY 10017, (800) 253-9646, Fax: (212) 963-4116, http://unstats.un.org; *Bulletin of Industrial Statistics for the Arab Countries; International Trade Statistics Yearbook;* and *Statistical Yearbook.*

The World Bank, 1818 H Street, NW, Washington, DC 20433, (202) 473-1000, Fax: (202) 477-6391, www.worldbank.org; *Bahrain* and *World Development Indicators (WDI) 2008.*

World Trade Organization (WTO), Centre William Rappard, Rue de Lausanne 154, CH-1211 Geneva 21, Switzerland, www.wto.org; *International Trade Statistics 2006.*

BAHRAIN - INTERNET USERS

International Telecommunication Union (ITU), Place des Nations, 1211 Geneva 20, Switzerland, www.itu.int; *World Telecommunication/ICT Indicators Database on CD-ROM; World Telecommunication/ICT Indicators Database Online;* and *Yearbook of Statistics - Telecommunication Services (Chronological Time Series 1997-2006).*

The World Bank, 1818 H Street, NW, Washington, DC 20433, (202) 473-1000, Fax: (202) 477-6391, www.worldbank.org; *Bahrain.*

BAHRAIN - IRON AND IRON ORE PRODUCTION

See BAHRAIN - MINERAL INDUSTRIES

BAHRAIN - IRRIGATION

Euromonitor International, Inc., 224 S. Michigan Avenue, Suite 1500, Chicago, IL 60604, (312) 922-1115, Fax: (312) 922-1157, www.euromonitor.com; *International Marketing Data and Statistics 2008.*

BAHRAIN - LABOR

Central Intelligence Agency, Office of Public Affairs, Washington, DC 20505, (703) 482-0623, Fax: (703) 482-1739, www.cia.gov; *The World Factbook.*

Euromonitor International, Inc., 224 S. Michigan Avenue, Suite 1500, Chicago, IL 60604, (312) 922-1115, Fax: (312) 922-1157, www.euromonitor.com; *International Marketing Data and Statistics 2008* and *World Marketing Data and Statistics.*

International Labour Office, I.L.O. Publications, 4 route des Morillons, CH-1211 Geneva 22, Switzerland, (Telephone in U.S. (202) 653-7652), (Fax in U.S. (202) 653-7687), www.ilo.org; *Yearbook of Labour Statistics 2006.*

M.E. Sharpe, 80 Business Park Drive, Armonk, NY 10504, (800) 541-6563, Fax: (914) 273-2106, www.mesharpe.com; *The Illustrated Book of World Rankings.*

Palgrave Macmillan Ltd., Houndmills, Basingstoke, Hampshire, RG21 6XS, England, (Telephone in U.S. (888) 330-8477), (Fax in U.S. (800) 672-2054), www.palgrave.com; *The Statesman's Yearbook 2008.*

Taylor and Francis Group, An Informa Business, 2 Park Square, Milton Park, Abingdon, Oxford OX14 4RN, United Kingdom, (Dial from U.S. (212) 216-7800), (Fax from U.S. (212) 564-7854), www.tandf.co.uk; *The Europa World Year Book.*

U.S. Department of Labor (DOL), Bureau of International Labor Affairs (ILAB), Frances Perkins Building, Room C-4325, 200 Constitution Avenue, NW, Washington, DC 20210, (202) 693-4770, Fax: (202) 693-4780, www.dol.gov/ilab; *Labor Rights Report.*

United Nations Economic and Social Commission for Western Asia (ESCWA), PO Box 11-8575, Riad el-Solh Square, Beirut, Lebanon, www.escwa.un.org; *Annual Report 2006* and *Statistical Abstract of the ESCWA Region 2007.*

United Nations Food and Agricultural Organization (FAO), Viale delle Terme di Caracalla, 00100 Rome, Italy, (Dial from U.S. (202) 653-2400), (Fax from U.S. (202) 653 5760), www.fao.org; *The State of Food and Agriculture (SOFA) 2006.*

United Nations Statistics Division, New York, NY 10017, (800) 253-9646, Fax: (212) 963-4116, http://unstats.un.org; *Human Development Report 2006.*

The World Bank, 1818 H Street, NW, Washington, DC 20433, (202) 473-1000, Fax: (202) 477-6391, www.worldbank.org; *The World Bank Atlas 2003-2004* and *World Development Indicators (WDI) 2008.*

BAHRAIN - LAND USE

Central Intelligence Agency, Office of Public Affairs, Washington, DC 20505, (703) 482-0623, Fax: (703) 482-1739, www.cia.gov; *The World Factbook.*

Euromonitor International, Inc., 224 S. Michigan Avenue, Suite 1500, Chicago, IL 60604, (312) 922-1115, Fax: (312) 922-1157, www.euromonitor.com; *International Marketing Data and Statistics 2008.*

M.E. Sharpe, 80 Business Park Drive, Armonk, NY 10504, (800) 541-6563, Fax: (914) 273-2106, www.mesharpe.com; *The Illustrated Book of World Rankings.*

United Nations Economic and Social Commission for Western Asia (ESCWA), PO Box 11-8575, Riad el-Solh Square, Beirut, Lebanon, www.escwa.un.org; *Annual Report 2006* and *Statistical Abstract of the ESCWA Region 2007.*

United Nations Food and Agricultural Organization (FAO), Viale delle Terme di Caracalla, 00100 Rome, Italy, (Dial from U.S. (202) 653-2400), (Fax from U.S. (202) 653 5760), www.fao.org; *FAO Production Yearbook 2002.*

BAHRAIN - LIBRARIES

M.E. Sharpe, 80 Business Park Drive, Armonk, NY 10504, (800) 541-6563, Fax: (914) 273-2106, www.mesharpe.com; *The Illustrated Book of World Rankings.*

UNESCO Institute for Statistics, C.P. 6128 Succursale Centre-Ville, Montreal, Quebec, H3C 3J7 Canada, (Dial from U.S. (514) 343-6880), (Fax from U.S. (514) 343 6882), www.uis.unesco.org; *Statistical Tables.*

BAHRAIN - LICENSES

International Monetary Fund (IMF), 700 Nineteenth Street, NW, Washington, DC 20431, (202) 623-7000, Fax: (202) 623-4661, www.imf.org; *Government Finance Statistics Yearbook (2008 Edition).*

BAHRAIN - LIFE EXPECTANCY

Euromonitor International, Inc., 224 S. Michigan Avenue, Suite 1500, Chicago, IL 60604, (312) 922-1115, Fax: (312) 922-1157, www.euromonitor.com; *The World Economic Factbook 2008.*

Palgrave Macmillan Ltd., Houndmills, Basingstoke, Hampshire, RG21 6XS, England, (Telephone in U.S. (888) 330-8477), (Fax in U.S. (800) 672-2054), www.palgrave.com; *The Statesman's Yearbook 2008.*

United Nations Statistics Division, New York, NY 10017, (800) 253-9646, Fax: (212) 963-4116, http://unstats.un.org; *Human Development Report 2006* and *World Statistics Pocketbook.*.

The World Bank, 1818 H Street, NW, Washington, DC 20433, (202) 473-1000, Fax: (202) 477-6391, www.worldbank.org; *The World Bank Atlas 2003-2004.*

BAHRAIN - LITERACY

Euromonitor International, Inc., 224 S. Michigan Avenue, Suite 1500, Chicago, IL 60604, (312) 922-1115, Fax: (312) 922-1157, www.euromonitor.com; *World Marketing Data and Statistics.*

BAHRAIN - LIVESTOCK

M.E. Sharpe, 80 Business Park Drive, Armonk, NY 10504, (800) 541-6563, Fax: (914) 273-2106, www.mesharpe.com; *The Illustrated Book of World Rankings.*

Palgrave Macmillan Ltd., Houndmills, Basingstoke, Hampshire, RG21 6XS, England, (Telephone in U.S. (888) 330-8477), (Fax in U.S. (800) 672-2054), www.palgrave.com; *The Statesman's Yearbook 2008.*

Taylor and Francis Group, An Informa Business, 2 Park Square, Milton Park, Abingdon, Oxford OX14 4RN, United Kingdom, (Dial from U.S. (212) 216-7800), (Fax from U.S. (212) 564-7854), www.tandf.co.uk; *The Europa World Year Book.*

United Nations Conference on Trade and Development (UNCTAD), DC2-1120, United Nations, New York, NY 10017, (212) 963-0027, www.unctad.org; *UNCTAD Commodity Yearbook.*

United Nations Food and Agricultural Organization (FAO), Viale delle Terme di Caracalla, 00100 Rome, Italy, (Dial from U.S. (202) 653-2400), (Fax from U.S. (202) 653 5760), www.fao.org; *FAO Production Yearbook 2002* and *The State of Food and Agriculture (SOFA) 2006.*

United Nations Statistics Division, New York, NY 10017, (800) 253-9646, Fax: (212) 963-4116, http://unstats.un.org; *Statistical Yearbook.*

BAHRAIN - LOCAL TAXATION

Euromonitor International, Inc., 224 S. Michigan Avenue, Suite 1500, Chicago, IL 60604, (312) 922-1115, Fax: (312) 922-1157, www.euromonitor.com; *International Marketing Data and Statistics 2008.*

BAHRAIN - MANUFACTURES

M.E. Sharpe, 80 Business Park Drive, Armonk, NY 10504, (800) 541-6563, Fax: (914) 273-2106, www.mesharpe.com; *The Illustrated Book of World Rankings.*

United Nations Statistics Division, New York, NY 10017, (800) 253-9646, Fax: (212) 963-4116, http://unstats.un.org; *Bulletin of Industrial Statistics for the Arab Countries.*

The World Bank, 1818 H Street, NW, Washington, DC 20433, (202) 473-1000, Fax: (202) 477-6391, www.worldbank.org; *World Development Indicators (WDI) 2008.*

BAHRAIN - MARRIAGE

M.E. Sharpe, 80 Business Park Drive, Armonk, NY 10504, (800) 541-6563, Fax: (914) 273-2106, www.mesharpe.com; *The Illustrated Book of World Rankings.*

Taylor and Francis Group, An Informa Business, 2 Park Square, Milton Park, Abingdon, Oxford OX14 4RN, United Kingdom, (Dial from U.S. (212) 216-7800), (Fax from U.S. (212) 564-7854), www.tandf.co.uk; *The Europa World Year Book.*

United Nations Statistics Division, New York, NY 10017, (800) 253-9646, Fax: (212) 963-4116, http://unstats.un.org; *Demographic Yearbook.*

BAHRAIN - MEAT PRODUCTION

See BAHRAIN - LIVESTOCK

BAHRAIN - MILK PRODUCTION

See BAHRAIN - DAIRY PROCESSING

BAHRAIN - MINERAL INDUSTRIES

International Monetary Fund (IMF), 700 Nineteenth Street, NW, Washington, DC 20431, (202) 623-7000, Fax: (202) 623-4661, www.imf.org; *International Financial Statistics Yearbook 2007.*

M.E. Sharpe, 80 Business Park Drive, Armonk, NY 10504, (800) 541-6563, Fax: (914) 273-2106, www.mesharpe.com; *The Illustrated Book of World Rankings.*

Organisation for Economic Cooperation and Development (OECD), 2 rue Andre Pascal, F-75775 Paris Cedex 16, France, (Telephone in U.S. (202) 785-6323), (Fax in U.S. (202) 785-0350), www.oecd.org; *World Energy Outlook 2007.*

Palgrave Macmillan Ltd., Houndmills, Basingstoke, Hampshire, RG21 6XS, England, (Telephone in U.S. (888) 330-8477), (Fax in U.S. (800) 672-2054), www.palgrave.com; *The Statesman's Yearbook 2008.*

Taylor and Francis Group, An Informa Business, 2 Park Square, Milton Park, Abingdon, Oxford OX14 4RN, United Kingdom, (Dial from U.S. (212) 216-7800), (Fax from U.S. (212) 564-7854), www.tandf.co.uk; *The Europa World Year Book.*

United Nations Conference on Trade and Development (UNCTAD), DC2-1120, United Nations, New York, NY 10017, (212) 963-0027, www.unctad.org; *UNCTAD Commodity Yearbook.*

United Nations Economic and Social Commission for Western Asia (ESCWA), PO Box 11-8575, Riad el-Solh Square, Beirut, Lebanon, www.escwa.un.org; *Annual Report 2006* and *Statistical Abstract of the ESCWA Region 2007.*

United Nations Statistics Division, New York, NY 10017, (800) 253-9646, Fax: (212) 963-4116, http://unstats.un.org; *Bulletin of Industrial Statistics for the Arab Countries* and *Statistical Yearbook.*

BAHRAIN - MONEY EXCHANGE RATES

See BAHRAIN - FOREIGN EXCHANGE RATES

BAHRAIN - MONEY SUPPLY

Economist Intelligence Unit, 111 West 57th Street, New York, NY 10019, (212) 554-0600, Fax: (212) 586-1181, www.eiu.com; *Bahrain Country Report.*

Euromonitor International, Inc., 224 S. Michigan Avenue, Suite 1500, Chicago, IL 60604, (312) 922-1115, Fax: (312) 922-1157, www.euromonitor.com; *International Marketing Data and Statistics 2008.*

International Monetary Fund (IMF), 700 Nineteenth Street, NW, Washington, DC 20431, (202) 623-7000, Fax: (202) 623-4661, www.imf.org; *International Financial Statistics Yearbook 2007.*

Taylor and Francis Group, An Informa Business, 2 Park Square, Milton Park, Abingdon, Oxford OX14 4RN, United Kingdom, (Dial from U.S. (212) 216-7800), (Fax from U.S. (212) 564-7854), www.tandf.co.uk; *The Europa World Year Book.*

United Nations Economic and Social Commission for Western Asia (ESCWA), PO Box 11-8575, Riad el-Solh Square, Beirut, Lebanon, www.escwa.un.org; *Annual Report 2006* and *Statistical Abstract of the ESCWA Region 2007.*

United Nations Statistics Division, New York, NY 10017, (800) 253-9646, Fax: (212) 963-4116, http://unstats.un.org; *Statistical Yearbook.*

The World Bank, 1818 H Street, NW, Washington, DC 20433, (202) 473-1000, Fax: (202) 477-6391, www.worldbank.org; *Bahrain* and *World Development Indicators (WDI) 2008.*

BAHRAIN - MORTALITY

Central Intelligence Agency, Office of Public Affairs, Washington, DC 20505, (703) 482-0623, Fax: (703) 482-1739, www.cia.gov; *The World Factbook.*

Euromonitor International, Inc., 224 S. Michigan Avenue, Suite 1500, Chicago, IL 60604, (312) 922-1115, Fax: (312) 922-1157, www.euromonitor.com; *International Marketing Data and Statistics 2008* and *The World Economic Factbook 2008.*

Palgrave Macmillan Ltd., Houndmills, Basingstoke, Hampshire, RG21 6XS, England, (Telephone in U.S. (888) 330-8477), (Fax in U.S. (800) 672-2054), www.palgrave.com; *The Statesman's Yearbook 2008.*

Taylor and Francis Group, An Informa Business, 2 Park Square, Milton Park, Abingdon, Oxford OX14 4RN, United Kingdom, (Dial from U.S. (212) 216-7800), (Fax from U.S. (212) 564-7854), www.tandf.co.uk; *The Europa World Year Book.*

United Nations Statistics Division, New York, NY 10017, (800) 253-9646, Fax: (212) 963-4116, http://unstats.un.org; *Demographic Yearbook; Human Development Report 2006;* and *World Statistics Pocketbook.*

The World Bank, 1818 H Street, NW, Washington, DC 20433, (202) 473-1000, Fax: (202) 477-6391, www.worldbank.org; *The World Bank Atlas 2003-2004.*

World Health Organization (WHO), Avenue Appia 20, 1211 Geneve 27, Switzerland, (Telephone in U.S. (212) 331-9081), www.who.int; The WHO Global Atlas of Infectious Diseases and *World Health Report 2006.*

BAHRAIN - MOTION PICTURES

Palgrave Macmillan Ltd., Houndmills, Basingstoke, Hampshire, RG21 6XS, England, (Telephone in U.S. (888) 330-8477), (Fax in U.S. (800) 672-2054), www.palgrave.com; *The Statesman's Yearbook 2008.*

United Nations Statistics Division, New York, NY 10017, (800) 253-9646, Fax: (212) 963-4116, http://unstats.un.org; *Statistical Yearbook.*

BAHRAIN - MOTOR VEHICLES

Taylor and Francis Group, An Informa Business, 2 Park Square, Milton Park, Abingdon, Oxford OX14 4RN, United Kingdom, (Dial from U.S. (212) 216-7800), (Fax from U.S. (212) 564-7854), www.tandf.co.uk; *The Europa World Year Book.*

United Nations Statistics Division, New York, NY 10017, (800) 253-9646, Fax: (212) 963-4116, http://unstats.un.org; *Statistical Yearbook.*

BAHRAIN - MUSEUMS

M.E. Sharpe, 80 Business Park Drive, Armonk, NY 10504, (800) 541-6563, Fax: (914) 273-2106, www.mesharpe.com; *The Illustrated Book of World Rankings.*

UNESCO Institute for Statistics, C.P. 6128 Succursale Centre-Ville, Montreal, Quebec, H3C 3J7 Canada, (Dial from U.S. (514) 343-6880), (Fax from U.S. (514) 343 6882), www.uis.unesco.org; *Statistical Tables.*

BAHRAIN - NATIONAL INCOME

United Nations Statistics Division, New York, NY 10017, (800) 253-9646, Fax: (212) 963-4116, http://unstats.un.org; *Statistical Yearbook.*

BAHRAIN - NATURAL GAS PRODUCTION

See BAHRAIN - MINERAL INDUSTRIES

BAHRAIN - NUTRITION

United Nations Food and Agricultural Organization (FAO), Viale delle Terme di Caracalla, 00100 Rome, Italy, (Dial from U.S. (202) 653-2400), (Fax from U.S. (202) 653 5760), www.fao.org; *The State of Food and Agriculture (SOFA) 2006.*

BAHRAIN - OLDER PEOPLE

M.E. Sharpe, 80 Business Park Drive, Armonk, NY 10504, (800) 541-6563, Fax: (914) 273-2106, www.mesharpe.com; *The Illustrated Book of World Rankings.*

BAHRAIN - PAPER

See BAHRAIN - FORESTS AND FORESTRY

BAHRAIN - PEANUT PRODUCTION

See BAHRAIN - CROPS

BAHRAIN - PESTICIDES

United Nations Food and Agricultural Organization (FAO), Viale delle Terme di Caracalla, 00100 Rome, Italy, (Dial from U.S. (202) 653-2400), (Fax from U.S. (202) 653 5760), www.fao.org; *The State of Food and Agriculture (SOFA) 2006.*

BAHRAIN - PETROLEUM INDUSTRY AND TRADE

International Monetary Fund (IMF), 700 Nineteenth Street, NW, Washington, DC 20431, (202) 623-7000, Fax: (202) 623-4661, www.imf.org; *International Financial Statistics Yearbook 2007.*

M.E. Sharpe, 80 Business Park Drive, Armonk, NY 10504, (800) 541-6563, Fax: (914) 273-2106, www.mesharpe.com; *The Illustrated Book of World Rankings.*

Organisation for Economic Cooperation and Development (OECD), 2 rue Andre Pascal, F-75775 Paris Cedex 16, France, (Telephone in U.S. (202) 785-6323), (Fax in U.S. (202) 785-0350), www.oecd.org; *World Energy Outlook 2007.*

Palgrave Macmillan Ltd., Houndmills, Basingstoke, Hampshire, RG21 6XS, England, (Telephone in U.S. (888) 330-8477), (Fax in U.S. (800) 672-2054), www.palgrave.com; *The Statesman's Yearbook 2008.*

PennWell Corporation, 1421 South Sheridan Road, Tulsa, OK 74112, (918) 835-3161, www.pennwell.com; *International Petroleum Encyclopedia 2007.*

U.S. Department of Energy (DOE), Energy Information Administration (EIA), 1000 Independence Avenue, SW, Washington, DC 20585, (202) 586-8800, www.eia.doe.gov; *International Energy Annual 2004* and *International Energy Outlook 2006.*

United Nations Conference on Trade and Development (UNCTAD), DC2-1120, United Nations, New York, NY 10017, (212) 963-0027, www.unctad.org; *UNCTAD Commodity Yearbook.*

United Nations Food and Agricultural Organization (FAO), Viale delle Terme di Caracalla, 00100 Rome, Italy, (Dial from U.S. (202) 653-2400), (Fax from U.S. (202) 653 5760), www.fao.org; *The State of Food and Agriculture (SOFA) 2006.*

United Nations Statistics Division, New York, NY 10017, (800) 253-9646, Fax: (212) 963-4116, http://unstats.un.org; *Statistical Yearbook.*

BAHRAIN - POLITICAL SCIENCE

Central Intelligence Agency, Office of Public Affairs, Washington, DC 20505, (703) 482-0623, Fax: (703) 482-1739, www.cia.gov; *The World Factbook.*

International Monetary Fund (IMF), 700 Nineteenth Street, NW, Washington, DC 20431, (202) 623-7000, Fax: (202) 623-4661, www.imf.org; *Government Finance Statistics Yearbook (2008 Edition).*

Palgrave Macmillan Ltd., Houndmills, Basingstoke, Hampshire, RG21 6XS, England, (Telephone in U.S. (888) 330-8477), (Fax in U.S. (800) 672-2054), www.palgrave.com; *The Statesman's Yearbook 2008.*

Taylor and Francis Group, An Informa Business, 2 Park Square, Milton Park, Abingdon, Oxford OX14 4RN, United Kingdom, (Dial from U.S. (212) 216-7800), (Fax from U.S. (212) 564-7854), www.tandf.co.uk; *The Europa World Year Book.*

United Nations Economic and Social Commission for Western Asia (ESCWA), PO Box 11-8575, Riad el-Solh Square, Beirut, Lebanon, www.escwa.un.org; *Annual Report 2006* and *Statistical Abstract of the ESCWA Region 2007.*

United Nations Statistics Division, New York, NY 10017, (800) 253-9646, Fax: (212) 963-4116, http://unstats.un.org; *National Accounts Statistics: Compendium of Income Distribution Statistics.*

The World Bank, 1818 H Street, NW, Washington, DC 20433, (202) 473-1000, Fax: (202) 477-6391, www.worldbank.org; *World Development Indicators (WDI) 2008.*

BAHRAIN - POPULATION

Central Intelligence Agency, Office of Public Affairs, Washington, DC 20505, (703) 482-0623, Fax: (703) 482-1739, www.cia.gov; *The World Factbook.*

Economist Intelligence Unit, 111 West 57th Street, New York, NY 10019, (212) 554-0600, Fax: (212) 586-1181, www.eiu.com; *Bahrain Country Report.*

Euromonitor International, Inc., 224 S. Michigan Avenue, Suite 1500, Chicago, IL 60604, (312) 922-1115, Fax: (312) 922-1157, www.euromonitor.com; *International Marketing Data and Statistics 2008* and *The World Economic Factbook 2008.*

International Labour Office, I.L.O. Publications, 4 route des Morillons, CH-1211 Geneva 22, Switzerland, (Telephone in U.S. (202) 653-7652), (Fax in U.S. (202) 653-7687), www.ilo.org; *Yearbook of Labour Statistics 2006.*

M.E. Sharpe, 80 Business Park Drive, Armonk, NY 10504, (800) 541-6563, Fax: (914) 273-2106, www.mesharpe.com; *The Illustrated Book of World Rankings.*

Palgrave Macmillan Ltd., Houndmills, Basingstoke, Hampshire, RG21 6XS, England, (Telephone in U.S. (888) 330-8477), (Fax in U.S. (800) 672-2054), www.palgrave.com; *The Statesman's Yearbook 2008.*

Taylor and Francis Group, An Informa Business, 2 Park Square, Milton Park, Abingdon, Oxford OX14 4RN, United Kingdom, (Dial from U.S. (212) 216-7800), (Fax from U.S. (212) 564-7854), www.tandf.co.uk; *The Europa World Year Book.*

U.S. Department of State (DOS), 2201 C Street NW, Washington, DC 20520, (202) 647-4000, www.state.gov; *World Military Expenditures and Arms Transfers (WMEAT).*

United Nations Economic and Social Commission for Western Asia (ESCWA), PO Box 11-8575, Riad el-Solh Square, Beirut, Lebanon, www.escwa.un.org; *Annual Report 2006* and *Statistical Abstract of the ESCWA Region 2007.*

United Nations Food and Agricultural Organization (FAO), Viale delle Terme di Caracalla, 00100 Rome, Italy, (Dial from U.S. (202) 653-2400), (Fax from U.S. (202) 653 5760), www.fao.org; *FAO Production Yearbook 2002.*

United Nations Statistics Division, New York, NY 10017, (800) 253-9646, Fax: (212) 963-4116, http://unstats.un.org; *Demographic Yearbook; Human Development Report 2006; Statistical Yearbook;* and *World Statistics Pocketbook.*

The World Bank, 1818 H Street, NW, Washington, DC 20433, (202) 473-1000, Fax: (202) 477-6391, www.worldbank.org; *Bahrain* and *The World Bank Atlas 2003-2004.*

World Health Organization (WHO), Avenue Appia 20, 1211 Geneve 27, Switzerland, (Telephone in U.S. (212) 331-9081), www.who.int; *World Health Report 2006.*

BAHRAIN - POPULATION DENSITY

Central Intelligence Agency, Office of Public Affairs, Washington, DC 20505, (703) 482-0623, Fax: (703) 482-1739, www.cia.gov; *The World Factbook.*

Euromonitor International, Inc., 224 S. Michigan Avenue, Suite 1500, Chicago, IL 60604, (312) 922-1115, Fax: (312) 922-1157, www.euromonitor.com; *International Marketing Data and Statistics 2008* and *The World Economic Factbook 2008.*

M.E. Sharpe, 80 Business Park Drive, Armonk, NY 10504, (800) 541-6563, Fax: (914) 273-2106, www.mesharpe.com; *The Illustrated Book of World Rankings.*

Palgrave Macmillan Ltd., Houndmills, Basingstoke, Hampshire, RG21 6XS, England, (Telephone in U.S. (888) 330-8477), (Fax in U.S. (800) 672-2054), www.palgrave.com; *The Statesman's Yearbook 2008.*

Taylor and Francis Group, An Informa Business, 2 Park Square, Milton Park, Abingdon, Oxford OX14 4RN, United Kingdom, (Dial from U.S. (212) 216-7800), (Fax from U.S. (212) 564-7854), www.tandf.co.uk; *The Europa World Year Book.*

United Nations Economic and Social Commission for Western Asia (ESCWA), PO Box 11-8575, Riad el-Solh Square, Beirut, Lebanon, www.escwa.un.org; *Annual Report 2006* and *Statistical Abstract of the ESCWA Region 2007.*

United Nations Food and Agricultural Organization (FAO), Viale delle Terme di Caracalla, 00100 Rome, Italy, (Dial from U.S. (202) 653-2400), (Fax from U.S. (202) 653 5760), www.fao.org; *The State of Food and Agriculture (SOFA) 2006.*

The World Bank, 1818 H Street, NW, Washington, DC 20433, (202) 473-1000, Fax: (202) 477-6391, www.worldbank.org; *Bahrain.*

BAHRAIN - POSTAL SERVICE

M.E. Sharpe, 80 Business Park Drive, Armonk, NY 10504, (800) 541-6563, Fax: (914) 273-2106, www.mesharpe.com; *The Illustrated Book of World Rankings.*

United Nations Statistics Division, New York, NY 10017, (800) 253-9646, Fax: (212) 963-4116, http://unstats.un.org; *Statistical Yearbook.*

BAHRAIN - POWER RESOURCES

Euromonitor International, Inc., 224 S. Michigan Avenue, Suite 1500, Chicago, IL 60604, (312) 922-1115, Fax: (312) 922-1157, www.euromonitor.com; *International Marketing Data and Statistics 2008; The World Economic Factbook 2008;* and *World Marketing Data and Statistics.*

M.E. Sharpe, 80 Business Park Drive, Armonk, NY 10504, (800) 541-6563, Fax: (914) 273-2106, www.mesharpe.com; *The Illustrated Book of World Rankings.*

Organisation for Economic Cooperation and Development (OECD), 2 rue Andre Pascal, F-75775 Paris Cedex 16, France, (Telephone in U.S. (202) 785-6323), (Fax in U.S. (202) 785-0350), www.oecd.org; *World Energy Outlook 2007.*

Palgrave Macmillan Ltd., Houndmills, Basingstoke, Hampshire, RG21 6XS, England, (Telephone in U.S. (888) 330-8477), (Fax in U.S. (800) 672-2054), www.palgrave.com; *The Statesman's Yearbook 2008.*

Platts, 2 Penn Plaza, 25th Floor, New York, NY 10121-2298, (212) 904-3070, www.platts.com; *Energy Economist.*

U.S. Department of Energy (DOE), Energy Information Administration (EIA), 1000 Independence Avenue, SW, Washington, DC 20585, (202) 586-8800, www.eia.doe.gov; *International Energy Annual 2004* and *International Energy Outlook 2006.*

United Nations Economic and Social Commission for Western Asia (ESCWA), PO Box 11-8575, Riad el-Solh Square, Beirut, Lebanon, www.escwa.un.org; *Annual Report 2006* and *Statistical Abstract of the ESCWA Region 2007.*

United Nations Food and Agricultural Organization (FAO), Viale delle Terme di Caracalla, 00100 Rome, Italy, (Dial from U.S. (202) 653-2400), (Fax from U.S. (202) 653 5760), www.fao.org; *The State of Food and Agriculture (SOFA) 2006.*

United Nations Statistics Division, New York, NY 10017, (800) 253-9646, Fax: (212) 963-4116, http://unstats.un.org; *Energy Statistics Yearbook 2003; Human Development Report 2006; Statistical Yearbook;* and *World Statistics Pocketbook.*

The World Bank, 1818 H Street, NW, Washington, DC 20433, (202) 473-1000, Fax: (202) 477-6391, www.worldbank.org; *The World Bank Atlas 2003-2004.*

BAHRAIN - PRICES

Euromonitor International, Inc., 224 S. Michigan Avenue, Suite 1500, Chicago, IL 60604, (312) 922-1115, Fax: (312) 922-1157, www.euromonitor.com; *World Marketing Data and Statistics.*

International Labour Office, I.L.O. Publications, 4 route des Morillons, CH-1211 Geneva 22, Switzerland, (Telephone in U.S. (202) 653-7652), (Fax in U.S. (202) 653-7687), www.ilo.org; *Yearbook of Labour Statistics 2006.*

International Monetary Fund (IMF), 700 Nineteenth Street, NW, Washington, DC 20431, (202) 623-7000, Fax: (202) 623-4661, www.imf.org; *International Financial Statistics Yearbook 2007.*

M.E. Sharpe, 80 Business Park Drive, Armonk, NY 10504, (800) 541-6563, Fax: (914) 273-2106, www.mesharpe.com; *The Illustrated Book of World Rankings.*

United Nations Food and Agricultural Organization (FAO), Viale delle Terme di Caracalla, 00100 Rome, Italy, (Dial from U.S. (202) 653-2400), (Fax from U.S. (202) 653 5760), www.fao.org; *FAO Production Yearbook 2002* and *The State of Food and Agriculture (SOFA) 2006.*

The World Bank, 1818 H Street, NW, Washington, DC 20433, (202) 473-1000, Fax: (202) 477-6391, www.worldbank.org; *Bahrain.*

BAHRAIN - PROFESSIONS

UNESCO Institute for Statistics, C.P. 6128 Succursale Centre-Ville, Montreal, Quebec, H3C 3J7 Canada, (Dial from U.S. (514) 343-6880), (Fax from U.S. (514) 343 6882), www.uis.unesco.org; *Statistical Tables.*

BAHRAIN - PUBLIC HEALTH

Euromonitor International, Inc., 224 S. Michigan Avenue, Suite 1500, Chicago, IL 60604, (312) 922-1115, Fax: (312) 922-1157, www.euromonitor.com; *World Marketing Data and Statistics.*

International Monetary Fund (IMF), 700 Nineteenth Street, NW, Washington, DC 20431, (202) 623-7000, Fax: (202) 623-4661, www.imf.org; *Government Finance Statistics Yearbook (2008 Edition).*

M.E. Sharpe, 80 Business Park Drive, Armonk, NY 10504, (800) 541-6563, Fax: (914) 273-2106, www.mesharpe.com; *The Illustrated Book of World Rankings.*

Palgrave Macmillan Ltd., Houndmills, Basingstoke, Hampshire, RG21 6XS, England, (Telephone in U.S. (888) 330-8477), (Fax in U.S. (800) 672-2054), www.palgrave.com; *The Statesman's Yearbook 2008.*

United Nations Economic and Social Commission for Western Asia (ESCWA), PO Box 11-8575, Riad el-Solh Square, Beirut, Lebanon, www.escwa.un.org; *Annual Report 2006* and *Statistical Abstract of the ESCWA Region 2007.*

United Nations Statistics Division, New York, NY 10017, (800) 253-9646, Fax: (212) 963-4116, http://unstats.un.org; *Human Development Report 2006* and *Statistical Yearbook.*

The World Bank, 1818 H Street, NW, Washington, DC 20433, (202) 473-1000, Fax: (202) 477-6391, www.worldbank.org; *Bahrain.*

World Health Organization (WHO), Avenue Appia 20, 1211 Geneve 27, Switzerland, (Telephone in U.S. (212) 331-9081), www.who.int; The WHO Global Atlas of Infectious Diseases and *World Health Report 2006.*

BAHRAIN - PUBLISHERS AND PUBLISHING

Taylor and Francis Group, An Informa Business, 2 Park Square, Milton Park, Abingdon, Oxford OX14 4RN, United Kingdom, (Dial from U.S. (212) 216-7800), (Fax from U.S. (212) 564-7854), www.tandf.co.uk; *The Europa World Year Book.*

BAHRAIN - RADIO BROADCASTING

Palgrave Macmillan Ltd., Houndmills, Basingstoke, Hampshire, RG21 6XS, England, (Telephone in U.S. (888) 330-8477), (Fax in U.S. (800) 672-2054), www.palgrave.com; *The Statesman's Yearbook 2008.*

BAHRAIN - RAILROADS

Taylor and Francis Group, An Informa Business, 2 Park Square, Milton Park, Abingdon, Oxford OX14 4RN, United Kingdom, (Dial from U.S. (212) 216-7800), (Fax from U.S. (212) 564-7854), www.tandf.co.uk; *The Europa World Year Book.*

BAHRAIN - RELIGION

Central Intelligence Agency, Office of Public Affairs, Washington, DC 20505, (703) 482-0623, Fax: (703) 482-1739, www.cia.gov; *The World Factbook.*

M.E. Sharpe, 80 Business Park Drive, Armonk, NY 10504, (800) 541-6563, Fax: (914) 273-2106, www.mesharpe.com; *The Illustrated Book of World Rankings.*

BAHRAIN - RENT CHARGES

International Labour Office, I.L.O. Publications, 4 route des Morillons, CH-1211 Geneva 22, Switzerland, (Telephone in U.S. (202) 653-7652), (Fax in U.S. (202) 653-7687), www.ilo.org; *Yearbook of Labour Statistics 2006.*

BAHRAIN - RESERVES (ACCOUNTING)

Euromonitor International, Inc., 224 S. Michigan Avenue, Suite 1500, Chicago, IL 60604, (312) 922-1115, Fax: (312) 922-1157, www.euromonitor.com; *International Marketing Data and Statistics 2008.*

The World Bank, 1818 H Street, NW, Washington, DC 20433, (202) 473-1000, Fax: (202) 477-6391, www.worldbank.org; *World Development Indicators (WDI) 2008.*

BAHRAIN - RETAIL TRADE

Euromonitor International, Inc., 224 S. Michigan Avenue, Suite 1500, Chicago, IL 60604, (312) 922-1115, Fax: (312) 922-1157, www.euromonitor.com; *World Marketing Data and Statistics.*

BAHRAIN - RICE PRODUCTION

See BAHRAIN - CROPS

BAHRAIN - ROADS

Central Intelligence Agency, Office of Public Affairs, Washington, DC 20505, (703) 482-0623, Fax: (703) 482-1739, www.cia.gov; *The World Factbook.*

Palgrave Macmillan Ltd., Houndmills, Basingstoke, Hampshire, RG21 6XS, England, (Telephone in U.S. (888) 330-8477), (Fax in U.S. (800) 672-2054), www.palgrave.com; *The Statesman's Yearbook 2008.*

BAHRAIN - RUBBER INDUSTRY AND TRADE

International Rubber Study Group (IRSG), 1st Floor, Heron House, 109/115 Wembley Hill Road, Wembley, Middlesex HA9 8DA, United Kingdom, www.rubberstudy.com; *Rubber Statistical Bulletin; Summary of World Rubber Statistics 2005; World Rubber Statistics Handbook (Volume 6, 1975-2001);* and *World Rubber Statistics Historic Handbook.*

M.E. Sharpe, 80 Business Park Drive, Armonk, NY 10504, (800) 541-6563, Fax: (914) 273-2106, www.mesharpe.com; *The Illustrated Book of World Rankings.*

BAHRAIN - SHEEP

See BAHRAIN - LIVESTOCK

BAHRAIN - SHIPPING

Palgrave Macmillan Ltd., Houndmills, Basingstoke, Hampshire, RG21 6XS, England, (Telephone in U.S. (888) 330-8477), (Fax in U.S. (800) 672-2054), www.palgrave.com; *The Statesman's Yearbook 2008.*

Taylor and Francis Group, An Informa Business, 2 Park Square, Milton Park, Abingdon, Oxford OX14 4RN, United Kingdom, (Dial from U.S. (212) 216-7800), (Fax from U.S. (212) 564-7854), www.tandf.co.uk; *The Europa World Year Book.*

United Nations Statistics Division, New York, NY 10017, (800) 253-9646, Fax: (212) 963-4116, http://unstats.un.org; *Statistical Yearbook.*

BAHRAIN - SILVER PRODUCTION

See BAHRAIN - MINERAL INDUSTRIES

BAHRAIN - SOCIAL ECOLOGY

M.E. Sharpe, 80 Business Park Drive, Armonk, NY 10504, (800) 541-6563, Fax: (914) 273-2106, www.mesharpe.com; *The Illustrated Book of World Rankings.*

United Nations Statistics Division, New York, NY 10017, (800) 253-9646, Fax: (212) 963-4116, http://unstats.un.org; *World Statistics Pocketbook.*

BAHRAIN - SOCIAL SECURITY

International Monetary Fund (IMF), 700 Nineteenth Street, NW, Washington, DC 20431, (202) 623-7000, Fax: (202) 623-4661, www.imf.org; *Government Finance Statistics Yearbook (2008 Edition).*

Palgrave Macmillan Ltd., Houndmills, Basingstoke, Hampshire, RG21 6XS, England, (Telephone in U.S. (888) 330-8477), (Fax in U.S. (800) 672-2054), www.palgrave.com; *The Statesman's Yearbook 2008.*

United Nations Statistics Division, New York, NY 10017, (800) 253-9646, Fax: (212) 963-4116, http://unstats.un.org; *National Accounts Statistics: Compendium of Income Distribution Statistics.*

BAHRAIN - STEEL PRODUCTION

See BAHRAIN - MINERAL INDUSTRIES

BAHRAIN - SUGAR PRODUCTION

See BAHRAIN - CROPS

BAHRAIN - TAXATION

International Monetary Fund (IMF), 700 Nineteenth Street, NW, Washington, DC 20431, (202) 623-7000, Fax: (202) 623-4661, www.imf.org; *Government Finance Statistics Yearbook (2008 Edition).*

Taylor and Francis Group, An Informa Business, 2 Park Square, Milton Park, Abingdon, Oxford OX14 4RN, United Kingdom, (Dial from U.S. (212) 216-7800), (Fax from U.S. (212) 564-7854), www.tandf.co.uk; *The Europa World Year Book.*

The World Bank, 1818 H Street, NW, Washington, DC 20433, (202) 473-1000, Fax: (202) 477-6391, www.worldbank.org; *World Development Indicators (WDI) 2008.*

BAHRAIN - TELEPHONE

International Telecommunication Union (ITU), Place des Nations, 1211 Geneva 20, Switzerland, www.itu.int; World Telecommunication Indicators Database.

Palgrave Macmillan Ltd., Houndmills, Basingstoke, Hampshire, RG21 6XS, England, (Telephone in U.S. (888) 330-8477), (Fax in U.S. (800) 672-2054), www.palgrave.com; *The Statesman's Yearbook 2008.*

Taylor and Francis Group, An Informa Business, 2 Park Square, Milton Park, Abingdon, Oxford OX14 4RN, United Kingdom, (Dial from U.S. (212) 216-7800), (Fax from U.S. (212) 564-7854), www.tandf.co.uk; *The Europa World Year Book.*

United Nations Statistics Division, New York, NY 10017, (800) 253-9646, Fax: (212) 963-4116, http://unstats.un.org; *Statistical Yearbook* and *World Statistics Pocketbook.*

BAHRAIN - TELEVISION BROADCASTING

M.E. Sharpe, 80 Business Park Drive, Armonk, NY 10504, (800) 541-6563, Fax: (914) 273-2106, www.mesharpe.com; *The Illustrated Book of World Rankings.*

UNESCO Institute for Statistics, C.P. 6128 Succursale Centre-Ville, Montreal, Quebec, H3C 3J7 Canada, (Dial from U.S. (514) 343-6880), (Fax from U.S. (514) 343 6882), www.uis.unesco.org; *Statistical Tables.*

BAHRAIN - TEXTILE INDUSTRY

M.E. Sharpe, 80 Business Park Drive, Armonk, NY 10504, (800) 541-6563, Fax: (914) 273-2106, www.mesharpe.com; *The Illustrated Book of World Rankings.*

Palgrave Macmillan Ltd., Houndmills, Basingstoke, Hampshire, RG21 6XS, England, (Telephone in U.S. (888) 330-8477), (Fax in U.S. (800) 672-2054), www.palgrave.com; *The Statesman's Yearbook 2008.*

United Nations Conference on Trade and Development (UNCTAD), DC2-1120, United Nations, New York, NY 10017, (212) 963-0027, www.unctad.org; *UNCTAD Commodity Yearbook.*

BAHRAIN - TOBACCO INDUSTRY

Foreign Agricultural Service (FAS), U.S. Department of Agriculture (USDA), 1400 Independence Avenue, SW, Washington, DC 20250, (202) 720-3935, www.fas.usda.gov; *Tobacco: World Markets and Trade.*

M.E. Sharpe, 80 Business Park Drive, Armonk, NY 10504, (800) 541-6563, Fax: (914) 273-2106, www.mesharpe.com; *The Illustrated Book of World Rankings.*

BAHRAIN - TOURISM

Euromonitor International, Inc., 224 S. Michigan Avenue, Suite 1500, Chicago, IL 60604, (312) 922-1115, Fax: (312) 922-1157, www.euromonitor.com; *The World Economic Factbook 2008* and *World Marketing Data and Statistics.*

M.E. Sharpe, 80 Business Park Drive, Armonk, NY 10504, (800) 541-6563, Fax: (914) 273-2106, www.mesharpe.com; *The Illustrated Book of World Rankings.*

Palgrave Macmillan Ltd., Houndmills, Basingstoke, Hampshire, RG21 6XS, England, (Telephone in U.S. (888) 330-8477), (Fax in U.S. (800) 672-2054), www.palgrave.com; *The Statesman's Yearbook 2008.*

Taylor and Francis Group, An Informa Business, 2 Park Square, Milton Park, Abingdon, Oxford OX14 4RN, United Kingdom, (Dial from U.S. (212) 216-7800), (Fax from U.S. (212) 564-7854), www.tandf.co.uk; *The Europa World Year Book.*

United Nations Economic and Social Commission for Western Asia (ESCWA), PO Box 11-8575, Riad el-Solh Square, Beirut, Lebanon, www.escwa.un.org; *Annual Report 2006* and *Statistical Abstract of the ESCWA Region 2007.*

The World Bank, 1818 H Street, NW, Washington, DC 20433, (202) 473-1000, Fax: (202) 477-6391, www.worldbank.org; *Bahrain.*

BAHRAIN - TRADE

See BAHRAIN - INTERNATIONAL TRADE

BAHRAIN - TRANSPORTATION

Central Intelligence Agency, Office of Public Affairs, Washington, DC 20505, (703) 482-0623, Fax: (703) 482-1739, www.cia.gov; *The World Factbook.*

Euromonitor International, Inc., 224 S. Michigan Avenue, Suite 1500, Chicago, IL 60604, (312) 922-1115, Fax: (312) 922-1157, www.euromonitor.com; *International Marketing Data and Statistics 2008* and *World Marketing Data and Statistics.*

M.E. Sharpe, 80 Business Park Drive, Armonk, NY 10504, (800) 541-6563, Fax: (914) 273-2106, www.mesharpe.com; *The Illustrated Book of World Rankings.*

Palgrave Macmillan Ltd., Houndmills, Basingstoke, Hampshire, RG21 6XS, England, (Telephone in U.S. (888) 330-8477), (Fax in U.S. (800) 672-2054), www.palgrave.com; *The Statesman's Yearbook 2008.*

Taylor and Francis Group, An Informa Business, 2 Park Square, Milton Park, Abingdon, Oxford OX14 4RN, United Kingdom, (Dial from U.S. (212) 216-7800), (Fax from U.S. (212) 564-7854), www.tandf.co.uk; *The Europa World Year Book.*

United Nations Economic and Social Commission for Western Asia (ESCWA), PO Box 11-8575, Riad el-Solh Square, Beirut, Lebanon, www.escwa.un.org; *Annual Report 2006* and *Statistical Abstract of the ESCWA Region 2007.*

United Nations Statistics Division, New York, NY 10017, (800) 253-9646, Fax: (212) 963-4116, http://unstats.un.org; *Human Development Report 2006.*

The World Bank, 1818 H Street, NW, Washington, DC 20433, (202) 473-1000, Fax: (202) 477-6391, www.worldbank.org; *Bahrain.*

BAHRAIN - UNEMPLOYMENT

Central Intelligence Agency, Office of Public Affairs, Washington, DC 20505, (703) 482-0623, Fax: (703) 482-1739, www.cia.gov; *The World Factbook.*

Euromonitor International, Inc., 224 S. Michigan Avenue, Suite 1500, Chicago, IL 60604, (312) 922-1115, Fax: (312) 922-1157, www.euromonitor.com; *International Marketing Data and Statistics 2008.*

International Labour Office, I.L.O. Publications, 4 route des Morillons, CH-1211 Geneva 22, Switzerland, (Telephone in U.S. (202) 653-7652), (Fax in U.S. (202) 653-7687), www.ilo.org; *Yearbook of Labour Statistics 2006.*

Palgrave Macmillan Ltd., Houndmills, Basingstoke, Hampshire, RG21 6XS, England, (Telephone in U.S. (888) 330-8477), (Fax in U.S. (800) 672-2054), www.palgrave.com; *The Statesman's Yearbook 2008.*

BAHRAIN - VITAL STATISTICS

Euromonitor International, Inc., 224 S. Michigan Avenue, Suite 1500, Chicago, IL 60604, (312) 922-1115, Fax: (312) 922-1157, www.euromonitor.com; *International Marketing Data and Statistics 2008.*

Palgrave Macmillan Ltd., Houndmills, Basingstoke, Hampshire, RG21 6XS, England, (Telephone in U.S. (888) 330-8477), (Fax in U.S. (800) 672-2054), www.palgrave.com; *The Statesman's Yearbook 2008.*

United Nations Economic and Social Commission for Western Asia (ESCWA), PO Box 11-8575, Riad el-Solh Square, Beirut, Lebanon, www.escwa.un.org; *Annual Report 2006; Bulletin on Population and Vital Statistics in the ESCWA Region;* and *Survey of Economic and Social Developments in the ESCWA Region 2006-2007.*

World Health Organization (WHO), Avenue Appia 20, 1211 Geneve 27, Switzerland, (Telephone in U.S. (212) 331-9081), www.who.int; *World Health Report 2006.*

BAHRAIN - WAGES

International Labour Office, I.L.O. Publications, 4 route des Morillons, CH-1211 Geneva 22, Switzerland, (Telephone in U.S. (202) 653-7652), (Fax in U.S. (202) 653-7687), www.ilo.org; *Yearbook of Labour Statistics 2006.*

The World Bank, 1818 H Street, NW, Washington, DC 20433, (202) 473-1000, Fax: (202) 477-6391, www.worldbank.org; *Bahrain.*

BAHRAIN - WEATHER

See BAHRAIN - CLIMATE

BAHRAIN - WELFARE STATE

International Monetary Fund (IMF), 700 Nineteenth Street, NW, Washington, DC 20431, (202) 623-7000, Fax: (202) 623-4661, www.imf.org; *Government Finance Statistics Yearbook (2008 Edition).*

Palgrave Macmillan Ltd., Houndmills, Basingstoke, Hampshire, RG21 6XS, England, (Telephone in U.S. (888) 330-8477), (Fax in U.S. (800) 672-2054), www.palgrave.com; *The Statesman's Yearbook 2008.*

BAHRAIN - WHEAT PRODUCTION

See BAHRAIN - CROPS

BAHRAIN - WINE PRODUCTION

See BAHRAIN - BEVERAGE INDUSTRY

BAHRAIN - WOOL PRODUCTION

See BAHRAIN - TEXTILE INDUSTRY

BAKERY PRODUCTS

Progressive Grocer, 770 Broadway, New York, NY 10003, (866) 890-8541, www.progressivegrocer.com; *Progressive Grocer 2006 Bakery Study.*

U.S. Bureau of Labor Statistics (BLS), Postal Square Building, 2 Massachusetts Avenue, NE, Washington, DC 20212-0001, (202) 691-5200, Fax: (202) 691-6325, www.bls.gov; *Consumer Price Index Detailed Report* and *Monthly Labor Review (MLR).*

BALANCE SHEET

Board of Governors of the Federal Reserve System, Constitution Avenue, NW, Washington, DC 20551, (202) 452-3000, www.federalreserve.gov; *Federal Reserve Board Statistical Release* and *Flow of Funds Accounts of the United States.*

U.S. Department of the Treasury (DOT), 1500 Pennsylvania Avenue, NW, Washington, DC 20220, (202) 622-2000, Fax: (202) 622-6415, www.ustreas.gov; *FY 2007 Performance and Accountability Report.*

U.S. Department of the Treasury (DOT), Internal Revenue Service (IRS), Statistics of Income Division (SIS), PO Box 2608, Washington, DC, 20013-2608, (202) 874-0410, Fax: (202) 874-0964, www.irs.ustreas.gov; *Statistics of Income Bulletin, Corporation Income Tax Returns.*

BALLET

National Endowment for the Arts (NEA), 1100 Pennsylvania Avenue, NW, Washington, DC 20506-0001, (202) 682-5400, www.arts.gov; *2007 Annual Report.*

BANANAS

Economic Research Service (ERS), U.S. Department of Agriculture (USDA), 1800 M Street, NW, Washington, DC 20036-5831, (202) 694-5050, Fax: (202) 694-5689, www.ers.usda.gov; *Agricultural Outlook; Food CPI, Prices, and Expenditures; Foreign Agricultural Trade of the United States (FATUS);* and *U.S. Agricultural Trade Update: 2006.*

U.S. Bureau of Labor Statistics (BLS), Postal Square Building, 2 Massachusetts Avenue, NE, Washington, DC 20212-0001, (202) 691-5200, Fax: (202) 691-6325, www.bls.gov; *Consumer Price Index Detailed Report* and *Monthly Labor Review (MLR).*

BANGLADESH - NATIONAL STATISTICAL OFFICE

Bangladesh Bureau of Statistics (BBS), Ministry of Planning, Statistics Wing, E-27/A, Agargaon, Sher-e-banglanagar, Dhaka-1207, Bangladesh, www.bbs.gov.bd; National Data Center.

BANGLADESH - PRIMARY STATISTICS SOURCES

Bangladesh Bureau of Statistics (BBS), Ministry of Planning, Statistics Wing, E-27/A, Agargaon, Sher-e-banglanagar, Dhaka-1207, Bangladesh, www.bbs.gov.bd; *Statistical Pocketbook Bangladesh - 2006* and *Statistical Yearbook of Bangladesh 2006.*

BANGLADESH - DATABASES

Bangladesh Bureau of Statistics (BBS), Ministry of Planning, Statistics Wing, E-27/A, Agargaon, Sher-e-banglanagar, Dhaka-1207, Bangladesh, www.bbs.gov.bd; Database. Subjects covered include essential macro, micro and local level data for all socio-economic sectors required for short and long term planning, policy formulation and implementation of development activities..

BANGLADESH - AGRICULTURE

Asian Development Bank (ADB), PO Box 789, 0980 Manila, Philippines, www.adb.org; *Key Indicators of Developing Asian and Pacific Countries 2006.*

Bangladesh Bureau of Statistics (BBS), Ministry of Planning, Statistics Wing, E-27/A, Agargaon, Sher-e-banglanagar, Dhaka-1207, Bangladesh, www.bbs.gov.bd; *Census at a Glance.*

Economist Intelligence Unit, 111 West 57th Street, New York, NY 10019, (212) 554-0600, Fax: (212) 586-1181, www.eiu.com; *Bangladesh Country Report.*

Euromonitor International, Inc., 224 S. Michigan Avenue, Suite 1500, Chicago, IL 60604, (312) 922-1115, Fax: (312) 922-1157, www.euromonitor.com; *International Marketing Data and Statistics 2008* and *World Marketing Data and Statistics.*

M.E. Sharpe, 80 Business Park Drive, Armonk, NY 10504, (800) 541-6563, Fax: (914) 273-2106, www.mesharpe.com; *The Illustrated Book of World Rankings.*

Palgrave Macmillan Ltd., Houndmills, Basingstoke, Hampshire, RG21 6XS, England, (Telephone in U.S. (888) 330-8477), (Fax in U.S. (800) 672-2054), www.palgrave.com; *The Statesman's Yearbook 2008.*

Taylor and Francis Group, An Informa Business, 2 Park Square, Milton Park, Abingdon, Oxford OX14 4RN, United Kingdom, (Dial from U.S. (212) 216-7800), (Fax from U.S. (212) 564-7854), www.tandf.co.uk; *The Europa World Year Book.*

United Nations Conference on Trade and Development (UNCTAD), DC2-1120, United Nations, New York, NY 10017, (212) 963-0027, www.unctad.org; *UNCTAD Commodity Yearbook.*

United Nations Food and Agricultural Organization (FAO), Viale delle Terme di Caracalla, 00100 Rome, Italy, (Dial from U.S. (202) 653-2400), (Fax from U.S. (202) 653 5760), www.fao.org; AQUASTAT; *FAO Production Yearbook 2002; FAO Trade Yearbook;* and *The State of Food and Agriculture (SOFA) 2006.*

United Nations Statistics Division, New York, NY 10017, (800) 253-9646, Fax: (212) 963-4116, http://unstats.un.org; *Asia-Pacific in Figures 2004; Statistical Yearbook;* and *Statistical Yearbook for Asia and the Pacific 2004.*

The World Bank, 1818 H Street, NW, Washington, DC 20433, (202) 473-1000, Fax: (202) 477-6391, www.worldbank.org; *Bangladesh* and *World Development Indicators (WDI) 2008.*

BANGLADESH - AIRLINES

Economist Intelligence Unit, 111 West 57th Street, New York, NY 10019, (212) 554-0600, Fax: (212) 586-1181, www.eiu.com; *Business Asia.*

International Civil Aviation Organization (ICAO), External Relations and Public Information Office (EPO), 999 University Street, Montreal, Quebec H3C 5H7, Canada, (Dial from U.S. (514) 954-8219), (Fax from U.S. (514) 954-6077), www.icao.int; *Civil Aviation Statistics of the World.*

M.E. Sharpe, 80 Business Park Drive, Armonk, NY 10504, (800) 541-6563, Fax: (914) 273-2106, www.mesharpe.com; *The Illustrated Book of World Rankings.*

Palgrave Macmillan Ltd., Houndmills, Basingstoke, Hampshire, RG21 6XS, England, (Telephone in U.S. (888) 330-8477), (Fax in U.S. (800) 672-2054), www.palgrave.com; *The Statesman's Yearbook 2008.*

BANGLADESH - AIRPORTS

Central Intelligence Agency, Office of Public Affairs, Washington, DC 20505, (703) 482-0623, Fax: (703) 482-1739, www.cia.gov; *The World Factbook.*

BANGLADESH - ALUMINUM PRODUCTION

See BANGLADESH - MINERAL INDUSTRIES

BANGLADESH - ARMED FORCES

Central Intelligence Agency, Office of Public Affairs, Washington, DC 20505, (703) 482-0623, Fax: (703) 482-1739, www.cia.gov; *The World Factbook.*

Economist Intelligence Unit, 111 West 57th Street, New York, NY 10019, (212) 554-0600, Fax: (212) 586-1181, www.eiu.com; *Business Asia.*

Euromonitor International, Inc., 224 S. Michigan Avenue, Suite 1500, Chicago, IL 60604, (312) 922-1115, Fax: (312) 922-1157, www.euromonitor.com; *World Marketing Data and Statistics.*

International Institute for Strategic Studies (IISS), Arundel House, 13-15 Arundel Street, Temple Place, London WC2R 3DX, England, www.iiss.org; *The Military Balance 2007.*

International Monetary Fund (IMF), 700 Nineteenth Street, NW, Washington, DC 20431, (202) 623-7000, Fax: (202) 623-4661, www.imf.org; *Government Finance Statistics Yearbook (2008 Edition).*

Palgrave Macmillan Ltd., Houndmills, Basingstoke, Hampshire, RG21 6XS, England, (Telephone in U.S. (888) 330-8477), (Fax in U.S. (800) 672-2054), www.palgrave.com; *The Statesman's Yearbook 2008.*

U.S. Department of State (DOS), 2201 C Street NW, Washington, DC 20520, (202) 647-4000, www.state.gov; *World Military Expenditures and Arms Transfers (WMEAT).*

United Nations Statistics Division, New York, NY 10017, (800) 253-9646, Fax: (212) 963-4116, http://unstats.un.org; *Human Development Report 2006.*

BANGLADESH - BALANCE OF PAYMENTS

Taylor and Francis Group, An Informa Business, 2 Park Square, Milton Park, Abingdon, Oxford OX14 4RN, United Kingdom, (Dial from U.S. (212) 216-7800), (Fax from U.S. (212) 564-7854), www.tandf.co.uk; *The Europa World Year Book.*

United Nations Conference on Trade and Development (UNCTAD), DC2-1120, United Nations, New York, NY 10017, (212) 963-0027, www.unctad.org; *Handbook of Statistics 2005.*

The World Bank, 1818 H Street, NW, Washington, DC 20433, (202) 473-1000, Fax: (202) 477-6391, www.worldbank.org; *Bangladesh; World Development Indicators (WDI) 2008;* and *World Development Report 2008.*

BANGLADESH - BANKS AND BANKING

Asian Development Bank (ADB), PO Box 789, 0980 Manila, Philippines, www.adb.org; *Key Indicators of Developing Asian and Pacific Countries 2006.*

Bangladesh Bureau of Statistics (BBS), Ministry of Planning, Statistics Wing, E-27/A, Agargaon, Sher-e-banglanagar, Dhaka-1207, Bangladesh, www.bbs.gov.bd; *Census at a Glance.*

Euromonitor International, Inc., 224 S. Michigan Avenue, Suite 1500, Chicago, IL 60604, (312) 922-1115, Fax: (312) 922-1157, www.euromonitor.com; *World Marketing Data and Statistics.*

International Monetary Fund (IMF), 700 Nineteenth Street, NW, Washington, DC 20431, (202) 623-7000, Fax: (202) 623-4661, www.imf.org; *Government Finance Statistics Yearbook (2008 Edition)* and *International Financial Statistics Yearbook 2007.*

M.E. Sharpe, 80 Business Park Drive, Armonk, NY 10504, (800) 541-6563, Fax: (914) 273-2106, www.mesharpe.com; *The Illustrated Book of World Rankings.*

Palgrave Macmillan Ltd., Houndmills, Basingstoke, Hampshire, RG21 6XS, England, (Telephone in U.S. (888) 330-8477), (Fax in U.S. (800) 672-2054), www.palgrave.com; *The Statesman's Yearbook 2008.*

Taylor and Francis Group, An Informa Business, 2 Park Square, Milton Park, Abingdon, Oxford OX14 4RN, United Kingdom, (Dial from U.S. (212) 216-7800), (Fax from U.S. (212) 564-7854), www.tandf.co.uk; *The Europa World Year Book.*

BANGLADESH - BARLEY PRODUCTION

See BANGLADESH - CROPS

BANGLADESH - BEVERAGE INDUSTRY

M.E. Sharpe, 80 Business Park Drive, Armonk, NY 10504, (800) 541-6563, Fax: (914) 273-2106, www.mesharpe.com; *The Illustrated Book of World Rankings.*

United Nations Statistics Division, New York, NY 10017, (800) 253-9646, Fax: (212) 963-4116, http://unstats.un.org; *Statistical Yearbook.*

BANGLADESH - BONDS

Asian Development Bank (ADB), PO Box 789, 0980 Manila, Philippines, www.adb.org; *Key Indicators of Developing Asian and Pacific Countries 2006.*

International Monetary Fund (IMF), 700 Nineteenth Street, NW, Washington, DC 20431, (202) 623-7000, Fax: (202) 623-4661, www.imf.org; *Government Finance Statistics Yearbook (2008 Edition).*

BANGLADESH - BROADCASTING

Central Intelligence Agency, Office of Public Affairs, Washington, DC 20505, (703) 482-0623, Fax: (703) 482-1739, www.cia.gov; *The World Factbook.*

Economist Intelligence Unit, 111 West 57th Street, New York, NY 10019, (212) 554-0600, Fax: (212) 586-1181, www.eiu.com; *Business Asia.*

Euromonitor International, Inc., 224 S. Michigan Avenue, Suite 1500, Chicago, IL 60604, (312) 922-1115, Fax: (312) 922-1157, www.euromonitor.com; *World Marketing Data and Statistics.*

M.E. Sharpe, 80 Business Park Drive, Armonk, NY 10504, (800) 541-6563, Fax: (914) 273-2106, www.mesharpe.com; *The Illustrated Book of World Rankings.*

Palgrave Macmillan Ltd., Houndmills, Basingstoke, Hampshire, RG21 6XS, England, (Telephone in U.S. (888) 330-8477), (Fax in U.S. (800) 672-2054), www.palgrave.com; *The Statesman's Yearbook 2008.*

UNESCO Institute for Statistics, C.P. 6128 Succursale Centre-Ville, Montreal, Quebec, H3C 3J7 Canada, (Dial from U.S. (514) 343-6880), (Fax from U.S. (514) 343 6882), www.uis.unesco.org; *Statistical Tables.*

WRTH Publications Limited, PO Box 290, Oxford OX2 7FT, UK, www.wrth.com; *World Radio TV Handbook 2007.*

BANGLADESH - BUDGET

Central Intelligence Agency, Office of Public Affairs, Washington, DC 20505, (703) 482-0623, Fax: (703) 482-1739, www.cia.gov; *The World Factbook.*

BANGLADESH - BUSINESS

United Nations Statistics Division, New York, NY 10017, (800) 253-9646, Fax: (212) 963-4116, http://unstats.un.org; *Statistical Yearbook for Asia and the Pacific 2004.*

BANGLADESH - CAPITAL INVESTMENTS

Asian Development Bank (ADB), PO Box 789, 0980 Manila, Philippines, www.adb.org; *Key Indicators of Developing Asian and Pacific Countries 2006.*

BANGLADESH - CAPITAL LEVY

Asian Development Bank (ADB), PO Box 789, 0980 Manila, Philippines, www.adb.org; *Key Indicators of Developing Asian and Pacific Countries 2006.*

International Monetary Fund (IMF), 700 Nineteenth Street, NW, Washington, DC 20431, (202) 623-7000, Fax: (202) 623-4661, www.imf.org; *Government Finance Statistics Yearbook (2008 Edition).*

BANGLADESH - CATTLE

See BANGLADESH - LIVESTOCK

BANGLADESH - CHICK PEA PRODUCTION

See BANGLADESH - CROPS

BANGLADESH - CHILDBIRTH - STATISTICS

Central Intelligence Agency, Office of Public Affairs, Washington, DC 20505, (703) 482-0623, Fax: (703) 482-1739, www.cia.gov; *The World Factbook.*

Economist Intelligence Unit, 111 West 57th Street, New York, NY 10019, (212) 554-0600, Fax: (212) 586-1181, www.eiu.com; *Business Asia.*

Euromonitor International, Inc., 224 S. Michigan Avenue, Suite 1500, Chicago, IL 60604, (312) 922-1115, Fax: (312) 922-1157, www.euromonitor.com; *International Marketing Data and Statistics 2008* and *The World Economic Factbook 2008.*

M.E. Sharpe, 80 Business Park Drive, Armonk, NY 10504, (800) 541-6563, Fax: (914) 273-2106, www.mesharpe.com; *The Illustrated Book of World Rankings.*

Palgrave Macmillan Ltd., Houndmills, Basingstoke, Hampshire, RG21 6XS, England, (Telephone in U.S. (888) 330-8477), (Fax in U.S. (800) 672-2054), www.palgrave.com; *The Statesman's Yearbook 2008.*

Taylor and Francis Group, An Informa Business, 2 Park Square, Milton Park, Abingdon, Oxford OX14 4RN, United Kingdom, (Dial from U.S. (212) 216-7800), (Fax from U.S. (212) 564-7854), www.tandf.co.uk; *The Europa World Year Book.*

United Nations Statistics Division, New York, NY 10017, (800) 253-9646, Fax: (212) 963-4116, http://unstats.un.org; *Asia-Pacific in Figures 2004; Demographic Yearbook;* and *Statistical Yearbook.*

The World Bank, 1818 H Street, NW, Washington, DC 20433, (202) 473-1000, Fax: (202) 477-6391, www.worldbank.org; *World Development Indicators (WDI) 2008.*

BANGLADESH - CLIMATE

International Institute for Environment and Development (IIED), 3 Endsleigh Street, London, England, WC1H 0DD, United Kingdom, www.iied.org; *Environment Urbanization.*

M.E. Sharpe, 80 Business Park Drive, Armonk, NY 10504, (800) 541-6563, Fax: (914) 273-2106, www.mesharpe.com; *The Illustrated Book of World Rankings.*

Palgrave Macmillan Ltd., Houndmills, Basingstoke, Hampshire, RG21 6XS, England, (Telephone in U.S. (888) 330-8477), (Fax in U.S. (800) 672-2054), www.palgrave.com; *The Statesman's Yearbook 2008.*

BANGLADESH - COAL PRODUCTION

See BANGLADESH - MINERAL INDUSTRIES

BANGLADESH - COFFEE

See BANGLADESH - CROPS

BANGLADESH - COMMERCE

Palgrave Macmillan Ltd., Houndmills, Basingstoke, Hampshire, RG21 6XS, England, (Telephone in U.S. (888) 330-8477), (Fax in U.S. (800) 672-2054), www.palgrave.com; *The Statesman's Yearbook 2008.*

BANGLADESH - COMMODITY EXCHANGES

Commodity Research Bureau, 330 South Wells Street, Suite 612, Chicago, IL 60606-7110, (800) 621-5271, Fax: (312) 939-4135, www.crbtrader.com; *2006 CRB Commodity Yearbook and CD.*

International Monetary Fund (IMF), 700 Nineteenth Street, NW, Washington, DC 20431, (202) 623-7000, Fax: (202) 623-4661, www.imf.org; *IMF Primary Commodity Prices.*

United Nations Food and Agricultural Organization (FAO), Viale delle Terme di Caracalla, 00100 Rome, Italy, (Dial from U.S. (202) 653-2400), (Fax from U.S. (202) 653 5760), www.fao.org; *The State of Food and Agriculture (SOFA) 2006.*

BANGLADESH - COMMUNICATION AND TRAFFIC

United Nations Statistics Division, New York, NY 10017, (800) 253-9646, Fax: (212) 963-4116, http://unstats.un.org; *Statistical Yearbook.*

BANGLADESH - CONSTRUCTION INDUSTRY

M.E. Sharpe, 80 Business Park Drive, Armonk, NY 10504, (800) 541-6563, Fax: (914) 273-2106, www.mesharpe.com; *The Illustrated Book of World Rankings.*

United Nations Statistics Division, New York, NY 10017, (800) 253-9646, Fax: (212) 963-4116, http://unstats.un.org; *Statistical Yearbook.*

BANGLADESH - CONSUMER PRICE INDEXES

Asian Development Bank (ADB), PO Box 789, 0980 Manila, Philippines, www.adb.org; *Key Indicators of Developing Asian and Pacific Countries 2006.*

Taylor and Francis Group, An Informa Business, 2 Park Square, Milton Park, Abingdon, Oxford OX14 4RN, United Kingdom, (Dial from U.S. (212) 216-7800), (Fax from U.S. (212) 564-7854), www.tandf.co.uk; *The Europa World Year Book.*

United Nations Statistics Division, New York, NY 10017, (800) 253-9646, Fax: (212) 963-4116, http://unstats.un.org; *Statistical Yearbook.*

The World Bank, 1818 H Street, NW, Washington, DC 20433, (202) 473-1000, Fax: (202) 477-6391, www.worldbank.org; *Bangladesh.*

BANGLADESH - CONSUMPTION (ECONOMICS)

The World Bank, 1818 H Street, NW, Washington, DC 20433, (202) 473-1000, Fax: (202) 477-6391, www.worldbank.org; *World Development Report 2008.*

BANGLADESH - COPPER INDUSTRY AND TRADE

See BANGLADESH - MINERAL INDUSTRIES

BANGLADESH - CORN INDUSTRY

See BANGLADESH - CROPS

BANGLADESH - COST AND STANDARD OF LIVING

International Monetary Fund (IMF), 700 Nineteenth Street, NW, Washington, DC 20431, (202) 623-7000, Fax: (202) 623-4661, www.imf.org; *Government Finance Statistics Yearbook (2008 Edition).*

BANGLADESH - COTTON

See BANGLADESH - CROPS

BANGLADESH - CROPS

Asian Development Bank (ADB), PO Box 789, 0980 Manila, Philippines, www.adb.org; *Key Indicators of Developing Asian and Pacific Countries 2006.*

International Monetary Fund (IMF), 700 Nineteenth Street, NW, Washington, DC 20431, (202) 623-7000, Fax: (202) 623-4661, www.imf.org; *International Financial Statistics Yearbook 2007.*

M.E. Sharpe, 80 Business Park Drive, Armonk, NY 10504, (800) 541-6563, Fax: (914) 273-2106, www.mesharpe.com; *The Illustrated Book of World Rankings.*

Palgrave Macmillan Ltd., Houndmills, Basingstoke, Hampshire, RG21 6XS, England, (Telephone in U.S. (888) 330-8477), (Fax in U.S. (800) 672-2054), www.palgrave.com; *The Statesman's Yearbook 2008.*

Taylor and Francis Group, An Informa Business, 2 Park Square, Milton Park, Abingdon, Oxford OX14 4RN, United Kingdom, (Dial from U.S. (212) 216-7800), (Fax from U.S. (212) 564-7854), www.tandf.co.uk; *The Europa World Year Book.*

United Nations Conference on Trade and Development (UNCTAD), DC2-1120, United Nations, New York, NY 10017, (212) 963-0027, www.unctad.org; *UNCTAD Commodity Yearbook.*

United Nations Food and Agricultural Organization (FAO), Viale delle Terme di Caracalla, 00100 Rome, Italy, (Dial from U.S. (202) 653-2400), (Fax from U.S. (202) 653 5760), www.fao.org; *The State of Food and Agriculture (SOFA) 2006.*

United Nations Statistics Division, New York, NY 10017, (800) 253-9646, Fax: (212) 963-4116, http://unstats.un.org; *Statistical Yearbook.*

BANGLADESH - CUSTOMS ADMINISTRATION

International Monetary Fund (IMF), 700 Nineteenth Street, NW, Washington, DC 20431, (202) 623-7000, Fax: (202) 623-4661, www.imf.org; *Government Finance Statistics Yearbook (2008 Edition).*

Palgrave Macmillan Ltd., Houndmills, Basingstoke, Hampshire, RG21 6XS, England, (Telephone in U.S. (888) 330-8477), (Fax in U.S. (800) 672-2054), www.palgrave.com; *The Statesman's Yearbook 2008.*

BANGLADESH - DAIRY PROCESSING

M.E. Sharpe, 80 Business Park Drive, Armonk, NY 10504, (800) 541-6563, Fax: (914) 273-2106, www.mesharpe.com; *The Illustrated Book of World Rankings.*

Palgrave Macmillan Ltd., Houndmills, Basingstoke, Hampshire, RG21 6XS, England, (Telephone in U.S. (888) 330-8477), (Fax in U.S. (800) 672-2054), www.palgrave.com; *The Statesman's Yearbook 2008.*

Taylor and Francis Group, An Informa Business, 2 Park Square, Milton Park, Abingdon, Oxford OX14 4RN, United Kingdom, (Dial from U.S. (212) 216-7800), (Fax from U.S. (212) 564-7854), www.tandf.co.uk; *The Europa World Year Book.*

United Nations Food and Agricultural Organization (FAO), Viale delle Terme di Caracalla, 00100 Rome, Italy, (Dial from U.S. (202) 653-2400), (Fax from U.S. (202) 653 5760), www.fao.org; *FAO Production Yearbook 2002* and *The State of Food and Agriculture (SOFA) 2006.*

United Nations Statistics Division, New York, NY 10017, (800) 253-9646, Fax: (212) 963-4116, http://unstats.un.org; *Statistical Yearbook.*

BANGLADESH - DEATH RATES

See BANGLADESH - MORTALITY

BANGLADESH - DEBTS, EXTERNAL

Asian Development Bank (ADB), PO Box 789, 0980 Manila, Philippines, www.adb.org; *Key Indicators of Developing Asian and Pacific Countries 2006.*

International Monetary Fund (IMF), 700 Nineteenth Street, NW, Washington, DC 20431, (202) 623-7000, Fax: (202) 623-4661, www.imf.org; *Government Finance Statistics Yearbook (2008 Edition).*

Palgrave Macmillan Ltd., Houndmills, Basingstoke, Hampshire, RG21 6XS, England, (Telephone in U.S. (888) 330-8477), (Fax in U.S. (800) 672-2054), www.palgrave.com; *The Statesman's Yearbook 2008.*

The World Bank, 1818 H Street, NW, Washington, DC 20433, (202) 473-1000, Fax: (202) 477-6391, www.worldbank.org; *Global Development Finance 2007; World Development Indicators (WDI) 2008;* and *World Development Report 2008.*

Worldinformation.com, 2 Market Street, Saffron Walden, Essex CB10 1HZ, United Kingdom, www.worldinformation.com; The World of Information (www.worldinformation.com).

BANGLADESH - DEFENSE EXPENDITURES

See BANGLADESH - ARMED FORCES

BANGLADESH - DEMOGRAPHY

Economist Intelligence Unit, 111 West 57th Street, New York, NY 10019, (212) 554-0600, Fax: (212) 586-1181, www.eiu.com; *Business Asia.*

Euromonitor International, Inc., 224 S. Michigan Avenue, Suite 1500, Chicago, IL 60604, (312) 922-1115, Fax: (312) 922-1157, www.euromonitor.com; *International Marketing Data and Statistics 2008; The World Economic Factbook 2008;* and *World Marketing Data and Statistics.*

M.E. Sharpe, 80 Business Park Drive, Armonk, NY 10504, (800) 541-6563, Fax: (914) 273-2106, www.mesharpe.com; *The Illustrated Book of World Rankings.*

United Nations Statistics Division, New York, NY 10017, (800) 253-9646, Fax: (212) 963-4116, http://unstats.un.org; *Asia-Pacific in Figures 2004* and *Human Development Report 2006.*

The World Bank, 1818 H Street, NW, Washington, DC 20433, (202) 473-1000, Fax: (202) 477-6391, www.worldbank.org; *Bangladesh.*

BANGLADESH - DIAMONDS

See BANGLADESH - MINERAL INDUSTRIES

BANGLADESH - DISPOSABLE INCOME

Bangladesh Bureau of Statistics (BBS), Ministry of Planning, Statistics Wing, E-27/A, Agargaon, Sher-e-banglanagar, Dhaka-1207, Bangladesh, www.bbs.gov.bd; *Census at a Glance.*

M.E. Sharpe, 80 Business Park Drive, Armonk, NY 10504, (800) 541-6563, Fax: (914) 273-2106, www.mesharpe.com; *The Illustrated Book of World Rankings.*

United Nations Statistics Division, New York, NY 10017, (800) 253-9646, Fax: (212) 963-4116, http://unstats.un.org; *National Accounts Statistics: Compendium of Income Distribution Statistics* and *Statistical Yearbook.*

BANGLADESH - DIVORCE

M.E. Sharpe, 80 Business Park Drive, Armonk, NY 10504, (800) 541-6563, Fax: (914) 273-2106, www.mesharpe.com; *The Illustrated Book of World Rankings.*

United Nations Statistics Division, New York, NY 10017, (800) 253-9646, Fax: (212) 963-4116, http://unstats.un.org; *Demographic Yearbook.*

BANGLADESH - ECONOMIC ASSISTANCE

Asian Development Bank (ADB), PO Box 789, 0980 Manila, Philippines, www.adb.org; *Key Indicators of Developing Asian and Pacific Countries 2006.*

United Nations Statistics Division, New York, NY 10017, (800) 253-9646, Fax: (212) 963-4116, http://unstats.un.org; *Statistical Yearbook.*

BANGLADESH - ECONOMIC CONDITIONS

Asian Development Bank (ADB), PO Box 789, 0980 Manila, Philippines, www.adb.org; *Key Indicators of Developing Asian and Pacific Countries 2006.*

Center for International Business Education Research (CIBER), Columbia Business School and School of International and Public Affairs, Uris Hall, Room 212, 3022 Broadway, New York, NY 10027-6902, Mr. Joshua Safier, (212) 854-4750, Fax: (212) 222-9821, www.columbia.edu/cu/ciber/; Datastream International.

Central Intelligence Agency, Office of Public Affairs, Washington, DC 20505, (703) 482-0623, Fax: (703) 482-1739, www.cia.gov; *The World Factbook.*

DSI Data Service Information, Xantener Strasse 51a, D-47495 Rheinberg, Germany, www.dsidata.com; *Campus Solution.*

Dun and Bradstreet (DB) Corporation, 103 JFK Parkway, Short Hills, NJ 07078, (973) 921-5500, www.dnb.com; *Country Report.*

Economist Intelligence Unit, 111 West 57th Street, New York, NY 10019, (212) 554-0600, Fax: (212) 586-1181, www.eiu.com; *Bangladesh Country Report.*

Euromonitor International, Inc., 224 S. Michigan Avenue, Suite 1500, Chicago, IL 60604, (312) 922-1115, Fax: (312) 922-1157, www.euromonitor.com; *International Marketing Data and Statistics 2008; The World Economic Factbook 2008;* and *World Marketing Data and Statistics.*

International Monetary Fund (IMF), 700 Nineteenth Street, NW, Washington, DC 20431, (202) 623-7000, Fax: (202) 623-4661, www.imf.org; *World Economic Outlook Reports.*

M.E. Sharpe, 80 Business Park Drive, Armonk, NY 10504, (800) 541-6563, Fax: (914) 273-2106, www.mesharpe.com; *The Illustrated Book of World Rankings.*

Nomura Research Institute (NRI), 2 World Financial Center, Building B, 19th Fl., New York, NY 10281-1198, (212) 667-1670, www.nri.co.jp/english; *Asian Economic Outlook 2003-2004.*

Palgrave Macmillan Ltd., Houndmills, Basingstoke, Hampshire, RG21 6XS, England, (Telephone in U.S. (888) 330-8477), (Fax in U.S. (800) 672-2054), www.palgrave.com; *The Statesman's Yearbook 2008.*

Taylor and Francis Group, An Informa Business, 2 Park Square, Milton Park, Abingdon, Oxford OX14 4RN, United Kingdom, (Dial from U.S. (212) 216-7800), (Fax from U.S. (212) 564-7854), www.tandf.co.uk; *The Europa World Year Book.*

United Nations Statistics Division, New York, NY 10017, (800) 253-9646, Fax: (212) 963-4116, http://unstats.un.org; *World Statistics Pocketbook.*

The World Bank, 1818 H Street, NW, Washington, DC 20433, (202) 473-1000, Fax: (202) 477-6391, www.worldbank.org; *Bangladesh; Global Economic Monitor (GEM); Global Economic Prospects 2008; The World Bank Atlas 2003-2004;* and *World Development Report 2008.*

BANGLADESH - EDUCATION

Bangladesh Bureau of Statistics (BBS), Ministry of Planning, Statistics Wing, E-27/A, Agargaon, Sher-e-banglanagar, Dhaka-1207, Bangladesh, www.bbs.gov.bd; *Census at a Glance.*

Economist Intelligence Unit, 111 West 57th Street, New York, NY 10019, (212) 554-0600, Fax: (212) 586-1181, www.eiu.com; *Business Asia.*

Euromonitor International, Inc., 224 S. Michigan Avenue, Suite 1500, Chicago, IL 60604, (312) 922-1115, Fax: (312) 922-1157, www.euromonitor.com; *International Marketing Data and Statistics 2008* and *World Marketing Data and Statistics.*

International Monetary Fund (IMF), 700 Nineteenth Street, NW, Washington, DC 20431, (202) 623-7000, Fax: (202) 623-4661, www.imf.org; *Government Finance Statistics Yearbook (2008 Edition).*

M.E. Sharpe, 80 Business Park Drive, Armonk, NY 10504, (800) 541-6563, Fax: (914) 273-2106, www.mesharpe.com; *The Illustrated Book of World Rankings.*

Palgrave Macmillan Ltd., Houndmills, Basingstoke, Hampshire, RG21 6XS, England, (Telephone in U.S. (888) 330-8477), (Fax in U.S. (800) 672-2054), www.palgrave.com; *The Statesman's Yearbook 2008.*

Taylor and Francis Group, An Informa Business, 2 Park Square, Milton Park, Abingdon, Oxford OX14 4RN, United Kingdom, (Dial from U.S. (212) 216-7800), (Fax from U.S. (212) 564-7854), www.tandf.co.uk; *The Europa World Year Book.*

UNESCO Institute for Statistics, C.P. 6128 Succursale Centre-Ville, Montreal, Quebec, H3C 3J7 Canada, (Dial from U.S. (514) 343-6880), (Fax from U.S. (514) 343 6882), www.uis.unesco.org; *Statistical Tables.*

United Nations Statistics Division, New York, NY 10017, (800) 253-9646, Fax: (212) 963-4116, http://unstats.un.org; *Asia-Pacific in Figures 2004; Human Development Report 2006;* and *Statistical Yearbook for Asia and the Pacific 2004.*

The World Bank, 1818 H Street, NW, Washington, DC 20433, (202) 473-1000, Fax: (202) 477-6391, www.worldbank.org; *Bangladesh; World Development Indicators (WDI) 2008;* and *World Development Report 2008.*

BANGLADESH - ELECTRICITY

Asian Development Bank (ADB), PO Box 789, 0980 Manila, Philippines, www.adb.org; *Key Indicators of Developing Asian and Pacific Countries 2006.*

M.E. Sharpe, 80 Business Park Drive, Armonk, NY 10504, (800) 541-6563, Fax: (914) 273-2106, www.mesharpe.com; *The Illustrated Book of World Rankings.*

Organisation for Economic Cooperation and Development (OECD), 2 rue Andre Pascal, F-75775 Paris Cedex 16, France, (Telephone in U.S. (202) 785-6323), (Fax in U.S. (202) 785-0350), www.oecd.org; *World Energy Outlook 2007.*

Palgrave Macmillan Ltd., Houndmills, Basingstoke, Hampshire, RG21 6XS, England, (Telephone in U.S. (888) 330-8477), (Fax in U.S. (800) 672-2054), www.palgrave.com; *The Statesman's Yearbook 2008.*

U.S. Department of Energy (DOE), Energy Information Administration (EIA), 1000 Independence Avenue, SW, Washington, DC 20585, (202) 586-8800, www.eia.doe.gov; *International Energy Annual 2004* and *International Energy Outlook 2006.*

United Nations Statistics Division, New York, NY 10017, (800) 253-9646, Fax: (212) 963-4116, http://unstats.un.org; *Electric Power in Asia and the Pacific 2001 and 2002* and *Human Development Report 2006.*

BANGLADESH - EMPLOYMENT

Euromonitor International, Inc., 224 S. Michigan Avenue, Suite 1500, Chicago, IL 60604, (312) 922-1115, Fax: (312) 922-1157, www.euromonitor.com; *International Marketing Data and Statistics 2008.*

International Labour Office, I.L.O. Publications, 4 route des Morillons, CH-1211 Geneva 22, Switzerland, (Telephone in U.S. (202) 653-7652), (Fax in U.S. (202) 653-7687), www.ilo.org; *Yearbook of Labour Statistics 2006.*

M.E. Sharpe, 80 Business Park Drive, Armonk, NY 10504, (800) 541-6563, Fax: (914) 273-2106, www.mesharpe.com; *The Illustrated Book of World Rankings.*

United Nations Statistics Division, New York, NY 10017, (800) 253-9646, Fax: (212) 963-4116, http://unstats.un.org; *Asia-Pacific in Figures 2004* and *Statistical Yearbook.*

The World Bank, 1818 H Street, NW, Washington, DC 20433, (202) 473-1000, Fax: (202) 477-6391, www.worldbank.org; *Bangladesh.*

BANGLADESH - ENERGY INDUSTRIES

Enerdata, 10 Rue Royale, 75008 Paris, France, www.enerdata.fr; *Global Energy Market Data.*

United Nations Statistics Division, New York, NY 10017, (800) 253-9646, Fax: (212) 963-4116, http://unstats.un.org; *Electric Power in Asia and the Pacific 2001 and 2002.*

BANGLADESH - ENVIRONMENTAL CONDITIONS

Bangladesh Bureau of Statistics (BBS), Ministry of Planning, Statistics Wing, E-27/A, Agargaon, Sher-e-banglanagar, Dhaka-1207, Bangladesh, www.bbs.gov.bd; *Census at a Glance.*

DSI Data Service Information, Xantener Strasse 51a, D-47495 Rheinberg, Germany, www.dsidata.com; *Campus Solution* and *DSI's Global Environmental Database.*

Economist Intelligence Unit, 111 West 57th Street, New York, NY 10019, (212) 554-0600, Fax: (212) 586-1181, www.eiu.com; *Bangladesh Country Report.*

International Institute for Environment and Development (IIED), 3 Endsleigh Street, London, England, WC1H 0DD, United Kingdom, www.iied.org; *Environment Urbanization.*

United Nations Statistics Division, New York, NY 10017, (800) 253-9646, Fax: (212) 963-4116, http://unstats.un.org; *World Statistics Pocketbook.*

BANGLADESH - EXCISE TAX

International Monetary Fund (IMF), 700 Nineteenth Street, NW, Washington, DC 20431, (202) 623-7000, Fax: (202) 623-4661, www.imf.org; *Government Finance Statistics Yearbook (2008 Edition).*

BANGLADESH - EXPORTS

Asian Development Bank (ADB), PO Box 789, 0980 Manila, Philippines, www.adb.org; *Key Indicators of Developing Asian and Pacific Countries 2006.*

Central Intelligence Agency, Office of Public Affairs, Washington, DC 20505, (703) 482-0623, Fax: (703) 482-1739, www.cia.gov; *The World Factbook.*

Economist Intelligence Unit, 111 West 57th Street, New York, NY 10019, (212) 554-0600, Fax: (212) 586-1181, www.eiu.com; *Bangladesh Country Report.*

Euromonitor International, Inc., 224 S. Michigan Avenue, Suite 1500, Chicago, IL 60604, (312) 922-1115, Fax: (312) 922-1157, www.euromonitor.com; *International Marketing Data and Statistics 2008* and *The World Economic Factbook 2008.*

International Monetary Fund (IMF), 700 Nineteenth Street, NW, Washington, DC 20431, (202) 623-7000, Fax: (202) 623-4661, www.imf.org; *Direction of Trade Statistics Yearbook 2007; Government Finance Statistics Yearbook (2008 Edition);* and *International Financial Statistics Yearbook 2007.*

Palgrave Macmillan Ltd., Houndmills, Basingstoke, Hampshire, RG21 6XS, England, (Telephone in U.S. (888) 330-8477), (Fax in U.S. (800) 672-2054), www.palgrave.com; *The Statesman's Yearbook 2008.*

Taylor and Francis Group, An Informa Business, 2 Park Square, Milton Park, Abingdon, Oxford OX14 4RN, United Kingdom, (Dial from U.S. (212) 216-7800), (Fax from U.S. (212) 564-7854), www.tandf.co.uk; *The Europa World Year Book.*

United Nations Conference on Trade and Development (UNCTAD), DC2-1120, United Nations, New York, NY 10017, (212) 963-0027, www.unctad.org; *Handbook of Statistics 2005.*

United Nations Food and Agricultural Organization (FAO), Viale delle Terme di Caracalla, 00100 Rome, Italy, (Dial from U.S. (202) 653-2400), (Fax from U.S. (202) 653 5760), www.fao.org; *The State of Food and Agriculture (SOFA) 2006.*

United Nations Statistics Division, New York, NY 10017, (800) 253-9646, Fax: (212) 963-4116, http://unstats.un.org; *Foreign Trade Statistics of Asia and the Pacific 1996-2000.*

The World Bank, 1818 H Street, NW, Washington, DC 20433, (202) 473-1000, Fax: (202) 477-6391, www.worldbank.org; *World Development Indicators (WDI) 2008* and *World Development Report 2008.*

Worldinformation.com, 2 Market Street, Saffron Walden, Essex CB10 1HZ, United Kingdom, www.worldinformation.com; The World of Information (www.worldinformation.com).

BANGLADESH - FEMALE WORKING POPULATION

See BANGLADESH - EMPLOYMENT

BANGLADESH - FERTILITY, HUMAN

Central Intelligence Agency, Office of Public Affairs, Washington, DC 20505, (703) 482-0623, Fax: (703) 482-1739, www.cia.gov; *The World Factbook.*

M.E. Sharpe, 80 Business Park Drive, Armonk, NY 10504, (800) 541-6563, Fax: (914) 273-2106, www.mesharpe.com; *The Illustrated Book of World Rankings.*

United Nations Statistics Division, New York, NY 10017, (800) 253-9646, Fax: (212) 963-4116, http://unstats.un.org; *Human Development Report 2006.*

The World Bank, 1818 H Street, NW, Washington, DC 20433, (202) 473-1000, Fax: (202) 477-6391, www.worldbank.org; *The World Bank Atlas 2003-2004; World Development Indicators (WDI) 2008;* and *World Development Report 2008.*

BANGLADESH - FERTILIZER INDUSTRY

United Nations Food and Agricultural Organization (FAO), Viale delle Terme di Caracalla, 00100 Rome, Italy, (Dial from U.S. (202) 653-2400), (Fax from U.S. (202) 653 5760), www.fao.org; *FAO Fertilizer Yearbook* and *The State of Food and Agriculture (SOFA) 2006.*

United Nations Statistics Division, New York, NY 10017, (800) 253-9646, Fax: (212) 963-4116, http://unstats.un.org; *Statistical Yearbook.*

BANGLADESH - FETAL MORTALITY

See BANGLADESH - MORTALITY

BANGLADESH - FINANCE

Taylor and Francis Group, An Informa Business, 2 Park Square, Milton Park, Abingdon, Oxford OX14 4RN, United Kingdom, (Dial from U.S. (212) 216-7800), (Fax from U.S. (212) 564-7854), www.tandf.co.uk; *The Europa World Year Book.*

United Nations Statistics Division, New York, NY 10017, (800) 253-9646, Fax: (212) 963-4116, http://unstats.un.org; *Asia-Pacific in Figures 2004; National Accounts Statistics: Compendium of Income Distribution Statistics; Statistical Yearbook;* and *Statistical Yearbook for Asia and the Pacific 2004.*

The World Bank, 1818 H Street, NW, Washington, DC 20433, (202) 473-1000, Fax: (202) 477-6391, www.worldbank.org; *Bangladesh.*

BANGLADESH - FINANCE, PUBLIC

Asian Development Bank (ADB), PO Box 789, 0980 Manila, Philippines, www.adb.org; *Key Indicators of Developing Asian and Pacific Countries 2006.*

Bangladesh Bureau of Statistics (BBS), Ministry of Planning, Statistics Wing, E-27/A, Agargaon, Sher-e-banglanagar, Dhaka-1207, Bangladesh, www.bbs.gov.bd; *Census at a Glance.*

Bernan Essential Government Publications, 4611-F Assembly Drive, Lanham MD, 20706-4391, (301) 459-2255, Fax: (800) 865-3450, www.bernan.com; *National Accounts Statistics.*

Economist Intelligence Unit, 111 West 57th Street, New York, NY 10019, (212) 554-0600, Fax: (212) 586-1181, www.eiu.com; *Bangladesh Country Report.*

International Monetary Fund (IMF), 700 Nineteenth Street, NW, Washington, DC 20431, (202) 623-7000, Fax: (202) 623-4661, www.imf.org; *Government Finance Statistics Yearbook (2008 Edition); International Financial Statistics; International Financial Statistics Online Service;* and *International Financial Statistics Yearbook 2007.*

M.E. Sharpe, 80 Business Park Drive, Armonk, NY 10504, (800) 541-6563, Fax: (914) 273-2106, www.mesharpe.com; *The Illustrated Book of World Rankings.*

Taylor and Francis Group, An Informa Business, 2 Park Square, Milton Park, Abingdon, Oxford OX14 4RN, United Kingdom, (Dial from U.S. (212) 216-7800), (Fax from U.S. (212) 564-7854), www.tandf.co.uk; *The Europa World Year Book.*

United Nations Statistics Division, New York, NY 10017, (800) 253-9646, Fax: (212) 963-4116, http://unstats.un.org; *Statistical Yearbook for Asia and the Pacific 2004.*

The World Bank, 1818 H Street, NW, Washington, DC 20433, (202) 473-1000, Fax: (202) 477-6391, www.worldbank.org; *Bangladesh.*

BANGLADESH - FISHERIES

Bangladesh Bureau of Statistics (BBS), Ministry of Planning, Statistics Wing, E-27/A, Agargaon, Sher-e-banglanagar, Dhaka-1207, Bangladesh, www.bbs.gov.bd; *Census at a Glance.*

M.E. Sharpe, 80 Business Park Drive, Armonk, NY 10504, (800) 541-6563, Fax: (914) 273-2106, www.mesharpe.com; *The Illustrated Book of World Rankings.*

Palgrave Macmillan Ltd., Houndmills, Basingstoke, Hampshire, RG21 6XS, England, (Telephone in U.S. (888) 330-8477), (Fax in U.S. (800) 672-2054), www.palgrave.com; *The Statesman's Yearbook 2008.*

Taylor and Francis Group, An Informa Business, 2 Park Square, Milton Park, Abingdon, Oxford OX14 4RN, United Kingdom, (Dial from U.S. (212) 216-7800), (Fax from U.S. (212) 564-7854), www.tandf.co.uk; *The Europa World Year Book.*

United Nations Conference on Trade and Development (UNCTAD), DC2-1120, United Nations, New York, NY 10017, (212) 963-0027, www.unctad.org; *UNCTAD Commodity Yearbook.*

United Nations Food and Agricultural Organization (FAO), Viale delle Terme di Caracalla, 00100 Rome, Italy, (Dial from U.S. (202) 653-2400), (Fax from U.S. (202) 653 5760), www.fao.org; *FAO Yearbook of Fishery Statistics;* Fishery Databases; FISHSTAT Database. Subjects covered include: Aquaculture production, capture production, fishery commodities; and *The State of Food and Agriculture (SOFA) 2006.*

United Nations Statistics Division, New York, NY 10017, (800) 253-9646, Fax: (212) 963-4116, http://unstats.un.org; *Statistical Yearbook.*

The World Bank, 1818 H Street, NW, Washington, DC 20433, (202) 473-1000, Fax: (202) 477-6391, www.worldbank.org; *Bangladesh.*

BANGLADESH - FOOD

United Nations Conference on Trade and Development (UNCTAD), DC2-1120, United Nations, New York, NY 10017, (212) 963-0027, www.unctad.org; *UNCTAD Commodity Yearbook.*

United Nations Food and Agricultural Organization (FAO), Viale delle Terme di Caracalla, 00100 Rome, Italy, (Dial from U.S. (202) 653-2400), (Fax from U.S. (202) 653 5760), www.fao.org; *FAO Production Yearbook 2002* and *The State of Food and Agriculture (SOFA) 2006.*

United Nations Statistics Division, New York, NY 10017, (800) 253-9646, Fax: (212) 963-4116, http://unstats.un.org; *Human Development Report 2006* and *Statistical Yearbook for Asia and the Pacific 2004.*

BANGLADESH - FOREIGN EXCHANGE RATES

Asian Development Bank (ADB), PO Box 789, 0980 Manila, Philippines, www.adb.org; *Key Indicators of Developing Asian and Pacific Countries 2006.*

Central Intelligence Agency, Office of Public Affairs, Washington, DC 20505, (703) 482-0623, Fax: (703) 482-1739, www.cia.gov; *The World Factbook.*

Economist Intelligence Unit, 111 West 57th Street, New York, NY 10019, (212) 554-0600, Fax: (212) 586-1181, www.eiu.com; *Business Asia.*

Euromonitor International, Inc., 224 S. Michigan Avenue, Suite 1500, Chicago, IL 60604, (312) 922-1115, Fax: (312) 922-1157, www.euromonitor.com; *International Marketing Data and Statistics 2008* and *The World Economic Factbook 2008.*

International Civil Aviation Organization (ICAO), External Relations and Public Information Office (EPO), 999 University Street, Montreal, Quebec H3C 5H7, Canada, (Dial from U.S. (514) 954-8219), (Fax from U.S. (514) 954-6077), www.icao.int; *Civil Aviation Statistics of the World.*

International Monetary Fund (IMF), 700 Nineteenth Street, NW, Washington, DC 20431, (202) 623-7000, Fax: (202) 623-4661, www.imf.org; *International Financial Statistics Yearbook 2007.*

Taylor and Francis Group, An Informa Business, 2 Park Square, Milton Park, Abingdon, Oxford OX14 4RN, United Kingdom, (Dial from U.S. (212) 216-7800), (Fax from U.S. (212) 564-7854), www.tandf.co.uk; *The Europa World Year Book.*

United Nations Statistics Division, New York, NY 10017, (800) 253-9646, Fax: (212) 963-4116, http://unstats.un.org; *Statistical Yearbook* and *World Statistics Pocketbook.*

Worldinformation.com, 2 Market Street, Saffron Walden, Essex CB10 1HZ, United Kingdom, www.worldinformation.com; The World of Information (www.worldinformation.com).

BANGLADESH - FORESTS AND FORESTRY

Bangladesh Bureau of Statistics (BBS), Ministry of Planning, Statistics Wing, E-27/A, Agargaon, Sher-e-banglanagar, Dhaka-1207, Bangladesh, www.bbs.gov.bd; *Census at a Glance.*

Economist Intelligence Unit, 111 West 57th Street, New York, NY 10019, (212) 554-0600, Fax: (212) 586-1181, www.eiu.com; *Business Asia.*

M.E. Sharpe, 80 Business Park Drive, Armonk, NY 10504, (800) 541-6563, Fax: (914) 273-2106, www.mesharpe.com; *The Illustrated Book of World Rankings.*

Palgrave Macmillan Ltd., Houndmills, Basingstoke, Hampshire, RG21 6XS, England, (Telephone in U.S. (888) 330-8477), (Fax in U.S. (800) 672-2054), www.palgrave.com; *The Statesman's Yearbook 2008.*

Taylor and Francis Group, An Informa Business, 2 Park Square, Milton Park, Abingdon, Oxford OX14 4RN, United Kingdom, (Dial from U.S. (212) 216-7800), (Fax from U.S. (212) 564-7854), www.tandf.co.uk; *The Europa World Year Book.*

UNESCO Institute for Statistics, C.P. 6128 Succursale Centre-Ville, Montreal, Quebec, H3C 3J7 Canada, (Dial from U.S. (514) 343-6880), (Fax from U.S. (514) 343 6882), www.uis.unesco.org; *Statistical Tables.*

United Nations Conference on Trade and Development (UNCTAD), DC2-1120, United Nations, New York, NY 10017, (212) 963-0027, www.unctad.org; *UNCTAD Commodity Yearbook.*

United Nations Food and Agricultural Organization (FAO), Viale delle Terme di Caracalla, 00100 Rome, Italy, (Dial from U.S. (202) 653-2400), (Fax from U.S. (202) 653 5760), www.fao.org; *FAO Yearbook of Forest Products* and *The State of Food and Agriculture (SOFA) 2006.*

United Nations Statistics Division, New York, NY 10017, (800) 253-9646, Fax: (212) 963-4116, http://unstats.un.org; *Statistical Yearbook.*

The World Bank, 1818 H Street, NW, Washington, DC 20433, (202) 473-1000, Fax: (202) 477-6391, www.worldbank.org; *Bangladesh* and *World Development Report 2008.*

BANGLADESH - GAS PRODUCTION

See BANGLADESH - MINERAL INDUSTRIES

BANGLADESH - GEOGRAPHIC INFORMATION SYSTEMS

M.E. Sharpe, 80 Business Park Drive, Armonk, NY 10504, (800) 541-6563, Fax: (914) 273-2106, www.mesharpe.com; *The Illustrated Book of World Rankings.*

The World Bank, 1818 H Street, NW, Washington, DC 20433, (202) 473-1000, Fax: (202) 477-6391, www.worldbank.org; *Bangladesh.*

BANGLADESH - GOLD INDUSTRY

International Monetary Fund (IMF), 700 Nineteenth Street, NW, Washington, DC 20431, (202) 623-7000, Fax: (202) 623-4661, www.imf.org; *International Financial Statistics Yearbook 2007.*

United Nations Statistics Division, New York, NY 10017, (800) 253-9646, Fax: (212) 963-4116, http://unstats.un.org; *Statistical Yearbook.*

The World Bank, 1818 H Street, NW, Washington, DC 20433, (202) 473-1000, Fax: (202) 477-6391, www.worldbank.org; *World Development Indicators (WDI) 2008.*

BANGLADESH - GOLD PRODUCTION

See BANGLADESH - MINERAL INDUSTRIES

BANGLADESH - GRANTS-IN-AID

International Monetary Fund (IMF), 700 Nineteenth Street, NW, Washington, DC 20431, (202) 623-7000, Fax: (202) 623-4661, www.imf.org; *Government Finance Statistics Yearbook (2008 Edition).*

BANGLADESH - GROSS DOMESTIC PRODUCT

Asian Development Bank (ADB), PO Box 789, 0980 Manila, Philippines, www.adb.org; *Key Indicators of Developing Asian and Pacific Countries 2006.*

Economist Intelligence Unit, 111 West 57th Street, New York, NY 10019, (212) 554-0600, Fax: (212) 586-1181, www.eiu.com; *Bangladesh Country Report* and *Business Asia.*

Euromonitor International, Inc., 224 S. Michigan Avenue, Suite 1500, Chicago, IL 60604, (312) 922-1115, Fax: (312) 922-1157, www.euromonitor.com; *International Marketing Data and Statistics 2008* and *The World Economic Factbook 2008.*

M.E. Sharpe, 80 Business Park Drive, Armonk, NY 10504, (800) 541-6563, Fax: (914) 273-2106, www.mesharpe.com; *The Illustrated Book of World Rankings.*

Taylor and Francis Group, An Informa Business, 2 Park Square, Milton Park, Abingdon, Oxford OX14 4RN, United Kingdom, (Dial from U.S. (212) 216-7800), (Fax from U.S. (212) 564-7854), www.tandf.co.uk; *The Europa World Year Book.*

United Nations Statistics Division, New York, NY 10017, (800) 253-9646, Fax: (212) 963-4116, http://unstats.un.org; *Human Development Report 2006; National Accounts Statistics: Compendium of Income Distribution Statistics;* and *Statistical Yearbook.*

The World Bank, 1818 H Street, NW, Washington, DC 20433, (202) 473-1000, Fax: (202) 477-6391, www.worldbank.org; *World Development Indicators (WDI) 2008* and *World Development Report 2008.*

BANGLADESH - GROSS NATIONAL PRODUCT

Asian Development Bank (ADB), PO Box 789, 0980 Manila, Philippines, www.adb.org; *Key Indicators of Developing Asian and Pacific Countries 2006.*

Euromonitor International, Inc., 224 S. Michigan Avenue, Suite 1500, Chicago, IL 60604, (312) 922-1115, Fax: (312) 922-1157, www.euromonitor.com; *International Marketing Data and Statistics 2008.*

M.E. Sharpe, 80 Business Park Drive, Armonk, NY 10504, (800) 541-6563, Fax: (914) 273-2106, www.mesharpe.com; *The Illustrated Book of World Rankings.*

Palgrave Macmillan Ltd., Houndmills, Basingstoke, Hampshire, RG21 6XS, England, (Telephone in U.S. (888) 330-8477), (Fax in U.S. (800) 672-2054), www.palgrave.com; *The Statesman's Yearbook 2008.*

U.S. Department of State (DOS), 2201 C Street NW, Washington, DC 20520, (202) 647-4000, www.state.gov; *World Military Expenditures and Arms Transfers (WMEAT).*

United Nations Statistics Division, New York, NY 10017, (800) 253-9646, Fax: (212) 963-4116, http://unstats.un.org; *Statistical Yearbook.*

The World Bank, 1818 H Street, NW, Washington, DC 20433, (202) 473-1000, Fax: (202) 477-6391, www.worldbank.org; *The World Bank Atlas 2003-2004; World Development Indicators (WDI) 2008;* and *World Development Report 2008.*

Worldinformation.com, 2 Market Street, Saffron Walden, Essex CB10 1HZ, United Kingdom, www.worldinformation.com; The World of Information (www.worldinformation.com).

BANGLADESH - HEMP FIBRE PRODUCTION

See BANGLADESH - TEXTILE INDUSTRY

BANGLADESH - HIDES AND SKINS INDUSTRY

United Nations Food and Agricultural Organization (FAO), Viale delle Terme di Caracalla, 00100 Rome, Italy, (Dial from U.S. (202) 653-2400), (Fax from U.S. (202) 653 5760), www.fao.org; *FAO Production Yearbook 2002.*

BANGLADESH - HOUSING

Bangladesh Bureau of Statistics (BBS), Ministry of Planning, Statistics Wing, E-27/A, Agargaon, Sher-e-banglanagar, Dhaka-1207, Bangladesh, www.bbs.gov.bd; *Census at a Glance.*

Euromonitor International, Inc., 224 S. Michigan Avenue, Suite 1500, Chicago, IL 60604, (312) 922-1115, Fax: (312) 922-1157, www.euromonitor.com; *World Marketing Data and Statistics.*

M.E. Sharpe, 80 Business Park Drive, Armonk, NY 10504, (800) 541-6563, Fax: (914) 273-2106, www.mesharpe.com; *The Illustrated Book of World Rankings.*

BANGLADESH - ILLITERATE PERSONS

Central Intelligence Agency, Office of Public Affairs, Washington, DC 20505, (703) 482-0623, Fax: (703) 482-1739, www.cia.gov; *The World Factbook.*

Euromonitor International, Inc., 224 S. Michigan Avenue, Suite 1500, Chicago, IL 60604, (312) 922-1115, Fax: (312) 922-1157, www.euromonitor.com; *The World Economic Factbook 2008.*

Palgrave Macmillan Ltd., Houndmills, Basingstoke, Hampshire, RG21 6XS, England, (Telephone in U.S. (888) 330-8477), (Fax in U.S. (800) 672-2054), www.palgrave.com; *The Statesman's Yearbook 2008.*

UNESCO Institute for Statistics, C.P. 6128 Succursale Centre-Ville, Montreal, Quebec, H3C 3J7 Canada, (Dial from U.S. (514) 343-6880), (Fax from U.S. (514) 343 6882), www.uis.unesco.org; *Statistical Tables.*

United Nations Statistics Division, New York, NY 10017, (800) 253-9646, Fax: (212) 963-4116, http://unstats.un.org; *Asia-Pacific in Figures 2004* and *Human Development Report 2006.*

BANGLADESH - IMPORTS

Asian Development Bank (ADB), PO Box 789, 0980 Manila, Philippines, www.adb.org; *Key Indicators of Developing Asian and Pacific Countries 2006.*

Central Intelligence Agency, Office of Public Affairs, Washington, DC 20505, (703) 482-0623, Fax: (703) 482-1739, www.cia.gov; *The World Factbook.*

Economist Intelligence Unit, 111 West 57th Street, New York, NY 10019, (212) 554-0600, Fax: (212) 586-1181, www.eiu.com; *Bangladesh Country Report.*

Euromonitor International, Inc., 224 S. Michigan Avenue, Suite 1500, Chicago, IL 60604, (312) 922-1115, Fax: (312) 922-1157, www.euromonitor.com; *International Marketing Data and Statistics 2008* and *The World Economic Factbook 2008.*

International Monetary Fund (IMF), 700 Nineteenth Street, NW, Washington, DC 20431, (202) 623-7000, Fax: (202) 623-4661, www.imf.org; *Direction of Trade Statistics Yearbook 2007; Government Finance Statistics Yearbook (2008 Edition);* and *International Financial Statistics Yearbook 2007.*

Palgrave Macmillan Ltd., Houndmills, Basingstoke, Hampshire, RG21 6XS, England, (Telephone in U.S. (888) 330-8477), (Fax in U.S. (800) 672-2054), www.palgrave.com; *The Statesman's Yearbook 2008.*

Taylor and Francis Group, An Informa Business, 2 Park Square, Milton Park, Abingdon, Oxford OX14 4RN, United Kingdom, (Dial from U.S. (212) 216-7800), (Fax from U.S. (212) 564-7854), www.tandf.co.uk; *The Europa World Year Book.*

United Nations Conference on Trade and Development (UNCTAD), DC2-1120, United Nations, New York, NY 10017, (212) 963-0027, www.unctad.org; *Handbook of Statistics 2005.*

United Nations Food and Agricultural Organization (FAO), Viale delle Terme di Caracalla, 00100 Rome, Italy, (Dial from U.S. (202) 653-2400), (Fax from U.S. (202) 653 5760), www.fao.org; *The State of Food and Agriculture (SOFA) 2006.*

United Nations Statistics Division, New York, NY 10017, (800) 253-9646, Fax: (212) 963-4116, http://unstats.un.org; *Foreign Trade Statistics of Asia and the Pacific 1996-2000.*

The World Bank, 1818 H Street, NW, Washington, DC 20433, (202) 473-1000, Fax: (202) 477-6391, www.worldbank.org; *World Development Indicators (WDI) 2008* and *World Development Report 2008.*

Worldinformation.com, 2 Market Street, Saffron Walden, Essex CB10 1HZ, United Kingdom, www.worldinformation.com; The World of Information (www.worldinformation.com).

BANGLADESH - INCOME TAXES

See BANGLADESH - TAXATION

BANGLADESH - INDUSTRIAL PRODUCTIVITY

Euromonitor International, Inc., 224 S. Michigan Avenue, Suite 1500, Chicago, IL 60604, (312) 922-1115, Fax: (312) 922-1157, www.euromonitor.com; *International Marketing Data and Statistics 2008.*

M.E. Sharpe, 80 Business Park Drive, Armonk, NY 10504, (800) 541-6563, Fax: (914) 273-2106, www.mesharpe.com; *The Illustrated Book of World Rankings.*

BANGLADESH - INDUSTRIAL PROPERTY

United Nations Statistics Division, New York, NY 10017, (800) 253-9646, Fax: (212) 963-4116, http://unstats.un.org; *Statistical Yearbook.*

BANGLADESH - INDUSTRIES

Bangladesh Bureau of Statistics (BBS), Ministry of Planning, Statistics Wing, E-27/A, Agargaon, Sher-e-banglanagar, Dhaka-1207, Bangladesh, www.bbs.gov.bd; *Census at a Glance.*

Central Intelligence Agency, Office of Public Affairs, Washington, DC 20505, (703) 482-0623, Fax: (703) 482-1739, www.cia.gov; *The World Factbook.*

Economist Intelligence Unit, 111 West 57th Street, New York, NY 10019, (212) 554-0600, Fax: (212) 586-1181, www.eiu.com; *Bangladesh Country Report.*

Euromonitor International, Inc., 224 S. Michigan Avenue, Suite 1500, Chicago, IL 60604, (312) 922-1115, Fax: (312) 922-1157, www.euromonitor.com; *International Marketing Data and Statistics 2008; The World Economic Factbook 2008;* and *World Marketing Data and Statistics.*

International Labour Office, I.L.O. Publications, 4 route des Morillons, CH-1211 Geneva 22, Switzerland, (Telephone in U.S. (202) 653-7652), (Fax in U.S. (202) 653-7687), www.ilo.org; *Yearbook of Labour Statistics 2006.*

M.E. Sharpe, 80 Business Park Drive, Armonk, NY 10504, (800) 541-6563, Fax: (914) 273-2106, www.mesharpe.com; *The Illustrated Book of World Rankings.*

Palgrave Macmillan Ltd., Houndmills, Basingstoke, Hampshire, RG21 6XS, England, (Telephone in U.S. (888) 330-8477), (Fax in U.S. (800) 672-2054), www.palgrave.com; *The Statesman's Yearbook 2008.*

Taylor and Francis Group, An Informa Business, 2 Park Square, Milton Park, Abingdon, Oxford OX14 4RN, United Kingdom, (Dial from U.S. (212) 216-7800), (Fax from U.S. (212) 564-7854), www.tandf.co.uk; *The Europa World Year Book.*

United Nations Industrial Development Organization (UNIDO), 1 United Nations Plaza, New York, NY 10017, (212) 963 6890, Fax: (212) 963-7904, http://unido.org; Industrial Statistics Database 2008 (INDSTAT) and *The International Yearbook of Industrial Statistics 2008.*

United Nations Statistics Division, New York, NY 10017, (800) 253-9646, Fax: (212) 963-4116, http://unstats.un.org; *Asia-Pacific in Figures 2004; 2004 Industrial Commodity Statistics Yearbook;* and *Statistical Yearbook for Asia and the Pacific 2004.*

The World Bank, 1818 H Street, NW, Washington, DC 20433, (202) 473-1000, Fax: (202) 477-6391, www.worldbank.org; *Bangladesh* and *World Development Indicators (WDI) 2008.*

BANGLADESH - INFANT AND MATERNAL MORTALITY

See BANGLADESH - MORTALITY

BANGLADESH - INORGANIC ACIDS

United Nations Statistics Division, New York, NY 10017, (800) 253-9646, Fax: (212) 963-4116, http://unstats.un.org; *Statistical Yearbook.*

BANGLADESH - INTERNATIONAL FINANCE

Asian Development Bank (ADB), PO Box 789, 0980 Manila, Philippines, www.adb.org; *Key Indicators of Developing Asian and Pacific Countries 2006.*

BANGLADESH - INTERNATIONAL LIQUIDITY

International Monetary Fund (IMF), 700 Nineteenth Street, NW, Washington, DC 20431, (202) 623-7000, Fax: (202) 623-4661, www.imf.org; *International Financial Statistics Yearbook 2007.*

BANGLADESH - INTERNATIONAL STATISTICS

Asian Development Bank (ADB), PO Box 789, 0980 Manila, Philippines, www.adb.org; *Key Indicators of Developing Asian and Pacific Countries 2006.*

BANGLADESH - INTERNATIONAL TRADE

Asian Development Bank (ADB), PO Box 789, 0980 Manila, Philippines, www.adb.org; *Key Indicators of Developing Asian and Pacific Countries 2006.*

Bangladesh Bureau of Statistics (BBS), Ministry of Planning, Statistics Wing, E-27/A, Agargaon, Sher-e-banglanagar, Dhaka-1207, Bangladesh, www.bbs.gov.bd; *Census at a Glance.*

Economist Intelligence Unit, 111 West 57th Street, New York, NY 10019, (212) 554-0600, Fax: (212) 586-1181, www.eiu.com; *Bangladesh Country Report* and *Business Asia.*

Euromonitor International, Inc., 224 S. Michigan Avenue, Suite 1500, Chicago, IL 60604, (312) 922-1115, Fax: (312) 922-1157, www.euromonitor.com; *International Marketing Data and Statistics 2008; The World Economic Factbook 2008;* and *World Marketing Data and Statistics.*

M.E. Sharpe, 80 Business Park Drive, Armonk, NY 10504, (800) 541-6563, Fax: (914) 273-2106, www.mesharpe.com; *The Illustrated Book of World Rankings.*

Organisation for Economic Cooperation and Development (OECD), 2 rue Andre Pascal, F-75775 Paris Cedex 16, France, (Telephone in U.S. (202) 785-6323), (Fax in U.S. (202) 785-0350), www.oecd.org; *International Trade by Commodity Statistics (ITCS).*

Palgrave Macmillan Ltd., Houndmills, Basingstoke, Hampshire, RG21 6XS, England, (Telephone in U.S. (888) 330-8477), (Fax in U.S. (800) 672-2054), www.palgrave.com; *The Statesman's Yearbook 2008.*

Taylor and Francis Group, An Informa Business, 2 Park Square, Milton Park, Abingdon, Oxford OX14 4RN, United Kingdom, (Dial from U.S. (212) 216-7800), (Fax from U.S. (212) 564-7854), www.tandf.co.uk; *The Europa World Year Book.*

United Nations Conference on Trade and Development (UNCTAD), DC2-1120, United Nations, New York, NY 10017, (212) 963-0027, www.unctad.org; *UNCTAD Commodity Yearbook.*

United Nations Food and Agricultural Organization (FAO), Viale delle Terme di Caracalla, 00100 Rome, Italy, (Dial from U.S. (202) 653-2400), (Fax from U.S. (202) 653 5760), www.fao.org; *FAO Trade Yearbook* and *The State of Food and Agriculture (SOFA) 2006.*

United Nations Statistics Division, New York, NY 10017, (800) 253-9646, Fax: (212) 963-4116, http://unstats.un.org; *Asia-Pacific in Figures 2004; International Trade Statistics Yearbook; Statistical Yearbook;* and *Statistical Yearbook for Asia and the Pacific 2004.*

The World Bank, 1818 H Street, NW, Washington, DC 20433, (202) 473-1000, Fax: (202) 477-6391, www.worldbank.org; *Bangladesh; World Development Indicators (WDI) 2008;* and *World Development Report 2008.*

World Trade Organization (WTO), Centre William Rappard, Rue de Lausanne 154, CH-1211 Geneva 21, Switzerland, www.wto.org; *International Trade Statistics 2006.*

BANGLADESH - INTERNET USERS

International Telecommunication Union (ITU), Place des Nations, 1211 Geneva 20, Switzerland, www.itu.int; *World Telecommunication/ICT Indicators Database on CD-ROM; World Telecommunication/ICT Indicators Database Online;* and *Yearbook of Statistics - Telecommunication Services (Chronological Time Series 1997-2006).*

The World Bank, 1818 H Street, NW, Washington, DC 20433, (202) 473-1000, Fax: (202) 477-6391, www.worldbank.org; *Bangladesh.*

BANGLADESH - IRON AND IRON ORE PRODUCTION

See BANGLADESH - MINERAL INDUSTRIES

BANGLADESH - IRRIGATION

Euromonitor International, Inc., 224 S. Michigan Avenue, Suite 1500, Chicago, IL 60604, (312) 922-1115, Fax: (312) 922-1157, www.euromonitor.com; *International Marketing Data and Statistics 2008.*

BANGLADESH - JUTE PRODUCTION

See BANGLADESH - CROPS

BANGLADESH - LABOR

Bangladesh Bureau of Statistics (BBS), Ministry of Planning, Statistics Wing, E-27/A, Agargaon, Sher-e-banglanagar, Dhaka-1207, Bangladesh, www.bbs.gov.bd; *Census at a Glance.*

Central Intelligence Agency, Office of Public Affairs, Washington, DC 20505, (703) 482-0623, Fax: (703) 482-1739, www.cia.gov; *The World Factbook.*

Economist Intelligence Unit, 111 West 57th Street, New York, NY 10019, (212) 554-0600, Fax: (212) 586-1181, www.eiu.com; *Business Asia.*

Euromonitor International, Inc., 224 S. Michigan Avenue, Suite 1500, Chicago, IL 60604, (312) 922-1115, Fax: (312) 922-1157, www.euromonitor.com; *International Marketing Data and Statistics 2008* and *World Marketing Data and Statistics.*

International Labour Office, I.L.O. Publications, 4 route des Morillons, CH-1211 Geneva 22, Switzerland, (Telephone in U.S. (202) 653-7652), (Fax in U.S. (202) 653-7687), www.ilo.org; *Yearbook of Labour Statistics 2006.*

M.E. Sharpe, 80 Business Park Drive, Armonk, NY 10504, (800) 541-6563, Fax: (914) 273-2106, www.mesharpe.com; *The Illustrated Book of World Rankings.*

Palgrave Macmillan Ltd., Houndmills, Basingstoke, Hampshire, RG21 6XS, England, (Telephone in U.S. (888) 330-8477), (Fax in U.S. (800) 672-2054), www.palgrave.com; *The Statesman's Yearbook 2008.*

Taylor and Francis Group, An Informa Business, 2 Park Square, Milton Park, Abingdon, Oxford OX14 4RN, United Kingdom, (Dial from U.S. (212) 216-7800), (Fax from U.S. (212) 564-7854), www.tandf.co.uk; *The Europa World Year Book.*

United Nations Food and Agricultural Organization (FAO), Viale delle Terme di Caracalla, 00100 Rome, Italy, (Dial from U.S. (202) 653-2400), (Fax from U.S. (202) 653 5760), www.fao.org; *The State of Food and Agriculture (SOFA) 2006.*

United Nations Statistics Division, New York, NY 10017, (800) 253-9646, Fax: (212) 963-4116, http://unstats.un.org; *Human Development Report 2006.*

The World Bank, 1818 H Street, NW, Washington, DC 20433, (202) 473-1000, Fax: (202) 477-6391, www.worldbank.org; *The World Bank Atlas 2003-2004; World Development Indicators (WDI) 2008;* and *World Development Report 2008.*

BANGLADESH - LAND USE

Central Intelligence Agency, Office of Public Affairs, Washington, DC 20505, (703) 482-0623, Fax: (703) 482-1739, www.cia.gov; *The World Factbook.*

Euromonitor International, Inc., 224 S. Michigan Avenue, Suite 1500, Chicago, IL 60604, (312) 922-1115, Fax: (312) 922-1157, www.euromonitor.com; *International Marketing Data and Statistics 2008.*

United Nations Food and Agricultural Organization (FAO), Viale delle Terme di Caracalla, 00100 Rome, Italy, (Dial from U.S. (202) 653-2400), (Fax from U.S. (202) 653 5760), www.fao.org; *FAO Production Yearbook 2002.*

The World Bank, 1818 H Street, NW, Washington, DC 20433, (202) 473-1000, Fax: (202) 477-6391, www.worldbank.org; *World Development Report 2008.*

BANGLADESH - LIBRARIES

M.E. Sharpe, 80 Business Park Drive, Armonk, NY 10504, (800) 541-6563, Fax: (914) 273-2106, www.mesharpe.com; *The Illustrated Book of World Rankings.*

BANGLADESH - LICENSES

International Monetary Fund (IMF), 700 Nineteenth Street, NW, Washington, DC 20431, (202) 623-7000, Fax: (202) 623-4661, www.imf.org; *Government Finance Statistics Yearbook (2008 Edition).*

BANGLADESH - LIFE EXPECTANCY

Central Intelligence Agency, Office of Public Affairs, Washington, DC 20505, (703) 482-0623, Fax: (703) 482-1739, www.cia.gov; *The World Factbook.*

Economist Intelligence Unit, 111 West 57th Street, New York, NY 10019, (212) 554-0600, Fax: (212) 586-1181, www.eiu.com; *Business Asia.*

Euromonitor International, Inc., 224 S. Michigan Avenue, Suite 1500, Chicago, IL 60604, (312) 922-1115, Fax: (312) 922-1157, www.euromonitor.com; *The World Economic Factbook 2008.*

Palgrave Macmillan Ltd., Houndmills, Basingstoke, Hampshire, RG21 6XS, England, (Telephone in U.S. (888) 330-8477), (Fax in U.S. (800) 672-2054), www.palgrave.com; *The Statesman's Yearbook 2008.*

United Nations Statistics Division, New York, NY 10017, (800) 253-9646, Fax: (212) 963-4116, http://unstats.un.org; *Asia-Pacific in Figures 2004; Human Development Report 2006;* and *World Statistics Pocketbook.*

The World Bank, 1818 H Street, NW, Washington, DC 20433, (202) 473-1000, Fax: (202) 477-6391, www.worldbank.org; *The World Bank Atlas 2003-2004* and *World Development Report 2008.*

BANGLADESH - LITERACY

Euromonitor International, Inc., 224 S. Michigan Avenue, Suite 1500, Chicago, IL 60604, (312) 922-1115, Fax: (312) 922-1157, www.euromonitor.com; *World Marketing Data and Statistics.*

BANGLADESH - LIVESTOCK

Bangladesh Bureau of Statistics (BBS), Ministry of Planning, Statistics Wing, E-27/A, Agargaon, Sher-e-banglanagar, Dhaka-1207, Bangladesh, www.bbs.gov.bd; *Census at a Glance.*

M.E. Sharpe, 80 Business Park Drive, Armonk, NY 10504, (800) 541-6563, Fax: (914) 273-2106, www.mesharpe.com; *The Illustrated Book of World Rankings.*

Palgrave Macmillan Ltd., Houndmills, Basingstoke, Hampshire, RG21 6XS, England, (Telephone in U.S. (888) 330-8477), (Fax in U.S. (800) 672-2054), www.palgrave.com; *The Statesman's Yearbook 2008.*

Taylor and Francis Group, An Informa Business, 2 Park Square, Milton Park, Abingdon, Oxford OX14 4RN, United Kingdom, (Dial from U.S. (212) 216-7800), (Fax from U.S. (212) 564-7854), www.tandf.co.uk; *The Europa World Year Book.*

United Nations Conference on Trade and Development (UNCTAD), DC2-1120, United Nations, New York, NY 10017, (212) 963-0027, www.unctad.org; *UNCTAD Commodity Yearbook.*

United Nations Food and Agricultural Organization (FAO), Viale delle Terme di Caracalla, 00100 Rome, Italy, (Dial from U.S. (202) 653-2400), (Fax from U.S. (202) 653 5760), www.fao.org; *FAO Production Yearbook 2002* and *The State of Food and Agriculture (SOFA) 2006.*

United Nations Statistics Division, New York, NY 10017, (800) 253-9646, Fax: (212) 963-4116, http://unstats.un.org; *Statistical Yearbook.*

BANGLADESH - LOCAL TAXATION

Euromonitor International, Inc., 224 S. Michigan Avenue, Suite 1500, Chicago, IL 60604, (312) 922-1115, Fax: (312) 922-1157, www.euromonitor.com; *International Marketing Data and Statistics 2008.*

BANGLADESH - MANPOWER

Bangladesh Bureau of Statistics (BBS), Ministry of Planning, Statistics Wing, E-27/A, Agargaon, Sher-e-banglanagar, Dhaka-1207, Bangladesh, www.bbs.gov.bd; *Census at a Glance.*

United Nations Statistics Division, New York, NY 10017, (800) 253-9646, Fax: (212) 963-4116, http://unstats.un.org; *Statistical Yearbook for Asia and the Pacific 2004.*

BANGLADESH - MANUFACTURES

Asian Development Bank (ADB), PO Box 789, 0980 Manila, Philippines, www.adb.org; *Key Indicators of Developing Asian and Pacific Countries 2006.*

M.E. Sharpe, 80 Business Park Drive, Armonk, NY 10504, (800) 541-6563, Fax: (914) 273-2106, www.mesharpe.com; *The Illustrated Book of World Rankings.*

United Nations Statistics Division, New York, NY 10017, (800) 253-9646, Fax: (212) 963-4116, http://unstats.un.org; *Statistical Yearbook.*

The World Bank, 1818 H Street, NW, Washington, DC 20433, (202) 473-1000, Fax: (202) 477-6391, www.worldbank.org; *World Development Indicators (WDI) 2008.*

BANGLADESH - MARRIAGE

M.E. Sharpe, 80 Business Park Drive, Armonk, NY 10504, (800) 541-6563, Fax: (914) 273-2106, www.mesharpe.com; *The Illustrated Book of World Rankings.*

United Nations Statistics Division, New York, NY 10017, (800) 253-9646, Fax: (212) 963-4116, http://unstats.un.org; *Demographic Yearbook.*

BANGLADESH - MEAT PRODUCTION

See BANGLADESH - LIVESTOCK

BANGLADESH - MILK PRODUCTION

See BANGLADESH - DAIRY PROCESSING

BANGLADESH - MINERAL INDUSTRIES

Asian Development Bank (ADB), PO Box 789, 0980 Manila, Philippines, www.adb.org; *Key Indicators of Developing Asian and Pacific Countries 2006.*

M.E. Sharpe, 80 Business Park Drive, Armonk, NY 10504, (800) 541-6563, Fax: (914) 273-2106, www.mesharpe.com; *The Illustrated Book of World Rankings.*

Organisation for Economic Cooperation and Development (OECD), 2 rue Andre Pascal, F-75775 Paris Cedex 16, France, (Telephone in U.S. (202) 785-6323), (Fax in U.S. (202) 785-0350), www.oecd.org; *World Energy Outlook 2007.*

Palgrave Macmillan Ltd., Houndmills, Basingstoke, Hampshire, RG21 6XS, England, (Telephone in U.S. (888) 330-8477), (Fax in U.S. (800) 672-2054), www.palgrave.com; *The Statesman's Yearbook 2008.*

Taylor and Francis Group, An Informa Business, 2 Park Square, Milton Park, Abingdon, Oxford OX14 4RN, United Kingdom, (Dial from U.S. (212) 216-7800), (Fax from U.S. (212) 564-7854), www.tandf.co.uk; *The Europa World Year Book.*

United Nations Conference on Trade and Development (UNCTAD), DC2-1120, United Nations, New York, NY 10017, (212) 963-0027, www.unctad.org; *UNCTAD Commodity Yearbook.*

United Nations Statistics Division, New York, NY 10017, (800) 253-9646, Fax: (212) 963-4116, http://unstats.un.org; *Statistical Yearbook.*

BANGLADESH - MONEY EXCHANGE RATES

See BANGLADESH - FOREIGN EXCHANGE RATES

BANGLADESH - MONEY SUPPLY

Asian Development Bank (ADB), PO Box 789, 0980 Manila, Philippines, www.adb.org; *Key Indicators of Developing Asian and Pacific Countries 2006.*

Economist Intelligence Unit, 111 West 57th Street, New York, NY 10019, (212) 554-0600, Fax: (212) 586-1181, www.eiu.com; *Bangladesh Country Report.*

Euromonitor International, Inc., 224 S. Michigan Avenue, Suite 1500, Chicago, IL 60604, (312) 922-1115, Fax: (312) 922-1157, www.euromonitor.com; *International Marketing Data and Statistics 2008.*

International Monetary Fund (IMF), 700 Nineteenth Street, NW, Washington, DC 20431, (202) 623-7000, Fax: (202) 623-4661, www.imf.org; *International Financial Statistics Yearbook 2007.*

Taylor and Francis Group, An Informa Business, 2 Park Square, Milton Park, Abingdon, Oxford OX14 4RN, United Kingdom, (Dial from U.S. (212) 216-7800), (Fax from U.S. (212) 564-7854), www.tandf.co.uk; *The Europa World Year Book.*

United Nations Statistics Division, New York, NY 10017, (800) 253-9646, Fax: (212) 963-4116, http://unstats.un.org; *Statistical Yearbook.*

The World Bank, 1818 H Street, NW, Washington, DC 20433, (202) 473-1000, Fax: (202) 477-6391, www.worldbank.org; *Bangladesh* and *World Development Indicators (WDI) 2008.*

BANGLADESH - MORTALITY

Central Intelligence Agency, Office of Public Affairs, Washington, DC 20505, (703) 482-0623, Fax: (703) 482-1739, www.cia.gov; *The World Factbook.*

Euromonitor International, Inc., 224 S. Michigan Avenue, Suite 1500, Chicago, IL 60604, (312) 922-1115, Fax: (312) 922-1157, www.euromonitor.com; *International Marketing Data and Statistics 2008* and *The World Economic Factbook 2008.*

Palgrave Macmillan Ltd., Houndmills, Basingstoke, Hampshire, RG21 6XS, England, (Telephone in U.S. (888) 330-8477), (Fax in U.S. (800) 672-2054), www.palgrave.com; *The Statesman's Yearbook 2008.*

Taylor and Francis Group, An Informa Business, 2 Park Square, Milton Park, Abingdon, Oxford OX14 4RN, United Kingdom, (Dial from U.S. (212) 216-7800), (Fax from U.S. (212) 564-7854), www.tandf.co.uk; *The Europa World Year Book.*

UNICEF, 3 United Nations Plaza, New York, NY 10017, (800) 253-9646, Fax: (212) 887-7465, www.unicef.org; *The State of the World's Children 2008.*

United Nations Statistics Division, New York, NY 10017, (800) 253-9646, Fax: (212) 963-4116, http://unstats.un.org; *Asia-Pacific in Figures 2004; Demographic Yearbook; Human Development Report 2006; Statistical Yearbook;* and *World Statistics Pocketbook.*

The World Bank, 1818 H Street, NW, Washington, DC 20433, (202) 473-1000, Fax: (202) 477-6391, www.worldbank.org; *The World Bank Atlas 2003-2004; World Development Indicators (WDI) 2008;* and *World Development Report 2008.*

World Health Organization (WHO), Avenue Appia 20, 1211 Geneve 27, Switzerland, (Telephone in U.S. (212) 331-9081), www.who.int; The WHO Global Atlas of Infectious Diseases and *World Health Report 2006.*

BANGLADESH - MOTION PICTURES

Palgrave Macmillan Ltd., Houndmills, Basingstoke, Hampshire, RG21 6XS, England, (Telephone in U.S.

(888) 330-8477), (Fax in U.S. (800) 672-2054), www.palgrave.com; *The Statesman's Yearbook 2008.*

BANGLADESH - MOTOR VEHICLES

Taylor and Francis Group, An Informa Business, 2 Park Square, Milton Park, Abingdon, Oxford OX14 4RN, United Kingdom, (Dial from U.S. (212) 216-7800), (Fax from U.S. (212) 564-7854), www.tandf.co.uk; *The Europa World Year Book.*

United Nations Statistics Division, New York, NY 10017, (800) 253-9646, Fax: (212) 963-4116, http://unstats.un.org; *Statistical Yearbook.*

BANGLADESH - MUSEUMS

M.E. Sharpe, 80 Business Park Drive, Armonk, NY 10504, (800) 541-6563, Fax: (914) 273-2106, www.mesharpe.com; *The Illustrated Book of World Rankings.*

UNESCO Institute for Statistics, C.P. 6128 Succursale Centre-Ville, Montreal, Quebec, H3C 3J7 Canada, (Dial from U.S. (514) 343-6880), (Fax from U.S. (514) 343 6882), www.uis.unesco.org; *Statistical Tables.*

BANGLADESH - NATIONAL INCOME

United Nations Statistics Division, New York, NY 10017, (800) 253-9646, Fax: (212) 963-4116, http://unstats.un.org; *Statistical Yearbook.*

BANGLADESH - NATURAL GAS PRODUCTION

See BANGLADESH - MINERAL INDUSTRIES

BANGLADESH - NUTRITION

Asian Development Bank (ADB), PO Box 789, 0980 Manila, Philippines, www.adb.org; *Key Indicators of Developing Asian and Pacific Countries 2006.*

United Nations Food and Agricultural Organization (FAO), Viale delle Terme di Caracalla, 00100 Rome, Italy, (Dial from U.S. (202) 653-2400), (Fax from U.S. (202) 653 5760), www.fao.org; *The State of Food and Agriculture (SOFA) 2006.*

BANGLADESH - OLDER PEOPLE

M.E. Sharpe, 80 Business Park Drive, Armonk, NY 10504, (800) 541-6563, Fax: (914) 273-2106, www.mesharpe.com; *The Illustrated Book of World Rankings.*

BANGLADESH - PAPER

See BANGLADESH - FORESTS AND FORESTRY

BANGLADESH - PEANUT PRODUCTION

See BANGLADESH - CROPS

BANGLADESH - PESTICIDES

United Nations Food and Agricultural Organization (FAO), Viale delle Terme di Caracalla, 00100 Rome, Italy, (Dial from U.S. (202) 653-2400), (Fax from U.S. (202) 653 5760), www.fao.org; *The State of Food and Agriculture (SOFA) 2006.*

BANGLADESH - PETROLEUM INDUSTRY AND TRADE

Asian Development Bank (ADB), PO Box 789, 0980 Manila, Philippines, www.adb.org; *Key Indicators of Developing Asian and Pacific Countries 2006.*

M.E. Sharpe, 80 Business Park Drive, Armonk, NY 10504, (800) 541-6563, Fax: (914) 273-2106, www.mesharpe.com; *The Illustrated Book of World Rankings.*

Organisation for Economic Cooperation and Development (OECD), 2 rue Andre Pascal, F-75775 Paris Cedex 16, France, (Telephone in U.S. (202) 785-6323), (Fax in U.S. (202) 785-0350), www.oecd.org; *World Energy Outlook 2007.*

Palgrave Macmillan Ltd., Houndmills, Basingstoke, Hampshire, RG21 6XS, England, (Telephone in U.S. (888) 330-8477), (Fax in U.S. (800) 672-2054), www.palgrave.com; *The Statesman's Yearbook 2008.*

PennWell Corporation, 1421 South Sheridan Road, Tulsa, OK 74112, (918) 835-3161, www.pennwell.com; *International Petroleum Encyclopedia 2007.*

U.S. Department of Energy (DOE), Energy Information Administration (EIA), 1000 Independence Avenue, SW, Washington, DC 20585, (202) 586-8800, www.eia.doe.gov; *International Energy Annual 2004* and *International Energy Outlook 2006.*

United Nations Conference on Trade and Development (UNCTAD), DC2-1120, United Nations, New York, NY 10017, (212) 963-0027, www.unctad.org; *UNCTAD Commodity Yearbook.*

United Nations Food and Agricultural Organization (FAO), Viale delle Terme di Caracalla, 00100 Rome, Italy, (Dial from U.S. (202) 653-2400), (Fax from U.S. (202) 653 5760), www.fao.org; *The State of Food and Agriculture (SOFA) 2006.*

United Nations Statistics Division, New York, NY 10017, (800) 253-9646, Fax: (212) 963-4116, http://unstats.un.org; *Statistical Yearbook.*

BANGLADESH - POLITICAL SCIENCE

Asian Development Bank (ADB), PO Box 789, 0980 Manila, Philippines, www.adb.org; *Key Indicators of Developing Asian and Pacific Countries 2006.*

Central Intelligence Agency, Office of Public Affairs, Washington, DC 20505, (703) 482-0623, Fax: (703) 482-1739, www.cia.gov; *The World Factbook.*

International Monetary Fund (IMF), 700 Nineteenth Street, NW, Washington, DC 20431, (202) 623-7000, Fax: (202) 623-4661, www.imf.org; *Government Finance Statistics Yearbook (2008 Edition).*

Palgrave Macmillan Ltd., Houndmills, Basingstoke, Hampshire, RG21 6XS, England, (Telephone in U.S. (888) 330-8477), (Fax in U.S. (800) 672-2054), www.palgrave.com; *The Statesman's Yearbook 2008.*

Taylor and Francis Group, An Informa Business, 2 Park Square, Milton Park, Abingdon, Oxford OX14 4RN, United Kingdom, (Dial from U.S. (212) 216-7800), (Fax from U.S. (212) 564-7854), www.tandf.co.uk; *The Europa World Year Book.*

United Nations Statistics Division, New York, NY 10017, (800) 253-9646, Fax: (212) 963-4116, http://unstats.un.org; *Asia-Pacific in Figures 2004* and *National Accounts Statistics: Compendium of Income Distribution Statistics.*

The World Bank, 1818 H Street, NW, Washington, DC 20433, (202) 473-1000, Fax: (202) 477-6391, www.worldbank.org; *World Development Indicators (WDI) 2008* and *World Development Report 2008.*

BANGLADESH - POPULATION

Asian Development Bank (ADB), PO Box 789, 0980 Manila, Philippines, www.adb.org; *Key Indicators of Developing Asian and Pacific Countries 2006.*

Bangladesh Bureau of Statistics (BBS), Ministry of Planning, Statistics Wing, E-27/A, Agargaon, Shere-banglanagar, Dhaka-1207, Bangladesh, www.bbs.gov.bd; *Census at a Glance.*

Central Intelligence Agency, Office of Public Affairs, Washington, DC 20505, (703) 482-0623, Fax: (703) 482-1739, www.cia.gov; *The World Factbook.*

Economist Intelligence Unit, 111 West 57th Street, New York, NY 10019, (212) 554-0600, Fax: (212) 586-1181, www.eiu.com; *Bangladesh Country Report* and *Business Asia.*

Euromonitor International, Inc., 224 S. Michigan Avenue, Suite 1500, Chicago, IL 60604, (312) 922-1115, Fax: (312) 922-1157, www.euromonitor.com; *International Marketing Data and Statistics 2008* and *The World Economic Factbook 2008.*

International Labour Office, I.L.O. Publications, 4 route des Morillons, CH-1211 Geneva 22, Switzerland, (Telephone in U.S. (202) 653-7652), (Fax in U.S. (202) 653-7687), www.ilo.org; *Yearbook of Labour Statistics 2006.*

M.E. Sharpe, 80 Business Park Drive, Armonk, NY 10504, (800) 541-6563, Fax: (914) 273-2106, www.mesharpe.com; *The Illustrated Book of World Rankings.*

Palgrave Macmillan Ltd., Houndmills, Basingstoke, Hampshire, RG21 6XS, England, (Telephone in U.S. (888) 330-8477), (Fax in U.S. (800) 672-2054), www.palgrave.com; *The Statesman's Yearbook 2008.*

Taylor and Francis Group, An Informa Business, 2 Park Square, Milton Park, Abingdon, Oxford OX14 4RN, United Kingdom, (Dial from U.S. (212) 216-7800), (Fax from U.S. (212) 564-7854), www.tandf.co.uk; *The Europa World Year Book.*

U.S. Department of State (DOS), 2201 C Street NW, Washington, DC 20520, (202) 647-4000, www.state.gov; *World Military Expenditures and Arms Transfers (WMEAT).*

United Nations Food and Agricultural Organization (FAO), Viale delle Terme di Caracalla, 00100 Rome, Italy, (Dial from U.S. (202) 653-2400), (Fax from U.S. (202) 653 5760), www.fao.org; *FAO Production Yearbook 2002.*

United Nations Statistics Division, New York, NY 10017, (800) 253-9646, Fax: (212) 963-4116, http://unstats.un.org; *Asia-Pacific in Figures 2004; Demographic Yearbook; Human Development Report 2006; Statistical Yearbook;* and *World Statistics Pocketbook.*

The World Bank, 1818 H Street, NW, Washington, DC 20433, (202) 473-1000, Fax: (202) 477-6391, www.worldbank.org; *Bangladesh; The World Bank Atlas 2003-2004;* and *World Development Report 2008.*

World Health Organization (WHO), Avenue Appia 20, 1211 Geneve 27, Switzerland, (Telephone in U.S. (212) 331-9081), www.who.int; *World Health Report 2006.*

Worldinformation.com, 2 Market Street, Saffron Walden, Essex CB10 1HZ, United Kingdom, www.worldinformation.com; The World of Information (www.worldinformation.com).

BANGLADESH - POPULATION DENSITY

Bangladesh Bureau of Statistics (BBS), Ministry of Planning, Statistics Wing, E-27/A, Agargaon, Shere-banglanagar, Dhaka-1207, Bangladesh, www.bbs.gov.bd; *Census at a Glance.*

Central Intelligence Agency, Office of Public Affairs, Washington, DC 20505, (703) 482-0623, Fax: (703) 482-1739, www.cia.gov; *The World Factbook.*

Euromonitor International, Inc., 224 S. Michigan Avenue, Suite 1500, Chicago, IL 60604, (312) 922-1115, Fax: (312) 922-1157, www.euromonitor.com; *International Marketing Data and Statistics 2008* and *The World Economic Factbook 2008.*

M.E. Sharpe, 80 Business Park Drive, Armonk, NY 10504, (800) 541-6563, Fax: (914) 273-2106, www.mesharpe.com; *The Illustrated Book of World Rankings.*

Palgrave Macmillan Ltd., Houndmills, Basingstoke, Hampshire, RG21 6XS, England, (Telephone in U.S. (888) 330-8477), (Fax in U.S. (800) 672-2054), www.palgrave.com; *The Statesman's Yearbook 2008.*

Taylor and Francis Group, An Informa Business, 2 Park Square, Milton Park, Abingdon, Oxford OX14 4RN, United Kingdom, (Dial from U.S. (212) 216-7800), (Fax from U.S. (212) 564-7854), www.tandf.co.uk; *The Europa World Year Book.*

United Nations Food and Agricultural Organization (FAO), Viale delle Terme di Caracalla, 00100 Rome, Italy, (Dial from U.S. (202) 653-2400), (Fax from U.S. (202) 653 5760), www.fao.org; *The State of Food and Agriculture (SOFA) 2006.*

United Nations Statistics Division, New York, NY 10017, (800) 253-9646, Fax: (212) 963-4116, http://unstats.un.org; *Statistical Yearbook.*

The World Bank, 1818 H Street, NW, Washington, DC 20433, (202) 473-1000, Fax: (202) 477-6391, www.worldbank.org; *Bangladesh* and *World Development Report 2008.*

BANGLADESH - POSTAL SERVICE

M.E. Sharpe, 80 Business Park Drive, Armonk, NY 10504, (800) 541-6563, Fax: (914) 273-2106, www.mesharpe.com; *The Illustrated Book of World Rankings.*

Palgrave Macmillan Ltd., Houndmills, Basingstoke, Hampshire, RG21 6XS, England, (Telephone in U.S. (888) 330-8477), (Fax in U.S. (800) 672-2054), www.palgrave.com; *The Statesman's Yearbook 2008.*

United Nations Statistics Division, New York, NY 10017, (800) 253-9646, Fax: (212) 963-4116, http://unstats.un.org; *Statistical Yearbook.*

BANGLADESH - POWER RESOURCES

Bangladesh Bureau of Statistics (BBS), Ministry of Planning, Statistics Wing, E-27/A, Agargaon, Sher-e-banglanagar, Dhaka-1207, Bangladesh, www.bbs.gov.bd; *Census at a Glance.*

Euromonitor International, Inc., 224 S. Michigan Avenue, Suite 1500, Chicago, IL 60604, (312) 922-1115, Fax: (312) 922-1157, www.euromonitor.com; *International Marketing Data and Statistics 2008; The World Economic Factbook 2008;* and *World Marketing Data and Statistics.*

M.E. Sharpe, 80 Business Park Drive, Armonk, NY 10504, (800) 541-6563, Fax: (914) 273-2106, www.mesharpe.com; *The Illustrated Book of World Rankings.*

Organisation for Economic Cooperation and Development (OECD), 2 rue Andre Pascal, F-75775 Paris Cedex 16, France, (Telephone in U.S. (202) 785-6323), (Fax in U.S. (202) 785-0350), www.oecd.org; *World Energy Outlook 2007.*

Palgrave Macmillan Ltd., Houndmills, Basingstoke, Hampshire, RG21 6XS, England, (Telephone in U.S. (888) 330-8477), (Fax in U.S. (800) 672-2054), www.palgrave.com; *The Statesman's Yearbook 2008.*

U.S. Department of Energy (DOE), Energy Information Administration (EIA), 1000 Independence Avenue, SW, Washington, DC 20585, (202) 586-8800, www.eia.doe.gov; *International Energy Annual 2004* and *International Energy Outlook 2006.*

United Nations Food and Agricultural Organization (FAO), Viale delle Terme di Caracalla, 00100 Rome, Italy, (Dial from U.S. (202) 653-2400), (Fax from U.S. (202) 653 5760), www.fao.org; *The State of Food and Agriculture (SOFA) 2006.*

United Nations Statistics Division, New York, NY 10017, (800) 253-9646, Fax: (212) 963-4116, http://unstats.un.org; *Asia-Pacific in Figures 2004; Human Development Report 2006; Statistical Yearbook; Statistical Yearbook for Asia and the Pacific 2004;* and *World Statistics Pocketbook.*

The World Bank, 1818 H Street, NW, Washington, DC 20433, (202) 473-1000, Fax: (202) 477-6391, www.worldbank.org; *The World Bank Atlas 2003-2004* and *World Development Report 2008.*

BANGLADESH - PRICES

Asian Development Bank (ADB), PO Box 789, 0980 Manila, Philippines, www.adb.org; *Key Indicators of Developing Asian and Pacific Countries 2006.*

Bangladesh Bureau of Statistics (BBS), Ministry of Planning, Statistics Wing, E-27/A, Agargaon, Sher-e-banglanagar, Dhaka-1207, Bangladesh, www.bbs.gov.bd; *Census at a Glance.*

Euromonitor International, Inc., 224 S. Michigan Avenue, Suite 1500, Chicago, IL 60604, (312) 922-1115, Fax: (312) 922-1157, www.euromonitor.com; *World Marketing Data and Statistics.*

International Labour Office, I.L.O. Publications, 4 route des Morillons, CH-1211 Geneva 22, Switzerland, (Telephone in U.S. (202) 653-7652), (Fax in U.S. (202) 653-7687), www.ilo.org; *Yearbook of Labour Statistics 2006.*

International Monetary Fund (IMF), 700 Nineteenth Street, NW, Washington, DC 20431, (202) 623-7000, Fax: (202) 623-4661, www.imf.org; *International Financial Statistics Yearbook 2007.*

M.E. Sharpe, 80 Business Park Drive, Armonk, NY 10504, (800) 541-6563, Fax: (914) 273-2106, www.mesharpe.com; *The Illustrated Book of World Rankings.*

United Nations Food and Agricultural Organization (FAO), Viale delle Terme di Caracalla, 00100 Rome, Italy, (Dial from U.S. (202) 653-2400), (Fax from U.S. (202) 653 5760), www.fao.org; *FAO Production Yearbook 2002* and *The State of Food and Agriculture (SOFA) 2006.*

The World Bank, 1818 H Street, NW, Washington, DC 20433, (202) 473-1000, Fax: (202) 477-6391, www.worldbank.org; *Bangladesh.*

BANGLADESH - PROFESSIONS

United Nations Statistics Division, New York, NY 10017, (800) 253-9646, Fax: (212) 963-4116, http://unstats.un.org; *Statistical Yearbook.*

BANGLADESH - PUBLIC HEALTH

Bangladesh Bureau of Statistics (BBS), Ministry of Planning, Statistics Wing, E-27/A, Agargaon, Sher-e-banglanagar, Dhaka-1207, Bangladesh, www.bbs.gov.bd; *Census at a Glance.*

Economist Intelligence Unit, 111 West 57th Street, New York, NY 10019, (212) 554-0600, Fax: (212) 586-1181, www.eiu.com; *Business Asia.*

Euromonitor International, Inc., 224 S. Michigan Avenue, Suite 1500, Chicago, IL 60604, (312) 922-1115, Fax: (312) 922-1157, www.euromonitor.com; *World Marketing Data and Statistics.*

International Monetary Fund (IMF), 700 Nineteenth Street, NW, Washington, DC 20431, (202) 623-7000, Fax: (202) 623-4661, www.imf.org; *Government Finance Statistics Yearbook (2008 Edition).*

M.E. Sharpe, 80 Business Park Drive, Armonk, NY 10504, (800) 541-6563, Fax: (914) 273-2106, www.mesharpe.com; *The Illustrated Book of World Rankings.*

Palgrave Macmillan Ltd., Houndmills, Basingstoke, Hampshire, RG21 6XS, England, (Telephone in U.S. (888) 330-8477), (Fax in U.S. (800) 672-2054), www.palgrave.com; *The Statesman's Yearbook 2008.*

UNICEF, 3 United Nations Plaza, New York, NY 10017, (800) 253-9646, Fax: (212) 887-7465, www.unicef.org; *The State of the World's Children 2008.*

United Nations Statistics Division, New York, NY 10017, (800) 253-9646, Fax: (212) 963-4116, http://unstats.un.org; *Asia-Pacific in Figures 2004; Human Development Report 2006;* and *Statistical Yearbook.*

The World Bank, 1818 H Street, NW, Washington, DC 20433, (202) 473-1000, Fax: (202) 477-6391, www.worldbank.org; *Bangladesh* and *World Development Report 2008.*

World Health Organization (WHO), Avenue Appia 20, 1211 Geneve 27, Switzerland, (Telephone in U.S. (212) 331-9081), www.who.int; The WHO Global Atlas of Infectious Diseases and *World Health Report 2006.*

BANGLADESH - PUBLIC UTILITIES

United Nations Statistics Division, New York, NY 10017, (800) 253-9646, Fax: (212) 963-4116, http://unstats.un.org; *Electric Power in Asia and the Pacific 2001 and 2002.*

BANGLADESH - PUBLISHERS AND PUBLISHING

Palgrave Macmillan Ltd., Houndmills, Basingstoke, Hampshire, RG21 6XS, England, (Telephone in U.S. (888) 330-8477), (Fax in U.S. (800) 672-2054), www.palgrave.com; *The Statesman's Yearbook 2008.*

Taylor and Francis Group, An Informa Business, 2 Park Square, Milton Park, Abingdon, Oxford OX14 4RN, United Kingdom, (Dial from U.S. (212) 216-7800), (Fax from U.S. (212) 564-7854), www.tandf.co.uk; *The Europa World Year Book.*

BANGLADESH - RADIO BROADCASTING

Palgrave Macmillan Ltd., Houndmills, Basingstoke, Hampshire, RG21 6XS, England, (Telephone in U.S. (888) 330-8477), (Fax in U.S. (800) 672-2054), www.palgrave.com; *The Statesman's Yearbook 2008.*

BANGLADESH - RAILROADS

Jane's Information Group, 110 North Royal Street, Suite 200, Alexandria, VA 22314, (703) 683-3700, Fax: (800) 836-0297, www.janes.com; *Jane's World Railways.*

Palgrave Macmillan Ltd., Houndmills, Basingstoke, Hampshire, RG21 6XS, England, (Telephone in U.S. (888) 330-8477), (Fax in U.S. (800) 672-2054), www.palgrave.com; *The Statesman's Yearbook 2008.*

Taylor and Francis Group, An Informa Business, 2 Park Square, Milton Park, Abingdon, Oxford OX14 4RN, United Kingdom, (Dial from U.S. (212) 216-7800), (Fax from U.S. (212) 564-7854), www.tandf.co.uk; *The Europa World Year Book.*

United Nations Statistics Division, New York, NY 10017, (800) 253-9646, Fax: (212) 963-4116, http://unstats.un.org; *Statistical Yearbook.*

BANGLADESH - RELIGION

Central Intelligence Agency, Office of Public Affairs, Washington, DC 20505, (703) 482-0623, Fax: (703) 482-1739, www.cia.gov; *The World Factbook.*

M.E. Sharpe, 80 Business Park Drive, Armonk, NY 10504, (800) 541-6563, Fax: (914) 273-2106, www.mesharpe.com; *The Illustrated Book of World Rankings.*

Palgrave Macmillan Ltd., Houndmills, Basingstoke, Hampshire, RG21 6XS, England, (Telephone in U.S. (888) 330-8477), (Fax in U.S. (800) 672-2054), www.palgrave.com; *The Statesman's Yearbook 2008.*

BANGLADESH - RENT CHARGES

International Labour Office, I.L.O. Publications, 4 route des Morillons, CH-1211 Geneva 22, Switzerland, (Telephone in U.S. (202) 653-7652), (Fax in U.S. (202) 653-7687), www.ilo.org; *Yearbook of Labour Statistics 2006.*

BANGLADESH - RESERVES (ACCOUNTING)

Asian Development Bank (ADB), PO Box 789, 0980 Manila, Philippines, www.adb.org; *Key Indicators of Developing Asian and Pacific Countries 2006.*

Euromonitor International, Inc., 224 S. Michigan Avenue, Suite 1500, Chicago, IL 60604, (312) 922-1115, Fax: (312) 922-1157, www.euromonitor.com; *International Marketing Data and Statistics 2008.*

The World Bank, 1818 H Street, NW, Washington, DC 20433, (202) 473-1000, Fax: (202) 477-6391, www.worldbank.org; *World Development Indicators (WDI) 2008.*

BANGLADESH - RETAIL TRADE

Euromonitor International, Inc., 224 S. Michigan Avenue, Suite 1500, Chicago, IL 60604, (312) 922-1115, Fax: (312) 922-1157, www.euromonitor.com; *World Marketing Data and Statistics.*

BANGLADESH - RICE PRODUCTION

See BANGLADESH - CROPS

BANGLADESH - ROADS

Central Intelligence Agency, Office of Public Affairs, Washington, DC 20505, (703) 482-0623, Fax: (703) 482-1739, www.cia.gov; *The World Factbook.*

Economist Intelligence Unit, 111 West 57th Street, New York, NY 10019, (212) 554-0600, Fax: (212) 586-1181, www.eiu.com; *Business Asia.*

Palgrave Macmillan Ltd., Houndmills, Basingstoke, Hampshire, RG21 6XS, England, (Telephone in U.S. (888) 330-8477), (Fax in U.S. (800) 672-2054), www.palgrave.com; *The Statesman's Yearbook 2008.*

BANGLADESH - RUBBER INDUSTRY AND TRADE

International Rubber Study Group (IRSG), 1st Floor, Heron House, 109/115 Wembley Hill Road, Wemb-

ley, Middlesex HA9 8DA, United Kingdom, www.rubberstudy.com; *Rubber Statistical Bulletin; Summary of World Rubber Statistics 2005; World Rubber Statistics Handbook (Volume 6, 1975-2001);* and *World Rubber Statistics Historic Handbook.*

M.E. Sharpe, 80 Business Park Drive, Armonk, NY 10504, (800) 541-6563, Fax: (914) 273-2106, www.mesharpe.com; *The Illustrated Book of World Rankings.*

BANGLADESH - SALT PRODUCTION

See BANGLADESH - MINERAL INDUSTRIES

BANGLADESH - SHEEP

M.E. Sharpe, 80 Business Park Drive, Armonk, NY 10504, (800) 541-6563, Fax: (914) 273-2106, www.mesharpe.com; *The Illustrated Book of World Rankings.*

United Nations Statistics Division, New York, NY 10017, (800) 253-9646, Fax: (212) 963-4116, http://unstats.un.org; *Statistical Yearbook.*

BANGLADESH - SHIPPING

Lloyd's Register - Fairplay, 8410 N.W. 53rd Terrace, Suite 207, Miami FL 33166, (305) 718-9929, Fax: (305) 718-9663, www.lrfairplay.com; *Register of Ships 2007-2008; World Casualty Statistics 2007; World Fleet Statistics 2006; World Marine Propulsion Report 2006-2010; World Shipbuilding Statistics 2007;* and The World Shipping Encyclopaedia.

Palgrave Macmillan Ltd., Houndmills, Basingstoke, Hampshire, RG21 6XS, England, (Telephone in U.S. (888) 330-8477), (Fax in U.S. (800) 672-2054), www.palgrave.com; *The Statesman's Yearbook 2008.*

Taylor and Francis Group, An Informa Business, 2 Park Square, Milton Park, Abingdon, Oxford OX14 4RN, United Kingdom, (Dial from U.S. (212) 216-7800), (Fax from U.S. (212) 564-7854), www.tandf.co.uk; *The Europa World Year Book.*

U.S. Department of Transportation (DOT), Maritime Administration (MARAD), West Building, Southeast Federal Center, 1200 New Jersey Avenue, SE, Washington, DC 20590, (800) 99-MARAD, www.marad.dot.gov; *World Merchant Fleet 2005.*

United Nations Statistics Division, New York, NY 10017, (800) 253-9646, Fax: (212) 963-4116, http://unstats.un.org; *Statistical Yearbook.*

BANGLADESH - SILVER PRODUCTION

See BANGLADESH - MINERAL INDUSTRIES

BANGLADESH - SOCIAL ECOLOGY

Asian Development Bank (ADB), PO Box 789, 0980 Manila, Philippines, www.adb.org; *Key Indicators of Developing Asian and Pacific Countries 2006.*

Bangladesh Bureau of Statistics (BBS), Ministry of Planning, Statistics Wing, E-27/A, Agargaon, Sher-e-banglanagar, Dhaka-1207, Bangladesh, www.bbs.gov.bd; *Census at a Glance.*

M.E. Sharpe, 80 Business Park Drive, Armonk, NY 10504, (800) 541-6563, Fax: (914) 273-2106, www.mesharpe.com; *The Illustrated Book of World Rankings.*

United Nations Statistics Division, New York, NY 10017, (800) 253-9646, Fax: (212) 963-4116, http://unstats.un.org; *World Statistics Pocketbook.*

BANGLADESH - SOCIAL SECURITY

International Monetary Fund (IMF), 700 Nineteenth Street, NW, Washington, DC 20431, (202) 623-7000, Fax: (202) 623-4661, www.imf.org; *Government Finance Statistics Yearbook (2008 Edition).*

United Nations Statistics Division, New York, NY 10017, (800) 253-9646, Fax: (212) 963-4116, http://unstats.un.org; *National Accounts Statistics: Compendium of Income Distribution Statistics.*

BANGLADESH - STEEL PRODUCTION

See BANGLADESH - MINERAL INDUSTRIES

BANGLADESH - SUGAR PRODUCTION

See BANGLADESH - CROPS

BANGLADESH - SULPHUR PRODUCTION

See BANGLADESH - MINERAL INDUSTRIES

BANGLADESH - TAXATION

International Monetary Fund (IMF), 700 Nineteenth Street, NW, Washington, DC 20431, (202) 623-7000, Fax: (202) 623-4661, www.imf.org; *Government Finance Statistics Yearbook (2008 Edition).*

Taylor and Francis Group, An Informa Business, 2 Park Square, Milton Park, Abingdon, Oxford OX14 4RN, United Kingdom, (Dial from U.S. (212) 216-7800), (Fax from U.S. (212) 564-7854), www.tandf.co.uk; *The Europa World Year Book.*

The World Bank, 1818 H Street, NW, Washington, DC 20433, (202) 473-1000, Fax: (202) 477-6391, www.worldbank.org; *World Development Indicators (WDI) 2008.*

BANGLADESH - TEA PRODUCTION

See BANGLADESH - CROPS

BANGLADESH - TELEPHONE

Economist Intelligence Unit, 111 West 57th Street, New York, NY 10019, (212) 554-0600, Fax: (212) 586-1181, www.eiu.com; *Business Asia.*

International Telecommunication Union (ITU), Place des Nations, 1211 Geneva 20, Switzerland, www.itu.int; World Telecommunication Indicators Database.

Palgrave Macmillan Ltd., Houndmills, Basingstoke, Hampshire, RG21 6XS, England, (Telephone in U.S. (888) 330-8477), (Fax in U.S. (800) 672-2054), www.palgrave.com; *The Statesman's Yearbook 2008.*

Taylor and Francis Group, An Informa Business, 2 Park Square, Milton Park, Abingdon, Oxford OX14 4RN, United Kingdom, (Dial from U.S. (212) 216-7800), (Fax from U.S. (212) 564-7854), www.tandf.co.uk; *The Europa World Year Book.*

United Nations Statistics Division, New York, NY 10017, (800) 253-9646, Fax: (212) 963-4116, http://unstats.un.org; *Statistical Yearbook* and *World Statistics Pocketbook.*

BANGLADESH - TEXTILE INDUSTRY

Palgrave Macmillan Ltd., Houndmills, Basingstoke, Hampshire, RG21 6XS, England, (Telephone in U.S. (888) 330-8477), (Fax in U.S. (800) 672-2054), www.palgrave.com; *The Statesman's Yearbook 2008.*

United Nations Conference on Trade and Development (UNCTAD), DC2-1120, United Nations, New York, NY 10017, (212) 963-0027, www.unctad.org; *UNCTAD Commodity Yearbook.*

United Nations Food and Agricultural Organization (FAO), Viale delle Terme di Caracalla, 00100 Rome, Italy, (Dial from U.S. (202) 653-2400), (Fax from U.S. (202) 653 5760), www.fao.org; *FAO Production Yearbook 2002.*

United Nations Statistics Division, New York, NY 10017, (800) 253-9646, Fax: (212) 963-4116, http://unstats.un.org; *Statistical Yearbook.*

BANGLADESH - TOBACCO INDUSTRY

Foreign Agricultural Service (FAS), U.S. Department of Agriculture (USDA), 1400 Independence Avenue, SW, Washington, DC 20250, (202) 720-3935, www.fas.usda.gov; *Tobacco: World Markets and Trade.*

M.E. Sharpe, 80 Business Park Drive, Armonk, NY 10504, (800) 541-6563, Fax: (914) 273-2106, www.mesharpe.com; *The Illustrated Book of World Rankings.*

United Nations Statistics Division, New York, NY 10017, (800) 253-9646, Fax: (212) 963-4116, http://unstats.un.org; *Statistical Yearbook.*

BANGLADESH - TOURISM

Euromonitor International, Inc., 224 S. Michigan Avenue, Suite 1500, Chicago, IL 60604, (312) 922-1115, Fax: (312) 922-1157, www.euromonitor.com; *The World Economic Factbook 2008* and *World Marketing Data and Statistics.*

M.E. Sharpe, 80 Business Park Drive, Armonk, NY 10504, (800) 541-6563, Fax: (914) 273-2106, www.mesharpe.com; *The Illustrated Book of World Rankings.*

Palgrave Macmillan Ltd., Houndmills, Basingstoke, Hampshire, RG21 6XS, England, (Telephone in U.S. (888) 330-8477), (Fax in U.S. (800) 672-2054), www.palgrave.com; *The Statesman's Yearbook 2008.*

Taylor and Francis Group, An Informa Business, 2 Park Square, Milton Park, Abingdon, Oxford OX14 4RN, United Kingdom, (Dial from U.S. (212) 216-7800), (Fax from U.S. (212) 564-7854), www.tandf.co.uk; *The Europa World Year Book.*

United Nations Statistics Division, New York, NY 10017, (800) 253-9646, Fax: (212) 963-4116, http://unstats.un.org; *Statistical Yearbook.*

United Nations World Tourism Organization (UNWTO), Capitan Haya 42, 28020 Madrid, Spain, www.world-tourism.org; *Yearbook of Tourism Statistics.*

The World Bank, 1818 H Street, NW, Washington, DC 20433, (202) 473-1000, Fax: (202) 477-6391, www.worldbank.org; *Bangladesh.*

BANGLADESH - TRADE

See BANGLADESH - INTERNATIONAL TRADE

BANGLADESH - TRANSPORTATION

Bangladesh Bureau of Statistics (BBS), Ministry of Planning, Statistics Wing, E-27/A, Agargaon, Sher-e-banglanagar, Dhaka-1207, Bangladesh, www.bbs.gov.bd; *Census at a Glance.*

Central Intelligence Agency, Office of Public Affairs, Washington, DC 20505, (703) 482-0623, Fax: (703) 482-1739, www.cia.gov; *The World Factbook.*

Economist Intelligence Unit, 111 West 57th Street, New York, NY 10019, (212) 554-0600, Fax: (212) 586-1181, www.eiu.com; *Business Asia.*

Euromonitor International, Inc., 224 S. Michigan Avenue, Suite 1500, Chicago, IL 60604, (312) 922-1115, Fax: (312) 922-1157, www.euromonitor.com; *International Marketing Data and Statistics 2008* and *World Marketing Data and Statistics.*

M.E. Sharpe, 80 Business Park Drive, Armonk, NY 10504, (800) 541-6563, Fax: (914) 273-2106, www.mesharpe.com; *The Illustrated Book of World Rankings.*

Palgrave Macmillan Ltd., Houndmills, Basingstoke, Hampshire, RG21 6XS, England, (Telephone in U.S. (888) 330-8477), (Fax in U.S. (800) 672-2054), www.palgrave.com; *The Statesman's Yearbook 2008.*

Taylor and Francis Group, An Informa Business, 2 Park Square, Milton Park, Abingdon, Oxford OX14 4RN, United Kingdom, (Dial from U.S. (212) 216-7800), (Fax from U.S. (212) 564-7854), www.tandf.co.uk; *The Europa World Year Book.*

United Nations Statistics Division, New York, NY 10017, (800) 253-9646, Fax: (212) 963-4116, http://unstats.un.org; *Human Development Report 2006* and *Statistical Yearbook for Asia and the Pacific 2004.*

The World Bank, 1818 H Street, NW, Washington, DC 20433, (202) 473-1000, Fax: (202) 477-6391, www.worldbank.org; *Bangladesh.*

BANGLADESH - TRAVEL COSTS

International Monetary Fund (IMF), 700 Nineteenth Street, NW, Washington, DC 20431, (202) 623-7000, Fax: (202) 623-4661, www.imf.org; *Government Finance Statistics Yearbook (2008 Edition).*

BANGLADESH - UNEMPLOYMENT

Central Intelligence Agency, Office of Public Affairs, Washington, DC 20505, (703) 482-0623, Fax: (703) 482-1739, www.cia.gov; *The World Factbook.*

Euromonitor International, Inc., 224 S. Michigan Avenue, Suite 1500, Chicago, IL 60604, (312) 922-

1115, Fax: (312) 922-1157, www.euromonitor.com; *International Marketing Data and Statistics 2008.*

International Labour Office, I.L.O. Publications, 4 route des Morillons, CH-1211 Geneva 22, Switzerland, (Telephone in U.S. (202) 653-7652), (Fax in U.S. (202) 653-7687), www.ilo.org; *Yearbook of Labour Statistics 2006.*

Palgrave Macmillan Ltd., Houndmills, Basingstoke, Hampshire, RG21 6XS, England, (Telephone in U.S. (888) 330-8477), (Fax in U.S. (800) 672-2054), www.palgrave.com; *The Statesman's Yearbook 2008.*

BANGLADESH - VITAL STATISTICS

Euromonitor International, Inc., 224 S. Michigan Avenue, Suite 1500, Chicago, IL 60604, (312) 922-1115, Fax: (312) 922-1157, www.euromonitor.com; *International Marketing Data and Statistics 2008.*

Palgrave Macmillan Ltd., Houndmills, Basingstoke, Hampshire, RG21 6XS, England, (Telephone in U.S. (888) 330-8477), (Fax in U.S. (800) 672-2054), www.palgrave.com; *The Statesman's Yearbook 2008.*

United Nations Statistics Division, New York, NY 10017, (800) 253-9646, Fax: (212) 963-4116, http://unstats.un.org; *Statistical Yearbook.*

World Health Organization (WHO), Avenue Appia 20, 1211 Geneve 27, Switzerland, (Telephone in U.S. (212) 331-9081), www.who.int; *World Health Report 2006.*

BANGLADESH - WAGES

Bangladesh Bureau of Statistics (BBS), Ministry of Planning, Statistics Wing, E-27/A, Agargaon, Sher-e-banglanagar, Dhaka-1207, Bangladesh, www.bbs.gov.bd; *Census at a Glance.*

International Labour Office, I.L.O. Publications, 4 route des Morillons, CH-1211 Geneva 22, Switzerland, (Telephone in U.S. (202) 653-7652), (Fax in U.S. (202) 653-7687), www.ilo.org; *Yearbook of Labour Statistics 2006.*

United Nations Statistics Division, New York, NY 10017, (800) 253-9646, Fax: (212) 963-4116, http://unstats.un.org; *Statistical Yearbook* and *Statistical Yearbook for Asia and the Pacific 2004.*

The World Bank, 1818 H Street, NW, Washington, DC 20433, (202) 473-1000, Fax: (202) 477-6391, www.worldbank.org; *Bangladesh.*

BANGLADESH - WEATHER

See BANGLADESH - CLIMATE

BANGLADESH - WELFARE STATE

International Monetary Fund (IMF), 700 Nineteenth Street, NW, Washington, DC 20431, (202) 623-7000, Fax: (202) 623-4661, www.imf.org; *Government Finance Statistics Yearbook (2008 Edition).*

BANGLADESH - WHEAT PRODUCTION

See BANGLADESH - CROPS

BANGLADESH - WHOLESALE PRICE INDEXES

Asian Development Bank (ADB), PO Box 789, 0980 Manila, Philippines, www.adb.org; *Key Indicators of Developing Asian and Pacific Countries 2006.*

BANGLADESH - WINE PRODUCTION

See BANGLADESH - BEVERAGE INDUSTRY

BANGLADESH - WOOL PRODUCTION

See BANGLADESH - TEXTILE INDUSTRY

BANGLADESH - YARN PRODUCTION

See BANGLADESH - TEXTILE INDUSTRY

BANKRUPTCIES

Office of Public Affairs, Administrative Office of the United States Courts, Washington, DC 20544, (202) 502-2600, www.uscourts.gov; *Statistical Tables for the Federal Judiciary* and unpublished data.

BANKS, COMMERCIAL

American Bankers Association, 1120 Connecticut Avenue, NW, Washington, DC 20036, (800) BANKERS, www.aba.com; *Quick Banking Facts.*

Bank for International Settlements (BIS), CH-4002, Basel, Switzerland, www.bis.org; *Annual Report 2006/07.*

Banque de France, 48 rue Croix des Petits champs, 75001 Paris, France, www.banque-france.fr/home.htm; Money and Banking Statistics.

British Bankers' Association (BBA), Pinners Hall, 105-108 Old Broad Street, London EC2N 1EX, United Kingdom, www.bba.org.uk; *Statistics Release.*

European Central Bank (ECB), Postfach 160319, D-60066 Frankfurt am Main, Germany, www.ecb.int; *Monetary Financial Institutions (MFI) Interest Rate Statistics (MIR).*

Federal Deposit Insurance Corporation (FDIC), 550 Seventeenth Street, NW, Washington, DC 20429-0002, (877) 275-3342, www.fdic.gov; *2007 Annual Report; Quarterly Banking Profile (QBP); State Banking Performance Summary;* and Statistics on Depository Institutions (SDI) (web app).

Federal Financial Institutions Examination Council (FFIEC), 3501 Fairfax Drive, Room D8073A, Arlington, VA 22226, (202) 872-7500, www.ffiec.gov; Trust Institutions Search.

Insurance Information Institute (III), 110 William Street, New York, NY 10038, (212) 346-5500, www.iii.org; *The Financial Services Fact Book 2008.*

Monetary and Financial Statistics Division, Bank of England, Threadneedle Street, London EC2R 8AH, United Kingdom, www.bankofengland.co.uk/statistics; *Statistical Interactive Database.*

Mortgage Bankers Association of America (MBA), 1919 Pennsylvania Avenue, NW, Washington, DC 20006-3404, (202) 557-2700, www.mbaa.org; *The Cost Study: Income and Cost for Origination and Servicing of One-to-Four-Unit Residential Loans* and *Mortgage Banking Compensation Survey.*

National Bureau of Statistics of China (NBS), No. 57, Yuetan Nanjie, Sanlihe, Xicheng District, Beijing 100826, China, www.stats.gov.cn/english; *Banking and Insurance.*

U.S. Census Bureau, Center for Economic Studies, 4600 Silver Hill Road, Washington DC 20233, (301) 457-1235, www.ces.census.gov; *2002 Economic Census, Management of Company and Enterprises.*

U.S. Census Bureau, Company Statistics Division, 4700 Silver Hill Road, Washington DC 20233-0001, (301) 763-3030, www.census.gov/csd/; *County Business Patterns 2004.*

BANKS, COMMERCIAL - ATM'S

Board of Governors of the Federal Reserve System, Constitution Avenue, NW, Washington, DC 20551, (202) 452-3000, www.federalreserve.gov; *Annual Report to the Congress on Retail Fees and Services of Depository Institutions.*

BANKS, COMMERCIAL - CHECKING ACCOUNTS

Board of Governors of the Federal Reserve System, Constitution Avenue, NW, Washington, DC 20551, (202) 452-3000, www.federalreserve.gov; *Annual Report to the Congress on Retail Fees and Services of Depository Institutions.*

BANKS, COMMERCIAL - CONSUMER CREDIT FINANCE RATES

Board of Governors of the Federal Reserve System, Constitution Avenue, NW, Washington, DC 20551, (202) 452-3000, www.federalreserve.gov; *Federal Reserve Bulletin.*

BANKS, COMMERCIAL - CREDIT CARDS

Federal Deposit Insurance Corporation (FDIC), 550 Seventeenth Street, NW, Washington, DC 20429-0002, (877) 275-3342, www.fdic.gov; *2007 Annual Report; Quarterly Banking Profile (QBP);* and *State Banking Performance Summary.*

Federal Financial Institutions Examination Council (FFIEC), 3501 Fairfax Drive, Room D8073A, Arlington, VA 22226, (202) 872-7500, www.ffiec.gov; *Uniform Bank Performance Report (UBPR).*

The Nilson Report, 1110 Eugenia Place, Suite 100, Carpinteria, CA 93013-9921, (805) 684-8800, Fax: (805) 684-8825, www.nilsonreport.com; *The Nilson Report.*

BANKS, COMMERCIAL - DEBIT CARDS

The Nilson Report, 1110 Eugenia Place, Suite 100, Carpinteria, CA 93013-9921, (805) 684-8800, Fax: (805) 684-8825, www.nilsonreport.com; *The Nilson Report.*

BANKS, COMMERCIAL - DELINQUENCY RATES, REPOSSESSIONS, LOANS

Federal Financial Institutions Examination Council (FFIEC), 3501 Fairfax Drive, Room D8073A, Arlington, VA 22226, (202) 872-7500, www.ffiec.gov; *Uniform Bank Performance Report (UBPR).*

BANKS, COMMERCIAL - DEPOSITS

Federal Deposit Insurance Corporation (FDIC), 550 Seventeenth Street, NW, Washington, DC 20429-0002, (877) 275-3342, www.fdic.gov; *2007 Annual Report; Quarterly Banking Profile (QBP);* and *State Banking Performance Summary.*

BANKS, COMMERCIAL - EARNINGS

U.S. Bureau of Labor Statistics (BLS), Postal Square Building, 2 Massachusetts Avenue, NE, Washington, DC 20212-0001, (202) 691-5200, Fax: (202) 691-6325, www.bls.gov; *Current Employment Statistics Survey (CES)* and *Employment and Earnings (EE).*

U.S. Census Bureau, Company Statistics Division, 4700 Silver Hill Road, Washington DC 20233-0001, (301) 763-3030, www.census.gov/csd/; *County Business Patterns 2004.*

BANKS, COMMERCIAL - EMPLOYEES

U.S. Bureau of Labor Statistics (BLS), Postal Square Building, 2 Massachusetts Avenue, NE, Washington, DC 20212-0001, (202) 691-5200, Fax: (202) 691-6325, www.bls.gov; *Current Employment Statistics Survey (CES)* and *Employment and Earnings (EE).*

U.S. Census Bureau, Company Statistics Division, 4700 Silver Hill Road, Washington DC 20233-0001, (301) 763-3030, www.census.gov/csd/; *County Business Patterns 2004.*

BANKS, COMMERCIAL - FEDERAL RESERVE BANKS

Federal Deposit Insurance Corporation (FDIC), 550 Seventeenth Street, NW, Washington, DC 20429-0002, (877) 275-3342, www.fdic.gov; *State Banking Performance Summary.*

BANKS, COMMERCIAL - FINANCES

Board of Governors of the Federal Reserve System, Constitution Avenue, NW, Washington, DC 20551, (202) 452-3000, www.federalreserve.gov; *Federal Reserve Board Statistical Release* and *Flow of Funds Accounts of the United States.*

Federal Deposit Insurance Corporation (FDIC), 550 Seventeenth Street, NW, Washington, DC 20429-0002, (877) 275-3342, www.fdic.gov; *2007 Annual Report; Quarterly Banking Profile (QBP);* and *State Banking Performance Summary.*

Federal Financial Institutions Examination Council (FFIEC), 3501 Fairfax Drive, Room D8073A, Arlington, VA 22226, (202) 872-7500, www.ffiec.gov; *Annual Report 2006* and Call Report and Thrift Financial Report (TFR) Data.

Reserve Bank of Australia (RBA), The Secretary, GPO Box 3947, Sydney NSW 2001, Australia, www.

rba.gov.au; *Reserve Bank of Australia Annual Report 2007* and *Statement on Monetary Policy.*

BANKS, COMMERCIAL - FLOW OF FUNDS

Board of Governors of the Federal Reserve System, Constitution Avenue, NW, Washington, DC 20551, (202) 452-3000, www.federalreserve.gov; *Federal Reserve Board Statistical Release* and *Flow of Funds Accounts of the United States.*

BANKS, COMMERCIAL - FOREIGN BANKING OFFICES IN THE UNITED STATES

Board of Governors of the Federal Reserve System, Constitution Avenue, NW, Washington, DC 20551, (202) 452-3000, www.federalreserve.gov; *Structure and Share Data for U.S. Banking Offices of Foreign Entities.*

BANKS, COMMERCIAL - FOREIGN LENDING

Federal Financial Institutions Examination Council (FFIEC), 3501 Fairfax Drive, Room D8073A, Arlington, VA 22226, (202) 872-7500, www.ffiec.gov; *Country Exposure Lending Survey.*

BANKS, COMMERCIAL - GROSS DOMESTIC PRODUCT

Bureau of Economic Analysis (BEA), U.S. Department of Commerce (DOC), 1441 L Street NW, Washington, DC 20230, (202) 606-9900, www.bea.gov; *Survey of Current Business (SCB).*

BANKS, COMMERCIAL - HOME EQUITY LOANS

Board of Governors of the Federal Reserve System, Constitution Avenue, NW, Washington, DC 20551, (202) 452-3000, www.federalreserve.gov; *Federal Reserve Bulletin* and unpublished data.

Federal Deposit Insurance Corporation (FDIC), 550 Seventeenth Street, NW, Washington, DC 20429-0002, (877) 275-3342, www.fdic.gov; *2007 Annual Report; Quarterly Banking Profile (QBP); State Banking Performance Summary;* and unpublished data.

BANKS, COMMERCIAL - INDIVIDUAL RETIREMENT ACCOUNTS - 401K PLANS

Investment Company Institute (ICI), 1401 H Street, NW, Suite 1200, Washington, DC 20005-2040, (202) 326-5800, www.ici.org; *IRA Ownership in 2004.*

BANKS, COMMERCIAL - INDUSTRIAL SAFETY

U.S. Bureau of Labor Statistics (BLS), Postal Square Building, 2 Massachusetts Avenue, NE, Washington, DC 20212-0001, (202) 691-5200, Fax: (202) 691-6325, www.bls.gov; *Injuries, Illnesses, and Fatalities (IIF).*

BANKS, COMMERCIAL - INSURED BANKS

Federal Deposit Insurance Corporation (FDIC), 550 Seventeenth Street, NW, Washington, DC 20429-0002, (877) 275-3342, www.fdic.gov; *State Banking Performance Summary.*

BANKS, COMMERCIAL - MERGERS AND ACQUISITIONS

Thomson Financial, 195 Broadway, New York, NY 10007, (646) 822-2000, www.thomson.com; Thomson Research.

BANKS, COMMERCIAL - PRODUCTIVITY

U.S. Bureau of Labor Statistics (BLS), Postal Square Building, 2 Massachusetts Avenue, NE, Washington, DC 20212-0001, (202) 691-5200, Fax: (202) 691-6325, www.bls.gov; *Industry Productivity and Costs.*

BANKS, COMMERCIAL - PROFITS

Federal Deposit Insurance Corporation (FDIC), 550 Seventeenth Street, NW, Washington, DC 20429-0002, (877) 275-3342, www.fdic.gov; *2007 Annual Report; Quarterly Banking Profile (QBP);* and *State Banking Performance Summary.*

BANKS, COMMERCIAL - ROBBERY

Federal Bureau of Investigation (FBI), J. Edgar Hoover Building, 935 Pennsylvania Avenue, NW, Washington, DC 20535-0001, (202) 324-3000, www.fbi.gov; *Crime in the United States (CIUS) 2007 (Preliminary).*

Justice Research and Statistics Association (JRSA), 777 N. Capitol Street, NE, Suite 801, Washington, DC 20002, (202) 842-9330, Fax: (202) 842-9329, www.jrsa.org; *Crime and Justice Atlas 2001.*

BANKS, COMMERCIAL - STOCK AND BOND PRICES AND YIELDS

Global Financial Data, Inc., 784 Fremont Villas, Los Angeles, CA 90042, (323) 924-1016, www.globalfindata.com; *Dow Jones Industrial Average* and *United States Government Bond Total Return Index.*

BARBADOS - NATIONAL STATISTICAL OFFICE

Barbados Statistical Service, Barbados Government Information Service (BGIS), National Insurance Building, Fairchild Street, Bridgetown, Barbados, Mrs. Angela Hunte, Director, (Dial from U.S. (246) 427-7396), (Fax from U.S. (246) 435-2198), www.barbados.gov.bb/bgis.htm; National Data Center.

BARBADOS - AGRICULTURE

Economist Intelligence Unit, 111 West 57th Street, New York, NY 10019, (212) 554-0600, Fax: (212) 586-1181, www.eiu.com; *Barbados Country Report.*

Euromonitor International, Inc., 224 S. Michigan Avenue, Suite 1500, Chicago, IL 60604, (312) 922-1115, Fax: (312) 922-1157, www.euromonitor.com; *World Marketing Data and Statistics.*

Inter-American Development Bank (IDB), 1300 New York Avenue, NW, Washington, DC 20577, (202) 623-1000, Fax: (202) 623-3096, www.iadb.org; *The Politics of Policies: Economic and Social Progress in Latin America - 2006 Report.*

M.E. Sharpe, 80 Business Park Drive, Armonk, NY 10504, (800) 541-6563, Fax: (914) 273-2106, www.mesharpe.com; *The Illustrated Book of World Rankings.*

Palgrave Macmillan Ltd., Houndmills, Basingstoke, Hampshire, RG21 6XS, England, (Telephone in U.S. (888) 330-8477), (Fax in U.S. (800) 672-2054), www.palgrave.com; *The Statesman's Yearbook 2008.*

Taylor and Francis Group, An Informa Business, 2 Park Square, Milton Park, Abingdon, Oxford OX14 4RN, United Kingdom, (Dial from U.S. (212) 216-7800), (Fax from U.S. (212) 564-7854), www.tandf.co.uk; *The Europa World Year Book.*

United Nations Conference on Trade and Development (UNCTAD), DC2-1120, United Nations, New York, NY 10017, (212) 963-0027, www.unctad.org; *UNCTAD Commodity Yearbook.*

United Nations Food and Agricultural Organization (FAO), Viale delle Terme di Caracalla, 00100 Rome, Italy, (Dial from U.S. (202) 653-2400), (Fax from U.S. (202) 653 5760), www.fao.org; AQUASTAT; *FAO Production Yearbook 2002; FAO Trade Yearbook;* and *The State of Food and Agriculture (SOFA) 2006.*

United Nations Statistics Division, New York, NY 10017, (800) 253-9646, Fax: (212) 963-4116, http://unstats.un.org; *Statistical Yearbook* and *Statistical Yearbook for Latin America and the Caribbean 2004.*

The World Bank, 1818 H Street, NW, Washington, DC 20433, (202) 473-1000, Fax: (202) 477-6391, www.worldbank.org; *Barbados* and *World Development Indicators (WDI) 2008.*

BARBADOS - AIRLINES

International Civil Aviation Organization (ICAO), External Relations and Public Information Office (EPO), 999 University Street, Montreal, Quebec H3C 5H7, Canada, (Dial from U.S. (514) 954-8219), (Fax from U.S. (514) 954-6077), www.icao.int; *Civil Aviation Statistics of the World.*

M.E. Sharpe, 80 Business Park Drive, Armonk, NY 10504, (800) 541-6563, Fax: (914) 273-2106, www.mesharpe.com; *The Illustrated Book of World Rankings.*

Palgrave Macmillan Ltd., Houndmills, Basingstoke, Hampshire, RG21 6XS, England, (Telephone in U.S. (888) 330-8477), (Fax in U.S. (800) 672-2054), www.palgrave.com; *The Statesman's Yearbook 2008.*

Taylor and Francis Group, An Informa Business, 2 Park Square, Milton Park, Abingdon, Oxford OX14 4RN, United Kingdom, (Dial from U.S. (212) 216-7800), (Fax from U.S. (212) 564-7854), www.tandf.co.uk; *The Europa World Year Book.*

BARBADOS - AIRPORTS

Central Intelligence Agency, Office of Public Affairs, Washington, DC 20505, (703) 482-0623, Fax: (703) 482-1739, www.cia.gov; *The World Factbook.*

BARBADOS - ALUMINUM PRODUCTION

See BARBADOS - MINERAL INDUSTRIES

BARBADOS - ARMED FORCES

Central Intelligence Agency, Office of Public Affairs, Washington, DC 20505, (703) 482-0623, Fax: (703) 482-1739, www.cia.gov; *The World Factbook.*

Euromonitor International, Inc., 224 S. Michigan Avenue, Suite 1500, Chicago, IL 60604, (312) 922-1115, Fax: (312) 922-1157, www.euromonitor.com; *World Marketing Data and Statistics.*

International Monetary Fund (IMF), 700 Nineteenth Street, NW, Washington, DC 20431, (202) 623-7000, Fax: (202) 623-4661, www.imf.org; *Government Finance Statistics Yearbook (2008 Edition).*

U.S. Department of State (DOS), 2201 C Street NW, Washington, DC 20520, (202) 647-4000, www.state.gov; *World Military Expenditures and Arms Transfers (WMEAT).*

United Nations Statistics Division, New York, NY 10017, (800) 253-9646, Fax: (212) 963-4116, http://unstats.un.org; *Human Development Report 2006.*

BARBADOS - BALANCE OF PAYMENTS

Inter-American Development Bank (IDB), 1300 New York Avenue, NW, Washington, DC 20577, (202) 623-1000, Fax: (202) 623-3096, www.iadb.org; *The Politics of Policies: Economic and Social Progress in Latin America - 2006 Report.*

International Monetary Fund (IMF), 700 Nineteenth Street, NW, Washington, DC 20431, (202) 623-7000, Fax: (202) 623-4661, www.imf.org; *Balance of Payments Statistics Newsletter* and *Balance of Payments Statistics Yearbook 2007.*

Organization of American States (OAS), 17th Street Constitution Avenue NW, Washington, DC 20006, (202) 458-3000, www.oas.org; *The OAS in Transition: 1994-2004.*

Taylor and Francis Group, An Informa Business, 2 Park Square, Milton Park, Abingdon, Oxford OX14 4RN, United Kingdom, (Dial from U.S. (212) 216-7800), (Fax from U.S. (212) 564-7854), www.tandf.co.uk; *The Europa World Year Book.*

United Nations Conference on Trade and Development (UNCTAD), DC2-1120, United Nations, New York, NY 10017, (212) 963-0027, www.unctad.org; *Handbook of Statistics 2005.*

United Nations Statistics Division, New York, NY 10017, (800) 253-9646, Fax: (212) 963-4116, http://unstats.un.org; *Economic Survey of Latin America and the Caribbean 2004-2005* and *Statistical Yearbook for Latin America and the Caribbean 2004.*

The World Bank, 1818 H Street, NW, Washington, DC 20433, (202) 473-1000, Fax: (202) 477-6391, www.worldbank.org; *Barbados* and *World Development Indicators (WDI) 2008.*

BARBADOS - BANKS AND BANKING

Euromonitor International, Inc., 224 S. Michigan Avenue, Suite 1500, Chicago, IL 60604, (312) 922-1115, Fax: (312) 922-1157, www.euromonitor.com; *World Marketing Data and Statistics.*

Inter-American Development Bank (IDB), 1300 New York Avenue, NW, Washington, DC 20577, (202) 623-1000, Fax: (202) 623-3096, www.iadb.org; *The Politics of Policies: Economic and Social Progress in Latin America - 2006 Report.*

International Monetary Fund (IMF), 700 Nineteenth Street, NW, Washington, DC 20431, (202) 623-7000, Fax: (202) 623-4661, www.imf.org; *Government Finance Statistics Yearbook (2008 Edition)* and *International Financial Statistics Yearbook 2007.*

M.E. Sharpe, 80 Business Park Drive, Armonk, NY 10504, (800) 541-6563, Fax: (914) 273-2106, www.mesharpe.com; *The Illustrated Book of World Rankings.*

Palgrave Macmillan Ltd., Houndmills, Basingstoke, Hampshire, RG21 6XS, England, (Telephone in U.S. (888) 330-8477), (Fax in U.S. (800) 672-2054), www.palgrave.com; *The Statesman's Yearbook 2008.*

Taylor and Francis Group, An Informa Business, 2 Park Square, Milton Park, Abingdon, Oxford OX14 4RN, United Kingdom, (Dial from U.S. (212) 216-7800), (Fax from U.S. (212) 564-7854), www.tandf.co.uk; *The Europa World Year Book.*

United Nations Statistics Division, New York, NY 10017, (800) 253-9646, Fax: (212) 963-4116, http://unstats.un.org; *Statistical Yearbook for Latin America and the Caribbean 2004.*

BARBADOS - BARLEY PRODUCTION

See BARBADOS - CROPS

BARBADOS - BEVERAGE INDUSTRY

M.E. Sharpe, 80 Business Park Drive, Armonk, NY 10504, (800) 541-6563, Fax: (914) 273-2106, www.mesharpe.com; *The Illustrated Book of World Rankings.*

United Nations Statistics Division, New York, NY 10017, (800) 253-9646, Fax: (212) 963-4116, http://unstats.un.org; *Statistical Yearbook.*

BARBADOS - BONDS

Inter-American Development Bank (IDB), 1300 New York Avenue, NW, Washington, DC 20577, (202) 623-1000, Fax: (202) 623-3096, www.iadb.org; *The Politics of Policies: Economic and Social Progress in Latin America - 2006 Report.*

International Monetary Fund (IMF), 700 Nineteenth Street, NW, Washington, DC 20431, (202) 623-7000, Fax: (202) 623-4661, www.imf.org; *Government Finance Statistics Yearbook (2008 Edition).*

BARBADOS - BROADCASTING

Central Intelligence Agency, Office of Public Affairs, Washington, DC 20505, (703) 482-0623, Fax: (703) 482-1739, www.cia.gov; *The World Factbook.*

Euromonitor International, Inc., 224 S. Michigan Avenue, Suite 1500, Chicago, IL 60604, (312) 922-1115, Fax: (312) 922-1157, www.euromonitor.com; *World Marketing Data and Statistics.*

M.E. Sharpe, 80 Business Park Drive, Armonk, NY 10504, (800) 541-6563, Fax: (914) 273-2106, www.mesharpe.com; *The Illustrated Book of World Rankings.*

Palgrave Macmillan Ltd., Houndmills, Basingstoke, Hampshire, RG21 6XS, England, (Telephone in U.S. (888) 330-8477), (Fax in U.S. (800) 672-2054), www.palgrave.com; *The Statesman's Yearbook 2008.*

UNESCO Institute for Statistics, C.P. 6128 Succursale Centre-Ville, Montreal, Quebec, H3C 3J7 Canada, (Dial from U.S. (514) 343-6880), (Fax from U.S. (514) 343 6882), www.uis.unesco.org; *Statistical Tables.*

WRTH Publications Limited, PO Box 290, Oxford OX2 7FT, UK, www.wrth.com; *World Radio TV Handbook 2007.*

BARBADOS - BUDGET

Central Intelligence Agency, Office of Public Affairs, Washington, DC 20505, (703) 482-0623, Fax: (703) 482-1739, www.cia.gov; *The World Factbook.*

BARBADOS - BUSINESS

Inter-American Development Bank (IDB), 1300 New York Avenue, NW, Washington, DC 20577, (202) 623-1000, Fax: (202) 623-3096, www.iadb.org; *The Politics of Policies: Economic and Social Progress in Latin America - 2006 Report.*

BARBADOS - CAPITAL INVESTMENTS

Inter-American Development Bank (IDB), 1300 New York Avenue, NW, Washington, DC 20577, (202) 623-1000, Fax: (202) 623-3096, www.iadb.org; *The Politics of Policies: Economic and Social Progress in Latin America - 2006 Report.*

BARBADOS - CAPITAL LEVY

Inter-American Development Bank (IDB), 1300 New York Avenue, NW, Washington, DC 20577, (202) 623-1000, Fax: (202) 623-3096, www.iadb.org; *The Politics of Policies: Economic and Social Progress in Latin America - 2006 Report.*

International Monetary Fund (IMF), 700 Nineteenth Street, NW, Washington, DC 20431, (202) 623-7000, Fax: (202) 623-4661, www.imf.org; *Government Finance Statistics Yearbook (2008 Edition).*

BARBADOS - CATTLE

See BARBADOS - LIVESTOCK

BARBADOS - CHILDBIRTH - STATISTICS

Central Intelligence Agency, Office of Public Affairs, Washington, DC 20505, (703) 482-0623, Fax: (703) 482-1739, www.cia.gov; *The World Factbook.*

Euromonitor International, Inc., 224 S. Michigan Avenue, Suite 1500, Chicago, IL 60604, (312) 922-1115, Fax: (312) 922-1157, www.euromonitor.com; *International Marketing Data and Statistics 2008* and *The World Economic Factbook 2008.*

M.E. Sharpe, 80 Business Park Drive, Armonk, NY 10504, (800) 541-6563, Fax: (914) 273-2106, www.mesharpe.com; *The Illustrated Book of World Rankings.*

Palgrave Macmillan Ltd., Houndmills, Basingstoke, Hampshire, RG21 6XS, England, (Telephone in U.S. (888) 330-8477), (Fax in U.S. (800) 672-2054), www.palgrave.com; *The Statesman's Yearbook 2008.*

Taylor and Francis Group, An Informa Business, 2 Park Square, Milton Park, Abingdon, Oxford OX14 4RN, United Kingdom, (Dial from U.S. (212) 216-7800), (Fax from U.S. (212) 564-7854), www.tandf.co.uk; *The Europa World Year Book.*

United Nations Statistics Division, New York, NY 10017, (800) 253-9646, Fax: (212) 963-4116, http://unstats.un.org; *Demographic Yearbook* and *Statistical Yearbook for Latin America and the Caribbean 2004.*

The World Bank, 1818 H Street, NW, Washington, DC 20433, (202) 473-1000, Fax: (202) 477-6391, www.worldbank.org; *World Development Indicators (WDI) 2008.*

BARBADOS - CLIMATE

M.E. Sharpe, 80 Business Park Drive, Armonk, NY 10504, (800) 541-6563, Fax: (914) 273-2106, www.mesharpe.com; *The Illustrated Book of World Rankings.*

Palgrave Macmillan Ltd., Houndmills, Basingstoke, Hampshire, RG21 6XS, England, (Telephone in U.S. (888) 330-8477), (Fax in U.S. (800) 672-2054), www.palgrave.com; *The Statesman's Yearbook 2008.*

BARBADOS - COAL PRODUCTION

See BARBADOS - MINERAL INDUSTRIES

BARBADOS - COFFEE

See BARBADOS - CROPS

BARBADOS - COMMERCE

Palgrave Macmillan Ltd., Houndmills, Basingstoke, Hampshire, RG21 6XS, England, (Telephone in U.S. (888) 330-8477), (Fax in U.S. (800) 672-2054), www.palgrave.com; *The Statesman's Yearbook 2008.*

BARBADOS - COMMODITY EXCHANGES

Commodity Research Bureau, 330 South Wells Street, Suite 612, Chicago, IL 60606-7110, (800) 621-5271, Fax: (312) 939-4135, www.crbtrader.com; *2006 CRB Commodity Yearbook and CD.*

International Monetary Fund (IMF), 700 Nineteenth Street, NW, Washington, DC 20431, (202) 623-7000, Fax: (202) 623-4661, www.imf.org; *IMF Primary Commodity Prices.*

United Nations Food and Agricultural Organization (FAO), Viale delle Terme di Caracalla, 00100 Rome, Italy, (Dial from U.S. (202) 653-2400), (Fax from U.S. (202) 653 5760), www.fao.org; *The State of Food and Agriculture (SOFA) 2006.*

BARBADOS - CONSTRUCTION INDUSTRY

Inter-American Development Bank (IDB), 1300 New York Avenue, NW, Washington, DC 20577, (202) 623-1000, Fax: (202) 623-3096, www.iadb.org; *The Politics of Policies: Economic and Social Progress in Latin America - 2006 Report.*

M.E. Sharpe, 80 Business Park Drive, Armonk, NY 10504, (800) 541-6563, Fax: (914) 273-2106, www.mesharpe.com; *The Illustrated Book of World Rankings.*

United Nations Statistics Division, New York, NY 10017, (800) 253-9646, Fax: (212) 963-4116, http://unstats.un.org; *Statistical Yearbook.*

BARBADOS - CONSUMER PRICE INDEXES

Taylor and Francis Group, An Informa Business, 2 Park Square, Milton Park, Abingdon, Oxford OX14 4RN, United Kingdom, (Dial from U.S. (212) 216-7800), (Fax from U.S. (212) 564-7854), www.tandf.co.uk; *The Europa World Year Book.*

United Nations Statistics Division, New York, NY 10017, (800) 253-9646, Fax: (212) 963-4116, http://unstats.un.org; *Statistical Yearbook.*

The World Bank, 1818 H Street, NW, Washington, DC 20433, (202) 473-1000, Fax: (202) 477-6391, www.worldbank.org; *Barbados.*

BARBADOS - CONSUMPTION (ECONOMICS)

Inter-American Development Bank (IDB), 1300 New York Avenue, NW, Washington, DC 20577, (202) 623-1000, Fax: (202) 623-3096, www.iadb.org; *The Politics of Policies: Economic and Social Progress in Latin America - 2006 Report.*

United Nations Statistics Division, New York, NY 10017, (800) 253-9646, Fax: (212) 963-4116, http://unstats.un.org; *Statistical Yearbook for Latin America and the Caribbean 2004.*

BARBADOS - COPPER INDUSTRY AND TRADE

See BARBADOS - MINERAL INDUSTRIES

BARBADOS - CORN INDUSTRY

See BARBADOS - CROPS

BARBADOS - COST AND STANDARD OF LIVING

International Monetary Fund (IMF), 700 Nineteenth Street, NW, Washington, DC 20431, (202) 623-7000, Fax: (202) 623-4661, www.imf.org; *Government Finance Statistics Yearbook (2008 Edition).*

BARBADOS - COTTON

See BARBADOS - CROPS

BARBADOS - CRIME

International Criminal Police Organization (INTERPOL), General Secretariat, 200 quai Charles de Gaulle, 69006 Lyon, France, www.interpol.int; *International Crime Statistics.*

BARBADOS - CROPS

International Monetary Fund (IMF), 700 Nineteenth Street, NW, Washington, DC 20431, (202) 623-7000, Fax: (202) 623-4661, www.imf.org; *International Financial Statistics Yearbook 2007.*

M.E. Sharpe, 80 Business Park Drive, Armonk, NY 10504, (800) 541-6563, Fax: (914) 273-2106, www.mesharpe.com; *The Illustrated Book of World Rankings.*

Organization of American States (OAS), 17th Street Constitution Avenue NW, Washington, DC 20006, (202) 458-3000, www.oas.org; *The OAS in Transition: 1994-2004.*

Palgrave Macmillan Ltd., Houndmills, Basingstoke, Hampshire, RG21 6XS, England, (Telephone in U.S. (888) 330-8477), (Fax in U.S. (800) 672-2054), www.palgrave.com; *The Statesman's Yearbook 2008.*

Taylor and Francis Group, An Informa Business, 2 Park Square, Milton Park, Abingdon, Oxford OX14 4RN, United Kingdom, (Dial from U.S. (212) 216-7800), (Fax from U.S. (212) 564-7854), www.tandf.co.uk; *The Europa World Year Book.*

United Nations Conference on Trade and Development (UNCTAD), DC2-1120, United Nations, New York, NY 10017, (212) 963-0027, www.unctad.org; *UNCTAD Commodity Yearbook.*

United Nations Food and Agricultural Organization (FAO), Viale delle Terme di Caracalla, 00100 Rome, Italy, (Dial from U.S. (202) 653-2400), (Fax from U.S. (202) 653 5760), www.fao.org; *FAO Production Yearbook 2002* and *The State of Food and Agriculture (SOFA) 2006.*

BARBADOS - CUSTOMS ADMINISTRATION

Inter-American Development Bank (IDB), 1300 New York Avenue, NW, Washington, DC 20577, (202) 623-1000, Fax: (202) 623-3096, www.iadb.org; *The Politics of Policies: Economic and Social Progress in Latin America - 2006 Report.*

International Monetary Fund (IMF), 700 Nineteenth Street, NW, Washington, DC 20431, (202) 623-7000, Fax: (202) 623-4661, www.imf.org; *Government Finance Statistics Yearbook (2008 Edition).*

Palgrave Macmillan Ltd., Houndmills, Basingstoke, Hampshire, RG21 6XS, England, (Telephone in U.S. (888) 330-8477), (Fax in U.S. (800) 672-2054), www.palgrave.com; *The Statesman's Yearbook 2008.*

BARBADOS - DAIRY PROCESSING

M.E. Sharpe, 80 Business Park Drive, Armonk, NY 10504, (800) 541-6563, Fax: (914) 273-2106, www.mesharpe.com; *The Illustrated Book of World Rankings.*

Palgrave Macmillan Ltd., Houndmills, Basingstoke, Hampshire, RG21 6XS, England, (Telephone in U.S. (888) 330-8477), (Fax in U.S. (800) 672-2054), www.palgrave.com; *The Statesman's Yearbook 2008.*

Taylor and Francis Group, An Informa Business, 2 Park Square, Milton Park, Abingdon, Oxford OX14 4RN, United Kingdom, (Dial from U.S. (212) 216-7800), (Fax from U.S. (212) 564-7854), www.tandf.co.uk; *The Europa World Year Book.*

United Nations Food and Agricultural Organization (FAO), Viale delle Terme di Caracalla, 00100 Rome, Italy, (Dial from U.S. (202) 653-2400), (Fax from U.S. (202) 653 5760), www.fao.org; *The State of Food and Agriculture (SOFA) 2006.*

BARBADOS - DEATH RATES

See BARBADOS - MORTALITY

BARBADOS - DEBTS, EXTERNAL

Inter-American Development Bank (IDB), 1300 New York Avenue, NW, Washington, DC 20577, (202) 623-1000, Fax: (202) 623-3096, www.iadb.org; *The Politics of Policies: Economic and Social Progress in Latin America - 2006 Report.*

International Monetary Fund (IMF), 700 Nineteenth Street, NW, Washington, DC 20431, (202) 623-7000, Fax: (202) 623-4661, www.imf.org; *Government Finance Statistics Yearbook (2008 Edition).*

Palgrave Macmillan Ltd., Houndmills, Basingstoke, Hampshire, RG21 6XS, England, (Telephone in U.S. (888) 330-8477), (Fax in U.S. (800) 672-2054), www.palgrave.com; *The Statesman's Yearbook 2008.*

United Nations Statistics Division, New York, NY 10017, (800) 253-9646, Fax: (212) 963-4116, http://unstats.un.org; *Economic Survey of Latin America and the Caribbean 2004-2005* and *Statistical Yearbook for Latin America and the Caribbean 2004.*

The World Bank, 1818 H Street, NW, Washington, DC 20433, (202) 473-1000, Fax: (202) 477-6391, www.worldbank.org; *Global Development Finance 2007* and *World Development Indicators (WDI) 2008.*

BARBADOS - DEFENSE EXPENDITURES

See BARBADOS - ARMED FORCES

BARBADOS - DEMOGRAPHY

Euromonitor International, Inc., 224 S. Michigan Avenue, Suite 1500, Chicago, IL 60604, (312) 922-1115, Fax: (312) 922-1157, www.euromonitor.com; *The World Economic Factbook 2008* and *World Marketing Data and Statistics.*

M.E. Sharpe, 80 Business Park Drive, Armonk, NY 10504, (800) 541-6563, Fax: (914) 273-2106, www.mesharpe.com; *The Illustrated Book of World Rankings.*

UCLA Latin American Institute, 10343 Bunche Hall, Box 951447, Los Angeles, CA 90095-1447, (310) 825-4571, Fax: (310) 206-6859, www.international.ucla.edu/lac; *Statistical Abstract of Latin America.*

United Nations Statistics Division, New York, NY 10017, (800) 253-9646, Fax: (212) 963-4116, http://unstats.un.org; *Human Development Report 2006.*

The World Bank, 1818 H Street, NW, Washington, DC 20433, (202) 473-1000, Fax: (202) 477-6391, www.worldbank.org; *Barbados.*

BARBADOS - DIAMONDS

See BARBADOS - MINERAL INDUSTRIES

BARBADOS - DISPOSABLE INCOME

Inter-American Development Bank (IDB), 1300 New York Avenue, NW, Washington, DC 20577, (202) 623-1000, Fax: (202) 623-3096, www.iadb.org; *The Politics of Policies: Economic and Social Progress in Latin America - 2006 Report.*

M.E. Sharpe, 80 Business Park Drive, Armonk, NY 10504, (800) 541-6563, Fax: (914) 273-2106, www.mesharpe.com; *The Illustrated Book of World Rankings.*

United Nations Statistics Division, New York, NY 10017, (800) 253-9646, Fax: (212) 963-4116, http://unstats.un.org; *National Accounts Statistics: Compendium of Income Distribution Statistics* and *Statistical Yearbook.*

BARBADOS - DIVORCE

M.E. Sharpe, 80 Business Park Drive, Armonk, NY 10504, (800) 541-6563, Fax: (914) 273-2106, www.mesharpe.com; *The Illustrated Book of World Rankings.*

United Nations Statistics Division, New York, NY 10017, (800) 253-9646, Fax: (212) 963-4116, http://unstats.un.org; *Demographic Yearbook* and *Statistical Yearbook.*

BARBADOS - ECONOMIC ASSISTANCE

Inter-American Development Bank (IDB), 1300 New York Avenue, NW, Washington, DC 20577, (202) 623-1000, Fax: (202) 623-3096, www.iadb.org; *The Politics of Policies: Economic and Social Progress in Latin America - 2006 Report.*

United Nations Statistics Division, New York, NY 10017, (800) 253-9646, Fax: (212) 963-4116, http://unstats.un.org; *Statistical Yearbook.*

BARBADOS - ECONOMIC CONDITIONS

Center for International Business Education Research (CIBER), Columbia Business School and School of International and Public Affairs, Uris Hall, Room 212, 3022 Broadway, New York, NY 10027-6902, Mr. Joshua Safier, (212) 854-4750, Fax: (212) 222-9821, www.columbia.edu/cu/ciber/; Datastream International.

Central Intelligence Agency, Office of Public Affairs, Washington, DC 20505, (703) 482-0623, Fax: (703) 482-1739, www.cia.gov; *The World Factbook.*

DSI Data Service Information, Xantener Strasse 51a, D-47495 Rheinberg, Germany, www.dsidata.com; *Campus Solution.*

Dun and Bradstreet (DB) Corporation, 103 JFK Parkway, Short Hills, NJ 07078, (973) 921-5500, www.dnb.com; *Country Report.*

Economist Intelligence Unit, 111 West 57th Street, New York, NY 10019, (212) 554-0600, Fax: (212) 586-1181, www.eiu.com; *Barbados Country Report.*

Euromonitor International, Inc., 224 S. Michigan Avenue, Suite 1500, Chicago, IL 60604, (312) 922-1115, Fax: (312) 922-1157, www.euromonitor.com; *The World Economic Factbook 2008* and *World Marketing Data and Statistics.*

Inter-American Development Bank (IDB), 1300 New York Avenue, NW, Washington, DC 20577, (202) 623-1000, Fax: (202) 623-3096, www.iadb.org; *The Politics of Policies: Economic and Social Progress in Latin America - 2006 Report.*

International Monetary Fund (IMF), 700 Nineteenth Street, NW, Washington, DC 20431, (202) 623-7000, Fax: (202) 623-4661, www.imf.org; *World Economic Outlook Reports.*

M.E. Sharpe, 80 Business Park Drive, Armonk, NY 10504, (800) 541-6563, Fax: (914) 273-2106, www.mesharpe.com; *The Illustrated Book of World Rankings.*

Organization of American States (OAS), 17th Street Constitution Avenue NW, Washington, DC 20006, (202) 458-3000, www.oas.org; *The OAS in Transition: 1994-2004.*

Palgrave Macmillan Ltd., Houndmills, Basingstoke, Hampshire, RG21 6XS, England, (Telephone in U.S. (888) 330-8477), (Fax in U.S. (800) 672-2054), www.palgrave.com; *The Statesman's Yearbook 2008.*

Taylor and Francis Group, An Informa Business, 2 Park Square, Milton Park, Abingdon, Oxford OX14 4RN, United Kingdom, (Dial from U.S. (212) 216-7800), (Fax from U.S. (212) 564-7854), www.tandf.co.uk; *The Europa World Year Book.*

United Nations Statistics Division, New York, NY 10017, (800) 253-9646, Fax: (212) 963-4116, http://unstats.un.org; *Economic Survey of Latin America and the Caribbean 2004-2005* and *World Statistics Pocketbook.*

The World Bank, 1818 H Street, NW, Washington, DC 20433, (202) 473-1000, Fax: (202) 477-6391, www.worldbank.org; *Barbados; Global Economic Monitor (GEM); Global Economic Prospects 2008;* and *The World Bank Atlas 2003-2004.*

BARBADOS - ECONOMICS - SOCIOLOGICAL ASPECTS

Inter-American Development Bank (IDB), 1300 New York Avenue, NW, Washington, DC 20577, (202) 623-1000, Fax: (202) 623-3096, www.iadb.org; *The Politics of Policies: Economic and Social Progress in Latin America - 2006 Report.*

BARBADOS - EDUCATION

Euromonitor International, Inc., 224 S. Michigan Avenue, Suite 1500, Chicago, IL 60604, (312) 922-1115, Fax: (312) 922-1157, www.euromonitor.com; *International Marketing Data and Statistics 2008* and *World Marketing Data and Statistics.*

International Monetary Fund (IMF), 700 Nineteenth Street, NW, Washington, DC 20431, (202) 623-7000, Fax: (202) 623-4661, www.imf.org; *Government Finance Statistics Yearbook (2008 Edition).*

M.E. Sharpe, 80 Business Park Drive, Armonk, NY 10504, (800) 541-6563, Fax: (914) 273-2106, www.mesharpe.com; *The Illustrated Book of World Rankings.*

Palgrave Macmillan Ltd., Houndmills, Basingstoke, Hampshire, RG21 6XS, England, (Telephone in U.S. (888) 330-8477), (Fax in U.S. (800) 672-2054), www.palgrave.com; *The Statesman's Yearbook 2008.*

Taylor and Francis Group, An Informa Business, 2 Park Square, Milton Park, Abingdon, Oxford OX14 4RN, United Kingdom, (Dial from U.S. (212) 216-7800), (Fax from U.S. (212) 564-7854), www.tandf.co.uk; *The Europa World Year Book.*

UNESCO Institute for Statistics, C.P. 6128 Succursale Centre-Ville, Montreal, Quebec, H3C 3J7 Canada, (Dial from U.S. (514) 343-6880), (Fax from U.S. (514) 343 6882), www.uis.unesco.org; *Statistical Tables.*

United Nations Statistics Division, New York, NY 10017, (800) 253-9646, Fax: (212) 963-4116, http://unstats.un.org; *Human Development Report 2006* and *Statistical Yearbook for Latin America and the Caribbean 2004.*

The World Bank, 1818 H Street, NW, Washington, DC 20433, (202) 473-1000, Fax: (202) 477-6391, www.worldbank.org; *Barbados* and *World Development Indicators (WDI) 2008.*

BARBADOS - ELECTRICITY

Inter-American Development Bank (IDB), 1300 New York Avenue, NW, Washington, DC 20577, (202) 623-1000, Fax: (202) 623-3096, www.iadb.org; *The Politics of Policies: Economic and Social Progress in Latin America - 2006 Report.*

M.E. Sharpe, 80 Business Park Drive, Armonk, NY 10504, (800) 541-6563, Fax: (914) 273-2106, www.mesharpe.com; *The Illustrated Book of World Rankings.*

Organisation for Economic Cooperation and Development (OECD), 2 rue Andre Pascal, F-75775 Paris Cedex 16, France, (Telephone in U.S. (202) 785-6323), (Fax in U.S. (202) 785-0350), www.oecd.org; *World Energy Outlook 2007.*

Organization of American States (OAS), 17th Street Constitution Avenue NW, Washington, DC 20006, (202) 458-3000, www.oas.org; *The OAS in Transition: 1994-2004.*

Palgrave Macmillan Ltd., Houndmills, Basingstoke, Hampshire, RG21 6XS, England, (Telephone in U.S. (888) 330-8477), (Fax in U.S. (800) 672-2054), www.palgrave.com; *The Statesman's Yearbook 2008.*

United Nations Statistics Division, New York, NY 10017, (800) 253-9646, Fax: (212) 963-4116, http://unstats.un.org; *Human Development Report 2006* and *Statistical Yearbook.*

BARBADOS - EMPLOYMENT

Euromonitor International, Inc., 224 S. Michigan Avenue, Suite 1500, Chicago, IL 60604, (312) 922-1115, Fax: (312) 922-1157, www.euromonitor.com; *International Marketing Data and Statistics 2008.*

International Labour Office, I.L.O. Publications, 4 route des Morillons, CH-1211 Geneva 22, Switzerland, (Telephone in U.S. (202) 653-7652), (Fax in U.S. (202) 653-7687), www.ilo.org; *Yearbook of Labour Statistics 2006.*

M.E. Sharpe, 80 Business Park Drive, Armonk, NY 10504, (800) 541-6563, Fax: (914) 273-2106, www.mesharpe.com; *The Illustrated Book of World Rankings.*

Organization of American States (OAS), 17th Street Constitution Avenue NW, Washington, DC 20006, (202) 458-3000, www.oas.org; *The OAS in Transition: 1994-2004.*

United Nations Statistics Division, New York, NY 10017, (800) 253-9646, Fax: (212) 963-4116, http://unstats.un.org; *Statistical Yearbook* and *Statistical Yearbook for Latin America and the Caribbean 2004.*

The World Bank, 1818 H Street, NW, Washington, DC 20433, (202) 473-1000, Fax: (202) 477-6391, www.worldbank.org; *Barbados.*

BARBADOS - ENERGY INDUSTRIES

Enerdata, 10 Rue Royale, 75008 Paris, France, www.enerdata.fr; *Global Energy Market Data.*

United Nations Statistics Division, New York, NY 10017, (800) 253-9646, Fax: (212) 963-4116, http://unstats.un.org; *Statistical Yearbook.*

BARBADOS - ENVIRONMENTAL CONDITIONS

DSI Data Service Information, Xantener Strasse 51a, D-47495 Rheinberg, Germany, www.dsidata.com; *Campus Solution* and *DSI's Global Environmental Database.*

Economist Intelligence Unit, 111 West 57th Street, New York, NY 10019, (212) 554-0600, Fax: (212) 586-1181, www.eiu.com; *Barbados Country Report.*

United Nations Statistics Division, New York, NY 10017, (800) 253-9646, Fax: (212) 963-4116, http://unstats.un.org; *World Statistics Pocketbook.*

BARBADOS - EXPENDITURES, PUBLIC

Inter-American Development Bank (IDB), 1300 New York Avenue, NW, Washington, DC 20577, (202) 623-1000, Fax: (202) 623-3096, www.iadb.org; *The Politics of Policies: Economic and Social Progress in Latin America - 2006 Report.*

Organization of American States (OAS), 17th Street Constitution Avenue NW, Washington, DC 20006, (202) 458-3000, www.oas.org; *The OAS in Transition: 1994-2004.*

United Nations Statistics Division, New York, NY 10017, (800) 253-9646, Fax: (212) 963-4116, http://unstats.un.org; *Statistical Yearbook for Latin America and the Caribbean 2004.*

BARBADOS - EXPORTS

Central Intelligence Agency, Office of Public Affairs, Washington, DC 20505, (703) 482-0623, Fax: (703) 482-1739, www.cia.gov; *The World Factbook.*

Economist Intelligence Unit, 111 West 57th Street, New York, NY 10019, (212) 554-0600, Fax: (212) 586-1181, www.eiu.com; *Barbados Country Report.*

Euromonitor International, Inc., 224 S. Michigan Avenue, Suite 1500, Chicago, IL 60604, (312) 922-1115, Fax: (312) 922-1157, www.euromonitor.com; *International Marketing Data and Statistics 2008* and *The World Economic Factbook 2008.*

Inter-American Development Bank (IDB), 1300 New York Avenue, NW, Washington, DC 20577, (202) 623-1000, Fax: (202) 623-3096, www.iadb.org; *The Politics of Policies: Economic and Social Progress in Latin America - 2006 Report.*

International Monetary Fund (IMF), 700 Nineteenth Street, NW, Washington, DC 20431, (202) 623-7000, Fax: (202) 623-4661, www.imf.org; *Direction of Trade Statistics Yearbook 2007; Government Finance Statistics Yearbook (2008 Edition);* and *International Financial Statistics Yearbook 2007.*

Organization of American States (OAS), 17th Street Constitution Avenue NW, Washington, DC 20006, (202) 458-3000, www.oas.org; *The OAS in Transition: 1994-2004.*

Palgrave Macmillan Ltd., Houndmills, Basingstoke, Hampshire, RG21 6XS, England, (Telephone in U.S. (888) 330-8477), (Fax in U.S. (800) 672-2054), www.palgrave.com; *The Statesman's Yearbook 2008.*

Taylor and Francis Group, An Informa Business, 2 Park Square, Milton Park, Abingdon, Oxford OX14 4RN, United Kingdom, (Dial from U.S. (212) 216-7800), (Fax from U.S. (212) 564-7854), www.tandf.co.uk; *The Europa World Year Book.*

United Nations Conference on Trade and Development (UNCTAD), DC2-1120, United Nations, New York, NY 10017, (212) 963-0027, www.unctad.org; *Handbook of Statistics 2005.*

United Nations Food and Agricultural Organization (FAO), Viale delle Terme di Caracalla, 00100 Rome, Italy, (Dial from U.S. (202) 653-2400), (Fax from U.S. (202) 653 5760), www.fao.org; *The State of Food and Agriculture (SOFA) 2006.*

United Nations Statistics Division, New York, NY 10017, (800) 253-9646, Fax: (212) 963-4116, http://unstats.un.org; *Statistical Yearbook for Latin America and the Caribbean 2004.*

The World Bank, 1818 H Street, NW, Washington, DC 20433, (202) 473-1000, Fax: (202) 477-6391, www.worldbank.org; *World Development Indicators (WDI) 2008.*

BARBADOS - FERTILITY, HUMAN

Central Intelligence Agency, Office of Public Affairs, Washington, DC 20505, (703) 482-0623, Fax: (703) 482-1739, www.cia.gov; *The World Factbook.*

United Nations Statistics Division, New York, NY 10017, (800) 253-9646, Fax: (212) 963-4116, http://unstats.un.org; *Human Development Report 2006.*

The World Bank, 1818 H Street, NW, Washington, DC 20433, (202) 473-1000, Fax: (202) 477-6391, www.worldbank.org; *The World Bank Atlas 2003-2004* and *World Development Indicators (WDI) 2008.*

BARBADOS - FERTILIZER INDUSTRY

M.E. Sharpe, 80 Business Park Drive, Armonk, NY 10504, (800) 541-6563, Fax: (914) 273-2106, www.mesharpe.com; *The Illustrated Book of World Rankings.*

United Nations Food and Agricultural Organization (FAO), Viale delle Terme di Caracalla, 00100 Rome, Italy, (Dial from U.S. (202) 653-2400), (Fax from U.S. (202) 653 5760), www.fao.org; *FAO Fertilizer Yearbook* and *The State of Food and Agriculture (SOFA) 2006.*

United Nations Statistics Division, New York, NY 10017, (800) 253-9646, Fax: (212) 963-4116, http://unstats.un.org; *Statistical Yearbook.*

The World Bank, 1818 H Street, NW, Washington, DC 20433, (202) 473-1000, Fax: (202) 477-6391, www.worldbank.org; *World Development Indicators (WDI) 2008.*

BARBADOS - FETAL MORTALITY

See BARBADOS - MORTALITY

BARBADOS - FINANCE

Inter-American Development Bank (IDB), 1300 New York Avenue, NW, Washington, DC 20577, (202) 623-1000, Fax: (202) 623-3096, www.iadb.org; *The Politics of Policies: Economic and Social Progress in Latin America - 2006 Report.*

Organization of American States (OAS), 17th Street Constitution Avenue NW, Washington, DC 20006, (202) 458-3000, www.oas.org; *The OAS in Transition: 1994-2004.*

United Nations Statistics Division, New York, NY 10017, (800) 253-9646, Fax: (212) 963-4116, http://unstats.un.org; *National Accounts Statistics: Compendium of Income Distribution Statistics* and *Statistical Yearbook.*

The World Bank, 1818 H Street, NW, Washington, DC 20433, (202) 473-1000, Fax: (202) 477-6391, www.worldbank.org; *Barbados.*

BARBADOS - FINANCE, PUBLIC

Bernan Essential Government Publications, 4611-F Assembly Drive, Lanham MD, 20706-4391, (301) 459-2255, Fax: (800) 865-3450, www.bernan.com; *National Accounts Statistics.*

Economist Intelligence Unit, 111 West 57th Street, New York, NY 10019, (212) 554-0600, Fax: (212) 586-1181, www.eiu.com; *Barbados Country Report.*

Inter-American Development Bank (IDB), 1300 New York Avenue, NW, Washington, DC 20577, (202) 623-1000, Fax: (202) 623-3096, www.iadb.org; *The Politics of Policies: Economic and Social Progress in Latin America - 2006 Report.*

International Monetary Fund (IMF), 700 Nineteenth Street, NW, Washington, DC 20431, (202) 623-7000, Fax: (202) 623-4661, www.imf.org; *Government Finance Statistics Yearbook (2008 Edition);*

International Financial Statistics; International Financial Statistics Online Service; and *International Financial Statistics Yearbook 2007.*

M.E. Sharpe, 80 Business Park Drive, Armonk, NY 10504, (800) 541-6563, Fax: (914) 273-2106, www.mesharpe.com; *The Illustrated Book of World Rankings.*

Organization of American States (OAS), 17th Street Constitution Avenue NW, Washington, DC 20006, (202) 458-3000, www.oas.org; *The OAS in Transition: 1994-2004.*

Palgrave Macmillan Ltd., Houndmills, Basingstoke, Hampshire, RG21 6XS, England, (Telephone in U.S. (888) 330-8477), (Fax in U.S. (800) 672-2054), www.palgrave.com; *The Statesman's Yearbook 2008.*

Taylor and Francis Group, An Informa Business, 2 Park Square, Milton Park, Abingdon, Oxford OX14 4RN, United Kingdom, (Dial from U.S. (212) 216-7800), (Fax from U.S. (212) 564-7854), www.tandf.co.uk; *The Europa World Year Book.*

The World Bank, 1818 H Street, NW, Washington, DC 20433, (202) 473-1000, Fax: (202) 477-6391, www.worldbank.org; *Barbados.*

BARBADOS - FISHERIES

Inter-American Development Bank (IDB), 1300 New York Avenue, NW, Washington, DC 20577, (202) 623-1000, Fax: (202) 623-3096, www.iadb.org; *The Politics of Policies: Economic and Social Progress in Latin America - 2006 Report.*

M.E. Sharpe, 80 Business Park Drive, Armonk, NY 10504, (800) 541-6563, Fax: (914) 273-2106, www.mesharpe.com; *The Illustrated Book of World Rankings.*

Palgrave Macmillan Ltd., Houndmills, Basingstoke, Hampshire, RG21 6XS, England, (Telephone in U.S. (888) 330-8477), (Fax in U.S. (800) 672-2054), www.palgrave.com; *The Statesman's Yearbook 2008.*

United Nations Conference on Trade and Development (UNCTAD), DC2-1120, United Nations, New York, NY 10017, (212) 963-0027, www.unctad.org; *UNCTAD Commodity Yearbook.*

United Nations Food and Agricultural Organization (FAO), Viale delle Terme di Caracalla, 00100 Rome, Italy, (Dial from U.S. (202) 653-2400), (Fax from U.S. (202) 653 5760), www.fao.org; *FAO Yearbook of Fishery Statistics;* Fishery Databases; FISHSTAT Database. Subjects covered include: Aquaculture production, capture production, fishery commodities; and *The State of Food and Agriculture (SOFA) 2006.*

United Nations Statistics Division, New York, NY 10017, (800) 253-9646, Fax: (212) 963-4116, http://unstats.un.org; *Statistical Yearbook.*

The World Bank, 1818 H Street, NW, Washington, DC 20433, (202) 473-1000, Fax: (202) 477-6391, www.worldbank.org; *Barbados.*

BARBADOS - FOOD

United Nations Conference on Trade and Development (UNCTAD), DC2-1120, United Nations, New York, NY 10017, (212) 963-0027, www.unctad.org; *UNCTAD Commodity Yearbook.*

United Nations Food and Agricultural Organization (FAO), Viale delle Terme di Caracalla, 00100 Rome, Italy, (Dial from U.S. (202) 653-2400), (Fax from U.S. (202) 653 5760), www.fao.org; *FAO Production Yearbook 2002* and *The State of Food and Agriculture (SOFA) 2006.*

United Nations Statistics Division, New York, NY 10017, (800) 253-9646, Fax: (212) 963-4116, http://unstats.un.org; *Human Development Report 2006.*

BARBADOS - FOREIGN EXCHANGE RATES

Central Intelligence Agency, Office of Public Affairs, Washington, DC 20505, (703) 482-0623, Fax: (703) 482-1739, www.cia.gov; *The World Factbook.*

Euromonitor International, Inc., 224 S. Michigan Avenue, Suite 1500, Chicago, IL 60604, (312) 922-1115, Fax: (312) 922-1157, www.euromonitor.com; *International Marketing Data and Statistics 2008* and *The World Economic Factbook 2008.*

Inter-American Development Bank (IDB), 1300 New York Avenue, NW, Washington, DC 20577, (202) 623-1000, Fax: (202) 623-3096, www.iadb.org; *The Politics of Policies: Economic and Social Progress in Latin America - 2006 Report.*

International Civil Aviation Organization (ICAO), External Relations and Public Information Office (EPO), 999 University Street, Montreal, Quebec H3C 5H7, Canada, (Dial from U.S. (514) 954-8219), (Fax from U.S. (514) 954-6077), www.icao.int; *Civil Aviation Statistics of the World.*

International Monetary Fund (IMF), 700 Nineteenth Street, NW, Washington, DC 20431, (202) 623-7000, Fax: (202) 623-4661, www.imf.org; *International Financial Statistics Yearbook 2007.*

Organization of American States (OAS), 17th Street Constitution Avenue NW, Washington, DC 20006, (202) 458-3000, www.oas.org; *The OAS in Transition: 1994-2004.*

Taylor and Francis Group, An Informa Business, 2 Park Square, Milton Park, Abingdon, Oxford OX14 4RN, United Kingdom, (Dial from U.S. (212) 216-7800), (Fax from U.S. (212) 564-7854), www.tandf.co.uk; *The Europa World Year Book.*

United Nations Statistics Division, New York, NY 10017, (800) 253-9646, Fax: (212) 963-4116, http://unstats.un.org; *Statistical Yearbook* and *World Statistics Pocketbook.*

BARBADOS - FORESTS AND FORESTRY

Inter-American Development Bank (IDB), 1300 New York Avenue, NW, Washington, DC 20577, (202) 623-1000, Fax: (202) 623-3096, www.iadb.org; *The Politics of Policies: Economic and Social Progress in Latin America - 2006 Report.*

M.E. Sharpe, 80 Business Park Drive, Armonk, NY 10504, (800) 541-6563, Fax: (914) 273-2106, www.mesharpe.com; *The Illustrated Book of World Rankings.*

UNESCO Institute for Statistics, C.P. 6128 Succursale Centre-Ville, Montreal, Quebec, H3C 3J7 Canada, (Dial from U.S. (514) 343-6880), (Fax from U.S. (514) 343 6882), www.uis.unesco.org; *Statistical Tables.*

United Nations Conference on Trade and Development (UNCTAD), DC2-1120, United Nations, New York, NY 10017, (212) 963-0027, www.unctad.org; *UNCTAD Commodity Yearbook.*

United Nations Food and Agricultural Organization (FAO), Viale delle Terme di Caracalla, 00100 Rome, Italy, (Dial from U.S. (202) 653-2400), (Fax from U.S. (202) 653 5760), www.fao.org; *FAO Yearbook of Forest Products* and *The State of Food and Agriculture (SOFA) 2006.*

United Nations Statistics Division, New York, NY 10017, (800) 253-9646, Fax: (212) 963-4116, http://unstats.un.org; *Statistical Yearbook.*

The World Bank, 1818 H Street, NW, Washington, DC 20433, (202) 473-1000, Fax: (202) 477-6391, www.worldbank.org; *Barbados.*

BARBADOS - GAS PRODUCTION

See BARBADOS - MINERAL INDUSTRIES

BARBADOS - GEOGRAPHIC INFORMATION SYSTEMS

M.E. Sharpe, 80 Business Park Drive, Armonk, NY 10504, (800) 541-6563, Fax: (914) 273-2106, www.mesharpe.com; *The Illustrated Book of World Rankings.*

The World Bank, 1818 H Street, NW, Washington, DC 20433, (202) 473-1000, Fax: (202) 477-6391, www.worldbank.org; *Barbados.*

BARBADOS - GOLD INDUSTRY

International Monetary Fund (IMF), 700 Nineteenth Street, NW, Washington, DC 20431, (202) 623-7000, Fax: (202) 623-4661, www.imf.org; *International Financial Statistics Yearbook 2007.*

United Nations Statistics Division, New York, NY 10017, (800) 253-9646, Fax: (212) 963-4116, http://unstats.un.org; *Statistical Yearbook.*

The World Bank, 1818 H Street, NW, Washington, DC 20433, (202) 473-1000, Fax: (202) 477-6391, www.worldbank.org; *World Development Indicators (WDI) 2008.*

BARBADOS - GOLD PRODUCTION

See BARBADOS - MINERAL INDUSTRIES

BARBADOS - GRANTS-IN-AID

International Monetary Fund (IMF), 700 Nineteenth Street, NW, Washington, DC 20431, (202) 623-7000, Fax: (202) 623-4661, www.imf.org; *Government Finance Statistics Yearbook (2008 Edition).*

BARBADOS - GROSS DOMESTIC PRODUCT

Economist Intelligence Unit, 111 West 57th Street, New York, NY 10019, (212) 554-0600, Fax: (212) 586-1181, www.eiu.com; *Barbados Country Report.*

Euromonitor International, Inc., 224 S. Michigan Avenue, Suite 1500, Chicago, IL 60604, (312) 922-1115, Fax: (312) 922-1157, www.euromonitor.com; *International Marketing Data and Statistics 2008* and *The World Economic Factbook 2008.*

Inter-American Development Bank (IDB), 1300 New York Avenue, NW, Washington, DC 20577, (202) 623-1000, Fax: (202) 623-3096, www.iadb.org; *The Politics of Policies: Economic and Social Progress in Latin America - 2006 Report.*

M.E. Sharpe, 80 Business Park Drive, Armonk, NY 10504, (800) 541-6563, Fax: (914) 273-2106, www.mesharpe.com; *The Illustrated Book of World Rankings.*

Organization of American States (OAS), 17th Street Constitution Avenue NW, Washington, DC 20006, (202) 458-3000, www.oas.org; *The OAS in Transition: 1994-2004.*

Taylor and Francis Group, An Informa Business, 2 Park Square, Milton Park, Abingdon, Oxford OX14 4RN, United Kingdom, (Dial from U.S. (212) 216-7800), (Fax from U.S. (212) 564-7854), www.tandf.co.uk; *The Europa World Year Book.*

United Nations Statistics Division, New York, NY 10017, (800) 253-9646, Fax: (212) 963-4116, http://unstats.un.org; *Human Development Report 2006; National Accounts Statistics: Compendium of Income Distribution Statistics; Statistical Yearbook;* and *Statistical Yearbook for Latin America and the Caribbean 2004.*

The World Bank, 1818 H Street, NW, Washington, DC 20433, (202) 473-1000, Fax: (202) 477-6391, www.worldbank.org; *World Development Indicators (WDI) 2008.*

BARBADOS - GROSS NATIONAL PRODUCT

Inter-American Development Bank (IDB), 1300 New York Avenue, NW, Washington, DC 20577, (202) 623-1000, Fax: (202) 623-3096, www.iadb.org; *The Politics of Policies: Economic and Social Progress in Latin America - 2006 Report.*

M.E. Sharpe, 80 Business Park Drive, Armonk, NY 10504, (800) 541-6563, Fax: (914) 273-2106, www.mesharpe.com; *The Illustrated Book of World Rankings.*

Palgrave Macmillan Ltd., Houndmills, Basingstoke, Hampshire, RG21 6XS, England, (Telephone in U.S. (888) 330-8477), (Fax in U.S. (800) 672-2054), www.palgrave.com; *The Statesman's Yearbook 2008.*

U.S. Department of State (DOS), 2201 C Street NW, Washington, DC 20520, (202) 647-4000, www.state.gov; *World Military Expenditures and Arms Transfers (WMEAT).*

United Nations Statistics Division, New York, NY 10017, (800) 253-9646, Fax: (212) 963-4116, http://unstats.un.org; *Statistical Yearbook.*

The World Bank, 1818 H Street, NW, Washington, DC 20433, (202) 473-1000, Fax: (202) 477-6391, www.worldbank.org; *The World Bank Atlas 2003-2004* and *World Development Indicators (WDI) 2008.*

BARBADOS - HIDES AND SKINS INDUSTRY

United Nations Food and Agricultural Organization (FAO), Viale delle Terme di Caracalla, 00100 Rome, Italy, (Dial from U.S. (202) 653-2400), (Fax from U.S. (202) 653 5760), www.fao.org; *FAO Production Yearbook 2002.*

BARBADOS - HOUSING

Euromonitor International, Inc., 224 S. Michigan Avenue, Suite 1500, Chicago, IL 60604, (312) 922-1115, Fax: (312) 922-1157, www.euromonitor.com; *World Marketing Data and Statistics.*

M.E. Sharpe, 80 Business Park Drive, Armonk, NY 10504, (800) 541-6563, Fax: (914) 273-2106, www.mesharpe.com; *The Illustrated Book of World Rankings.*

United Nations Statistics Division, New York, NY 10017, (800) 253-9646, Fax: (212) 963-4116, http://unstats.un.org; *Statistical Yearbook for Latin America and the Caribbean 2004.*

BARBADOS - ILLITERATE PERSONS

Euromonitor International, Inc., 224 S. Michigan Avenue, Suite 1500, Chicago, IL 60604, (312) 922-1115, Fax: (312) 922-1157, www.euromonitor.com; *The World Economic Factbook 2008.*

UNESCO Institute for Statistics, C.P. 6128 Succursale Centre-Ville, Montreal, Quebec, H3C 3J7 Canada, (Dial from U.S. (514) 343-6880), (Fax from U.S. (514) 343 6882), www.uis.unesco.org; *Statistical Tables.*

United Nations Statistics Division, New York, NY 10017, (800) 253-9646, Fax: (212) 963-4116, http://unstats.un.org; *Human Development Report 2006* and *Statistical Yearbook for Latin America and the Caribbean 2004.*

BARBADOS - IMPORTS

Central Intelligence Agency, Office of Public Affairs, Washington, DC 20505, (703) 482-0623, Fax: (703) 482-1739, www.cia.gov; *The World Factbook.*

Economist Intelligence Unit, 111 West 57th Street, New York, NY 10019, (212) 554-0600, Fax: (212) 586-1181, www.eiu.com; *Barbados Country Report.*

Euromonitor International, Inc., 224 S. Michigan Avenue, Suite 1500, Chicago, IL 60604, (312) 922-1115, Fax: (312) 922-1157, www.euromonitor.com; *International Marketing Data and Statistics 2008* and *The World Economic Factbook 2008.*

Inter-American Development Bank (IDB), 1300 New York Avenue, NW, Washington, DC 20577, (202) 623-1000, Fax: (202) 623-3096, www.iadb.org; *The Politics of Policies: Economic and Social Progress in Latin America - 2006 Report.*

International Monetary Fund (IMF), 700 Nineteenth Street, NW, Washington, DC 20431, (202) 623-7000, Fax: (202) 623-4661, www.imf.org; *Direction of Trade Statistics Yearbook 2007* and *International Financial Statistics Yearbook 2007.*

Organization of American States (OAS), 17th Street Constitution Avenue NW, Washington, DC 20006, (202) 458-3000, www.oas.org; *The OAS in Transition: 1994-2004.*

Palgrave Macmillan Ltd., Houndmills, Basingstoke, Hampshire, RG21 6XS, England, (Telephone in U.S. (888) 330-8477), (Fax in U.S. (800) 672-2054), www.palgrave.com; *The Statesman's Yearbook 2008.*

Taylor and Francis Group, An Informa Business, 2 Park Square, Milton Park, Abingdon, Oxford OX14 4RN, United Kingdom, (Dial from U.S. (212) 216-7800), (Fax from U.S. (212) 564-7854), www.tandf.co.uk; *The Europa World Year Book.*

United Nations Conference on Trade and Development (UNCTAD), DC2-1120, United Nations, New York, NY 10017, (212) 963-0027, www.unctad.org; *Handbook of Statistics 2005.*

United Nations Food and Agricultural Organization (FAO), Viale delle Terme di Caracalla, 00100 Rome, Italy, (Dial from U.S. (202) 653-2400), (Fax from U.S. (202) 653 5760), www.fao.org; *The State of Food and Agriculture (SOFA) 2006.*

United Nations Statistics Division, New York, NY 10017, (800) 253-9646, Fax: (212) 963-4116, http://unstats.un.org; *Statistical Yearbook for Latin America and the Caribbean 2004.*

The World Bank, 1818 H Street, NW, Washington, DC 20433, (202) 473-1000, Fax: (202) 477-6391, www.worldbank.org; *World Development Indicators (WDI) 2008.*

BARBADOS - INCOME DISTRIBUTION

United Nations Statistics Division, New York, NY 10017, (800) 253-9646, Fax: (212) 963-4116, http://unstats.un.org; *Statistical Yearbook for Latin America and the Caribbean 2004.*

BARBADOS - INCOME TAXES

See BARBADOS - TAXATION

BARBADOS - INDUSTRIAL PRODUCTIVITY

M.E. Sharpe, 80 Business Park Drive, Armonk, NY 10504, (800) 541-6563, Fax: (914) 273-2106, www.mesharpe.com; *The Illustrated Book of World Rankings.*

BARBADOS - INDUSTRIAL PROPERTY

United Nations Statistics Division, New York, NY 10017, (800) 253-9646, Fax: (212) 963-4116, http://unstats.un.org; *Statistical Yearbook.*

BARBADOS - INDUSTRIES

Central Intelligence Agency, Office of Public Affairs, Washington, DC 20505, (703) 482-0623, Fax: (703) 482-1739, www.cia.gov; *The World Factbook.*

Economist Intelligence Unit, 111 West 57th Street, New York, NY 10019, (212) 554-0600, Fax: (212) 586-1181, www.eiu.com; *Barbados Country Report.*

Euromonitor International, Inc., 224 S. Michigan Avenue, Suite 1500, Chicago, IL 60604, (312) 922-1115, Fax: (312) 922-1157, www.euromonitor.com; *The World Economic Factbook 2008* and *World Marketing Data and Statistics.*

International Labour Office, I.L.O. Publications, 4 route des Morillons, CH-1211 Geneva 22, Switzerland, (Telephone in U.S. (202) 653-7652), (Fax in U.S. (202) 653-7687), www.ilo.org; *Yearbook of Labour Statistics 2006.*

M.E. Sharpe, 80 Business Park Drive, Armonk, NY 10504, (800) 541-6563, Fax: (914) 273-2106, www.mesharpe.com; *The Illustrated Book of World Rankings.*

Palgrave Macmillan Ltd., Houndmills, Basingstoke, Hampshire, RG21 6XS, England, (Telephone in U.S. (888) 330-8477), (Fax in U.S. (800) 672-2054), www.palgrave.com; *The Statesman's Yearbook 2008.*

Taylor and Francis Group, An Informa Business, 2 Park Square, Milton Park, Abingdon, Oxford OX14 4RN, United Kingdom, (Dial from U.S. (212) 216-7800), (Fax from U.S. (212) 564-7854), www.tandf.co.uk; *The Europa World Year Book.*

United Nations Industrial Development Organization (UNIDO), 1 United Nations Plaza, New York, NY 10017, (212) 963 6890, Fax: (212) 963-7904, http://unido.org; Industrial Statistics Database 2008 (INDSTAT) and *The International Yearbook of Industrial Statistics 2008.*

United Nations Statistics Division, New York, NY 10017, (800) 253-9646, Fax: (212) 963-4116, http://unstats.un.org; *Economic Survey of Latin America and the Caribbean 2004-2005* and *Statistical Yearbook.*

The World Bank, 1818 H Street, NW, Washington, DC 20433, (202) 473-1000, Fax: (202) 477-6391, www.worldbank.org; *Barbados* and *World Development Indicators (WDI) 2008.*

BARBADOS - INFANT AND MATERNAL MORTALITY

See BARBADOS - MORTALITY

BARBADOS - INFLATION (FINANCE)

United Nations Statistics Division, New York, NY 10017, (800) 253-9646, Fax: (212) 963-4116, http://unstats.un.org; *Economic Survey of Latin America and the Caribbean 2004-2005.*

BARBADOS - INTEREST RATES

Inter-American Development Bank (IDB), 1300 New York Avenue, NW, Washington, DC 20577, (202) 623-1000, Fax: (202) 623-3096, www.iadb.org; *The Politics of Policies: Economic and Social Progress in Latin America - 2006 Report.*

Organization of American States (OAS), 17th Street Constitution Avenue NW, Washington, DC 20006, (202) 458-3000, www.oas.org; *The OAS in Transition: 1994-2004.*

United Nations Statistics Division, New York, NY 10017, (800) 253-9646, Fax: (212) 963-4116, http://unstats.un.org; *Statistical Yearbook.*

BARBADOS - INTERNAL REVENUE

Inter-American Development Bank (IDB), 1300 New York Avenue, NW, Washington, DC 20577, (202) 623-1000, Fax: (202) 623-3096, www.iadb.org; *The Politics of Policies: Economic and Social Progress in Latin America - 2006 Report.*

Organization of American States (OAS), 17th Street Constitution Avenue NW, Washington, DC 20006, (202) 458-3000, www.oas.org; *The OAS in Transition: 1994-2004.*

BARBADOS - INTERNATIONAL FINANCE

Inter-American Development Bank (IDB), 1300 New York Avenue, NW, Washington, DC 20577, (202) 623-1000, Fax: (202) 623-3096, www.iadb.org; *The Politics of Policies: Economic and Social Progress in Latin America - 2006 Report.*

United Nations Statistics Division, New York, NY 10017, (800) 253-9646, Fax: (212) 963-4116, http://unstats.un.org; *Statistical Yearbook for Latin America and the Caribbean 2004.*

BARBADOS - INTERNATIONAL LIQUIDITY

Inter-American Development Bank (IDB), 1300 New York Avenue, NW, Washington, DC 20577, (202) 623-1000, Fax: (202) 623-3096, www.iadb.org; *The Politics of Policies: Economic and Social Progress in Latin America - 2006 Report.*

International Monetary Fund (IMF), 700 Nineteenth Street, NW, Washington, DC 20431, (202) 623-7000, Fax: (202) 623-4661, www.imf.org; *International Financial Statistics Yearbook 2007.*

BARBADOS - INTERNATIONAL STATISTICS

Inter-American Development Bank (IDB), 1300 New York Avenue, NW, Washington, DC 20577, (202) 623-1000, Fax: (202) 623-3096, www.iadb.org; *The Politics of Policies: Economic and Social Progress in Latin America - 2006 Report.*

BARBADOS - INTERNATIONAL TRADE

Economist Intelligence Unit, 111 West 57th Street, New York, NY 10019, (212) 554-0600, Fax: (212) 586-1181, www.eiu.com; *Barbados Country Report.*

Euromonitor International, Inc., 224 S. Michigan Avenue, Suite 1500, Chicago, IL 60604, (312) 922-1115, Fax: (312) 922-1157, www.euromonitor.com; *The World Economic Factbook 2008* and *World Marketing Data and Statistics.*

Inter-American Development Bank (IDB), 1300 New York Avenue, NW, Washington, DC 20577, (202) 623-1000, Fax: (202) 623-3096, www.iadb.org; *The*

Politics of Policies: Economic and Social Progress in Latin America - 2006 Report.

M.E. Sharpe, 80 Business Park Drive, Armonk, NY 10504, (800) 541-6563, Fax: (914) 273-2106, www.mesharpe.com; *The Illustrated Book of World Rankings.*

Organisation for Economic Cooperation and Development (OECD), 2 rue Andre Pascal, F-75775 Paris Cedex 16, France, (Telephone in U.S. (202) 785-6323), (Fax in U.S. (202) 785-0350), www.oecd.org; *International Trade by Commodity Statistics (ITCS).*

Palgrave Macmillan Ltd., Houndmills, Basingstoke, Hampshire, RG21 6XS, England, (Telephone in U.S. (888) 330-8477), (Fax in U.S. (800) 672-2054), www.palgrave.com; *The Statesman's Yearbook 2008.*

Taylor and Francis Group, An Informa Business, 2 Park Square, Milton Park, Abingdon, Oxford OX14 4RN, United Kingdom, (Dial from U.S. (212) 216-7800), (Fax from U.S. (212) 564-7854), www.tandf.co.uk; *The Europa World Year Book.*

United Nations Conference on Trade and Development (UNCTAD), DC2-1120, United Nations, New York, NY 10017, (212) 963-0027, www.unctad.org; *UNCTAD Commodity Yearbook.*

United Nations Food and Agricultural Organization (FAO), Viale delle Terme di Caracalla, 00100 Rome, Italy, (Dial from U.S. (202) 653-2400), (Fax from U.S. (202) 653 5760), www.fao.org; *The State of Food and Agriculture (SOFA) 2006.*

United Nations Statistics Division, New York, NY 10017, (800) 253-9646, Fax: (212) 963-4116, http://unstats.un.org; *Economic Survey of Latin America and the Caribbean 2004-2005; International Trade Statistics Yearbook; Statistical Yearbook;* and *Statistical Yearbook for Latin America and the Caribbean 2004.*

The World Bank, 1818 H Street, NW, Washington, DC 20433, (202) 473-1000, Fax: (202) 477-6391, www.worldbank.org; *Barbados* and *World Development Indicators (WDI) 2008.*

World Trade Organization (WTO), Centre William Rappard, Rue de Lausanne 154, CH-1211 Geneva 21, Switzerland, www.wto.org; *International Trade Statistics 2006.*

BARBADOS - INTERNET USERS

International Telecommunication Union (ITU), Place des Nations, 1211 Geneva 20, Switzerland, www.itu.int; *World Telecommunication/ICT Indicators Database on CD-ROM; World Telecommunication/ICT Indicators Database Online;* and *Yearbook of Statistics - Telecommunication Services (Chronological Time Series 1997-2006).*

The World Bank, 1818 H Street, NW, Washington, DC 20433, (202) 473-1000, Fax: (202) 477-6391, www.worldbank.org; *Barbados.*

BARBADOS - INVESTMENTS

Inter-American Development Bank (IDB), 1300 New York Avenue, NW, Washington, DC 20577, (202) 623-1000, Fax: (202) 623-3096, www.iadb.org; *The Politics of Policies: Economic and Social Progress in Latin America - 2006 Report.*

United Nations Statistics Division, New York, NY 10017, (800) 253-9646, Fax: (212) 963-4116, http://unstats.un.org; *Statistical Yearbook for Latin America and the Caribbean 2004.*

BARBADOS - IRON AND IRON ORE PRODUCTION

See BARBADOS - MINERAL INDUSTRIES

BARBADOS - IRRIGATION

Inter-American Development Bank (IDB), 1300 New York Avenue, NW, Washington, DC 20577, (202) 623-1000, Fax: (202) 623-3096, www.iadb.org; *The Politics of Policies: Economic and Social Progress in Latin America - 2006 Report.*

BARBADOS - LABOR

Central Intelligence Agency, Office of Public Affairs, Washington, DC 20505, (703) 482-0623, Fax: (703) 482-1739, www.cia.gov; *The World Factbook.*

Euromonitor International, Inc., 224 S. Michigan Avenue, Suite 1500, Chicago, IL 60604, (312) 922-1115, Fax: (312) 922-1157, www.euromonitor.com; *International Marketing Data and Statistics 2008* and *World Marketing Data and Statistics.*

International Labour Office, I.L.O. Publications, 4 route des Morillons, CH-1211 Geneva 22, Switzerland, (Telephone in U.S. (202) 653-7652), (Fax in U.S. (202) 653-7687), www.ilo.org; *Yearbook of Labour Statistics 2006.*

M.E. Sharpe, 80 Business Park Drive, Armonk, NY 10504, (800) 541-6563, Fax: (914) 273-2106, www.mesharpe.com; *The Illustrated Book of World Rankings.*

Palgrave Macmillan Ltd., Houndmills, Basingstoke, Hampshire, RG21 6XS, England, (Telephone in U.S. (888) 330-8477), (Fax in U.S. (800) 672-2054), www.palgrave.com; *The Statesman's Yearbook 2008.*

Taylor and Francis Group, An Informa Business, 2 Park Square, Milton Park, Abingdon, Oxford OX14 4RN, United Kingdom, (Dial from U.S. (212) 216-7800), (Fax from U.S. (212) 564-7854), www.tandf.co.uk; *The Europa World Year Book.*

United Nations Food and Agricultural Organization (FAO), Viale delle Terme di Caracalla, 00100 Rome, Italy, (Dial from U.S. (202) 653-2400), (Fax from U.S. (202) 653 5760), www.fao.org; *The State of Food and Agriculture (SOFA) 2006.*

United Nations Statistics Division, New York, NY 10017, (800) 253-9646, Fax: (212) 963-4116, http://unstats.un.org; *Human Development Report 2006.*

The World Bank, 1818 H Street, NW, Washington, DC 20433, (202) 473-1000, Fax: (202) 477-6391, www.worldbank.org; *The World Bank Atlas 2003-2004* and *World Development Indicators (WDI) 2008.*

BARBADOS - LAND USE

Central Intelligence Agency, Office of Public Affairs, Washington, DC 20505, (703) 482-0623, Fax: (703) 482-1739, www.cia.gov; *The World Factbook.*

Euromonitor International, Inc., 224 S. Michigan Avenue, Suite 1500, Chicago, IL 60604, (312) 922-1115, Fax: (312) 922-1157, www.euromonitor.com; *International Marketing Data and Statistics 2008.*

Inter-American Development Bank (IDB), 1300 New York Avenue, NW, Washington, DC 20577, (202) 623-1000, Fax: (202) 623-3096, www.iadb.org; *The Politics of Policies: Economic and Social Progress in Latin America - 2006 Report.*

United Nations Food and Agricultural Organization (FAO), Viale delle Terme di Caracalla, 00100 Rome, Italy, (Dial from U.S. (202) 653-2400), (Fax from U.S. (202) 653 5760), www.fao.org; *FAO Production Yearbook 2002.*

BARBADOS - LIBRARIES

M.E. Sharpe, 80 Business Park Drive, Armonk, NY 10504, (800) 541-6563, Fax: (914) 273-2106, www.mesharpe.com; *The Illustrated Book of World Rankings.*

UNESCO Institute for Statistics, C.P. 6128 Succursale Centre-Ville, Montreal, Quebec, H3C 3J7 Canada, (Dial from U.S. (514) 343-6880), (Fax from U.S. (514) 343 6882), www.uis.unesco.org; *Statistical Tables.*

BARBADOS - LICENSES

International Monetary Fund (IMF), 700 Nineteenth Street, NW, Washington, DC 20431, (202) 623-7000, Fax: (202) 623-4661, www.imf.org; *Government Finance Statistics Yearbook (2008 Edition).*

BARBADOS - LIFE EXPECTANCY

Central Intelligence Agency, Office of Public Affairs, Washington, DC 20505, (703) 482-0623, Fax: (703) 482-1739, www.cia.gov; *The World Factbook.*

Euromonitor International, Inc., 224 S. Michigan Avenue, Suite 1500, Chicago, IL 60604, (312) 922-1115, Fax: (312) 922-1157, www.euromonitor.com; *The World Economic Factbook 2008.*

Palgrave Macmillan Ltd., Houndmills, Basingstoke, Hampshire, RG21 6XS, England, (Telephone in U.S. (888) 330-8477), (Fax in U.S. (800) 672-2054), www.palgrave.com; *The Statesman's Yearbook 2008.*

United Nations Statistics Division, New York, NY 10017, (800) 253-9646, Fax: (212) 963-4116, http://unstats.un.org; *Human Development Report 2006; Statistical Yearbook for Latin America and the Caribbean 2004;* and *World Statistics Pocketbook.*

The World Bank, 1818 H Street, NW, Washington, DC 20433, (202) 473-1000, Fax: (202) 477-6391, www.worldbank.org; *The World Bank Atlas 2003-2004.*

BARBADOS - LITERACY

Euromonitor International, Inc., 224 S. Michigan Avenue, Suite 1500, Chicago, IL 60604, (312) 922-1115, Fax: (312) 922-1157, www.euromonitor.com; *World Marketing Data and Statistics.*

BARBADOS - LIVESTOCK

M.E. Sharpe, 80 Business Park Drive, Armonk, NY 10504, (800) 541-6563, Fax: (914) 273-2106, www.mesharpe.com; *The Illustrated Book of World Rankings.*

Palgrave Macmillan Ltd., Houndmills, Basingstoke, Hampshire, RG21 6XS, England, (Telephone in U.S. (888) 330-8477), (Fax in U.S. (800) 672-2054), www.palgrave.com; *The Statesman's Yearbook 2008.*

Taylor and Francis Group, An Informa Business, 2 Park Square, Milton Park, Abingdon, Oxford OX14 4RN, United Kingdom, (Dial from U.S. (212) 216-7800), (Fax from U.S. (212) 564-7854), www.tandf.co.uk; *The Europa World Year Book.*

United Nations Conference on Trade and Development (UNCTAD), DC2-1120, United Nations, New York, NY 10017, (212) 963-0027, www.unctad.org; *UNCTAD Commodity Yearbook.*

United Nations Food and Agricultural Organization (FAO), Viale delle Terme di Caracalla, 00100 Rome, Italy, (Dial from U.S. (202) 653-2400), (Fax from U.S. (202) 653 5760), www.fao.org; *FAO Production Yearbook 2002* and *The State of Food and Agriculture (SOFA) 2006.*

United Nations Statistics Division, New York, NY 10017, (800) 253-9646, Fax: (212) 963-4116, http://unstats.un.org; *Statistical Yearbook.*

BARBADOS - LOCAL TAXATION

Inter-American Development Bank (IDB), 1300 New York Avenue, NW, Washington, DC 20577, (202) 623-1000, Fax: (202) 623-3096, www.iadb.org; *The Politics of Policies: Economic and Social Progress in Latin America - 2006 Report.*

BARBADOS - MANUFACTURES

Inter-American Development Bank (IDB), 1300 New York Avenue, NW, Washington, DC 20577, (202) 623-1000, Fax: (202) 623-3096, www.iadb.org; *The Politics of Policies: Economic and Social Progress in Latin America - 2006 Report.*

M.E. Sharpe, 80 Business Park Drive, Armonk, NY 10504, (800) 541-6563, Fax: (914) 273-2106, www.mesharpe.com; *The Illustrated Book of World Rankings.*

Organization of American States (OAS), 17th Street Constitution Avenue NW, Washington, DC 20006, (202) 458-3000, www.oas.org; *The OAS in Transition: 1994-2004.*

United Nations Statistics Division, New York, NY 10017, (800) 253-9646, Fax: (212) 963-4116, http://unstats.un.org; *Statistical Yearbook* and *Statistical Yearbook for Latin America and the Caribbean 2004.*

The World Bank, 1818 H Street, NW, Washington, DC 20433, (202) 473-1000, Fax: (202) 477-6391, www.worldbank.org; *World Development Indicators (WDI) 2008.*

BARBADOS - MARRIAGE

M.E. Sharpe, 80 Business Park Drive, Armonk, NY 10504, (800) 541-6563, Fax: (914) 273-2106, www.mesharpe.com; *The Illustrated Book of World Rankings.*

Taylor and Francis Group, An Informa Business, 2 Park Square, Milton Park, Abingdon, Oxford OX14 4RN, United Kingdom, (Dial from U.S. (212) 216-7800), (Fax from U.S. (212) 564-7854), www.tandf.co.uk; *The Europa World Year Book.*

United Nations Statistics Division, New York, NY 10017, (800) 253-9646, Fax: (212) 963-4116, http://unstats.un.org; *Demographic Yearbook* and *Statistical Yearbook.*

BARBADOS - MEAT PRODUCTION

See BARBADOS - LIVESTOCK

BARBADOS - MILK PRODUCTION

See BARBADOS - DAIRY PROCESSING

BARBADOS - MINERAL INDUSTRIES

Inter-American Development Bank (IDB), 1300 New York Avenue, NW, Washington, DC 20577, (202) 623-1000, Fax: (202) 623-3096, www.iadb.org; *The Politics of Policies: Economic and Social Progress in Latin America - 2006 Report.*

M.E. Sharpe, 80 Business Park Drive, Armonk, NY 10504, (800) 541-6563, Fax: (914) 273-2106, www.mesharpe.com; *The Illustrated Book of World Rankings.*

Organisation for Economic Cooperation and Development (OECD), 2 rue Andre Pascal, F-75775 Paris Cedex 16, France, (Telephone in U.S. (202) 785-6323), (Fax in U.S. (202) 785-0350), www.oecd.org; *World Energy Outlook 2007.*

Organization of American States (OAS), 17th Street Constitution Avenue NW, Washington, DC 20006, (202) 458-3000, www.oas.org; *The OAS in Transition: 1994-2004.*

Taylor and Francis Group, An Informa Business, 2 Park Square, Milton Park, Abingdon, Oxford OX14 4RN, United Kingdom, (Dial from U.S. (212) 216-7800), (Fax from U.S. (212) 564-7854), www.tandf.co.uk; *The Europa World Year Book.*

United Nations Conference on Trade and Development (UNCTAD), DC2-1120, United Nations, New York, NY 10017, (212) 963-0027, www.unctad.org; *UNCTAD Commodity Yearbook.*

United Nations Statistics Division, New York, NY 10017, (800) 253-9646, Fax: (212) 963-4116, http://unstats.un.org; *Statistical Yearbook* and *Statistical Yearbook for Latin America and the Caribbean 2004.*

BARBADOS - MONEY EXCHANGE RATES

See BARBADOS - FOREIGN EXCHANGE RATES

BARBADOS - MONEY SUPPLY

Economist Intelligence Unit, 111 West 57th Street, New York, NY 10019, (212) 554-0600, Fax: (212) 586-1181, www.eiu.com; *Barbados Country Report.*

Inter-American Development Bank (IDB), 1300 New York Avenue, NW, Washington, DC 20577, (202) 623-1000, Fax: (202) 623-3096, www.iadb.org; *The Politics of Policies: Economic and Social Progress in Latin America - 2006 Report.*

International Monetary Fund (IMF), 700 Nineteenth Street, NW, Washington, DC 20431, (202) 623-7000, Fax: (202) 623-4661, www.imf.org; *International Financial Statistics Yearbook 2007.*

Taylor and Francis Group, An Informa Business, 2 Park Square, Milton Park, Abingdon, Oxford OX14 4RN, United Kingdom, (Dial from U.S. (212) 216-7800), (Fax from U.S. (212) 564-7854), www.tandf.co.uk; *The Europa World Year Book.*

United Nations Statistics Division, New York, NY 10017, (800) 253-9646, Fax: (212) 963-4116, http://unstats.un.org; *Statistical Yearbook.*

The World Bank, 1818 H Street, NW, Washington, DC 20433, (202) 473-1000, Fax: (202) 477-6391, www.worldbank.org; *Barbados* and *World Development Indicators (WDI) 2008.*

BARBADOS - MORTALITY

Central Intelligence Agency, Office of Public Affairs, Washington, DC 20505, (703) 482-0623, Fax: (703) 482-1739, www.cia.gov; *The World Factbook.*

Euromonitor International, Inc., 224 S. Michigan Avenue, Suite 1500, Chicago, IL 60604, (312) 922-1115, Fax: (312) 922-1157, www.euromonitor.com; *International Marketing Data and Statistics 2008* and *The World Economic Factbook 2008.*

Palgrave Macmillan Ltd., Houndmills, Basingstoke, Hampshire, RG21 6XS, England, (Telephone in U.S. (888) 330-8477), (Fax in U.S. (800) 672-2054), www.palgrave.com; *The Statesman's Yearbook 2008.*

Taylor and Francis Group, An Informa Business, 2 Park Square, Milton Park, Abingdon, Oxford OX14 4RN, United Kingdom, (Dial from U.S. (212) 216-7800), (Fax from U.S. (212) 564-7854), www.tandf.co.uk; *The Europa World Year Book.*

United Nations Statistics Division, New York, NY 10017, (800) 253-9646, Fax: (212) 963-4116, http://unstats.un.org; *Demographic Yearbook; Human Development Report 2006; Statistical Yearbook; Statistical Yearbook for Latin America and the Caribbean 2004;* and *World Statistics Pocketbook.*

The World Bank, 1818 H Street, NW, Washington, DC 20433, (202) 473-1000, Fax: (202) 477-6391, www.worldbank.org; *The World Bank Atlas 2003-2004* and *World Development Indicators (WDI) 2008.*

World Health Organization (WHO), Avenue Appia 20, 1211 Geneve 27, Switzerland, (Telephone in U.S. (212) 331-9081), www.who.int; The WHO Global Atlas of Infectious Diseases and *World Health Report 2006.*

BARBADOS - MOTION PICTURES

Palgrave Macmillan Ltd., Houndmills, Basingstoke, Hampshire, RG21 6XS, England, (Telephone in U.S. (888) 330-8477), (Fax in U.S. (800) 672-2054), www.palgrave.com; *The Statesman's Yearbook 2008.*

BARBADOS - MOTOR VEHICLES

Taylor and Francis Group, An Informa Business, 2 Park Square, Milton Park, Abingdon, Oxford OX14 4RN, United Kingdom, (Dial from U.S. (212) 216-7800), (Fax from U.S. (212) 564-7854), www.tandf.co.uk; *The Europa World Year Book.*

United Nations Statistics Division, New York, NY 10017, (800) 253-9646, Fax: (212) 963-4116, http://unstats.un.org; *Statistical Yearbook.*

BARBADOS - MUSEUMS

M.E. Sharpe, 80 Business Park Drive, Armonk, NY 10504, (800) 541-6563, Fax: (914) 273-2106, www.mesharpe.com; *The Illustrated Book of World Rankings.*

UNESCO Institute for Statistics, C.P. 6128 Succursale Centre-Ville, Montreal, Quebec, H3C 3J7 Canada, (Dial from U.S. (514) 343-6880), (Fax from U.S. (514) 343 6882), www.uis.unesco.org; *Statistical Tables.*

BARBADOS - NATIONAL INCOME

United Nations Statistics Division, New York, NY 10017, (800) 253-9646, Fax: (212) 963-4116, http://unstats.un.org; *Statistical Yearbook.*

BARBADOS - NATURAL GAS PRODUCTION

See BARBADOS - MINERAL INDUSTRIES

BARBADOS - NUTRITION

United Nations Food and Agricultural Organization (FAO), Viale delle Terme di Caracalla, 00100 Rome, Italy, (Dial from U.S. (202) 653-2400), (Fax from U.S. (202) 653 5760), www.fao.org; *The State of Food and Agriculture (SOFA) 2006.*

United Nations Statistics Division, New York, NY 10017, (800) 253-9646, Fax: (212) 963-4116, http://unstats.un.org; *Statistical Yearbook for Latin America and the Caribbean 2004.*

BARBADOS - OLDER PEOPLE

M.E. Sharpe, 80 Business Park Drive, Armonk, NY 10504, (800) 541-6563, Fax: (914) 273-2106, www.mesharpe.com; *The Illustrated Book of World Rankings.*

BARBADOS - PAPER

See BARBADOS - FORESTS AND FORESTRY

BARBADOS - PEANUT PRODUCTION

See BARBADOS - CROPS

BARBADOS - PERIODICALS

UNESCO Institute for Statistics, C.P. 6128 Succursale Centre-Ville, Montreal, Quebec, H3C 3J7 Canada, (Dial from U.S. (514) 343-6880), (Fax from U.S. (514) 343 6882), www.uis.unesco.org; *Statistical Tables.*

BARBADOS - PESTICIDES

United Nations Food and Agricultural Organization (FAO), Viale delle Terme di Caracalla, 00100 Rome, Italy, (Dial from U.S. (202) 653-2400), (Fax from U.S. (202) 653 5760), www.fao.org; *The State of Food and Agriculture (SOFA) 2006.*

BARBADOS - PETROLEUM INDUSTRY AND TRADE

Inter-American Development Bank (IDB), 1300 New York Avenue, NW, Washington, DC 20577, (202) 623-1000, Fax: (202) 623-3096, www.iadb.org; *The Politics of Policies: Economic and Social Progress in Latin America - 2006 Report.*

M.E. Sharpe, 80 Business Park Drive, Armonk, NY 10504, (800) 541-6563, Fax: (914) 273-2106, www.mesharpe.com; *The Illustrated Book of World Rankings.*

Organisation for Economic Cooperation and Development (OECD), 2 rue Andre Pascal, F-75775 Paris Cedex 16, France, (Telephone in U.S. (202) 785-6323), (Fax in U.S. (202) 785-0350), www.oecd.org; *World Energy Outlook 2007.*

Palgrave Macmillan Ltd., Houndmills, Basingstoke, Hampshire, RG21 6XS, England, (Telephone in U.S. (888) 330-8477), (Fax in U.S. (800) 672-2054), www.palgrave.com; *The Statesman's Yearbook 2008.*

PennWell Corporation, 1421 South Sheridan Road, Tulsa, OK 74112, (918) 835-3161, www.pennwell.com; *International Petroleum Encyclopedia 2007.*

United Nations Conference on Trade and Development (UNCTAD), DC2-1120, United Nations, New York, NY 10017, (212) 963-0027, www.unctad.org; *UNCTAD Commodity Yearbook.*

United Nations Food and Agricultural Organization (FAO), Viale delle Terme di Caracalla, 00100 Rome, Italy, (Dial from U.S. (202) 653-2400), (Fax from U.S. (202) 653 5760), www.fao.org; *The State of Food and Agriculture (SOFA) 2006.*

United Nations Statistics Division, New York, NY 10017, (800) 253-9646, Fax: (212) 963-4116, http://unstats.un.org; *Statistical Yearbook.*

BARBADOS - POLITICAL SCIENCE

Central Intelligence Agency, Office of Public Affairs, Washington, DC 20505, (703) 482-0623, Fax: (703) 482-1739, www.cia.gov; *The World Factbook.*

Inter-American Development Bank (IDB), 1300 New York Avenue, NW, Washington, DC 20577, (202) 623-1000, Fax: (202) 623-3096, www.iadb.org; *The Politics of Policies: Economic and Social Progress in Latin America - 2006 Report.*

International Monetary Fund (IMF), 700 Nineteenth Street, NW, Washington, DC 20431, (202) 623-7000, Fax: (202) 623-4661, www.imf.org; *Government Finance Statistics Yearbook (2008 Edition).*

Palgrave Macmillan Ltd., Houndmills, Basingstoke, Hampshire, RG21 6XS, England, (Telephone in U.S. (888) 330-8477), (Fax in U.S. (800) 672-2054), www.palgrave.com; *The Statesman's Yearbook 2008.*

Taylor and Francis Group, An Informa Business, 2 Park Square, Milton Park, Abingdon, Oxford OX14 4RN, United Kingdom, (Dial from U.S. (212) 216-7800), (Fax from U.S. (212) 564-7854), www.tandf.co.uk; *The Europa World Year Book.*

United Nations Statistics Division, New York, NY 10017, (800) 253-9646, Fax: (212) 963-4116, http://

unstats.un.org; *National Accounts Statistics: Compendium of Income Distribution Statistics.*

The World Bank, 1818 H Street, NW, Washington, DC 20433, (202) 473-1000, Fax: (202) 477-6391, www.worldbank.org; *World Development Indicators (WDI) 2008.*

BARBADOS - POPULATION

Caribbean Epidemiology Centre (CAREC), 16-18 Jamaica Boulevard, Federation Park, PO Box 164, Port of Spain, Republic of Trinidad and Tobago, (Dial from U.S. (868) 622-4261), (Fax from U.S. (868) 622-2792), www.carec.org; *Population Data.*

Central Intelligence Agency, Office of Public Affairs, Washington, DC 20505, (703) 482-0623, Fax: (703) 482-1739, www.cia.gov; *The World Factbook.*

Economist Intelligence Unit, 111 West 57th Street, New York, NY 10019, (212) 554-0600, Fax: (212) 586-1181, www.eiu.com; *Barbados Country Report.*

Euromonitor International, Inc., 224 S. Michigan Avenue, Suite 1500, Chicago, IL 60604, (312) 922-1115, Fax: (312) 922-1157, www.euromonitor.com; *International Marketing Data and Statistics 2008* and *The World Economic Factbook 2008.*

Eurostat, Batiment Jean Monnet, Rue Alcide de Gasperi, L-2920 Luxembourg, http://epp.eurostat.ec.europa.eu; *Demographic Indicators - Population by Age-Classes.*

Inter-American Development Bank (IDB), 1300 New York Avenue, NW, Washington, DC 20577, (202) 623-1000, Fax: (202) 623-3096, www.iadb.org; *The Politics of Policies: Economic and Social Progress in Latin America - 2006 Report.*

International Labour Office, I.L.O. Publications, 4 route des Morillons, CH-1211 Geneva 22, Switzerland, (Telephone in U.S. (202) 653-7652), (Fax in U.S. (202) 653-7687), www.ilo.org; *Yearbook of Labour Statistics 2006.*

M.E. Sharpe, 80 Business Park Drive, Armonk, NY 10504, (800) 541-6563, Fax: (914) 273-2106, www.mesharpe.com; *The Illustrated Book of World Rankings.*

Organization of American States (OAS), 17th Street Constitution Avenue NW, Washington, DC 20006, (202) 458-3000, www.oas.org; *The OAS in Transition: 1994-2004.*

Palgrave Macmillan Ltd., Houndmills, Basingstoke, Hampshire, RG21 6XS, England, (Telephone in U.S. (888) 330-8477), (Fax in U.S. (800) 672-2054), www.palgrave.com; *The Statesman's Yearbook 2008.*

Taylor and Francis Group, An Informa Business, 2 Park Square, Milton Park, Abingdon, Oxford OX14 4RN, United Kingdom, (Dial from U.S. (212) 216-7800), (Fax from U.S. (212) 564-7854), www.tandf.co.uk; *The Europa World Year Book.*

U.S. Department of State (DOS), 2201 C Street NW, Washington, DC 20520, (202) 647-4000, www.state.gov; *World Military Expenditures and Arms Transfers (WMEAT).*

United Nations Food and Agricultural Organization (FAO), Viale delle Terme di Caracalla, 00100 Rome, Italy, (Dial from U.S. (202) 653-2400), (Fax from U.S. (202) 653 5760), www.fao.org; *FAO Production Yearbook 2002.*

United Nations Statistics Division, New York, NY 10017, (800) 253-9646, Fax: (212) 963-4116, http://unstats.un.org; *Demographic Yearbook; Human Development Report 2006; Statistical Yearbook; Statistical Yearbook for Latin America and the Caribbean 2004;* and *World Statistics Pocketbook.*

The World Bank, 1818 H Street, NW, Washington, DC 20433, (202) 473-1000, Fax: (202) 477-6391, www.worldbank.org; *Barbados* and *The World Bank Atlas 2003-2004.*

World Health Organization (WHO), Avenue Appia 20, 1211 Geneve 27, Switzerland, (Telephone in U.S. (212) 331-9081), www.who.int; *World Health Report 2006.*

BARBADOS - POPULATION DENSITY

Central Intelligence Agency, Office of Public Affairs, Washington, DC 20505, (703) 482-0623, Fax: (703) 482-1739, www.cia.gov; *The World Factbook.*

Euromonitor International, Inc., 224 S. Michigan Avenue, Suite 1500, Chicago, IL 60604, (312) 922-1115, Fax: (312) 922-1157, www.euromonitor.com; *The World Economic Factbook 2008.*

Inter-American Development Bank (IDB), 1300 New York Avenue, NW, Washington, DC 20577, (202) 623-1000, Fax: (202) 623-3096, www.iadb.org; *The Politics of Policies: Economic and Social Progress in Latin America - 2006 Report.*

M.E. Sharpe, 80 Business Park Drive, Armonk, NY 10504, (800) 541-6563, Fax: (914) 273-2106, www.mesharpe.com; *The Illustrated Book of World Rankings.*

Palgrave Macmillan Ltd., Houndmills, Basingstoke, Hampshire, RG21 6XS, England, (Telephone in U.S. (888) 330-8477), (Fax in U.S. (800) 672-2054), www.palgrave.com; *The Statesman's Yearbook 2008.*

Taylor and Francis Group, An Informa Business, 2 Park Square, Milton Park, Abingdon, Oxford OX14 4RN, United Kingdom, (Dial from U.S. (212) 216-7800), (Fax from U.S. (212) 564-7854), www.tandf.co.uk; *The Europa World Year Book.*

United Nations Food and Agricultural Organization (FAO), Viale delle Terme di Caracalla, 00100 Rome, Italy, (Dial from U.S. (202) 653-2400), (Fax from U.S. (202) 653 5760), www.fao.org; *The State of Food and Agriculture (SOFA) 2006.*

United Nations Statistics Division, New York, NY 10017, (800) 253-9646, Fax: (212) 963-4116, http://unstats.un.org; *Statistical Yearbook.*

The World Bank, 1818 H Street, NW, Washington, DC 20433, (202) 473-1000, Fax: (202) 477-6391, www.worldbank.org; *Barbados.*

BARBADOS - POSTAL SERVICE

M.E. Sharpe, 80 Business Park Drive, Armonk, NY 10504, (800) 541-6563, Fax: (914) 273-2106, www.mesharpe.com; *The Illustrated Book of World Rankings.*

Palgrave Macmillan Ltd., Houndmills, Basingstoke, Hampshire, RG21 6XS, England, (Telephone in U.S. (888) 330-8477), (Fax in U.S. (800) 672-2054), www.palgrave.com; *The Statesman's Yearbook 2008.*

United Nations Statistics Division, New York, NY 10017, (800) 253-9646, Fax: (212) 963-4116, http://unstats.un.org; *Statistical Yearbook.*

BARBADOS - POWER RESOURCES

Euromonitor International, Inc., 224 S. Michigan Avenue, Suite 1500, Chicago, IL 60604, (312) 922-1115, Fax: (312) 922-1157, www.euromonitor.com; *International Marketing Data and Statistics 2008; The World Economic Factbook 2008;* and *World Marketing Data and Statistics.*

M.E. Sharpe, 80 Business Park Drive, Armonk, NY 10504, (800) 541-6563, Fax: (914) 273-2106, www.mesharpe.com; *The Illustrated Book of World Rankings.*

Organisation for Economic Cooperation and Development (OECD), 2 rue Andre Pascal, F-75775 Paris Cedex 16, France, (Telephone in U.S. (202) 785-6323), (Fax in U.S. (202) 785-0350), www.oecd.org; *World Energy Outlook 2007.*

Palgrave Macmillan Ltd., Houndmills, Basingstoke, Hampshire, RG21 6XS, England, (Telephone in U.S. (888) 330-8477), (Fax in U.S. (800) 672-2054), www.palgrave.com; *The Statesman's Yearbook 2008.*

Platts, 2 Penn Plaza, 25th Floor, New York, NY 10121-2298, (212) 904-3070, www.platts.com; *Energy Economist.*

United Nations Food and Agricultural Organization (FAO), Viale delle Terme di Caracalla, 00100 Rome, Italy, (Dial from U.S. (202) 653-2400), (Fax from U.S. (202) 653 5760), www.fao.org; *The State of Food and Agriculture (SOFA) 2006.*

United Nations Statistics Division, New York, NY 10017, (800) 253-9646, Fax: (212) 963-4116, http://unstats.un.org; *Energy Statistics Yearbook 2003; Human Development Report 2006; Statistical Yearbook; Statistical Yearbook for Latin America and the Caribbean 2004;* and *World Statistics Pocketbook.*

The World Bank, 1818 H Street, NW, Washington, DC 20433, (202) 473-1000, Fax: (202) 477-6391, www.worldbank.org; *The World Bank Atlas 2003-2004.*

BARBADOS - PRICES

Euromonitor International, Inc., 224 S. Michigan Avenue, Suite 1500, Chicago, IL 60604, (312) 922-1115, Fax: (312) 922-1157, www.euromonitor.com; *World Marketing Data and Statistics.*

International Labour Office, I.L.O. Publications, 4 route des Morillons, CH-1211 Geneva 22, Switzerland, (Telephone in U.S. (202) 653-7652), (Fax in U.S. (202) 653-7687), www.ilo.org; *Yearbook of Labour Statistics 2006.*

International Monetary Fund (IMF), 700 Nineteenth Street, NW, Washington, DC 20431, (202) 623-7000, Fax: (202) 623-4661, www.imf.org; *International Financial Statistics Yearbook 2007.*

M.E. Sharpe, 80 Business Park Drive, Armonk, NY 10504, (800) 541-6563, Fax: (914) 273-2106, www.mesharpe.com; *The Illustrated Book of World Rankings.*

Organization of American States (OAS), 17th Street Constitution Avenue NW, Washington, DC 20006, (202) 458-3000, www.oas.org; *The OAS in Transition: 1994-2004.*

United Nations Food and Agricultural Organization (FAO), Viale delle Terme di Caracalla, 00100 Rome, Italy, (Dial from U.S. (202) 653-2400), (Fax from U.S. (202) 653 5760), www.fao.org; *FAO Production Yearbook 2002* and *The State of Food and Agriculture (SOFA) 2006.*

United Nations Statistics Division, New York, NY 10017, (800) 253-9646, Fax: (212) 963-4116, http://unstats.un.org; *Statistical Yearbook for Latin America and the Caribbean 2004.*

The World Bank, 1818 H Street, NW, Washington, DC 20433, (202) 473-1000, Fax: (202) 477-6391, www.worldbank.org; *Barbados.*

BARBADOS - PUBLIC HEALTH

Euromonitor International, Inc., 224 S. Michigan Avenue, Suite 1500, Chicago, IL 60604, (312) 922-1115, Fax: (312) 922-1157, www.euromonitor.com; *World Marketing Data and Statistics.*

International Monetary Fund (IMF), 700 Nineteenth Street, NW, Washington, DC 20431, (202) 623-7000, Fax: (202) 623-4661, www.imf.org; *Government Finance Statistics Yearbook (2008 Edition).*

M.E. Sharpe, 80 Business Park Drive, Armonk, NY 10504, (800) 541-6563, Fax: (914) 273-2106, www.mesharpe.com; *The Illustrated Book of World Rankings.*

Palgrave Macmillan Ltd., Houndmills, Basingstoke, Hampshire, RG21 6XS, England, (Telephone in U.S. (888) 330-8477), (Fax in U.S. (800) 672-2054), www.palgrave.com; *The Statesman's Yearbook 2008.*

United Nations Statistics Division, New York, NY 10017, (800) 253-9646, Fax: (212) 963-4116, http://unstats.un.org; *Human Development Report 2006* and *Statistical Yearbook.*

The World Bank, 1818 H Street, NW, Washington, DC 20433, (202) 473-1000, Fax: (202) 477-6391, www.worldbank.org; *Barbados.*

World Health Organization (WHO), Avenue Appia 20, 1211 Geneve 27, Switzerland, (Telephone in U.S. (212) 331-9081), www.who.int; The WHO Global Atlas of Infectious Diseases and *World Health Report 2006.*

BARBADOS - PUBLISHERS AND PUBLISHING

Taylor and Francis Group, An Informa Business, 2 Park Square, Milton Park, Abingdon, Oxford OX14

4RN, United Kingdom, (Dial from U.S. (212) 216-7800), (Fax from U.S. (212) 564-7854), www.tandf.co.uk; *The Europa World Year Book.*

UNESCO Institute for Statistics, C.P. 6128 Succursale Centre-Ville, Montreal, Quebec, H3C 3J7 Canada, (Dial from U.S. (514) 343-6880), (Fax from U.S. (514) 343 6882), www.uis.unesco.org; *Statistical Tables.*

BARBADOS - RADIO BROADCASTING

Palgrave Macmillan Ltd., Houndmills, Basingstoke, Hampshire, RG21 6XS, England, (Telephone in U.S. (888) 330-8477), (Fax in U.S. (800) 672-2054), www.palgrave.com; *The Statesman's Yearbook 2008.*

BARBADOS - RELIGION

Central Intelligence Agency, Office of Public Affairs, Washington, DC 20505, (703) 482-0623, Fax: (703) 482-1739, www.cia.gov; *The World Factbook.*

M.E. Sharpe, 80 Business Park Drive, Armonk, NY 10504, (800) 541-6563, Fax: (914) 273-2106, www.mesharpe.com; *The Illustrated Book of World Rankings.*

Palgrave Macmillan Ltd., Houndmills, Basingstoke, Hampshire, RG21 6XS, England, (Telephone in U.S. (888) 330-8477), (Fax in U.S. (800) 672-2054), www.palgrave.com; *The Statesman's Yearbook 2008.*

BARBADOS - RENT CHARGES

International Labour Office, I.L.O. Publications, 4 route des Morillons, CH-1211 Geneva 22, Switzerland, (Telephone in U.S. (202) 653-7652), (Fax in U.S. (202) 653-7687), www.ilo.org; *Yearbook of Labour Statistics 2006.*

BARBADOS - RESERVES (ACCOUNTING)

Inter-American Development Bank (IDB), 1300 New York Avenue, NW, Washington, DC 20577, (202) 623-1000, Fax: (202) 623-3096, www.iadb.org; *The Politics of Policies: Economic and Social Progress in Latin America - 2006 Report.*

Organization of American States (OAS), 17th Street Constitution Avenue NW, Washington, DC 20006, (202) 458-3000, www.oas.org; *The OAS in Transition: 1994-2004.*

The World Bank, 1818 H Street, NW, Washington, DC 20433, (202) 473-1000, Fax: (202) 477-6391, www.worldbank.org; *World Development Indicators (WDI) 2008.*

BARBADOS - RETAIL TRADE

Euromonitor International, Inc., 224 S. Michigan Avenue, Suite 1500, Chicago, IL 60604, (312) 922-1115, Fax: (312) 922-1157, www.euromonitor.com; *World Marketing Data and Statistics.*

Inter-American Development Bank (IDB), 1300 New York Avenue, NW, Washington, DC 20577, (202) 623-1000, Fax: (202) 623-3096, www.iadb.org; *The Politics of Policies: Economic and Social Progress in Latin America - 2006 Report.*

BARBADOS - RICE PRODUCTION

See BARBADOS - CROPS

BARBADOS - ROADS

Central Intelligence Agency, Office of Public Affairs, Washington, DC 20505, (703) 482-0623, Fax: (703) 482-1739, www.cia.gov; *The World Factbook.*

Palgrave Macmillan Ltd., Houndmills, Basingstoke, Hampshire, RG21 6XS, England, (Telephone in U.S. (888) 330-8477), (Fax in U.S. (800) 672-2054), www.palgrave.com; *The Statesman's Yearbook 2008.*

BARBADOS - RUBBER INDUSTRY AND TRADE

International Rubber Study Group (IRSG), 1st Floor, Heron House, 109/115 Wembley Hill Road, Wembley, Middlesex HA9 8DA, United Kingdom, www.rubberstudy.com; *Rubber Statistical Bulletin; Summary of World Rubber Statistics 2005; World Rubber Statistics Handbook (Volume 6, 1975-2001);* and *World Rubber Statistics Historic Handbook.*

M.E. Sharpe, 80 Business Park Drive, Armonk, NY 10504, (800) 541-6563, Fax: (914) 273-2106, www.mesharpe.com; *The Illustrated Book of World Rankings.*

BARBADOS - SHEEP

See BARBADOS - LIVESTOCK

BARBADOS - SHIPPING

Palgrave Macmillan Ltd., Houndmills, Basingstoke, Hampshire, RG21 6XS, England, (Telephone in U.S. (888) 330-8477), (Fax in U.S. (800) 672-2054), www.palgrave.com; *The Statesman's Yearbook 2008.*

Taylor and Francis Group, An Informa Business, 2 Park Square, Milton Park, Abingdon, Oxford OX14 4RN, United Kingdom, (Dial from U.S. (212) 216-7800), (Fax from U.S. (212) 564-7854), www.tandf.co.uk; *The Europa World Year Book.*

United Nations Statistics Division, New York, NY 10017, (800) 253-9646, Fax: (212) 963-4116, http://unstats.un.org; *Statistical Yearbook.*

BARBADOS - SILVER PRODUCTION

See BARBADOS - MINERAL INDUSTRIES

BARBADOS - SOCIAL ECOLOGY

M.E. Sharpe, 80 Business Park Drive, Armonk, NY 10504, (800) 541-6563, Fax: (914) 273-2106, www.mesharpe.com; *The Illustrated Book of World Rankings.*

BARBADOS - SOCIAL SECURITY

Inter-American Development Bank (IDB), 1300 New York Avenue, NW, Washington, DC 20577, (202) 623-1000, Fax: (202) 623-3096, www.iadb.org; *The Politics of Policies: Economic and Social Progress in Latin America - 2006 Report.*

International Monetary Fund (IMF), 700 Nineteenth Street, NW, Washington, DC 20431, (202) 623-7000, Fax: (202) 623-4661, www.imf.org; *Government Finance Statistics Yearbook (2008 Edition).*

United Nations Statistics Division, New York, NY 10017, (800) 253-9646, Fax: (212) 963-4116, http://unstats.un.org; *National Accounts Statistics: Compendium of Income Distribution Statistics* and *World Statistics Pocketbook.*

BARBADOS - STEEL PRODUCTION

See BARBADOS - MINERAL INDUSTRIES

BARBADOS - SUGAR PRODUCTION

See BARBADOS - CROPS

BARBADOS - TAXATION

Inter-American Development Bank (IDB), 1300 New York Avenue, NW, Washington, DC 20577, (202) 623-1000, Fax: (202) 623-3096, www.iadb.org; *The Politics of Policies: Economic and Social Progress in Latin America - 2006 Report.*

International Monetary Fund (IMF), 700 Nineteenth Street, NW, Washington, DC 20431, (202) 623-7000, Fax: (202) 623-4661, www.imf.org; *Government Finance Statistics Yearbook (2008 Edition).*

Taylor and Francis Group, An Informa Business, 2 Park Square, Milton Park, Abingdon, Oxford OX14 4RN, United Kingdom, (Dial from U.S. (212) 216-7800), (Fax from U.S. (212) 564-7854), www.tandf.co.uk; *The Europa World Year Book.*

United Nations Statistics Division, New York, NY 10017, (800) 253-9646, Fax: (212) 963-4116, http://unstats.un.org; *Statistical Yearbook for Latin America and the Caribbean 2004.*

The World Bank, 1818 H Street, NW, Washington, DC 20433, (202) 473-1000, Fax: (202) 477-6391, www.worldbank.org; *World Development Indicators (WDI) 2008.*

BARBADOS - TELEPHONE

International Telecommunication Union (ITU), Place des Nations, 1211 Geneva 20, Switzerland, www.itu.int; World Telecommunication Indicators Database.

Palgrave Macmillan Ltd., Houndmills, Basingstoke, Hampshire, RG21 6XS, England, (Telephone in U.S. (888) 330-8477), (Fax in U.S. (800) 672-2054), www.palgrave.com; *The Statesman's Yearbook 2008.*

Taylor and Francis Group, An Informa Business, 2 Park Square, Milton Park, Abingdon, Oxford OX14 4RN, United Kingdom, (Dial from U.S. (212) 216-7800), (Fax from U.S. (212) 564-7854), www.tandf.co.uk; *The Europa World Year Book.*

United Nations Statistics Division, New York, NY 10017, (800) 253-9646, Fax: (212) 963-4116, http://unstats.un.org; *Statistical Yearbook* and *World Statistics Pocketbook.*

BARBADOS - TEXTILE INDUSTRY

M.E. Sharpe, 80 Business Park Drive, Armonk, NY 10504, (800) 541-6563, Fax: (914) 273-2106, www.mesharpe.com; *The Illustrated Book of World Rankings.*

Palgrave Macmillan Ltd., Houndmills, Basingstoke, Hampshire, RG21 6XS, England, (Telephone in U.S. (888) 330-8477), (Fax in U.S. (800) 672-2054), www.palgrave.com; *The Statesman's Yearbook 2008.*

United Nations Conference on Trade and Development (UNCTAD), DC2-1120, United Nations, New York, NY 10017, (212) 963-0027, www.unctad.org; *UNCTAD Commodity Yearbook.*

BARBADOS - THEATER

UNESCO Institute for Statistics, C.P. 6128 Succursale Centre-Ville, Montreal, Quebec, H3C 3J7 Canada, (Dial from U.S. (514) 343-6880), (Fax from U.S. (514) 343 6882), www.uis.unesco.org; *Statistical Tables.*

BARBADOS - TOBACCO INDUSTRY

Foreign Agricultural Service (FAS), U.S. Department of Agriculture (USDA), 1400 Independence Avenue, SW, Washington, DC 20250, (202) 720-3935, www.fas.usda.gov; *Tobacco: World Markets and Trade.*

M.E. Sharpe, 80 Business Park Drive, Armonk, NY 10504, (800) 541-6563, Fax: (914) 273-2106, www.mesharpe.com; *The Illustrated Book of World Rankings.*

United Nations Statistics Division, New York, NY 10017, (800) 253-9646, Fax: (212) 963-4116, http://unstats.un.org; *Statistical Yearbook.*

BARBADOS - TOURISM

Euromonitor International, Inc., 224 S. Michigan Avenue, Suite 1500, Chicago, IL 60604, (312) 922-1115, Fax: (312) 922-1157, www.euromonitor.com; *The World Economic Factbook 2008* and *World Marketing Data and Statistics.*

M.E. Sharpe, 80 Business Park Drive, Armonk, NY 10504, (800) 541-6563, Fax: (914) 273-2106, www.mesharpe.com; *The Illustrated Book of World Rankings.*

Organization of American States (OAS), 17th Street Constitution Avenue NW, Washington, DC 20006, (202) 458-3000, www.oas.org; *The OAS in Transition: 1994-2004.*

Palgrave Macmillan Ltd., Houndmills, Basingstoke, Hampshire, RG21 6XS, England, (Telephone in U.S. (888) 330-8477), (Fax in U.S. (800) 672-2054), www.palgrave.com; *The Statesman's Yearbook 2008.*

Taylor and Francis Group, An Informa Business, 2 Park Square, Milton Park, Abingdon, Oxford OX14 4RN, United Kingdom, (Dial from U.S. (212) 216-7800), (Fax from U.S. (212) 564-7854), www.tandf.co.uk; *The Europa World Year Book.*

United Nations Statistics Division, New York, NY 10017, (800) 253-9646, Fax: (212) 963-4116, http://unstats.un.org; *Statistical Yearbook* and *Statistical Yearbook for Latin America and the Caribbean 2004.*

United Nations World Tourism Organization (UNWTO), Capitan Haya 42, 28020 Madrid, Spain, www.world-tourism.org; *Yearbook of Tourism Statistics*.

The World Bank, 1818 H Street, NW, Washington, DC 20433, (202) 473-1000, Fax: (202) 477-6391, www.worldbank.org; *Barbados*.

BARBADOS - TRADE

See BARBADOS - INTERNATIONAL TRADE

BARBADOS - TRANSPORTATION

Central Intelligence Agency, Office of Public Affairs, Washington, DC 20505, (703) 482-0623, Fax: (703) 482-1739, www.cia.gov; *The World Factbook*.

Euromonitor International, Inc., 224 S. Michigan Avenue, Suite 1500, Chicago, IL 60604, (312) 922-1115, Fax: (312) 922-1157, www.euromonitor.com; *International Marketing Data and Statistics 2008* and *World Marketing Data and Statistics*.

Inter-American Development Bank (IDB), 1300 New York Avenue, NW, Washington, DC 20577, (202) 623-1000, Fax: (202) 623-3096, www.iadb.org; *The Politics of Policies: Economic and Social Progress in Latin America - 2006 Report*.

M.E. Sharpe, 80 Business Park Drive, Armonk, NY 10504, (800) 541-6563, Fax: (914) 273-2106, www.mesharpe.com; *The Illustrated Book of World Rankings*.

Palgrave Macmillan Ltd., Houndmills, Basingstoke, Hampshire, RG21 6XS, England, (Telephone in U.S. (888) 330-8477), (Fax in U.S. (800) 672-2054), www.palgrave.com; *The Statesman's Yearbook 2008*.

Taylor and Francis Group, An Informa Business, 2 Park Square, Milton Park, Abingdon, Oxford OX14 4RN, United Kingdom, (Dial from U.S. (212) 216-7800), (Fax from U.S. (212) 564-7854), www.tandf.co.uk; *The Europa World Year Book*.

United Nations Statistics Division, New York, NY 10017, (800) 253-9646, Fax: (212) 963-4116, http://unstats.un.org; *Human Development Report 2006* and *Statistical Yearbook for Latin America and the Caribbean 2004*.

The World Bank, 1818 H Street, NW, Washington, DC 20433, (202) 473-1000, Fax: (202) 477-6391, www.worldbank.org; *Barbados*.

BARBADOS - TRAVEL COSTS

International Monetary Fund (IMF), 700 Nineteenth Street, NW, Washington, DC 20431, (202) 623-7000, Fax: (202) 623-4661, www.imf.org; *Government Finance Statistics Yearbook (2008 Edition)*.

BARBADOS - UNEMPLOYMENT

Central Intelligence Agency, Office of Public Affairs, Washington, DC 20505, (703) 482-0623, Fax: (703) 482-1739, www.cia.gov; *The World Factbook*.

International Labour Office, I.L.O. Publications, 4 route des Morillons, CH-1211 Geneva 22, Switzerland, (Telephone in U.S. (202) 653-7652), (Fax in U.S. (202) 653-7687), www.ilo.org; *Yearbook of Labour Statistics 2006*.

Organization of American States (OAS), 17th Street Constitution Avenue NW, Washington, DC 20006, (202) 458-3000, www.oas.org; *The OAS in Transition: 1994-2004*.

United Nations Statistics Division, New York, NY 10017, (800) 253-9646, Fax: (212) 963-4116, http://unstats.un.org; *Statistical Yearbook*.

BARBADOS - VITAL STATISTICS

Palgrave Macmillan Ltd., Houndmills, Basingstoke, Hampshire, RG21 6XS, England, (Telephone in U.S. (888) 330-8477), (Fax in U.S. (800) 672-2054), www.palgrave.com; *The Statesman's Yearbook 2008*.

United Nations Statistics Division, New York, NY 10017, (800) 253-9646, Fax: (212) 963-4116, http://unstats.un.org; *Statistical Yearbook*.

BARBADOS - WAGES

International Labour Office, I.L.O. Publications, 4 route des Morillons, CH-1211 Geneva 22, Switzerland, (Telephone in U.S. (202) 653-7652), (Fax in U.S. (202) 653-7687), www.ilo.org; *Yearbook of Labour Statistics 2006*.

United Nations Statistics Division, New York, NY 10017, (800) 253-9646, Fax: (212) 963-4116, http://unstats.un.org; *Statistical Yearbook*.

The World Bank, 1818 H Street, NW, Washington, DC 20433, (202) 473-1000, Fax: (202) 477-6391, www.worldbank.org; *Barbados*.

BARBADOS - WEATHER

See BARBADOS - CLIMATE

BARBADOS - WELFARE STATE

Inter-American Development Bank (IDB), 1300 New York Avenue, NW, Washington, DC 20577, (202) 623-1000, Fax: (202) 623-3096, www.iadb.org; *The Politics of Policies: Economic and Social Progress in Latin America - 2006 Report*.

International Monetary Fund (IMF), 700 Nineteenth Street, NW, Washington, DC 20431, (202) 623-7000, Fax: (202) 623-4661, www.imf.org; *Government Finance Statistics Yearbook (2008 Edition)*.

BARBADOS - WHEAT PRODUCTION

See BARBADOS - CROPS

BARBADOS - WHOLESALE PRICE INDEXES

Inter-American Development Bank (IDB), 1300 New York Avenue, NW, Washington, DC 20577, (202) 623-1000, Fax: (202) 623-3096, www.iadb.org; *The Politics of Policies: Economic and Social Progress in Latin America - 2006 Report*.

BARBADOS - WHOLESALE TRADE

Inter-American Development Bank (IDB), 1300 New York Avenue, NW, Washington, DC 20577, (202) 623-1000, Fax: (202) 623-3096, www.iadb.org; *The Politics of Policies: Economic and Social Progress in Latin America - 2006 Report*.

BARBADOS - WINE PRODUCTION

See BARBADOS - BEVERAGE INDUSTRY

BARBADOS - WOOL PRODUCTION

See BARBADOS - TEXTILE INDUSTRY

BARBECUING

Mediamark Research, Inc., 75 Ninth Avenue, 5th Floor, New York, NY 10011, (212) 884-9200, Fax: (212) 884-9339, www.mediamark.com; MRI+.

BARBER SHOPS

U.S. Bureau of Labor Statistics (BLS), Postal Square Building, 2 Massachusetts Avenue, NE, Washington, DC 20212-0001, (202) 691-5200, Fax: (202) 691-6325, www.bls.gov; *Industry Productivity and Costs*.

U.S. Census Bureau, Center for Economic Studies, 4600 Silver Hill Road, Washington DC 20233, (301) 457-1235, www.ces.census.gov; *2002 Economic Census, Other Services (except Public Administration)*.

BARITE

U.S. Department of the Interior (DOI), U.S. Geological Survey (USGS), Office of Minerals Information, 12201 Sunrise Valley Drive, Reston, VA 20192, Mr. Kenneth A. Beckman, (703) 648-4916, Fax: (703) 648-4995, http://minerals.usgs.gov/minerals; *Mineral Commodity Summaries*.

BARIUM

U.S. Department of the Interior (DOI), U.S. Geological Survey (USGS), Office of Minerals Information, 12201 Sunrise Valley Drive, Reston, VA 20192, Mr. Kenneth A. Beckman, (703) 648-4916, Fax: (703) 648-4995, http://minerals.usgs.gov/minerals; *Mineral Commodity Summaries*.

BARLEY

Economic Research Service (ERS), U.S. Department of Agriculture (USDA), 1800 M Street, NW, Washington, DC 20036-5831, (202) 694-5050, Fax: (202) 694-5689, www.ers.usda.gov; *Agricultural Income and Finance Outlook; Farm Income: Data Files;* and *Organic Production*.

National Agricultural Statistics Service (NASS), U.S. Department of Agriculture (USDA), 1400 Independence Avenue, SW, Washington, DC 20250, (800) 727-9540, Fax: (202) 690-2090, www.nass.usda.gov; *Grain Stocks*.

BARS

See FOOD SERVICE AND DRINKING PLACES

BASEBALL

The Baseball Archive, 48 Cedarwood Road, Rochester, NY 14617, www.baseball1.com; The Lahman Baseball Database.

Elias Sports Bureau, Inc., 500 Fifth Avenue, Number 2140, New York, NY 10110, (212) 869-1530, www.esb.com; *The Elias Book of Baseball Records 2006*.

Major League Baseball (MLB), 245 Park Ave #31, New York, NY 10167-0002, (212) 931-7800, www.mlb.com; unpublished data.

Mediamark Research, Inc., 75 Ninth Avenue, 5th Floor, New York, NY 10011, (212) 884-9200, Fax: (212) 884-9339, www.mediamark.com; MRI+.

National Collegiate Athletic Association (NCAA), 700 West Washington Street, PO Box 6222, Indianapolis, IN 46206-6222, (317) 917-6222, Fax: (317) 917-6888, www.ncaa.org; *1982-2003 Sports Sponsorship and Participation Rates Report*.

National Federation of State High School Associations, PO Box 690, Indianapolis, IN 46206, (317) 972-6900, Fax: (317) 822-5700, www.nfhs.org; *2005-06 High School Athletics Participation Survey*.

National Sporting Goods Association (NSGA), 1601 Feehanville Drive, Suite 300, Mount Prospect, IL 60056, (847) 296-6742, Fax: (847) 391-9827, www.nsga.org; *2006 Sports Participation* and *Ten-Year History of Selected Sports Participation, 1996-2006*.

Sports Reference LLC, 6757 Greene Street, Suite 315, Philadelphia PA 19119, (215) 301-9181, www.sports-reference.com; *Baseball-Reference.com*.

BASKETBALL

Mediamark Research, Inc., 75 Ninth Avenue, 5th Floor, New York, NY 10011, (212) 884-9200, Fax: (212) 884-9339, www.mediamark.com; MRI+.

National Basketball Association (NBA), 645 Fifth Avenue, New York, NY 10022, (212) 407-8000, www.nba.com; unpublished data.

National Collegiate Athletic Association (NCAA), 700 West Washington Street, PO Box 6222, Indianapolis, IN 46206-6222, (317) 917-6222, Fax: (317) 917-6888, www.ncaa.org; *1982-2003 Sports Sponsorship and Participation Rates Report*.

National Federation of State High School Associations, PO Box 690, Indianapolis, IN 46206, (317) 972-6900, Fax: (317) 822-5700, www.nfhs.org; *2005-06 High School Athletics Participation Survey*.

National Sporting Goods Association (NSGA), 1601 Feehanville Drive, Suite 300, Mount Prospect, IL 60056, (847) 296-6742, Fax: (847) 391-9827, www.nsga.org; *2006 Sports Participation* and *Ten-Year History of Selected Sports Participation, 1996-2006*.

Sports Reference LLC, 6757 Greene Street, Suite 315, Philadelphia PA 19119, (215) 301-9181, www.sports-reference.com; *Basketball-Reference.com*.

BAUXITE

U.S. Department of the Interior (DOI), U.S. Geological Survey (USGS), Office of Minerals Information, 12201 Sunrise Valley Drive, Reston, VA 20192, Mr. Kenneth A. Beckman, (703) 648-4916, Fax: (703) 648-4995, http://minerals.usgs.gov/minerals; *Mineral Commodity Summaries* and *Minerals Yearbook*.

BAUXITE - CONSUMPTION

U.S. Department of the Interior (DOI), U.S. Geological Survey (USGS), Office of Minerals Information, 12201 Sunrise Valley Drive, Reston, VA 20192, Mr. Kenneth A. Beckman, (703) 648-4916, Fax: (703) 648-4995, http://minerals.usgs.gov/minerals; *Mineral Commodity Summaries.*

BAUXITE - EMPLOYMENT

U.S. Department of the Interior (DOI), U.S. Geological Survey (USGS), Office of Minerals Information, 12201 Sunrise Valley Drive, Reston, VA 20192, Mr. Kenneth A. Beckman, (703) 648-4916, Fax: (703) 648-4995, http://minerals.usgs.gov/minerals; *Mineral Commodity Summaries.*

BAUXITE - INTERNATIONAL TRADE

U.S. Department of the Interior (DOI), U.S. Geological Survey (USGS), Office of Minerals Information, 12201 Sunrise Valley Drive, Reston, VA 20192, Mr. Kenneth A. Beckman, (703) 648-4916, Fax: (703) 648-4995, http://minerals.usgs.gov/minerals; *Mineral Commodity Summaries.*

BAUXITE - PRICES

U.S. Department of the Interior (DOI), U.S. Geological Survey (USGS), Office of Minerals Information, 12201 Sunrise Valley Drive, Reston, VA 20192, Mr. Kenneth A. Beckman, (703) 648-4916, Fax: (703) 648-4995, http://minerals.usgs.gov/minerals; *Mineral Commodity Summaries.*

BAUXITE - PRODUCTION

U.S. Department of the Interior (DOI), U.S. Geological Survey (USGS), Office of Minerals Information, 12201 Sunrise Valley Drive, Reston, VA 20192, Mr. Kenneth A. Beckman, (703) 648-4916, Fax: (703) 648-4995, http://minerals.usgs.gov/minerals; *Mineral Commodity Summaries* and *Minerals Yearbook.*

BAUXITE - STRATEGIC AND CRITICAL MATERIALS

U.S. Department of Defense (DOD), Defense Logistics Agency (DLA), 8725 John J. Kingman Road, Fort Belvoir, VA 22060, (703) 767-6666, www.dla.mil; *Stockpile Report to the Congress 2002.*

BAUXITE - WORLD PRODUCTION

U.S. Department of the Interior (DOI), U.S. Geological Survey (USGS), Office of Minerals Information, 12201 Sunrise Valley Drive, Reston, VA 20192, Mr. Kenneth A. Beckman, (703) 648-4916, Fax: (703) 648-4995, http://minerals.usgs.gov/minerals; *Mineral Commodity Summaries* and *Minerals Yearbook.*

BEANS

Economic Research Service (ERS), U.S. Department of Agriculture (USDA), 1800 M Street, NW, Washington, DC 20036-5831, (202) 694-5050, Fax: (202) 694-5689, www.ers.usda.gov; *Agricultural Outlook* and *Agricultural Statistics.*

National Agricultural Statistics Service (NASS), U.S. Department of Agriculture (USDA), 1400 Independence Avenue, SW, Washington, DC 20250, (800) 727-9540, Fax: (202) 690-2090, www.nass.usda.gov; *Agricultural Prices* and *Vegetables: 2004 Annual Summary.*

BEAUTY SHOPS

The NPD Group, Port Washington, 900 West Shore Road, Port Washington, NY 11050, (866) 444-1411, www.npd.com; *Market Research for the Beauty Industry.*

U.S. Bureau of Labor Statistics (BLS), Postal Square Building, 2 Massachusetts Avenue, NE, Washington, DC 20212-0001, (202) 691-5200, Fax: (202) 691-6325, www.bls.gov; *Industry Productivity and Costs.*

U.S. Census Bureau, Center for Economic Studies, 4600 Silver Hill Road, Washington DC 20233, (301) 457-1235, www.ces.census.gov; *2002 Economic Census, Other Services (except Public Administration).*

BEAUTY SHOPS - PRICE INDEXES

The NPD Group, Port Washington, 900 West Shore Road, Port Washington, NY 11050, (866) 444-1411, www.npd.com; *Market Research for the Beauty Industry.*

U.S. Bureau of Labor Statistics (BLS), Postal Square Building, 2 Massachusetts Avenue, NE, Washington, DC 20212-0001, (202) 691-5200, Fax: (202) 691-6325, www.bls.gov; *Consumer Price Index Detailed Report* and *Monthly Labor Review (MLR).*

BEEF

See also MEAT INDUSTRY AND TRADE

National Agricultural Statistics Service (NASS), U.S. Department of Agriculture (USDA), 1400 Independence Avenue, SW, Washington, DC 20250, (800) 727-9540, Fax: (202) 690-2090, www.nass.usda.gov; *Cold Storage.*

Progressive Grocer, 770 Broadway, New York, NY 10003, (866) 890-8541, www.progressivegrocer.com; *Meat Operations Review 2008: Leaner Times.*

BEEF - CONSUMER EXPENDITURES

U.S. Bureau of Labor Statistics (BLS), Postal Square Building, 2 Massachusetts Avenue, NE, Washington, DC 20212-0001, (202) 691-5200, Fax: (202) 691-6325, www.bls.gov; *Consumer Expenditures in 2006.*

BEEF - CONSUMPTION

Economic Research Service (ERS), U.S. Department of Agriculture (USDA), 1800 M Street, NW, Washington, DC 20036-5831, (202) 694-5050, Fax: (202) 694-5689, www.ers.usda.gov; *Agricultural Outlook* and *Food CPI, Prices, and Expenditures.*

Foreign Agricultural Service (FAS), U.S. Department of Agriculture (USDA), 1400 Independence Avenue, SW, Washington, DC 20250, (202) 720-3935, www.fas.usda.gov; *Livestock and Poultry: World Markets and Trade.*

BEEF - CONSUMPTION - FOREIGN COUNTRIES

Foreign Agricultural Service (FAS), U.S. Department of Agriculture (USDA), 1400 Independence Avenue, SW, Washington, DC 20250, (202) 720-3935, www.fas.usda.gov; *Livestock and Poultry: World Markets and Trade.*

BEEF - INTERNATIONAL TRADE

Economic Research Service (ERS), U.S. Department of Agriculture (USDA), 1800 M Street, NW, Washington, DC 20036-5831, (202) 694-5050, Fax: (202) 694-5689, www.ers.usda.gov; *Agricultural Outlook; Food CPI, Prices, and Expenditures; Foreign Agricultural Trade of the United States (FATUS);* and *U.S. Agricultural Trade Update: 2006.*

BEEF - PRICE INDEXES

U.S. Bureau of Labor Statistics (BLS), Postal Square Building, 2 Massachusetts Avenue, NE, Washington, DC 20212-0001, (202) 691-5200, Fax: (202) 691-6325, www.bls.gov; *Consumer Price Index Detailed Report* and *Monthly Labor Review (MLR).*

BEEF - PRICES

U.S. Bureau of Labor Statistics (BLS), Postal Square Building, 2 Massachusetts Avenue, NE, Washington, DC 20212-0001, (202) 691-5200, Fax: (202) 691-6325, www.bls.gov; *Consumer Price Index Detailed Report* and *Monthly Labor Review (MLR).*

BEEF - PRODUCTION

Economic Research Service (ERS), U.S. Department of Agriculture (USDA), 1800 M Street, NW, Washington, DC 20036-5831, (202) 694-5050, Fax: (202) 694-5689, www.ers.usda.gov; *Agricultural Outlook.*

National Agricultural Statistics Service (NASS), U.S. Department of Agriculture (USDA), 1400 Independence Avenue, SW, Washington, DC 20250, (800) 727-9540, Fax: (202) 690-2090, www.nass.usda.gov; *Agricultural Prices; Cold Storage;* and *Livestock Slaughter.*

Teagasc, Oak Park, Carlow, Ireland, www.teagasc.ie; *Beef and Sheep Production Research.*

BEEF - PRODUCTION - FOREIGN COUNTRIES

Economic Research Service (ERS), U.S. Department of Agriculture (USDA), 1800 M Street, NW, Washington, DC 20036-5831, (202) 694-5050, Fax: (202) 694-5689, www.ers.usda.gov; *Agricultural Statistics.*

BEEF - SUPPLY

Economic Research Service (ERS), U.S. Department of Agriculture (USDA), 1800 M Street, NW, Washington, DC 20036-5831, (202) 694-5050, Fax: (202) 694-5689, www.ers.usda.gov; *Agricultural Outlook* and *Food CPI, Prices, and Expenditures.*

BEER

See BEVERAGES - CONSUMPTION

BEER, WINE, AND LIQUOR STORES - EARNINGS

Office of Trade and Industry Information (OTII), Manufacturing and Services, International Trade Administration, U.S. Department of Commerce, 1401 Constitution Ave, NW, Washington, DC 20230, (800) USA TRAD(E), http://trade.gov/index.asp; *TradeStats Express.*

U.S. Census Bureau, Center for Economic Studies, 4600 Silver Hill Road, Washington DC 20233, (301) 457-1235, www.ces.census.gov; *2002 Economic Census, Retail Trade* and *2002 Economic Census, Wholesale Trade.*

U.S. Census Bureau, Company Statistics Division, 4700 Silver Hill Road, Washington DC 20233-0001, (301) 763-3030, www.census.gov/csd/; *County Business Patterns 2004.*

BEER, WINE, AND LIQUOR STORES - EMPLOYEES

U.S. Census Bureau, Center for Economic Studies, 4600 Silver Hill Road, Washington DC 20233, (301) 457-1235, www.ces.census.gov; *2002 Economic Census, Retail Trade* and *2002 Economic Census, Wholesale Trade.*

U.S. Census Bureau, Company Statistics Division, 4700 Silver Hill Road, Washington DC 20233-0001, (301) 763-3030, www.census.gov/csd/; *County Business Patterns 2004.*

BEER, WINE, AND LIQUOR STORES - ESTABLISHMENTS

Office of Trade and Industry Information (OTII), Manufacturing and Services, International Trade Administration, U.S. Department of Commerce, 1401 Constitution Ave, NW, Washington, DC 20230, (800) USA TRAD(E), http://trade.gov/index.asp; *TradeStats Express.*

U.S. Census Bureau, 4700 Silver Hill Road, Washington DC 20233-0001, (301) 763-3030, www.census.gov; *2002 Economic Census, Nonemployer Statistics.*

U.S. Census Bureau, Center for Economic Studies, 4600 Silver Hill Road, Washington DC 20233, (301) 457-1235, www.ces.census.gov; *2002 Economic Census, Retail Trade* and *2002 Economic Census, Wholesale Trade.*

U.S. Census Bureau, Company Statistics Division, 4700 Silver Hill Road, Washington DC 20233-0001, (301) 763-3030, www.census.gov/csd/; *County Business Patterns 2004.*

BEER, WINE, AND LIQUOR STORES - NONEMPLOYERS

Office of Trade and Industry Information (OTII), Manufacturing and Services, International Trade

Administration, U.S. Department of Commerce, 1401 Constitution Ave, NW, Washington, DC 20230, (800) USA TRAD(E), http://trade.gov/index.asp; *TradeStats Express.*

U.S. Census Bureau, 4700 Silver Hill Road, Washington DC 20233-0001, (301) 763-3030, www.census.gov; *2002 Economic Census, Nonemployer Statistics.*

U.S. Census Bureau, Center for Economic Studies, 4600 Silver Hill Road, Washington DC 20233, (301) 457-1235, www.ces.census.gov; *2002 Economic Census, Retail Trade* and *2002 Economic Census, Wholesale Trade.*

U.S. Census Bureau, Company Statistics Division, 4700 Silver Hill Road, Washington DC 20233-0001, (301) 763-3030, www.census.gov/csd/; *County Business Patterns 2004.*

BEER, WINE, AND LIQUOR STORES - PRODUCTIVITY

U.S. Bureau of Labor Statistics (BLS), Postal Square Building, 2 Massachusetts Avenue, NE, Washington, DC 20212-0001, (202) 691-5200, Fax: (202) 691-6325, www.bls.gov; *Industry Productivity and Costs.*

BEER, WINE, AND LIQUOR STORES - SALES

Department of Finance, Government of the Northwest Territories (GNWT), PO Box 1320, Yellowknife, Northwest Territories X1A 2L9, Canada, (Dial from U.S. (867) 873-7158), (Fax from U.S. (867) 873-0325), www.fin.gov.nt.ca; *NWT Liquor Commission/ NWT Liquor Licensing Board Annual Report 2004-2005.*

Office of Trade and Industry Information (OTII), Manufacturing and Services, International Trade Administration, U.S. Department of Commerce, 1401 Constitution Ave, NW, Washington, DC 20230, (800) USA TRAD(E), http://trade.gov/index.asp; *TradeStats Express.*

U.S. Census Bureau, 4700 Silver Hill Road, Washington DC 20233-0001, (301) 763-3030, www.census.gov; *2002 Economic Census, Nonemployer Statistics.*

U.S. Census Bureau, Center for Economic Studies, 4600 Silver Hill Road, Washington DC 20233, (301) 457-1235, www.ces.census.gov; *2002 Economic Census, Retail Trade* and *2002 Economic Census, Wholesale Trade.*

U.S. Census Bureau, Company Statistics Division, 4700 Silver Hill Road, Washington DC 20233-0001, (301) 763-3030, www.census.gov/csd/; *Current Business Reports.*

BELARUS - NATIONAL STATISTICAL OFFICE

Ministry of Statistics and Analysis of the Republic of Belarus, 12 Partizansky Avenue, Minsk 220070, Belarus, www.belstat.gov.by; National Data Center.

BELARUS - PRIMARY STATISTICS SOURCES

Ministry of Statistics and Analysis of the Republic of Belarus, 12 Partizansky Avenue, Minsk 220070, Belarus, www.belstat.gov.by; *Belarus in Figures, 2008; Regions of the Republic of Belarus, 2008; Statistical Bulletin;* and *Statistical Yearbook of the Republic of Belarus, 2008.*

BELARUS - ABORTION

United Nations Statistics Division, New York, NY 10017, (800) 253-9646, Fax: (212) 963-4116, http://unstats.un.org; *Demographic Yearbook* and *Trends in Europe and North America: The Statistical Yearbook of the ECE 2005.*

BELARUS - AGRICULTURE

Academic International Press, PO Box 1111, Gulf Breeze, FL 32562-1111, Fax: (850) 934-0953, www.ai-press.com; *Russia and Eurasia Facts and Figures Annual.*

Economist Intelligence Unit, 111 West 57th Street, New York, NY 10019, (212) 554-0600, Fax: (212) 586-1181, www.eiu.com; *Belarus Country Report.*

Euromonitor International, Inc., 224 S. Michigan Avenue, Suite 1500, Chicago, IL 60604, (312) 922-1115, Fax: (312) 922-1157, www.euromonitor.com; *World Marketing Data and Statistics.*

Palgrave Macmillan Ltd., Houndmills, Basingstoke, Hampshire, RG21 6XS, England, (Telephone in U.S. (888) 330-8477), (Fax in U.S. (800) 672-2054), www.palgrave.com; *The Statesman's Yearbook 2008.*

Taylor and Francis Group, An Informa Business, 2 Park Square, Milton Park, Abingdon, Oxford OX14 4RN, United Kingdom, (Dial from U.S. (212) 216-7800), (Fax from U.S. (212) 564-7854), www.tandf.co.uk; *The Europa World Year Book.*

United Nations Food and Agricultural Organization (FAO), Viale delle Terme di Caracalla, 00100 Rome, Italy, (Dial from U.S. (202) 653-2400), (Fax from U.S. (202) 653 5760), www.fao.org; AQUASTAT; *FAO Production Yearbook 2002; FAO Trade Yearbook;* and *The State of Food and Agriculture (SOFA) 2006.*

United Nations Statistics Division, New York, NY 10017, (800) 253-9646, Fax: (212) 963-4116, http://unstats.un.org; *2004 Industrial Commodity Statistics Yearbook* and *Statistical Yearbook.*

The World Bank, 1818 H Street, NW, Washington, DC 20433, (202) 473-1000, Fax: (202) 477-6391, www.worldbank.org; *Belarus; Statistical Handbook: States of the Former USSR;* and *World Development Indicators (WDI) 2008.*

BELARUS - AIRLINES

International Civil Aviation Organization (ICAO), External Relations and Public Information Office (EPO), 999 University Street, Montreal, Quebec H3C 5H7, Canada, (Dial from U.S. (514) 954-8219), (Fax from U.S. (514) 954-6077), www.icao.int; *Civil Aviation Statistics of the World.*

United Nations Statistics Division, New York, NY 10017, (800) 253-9646, Fax: (212) 963-4116, http://unstats.un.org; *Statistical Yearbook.*

BELARUS - AIRPORTS

Central Intelligence Agency, Office of Public Affairs, Washington, DC 20505, (703) 482-0623, Fax: (703) 482-1739, www.cia.gov; *The World Factbook.*

BELARUS - ARMED FORCES

Academic International Press, PO Box 1111, Gulf Breeze, FL 32562-1111, Fax: (850) 934-0953, www.ai-press.com; *Russia and Eurasia Facts and Figures Annual.*

Central Intelligence Agency, Office of Public Affairs, Washington, DC 20505, (703) 482-0623, Fax: (703) 482-1739, www.cia.gov; *The World Factbook.*

Euromonitor International, Inc., 224 S. Michigan Avenue, Suite 1500, Chicago, IL 60604, (312) 922-1115, Fax: (312) 922-1157, www.euromonitor.com; *World Marketing Data and Statistics.*

International Institute for Strategic Studies (IISS), Arundel House, 13-15 Arundel Street, Temple Place, London WC2R 3DX, England, www.iiss.org; *The Military Balance 2007.*

Palgrave Macmillan Ltd., Houndmills, Basingstoke, Hampshire, RG21 6XS, England, (Telephone in U.S. (888) 330-8477), (Fax in U.S. (800) 672-2054), www.palgrave.com; *The Statesman's Yearbook 2008.*

United Nations Statistics Division, New York, NY 10017, (800) 253-9646, Fax: (212) 963-4116, http://unstats.un.org; *Human Development Report 2006.*

BELARUS - AUTOMOBILE INDUSTRY AND TRADE

United Nations Statistics Division, New York, NY 10017, (800) 253-9646, Fax: (212) 963-4116, http://unstats.un.org; *Statistical Yearbook.*

BELARUS - BALANCE OF PAYMENTS

The World Bank, 1818 H Street, NW, Washington, DC 20433, (202) 473-1000, Fax: (202) 477-6391, www.worldbank.org; *Belarus; World Development Indicators (WDI) 2008;* and *World Development Report 2008.*

BELARUS - BANKS AND BANKING

Euromonitor International, Inc., 224 S. Michigan Avenue, Suite 1500, Chicago, IL 60604, (312) 922-1115, Fax: (312) 922-1157, www.euromonitor.com; *World Marketing Data and Statistics.*

Palgrave Macmillan Ltd., Houndmills, Basingstoke, Hampshire, RG21 6XS, England, (Telephone in U.S. (888) 330-8477), (Fax in U.S. (800) 672-2054), www.palgrave.com; *The Statesman's Yearbook 2008.*

BELARUS - BEVERAGE INDUSTRY

United Nations Statistics Division, New York, NY 10017, (800) 253-9646, Fax: (212) 963-4116, http://unstats.un.org; *Statistical Yearbook.*

BELARUS - BROADCASTING

Central Intelligence Agency, Office of Public Affairs, Washington, DC 20505, (703) 482-0623, Fax: (703) 482-1739, www.cia.gov; *The World Factbook.*

Euromonitor International, Inc., 224 S. Michigan Avenue, Suite 1500, Chicago, IL 60604, (312) 922-1115, Fax: (312) 922-1157, www.euromonitor.com; *World Marketing Data and Statistics.*

Palgrave Macmillan Ltd., Houndmills, Basingstoke, Hampshire, RG21 6XS, England, (Telephone in U.S. (888) 330-8477), (Fax in U.S. (800) 672-2054), www.palgrave.com; *The Statesman's Yearbook 2008.*

UNESCO Institute for Statistics, C.P. 6128 Succursale Centre-Ville, Montreal, Quebec, H3C 3J7 Canada, (Dial from U.S. (514) 343-6880), (Fax from U.S. (514) 343 6882), www.uis.unesco.org; *Statistical Tables.*

United Nations Statistics Division, New York, NY 10017, (800) 253-9646, Fax: (212) 963-4116, http://unstats.un.org; *Trends in Europe and North America: The Statistical Yearbook of the ECE 2005.*

BELARUS - BUDGET

Central Intelligence Agency, Office of Public Affairs, Washington, DC 20505, (703) 482-0623, Fax: (703) 482-1739, www.cia.gov; *The World Factbook.*

BELARUS - BUSINESS

Economist Intelligence Unit, 111 West 57th Street, New York, NY 10019, (212) 554-0600, Fax: (212) 586-1181, www.eiu.com; *Business Eastern Europe* and *Business Eastern Europe.*

United Nations Statistics Division, New York, NY 10017, (800) 253-9646, Fax: (212) 963-4116, http://unstats.un.org; *Statistical Yearbook.*

BELARUS - CAPITAL INVESTMENTS

The World Bank, 1818 H Street, NW, Washington, DC 20433, (202) 473-1000, Fax: (202) 477-6391, www.worldbank.org; *Statistical Handbook: States of the Former USSR.*

BELARUS - CATTLE

See BELARUS - LIVESTOCK

BELARUS - CHILDBIRTH - STATISTICS

Central Intelligence Agency, Office of Public Affairs, Washington, DC 20505, (703) 482-0623, Fax: (703) 482-1739, www.cia.gov; *The World Factbook.*

Euromonitor International, Inc., 224 S. Michigan Avenue, Suite 1500, Chicago, IL 60604, (312) 922-1115, Fax: (312) 922-1157, www.euromonitor.com; *The World Economic Factbook 2008.*

Palgrave Macmillan Ltd., Houndmills, Basingstoke, Hampshire, RG21 6XS, England, (Telephone in U.S. (888) 330-8477), (Fax in U.S. (800) 672-2054), www.palgrave.com; *The Statesman's Yearbook 2008.*

Taylor and Francis Group, An Informa Business, 2 Park Square, Milton Park, Abingdon, Oxford OX14 4RN, United Kingdom, (Dial from U.S. (212) 216-

7800), (Fax from U.S. (212) 564-7854), www.tandf.co.uk; *The Europa World Year Book.*

United Nations Statistics Division, New York, NY 10017, (800) 253-9646, Fax: (212) 963-4116, http://unstats.un.org; *Demographic Yearbook* and *Statistical Yearbook.*

World Health Organization (WHO), Avenue Appia 20, 1211 Geneve 27, Switzerland, (Telephone in U.S. (212) 331-9081), www.who.int; *World Health Report 2006.*

BELARUS - COAL PRODUCTION

See BELARUS - MINERAL INDUSTRIES

BELARUS - COMMERCE

Palgrave Macmillan Ltd., Houndmills, Basingstoke, Hampshire, RG21 6XS, England, (Telephone in U.S. (888) 330-8477), (Fax in U.S. (800) 672-2054), www.palgrave.com; *The Statesman's Yearbook 2008.*

BELARUS - COMMUNICATION AND TRAFFIC

United Nations Statistics Division, New York, NY 10017, (800) 253-9646, Fax: (212) 963-4116, http://unstats.un.org; *Statistical Yearbook.*

BELARUS - CONSTRUCTION INDUSTRY

Academic International Press, PO Box 1111, Gulf Breeze, FL 32562-1111, Fax: (850) 934-0953, www.ai-press.com; *Russia and Eurasia Facts and Figures Annual.*

United Nations Statistics Division, New York, NY 10017, (800) 253-9646, Fax: (212) 963-4116, http://unstats.un.org; *Statistical Yearbook.*

BELARUS - CONSUMER PRICE INDEXES

Taylor and Francis Group, An Informa Business, 2 Park Square, Milton Park, Abingdon, Oxford OX14 4RN, United Kingdom, (Dial from U.S. (212) 216-7800), (Fax from U.S. (212) 564-7854), www.tandf.co.uk; *The Europa World Year Book.*

United Nations Statistics Division, New York, NY 10017, (800) 253-9646, Fax: (212) 963-4116, http://unstats.un.org; *Statistical Yearbook* and *Trends in Europe and North America: The Statistical Yearbook of the ECE 2005.*

The World Bank, 1818 H Street, NW, Washington, DC 20433, (202) 473-1000, Fax: (202) 477-6391, www.worldbank.org; *Belarus.*

BELARUS - CONSUMPTION (ECONOMICS)

The World Bank, 1818 H Street, NW, Washington, DC 20433, (202) 473-1000, Fax: (202) 477-6391, www.worldbank.org; *Statistical Handbook: States of the Former USSR* and *World Development Report 2008.*

BELARUS - COTTON

See BELARUS - CROPS

BELARUS - CRIME

Academic International Press, PO Box 1111, Gulf Breeze, FL 32562-1111, Fax: (850) 934-0953, www.ai-press.com; *Russia and Eurasia Facts and Figures Annual.*

United Nations Statistics Division, New York, NY 10017, (800) 253-9646, Fax: (212) 963-4116, http://unstats.un.org; *Trends in Europe and North America: The Statistical Yearbook of the ECE 2005.*

BELARUS - CROPS

Palgrave Macmillan Ltd., Houndmills, Basingstoke, Hampshire, RG21 6XS, England, (Telephone in U.S. (888) 330-8477), (Fax in U.S. (800) 672-2054), www.palgrave.com; *The Statesman's Yearbook 2008.*

Taylor and Francis Group, An Informa Business, 2 Park Square, Milton Park, Abingdon, Oxford OX14 4RN, United Kingdom, (Dial from U.S. (212) 216-7800), (Fax from U.S. (212) 564-7854), www.tandf.co.uk; *The Europa World Year Book.*

United Nations Food and Agricultural Organization (FAO), Viale delle Terme di Caracalla, 00100 Rome, Italy, (Dial from U.S. (202) 653-2400), (Fax from U.S. (202) 653 5760), www.fao.org; *FAO Production Yearbook 2002* and *The State of Food and Agriculture (SOFA) 2006.*

United Nations Statistics Division, New York, NY 10017, (800) 253-9646, Fax: (212) 963-4116, http://unstats.un.org; *2004 Industrial Commodity Statistics Yearbook* and *Statistical Yearbook.*

The World Bank, 1818 H Street, NW, Washington, DC 20433, (202) 473-1000, Fax: (202) 477-6391, www.worldbank.org; *Statistical Handbook: States of the Former USSR.*

BELARUS - DAIRY PROCESSING

Palgrave Macmillan Ltd., Houndmills, Basingstoke, Hampshire, RG21 6XS, England, (Telephone in U.S. (888) 330-8477), (Fax in U.S. (800) 672-2054), www.palgrave.com; *The Statesman's Yearbook 2008.*

Taylor and Francis Group, An Informa Business, 2 Park Square, Milton Park, Abingdon, Oxford OX14 4RN, United Kingdom, (Dial from U.S. (212) 216-7800), (Fax from U.S. (212) 564-7854), www.tandf.co.uk; *The Europa World Year Book.*

United Nations Food and Agricultural Organization (FAO), Viale delle Terme di Caracalla, 00100 Rome, Italy, (Dial from U.S. (202) 653-2400), (Fax from U.S. (202) 653 5760), www.fao.org; *FAO Production Yearbook 2002* and *The State of Food and Agriculture (SOFA) 2006.*

United Nations Statistics Division, New York, NY 10017, (800) 253-9646, Fax: (212) 963-4116, http://unstats.un.org; *2004 Industrial Commodity Statistics Yearbook* and *Statistical Yearbook.*

BELARUS - DEATH RATES

See BELARUS - MORTALITY

BELARUS - DEBTS, EXTERNAL

The World Bank, 1818 H Street, NW, Washington, DC 20433, (202) 473-1000, Fax: (202) 477-6391, www.worldbank.org; *Global Development Finance 2007; World Development Indicators (WDI) 2008;* and *World Development Report 2008.*

BELARUS - DEMOGRAPHY

Euromonitor International, Inc., 224 S. Michigan Avenue, Suite 1500, Chicago, IL 60604, (312) 922-1115, Fax: (312) 922-1157, www.euromonitor.com; *The World Economic Factbook 2008* and *World Marketing Data and Statistics.*

United Nations Statistics Division, New York, NY 10017, (800) 253-9646, Fax: (212) 963-4116, http://unstats.un.org; *Demographic Yearbook* and *Human Development Report 2006.*

The World Bank, 1818 H Street, NW, Washington, DC 20433, (202) 473-1000, Fax: (202) 477-6391, www.worldbank.org; *Belarus* and *Statistical Handbook: States of the Former USSR.*

BELARUS - DISPOSABLE INCOME

United Nations Statistics Division, New York, NY 10017, (800) 253-9646, Fax: (212) 963-4116, http://unstats.un.org; *National Accounts Statistics: Compendium of Income Distribution Statistics* and *Statistical Yearbook.*

BELARUS - DIVORCE

United Nations Statistics Division, New York, NY 10017, (800) 253-9646, Fax: (212) 963-4116, http://unstats.un.org; *Demographic Yearbook; Statistical Yearbook;* and *Trends in Europe and North America: The Statistical Yearbook of the ECE 2005.*

BELARUS - ECONOMIC CONDITIONS

Academic International Press, PO Box 1111, Gulf Breeze, FL 32562-1111, Fax: (850) 934-0953, www.ai-press.com; *Russia and Eurasia Facts and Figures Annual.*

Center for International Business Education Research (CIBER), Columbia Business School and School of International and Public Affairs, Uris Hall, Room 212, 3022 Broadway, New York, NY 10027-6902, Mr. Joshua Safier, (212) 854-4750, Fax: (212) 222-9821, www.columbia.edu/cu/ciber/; Datastream International.

Central Intelligence Agency, Office of Public Affairs, Washington, DC 20505, (703) 482-0623, Fax: (703) 482-1739, www.cia.gov; *The World Factbook.*

DSI Data Service Information, Xantener Strasse 51a, D-47495 Rheinberg, Germany, www.dsidata.com; *Campus Solution.*

Dun and Bradstreet (DB) Corporation, 103 JFK Parkway, Short Hills, NJ 07078, (973) 921-5500, www.dnb.com; *Country Report.*

Economist Intelligence Unit, 111 West 57th Street, New York, NY 10019, (212) 554-0600, Fax: (212) 586-1181, www.eiu.com; *Belarus Country Report.*

Euromonitor International, Inc., 224 S. Michigan Avenue, Suite 1500, Chicago, IL 60604, (312) 922-1115, Fax: (312) 922-1157, www.euromonitor.com; *The World Economic Factbook 2008* and *World Marketing Data and Statistics.*

International Monetary Fund (IMF), 700 Nineteenth Street, NW, Washington, DC 20431, (202) 623-7000, Fax: (202) 623-4661, www.imf.org; *World Economic Outlook Reports.*

Ministry of Statistics and Analysis of the Republic of Belarus, 12 Partizansky Avenue, Minsk 220070, Belarus, www.belstat.gov.by; *National Accounts of the Republic of Belarus* and *Socio-Economic Conditions of Households in the Republic of Belarus.*

Palgrave Macmillan Ltd., Houndmills, Basingstoke, Hampshire, RG21 6XS, England, (Telephone in U.S. (888) 330-8477), (Fax in U.S. (800) 672-2054), www.palgrave.com; *The Statesman's Yearbook 2008.*

Taylor and Francis Group, An Informa Business, 2 Park Square, Milton Park, Abingdon, Oxford OX14 4RN, United Kingdom, (Dial from U.S. (212) 216-7800), (Fax from U.S. (212) 564-7854), www.tandf.co.uk; *The Europa World Year Book.*

United Nations Statistics Division, New York, NY 10017, (800) 253-9646, Fax: (212) 963-4116, http://unstats.un.org; *World Statistics Pocketbook.*

The World Bank, 1818 H Street, NW, Washington, DC 20433, (202) 473-1000, Fax: (202) 477-6391, www.worldbank.org; *Belarus; Global Economic Monitor (GEM); Global Economic Prospects 2008; The World Bank Atlas 2003-2004;* and *World Development Report 2008.*

BELARUS - EDUCATION

Academic International Press, PO Box 1111, Gulf Breeze, FL 32562-1111, Fax: (850) 934-0953, www.ai-press.com; *Russia and Eurasia Facts and Figures Annual.*

Euromonitor International, Inc., 224 S. Michigan Avenue, Suite 1500, Chicago, IL 60604, (312) 922-1115, Fax: (312) 922-1157, www.euromonitor.com; *World Marketing Data and Statistics.*

European Union, Delegation of the European Commission to the United States, 2300 M Street, NW, Washington, DC 20037, (202) 862-9500, Fax: (202) 429-1766, www.eurunion.org; *Education across Europe 2003.*

Ministry of Statistics and Analysis of the Republic of Belarus, 12 Partizansky Avenue, Minsk 220070, Belarus, www.belstat.gov.by; *Education in the Republic of Belarus.*

Palgrave Macmillan Ltd., Houndmills, Basingstoke, Hampshire, RG21 6XS, England, (Telephone in U.S. (888) 330-8477), (Fax in U.S. (800) 672-2054), www.palgrave.com; *The Statesman's Yearbook 2008.*

Taylor and Francis Group, An Informa Business, 2 Park Square, Milton Park, Abingdon, Oxford OX14 4RN, United Kingdom, (Dial from U.S. (212) 216-7800), (Fax from U.S. (212) 564-7854), www.tandf.co.uk; *The Europa World Year Book.*

UNESCO Institute for Statistics, C.P. 6128 Succursale Centre-Ville, Montreal, Quebec, H3C 3J7 Canada, (Dial from U.S. (514) 343-6880), (Fax from U.S. (514) 343 6882), www.uis.unesco.org; *Statistical Tables.*

United Nations Statistics Division, New York, NY 10017, (800) 253-9646, Fax: (212) 963-4116, http://unstats.un.org; *Human Development Report 2006* and *Trends in Europe and North America: The Statistical Yearbook of the ECE 2005.*

The World Bank, 1818 H Street, NW, Washington, DC 20433, (202) 473-1000, Fax: (202) 477-6391, www.worldbank.org; *Belarus* and *World Development Report 2008.*

BELARUS - ELECTRICITY

Palgrave Macmillan Ltd., Houndmills, Basingstoke, Hampshire, RG21 6XS, England, (Telephone in U.S. (888) 330-8477), (Fax in U.S. (800) 672-2054), www.palgrave.com; *The Statesman's Yearbook 2008.*

Platts, 2 Penn Plaza, 25th Floor, New York, NY 10121-2298, (212) 904-3070, www.platts.com; *Energy Economist* and *European Electricity Review 2004.*

U.S. Department of Energy (DOE), Energy Information Administration (EIA), 1000 Independence Avenue, SW, Washington, DC 20585, (202) 586-8800, www.eia.doe.gov; *International Energy Annual 2004* and *International Energy Outlook 2006.*

United Nations Statistics Division, New York, NY 10017, (800) 253-9646, Fax: (212) 963-4116, http://unstats.un.org; *Energy Statistics Yearbook 2003; Human Development Report 2006; Statistical Yearbook;* and *Trends in Europe and North America: The Statistical Yearbook of the ECE 2005.*

The World Bank, 1818 H Street, NW, Washington, DC 20433, (202) 473-1000, Fax: (202) 477-6391, www.worldbank.org; *Statistical Handbook: States of the Former USSR.*

BELARUS - EMPLOYMENT

International Labour Office, I.L.O. Publications, 4 route des Morillons, CH-1211 Geneva 22, Switzerland, (Telephone in U.S. (202) 653-7652), (Fax in U.S. (202) 653-7687), www.ilo.org; *Yearbook of Labour Statistics 2006.*

United Nations Statistics Division, New York, NY 10017, (800) 253-9646, Fax: (212) 963-4116, http://unstats.un.org; *Statistical Yearbook* and *Trends in Europe and North America: The Statistical Yearbook of the ECE 2005.*

The World Bank, 1818 H Street, NW, Washington, DC 20433, (202) 473-1000, Fax: (202) 477-6391, www.worldbank.org; *Belarus* and *Statistical Handbook: States of the Former USSR.*

BELARUS - ENERGY INDUSTRIES

Platts, 2 Penn Plaza, 25th Floor, New York, NY 10121-2298, (212) 904-3070, www.platts.com; *Energy in East Europe.*

BELARUS - ENVIRONMENTAL CONDITIONS

Center for Research on the Epidemiology of Disasters (CRED), Universite Catholique de Louvain, Ecole de Sante Publique, 30.94 Clos Chapelle-aux-Champs, 1200 Brussels, Belgium, www.cred.be; *Three Decades of Floods in Europe: A Preliminary Analysis of EMDAT Data.*

DSI Data Service Information, Xantener Strasse 51a, D-47495 Rheinberg, Germany, www.dsidata.com; *Campus Solution* and *DSI's Global Environmental Database.*

Economist Intelligence Unit, 111 West 57th Street, New York, NY 10019, (212) 554-0600, Fax: (212) 586-1181, www.eiu.com; *Belarus Country Report.*

Eurostat, Batiment Jean Monnet, Rue Alcide de Gasperi, L-2920 Luxembourg, http://epp.eurostat.ec.europa.eu; *Environmental Protection Expenditure in Europe.*

Ministry of Statistics and Analysis of the Republic of Belarus, 12 Partizansky Avenue, Minsk 220070, Belarus, www.belstat.gov.by; *Environment and Natural Resources in the Republic of Belarus.*

United Nations Statistics Division, New York, NY 10017, (800) 253-9646, Fax: (212) 963-4116, http://unstats.un.org; *Statistical Yearbook; Trends in Europe and North America: The Statistical Yearbook of the ECE 2005;* and *World Statistics Pocketbook.*

BELARUS - EXPORTS

Academic International Press, PO Box 1111, Gulf Breeze, FL 32562-1111, Fax: (850) 934-0953, www.ai-press.com; *Russia and Eurasia Facts and Figures Annual.*

Central Intelligence Agency, Office of Public Affairs, Washington, DC 20505, (703) 482-0623, Fax: (703) 482-1739, www.cia.gov; *The World Factbook.*

Economist Intelligence Unit, 111 West 57th Street, New York, NY 10019, (212) 554-0600, Fax: (212) 586-1181, www.eiu.com; *Belarus Country Report.*

Euromonitor International, Inc., 224 S. Michigan Avenue, Suite 1500, Chicago, IL 60604, (312) 922-1115, Fax: (312) 922-1157, www.euromonitor.com; *The World Economic Factbook 2008.*

International Monetary Fund (IMF), 700 Nineteenth Street, NW, Washington, DC 20431, (202) 623-7000, Fax: (202) 623-4661, www.imf.org; *Direction of Trade Statistics Yearbook 2007.*

Palgrave Macmillan Ltd., Houndmills, Basingstoke, Hampshire, RG21 6XS, England, (Telephone in U.S. (888) 330-8477), (Fax in U.S. (800) 672-2054), www.palgrave.com; *The Statesman's Yearbook 2008.*

Taylor and Francis Group, An Informa Business, 2 Park Square, Milton Park, Abingdon, Oxford OX14 4RN, United Kingdom, (Dial from U.S. (212) 216-7800), (Fax from U.S. (212) 564-7854), www.tandf.co.uk; *The Europa World Year Book.*

United Nations Statistics Division, New York, NY 10017, (800) 253-9646, Fax: (212) 963-4116, http://unstats.un.org; *International Trade Statistics Yearbook* and *Trends in Europe and North America: The Statistical Yearbook of the ECE 2005.*

The World Bank, 1818 H Street, NW, Washington, DC 20433, (202) 473-1000, Fax: (202) 477-6391, www.worldbank.org; *Statistical Handbook: States of the Former USSR; World Development Indicators (WDI) 2008;* and *World Development Report 2008.*

BELARUS - FERTILITY, HUMAN

Central Intelligence Agency, Office of Public Affairs, Washington, DC 20505, (703) 482-0623, Fax: (703) 482-1739, www.cia.gov; *The World Factbook.*

United Nations Statistics Division, New York, NY 10017, (800) 253-9646, Fax: (212) 963-4116, http://unstats.un.org; *Demographic Yearbook* and *Trends in Europe and North America: The Statistical Yearbook of the ECE 2005.*

The World Bank, 1818 H Street, NW, Washington, DC 20433, (202) 473-1000, Fax: (202) 477-6391, www.worldbank.org; *Statistical Handbook: States of the Former USSR; The World Bank Atlas 2003-2004; World Development Indicators (WDI) 2008;* and *World Development Report 2008.*

World Health Organization (WHO), Avenue Appia 20, 1211 Geneve 27, Switzerland, (Telephone in U.S. (212) 331-9081), www.who.int; *World Health Report 2006.*

BELARUS - FERTILIZER INDUSTRY

United Nations Food and Agricultural Organization (FAO), Viale delle Terme di Caracalla, 00100 Rome, Italy, (Dial from U.S. (202) 653-2400), (Fax from U.S. (202) 653 5760), www.fao.org; *FAO Fertilizer Yearbook.*

United Nations Statistics Division, New York, NY 10017, (800) 253-9646, Fax: (212) 963-4116, http://unstats.un.org; *Human Development Report 2006; 2004 Industrial Commodity Statistics Yearbook;* and *Statistical Yearbook.*

BELARUS - FETAL MORTALITY

See BELARUS - MORTALITY

BELARUS - FILM

See BELARUS - MOTION PICTURES

BELARUS - FINANCE

Ministry of Statistics and Analysis of the Republic of Belarus, 12 Partizansky Avenue, Minsk 220070, Belarus, www.belstat.gov.by; *National Accounts of the Republic of Belarus.*

Taylor and Francis Group, An Informa Business, 2 Park Square, Milton Park, Abingdon, Oxford OX14 4RN, United Kingdom, (Dial from U.S. (212) 216-7800), (Fax from U.S. (212) 564-7854), www.tandf.co.uk; *The Europa World Year Book.*

United Nations Statistics Division, New York, NY 10017, (800) 253-9646, Fax: (212) 963-4116, http://unstats.un.org; *National Accounts Statistics: Compendium of Income Distribution Statistics* and *Statistical Yearbook.*

The World Bank, 1818 H Street, NW, Washington, DC 20433, (202) 473-1000, Fax: (202) 477-6391, www.worldbank.org; *Belarus* and *Statistical Handbook: States of the Former USSR.*

BELARUS - FINANCE, PUBLIC

Banque de France, 48 rue Croix des Petits champs, 75001 Paris, France, www.banque-france.fr/home.htm; *Public Finance.*

Bernan Essential Government Publications, 4611-F Assembly Drive, Lanham MD, 20706-4391, (301) 459-2255, Fax: (800) 865-3450, www.bernan.com; *National Accounts Statistics.*

Economist Intelligence Unit, 111 West 57th Street, New York, NY 10019, (212) 554-0600, Fax: (212) 586-1181, www.eiu.com; *Belarus Country Report.*

International Monetary Fund (IMF), 700 Nineteenth Street, NW, Washington, DC 20431, (202) 623-7000, Fax: (202) 623-4661, www.imf.org; *International Financial Statistics* and *International Financial Statistics Online Service.*

Palgrave Macmillan Ltd., Houndmills, Basingstoke, Hampshire, RG21 6XS, England, (Telephone in U.S. (888) 330-8477), (Fax in U.S. (800) 672-2054), www.palgrave.com; *The Statesman's Yearbook 2008.*

Taylor and Francis Group, An Informa Business, 2 Park Square, Milton Park, Abingdon, Oxford OX14 4RN, United Kingdom, (Dial from U.S. (212) 216-7800), (Fax from U.S. (212) 564-7854), www.tandf.co.uk; *The Europa World Year Book.*

The World Bank, 1818 H Street, NW, Washington, DC 20433, (202) 473-1000, Fax: (202) 477-6391, www.worldbank.org; *Belarus* and *Statistical Handbook: States of the Former USSR.*

BELARUS - FISHERIES

United Nations Food and Agricultural Organization (FAO), Viale delle Terme di Caracalla, 00100 Rome, Italy, (Dial from U.S. (202) 653-2400), (Fax from U.S. (202) 653 5760), www.fao.org; *FAO Yearbook of Fishery Statistics;* Fishery Databases; FISHSTAT Database. Subjects covered include: Aquaculture production, capture production, fishery commodities; and *The State of Food and Agriculture (SOFA) 2006.*

United Nations Statistics Division, New York, NY 10017, (800) 253-9646, Fax: (212) 963-4116, http://unstats.un.org; *2004 Industrial Commodity Statistics Yearbook* and *Statistical Yearbook.*

The World Bank, 1818 H Street, NW, Washington, DC 20433, (202) 473-1000, Fax: (202) 477-6391, www.worldbank.org; *Belarus.*

BELARUS - FLOUR PRODUCTION

See BELARUS - CROPS

BELARUS - FOOD

United Nations Food and Agricultural Organization (FAO), Viale delle Terme di Caracalla, 00100 Rome, Italy, (Dial from U.S. (202) 653-2400), (Fax from U.S. (202) 653 5760), www.fao.org; *FAO Production Yearbook 2002* and *The State of Food and Agriculture (SOFA) 2006.*

United Nations Statistics Division, New York, NY 10017, (800) 253-9646, Fax: (212) 963-4116, http://unstats.un.org; *Human Development Report 2006* and *2004 Industrial Commodity Statistics Yearbook*.

BELARUS - FOREIGN EXCHANGE RATES

Central Intelligence Agency, Office of Public Affairs, Washington, DC 20505, (703) 482-0623, Fax: (703) 482-1739, www.cia.gov; *The World Factbook*.

Euromonitor International, Inc., 224 S. Michigan Avenue, Suite 1500, Chicago, IL 60604, (312) 922-1115, Fax: (312) 922-1157, www.euromonitor.com; *The World Economic Factbook 2008*.

Taylor and Francis Group, An Informa Business, 2 Park Square, Milton Park, Abingdon, Oxford OX14 4RN, United Kingdom, (Dial from U.S. (212) 216-7800), (Fax from U.S. (212) 564-7854), www.tandf.co.uk; *The Europa World Year Book*.

United Nations Statistics Division, New York, NY 10017, (800) 253-9646, Fax: (212) 963-4116, http://unstats.un.org; *Statistical Yearbook; Trends in Europe and North America: The Statistical Yearbook of the ECE 2005;* and *World Statistics Pocketbook*.

BELARUS - FORESTS AND FORESTRY

Academic International Press, PO Box 1111, Gulf Breeze, FL 32562-1111, Fax: (850) 934-0953, www.ai-press.com; *Russia and Eurasia Facts and Figures Annual*.

Ministry of Statistics and Analysis of the Republic of Belarus, 12 Partizansky Avenue, Minsk 220070, Belarus, www.belstat.gov.by; *Environment and Natural Resources in the Republic of Belarus*.

Palgrave Macmillan Ltd., Houndmills, Basingstoke, Hampshire, RG21 6XS, England, (Telephone in U.S. (888) 330-8477), (Fax in U.S. (800) 672-2054), www.palgrave.com; *The Statesman's Yearbook 2008*.

UNESCO Institute for Statistics, C.P. 6128 Succursale Centre-Ville, Montreal, Quebec, H3C 3J7 Canada, (Dial from U.S. (514) 343-6880), (Fax from U.S. (514) 343 6882), www.uis.unesco.org; *Statistical Tables*.

United Nations Food and Agricultural Organization (FAO), Viale delle Terme di Caracalla, 00100 Rome, Italy, (Dial from U.S. (202) 653-2400), (Fax from U.S. (202) 653 5760), www.fao.org; *FAO Yearbook of Forest Products* and *The State of Food and Agriculture (SOFA) 2006*.

United Nations Statistics Division, New York, NY 10017, (800) 253-9646, Fax: (212) 963-4116, http://unstats.un.org; *2004 Industrial Commodity Statistics Yearbook; Statistical Yearbook;* and *Trends in Europe and North America: The Statistical Yearbook of the ECE 2005*.

The World Bank, 1818 H Street, NW, Washington, DC 20433, (202) 473-1000, Fax: (202) 477-6391, www.worldbank.org; *Belarus* and *World Development Report 2008*.

BELARUS - GAS PRODUCTION

See BELARUS - MINERAL INDUSTRIES

BELARUS - GROSS DOMESTIC PRODUCT

Academic International Press, PO Box 1111, Gulf Breeze, FL 32562-1111, Fax: (850) 934-0953, www.ai-press.com; *Russia and Eurasia Facts and Figures Annual*.

Economist Intelligence Unit, 111 West 57th Street, New York, NY 10019, (212) 554-0600, Fax: (212) 586-1181, www.eiu.com; *Belarus Country Report*.

Euromonitor International, Inc., 224 S. Michigan Avenue, Suite 1500, Chicago, IL 60604, (312) 922-1115, Fax: (312) 922-1157, www.euromonitor.com; *The World Economic Factbook 2008*.

United Nations Statistics Division, New York, NY 10017, (800) 253-9646, Fax: (212) 963-4116, http://unstats.un.org; *Human Development Report 2006; National Accounts Statistics: Compendium of Income Distribution Statistics; Statistical Yearbook;* and *Trends in Europe and North America: The Statistical Yearbook of the ECE 2005*.

The World Bank, 1818 H Street, NW, Washington, DC 20433, (202) 473-1000, Fax: (202) 477-6391, www.worldbank.org; *Statistical Handbook: States of the Former USSR; World Development Indicators (WDI) 2008;* and *World Development Report 2008*.

BELARUS - GROSS NATIONAL PRODUCT

Palgrave Macmillan Ltd., Houndmills, Basingstoke, Hampshire, RG21 6XS, England, (Telephone in U.S. (888) 330-8477), (Fax in U.S. (800) 672-2054), www.palgrave.com; *The Statesman's Yearbook 2008*.

United Nations Statistics Division, New York, NY 10017, (800) 253-9646, Fax: (212) 963-4116, http://unstats.un.org; *Statistical Yearbook*.

The World Bank, 1818 H Street, NW, Washington, DC 20433, (202) 473-1000, Fax: (202) 477-6391, www.worldbank.org; *The World Bank Atlas 2003-2004; World Development Indicators (WDI) 2008;* and *World Development Report 2008*.

BELARUS - HOUSING

Euromonitor International, Inc., 224 S. Michigan Avenue, Suite 1500, Chicago, IL 60604, (312) 922-1115, Fax: (312) 922-1157, www.euromonitor.com; *World Marketing Data and Statistics*.

United Nations Statistics Division, New York, NY 10017, (800) 253-9646, Fax: (212) 963-4116, http://unstats.un.org; *Trends in Europe and North America: The Statistical Yearbook of the ECE 2005*.

BELARUS - ILLITERATE PERSONS

Euromonitor International, Inc., 224 S. Michigan Avenue, Suite 1500, Chicago, IL 60604, (312) 922-1115, Fax: (312) 922-1157, www.euromonitor.com; *The World Economic Factbook 2008*.

UNESCO Institute for Statistics, C.P. 6128 Succursale Centre-Ville, Montreal, Quebec H3C 3J7 Canada, (Dial from U.S. (514) 343-6880), (Fax from U.S. (514) 343 6882), www.uis.unesco.org; *Statistical Tables*.

United Nations Statistics Division, New York, NY 10017, (800) 253-9646, Fax: (212) 963-4116, http://unstats.un.org; *Human Development Report 2006*.

BELARUS - IMPORTS

Academic International Press, PO Box 1111, Gulf Breeze, FL 32562-1111, Fax: (850) 934-0953, www.ai-press.com; *Russia and Eurasia Facts and Figures Annual*.

Central Intelligence Agency, Office of Public Affairs, Washington, DC 20505, (703) 482-0623, Fax: (703) 482-1739, www.cia.gov; *The World Factbook*.

Economist Intelligence Unit, 111 West 57th Street, New York, NY 10019, (212) 554-0600, Fax: (212) 586-1181, www.eiu.com; *Belarus Country Report*.

Euromonitor International, Inc., 224 S. Michigan Avenue, Suite 1500, Chicago, IL 60604, (312) 922-1115, Fax: (312) 922-1157, www.euromonitor.com; *The World Economic Factbook 2008*.

International Monetary Fund (IMF), 700 Nineteenth Street, NW, Washington, DC 20431, (202) 623-7000, Fax: (202) 623-4661, www.imf.org; *Direction of Trade Statistics Yearbook 2007*.

Palgrave Macmillan Ltd., Houndmills, Basingstoke, Hampshire, RG21 6XS, England, (Telephone in U.S. (888) 330-8477), (Fax in U.S. (800) 672-2054), www.palgrave.com; *The Statesman's Yearbook 2008*.

Taylor and Francis Group, An Informa Business, 2 Park Square, Milton Park, Abingdon, Oxford OX14 4RN, United Kingdom, (Dial from U.S. (212) 216-7800), (Fax from U.S. (212) 564-7854), www.tandf.co.uk; *The Europa World Year Book*.

United Nations Statistics Division, New York, NY 10017, (800) 253-9646, Fax: (212) 963-4116, http://unstats.un.org; *International Trade Statistics Yearbook* and *Trends in Europe and North America: The Statistical Yearbook of the ECE 2005*.

The World Bank, 1818 H Street, NW, Washington, DC 20433, (202) 473-1000, Fax: (202) 477-6391, www.worldbank.org; *Statistical Handbook: States of the Former USSR; World Development Indicators (WDI) 2008;* and *World Development Report 2008*.

BELARUS - INDUSTRIAL PRODUCTIVITY

The World Bank, 1818 H Street, NW, Washington, DC 20433, (202) 473-1000, Fax: (202) 477-6391, www.worldbank.org; *Statistical Handbook: States of the Former USSR*.

BELARUS - INDUSTRIAL PROPERTY

United Nations Statistics Division, New York, NY 10017, (800) 253-9646, Fax: (212) 963-4116, http://unstats.un.org; *Statistical Yearbook*.

BELARUS - INDUSTRIES

Academic International Press, PO Box 1111, Gulf Breeze, FL 32562-1111, Fax: (850) 934-0953, www.ai-press.com; *Russia and Eurasia Facts and Figures Annual*.

Central Intelligence Agency, Office of Public Affairs, Washington, DC 20505, (703) 482-0623, Fax: (703) 482-1739, www.cia.gov; *The World Factbook*.

Economist Intelligence Unit, 111 West 57th Street, New York, NY 10019, (212) 554-0600, Fax: (212) 586-1181, www.eiu.com; *Belarus Country Report*.

Euromonitor International, Inc., 224 S. Michigan Avenue, Suite 1500, Chicago, IL 60604, (312) 922-1115, Fax: (312) 922-1157, www.euromonitor.com; *The World Economic Factbook 2008* and *World Marketing Data and Statistics*.

International Labour Office, I.L.O. Publications, 4 route des Morillons, CH-1211 Geneva 22, Switzerland, (Telephone in U.S. (202) 653-7652), (Fax in U.S. (202) 653-7687), www.ilo.org; *Yearbook of Labour Statistics 2006*.

Palgrave Macmillan Ltd., Houndmills, Basingstoke, Hampshire, RG21 6XS, England, (Telephone in U.S. (888) 330-8477), (Fax in U.S. (800) 672-2054), www.palgrave.com; *The Statesman's Yearbook 2008*.

Taylor and Francis Group, An Informa Business, 2 Park Square, Milton Park, Abingdon, Oxford OX14 4RN, United Kingdom, (Dial from U.S. (212) 216-7800), (Fax from U.S. (212) 564-7854), www.tandf.co.uk; *The Europa World Year Book*.

United Nations Industrial Development Organization (UNIDO), 1 United Nations Plaza, New York, NY 10017, (212) 963 6890, Fax: (212) 963-7904, http://unido.org; Industrial Statistics Database 2008 (INDSTAT) and *The International Yearbook of Industrial Statistics 2008*.

United Nations Statistics Division, New York, NY 10017, (800) 253-9646, Fax: (212) 963-4116, http://unstats.un.org; *2004 Industrial Commodity Statistics Yearbook; Statistical Yearbook;* and *Trends in Europe and North America: The Statistical Yearbook of the ECE 2005*.

The World Bank, 1818 H Street, NW, Washington, DC 20433, (202) 473-1000, Fax: (202) 477-6391, www.worldbank.org; *Belarus; Statistical Handbook: States of the Former USSR;* and *World Development Indicators (WDI) 2008*.

BELARUS - INFANT AND MATERNAL MORTALITY

See BELARUS - MORTALITY

BELARUS - INTERNATIONAL TRADE

Academic International Press, PO Box 1111, Gulf Breeze, FL 32562-1111, Fax: (850) 934-0953, www.ai-press.com; *Russia and Eurasia Facts and Figures Annual*.

Banque de France, 48 rue Croix des Petits champs, 75001 Paris, France, www.banque-france.fr/home.htm; *Monthly Business Survey Overview*.

Economist Intelligence Unit, 111 West 57th Street, New York, NY 10019, (212) 554-0600, Fax: (212) 586-1181, www.eiu.com; *Belarus Country Report*.

Euromonitor International, Inc., 224 S. Michigan Avenue, Suite 1500, Chicago, IL 60604, (312) 922-

1115, Fax: (312) 922-1157, www.euromonitor.com; *The World Economic Factbook 2008* and *World Marketing Data and Statistics.*

International Monetary Fund (IMF), 700 Nineteenth Street, NW, Washington, DC 20431, (202) 623-7000, Fax: (202) 623-4661, www.imf.org; *Direction of Trade Statistics Yearbook 2007.*

United Nations Food and Agricultural Organization (FAO), Viale delle Terme di Caracalla, 00100 Rome, Italy, (Dial from U.S. (202) 653-2400), (Fax from U.S. (202) 653 5760), www.fao.org; *FAO Trade Yearbook.*

United Nations Statistics Division, New York, NY 10017, (800) 253-9646, Fax: (212) 963-4116, http://unstats.un.org; *International Trade Statistics Yearbook* and *Statistical Yearbook.*

The World Bank, 1818 H Street, NW, Washington, DC 20433, (202) 473-1000, Fax: (202) 477-6391, www.worldbank.org; *Belarus; Statistical Handbook: States of the Former USSR; World Development Indicators (WDI) 2008;* and *World Development Report 2008.*

World Trade Organization (WTO), Centre William Rappard, Rue de Lausanne 154, CH-1211 Geneva 21, Switzerland, www.wto.org; *International Trade Statistics 2006.*

BELARUS - INTERNET USERS

International Telecommunication Union (ITU), Place des Nations, 1211 Geneva 20, Switzerland, www.itu.int; *World Telecommunication/ICT Indicators Database on CD-ROM; World Telecommunication/ICT Indicators Database Online;* and *Yearbook of Statistics - Telecommunication Services (Chronological Time Series 1997-2006).*

The World Bank, 1818 H Street, NW, Washington, DC 20433, (202) 473-1000, Fax: (202) 477-6391, www.worldbank.org; *Belarus.*

BELARUS - LABOR

Academic International Press, PO Box 1111, Gulf Breeze, FL 32562-1111, Fax: (850) 934-0953, www.ai-press.com; *Russia and Eurasia Facts and Figures Annual.*

Central Intelligence Agency, Office of Public Affairs, Washington, DC 20505, (703) 482-0623, Fax: (703) 482-1739, www.cia.gov; *The World Factbook.*

Euromonitor International, Inc., 224 S. Michigan Avenue, Suite 1500, Chicago, IL 60604, (312) 922-1115, Fax: (312) 922-1157, www.euromonitor.com; *World Marketing Data and Statistics.*

International Labour Office, I.L.O. Publications, 4 route des Morillons, CH-1211 Geneva 22, Switzerland, (Telephone in U.S. (202) 653-7652), (Fax in U.S. (202) 653-7687), www.ilo.org; *Yearbook of Labour Statistics 2006.*

Palgrave Macmillan Ltd., Houndmills, Basingstoke, Hampshire, RG21 6XS, England, (Telephone in U.S. (888) 330-8477), (Fax in U.S. (800) 672-2054), www.palgrave.com; *The Statesman's Yearbook 2008.*

United Nations Statistics Division, New York, NY 10017, (800) 253-9646, Fax: (212) 963-4116, http://unstats.un.org; *Human Development Report 2006* and *Statistical Yearbook.*

The World Bank, 1818 H Street, NW, Washington, DC 20433, (202) 473-1000, Fax: (202) 477-6391, www.worldbank.org; *Statistical Handbook: States of the Former USSR; The World Bank Atlas 2003-2004; World Development Indicators (WDI) 2008;* and *World Development Report 2008.*

BELARUS - LAND USE

Central Intelligence Agency, Office of Public Affairs, Washington, DC 20505, (703) 482-0623, Fax: (703) 482-1739, www.cia.gov; *The World Factbook.*

United Nations Food and Agricultural Organization (FAO), Viale delle Terme di Caracalla, 00100 Rome, Italy, (Dial from U.S. (202) 653-2400), (Fax from U.S. (202) 653 5760), www.fao.org; *FAO Production Yearbook 2002.*

The World Bank, 1818 H Street, NW, Washington, DC 20433, (202) 473-1000, Fax: (202) 477-6391, www.worldbank.org; *World Development Report 2008.*

BELARUS - LIBRARIES

UNESCO Institute for Statistics, C.P. 6128 Succursale Centre-Ville, Montreal, Quebec, H3C 3J7 Canada, (Dial from U.S. (514) 343-6880), (Fax from U.S. (514) 343 6882), www.uis.unesco.org; *Statistical Tables.*

United Nations Statistics Division, New York, NY 10017, (800) 253-9646, Fax: (212) 963-4116, http://unstats.un.org; *Trends in Europe and North America: The Statistical Yearbook of the ECE 2005.*

BELARUS - LIFE EXPECTANCY

Central Intelligence Agency, Office of Public Affairs, Washington, DC 20505, (703) 482-0623, Fax: (703) 482-1739, www.cia.gov; *The World Factbook.*

Euromonitor International, Inc., 224 S. Michigan Avenue, Suite 1500, Chicago, IL 60604, (312) 922-1115, Fax: (312) 922-1157, www.euromonitor.com; *The World Economic Factbook 2008.*

United Nations Statistics Division, New York, NY 10017, (800) 253-9646, Fax: (212) 963-4116, http://unstats.un.org; *Demographic Yearbook; Human Development Report 2006; Trends in Europe and North America: The Statistical Yearbook of the ECE 2005;* and *World Statistics Pocketbook.*

The World Bank, 1818 H Street, NW, Washington, DC 20433, (202) 473-1000, Fax: (202) 477-6391, www.worldbank.org; *The World Bank Atlas 2003-2004; World Development Indicators (WDI) 2008;* and *World Development Report 2008.*

World Health Organization (WHO), Avenue Appia 20, 1211 Geneve 27, Switzerland, (Telephone in U.S. (212) 331-9081), www.who.int; *World Health Report 2006.*

BELARUS - LITERACY

Euromonitor International, Inc., 224 S. Michigan Avenue, Suite 1500, Chicago, IL 60604, (312) 922-1115, Fax: (312) 922-1157, www.euromonitor.com; *World Marketing Data and Statistics.*

BELARUS - LIVESTOCK

Academic International Press, PO Box 1111, Gulf Breeze, FL 32562-1111, Fax: (850) 934-0953, www.ai-press.com; *Russia and Eurasia Facts and Figures Annual.*

Palgrave Macmillan Ltd., Houndmills, Basingstoke, Hampshire, RG21 6XS, England, (Telephone in U.S. (888) 330-8477), (Fax in U.S. (800) 672-2054), www.palgrave.com; *The Statesman's Yearbook 2008.*

Taylor and Francis Group, An Informa Business, 2 Park Square, Milton Park, Abingdon, Oxford OX14 4RN, United Kingdom, (Dial from U.S. (212) 216-7800), (Fax from U.S. (212) 564-7854), www.tandf.co.uk; *The Europa World Year Book.*

United Nations Food and Agricultural Organization (FAO), Viale delle Terme di Caracalla, 00100 Rome, Italy, (Dial from U.S. (202) 653-2400), (Fax from U.S. (202) 653 5760), www.fao.org; *FAO Production Yearbook 2002* and *The State of Food and Agriculture (SOFA) 2006.*

United Nations Statistics Division, New York, NY 10017, (800) 253-9646, Fax: (212) 963-4116, http://unstats.un.org; *2004 Industrial Commodity Statistics Yearbook.*

BELARUS - MACHINERY

United Nations Statistics Division, New York, NY 10017, (800) 253-9646, Fax: (212) 963-4116, http://unstats.un.org; *2004 Industrial Commodity Statistics Yearbook.*

BELARUS - MANUFACTURES

United Nations Statistics Division, New York, NY 10017, (800) 253-9646, Fax: (212) 963-4116, http://unstats.un.org; *2004 Industrial Commodity Statistics Yearbook* and *Statistical Yearbook.*

The World Bank, 1818 H Street, NW, Washington, DC 20433, (202) 473-1000, Fax: (202) 477-6391, www.worldbank.org; *World Development Indicators (WDI) 2008.*

BELARUS - MARRIAGE

Taylor and Francis Group, An Informa Business, 2 Park Square, Milton Park, Abingdon, Oxford OX14 4RN, United Kingdom, (Dial from U.S. (212) 216-7800), (Fax from U.S. (212) 564-7854), www.tandf.co.uk; *The Europa World Year Book.*

United Nations Statistics Division, New York, NY 10017, (800) 253-9646, Fax: (212) 963-4116, http://unstats.un.org; *Demographic Yearbook; Statistical Yearbook;* and *Trends in Europe and North America: The Statistical Yearbook of the ECE 2005.*

BELARUS - MEAT PRODUCTION

See BELARUS - LIVESTOCK

BELARUS - MILK PRODUCTION

See BELARUS - DAIRY PROCESSING

BELARUS - MINERAL INDUSTRIES

Academic International Press, PO Box 1111, Gulf Breeze, FL 32562-1111, Fax: (850) 934-0953, www.ai-press.com; *Russia and Eurasia Facts and Figures Annual.*

Palgrave Macmillan Ltd., Houndmills, Basingstoke, Hampshire, RG21 6XS, England, (Telephone in U.S. (888) 330-8477), (Fax in U.S. (800) 672-2054), www.palgrave.com; *The Statesman's Yearbook 2008.*

Platts, 2 Penn Plaza, 25th Floor, New York, NY 10121-2298, (212) 904-3070, www.platts.com; *Energy Economist* and *Energy in East Europe.*

Taylor and Francis Group, An Informa Business, 2 Park Square, Milton Park, Abingdon, Oxford OX14 4RN, United Kingdom, (Dial from U.S. (212) 216-7800), (Fax from U.S. (212) 564-7854), www.tandf.co.uk; *The Europa World Year Book.*

United Nations Statistics Division, New York, NY 10017, (800) 253-9646, Fax: (212) 963-4116, http://unstats.un.org; *Energy Statistics Yearbook 2003; 2004 Industrial Commodity Statistics Yearbook;* and *Statistical Yearbook.*

The World Bank, 1818 H Street, NW, Washington, DC 20433, (202) 473-1000, Fax: (202) 477-6391, www.worldbank.org; *Belarus.*

BELARUS - MONEY SUPPLY

Economist Intelligence Unit, 111 West 57th Street, New York, NY 10019, (212) 554-0600, Fax: (212) 586-1181, www.eiu.com; *Belarus Country Report.*

Taylor and Francis Group, An Informa Business, 2 Park Square, Milton Park, Abingdon, Oxford OX14 4RN, United Kingdom, (Dial from U.S. (212) 216-7800), (Fax from U.S. (212) 564-7854), www.tandf.co.uk; *The Europa World Year Book.*

The World Bank, 1818 H Street, NW, Washington, DC 20433, (202) 473-1000, Fax: (202) 477-6391, www.worldbank.org; *Belarus.*

BELARUS - MORTALITY

Central Intelligence Agency, Office of Public Affairs, Washington, DC 20505, (703) 482-0623, Fax: (703) 482-1739, www.cia.gov; *The World Factbook.*

Euromonitor International, Inc., 224 S. Michigan Avenue, Suite 1500, Chicago, IL 60604, (312) 922-1115, Fax: (312) 922-1157, www.euromonitor.com; *The World Economic Factbook 2008.*

Palgrave Macmillan Ltd., Houndmills, Basingstoke, Hampshire, RG21 6XS, England, (Telephone in U.S. (888) 330-8477), (Fax in U.S. (800) 672-2054), www.palgrave.com; *The Statesman's Yearbook 2008.*

Taylor and Francis Group, An Informa Business, 2 Park Square, Milton Park, Abingdon, Oxford OX14 4RN, United Kingdom, (Dial from U.S. (212) 216-

7800), (Fax from U.S. (212) 564-7854), www.tandf.co.uk; *The Europa World Year Book.*

UNICEF, 3 United Nations Plaza, New York, NY 10017, (800) 253-9646, Fax: (212) 887-7465, www.unicef.org; *The State of the World's Children 2008.*

United Nations Statistics Division, New York, NY 10017, (800) 253-9646, Fax: (212) 963-4116, http://unstats.un.org; *Demographic Yearbook; Human Development Report 2006; Statistical Yearbook; Trends in Europe and North America: The Statistical Yearbook of the ECE 2005;* and *World Statistics Pocketbook.*

The World Bank, 1818 H Street, NW, Washington, DC 20433, (202) 473-1000, Fax: (202) 477-6391, www.worldbank.org; *The World Bank Atlas 2003-2004; World Development Indicators (WDI) 2008;* and *World Development Report 2008.*

World Health Organization (WHO), Avenue Appia 20, 1211 Geneve 27, Switzerland, (Telephone in U.S. (212) 331-9081), www.who.int; The WHO Global Atlas of Infectious Diseases and *World Health Report 2006.*

BELARUS - MOTION PICTURES

Palgrave Macmillan Ltd., Houndmills, Basingstoke, Hampshire, RG21 6XS, England, (Telephone in U.S. (888) 330-8477), (Fax in U.S. (800) 672-2054), www.palgrave.com; *The Statesman's Yearbook 2008.*

UNESCO Institute for Statistics, C.P. 6128 Succursale Centre-Ville, Montreal, Quebec, H3C 3J7 Canada, (Dial from U.S. (514) 343-6880), (Fax from U.S. (514) 343 6882), www.uis.unesco.org; *Statistical Tables.*

United Nations Statistics Division, New York, NY 10017, (800) 253-9646, Fax: (212) 963-4116, http://unstats.un.org; *Statistical Yearbook.*

BELARUS - MUSEUMS

UNESCO Institute for Statistics, C.P. 6128 Succursale Centre-Ville, Montreal, Quebec, H3C 3J7 Canada, (Dial from U.S. (514) 343-6880), (Fax from U.S. (514) 343 6882), www.uis.unesco.org; *Statistical Tables.*

BELARUS - NATIONAL INCOME

United Nations Statistics Division, New York, NY 10017, (800) 253-9646, Fax: (212) 963-4116, http://unstats.un.org; *Statistical Yearbook.*

BELARUS - NATURAL GAS PRODUCTION

See BELARUS - MINERAL INDUSTRIES

BELARUS - PAPER

See BELARUS - FORESTS AND FORESTRY

BELARUS - PERIODICALS

UNESCO Institute for Statistics, C.P. 6128 Succursale Centre-Ville, Montreal, Quebec, H3C 3J7 Canada, (Dial from U.S. (514) 343-6880), (Fax from U.S. (514) 343 6882), www.uis.unesco.org; *Statistical Tables.*

BELARUS - PETROLEUM INDUSTRY AND TRADE

Palgrave Macmillan Ltd., Houndmills, Basingstoke, Hampshire, RG21 6XS, England, (Telephone in U.S. (888) 330-8477), (Fax in U.S. (800) 672-2054), www.palgrave.com; *The Statesman's Yearbook 2008.*

PennWell Corporation, 1421 South Sheridan Road, Tulsa, OK 74112, (918) 835-3161, www.pennwell.com; *International Petroleum Encyclopedia 2007.*

Platts, 2 Penn Plaza, 25th Floor, New York, NY 10121-2298, (212) 904-3070, www.platts.com; *Energy Economist.*

U.S. Department of Energy (DOE), Energy Information Administration (EIA), 1000 Independence Avenue, SW, Washington, DC 20585, (202) 586-8800, www.eia.doe.gov; *International Energy Annual 2004* and *International Energy Outlook 2006.*

United Nations Food and Agricultural Organization (FAO), Viale delle Terme di Caracalla, 00100 Rome, Italy, (Dial from U.S. (202) 653-2400), (Fax from U.S. (202) 653 5760), www.fao.org; *The State of Food and Agriculture (SOFA) 2006.*

United Nations Statistics Division, New York, NY 10017, (800) 253-9646, Fax: (212) 963-4116, http://unstats.un.org; *Energy Statistics Yearbook 2003; 2004 Industrial Commodity Statistics Yearbook; Statistical Yearbook;* and *Trends in Europe and North America: The Statistical Yearbook of the ECE 2005.*

BELARUS - PIPELINES

United Nations Statistics Division, New York, NY 10017, (800) 253-9646, Fax: (212) 963-4116, http://unstats.un.org; *Annual Bulletin of Transport Statistics for Europe and North America 2004.*

BELARUS - POLITICAL SCIENCE

Academic International Press, PO Box 1111, Gulf Breeze, FL 32562-1111, Fax: (850) 934-0953, www.ai-press.com; *Russia and Eurasia Facts and Figures Annual.*

Central Intelligence Agency, Office of Public Affairs, Washington, DC 20505, (703) 482-0623, Fax: (703) 482-1739, www.cia.gov; *The World Factbook.*

Palgrave Macmillan Ltd., Houndmills, Basingstoke, Hampshire, RG21 6XS, England, (Telephone in U.S. (888) 330-8477), (Fax in U.S. (800) 672-2054), www.palgrave.com; *The Statesman's Yearbook 2008.*

Taylor and Francis Group, An Informa Business, 2 Park Square, Milton Park, Abingdon, Oxford OX14 4RN, United Kingdom, (Dial from U.S. (212) 216-7800), (Fax from U.S. (212) 564-7854), www.tandf.co.uk; *The Europa World Year Book.*

United Nations Statistics Division, New York, NY 10017, (800) 253-9646, Fax: (212) 963-4116, http://unstats.un.org; *National Accounts Statistics: Compendium of Income Distribution Statistics* and *Statistical Yearbook.*

The World Bank, 1818 H Street, NW, Washington, DC 20433, (202) 473-1000, Fax: (202) 477-6391, www.worldbank.org; *Statistical Handbook: States of the Former USSR* and *World Development Report 2008.*

BELARUS - POPULATION

Academic International Press, PO Box 1111, Gulf Breeze, FL 32562-1111, Fax: (850) 934-0953, www.ai-press.com; *Russia and Eurasia Facts and Figures Annual.*

Central Intelligence Agency, Office of Public Affairs, Washington, DC 20505, (703) 482-0623, Fax: (703) 482-1739, www.cia.gov; *The World Factbook.*

Economist Intelligence Unit, 111 West 57th Street, New York, NY 10019, (212) 554-0600, Fax: (212) 586-1181, www.eiu.com; *Belarus Country Report.*

Euromonitor International, Inc., 224 S. Michigan Avenue, Suite 1500, Chicago, IL 60604, (312) 922-1115, Fax: (312) 922-1157, www.euromonitor.com; *The World Economic Factbook 2008.*

International Labour Office, I.L.O. Publications, 4 route des Morillons, CH-1211 Geneva 22, Switzerland, (Telephone in U.S. (202) 653-7652), (Fax in U.S. (202) 653-7687), www.ilo.org; *Yearbook of Labour Statistics 2006.*

Ministry of Statistics and Analysis of the Republic of Belarus, 12 Partizansky Avenue, Minsk 220070, Belarus, www.belstat.gov.by; *Socio-Economic Conditions of Households in the Republic of Belarus.*

Palgrave Macmillan Ltd., Houndmills, Basingstoke, Hampshire, RG21 6XS, England, (Telephone in U.S. (888) 330-8477), (Fax in U.S. (800) 672-2054), www.palgrave.com; *The Statesman's Yearbook 2008.*

Taylor and Francis Group, An Informa Business, 2 Park Square, Milton Park, Abingdon, Oxford OX14 4RN, United Kingdom, (Dial from U.S. (212) 216-7800), (Fax from U.S. (212) 564-7854), www.tandf.co.uk; *The Europa World Year Book.*

United Nations Food and Agricultural Organization (FAO), Viale delle Terme di Caracalla, 00100 Rome, Italy, (Dial from U.S. (202) 653-2400), (Fax from U.S. (202) 653 5760), www.fao.org; *FAO Production Yearbook 2002.*

United Nations Statistics Division, New York, NY 10017, (800) 253-9646, Fax: (212) 963-4116, http://unstats.un.org; *Demographic Yearbook; Human Development Report 2006; Statistical Yearbook; Trends in Europe and North America: The Statistical Yearbook of the ECE 2005;* and *World Statistics Pocketbook.*

The World Bank, 1818 H Street, NW, Washington, DC 20433, (202) 473-1000, Fax: (202) 477-6391, www.worldbank.org; *Belarus; Statistical Handbook: States of the Former USSR; The World Bank Atlas 2003-2004; World Development Indicators (WDI) 2008;* and *World Development Report 2008.*

World Health Organization (WHO), Avenue Appia 20, 1211 Geneve 27, Switzerland, (Telephone in U.S. (212) 331-9081), www.who.int; *World Health Report 2006.*

BELARUS - POPULATION DENSITY

Central Intelligence Agency, Office of Public Affairs, Washington, DC 20505, (703) 482-0623, Fax: (703) 482-1739, www.cia.gov; *The World Factbook.*

Euromonitor International, Inc., 224 S. Michigan Avenue, Suite 1500, Chicago, IL 60604, (312) 922-1115, Fax: (312) 922-1157, www.euromonitor.com; *The World Economic Factbook 2008.*

Palgrave Macmillan Ltd., Houndmills, Basingstoke, Hampshire, RG21 6XS, England, (Telephone in U.S. (888) 330-8477), (Fax in U.S. (800) 672-2054), www.palgrave.com; *The Statesman's Yearbook 2008.*

Taylor and Francis Group, An Informa Business, 2 Park Square, Milton Park, Abingdon, Oxford OX14 4RN, United Kingdom, (Dial from U.S. (212) 216-7800), (Fax from U.S. (212) 564-7854), www.tandf.co.uk; *The Europa World Year Book.*

UNESCO Institute for Statistics, C.P. 6128 Succursale Centre-Ville, Montreal, Quebec, H3C 3J7 Canada, (Dial from U.S. (514) 343-6880), (Fax from U.S. (514) 343 6882), www.uis.unesco.org; *Statistical Tables.*

United Nations Statistics Division, New York, NY 10017, (800) 253-9646, Fax: (212) 963-4116, http://unstats.un.org; *Statistical Yearbook* and *Trends in Europe and North America: The Statistical Yearbook of the ECE 2005.*

The World Bank, 1818 H Street, NW, Washington, DC 20433, (202) 473-1000, Fax: (202) 477-6391, www.worldbank.org; *Belarus* and *World Development Report 2008.*

BELARUS - POSTAL SERVICE

United Nations Statistics Division, New York, NY 10017, (800) 253-9646, Fax: (212) 963-4116, http://unstats.un.org; *Statistical Yearbook* and *Trends in Europe and North America: The Statistical Yearbook of the ECE 2005.*

BELARUS - POULTRY

See BELARUS - LIVESTOCK

BELARUS - POWER RESOURCES

Academic International Press, PO Box 1111, Gulf Breeze, FL 32562-1111, Fax: (850) 934-0953, www.ai-press.com; *Russia and Eurasia Facts and Figures Annual.*

Euromonitor International, Inc., 224 S. Michigan Avenue, Suite 1500, Chicago, IL 60604, (312) 922-1115, Fax: (312) 922-1157, www.euromonitor.com; *The World Economic Factbook 2008* and *World Marketing Data and Statistics.*

Palgrave Macmillan Ltd., Houndmills, Basingstoke, Hampshire, RG21 6XS, England, (Telephone in U.S. (888) 330-8477), (Fax in U.S. (800) 672-2054), www.palgrave.com; *The Statesman's Yearbook 2008.*

Platts, 2 Penn Plaza, 25th Floor, New York, NY 10121-2298, (212) 904-3070, www.platts.com; *Energy Economist* and *European Power Daily.*

U.S. Department of Energy (DOE), Energy Information Administration (EIA), 1000 Independence Avenue, SW, Washington, DC 20585, (202) 586-8800, www.eia.doe.gov; *International Energy Annual 2004* and *International Energy Outlook 2006.*

United Nations Statistics Division, New York, NY 10017, (800) 253-9646, Fax: (212) 963-4116, http://unstats.un.org; *Energy Statistics Yearbook 2003; Human Development Report 2006; Statistical Yearbook; Trends in Europe and North America: The Statistical Yearbook of the ECE 2005;* and *World Statistics Pocketbook.*

The World Bank, 1818 H Street, NW, Washington, DC 20433, (202) 473-1000, Fax: (202) 477-6391, www.worldbank.org; *Statistical Handbook: States of the Former USSR; The World Bank Atlas 2003-2004;* and *World Development Report 2008.*

BELARUS - PRICES

Euromonitor International, Inc., 224 S. Michigan Avenue, Suite 1500, Chicago, IL 60604, (312) 922-1115, Fax: (312) 922-1157, www.euromonitor.com; *World Marketing Data and Statistics.*

International Labour Office, I.L.O. Publications, 4 route des Morillons, CH-1211 Geneva 22, Switzerland, (Telephone in U.S. (202) 653-7652), (Fax in U.S. (202) 653-7687), www.ilo.org; *Yearbook of Labour Statistics 2006.*

United Nations Food and Agricultural Organization (FAO), Viale delle Terme di Caracalla, 00100 Rome, Italy, (Dial from U.S. (202) 653-2400), (Fax from U.S. (202) 653 5760), www.fao.org; *FAO Production Yearbook 2002.*

The World Bank, 1818 H Street, NW, Washington, DC 20433, (202) 473-1000, Fax: (202) 477-6391, www.worldbank.org; *Belarus* and *Statistical Handbook: States of the Former USSR.*

BELARUS - PROFESSIONS

United Nations Statistics Division, New York, NY 10017, (800) 253-9646, Fax: (212) 963-4116, http://unstats.un.org; *Statistical Yearbook.*

BELARUS - PUBLIC HEALTH

Academic International Press, PO Box 1111, Gulf Breeze, FL 32562-1111, Fax: (850) 934-0953, www.ai-press.com; *Russia and Eurasia Facts and Figures Annual.*

Euromonitor International, Inc., 224 S. Michigan Avenue, Suite 1500, Chicago, IL 60604, (312) 922-1115, Fax: (312) 922-1157, www.euromonitor.com; *World Health Databook 2007/2008* and *World Marketing Data and Statistics.*

Palgrave Macmillan Ltd., Houndmills, Basingstoke, Hampshire, RG21 6XS, England, (Telephone in U.S. (888) 330-8477), (Fax in U.S. (800) 672-2054), www.palgrave.com; *The Statesman's Yearbook 2008.*

UNICEF, 3 United Nations Plaza, New York, NY 10017, (800) 253-9646, Fax: (212) 887-7465, www.unicef.org; *The State of the World's Children 2008.*

United Nations Statistics Division, New York, NY 10017, (800) 253-9646, Fax: (212) 963-4116, http://unstats.un.org; *Human Development Report 2006; Statistical Yearbook;* and *Trends in Europe and North America: The Statistical Yearbook of the ECE 2005.*

The World Bank, 1818 H Street, NW, Washington, DC 20433, (202) 473-1000, Fax: (202) 477-6391, www.worldbank.org; *Belarus* and *World Development Report 2008.*

World Health Organization (WHO), Avenue Appia 20, 1211 Geneve 27, Switzerland, (Telephone in U.S. (212) 331-9081), www.who.int; The WHO Global Atlas of Infectious Diseases and *World Health Report 2006.*

BELARUS - PUBLISHERS AND PUBLISHING

Taylor and Francis Group, An Informa Business, 2 Park Square, Milton Park, Abingdon, Oxford OX14 4RN, United Kingdom, (Dial from U.S. (212) 216-7800), (Fax from U.S. (212) 564-7854), www.tandf.co.uk; *The Europa World Year Book.*

UNESCO Institute for Statistics, C.P. 6128 Succursale Centre-Ville, Montreal, Quebec, H3C 3J7 Canada, (Dial from U.S. (514) 343-6880), (Fax from U.S. (514) 343 6882), www.uis.unesco.org; *Statistical Tables.*

United Nations Statistics Division, New York, NY 10017, (800) 253-9646, Fax: (212) 963-4116, http://unstats.un.org; *Trends in Europe and North America: The Statistical Yearbook of the ECE 2005.*

BELARUS - RADIO - RECEIVERS AND RECEPTION

Palgrave Macmillan Ltd., Houndmills, Basingstoke, Hampshire, RG21 6XS, England, (Telephone in U.S. (888) 330-8477), (Fax in U.S. (800) 672-2054), www.palgrave.com; *The Statesman's Yearbook 2008.*

United Nations Statistics Division, New York, NY 10017, (800) 253-9646, Fax: (212) 963-4116, http://unstats.un.org; *Statistical Yearbook.*

BELARUS - RAILROADS

Palgrave Macmillan Ltd., Houndmills, Basingstoke, Hampshire, RG21 6XS, England, (Telephone in U.S. (888) 330-8477), (Fax in U.S. (800) 672-2054), www.palgrave.com; *The Statesman's Yearbook 2008.*

Taylor and Francis Group, An Informa Business, 2 Park Square, Milton Park, Abingdon, Oxford OX14 4RN, United Kingdom, (Dial from U.S. (212) 216-7800), (Fax from U.S. (212) 564-7854), www.tandf.co.uk; *The Europa World Year Book.*

United Nations Statistics Division, New York, NY 10017, (800) 253-9646, Fax: (212) 963-4116, http://unstats.un.org; *Annual Bulletin of Transport Statistics for Europe and North America 2004; Statistical Yearbook;* and *Trends in Europe and North America: The Statistical Yearbook of the ECE 2005.*

BELARUS - RELIGION

Academic International Press, PO Box 1111, Gulf Breeze, FL 32562-1111, Fax: (850) 934-0953, www.ai-press.com; *Russia and Eurasia Facts and Figures Annual.*

Central Intelligence Agency, Office of Public Affairs, Washington, DC 20505, (703) 482-0623, Fax: (703) 482-1739, www.cia.gov; *The World Factbook.*

Palgrave Macmillan Ltd., Houndmills, Basingstoke, Hampshire, RG21 6XS, England, (Telephone in U.S. (888) 330-8477), (Fax in U.S. (800) 672-2054), www.palgrave.com; *The Statesman's Yearbook 2008.*

BELARUS - RENT CHARGES

International Labour Office, I.L.O. Publications, 4 route des Morillons, CH-1211 Geneva 22, Switzerland, (Telephone in U.S. (202) 653-7652), (Fax in U.S. (202) 653-7687), www.ilo.org; *Yearbook of Labour Statistics 2006.*

BELARUS - RETAIL TRADE

Banque de France, 48 rue Croix des Petits champs, 75001 Paris, France, www.banque-france.fr/home.htm; *Monthly Business Survey Overview.*

Euromonitor International, Inc., 224 S. Michigan Avenue, Suite 1500, Chicago, IL 60604, (312) 922-1115, Fax: (312) 922-1157, www.euromonitor.com; *World Marketing Data and Statistics.*

United Nations Statistics Division, New York, NY 10017, (800) 253-9646, Fax: (212) 963-4116, http://unstats.un.org; *Statistical Yearbook.*

BELARUS - ROADS

Central Intelligence Agency, Office of Public Affairs, Washington, DC 20505, (703) 482-0623, Fax: (703) 482-1739, www.cia.gov; *The World Factbook.*

Palgrave Macmillan Ltd., Houndmills, Basingstoke, Hampshire, RG21 6XS, England, (Telephone in U.S. (888) 330-8477), (Fax in U.S. (800) 672-2054), www.palgrave.com; *The Statesman's Yearbook 2008.*

United Nations Statistics Division, New York, NY 10017, (800) 253-9646, Fax: (212) 963-4116, http://unstats.un.org; *Annual Bulletin of Transport Statistics for Europe and North America 2004* and *Trends in Europe and North America: The Statistical Yearbook of the ECE 2005.*

BELARUS - RUBBER INDUSTRY AND TRADE

International Rubber Study Group (IRSG), 1st Floor, Heron House, 109/115 Wembley Hill Road, Wembley, Middlesex HA9 8DA, United Kingdom, www.rubberstudy.com; *Rubber Statistical Bulletin; Summary of World Rubber Statistics 2005; World Rubber Statistics Handbook (Volume 6, 1975-2001);* and *World Rubber Statistics Historic Handbook.*

United Nations Statistics Division, New York, NY 10017, (800) 253-9646, Fax: (212) 963-4116, http://unstats.un.org; *Statistical Yearbook.*

BELARUS - SHEEP

See BELARUS - LIVESTOCK

BELARUS - SHIPPING

Palgrave Macmillan Ltd., Houndmills, Basingstoke, Hampshire, RG21 6XS, England, (Telephone in U.S. (888) 330-8477), (Fax in U.S. (800) 672-2054), www.palgrave.com; *The Statesman's Yearbook 2008.*

United Nations Statistics Division, New York, NY 10017, (800) 253-9646, Fax: (212) 963-4116, http://unstats.un.org; *Annual Bulletin of Transport Statistics for Europe and North America 2004* and *Statistical Yearbook.*

BELARUS - SOCIAL ECOLOGY

United Nations Statistics Division, New York, NY 10017, (800) 253-9646, Fax: (212) 963-4116, http://unstats.un.org; *World Statistics Pocketbook.*

BELARUS - SOCIAL SECURITY

United Nations Statistics Division, New York, NY 10017, (800) 253-9646, Fax: (212) 963-4116, http://unstats.un.org; *National Accounts Statistics: Compendium of Income Distribution Statistics.*

BELARUS - STEEL PRODUCTION

See BELARUS - MINERAL INDUSTRIES

BELARUS - SUGAR PRODUCTION

See BELARUS - CROPS

BELARUS - SULPHUR PRODUCTION

See BELARUS - MINERAL INDUSTRIES

BELARUS - TAXATION

Taylor and Francis Group, An Informa Business, 2 Park Square, Milton Park, Abingdon, Oxford OX14 4RN, United Kingdom, (Dial from U.S. (212) 216-7800), (Fax from U.S. (212) 564-7854), www.tandf.co.uk; *The Europa World Year Book.*

BELARUS - TELEPHONE

United Nations Statistics Division, New York, NY 10017, (800) 253-9646, Fax: (212) 963-4116, http://unstats.un.org; *Statistical Yearbook; Trends in Europe and North America: The Statistical Yearbook of the ECE 2005;* and *World Statistics Pocketbook.*

BELARUS - TELEVISION - RECEIVERS AND RECEPTION

United Nations Statistics Division, New York, NY 10017, (800) 253-9646, Fax: (212) 963-4116, http://unstats.un.org; *Statistical Yearbook.*

BELARUS - TEXTILE INDUSTRY

United Nations Statistics Division, New York, NY 10017, (800) 253-9646, Fax: (212) 963-4116, http://unstats.un.org; *2004 Industrial Commodity Statistics Yearbook* and *Statistical Yearbook.*

BELARUS - THEATER

UNESCO Institute for Statistics, C.P. 6128 Succursale Centre-Ville, Montreal, Quebec, H3C 3J7

Canada, (Dial from U.S. (514) 343-6880), (Fax from U.S. (514) 343 6882), www.uis.unesco.org; *Statistical Tables.*

BELARUS - TIRE INDUSTRY

United Nations Statistics Division, New York, NY 10017, (800) 253-9646, Fax: (212) 963-4116, http://unstats.un.org; *Statistical Yearbook.*

BELARUS - TOBACCO INDUSTRY

Foreign Agricultural Service (FAS), U.S. Department of Agriculture (USDA), 1400 Independence Avenue, SW, Washington, DC 20250, (202) 720-3935, www.fas.usda.gov; *Tobacco: World Markets and Trade.*

United Nations Statistics Division, New York, NY 10017, (800) 253-9646, Fax: (212) 963-4116, http://unstats.un.org; *Statistical Yearbook.*

BELARUS - TOURISM

Euromonitor International, Inc., 224 S. Michigan Avenue, Suite 1500, Chicago, IL 60604, (312) 922-1115, Fax: (312) 922-1157, www.euromonitor.com; *The World Economic Factbook 2008* and *World Marketing Data and Statistics.*

United Nations Statistics Division, New York, NY 10017, (800) 253-9646, Fax: (212) 963-4116, http://unstats.un.org; *Statistical Yearbook* and *Trends in Europe and North America: The Statistical Yearbook of the ECE 2005.*

The World Bank, 1818 H Street, NW, Washington, DC 20433, (202) 473-1000, Fax: (202) 477-6391, www.worldbank.org; *Belarus.*

BELARUS - TRANSPORTATION

Academic International Press, PO Box 1111, Gulf Breeze, FL 32562-1111, Fax: (850) 934-0953, www.ai-press.com; *Russia and Eurasia Facts and Figures Annual.*

Central Intelligence Agency, Office of Public Affairs, Washington, DC 20505, (703) 482-0623, Fax: (703) 482-1739, www.cia.gov; *The World Factbook.*

Euromonitor International, Inc., 224 S. Michigan Avenue, Suite 1500, Chicago, IL 60604, (312) 922-1115, Fax: (312) 922-1157, www.euromonitor.com; *World Marketing Data and Statistics.*

Palgrave Macmillan Ltd., Houndmills, Basingstoke, Hampshire, RG21 6XS, England, (Telephone in U.S. (888) 330-8477), (Fax in U.S. (800) 672-2054), www.palgrave.com; *The Statesman's Yearbook 2008.*

Taylor and Francis Group, An Informa Business, 2 Park Square, Milton Park, Abingdon, Oxford OX14 4RN, United Kingdom, (Dial from U.S. (212) 216-7800), (Fax from U.S. (212) 564-7854), www.tandf.co.uk; *The Europa World Year Book.*

United Nations Statistics Division, New York, NY 10017, (800) 253-9646, Fax: (212) 963-4116, http://unstats.un.org; *Annual Bulletin of Transport Statistics for Europe and North America 2004; Human Development Report 2006;* and *Trends in Europe and North America: The Statistical Yearbook of the ECE 2005.*

The World Bank, 1818 H Street, NW, Washington, DC 20433, (202) 473-1000, Fax: (202) 477-6391, www.worldbank.org; *Belarus.*

BELARUS - UNEMPLOYMENT

Central Intelligence Agency, Office of Public Affairs, Washington, DC 20505, (703) 482-0623, Fax: (703) 482-1739, www.cia.gov; *The World Factbook.*

International Labour Office, I.L.O. Publications, 4 route des Morillons, CH-1211 Geneva 22, Switzerland, (Telephone in U.S. (202) 653-7652), (Fax in U.S. (202) 653-7687), www.ilo.org; *Yearbook of Labour Statistics 2006.*

Palgrave Macmillan Ltd., Houndmills, Basingstoke, Hampshire, RG21 6XS, England, (Telephone in U.S. (888) 330-8477), (Fax in U.S. (800) 672-2054), www.palgrave.com; *The Statesman's Yearbook 2008.*

United Nations Statistics Division, New York, NY 10017, (800) 253-9646, Fax: (212) 963-4116, http://unstats.un.org; *Statistical Yearbook* and *Trends in Europe and North America: The Statistical Yearbook of the ECE 2005.*

The World Bank, 1818 H Street, NW, Washington, DC 20433, (202) 473-1000, Fax: (202) 477-6391, www.worldbank.org; *Belarus.*

BELARUS - VITAL STATISTICS

Ministry of Statistics and Analysis of the Republic of Belarus, 12 Partizansky Avenue, Minsk 220070, Belarus, www.belstat.gov.by; *Belarus in Figures, 2008; Regions of the Republic of Belarus, 2008; Socio-Economic Conditions of Households in the Republic of Belarus; Statistical Bulletin;* and *Statistical Yearbook of the Republic of Belarus, 2008.*

Palgrave Macmillan Ltd., Houndmills, Basingstoke, Hampshire, RG21 6XS, England, (Telephone in U.S. (888) 330-8477), (Fax in U.S. (800) 672-2054), www.palgrave.com; *The Statesman's Yearbook 2008.*

United Nations Statistics Division, New York, NY 10017, (800) 253-9646, Fax: (212) 963-4116, http://unstats.un.org; *Statistical Yearbook.*

World Health Organization (WHO), Avenue Appia 20, 1211 Geneve 27, Switzerland, (Telephone in U.S. (212) 331-9081), www.who.int; *World Health Report 2006.*

BELARUS - WAGES

International Labour Office, I.L.O. Publications, 4 route des Morillons, CH-1211 Geneva 22, Switzerland, (Telephone in U.S. (202) 653-7652), (Fax in U.S. (202) 653-7687), www.ilo.org; *Yearbook of Labour Statistics 2006.*

United Nations Statistics Division, New York, NY 10017, (800) 253-9646, Fax: (212) 963-4116, http://unstats.un.org; *Statistical Yearbook.*

The World Bank, 1818 H Street, NW, Washington, DC 20433, (202) 473-1000, Fax: (202) 477-6391, www.worldbank.org; *Belarus* and *Statistical Handbook: States of the Former USSR.*

BELARUS - WATERWAYS

United Nations Statistics Division, New York, NY 10017, (800) 253-9646, Fax: (212) 963-4116, http://unstats.un.org; *Annual Bulletin of Transport Statistics for Europe and North America 2004.*

BELARUS - WELFARE STATE

Palgrave Macmillan Ltd., Houndmills, Basingstoke, Hampshire, RG21 6XS, England, (Telephone in U.S. (888) 330-8477), (Fax in U.S. (800) 672-2054), www.palgrave.com; *The Statesman's Yearbook 2008.*

BELARUS - WHEAT PRODUCTION

See BELARUS - CROPS

BELARUS - WHOLESALE TRADE

United Nations Statistics Division, New York, NY 10017, (800) 253-9646, Fax: (212) 963-4116, http://unstats.un.org; *Statistical Yearbook.*

BELARUS - WINE PRODUCTION

See BELARUS - BEVERAGE INDUSTRY

BELARUS - WOOL PRODUCTION

See BELARUS - TEXTILE INDUSTRY

BELARUS - YARN PRODUCTION

See BELARUS - TEXTILE INDUSTRY

BELGIUM - NATIONAL STATISTICAL OFFICE

Statistics Belgium, Rue du Progres, 50 - 1210 Brussels, Belgium, www.statbel.fgov.be; National Data Center.

BELGIUM - PRIMARY STATISTICS SOURCES

Eurostat, Batiment Jean Monnet, Rue Alcide de Gasperi, L-2920 Luxembourg, http://epp.eurostat.ec.europa.eu; *Pocketbook on Candidate and Potential Candidate Countries.*

Statistics Belgium, Rue du Progres, 50 - 1210 Brussels, Belgium, www.statbel.fgov.be; *Bulletin de Statistique.*

BELGIUM - DATABASES

Fonds Quetelet Library, Federal Public Service Economy, City Atrium - 2nd floor, Rue du Progres, 50, 1210 Brussels, Belgium, http://economie.fgov.be; *Database: Belgian Yearbook Corporate Finance 2004.*

BELGIUM - ABORTION

European Union, Delegation of the European Commission to the United States, 2300 M Street, NW, Washington, DC 20037, (202) 862-9500, Fax: (202) 429-1766, www.eurunion.org; *First Demographic Estimates for 2006.*

United Nations Statistics Division, New York, NY 10017, (800) 253-9646, Fax: (212) 963-4116, http://unstats.un.org; *Trends in Europe and North America: The Statistical Yearbook of the ECE 2005.*

BELGIUM - AGRICULTURAL MACHINERY

European Union, Delegation of the European Commission to the United States, 2300 M Street, NW, Washington, DC 20037, (202) 862-9500, Fax: (202) 429-1766, www.eurunion.org; *Statistical Overview of Transport in the European Union (Data 1970-2001).*

BELGIUM - AGRICULTURE

Economist Intelligence Unit, 111 West 57th Street, New York, NY 10019, (212) 554-0600, Fax: (212) 586-1181, www.eiu.com; *Belgium Country Report.*

Euromonitor International, Inc., 224 S. Michigan Avenue, Suite 1500, Chicago, IL 60604, (312) 922-1115, Fax: (312) 922-1157, www.euromonitor.com; *World Marketing Data and Statistics.*

European Union, Delegation of the European Commission to the United States, 2300 M Street, NW, Washington, DC 20037, (202) 862-9500, Fax: (202) 429-1766, www.eurunion.org; *Agricultural Statistics: Data 1995-2005; European Union Labour Force Survey; Eurostatistics: Data for Short-Term Economic Analysis (2007 edition);* and *Regions - Statistical Yearbook 2006.*

Eurostat, Batiment Jean Monnet, Rue Alcide de Gasperi, L-2920 Luxembourg, http://epp.eurostat.ec.europa.eu; *EU Agricultural Prices in 2007* and *Eurostat Yearbook 2006-2007.*

M.E. Sharpe, 80 Business Park Drive, Armonk, NY 10504, (800) 541-6563, Fax: (914) 273-2106, www.mesharpe.com; *The Illustrated Book of World Rankings.*

Organisation for Economic Cooperation and Development (OECD), 2 rue Andre Pascal, F-75775 Paris Cedex 16, France, (Telephone in U.S. (202) 785-6323), (Fax in U.S. (202) 785-0350), www.oecd.org; *Indicators of Industrial Activity; 2005 OECD Agricultural Outlook Tables, 1970-2014; OECD Agricultural Outlook: 2007-2016; OECD Economic Survey - Belgium 2007;* and STructural ANalysis (STAN) database.

Palgrave Macmillan Ltd., Houndmills, Basingstoke, Hampshire, RG21 6XS, England, (Telephone in U.S. (888) 330-8477), (Fax in U.S. (800) 672-2054), www.palgrave.com; *The Statesman's Yearbook 2008.*

Taylor and Francis Group, An Informa Business, 2 Park Square, Milton Park, Abingdon, Oxford OX14 4RN, United Kingdom, (Dial from U.S. (212) 216-7800), (Fax from U.S. (212) 564-7854), www.tandf.co.uk; *The Europa World Year Book.*

United Nations Conference on Trade and Development (UNCTAD), DC2-1120, United Nations, New York, NY 10017, (212) 963-0027, www.unctad.org; *UNCTAD Commodity Yearbook.*

United Nations Food and Agricultural Organization (FAO), Viale delle Terme di Caracalla, 00100 Rome, Italy, (Dial from U.S. (202) 653-2400), (Fax from U.S. (202) 653 5760), www.fao.org; AQUASTAT;

FAO Production Yearbook 2002; FAO Trade Yearbook; and *The State of Food and Agriculture (SOFA) 2006.*

United Nations Statistics Division, New York, NY 10017, (800) 253-9646, Fax: (212) 963-4116, http://unstats.un.org; *Statistical Yearbook.*

The World Bank, 1818 H Street, NW, Washington, DC 20433, (202) 473-1000, Fax: (202) 477-6391, www.worldbank.org; *Belgium* and *World Development Indicators (WDI) 2008.*

BELGIUM - AIRLINES

European Union, Delegation of the European Commission to the United States, 2300 M Street, NW, Washington, DC 20037, (202) 862-9500, Fax: (202) 429-1766, www.eurunion.org; *Regions - Statistical Yearbook 2006* and *Statistical Overview of Transport in the European Union (Data 1970-2001).*

Eurostat, Batiment Jean Monnet, Rue Alcide de Gasperi, L-2920 Luxembourg, http://epp.eurostat.ec.europa.eu; *Eurostat Yearbook 2006-2007* and *Regional Passenger and Freight Air Transport in Europe in 2006.*

International Civil Aviation Organization (ICAO), External Relations and Public Information Office (EPO), 999 University Street, Montreal, Quebec H3C 5H7, Canada, (Dial from U.S. (514) 954-8219), (Fax from U.S. (514) 954-6077), www.icao.int; *Civil Aviation Statistics of the World.*

M.E. Sharpe, 80 Business Park Drive, Armonk, NY 10504, (800) 541-6563, Fax: (914) 273-2106, www.mesharpe.com; *The Illustrated Book of World Rankings.*

Organisation for Economic Cooperation and Development (OECD), 2 rue Andre Pascal, F-75775 Paris Cedex 16, France, (Telephone in U.S. (202) 785-6323), (Fax in U.S. (202) 785-0350), www.oecd.org; *Household, Tourism, Travel: Trends, Environmental Impacts and Policy Responses.*

Palgrave Macmillan Ltd., Houndmills, Basingstoke, Hampshire, RG21 6XS, England, (Telephone in U.S. (888) 330-8477), (Fax in U.S. (800) 672-2054), www.palgrave.com; *The Statesman's Yearbook 2008.*

Taylor and Francis Group, An Informa Business, 2 Park Square, Milton Park, Abingdon, Oxford OX14 4RN, United Kingdom, (Dial from U.S. (212) 216-7800), (Fax from U.S. (212) 564-7854), www.tandf.co.uk; *The Europa World Year Book.*

United Nations Statistics Division, New York, NY 10017, (800) 253-9646, Fax: (212) 963-4116, http://unstats.un.org; *Statistical Yearbook.*

BELGIUM - AIRPORTS

Central Intelligence Agency, Office of Public Affairs, Washington, DC 20505, (703) 482-0623, Fax: (703) 482-1739, www.cia.gov; *The World Factbook.*

BELGIUM - ALMOND PRODUCTION

See BELGIUM - CROPS

BELGIUM - ALUMINUM PRODUCTION

See BELGIUM - MINERAL INDUSTRIES

BELGIUM - ANIMAL FEEDING

Organisation for Economic Cooperation and Development (OECD), 2 rue Andre Pascal, F-75775 Paris Cedex 16, France, (Telephone in U.S. (202) 785-6323), (Fax in U.S. (202) 785-0350), www.oecd.org; *International Trade by Commodity Statistics (ITCS).*

United Nations Statistics Division, New York, NY 10017, (800) 253-9646, Fax: (212) 963-4116, http://unstats.un.org; *Statistical Yearbook.*

BELGIUM - APPLE PRODUCTION

See BELGIUM - CROPS

BELGIUM - ARMED FORCES

Central Intelligence Agency, Office of Public Affairs, Washington, DC 20505, (703) 482-0623, Fax: (703) 482-1739, www.cia.gov; *The World Factbook.*

Euromonitor International, Inc., 224 S. Michigan Avenue, Suite 1500, Chicago, IL 60604, (312) 922-1115, Fax: (312) 922-1157, www.euromonitor.com; *World Marketing Data and Statistics.*

European Union, Delegation of the European Commission to the United States, 2300 M Street, NW, Washington, DC 20037, (202) 862-9500, Fax: (202) 429-1766, www.eurunion.org; *RD Expenditure in Europe (2006 edition).*

International Institute for Strategic Studies (IISS), Arundel House, 13-15 Arundel Street, Temple Place, London WC2R 3DX, England, www.iiss.org; *The Military Balance 2007.*

International Monetary Fund (IMF), 700 Nineteenth Street, NW, Washington, DC 20431, (202) 623-7000, Fax: (202) 623-4661, www.imf.org; *Government Finance Statistics Yearbook (2008 Edition).*

Palgrave Macmillan Ltd., Houndmills, Basingstoke, Hampshire, RG21 6XS, England, (Telephone in U.S. (888) 330-8477), (Fax in U.S. (800) 672-2054), www.palgrave.com; *The Statesman's Yearbook 2008.*

U.S. Department of State (DOS), 2201 C Street NW, Washington, DC 20520, (202) 647-4000, www.state.gov; *World Military Expenditures and Arms Transfers (WMEAT).*

United Nations Statistics Division, New York, NY 10017, (800) 253-9646, Fax: (212) 963-4116, http://unstats.un.org; *Human Development Report 2006.*

BELGIUM - AUTOMOBILE INDUSTRY AND TRADE

European Union, Delegation of the European Commission to the United States, 2300 M Street, NW, Washington, DC 20037, (202) 862-9500, Fax: (202) 429-1766, www.eurunion.org; *Eurostatistics: Data for Short-Term Economic Analysis (2007 edition).*

Eurostat, Batiment Jean Monnet, Rue Alcide de Gasperi, L-2920 Luxembourg, http://epp.eurostat.ec.europa.eu; *Eurostat Yearbook 2006-2007.*

Organisation for Economic Cooperation and Development (OECD), 2 rue Andre Pascal, F-75775 Paris Cedex 16, France, (Telephone in U.S. (202) 785-6323), (Fax in U.S. (202) 785-0350), www.oecd.org; *Indicators of Industrial Activity* and *International Trade by Commodity Statistics (ITCS).*

United Nations Statistics Division, New York, NY 10017, (800) 253-9646, Fax: (212) 963-4116, http://unstats.un.org; *Statistical Yearbook.*

BELGIUM - BALANCE OF PAYMENTS

European Union, Delegation of the European Commission to the United States, 2300 M Street, NW, Washington, DC 20037, (202) 862-9500, Fax: (202) 429-1766, www.eurunion.org; *Eurostatistics: Data for Short-Term Economic Analysis (2007 edition).*

Eurostat, Batiment Jean Monnet, Rue Alcide de Gasperi, L-2920 Luxembourg, http://epp.eurostat.ec.europa.eu; *Eurostat Yearbook 2006-2007.*

International Monetary Fund (IMF), 700 Nineteenth Street, NW, Washington, DC 20431, (202) 623-7000, Fax: (202) 623-4661, www.imf.org; *Balance of Payments Statistics Newsletter; Balance of Payments Statistics Yearbook 2007;* and *International Financial Statistics Yearbook 2007.*

Organisation for Economic Cooperation and Development (OECD), 2 rue Andre Pascal, F-75775 Paris Cedex 16, France, (Telephone in U.S. (202) 785-6323), (Fax in U.S. (202) 785-0350), www.oecd.org; *Geographical Distribution of Financial Flows to Aid Recipients 2002-2006; OECD Economic Outlook 2008;* and *OECD Economic Survey - Belgium 2007.*

Platts, 2 Penn Plaza, 25th Floor, New York, NY 10121-2298, (212) 904-3070, www.platts.com; *Energy Economist.*

Taylor and Francis Group, An Informa Business, 2 Park Square, Milton Park, Abingdon, Oxford OX14 4RN, United Kingdom, (Dial from U.S. (212) 216-7800), (Fax from U.S. (212) 564-7854), www.tandf.co.uk; *The Europa World Year Book.*

United Nations Conference on Trade and Development (UNCTAD), DC2-1120, United Nations, New York, NY 10017, (212) 963-0027, www.unctad.org; *Handbook of Statistics 2005.*

United Nations Statistics Division, New York, NY 10017, (800) 253-9646, Fax: (212) 963-4116, http://unstats.un.org; *Energy Statistics Yearbook 2003.*

The World Bank, 1818 H Street, NW, Washington, DC 20433, (202) 473-1000, Fax: (202) 477-6391, www.worldbank.org; *Belgium; World Development Indicators (WDI) 2008;* and *World Development Report 2008.*

BELGIUM - BANANAS

See BELGIUM - CROPS

BELGIUM - BANKS AND BANKING

Euromonitor International, Inc., 224 S. Michigan Avenue, Suite 1500, Chicago, IL 60604, (312) 922-1115, Fax: (312) 922-1157, www.euromonitor.com; *World Marketing Data and Statistics.*

European Union, Delegation of the European Commission to the United States, 2300 M Street, NW, Washington, DC 20037, (202) 862-9500, Fax: (202) 429-1766, www.eurunion.org; *The EU Economy, 2007 Review: Moving Europe's Productivity Frontier* and *Eurostatistics: Data for Short-Term Economic Analysis (2007 edition).*

Eurostat, Batiment Jean Monnet, Rue Alcide de Gasperi, L-2920 Luxembourg, http://epp.eurostat.ec.europa.eu; *Eurostat Yearbook 2006-2007.*

International Monetary Fund (IMF), 700 Nineteenth Street, NW, Washington, DC 20431, (202) 623-7000, Fax: (202) 623-4661, www.imf.org; *Government Finance Statistics Yearbook (2008 Edition)* and *International Financial Statistics Yearbook 2007.*

M.E. Sharpe, 80 Business Park Drive, Armonk, NY 10504, (800) 541-6563, Fax: (914) 273-2106, www.mesharpe.com; *The Illustrated Book of World Rankings.*

Organisation for Economic Cooperation and Development (OECD), 2 rue Andre Pascal, F-75775 Paris Cedex 16, France, (Telephone in U.S. (202) 785-6323), (Fax in U.S. (202) 785-0350), www.oecd.org; *Financial Market Trends: OECD Periodical; OECD Economic Outlook 2008;* and *OECD Economic Survey - Belgium 2007.*

Palgrave Macmillan Ltd., Houndmills, Basingstoke, Hampshire, RG21 6XS, England, (Telephone in U.S. (888) 330-8477), (Fax in U.S. (800) 672-2054), www.palgrave.com; *The Statesman's Yearbook 2008.*

Taylor and Francis Group, An Informa Business, 2 Park Square, Milton Park, Abingdon, Oxford OX14 4RN, United Kingdom, (Dial from U.S. (212) 216-7800), (Fax from U.S. (212) 564-7854), www.tandf.co.uk; *The Europa World Year Book.*

United Nations Statistics Division, New York, NY 10017, (800) 253-9646, Fax: (212) 963-4116, http://unstats.un.org; *Statistical Yearbook.*

BELGIUM - BARLEY PRODUCTION

See BELGIUM - CROPS

BELGIUM - BEVERAGE INDUSTRY

Eurostat, Batiment Jean Monnet, Rue Alcide de Gasperi, L-2920 Luxembourg, http://epp.eurostat.ec.europa.eu; *Eurostat Yearbook 2006-2007.*

M.E. Sharpe, 80 Business Park Drive, Armonk, NY 10504, (800) 541-6563, Fax: (914) 273-2106, www.mesharpe.com; *The Illustrated Book of World Rankings.*

Organisation for Economic Cooperation and Development (OECD), 2 rue Andre Pascal, F-75775 Paris Cedex 16, France, (Telephone in U.S. (202) 785-6323), (Fax in U.S. (202) 785-0350), www.oecd.org; *Indicators of Industrial Activity.*

United Nations Statistics Division, New York, NY 10017, (800) 253-9646, Fax: (212) 963-4116, http://unstats.un.org; *Statistical Yearbook.*

BELGIUM - BONDS

Eurostat, Batiment Jean Monnet, Rue Alcide de Gasperi, L-2920 Luxembourg, http://epp.eurostat.ec.europa.eu; *Eurostat Yearbook 2006-2007.*

International Monetary Fund (IMF), 700 Nineteenth Street, NW, Washington, DC 20431, (202) 623-7000, Fax: (202) 623-4661, www.imf.org; *Government Finance Statistics Yearbook (2008 Edition).*

Organisation for Economic Cooperation and Development (OECD), 2 rue Andre Pascal, F-75775 Paris Cedex 16, France, (Telephone in U.S. (202) 785-6323), (Fax in U.S. (202) 785-0350), www.oecd.org; *Financial Market Trends: OECD Periodical.*

United Nations Statistics Division, New York, NY 10017, (800) 253-9646, Fax: (212) 963-4116, http://unstats.un.org; *Statistical Yearbook.*

BELGIUM - BROADCASTING

Central Intelligence Agency, Office of Public Affairs, Washington, DC 20505, (703) 482-0623, Fax: (703) 482-1739, www.cia.gov; *The World Factbook.*

Euromonitor International, Inc., 224 S. Michigan Avenue, Suite 1500, Chicago, IL 60604, (312) 922-1115, Fax: (312) 922-1157, www.euromonitor.com; *World Marketing Data and Statistics.*

Eurostat, Batiment Jean Monnet, Rue Alcide de Gasperi, L-2920 Luxembourg, http://epp.eurostat.ec.europa.eu; *Eurostat Yearbook 2006-2007.*

M.E. Sharpe, 80 Business Park Drive, Armonk, NY 10504, (800) 541-6563, Fax: (914) 273-2106, www.mesharpe.com; *The Illustrated Book of World Rankings.*

Palgrave Macmillan Ltd., Houndmills, Basingstoke, Hampshire, RG21 6XS, England, (Telephone in U.S. (888) 330-8477), (Fax in U.S. (800) 672-2054), www.palgrave.com; *The Statesman's Yearbook 2008.*

UNESCO Institute for Statistics, C.P. 6128 Succursale Centre-Ville, Montreal, Quebec, H3C 3J7 Canada, (Dial from U.S. (514) 343-6880), (Fax from U.S. (514) 343 6882), www.uis.unesco.org; *Statistical Tables.*

United Nations Statistics Division, New York, NY 10017, (800) 253-9646, Fax: (212) 963-4116, http://unstats.un.org; *Trends in Europe and North America: The Statistical Yearbook of the ECE 2005.*

WRTH Publications Limited, PO Box 290, Oxford OX2 7FT, UK, www.wrth.com; *World Radio TV Handbook 2007.*

BELGIUM - BUDGET

Central Intelligence Agency, Office of Public Affairs, Washington, DC 20505, (703) 482-0623, Fax: (703) 482-1739, www.cia.gov; *The World Factbook.*

Eurostat, Batiment Jean Monnet, Rue Alcide de Gasperi, L-2920 Luxembourg, http://epp.eurostat.ec.europa.eu; *Government Budgets.*

BELGIUM - BUSINESS

Eurostat, Batiment Jean Monnet, Rue Alcide de Gasperi, L-2920 Luxembourg, http://epp.eurostat.ec.europa.eu; *Eurostat Yearbook 2006-2007.*

Fonds Quetelet Library, Federal Public Service Economy, City Atrium - 2nd floor, Rue du Progres, 50, 1210 Brussels, Belgium, http://economie.fgov.be; *Database: Belgian Yearbook Corporate Finance 2004.*

Organisation for Economic Cooperation and Development (OECD), 2 rue Andre Pascal, F-75775 Paris Cedex 16, France, (Telephone in U.S. (202) 785-6323), (Fax in U.S. (202) 785-0350), www.oecd.org; *OECD Main Economic Indicators (MEI).*

BELGIUM - CADMIUM PRODUCTION

See BELGIUM - MINERAL INDUSTRIES

BELGIUM - CAPITAL INVESTMENTS

Organisation for Economic Cooperation and Development (OECD), 2 rue Andre Pascal, F-75775 Paris Cedex 16, France, (Telephone in U.S. (202) 785-6323), (Fax in U.S. (202) 785-0350), www.oecd.org; *Financial Market Trends: OECD Periodical* and *OECD Economic Outlook 2008.*

BELGIUM - CAPITAL LEVY

International Monetary Fund (IMF), 700 Nineteenth Street, NW, Washington, DC 20431, (202) 623-7000, Fax: (202) 623-4661, www.imf.org; *Government Finance Statistics Yearbook (2008 Edition).*

Organisation for Economic Cooperation and Development (OECD), 2 rue Andre Pascal, F-75775 Paris Cedex 16, France, (Telephone in U.S. (202) 785-6323), (Fax in U.S. (202) 785-0350), www.oecd.org; *Financial Market Trends: OECD Periodical* and *OECD Economic Outlook 2008.*

BELGIUM - CATTLE

See BELGIUM - LIVESTOCK

BELGIUM - CHESTNUT INDUSTRY

Eurostat, Batiment Jean Monnet, Rue Alcide de Gasperi, L-2920 Luxembourg, http://epp.eurostat.ec.europa.eu; *Eurostat Yearbook 2006-2007.*

BELGIUM - CHICKENS

See BELGIUM - LIVESTOCK

BELGIUM - CHILDBIRTH - STATISTICS

Central Intelligence Agency, Office of Public Affairs, Washington, DC 20505, (703) 482-0623, Fax: (703) 482-1739, www.cia.gov; *The World Factbook.*

Euromonitor International, Inc., 224 S. Michigan Avenue, Suite 1500, Chicago, IL 60604, (312) 922-1115, Fax: (312) 922-1157, www.euromonitor.com; *The World Economic Factbook 2008.*

European Union, Delegation of the European Commission to the United States, 2300 M Street, NW, Washington, DC 20037, (202) 862-9500, Fax: (202) 429-1766, www.eurunion.org; *First Demographic Estimates for 2006.*

Eurostat, Batiment Jean Monnet, Rue Alcide de Gasperi, L-2920 Luxembourg, http://epp.eurostat.ec.europa.eu; *Eurostat Yearbook 2006-2007.*

M.E. Sharpe, 80 Business Park Drive, Armonk, NY 10504, (800) 541-6563, Fax: (914) 273-2106, www.mesharpe.com; *The Illustrated Book of World Rankings.*

Palgrave Macmillan Ltd., Houndmills, Basingstoke, Hampshire, RG21 6XS, England, (Telephone in U.S. (888) 330-8477), (Fax in U.S. (800) 672-2054), www.palgrave.com; *The Statesman's Yearbook 2008.*

Taylor and Francis Group, An Informa Business, 2 Park Square, Milton Park, Abingdon, Oxford OX14 4RN, United Kingdom, (Dial from U.S. (212) 216-7800), (Fax from U.S. (212) 564-7854), www.tandf.co.uk; *The Europa World Year Book.*

United Nations Statistics Division, New York, NY 10017, (800) 253-9646, Fax: (212) 963-4116, http://unstats.un.org; *Demographic Yearbook* and *Statistical Yearbook.*

The World Bank, 1818 H Street, NW, Washington, DC 20433, (202) 473-1000, Fax: (202) 477-6391, www.worldbank.org; *World Development Indicators (WDI) 2008.*

World Health Organization (WHO), Avenue Appia 20, 1211 Geneve 27, Switzerland, (Telephone in U.S. (212) 331-9081), www.who.int; *World Health Report 2006.*

BELGIUM - CLIMATE

M.E. Sharpe, 80 Business Park Drive, Armonk, NY 10504, (800) 541-6563, Fax: (914) 273-2106, www.mesharpe.com; *The Illustrated Book of World Rankings.*

Palgrave Macmillan Ltd., Houndmills, Basingstoke, Hampshire, RG21 6XS, England, (Telephone in U.S. (888) 330-8477), (Fax in U.S. (800) 672-2054), www.palgrave.com; *The Statesman's Yearbook 2008.*

BELGIUM - CLOTHING EXPORTS AND IMPORTS

See BELGIUM - TEXTILE INDUSTRY

BELGIUM - COAL PRODUCTION

See BELGIUM - MINERAL INDUSTRIES

BELGIUM - COBALT PRODUCTION

See BELGIUM - MINERAL INDUSTRIES

BELGIUM - COCOA PRODUCTION

See BELGIUM - CROPS

BELGIUM - COFFEE

See BELGIUM - CROPS

BELGIUM - COMMERCE

Palgrave Macmillan Ltd., Houndmills, Basingstoke, Hampshire, RG21 6XS, England, (Telephone in U.S. (888) 330-8477), (Fax in U.S. (800) 672-2054), www.palgrave.com; *The Statesman's Yearbook 2008.*

BELGIUM - COMMODITY EXCHANGES

Commodity Research Bureau, 330 South Wells Street, Suite 612, Chicago, IL 60606-7110, (800) 621-5271, Fax: (312) 939-4135, www.crbtrader.com; *2006 CRB Commodity Yearbook and CD.*

International Lead and Zinc Study Group (ILZSG), Rua Almirante Barroso 38, 5th Floor, Lisbon 1000 - 013, Portugal, www.ilzsg.org; Interactive Statistical Database.

International Monetary Fund (IMF), 700 Nineteenth Street, NW, Washington, DC 20431, (202) 623-7000, Fax: (202) 623-4661, www.imf.org; *IMF Primary Commodity Prices.*

United Nations Food and Agricultural Organization (FAO), Viale delle Terme di Caracalla, 00100 Rome, Italy, (Dial from U.S. (202) 653-2400), (Fax from U.S. (202) 653 5760), www.fao.org; *The State of Food and Agriculture (SOFA) 2006.*

United Nations Statistics Division, New York, NY 10017, (800) 253-9646, Fax: (212) 963-4116, http://unstats.un.org; *Statistical Yearbook.*

World Bureau of Metal Statistics (WBMS), 27a High Street, Ware, Hertfordshire, SG12 9BA, United Kingdom, www.world-bureau.com; *Annual Stainless Steel Statistics; World Flow Charts; World Metal Statistics; World Nickel Statistics;* and *World Tin Statistics.*

BELGIUM - COMMUNICATION AND TRAFFIC

European Union, Delegation of the European Commission to the United States, 2300 M Street, NW, Washington, DC 20037, (202) 862-9500, Fax: (202) 429-1766, www.eurunion.org; *Statistical Overview of Transport in the European Union (Data 1970-2001).*

United Nations Statistics Division, New York, NY 10017, (800) 253-9646, Fax: (212) 963-4116, http://unstats.un.org; *Statistical Yearbook.*

BELGIUM - CONSTRUCTION INDUSTRY

European Union, Delegation of the European Commission to the United States, 2300 M Street, NW, Washington, DC 20037, (202) 862-9500, Fax: (202) 429-1766, www.eurunion.org; *European Union Labour Force Survey.*

Eurostat, Batiment Jean Monnet, Rue Alcide de Gasperi, L-2920 Luxembourg, http://epp.eurostat.ec.europa.eu; *Eurostat Yearbook 2006-2007.*

M.E. Sharpe, 80 Business Park Drive, Armonk, NY 10504, (800) 541-6563, Fax: (914) 273-2106, www.mesharpe.com; *The Illustrated Book of World Rankings.*

Organisation for Economic Cooperation and Development (OECD), 2 rue Andre Pascal, F-75775 Paris Cedex 16, France, (Telephone in U.S. (202) 785-6323), (Fax in U.S. (202) 785-0350), www.oecd.org; *Iron and Steel Industry in 2004 (2006 Edition)* and *OECD Economic Survey - Belgium 2007.*

Palgrave Macmillan Ltd., Houndmills, Basingstoke, Hampshire, RG21 6XS, England, (Telephone in U.S. (888) 330-8477), (Fax in U.S. (800) 672-2054), www.palgrave.com; *The Statesman's Yearbook 2008.*

United Nations Statistics Division, New York, NY 10017, (800) 253-9646, Fax: (212) 963-4116, http://unstats.un.org; *Statistical Yearbook.*

BELGIUM - CONSUMER PRICE INDEXES

Eurostat, Batiment Jean Monnet, Rue Alcide de Gasperi, L-2920 Luxembourg, http://epp.eurostat.ec.europa.eu; *Eurostat Yearbook 2006-2007.*

Organisation for Economic Cooperation and Development (OECD), 2 rue Andre Pascal, F-75775 Paris Cedex 16, France, (Telephone in U.S. (202) 785-6323), (Fax in U.S. (202) 785-0350), www.oecd.org; *OECD Economic Outlook 2008.*

Taylor and Francis Group, An Informa Business, 2 Park Square, Milton Park, Abingdon, Oxford OX14 4RN, United Kingdom, (Dial from U.S. (212) 216-7800), (Fax from U.S. (212) 564-7854), www.tandf.co.uk; *The Europa World Year Book.*

United Nations Statistics Division, New York, NY 10017, (800) 253-9646, Fax: (212) 963-4116, http://unstats.un.org; *Statistical Yearbook* and *Trends in Europe and North America: The Statistical Yearbook of the ECE 2005.*

The World Bank, 1818 H Street, NW, Washington, DC 20433, (202) 473-1000, Fax: (202) 477-6391, www.worldbank.org; *Belgium.*

BELGIUM - CONSUMPTION (ECONOMICS)

Eurostat, Batiment Jean Monnet, Rue Alcide de Gasperi, L-2920 Luxembourg, http://epp.eurostat.ec.europa.eu; *Eurostat Yearbook 2006-2007.*

International Iron and Steel Institute (IISI), Rue Colonel Bourg 120, B-1140 Brussels, Belgium, www.worldsteel.org; *Steel Statistical Yearbook 2006.*

Organisation for Economic Cooperation and Development (OECD), 2 rue Andre Pascal, F-75775 Paris Cedex 16, France, (Telephone in U.S. (202) 785-6323), (Fax in U.S. (202) 785-0350), www.oecd.org; *Environmental Impacts of Foreign Direct Investment in the Mining Sector in the Newly Independent States (NIS); Iron and Steel Industry in 2004 (2006 Edition); A New World Map in Textiles and Clothing: Adjusting to Change; 2005 OECD Agricultural Outlook Tables, 1970-2014; Revenue Statistics 1965-2006 - 2007 Edition;* and *Towards Sustainable Household Consumption?: Trends and Policies in OECD Countries.*

Technical Association of the Pulp and Paper Industry (TAPPI), 15 Technology Parkway South, Norcross, GA 30092, (770) 446-1400, Fax: (770) 446-6947, www.tappi.org; *TAPPI Annual Report.*

The World Bank, 1818 H Street, NW, Washington, DC 20433, (202) 473-1000, Fax: (202) 477-6391, www.worldbank.org; *World Development Report 2008.*

BELGIUM - COPPER INDUSTRY AND TRADE

See BELGIUM - MINERAL INDUSTRIES

BELGIUM - CORN INDUSTRY

See BELGIUM - CROPS

BELGIUM - COST AND STANDARD OF LIVING

Eurostat, Batiment Jean Monnet, Rue Alcide de Gasperi, L-2920 Luxembourg, http://epp.eurostat.ec.europa.eu; *Eurostat Yearbook 2006-2007.*

International Monetary Fund (IMF), 700 Nineteenth Street, NW, Washington, DC 20431, (202) 623-7000, Fax: (202) 623-4661, www.imf.org; *Government Finance Statistics Yearbook (2008 Edition).*

BELGIUM - COTTON

See BELGIUM - CROPS

BELGIUM - CRIME

Eurostat, Batiment Jean Monnet, Rue Alcide de Gasperi, L-2920 Luxembourg, http://epp.eurostat.ec.europa.eu; *Crime and Criminal Justice; General Government Expenditure and Revenue in the EU, 2006;* and *Study on Crime Victimisation.*

International Criminal Police Organization (INTERPOL), General Secretariat, 200 quai Charles de Gaulle, 69006 Lyon, France, www.interpol.int; *International Crime Statistics.*

United Nations Statistics Division, New York, NY 10017, (800) 253-9646, Fax: (212) 963-4116, http://unstats.un.org; *Trends in Europe and North America: The Statistical Yearbook of the ECE 2005.*

Yale University Press, PO Box 209040, New Haven, CT 06520-9040, (203) 432-0960, Fax: (203) 432-0948, http://yalepress.yale.edu/yupbooks; *Violence and Crime in Cross-National Perspective.*

BELGIUM - CROPS

Euromonitor International, Inc., 224 S. Michigan Avenue, Suite 1500, Chicago, IL 60604, (312) 922-1115, Fax: (312) 922-1157, www.euromonitor.com; *European Marketing Data and Statistics 2008.*

European Union, Delegation of the European Commission to the United States, 2300 M Street, NW, Washington, DC 20037, (202) 862-9500, Fax: (202) 429-1766, www.eurunion.org; *Agricultural Statistics: Data 1995-2005; Agriculture in the European Union: Statistical and Economic Information 2006; Eurostatistics: Data for Short-Term Economic Analysis (2007 edition);* and *Regions - Statistical Yearbook 2006.*

Eurostat, Batiment Jean Monnet, Rue Alcide de Gasperi, L-2920 Luxembourg, http://epp.eurostat.ec.europa.eu; *Eurostat Yearbook 2006-2007.*

M.E. Sharpe, 80 Business Park Drive, Armonk, NY 10504, (800) 541-6563, Fax: (914) 273-2106, www.mesharpe.com; *The Illustrated Book of World Rankings.*

Organisation for Economic Cooperation and Development (OECD), 2 rue Andre Pascal, F-75775 Paris Cedex 16, France, (Telephone in U.S. (202) 785-6323), (Fax in U.S. (202) 785-0350), www.oecd.org; *International Trade by Commodity Statistics (ITCS)* and *2005 OECD Agricultural Outlook Tables, 1970-2014.*

Palgrave Macmillan Ltd., Houndmills, Basingstoke, Hampshire, RG21 6XS, England, (Telephone in U.S. (888) 330-8477), (Fax in U.S. (800) 672-2054), www.palgrave.com; *The Statesman's Yearbook 2008.*

Taylor and Francis Group, An Informa Business, 2 Park Square, Milton Park, Abingdon, Oxford OX14 4RN, United Kingdom, (Dial from U.S. (212) 216-7800), (Fax from U.S. (212) 564-7854), www.tandf.co.uk; *The Europa World Year Book.*

United Nations Conference on Trade and Development (UNCTAD), DC2-1120, United Nations, New York, NY 10017, (212) 963-0027, www.unctad.org; *UNCTAD Commodity Yearbook.*

United Nations Food and Agricultural Organization (FAO), Viale delle Terme di Caracalla, 00100 Rome, Italy, (Dial from U.S. (202) 653-2400), (Fax from U.S. (202) 653 5760), www.fao.org; *FAO Production Yearbook 2002* and *The State of Food and Agriculture (SOFA) 2006.*

United Nations Statistics Division, New York, NY 10017, (800) 253-9646, Fax: (212) 963-4116, http://unstats.un.org; *Statistical Yearbook.*

BELGIUM - CUSTOMS ADMINISTRATION

Eurostat, Batiment Jean Monnet, Rue Alcide de Gasperi, L-2920 Luxembourg, http://epp.eurostat.ec.europa.eu; *Eurostat Yearbook 2006-2007.*

International Monetary Fund (IMF), 700 Nineteenth Street, NW, Washington, DC 20431, (202) 623-7000, Fax: (202) 623-4661, www.imf.org; *Government Finance Statistics Yearbook (2008 Edition).*

Organisation for Economic Cooperation and Development (OECD), 2 rue Andre Pascal, F-75775 Paris Cedex 16, France, (Telephone in U.S. (202) 785-6323), (Fax in U.S. (202) 785-0350), www.oecd.org; *Environmental Impacts of Foreign Direct Investment in the Mining Sector in the Newly Independent States (NIS).*

Palgrave Macmillan Ltd., Houndmills, Basingstoke, Hampshire, RG21 6XS, England, (Telephone in U.S. (888) 330-8477), (Fax in U.S. (800) 672-2054), www.palgrave.com; *The Statesman's Yearbook 2008.*

BELGIUM - DAIRY PROCESSING

European Union, Delegation of the European Commission to the United States, 2300 M Street, NW, Washington, DC 20037, (202) 862-9500, Fax: (202) 429-1766, www.eurunion.org; *Eurostatistics: Data for Short-Term Economic Analysis (2007 edition).*

Eurostat, Batiment Jean Monnet, Rue Alcide de Gasperi, L-2920 Luxembourg, http://epp.eurostat.ec.europa.eu; *Eurostat Yearbook 2006-2007.*

M.E. Sharpe, 80 Business Park Drive, Armonk, NY 10504, (800) 541-6563, Fax: (914) 273-2106, www.mesharpe.com; *The Illustrated Book of World Rankings.*

Organisation for Economic Cooperation and Development (OECD), 2 rue Andre Pascal, F-75775 Paris Cedex 16, France, (Telephone in U.S. (202) 785-6323), (Fax in U.S. (202) 785-0350), www.oecd.org; *2005 OECD Agricultural Outlook Tables, 1970-2014.*

Palgrave Macmillan Ltd., Houndmills, Basingstoke, Hampshire, RG21 6XS, England, (Telephone in U.S. (888) 330-8477), (Fax in U.S. (800) 672-2054), www.palgrave.com; *The Statesman's Yearbook 2008.*

Taylor and Francis Group, An Informa Business, 2 Park Square, Milton Park, Abingdon, Oxford OX14 4RN, United Kingdom, (Dial from U.S. (212) 216-7800), (Fax from U.S. (212) 564-7854), www.tandf.co.uk; *The Europa World Year Book.*

United Nations Food and Agricultural Organization (FAO), Viale delle Terme di Caracalla, 00100 Rome, Italy, (Dial from U.S. (202) 653-2400), (Fax from U.S. (202) 653 5760), www.fao.org; *FAO Production Yearbook 2002* and *The State of Food and Agriculture (SOFA) 2006.*

United Nations Statistics Division, New York, NY 10017, (800) 253-9646, Fax: (212) 963-4116, http://unstats.un.org; *Statistical Yearbook.*

BELGIUM - DEATH RATES

See BELGIUM - MORTALITY

BELGIUM - DEBTS, EXTERNAL

International Monetary Fund (IMF), 700 Nineteenth Street, NW, Washington, DC 20431, (202) 623-7000, Fax: (202) 623-4661, www.imf.org; *Government Finance Statistics Yearbook (2008 Edition).*

Organisation for Economic Cooperation and Development (OECD), 2 rue Andre Pascal, F-75775 Paris Cedex 16, France, (Telephone in U.S. (202) 785-6323), (Fax in U.S. (202) 785-0350), www.oecd.org; *Financial Market Trends: OECD Periodical; Geographical Distribution of Financial Flows to Aid Recipients 2002-2006;* and *OECD Economic Outlook 2008.*

Palgrave Macmillan Ltd., Houndmills, Basingstoke, Hampshire, RG21 6XS, England, (Telephone in U.S. (888) 330-8477), (Fax in U.S. (800) 672-2054), www.palgrave.com; *The Statesman's Yearbook 2008.*

The World Bank, 1818 H Street, NW, Washington, DC 20433, (202) 473-1000, Fax: (202) 477-6391, www.worldbank.org; *Global Development Finance 2007; World Development Indicators (WDI) 2008;* and *World Development Report 2008.*

BELGIUM - DEFENSE EXPENDITURES

See BELGIUM - ARMED FORCES

BELGIUM - DEMOGRAPHY

Euromonitor International, Inc., 224 S. Michigan Avenue, Suite 1500, Chicago, IL 60604, (312) 922-1115, Fax: (312) 922-1157, www.euromonitor.com; *The World Economic Factbook 2008* and *World Marketing Data and Statistics.*

European Union, Delegation of the European Commission to the United States, 2300 M Street, NW, Washington, DC 20037, (202) 862-9500, Fax: (202) 429-1766, www.eurunion.org; *First Demographic Estimates for 2006* and *Regions - Statistical Yearbook 2006.*

Eurostat, Batiment Jean Monnet, Rue Alcide de Gasperi, L-2920 Luxembourg, http://epp.eurostat.

ec.europa.eu; *Demographic Outlook - National Reports on the Demographic Developments in 2006* and *Eurostat Yearbook 2006-2007*.

M.E. Sharpe, 80 Business Park Drive, Armonk, NY 10504, (800) 541-6563, Fax: (914) 273-2106, www.mesharpe.com; *The Illustrated Book of World Rankings*.

United Nations Statistics Division, New York, NY 10017, (800) 253-9646, Fax: (212) 963-4116, http://unstats.un.org; *Human Development Report 2006*.

The World Bank, 1818 H Street, NW, Washington, DC 20433, (202) 473-1000, Fax: (202) 477-6391, www.worldbank.org; *Belgium*.

BELGIUM - DIAMONDS

See BELGIUM - MINERAL INDUSTRIES

BELGIUM - DISPOSABLE INCOME

M.E. Sharpe, 80 Business Park Drive, Armonk, NY 10504, (800) 541-6563, Fax: (914) 273-2106, www.mesharpe.com; *The Illustrated Book of World Rankings*.

Organisation for Economic Cooperation and Development (OECD), 2 rue Andre Pascal, F-75775 Paris Cedex 16, France, (Telephone in U.S. (202) 785-6323), (Fax in U.S. (202) 785-0350), www.oecd.org; *OECD Economic Outlook 2008*.

United Nations Statistics Division, New York, NY 10017, (800) 253-9646, Fax: (212) 963-4116, http://unstats.un.org; *National Accounts Statistics: Compendium of Income Distribution Statistics* and *Statistical Yearbook*.

BELGIUM - DIVORCE

European Union, Delegation of the European Commission to the United States, 2300 M Street, NW, Washington, DC 20037, (202) 862-9500, Fax: (202) 429-1766, www.eurunion.org; *First Demographic Estimates for 2006*.

M.E. Sharpe, 80 Business Park Drive, Armonk, NY 10504, (800) 541-6563, Fax: (914) 273-2106, www.mesharpe.com; *The Illustrated Book of World Rankings*.

United Nations Statistics Division, New York, NY 10017, (800) 253-9646, Fax: (212) 963-4116, http://unstats.un.org; *Demographic Yearbook; Statistical Yearbook;* and *Trends in Europe and North America: The Statistical Yearbook of the ECE 2005*.

BELGIUM - ECONOMIC ASSISTANCE

European Union, Delegation of the European Commission to the United States, 2300 M Street, NW, Washington, DC 20037, (202) 862-9500, Fax: (202) 429-1766, www.eurunion.org; *RD Expenditure in Europe (2006 edition)*.

Eurostat, Batiment Jean Monnet, Rue Alcide de Gasperi, L-2920 Luxembourg, http://epp.eurostat.ec.europa.eu; *Eurostat Yearbook 2006-2007*.

Organisation for Economic Cooperation and Development (OECD), 2 rue Andre Pascal, F-75775 Paris Cedex 16, France, (Telephone in U.S. (202) 785-6323), (Fax in U.S. (202) 785-0350), www.oecd.org; *Geographical Distribution of Financial Flows to Aid Recipients 2002-2006*.

United Nations Statistics Division, New York, NY 10017, (800) 253-9646, Fax: (212) 963-4116, http://unstats.un.org; *Statistical Yearbook*.

BELGIUM - ECONOMIC CONDITIONS

Banque de France, 48 rue Croix des Petits champs, 75001 Paris, France, www.banque-france.fr/home.htm; *Key Data for the Euro Area*.

Center for International Business Education Research (CIBER), Columbia Business School and School of International and Public Affairs, Uris Hall, Room 212, 3022 Broadway, New York, NY 10027-6902, Mr. Joshua Safier, (212) 854-4750, Fax: (212) 222-9821, www.columbia.edu/cu/ciber/; Datastream International.

Central Intelligence Agency, Office of Public Affairs, Washington, DC 20505, (703) 482-0623, Fax: (703) 482-1739, www.cia.gov; *The World Factbook*.

DSI Data Service Information, Xantener Strasse 51a, D-47495 Rheinberg, Germany, www.dsidata.com; *Campus Solution*.

Dun and Bradstreet (DB) Corporation, 103 JFK Parkway, Short Hills, NJ 07078, (973) 921-5500, www.dnb.com; *Country Report*.

Economist Intelligence Unit, 111 West 57th Street, New York, NY 10019, (212) 554-0600, Fax: (212) 586-1181, www.eiu.com; *Belgium Country Report*.

Euromonitor International, Inc., 224 S. Michigan Avenue, Suite 1500, Chicago, IL 60604, (312) 922-1115, Fax: (312) 922-1157, www.euromonitor.com; *European Marketing Data and Statistics 2008; The World Economic Factbook 2008;* and *World Marketing Data and Statistics*.

European Union, Delegation of the European Commission to the United States, 2300 M Street, NW, Washington, DC 20037, (202) 862-9500, Fax: (202) 429-1766, www.eurunion.org; *The EU Economy, 2007 Review: Moving Europe's Productivity Frontier* and *European Union Labour Force Survey*.

Eurostat, Batiment Jean Monnet, Rue Alcide de Gasperi, L-2920 Luxembourg, http://epp.eurostat.ec.europa.eu; *Consumers in Europe - Facts and Figures on Services of General Interest; EU Economic Data Pocketbook;* and *Eurostat Yearbook 2006-2007*.

International Monetary Fund (IMF), 700 Nineteenth Street, NW, Washington, DC 20431, (202) 623-7000, Fax: (202) 623-4661, www.imf.org; *World Economic Outlook Reports*.

M.E. Sharpe, 80 Business Park Drive, Armonk, NY 10504, (800) 541-6563, Fax: (914) 273-2106, www.mesharpe.com; *The Illustrated Book of World Rankings*.

Organisation for Economic Cooperation and Development (OECD), 2 rue Andre Pascal, F-75775 Paris Cedex 16, France, (Telephone in U.S. (202) 785-6323), (Fax in U.S. (202) 785-0350), www.oecd.org; *Geographical Distribution of Financial Flows to Aid Recipients 2002-2006; ICT Sector Data and Metadata by Country; Labour Force Statistics: 1986-2005, 2007 Edition; OECD Composite Leading Indicators (CLIs), Updated September 2007; OECD Economic Outlook 2008; OECD Economic Survey - Belgium 2007; OECD Employment Outlook 2007;* and *OECD in Figures 2007*.

Palgrave Macmillan Ltd., Houndmills, Basingstoke, Hampshire, RG21 6XS, England, (Telephone in U.S. (888) 330-8477), (Fax in U.S. (800) 672-2054), www.palgrave.com; *The Statesman's Yearbook 2008*.

Platts, 2 Penn Plaza, 25th Floor, New York, NY 10121-2298, (212) 904-3070, www.platts.com; *Energy Economist*.

Taylor and Francis Group, An Informa Business, 2 Park Square, Milton Park, Abingdon, Oxford OX14 4RN, United Kingdom, (Dial from U.S. (212) 216-7800), (Fax from U.S. (212) 564-7854), www.tandf.co.uk; *The Europa World Year Book*.

United Nations Statistics Division, New York, NY 10017, (800) 253-9646, Fax: (212) 963-4116, http://unstats.un.org; *Energy Statistics Yearbook 2003* and *World Statistics Pocketbook*.

The World Bank, 1818 H Street, NW, Washington, DC 20433, (202) 473-1000, Fax: (202) 477-6391, www.worldbank.org; *Belgium; Global Economic Monitor (GEM); Global Economic Prospects 2008; The World Bank Atlas 2003-2004;* and *World Development Report 2008*.

BELGIUM - ECONOMICS - SOCIOLOGICAL ASPECTS

Eurostat, Batiment Jean Monnet, Rue Alcide de Gasperi, L-2920 Luxembourg, http://epp.eurostat.ec.europa.eu; *Eurostat Yearbook 2006-2007*.

Organisation for Economic Cooperation and Development (OECD), 2 rue Andre Pascal, F-75775 Paris Cedex 16, France, (Telephone in U.S. (202) 785-6323), (Fax in U.S. (202) 785-0350), www.oecd.org; *OECD Economic Outlook 2008*.

BELGIUM - EDUCATION

Euromonitor International, Inc., 224 S. Michigan Avenue, Suite 1500, Chicago, IL 60604, (312) 922-1115, Fax: (312) 922-1157, www.euromonitor.com; *European Marketing Data and Statistics 2008* and *World Marketing Data and Statistics*.

European Union, Delegation of the European Commission to the United States, 2300 M Street, NW, Washington, DC 20037, (202) 862-9500, Fax: (202) 429-1766, www.eurunion.org; *Education across Europe 2003* and *Regions - Statistical Yearbook 2006*.

Eurostat, Batiment Jean Monnet, Rue Alcide de Gasperi, L-2920 Luxembourg, http://epp.eurostat.ec.europa.eu; *Education, Science and Culture Statistics* and *Eurostat Yearbook 2006-2007*.

International Monetary Fund (IMF), 700 Nineteenth Street, NW, Washington, DC 20431, (202) 623-7000, Fax: (202) 623-4661, www.imf.org; *Government Finance Statistics Yearbook (2008 Edition)*.

M.E. Sharpe, 80 Business Park Drive, Armonk, NY 10504, (800) 541-6563, Fax: (914) 273-2106, www.mesharpe.com; *The Illustrated Book of World Rankings*.

Organisation for Economic Cooperation and Development (OECD), 2 rue Andre Pascal, F-75775 Paris Cedex 16, France, (Telephone in U.S. (202) 785-6323), (Fax in U.S. (202) 785-0350), www.oecd.org; *Education at a Glance* (2007 Edition).

Palgrave Macmillan Ltd., Houndmills, Basingstoke, Hampshire, RG21 6XS, England, (Telephone in U.S. (888) 330-8477), (Fax in U.S. (800) 672-2054), www.palgrave.com; *The Statesman's Yearbook 2008*.

Taylor and Francis Group, An Informa Business, 2 Park Square, Milton Park, Abingdon, Oxford OX14 4RN, United Kingdom, (Dial from U.S. (212) 216-7800), (Fax from U.S. (212) 564-7854), www.tandf.co.uk; *The Europa World Year Book*.

UNESCO Institute for Statistics, C.P. 6128 Succursale Centre-Ville, Montreal, Quebec, H3C 3J7 Canada, (Dial from U.S. (514) 343-6880), (Fax from U.S. (514) 343 6882), www.uis.unesco.org; *Statistical Tables*.

United Nations Statistics Division, New York, NY 10017, (800) 253-9646, Fax: (212) 963-4116, http://unstats.un.org; *Human Development Report 2006* and *Trends in Europe and North America: The Statistical Yearbook of the ECE 2005*.

The World Bank, 1818 H Street, NW, Washington, DC 20433, (202) 473-1000, Fax: (202) 477-6391, www.worldbank.org; *Belgium; World Development Indicators (WDI) 2008;* and *World Development Report 2008*.

BELGIUM - ELECTRICITY

European Union, Delegation of the European Commission to the United States, 2300 M Street, NW, Washington, DC 20037, (202) 862-9500, Fax: (202) 429-1766, www.eurunion.org; *European Union Energy Transport in Figures 2006; Eurostatistics: Data for Short-Term Economic Analysis (2007 edition);* and *Regions - Statistical Yearbook 2006*.

Eurostat, Batiment Jean Monnet, Rue Alcide de Gasperi, L-2920 Luxembourg, http://epp.eurostat.ec.europa.eu; *Energy - Monthly Statistics; Eurostat Yearbook 2006-2007;* and *Panorama of Energy - 2007 Edition*.

M.E. Sharpe, 80 Business Park Drive, Armonk, NY 10504, (800) 541-6563, Fax: (914) 273-2106, www.mesharpe.com; *The Illustrated Book of World Rankings*.

Organisation for Economic Cooperation and Development (OECD), 2 rue Andre Pascal, F-75775 Paris Cedex 16, France, (Telephone in U.S. (202) 785-6323), (Fax in U.S. (202) 785-0350), www.oecd.org; *Coal Information: 2007 Edition; Energy Statistics of OECD Countries* (2007 Edition); *Indicators of Industrial Activity;* and STructural ANalysis (STAN) database.

Palgrave Macmillan Ltd., Houndmills, Basingstoke, Hampshire, RG21 6XS, England, (Telephone in U.S.

(888) 330-8477), (Fax in U.S. (800) 672-2054), www.palgrave.com; *The Statesman's Yearbook 2008.*

Platts, 2 Penn Plaza, 25th Floor, New York, NY 10121-2298, (212) 904-3070, www.platts.com; *Energy Economist; EU Energy;* and *European Electricity Review 2004.*

U.S. Department of Energy (DOE), Energy Information Administration (EIA), 1000 Independence Avenue, SW, Washington, DC 20585, (202) 586-8800, www.eia.doe.gov; *International Energy Annual 2004* and *International Energy Outlook 2006.*

United Nations Statistics Division, New York, NY 10017, (800) 253-9646, Fax: (212) 963-4116, http://unstats.un.org; *Energy Statistics Yearbook 2003; Human Development Report 2006; Statistical Yearbook;* and *Trends in Europe and North America: The Statistical Yearbook of the ECE 2005.*

BELGIUM - EMPLOYMENT

Bernan Essential Government Publications, 4611-F Assembly Drive, Lanham MD, 20706-4391, (301) 459-2255, Fax: (800) 865-3450, www.bernan.com; *OECD Factbook 2006.*

Euromonitor International, Inc., 224 S. Michigan Avenue, Suite 1500, Chicago, IL 60604, (312) 922-1115, Fax: (312) 922-1157, www.euromonitor.com; *European Marketing Data and Statistics 2008.*

European Union, Delegation of the European Commission to the United States, 2300 M Street, NW, Washington, DC 20037, (202) 862-9500, Fax: (202) 429-1766, www.eurunion.org; *Agriculture in the European Union: Statistical and Economic Information 2006; European Union Labour Force Survey; Eurostatistics: Data for Short-Term Economic Analysis (2007 edition);* and *Iron and Steel.*

Eurostat, Batiment Jean Monnet, Rue Alcide de Gasperi, L-2920 Luxembourg, http://epp.eurostat.ec.europa.eu; *Eurostat Yearbook 2006-2007.*

International Labour Office, I.L.O. Publications, 4 route des Morillons, CH-1211 Geneva 22, Switzerland, (Telephone in U.S. (202) 653-7652), (Fax in U.S. (202) 653-7687), www.ilo.org; *Yearbook of Labour Statistics 2006.*

M.E. Sharpe, 80 Business Park Drive, Armonk, NY 10504, (800) 541-6563, Fax: (914) 273-2106, www.mesharpe.com; *The Illustrated Book of World Rankings.*

Organisation for Economic Cooperation and Development (OECD), 2 rue Andre Pascal, F-75775 Paris Cedex 16, France, (Telephone in U.S. (202) 785-6323), (Fax in U.S. (202) 785-0350), www.oecd.org; *Coal Information: 2007 Edition; ICT Sector Data and Metadata by Country; Iron and Steel Industry in 2004 (2006 Edition); Labour Force Statistics: 1986-2005, 2007 Edition; OECD Composite Leading Indicators (CLIs), Updated September 2007; OECD Economic Outlook 2008; OECD Economic Survey - Belgium 2007; OECD Employment Outlook 2007;* and *OECD in Figures 2007.*

United Nations Statistics Division, New York, NY 10017, (800) 253-9646, Fax: (212) 963-4116, http://unstats.un.org; *Statistical Yearbook* and *Trends in Europe and North America: The Statistical Yearbook of the ECE 2005.*

The World Bank, 1818 H Street, NW, Washington, DC 20433, (202) 473-1000, Fax: (202) 477-6391, www.worldbank.org; *Belgium.*

BELGIUM - ENERGY INDUSTRIES

Enerdata, 10 Rue Royale, 75008 Paris, France, www.enerdata.fr; *Global Energy Market Data.*

Eurostat, Batiment Jean Monnet, Rue Alcide de Gasperi, L-2920 Luxembourg, http://epp.eurostat.ec.europa.eu; *Energy - Monthly Statistics; Eurostat Yearbook 2006-2007;* and *Panorama of Energy - 2007 Edition.*

International Energy Agency (IEA), 9, rue de la Federation, 75739 Paris Cedex 15, France, www.iea.org; *Key World Energy Statistics 2007.*

Organisation for Economic Cooperation and Development (OECD), 2 rue Andre Pascal, F-75775 Paris Cedex 16, France, (Telephone in U.S. (202) 785-6323), (Fax in U.S. (202) 785-0350), www.oecd.org; *Towards Sustainable Household Consumption?: Trends and Policies in OECD Countries.*

Platts, 2 Penn Plaza, 25th Floor, New York, NY 10121-2298, (212) 904-3070, www.platts.com; *EU Energy* and *European Power Daily.*

United Nations Statistics Division, New York, NY 10017, (800) 253-9646, Fax: (212) 963-4116, http://unstats.un.org; *Statistical Yearbook.*

BELGIUM - ENVIRONMENTAL CONDITIONS

Center for Research on the Epidemiology of Disasters (CRED), Universite Catholique de Louvain, Ecole de Sante Publique, 30.94 Clos Chapelle-aux-Champs, 1200 Brussels, Belgium, www.cred.be; *Three Decades of Floods in Europe: A Preliminary Analysis of EMDAT Data.*

DSI Data Service Information, Xantener Strasse 51a, D-47495 Rheinberg, Germany, www.dsidata.com; *Campus Solution* and *DSI's Global Environmental Database.*

Economist Intelligence Unit, 111 West 57th Street, New York, NY 10019, (212) 554-0600, Fax: (212) 586-1181, www.eiu.com; *Belgium Country Report.*

Eurostat, Batiment Jean Monnet, Rue Alcide de Gasperi, L-2920 Luxembourg, http://epp.eurostat.ec.europa.eu; *Environmental Protection Expenditure in Europe.*

Organisation for Economic Cooperation and Development (OECD), 2 rue Andre Pascal, F-75775 Paris Cedex 16, France, (Telephone in U.S. (202) 785-6323), (Fax in U.S. (202) 785-0350), www.oecd.org; *Key Environmental Indicators 2004.*

Platts, 2 Penn Plaza, 25th Floor, New York, NY 10121-2298, (212) 904-3070, www.platts.com; *Emissions Daily.*

United Nations Statistics Division, New York, NY 10017, (800) 253-9646, Fax: (212) 963-4116, http://unstats.un.org; *Trends in Europe and North America: The Statistical Yearbook of the ECE 2005* and *World Statistics Pocketbook.*

BELGIUM - EXPENDITURES, PUBLIC

Eurostat, Batiment Jean Monnet, Rue Alcide de Gasperi, L-2920 Luxembourg, http://epp.eurostat.ec.europa.eu; *European Social Statistics - Social Protection Expenditure and Receipts - Data 1997-2005* and *Eurostat Yearbook 2006-2007.*

Organisation for Economic Cooperation and Development (OECD), 2 rue Andre Pascal, F-75775 Paris Cedex 16, France, (Telephone in U.S. (202) 785-6323), (Fax in U.S. (202) 785-0350), www.oecd.org; *Revenue Statistics 1965-2006 - 2007 Edition.*

BELGIUM - EXPORTS

Central Intelligence Agency, Office of Public Affairs, Washington, DC 20505, (703) 482-0623, Fax: (703) 482-1739, www.cia.gov; *The World Factbook.*

Economist Intelligence Unit, 111 West 57th Street, New York, NY 10019, (212) 554-0600, Fax: (212) 586-1181, www.eiu.com; *Belgium Country Report.*

Euromonitor International, Inc., 224 S. Michigan Avenue, Suite 1500, Chicago, IL 60604, (312) 922-1115, Fax: (312) 922-1157, www.euromonitor.com; *The World Economic Factbook 2008.*

European Union, Delegation of the European Commission to the United States, 2300 M Street, NW, Washington, DC 20037, (202) 862-9500, Fax: (202) 429-1766, www.eurunion.org; *European Union Energy Transport in Figures 2006; Eurostatistics: Data for Short-Term Economic Analysis (2007 edition); External and Intra-European Union Trade: Data 1958-2002; External and Intra-European Union Trade: Data 1999-2004;* and *Fishery Statistics - 1990-2006.*

Eurostat, Batiment Jean Monnet, Rue Alcide de Gasperi, L-2920 Luxembourg, http://epp.eurostat.ec.europa.eu; *Eurostat Yearbook 2006-2007.*

International Iron and Steel Institute (IISI), Rue Colonel Bourg 120, B-1140 Brussels, Belgium, www.worldsteel.org; *Steel Statistical Yearbook 2006.*

International Lead and Zinc Study Group (ILZSG), Rua Almirante Barroso 38, 5th Floor, Lisbon 1000 - 013, Portugal, www.ilzsg.org; Interactive Statistical Database.

International Monetary Fund (IMF), 700 Nineteenth Street, NW, Washington, DC 20431, (202) 623-7000, Fax: (202) 623-4661, www.imf.org; *Direction of Trade Statistics Yearbook 2007* and *International Financial Statistics Yearbook 2007.*

Organisation for Economic Cooperation and Development (OECD), 2 rue Andre Pascal, F-75775 Paris Cedex 16, France, (Telephone in U.S. (202) 785-6323), (Fax in U.S. (202) 785-0350), www.oecd.org; *Geographical Distribution of Financial Flows to Aid Recipients 2002-2006; International Trade by Commodity Statistics (ITCS); Iron and Steel Industry in 2004 (2006 Edition); 2005 OECD Agricultural Outlook Tables, 1970-2014; OECD Economic Outlook 2008; OECD Economic Survey - Belgium 2007; Review of Fisheries in OECD Countries: Country Statistics 2001 to 2003 - 2005 Edition;* and STructural ANalysis (STAN) database.

Palgrave Macmillan Ltd., Houndmills, Basingstoke, Hampshire, RG21 6XS, England, (Telephone in U.S. (888) 330-8477), (Fax in U.S. (800) 672-2054), www.palgrave.com; *The Statesman's Yearbook 2008.*

Platts, 2 Penn Plaza, 25th Floor, New York, NY 10121-2298, (212) 904-3070, www.platts.com; *Energy Economist.*

Taylor and Francis Group, An Informa Business, 2 Park Square, Milton Park, Abingdon, Oxford OX14 4RN, United Kingdom, (Dial from U.S. (212) 216-7800), (Fax from U.S. (212) 564-7854), www.tandf.co.uk; *The Europa World Year Book.*

Technical Association of the Pulp and Paper Industry (TAPPI), 15 Technology Parkway South, Norcross, GA 30092, (770) 446-1400, Fax: (770) 446-6947, www.tappi.org; *TAPPI Annual Report.*

United Nations Conference on Trade and Development (UNCTAD), DC2-1120, United Nations, New York, NY 10017, (212) 963-0027, www.unctad.org; *Handbook of Statistics 2005.*

United Nations Food and Agricultural Organization (FAO), Viale delle Terme di Caracalla, 00100 Rome, Italy, (Dial from U.S. (202) 653-2400), (Fax from U.S. (202) 653 5760), www.fao.org; *The State of Food and Agriculture (SOFA) 2006.*

United Nations Statistics Division, New York, NY 10017, (800) 253-9646, Fax: (212) 963-4116, http://unstats.un.org; *Energy Statistics Yearbook 2003* and *Trends in Europe and North America: The Statistical Yearbook of the ECE 2005.*

The World Bank, 1818 H Street, NW, Washington, DC 20433, (202) 473-1000, Fax: (202) 477-6391, www.worldbank.org; *World Development Indicators (WDI) 2008* and *World Development Report 2008.*

BELGIUM - FEMALE WORKING POPULATION

See BELGIUM - EMPLOYMENT

BELGIUM - FERTILITY, HUMAN

Central Intelligence Agency, Office of Public Affairs, Washington, DC 20505, (703) 482-0623, Fax: (703) 482-1739, www.cia.gov; *The World Factbook.*

European Union, Delegation of the European Commission to the United States, 2300 M Street, NW, Washington, DC 20037, (202) 862-9500, Fax: (202) 429-1766, www.eurunion.org; *First Demographic Estimates for 2006.*

M.E. Sharpe, 80 Business Park Drive, Armonk, NY 10504, (800) 541-6563, Fax: (914) 273-2106, www.mesharpe.com; *The Illustrated Book of World Rankings.*

United Nations Statistics Division, New York, NY 10017, (800) 253-9646, Fax: (212) 963-4116, http://unstats.un.org; *Human Development Report 2006* and *Trends in Europe and North America: The Statistical Yearbook of the ECE 2005.*

The World Bank, 1818 H Street, NW, Washington, DC 20433, (202) 473-1000, Fax: (202) 477-6391, www.worldbank.org; *The World Bank Atlas 2003-2004; World Development Indicators (WDI) 2008;* and *World Development Report 2008.*

BELGIUM - FERTILIZER INDUSTRY

Eurostat, Batiment Jean Monnet, Rue Alcide de Gasperi, L-2920 Luxembourg, http://epp.eurostat.ec.europa.eu; *Eurostat Yearbook 2006-2007.*

Organisation for Economic Cooperation and Development (OECD), 2 rue Andre Pascal, F-75775 Paris Cedex 16, France, (Telephone in U.S. (202) 785-6323), (Fax in U.S. (202) 785-0350), www.oecd.org; *International Trade by Commodity Statistics (ITCS)* and *2005 OECD Agricultural Outlook Tables, 1970-2014.*

United Nations Food and Agricultural Organization (FAO), Viale delle Terme di Caracalla, 00100 Rome, Italy, (Dial from U.S. (202) 653-2400), (Fax from U.S. (202) 653 5760), www.fao.org; *FAO Fertilizer Yearbook* and *The State of Food and Agriculture (SOFA) 2006.*

United Nations Statistics Division, New York, NY 10017, (800) 253-9646, Fax: (212) 963-4116, http://unstats.un.org; *Statistical Yearbook.*

BELGIUM - FETAL MORTALITY

See BELGIUM - MORTALITY

BELGIUM - FILM

See BELGIUM - MOTION PICTURES

BELGIUM - FINANCE

European Union, Delegation of the European Commission to the United States, 2300 M Street, NW, Washington, DC 20037, (202) 862-9500, Fax: (202) 429-1766, www.eurunion.org; *Eurostatistics: Data for Short-Term Economic Analysis (2007 edition).*

Eurostat, Batiment Jean Monnet, Rue Alcide de Gasperi, L-2920 Luxembourg, http://epp.eurostat.ec.europa.eu; *Eurostat Yearbook 2006-2007.*

International Monetary Fund (IMF), 700 Nineteenth Street, NW, Washington, DC 20431, (202) 623-7000, Fax: (202) 623-4661, www.imf.org; *International Financial Statistics Yearbook 2007.*

Organisation for Economic Cooperation and Development (OECD), 2 rue Andre Pascal, F-75775 Paris Cedex 16, France, (Telephone in U.S. (202) 785-6323), (Fax in U.S. (202) 785-0350), www.oecd.org; *OECD Economic Outlook 2008.*

Taylor and Francis Group, An Informa Business, 2 Park Square, Milton Park, Abingdon, Oxford OX14 4RN, United Kingdom, (Dial from U.S. (212) 216-7800), (Fax from U.S. (212) 564-7854), www.tandf.co.uk; *The Europa World Year Book.*

United Nations Statistics Division, New York, NY 10017, (800) 253-9646, Fax: (212) 963-4116, http://unstats.un.org; *National Accounts Statistics: Compendium of Income Distribution Statistics* and *Statistical Yearbook.*

The World Bank, 1818 H Street, NW, Washington, DC 20433, (202) 473-1000, Fax: (202) 477-6391, www.worldbank.org; *Belgium.*

BELGIUM - FINANCE, PUBLIC

Banque de France, 48 rue Croix des Petits champs, 75001 Paris, France, www.banque-france.fr/home.htm; *Key Data for the Euro Area* and *Public Finance.*

Bernan Essential Government Publications, 4611-F Assembly Drive, Lanham MD, 20706-4391, (301) 459-2255, Fax: (800) 865-3450, www.bernan.com; *National Accounts Statistics.*

Economist Intelligence Unit, 111 West 57th Street, New York, NY 10019, (212) 554-0600, Fax: (212) 586-1181, www.eiu.com; *Belgium Country Report.*

European Union, Delegation of the European Commission to the United States, 2300 M Street, NW, Washington, DC 20037, (202) 862-9500, Fax: (202) 429-1766, www.eurunion.org; *Eurostatistics: Data for Short-Term Economic Analysis (2007 edition).*

Eurostat, Batiment Jean Monnet, Rue Alcide de Gasperi, L-2920 Luxembourg, http://epp.eurostat.ec.europa.eu; *Eurostat Yearbook 2006-2007.*

International Monetary Fund (IMF), 700 Nineteenth Street, NW, Washington, DC 20431, (202) 623-7000, Fax: (202) 623-4661, www.imf.org; *Government Finance Statistics Yearbook (2008 Edition); International Financial Statistics; International Financial Statistics Online Service;* and *International Financial Statistics Yearbook 2007.*

M.E. Sharpe, 80 Business Park Drive, Armonk, NY 10504, (800) 541-6563, Fax: (914) 273-2106, www.mesharpe.com; *The Illustrated Book of World Rankings.*

Organisation for Economic Cooperation and Development (OECD), 2 rue Andre Pascal, F-75775 Paris Cedex 16, France, (Telephone in U.S. (202) 785-6323), (Fax in U.S. (202) 785-0350), www.oecd.org; *Financial Market Trends: OECD Periodical; Geographical Distribution of Financial Flows to Aid Recipients 2002-2006; OECD Economic Outlook 2008;* and *Revenue Statistics 1965-2006 - 2007 Edition.*

Palgrave Macmillan Ltd., Houndmills, Basingstoke, Hampshire, RG21 6XS, England, (Telephone in U.S. (888) 330-8477), (Fax in U.S. (800) 672-2054), www.palgrave.com; *The Statesman's Yearbook 2008.*

Taylor and Francis Group, An Informa Business, 2 Park Square, Milton Park, Abingdon, Oxford OX14 4RN, United Kingdom, (Dial from U.S. (212) 216-7800), (Fax from U.S. (212) 564-7854), www.tandf.co.uk; *The Europa World Year Book.*

The World Bank, 1818 H Street, NW, Washington, DC 20433, (202) 473-1000, Fax: (202) 477-6391, www.worldbank.org; *Belgium.*

BELGIUM - FISHERIES

Euromonitor International, Inc., 224 S. Michigan Avenue, Suite 1500, Chicago, IL 60604, (312) 922-1115, Fax: (312) 922-1157, www.euromonitor.com; *European Marketing Data and Statistics 2008.*

European Union, Delegation of the European Commission to the United States, 2300 M Street, NW, Washington, DC 20037, (202) 862-9500, Fax: (202) 429-1766, www.eurunion.org; *Agricultural Statistics: Data 1995-2005* and *Fishery Statistics - 1990-2006.*

Eurostat, Batiment Jean Monnet, Rue Alcide de Gasperi, L-2920 Luxembourg, http://epp.eurostat.ec.europa.eu; *Eurostat Yearbook 2006-2007.*

M.E. Sharpe, 80 Business Park Drive, Armonk, NY 10504, (800) 541-6563, Fax: (914) 273-2106, www.mesharpe.com; *The Illustrated Book of World Rankings.*

Organisation for Economic Cooperation and Development (OECD), 2 rue Andre Pascal, F-75775 Paris Cedex 16, France, (Telephone in U.S. (202) 785-6323), (Fax in U.S. (202) 785-0350), www.oecd.org; *International Trade by Commodity Statistics (ITCS); Review of Fisheries in OECD Countries: Country Statistics 2001 to 2003 - 2005 Edition;* and STructural ANalysis (STAN) database.

Palgrave Macmillan Ltd., Houndmills, Basingstoke, Hampshire, RG21 6XS, England, (Telephone in U.S. (888) 330-8477), (Fax in U.S. (800) 672-2054), www.palgrave.com; *The Statesman's Yearbook 2008.*

Taylor and Francis Group, An Informa Business, 2 Park Square, Milton Park, Abingdon, Oxford OX14 4RN, United Kingdom, (Dial from U.S. (212) 216-7800), (Fax from U.S. (212) 564-7854), www.tandf.co.uk; *The Europa World Year Book.*

United Nations Conference on Trade and Development (UNCTAD), DC2-1120, United Nations, New York, NY 10017, (212) 963-0027, www.unctad.org; *UNCTAD Commodity Yearbook.*

United Nations Food and Agricultural Organization (FAO), Viale delle Terme di Caracalla, 00100 Rome, Italy, (Dial from U.S. (202) 653-2400), (Fax from U.S. (202) 653 5760), www.fao.org; *FAO Yearbook of Fishery Statistics;* Fishery Databases; FISHSTAT Database. Subjects covered include: Aquaculture production, capture production, fishery commodities; and *The State of Food and Agriculture (SOFA) 2006.*

United Nations Statistics Division, New York, NY 10017, (800) 253-9646, Fax: (212) 963-4116, http://unstats.un.org; *Statistical Yearbook.*

The World Bank, 1818 H Street, NW, Washington, DC 20433, (202) 473-1000, Fax: (202) 477-6391, www.worldbank.org; *Belgium.*

BELGIUM - FLOUR INDUSTRY

Eurostat, Batiment Jean Monnet, Rue Alcide de Gasperi, L-2920 Luxembourg, http://epp.eurostat.ec.europa.eu; *Eurostat Yearbook 2006-2007.*

United Nations Statistics Division, New York, NY 10017, (800) 253-9646, Fax: (212) 963-4116, http://unstats.un.org; *Statistical Yearbook.*

BELGIUM - FOOD

Euromonitor International, Inc., 224 S. Michigan Avenue, Suite 1500, Chicago, IL 60604, (312) 922-1115, Fax: (312) 922-1157, www.euromonitor.com; *World Marketing Data and Statistics.*

Eurostat, Batiment Jean Monnet, Rue Alcide de Gasperi, L-2920 Luxembourg, http://epp.eurostat.ec.europa.eu; *Eurostat Yearbook 2006-2007.*

Organisation for Economic Cooperation and Development (OECD), 2 rue Andre Pascal, F-75775 Paris Cedex 16, France, (Telephone in U.S. (202) 785-6323), (Fax in U.S. (202) 785-0350), www.oecd.org; *International Trade by Commodity Statistics (ITCS)* and *Towards Sustainable Household Consumption?: Trends and Policies in OECD Countries.*

United Nations Conference on Trade and Development (UNCTAD), DC2-1120, United Nations, New York, NY 10017, (212) 963-0027, www.unctad.org; *UNCTAD Commodity Yearbook.*

United Nations Food and Agricultural Organization (FAO), Viale delle Terme di Caracalla, 00100 Rome, Italy, (Dial from U.S. (202) 653-2400), (Fax from U.S. (202) 653 5760), www.fao.org; *FAO Production Yearbook 2002* and *The State of Food and Agriculture (SOFA) 2006.*

United Nations Statistics Division, New York, NY 10017, (800) 253-9646, Fax: (212) 963-4116, http://unstats.un.org; *Human Development Report 2006.*

BELGIUM - FOOTWEAR

Organisation for Economic Cooperation and Development (OECD), 2 rue Andre Pascal, F-75775 Paris Cedex 16, France, (Telephone in U.S. (202) 785-6323), (Fax in U.S. (202) 785-0350), www.oecd.org; *Indicators of Industrial Activity.*

BELGIUM - FOREIGN EXCHANGE RATES

Central Intelligence Agency, Office of Public Affairs, Washington, DC 20505, (703) 482-0623, Fax: (703) 482-1739, www.cia.gov; *The World Factbook.*

Euromonitor International, Inc., 224 S. Michigan Avenue, Suite 1500, Chicago, IL 60604, (312) 922-1115, Fax: (312) 922-1157, www.euromonitor.com; *The World Economic Factbook 2008.*

European Union, Delegation of the European Commission to the United States, 2300 M Street, NW, Washington, DC 20037, (202) 862-9500, Fax: (202) 429-1766, www.eurunion.org; *Eurostatistics: Data for Short-Term Economic Analysis (2007 edition).*

Eurostat, Batiment Jean Monnet, Rue Alcide de Gasperi, L-2920 Luxembourg, http://epp.eurostat.ec.europa.eu; *Eurostat Yearbook 2006-2007.*

International Civil Aviation Organization (ICAO), External Relations and Public Information Office (EPO), 999 University Street, Montreal, Quebec H3C 5H7, Canada, (Dial from U.S. (514) 954-8219), (Fax from U.S. (514) 954-6077), www.icao.int; *Civil Aviation Statistics of the World.*

International Monetary Fund (IMF), 700 Nineteenth Street, NW, Washington, DC 20431, (202) 623-7000, Fax: (202) 623-4661, www.imf.org; *International Financial Statistics Yearbook 2007.*

Organisation for Economic Cooperation and Development (OECD), 2 rue Andre Pascal, F-75775 Paris Cedex 16, France, (Telephone in U.S. (202) 785-6323), (Fax in U.S. (202) 785-0350), www.oecd.org; *Financial Market Trends: OECD Periodical; Household, Tourism, Travel: Trends, Environmental Impacts and Policy Responses; OECD Economic Outlook 2008;* and *Revenue Statistics 1965-2006 - 2007 Edition.*

Taylor and Francis Group, An Informa Business, 2 Park Square, Milton Park, Abingdon, Oxford OX14 4RN, United Kingdom, (Dial from U.S. (212) 216-7800), (Fax from U.S. (212) 564-7854), www.tandf.co.uk; *The Europa World Year Book.*

United Nations Statistics Division, New York, NY 10017, (800) 253-9646, Fax: (212) 963-4116, http://unstats.un.org; *Statistical Yearbook; Trends in Europe and North America: The Statistical Yearbook of the ECE 2005;* and *World Statistics Pocketbook.*

BELGIUM - FORESTS AND FORESTRY

American Forest Paper Association (AFPA), 1111 Nineteenth Street, NW, Suite 800, Washington, DC 20036, (800) 878-8878, www.afandpa.org; *2007 Annual Statistics of Paper, Paperboard, and Wood Pulp.*

Euromonitor International, Inc., 224 S. Michigan Avenue, Suite 1500, Chicago, IL 60604, (312) 922-1115, Fax: (312) 922-1157, www.euromonitor.com; *European Marketing Data and Statistics 2008.*

European Union, Delegation of the European Commission to the United States, 2300 M Street, NW, Washington, DC 20037, (202) 862-9500, Fax: (202) 429-1766, www.eurunion.org; *Agricultural Statistics: Data 1995-2005.*

Eurostat, Batiment Jean Monnet, Rue Alcide de Gasperi, L-2920 Luxembourg, http://epp.eurostat.ec.europa.eu; *Eurostat Yearbook 2006-2007.*

M.E. Sharpe, 80 Business Park Drive, Armonk, NY 10504, (800) 541-6563, Fax: (914) 273-2106, www.mesharpe.com; *The Illustrated Book of World Rankings.*

Organisation for Economic Cooperation and Development (OECD), 2 rue Andre Pascal, F-75775 Paris Cedex 16, France, (Telephone in U.S. (202) 785-6323), (Fax in U.S. (202) 785-0350), www.oecd.org; *Indicators of Industrial Activity* and STructural ANalysis (STAN) database.

Palgrave Macmillan Ltd., Houndmills, Basingstoke, Hampshire, RG21 6XS, England, (Telephone in U.S. (888) 330-8477), (Fax in U.S. (800) 672-2054), www.palgrave.com; *The Statesman's Yearbook 2008.*

Technical Association of the Pulp and Paper Industry (TAPPI), 15 Technology Parkway South, Norcross, GA 30092, (770) 446-1400, Fax: (770) 446-6947, www.tappi.org; *TAPPI Annual Report.*

UNESCO Institute for Statistics, C.P. 6128 Succursale Centre-Ville, Montreal, Quebec, H3C 3J7 Canada, (Dial from U.S. (514) 343-6880), (Fax from U.S. (514) 343 6882), www.uis.unesco.org; *Statistical Tables.*

United Nations Conference on Trade and Development (UNCTAD), DC2-1120, United Nations, New York, NY 10017, (212) 963-0027, www.unctad.org; *UNCTAD Commodity Yearbook.*

United Nations Food and Agricultural Organization (FAO), Viale delle Terme di Caracalla, 00100 Rome, Italy, (Dial from U.S. (202) 653-2400), (Fax from U.S. (202) 653 5760), www.fao.org; *FAO Yearbook of Forest Products* and *The State of Food and Agriculture (SOFA) 2006.*

United Nations Statistics Division, New York, NY 10017, (800) 253-9646, Fax: (212) 963-4116, http://unstats.un.org; *Trends in Europe and North America: The Statistical Yearbook of the ECE 2005.*

The World Bank, 1818 H Street, NW, Washington, DC 20433, (202) 473-1000, Fax: (202) 477-6391, www.worldbank.org; *Belgium* and *World Development Report 2008.*

BELGIUM - FRUIT PRODUCTION

See BELGIUM - CROPS

BELGIUM - GAS PRODUCTION

See BELGIUM - MINERAL INDUSTRIES

BELGIUM - GEOGRAPHIC INFORMATION SYSTEMS

Eurostat, Batiment Jean Monnet, Rue Alcide de Gasperi, L-2920 Luxembourg, http://epp.eurostat.ec.europa.eu; *Eurostat Yearbook 2006-2007.*

M.E. Sharpe, 80 Business Park Drive, Armonk, NY 10504, (800) 541-6563, Fax: (914) 273-2106, www.mesharpe.com; *The Illustrated Book of World Rankings.*

The World Bank, 1818 H Street, NW, Washington, DC 20433, (202) 473-1000, Fax: (202) 477-6391, www.worldbank.org; *Belgium.*

BELGIUM - GLASS AND GLASS PRODUCTS

See BELGIUM - MINERAL INDUSTRIES

BELGIUM - GOLD INDUSTRY

International Monetary Fund (IMF), 700 Nineteenth Street, NW, Washington, DC 20431, (202) 623-7000, Fax: (202) 623-4661, www.imf.org; *International Financial Statistics Yearbook 2007.*

United Nations Statistics Division, New York, NY 10017, (800) 253-9646, Fax: (212) 963-4116, http://unstats.un.org; *Statistical Yearbook.*

The World Bank, 1818 H Street, NW, Washington, DC 20433, (202) 473-1000, Fax: (202) 477-6391, www.worldbank.org; *World Development Indicators (WDI) 2008.*

BELGIUM - GOLD PRODUCTION

See BELGIUM - MINERAL INDUSTRIES

BELGIUM - GRANTS-IN-AID

International Monetary Fund (IMF), 700 Nineteenth Street, NW, Washington, DC 20431, (202) 623-7000, Fax: (202) 623-4661, www.imf.org; *Government Finance Statistics Yearbook (2008 Edition).*

Organisation for Economic Cooperation and Development (OECD), 2 rue Andre Pascal, F-75775 Paris Cedex 16, France, (Telephone in U.S. (202) 785-6323), (Fax in U.S. (202) 785-0350), www.oecd.org; *Geographical Distribution of Financial Flows to Aid Recipients 2002-2006.*

BELGIUM - GREEN PEPPER AND CHILIE PRODUCTION

See BELGIUM - CROPS

BELGIUM - GROSS DOMESTIC PRODUCT

Economist Intelligence Unit, 111 West 57th Street, New York, NY 10019, (212) 554-0600, Fax: (212) 586-1181, www.eiu.com; *Belgium Country Report.*

Euromonitor International, Inc., 224 S. Michigan Avenue, Suite 1500, Chicago, IL 60604, (312) 922-1115, Fax: (312) 922-1157, www.euromonitor.com; *The World Economic Factbook 2008.*

European Union, Delegation of the European Commission to the United States, 2300 M Street, NW, Washington, DC 20037, (202) 862-9500, Fax: (202) 429-1766, www.eurunion.org; *Eurostatistics: Data for Short-Term Economic Analysis (2007 edition); Iron and Steel;* and *RD Expenditure in Europe (2006 edition).*

Eurostat, Batiment Jean Monnet, Rue Alcide de Gasperi, L-2920 Luxembourg, http://epp.eurostat.ec.europa.eu; *Eurostat Yearbook 2006-2007.*

M.E. Sharpe, 80 Business Park Drive, Armonk, NY 10504, (800) 541-6563, Fax: (914) 273-2106, www.mesharpe.com; *The Illustrated Book of World Rankings.*

Organisation for Economic Cooperation and Development (OECD), 2 rue Andre Pascal, F-75775 Paris Cedex 16, France, (Telephone in U.S. (202) 785-6323), (Fax in U.S. (202) 785-0350), www.oecd.org; *Comparison of Gross Domestic Product (GDP) for OECD Countries; Geographical Distribution of Financial Flows to Aid Recipients 2002-2006; OECD Economic Outlook 2008;* and *Revenue Statistics 1965-2006 - 2007 Edition.*

Taylor and Francis Group, An Informa Business, 2 Park Square, Milton Park, Abingdon, Oxford OX14 4RN, United Kingdom, (Dial from U.S. (212) 216-7800), (Fax from U.S. (212) 564-7854), www.tandf.co.uk; *The Europa World Year Book.*

United Nations Statistics Division, New York, NY 10017, (800) 253-9646, Fax: (212) 963-4116, http://unstats.un.org; *Human Development Report 2006; Statistical Yearbook;* and *Trends in Europe and North America: The Statistical Yearbook of the ECE 2005.*

The World Bank, 1818 H Street, NW, Washington, DC 20433, (202) 473-1000, Fax: (202) 477-6391, www.worldbank.org; *World Development Indicators (WDI) 2008* and *World Development Report 2008.*

BELGIUM - GROSS NATIONAL PRODUCT

European Union, Delegation of the European Commission to the United States, 2300 M Street, NW, Washington, DC 20037, (202) 862-9500, Fax: (202) 429-1766, www.eurunion.org; *The EU Economy, 2007 Review: Moving Europe's Productivity Frontier.*

Eurostat, Batiment Jean Monnet, Rue Alcide de Gasperi, L-2920 Luxembourg, http://epp.eurostat.ec.europa.eu; *Eurostat Yearbook 2006-2007.*

M.E. Sharpe, 80 Business Park Drive, Armonk, NY 10504, (800) 541-6563, Fax: (914) 273-2106, www.mesharpe.com; *The Illustrated Book of World Rankings.*

Organisation for Economic Cooperation and Development (OECD), 2 rue Andre Pascal, F-75775 Paris Cedex 16, France, (Telephone in U.S. (202) 785-6323), (Fax in U.S. (202) 785-0350), www.oecd.org; *Geographical Distribution of Financial Flows to Aid Recipients 2002-2006; OECD Composite Leading Indicators (CLIs), Updated September 2007;* and *OECD Economic Outlook 2008.*

Palgrave Macmillan Ltd., Houndmills, Basingstoke, Hampshire, RG21 6XS, England, (Telephone in U.S. (888) 330-8477), (Fax in U.S. (800) 672-2054), www.palgrave.com; *The Statesman's Yearbook 2008.*

U.S. Department of State (DOS), 2201 C Street NW, Washington, DC 20520, (202) 647-4000, www.state.gov; *World Military Expenditures and Arms Transfers (WMEAT).*

United Nations Statistics Division, New York, NY 10017, (800) 253-9646, Fax: (212) 963-4116, http://unstats.un.org; *Statistical Yearbook.*

The World Bank, 1818 H Street, NW, Washington, DC 20433, (202) 473-1000, Fax: (202) 477-6391, www.worldbank.org; *The World Bank Atlas 2003-2004; World Development Indicators (WDI) 2008;* and *World Development Report 2008.*

BELGIUM - HAY PRODUCTION

See BELGIUM - CROPS

BELGIUM - HAZELNUT PRODUCTION

See BELGIUM - CROPS

BELGIUM - HEALTH

See BELGIUM - PUBLIC HEALTH

BELGIUM - HEMP FIBRE PRODUCTION

See BELGIUM - TEXTILE INDUSTRY

BELGIUM - HIDES AND SKINS INDUSTRY

Organisation for Economic Cooperation and Development (OECD), 2 rue Andre Pascal, F-75775 Paris Cedex 16, France, (Telephone in U.S. (202) 785-6323), (Fax in U.S. (202) 785-0350), www.oecd.org; *Indicators of Industrial Activity* and *International Trade by Commodity Statistics (ITCS).*

United Nations Food and Agricultural Organization (FAO), Viale delle Terme di Caracalla, 00100 Rome,

Italy, (Dial from U.S. (202) 653-2400), (Fax from U.S. (202) 653 5760), www.fao.org; *FAO Production Yearbook 2002.*

BELGIUM - HOPS PRODUCTION

See BELGIUM - CROPS

BELGIUM - HOUSING

Euromonitor International, Inc., 224 S. Michigan Avenue, Suite 1500, Chicago, IL 60604, (312) 922-1115, Fax: (312) 922-1157, www.euromonitor.com; *World Marketing Data and Statistics.*

European Union, Delegation of the European Commission to the United States, 2300 M Street, NW, Washington, DC 20037, (202) 862-9500, Fax: (202) 429-1766, www.eurunion.org; *European Union Labour Force Survey* and *Regions - Statistical Yearbook 2006.*

Eurostat, Batiment Jean Monnet, Rue Alcide de Gasperi, L-2920 Luxembourg, http://epp.eurostat.ec.europa.eu; *Eurostat Yearbook 2006-2007.*

M.E. Sharpe, 80 Business Park Drive, Armonk, NY 10504, (800) 541-6563, Fax: (914) 273-2106, www.mesharpe.com; *The Illustrated Book of World Rankings.*

United Nations Statistics Division, New York, NY 10017, (800) 253-9646, Fax: (212) 963-4116, http://unstats.un.org; *Trends in Europe and North America: The Statistical Yearbook of the ECE 2005.*

BELGIUM - HOUSING - FINANCE

Organisation for Economic Cooperation and Development (OECD), 2 rue Andre Pascal, F-75775 Paris Cedex 16, France, (Telephone in U.S. (202) 785-6323), (Fax in U.S. (202) 785-0350), www.oecd.org; *OECD Main Economic Indicators (MEI).*

BELGIUM - HOUSING CONSTRUCTION

See BELGIUM - CONSTRUCTION INDUSTRY

BELGIUM - ILLITERATE PERSONS

Euromonitor International, Inc., 224 S. Michigan Avenue, Suite 1500, Chicago, IL 60604, (312) 922-1115, Fax: (312) 922-1157, www.euromonitor.com; *The World Economic Factbook 2008.*

UNESCO Institute for Statistics, C.P. 6128 Succursale Centre-Ville, Montreal, Quebec, H3C 3J7 Canada, (Dial from U.S. (514) 343-6880), (Fax from U.S. (514) 343 6882), www.uis.unesco.org; *Statistical Tables.*

United Nations Statistics Division, New York, NY 10017, (800) 253-9646, Fax: (212) 963-4116, http://unstats.un.org; *Human Development Report 2006.*

BELGIUM - IMPORTS

Central Intelligence Agency, Office of Public Affairs, Washington, DC 20505, (703) 482-0623, Fax: (703) 482-1739, www.cia.gov; *The World Factbook.*

Economist Intelligence Unit, 111 West 57th Street, New York, NY 10019, (212) 554-0600, Fax: (212) 586-1181, www.eiu.com; *Belgium Country Report.*

Euromonitor International, Inc., 224 S. Michigan Avenue, Suite 1500, Chicago, IL 60604, (312) 922-1115, Fax: (312) 922-1157, www.euromonitor.com; *The World Economic Factbook 2008.*

European Union, Delegation of the European Commission to the United States, 2300 M Street, NW, Washington, DC 20037, (202) 862-9500, Fax: (202) 429-1766, www.eurunion.org; *Eurostatistics: Data for Short-Term Economic Analysis (2007 edition); External and Intra-European Union Trade: Data 1958-2002; External and Intra-European Union Trade: Data 1999-2004;* and *Fishery Statistics - 1990-2006.*

Eurostat, Batiment Jean Monnet, Rue Alcide de Gasperi, L-2920 Luxembourg, http://epp.eurostat.ec.europa.eu; *Eurostat Yearbook 2006-2007.*

International Iron and Steel Institute (IISI), Rue Colonel Bourg 120, B-1140 Brussels, Belgium, www.worldsteel.org; *Steel Statistical Yearbook 2006.*

International Lead and Zinc Study Group (ILZSG), Rua Almirante Barroso 38, 5th Floor, Lisbon 1000 - 013, Portugal, www.ilzsg.org; Interactive Statistical Database.

International Monetary Fund (IMF), 700 Nineteenth Street, NW, Washington, DC 20431, (202) 623-7000, Fax: (202) 623-4661, www.imf.org; *Direction of Trade Statistics Yearbook 2007* and *Government Finance Statistics Yearbook (2008 Edition).*

Organisation for Economic Cooperation and Development (OECD), 2 rue Andre Pascal, F-75775 Paris Cedex 16, France, (Telephone in U.S. (202) 785-6323), (Fax in U.S. (202) 785-0350), www.oecd.org; *Iron and Steel Industry in 2004 (2006 Edition); 2005 OECD Agricultural Outlook Tables, 1970-2014; OECD Economic Outlook 2008; Review of Fisheries in OECD Countries: Country Statistics 2001 to 2003 - 2005 Edition;* and STructural ANalysis (STAN) database.

Palgrave Macmillan Ltd., Houndmills, Basingstoke, Hampshire, RG21 6XS, England, (Telephone in U.S. (888) 330-8477), (Fax in U.S. (800) 672-2054), www.palgrave.com; *The Statesman's Yearbook 2008.*

Platts, 2 Penn Plaza, 25th Floor, New York, NY 10121-2298, (212) 904-3070, www.platts.com; *Energy Economist.*

Taylor and Francis Group, An Informa Business, 2 Park Square, Milton Park, Abingdon, Oxford OX14 4RN, United Kingdom, (Dial from U.S. (212) 216-7800), (Fax from U.S. (212) 564-7854), www.tandf.co.uk; *The Europa World Year Book.*

Technical Association of the Pulp and Paper Industry (TAPPI), 15 Technology Parkway South, Norcross, GA 30092, (770) 446-1400, Fax: (770) 446-6947, www.tappi.org; *TAPPI Annual Report.*

United Nations Conference on Trade and Development (UNCTAD), DC2-1120, United Nations, New York, NY 10017, (212) 963-0027, www.unctad.org; *Handbook of Statistics 2005.*

United Nations Food and Agricultural Organization (FAO), Viale delle Terme di Caracalla, 00100 Rome, Italy, (Dial from U.S. (202) 653-2400), (Fax from U.S. (202) 653 5760), www.fao.org; *The State of Food and Agriculture (SOFA) 2006.*

United Nations Statistics Division, New York, NY 10017, (800) 253-9646, Fax: (212) 963-4116, http://unstats.un.org; *Energy Statistics Yearbook 2003* and *Trends in Europe and North America: The Statistical Yearbook of the ECE 2005.*

The World Bank, 1818 H Street, NW, Washington, DC 20433, (202) 473-1000, Fax: (202) 477-6391, www.worldbank.org; *World Development Indicators (WDI) 2008* and *World Development Report 2008.*

BELGIUM - INCOME TAXES

See BELGIUM - TAXATION

BELGIUM - INDUSTRIAL METALS PRODUCTION

See BELGIUM - MINERAL INDUSTRIES

BELGIUM - INDUSTRIAL PRODUCTIVITY

European Union, Delegation of the European Commission to the United States, 2300 M Street, NW, Washington, DC 20037, (202) 862-9500, Fax: (202) 429-1766, www.eurunion.org; *Eurostatistics: Data for Short-Term Economic Analysis (2007 edition); Fishery Statistics - 1990-2006;* and *RD Expenditure in Europe (2006 edition).*

Eurostat, Batiment Jean Monnet, Rue Alcide de Gasperi, L-2920 Luxembourg, http://epp.eurostat.ec.europa.eu; *Eurostat Yearbook 2006-2007.*

International Iron and Steel Institute (IISI), Rue Colonel Bourg 120, B-1140 Brussels, Belgium, www.worldsteel.org; *Steel Statistical Yearbook 2006.*

M.E. Sharpe, 80 Business Park Drive, Armonk, NY 10504, (800) 541-6563, Fax: (914) 273-2106, www.mesharpe.com; *The Illustrated Book of World Rankings.*

Organisation for Economic Cooperation and Development (OECD), 2 rue Andre Pascal, F-75775 Paris Cedex 16, France, (Telephone in U.S. (202) 785-6323), (Fax in U.S. (202) 785-0350), www.oecd.org; *Environmental Impacts of Foreign Direct Investment in the Mining Sector in the Newly Independent States (NIS); Indicators of Industrial Activity; Iron and Steel Industry in 2004 (2006 Edition); A New World Map in Textiles and Clothing: Adjusting to Change; 2005 OECD Agricultural Outlook Tables, 1970-2014; OECD Economic Outlook 2008;* and STructural ANalysis (STAN) database.

Technical Association of the Pulp and Paper Industry (TAPPI), 15 Technology Parkway South, Norcross, GA 30092, (770) 446-1400, Fax: (770) 446-6947, www.tappi.org; *TAPPI Annual Report.*

BELGIUM - INDUSTRIAL PROPERTY

United Nations Statistics Division, New York, NY 10017, (800) 253-9646, Fax: (212) 963-4116, http://unstats.un.org; *Statistical Yearbook.*

BELGIUM - INDUSTRIES

Central Intelligence Agency, Office of Public Affairs, Washington, DC 20505, (703) 482-0623, Fax: (703) 482-1739, www.cia.gov; *The World Factbook.*

Economist Intelligence Unit, 111 West 57th Street, New York, NY 10019, (212) 554-0600, Fax: (212) 586-1181, www.eiu.com; *Belgium Country Report.*

Euromonitor International, Inc., 224 S. Michigan Avenue, Suite 1500, Chicago, IL 60604, (312) 922-1115, Fax: (312) 922-1157, www.euromonitor.com; *The World Economic Factbook 2008* and *World Marketing Data and Statistics.*

European Union, Delegation of the European Commission to the United States, 2300 M Street, NW, Washington, DC 20037, (202) 862-9500, Fax: (202) 429-1766, www.eurunion.org; *European Union Labour Force Survey* and *Eurostatistics: Data for Short-Term Economic Analysis (2007 edition).*

Eurostat, Batiment Jean Monnet, Rue Alcide de Gasperi, L-2920 Luxembourg, http://epp.eurostat.ec.europa.eu; *Eurostat Yearbook 2006-2007.*

International Labour Office, I.L.O. Publications, 4 route des Morillons, CH-1211 Geneva 22, Switzerland, (Telephone in U.S. (202) 653-7652), (Fax in U.S. (202) 653-7687), www.ilo.org; *Yearbook of Labour Statistics 2006.*

M.E. Sharpe, 80 Business Park Drive, Armonk, NY 10504, (800) 541-6563, Fax: (914) 273-2106, www.mesharpe.com; *The Illustrated Book of World Rankings.*

Organisation for Economic Cooperation and Development (OECD), 2 rue Andre Pascal, F-75775 Paris Cedex 16, France, (Telephone in U.S. (202) 785-6323), (Fax in U.S. (202) 785-0350), www.oecd.org; *Indicators of Industrial Activity; Key Environmental Indicators 2004; OECD Economic Outlook 2008; OECD Main Economic Indicators (MEI);* and STructural ANalysis (STAN) database.

Palgrave Macmillan Ltd., Houndmills, Basingstoke, Hampshire, RG21 6XS, England, (Telephone in U.S. (888) 330-8477), (Fax in U.S. (800) 672-2054), www.palgrave.com; *The Statesman's Yearbook 2008.*

Taylor and Francis Group, An Informa Business, 2 Park Square, Milton Park, Abingdon, Oxford OX14 4RN, United Kingdom, (Dial from U.S. (212) 216-7800), (Fax from U.S. (212) 564-7854), www.tandf.co.uk; *The Europa World Year Book.*

United Nations Industrial Development Organization (UNIDO), 1 United Nations Plaza, New York, NY 10017, (212) 963 6890, Fax: (212) 963-7904, http://unido.org; Industrial Statistics Database 2008 (INDSTAT) and *The International Yearbook of Industrial Statistics 2008.*

United Nations Statistics Division, New York, NY 10017, (800) 253-9646, Fax: (212) 963-4116, http://unstats.un.org; *2004 Industrial Commodity Statistics Yearbook; Statistical Yearbook;* and *Trends in Europe and North America: The Statistical Yearbook of the ECE 2005.*

The World Bank, 1818 H Street, NW, Washington, DC 20433, (202) 473-1000, Fax: (202) 477-6391,

www.worldbank.org; *Belgium* and *World Development Indicators (WDI) 2008.*

BELGIUM - INFANT AND MATERNAL MORTALITY

See BELGIUM - MORTALITY

BELGIUM - INORGANIC ACIDS

Eurostat, Batiment Jean Monnet, Rue Alcide de Gasperi, L-2920 Luxembourg, http://epp.eurostat.ec.europa.eu; *Eurostat Yearbook 2006-2007.*

BELGIUM - INTEREST RATES

Eurostat, Batiment Jean Monnet, Rue Alcide de Gasperi, L-2920 Luxembourg, http://epp.eurostat.ec.europa.eu; *Eurostat Yearbook 2006-2007.*

Organisation for Economic Cooperation and Development (OECD), 2 rue Andre Pascal, F-75775 Paris Cedex 16, France, (Telephone in U.S. (202) 785-6323), (Fax in U.S. (202) 785-0350), www.oecd.org; *Financial Market Trends: OECD Periodical; OECD Economic Outlook 2008;* and *OECD Main Economic Indicators (MEI).*

United Nations Statistics Division, New York, NY 10017, (800) 253-9646, Fax: (212) 963-4116, http://unstats.un.org; *Statistical Yearbook.*

BELGIUM - INTERNAL REVENUE

Organisation for Economic Cooperation and Development (OECD), 2 rue Andre Pascal, F-75775 Paris Cedex 16, France, (Telephone in U.S. (202) 785-6323), (Fax in U.S. (202) 785-0350), www.oecd.org; *Revenue Statistics 1965-2006 - 2007 Edition.*

BELGIUM - INTERNATIONAL FINANCE

Eurostat, Batiment Jean Monnet, Rue Alcide de Gasperi, L-2920 Luxembourg, http://epp.eurostat.ec.europa.eu; *Eurostat Yearbook 2006-2007.*

Inter-American Development Bank (IDB), 1300 New York Avenue, NW, Washington, DC 20577, (202) 623-1000, Fax: (202) 623-3096, www.iadb.org; *The Politics of Policies: Economic and Social Progress in Latin America - 2006 Report.*

International Finance Corporation (IFC), 2121 Pennsylvania Avenue, NW, Washington, DC 20433 USA, (202) 473-1000, Fax: (202) 974-4384, www.ifc.org; *Annual Report 2007.*

Organisation for Economic Cooperation and Development (OECD), 2 rue Andre Pascal, F-75775 Paris Cedex 16, France, (Telephone in U.S. (202) 785-6323), (Fax in U.S. (202) 785-0350), www.oecd.org; *Financial Market Trends: OECD Periodical; OECD Economic Outlook 2008;* and *OECD Main Economic Indicators (MEI).*

BELGIUM - INTERNATIONAL LIQUIDITY

International Monetary Fund (IMF), 700 Nineteenth Street, NW, Washington, DC 20431, (202) 623-7000, Fax: (202) 623-4661, www.imf.org; *International Financial Statistics Yearbook 2007.*

Organisation for Economic Cooperation and Development (OECD), 2 rue Andre Pascal, F-75775 Paris Cedex 16, France, (Telephone in U.S. (202) 785-6323), (Fax in U.S. (202) 785-0350), www.oecd.org; *Financial Market Trends: OECD Periodical* and *OECD Economic Outlook 2008.*

BELGIUM - INTERNATIONAL STATISTICS

Organisation for Economic Cooperation and Development (OECD), 2 rue Andre Pascal, F-75775 Paris Cedex 16, France, (Telephone in U.S. (202) 785-6323), (Fax in U.S. (202) 785-0350), www.oecd.org; *Financial Market Trends: OECD Periodical* and *Household, Tourism, Travel: Trends, Environmental Impacts and Policy Responses.*

BELGIUM - INTERNATIONAL TRADE

Banque de France, 48 rue Croix des Petits champs, 75001 Paris, France, www.banque-france.fr/home.htm; *Monthly Business Survey Overview.*

Bernan Essential Government Publications, 4611-F Assembly Drive, Lanham MD, 20706-4391, (301) 459-2255, Fax: (800) 865-3450, www.bernan.com; *OECD Factbook 2006.*

Economist Intelligence Unit, 111 West 57th Street, New York, NY 10019, (212) 554-0600, Fax: (212) 586-1181, www.eiu.com; *Belgium Country Report.*

Euromonitor International, Inc., 224 S. Michigan Avenue, Suite 1500, Chicago, IL 60604, (312) 922-1115, Fax: (312) 922-1157, www.euromonitor.com; *European Marketing Data and Statistics 2008; The World Economic Factbook 2008;* and *World Marketing Data and Statistics.*

European Union, Delegation of the European Commission to the United States, 2300 M Street, NW, Washington, DC 20037, (202) 862-9500, Fax: (202) 429-1766, www.eurunion.org; *Eurostatistics: Data for Short-Term Economic Analysis (2007 edition); External and Intra-European Union Trade: Data 1958-2002; External and Intra-European Union Trade: Data 1999-2004;* and *Iron and Steel.*

Eurostat, Batiment Jean Monnet, Rue Alcide de Gasperi, L-2920 Luxembourg, http://epp.eurostat.ec.europa.eu; *Eurostat Yearbook 2006-2007* and Intra- and Extra-EU Trade.

International Iron and Steel Institute (IISI), Rue Colonel Bourg 120, B-1140 Brussels, Belgium, www.worldsteel.org; *Steel Statistical Yearbook 2006.*

M.E. Sharpe, 80 Business Park Drive, Armonk, NY 10504, (800) 541-6563, Fax: (914) 273-2106, www.mesharpe.com; *The Illustrated Book of World Rankings.*

Organisation for Economic Cooperation and Development (OECD), 2 rue Andre Pascal, F-75775 Paris Cedex 16, France, (Telephone in U.S. (202) 785-6323), (Fax in U.S. (202) 785-0350), www.oecd.org; *International Trade by Commodity Statistics (ITCS); 2005 OECD Agricultural Outlook Tables, 1970-2014; OECD Economic Outlook 2008; OECD Economic Survey - Belgium 2007; OECD in Figures 2007; OECD Main Economic Indicators (MEI);* and *Statistics on Ship Production, Exports and Orders in 2004.*

Palgrave Macmillan Ltd., Houndmills, Basingstoke, Hampshire, RG21 6XS, England, (Telephone in U.S. (888) 330-8477), (Fax in U.S. (800) 672-2054), www.palgrave.com; *The Statesman's Yearbook 2008.*

Taylor and Francis Group, An Informa Business, 2 Park Square, Milton Park, Abingdon, Oxford OX14 4RN, United Kingdom, (Dial from U.S. (212) 216-7800), (Fax from U.S. (212) 564-7854), www.tandf.co.uk; *The Europa World Year Book.*

United Nations Conference on Trade and Development (UNCTAD), DC2-1120, United Nations, New York, NY 10017, (212) 963-0027, www.unctad.org; *UNCTAD Commodity Yearbook.*

United Nations Food and Agricultural Organization (FAO), Viale delle Terme di Caracalla, 00100 Rome, Italy, (Dial from U.S. (202) 653-2400), (Fax from U.S. (202) 653 5760), www.fao.org; *FAO Trade Yearbook* and *The State of Food and Agriculture (SOFA) 2006.*

United Nations Statistics Division, New York, NY 10017, (800) 253-9646, Fax: (212) 963-4116, http://unstats.un.org; *International Trade Statistics Yearbook* and *Statistical Yearbook.*

The World Bank, 1818 H Street, NW, Washington, DC 20433, (202) 473-1000, Fax: (202) 477-6391, www.worldbank.org; *Belgium; World Development Indicators (WDI) 2008;* and *World Development Report 2008.*

World Bureau of Metal Statistics (WBMS), 27a High Street, Ware, Hertfordshire, SG12 9BA, United Kingdom, www.world-bureau.com; *World Flow Charts* and *World Metal Statistics.*

World Trade Organization (WTO), Centre William Rappard, Rue de Lausanne 154, CH-1211 Geneva 21, Switzerland, www.wto.org; *International Trade Statistics 2006.*

BELGIUM - INTERNET USERS

Eurostat, Batiment Jean Monnet, Rue Alcide de Gasperi, L-2920 Luxembourg, http://epp.eurostat.ec.europa.eu; *Internet Usage by Enterprises 2007.*

International Telecommunication Union (ITU), Place des Nations, 1211 Geneva 20, Switzerland, www.itu.int; *World Telecommunication/ICT Indicators Database on CD-ROM; World Telecommunication/ICT Indicators Database Online;* and *Yearbook of Statistics - Telecommunication Services (Chronological Time Series 1997-2006).*

The World Bank, 1818 H Street, NW, Washington, DC 20433, (202) 473-1000, Fax: (202) 477-6391, www.worldbank.org; *Belgium.*

BELGIUM - INVESTMENTS

International Monetary Fund (IMF), 700 Nineteenth Street, NW, Washington, DC 20431, (202) 623-7000, Fax: (202) 623-4661, www.imf.org; *International Financial Statistics Yearbook 2007.*

Organisation for Economic Cooperation and Development (OECD), 2 rue Andre Pascal, F-75775 Paris Cedex 16, France, (Telephone in U.S. (202) 785-6323), (Fax in U.S. (202) 785-0350), www.oecd.org; *Financial Market Trends: OECD Periodical; Iron and Steel Industry in 2004 (2006 Edition); A New World Map in Textiles and Clothing: Adjusting to Change; OECD Economic Outlook 2008;* and STructural ANalysis (STAN) database.

BELGIUM - IRON AND IRON ORE PRODUCTION

See BELGIUM - MINERAL INDUSTRIES

BELGIUM - JUTE PRODUCTION

See BELGIUM - CROPS

BELGIUM - LABOR

Central Intelligence Agency, Office of Public Affairs, Washington, DC 20505, (703) 482-0623, Fax: (703) 482-1739, www.cia.gov; *The World Factbook.*

Euromonitor International, Inc., 224 S. Michigan Avenue, Suite 1500, Chicago, IL 60604, (312) 922-1115, Fax: (312) 922-1157, www.euromonitor.com; *World Marketing Data and Statistics.*

European Union, Delegation of the European Commission to the United States, 2300 M Street, NW, Washington, DC 20037, (202) 862-9500, Fax: (202) 429-1766, www.eurunion.org; *European Union Labour Force Survey* and *Regions - Statistical Yearbook 2006.*

Eurostat, Batiment Jean Monnet, Rue Alcide de Gasperi, L-2920 Luxembourg, http://epp.eurostat.ec.europa.eu; *Eurostat Yearbook 2006-2007.*

International Labour Office, I.L.O. Publications, 4 route des Morillons, CH-1211 Geneva 22, Switzerland, (Telephone in U.S. (202) 653-7652), (Fax in U.S. (202) 653-7687), www.ilo.org; *Yearbook of Labour Statistics 2006.*

M.E. Sharpe, 80 Business Park Drive, Armonk, NY 10504, (800) 541-6563, Fax: (914) 273-2106, www.mesharpe.com; *The Illustrated Book of World Rankings.*

Organisation for Economic Cooperation and Development (OECD), 2 rue Andre Pascal, F-75775 Paris Cedex 16, France, (Telephone in U.S. (202) 785-6323), (Fax in U.S. (202) 785-0350), www.oecd.org; *Iron and Steel Industry in 2004 (2006 Edition); OECD Economic Outlook 2008; OECD Economic Survey - Belgium 2007; OECD Employment Outlook 2007; OECD Main Economic Indicators (MEI);* and *Statistics on Ship Production, Exports and Orders in 2004.*

Palgrave Macmillan Ltd., Houndmills, Basingstoke, Hampshire, RG21 6XS, England, (Telephone in U.S. (888) 330-8477), (Fax in U.S. (800) 672-2054), www.palgrave.com; *The Statesman's Yearbook 2008.*

United Nations Food and Agricultural Organization (FAO), Viale delle Terme di Caracalla, 00100 Rome, Italy, (Dial from U.S. (202) 653-2400), (Fax from

U.S. (202) 653 5760), www.fao.org; *The State of Food and Agriculture (SOFA) 2006.*

United Nations Statistics Division, New York, NY 10017, (800) 253-9646, Fax: (212) 963-4116, http://unstats.un.org; *Human Development Report 2006.*

The World Bank, 1818 H Street, NW, Washington, DC 20433, (202) 473-1000, Fax: (202) 477-6391, www.worldbank.org; *The World Bank Atlas 2003-2004; World Development Indicators (WDI) 2008;* and *World Development Report 2008.*

BELGIUM - LAND USE

Central Intelligence Agency, Office of Public Affairs, Washington, DC 20505, (703) 482-0623, Fax: (703) 482-1739, www.cia.gov; *The World Factbook.*

Euromonitor International, Inc., 224 S. Michigan Avenue, Suite 1500, Chicago, IL 60604, (312) 922-1115, Fax: (312) 922-1157, www.euromonitor.com; *European Marketing Data and Statistics 2008.*

European Union, Delegation of the European Commission to the United States, 2300 M Street, NW, Washington, DC 20037, (202) 862-9500, Fax: (202) 429-1766, www.eurunion.org; *Agricultural Statistics: Data 1995-2005; Agriculture in the European Union: Statistical and Economic Information 2006;* and *Regions - Statistical Yearbook 2006.*

Eurostat, Batiment Jean Monnet, Rue Alcide de Gasperi, L-2920 Luxembourg, http://epp.eurostat.ec.europa.eu; *Eurostat Yearbook 2006-2007.*

United Nations Food and Agricultural Organization (FAO), Viale delle Terme di Caracalla, 00100 Rome, Italy, (Dial from U.S. (202) 653-2400), (Fax from U.S. (202) 653 5760), www.fao.org; *FAO Production Yearbook 2002.*

The World Bank, 1818 H Street, NW, Washington, DC 20433, (202) 473-1000, Fax: (202) 477-6391, www.worldbank.org; *World Development Report 2008.*

BELGIUM - LEATHER INDUSTRY AND TRADE

Eurostat, Batiment Jean Monnet, Rue Alcide de Gasperi, L-2920 Luxembourg, http://epp.eurostat.ec.europa.eu; *Eurostat Yearbook 2006-2007.*

Organisation for Economic Cooperation and Development (OECD), 2 rue Andre Pascal, F-75775 Paris Cedex 16, France, (Telephone in U.S. (202) 785-6323), (Fax in U.S. (202) 785-0350), www.oecd.org; *Indicators of Industrial Activity.*

BELGIUM - LIBRARIES

Euromonitor International, Inc., 224 S. Michigan Avenue, Suite 1500, Chicago, IL 60604, (312) 922-1115, Fax: (312) 922-1157, www.euromonitor.com; *European Marketing Data and Statistics 2008.*

M.E. Sharpe, 80 Business Park Drive, Armonk, NY 10504, (800) 541-6563, Fax: (914) 273-2106, www.mesharpe.com; *The Illustrated Book of World Rankings.*

UNESCO Institute for Statistics, C.P. 6128 Succursale Centre-Ville, Montreal, Quebec, H3C 3J7 Canada, (Dial from U.S. (514) 343-6880), (Fax from U.S. (514) 343 6882), www.uis.unesco.org; *Statistical Tables.*

United Nations Statistics Division, New York, NY 10017, (800) 253-9646, Fax: (212) 963-4116, http://unstats.un.org; *Trends in Europe and North America: The Statistical Yearbook of the ECE 2005.*

BELGIUM - LICENSES

International Monetary Fund (IMF), 700 Nineteenth Street, NW, Washington, DC 20431, (202) 623-7000, Fax: (202) 623-4661, www.imf.org; *Government Finance Statistics Yearbook (2008 Edition).*

BELGIUM - LIFE EXPECTANCY

Central Intelligence Agency, Office of Public Affairs, Washington, DC 20505, (703) 482-0623, Fax: (703) 482-1739, www.cia.gov; *The World Factbook.*

Euromonitor International, Inc., 224 S. Michigan Avenue, Suite 1500, Chicago, IL 60604, (312) 922-1115, Fax: (312) 922-1157, www.euromonitor.com; *The World Economic Factbook 2008.*

Organisation for Economic Cooperation and Development (OECD), 2 rue Andre Pascal, F-75775 Paris Cedex 16, France, (Telephone in U.S. (202) 785-6323), (Fax in U.S. (202) 785-0350), www.oecd.org; *OECD Economic Outlook 2008.*

Palgrave Macmillan Ltd., Houndmills, Basingstoke, Hampshire, RG21 6XS, England, (Telephone in U.S. (888) 330-8477), (Fax in U.S. (800) 672-2054), www.palgrave.com; *The Statesman's Yearbook 2008.*

United Nations Statistics Division, New York, NY 10017, (800) 253-9646, Fax: (212) 963-4116, http://unstats.un.org; *Human Development Report 2006; Trends in Europe and North America: The Statistical Yearbook of the ECE 2005;* and *World Statistics Pocketbook.*

The World Bank, 1818 H Street, NW, Washington, DC 20433, (202) 473-1000, Fax: (202) 477-6391, www.worldbank.org; *The World Bank Atlas 2003-2004* and *World Development Report 2008.*

BELGIUM - LITERACY

Euromonitor International, Inc., 224 S. Michigan Avenue, Suite 1500, Chicago, IL 60604, (312) 922-1115, Fax: (312) 922-1157, www.euromonitor.com; *World Marketing Data and Statistics.*

BELGIUM - LIVESTOCK

Euromonitor International, Inc., 224 S. Michigan Avenue, Suite 1500, Chicago, IL 60604, (312) 922-1115, Fax: (312) 922-1157, www.euromonitor.com; *European Marketing Data and Statistics 2008.*

European Union, Delegation of the European Commission to the United States, 2300 M Street, NW, Washington, DC 20037, (202) 862-9500, Fax: (202) 429-1766, www.eurunion.org; *Agricultural Statistics: Data 1995-2005; Eurostatistics: Data for Short-Term Economic Analysis (2007 edition);* and *Regions - Statistical Yearbook 2006.*

Eurostat, Batiment Jean Monnet, Rue Alcide de Gasperi, L-2920 Luxembourg, http://epp.eurostat.ec.europa.eu; *Eurostat Yearbook 2006-2007.*

M.E. Sharpe, 80 Business Park Drive, Armonk, NY 10504, (800) 541-6563, Fax: (914) 273-2106, www.mesharpe.com; *The Illustrated Book of World Rankings.*

Organisation for Economic Cooperation and Development (OECD), 2 rue Andre Pascal, F-75775 Paris Cedex 16, France, (Telephone in U.S. (202) 785-6323), (Fax in U.S. (202) 785-0350), www.oecd.org; *2005 OECD Agricultural Outlook Tables, 1970-2014.*

Palgrave Macmillan Ltd., Houndmills, Basingstoke, Hampshire, RG21 6XS, England, (Telephone in U.S. (888) 330-8477), (Fax in U.S. (800) 672-2054), www.palgrave.com; *The Statesman's Yearbook 2008.*

Taylor and Francis Group, An Informa Business, 2 Park Square, Milton Park, Abingdon, Oxford OX14 4RN, United Kingdom, (Dial from U.S. (212) 216-7800), (Fax from U.S. (212) 564-7854), www.tandf.co.uk; *The Europa World Year Book.*

United Nations Conference on Trade and Development (UNCTAD), DC2-1120, United Nations, New York, NY 10017, (212) 963-0027, www.unctad.org; *UNCTAD Commodity Yearbook.*

United Nations Food and Agricultural Organization (FAO), Viale delle Terme di Caracalla, 00100 Rome, Italy, (Dial from U.S. (202) 653-2400), (Fax from U.S. (202) 653 5760), www.fao.org; *FAO Production Yearbook 2002* and *The State of Food and Agriculture (SOFA) 2006.*

United Nations Statistics Division, New York, NY 10017, (800) 253-9646, Fax: (212) 963-4116, http://unstats.un.org; *Statistical Yearbook.*

BELGIUM - MACHINERY

Organisation for Economic Cooperation and Development (OECD), 2 rue Andre Pascal, F-75775 Paris Cedex 16, France, (Telephone in U.S. (202) 785-6323), (Fax in U.S. (202) 785-0350), www.oecd.org; *Indicators of Industrial Activity.*

BELGIUM - MAGNESIUM PRODUCTION AND CONSUMPTION

See BELGIUM - MINERAL INDUSTRIES

BELGIUM - MANUFACTURES

European Union, Delegation of the European Commission to the United States, 2300 M Street, NW, Washington, DC 20037, (202) 862-9500, Fax: (202) 429-1766, www.eurunion.org; *Eurostatistics: Data for Short-Term Economic Analysis (2007 edition)* and *The Textile Industry in the EU.*

Eurostat, Batiment Jean Monnet, Rue Alcide de Gasperi, L-2920 Luxembourg, http://epp.eurostat.ec.europa.eu; *Eurostat Yearbook 2006-2007.*

M.E. Sharpe, 80 Business Park Drive, Armonk, NY 10504, (800) 541-6563, Fax: (914) 273-2106, www.mesharpe.com; *The Illustrated Book of World Rankings.*

Organisation for Economic Cooperation and Development (OECD), 2 rue Andre Pascal, F-75775 Paris Cedex 16, France, (Telephone in U.S. (202) 785-6323), (Fax in U.S. (202) 785-0350), www.oecd.org; *Indicators of Industrial Activity; International Trade by Commodity Statistics (ITCS); OECD Economic Survey - Belgium 2007;* and STructural ANalysis (STAN) database.

United Nations Statistics Division, New York, NY 10017, (800) 253-9646, Fax: (212) 963-4116, http://unstats.un.org; *Statistical Yearbook.*

The World Bank, 1818 H Street, NW, Washington, DC 20433, (202) 473-1000, Fax: (202) 477-6391, www.worldbank.org; *World Development Indicators (WDI) 2008.*

BELGIUM - MARRIAGE

Eurostat, Batiment Jean Monnet, Rue Alcide de Gasperi, L-2920 Luxembourg, http://epp.eurostat.ec.europa.eu; *Eurostat Yearbook 2006-2007.*

M.E. Sharpe, 80 Business Park Drive, Armonk, NY 10504, (800) 541-6563, Fax: (914) 273-2106, www.mesharpe.com; *The Illustrated Book of World Rankings.*

Taylor and Francis Group, An Informa Business, 2 Park Square, Milton Park, Abingdon, Oxford OX14 4RN, United Kingdom, (Dial from U.S. (212) 216-7800), (Fax from U.S. (212) 564-7854), www.tandf.co.uk; *The Europa World Year Book.*

United Nations Statistics Division, New York, NY 10017, (800) 253-9646, Fax: (212) 963-4116, http://unstats.un.org; *Demographic Yearbook; Statistical Yearbook;* and *Trends in Europe and North America: The Statistical Yearbook of the ECE 2005.*

BELGIUM - MEAT PRODUCTION

See BELGIUM - LIVESTOCK

BELGIUM - MERCURY PRODUCTION

See BELGIUM - MINERAL INDUSTRIES

BELGIUM - METAL PRODUCTS

Eurostat, Batiment Jean Monnet, Rue Alcide de Gasperi, L-2920 Luxembourg, http://epp.eurostat.ec.europa.eu; *Eurostat Yearbook 2006-2007.*

BELGIUM - MILK PRODUCTION

See BELGIUM - DAIRY PROCESSING

BELGIUM - MINERAL INDUSTRIES

Commodity Research Bureau, 330 South Wells Street, Suite 612, Chicago, IL 60606-7110, (800) 621-5271, Fax: (312) 939-4135, www.crbtrader.com; *2006 CRB Commodity Yearbook and CD.*

European Union, Delegation of the European Commission to the United States, 2300 M Street, NW, Washington, DC 20037, (202) 862-9500, Fax: (202) 429-1766, www.eurunion.org; *European Union Energy Transport in Figures 2006; Eurostatistics; Data for Short-Term Economic Analysis (2007 edition); Iron and Steel;* and *Regions - Statistical Yearbook 2006.*

Eurostat, Batiment Jean Monnet, Rue Alcide de Gasperi, L-2920 Luxembourg, http://epp.eurostat.ec.europa.eu; *Energy - Monthly Statistics; Eurostat Yearbook 2006-2007;* and *Panorama of Energy - 2007 Edition.*

International Energy Agency (IEA), 9, rue de la Federation, 75739 Paris Cedex 15, France, www.iea.org; *Key World Energy Statistics 2007.*

International Iron and Steel Institute (IISI), Rue Colonel Bourg 120, B-1140 Brussels, Belgium, www.worldsteel.org; *Steel Statistical Yearbook 2006.*

International Lead and Zinc Study Group (ILZSG), Rua Almirante Barroso 38, 5th Floor, Lisbon 1000 - 013, Portugal, www.ilzsg.org; Interactive Statistical Database.

M.E. Sharpe, 80 Business Park Drive, Armonk, NY 10504, (800) 541-6563, Fax: (914) 273-2106, www.mesharpe.com; *The Illustrated Book of World Rankings.*

Organisation for Economic Cooperation and Development (OECD), 2 rue Andre Pascal, F-75775 Paris Cedex 16, France, (Telephone in U.S. (202) 785-6323), (Fax in U.S. (202) 785-0350), www.oecd.org; *Coal Information: 2007 Edition; Energy Statistics of OECD Countries* (2007 Edition); *Environmental Impacts of Foreign Direct Investment in the Mining Sector in the Newly Independent States (NIS); Indicators of Industrial Activity; International Trade by Commodity Statistics (ITCS); Iron and Steel Industry in 2004 (2006 Edition); OECD Economic Survey - Belgium 2007; OECD Main Economic Indicators (MEI);* and STructural ANalysis (STAN) database.

Palgrave Macmillan Ltd., Houndmills, Basingstoke, Hampshire, RG21 6XS, England, (Telephone in U.S. (888) 330-8477), (Fax in U.S. (800) 672-2054), www.palgrave.com; *The Statesman's Yearbook 2008.*

Platts, 2 Penn Plaza, 25th Floor, New York, NY 10121-2298, (212) 904-3070, www.platts.com; *Energy Economist* and *EU Energy.*

Taylor and Francis Group, An Informa Business, 2 Park Square, Milton Park, Abingdon, Oxford OX14 4RN, United Kingdom, (Dial from U.S. (212) 216-7800), (Fax from U.S. (212) 564-7854), www.tandf.co.uk; *The Europa World Year Book.*

United Nations Conference on Trade and Development (UNCTAD), DC2-1120, United Nations, New York, NY 10017, (212) 963-0027, www.unctad.org; *UNCTAD Commodity Yearbook.*

United Nations Statistics Division, New York, NY 10017, (800) 253-9646, Fax: (212) 963-4116, http://unstats.un.org; *Energy Statistics Yearbook 2003* and *Statistical Yearbook.*

World Bureau of Metal Statistics (WBMS), 27a High Street, Ware, Hertfordshire, SG12 9BA, United Kingdom, www.world-bureau.com; *Annual Stainless Steel Statistics; World Flow Charts; World Metal Statistics; World Nickel Statistics;* and *World Tin Statistics.*

BELGIUM - MONEY

European Central Bank (ECB), Postfach 160319, D-60066 Frankfurt am Main, Germany, www.ecb.int; *Monetary Developments in the Euro Area; Monthly Bulletin;* and *Statistics Pocket Book.*

Organisation for Economic Cooperation and Development (OECD), 2 rue Andre Pascal, F-75775 Paris Cedex 16, France, (Telephone in U.S. (202) 785-6323), (Fax in U.S. (202) 785-0350), www.oecd.org; *OECD Economic Survey - Belgium 2007.*

BELGIUM - MONEY EXCHANGE RATES

See BELGIUM - FOREIGN EXCHANGE RATES

BELGIUM - MONEY SUPPLY

Economist Intelligence Unit, 111 West 57th Street, New York, NY 10019, (212) 554-0600, Fax: (212) 586-1181, www.eiu.com; *Belgium Country Report.*

European Union, Delegation of the European Commission to the United States, 2300 M Street, NW, Washington, DC 20037, (202) 862-9500, Fax: (202) 429-1766, www.eurunion.org; *Eurostatistics: Data for Short-Term Economic Analysis (2007 edition).*

Eurostat, Batiment Jean Monnet, Rue Alcide de Gasperi, L-2920 Luxembourg, http://epp.eurostat.ec.europa.eu; *Eurostat Yearbook 2006-2007.*

International Monetary Fund (IMF), 700 Nineteenth Street, NW, Washington, DC 20431, (202) 623-7000, Fax: (202) 623-4661, www.imf.org; *International Financial Statistics Yearbook 2007.*

Organisation for Economic Cooperation and Development (OECD), 2 rue Andre Pascal, F-75775 Paris Cedex 16, France, (Telephone in U.S. (202) 785-6323), (Fax in U.S. (202) 785-0350), www.oecd.org; *OECD Economic Outlook 2008.*

Taylor and Francis Group, An Informa Business, 2 Park Square, Milton Park, Abingdon, Oxford OX14 4RN, United Kingdom, (Dial from U.S. (212) 216-7800), (Fax from U.S. (212) 564-7854), www.tandf.co.uk; *The Europa World Year Book.*

United Nations Statistics Division, New York, NY 10017, (800) 253-9646, Fax: (212) 963-4116, http://unstats.un.org; *Statistical Yearbook.*

The World Bank, 1818 H Street, NW, Washington, DC 20433, (202) 473-1000, Fax: (202) 477-6391, www.worldbank.org; *Belgium* and *World Development Indicators (WDI) 2008.*

BELGIUM - MORTALITY

Central Intelligence Agency, Office of Public Affairs, Washington, DC 20505, (703) 482-0623, Fax: (703) 482-1739, www.cia.gov; *The World Factbook.*

Euromonitor International, Inc., 224 S. Michigan Avenue, Suite 1500, Chicago, IL 60604, (312) 922-1115, Fax: (312) 922-1157, www.euromonitor.com; *The World Economic Factbook 2008.*

European Union, Delegation of the European Commission to the United States, 2300 M Street, NW, Washington, DC 20037, (202) 862-9500, Fax: (202) 429-1766, www.eurunion.org; *First Demographic Estimates for 2006.*

Eurostat, Batiment Jean Monnet, Rue Alcide de Gasperi, L-2920 Luxembourg, http://epp.eurostat.ec.europa.eu; *Eurostat Yearbook 2006-2007.*

Palgrave Macmillan Ltd., Houndmills, Basingstoke, Hampshire, RG21 6XS, England, (Telephone in U.S. (888) 330-8477), (Fax in U.S. (800) 672-2054), www.palgrave.com; *The Statesman's Yearbook 2008.*

Taylor and Francis Group, An Informa Business, 2 Park Square, Milton Park, Abingdon, Oxford OX14 4RN, United Kingdom, (Dial from U.S. (212) 216-7800), (Fax from U.S. (212) 564-7854), www.tandf.co.uk; *The Europa World Year Book.*

United Nations Statistics Division, New York, NY 10017, (800) 253-9646, Fax: (212) 963-4116, http://unstats.un.org; *Demographic Yearbook; Human Development Report 2006; Statistical Yearbook; Trends in Europe and North America: The Statistical Yearbook of the ECE 2005;* and *World Statistics Pocketbook.*

The World Bank, 1818 H Street, NW, Washington, DC 20433, (202) 473-1000, Fax: (202) 477-6391, www.worldbank.org; *The World Bank Atlas 2003-2004* and *World Development Report 2008.*

World Health Organization (WHO), Avenue Appia 20, 1211 Geneve 27, Switzerland, (Telephone in U.S. (212) 331-9081), www.who.int; The WHO Global Atlas of Infectious Diseases and *World Health Report 2006.*

BELGIUM - MOTION PICTURES

Palgrave Macmillan Ltd., Houndmills, Basingstoke, Hampshire, RG21 6XS, England, (Telephone in U.S. (888) 330-8477), (Fax in U.S. (800) 672-2054), www.palgrave.com; *The Statesman's Yearbook 2008.*

UNESCO Institute for Statistics, C.P. 6128 Succursale Centre-Ville, Montreal, Quebec, H3C 3J7 Canada, (Dial from U.S. (514) 343-6880), (Fax from U.S. (514) 343 6882), www.uis.unesco.org; *Statistical Tables.*

United Nations Statistics Division, New York, NY 10017, (800) 253-9646, Fax: (212) 963-4116, http://unstats.un.org; *Statistical Yearbook.*

BELGIUM - MOTOR VEHICLES

European Union, Delegation of the European Commission to the United States, 2300 M Street, NW, Washington, DC 20037, (202) 862-9500, Fax: (202) 429-1766, www.eurunion.org; *Statistical Overview of Transport in the European Union (Data 1970-2001).*

International Road Federation (IFR), Madison Place, 500 Montgomery Street, 5th Floor, Alexandria, VA 22314, (703) 535-1001, Fax: (703) 535-1007, www.irfnet.org; *World Road Statistics 2006.*

Taylor and Francis Group, An Informa Business, 2 Park Square, Milton Park, Abingdon, Oxford OX14 4RN, United Kingdom, (Dial from U.S. (212) 216-7800), (Fax from U.S. (212) 564-7854), www.tandf.co.uk; *The Europa World Year Book.*

United Nations Statistics Division, New York, NY 10017, (800) 253-9646, Fax: (212) 963-4116, http://unstats.un.org; *Statistical Yearbook.*

BELGIUM - MUSEUMS

M.E. Sharpe, 80 Business Park Drive, Armonk, NY 10504, (800) 541-6563, Fax: (914) 273-2106, www.mesharpe.com; *The Illustrated Book of World Rankings.*

UNESCO Institute for Statistics, C.P. 6128 Succursale Centre-Ville, Montreal, Quebec, H3C 3J7 Canada, (Dial from U.S. (514) 343-6880), (Fax from U.S. (514) 343 6882), www.uis.unesco.org; *Statistical Tables.*

BELGIUM - NATIONAL INCOME

United Nations Statistics Division, New York, NY 10017, (800) 253-9646, Fax: (212) 963-4116, http://unstats.un.org; *Statistical Yearbook.*

BELGIUM - NATURAL GAS PRODUCTION

See BELGIUM - MINERAL INDUSTRIES

BELGIUM - NICKEL AND NICKEL ORE

See BELGIUM - MINERAL INDUSTRIES

BELGIUM - NUTRITION

United Nations Food and Agricultural Organization (FAO), Viale delle Terme di Caracalla, 00100 Rome, Italy, (Dial from U.S. (202) 653-2400), (Fax from U.S. (202) 653 5760), www.fao.org; *The State of Food and Agriculture (SOFA) 2006.*

BELGIUM - OATS PRODUCTION

See BELGIUM - CROPS

BELGIUM - OILSEED PLANTS

Eurostat, Batiment Jean Monnet, Rue Alcide de Gasperi, L-2920 Luxembourg, http://epp.eurostat.ec.europa.eu; *Eurostat Yearbook 2006-2007.*

Organisation for Economic Cooperation and Development (OECD), 2 rue Andre Pascal, F-75775 Paris Cedex 16, France, (Telephone in U.S. (202) 785-6323), (Fax in U.S. (202) 785-0350), www.oecd.org; *International Trade by Commodity Statistics (ITCS).*

BELGIUM - OLDER PEOPLE

M.E. Sharpe, 80 Business Park Drive, Armonk, NY 10504, (800) 541-6563, Fax: (914) 273-2106, www.mesharpe.com; *The Illustrated Book of World Rankings.*

BELGIUM - ONION PRODUCTION

See BELGIUM - CROPS

BELGIUM - PALM OIL PRODUCTION

See BELGIUM - CROPS

BELGIUM - PAPER

See BELGIUM - FORESTS AND FORESTRY

BELGIUM - PEANUT PRODUCTION

See BELGIUM - CROPS

BELGIUM - PEPPER PRODUCTION

See BELGIUM - CROPS

BELGIUM - PERIODICALS

UNESCO Institute for Statistics, C.P. 6128 Succursale Centre-Ville, Montreal, Quebec, H3C 3J7 Canada, (Dial from U.S. (514) 343-6880), (Fax from U.S. (514) 343 6882), www.uis.unesco.org; *Statistical Tables.*

BELGIUM - PESTICIDES

United Nations Food and Agricultural Organization (FAO), Viale delle Terme di Caracalla, 00100 Rome, Italy, (Dial from U.S. (202) 653-2400), (Fax from U.S. (202) 653 5760), www.fao.org; *The State of Food and Agriculture (SOFA) 2006.*

BELGIUM - PETROLEUM INDUSTRY AND TRADE

Euromonitor International, Inc., 224 S. Michigan Avenue, Suite 1500, Chicago, IL 60604, (312) 922-1115, Fax: (312) 922-1157, www.euromonitor.com; *European Marketing Data and Statistics 2008.*

Eurostat, Batiment Jean Monnet, Rue Alcide de Gasperi, L-2920 Luxembourg, http://epp.eurostat.ec.europa.eu; *Eurostat Yearbook 2006-2007.*

International Energy Agency (IEA), 9, rue de la Federation, 75739 Paris Cedex 15, France, www.iea.org; *Key World Energy Statistics 2007.*

M.E. Sharpe, 80 Business Park Drive, Armonk, NY 10504, (800) 541-6563, Fax: (914) 273-2106, www.mesharpe.com; *The Illustrated Book of World Rankings.*

Organisation for Economic Cooperation and Development (OECD), 2 rue Andre Pascal, F-75775 Paris Cedex 16, France, (Telephone in U.S. (202) 785-6323), (Fax in U.S. (202) 785-0350), www.oecd.org; *Energy Statistics of OECD Countries* (2007 Edition); *Indicators of Industrial Activity; International Trade by Commodity Statistics (ITCS);* and *Oil Information 2006 Edition.*

Palgrave Macmillan Ltd., Houndmills, Basingstoke, Hampshire, RG21 6XS, England, (Telephone in U.S. (888) 330-8477), (Fax in U.S. (800) 672-2054), www.palgrave.com; *The Statesman's Yearbook 2008.*

PennWell Corporation, 1421 South Sheridan Road, Tulsa, OK 74112, (918) 835-3161, www.pennwell.com; *International Petroleum Encyclopedia 2007.*

Platts, 2 Penn Plaza, 25th Floor, New York, NY 10121-2298, (212) 904-3070, www.platts.com; *Energy Economist.*

U.S. Department of Energy (DOE), Energy Information Administration (EIA), 1000 Independence Avenue, SW, Washington, DC 20585, (202) 586-8800, www.eia.doe.gov; *International Energy Annual 2004* and *International Energy Outlook 2006.*

United Nations Conference on Trade and Development (UNCTAD), DC2-1120, United Nations, New York, NY 10017, (212) 963-0027, www.unctad.org; *UNCTAD Commodity Yearbook.*

United Nations Food and Agricultural Organization (FAO), Viale delle Terme di Caracalla, 00100 Rome, Italy, (Dial from U.S. (202) 653-2400), (Fax from U.S. (202) 653 5760), www.fao.org; *The State of Food and Agriculture (SOFA) 2006.*

United Nations Statistics Division, New York, NY 10017, (800) 253-9646, Fax: (212) 963-4116, http://unstats.un.org; *Energy Statistics Yearbook 2003; Statistical Yearbook;* and *Trends in Europe and North America: The Statistical Yearbook of the ECE 2005.*

BELGIUM - PHOSPHATES PRODUCTION

See BELGIUM - MINERAL INDUSTRIES

BELGIUM - PIPELINES

European Union, Delegation of the European Commission to the United States, 2300 M Street, NW, Washington, DC 20037, (202) 862-9500, Fax: (202) 429-1766, www.eurunion.org; *Statistical Overview of Transport in the European Union (Data 1970-2001).*

United Nations Statistics Division, New York, NY 10017, (800) 253-9646, Fax: (212) 963-4116, http://unstats.un.org; *Annual Bulletin of Transport Statistics for Europe and North America 2004.*

BELGIUM - PLASTICS INDUSTRY AND TRADE

Eurostat, Batiment Jean Monnet, Rue Alcide de Gasperi, L-2920 Luxembourg, http://epp.eurostat.ec.europa.eu; *Eurostat Yearbook 2006-2007.*

Organisation for Economic Cooperation and Development (OECD), 2 rue Andre Pascal, F-75775 Paris Cedex 16, France, (Telephone in U.S. (202) 785-6323), (Fax in U.S. (202) 785-0350), www.oecd.org; *International Trade by Commodity Statistics (ITCS).*

United Nations Statistics Division, New York, NY 10017, (800) 253-9646, Fax: (212) 963-4116, http://unstats.un.org; *Statistical Yearbook.*

BELGIUM - PLATINUM PRODUCTION

See BELGIUM - MINERAL INDUSTRIES

BELGIUM - POLITICAL SCIENCE

Central Intelligence Agency, Office of Public Affairs, Washington, DC 20505, (703) 482-0623, Fax: (703) 482-1739, www.cia.gov; *The World Factbook.*

European Union, Delegation of the European Commission to the United States, 2300 M Street, NW, Washington, DC 20037, (202) 862-9500, Fax: (202) 429-1766, www.eurunion.org; *RD Expenditure in Europe (2006 edition).*

Eurostat, Batiment Jean Monnet, Rue Alcide de Gasperi, L-2920 Luxembourg, http://epp.eurostat.ec.europa.eu; *Eurostat Yearbook 2006-2007.*

International Monetary Fund (IMF), 700 Nineteenth Street, NW, Washington, DC 20431, (202) 623-7000, Fax: (202) 623-4661, www.imf.org; *Government Finance Statistics Yearbook (2008 Edition).*

Organisation for Economic Cooperation and Development (OECD), 2 rue Andre Pascal, F-75775 Paris Cedex 16, France, (Telephone in U.S. (202) 785-6323), (Fax in U.S. (202) 785-0350), www.oecd.org; *OECD Economic Outlook 2008* and *Revenue Statistics 1965-2006 - 2007 Edition.*

Palgrave Macmillan Ltd., Houndmills, Basingstoke, Hampshire, RG21 6XS, England, (Telephone in U.S. (888) 330-8477), (Fax in U.S. (800) 672-2054), www.palgrave.com; *The Statesman's Yearbook 2008.*

Taylor and Francis Group, An Informa Business, 2 Park Square, Milton Park, Abingdon, Oxford OX14 4RN, United Kingdom, (Dial from U.S. (212) 216-7800), (Fax from U.S. (212) 564-7854), www.tandf.co.uk; *The Europa World Year Book.*

United Nations Statistics Division, New York, NY 10017, (800) 253-9646, Fax: (212) 963-4116, http://unstats.un.org; *National Accounts Statistics: Compendium of Income Distribution Statistics* and *Statistical Yearbook.*

The World Bank, 1818 H Street, NW, Washington, DC 20433, (202) 473-1000, Fax: (202) 477-6391, www.worldbank.org; *World Development Indicators (WDI) 2008* and *World Development Report 2008.*

BELGIUM - POPULATION

Banque de France, 48 rue Croix des Petits champs, 75001 Paris, France, www.banque-france.fr/home.htm; *Key Data for the Euro Area.*

Central Intelligence Agency, Office of Public Affairs, Washington, DC 20505, (703) 482-0623, Fax: (703) 482-1739, www.cia.gov; *The World Factbook.*

Economist Intelligence Unit, 111 West 57th Street, New York, NY 10019, (212) 554-0600, Fax: (212) 586-1181, www.eiu.com; *Belgium Country Report.*

Euromonitor International, Inc., 224 S. Michigan Avenue, Suite 1500, Chicago, IL 60604, (312) 922-1115, Fax: (312) 922-1157, www.euromonitor.com; *European Marketing Data and Statistics 2008* and *The World Economic Factbook 2008.*

European Union, Delegation of the European Commission to the United States, 2300 M Street, NW, Washington, DC 20037, (202) 862-9500, Fax: (202) 429-1766, www.eurunion.org; *European Union Labour Force Survey; First Demographic Estimates for 2006;* and *Regions - Statistical Yearbook 2006.*

Eurostat, Batiment Jean Monnet, Rue Alcide de Gasperi, L-2920 Luxembourg, http://epp.eurostat.ec.europa.eu; *Eurostat Yearbook 2006-2007* and *The Life of Women and Men in Europe - A Statistical Portrait.*

International Labour Office, I.L.O. Publications, 4 route des Morillons, CH-1211 Geneva 22, Switzerland, (Telephone in U.S. (202) 653-7652), (Fax in U.S. (202) 653-7687), www.ilo.org; *Yearbook of Labour Statistics 2006.*

M.E. Sharpe, 80 Business Park Drive, Armonk, NY 10504, (800) 541-6563, Fax: (914) 273-2106, www.mesharpe.com; *The Illustrated Book of World Rankings.*

Organisation for Economic Cooperation and Development (OECD), 2 rue Andre Pascal, F-75775 Paris Cedex 16, France, (Telephone in U.S. (202) 785-6323), (Fax in U.S. (202) 785-0350), www.oecd.org; *Labour Force Statistics: 1986-2005, 2007 Edition.*

Palgrave Macmillan Ltd., Houndmills, Basingstoke, Hampshire, RG21 6XS, England, (Telephone in U.S. (888) 330-8477), (Fax in U.S. (800) 672-2054), www.palgrave.com; *The Statesman's Yearbook 2008.*

Taylor and Francis Group, An Informa Business, 2 Park Square, Milton Park, Abingdon, Oxford OX14 4RN, United Kingdom, (Dial from U.S. (212) 216-7800), (Fax from U.S. (212) 564-7854), www.tandf.co.uk; *The Europa World Year Book.*

U.S. Department of State (DOS), 2201 C Street NW, Washington, DC 20520, (202) 647-4000, www.state.gov; *World Military Expenditures and Arms Transfers (WMEAT).*

UNESCO Institute for Statistics, C.P. 6128 Succursale Centre-Ville, Montreal, Quebec, H3C 3J7 Canada, (Dial from U.S. (514) 343-6880), (Fax from U.S. (514) 343 6882), www.uis.unesco.org; *Statistical Tables.*

United Nations Food and Agricultural Organization (FAO), Viale delle Terme di Caracalla, 00100 Rome, Italy, (Dial from U.S. (202) 653-2400), (Fax from U.S. (202) 653 5760), www.fao.org; *FAO Production Yearbook 2002.*

United Nations Statistics Division, New York, NY 10017, (800) 253-9646, Fax: (212) 963-4116, http://unstats.un.org; *Demographic Yearbook; Human Development Report 2006; Statistical Yearbook; Trends in Europe and North America: The Statistical Yearbook of the ECE 2005;* and *World Statistics Pocketbook.*

The World Bank, 1818 H Street, NW, Washington, DC 20433, (202) 473-1000, Fax: (202) 477-6391, www.worldbank.org; *Belgium; The World Bank Atlas 2003-2004;* and *World Development Report 2008.*

World Health Organization (WHO), Avenue Appia 20, 1211 Geneve 27, Switzerland, (Telephone in U.S. (212) 331-9081), www.who.int; *World Health Report 2006.*

BELGIUM - POPULATION DENSITY

Central Intelligence Agency, Office of Public Affairs, Washington, DC 20505, (703) 482-0623, Fax: (703) 482-1739, www.cia.gov; *The World Factbook.*

Euromonitor International, Inc., 224 S. Michigan Avenue, Suite 1500, Chicago, IL 60604, (312) 922-1115, Fax: (312) 922-1157, www.euromonitor.com; *The World Economic Factbook 2008.*

European Union, Delegation of the European Commission to the United States, 2300 M Street, NW, Washington, DC 20037, (202) 862-9500, Fax: (202) 429-1766, www.eurunion.org; *First Demographic Estimates for 2006.*

Eurostat, Batiment Jean Monnet, Rue Alcide de Gasperi, L-2920 Luxembourg, http://epp.eurostat.ec.europa.eu; *Eurostat Yearbook 2006-2007.*

M.E. Sharpe, 80 Business Park Drive, Armonk, NY 10504, (800) 541-6563, Fax: (914) 273-2106, www.mesharpe.com; *The Illustrated Book of World Rankings.*

Palgrave Macmillan Ltd., Houndmills, Basingstoke, Hampshire, RG21 6XS, England, (Telephone in U.S. (888) 330-8477), (Fax in U.S. (800) 672-2054), www.palgrave.com; *The Statesman's Yearbook 2008.*

Taylor and Francis Group, An Informa Business, 2 Park Square, Milton Park, Abingdon, Oxford OX14 4RN, United Kingdom, (Dial from U.S. (212) 216-7800), (Fax from U.S. (212) 564-7854), www.tandf.co.uk; *The Europa World Year Book.*

United Nations Food and Agricultural Organization (FAO), Viale delle Terme di Caracalla, 00100 Rome, Italy, (Dial from U.S. (202) 653-2400), (Fax from U.S. (202) 653 5760), www.fao.org; *The State of Food and Agriculture (SOFA) 2006.*

United Nations Statistics Division, New York, NY 10017, (800) 253-9646, Fax: (212) 963-4116, http://unstats.un.org; *Statistical Yearbook* and *Trends in Europe and North America: The Statistical Yearbook of the ECE 2005.*

The World Bank, 1818 H Street, NW, Washington, DC 20433, (202) 473-1000, Fax: (202) 477-6391, www.worldbank.org; *Belgium* and *World Development Report 2008.*

BELGIUM - POSTAL SERVICE

European Union, Delegation of the European Commission to the United States, 2300 M Street, NW, Washington, DC 20037, (202) 862-9500, Fax: (202) 429-1766, www.eurunion.org; *Statistical Overview of Transport in the European Union (Data 1970-2001).*

M.E. Sharpe, 80 Business Park Drive, Armonk, NY 10504, (800) 541-6563, Fax: (914) 273-2106, www.mesharpe.com; *The Illustrated Book of World Rankings.*

Palgrave Macmillan Ltd., Houndmills, Basingstoke, Hampshire, RG21 6XS, England, (Telephone in U.S. (888) 330-8477), (Fax in U.S. (800) 672-2054), www.palgrave.com; *The Statesman's Yearbook 2008.*

United Nations Statistics Division, New York, NY 10017, (800) 253-9646, Fax: (212) 963-4116, http://unstats.un.org; *Statistical Yearbook* and *Trends in Europe and North America: The Statistical Yearbook of the ECE 2005.*

BELGIUM - POULTRY

See BELGIUM - LIVESTOCK

BELGIUM - POWER RESOURCES

Euromonitor International, Inc., 224 S. Michigan Avenue, Suite 1500, Chicago, IL 60604, (312) 922-1115, Fax: (312) 922-1157, www.euromonitor.com; *European Marketing Data and Statistics 2008; The World Economic Factbook 2008;* and *World Marketing Data and Statistics.*

European Union, Delegation of the European Commission to the United States, 2300 M Street, NW, Washington, DC 20037, (202) 862-9500, Fax: (202) 429-1766, www.eurunion.org; *European Union Energy Transport in Figures 2006; Regions - Statistical Yearbook 2006;* and *Statistical Overview of Transport in the European Union (Data 1970-2001).*

Eurostat, Batiment Jean Monnet, Rue Alcide de Gasperi, L-2920 Luxembourg, http://epp.eurostat.ec.europa.eu; *Eurostat Yearbook 2006-2007.*

M.E. Sharpe, 80 Business Park Drive, Armonk, NY 10504, (800) 541-6563, Fax: (914) 273-2106, www.mesharpe.com; *The Illustrated Book of World Rankings.*

Organisation for Economic Cooperation and Development (OECD), 2 rue Andre Pascal, F-75775 Paris Cedex 16, France, (Telephone in U.S. (202) 785-6323), (Fax in U.S. (202) 785-0350), www.oecd.org; *Coal Information: 2007 Edition; Energy Statistics of OECD Countries* (2007 Edition); *Key Environmental Indicators 2004;* and *Oil Information 2006 Edition.*

Palgrave Macmillan Ltd., Houndmills, Basingstoke, Hampshire, RG21 6XS, England, (Telephone in U.S. (888) 330-8477), (Fax in U.S. (800) 672-2054), www.palgrave.com; *The Statesman's Yearbook 2008.*

Platts, 2 Penn Plaza, 25th Floor, New York, NY 10121-2298, (212) 904-3070, www.platts.com; *Energy Economist* and *European Power Daily.*

U.S. Department of Energy (DOE), Energy Information Administration (EIA), 1000 Independence Avenue, SW, Washington, DC 20585, (202) 586-8800, www.eia.doe.gov; *International Energy Annual 2004* and *International Energy Outlook 2006.*

United Nations Food and Agricultural Organization (FAO), Viale delle Terme di Caracalla, 00100 Rome, Italy, (Dial from U.S. (202) 653-2400), (Fax from U.S. (202) 653 5760), www.fao.org; *The State of Food and Agriculture (SOFA) 2006.*

United Nations Statistics Division, New York, NY 10017, (800) 253-9646, Fax: (212) 963-4116, http://unstats.un.org; *Energy Statistics Yearbook 2003; Human Development Report 2006; Statistical Yearbook; Trends in Europe and North America: The Statistical Yearbook of the ECE 2005;* and *World Statistics Pocketbook.*

The World Bank, 1818 H Street, NW, Washington, DC 20433, (202) 473-1000, Fax: (202) 477-6391, www.worldbank.org; *The World Bank Atlas 2003-2004* and *World Development Report 2008.*

BELGIUM - PRICES

Euromonitor International, Inc., 224 S. Michigan Avenue, Suite 1500, Chicago, IL 60604, (312) 922-1115, Fax: (312) 922-1157, www.euromonitor.com; *European Marketing Data and Statistics 2008* and *World Marketing Data and Statistics.*

European Union, Delegation of the European Commission to the United States, 2300 M Street, NW, Washington, DC 20037, (202) 862-9500, Fax: (202) 429-1766, www.eurunion.org; *Eurostatistics: Data for Short-Term Economic Analysis (2007 edition).*

Eurostat, Batiment Jean Monnet, Rue Alcide de Gasperi, L-2920 Luxembourg, http://epp.eurostat.ec.europa.eu; *Eurostat Yearbook 2006-2007.*

International Labour Office, I.L.O. Publications, 4 route des Morillons, CH-1211 Geneva 22, Switzerland, (Telephone in U.S. (202) 653-7652), (Fax in U.S. (202) 653-7687), www.ilo.org; *Yearbook of Labour Statistics 2006.*

International Lead and Zinc Study Group (ILZSG), Rua Almirante Barroso 38, 5th Floor, Lisbon 1000 - 013, Portugal, www.ilzsg.org; Interactive Statistical Database.

M.E. Sharpe, 80 Business Park Drive, Armonk, NY 10504, (800) 541-6563, Fax: (914) 273-2106, www.mesharpe.com; *The Illustrated Book of World Rankings.*

Organisation for Economic Cooperation and Development (OECD), 2 rue Andre Pascal, F-75775 Paris Cedex 16, France, (Telephone in U.S. (202) 785-6323), (Fax in U.S. (202) 785-0350), www.oecd.org; *Indicators of Industrial Activity; Iron and Steel Industry in 2004 (2006 Edition); OECD Economic Outlook 2008;* and *OECD Main Economic Indicators (MEI).*

Technical Association of the Pulp and Paper Industry (TAPPI), 15 Technology Parkway South, Norcross, GA 30092, (770) 446-1400, Fax: (770) 446-6947, www.tappi.org; *TAPPI Annual Report.*

United Nations Food and Agricultural Organization (FAO), Viale delle Terme di Caracalla, 00100 Rome, Italy, (Dial from U.S. (202) 653-2400), (Fax from U.S. (202) 653 5760), www.fao.org; *FAO Production Yearbook 2002* and *The State of Food and Agriculture (SOFA) 2006.*

The World Bank, 1818 H Street, NW, Washington, DC 20433, (202) 473-1000, Fax: (202) 477-6391, www.worldbank.org; *Belgium.*

World Bureau of Metal Statistics (WBMS), 27a High Street, Ware, Hertfordshire, SG12 9BA, United Kingdom, www.world-bureau.com; *World Flow Charts* and *World Metal Statistics.*

BELGIUM - PROFESSIONS

Eurostat, Batiment Jean Monnet, Rue Alcide de Gasperi, L-2920 Luxembourg, http://epp.eurostat.ec.europa.eu; *Eurostat Yearbook 2006-2007.*

UNESCO Institute for Statistics, C.P. 6128 Succursale Centre-Ville, Montreal, Quebec, H3C 3J7 Canada, (Dial from U.S. (514) 343-6880), (Fax from U.S. (514) 343 6882), www.uis.unesco.org; *Statistical Tables.*

United Nations Statistics Division, New York, NY 10017, (800) 253-9646, Fax: (212) 963-4116, http://unstats.un.org; *Statistical Yearbook.*

BELGIUM - PUBLIC HEALTH

Euromonitor International, Inc., 224 S. Michigan Avenue, Suite 1500, Chicago, IL 60604, (312) 922-1115, Fax: (312) 922-1157, www.euromonitor.com; *World Health Databook 2007/2008* and *World Marketing Data and Statistics.*

European Centre for Disease Prevention and Control (ECDC), 171 83 Stockholm, Sweden, www.ecdc.europa.eu; *Eurosurveillance.*

European Union, Delegation of the European Commission to the United States, 2300 M Street, NW, Washington, DC 20037, (202) 862-9500, Fax: (202) 429-1766, www.eurunion.org; *Regions - Statistical Yearbook 2006.*

Eurostat, Batiment Jean Monnet, Rue Alcide de Gasperi, L-2920 Luxembourg, http://epp.eurostat.ec.europa.eu; *Eurostat Yearbook 2006-2007.*

International Monetary Fund (IMF), 700 Nineteenth Street, NW, Washington, DC 20431, (202) 623-7000, Fax: (202) 623-4661, www.imf.org; *Government Finance Statistics Yearbook (2008 Edition).*

M.E. Sharpe, 80 Business Park Drive, Armonk, NY 10504, (800) 541-6563, Fax: (914) 273-2106, www.mesharpe.com; *The Illustrated Book of World Rankings.*

Organisation for Economic Cooperation and Development (OECD), 2 rue Andre Pascal, F-75775 Paris Cedex 16, France, (Telephone in U.S. (202) 785-6323), (Fax in U.S. (202) 785-0350), www.oecd.org; *Health at a Glance 2007 - OECD Indicators.*

Palgrave Macmillan Ltd., Houndmills, Basingstoke, Hampshire, RG21 6XS, England, (Telephone in U.S. (888) 330-8477), (Fax in U.S. (800) 672-2054), www.palgrave.com; *The Statesman's Yearbook 2008.*

UNICEF, 3 United Nations Plaza, New York, NY 10017, (800) 253-9646, Fax: (212) 887-7465, www.unicef.org; *The State of the World's Children 2008.*

United Nations Statistics Division, New York, NY 10017, (800) 253-9646, Fax: (212) 963-4116, http://unstats.un.org; *Human Development Report 2006; Statistical Yearbook;* and *Trends in Europe and North America: The Statistical Yearbook of the ECE 2005.*

The World Bank, 1818 H Street, NW, Washington, DC 20433, (202) 473-1000, Fax: (202) 477-6391, www.worldbank.org; *Belgium* and *World Development Report 2008.*

World Health Organization (WHO), Avenue Appia 20, 1211 Geneve 27, Switzerland, (Telephone in U.S. (212) 331-9081), www.who.int; The WHO Global Atlas of Infectious Diseases and *World Health Report 2006.*

BELGIUM - PUBLIC UTILITIES

Eurostat, Batiment Jean Monnet, Rue Alcide de Gasperi, L-2920 Luxembourg, http://epp.eurostat.ec.europa.eu; *Eurostat Yearbook 2006-2007.*

BELGIUM - PUBLISHERS AND PUBLISHING

Organisation for Economic Cooperation and Development (OECD), 2 rue Andre Pascal, F-75775 Paris Cedex 16, France, (Telephone in U.S. (202) 785-6323), (Fax in U.S. (202) 785-0350), www.oecd.org; *Indicators of Industrial Activity.*

Taylor and Francis Group, An Informa Business, 2 Park Square, Milton Park, Abingdon, Oxford OX14 4RN, United Kingdom, (Dial from U.S. (212) 216-7800), (Fax from U.S. (212) 564-7854), www.tandf.co.uk; *The Europa World Year Book.*

UNESCO Institute for Statistics, C.P. 6128 Succursale Centre-Ville, Montreal, Quebec, H3C 3J7 Canada, (Dial from U.S. (514) 343-6880), (Fax from U.S. (514) 343 6882), www.uis.unesco.org; *Statistical Tables.*

United Nations Statistics Division, New York, NY 10017, (800) 253-9646, Fax: (212) 963-4116, http://unstats.un.org; *Trends in Europe and North America: The Statistical Yearbook of the ECE 2005.*

BELGIUM - RADIO - RECEIVERS AND RECEPTION

Palgrave Macmillan Ltd., Houndmills, Basingstoke, Hampshire, RG21 6XS, England, (Telephone in U.S. (888) 330-8477), (Fax in U.S. (800) 672-2054), www.palgrave.com; *The Statesman's Yearbook 2008.*

United Nations Statistics Division, New York, NY 10017, (800) 253-9646, Fax: (212) 963-4116, http://unstats.un.org; *Statistical Yearbook.*

BELGIUM - RAILROADS

Euromonitor International, Inc., 224 S. Michigan Avenue, Suite 1500, Chicago, IL 60604, (312) 922-1115, Fax: (312) 922-1157, www.euromonitor.com; *European Marketing Data and Statistics 2008.*

European Union, Delegation of the European Commission to the United States, 2300 M Street, NW, Washington, DC 20037, (202) 862-9500, Fax: (202) 429-1766, www.eurunion.org; *Regions - Statistical Yearbook 2006* and *Statistical Overview of Transport in the European Union (Data 1970-2001).*

Eurostat, Batiment Jean Monnet, Rue Alcide de Gasperi, L-2920 Luxembourg, http://epp.eurostat.ec.europa.eu; *Eurostat Yearbook 2006-2007.*

Jane's Information Group, 110 North Royal Street, Suite 200, Alexandria, VA 22314, (703) 683-3700, Fax: (800) 836-0297, www.janes.com; *Jane's World Railways.*

Palgrave Macmillan Ltd., Houndmills, Basingstoke, Hampshire, RG21 6XS, England, (Telephone in U.S. (888) 330-8477), (Fax in U.S. (800) 672-2054), www.palgrave.com; *The Statesman's Yearbook 2008.*

Taylor and Francis Group, An Informa Business, 2 Park Square, Milton Park, Abingdon, Oxford OX14 4RN, United Kingdom, (Dial from U.S. (212) 216-7800), (Fax from U.S. (212) 564-7854), www.tandf.co.uk; *The Europa World Year Book.*

United Nations Statistics Division, New York, NY 10017, (800) 253-9646, Fax: (212) 963-4116, http://unstats.un.org; *Annual Bulletin of Transport Statistics for Europe and North America 2004; Statistical Yearbook;* and *Trends in Europe and North America: The Statistical Yearbook of the ECE 2005.*

BELGIUM - RANCHING

Eurostat, Batiment Jean Monnet, Rue Alcide de Gasperi, L-2920 Luxembourg, http://epp.eurostat.ec.europa.eu; *Eurostat Yearbook 2006-2007.*

BELGIUM - RELIGION

Central Intelligence Agency, Office of Public Affairs, Washington, DC 20505, (703) 482-0623, Fax: (703) 482-1739, www.cia.gov; *The World Factbook.*

M.E. Sharpe, 80 Business Park Drive, Armonk, NY 10504, (800) 541-6563, Fax: (914) 273-2106, www.mesharpe.com; *The Illustrated Book of World Rankings.*

Palgrave Macmillan Ltd., Houndmills, Basingstoke, Hampshire, RG21 6XS, England, (Telephone in U.S. (888) 330-8477), (Fax in U.S. (800) 672-2054), www.palgrave.com; *The Statesman's Yearbook 2008.*

BELGIUM - RENT CHARGES

International Labour Office, I.L.O. Publications, 4 route des Morillons, CH-1211 Geneva 22, Switzerland, (Telephone in U.S. (202) 653-7652), (Fax in U.S. (202) 653-7687), www.ilo.org; *Yearbook of Labour Statistics 2006.*

BELGIUM - RESERVES (ACCOUNTING)

Eurostat, Batiment Jean Monnet, Rue Alcide de Gasperi, L-2920 Luxembourg, http://epp.eurostat.ec.europa.eu; *Eurostat Yearbook 2006-2007.*

Organisation for Economic Cooperation and Development (OECD), 2 rue Andre Pascal, F-75775 Paris Cedex 16, France, (Telephone in U.S. (202) 785-6323), (Fax in U.S. (202) 785-0350), www.oecd.org; *Financial Market Trends: OECD Periodical* and *OECD Economic Outlook 2008.*

The World Bank, 1818 H Street, NW, Washington, DC 20433, (202) 473-1000, Fax: (202) 477-6391, www.worldbank.org; *World Development Indicators (WDI) 2008.*

BELGIUM - RETAIL TRADE

Banque de France, 48 rue Croix des Petits champs, 75001 Paris, France, www.banque-france.fr/home.htm; *Monthly Business Survey Overview.*

Euromonitor International, Inc., 224 S. Michigan Avenue, Suite 1500, Chicago, IL 60604, (312) 922-1115, Fax: (312) 922-1157, www.euromonitor.com; *Retail Trade International 2007* and *World Marketing Data and Statistics.*

European Union, Delegation of the European Commission to the United States, 2300 M Street, NW, Washington, DC 20037, (202) 862-9500, Fax: (202) 429-1766, www.eurunion.org; *Eurostatistics: Data for Short-Term Economic Analysis (2007 edition).*

Eurostat, Batiment Jean Monnet, Rue Alcide de Gasperi, L-2920 Luxembourg, http://epp.eurostat.ec.europa.eu; *Eurostat Yearbook 2006-2007.*

United Nations Statistics Division, New York, NY 10017, (800) 253-9646, Fax: (212) 963-4116, http://unstats.un.org; *Statistical Yearbook.*

BELGIUM - RICE PRODUCTION

See BELGIUM - CROPS

BELGIUM - ROADS

Central Intelligence Agency, Office of Public Affairs, Washington, DC 20505, (703) 482-0623, Fax: (703) 482-1739, www.cia.gov; *The World Factbook.*

European Union, Delegation of the European Commission to the United States, 2300 M Street, NW, Washington, DC 20037, (202) 862-9500, Fax: (202) 429-1766, www.eurunion.org; *Statistical Overview of Transport in the European Union (Data 1970-2001).*

Eurostat, Batiment Jean Monnet, Rue Alcide de Gasperi, L-2920 Luxembourg, http://epp.eurostat.ec.europa.eu; *Eurostat Yearbook 2006-2007.*

International Road Federation (IFR), Madison Place, 500 Montgomery Street, 5th Floor, Alexandria, VA 22314, (703) 535-1001, Fax: (703) 535-1007, www.irfnet.org; *World Road Statistics 2006.*

Palgrave Macmillan Ltd., Houndmills, Basingstoke, Hampshire, RG21 6XS, England, (Telephone in U.S. (888) 330-8477), (Fax in U.S. (800) 672-2054), www.palgrave.com; *The Statesman's Yearbook 2008.*

United Nations Statistics Division, New York, NY 10017, (800) 253-9646, Fax: (212) 963-4116, http://unstats.un.org; *Annual Bulletin of Transport Statistics for Europe and North America 2004* and *Trends in Europe and North America: The Statistical Yearbook of the ECE 2005.*

BELGIUM - RUBBER INDUSTRY AND TRADE

Eurostat, Batiment Jean Monnet, Rue Alcide de Gasperi, L-2920 Luxembourg, http://epp.eurostat.ec.europa.eu; *Eurostat Yearbook 2006-2007.*

International Rubber Study Group (IRSG), 1st Floor, Heron House, 109/115 Wembley Hill Road, Wembley, Middlesex HA9 8DA, United Kingdom, www.rubberstudy.com; *Rubber Statistical Bulletin; Summary of World Rubber Statistics 2005; World Rubber Statistics Handbook (Volume 6, 1975-2001);* and *World Rubber Statistics Historic Handbook.*

M.E. Sharpe, 80 Business Park Drive, Armonk, NY 10504, (800) 541-6563, Fax: (914) 273-2106, www.mesharpe.com; *The Illustrated Book of World Rankings.*

Organisation for Economic Cooperation and Development (OECD), 2 rue Andre Pascal, F-75775 Paris Cedex 16, France, (Telephone in U.S. (202) 785-6323), (Fax in U.S. (202) 785-0350), www.oecd.org; *International Trade by Commodity Statistics (ITCS).*

United Nations Statistics Division, New York, NY 10017, (800) 253-9646, Fax: (212) 963-4116, http://unstats.un.org; *Statistical Yearbook.*

BELGIUM - RYE PRODUCTION

See BELGIUM - CROPS

BELGIUM - SAFFLOWER SEED PRODUCTION

See BELGIUM - CROPS

BELGIUM - SALT PRODUCTION

See BELGIUM - MINERAL INDUSTRIES

BELGIUM - SAVING AND INVESTMENT

Organisation for Economic Cooperation and Development (OECD), 2 rue Andre Pascal, F-75775 Paris Cedex 16, France, (Telephone in U.S. (202) 785-6323), (Fax in U.S. (202) 785-0350), www.oecd.org; *OECD Economic Outlook 2008.*

BELGIUM - SAVINGS ACCOUNT DEPOSITS

See BELGIUM - BANKS AND BANKING

BELGIUM - SHEEP

See BELGIUM - LIVESTOCK

BELGIUM - SHIPBUILDING

Organisation for Economic Cooperation and Development (OECD), 2 rue Andre Pascal, F-75775 Paris Cedex 16, France, (Telephone in U.S. (202) 785-6323), (Fax in U.S. (202) 785-0350), www.oecd.org; *Indicators of Industrial Activity.*

BELGIUM - SHIPPING

European Union, Delegation of the European Commission to the United States, 2300 M Street, NW, Washington, DC 20037, (202) 862-9500, Fax: (202) 429-1766, www.eurunion.org; *Fishery Statistics - 1990-2006; Regions - Statistical Yearbook 2006;* and *Statistical Overview of Transport in the European Union (Data 1970-2001).*

Eurostat, Batiment Jean Monnet, Rue Alcide de Gasperi, L-2920 Luxembourg, http://epp.eurostat.ec.europa.eu; *Eurostat Yearbook 2006-2007.*

Lloyd's Register - Fairplay, 8410 N.W. 53rd Terrace, Suite 207, Miami FL 33166, (305) 718-9929, Fax: (305) 718-9663, www.lrfairplay.com; *Register of Ships 2007-2008; World Casualty Statistics 2007; World Fleet Statistics 2006; World Marine Propulsion Report 2006-2010; World Shipbuilding Statistics 2007;* and The World Shipping Encyclopaedia.

Organisation for Economic Cooperation and Development (OECD), 2 rue Andre Pascal, F-75775 Paris Cedex 16, France, (Telephone in U.S. (202) 785-6323), (Fax in U.S. (202) 785-0350), www.oecd.org; *Statistics on Ship Production, Exports and Orders in 2004.*

Palgrave Macmillan Ltd., Houndmills, Basingstoke, Hampshire, RG21 6XS, England, (Telephone in U.S. (888) 330-8477), (Fax in U.S. (800) 672-2054), www.palgrave.com; *The Statesman's Yearbook 2008.*

Taylor and Francis Group, An Informa Business, 2 Park Square, Milton Park, Abingdon, Oxford OX14 4RN, United Kingdom, (Dial from U.S. (212) 216-7800), (Fax from U.S. (212) 564-7854), www.tandf.co.uk; *The Europa World Year Book.*

United Nations Statistics Division, New York, NY 10017, (800) 253-9646, Fax: (212) 963-4116, http://unstats.un.org; *Annual Bulletin of Transport Statistics for Europe and North America 2004* and *Statistical Yearbook.*

BELGIUM - SILVER PRODUCTION

See BELGIUM - MINERAL INDUSTRIES

BELGIUM - SOCIAL CLASSES

European Union, Delegation of the European Commission to the United States, 2300 M Street, NW, Washington, DC 20037, (202) 862-9500, Fax: (202) 429-1766, www.eurunion.org; *European Union Labour Force Survey.*

Eurostat, Batiment Jean Monnet, Rue Alcide de Gasperi, L-2920 Luxembourg, http://epp.eurostat.ec.europa.eu; *Eurostat Yearbook 2006-2007.*

BELGIUM - SOCIAL ECOLOGY

Eurostat, Batiment Jean Monnet, Rue Alcide de Gasperi, L-2920 Luxembourg, http://epp.eurostat.ec.europa.eu; *Eurostat Yearbook 2006-2007.*

M.E. Sharpe, 80 Business Park Drive, Armonk, NY 10504, (800) 541-6563, Fax: (914) 273-2106, www.mesharpe.com; *The Illustrated Book of World Rankings.*

United Nations Statistics Division, New York, NY 10017, (800) 253-9646, Fax: (212) 963-4116, http://unstats.un.org; *World Statistics Pocketbook.*

BELGIUM - SOCIAL SECURITY

Eurostat, Batiment Jean Monnet, Rue Alcide de Gasperi, L-2920 Luxembourg, http://epp.eurostat.ec.europa.eu; *Eurostat Yearbook 2006-2007.*

International Monetary Fund (IMF), 700 Nineteenth Street, NW, Washington, DC 20431, (202) 623-7000, Fax: (202) 623-4661, www.imf.org; *Government Finance Statistics Yearbook (2008 Edition).*

Organisation for Economic Cooperation and Development (OECD), 2 rue Andre Pascal, F-75775 Paris Cedex 16, France, (Telephone in U.S. (202) 785-6323), (Fax in U.S. (202) 785-0350), www.oecd.org; *Revenue Statistics 1965-2006 - 2007 Edition.*

Palgrave Macmillan Ltd., Houndmills, Basingstoke, Hampshire, RG21 6XS, England, (Telephone in U.S. (888) 330-8477), (Fax in U.S. (800) 672-2054), www.palgrave.com; *The Statesman's Yearbook 2008.*

United Nations Statistics Division, New York, NY 10017, (800) 253-9646, Fax: (212) 963-4116, http://unstats.un.org; *National Accounts Statistics: Compendium of Income Distribution Statistics.*

BELGIUM - SOYBEAN PRODUCTION

See BELGIUM - CROPS

BELGIUM - STEEL PRODUCTION

See BELGIUM - MINERAL INDUSTRIES

BELGIUM - STRAW PRODUCTION

See BELGIUM - CROPS

BELGIUM - SUGAR PRODUCTION

See BELGIUM - CROPS

BELGIUM - SULPHUR PRODUCTION

See BELGIUM - MINERAL INDUSTRIES

BELGIUM - SUNFLOWER PRODUCTION

See BELGIUM - CROPS

BELGIUM - TAXATION

Eurostat, Batiment Jean Monnet, Rue Alcide de Gasperi, L-2920 Luxembourg, http://epp.eurostat.ec.europa.eu; *Eurostat Yearbook 2006-2007* and *Taxation Trends in the European Union - Data for the EU Member States and Norway.*

International Monetary Fund (IMF), 700 Nineteenth Street, NW, Washington, DC 20431, (202) 623-7000, Fax: (202) 623-4661, www.imf.org; *Government Finance Statistics Yearbook (2008 Edition).*

International Road Federation (IFR), Madison Place, 500 Montgomery Street, 5th Floor, Alexandria, VA 22314, (703) 535-1001, Fax: (703) 535-1007, www.irfnet.org; *World Road Statistics 2006.*

Organisation for Economic Cooperation and Development (OECD), 2 rue Andre Pascal, F-75775 Paris Cedex 16, France, (Telephone in U.S. (202) 785-6323), (Fax in U.S. (202) 785-0350), www.oecd.org; *Revenue Statistics 1965-2006 - 2007 Edition.*

Taylor and Francis Group, An Informa Business, 2 Park Square, Milton Park, Abingdon, Oxford OX14 4RN, United Kingdom, (Dial from U.S. (212) 216-7800), (Fax from U.S. (212) 564-7854), www.tandf.co.uk; *The Europa World Year Book.*

The World Bank, 1818 H Street, NW, Washington, DC 20433, (202) 473-1000, Fax: (202) 477-6391, www.worldbank.org; *World Development Indicators (WDI) 2008.*

BELGIUM - TEA PRODUCTION

See BELGIUM - CROPS

BELGIUM - TELEPHONE

European Union, Delegation of the European Commission to the United States, 2300 M Street, NW, Washington, DC 20037, (202) 862-9500, Fax: (202) 429-1766, www.eurunion.org; *Statistical Overview of Transport in the European Union (Data 1970-2001).*

Eurostat, Batiment Jean Monnet, Rue Alcide de Gasperi, L-2920 Luxembourg, http://epp.eurostat.ec.europa.eu; *Eurostat Yearbook 2006-2007.*

International Telecommunication Union (ITU), Place des Nations, 1211 Geneva 20, Switzerland, www.itu.int; World Telecommunication Indicators Database.

Palgrave Macmillan Ltd., Houndmills, Basingstoke, Hampshire, RG21 6XS, England, (Telephone in U.S. (888) 330-8477), (Fax in U.S. (800) 672-2054), www.palgrave.com; *The Statesman's Yearbook 2008.*

Taylor and Francis Group, An Informa Business, 2 Park Square, Milton Park, Abingdon, Oxford OX14 4RN, United Kingdom, (Dial from U.S. (212) 216-7800), (Fax from U.S. (212) 564-7854), www.tandf.co.uk; *The Europa World Year Book.*

United Nations Statistics Division, New York, NY 10017, (800) 253-9646, Fax: (212) 963-4116, http://unstats.un.org; *Statistical Yearbook; Trends in Europe and North America: The Statistical Yearbook of the ECE 2005;* and *World Statistics Pocketbook.*

BELGIUM - TELEVISION - RECEIVERS AND RECEPTION

Eurostat, Batiment Jean Monnet, Rue Alcide de Gasperi, L-2920 Luxembourg, http://epp.eurostat.ec.europa.eu; *Eurostat Yearbook 2006-2007.*

United Nations Statistics Division, New York, NY 10017, (800) 253-9646, Fax: (212) 963-4116, http://unstats.un.org; *Statistical Yearbook.*

BELGIUM - TEXTILE INDUSTRY

Euromonitor International, Inc., 224 S. Michigan Avenue, Suite 1500, Chicago, IL 60604, (312) 922-1115, Fax: (312) 922-1157, www.euromonitor.com; *Retail Trade International 2007.*

European Union, Delegation of the European Commission to the United States, 2300 M Street, NW, Washington, DC 20037, (202) 862-9500, Fax: (202) 429-1766, www.eurunion.org; *Agriculture in the European Union: Statistical and Economic Information 2006; Eurostatistics: Data for Short-Term Economic Analysis (2007 edition);* and *The Textile Industry in the EU.*

Eurostat, Batiment Jean Monnet, Rue Alcide de Gasperi, L-2920 Luxembourg, http://epp.eurostat.ec.europa.eu; *Eurostat Yearbook 2006-2007.*

Organisation for Economic Cooperation and Development (OECD), 2 rue Andre Pascal, F-75775 Paris Cedex 16, France, (Telephone in U.S. (202) 785-6323), (Fax in U.S. (202) 785-0350), www.oecd.org; *Indicators of Industrial Activity; International Trade by Commodity Statistics (ITCS); A New World Map in Textiles and Clothing: Adjusting to Change;* and STructural ANalysis (STAN) database.

Palgrave Macmillan Ltd., Houndmills, Basingstoke, Hampshire, RG21 6XS, England, (Telephone in U.S. (888) 330-8477), (Fax in U.S. (800) 672-2054), www.palgrave.com; *The Statesman's Yearbook 2008.*

United Nations Conference on Trade and Development (UNCTAD), DC2-1120, United Nations, New York, NY 10017, (212) 963-0027, www.unctad.org; *UNCTAD Commodity Yearbook.*

United Nations Food and Agricultural Organization (FAO), Viale delle Terme di Caracalla, 00100 Rome, Italy, (Dial from U.S. (202) 653-2400), (Fax from U.S. (202) 653 5760), www.fao.org; *The State of Food and Agriculture (SOFA) 2006.*

United Nations Statistics Division, New York, NY 10017, (800) 253-9646, Fax: (212) 963-4116, http://unstats.un.org; *Statistical Yearbook.*

BELGIUM - TIMBER

See BELGIUM - FORESTS AND FORESTRY

BELGIUM - TIN PRODUCTION

See BELGIUM - MINERAL INDUSTRIES

BELGIUM - TIRE INDUSTRY

United Nations Statistics Division, New York, NY 10017, (800) 253-9646, Fax: (212) 963-4116, http://unstats.un.org; *Statistical Yearbook.*

BELGIUM - TOBACCO INDUSTRY

Euromonitor International, Inc., 224 S. Michigan Avenue, Suite 1500, Chicago, IL 60604, (312) 922-1115, Fax: (312) 922-1157, www.euromonitor.com; *European Marketing Data and Statistics 2008.*

Eurostat, Batiment Jean Monnet, Rue Alcide de Gasperi, L-2920 Luxembourg, http://epp.eurostat.ec.europa.eu; *Eurostat Yearbook 2006-2007.*

Foreign Agricultural Service (FAS), U.S. Department of Agriculture (USDA), 1400 Independence Avenue, SW, Washington, DC 20250, (202) 720-3935, www.fas.usda.gov; *Tobacco: World Markets and Trade.*

M.E. Sharpe, 80 Business Park Drive, Armonk, NY 10504, (800) 541-6563, Fax: (914) 273-2106, www.mesharpe.com; *The Illustrated Book of World Rankings.*

Organisation for Economic Cooperation and Development (OECD), 2 rue Andre Pascal, F-75775 Paris Cedex 16, France, (Telephone in U.S. (202) 785-6323), (Fax in U.S. (202) 785-0350), www.oecd.org; *Indicators of Industrial Activity; International Trade by Commodity Statistics (ITCS);* and STructural ANalysis (STAN) database.

United Nations Statistics Division, New York, NY 10017, (800) 253-9646, Fax: (212) 963-4116, http://unstats.un.org; *Statistical Yearbook.*

BELGIUM - TOURISM

Euromonitor International, Inc., 224 S. Michigan Avenue, Suite 1500, Chicago, IL 60604, (312) 922-1115, Fax: (312) 922-1157, www.euromonitor.com; *European Marketing Data and Statistics 2008; The World Economic Factbook 2008;* and *World Marketing Data and Statistics.*

European Union, Delegation of the European Commission to the United States, 2300 M Street, NW, Washington, DC 20037, (202) 862-9500, Fax: (202) 429-1766, www.eurunion.org; *Statistical Overview of Transport in the European Union (Data 1970-2001).*

Eurostat, Batiment Jean Monnet, Rue Alcide de Gasperi, L-2920 Luxembourg, http://epp.eurostat.ec.europa.eu; *Tourism in Europe: First Results for 2007* and *Tourism in Europe: First Results for 2007.*

M.E. Sharpe, 80 Business Park Drive, Armonk, NY 10504, (800) 541-6563, Fax: (914) 273-2106, www.mesharpe.com; *The Illustrated Book of World Rankings.*

Organisation for Economic Cooperation and Development (OECD), 2 rue Andre Pascal, F-75775 Paris Cedex 16, France, (Telephone in U.S. (202) 785-6323), (Fax in U.S. (202) 785-0350), www.oecd.org; *Household, Tourism, Travel: Trends, Environmental Impacts and Policy Responses.*

Palgrave Macmillan Ltd., Houndmills, Basingstoke, Hampshire, RG21 6XS, England, (Telephone in U.S. (888) 330-8477), (Fax in U.S. (800) 672-2054), www.palgrave.com; *The Statesman's Yearbook 2008.*

Taylor and Francis Group, An Informa Business, 2 Park Square, Milton Park, Abingdon, Oxford OX14 4RN, United Kingdom, (Dial from U.S. (212) 216-7800), (Fax from U.S. (212) 564-7854), www.tandf.co.uk; *The Europa World Year Book.*

United Nations Statistics Division, New York, NY 10017, (800) 253-9646, Fax: (212) 963-4116, http://unstats.un.org; *Statistical Yearbook* and *Trends in Europe and North America: The Statistical Yearbook of the ECE 2005.*

United Nations World Tourism Organization (UNWTO), Capitan Haya 42, 28020 Madrid, Spain, www.world-tourism.org; *Tourism Market Trends 2004 - Europe; Tourism Market Trends 2004 - Europe;* and *Yearbook of Tourism Statistics.*

The World Bank, 1818 H Street, NW, Washington, DC 20433, (202) 473-1000, Fax: (202) 477-6391, www.worldbank.org; *Belgium.*

BELGIUM - TRADE

See BELGIUM - INTERNATIONAL TRADE

BELGIUM - TRANSPORTATION

Central Intelligence Agency, Office of Public Affairs, Washington, DC 20505, (703) 482-0623, Fax: (703) 482-1739, www.cia.gov; *The World Factbook.*

Euromonitor International, Inc., 224 S. Michigan Avenue, Suite 1500, Chicago, IL 60604, (312) 922-1115, Fax: (312) 922-1157, www.euromonitor.com; *World Marketing Data and Statistics.*

European Union, Delegation of the European Commission to the United States, 2300 M Street, NW, Washington, DC 20037, (202) 862-9500, Fax: (202) 429-1766, www.eurunion.org; *Regions - Statistical Yearbook 2006* and *Statistical Overview of Transport in the European Union (Data 1970-2001).*

Eurostat, Batiment Jean Monnet, Rue Alcide de Gasperi, L-2920 Luxembourg, http://epp.eurostat.ec.europa.eu; *Eurostat Yearbook 2006-2007; Regional Passenger and Freight Air Transport in Europe in 2006;* and *Regional Road and Rail Transport Networks.*

M.E. Sharpe, 80 Business Park Drive, Armonk, NY 10504, (800) 541-6563, Fax: (914) 273-2106, www.mesharpe.com; *The Illustrated Book of World Rankings.*

Palgrave Macmillan Ltd., Houndmills, Basingstoke, Hampshire, RG21 6XS, England, (Telephone in U.S. (888) 330-8477), (Fax in U.S. (800) 672-2054), www.palgrave.com; *The Statesman's Yearbook 2008.*

Platts, 2 Penn Plaza, 25th Floor, New York, NY 10121-2298, (212) 904-3070, www.platts.com; *Energy Economist.*

Taylor and Francis Group, An Informa Business, 2 Park Square, Milton Park, Abingdon, Oxford OX14 4RN, United Kingdom, (Dial from U.S. (212) 216-7800), (Fax from U.S. (212) 564-7854), www.tandf.co.uk; *The Europa World Year Book.*

United Nations Statistics Division, New York, NY 10017, (800) 253-9646, Fax: (212) 963-4116, http://unstats.un.org; *Energy Statistics Yearbook 2003; Human Development Report 2006;* and *Trends in Europe and North America: The Statistical Yearbook of the ECE 2005.*

The World Bank, 1818 H Street, NW, Washington, DC 20433, (202) 473-1000, Fax: (202) 477-6391, www.worldbank.org; *Belgium.*

BELGIUM - TURKEYS

See BELGIUM - LIVESTOCK

BELGIUM - UNEMPLOYMENT

Central Intelligence Agency, Office of Public Affairs, Washington, DC 20505, (703) 482-0623, Fax: (703) 482-1739, www.cia.gov; *The World Factbook.*

Euromonitor International, Inc., 224 S. Michigan Avenue, Suite 1500, Chicago, IL 60604, (312) 922-1115, Fax: (312) 922-1157, www.euromonitor.com; *European Marketing Data and Statistics 2008.*

European Union, Delegation of the European Commission to the United States, 2300 M Street, NW, Washington, DC 20037, (202) 862-9500, Fax: (202) 429-1766, www.eurunion.org; *European Union Labour Force Survey; Eurostatistics: Data for Short-Term Economic Analysis (2007 edition);* and *Regions - Statistical Yearbook 2006.*

Eurostat, Batiment Jean Monnet, Rue Alcide de Gasperi, L-2920 Luxembourg, http://epp.eurostat.ec.europa.eu; *Eurostat Yearbook 2006-2007.*

International Labour Office, I.L.O. Publications, 4 route des Morillons, CH-1211 Geneva 22, Switzerland, (Telephone in U.S. (202) 653-7652), (Fax in U.S. (202) 653-7687), www.ilo.org; *Yearbook of Labour Statistics 2006.*

Organisation for Economic Cooperation and Development (OECD), 2 rue Andre Pascal, F-75775 Paris Cedex 16, France, (Telephone in U.S. (202) 785-6323), (Fax in U.S. (202) 785-0350), www.oecd.org; *Labour Force Statistics: 1986-2005, 2007 Edition; OECD Composite Leading Indicators (CLIs), Updated September 2007; OECD Economic Outlook 2008; OECD Economic Survey - Belgium 2007;* and *OECD Employment Outlook 2007.*

Palgrave Macmillan Ltd., Houndmills, Basingstoke, Hampshire, RG21 6XS, England, (Telephone in U.S. (888) 330-8477), (Fax in U.S. (800) 672-2054), www.palgrave.com; *The Statesman's Yearbook 2008.*

United Nations Statistics Division, New York, NY 10017, (800) 253-9646, Fax: (212) 963-4116, http://unstats.un.org; *Statistical Yearbook* and *Trends in Europe and North America: The Statistical Yearbook of the ECE 2005.*

BELGIUM - URANIUM PRODUCTION AND CONSUMPTION

See BELGIUM - MINERAL INDUSTRIES

BELGIUM - VITAL STATISTICS

Belgian Statistical Society, National Statistical Institute, Rue de Louvain, 44, 1000 Brussels, Belgium, www.sbs-bvs.be; *B-Stat News.*

Eurostat, Batiment Jean Monnet, Rue Alcide de Gasperi, L-2920 Luxembourg, http://epp.eurostat.ec.europa.eu; *Eurostat Yearbook 2006-2007.*

Palgrave Macmillan Ltd., Houndmills, Basingstoke, Hampshire, RG21 6XS, England, (Telephone in U.S. (888) 330-8477), (Fax in U.S. (800) 672-2054), www.palgrave.com; *The Statesman's Yearbook 2008.*

United Nations Statistics Division, New York, NY 10017, (800) 253-9646, Fax: (212) 963-4116, http://unstats.un.org; *Statistical Yearbook.*

BELGIUM - WAGES

Euromonitor International, Inc., 224 S. Michigan Avenue, Suite 1500, Chicago, IL 60604, (312) 922-1115, Fax: (312) 922-1157, www.euromonitor.com; *European Marketing Data and Statistics 2008.*

European Union, Delegation of the European Commission to the United States, 2300 M Street, NW, Washington, DC 20037, (202) 862-9500, Fax: (202) 429-1766, www.eurunion.org; *Agriculture in the European Union: Statistical and Economic Information 2006* and *Eurostatistics: Data for Short-Term Economic Analysis (2007 edition).*

Eurostat, Batiment Jean Monnet, Rue Alcide de Gasperi, L-2920 Luxembourg, http://epp.eurostat.ec.europa.eu; *Eurostat Yearbook 2006-2007.*

International Labour Office, I.L.O. Publications, 4 route des Morillons, CH-1211 Geneva 22, Switzerland, (Telephone in U.S. (202) 653-7652), (Fax in U.S. (202) 653-7687), www.ilo.org; *Yearbook of Labour Statistics 2006.*

Organisation for Economic Cooperation and Development (OECD), 2 rue Andre Pascal, F-75775 Paris Cedex 16, France, (Telephone in U.S. (202) 785-6323), (Fax in U.S. (202) 785-0350), www.oecd.org; *ICT Sector Data and Metadata by Country; OECD Economic Outlook 2008; OECD Main Economic Indicators (MEI);* and STructural ANalysis (STAN) database.

United Nations Statistics Division, New York, NY 10017, (800) 253-9646, Fax: (212) 963-4116, http://unstats.un.org; *Statistical Yearbook.*

The World Bank, 1818 H Street, NW, Washington, DC 20433, (202) 473-1000, Fax: (202) 477-6391, www.worldbank.org; *Belgium.*

BELGIUM - WALNUT PRODUCTION

See BELGIUM - CROPS

BELGIUM - WEATHER

See BELGIUM - CLIMATE

BELGIUM - WELFARE STATE

Eurostat, Batiment Jean Monnet, Rue Alcide de Gasperi, L-2920 Luxembourg, http://epp.eurostat.ec.europa.eu; *Eurostat Yearbook 2006-2007.*

International Monetary Fund (IMF), 700 Nineteenth Street, NW, Washington, DC 20431, (202) 623-7000, Fax: (202) 623-4661, www.imf.org; *Government Finance Statistics Yearbook (2008 Edition).*

Palgrave Macmillan Ltd., Houndmills, Basingstoke, Hampshire, RG21 6XS, England, (Telephone in U.S. (888) 330-8477), (Fax in U.S. (800) 672-2054), www.palgrave.com; *The Statesman's Yearbook 2008.*

BELGIUM - WHEAT PRODUCTION

See BELGIUM - CROPS

BELGIUM - WHOLESALE PRICE INDEXES

Eurostat, Batiment Jean Monnet, Rue Alcide de Gasperi, L-2920 Luxembourg, http://epp.eurostat.ec.europa.eu; *Eurostat Yearbook 2006-2007.*

International Monetary Fund (IMF), 700 Nineteenth Street, NW, Washington, DC 20431, (202) 623-7000, Fax: (202) 623-4661, www.imf.org; *International Financial Statistics Yearbook 2007.*

United Nations Statistics Division, New York, NY 10017, (800) 253-9646, Fax: (212) 963-4116, http://unstats.un.org; *Statistical Yearbook.*

BELGIUM - WHOLESALE TRADE

Eurostat, Batiment Jean Monnet, Rue Alcide de Gasperi, L-2920 Luxembourg, http://epp.eurostat.ec.europa.eu; *Eurostat Yearbook 2006-2007.*

United Nations Statistics Division, New York, NY 10017, (800) 253-9646, Fax: (212) 963-4116, http://unstats.un.org; *Statistical Yearbook.*

BELGIUM - WINE PRODUCTION

See BELGIUM - BEVERAGE INDUSTRY

BELGIUM - WOOD AND WOOD PULP

See BELGIUM - FORESTS AND FORESTRY

BELGIUM - WOOD PRODUCTS

Eurostat, Batiment Jean Monnet, Rue Alcide de Gasperi, L-2920 Luxembourg, http://epp.eurostat.ec.europa.eu; *Eurostat Yearbook 2006-2007.*

Organisation for Economic Cooperation and Development (OECD), 2 rue Andre Pascal, F-75775 Paris Cedex 16, France, (Telephone in U.S. (202) 785-6323), (Fax in U.S. (202) 785-0350), www.oecd.org; *International Trade by Commodity Statistics (ITCS); OECD Economic Survey - Belgium 2007;* and STructural ANalysis (STAN) database.

BELGIUM - WOOL PRODUCTION

See BELGIUM - TEXTILE INDUSTRY

BELGIUM - YARN PRODUCTION

See BELGIUM - TEXTILE INDUSTRY

BELGIUM - ZINC AND ZINC ORE

See BELGIUM - MINERAL INDUSTRIES

BELGIUM - ZOOS

UNESCO Institute for Statistics, C.P. 6128 Succursale Centre-Ville, Montreal, Quebec, H3C 3J7 Canada, (Dial from U.S. (514) 343-6880), (Fax from U.S. (514) 343 6882), www.uis.unesco.org; *Statistical Tables.*

BELIZE - NATIONAL STATISTICAL OFFICE

Central Statistical Office (CSO), Corner Culvert Road Mountain View Boulevard, Belmopan City, Belize, www.cso.gov.bz/welcome.html; National Data Center.

BELIZE - PRIMARY STATISTICS SOURCES

Central Statistical Office (CSO), Corner Culvert Road Mountain View Boulevard, Belmopan City, Belize, www.cso.gov.bz/welcome.html; *Abstract of Statistics 2004.*

BELIZE - AGRICULTURAL MACHINERY

United Nations Statistics Division, New York, NY 10017, (800) 253-9646, Fax: (212) 963-4116, http://unstats.un.org; *Statistical Yearbook.*

BELIZE - AGRICULTURE

Economist Intelligence Unit, 111 West 57th Street, New York, NY 10019, (212) 554-0600, Fax: (212) 586-1181, www.eiu.com; *Belize Country Report.*

Euromonitor International, Inc., 224 S. Michigan Avenue, Suite 1500, Chicago, IL 60604, (312) 922-1115, Fax: (312) 922-1157, www.euromonitor.com; *World Marketing Data and Statistics.*

Palgrave Macmillan Ltd., Houndmills, Basingstoke, Hampshire, RG21 6XS, England, (Telephone in U.S. (888) 330-8477), (Fax in U.S. (800) 672-2054), www.palgrave.com; *The Statesman's Yearbook 2008.*

Taylor and Francis Group, An Informa Business, 2 Park Square, Milton Park, Abingdon, Oxford OX14 4RN, United Kingdom, (Dial from U.S. (212) 216-7800), (Fax from U.S. (212) 564-7854), www.tandf.co.uk; *The Europa World Year Book.*

United Nations Conference on Trade and Development (UNCTAD), DC2-1120, United Nations, New York, NY 10017, (212) 963-0027, www.unctad.org; *UNCTAD Commodity Yearbook.*

United Nations Food and Agricultural Organization (FAO), Viale delle Terme di Caracalla, 00100 Rome, Italy, (Dial from U.S. (202) 653-2400), (Fax from U.S. (202) 653 5760), www.fao.org; AQUASTAT; *FAO Production Yearbook 2002; FAO Trade Yearbook;* and *The State of Food and Agriculture (SOFA) 2006.*

United Nations Statistics Division, New York, NY 10017, (800) 253-9646, Fax: (212) 963-4116, http://unstats.un.org; *Statistical Yearbook.*

The World Bank, 1818 H Street, NW, Washington, DC 20433, (202) 473-1000, Fax: (202) 477-6391, www.worldbank.org; *Belize* and *World Development Indicators (WDI) 2008.*

BELIZE - AIRLINES

Palgrave Macmillan Ltd., Houndmills, Basingstoke, Hampshire, RG21 6XS, England, (Telephone in U.S. (888) 330-8477), (Fax in U.S. (800) 672-2054), www.palgrave.com; *The Statesman's Yearbook 2008.*

Taylor and Francis Group, An Informa Business, 2 Park Square, Milton Park, Abingdon, Oxford OX14 4RN, United Kingdom, (Dial from U.S. (212) 216-7800), (Fax from U.S. (212) 564-7854), www.tandf.co.uk; *The Europa World Year Book.*

BELIZE - AIRPORTS

Central Intelligence Agency, Office of Public Affairs, Washington, DC 20505, (703) 482-0623, Fax: (703) 482-1739, www.cia.gov; *The World Factbook.*

BELIZE - ARMED FORCES

Central Intelligence Agency, Office of Public Affairs, Washington, DC 20505, (703) 482-0623, Fax: (703) 482-1739, www.cia.gov; *The World Factbook.*

Euromonitor International, Inc., 224 S. Michigan Avenue, Suite 1500, Chicago, IL 60604, (312) 922-1115, Fax: (312) 922-1157, www.euromonitor.com; *World Marketing Data and Statistics.*

International Institute for Strategic Studies (IISS), Arundel House, 13-15 Arundel Street, Temple Place, London WC2R 3DX, England, www.iiss.org; *The Military Balance 2007.*

Palgrave Macmillan Ltd., Houndmills, Basingstoke, Hampshire, RG21 6XS, England, (Telephone in U.S. (888) 330-8477), (Fax in U.S. (800) 672-2054), www.palgrave.com; *The Statesman's Yearbook 2008.*

United Nations Statistics Division, New York, NY 10017, (800) 253-9646, Fax: (212) 963-4116, http://unstats.un.org; *Human Development Report 2006.*

BELIZE - BALANCE OF PAYMENTS

Taylor and Francis Group, An Informa Business, 2 Park Square, Milton Park, Abingdon, Oxford OX14 4RN, United Kingdom, (Dial from U.S. (212) 216-7800), (Fax from U.S. (212) 564-7854), www.tandf.co.uk; *The Europa World Year Book.*

United Nations Conference on Trade and Development (UNCTAD), DC2-1120, United Nations, New York, NY 10017, (212) 963-0027, www.unctad.org; *Handbook of Statistics 2005.*

United Nations Statistics Division, New York, NY 10017, (800) 253-9646, Fax: (212) 963-4116, http://unstats.un.org; *Economic Survey of Latin America and the Caribbean 2004-2005.*

The World Bank, 1818 H Street, NW, Washington, DC 20433, (202) 473-1000, Fax: (202) 477-6391, www.worldbank.org; *Belize* and *World Development Indicators (WDI) 2008.*

BELIZE - BANKS AND BANKING

Euromonitor International, Inc., 224 S. Michigan Avenue, Suite 1500, Chicago, IL 60604, (312) 922-1115, Fax: (312) 922-1157, www.euromonitor.com; *World Marketing Data and Statistics.*

Palgrave Macmillan Ltd., Houndmills, Basingstoke, Hampshire, RG21 6XS, England, (Telephone in U.S. (888) 330-8477), (Fax in U.S. (800) 672-2054), www.palgrave.com; *The Statesman's Yearbook 2008.*

Taylor and Francis Group, An Informa Business, 2 Park Square, Milton Park, Abingdon, Oxford OX14 4RN, United Kingdom, (Dial from U.S. (212) 216-7800), (Fax from U.S. (212) 564-7854), www.tandf.co.uk; *The Europa World Year Book.*

BELIZE - BROADCASTING

Central Intelligence Agency, Office of Public Affairs, Washington, DC 20505, (703) 482-0623, Fax: (703) 482-1739, www.cia.gov; *The World Factbook.*

Euromonitor International, Inc., 224 S. Michigan Avenue, Suite 1500, Chicago, IL 60604, (312) 922-1115, Fax: (312) 922-1157, www.euromonitor.com; *World Marketing Data and Statistics.*

Palgrave Macmillan Ltd., Houndmills, Basingstoke, Hampshire, RG21 6XS, England, (Telephone in U.S. (888) 330-8477), (Fax in U.S. (800) 672-2054), www.palgrave.com; *The Statesman's Yearbook 2008.*

WRTH Publications Limited, PO Box 290, Oxford OX2 7FT, UK, www.wrth.com; *World Radio TV Handbook 2007.*

BELIZE - BUDGET

Central Intelligence Agency, Office of Public Affairs, Washington, DC 20505, (703) 482-0623, Fax: (703) 482-1739, www.cia.gov; *The World Factbook.*

BELIZE - CATTLE

See BELIZE - LIVESTOCK

BELIZE - CHILDBIRTH - STATISTICS

Central Intelligence Agency, Office of Public Affairs, Washington, DC 20505, (703) 482-0623, Fax: (703) 482-1739, www.cia.gov; *The World Factbook.*

Euromonitor International, Inc., 224 S. Michigan Avenue, Suite 1500, Chicago, IL 60604, (312) 922-1115, Fax: (312) 922-1157, www.euromonitor.com; *International Marketing Data and Statistics 2008* and *The World Economic Factbook 2008.*

Palgrave Macmillan Ltd., Houndmills, Basingstoke, Hampshire, RG21 6XS, England, (Telephone in U.S. (888) 330-8477), (Fax in U.S. (800) 672-2054), www.palgrave.com; *The Statesman's Yearbook 2008.*

Taylor and Francis Group, An Informa Business, 2 Park Square, Milton Park, Abingdon, Oxford OX14 4RN, United Kingdom, (Dial from U.S. (212) 216-7800), (Fax from U.S. (212) 564-7854), www.tandf.co.uk; *The Europa World Year Book.*

United Nations Statistics Division, New York, NY 10017, (800) 253-9646, Fax: (212) 963-4116, http://unstats.un.org; *Demographic Yearbook* and *Statistical Yearbook.*

The World Bank, 1818 H Street, NW, Washington, DC 20433, (202) 473-1000, Fax: (202) 477-6391, www.worldbank.org; *World Development Indicators (WDI) 2008.*

World Health Organization (WHO), Avenue Appia 20, 1211 Geneve 27, Switzerland, (Telephone in U.S. (212) 331-9081), www.who.int; *World Health Report 2006.*

BELIZE - CLIMATE

Palgrave Macmillan Ltd., Houndmills, Basingstoke, Hampshire, RG21 6XS, England, (Telephone in U.S. (888) 330-8477), (Fax in U.S. (800) 672-2054), www.palgrave.com; *The Statesman's Yearbook 2008.*

BELIZE - COMMERCE

Palgrave Macmillan Ltd., Houndmills, Basingstoke, Hampshire, RG21 6XS, England, (Telephone in U.S. (888) 330-8477), (Fax in U.S. (800) 672-2054), www.palgrave.com; *The Statesman's Yearbook 2008.*

BELIZE - COMMODITY EXCHANGES

Commodity Research Bureau, 330 South Wells Street, Suite 612, Chicago, IL 60606-7110, (800) 621-5271, Fax: (312) 939-4135, www.crbtrader.com; *2006 CRB Commodity Yearbook and CD.*

International Monetary Fund (IMF), 700 Nineteenth Street, NW, Washington, DC 20431, (202) 623-7000, Fax: (202) 623-4661, www.imf.org; *IMF Primary Commodity Prices.*

United Nations Food and Agricultural Organization (FAO), Viale delle Terme di Caracalla, 00100 Rome, Italy, (Dial from U.S. (202) 653-2400), (Fax from U.S. (202) 653 5760), www.fao.org; *The State of Food and Agriculture (SOFA) 2006.*

BELIZE - CONSTRUCTION INDUSTRY

United Nations Statistics Division, New York, NY 10017, (800) 253-9646, Fax: (212) 963-4116, http://unstats.un.org; *Statistical Yearbook.*

BELIZE - CONSUMER PRICE INDEXES

Euromonitor International, Inc., 224 S. Michigan Avenue, Suite 1500, Chicago, IL 60604, (312) 922-1115, Fax: (312) 922-1157, www.euromonitor.com; *World Marketing Data and Statistics.*

Taylor and Francis Group, An Informa Business, 2 Park Square, Milton Park, Abingdon, Oxford OX14 4RN, United Kingdom, (Dial from U.S. (212) 216-7800), (Fax from U.S. (212) 564-7854), www.tandf.co.uk; *The Europa World Year Book.*

United Nations Statistics Division, New York, NY 10017, (800) 253-9646, Fax: (212) 963-4116, http://unstats.un.org; *Statistical Yearbook.*

The World Bank, 1818 H Street, NW, Washington, DC 20433, (202) 473-1000, Fax: (202) 477-6391, www.worldbank.org; *Belize.*

BELIZE - CORN INDUSTRY

See BELIZE - CROPS

BELIZE - CROPS

Palgrave Macmillan Ltd., Houndmills, Basingstoke, Hampshire, RG21 6XS, England, (Telephone in U.S. (888) 330-8477), (Fax in U.S. (800) 672-2054), www.palgrave.com; *The Statesman's Yearbook 2008.*

Taylor and Francis Group, An Informa Business, 2 Park Square, Milton Park, Abingdon, Oxford OX14 4RN, United Kingdom, (Dial from U.S. (212) 216-7800), (Fax from U.S. (212) 564-7854), www.tandf.co.uk; *The Europa World Year Book.*

United Nations Conference on Trade and Development (UNCTAD), DC2-1120, United Nations, New York, NY 10017, (212) 963-0027, www.unctad.org; *UNCTAD Commodity Yearbook.*

United Nations Food and Agricultural Organization (FAO), Viale delle Terme di Caracalla, 00100 Rome, Italy, (Dial from U.S. (202) 653-2400), (Fax from U.S. (202) 653 5760), www.fao.org; *The State of Food and Agriculture (SOFA) 2006.*

United Nations Statistics Division, New York, NY 10017, (800) 253-9646, Fax: (212) 963-4116, http://unstats.un.org; *Statistical Yearbook.*

BELIZE - CUSTOMS ADMINISTRATION

Palgrave Macmillan Ltd., Houndmills, Basingstoke, Hampshire, RG21 6XS, England, (Telephone in U.S. (888) 330-8477), (Fax in U.S. (800) 672-2054), www.palgrave.com; *The Statesman's Yearbook 2008.*

BELIZE - DAIRY PROCESSING

Palgrave Macmillan Ltd., Houndmills, Basingstoke, Hampshire, RG21 6XS, England, (Telephone in U.S. (888) 330-8477), (Fax in U.S. (800) 672-2054), www.palgrave.com; *The Statesman's Yearbook 2008.*

Taylor and Francis Group, An Informa Business, 2 Park Square, Milton Park, Abingdon, Oxford OX14 4RN, United Kingdom, (Dial from U.S. (212) 216-7800), (Fax from U.S. (212) 564-7854), www.tandf.co.uk; *The Europa World Year Book.*

United Nations Food and Agricultural Organization (FAO), Viale delle Terme di Caracalla, 00100 Rome, Italy, (Dial from U.S. (202) 653-2400), (Fax from U.S. (202) 653 5760), www.fao.org; *The State of Food and Agriculture (SOFA) 2006.*

BELIZE - DEATH RATES

See BELIZE - MORTALITY

BELIZE - DEBTS, EXTERNAL

Palgrave Macmillan Ltd., Houndmills, Basingstoke, Hampshire, RG21 6XS, England, (Telephone in U.S. (888) 330-8477), (Fax in U.S. (800) 672-2054), www.palgrave.com; *The Statesman's Yearbook 2008.*

United Nations Statistics Division, New York, NY 10017, (800) 253-9646, Fax: (212) 963-4116, http://unstats.un.org; *Economic Survey of Latin America and the Caribbean 2004-2005.*

The World Bank, 1818 H Street, NW, Washington, DC 20433, (202) 473-1000, Fax: (202) 477-6391, www.worldbank.org; *Global Development Finance 2007* and *World Development Indicators (WDI) 2008.*

BELIZE - DEMOGRAPHY

Euromonitor International, Inc., 224 S. Michigan Avenue, Suite 1500, Chicago, IL 60604, (312) 922-1115, Fax: (312) 922-1157, www.euromonitor.com; *International Marketing Data and Statistics 2008; The World Economic Factbook 2008;* and *World Marketing Data and Statistics.*

United Nations Statistics Division, New York, NY 10017, (800) 253-9646, Fax: (212) 963-4116, http://unstats.un.org; *Human Development Report 2006.*

The World Bank, 1818 H Street, NW, Washington, DC 20433, (202) 473-1000, Fax: (202) 477-6391, www.worldbank.org; *Belize.*

BELIZE - DISPOSABLE INCOME

United Nations Statistics Division, New York, NY 10017, (800) 253-9646, Fax: (212) 963-4116, http://unstats.un.org; *National Accounts Statistics: Compendium of Income Distribution Statistics* and *Statistical Yearbook.*

BELIZE - DIVORCE

United Nations Statistics Division, New York, NY 10017, (800) 253-9646, Fax: (212) 963-4116, http://unstats.un.org; *Demographic Yearbook* and *Statistical Yearbook.*

BELIZE - ECONOMIC ASSISTANCE

United Nations Statistics Division, New York, NY 10017, (800) 253-9646, Fax: (212) 963-4116, http://unstats.un.org; *Statistical Yearbook.*

BELIZE - ECONOMIC CONDITIONS

Center for International Business Education Research (CIBER), Columbia Business School and School of International and Public Affairs, Uris Hall, Room 212, 3022 Broadway, New York, NY 10027-6902, Mr. Joshua Safier, (212) 854-4750, Fax: (212) 222-9821, www.columbia.edu/cu/ciber/; Datastream International.

Central Intelligence Agency, Office of Public Affairs, Washington, DC 20505, (703) 482-0623, Fax: (703) 482-1739, www.cia.gov; *The World Factbook.*

DSI Data Service Information, Xantener Strasse 51a, D-47495 Rheinberg, Germany, www.dsidata.com; *Campus Solution.*

Dun and Bradstreet (DB) Corporation, 103 JFK Parkway, Short Hills, NJ 07078, (973) 921-5500, www.dnb.com; *Country Report.*

Economist Intelligence Unit, 111 West 57th Street, New York, NY 10019, (212) 554-0600, Fax: (212) 586-1181, www.eiu.com; *Belize Country Report.*

Euromonitor International, Inc., 224 S. Michigan Avenue, Suite 1500, Chicago, IL 60604, (312) 922-1115, Fax: (312) 922-1157, www.euromonitor.com; *The World Economic Factbook 2008* and *World Marketing Data and Statistics.*

International Monetary Fund (IMF), 700 Nineteenth Street, NW, Washington, DC 20431, (202) 623-7000, Fax: (202) 623-4661, www.imf.org; *World Economic Outlook Reports.*

Palgrave Macmillan Ltd., Houndmills, Basingstoke, Hampshire, RG21 6XS, England, (Telephone in U.S. (888) 330-8477), (Fax in U.S. (800) 672-2054), www.palgrave.com; *The Statesman's Yearbook 2008.*

Taylor and Francis Group, An Informa Business, 2 Park Square, Milton Park, Abingdon, Oxford OX14 4RN, United Kingdom, (Dial from U.S. (212) 216-7800), (Fax from U.S. (212) 564-7854), www.tandf.co.uk; *The Europa World Year Book.*

United Nations Statistics Division, New York, NY 10017, (800) 253-9646, Fax: (212) 963-4116, http://unstats.un.org; *Economic Survey of Latin America and the Caribbean 2004-2005* and *World Statistics Pocketbook.*

The World Bank, 1818 H Street, NW, Washington, DC 20433, (202) 473-1000, Fax: (202) 477-6391, www.worldbank.org; *Belize; Global Economic Monitor (GEM); Global Economic Prospects 2008;* and *The World Bank Atlas 2003-2004.*

BELIZE - EDUCATION

Euromonitor International, Inc., 224 S. Michigan Avenue, Suite 1500, Chicago, IL 60604, (312) 922-1115, Fax: (312) 922-1157, www.euromonitor.com; *International Marketing Data and Statistics 2008* and *World Marketing Data and Statistics.*

Organisation for Economic Cooperation and Development (OECD), 2 rue Andre Pascal, F-75775 Paris Cedex 16, France, (Telephone in U.S. (202) 785-6323), (Fax in U.S. (202) 785-0350), www.oecd.org; *Education at a Glance* (2007 Edition).

Palgrave Macmillan Ltd., Houndmills, Basingstoke, Hampshire, RG21 6XS, England, (Telephone in U.S. (888) 330-8477), (Fax in U.S. (800) 672-2054), www.palgrave.com; *The Statesman's Yearbook 2008.*

Taylor and Francis Group, An Informa Business, 2 Park Square, Milton Park, Abingdon, Oxford OX14 4RN, United Kingdom, (Dial from U.S. (212) 216-7800), (Fax from U.S. (212) 564-7854), www.tandf.co.uk; *The Europa World Year Book.*

UNESCO Institute for Statistics, C.P. 6128 Succursale Centre-Ville, Montreal, Quebec, H3C 3J7 Canada, (Dial from U.S. (514) 343-6880), (Fax from U.S. (514) 343 6882), www.uis.unesco.org; *Statistical Tables.*

United Nations Statistics Division, New York, NY 10017, (800) 253-9646, Fax: (212) 963-4116, http://unstats.un.org; *Human Development Report 2006.*

The World Bank, 1818 H Street, NW, Washington, DC 20433, (202) 473-1000, Fax: (202) 477-6391, www.worldbank.org; *Belize* and *World Development Indicators (WDI) 2008.*

BELIZE - ELECTRICITY

Palgrave Macmillan Ltd., Houndmills, Basingstoke, Hampshire, RG21 6XS, England, (Telephone in U.S. (888) 330-8477), (Fax in U.S. (800) 672-2054), www.palgrave.com; *The Statesman's Yearbook 2008.*

United Nations Statistics Division, New York, NY 10017, (800) 253-9646, Fax: (212) 963-4116, http://unstats.un.org; *Human Development Report 2006* and *Statistical Yearbook.*

BELIZE - EMPLOYMENT

Euromonitor International, Inc., 224 S. Michigan Avenue, Suite 1500, Chicago, IL 60604, (312) 922-1115, Fax: (312) 922-1157, www.euromonitor.com; *International Marketing Data and Statistics 2008.*

United Nations Statistics Division, New York, NY 10017, (800) 253-9646, Fax: (212) 963-4116, http://unstats.un.org; *Statistical Yearbook.*

The World Bank, 1818 H Street, NW, Washington, DC 20433, (202) 473-1000, Fax: (202) 477-6391, www.worldbank.org; *Belize.*

BELIZE - ENVIRONMENTAL CONDITIONS

DSI Data Service Information, Xantener Strasse 51a, D-47495 Rheinberg, Germany, www.dsidata.com; *Campus Solution* and *DSI's Global Environmental Database.*

Economist Intelligence Unit, 111 West 57th Street, New York, NY 10019, (212) 554-0600, Fax: (212) 586-1181, www.eiu.com; *Belize Country Report.*

United Nations Statistics Division, New York, NY 10017, (800) 253-9646, Fax: (212) 963-4116, http://unstats.un.org; *World Statistics Pocketbook.*

BELIZE - EXPORTS

Central Intelligence Agency, Office of Public Affairs, Washington, DC 20505, (703) 482-0623, Fax: (703) 482-1739, www.cia.gov; *The World Factbook.*

Economist Intelligence Unit, 111 West 57th Street, New York, NY 10019, (212) 554-0600, Fax: (212) 586-1181, www.eiu.com; *Belize Country Report.*

Euromonitor International, Inc., 224 S. Michigan Avenue, Suite 1500, Chicago, IL 60604, (312) 922-1115, Fax: (312) 922-1157, www.euromonitor.com; *International Marketing Data and Statistics 2008* and *The World Economic Factbook 2008.*

Palgrave Macmillan Ltd., Houndmills, Basingstoke, Hampshire, RG21 6XS, England, (Telephone in U.S. (888) 330-8477), (Fax in U.S. (800) 672-2054), www.palgrave.com; *The Statesman's Yearbook 2008.*

Taylor and Francis Group, An Informa Business, 2 Park Square, Milton Park, Abingdon, Oxford OX14 4RN, United Kingdom, (Dial from U.S. (212) 216-7800), (Fax from U.S. (212) 564-7854), www.tandf.co.uk; *The Europa World Year Book.*

United Nations Conference on Trade and Development (UNCTAD), DC2-1120, United Nations, New York, NY 10017, (212) 963-0027, www.unctad.org; *Handbook of Statistics 2005.*

United Nations Food and Agricultural Organization (FAO), Viale delle Terme di Caracalla, 00100 Rome, Italy, (Dial from U.S. (202) 653-2400), (Fax from U.S. (202) 653 5760), www.fao.org; *The State of Food and Agriculture (SOFA) 2006.*

The World Bank, 1818 H Street, NW, Washington, DC 20433, (202) 473-1000, Fax: (202) 477-6391, www.worldbank.org; *World Development Indicators (WDI) 2008.*

BELIZE - FERTILITY, HUMAN

Central Intelligence Agency, Office of Public Affairs, Washington, DC 20505, (703) 482-0623, Fax: (703) 482-1739, www.cia.gov; *The World Factbook.*

United Nations Statistics Division, New York, NY 10017, (800) 253-9646, Fax: (212) 963-4116, http://unstats.un.org; *Human Development Report 2006.*

The World Bank, 1818 H Street, NW, Washington, DC 20433, (202) 473-1000, Fax: (202) 477-6391, www.worldbank.org; *The World Bank Atlas 2003-2004* and *World Development Indicators (WDI) 2008.*

BELIZE - FERTILIZER INDUSTRY

United Nations Food and Agricultural Organization (FAO), Viale delle Terme di Caracalla, 00100 Rome, Italy, (Dial from U.S. (202) 653-2400), (Fax from U.S. (202) 653 5760), www.fao.org; *FAO Fertilizer Yearbook* and *The State of Food and Agriculture (SOFA) 2006.*

United Nations Statistics Division, New York, NY 10017, (800) 253-9646, Fax: (212) 963-4116, http://unstats.un.org; *Statistical Yearbook.*

BELIZE - FETAL MORTALITY

See BELIZE - MORTALITY

BELIZE - FINANCE

United Nations Statistics Division, New York, NY 10017, (800) 253-9646, Fax: (212) 963-4116, http://unstats.un.org; *National Accounts Statistics: Compendium of Income Distribution Statistics* and *Statistical Yearbook.*

The World Bank, 1818 H Street, NW, Washington, DC 20433, (202) 473-1000, Fax: (202) 477-6391, www.worldbank.org; *Belize.*

BELIZE - FINANCE, PUBLIC

Bernan Essential Government Publications, 4611-F Assembly Drive, Lanham MD, 20706-4391, (301) 459-2255, Fax: (800) 865-3450, www.bernan.com; *National Accounts Statistics.*

Economist Intelligence Unit, 111 West 57th Street, New York, NY 10019, (212) 554-0600, Fax: (212) 586-1181, www.eiu.com; *Belize Country Report.*

International Monetary Fund (IMF), 700 Nineteenth Street, NW, Washington, DC 20431, (202) 623-7000, Fax: (202) 623-4661, www.imf.org; *International Financial Statistics* and *International Financial Statistics Online Service.*

Palgrave Macmillan Ltd., Houndmills, Basingstoke, Hampshire, RG21 6XS, England, (Telephone in U.S. (888) 330-8477), (Fax in U.S. (800) 672-2054), www.palgrave.com; *The Statesman's Yearbook 2008.*

Taylor and Francis Group, An Informa Business, 2 Park Square, Milton Park, Abingdon, Oxford OX14 4RN, United Kingdom, (Dial from U.S. (212) 216-7800), (Fax from U.S. (212) 564-7854), www.tandf.co.uk; *The Europa World Year Book.*

The World Bank, 1818 H Street, NW, Washington, DC 20433, (202) 473-1000, Fax: (202) 477-6391, www.worldbank.org; *Belize.*

BELIZE - FISHERIES

Taylor and Francis Group, An Informa Business, 2 Park Square, Milton Park, Abingdon, Oxford OX14 4RN, United Kingdom, (Dial from U.S. (212) 216-7800), (Fax from U.S. (212) 564-7854), www.tandf.co.uk; *The Europa World Year Book.*

United Nations Conference on Trade and Development (UNCTAD), DC2-1120, United Nations, New York, NY 10017, (212) 963-0027, www.unctad.org; *UNCTAD Commodity Yearbook.*

United Nations Food and Agricultural Organization (FAO), Viale delle Terme di Caracalla, 00100 Rome, Italy, (Dial from U.S. (202) 653-2400), (Fax from U.S. (202) 653 5760), www.fao.org; *FAO Yearbook of Fishery Statistics;* Fishery Databases; FISHSTAT Database. Subjects covered include: Aquaculture production, capture production, fishery commodities; and *The State of Food and Agriculture (SOFA) 2006.*

United Nations Statistics Division, New York, NY 10017, (800) 253-9646, Fax: (212) 963-4116, http://unstats.un.org; *Statistical Yearbook.*

The World Bank, 1818 H Street, NW, Washington, DC 20433, (202) 473-1000, Fax: (202) 477-6391, www.worldbank.org; *Belize.*

BELIZE - FOOD

United Nations Conference on Trade and Development (UNCTAD), DC2-1120, United Nations, New York, NY 10017, (212) 963-0027, www.unctad.org; *UNCTAD Commodity Yearbook.*

United Nations Food and Agricultural Organization (FAO), Viale delle Terme di Caracalla, 00100 Rome, Italy, (Dial from U.S. (202) 653-2400), (Fax from U.S. (202) 653 5760), www.fao.org; *FAO Production Yearbook 2002* and *The State of Food and Agriculture (SOFA) 2006.*

United Nations Statistics Division, New York, NY 10017, (800) 253-9646, Fax: (212) 963-4116, http://unstats.un.org; *Human Development Report 2006.*

BELIZE - FOREIGN EXCHANGE RATES

Central Intelligence Agency, Office of Public Affairs, Washington, DC 20505, (703) 482-0623, Fax: (703) 482-1739, www.cia.gov; *The World Factbook.*

Euromonitor International, Inc., 224 S. Michigan Avenue, Suite 1500, Chicago, IL 60604, (312) 922-1115, Fax: (312) 922-1157, www.euromonitor.com; *International Marketing Data and Statistics 2008* and *The World Economic Factbook 2008.*

Taylor and Francis Group, An Informa Business, 2 Park Square, Milton Park, Abingdon, Oxford OX14 4RN, United Kingdom, (Dial from U.S. (212) 216-7800), (Fax from U.S. (212) 564-7854), www.tandf.co.uk; *The Europa World Year Book.*

United Nations Statistics Division, New York, NY 10017, (800) 253-9646, Fax: (212) 963-4116, http://unstats.un.org; *World Statistics Pocketbook.*

BELIZE - FORESTS AND FORESTRY

Palgrave Macmillan Ltd., Houndmills, Basingstoke, Hampshire, RG21 6XS, England, (Telephone in U.S. (888) 330-8477), (Fax in U.S. (800) 672-2054), www.palgrave.com; *The Statesman's Yearbook 2008.*

Taylor and Francis Group, An Informa Business, 2 Park Square, Milton Park, Abingdon, Oxford OX14 4RN, United Kingdom, (Dial from U.S. (212) 216-7800), (Fax from U.S. (212) 564-7854), www.tandf.co.uk; *The Europa World Year Book.*

UNESCO Institute for Statistics, C.P. 6128 Succursale Centre-Ville, Montreal, Quebec, H3C 3J7 Canada, (Dial from U.S. (514) 343-6880), (Fax from U.S. (514) 343 6882), www.uis.unesco.org; *Statistical Tables.*

United Nations Conference on Trade and Development (UNCTAD), DC2-1120, United Nations, New York, NY 10017, (212) 963-0027, www.unctad.org; *UNCTAD Commodity Yearbook.*

United Nations Food and Agricultural Organization (FAO), Viale delle Terme di Caracalla, 00100 Rome, Italy, (Dial from U.S. (202) 653-2400), (Fax from U.S. (202) 653 5760), www.fao.org; *FAO Yearbook of Forest Products* and *The State of Food and Agriculture (SOFA) 2006.*

United Nations Statistics Division, New York, NY 10017, (800) 253-9646, Fax: (212) 963-4116, http://unstats.un.org; *Statistical Yearbook.*

The World Bank, 1818 H Street, NW, Washington, DC 20433, (202) 473-1000, Fax: (202) 477-6391, www.worldbank.org; *Belize.*

BELIZE - GEOGRAPHIC INFORMATION SYSTEMS

The World Bank, 1818 H Street, NW, Washington, DC 20433, (202) 473-1000, Fax: (202) 477-6391, www.worldbank.org; *Belize.*

BELIZE - GOLD INDUSTRY

The World Bank, 1818 H Street, NW, Washington, DC 20433, (202) 473-1000, Fax: (202) 477-6391, www.worldbank.org; *World Development Indicators (WDI) 2008.*

BELIZE - GROSS DOMESTIC PRODUCT

Economist Intelligence Unit, 111 West 57th Street, New York, NY 10019, (212) 554-0600, Fax: (212) 586-1181, www.eiu.com; *Belize Country Report.*

Euromonitor International, Inc., 224 S. Michigan Avenue, Suite 1500, Chicago, IL 60604, (312) 922-1115, Fax: (312) 922-1157, www.euromonitor.com; *International Marketing Data and Statistics 2008* and *The World Economic Factbook 2008.*

Taylor and Francis Group, An Informa Business, 2 Park Square, Milton Park, Abingdon, Oxford OX14 4RN, United Kingdom, (Dial from U.S. (212) 216-7800), (Fax from U.S. (212) 564-7854), www.tandf.co.uk; *The Europa World Year Book.*

United Nations Statistics Division, New York, NY 10017, (800) 253-9646, Fax: (212) 963-4116, http://unstats.un.org; *Human Development Report 2006; National Accounts Statistics: Compendium of Income Distribution Statistics;* and *Statistical Yearbook.*

The World Bank, 1818 H Street, NW, Washington, DC 20433, (202) 473-1000, Fax: (202) 477-6391, www.worldbank.org; *World Development Indicators (WDI) 2008.*

BELIZE - GROSS NATIONAL PRODUCT

Palgrave Macmillan Ltd., Houndmills, Basingstoke, Hampshire, RG21 6XS, England, (Telephone in U.S. (888) 330-8477), (Fax in U.S. (800) 672-2054), www.palgrave.com; *The Statesman's Yearbook 2008.*

United Nations Statistics Division, New York, NY 10017, (800) 253-9646, Fax: (212) 963-4116, http://unstats.un.org; *Statistical Yearbook.*

The World Bank, 1818 H Street, NW, Washington, DC 20433, (202) 473-1000, Fax: (202) 477-6391, www.worldbank.org; *The World Bank Atlas 2003-2004* and *World Development Indicators (WDI) 2008.*

BELIZE - HIDES AND SKINS INDUSTRY

United Nations Food and Agricultural Organization (FAO), Viale delle Terme di Caracalla, 00100 Rome, Italy, (Dial from U.S. (202) 653-2400), (Fax from U.S. (202) 653 5760), www.fao.org; *FAO Production Yearbook 2002.*

BELIZE - HOUSING

Euromonitor International, Inc., 224 S. Michigan Avenue, Suite 1500, Chicago, IL 60604, (312) 922-1115, Fax: (312) 922-1157, www.euromonitor.com; *World Marketing Data and Statistics.*

BELIZE - ILLITERATE PERSONS

Euromonitor International, Inc., 224 S. Michigan Avenue, Suite 1500, Chicago, IL 60604, (312) 922-1115, Fax: (312) 922-1157, www.euromonitor.com; *The World Economic Factbook 2008.*

Palgrave Macmillan Ltd., Houndmills, Basingstoke, Hampshire, RG21 6XS, England, (Telephone in U.S. (888) 330-8477), (Fax in U.S. (800) 672-2054), www.palgrave.com; *The Statesman's Yearbook 2008.*

UNESCO Institute for Statistics, C.P. 6128 Succursale Centre-Ville, Montreal, Quebec, H3C 3J7 Canada, (Dial from U.S. (514) 343-6880), (Fax from U.S. (514) 343 6882), www.uis.unesco.org; *Statistical Tables.*

United Nations Statistics Division, New York, NY 10017, (800) 253-9646, Fax: (212) 963-4116, http://unstats.un.org; *Human Development Report 2006.*

BELIZE - IMPORTS

Central Intelligence Agency, Office of Public Affairs, Washington, DC 20505, (703) 482-0623, Fax: (703) 482-1739, www.cia.gov; *The World Factbook.*

Economist Intelligence Unit, 111 West 57th Street, New York, NY 10019, (212) 554-0600, Fax: (212) 586-1181, www.eiu.com; *Belize Country Report.*

Euromonitor International, Inc., 224 S. Michigan Avenue, Suite 1500, Chicago, IL 60604, (312) 922-1115, Fax: (312) 922-1157, www.euromonitor.com; *International Marketing Data and Statistics 2008* and *The World Economic Factbook 2008.*

International Monetary Fund (IMF), 700 Nineteenth Street, NW, Washington, DC 20431, (202) 623-7000, Fax: (202) 623-4661, www.imf.org; *Direction of Trade Statistics Yearbook 2007.*

Palgrave Macmillan Ltd., Houndmills, Basingstoke, Hampshire, RG21 6XS, England, (Telephone in U.S. (888) 330-8477), (Fax in U.S. (800) 672-2054), www.palgrave.com; *The Statesman's Yearbook 2008.*

Taylor and Francis Group, An Informa Business, 2 Park Square, Milton Park, Abingdon, Oxford OX14 4RN, United Kingdom, (Dial from U.S. (212) 216-7800), (Fax from U.S. (212) 564-7854), www.tandf.co.uk; *The Europa World Year Book.*

United Nations Conference on Trade and Development (UNCTAD), DC2-1120, United Nations, New York, NY 10017, (212) 963-0027, www.unctad.org; *Handbook of Statistics 2005.*

United Nations Food and Agricultural Organization (FAO), Viale delle Terme di Caracalla, 00100 Rome, Italy, (Dial from U.S. (202) 653-2400), (Fax from U.S. (202) 653 5760), www.fao.org; *The State of Food and Agriculture (SOFA) 2006.*

The World Bank, 1818 H Street, NW, Washington, DC 20433, (202) 473-1000, Fax: (202) 477-6391, www.worldbank.org; *World Development Indicators (WDI) 2008.*

BELIZE - INDUSTRIES

Central Intelligence Agency, Office of Public Affairs, Washington, DC 20505, (703) 482-0623, Fax: (703) 482-1739, www.cia.gov; *The World Factbook.*

Economist Intelligence Unit, 111 West 57th Street, New York, NY 10019, (212) 554-0600, Fax: (212) 586-1181, www.eiu.com; *Belize Country Report.*

Euromonitor International, Inc., 224 S. Michigan Avenue, Suite 1500, Chicago, IL 60604, (312) 922-1115, Fax: (312) 922-1157, www.euromonitor.com; *The World Economic Factbook 2008* and *World Marketing Data and Statistics.*

Palgrave Macmillan Ltd., Houndmills, Basingstoke, Hampshire, RG21 6XS, England, (Telephone in U.S. (888) 330-8477), (Fax in U.S. (800) 672-2054), www.palgrave.com; *The Statesman's Yearbook 2008.*

Taylor and Francis Group, An Informa Business, 2 Park Square, Milton Park, Abingdon, Oxford OX14 4RN, United Kingdom, (Dial from U.S. (212) 216-7800), (Fax from U.S. (212) 564-7854), www.tandf.co.uk; *The Europa World Year Book.*

United Nations Industrial Development Organization (UNIDO), 1 United Nations Plaza, New York, NY 10017, (212) 963 6890, Fax: (212) 963-7904, http://unido.org; Industrial Statistics Database 2008 (INDSTAT) and *The International Yearbook of Industrial Statistics 2008.*

United Nations Statistics Division, New York, NY 10017, (800) 253-9646, Fax: (212) 963-4116, http://unstats.un.org; *Economic Survey of Latin America and the Caribbean 2004-2005.*

The World Bank, 1818 H Street, NW, Washington, DC 20433, (202) 473-1000, Fax: (202) 477-6391, www.worldbank.org; *Belize* and *World Development Indicators (WDI) 2008.*

BELIZE - INFANT AND MATERNAL MORTALITY

See BELIZE - MORTALITY

BELIZE - INFLATION (FINANCE)

United Nations Statistics Division, New York, NY 10017, (800) 253-9646, Fax: (212) 963-4116, http://unstats.un.org; *Economic Survey of Latin America and the Caribbean 2004-2005.*

BELIZE - INTERNATIONAL TRADE

Economist Intelligence Unit, 111 West 57th Street, New York, NY 10019, (212) 554-0600, Fax: (212) 586-1181, www.eiu.com; *Belize Country Report.*

Euromonitor International, Inc., 224 S. Michigan Avenue, Suite 1500, Chicago, IL 60604, (312) 922-1115, Fax: (312) 922-1157, www.euromonitor.com; *The World Economic Factbook 2008* and *World Marketing Data and Statistics.*

Palgrave Macmillan Ltd., Houndmills, Basingstoke, Hampshire, RG21 6XS, England, (Telephone in U.S. (888) 330-8477), (Fax in U.S. (800) 672-2054), www.palgrave.com; *The Statesman's Yearbook 2008.*

Taylor and Francis Group, An Informa Business, 2 Park Square, Milton Park, Abingdon, Oxford OX14 4RN, United Kingdom, (Dial from U.S. (212) 216-7800), (Fax from U.S. (212) 564-7854), www.tandf.co.uk; *The Europa World Year Book.*

United Nations Conference on Trade and Development (UNCTAD), DC2-1120, United Nations, New York, NY 10017, (212) 963-0027, www.unctad.org; *UNCTAD Commodity Yearbook.*

United Nations Food and Agricultural Organization (FAO), Viale delle Terme di Caracalla, 00100 Rome, Italy, (Dial from U.S. (202) 653-2400), (Fax from U.S. (202) 653 5760), www.fao.org; *FAO Trade Yearbook* and *The State of Food and Agriculture (SOFA) 2006.*

United Nations Statistics Division, New York, NY 10017, (800) 253-9646, Fax: (212) 963-4116, http://unstats.un.org; *Economic Survey of Latin America and the Caribbean 2004-2005; International Trade Statistics Yearbook;* and *Statistical Yearbook.*

The World Bank, 1818 H Street, NW, Washington, DC 20433, (202) 473-1000, Fax: (202) 477-6391, www.worldbank.org; *Belize* and *World Development Indicators (WDI) 2008.*

World Trade Organization (WTO), Centre William Rappard, Rue de Lausanne 154, CH-1211 Geneva 21, Switzerland, www.wto.org; *International Trade Statistics 2006.*

BELIZE - INTERNET USERS

International Telecommunication Union (ITU), Place des Nations, 1211 Geneva 20, Switzerland, www.itu.int; *World Telecommunication/ICT Indicators Database on CD-ROM; World Telecommunication/ICT Indicators Database Online;* and *Yearbook of Statistics - Telecommunication Services (Chronological Time Series 1997-2006).*

The World Bank, 1818 H Street, NW, Washington, DC 20433, (202) 473-1000, Fax: (202) 477-6391, www.worldbank.org; *Belize.*

BELIZE - LABOR

Central Intelligence Agency, Office of Public Affairs, Washington, DC 20505, (703) 482-0623, Fax: (703) 482-1739, www.cia.gov; *The World Factbook.*

Euromonitor International, Inc., 224 S. Michigan Avenue, Suite 1500, Chicago, IL 60604, (312) 922-1115, Fax: (312) 922-1157, www.euromonitor.com; *International Marketing Data and Statistics 2008* and *World Marketing Data and Statistics.*

Palgrave Macmillan Ltd., Houndmills, Basingstoke, Hampshire, RG21 6XS, England, (Telephone in U.S. (888) 330-8477), (Fax in U.S. (800) 672-2054), www.palgrave.com; *The Statesman's Yearbook 2008.*

United Nations Food and Agricultural Organization (FAO), Viale delle Terme di Caracalla, 00100 Rome, Italy, (Dial from U.S. (202) 653-2400), (Fax from U.S. (202) 653 5760), www.fao.org; *The State of Food and Agriculture (SOFA) 2006.*

United Nations Statistics Division, New York, NY 10017, (800) 253-9646, Fax: (212) 963-4116, http://unstats.un.org; *Human Development Report 2006.*

The World Bank, 1818 H Street, NW, Washington, DC 20433, (202) 473-1000, Fax: (202) 477-6391, www.worldbank.org; *The World Bank Atlas 2003-2004* and *World Development Indicators (WDI) 2008.*

BELIZE - LAND USE

Central Intelligence Agency, Office of Public Affairs, Washington, DC 20505, (703) 482-0623, Fax: (703) 482-1739, www.cia.gov; *The World Factbook.*

Euromonitor International, Inc., 224 S. Michigan Avenue, Suite 1500, Chicago, IL 60604, (312) 922-1115, Fax: (312) 922-1157, www.euromonitor.com; *International Marketing Data and Statistics 2008.*

United Nations Food and Agricultural Organization (FAO), Viale delle Terme di Caracalla, 00100 Rome, Italy, (Dial from U.S. (202) 653-2400), (Fax from U.S. (202) 653 5760), www.fao.org; *FAO Production Yearbook 2002.*

BELIZE - LIBRARIES

UNESCO Institute for Statistics, C.P. 6128 Succursale Centre-Ville, Montreal, Quebec, H3C 3J7 Canada, (Dial from U.S. (514) 343-6880), (Fax from U.S. (514) 343 6882), www.uis.unesco.org; *Statistical Tables.*

BELIZE - LIFE EXPECTANCY

Central Intelligence Agency, Office of Public Affairs, Washington, DC 20505, (703) 482-0623, Fax: (703) 482-1739, www.cia.gov; *The World Factbook.*

Euromonitor International, Inc., 224 S. Michigan Avenue, Suite 1500, Chicago, IL 60604, (312) 922-1115, Fax: (312) 922-1157, www.euromonitor.com; *The World Economic Factbook 2008.*

Palgrave Macmillan Ltd., Houndmills, Basingstoke, Hampshire, RG21 6XS, England, (Telephone in U.S. (888) 330-8477), (Fax in U.S. (800) 672-2054), www.palgrave.com; *The Statesman's Yearbook 2008.*

United Nations Statistics Division, New York, NY 10017, (800) 253-9646, Fax: (212) 963-4116, http://unstats.un.org; *Human Development Report 2006* and *World Statistics Pocketbook.*

The World Bank, 1818 H Street, NW, Washington, DC 20433, (202) 473-1000, Fax: (202) 477-6391, www.worldbank.org; *The World Bank Atlas 2003-2004.*

BELIZE - LITERACY

Euromonitor International, Inc., 224 S. Michigan Avenue, Suite 1500, Chicago, IL 60604, (312) 922-1115, Fax: (312) 922-1157, www.euromonitor.com; *World Marketing Data and Statistics.*

BELIZE - LIVESTOCK

Palgrave Macmillan Ltd., Houndmills, Basingstoke, Hampshire, RG21 6XS, England, (Telephone in U.S. (888) 330-8477), (Fax in U.S. (800) 672-2054), www.palgrave.com; *The Statesman's Yearbook 2008.*

Taylor and Francis Group, An Informa Business, 2 Park Square, Milton Park, Abingdon, Oxford OX14 4RN, United Kingdom, (Dial from U.S. (212) 216-7800), (Fax from U.S. (212) 564-7854), www.tandf.co.uk; *The Europa World Year Book.*

United Nations Conference on Trade and Development (UNCTAD), DC2-1120, United Nations, New York, NY 10017, (212) 963-0027, www.unctad.org; *UNCTAD Commodity Yearbook.*

United Nations Food and Agricultural Organization (FAO), Viale delle Terme di Caracalla, 00100 Rome,

Italy, (Dial from U.S. (202) 653-2400), (Fax from U.S. (202) 653 5760), www.fao.org; *FAO Production Yearbook 2002* and *The State of Food and Agriculture (SOFA) 2006.*

United Nations Statistics Division, New York, NY 10017, (800) 253-9646, Fax: (212) 963-4116, http://unstats.un.org; *Statistical Yearbook.*

BELIZE - MANUFACTURES

The World Bank, 1818 H Street, NW, Washington, DC 20433, (202) 473-1000, Fax: (202) 477-6391, www.worldbank.org; *World Development Indicators (WDI) 2008.*

BELIZE - MARRIAGE

Taylor and Francis Group, An Informa Business, 2 Park Square, Milton Park, Abingdon, Oxford OX14 4RN, United Kingdom, (Dial from U.S. (212) 216-7800), (Fax from U.S. (212) 564-7854), www.tandf.co.uk; *The Europa World Year Book.*

United Nations Statistics Division, New York, NY 10017, (800) 253-9646, Fax: (212) 963-4116, http://unstats.un.org; *Demographic Yearbook* and *Statistical Yearbook.*

BELIZE - MEAT PRODUCTION

See BELIZE - LIVESTOCK

BELIZE - MINERAL INDUSTRIES

Palgrave Macmillan Ltd., Houndmills, Basingstoke, Hampshire, RG21 6XS, England, (Telephone in U.S. (888) 330-8477), (Fax in U.S. (800) 672-2054), www.palgrave.com; *The Statesman's Yearbook 2008.*

United Nations Conference on Trade and Development (UNCTAD), DC2-1120, United Nations, New York, NY 10017, (212) 963-0027, www.unctad.org; *UNCTAD Commodity Yearbook.*

BELIZE - MONEY SUPPLY

Economist Intelligence Unit, 111 West 57th Street, New York, NY 10019, (212) 554-0600, Fax: (212) 586-1181, www.eiu.com; *Belize Country Report.*

Taylor and Francis Group, An Informa Business, 2 Park Square, Milton Park, Abingdon, Oxford OX14 4RN, United Kingdom, (Dial from U.S. (212) 216-7800), (Fax from U.S. (212) 564-7854), www.tandf.co.uk; *The Europa World Year Book.*

The World Bank, 1818 H Street, NW, Washington, DC 20433, (202) 473-1000, Fax: (202) 477-6391, www.worldbank.org; *Belize* and *World Development Indicators (WDI) 2008.*

BELIZE - MONUMENTS AND HISTORIC SITES

UNESCO Institute for Statistics, C.P. 6128 Succursale Centre-Ville, Montreal, Quebec, H3C 3J7 Canada, (Dial from U.S. (514) 343-6880), (Fax from U.S. (514) 343 6882), www.uis.unesco.org; *Statistical Tables.*

BELIZE - MORTALITY

Central Intelligence Agency, Office of Public Affairs, Washington, DC 20505, (703) 482-0623, Fax: (703) 482-1739, www.cia.gov; *The World Factbook.*

Euromonitor International, Inc., 224 S. Michigan Avenue, Suite 1500, Chicago, IL 60604, (312) 922-1115, Fax: (312) 922-1157, www.euromonitor.com; *International Marketing Data and Statistics 2008* and *The World Economic Factbook 2008.*

Palgrave Macmillan Ltd., Houndmills, Basingstoke, Hampshire, RG21 6XS, England, (Telephone in U.S. (888) 330-8477), (Fax in U.S. (800) 672-2054), www.palgrave.com; *The Statesman's Yearbook 2008.*

Taylor and Francis Group, An Informa Business, 2 Park Square, Milton Park, Abingdon, Oxford OX14 4RN, United Kingdom, (Dial from U.S. (212) 216-7800), (Fax from U.S. (212) 564-7854), www.tandf.co.uk; *The Europa World Year Book.*

United Nations Statistics Division, New York, NY 10017, (800) 253-9646, Fax: (212) 963-4116, http://unstats.un.org; *Demographic Yearbook; Human Development Report 2006; Statistical Yearbook;* and *World Statistics Pocketbook.*

The World Bank, 1818 H Street, NW, Washington, DC 20433, (202) 473-1000, Fax: (202) 477-6391, www.worldbank.org; *World Development Report 2008.*

World Health Organization (WHO), Avenue Appia 20, 1211 Geneve 27, Switzerland, (Telephone in U.S. (212) 331-9081), www.who.int; The WHO Global Atlas of Infectious Diseases and *World Health Report 2006.*

BELIZE - MOTION PICTURES

Palgrave Macmillan Ltd., Houndmills, Basingstoke, Hampshire, RG21 6XS, England, (Telephone in U.S. (888) 330-8477), (Fax in U.S. (800) 672-2054), www.palgrave.com; *The Statesman's Yearbook 2008.*

United Nations Statistics Division, New York, NY 10017, (800) 253-9646, Fax: (212) 963-4116, http://unstats.un.org; *Statistical Yearbook.*

BELIZE - MOTOR VEHICLES

Taylor and Francis Group, An Informa Business, 2 Park Square, Milton Park, Abingdon, Oxford OX14 4RN, United Kingdom, (Dial from U.S. (212) 216-7800), (Fax from U.S. (212) 564-7854), www.tandf.co.uk; *The Europa World Year Book.*

United Nations Statistics Division, New York, NY 10017, (800) 253-9646, Fax: (212) 963-4116, http://unstats.un.org; *Statistical Yearbook.*

BELIZE - MUSEUMS

UNESCO Institute for Statistics, C.P. 6128 Succursale Centre-Ville, Montreal, Quebec, H3C 3J7 Canada, (Dial from U.S. (514) 343-6880), (Fax from U.S. (514) 343 6882), www.uis.unesco.org; *Statistical Tables.*

BELIZE - NATIONAL INCOME

United Nations Statistics Division, New York, NY 10017, (800) 253-9646, Fax: (212) 963-4116, http://unstats.un.org; *Statistical Yearbook.*

BELIZE - NUTRITION

United Nations Food and Agricultural Organization (FAO), Viale delle Terme di Caracalla, 00100 Rome, Italy, (Dial from U.S. (202) 653-2400), (Fax from U.S. (202) 653 5760), www.fao.org; *The State of Food and Agriculture (SOFA) 2006.*

BELIZE - PAPER

See BELIZE - FORESTS AND FORESTRY

BELIZE - PERIODICALS

UNESCO Institute for Statistics, C.P. 6128 Succursale Centre-Ville, Montreal, Quebec, H3C 3J7 Canada, (Dial from U.S. (514) 343-6880), (Fax from U.S. (514) 343 6882), www.uis.unesco.org; *Statistical Tables.*

BELIZE - PESTICIDES

United Nations Food and Agricultural Organization (FAO), Viale delle Terme di Caracalla, 00100 Rome, Italy, (Dial from U.S. (202) 653-2400), (Fax from U.S. (202) 653 5760), www.fao.org; *The State of Food and Agriculture (SOFA) 2006.*

BELIZE - PETROLEUM INDUSTRY AND TRADE

PennWell Corporation, 1421 South Sheridan Road, Tulsa, OK 74112, (918) 835-3161, www.pennwell.com; *International Petroleum Encyclopedia 2007.*

United Nations Conference on Trade and Development (UNCTAD), DC2-1120, United Nations, New York, NY 10017, (212) 963-0027, www.unctad.org; *UNCTAD Commodity Yearbook.*

United Nations Food and Agricultural Organization (FAO), Viale delle Terme di Caracalla, 00100 Rome, Italy, (Dial from U.S. (202) 653-2400), (Fax from U.S. (202) 653 5760), www.fao.org; *The State of Food and Agriculture (SOFA) 2006.*

BELIZE - POLITICAL SCIENCE

Central Intelligence Agency, Office of Public Affairs, Washington, DC 20505, (703) 482-0623, Fax: (703) 482-1739, www.cia.gov; *The World Factbook.*

Palgrave Macmillan Ltd., Houndmills, Basingstoke, Hampshire, RG21 6XS, England, (Telephone in U.S. (888) 330-8477), (Fax in U.S. (800) 672-2054), www.palgrave.com; *The Statesman's Yearbook 2008.*

Taylor and Francis Group, An Informa Business, 2 Park Square, Milton Park, Abingdon, Oxford OX14 4RN, United Kingdom, (Dial from U.S. (212) 216-7800), (Fax from U.S. (212) 564-7854), www.tandf.co.uk; *The Europa World Year Book.*

United Nations Statistics Division, New York, NY 10017, (800) 253-9646, Fax: (212) 963-4116, http://unstats.un.org; *National Accounts Statistics: Compendium of Income Distribution Statistics.*

The World Bank, 1818 H Street, NW, Washington, DC 20433, (202) 473-1000, Fax: (202) 477-6391, www.worldbank.org; *World Development Indicators (WDI) 2008.*

BELIZE - POPULATION

Caribbean Epidemiology Centre (CAREC), 16-18 Jamaica Boulevard, Federation Park, PO Box 164, Port of Spain, Republic of Trinidad and Tobago, (Dial from U.S. (868) 622-4261), (Fax from U.S. (868) 622-2792), www.carec.org; *Population Data.*

Central Intelligence Agency, Office of Public Affairs, Washington, DC 20505, (703) 482-0623, Fax: (703) 482-1739, www.cia.gov; *The World Factbook.*

Economist Intelligence Unit, 111 West 57th Street, New York, NY 10019, (212) 554-0600, Fax: (212) 586-1181, www.eiu.com; *Belize Country Report.*

Euromonitor International, Inc., 224 S. Michigan Avenue, Suite 1500, Chicago, IL 60604, (312) 922-1115, Fax: (312) 922-1157, www.euromonitor.com; *International Marketing Data and Statistics 2008* and *The World Economic Factbook 2008.*

Palgrave Macmillan Ltd., Houndmills, Basingstoke, Hampshire, RG21 6XS, England, (Telephone in U.S. (888) 330-8477), (Fax in U.S. (800) 672-2054), www.palgrave.com; *The Statesman's Yearbook 2008.*

Taylor and Francis Group, An Informa Business, 2 Park Square, Milton Park, Abingdon, Oxford OX14 4RN, United Kingdom, (Dial from U.S. (212) 216-7800), (Fax from U.S. (212) 564-7854), www.tandf.co.uk; *The Europa World Year Book.*

UNESCO Institute for Statistics, C.P. 6128 Succursale Centre-Ville, Montreal, Quebec, H3C 3J7 Canada, (Dial from U.S. (514) 343-6880), (Fax from U.S. (514) 343 6882), www.uis.unesco.org; *Statistical Tables.*

United Nations Food and Agricultural Organization (FAO), Viale delle Terme di Caracalla, 00100 Rome, Italy, (Dial from U.S. (202) 653-2400), (Fax from U.S. (202) 653 5760), www.fao.org; *FAO Production Yearbook 2002.*

United Nations Statistics Division, New York, NY 10017, (800) 253-9646, Fax: (212) 963-4116, http://unstats.un.org; *Demographic Yearbook; Human Development Report 2006; Statistical Yearbook;* and *World Statistics Pocketbook.*

The World Bank, 1818 H Street, NW, Washington, DC 20433, (202) 473-1000, Fax: (202) 477-6391, www.worldbank.org; *Belize* and *World Development Report 2008.*

World Health Organization (WHO), Avenue Appia 20, 1211 Geneve 27, Switzerland, (Telephone in U.S. (212) 331-9081), www.who.int; *World Health Report 2006.*

BELIZE - POPULATION DENSITY

Central Intelligence Agency, Office of Public Affairs, Washington, DC 20505, (703) 482-0623, Fax: (703) 482-1739, www.cia.gov; *The World Factbook.*

Euromonitor International, Inc., 224 S. Michigan Avenue, Suite 1500, Chicago, IL 60604, (312) 922-

1115, Fax: (312) 922-1157, www.euromonitor.com; *The World Economic Factbook 2008.*

Palgrave Macmillan Ltd., Houndmills, Basingstoke, Hampshire, RG21 6XS, England, (Telephone in U.S. (888) 330-8477), (Fax in U.S. (800) 672-2054), www.palgrave.com; *The Statesman's Yearbook 2008.*

Taylor and Francis Group, An Informa Business, 2 Park Square, Milton Park, Abingdon, Oxford OX14 4RN, United Kingdom, (Dial from U.S. (212) 216-7800), (Fax from U.S. (212) 564-7854), www.tandf.co.uk; *The Europa World Year Book.*

United Nations Food and Agricultural Organization (FAO), Viale delle Terme di Caracalla, 00100 Rome, Italy, (Dial from U.S. (202) 653-2400), (Fax from U.S. (202) 653 5760), www.fao.org; *The State of Food and Agriculture (SOFA) 2006.*

United Nations Statistics Division, New York, NY 10017, (800) 253-9646, Fax: (212) 963-4116, http://unstats.un.org; *Statistical Yearbook.*

The World Bank, 1818 H Street, NW, Washington, DC 20433, (202) 473-1000, Fax: (202) 477-6391, www.worldbank.org; *Belize.*

BELIZE - POSTAL SERVICE

Palgrave Macmillan Ltd., Houndmills, Basingstoke, Hampshire, RG21 6XS, England, (Telephone in U.S. (888) 330-8477), (Fax in U.S. (800) 672-2054), www.palgrave.com; *The Statesman's Yearbook 2008.*

United Nations Statistics Division, New York, NY 10017, (800) 253-9646, Fax: (212) 963-4116, http://unstats.un.org; *Statistical Yearbook.*

BELIZE - POWER RESOURCES

Euromonitor International, Inc., 224 S. Michigan Avenue, Suite 1500, Chicago, IL 60604, (312) 922-1115, Fax: (312) 922-1157, www.euromonitor.com; *International Marketing Data and Statistics 2008; The World Economic Factbook 2008;* and *World Marketing Data and Statistics.*

Palgrave Macmillan Ltd., Houndmills, Basingstoke, Hampshire, RG21 6XS, England, (Telephone in U.S. (888) 330-8477), (Fax in U.S. (800) 672-2054), www.palgrave.com; *The Statesman's Yearbook 2008.*

Platts, 2 Penn Plaza, 25th Floor, New York, NY 10121-2298, (212) 904-3070, www.platts.com; *Energy Economist.*

United Nations Food and Agricultural Organization (FAO), Viale delle Terme di Caracalla, 00100 Rome, Italy, (Dial from U.S. (202) 653-2400), (Fax from U.S. (202) 653 5760), www.fao.org; *The State of Food and Agriculture (SOFA) 2006.*

United Nations Statistics Division, New York, NY 10017, (800) 253-9646, Fax: (212) 963-4116, http://unstats.un.org; *Energy Statistics Yearbook 2003; Human Development Report 2006; Statistical Yearbook;* and *World Statistics Pocketbook.*

The World Bank, 1818 H Street, NW, Washington, DC 20433, (202) 473-1000, Fax: (202) 477-6391, www.worldbank.org; *The World Bank Atlas 2003-2004.*

BELIZE - PRICES

United Nations Food and Agricultural Organization (FAO), Viale delle Terme di Caracalla, 00100 Rome, Italy, (Dial from U.S. (202) 653-2400), (Fax from U.S. (202) 653 5760), www.fao.org; *FAO Production Yearbook 2002* and *The State of Food and Agriculture (SOFA) 2006.*

United Nations Statistics Division, New York, NY 10017, (800) 253-9646, Fax: (212) 963-4116, http://unstats.un.org; *Economic Survey of Latin America and the Caribbean 2004-2005.*

The World Bank, 1818 H Street, NW, Washington, DC 20433, (202) 473-1000, Fax: (202) 477-6391, www.worldbank.org; *Belize.*

BELIZE - PROFESSIONS

UNESCO Institute for Statistics, C.P. 6128 Succursale Centre-Ville, Montreal, Quebec, H3C 3J7 Canada, (Dial from U.S. (514) 343-6880), (Fax from U.S. (514) 343 6882), www.uis.unesco.org; *Statistical Tables.*

United Nations Statistics Division, New York, NY 10017, (800) 253-9646, Fax: (212) 963-4116, http://unstats.un.org; *Statistical Yearbook.*

BELIZE - PUBLIC HEALTH

Euromonitor International, Inc., 224 S. Michigan Avenue, Suite 1500, Chicago, IL 60604, (312) 922-1115, Fax: (312) 922-1157, www.euromonitor.com; *World Marketing Data and Statistics.*

Palgrave Macmillan Ltd., Houndmills, Basingstoke, Hampshire, RG21 6XS, England, (Telephone in U.S. (888) 330-8477), (Fax in U.S. (800) 672-2054), www.palgrave.com; *The Statesman's Yearbook 2008.*

United Nations Statistics Division, New York, NY 10017, (800) 253-9646, Fax: (212) 963-4116, http://unstats.un.org; *Human Development Report 2006* and *Statistical Yearbook.*

The World Bank, 1818 H Street, NW, Washington, DC 20433, (202) 473-1000, Fax: (202) 477-6391, www.worldbank.org; *Belize.*

World Health Organization (WHO), Avenue Appia 20, 1211 Geneve 27, Switzerland, (Telephone in U.S. (212) 331-9081), www.who.int; The WHO Global Atlas of Infectious Diseases and *World Health Report 2006.*

BELIZE - RADIO BROADCASTING

Palgrave Macmillan Ltd., Houndmills, Basingstoke, Hampshire, RG21 6XS, England, (Telephone in U.S. (888) 330-8477), (Fax in U.S. (800) 672-2054), www.palgrave.com; *The Statesman's Yearbook 2008.*

BELIZE - RELIGION

Central Intelligence Agency, Office of Public Affairs, Washington, DC 20505, (703) 482-0623, Fax: (703) 482-1739, www.cia.gov; *The World Factbook.*

Palgrave Macmillan Ltd., Houndmills, Basingstoke, Hampshire, RG21 6XS, England, (Telephone in U.S. (888) 330-8477), (Fax in U.S. (800) 672-2054), www.palgrave.com; *The Statesman's Yearbook 2008.*

BELIZE - RESERVES (ACCOUNTING)

The World Bank, 1818 H Street, NW, Washington, DC 20433, (202) 473-1000, Fax: (202) 477-6391, www.worldbank.org; *World Development Indicators (WDI) 2008.*

BELIZE - RETAIL TRADE

Euromonitor International, Inc., 224 S. Michigan Avenue, Suite 1500, Chicago, IL 60604, (312) 922-1115, Fax: (312) 922-1157, www.euromonitor.com; *World Marketing Data and Statistics.*

BELIZE - RICE PRODUCTION

See BELIZE - CROPS

BELIZE - ROADS

Central Intelligence Agency, Office of Public Affairs, Washington, DC 20505, (703) 482-0623, Fax: (703) 482-1739, www.cia.gov; *The World Factbook.*

Palgrave Macmillan Ltd., Houndmills, Basingstoke, Hampshire, RG21 6XS, England, (Telephone in U.S. (888) 330-8477), (Fax in U.S. (800) 672-2054), www.palgrave.com; *The Statesman's Yearbook 2008.*

BELIZE - SHEEP

See BELIZE - LIVESTOCK

BELIZE - SHIPPING

Palgrave Macmillan Ltd., Houndmills, Basingstoke, Hampshire, RG21 6XS, England, (Telephone in U.S. (888) 330-8477), (Fax in U.S. (800) 672-2054), www.palgrave.com; *The Statesman's Yearbook 2008.*

Taylor and Francis Group, An Informa Business, 2 Park Square, Milton Park, Abingdon, Oxford OX14 4RN, United Kingdom, (Dial from U.S. (212) 216-7800), (Fax from U.S. (212) 564-7854), www.tandf.co.uk; *The Europa World Year Book.*

United Nations Statistics Division, New York, NY 10017, (800) 253-9646, Fax: (212) 963-4116, http://unstats.un.org; *Statistical Yearbook.*

BELIZE - SOCIAL SECURITY

United Nations Statistics Division, New York, NY 10017, (800) 253-9646, Fax: (212) 963-4116, http://unstats.un.org; *National Accounts Statistics: Compendium of Income Distribution Statistics* and *World Statistics Pocketbook.*

BELIZE - SUGAR PRODUCTION

See BELIZE - CROPS

BELIZE - TAXATION

Taylor and Francis Group, An Informa Business, 2 Park Square, Milton Park, Abingdon, Oxford OX14 4RN, United Kingdom, (Dial from U.S. (212) 216-7800), (Fax from U.S. (212) 564-7854), www.tandf.co.uk; *The Europa World Year Book.*

The World Bank, 1818 H Street, NW, Washington, DC 20433, (202) 473-1000, Fax: (202) 477-6391, www.worldbank.org; *World Development Indicators (WDI) 2008.*

BELIZE - TELEPHONE

Central Intelligence Agency, Office of Public Affairs, Washington, DC 20505, (703) 482-0623, Fax: (703) 482-1739, www.cia.gov; *The World Factbook.*

International Telecommunication Union (ITU), Place des Nations, 1211 Geneva 20, Switzerland, www.itu.int; World Telecommunication Indicators Database.

Palgrave Macmillan Ltd., Houndmills, Basingstoke, Hampshire, RG21 6XS, England, (Telephone in U.S. (888) 330-8477), (Fax in U.S. (800) 672-2054), www.palgrave.com; *The Statesman's Yearbook 2008.*

Taylor and Francis Group, An Informa Business, 2 Park Square, Milton Park, Abingdon, Oxford OX14 4RN, United Kingdom, (Dial from U.S. (212) 216-7800), (Fax from U.S. (212) 564-7854), www.tandf.co.uk; *The Europa World Year Book.*

United Nations Statistics Division, New York, NY 10017, (800) 253-9646, Fax: (212) 963-4116, http://unstats.un.org; *Statistical Yearbook* and *World Statistics Pocketbook.*

BELIZE - TEXTILE INDUSTRY

United Nations Conference on Trade and Development (UNCTAD), DC2-1120, United Nations, New York, NY 10017, (212) 963-0027, www.unctad.org; *UNCTAD Commodity Yearbook.*

BELIZE - TOBACCO INDUSTRY

Foreign Agricultural Service (FAS), U.S. Department of Agriculture (USDA), 1400 Independence Avenue, SW, Washington, DC 20250, (202) 720-3935, www.fas.usda.gov; *Tobacco: World Markets and Trade.*

United Nations Statistics Division, New York, NY 10017, (800) 253-9646, Fax: (212) 963-4116, http://unstats.un.org; *Statistical Yearbook.*

BELIZE - TOURISM

Euromonitor International, Inc., 224 S. Michigan Avenue, Suite 1500, Chicago, IL 60604, (312) 922-1115, Fax: (312) 922-1157, www.euromonitor.com; *The World Economic Factbook 2008* and *World Marketing Data and Statistics.*

International Institute for Strategic Studies (IISS), Arundel House, 13-15 Arundel Street, Temple Place, London WC2R 3DX, England, www.iiss.org; *The Military Balance 2007.*

Palgrave Macmillan Ltd., Houndmills, Basingstoke, Hampshire, RG21 6XS, England, (Telephone in U.S. (888) 330-8477), (Fax in U.S. (800) 672-2054), www.palgrave.com; *The Statesman's Yearbook 2008.*

Taylor and Francis Group, An Informa Business, 2 Park Square, Milton Park, Abingdon, Oxford OX14 4RN, United Kingdom, (Dial from U.S. (212) 216-7800), (Fax from U.S. (212) 564-7854), www.tandf.co.uk; *The Europa World Year Book.*

United Nations World Tourism Organization (UNWTO), Capitan Haya 42, 28020 Madrid, Spain, www.world-tourism.org; *Yearbook of Tourism Statistics.*

The World Bank, 1818 H Street, NW, Washington, DC 20433, (202) 473-1000, Fax: (202) 477-6391, www.worldbank.org; *Belize.*

BELIZE - TRADE

See BELIZE - INTERNATIONAL TRADE

BELIZE - TRANSPORTATION

Central Intelligence Agency, Office of Public Affairs, Washington, DC 20505, (703) 482-0623, Fax: (703) 482-1739, www.cia.gov; *The World Factbook.*

Euromonitor International, Inc., 224 S. Michigan Avenue, Suite 1500, Chicago, IL 60604, (312) 922-1115, Fax: (312) 922-1157, www.euromonitor.com; *International Marketing Data and Statistics 2008* and *World Marketing Data and Statistics.*

Palgrave Macmillan Ltd., Houndmills, Basingstoke, Hampshire, RG21 6XS, England, (Telephone in U.S. (888) 330-8477), (Fax in U.S. (800) 672-2054), www.palgrave.com; *The Statesman's Yearbook 2008.*

Taylor and Francis Group, An Informa Business, 2 Park Square, Milton Park, Abingdon, Oxford OX14 4RN, United Kingdom, (Dial from U.S. (212) 216-7800), (Fax from U.S. (212) 564-7854), www.tandf.co.uk; *The Europa World Year Book.*

United Nations Statistics Division, New York, NY 10017, (800) 253-9646, Fax: (212) 963-4116, http://unstats.un.org; *Human Development Report 2006.*

The World Bank, 1818 H Street, NW, Washington, DC 20433, (202) 473-1000, Fax: (202) 477-6391, www.worldbank.org; *Belize.*

BELIZE - TURKEYS

See BELIZE - LIVESTOCK

BELIZE - UNEMPLOYMENT

Central Intelligence Agency, Office of Public Affairs, Washington, DC 20505, (703) 482-0623, Fax: (703) 482-1739, www.cia.gov; *The World Factbook.*

BELIZE - VITAL STATISTICS

Palgrave Macmillan Ltd., Houndmills, Basingstoke, Hampshire, RG21 6XS, England, (Telephone in U.S. (888) 330-8477), (Fax in U.S. (800) 672-2054), www.palgrave.com; *The Statesman's Yearbook 2008.*

United Nations Statistics Division, New York, NY 10017, (800) 253-9646, Fax: (212) 963-4116, http://unstats.un.org; *Statistical Yearbook.*

World Health Organization (WHO), Avenue Appia 20, 1211 Geneve 27, Switzerland, (Telephone in U.S. (212) 331-9081), www.who.int; *World Health Report 2006.*

BELIZE - WAGES

The World Bank, 1818 H Street, NW, Washington, DC 20433, (202) 473-1000, Fax: (202) 477-6391, www.worldbank.org; *Belize.*

BENIN - NATIONAL STATISTICAL OFFICE

Institut National de la Statistique et de l'Analyse Economique (INSAE), 01 BP 323, Cotonou, Benin, www.insae-bj.org; National Data Center.

BENIN - PRIMARY STATISTICS SOURCES

Institut National de la Statistique et de l'Analyse Economique (INSAE), 01 BP 323, Cotonou, Benin, www.insae-bj.org; *Annuaire Statistique* (Statistical Yearbook) and *Bulletin de Statistique* (Bulletin of Statistics).

BENIN - AGRICULTURAL MACHINERY

United Nations Statistics Division, New York, NY 10017, (800) 253-9646, Fax: (212) 963-4116, http://unstats.un.org; *Statistical Yearbook.*

BENIN - AGRICULTURE

Economist Intelligence Unit, 111 West 57th Street, New York, NY 10019, (212) 554-0600, Fax: (212) 586-1181, www.eiu.com; *Benin Country Report.*

Euromonitor International, Inc., 224 S. Michigan Avenue, Suite 1500, Chicago, IL 60604, (312) 922-1115, Fax: (312) 922-1157, www.euromonitor.com; *International Marketing Data and Statistics 2008* and *World Marketing Data and Statistics.*

M.E. Sharpe, 80 Business Park Drive, Armonk, NY 10504, (800) 541-6563, Fax: (914) 273-2106, www.mesharpe.com; *The Illustrated Book of World Rankings.*

Palgrave Macmillan Ltd., Houndmills, Basingstoke, Hampshire, RG21 6XS, England, (Telephone in U.S. (888) 330-8477), (Fax in U.S. (800) 672-2054), www.palgrave.com; *The Statesman's Yearbook 2008.*

Taylor and Francis Group, An Informa Business, 2 Park Square, Milton Park, Abingdon, Oxford OX14 4RN, United Kingdom, (Dial from U.S. (212) 216-7800), (Fax from U.S. (212) 564-7854), www.tandf.co.uk; *The Europa World Year Book.*

United Nations Conference on Trade and Development (UNCTAD), DC2-1120, United Nations, New York, NY 10017, (212) 963-0027, www.unctad.org; *UNCTAD Commodity Yearbook.*

United Nations Economic Commission for Africa (ECA), PO Box 3001, Addis Ababa, Ethiopia, (Telephone in U.S. (212) 963-4957), www.uneca.org; *African Statistical Yearbook 2006.*

United Nations Food and Agricultural Organization (FAO), Viale delle Terme di Caracalla, 00100 Rome, Italy, (Dial from U.S. (202) 653-2400), (Fax from U.S. (202) 653 5760), www.fao.org; AQUASTAT; *FAO Production Yearbook 2002; FAO Trade Yearbook;* and *The State of Food and Agriculture (SOFA) 2006.*

United Nations Statistics Division, New York, NY 10017, (800) 253-9646, Fax: (212) 963-4116, http://unstats.un.org; *Statistical Yearbook* and *Survey of Economic and Social Conditions in Africa 2005.*

The World Bank, 1818 H Street, NW, Washington, DC 20433, (202) 473-1000, Fax: (202) 477-6391, www.worldbank.org; *Africa Live Database (LDB); African Development Indicators (ADI) 2007; Benin;* and *World Development Indicators (WDI) 2008.*

BENIN - AIRLINES

M.E. Sharpe, 80 Business Park Drive, Armonk, NY 10504, (800) 541-6563, Fax: (914) 273-2106, www.mesharpe.com; *The Illustrated Book of World Rankings.*

Palgrave Macmillan Ltd., Houndmills, Basingstoke, Hampshire, RG21 6XS, England, (Telephone in U.S. (888) 330-8477), (Fax in U.S. (800) 672-2054), www.palgrave.com; *The Statesman's Yearbook 2008.*

Taylor and Francis Group, An Informa Business, 2 Park Square, Milton Park, Abingdon, Oxford OX14 4RN, United Kingdom, (Dial from U.S. (212) 216-7800), (Fax from U.S. (212) 564-7854), www.tandf.co.uk; *The Europa World Year Book.*

United Nations Economic Commission for Africa (ECA), PO Box 3001, Addis Ababa, Ethiopia, (Telephone in U.S. (212) 963-4957), www.uneca.org; *African Statistical Yearbook 2006.*

United Nations Statistics Division, New York, NY 10017, (800) 253-9646, Fax: (212) 963-4116, http://unstats.un.org; *Statistical Yearbook.*

BENIN - AIRPORTS

Central Intelligence Agency, Office of Public Affairs, Washington, DC 20505, (703) 482-0623, Fax: (703) 482-1739, www.cia.gov; *The World Factbook.*

BENIN - ALUMINUM PRODUCTION

See BENIN - MINERAL INDUSTRIES

BENIN - ARMED FORCES

Central Intelligence Agency, Office of Public Affairs, Washington, DC 20505, (703) 482-0623, Fax: (703) 482-1739, www.cia.gov; *The World Factbook.*

Euromonitor International, Inc., 224 S. Michigan Avenue, Suite 1500, Chicago, IL 60604, (312) 922-1115, Fax: (312) 922-1157, www.euromonitor.com; *World Marketing Data and Statistics.*

International Institute for Strategic Studies (IISS), Arundel House, 13-15 Arundel Street, Temple Place, London WC2R 3DX, England, www.iiss.org; *The Military Balance 2007.*

Palgrave Macmillan Ltd., Houndmills, Basingstoke, Hampshire, RG21 6XS, England, (Telephone in U.S. (888) 330-8477), (Fax in U.S. (800) 672-2054), www.palgrave.com; *The Statesman's Yearbook 2008.*

U.S. Department of State (DOS), 2201 C Street NW, Washington, DC 20520, (202) 647-4000, www.state.gov; *World Military Expenditures and Arms Transfers (WMEAT).*

United Nations Statistics Division, New York, NY 10017, (800) 253-9646, Fax: (212) 963-4116, http://unstats.un.org; *Human Development Report 2006.*

BENIN - BALANCE OF PAYMENTS

African Development Bank Group, Rue Joseph Anoma, 01 BP 1387 Abidjan 01, Cote d'Ivoire, www.afdb.org; *Statistics Pocketbook 2008.*

International Monetary Fund (IMF), 700 Nineteenth Street, NW, Washington, DC 20431, (202) 623-7000, Fax: (202) 623-4661, www.imf.org; *Balance of Payments Statistics Newsletter; Balance of Payments Statistics Yearbook 2007;* and *International Financial Statistics Yearbook 2007.*

M.E. Sharpe, 80 Business Park Drive, Armonk, NY 10504, (800) 541-6563, Fax: (914) 273-2106, www.mesharpe.com; *The Illustrated Book of World Rankings.*

Taylor and Francis Group, An Informa Business, 2 Park Square, Milton Park, Abingdon, Oxford OX14 4RN, United Kingdom, (Dial from U.S. (212) 216-7800), (Fax from U.S. (212) 564-7854), www.tandf.co.uk; *The Europa World Year Book.*

United Nations Conference on Trade and Development (UNCTAD), DC2-1120, United Nations, New York, NY 10017, (212) 963-0027, www.unctad.org; *Handbook of Statistics 2005.*

United Nations Economic Commission for Africa (ECA), PO Box 3001, Addis Ababa, Ethiopia, (Telephone in U.S. (212) 963-4957), www.uneca.org; *African Statistical Yearbook 2006.*

The World Bank, 1818 H Street, NW, Washington, DC 20433, (202) 473-1000, Fax: (202) 477-6391, www.worldbank.org; *Benin; World Development Indicators (WDI) 2008;* and *World Development Report 2008.*

BENIN - BANKS AND BANKING

Euromonitor International, Inc., 224 S. Michigan Avenue, Suite 1500, Chicago, IL 60604, (312) 922-1115, Fax: (312) 922-1157, www.euromonitor.com; *World Marketing Data and Statistics.*

International Monetary Fund (IMF), 700 Nineteenth Street, NW, Washington, DC 20431, (202) 623-7000, Fax: (202) 623-4661, www.imf.org; *International Financial Statistics Yearbook 2007.*

M.E. Sharpe, 80 Business Park Drive, Armonk, NY 10504, (800) 541-6563, Fax: (914) 273-2106, www.mesharpe.com; *The Illustrated Book of World Rankings.*

Palgrave Macmillan Ltd., Houndmills, Basingstoke, Hampshire, RG21 6XS, England, (Telephone in U.S. (888) 330-8477), (Fax in U.S. (800) 672-2054), www.palgrave.com; *The Statesman's Yearbook 2008.*

Taylor and Francis Group, An Informa Business, 2 Park Square, Milton Park, Abingdon, Oxford OX14 4RN, United Kingdom, (Dial from U.S. (212) 216-7800), (Fax from U.S. (212) 564-7854), www.tandf.co.uk; *The Europa World Year Book.*

United Nations Statistics Division, New York, NY 10017, (800) 253-9646, Fax: (212) 963-4116, http://unstats.un.org; *Statistical Yearbook.*

BENIN - BARLEY PRODUCTION

See BENIN - CROPS

BENIN - BEVERAGE INDUSTRY

M.E. Sharpe, 80 Business Park Drive, Armonk, NY 10504, (800) 541-6563, Fax: (914) 273-2106, www.mesharpe.com; *The Illustrated Book of World Rankings.*

United Nations Statistics Division, New York, NY 10017, (800) 253-9646, Fax: (212) 963-4116, http://unstats.un.org; *Statistical Yearbook.*

BENIN - BROADCASTING

Central Intelligence Agency, Office of Public Affairs, Washington, DC 20505, (703) 482-0623, Fax: (703) 482-1739, www.cia.gov; *The World Factbook.*

Euromonitor International, Inc., 224 S. Michigan Avenue, Suite 1500, Chicago, IL 60604, (312) 922-1115, Fax: (312) 922-1157, www.euromonitor.com; *World Marketing Data and Statistics.*

M.E. Sharpe, 80 Business Park Drive, Armonk, NY 10504, (800) 541-6563, Fax: (914) 273-2106, www.mesharpe.com; *The Illustrated Book of World Rankings.*

WRTH Publications Limited, PO Box 290, Oxford OX2 7FT, UK, www.wrth.com; *World Radio TV Handbook 2007.*

BENIN - BUDGET

Central Intelligence Agency, Office of Public Affairs, Washington, DC 20505, (703) 482-0623, Fax: (703) 482-1739, www.cia.gov; *The World Factbook.*

BENIN - CAPITAL LEVY

International Monetary Fund (IMF), 700 Nineteenth Street, NW, Washington, DC 20431, (202) 623-7000, Fax: (202) 623-4661, www.imf.org; *Government Finance Statistics Yearbook (2008 Edition).*

BENIN - CATTLE

See BENIN - LIVESTOCK

BENIN - CHICKENS

See BENIN - LIVESTOCK

BENIN - CHILDBIRTH - STATISTICS

Central Intelligence Agency, Office of Public Affairs, Washington, DC 20505, (703) 482-0623, Fax: (703) 482-1739, www.cia.gov; *The World Factbook.*

Euromonitor International, Inc., 224 S. Michigan Avenue, Suite 1500, Chicago, IL 60604, (312) 922-1115, Fax: (312) 922-1157, www.euromonitor.com; *International Marketing Data and Statistics 2008* and *The World Economic Factbook 2008.*

M.E. Sharpe, 80 Business Park Drive, Armonk, NY 10504, (800) 541-6563, Fax: (914) 273-2106, www.mesharpe.com; *The Illustrated Book of World Rankings.*

Palgrave Macmillan Ltd., Houndmills, Basingstoke, Hampshire, RG21 6XS, England, (Telephone in U.S. (888) 330-8477), (Fax in U.S. (800) 672-2054), www.palgrave.com; *The Statesman's Yearbook 2008.*

Taylor and Francis Group, An Informa Business, 2 Park Square, Milton Park, Abingdon, Oxford OX14 4RN, United Kingdom, (Dial from U.S. (212) 216-7800), (Fax from U.S. (212) 564-7854), www.tandf.co.uk; *The Europa World Year Book.*

United Nations Statistics Division, New York, NY 10017, (800) 253-9646, Fax: (212) 963-4116, http://unstats.un.org; *Demographic Yearbook; Statistical Yearbook;* and *Survey of Economic and Social Conditions in Africa 2005.*

The World Bank, 1818 H Street, NW, Washington, DC 20433, (202) 473-1000, Fax: (202) 477-6391, www.worldbank.org; *World Development Indicators (WDI) 2008.*

BENIN - CLIMATE

International Institute for Environment and Development (IIED), 3 Endsleigh Street, London, England, WC1H 0DD, United Kingdom, www.iied.org; *Environment Urbanization* and *Haramata - Bulletin of the Drylands.*

M.E. Sharpe, 80 Business Park Drive, Armonk, NY 10504, (800) 541-6563, Fax: (914) 273-2106, www.mesharpe.com; *The Illustrated Book of World Rankings.*

Palgrave Macmillan Ltd., Houndmills, Basingstoke, Hampshire, RG21 6XS, England, (Telephone in U.S. (888) 330-8477), (Fax in U.S. (800) 672-2054), www.palgrave.com; *The Statesman's Yearbook 2008.*

BENIN - COAL PRODUCTION

See BENIN - MINERAL INDUSTRIES

BENIN - COFFEE

See BENIN - CROPS

BENIN - COMMERCE

Palgrave Macmillan Ltd., Houndmills, Basingstoke, Hampshire, RG21 6XS, England, (Telephone in U.S. (888) 330-8477), (Fax in U.S. (800) 672-2054), www.palgrave.com; *The Statesman's Yearbook 2008.*

BENIN - COMMODITY EXCHANGES

Commodity Research Bureau, 330 South Wells Street, Suite 612, Chicago, IL 60606-7110, (800) 621-5271, Fax: (312) 939-4135, www.crbtrader.com; *2006 CRB Commodity Yearbook and CD.*

International Monetary Fund (IMF), 700 Nineteenth Street, NW, Washington, DC 20431, (202) 623-7000, Fax: (202) 623-4661, www.imf.org; *IMF Primary Commodity Prices.*

United Nations Food and Agricultural Organization (FAO), Viale delle Terme di Caracalla, 00100 Rome, Italy, (Dial from U.S. (202) 653-2400), (Fax from U.S. (202) 653 5760), www.fao.org; *The State of Food and Agriculture (SOFA) 2006.*

BENIN - COMMUNICATION AND TRAFFIC

United Nations Statistics Division, New York, NY 10017, (800) 253-9646, Fax: (212) 963-4116, http://unstats.un.org; *Statistical Yearbook.*

BENIN - CONSTRUCTION INDUSTRY

M.E. Sharpe, 80 Business Park Drive, Armonk, NY 10504, (800) 541-6563, Fax: (914) 273-2106, www.mesharpe.com; *The Illustrated Book of World Rankings.*

United Nations Economic Commission for Africa (ECA), PO Box 3001, Addis Ababa, Ethiopia, (Telephone in U.S. (212) 963-4957), www.uneca.org; *African Statistical Yearbook 2006.*

BENIN - CONSUMER PRICE INDEXES

Euromonitor International, Inc., 224 S. Michigan Avenue, Suite 1500, Chicago, IL 60604, (312) 922-1115, Fax: (312) 922-1157, www.euromonitor.com; *World Marketing Data and Statistics.*

United Nations Statistics Division, New York, NY 10017, (800) 253-9646, Fax: (212) 963-4116, http://unstats.un.org; *Survey of Economic and Social Conditions in Africa 2005.*

The World Bank, 1818 H Street, NW, Washington, DC 20433, (202) 473-1000, Fax: (202) 477-6391, www.worldbank.org; *Benin.*

BENIN - CONSUMPTION (ECONOMICS)

African Development Bank Group, Rue Joseph Anoma, 01 BP 1387 Abidjan 01, Cote d'Ivoire, www.afdb.org; *Statistics Pocketbook 2008.*

United Nations Statistics Division, New York, NY 10017, (800) 253-9646, Fax: (212) 963-4116, http://unstats.un.org; *Survey of Economic and Social Conditions in Africa 2005.*

The World Bank, 1818 H Street, NW, Washington, DC 20433, (202) 473-1000, Fax: (202) 477-6391, www.worldbank.org; *World Development Report 2008.*

BENIN - COPPER INDUSTRY AND TRADE

See BENIN - MINERAL INDUSTRIES

BENIN - CORN INDUSTRY

See BENIN - CROPS

BENIN - COTTON

See BENIN - CROPS

BENIN - CROPS

M.E. Sharpe, 80 Business Park Drive, Armonk, NY 10504, (800) 541-6563, Fax: (914) 273-2106, www.mesharpe.com; *The Illustrated Book of World Rankings.*

Palgrave Macmillan Ltd., Houndmills, Basingstoke, Hampshire, RG21 6XS, England, (Telephone in U.S. (888) 330-8477), (Fax in U.S. (800) 672-2054), www.palgrave.com; *The Statesman's Yearbook 2008.*

Taylor and Francis Group, An Informa Business, 2 Park Square, Milton Park, Abingdon, Oxford OX14 4RN, United Kingdom, (Dial from U.S. (212) 216-7800), (Fax from U.S. (212) 564-7854), www.tandf.co.uk; *The Europa World Year Book.*

United Nations Conference on Trade and Development (UNCTAD), DC2-1120, United Nations, New York, NY 10017, (212) 963-0027, www.unctad.org; *UNCTAD Commodity Yearbook.*

United Nations Economic Commission for Africa (ECA), PO Box 3001, Addis Ababa, Ethiopia, (Telephone in U.S. (212) 963-4957), www.uneca.org; *African Statistical Yearbook 2006.*

United Nations Food and Agricultural Organization (FAO), Viale delle Terme di Caracalla, 00100 Rome, Italy, (Dial from U.S. (202) 653-2400), (Fax from U.S. (202) 653 5760), www.fao.org; *FAO Production Yearbook 2002* and *The State of Food and Agriculture (SOFA) 2006.*

United Nations Statistics Division, New York, NY 10017, (800) 253-9646, Fax: (212) 963-4116, http://unstats.un.org; *Statistical Yearbook.*

BENIN - CUSTOMS ADMINISTRATION

International Monetary Fund (IMF), 700 Nineteenth Street, NW, Washington, DC 20431, (202) 623-7000, Fax: (202) 623-4661, www.imf.org; *Government Finance Statistics Yearbook (2008 Edition).*

Palgrave Macmillan Ltd., Houndmills, Basingstoke, Hampshire, RG21 6XS, England, (Telephone in U.S. (888) 330-8477), (Fax in U.S. (800) 672-2054), www.palgrave.com; *The Statesman's Yearbook 2008.*

BENIN - DAIRY PROCESSING

M.E. Sharpe, 80 Business Park Drive, Armonk, NY 10504, (800) 541-6563, Fax: (914) 273-2106, www.mesharpe.com; *The Illustrated Book of World Rankings.*

Palgrave Macmillan Ltd., Houndmills, Basingstoke, Hampshire, RG21 6XS, England, (Telephone in U.S. (888) 330-8477), (Fax in U.S. (800) 672-2054), www.palgrave.com; *The Statesman's Yearbook 2008.*

Taylor and Francis Group, An Informa Business, 2 Park Square, Milton Park, Abingdon, Oxford OX14 4RN, United Kingdom, (Dial from U.S. (212) 216-7800), (Fax from U.S. (212) 564-7854), www.tandf.co.uk; *The Europa World Year Book.*

United Nations Food and Agricultural Organization (FAO), Viale delle Terme di Caracalla, 00100 Rome, Italy, (Dial from U.S. (202) 653-2400), (Fax from U.S. (202) 653 5760), www.fao.org; *FAO Production Yearbook 2002* and *The State of Food and Agriculture (SOFA) 2006.*

United Nations Statistics Division, New York, NY 10017, (800) 253-9646, Fax: (212) 963-4116, http://unstats.un.org; *Statistical Yearbook.*

BENIN - DEATH RATES

See BENIN - MORTALITY

BENIN - DEBTS, EXTERNAL

African Development Bank Group, Rue Joseph Anoma, 01 BP 1387 Abidjan 01, Cote d'Ivoire, www.afdb.org; *Statistics Pocketbook 2008.*

Palgrave Macmillan Ltd., Houndmills, Basingstoke, Hampshire, RG21 6XS, England, (Telephone in U.S. (888) 330-8477), (Fax in U.S. (800) 672-2054), www.palgrave.com; *The Statesman's Yearbook 2008.*

United Nations Statistics Division, New York, NY 10017, (800) 253-9646, Fax: (212) 963-4116, http://unstats.un.org; *Survey of Economic and Social Conditions in Africa 2005.*

The World Bank, 1818 H Street, NW, Washington, DC 20433, (202) 473-1000, Fax: (202) 477-6391, www.worldbank.org; *Africa Live Database (LDB); African Development Indicators (ADI) 2007; Global Development Finance 2007; World Development Indicators (WDI) 2008;* and *World Development Report 2008.*

BENIN - DEFENSE EXPENDITURES

See BENIN - ARMED FORCES

BENIN - DEMOGRAPHY

Euromonitor International, Inc., 224 S. Michigan Avenue, Suite 1500, Chicago, IL 60604, (312) 922-1115, Fax: (312) 922-1157, www.euromonitor.com; *International Marketing Data and Statistics 2008; The World Economic Factbook 2008;* and *World Marketing Data and Statistics.*

M.E. Sharpe, 80 Business Park Drive, Armonk, NY 10504, (800) 541-6563, Fax: (914) 273-2106, www.mesharpe.com; *The Illustrated Book of World Rankings.*

United Nations Statistics Division, New York, NY 10017, (800) 253-9646, Fax: (212) 963-4116, http://unstats.un.org; *Human Development Report 2006* and *Survey of Economic and Social Conditions in Africa 2005.*

The World Bank, 1818 H Street, NW, Washington, DC 20433, (202) 473-1000, Fax: (202) 477-6391, www.worldbank.org; *Benin.*

BENIN - DIAMONDS

See BENIN - MINERAL INDUSTRIES

BENIN - DISEASES

World Health Organization (WHO), Avenue Appia 20, 1211 Geneve 27, Switzerland, (Telephone in U.S. (212) 331-9081), www.who.int; *World Health Report 2006.*

BENIN - DISPOSABLE INCOME

M.E. Sharpe, 80 Business Park Drive, Armonk, NY 10504, (800) 541-6563, Fax: (914) 273-2106, www.mesharpe.com; *The Illustrated Book of World Rankings.*

United Nations Statistics Division, New York, NY 10017, (800) 253-9646, Fax: (212) 963-4116, http://unstats.un.org; *National Accounts Statistics: Compendium of Income Distribution Statistics* and *Statistical Yearbook.*

BENIN - DIVORCE

M.E. Sharpe, 80 Business Park Drive, Armonk, NY 10504, (800) 541-6563, Fax: (914) 273-2106, www.mesharpe.com; *The Illustrated Book of World Rankings.*

BENIN - ECONOMIC ASSISTANCE

United Nations Statistics Division, New York, NY 10017, (800) 253-9646, Fax: (212) 963-4116, http://unstats.un.org; *Statistical Yearbook.*

BENIN - ECONOMIC CONDITIONS

African Development Bank Group, Rue Joseph Anoma, 01 BP 1387 Abidjan 01, Cote d'Ivoire, www.afdb.org; *The African Statistical Journal; Gender, Poverty and Environmental Indicators on African Countries 2007; Selected Statistics on African Countries 2007;* and *Statistics Pocketbook 2008.*

Center for International Business Education Research (CIBER), Columbia Business School and School of International and Public Affairs, Uris Hall, Room 212, 3022 Broadway, New York, NY 10027-6902, Mr. Joshua Safier, (212) 854-4750, Fax: (212) 222-9821, www.columbia.edu/cu/ciber/; Datastream International.

Central Intelligence Agency, Office of Public Affairs, Washington, DC 20505, (703) 482-0623, Fax: (703) 482-1739, www.cia.gov; *The World Factbook.*

DSI Data Service Information, Xantener Strasse 51a, D-47495 Rheinberg, Germany, www.dsidata.com; *Campus Solution.*

Dun and Bradstreet (DB) Corporation, 103 JFK Parkway, Short Hills, NJ 07078, (973) 921-5500, www.dnb.com; *Country Report.*

Economist Intelligence Unit, 111 West 57th Street, New York, NY 10019, (212) 554-0600, Fax: (212) 586-1181, www.eiu.com; *Benin Country Report* and *Business Africa.*

Euromonitor International, Inc., 224 S. Michigan Avenue, Suite 1500, Chicago, IL 60604, (312) 922-1115, Fax: (312) 922-1157, www.euromonitor.com; *International Marketing Data and Statistics 2008; The World Economic Factbook 2008;* and *World Marketing Data and Statistics.*

International Monetary Fund (IMF), 700 Nineteenth Street, NW, Washington, DC 20431, (202) 623-7000, Fax: (202) 623-4661, www.imf.org; *World Economic Outlook Reports.*

M.E. Sharpe, 80 Business Park Drive, Armonk, NY 10504, (800) 541-6563, Fax: (914) 273-2106, www.mesharpe.com; *The Illustrated Book of World Rankings.*

Palgrave Macmillan Ltd., Houndmills, Basingstoke, Hampshire, RG21 6XS, England, (Telephone in U.S. (888) 330-8477), (Fax in U.S. (800) 672-2054), www.palgrave.com; *The Statesman's Yearbook 2008.*

Taylor and Francis Group, An Informa Business, 2 Park Square, Milton Park, Abingdon, Oxford OX14 4RN, United Kingdom, (Dial from U.S. (212) 216-7800), (Fax from U.S. (212) 564-7854), www.tandf.co.uk; *The Europa World Year Book.*

United Nations Statistics Division, New York, NY 10017, (800) 253-9646, Fax: (212) 963-4116, http://unstats.un.org; *Compendium of Intra-African and Related Foreign Trade Statistics 2003* and *World Statistics Pocketbook.*

The World Bank, 1818 H Street, NW, Washington, DC 20433, (202) 473-1000, Fax: (202) 477-6391, www.worldbank.org; *Africa Household Survey Databank; Africa Live Database (LDB); Africa Standardized Files and Indicators; African Development Indicators (ADI) 2007; Benin; Global Economic Monitor (GEM); Global Economic Prospects 2008; The World Bank Atlas 2003-2004;* and *World Development Report 2008.*

BENIN - EDUCATION

African Development Bank Group, Rue Joseph Anoma, 01 BP 1387 Abidjan 01, Cote d'Ivoire, www.afdb.org; *Statistics Pocketbook 2008.*

Euromonitor International, Inc., 224 S. Michigan Avenue, Suite 1500, Chicago, IL 60604, (312) 922-1115, Fax: (312) 922-1157, www.euromonitor.com; *International Marketing Data and Statistics 2008* and *World Marketing Data and Statistics.*

M.E. Sharpe, 80 Business Park Drive, Armonk, NY 10504, (800) 541-6563, Fax: (914) 273-2106, www.mesharpe.com; *The Illustrated Book of World Rankings.*

Palgrave Macmillan Ltd., Houndmills, Basingstoke, Hampshire, RG21 6XS, England, (Telephone in U.S. (888) 330-8477), (Fax in U.S. (800) 672-2054), www.palgrave.com; *The Statesman's Yearbook 2008.*

Taylor and Francis Group, An Informa Business, 2 Park Square, Milton Park, Abingdon, Oxford OX14 4RN, United Kingdom, (Dial from U.S. (212) 216-7800), (Fax from U.S. (212) 564-7854), www.tandf.co.uk; *The Europa World Year Book.*

UNESCO Institute for Statistics, C.P. 6128 Succursale Centre-Ville, Montreal, Quebec, H3C 3J7 Canada, (Dial from U.S. (514) 343-6880), (Fax from U.S. (514) 343 6882), www.uis.unesco.org; *Statistical Tables.*

United Nations Economic Commission for Africa (ECA), PO Box 3001, Addis Ababa, Ethiopia, (Telephone in U.S. (212) 963-4957), www.uneca.org; *African Statistical Yearbook 2006.*

United Nations Statistics Division, New York, NY 10017, (800) 253-9646, Fax: (212) 963-4116, http://unstats.un.org; *Human Development Report 2006* and *Survey of Economic and Social Conditions in Africa 2005.*

The World Bank, 1818 H Street, NW, Washington, DC 20433, (202) 473-1000, Fax: (202) 477-6391, www.worldbank.org; *Benin; World Development Indicators (WDI) 2008;* and *World Development Report 2008.*

BENIN - ELECTRICITY

M.E. Sharpe, 80 Business Park Drive, Armonk, NY 10504, (800) 541-6563, Fax: (914) 273-2106, www.mesharpe.com; *The Illustrated Book of World Rankings.*

Organisation for Economic Cooperation and Development (OECD), 2 rue Andre Pascal, F-75775 Paris Cedex 16, France, (Telephone in U.S. (202) 785-6323), (Fax in U.S. (202) 785-0350), www.oecd.org; *World Energy Outlook 2007.*

Palgrave Macmillan Ltd., Houndmills, Basingstoke, Hampshire, RG21 6XS, England, (Telephone in U.S. (888) 330-8477), (Fax in U.S. (800) 672-2054), www.palgrave.com; *The Statesman's Yearbook 2008.*

United Nations Economic Commission for Africa (ECA), PO Box 3001, Addis Ababa, Ethiopia, (Telephone in U.S. (212) 963-4957), www.uneca.org; *African Statistical Yearbook 2006.*

United Nations Statistics Division, New York, NY 10017, (800) 253-9646, Fax: (212) 963-4116, http://unstats.un.org; *Human Development Report 2006; Statistical Yearbook;* and *Survey of Economic and Social Conditions in Africa 2005.*

BENIN - EMPLOYMENT

Euromonitor International, Inc., 224 S. Michigan Avenue, Suite 1500, Chicago, IL 60604, (312) 922-1115, Fax: (312) 922-1157, www.euromonitor.com; *International Marketing Data and Statistics 2008.*

International Labour Office, I.L.O. Publications, 4 route des Morillons, CH-1211 Geneva 22, Switzerland, (Telephone in U.S. (202) 653-7652), (Fax in U.S. (202) 653-7687), www.ilo.org; *Yearbook of Labour Statistics 2006.*

M.E. Sharpe, 80 Business Park Drive, Armonk, NY 10504, (800) 541-6563, Fax: (914) 273-2106, www.mesharpe.com; *The Illustrated Book of World Rankings.*

United Nations Economic Commission for Africa (ECA), PO Box 3001, Addis Ababa, Ethiopia, (Telephone in U.S. (212) 963-4957), www.uneca.org; *African Statistical Yearbook 2006.*

United Nations Statistics Division, New York, NY 10017, (800) 253-9646, Fax: (212) 963-4116, http://unstats.un.org; *Survey of Economic and Social Conditions in Africa 2005.*

The World Bank, 1818 H Street, NW, Washington, DC 20433, (202) 473-1000, Fax: (202) 477-6391, www.worldbank.org; *Benin.*

BENIN - ENVIRONMENTAL CONDITIONS

DSI Data Service Information, Xantener Strasse 51a, D-47495 Rheinberg, Germany, www.dsidata.com; *Campus Solution* and *DSI's Global Environmental Database.*

Economist Intelligence Unit, 111 West 57th Street, New York, NY 10019, (212) 554-0600, Fax: (212) 586-1181, www.eiu.com; *Benin Country Report.*

International Institute for Environment and Development (IIED), 3 Endsleigh Street, London, England, WC1H 0DD, United Kingdom, www.iied.org; *Environment Urbanization* and *Haramata - Bulletin of the Drylands.*

United Nations Statistics Division, New York, NY 10017, (800) 253-9646, Fax: (212) 963-4116, http://unstats.un.org; *World Statistics Pocketbook.*

BENIN - EXPORTS

African Development Bank Group, Rue Joseph Anoma, 01 BP 1387 Abidjan 01, Cote d'Ivoire, www.afdb.org; *Statistics Pocketbook 2008.*

Central Intelligence Agency, Office of Public Affairs, Washington, DC 20505, (703) 482-0623, Fax: (703) 482-1739, www.cia.gov; *The World Factbook.*

Economist Intelligence Unit, 111 West 57th Street, New York, NY 10019, (212) 554-0600, Fax: (212) 586-1181, www.eiu.com; *Benin Country Report.*

Euromonitor International, Inc., 224 S. Michigan Avenue, Suite 1500, Chicago, IL 60604, (312) 922-1115, Fax: (312) 922-1157, www.euromonitor.com; *International Marketing Data and Statistics 2008* and *The World Economic Factbook 2008.*

International Monetary Fund (IMF), 700 Nineteenth Street, NW, Washington, DC 20431, (202) 623-7000, Fax: (202) 623-4661, www.imf.org; *Direction of Trade Statistics Yearbook 2007.*

Palgrave Macmillan Ltd., Houndmills, Basingstoke, Hampshire, RG21 6XS, England, (Telephone in U.S. (888) 330-8477), (Fax in U.S. (800) 672-2054), www.palgrave.com; *The Statesman's Yearbook 2008.*

Taylor and Francis Group, An Informa Business, 2 Park Square, Milton Park, Abingdon, Oxford OX14 4RN, United Kingdom, (Dial from U.S. (212) 216-7800), (Fax from U.S. (212) 564-7854), www.tandf.co.uk; *The Europa World Year Book.*

United Nations Conference on Trade and Development (UNCTAD), DC2-1120, United Nations, New York, NY 10017, (212) 963-0027, www.unctad.org; *Handbook of Statistics 2005.*

United Nations Economic Commission for Africa (ECA), PO Box 3001, Addis Ababa, Ethiopia, (Telephone in U.S. (212) 963-4957), www.uneca.org; *African Statistical Yearbook 2006.*

United Nations Food and Agricultural Organization (FAO), Viale delle Terme di Caracalla, 00100 Rome, Italy, (Dial from U.S. (202) 653-2400), (Fax from U.S. (202) 653 5760), www.fao.org; *The State of Food and Agriculture (SOFA) 2006.*

United Nations Statistics Division, New York, NY 10017, (800) 253-9646, Fax: (212) 963-4116, http://unstats.un.org; *Compendium of Intra-African and Related Foreign Trade Statistics 2003* and *Survey of Economic and Social Conditions in Africa 2005.*

The World Bank, 1818 H Street, NW, Washington, DC 20433, (202) 473-1000, Fax: (202) 477-6391, www.worldbank.org; *World Development Indicators (WDI) 2008* and *World Development Report 2008.*

BENIN - FEMALE WORKING POPULATION

See BENIN - EMPLOYMENT

BENIN - FERTILITY, HUMAN

Central Intelligence Agency, Office of Public Affairs, Washington, DC 20505, (703) 482-0623, Fax: (703) 482-1739, www.cia.gov; *The World Factbook.*

M.E. Sharpe, 80 Business Park Drive, Armonk, NY 10504, (800) 541-6563, Fax: (914) 273-2106, www.mesharpe.com; *The Illustrated Book of World Rankings.*

United Nations Statistics Division, New York, NY 10017, (800) 253-9646, Fax: (212) 963-4116, http://unstats.un.org; *Human Development Report 2006* and *Survey of Economic and Social Conditions in Africa 2005.*

The World Bank, 1818 H Street, NW, Washington, DC 20433, (202) 473-1000, Fax: (202) 477-6391, www.worldbank.org; *The World Bank Atlas 2003-2004; World Development Indicators (WDI) 2008;* and *World Development Report 2008.*

BENIN - FERTILIZER INDUSTRY

United Nations Food and Agricultural Organization (FAO), Viale delle Terme di Caracalla, 00100 Rome, Italy, (Dial from U.S. (202) 653-2400), (Fax from U.S. (202) 653 5760), www.fao.org; *FAO Fertilizer Yearbook* and *The State of Food and Agriculture (SOFA) 2006.*

United Nations Statistics Division, New York, NY 10017, (800) 253-9646, Fax: (212) 963-4116, http://unstats.un.org; *Statistical Yearbook.*

BENIN - FINANCE

Taylor and Francis Group, An Informa Business, 2 Park Square, Milton Park, Abingdon, Oxford OX14 4RN, United Kingdom, (Dial from U.S. (212) 216-7800), (Fax from U.S. (212) 564-7854), www.tandf.co.uk; *The Europa World Year Book.*

United Nations Economic Commission for Africa (ECA), PO Box 3001, Addis Ababa, Ethiopia, (Telephone in U.S. (212) 963-4957), www.uneca.org; *African Statistical Yearbook 2006.*

United Nations Statistics Division, New York, NY 10017, (800) 253-9646, Fax: (212) 963-4116, http://unstats.un.org; *National Accounts Statistics: Compendium of Income Distribution Statistics* and *Statistical Yearbook.*

The World Bank, 1818 H Street, NW, Washington, DC 20433, (202) 473-1000, Fax: (202) 477-6391, www.worldbank.org; *Benin.*

BENIN - FINANCE, PUBLIC

African Development Bank Group, Rue Joseph Anoma, 01 BP 1387 Abidjan 01, Cote d'Ivoire, www.afdb.org; *Statistics Pocketbook 2008.*

Bernan Essential Government Publications, 4611-F Assembly Drive, Lanham MD, 20706-4391, (301) 459-2255, Fax: (800) 865-3450, www.bernan.com; *National Accounts Statistics.*

Economist Intelligence Unit, 111 West 57th Street, New York, NY 10019, (212) 554-0600, Fax: (212) 586-1181, www.eiu.com; *Benin Country Report.*

International Monetary Fund (IMF), 700 Nineteenth Street, NW, Washington, DC 20431, (202) 623-7000, Fax: (202) 623-4661, www.imf.org; *International Financial Statistics* and *International Financial Statistics Online Service.*

M.E. Sharpe, 80 Business Park Drive, Armonk, NY 10504, (800) 541-6563, Fax: (914) 273-2106, www.mesharpe.com; *The Illustrated Book of World Rankings.*

Palgrave Macmillan Ltd., Houndmills, Basingstoke, Hampshire, RG21 6XS, England, (Telephone in U.S. (888) 330-8477), (Fax in U.S. (800) 672-2054), www.palgrave.com; *The Statesman's Yearbook 2008.*

Taylor and Francis Group, An Informa Business, 2 Park Square, Milton Park, Abingdon, Oxford OX14 4RN, United Kingdom, (Dial from U.S. (212) 216-7800), (Fax from U.S. (212) 564-7854), www.tandf.co.uk; *The Europa World Year Book.*

United Nations Economic Commission for Africa (ECA), PO Box 3001, Addis Ababa, Ethiopia, (Telephone in U.S. (212) 963-4957), www.uneca.org; *African Statistical Yearbook 2006.*

The World Bank, 1818 H Street, NW, Washington, DC 20433, (202) 473-1000, Fax: (202) 477-6391, www.worldbank.org; *Benin.*

BENIN - FISHERIES

M.E. Sharpe, 80 Business Park Drive, Armonk, NY 10504, (800) 541-6563, Fax: (914) 273-2106, www.mesharpe.com; *The Illustrated Book of World Rankings.*

Palgrave Macmillan Ltd., Houndmills, Basingstoke, Hampshire, RG21 6XS, England, (Telephone in U.S. (888) 330-8477), (Fax in U.S. (800) 672-2054), www.palgrave.com; *The Statesman's Yearbook 2008.*

Taylor and Francis Group, An Informa Business, 2 Park Square, Milton Park, Abingdon, Oxford OX14 4RN, United Kingdom, (Dial from U.S. (212) 216-7800), (Fax from U.S. (212) 564-7854), www.tandf.co.uk; *The Europa World Year Book.*

United Nations Conference on Trade and Development (UNCTAD), DC2-1120, United Nations, New York, NY 10017, (212) 963-0027, www.unctad.org; *UNCTAD Commodity Yearbook.*

United Nations Economic Commission for Africa (ECA), PO Box 3001, Addis Ababa, Ethiopia, (Telephone in U.S. (212) 963-4957), www.uneca.org; *African Statistical Yearbook 2006.*

United Nations Food and Agricultural Organization (FAO), Viale delle Terme di Caracalla, 00100 Rome, Italy, (Dial from U.S. (202) 653-2400), (Fax from U.S. (202) 653 5760), www.fao.org; *FAO Yearbook of Fishery Statistics;* Fishery Databases; FISHSTAT Database. Subjects covered include: Aquaculture production, capture production, fishery commodities; and *The State of Food and Agriculture (SOFA) 2006.*

United Nations Statistics Division, New York, NY 10017, (800) 253-9646, Fax: (212) 963-4116, http://unstats.un.org; *Statistical Yearbook* and *Survey of Economic and Social Conditions in Africa 2005.*

The World Bank, 1818 H Street, NW, Washington, DC 20433, (202) 473-1000, Fax: (202) 477-6391, www.worldbank.org; *Benin.*

BENIN - FOOD

African Development Bank Group, Rue Joseph Anoma, 01 BP 1387 Abidjan 01, Cote d'Ivoire, www.afdb.org; *Statistics Pocketbook 2008.*

United Nations Conference on Trade and Development (UNCTAD), DC2-1120, United Nations, New York, NY 10017, (212) 963-0027, www.unctad.org; *UNCTAD Commodity Yearbook.*

United Nations Food and Agricultural Organization (FAO), Viale delle Terme di Caracalla, 00100 Rome, Italy, (Dial from U.S. (202) 653-2400), (Fax from U.S. (202) 653 5760), www.fao.org; *FAO Production Yearbook 2002* and *The State of Food and Agriculture (SOFA) 2006.*

United Nations Statistics Division, New York, NY 10017, (800) 253-9646, Fax: (212) 963-4116, http://unstats.un.org; *Human Development Report 2006.*

BENIN - FOREIGN EXCHANGE RATES

African Development Bank Group, Rue Joseph Anoma, 01 BP 1387 Abidjan 01, Cote d'Ivoire, www.afdb.org; *Statistics Pocketbook 2008.*

Central Intelligence Agency, Office of Public Affairs, Washington, DC 20505, (703) 482-0623, Fax: (703) 482-1739, www.cia.gov; *The World Factbook.*

Euromonitor International, Inc., 224 S. Michigan Avenue, Suite 1500, Chicago, IL 60604, (312) 922-1115, Fax: (312) 922-1157, www.euromonitor.com; *International Marketing Data and Statistics 2008* and *The World Economic Factbook 2008.*

International Monetary Fund (IMF), 700 Nineteenth Street, NW, Washington, DC 20431, (202) 623-7000, Fax: (202) 623-4661, www.imf.org; *International Financial Statistics Yearbook 2007.*

Taylor and Francis Group, An Informa Business, 2 Park Square, Milton Park, Abingdon, Oxford OX14 4RN, United Kingdom, (Dial from U.S. (212) 216-7800), (Fax from U.S. (212) 564-7854), www.tandf.co.uk; *The Europa World Year Book.*

United Nations Statistics Division, New York, NY 10017, (800) 253-9646, Fax: (212) 963-4116, http://unstats.un.org; *Compendium of Intra-African and Related Foreign Trade Statistics 2003* and *World Statistics Pocketbook.*

BENIN - FORESTS AND FORESTRY

M.E. Sharpe, 80 Business Park Drive, Armonk, NY 10504, (800) 541-6563, Fax: (914) 273-2106, www.mesharpe.com; *The Illustrated Book of World Rankings.*

Palgrave Macmillan Ltd., Houndmills, Basingstoke, Hampshire, RG21 6XS, England, (Telephone in U.S. (888) 330-8477), (Fax in U.S. (800) 672-2054), www.palgrave.com; *The Statesman's Yearbook 2008.*

Taylor and Francis Group, An Informa Business, 2 Park Square, Milton Park, Abingdon, Oxford OX14 4RN, United Kingdom, (Dial from U.S. (212) 216-7800), (Fax from U.S. (212) 564-7854), www.tandf.co.uk; *The Europa World Year Book.*

UNESCO Institute for Statistics, C.P. 6128 Succursale Centre-Ville, Montreal, Quebec, H3C 3J7

Canada, (Dial from U.S. (514) 343-6880), (Fax from U.S. (514) 343 6882), www.uis.unesco.org; *Statistical Tables.*

United Nations Conference on Trade and Development (UNCTAD), DC2-1120, United Nations, New York, NY 10017, (212) 963-0027, www.unctad.org; *UNCTAD Commodity Yearbook.*

United Nations Economic Commission for Africa (ECA), PO Box 3001, Addis Ababa, Ethiopia, (Telephone in U.S. (212) 963-4957), www.uneca.org; *African Statistical Yearbook 2006.*

United Nations Food and Agricultural Organization (FAO), Viale delle Terme di Caracalla, 00100 Rome, Italy, (Dial from U.S. (202) 653-2400), (Fax from U.S. (202) 653 5760), www.fao.org; *FAO Yearbook of Forest Products* and *The State of Food and Agriculture (SOFA) 2006.*

United Nations Statistics Division, New York, NY 10017, (800) 253-9646, Fax: (212) 963-4116, http://unstats.un.org; *Statistical Yearbook.*

The World Bank, 1818 H Street, NW, Washington, DC 20433, (202) 473-1000, Fax: (202) 477-6391, www.worldbank.org; *Benin* and *World Development Report 2008.*

BENIN - GAS PRODUCTION

See BENIN - MINERAL INDUSTRIES

BENIN - GEOGRAPHIC INFORMATION SYSTEMS

M.E. Sharpe, 80 Business Park Drive, Armonk, NY 10504, (800) 541-6563, Fax: (914) 273-2106, www.mesharpe.com; *The Illustrated Book of World Rankings.*

The World Bank, 1818 H Street, NW, Washington, DC 20433, (202) 473-1000, Fax: (202) 477-6391, www.worldbank.org; *Benin.*

BENIN - GOLD INDUSTRY

International Monetary Fund (IMF), 700 Nineteenth Street, NW, Washington, DC 20431, (202) 623-7000, Fax: (202) 623-4661, www.imf.org; *International Financial Statistics Yearbook 2007.*

United Nations Statistics Division, New York, NY 10017, (800) 253-9646, Fax: (212) 963-4116, http://unstats.un.org; *Statistical Yearbook.*

The World Bank, 1818 H Street, NW, Washington, DC 20433, (202) 473-1000, Fax: (202) 477-6391, www.worldbank.org; *World Development Indicators (WDI) 2008.*

BENIN - GOLD PRODUCTION

See BENIN - MINERAL INDUSTRIES

BENIN - GRANTS-IN-AID

International Monetary Fund (IMF), 700 Nineteenth Street, NW, Washington, DC 20431, (202) 623-7000, Fax: (202) 623-4661, www.imf.org; *Government Finance Statistics Yearbook (2008 Edition).*

BENIN - GROSS DOMESTIC PRODUCT

African Development Bank Group, Rue Joseph Anoma, 01 BP 1387 Abidjan 01, Cote d'Ivoire, www.afdb.org; *Statistics Pocketbook 2008.*

Economist Intelligence Unit, 111 West 57th Street, New York, NY 10019, (212) 554-0600, Fax: (212) 586-1181, www.eiu.com; *Benin Country Report.*

Euromonitor International, Inc., 224 S. Michigan Avenue, Suite 1500, Chicago, IL 60604, (312) 922-1115, Fax: (312) 922-1157, www.euromonitor.com; *International Marketing Data and Statistics 2008* and *The World Economic Factbook 2008.*

M.E. Sharpe, 80 Business Park Drive, Armonk, NY 10504, (800) 541-6563, Fax: (914) 273-2106, www.mesharpe.com; *The Illustrated Book of World Rankings.*

Taylor and Francis Group, An Informa Business, 2 Park Square, Milton Park, Abingdon, Oxford OX14 4RN, United Kingdom, (Dial from U.S. (212) 216-7800), (Fax from U.S. (212) 564-7854), www.tandf.co.uk; *The Europa World Year Book.*

United Nations Economic Commission for Africa (ECA), PO Box 3001, Addis Ababa, Ethiopia, (Telephone in U.S. (212) 963-4957), www.uneca.org; *African Statistical Yearbook 2006.*

United Nations Statistics Division, New York, NY 10017, (800) 253-9646, Fax: (212) 963-4116, http://unstats.un.org; *National Accounts Statistics: Compendium of Income Distribution Statistics; Statistical Yearbook;* and *Survey of Economic and Social Conditions in Africa 2005.*

The World Bank, 1818 H Street, NW, Washington, DC 20433, (202) 473-1000, Fax: (202) 477-6391, www.worldbank.org; *World Development Indicators (WDI) 2008* and *World Development Report 2008.*

BENIN - GROSS NATIONAL PRODUCT

Euromonitor International, Inc., 224 S. Michigan Avenue, Suite 1500, Chicago, IL 60604, (312) 922-1115, Fax: (312) 922-1157, www.euromonitor.com; *International Marketing Data and Statistics 2008.*

M.E. Sharpe, 80 Business Park Drive, Armonk, NY 10504, (800) 541-6563, Fax: (914) 273-2106, www.mesharpe.com; *The Illustrated Book of World Rankings.*

Palgrave Macmillan Ltd., Houndmills, Basingstoke, Hampshire, RG21 6XS, England, (Telephone in U.S. (888) 330-8477), (Fax in U.S. (800) 672-2054), www.palgrave.com; *The Statesman's Yearbook 2008.*

Taylor and Francis Group, An Informa Business, 2 Park Square, Milton Park, Abingdon, Oxford OX14 4RN, United Kingdom, (Dial from U.S. (212) 216-7800), (Fax from U.S. (212) 564-7854), www.tandf.co.uk; *The Europa World Year Book.*

U.S. Department of State (DOS), 2201 C Street NW, Washington, DC 20520, (202) 647-4000, www.state.gov; *World Military Expenditures and Arms Transfers (WMEAT).*

United Nations Statistics Division, New York, NY 10017, (800) 253-9646, Fax: (212) 963-4116, http://unstats.un.org; *Human Development Report 2006* and *Statistical Yearbook.*

The World Bank, 1818 H Street, NW, Washington, DC 20433, (202) 473-1000, Fax: (202) 477-6391, www.worldbank.org; *The World Bank Atlas 2003-2004; World Development Indicators (WDI) 2008;* and *World Development Report 2008.*

BENIN - HIDES AND SKINS INDUSTRY

United Nations Food and Agricultural Organization (FAO), Viale delle Terme di Caracalla, 00100 Rome, Italy, (Dial from U.S. (202) 653-2400), (Fax from U.S. (202) 653 5760), www.fao.org; *FAO Production Yearbook 2002.*

BENIN - HOUSING

M.E. Sharpe, 80 Business Park Drive, Armonk, NY 10504, (800) 541-6563, Fax: (914) 273-2106, www.mesharpe.com; *The Illustrated Book of World Rankings.*

BENIN - ILLITERATE PERSONS

Euromonitor International, Inc., 224 S. Michigan Avenue, Suite 1500, Chicago, IL 60604, (312) 922-1115, Fax: (312) 922-1157, www.euromonitor.com; *The World Economic Factbook 2008.*

Palgrave Macmillan Ltd., Houndmills, Basingstoke, Hampshire, RG21 6XS, England, (Telephone in U.S. (888) 330-8477), (Fax in U.S. (800) 672-2054), www.palgrave.com; *The Statesman's Yearbook 2008.*

UNESCO Institute for Statistics, C.P. 6128 Succursale Centre-Ville, Montreal, Quebec, H3C 3J7 Canada, (Dial from U.S. (514) 343-6880), (Fax from U.S. (514) 343 6882), www.uis.unesco.org; *Statistical Tables.*

United Nations Statistics Division, New York, NY 10017, (800) 253-9646, Fax: (212) 963-4116, http://unstats.un.org; *Human Development Report 2006.*

BENIN - IMPORTS

Central Intelligence Agency, Office of Public Affairs, Washington, DC 20505, (703) 482-0623, Fax: (703) 482-1739, www.cia.gov; *The World Factbook.*

Economist Intelligence Unit, 111 West 57th Street, New York, NY 10019, (212) 554-0600, Fax: (212) 586-1181, www.eiu.com; *Benin Country Report.*

Euromonitor International, Inc., 224 S. Michigan Avenue, Suite 1500, Chicago, IL 60604, (312) 922-1115, Fax: (312) 922-1157, www.euromonitor.com; *International Marketing Data and Statistics 2008* and *The World Economic Factbook 2008.*

International Monetary Fund (IMF), 700 Nineteenth Street, NW, Washington, DC 20431, (202) 623-7000, Fax: (202) 623-4661, www.imf.org; *Direction of Trade Statistics Yearbook 2007* and *Government Finance Statistics Yearbook (2008 Edition).*

Palgrave Macmillan Ltd., Houndmills, Basingstoke, Hampshire, RG21 6XS, England, (Telephone in U.S. (888) 330-8477), (Fax in U.S. (800) 672-2054), www.palgrave.com; *The Statesman's Yearbook 2008.*

Taylor and Francis Group, An Informa Business, 2 Park Square, Milton Park, Abingdon, Oxford OX14 4RN, United Kingdom, (Dial from U.S. (212) 216-7800), (Fax from U.S. (212) 564-7854), www.tandf.co.uk; *The Europa World Year Book.*

United Nations Conference on Trade and Development (UNCTAD), DC2-1120, United Nations, New York, NY 10017, (212) 963-0027, www.unctad.org; *Handbook of Statistics 2005.*

United Nations Economic Commission for Africa (ECA), PO Box 3001, Addis Ababa, Ethiopia, (Telephone in U.S. (212) 963-4957), www.uneca.org; *African Statistical Yearbook 2006.*

United Nations Food and Agricultural Organization (FAO), Viale delle Terme di Caracalla, 00100 Rome, Italy, (Dial from U.S. (202) 653-2400), (Fax from U.S. (202) 653 5760), www.fao.org; *The State of Food and Agriculture (SOFA) 2006.*

United Nations Statistics Division, New York, NY 10017, (800) 253-9646, Fax: (212) 963-4116, http://unstats.un.org; *Compendium of Intra-African and Related Foreign Trade Statistics 2003* and *Survey of Economic and Social Conditions in Africa 2005.*

The World Bank, 1818 H Street, NW, Washington, DC 20433, (202) 473-1000, Fax: (202) 477-6391, www.worldbank.org; *World Development Indicators (WDI) 2008* and *World Development Report 2008.*

BENIN - INCOME TAXES

See BENIN - TAXATION

BENIN - INDUSTRIAL PRODUCTIVITY

Euromonitor International, Inc., 224 S. Michigan Avenue, Suite 1500, Chicago, IL 60604, (312) 922-1115, Fax: (312) 922-1157, www.euromonitor.com; *International Marketing Data and Statistics 2008.*

M.E. Sharpe, 80 Business Park Drive, Armonk, NY 10504, (800) 541-6563, Fax: (914) 273-2106, www.mesharpe.com; *The Illustrated Book of World Rankings.*

BENIN - INDUSTRIES

Central Intelligence Agency, Office of Public Affairs, Washington, DC 20505, (703) 482-0623, Fax: (703) 482-1739, www.cia.gov; *The World Factbook.*

Economist Intelligence Unit, 111 West 57th Street, New York, NY 10019, (212) 554-0600, Fax: (212) 586-1181, www.eiu.com; *Benin Country Report.*

Euromonitor International, Inc., 224 S. Michigan Avenue, Suite 1500, Chicago, IL 60604, (312) 922-1115, Fax: (312) 922-1157, www.euromonitor.com; *International Marketing Data and Statistics 2008; The World Economic Factbook 2008;* and *World Marketing Data and Statistics.*

International Labour Office, I.L.O. Publications, 4 route des Morillons, CH-1211 Geneva 22, Switzerland, (Telephone in U.S. (202) 653-7652), (Fax in U.S. (202) 653-7687), www.ilo.org; *Yearbook of Labour Statistics 2006.*

M.E. Sharpe, 80 Business Park Drive, Armonk, NY 10504, (800) 541-6563, Fax: (914) 273-2106, www.mesharpe.com; *The Illustrated Book of World Rankings.*

Palgrave Macmillan Ltd., Houndmills, Basingstoke, Hampshire, RG21 6XS, England, (Telephone in U.S. (888) 330-8477), (Fax in U.S. (800) 672-2054), www.palgrave.com; *The Statesman's Yearbook 2008.*

Taylor and Francis Group, An Informa Business, 2 Park Square, Milton Park, Abingdon, Oxford OX14 4RN, United Kingdom, (Dial from U.S. (212) 216-7800), (Fax from U.S. (212) 564-7854), www.tandf.co.uk; *The Europa World Year Book.*

United Nations Economic Commission for Africa (ECA), PO Box 3001, Addis Ababa, Ethiopia, (Telephone in U.S. (212) 963-4957), www.uneca.org; *African Statistical Yearbook 2006.*

United Nations Industrial Development Organization (UNIDO), 1 United Nations Plaza, New York, NY 10017, (212) 963 6890, Fax: (212) 963-7904, http://unido.org; Industrial Statistics Database 2008 (INDSTAT) and *The International Yearbook of Industrial Statistics 2008.*

United Nations Statistics Division, New York, NY 10017, (800) 253-9646, Fax: (212) 963-4116, http://unstats.un.org; *Survey of Economic and Social Conditions in Africa 2005.*

The World Bank, 1818 H Street, NW, Washington, DC 20433, (202) 473-1000, Fax: (202) 477-6391, www.worldbank.org; *Benin* and *World Development Indicators (WDI) 2008.*

BENIN - INFANT AND MATERNAL MORTALITY

See BENIN - MORTALITY

BENIN - INTERNATIONAL TRADE

African Development Bank Group, Rue Joseph Anoma, 01 BP 1387 Abidjan 01, Cote d'Ivoire, www.afdb.org; *Statistics Pocketbook 2008.*

Economist Intelligence Unit, 111 West 57th Street, New York, NY 10019, (212) 554-0600, Fax: (212) 586-1181, www.eiu.com; *Benin Country Report.*

Euromonitor International, Inc., 224 S. Michigan Avenue, Suite 1500, Chicago, IL 60604, (312) 922-1115, Fax: (312) 922-1157, www.euromonitor.com; *International Marketing Data and Statistics 2008; The World Economic Factbook 2008;* and *World Marketing Data and Statistics.*

M.E. Sharpe, 80 Business Park Drive, Armonk, NY 10504, (800) 541-6563, Fax: (914) 273-2106, www.mesharpe.com; *The Illustrated Book of World Rankings.*

Organisation for Economic Cooperation and Development (OECD), 2 rue Andre Pascal, F-75775 Paris Cedex 16, France, (Telephone in U.S. (202) 785-6323), (Fax in U.S. (202) 785-0350), www.oecd.org; *International Trade by Commodity Statistics (ITCS).*

Palgrave Macmillan Ltd., Houndmills, Basingstoke, Hampshire, RG21 6XS, England, (Telephone in U.S. (888) 330-8477), (Fax in U.S. (800) 672-2054), www.palgrave.com; *The Statesman's Yearbook 2008.*

Taylor and Francis Group, An Informa Business, 2 Park Square, Milton Park, Abingdon, Oxford OX14 4RN, United Kingdom, (Dial from U.S. (212) 216-7800), (Fax from U.S. (212) 564-7854), www.tandf.co.uk; *The Europa World Year Book.*

United Nations Conference on Trade and Development (UNCTAD), DC2-1120, United Nations, New York, NY 10017, (212) 963-0027, www.unctad.org; *UNCTAD Commodity Yearbook.*

United Nations Economic Commission for Africa (ECA), PO Box 3001, Addis Ababa, Ethiopia, (Telephone in U.S. (212) 963-4957), www.uneca.org; *African Statistical Yearbook 2006.*

United Nations Food and Agricultural Organization (FAO), Viale delle Terme di Caracalla, 00100 Rome, Italy, (Dial from U.S. (202) 653-2400), (Fax from U.S. (202) 653 5760), www.fao.org; *FAO Trade Yearbook* and *The State of Food and Agriculture (SOFA) 2006.*

United Nations Statistics Division, New York, NY 10017, (800) 253-9646, Fax: (212) 963-4116, http://unstats.un.org; *Compendium of Intra-African and Related Foreign Trade Statistics 2003; International Trade Statistics Yearbook;* and *Statistical Yearbook.*

The World Bank, 1818 H Street, NW, Washington, DC 20433, (202) 473-1000, Fax: (202) 477-6391, www.worldbank.org; *Benin; World Development Indicators (WDI) 2008;* and *World Development Report 2008.*

World Trade Organization (WTO), Centre William Rappard, Rue de Lausanne 154, CH-1211 Geneva 21, Switzerland, www.wto.org; *International Trade Statistics 2006.*

BENIN - INTERNET USERS

International Telecommunication Union (ITU), Place des Nations, 1211 Geneva 20, Switzerland, www.itu.int; *World Telecommunication/ICT Indicators Database on CD-ROM; World Telecommunication/ICT Indicators Database Online;* and *Yearbook of Statistics - Telecommunication Services (Chronological Time Series 1997-2006).*

The World Bank, 1818 H Street, NW, Washington, DC 20433, (202) 473-1000, Fax: (202) 477-6391, www.worldbank.org; *Benin.*

BENIN - IRON AND IRON ORE PRODUCTION

See BENIN - MINERAL INDUSTRIES

BENIN - IRRIGATION

Euromonitor International, Inc., 224 S. Michigan Avenue, Suite 1500, Chicago, IL 60604, (312) 922-1115, Fax: (312) 922-1157, www.euromonitor.com; *International Marketing Data and Statistics 2008.*

BENIN - LABOR

African Development Bank Group, Rue Joseph Anoma, 01 BP 1387 Abidjan 01, Cote d'Ivoire, www.afdb.org; *Statistics Pocketbook 2008.*

Central Intelligence Agency, Office of Public Affairs, Washington, DC 20505, (703) 482-0623, Fax: (703) 482-1739, www.cia.gov; *The World Factbook.*

Euromonitor International, Inc., 224 S. Michigan Avenue, Suite 1500, Chicago, IL 60604, (312) 922-1115, Fax: (312) 922-1157, www.euromonitor.com; *International Marketing Data and Statistics 2008* and *World Marketing Data and Statistics.*

International Labour Office, I.L.O. Publications, 4 route des Morillons, CH-1211 Geneva 22, Switzerland, (Telephone in U.S. (202) 653-7652), (Fax in U.S. (202) 653-7687), www.ilo.org; *Yearbook of Labour Statistics 2006.*

M.E. Sharpe, 80 Business Park Drive, Armonk, NY 10504, (800) 541-6563, Fax: (914) 273-2106, www.mesharpe.com; *The Illustrated Book of World Rankings.*

Palgrave Macmillan Ltd., Houndmills, Basingstoke, Hampshire, RG21 6XS, England, (Telephone in U.S. (888) 330-8477), (Fax in U.S. (800) 672-2054), www.palgrave.com; *The Statesman's Yearbook 2008.*

United Nations Food and Agricultural Organization (FAO), Viale delle Terme di Caracalla, 00100 Rome, Italy, (Dial from U.S. (202) 653-2400), (Fax from U.S. (202) 653 5760), www.fao.org; *The State of Food and Agriculture (SOFA) 2006.*

United Nations Statistics Division, New York, NY 10017, (800) 253-9646, Fax: (212) 963-4116, http://unstats.un.org; *Human Development Report 2006.*

The World Bank, 1818 H Street, NW, Washington, DC 20433, (202) 473-1000, Fax: (202) 477-6391, www.worldbank.org; *The World Bank Atlas 2003-2004; World Development Indicators (WDI) 2008;* and *World Development Report 2008.*

BENIN - LAND USE

Central Intelligence Agency, Office of Public Affairs, Washington, DC 20505, (703) 482-0623, Fax: (703) 482-1739, www.cia.gov; *The World Factbook.*

Euromonitor International, Inc., 224 S. Michigan Avenue, Suite 1500, Chicago, IL 60604, (312) 922-1115, Fax: (312) 922-1157, www.euromonitor.com; *International Marketing Data and Statistics 2008.*

United Nations Food and Agricultural Organization (FAO), Viale delle Terme di Caracalla, 00100 Rome, Italy, (Dial from U.S. (202) 653-2400), (Fax from U.S. (202) 653 5760), www.fao.org; *FAO Production Yearbook 2002.*

The World Bank, 1818 H Street, NW, Washington, DC 20433, (202) 473-1000, Fax: (202) 477-6391, www.worldbank.org; *World Development Report 2008.*

BENIN - LIBRARIES

M.E. Sharpe, 80 Business Park Drive, Armonk, NY 10504, (800) 541-6563, Fax: (914) 273-2106, www.mesharpe.com; *The Illustrated Book of World Rankings.*

UNESCO Institute for Statistics, C.P. 6128 Succursale Centre-Ville, Montreal, Quebec, H3C 3J7 Canada, (Dial from U.S. (514) 343-6880), (Fax from U.S. (514) 343 6882), www.uis.unesco.org; *Statistical Tables.*

BENIN - LICENSES

International Monetary Fund (IMF), 700 Nineteenth Street, NW, Washington, DC 20431, (202) 623-7000, Fax: (202) 623-4661, www.imf.org; *Government Finance Statistics Yearbook (2008 Edition).*

BENIN - LIFE EXPECTANCY

African Development Bank Group, Rue Joseph Anoma, 01 BP 1387 Abidjan 01, Cote d'Ivoire, www.afdb.org; *Statistics Pocketbook 2008.*

Central Intelligence Agency, Office of Public Affairs, Washington, DC 20505, (703) 482-0623, Fax: (703) 482-1739, www.cia.gov; *The World Factbook.*

Euromonitor International, Inc., 224 S. Michigan Avenue, Suite 1500, Chicago, IL 60604, (312) 922-1115, Fax: (312) 922-1157, www.euromonitor.com; *The World Economic Factbook 2008.*

Palgrave Macmillan Ltd., Houndmills, Basingstoke, Hampshire, RG21 6XS, England, (Telephone in U.S. (888) 330-8477), (Fax in U.S. (800) 672-2054), www.palgrave.com; *The Statesman's Yearbook 2008.*

United Nations Statistics Division, New York, NY 10017, (800) 253-9646, Fax: (212) 963-4116, http://unstats.un.org; *Human Development Report 2006* and *World Statistics Pocketbook.*

The World Bank, 1818 H Street, NW, Washington, DC 20433, (202) 473-1000, Fax: (202) 477-6391, www.worldbank.org; *The World Bank Atlas 2003-2004* and *World Development Report 2008.*

BENIN - LITERACY

Euromonitor International, Inc., 224 S. Michigan Avenue, Suite 1500, Chicago, IL 60604, (312) 922-1115, Fax: (312) 922-1157, www.euromonitor.com; *World Marketing Data and Statistics.*

United Nations Statistics Division, New York, NY 10017, (800) 253-9646, Fax: (212) 963-4116, http://unstats.un.org; *Survey of Economic and Social Conditions in Africa 2005.*

BENIN - LIVESTOCK

Euromonitor International, Inc., 224 S. Michigan Avenue, Suite 1500, Chicago, IL 60604, (312) 922-1115, Fax: (312) 922-1157, www.euromonitor.com; *International Marketing Data and Statistics 2008.*

M.E. Sharpe, 80 Business Park Drive, Armonk, NY 10504, (800) 541-6563, Fax: (914) 273-2106, www.mesharpe.com; *The Illustrated Book of World Rankings.*

Palgrave Macmillan Ltd., Houndmills, Basingstoke, Hampshire, RG21 6XS, England, (Telephone in U.S. (888) 330-8477), (Fax in U.S. (800) 672-2054), www.palgrave.com; *The Statesman's Yearbook 2008.*

Taylor and Francis Group, An Informa Business, 2 Park Square, Milton Park, Abingdon, Oxford OX14

4RN, United Kingdom, (Dial from U.S. (212) 216-7800), (Fax from U.S. (212) 564-7854), www.tandf.co.uk; *The Europa World Year Book.*

United Nations Conference on Trade and Development (UNCTAD), DC2-1120, United Nations, New York, NY 10017, (212) 963-0027, www.unctad.org; *UNCTAD Commodity Yearbook.*

United Nations Economic Commission for Africa (ECA), PO Box 3001, Addis Ababa, Ethiopia, (Telephone in U.S. (212) 963-4957), www.uneca.org; *African Statistical Yearbook 2006.*

United Nations Food and Agricultural Organization (FAO), Viale delle Terme di Caracalla, 00100 Rome, Italy, (Dial from U.S. (202) 653-2400), (Fax from U.S. (202) 653 5760), www.fao.org; *FAO Production Yearbook 2002* and *The State of Food and Agriculture (SOFA) 2006.*

United Nations Statistics Division, New York, NY 10017, (800) 253-9646, Fax: (212) 963-4116, http://unstats.un.org; *Statistical Yearbook* and *Survey of Economic and Social Conditions in Africa 2005.*

BENIN - LOCAL TAXATION

Euromonitor International, Inc., 224 S. Michigan Avenue, Suite 1500, Chicago, IL 60604, (312) 922-1115, Fax: (312) 922-1157, www.euromonitor.com; *International Marketing Data and Statistics 2008.*

BENIN - MANUFACTURES

M.E. Sharpe, 80 Business Park Drive, Armonk, NY 10504, (800) 541-6563, Fax: (914) 273-2106, www.mesharpe.com; *The Illustrated Book of World Rankings.*

United Nations Economic Commission for Africa (ECA), PO Box 3001, Addis Ababa, Ethiopia, (Telephone in U.S. (212) 963-4957), www.uneca.org; *African Statistical Yearbook 2006.*

United Nations Statistics Division, New York, NY 10017, (800) 253-9646, Fax: (212) 963-4116, http://unstats.un.org; *Survey of Economic and Social Conditions in Africa 2005.*

The World Bank, 1818 H Street, NW, Washington, DC 20433, (202) 473-1000, Fax: (202) 477-6391, www.worldbank.org; *World Development Indicators (WDI) 2008.*

BENIN - MARRIAGE

M.E. Sharpe, 80 Business Park Drive, Armonk, NY 10504, (800) 541-6563, Fax: (914) 273-2106, www.mesharpe.com; *The Illustrated Book of World Rankings.*

BENIN - MEAT PRODUCTION

See BENIN - LIVESTOCK

BENIN - MILK PRODUCTION

See BENIN - DAIRY PROCESSING

BENIN - MINERAL INDUSTRIES

M.E. Sharpe, 80 Business Park Drive, Armonk, NY 10504, (800) 541-6563, Fax: (914) 273-2106, www.mesharpe.com; *The Illustrated Book of World Rankings.*

Organisation for Economic Cooperation and Development (OECD), 2 rue Andre Pascal, F-75775 Paris Cedex 16, France, (Telephone in U.S. (202) 785-6323), (Fax in U.S. (202) 785-0350), www.oecd.org; *World Energy Outlook 2007.*

Taylor and Francis Group, An Informa Business, 2 Park Square, Milton Park, Abingdon, Oxford OX14 4RN, United Kingdom, (Dial from U.S. (212) 216-7800), (Fax from U.S. (212) 564-7854), www.tandf.co.uk; *The Europa World Year Book.*

United Nations Conference on Trade and Development (UNCTAD), DC2-1120, United Nations, New York, NY 10017, (212) 963-0027, www.unctad.org; *UNCTAD Commodity Yearbook.*

United Nations Economic Commission for Africa (ECA), PO Box 3001, Addis Ababa, Ethiopia, (Telephone in U.S. (212) 963-4957), www.uneca.org; *African Statistical Yearbook 2006.*

United Nations Statistics Division, New York, NY 10017, (800) 253-9646, Fax: (212) 963-4116, http://unstats.un.org; *Statistical Yearbook.*

BENIN - MONEY EXCHANGE RATES

See BENIN - FOREIGN EXCHANGE RATES

BENIN - MONEY SUPPLY

African Development Bank Group, Rue Joseph Anoma, 01 BP 1387 Abidjan 01, Cote d'Ivoire, www.afdb.org; *Statistics Pocketbook 2008.*

Economist Intelligence Unit, 111 West 57th Street, New York, NY 10019, (212) 554-0600, Fax: (212) 586-1181, www.eiu.com; *Benin Country Report.*

Euromonitor International, Inc., 224 S. Michigan Avenue, Suite 1500, Chicago, IL 60604, (312) 922-1115, Fax: (312) 922-1157, www.euromonitor.com; *International Marketing Data and Statistics 2008.*

International Monetary Fund (IMF), 700 Nineteenth Street, NW, Washington, DC 20431, (202) 623-7000, Fax: (202) 623-4661, www.imf.org; *International Financial Statistics Yearbook 2007.*

Taylor and Francis Group, An Informa Business, 2 Park Square, Milton Park, Abingdon, Oxford OX14 4RN, United Kingdom, (Dial from U.S. (212) 216-7800), (Fax from U.S. (212) 564-7854), www.tandf.co.uk; *The Europa World Year Book.*

United Nations Statistics Division, New York, NY 10017, (800) 253-9646, Fax: (212) 963-4116, http://unstats.un.org; *Statistical Yearbook.*

The World Bank, 1818 H Street, NW, Washington, DC 20433, (202) 473-1000, Fax: (202) 477-6391, www.worldbank.org; *Benin* and *World Development Indicators (WDI) 2008.*

BENIN - MORTALITY

Central Intelligence Agency, Office of Public Affairs, Washington, DC 20505, (703) 482-0623, Fax: (703) 482-1739, www.cia.gov; *The World Factbook.*

Euromonitor International, Inc., 224 S. Michigan Avenue, Suite 1500, Chicago, IL 60604, (312) 922-1115, Fax: (312) 922-1157, www.euromonitor.com; *International Marketing Data and Statistics 2008* and *The World Economic Factbook 2008.*

Palgrave Macmillan Ltd., Houndmills, Basingstoke, Hampshire, RG21 6XS, England, (Telephone in U.S. (888) 330-8477), (Fax in U.S. (800) 672-2054), www.palgrave.com; *The Statesman's Yearbook 2008.*

Taylor and Francis Group, An Informa Business, 2 Park Square, Milton Park, Abingdon, Oxford OX14 4RN, United Kingdom, (Dial from U.S. (212) 216-7800), (Fax from U.S. (212) 564-7854), www.tandf.co.uk; *The Europa World Year Book.*

United Nations Statistics Division, New York, NY 10017, (800) 253-9646, Fax: (212) 963-4116, http://unstats.un.org; *Demographic Yearbook; Human Development Report 2006; Statistical Yearbook; Survey of Economic and Social Conditions in Africa 2005;* and *World Statistics Pocketbook.*

The World Bank, 1818 H Street, NW, Washington, DC 20433, (202) 473-1000, Fax: (202) 477-6391, www.worldbank.org; *The World Bank Atlas 2003-2004; World Development Indicators (WDI) 2008;* and *World Development Report 2008.*

World Health Organization (WHO), Avenue Appia 20, 1211 Geneve 27, Switzerland, (Telephone in U.S. (212) 331-9081), www.who.int; The WHO Global Atlas of Infectious Diseases and *World Health Report 2006.*

BENIN - MOTION PICTURES

United Nations Statistics Division, New York, NY 10017, (800) 253-9646, Fax: (212) 963-4116, http://unstats.un.org; *Statistical Yearbook.*

BENIN - MOTOR VEHICLES

International Road Federation (IFR), Madison Place, 500 Montgomery Street, 5th Floor, Alexandria, VA 22314, (703) 535-1001, Fax: (703) 535-1007, www.irfnet.org; *World Road Statistics 2006.*

Taylor and Francis Group, An Informa Business, 2 Park Square, Milton Park, Abingdon, Oxford OX14 4RN, United Kingdom, (Dial from U.S. (212) 216-7800), (Fax from U.S. (212) 564-7854), www.tandf.co.uk; *The Europa World Year Book.*

United Nations Statistics Division, New York, NY 10017, (800) 253-9646, Fax: (212) 963-4116, http://unstats.un.org; *Statistical Yearbook* and *Survey of Economic and Social Conditions in Africa 2005.*

BENIN - MUSEUMS

M.E. Sharpe, 80 Business Park Drive, Armonk, NY 10504, (800) 541-6563, Fax: (914) 273-2106, www.mesharpe.com; *The Illustrated Book of World Rankings.*

UNESCO Institute for Statistics, C.P. 6128 Succursale Centre-Ville, Montreal, Quebec, H3C 3J7 Canada, (Dial from U.S. (514) 343-6880), (Fax from U.S. (514) 343 6882), www.uis.unesco.org; *Statistical Tables.*

BENIN - NATIONAL INCOME

United Nations Statistics Division, New York, NY 10017, (800) 253-9646, Fax: (212) 963-4116, http://unstats.un.org; *Statistical Yearbook.*

BENIN - NATURAL GAS PRODUCTION

See BENIN - MINERAL INDUSTRIES

BENIN - NUTRITION

African Development Bank Group, Rue Joseph Anoma, 01 BP 1387 Abidjan 01, Cote d'Ivoire, www.afdb.org; *Statistics Pocketbook 2008.*

United Nations Food and Agricultural Organization (FAO), Viale delle Terme di Caracalla, 00100 Rome, Italy, (Dial from U.S. (202) 653-2400), (Fax from U.S. (202) 653 5760), www.fao.org; *The State of Food and Agriculture (SOFA) 2006.*

BENIN - OLDER PEOPLE

M.E. Sharpe, 80 Business Park Drive, Armonk, NY 10504, (800) 541-6563, Fax: (914) 273-2106, www.mesharpe.com; *The Illustrated Book of World Rankings.*

BENIN - PAPER

See BENIN - FORESTS AND FORESTRY

BENIN - PEANUT PRODUCTION

See BENIN - CROPS

BENIN - PERIODICALS

UNESCO Institute for Statistics, C.P. 6128 Succursale Centre-Ville, Montreal, Quebec, H3C 3J7 Canada, (Dial from U.S. (514) 343-6880), (Fax from U.S. (514) 343 6882), www.uis.unesco.org; *Statistical Tables.*

BENIN - PESTICIDES

United Nations Food and Agricultural Organization (FAO), Viale delle Terme di Caracalla, 00100 Rome, Italy, (Dial from U.S. (202) 653-2400), (Fax from U.S. (202) 653 5760), www.fao.org; *The State of Food and Agriculture (SOFA) 2006.*

BENIN - PETROLEUM INDUSTRY AND TRADE

M.E. Sharpe, 80 Business Park Drive, Armonk, NY 10504, (800) 541-6563, Fax: (914) 273-2106, www.mesharpe.com; *The Illustrated Book of World Rankings.*

Organisation for Economic Cooperation and Development (OECD), 2 rue Andre Pascal, F-75775 Paris Cedex 16, France, (Telephone in U.S. (202) 785-6323), (Fax in U.S. (202) 785-0350), www.oecd.org; *World Energy Outlook 2007.*

Palgrave Macmillan Ltd., Houndmills, Basingstoke, Hampshire, RG21 6XS, England, (Telephone in U.S.

(888) 330-8477), (Fax in U.S. (800) 672-2054), www.palgrave.com; *The Statesman's Yearbook 2008.*

PennWell Corporation, 1421 South Sheridan Road, Tulsa, OK 74112, (918) 835-3161, www.pennwell.com; *International Petroleum Encyclopedia 2007.*

United Nations Conference on Trade and Development (UNCTAD), DC2-1120, United Nations, New York, NY 10017, (212) 963-0027, www.unctad.org; *UNCTAD Commodity Yearbook.*

United Nations Food and Agricultural Organization (FAO), Viale delle Terme di Caracalla, 00100 Rome, Italy, (Dial from U.S. (202) 653-2400), (Fax from U.S. (202) 653 5760), www.fao.org; *The State of Food and Agriculture (SOFA) 2006.*

BENIN - POLITICAL SCIENCE

Central Intelligence Agency, Office of Public Affairs, Washington, DC 20505, (703) 482-0623, Fax: (703) 482-1739, www.cia.gov; *The World Factbook.*

International Monetary Fund (IMF), 700 Nineteenth Street, NW, Washington, DC 20431, (202) 623-7000, Fax: (202) 623-4661, www.imf.org; *Government Finance Statistics Yearbook (2008 Edition).*

Palgrave Macmillan Ltd., Houndmills, Basingstoke, Hampshire, RG21 6XS, England, (Telephone in U.S. (888) 330-8477), (Fax in U.S. (800) 672-2054), www.palgrave.com; *The Statesman's Yearbook 2008.*

Taylor and Francis Group, An Informa Business, 2 Park Square, Milton Park, Abingdon, Oxford OX14 4RN, United Kingdom, (Dial from U.S. (212) 216-7800), (Fax from U.S. (212) 564-7854), www.tandf.co.uk; *The Europa World Year Book.*

United Nations Statistics Division, New York, NY 10017, (800) 253-9646, Fax: (212) 963-4116, http://unstats.un.org; *National Accounts Statistics: Compendium of Income Distribution Statistics* and *Survey of Economic and Social Conditions in Africa 2005.*

The World Bank, 1818 H Street, NW, Washington, DC 20433, (202) 473-1000, Fax: (202) 477-6391, www.worldbank.org; *World Development Indicators (WDI) 2008* and *World Development Report 2008.*

BENIN - POPULATION

African Development Bank Group, Rue Joseph Anoma, 01 BP 1387 Abidjan 01, Cote d'Ivoire, www.afdb.org; *The African Statistical Journal; Gender, Poverty and Environmental Indicators on African Countries 2007; Selected Statistics on African Countries 2007;* and *Statistics Pocketbook 2008.*

Central Intelligence Agency, Office of Public Affairs, Washington, DC 20505, (703) 482-0623, Fax: (703) 482-1739, www.cia.gov; *The World Factbook.*

Economist Intelligence Unit, 111 West 57th Street, New York, NY 10019, (212) 554-0600, Fax: (212) 586-1181, www.eiu.com; *Benin Country Report.*

Euromonitor International, Inc., 224 S. Michigan Avenue, Suite 1500, Chicago, IL 60604, (312) 922-1115, Fax: (312) 922-1157, www.euromonitor.com; *International Marketing Data and Statistics 2008* and *The World Economic Factbook 2008.*

Eurostat, Batiment Jean Monnet, Rue Alcide de Gasperi, L-2920 Luxembourg, http://epp.eurostat.ec.europa.eu; *Demographic Indicators - Population by Age-Classes.*

International Labour Office, I.L.O. Publications, 4 route des Morillons, CH-1211 Geneva 22, Switzerland, (Telephone in U.S. (202) 653-7652), (Fax in U.S. (202) 653-7687), www.ilo.org; *Yearbook of Labour Statistics 2006.*

M.E. Sharpe, 80 Business Park Drive, Armonk, NY 10504, (800) 541-6563, Fax: (914) 273-2106, www.mesharpe.com; *The Illustrated Book of World Rankings.*

Palgrave Macmillan Ltd., Houndmills, Basingstoke, Hampshire, RG21 6XS, England, (Telephone in U.S. (888) 330-8477), (Fax in U.S. (800) 672-2054), www.palgrave.com; *The Statesman's Yearbook 2008.*

Taylor and Francis Group, An Informa Business, 2 Park Square, Milton Park, Abingdon, Oxford OX14 4RN, United Kingdom, (Dial from U.S. (212) 216-7800), (Fax from U.S. (212) 564-7854), www.tandf.co.uk; *The Europa World Year Book.*

U.S. Department of State (DOS), 2201 C Street NW, Washington, DC 20520, (202) 647-4000, www.state.gov; *World Military Expenditures and Arms Transfers (WMEAT).*

UNESCO Institute for Statistics, C.P. 6128 Succursale Centre-Ville, Montreal, Quebec, H3C 3J7 Canada, (Dial from U.S. (514) 343-6880), (Fax from U.S. (514) 343 6882), www.uis.unesco.org; *Statistical Tables.*

United Nations Food and Agricultural Organization (FAO), Viale delle Terme di Caracalla, 00100 Rome, Italy, (Dial from U.S. (202) 653-2400), (Fax from U.S. (202) 653 5760), www.fao.org; *FAO Production Yearbook 2002.*

United Nations Statistics Division, New York, NY 10017, (800) 253-9646, Fax: (212) 963-4116, http://unstats.un.org; *Demographic Yearbook; Human Development Report 2006; Statistical Yearbook; Survey of Economic and Social Conditions in Africa 2005;* and *World Statistics Pocketbook.*

The World Bank, 1818 H Street, NW, Washington, DC 20433, (202) 473-1000, Fax: (202) 477-6391, www.worldbank.org; *Benin; The World Bank Atlas 2003-2004;* and *World Development Report 2008.*

World Health Organization (WHO), Avenue Appia 20, 1211 Geneve 27, Switzerland, (Telephone in U.S. (212) 331-9081), www.who.int; *World Health Report 2006.*

BENIN - POPULATION DENSITY

African Development Bank Group, Rue Joseph Anoma, 01 BP 1387 Abidjan 01, Cote d'Ivoire, www.afdb.org; *Statistics Pocketbook 2008.*

Central Intelligence Agency, Office of Public Affairs, Washington, DC 20505, (703) 482-0623, Fax: (703) 482-1739, www.cia.gov; *The World Factbook.*

Euromonitor International, Inc., 224 S. Michigan Avenue, Suite 1500, Chicago, IL 60604, (312) 922-1115, Fax: (312) 922-1157, www.euromonitor.com; *International Marketing Data and Statistics 2008* and *The World Economic Factbook 2008.*

M.E. Sharpe, 80 Business Park Drive, Armonk, NY 10504, (800) 541-6563, Fax: (914) 273-2106, www.mesharpe.com; *The Illustrated Book of World Rankings.*

Palgrave Macmillan Ltd., Houndmills, Basingstoke, Hampshire, RG21 6XS, England, (Telephone in U.S. (888) 330-8477), (Fax in U.S. (800) 672-2054), www.palgrave.com; *The Statesman's Yearbook 2008.*

Taylor and Francis Group, An Informa Business, 2 Park Square, Milton Park, Abingdon, Oxford OX14 4RN, United Kingdom, (Dial from U.S. (212) 216-7800), (Fax from U.S. (212) 564-7854), www.tandf.co.uk; *The Europa World Year Book.*

UNESCO Institute for Statistics, C.P. 6128 Succursale Centre-Ville, Montreal, Quebec, H3C 3J7 Canada, (Dial from U.S. (514) 343-6880), (Fax from U.S. (514) 343 6882), www.uis.unesco.org; *Statistical Tables.*

United Nations Food and Agricultural Organization (FAO), Viale delle Terme di Caracalla, 00100 Rome, Italy, (Dial from U.S. (202) 653-2400), (Fax from U.S. (202) 653 5760), www.fao.org; *The State of Food and Agriculture (SOFA) 2006.*

United Nations Statistics Division, New York, NY 10017, (800) 253-9646, Fax: (212) 963-4116, http://unstats.un.org; *Statistical Yearbook* and *Survey of Economic and Social Conditions in Africa 2005.*

The World Bank, 1818 H Street, NW, Washington, DC 20433, (202) 473-1000, Fax: (202) 477-6391, www.worldbank.org; *Benin* and *World Development Report 2008.*

BENIN - POSTAL SERVICE

M.E. Sharpe, 80 Business Park Drive, Armonk, NY 10504, (800) 541-6563, Fax: (914) 273-2106, www.mesharpe.com; *The Illustrated Book of World Rankings.*

United Nations Statistics Division, New York, NY 10017, (800) 253-9646, Fax: (212) 963-4116, http://unstats.un.org; *Statistical Yearbook.*

BENIN - POWER RESOURCES

Euromonitor International, Inc., 224 S. Michigan Avenue, Suite 1500, Chicago, IL 60604, (312) 922-1115, Fax: (312) 922-1157, www.euromonitor.com; *International Marketing Data and Statistics 2008; The World Economic Factbook 2008;* and *World Marketing Data and Statistics.*

M.E. Sharpe, 80 Business Park Drive, Armonk, NY 10504, (800) 541-6563, Fax: (914) 273-2106, www.mesharpe.com; *The Illustrated Book of World Rankings.*

Organisation for Economic Cooperation and Development (OECD), 2 rue Andre Pascal, F-75775 Paris Cedex 16, France, (Telephone in U.S. (202) 785-6323), (Fax in U.S. (202) 785-0350), www.oecd.org; *World Energy Outlook 2007.*

Palgrave Macmillan Ltd., Houndmills, Basingstoke, Hampshire, RG21 6XS, England, (Telephone in U.S. (888) 330-8477), (Fax in U.S. (800) 672-2054), www.palgrave.com; *The Statesman's Yearbook 2008.*

United Nations Economic Commission for Africa (ECA), PO Box 3001, Addis Ababa, Ethiopia, (Telephone in U.S. (212) 963-4957), www.uneca.org; *African Statistical Yearbook 2006.*

United Nations Food and Agricultural Organization (FAO), Viale delle Terme di Caracalla, 00100 Rome, Italy, (Dial from U.S. (202) 653-2400), (Fax from U.S. (202) 653 5760), www.fao.org; *The State of Food and Agriculture (SOFA) 2006.*

United Nations Statistics Division, New York, NY 10017, (800) 253-9646, Fax: (212) 963-4116, http://unstats.un.org; *Human Development Report 2006* and *World Statistics Pocketbook.*

The World Bank, 1818 H Street, NW, Washington, DC 20433, (202) 473-1000, Fax: (202) 477-6391, www.worldbank.org; *The World Bank Atlas 2003-2004* and *World Development Report 2008.*

BENIN - PRICES

Euromonitor International, Inc., 224 S. Michigan Avenue, Suite 1500, Chicago, IL 60604, (312) 922-1115, Fax: (312) 922-1157, www.euromonitor.com; *World Marketing Data and Statistics.*

International Labour Office, I.L.O. Publications, 4 route des Morillons, CH-1211 Geneva 22, Switzerland, (Telephone in U.S. (202) 653-7652), (Fax in U.S. (202) 653-7687), www.ilo.org; *Yearbook of Labour Statistics 2006.*

M.E. Sharpe, 80 Business Park Drive, Armonk, NY 10504, (800) 541-6563, Fax: (914) 273-2106, www.mesharpe.com; *The Illustrated Book of World Rankings.*

United Nations Food and Agricultural Organization (FAO), Viale delle Terme di Caracalla, 00100 Rome, Italy, (Dial from U.S. (202) 653-2400), (Fax from U.S. (202) 653 5760), www.fao.org; *FAO Production Yearbook 2002* and *The State of Food and Agriculture (SOFA) 2006.*

The World Bank, 1818 H Street, NW, Washington, DC 20433, (202) 473-1000, Fax: (202) 477-6391, www.worldbank.org; *Benin.*

BENIN - PUBLIC HEALTH

African Development Bank Group, Rue Joseph Anoma, 01 BP 1387 Abidjan 01, Cote d'Ivoire, www.afdb.org; *Statistics Pocketbook 2008.*

Euromonitor International, Inc., 224 S. Michigan Avenue, Suite 1500, Chicago, IL 60604, (312) 922-1115, Fax: (312) 922-1157, www.euromonitor.com; *World Marketing Data and Statistics.*

M.E. Sharpe, 80 Business Park Drive, Armonk, NY 10504, (800) 541-6563, Fax: (914) 273-2106, www.mesharpe.com; *The Illustrated Book of World Rankings.*

Palgrave Macmillan Ltd., Houndmills, Basingstoke, Hampshire, RG21 6XS, England, (Telephone in U.S.

(888) 330-8477), (Fax in U.S. (800) 672-2054), www.palgrave.com; *The Statesman's Yearbook 2008.*

United Nations Economic Commission for Africa (ECA), PO Box 3001, Addis Ababa, Ethiopia, (Telephone in U.S. (212) 963-4957), www.uneca.org; *African Statistical Yearbook 2006.*

United Nations Statistics Division, New York, NY 10017, (800) 253-9646, Fax: (212) 963-4116, http://unstats.un.org; *Human Development Report 2006* and *Statistical Yearbook.*

The World Bank, 1818 H Street, NW, Washington, DC 20433, (202) 473-1000, Fax: (202) 477-6391, www.worldbank.org; *Benin* and *World Development Report 2008.*

World Health Organization (WHO), Avenue Appia 20, 1211 Geneve 27, Switzerland, (Telephone in U.S. (212) 331-9081), www.who.int; The WHO Global Atlas of Infectious Diseases and *World Health Report 2006.*

BENIN - PUBLISHERS AND PUBLISHING

UNESCO Institute for Statistics, C.P. 6128 Succursale Centre-Ville, Montreal, Quebec, H3C 3J7 Canada, (Dial from U.S. (514) 343-6880), (Fax from U.S. (514) 343 6882), www.uis.unesco.org; *Statistical Tables.*

BENIN - RADIO BROADCASTING

Palgrave Macmillan Ltd., Houndmills, Basingstoke, Hampshire, RG21 6XS, England, (Telephone in U.S. (888) 330-8477), (Fax in U.S. (800) 672-2054), www.palgrave.com; *The Statesman's Yearbook 2008.*

BENIN - RAILROADS

Jane's Information Group, 110 North Royal Street, Suite 200, Alexandria, VA 22314, (703) 683-3700, Fax: (800) 836-0297, www.janes.com; *Jane's World Railways.*

Palgrave Macmillan Ltd., Houndmills, Basingstoke, Hampshire, RG21 6XS, England, (Telephone in U.S. (888) 330-8477), (Fax in U.S. (800) 672-2054), www.palgrave.com; *The Statesman's Yearbook 2008.*

Taylor and Francis Group, An Informa Business, 2 Park Square, Milton Park, Abingdon, Oxford OX14 4RN, United Kingdom, (Dial from U.S. (212) 216-7800), (Fax from U.S. (212) 564-7854), www.tandf.co.uk; *The Europa World Year Book.*

United Nations Economic Commission for Africa (ECA), PO Box 3001, Addis Ababa, Ethiopia, (Telephone in U.S. (212) 963-4957), www.uneca.org; *African Statistical Yearbook 2006.*

United Nations Statistics Division, New York, NY 10017, (800) 253-9646, Fax: (212) 963-4116, http://unstats.un.org; *Statistical Yearbook* and *Survey of Economic and Social Conditions in Africa 2005.*

BENIN - RELIGION

Central Intelligence Agency, Office of Public Affairs, Washington, DC 20505, (703) 482-0623, Fax: (703) 482-1739, www.cia.gov; *The World Factbook.*

M.E. Sharpe, 80 Business Park Drive, Armonk, NY 10504, (800) 541-6563, Fax: (914) 273-2106, www.mesharpe.com; *The Illustrated Book of World Rankings.*

Palgrave Macmillan Ltd., Houndmills, Basingstoke, Hampshire, RG21 6XS, England, (Telephone in U.S. (888) 330-8477), (Fax in U.S. (800) 672-2054), www.palgrave.com; *The Statesman's Yearbook 2008.*

BENIN - RENT CHARGES

International Labour Office, I.L.O. Publications, 4 route des Morillons, CH-1211 Geneva 22, Switzerland, (Telephone in U.S. (202) 653-7652), (Fax in U.S. (202) 653-7687), www.ilo.org; *Yearbook of Labour Statistics 2006.*

BENIN - RESERVES (ACCOUNTING)

African Development Bank Group, Rue Joseph Anoma, 01 BP 1387 Abidjan 01, Cote d'Ivoire, www.afdb.org; *Statistics Pocketbook 2008.*

Euromonitor International, Inc., 224 S. Michigan Avenue, Suite 1500, Chicago, IL 60604, (312) 922-1115, Fax: (312) 922-1157, www.euromonitor.com; *International Marketing Data and Statistics 2008.*

The World Bank, 1818 H Street, NW, Washington, DC 20433, (202) 473-1000, Fax: (202) 477-6391, www.worldbank.org; *World Development Indicators (WDI) 2008.*

BENIN - RETAIL TRADE

Euromonitor International, Inc., 224 S. Michigan Avenue, Suite 1500, Chicago, IL 60604, (312) 922-1115, Fax: (312) 922-1157, www.euromonitor.com; *World Marketing Data and Statistics.*

BENIN - RICE PRODUCTION

See BENIN - CROPS

BENIN - ROADS

Central Intelligence Agency, Office of Public Affairs, Washington, DC 20505, (703) 482-0623, Fax: (703) 482-1739, www.cia.gov; *The World Factbook.*

International Road Federation (IFR), Madison Place, 500 Montgomery Street, 5th Floor, Alexandria, VA 22314, (703) 535-1001, Fax: (703) 535-1007, www.irfnet.org; *World Road Statistics 2006.*

Palgrave Macmillan Ltd., Houndmills, Basingstoke, Hampshire, RG21 6XS, England, (Telephone in U.S. (888) 330-8477), (Fax in U.S. (800) 672-2054), www.palgrave.com; *The Statesman's Yearbook 2008.*

United Nations Economic Commission for Africa (ECA), PO Box 3001, Addis Ababa, Ethiopia, (Telephone in U.S. (212) 963-4957), www.uneca.org; *African Statistical Yearbook 2006.*

United Nations Statistics Division, New York, NY 10017, (800) 253-9646, Fax: (212) 963-4116, http://unstats.un.org; *Survey of Economic and Social Conditions in Africa 2005.*

BENIN - RUBBER INDUSTRY AND TRADE

International Rubber Study Group (IRSG), 1st Floor, Heron House, 109/115 Wembley Hill Road, Wembley, Middlesex HA9 8DA, United Kingdom, www.rubberstudy.com; *Rubber Statistical Bulletin; Summary of World Rubber Statistics 2005; World Rubber Statistics Handbook (Volume 6, 1975-2001);* and *World Rubber Statistics Historic Handbook.*

M.E. Sharpe, 80 Business Park Drive, Armonk, NY 10504, (800) 541-6563, Fax: (914) 273-2106, www.mesharpe.com; *The Illustrated Book of World Rankings.*

BENIN - SAVING AND INVESTMENT

International Monetary Fund (IMF), 700 Nineteenth Street, NW, Washington, DC 20431, (202) 623-7000, Fax: (202) 623-4661, www.imf.org; *International Financial Statistics Yearbook 2007.*

BENIN - SHEEP

See BENIN - LIVESTOCK

BENIN - SHIPPING

Taylor and Francis Group, An Informa Business, 2 Park Square, Milton Park, Abingdon, Oxford OX14 4RN, United Kingdom, (Dial from U.S. (212) 216-7800), (Fax from U.S. (212) 564-7854), www.tandf.co.uk; *The Europa World Year Book.*

United Nations Economic Commission for Africa (ECA), PO Box 3001, Addis Ababa, Ethiopia, (Telephone in U.S. (212) 963-4957), www.uneca.org; *African Statistical Yearbook 2006.*

United Nations Statistics Division, New York, NY 10017, (800) 253-9646, Fax: (212) 963-4116, http://unstats.un.org; *Statistical Yearbook.*

BENIN - SILVER PRODUCTION

See BENIN - MINERAL INDUSTRIES

BENIN - SOCIAL ECOLOGY

M.E. Sharpe, 80 Business Park Drive, Armonk, NY 10504, (800) 541-6563, Fax: (914) 273-2106, www.mesharpe.com; *The Illustrated Book of World Rankings.*

United Nations Statistics Division, New York, NY 10017, (800) 253-9646, Fax: (212) 963-4116, http://unstats.un.org; *World Statistics Pocketbook.*

BENIN - SOCIAL SECURITY

United Nations Statistics Division, New York, NY 10017, (800) 253-9646, Fax: (212) 963-4116, http://unstats.un.org; *National Accounts Statistics: Compendium of Income Distribution Statistics.*

BENIN - STEEL PRODUCTION

See BENIN - MINERAL INDUSTRIES

BENIN - SUGAR PRODUCTION

See BENIN - CROPS

BENIN - TAXATION

International Monetary Fund (IMF), 700 Nineteenth Street, NW, Washington, DC 20431, (202) 623-7000, Fax: (202) 623-4661, www.imf.org; *Government Finance Statistics Yearbook (2008 Edition).*

International Road Federation (IFR), Madison Place, 500 Montgomery Street, 5th Floor, Alexandria, VA 22314, (703) 535-1001, Fax: (703) 535-1007, www.irfnet.org; *World Road Statistics 2006.*

Taylor and Francis Group, An Informa Business, 2 Park Square, Milton Park, Abingdon, Oxford OX14 4RN, United Kingdom, (Dial from U.S. (212) 216-7800), (Fax from U.S. (212) 564-7854), www.tandf.co.uk; *The Europa World Year Book.*

The World Bank, 1818 H Street, NW, Washington, DC 20433, (202) 473-1000, Fax: (202) 477-6391, www.worldbank.org; *World Development Indicators (WDI) 2008.*

BENIN - TELEPHONE

International Telecommunication Union (ITU), Place des Nations, 1211 Geneva 20, Switzerland, www.itu.int; World Telecommunication Indicators Database.

Palgrave Macmillan Ltd., Houndmills, Basingstoke, Hampshire, RG21 6XS, England, (Telephone in U.S. (888) 330-8477), (Fax in U.S. (800) 672-2054), www.palgrave.com; *The Statesman's Yearbook 2008.*

Taylor and Francis Group, An Informa Business, 2 Park Square, Milton Park, Abingdon, Oxford OX14 4RN, United Kingdom, (Dial from U.S. (212) 216-7800), (Fax from U.S. (212) 564-7854), www.tandf.co.uk; *The Europa World Year Book.*

United Nations Statistics Division, New York, NY 10017, (800) 253-9646, Fax: (212) 963-4116, http://unstats.un.org; *Statistical Yearbook* and *World Statistics Pocketbook.*

BENIN - TEXTILE INDUSTRY

M.E. Sharpe, 80 Business Park Drive, Armonk, NY 10504, (800) 541-6563, Fax: (914) 273-2106, www.mesharpe.com; *The Illustrated Book of World Rankings.*

United Nations Conference on Trade and Development (UNCTAD), DC2-1120, United Nations, New York, NY 10017, (212) 963-0027, www.unctad.org; *UNCTAD Commodity Yearbook.*

BENIN - TOBACCO INDUSTRY

Foreign Agricultural Service (FAS), U.S. Department of Agriculture (USDA), 1400 Independence Avenue, SW, Washington, DC 20250, (202) 720-3935, www.fas.usda.gov; *Tobacco: World Markets and Trade.*

M.E. Sharpe, 80 Business Park Drive, Armonk, NY 10504, (800) 541-6563, Fax: (914) 273-2106, www.mesharpe.com; *The Illustrated Book of World Rankings.*

United Nations Statistics Division, New York, NY 10017, (800) 253-9646, Fax: (212) 963-4116, http://unstats.un.org; *Statistical Yearbook.*

BENIN - TOURISM

Euromonitor International, Inc., 224 S. Michigan Avenue, Suite 1500, Chicago, IL 60604, (312) 922-

1115, Fax: (312) 922-1157, www.euromonitor.com; *The World Economic Factbook 2008* and *World Marketing Data and Statistics.*

M.E. Sharpe, 80 Business Park Drive, Armonk, NY 10504, (800) 541-6563, Fax: (914) 273-2106, www.mesharpe.com; *The Illustrated Book of World Rankings.*

Taylor and Francis Group, An Informa Business, 2 Park Square, Milton Park, Abingdon, Oxford OX14 4RN, United Kingdom, (Dial from U.S. (212) 216-7800), (Fax from U.S. (212) 564-7854), www.tandf.co.uk; *The Europa World Year Book.*

United Nations Economic Commission for Africa (ECA), PO Box 3001, Addis Ababa, Ethiopia, (Telephone in U.S. (212) 963-4957), www.uneca.org; *African Statistical Yearbook 2006.*

United Nations Statistics Division, New York, NY 10017, (800) 253-9646, Fax: (212) 963-4116, http://unstats.un.org; *Statistical Yearbook.*

The World Bank, 1818 H Street, NW, Washington, DC 20433, (202) 473-1000, Fax: (202) 477-6391, www.worldbank.org; *Benin.*

BENIN - TRADE

See BENIN - INTERNATIONAL TRADE

BENIN - TRANSPORTATION

Central Intelligence Agency, Office of Public Affairs, Washington, DC 20505, (703) 482-0623, Fax: (703) 482-1739, www.cia.gov; *The World Factbook.*

Euromonitor International, Inc., 224 S. Michigan Avenue, Suite 1500, Chicago, IL 60604, (312) 922-1115, Fax: (312) 922-1157, www.euromonitor.com; *International Marketing Data and Statistics 2008* and *World Marketing Data and Statistics.*

M.E. Sharpe, 80 Business Park Drive, Armonk, NY 10504, (800) 541-6563, Fax: (914) 273-2106, www.mesharpe.com; *The Illustrated Book of World Rankings.*

Palgrave Macmillan Ltd., Houndmills, Basingstoke, Hampshire, RG21 6XS, England, (Telephone in U.S. (888) 330-8477), (Fax in U.S. (800) 672-2054), www.palgrave.com; *The Statesman's Yearbook 2008.*

Taylor and Francis Group, An Informa Business, 2 Park Square, Milton Park, Abingdon, Oxford OX14 4RN, United Kingdom, (Dial from U.S. (212) 216-7800), (Fax from U.S. (212) 564-7854), www.tandf.co.uk; *The Europa World Year Book.*

United Nations Economic Commission for Africa (ECA), PO Box 3001, Addis Ababa, Ethiopia, (Telephone in U.S. (212) 963-4957), www.uneca.org; *African Statistical Yearbook 2006.*

United Nations Statistics Division, New York, NY 10017, (800) 253-9646, Fax: (212) 963-4116, http://unstats.un.org; *Human Development Report 2006.*

The World Bank, 1818 H Street, NW, Washington, DC 20433, (202) 473-1000, Fax: (202) 477-6391, www.worldbank.org; *Africa Live Database (LDB)* and *Benin.*

BENIN - TRAVEL COSTS

International Monetary Fund (IMF), 700 Nineteenth Street, NW, Washington, DC 20431, (202) 623-7000, Fax: (202) 623-4661, www.imf.org; *Government Finance Statistics Yearbook (2008 Edition).*

BENIN - UNEMPLOYMENT

Central Intelligence Agency, Office of Public Affairs, Washington, DC 20505, (703) 482-0623, Fax: (703) 482-1739, www.cia.gov; *The World Factbook.*

Euromonitor International, Inc., 224 S. Michigan Avenue, Suite 1500, Chicago, IL 60604, (312) 922-1115, Fax: (312) 922-1157, www.euromonitor.com; *International Marketing Data and Statistics 2008.*

International Labour Office, I.L.O. Publications, 4 route des Morillons, CH-1211 Geneva 22, Switzerland, (Telephone in U.S. (202) 653-7652), (Fax in U.S. (202) 653-7687), www.ilo.org; *Yearbook of Labour Statistics 2006.*

BENIN - VITAL STATISTICS

Euromonitor International, Inc., 224 S. Michigan Avenue, Suite 1500, Chicago, IL 60604, (312) 922-1115, Fax: (312) 922-1157, www.euromonitor.com; *International Marketing Data and Statistics 2008.*

Palgrave Macmillan Ltd., Houndmills, Basingstoke, Hampshire, RG21 6XS, England, (Telephone in U.S. (888) 330-8477), (Fax in U.S. (800) 672-2054), www.palgrave.com; *The Statesman's Yearbook 2008.*

United Nations Statistics Division, New York, NY 10017, (800) 253-9646, Fax: (212) 963-4116, http://unstats.un.org; *Statistical Yearbook.*

World Health Organization (WHO), Avenue Appia 20, 1211 Geneve 27, Switzerland, (Telephone in U.S. (212) 331-9081), www.who.int; *World Health Report 2006.*

BENIN - WAGES

International Labour Office, I.L.O. Publications, 4 route des Morillons, CH-1211 Geneva 22, Switzerland, (Telephone in U.S. (202) 653-7652), (Fax in U.S. (202) 653-7687), www.ilo.org; *Yearbook of Labour Statistics 2006.*

The World Bank, 1818 H Street, NW, Washington, DC 20433, (202) 473-1000, Fax: (202) 477-6391, www.worldbank.org; *Benin.*

BENIN - WEATHER

See BENIN - CLIMATE

BENIN - WHEAT PRODUCTION

See BENIN - CROPS

BENIN - WINE PRODUCTION

See BENIN - BEVERAGE INDUSTRY

BENIN - WOOL PRODUCTION

See BENIN - TEXTILE INDUSTRY

BERMUDA - NATIONAL STATISTICAL OFFICE

Department of Statistics, Bermuda Government, PO Box HM 3015, Hamilton HM MX, Bermuda, (Dial from U.S. (441) 297-7761), (Fax from U.S. (441) 295-8390), www.gov.bm; National Data Center.

BERMUDA - PRIMARY STATISTICS SOURCES

Department of Statistics, Bermuda Government, PO Box HM 3015, Hamilton HM MX, Bermuda, (Dial from U.S. (441) 297-7761), (Fax from U.S. (441) 295-8390), www.gov.bm; *Facts and Figures 2006.*

BERMUDA - AGRICULTURAL MACHINERY

United Nations Statistics Division, New York, NY 10017, (800) 253-9646, Fax: (212) 963-4116, http://unstats.un.org; *Statistical Yearbook.*

BERMUDA - AGRICULTURE

Economist Intelligence Unit, 111 West 57th Street, New York, NY 10019, (212) 554-0600, Fax: (212) 586-1181, www.eiu.com; *Bermuda Country Report.*

Euromonitor International, Inc., 224 S. Michigan Avenue, Suite 1500, Chicago, IL 60604, (312) 922-1115, Fax: (312) 922-1157, www.euromonitor.com; *World Marketing Data and Statistics.*

M.E. Sharpe, 80 Business Park Drive, Armonk, NY 10504, (800) 541-6563, Fax: (914) 273-2106, www.mesharpe.com; *The Illustrated Book of World Rankings.*

Palgrave Macmillan Ltd., Houndmills, Basingstoke, Hampshire, RG21 6XS, England, (Telephone in U.S. (888) 330-8477), (Fax in U.S. (800) 672-2054), www.palgrave.com; *The Statesman's Yearbook 2008.*

Taylor and Francis Group, An Informa Business, 2 Park Square, Milton Park, Abingdon, Oxford OX14 4RN, United Kingdom, (Dial from U.S. (212) 216-7800), (Fax from U.S. (212) 564-7854), www.tandf.co.uk; *The Europa World Year Book.*

United Nations Conference on Trade and Development (UNCTAD), DC2-1120, United Nations, New York, NY 10017, (212) 963-0027, www.unctad.org; *UNCTAD Commodity Yearbook.*

United Nations Food and Agricultural Organization (FAO), Viale delle Terme di Caracalla, 00100 Rome, Italy, (Dial from U.S. (202) 653-2400), (Fax from U.S. (202) 653 5760), www.fao.org; AQUASTAT; *FAO Production Yearbook 2002; FAO Trade Yearbook;* and *The State of Food and Agriculture (SOFA) 2006.*

United Nations Statistics Division, New York, NY 10017, (800) 253-9646, Fax: (212) 963-4116, http://unstats.un.org; *Statistical Yearbook.*

BERMUDA - AIRLINES

M.E. Sharpe, 80 Business Park Drive, Armonk, NY 10504, (800) 541-6563, Fax: (914) 273-2106, www.mesharpe.com; *The Illustrated Book of World Rankings.*

Palgrave Macmillan Ltd., Houndmills, Basingstoke, Hampshire, RG21 6XS, England, (Telephone in U.S. (888) 330-8477), (Fax in U.S. (800) 672-2054), www.palgrave.com; *The Statesman's Yearbook 2008.*

Taylor and Francis Group, An Informa Business, 2 Park Square, Milton Park, Abingdon, Oxford OX14 4RN, United Kingdom, (Dial from U.S. (212) 216-7800), (Fax from U.S. (212) 564-7854), www.tandf.co.uk; *The Europa World Year Book.*

BERMUDA - AIRPORTS

Central Intelligence Agency, Office of Public Affairs, Washington, DC 20505, (703) 482-0623, Fax: (703) 482-1739, www.cia.gov; *The World Factbook.*

BERMUDA - ALUMINUM PRODUCTION

See BERMUDA - MINERAL INDUSTRIES

BERMUDA - ARMED FORCES

Central Intelligence Agency, Office of Public Affairs, Washington, DC 20505, (703) 482-0623, Fax: (703) 482-1739, www.cia.gov; *The World Factbook.*

Euromonitor International, Inc., 224 S. Michigan Avenue, Suite 1500, Chicago, IL 60604, (312) 922-1115, Fax: (312) 922-1157, www.euromonitor.com; *World Marketing Data and Statistics.*

Palgrave Macmillan Ltd., Houndmills, Basingstoke, Hampshire, RG21 6XS, England, (Telephone in U.S. (888) 330-8477), (Fax in U.S. (800) 672-2054), www.palgrave.com; *The Statesman's Yearbook 2008.*

BERMUDA - BALANCE OF PAYMENTS

Taylor and Francis Group, An Informa Business, 2 Park Square, Milton Park, Abingdon, Oxford OX14 4RN, United Kingdom, (Dial from U.S. (212) 216-7800), (Fax from U.S. (212) 564-7854), www.tandf.co.uk; *The Europa World Year Book.*

BERMUDA - BANKS AND BANKING

Euromonitor International, Inc., 224 S. Michigan Avenue, Suite 1500, Chicago, IL 60604, (312) 922-1115, Fax: (312) 922-1157, www.euromonitor.com; *World Marketing Data and Statistics.*

M.E. Sharpe, 80 Business Park Drive, Armonk, NY 10504, (800) 541-6563, Fax: (914) 273-2106, www.mesharpe.com; *The Illustrated Book of World Rankings.*

Palgrave Macmillan Ltd., Houndmills, Basingstoke, Hampshire, RG21 6XS, England, (Telephone in U.S. (888) 330-8477), (Fax in U.S. (800) 672-2054), www.palgrave.com; *The Statesman's Yearbook 2008.*

BERMUDA - BARLEY PRODUCTION

See BERMUDA - CROPS

BERMUDA - BEVERAGE INDUSTRY

M.E. Sharpe, 80 Business Park Drive, Armonk, NY 10504, (800) 541-6563, Fax: (914) 273-2106, www.mesharpe.com; *The Illustrated Book of World Rankings.*

BERMUDA - BROADCASTING

Central Intelligence Agency, Office of Public Affairs, Washington, DC 20505, (703) 482-0623, Fax: (703) 482-1739, www.cia.gov; *The World Factbook.*

Euromonitor International, Inc., 224 S. Michigan Avenue, Suite 1500, Chicago, IL 60604, (312) 922-1115, Fax: (312) 922-1157, www.euromonitor.com; *World Marketing Data and Statistics.*

M.E. Sharpe, 80 Business Park Drive, Armonk, NY 10504, (800) 541-6563, Fax: (914) 273-2106, www.mesharpe.com; *The Illustrated Book of World Rankings.*

Palgrave Macmillan Ltd., Houndmills, Basingstoke, Hampshire, RG21 6XS, England, (Telephone in U.S. (888) 330-8477), (Fax in U.S. (800) 672-2054), www.palgrave.com; *The Statesman's Yearbook 2008.*

WRTH Publications Limited, PO Box 290, Oxford OX2 7FT, UK, www.wrth.com; *World Radio TV Handbook 2007.*

BERMUDA - BUDGET

Central Intelligence Agency, Office of Public Affairs, Washington, DC 20505, (703) 482-0623, Fax: (703) 482-1739, www.cia.gov; *The World Factbook.*

BERMUDA - CATTLE

See BERMUDA - LIVESTOCK

BERMUDA - CHILDBIRTH - STATISTICS

Central Intelligence Agency, Office of Public Affairs, Washington, DC 20505, (703) 482-0623, Fax: (703) 482-1739, www.cia.gov; *The World Factbook.*

Euromonitor International, Inc., 224 S. Michigan Avenue, Suite 1500, Chicago, IL 60604, (312) 922-1115, Fax: (312) 922-1157, www.euromonitor.com; *International Marketing Data and Statistics 2008* and *The World Economic Factbook 2008.*

M.E. Sharpe, 80 Business Park Drive, Armonk, NY 10504, (800) 541-6563, Fax: (914) 273-2106, www.mesharpe.com; *The Illustrated Book of World Rankings.*

Palgrave Macmillan Ltd., Houndmills, Basingstoke, Hampshire, RG21 6XS, England, (Telephone in U.S. (888) 330-8477), (Fax in U.S. (800) 672-2054), www.palgrave.com; *The Statesman's Yearbook 2008.*

Taylor and Francis Group, An Informa Business, 2 Park Square, Milton Park, Abingdon, Oxford OX14 4RN, United Kingdom, (Dial from U.S. (212) 216-7800), (Fax from U.S. (212) 564-7854), www.tandf.co.uk; *The Europa World Year Book.*

United Nations Statistics Division, New York, NY 10017, (800) 253-9646, Fax: (212) 963-4116, http://unstats.un.org; *Demographic Yearbook* and *Statistical Yearbook.*

World Health Organization (WHO), Avenue Appia 20, 1211 Geneve 27, Switzerland, (Telephone in U.S. (212) 331-9081), www.who.int; *World Health Report 2006.*

BERMUDA - CLIMATE

M.E. Sharpe, 80 Business Park Drive, Armonk, NY 10504, (800) 541-6563, Fax: (914) 273-2106, www.mesharpe.com; *The Illustrated Book of World Rankings.*

Palgrave Macmillan Ltd., Houndmills, Basingstoke, Hampshire, RG21 6XS, England, (Telephone in U.S. (888) 330-8477), (Fax in U.S. (800) 672-2054), www.palgrave.com; *The Statesman's Yearbook 2008.*

BERMUDA - COAL PRODUCTION

See BERMUDA - MINERAL INDUSTRIES

BERMUDA - COFFEE

See BERMUDA - CROPS

BERMUDA - COMMERCE

Palgrave Macmillan Ltd., Houndmills, Basingstoke, Hampshire, RG21 6XS, England, (Telephone in U.S. (888) 330-8477), (Fax in U.S. (800) 672-2054), www.palgrave.com; *The Statesman's Yearbook 2008.*

BERMUDA - COMMODITY EXCHANGES

Commodity Research Bureau, 330 South Wells Street, Suite 612, Chicago, IL 60606-7110, (800) 621-5271, Fax: (312) 939-4135, www.crbtrader.com; *2006 CRB Commodity Yearbook and CD.*

International Monetary Fund (IMF), 700 Nineteenth Street, NW, Washington, DC 20431, (202) 623-7000, Fax: (202) 623-4661, www.imf.org; *IMF Primary Commodity Prices.*

United Nations Food and Agricultural Organization (FAO), Viale delle Terme di Caracalla, 00100 Rome, Italy, (Dial from U.S. (202) 653-2400), (Fax from U.S. (202) 653 5760), www.fao.org; *The State of Food and Agriculture (SOFA) 2006.*

BERMUDA - CONSTRUCTION INDUSTRY

M.E. Sharpe, 80 Business Park Drive, Armonk, NY 10504, (800) 541-6563, Fax: (914) 273-2106, www.mesharpe.com; *The Illustrated Book of World Rankings.*

United Nations Statistics Division, New York, NY 10017, (800) 253-9646, Fax: (212) 963-4116, http://unstats.un.org; *Statistical Yearbook.*

BERMUDA - CONSUMER PRICE INDEXES

Taylor and Francis Group, An Informa Business, 2 Park Square, Milton Park, Abingdon, Oxford OX14 4RN, United Kingdom, (Dial from U.S. (212) 216-7800), (Fax from U.S. (212) 564-7854), www.tandf.co.uk; *The Europa World Year Book.*

United Nations Statistics Division, New York, NY 10017, (800) 253-9646, Fax: (212) 963-4116, http://unstats.un.org; *Statistical Yearbook.*

BERMUDA - COPPER INDUSTRY AND TRADE

See BERMUDA - MINERAL INDUSTRIES

BERMUDA - CORN INDUSTRY

See BERMUDA - CROPS

BERMUDA - COTTON

See BERMUDA - CROPS

BERMUDA - CRIME

Yale University Press, PO Box 209040, New Haven, CT 06520-9040, (203) 432-0960, Fax: (203) 432-0948, http://yalepress.yale.edu/yupbooks; *Violence and Crime in Cross-National Perspective.*

BERMUDA - CROPS

M.E. Sharpe, 80 Business Park Drive, Armonk, NY 10504, (800) 541-6563, Fax: (914) 273-2106, www.mesharpe.com; *The Illustrated Book of World Rankings.*

Palgrave Macmillan Ltd., Houndmills, Basingstoke, Hampshire, RG21 6XS, England, (Telephone in U.S. (888) 330-8477), (Fax in U.S. (800) 672-2054), www.palgrave.com; *The Statesman's Yearbook 2008.*

Taylor and Francis Group, An Informa Business, 2 Park Square, Milton Park, Abingdon, Oxford OX14 4RN, United Kingdom, (Dial from U.S. (212) 216-7800), (Fax from U.S. (212) 564-7854), www.tandf.co.uk; *The Europa World Year Book.*

United Nations Conference on Trade and Development (UNCTAD), DC2-1120, United Nations, New York, NY 10017, (212) 963-0027, www.unctad.org; *UNCTAD Commodity Yearbook.*

United Nations Food and Agricultural Organization (FAO), Viale delle Terme di Caracalla, 00100 Rome, Italy, (Dial from U.S. (202) 653-2400), (Fax from U.S. (202) 653 5760), www.fao.org; *The State of Food and Agriculture (SOFA) 2006.*

BERMUDA - CUSTOMS ADMINISTRATION

Palgrave Macmillan Ltd., Houndmills, Basingstoke, Hampshire, RG21 6XS, England, (Telephone in U.S. (888) 330-8477), (Fax in U.S. (800) 672-2054), www.palgrave.com; *The Statesman's Yearbook 2008.*

BERMUDA - DAIRY PROCESSING

M.E. Sharpe, 80 Business Park Drive, Armonk, NY 10504, (800) 541-6563, Fax: (914) 273-2106, www.mesharpe.com; *The Illustrated Book of World Rankings.*

Taylor and Francis Group, An Informa Business, 2 Park Square, Milton Park, Abingdon, Oxford OX14 4RN, United Kingdom, (Dial from U.S. (212) 216-7800), (Fax from U.S. (212) 564-7854), www.tandf.co.uk; *The Europa World Year Book.*

United Nations Food and Agricultural Organization (FAO), Viale delle Terme di Caracalla, 00100 Rome, Italy, (Dial from U.S. (202) 653-2400), (Fax from U.S. (202) 653 5760), www.fao.org; *The State of Food and Agriculture (SOFA) 2006.*

BERMUDA - DEATH RATES

See BERMUDA - MORTALITY

BERMUDA - DEBTS, EXTERNAL

Palgrave Macmillan Ltd., Houndmills, Basingstoke, Hampshire, RG21 6XS, England, (Telephone in U.S. (888) 330-8477), (Fax in U.S. (800) 672-2054), www.palgrave.com; *The Statesman's Yearbook 2008.*

The World Bank, 1818 H Street, NW, Washington, DC 20433, (202) 473-1000, Fax: (202) 477-6391, www.worldbank.org; *Global Development Finance 2007.*

BERMUDA - DEMOGRAPHY

Euromonitor International, Inc., 224 S. Michigan Avenue, Suite 1500, Chicago, IL 60604, (312) 922-1115, Fax: (312) 922-1157, www.euromonitor.com; *International Marketing Data and Statistics 2008; The World Economic Factbook 2008;* and *World Marketing Data and Statistics.*

M.E. Sharpe, 80 Business Park Drive, Armonk, NY 10504, (800) 541-6563, Fax: (914) 273-2106, www.mesharpe.com; *The Illustrated Book of World Rankings.*

BERMUDA - DIAMONDS

See BERMUDA - MINERAL INDUSTRIES

BERMUDA - DISPOSABLE INCOME

M.E. Sharpe, 80 Business Park Drive, Armonk, NY 10504, (800) 541-6563, Fax: (914) 273-2106, www.mesharpe.com; *The Illustrated Book of World Rankings.*

United Nations Statistics Division, New York, NY 10017, (800) 253-9646, Fax: (212) 963-4116, http://unstats.un.org; *National Accounts Statistics: Compendium of Income Distribution Statistics.*

BERMUDA - DIVORCE

M.E. Sharpe, 80 Business Park Drive, Armonk, NY 10504, (800) 541-6563, Fax: (914) 273-2106, www.mesharpe.com; *The Illustrated Book of World Rankings.*

United Nations Statistics Division, New York, NY 10017, (800) 253-9646, Fax: (212) 963-4116, http://unstats.un.org; *Demographic Yearbook* and *Statistical Yearbook.*

BERMUDA - ECONOMIC ASSISTANCE

United Nations Statistics Division, New York, NY 10017, (800) 253-9646, Fax: (212) 963-4116, http://unstats.un.org; *Statistical Yearbook.*

BERMUDA - ECONOMIC CONDITIONS

Center for International Business Education Research (CIBER), Columbia Business School and School of International and Public Affairs, Uris Hall, Room 212, 3022 Broadway, New York, NY 10027-

6902, Mr. Joshua Safier, (212) 854-4750, Fax: (212) 222-9821, www.columbia.edu/cu/ciber/; Datastream International.

Central Intelligence Agency, Office of Public Affairs, Washington, DC 20505, (703) 482-0623, Fax: (703) 482-1739, www.cia.gov; *The World Factbook.*

Department of Statistics, Bermuda Government, PO Box HM 3015, Hamilton HM MX, Bermuda, (Dial from U.S. (441) 297-7761), (Fax from U.S. (441) 295-8390), www.gov.bm; *2006 Economic Activity Survey Press Release* and *Labour Market Indicators 2006.*

DSI Data Service Information, Xantener Strasse 51a, D-47495 Rheinberg, Germany, www.dsidata.com; *Campus Solution.*

Dun and Bradstreet (DB) Corporation, 103 JFK Parkway, Short Hills, NJ 07078, (973) 921-5500, www.dnb.com; *Country Report.*

Economist Intelligence Unit, 111 West 57th Street, New York, NY 10019, (212) 554-0600, Fax: (212) 586-1181, www.eiu.com; *Bermuda Country Report.*

Euromonitor International, Inc., 224 S. Michigan Avenue, Suite 1500, Chicago, IL 60604, (312) 922-1115, Fax: (312) 922-1157, www.euromonitor.com; *The World Economic Factbook 2008* and *World Marketing Data and Statistics.*

International Monetary Fund (IMF), 700 Nineteenth Street, NW, Washington, DC 20431, (202) 623-7000, Fax: (202) 623-4661, www.imf.org; *World Economic Outlook Reports.*

M.E. Sharpe, 80 Business Park Drive, Armonk, NY 10504, (800) 541-6563, Fax: (914) 273-2106, www.mesharpe.com; *The Illustrated Book of World Rankings.*

Palgrave Macmillan Ltd., Houndmills, Basingstoke, Hampshire, RG21 6XS, England, (Telephone in U.S. (888) 330-8477), (Fax in U.S. (800) 672-2054), www.palgrave.com; *The Statesman's Yearbook 2008.*

Taylor and Francis Group, An Informa Business, 2 Park Square, Milton Park, Abingdon, Oxford OX14 4RN, United Kingdom, (Dial from U.S. (212) 216-7800), (Fax from U.S. (212) 564-7854), www.tandf.co.uk; *The Europa World Year Book.*

United Nations Statistics Division, New York, NY 10017, (800) 253-9646, Fax: (212) 963-4116, http://unstats.un.org; *World Statistics Pocketbook.*

The World Bank, 1818 H Street, NW, Washington, DC 20433, (202) 473-1000, Fax: (202) 477-6391, www.worldbank.org; *Global Economic Monitor (GEM); Global Economic Prospects 2008;* and *The World Bank Atlas 2003-2004.*

BERMUDA - EDUCATION

Euromonitor International, Inc., 224 S. Michigan Avenue, Suite 1500, Chicago, IL 60604, (312) 922-1115, Fax: (312) 922-1157, www.euromonitor.com; *International Marketing Data and Statistics 2008* and *World Marketing Data and Statistics.*

M.E. Sharpe, 80 Business Park Drive, Armonk, NY 10504, (800) 541-6563, Fax: (914) 273-2106, www.mesharpe.com; *The Illustrated Book of World Rankings.*

Palgrave Macmillan Ltd., Houndmills, Basingstoke, Hampshire, RG21 6XS, England, (Telephone in U.S. (888) 330-8477), (Fax in U.S. (800) 672-2054), www.palgrave.com; *The Statesman's Yearbook 2008.*

Taylor and Francis Group, An Informa Business, 2 Park Square, Milton Park, Abingdon, Oxford OX14 4RN, United Kingdom, (Dial from U.S. (212) 216-7800), (Fax from U.S. (212) 564-7854), www.tandf.co.uk; *The Europa World Year Book.*

UNESCO Institute for Statistics, C.P. 6128 Succursale Centre-Ville, Montreal, Quebec, H3C 3J7 Canada, (Dial from U.S. (514) 343-6880), (Fax from U.S. (514) 343 6882), www.uis.unesco.org; *Statistical Tables.*

BERMUDA - ELECTRICITY

M.E. Sharpe, 80 Business Park Drive, Armonk, NY 10504, (800) 541-6563, Fax: (914) 273-2106, www.mesharpe.com; *The Illustrated Book of World Rankings.*

Palgrave Macmillan Ltd., Houndmills, Basingstoke, Hampshire, RG21 6XS, England, (Telephone in U.S. (888) 330-8477), (Fax in U.S. (800) 672-2054), www.palgrave.com; *The Statesman's Yearbook 2008.*

United Nations Statistics Division, New York, NY 10017, (800) 253-9646, Fax: (212) 963-4116, http://unstats.un.org; *Statistical Yearbook.*

BERMUDA - EMPLOYMENT

Euromonitor International, Inc., 224 S. Michigan Avenue, Suite 1500, Chicago, IL 60604, (312) 922-1115, Fax: (312) 922-1157, www.euromonitor.com; *International Marketing Data and Statistics 2008.*

International Labour Office, I.L.O. Publications, 4 route des Morillons, CH-1211 Geneva 22, Switzerland, (Telephone in U.S. (202) 653-7652), (Fax in U.S. (202) 653-7687), www.ilo.org; *Yearbook of Labour Statistics 2006.*

M.E. Sharpe, 80 Business Park Drive, Armonk, NY 10504, (800) 541-6563, Fax: (914) 273-2106, www.mesharpe.com; *The Illustrated Book of World Rankings.*

BERMUDA - ENVIRONMENTAL CONDITIONS

DSI Data Service Information, Xantener Strasse 51a, D-47495 Rheinberg, Germany, www.dsidata.com; *Campus Solution* and *DSI's Global Environmental Database.*

Economist Intelligence Unit, 111 West 57th Street, New York, NY 10019, (212) 554-0600, Fax: (212) 586-1181, www.eiu.com; *Bermuda Country Report.*

United Nations Statistics Division, New York, NY 10017, (800) 253-9646, Fax: (212) 963-4116, http://unstats.un.org; *World Statistics Pocketbook.*

BERMUDA - EXPORTS

Central Intelligence Agency, Office of Public Affairs, Washington, DC 20505, (703) 482-0623, Fax: (703) 482-1739, www.cia.gov; *The World Factbook.*

Economist Intelligence Unit, 111 West 57th Street, New York, NY 10019, (212) 554-0600, Fax: (212) 586-1181, www.eiu.com; *Bermuda Country Report.*

Euromonitor International, Inc., 224 S. Michigan Avenue, Suite 1500, Chicago, IL 60604, (312) 922-1115, Fax: (312) 922-1157, www.euromonitor.com; *International Marketing Data and Statistics 2008* and *The World Economic Factbook 2008.*

International Monetary Fund (IMF), 700 Nineteenth Street, NW, Washington, DC 20431, (202) 623-7000, Fax: (202) 623-4661, www.imf.org; *Direction of Trade Statistics Yearbook 2007.*

Palgrave Macmillan Ltd., Houndmills, Basingstoke, Hampshire, RG21 6XS, England, (Telephone in U.S. (888) 330-8477), (Fax in U.S. (800) 672-2054), www.palgrave.com; *The Statesman's Yearbook 2008.*

Taylor and Francis Group, An Informa Business, 2 Park Square, Milton Park, Abingdon, Oxford OX14 4RN, United Kingdom, (Dial from U.S. (212) 216-7800), (Fax from U.S. (212) 564-7854), www.tandf.co.uk; *The Europa World Year Book.*

United Nations Food and Agricultural Organization (FAO), Viale delle Terme di Caracalla, 00100 Rome, Italy, (Dial from U.S. (202) 653-2400), (Fax from U.S. (202) 653 5760), www.fao.org; *The State of Food and Agriculture (SOFA) 2006.*

BERMUDA - FERTILITY, HUMAN

Central Intelligence Agency, Office of Public Affairs, Washington, DC 20505, (703) 482-0623, Fax: (703) 482-1739, www.cia.gov; *The World Factbook.*

M.E. Sharpe, 80 Business Park Drive, Armonk, NY 10504, (800) 541-6563, Fax: (914) 273-2106, www.mesharpe.com; *The Illustrated Book of World Rankings.*

The World Bank, 1818 H Street, NW, Washington, DC 20433, (202) 473-1000, Fax: (202) 477-6391, www.worldbank.org; *The World Bank Atlas 2003-2004.*

BERMUDA - FERTILIZER INDUSTRY

Organisation for Economic Cooperation and Development (OECD), 2 rue Andre Pascal, F-75775 Paris Cedex 16, France, (Telephone in U.S. (202) 785-6323), (Fax in U.S. (202) 785-0350), www.oecd.org; *Indicators of Industrial Activity.*

United Nations Food and Agricultural Organization (FAO), Viale delle Terme di Caracalla, 00100 Rome, Italy, (Dial from U.S. (202) 653-2400), (Fax from U.S. (202) 653 5760), www.fao.org; *The State of Food and Agriculture (SOFA) 2006.*

BERMUDA - FETAL MORTALITY

See BERMUDA - MORTALITY

BERMUDA - FINANCE, PUBLIC

Bernan Essential Government Publications, 4611-F Assembly Drive, Lanham MD, 20706-4391, (301) 459-2255, Fax: (800) 865-3450, www.bernan.com; *National Accounts Statistics.*

Economist Intelligence Unit, 111 West 57th Street, New York, NY 10019, (212) 554-0600, Fax: (212) 586-1181, www.eiu.com; *Bermuda Country Report.*

International Monetary Fund (IMF), 700 Nineteenth Street, NW, Washington, DC 20431, (202) 623-7000, Fax: (202) 623-4661, www.imf.org; *International Financial Statistics* and *International Financial Statistics Online Service.*

M.E. Sharpe, 80 Business Park Drive, Armonk, NY 10504, (800) 541-6563, Fax: (914) 273-2106, www.mesharpe.com; *The Illustrated Book of World Rankings.*

Palgrave Macmillan Ltd., Houndmills, Basingstoke, Hampshire, RG21 6XS, England, (Telephone in U.S. (888) 330-8477), (Fax in U.S. (800) 672-2054), www.palgrave.com; *The Statesman's Yearbook 2008.*

Taylor and Francis Group, An Informa Business, 2 Park Square, Milton Park, Abingdon, Oxford OX14 4RN, United Kingdom, (Dial from U.S. (212) 216-7800), (Fax from U.S. (212) 564-7854), www.tandf.co.uk; *The Europa World Year Book.*

BERMUDA - FISHERIES

M.E. Sharpe, 80 Business Park Drive, Armonk, NY 10504, (800) 541-6563, Fax: (914) 273-2106, www.mesharpe.com; *The Illustrated Book of World Rankings.*

Palgrave Macmillan Ltd., Houndmills, Basingstoke, Hampshire, RG21 6XS, England, (Telephone in U.S. (888) 330-8477), (Fax in U.S. (800) 672-2054), www.palgrave.com; *The Statesman's Yearbook 2008.*

Taylor and Francis Group, An Informa Business, 2 Park Square, Milton Park, Abingdon, Oxford OX14 4RN, United Kingdom, (Dial from U.S. (212) 216-7800), (Fax from U.S. (212) 564-7854), www.tandf.co.uk; *The Europa World Year Book.*

United Nations Conference on Trade and Development (UNCTAD), DC2-1120, United Nations, New York, NY 10017, (212) 963-0027, www.unctad.org; *UNCTAD Commodity Yearbook.*

United Nations Food and Agricultural Organization (FAO), Viale delle Terme di Caracalla, 00100 Rome, Italy, (Dial from U.S. (202) 653-2400), (Fax from U.S. (202) 653 5760), www.fao.org; *FAO Yearbook of Fishery Statistics;* Fishery Databases; FISHSTAT Database. Subjects covered include: Aquaculture production, capture production, fishery commodities; and *The State of Food and Agriculture (SOFA) 2006.*

United Nations Statistics Division, New York, NY 10017, (800) 253-9646, Fax: (212) 963-4116, http://unstats.un.org; *Statistical Yearbook.*

BERMUDA - FOOD

United Nations Conference on Trade and Development (UNCTAD), DC2-1120, United Nations, New

York, NY 10017, (212) 963-0027, www.unctad.org; *UNCTAD Commodity Yearbook.*

United Nations Food and Agricultural Organization (FAO), Viale delle Terme di Caracalla, 00100 Rome, Italy, (Dial from U.S. (202) 653-2400), (Fax from U.S. (202) 653 5760), www.fao.org; *FAO Production Yearbook 2002* and *The State of Food and Agriculture (SOFA) 2006.*

BERMUDA - FOREIGN EXCHANGE RATES

Central Intelligence Agency, Office of Public Affairs, Washington, DC 20505, (703) 482-0623, Fax: (703) 482-1739, www.cia.gov; *The World Factbook.*

Euromonitor International, Inc., 224 S. Michigan Avenue, Suite 1500, Chicago, IL 60604, (312) 922-1115, Fax: (312) 922-1157, www.euromonitor.com; *International Marketing Data and Statistics 2008* and *The World Economic Factbook 2008.*

Taylor and Francis Group, An Informa Business, 2 Park Square, Milton Park, Abingdon, Oxford OX14 4RN, United Kingdom, (Dial from U.S. (212) 216-7800), (Fax from U.S. (212) 564-7854), www.tandf.co.uk; *The Europa World Year Book.*

United Nations Statistics Division, New York, NY 10017, (800) 253-9646, Fax: (212) 963-4116, http://unstats.un.org; *World Statistics Pocketbook.*

BERMUDA - FORESTS AND FORESTRY

M.E. Sharpe, 80 Business Park Drive, Armonk, NY 10504, (800) 541-6563, Fax: (914) 273-2106, www.mesharpe.com; *The Illustrated Book of World Rankings.*

UNESCO Institute for Statistics, C.P. 6128 Succursale Centre-Ville, Montreal, Quebec, H3C 3J7 Canada, (Dial from U.S. (514) 343-6880), (Fax from U.S. (514) 343 6882), www.uis.unesco.org; *Statistical Tables.*

United Nations Conference on Trade and Development (UNCTAD), DC2-1120, United Nations, New York, NY 10017, (212) 963-0027, www.unctad.org; *UNCTAD Commodity Yearbook.*

United Nations Food and Agricultural Organization (FAO), Viale delle Terme di Caracalla, 00100 Rome, Italy, (Dial from U.S. (202) 653-2400), (Fax from U.S. (202) 653 5760), www.fao.org; *The State of Food and Agriculture (SOFA) 2006.*

BERMUDA - GAS PRODUCTION

See BERMUDA - MINERAL INDUSTRIES

BERMUDA - GEOGRAPHIC INFORMATION SYSTEMS

M.E. Sharpe, 80 Business Park Drive, Armonk, NY 10504, (800) 541-6563, Fax: (914) 273-2106, www.mesharpe.com; *The Illustrated Book of World Rankings.*

BERMUDA - GOLD PRODUCTION

See BERMUDA - MINERAL INDUSTRIES

BERMUDA - GROSS DOMESTIC PRODUCT

Economist Intelligence Unit, 111 West 57th Street, New York, NY 10019, (212) 554-0600, Fax: (212) 586-1181, www.eiu.com; *Bermuda Country Report.*

Euromonitor International, Inc., 224 S. Michigan Avenue, Suite 1500, Chicago, IL 60604, (312) 922-1115, Fax: (312) 922-1157, www.euromonitor.com; *International Marketing Data and Statistics 2008* and *The World Economic Factbook 2008.*

M.E. Sharpe, 80 Business Park Drive, Armonk, NY 10504, (800) 541-6563, Fax: (914) 273-2106, www.mesharpe.com; *The Illustrated Book of World Rankings.*

Taylor and Francis Group, An Informa Business, 2 Park Square, Milton Park, Abingdon, Oxford OX14 4RN, United Kingdom, (Dial from U.S. (212) 216-7800), (Fax from U.S. (212) 564-7854), www.tandf.co.uk; *The Europa World Year Book.*

United Nations Statistics Division, New York, NY 10017, (800) 253-9646, Fax: (212) 963-4116, http://unstats.un.org; *National Accounts Statistics: Compendium of Income Distribution Statistics.*

BERMUDA - GROSS NATIONAL PRODUCT

M.E. Sharpe, 80 Business Park Drive, Armonk, NY 10504, (800) 541-6563, Fax: (914) 273-2106, www.mesharpe.com; *The Illustrated Book of World Rankings.*

Palgrave Macmillan Ltd., Houndmills, Basingstoke, Hampshire, RG21 6XS, England, (Telephone in U.S. (888) 330-8477), (Fax in U.S. (800) 672-2054), www.palgrave.com; *The Statesman's Yearbook 2008.*

The World Bank, 1818 H Street, NW, Washington, DC 20433, (202) 473-1000, Fax: (202) 477-6391, www.worldbank.org; *The World Bank Atlas 2003-2004.*

BERMUDA - HIDES AND SKINS INDUSTRY

United Nations Food and Agricultural Organization (FAO), Viale delle Terme di Caracalla, 00100 Rome, Italy, (Dial from U.S. (202) 653-2400), (Fax from U.S. (202) 653 5760), www.fao.org; *FAO Production Yearbook 2002.*

BERMUDA - HOUSING

Euromonitor International, Inc., 224 S. Michigan Avenue, Suite 1500, Chicago, IL 60604, (312) 922-1115, Fax: (312) 922-1157, www.euromonitor.com; *World Marketing Data and Statistics.*

M.E. Sharpe, 80 Business Park Drive, Armonk, NY 10504, (800) 541-6563, Fax: (914) 273-2106, www.mesharpe.com; *The Illustrated Book of World Rankings.*

BERMUDA - ILLITERATE PERSONS

Euromonitor International, Inc., 224 S. Michigan Avenue, Suite 1500, Chicago, IL 60604, (312) 922-1115, Fax: (312) 922-1157, www.euromonitor.com; *The World Economic Factbook 2008.*

UNESCO Institute for Statistics, C.P. 6128 Succursale Centre-Ville, Montreal, Quebec, H3C 3J7 Canada, (Dial from U.S. (514) 343-6880), (Fax from U.S. (514) 343 6882), www.uis.unesco.org; *Statistical Tables.*

BERMUDA - IMPORTS

Central Intelligence Agency, Office of Public Affairs, Washington, DC 20505, (703) 482-0623, Fax: (703) 482-1739, www.cia.gov; *The World Factbook.*

Economist Intelligence Unit, 111 West 57th Street, New York, NY 10019, (212) 554-0600, Fax: (212) 586-1181, www.eiu.com; *Bermuda Country Report.*

Euromonitor International, Inc., 224 S. Michigan Avenue, Suite 1500, Chicago, IL 60604, (312) 922-1115, Fax: (312) 922-1157, www.euromonitor.com; *International Marketing Data and Statistics 2008* and *The World Economic Factbook 2008.*

International Monetary Fund (IMF), 700 Nineteenth Street, NW, Washington, DC 20431, (202) 623-7000, Fax: (202) 623-4661, www.imf.org; *Direction of Trade Statistics Yearbook 2007.*

Palgrave Macmillan Ltd., Houndmills, Basingstoke, Hampshire, RG21 6XS, England, (Telephone in U.S. (888) 330-8477), (Fax in U.S. (800) 672-2054), www.palgrave.com; *The Statesman's Yearbook 2008.*

Taylor and Francis Group, An Informa Business, 2 Park Square, Milton Park, Abingdon, Oxford OX14 4RN, United Kingdom, (Dial from U.S. (212) 216-7800), (Fax from U.S. (212) 564-7854), www.tandf.co.uk; *The Europa World Year Book.*

United Nations Food and Agricultural Organization (FAO), Viale delle Terme di Caracalla, 00100 Rome, Italy, (Dial from U.S. (202) 653-2400), (Fax from U.S. (202) 653 5760), www.fao.org; *The State of Food and Agriculture (SOFA) 2006.*

BERMUDA - INDUSTRIAL PRODUCTIVITY

M.E. Sharpe, 80 Business Park Drive, Armonk, NY 10504, (800) 541-6563, Fax: (914) 273-2106, www.mesharpe.com; *The Illustrated Book of World Rankings.*

BERMUDA - INDUSTRIES

Central Intelligence Agency, Office of Public Affairs, Washington, DC 20505, (703) 482-0623, Fax: (703) 482-1739, www.cia.gov; *The World Factbook.*

Economist Intelligence Unit, 111 West 57th Street, New York, NY 10019, (212) 554-0600, Fax: (212) 586-1181, www.eiu.com; *Bermuda Country Report.*

Euromonitor International, Inc., 224 S. Michigan Avenue, Suite 1500, Chicago, IL 60604, (312) 922-1115, Fax: (312) 922-1157, www.euromonitor.com; *The World Economic Factbook 2008* and *World Marketing Data and Statistics.*

International Labour Office, I.L.O. Publications, 4 route des Morillons, CH-1211 Geneva 22, Switzerland, (Telephone in U.S. (202) 653-7652), (Fax in U.S. (202) 653-7687), www.ilo.org; *Yearbook of Labour Statistics 2006.*

M.E. Sharpe, 80 Business Park Drive, Armonk, NY 10504, (800) 541-6563, Fax: (914) 273-2106, www.mesharpe.com; *The Illustrated Book of World Rankings.*

Palgrave Macmillan Ltd., Houndmills, Basingstoke, Hampshire, RG21 6XS, England, (Telephone in U.S. (888) 330-8477), (Fax in U.S. (800) 672-2054), www.palgrave.com; *The Statesman's Yearbook 2008.*

Taylor and Francis Group, An Informa Business, 2 Park Square, Milton Park, Abingdon, Oxford OX14 4RN, United Kingdom, (Dial from U.S. (212) 216-7800), (Fax from U.S. (212) 564-7854), www.tandf.co.uk; *The Europa World Year Book.*

United Nations Industrial Development Organization (UNIDO), 1 United Nations Plaza, New York, NY 10017, (212) 963 6890, Fax: (212) 963-7904, http://unido.org; Industrial Statistics Database 2008 (INDSTAT) and *The International Yearbook of Industrial Statistics 2008.*

BERMUDA - INFANT AND MATERNAL MORTALITY

See BERMUDA - MORTALITY

BERMUDA - INTERNATIONAL TRADE

Economist Intelligence Unit, 111 West 57th Street, New York, NY 10019, (212) 554-0600, Fax: (212) 586-1181, www.eiu.com; *Bermuda Country Report.*

Euromonitor International, Inc., 224 S. Michigan Avenue, Suite 1500, Chicago, IL 60604, (312) 922-1115, Fax: (312) 922-1157, www.euromonitor.com; *The World Economic Factbook 2008* and *World Marketing Data and Statistics.*

M.E. Sharpe, 80 Business Park Drive, Armonk, NY 10504, (800) 541-6563, Fax: (914) 273-2106, www.mesharpe.com; *The Illustrated Book of World Rankings.*

Organisation for Economic Cooperation and Development (OECD), 2 rue Andre Pascal, F-75775 Paris Cedex 16, France, (Telephone in U.S. (202) 785-6323), (Fax in U.S. (202) 785-0350), www.oecd.org; *International Trade by Commodity Statistics (ITCS).*

Palgrave Macmillan Ltd., Houndmills, Basingstoke, Hampshire, RG21 6XS, England, (Telephone in U.S. (888) 330-8477), (Fax in U.S. (800) 672-2054), www.palgrave.com; *The Statesman's Yearbook 2008.*

Taylor and Francis Group, An Informa Business, 2 Park Square, Milton Park, Abingdon, Oxford OX14 4RN, United Kingdom, (Dial from U.S. (212) 216-7800), (Fax from U.S. (212) 564-7854), www.tandf.co.uk; *The Europa World Year Book.*

United Nations Conference on Trade and Development (UNCTAD), DC2-1120, United Nations, New York, NY 10017, (212) 963-0027, www.unctad.org; *UNCTAD Commodity Yearbook.*

United Nations Food and Agricultural Organization (FAO), Viale delle Terme di Caracalla, 00100 Rome,

Italy, (Dial from U.S. (202) 653-2400), (Fax from U.S. (202) 653 5760), www.fao.org; *FAO Trade Yearbook* and *The State of Food and Agriculture (SOFA) 2006.*

United Nations Statistics Division, New York, NY 10017, (800) 253-9646, Fax: (212) 963-4116, http://unstats.un.org; *International Trade Statistics Yearbook* and *Statistical Yearbook.*

World Trade Organization (WTO), Centre William Rappard, Rue de Lausanne 154, CH-1211 Geneva 21, Switzerland, www.wto.org; *International Trade Statistics 2006.*

BERMUDA - INTERNET USERS

International Telecommunication Union (ITU), Place des Nations, 1211 Geneva 20, Switzerland, www.itu.int; *World Telecommunication/ICT Indicators Database on CD-ROM; World Telecommunication/ICT Indicators Database Online;* and *Yearbook of Statistics - Telecommunication Services (Chronological Time Series 1997-2006).*

BERMUDA - IRON AND IRON ORE PRODUCTION

See BERMUDA - MINERAL INDUSTRIES

BERMUDA - LABOR

Central Intelligence Agency, Office of Public Affairs, Washington, DC 20505, (703) 482-0623, Fax: (703) 482-1739, www.cia.gov; *The World Factbook.*

Department of Statistics, Bermuda Government, PO Box HM 3015, Hamilton HM MX, Bermuda, (Dial from U.S. (441) 297-7761), (Fax from U.S. (441) 295-8390), www.gov.bm; *Labour Market Indicators 2006.*

Euromonitor International, Inc., 224 S. Michigan Avenue, Suite 1500, Chicago, IL 60604, (312) 922-1115, Fax: (312) 922-1157, www.euromonitor.com; *International Marketing Data and Statistics 2008* and *World Marketing Data and Statistics.*

International Labour Office, I.L.O. Publications, 4 route des Morillons, CH-1211 Geneva 22, Switzerland, (Telephone in U.S. (202) 653-7652), (Fax in U.S. (202) 653-7687), www.ilo.org; *Yearbook of Labour Statistics 2006.*

M.E. Sharpe, 80 Business Park Drive, Armonk, NY 10504, (800) 541-6563, Fax: (914) 273-2106, www.mesharpe.com; *The Illustrated Book of World Rankings.*

Palgrave Macmillan Ltd., Houndmills, Basingstoke, Hampshire, RG21 6XS, England, (Telephone in U.S. (888) 330-8477), (Fax in U.S. (800) 672-2054), www.palgrave.com; *The Statesman's Yearbook 2008.*

Taylor and Francis Group, An Informa Business, 2 Park Square, Milton Park, Abingdon, Oxford OX14 4RN, United Kingdom, (Dial from U.S. (212) 216-7800), (Fax from U.S. (212) 564-7854), www.tandf.co.uk; *The Europa World Year Book.*

United Nations Food and Agricultural Organization (FAO), Viale delle Terme di Caracalla, 00100 Rome, Italy, (Dial from U.S. (202) 653-2400), (Fax from U.S. (202) 653 5760), www.fao.org; *The State of Food and Agriculture (SOFA) 2006.*

The World Bank, 1818 H Street, NW, Washington, DC 20433, (202) 473-1000, Fax: (202) 477-6391, www.worldbank.org; *The World Bank Atlas 2003-2004.*

BERMUDA - LAND USE

Central Intelligence Agency, Office of Public Affairs, Washington, DC 20505, (703) 482-0623, Fax: (703) 482-1739, www.cia.gov; *The World Factbook.*

Euromonitor International, Inc., 224 S. Michigan Avenue, Suite 1500, Chicago, IL 60604, (312) 922-1115, Fax: (312) 922-1157, www.euromonitor.com; *International Marketing Data and Statistics 2008.*

United Nations Food and Agricultural Organization (FAO), Viale delle Terme di Caracalla, 00100 Rome, Italy, (Dial from U.S. (202) 653-2400), (Fax from U.S. (202) 653 5760), www.fao.org; *FAO Production Yearbook 2002.*

BERMUDA - LIBRARIES

M.E. Sharpe, 80 Business Park Drive, Armonk, NY 10504, (800) 541-6563, Fax: (914) 273-2106, www.mesharpe.com; *The Illustrated Book of World Rankings.*

UNESCO Institute for Statistics, C.P. 6128 Succursale Centre-Ville, Montreal, Quebec, H3C 3J7 Canada, (Dial from U.S. (514) 343-6880), (Fax from U.S. (514) 343 6882), www.uis.unesco.org; *Statistical Tables.*

BERMUDA - LIFE EXPECTANCY

Central Intelligence Agency, Office of Public Affairs, Washington, DC 20505, (703) 482-0623, Fax: (703) 482-1739, www.cia.gov; *The World Factbook.*

Euromonitor International, Inc., 224 S. Michigan Avenue, Suite 1500, Chicago, IL 60604, (312) 922-1115, Fax: (312) 922-1157, www.euromonitor.com; *The World Economic Factbook 2008.*

United Nations Statistics Division, New York, NY 10017, (800) 253-9646, Fax: (212) 963-4116, http://unstats.un.org; *World Statistics Pocketbook.*

The World Bank, 1818 H Street, NW, Washington, DC 20433, (202) 473-1000, Fax: (202) 477-6391, www.worldbank.org; *The World Bank Atlas 2003-2004.*

BERMUDA - LITERACY

Department of Statistics, Bermuda Government, PO Box HM 3015, Hamilton HM MX, Bermuda, (Dial from U.S. (441) 297-7761), (Fax from U.S. (441) 295-8390), www.gov.bm; *Literacy in Bermuda.*

Euromonitor International, Inc., 224 S. Michigan Avenue, Suite 1500, Chicago, IL 60604, (312) 922-1115, Fax: (312) 922-1157, www.euromonitor.com; *World Marketing Data and Statistics.*

BERMUDA - LIVESTOCK

M.E. Sharpe, 80 Business Park Drive, Armonk, NY 10504, (800) 541-6563, Fax: (914) 273-2106, www.mesharpe.com; *The Illustrated Book of World Rankings.*

Taylor and Francis Group, An Informa Business, 2 Park Square, Milton Park, Abingdon, Oxford OX14 4RN, United Kingdom, (Dial from U.S. (212) 216-7800), (Fax from U.S. (212) 564-7854), www.tandf.co.uk; *The Europa World Year Book.*

United Nations Conference on Trade and Development (UNCTAD), DC2-1120, United Nations, New York, NY 10017, (212) 963-0027, www.unctad.org; *UNCTAD Commodity Yearbook.*

United Nations Food and Agricultural Organization (FAO), Viale delle Terme di Caracalla, 00100 Rome, Italy, (Dial from U.S. (202) 653-2400), (Fax from U.S. (202) 653 5760), www.fao.org; *FAO Production Yearbook 2002* and *The State of Food and Agriculture (SOFA) 2006.*

United Nations Statistics Division, New York, NY 10017, (800) 253-9646, Fax: (212) 963-4116, http://unstats.un.org; *Statistical Yearbook.*

BERMUDA - MANUFACTURES

M.E. Sharpe, 80 Business Park Drive, Armonk, NY 10504, (800) 541-6563, Fax: (914) 273-2106, www.mesharpe.com; *The Illustrated Book of World Rankings.*

BERMUDA - MARRIAGE

M.E. Sharpe, 80 Business Park Drive, Armonk, NY 10504, (800) 541-6563, Fax: (914) 273-2106, www.mesharpe.com; *The Illustrated Book of World Rankings.*

Taylor and Francis Group, An Informa Business, 2 Park Square, Milton Park, Abingdon, Oxford OX14 4RN, United Kingdom, (Dial from U.S. (212) 216-7800), (Fax from U.S. (212) 564-7854), www.tandf.co.uk; *The Europa World Year Book.*

United Nations Statistics Division, New York, NY 10017, (800) 253-9646, Fax: (212) 963-4116, http://unstats.un.org; *Demographic Yearbook* and *Statistical Yearbook.*

BERMUDA - MEAT PRODUCTION

See BERMUDA - LIVESTOCK

BERMUDA - MILK PRODUCTION

See BERMUDA - DAIRY PROCESSING

BERMUDA - MINERAL INDUSTRIES

M.E. Sharpe, 80 Business Park Drive, Armonk, NY 10504, (800) 541-6563, Fax: (914) 273-2106, www.mesharpe.com; *The Illustrated Book of World Rankings.*

United Nations Conference on Trade and Development (UNCTAD), DC2-1120, United Nations, New York, NY 10017, (212) 963-0027, www.unctad.org; *UNCTAD Commodity Yearbook.*

BERMUDA - MONEY SUPPLY

Economist Intelligence Unit, 111 West 57th Street, New York, NY 10019, (212) 554-0600, Fax: (212) 586-1181, www.eiu.com; *Bermuda Country Report.*

BERMUDA - MORTALITY

Central Intelligence Agency, Office of Public Affairs, Washington, DC 20505, (703) 482-0623, Fax: (703) 482-1739, www.cia.gov; *The World Factbook.*

Euromonitor International, Inc., 224 S. Michigan Avenue, Suite 1500, Chicago, IL 60604, (312) 922-1115, Fax: (312) 922-1157, www.euromonitor.com; *International Marketing Data and Statistics 2008* and *The World Economic Factbook 2008.*

Palgrave Macmillan Ltd., Houndmills, Basingstoke, Hampshire, RG21 6XS, England, (Telephone in U.S. (888) 330-8477), (Fax in U.S. (800) 672-2054), www.palgrave.com; *The Statesman's Yearbook 2008.*

Taylor and Francis Group, An Informa Business, 2 Park Square, Milton Park, Abingdon, Oxford OX14 4RN, United Kingdom, (Dial from U.S. (212) 216-7800), (Fax from U.S. (212) 564-7854), www.tandf.co.uk; *The Europa World Year Book.*

United Nations Statistics Division, New York, NY 10017, (800) 253-9646, Fax: (212) 963-4116, http://unstats.un.org; *Demographic Yearbook; Statistical Yearbook;* and *World Statistics Pocketbook.*

The World Bank, 1818 H Street, NW, Washington, DC 20433, (202) 473-1000, Fax: (202) 477-6391, www.worldbank.org; *The World Bank Atlas 2003-2004.*

World Health Organization (WHO), Avenue Appia 20, 1211 Geneve 27, Switzerland, (Telephone in U.S. (212) 331-9081), www.who.int; The WHO Global Atlas of Infectious Diseases and *World Health Report 2006.*

BERMUDA - MOTION PICTURES

United Nations Statistics Division, New York, NY 10017, (800) 253-9646, Fax: (212) 963-4116, http://unstats.un.org; *Statistical Yearbook.*

BERMUDA - MOTOR VEHICLES

Taylor and Francis Group, An Informa Business, 2 Park Square, Milton Park, Abingdon, Oxford OX14 4RN, United Kingdom, (Dial from U.S. (212) 216-7800), (Fax from U.S. (212) 564-7854), www.tandf.co.uk; *The Europa World Year Book.*

United Nations Statistics Division, New York, NY 10017, (800) 253-9646, Fax: (212) 963-4116, http://unstats.un.org; *Statistical Yearbook.*

BERMUDA - MUSEUMS

M.E. Sharpe, 80 Business Park Drive, Armonk, NY 10504, (800) 541-6563, Fax: (914) 273-2106, www.mesharpe.com; *The Illustrated Book of World Rankings.*

UNESCO Institute for Statistics, C.P. 6128 Succursale Centre-Ville, Montreal, Quebec, H3C 3J7 Canada, (Dial from U.S. (514) 343-6880), (Fax from U.S. (514) 343 6882), www.uis.unesco.org; *Statistical Tables.*

BERMUDA - NATURAL GAS PRODUCTION

See BERMUDA - MINERAL INDUSTRIES

BERMUDA - NUTRITION

United Nations Food and Agricultural Organization (FAO), Viale delle Terme di Caracalla, 00100 Rome, Italy, (Dial from U.S. (202) 653-2400), (Fax from U.S. (202) 653 5760), www.fao.org; *The State of Food and Agriculture (SOFA) 2006.*

BERMUDA - OLDER PEOPLE

M.E. Sharpe, 80 Business Park Drive, Armonk, NY 10504, (800) 541-6563, Fax: (914) 273-2106, www.mesharpe.com; *The Illustrated Book of World Rankings.*

BERMUDA - PEANUT PRODUCTION

See BERMUDA - CROPS

BERMUDA - PESTICIDES

United Nations Food and Agricultural Organization (FAO), Viale delle Terme di Caracalla, 00100 Rome, Italy, (Dial from U.S. (202) 653-2400), (Fax from U.S. (202) 653 5760), www.fao.org; *The State of Food and Agriculture (SOFA) 2006.*

BERMUDA - PETROLEUM INDUSTRY AND TRADE

M.E. Sharpe, 80 Business Park Drive, Armonk, NY 10504, (800) 541-6563, Fax: (914) 273-2106, www.mesharpe.com; *The Illustrated Book of World Rankings.*

PennWell Corporation, 1421 South Sheridan Road, Tulsa, OK 74112, (918) 835-3161, www.pennwell.com; *International Petroleum Encyclopedia 2007.*

United Nations Conference on Trade and Development (UNCTAD), DC2-1120, United Nations, New York, NY 10017, (212) 963-0027, www.unctad.org; *UNCTAD Commodity Yearbook.*

United Nations Food and Agricultural Organization (FAO), Viale delle Terme di Caracalla, 00100 Rome, Italy, (Dial from U.S. (202) 653-2400), (Fax from U.S. (202) 653 5760), www.fao.org; *The State of Food and Agriculture (SOFA) 2006.*

BERMUDA - POLITICAL SCIENCE

Central Intelligence Agency, Office of Public Affairs, Washington, DC 20505, (703) 482-0623, Fax: (703) 482-1739, www.cia.gov; *The World Factbook.*

Palgrave Macmillan Ltd., Houndmills, Basingstoke, Hampshire, RG21 6XS, England, (Telephone in U.S. (888) 330-8477), (Fax in U.S. (800) 672-2054), www.palgrave.com; *The Statesman's Yearbook 2008.*

Taylor and Francis Group, An Informa Business, 2 Park Square, Milton Park, Abingdon, Oxford OX14 4RN, United Kingdom, (Dial from U.S. (212) 216-7800), (Fax from U.S. (212) 564-7854), www.tandf.co.uk; *The Europa World Year Book.*

United Nations Statistics Division, New York, NY 10017, (800) 253-9646, Fax: (212) 963-4116, http://unstats.un.org; *National Accounts Statistics: Compendium of Income Distribution Statistics.*

BERMUDA - POPULATION

Caribbean Epidemiology Centre (CAREC), 16-18 Jamaica Boulevard, Federation Park, PO Box 164, Port of Spain, Republic of Trinidad and Tobago, (Dial from U.S. (868) 622-4261), (Fax from U.S. (868) 622-2792), www.carec.org; *Population Data.*

Central Intelligence Agency, Office of Public Affairs, Washington, DC 20505, (703) 482-0623, Fax: (703) 482-1739, www.cia.gov; *The World Factbook.*

Department of Statistics, Bermuda Government, PO Box HM 3015, Hamilton HM MX, Bermuda, (Dial from U.S. (441) 297-7761), (Fax from U.S. (441) 295-8390), www.gov.bm; *Literacy in Bermuda* and *A Profile of Bermuda's Disabled Population.*

Economist Intelligence Unit, 111 West 57th Street, New York, NY 10019, (212) 554-0600, Fax: (212) 586-1181, www.eiu.com; *Bermuda Country Report.*

Euromonitor International, Inc., 224 S. Michigan Avenue, Suite 1500, Chicago, IL 60604, (312) 922-1115, Fax: (312) 922-1157, www.euromonitor.com; *International Marketing Data and Statistics 2008* and *The World Economic Factbook 2008.*

International Labour Office, I.L.O. Publications, 4 route des Morillons, CH-1211 Geneva 22, Switzerland, (Telephone in U.S. (202) 653-7652), (Fax in U.S. (202) 653-7687), www.ilo.org; *Yearbook of Labour Statistics 2006.*

M.E. Sharpe, 80 Business Park Drive, Armonk, NY 10504, (800) 541-6563, Fax: (914) 273-2106, www.mesharpe.com; *The Illustrated Book of World Rankings.*

Palgrave Macmillan Ltd., Houndmills, Basingstoke, Hampshire, RG21 6XS, England, (Telephone in U.S. (888) 330-8477), (Fax in U.S. (800) 672-2054), www.palgrave.com; *The Statesman's Yearbook 2008.*

Taylor and Francis Group, An Informa Business, 2 Park Square, Milton Park, Abingdon, Oxford OX14 4RN, United Kingdom, (Dial from U.S. (212) 216-7800), (Fax from U.S. (212) 564-7854), www.tandf.co.uk; *The Europa World Year Book.*

United Nations Food and Agricultural Organization (FAO), Viale delle Terme di Caracalla, 00100 Rome, Italy, (Dial from U.S. (202) 653-2400), (Fax from U.S. (202) 653 5760), www.fao.org; *FAO Production Yearbook 2002.*

United Nations Statistics Division, New York, NY 10017, (800) 253-9646, Fax: (212) 963-4116, http://unstats.un.org; *Demographic Yearbook; Statistical Yearbook;* and *World Statistics Pocketbook.*

The World Bank, 1818 H Street, NW, Washington, DC 20433, (202) 473-1000, Fax: (202) 477-6391, www.worldbank.org; *The World Bank Atlas 2003-2004.*

World Health Organization (WHO), Avenue Appia 20, 1211 Geneve 27, Switzerland, (Telephone in U.S. (212) 331-9081), www.who.int; *World Health Report 2006.*

BERMUDA - POPULATION DENSITY

Central Intelligence Agency, Office of Public Affairs, Washington, DC 20505, (703) 482-0623, Fax: (703) 482-1739, www.cia.gov; *The World Factbook.*

Euromonitor International, Inc., 224 S. Michigan Avenue, Suite 1500, Chicago, IL 60604, (312) 922-1115, Fax: (312) 922-1157, www.euromonitor.com; *The World Economic Factbook 2008.*

M.E. Sharpe, 80 Business Park Drive, Armonk, NY 10504, (800) 541-6563, Fax: (914) 273-2106, www.mesharpe.com; *The Illustrated Book of World Rankings.*

Palgrave Macmillan Ltd., Houndmills, Basingstoke, Hampshire, RG21 6XS, England, (Telephone in U.S. (888) 330-8477), (Fax in U.S. (800) 672-2054), www.palgrave.com; *The Statesman's Yearbook 2008.*

Taylor and Francis Group, An Informa Business, 2 Park Square, Milton Park, Abingdon, Oxford OX14 4RN, United Kingdom, (Dial from U.S. (212) 216-7800), (Fax from U.S. (212) 564-7854), www.tandf.co.uk; *The Europa World Year Book.*

United Nations Food and Agricultural Organization (FAO), Viale delle Terme di Caracalla, 00100 Rome, Italy, (Dial from U.S. (202) 653-2400), (Fax from U.S. (202) 653 5760), www.fao.org; *The State of Food and Agriculture (SOFA) 2006.*

United Nations Statistics Division, New York, NY 10017, (800) 253-9646, Fax: (212) 963-4116, http://unstats.un.org; *Statistical Yearbook.*

BERMUDA - POSTAL SERVICE

M.E. Sharpe, 80 Business Park Drive, Armonk, NY 10504, (800) 541-6563, Fax: (914) 273-2106, www.mesharpe.com; *The Illustrated Book of World Rankings.*

Palgrave Macmillan Ltd., Houndmills, Basingstoke, Hampshire, RG21 6XS, England, (Telephone in U.S. (888) 330-8477), (Fax in U.S. (800) 672-2054), www.palgrave.com; *The Statesman's Yearbook 2008.*

United Nations Statistics Division, New York, NY 10017, (800) 253-9646, Fax: (212) 963-4116, http://unstats.un.org; *Statistical Yearbook.*

BERMUDA - POWER RESOURCES

Euromonitor International, Inc., 224 S. Michigan Avenue, Suite 1500, Chicago, IL 60604, (312) 922-1115, Fax: (312) 922-1157, www.euromonitor.com; *International Marketing Data and Statistics 2008; The World Economic Factbook 2008;* and *World Marketing Data and Statistics.*

M.E. Sharpe, 80 Business Park Drive, Armonk, NY 10504, (800) 541-6563, Fax: (914) 273-2106, www.mesharpe.com; *The Illustrated Book of World Rankings.*

Palgrave Macmillan Ltd., Houndmills, Basingstoke, Hampshire, RG21 6XS, England, (Telephone in U.S. (888) 330-8477), (Fax in U.S. (800) 672-2054), www.palgrave.com; *The Statesman's Yearbook 2008.*

Platts, 2 Penn Plaza, 25th Floor, New York, NY 10121-2298, (212) 904-3070, www.platts.com; *Energy Economist.*

United Nations Food and Agricultural Organization (FAO), Viale delle Terme di Caracalla, 00100 Rome, Italy, (Dial from U.S. (202) 653-2400), (Fax from U.S. (202) 653 5760), www.fao.org; *The State of Food and Agriculture (SOFA) 2006.*

United Nations Statistics Division, New York, NY 10017, (800) 253-9646, Fax: (212) 963-4116, http://unstats.un.org; *Energy Statistics Yearbook 2003* and *World Statistics Pocketbook.*

The World Bank, 1818 H Street, NW, Washington, DC 20433, (202) 473-1000, Fax: (202) 477-6391, www.worldbank.org; *The World Bank Atlas 2003-2004.*

BERMUDA - PRICES

Euromonitor International, Inc., 224 S. Michigan Avenue, Suite 1500, Chicago, IL 60604, (312) 922-1115, Fax: (312) 922-1157, www.euromonitor.com; *World Marketing Data and Statistics.*

International Labour Office, I.L.O. Publications, 4 route des Morillons, CH-1211 Geneva 22, Switzerland, (Telephone in U.S. (202) 653-7652), (Fax in U.S. (202) 653-7687), www.ilo.org; *Yearbook of Labour Statistics 2006.*

M.E. Sharpe, 80 Business Park Drive, Armonk, NY 10504, (800) 541-6563, Fax: (914) 273-2106, www.mesharpe.com; *The Illustrated Book of World Rankings.*

United Nations Food and Agricultural Organization (FAO), Viale delle Terme di Caracalla, 00100 Rome, Italy, (Dial from U.S. (202) 653-2400), (Fax from U.S. (202) 653 5760), www.fao.org; *FAO Production Yearbook 2002* and *The State of Food and Agriculture (SOFA) 2006.*

BERMUDA - PROFESSIONS

United Nations Statistics Division, New York, NY 10017, (800) 253-9646, Fax: (212) 963-4116, http://unstats.un.org; *Statistical Yearbook.*

BERMUDA - PUBLIC HEALTH

Department of Statistics, Bermuda Government, PO Box HM 3015, Hamilton HM MX, Bermuda, (Dial from U.S. (441) 297-7761), (Fax from U.S. (441) 295-8390), www.gov.bm; *A Profile of Bermuda's Disabled Population.*

Euromonitor International, Inc., 224 S. Michigan Avenue, Suite 1500, Chicago, IL 60604, (312) 922-1115, Fax: (312) 922-1157, www.euromonitor.com; *World Marketing Data and Statistics.*

M.E. Sharpe, 80 Business Park Drive, Armonk, NY 10504, (800) 541-6563, Fax: (914) 273-2106, www.mesharpe.com; *The Illustrated Book of World Rankings.*

Palgrave Macmillan Ltd., Houndmills, Basingstoke, Hampshire, RG21 6XS, England, (Telephone in U.S. (888) 330-8477), (Fax in U.S. (800) 672-2054), www.palgrave.com; *The Statesman's Yearbook 2008.*

United Nations Statistics Division, New York, NY 10017, (800) 253-9646, Fax: (212) 963-4116, http://unstats.un.org; *Statistical Yearbook.*

World Health Organization (WHO), Avenue Appia 20, 1211 Geneve 27, Switzerland, (Telephone in

U.S. (212) 331-9081), www.who.int; The WHO Global Atlas of Infectious Diseases and *World Health Report 2006.*

BERMUDA - RADIO BROADCASTING

Palgrave Macmillan Ltd., Houndmills, Basingstoke, Hampshire, RG21 6XS, England, (Telephone in U.S. (888) 330-8477), (Fax in U.S. (800) 672-2054), www.palgrave.com; *The Statesman's Yearbook 2008.*

BERMUDA - RELIGION

Central Intelligence Agency, Office of Public Affairs, Washington, DC 20505, (703) 482-0623, Fax: (703) 482-1739, www.cia.gov; *The World Factbook.*

M.E. Sharpe, 80 Business Park Drive, Armonk, NY 10504, (800) 541-6563, Fax: (914) 273-2106, www.mesharpe.com; *The Illustrated Book of World Rankings.*

BERMUDA - RENT CHARGES

International Labour Office, I.L.O. Publications, 4 route des Morillons, CH-1211 Geneva 22, Switzerland, (Telephone in U.S. (202) 653-7652), (Fax in U.S. (202) 653-7687), www.ilo.org; *Yearbook of Labour Statistics 2006.*

BERMUDA - RETAIL TRADE

Euromonitor International, Inc., 224 S. Michigan Avenue, Suite 1500, Chicago, IL 60604, (312) 922-1115, Fax: (312) 922-1157, www.euromonitor.com; *World Marketing Data and Statistics.*

BERMUDA - RICE PRODUCTION

See BERMUDA - CROPS

BERMUDA - ROADS

Central Intelligence Agency, Office of Public Affairs, Washington, DC 20505, (703) 482-0623, Fax: (703) 482-1739, www.cia.gov; *The World Factbook.*

Palgrave Macmillan Ltd., Houndmills, Basingstoke, Hampshire, RG21 6XS, England, (Telephone in U.S. (888) 330-8477), (Fax in U.S. (800) 672-2054), www.palgrave.com; *The Statesman's Yearbook 2008.*

BERMUDA - RUBBER INDUSTRY AND TRADE

International Rubber Study Group (IRSG), 1st Floor, Heron House, 109/115 Wembley Hill Road, Wembley, Middlesex HA9 8DA, United Kingdom, www.rubberstudy.com; *Rubber Statistical Bulletin; Summary of World Rubber Statistics 2005; World Rubber Statistics Handbook (Volume 6, 1975-2001);* and *World Rubber Statistics Historic Handbook.*

M.E. Sharpe, 80 Business Park Drive, Armonk, NY 10504, (800) 541-6563, Fax: (914) 273-2106, www.mesharpe.com; *The Illustrated Book of World Rankings.*

BERMUDA - SHEEP

See BERMUDA - LIVESTOCK

BERMUDA - SHIPPING

Palgrave Macmillan Ltd., Houndmills, Basingstoke, Hampshire, RG21 6XS, England, (Telephone in U.S. (888) 330-8477), (Fax in U.S. (800) 672-2054), www.palgrave.com; *The Statesman's Yearbook 2008.*

Taylor and Francis Group, An Informa Business, 2 Park Square, Milton Park, Abingdon, Oxford OX14 4RN, United Kingdom, (Dial from U.S. (212) 216-7800), (Fax from U.S. (212) 564-7854), www.tandf.co.uk; *The Europa World Year Book.*

United Nations Statistics Division, New York, NY 10017, (800) 253-9646, Fax: (212) 963-4116, http://unstats.un.org; *Statistical Yearbook.*

BERMUDA - SILVER PRODUCTION

See BERMUDA - MINERAL INDUSTRIES

BERMUDA - SOCIAL ECOLOGY

M.E. Sharpe, 80 Business Park Drive, Armonk, NY 10504, (800) 541-6563, Fax: (914) 273-2106, www.mesharpe.com; *The Illustrated Book of World Rankings.*

United Nations Statistics Division, New York, NY 10017, (800) 253-9646, Fax: (212) 963-4116, http://unstats.un.org; *World Statistics Pocketbook.*

BERMUDA - SOCIAL SECURITY

United Nations Statistics Division, New York, NY 10017, (800) 253-9646, Fax: (212) 963-4116, http://unstats.un.org; *National Accounts Statistics: Compendium of Income Distribution Statistics.*

BERMUDA - STEEL PRODUCTION

See BERMUDA - MINERAL INDUSTRIES

BERMUDA - SUGAR PRODUCTION

See BERMUDA - CROPS

BERMUDA - TAXATION

Palgrave Macmillan Ltd., Houndmills, Basingstoke, Hampshire, RG21 6XS, England, (Telephone in U.S. (888) 330-8477), (Fax in U.S. (800) 672-2054), www.palgrave.com; *The Statesman's Yearbook 2008.*

BERMUDA - TELEPHONE

International Telecommunication Union (ITU), Place des Nations, 1211 Geneva 20, Switzerland, www.itu.int; World Telecommunication Indicators Database.

Palgrave Macmillan Ltd., Houndmills, Basingstoke, Hampshire, RG21 6XS, England, (Telephone in U.S. (888) 330-8477), (Fax in U.S. (800) 672-2054), www.palgrave.com; *The Statesman's Yearbook 2008.*

Taylor and Francis Group, An Informa Business, 2 Park Square, Milton Park, Abingdon, Oxford OX14 4RN, United Kingdom, (Dial from U.S. (212) 216-7800), (Fax from U.S. (212) 564-7854), www.tandf.co.uk; *The Europa World Year Book.*

United Nations Statistics Division, New York, NY 10017, (800) 253-9646, Fax: (212) 963-4116, http://unstats.un.org; *Statistical Yearbook* and *World Statistics Pocketbook.*

BERMUDA - TEXTILE INDUSTRY

M.E. Sharpe, 80 Business Park Drive, Armonk, NY 10504, (800) 541-6563, Fax: (914) 273-2106, www.mesharpe.com; *The Illustrated Book of World Rankings.*

Palgrave Macmillan Ltd., Houndmills, Basingstoke, Hampshire, RG21 6XS, England, (Telephone in U.S. (888) 330-8477), (Fax in U.S. (800) 672-2054), www.palgrave.com; *The Statesman's Yearbook 2008.*

United Nations Conference on Trade and Development (UNCTAD), DC2-1120, United Nations, New York, NY 10017, (212) 963-0027, www.unctad.org; *UNCTAD Commodity Yearbook.*

BERMUDA - THEATER

UNESCO Institute for Statistics, C.P. 6128 Succursale Centre-Ville, Montreal, Quebec, H3C 3J7 Canada, (Dial from U.S. (514) 343-6880), (Fax from U.S. (514) 343 6882), www.uis.unesco.org; *Statistical Tables.*

BERMUDA - TOBACCO INDUSTRY

Foreign Agricultural Service (FAS), U.S. Department of Agriculture (USDA), 1400 Independence Avenue, SW, Washington, DC 20250, (202) 720-3935, www.fas.usda.gov; *Tobacco: World Markets and Trade.*

M.E. Sharpe, 80 Business Park Drive, Armonk, NY 10504, (800) 541-6563, Fax: (914) 273-2106, www.mesharpe.com; *The Illustrated Book of World Rankings.*

BERMUDA - TOURISM

Euromonitor International, Inc., 224 S. Michigan Avenue, Suite 1500, Chicago, IL 60604, (312) 922-1115, Fax: (312) 922-1157, www.euromonitor.com; *The World Economic Factbook 2008* and *World Marketing Data and Statistics.*

M.E. Sharpe, 80 Business Park Drive, Armonk, NY 10504, (800) 541-6563, Fax: (914) 273-2106, www.mesharpe.com; *The Illustrated Book of World Rankings.*

Palgrave Macmillan Ltd., Houndmills, Basingstoke, Hampshire, RG21 6XS, England, (Telephone in U.S. (888) 330-8477), (Fax in U.S. (800) 672-2054), www.palgrave.com; *The Statesman's Yearbook 2008.*

Taylor and Francis Group, An Informa Business, 2 Park Square, Milton Park, Abingdon, Oxford OX14 4RN, United Kingdom, (Dial from U.S. (212) 216-7800), (Fax from U.S. (212) 564-7854), www.tandf.co.uk; *The Europa World Year Book.*

United Nations Statistics Division, New York, NY 10017, (800) 253-9646, Fax: (212) 963-4116, http://unstats.un.org; *Statistical Yearbook.*

United Nations World Tourism Organization (UNWTO), Capitan Haya 42, 28020 Madrid, Spain, www.world-tourism.org; *Yearbook of Tourism Statistics.*

BERMUDA - TRADE

See BERMUDA - INTERNATIONAL TRADE

BERMUDA - TRANSPORTATION

Central Intelligence Agency, Office of Public Affairs, Washington, DC 20505, (703) 482-0623, Fax: (703) 482-1739, www.cia.gov; *The World Factbook.*

Euromonitor International, Inc., 224 S. Michigan Avenue, Suite 1500, Chicago, IL 60604, (312) 922-1115, Fax: (312) 922-1157, www.euromonitor.com; *International Marketing Data and Statistics 2008* and *World Marketing Data and Statistics.*

M.E. Sharpe, 80 Business Park Drive, Armonk, NY 10504, (800) 541-6563, Fax: (914) 273-2106, www.mesharpe.com; *The Illustrated Book of World Rankings.*

Palgrave Macmillan Ltd., Houndmills, Basingstoke, Hampshire, RG21 6XS, England, (Telephone in U.S. (888) 330-8477), (Fax in U.S. (800) 672-2054), www.palgrave.com; *The Statesman's Yearbook 2008.*

Taylor and Francis Group, An Informa Business, 2 Park Square, Milton Park, Abingdon, Oxford OX14 4RN, United Kingdom, (Dial from U.S. (212) 216-7800), (Fax from U.S. (212) 564-7854), www.tandf.co.uk; *The Europa World Year Book.*

BERMUDA - UNEMPLOYMENT

Central Intelligence Agency, Office of Public Affairs, Washington, DC 20505, (703) 482-0623, Fax: (703) 482-1739, www.cia.gov; *The World Factbook.*

International Labour Office, I.L.O. Publications, 4 route des Morillons, CH-1211 Geneva 22, Switzerland, (Telephone in U.S. (202) 653-7652), (Fax in U.S. (202) 653-7687), www.ilo.org; *Yearbook of Labour Statistics 2006.*

BERMUDA - VITAL STATISTICS

Palgrave Macmillan Ltd., Houndmills, Basingstoke, Hampshire, RG21 6XS, England, (Telephone in U.S. (888) 330-8477), (Fax in U.S. (800) 672-2054), www.palgrave.com; *The Statesman's Yearbook 2008.*

United Nations Statistics Division, New York, NY 10017, (800) 253-9646, Fax: (212) 963-4116, http://unstats.un.org; *Statistical Yearbook.*

World Health Organization (WHO), Avenue Appia 20, 1211 Geneve 27, Switzerland, (Telephone in U.S. (212) 331-9081), www.who.int; *World Health Report 2006.*

BERMUDA - WAGES

International Labour Office, I.L.O. Publications, 4 route des Morillons, CH-1211 Geneva 22, Switzerland, (Telephone in U.S. (202) 653-7652), (Fax in U.S. (202) 653-7687), www.ilo.org; *Yearbook of Labour Statistics 2006.*

BERMUDA - WEATHER

See BERMUDA - CLIMATE

BERMUDA - WHEAT PRODUCTION

See BERMUDA - CROPS

BERMUDA - WINE PRODUCTION

See BERMUDA - BEVERAGE INDUSTRY

BERMUDA - WOOL PRODUCTION

See BERMUDA - TEXTILE INDUSTRY

BERYLLIUM

U.S. Department of the Interior (DOI), U.S. Geological Survey (USGS), Office of Minerals Information, 12201 Sunrise Valley Drive, Reston, VA 20192, Mr. Kenneth A. Beckman, (703) 648-4916, Fax: (703) 648-4995, http://minerals.usgs.gov/minerals; *Mineral Commodity Summaries.*

BEVERAGES

See also ALCOHOLIC BEVERAGES

BEVERAGES - CONSUMPTION

Economic Research Service (ERS), U.S. Department of Agriculture (USDA), 1800 M Street, NW, Washington, DC 20036-5831, (202) 694-5050, Fax: (202) 694-5689, www.ers.usda.gov; *Agricultural Outlook* and *Food CPI, Prices, and Expenditures.*

BEVERAGES - PRICE INDEXES

U.S. Bureau of Labor Statistics (BLS), Postal Square Building, 2 Massachusetts Avenue, NE, Washington, DC 20212-0001, (202) 691-5200, Fax: (202) 691-6325, www.bls.gov; *Consumer Price Index Detailed Report* and *Monthly Labor Review (MLR).*

U.S. Department of Labor (DOL), Bureau of Labor Statistics (BLS), Postal Square Building, 2 Massachusetts Avenue, NE, Washington, DC 20212-0001, (202) 691-5200, Fax: (202) 691-6325, www.bls.gov; *Consumer Price Indexes (CPI).*

BEVERAGES - WHISKEY

U.S. Bureau of Labor Statistics (BLS), Postal Square Building, 2 Massachusetts Avenue, NE, Washington, DC 20212-0001, (202) 691-5200, Fax: (202) 691-6325, www.bls.gov; *Consumer Price Index Detailed Report* and *Monthly Labor Review (MLR).*

BEVERAGES - WINE

U.S. Bureau of Labor Statistics (BLS), Postal Square Building, 2 Massachusetts Avenue, NE, Washington, DC 20212-0001, (202) 691-5200, Fax: (202) 691-6325, www.bls.gov; *Consumer Price Index Detailed Report* and *Monthly Labor Review (MLR).*

BEVERAGES AND TOBACCO PRODUCT MANUFACTURING - EARNINGS

U.S. Bureau of Labor Statistics (BLS), Postal Square Building, 2 Massachusetts Avenue, NE, Washington, DC 20212-0001, (202) 691-5200, Fax: (202) 691-6325, www.bls.gov; *Current Employment Statistics Survey (CES)* and *Employment and Earnings (EE).*

BEVERAGES AND TOBACCO PRODUCT MANUFACTURING - EMPLOYEES

U.S. Bureau of Labor Statistics (BLS), Postal Square Building, 2 Massachusetts Avenue, NE, Washington, DC 20212-0001, (202) 691-5200, Fax: (202) 691-6325, www.bls.gov; *Current Employment Statistics Survey (CES)* and *Employment and Earnings (EE).*

BEVERAGES AND TOBACCO PRODUCT MANUFACTURING - PRODUCTIVITY

U.S. Bureau of Labor Statistics (BLS), Postal Square Building, 2 Massachusetts Avenue, NE, Washington, DC 20212-0001, (202) 691-5200, Fax: (202) 691-6325, www.bls.gov; *Industry Productivity and Costs.*

BEVERAGES AND TOBACCO PRODUCT MANUFACTURING - SHIPMENTS

U.S. Census Bureau, Manufacturing and Construction Division, 4600 Silver Hill Road, Washington DC 20233, (301) 763-4673, www.census.gov/mcd; *Annual Survey of Manufactures, Statistics for Industry Groups and Industries; Current Industrial Reports;* and *Manufacturers Shipments, Inventories and Orders.*

BHUTAN - NATIONAL STATISTICAL OFFICE

National Statistical Bureau, Department of Planning, Ministry of Finance, Post Box 127, Thimphu, Bhutan, www.nsb.gov.bt; National Data Center.

BHUTAN - PRIMARY STATISTICS SOURCES

National Statistical Bureau, Department of Planning, Ministry of Finance, Post Box 127, Thimphu, Bhutan, www.nsb.gov.bt; *Bhutan at a Glance* and *Statistical Yearbook of Bhutan 2004.*

BHUTAN - AGRICULTURE

Asian Development Bank (ADB), PO Box 789, 0980 Manila, Philippines, www.adb.org; *Key Indicators of Developing Asian and Pacific Countries 2006.*

Economist Intelligence Unit, 111 West 57th Street, New York, NY 10019, (212) 554-0600, Fax: (212) 586-1181, www.eiu.com; *Bhutan Country Report.*

Euromonitor International, Inc., 224 S. Michigan Avenue, Suite 1500, Chicago, IL 60604, (312) 922-1115, Fax: (312) 922-1157, www.euromonitor.com; *International Marketing Data and Statistics 2008* and *World Marketing Data and Statistics.*

M.E. Sharpe, 80 Business Park Drive, Armonk, NY 10504, (800) 541-6563, Fax: (914) 273-2106, www.mesharpe.com; *The Illustrated Book of World Rankings.*

Palgrave Macmillan Ltd., Houndmills, Basingstoke, Hampshire, RG21 6XS, England, (Telephone in U.S. (888) 330-8477), (Fax in U.S. (800) 672-2054), www.palgrave.com; *The Statesman's Yearbook 2008.*

Taylor and Francis Group, An Informa Business, 2 Park Square, Milton Park, Abingdon, Oxford OX14 4RN, United Kingdom, (Dial from U.S. (212) 216-7800), (Fax from U.S. (212) 564-7854), www.tandf.co.uk; *The Europa World Year Book.*

United Nations Conference on Trade and Development (UNCTAD), DC2-1120, United Nations, New York, NY 10017, (212) 963-0027, www.unctad.org; *UNCTAD Commodity Yearbook.*

United Nations Food and Agricultural Organization (FAO), Viale delle Terme di Caracalla, 00100 Rome, Italy, (Dial from U.S. (202) 653-2400), (Fax from U.S. (202) 653 5760), www.fao.org; AQUASTAT; *FAO Production Yearbook 2002; FAO Trade Yearbook;* and *The State of Food and Agriculture (SOFA) 2006.*

United Nations Statistics Division, New York, NY 10017, (800) 253-9646, Fax: (212) 963-4116, http://unstats.un.org; *Asia-Pacific in Figures 2004* and *Statistical Yearbook for Asia and the Pacific 2004.*

The World Bank, 1818 H Street, NW, Washington, DC 20433, (202) 473-1000, Fax: (202) 477-6391, www.worldbank.org; *Bhutan* and *World Development Indicators (WDI) 2008.*

BHUTAN - AIRLINES

Economist Intelligence Unit, 111 West 57th Street, New York, NY 10019, (212) 554-0600, Fax: (212) 586-1181, www.eiu.com; *Business Asia.*

M.E. Sharpe, 80 Business Park Drive, Armonk, NY 10504, (800) 541-6563, Fax: (914) 273-2106, www.mesharpe.com; *The Illustrated Book of World Rankings.*

Palgrave Macmillan Ltd., Houndmills, Basingstoke, Hampshire, RG21 6XS, England, (Telephone in U.S. (888) 330-8477), (Fax in U.S. (800) 672-2054), www.palgrave.com; *The Statesman's Yearbook 2008.*

Taylor and Francis Group, An Informa Business, 2 Park Square, Milton Park, Abingdon, Oxford OX14 4RN, United Kingdom, (Dial from U.S. (212) 216-7800), (Fax from U.S. (212) 564-7854), www.tandf.co.uk; *The Europa World Year Book.*

BHUTAN - AIRPORTS

Central Intelligence Agency, Office of Public Affairs, Washington, DC 20505, (703) 482-0623, Fax: (703) 482-1739, www.cia.gov; *The World Factbook.*

BHUTAN - ALUMINUM PRODUCTION

See BHUTAN - MINERAL INDUSTRIES

BHUTAN - ARMED FORCES

Central Intelligence Agency, Office of Public Affairs, Washington, DC 20505, (703) 482-0623, Fax: (703) 482-1739, www.cia.gov; *The World Factbook.*

Economist Intelligence Unit, 111 West 57th Street, New York, NY 10019, (212) 554-0600, Fax: (212) 586-1181, www.eiu.com; *Business Asia.*

Euromonitor International, Inc., 224 S. Michigan Avenue, Suite 1500, Chicago, IL 60604, (312) 922-1115, Fax: (312) 922-1157, www.euromonitor.com; *World Marketing Data and Statistics.*

Palgrave Macmillan Ltd., Houndmills, Basingstoke, Hampshire, RG21 6XS, England, (Telephone in U.S. (888) 330-8477), (Fax in U.S. (800) 672-2054), www.palgrave.com; *The Statesman's Yearbook 2008.*

United Nations Statistics Division, New York, NY 10017, (800) 253-9646, Fax: (212) 963-4116, http://unstats.un.org; *Human Development Report 2006.*

BHUTAN - BALANCE OF PAYMENTS

Taylor and Francis Group, An Informa Business, 2 Park Square, Milton Park, Abingdon, Oxford OX14 4RN, United Kingdom, (Dial from U.S. (212) 216-7800), (Fax from U.S. (212) 564-7854), www.tandf.co.uk; *The Europa World Year Book.*

The World Bank, 1818 H Street, NW, Washington, DC 20433, (202) 473-1000, Fax: (202) 477-6391, www.worldbank.org; *Bhutan* and *World Development Indicators (WDI) 2008.*

BHUTAN - BANKS AND BANKING

Asian Development Bank (ADB), PO Box 789, 0980 Manila, Philippines, www.adb.org; *Key Indicators of Developing Asian and Pacific Countries 2006.*

Euromonitor International, Inc., 224 S. Michigan Avenue, Suite 1500, Chicago, IL 60604, (312) 922-1115, Fax: (312) 922-1157, www.euromonitor.com; *World Marketing Data and Statistics.*

M.E. Sharpe, 80 Business Park Drive, Armonk, NY 10504, (800) 541-6563, Fax: (914) 273-2106, www.mesharpe.com; *The Illustrated Book of World Rankings.*

Palgrave Macmillan Ltd., Houndmills, Basingstoke, Hampshire, RG21 6XS, England, (Telephone in U.S. (888) 330-8477), (Fax in U.S. (800) 672-2054), www.palgrave.com; *The Statesman's Yearbook 2008.*

Taylor and Francis Group, An Informa Business, 2 Park Square, Milton Park, Abingdon, Oxford OX14 4RN, United Kingdom, (Dial from U.S. (212) 216-7800), (Fax from U.S. (212) 564-7854), www.tandf.co.uk; *The Europa World Year Book.*

BHUTAN - BARLEY PRODUCTION

See BHUTAN - CROPS

BHUTAN - BEVERAGE INDUSTRY

M.E. Sharpe, 80 Business Park Drive, Armonk, NY 10504, (800) 541-6563, Fax: (914) 273-2106, www.mesharpe.com; *The Illustrated Book of World Rankings.*

BHUTAN - BONDS

Asian Development Bank (ADB), PO Box 789, 0980 Manila, Philippines, www.adb.org; *Key Indicators of Developing Asian and Pacific Countries 2006.*

BHUTAN - BROADCASTING

Central Intelligence Agency, Office of Public Affairs, Washington, DC 20505, (703) 482-0623, Fax: (703) 482-1739, www.cia.gov; *The World Factbook.*

Economist Intelligence Unit, 111 West 57th Street, New York, NY 10019, (212) 554-0600, Fax: (212) 586-1181, www.eiu.com; *Business Asia.*

Euromonitor International, Inc., 224 S. Michigan Avenue, Suite 1500, Chicago, IL 60604, (312) 922-1115, Fax: (312) 922-1157, www.euromonitor.com; *World Marketing Data and Statistics.*

M.E. Sharpe, 80 Business Park Drive, Armonk, NY 10504, (800) 541-6563, Fax: (914) 273-2106, www.mesharpe.com; *The Illustrated Book of World Rankings.*

Palgrave Macmillan Ltd., Houndmills, Basingstoke, Hampshire, RG21 6XS, England, (Telephone in U.S. (888) 330-8477), (Fax in U.S. (800) 672-2054), www.palgrave.com; *The Statesman's Yearbook 2008.*

WRTH Publications Limited, PO Box 290, Oxford OX2 7FT, UK, www.wrth.com; *World Radio TV Handbook 2007.*

BHUTAN - BUDGET

Central Intelligence Agency, Office of Public Affairs, Washington, DC 20505, (703) 482-0623, Fax: (703) 482-1739, www.cia.gov; *The World Factbook.*

BHUTAN - BUSINESS

United Nations Statistics Division, New York, NY 10017, (800) 253-9646, Fax: (212) 963-4116, http://unstats.un.org; *Statistical Yearbook for Asia and the Pacific 2004.*

BHUTAN - CAPITAL INVESTMENTS

Asian Development Bank (ADB), PO Box 789, 0980 Manila, Philippines, www.adb.org; *Key Indicators of Developing Asian and Pacific Countries 2006.*

BHUTAN - CAPITAL LEVY

Asian Development Bank (ADB), PO Box 789, 0980 Manila, Philippines, www.adb.org; *Key Indicators of Developing Asian and Pacific Countries 2006.*

BHUTAN - CATTLE

See BHUTAN - LIVESTOCK

BHUTAN - CHICKENS

See BHUTAN - LIVESTOCK

BHUTAN - CHILDBIRTH - STATISTICS

Central Intelligence Agency, Office of Public Affairs, Washington, DC 20505, (703) 482-0623, Fax: (703) 482-1739, www.cia.gov; *The World Factbook.*

Economist Intelligence Unit, 111 West 57th Street, New York, NY 10019, (212) 554-0600, Fax: (212) 586-1181, www.eiu.com; *Business Asia.*

Euromonitor International, Inc., 224 S. Michigan Avenue, Suite 1500, Chicago, IL 60604, (312) 922-1115, Fax: (312) 922-1157, www.euromonitor.com; *International Marketing Data and Statistics 2008* and *The World Economic Factbook 2008.*

M.E. Sharpe, 80 Business Park Drive, Armonk, NY 10504, (800) 541-6563, Fax: (914) 273-2106, www.mesharpe.com; *The Illustrated Book of World Rankings.*

Taylor and Francis Group, An Informa Business, 2 Park Square, Milton Park, Abingdon, Oxford OX14 4RN, United Kingdom, (Dial from U.S. (212) 216-7800), (Fax from U.S. (212) 564-7854), www.tandf.co.uk; *The Europa World Year Book.*

United Nations Statistics Division, New York, NY 10017, (800) 253-9646, Fax: (212) 963-4116, http://unstats.un.org; *Asia-Pacific in Figures 2004; Demographic Yearbook;* and *Statistical Yearbook.*

The World Bank, 1818 H Street, NW, Washington, DC 20433, (202) 473-1000, Fax: (202) 477-6391, www.worldbank.org; *World Development Indicators (WDI) 2008.*

BHUTAN - CLIMATE

International Institute for Environment and Development (IIED), 3 Endsleigh Street, London, England, WC1H 0DD, United Kingdom, www.iied.org; *Environment Urbanization.*

M.E. Sharpe, 80 Business Park Drive, Armonk, NY 10504, (800) 541-6563, Fax: (914) 273-2106, www.mesharpe.com; *The Illustrated Book of World Rankings.*

Palgrave Macmillan Ltd., Houndmills, Basingstoke, Hampshire, RG21 6XS, England, (Telephone in U.S. (888) 330-8477), (Fax in U.S. (800) 672-2054), www.palgrave.com; *The Statesman's Yearbook 2008.*

BHUTAN - COAL PRODUCTION

See BHUTAN - MINERAL INDUSTRIES

BHUTAN - COFFEE

See BHUTAN - CROPS

BHUTAN - COMMERCE

Palgrave Macmillan Ltd., Houndmills, Basingstoke, Hampshire, RG21 6XS, England, (Telephone in U.S. (888) 330-8477), (Fax in U.S. (800) 672-2054), www.palgrave.com; *The Statesman's Yearbook 2008.*

BHUTAN - COMMODITY EXCHANGES

United Nations Food and Agricultural Organization (FAO), Viale delle Terme di Caracalla, 00100 Rome, Italy, (Dial from U.S. (202) 653-2400), (Fax from U.S. (202) 653 5760), www.fao.org; *The State of Food and Agriculture (SOFA) 2006.*

BHUTAN - CONSTRUCTION INDUSTRY

M.E. Sharpe, 80 Business Park Drive, Armonk, NY 10504, (800) 541-6563, Fax: (914) 273-2106, www.mesharpe.com; *The Illustrated Book of World Rankings.*

BHUTAN - CONSUMER PRICE INDEXES

Asian Development Bank (ADB), PO Box 789, 0980 Manila, Philippines, www.adb.org; *Key Indicators of Developing Asian and Pacific Countries 2006.*

Taylor and Francis Group, An Informa Business, 2 Park Square, Milton Park, Abingdon, Oxford OX14 4RN, United Kingdom, (Dial from U.S. (212) 216-7800), (Fax from U.S. (212) 564-7854), www.tandf.co.uk; *The Europa World Year Book.*

The World Bank, 1818 H Street, NW, Washington, DC 20433, (202) 473-1000, Fax: (202) 477-6391, www.worldbank.org; *Bhutan.*

BHUTAN - COPPER INDUSTRY AND TRADE

See BHUTAN - MINERAL INDUSTRIES

BHUTAN - CORN INDUSTRY

See BHUTAN - CROPS

BHUTAN - COTTON

See BHUTAN - CROPS

BHUTAN - CROPS

Asian Development Bank (ADB), PO Box 789, 0980 Manila, Philippines, www.adb.org; *Key Indicators of Developing Asian and Pacific Countries 2006.*

M.E. Sharpe, 80 Business Park Drive, Armonk, NY 10504, (800) 541-6563, Fax: (914) 273-2106, www.mesharpe.com; *The Illustrated Book of World Rankings.*

Palgrave Macmillan Ltd., Houndmills, Basingstoke, Hampshire, RG21 6XS, England, (Telephone in U.S. (888) 330-8477), (Fax in U.S. (800) 672-2054), www.palgrave.com; *The Statesman's Yearbook 2008.*

Taylor and Francis Group, An Informa Business, 2 Park Square, Milton Park, Abingdon, Oxford OX14 4RN, United Kingdom, (Dial from U.S. (212) 216-7800), (Fax from U.S. (212) 564-7854), www.tandf.co.uk; *The Europa World Year Book.*

United Nations Conference on Trade and Development (UNCTAD), DC2-1120, United Nations, New York, NY 10017, (212) 963-0027, www.unctad.org; *UNCTAD Commodity Yearbook.*

United Nations Food and Agricultural Organization (FAO), Viale delle Terme di Caracalla, 00100 Rome, Italy, (Dial from U.S. (202) 653-2400), (Fax from U.S. (202) 653 5760), www.fao.org; *The State of Food and Agriculture (SOFA) 2006.*

United Nations Statistics Division, New York, NY 10017, (800) 253-9646, Fax: (212) 963-4116, http://unstats.un.org; *Statistical Yearbook.*

BHUTAN - DAIRY PROCESSING

M.E. Sharpe, 80 Business Park Drive, Armonk, NY 10504, (800) 541-6563, Fax: (914) 273-2106, www.mesharpe.com; *The Illustrated Book of World Rankings.*

Taylor and Francis Group, An Informa Business, 2 Park Square, Milton Park, Abingdon, Oxford OX14 4RN, United Kingdom, (Dial from U.S. (212) 216-7800), (Fax from U.S. (212) 564-7854), www.tandf.co.uk; *The Europa World Year Book.*

United Nations Food and Agricultural Organization (FAO), Viale delle Terme di Caracalla, 00100 Rome, Italy, (Dial from U.S. (202) 653-2400), (Fax from U.S. (202) 653 5760), www.fao.org; *FAO Production Yearbook 2002* and *The State of Food and Agriculture (SOFA) 2006.*

BHUTAN - DEATH RATES

See BHUTAN - MORTALITY

BHUTAN - DEBTS, EXTERNAL

Asian Development Bank (ADB), PO Box 789, 0980 Manila, Philippines, www.adb.org; *Key Indicators of Developing Asian and Pacific Countries 2006.*

The World Bank, 1818 H Street, NW, Washington, DC 20433, (202) 473-1000, Fax: (202) 477-6391, www.worldbank.org; *World Development Indicators (WDI) 2008.*

Worldinformation.com, 2 Market Street, Saffron Walden, Essex CB10 1HZ, United Kingdom, www.worldinformation.com; The World of Information (www.worldinformation.com).

BHUTAN - DEMOGRAPHY

Economist Intelligence Unit, 111 West 57th Street, New York, NY 10019, (212) 554-0600, Fax: (212) 586-1181, www.eiu.com; *Business Asia.*

Euromonitor International, Inc., 224 S. Michigan Avenue, Suite 1500, Chicago, IL 60604, (312) 922-1115, Fax: (312) 922-1157, www.euromonitor.com; *International Marketing Data and Statistics 2008; The World Economic Factbook 2008;* and *World Marketing Data and Statistics.*

M.E. Sharpe, 80 Business Park Drive, Armonk, NY 10504, (800) 541-6563, Fax: (914) 273-2106, www.mesharpe.com; *The Illustrated Book of World Rankings.*

United Nations Statistics Division, New York, NY 10017, (800) 253-9646, Fax: (212) 963-4116, http://unstats.un.org; *Asia-Pacific in Figures 2004* and *Human Development Report 2006.*

The World Bank, 1818 H Street, NW, Washington, DC 20433, (202) 473-1000, Fax: (202) 477-6391, www.worldbank.org; *Bhutan.*

BHUTAN - DIAMONDS

See BHUTAN - MINERAL INDUSTRIES

BHUTAN - DISPOSABLE INCOME

M.E. Sharpe, 80 Business Park Drive, Armonk, NY 10504, (800) 541-6563, Fax: (914) 273-2106, www.mesharpe.com; *The Illustrated Book of World Rankings.*

United Nations Statistics Division, New York, NY 10017, (800) 253-9646, Fax: (212) 963-4116, http://unstats.un.org; *National Accounts Statistics: Compendium of Income Distribution Statistics* and *Statistical Yearbook.*

BHUTAN - DIVORCE

M.E. Sharpe, 80 Business Park Drive, Armonk, NY 10504, (800) 541-6563, Fax: (914) 273-2106, www.mesharpe.com; *The Illustrated Book of World Rankings.*

United Nations Statistics Division, New York, NY 10017, (800) 253-9646, Fax: (212) 963-4116, http://unstats.un.org; *Demographic Yearbook.*

BHUTAN - ECONOMIC ASSISTANCE

Asian Development Bank (ADB), PO Box 789, 0980 Manila, Philippines, www.adb.org; *Key Indicators of Developing Asian and Pacific Countries 2006.*

United Nations Statistics Division, New York, NY 10017, (800) 253-9646, Fax: (212) 963-4116, http://unstats.un.org; *Statistical Yearbook.*

BHUTAN - ECONOMIC CONDITIONS

Asian Development Bank (ADB), PO Box 789, 0980 Manila, Philippines, www.adb.org; *Key Indicators of Developing Asian and Pacific Countries 2006.*

Central Intelligence Agency, Office of Public Affairs, Washington, DC 20505, (703) 482-0623, Fax: (703) 482-1739, www.cia.gov; *The World Factbook.*

Economist Intelligence Unit, 111 West 57th Street, New York, NY 10019, (212) 554-0600, Fax: (212) 586-1181, www.eiu.com; *Bhutan Country Report.*

Euromonitor International, Inc., 224 S. Michigan Avenue, Suite 1500, Chicago, IL 60604, (312) 922-1115, Fax: (312) 922-1157, www.euromonitor.com; *International Marketing Data and Statistics 2008; The World Economic Factbook 2008;* and *World Marketing Data and Statistics.*

M.E. Sharpe, 80 Business Park Drive, Armonk, NY 10504, (800) 541-6563, Fax: (914) 273-2106, www.mesharpe.com; *The Illustrated Book of World Rankings.*

Palgrave Macmillan Ltd., Houndmills, Basingstoke, Hampshire, RG21 6XS, England, (Telephone in U.S. (888) 330-8477), (Fax in U.S. (800) 672-2054), www.palgrave.com; *The Statesman's Yearbook 2008.*

Taylor and Francis Group, An Informa Business, 2 Park Square, Milton Park, Abingdon, Oxford OX14 4RN, United Kingdom, (Dial from U.S. (212) 216-7800), (Fax from U.S. (212) 564-7854), www.tandf.co.uk; *The Europa World Year Book.*

United Nations Statistics Division, New York, NY 10017, (800) 253-9646, Fax: (212) 963-4116, http://unstats.un.org; *World Statistics Pocketbook.*

The World Bank, 1818 H Street, NW, Washington, DC 20433, (202) 473-1000, Fax: (202) 477-6391, www.worldbank.org; *Bhutan* and *The World Bank Atlas 2003-2004.*

BHUTAN - EDUCATION

Economist Intelligence Unit, 111 West 57th Street, New York, NY 10019, (212) 554-0600, Fax: (212) 586-1181, www.eiu.com; *Business Asia.*

Euromonitor International, Inc., 224 S. Michigan Avenue, Suite 1500, Chicago, IL 60604, (312) 922-1115, Fax: (312) 922-1157, www.euromonitor.com; *International Marketing Data and Statistics 2008* and *World Marketing Data and Statistics.*

M.E. Sharpe, 80 Business Park Drive, Armonk, NY 10504, (800) 541-6563, Fax: (914) 273-2106, www.mesharpe.com; *The Illustrated Book of World Rankings.*

Palgrave Macmillan Ltd., Houndmills, Basingstoke, Hampshire, RG21 6XS, England, (Telephone in U.S. (888) 330-8477), (Fax in U.S. (800) 672-2054), www.palgrave.com; *The Statesman's Yearbook 2008.*

Taylor and Francis Group, An Informa Business, 2 Park Square, Milton Park, Abingdon, Oxford OX14 4RN, United Kingdom, (Dial from U.S. (212) 216-7800), (Fax from U.S. (212) 564-7854), www.tandf.co.uk; *The Europa World Year Book.*

UNESCO Institute for Statistics, C.P. 6128 Succursale Centre-Ville, Montreal, Quebec, H3C 3J7 Canada, (Dial from U.S. (514) 343-6880), (Fax from U.S. (514) 343 6882), www.uis.unesco.org; *Statistical Tables.*

United Nations Statistics Division, New York, NY 10017, (800) 253-9646, Fax: (212) 963-4116, http://unstats.un.org; *Asia-Pacific in Figures 2004; Human Development Report 2006;* and *Statistical Yearbook for Asia and the Pacific 2004.*

The World Bank, 1818 H Street, NW, Washington, DC 20433, (202) 473-1000, Fax: (202) 477-6391, www.worldbank.org; *Bhutan* and *World Development Indicators (WDI) 2008.*

BHUTAN - ELECTRICITY

Asian Development Bank (ADB), PO Box 789, 0980 Manila, Philippines, www.adb.org; *Key Indicators of Developing Asian and Pacific Countries 2006.*

M.E. Sharpe, 80 Business Park Drive, Armonk, NY 10504, (800) 541-6563, Fax: (914) 273-2106, www.mesharpe.com; *The Illustrated Book of World Rankings.*

Palgrave Macmillan Ltd., Houndmills, Basingstoke, Hampshire, RG21 6XS, England, (Telephone in U.S. (888) 330-8477), (Fax in U.S. (800) 672-2054), www.palgrave.com; *The Statesman's Yearbook 2008.*

U.S. Department of Energy (DOE), Energy Information Administration (EIA), 1000 Independence Avenue, SW, Washington, DC 20585, (202) 586-8800, www.eia.doe.gov; *International Energy Annual 2004* and *International Energy Outlook 2006.*

United Nations Statistics Division, New York, NY 10017, (800) 253-9646, Fax: (212) 963-4116, http://unstats.un.org; *Human Development Report 2006.*

BHUTAN - EMPLOYMENT

Euromonitor International, Inc., 224 S. Michigan Avenue, Suite 1500, Chicago, IL 60604, (312) 922-1115, Fax: (312) 922-1157, www.euromonitor.com; *International Marketing Data and Statistics 2008.*

M.E. Sharpe, 80 Business Park Drive, Armonk, NY 10504, (800) 541-6563, Fax: (914) 273-2106, www.mesharpe.com; *The Illustrated Book of World Rankings.*

United Nations Statistics Division, New York, NY 10017, (800) 253-9646, Fax: (212) 963-4116, http://unstats.un.org; *Asia-Pacific in Figures 2004.*

The World Bank, 1818 H Street, NW, Washington, DC 20433, (202) 473-1000, Fax: (202) 477-6391, www.worldbank.org; *Bhutan.*

BHUTAN - ENVIRONMENTAL CONDITIONS

DSI Data Service Information, Xantener Strasse 51a, D-47495 Rheinberg, Germany, www.dsidata.com; *Campus Solution.*

Economist Intelligence Unit, 111 West 57th Street, New York, NY 10019, (212) 554-0600, Fax: (212) 586-1181, www.eiu.com; *Bhutan Country Report.*

International Institute for Environment and Development (IIED), 3 Endsleigh Street, London, England, WC1H 0DD, United Kingdom, www.iied.org; *Environment Urbanization.*

United Nations Statistics Division, New York, NY 10017, (800) 253-9646, Fax: (212) 963-4116, http://unstats.un.org; *World Statistics Pocketbook.*

BHUTAN - EXPORTS

Asian Development Bank (ADB), PO Box 789, 0980 Manila, Philippines, www.adb.org; *Key Indicators of Developing Asian and Pacific Countries 2006.*

Central Intelligence Agency, Office of Public Affairs, Washington, DC 20505, (703) 482-0623, Fax: (703) 482-1739, www.cia.gov; *The World Factbook.*

Economist Intelligence Unit, 111 West 57th Street, New York, NY 10019, (212) 554-0600, Fax: (212) 586-1181, www.eiu.com; *Bhutan Country Report.*

Euromonitor International, Inc., 224 S. Michigan Avenue, Suite 1500, Chicago, IL 60604, (312) 922-1115, Fax: (312) 922-1157, www.euromonitor.com; *International Marketing Data and Statistics 2008* and *The World Economic Factbook 2008.*

Palgrave Macmillan Ltd., Houndmills, Basingstoke, Hampshire, RG21 6XS, England, (Telephone in U.S. (888) 330-8477), (Fax in U.S. (800) 672-2054), www.palgrave.com; *The Statesman's Yearbook 2008.*

Taylor and Francis Group, An Informa Business, 2 Park Square, Milton Park, Abingdon, Oxford OX14 4RN, United Kingdom, (Dial from U.S. (212) 216-7800), (Fax from U.S. (212) 564-7854), www.tandf.co.uk; *The Europa World Year Book.*

United Nations Food and Agricultural Organization (FAO), Viale delle Terme di Caracalla, 00100 Rome, Italy, (Dial from U.S. (202) 653-2400), (Fax from U.S. (202) 653 5760), www.fao.org; *The State of Food and Agriculture (SOFA) 2006.*

The World Bank, 1818 H Street, NW, Washington, DC 20433, (202) 473-1000, Fax: (202) 477-6391, www.worldbank.org; *World Development Indicators (WDI) 2008.*

Worldinformation.com, 2 Market Street, Saffron Walden, Essex CB10 1HZ, United Kingdom, www.worldinformation.com; The World of Information (www.worldinformation.com).

BHUTAN - FEMALE WORKING POPULATION

See BHUTAN - EMPLOYMENT

BHUTAN - FERTILITY, HUMAN

Central Intelligence Agency, Office of Public Affairs, Washington, DC 20505, (703) 482-0623, Fax: (703) 482-1739, www.cia.gov; *The World Factbook.*

M.E. Sharpe, 80 Business Park Drive, Armonk, NY 10504, (800) 541-6563, Fax: (914) 273-2106, www.mesharpe.com; *The Illustrated Book of World Rankings.*

United Nations Statistics Division, New York, NY 10017, (800) 253-9646, Fax: (212) 963-4116, http://unstats.un.org; *Human Development Report 2006.*

The World Bank, 1818 H Street, NW, Washington, DC 20433, (202) 473-1000, Fax: (202) 477-6391, www.worldbank.org; *The World Bank Atlas 2003-2004* and *World Development Indicators (WDI) 2008.*

BHUTAN - FERTILIZER INDUSTRY

United Nations Food and Agricultural Organization (FAO), Viale delle Terme di Caracalla, 00100 Rome, Italy, (Dial from U.S. (202) 653-2400), (Fax from U.S. (202) 653 5760), www.fao.org; *The State of Food and Agriculture (SOFA) 2006.*

BHUTAN - FETAL MORTALITY

See BHUTAN - MORTALITY

BHUTAN - FINANCE

Taylor and Francis Group, An Informa Business, 2 Park Square, Milton Park, Abingdon, Oxford OX14 4RN, United Kingdom, (Dial from U.S. (212) 216-7800), (Fax from U.S. (212) 564-7854), www.tandf.co.uk; *The Europa World Year Book.*

United Nations Statistics Division, New York, NY 10017, (800) 253-9646, Fax: (212) 963-4116, http://unstats.un.org; *Asia-Pacific in Figures 2004* and *Statistical Yearbook for Asia and the Pacific 2004.*

The World Bank, 1818 H Street, NW, Washington, DC 20433, (202) 473-1000, Fax: (202) 477-6391, www.worldbank.org; *Bhutan.*

BHUTAN - FINANCE, PUBLIC

Asian Development Bank (ADB), PO Box 789, 0980 Manila, Philippines, www.adb.org; *Key Indicators of Developing Asian and Pacific Countries 2006.*

Economist Intelligence Unit, 111 West 57th Street, New York, NY 10019, (212) 554-0600, Fax: (212) 586-1181, www.eiu.com; *Bhutan Country Report.*

M.E. Sharpe, 80 Business Park Drive, Armonk, NY 10504, (800) 541-6563, Fax: (914) 273-2106, www.mesharpe.com; *The Illustrated Book of World Rankings.*

Palgrave Macmillan Ltd., Houndmills, Basingstoke, Hampshire, RG21 6XS, England, (Telephone in U.S. (888) 330-8477), (Fax in U.S. (800) 672-2054), www.palgrave.com; *The Statesman's Yearbook 2008.*

Taylor and Francis Group, An Informa Business, 2 Park Square, Milton Park, Abingdon, Oxford OX14

4RN, United Kingdom, (Dial from U.S. (212) 216-7800), (Fax from U.S. (212) 564-7854), www.tandf.co.uk; *The Europa World Year Book.*

United Nations Statistics Division, New York, NY 10017, (800) 253-9646, Fax: (212) 963-4116, http://unstats.un.org; *Statistical Yearbook for Asia and the Pacific 2004.*

The World Bank, 1818 H Street, NW, Washington, DC 20433, (202) 473-1000, Fax: (202) 477-6391, www.worldbank.org; *Bhutan.*

BHUTAN - FISHERIES

M.E. Sharpe, 80 Business Park Drive, Armonk, NY 10504, (800) 541-6563, Fax: (914) 273-2106, www.mesharpe.com; *The Illustrated Book of World Rankings.*

Taylor and Francis Group, An Informa Business, 2 Park Square, Milton Park, Abingdon, Oxford OX14 4RN, United Kingdom, (Dial from U.S. (212) 216-7800), (Fax from U.S. (212) 564-7854), www.tandf.co.uk; *The Europa World Year Book.*

United Nations Conference on Trade and Development (UNCTAD), DC2-1120, United Nations, New York, NY 10017, (212) 963-0027, www.unctad.org; *UNCTAD Commodity Yearbook.*

United Nations Food and Agricultural Organization (FAO), Viale delle Terme di Caracalla, 00100 Rome, Italy, (Dial from U.S. (202) 653-2400), (Fax from U.S. (202) 653 5760), www.fao.org; *FAO Yearbook of Fishery Statistics;* Fishery Databases; FISHSTAT Database. Subjects covered include: Aquaculture production, capture production, fishery commodities; and *The State of Food and Agriculture (SOFA) 2006.*

United Nations Statistics Division, New York, NY 10017, (800) 253-9646, Fax: (212) 963-4116, http://unstats.un.org; *Statistical Yearbook.*

The World Bank, 1818 H Street, NW, Washington, DC 20433, (202) 473-1000, Fax: (202) 477-6391, www.worldbank.org; *Bhutan.*

BHUTAN - FOOD

United Nations Conference on Trade and Development (UNCTAD), DC2-1120, United Nations, New York, NY 10017, (212) 963-0027, www.unctad.org; *UNCTAD Commodity Yearbook.*

United Nations Food and Agricultural Organization (FAO), Viale delle Terme di Caracalla, 00100 Rome, Italy, (Dial from U.S. (202) 653-2400), (Fax from U.S. (202) 653 5760), www.fao.org; *FAO Production Yearbook 2002* and *The State of Food and Agriculture (SOFA) 2006.*

United Nations Statistics Division, New York, NY 10017, (800) 253-9646, Fax: (212) 963-4116, http://unstats.un.org; *Human Development Report 2006* and *Statistical Yearbook for Asia and the Pacific 2004.*

BHUTAN - FOREIGN EXCHANGE RATES

Asian Development Bank (ADB), PO Box 789, 0980 Manila, Philippines, www.adb.org; *Key Indicators of Developing Asian and Pacific Countries 2006.*

Central Intelligence Agency, Office of Public Affairs, Washington, DC 20505, (703) 482-0623, Fax: (703) 482-1739, www.cia.gov; *The World Factbook.*

Economist Intelligence Unit, 111 West 57th Street, New York, NY 10019, (212) 554-0600, Fax: (212) 586-1181, www.eiu.com; *Business Asia.*

Euromonitor International, Inc., 224 S. Michigan Avenue, Suite 1500, Chicago, IL 60604, (312) 922-1115, Fax: (312) 922-1157, www.euromonitor.com; *International Marketing Data and Statistics 2008* and *The World Economic Factbook 2008.*

Taylor and Francis Group, An Informa Business, 2 Park Square, Milton Park, Abingdon, Oxford OX14 4RN, United Kingdom, (Dial from U.S. (212) 216-7800), (Fax from U.S. (212) 564-7854), www.tandf.co.uk; *The Europa World Year Book.*

United Nations Statistics Division, New York, NY 10017, (800) 253-9646, Fax: (212) 963-4116, http://unstats.un.org; *World Statistics Pocketbook.*

Worldinformation.com, 2 Market Street, Saffron Walden, Essex CB10 1HZ, United Kingdom, www.worldinformation.com; The World of Information (www.worldinformation.com).

BHUTAN - FORESTS AND FORESTRY

Economist Intelligence Unit, 111 West 57th Street, New York, NY 10019, (212) 554-0600, Fax: (212) 586-1181, www.eiu.com; *Business Asia.*

M.E. Sharpe, 80 Business Park Drive, Armonk, NY 10504, (800) 541-6563, Fax: (914) 273-2106, www.mesharpe.com; *The Illustrated Book of World Rankings.*

Palgrave Macmillan Ltd., Houndmills, Basingstoke, Hampshire, RG21 6XS, England, (Telephone in U.S. (888) 330-8477), (Fax in U.S. (800) 672-2054), www.palgrave.com; *The Statesman's Yearbook 2008.*

Taylor and Francis Group, An Informa Business, 2 Park Square, Milton Park, Abingdon, Oxford OX14 4RN, United Kingdom, (Dial from U.S. (212) 216-7800), (Fax from U.S. (212) 564-7854), www.tandf.co.uk; *The Europa World Year Book.*

United Nations Conference on Trade and Development (UNCTAD), DC2-1120, United Nations, New York, NY 10017, (212) 963-0027, www.unctad.org; *UNCTAD Commodity Yearbook.*

United Nations Food and Agricultural Organization (FAO), Viale delle Terme di Caracalla, 00100 Rome, Italy, (Dial from U.S. (202) 653-2400), (Fax from U.S. (202) 653 5760), www.fao.org; *The State of Food and Agriculture (SOFA) 2006.*

The World Bank, 1818 H Street, NW, Washington, DC 20433, (202) 473-1000, Fax: (202) 477-6391, www.worldbank.org; *Bhutan.*

BHUTAN - GAS PRODUCTION

See BHUTAN - MINERAL INDUSTRIES

BHUTAN - GEOGRAPHIC INFORMATION SYSTEMS

M.E. Sharpe, 80 Business Park Drive, Armonk, NY 10504, (800) 541-6563, Fax: (914) 273-2106, www.mesharpe.com; *The Illustrated Book of World Rankings.*

The World Bank, 1818 H Street, NW, Washington, DC 20433, (202) 473-1000, Fax: (202) 477-6391, www.worldbank.org; *Bhutan.*

BHUTAN - GOLD INDUSTRY

The World Bank, 1818 H Street, NW, Washington, DC 20433, (202) 473-1000, Fax: (202) 477-6391, www.worldbank.org; *World Development Indicators (WDI) 2008.*

BHUTAN - GOLD PRODUCTION

See BHUTAN - MINERAL INDUSTRIES

BHUTAN - GROSS DOMESTIC PRODUCT

Asian Development Bank (ADB), PO Box 789, 0980 Manila, Philippines, www.adb.org; *Key Indicators of Developing Asian and Pacific Countries 2006.*

Economist Intelligence Unit, 111 West 57th Street, New York, NY 10019, (212) 554-0600, Fax: (212) 586-1181, www.eiu.com; *Bhutan Country Report* and *Business Asia.*

Euromonitor International, Inc., 224 S. Michigan Avenue, Suite 1500, Chicago, IL 60604, (312) 922-1115, Fax: (312) 922-1157, www.euromonitor.com; *International Marketing Data and Statistics 2008* and *The World Economic Factbook 2008.*

M.E. Sharpe, 80 Business Park Drive, Armonk, NY 10504, (800) 541-6563, Fax: (914) 273-2106, www.mesharpe.com; *The Illustrated Book of World Rankings.*

Taylor and Francis Group, An Informa Business, 2 Park Square, Milton Park, Abingdon, Oxford OX14 4RN, United Kingdom, (Dial from U.S. (212) 216-7800), (Fax from U.S. (212) 564-7854), www.tandf.co.uk; *The Europa World Year Book.*

United Nations Statistics Division, New York, NY 10017, (800) 253-9646, Fax: (212) 963-4116, http://unstats.un.org; *Human Development Report 2006; National Accounts Statistics: Compendium of Income Distribution Statistics;* and *Statistical Yearbook.*

The World Bank, 1818 H Street, NW, Washington, DC 20433, (202) 473-1000, Fax: (202) 477-6391, www.worldbank.org; *World Development Indicators (WDI) 2008.*

BHUTAN - GROSS NATIONAL PRODUCT

Asian Development Bank (ADB), PO Box 789, 0980 Manila, Philippines, www.adb.org; *Key Indicators of Developing Asian and Pacific Countries 2006.*

Euromonitor International, Inc., 224 S. Michigan Avenue, Suite 1500, Chicago, IL 60604, (312) 922-1115, Fax: (312) 922-1157, www.euromonitor.com; *International Marketing Data and Statistics 2008.*

M.E. Sharpe, 80 Business Park Drive, Armonk, NY 10504, (800) 541-6563, Fax: (914) 273-2106, www.mesharpe.com; *The Illustrated Book of World Rankings.*

Palgrave Macmillan Ltd., Houndmills, Basingstoke, Hampshire, RG21 6XS, England, (Telephone in U.S. (888) 330-8477), (Fax in U.S. (800) 672-2054), www.palgrave.com; *The Statesman's Yearbook 2008.*

The World Bank, 1818 H Street, NW, Washington, DC 20433, (202) 473-1000, Fax: (202) 477-6391, www.worldbank.org; *The World Bank Atlas 2003-2004* and *World Development Indicators (WDI) 2008.*

Worldinformation.com, 2 Market Street, Saffron Walden, Essex CB10 1HZ, United Kingdom, www.worldinformation.com; The World of Information (www.worldinformation.com).

BHUTAN - HIDES AND SKINS INDUSTRY

United Nations Food and Agricultural Organization (FAO), Viale delle Terme di Caracalla, 00100 Rome, Italy, (Dial from U.S. (202) 653-2400), (Fax from U.S. (202) 653 5760), www.fao.org; *FAO Production Yearbook 2002.*

BHUTAN - HOUSING

Euromonitor International, Inc., 224 S. Michigan Avenue, Suite 1500, Chicago, IL 60604, (312) 922-1115, Fax: (312) 922-1157, www.euromonitor.com; *World Marketing Data and Statistics.*

M.E. Sharpe, 80 Business Park Drive, Armonk, NY 10504, (800) 541-6563, Fax: (914) 273-2106, www.mesharpe.com; *The Illustrated Book of World Rankings.*

BHUTAN - ILLITERATE PERSONS

Euromonitor International, Inc., 224 S. Michigan Avenue, Suite 1500, Chicago, IL 60604, (312) 922-1115, Fax: (312) 922-1157, www.euromonitor.com; *The World Economic Factbook 2008.*

United Nations Statistics Division, New York, NY 10017, (800) 253-9646, Fax: (212) 963-4116, http://unstats.un.org; *Asia-Pacific in Figures 2004* and *Human Development Report 2006.*

BHUTAN - IMPORTS

Asian Development Bank (ADB), PO Box 789, 0980 Manila, Philippines, www.adb.org; *Key Indicators of Developing Asian and Pacific Countries 2006.*

Central Intelligence Agency, Office of Public Affairs, Washington, DC 20505, (703) 482-0623, Fax: (703) 482-1739, www.cia.gov; *The World Factbook.*

Economist Intelligence Unit, 111 West 57th Street, New York, NY 10019, (212) 554-0600, Fax: (212) 586-1181, www.eiu.com; *Bhutan Country Report.*

Euromonitor International, Inc., 224 S. Michigan Avenue, Suite 1500, Chicago, IL 60604, (312) 922-1115, Fax: (312) 922-1157, www.euromonitor.com; *International Marketing Data and Statistics 2008* and *The World Economic Factbook 2008.*

Palgrave Macmillan Ltd., Houndmills, Basingstoke, Hampshire, RG21 6XS, England, (Telephone in U.S.

(888) 330-8477), (Fax in U.S. (800) 672-2054), www.palgrave.com; *The Statesman's Yearbook 2008.*

Taylor and Francis Group, An Informa Business, 2 Park Square, Milton Park, Abingdon, Oxford OX14 4RN, United Kingdom, (Dial from U.S. (212) 216-7800), (Fax from U.S. (212) 564-7854), www.tandf.co.uk; *The Europa World Year Book.*

United Nations Food and Agricultural Organization (FAO), Viale delle Terme di Caracalla, 00100 Rome, Italy, (Dial from U.S. (202) 653-2400), (Fax from U.S. (202) 653 5760), www.fao.org; *The State of Food and Agriculture (SOFA) 2006.*

The World Bank, 1818 H Street, NW, Washington, DC 20433, (202) 473-1000, Fax: (202) 477-6391, www.worldbank.org; *World Development Indicators (WDI) 2008.*

Worldinformation.com, 2 Market Street, Saffron Walden, Essex CB10 1HZ, United Kingdom, www.worldinformation.com; The World of Information (www.worldinformation.com).

BHUTAN - INDUSTRIAL PRODUCTIVITY

Euromonitor International, Inc., 224 S. Michigan Avenue, Suite 1500, Chicago, IL 60604, (312) 922-1115, Fax: (312) 922-1157, www.euromonitor.com; *International Marketing Data and Statistics 2008.*

M.E. Sharpe, 80 Business Park Drive, Armonk, NY 10504, (800) 541-6563, Fax: (914) 273-2106, www.mesharpe.com; *The Illustrated Book of World Rankings.*

BHUTAN - INDUSTRIES

Central Intelligence Agency, Office of Public Affairs, Washington, DC 20505, (703) 482-0623, Fax: (703) 482-1739, www.cia.gov; *The World Factbook.*

Economist Intelligence Unit, 111 West 57th Street, New York, NY 10019, (212) 554-0600, Fax: (212) 586-1181, www.eiu.com; *Bhutan Country Report.*

Euromonitor International, Inc., 224 S. Michigan Avenue, Suite 1500, Chicago, IL 60604, (312) 922-1115, Fax: (312) 922-1157, www.euromonitor.com; *International Marketing Data and Statistics 2008* and *World Marketing Data and Statistics.*

M.E. Sharpe, 80 Business Park Drive, Armonk, NY 10504, (800) 541-6563, Fax: (914) 273-2106, www.mesharpe.com; *The Illustrated Book of World Rankings.*

Palgrave Macmillan Ltd., Houndmills, Basingstoke, Hampshire, RG21 6XS, England, (Telephone in U.S. (888) 330-8477), (Fax in U.S. (800) 672-2054), www.palgrave.com; *The Statesman's Yearbook 2008.*

Taylor and Francis Group, An Informa Business, 2 Park Square, Milton Park, Abingdon, Oxford OX14 4RN, United Kingdom, (Dial from U.S. (212) 216-7800), (Fax from U.S. (212) 564-7854), www.tandf.co.uk; *The Europa World Year Book.*

United Nations Statistics Division, New York, NY 10017, (800) 253-9646, Fax: (212) 963-4116, http://unstats.un.org; *Asia-Pacific in Figures 2004* and *Statistical Yearbook for Asia and the Pacific 2004.*

The World Bank, 1818 H Street, NW, Washington, DC 20433, (202) 473-1000, Fax: (202) 477-6391, www.worldbank.org; *Bhutan* and *World Development Indicators (WDI) 2008.*

BHUTAN - INFANT AND MATERNAL MORTALITY

See BHUTAN - MORTALITY

BHUTAN - INTERNATIONAL FINANCE

Asian Development Bank (ADB), PO Box 789, 0980 Manila, Philippines, www.adb.org; *Key Indicators of Developing Asian and Pacific Countries 2006.*

The World Bank, 1818 H Street, NW, Washington, DC 20433, (202) 473-1000, Fax: (202) 477-6391, www.worldbank.org; *Bhutan.*

BHUTAN - INTERNATIONAL STATISTICS

Asian Development Bank (ADB), PO Box 789, 0980 Manila, Philippines, www.adb.org; *Key Indicators of Developing Asian and Pacific Countries 2006.*

BHUTAN - INTERNATIONAL TRADE

Asian Development Bank (ADB), PO Box 789, 0980 Manila, Philippines, www.adb.org; *Key Indicators of Developing Asian and Pacific Countries 2006.*

Economist Intelligence Unit, 111 West 57th Street, New York, NY 10019, (212) 554-0600, Fax: (212) 586-1181, www.eiu.com; *Bhutan Country Report* and *Business Asia.*

Euromonitor International, Inc., 224 S. Michigan Avenue, Suite 1500, Chicago, IL 60604, (312) 922-1115, Fax: (312) 922-1157, www.euromonitor.com; *International Marketing Data and Statistics 2008; The World Economic Factbook 2008;* and *World Marketing Data and Statistics.*

M.E. Sharpe, 80 Business Park Drive, Armonk, NY 10504, (800) 541-6563, Fax: (914) 273-2106, www.mesharpe.com; *The Illustrated Book of World Rankings.*

Organisation for Economic Cooperation and Development (OECD), 2 rue Andre Pascal, F-75775 Paris Cedex 16, France, (Telephone in U.S. (202) 785-6323), (Fax in U.S. (202) 785-0350), www.oecd.org; *International Trade by Commodity Statistics (ITCS).*

Palgrave Macmillan Ltd., Houndmills, Basingstoke, Hampshire, RG21 6XS, England, (Telephone in U.S. (888) 330-8477), (Fax in U.S. (800) 672-2054), www.palgrave.com; *The Statesman's Yearbook 2008.*

Taylor and Francis Group, An Informa Business, 2 Park Square, Milton Park, Abingdon, Oxford OX14 4RN, United Kingdom, (Dial from U.S. (212) 216-7800), (Fax from U.S. (212) 564-7854), www.tandf.co.uk; *The Europa World Year Book.*

United Nations Conference on Trade and Development (UNCTAD), DC2-1120, United Nations, New York, NY 10017, (212) 963-0027, www.unctad.org; *UNCTAD Commodity Yearbook.*

United Nations Food and Agricultural Organization (FAO), Viale delle Terme di Caracalla, 00100 Rome, Italy, (Dial from U.S. (202) 653-2400), (Fax from U.S. (202) 653 5760), www.fao.org; *FAO Trade Yearbook* and *The State of Food and Agriculture (SOFA) 2006.*

United Nations Statistics Division, New York, NY 10017, (800) 253-9646, Fax: (212) 963-4116, http://unstats.un.org; *Asia-Pacific in Figures 2004* and *Statistical Yearbook for Asia and the Pacific 2004.*

The World Bank, 1818 H Street, NW, Washington, DC 20433, (202) 473-1000, Fax: (202) 477-6391, www.worldbank.org; *Bhutan* and *World Development Indicators (WDI) 2008.*

World Trade Organization (WTO), Centre William Rappard, Rue de Lausanne 154, CH-1211 Geneva 21, Switzerland, www.wto.org; *International Trade Statistics 2006.*

BHUTAN - IRON AND IRON ORE PRODUCTION

See BHUTAN - MINERAL INDUSTRIES

BHUTAN - IRRIGATION

Euromonitor International, Inc., 224 S. Michigan Avenue, Suite 1500, Chicago, IL 60604, (312) 922-1115, Fax: (312) 922-1157, www.euromonitor.com; *International Marketing Data and Statistics 2008.*

BHUTAN - JUTE PRODUCTION

See BHUTAN - CROPS

BHUTAN - LABOR

Central Intelligence Agency, Office of Public Affairs, Washington, DC 20505, (703) 482-0623, Fax: (703) 482-1739, www.cia.gov; *The World Factbook.*

Economist Intelligence Unit, 111 West 57th Street, New York, NY 10019, (212) 554-0600, Fax: (212) 586-1181, www.eiu.com; *Business Asia.*

Euromonitor International, Inc., 224 S. Michigan Avenue, Suite 1500, Chicago, IL 60604, (312) 922-1115, Fax: (312) 922-1157, www.euromonitor.com; *International Marketing Data and Statistics 2008* and *World Marketing Data and Statistics.*

M.E. Sharpe, 80 Business Park Drive, Armonk, NY 10504, (800) 541-6563, Fax: (914) 273-2106, www.mesharpe.com; *The Illustrated Book of World Rankings.*

Palgrave Macmillan Ltd., Houndmills, Basingstoke, Hampshire, RG21 6XS, England, (Telephone in U.S. (888) 330-8477), (Fax in U.S. (800) 672-2054), www.palgrave.com; *The Statesman's Yearbook 2008.*

United Nations Food and Agricultural Organization (FAO), Viale delle Terme di Caracalla, 00100 Rome, Italy, (Dial from U.S. (202) 653-2400), (Fax from U.S. (202) 653 5760), www.fao.org; *The State of Food and Agriculture (SOFA) 2006.*

United Nations Statistics Division, New York, NY 10017, (800) 253-9646, Fax: (212) 963-4116, http://unstats.un.org; *Human Development Report 2006.*

The World Bank, 1818 H Street, NW, Washington, DC 20433, (202) 473-1000, Fax: (202) 477-6391, www.worldbank.org; *The World Bank Atlas 2003-2004* and *World Development Indicators (WDI) 2008.*

BHUTAN - LAND USE

Central Intelligence Agency, Office of Public Affairs, Washington, DC 20505, (703) 482-0623, Fax: (703) 482-1739, www.cia.gov; *The World Factbook.*

Euromonitor International, Inc., 224 S. Michigan Avenue, Suite 1500, Chicago, IL 60604, (312) 922-1115, Fax: (312) 922-1157, www.euromonitor.com; *International Marketing Data and Statistics 2008.*

United Nations Food and Agricultural Organization (FAO), Viale delle Terme di Caracalla, 00100 Rome, Italy, (Dial from U.S. (202) 653-2400), (Fax from U.S. (202) 653 5760), www.fao.org; *FAO Production Yearbook 2002.*

BHUTAN - LIBRARIES

M.E. Sharpe, 80 Business Park Drive, Armonk, NY 10504, (800) 541-6563, Fax: (914) 273-2106, www.mesharpe.com; *The Illustrated Book of World Rankings.*

BHUTAN - LIFE EXPECTANCY

Central Intelligence Agency, Office of Public Affairs, Washington, DC 20505, (703) 482-0623, Fax: (703) 482-1739, www.cia.gov; *The World Factbook.*

Economist Intelligence Unit, 111 West 57th Street, New York, NY 10019, (212) 554-0600, Fax: (212) 586-1181, www.eiu.com; *Business Asia.*

Euromonitor International, Inc., 224 S. Michigan Avenue, Suite 1500, Chicago, IL 60604, (312) 922-1115, Fax: (312) 922-1157, www.euromonitor.com; *The World Economic Factbook 2008.*

Palgrave Macmillan Ltd., Houndmills, Basingstoke, Hampshire, RG21 6XS, England, (Telephone in U.S. (888) 330-8477), (Fax in U.S. (800) 672-2054), www.palgrave.com; *The Statesman's Yearbook 2008.*

United Nations Statistics Division, New York, NY 10017, (800) 253-9646, Fax: (212) 963-4116, http://unstats.un.org; *Asia-Pacific in Figures 2004; Human Development Report 2006;* and *World Statistics Pocketbook.*

The World Bank, 1818 H Street, NW, Washington, DC 20433, (202) 473-1000, Fax: (202) 477-6391, www.worldbank.org; *The World Bank Atlas 2003-2004.*

BHUTAN - LITERACY

Euromonitor International, Inc., 224 S. Michigan Avenue, Suite 1500, Chicago, IL 60604, (312) 922-1115, Fax: (312) 922-1157, www.euromonitor.com; *World Marketing Data and Statistics.*

BHUTAN - LIVESTOCK

Euromonitor International, Inc., 224 S. Michigan Avenue, Suite 1500, Chicago, IL 60604, (312) 922-1115, Fax: (312) 922-1157, www.euromonitor.com; *International Marketing Data and Statistics 2008.*

M.E. Sharpe, 80 Business Park Drive, Armonk, NY 10504, (800) 541-6563, Fax: (914) 273-2106, www.mesharpe.com; *The Illustrated Book of World Rankings.*

Palgrave Macmillan Ltd., Houndmills, Basingstoke, Hampshire, RG21 6XS, England, (Telephone in U.S. (888) 330-8477), (Fax in U.S. (800) 672-2054), www.palgrave.com; *The Statesman's Yearbook 2008.*

Taylor and Francis Group, An Informa Business, 2 Park Square, Milton Park, Abingdon, Oxford OX14 4RN, United Kingdom, (Dial from U.S. (212) 216-7800), (Fax from U.S. (212) 564-7854), www.tandf.co.uk; *The Europa World Year Book.*

United Nations Conference on Trade and Development (UNCTAD), DC2-1120, United Nations, New York, NY 10017, (212) 963-0027, www.unctad.org; *UNCTAD Commodity Yearbook.*

United Nations Food and Agricultural Organization (FAO), Viale delle Terme di Caracalla, 00100 Rome, Italy, (Dial from U.S. (202) 653-2400), (Fax from U.S. (202) 653 5760), www.fao.org; *FAO Production Yearbook 2002* and *The State of Food and Agriculture (SOFA) 2006.*

United Nations Statistics Division, New York, NY 10017, (800) 253-9646, Fax: (212) 963-4116, http://unstats.un.org; *Statistical Yearbook.*

BHUTAN - LOCAL TAXATION

Euromonitor International, Inc., 224 S. Michigan Avenue, Suite 1500, Chicago, IL 60604, (312) 922-1115, Fax: (312) 922-1157, www.euromonitor.com; *International Marketing Data and Statistics 2008.*

BHUTAN - MANPOWER

United Nations Statistics Division, New York, NY 10017, (800) 253-9646, Fax: (212) 963-4116, http://unstats.un.org; *Statistical Yearbook for Asia and the Pacific 2004.*

BHUTAN - MANUFACTURES

Asian Development Bank (ADB), PO Box 789, 0980 Manila, Philippines, www.adb.org; *Key Indicators of Developing Asian and Pacific Countries 2006.*

M.E. Sharpe, 80 Business Park Drive, Armonk, NY 10504, (800) 541-6563, Fax: (914) 273-2106, www.mesharpe.com; *The Illustrated Book of World Rankings.*

The World Bank, 1818 H Street, NW, Washington, DC 20433, (202) 473-1000, Fax: (202) 477-6391, www.worldbank.org; *World Development Indicators (WDI) 2008.*

BHUTAN - MARRIAGE

M.E. Sharpe, 80 Business Park Drive, Armonk, NY 10504, (800) 541-6563, Fax: (914) 273-2106, www.mesharpe.com; *The Illustrated Book of World Rankings.*

United Nations Statistics Division, New York, NY 10017, (800) 253-9646, Fax: (212) 963-4116, http://unstats.un.org; *Demographic Yearbook.*

BHUTAN - MEAT PRODUCTION

See BHUTAN - LIVESTOCK

BHUTAN - MILK PRODUCTION

See BHUTAN - DAIRY PROCESSING

BHUTAN - MINERAL INDUSTRIES

Asian Development Bank (ADB), PO Box 789, 0980 Manila, Philippines, www.adb.org; *Key Indicators of Developing Asian and Pacific Countries 2006.*

M.E. Sharpe, 80 Business Park Drive, Armonk, NY 10504, (800) 541-6563, Fax: (914) 273-2106, www.mesharpe.com; *The Illustrated Book of World Rankings.*

Palgrave Macmillan Ltd., Houndmills, Basingstoke, Hampshire, RG21 6XS, England, (Telephone in U.S. (888) 330-8477), (Fax in U.S. (800) 672-2054), www.palgrave.com; *The Statesman's Yearbook 2008.*

Taylor and Francis Group, An Informa Business, 2 Park Square, Milton Park, Abingdon, Oxford OX14 4RN, United Kingdom, (Dial from U.S. (212) 216-7800), (Fax from U.S. (212) 564-7854), www.tandf.co.uk; *The Europa World Year Book.*

United Nations Conference on Trade and Development (UNCTAD), DC2-1120, United Nations, New York, NY 10017, (212) 963-0027, www.unctad.org; *UNCTAD Commodity Yearbook.*

The World Bank, 1818 H Street, NW, Washington, DC 20433, (202) 473-1000, Fax: (202) 477-6391, www.worldbank.org; *Bhutan.*

BHUTAN - MONEY EXCHANGE RATES

See BHUTAN - FOREIGN EXCHANGE RATES

BHUTAN - MONEY SUPPLY

Asian Development Bank (ADB), PO Box 789, 0980 Manila, Philippines, www.adb.org; *Key Indicators of Developing Asian and Pacific Countries 2006.*

Economist Intelligence Unit, 111 West 57th Street, New York, NY 10019, (212) 554-0600, Fax: (212) 586-1181, www.eiu.com; *Bhutan Country Report.*

Euromonitor International, Inc., 224 S. Michigan Avenue, Suite 1500, Chicago, IL 60604, (312) 922-1115, Fax: (312) 922-1157, www.euromonitor.com; *International Marketing Data and Statistics 2008.*

Taylor and Francis Group, An Informa Business, 2 Park Square, Milton Park, Abingdon, Oxford OX14 4RN, United Kingdom, (Dial from U.S. (212) 216-7800), (Fax from U.S. (212) 564-7854), www.tandf.co.uk; *The Europa World Year Book.*

The World Bank, 1818 H Street, NW, Washington, DC 20433, (202) 473-1000, Fax: (202) 477-6391, www.worldbank.org; *Bhutan* and *World Development Indicators (WDI) 2008.*

BHUTAN - MORTALITY

Central Intelligence Agency, Office of Public Affairs, Washington, DC 20505, (703) 482-0623, Fax: (703) 482-1739, www.cia.gov; *The World Factbook.*

Euromonitor International, Inc., 224 S. Michigan Avenue, Suite 1500, Chicago, IL 60604, (312) 922-1115, Fax: (312) 922-1157, www.euromonitor.com; *International Marketing Data and Statistics 2008* and *The World Economic Factbook 2008.*

Taylor and Francis Group, An Informa Business, 2 Park Square, Milton Park, Abingdon, Oxford OX14 4RN, United Kingdom, (Dial from U.S. (212) 216-7800), (Fax from U.S. (212) 564-7854), www.tandf.co.uk; *The Europa World Year Book.*

UNICEF, 3 United Nations Plaza, New York, NY 10017, (800) 253-9646, Fax: (212) 887-7465, www.unicef.org; *The State of the World's Children 2008.*

United Nations Statistics Division, New York, NY 10017, (800) 253-9646, Fax: (212) 963-4116, http://unstats.un.org; *Asia-Pacific in Figures 2004; Demographic Yearbook; Human Development Report 2006; Statistical Yearbook;* and *World Statistics Pocketbook.*

The World Bank, 1818 H Street, NW, Washington, DC 20433, (202) 473-1000, Fax: (202) 477-6391, www.worldbank.org; *The World Bank Atlas 2003-2004.*

BHUTAN - MOTION PICTURES

Palgrave Macmillan Ltd., Houndmills, Basingstoke, Hampshire, RG21 6XS, England, (Telephone in U.S. (888) 330-8477), (Fax in U.S. (800) 672-2054), www.palgrave.com; *The Statesman's Yearbook 2008.*

BHUTAN - MOTOR VEHICLES

Taylor and Francis Group, An Informa Business, 2 Park Square, Milton Park, Abingdon, Oxford OX14 4RN, United Kingdom, (Dial from U.S. (212) 216-7800), (Fax from U.S. (212) 564-7854), www.tandf.co.uk; *The Europa World Year Book.*

BHUTAN - MUSEUMS

M.E. Sharpe, 80 Business Park Drive, Armonk, NY 10504, (800) 541-6563, Fax: (914) 273-2106, www.mesharpe.com; *The Illustrated Book of World Rankings.*

UNESCO Institute for Statistics, C.P. 6128 Succursale Centre-Ville, Montreal, Quebec, H3C 3J7 Canada, (Dial from U.S. (514) 343-6880), (Fax from U.S. (514) 343 6882), www.uis.unesco.org; *Statistical Tables.*

BHUTAN - NATURAL GAS PRODUCTION

See BHUTAN - MINERAL INDUSTRIES

BHUTAN - NUTRITION

Asian Development Bank (ADB), PO Box 789, 0980 Manila, Philippines, www.adb.org; *Key Indicators of Developing Asian and Pacific Countries 2006.*

United Nations Food and Agricultural Organization (FAO), Viale delle Terme di Caracalla, 00100 Rome, Italy, (Dial from U.S. (202) 653-2400), (Fax from U.S. (202) 653 5760), www.fao.org; *The State of Food and Agriculture (SOFA) 2006.*

BHUTAN - OLDER PEOPLE

M.E. Sharpe, 80 Business Park Drive, Armonk, NY 10504, (800) 541-6563, Fax: (914) 273-2106, www.mesharpe.com; *The Illustrated Book of World Rankings.*

BHUTAN - PEANUT PRODUCTION

See BHUTAN - CROPS

BHUTAN - PESTICIDES

United Nations Food and Agricultural Organization (FAO), Viale delle Terme di Caracalla, 00100 Rome, Italy, (Dial from U.S. (202) 653-2400), (Fax from U.S. (202) 653 5760), www.fao.org; *The State of Food and Agriculture (SOFA) 2006.*

BHUTAN - PETROLEUM INDUSTRY AND TRADE

Asian Development Bank (ADB), PO Box 789, 0980 Manila, Philippines, www.adb.org; *Key Indicators of Developing Asian and Pacific Countries 2006.*

M.E. Sharpe, 80 Business Park Drive, Armonk, NY 10504, (800) 541-6563, Fax: (914) 273-2106, www.mesharpe.com; *The Illustrated Book of World Rankings.*

PennWell Corporation, 1421 South Sheridan Road, Tulsa, OK 74112, (918) 835-3161, www.pennwell.com; *International Petroleum Encyclopedia 2007.*

U.S. Department of Energy (DOE), Energy Information Administration (EIA), 1000 Independence Avenue, SW, Washington, DC 20585, (202) 586-8800, www.eia.doe.gov; *International Energy Annual 2004* and *International Energy Outlook 2006.*

United Nations Conference on Trade and Development (UNCTAD), DC2-1120, United Nations, New York, NY 10017, (212) 963-0027, www.unctad.org; *UNCTAD Commodity Yearbook.*

United Nations Food and Agricultural Organization (FAO), Viale delle Terme di Caracalla, 00100 Rome, Italy, (Dial from U.S. (202) 653-2400), (Fax from U.S. (202) 653 5760), www.fao.org; *The State of Food and Agriculture (SOFA) 2006.*

BHUTAN - POLITICAL SCIENCE

Asian Development Bank (ADB), PO Box 789, 0980 Manila, Philippines, www.adb.org; *Key Indicators of Developing Asian and Pacific Countries 2006.*

Central Intelligence Agency, Office of Public Affairs, Washington, DC 20505, (703) 482-0623, Fax: (703) 482-1739, www.cia.gov; *The World Factbook.*

Palgrave Macmillan Ltd., Houndmills, Basingstoke, Hampshire, RG21 6XS, England, (Telephone in U.S. (888) 330-8477), (Fax in U.S. (800) 672-2054), www.palgrave.com; *The Statesman's Yearbook 2008.*

Taylor and Francis Group, An Informa Business, 2 Park Square, Milton Park, Abingdon, Oxford OX14 4RN, United Kingdom, (Dial from U.S. (212) 216-7800), (Fax from U.S. (212) 564-7854), www.tandf.co.uk; *The Europa World Year Book.*

United Nations Statistics Division, New York, NY 10017, (800) 253-9646, Fax: (212) 963-4116, http://unstats.un.org; *Asia-Pacific in Figures 2004* and *National Accounts Statistics: Compendium of Income Distribution Statistics.*

The World Bank, 1818 H Street, NW, Washington, DC 20433, (202) 473-1000, Fax: (202) 477-6391, www.worldbank.org; *World Development Indicators (WDI) 2008.*

BHUTAN - POPULATION

Asian Development Bank (ADB), PO Box 789, 0980 Manila, Philippines, www.adb.org; *Key Indicators of Developing Asian and Pacific Countries 2006.*

Central Intelligence Agency, Office of Public Affairs, Washington, DC 20505, (703) 482-0623, Fax: (703) 482-1739, www.cia.gov; *The World Factbook.*

Economist Intelligence Unit, 111 West 57th Street, New York, NY 10019, (212) 554-0600, Fax: (212) 586-1181, www.eiu.com; *Bhutan Country Report* and *Business Asia.*

Euromonitor International, Inc., 224 S. Michigan Avenue, Suite 1500, Chicago, IL 60604, (312) 922-1115, Fax: (312) 922-1157, www.euromonitor.com; *International Marketing Data and Statistics 2008* and *The World Economic Factbook 2008.*

M.E. Sharpe, 80 Business Park Drive, Armonk, NY 10504, (800) 541-6563, Fax: (914) 273-2106, www.mesharpe.com; *The Illustrated Book of World Rankings.*

Palgrave Macmillan Ltd., Houndmills, Basingstoke, Hampshire, RG21 6XS, England, (Telephone in U.S. (888) 330-8477), (Fax in U.S. (800) 672-2054), www.palgrave.com; *The Statesman's Yearbook 2008.*

Taylor and Francis Group, An Informa Business, 2 Park Square, Milton Park, Abingdon, Oxford OX14 4RN, United Kingdom, (Dial from U.S. (212) 216-7800), (Fax from U.S. (212) 564-7854), www.tandf.co.uk; *The Europa World Year Book.*

United Nations Food and Agricultural Organization (FAO), Viale delle Terme di Caracalla, 00100 Rome, Italy, (Dial from U.S. (202) 653-2400), (Fax from U.S. (202) 653 5760), www.fao.org; *FAO Production Yearbook 2002.*

United Nations Statistics Division, New York, NY 10017, (800) 253-9646, Fax: (212) 963-4116, http://unstats.un.org; *Asia-Pacific in Figures 2004; Demographic Yearbook; Human Development Report 2006; Statistical Yearbook; Statistical Yearbook for Asia and the Pacific 2004;* and *World Statistics Pocketbook.*

The World Bank, 1818 H Street, NW, Washington, DC 20433, (202) 473-1000, Fax: (202) 477-6391, www.worldbank.org; *Bhutan* and *The World Bank Atlas 2003-2004.*

World Health Organization (WHO), Avenue Appia 20, 1211 Geneve 27, Switzerland, (Telephone in U.S. (212) 331-9081), www.who.int; *World Health Report 2006.*

Worldinformation.com, 2 Market Street, Saffron Walden, Essex CB10 1HZ, United Kingdom, www.worldinformation.com; The World of Information (www.worldinformation.com).

BHUTAN - POPULATION DENSITY

Central Intelligence Agency, Office of Public Affairs, Washington, DC 20505, (703) 482-0623, Fax: (703) 482-1739, www.cia.gov; *The World Factbook.*

Euromonitor International, Inc., 224 S. Michigan Avenue, Suite 1500, Chicago, IL 60604, (312) 922-1115, Fax: (312) 922-1157, www.euromonitor.com; *International Marketing Data and Statistics 2008* and *The World Economic Factbook 2008.*

M.E. Sharpe, 80 Business Park Drive, Armonk, NY 10504, (800) 541-6563, Fax: (914) 273-2106, www.mesharpe.com; *The Illustrated Book of World Rankings.*

Palgrave Macmillan Ltd., Houndmills, Basingstoke, Hampshire, RG21 6XS, England, (Telephone in U.S. (888) 330-8477), (Fax in U.S. (800) 672-2054), www.palgrave.com; *The Statesman's Yearbook 2008.*

Taylor and Francis Group, An Informa Business, 2 Park Square, Milton Park, Abingdon, Oxford OX14 4RN, United Kingdom, (Dial from U.S. (212) 216-7800), (Fax from U.S. (212) 564-7854), www.tandf.co.uk; *The Europa World Year Book.*

United Nations Food and Agricultural Organization (FAO), Viale delle Terme di Caracalla, 00100 Rome, Italy, (Dial from U.S. (202) 653-2400), (Fax from U.S. (202) 653 5760), www.fao.org; *The State of Food and Agriculture (SOFA) 2006.*

United Nations Statistics Division, New York, NY 10017, (800) 253-9646, Fax: (212) 963-4116, http://unstats.un.org; *Statistical Yearbook.*

The World Bank, 1818 H Street, NW, Washington, DC 20433, (202) 473-1000, Fax: (202) 477-6391, www.worldbank.org; *Bhutan.*

BHUTAN - POSTAL SERVICE

M.E. Sharpe, 80 Business Park Drive, Armonk, NY 10504, (800) 541-6563, Fax: (914) 273-2106, www.mesharpe.com; *The Illustrated Book of World Rankings.*

Palgrave Macmillan Ltd., Houndmills, Basingstoke, Hampshire, RG21 6XS, England, (Telephone in U.S. (888) 330-8477), (Fax in U.S. (800) 672-2054), www.palgrave.com; *The Statesman's Yearbook 2008.*

United Nations Statistics Division, New York, NY 10017, (800) 253-9646, Fax: (212) 963-4116, http://unstats.un.org; *Statistical Yearbook.*

BHUTAN - POWER RESOURCES

Euromonitor International, Inc., 224 S. Michigan Avenue, Suite 1500, Chicago, IL 60604, (312) 922-1115, Fax: (312) 922-1157, www.euromonitor.com; *International Marketing Data and Statistics 2008; The World Economic Factbook 2008;* and *World Marketing Data and Statistics.*

M.E. Sharpe, 80 Business Park Drive, Armonk, NY 10504, (800) 541-6563, Fax: (914) 273-2106, www.mesharpe.com; *The Illustrated Book of World Rankings.*

Palgrave Macmillan Ltd., Houndmills, Basingstoke, Hampshire, RG21 6XS, England, (Telephone in U.S. (888) 330-8477), (Fax in U.S. (800) 672-2054), www.palgrave.com; *The Statesman's Yearbook 2008.*

U.S. Department of Energy (DOE), Energy Information Administration (EIA), 1000 Independence Avenue, SW, Washington, DC 20585, (202) 586-8800, www.eia.doe.gov; *International Energy Annual 2004* and *International Energy Outlook 2006.*

United Nations Food and Agricultural Organization (FAO), Viale delle Terme di Caracalla, 00100 Rome, Italy, (Dial from U.S. (202) 653-2400), (Fax from U.S. (202) 653 5760), www.fao.org; *The State of Food and Agriculture (SOFA) 2006.*

United Nations Statistics Division, New York, NY 10017, (800) 253-9646, Fax: (212) 963-4116, http://unstats.un.org; *Asia-Pacific in Figures 2004; Human Development Report 2006; Statistical Yearbook for Asia and the Pacific 2004;* and *World Statistics Pocketbook.*

The World Bank, 1818 H Street, NW, Washington, DC 20433, (202) 473-1000, Fax: (202) 477-6391, www.worldbank.org; *The World Bank Atlas 2003-2004.*

BHUTAN - PRICES

Asian Development Bank (ADB), PO Box 789, 0980 Manila, Philippines, www.adb.org; *Key Indicators of Developing Asian and Pacific Countries 2006.*

Euromonitor International, Inc., 224 S. Michigan Avenue, Suite 1500, Chicago, IL 60604, (312) 922-1115, Fax: (312) 922-1157, www.euromonitor.com; *World Marketing Data and Statistics.*

M.E. Sharpe, 80 Business Park Drive, Armonk, NY 10504, (800) 541-6563, Fax: (914) 273-2106, www.mesharpe.com; *The Illustrated Book of World Rankings.*

United Nations Food and Agricultural Organization (FAO), Viale delle Terme di Caracalla, 00100 Rome, Italy, (Dial from U.S. (202) 653-2400), (Fax from U.S. (202) 653 5760), www.fao.org; *FAO Production Yearbook 2002* and *The State of Food and Agriculture (SOFA) 2006.*

The World Bank, 1818 H Street, NW, Washington, DC 20433, (202) 473-1000, Fax: (202) 477-6391, www.worldbank.org; *Bhutan.*

BHUTAN - PUBLIC HEALTH

Economist Intelligence Unit, 111 West 57th Street, New York, NY 10019, (212) 554-0600, Fax: (212) 586-1181, www.eiu.com; *Business Asia.*

Euromonitor International, Inc., 224 S. Michigan Avenue, Suite 1500, Chicago, IL 60604, (312) 922-1115, Fax: (312) 922-1157, www.euromonitor.com; *World Marketing Data and Statistics.*

M.E. Sharpe, 80 Business Park Drive, Armonk, NY 10504, (800) 541-6563, Fax: (914) 273-2106, www.mesharpe.com; *The Illustrated Book of World Rankings.*

Palgrave Macmillan Ltd., Houndmills, Basingstoke, Hampshire, RG21 6XS, England, (Telephone in U.S. (888) 330-8477), (Fax in U.S. (800) 672-2054), www.palgrave.com; *The Statesman's Yearbook 2008.*

UNICEF, 3 United Nations Plaza, New York, NY 10017, (800) 253-9646, Fax: (212) 887-7465, www.unicef.org; *The State of the World's Children 2008.*

United Nations Statistics Division, New York, NY 10017, (800) 253-9646, Fax: (212) 963-4116, http://unstats.un.org; *Asia-Pacific in Figures 2004* and *Human Development Report 2006.*

The World Bank, 1818 H Street, NW, Washington, DC 20433, (202) 473-1000, Fax: (202) 477-6391, www.worldbank.org; *Bhutan.*

BHUTAN - RADIO BROADCASTING

Palgrave Macmillan Ltd., Houndmills, Basingstoke, Hampshire, RG21 6XS, England, (Telephone in U.S. (888) 330-8477), (Fax in U.S. (800) 672-2054), www.palgrave.com; *The Statesman's Yearbook 2008.*

BHUTAN - RELIGION

Central Intelligence Agency, Office of Public Affairs, Washington, DC 20505, (703) 482-0623, Fax: (703) 482-1739, www.cia.gov; *The World Factbook.*

M.E. Sharpe, 80 Business Park Drive, Armonk, NY 10504, (800) 541-6563, Fax: (914) 273-2106, www.mesharpe.com; *The Illustrated Book of World Rankings.*

Palgrave Macmillan Ltd., Houndmills, Basingstoke, Hampshire, RG21 6XS, England, (Telephone in U.S. (888) 330-8477), (Fax in U.S. (800) 672-2054), www.palgrave.com; *The Statesman's Yearbook 2008.*

BHUTAN - RESERVES (ACCOUNTING)

Asian Development Bank (ADB), PO Box 789, 0980 Manila, Philippines, www.adb.org; *Key Indicators of Developing Asian and Pacific Countries 2006.*

Euromonitor International, Inc., 224 S. Michigan Avenue, Suite 1500, Chicago, IL 60604, (312) 922-1115, Fax: (312) 922-1157, www.euromonitor.com; *International Marketing Data and Statistics 2008.*

The World Bank, 1818 H Street, NW, Washington, DC 20433, (202) 473-1000, Fax: (202) 477-6391, www.worldbank.org; *World Development Indicators (WDI) 2008.*

BHUTAN - RETAIL TRADE

Euromonitor International, Inc., 224 S. Michigan Avenue, Suite 1500, Chicago, IL 60604, (312) 922-1115, Fax: (312) 922-1157, www.euromonitor.com; *World Marketing Data and Statistics.*

BHUTAN - RICE PRODUCTION

See BHUTAN - CROPS

BHUTAN - ROADS

Central Intelligence Agency, Office of Public Affairs, Washington, DC 20505, (703) 482-0623, Fax: (703) 482-1739, www.cia.gov; *The World Factbook.*

Economist Intelligence Unit, 111 West 57th Street, New York, NY 10019, (212) 554-0600, Fax: (212) 586-1181, www.eiu.com; *Business Asia.*

Palgrave Macmillan Ltd., Houndmills, Basingstoke, Hampshire, RG21 6XS, England, (Telephone in U.S. (888) 330-8477), (Fax in U.S. (800) 672-2054), www.palgrave.com; *The Statesman's Yearbook 2008.*

BHUTAN - RUBBER INDUSTRY AND TRADE

International Rubber Study Group (IRSG), 1st Floor, Heron House, 109/115 Wembley Hill Road, Wembley, Middlesex HA9 8DA, United Kingdom, www.rubberstudy.com; *Rubber Statistical Bulletin; Summary of World Rubber Statistics 2005; World Rubber Statistics Handbook (Volume 6, 1975-2001);* and *World Rubber Statistics Historic Handbook.*

M.E. Sharpe, 80 Business Park Drive, Armonk, NY 10504, (800) 541-6563, Fax: (914) 273-2106, www.mesharpe.com; *The Illustrated Book of World Rankings.*

BHUTAN - SHEEP

See BHUTAN - LIVESTOCK

BHUTAN - SILVER PRODUCTION

See BHUTAN - MINERAL INDUSTRIES

BHUTAN - SOCIAL ECOLOGY

Asian Development Bank (ADB), PO Box 789, 0980 Manila, Philippines, www.adb.org; *Key Indicators of Developing Asian and Pacific Countries 2006.*

M.E. Sharpe, 80 Business Park Drive, Armonk, NY 10504, (800) 541-6563, Fax: (914) 273-2106, www.mesharpe.com; *The Illustrated Book of World Rankings.*

United Nations Statistics Division, New York, NY 10017, (800) 253-9646, Fax: (212) 963-4116, http://unstats.un.org; *World Statistics Pocketbook.*

BHUTAN - SOCIAL SECURITY

United Nations Statistics Division, New York, NY 10017, (800) 253-9646, Fax: (212) 963-4116, http://unstats.un.org; *National Accounts Statistics: Compendium of Income Distribution Statistics.*

BHUTAN - STEEL PRODUCTION

See BHUTAN - MINERAL INDUSTRIES

BHUTAN - SUGAR PRODUCTION

See BHUTAN - CROPS

BHUTAN - TAXATION

Taylor and Francis Group, An Informa Business, 2 Park Square, Milton Park, Abingdon, Oxford OX14 4RN, United Kingdom, (Dial from U.S. (212) 216-7800), (Fax from U.S. (212) 564-7854), www.tandf.co.uk; *The Europa World Year Book.*

The World Bank, 1818 H Street, NW, Washington, DC 20433, (202) 473-1000, Fax: (202) 477-6391, www.worldbank.org; *World Development Indicators (WDI) 2008.*

BHUTAN - TELEPHONE

Economist Intelligence Unit, 111 West 57th Street, New York, NY 10019, (212) 554-0600, Fax: (212) 586-1181, www.eiu.com; *Business Asia.*

International Telecommunication Union (ITU), Place des Nations, 1211 Geneva 20, Switzerland, www.itu.int; World Telecommunication Indicators Database.

Palgrave Macmillan Ltd., Houndmills, Basingstoke, Hampshire, RG21 6XS, England, (Telephone in U.S. (888) 330-8477), (Fax in U.S. (800) 672-2054), www.palgrave.com; *The Statesman's Yearbook 2008.*

Taylor and Francis Group, An Informa Business, 2 Park Square, Milton Park, Abingdon, Oxford OX14 4RN, United Kingdom, (Dial from U.S. (212) 216-7800), (Fax from U.S. (212) 564-7854), www.tandf.co.uk; *The Europa World Year Book.*

United Nations Statistics Division, New York, NY 10017, (800) 253-9646, Fax: (212) 963-4116, http://unstats.un.org; *World Statistics Pocketbook.*

BHUTAN - TEXTILE INDUSTRY

M.E. Sharpe, 80 Business Park Drive, Armonk, NY 10504, (800) 541-6563, Fax: (914) 273-2106, www.mesharpe.com; *The Illustrated Book of World Rankings.*

United Nations Conference on Trade and Development (UNCTAD), DC2-1120, United Nations, New York, NY 10017, (212) 963-0027, www.unctad.org; *UNCTAD Commodity Yearbook.*

BHUTAN - TOBACCO INDUSTRY

Foreign Agricultural Service (FAS), U.S. Department of Agriculture (USDA), 1400 Independence Avenue, SW, Washington, DC 20250, (202) 720-3935, www.fas.usda.gov; *Tobacco: World Markets and Trade.*

M.E. Sharpe, 80 Business Park Drive, Armonk, NY 10504, (800) 541-6563, Fax: (914) 273-2106, www.mesharpe.com; *The Illustrated Book of World Rankings.*

United Nations Statistics Division, New York, NY 10017, (800) 253-9646, Fax: (212) 963-4116, http://unstats.un.org; *Statistical Yearbook.*

BHUTAN - TOURISM

Euromonitor International, Inc., 224 S. Michigan Avenue, Suite 1500, Chicago, IL 60604, (312) 922-1115, Fax: (312) 922-1157, www.euromonitor.com; *The World Economic Factbook 2008* and *World Marketing Data and Statistics.*

M.E. Sharpe, 80 Business Park Drive, Armonk, NY 10504, (800) 541-6563, Fax: (914) 273-2106, www.mesharpe.com; *The Illustrated Book of World Rankings.*

Palgrave Macmillan Ltd., Houndmills, Basingstoke, Hampshire, RG21 6XS, England, (Telephone in U.S. (888) 330-8477), (Fax in U.S. (800) 672-2054), www.palgrave.com; *The Statesman's Yearbook 2008.*

Taylor and Francis Group, An Informa Business, 2 Park Square, Milton Park, Abingdon, Oxford OX14 4RN, United Kingdom, (Dial from U.S. (212) 216-7800), (Fax from U.S. (212) 564-7854), www.tandf.co.uk; *The Europa World Year Book.*

United Nations World Tourism Organization (UNWTO), Capitan Haya 42, 28020 Madrid, Spain, www.world-tourism.org; *Yearbook of Tourism Statistics.*

The World Bank, 1818 H Street, NW, Washington, DC 20433, (202) 473-1000, Fax: (202) 477-6391, www.worldbank.org; *Bhutan.*

BHUTAN - TRADE

See BHUTAN - INTERNATIONAL TRADE

BHUTAN - TRANSPORTATION

Central Intelligence Agency, Office of Public Affairs, Washington, DC 20505, (703) 482-0623, Fax: (703) 482-1739, www.cia.gov; *The World Factbook.*

Economist Intelligence Unit, 111 West 57th Street, New York, NY 10019, (212) 554-0600, Fax: (212) 586-1181, www.eiu.com; *Business Asia.*

Euromonitor International, Inc., 224 S. Michigan Avenue, Suite 1500, Chicago, IL 60604, (312) 922-1115, Fax: (312) 922-1157, www.euromonitor.com; *International Marketing Data and Statistics 2008* and *World Marketing Data and Statistics.*

M.E. Sharpe, 80 Business Park Drive, Armonk, NY 10504, (800) 541-6563, Fax: (914) 273-2106, www.mesharpe.com; *The Illustrated Book of World Rankings.*

Palgrave Macmillan Ltd., Houndmills, Basingstoke, Hampshire, RG21 6XS, England, (Telephone in U.S. (888) 330-8477), (Fax in U.S. (800) 672-2054), www.palgrave.com; *The Statesman's Yearbook 2008.*

Taylor and Francis Group, An Informa Business, 2 Park Square, Milton Park, Abingdon, Oxford OX14 4RN, United Kingdom, (Dial from U.S. (212) 216-7800), (Fax from U.S. (212) 564-7854), www.tandf.co.uk; *The Europa World Year Book.*

United Nations Statistics Division, New York, NY 10017, (800) 253-9646, Fax: (212) 963-4116, http://unstats.un.org; *Human Development Report 2006* and *Statistical Yearbook for Asia and the Pacific 2004.*

The World Bank, 1818 H Street, NW, Washington, DC 20433, (202) 473-1000, Fax: (202) 477-6391, www.worldbank.org; *Bhutan.*

BHUTAN - UNEMPLOYMENT

Central Intelligence Agency, Office of Public Affairs, Washington, DC 20505, (703) 482-0623, Fax: (703) 482-1739, www.cia.gov; *The World Factbook.*

Euromonitor International, Inc., 224 S. Michigan Avenue, Suite 1500, Chicago, IL 60604, (312) 922-1115, Fax: (312) 922-1157, www.euromonitor.com; *International Marketing Data and Statistics 2008.*

The World Bank, 1818 H Street, NW, Washington, DC 20433, (202) 473-1000, Fax: (202) 477-6391, www.worldbank.org; *Bhutan.*

BHUTAN - VITAL STATISTICS

Euromonitor International, Inc., 224 S. Michigan Avenue, Suite 1500, Chicago, IL 60604, (312) 922-1115, Fax: (312) 922-1157, www.euromonitor.com; *International Marketing Data and Statistics 2008.*

Palgrave Macmillan Ltd., Houndmills, Basingstoke, Hampshire, RG21 6XS, England, (Telephone in U.S. (888) 330-8477), (Fax in U.S. (800) 672-2054), www.palgrave.com; *The Statesman's Yearbook 2008.*

World Health Organization (WHO), Avenue Appia 20, 1211 Geneve 27, Switzerland, (Telephone in U.S. (212) 331-9081), www.who.int; *World Health Report 2006.*

BHUTAN - WAGES

United Nations Statistics Division, New York, NY 10017, (800) 253-9646, Fax: (212) 963-4116, http://unstats.un.org; *Statistical Yearbook for Asia and the Pacific 2004.*

The World Bank, 1818 H Street, NW, Washington, DC 20433, (202) 473-1000, Fax: (202) 477-6391, www.worldbank.org; *Bhutan.*

BHUTAN - WEATHER

See BHUTAN - CLIMATE

BHUTAN - WHEAT PRODUCTION

See BHUTAN - CROPS

BHUTAN - WHOLESALE PRICE INDEXES

Asian Development Bank (ADB), PO Box 789, 0980 Manila, Philippines, www.adb.org; *Key Indicators of Developing Asian and Pacific Countries 2006.*

BHUTAN - WINE PRODUCTION

See BHUTAN - BEVERAGE INDUSTRY

BHUTAN - WOOL PRODUCTION

See BHUTAN - TEXTILE INDUSTRY

BICYCLES

National Center for Statistics and Analysis (NCSA) of the National Highway Traffic Safety Administration, West Building, 1200 New Jersey Avenue, S.E., Washington, DC 20590, (202) 366-1503, Fax: (202) 366-7078, www.nhtsa.gov; *Traffic Safety Fact Sheets, 2006 Data - Bicyclists and Other Cyclists.*

National Sporting Goods Association (NSGA), 1601 Feehanville Drive, Suite 300, Mount Prospect, IL 60056, (847) 296-6742, Fax: (847) 391-9827, www.nsga.org; *2006 Sports Participation* and *Ten-Year History of Selected Sports Participation, 1996-2006.*

BICYCLES - THEFT

Federal Bureau of Investigation (FBI), J. Edgar Hoover Building, 935 Pennsylvania Avenue, NW, Washington, DC 20535-0001, (202) 324-3000, www.fbi.gov; *Crime in the United States (CIUS) 2007 (Preliminary).*

Justice Research and Statistics Association (JRSA), 777 N. Capitol Street, NE, Suite 801, Washington, DC 20002, (202) 842-9330, Fax: (202) 842-9329, www.jrsa.org; *Crime and Justice Atlas 2001.*

BILLIARDS

National Sporting Goods Association (NSGA), 1601 Feehanville Drive, Suite 300, Mount Prospect, IL

60056, (847) 296-6742, Fax: (847) 391-9827, www.nsga.org; *2006 Sports Participation* and *Ten-Year History of Selected Sports Participation, 1996-2006.*

BIOLOGICAL SCIENCES - DEGREES CONFERRED

National Science Foundation, Division of Science Resources Statistics (SRS), 4201 Wilson Boulevard, Arlington, VA 22230, (703) 292-8780, Fax: (703) 292-9092, www.nsf.gov; *Selected Data on Science and Engineering Doctorate Awards* and *Survey of Earned Doctorates 2006.*

BIOLOGICAL SCIENCES - EMPLOYMENT

U.S. Bureau of Labor Statistics (BLS), Postal Square Building, 2 Massachusetts Avenue, NE, Washington, DC 20212-0001, (202) 691-5200, Fax: (202) 691-6325, www.bls.gov; *Employment and Earnings (EE)* and unpublished data.

BIRD OWNERSHIP

American Veterinary Medical Association (AVMA), 1931 North Meacham Road, Suite 100, Schaumburg, IL 60173, (847) 925-8070, Fax: (847) 925-1329, www.avma.org; *U.S. Pet Ownership and Demographics Sourcebook.*

BIRTH COMPLICATIONS

National Center for Health Statistics (NCHS), Centers for Disease Control and Prevention (CDC), U.S. Department of Health and Human Services (HHS), 3311 Toledo Road, Hyattsville, MD 20782, (866) 232-4636, www.cdc.gov/nchs; *Faststats A to Z; Vital Statistics of the United States (VSUS);* and unpublished data.

BIRTH CONTROL

Alan Guttmacher Institute, 125 Maiden Lane, 7th Floor, New York, NY 10038, (212) 248-1111, Fax: (212) 248-1951, www.agi-usa.org; *Contraceptive Needs and Services, 2001-2006* and *Public Funding for Contraceptive, Sterilization and Abortion Services, FY 1980-2001.*

National Center for Health Statistics (NCHS), Centers for Disease Control and Prevention (CDC), U.S. Department of Health and Human Services (HHS), 3311 Toledo Road, Hyattsville, MD 20782, (866) 232-4636, www.cdc.gov/nchs; *Faststats A to Z* and *National Survey of Family Growth (NSFG).*

BIRTH WEIGHTS

Bernan Essential Government Publications, 4611-F Assembly Drive, Lanham MD, 20706-4391, (301) 459-2255, Fax: (800) 865-3450, www.bernan.com; *Vital Statistics of the United States: Births, Life Expectancy, Deaths, and Selected Health Data.*

National Center for Health Statistics (NCHS), Centers for Disease Control and Prevention (CDC), U.S. Department of Health and Human Services (HHS), 3311 Toledo Road, Hyattsville, MD 20782, (866) 232-4636, www.cdc.gov/nchs; *National Vital Statistics Reports (NVSR); Vital Statistics of the United States (VSUS);* and unpublished data.

BISMUTH

U.S. Department of the Interior (DOI), U.S. Geological Survey (USGS), Office of Minerals Information, 12201 Sunrise Valley Drive, Reston, VA 20192, Mr. Kenneth A. Beckman, (703) 648-4916, Fax: (703) 648-4995, http://minerals.usgs.gov/minerals; *Mineral Commodity Summaries.*

BLACK LUNG BENEFIT PROGRAM

National Academy of Social Insurance (NASI), 1776 Massachusetts Avenue, NW, Suite 615, Washington, DC 20036, (202) 452-8097, Fax: (202) 452-8111, www.nasi.org; *Workers' Compensation: Benefits, Coverage, and Costs, 2004.*

Social Security Administration (SSA), Office of Public Inquiries, Windsor Park Building, 6401 Security Boulevard, Baltimore, MD 21235, (800) 772-1213, www.ssa.gov; *Social Security Bulletin.*

BLACK POPULATION

The Annie E. Casey Foundation, 701 Saint Paul Street, Baltimore, MD 21202, (410) 547-6600, Fax: (410) 547-3610, www.aecf.org; *Faith Matters: Race/Ethnicity, Religion, and Substance Abuse.*

National Center for Health Statistics (NCHS), Centers for Disease Control and Prevention (CDC), U.S. Department of Health and Human Services (HHS), 3311 Toledo Road, Hyattsville, MD 20782, (866) 232-4636, www.cdc.gov/nchs; *Indicators of Social and Economic Well-Being by Race and Hispanic Origin.*

National Center for Statistics and Analysis (NCSA) of the National Highway Traffic Safety Administration, West Building, 1200 New Jersey Avenue, S.E., Washington, DC 20590, (202) 366-1503, Fax: (202) 366-7078, www.nhtsa.gov; *Race and Ethnicity in Fatal Motor Vehicle Traffic Crashes 1999-2004.*

U.S. Census Bureau, 4700 Silver Hill Road, Washington DC 20233-0001, (301) 763-3030, www.census.gov; American FactFinder (web app); *County and City Data Book 2007;* and *State and County QuickFacts.*

U.S. Census Bureau, Population Division, 4700 Silver Hill Road, Washington DC 20233-0001, (301) 763-3030, www.census.gov/population/www/; *Current Population Reports.*

BLACK POPULATION - ABORTION

Alan Guttmacher Institute, 125 Maiden Lane, 7th Floor, New York, NY 10038, (212) 248-1111, Fax: (212) 248-1951, www.agi-usa.org; *Estimates of U.S. Abortion Incidence, 2001-2003; Public Funding for Contraceptive, Sterilization and Abortion Services, FY 1980-2001; State Facts About Abortion; Three Decades of Legal Abortion: New Research and Analysis;* and unpublished data.

BLACK POPULATION - ACTIVITY LIMITATION

National Center for Health Statistics (NCHS), Centers for Disease Control and Prevention (CDC), U.S. Department of Health and Human Services (HHS), 3311 Toledo Road, Hyattsville, MD 20782, (866) 232-4636, www.cdc.gov/nchs; *Health, United States, 2006, with Chartbook on Trends in the Health of Americans with Special Feature on Pain.*

BLACK POPULATION - ADULT EDUCATION

National Center for Education Statistics (NCES), 1990 K Street, NW, Washington, DC 20006, (202) 502-7300, http://nces.ed.gov; *The National Household Education Surveys Program (NHES).*

BLACK POPULATION - AGE AND/OR SEX

U.S. Census Bureau, Population Division, 4700 Silver Hill Road, Washington DC 20233-0001, (301) 763-3030, www.census.gov/population/www/; *The Black Population in the United States.*

BLACK POPULATION - AIDS

Centers for Disease Control and Prevention (CDC), U.S. Department of Health and Human Services (HHS), 1600 Clifton Road, Atlanta, GA 30333, (800) 311-3435, www.cdc.gov; *HIV/AIDS Surveillance Report.*

BLACK POPULATION - BUSINESS OWNERS

U.S. Census Bureau, Company Statistics Division, 4700 Silver Hill Road, Washington DC 20233-0001, (301) 763-3030, www.census.gov/csd/; *2002 Survey of Business Owners (SBO).*

U.S. Census Bureau, Population Division, 4700 Silver Hill Road, Washington DC 20233-0001, (301) 763-3030, www.census.gov/population/www/; *The Black Population in the United States.*

BLACK POPULATION - CANCER

American Cancer Society, 1599 Clifton Road, NE, Atlanta, GA 30329-4250, (404) 320-3333, www.cancer.org; *Cancer Facts and Figures 2008* and *Cancer Facts and Figures for African Americans 2007-2008.*

Bernan Essential Government Publications, 4611-F Assembly Drive, Lanham MD, 20706-4391, (301) 459-2255, Fax: (800) 865-3450, www.bernan.com; *Vital Statistics of the United States: Births, Life Expectancy, Deaths, and Selected Health Data.*

National Cancer Institute (NCI), National Institutes of Health (NIH), Public Inquiries Office, 6116 Executive Boulevard, Room 3036A, Bethesda, MD 20892-8322, (800) 422-6237, www.cancer.gov; *2006-2007 Annual Report to the Nation; Assessing Progress, Advancing Change: 2005-2006 Annual President's Cancer Panel;* and *SEER Cancer Statistics Review, 1975-2005.*

National Center for Health Statistics (NCHS), Centers for Disease Control and Prevention (CDC), U.S. Department of Health and Human Services (HHS), 3311 Toledo Road, Hyattsville, MD 20782, (866) 232-4636, www.cdc.gov/nchs; *National Vital Statistics Reports (NVSR); Vital Statistics of the United States (VSUS);* and unpublished data.

BLACK POPULATION - CHARITY CONTRIBUTIONS

Independent Sector, 1200 Eighteenth Street, NW, Suite 200, Washington, DC 20036, (202) 467-6100, Fax: (202) 467-6101, www.independentsector.org; *Giving and Volunteering in the United States 2001.*

BLACK POPULATION - CHILD CARE

National Center for Education Statistics (NCES), 1990 K Street, NW, Washington, DC 20006, (202) 502-7300, http://nces.ed.gov; *Digest of Education Statistics 2007.*

BLACK POPULATION - CHILDBIRTH - STATISTICS

Alan Guttmacher Institute, 125 Maiden Lane, 7th Floor, New York, NY 10038, (212) 248-1111, Fax: (212) 248-1951, www.agi-usa.org; *U.S. Teenage Pregnancy Statistics: Overall Trends, Trends by Race and Ethnicity and State-by-State Information* and *U.S. Teenage Pregnancy Statistics: Overall Trends, Trends by Race and Ethnicity and State-by-State Information.*

Bernan Essential Government Publications, 4611-F Assembly Drive, Lanham MD, 20706-4391, (301) 459-2255, Fax: (800) 865-3450, www.bernan.com; *Vital Statistics of the United States: Births, Life Expectancy, Deaths, and Selected Health Data.*

National Center for Health Statistics (NCHS), Centers for Disease Control and Prevention (CDC), U.S. Department of Health and Human Services (HHS), 3311 Toledo Road, Hyattsville, MD 20782, (866) 232-4636, www.cdc.gov/nchs; *National Vital Statistics Reports (NVSR); Vital Statistics of the United States (VSUS);* and unpublished data.

U.S. Census Bureau, 4700 Silver Hill Road, Washington DC 20233-0001, (301) 763-3030, www.census.gov; unpublished data.

U.S. Census Bureau, Population Division, 4700 Silver Hill Road, Washington DC 20233-0001, (301) 763-3030, www.census.gov/population/www/; *The Black Population in the United States.*

BLACK POPULATION - CHILDREN UNDER EIGHTEEN YEARS OLD

Federal Interagency Forum on Child and Family Statistics, 2070 Chain Bridge Road, Suite 450, Vienna, VA 22182-2536, (888) ASK-HRSA, www.childstats.gov; *America's Children: Key National Indicators of Well-Being 2006.*

U.S. Census Bureau, 4700 Silver Hill Road, Washington DC 20233-0001, (301) 763-3030, www.census.gov; unpublished data.

U.S. Census Bureau, Population Division, 4700 Silver Hill Road, Washington DC 20233-0001, (301) 763-3030, www.census.gov/population/www/; *The Black Population in the United States.*

BLACK POPULATION - CHILDREN UNDER EIGHTEEN YEARS OLD - LITERACY ACTIVITIES

National Center for Education Statistics (NCES), 1990 K Street, NW, Washington, DC 20006, (202) 502-7300, http://nces.ed.gov; *Home Literacy Activities and Signs of Children's Emerging Literacy* and various fact sheets.

BLACK POPULATION - CHILDREN UNDER EIGHTEEN YEARS OLD - POVERTY

National Center for Children in Poverty (NCCP), 215 W. 125th Street, 3rd Floor, New York, NY 10027, (646) 284-9600, Fax: (646) 284-9623, www.nccp.org; *Basic Facts About Low-Income Children; Child Poverty in 21st Century America; Child Poverty in States Hit by Hurricane Katrina; Low-Income Children in the United States: National and State Trend Data, 1996-2006;* and *Predictors of Child Care Subsidy Use.*

Population Reference Bureau, 1875 Connecticut Avenue, NW, Suite 520, Washington, DC, 20009-5728, (800) 877-9881, Fax: (202) 328-3937, www.prb.org; *Child Poverty in Rural America* and *Strengthening Rural Families: America's Rural Children.*

U.S. Census Bureau, 4700 Silver Hill Road, Washington DC 20233-0001, (301) 763-3030, www.census.gov; unpublished data.

U.S. Census Bureau, Housing and Household Economics Statistics Division, 4700 Silver Hill Road, Washington DC 20233-0001, (301) 763-3030, www.census.gov/hhes/www; *Historical Poverty Tables.*

U.S. Census Bureau, Population Division, 4700 Silver Hill Road, Washington DC 20233-0001, (301) 763-3030, www.census.gov/population/www/; *The Black Population in the United States.*

BLACK POPULATION - CHILDREN UNDER EIGHTEEN YEARS OLD - SCHOOL READINESS

The Annie E. Casey Foundation, 701 Saint Paul Street, Baltimore, MD 21202, (410) 547-6600, Fax: (410) 547-3610, www.aecf.org; *Improving School Readiness Outcomes.*

National Center for Education Statistics (NCES), 1990 K Street, NW, Washington, DC 20006, (202) 502-7300, http://nces.ed.gov; *Home Literacy Activities and Signs of Children's Emerging Literacy* and various fact sheets.

BLACK POPULATION - CIGARETTE SMOKING

National Center for Health Statistics (NCHS), Centers for Disease Control and Prevention (CDC), U.S. Department of Health and Human Services (HHS), 3311 Toledo Road, Hyattsville, MD 20782, (866) 232-4636, www.cdc.gov/nchs; *Health, United States, 2006, with Chartbook on Trends in the Health of Americans with Special Feature on Pain.*

BLACK POPULATION - CITIES

Population Reference Bureau, 1875 Connecticut Avenue, NW, Suite 520, Washington, DC, 20009-5728, (800) 877-9881, Fax: (202) 328-3937, www.prb.org; *The American People Series.*

U.S. Census Bureau, 4700 Silver Hill Road, Washington DC 20233-0001, (301) 763-3030, www.census.gov; American FactFinder (web app); *County and City Data Book 2007;* and *State and County QuickFacts.*

U.S. Census Bureau, Population Division, 4700 Silver Hill Road, Washington DC 20233-0001, (301) 763-3030, www.census.gov/population/www/; *Census 2000 Profiles of General Demographic Characteristics.*

BLACK POPULATION - COHABITATION EXPERIENCE

National Center for Health Statistics (NCHS), Centers for Disease Control and Prevention (CDC), U.S. Department of Health and Human Services (HHS), 3311 Toledo Road, Hyattsville, MD 20782, (866) 232-4636, www.cdc.gov/nchs; *National Survey of Family Growth (NSFG).*

BLACK POPULATION - COMMUNITY SERVICE (STUDENTS)

National Center for Education Statistics (NCES), 1990 K Street, NW, Washington, DC 20006, (202) 502-7300, http://nces.ed.gov; various fact sheets.

BLACK POPULATION - COMPUTER USE

National Center for Education Statistics (NCES), 1990 K Street, NW, Washington, DC 20006, (202) 502-7300, http://nces.ed.gov; *Digest of Education Statistics 2007.*

National Telecommunications and Information Administration (NTIA), U.S. Department of Commerce (DOC), 1401 Constitution Avenue, NW, Washington, DC 20230, (202) 482-7002, www.ntia.doc.gov; *A Nation Online: Entering the Broadband Age.*

U.S. Census Bureau, Population Division, 4700 Silver Hill Road, Washington DC 20233-0001, (301) 763-3030, www.census.gov/population/www/; *The Black Population in the United States.*

BLACK POPULATION - CONGRESS, MEMBERS OF

U.S. Government Printing Office (GPO), Office of Congressional Publishing Services (OCPS), 732 North Capitol Street NW, Washington, DC 20401, (202) 512-0224, www.gpo.gov/customerservices/cps.htm; *Congressional Directory.*

BLACK POPULATION - CONSUMER EXPENDITURES

Book Industry Study Group (BISG), 370 Lexington Avenue, Suite 900, New York, NY 10017, (646) 336-7141, Fax: (646) 336-6214, www.bisg.org; *The African-American Book Buyers Study.*

Selig Center for Economic Growth, Terry College of Business, University of Georgia, Athens, GA 30602-6269, Mr. Jeffrey M. Humphreys, Director, (706) 425-2962, www.selig.uga.edu; *The Multicultural Economy: Minority Buying Power in 2006.*

U.S. Bureau of Labor Statistics (BLS), Postal Square Building, 2 Massachusetts Avenue, NE, Washington, DC 20212-0001, (202) 691-5200, Fax: (202) 691-6325, www.bls.gov; *Consumer Expenditures in 2006.*

BLACK POPULATION - CONTRACEPTIVE USE

Alan Guttmacher Institute, 125 Maiden Lane, 7th Floor, New York, NY 10038, (212) 248-1111, Fax: (212) 248-1951, www.agi-usa.org; *Contraceptive Needs and Services, 2001-2006.*

National Center for Health Statistics (NCHS), Centers for Disease Control and Prevention (CDC), U.S. Department of Health and Human Services (HHS), 3311 Toledo Road, Hyattsville, MD 20782, (866) 232-4636, www.cdc.gov/nchs; *National Survey of Family Growth (NSFG).*

BLACK POPULATION - CRIMINAL STATISTICS

Federal Bureau of Investigation (FBI), J. Edgar Hoover Building, 935 Pennsylvania Avenue, NW, Washington, DC 20535-0001, (202) 324-3000, www.fbi.gov; *Crime in the United States (CIUS) 2007 (Preliminary).*

Justice Research and Statistics Association (JRSA), 777 N. Capitol Street, NE, Suite 801, Washington, DC 20002, (202) 842-9330, Fax: (202) 842-9329, www.jrsa.org; *Crime and Justice Atlas 2001.*

RAND Corporation, 1776 Main Street, PO Box 2138, Santa Monica, CA 90407-2138, (310) 393-0411, www.rand.org; *Analysis of Racial Disparities in the New York Police Department's Stop, Question, and Frisk Practices.*

U.S. Department of Justice (DOJ), Bureau of Justice Statistics, 810 Seventh Street, NW, Washington, DC 20531, (202) 307-0765, www.ojp.usdoj.gov/bjs/; *Census of Jails; Crime and the Nation's Households, 2004; Criminal Victimization, 2005; Mental Health Problems of Prison and Jail Inmates; Substance Dependence, Abuse, and Treatment of Jail Inmates, 2002; Violence by Gang Members, 1993-2003;* and *Violent Felons in Large Urban Counties.*

BLACK POPULATION - CRIMINAL VICTIMIZATION

National Center for Education Statistics (NCES), 1990 K Street, NW, Washington, DC 20006, (202) 502-7300, http://nces.ed.gov; *Indicators of School Crime and Safety: 2007.*

U.S. Department of Justice (DOJ), Bureau of Justice Statistics, 810 Seventh Street, NW, Washington, DC 20531, (202) 307-0765, www.ojp.usdoj.gov/bjs/; *Criminal Victimization, 2005* and *Weapon Use and Violent Crime, 1993-2001.*

BLACK POPULATION - DEATHS AND DEATH RATES

Bernan Essential Government Publications, 4611-F Assembly Drive, Lanham MD, 20706-4391, (301) 459-2255, Fax: (800) 865-3450, www.bernan.com; *Vital Statistics of the United States: Births, Life Expectancy, Deaths, and Selected Health Data.*

Centers for Disease Control and Prevention (CDC), U.S. Department of Health and Human Services (HHS), 1600 Clifton Road, Atlanta, GA 30333, (800) 311-3435, www.cdc.gov; unpublished data.

National Center for Health Statistics (NCHS), Centers for Disease Control and Prevention (CDC), U.S. Department of Health and Human Services (HHS), 3311 Toledo Road, Hyattsville, MD 20782, (866) 232-4636, www.cdc.gov/nchs; *National Vital Statistics Reports (NVSR); Vital Statistics of the United States (VSUS);* and unpublished data.

National Center for Statistics and Analysis (NCSA) of the National Highway Traffic Safety Administration, West Building, 1200 New Jersey Avenue, S.E., Washington, DC 20590, (202) 366-1503, Fax: (202) 366-7078, www.nhtsa.gov; *Motor Vehicle Traffic Crashes as a Leading Cause of Death in the U.S., 2002 - A Demographic Perspective* and *Race and Ethnicity in Fatal Motor Vehicle Traffic Crashes 1999-2004.*

BLACK POPULATION - DISABLED PERSONS

U.S. Census Bureau, 4700 Silver Hill Road, Washington DC 20233-0001, (301) 763-3030, www.census.gov; unpublished data.

BLACK POPULATION - EDUCATIONAL ATTAINMENT

Robert Wood Johnson Foundation, PO Box 2316, College Road East and Route 1, Princeton, NJ 08543, (877) 843-7953, www.rwjf.org; *Race Ethnicity, and the Education Gradient in Health.*

BLACK POPULATION - ELECTED OFFICIALS

Joint Center for Political and Economic Studies, 1090 Vermont Avenue, NW, Suite 1100, Washington, DC 20005-4928, (202) 789-3500, Fax: (202) 789-6390, www.jointcenter.org; *Black Elected Officials: A Statistical Summary.*

U.S. Government Printing Office (GPO), Office of Congressional Publishing Services (OCPS), 732 North Capitol Street NW, Washington, DC 20401, (202) 512-0224, www.gpo.gov/customerservices/cps.htm; *Congressional Directory.*

BLACK POPULATION - ELECTIONS, VOTER REGISTRATION AND TURNOUT

Congressional Quarterly, Inc., 1255 22nd Street, NW, Washington, DC 20037, (202) 419-8500, www.cq.com; *Vital Statistics on American Politics 2007-2008.*

The Eagleton Institute of Politics, Rutgers, The State University of New Jersey, 191 Ryders Lane, New

Brunswick, NJ 08901-8557, (732) 932-9384, Fax: (732) 932-6778, www.eagleton.rutgers.edu; *America's Newest Voters: Understanding Immigrant and Minority Voting Behavior.*

U.S. Census Bureau, 4700 Silver Hill Road, Washington DC 20233-0001, (301) 763-3030, www.census.gov; unpublished data.

U.S. Census Bureau, Population Division, 4700 Silver Hill Road, Washington DC 20233-0001, (301) 763-3030, www.census.gov/population/www/; *The Black Population in the United States.*

BLACK POPULATION - EMPLOYMENT STATUS

U.S. Bureau of Labor Statistics (BLS), Postal Square Building, 2 Massachusetts Avenue, NE, Washington, DC 20212-0001, (202) 691-5200, Fax: (202) 691-6325, www.bls.gov; *Current Population Survey (CPS)* and *Employment and Earnings (EE).*

BLACK POPULATION - EMPLOYMENT STATUS - EDUCATIONAL ATTAINMENT

U.S. Bureau of Labor Statistics (BLS), Postal Square Building, 2 Massachusetts Avenue, NE, Washington, DC 20212-0001, (202) 691-5200, Fax: (202) 691-6325, www.bls.gov; unpublished data.

BLACK POPULATION - EMPLOYMENT STATUS - HIGH SCHOOL GRADUATES AND DROPOUTS

U.S. Bureau of Labor Statistics (BLS), Postal Square Building, 2 Massachusetts Avenue, NE, Washington, DC 20212-0001, (202) 691-5200, Fax: (202) 691-6325, www.bls.gov; *Current Population Survey (CPS); Monthly Labor Review (MLR);* and unpublished data.

BLACK POPULATION - EMPLOYMENT STATUS - SCHOOL ENROLLMENT

U.S. Bureau of Labor Statistics (BLS), Postal Square Building, 2 Massachusetts Avenue, NE, Washington, DC 20212-0001, (202) 691-5200, Fax: (202) 691-6325, www.bls.gov; *Current Population Survey (CPS); Monthly Labor Review (MLR);* and unpublished data.

BLACK POPULATION - EMPLOYMENT STATUS - UNEMPLOYED

U.S. Bureau of Labor Statistics (BLS), Postal Square Building, 2 Massachusetts Avenue, NE, Washington, DC 20212-0001, (202) 691-5200, Fax: (202) 691-6325, www.bls.gov; *Employment and Earnings (EE)* and unpublished data.

BLACK POPULATION - FAMILIES - CHARACTERISTICS

U.S. Census Bureau, 4700 Silver Hill Road, Washington DC 20233-0001, (301) 763-3030, www.census.gov; unpublished data.

U.S. Census Bureau, Population Division, 4700 Silver Hill Road, Washington DC 20233-0001, (301) 763-3030, www.census.gov/population/www/; *The Black Population in the United States.*

BLACK POPULATION - FARM OPERATORS AND WORKERS

National Agricultural Statistics Service (NASS), U.S. Department of Agriculture (USDA), 1400 Independence Avenue, SW, Washington, DC 20250, (800) 727-9540, Fax: (202) 690-2090, www.nass.usda.gov; *2007 Census of Agriculture.*

BLACK POPULATION - FERTILITY RATE

National Center for Health Statistics (NCHS), Centers for Disease Control and Prevention (CDC), U.S. Department of Health and Human Services (HHS), 3311 Toledo Road, Hyattsville, MD 20782, (866) 232-4636, www.cdc.gov/nchs; *Vital Statistics of the United States (VSUS)* and unpublished data.

U.S. Census Bureau, Population Division, 4700 Silver Hill Road, Washington DC 20233-0001, (301) 763-3030, www.census.gov/population/www/; *The Black Population in the United States.*

BLACK POPULATION - FOOD STAMP PARTICIPANTS

Food and Nutrition Service (FNS), U.S. Department of Agriculture (USDA), 3101 Park Center Drive, Alexandria, VA 22302, (703) 305-2062, www.fns.usda.gov/fns; *Characteristics of Food Stamp Households: Fiscal Year 2005.*

BLACK POPULATION - FOREIGN BORN POPULATION

Migration Information Source, Migration Policy Institute (MPI), 1400 16th Street NW, Suite 300, Washington, DC 20036-2257, (202) 266-1940, Fax: (202) 266-1900, www.migrationinformation.org; *Maps of the Foreign Born in the United States; US Census Data on the Foreign Born; US Historical Trends;* and *Who's Where in the United States?*

U.S. Census Bureau, Population Division, 4700 Silver Hill Road, Washington DC 20233-0001, (301) 763-3030, www.census.gov/population/www/; *The Black Population in the United States* and *Foreign-Born Population in the U.S. 2003.*

BLACK POPULATION - HEALTH CARE VISITS TO PROFESSIONALS

National Center for Health Statistics (NCHS), Centers for Disease Control and Prevention (CDC), U.S. Department of Health and Human Services (HHS), 3311 Toledo Road, Hyattsville, MD 20782, (866) 232-4636, www.cdc.gov/nchs; *Health, United States, 2006, with Chartbook on Trends in the Health of Americans with Special Feature on Pain.*

BLACK POPULATION - HEALTH INSURANCE COVERAGE

National Center for Health Statistics (NCHS), Centers for Disease Control and Prevention (CDC), U.S. Department of Health and Human Services (HHS), 3311 Toledo Road, Hyattsville, MD 20782, (866) 232-4636, www.cdc.gov/nchs; *Faststats A to Z.*

Robert Wood Johnson Foundation, PO Box 2316, College Road East and Route 1, Princeton, NJ 08543, (877) 843-7953, www.rwjf.org; *Medicare Race and Ethnicity Data: Prepared for the Study Panel on Sharpening Medicare's Tools to Reduce Racial and Ethnic Disparities.*

U.S. Census Bureau, Population Division, 4700 Silver Hill Road, Washington DC 20233-0001, (301) 763-3030, www.census.gov/population/www/; *The Black Population in the United States.*

BLACK POPULATION - HIGH SCHOOL GRADUATES AND DROPOUTS

U.S. Census Bureau, Population Division, 4700 Silver Hill Road, Washington DC 20233-0001, (301) 763-3030, www.census.gov/population/www/; *The Black Population in the United States.*

BLACK POPULATION - HOME HEALTH AND HOSPICE CARE

National Center for Health Statistics (NCHS), Centers for Disease Control and Prevention (CDC), U.S. Department of Health and Human Services (HHS), 3311 Toledo Road, Hyattsville, MD 20782, (866) 232-4636, www.cdc.gov/nchs; *Health, United States, 2006, with Chartbook on Trends in the Health of Americans with Special Feature on Pain.*

BLACK POPULATION - HOMESCHOOLED

National Center for Education Statistics (NCES), 1990 K Street, NW, Washington, DC 20006, (202) 502-7300, http://nces.ed.gov; *Homeschooling in the United States: 2003.*

BLACK POPULATION - HOMICIDES

Bernan Essential Government Publications, 4611-F Assembly Drive, Lanham MD, 20706-4391, (301) 459-2255, Fax: (800) 865-3450, www.bernan.com; *Vital Statistics of the United States: Births, Life Expectancy, Deaths, and Selected Health Data.*

National Center for Health Statistics (NCHS), Centers for Disease Control and Prevention (CDC), U.S. Department of Health and Human Services (HHS), 3311 Toledo Road, Hyattsville, MD 20782, (866) 232-4636, www.cdc.gov/nchs; *National Vital Statistics Reports (NVSR)* and *Vital Statistics of the United States (VSUS).*

BLACK POPULATION - HOUSEHOLDS - CHARACTERISTICS

U.S. Census Bureau, 4700 Silver Hill Road, Washington DC 20233-0001, (301) 763-3030, www.census.gov; unpublished data.

U.S. Census Bureau, Population Division, 4700 Silver Hill Road, Washington DC 20233-0001, (301) 763-3030, www.census.gov/population/www/; *The Black Population in the United States.*

BLACK POPULATION - HOUSING

U.S. Census Bureau, Housing and Household Economics Statistics Division, 4700 Silver Hill Road, Washington DC 20233-0001, (301) 763-3030, www.census.gov/hhes/www; *2006 American Community Survey (ACS); American Housing Survey (AHS); American Housing Survey (AHS);* and *Housing Characteristics: 2000.*

BLACK POPULATION - IMMUNIZATION OF CHILDREN

Centers for Disease Control and Prevention (CDC), U.S. Department of Health and Human Services (HHS), 1600 Clifton Road, Atlanta, GA 30333, (800) 311-3435, www.cdc.gov; *Morbidity and Mortality Weekly Report (MMWR).*

National Center for Health Statistics (NCHS), Centers for Disease Control and Prevention (CDC), U.S. Department of Health and Human Services (HHS), 3311 Toledo Road, Hyattsville, MD 20782, (866) 232-4636, www.cdc.gov/nchs; *2006 National Health Interview Survey (NHIS).*

BLACK POPULATION - INCOME

Selig Center for Economic Growth, Terry College of Business, University of Georgia, Athens, GA 30602-6269, Mr. Jeffrey M. Humphreys, Director, (706) 425-2962, www.selig.uga.edu; *The Multicultural Economy: Minority Buying Power in 2006.*

U.S. Census Bureau, Population Division, 4700 Silver Hill Road, Washington DC 20233-0001, (301) 763-3030, www.census.gov/population/www/; *The Black Population in the United States.*

BLACK POPULATION - INFANT DEATHS

Bernan Essential Government Publications, 4611-F Assembly Drive, Lanham MD, 20706-4391, (301) 459-2255, Fax: (800) 865-3450, www.bernan.com; *Vital Statistics of the United States: Births, Life Expectancy, Deaths, and Selected Health Data.*

National Center for Health Statistics (NCHS), Centers for Disease Control and Prevention (CDC), U.S. Department of Health and Human Services (HHS), 3311 Toledo Road, Hyattsville, MD 20782, (866) 232-4636, www.cdc.gov/nchs; *National Vital Statistics Reports (NVSR); Vital Statistics of the United States (VSUS);* and unpublished data.

BLACK POPULATION - INTERNET ACCESS

Mediamark Research, Inc., 75 Ninth Avenue, 5th Floor, New York, NY 10011, (212) 884-9200, Fax: (212) 884-9339, www.mediamark.com; MRI+.

National Telecommunications and Information Administration (NTIA), U.S. Department of Commerce (DOC), 1401 Constitution Avenue, NW, Washington, DC 20230, (202) 482-7002, www.ntia.doc.gov; *A Nation Online: Entering the Broadband Age.*

U.S. Census Bureau, Population Division, 4700 Silver Hill Road, Washington DC 20233-0001, (301)

763-3030, www.census.gov/population/www/; *The Black Population in the United States.*

BLACK POPULATION - LABOR FORCE

Higher Education Research Institute (HERI), University of California, Los Angeles, 3005 Moore Hall/Box 951521, Los Angeles, CA 90095-1521, (310) 825-1925, Fax: (310) 206-2228, www.gseis.ucla.edu/heri/index.php; *Race and Ethnicity in the American Professoriate.*

U.S. Bureau of Labor Statistics (BLS), Postal Square Building, 2 Massachusetts Avenue, NE, Washington, DC 20212-0001, (202) 691-5200, Fax: (202) 691-6325, www.bls.gov; *Current Population Survey (CPS); Employment and Earnings (EE); Monthly Labor Review (MLR);* and unpublished data.

BLACK POPULATION - LABOR FORCE - DISPLACED WORKERS

U.S. Bureau of Labor Statistics (BLS), Postal Square Building, 2 Massachusetts Avenue, NE, Washington, DC 20212-0001, (202) 691-5200, Fax: (202) 691-6325, www.bls.gov; *Monthly Labor Review (MLR)* and unpublished data.

BLACK POPULATION - LABOR FORCE - EARNINGS

U.S. Bureau of Labor Statistics (BLS), Postal Square Building, 2 Massachusetts Avenue, NE, Washington, DC 20212-0001, (202) 691-5200, Fax: (202) 691-6325, www.bls.gov; *Current Population Survey (CPS); Employment and Earnings (EE);* and unpublished data.

BLACK POPULATION - LABOR FORCE - EMPLOYED

U.S. Bureau of Labor Statistics (BLS), Postal Square Building, 2 Massachusetts Avenue, NE, Washington, DC 20212-0001, (202) 691-5200, Fax: (202) 691-6325, www.bls.gov; *Current Population Survey (CPS); Employment and Earnings (EE);* and unpublished data.

BLACK POPULATION - LABOR FORCE - JOB SEARCH

U.S. Bureau of Labor Statistics (BLS), Postal Square Building, 2 Massachusetts Avenue, NE, Washington, DC 20212-0001, (202) 691-5200, Fax: (202) 691-6325, www.bls.gov; *Monthly Labor Review (MLR).*

BLACK POPULATION - LABOR FORCE - PERSONS WORKING AT HOME

U.S. Bureau of Labor Statistics (BLS), Postal Square Building, 2 Massachusetts Avenue, NE, Washington, DC 20212-0001, (202) 691-5200, Fax: (202) 691-6325, www.bls.gov; *Monthly Labor Review (MLR)* and *Work at Home.*

BLACK POPULATION - LIFE EXPECTANCY

Bernan Essential Government Publications, 4611-F Assembly Drive, Lanham MD, 20706-4391, (301) 459-2255, Fax: (800) 865-3450, www.bernan.com; *Vital Statistics of the United States: Births, Life Expectancy, Deaths, and Selected Health Data.*

National Center for Health Statistics (NCHS), Centers for Disease Control and Prevention (CDC), U.S. Department of Health and Human Services (HHS), 3311 Toledo Road, Hyattsville, MD 20782, (866) 232-4636, www.cdc.gov/nchs; *National Vital Statistics Reports (NVSR); United States Life Tables, 2004; Vital Statistics of the United States (VSUS);* and unpublished data.

BLACK POPULATION - LIVING ARRANGEMENTS

U.S. Census Bureau, 4700 Silver Hill Road, Washington DC 20233-0001, (301) 763-3030, www.census.gov; unpublished data.

U.S. Census Bureau, Housing and Household Economics Statistics Division, 4700 Silver Hill Road, Washington DC 20233-0001, (301) 763-3030, www.census.gov/hhes/www; *Families and Living Arrangements.*

U.S. Census Bureau, Population Division, 4700 Silver Hill Road, Washington DC 20233-0001, (301) 763-3030, www.census.gov/population/www/; *The Black Population in the United States.*

BLACK POPULATION - MARITAL STATUS

U.S. Census Bureau, 4700 Silver Hill Road, Washington DC 20233-0001, (301) 763-3030, www.census.gov; unpublished data.

U.S. Census Bureau, Population Division, 4700 Silver Hill Road, Washington DC 20233-0001, (301) 763-3030, www.census.gov/population/www/; *The Black Population in the United States.*

BLACK POPULATION - MEDIA USERS

Mediamark Research, Inc., 75 Ninth Avenue, 5th Floor, New York, NY 10011, (212) 884-9200, Fax: (212) 884-9339, www.mediamark.com; MRI+.

BLACK POPULATION - MEDICAL CARE

American Cancer Society, 1599 Clifton Road, NE, Atlanta, GA 30329-4250, (404) 320-3333, www.cancer.org; *Cancer Facts and Figures for African Americans 2007-2008.*

National Center for Chronic Disease Prevention and Health Promotion (NCCDPHP), Centers for Disease Control and Prevention (CDC), 4770 Buford Hwy, NE, MS K-40, Atlanta, GA 30341-3717, (404) 639-3311, www.cdc.gov/nccdphp; *Racial and Ethnic Approaches to Community Health (REACH 2010): Addressing Disparities in Health.*

National Center for Health Statistics (NCHS), Centers for Disease Control and Prevention (CDC), U.S. Department of Health and Human Services (HHS), 3311 Toledo Road, Hyattsville, MD 20782, (866) 232-4636, www.cdc.gov/nchs; *Faststats A to Z* and *Women's Health and Mortality Chartbook (2004 Edition).*

Robert Wood Johnson Foundation, PO Box 2316, College Road East and Route 1, Princeton, NJ 08543, (877) 843-7953, www.rwjf.org; *First-Year Achievements Signal Big Improvements in Heart Care for Minority Patients; Medicare Race and Ethnicity Data: Prepared for the Study Panel on Sharpening Medicare's Tools to Reduce Racial and Ethnic Disparities; Race Ethnicity, and the Education Gradient in Health;* and *Reducing Racial and Ethnic Disparities and Improving Quality of Health Care.*

U.S. Department of Health and Human Services, 200 Independence Avenue, S.W., Washington, D.C. 20201, (202) 619-0257, www.hhs.gov; *Eliminating Health Disparities: Strengthening Data on Race, Ethnicity, and Primary Language in the United States.*

U.S. Department of Justice (DOJ), Bureau of Justice Statistics, 810 Seventh Street, NW, Washington, DC 20531, (202) 307-0765, www.ojp.usdoj.gov/bjs/; *Mental Health Problems of Prison and Jail Inmates.*

BLACK POPULATION - MINIMUM WAGE WORKERS

U.S. Bureau of Labor Statistics (BLS), Postal Square Building, 2 Massachusetts Avenue, NE, Washington, DC 20212-0001, (202) 691-5200, Fax: (202) 691-6325, www.bls.gov; unpublished data.

BLACK POPULATION - NURSES

Health Resources and Services Administration (HRSA), National Center for Health Workforce Analysis (NCHWA), 5600 Fishers Lane, Rockville, MD 20857, (301) 443-2216, www.hrsa.gov; Registered Nurse Population: Findings from the 2004 National Sample Survey of Registered Nurses.

BLACK POPULATION - OLDER PEOPLE

U.S. Census Bureau, 4700 Silver Hill Road, Washington DC 20233-0001, (301) 763-3030, www.census.gov; unpublished data.

U.S. Census Bureau, Population Division, 4700 Silver Hill Road, Washington DC 20233-0001, (301) 763-3030, www.census.gov/population/www/; *The Black Population in the United States.*

BLACK POPULATION - OVERWEIGHT

National Center for Health Statistics (NCHS), Centers for Disease Control and Prevention (CDC), U.S. Department of Health and Human Services (HHS), 3311 Toledo Road, Hyattsville, MD 20782, (866) 232-4636, www.cdc.gov/nchs; unpublished data.

BLACK POPULATION - PHYSICAL ACTIVITY

Centers for Disease Control and Prevention (CDC), U.S. Department of Health and Human Services (HHS), 1600 Clifton Road, Atlanta, GA 30333, (800) 311-3435, www.cdc.gov; unpublished data.

National Center for Health Statistics (NCHS), Centers for Disease Control and Prevention (CDC), U.S. Department of Health and Human Services (HHS), 3311 Toledo Road, Hyattsville, MD 20782, (866) 232-4636, www.cdc.gov/nchs; *2006 National Health Interview Survey (NHIS).*

Robert Wood Johnson Foundation, PO Box 2316, College Road East and Route 1, Princeton, NJ 08543, (877) 843-7953, www.rwjf.org; *First-Year Achievements Signal Big Improvements in Heart Care for Minority Patients.*

BLACK POPULATION - POLICE CONTACT

RAND Corporation, 1776 Main Street, PO Box 2138, Santa Monica, CA 90407-2138, (310) 393-0411, www.rand.org; *Analysis of Racial Disparities in the New York Police Department's Stop, Question, and Frisk Practices.*

U.S. Department of Justice (DOJ), Bureau of Justice Statistics, 810 Seventh Street, NW, Washington, DC 20531, (202) 307-0765, www.ojp.usdoj.gov/bjs/; *Contacts between Police and the Public: Findings from the 2002 National Survey.*

BLACK POPULATION - POVERTY

National Center for Children in Poverty (NCCP), 215 W. 125th Street, 3rd Floor, New York, NY 10027, (646) 284-9600, Fax: (646) 284-9623, www.nccp.org; *Child Poverty in States Hit by Hurricane Katrina.*

U.S. Census Bureau, Housing and Household Economics Statistics Division, 4700 Silver Hill Road, Washington DC 20233-0001, (301) 763-3030, www.census.gov/hhes/www; *Historical Poverty Tables.*

U.S. Census Bureau, Population Division, 4700 Silver Hill Road, Washington DC 20233-0001, (301) 763-3030, www.census.gov/population/www/; *The Black Population in the United States.*

BLACK POPULATION - PRISONERS

U.S. Department of Justice (DOJ), Bureau of Justice Statistics, 810 Seventh Street, NW, Washington, DC 20531, (202) 307-0765, www.ojp.usdoj.gov/bjs/; *Census of Jails; Drug Use and Dependence, State and Federal Prisoners, 2004; Mental Health Problems of Prison and Jail Inmates; National Corrections Reporting Program; Prison and Jail Inmates at Midyear 2005; Prisoners in 2004; Probation and Parole in the United States, 2004; Profile of Jail Inmates, 2002;* and *Veterans in Prison or Jail.*

BLACK POPULATION - PROJECTIONS

U.S. Census Bureau, Population Division, 4700 Silver Hill Road, Washington DC 20233-0001, (301) 763-3030, www.census.gov/population/www/; *The Black Population in the United States.*

BLACK POPULATION - PROPERTY OWNERS

U.S. Census Bureau, Housing and Household Economics Statistics Division, 4700 Silver Hill Road, Washington DC 20233-0001, (301) 763-3030, www.

census.gov/hhes/www; *2006 American Community Survey (ACS); American Housing Survey (AHS);* and *American Housing Survey (AHS).*

BLACK POPULATION - RECREATIONAL ACTIVITIES

National Endowment for the Arts (NEA), 1100 Pennsylvania Avenue, NW, Washington, DC 20506-0001, (202) 682-5400, www.arts.gov; *2002 Survey of Public Participation in the Arts.*

Robert Wood Johnson Foundation, PO Box 2316, College Road East and Route 1, Princeton, NJ 08543, (877) 843-7953, www.rwjf.org; *First-Year Achievements Signal Big Improvements in Heart Care for Minority Patients.*

BLACK POPULATION - SCHOOL DROPOUTS - HIGH SCHOOL

U.S. Bureau of Labor Statistics (BLS), Postal Square Building, 2 Massachusetts Avenue, NE, Washington, DC 20212-0001, (202) 691-5200, Fax: (202) 691-6325, www.bls.gov; *Current Population Survey (CPS)* and unpublished data.

U.S. Census Bureau, Population Division, 4700 Silver Hill Road, Washington DC 20233-0001, (301) 763-3030, www.census.gov/population/www/; *The Black Population in the United States.*

BLACK POPULATION - SCHOOLS AND EDUCATION - ADULT EDUCATION

National Center for Education Statistics (NCES), 1990 K Street, NW, Washington, DC 20006, (202) 502-7300, http://nces.ed.gov; *The National Household Education Surveys Program (NHES).*

BLACK POPULATION - SCHOOLS AND EDUCATION - AMERICAN COLLEGE TESTING PROGRAM

ACT, 500 ACT Drive, Box 168, Iowa City, IA 52243-0168, (319) 337-1000, Fax: (319) 339-3020, www.act.org; *ACT National and State Scores.*

BLACK POPULATION - SCHOOLS AND EDUCATION - ATTAINMENT

U.S. Census Bureau, 4700 Silver Hill Road, Washington DC 20233-0001, (301) 763-3030, www.census.gov; unpublished data.

U.S. Census Bureau, Population Division, 4700 Silver Hill Road, Washington DC 20233-0001, (301) 763-3030, www.census.gov/population/www/; *The Black Population in the United States.*

BLACK POPULATION - SCHOOLS AND EDUCATION - EMPLOYED STUDENTS

U.S. Bureau of Labor Statistics (BLS), Postal Square Building, 2 Massachusetts Avenue, NE, Washington, DC 20212-0001, (202) 691-5200, Fax: (202) 691-6325, www.bls.gov; *Employment Experience of Youths: Results From a Longitudinal Survey.*

BLACK POPULATION - SCHOOLS AND EDUCATION - ENROLLMENT

U.S. Census Bureau, 4700 Silver Hill Road, Washington DC 20233-0001, (301) 763-3030, www.census.gov; unpublished data.

U.S. Census Bureau, Population Division, 4700 Silver Hill Road, Washington DC 20233-0001, (301) 763-3030, www.census.gov/population/www/; *The Black Population in the United States.*

BLACK POPULATION - SCHOOLS AND EDUCATION - ENROLLMENT - COLLEGE ENROLLMENT

National Center for Education Statistics (NCES), 1990 K Street, NW, Washington, DC 20006, (202) 502-7300, http://nces.ed.gov; *Digest of Education Statistics 2007.*

U.S. Census Bureau, Population Division, 4700 Silver Hill Road, Washington DC 20233-0001, (301) 763-3030, www.census.gov/population/www/; *The Black Population in the United States.*

BLACK POPULATION - SCHOOLS AND EDUCATION - ENROLLMENT - CREDIT CARD USE

National Center for Education Statistics (NCES), 1990 K Street, NW, Washington, DC 20006, (202) 502-7300, http://nces.ed.gov; *Profile of Undergraduates in U.S. Postsecondary Education Institutions: 2003-04, With a Special Analysis of Community College Students.*

BLACK POPULATION - SCHOOLS AND EDUCATION - ENROLLMENT - DISABILITY

National Center for Education Statistics (NCES), 1990 K Street, NW, Washington, DC 20006, (202) 502-7300, http://nces.ed.gov; *Profile of Undergraduates in U.S. Postsecondary Education Institutions: 2003-04, With a Special Analysis of Community College Students.*

BLACK POPULATION - SCHOOLS AND EDUCATION - ENROLLMENT - DISTANCE EDUCATION

National Center for Education Statistics (NCES), 1990 K Street, NW, Washington, DC 20006, (202) 502-7300, http://nces.ed.gov; *Profile of Undergraduates in U.S. Postsecondary Education Institutions: 2003-04, With a Special Analysis of Community College Students.*

BLACK POPULATION - SCHOOLS AND EDUCATION - ENROLLMENT - PREPRIMARY

U.S. Census Bureau, Population Division, 4700 Silver Hill Road, Washington DC 20233-0001, (301) 763-3030, www.census.gov/population/www/; *The Black Population in the United States.*

BLACK POPULATION - SCHOOLS AND EDUCATION - HIGH SCHOOL DROPOUTS

U.S. Bureau of Labor Statistics (BLS), Postal Square Building, 2 Massachusetts Avenue, NE, Washington, DC 20212-0001, (202) 691-5200, Fax: (202) 691-6325, www.bls.gov; *Current Population Survey (CPS)* and unpublished data.

U.S. Census Bureau, Population Division, 4700 Silver Hill Road, Washington DC 20233-0001, (301) 763-3030, www.census.gov/population/www/; *The Black Population in the United States.*

BLACK POPULATION - SCHOOLS AND EDUCATION - HIGH SCHOOL GRADUATES

U.S. Bureau of Labor Statistics (BLS), Postal Square Building, 2 Massachusetts Avenue, NE, Washington, DC 20212-0001, (202) 691-5200, Fax: (202) 691-6325, www.bls.gov; *Current Population Survey (CPS)* and unpublished data.

BLACK POPULATION - SCHOOLS AND EDUCATION - HIGHER EDUCATION INSTITUTIONS - DEGREES CONFERRED

National Science Foundation, Division of Science Resources Statistics (SRS), 4201 Wilson Boulevard, Arlington, VA 22230, (703) 292-8780, Fax: (703) 292-9092, www.nsf.gov; *Selected Data on Science and Engineering Doctorate Awards* and *Survey of Earned Doctorates 2006.*

BLACK POPULATION - SCHOOLS AND EDUCATION - HIGHER EDUCATION INSTITUTIONS - ENROLLMENT

National Center for Education Statistics (NCES), 1990 K Street, NW, Washington, DC 20006, (202) 502-7300, http://nces.ed.gov; *Digest of Education Statistics 2007.*

U.S. Census Bureau, Population Division, 4700 Silver Hill Road, Washington DC 20233-0001, (301) 763-3030, www.census.gov/population/www/; *The Black Population in the United States.*

BLACK POPULATION - SCHOOLS AND EDUCATION - HOMESCHOOLED

National Center for Education Statistics (NCES), 1990 K Street, NW, Washington, DC 20006, (202) 502-7300, http://nces.ed.gov; *Homeschooling in the United States: 2003.*

BLACK POPULATION - SCHOOLS AND EDUCATION - SCHOLASTIC APTITUDE TEST

College Board, 45 Columbus Avenue, New York, NY 10023, (212) 713-8000, www.collegeboard.com; *College-Bound Seniors 2006.*

BLACK POPULATION - SCHOOLS AND EDUCATION - SPORTS PARTICIPATION

Centers for Disease Control and Prevention (CDC), U.S. Department of Health and Human Services (HHS), 1600 Clifton Road, Atlanta, GA 30333, (800) 311-3435, www.cdc.gov; *Morbidity and Mortality Weekly Report (MMWR)* and *Youth Risk Behavior Surveillance - United States, 2007.*

BLACK POPULATION - SCHOOLS AND EDUCATION - TEACHERS

National Center for Education Statistics (NCES), 1990 K Street, NW, Washington, DC 20006, (202) 502-7300, http://nces.ed.gov; unpublished data.

U.S. Bureau of Labor Statistics (BLS), Postal Square Building, 2 Massachusetts Avenue, NE, Washington, DC 20212-0001, (202) 691-5200, Fax: (202) 691-6325, www.bls.gov; *Employment and Earnings (EE)* and unpublished data.

BLACK POPULATION - SENIOR CITIZEN COMMUNITIES

U.S. Census Bureau, Housing and Household Economics Statistics Division, 4700 Silver Hill Road, Washington DC 20233-0001, (301) 763-3030, www.census.gov/hhes/www; *2006 American Community Survey (ACS)* and *American Housing Survey (AHS).*

BLACK POPULATION - SINGLE MOTHERS

Bernan Essential Government Publications, 4611-F Assembly Drive, Lanham MD, 20706-4391, (301) 459-2255, Fax: (800) 865-3450, www.bernan.com; *Vital Statistics of the United States: Births, Life Expectancy, Deaths, and Selected Health Data.*

National Center for Health Statistics (NCHS), Centers for Disease Control and Prevention (CDC), U.S. Department of Health and Human Services (HHS), 3311 Toledo Road, Hyattsville, MD 20782, (866) 232-4636, www.cdc.gov/nchs; *National Vital Statistics Reports (NVSR); Vital Statistics of the United States (VSUS);* and unpublished data.

U.S. Census Bureau, Population Division, 4700 Silver Hill Road, Washington DC 20233-0001, (301) 763-3030, www.census.gov/population/www/; *The Black Population in the United States.*

BLACK POPULATION - SUICIDES

Bernan Essential Government Publications, 4611-F Assembly Drive, Lanham, MD, 20706-4391, (301) 459-2255, Fax: (800) 865-3450, www.bernan.com; *Vital Statistics of the United States: Births, Life Expectancy, Deaths, and Selected Health Data.*

National Center for Health Statistics (NCHS), Centers for Disease Control and Prevention (CDC), U.S. Department of Health and Human Services (HHS), 3311 Toledo Road, Hyattsville, MD 20782, (866) 232-4636, www.cdc.gov/nchs; *National Vital Statistics Reports (NVSR); Vital Statistics of the United States (VSUS);* and unpublished data.

U.S. Department of Justice (DOJ), Bureau of Justice Statistics, 810 Seventh Street, NW, Washington, DC 20531, (202) 307-0765, www.ojp.usdoj.gov/bjs/; *Suicide and Homicide in State Prisons and Local Jails.*

BLACK POPULATION - TEENAGE MOTHERS

Bernan Essential Government Publications, 4611-F Assembly Drive, Lanham MD, 20706-4391, (301) 459-2255, Fax: (800) 865-3450, www.bernan.com; *Vital Statistics of the United States: Births, Life Expectancy, Deaths, and Selected Health Data.*

National Center for Health Statistics (NCHS), Centers for Disease Control and Prevention (CDC), U.S. Department of Health and Human Services

(HHS), 3311 Toledo Road, Hyattsville, MD 20782, (866) 232-4636, www.cdc.gov/nchs; *National Vital Statistics Reports (NVSR)* and *Vital Statistics of the United States (VSUS).*

BLACK POPULATION - UNION MEMBERSHIP

U.S. Bureau of Labor Statistics (BLS), Postal Square Building, 2 Massachusetts Avenue, NE, Washington, DC 20212-0001, (202) 691-5200, Fax: (202) 691-6325, www.bls.gov; *Employment and Earnings (EE).*

BLACK POPULATION - VOLUNTEERS

Independent Sector, 1200 Eighteenth Street, NW, Suite 200, Washington, DC 20036, (202) 467-6100, Fax: (202) 467-6101, www.independentsector.org; *Giving and Volunteering in the United States 2001.*

BLACK POPULATION - VOTER REGISTRATION AND TURNOUT

The Eagleton Institute of Politics, Rutgers, The State University of New Jersey, 191 Ryders Lane, New Brunswick, NJ 08901-8557, (732) 932-9384, Fax: (732) 932-6778, www.eagleton.rutgers.edu; *America's Newest Voters: Understanding Immigrant and Minority Voting Behavior.*

U.S. Census Bureau, 4700 Silver Hill Road, Washington DC 20233-0001, (301) 763-3030, www.census.gov; unpublished data.

U.S. Census Bureau, Population Division, 4700 Silver Hill Road, Washington DC 20233-0001, (301) 763-3030, www.census.gov/population/www/; *The Black Population in the United States.*

BLAST FURNACE AND BASIC STEEL PRODUCTS

See IRON AND STEEL

BLIND PERSONS

LISU, Holywell Park, Loughborough University, Leicestershire, LE11 3TU, United Kingdom, www.lboro.ac.uk/departments/dis/lisu; *Availability of Accessible Publications.*

Social Security Administration (SSA), Office of Public Inquiries, Windsor Park Building, 6401 Security Boulevard, Baltimore, MD 21235, (800) 772-1213, www.ssa.gov; *Annual Statistical Supplement, 2007* and *Social Security Bulletin.*

BLIND PERSONS - MEDICAID PAYMENTS AND RECIPIENTS

Centers for Medicare and Medicaid Services (CMS), U.S. Department of Health and Human Services (HHS), 7500 Security Boulevard, Baltimore, MD 21244-1850, (410) 786-3000, http://cms.hhs.gov; The Medicare Current Beneficiary Survey (MCBS) (web app).

BLOOD ALCOHOL CONCENTRATION

Center for Substance Abuse Research (CESAR), 4321 Hartwick Road, Suite 501, College Park, MD 20740, (301) 405-9770, Fax: (301) 403-8342, www.cesar.umd.edu; *Assessment and Treatment of DWI Offenders in Maryland, 1995-2003: Current Findings.*

National Center for Statistics and Analysis (NCSA) of the National Highway Traffic Safety Administration, West Building, 1200 New Jersey Avenue, S.E., Washington, DC 20590, (202) 366-1503, Fax: (202) 366-7078, www.nhtsa.gov; *Alcohol Involvement in Fatal Motor Vehicle Traffic Crashes, 2003; Impaired Motorcycle Operators Involved in Fatal Crashes; Individual State Data from the State Alcohol Related Fatality Report; Large-Truck Crash Causation Study: An Initial Overview; Recent Trends in Fatal Motorcycle Crashes: An Update; State Alcohol-Related Fatality Rates 2003; Total and Alcohol-Related Fatality Rates by State, 2003-2004; Traffic Safety Fact Sheets, 2005 Data - State Alcohol Estimates; Traffic Safety Fact Sheets, 2006 Data - Alcohol-Impaired Driving;* and *Traffic Safety Facts Annual Report: 2005.*

National Criminal Justice Reference Service (NCJRS), PO Box 6000, Rockville, MD 20849-6000, (800) 851-3420, Fax: (301) 519-5212, www.ncjrs.org; *Driving Under the Influence in the City and County of Honolulu.*

BLUE-COLLAR WORKERS

U.S. Bureau of Labor Statistics (BLS), Postal Square Building, 2 Massachusetts Avenue, NE, Washington, DC 20212-0001, (202) 691-5200, Fax: (202) 691-6325, www.bls.gov; *Employment Cost Index; National Compensation Survey; National Compensation Survey - Wages;* and unpublished data.

BLUEFISH

National Marine Fisheries Service (NMFS), National Oceanic and Atmospheric Administration (NOAA), Office of Constituent Services, 1315 East West Highway, 9th Floor, Silver Spring, MD 20910, (301) 713-2379, Fax: (301) 713-2385, www.nmfs.noaa.gov; *Fisheries of the United States - 2006.*

BOARD GAMES

Unites States Chess Federation (USCF), PO Box 3967, Crossville, TN 38557, (931) 787-1234, Fax: (931) 787-1200, www.uschess.org; *Chess and Cognitive Development* and unpublished data.

BOATING, CANOEING, ETC

National Marine Manufacturers Association (NMMA), 200 East Randolph Drive, Suite 5100, Chicago, IL 60601, (312) 946-6200, www.nmma.org; *Boating Industry Facts and Figures* and *2004 Recreational Boating Statistical Abstract.*

National Sporting Goods Association (NSGA), 1601 Feehanville Drive, Suite 300, Mount Prospect, IL 60056, (847) 296-6742, Fax: (847) 391-9827, www.nsga.org; *2006 Sports Participation* and *Ten-Year History of Selected Sports Participation, 1996-2006.*

BOATING, CANOEING, ETC. - ACCIDENTS

U.S. Department of Transportation (DOT), Research and Innovative Technology Administration (RITA), Bureau of Transportation Statistics (BTS), 1200 New Jersey Avenue, SE, Washington, DC 20590, (800) 853-1351, www.bts.gov; *TranStats.*

BOLIVIA - NATIONAL STATISTICAL OFFICE

Instituto Nacional de Estadistica (INE), Calle Jose Carrasco No. 1391, Casilla Postal 6129, Bolivia, www.ine.gov.bo; National Data Center.

BOLIVIA - PRIMARY STATISTICS SOURCES

Instituto Nacional de Estadistica (INE), Calle Jose Carrasco No. 1391, Casilla Postal 6129, Bolivia, www.ine.gov.bo; *Analisis de la Actividad Economica - Ano 2006; Anuario Estadistico 2005;* and *Bolivia: Indicadores demograficos.*

Instituto Nacional de Estadistica (INE), Av. Boyaca Edif, Fundacion La Salle, Piso 4, Mariperez, Caracas, Venezuela, www.ine.gov.ve; *Republica Bolivariana en Cifras, 1998-2006.*

BOLIVIA - AGRICULTURAL MACHINERY

Economist Intelligence Unit, 111 West 57th Street, New York, NY 10019, (212) 554-0600, Fax: (212) 586-1181, www.eiu.com; *Business Latin America.*

United Nations Statistics Division, New York, NY 10017, (800) 253-9646, Fax: (212) 963-4116, http://unstats.un.org; *Statistical Yearbook.*

BOLIVIA - AGRICULTURE

Economist Intelligence Unit, 111 West 57th Street, New York, NY 10019, (212) 554-0600, Fax: (212) 586-1181, www.eiu.com; *Bolivia Country Report* and *Business Latin America.*

Euromonitor International, Inc., 224 S. Michigan Avenue, Suite 1500, Chicago, IL 60604, (312) 922-1115, Fax: (312) 922-1157, www.euromonitor.com; *International Marketing Data and Statistics 2008* and *World Marketing Data and Statistics.*

Inter-American Development Bank (IDB), 1300 New York Avenue, NW, Washington, DC 20577, (202) 623-1000, Fax: (202) 623-3096, www.iadb.org; *The Politics of Policies: Economic and Social Progress in Latin America - 2006 Report.*

M.E. Sharpe, 80 Business Park Drive, Armonk, NY 10504, (800) 541-6563, Fax: (914) 273-2106, www.mesharpe.com; *The Illustrated Book of World Rankings.*

Palgrave Macmillan Ltd., Houndmills, Basingstoke, Hampshire, RG21 6XS, England, (Telephone in U.S. (888) 330-8477), (Fax in U.S. (800) 672-2054), www.palgrave.com; *The Statesman's Yearbook 2008.*

Taylor and Francis Group, An Informa Business, 2 Park Square, Milton Park, Abingdon, Oxford OX14 4RN, United Kingdom, (Dial from U.S. (212) 216-7800), (Fax from U.S. (212) 564-7854), www.tandf.co.uk; *The Europa World Year Book.*

UCLA Latin American Institute, 10343 Bunche Hall, Box 951447, Los Angeles, CA 90095-1447, (310) 825-4571, Fax: (310) 206-6859, www.international.ucla.edu/lac; *Statistical Abstract of Latin America.*

United Nations Conference on Trade and Development (UNCTAD), DC2-1120, United Nations, New York, NY 10017, (212) 963-0027, www.unctad.org; *UNCTAD Commodity Yearbook.*

United Nations Food and Agricultural Organization (FAO), Viale delle Terme di Caracalla, 00100 Rome, Italy, (Dial from U.S. (202) 653-2400), (Fax from U.S. (202) 653 5760), www.fao.org; AQUASTAT; *FAO Production Yearbook 2002; FAO Trade Yearbook;* and *The State of Food and Agriculture (SOFA) 2006.*

United Nations Statistics Division, New York, NY 10017, (800) 253-9646, Fax: (212) 963-4116, http://unstats.un.org; *Statistical Yearbook* and *Statistical Yearbook for Latin America and the Caribbean 2004.*

The World Bank, 1818 H Street, NW, Washington, DC 20433, (202) 473-1000, Fax: (202) 477-6391, www.worldbank.org; *Bolivia* and *World Development Indicators (WDI) 2008.*

BOLIVIA - AIRLINES

Economist Intelligence Unit, 111 West 57th Street, New York, NY 10019, (212) 554-0600, Fax: (212) 586-1181, www.eiu.com; *Business Latin America.*

International Civil Aviation Organization (ICAO), External Relations and Public Information Office (EPO), 999 University Street, Montreal, Quebec H3C 5H7, Canada, (Dial from U.S. (514) 954-8219), (Fax from U.S. (514) 954-6077), www.icao.int; *Civil Aviation Statistics of the World.*

M.E. Sharpe, 80 Business Park Drive, Armonk, NY 10504, (800) 541-6563, Fax: (914) 273-2106, www.mesharpe.com; *The Illustrated Book of World Rankings.*

Palgrave Macmillan Ltd., Houndmills, Basingstoke, Hampshire, RG21 6XS, England, (Telephone in U.S. (888) 330-8477), (Fax in U.S. (800) 672-2054), www.palgrave.com; *The Statesman's Yearbook 2008.*

Taylor and Francis Group, An Informa Business, 2 Park Square, Milton Park, Abingdon, Oxford OX14 4RN, United Kingdom, (Dial from U.S. (212) 216-7800), (Fax from U.S. (212) 564-7854), www.tandf.co.uk; *The Europa World Year Book.*

United Nations Statistics Division, New York, NY 10017, (800) 253-9646, Fax: (212) 963-4116, http://unstats.un.org; *Statistical Yearbook.*

BOLIVIA - AIRPORTS

Central Intelligence Agency, Office of Public Affairs, Washington, DC 20505, (703) 482-0623, Fax: (703) 482-1739, www.cia.gov; *The World Factbook.*

BOLIVIA - ALUMINUM PRODUCTION

See BOLIVIA - MINERAL INDUSTRIES

BOLIVIA - AREA

Economist Intelligence Unit, 111 West 57th Street, New York, NY 10019, (212) 554-0600, Fax: (212) 586-1181, www.eiu.com; *Business Latin America.*

BOLIVIA - ARMED FORCES

Central Intelligence Agency, Office of Public Affairs, Washington, DC 20505, (703) 482-0623, Fax: (703) 482-1739, www.cia.gov; *The World Factbook.*

Economist Intelligence Unit, 111 West 57th Street, New York, NY 10019, (212) 554-0600, Fax: (212) 586-1181, www.eiu.com; *Business Latin America.*

Euromonitor International, Inc., 224 S. Michigan Avenue, Suite 1500, Chicago, IL 60604, (312) 922-1115, Fax: (312) 922-1157, www.euromonitor.com; *World Marketing Data and Statistics.*

International Institute for Strategic Studies (IISS), Arundel House, 13-15 Arundel Street, Temple Place, London WC2R 3DX, England, www.iiss.org; *The Military Balance 2007.*

International Monetary Fund (IMF), 700 Nineteenth Street, NW, Washington, DC 20431, (202) 623-7000, Fax: (202) 623-4661, www.imf.org; *Government Finance Statistics Yearbook (2008 Edition).*

Palgrave Macmillan Ltd., Houndmills, Basingstoke, Hampshire, RG21 6XS, England, (Telephone in U.S. (888) 330-8477), (Fax in U.S. (800) 672-2054), www.palgrave.com; *The Statesman's Yearbook 2008.*

U.S. Department of State (DOS), 2201 C Street NW, Washington, DC 20520, (202) 647-4000, www.state.gov; *World Military Expenditures and Arms Transfers (WMEAT).*

UCLA Latin American Institute, 10343 Bunche Hall, Box 951447, Los Angeles, CA 90095-1447, (310) 825-4571, Fax: (310) 206-6859, www.international.ucla.edu/lac; *Statistical Abstract of Latin America.*

United Nations Statistics Division, New York, NY 10017, (800) 253-9646, Fax: (212) 963-4116, http://unstats.un.org; *Human Development Report 2006.*

BOLIVIA - BALANCE OF PAYMENTS

Economist Intelligence Unit, 111 West 57th Street, New York, NY 10019, (212) 554-0600, Fax: (212) 586-1181, www.eiu.com; *Business Latin America.*

Inter-American Development Bank (IDB), 1300 New York Avenue, NW, Washington, DC 20577, (202) 623-1000, Fax: (202) 623-3096, www.iadb.org; *The Politics of Policies: Economic and Social Progress in Latin America - 2006 Report.*

International Monetary Fund (IMF), 700 Nineteenth Street, NW, Washington, DC 20431, (202) 623-7000, Fax: (202) 623-4661, www.imf.org; *Balance of Payments Statistics Newsletter; Balance of Payments Statistics Yearbook 2007;* and *International Financial Statistics Yearbook 2007.*

Organization of American States (OAS), 17th Street Constitution Avenue NW, Washington, DC 20006, (202) 458-3000, www.oas.org; *The OAS in Transition: 1994-2004.*

Taylor and Francis Group, An Informa Business, 2 Park Square, Milton Park, Abingdon, Oxford OX14 4RN, United Kingdom, (Dial from U.S. (212) 216-7800), (Fax from U.S. (212) 564-7854), www.tandf.co.uk; *The Europa World Year Book.*

UCLA Latin American Institute, 10343 Bunche Hall, Box 951447, Los Angeles, CA 90095-1447, (310) 825-4571, Fax: (310) 206-6859, www.international.ucla.edu/lac; *Statistical Abstract of Latin America.*

United Nations Conference on Trade and Development (UNCTAD), DC2-1120, United Nations, New York, NY 10017, (212) 963-0027, www.unctad.org; *Handbook of Statistics 2005.*

United Nations Statistics Division, New York, NY 10017, (800) 253-9646, Fax: (212) 963-4116, http://unstats.un.org; *Economic Survey of Latin America and the Caribbean 2004-2005* and *Statistical Yearbook for Latin America and the Caribbean 2004.*

The World Bank, 1818 H Street, NW, Washington, DC 20433, (202) 473-1000, Fax: (202) 477-6391, www.worldbank.org; *Bolivia; World Development Indicators (WDI) 2008;* and *World Development Report 2008.*

BOLIVIA - BANKS AND BANKING

Euromonitor International, Inc., 224 S. Michigan Avenue, Suite 1500, Chicago, IL 60604, (312) 922-1115, Fax: (312) 922-1157, www.euromonitor.com; *World Marketing Data and Statistics.*

Inter-American Development Bank (IDB), 1300 New York Avenue, NW, Washington, DC 20577, (202) 623-1000, Fax: (202) 623-3096, www.iadb.org; *The Politics of Policies: Economic and Social Progress in Latin America - 2006 Report.*

International Monetary Fund (IMF), 700 Nineteenth Street, NW, Washington, DC 20431, (202) 623-7000, Fax: (202) 623-4661, www.imf.org; *Government Finance Statistics Yearbook (2008 Edition)* and *International Financial Statistics Yearbook 2007.*

M.E. Sharpe, 80 Business Park Drive, Armonk, NY 10504, (800) 541-6563, Fax: (914) 273-2106, www.mesharpe.com; *The Illustrated Book of World Rankings.*

Palgrave Macmillan Ltd., Houndmills, Basingstoke, Hampshire, RG21 6XS, England, (Telephone in U.S. (888) 330-8477), (Fax in U.S. (800) 672-2054), www.palgrave.com; *The Statesman's Yearbook 2008.*

Taylor and Francis Group, An Informa Business, 2 Park Square, Milton Park, Abingdon, Oxford OX14 4RN, United Kingdom, (Dial from U.S. (212) 216-7800), (Fax from U.S. (212) 564-7854), www.tandf.co.uk; *The Europa World Year Book.*

United Nations Statistics Division, New York, NY 10017, (800) 253-9646, Fax: (212) 963-4116, http://unstats.un.org; *Statistical Yearbook for Latin America and the Caribbean 2004.*

BOLIVIA - BARLEY PRODUCTION

See BOLIVIA - CROPS

BOLIVIA - BEVERAGE INDUSTRY

M.E. Sharpe, 80 Business Park Drive, Armonk, NY 10504, (800) 541-6563, Fax: (914) 273-2106, www.mesharpe.com; *The Illustrated Book of World Rankings.*

United Nations Statistics Division, New York, NY 10017, (800) 253-9646, Fax: (212) 963-4116, http://unstats.un.org; *Statistical Yearbook.*

BOLIVIA - BIRTH CONTROL

UCLA Latin American Institute, 10343 Bunche Hall, Box 951447, Los Angeles, CA 90095-1447, (310) 825-4571, Fax: (310) 206-6859, www.international.ucla.edu/lac; *Statistical Abstract of Latin America.*

BOLIVIA - BONDS

Inter-American Development Bank (IDB), 1300 New York Avenue, NW, Washington, DC 20577, (202) 623-1000, Fax: (202) 623-3096, www.iadb.org; *The Politics of Policies: Economic and Social Progress in Latin America - 2006 Report.*

International Monetary Fund (IMF), 700 Nineteenth Street, NW, Washington, DC 20431, (202) 623-7000, Fax: (202) 623-4661, www.imf.org; *Government Finance Statistics Yearbook (2008 Edition).*

BOLIVIA - BROADCASTING

Central Intelligence Agency, Office of Public Affairs, Washington, DC 20505, (703) 482-0623, Fax: (703) 482-1739, www.cia.gov; *The World Factbook.*

Euromonitor International, Inc., 224 S. Michigan Avenue, Suite 1500, Chicago, IL 60604, (312) 922-1115, Fax: (312) 922-1157, www.euromonitor.com; *World Marketing Data and Statistics.*

M.E. Sharpe, 80 Business Park Drive, Armonk, NY 10504, (800) 541-6563, Fax: (914) 273-2106, www.mesharpe.com; *The Illustrated Book of World Rankings.*

Palgrave Macmillan Ltd., Houndmills, Basingstoke, Hampshire, RG21 6XS, England, (Telephone in U.S. (888) 330-8477), (Fax in U.S. (800) 672-2054), www.palgrave.com; *The Statesman's Yearbook 2008.*

WRTH Publications Limited, PO Box 290, Oxford OX2 7FT, UK, www.wrth.com; *World Radio TV Handbook 2007.*

BOLIVIA - BUDGET

Central Intelligence Agency, Office of Public Affairs, Washington, DC 20505, (703) 482-0623, Fax: (703) 482-1739, www.cia.gov; *The World Factbook.*

BOLIVIA - BUSINESS

Inter-American Development Bank (IDB), 1300 New York Avenue, NW, Washington, DC 20577, (202) 623-1000, Fax: (202) 623-3096, www.iadb.org; *The Politics of Policies: Economic and Social Progress in Latin America - 2006 Report.*

BOLIVIA - CAPITAL INVESTMENTS

Inter-American Development Bank (IDB), 1300 New York Avenue, NW, Washington, DC 20577, (202) 623-1000, Fax: (202) 623-3096, www.iadb.org; *The Politics of Policies: Economic and Social Progress in Latin America - 2006 Report.*

BOLIVIA - CAPITAL LEVY

Inter-American Development Bank (IDB), 1300 New York Avenue, NW, Washington, DC 20577, (202) 623-1000, Fax: (202) 623-3096, www.iadb.org; *The Politics of Policies: Economic and Social Progress in Latin America - 2006 Report.*

International Monetary Fund (IMF), 700 Nineteenth Street, NW, Washington, DC 20431, (202) 623-7000, Fax: (202) 623-4661, www.imf.org; *Government Finance Statistics Yearbook (2008 Edition).*

BOLIVIA - CATTLE

See BOLIVIA - LIVESTOCK

BOLIVIA - CHESTNUT PRODUCTION

See BOLIVIA - CROPS

BOLIVIA - CHICK PEA PRODUCTION

See BOLIVIA - CROPS

BOLIVIA - CHICKENS

See BOLIVIA - LIVESTOCK

BOLIVIA - CHILDBIRTH - STATISTICS

Central Intelligence Agency, Office of Public Affairs, Washington, DC 20505, (703) 482-0623, Fax: (703) 482-1739, www.cia.gov; *The World Factbook.*

Euromonitor International, Inc., 224 S. Michigan Avenue, Suite 1500, Chicago, IL 60604, (312) 922-1115, Fax: (312) 922-1157, www.euromonitor.com; *International Marketing Data and Statistics 2008* and *The World Economic Factbook 2008.*

M.E. Sharpe, 80 Business Park Drive, Armonk, NY 10504, (800) 541-6563, Fax: (914) 273-2106, www.mesharpe.com; *The Illustrated Book of World Rankings.*

Taylor and Francis Group, An Informa Business, 2 Park Square, Milton Park, Abingdon, Oxford OX14 4RN, United Kingdom, (Dial from U.S. (212) 216-7800), (Fax from U.S. (212) 564-7854), www.tandf.co.uk; *The Europa World Year Book.*

United Nations Statistics Division, New York, NY 10017, (800) 253-9646, Fax: (212) 963-4116, http://unstats.un.org; *Demographic Yearbook; Statistical Yearbook;* and *Statistical Yearbook for Latin America and the Caribbean 2004.*

The World Bank, 1818 H Street, NW, Washington, DC 20433, (202) 473-1000, Fax: (202) 477-6391, www.worldbank.org; *World Development Indicators (WDI) 2008.*

World Health Organization (WHO), Avenue Appia 20, 1211 Geneve 27, Switzerland, (Telephone in U.S. (212) 331-9081), www.who.int; *World Health Report 2006.*

BOLIVIA - CLIMATE

M.E. Sharpe, 80 Business Park Drive, Armonk, NY 10504, (800) 541-6563, Fax: (914) 273-2106, www.mesharpe.com; *The Illustrated Book of World Rankings.*

Palgrave Macmillan Ltd., Houndmills, Basingstoke, Hampshire, RG21 6XS, England, (Telephone in U.S. (888) 330-8477), (Fax in U.S. (800) 672-2054), www.palgrave.com; *The Statesman's Yearbook 2008.*

BOLIVIA - COAL PRODUCTION

See BOLIVIA - MINERAL INDUSTRIES

BOLIVIA - COCOA PRODUCTION

See BOLIVIA - CROPS

BOLIVIA - COFFEE

See BOLIVIA - CROPS

BOLIVIA - COMMERCE

Palgrave Macmillan Ltd., Houndmills, Basingstoke, Hampshire, RG21 6XS, England, (Telephone in U.S. (888) 330-8477), (Fax in U.S. (800) 672-2054), www.palgrave.com; *The Statesman's Yearbook 2008.*

BOLIVIA - COMMODITY EXCHANGES

Commodity Research Bureau, 330 South Wells Street, Suite 612, Chicago, IL 60606-7110, (800) 621-5271, Fax: (312) 939-4135, www.crbtrader.com; *2006 CRB Commodity Yearbook and CD.*

International Monetary Fund (IMF), 700 Nineteenth Street, NW, Washington, DC 20431, (202) 623-7000, Fax: (202) 623-4661, www.imf.org; *IMF Primary Commodity Prices.*

United Nations Food and Agricultural Organization (FAO), Viale delle Terme di Caracalla, 00100 Rome, Italy, (Dial from U.S. (202) 653-2400), (Fax from U.S. (202) 653 5760), www.fao.org; *The State of Food and Agriculture (SOFA) 2006.*

BOLIVIA - CONSTRUCTION INDUSTRY

Economist Intelligence Unit, 111 West 57th Street, New York, NY 10019, (212) 554-0600, Fax: (212) 586-1181, www.eiu.com; *Business Latin America.*

Inter-American Development Bank (IDB), 1300 New York Avenue, NW, Washington, DC 20577, (202) 623-1000, Fax: (202) 623-3096, www.iadb.org; *The Politics of Policies: Economic and Social Progress in Latin America - 2006 Report.*

M.E. Sharpe, 80 Business Park Drive, Armonk, NY 10504, (800) 541-6563, Fax: (914) 273-2106, www.mesharpe.com; *The Illustrated Book of World Rankings.*

UCLA Latin American Institute, 10343 Bunche Hall, Box 951447, Los Angeles, CA 90095-1447, (310) 825-4571, Fax: (310) 206-6859, www.international.ucla.edu/lac; *Statistical Abstract of Latin America.*

United Nations Statistics Division, New York, NY 10017, (800) 253-9646, Fax: (212) 963-4116, http://unstats.un.org; *Statistical Yearbook.*

BOLIVIA - CONSUMER COOPERATIVES

UCLA Latin American Institute, 10343 Bunche Hall, Box 951447, Los Angeles, CA 90095-1447, (310) 825-4571, Fax: (310) 206-6859, www.international.ucla.edu/lac; *Statistical Abstract of Latin America.*

BOLIVIA - CONSUMER PRICE INDEXES

Taylor and Francis Group, An Informa Business, 2 Park Square, Milton Park, Abingdon, Oxford OX14 4RN, United Kingdom, (Dial from U.S. (212) 216-7800), (Fax from U.S. (212) 564-7854), www.tandf.co.uk; *The Europa World Year Book.*

United Nations Statistics Division, New York, NY 10017, (800) 253-9646, Fax: (212) 963-4116, http://unstats.un.org; *Statistical Yearbook.*

The World Bank, 1818 H Street, NW, Washington, DC 20433, (202) 473-1000, Fax: (202) 477-6391, www.worldbank.org; *Bolivia.*

BOLIVIA - CONSUMPTION (ECONOMICS)

Economist Intelligence Unit, 111 West 57th Street, New York, NY 10019, (212) 554-0600, Fax: (212) 586-1181, www.eiu.com; *Business Latin America.*

Inter-American Development Bank (IDB), 1300 New York Avenue, NW, Washington, DC 20577, (202) 623-1000, Fax: (202) 623-3096, www.iadb.org; *The Politics of Policies: Economic and Social Progress in Latin America - 2006 Report.*

United Nations Statistics Division, New York, NY 10017, (800) 253-9646, Fax: (212) 963-4116, http://unstats.un.org; *Statistical Yearbook for Latin America and the Caribbean 2004.*

The World Bank, 1818 H Street, NW, Washington, DC 20433, (202) 473-1000, Fax: (202) 477-6391, www.worldbank.org; *World Development Report 2008.*

BOLIVIA - COPPER INDUSTRY AND TRADE

See BOLIVIA - MINERAL INDUSTRIES

BOLIVIA - CORN INDUSTRY

See BOLIVIA - CROPS

BOLIVIA - COST AND STANDARD OF LIVING

International Monetary Fund (IMF), 700 Nineteenth Street, NW, Washington, DC 20431, (202) 623-7000, Fax: (202) 623-4661, www.imf.org; *Government Finance Statistics Yearbook (2008 Edition).*

United Nations Statistics Division, New York, NY 10017, (800) 253-9646, Fax: (212) 963-4116, http://unstats.un.org; *Statistical Yearbook for Latin America and the Caribbean 2004.*

BOLIVIA - COTTON

See BOLIVIA - CROPS

BOLIVIA - CRIME

Yale University Press, PO Box 209040, New Haven, CT 06520-9040, (203) 432-0960, Fax: (203) 432-0948, http://yalepress.yale.edu/yupbooks; *Violence and Crime in Cross-National Perspective.*

BOLIVIA - CROPS

Economist Intelligence Unit, 111 West 57th Street, New York, NY 10019, (212) 554-0600, Fax: (212) 586-1181, www.eiu.com; *Business Latin America.*

Inter-American Development Bank (IDB), 1300 New York Avenue, NW, Washington, DC 20577, (202) 623-1000, Fax: (202) 623-3096, www.iadb.org; *The Politics of Policies: Economic and Social Progress in Latin America - 2006 Report.*

M.E. Sharpe, 80 Business Park Drive, Armonk, NY 10504, (800) 541-6563, Fax: (914) 273-2106, www.mesharpe.com; *The Illustrated Book of World Rankings.*

Palgrave Macmillan Ltd., Houndmills, Basingstoke, Hampshire, RG21 6XS, England, (Telephone in U.S. (888) 330-8477), (Fax in U.S. (800) 672-2054), www.palgrave.com; *The Statesman's Yearbook 2008.*

Taylor and Francis Group, An Informa Business, 2 Park Square, Milton Park, Abingdon, Oxford OX14 4RN, United Kingdom, (Dial from U.S. (212) 216-7800), (Fax from U.S. (212) 564-7854), www.tandf.co.uk; *The Europa World Year Book.*

United Nations Conference on Trade and Development (UNCTAD), DC2-1120, United Nations, New York, NY 10017, (212) 963-0027, www.unctad.org; *UNCTAD Commodity Yearbook.*

United Nations Food and Agricultural Organization (FAO), Viale delle Terme di Caracalla, 00100 Rome, Italy, (Dial from U.S. (202) 653-2400), (Fax from U.S. (202) 653 5760), www.fao.org; *The State of Food and Agriculture (SOFA) 2006.*

United Nations Statistics Division, New York, NY 10017, (800) 253-9646, Fax: (212) 963-4116, http://unstats.un.org; *Statistical Yearbook.*

BOLIVIA - CUSTOMS ADMINISTRATION

Inter-American Development Bank (IDB), 1300 New York Avenue, NW, Washington, DC 20577, (202) 623-1000, Fax: (202) 623-3096, www.iadb.org; *The Politics of Policies: Economic and Social Progress in Latin America - 2006 Report.*

International Monetary Fund (IMF), 700 Nineteenth Street, NW, Washington, DC 20431, (202) 623-7000, Fax: (202) 623-4661, www.imf.org; *Government Finance Statistics Yearbook (2008 Edition).*

Palgrave Macmillan Ltd., Houndmills, Basingstoke, Hampshire, RG21 6XS, England, (Telephone in U.S. (888) 330-8477), (Fax in U.S. (800) 672-2054), www.palgrave.com; *The Statesman's Yearbook 2008.*

BOLIVIA - DAIRY PROCESSING

M.E. Sharpe, 80 Business Park Drive, Armonk, NY 10504, (800) 541-6563, Fax: (914) 273-2106, www.mesharpe.com; *The Illustrated Book of World Rankings.*

Palgrave Macmillan Ltd., Houndmills, Basingstoke, Hampshire, RG21 6XS, England, (Telephone in U.S. (888) 330-8477), (Fax in U.S. (800) 672-2054), www.palgrave.com; *The Statesman's Yearbook 2008.*

Taylor and Francis Group, An Informa Business, 2 Park Square, Milton Park, Abingdon, Oxford OX14 4RN, United Kingdom, (Dial from U.S. (212) 216-7800), (Fax from U.S. (212) 564-7854), www.tandf.co.uk; *The Europa World Year Book.*

United Nations Food and Agricultural Organization (FAO), Viale delle Terme di Caracalla, 00100 Rome, Italy, (Dial from U.S. (202) 653-2400), (Fax from U.S. (202) 653 5760), www.fao.org; *FAO Production Yearbook 2002* and *The State of Food and Agriculture (SOFA) 2006.*

United Nations Statistics Division, New York, NY 10017, (800) 253-9646, Fax: (212) 963-4116, http://unstats.un.org; *Statistical Yearbook.*

BOLIVIA - DEATH RATES

See BOLIVIA - MORTALITY

BOLIVIA - DEBT

Economist Intelligence Unit, 111 West 57th Street, New York, NY 10019, (212) 554-0600, Fax: (212) 586-1181, www.eiu.com; *Business Latin America.*

The World Bank, 1818 H Street, NW, Washington, DC 20433, (202) 473-1000, Fax: (202) 477-6391, www.worldbank.org; *Global Development Finance 2007.*

BOLIVIA - DEBTS, EXTERNAL

Economist Intelligence Unit, 111 West 57th Street, New York, NY 10019, (212) 554-0600, Fax: (212) 586-1181, www.eiu.com; *Business Latin America.*

Inter-American Development Bank (IDB), 1300 New York Avenue, NW, Washington, DC 20577, (202) 623-1000, Fax: (202) 623-3096, www.iadb.org; *The Politics of Policies: Economic and Social Progress in Latin America - 2006 Report.*

International Monetary Fund (IMF), 700 Nineteenth Street, NW, Washington, DC 20431, (202) 623-7000, Fax: (202) 623-4661, www.imf.org; *Government Finance Statistics Yearbook (2008 Edition).*

Palgrave Macmillan Ltd., Houndmills, Basingstoke, Hampshire, RG21 6XS, England, (Telephone in U.S. (888) 330-8477), (Fax in U.S. (800) 672-2054), www.palgrave.com; *The Statesman's Yearbook 2008.*

United Nations Statistics Division, New York, NY 10017, (800) 253-9646, Fax: (212) 963-4116, http://unstats.un.org; *Economic Survey of Latin America and the Caribbean 2004-2005* and *Statistical Yearbook for Latin America and the Caribbean 2004.*

The World Bank, 1818 H Street, NW, Washington, DC 20433, (202) 473-1000, Fax: (202) 477-6391, www.worldbank.org; *Global Development Finance 2007; World Development Indicators (WDI) 2008;* and *World Development Report 2008.*

BOLIVIA - DEFENSE EXPENDITURES

See BOLIVIA - ARMED FORCES

BOLIVIA - DEMOGRAPHY

Euromonitor International, Inc., 224 S. Michigan Avenue, Suite 1500, Chicago, IL 60604, (312) 922-1115, Fax: (312) 922-1157, www.euromonitor.com; *International Marketing Data and Statistics 2008; The World Economic Factbook 2008;* and *World Marketing Data and Statistics.*

M.E. Sharpe, 80 Business Park Drive, Armonk, NY 10504, (800) 541-6563, Fax: (914) 273-2106, www.mesharpe.com; *The Illustrated Book of World Rankings.*

United Nations Statistics Division, New York, NY 10017, (800) 253-9646, Fax: (212) 963-4116, http://unstats.un.org; *Human Development Report 2006.*

The World Bank, 1818 H Street, NW, Washington, DC 20433, (202) 473-1000, Fax: (202) 477-6391, www.worldbank.org; *Bolivia.*

BOLIVIA - DIAMONDS

See BOLIVIA - MINERAL INDUSTRIES

BOLIVIA - DISPOSABLE INCOME

Inter-American Development Bank (IDB), 1300 New York Avenue, NW, Washington, DC 20577, (202) 623-1000, Fax: (202) 623-3096, www.iadb.org; *The Politics of Policies: Economic and Social Progress in Latin America - 2006 Report.*

M.E. Sharpe, 80 Business Park Drive, Armonk, NY 10504, (800) 541-6563, Fax: (914) 273-2106, www.mesharpe.com; *The Illustrated Book of World Rankings.*

United Nations Statistics Division, New York, NY 10017, (800) 253-9646, Fax: (212) 963-4116, http://unstats.un.org; *National Accounts Statistics: Compendium of Income Distribution Statistics; Statistical Yearbook;* and *Statistical Yearbook for Latin America and the Caribbean 2004.*

BOLIVIA - DIVORCE

M.E. Sharpe, 80 Business Park Drive, Armonk, NY 10504, (800) 541-6563, Fax: (914) 273-2106, www.mesharpe.com; *The Illustrated Book of World Rankings.*

United Nations Statistics Division, New York, NY 10017, (800) 253-9646, Fax: (212) 963-4116, http://unstats.un.org; *Demographic Yearbook.*

BOLIVIA - ECONOMIC ASSISTANCE

Inter-American Development Bank (IDB), 1300 New York Avenue, NW, Washington, DC 20577, (202) 623-1000, Fax: (202) 623-3096, www.iadb.org; *The Politics of Policies: Economic and Social Progress in Latin America - 2006 Report.*

United Nations Statistics Division, New York, NY 10017, (800) 253-9646, Fax: (212) 963-4116, http://unstats.un.org; *Statistical Yearbook.*

BOLIVIA - ECONOMIC CONDITIONS

Center for International Business Education Research (CIBER), Columbia Business School and School of International and Public Affairs, Uris Hall, Room 212, 3022 Broadway, New York, NY 10027-6902, Mr. Joshua Safier, (212) 854-4750, Fax: (212) 222-9821, www.columbia.edu/cu/ciber/; Datastream International.

Central Intelligence Agency, Office of Public Affairs, Washington, DC 20505, (703) 482-0623, Fax: (703) 482-1739, www.cia.gov; *The World Factbook.*

DSI Data Service Information, Xantener Strasse 51a, D-47495 Rheinberg, Germany, www.dsidata.com; *Campus Solution.*

Dun and Bradstreet (DB) Corporation, 103 JFK Parkway, Short Hills, NJ 07078, (973) 921-5500, www.dnb.com; *Country Report.*

Economist Intelligence Unit, 111 West 57th Street, New York, NY 10019, (212) 554-0600, Fax: (212) 586-1181, www.eiu.com; *Bolivia Country Report.*

Euromonitor International, Inc., 224 S. Michigan Avenue, Suite 1500, Chicago, IL 60604, (312) 922-1115, Fax: (312) 922-1157, www.euromonitor.com; *International Marketing Data and Statistics 2008; The World Economic Factbook 2008;* and *World Marketing Data and Statistics.*

Inter-American Development Bank (IDB), 1300 New York Avenue, NW, Washington, DC 20577, (202) 623-1000, Fax: (202) 623-3096, www.iadb.org; *The Politics of Policies: Economic and Social Progress in Latin America - 2006 Report.*

International Monetary Fund (IMF), 700 Nineteenth Street, NW, Washington, DC 20431, (202) 623-7000, Fax: (202) 623-4661, www.imf.org; *World Economic Outlook Reports.*

M.E. Sharpe, 80 Business Park Drive, Armonk, NY 10504, (800) 541-6563, Fax: (914) 273-2106, www.mesharpe.com; *The Illustrated Book of World Rankings.*

Organization of American States (OAS), 17th Street Constitution Avenue NW, Washington, DC 20006, (202) 458-3000, www.oas.org; *The OAS in Transition: 1994-2004.*

Palgrave Macmillan Ltd., Houndmills, Basingstoke, Hampshire, RG21 6XS, England, (Telephone in U.S. (888) 330-8477), (Fax in U.S. (800) 672-2054), www.palgrave.com; *The Statesman's Yearbook 2008.*

Taylor and Francis Group, An Informa Business, 2 Park Square, Milton Park, Abingdon, Oxford OX14 4RN, United Kingdom, (Dial from U.S. (212) 216-7800), (Fax from U.S. (212) 564-7854), www.tandf.co.uk; *The Europa World Year Book.*

UCLA Latin American Institute, 10343 Bunche Hall, Box 951447, Los Angeles, CA 90095-1447, (310) 825-4571, Fax: (310) 206-6859, www.international.ucla.edu/lac; *Statistical Abstract of Latin America.*

United Nations Statistics Division, New York, NY 10017, (800) 253-9646, Fax: (212) 963-4116, http://unstats.un.org; *Economic Survey of Latin America and the Caribbean 2004-2005* and *World Statistics Pocketbook.*

The World Bank, 1818 H Street, NW, Washington, DC 20433, (202) 473-1000, Fax: (202) 477-6391, www.worldbank.org; *Bolivia; Global Economic Monitor (GEM); Global Economic Prospects 2008; The World Bank Atlas 2003-2004;* and *World Development Report 2008.*

BOLIVIA - ECONOMICS - SOCIOLOGICAL ASPECTS

Inter-American Development Bank (IDB), 1300 New York Avenue, NW, Washington, DC 20577, (202) 623-1000, Fax: (202) 623-3096, www.iadb.org; *The Politics of Policies: Economic and Social Progress in Latin America - 2006 Report.*

UCLA Latin American Institute, 10343 Bunche Hall, Box 951447, Los Angeles, CA 90095-1447, (310) 825-4571, Fax: (310) 206-6859, www.international.ucla.edu/lac; *Statistical Abstract of Latin America.*

BOLIVIA - EDUCATION

Economist Intelligence Unit, 111 West 57th Street, New York, NY 10019, (212) 554-0600, Fax: (212) 586-1181, www.eiu.com; *Business Latin America.*

Euromonitor International, Inc., 224 S. Michigan Avenue, Suite 1500, Chicago, IL 60604, (312) 922-1115, Fax: (312) 922-1157, www.euromonitor.com; *International Marketing Data and Statistics 2008* and *World Marketing Data and Statistics.*

International Monetary Fund (IMF), 700 Nineteenth Street, NW, Washington, DC 20431, (202) 623-7000, Fax: (202) 623-4661, www.imf.org; *Government Finance Statistics Yearbook (2008 Edition).*

M.E. Sharpe, 80 Business Park Drive, Armonk, NY 10504, (800) 541-6563, Fax: (914) 273-2106, www.mesharpe.com; *The Illustrated Book of World Rankings.*

Palgrave Macmillan Ltd., Houndmills, Basingstoke, Hampshire, RG21 6XS, England, (Telephone in U.S. (888) 330-8477), (Fax in U.S. (800) 672-2054), www.palgrave.com; *The Statesman's Yearbook 2008.*

Taylor and Francis Group, An Informa Business, 2 Park Square, Milton Park, Abingdon, Oxford OX14 4RN, United Kingdom, (Dial from U.S. (212) 216-7800), (Fax from U.S. (212) 564-7854), www.tandf.co.uk; *The Europa World Year Book.*

UCLA Latin American Institute, 10343 Bunche Hall, Box 951447, Los Angeles, CA 90095-1447, (310) 825-4571, Fax: (310) 206-6859, www.international.ucla.edu/lac; *Statistical Abstract of Latin America.*

UNESCO Institute for Statistics, C.P. 6128 Succursale Centre-Ville, Montreal, Quebec, H3C 3J7 Canada, (Dial from U.S. (514) 343-6880), (Fax from U.S. (514) 343 6882), www.uis.unesco.org; *Statistical Tables.*

United Nations Statistics Division, New York, NY 10017, (800) 253-9646, Fax: (212) 963-4116, http://unstats.un.org; *Human Development Report 2006* and *Statistical Yearbook for Latin America and the Caribbean 2004.*

The World Bank, 1818 H Street, NW, Washington, DC 20433, (202) 473-1000, Fax: (202) 477-6391, www.worldbank.org; *Bolivia; World Development Indicators (WDI) 2008;* and *World Development Report 2008.*

BOLIVIA - ELECTRICITY

Economist Intelligence Unit, 111 West 57th Street, New York, NY 10019, (212) 554-0600, Fax: (212) 586-1181, www.eiu.com; *Business Latin America.*

Inter-American Development Bank (IDB), 1300 New York Avenue, NW, Washington, DC 20577, (202) 623-1000, Fax: (202) 623-3096, www.iadb.org; *The Politics of Policies: Economic and Social Progress in Latin America - 2006 Report.*

M.E. Sharpe, 80 Business Park Drive, Armonk, NY 10504, (800) 541-6563, Fax: (914) 273-2106, www.mesharpe.com; *The Illustrated Book of World Rankings.*

Organisation for Economic Cooperation and Development (OECD), 2 rue Andre Pascal, F-75775 Paris Cedex 16, France, (Telephone in U.S. (202) 785-6323), (Fax in U.S. (202) 785-0350), www.oecd.org; *World Energy Outlook 2007.*

Palgrave Macmillan Ltd., Houndmills, Basingstoke, Hampshire, RG21 6XS, England, (Telephone in U.S. (888) 330-8477), (Fax in U.S. (800) 672-2054), www.palgrave.com; *The Statesman's Yearbook 2008.*

U.S. Department of Energy (DOE), Energy Information Administration (EIA), 1000 Independence Avenue, SW, Washington, DC 20585, (202) 586-8800, www.eia.doe.gov; *International Energy Annual 2004* and *International Energy Outlook 2006.*

United Nations Statistics Division, New York, NY 10017, (800) 253-9646, Fax: (212) 963-4116, http://unstats.un.org; *Human Development Report 2006* and *Statistical Yearbook.*

BOLIVIA - EMIGRATION AND IMMIGRATION

UCLA Latin American Institute, 10343 Bunche Hall, Box 951447, Los Angeles, CA 90095-1447, (310) 825-4571, Fax: (310) 206-6859, www.international.ucla.edu/lac; *Statistical Abstract of Latin America.*

BOLIVIA - EMPLOYMENT

Euromonitor International, Inc., 224 S. Michigan Avenue, Suite 1500, Chicago, IL 60604, (312) 922-1115, Fax: (312) 922-1157, www.euromonitor.com; *International Marketing Data and Statistics 2008.*

International Labour Office, I.L.O. Publications, 4 route des Morillons, CH-1211 Geneva 22, Switzerland, (Telephone in U.S. (202) 653-7652), (Fax in U.S. (202) 653-7687), www.ilo.org; *Yearbook of Labour Statistics 2006.*

M.E. Sharpe, 80 Business Park Drive, Armonk, NY 10504, (800) 541-6563, Fax: (914) 273-2106, www.mesharpe.com; *The Illustrated Book of World Rankings.*

UCLA Latin American Institute, 10343 Bunche Hall, Box 951447, Los Angeles, CA 90095-1447, (310) 825-4571, Fax: (310) 206-6859, www.international.ucla.edu/lac; *Statistical Abstract of Latin America.*

United Nations Statistics Division, New York, NY 10017, (800) 253-9646, Fax: (212) 963-4116, http://

unstats.un.org; *Statistical Yearbook* and *Statistical Yearbook for Latin America and the Caribbean 2004*.

The World Bank, 1818 H Street, NW, Washington, DC 20433, (202) 473-1000, Fax: (202) 477-6391, www.worldbank.org; *Bolivia*.

BOLIVIA - ENERGY INDUSTRIES

Enerdata, 10 Rue Royale, 75008 Paris, France, www.enerdata.fr; *Global Energy Market Data*.

United Nations Statistics Division, New York, NY 10017, (800) 253-9646, Fax: (212) 963-4116, http://unstats.un.org; *Statistical Yearbook*.

BOLIVIA - ENVIRONMENTAL CONDITIONS

DSI Data Service Information, Xantener Strasse 51a, D-47495 Rheinberg, Germany, www.dsidata.com; *Campus Solution* and *DSI's Global Environmental Database*.

Economist Intelligence Unit, 111 West 57th Street, New York, NY 10019, (212) 554-0600, Fax: (212) 586-1181, www.eiu.com; *Bolivia Country Report*.

United Nations Statistics Division, New York, NY 10017, (800) 253-9646, Fax: (212) 963-4116, http://unstats.un.org; *World Statistics Pocketbook*.

BOLIVIA - EXPENDITURES, PUBLIC

Inter-American Development Bank (IDB), 1300 New York Avenue, NW, Washington, DC 20577, (202) 623-1000, Fax: (202) 623-3096, www.iadb.org; *The Politics of Policies: Economic and Social Progress in Latin America - 2006 Report*.

Organization of American States (OAS), 17th Street Constitution Avenue NW, Washington, DC 20006, (202) 458-3000, www.oas.org; *The OAS in Transition: 1994-2004*.

United Nations Statistics Division, New York, NY 10017, (800) 253-9646, Fax: (212) 963-4116, http://unstats.un.org; *Statistical Yearbook for Latin America and the Caribbean 2004*.

BOLIVIA - EXPORTS

Central Intelligence Agency, Office of Public Affairs, Washington, DC 20505, (703) 482-0623, Fax: (703) 482-1739, www.cia.gov; *The World Factbook*.

Economist Intelligence Unit, 111 West 57th Street, New York, NY 10019, (212) 554-0600, Fax: (212) 586-1181, www.eiu.com; *Bolivia Country Report* and *Business Latin America*.

Euromonitor International, Inc., 224 S. Michigan Avenue, Suite 1500, Chicago, IL 60604, (312) 922-1115, Fax: (312) 922-1157, www.euromonitor.com; *International Marketing Data and Statistics 2008* and *The World Economic Factbook 2008*.

Inter-American Development Bank (IDB), 1300 New York Avenue, NW, Washington, DC 20577, (202) 623-1000, Fax: (202) 623-3096, www.iadb.org; *The Politics of Policies: Economic and Social Progress in Latin America - 2006 Report*.

International Monetary Fund (IMF), 700 Nineteenth Street, NW, Washington, DC 20431, (202) 623-7000, Fax: (202) 623-4661, www.imf.org; *Direction of Trade Statistics Yearbook 2007* and *International Financial Statistics Yearbook 2007*.

Organization of American States (OAS), 17th Street Constitution Avenue NW, Washington, DC 20006, (202) 458-3000, www.oas.org; *The OAS in Transition: 1994-2004*.

Palgrave Macmillan Ltd., Houndmills, Basingstoke, Hampshire, RG21 6XS, England, (Telephone in U.S. (888) 330-8477), (Fax in U.S. (800) 672-2054), www.palgrave.com; *The Statesman's Yearbook 2008*.

Taylor and Francis Group, An Informa Business, 2 Park Square, Milton Park, Abingdon, Oxford OX14 4RN, United Kingdom, (Dial from U.S. (212) 216-7800), (Fax from U.S. (212) 564-7854), www.tandf.co.uk; *The Europa World Year Book*.

United Nations Conference on Trade and Development (UNCTAD), DC2-1120, United Nations, New York, NY 10017, (212) 963-0027, www.unctad.org; *Handbook of Statistics 2005*.

United Nations Food and Agricultural Organization (FAO), Viale delle Terme di Caracalla, 00100 Rome, Italy, (Dial from U.S. (202) 653-2400), (Fax from U.S. (202) 653 5760), www.fao.org; *The State of Food and Agriculture (SOFA) 2006*.

United Nations Statistics Division, New York, NY 10017, (800) 253-9646, Fax: (212) 963-4116, http://unstats.un.org; *Statistical Yearbook for Latin America and the Caribbean 2004*.

The World Bank, 1818 H Street, NW, Washington, DC 20433, (202) 473-1000, Fax: (202) 477-6391, www.worldbank.org; *World Development Indicators (WDI) 2008* and *World Development Report 2008*.

BOLIVIA - FEMALE WORKING POPULATION

See BOLIVIA - EMPLOYMENT

BOLIVIA - FERTILITY, HUMAN

Central Intelligence Agency, Office of Public Affairs, Washington, DC 20505, (703) 482-0623, Fax: (703) 482-1739, www.cia.gov; *The World Factbook*.

M.E. Sharpe, 80 Business Park Drive, Armonk, NY 10504, (800) 541-6563, Fax: (914) 273-2106, www.mesharpe.com; *The Illustrated Book of World Rankings*.

United Nations Statistics Division, New York, NY 10017, (800) 253-9646, Fax: (212) 963-4116, http://unstats.un.org; *Human Development Report 2006*.

The World Bank, 1818 H Street, NW, Washington, DC 20433, (202) 473-1000, Fax: (202) 477-6391, www.worldbank.org; *The World Bank Atlas 2003-2004; World Development Indicators (WDI) 2008;* and *World Development Report 2008*.

BOLIVIA - FERTILIZER INDUSTRY

Economist Intelligence Unit, 111 West 57th Street, New York, NY 10019, (212) 554-0600, Fax: (212) 586-1181, www.eiu.com; *Business Latin America*.

United Nations Food and Agricultural Organization (FAO), Viale delle Terme di Caracalla, 00100 Rome, Italy, (Dial from U.S. (202) 653-2400), (Fax from U.S. (202) 653 5760), www.fao.org; *FAO Fertilizer Yearbook* and *The State of Food and Agriculture (SOFA) 2006*.

United Nations Statistics Division, New York, NY 10017, (800) 253-9646, Fax: (212) 963-4116, http://unstats.un.org; *Statistical Yearbook*.

BOLIVIA - FETAL MORTALITY

See BOLIVIA - MORTALITY

BOLIVIA - FILM

See BOLIVIA - MOTION PICTURES

BOLIVIA - FINANCE

Inter-American Development Bank (IDB), 1300 New York Avenue, NW, Washington, DC 20577, (202) 623-1000, Fax: (202) 623-3096, www.iadb.org; *The Politics of Policies: Economic and Social Progress in Latin America - 2006 Report*.

Organization of American States (OAS), 17th Street Constitution Avenue NW, Washington, DC 20006, (202) 458-3000, www.oas.org; *The OAS in Transition: 1994-2004*.

Taylor and Francis Group, An Informa Business, 2 Park Square, Milton Park, Abingdon, Oxford OX14 4RN, United Kingdom, (Dial from U.S. (212) 216-7800), (Fax from U.S. (212) 564-7854), www.tandf.co.uk; *The Europa World Year Book*.

UCLA Latin American Institute, 10343 Bunche Hall, Box 951447, Los Angeles, CA 90095-1447, (310) 825-4571, Fax: (310) 206-6859, www.international.ucla.edu/lac; *Statistical Abstract of Latin America*.

United Nations Statistics Division, New York, NY 10017, (800) 253-9646, Fax: (212) 963-4116, http://unstats.un.org; *National Accounts Statistics: Compendium of Income Distribution Statistics*.

The World Bank, 1818 H Street, NW, Washington, DC 20433, (202) 473-1000, Fax: (202) 477-6391, www.worldbank.org; *Bolivia*.

BOLIVIA - FINANCE, PUBLIC

Bernan Essential Government Publications, 4611-F Assembly Drive, Lanham MD, 20706-4391, (301) 459-2255, Fax: (800) 865-3450, www.bernan.com; *National Accounts Statistics*.

Economist Intelligence Unit, 111 West 57th Street, New York, NY 10019, (212) 554-0600, Fax: (212) 586-1181, www.eiu.com; *Bolivia Country Report*.

Inter-American Development Bank (IDB), 1300 New York Avenue, NW, Washington, DC 20577, (202) 623-1000, Fax: (202) 623-3096, www.iadb.org; *The Politics of Policies: Economic and Social Progress in Latin America - 2006 Report*.

International Monetary Fund (IMF), 700 Nineteenth Street, NW, Washington, DC 20431, (202) 623-7000, Fax: (202) 623-4661, www.imf.org; *Government Finance Statistics Yearbook (2008 Edition); International Financial Statistics; International Financial Statistics Online Service;* and *International Financial Statistics Yearbook 2007*.

M.E. Sharpe, 80 Business Park Drive, Armonk, NY 10504, (800) 541-6563, Fax: (914) 273-2106, www.mesharpe.com; *The Illustrated Book of World Rankings*.

Organization of American States (OAS), 17th Street Constitution Avenue NW, Washington, DC 20006, (202) 458-3000, www.oas.org; *The OAS in Transition: 1994-2004*.

Palgrave Macmillan Ltd., Houndmills, Basingstoke, Hampshire, RG21 6XS, England, (Telephone in U.S. (888) 330-8477), (Fax in U.S. (800) 672-2054), www.palgrave.com; *The Statesman's Yearbook 2008*.

Taylor and Francis Group, An Informa Business, 2 Park Square, Milton Park, Abingdon, Oxford OX14 4RN, United Kingdom, (Dial from U.S. (212) 216-7800), (Fax from U.S. (212) 564-7854), www.tandf.co.uk; *The Europa World Year Book*.

UCLA Latin American Institute, 10343 Bunche Hall, Box 951447, Los Angeles, CA 90095-1447, (310) 825-4571, Fax: (310) 206-6859, www.international.ucla.edu/lac; *Statistical Abstract of Latin America*.

The World Bank, 1818 H Street, NW, Washington, DC 20433, (202) 473-1000, Fax: (202) 477-6391, www.worldbank.org; *Bolivia*.

BOLIVIA - FISHERIES

Inter-American Development Bank (IDB), 1300 New York Avenue, NW, Washington, DC 20577, (202) 623-1000, Fax: (202) 623-3096, www.iadb.org; *The Politics of Policies: Economic and Social Progress in Latin America - 2006 Report*.

M.E. Sharpe, 80 Business Park Drive, Armonk, NY 10504, (800) 541-6563, Fax: (914) 273-2106, www.mesharpe.com; *The Illustrated Book of World Rankings*.

Taylor and Francis Group, An Informa Business, 2 Park Square, Milton Park, Abingdon, Oxford OX14 4RN, United Kingdom, (Dial from U.S. (212) 216-7800), (Fax from U.S. (212) 564-7854), www.tandf.co.uk; *The Europa World Year Book*.

UCLA Latin American Institute, 10343 Bunche Hall, Box 951447, Los Angeles, CA 90095-1447, (310) 825-4571, Fax: (310) 206-6859, www.international.ucla.edu/lac; *Statistical Abstract of Latin America*.

United Nations Conference on Trade and Development (UNCTAD), DC2-1120, United Nations, New York, NY 10017, (212) 963-0027, www.unctad.org; *UNCTAD Commodity Yearbook*.

United Nations Food and Agricultural Organization (FAO), Viale delle Terme di Caracalla, 00100 Rome, Italy, (Dial from U.S. (202) 653-2400), (Fax from U.S. (202) 653 5760), www.fao.org; *FAO Yearbook of Fishery Statistics;* Fishery Databases; FISHSTAT Database. Subjects covered include: Aquaculture production, capture production, fishery commodities; and *The State of Food and Agriculture (SOFA) 2006*.

United Nations Statistics Division, New York, NY 10017, (800) 253-9646, Fax: (212) 963-4116, http://unstats.un.org; *Statistical Yearbook.*

The World Bank, 1818 H Street, NW, Washington, DC 20433, (202) 473-1000, Fax: (202) 477-6391, www.worldbank.org; *Bolivia.*

BOLIVIA - FLOUR INDUSTRY

United Nations Statistics Division, New York, NY 10017, (800) 253-9646, Fax: (212) 963-4116, http://unstats.un.org; *Statistical Yearbook.*

BOLIVIA - FOOD

United Nations Conference on Trade and Development (UNCTAD), DC2-1120, United Nations, New York, NY 10017, (212) 963-0027, www.unctad.org; *UNCTAD Commodity Yearbook.*

United Nations Food and Agricultural Organization (FAO), Viale delle Terme di Caracalla, 00100 Rome, Italy, (Dial from U.S. (202) 653-2400), (Fax from U.S. (202) 653 5760), www.fao.org; *FAO Production Yearbook 2002* and *The State of Food and Agriculture (SOFA) 2006.*

United Nations Statistics Division, New York, NY 10017, (800) 253-9646, Fax: (212) 963-4116, http://unstats.un.org; *Human Development Report 2006.*

BOLIVIA - FOREIGN EXCHANGE RATES

Central Intelligence Agency, Office of Public Affairs, Washington, DC 20505, (703) 482-0623, Fax: (703) 482-1739, www.cia.gov; *The World Factbook.*

Euromonitor International, Inc., 224 S. Michigan Avenue, Suite 1500, Chicago, IL 60604, (312) 922-1115, Fax: (312) 922-1157, www.euromonitor.com; *International Marketing Data and Statistics 2008* and *The World Economic Factbook 2008.*

Inter-American Development Bank (IDB), 1300 New York Avenue, NW, Washington, DC 20577, (202) 623-1000, Fax: (202) 623-3096, www.iadb.org; *The Politics of Policies: Economic and Social Progress in Latin America - 2006 Report.*

International Civil Aviation Organization (ICAO), External Relations and Public Information Office (EPO), 999 University Street, Montreal, Quebec H3C 5H7, Canada, (Dial from U.S. (514) 954-8219), (Fax from U.S. (514) 954-6077), www.icao.int; *Civil Aviation Statistics of the World.*

International Monetary Fund (IMF), 700 Nineteenth Street, NW, Washington, DC 20431, (202) 623-7000, Fax: (202) 623-4661, www.imf.org; *International Financial Statistics Yearbook 2007.*

Organization of American States (OAS), 17th Street Constitution Avenue NW, Washington, DC 20006, (202) 458-3000, www.oas.org; *The OAS in Transition: 1994-2004.*

Taylor and Francis Group, An Informa Business, 2 Park Square, Milton Park, Abingdon, Oxford OX14 4RN, United Kingdom, (Dial from U.S. (212) 216-7800), (Fax from U.S. (212) 564-7854), www.tandf.co.uk; *The Europa World Year Book.*

UCLA Latin American Institute, 10343 Bunche Hall, Box 951447, Los Angeles, CA 90095-1447, (310) 825-4571, Fax: (310) 206-6859, www.international.ucla.edu/lac; *Statistical Abstract of Latin America.*

United Nations Statistics Division, New York, NY 10017, (800) 253-9646, Fax: (212) 963-4116, http://unstats.un.org; *Statistical Yearbook* and *World Statistics Pocketbook.*

BOLIVIA - FORESTS AND FORESTRY

Economist Intelligence Unit, 111 West 57th Street, New York, NY 10019, (212) 554-0600, Fax: (212) 586-1181, www.eiu.com; *Business Latin America.*

Inter-American Development Bank (IDB), 1300 New York Avenue, NW, Washington, DC 20577, (202) 623-1000, Fax: (202) 623-3096, www.iadb.org; *The Politics of Policies: Economic and Social Progress in Latin America - 2006 Report.*

M.E. Sharpe, 80 Business Park Drive, Armonk, NY 10504, (800) 541-6563, Fax: (914) 273-2106, www.mesharpe.com; *The Illustrated Book of World Rankings.*

Palgrave Macmillan Ltd., Houndmills, Basingstoke, Hampshire, RG21 6XS, England, (Telephone in U.S. (888) 330-8477), (Fax in U.S. (800) 672-2054), www.palgrave.com; *The Statesman's Yearbook 2008.*

Taylor and Francis Group, An Informa Business, 2 Park Square, Milton Park, Abingdon, Oxford OX14 4RN, United Kingdom, (Dial from U.S. (212) 216-7800), (Fax from U.S. (212) 564-7854), www.tandf.co.uk; *The Europa World Year Book.*

UCLA Latin American Institute, 10343 Bunche Hall, Box 951447, Los Angeles, CA 90095-1447, (310) 825-4571, Fax: (310) 206-6859, www.international.ucla.edu/lac; *Statistical Abstract of Latin America.*

United Nations Conference on Trade and Development (UNCTAD), DC2-1120, United Nations, New York, NY 10017, (212) 963-0027, www.unctad.org; *UNCTAD Commodity Yearbook.*

United Nations Food and Agricultural Organization (FAO), Viale delle Terme di Caracalla, 00100 Rome, Italy, (Dial from U.S. (202) 653-2400), (Fax from U.S. (202) 653 5760), www.fao.org; *FAO Yearbook of Forest Products* and *The State of Food and Agriculture (SOFA) 2006.*

United Nations Statistics Division, New York, NY 10017, (800) 253-9646, Fax: (212) 963-4116, http://unstats.un.org; *Statistical Yearbook.*

The World Bank, 1818 H Street, NW, Washington, DC 20433, (202) 473-1000, Fax: (202) 477-6391, www.worldbank.org; *Bolivia* and *World Development Report 2008.*

BOLIVIA - GAS PRODUCTION

See BOLIVIA - MINERAL INDUSTRIES

BOLIVIA - GEOGRAPHIC INFORMATION SYSTEMS

M.E. Sharpe, 80 Business Park Drive, Armonk, NY 10504, (800) 541-6563, Fax: (914) 273-2106, www.mesharpe.com; *The Illustrated Book of World Rankings.*

UCLA Latin American Institute, 10343 Bunche Hall, Box 951447, Los Angeles, CA 90095-1447, (310) 825-4571, Fax: (310) 206-6859, www.international.ucla.edu/lac; *Statistical Abstract of Latin America.*

The World Bank, 1818 H Street, NW, Washington, DC 20433, (202) 473-1000, Fax: (202) 477-6391, www.worldbank.org; *Bolivia.*

BOLIVIA - GOLD INDUSTRY

Economist Intelligence Unit, 111 West 57th Street, New York, NY 10019, (212) 554-0600, Fax: (212) 586-1181, www.eiu.com; *Business Latin America.*

International Monetary Fund (IMF), 700 Nineteenth Street, NW, Washington, DC 20431, (202) 623-7000, Fax: (202) 623-4661, www.imf.org; *International Financial Statistics Yearbook 2007.*

United Nations Statistics Division, New York, NY 10017, (800) 253-9646, Fax: (212) 963-4116, http://unstats.un.org; *Statistical Yearbook.*

The World Bank, 1818 H Street, NW, Washington, DC 20433, (202) 473-1000, Fax: (202) 477-6391, www.worldbank.org; *World Development Indicators (WDI) 2008.*

BOLIVIA - GOLD PRODUCTION

See BOLIVIA - MINERAL INDUSTRIES

BOLIVIA - GRANTS-IN-AID

International Monetary Fund (IMF), 700 Nineteenth Street, NW, Washington, DC 20431, (202) 623-7000, Fax: (202) 623-4661, www.imf.org; *Government Finance Statistics Yearbook (2008 Edition).*

BOLIVIA - GREEN PEPPER AND CHILIE PRODUCTION

See BOLIVIA - CROPS

BOLIVIA - GROSS DOMESTIC PRODUCT

Economist Intelligence Unit, 111 West 57th Street, New York, NY 10019, (212) 554-0600, Fax: (212) 586-1181, www.eiu.com; *Bolivia Country Report* and *Business Latin America.*

Euromonitor International, Inc., 224 S. Michigan Avenue, Suite 1500, Chicago, IL 60604, (312) 922-1115, Fax: (312) 922-1157, www.euromonitor.com; *International Marketing Data and Statistics 2008* and *The World Economic Factbook 2008.*

Inter-American Development Bank (IDB), 1300 New York Avenue, NW, Washington, DC 20577, (202) 623-1000, Fax: (202) 623-3096, www.iadb.org; *The Politics of Policies: Economic and Social Progress in Latin America - 2006 Report.*

M.E. Sharpe, 80 Business Park Drive, Armonk, NY 10504, (800) 541-6563, Fax: (914) 273-2106, www.mesharpe.com; *The Illustrated Book of World Rankings.*

Organization of American States (OAS), 17th Street Constitution Avenue NW, Washington, DC 20006, (202) 458-3000, www.oas.org; *The OAS in Transition: 1994-2004.*

Taylor and Francis Group, An Informa Business, 2 Park Square, Milton Park, Abingdon, Oxford OX14 4RN, United Kingdom, (Dial from U.S. (212) 216-7800), (Fax from U.S. (212) 564-7854), www.tandf.co.uk; *The Europa World Year Book.*

UCLA Latin American Institute, 10343 Bunche Hall, Box 951447, Los Angeles, CA 90095-1447, (310) 825-4571, Fax: (310) 206-6859, www.international.ucla.edu/lac; *Statistical Abstract of Latin America.*

United Nations Statistics Division, New York, NY 10017, (800) 253-9646, Fax: (212) 963-4116, http://unstats.un.org; *Human Development Report 2006; National Accounts Statistics: Compendium of Income Distribution Statistics; Statistical Yearbook;* and *Statistical Yearbook for Latin America and the Caribbean 2004.*

The World Bank, 1818 H Street, NW, Washington, DC 20433, (202) 473-1000, Fax: (202) 477-6391, www.worldbank.org; *World Development Indicators (WDI) 2008* and *World Development Report 2008.*

BOLIVIA - GROSS NATIONAL PRODUCT

Euromonitor International, Inc., 224 S. Michigan Avenue, Suite 1500, Chicago, IL 60604, (312) 922-1115, Fax: (312) 922-1157, www.euromonitor.com; *International Marketing Data and Statistics 2008.*

Inter-American Development Bank (IDB), 1300 New York Avenue, NW, Washington, DC 20577, (202) 623-1000, Fax: (202) 623-3096, www.iadb.org; *The Politics of Policies: Economic and Social Progress in Latin America - 2006 Report.*

M.E. Sharpe, 80 Business Park Drive, Armonk, NY 10504, (800) 541-6563, Fax: (914) 273-2106, www.mesharpe.com; *The Illustrated Book of World Rankings.*

Palgrave Macmillan Ltd., Houndmills, Basingstoke, Hampshire, RG21 6XS, England, (Telephone in U.S. (888) 330-8477), (Fax in U.S. (800) 672-2054), www.palgrave.com; *The Statesman's Yearbook 2008.*

U.S. Department of State (DOS), 2201 C Street NW, Washington, DC 20520, (202) 647-4000, www.state.gov; *World Military Expenditures and Arms Transfers (WMEAT).*

United Nations Statistics Division, New York, NY 10017, (800) 253-9646, Fax: (212) 963-4116, http://unstats.un.org; *Statistical Yearbook.*

The World Bank, 1818 H Street, NW, Washington, DC 20433, (202) 473-1000, Fax: (202) 477-6391, www.worldbank.org; *The World Bank Atlas 2003-2004; World Development Indicators (WDI) 2008;* and *World Development Report 2008.*

BOLIVIA - HIDES AND SKINS INDUSTRY

United Nations Food and Agricultural Organization (FAO), Viale delle Terme di Caracalla, 00100 Rome, Italy, (Dial from U.S. (202) 653-2400), (Fax from U.S. (202) 653 5760), www.fao.org; *FAO Production Yearbook 2002.*

BOLIVIA - HOUSING

Euromonitor International, Inc., 224 S. Michigan Avenue, Suite 1500, Chicago, IL 60604, (312) 922-1115, Fax: (312) 922-1157, www.euromonitor.com; *World Marketing Data and Statistics.*

M.E. Sharpe, 80 Business Park Drive, Armonk, NY 10504, (800) 541-6563, Fax: (914) 273-2106, www.mesharpe.com; *The Illustrated Book of World Rankings.*

BOLIVIA - ILLITERATE PERSONS

Euromonitor International, Inc., 224 S. Michigan Avenue, Suite 1500, Chicago, IL 60604, (312) 922-1115, Fax: (312) 922-1157, www.euromonitor.com; *The World Economic Factbook 2008.*

UNESCO Institute for Statistics, C.P. 6128 Succursale Centre-Ville, Montreal, Quebec, H3C 3J7 Canada, (Dial from U.S. (514) 343-6880), (Fax from U.S. (514) 343 6882), www.uis.unesco.org; *Statistical Tables.*

United Nations Statistics Division, New York, NY 10017, (800) 253-9646, Fax: (212) 963-4116, http://unstats.un.org; *Human Development Report 2006* and *Statistical Yearbook for Latin America and the Caribbean 2004.*

BOLIVIA - IMPORTS

Central Intelligence Agency, Office of Public Affairs, Washington, DC 20505, (703) 482-0623, Fax: (703) 482-1739, www.cia.gov; *The World Factbook.*

Economist Intelligence Unit, 111 West 57th Street, New York, NY 10019, (212) 554-0600, Fax: (212) 586-1181, www.eiu.com; *Bolivia Country Report* and *Business Latin America.*

Euromonitor International, Inc., 224 S. Michigan Avenue, Suite 1500, Chicago, IL 60604, (312) 922-1115, Fax: (312) 922-1157, www.euromonitor.com; *International Marketing Data and Statistics 2008* and *The World Economic Factbook 2008.*

Inter-American Development Bank (IDB), 1300 New York Avenue, NW, Washington, DC 20577, (202) 623-1000, Fax: (202) 623-3096, www.iadb.org; *The Politics of Policies: Economic and Social Progress in Latin America - 2006 Report.*

International Monetary Fund (IMF), 700 Nineteenth Street, NW, Washington, DC 20431, (202) 623-7000, Fax: (202) 623-4661, www.imf.org; *Direction of Trade Statistics Yearbook 2007; Government Finance Statistics Yearbook (2008 Edition);* and *International Financial Statistics Yearbook 2007.*

Organization of American States (OAS), 17th Street Constitution Avenue NW, Washington, DC 20006, (202) 458-3000, www.oas.org; *The OAS in Transition: 1994-2004.*

Palgrave Macmillan Ltd., Houndmills, Basingstoke, Hampshire, RG21 6XS, England, (Telephone in U.S. (888) 330-8477), (Fax in U.S. (800) 672-2054), www.palgrave.com; *The Statesman's Yearbook 2008.*

Taylor and Francis Group, An Informa Business, 2 Park Square, Milton Park, Abingdon, Oxford OX14 4RN, United Kingdom, (Dial from U.S. (212) 216-7800), (Fax from U.S. (212) 564-7854), www.tandf.co.uk; *The Europa World Year Book.*

United Nations Conference on Trade and Development (UNCTAD), DC2-1120, United Nations, New York, NY 10017, (212) 963-0027, www.unctad.org; *Handbook of Statistics 2005.*

United Nations Food and Agricultural Organization (FAO), Viale delle Terme di Caracalla, 00100 Rome, Italy, (Dial from U.S. (202) 653-2400), (Fax from U.S. (202) 653 5760), www.fao.org; *The State of Food and Agriculture (SOFA) 2006.*

United Nations Statistics Division, New York, NY 10017, (800) 253-9646, Fax: (212) 963-4116, http://unstats.un.org; *Statistical Yearbook for Latin America and the Caribbean 2004.*

The World Bank, 1818 H Street, NW, Washington, DC 20433, (202) 473-1000, Fax: (202) 477-6391, www.worldbank.org; *World Development Indicators (WDI) 2008* and *World Development Report 2008.*

BOLIVIA - INCOME DISTRIBUTION

UCLA Latin American Institute, 10343 Bunche Hall, Box 951447, Los Angeles, CA 90095-1447, (310) 825-4571, Fax: (310) 206-6859, www.international.ucla.edu/lac; *Statistical Abstract of Latin America.*

United Nations Statistics Division, New York, NY 10017, (800) 253-9646, Fax: (212) 963-4116, http://unstats.un.org; *Statistical Yearbook for Latin America and the Caribbean 2004.*

BOLIVIA - INCOME TAXES

See BOLIVIA - TAXATION

BOLIVIA - INDUSTRIAL PRODUCTIVITY

Euromonitor International, Inc., 224 S. Michigan Avenue, Suite 1500, Chicago, IL 60604, (312) 922-1115, Fax: (312) 922-1157, www.euromonitor.com; *International Marketing Data and Statistics 2008.*

M.E. Sharpe, 80 Business Park Drive, Armonk, NY 10504, (800) 541-6563, Fax: (914) 273-2106, www.mesharpe.com; *The Illustrated Book of World Rankings.*

BOLIVIA - INDUSTRIAL PROPERTY

United Nations Statistics Division, New York, NY 10017, (800) 253-9646, Fax: (212) 963-4116, http://unstats.un.org; *Statistical Yearbook.*

BOLIVIA - INDUSTRIES

Central Intelligence Agency, Office of Public Affairs, Washington, DC 20505, (703) 482-0623, Fax: (703) 482-1739, www.cia.gov; *The World Factbook.*

Economist Intelligence Unit, 111 West 57th Street, New York, NY 10019, (212) 554-0600, Fax: (212) 586-1181, www.eiu.com; *Bolivia Country Report.*

Euromonitor International, Inc., 224 S. Michigan Avenue, Suite 1500, Chicago, IL 60604, (312) 922-1115, Fax: (312) 922-1157, www.euromonitor.com; *International Marketing Data and Statistics 2008; The World Economic Factbook 2008;* and *World Marketing Data and Statistics.*

International Labour Office, I.L.O. Publications, 4 route des Morillons, CH-1211 Geneva 22, Switzerland, (Telephone in U.S. (202) 653-7652), (Fax in U.S. (202) 653-7687), www.ilo.org; *Yearbook of Labour Statistics 2006.*

M.E. Sharpe, 80 Business Park Drive, Armonk, NY 10504, (800) 541-6563, Fax: (914) 273-2106, www.mesharpe.com; *The Illustrated Book of World Rankings.*

Palgrave Macmillan Ltd., Houndmills, Basingstoke, Hampshire, RG21 6XS, England, (Telephone in U.S. (888) 330-8477), (Fax in U.S. (800) 672-2054), www.palgrave.com; *The Statesman's Yearbook 2008.*

Taylor and Francis Group, An Informa Business, 2 Park Square, Milton Park, Abingdon, Oxford OX14 4RN, United Kingdom, (Dial from U.S. (212) 216-7800), (Fax from U.S. (212) 564-7854), www.tandf.co.uk; *The Europa World Year Book.*

UCLA Latin American Institute, 10343 Bunche Hall, Box 951447, Los Angeles, CA 90095-1447, (310) 825-4571, Fax: (310) 206-6859, www.international.ucla.edu/lac; *Statistical Abstract of Latin America.*

United Nations Industrial Development Organization (UNIDO), 1 United Nations Plaza, New York, NY 10017, (212) 963 6890, Fax: (212) 963-7904, http://unido.org; Industrial Statistics Database 2008 (INDSTAT) and *The International Yearbook of Industrial Statistics 2008.*

United Nations Statistics Division, New York, NY 10017, (800) 253-9646, Fax: (212) 963-4116, http://unstats.un.org; *Economic Survey of Latin America and the Caribbean 2004-2005* and *2004 Industrial Commodity Statistics Yearbook.*

The World Bank, 1818 H Street, NW, Washington, DC 20433, (202) 473-1000, Fax: (202) 477-6391, www.worldbank.org; *Bolivia* and *World Development Indicators (WDI) 2008.*

BOLIVIA - INFANT AND MATERNAL MORTALITY

See BOLIVIA - MORTALITY

BOLIVIA - INFLATION (FINANCE)

United Nations Statistics Division, New York, NY 10017, (800) 253-9646, Fax: (212) 963-4116, http://unstats.un.org; *Economic Survey of Latin America and the Caribbean 2004-2005.*

BOLIVIA - INORGANIC ACIDS

United Nations Statistics Division, New York, NY 10017, (800) 253-9646, Fax: (212) 963-4116, http://unstats.un.org; *Statistical Yearbook.*

BOLIVIA - INTEREST RATES

Inter-American Development Bank (IDB), 1300 New York Avenue, NW, Washington, DC 20577, (202) 623-1000, Fax: (202) 623-3096, www.iadb.org; *The Politics of Policies: Economic and Social Progress in Latin America - 2006 Report.*

BOLIVIA - INTERNAL REVENUE

Inter-American Development Bank (IDB), 1300 New York Avenue, NW, Washington, DC 20577, (202) 623-1000, Fax: (202) 623-3096, www.iadb.org; *The Politics of Policies: Economic and Social Progress in Latin America - 2006 Report.*

Organization of American States (OAS), 17th Street Constitution Avenue NW, Washington, DC 20006, (202) 458-3000, www.oas.org; *The OAS in Transition: 1994-2004.*

BOLIVIA - INTERNATIONAL FINANCE

Inter-American Development Bank (IDB), 1300 New York Avenue, NW, Washington, DC 20577, (202) 623-1000, Fax: (202) 623-3096, www.iadb.org; *The Politics of Policies: Economic and Social Progress in Latin America - 2006 Report.*

UCLA Latin American Institute, 10343 Bunche Hall, Box 951447, Los Angeles, CA 90095-1447, (310) 825-4571, Fax: (310) 206-6859, www.international.ucla.edu/lac; *Statistical Abstract of Latin America.*

United Nations Statistics Division, New York, NY 10017, (800) 253-9646, Fax: (212) 963-4116, http://unstats.un.org; *Statistical Yearbook for Latin America and the Caribbean 2004.*

BOLIVIA - INTERNATIONAL LIQUIDITY

Inter-American Development Bank (IDB), 1300 New York Avenue, NW, Washington, DC 20577, (202) 623-1000, Fax: (202) 623-3096, www.iadb.org; *The Politics of Policies: Economic and Social Progress in Latin America - 2006 Report.*

International Monetary Fund (IMF), 700 Nineteenth Street, NW, Washington, DC 20431, (202) 623-7000, Fax: (202) 623-4661, www.imf.org; *International Financial Statistics Yearbook 2007.*

BOLIVIA - INTERNATIONAL STATISTICS

Inter-American Development Bank (IDB), 1300 New York Avenue, NW, Washington, DC 20577, (202) 623-1000, Fax: (202) 623-3096, www.iadb.org; *The Politics of Policies: Economic and Social Progress in Latin America - 2006 Report.*

UCLA Latin American Institute, 10343 Bunche Hall, Box 951447, Los Angeles, CA 90095-1447, (310) 825-4571, Fax: (310) 206-6859, www.international.ucla.edu/lac; *Statistical Abstract of Latin America.*

BOLIVIA - INTERNATIONAL TRADE

Economist Intelligence Unit, 111 West 57th Street, New York, NY 10019, (212) 554-0600, Fax: (212) 586-1181, www.eiu.com; *Bolivia Country Report* and *Business Latin America.*

Euromonitor International, Inc., 224 S. Michigan Avenue, Suite 1500, Chicago, IL 60604, (312) 922-1115, Fax: (312) 922-1157, www.euromonitor.com; *International Marketing Data and Statistics 2008; The World Economic Factbook 2008;* and *World Marketing Data and Statistics.*

Inter-American Development Bank (IDB), 1300 New York Avenue, NW, Washington, DC 20577, (202) 623-1000, Fax: (202) 623-3096, www.iadb.org; *The Politics of Policies: Economic and Social Progress in Latin America - 2006 Report.*

M.E. Sharpe, 80 Business Park Drive, Armonk, NY 10504, (800) 541-6563, Fax: (914) 273-2106, www.mesharpe.com; *The Illustrated Book of World Rankings.*

Organisation for Economic Cooperation and Development (OECD), 2 rue Andre Pascal, F-75775 Paris Cedex 16, France, (Telephone in U.S. (202) 785-6323), (Fax in U.S. (202) 785-0350), www.oecd.org; *International Trade by Commodity Statistics (ITCS).*

Palgrave Macmillan Ltd., Houndmills, Basingstoke, Hampshire, RG21 6XS, England, (Telephone in U.S. (888) 330-8477), (Fax in U.S. (800) 672-2054), www.palgrave.com; *The Statesman's Yearbook 2008.*

Taylor and Francis Group, An Informa Business, 2 Park Square, Milton Park, Abingdon, Oxford OX14 4RN, United Kingdom, (Dial from U.S. (212) 216-7800), (Fax from U.S. (212) 564-7854), www.tandf.co.uk; *The Europa World Year Book.*

UCLA Latin American Institute, 10343 Bunche Hall, Box 951447, Los Angeles, CA 90095-1447, (310) 825-4571, Fax: (310) 206-6859, www.international.ucla.edu/lac; *Statistical Abstract of Latin America.*

United Nations Conference on Trade and Development (UNCTAD), DC2-1120, United Nations, New York, NY 10017, (212) 963-0027, www.unctad.org; *UNCTAD Commodity Yearbook.*

United Nations Food and Agricultural Organization (FAO), Viale delle Terme di Caracalla, 00100 Rome, Italy, (Dial from U.S. (202) 653-2400), (Fax from U.S. (202) 653 5760), www.fao.org; *FAO Trade Yearbook* and *The State of Food and Agriculture (SOFA) 2006.*

United Nations Statistics Division, New York, NY 10017, (800) 253-9646, Fax: (212) 963-4116, http://unstats.un.org; *Economic Survey of Latin America and the Caribbean 2004-2005; International Trade Statistics Yearbook; Statistical Yearbook;* and *Statistical Yearbook for Latin America and the Caribbean 2004.*

The World Bank, 1818 H Street, NW, Washington, DC 20433, (202) 473-1000, Fax: (202) 477-6391, www.worldbank.org; *Bolivia; World Development Indicators (WDI) 2008;* and *World Development Report 2008.*

World Trade Organization (WTO), Centre William Rappard, Rue de Lausanne 154, CH-1211 Geneva 21, Switzerland, www.wto.org; *International Trade Statistics 2006.*

BOLIVIA - INTERNET USERS

International Telecommunication Union (ITU), Place des Nations, 1211 Geneva 20, Switzerland, www.itu.int; *World Telecommunication/ICT Indicators Database on CD-ROM; World Telecommunication/ICT Indicators Database Online;* and *Yearbook of Statistics - Telecommunication Services (Chronological Time Series 1997-2006).*

The World Bank, 1818 H Street, NW, Washington, DC 20433, (202) 473-1000, Fax: (202) 477-6391, www.worldbank.org; *Bolivia.*

BOLIVIA - INVESTMENTS

Inter-American Development Bank (IDB), 1300 New York Avenue, NW, Washington, DC 20577, (202) 623-1000, Fax: (202) 623-3096, www.iadb.org; *The Politics of Policies: Economic and Social Progress in Latin America - 2006 Report.*

International Monetary Fund (IMF), 700 Nineteenth Street, NW, Washington, DC 20431, (202) 623-7000, Fax: (202) 623-4661, www.imf.org; *International Financial Statistics Yearbook 2007.*

United Nations Statistics Division, New York, NY 10017, (800) 253-9646, Fax: (212) 963-4116, http://unstats.un.org; *Statistical Yearbook for Latin America and the Caribbean 2004.*

BOLIVIA - INVESTMENTS, FOREIGN

Economist Intelligence Unit, 111 West 57th Street, New York, NY 10019, (212) 554-0600, Fax: (212) 586-1181, www.eiu.com; *Business Latin America.*

BOLIVIA - IRON AND IRON ORE PRODUCTION

See BOLIVIA - MINERAL INDUSTRIES

BOLIVIA - IRRIGATION

Euromonitor International, Inc., 224 S. Michigan Avenue, Suite 1500, Chicago, IL 60604, (312) 922-1115, Fax: (312) 922-1157, www.euromonitor.com; *International Marketing Data and Statistics 2008.*

Inter-American Development Bank (IDB), 1300 New York Avenue, NW, Washington, DC 20577, (202) 623-1000, Fax: (202) 623-3096, www.iadb.org; *The Politics of Policies: Economic and Social Progress in Latin America - 2006 Report.*

BOLIVIA - LABOR

Central Intelligence Agency, Office of Public Affairs, Washington, DC 20505, (703) 482-0623, Fax: (703) 482-1739, www.cia.gov; *The World Factbook.*

Economist Intelligence Unit, 111 West 57th Street, New York, NY 10019, (212) 554-0600, Fax: (212) 586-1181, www.eiu.com; *Business Latin America.*

Euromonitor International, Inc., 224 S. Michigan Avenue, Suite 1500, Chicago, IL 60604, (312) 922-1115, Fax: (312) 922-1157, www.euromonitor.com; *International Marketing Data and Statistics 2008* and *World Marketing Data and Statistics.*

International Labour Office, I.L.O. Publications, 4 route des Morillons, CH-1211 Geneva 22, Switzerland, (Telephone in U.S. (202) 653-7652), (Fax in U.S. (202) 653-7687), www.ilo.org; *Yearbook of Labour Statistics 2006.*

M.E. Sharpe, 80 Business Park Drive, Armonk, NY 10504, (800) 541-6563, Fax: (914) 273-2106, www.mesharpe.com; *The Illustrated Book of World Rankings.*

Palgrave Macmillan Ltd., Houndmills, Basingstoke, Hampshire, RG21 6XS, England, (Telephone in U.S. (888) 330-8477), (Fax in U.S. (800) 672-2054), www.palgrave.com; *The Statesman's Yearbook 2008.*

Taylor and Francis Group, An Informa Business, 2 Park Square, Milton Park, Abingdon, Oxford OX14 4RN, United Kingdom, (Dial from U.S. (212) 216-7800), (Fax from U.S. (212) 564-7854), www.tandf.co.uk; *The Europa World Year Book.*

United Nations Food and Agricultural Organization (FAO), Viale delle Terme di Caracalla, 00100 Rome, Italy, (Dial from U.S. (202) 653-2400), (Fax from U.S. (202) 653 5760), www.fao.org; *The State of Food and Agriculture (SOFA) 2006.*

United Nations Statistics Division, New York, NY 10017, (800) 253-9646, Fax: (212) 963-4116, http://unstats.un.org; *Human Development Report 2006.*

The World Bank, 1818 H Street, NW, Washington, DC 20433, (202) 473-1000, Fax: (202) 477-6391, www.worldbank.org; *The World Bank Atlas 2003-2004; World Development Indicators (WDI) 2008;* and *World Development Report 2008.*

BOLIVIA - LAND USE

Central Intelligence Agency, Office of Public Affairs, Washington, DC 20505, (703) 482-0623, Fax: (703) 482-1739, www.cia.gov; *The World Factbook.*

Euromonitor International, Inc., 224 S. Michigan Avenue, Suite 1500, Chicago, IL 60604, (312) 922-1115, Fax: (312) 922-1157, www.euromonitor.com; *International Marketing Data and Statistics 2008.*

Inter-American Development Bank (IDB), 1300 New York Avenue, NW, Washington, DC 20577, (202) 623-1000, Fax: (202) 623-3096, www.iadb.org; *The Politics of Policies: Economic and Social Progress in Latin America - 2006 Report.*

United Nations Food and Agricultural Organization (FAO), Viale delle Terme di Caracalla, 00100 Rome, Italy, (Dial from U.S. (202) 653-2400), (Fax from U.S. (202) 653 5760), www.fao.org; *FAO Production Yearbook 2002.*

The World Bank, 1818 H Street, NW, Washington, DC 20433, (202) 473-1000, Fax: (202) 477-6391, www.worldbank.org; *World Development Report 2008.*

BOLIVIA - LIBRARIES

M.E. Sharpe, 80 Business Park Drive, Armonk, NY 10504, (800) 541-6563, Fax: (914) 273-2106, www.mesharpe.com; *The Illustrated Book of World Rankings.*

BOLIVIA - LICENSES

International Monetary Fund (IMF), 700 Nineteenth Street, NW, Washington, DC 20431, (202) 623-7000, Fax: (202) 623-4661, www.imf.org; *Government Finance Statistics Yearbook (2008 Edition).*

BOLIVIA - LIFE EXPECTANCY

Central Intelligence Agency, Office of Public Affairs, Washington, DC 20505, (703) 482-0623, Fax: (703) 482-1739, www.cia.gov; *The World Factbook.*

Economist Intelligence Unit, 111 West 57th Street, New York, NY 10019, (212) 554-0600, Fax: (212) 586-1181, www.eiu.com; *Business Latin America.*

Euromonitor International, Inc., 224 S. Michigan Avenue, Suite 1500, Chicago, IL 60604, (312) 922-1115, Fax: (312) 922-1157, www.euromonitor.com; *The World Economic Factbook 2008.*

United Nations Statistics Division, New York, NY 10017, (800) 253-9646, Fax: (212) 963-4116, http://unstats.un.org; *Human Development Report 2006* and *World Statistics Pocketbook.*

The World Bank, 1818 H Street, NW, Washington, DC 20433, (202) 473-1000, Fax: (202) 477-6391, www.worldbank.org; *The World Bank Atlas 2003-2004* and *World Development Report 2008.*

BOLIVIA - LITERACY

Central Intelligence Agency, Office of Public Affairs, Washington, DC 20505, (703) 482-0623, Fax: (703) 482-1739, www.cia.gov; *The World Factbook.*

Economist Intelligence Unit, 111 West 57th Street, New York, NY 10019, (212) 554-0600, Fax: (212) 586-1181, www.eiu.com; *Business Latin America.*

Euromonitor International, Inc., 224 S. Michigan Avenue, Suite 1500, Chicago, IL 60604, (312) 922-1115, Fax: (312) 922-1157, www.euromonitor.com; *World Marketing Data and Statistics.*

BOLIVIA - LIVESTOCK

Euromonitor International, Inc., 224 S. Michigan Avenue, Suite 1500, Chicago, IL 60604, (312) 922-1115, Fax: (312) 922-1157, www.euromonitor.com; *International Marketing Data and Statistics 2008.*

M.E. Sharpe, 80 Business Park Drive, Armonk, NY 10504, (800) 541-6563, Fax: (914) 273-2106, www.mesharpe.com; *The Illustrated Book of World Rankings.*

Palgrave Macmillan Ltd., Houndmills, Basingstoke, Hampshire, RG21 6XS, England, (Telephone in U.S. (888) 330-8477), (Fax in U.S. (800) 672-2054), www.palgrave.com; *The Statesman's Yearbook 2008.*

Taylor and Francis Group, An Informa Business, 2 Park Square, Milton Park, Abingdon, Oxford OX14 4RN, United Kingdom, (Dial from U.S. (212) 216-7800), (Fax from U.S. (212) 564-7854), www.tandf.co.uk; *The Europa World Year Book.*

United Nations Conference on Trade and Development (UNCTAD), DC2-1120, United Nations, New York, NY 10017, (212) 963-0027, www.unctad.org; *UNCTAD Commodity Yearbook.*

United Nations Food and Agricultural Organization (FAO), Viale delle Terme di Caracalla, 00100 Rome, Italy, (Dial from U.S. (202) 653-2400), (Fax from U.S. (202) 653 5760), www.fao.org; *FAO Production Yearbook 2002* and *The State of Food and Agriculture (SOFA) 2006.*

United Nations Statistics Division, New York, NY 10017, (800) 253-9646, Fax: (212) 963-4116, http://unstats.un.org; *Statistical Yearbook.*

BOLIVIA - LOCAL TAXATION

Euromonitor International, Inc., 224 S. Michigan Avenue, Suite 1500, Chicago, IL 60604, (312) 922-

1115, Fax: (312) 922-1157, www.euromonitor.com; *International Marketing Data and Statistics 2008.*

Inter-American Development Bank (IDB), 1300 New York Avenue, NW, Washington, DC 20577, (202) 623-1000, Fax: (202) 623-3096, www.iadb.org; *The Politics of Policies: Economic and Social Progress in Latin America - 2006 Report.*

BOLIVIA - MANUFACTURES

Economist Intelligence Unit, 111 West 57th Street, New York, NY 10019, (212) 554-0600, Fax: (212) 586-1181, www.eiu.com; *Business Latin America.*

Inter-American Development Bank (IDB), 1300 New York Avenue, NW, Washington, DC 20577, (202) 623-1000, Fax: (202) 623-3096, www.iadb.org; *The Politics of Policies: Economic and Social Progress in Latin America - 2006 Report.*

M.E. Sharpe, 80 Business Park Drive, Armonk, NY 10504, (800) 541-6563, Fax: (914) 273-2106, www.mesharpe.com; *The Illustrated Book of World Rankings.*

United Nations Statistics Division, New York, NY 10017, (800) 253-9646, Fax: (212) 963-4116, http://unstats.un.org; *Statistical Yearbook* and *Statistical Yearbook for Latin America and the Caribbean 2004.*

The World Bank, 1818 H Street, NW, Washington, DC 20433, (202) 473-1000, Fax: (202) 477-6391, www.worldbank.org; *World Development Indicators (WDI) 2008.*

BOLIVIA - MARRIAGE

M.E. Sharpe, 80 Business Park Drive, Armonk, NY 10504, (800) 541-6563, Fax: (914) 273-2106, www.mesharpe.com; *The Illustrated Book of World Rankings.*

United Nations Statistics Division, New York, NY 10017, (800) 253-9646, Fax: (212) 963-4116, http://unstats.un.org; *Demographic Yearbook* and *Statistical Yearbook.*

BOLIVIA - MEAT PRODUCTION

See BOLIVIA - LIVESTOCK

BOLIVIA - MEDICAL CARE, COST OF

International Monetary Fund (IMF), 700 Nineteenth Street, NW, Washington, DC 20431, (202) 623-7000, Fax: (202) 623-4661, www.imf.org; *Government Finance Statistics Yearbook (2008 Edition).*

United Nations Statistics Division, New York, NY 10017, (800) 253-9646, Fax: (212) 963-4116, http://unstats.un.org; *Statistical Yearbook for Latin America and the Caribbean 2004.*

BOLIVIA - MEDICAL PERSONNEL

UCLA Latin American Institute, 10343 Bunche Hall, Box 951447, Los Angeles, CA 90095-1447, (310) 825-4571, Fax: (310) 206-6859, www.international.ucla.edu/lac; *Statistical Abstract of Latin America.*

BOLIVIA - MERCURY PRODUCTION

See BOLIVIA - MINERAL INDUSTRIES

BOLIVIA - MILK PRODUCTION

See BOLIVIA - DAIRY PROCESSING

BOLIVIA - MINERAL INDUSTRIES

Commodity Research Bureau, 330 South Wells Street, Suite 612, Chicago, IL 60606-7110, (800) 621-5271, Fax: (312) 939-4135, www.crbtrader.com; *2006 CRB Commodity Yearbook and CD.*

Economist Intelligence Unit, 111 West 57th Street, New York, NY 10019, (212) 554-0600, Fax: (212) 586-1181, www.eiu.com; *Business Latin America.*

Inter-American Development Bank (IDB), 1300 New York Avenue, NW, Washington, DC 20577, (202) 623-1000, Fax: (202) 623-3096, www.iadb.org; *The Politics of Policies: Economic and Social Progress in Latin America - 2006 Report.*

International Monetary Fund (IMF), 700 Nineteenth Street, NW, Washington, DC 20431, (202) 623-7000, Fax: (202) 623-4661, www.imf.org; *International Financial Statistics Yearbook 2007.*

M.E. Sharpe, 80 Business Park Drive, Armonk, NY 10504, (800) 541-6563, Fax: (914) 273-2106, www.mesharpe.com; *The Illustrated Book of World Rankings.*

Organisation for Economic Cooperation and Development (OECD), 2 rue Andre Pascal, F-75775 Paris Cedex 16, France, (Telephone in U.S. (202) 785-6323), (Fax in U.S. (202) 785-0350), www.oecd.org; *World Energy Outlook 2007.*

Palgrave Macmillan Ltd., Houndmills, Basingstoke, Hampshire, RG21 6XS, England, (Telephone in U.S. (888) 330-8477), (Fax in U.S. (800) 672-2054), www.palgrave.com; *The Statesman's Yearbook 2008.*

PennWell Corporation, 1421 South Sheridan Road, Tulsa, OK 74112, (918) 835-3161, www.pennwell.com; *Oil Gas Journal Latinoamericana.*

Taylor and Francis Group, An Informa Business, 2 Park Square, Milton Park, Abingdon, Oxford OX14 4RN, United Kingdom, (Dial from U.S. (212) 216-7800), (Fax from U.S. (212) 564-7854), www.tandf.co.uk; *The Europa World Year Book.*

UCLA Latin American Institute, 10343 Bunche Hall, Box 951447, Los Angeles, CA 90095-1447, (310) 825-4571, Fax: (310) 206-6859, www.international.ucla.edu/lac; *Statistical Abstract of Latin America.*

United Nations Conference on Trade and Development (UNCTAD), DC2-1120, United Nations, New York, NY 10017, (212) 963-0027, www.unctad.org; *UNCTAD Commodity Yearbook.*

United Nations Statistics Division, New York, NY 10017, (800) 253-9646, Fax: (212) 963-4116, http://unstats.un.org; *Statistical Yearbook* and *Statistical Yearbook for Latin America and the Caribbean 2004.*

BOLIVIA - MONEY EXCHANGE RATES

See BOLIVIA - FOREIGN EXCHANGE RATES

BOLIVIA - MONEY SUPPLY

Economist Intelligence Unit, 111 West 57th Street, New York, NY 10019, (212) 554-0600, Fax: (212) 586-1181, www.eiu.com; *Bolivia Country Report.*

Euromonitor International, Inc., 224 S. Michigan Avenue, Suite 1500, Chicago, IL 60604, (312) 922-1115, Fax: (312) 922-1157, www.euromonitor.com; *International Marketing Data and Statistics 2008.*

Inter-American Development Bank (IDB), 1300 New York Avenue, NW, Washington, DC 20577, (202) 623-1000, Fax: (202) 623-3096, www.iadb.org; *The Politics of Policies: Economic and Social Progress in Latin America - 2006 Report.*

International Monetary Fund (IMF), 700 Nineteenth Street, NW, Washington, DC 20431, (202) 623-7000, Fax: (202) 623-4661, www.imf.org; *International Financial Statistics Yearbook 2007.*

Taylor and Francis Group, An Informa Business, 2 Park Square, Milton Park, Abingdon, Oxford OX14 4RN, United Kingdom, (Dial from U.S. (212) 216-7800), (Fax from U.S. (212) 564-7854), www.tandf.co.uk; *The Europa World Year Book.*

UCLA Latin American Institute, 10343 Bunche Hall, Box 951447, Los Angeles, CA 90095-1447, (310) 825-4571, Fax: (310) 206-6859, www.international.ucla.edu/lac; *Statistical Abstract of Latin America.*

United Nations Statistics Division, New York, NY 10017, (800) 253-9646, Fax: (212) 963-4116, http://unstats.un.org; *Statistical Yearbook.*

The World Bank, 1818 H Street, NW, Washington, DC 20433, (202) 473-1000, Fax: (202) 477-6391, www.worldbank.org; *Bolivia* and *World Development Indicators (WDI) 2008.*

BOLIVIA - MORTALITY

Central Intelligence Agency, Office of Public Affairs, Washington, DC 20505, (703) 482-0623, Fax: (703) 482-1739, www.cia.gov; *The World Factbook.*

Economist Intelligence Unit, 111 West 57th Street, New York, NY 10019, (212) 554-0600, Fax: (212) 586-1181, www.eiu.com; *Business Latin America.*

Euromonitor International, Inc., 224 S. Michigan Avenue, Suite 1500, Chicago, IL 60604, (312) 922-1115, Fax: (312) 922-1157, www.euromonitor.com; *International Marketing Data and Statistics 2008* and *The World Economic Factbook 2008.*

Taylor and Francis Group, An Informa Business, 2 Park Square, Milton Park, Abingdon, Oxford OX14 4RN, United Kingdom, (Dial from U.S. (212) 216-7800), (Fax from U.S. (212) 564-7854), www.tandf.co.uk; *The Europa World Year Book.*

UNICEF, 3 United Nations Plaza, New York, NY 10017, (800) 253-9646, Fax: (212) 887-7465, www.unicef.org; *The State of the World's Children 2008.*

United Nations Statistics Division, New York, NY 10017, (800) 253-9646, Fax: (212) 963-4116, http://unstats.un.org; *Demographic Yearbook; Human Development Report 2006; Statistical Yearbook; Statistical Yearbook for Latin America and the Caribbean 2004;* and *World Statistics Pocketbook.*

The World Bank, 1818 H Street, NW, Washington, DC 20433, (202) 473-1000, Fax: (202) 477-6391, www.worldbank.org; *The World Bank Atlas 2003-2004; World Development Indicators (WDI) 2008;* and *World Development Report 2008.*

World Health Organization (WHO), Avenue Appia 20, 1211 Geneve 27, Switzerland, (Telephone in U.S. (212) 331-9081), www.who.int; The WHO Global Atlas of Infectious Diseases and *World Health Report 2006.*

BOLIVIA - MOTION PICTURES

Palgrave Macmillan Ltd., Houndmills, Basingstoke, Hampshire, RG21 6XS, England, (Telephone in U.S. (888) 330-8477), (Fax in U.S. (800) 672-2054), www.palgrave.com; *The Statesman's Yearbook 2008.*

UNESCO Institute for Statistics, C.P. 6128 Succursale Centre-Ville, Montreal, Quebec, H3C 3J7 Canada, (Dial from U.S. (514) 343-6880), (Fax from U.S. (514) 343 6882), www.uis.unesco.org; *Statistical Tables.*

BOLIVIA - MOTOR VEHICLES

Economist Intelligence Unit, 111 West 57th Street, New York, NY 10019, (212) 554-0600, Fax: (212) 586-1181, www.eiu.com; *Business Latin America.*

International Road Federation (IFR), Madison Place, 500 Montgomery Street, 5th Floor, Alexandria, VA 22314, (703) 535-1001, Fax: (703) 535-1007, www.irfnet.org; *World Road Statistics 2006.*

Taylor and Francis Group, An Informa Business, 2 Park Square, Milton Park, Abingdon, Oxford OX14 4RN, United Kingdom, (Dial from U.S. (212) 216-7800), (Fax from U.S. (212) 564-7854), www.tandf.co.uk; *The Europa World Year Book.*

United Nations Statistics Division, New York, NY 10017, (800) 253-9646, Fax: (212) 963-4116, http://unstats.un.org; *Statistical Yearbook.*

BOLIVIA - MUSEUMS

M.E. Sharpe, 80 Business Park Drive, Armonk, NY 10504, (800) 541-6563, Fax: (914) 273-2106, www.mesharpe.com; *The Illustrated Book of World Rankings.*

BOLIVIA - NATIONAL INCOME

United Nations Statistics Division, New York, NY 10017, (800) 253-9646, Fax: (212) 963-4116, http://unstats.un.org; *Statistical Yearbook.*

BOLIVIA - NATURAL GAS PRODUCTION

See BOLIVIA - MINERAL INDUSTRIES

BOLIVIA - NATURAL RESOURCES

UCLA Latin American Institute, 10343 Bunche Hall, Box 951447, Los Angeles, CA 90095-1447, (310) 825-4571, Fax: (310) 206-6859, www.international.ucla.edu/lac; *Statistical Abstract of Latin America.*

United Nations Statistics Division, New York, NY 10017, (800) 253-9646, Fax: (212) 963-4116, http://unstats.un.org; *Statistical Yearbook for Latin America and the Caribbean 2004.*

BOLIVIA - NUTRITION

United Nations Food and Agricultural Organization (FAO), Viale delle Terme di Caracalla, 00100 Rome, Italy, (Dial from U.S. (202) 653-2400), (Fax from U.S. (202) 653 5760), www.fao.org; *The State of Food and Agriculture (SOFA) 2006.*

United Nations Statistics Division, New York, NY 10017, (800) 253-9646, Fax: (212) 963-4116, http://unstats.un.org; *Statistical Yearbook for Latin America and the Caribbean 2004.*

BOLIVIA - OATS PRODUCTION

See BOLIVIA - CROPS

BOLIVIA - OLDER PEOPLE

M.E. Sharpe, 80 Business Park Drive, Armonk, NY 10504, (800) 541-6563, Fax: (914) 273-2106, www.mesharpe.com; *The Illustrated Book of World Rankings.*

BOLIVIA - PAPER

See BOLIVIA - FORESTS AND FORESTRY

BOLIVIA - PEANUT PRODUCTION

See BOLIVIA - CROPS

BOLIVIA - PESTICIDES

United Nations Food and Agricultural Organization (FAO), Viale delle Terme di Caracalla, 00100 Rome, Italy, (Dial from U.S. (202) 653-2400), (Fax from U.S. (202) 653 5760), www.fao.org; *The State of Food and Agriculture (SOFA) 2006.*

BOLIVIA - PETROLEUM INDUSTRY AND TRADE

Economist Intelligence Unit, 111 West 57th Street, New York, NY 10019, (212) 554-0600, Fax: (212) 586-1181, www.eiu.com; *Business Latin America.*

Inter-American Development Bank (IDB), 1300 New York Avenue, NW, Washington, DC 20577, (202) 623-1000, Fax: (202) 623-3096, www.iadb.org; *The Politics of Policies: Economic and Social Progress in Latin America - 2006 Report.*

International Monetary Fund (IMF), 700 Nineteenth Street, NW, Washington, DC 20431, (202) 623-7000, Fax: (202) 623-4661, www.imf.org; *International Financial Statistics Yearbook 2007.*

M.E. Sharpe, 80 Business Park Drive, Armonk, NY 10504, (800) 541-6563, Fax: (914) 273-2106, www.mesharpe.com; *The Illustrated Book of World Rankings.*

Organisation for Economic Cooperation and Development (OECD), 2 rue Andre Pascal, F-75775 Paris Cedex 16, France, (Telephone in U.S. (202) 785-6323), (Fax in U.S. (202) 785-0350), www.oecd.org; *World Energy Outlook 2007.*

Organization of American States (OAS), 17th Street Constitution Avenue NW, Washington, DC 20006, (202) 458-3000, www.oas.org; *The OAS in Transition: 1994-2004.*

Palgrave Macmillan Ltd., Houndmills, Basingstoke, Hampshire, RG21 6XS, England, (Telephone in U.S. (888) 330-8477), (Fax in U.S. (800) 672-2054), www.palgrave.com; *The Statesman's Yearbook 2008.*

PennWell Corporation, 1421 South Sheridan Road, Tulsa, OK 74112, (918) 835-3161, www.pennwell.com; *International Petroleum Encyclopedia 2007* and *Oil Gas Journal Latinoamericana.*

U.S. Department of Energy (DOE), Energy Information Administration (EIA), 1000 Independence Avenue, SW, Washington, DC 20585, (202) 586-8800, www.eia.doe.gov; *International Energy Annual 2004* and *International Energy Outlook 2006.*

United Nations Conference on Trade and Development (UNCTAD), DC2-1120, United Nations, New York, NY 10017, (212) 963-0027, www.unctad.org; *UNCTAD Commodity Yearbook.*

United Nations Statistics Division, New York, NY 10017, (800) 253-9646, Fax: (212) 963-4116, http://unstats.un.org; *Statistical Yearbook.*

BOLIVIA - POLITICAL SCIENCE

Central Intelligence Agency, Office of Public Affairs, Washington, DC 20505, (703) 482-0623, Fax: (703) 482-1739, www.cia.gov; *The World Factbook.*

Inter-American Development Bank (IDB), 1300 New York Avenue, NW, Washington, DC 20577, (202) 623-1000, Fax: (202) 623-3096, www.iadb.org; *The Politics of Policies: Economic and Social Progress in Latin America - 2006 Report.*

International Monetary Fund (IMF), 700 Nineteenth Street, NW, Washington, DC 20431, (202) 623-7000, Fax: (202) 623-4661, www.imf.org; *Government Finance Statistics Yearbook (2008 Edition)* and *International Financial Statistics Yearbook 2007.*

Palgrave Macmillan Ltd., Houndmills, Basingstoke, Hampshire, RG21 6XS, England, (Telephone in U.S. (888) 330-8477), (Fax in U.S. (800) 672-2054), www.palgrave.com; *The Statesman's Yearbook 2008.*

Taylor and Francis Group, An Informa Business, 2 Park Square, Milton Park, Abingdon, Oxford OX14 4RN, United Kingdom, (Dial from U.S. (212) 216-7800), (Fax from U.S. (212) 564-7854), www.tandf.co.uk; *The Europa World Year Book.*

UCLA Latin American Institute, 10343 Bunche Hall, Box 951447, Los Angeles, CA 90095-1447, (310) 825-4571, Fax: (310) 206-6859, www.international.ucla.edu/lac; *Statistical Abstract of Latin America.*

United Nations Statistics Division, New York, NY 10017, (800) 253-9646, Fax: (212) 963-4116, http://unstats.un.org; *National Accounts Statistics: Compendium of Income Distribution Statistics* and *Statistical Yearbook.*

The World Bank, 1818 H Street, NW, Washington, DC 20433, (202) 473-1000, Fax: (202) 477-6391, www.worldbank.org; *World Development Indicators (WDI) 2008* and *World Development Report 2008.*

BOLIVIA - POPULATION

Central Intelligence Agency, Office of Public Affairs, Washington, DC 20505, (703) 482-0623, Fax: (703) 482-1739, www.cia.gov; *The World Factbook.*

Economist Intelligence Unit, 111 West 57th Street, New York, NY 10019, (212) 554-0600, Fax: (212) 586-1181, www.eiu.com; *Bolivia Country Report* and *Business Latin America.*

Euromonitor International, Inc., 224 S. Michigan Avenue, Suite 1500, Chicago, IL 60604, (312) 922-1115, Fax: (312) 922-1157, www.euromonitor.com; *International Marketing Data and Statistics 2008* and *The World Economic Factbook 2008.*

Inter-American Development Bank (IDB), 1300 New York Avenue, NW, Washington, DC 20577, (202) 623-1000, Fax: (202) 623-3096, www.iadb.org; *The Politics of Policies: Economic and Social Progress in Latin America - 2006 Report.*

International Labour Office, I.L.O. Publications, 4 route des Morillons, CH-1211 Geneva 22, Switzerland, (Telephone in U.S. (202) 653-7652), (Fax in U.S. (202) 653-7687), www.ilo.org; *Yearbook of Labour Statistics 2006.*

M.E. Sharpe, 80 Business Park Drive, Armonk, NY 10504, (800) 541-6563, Fax: (914) 273-2106, www.mesharpe.com; *The Illustrated Book of World Rankings.*

Organization of American States (OAS), 17th Street Constitution Avenue NW, Washington, DC 20006, (202) 458-3000, www.oas.org; *The OAS in Transition: 1994-2004.*

Palgrave Macmillan Ltd., Houndmills, Basingstoke, Hampshire, RG21 6XS, England, (Telephone in U.S. (888) 330-8477), (Fax in U.S. (800) 672-2054), www.palgrave.com; *The Statesman's Yearbook 2008.*

Taylor and Francis Group, An Informa Business, 2 Park Square, Milton Park, Abingdon, Oxford OX14 4RN, United Kingdom, (Dial from U.S. (212) 216-7800), (Fax from U.S. (212) 564-7854), www.tandf.co.uk; *The Europa World Year Book.*

U.S. Department of State (DOS), 2201 C Street NW, Washington, DC 20520, (202) 647-4000, www.state.gov; *World Military Expenditures and Arms Transfers (WMEAT).*

UCLA Latin American Institute, 10343 Bunche Hall, Box 951447, Los Angeles, CA 90095-1447, (310) 825-4571, Fax: (310) 206-6859, www.international.ucla.edu/lac; *Statistical Abstract of Latin America.*

UNESCO Institute for Statistics, C.P. 6128 Succursale Centre-Ville, Montreal, Quebec, H3C 3J7 Canada, (Dial from U.S. (514) 343-6880), (Fax from U.S. (514) 343 6882), www.uis.unesco.org; *Statistical Tables.*

United Nations Food and Agricultural Organization (FAO), Viale delle Terme di Caracalla, 00100 Rome, Italy, (Dial from U.S. (202) 653-2400), (Fax from U.S. (202) 653 5760), www.fao.org; *FAO Production Yearbook 2002.*

United Nations Statistics Division, New York, NY 10017, (800) 253-9646, Fax: (212) 963-4116, http://unstats.un.org; *Demographic Yearbook; Human Development Report 2006; Statistical Yearbook;* and *World Statistics Pocketbook.*

The World Bank, 1818 H Street, NW, Washington, DC 20433, (202) 473-1000, Fax: (202) 477-6391, www.worldbank.org; *Bolivia; The World Bank Atlas 2003-2004;* and *World Development Report 2008.*

World Health Organization (WHO), Avenue Appia 20, 1211 Geneve 27, Switzerland, (Telephone in U.S. (212) 331-9081), www.who.int; *World Health Report 2006.*

BOLIVIA - POPULATION DENSITY

Central Intelligence Agency, Office of Public Affairs, Washington, DC 20505, (703) 482-0623, Fax: (703) 482-1739, www.cia.gov; *The World Factbook.*

Euromonitor International, Inc., 224 S. Michigan Avenue, Suite 1500, Chicago, IL 60604, (312) 922-1115, Fax: (312) 922-1157, www.euromonitor.com; *International Marketing Data and Statistics 2008* and *The World Economic Factbook 2008.*

Inter-American Development Bank (IDB), 1300 New York Avenue, NW, Washington, DC 20577, (202) 623-1000, Fax: (202) 623-3096, www.iadb.org; *The Politics of Policies: Economic and Social Progress in Latin America - 2006 Report.*

M.E. Sharpe, 80 Business Park Drive, Armonk, NY 10504, (800) 541-6563, Fax: (914) 273-2106, www.mesharpe.com; *The Illustrated Book of World Rankings.*

Palgrave Macmillan Ltd., Houndmills, Basingstoke, Hampshire, RG21 6XS, England, (Telephone in U.S. (888) 330-8477), (Fax in U.S. (800) 672-2054), www.palgrave.com; *The Statesman's Yearbook 2008.*

Taylor and Francis Group, An Informa Business, 2 Park Square, Milton Park, Abingdon, Oxford OX14 4RN, United Kingdom, (Dial from U.S. (212) 216-7800), (Fax from U.S. (212) 564-7854), www.tandf.co.uk; *The Europa World Year Book.*

United Nations Food and Agricultural Organization (FAO), Viale delle Terme di Caracalla, 00100 Rome, Italy, (Dial from U.S. (202) 653-2400), (Fax from U.S. (202) 653 5760), www.fao.org; *The State of Food and Agriculture (SOFA) 2006.*

United Nations Statistics Division, New York, NY 10017, (800) 253-9646, Fax: (212) 963-4116, http://unstats.un.org; *Statistical Yearbook.*

The World Bank, 1818 H Street, NW, Washington, DC 20433, (202) 473-1000, Fax: (202) 477-6391, www.worldbank.org; *Bolivia* and *World Development Report 2008.*

BOLIVIA - POSTAL SERVICE

M.E. Sharpe, 80 Business Park Drive, Armonk, NY 10504, (800) 541-6563, Fax: (914) 273-2106, www.mesharpe.com; *The Illustrated Book of World Rankings.*

United Nations Statistics Division, New York, NY 10017, (800) 253-9646, Fax: (212) 963-4116, http://unstats.un.org; *Statistical Yearbook.*

BOLIVIA - POWER RESOURCES

Economist Intelligence Unit, 111 West 57th Street, New York, NY 10019, (212) 554-0600, Fax: (212) 586-1181, www.eiu.com; *Business Latin America.*

Euromonitor International, Inc., 224 S. Michigan Avenue, Suite 1500, Chicago, IL 60604, (312) 922-1115, Fax: (312) 922-1157, www.euromonitor.com; *International Marketing Data and Statistics 2008; The World Economic Factbook 2008;* and *World Marketing Data and Statistics.*

M.E. Sharpe, 80 Business Park Drive, Armonk, NY 10504, (800) 541-6563, Fax: (914) 273-2106, www.mesharpe.com; *The Illustrated Book of World Rankings.*

Organisation for Economic Cooperation and Development (OECD), 2 rue Andre Pascal, F-75775 Paris Cedex 16, France, (Telephone in U.S. (202) 785-6323), (Fax in U.S. (202) 785-0350), www.oecd.org; *World Energy Outlook 2007.*

Palgrave Macmillan Ltd., Houndmills, Basingstoke, Hampshire, RG21 6XS, England, (Telephone in U.S. (888) 330-8477), (Fax in U.S. (800) 672-2054), www.palgrave.com; *The Statesman's Yearbook 2008.*

Platts, 2 Penn Plaza, 25th Floor, New York, NY 10121-2298, (212) 904-3070, www.platts.com; *Energy Economist.*

U.S. Department of Energy (DOE), Energy Information Administration (EIA), 1000 Independence Avenue, SW, Washington, DC 20585, (202) 586-8800, www.eia.doe.gov; *International Energy Annual 2004* and *International Energy Outlook 2006.*

UCLA Latin American Institute, 10343 Bunche Hall, Box 951447, Los Angeles, CA 90095-1447, (310) 825-4571, Fax: (310) 206-6859, www.international.ucla.edu/lac; *Statistical Abstract of Latin America.*

United Nations Statistics Division, New York, NY 10017, (800) 253-9646, Fax: (212) 963-4116, http://unstats.un.org; *Energy Statistics Yearbook 2003; Human Development Report 2006; Statistical Yearbook for Latin America and the Caribbean 2004;* and *World Statistics Pocketbook.*

The World Bank, 1818 H Street, NW, Washington, DC 20433, (202) 473-1000, Fax: (202) 477-6391, www.worldbank.org; *The World Bank Atlas 2003-2004* and *World Development Report 2008.*

BOLIVIA - PRICES

Economist Intelligence Unit, 111 West 57th Street, New York, NY 10019, (212) 554-0600, Fax: (212) 586-1181, www.eiu.com; *Business Latin America.*

Euromonitor International, Inc., 224 S. Michigan Avenue, Suite 1500, Chicago, IL 60604, (312) 922-1115, Fax: (312) 922-1157, www.euromonitor.com; *World Marketing Data and Statistics.*

International Labour Office, I.L.O. Publications, 4 route des Morillons, CH-1211 Geneva 22, Switzerland, (Telephone in U.S. (202) 653-7652), (Fax in U.S. (202) 653-7687), www.ilo.org; *Yearbook of Labour Statistics 2006.*

International Monetary Fund (IMF), 700 Nineteenth Street, NW, Washington, DC 20431, (202) 623-7000, Fax: (202) 623-4661, www.imf.org; *International Financial Statistics Yearbook 2007.*

M.E. Sharpe, 80 Business Park Drive, Armonk, NY 10504, (800) 541-6563, Fax: (914) 273-2106, www.mesharpe.com; *The Illustrated Book of World Rankings.*

Organization of American States (OAS), 17th Street Constitution Avenue NW, Washington, DC 20006, (202) 458-3000, www.oas.org; *The OAS in Transition: 1994-2004.*

United Nations Food and Agricultural Organization (FAO), Viale delle Terme di Caracalla, 00100 Rome, Italy, (Dial from U.S. (202) 653-2400), (Fax from U.S. (202) 653 5760), www.fao.org; *FAO Production Yearbook 2002* and *The State of Food and Agriculture (SOFA) 2006.*

United Nations Statistics Division, New York, NY 10017, (800) 253-9646, Fax: (212) 963-4116, http://unstats.un.org; *Statistical Yearbook for Latin America and the Caribbean 2004.*

The World Bank, 1818 H Street, NW, Washington, DC 20433, (202) 473-1000, Fax: (202) 477-6391, www.worldbank.org; *Bolivia.*

BOLIVIA - PROFESSIONS

UNESCO Institute for Statistics, C.P. 6128 Succursale Centre-Ville, Montreal, Quebec, H3C 3J7 Canada, (Dial from U.S. (514) 343-6880), (Fax from U.S. (514) 343 6882), www.uis.unesco.org; *Statistical Tables.*

United Nations Statistics Division, New York, NY 10017, (800) 253-9646, Fax: (212) 963-4116, http://unstats.un.org; *Statistical Yearbook for Latin America and the Caribbean 2004.*

BOLIVIA - PUBLIC HEALTH

Economist Intelligence Unit, 111 West 57th Street, New York, NY 10019, (212) 554-0600, Fax: (212) 586-1181, www.eiu.com; *Business Latin America.*

Euromonitor International, Inc., 224 S. Michigan Avenue, Suite 1500, Chicago, IL 60604, (312) 922-1115, Fax: (312) 922-1157, www.euromonitor.com; *World Health Databook 2007/2008* and *World Marketing Data and Statistics.*

M.E. Sharpe, 80 Business Park Drive, Armonk, NY 10504, (800) 541-6563, Fax: (914) 273-2106, www.mesharpe.com; *The Illustrated Book of World Rankings.*

Palgrave Macmillan Ltd., Houndmills, Basingstoke, Hampshire, RG21 6XS, England, (Telephone in U.S. (888) 330-8477), (Fax in U.S. (800) 672-2054), www.palgrave.com; *The Statesman's Yearbook 2008.*

UNICEF, 3 United Nations Plaza, New York, NY 10017, (800) 253-9646, Fax: (212) 887-7465, www.unicef.org; *The State of the World's Children 2008.*

United Nations Statistics Division, New York, NY 10017, (800) 253-9646, Fax: (212) 963-4116, http://unstats.un.org; *Human Development Report 2006* and *Statistical Yearbook.*

The World Bank, 1818 H Street, NW, Washington, DC 20433, (202) 473-1000, Fax: (202) 477-6391, www.worldbank.org; *Bolivia* and *World Development Report 2008.*

World Health Organization (WHO), Avenue Appia 20, 1211 Geneve 27, Switzerland, (Telephone in U.S. (212) 331-9081), www.who.int; The WHO Global Atlas of Infectious Diseases and *World Health Report 2006.*

BOLIVIA - PUBLIC UTILITIES

UCLA Latin American Institute, 10343 Bunche Hall, Box 951447, Los Angeles, CA 90095-1447, (310) 825-4571, Fax: (310) 206-6859, www.international.ucla.edu/lac; *Statistical Abstract of Latin America.*

BOLIVIA - PUBLISHERS AND PUBLISHING

Taylor and Francis Group, An Informa Business, 2 Park Square, Milton Park, Abingdon, Oxford OX14 4RN, United Kingdom, (Dial from U.S. (212) 216-7800), (Fax from U.S. (212) 564-7854), www.tandf.co.uk; *The Europa World Year Book.*

BOLIVIA - RADIO BROADCASTING

Palgrave Macmillan Ltd., Houndmills, Basingstoke, Hampshire, RG21 6XS, England, (Telephone in U.S. (888) 330-8477), (Fax in U.S. (800) 672-2054), www.palgrave.com; *The Statesman's Yearbook 2008.*

BOLIVIA - RAILROADS

Economist Intelligence Unit, 111 West 57th Street, New York, NY 10019, (212) 554-0600, Fax: (212) 586-1181, www.eiu.com; *Business Latin America.*

Jane's Information Group, 110 North Royal Street, Suite 200, Alexandria, VA 22314, (703) 683-3700, Fax: (800) 836-0297, www.janes.com; *Jane's World Railways.*

Palgrave Macmillan Ltd., Houndmills, Basingstoke, Hampshire, RG21 6XS, England, (Telephone in U.S. (888) 330-8477), (Fax in U.S. (800) 672-2054), www.palgrave.com; *The Statesman's Yearbook 2008.*

Taylor and Francis Group, An Informa Business, 2 Park Square, Milton Park, Abingdon, Oxford OX14 4RN, United Kingdom, (Dial from U.S. (212) 216-7800), (Fax from U.S. (212) 564-7854), www.tandf.co.uk; *The Europa World Year Book.*

United Nations Statistics Division, New York, NY 10017, (800) 253-9646, Fax: (212) 963-4116, http://unstats.un.org; *Statistical Yearbook.*

BOLIVIA - RANCHING

UCLA Latin American Institute, 10343 Bunche Hall, Box 951447, Los Angeles, CA 90095-1447, (310) 825-4571, Fax: (310) 206-6859, www.international.ucla.edu/lac; *Statistical Abstract of Latin America.*

BOLIVIA - RELIGION

Central Intelligence Agency, Office of Public Affairs, Washington, DC 20505, (703) 482-0623, Fax: (703) 482-1739, www.cia.gov; *The World Factbook.*

M.E. Sharpe, 80 Business Park Drive, Armonk, NY 10504, (800) 541-6563, Fax: (914) 273-2106, www.mesharpe.com; *The Illustrated Book of World Rankings.*

Palgrave Macmillan Ltd., Houndmills, Basingstoke, Hampshire, RG21 6XS, England, (Telephone in U.S. (888) 330-8477), (Fax in U.S. (800) 672-2054), www.palgrave.com; *The Statesman's Yearbook 2008.*

UCLA Latin American Institute, 10343 Bunche Hall, Box 951447, Los Angeles, CA 90095-1447, (310) 825-4571, Fax: (310) 206-6859, www.international.ucla.edu/lac; *Statistical Abstract of Latin America.*

BOLIVIA - RENT CHARGES

International Labour Office, I.L.O. Publications, 4 route des Morillons, CH-1211 Geneva 22, Switzerland, (Telephone in U.S. (202) 653-7652), (Fax in U.S. (202) 653-7687), www.ilo.org; *Yearbook of Labour Statistics 2006.*

BOLIVIA - RESERVES (ACCOUNTING)

Economist Intelligence Unit, 111 West 57th Street, New York, NY 10019, (212) 554-0600, Fax: (212) 586-1181, www.eiu.com; *Business Latin America.*

Euromonitor International, Inc., 224 S. Michigan Avenue, Suite 1500, Chicago, IL 60604, (312) 922-1115, Fax: (312) 922-1157, www.euromonitor.com; *International Marketing Data and Statistics 2008.*

Inter-American Development Bank (IDB), 1300 New York Avenue, NW, Washington, DC 20577, (202) 623-1000, Fax: (202) 623-3096, www.iadb.org; *The Politics of Policies: Economic and Social Progress in Latin America - 2006 Report.*

Organization of American States (OAS), 17th Street Constitution Avenue NW, Washington, DC 20006, (202) 458-3000, www.oas.org; *The OAS in Transition: 1994-2004.*

The World Bank, 1818 H Street, NW, Washington, DC 20433, (202) 473-1000, Fax: (202) 477-6391, www.worldbank.org; *World Development Indicators (WDI) 2008.*

BOLIVIA - RETAIL TRADE

Euromonitor International, Inc., 224 S. Michigan Avenue, Suite 1500, Chicago, IL 60604, (312) 922-1115, Fax: (312) 922-1157, www.euromonitor.com; *World Marketing Data and Statistics.*

Inter-American Development Bank (IDB), 1300 New York Avenue, NW, Washington, DC 20577, (202) 623-1000, Fax: (202) 623-3096, www.iadb.org; *The Politics of Policies: Economic and Social Progress in Latin America - 2006 Report.*

BOLIVIA - RICE PRODUCTION

See BOLIVIA - CROPS

BOLIVIA - ROADS

Central Intelligence Agency, Office of Public Affairs, Washington, DC 20505, (703) 482-0623, Fax: (703) 482-1739, www.cia.gov; *The World Factbook.*

Economist Intelligence Unit, 111 West 57th Street, New York, NY 10019, (212) 554-0600, Fax: (212) 586-1181, www.eiu.com; *Business Latin America.*

International Road Federation (IFR), Madison Place, 500 Montgomery Street, 5th Floor, Alexandria, VA 22314, (703) 535-1001, Fax: (703) 535-1007, www.irfnet.org; *World Road Statistics 2006.*

Palgrave Macmillan Ltd., Houndmills, Basingstoke, Hampshire, RG21 6XS, England, (Telephone in U.S. (888) 330-8477), (Fax in U.S. (800) 672-2054), www.palgrave.com; *The Statesman's Yearbook 2008.*

BOLIVIA - RUBBER INDUSTRY AND TRADE

International Rubber Study Group (IRSG), 1st Floor, Heron House, 109/115 Wembley Hill Road, Wembley, Middlesex HA9 8DA, United Kingdom, www.rubberstudy.com; *Rubber Statistical Bulletin; Summary of World Rubber Statistics 2005; World Rubber Statistics Handbook (Volume 6, 1975-2001);* and *World Rubber Statistics Historic Handbook.*

M.E. Sharpe, 80 Business Park Drive, Armonk, NY 10504, (800) 541-6563, Fax: (914) 273-2106, www.mesharpe.com; *The Illustrated Book of World Rankings.*

BOLIVIA - SHEEP

See BOLIVIA - LIVESTOCK

BOLIVIA - SILVER PRODUCTION

See BOLIVIA - MINERAL INDUSTRIES

BOLIVIA - SOCIAL ECOLOGY

M.E. Sharpe, 80 Business Park Drive, Armonk, NY 10504, (800) 541-6563, Fax: (914) 273-2106, www.mesharpe.com; *The Illustrated Book of World Rankings.*

UCLA Latin American Institute, 10343 Bunche Hall, Box 951447, Los Angeles, CA 90095-1447, (310) 825-4571, Fax: (310) 206-6859, www.international.ucla.edu/lac; *Statistical Abstract of Latin America.*

United Nations Statistics Division, New York, NY 10017, (800) 253-9646, Fax: (212) 963-4116, http://unstats.un.org; *World Statistics Pocketbook.*

BOLIVIA - SOCIAL SECURITY

Inter-American Development Bank (IDB), 1300 New York Avenue, NW, Washington, DC 20577, (202) 623-1000, Fax: (202) 623-3096, www.iadb.org; *The Politics of Policies: Economic and Social Progress in Latin America - 2006 Report.*

International Monetary Fund (IMF), 700 Nineteenth Street, NW, Washington, DC 20431, (202) 623-7000, Fax: (202) 623-4661, www.imf.org; *Government Finance Statistics Yearbook (2008 Edition).*

United Nations Statistics Division, New York, NY 10017, (800) 253-9646, Fax: (212) 963-4116, http://unstats.un.org; *National Accounts Statistics: Compendium of Income Distribution Statistics.*

BOLIVIA - SOYBEAN PRODUCTION

See BOLIVIA - CROPS

BOLIVIA - STEEL PRODUCTION

See BOLIVIA - MINERAL INDUSTRIES

BOLIVIA - SUGAR PRODUCTION

See BOLIVIA - CROPS

BOLIVIA - SULPHUR PRODUCTION

See BOLIVIA - MINERAL INDUSTRIES

BOLIVIA - TAXATION

Inter-American Development Bank (IDB), 1300 New York Avenue, NW, Washington, DC 20577, (202) 623-1000, Fax: (202) 623-3096, www.iadb.org; *The Politics of Policies: Economic and Social Progress in Latin America - 2006 Report.*

International Monetary Fund (IMF), 700 Nineteenth Street, NW, Washington, DC 20431, (202) 623-7000, Fax: (202) 623-4661, www.imf.org; *Government Finance Statistics Yearbook (2008 Edition).*

International Road Federation (IFR), Madison Place, 500 Montgomery Street, 5th Floor, Alexandria, VA 22314, (703) 535-1001, Fax: (703) 535-1007, www.irfnet.org; *World Road Statistics 2006.*

Taylor and Francis Group, An Informa Business, 2 Park Square, Milton Park, Abingdon, Oxford OX14 4RN, United Kingdom, (Dial from U.S. (212) 216-7800), (Fax from U.S. (212) 564-7854), www.tandf.co.uk; *The Europa World Year Book.*

United Nations Statistics Division, New York, NY 10017, (800) 253-9646, Fax: (212) 963-4116, http://unstats.un.org; *Statistical Yearbook for Latin America and the Caribbean 2004.*

The World Bank, 1818 H Street, NW, Washington, DC 20433, (202) 473-1000, Fax: (202) 477-6391, www.worldbank.org; *World Development Report 2008.*

BOLIVIA - TELEPHONE

Economist Intelligence Unit, 111 West 57th Street, New York, NY 10019, (212) 554-0600, Fax: (212) 586-1181, www.eiu.com; *Business Latin America.*

International Telecommunication Union (ITU), Place des Nations, 1211 Geneva 20, Switzerland, www.itu.int; World Telecommunication Indicators Database.

Palgrave Macmillan Ltd., Houndmills, Basingstoke, Hampshire, RG21 6XS, England, (Telephone in U.S. (888) 330-8477), (Fax in U.S. (800) 672-2054), www.palgrave.com; *The Statesman's Yearbook 2008.*

Taylor and Francis Group, An Informa Business, 2 Park Square, Milton Park, Abingdon, Oxford OX14 4RN, United Kingdom, (Dial from U.S. (212) 216-7800), (Fax from U.S. (212) 564-7854), www.tandf.co.uk; *The Europa World Year Book.*

United Nations Statistics Division, New York, NY 10017, (800) 253-9646, Fax: (212) 963-4116, http://unstats.un.org; *World Statistics Pocketbook.*

BOLIVIA - TEXTILE INDUSTRY

M.E. Sharpe, 80 Business Park Drive, Armonk, NY 10504, (800) 541-6563, Fax: (914) 273-2106, www.mesharpe.com; *The Illustrated Book of World Rankings.*

United Nations Conference on Trade and Development (UNCTAD), DC2-1120, United Nations, New York, NY 10017, (212) 963-0027, www.unctad.org; *UNCTAD Commodity Yearbook.*

United Nations Statistics Division, New York, NY 10017, (800) 253-9646, Fax: (212) 963-4116, http://unstats.un.org; *Statistical Yearbook.*

BOLIVIA - TIN PRODUCTION

See BOLIVIA - MINERAL INDUSTRIES

BOLIVIA - TOBACCO INDUSTRY

Foreign Agricultural Service (FAS), U.S. Department of Agriculture (USDA), 1400 Independence Avenue, SW, Washington, DC 20250, (202) 720-3935, www.fas.usda.gov; *Tobacco: World Markets and Trade.*

M.E. Sharpe, 80 Business Park Drive, Armonk, NY 10504, (800) 541-6563, Fax: (914) 273-2106, www.mesharpe.com; *The Illustrated Book of World Rankings.*

United Nations Statistics Division, New York, NY 10017, (800) 253-9646, Fax: (212) 963-4116, http://unstats.un.org; *Statistical Yearbook.*

BOLIVIA - TOURISM

Economist Intelligence Unit, 111 West 57th Street, New York, NY 10019, (212) 554-0600, Fax: (212) 586-1181, www.eiu.com; *Business Latin America.*

Euromonitor International, Inc., 224 S. Michigan Avenue, Suite 1500, Chicago, IL 60604, (312) 922-1115, Fax: (312) 922-1157, www.euromonitor.com; *The World Economic Factbook 2008* and *World Marketing Data and Statistics.*

M.E. Sharpe, 80 Business Park Drive, Armonk, NY 10504, (800) 541-6563, Fax: (914) 273-2106, www.mesharpe.com; *The Illustrated Book of World Rankings.*

Palgrave Macmillan Ltd., Houndmills, Basingstoke, Hampshire, RG21 6XS, England, (Telephone in U.S. (888) 330-8477), (Fax in U.S. (800) 672-2054), www.palgrave.com; *The Statesman's Yearbook 2008.*

Taylor and Francis Group, An Informa Business, 2 Park Square, Milton Park, Abingdon, Oxford OX14 4RN, United Kingdom, (Dial from U.S. (212) 216-7800), (Fax from U.S. (212) 564-7854), www.tandf.co.uk; *The Europa World Year Book.*

UCLA Latin American Institute, 10343 Bunche Hall, Box 951447, Los Angeles, CA 90095-1447, (310) 825-4571, Fax: (310) 206-6859, www.international.ucla.edu/lac; *Statistical Abstract of Latin America.*

United Nations Statistics Division, New York, NY 10017, (800) 253-9646, Fax: (212) 963-4116, http://unstats.un.org; *Statistical Yearbook* and *Statistical Yearbook for Latin America and the Caribbean 2004.*

United Nations World Tourism Organization (UNWTO), Capitan Haya 42, 28020 Madrid, Spain, www.world-tourism.org; *Yearbook of Tourism Statistics.*

The World Bank, 1818 H Street, NW, Washington, DC 20433, (202) 473-1000, Fax: (202) 477-6391, www.worldbank.org; *Bolivia.*

BOLIVIA - TRADE

See BOLIVIA - INTERNATIONAL TRADE

BOLIVIA - TRANSPORTATION

Central Intelligence Agency, Office of Public Affairs, Washington, DC 20505, (703) 482-0623, Fax: (703) 482-1739, www.cia.gov; *The World Factbook.*

Economist Intelligence Unit, 111 West 57th Street, New York, NY 10019, (212) 554-0600, Fax: (212) 586-1181, www.eiu.com; *Business Latin America.*

Euromonitor International, Inc., 224 S. Michigan Avenue, Suite 1500, Chicago, IL 60604, (312) 922-1115, Fax: (312) 922-1157, www.euromonitor.com; *International Marketing Data and Statistics 2008* and *World Marketing Data and Statistics.*

Inter-American Development Bank (IDB), 1300 New York Avenue, NW, Washington, DC 20577, (202) 623-1000, Fax: (202) 623-3096, www.iadb.org; *The Politics of Policies: Economic and Social Progress in Latin America - 2006 Report.*

M.E. Sharpe, 80 Business Park Drive, Armonk, NY 10504, (800) 541-6563, Fax: (914) 273-2106, www.mesharpe.com; *The Illustrated Book of World Rankings.*

Palgrave Macmillan Ltd., Houndmills, Basingstoke, Hampshire, RG21 6XS, England, (Telephone in U.S. (888) 330-8477), (Fax in U.S. (800) 672-2054), www.palgrave.com; *The Statesman's Yearbook 2008.*

Taylor and Francis Group, An Informa Business, 2 Park Square, Milton Park, Abingdon, Oxford OX14 4RN, United Kingdom, (Dial from U.S. (212) 216-7800), (Fax from U.S. (212) 564-7854), www.tandf.co.uk; *The Europa World Year Book.*

UCLA Latin American Institute, 10343 Bunche Hall, Box 951447, Los Angeles, CA 90095-1447, (310) 825-4571, Fax: (310) 206-6859, www.international.ucla.edu/lac; *Statistical Abstract of Latin America.*

United Nations Statistics Division, New York, NY 10017, (800) 253-9646, Fax: (212) 963-4116, http://unstats.un.org; *Human Development Report 2006* and *Statistical Yearbook for Latin America and the Caribbean 2004.*

The World Bank, 1818 H Street, NW, Washington, DC 20433, (202) 473-1000, Fax: (202) 477-6391, www.worldbank.org; *Bolivia.*

BOLIVIA - TRAVEL COSTS

International Monetary Fund (IMF), 700 Nineteenth Street, NW, Washington, DC 20431, (202) 623-

7000, Fax: (202) 623-4661, www.imf.org; *Government Finance Statistics Yearbook (2008 Edition).*

BOLIVIA - TURKEYS

See BOLIVIA - LIVESTOCK

BOLIVIA - UNEMPLOYMENT

Central Intelligence Agency, Office of Public Affairs, Washington, DC 20505, (703) 482-0623, Fax: (703) 482-1739, www.cia.gov; *The World Factbook.*

Economist Intelligence Unit, 111 West 57th Street, New York, NY 10019, (212) 554-0600, Fax: (212) 586-1181, www.eiu.com; *Business Latin America.*

Euromonitor International, Inc., 224 S. Michigan Avenue, Suite 1500, Chicago, IL 60604, (312) 922-1115, Fax: (312) 922-1157, www.euromonitor.com; *International Marketing Data and Statistics 2008.*

International Labour Office, I.L.O. Publications, 4 route des Morillons, CH-1211 Geneva 22, Switzerland, (Telephone in U.S. (202) 653-7652), (Fax in U.S. (202) 653-7687), www.ilo.org; *Yearbook of Labour Statistics 2006.*

UCLA Latin American Institute, 10343 Bunche Hall, Box 951447, Los Angeles, CA 90095-1447, (310) 825-4571, Fax: (310) 206-6859, www.international.ucla.edu/lac; *Statistical Abstract of Latin America.*

United Nations Statistics Division, New York, NY 10017, (800) 253-9646, Fax: (212) 963-4116, http://unstats.un.org; *Statistical Yearbook.*

BOLIVIA - VITAL STATISTICS

Euromonitor International, Inc., 224 S. Michigan Avenue, Suite 1500, Chicago, IL 60604, (312) 922-1115, Fax: (312) 922-1157, www.euromonitor.com; *International Marketing Data and Statistics 2008.*

Palgrave Macmillan Ltd., Houndmills, Basingstoke, Hampshire, RG21 6XS, England, (Telephone in U.S. (888) 330-8477), (Fax in U.S. (800) 672-2054), www.palgrave.com; *The Statesman's Yearbook 2008.*

World Health Organization (WHO), Avenue Appia 20, 1211 Geneve 27, Switzerland, (Telephone in U.S. (212) 331-9081), www.who.int; *World Health Report 2006.*

BOLIVIA - WAGES

International Labour Office, I.L.O. Publications, 4 route des Morillons, CH-1211 Geneva 22, Switzerland, (Telephone in U.S. (202) 653-7652), (Fax in U.S. (202) 653-7687), www.ilo.org; *Yearbook of Labour Statistics 2006.*

UCLA Latin American Institute, 10343 Bunche Hall, Box 951447, Los Angeles, CA 90095-1447, (310) 825-4571, Fax: (310) 206-6859, www.international.ucla.edu/lac; *Statistical Abstract of Latin America.*

United Nations Statistics Division, New York, NY 10017, (800) 253-9646, Fax: (212) 963-4116, http://unstats.un.org; *Statistical Yearbook.*

The World Bank, 1818 H Street, NW, Washington, DC 20433, (202) 473-1000, Fax: (202) 477-6391, www.worldbank.org; *Bolivia.*

BOLIVIA - WEATHER

See BOLIVIA - CLIMATE

BOLIVIA - WELFARE STATE

Inter-American Development Bank (IDB), 1300 New York Avenue, NW, Washington, DC 20577, (202) 623-1000, Fax: (202) 623-3096, www.iadb.org; *The Politics of Policies: Economic and Social Progress in Latin America - 2006 Report.*

International Monetary Fund (IMF), 700 Nineteenth Street, NW, Washington, DC 20431, (202) 623-7000, Fax: (202) 623-4661, www.imf.org; *Government Finance Statistics Yearbook (2008 Edition).*

BOLIVIA - WHEAT PRODUCTION

See BOLIVIA - CROPS

BOLIVIA - WHOLESALE PRICE INDEXES

Inter-American Development Bank (IDB), 1300 New York Avenue, NW, Washington, DC 20577, (202) 623-1000, Fax: (202) 623-3096, www.iadb.org; *The Politics of Policies: Economic and Social Progress in Latin America - 2006 Report.*

BOLIVIA - WHOLESALE TRADE

Inter-American Development Bank (IDB), 1300 New York Avenue, NW, Washington, DC 20577, (202) 623-1000, Fax: (202) 623-3096, www.iadb.org; *The Politics of Policies: Economic and Social Progress in Latin America - 2006 Report.*

BOLIVIA - WINE PRODUCTION

See BOLIVIA - BEVERAGE INDUSTRY

BOLIVIA - WOOL PRODUCTION

See BOLIVIA - TEXTILE INDUSTRY

BOLIVIA - YARN PRODUCTION

See BOLIVIA - TEXTILE INDUSTRY

BOLIVIA - ZINC AND ZINC ORE

See BOLIVIA - MINERAL INDUSTRIES

BOMBS

Bureau of Alcohol, Tobacco, Firearms and Explosives (ATF), Office of Public and Governmental Affairs, 99 New York Avenue, NE, Mail Stop 5S144, Washington, DC 20226, (202) 927-7890, www.atf.gov; *Explosive Incident Reports For Bombing.*

BONDS - FOREIGN - UNITED STATES PURCHASES AND SALES OF

Bureau of Economic Analysis (BEA), U.S. Department of Commerce (DOC), 1441 L Street NW, Washington, DC 20230, (202) 606-9900, www.bea.gov; *Survey of Current Business (SCB).*

U.S. Department of the Treasury (DOT), 1500 Pennsylvania Avenue, NW, Washington, DC 20220, (202) 622-2000, Fax: (202) 622-6415, www.ustreas.gov; *Treasury Bulletin.*

BONDS - HOLDINGS BY SECTOR

Board of Governors of the Federal Reserve System, Constitution Avenue, NW, Washington, DC 20551, (202) 452-3000, www.federalreserve.gov; *Federal Reserve Board Statistical Release* and *Flow of Funds Accounts of the United States.*

BONDS - LIFE INSURANCE COMPANIES

American Council of Life Insurers (ACLI), 101 Constitution Avenue, NW, Washington, DC 20001-2133, (202) 624-2000, www.acli.com; *Life Insurers Fact Book 2007.*

Board of Governors of the Federal Reserve System, Constitution Avenue, NW, Washington, DC 20551, (202) 452-3000, www.federalreserve.gov; *Federal Reserve Board Statistical Release* and *Flow of Funds Accounts of the United States.*

BONDS - NEW ISSUES

Board of Governors of the Federal Reserve System, Constitution Avenue, NW, Washington, DC 20551, (202) 452-3000, www.federalreserve.gov; *Federal Reserve Bulletin.*

BONDS - OWNERSHIP BY EQUITY HOLDERS

Investment Company Institute (ICI), 1401 H Street, NW, Suite 1200, Washington, DC 20005-2040, (202) 326-5800, www.ici.org; *Equity Ownership in America, 2005.*

BONDS - PRICES, YIELDS, SALES, AND ISSUES

Board of Governors of the Federal Reserve System, Constitution Avenue, NW, Washington, DC 20551, (202) 452-3000, www.federalreserve.gov; *Federal Reserve Bulletin.*

Bond Market Association, 360 Madison Avenue, New York, NY 10017-7111, (646) 637-9200, Fax: (646) 637-9126, www.bondmarket.com; *Statistical Tables by Market.*

Global Financial Data, Inc., 784 Fremont Villas, Los Angeles, CA 90042, (323) 924-1016, www.globalfindata.com; *Global Stock Market Indices; United States Government Bond Total Return Index;* and unpublished data.

New York Stock Exchange (NYSE), 11 Wall Street, New York, NY 10005, (212) 656-3000, www.nyse.com; *NYSE Facts and Figures.*

U.S. Department of the Treasury (DOT), 1500 Pennsylvania Avenue, NW, Washington, DC 20220, (202) 622-2000, Fax: (202) 622-6415, www.ustreas.gov; *Treasury Bulletin.*

BONDS - RATINGS

Moody's Investors Service, 99 Church Street, New York, NY 10007, (212) 553-0300, www.moodys.com; unpublished data.

Standard and Poor's Corporation, 55 Water Street, New York, NY 10041, (212) 438-1000, www.standardandpoors.com; *Bond Fund Ratings.*

BONDS - UNITED STATES SAVINGS

Board of Governors of the Federal Reserve System, Constitution Avenue, NW, Washington, DC 20551, (202) 452-3000, www.federalreserve.gov; *Federal Reserve Bulletin* and unpublished data.

U.S. Department of the Treasury (DOT), 1500 Pennsylvania Avenue, NW, Washington, DC 20220, (202) 622-2000, Fax: (202) 622-6415, www.ustreas.gov; *Treasury Bulletin.*

BOOK PUBLISHING INDUSTRY

Book Industry Study Group (BISG), 370 Lexington Avenue, Suite 900, New York, NY 10017, (646) 336-7141, Fax: (646) 336-6214, www.bisg.org; *Used-Book Sales.*

LISU, Holywell Park, Loughborough University, Leicestershire, LE11 3TU, United Kingdom, www.lboro.ac.uk/departments/dis/lisu; *Availability of Accessible Publications* and *Average Prices of British and USA Academic Books.*

U.S. Census Bureau, Center for Economic Studies, 4600 Silver Hill Road, Washington DC 20233, (301) 457-1235, www.ces.census.gov; *2002 Economic Census, Information.*

U.S. Census Bureau, Service Sector Statistics Division, 4700 Silver Hill Road, Washington DC 20233-0001, (301) 763-3030, www.census.gov/svsd/www/economic.html; *2004 Service Annual Survey.*

BOOKKEEPING

See ACCOUNTING, TAX PREPARATION, BOOKKEEPING, AND PAYROLL SERVICES

BOOKS

See also INFORMATION INDUSTRY and PUBLISHING INDUSTRIES

BOOKS - PRICES

Information Today, Inc., 143 Old Marlton Pike, Medford, NJ 08055-8750, (609) 654-6266, Fax: (609) 654-4309, www.infotoday.com; *The Bowker Annual Library and Book Trade Almanac 2006.*

LISU, Holywell Park, Loughborough University, Leicestershire, LE11 3TU, United Kingdom, www.lboro.ac.uk/departments/dis/lisu; *Average Prices of British and USA Academic Books.*

BOOKS - PRODUCTION

Information Today, Inc., 143 Old Marlton Pike, Medford, NJ 08055-8750, (609) 654-6266, Fax: (609) 654-4309, www.infotoday.com; *The Bowker Annual Library and Book Trade Almanac 2006.*

BOOKS - READING

National Endowment for the Arts (NEA), 1100 Pennsylvania Avenue, NW, Washington, DC 20506-0001, (202) 682-5400, www.arts.gov; *Reading at Risk: A Survey of Literary Reading in America.*

Veronis Suhler Stevenson Partners LLC, 350 Park Avenue, New York, NY 10022, (212) 935-4990, Fax: (212) 381-8168, www.vss.com; Communications Industry Report.

BOOKS - SALES

Book Industry Study Group (BISG), 370 Lexington Avenue, Suite 900, New York, NY 10017, (646) 336-7141, Fax: (646) 336-6214, www.bisg.org; *The African-American Book Buyers Study; Book Industry Trends 2007; Consumer Research Study on Book Purchasing;* and *Used-Book Sales.*

Bureau of Economic Analysis (BEA), U.S. Department of Commerce (DOC), 1441 L Street NW, Washington, DC 20230, (202) 606-9900, www.bea.gov; *2007 Annual Revision of the National Income and Product Accounts (NIPA)* and *Survey of Current Business (SCB).*

Forrester Research, Inc., 400 Technology Square, Cambridge, MA 02139, (617) 613-6000, www.forrester.com; *US Online Retail.*

U.S. Census Bureau, 4700 Silver Hill Road, Washington DC 20233-0001, (301) 763-3030, www.census.gov; *2006 E-Commerce Multi-Sector Report* and *E-Stats - Measuring the Electronic Economy.*

BOOTS

See FOOTWEAR

BORDER PATROL ACTIVITIES

U.S. Citizenship and Immigration Services (USCIS), Washington District Office, 2675 Prosperity Avenue, Fairfax, VA 22031, (800) 375-5283, http://uscis.gov; *2005 Yearbook of Immigration Statistics.*

U.S. Customs and Border Protection (CBP), U.S. Department of Homeland Security (DHS), 1300 Pennsylvania Avenue, NW Washington, DC 20004-3002, (202) 354-1000, www.cbp.gov; *FY04 Year-End Import Trade Trends Report* and *National Workload Statistics.*

U.S. Department of Homeland Security (DHS), Office of Immigration Statistics, Washington, DC 20528, (202) 282-8000, www.dhs.gov; *Immigration Enforcement Actions: 2005.*

U.S. Library of Congress (LOC), Congressional Research Service (CRS), The Library of Congress, 101 Independence Avenue, SE, Washington, DC 20540-7500, (202) 707-5700, www.loc.gov/crsinfo; *Border Security: The Role of the U.S. Border Patrol* and *Immigration Fraud: Policies, Investigations, and Issues.*

BORON

U.S. Department of the Interior (DOI), U.S. Geological Survey (USGS), Office of Minerals Information, 12201 Sunrise Valley Drive, Reston, VA 20192, Mr. Kenneth A. Beckman, (703) 648-4916, Fax: (703) 648-4995, http://minerals.usgs.gov/minerals; *Mineral Commodity Summaries* and *Minerals Yearbook.*

BOSNIA AND HERZEGOVINA - NATIONAL STATISTICAL OFFICE

Agency for Statistics of Bosnia and Herzegovina, Zelenih Beretki 26, 71000 Sarajevo, Bosnia and Herzegovina, www.bhas.ba; National Data Center.

BOSNIA AND HERZEGOVINA - PRIMARY STATISTICS SOURCES

Agency for Statistics of Bosnia and Herzegovina, Zelenih Beretki 26, 71000 Sarajevo, Bosnia and Herzegovina, www.bhas.ba; *Thematic Bulletin 2007.*

BOSNIA AND HERZEGOVINA - ABORTION

United Nations Statistics Division, New York, NY 10017, (800) 253-9646, Fax: (212) 963-4116, http://unstats.un.org; *Trends in Europe and North America: The Statistical Yearbook of the ECE 2005.*

BOSNIA AND HERZEGOVINA - AGRICULTURE

Economist Intelligence Unit, 111 West 57th Street, New York, NY 10019, (212) 554-0600, Fax: (212) 586-1181, www.eiu.com; *Bosnia Herzegovina Country Report.*

Euromonitor International, Inc., 224 S. Michigan Avenue, Suite 1500, Chicago, IL 60604, (312) 922-1115, Fax: (312) 922-1157, www.euromonitor.com; *World Marketing Data and Statistics.*

Palgrave Macmillan Ltd., Houndmills, Basingstoke, Hampshire, RG21 6XS, England, (Telephone in U.S. (888) 330-8477), (Fax in U.S. (800) 672-2054), www.palgrave.com; *The Statesman's Yearbook 2008.*

Taylor and Francis Group, An Informa Business, 2 Park Square, Milton Park, Abingdon, Oxford OX14 4RN, United Kingdom, (Dial from U.S. (212) 216-7800), (Fax from U.S. (212) 564-7854), www.tandf.co.uk; *The Europa World Year Book.*

United Nations Food and Agricultural Organization (FAO), Viale delle Terme di Caracalla, 00100 Rome, Italy, (Dial from U.S. (202) 653-2400), (Fax from U.S. (202) 653 5760), www.fao.org; AQUASTAT; *FAO Production Yearbook 2002; FAO Trade Yearbook;* and *The State of Food and Agriculture (SOFA) 2006.*

United Nations Statistics Division, New York, NY 10017, (800) 253-9646, Fax: (212) 963-4116, http://unstats.un.org; *2004 Industrial Commodity Statistics Yearbook* and *Statistical Yearbook.*

The World Bank, 1818 H Street, NW, Washington, DC 20433, (202) 473-1000, Fax: (202) 477-6391, www.worldbank.org; *Bosnia and Herzegovina.*

BOSNIA AND HERZEGOVINA - AIRLINES

International Civil Aviation Organization (ICAO), External Relations and Public Information Office (EPO), 999 University Street, Montreal, Quebec H3C 5H7, Canada, (Dial from U.S. (514) 954-8219), (Fax from U.S. (514) 954-6077), www.icao.int; *Civil Aviation Statistics of the World.*

United Nations Statistics Division, New York, NY 10017, (800) 253-9646, Fax: (212) 963-4116, http://unstats.un.org; *Statistical Yearbook.*

BOSNIA AND HERZEGOVINA - AIRPORTS

Central Intelligence Agency, Office of Public Affairs, Washington, DC 20505, (703) 482-0623, Fax: (703) 482-1739, www.cia.gov; *The World Factbook.*

BOSNIA AND HERZEGOVINA - ARMED FORCES

Central Intelligence Agency, Office of Public Affairs, Washington, DC 20505, (703) 482-0623, Fax: (703) 482-1739, www.cia.gov; *The World Factbook.*

Euromonitor International, Inc., 224 S. Michigan Avenue, Suite 1500, Chicago, IL 60604, (312) 922-1115, Fax: (312) 922-1157, www.euromonitor.com; *World Marketing Data and Statistics.*

BOSNIA AND HERZEGOVINA - AUTOMOBILE INDUSTRY AND TRADE

United Nations Statistics Division, New York, NY 10017, (800) 253-9646, Fax: (212) 963-4116, http://unstats.un.org; *Statistical Yearbook.*

BOSNIA AND HERZEGOVINA - BANKS AND BANKING

Euromonitor International, Inc., 224 S. Michigan Avenue, Suite 1500, Chicago, IL 60604, (312) 922-1115, Fax: (312) 922-1157, www.euromonitor.com; *World Marketing Data and Statistics.*

Palgrave Macmillan Ltd., Houndmills, Basingstoke, Hampshire, RG21 6XS, England, (Telephone in U.S. (888) 330-8477), (Fax in U.S. (800) 672-2054), www.palgrave.com; *The Statesman's Yearbook 2008.*

BOSNIA AND HERZEGOVINA - BEVERAGE INDUSTRY

United Nations Statistics Division, New York, NY 10017, (800) 253-9646, Fax: (212) 963-4116, http://unstats.un.org; *Statistical Yearbook.*

BOSNIA AND HERZEGOVINA - BROADCASTING

Central Intelligence Agency, Office of Public Affairs, Washington, DC 20505, (703) 482-0623, Fax: (703) 482-1739, www.cia.gov; *The World Factbook.*

Euromonitor International, Inc., 224 S. Michigan Avenue, Suite 1500, Chicago, IL 60604, (312) 922-1115, Fax: (312) 922-1157, www.euromonitor.com; *World Marketing Data and Statistics.*

UNESCO Institute for Statistics, C.P. 6128 Succursale Centre-Ville, Montreal, Quebec, H3C 3J7 Canada, (Dial from U.S. (514) 343-6880), (Fax from U.S. (514) 343 6882), www.uis.unesco.org; *Statistical Tables.*

United Nations Statistics Division, New York, NY 10017, (800) 253-9646, Fax: (212) 963-4116, http://unstats.un.org; *Trends in Europe and North America: The Statistical Yearbook of the ECE 2005.*

BOSNIA AND HERZEGOVINA - BUDGET

Central Intelligence Agency, Office of Public Affairs, Washington, DC 20505, (703) 482-0623, Fax: (703) 482-1739, www.cia.gov; *The World Factbook.*

BOSNIA AND HERZEGOVINA - BUSINESS

Economist Intelligence Unit, 111 West 57th Street, New York, NY 10019, (212) 554-0600, Fax: (212) 586-1181, www.eiu.com; *Business Eastern Europe.*

United Nations Statistics Division, New York, NY 10017, (800) 253-9646, Fax: (212) 963-4116, http://unstats.un.org; *Statistical Yearbook.*

BOSNIA AND HERZEGOVINA - CHILDBIRTH - STATISTICS

Central Intelligence Agency, Office of Public Affairs, Washington, DC 20505, (703) 482-0623, Fax: (703) 482-1739, www.cia.gov; *The World Factbook.*

Euromonitor International, Inc., 224 S. Michigan Avenue, Suite 1500, Chicago, IL 60604, (312) 922-1115, Fax: (312) 922-1157, www.euromonitor.com; *The World Economic Factbook 2008.*

Palgrave Macmillan Ltd., Houndmills, Basingstoke, Hampshire, RG21 6XS, England, (Telephone in U.S. (888) 330-8477), (Fax in U.S. (800) 672-2054), www.palgrave.com; *The Statesman's Yearbook 2008.*

United Nations Statistics Division, New York, NY 10017, (800) 253-9646, Fax: (212) 963-4116, http://unstats.un.org; *Statistical Yearbook.*

BOSNIA AND HERZEGOVINA - COMMERCE

Palgrave Macmillan Ltd., Houndmills, Basingstoke, Hampshire, RG21 6XS, England, (Telephone in U.S. (888) 330-8477), (Fax in U.S. (800) 672-2054), www.palgrave.com; *The Statesman's Yearbook 2008.*

BOSNIA AND HERZEGOVINA - CONSTRUCTION INDUSTRY

United Nations Statistics Division, New York, NY 10017, (800) 253-9646, Fax: (212) 963-4116, http://unstats.un.org; *Statistical Yearbook.*

BOSNIA AND HERZEGOVINA - CONSUMER PRICE INDEXES

Euromonitor International, Inc., 224 S. Michigan Avenue, Suite 1500, Chicago, IL 60604, (312) 922-1115, Fax: (312) 922-1157, www.euromonitor.com; *World Marketing Data and Statistics.*

United Nations Statistics Division, New York, NY 10017, (800) 253-9646, Fax: (212) 963-4116, http://unstats.un.org; *Statistical Yearbook* and *Trends in Europe and North America: The Statistical Yearbook of the ECE 2005.*

The World Bank, 1818 H Street, NW, Washington, DC 20433, (202) 473-1000, Fax: (202) 477-6391, www.worldbank.org; *Bosnia and Herzegovina.*

BOSNIA AND HERZEGOVINA - CRIME

United Nations Statistics Division, New York, NY 10017, (800) 253-9646, Fax: (212) 963-4116, http://unstats.un.org; *Trends in Europe and North America: The Statistical Yearbook of the ECE 2005.*

BOSNIA AND HERZEGOVINA - CROPS

Palgrave Macmillan Ltd., Houndmills, Basingstoke, Hampshire, RG21 6XS, England, (Telephone in U.S. (888) 330-8477), (Fax in U.S. (800) 672-2054), www.palgrave.com; *The Statesman's Yearbook 2008.*

Taylor and Francis Group, An Informa Business, 2 Park Square, Milton Park, Abingdon, Oxford OX14 4RN, United Kingdom, (Dial from U.S. (212) 216-7800), (Fax from U.S. (212) 564-7854), www.tandf.co.uk; *The Europa World Year Book.*

United Nations Food and Agricultural Organization (FAO), Viale delle Terme di Caracalla, 00100 Rome, Italy, (Dial from U.S. (202) 653-2400), (Fax from U.S. (202) 653 5760), www.fao.org; *FAO Production Yearbook 2002* and *The State of Food and Agriculture (SOFA) 2006.*

United Nations Statistics Division, New York, NY 10017, (800) 253-9646, Fax: (212) 963-4116, http://unstats.un.org; *2004 Industrial Commodity Statistics Yearbook* and *Statistical Yearbook.*

BOSNIA AND HERZEGOVINA - DAIRY PROCESSING

Palgrave Macmillan Ltd., Houndmills, Basingstoke, Hampshire, RG21 6XS, England, (Telephone in U.S. (888) 330-8477), (Fax in U.S. (800) 672-2054), www.palgrave.com; *The Statesman's Yearbook 2008.*

Taylor and Francis Group, An Informa Business, 2 Park Square, Milton Park, Abingdon, Oxford OX14 4RN, United Kingdom, (Dial from U.S. (212) 216-7800), (Fax from U.S. (212) 564-7854), www.tandf.co.uk; *The Europa World Year Book.*

United Nations Food and Agricultural Organization (FAO), Viale delle Terme di Caracalla, 00100 Rome, Italy, (Dial from U.S. (202) 653-2400), (Fax from U.S. (202) 653 5760), www.fao.org; *FAO Production Yearbook 2002* and *The State of Food and Agriculture (SOFA) 2006.*

United Nations Statistics Division, New York, NY 10017, (800) 253-9646, Fax: (212) 963-4116, http://unstats.un.org; *2004 Industrial Commodity Statistics Yearbook* and *Statistical Yearbook.*

BOSNIA AND HERZEGOVINA - DEMOGRAPHY

Euromonitor International, Inc., 224 S. Michigan Avenue, Suite 1500, Chicago, IL 60604, (312) 922-1115, Fax: (312) 922-1157, www.euromonitor.com; *The World Economic Factbook 2008* and *World Marketing Data and Statistics.*

United Nations Statistics Division, New York, NY 10017, (800) 253-9646, Fax: (212) 963-4116, http://unstats.un.org; *Demographic Yearbook.*

The World Bank, 1818 H Street, NW, Washington, DC 20433, (202) 473-1000, Fax: (202) 477-6391, www.worldbank.org; *Bosnia and Herzegovina.*

BOSNIA AND HERZEGOVINA - DISPOSABLE INCOME

United Nations Statistics Division, New York, NY 10017, (800) 253-9646, Fax: (212) 963-4116, http://unstats.un.org; *Statistical Yearbook.*

BOSNIA AND HERZEGOVINA - DIVORCE

United Nations Statistics Division, New York, NY 10017, (800) 253-9646, Fax: (212) 963-4116, http://unstats.un.org; *Demographic Yearbook; Statistical Yearbook;* and *Trends in Europe and North America: The Statistical Yearbook of the ECE 2005.*

BOSNIA AND HERZEGOVINA - ECONOMIC CONDITIONS

Center for International Business Education Research (CIBER), Columbia Business School and School of International and Public Affairs, Uris Hall, Room 212, 3022 Broadway, New York, NY 10027-6902, Mr. Joshua Safier, (212) 854-4750, Fax: (212) 222-9821, www.columbia.edu/cu/ciber/; Datastream International.

Central Intelligence Agency, Office of Public Affairs, Washington, DC 20505, (703) 482-0623, Fax: (703) 482-1739, www.cia.gov; *The World Factbook.*

DSI Data Service Information, Xantener Strasse 51a, D-47495 Rheinberg, Germany, www.dsidata.com; *Campus Solution.*

Dun and Bradstreet (DB) Corporation, 103 JFK Parkway, Short Hills, NJ 07078, (973) 921-5500, www.dnb.com; *Country Report.*

Economist Intelligence Unit, 111 West 57th Street, New York, NY 10019, (212) 554-0600, Fax: (212) 586-1181, www.eiu.com; *Bosnia Herzegovina Country Report.*

Euromonitor International, Inc., 224 S. Michigan Avenue, Suite 1500, Chicago, IL 60604, (312) 922-1115, Fax: (312) 922-1157, www.euromonitor.com; *The World Economic Factbook 2008* and *World Marketing Data and Statistics.*

International Monetary Fund (IMF), 700 Nineteenth Street, NW, Washington, DC 20431, (202) 623-7000, Fax: (202) 623-4661, www.imf.org; *World Economic Outlook Reports.*

Palgrave Macmillan Ltd., Houndmills, Basingstoke, Hampshire, RG21 6XS, England, (Telephone in U.S. (888) 330-8477), (Fax in U.S. (800) 672-2054), www.palgrave.com; *The Statesman's Yearbook 2008.*

United Nations Statistics Division, New York, NY 10017, (800) 253-9646, Fax: (212) 963-4116, http://unstats.un.org; *World Statistics Pocketbook.*

The World Bank, 1818 H Street, NW, Washington, DC 20433, (202) 473-1000, Fax: (202) 477-6391, www.worldbank.org; *Bosnia and Herzegovina; Global Economic Monitor (GEM); Global Economic Prospects 2008;* and *The World Bank Atlas 2003-2004.*

BOSNIA AND HERZEGOVINA - EDUCATION

Euromonitor International, Inc., 224 S. Michigan Avenue, Suite 1500, Chicago, IL 60604, (312) 922-1115, Fax: (312) 922-1157, www.euromonitor.com; *World Marketing Data and Statistics.*

Palgrave Macmillan Ltd., Houndmills, Basingstoke, Hampshire, RG21 6XS, England, (Telephone in U.S. (888) 330-8477), (Fax in U.S. (800) 672-2054), www.palgrave.com; *The Statesman's Yearbook 2008.*

UNESCO Institute for Statistics, C.P. 6128 Succursale Centre-Ville, Montreal, Quebec, H3C 3J7 Canada, (Dial from U.S. (514) 343-6880), (Fax from U.S. (514) 343 6882), www.uis.unesco.org; *Statistical Tables.*

United Nations Statistics Division, New York, NY 10017, (800) 253-9646, Fax: (212) 963-4116, http://unstats.un.org; *Trends in Europe and North America: The Statistical Yearbook of the ECE 2005.*

The World Bank, 1818 H Street, NW, Washington, DC 20433, (202) 473-1000, Fax: (202) 477-6391, www.worldbank.org; *Bosnia and Herzegovina.*

BOSNIA AND HERZEGOVINA - ELECTRICITY

Palgrave Macmillan Ltd., Houndmills, Basingstoke, Hampshire, RG21 6XS, England, (Telephone in U.S. (888) 330-8477), (Fax in U.S. (800) 672-2054), www.palgrave.com; *The Statesman's Yearbook 2008.*

Platts, 2 Penn Plaza, 25th Floor, New York, NY 10121-2298, (212) 904-3070, www.platts.com; *Energy Economist* and *European Electricity Review 2004.*

U.S. Department of Energy (DOE), Energy Information Administration (EIA), 1000 Independence Avenue, SW, Washington, DC 20585, (202) 586-8800, www.eia.doe.gov; *International Energy Annual 2004* and *International Energy Outlook 2006.*

United Nations Statistics Division, New York, NY 10017, (800) 253-9646, Fax: (212) 963-4116, http://unstats.un.org; *Energy Statistics Yearbook 2003; Statistical Yearbook;* and *Trends in Europe and North America: The Statistical Yearbook of the ECE 2005.*

BOSNIA AND HERZEGOVINA - EMPLOYMENT

United Nations Statistics Division, New York, NY 10017, (800) 253-9646, Fax: (212) 963-4116, http://unstats.un.org; *Statistical Yearbook* and *Trends in Europe and North America: The Statistical Yearbook of the ECE 2005.*

The World Bank, 1818 H Street, NW, Washington, DC 20433, (202) 473-1000, Fax: (202) 477-6391, www.worldbank.org; *Bosnia and Herzegovina.*

BOSNIA AND HERZEGOVINA - ENERGY INDUSTRIES

Platts, 2 Penn Plaza, 25th Floor, New York, NY 10121-2298, (212) 904-3070, www.platts.com; *Energy in East Europe.*

BOSNIA AND HERZEGOVINA - ENVIRONMENTAL CONDITIONS

DSI Data Service Information, Xantener Strasse 51a, D-47495 Rheinberg, Germany, www.dsidata.com; *Campus Solution* and *DSI's Global Environmental Database.*

Economist Intelligence Unit, 111 West 57th Street, New York, NY 10019, (212) 554-0600, Fax: (212) 586-1181, www.eiu.com; *Bosnia Herzegovina Country Report.*

United Nations Statistics Division, New York, NY 10017, (800) 253-9646, Fax: (212) 963-4116, http://unstats.un.org; *Statistical Yearbook; Trends in Europe and North America: The Statistical Yearbook of the ECE 2005;* and *World Statistics Pocketbook.*

BOSNIA AND HERZEGOVINA - EXPORTS

Central Intelligence Agency, Office of Public Affairs, Washington, DC 20505, (703) 482-0623, Fax: (703) 482-1739, www.cia.gov; *The World Factbook.*

Economist Intelligence Unit, 111 West 57th Street, New York, NY 10019, (212) 554-0600, Fax: (212) 586-1181, www.eiu.com; *Bosnia Herzegovina Country Report.*

Euromonitor International, Inc., 224 S. Michigan Avenue, Suite 1500, Chicago, IL 60604, (312) 922-1115, Fax: (312) 922-1157, www.euromonitor.com; *The World Economic Factbook 2008.*

Palgrave Macmillan Ltd., Houndmills, Basingstoke, Hampshire, RG21 6XS, England, (Telephone in U.S. (888) 330-8477), (Fax in U.S. (800) 672-2054), www.palgrave.com; *The Statesman's Yearbook 2008.*

United Nations Statistics Division, New York, NY 10017, (800) 253-9646, Fax: (212) 963-4116, http://unstats.un.org; *International Trade Statistics Yearbook* and *Trends in Europe and North America: The Statistical Yearbook of the ECE 2005.*

BOSNIA AND HERZEGOVINA - FERTILITY, HUMAN

Central Intelligence Agency, Office of Public Affairs, Washington, DC 20505, (703) 482-0623, Fax: (703) 482-1739, www.cia.gov; *The World Factbook.*

United Nations Statistics Division, New York, NY 10017, (800) 253-9646, Fax: (212) 963-4116, http://unstats.un.org; *Trends in Europe and North America: The Statistical Yearbook of the ECE 2005.*

The World Bank, 1818 H Street, NW, Washington, DC 20433, (202) 473-1000, Fax: (202) 477-6391, www.worldbank.org; *The World Bank Atlas 2003-2004.*

BOSNIA AND HERZEGOVINA - FERTILIZER INDUSTRY

United Nations Food and Agricultural Organization (FAO), Viale delle Terme di Caracalla, 00100 Rome, Italy, (Dial from U.S. (202) 653-2400), (Fax from U.S. (202) 653 5760), www.fao.org; *FAO Production Yearbook 2002.*

United Nations Statistics Division, New York, NY 10017, (800) 253-9646, Fax: (212) 963-4116, http://unstats.un.org; *2004 Industrial Commodity Statistics Yearbook* and *Statistical Yearbook.*

BOSNIA AND HERZEGOVINA - FINANCE

United Nations Statistics Division, New York, NY 10017, (800) 253-9646, Fax: (212) 963-4116, http://unstats.un.org; *National Accounts Statistics: Compendium of Income Distribution Statistics* and *Statistical Yearbook.*

The World Bank, 1818 H Street, NW, Washington, DC 20433, (202) 473-1000, Fax: (202) 477-6391, www.worldbank.org; *Bosnia and Herzegovina.*

BOSNIA AND HERZEGOVINA - FINANCE, PUBLIC

Bernan Essential Government Publications, 4611-F Assembly Drive, Lanham MD, 20706-4391, (301) 459-2255, Fax: (800) 865-3450, www.bernan.com; *National Accounts Statistics.*

Economist Intelligence Unit, 111 West 57th Street, New York, NY 10019, (212) 554-0600, Fax: (212) 586-1181, www.eiu.com; *Bosnia Herzegovina Country Report.*

International Monetary Fund (IMF), 700 Nineteenth Street, NW, Washington, DC 20431, (202) 623-7000, Fax: (202) 623-4661, www.imf.org; *International Financial Statistics* and *International Financial Statistics Online Service.*

Taylor and Francis Group, An Informa Business, 2 Park Square, Milton Park, Abingdon, Oxford OX14 4RN, United Kingdom, (Dial from U.S. (212) 216-7800), (Fax from U.S. (212) 564-7854), www.tandf.co.uk; *The Europa World Year Book.*

The World Bank, 1818 H Street, NW, Washington, DC 20433, (202) 473-1000, Fax: (202) 477-6391, www.worldbank.org; *Bosnia and Herzegovina.*

BOSNIA AND HERZEGOVINA - FISHERIES

United Nations Food and Agricultural Organization (FAO), Viale delle Terme di Caracalla, 00100 Rome, Italy, (Dial from U.S. (202) 653-2400), (Fax from U.S. (202) 653 5760), www.fao.org; *FAO Yearbook of Fishery Statistics;* Fishery Databases; FISHSTAT Database. Subjects covered include: Aquaculture production, capture production, fishery commodities; and *The State of Food and Agriculture (SOFA) 2006.*

United Nations Statistics Division, New York, NY 10017, (800) 253-9646, Fax: (212) 963-4116, http://unstats.un.org; *2004 Industrial Commodity Statistics Yearbook* and *Statistical Yearbook.*

The World Bank, 1818 H Street, NW, Washington, DC 20433, (202) 473-1000, Fax: (202) 477-6391, www.worldbank.org; *Bosnia and Herzegovina.*

BOSNIA AND HERZEGOVINA - FOOD

United Nations Food and Agricultural Organization (FAO), Viale delle Terme di Caracalla, 00100 Rome, Italy, (Dial from U.S. (202) 653-2400), (Fax from U.S. (202) 653 5760), www.fao.org; *FAO Production Yearbook 2002* and *The State of Food and Agriculture (SOFA) 2006.*

United Nations Statistics Division, New York, NY 10017, (800) 253-9646, Fax: (212) 963-4116, http://unstats.un.org; *2004 Industrial Commodity Statistics Yearbook.*

BOSNIA AND HERZEGOVINA - FOREIGN EXCHANGE RATES

Central Intelligence Agency, Office of Public Affairs, Washington, DC 20505, (703) 482-0623, Fax: (703) 482-1739, www.cia.gov; *The World Factbook.*

Euromonitor International, Inc., 224 S. Michigan Avenue, Suite 1500, Chicago, IL 60604, (312) 922-1115, Fax: (312) 922-1157, www.euromonitor.com; *The World Economic Factbook 2008.*

Taylor and Francis Group, An Informa Business, 2 Park Square, Milton Park, Abingdon, Oxford OX14 4RN, United Kingdom, (Dial from U.S. (212) 216-7800), (Fax from U.S. (212) 564-7854), www.tandf.co.uk; *The Europa World Year Book.*

United Nations Statistics Division, New York, NY 10017, (800) 253-9646, Fax: (212) 963-4116, http://unstats.un.org; *Statistical Yearbook; Trends in Europe and North America: The Statistical Yearbook of the ECE 2005;* and *World Statistics Pocketbook.*

BOSNIA AND HERZEGOVINA - FORESTS AND FORESTRY

UNESCO Institute for Statistics, C.P. 6128 Succursale Centre-Ville, Montreal, Quebec, H3C 3J7 Canada, (Dial from U.S. (514) 343-6880), (Fax from U.S. (514) 343 6882), www.uis.unesco.org; *Statistical Tables.*

United Nations Food and Agricultural Organization (FAO), Viale delle Terme di Caracalla, 00100 Rome, Italy, (Dial from U.S. (202) 653-2400), (Fax from U.S. (202) 653 5760), www.fao.org; *FAO Yearbook of Forest Products* and *The State of Food and Agriculture (SOFA) 2006.*

United Nations Statistics Division, New York, NY 10017, (800) 253-9646, Fax: (212) 963-4116, http://unstats.un.org; *2004 Industrial Commodity Statistics Yearbook; Statistical Yearbook;* and *Trends in Europe and North America: The Statistical Yearbook of the ECE 2005.*

The World Bank, 1818 H Street, NW, Washington, DC 20433, (202) 473-1000, Fax: (202) 477-6391, www.worldbank.org; *Bosnia and Herzegovina.*

BOSNIA AND HERZEGOVINA - GROSS DOMESTIC PRODUCT

Economist Intelligence Unit, 111 West 57th Street, New York, NY 10019, (212) 554-0600, Fax: (212) 586-1181, www.eiu.com; *Bosnia Herzegovina Country Report.*

Euromonitor International, Inc., 224 S. Michigan Avenue, Suite 1500, Chicago, IL 60604, (312) 922-1115, Fax: (312) 922-1157, www.euromonitor.com; *The World Economic Factbook 2008.*

United Nations Statistics Division, New York, NY 10017, (800) 253-9646, Fax: (212) 963-4116, http://unstats.un.org; *National Accounts Statistics: Compendium of Income Distribution Statistics; Statistical Yearbook;* and *Trends in Europe and North America: The Statistical Yearbook of the ECE 2005.*

BOSNIA AND HERZEGOVINA - GROSS NATIONAL PRODUCT

United Nations Statistics Division, New York, NY 10017, (800) 253-9646, Fax: (212) 963-4116, http://unstats.un.org; *Statistical Yearbook.*

The World Bank, 1818 H Street, NW, Washington, DC 20433, (202) 473-1000, Fax: (202) 477-6391, www.worldbank.org; *The World Bank Atlas 2003-2004.*

BOSNIA AND HERZEGOVINA - HOUSING

Euromonitor International, Inc., 224 S. Michigan Avenue, Suite 1500, Chicago, IL 60604, (312) 922-1115, Fax: (312) 922-1157, www.euromonitor.com; *World Marketing Data and Statistics.*

United Nations Statistics Division, New York, NY 10017, (800) 253-9646, Fax: (212) 963-4116, http://unstats.un.org; *Trends in Europe and North America: The Statistical Yearbook of the ECE 2005.*

BOSNIA AND HERZEGOVINA - ILLITERATE PERSONS

Central Intelligence Agency, Office of Public Affairs, Washington, DC 20505, (703) 482-0623, Fax: (703) 482-1739, www.cia.gov; *The World Factbook.*

Euromonitor International, Inc., 224 S. Michigan Avenue, Suite 1500, Chicago, IL 60604, (312) 922-1115, Fax: (312) 922-1157, www.euromonitor.com; *The World Economic Factbook 2008.*

UNESCO Institute for Statistics, C.P. 6128 Succursale Centre-Ville, Montreal, Quebec, H3C 3J7 Canada, (Dial from U.S. (514) 343-6880), (Fax from U.S. (514) 343 6882), www.uis.unesco.org; *Statistical Tables.*

BOSNIA AND HERZEGOVINA - IMPORTS

Central Intelligence Agency, Office of Public Affairs, Washington, DC 20505, (703) 482-0623, Fax: (703) 482-1739, www.cia.gov; *The World Factbook.*

Economist Intelligence Unit, 111 West 57th Street, New York, NY 10019, (212) 554-0600, Fax: (212) 586-1181, www.eiu.com; *Bosnia Herzegovina Country Report.*

Euromonitor International, Inc., 224 S. Michigan Avenue, Suite 1500, Chicago, IL 60604, (312) 922-1115, Fax: (312) 922-1157, www.euromonitor.com; *The World Economic Factbook 2008.*

Palgrave Macmillan Ltd., Houndmills, Basingstoke, Hampshire, RG21 6XS, England, (Telephone in U.S. (888) 330-8477), (Fax in U.S. (800) 672-2054), www.palgrave.com; *The Statesman's Yearbook 2008.*

United Nations Statistics Division, New York, NY 10017, (800) 253-9646, Fax: (212) 963-4116, http://unstats.un.org; *International Trade Statistics Yearbook* and *Trends in Europe and North America: The Statistical Yearbook of the ECE 2005.*

BOSNIA AND HERZEGOVINA - INDUSTRIAL PROPERTY

United Nations Statistics Division, New York, NY 10017, (800) 253-9646, Fax: (212) 963-4116, http://unstats.un.org; *Statistical Yearbook.*

BOSNIA AND HERZEGOVINA - INDUSTRIES

Central Intelligence Agency, Office of Public Affairs, Washington, DC 20505, (703) 482-0623, Fax: (703) 482-1739, www.cia.gov; *The World Factbook.*

Economist Intelligence Unit, 111 West 57th Street, New York, NY 10019, (212) 554-0600, Fax: (212) 586-1181, www.eiu.com; *Bosnia Herzegovina Country Report.*

Euromonitor International, Inc., 224 S. Michigan Avenue, Suite 1500, Chicago, IL 60604, (312) 922-1115, Fax: (312) 922-1157, www.euromonitor.com; *The World Economic Factbook 2008* and *World Marketing Data and Statistics.*

Palgrave Macmillan Ltd., Houndmills, Basingstoke, Hampshire, RG21 6XS, England, (Telephone in U.S. (888) 330-8477), (Fax in U.S. (800) 672-2054), www.palgrave.com; *The Statesman's Yearbook 2008.*

Taylor and Francis Group, An Informa Business, 2 Park Square, Milton Park, Abingdon, Oxford OX14 4RN, United Kingdom, (Dial from U.S. (212) 216-7800), (Fax from U.S. (212) 564-7854), www.tandf.co.uk; *The Europa World Year Book.*

United Nations Industrial Development Organization (UNIDO), 1 United Nations Plaza, New York, NY 10017, (212) 963 6890, Fax: (212) 963-7904, http://unido.org; Industrial Statistics Database 2008 (INDSTAT) and *The International Yearbook of Industrial Statistics 2008.*

United Nations Statistics Division, New York, NY 10017, (800) 253-9646, Fax: (212) 963-4116, http://unstats.un.org; *2004 Industrial Commodity Statistics Yearbook; Statistical Yearbook;* and *Trends in Europe and North America: The Statistical Yearbook of the ECE 2005.*

The World Bank, 1818 H Street, NW, Washington, DC 20433, (202) 473-1000, Fax: (202) 477-6391, www.worldbank.org; *Bosnia and Herzegovina.*

BOSNIA AND HERZEGOVINA - INTERNATIONAL TRADE

Economist Intelligence Unit, 111 West 57th Street, New York, NY 10019, (212) 554-0600, Fax: (212) 586-1181, www.eiu.com; *Bosnia Herzegovina Country Report.*

Euromonitor International, Inc., 224 S. Michigan Avenue, Suite 1500, Chicago, IL 60604, (312) 922-1115, Fax: (312) 922-1157, www.euromonitor.com; *The World Economic Factbook 2008* and *World Marketing Data and Statistics.*

United Nations Food and Agricultural Organization (FAO), Viale delle Terme di Caracalla, 00100 Rome,

Italy, (Dial from U.S. (202) 653-2400), (Fax from U.S. (202) 653 5760), www.fao.org; *FAO Trade Yearbook.*

United Nations Statistics Division, New York, NY 10017, (800) 253-9646, Fax: (212) 963-4116, http://unstats.un.org; *International Trade Statistics Yearbook* and *Statistical Yearbook.*

The World Bank, 1818 H Street, NW, Washington, DC 20433, (202) 473-1000, Fax: (202) 477-6391, www.worldbank.org; *Bosnia and Herzegovina.*

World Trade Organization (WTO), Centre William Rappard, Rue de Lausanne 154, CH-1211 Geneva 21, Switzerland, www.wto.org; *International Trade Statistics 2006.*

BOSNIA AND HERZEGOVINA - INTERNET USERS

International Telecommunication Union (ITU), Place des Nations, 1211 Geneva 20, Switzerland, www.itu.int; *World Telecommunication/ICT Indicators Database on CD-ROM; World Telecommunication/ICT Indicators Database Online;* and *Yearbook of Statistics - Telecommunication Services (Chronological Time Series 1997-2006).*

The World Bank, 1818 H Street, NW, Washington, DC 20433, (202) 473-1000, Fax: (202) 477-6391, www.worldbank.org; *Bosnia and Herzegovina.*

BOSNIA AND HERZEGOVINA - LABOR

Central Intelligence Agency, Office of Public Affairs, Washington, DC 20505, (703) 482-0623, Fax: (703) 482-1739, www.cia.gov; *The World Factbook.*

Euromonitor International, Inc., 224 S. Michigan Avenue, Suite 1500, Chicago, IL 60604, (312) 922-1115, Fax: (312) 922-1157, www.euromonitor.com; *World Marketing Data and Statistics.*

Palgrave Macmillan Ltd., Houndmills, Basingstoke, Hampshire, RG21 6XS, England, (Telephone in U.S. (888) 330-8477), (Fax in U.S. (800) 672-2054), www.palgrave.com; *The Statesman's Yearbook 2008.*

United Nations Statistics Division, New York, NY 10017, (800) 253-9646, Fax: (212) 963-4116, http://unstats.un.org; *Statistical Yearbook.*

The World Bank, 1818 H Street, NW, Washington, DC 20433, (202) 473-1000, Fax: (202) 477-6391, www.worldbank.org; *The World Bank Atlas 2003-2004.*

BOSNIA AND HERZEGOVINA - LAND USE

Central Intelligence Agency, Office of Public Affairs, Washington, DC 20505, (703) 482-0623, Fax: (703) 482-1739, www.cia.gov; *The World Factbook.*

United Nations Food and Agricultural Organization (FAO), Viale delle Terme di Caracalla, 00100 Rome, Italy, (Dial from U.S. (202) 653-2400), (Fax from U.S. (202) 653 5760), www.fao.org; *FAO Production Yearbook 2002.*

BOSNIA AND HERZEGOVINA - LIBRARIES

UNESCO Institute for Statistics, C.P. 6128 Succursale Centre-Ville, Montreal, Quebec, H3C 3J7 Canada, (Dial from U.S. (514) 343-6880), (Fax from U.S. (514) 343 6882), www.uis.unesco.org; *Statistical Tables.*

United Nations Statistics Division, New York, NY 10017, (800) 253-9646, Fax: (212) 963-4116, http://unstats.un.org; *Trends in Europe and North America: The Statistical Yearbook of the ECE 2005.*

BOSNIA AND HERZEGOVINA - LIFE EXPECTANCY

Central Intelligence Agency, Office of Public Affairs, Washington, DC 20505, (703) 482-0623, Fax: (703) 482-1739, www.cia.gov; *The World Factbook.*

Euromonitor International, Inc., 224 S. Michigan Avenue, Suite 1500, Chicago, IL 60604, (312) 922-1115, Fax: (312) 922-1157, www.euromonitor.com; *The World Economic Factbook 2008.*

United Nations Statistics Division, New York, NY 10017, (800) 253-9646, Fax: (212) 963-4116, http://unstats.un.org; *Demographic Yearbook; Trends in Europe and North America: The Statistical Yearbook of the ECE 2005;* and *World Statistics Pocketbook.*

The World Bank, 1818 H Street, NW, Washington, DC 20433, (202) 473-1000, Fax: (202) 477-6391, www.worldbank.org; *The World Bank Atlas 2003-2004.*

BOSNIA AND HERZEGOVINA - LITERACY

Euromonitor International, Inc., 224 S. Michigan Avenue, Suite 1500, Chicago, IL 60604, (312) 922-1115, Fax: (312) 922-1157, www.euromonitor.com; *World Marketing Data and Statistics.*

BOSNIA AND HERZEGOVINA - LIVESTOCK

Palgrave Macmillan Ltd., Houndmills, Basingstoke, Hampshire, RG21 6XS, England, (Telephone in U.S. (888) 330-8477), (Fax in U.S. (800) 672-2054), www.palgrave.com; *The Statesman's Yearbook 2008.*

Taylor and Francis Group, An Informa Business, 2 Park Square, Milton Park, Abingdon, Oxford OX14 4RN, United Kingdom, (Dial from U.S. (212) 216-7800), (Fax from U.S. (212) 564-7854), www.tandf.co.uk; *The Europa World Year Book.*

United Nations Food and Agricultural Organization (FAO), Viale delle Terme di Caracalla, 00100 Rome, Italy, (Dial from U.S. (202) 653-2400), (Fax from U.S. (202) 653 5760), www.fao.org; *FAO Production Yearbook 2002* and *The State of Food and Agriculture (SOFA) 2006.*

United Nations Statistics Division, New York, NY 10017, (800) 253-9646, Fax: (212) 963-4116, http://unstats.un.org; *2004 Industrial Commodity Statistics Yearbook* and *Statistical Yearbook.*

BOSNIA AND HERZEGOVINA - MACHINERY

United Nations Statistics Division, New York, NY 10017, (800) 253-9646, Fax: (212) 963-4116, http://unstats.un.org; *2004 Industrial Commodity Statistics Yearbook.*

BOSNIA AND HERZEGOVINA - MANUFACTURES

United Nations Statistics Division, New York, NY 10017, (800) 253-9646, Fax: (212) 963-4116, http://unstats.un.org; *2004 Industrial Commodity Statistics Yearbook* and *Statistical Yearbook.*

BOSNIA AND HERZEGOVINA - MARRIAGE

United Nations Statistics Division, New York, NY 10017, (800) 253-9646, Fax: (212) 963-4116, http://unstats.un.org; *Demographic Yearbook; Statistical Yearbook;* and *Trends in Europe and North America: The Statistical Yearbook of the ECE 2005.*

BOSNIA AND HERZEGOVINA - MINERAL INDUSTRIES

Platts, 2 Penn Plaza, 25th Floor, New York, NY 10121-2298, (212) 904-3070, www.platts.com; *Energy Economist* and *Energy in East Europe.*

Taylor and Francis Group, An Informa Business, 2 Park Square, Milton Park, Abingdon, Oxford OX14 4RN, United Kingdom, (Dial from U.S. (212) 216-7800), (Fax from U.S. (212) 564-7854), www.tandf.co.uk; *The Europa World Year Book.*

United Nations Statistics Division, New York, NY 10017, (800) 253-9646, Fax: (212) 963-4116, http://unstats.un.org; *Energy Statistics Yearbook 2003; 2004 Industrial Commodity Statistics Yearbook;* and *Statistical Yearbook.*

The World Bank, 1818 H Street, NW, Washington, DC 20433, (202) 473-1000, Fax: (202) 477-6391, www.worldbank.org; *Bosnia and Herzegovina.*

BOSNIA AND HERZEGOVINA - MONEY SUPPLY

Economist Intelligence Unit, 111 West 57th Street, New York, NY 10019, (212) 554-0600, Fax: (212) 586-1181, www.eiu.com; *Bosnia Herzegovina Country Report.*

The World Bank, 1818 H Street, NW, Washington, DC 20433, (202) 473-1000, Fax: (202) 477-6391, www.worldbank.org; *Bosnia and Herzegovina.*

BOSNIA AND HERZEGOVINA - MONUMENTS AND HISTORIC SITES

UNESCO Institute for Statistics, C.P. 6128 Succursale Centre-Ville, Montreal, Quebec, H3C 3J7 Canada, (Dial from U.S. (514) 343-6880), (Fax from U.S. (514) 343 6882), www.uis.unesco.org; *Statistical Tables.*

BOSNIA AND HERZEGOVINA - MORTALITY

Central Intelligence Agency, Office of Public Affairs, Washington, DC 20505, (703) 482-0623, Fax: (703) 482-1739, www.cia.gov; *The World Factbook.*

Euromonitor International, Inc., 224 S. Michigan Avenue, Suite 1500, Chicago, IL 60604, (312) 922-1115, Fax: (312) 922-1157, www.euromonitor.com; *The World Economic Factbook 2008.*

Palgrave Macmillan Ltd., Houndmills, Basingstoke, Hampshire, RG21 6XS, England, (Telephone in U.S. (888) 330-8477), (Fax in U.S. (800) 672-2054), www.palgrave.com; *The Statesman's Yearbook 2008.*

UNICEF, 3 United Nations Plaza, New York, NY 10017, (800) 253-9646, Fax: (212) 887-7465, www.unicef.org; *The State of the World's Children 2008.*

United Nations Statistics Division, New York, NY 10017, (800) 253-9646, Fax: (212) 963-4116, http://unstats.un.org; *Demographic Yearbook; Statistical Yearbook; Trends in Europe and North America: The Statistical Yearbook of the ECE 2005;* and *World Statistics Pocketbook.*

The World Bank, 1818 H Street, NW, Washington, DC 20433, (202) 473-1000, Fax: (202) 477-6391, www.worldbank.org; *The World Bank Atlas 2003-2004.*

World Health Organization (WHO), Avenue Appia 20, 1211 Geneve 27, Switzerland, (Telephone in U.S. (212) 331-9081), www.who.int; The WHO Global Atlas of Infectious Diseases.

BOSNIA AND HERZEGOVINA - MOTION PICTURES

UNESCO Institute for Statistics, C.P. 6128 Succursale Centre-Ville, Montreal, Quebec, H3C 3J7 Canada, (Dial from U.S. (514) 343-6880), (Fax from U.S. (514) 343 6882), www.uis.unesco.org; *Statistical Tables.*

United Nations Statistics Division, New York, NY 10017, (800) 253-9646, Fax: (212) 963-4116, http://unstats.un.org; *Statistical Yearbook.*

BOSNIA AND HERZEGOVINA - MUSEUMS

UNESCO Institute for Statistics, C.P. 6128 Succursale Centre-Ville, Montreal, Quebec, H3C 3J7 Canada, (Dial from U.S. (514) 343-6880), (Fax from U.S. (514) 343 6882), www.uis.unesco.org; *Statistical Tables.*

BOSNIA AND HERZEGOVINA - PERIODICALS

UNESCO Institute for Statistics, C.P. 6128 Succursale Centre-Ville, Montreal, Quebec, H3C 3J7 Canada, (Dial from U.S. (514) 343-6880), (Fax from U.S. (514) 343 6882), www.uis.unesco.org; *Statistical Tables.*

BOSNIA AND HERZEGOVINA - PETROLEUM INDUSTRY AND TRADE

PennWell Corporation, 1421 South Sheridan Road, Tulsa, OK 74112, (918) 835-3161, www.pennwell.com; *International Petroleum Encyclopedia 2007.*

Platts, 2 Penn Plaza, 25th Floor, New York, NY 10121-2298, (212) 904-3070, www.platts.com; *Energy Economist.*

U.S. Department of Energy (DOE), Energy Information Administration (EIA), 1000 Independence Avenue, SW, Washington, DC 20585, (202) 586-

8800, www.eia.doe.gov; *International Energy Annual 2004* and *International Energy Outlook 2006.*

United Nations Food and Agricultural Organization (FAO), Viale delle Terme di Caracalla, 00100 Rome, Italy, (Dial from U.S. (202) 653-2400), (Fax from U.S. (202) 653 5760), www.fao.org; *The State of Food and Agriculture (SOFA) 2006.*

United Nations Statistics Division, New York, NY 10017, (800) 253-9646, Fax: (212) 963-4116, http://unstats.un.org; *Energy Statistics Yearbook 2003; 2004 Industrial Commodity Statistics Yearbook; Statistical Yearbook;* and *Trends in Europe and North America: The Statistical Yearbook of the ECE 2005.*

BOSNIA AND HERZEGOVINA - POLITICAL SCIENCE

Central Intelligence Agency, Office of Public Affairs, Washington, DC 20505, (703) 482-0623, Fax: (703) 482-1739, www.cia.gov; *The World Factbook.*

Palgrave Macmillan Ltd., Houndmills, Basingstoke, Hampshire, RG21 6XS, England, (Telephone in U.S. (888) 330-8477), (Fax in U.S. (800) 672-2054), www.palgrave.com; *The Statesman's Yearbook 2008.*

United Nations Statistics Division, New York, NY 10017, (800) 253-9646, Fax: (212) 963-4116, http://unstats.un.org; *Statistical Yearbook.*

BOSNIA AND HERZEGOVINA - POPULATION

Central Intelligence Agency, Office of Public Affairs, Washington, DC 20505, (703) 482-0623, Fax: (703) 482-1739, www.cia.gov; *The World Factbook.*

Economist Intelligence Unit, 111 West 57th Street, New York, NY 10019, (212) 554-0600, Fax: (212) 586-1181, www.eiu.com; *Bosnia Herzegovina Country Report.*

Euromonitor International, Inc., 224 S. Michigan Avenue, Suite 1500, Chicago, IL 60604, (312) 922-1115, Fax: (312) 922-1157, www.euromonitor.com; *The World Economic Factbook 2008.*

Palgrave Macmillan Ltd., Houndmills, Basingstoke, Hampshire, RG21 6XS, England, (Telephone in U.S. (888) 330-8477), (Fax in U.S. (800) 672-2054), www.palgrave.com; *The Statesman's Yearbook 2008.*

Taylor and Francis Group, An Informa Business, 2 Park Square, Milton Park, Abingdon, Oxford OX14 4RN, United Kingdom, (Dial from U.S. (212) 216-7800), (Fax from U.S. (212) 564-7854), www.tandf.co.uk; *The Europa World Year Book.*

UNESCO Institute for Statistics, C.P. 6128 Succursale Centre-Ville, Montreal, Quebec, H3C 3J7 Canada, (Dial from U.S. (514) 343-6880), (Fax from U.S. (514) 343 6882), www.uis.unesco.org; *Statistical Tables.*

United Nations Food and Agricultural Organization (FAO), Viale delle Terme di Caracalla, 00100 Rome, Italy, (Dial from U.S. (202) 653-2400), (Fax from U.S. (202) 653 5760), www.fao.org; *FAO Production Yearbook 2002.*

United Nations Statistics Division, New York, NY 10017, (800) 253-9646, Fax: (212) 963-4116, http://unstats.un.org; *Demographic Yearbook; Statistical Yearbook; Trends in Europe and North America: The Statistical Yearbook of the ECE 2005;* and *World Statistics Pocketbook.*

The World Bank, 1818 H Street, NW, Washington, DC 20433, (202) 473-1000, Fax: (202) 477-6391, www.worldbank.org; *Bosnia and Herzegovina* and *The World Bank Atlas 2003-2004.*

BOSNIA AND HERZEGOVINA - POPULATION DENSITY

Central Intelligence Agency, Office of Public Affairs, Washington, DC 20505, (703) 482-0623, Fax: (703) 482-1739, www.cia.gov; *The World Factbook.*

Euromonitor International, Inc., 224 S. Michigan Avenue, Suite 1500, Chicago, IL 60604, (312) 922-1115, Fax: (312) 922-1157, www.euromonitor.com; *The World Economic Factbook 2008.*

Palgrave Macmillan Ltd., Houndmills, Basingstoke, Hampshire, RG21 6XS, England, (Telephone in U.S. (888) 330-8477), (Fax in U.S. (800) 672-2054), www.palgrave.com; *The Statesman's Yearbook 2008.*

Taylor and Francis Group, An Informa Business, 2 Park Square, Milton Park, Abingdon, Oxford OX14 4RN, United Kingdom, (Dial from U.S. (212) 216-7800), (Fax from U.S. (212) 564-7854), www.tandf.co.uk; *The Europa World Year Book.*

UNESCO Institute for Statistics, C.P. 6128 Succursale Centre-Ville, Montreal, Quebec, H3C 3J7 Canada, (Dial from U.S. (514) 343-6880), (Fax from U.S. (514) 343 6882), www.uis.unesco.org; *Statistical Tables.*

United Nations Statistics Division, New York, NY 10017, (800) 253-9646, Fax: (212) 963-4116, http://unstats.un.org; *Statistical Yearbook* and *Trends in Europe and North America: The Statistical Yearbook of the ECE 2005.*

The World Bank, 1818 H Street, NW, Washington, DC 20433, (202) 473-1000, Fax: (202) 477-6391, www.worldbank.org; *Bosnia and Herzegovina.*

BOSNIA AND HERZEGOVINA - POSTAL SERVICE

United Nations Statistics Division, New York, NY 10017, (800) 253-9646, Fax: (212) 963-4116, http://unstats.un.org; *Statistical Yearbook* and *Trends in Europe and North America: The Statistical Yearbook of the ECE 2005.*

BOSNIA AND HERZEGOVINA - POWER RESOURCES

Euromonitor International, Inc., 224 S. Michigan Avenue, Suite 1500, Chicago, IL 60604, (312) 922-1115, Fax: (312) 922-1157, www.euromonitor.com; *The World Economic Factbook 2008* and *World Marketing Data and Statistics.*

Platts, 2 Penn Plaza, 25th Floor, New York, NY 10121-2298, (212) 904-3070, www.platts.com; *Energy Economist* and *European Power Daily.*

U.S. Department of Energy (DOE), Energy Information Administration (EIA), 1000 Independence Avenue, SW, Washington, DC 20585, (202) 586-8800, www.eia.doe.gov; *International Energy Annual 2004* and *International Energy Outlook 2006.*

United Nations Statistics Division, New York, NY 10017, (800) 253-9646, Fax: (212) 963-4116, http://unstats.un.org; *Energy Statistics Yearbook 2003; Statistical Yearbook; Trends in Europe and North America: The Statistical Yearbook of the ECE 2005;* and *World Statistics Pocketbook.*

The World Bank, 1818 H Street, NW, Washington, DC 20433, (202) 473-1000, Fax: (202) 477-6391, www.worldbank.org; *The World Bank Atlas 2003-2004.*

BOSNIA AND HERZEGOVINA - PRICES

United Nations Food and Agricultural Organization (FAO), Viale delle Terme di Caracalla, 00100 Rome, Italy, (Dial from U.S. (202) 653-2400), (Fax from U.S. (202) 653 5760), www.fao.org; *FAO Production Yearbook 2002.*

The World Bank, 1818 H Street, NW, Washington, DC 20433, (202) 473-1000, Fax: (202) 477-6391, www.worldbank.org; *Bosnia and Herzegovina.*

BOSNIA AND HERZEGOVINA - PROFESSIONS

United Nations Statistics Division, New York, NY 10017, (800) 253-9646, Fax: (212) 963-4116, http://unstats.un.org; *Statistical Yearbook.*

BOSNIA AND HERZEGOVINA - PUBLIC HEALTH

Euromonitor International, Inc., 224 S. Michigan Avenue, Suite 1500, Chicago, IL 60604, (312) 922-1115, Fax: (312) 922-1157, www.euromonitor.com; *World Marketing Data and Statistics.*

Palgrave Macmillan Ltd., Houndmills, Basingstoke, Hampshire, RG21 6XS, England, (Telephone in U.S. (888) 330-8477), (Fax in U.S. (800) 672-2054), www.palgrave.com; *The Statesman's Yearbook 2008.*

UNICEF, 3 United Nations Plaza, New York, NY 10017, (800) 253-9646, Fax: (212) 887-7465, www.unicef.org; *The State of the World's Children 2008.*

United Nations Statistics Division, New York, NY 10017, (800) 253-9646, Fax: (212) 963-4116, http://unstats.un.org; *Statistical Yearbook* and *Trends in Europe and North America: The Statistical Yearbook of the ECE 2005.*

The World Bank, 1818 H Street, NW, Washington, DC 20433, (202) 473-1000, Fax: (202) 477-6391, www.worldbank.org; *Bosnia and Herzegovina.*

World Health Organization (WHO), Avenue Appia 20, 1211 Geneve 27, Switzerland, (Telephone in U.S. (212) 331-9081), www.who.int; The WHO Global Atlas of Infectious Diseases.

BOSNIA AND HERZEGOVINA - PUBLISHERS AND PUBLISHING

UNESCO Institute for Statistics, C.P. 6128 Succursale Centre-Ville, Montreal, Quebec, H3C 3J7 Canada, (Dial from U.S. (514) 343-6880), (Fax from U.S. (514) 343 6882), www.uis.unesco.org; *Statistical Tables.*

United Nations Statistics Division, New York, NY 10017, (800) 253-9646, Fax: (212) 963-4116, http://unstats.un.org; *Trends in Europe and North America: The Statistical Yearbook of the ECE 2005.*

BOSNIA AND HERZEGOVINA - RADIO - RECEIVERS AND RECEPTION

United Nations Statistics Division, New York, NY 10017, (800) 253-9646, Fax: (212) 963-4116, http://unstats.un.org; *Statistical Yearbook.*

BOSNIA AND HERZEGOVINA - RAILROADS

Palgrave Macmillan Ltd., Houndmills, Basingstoke, Hampshire, RG21 6XS, England, (Telephone in U.S. (888) 330-8477), (Fax in U.S. (800) 672-2054), www.palgrave.com; *The Statesman's Yearbook 2008.*

United Nations Statistics Division, New York, NY 10017, (800) 253-9646, Fax: (212) 963-4116, http://unstats.un.org; *Annual Bulletin of Transport Statistics for Europe and North America 2004; Statistical Yearbook;* and *Trends in Europe and North America: The Statistical Yearbook of the ECE 2005.*

BOSNIA AND HERZEGOVINA - RELIGION

Central Intelligence Agency, Office of Public Affairs, Washington, DC 20505, (703) 482-0623, Fax: (703) 482-1739, www.cia.gov; *The World Factbook.*

BOSNIA AND HERZEGOVINA - RETAIL TRADE

Euromonitor International, Inc., 224 S. Michigan Avenue, Suite 1500, Chicago, IL 60604, (312) 922-1115, Fax: (312) 922-1157, www.euromonitor.com; *World Marketing Data and Statistics.*

United Nations Statistics Division, New York, NY 10017, (800) 253-9646, Fax: (212) 963-4116, http://unstats.un.org; *Statistical Yearbook.*

BOSNIA AND HERZEGOVINA - ROADS

Central Intelligence Agency, Office of Public Affairs, Washington, DC 20505, (703) 482-0623, Fax: (703) 482-1739, www.cia.gov; *The World Factbook.*

Palgrave Macmillan Ltd., Houndmills, Basingstoke, Hampshire, RG21 6XS, England, (Telephone in U.S. (888) 330-8477), (Fax in U.S. (800) 672-2054), www.palgrave.com; *The Statesman's Yearbook 2008.*

United Nations Statistics Division, New York, NY 10017, (800) 253-9646, Fax: (212) 963-4116, http://unstats.un.org; *Annual Bulletin of Transport Statistics for Europe and North America 2004* and *Trends in Europe and North America: The Statistical Yearbook of the ECE 2005.*

BOSNIA AND HERZEGOVINA - RUBBER INDUSTRY AND TRADE

International Rubber Study Group (IRSG), 1st Floor, Heron House, 109/115 Wembley Hill Road, Wemb-

ley, Middlesex HA9 8DA, United Kingdom, www.rubberstudy.com; *Rubber Statistical Bulletin; Summary of World Rubber Statistics 2005; World Rubber Statistics Handbook (Volume 6, 1975-2001);* and *World Rubber Statistics Historic Handbook.*

United Nations Statistics Division, New York, NY 10017, (800) 253-9646, Fax: (212) 963-4116, http://unstats.un.org; *Statistical Yearbook.*

BOSNIA AND HERZEGOVINA - SHIPPING

United Nations Statistics Division, New York, NY 10017, (800) 253-9646, Fax: (212) 963-4116, http://unstats.un.org; *Annual Bulletin of Transport Statistics for Europe and North America 2004* and *Statistical Yearbook.*

BOSNIA AND HERZEGOVINA - SOCIAL ECOLOGY

United Nations Statistics Division, New York, NY 10017, (800) 253-9646, Fax: (212) 963-4116, http://unstats.un.org; *World Statistics Pocketbook.*

BOSNIA AND HERZEGOVINA - TELEPHONE

United Nations Statistics Division, New York, NY 10017, (800) 253-9646, Fax: (212) 963-4116, http://unstats.un.org; *Statistical Yearbook; Trends in Europe and North America: The Statistical Yearbook of the ECE 2005;* and *World Statistics Pocketbook.*

BOSNIA AND HERZEGOVINA - TEXTILE INDUSTRY

Palgrave Macmillan Ltd., Houndmills, Basingstoke, Hampshire, RG21 6XS, England, (Telephone in U.S. (888) 330-8477), (Fax in U.S. (800) 672-2054), www.palgrave.com; *The Statesman's Yearbook 2008.*

United Nations Statistics Division, New York, NY 10017, (800) 253-9646, Fax: (212) 963-4116, http://unstats.un.org; *2004 Industrial Commodity Statistics Yearbook* and *Statistical Yearbook.*

BOSNIA AND HERZEGOVINA - THEATER

UNESCO Institute for Statistics, C.P. 6128 Succursale Centre-Ville, Montreal, Quebec, H3C 3J7 Canada, (Dial from U.S. (514) 343-6880), (Fax from U.S. (514) 343 6882), www.uis.unesco.org; *Statistical Tables.*

BOSNIA AND HERZEGOVINA - TIRE INDUSTRY

United Nations Statistics Division, New York, NY 10017, (800) 253-9646, Fax: (212) 963-4116, http://unstats.un.org; *Statistical Yearbook.*

BOSNIA AND HERZEGOVINA - TOBACCO INDUSTRY

Foreign Agricultural Service (FAS), U.S. Department of Agriculture (USDA), 1400 Independence Avenue, SW, Washington, DC 20250, (202) 720-3935, www.fas.usda.gov; *Tobacco: World Markets and Trade.*

United Nations Statistics Division, New York, NY 10017, (800) 253-9646, Fax: (212) 963-4116, http://unstats.un.org; *Statistical Yearbook.*

BOSNIA AND HERZEGOVINA - TOURISM

Euromonitor International, Inc., 224 S. Michigan Avenue, Suite 1500, Chicago, IL 60604, (312) 922-1115, Fax: (312) 922-1157, www.euromonitor.com; *The World Economic Factbook 2008* and *World Marketing Data and Statistics.*

United Nations Statistics Division, New York, NY 10017, (800) 253-9646, Fax: (212) 963-4116, http://unstats.un.org; *Statistical Yearbook* and *Trends in Europe and North America: The Statistical Yearbook of the ECE 2005.*

The World Bank, 1818 H Street, NW, Washington, DC 20433, (202) 473-1000, Fax: (202) 477-6391, www.worldbank.org; *Bosnia and Herzegovina.*

BOSNIA AND HERZEGOVINA - TRANSPORTATION

Central Intelligence Agency, Office of Public Affairs, Washington, DC 20505, (703) 482-0623, Fax: (703) 482-1739, www.cia.gov; *The World Factbook.*

Euromonitor International, Inc., 224 S. Michigan Avenue, Suite 1500, Chicago, IL 60604, (312) 922-1115, Fax: (312) 922-1157, www.euromonitor.com; *World Marketing Data and Statistics.*

Palgrave Macmillan Ltd., Houndmills, Basingstoke, Hampshire, RG21 6XS, England, (Telephone in U.S. (888) 330-8477), (Fax in U.S. (800) 672-2054), www.palgrave.com; *The Statesman's Yearbook 2008.*

United Nations Statistics Division, New York, NY 10017, (800) 253-9646, Fax: (212) 963-4116, http://unstats.un.org; *Annual Bulletin of Transport Statistics for Europe and North America 2004* and *Trends in Europe and North America: The Statistical Yearbook of the ECE 2005.*

The World Bank, 1818 H Street, NW, Washington, DC 20433, (202) 473-1000, Fax: (202) 477-6391, www.worldbank.org; *Bosnia and Herzegovina.*

BOSNIA AND HERZEGOVINA - UNEMPLOYMENT

Central Intelligence Agency, Office of Public Affairs, Washington, DC 20505, (703) 482-0623, Fax: (703) 482-1739, www.cia.gov; *The World Factbook.*

Palgrave Macmillan Ltd., Houndmills, Basingstoke, Hampshire, RG21 6XS, England, (Telephone in U.S. (888) 330-8477), (Fax in U.S. (800) 672-2054), www.palgrave.com; *The Statesman's Yearbook 2008.*

United Nations Statistics Division, New York, NY 10017, (800) 253-9646, Fax: (212) 963-4116, http://unstats.un.org; *Statistical Yearbook* and *Trends in Europe and North America: The Statistical Yearbook of the ECE 2005.*

The World Bank, 1818 H Street, NW, Washington, DC 20433, (202) 473-1000, Fax: (202) 477-6391, www.worldbank.org; *Bosnia and Herzegovina.*

BOSNIA AND HERZEGOVINA - VITAL STATISTICS

Palgrave Macmillan Ltd., Houndmills, Basingstoke, Hampshire, RG21 6XS, England, (Telephone in U.S. (888) 330-8477), (Fax in U.S. (800) 672-2054), www.palgrave.com; *The Statesman's Yearbook 2008.*

United Nations Statistics Division, New York, NY 10017, (800) 253-9646, Fax: (212) 963-4116, http://unstats.un.org; *Statistical Yearbook.*

BOSNIA AND HERZEGOVINA - WAGES

United Nations Statistics Division, New York, NY 10017, (800) 253-9646, Fax: (212) 963-4116, http://unstats.un.org; *Statistical Yearbook.*

The World Bank, 1818 H Street, NW, Washington, DC 20433, (202) 473-1000, Fax: (202) 477-6391, www.worldbank.org; *Bosnia and Herzegovina.*

BOSNIA AND HERZEGOVINA - WELFARE STATE

Palgrave Macmillan Ltd., Houndmills, Basingstoke, Hampshire, RG21 6XS, England, (Telephone in U.S. (888) 330-8477), (Fax in U.S. (800) 672-2054), www.palgrave.com; *The Statesman's Yearbook 2008.*

BOSNIA AND HERZEGOVINA - WHOLESALE PRICE INDEXES

United Nations Statistics Division, New York, NY 10017, (800) 253-9646, Fax: (212) 963-4116, http://unstats.un.org; *Statistical Yearbook.*

BOSNIA AND HERZEGOVINA - WHOLESALE TRADE

United Nations Statistics Division, New York, NY 10017, (800) 253-9646, Fax: (212) 963-4116, http://unstats.un.org; *Statistical Yearbook.*

BOTSWANA - NATIONAL STATISTICAL OFFICE

Central Statistics Office (CSO), Ministry of Finance and Development Planning, Private Bag 0024, Gaborone, Botswana, www.cso.gov.bw; National Data Center.

BOTSWANA - PRIMARY STATISTICS SOURCES

Central Statistics Office (CSO), Ministry of Finance and Development Planning, Private Bag 0024, Gaborone, Botswana, www.cso.gov.bw; *Statistical Year Book* and *Stats Update.*

BOTSWANA - AGRICULTURAL MACHINERY

United Nations Statistics Division, New York, NY 10017, (800) 253-9646, Fax: (212) 963-4116, http://unstats.un.org; *Statistical Yearbook.*

BOTSWANA - AGRICULTURE

Economist Intelligence Unit, 111 West 57th Street, New York, NY 10019, (212) 554-0600, Fax: (212) 586-1181, www.eiu.com; *Botswana Country Report.*

Euromonitor International, Inc., 224 S. Michigan Avenue, Suite 1500, Chicago, IL 60604, (312) 922-1115, Fax: (312) 922-1157, www.euromonitor.com; *World Marketing Data and Statistics.*

M.E. Sharpe, 80 Business Park Drive, Armonk, NY 10504, (800) 541-6563, Fax: (914) 273-2106, www.mesharpe.com; *The Illustrated Book of World Rankings.*

Palgrave Macmillan Ltd., Houndmills, Basingstoke, Hampshire, RG21 6XS, England, (Telephone in U.S. (888) 330-8477), (Fax in U.S. (800) 672-2054), www.palgrave.com; *The Statesman's Yearbook 2008.*

Taylor and Francis Group, An Informa Business, 2 Park Square, Milton Park, Abingdon, Oxford OX14 4RN, United Kingdom, (Dial from U.S. (212) 216-7800), (Fax from U.S. (212) 564-7854), www.tandf.co.uk; *The Europa World Year Book.*

United Nations Conference on Trade and Development (UNCTAD), DC2-1120, United Nations, New York, NY 10017, (212) 963-0027, www.unctad.org; *UNCTAD Commodity Yearbook.*

United Nations Economic Commission for Africa (ECA), PO Box 3001, Addis Ababa, Ethiopia, (Telephone in U.S. (212) 963-4957), www.uneca.org; *African Statistical Yearbook 2006.*

United Nations Food and Agricultural Organization (FAO), Viale delle Terme di Caracalla, 00100 Rome, Italy, (Dial from U.S. (202) 653-2400), (Fax from U.S. (202) 653 5760), www.fao.org; AQUASTAT; *FAO Production Yearbook 2002; FAO Trade Yearbook;* and *The State of Food and Agriculture (SOFA) 2006.*

United Nations Statistics Division, New York, NY 10017, (800) 253-9646, Fax: (212) 963-4116, http://unstats.un.org; *Statistical Yearbook* and *Survey of Economic and Social Conditions in Africa 2005.*

The World Bank, 1818 H Street, NW, Washington, DC 20433, (202) 473-1000, Fax: (202) 477-6391, www.worldbank.org; *Africa Live Database (LDB); African Development Indicators (ADI) 2007; Botswana;* and *World Development Indicators (WDI) 2008.*

BOTSWANA - AIRLINES

M.E. Sharpe, 80 Business Park Drive, Armonk, NY 10504, (800) 541-6563, Fax: (914) 273-2106, www.mesharpe.com; *The Illustrated Book of World Rankings.*

Palgrave Macmillan Ltd., Houndmills, Basingstoke, Hampshire, RG21 6XS, England, (Telephone in U.S. (888) 330-8477), (Fax in U.S. (800) 672-2054), www.palgrave.com; *The Statesman's Yearbook 2008.*

Taylor and Francis Group, An Informa Business, 2 Park Square, Milton Park, Abingdon, Oxford OX14 4RN, United Kingdom, (Dial from U.S. (212) 216-7800), (Fax from U.S. (212) 564-7854), www.tandf.co.uk; *The Europa World Year Book.*

United Nations Economic Commission for Africa (ECA), PO Box 3001, Addis Ababa, Ethiopia, (Telephone in U.S. (212) 963-4957), www.uneca.org; *African Statistical Yearbook 2006.*

BOTSWANA - AIRPORTS

Central Intelligence Agency, Office of Public Affairs, Washington, DC 20505, (703) 482-0623, Fax: (703) 482-1739, www.cia.gov; *The World Factbook.*

BOTSWANA - ALUMINUM PRODUCTION

See BOTSWANA - MINERAL INDUSTRIES

BOTSWANA - ARMED FORCES

Central Intelligence Agency, Office of Public Affairs, Washington, DC 20505, (703) 482-0623, Fax: (703) 482-1739, www.cia.gov; *The World Factbook.*

Euromonitor International, Inc., 224 S. Michigan Avenue, Suite 1500, Chicago, IL 60604, (312) 922-1115, Fax: (312) 922-1157, www.euromonitor.com; *World Marketing Data and Statistics.*

International Institute for Strategic Studies (IISS), Arundel House, 13-15 Arundel Street, Temple Place, London WC2R 3DX, England, www.iiss.org; *The Military Balance 2007.*

International Monetary Fund (IMF), 700 Nineteenth Street, NW, Washington, DC 20431, (202) 623-7000, Fax: (202) 623-4661, www.imf.org; *Government Finance Statistics Yearbook (2008 Edition).*

Palgrave Macmillan Ltd., Houndmills, Basingstoke, Hampshire, RG21 6XS, England, (Telephone in U.S. (888) 330-8477), (Fax in U.S. (800) 672-2054), www.palgrave.com; *The Statesman's Yearbook 2008.*

U.S. Department of State (DOS), 2201 C Street NW, Washington, DC 20520, (202) 647-4000, www.state.gov; *World Military Expenditures and Arms Transfers (WMEAT).*

United Nations Statistics Division, New York, NY 10017, (800) 253-9646, Fax: (212) 963-4116, http://unstats.un.org; *Human Development Report 2006.*

BOTSWANA - BALANCE OF PAYMENTS

African Development Bank Group, Rue Joseph Anoma, 01 BP 1387 Abidjan 01, Cote d'Ivoire, www.afdb.org; *Statistics Pocketbook 2008.*

International Monetary Fund (IMF), 700 Nineteenth Street, NW, Washington, DC 20431, (202) 623-7000, Fax: (202) 623-4661, www.imf.org; *Balance of Payments Statistics Newsletter* and *Balance of Payments Statistics Yearbook 2007.*

Taylor and Francis Group, An Informa Business, 2 Park Square, Milton Park, Abingdon, Oxford OX14 4RN, United Kingdom, (Dial from U.S. (212) 216-7800), (Fax from U.S. (212) 564-7854), www.tandf.co.uk; *The Europa World Year Book.*

United Nations Conference on Trade and Development (UNCTAD), DC2-1120, United Nations, New York, NY 10017, (212) 963-0027, www.unctad.org; *Handbook of Statistics 2005.*

United Nations Economic Commission for Africa (ECA), PO Box 3001, Addis Ababa, Ethiopia, (Telephone in U.S. (212) 963-4957), www.uneca.org; *African Statistical Yearbook 2006.*

The World Bank, 1818 H Street, NW, Washington, DC 20433, (202) 473-1000, Fax: (202) 477-6391, www.worldbank.org; *Botswana; World Development Indicators (WDI) 2008;* and *World Development Report 2008.*

BOTSWANA - BANKS AND BANKING

Euromonitor International, Inc., 224 S. Michigan Avenue, Suite 1500, Chicago, IL 60604, (312) 922-1115, Fax: (312) 922-1157, www.euromonitor.com; *World Marketing Data and Statistics.*

International Monetary Fund (IMF), 700 Nineteenth Street, NW, Washington, DC 20431, (202) 623-7000, Fax: (202) 623-4661, www.imf.org; *Government Finance Statistics Yearbook (2008 Edition)* and *International Financial Statistics Yearbook 2007.*

M.E. Sharpe, 80 Business Park Drive, Armonk, NY 10504, (800) 541-6563, Fax: (914) 273-2106, www.mesharpe.com; *The Illustrated Book of World Rankings.*

Palgrave Macmillan Ltd., Houndmills, Basingstoke, Hampshire, RG21 6XS, England, (Telephone in U.S. (888) 330-8477), (Fax in U.S. (800) 672-2054), www.palgrave.com; *The Statesman's Yearbook 2008.*

Taylor and Francis Group, An Informa Business, 2 Park Square, Milton Park, Abingdon, Oxford OX14 4RN, United Kingdom, (Dial from U.S. (212) 216-7800), (Fax from U.S. (212) 564-7854), www.tandf.co.uk; *The Europa World Year Book.*

United Nations Economic Commission for Africa (ECA), PO Box 3001, Addis Ababa, Ethiopia, (Telephone in U.S. (212) 963-4957), www.uneca.org; *African Statistical Yearbook 2006.*

BOTSWANA - BARLEY PRODUCTION

See BOTSWANA - CROPS

BOTSWANA - BEVERAGE INDUSTRY

M.E. Sharpe, 80 Business Park Drive, Armonk, NY 10504, (800) 541-6563, Fax: (914) 273-2106, www.mesharpe.com; *The Illustrated Book of World Rankings.*

United Nations Statistics Division, New York, NY 10017, (800) 253-9646, Fax: (212) 963-4116, http://unstats.un.org; *Statistical Yearbook.*

BOTSWANA - BONDS

International Monetary Fund (IMF), 700 Nineteenth Street, NW, Washington, DC 20431, (202) 623-7000, Fax: (202) 623-4661, www.imf.org; *Government Finance Statistics Yearbook (2008 Edition).*

BOTSWANA - BROADCASTING

Central Intelligence Agency, Office of Public Affairs, Washington, DC 20505, (703) 482-0623, Fax: (703) 482-1739, www.cia.gov; *The World Factbook.*

Euromonitor International, Inc., 224 S. Michigan Avenue, Suite 1500, Chicago, IL 60604, (312) 922-1115, Fax: (312) 922-1157, www.euromonitor.com; *World Marketing Data and Statistics.*

M.E. Sharpe, 80 Business Park Drive, Armonk, NY 10504, (800) 541-6563, Fax: (914) 273-2106, www.mesharpe.com; *The Illustrated Book of World Rankings.*

Palgrave Macmillan Ltd., Houndmills, Basingstoke, Hampshire, RG21 6XS, England, (Telephone in U.S. (888) 330-8477), (Fax in U.S. (800) 672-2054), www.palgrave.com; *The Statesman's Yearbook 2008.*

WRTH Publications Limited, PO Box 290, Oxford OX2 7FT, UK, www.wrth.com; *World Radio TV Handbook 2007.*

BOTSWANA - BUDGET

Central Intelligence Agency, Office of Public Affairs, Washington, DC 20505, (703) 482-0623, Fax: (703) 482-1739, www.cia.gov; *The World Factbook.*

BOTSWANA - CAPITAL LEVY

International Monetary Fund (IMF), 700 Nineteenth Street, NW, Washington, DC 20431, (202) 623-7000, Fax: (202) 623-4661, www.imf.org; *Government Finance Statistics Yearbook (2008 Edition).*

BOTSWANA - CATTLE

See BOTSWANA - LIVESTOCK

BOTSWANA - CHICKENS

See BOTSWANA - LIVESTOCK

BOTSWANA - CHILDBIRTH - STATISTICS

Central Intelligence Agency, Office of Public Affairs, Washington, DC 20505, (703) 482-0623, Fax: (703) 482-1739, www.cia.gov; *The World Factbook.*

Euromonitor International, Inc., 224 S. Michigan Avenue, Suite 1500, Chicago, IL 60604, (312) 922-1115, Fax: (312) 922-1157, www.euromonitor.com; *International Marketing Data and Statistics 2008* and *The World Economic Factbook 2008.*

M.E. Sharpe, 80 Business Park Drive, Armonk, NY 10504, (800) 541-6563, Fax: (914) 273-2106, www.mesharpe.com; *The Illustrated Book of World Rankings.*

Taylor and Francis Group, An Informa Business, 2 Park Square, Milton Park, Abingdon, Oxford OX14 4RN, United Kingdom, (Dial from U.S. (212) 216-7800), (Fax from U.S. (212) 564-7854), www.tandf.co.uk; *The Europa World Year Book.*

United Nations Statistics Division, New York, NY 10017, (800) 253-9646, Fax: (212) 963-4116, http://unstats.un.org; *Demographic Yearbook; Statistical Yearbook;* and *Survey of Economic and Social Conditions in Africa 2005.*

The World Bank, 1818 H Street, NW, Washington, DC 20433, (202) 473-1000, Fax: (202) 477-6391, www.worldbank.org; *World Development Indicators (WDI) 2008.*

BOTSWANA - CLIMATE

International Institute for Environment and Development (IIED), 3 Endsleigh Street, London, England, WC1H 0DD, United Kingdom, www.iied.org; *Environment Urbanization* and *Haramata - Bulletin of the Drylands.*

M.E. Sharpe, 80 Business Park Drive, Armonk, NY 10504, (800) 541-6563, Fax: (914) 273-2106, www.mesharpe.com; *The Illustrated Book of World Rankings.*

Palgrave Macmillan Ltd., Houndmills, Basingstoke, Hampshire, RG21 6XS, England, (Telephone in U.S. (888) 330-8477), (Fax in U.S. (800) 672-2054), www.palgrave.com; *The Statesman's Yearbook 2008.*

BOTSWANA - COAL PRODUCTION

See BOTSWANA - MINERAL INDUSTRIES

BOTSWANA - COFFEE

See BOTSWANA - CROPS

BOTSWANA - COMMERCE

Palgrave Macmillan Ltd., Houndmills, Basingstoke, Hampshire, RG21 6XS, England, (Telephone in U.S. (888) 330-8477), (Fax in U.S. (800) 672-2054), www.palgrave.com; *The Statesman's Yearbook 2008.*

BOTSWANA - COMMODITY EXCHANGES

Commodity Research Bureau, 330 South Wells Street, Suite 612, Chicago, IL 60606-7110, (800) 621-5271, Fax: (312) 939-4135, www.crbtrader.com; *2006 CRB Commodity Yearbook and CD.*

International Monetary Fund (IMF), 700 Nineteenth Street, NW, Washington, DC 20431, (202) 623-7000, Fax: (202) 623-4661, www.imf.org; *IMF Primary Commodity Prices.*

United Nations Food and Agricultural Organization (FAO), Viale delle Terme di Caracalla, 00100 Rome, Italy, (Dial from U.S. (202) 653-2400), (Fax from U.S. (202) 653 5760), www.fao.org; *The State of Food and Agriculture (SOFA) 2006.*

BOTSWANA - CONSTRUCTION INDUSTRY

M.E. Sharpe, 80 Business Park Drive, Armonk, NY 10504, (800) 541-6563, Fax: (914) 273-2106, www.mesharpe.com; *The Illustrated Book of World Rankings.*

United Nations Economic Commission for Africa (ECA), PO Box 3001, Addis Ababa, Ethiopia, (Telephone in U.S. (212) 963-4957), www.uneca.org; *African Statistical Yearbook 2006.*

United Nations Statistics Division, New York, NY 10017, (800) 253-9646, Fax: (212) 963-4116, http://unstats.un.org; *Statistical Yearbook.*

BOTSWANA - CONSUMER PRICE INDEXES

Taylor and Francis Group, An Informa Business, 2 Park Square, Milton Park, Abingdon, Oxford OX14 4RN, United Kingdom, (Dial from U.S. (212) 216-7800), (Fax from U.S. (212) 564-7854), www.tandf.co.uk; *The Europa World Year Book.*

United Nations Economic Commission for Africa (ECA), PO Box 3001, Addis Ababa, Ethiopia,

(Telephone in U.S. (212) 963-4957), www.uneca.org; *African Statistical Yearbook 2006*.

United Nations Statistics Division, New York, NY 10017, (800) 253-9646, Fax: (212) 963-4116, http://unstats.un.org; *Statistical Yearbook* and *Survey of Economic and Social Conditions in Africa 2005*.

The World Bank, 1818 H Street, NW, Washington, DC 20433, (202) 473-1000, Fax: (202) 477-6391, www.worldbank.org; *Botswana*.

BOTSWANA - CONSUMPTION (ECONOMICS)

African Development Bank Group, Rue Joseph Anoma, 01 BP 1387 Abidjan 01, Cote d'Ivoire, www.afdb.org; *Statistics Pocketbook 2008*.

United Nations Statistics Division, New York, NY 10017, (800) 253-9646, Fax: (212) 963-4116, http://unstats.un.org; *Survey of Economic and Social Conditions in Africa 2005*.

The World Bank, 1818 H Street, NW, Washington, DC 20433, (202) 473-1000, Fax: (202) 477-6391, www.worldbank.org; *World Development Report 2008*.

BOTSWANA - COPPER INDUSTRY AND TRADE

See BOTSWANA - MINERAL INDUSTRIES

BOTSWANA - CORN INDUSTRY

See BOTSWANA - CROPS

BOTSWANA - COST AND STANDARD OF LIVING

International Monetary Fund (IMF), 700 Nineteenth Street, NW, Washington, DC 20431, (202) 623-7000, Fax: (202) 623-4661, www.imf.org; *Government Finance Statistics Yearbook (2008 Edition)*.

BOTSWANA - COTTON

See BOTSWANA - CROPS

BOTSWANA - CRIME

Yale University Press, PO Box 209040, New Haven, CT 06520-9040, (203) 432-0960, Fax: (203) 432-0948, http://yalepress.yale.edu/yupbooks; *Violence and Crime in Cross-National Perspective*.

BOTSWANA - CROPS

M.E. Sharpe, 80 Business Park Drive, Armonk, NY 10504, (800) 541-6563, Fax: (914) 273-2106, www.mesharpe.com; *The Illustrated Book of World Rankings*.

Palgrave Macmillan Ltd., Houndmills, Basingstoke, Hampshire, RG21 6XS, England, (Telephone in U.S. (888) 330-8477), (Fax in U.S. (800) 672-2054), www.palgrave.com; *The Statesman's Yearbook 2008*.

Taylor and Francis Group, An Informa Business, 2 Park Square, Milton Park, Abingdon, Oxford OX14 4RN, United Kingdom, (Dial from U.S. (212) 216-7800), (Fax from U.S. (212) 564-7854), www.tandf.co.uk; *The Europa World Year Book*.

United Nations Conference on Trade and Development (UNCTAD), DC2-1120, United Nations, New York, NY 10017, (212) 963-0027, www.unctad.org; *UNCTAD Commodity Yearbook*.

United Nations Economic Commission for Africa (ECA), PO Box 3001, Addis Ababa, Ethiopia, (Telephone in U.S. (212) 963-4957), www.uneca.org; *African Statistical Yearbook 2006*.

United Nations Food and Agricultural Organization (FAO), Viale delle Terme di Caracalla, 00100 Rome, Italy, (Dial from U.S. (202) 653-2400), (Fax from U.S. (202) 653 5760), www.fao.org; *FAO Production Yearbook 2002* and *The State of Food and Agriculture (SOFA) 2006*.

United Nations Statistics Division, New York, NY 10017, (800) 253-9646, Fax: (212) 963-4116, http://unstats.un.org; *Statistical Yearbook*.

BOTSWANA - CUSTOMS ADMINISTRATION

International Monetary Fund (IMF), 700 Nineteenth Street, NW, Washington, DC 20431, (202) 623-7000, Fax: (202) 623-4661, www.imf.org; *Government Finance Statistics Yearbook (2008 Edition)*.

Palgrave Macmillan Ltd., Houndmills, Basingstoke, Hampshire, RG21 6XS, England, (Telephone in U.S. (888) 330-8477), (Fax in U.S. (800) 672-2054), www.palgrave.com; *The Statesman's Yearbook 2008*.

BOTSWANA - DAIRY PROCESSING

M.E. Sharpe, 80 Business Park Drive, Armonk, NY 10504, (800) 541-6563, Fax: (914) 273-2106, www.mesharpe.com; *The Illustrated Book of World Rankings*.

Palgrave Macmillan Ltd., Houndmills, Basingstoke, Hampshire, RG21 6XS, England, (Telephone in U.S. (888) 330-8477), (Fax in U.S. (800) 672-2054), www.palgrave.com; *The Statesman's Yearbook 2008*.

Taylor and Francis Group, An Informa Business, 2 Park Square, Milton Park, Abingdon, Oxford OX14 4RN, United Kingdom, (Dial from U.S. (212) 216-7800), (Fax from U.S. (212) 564-7854), www.tandf.co.uk; *The Europa World Year Book*.

United Nations Food and Agricultural Organization (FAO), Viale delle Terme di Caracalla, 00100 Rome, Italy, (Dial from U.S. (202) 653-2400), (Fax from U.S. (202) 653 5760), www.fao.org; *The State of Food and Agriculture (SOFA) 2006*.

United Nations Statistics Division, New York, NY 10017, (800) 253-9646, Fax: (212) 963-4116, http://unstats.un.org; *Statistical Yearbook*.

BOTSWANA - DEATH RATES

See BOTSWANA - MORTALITY

BOTSWANA - DEBTS, EXTERNAL

African Development Bank Group, Rue Joseph Anoma, 01 BP 1387 Abidjan 01, Cote d'Ivoire, www.afdb.org; *Statistics Pocketbook 2008*.

International Monetary Fund (IMF), 700 Nineteenth Street, NW, Washington, DC 20431, (202) 623-7000, Fax: (202) 623-4661, www.imf.org; *Government Finance Statistics Yearbook (2008 Edition)*.

Palgrave Macmillan Ltd., Houndmills, Basingstoke, Hampshire, RG21 6XS, England, (Telephone in U.S. (888) 330-8477), (Fax in U.S. (800) 672-2054), www.palgrave.com; *The Statesman's Yearbook 2008*.

United Nations Statistics Division, New York, NY 10017, (800) 253-9646, Fax: (212) 963-4116, http://unstats.un.org; *Survey of Economic and Social Conditions in Africa 2005*.

The World Bank, 1818 H Street, NW, Washington, DC 20433, (202) 473-1000, Fax: (202) 477-6391, www.worldbank.org; *Africa Live Database (LDB); African Development Indicators (ADI) 2007; Global Development Finance 2007; World Development Indicators (WDI) 2008;* and *World Development Report 2008*.

BOTSWANA - DEFENSE EXPENDITURES

See BOTSWANA - ARMED FORCES

BOTSWANA - DEMOGRAPHY

Euromonitor International, Inc., 224 S. Michigan Avenue, Suite 1500, Chicago, IL 60604, (312) 922-1115, Fax: (312) 922-1157, www.euromonitor.com; *International Marketing Data and Statistics 2008; The World Economic Factbook 2008;* and *World Marketing Data and Statistics*.

M.E. Sharpe, 80 Business Park Drive, Armonk, NY 10504, (800) 541-6563, Fax: (914) 273-2106, www.mesharpe.com; *The Illustrated Book of World Rankings*.

United Nations Statistics Division, New York, NY 10017, (800) 253-9646, Fax: (212) 963-4116, http://unstats.un.org; *Human Development Report 2006* and *Survey of Economic and Social Conditions in Africa 2005*.

The World Bank, 1818 H Street, NW, Washington, DC 20433, (202) 473-1000, Fax: (202) 477-6391, www.worldbank.org; *Botswana*.

BOTSWANA - DIAMONDS

See BOTSWANA - MINERAL INDUSTRIES

BOTSWANA - DISPOSABLE INCOME

M.E. Sharpe, 80 Business Park Drive, Armonk, NY 10504, (800) 541-6563, Fax: (914) 273-2106, www.mesharpe.com; *The Illustrated Book of World Rankings*.

United Nations Statistics Division, New York, NY 10017, (800) 253-9646, Fax: (212) 963-4116, http://unstats.un.org; *National Accounts Statistics: Compendium of Income Distribution Statistics* and *Statistical Yearbook*.

BOTSWANA - DIVORCE

M.E. Sharpe, 80 Business Park Drive, Armonk, NY 10504, (800) 541-6563, Fax: (914) 273-2106, www.mesharpe.com; *The Illustrated Book of World Rankings*.

United Nations Statistics Division, New York, NY 10017, (800) 253-9646, Fax: (212) 963-4116, http://unstats.un.org; *Demographic Yearbook*.

BOTSWANA - ECONOMIC ASSISTANCE

United Nations Statistics Division, New York, NY 10017, (800) 253-9646, Fax: (212) 963-4116, http://unstats.un.org; *Statistical Yearbook*.

BOTSWANA - ECONOMIC CONDITIONS

African Development Bank Group, Rue Joseph Anoma, 01 BP 1387 Abidjan 01, Cote d'Ivoire, www.afdb.org; *The African Statistical Journal; Gender, Poverty and Environmental Indicators on African Countries 2007; Selected Statistics on African Countries 2007;* and *Statistics Pocketbook 2008*.

Center for International Business Education Research (CIBER), Columbia Business School and School of International and Public Affairs, Uris Hall, Room 212, 3022 Broadway, New York, NY 10027-6902, Mr. Joshua Safier, (212) 854-4750, Fax: (212) 222-9821, www.columbia.edu/cu/ciber/; Datastream International.

Central Intelligence Agency, Office of Public Affairs, Washington, DC 20505, (703) 482-0623, Fax: (703) 482-1739, www.cia.gov; *The World Factbook*.

DSI Data Service Information, Xantener Strasse 51a, D-47495 Rheinberg, Germany, www.dsidata.com; *Campus Solution*.

Dun and Bradstreet (DB) Corporation, 103 JFK Parkway, Short Hills, NJ 07078, (973) 921-5500, www.dnb.com; *Country Report*.

Economist Intelligence Unit, 111 West 57th Street, New York, NY 10019, (212) 554-0600, Fax: (212) 586-1181, www.eiu.com; *Botswana Country Report* and *Business Africa*.

Euromonitor International, Inc., 224 S. Michigan Avenue, Suite 1500, Chicago, IL 60604, (312) 922-1115, Fax: (312) 922-1157, www.euromonitor.com; *The World Economic Factbook 2008* and *World Marketing Data and Statistics*.

International Monetary Fund (IMF), 700 Nineteenth Street, NW, Washington, DC 20431, (202) 623-7000, Fax: (202) 623-4661, www.imf.org; *World Economic Outlook Reports*.

M.E. Sharpe, 80 Business Park Drive, Armonk, NY 10504, (800) 541-6563, Fax: (914) 273-2106, www.mesharpe.com; *The Illustrated Book of World Rankings*.

Palgrave Macmillan Ltd., Houndmills, Basingstoke, Hampshire, RG21 6XS, England, (Telephone in U.S. (888) 330-8477), (Fax in U.S. (800) 672-2054), www.palgrave.com; *The Statesman's Yearbook 2008*.

Taylor and Francis Group, An Informa Business, 2 Park Square, Milton Park, Abingdon, Oxford OX14 4RN, United Kingdom, (Dial from U.S. (212) 216-7800), (Fax from U.S. (212) 564-7854), www.tandf.co.uk; *The Europa World Year Book*.

United Nations Statistics Division, New York, NY 10017, (800) 253-9646, Fax: (212) 963-4116, http://unstats.un.org; *World Statistics Pocketbook*.

The World Bank, 1818 H Street, NW, Washington, DC 20433, (202) 473-1000, Fax: (202) 477-6391, www.worldbank.org; *Africa Household Survey Databank; Africa Live Database (LDB); Africa Standardized Files and Indicators; African Development Indicators (ADI) 2007; Botswana; Global Economic Monitor (GEM); Global Economic Prospects 2008; The World Bank Atlas 2003-2004;* and *World Development Report 2008.*

BOTSWANA - EDUCATION

African Development Bank Group, Rue Joseph Anoma, 01 BP 1387 Abidjan 01, Cote d'Ivoire, www.afdb.org; *Statistics Pocketbook 2008.*

Euromonitor International, Inc., 224 S. Michigan Avenue, Suite 1500, Chicago, IL 60604, (312) 922-1115, Fax: (312) 922-1157, www.euromonitor.com; *International Marketing Data and Statistics 2008* and *World Marketing Data and Statistics.*

International Monetary Fund (IMF), 700 Nineteenth Street, NW, Washington, DC 20431, (202) 623-7000, Fax: (202) 623-4661, www.imf.org; *Government Finance Statistics Yearbook (2008 Edition).*

M.E. Sharpe, 80 Business Park Drive, Armonk, NY 10504, (800) 541-6563, Fax: (914) 273-2106, www.mesharpe.com; *The Illustrated Book of World Rankings.*

Palgrave Macmillan Ltd., Houndmills, Basingstoke, Hampshire, RG21 6XS, England, (Telephone in U.S. (888) 330-8477), (Fax in U.S. (800) 672-2054), www.palgrave.com; *The Statesman's Yearbook 2008.*

Taylor and Francis Group, An Informa Business, 2 Park Square, Milton Park, Abingdon, Oxford OX14 4RN, United Kingdom, (Dial from U.S. (212) 216-7800), (Fax from U.S. (212) 564-7854), www.tandf.co.uk; *The Europa World Year Book.*

UNESCO Institute for Statistics, C.P. 6128 Succursale Centre-Ville, Montreal, Quebec, H3C 3J7 Canada, (Dial from U.S. (514) 343-6880), (Fax from U.S. (514) 343 6882), www.uis.unesco.org; *Statistical Tables.*

United Nations Economic Commission for Africa (ECA), PO Box 3001, Addis Ababa, Ethiopia, (Telephone in U.S. (212) 963-4957), www.uneca.org; *African Statistical Yearbook 2006.*

United Nations Statistics Division, New York, NY 10017, (800) 253-9646, Fax: (212) 963-4116, http://unstats.un.org; *Human Development Report 2006* and *Survey of Economic and Social Conditions in Africa 2005.*

The World Bank, 1818 H Street, NW, Washington, DC 20433, (202) 473-1000, Fax: (202) 477-6391, www.worldbank.org; *Botswana; World Development Indicators (WDI) 2008;* and *World Development Report 2008.*

BOTSWANA - ELECTRICITY

Central Intelligence Agency, Office of Public Affairs, Washington, DC 20505, (703) 482-0623, Fax: (703) 482-1739, www.cia.gov; *The World Factbook.*

M.E. Sharpe, 80 Business Park Drive, Armonk, NY 10504, (800) 541-6563, Fax: (914) 273-2106, www.mesharpe.com; *The Illustrated Book of World Rankings.*

Palgrave Macmillan Ltd., Houndmills, Basingstoke, Hampshire, RG21 6XS, England, (Telephone in U.S. (888) 330-8477), (Fax in U.S. (800) 672-2054), www.palgrave.com; *The Statesman's Yearbook 2008.*

U.S. Department of Energy (DOE), Energy Information Administration (EIA), 1000 Independence Avenue, SW, Washington, DC 20585, (202) 586-8800, www.eia.doe.gov; *International Energy Annual 2004* and *International Energy Outlook 2006.*

United Nations Economic Commission for Africa (ECA), PO Box 3001, Addis Ababa, Ethiopia, (Telephone in U.S. (212) 963-4957), www.uneca.org; *African Statistical Yearbook 2006.*

United Nations Statistics Division, New York, NY 10017, (800) 253-9646, Fax: (212) 963-4116, http://unstats.un.org; *Human Development Report 2006* and *Survey of Economic and Social Conditions in Africa 2005.*

BOTSWANA - EMPLOYMENT

Euromonitor International, Inc., 224 S. Michigan Avenue, Suite 1500, Chicago, IL 60604, (312) 922-1115, Fax: (312) 922-1157, www.euromonitor.com; *International Marketing Data and Statistics 2008.*

International Labour Office, I.L.O. Publications, 4 route des Morillons, CH-1211 Geneva 22, Switzerland, (Telephone in U.S. (202) 653-7652), (Fax in U.S. (202) 653-7687), www.ilo.org; *Yearbook of Labour Statistics 2006.*

M.E. Sharpe, 80 Business Park Drive, Armonk, NY 10504, (800) 541-6563, Fax: (914) 273-2106, www.mesharpe.com; *The Illustrated Book of World Rankings.*

United Nations Economic Commission for Africa (ECA), PO Box 3001, Addis Ababa, Ethiopia, (Telephone in U.S. (212) 963-4957), www.uneca.org; *African Statistical Yearbook 2006.*

United Nations Statistics Division, New York, NY 10017, (800) 253-9646, Fax: (212) 963-4116, http://unstats.un.org; *Statistical Yearbook* and *Survey of Economic and Social Conditions in Africa 2005.*

The World Bank, 1818 H Street, NW, Washington, DC 20433, (202) 473-1000, Fax: (202) 477-6391, www.worldbank.org; *Botswana.*

BOTSWANA - ENVIRONMENTAL CONDITIONS

DSI Data Service Information, Xantener Strasse 51a, D-47495 Rheinberg, Germany, www.dsidata.com; *Campus Solution* and *DSI's Global Environmental Database.*

Economist Intelligence Unit, 111 West 57th Street, New York, NY 10019, (212) 554-0600, Fax: (212) 586-1181, www.eiu.com; *Botswana Country Report.*

International Institute for Environment and Development (IIED), 3 Endsleigh Street, London, England, WC1H 0DD, United Kingdom, www.iied.org; *Environment Urbanization* and *Haramata - Bulletin of the Drylands.*

United Nations Statistics Division, New York, NY 10017, (800) 253-9646, Fax: (212) 963-4116, http://unstats.un.org; *World Statistics Pocketbook.*

BOTSWANA - EXPORTS

African Development Bank Group, Rue Joseph Anoma, 01 BP 1387 Abidjan 01, Cote d'Ivoire, www.afdb.org; *Statistics Pocketbook 2008.*

Central Intelligence Agency, Office of Public Affairs, Washington, DC 20505, (703) 482-0623, Fax: (703) 482-1739, www.cia.gov; *The World Factbook.*

Economist Intelligence Unit, 111 West 57th Street, New York, NY 10019, (212) 554-0600, Fax: (212) 586-1181, www.eiu.com; *Botswana Country Report.*

Euromonitor International, Inc., 224 S. Michigan Avenue, Suite 1500, Chicago, IL 60604, (312) 922-1115, Fax: (312) 922-1157, www.euromonitor.com; *International Marketing Data and Statistics 2008* and *The World Economic Factbook 2008.*

International Monetary Fund (IMF), 700 Nineteenth Street, NW, Washington, DC 20431, (202) 623-7000, Fax: (202) 623-4661, www.imf.org; *Direction of Trade Statistics Yearbook 2007; Government Finance Statistics Yearbook (2008 Edition);* and *International Financial Statistics Yearbook 2007.*

Palgrave Macmillan Ltd., Houndmills, Basingstoke, Hampshire, RG21 6XS, England, (Telephone in U.S. (888) 330-8477), (Fax in U.S. (800) 672-2054), www.palgrave.com; *The Statesman's Yearbook 2008.*

Taylor and Francis Group, An Informa Business, 2 Park Square, Milton Park, Abingdon, Oxford OX14 4RN, United Kingdom, (Dial from U.S. (212) 216-7800), (Fax from U.S. (212) 564-7854), www.tandf.co.uk; *The Europa World Year Book.*

United Nations Conference on Trade and Development (UNCTAD), DC2-1120, United Nations, New York, NY 10017, (212) 963-0027, www.unctad.org; *Handbook of Statistics 2005.*

United Nations Economic Commission for Africa (ECA), PO Box 3001, Addis Ababa, Ethiopia, (Telephone in U.S. (212) 963-4957), www.uneca.org; *African Statistical Yearbook 2006.*

United Nations Food and Agricultural Organization (FAO), Viale delle Terme di Caracalla, 00100 Rome, Italy, (Dial from U.S. (202) 653-2400), (Fax from U.S. (202) 653 5760), www.fao.org; *The State of Food and Agriculture (SOFA) 2006.*

United Nations Statistics Division, New York, NY 10017, (800) 253-9646, Fax: (212) 963-4116, http://unstats.un.org; *Survey of Economic and Social Conditions in Africa 2005.*

The World Bank, 1818 H Street, NW, Washington, DC 20433, (202) 473-1000, Fax: (202) 477-6391, www.worldbank.org; *World Development Indicators (WDI) 2008* and *World Development Report 2008.*

BOTSWANA - FERTILITY, HUMAN

Central Intelligence Agency, Office of Public Affairs, Washington, DC 20505, (703) 482-0623, Fax: (703) 482-1739, www.cia.gov; *The World Factbook.*

M.E. Sharpe, 80 Business Park Drive, Armonk, NY 10504, (800) 541-6563, Fax: (914) 273-2106, www.mesharpe.com; *The Illustrated Book of World Rankings.*

United Nations Statistics Division, New York, NY 10017, (800) 253-9646, Fax: (212) 963-4116, http://unstats.un.org; *Human Development Report 2006* and *Survey of Economic and Social Conditions in Africa 2005.*

The World Bank, 1818 H Street, NW, Washington, DC 20433, (202) 473-1000, Fax: (202) 477-6391, www.worldbank.org; *The World Bank Atlas 2003-2004; World Development Indicators (WDI) 2008;* and *World Development Report 2008.*

BOTSWANA - FERTILIZER INDUSTRY

United Nations Food and Agricultural Organization (FAO), Viale delle Terme di Caracalla, 00100 Rome, Italy, (Dial from U.S. (202) 653-2400), (Fax from U.S. (202) 653 5760), www.fao.org; *FAO Fertilizer Yearbook* and *The State of Food and Agriculture (SOFA) 2006.*

United Nations Statistics Division, New York, NY 10017, (800) 253-9646, Fax: (212) 963-4116, http://unstats.un.org; *Statistical Yearbook.*

BOTSWANA - FETAL MORTALITY

See BOTSWANA - MORTALITY

BOTSWANA - FINANCE

Taylor and Francis Group, An Informa Business, 2 Park Square, Milton Park, Abingdon, Oxford OX14 4RN, United Kingdom, (Dial from U.S. (212) 216-7800), (Fax from U.S. (212) 564-7854), www.tandf.co.uk; *The Europa World Year Book.*

United Nations Economic Commission for Africa (ECA), PO Box 3001, Addis Ababa, Ethiopia, (Telephone in U.S. (212) 963-4957), www.uneca.org; *African Statistical Yearbook 2006.*

United Nations Statistics Division, New York, NY 10017, (800) 253-9646, Fax: (212) 963-4116, http://unstats.un.org; *National Accounts Statistics: Compendium of Income Distribution Statistics* and *Statistical Yearbook.*

The World Bank, 1818 H Street, NW, Washington, DC 20433, (202) 473-1000, Fax: (202) 477-6391, www.worldbank.org; *Botswana.*

BOTSWANA - FINANCE, PUBLIC

African Development Bank Group, Rue Joseph Anoma, 01 BP 1387 Abidjan 01, Cote d'Ivoire, www.afdb.org; *Statistics Pocketbook 2008.*

Bernan Essential Government Publications, 4611-F Assembly Drive, Lanham MD, 20706-4391, (301) 459-2255, Fax: (800) 865-3450, www.bernan.com; *National Accounts Statistics.*

Economist Intelligence Unit, 111 West 57th Street, New York, NY 10019, (212) 554-0600, Fax: (212) 586-1181, www.eiu.com; *Botswana Country Report.*

International Monetary Fund (IMF), 700 Nineteenth Street, NW, Washington, DC 20431, (202) 623-7000, Fax: (202) 623-4661, www.imf.org; *Government Finance Statistics Yearbook (2008 Edition); International Financial Statistics; International Financial Statistics Online Service;* and *International Financial Statistics Yearbook 2007.*

M.E. Sharpe, 80 Business Park Drive, Armonk, NY 10504, (800) 541-6563, Fax: (914) 273-2106, www.mesharpe.com; *The Illustrated Book of World Rankings.*

Palgrave Macmillan Ltd., Houndmills, Basingstoke, Hampshire, RG21 6XS, England, (Telephone in U.S. (888) 330-8477), (Fax in U.S. (800) 672-2054), www.palgrave.com; *The Statesman's Yearbook 2008.*

Taylor and Francis Group, An Informa Business, 2 Park Square, Milton Park, Abingdon, Oxford OX14 4RN, United Kingdom, (Dial from U.S. (212) 216-7800), (Fax from U.S. (212) 564-7854), www.tandf.co.uk; *The Europa World Year Book.*

United Nations Economic Commission for Africa (ECA), PO Box 3001, Addis Ababa, Ethiopia, (Telephone in U.S. (212) 963-4957), www.uneca.org; *African Statistical Yearbook 2006.*

The World Bank, 1818 H Street, NW, Washington, DC 20433, (202) 473-1000, Fax: (202) 477-6391, www.worldbank.org; *Botswana.*

BOTSWANA - FISHERIES

M.E. Sharpe, 80 Business Park Drive, Armonk, NY 10504, (800) 541-6563, Fax: (914) 273-2106, www.mesharpe.com; *The Illustrated Book of World Rankings.*

Taylor and Francis Group, An Informa Business, 2 Park Square, Milton Park, Abingdon, Oxford OX14 4RN, United Kingdom, (Dial from U.S. (212) 216-7800), (Fax from U.S. (212) 564-7854), www.tandf.co.uk; *The Europa World Year Book.*

United Nations Conference on Trade and Development (UNCTAD), DC2-1120, United Nations, New York, NY 10017, (212) 963-0027, www.unctad.org; *UNCTAD Commodity Yearbook.*

United Nations Economic Commission for Africa (ECA), PO Box 3001, Addis Ababa, Ethiopia, (Telephone in U.S. (212) 963-4957), www.uneca.org; *African Statistical Yearbook 2006.*

United Nations Food and Agricultural Organization (FAO), Viale delle Terme di Caracalla, 00100 Rome, Italy, (Dial from U.S. (202) 653-2400), (Fax from U.S. (202) 653 5760), www.fao.org; *FAO Yearbook of Fishery Statistics;* Fishery Databases; FISHSTAT Database. Subjects covered include: Aquaculture production, capture production, fishery commodities; and *The State of Food and Agriculture (SOFA) 2006.*

United Nations Statistics Division, New York, NY 10017, (800) 253-9646, Fax: (212) 963-4116, http://unstats.un.org; *Statistical Yearbook* and *Survey of Economic and Social Conditions in Africa 2005.*

The World Bank, 1818 H Street, NW, Washington, DC 20433, (202) 473-1000, Fax: (202) 477-6391, www.worldbank.org; *Botswana.*

BOTSWANA - FOOD

African Development Bank Group, Rue Joseph Anoma, 01 BP 1387 Abidjan 01, Cote d'Ivoire, www.afdb.org; *Statistics Pocketbook 2008.*

United Nations Food and Agricultural Organization (FAO), Viale delle Terme di Caracalla, 00100 Rome, Italy, (Dial from U.S. (202) 653-2400), (Fax from U.S. (202) 653 5760), www.fao.org; *FAO Production Yearbook 2002* and *The State of Food and Agriculture (SOFA) 2006.*

United Nations Statistics Division, New York, NY 10017, (800) 253-9646, Fax: (212) 963-4116, http://unstats.un.org; *Human Development Report 2006.*

BOTSWANA - FOREIGN EXCHANGE RATES

African Development Bank Group, Rue Joseph Anoma, 01 BP 1387 Abidjan 01, Cote d'Ivoire, www.afdb.org; *Statistics Pocketbook 2008.*

Central Intelligence Agency, Office of Public Affairs, Washington, DC 20505, (703) 482-0623, Fax: (703) 482-1739, www.cia.gov; *The World Factbook.*

Euromonitor International, Inc., 224 S. Michigan Avenue, Suite 1500, Chicago, IL 60604, (312) 922-1115, Fax: (312) 922-1157, www.euromonitor.com; *International Marketing Data and Statistics 2008* and *The World Economic Factbook 2008.*

International Monetary Fund (IMF), 700 Nineteenth Street, NW, Washington, DC 20431, (202) 623-7000, Fax: (202) 623-4661, www.imf.org; *International Financial Statistics Yearbook 2007.*

Taylor and Francis Group, An Informa Business, 2 Park Square, Milton Park, Abingdon, Oxford OX14 4RN, United Kingdom, (Dial from U.S. (212) 216-7800), (Fax from U.S. (212) 564-7854), www.tandf.co.uk; *The Europa World Year Book.*

United Nations Statistics Division, New York, NY 10017, (800) 253-9646, Fax: (212) 963-4116, http://unstats.un.org; *Statistical Yearbook* and *World Statistics Pocketbook.*

BOTSWANA - FORESTS AND FORESTRY

M.E. Sharpe, 80 Business Park Drive, Armonk, NY 10504, (800) 541-6563, Fax: (914) 273-2106, www.mesharpe.com; *The Illustrated Book of World Rankings.*

Palgrave Macmillan Ltd., Houndmills, Basingstoke, Hampshire, RG21 6XS, England, (Telephone in U.S. (888) 330-8477), (Fax in U.S. (800) 672-2054), www.palgrave.com; *The Statesman's Yearbook 2008.*

Taylor and Francis Group, An Informa Business, 2 Park Square, Milton Park, Abingdon, Oxford OX14 4RN, United Kingdom, (Dial from U.S. (212) 216-7800), (Fax from U.S. (212) 564-7854), www.tandf.co.uk; *The Europa World Year Book.*

UNESCO Institute for Statistics, C.P. 6128 Succursale Centre-Ville, Montreal, Quebec, H3C 3J7 Canada, (Dial from U.S. (514) 343-6880), (Fax from U.S. (514) 343 6882), www.uis.unesco.org; *Statistical Tables.*

United Nations Conference on Trade and Development (UNCTAD), DC2-1120, United Nations, New York, NY 10017, (212) 963-0027, www.unctad.org; *UNCTAD Commodity Yearbook.*

United Nations Economic Commission for Africa (ECA), PO Box 3001, Addis Ababa, Ethiopia, (Telephone in U.S. (212) 963-4957), www.uneca.org; *African Statistical Yearbook 2006.*

United Nations Food and Agricultural Organization (FAO), Viale delle Terme di Caracalla, 00100 Rome, Italy, (Dial from U.S. (202) 653-2400), (Fax from U.S. (202) 653 5760), www.fao.org; *FAO Yearbook of Forest Products* and *The State of Food and Agriculture (SOFA) 2006.*

United Nations Statistics Division, New York, NY 10017, (800) 253-9646, Fax: (212) 963-4116, http://unstats.un.org; *Statistical Yearbook.*

The World Bank, 1818 H Street, NW, Washington, DC 20433, (202) 473-1000, Fax: (202) 477-6391, www.worldbank.org; *Botswana* and *World Development Report 2008.*

BOTSWANA - GAS PRODUCTION

See BOTSWANA - MINERAL INDUSTRIES

BOTSWANA - GEOGRAPHIC INFORMATION SYSTEMS

M.E. Sharpe, 80 Business Park Drive, Armonk, NY 10504, (800) 541-6563, Fax: (914) 273-2106, www.mesharpe.com; *The Illustrated Book of World Rankings.*

The World Bank, 1818 H Street, NW, Washington, DC 20433, (202) 473-1000, Fax: (202) 477-6391, www.worldbank.org; *Botswana.*

BOTSWANA - GOLD INDUSTRY

International Monetary Fund (IMF), 700 Nineteenth Street, NW, Washington, DC 20431, (202) 623-7000, Fax: (202) 623-4661, www.imf.org; *International Financial Statistics Yearbook 2007.*

The World Bank, 1818 H Street, NW, Washington, DC 20433, (202) 473-1000, Fax: (202) 477-6391, www.worldbank.org; *World Development Indicators (WDI) 2008.*

BOTSWANA - GOLD PRODUCTION

See BOTSWANA - MINERAL INDUSTRIES

BOTSWANA - GRANTS-IN-AID

International Monetary Fund (IMF), 700 Nineteenth Street, NW, Washington, DC 20431, (202) 623-7000, Fax: (202) 623-4661, www.imf.org; *Government Finance Statistics Yearbook (2008 Edition).*

BOTSWANA - GROSS DOMESTIC PRODUCT

African Development Bank Group, Rue Joseph Anoma, 01 BP 1387 Abidjan 01, Cote d'Ivoire, www.afdb.org; *Statistics Pocketbook 2008.*

Economist Intelligence Unit, 111 West 57th Street, New York, NY 10019, (212) 554-0600, Fax: (212) 586-1181, www.eiu.com; *Botswana Country Report.*

Euromonitor International, Inc., 224 S. Michigan Avenue, Suite 1500, Chicago, IL 60604, (312) 922-1115, Fax: (312) 922-1157, www.euromonitor.com; *International Marketing Data and Statistics 2008* and *The World Economic Factbook 2008.*

M.E. Sharpe, 80 Business Park Drive, Armonk, NY 10504, (800) 541-6563, Fax: (914) 273-2106, www.mesharpe.com; *The Illustrated Book of World Rankings.*

Taylor and Francis Group, An Informa Business, 2 Park Square, Milton Park, Abingdon, Oxford OX14 4RN, United Kingdom, (Dial from U.S. (212) 216-7800), (Fax from U.S. (212) 564-7854), www.tandf.co.uk; *The Europa World Year Book.*

United Nations Economic Commission for Africa (ECA), PO Box 3001, Addis Ababa, Ethiopia, (Telephone in U.S. (212) 963-4957), www.uneca.org; *African Statistical Yearbook 2006.*

United Nations Statistics Division, New York, NY 10017, (800) 253-9646, Fax: (212) 963-4116, http://unstats.un.org; *Human Development Report 2006; National Accounts Statistics: Compendium of Income Distribution Statistics; Statistical Yearbook;* and *Survey of Economic and Social Conditions in Africa 2005.*

The World Bank, 1818 H Street, NW, Washington, DC 20433, (202) 473-1000, Fax: (202) 477-6391, www.worldbank.org; *World Development Indicators (WDI) 2008* and *World Development Report 2008.*

BOTSWANA - GROSS NATIONAL PRODUCT

M.E. Sharpe, 80 Business Park Drive, Armonk, NY 10504, (800) 541-6563, Fax: (914) 273-2106, www.mesharpe.com; *The Illustrated Book of World Rankings.*

Palgrave Macmillan Ltd., Houndmills, Basingstoke, Hampshire, RG21 6XS, England, (Telephone in U.S. (888) 330-8477), (Fax in U.S. (800) 672-2054), www.palgrave.com; *The Statesman's Yearbook 2008.*

Taylor and Francis Group, An Informa Business, 2 Park Square, Milton Park, Abingdon, Oxford OX14 4RN, United Kingdom, (Dial from U.S. (212) 216-7800), (Fax from U.S. (212) 564-7854), www.tandf.co.uk; *The Europa World Year Book.*

U.S. Department of State (DOS), 2201 C Street NW, Washington, DC 20520, (202) 647-4000, www.state.gov; *World Military Expenditures and Arms Transfers (WMEAT).*

The World Bank, 1818 H Street, NW, Washington, DC 20433, (202) 473-1000, Fax: (202) 477-6391, www.worldbank.org; *The World Bank Atlas 2003-2004; World Development Indicators (WDI) 2008;* and *World Development Report 2008.*

BOTSWANA - HIDES AND SKINS INDUSTRY

United Nations Food and Agricultural Organization (FAO), Viale delle Terme di Caracalla, 00100 Rome,

Italy, (Dial from U.S. (202) 653-2400), (Fax from U.S. (202) 653 5760), www.fao.org; *FAO Production Yearbook 2002.*

BOTSWANA - HOURS OF LABOR

International Labour Office, I.L.O. Publications, 4 route des Morillons, CH-1211 Geneva 22, Switzerland, (Telephone in U.S. (202) 653-7652), (Fax in U.S. (202) 653-7687), www.ilo.org; *Yearbook of Labour Statistics 2006.*

BOTSWANA - HOUSING

Euromonitor International, Inc., 224 S. Michigan Avenue, Suite 1500, Chicago, IL 60604, (312) 922-1115, Fax: (312) 922-1157, www.euromonitor.com; *World Marketing Data and Statistics.*

M.E. Sharpe, 80 Business Park Drive, Armonk, NY 10504, (800) 541-6563, Fax: (914) 273-2106, www.mesharpe.com; *The Illustrated Book of World Rankings.*

BOTSWANA - ILLITERATE PERSONS

Euromonitor International, Inc., 224 S. Michigan Avenue, Suite 1500, Chicago, IL 60604, (312) 922-1115, Fax: (312) 922-1157, www.euromonitor.com; *The World Economic Factbook 2008.*

Palgrave Macmillan Ltd., Houndmills, Basingstoke, Hampshire, RG21 6XS, England, (Telephone in U.S. (888) 330-8477), (Fax in U.S. (800) 672-2054), www.palgrave.com; *The Statesman's Yearbook 2008.*

UNESCO Institute for Statistics, C.P. 6128 Succursale Centre-Ville, Montreal, Quebec, H3C 3J7 Canada, (Dial from U.S. (514) 343-6880), (Fax from U.S. (514) 343 6882), www.uis.unesco.org; *Statistical Tables.*

United Nations Statistics Division, New York, NY 10017, (800) 253-9646, Fax: (212) 963-4116, http://unstats.un.org; *Human Development Report 2006.*

BOTSWANA - IMPORTS

Central Intelligence Agency, Office of Public Affairs, Washington, DC 20505, (703) 482-0623, Fax: (703) 482-1739, www.cia.gov; *The World Factbook.*

Economist Intelligence Unit, 111 West 57th Street, New York, NY 10019, (212) 554-0600, Fax: (212) 586-1181, www.eiu.com; *Botswana Country Report.*

Euromonitor International, Inc., 224 S. Michigan Avenue, Suite 1500, Chicago, IL 60604, (312) 922-1115, Fax: (312) 922-1157, www.euromonitor.com; *International Marketing Data and Statistics 2008* and *The World Economic Factbook 2008.*

International Monetary Fund (IMF), 700 Nineteenth Street, NW, Washington, DC 20431, (202) 623-7000, Fax: (202) 623-4661, www.imf.org; *Direction of Trade Statistics Yearbook 2007* and *International Financial Statistics Yearbook 2007.*

Taylor and Francis Group, An Informa Business, 2 Park Square, Milton Park, Abingdon, Oxford OX14 4RN, United Kingdom, (Dial from U.S. (212) 216-7800), (Fax from U.S. (212) 564-7854), www.tandf.co.uk; *The Europa World Year Book.*

United Nations Conference on Trade and Development (UNCTAD), DC2-1120, United Nations, New York, NY 10017, (212) 963-0027, www.unctad.org; *Handbook of Statistics 2005.*

United Nations Economic Commission for Africa (ECA), PO Box 3001, Addis Ababa, Ethiopia, (Telephone in U.S. (212) 963-4957), www.uneca.org; *African Statistical Yearbook 2006.*

United Nations Food and Agricultural Organization (FAO), Viale delle Terme di Caracalla, 00100 Rome, Italy, (Dial from U.S. (202) 653-2400), (Fax from U.S. (202) 653 5760), www.fao.org; *The State of Food and Agriculture (SOFA) 2006.*

United Nations Statistics Division, New York, NY 10017, (800) 253-9646, Fax: (212) 963-4116, http://unstats.un.org; *Survey of Economic and Social Conditions in Africa 2005.*

The World Bank, 1818 H Street, NW, Washington, DC 20433, (202) 473-1000, Fax: (202) 477-6391, www.worldbank.org; *World Development Indicators (WDI) 2008* and *World Development Report 2008.*

BOTSWANA - INCOME TAXES

See BOTSWANA - TAXATION

BOTSWANA - INDUSTRIAL PRODUCTIVITY

M.E. Sharpe, 80 Business Park Drive, Armonk, NY 10504, (800) 541-6563, Fax: (914) 273-2106, www.mesharpe.com; *The Illustrated Book of World Rankings.*

BOTSWANA - INDUSTRIAL PROPERTY

World Intellectual Property Organization (WIPO), PO Box 18, CH-1211 Geneva 20, Switzerland, www.wipo.int; *Industrial Property Statistics* and *Industrial Property Statistics Online Directory.*

BOTSWANA - INDUSTRIES

Central Intelligence Agency, Office of Public Affairs, Washington, DC 20505, (703) 482-0623, Fax: (703) 482-1739, www.cia.gov; *The World Factbook.*

Economist Intelligence Unit, 111 West 57th Street, New York, NY 10019, (212) 554-0600, Fax: (212) 586-1181, www.eiu.com; *Botswana Country Report.*

Euromonitor International, Inc., 224 S. Michigan Avenue, Suite 1500, Chicago, IL 60604, (312) 922-1115, Fax: (312) 922-1157, www.euromonitor.com; *The World Economic Factbook 2008* and *World Marketing Data and Statistics.*

International Labour Office, I.L.O. Publications, 4 route des Morillons, CH-1211 Geneva 22, Switzerland, (Telephone in U.S. (202) 653-7652), (Fax in U.S. (202) 653-7687), www.ilo.org; *Yearbook of Labour Statistics 2006.*

M.E. Sharpe, 80 Business Park Drive, Armonk, NY 10504, (800) 541-6563, Fax: (914) 273-2106, www.mesharpe.com; *The Illustrated Book of World Rankings.*

Palgrave Macmillan Ltd., Houndmills, Basingstoke, Hampshire, RG21 6XS, England, (Telephone in U.S. (888) 330-8477), (Fax in U.S. (800) 672-2054), www.palgrave.com; *The Statesman's Yearbook 2008.*

Taylor and Francis Group, An Informa Business, 2 Park Square, Milton Park, Abingdon, Oxford OX14 4RN, United Kingdom, (Dial from U.S. (212) 216-7800), (Fax from U.S. (212) 564-7854), www.tandf.co.uk; *The Europa World Year Book.*

United Nations Economic Commission for Africa (ECA), PO Box 3001, Addis Ababa, Ethiopia, (Telephone in U.S. (212) 963-4957), www.uneca.org; *African Statistical Yearbook 2006.*

United Nations Industrial Development Organization (UNIDO), 1 United Nations Plaza, New York, NY 10017, (212) 963 6890, Fax: (212) 963-7904, http://unido.org; Industrial Statistics Database 2008 (INDSTAT) and *The International Yearbook of Industrial Statistics 2008.*

United Nations Statistics Division, New York, NY 10017, (800) 253-9646, Fax: (212) 963-4116, http://unstats.un.org; *Survey of Economic and Social Conditions in Africa 2005.*

The World Bank, 1818 H Street, NW, Washington, DC 20433, (202) 473-1000, Fax: (202) 477-6391, www.worldbank.org; *Botswana* and *World Development Indicators (WDI) 2008.*

World Intellectual Property Organization (WIPO), PO Box 18, CH-1211 Geneva 20, Switzerland, www.wipo.int; *Industrial Property Statistics* and *Industrial Property Statistics Online Directory.*

BOTSWANA - INFANT AND MATERNAL MORTALITY

See BOTSWANA - MORTALITY

BOTSWANA - INTERNATIONAL LIQUIDITY

International Monetary Fund (IMF), 700 Nineteenth Street, NW, Washington, DC 20431, (202) 623-7000, Fax: (202) 623-4661, www.imf.org; *International Financial Statistics Yearbook 2007.*

BOTSWANA - INTERNATIONAL TRADE

African Development Bank Group, Rue Joseph Anoma, 01 BP 1387 Abidjan 01, Cote d'Ivoire, www.afdb.org; *Statistics Pocketbook 2008.*

Economist Intelligence Unit, 111 West 57th Street, New York, NY 10019, (212) 554-0600, Fax: (212) 586-1181, www.eiu.com; *Botswana Country Report.*

Euromonitor International, Inc., 224 S. Michigan Avenue, Suite 1500, Chicago, IL 60604, (312) 922-1115, Fax: (312) 922-1157, www.euromonitor.com; *The World Economic Factbook 2008* and *World Marketing Data and Statistics.*

M.E. Sharpe, 80 Business Park Drive, Armonk, NY 10504, (800) 541-6563, Fax: (914) 273-2106, www.mesharpe.com; *The Illustrated Book of World Rankings.*

Organisation for Economic Cooperation and Development (OECD), 2 rue Andre Pascal, F-75775 Paris Cedex 16, France, (Telephone in U.S. (202) 785-6323), (Fax in U.S. (202) 785-0350), www.oecd.org; *International Trade by Commodity Statistics (ITCS).*

Taylor and Francis Group, An Informa Business, 2 Park Square, Milton Park, Abingdon, Oxford OX14 4RN, United Kingdom, (Dial from U.S. (212) 216-7800), (Fax from U.S. (212) 564-7854), www.tandf.co.uk; *The Europa World Year Book.*

United Nations Conference on Trade and Development (UNCTAD), DC2-1120, United Nations, New York, NY 10017, (212) 963-0027, www.unctad.org; *UNCTAD Commodity Yearbook.*

United Nations Economic Commission for Africa (ECA), PO Box 3001, Addis Ababa, Ethiopia, (Telephone in U.S. (212) 963-4957), www.uneca.org; *African Statistical Yearbook 2006.*

United Nations Food and Agricultural Organization (FAO), Viale delle Terme di Caracalla, 00100 Rome, Italy, (Dial from U.S. (202) 653-2400), (Fax from U.S. (202) 653 5760), www.fao.org; *FAO Trade Yearbook* and *The State of Food and Agriculture (SOFA) 2006.*

The World Bank, 1818 H Street, NW, Washington, DC 20433, (202) 473-1000, Fax: (202) 477-6391, www.worldbank.org; *Botswana; World Development Indicators (WDI) 2008;* and *World Development Report 2008.*

World Trade Organization (WTO), Centre William Rappard, Rue de Lausanne 154, CH-1211 Geneva 21, Switzerland, www.wto.org; *International Trade Statistics 2006.*

BOTSWANA - INTERNET USERS

International Telecommunication Union (ITU), Place des Nations, 1211 Geneva 20, Switzerland, www.itu.int; *World Telecommunication/ICT Indicators Database on CD-ROM; World Telecommunication/ICT Indicators Database Online;* and *Yearbook of Statistics - Telecommunication Services (Chronological Time Series 1997-2006).*

The World Bank, 1818 H Street, NW, Washington, DC 20433, (202) 473-1000, Fax: (202) 477-6391, www.worldbank.org; *Botswana.*

BOTSWANA - IRON AND IRON ORE PRODUCTION

See BOTSWANA - MINERAL INDUSTRIES

BOTSWANA - LABOR

African Development Bank Group, Rue Joseph Anoma, 01 BP 1387 Abidjan 01, Cote d'Ivoire, www.afdb.org; *Statistics Pocketbook 2008.*

Central Intelligence Agency, Office of Public Affairs, Washington, DC 20505, (703) 482-0623, Fax: (703) 482-1739, www.cia.gov; *The World Factbook.*

Euromonitor International, Inc., 224 S. Michigan Avenue, Suite 1500, Chicago, IL 60604, (312) 922-1115, Fax: (312) 922-1157, www.euromonitor.com; *International Marketing Data and Statistics 2008* and *World Marketing Data and Statistics.*

International Labour Office, I.L.O. Publications, 4 route des Morillons, CH-1211 Geneva 22, Switzerland, (Telephone in U.S. (202) 653-7652), (Fax in U.S. (202) 653-7687), www.ilo.org; *Yearbook of Labour Statistics 2006*.

M.E. Sharpe, 80 Business Park Drive, Armonk, NY 10504, (800) 541-6563, Fax: (914) 273-2106, www.mesharpe.com; *The Illustrated Book of World Rankings*.

Palgrave Macmillan Ltd., Houndmills, Basingstoke, Hampshire, RG21 6XS, England, (Telephone in U.S. (888) 330-8477), (Fax in U.S. (800) 672-2054), www.palgrave.com; *The Statesman's Yearbook 2008*.

Taylor and Francis Group, An Informa Business, 2 Park Square, Milton Park, Abingdon, Oxford OX14 4RN, United Kingdom, (Dial from U.S. (212) 216-7800), (Fax from U.S. (212) 564-7854), www.tandf.co.uk; *The Europa World Year Book*.

United Nations Food and Agricultural Organization (FAO), Viale delle Terme di Caracalla, 00100 Rome, Italy, (Dial from U.S. (202) 653-2400), (Fax from U.S. (202) 653 5760), www.fao.org; *The State of Food and Agriculture (SOFA) 2006*.

United Nations Statistics Division, New York, NY 10017, (800) 253-9646, Fax: (212) 963-4116, http://unstats.un.org; *Human Development Report 2006*.

The World Bank, 1818 H Street, NW, Washington, DC 20433, (202) 473-1000, Fax: (202) 477-6391, www.worldbank.org; *The World Bank Atlas 2003-2004; World Development Indicators (WDI) 2008;* and *World Development Report 2008*.

BOTSWANA - LAND USE

Central Intelligence Agency, Office of Public Affairs, Washington, DC 20505, (703) 482-0623, Fax: (703) 482-1739, www.cia.gov; *The World Factbook*.

Euromonitor International, Inc., 224 S. Michigan Avenue, Suite 1500, Chicago, IL 60604, (312) 922-1115, Fax: (312) 922-1157, www.euromonitor.com; *International Marketing Data and Statistics 2008*.

United Nations Food and Agricultural Organization (FAO), Viale delle Terme di Caracalla, 00100 Rome, Italy, (Dial from U.S. (202) 653-2400), (Fax from U.S. (202) 653 5760), www.fao.org; *FAO Production Yearbook 2002*.

The World Bank, 1818 H Street, NW, Washington, DC 20433, (202) 473-1000, Fax: (202) 477-6391, www.worldbank.org; *World Development Report 2008*.

BOTSWANA - LIBRARIES

M.E. Sharpe, 80 Business Park Drive, Armonk, NY 10504, (800) 541-6563, Fax: (914) 273-2106, www.mesharpe.com; *The Illustrated Book of World Rankings*.

BOTSWANA - LICENSES

International Monetary Fund (IMF), 700 Nineteenth Street, NW, Washington, DC 20431, (202) 623-7000, Fax: (202) 623-4661, www.imf.org; *Government Finance Statistics Yearbook (2008 Edition)*.

BOTSWANA - LIFE EXPECTANCY

African Development Bank Group, Rue Joseph Anoma, 01 BP 1387 Abidjan 01, Cote d'Ivoire, www.afdb.org; *Statistics Pocketbook 2008*.

Central Intelligence Agency, Office of Public Affairs, Washington, DC 20505, (703) 482-0623, Fax: (703) 482-1739, www.cia.gov; *The World Factbook*.

Euromonitor International, Inc., 224 S. Michigan Avenue, Suite 1500, Chicago, IL 60604, (312) 922-1115, Fax: (312) 922-1157, www.euromonitor.com; *The World Economic Factbook 2008*.

United Nations Statistics Division, New York, NY 10017, (800) 253-9646, Fax: (212) 963-4116, http://unstats.un.org; *Human Development Report 2006* and *World Statistics Pocketbook*.

The World Bank, 1818 H Street, NW, Washington, DC 20433, (202) 473-1000, Fax: (202) 477-6391, www.worldbank.org; *The World Bank Atlas 2003-2004* and *World Development Report 2008*.

BOTSWANA - LITERACY

Euromonitor International, Inc., 224 S. Michigan Avenue, Suite 1500, Chicago, IL 60604, (312) 922-1115, Fax: (312) 922-1157, www.euromonitor.com; *World Marketing Data and Statistics*.

United Nations Statistics Division, New York, NY 10017, (800) 253-9646, Fax: (212) 963-4116, http://unstats.un.org; *Survey of Economic and Social Conditions in Africa 2005*.

BOTSWANA - LIVESTOCK

M.E. Sharpe, 80 Business Park Drive, Armonk, NY 10504, (800) 541-6563, Fax: (914) 273-2106, www.mesharpe.com; *The Illustrated Book of World Rankings*.

Palgrave Macmillan Ltd., Houndmills, Basingstoke, Hampshire, RG21 6XS, England, (Telephone in U.S. (888) 330-8477), (Fax in U.S. (800) 672-2054), www.palgrave.com; *The Statesman's Yearbook 2008*.

Taylor and Francis Group, An Informa Business, 2 Park Square, Milton Park, Abingdon, Oxford OX14 4RN, United Kingdom, (Dial from U.S. (212) 216-7800), (Fax from U.S. (212) 564-7854), www.tandf.co.uk; *The Europa World Year Book*.

United Nations Conference on Trade and Development (UNCTAD), DC2-1120, United Nations, New York, NY 10017, (212) 963-0027, www.unctad.org; *UNCTAD Commodity Yearbook*.

United Nations Economic Commission for Africa (ECA), PO Box 3001, Addis Ababa, Ethiopia, (Telephone in U.S. (212) 963-4957), www.uneca.org; *African Statistical Yearbook 2006*.

United Nations Food and Agricultural Organization (FAO), Viale delle Terme di Caracalla, 00100 Rome, Italy, (Dial from U.S. (202) 653-2400), (Fax from U.S. (202) 653 5760), www.fao.org; *FAO Production Yearbook 2002* and *The State of Food and Agriculture (SOFA) 2006*.

United Nations Statistics Division, New York, NY 10017, (800) 253-9646, Fax: (212) 963-4116, http://unstats.un.org; *Statistical Yearbook* and *Survey of Economic and Social Conditions in Africa 2005*.

BOTSWANA - MANUFACTURES

M.E. Sharpe, 80 Business Park Drive, Armonk, NY 10504, (800) 541-6563, Fax: (914) 273-2106, www.mesharpe.com; *The Illustrated Book of World Rankings*.

United Nations Economic Commission for Africa (ECA), PO Box 3001, Addis Ababa, Ethiopia, (Telephone in U.S. (212) 963-4957), www.uneca.org; *African Statistical Yearbook 2006*.

United Nations Statistics Division, New York, NY 10017, (800) 253-9646, Fax: (212) 963-4116, http://unstats.un.org; *Statistical Yearbook* and *Survey of Economic and Social Conditions in Africa 2005*.

The World Bank, 1818 H Street, NW, Washington, DC 20433, (202) 473-1000, Fax: (202) 477-6391, www.worldbank.org; *World Development Indicators (WDI) 2008*.

BOTSWANA - MARRIAGE

M.E. Sharpe, 80 Business Park Drive, Armonk, NY 10504, (800) 541-6563, Fax: (914) 273-2106, www.mesharpe.com; *The Illustrated Book of World Rankings*.

United Nations Statistics Division, New York, NY 10017, (800) 253-9646, Fax: (212) 963-4116, http://unstats.un.org; *Demographic Yearbook*.

BOTSWANA - MEAT PRODUCTION

See BOTSWANA - LIVESTOCK

BOTSWANA - MEDICAL CARE, COST OF

International Monetary Fund (IMF), 700 Nineteenth Street, NW, Washington, DC 20431, (202) 623-7000, Fax: (202) 623-4661, www.imf.org; *Government Finance Statistics Yearbook (2008 Edition)*.

BOTSWANA - MILK PRODUCTION

See BOTSWANA - DAIRY PROCESSING

BOTSWANA - MINERAL INDUSTRIES

International Monetary Fund (IMF), 700 Nineteenth Street, NW, Washington, DC 20431, (202) 623-7000, Fax: (202) 623-4661, www.imf.org; *International Financial Statistics Yearbook 2007*.

M.E. Sharpe, 80 Business Park Drive, Armonk, NY 10504, (800) 541-6563, Fax: (914) 273-2106, www.mesharpe.com; *The Illustrated Book of World Rankings*.

Palgrave Macmillan Ltd., Houndmills, Basingstoke, Hampshire, RG21 6XS, England, (Telephone in U.S. (888) 330-8477), (Fax in U.S. (800) 672-2054), www.palgrave.com; *The Statesman's Yearbook 2008*.

Taylor and Francis Group, An Informa Business, 2 Park Square, Milton Park, Abingdon, Oxford OX14 4RN, United Kingdom, (Dial from U.S. (212) 216-7800), (Fax from U.S. (212) 564-7854), www.tandf.co.uk; *The Europa World Year Book*.

United Nations Conference on Trade and Development (UNCTAD), DC2-1120, United Nations, New York, NY 10017, (212) 963-0027, www.unctad.org; *UNCTAD Commodity Yearbook*.

United Nations Economic Commission for Africa (ECA), PO Box 3001, Addis Ababa, Ethiopia, (Telephone in U.S. (212) 963-4957), www.uneca.org; *African Statistical Yearbook 2006*.

United Nations Statistics Division, New York, NY 10017, (800) 253-9646, Fax: (212) 963-4116, http://unstats.un.org; *Statistical Yearbook*.

BOTSWANA - MONEY EXCHANGE RATES

See BOTSWANA - FOREIGN EXCHANGE RATES

BOTSWANA - MONEY SUPPLY

African Development Bank Group, Rue Joseph Anoma, 01 BP 1387 Abidjan 01, Cote d'Ivoire, www.afdb.org; *Statistics Pocketbook 2008*.

Economist Intelligence Unit, 111 West 57th Street, New York, NY 10019, (212) 554-0600, Fax: (212) 586-1181, www.eiu.com; *Botswana Country Report*.

International Monetary Fund (IMF), 700 Nineteenth Street, NW, Washington, DC 20431, (202) 623-7000, Fax: (202) 623-4661, www.imf.org; *International Financial Statistics Yearbook 2007*.

Taylor and Francis Group, An Informa Business, 2 Park Square, Milton Park, Abingdon, Oxford OX14 4RN, United Kingdom, (Dial from U.S. (212) 216-7800), (Fax from U.S. (212) 564-7854), www.tandf.co.uk; *The Europa World Year Book*.

The World Bank, 1818 H Street, NW, Washington, DC 20433, (202) 473-1000, Fax: (202) 477-6391, www.worldbank.org; *Botswana* and *World Development Indicators (WDI) 2008*.

BOTSWANA - MONUMENTS AND HISTORIC SITES

UNESCO Institute for Statistics, C.P. 6128 Succursale Centre-Ville, Montreal, Quebec, H3C 3J7 Canada, (Dial from U.S. (514) 343-6880), (Fax from U.S. (514) 343 6882), www.uis.unesco.org; *Statistical Tables*.

BOTSWANA - MORTALITY

Central Intelligence Agency, Office of Public Affairs, Washington, DC 20505, (703) 482-0623, Fax: (703) 482-1739, www.cia.gov; *The World Factbook*.

Euromonitor International, Inc., 224 S. Michigan Avenue, Suite 1500, Chicago, IL 60604, (312) 922-1115, Fax: (312) 922-1157, www.euromonitor.com; *International Marketing Data and Statistics 2008* and *The World Economic Factbook 2008*.

Taylor and Francis Group, An Informa Business, 2 Park Square, Milton Park, Abingdon, Oxford OX14 4RN, United Kingdom, (Dial from U.S. (212) 216-7800), (Fax from U.S. (212) 564-7854), www.tandf.co.uk; *The Europa World Year Book*.

UNICEF, 3 United Nations Plaza, New York, NY 10017, (800) 253-9646, Fax: (212) 887-7465, www.unicef.org; *The State of the World's Children 2008*.

United Nations Statistics Division, New York, NY 10017, (800) 253-9646, Fax: (212) 963-4116, http://unstats.un.org; *Demographic Yearbook; Human Development Report 2006; Statistical Yearbook; Survey of Economic and Social Conditions in Africa 2005;* and *World Statistics Pocketbook.*

The World Bank, 1818 H Street, NW, Washington, DC 20433, (202) 473-1000, Fax: (202) 477-6391, www.worldbank.org; *The World Bank Atlas 2003-2004; World Development Indicators (WDI) 2008;* and *World Development Report 2008.*

World Health Organization (WHO), Avenue Appia 20, 1211 Geneve 27, Switzerland, (Telephone in U.S. (212) 331-9081), www.who.int; The WHO Global Atlas of Infectious Diseases.

BOTSWANA - MOTION PICTURES

United Nations Statistics Division, New York, NY 10017, (800) 253-9646, Fax: (212) 963-4116, http://unstats.un.org; *Statistical Yearbook.*

BOTSWANA - MOTOR VEHICLES

International Road Federation (IFR), Madison Place, 500 Montgomery Street, 5th Floor, Alexandria, VA 22314, (703) 535-1001, Fax: (703) 535-1007, www.irfnet.org; *World Road Statistics 2006.*

Taylor and Francis Group, An Informa Business, 2 Park Square, Milton Park, Abingdon, Oxford OX14 4RN, United Kingdom, (Dial from U.S. (212) 216-7800), (Fax from U.S. (212) 564-7854), www.tandf.co.uk; *The Europa World Year Book.*

United Nations Statistics Division, New York, NY 10017, (800) 253-9646, Fax: (212) 963-4116, http://unstats.un.org; *Statistical Yearbook* and *Survey of Economic and Social Conditions in Africa 2005.*

BOTSWANA - MUSEUMS

M.E. Sharpe, 80 Business Park Drive, Armonk, NY 10504, (800) 541-6563, Fax: (914) 273-2106, www.mesharpe.com; *The Illustrated Book of World Rankings.*

UNESCO Institute for Statistics, C.P. 6128 Succursale Centre-Ville, Montreal, Quebec, H3C 3J7 Canada, (Dial from U.S. (514) 343-6880), (Fax from U.S. (514) 343 6882), www.uis.unesco.org; *Statistical Tables.*

BOTSWANA - NATIONAL INCOME

United Nations Statistics Division, New York, NY 10017, (800) 253-9646, Fax: (212) 963-4116, http://unstats.un.org; *Statistical Yearbook.*

BOTSWANA - NATURAL GAS PRODUCTION

See BOTSWANA - MINERAL INDUSTRIES

BOTSWANA - NICKEL AND NICKEL ORE

See BOTSWANA - MINERAL INDUSTRIES

BOTSWANA - NUTRITION

African Development Bank Group, Rue Joseph Anoma, 01 BP 1387 Abidjan 01, Cote d'Ivoire, www.afdb.org; *Statistics Pocketbook 2008.*

United Nations Food and Agricultural Organization (FAO), Viale delle Terme di Caracalla, 00100 Rome, Italy, (Dial from U.S. (202) 653-2400), (Fax from U.S. (202) 653 5760), www.fao.org; *The State of Food and Agriculture (SOFA) 2006.*

BOTSWANA - OLDER PEOPLE

M.E. Sharpe, 80 Business Park Drive, Armonk, NY 10504, (800) 541-6563, Fax: (914) 273-2106, www.mesharpe.com; *The Illustrated Book of World Rankings.*

BOTSWANA - PEANUT PRODUCTION

See BOTSWANA - CROPS

BOTSWANA - PESTICIDES

United Nations Food and Agricultural Organization (FAO), Viale delle Terme di Caracalla, 00100 Rome, Italy, (Dial from U.S. (202) 653-2400), (Fax from U.S. (202) 653 5760), www.fao.org; *The State of Food and Agriculture (SOFA) 2006.*

BOTSWANA - PETROLEUM INDUSTRY AND TRADE

M.E. Sharpe, 80 Business Park Drive, Armonk, NY 10504, (800) 541-6563, Fax: (914) 273-2106, www.mesharpe.com; *The Illustrated Book of World Rankings.*

PennWell Corporation, 1421 South Sheridan Road, Tulsa, OK 74112, (918) 835-3161, www.pennwell.com; *International Petroleum Encyclopedia 2007.*

U.S. Department of Energy (DOE), Energy Information Administration (EIA), 1000 Independence Avenue, SW, Washington, DC 20585, (202) 586-8800, www.eia.doe.gov; *International Energy Annual 2004* and *International Energy Outlook 2006.*

United Nations Conference on Trade and Development (UNCTAD), DC2-1120, United Nations, New York, NY 10017, (212) 963-0027, www.unctad.org; *UNCTAD Commodity Yearbook.*

United Nations Food and Agricultural Organization (FAO), Viale delle Terme di Caracalla, 00100 Rome, Italy, (Dial from U.S. (202) 653-2400), (Fax from U.S. (202) 653 5760), www.fao.org; *The State of Food and Agriculture (SOFA) 2006.*

BOTSWANA - POLITICAL SCIENCE

Central Intelligence Agency, Office of Public Affairs, Washington, DC 20505, (703) 482-0623, Fax: (703) 482-1739, www.cia.gov; *The World Factbook.*

International Monetary Fund (IMF), 700 Nineteenth Street, NW, Washington, DC 20431, (202) 623-7000, Fax: (202) 623-4661, www.imf.org; *Government Finance Statistics Yearbook (2008 Edition)* and *International Financial Statistics Yearbook 2007.*

Palgrave Macmillan Ltd., Houndmills, Basingstoke, Hampshire, RG21 6XS, England, (Telephone in U.S. (888) 330-8477), (Fax in U.S. (800) 672-2054), www.palgrave.com; *The Statesman's Yearbook 2008.*

Taylor and Francis Group, An Informa Business, 2 Park Square, Milton Park, Abingdon, Oxford OX14 4RN, United Kingdom, (Dial from U.S. (212) 216-7800), (Fax from U.S. (212) 564-7854), www.tandf.co.uk; *The Europa World Year Book.*

United Nations Statistics Division, New York, NY 10017, (800) 253-9646, Fax: (212) 963-4116, http://unstats.un.org; *National Accounts Statistics: Compendium of Income Distribution Statistics* and *Survey of Economic and Social Conditions in Africa 2005.*

The World Bank, 1818 H Street, NW, Washington, DC 20433, (202) 473-1000, Fax: (202) 477-6391, www.worldbank.org; *World Development Indicators (WDI) 2008* and *World Development Report 2008.*

BOTSWANA - POPULATION

African Development Bank Group, Rue Joseph Anoma, 01 BP 1387 Abidjan 01, Cote d'Ivoire, www.afdb.org; *The African Statistical Journal; Gender, Poverty and Environmental Indicators on African Countries 2007; Selected Statistics on African Countries 2007;* and *Statistics Pocketbook 2008.*

Central Intelligence Agency, Office of Public Affairs, Washington, DC 20505, (703) 482-0623, Fax: (703) 482-1739, www.cia.gov; *The World Factbook.*

Economist Intelligence Unit, 111 West 57th Street, New York, NY 10019, (212) 554-0600, Fax: (212) 586-1181, www.eiu.com; *Botswana Country Report.*

Euromonitor International, Inc., 224 S. Michigan Avenue, Suite 1500, Chicago, IL 60604, (312) 922-1115, Fax: (312) 922-1157, www.euromonitor.com; *International Marketing Data and Statistics 2008* and *The World Economic Factbook 2008.*

Eurostat, Batiment Jean Monnet, Rue Alcide de Gasperi, L-2920 Luxembourg, http://epp.eurostat.ec.europa.eu; *Demographic Indicators - Population by Age-Classes.*

International Labour Office, I.L.O. Publications, 4 route des Morillons, CH-1211 Geneva 22, Switzerland, (Telephone in U.S. (202) 653-7652), (Fax in U.S. (202) 653-7687), www.ilo.org; *Yearbook of Labour Statistics 2006.*

M.E. Sharpe, 80 Business Park Drive, Armonk, NY 10504, (800) 541-6563, Fax: (914) 273-2106, www.mesharpe.com; *The Illustrated Book of World Rankings.*

Palgrave Macmillan Ltd., Houndmills, Basingstoke, Hampshire, RG21 6XS, England, (Telephone in U.S. (888) 330-8477), (Fax in U.S. (800) 672-2054), www.palgrave.com; *The Statesman's Yearbook 2008.*

Taylor and Francis Group, An Informa Business, 2 Park Square, Milton Park, Abingdon, Oxford OX14 4RN, United Kingdom, (Dial from U.S. (212) 216-7800), (Fax from U.S. (212) 564-7854), www.tandf.co.uk; *The Europa World Year Book.*

U.S. Department of State (DOS), 2201 C Street NW, Washington, DC 20520, (202) 647-4000, www.state.gov; *World Military Expenditures and Arms Transfers (WMEAT).*

UNESCO Institute for Statistics, C.P. 6128 Succursale Centre-Ville, Montreal, Quebec, H3C 3J7 Canada, (Dial from U.S. (514) 343-6880), (Fax from U.S. (514) 343 6882), www.uis.unesco.org; *Statistical Tables.*

United Nations Food and Agricultural Organization (FAO), Viale delle Terme di Caracalla, 00100 Rome, Italy, (Dial from U.S. (202) 653-2400), (Fax from U.S. (202) 653 5760), www.fao.org; *FAO Production Yearbook 2002.*

United Nations Statistics Division, New York, NY 10017, (800) 253-9646, Fax: (212) 963-4116, http://unstats.un.org; *Demographic Yearbook; Human Development Report 2006; Statistical Yearbook; Survey of Economic and Social Conditions in Africa 2005;* and *World Statistics Pocketbook.*

The World Bank, 1818 H Street, NW, Washington, DC 20433, (202) 473-1000, Fax: (202) 477-6391, www.worldbank.org; *Botswana; The World Bank Atlas 2003-2004;* and *World Development Report 2008.*

World Health Organization (WHO), Avenue Appia 20, 1211 Geneve 27, Switzerland, (Telephone in U.S. (212) 331-9081), www.who.int; *World Health Report 2006.*

BOTSWANA - POPULATION DENSITY

African Development Bank Group, Rue Joseph Anoma, 01 BP 1387 Abidjan 01, Cote d'Ivoire, www.afdb.org; *Statistics Pocketbook 2008.*

Central Intelligence Agency, Office of Public Affairs, Washington, DC 20505, (703) 482-0623, Fax: (703) 482-1739, www.cia.gov; *The World Factbook.*

Euromonitor International, Inc., 224 S. Michigan Avenue, Suite 1500, Chicago, IL 60604, (312) 922-1115, Fax: (312) 922-1157, www.euromonitor.com; *The World Economic Factbook 2008.*

M.E. Sharpe, 80 Business Park Drive, Armonk, NY 10504, (800) 541-6563, Fax: (914) 273-2106, www.mesharpe.com; *The Illustrated Book of World Rankings.*

Palgrave Macmillan Ltd., Houndmills, Basingstoke, Hampshire, RG21 6XS, England, (Telephone in U.S. (888) 330-8477), (Fax in U.S. (800) 672-2054), www.palgrave.com; *The Statesman's Yearbook 2008.*

Taylor and Francis Group, An Informa Business, 2 Park Square, Milton Park, Abingdon, Oxford OX14 4RN, United Kingdom, (Dial from U.S. (212) 216-7800), (Fax from U.S. (212) 564-7854), www.tandf.co.uk; *The Europa World Year Book.*

United Nations Food and Agricultural Organization (FAO), Viale delle Terme di Caracalla, 00100 Rome, Italy, (Dial from U.S. (202) 653-2400), (Fax from U.S. (202) 653 5760), www.fao.org; *The State of Food and Agriculture (SOFA) 2006.*

United Nations Statistics Division, New York, NY 10017, (800) 253-9646, Fax: (212) 963-4116, http://unstats.un.org; *Statistical Yearbook* and *Survey of Economic and Social Conditions in Africa 2005.*

The World Bank, 1818 H Street, NW, Washington, DC 20433, (202) 473-1000, Fax: (202) 477-6391, www.worldbank.org; *Botswana* and *World Development Report 2008.*

BOTSWANA - POSTAL SERVICE

M.E. Sharpe, 80 Business Park Drive, Armonk, NY 10504, (800) 541-6563, Fax: (914) 273-2106, www.mesharpe.com; *The Illustrated Book of World Rankings.*

Palgrave Macmillan Ltd., Houndmills, Basingstoke, Hampshire, RG21 6XS, England, (Telephone in U.S. (888) 330-8477), (Fax in U.S. (800) 672-2054), www.palgrave.com; *The Statesman's Yearbook 2008.*

United Nations Statistics Division, New York, NY 10017, (800) 253-9646, Fax: (212) 963-4116, http://unstats.un.org; *Statistical Yearbook.*

BOTSWANA - POWER RESOURCES

Euromonitor International, Inc., 224 S. Michigan Avenue, Suite 1500, Chicago, IL 60604, (312) 922-1115, Fax: (312) 922-1157, www.euromonitor.com; *International Marketing Data and Statistics 2008; The World Economic Factbook 2008;* and *World Marketing Data and Statistics.*

M.E. Sharpe, 80 Business Park Drive, Armonk, NY 10504, (800) 541-6563, Fax: (914) 273-2106, www.mesharpe.com; *The Illustrated Book of World Rankings.*

Palgrave Macmillan Ltd., Houndmills, Basingstoke, Hampshire, RG21 6XS, England, (Telephone in U.S. (888) 330-8477), (Fax in U.S. (800) 672-2054), www.palgrave.com; *The Statesman's Yearbook 2008.*

Platts, 2 Penn Plaza, 25th Floor, New York, NY 10121-2298, (212) 904-3070, www.platts.com; *Energy Economist.*

U.S. Department of Energy (DOE), Energy Information Administration (EIA), 1000 Independence Avenue, SW, Washington, DC 20585, (202) 586-8800, www.eia.doe.gov; *International Energy Annual 2004* and *International Energy Outlook 2006.*

United Nations Economic Commission for Africa (ECA), PO Box 3001, Addis Ababa, Ethiopia, (Telephone in U.S. (212) 963-4957), www.uneca.org; *African Statistical Yearbook 2006.*

United Nations Food and Agricultural Organization (FAO), Viale delle Terme di Caracalla, 00100 Rome, Italy, (Dial from U.S. (202) 653-2400), (Fax from U.S. (202) 653 5760), www.fao.org; *The State of Food and Agriculture (SOFA) 2006.*

United Nations Statistics Division, New York, NY 10017, (800) 253-9646, Fax: (212) 963-4116, http://unstats.un.org; *Energy Statistics Yearbook 2003; Human Development Report 2006; Statistical Yearbook;* and *World Statistics Pocketbook.*

The World Bank, 1818 H Street, NW, Washington, DC 20433, (202) 473-1000, Fax: (202) 477-6391, www.worldbank.org; *The World Bank Atlas 2003-2004* and *World Development Report 2008.*

BOTSWANA - PRICES

Euromonitor International, Inc., 224 S. Michigan Avenue, Suite 1500, Chicago, IL 60604, (312) 922-1115, Fax: (312) 922-1157, www.euromonitor.com; *World Marketing Data and Statistics.*

International Labour Office, I.L.O. Publications, 4 route des Morillons, CH-1211 Geneva 22, Switzerland, (Telephone in U.S. (202) 653-7652), (Fax in U.S. (202) 653-7687), www.ilo.org; *Yearbook of Labour Statistics 2006.*

International Monetary Fund (IMF), 700 Nineteenth Street, NW, Washington, DC 20431, (202) 623-7000, Fax: (202) 623-4661, www.imf.org; *International Financial Statistics Yearbook 2007.*

M.E. Sharpe, 80 Business Park Drive, Armonk, NY 10504, (800) 541-6563, Fax: (914) 273-2106, www.mesharpe.com; *The Illustrated Book of World Rankings.*

United Nations Economic Commission for Africa (ECA), PO Box 3001, Addis Ababa, Ethiopia, (Telephone in U.S. (212) 963-4957), www.uneca.org; *African Statistical Yearbook 2006.*

United Nations Food and Agricultural Organization (FAO), Viale delle Terme di Caracalla, 00100 Rome, Italy, (Dial from U.S. (202) 653-2400), (Fax from U.S. (202) 653 5760), www.fao.org; *FAO Production Yearbook 2002.*

The World Bank, 1818 H Street, NW, Washington, DC 20433, (202) 473-1000, Fax: (202) 477-6391, www.worldbank.org; *Botswana.*

BOTSWANA - PROFESSIONS

UNESCO Institute for Statistics, C.P. 6128 Succursale Centre-Ville, Montreal, Quebec, H3C 3J7 Canada, (Dial from U.S. (514) 343-6880), (Fax from U.S. (514) 343 6882), www.uis.unesco.org; *Statistical Tables.*

United Nations Statistics Division, New York, NY 10017, (800) 253-9646, Fax: (212) 963-4116, http://unstats.un.org; *Statistical Yearbook.*

BOTSWANA - PUBLIC HEALTH

African Development Bank Group, Rue Joseph Anoma, 01 BP 1387 Abidjan 01, Cote d'Ivoire, www.afdb.org; *Statistics Pocketbook 2008.*

Euromonitor International, Inc., 224 S. Michigan Avenue, Suite 1500, Chicago, IL 60604, (312) 922-1115, Fax: (312) 922-1157, www.euromonitor.com; *World Marketing Data and Statistics.*

M.E. Sharpe, 80 Business Park Drive, Armonk, NY 10504, (800) 541-6563, Fax: (914) 273-2106, www.mesharpe.com; *The Illustrated Book of World Rankings.*

Palgrave Macmillan Ltd., Houndmills, Basingstoke, Hampshire, RG21 6XS, England, (Telephone in U.S. (888) 330-8477), (Fax in U.S. (800) 672-2054), www.palgrave.com; *The Statesman's Yearbook 2008.*

UNICEF, 3 United Nations Plaza, New York, NY 10017, (800) 253-9646, Fax: (212) 887-7465, www.unicef.org; *The State of the World's Children 2008.*

United Nations Economic Commission for Africa (ECA), PO Box 3001, Addis Ababa, Ethiopia, (Telephone in U.S. (212) 963-4957), www.uneca.org; *African Statistical Yearbook 2006.*

United Nations Statistics Division, New York, NY 10017, (800) 253-9646, Fax: (212) 963-4116, http://unstats.un.org; *Human Development Report 2006* and *Statistical Yearbook.*

The World Bank, 1818 H Street, NW, Washington, DC 20433, (202) 473-1000, Fax: (202) 477-6391, www.worldbank.org; *Botswana* and *World Development Report 2008.*

World Health Organization (WHO), Avenue Appia 20, 1211 Geneve 27, Switzerland, (Telephone in U.S. (212) 331-9081), www.who.int; The WHO Global Atlas of Infectious Diseases.

BOTSWANA - PUBLISHERS AND PUBLISHING

Taylor and Francis Group, An Informa Business, 2 Park Square, Milton Park, Abingdon, Oxford OX14 4RN, United Kingdom, (Dial from U.S. (212) 216-7800), (Fax from U.S. (212) 564-7854), www.tandf.co.uk; *The Europa World Year Book.*

UNESCO Institute for Statistics, C.P. 6128 Succursale Centre-Ville, Montreal, Quebec, H3C 3J7 Canada, (Dial from U.S. (514) 343-6880), (Fax from U.S. (514) 343 6882), www.uis.unesco.org; *Statistical Tables.*

BOTSWANA - RADIO BROADCASTING

Palgrave Macmillan Ltd., Houndmills, Basingstoke, Hampshire, RG21 6XS, England, (Telephone in U.S. (888) 330-8477), (Fax in U.S. (800) 672-2054), www.palgrave.com; *The Statesman's Yearbook 2008.*

BOTSWANA - RAILROADS

Jane's Information Group, 110 North Royal Street, Suite 200, Alexandria, VA 22314, (703) 683-3700, Fax: (800) 836-0297, www.janes.com; *Jane's World Railways.*

Palgrave Macmillan Ltd., Houndmills, Basingstoke, Hampshire, RG21 6XS, England, (Telephone in U.S. (888) 330-8477), (Fax in U.S. (800) 672-2054), www.palgrave.com; *The Statesman's Yearbook 2008.*

Taylor and Francis Group, An Informa Business, 2 Park Square, Milton Park, Abingdon, Oxford OX14 4RN, United Kingdom, (Dial from U.S. (212) 216-7800), (Fax from U.S. (212) 564-7854), www.tandf.co.uk; *The Europa World Year Book.*

United Nations Economic Commission for Africa (ECA), PO Box 3001, Addis Ababa, Ethiopia, (Telephone in U.S. (212) 963-4957), www.uneca.org; *African Statistical Yearbook 2006.*

United Nations Statistics Division, New York, NY 10017, (800) 253-9646, Fax: (212) 963-4116, http://unstats.un.org; *Statistical Yearbook* and *Survey of Economic and Social Conditions in Africa 2005.*

BOTSWANA - RELIGION

Central Intelligence Agency, Office of Public Affairs, Washington, DC 20505, (703) 482-0623, Fax: (703) 482-1739, www.cia.gov; *The World Factbook.*

M.E. Sharpe, 80 Business Park Drive, Armonk, NY 10504, (800) 541-6563, Fax: (914) 273-2106, www.mesharpe.com; *The Illustrated Book of World Rankings.*

Palgrave Macmillan Ltd., Houndmills, Basingstoke, Hampshire, RG21 6XS, England, (Telephone in U.S. (888) 330-8477), (Fax in U.S. (800) 672-2054), www.palgrave.com; *The Statesman's Yearbook 2008.*

BOTSWANA - RENT CHARGES

International Labour Office, I.L.O. Publications, 4 route des Morillons, CH-1211 Geneva 22, Switzerland, (Telephone in U.S. (202) 653-7652), (Fax in U.S. (202) 653-7687), www.ilo.org; *Yearbook of Labour Statistics 2006.*

BOTSWANA - RESERVES (ACCOUNTING)

African Development Bank Group, Rue Joseph Anoma, 01 BP 1387 Abidjan 01, Cote d'Ivoire, www.afdb.org; *Statistics Pocketbook 2008.*

The World Bank, 1818 H Street, NW, Washington, DC 20433, (202) 473-1000, Fax: (202) 477-6391, www.worldbank.org; *World Development Indicators (WDI) 2008.*

BOTSWANA - RETAIL TRADE

Euromonitor International, Inc., 224 S. Michigan Avenue, Suite 1500, Chicago, IL 60604, (312) 922-1115, Fax: (312) 922-1157, www.euromonitor.com; *World Marketing Data and Statistics.*

BOTSWANA - RICE PRODUCTION

See BOTSWANA - CROPS

BOTSWANA - ROADS

Central Intelligence Agency, Office of Public Affairs, Washington, DC 20505, (703) 482-0623, Fax: (703) 482-1739, www.cia.gov; *The World Factbook.*

International Road Federation (IFR), Madison Place, 500 Montgomery Street, 5th Floor, Alexandria, VA 22314, (703) 535-1001, Fax: (703) 535-1007, www.irfnet.org; *World Road Statistics 2006.*

Palgrave Macmillan Ltd., Houndmills, Basingstoke, Hampshire, RG21 6XS, England, (Telephone in U.S. (888) 330-8477), (Fax in U.S. (800) 672-2054), www.palgrave.com; *The Statesman's Yearbook 2008.*

United Nations Economic Commission for Africa (ECA), PO Box 3001, Addis Ababa, Ethiopia, (Telephone in U.S. (212) 963-4957), www.uneca.org; *African Statistical Yearbook 2006.*

United Nations Statistics Division, New York, NY 10017, (800) 253-9646, Fax: (212) 963-4116, http://unstats.un.org; *Survey of Economic and Social Conditions in Africa 2005.*

BOTSWANA - RUBBER INDUSTRY AND TRADE

International Rubber Study Group (IRSG), 1st Floor, Heron House, 109/115 Wembley Hill Road, Wemb-

ley, Middlesex HA9 8DA, United Kingdom, www.rubberstudy.com; *Rubber Statistical Bulletin; Summary of World Rubber Statistics 2005; World Rubber Statistics Handbook (Volume 6, 1975-2001);* and *World Rubber Statistics Historic Handbook.*

M.E. Sharpe, 80 Business Park Drive, Armonk, NY 10504, (800) 541-6563, Fax: (914) 273-2106, www.mesharpe.com; *The Illustrated Book of World Rankings.*

BOTSWANA - SHEEP

See BOTSWANA - LIVESTOCK

BOTSWANA - SHIPPING

United Nations Economic Commission for Africa (ECA), PO Box 3001, Addis Ababa, Ethiopia, (Telephone in U.S. (212) 963-4957), www.uneca.org; *African Statistical Yearbook 2006.*

BOTSWANA - SILVER PRODUCTION

See BOTSWANA - MINERAL INDUSTRIES

BOTSWANA - SOCIAL ECOLOGY

M.E. Sharpe, 80 Business Park Drive, Armonk, NY 10504, (800) 541-6563, Fax: (914) 273-2106, www.mesharpe.com; *The Illustrated Book of World Rankings.*

United Nations Statistics Division, New York, NY 10017, (800) 253-9646, Fax: (212) 963-4116, http://unstats.un.org; *World Statistics Pocketbook.*

BOTSWANA - SOCIAL SECURITY

International Monetary Fund (IMF), 700 Nineteenth Street, NW, Washington, DC 20431, (202) 623-7000, Fax: (202) 623-4661, www.imf.org; *Government Finance Statistics Yearbook (2008 Edition).*

United Nations Statistics Division, New York, NY 10017, (800) 253-9646, Fax: (212) 963-4116, http://unstats.un.org; *National Accounts Statistics: Compendium of Income Distribution Statistics.*

BOTSWANA - STEEL PRODUCTION

See BOTSWANA - MINERAL INDUSTRIES

BOTSWANA - SUGAR PRODUCTION

See BOTSWANA - CROPS

BOTSWANA - TAXATION

International Monetary Fund (IMF), 700 Nineteenth Street, NW, Washington, DC 20431, (202) 623-7000, Fax: (202) 623-4661, www.imf.org; *Government Finance Statistics Yearbook (2008 Edition).*

International Road Federation (IFR), Madison Place, 500 Montgomery Street, 5th Floor, Alexandria, VA 22314, (703) 535-1001, Fax: (703) 535-1007, www.irfnet.org; *World Road Statistics 2006.*

Taylor and Francis Group, An Informa Business, 2 Park Square, Milton Park, Abingdon, Oxford OX14 4RN, United Kingdom, (Dial from U.S. (212) 216-7800), (Fax from U.S. (212) 564-7854), www.tandf.co.uk; *The Europa World Year Book.*

The World Bank, 1818 H Street, NW, Washington, DC 20433, (202) 473-1000, Fax: (202) 477-6391, www.worldbank.org; *World Development Indicators (WDI) 2008.*

BOTSWANA - TELEPHONE

International Telecommunication Union (ITU), Place des Nations, 1211 Geneva 20, Switzerland, www.itu.int; World Telecommunication Indicators Database.

Palgrave Macmillan Ltd., Houndmills, Basingstoke, Hampshire, RG21 6XS, England, (Telephone in U.S. (888) 330-8477), (Fax in U.S. (800) 672-2054), www.palgrave.com; *The Statesman's Yearbook 2008.*

Taylor and Francis Group, An Informa Business, 2 Park Square, Milton Park, Abingdon, Oxford OX14 4RN, United Kingdom, (Dial from U.S. (212) 216-7800), (Fax from U.S. (212) 564-7854), www.tandf.co.uk; *The Europa World Year Book.*

United Nations Statistics Division, New York, NY 10017, (800) 253-9646, Fax: (212) 963-4116, http://unstats.un.org; *Statistical Yearbook* and *World Statistics Pocketbook.*

BOTSWANA - TEXTILE INDUSTRY

M.E. Sharpe, 80 Business Park Drive, Armonk, NY 10504, (800) 541-6563, Fax: (914) 273-2106, www.mesharpe.com; *The Illustrated Book of World Rankings.*

Palgrave Macmillan Ltd., Houndmills, Basingstoke, Hampshire, RG21 6XS, England, (Telephone in U.S. (888) 330-8477), (Fax in U.S. (800) 672-2054), www.palgrave.com; *The Statesman's Yearbook 2008.*

United Nations Conference on Trade and Development (UNCTAD), DC2-1120, United Nations, New York, NY 10017, (212) 963-0027, www.unctad.org; *UNCTAD Commodity Yearbook.*

BOTSWANA - THEATER

UNESCO Institute for Statistics, C.P. 6128 Succursale Centre-Ville, Montreal, Quebec, H3C 3J7 Canada, (Dial from U.S. (514) 343-6880), (Fax from U.S. (514) 343 6882), www.uis.unesco.org; *Statistical Tables.*

BOTSWANA - TOBACCO INDUSTRY

Foreign Agricultural Service (FAS), U.S. Department of Agriculture (USDA), 1400 Independence Avenue, SW, Washington, DC 20250, (202) 720-3935, www.fas.usda.gov; *Tobacco: World Markets and Trade.*

M.E. Sharpe, 80 Business Park Drive, Armonk, NY 10504, (800) 541-6563, Fax: (914) 273-2106, www.mesharpe.com; *The Illustrated Book of World Rankings.*

BOTSWANA - TOURISM

Euromonitor International, Inc., 224 S. Michigan Avenue, Suite 1500, Chicago, IL 60604, (312) 922-1115, Fax: (312) 922-1157, www.euromonitor.com; *The World Economic Factbook 2008* and *World Marketing Data and Statistics.*

M.E. Sharpe, 80 Business Park Drive, Armonk, NY 10504, (800) 541-6563, Fax: (914) 273-2106, www.mesharpe.com; *The Illustrated Book of World Rankings.*

Palgrave Macmillan Ltd., Houndmills, Basingstoke, Hampshire, RG21 6XS, England, (Telephone in U.S. (888) 330-8477), (Fax in U.S. (800) 672-2054), www.palgrave.com; *The Statesman's Yearbook 2008.*

Taylor and Francis Group, An Informa Business, 2 Park Square, Milton Park, Abingdon, Oxford OX14 4RN, United Kingdom, (Dial from U.S. (212) 216-7800), (Fax from U.S. (212) 564-7854), www.tandf.co.uk; *The Europa World Year Book.*

United Nations Economic Commission for Africa (ECA), PO Box 3001, Addis Ababa, Ethiopia, (Telephone in U.S. (212) 963-4957), www.uneca.org; *African Statistical Yearbook 2006.*

United Nations World Tourism Organization (UNWTO), Capitan Haya 42, 28020 Madrid, Spain, www.world-tourism.org; *Yearbook of Tourism Statistics.*

The World Bank, 1818 H Street, NW, Washington, DC 20433, (202) 473-1000, Fax: (202) 477-6391, www.worldbank.org; *Botswana.*

BOTSWANA - TRADE

See BOTSWANA - INTERNATIONAL TRADE

BOTSWANA - TRANSPORTATION

Central Intelligence Agency, Office of Public Affairs, Washington, DC 20505, (703) 482-0623, Fax: (703) 482-1739, www.cia.gov; *The World Factbook.*

Euromonitor International, Inc., 224 S. Michigan Avenue, Suite 1500, Chicago, IL 60604, (312) 922-1115, Fax: (312) 922-1157, www.euromonitor.com; *International Marketing Data and Statistics 2008* and *World Marketing Data and Statistics.*

M.E. Sharpe, 80 Business Park Drive, Armonk, NY 10504, (800) 541-6563, Fax: (914) 273-2106, www.mesharpe.com; *The Illustrated Book of World Rankings.*

Palgrave Macmillan Ltd., Houndmills, Basingstoke, Hampshire, RG21 6XS, England, (Telephone in U.S. (888) 330-8477), (Fax in U.S. (800) 672-2054), www.palgrave.com; *The Statesman's Yearbook 2008.*

Taylor and Francis Group, An Informa Business, 2 Park Square, Milton Park, Abingdon, Oxford OX14 4RN, United Kingdom, (Dial from U.S. (212) 216-7800), (Fax from U.S. (212) 564-7854), www.tandf.co.uk; *The Europa World Year Book.*

United Nations Economic Commission for Africa (ECA), PO Box 3001, Addis Ababa, Ethiopia, (Telephone in U.S. (212) 963-4957), www.uneca.org; *African Statistical Yearbook 2006.*

United Nations Statistics Division, New York, NY 10017, (800) 253-9646, Fax: (212) 963-4116, http://unstats.un.org; *Human Development Report 2006.*

The World Bank, 1818 H Street, NW, Washington, DC 20433, (202) 473-1000, Fax: (202) 477-6391, www.worldbank.org; *Africa Live Database (LDB)* and *Botswana.*

BOTSWANA - UNEMPLOYMENT

Central Intelligence Agency, Office of Public Affairs, Washington, DC 20505, (703) 482-0623, Fax: (703) 482-1739, www.cia.gov; *The World Factbook.*

International Labour Office, I.L.O. Publications, 4 route des Morillons, CH-1211 Geneva 22, Switzerland, (Telephone in U.S. (202) 653-7652), (Fax in U.S. (202) 653-7687), www.ilo.org; *Yearbook of Labour Statistics 2006.*

Palgrave Macmillan Ltd., Houndmills, Basingstoke, Hampshire, RG21 6XS, England, (Telephone in U.S. (888) 330-8477), (Fax in U.S. (800) 672-2054), www.palgrave.com; *The Statesman's Yearbook 2008.*

BOTSWANA - VITAL STATISTICS

Palgrave Macmillan Ltd., Houndmills, Basingstoke, Hampshire, RG21 6XS, England, (Telephone in U.S. (888) 330-8477), (Fax in U.S. (800) 672-2054), www.palgrave.com; *The Statesman's Yearbook 2008.*

World Health Organization (WHO), Avenue Appia 20, 1211 Geneve 27, Switzerland, (Telephone in U.S. (212) 331-9081), www.who.int; *World Health Report 2006.*

BOTSWANA - WAGES

International Labour Office, I.L.O. Publications, 4 route des Morillons, CH-1211 Geneva 22, Switzerland, (Telephone in U.S. (202) 653-7652), (Fax in U.S. (202) 653-7687), www.ilo.org; *Yearbook of Labour Statistics 2006.*

The World Bank, 1818 H Street, NW, Washington, DC 20433, (202) 473-1000, Fax: (202) 477-6391, www.worldbank.org; *Botswana.*

BOTSWANA - WEATHER

See BOTSWANA - CLIMATE

BOTSWANA - WELFARE STATE

International Monetary Fund (IMF), 700 Nineteenth Street, NW, Washington, DC 20431, (202) 623-7000, Fax: (202) 623-4661, www.imf.org; *Government Finance Statistics Yearbook (2008 Edition).*

BOTSWANA - WHEAT PRODUCTION

See BOTSWANA - CROPS

BOTSWANA - WINE PRODUCTION

See BOTSWANA - BEVERAGE INDUSTRY

BOTSWANA - WOOL PRODUCTION

See BOTSWANA - TEXTILE INDUSTRY

BOTULISM

Centers for Disease Control and Prevention (CDC), U.S. Department of Health and Human Services (HHS), 1600 Clifton Road, Atlanta, GA 30333, (800) 311-3435, www.cdc.gov; *Morbidity and Mortality Weekly Report (MMWR)* and *Summary of Notifiable Diseases, United States, 2006.*

BOWLING

American Bowling Congress, 5301 South 76th Street, Greendale, WI 53129, (800) 514-BOWL, www.bowl.com; unpublished data.

National Sporting Goods Association (NSGA), 1601 Feehanville Drive, Suite 300, Mount Prospect, IL 60056, (847) 296-6742, Fax: (847) 391-9827, www.nsga.org; *2006 Sports Participation* and *Ten-Year History of Selected Sports Participation, 1996-2006*.

BOWLING CENTER INDUSTRY RECEIPTS

U.S. Census Bureau, Center for Economic Studies, 4600 Silver Hill Road, Washington DC 20233, (301) 457-1235, www.ces.census.gov; *2002 Economic Census, Information*.

U.S. Census Bureau, Service Sector Statistics Division, 4700 Silver Hill Road, Washington DC 20233-0001, (301) 763-3030, www.census.gov/svsd/www/economic.html; *2004 Service Annual Survey: Arts, Entertainment, and Recreation*.

BOXING

Mediamark Research, Inc., 75 Ninth Avenue, 5th Floor, New York, NY 10011, (212) 884-9200, Fax: (212) 884-9339, www.mediamark.com; MRI+.

BOY SCOUTS - MEMBERSHIP AND UNITS

Boy Scouts of America, PO Box 152079, Irving, TX 75015-2079, (972) 580-2204, www.scouting.org; *Annual Report*.

BRAZIL - NATIONAL STATISTICAL OFFICE

Brazilian Statistical and Geographic Institute (Instituto Brasileiro de Geografia e Estatistica (IBGE)), Rua General Canabarro, 706 - Maracana, Rio de Janeiro, RJ 20271-201, Brazil, www.ibge.gov.br/english/default.php; National Data Center.

BRAZIL - PRIMARY STATISTICS SOURCES

Brazilian Statistical and Geographic Institute (Instituto Brasileiro de Geografia e Estatistica (IBGE)), Rua General Canabarro, 706 - Maracana, Rio de Janeiro, RJ 20271-201, Brazil, www.ibge.gov.br/english/default.php; *Anuario estatistico do Brasil* (Statistical Yearbook of Brazil) and *Summary of Social Indicators, 2004*.

BRAZIL - AGRICULTURAL MACHINERY

Economist Intelligence Unit, 111 West 57th Street, New York, NY 10019, (212) 554-0600, Fax: (212) 586-1181, www.eiu.com; *Business Latin America*.

United Nations Statistics Division, New York, NY 10017, (800) 253-9646, Fax: (212) 963-4116, http://unstats.un.org; *Statistical Yearbook*.

BRAZIL - AGRICULTURE

Economist Intelligence Unit, 111 West 57th Street, New York, NY 10019, (212) 554-0600, Fax: (212) 586-1181, www.eiu.com; *Brazil Country Report* and *Business Latin America*.

Euromonitor International, Inc., 224 S. Michigan Avenue, Suite 1500, Chicago, IL 60604, (312) 922-1115, Fax: (312) 922-1157, www.euromonitor.com; *International Marketing Data and Statistics 2008* and *World Marketing Data and Statistics*.

Federal Statistical Office Germany, D-65180 Wiesbaden, Germany, www.destatis.de; *Brazil 2006*.

Inter-American Development Bank (IDB), 1300 New York Avenue, NW, Washington, DC 20577, (202) 623-1000, Fax: (202) 623-3096, www.iadb.org; *The Politics of Policies: Economic and Social Progress in Latin America - 2006 Report*.

M.E. Sharpe, 80 Business Park Drive, Armonk, NY 10504, (800) 541-6563, Fax: (914) 273-2106, www.mesharpe.com; *The Illustrated Book of World Rankings*.

Organisation for Economic Cooperation and Development (OECD), 2 rue Andre Pascal, F-75775 Paris Cedex 16, France, (Telephone in U.S. (202) 785-6323), (Fax in U.S. (202) 785-0350), www.oecd.org; *OECD Economic Survey - Brazil 2006*.

Palgrave Macmillan Ltd., Houndmills, Basingstoke, Hampshire, RG21 6XS, England, (Telephone in U.S. (888) 330-8477), (Fax in U.S. (800) 672-2054), www.palgrave.com; *The Statesman's Yearbook 2008*.

Taylor and Francis Group, An Informa Business, 2 Park Square, Milton Park, Abingdon, Oxford OX14 4RN, United Kingdom, (Dial from U.S. (212) 216-7800), (Fax from U.S. (212) 564-7854), www.tandf.co.uk; *The Europa World Year Book*.

UCLA Latin American Institute, 10343 Bunche Hall, Box 951447, Los Angeles, CA 90095-1447, (310) 825-4571, Fax: (310) 206-6859, www.international.ucla.edu/lac; *Statistical Abstract of Latin America*.

United Nations Conference on Trade and Development (UNCTAD), DC2-1120, United Nations, New York, NY 10017, (212) 963-0027, www.unctad.org; *UNCTAD Commodity Yearbook*.

United Nations Food and Agricultural Organization (FAO), Viale delle Terme di Caracalla, 00100 Rome, Italy, (Dial from U.S. (202) 653-2400), (Fax from U.S. (202) 653 5760), www.fao.org; AQUASTAT; *FAO Production Yearbook 2002; FAO Trade Yearbook;* and *The State of Food and Agriculture (SOFA) 2006*.

United Nations Statistics Division, New York, NY 10017, (800) 253-9646, Fax: (212) 963-4116, http://unstats.un.org; *Statistical Yearbook* and *Statistical Yearbook for Latin America and the Caribbean 2004*.

The World Bank, 1818 H Street, NW, Washington, DC 20433, (202) 473-1000, Fax: (202) 477-6391, www.worldbank.org; *Brazil* and *World Development Indicators (WDI) 2008*.

BRAZIL - AIRLINES

Economist Intelligence Unit, 111 West 57th Street, New York, NY 10019, (212) 554-0600, Fax: (212) 586-1181, www.eiu.com; *Business Latin America*.

International Civil Aviation Organization (ICAO), External Relations and Public Information Office (EPO), 999 University Street, Montreal, Quebec H3C 5H7, Canada, (Dial from U.S. (514) 954-8219), (Fax from U.S. (514) 954-6077), www.icao.int; *Civil Aviation Statistics of the World*.

M.E. Sharpe, 80 Business Park Drive, Armonk, NY 10504, (800) 541-6563, Fax: (914) 273-2106, www.mesharpe.com; *The Illustrated Book of World Rankings*.

Palgrave Macmillan Ltd., Houndmills, Basingstoke, Hampshire, RG21 6XS, England, (Telephone in U.S. (888) 330-8477), (Fax in U.S. (800) 672-2054), www.palgrave.com; *The Statesman's Yearbook 2008*.

Taylor and Francis Group, An Informa Business, 2 Park Square, Milton Park, Abingdon, Oxford OX14 4RN, United Kingdom, (Dial from U.S. (212) 216-7800), (Fax from U.S. (212) 564-7854), www.tandf.co.uk; *The Europa World Year Book*.

United Nations Statistics Division, New York, NY 10017, (800) 253-9646, Fax: (212) 963-4116, http://unstats.un.org; *Statistical Yearbook*.

BRAZIL - AIRPORTS

Central Intelligence Agency, Office of Public Affairs, Washington, DC 20505, (703) 482-0623, Fax: (703) 482-1739, www.cia.gov; *The World Factbook*.

BRAZIL - ALUMINUM PRODUCTION

See BRAZIL - MINERAL INDUSTRIES

BRAZIL - ANIMAL FEEDING

United Nations Statistics Division, New York, NY 10017, (800) 253-9646, Fax: (212) 963-4116, http://unstats.un.org; *Statistical Yearbook*.

BRAZIL - AREA

Economist Intelligence Unit, 111 West 57th Street, New York, NY 10019, (212) 554-0600, Fax: (212) 586-1181, www.eiu.com; *Business Latin America*.

BRAZIL - ARMED FORCES

Central Intelligence Agency, Office of Public Affairs, Washington, DC 20505, (703) 482-0623, Fax: (703) 482-1739, www.cia.gov; *The World Factbook*.

Economist Intelligence Unit, 111 West 57th Street, New York, NY 10019, (212) 554-0600, Fax: (212) 586-1181, www.eiu.com; *Business Latin America*.

Euromonitor International, Inc., 224 S. Michigan Avenue, Suite 1500, Chicago, IL 60604, (312) 922-1115, Fax: (312) 922-1157, www.euromonitor.com; *World Marketing Data and Statistics*.

International Institute for Strategic Studies (IISS), Arundel House, 13-15 Arundel Street, Temple Place, London WC2R 3DX, England, www.iiss.org; *The Military Balance 2007*.

International Monetary Fund (IMF), 700 Nineteenth Street, NW, Washington, DC 20431, (202) 623-7000, Fax: (202) 623-4661, www.imf.org; *Government Finance Statistics Yearbook (2008 Edition)*.

Palgrave Macmillan Ltd., Houndmills, Basingstoke, Hampshire, RG21 6XS, England, (Telephone in U.S. (888) 330-8477), (Fax in U.S. (800) 672-2054), www.palgrave.com; *The Statesman's Yearbook 2008*.

U.S. Department of State (DOS), 2201 C Street NW, Washington, DC 20520, (202) 647-4000, www.state.gov; *World Military Expenditures and Arms Transfers (WMEAT)*.

UCLA Latin American Institute, 10343 Bunche Hall, Box 951447, Los Angeles, CA 90095-1447, (310) 825-4571, Fax: (310) 206-6859, www.international.ucla.edu/lac; *Statistical Abstract of Latin America*.

BRAZIL - AUTOMOBILE INDUSTRY AND TRADE

United Nations Statistics Division, New York, NY 10017, (800) 253-9646, Fax: (212) 963-4116, http://unstats.un.org; *Statistical Yearbook*.

BRAZIL - BALANCE OF PAYMENTS

Economist Intelligence Unit, 111 West 57th Street, New York, NY 10019, (212) 554-0600, Fax: (212) 586-1181, www.eiu.com; *Business Latin America*.

Federal Statistical Office Germany, D-65180 Wiesbaden, Germany, www.destatis.de; *Brazil 2006*.

Inter-American Development Bank (IDB), 1300 New York Avenue, NW, Washington, DC 20577, (202) 623-1000, Fax: (202) 623-3096, www.iadb.org; *The Politics of Policies: Economic and Social Progress in Latin America - 2006 Report*.

International Monetary Fund (IMF), 700 Nineteenth Street, NW, Washington, DC 20431, (202) 623-7000, Fax: (202) 623-4661, www.imf.org; *Balance of Payments Statistics Newsletter; Balance of Payments Statistics Yearbook 2007;* and *International Financial Statistics Yearbook 2007*.

Organisation for Economic Cooperation and Development (OECD), 2 rue Andre Pascal, F-75775 Paris Cedex 16, France, (Telephone in U.S. (202) 785-6323), (Fax in U.S. (202) 785-0350), www.oecd.org; *OECD Economic Survey - Brazil 2006*.

Organization of American States (OAS), 17th Street Constitution Avenue NW, Washington, DC 20006, (202) 458-3000, www.oas.org; *The OAS in Transition: 1994-2004*.

Taylor and Francis Group, An Informa Business, 2 Park Square, Milton Park, Abingdon, Oxford OX14 4RN, United Kingdom, (Dial from U.S. (212) 216-7800), (Fax from U.S. (212) 564-7854), www.tandf.co.uk; *The Europa World Year Book*.

UCLA Latin American Institute, 10343 Bunche Hall, Box 951447, Los Angeles, CA 90095-1447, (310) 825-4571, Fax: (310) 206-6859, www.international.ucla.edu/lac; *Statistical Abstract of Latin America*.

United Nations Conference on Trade and Development (UNCTAD), DC2-1120, United Nations, New York, NY 10017, (212) 963-0027, www.unctad.org; *Handbook of Statistics 2005*.

United Nations Statistics Division, New York, NY 10017, (800) 253-9646, Fax: (212) 963-4116, http://

unstats.un.org; *Economic Survey of Latin America and the Caribbean 2004-2005* and *Statistical Yearbook for Latin America and the Caribbean 2004.*

The World Bank, 1818 H Street, NW, Washington, DC 20433, (202) 473-1000, Fax: (202) 477-6391, www.worldbank.org; *Brazil; World Development Indicators (WDI) 2008;* and *World Development Report 2008.*

BRAZIL - BANKS AND BANKING

Euromonitor International, Inc., 224 S. Michigan Avenue, Suite 1500, Chicago, IL 60604, (312) 922-1115, Fax: (312) 922-1157, www.euromonitor.com; *World Marketing Data and Statistics.*

Inter-American Development Bank (IDB), 1300 New York Avenue, NW, Washington, DC 20577, (202) 623-1000, Fax: (202) 623-3096, www.iadb.org; *The Politics of Policies: Economic and Social Progress in Latin America - 2006 Report.*

International Monetary Fund (IMF), 700 Nineteenth Street, NW, Washington, DC 20431, (202) 623-7000, Fax: (202) 623-4661, www.imf.org; *Government Finance Statistics Yearbook (2008 Edition)* and *International Financial Statistics Yearbook 2007.*

M.E. Sharpe, 80 Business Park Drive, Armonk, NY 10504, (800) 541-6563, Fax: (914) 273-2106, www.mesharpe.com; *The Illustrated Book of World Rankings.*

Organisation for Economic Cooperation and Development (OECD), 2 rue Andre Pascal, F-75775 Paris Cedex 16, France, (Telephone in U.S. (202) 785-6323), (Fax in U.S. (202) 785-0350), www.oecd.org; *OECD Economic Survey - Brazil 2006.*

Palgrave Macmillan Ltd., Houndmills, Basingstoke, Hampshire, RG21 6XS, England, (Telephone in U.S. (888) 330-8477), (Fax in U.S. (800) 672-2054), www.palgrave.com; *The Statesman's Yearbook 2008.*

Taylor and Francis Group, An Informa Business, 2 Park Square, Milton Park, Abingdon, Oxford OX14 4RN, United Kingdom, (Dial from U.S. (212) 216-7800), (Fax from U.S. (212) 564-7854), www.tandf.co.uk; *The Europa World Year Book.*

United Nations Statistics Division, New York, NY 10017, (800) 253-9646, Fax: (212) 963-4116, http://unstats.un.org; *Statistical Yearbook* and *Statistical Yearbook for Latin America and the Caribbean 2004.*

BRAZIL - BARLEY PRODUCTION

See BRAZIL - CROPS

BRAZIL - BEVERAGE INDUSTRY

M.E. Sharpe, 80 Business Park Drive, Armonk, NY 10504, (800) 541-6563, Fax: (914) 273-2106, www.mesharpe.com; *The Illustrated Book of World Rankings.*

United Nations Statistics Division, New York, NY 10017, (800) 253-9646, Fax: (212) 963-4116, http://unstats.un.org; *Statistical Yearbook.*

BRAZIL - BIRTH CONTROL

UCLA Latin American Institute, 10343 Bunche Hall, Box 951447, Los Angeles, CA 90095-1447, (310) 825-4571, Fax: (310) 206-6859, www.international.ucla.edu/lac; *Statistical Abstract of Latin America.*

BRAZIL - BONDS

Inter-American Development Bank (IDB), 1300 New York Avenue, NW, Washington, DC 20577, (202) 623-1000, Fax: (202) 623-3096, www.iadb.org; *The Politics of Policies: Economic and Social Progress in Latin America - 2006 Report.*

International Monetary Fund (IMF), 700 Nineteenth Street, NW, Washington, DC 20431, (202) 623-7000, Fax: (202) 623-4661, www.imf.org; *Government Finance Statistics Yearbook (2008 Edition).*

BRAZIL - BROADCASTING

Central Intelligence Agency, Office of Public Affairs, Washington, DC 20505, (703) 482-0623, Fax: (703) 482-1739, www.cia.gov; *The World Factbook.*

Euromonitor International, Inc., 224 S. Michigan Avenue, Suite 1500, Chicago, IL 60604, (312) 922-1115, Fax: (312) 922-1157, www.euromonitor.com; *World Marketing Data and Statistics.*

M.E. Sharpe, 80 Business Park Drive, Armonk, NY 10504, (800) 541-6563, Fax: (914) 273-2106, www.mesharpe.com; *The Illustrated Book of World Rankings.*

Palgrave Macmillan Ltd., Houndmills, Basingstoke, Hampshire, RG21 6XS, England, (Telephone in U.S. (888) 330-8477), (Fax in U.S. (800) 672-2054), www.palgrave.com; *The Statesman's Yearbook 2008.*

UNESCO Institute for Statistics, C.P. 6128 Succursale Centre-Ville, Montreal, Quebec, H3C 3J7 Canada, (Dial from U.S. (514) 343-6880), (Fax from U.S. (514) 343 6882), www.uis.unesco.org; *Statistical Tables.*

WRTH Publications Limited, PO Box 290, Oxford OX2 7FT, UK, www.wrth.com; *World Radio TV Handbook 2007.*

BRAZIL - BUDGET

Central Intelligence Agency, Office of Public Affairs, Washington, DC 20505, (703) 482-0623, Fax: (703) 482-1739, www.cia.gov; *The World Factbook.*

BRAZIL - BUSINESS

Inter-American Development Bank (IDB), 1300 New York Avenue, NW, Washington, DC 20577, (202) 623-1000, Fax: (202) 623-3096, www.iadb.org; *The Politics of Policies: Economic and Social Progress in Latin America - 2006 Report.*

United Nations Statistics Division, New York, NY 10017, (800) 253-9646, Fax: (212) 963-4116, http://unstats.un.org; *Statistical Yearbook.*

BRAZIL - CADMIUM PRODUCTION

See BRAZIL - MINERAL INDUSTRIES

BRAZIL - CAPITAL INVESTMENTS

Inter-American Development Bank (IDB), 1300 New York Avenue, NW, Washington, DC 20577, (202) 623-1000, Fax: (202) 623-3096, www.iadb.org; *The Politics of Policies: Economic and Social Progress in Latin America - 2006 Report.*

BRAZIL - CAPITAL LEVY

Inter-American Development Bank (IDB), 1300 New York Avenue, NW, Washington, DC 20577, (202) 623-1000, Fax: (202) 623-3096, www.iadb.org; *The Politics of Policies: Economic and Social Progress in Latin America - 2006 Report.*

International Monetary Fund (IMF), 700 Nineteenth Street, NW, Washington, DC 20431, (202) 623-7000, Fax: (202) 623-4661, www.imf.org; *Government Finance Statistics Yearbook (2008 Edition).*

BRAZIL - CATTLE

See BRAZIL - LIVESTOCK

BRAZIL - CHESTNUT PRODUCTION

See BRAZIL - CROPS

BRAZIL - CHICKENS

See BRAZIL - LIVESTOCK

BRAZIL - CHILDBIRTH - STATISTICS

Central Intelligence Agency, Office of Public Affairs, Washington, DC 20505, (703) 482-0623, Fax: (703) 482-1739, www.cia.gov; *The World Factbook.*

Euromonitor International, Inc., 224 S. Michigan Avenue, Suite 1500, Chicago, IL 60604, (312) 922-1115, Fax: (312) 922-1157, www.euromonitor.com; *International Marketing Data and Statistics 2008* and *The World Economic Factbook 2008.*

M.E. Sharpe, 80 Business Park Drive, Armonk, NY 10504, (800) 541-6563, Fax: (914) 273-2106, www.mesharpe.com; *The Illustrated Book of World Rankings.*

Taylor and Francis Group, An Informa Business, 2 Park Square, Milton Park, Abingdon, Oxford OX14 4RN, United Kingdom, (Dial from U.S. (212) 216-7800), (Fax from U.S. (212) 564-7854), www.tandf.co.uk; *The Europa World Year Book.*

United Nations Statistics Division, New York, NY 10017, (800) 253-9646, Fax: (212) 963-4116, http://unstats.un.org; *Demographic Yearbook; Statistical Yearbook;* and *Statistical Yearbook for Latin America and the Caribbean 2004.*

The World Bank, 1818 H Street, NW, Washington, DC 20433, (202) 473-1000, Fax: (202) 477-6391, www.worldbank.org; *World Development Indicators (WDI) 2008.*

World Health Organization (WHO), Avenue Appia 20, 1211 Geneve 27, Switzerland, (Telephone in U.S. (212) 331-9081), www.who.int; *World Health Report 2006.*

BRAZIL - CLIMATE

M.E. Sharpe, 80 Business Park Drive, Armonk, NY 10504, (800) 541-6563, Fax: (914) 273-2106, www.mesharpe.com; *The Illustrated Book of World Rankings.*

Palgrave Macmillan Ltd., Houndmills, Basingstoke, Hampshire, RG21 6XS, England, (Telephone in U.S. (888) 330-8477), (Fax in U.S. (800) 672-2054), www.palgrave.com; *The Statesman's Yearbook 2008.*

BRAZIL - COAL PRODUCTION

See BRAZIL - MINERAL INDUSTRIES

BRAZIL - COCOA PRODUCTION

See BRAZIL - CROPS

BRAZIL - COFFEE

See BRAZIL - CROPS

BRAZIL - COMMERCE

Palgrave Macmillan Ltd., Houndmills, Basingstoke, Hampshire, RG21 6XS, England, (Telephone in U.S. (888) 330-8477), (Fax in U.S. (800) 672-2054), www.palgrave.com; *The Statesman's Yearbook 2008.*

BRAZIL - COMMODITY EXCHANGES

Commodity Research Bureau, 330 South Wells Street, Suite 612, Chicago, IL 60606-7110, (800) 621-5271, Fax: (312) 939-4135, www.crbtrader.com; *2006 CRB Commodity Yearbook and CD.*

International Monetary Fund (IMF), 700 Nineteenth Street, NW, Washington, DC 20431, (202) 623-7000, Fax: (202) 623-4661, www.imf.org; *IMF Primary Commodity Prices.*

United Nations Food and Agricultural Organization (FAO), Viale delle Terme di Caracalla, 00100 Rome, Italy, (Dial from U.S. (202) 653-2400), (Fax from U.S. (202) 653 5760), www.fao.org; *The State of Food and Agriculture (SOFA) 2006.*

World Bureau of Metal Statistics (WBMS), 27a High Street, Ware, Hertfordshire, SG12 9BA, United Kingdom, www.world-bureau.com; *Annual Stainless Steel Statistics; World Flow Charts; World Metal Statistics; World Nickel Statistics;* and *World Tin Statistics.*

BRAZIL - COMMUNICATION AND TRAFFIC

United Nations Statistics Division, New York, NY 10017, (800) 253-9646, Fax: (212) 963-4116, http://unstats.un.org; *Statistical Yearbook.*

BRAZIL - CONSTRUCTION INDUSTRY

Economist Intelligence Unit, 111 West 57th Street, New York, NY 10019, (212) 554-0600, Fax: (212) 586-1181, www.eiu.com; *Business Latin America.*

Inter-American Development Bank (IDB), 1300 New York Avenue, NW, Washington, DC 20577, (202) 623-1000, Fax: (202) 623-3096, www.iadb.org; *The Politics of Policies: Economic and Social Progress in Latin America - 2006 Report.*

M.E. Sharpe, 80 Business Park Drive, Armonk, NY 10504, (800) 541-6563, Fax: (914) 273-2106, www.mesharpe.com; *The Illustrated Book of World Rankings.*

Organisation for Economic Cooperation and Development (OECD), 2 rue Andre Pascal, F-75775 Paris Cedex 16, France, (Telephone in U.S. (202) 785-6323), (Fax in U.S. (202) 785-0350), www.oecd.org; *OECD Economic Survey - Brazil 2006.*

Organization of American States (OAS), 17th Street Constitution Avenue NW, Washington, DC 20006, (202) 458-3000, www.oas.org; *The OAS in Transition: 1994-2004.*

Palgrave Macmillan Ltd., Houndmills, Basingstoke, Hampshire, RG21 6XS, England, (Telephone in U.S. (888) 330-8477), (Fax in U.S. (800) 672-2054), www.palgrave.com; *The Statesman's Yearbook 2008.*

UCLA Latin American Institute, 10343 Bunche Hall, Box 951447, Los Angeles, CA 90095-1447, (310) 825-4571, Fax: (310) 206-6859, www.international.ucla.edu/lac; *Statistical Abstract of Latin America.*

United Nations Statistics Division, New York, NY 10017, (800) 253-9646, Fax: (212) 963-4116, http://unstats.un.org; *Statistical Yearbook.*

BRAZIL - CONSUMER COOPERATIVES

UCLA Latin American Institute, 10343 Bunche Hall, Box 951447, Los Angeles, CA 90095-1447, (310) 825-4571, Fax: (310) 206-6859, www.international.ucla.edu/lac; *Statistical Abstract of Latin America.*

BRAZIL - CONSUMER PRICE INDEXES

Federal Statistical Office Germany, D-65180 Wiesbaden, Germany, www.destatis.de; *Brazil 2006.*

Taylor and Francis Group, An Informa Business, 2 Park Square, Milton Park, Abingdon, Oxford OX14 4RN, United Kingdom, (Dial from U.S. (212) 216-7800), (Fax from U.S. (212) 564-7854), www.tandf.co.uk; *The Europa World Year Book.*

United Nations Statistics Division, New York, NY 10017, (800) 253-9646, Fax: (212) 963-4116, http://unstats.un.org; *Statistical Yearbook.*

The World Bank, 1818 H Street, NW, Washington, DC 20433, (202) 473-1000, Fax: (202) 477-6391, www.worldbank.org; *Brazil.*

BRAZIL - CONSUMPTION (ECONOMICS)

Economist Intelligence Unit, 111 West 57th Street, New York, NY 10019, (212) 554-0600, Fax: (212) 586-1181, www.eiu.com; *Business Latin America.*

Inter-American Development Bank (IDB), 1300 New York Avenue, NW, Washington, DC 20577, (202) 623-1000, Fax: (202) 623-3096, www.iadb.org; *The Politics of Policies: Economic and Social Progress in Latin America - 2006 Report.*

United Nations Statistics Division, New York, NY 10017, (800) 253-9646, Fax: (212) 963-4116, http://unstats.un.org; *Statistical Yearbook for Latin America and the Caribbean 2004.*

The World Bank, 1818 H Street, NW, Washington, DC 20433, (202) 473-1000, Fax: (202) 477-6391, www.worldbank.org; *World Development Report 2008.*

BRAZIL - COPPER INDUSTRY AND TRADE

See BRAZIL - MINERAL INDUSTRIES

BRAZIL - CORN INDUSTRY

See BRAZIL - CROPS

BRAZIL - COST AND STANDARD OF LIVING

International Monetary Fund (IMF), 700 Nineteenth Street, NW, Washington, DC 20431, (202) 623-7000, Fax: (202) 623-4661, www.imf.org; *Government Finance Statistics Yearbook (2008 Edition).*

BRAZIL - COTTON

See BRAZIL - CROPS

BRAZIL - CRIME

U.S. Department of Justice (DOJ), Bureau of Justice Statistics, 810 Seventh Street, NW, Washington, DC 20531, (202) 307-0765, www.ojp.usdoj.gov/bjs/; *The World Factbook of Criminal Justice Systems.*

BRAZIL - CROPS

Economist Intelligence Unit, 111 West 57th Street, New York, NY 10019, (212) 554-0600, Fax: (212) 586-1181, www.eiu.com; *Business Latin America.*

International Monetary Fund (IMF), 700 Nineteenth Street, NW, Washington, DC 20431, (202) 623-7000, Fax: (202) 623-4661, www.imf.org; *Government Finance Statistics Yearbook (2008 Edition).*

M.E. Sharpe, 80 Business Park Drive, Armonk, NY 10504, (800) 541-6563, Fax: (914) 273-2106, www.mesharpe.com; *The Illustrated Book of World Rankings.*

Organization of American States (OAS), 17th Street Constitution Avenue NW, Washington, DC 20006, (202) 458-3000, www.oas.org; *The OAS in Transition: 1994-2004.*

Palgrave Macmillan Ltd., Houndmills, Basingstoke, Hampshire, RG21 6XS, England, (Telephone in U.S. (888) 330-8477), (Fax in U.S. (800) 672-2054), www.palgrave.com; *The Statesman's Yearbook 2008.*

Taylor and Francis Group, An Informa Business, 2 Park Square, Milton Park, Abingdon, Oxford OX14 4RN, United Kingdom, (Dial from U.S. (212) 216-7800), (Fax from U.S. (212) 564-7854), www.tandf.co.uk; *The Europa World Year Book.*

United Nations Conference on Trade and Development (UNCTAD), DC2-1120, United Nations, New York, NY 10017, (212) 963-0027, www.unctad.org; *UNCTAD Commodity Yearbook.*

United Nations Food and Agricultural Organization (FAO), Viale delle Terme di Caracalla, 00100 Rome, Italy, (Dial from U.S. (202) 653-2400), (Fax from U.S. (202) 653 5760), www.fao.org; *FAO Production Yearbook 2002* and *The State of Food and Agriculture (SOFA) 2006.*

United Nations Statistics Division, New York, NY 10017, (800) 253-9646, Fax: (212) 963-4116, http://unstats.un.org; *Statistical Yearbook.*

BRAZIL - CUSTOMS ADMINISTRATION

Inter-American Development Bank (IDB), 1300 New York Avenue, NW, Washington, DC 20577, (202) 623-1000, Fax: (202) 623-3096, www.iadb.org; *The Politics of Policies: Economic and Social Progress in Latin America - 2006 Report.*

International Monetary Fund (IMF), 700 Nineteenth Street, NW, Washington, DC 20431, (202) 623-7000, Fax: (202) 623-4661, www.imf.org; *Government Finance Statistics Yearbook (2008 Edition).*

Palgrave Macmillan Ltd., Houndmills, Basingstoke, Hampshire, RG21 6XS, England, (Telephone in U.S. (888) 330-8477), (Fax in U.S. (800) 672-2054), www.palgrave.com; *The Statesman's Yearbook 2008.*

BRAZIL - DAIRY PROCESSING

M.E. Sharpe, 80 Business Park Drive, Armonk, NY 10504, (800) 541-6563, Fax: (914) 273-2106, www.mesharpe.com; *The Illustrated Book of World Rankings.*

Palgrave Macmillan Ltd., Houndmills, Basingstoke, Hampshire, RG21 6XS, England, (Telephone in U.S. (888) 330-8477), (Fax in U.S. (800) 672-2054), www.palgrave.com; *The Statesman's Yearbook 2008.*

Taylor and Francis Group, An Informa Business, 2 Park Square, Milton Park, Abingdon, Oxford OX14 4RN, United Kingdom, (Dial from U.S. (212) 216-7800), (Fax from U.S. (212) 564-7854), www.tandf.co.uk; *The Europa World Year Book.*

United Nations Food and Agricultural Organization (FAO), Viale delle Terme di Caracalla, 00100 Rome, Italy, (Dial from U.S. (202) 653-2400), (Fax from U.S. (202) 653 5760), www.fao.org; *FAO Production Yearbook 2002* and *The State of Food and Agriculture (SOFA) 2006.*

United Nations Statistics Division, New York, NY 10017, (800) 253-9646, Fax: (212) 963-4116, http://unstats.un.org; *Statistical Yearbook.*

BRAZIL - DEATH RATES

See BRAZIL - MORTALITY

BRAZIL - DEBT

Economist Intelligence Unit, 111 West 57th Street, New York, NY 10019, (212) 554-0600, Fax: (212) 586-1181, www.eiu.com; *Business Latin America.*

The World Bank, 1818 H Street, NW, Washington, DC 20433, (202) 473-1000, Fax: (202) 477-6391, www.worldbank.org; *Global Development Finance 2007.*

BRAZIL - DEBTS, EXTERNAL

Economist Intelligence Unit, 111 West 57th Street, New York, NY 10019, (212) 554-0600, Fax: (212) 586-1181, www.eiu.com; *Business Latin America.*

Inter-American Development Bank (IDB), 1300 New York Avenue, NW, Washington, DC 20577, (202) 623-1000, Fax: (202) 623-3096, www.iadb.org; *The Politics of Policies: Economic and Social Progress in Latin America - 2006 Report.*

International Monetary Fund (IMF), 700 Nineteenth Street, NW, Washington, DC 20431, (202) 623-7000, Fax: (202) 623-4661, www.imf.org; *Government Finance Statistics Yearbook (2008 Edition).*

Palgrave Macmillan Ltd., Houndmills, Basingstoke, Hampshire, RG21 6XS, England, (Telephone in U.S. (888) 330-8477), (Fax in U.S. (800) 672-2054), www.palgrave.com; *The Statesman's Yearbook 2008.*

United Nations Statistics Division, New York, NY 10017, (800) 253-9646, Fax: (212) 963-4116, http://unstats.un.org; *Economic Survey of Latin America and the Caribbean 2004-2005* and *Statistical Yearbook for Latin America and the Caribbean 2004.*

The World Bank, 1818 H Street, NW, Washington, DC 20433, (202) 473-1000, Fax: (202) 477-6391, www.worldbank.org; *Global Development Finance 2007; World Development Indicators (WDI) 2008;* and *World Development Report 2008.*

BRAZIL - DEFENSE EXPENDITURES

See BRAZIL - ARMED FORCES

BRAZIL - DEMOGRAPHY

Euromonitor International, Inc., 224 S. Michigan Avenue, Suite 1500, Chicago, IL 60604, (312) 922-1115, Fax: (312) 922-1157, www.euromonitor.com; *International Marketing Data and Statistics 2008; The World Economic Factbook 2008;* and *World Marketing Data and Statistics.*

Federal Statistical Office Germany, D-65180 Wiesbaden, Germany, www.destatis.de; *Brazil 2006.*

M.E. Sharpe, 80 Business Park Drive, Armonk, NY 10504, (800) 541-6563, Fax: (914) 273-2106, www.mesharpe.com; *The Illustrated Book of World Rankings.*

UCLA Latin American Institute, 10343 Bunche Hall, Box 951447, Los Angeles, CA 90095-1447, (310) 825-4571, Fax: (310) 206-6859, www.international.ucla.edu/lac; *Statistical Abstract of Latin America.*

United Nations Statistics Division, New York, NY 10017, (800) 253-9646, Fax: (212) 963-4116, http://unstats.un.org; *Human Development Report 2006.*

The World Bank, 1818 H Street, NW, Washington, DC 20433, (202) 473-1000, Fax: (202) 477-6391, www.worldbank.org; *Brazil.*

BRAZIL - DIAMONDS

See BRAZIL - MINERAL INDUSTRIES

BRAZIL - DISPOSABLE INCOME

Inter-American Development Bank (IDB), 1300 New York Avenue, NW, Washington, DC 20577, (202) 623-1000, Fax: (202) 623-3096, www.iadb.org; *The*

Politics of Policies: Economic and Social Progress in Latin America - 2006 Report.

M.E. Sharpe, 80 Business Park Drive, Armonk, NY 10504, (800) 541-6563, Fax: (914) 273-2106, www.mesharpe.com; *The Illustrated Book of World Rankings.*

United Nations Statistics Division, New York, NY 10017, (800) 253-9646, Fax: (212) 963-4116, http://unstats.un.org; *National Accounts Statistics: Compendium of Income Distribution Statistics; Statistical Yearbook;* and *Statistical Yearbook for Latin America and the Caribbean 2004.*

BRAZIL - DIVORCE

M.E. Sharpe, 80 Business Park Drive, Armonk, NY 10504, (800) 541-6563, Fax: (914) 273-2106, www.mesharpe.com; *The Illustrated Book of World Rankings.*

United Nations Statistics Division, New York, NY 10017, (800) 253-9646, Fax: (212) 963-4116, http://unstats.un.org; *Demographic Yearbook.*

BRAZIL - ECONOMIC ASSISTANCE

Inter-American Development Bank (IDB), 1300 New York Avenue, NW, Washington, DC 20577, (202) 623-1000, Fax: (202) 623-3096, www.iadb.org; *The Politics of Policies: Economic and Social Progress in Latin America - 2006 Report.*

United Nations Statistics Division, New York, NY 10017, (800) 253-9646, Fax: (212) 963-4116, http://unstats.un.org; *Statistical Yearbook.*

BRAZIL - ECONOMIC CONDITIONS

Brazilian Statistical and Geographic Institute (Instituto Brasileiro de Geografia e Estatistica (IBGE)), Rua General Canabarro, 706 - Maracana, Rio de Janeiro, RJ 20271-201, Brazil, www.ibge.gov.br/english/default.php; *Urban Informal Economy - Brazil and Major Regions.*

Center for International Business Education Research (CIBER), Columbia Business School and School of International and Public Affairs, Uris Hall, Room 212, 3022 Broadway, New York, NY 10027-6902, Mr. Joshua Safier, (212) 854-4750, Fax: (212) 222-9821, www.columbia.edu/cu/ciber/; Datastream International.

Central Intelligence Agency, Office of Public Affairs, Washington, DC 20505, (703) 482-0623, Fax: (703) 482-1739, www.cia.gov; *The World Factbook.*

DSI Data Service Information, Xantener Strasse 51a, D-47495 Rheinberg, Germany, www.dsidata.com; *Campus Solution.*

Dun and Bradstreet (DB) Corporation, 103 JFK Parkway, Short Hills, NJ 07078, (973) 921-5500, www.dnb.com; *Country Report.*

Economist Intelligence Unit, 111 West 57th Street, New York, NY 10019, (212) 554-0600, Fax: (212) 586-1181, www.eiu.com; *Brazil Country Report.*

Euromonitor International, Inc., 224 S. Michigan Avenue, Suite 1500, Chicago, IL 60604, (312) 922-1115, Fax: (312) 922-1157, www.euromonitor.com; *International Marketing Data and Statistics 2008; The World Economic Factbook 2008;* and *World Marketing Data and Statistics.*

Federal Statistical Office Germany, D-65180 Wiesbaden, Germany, www.destatis.de; *Brazil 2006.*

Inter-American Development Bank (IDB), 1300 New York Avenue, NW, Washington, DC 20577, (202) 623-1000, Fax: (202) 623-3096, www.iadb.org; *The Politics of Policies: Economic and Social Progress in Latin America - 2006 Report.*

International Monetary Fund (IMF), 700 Nineteenth Street, NW, Washington, DC 20431, (202) 623-7000, Fax: (202) 623-4661, www.imf.org; *World Economic Outlook Reports.*

M.E. Sharpe, 80 Business Park Drive, Armonk, NY 10504, (800) 541-6563, Fax: (914) 273-2106, www.mesharpe.com; *The Illustrated Book of World Rankings.*

Organisation for Economic Cooperation and Development (OECD), 2 rue Andre Pascal, F-75775 Paris Cedex 16, France, (Telephone in U.S. (202) 785-6323), (Fax in U.S. (202) 785-0350), www.oecd.org; *OECD Economic Survey - Brazil 2006.*

Organization of American States (OAS), 17th Street Constitution Avenue NW, Washington, DC 20006, (202) 458-3000, www.oas.org; *The OAS in Transition: 1994-2004.*

Palgrave Macmillan Ltd., Houndmills, Basingstoke, Hampshire, RG21 6XS, England, (Telephone in U.S. (888) 330-8477), (Fax in U.S. (800) 672-2054), www.palgrave.com; *The Statesman's Yearbook 2008.*

Taylor and Francis Group, An Informa Business, 2 Park Square, Milton Park, Abingdon, Oxford OX14 4RN, United Kingdom, (Dial from U.S. (212) 216-7800), (Fax from U.S. (212) 564-7854), www.tandf.co.uk; *The Europa World Year Book.*

UCLA Latin American Institute, 10343 Bunche Hall, Box 951447, Los Angeles, CA 90095-1447, (310) 825-4571, Fax: (310) 206-6859, www.international.ucla.edu/lac; *Statistical Abstract of Latin America.*

United Nations Statistics Division, New York, NY 10017, (800) 253-9646, Fax: (212) 963-4116, http://unstats.un.org; *Economic Survey of Latin America and the Caribbean 2004-2005* and *World Statistics Pocketbook.*

The World Bank, 1818 H Street, NW, Washington, DC 20433, (202) 473-1000, Fax: (202) 477-6391, www.worldbank.org; *Brazil; Global Economic Monitor (GEM); Global Economic Prospects 2008; The World Bank Atlas 2003-2004;* and *World Development Report 2008.*

BRAZIL - ECONOMICS - SOCIOLOGICAL ASPECTS

Inter-American Development Bank (IDB), 1300 New York Avenue, NW, Washington, DC 20577, (202) 623-1000, Fax: (202) 623-3096, www.iadb.org; *The Politics of Policies: Economic and Social Progress in Latin America - 2006 Report.*

UCLA Latin American Institute, 10343 Bunche Hall, Box 951447, Los Angeles, CA 90095-1447, (310) 825-4571, Fax: (310) 206-6859, www.international.ucla.edu/lac; *Statistical Abstract of Latin America.*

BRAZIL - EDUCATION

Economist Intelligence Unit, 111 West 57th Street, New York, NY 10019, (212) 554-0600, Fax: (212) 586-1181, www.eiu.com; *Business Latin America.*

Euromonitor International, Inc., 224 S. Michigan Avenue, Suite 1500, Chicago, IL 60604, (312) 922-1115, Fax: (312) 922-1157, www.euromonitor.com; *International Marketing Data and Statistics 2008* and *World Marketing Data and Statistics.*

Federal Statistical Office Germany, D-65180 Wiesbaden, Germany, www.destatis.de; *Brazil 2006.*

International Monetary Fund (IMF), 700 Nineteenth Street, NW, Washington, DC 20431, (202) 623-7000, Fax: (202) 623-4661, www.imf.org; *Government Finance Statistics Yearbook (2008 Edition).*

M.E. Sharpe, 80 Business Park Drive, Armonk, NY 10504, (800) 541-6563, Fax: (914) 273-2106, www.mesharpe.com; *The Illustrated Book of World Rankings.*

Palgrave Macmillan Ltd., Houndmills, Basingstoke, Hampshire, RG21 6XS, England, (Telephone in U.S. (888) 330-8477), (Fax in U.S. (800) 672-2054), www.palgrave.com; *The Statesman's Yearbook 2008.*

Taylor and Francis Group, An Informa Business, 2 Park Square, Milton Park, Abingdon, Oxford OX14 4RN, United Kingdom, (Dial from U.S. (212) 216-7800), (Fax from U.S. (212) 564-7854), www.tandf.co.uk; *The Europa World Year Book.*

UCLA Latin American Institute, 10343 Bunche Hall, Box 951447, Los Angeles, CA 90095-1447, (310) 825-4571, Fax: (310) 206-6859, www.international.ucla.edu/lac; *Statistical Abstract of Latin America.*

UNESCO Institute for Statistics, C.P. 6128 Succursale Centre-Ville, Montreal, Quebec, H3C 3J7 Canada, (Dial from U.S. (514) 343-6880), (Fax from U.S. (514) 343 6882), www.uis.unesco.org; *Statistical Tables.*

United Nations Statistics Division, New York, NY 10017, (800) 253-9646, Fax: (212) 963-4116, http://unstats.un.org; *Human Development Report 2006* and *Statistical Yearbook for Latin America and the Caribbean 2004.*

The World Bank, 1818 H Street, NW, Washington, DC 20433, (202) 473-1000, Fax: (202) 477-6391, www.worldbank.org; *Brazil; World Development Indicators (WDI) 2008;* and *World Development Report 2008.*

BRAZIL - ELECTRICITY

Economist Intelligence Unit, 111 West 57th Street, New York, NY 10019, (212) 554-0600, Fax: (212) 586-1181, www.eiu.com; *Business Latin America.*

Inter-American Development Bank (IDB), 1300 New York Avenue, NW, Washington, DC 20577, (202) 623-1000, Fax: (202) 623-3096, www.iadb.org; *The Politics of Policies: Economic and Social Progress in Latin America - 2006 Report.*

M.E. Sharpe, 80 Business Park Drive, Armonk, NY 10504, (800) 541-6563, Fax: (914) 273-2106, www.mesharpe.com; *The Illustrated Book of World Rankings.*

Organisation for Economic Cooperation and Development (OECD), 2 rue Andre Pascal, F-75775 Paris Cedex 16, France, (Telephone in U.S. (202) 785-6323), (Fax in U.S. (202) 785-0350), www.oecd.org; *World Energy Outlook 2007.*

Organization of American States (OAS), 17th Street Constitution Avenue NW, Washington, DC 20006, (202) 458-3000, www.oas.org; *The OAS in Transition: 1994-2004.*

Palgrave Macmillan Ltd., Houndmills, Basingstoke, Hampshire, RG21 6XS, England, (Telephone in U.S. (888) 330-8477), (Fax in U.S. (800) 672-2054), www.palgrave.com; *The Statesman's Yearbook 2008.*

U.S. Department of Energy (DOE), Energy Information Administration (EIA), 1000 Independence Avenue, SW, Washington, DC 20585, (202) 586-8800, www.eia.doe.gov; *International Energy Annual 2004* and *International Energy Outlook 2006.*

United Nations Statistics Division, New York, NY 10017, (800) 253-9646, Fax: (212) 963-4116, http://unstats.un.org; *Human Development Report 2006* and *Statistical Yearbook.*

BRAZIL - EMIGRATION AND IMMIGRATION

UCLA Latin American Institute, 10343 Bunche Hall, Box 951447, Los Angeles, CA 90095-1447, (310) 825-4571, Fax: (310) 206-6859, www.international.ucla.edu/lac; *Statistical Abstract of Latin America.*

BRAZIL - EMPLOYMENT

Euromonitor International, Inc., 224 S. Michigan Avenue, Suite 1500, Chicago, IL 60604, (312) 922-1115, Fax: (312) 922-1157, www.euromonitor.com; *International Marketing Data and Statistics 2008.*

Federal Statistical Office Germany, D-65180 Wiesbaden, Germany, www.destatis.de; *Brazil 2006.*

International Labour Office, I.L.O. Publications, 4 route des Morillons, CH-1211 Geneva 22, Switzerland, (Telephone in U.S. (202) 653-7652), (Fax in U.S. (202) 653-7687), www.ilo.org; *Yearbook of Labour Statistics 2006.*

M.E. Sharpe, 80 Business Park Drive, Armonk, NY 10504, (800) 541-6563, Fax: (914) 273-2106, www.mesharpe.com; *The Illustrated Book of World Rankings.*

Organisation for Economic Cooperation and Development (OECD), 2 rue Andre Pascal, F-75775 Paris Cedex 16, France, (Telephone in U.S. (202) 785-6323), (Fax in U.S. (202) 785-0350), www.oecd.org; *OECD Economic Survey - Brazil 2006.*

Organization of American States (OAS), 17th Street Constitution Avenue NW, Washington, DC 20006, (202) 458-3000, www.oas.org; *The OAS in Transition: 1994-2004.*

UCLA Latin American Institute, 10343 Bunche Hall, Box 951447, Los Angeles, CA 90095-1447, (310)

825-4571, Fax: (310) 206-6859, www.international.ucla.edu/lac; *Statistical Abstract of Latin America.*

United Nations Statistics Division, New York, NY 10017, (800) 253-9646, Fax: (212) 963-4116, http://unstats.un.org; *Statistical Yearbook* and *Statistical Yearbook for Latin America and the Caribbean 2004.*

The World Bank, 1818 H Street, NW, Washington, DC 20433, (202) 473-1000, Fax: (202) 477-6391, www.worldbank.org; *Brazil.*

BRAZIL - ENVIRONMENTAL CONDITIONS

Brazilian Statistical and Geographic Institute (Instituto Brasileiro de Geografia e Estatistica (IBGE)), Rua General Canabarro, 706 - Maracana, Rio de Janeiro, RJ 20271-201, Brazil, www.ibge.gov.br/english/default.php; *Profile of Brazilian Municipalities - Environment.*

DSI Data Service Information, Xantener Strasse 51a, D-47495 Rheinberg, Germany, www.dsidata.com; *Campus Solution* and *DSI's Global Environmental Database.*

Economist Intelligence Unit, 111 West 57th Street, New York, NY 10019, (212) 554-0600, Fax: (212) 586-1181, www.eiu.com; *Brazil Country Report.*

United Nations Statistics Division, New York, NY 10017, (800) 253-9646, Fax: (212) 963-4116, http://unstats.un.org; *World Statistics Pocketbook.*

BRAZIL - EXPENDITURES, PUBLIC

Inter-American Development Bank (IDB), 1300 New York Avenue, NW, Washington, DC 20577, (202) 623-1000, Fax: (202) 623-3096, www.iadb.org; *The Politics of Policies: Economic and Social Progress in Latin America - 2006 Report.*

Organization of American States (OAS), 17th Street Constitution Avenue NW, Washington, DC 20006, (202) 458-3000, www.oas.org; *The OAS in Transition: 1994-2004.*

United Nations Statistics Division, New York, NY 10017, (800) 253-9646, Fax: (212) 963-4116, http://unstats.un.org; *Statistical Yearbook for Latin America and the Caribbean 2004.*

BRAZIL - EXPORTS

Central Intelligence Agency, Office of Public Affairs, Washington, DC 20505, (703) 482-0623, Fax: (703) 482-1739, www.cia.gov; *The World Factbook.*

Economist Intelligence Unit, 111 West 57th Street, New York, NY 10019, (212) 554-0600, Fax: (212) 586-1181, www.eiu.com; *Brazil Country Report* and *Business Latin America.*

Euromonitor International, Inc., 224 S. Michigan Avenue, Suite 1500, Chicago, IL 60604, (312) 922-1115, Fax: (312) 922-1157, www.euromonitor.com; *International Marketing Data and Statistics 2008; The World Economic Factbook 2008;* and *World Marketing Data and Statistics.*

Inter-American Development Bank (IDB), 1300 New York Avenue, NW, Washington, DC 20577, (202) 623-1000, Fax: (202) 623-3096, www.iadb.org; *The Politics of Policies: Economic and Social Progress in Latin America - 2006 Report.*

International Monetary Fund (IMF), 700 Nineteenth Street, NW, Washington, DC 20431, (202) 623-7000, Fax: (202) 623-4661, www.imf.org; *Direction of Trade Statistics Yearbook 2007* and *International Financial Statistics Yearbook 2007.*

Organisation for Economic Cooperation and Development (OECD), 2 rue Andre Pascal, F-75775 Paris Cedex 16, France, (Telephone in U.S. (202) 785-6323), (Fax in U.S. (202) 785-0350), www.oecd.org; *OECD Economic Survey - Brazil 2006.*

Organization of American States (OAS), 17th Street Constitution Avenue NW, Washington, DC 20006, (202) 458-3000, www.oas.org; *The OAS in Transition: 1994-2004.*

Palgrave Macmillan Ltd., Houndmills, Basingstoke, Hampshire, RG21 6XS, England, (Telephone in U.S. (888) 330-8477), (Fax in U.S. (800) 672-2054), www.palgrave.com; *The Statesman's Yearbook 2008.*

Taylor and Francis Group, An Informa Business, 2 Park Square, Milton Park, Abingdon, Oxford OX14 4RN, United Kingdom, (Dial from U.S. (212) 216-7800), (Fax from U.S. (212) 564-7854), www.tandf.co.uk; *The Europa World Year Book.*

United Nations Food and Agricultural Organization (FAO), Viale delle Terme di Caracalla, 00100 Rome, Italy, (Dial from U.S. (202) 653-2400), (Fax from U.S. (202) 653 5760), www.fao.org; *The State of Food and Agriculture (SOFA) 2006.*

United Nations Statistics Division, New York, NY 10017, (800) 253-9646, Fax: (212) 963-4116, http://unstats.un.org; *Statistical Yearbook for Latin America and the Caribbean 2004.*

The World Bank, 1818 H Street, NW, Washington, DC 20433, (202) 473-1000, Fax: (202) 477-6391, www.worldbank.org; *World Development Indicators (WDI) 2008* and *World Development Report 2008.*

BRAZIL - FEMALE WORKING POPULATION

See BRAZIL - EMPLOYMENT

BRAZIL - FERTILITY, HUMAN

Central Intelligence Agency, Office of Public Affairs, Washington, DC 20505, (703) 482-0623, Fax: (703) 482-1739, www.cia.gov; *The World Factbook.*

M.E. Sharpe, 80 Business Park Drive, Armonk, NY 10504, (800) 541-6563, Fax: (914) 273-2106, www.mesharpe.com; *The Illustrated Book of World Rankings.*

United Nations Statistics Division, New York, NY 10017, (800) 253-9646, Fax: (212) 963-4116, http://unstats.un.org; *Human Development Report 2006.*

The World Bank, 1818 H Street, NW, Washington, DC 20433, (202) 473-1000, Fax: (202) 477-6391, www.worldbank.org; *The World Bank Atlas 2003-2004; World Development Indicators (WDI) 2008;* and *World Development Report 2008.*

BRAZIL - FERTILIZER INDUSTRY

Economist Intelligence Unit, 111 West 57th Street, New York, NY 10019, (212) 554-0600, Fax: (212) 586-1181, www.eiu.com; *Business Latin America.*

United Nations Food and Agricultural Organization (FAO), Viale delle Terme di Caracalla, 00100 Rome, Italy, (Dial from U.S. (202) 653-2400), (Fax from U.S. (202) 653 5760), www.fao.org; *FAO Fertilizer Yearbook* and *The State of Food and Agriculture (SOFA) 2006.*

United Nations Statistics Division, New York, NY 10017, (800) 253-9646, Fax: (212) 963-4116, http://unstats.un.org; *Statistical Yearbook.*

BRAZIL - FETAL MORTALITY

See BRAZIL - MORTALITY

BRAZIL - FILM

See BRAZIL - MOTION PICTURES

BRAZIL - FINANCE

Federal Statistical Office Germany, D-65180 Wiesbaden, Germany, www.destatis.de; *Brazil 2006.*

Inter-American Development Bank (IDB), 1300 New York Avenue, NW, Washington, DC 20577, (202) 623-1000, Fax: (202) 623-3096, www.iadb.org; *The Politics of Policies: Economic and Social Progress in Latin America - 2006 Report.*

Organization of American States (OAS), 17th Street Constitution Avenue NW, Washington, DC 20006, (202) 458-3000, www.oas.org; *The OAS in Transition: 1994-2004.*

Taylor and Francis Group, An Informa Business, 2 Park Square, Milton Park, Abingdon, Oxford OX14 4RN, United Kingdom, (Dial from U.S. (212) 216-7800), (Fax from U.S. (212) 564-7854), www.tandf.co.uk; *The Europa World Year Book.*

UCLA Latin American Institute, 10343 Bunche Hall, Box 951447, Los Angeles, CA 90095-1447, (310) 825-4571, Fax: (310) 206-6859, www.international.ucla.edu/lac; *Statistical Abstract of Latin America.*

United Nations Statistics Division, New York, NY 10017, (800) 253-9646, Fax: (212) 963-4116, http://unstats.un.org; *National Accounts Statistics: Compendium of Income Distribution Statistics* and *Statistical Yearbook.*

The World Bank, 1818 H Street, NW, Washington, DC 20433, (202) 473-1000, Fax: (202) 477-6391, www.worldbank.org; *Brazil.*

BRAZIL - FINANCE, PUBLIC

Bernan Essential Government Publications, 4611-F Assembly Drive, Lanham MD, 20706-4391, (301) 459-2255, Fax: (800) 865-3450, www.bernan.com; *National Accounts Statistics.*

Economist Intelligence Unit, 111 West 57th Street, New York, NY 10019, (212) 554-0600, Fax: (212) 586-1181, www.eiu.com; *Brazil Country Report.*

Federal Statistical Office Germany, D-65180 Wiesbaden, Germany, www.destatis.de; *Brazil 2006.*

Inter-American Development Bank (IDB), 1300 New York Avenue, NW, Washington, DC 20577, (202) 623-1000, Fax: (202) 623-3096, www.iadb.org; *The Politics of Policies: Economic and Social Progress in Latin America - 2006 Report.*

International Monetary Fund (IMF), 700 Nineteenth Street, NW, Washington, DC 20431, (202) 623-7000, Fax: (202) 623-4661, www.imf.org; *Government Finance Statistics Yearbook (2008 Edition); International Financial Statistics; International Financial Statistics Online Service;* and *International Financial Statistics Yearbook 2007.*

M.E. Sharpe, 80 Business Park Drive, Armonk, NY 10504, (800) 541-6563, Fax: (914) 273-2106, www.mesharpe.com; *The Illustrated Book of World Rankings.*

Organization of American States (OAS), 17th Street Constitution Avenue NW, Washington, DC 20006, (202) 458-3000, www.oas.org; *The OAS in Transition: 1994-2004.*

Palgrave Macmillan Ltd., Houndmills, Basingstoke, Hampshire, RG21 6XS, England, (Telephone in U.S. (888) 330-8477), (Fax in U.S. (800) 672-2054), www.palgrave.com; *The Statesman's Yearbook 2008.*

Taylor and Francis Group, An Informa Business, 2 Park Square, Milton Park, Abingdon, Oxford OX14 4RN, United Kingdom, (Dial from U.S. (212) 216-7800), (Fax from U.S. (212) 564-7854), www.tandf.co.uk; *The Europa World Year Book.*

UCLA Latin American Institute, 10343 Bunche Hall, Box 951447, Los Angeles, CA 90095-1447, (310) 825-4571, Fax: (310) 206-6859, www.international.ucla.edu/lac; *Statistical Abstract of Latin America.*

The World Bank, 1818 H Street, NW, Washington, DC 20433, (202) 473-1000, Fax: (202) 477-6391, www.worldbank.org; *Brazil.*

BRAZIL - FISHERIES

Federal Statistical Office Germany, D-65180 Wiesbaden, Germany, www.destatis.de; *Brazil 2006.*

Inter-American Development Bank (IDB), 1300 New York Avenue, NW, Washington, DC 20577, (202) 623-1000, Fax: (202) 623-3096, www.iadb.org; *The Politics of Policies: Economic and Social Progress in Latin America - 2006 Report.*

M.E. Sharpe, 80 Business Park Drive, Armonk, NY 10504, (800) 541-6563, Fax: (914) 273-2106, www.mesharpe.com; *The Illustrated Book of World Rankings.*

Palgrave Macmillan Ltd., Houndmills, Basingstoke, Hampshire, RG21 6XS, England, (Telephone in U.S. (888) 330-8477), (Fax in U.S. (800) 672-2054), www.palgrave.com; *The Statesman's Yearbook 2008.*

Taylor and Francis Group, An Informa Business, 2 Park Square, Milton Park, Abingdon, Oxford OX14 4RN, United Kingdom, (Dial from U.S. (212) 216-7800), (Fax from U.S. (212) 564-7854), www.tandf.co.uk; *The Europa World Year Book.*

UCLA Latin American Institute, 10343 Bunche Hall, Box 951447, Los Angeles, CA 90095-1447, (310) 825-4571, Fax: (310) 206-6859, www.international.ucla.edu/lac; *Statistical Abstract of Latin America.*

United Nations Conference on Trade and Development (UNCTAD), DC2-1120, United Nations, New York, NY 10017, (212) 963-0027, www.unctad.org; *UNCTAD Commodity Yearbook.*

United Nations Food and Agricultural Organization (FAO), Viale delle Terme di Caracalla, 00100 Rome, Italy, (Dial from U.S. (202) 653-2400), (Fax from U.S. (202) 653 5760), www.fao.org; *FAO Yearbook of Fishery Statistics;* Fishery Databases; FISHSTAT Database. Subjects covered include: Aquaculture production, capture production, fishery commodities; and *The State of Food and Agriculture (SOFA) 2006.*

United Nations Statistics Division, New York, NY 10017, (800) 253-9646, Fax: (212) 963-4116, http://unstats.un.org; *Statistical Yearbook.*

The World Bank, 1818 H Street, NW, Washington, DC 20433, (202) 473-1000, Fax: (202) 477-6391, www.worldbank.org; *Brazil.*

BRAZIL - FLOUR INDUSTRY

United Nations Statistics Division, New York, NY 10017, (800) 253-9646, Fax: (212) 963-4116, http://unstats.un.org; *Statistical Yearbook.*

BRAZIL - FOOD

Euromonitor International, Inc., 224 S. Michigan Avenue, Suite 1500, Chicago, IL 60604, (312) 922-1115, Fax: (312) 922-1157, www.euromonitor.com; *Retail Trade International 2007.*

United Nations Conference on Trade and Development (UNCTAD), DC2-1120, United Nations, New York, NY 10017, (212) 963-0027, www.unctad.org; *UNCTAD Commodity Yearbook.*

United Nations Food and Agricultural Organization (FAO), Viale delle Terme di Caracalla, 00100 Rome, Italy, (Dial from U.S. (202) 653-2400), (Fax from U.S. (202) 653 5760), www.fao.org; *FAO Production Yearbook 2002* and *The State of Food and Agriculture (SOFA) 2006.*

United Nations Statistics Division, New York, NY 10017, (800) 253-9646, Fax: (212) 963-4116, http://unstats.un.org; *Human Development Report 2006.*

BRAZIL - FOREIGN EXCHANGE RATES

Central Intelligence Agency, Office of Public Affairs, Washington, DC 20505, (703) 482-0623, Fax: (703) 482-1739, www.cia.gov; *The World Factbook.*

Euromonitor International, Inc., 224 S. Michigan Avenue, Suite 1500, Chicago, IL 60604, (312) 922-1115, Fax: (312) 922-1157, www.euromonitor.com; *International Marketing Data and Statistics 2008* and *The World Economic Factbook 2008.*

Inter-American Development Bank (IDB), 1300 New York Avenue, NW, Washington, DC 20577, (202) 623-1000, Fax: (202) 623-3096, www.iadb.org; *The Politics of Policies: Economic and Social Progress in Latin America - 2006 Report.*

International Civil Aviation Organization (ICAO), External Relations and Public Information Office (EPO), 999 University Street, Montreal, Quebec H3C 5H7, Canada, (Dial from U.S. (514) 954-8219), (Fax from U.S. (514) 954-6077), www.icao.int; *Civil Aviation Statistics of the World.*

International Monetary Fund (IMF), 700 Nineteenth Street, NW, Washington, DC 20431, (202) 623-7000, Fax: (202) 623-4661, www.imf.org; *International Financial Statistics Yearbook 2007.*

Organization of American States (OAS), 17th Street Constitution Avenue NW, Washington, DC 20006, (202) 458-3000, www.oas.org; *The OAS in Transition: 1994-2004.*

Taylor and Francis Group, An Informa Business, 2 Park Square, Milton Park, Abingdon, Oxford OX14 4RN, United Kingdom, (Dial from U.S. (212) 216-7800), (Fax from U.S. (212) 564-7854), www.tandf.co.uk; *The Europa World Year Book.*

UCLA Latin American Institute, 10343 Bunche Hall, Box 951447, Los Angeles, CA 90095-1447, (310) 825-4571, Fax: (310) 206-6859, www.international.ucla.edu/lac; *Statistical Abstract of Latin America.*

United Nations Statistics Division, New York, NY 10017, (800) 253-9646, Fax: (212) 963-4116, http://unstats.un.org; *Statistical Yearbook* and *World Statistics Pocketbook.*

BRAZIL - FORESTS AND FORESTRY

American Forest Paper Association (AFPA), 1111 Nineteenth Street, NW, Suite 800, Washington, DC 20036, (800) 878-8878, www.afandpa.org; *2007 Annual Statistics of Paper, Paperboard, and Wood Pulp.*

Economist Intelligence Unit, 111 West 57th Street, New York, NY 10019, (212) 554-0600, Fax: (212) 586-1181, www.eiu.com; *Business Latin America.*

Federal Statistical Office Germany, D-65180 Wiesbaden, Germany, www.destatis.de; *Brazil 2006.*

Inter-American Development Bank (IDB), 1300 New York Avenue, NW, Washington, DC 20577, (202) 623-1000, Fax: (202) 623-3096, www.iadb.org; *The Politics of Policies: Economic and Social Progress in Latin America - 2006 Report.*

M.E. Sharpe, 80 Business Park Drive, Armonk, NY 10504, (800) 541-6563, Fax: (914) 273-2106, www.mesharpe.com; *The Illustrated Book of World Rankings.*

Palgrave Macmillan Ltd., Houndmills, Basingstoke, Hampshire, RG21 6XS, England, (Telephone in U.S. (888) 330-8477), (Fax in U.S. (800) 672-2054), www.palgrave.com; *The Statesman's Yearbook 2008.*

Taylor and Francis Group, An Informa Business, 2 Park Square, Milton Park, Abingdon, Oxford OX14 4RN, United Kingdom, (Dial from U.S. (212) 216-7800), (Fax from U.S. (212) 564-7854), www.tandf.co.uk; *The Europa World Year Book.*

UCLA Latin American Institute, 10343 Bunche Hall, Box 951447, Los Angeles, CA 90095-1447, (310) 825-4571, Fax: (310) 206-6859, www.international.ucla.edu/lac; *Statistical Abstract of Latin America.*

UNESCO Institute for Statistics, C.P. 6128 Succursale Centre-Ville, Montreal, Quebec, H3C 3J7 Canada, (Dial from U.S. (514) 343-6880), (Fax from U.S. (514) 343 6882), www.uis.unesco.org; *Statistical Tables.*

United Nations Conference on Trade and Development (UNCTAD), DC2-1120, United Nations, New York, NY 10017, (212) 963-0027, www.unctad.org; *UNCTAD Commodity Yearbook.*

United Nations Food and Agricultural Organization (FAO), Viale delle Terme di Caracalla, 00100 Rome, Italy, (Dial from U.S. (202) 653-2400), (Fax from U.S. (202) 653 5760), www.fao.org; *FAO Yearbook of Forest Products* and *The State of Food and Agriculture (SOFA) 2006.*

The World Bank, 1818 H Street, NW, Washington, DC 20433, (202) 473-1000, Fax: (202) 477-6391, www.worldbank.org; *Brazil* and *World Development Report 2008.*

BRAZIL - GAS PRODUCTION

See BRAZIL - MINERAL INDUSTRIES

BRAZIL - GEOGRAPHIC INFORMATION SYSTEMS

Federal Statistical Office Germany, D-65180 Wiesbaden, Germany, www.destatis.de; *Brazil 2006.*

M.E. Sharpe, 80 Business Park Drive, Armonk, NY 10504, (800) 541-6563, Fax: (914) 273-2106, www.mesharpe.com; *The Illustrated Book of World Rankings.*

UCLA Latin American Institute, 10343 Bunche Hall, Box 951447, Los Angeles, CA 90095-1447, (310) 825-4571, Fax: (310) 206-6859, www.international.ucla.edu/lac; *Statistical Abstract of Latin America.*

The World Bank, 1818 H Street, NW, Washington, DC 20433, (202) 473-1000, Fax: (202) 477-6391, www.worldbank.org; *Brazil.*

BRAZIL - GOLD INDUSTRY

Economist Intelligence Unit, 111 West 57th Street, New York, NY 10019, (212) 554-0600, Fax: (212) 586-1181, www.eiu.com; *Business Latin America.*

International Monetary Fund (IMF), 700 Nineteenth Street, NW, Washington, DC 20431, (202) 623-7000, Fax: (202) 623-4661, www.imf.org; *International Financial Statistics Yearbook 2007.*

United Nations Statistics Division, New York, NY 10017, (800) 253-9646, Fax: (212) 963-4116, http://unstats.un.org; *Statistical Yearbook.*

The World Bank, 1818 H Street, NW, Washington, DC 20433, (202) 473-1000, Fax: (202) 477-6391, www.worldbank.org; *World Development Indicators (WDI) 2008.*

BRAZIL - GOLD PRODUCTION

See BRAZIL - MINERAL INDUSTRIES

BRAZIL - GRANTS-IN-AID

International Monetary Fund (IMF), 700 Nineteenth Street, NW, Washington, DC 20431, (202) 623-7000, Fax: (202) 623-4661, www.imf.org; *Government Finance Statistics Yearbook (2008 Edition).*

BRAZIL - GROSS DOMESTIC PRODUCT

Economist Intelligence Unit, 111 West 57th Street, New York, NY 10019, (212) 554-0600, Fax: (212) 586-1181, www.eiu.com; *Brazil Country Report* and *Business Latin America.*

Euromonitor International, Inc., 224 S. Michigan Avenue, Suite 1500, Chicago, IL 60604, (312) 922-1115, Fax: (312) 922-1157, www.euromonitor.com; *International Marketing Data and Statistics 2008* and *The World Economic Factbook 2008.*

Inter-American Development Bank (IDB), 1300 New York Avenue, NW, Washington, DC 20577, (202) 623-1000, Fax: (202) 623-3096, www.iadb.org; *The Politics of Policies: Economic and Social Progress in Latin America - 2006 Report.*

M.E. Sharpe, 80 Business Park Drive, Armonk, NY 10504, (800) 541-6563, Fax: (914) 273-2106, www.mesharpe.com; *The Illustrated Book of World Rankings.*

Organization of American States (OAS), 17th Street Constitution Avenue NW, Washington, DC 20006, (202) 458-3000, www.oas.org; *The OAS in Transition: 1994-2004.*

Taylor and Francis Group, An Informa Business, 2 Park Square, Milton Park, Abingdon, Oxford OX14 4RN, United Kingdom, (Dial from U.S. (212) 216-7800), (Fax from U.S. (212) 564-7854), www.tandf.co.uk; *The Europa World Year Book.*

UCLA Latin American Institute, 10343 Bunche Hall, Box 951447, Los Angeles, CA 90095-1447, (310) 825-4571, Fax: (310) 206-6859, www.international.ucla.edu/lac; *Statistical Abstract of Latin America.*

United Nations Statistics Division, New York, NY 10017, (800) 253-9646, Fax: (212) 963-4116, http://unstats.un.org; *Human Development Report 2006; National Accounts Statistics: Compendium of Income Distribution Statistics; Statistical Yearbook;* and *Statistical Yearbook for Latin America and the Caribbean 2004.*

The World Bank, 1818 H Street, NW, Washington, DC 20433, (202) 473-1000, Fax: (202) 477-6391, www.worldbank.org; *World Development Indicators (WDI) 2008* and *World Development Report 2008.*

BRAZIL - GROSS NATIONAL PRODUCT

Euromonitor International, Inc., 224 S. Michigan Avenue, Suite 1500, Chicago, IL 60604, (312) 922-1115, Fax: (312) 922-1157, www.euromonitor.com; *International Marketing Data and Statistics 2008.*

Inter-American Development Bank (IDB), 1300 New York Avenue, NW, Washington, DC 20577, (202) 623-1000, Fax: (202) 623-3096, www.iadb.org; *The Politics of Policies: Economic and Social Progress in Latin America - 2006 Report.*

M.E. Sharpe, 80 Business Park Drive, Armonk, NY 10504, (800) 541-6563, Fax: (914) 273-2106, www.mesharpe.com; *The Illustrated Book of World Rankings.*

Palgrave Macmillan Ltd., Houndmills, Basingstoke, Hampshire, RG21 6XS, England, (Telephone in U.S. (888) 330-8477), (Fax in U.S. (800) 672-2054), www.palgrave.com; *The Statesman's Yearbook 2008.*

Taylor and Francis Group, An Informa Business, 2 Park Square, Milton Park, Abingdon, Oxford OX14 4RN, United Kingdom, (Dial from U.S. (212) 216-7800), (Fax from U.S. (212) 564-7854), www.tandf.co.uk; *The Europa World Year Book.*

U.S. Department of State (DOS), 2201 C Street NW, Washington, DC 20520, (202) 647-4000, www.state.gov; *World Military Expenditures and Arms Transfers (WMEAT).*

United Nations Statistics Division, New York, NY 10017, (800) 253-9646, Fax: (212) 963-4116, http://unstats.un.org; *Statistical Yearbook.*

The World Bank, 1818 H Street, NW, Washington, DC 20433, (202) 473-1000, Fax: (202) 477-6391, www.worldbank.org; *The World Bank Atlas 2003-2004; World Development Indicators (WDI) 2008;* and *World Development Report 2008.*

BRAZIL - HIDES AND SKINS INDUSTRY

United Nations Food and Agricultural Organization (FAO), Viale delle Terme di Caracalla, 00100 Rome, Italy, (Dial from U.S. (202) 653-2400), (Fax from U.S. (202) 653 5760), www.fao.org; *FAO Production Yearbook 2002.*

BRAZIL - HOUSING

Euromonitor International, Inc., 224 S. Michigan Avenue, Suite 1500, Chicago, IL 60604, (312) 922-1115, Fax: (312) 922-1157, www.euromonitor.com; *World Marketing Data and Statistics.*

M.E. Sharpe, 80 Business Park Drive, Armonk, NY 10504, (800) 541-6563, Fax: (914) 273-2106, www.mesharpe.com; *The Illustrated Book of World Rankings.*

UCLA Latin American Institute, 10343 Bunche Hall, Box 951447, Los Angeles, CA 90095-1447, (310) 825-4571, Fax: (310) 206-6859, www.international.ucla.edu/lac; *Statistical Abstract of Latin America.*

United Nations Statistics Division, New York, NY 10017, (800) 253-9646, Fax: (212) 963-4116, http://unstats.un.org; *Statistical Yearbook for Latin America and the Caribbean 2004.*

BRAZIL - ILLITERATE PERSONS

Euromonitor International, Inc., 224 S. Michigan Avenue, Suite 1500, Chicago, IL 60604, (312) 922-1115, Fax: (312) 922-1157, www.euromonitor.com; *The World Economic Factbook 2008.*

UNESCO Institute for Statistics, C.P. 6128 Succursale Centre-Ville, Montreal, Quebec, H3C 3J7 Canada, (Dial from U.S. (514) 343-6880), (Fax from U.S. (514) 343 6882), www.uis.unesco.org; *Statistical Tables.*

United Nations Statistics Division, New York, NY 10017, (800) 253-9646, Fax: (212) 963-4116, http://unstats.un.org; *Human Development Report 2006* and *Statistical Yearbook for Latin America and the Caribbean 2004.*

BRAZIL - IMPORTS

Central Intelligence Agency, Office of Public Affairs, Washington, DC 20505, (703) 482-0623, Fax: (703) 482-1739, www.cia.gov; *The World Factbook.*

Economist Intelligence Unit, 111 West 57th Street, New York, NY 10019, (212) 554-0600, Fax: (212) 586-1181, www.eiu.com; *Brazil Country Report* and *Business Latin America.*

Euromonitor International, Inc., 224 S. Michigan Avenue, Suite 1500, Chicago, IL 60604, (312) 922-1115, Fax: (312) 922-1157, www.euromonitor.com; *International Marketing Data and Statistics 2008; The World Economic Factbook 2008;* and *World Marketing Data and Statistics.*

Inter-American Development Bank (IDB), 1300 New York Avenue, NW, Washington, DC 20577, (202) 623-1000, Fax: (202) 623-3096, www.iadb.org; *The Politics of Policies: Economic and Social Progress in Latin America - 2006 Report.*

International Monetary Fund (IMF), 700 Nineteenth Street, NW, Washington, DC 20431, (202) 623-7000, Fax: (202) 623-4661, www.imf.org; *Direction of Trade Statistics Yearbook 2007; Government Finance Statistics Yearbook (2008 Edition);* and *International Financial Statistics Yearbook 2007.*

Organisation for Economic Cooperation and Development (OECD), 2 rue Andre Pascal, F-75775 Paris Cedex 16, France, (Telephone in U.S. (202) 785-6323), (Fax in U.S. (202) 785-0350), www.oecd.org; *OECD Economic Survey - Brazil 2006.*

Organization of American States (OAS), 17th Street Constitution Avenue NW, Washington, DC 20006, (202) 458-3000, www.oas.org; *The OAS in Transition: 1994-2004.*

Palgrave Macmillan Ltd., Houndmills, Basingstoke, Hampshire, RG21 6XS, England, (Telephone in U.S. (888) 330-8477), (Fax in U.S. (800) 672-2054), www.palgrave.com; *The Statesman's Yearbook 2008.*

Taylor and Francis Group, An Informa Business, 2 Park Square, Milton Park, Abingdon, Oxford OX14 4RN, United Kingdom, (Dial from U.S. (212) 216-7800), (Fax from U.S. (212) 564-7854), www.tandf.co.uk; *The Europa World Year Book.*

United Nations Conference on Trade and Development (UNCTAD), DC2-1120, United Nations, New York, NY 10017, (212) 963-0027, www.unctad.org; *Handbook of Statistics 2005.*

United Nations Food and Agricultural Organization (FAO), Viale delle Terme di Caracalla, 00100 Rome, Italy, (Dial from U.S. (202) 653-2400), (Fax from U.S. (202) 653 5760), www.fao.org; *The State of Food and Agriculture (SOFA) 2006.*

United Nations Statistics Division, New York, NY 10017, (800) 253-9646, Fax: (212) 963-4116, http://unstats.un.org; *Statistical Yearbook for Latin America and the Caribbean 2004.*

The World Bank, 1818 H Street, NW, Washington, DC 20433, (202) 473-1000, Fax: (202) 477-6391, www.worldbank.org; *World Development Indicators (WDI) 2008* and *World Development Report 2008.*

BRAZIL - INCOME DISTRIBUTION

UCLA Latin American Institute, 10343 Bunche Hall, Box 951447, Los Angeles, CA 90095-1447, (310) 825-4571, Fax: (310) 206-6859, www.international.ucla.edu/lac; *Statistical Abstract of Latin America.*

United Nations Statistics Division, New York, NY 10017, (800) 253-9646, Fax: (212) 963-4116, http://unstats.un.org; *Statistical Yearbook for Latin America and the Caribbean 2004.*

BRAZIL - INCOME TAXES

See BRAZIL - TAXATION

BRAZIL - INDUSTRIAL METALS PRODUCTION

See BRAZIL - MINERAL INDUSTRIES

BRAZIL - INDUSTRIAL PRODUCTIVITY

Euromonitor International, Inc., 224 S. Michigan Avenue, Suite 1500, Chicago, IL 60604, (312) 922-1115, Fax: (312) 922-1157, www.euromonitor.com; *International Marketing Data and Statistics 2008.*

M.E. Sharpe, 80 Business Park Drive, Armonk, NY 10504, (800) 541-6563, Fax: (914) 273-2106, www.mesharpe.com; *The Illustrated Book of World Rankings.*

BRAZIL - INDUSTRIAL PROPERTY

United Nations Statistics Division, New York, NY 10017, (800) 253-9646, Fax: (212) 963-4116, http://unstats.un.org; *Statistical Yearbook.*

World Intellectual Property Organization (WIPO), PO Box 18, CH-1211 Geneva 20, Switzerland, www.wipo.int; *Industrial Property Statistics* and *Industrial Property Statistics Online Directory.*

BRAZIL - INDUSTRIES

Central Intelligence Agency, Office of Public Affairs, Washington, DC 20505, (703) 482-0623, Fax: (703) 482-1739, www.cia.gov; *The World Factbook.*

Economist Intelligence Unit, 111 West 57th Street, New York, NY 10019, (212) 554-0600, Fax: (212) 586-1181, www.eiu.com; *Brazil Country Report.*

Euromonitor International, Inc., 224 S. Michigan Avenue, Suite 1500, Chicago, IL 60604, (312) 922-1115, Fax: (312) 922-1157, www.euromonitor.com; *The World Economic Factbook 2008* and *World Marketing Data and Statistics.*

Federal Statistical Office Germany, D-65180 Wiesbaden, Germany, www.destatis.de; *Brazil 2006.*

International Labour Office, I.L.O. Publications, 4 route des Morillons, CH-1211 Geneva 22, Switzerland, (Telephone in U.S. (202) 653-7652), (Fax in U.S. (202) 653-7687), www.ilo.org; *Yearbook of Labour Statistics 2006.*

M.E. Sharpe, 80 Business Park Drive, Armonk, NY 10504, (800) 541-6563, Fax: (914) 273-2106, www.mesharpe.com; *The Illustrated Book of World Rankings.*

Palgrave Macmillan Ltd., Houndmills, Basingstoke, Hampshire, RG21 6XS, England, (Telephone in U.S. (888) 330-8477), (Fax in U.S. (800) 672-2054), www.palgrave.com; *The Statesman's Yearbook 2008.*

Taylor and Francis Group, An Informa Business, 2 Park Square, Milton Park, Abingdon, Oxford OX14 4RN, United Kingdom, (Dial from U.S. (212) 216-7800), (Fax from U.S. (212) 564-7854), www.tandf.co.uk; *The Europa World Year Book.*

UCLA Latin American Institute, 10343 Bunche Hall, Box 951447, Los Angeles, CA 90095-1447, (310) 825-4571, Fax: (310) 206-6859, www.international.ucla.edu/lac; *Statistical Abstract of Latin America.*

United Nations Industrial Development Organization (UNIDO), 1 United Nations Plaza, New York, NY 10017, (212) 963 6890, Fax: (212) 963-7904, http://unido.org; Industrial Statistics Database 2008 (INDSTAT) and *The International Yearbook of Industrial Statistics 2008.*

United Nations Statistics Division, New York, NY 10017, (800) 253-9646, Fax: (212) 963-4116, http://unstats.un.org; *Economic Survey of Latin America and the Caribbean 2004-2005* and *2004 Industrial Commodity Statistics Yearbook.*

The World Bank, 1818 H Street, NW, Washington, DC 20433, (202) 473-1000, Fax: (202) 477-6391, www.worldbank.org; *Brazil* and *World Development Indicators (WDI) 2008.*

World Intellectual Property Organization (WIPO), PO Box 18, CH-1211 Geneva 20, Switzerland, www.wipo.int; *Industrial Property Statistics* and *Industrial Property Statistics Online Directory.*

BRAZIL - INFANT AND MATERNAL MORTALITY

See BRAZIL - MORTALITY

BRAZIL - INFLATION (FINANCE)

United Nations Statistics Division, New York, NY 10017, (800) 253-9646, Fax: (212) 963-4116, http://unstats.un.org; *Economic Survey of Latin America and the Caribbean 2004-2005.*

BRAZIL - INORGANIC ACIDS

United Nations Statistics Division, New York, NY 10017, (800) 253-9646, Fax: (212) 963-4116, http://unstats.un.org; *Statistical Yearbook.*

BRAZIL - INTEREST RATES

Inter-American Development Bank (IDB), 1300 New York Avenue, NW, Washington, DC 20577, (202) 623-1000, Fax: (202) 623-3096, www.iadb.org; *The Politics of Policies: Economic and Social Progress in Latin America - 2006 Report.*

Organization of American States (OAS), 17th Street Constitution Avenue NW, Washington, DC 20006, (202) 458-3000, www.oas.org; *The OAS in Transition: 1994-2004.*

BRAZIL - INTERNAL REVENUE

Inter-American Development Bank (IDB), 1300 New York Avenue, NW, Washington, DC 20577, (202) 623-1000, Fax: (202) 623-3096, www.iadb.org; *The Politics of Policies: Economic and Social Progress in Latin America - 2006 Report.*

Organization of American States (OAS), 17th Street Constitution Avenue NW, Washington, DC 20006, (202) 458-3000, www.oas.org; *The OAS in Transition: 1994-2004.*

BRAZIL - INTERNATIONAL FINANCE

Federal Statistical Office Germany, D-65180 Wiesbaden, Germany, www.destatis.de; *Brazil 2006.*

Inter-American Development Bank (IDB), 1300 New York Avenue, NW, Washington, DC 20577, (202) 623-1000, Fax: (202) 623-3096, www.iadb.org; *The Politics of Policies: Economic and Social Progress in Latin America - 2006 Report.*

UCLA Latin American Institute, 10343 Bunche Hall, Box 951447, Los Angeles, CA 90095-1447, (310) 825-4571, Fax: (310) 206-6859, www.international.ucla.edu/lac; *Statistical Abstract of Latin America.*

United Nations Statistics Division, New York, NY 10017, (800) 253-9646, Fax: (212) 963-4116, http://unstats.un.org; *Statistical Yearbook for Latin America and the Caribbean 2004.*

BRAZIL - INTERNATIONAL LIQUIDITY

Inter-American Development Bank (IDB), 1300 New York Avenue, NW, Washington, DC 20577, (202) 623-1000, Fax: (202) 623-3096, www.iadb.org; *The Politics of Policies: Economic and Social Progress in Latin America - 2006 Report.*

International Monetary Fund (IMF), 700 Nineteenth Street, NW, Washington, DC 20431, (202) 623-7000, Fax: (202) 623-4661, www.imf.org; *International Financial Statistics Yearbook 2007.*

BRAZIL - INTERNATIONAL STATISTICS

Inter-American Development Bank (IDB), 1300 New York Avenue, NW, Washington, DC 20577, (202) 623-1000, Fax: (202) 623-3096, www.iadb.org; *The Politics of Policies: Economic and Social Progress in Latin America - 2006 Report.*

UCLA Latin American Institute, 10343 Bunche Hall, Box 951447, Los Angeles, CA 90095-1447, (310) 825-4571, Fax: (310) 206-6859, www.international.ucla.edu/lac; *Statistical Abstract of Latin America.*

BRAZIL - INTERNATIONAL TRADE

Economist Intelligence Unit, 111 West 57th Street, New York, NY 10019, (212) 554-0600, Fax: (212) 586-1181, www.eiu.com; *Brazil Country Report* and *Business Latin America.*

Euromonitor International, Inc., 224 S. Michigan Avenue, Suite 1500, Chicago, IL 60604, (312) 922-1115, Fax: (312) 922-1157, www.euromonitor.com; *International Marketing Data and Statistics 2008; The World Economic Factbook 2008;* and *World Marketing Data and Statistics.*

Federal Statistical Office Germany, D-65180 Wiesbaden, Germany, www.destatis.de; *Brazil 2006.*

Inter-American Development Bank (IDB), 1300 New York Avenue, NW, Washington, DC 20577, (202) 623-1000, Fax: (202) 623-3096, www.iadb.org; *The Politics of Policies: Economic and Social Progress in Latin America - 2006 Report.*

M.E. Sharpe, 80 Business Park Drive, Armonk, NY 10504, (800) 541-6563, Fax: (914) 273-2106, www.mesharpe.com; *The Illustrated Book of World Rankings.*

Organisation for Economic Cooperation and Development (OECD), 2 rue Andre Pascal, F-75775 Paris Cedex 16, France, (Telephone in U.S. (202) 785-6323), (Fax in U.S. (202) 785-0350), www.oecd.org; *OECD Economic Survey - Brazil 2006.*

Palgrave Macmillan Ltd., Houndmills, Basingstoke, Hampshire, RG21 6XS, England, (Telephone in U.S. (888) 330-8477), (Fax in U.S. (800) 672-2054), www.palgrave.com; *The Statesman's Yearbook 2008.*

Taylor and Francis Group, An Informa Business, 2 Park Square, Milton Park, Abingdon, Oxford OX14 4RN, United Kingdom, (Dial from U.S. (212) 216-7800), (Fax from U.S. (212) 564-7854), www.tandf.co.uk; *The Europa World Year Book.*

UCLA Latin American Institute, 10343 Bunche Hall, Box 951447, Los Angeles, CA 90095-1447, (310) 825-4571, Fax: (310) 206-6859, www.international.ucla.edu/lac; *Statistical Abstract of Latin America.*

United Nations Conference on Trade and Development (UNCTAD), DC2-1120, United Nations, New York, NY 10017, (212) 963-0027, www.unctad.org; *UNCTAD Commodity Yearbook.*

United Nations Food and Agricultural Organization (FAO), Viale delle Terme di Caracalla, 00100 Rome, Italy, (Dial from U.S. (202) 653-2400), (Fax from U.S. (202) 653 5760), www.fao.org; *FAO Trade Yearbook* and *The State of Food and Agriculture (SOFA) 2006.*

United Nations Statistics Division, New York, NY 10017, (800) 253-9646, Fax: (212) 963-4116, http://unstats.un.org; *Economic Survey of Latin America and the Caribbean 2004-2005; International Trade Statistics Yearbook; Statistical Yearbook;* and *Statistical Yearbook for Latin America and the Caribbean 2004.*

The World Bank, 1818 H Street, NW, Washington, DC 20433, (202) 473-1000, Fax: (202) 477-6391, www.worldbank.org; *Brazil; World Development Indicators (WDI) 2008;* and *World Development Report 2008.*

World Bureau of Metal Statistics (WBMS), 27a High Street, Ware, Hertfordshire, SG12 9BA, United Kingdom, www.world-bureau.com; *Annual Stainless Steel Statistics; World Flow Charts; World Metal Statistics; World Nickel Statistics;* and *World Tin Statistics.*

World Trade Organization (WTO), Centre William Rappard, Rue de Lausanne 154, CH-1211 Geneva 21, Switzerland, www.wto.org; *International Trade Statistics 2006.*

BRAZIL - INTERNET USERS

Federal Statistical Office Germany, D-65180 Wiesbaden, Germany, www.destatis.de; *Brazil 2006.*

International Telecommunication Union (ITU), Place des Nations, 1211 Geneva 20, Switzerland, www.itu.int; *World Telecommunication/ICT Indicators Database on CD-ROM; World Telecommunication/ICT Indicators Database Online;* and *Yearbook of Statistics - Telecommunication Services (Chronological Time Series 1997-2006).*

The World Bank, 1818 H Street, NW, Washington, DC 20433, (202) 473-1000, Fax: (202) 477-6391, www.worldbank.org; *Brazil.*

BRAZIL - INVESTMENTS

Inter-American Development Bank (IDB), 1300 New York Avenue, NW, Washington, DC 20577, (202) 623-1000, Fax: (202) 623-3096, www.iadb.org; *The Politics of Policies: Economic and Social Progress in Latin America - 2006 Report.*

International Monetary Fund (IMF), 700 Nineteenth Street, NW, Washington, DC 20431, (202) 623-7000, Fax: (202) 623-4661, www.imf.org; *International Financial Statistics Yearbook 2007.*

United Nations Statistics Division, New York, NY 10017, (800) 253-9646, Fax: (212) 963-4116, http://unstats.un.org; *Statistical Yearbook for Latin America and the Caribbean 2004.*

BRAZIL - INVESTMENTS, FOREIGN

Economist Intelligence Unit, 111 West 57th Street, New York, NY 10019, (212) 554-0600, Fax: (212) 586-1181, www.eiu.com; *Business Latin America.*

BRAZIL - IRON AND IRON ORE PRODUCTION

See BRAZIL - MINERAL INDUSTRIES

BRAZIL - IRRIGATION

Euromonitor International, Inc., 224 S. Michigan Avenue, Suite 1500, Chicago, IL 60604, (312) 922-1115, Fax: (312) 922-1157, www.euromonitor.com; *International Marketing Data and Statistics 2008.*

Inter-American Development Bank (IDB), 1300 New York Avenue, NW, Washington, DC 20577, (202) 623-1000, Fax: (202) 623-3096, www.iadb.org; *The Politics of Policies: Economic and Social Progress in Latin America - 2006 Report.*

BRAZIL - JUTE PRODUCTION

See BRAZIL - CROPS

BRAZIL - LABOR

Central Intelligence Agency, Office of Public Affairs, Washington, DC 20505, (703) 482-0623, Fax: (703) 482-1739, www.cia.gov; *The World Factbook.*

Economist Intelligence Unit, 111 West 57th Street, New York, NY 10019, (212) 554-0600, Fax: (212) 586-1181, www.eiu.com; *Business Latin America.*

Euromonitor International, Inc., 224 S. Michigan Avenue, Suite 1500, Chicago, IL 60604, (312) 922-1115, Fax: (312) 922-1157, www.euromonitor.com; *International Marketing Data and Statistics 2008* and *World Marketing Data and Statistics.*

International Labour Office, I.L.O. Publications, 4 route des Morillons, CH-1211 Geneva 22, Switzerland, (Telephone in U.S. (202) 653-7652), (Fax in U.S. (202) 653-7687), www.ilo.org; *Yearbook of Labour Statistics 2006.*

M.E. Sharpe, 80 Business Park Drive, Armonk, NY 10504, (800) 541-6563, Fax: (914) 273-2106, www.mesharpe.com; *The Illustrated Book of World Rankings.*

Organisation for Economic Cooperation and Development (OECD), 2 rue Andre Pascal, F-75775 Paris Cedex 16, France, (Telephone in U.S. (202) 785-6323), (Fax in U.S. (202) 785-0350), www.oecd.org; *OECD Economic Survey - Brazil 2006.*

Palgrave Macmillan Ltd., Houndmills, Basingstoke, Hampshire, RG21 6XS, England, (Telephone in U.S. (888) 330-8477), (Fax in U.S. (800) 672-2054), www.palgrave.com; *The Statesman's Yearbook 2008.*

Taylor and Francis Group, An Informa Business, 2 Park Square, Milton Park, Abingdon, Oxford OX14 4RN, United Kingdom, (Dial from U.S. (212) 216-7800), (Fax from U.S. (212) 564-7854), www.tandf.co.uk; *The Europa World Year Book.*

United Nations Food and Agricultural Organization (FAO), Viale delle Terme di Caracalla, 00100 Rome, Italy, (Dial from U.S. (202) 653-2400), (Fax from U.S. (202) 653 5760), www.fao.org; *The State of Food and Agriculture (SOFA) 2006.*

The World Bank, 1818 H Street, NW, Washington, DC 20433, (202) 473-1000, Fax: (202) 477-6391, www.worldbank.org; *The World Bank Atlas 2003-2004; World Development Indicators (WDI) 2008;* and *World Development Report 2008.*

BRAZIL - LAND USE

Central Intelligence Agency, Office of Public Affairs, Washington, DC 20505, (703) 482-0623, Fax: (703) 482-1739, www.cia.gov; *The World Factbook.*

Euromonitor International, Inc., 224 S. Michigan Avenue, Suite 1500, Chicago, IL 60604, (312) 922-1115, Fax: (312) 922-1157, www.euromonitor.com; *International Marketing Data and Statistics 2008.*

Inter-American Development Bank (IDB), 1300 New York Avenue, NW, Washington, DC 20577, (202) 623-1000, Fax: (202) 623-3096, www.iadb.org; *The Politics of Policies: Economic and Social Progress in Latin America - 2006 Report.*

United Nations Food and Agricultural Organization (FAO), Viale delle Terme di Caracalla, 00100 Rome,

Italy, (Dial from U.S. (202) 653-2400), (Fax from U.S. (202) 653 5760), www.fao.org; *FAO Production Yearbook 2002.*

The World Bank, 1818 H Street, NW, Washington, DC 20433, (202) 473-1000, Fax: (202) 477-6391, www.worldbank.org; *World Development Report 2008.*

BRAZIL - LIBRARIES

M.E. Sharpe, 80 Business Park Drive, Armonk, NY 10504, (800) 541-6563, Fax: (914) 273-2106, www.mesharpe.com; *The Illustrated Book of World Rankings.*

UNESCO Institute for Statistics, C.P. 6128 Succursale Centre-Ville, Montreal, Quebec, H3C 3J7 Canada, (Dial from U.S. (514) 343-6880), (Fax from U.S. (514) 343 6882), www.uis.unesco.org; *Statistical Tables.*

BRAZIL - LICENSES

International Monetary Fund (IMF), 700 Nineteenth Street, NW, Washington, DC 20431, (202) 623-7000, Fax: (202) 623-4661, www.imf.org; *Government Finance Statistics Yearbook (2008 Edition).*

BRAZIL - LIFE EXPECTANCY

Central Intelligence Agency, Office of Public Affairs, Washington, DC 20505, (703) 482-0623, Fax: (703) 482-1739, www.cia.gov; *The World Factbook.*

Economist Intelligence Unit, 111 West 57th Street, New York, NY 10019, (212) 554-0600, Fax: (212) 586-1181, www.eiu.com; *Business Latin America.*

Euromonitor International, Inc., 224 S. Michigan Avenue, Suite 1500, Chicago, IL 60604, (312) 922-1115, Fax: (312) 922-1157, www.euromonitor.com; *The World Economic Factbook 2008.*

Palgrave Macmillan Ltd., Houndmills, Basingstoke, Hampshire, RG21 6XS, England, (Telephone in U.S. (888) 330-8477), (Fax in U.S. (800) 672-2054), www.palgrave.com; *The Statesman's Yearbook 2008.*

United Nations Statistics Division, New York, NY 10017, (800) 253-9646, Fax: (212) 963-4116, http://unstats.un.org; *Statistical Yearbook for Latin America and the Caribbean 2004* and *World Statistics Pocketbook.*

The World Bank, 1818 H Street, NW, Washington, DC 20433, (202) 473-1000, Fax: (202) 477-6391, www.worldbank.org; *The World Bank Atlas 2003-2004* and *World Development Report 2008.*

BRAZIL - LITERACY

Economist Intelligence Unit, 111 West 57th Street, New York, NY 10019, (212) 554-0600, Fax: (212) 586-1181, www.eiu.com; *Business Latin America.*

Euromonitor International, Inc., 224 S. Michigan Avenue, Suite 1500, Chicago, IL 60604, (312) 922-1115, Fax: (312) 922-1157, www.euromonitor.com; *World Marketing Data and Statistics.*

BRAZIL - LIVESTOCK

Euromonitor International, Inc., 224 S. Michigan Avenue, Suite 1500, Chicago, IL 60604, (312) 922-1115, Fax: (312) 922-1157, www.euromonitor.com; *International Marketing Data and Statistics 2008.*

M.E. Sharpe, 80 Business Park Drive, Armonk, NY 10504, (800) 541-6563, Fax: (914) 273-2106, www.mesharpe.com; *The Illustrated Book of World Rankings.*

Palgrave Macmillan Ltd., Houndmills, Basingstoke, Hampshire, RG21 6XS, England, (Telephone in U.S. (888) 330-8477), (Fax in U.S. (800) 672-2054), www.palgrave.com; *The Statesman's Yearbook 2008.*

Taylor and Francis Group, An Informa Business, 2 Park Square, Milton Park, Abingdon, Oxford OX14 4RN, United Kingdom, (Dial from U.S. (212) 216-7800), (Fax from U.S. (212) 564-7854), www.tandf.co.uk; *The Europa World Year Book.*

United Nations Conference on Trade and Development (UNCTAD), DC2-1120, United Nations, New York, NY 10017, (212) 963-0027, www.unctad.org; *UNCTAD Commodity Yearbook.*

United Nations Food and Agricultural Organization (FAO), Viale delle Terme di Caracalla, 00100 Rome, Italy, (Dial from U.S. (202) 653-2400), (Fax from U.S. (202) 653 5760), www.fao.org; *FAO Production Yearbook 2002* and *The State of Food and Agriculture (SOFA) 2006.*

United Nations Statistics Division, New York, NY 10017, (800) 253-9646, Fax: (212) 963-4116, http://unstats.un.org; *Statistical Yearbook.*

BRAZIL - LOCAL TAXATION

Euromonitor International, Inc., 224 S. Michigan Avenue, Suite 1500, Chicago, IL 60604, (312) 922-1115, Fax: (312) 922-1157, www.euromonitor.com; *International Marketing Data and Statistics 2008.*

Inter-American Development Bank (IDB), 1300 New York Avenue, NW, Washington, DC 20577, (202) 623-1000, Fax: (202) 623-3096, www.iadb.org; *The Politics of Policies: Economic and Social Progress in Latin America - 2006 Report.*

BRAZIL - MANUFACTURES

Economist Intelligence Unit, 111 West 57th Street, New York, NY 10019, (212) 554-0600, Fax: (212) 586-1181, www.eiu.com; *Business Latin America.*

Inter-American Development Bank (IDB), 1300 New York Avenue, NW, Washington, DC 20577, (202) 623-1000, Fax: (202) 623-3096, www.iadb.org; *The Politics of Policies: Economic and Social Progress in Latin America - 2006 Report.*

M.E. Sharpe, 80 Business Park Drive, Armonk, NY 10504, (800) 541-6563, Fax: (914) 273-2106, www.mesharpe.com; *The Illustrated Book of World Rankings.*

Organisation for Economic Cooperation and Development (OECD), 2 rue Andre Pascal, F-75775 Paris Cedex 16, France, (Telephone in U.S. (202) 785-6323), (Fax in U.S. (202) 785-0350), www.oecd.org; *OECD Economic Survey - Brazil 2006.*

United Nations Statistics Division, New York, NY 10017, (800) 253-9646, Fax: (212) 963-4116, http://unstats.un.org; *Statistical Yearbook* and *Statistical Yearbook for Latin America and the Caribbean 2004.*

The World Bank, 1818 H Street, NW, Washington, DC 20433, (202) 473-1000, Fax: (202) 477-6391, www.worldbank.org; *World Development Indicators (WDI) 2008.*

BRAZIL - MARRIAGE

M.E. Sharpe, 80 Business Park Drive, Armonk, NY 10504, (800) 541-6563, Fax: (914) 273-2106, www.mesharpe.com; *The Illustrated Book of World Rankings.*

United Nations Statistics Division, New York, NY 10017, (800) 253-9646, Fax: (212) 963-4116, http://unstats.un.org; *Demographic Yearbook.*

BRAZIL - MEAT PRODUCTION

See BRAZIL - LIVESTOCK

BRAZIL - MEDICAL PERSONNEL

UCLA Latin American Institute, 10343 Bunche Hall, Box 951447, Los Angeles, CA 90095-1447, (310) 825-4571, Fax: (310) 206-6859, www.international.ucla.edu/lac; *Statistical Abstract of Latin America.*

BRAZIL - MILK PRODUCTION

See BRAZIL - DAIRY PROCESSING

BRAZIL - MINERAL INDUSTRIES

Commodity Research Bureau, 330 South Wells Street, Suite 612, Chicago, IL 60606-7110, (800) 621-5271, Fax: (312) 939-4135, www.crbtrader.com; *2006 CRB Commodity Yearbook and CD.*

Economist Intelligence Unit, 111 West 57th Street, New York, NY 10019, (212) 554-0600, Fax: (212) 586-1181, www.eiu.com; *Business Latin America.*

Federal Statistical Office Germany, D-65180 Wiesbaden, Germany, www.destatis.de; *Brazil 2006.*

Inter-American Development Bank (IDB), 1300 New York Avenue, NW, Washington, DC 20577, (202) 623-1000, Fax: (202) 623-3096, www.iadb.org; *The Politics of Policies: Economic and Social Progress in Latin America - 2006 Report.*

International Monetary Fund (IMF), 700 Nineteenth Street, NW, Washington, DC 20431, (202) 623-7000, Fax: (202) 623-4661, www.imf.org; *International Financial Statistics Yearbook 2007.*

M.E. Sharpe, 80 Business Park Drive, Armonk, NY 10504, (800) 541-6563, Fax: (914) 273-2106, www.mesharpe.com; *The Illustrated Book of World Rankings.*

Organisation for Economic Cooperation and Development (OECD), 2 rue Andre Pascal, F-75775 Paris Cedex 16, France, (Telephone in U.S. (202) 785-6323), (Fax in U.S. (202) 785-0350), www.oecd.org; *OECD Economic Survey - Brazil 2006* and *World Energy Outlook 2007.*

Organization of American States (OAS), 17th Street Constitution Avenue NW, Washington, DC 20006, (202) 458-3000, www.oas.org; *The OAS in Transition: 1994-2004.*

Palgrave Macmillan Ltd., Houndmills, Basingstoke, Hampshire, RG21 6XS, England, (Telephone in U.S. (888) 330-8477), (Fax in U.S. (800) 672-2054), www.palgrave.com; *The Statesman's Yearbook 2008.*

Taylor and Francis Group, An Informa Business, 2 Park Square, Milton Park, Abingdon, Oxford OX14 4RN, United Kingdom, (Dial from U.S. (212) 216-7800), (Fax from U.S. (212) 564-7854), www.tandf.co.uk; *The Europa World Year Book.*

UCLA Latin American Institute, 10343 Bunche Hall, Box 951447, Los Angeles, CA 90095-1447, (310) 825-4571, Fax: (310) 206-6859, www.international.ucla.edu/lac; *Statistical Abstract of Latin America.*

United Nations Conference on Trade and Development (UNCTAD), DC2-1120, United Nations, New York, NY 10017, (212) 963-0027, www.unctad.org; *UNCTAD Commodity Yearbook.*

United Nations Statistics Division, New York, NY 10017, (800) 253-9646, Fax: (212) 963-4116, http://unstats.un.org; *Statistical Yearbook* and *Statistical Yearbook for Latin America and the Caribbean 2004.*

World Bureau of Metal Statistics (WBMS), 27a High Street, Ware, Hertfordshire, SG12 9BA, United Kingdom, www.world-bureau.com; *Annual Stainless Steel Statistics; World Flow Charts; World Metal Statistics; World Nickel Statistics;* and *World Tin Statistics.*

BRAZIL - MOLASSES PRODUCTION

See BRAZIL - CROPS

BRAZIL - MONEY EXCHANGE RATES

See BRAZIL - FOREIGN EXCHANGE RATES

BRAZIL - MONEY SUPPLY

Economist Intelligence Unit, 111 West 57th Street, New York, NY 10019, (212) 554-0600, Fax: (212) 586-1181, www.eiu.com; *Brazil Country Report.*

Euromonitor International, Inc., 224 S. Michigan Avenue, Suite 1500, Chicago, IL 60604, (312) 922-1115, Fax: (312) 922-1157, www.euromonitor.com; *International Marketing Data and Statistics 2008.*

Federal Statistical Office Germany, D-65180 Wiesbaden, Germany, www.destatis.de; *Brazil 2006.*

Inter-American Development Bank (IDB), 1300 New York Avenue, NW, Washington, DC 20577, (202) 623-1000, Fax: (202) 623-3096, www.iadb.org; *The Politics of Policies: Economic and Social Progress in Latin America - 2006 Report.*

International Monetary Fund (IMF), 700 Nineteenth Street, NW, Washington, DC 20431, (202) 623-7000, Fax: (202) 623-4661, www.imf.org; *International Financial Statistics Yearbook 2007.*

Organisation for Economic Cooperation and Development (OECD), 2 rue Andre Pascal, F-75775 Paris

Cedex 16, France, (Telephone in U.S. (202) 785-6323), (Fax in U.S. (202) 785-0350), www.oecd.org; *OECD Economic Survey - Brazil 2006.*

Taylor and Francis Group, An Informa Business, 2 Park Square, Milton Park, Abingdon, Oxford OX14 4RN, United Kingdom, (Dial from U.S. (212) 216-7800), (Fax from U.S. (212) 564-7854), www.tandf.co.uk; *The Europa World Year Book.*

UCLA Latin American Institute, 10343 Bunche Hall, Box 951447, Los Angeles, CA 90095-1447, (310) 825-4571, Fax: (310) 206-6859, www.international.ucla.edu/lac; *Statistical Abstract of Latin America.*

United Nations Statistics Division, New York, NY 10017, (800) 253-9646, Fax: (212) 963-4116, http://unstats.un.org; *Statistical Yearbook.*

The World Bank, 1818 H Street, NW, Washington, DC 20433, (202) 473-1000, Fax: (202) 477-6391, www.worldbank.org; *Brazil* and *World Development Indicators (WDI) 2008.*

BRAZIL - MORTALITY

Central Intelligence Agency, Office of Public Affairs, Washington, DC 20505, (703) 482-0623, Fax: (703) 482-1739, www.cia.gov; *The World Factbook.*

Economist Intelligence Unit, 111 West 57th Street, New York, NY 10019, (212) 554-0600, Fax: (212) 586-1181, www.eiu.com; *Business Latin America.*

Euromonitor International, Inc., 224 S. Michigan Avenue, Suite 1500, Chicago, IL 60604, (312) 922-1115, Fax: (312) 922-1157, www.euromonitor.com; *International Marketing Data and Statistics 2008.*

Taylor and Francis Group, An Informa Business, 2 Park Square, Milton Park, Abingdon, Oxford OX14 4RN, United Kingdom, (Dial from U.S. (212) 216-7800), (Fax from U.S. (212) 564-7854), www.tandf.co.uk; *The Europa World Year Book.*

UNICEF, 3 United Nations Plaza, New York, NY 10017, (800) 253-9646, Fax: (212) 887-7465, www.unicef.org; *The State of the World's Children 2008.*

United Nations Statistics Division, New York, NY 10017, (800) 253-9646, Fax: (212) 963-4116, http://unstats.un.org; *Demographic Yearbook; Statistical Yearbook; Statistical Yearbook for Latin America and the Caribbean 2004;* and *World Statistics Pocketbook.*

The World Bank, 1818 H Street, NW, Washington, DC 20433, (202) 473-1000, Fax: (202) 477-6391, www.worldbank.org; *The World Bank Atlas 2003-2004; World Development Indicators (WDI) 2008;* and *World Development Report 2008.*

World Health Organization (WHO), Avenue Appia 20, 1211 Geneve 27, Switzerland, (Telephone in U.S. (212) 331-9081), www.who.int; The WHO Global Atlas of Infectious Diseases and *World Health Report 2006.*

BRAZIL - MOTION PICTURES

Palgrave Macmillan Ltd., Houndmills, Basingstoke, Hampshire, RG21 6XS, England, (Telephone in U.S. (888) 330-8477), (Fax in U.S. (800) 672-2054), www.palgrave.com; *The Statesman's Yearbook 2008.*

UNESCO Institute for Statistics, C.P. 6128 Succursale Centre-Ville, Montreal, Quebec, H3C 3J7 Canada, (Dial from U.S. (514) 343-6880), (Fax from U.S. (514) 343 6882), www.uis.unesco.org; *Statistical Tables.*

United Nations Statistics Division, New York, NY 10017, (800) 253-9646, Fax: (212) 963-4116, http://unstats.un.org; *Statistical Yearbook.*

BRAZIL - MOTOR VEHICLES

Economist Intelligence Unit, 111 West 57th Street, New York, NY 10019, (212) 554-0600, Fax: (212) 586-1181, www.eiu.com; *Business Latin America.*

International Road Federation (IFR), Madison Place, 500 Montgomery Street, 5th Floor, Alexandria, VA 22314, (703) 535-1001, Fax: (703) 535-1007, www.irfnet.org; *World Road Statistics 2006.*

Taylor and Francis Group, An Informa Business, 2 Park Square, Milton Park, Abingdon, Oxford OX14 4RN, United Kingdom, (Dial from U.S. (212) 216-7800), (Fax from U.S. (212) 564-7854), www.tandf.co.uk; *The Europa World Year Book.*

United Nations Statistics Division, New York, NY 10017, (800) 253-9646, Fax: (212) 963-4116, http://unstats.un.org; *Statistical Yearbook.*

BRAZIL - MUSEUMS

M.E. Sharpe, 80 Business Park Drive, Armonk, NY 10504, (800) 541-6563, Fax: (914) 273-2106, www.mesharpe.com; *The Illustrated Book of World Rankings.*

UNESCO Institute for Statistics, C.P. 6128 Succursale Centre-Ville, Montreal, Quebec, H3C 3J7 Canada, (Dial from U.S. (514) 343-6880), (Fax from U.S. (514) 343 6882), www.uis.unesco.org; *Statistical Tables.*

BRAZIL - NATIONAL INCOME

United Nations Statistics Division, New York, NY 10017, (800) 253-9646, Fax: (212) 963-4116, http://unstats.un.org; *Statistical Yearbook.*

BRAZIL - NATURAL GAS PRODUCTION

See BRAZIL - MINERAL INDUSTRIES

BRAZIL - NICKEL AND NICKEL ORE

See BRAZIL - MINERAL INDUSTRIES

BRAZIL - NUTRITION

United Nations Food and Agricultural Organization (FAO), Viale delle Terme di Caracalla, 00100 Rome, Italy, (Dial from U.S. (202) 653-2400), (Fax from U.S. (202) 653 5760), www.fao.org; *The State of Food and Agriculture (SOFA) 2006.*

United Nations Statistics Division, New York, NY 10017, (800) 253-9646, Fax: (212) 963-4116, http://unstats.un.org; *Statistical Yearbook for Latin America and the Caribbean 2004.*

BRAZIL - OATS PRODUCTION

See BRAZIL - CROPS

BRAZIL - OLDER PEOPLE

M.E. Sharpe, 80 Business Park Drive, Armonk, NY 10504, (800) 541-6563, Fax: (914) 273-2106, www.mesharpe.com; *The Illustrated Book of World Rankings.*

BRAZIL - ONION PRODUCTION

See BRAZIL - CROPS

BRAZIL - ORANGES PRODUCTION

See BRAZIL - CROPS

BRAZIL - PALM OIL PRODUCTION

See BRAZIL - CROPS

BRAZIL - PAPER

See BRAZIL - FORESTS AND FORESTRY

BRAZIL - PEANUT PRODUCTION

See BRAZIL - CROPS

BRAZIL - PEPPER PRODUCTION

See BRAZIL - CROPS

BRAZIL - PERIODICALS

UNESCO Institute for Statistics, C.P. 6128 Succursale Centre-Ville, Montreal, Quebec, H3C 3J7 Canada, (Dial from U.S. (514) 343-6880), (Fax from U.S. (514) 343 6882), www.uis.unesco.org; *Statistical Tables.*

BRAZIL - PESTICIDES

United Nations Food and Agricultural Organization (FAO), Viale delle Terme di Caracalla, 00100 Rome, Italy, (Dial from U.S. (202) 653-2400), (Fax from U.S. (202) 653 5760), www.fao.org; *The State of Food and Agriculture (SOFA) 2006.*

BRAZIL - PETROLEUM INDUSTRY AND TRADE

Economist Intelligence Unit, 111 West 57th Street, New York, NY 10019, (212) 554-0600, Fax: (212) 586-1181, www.eiu.com; *Business Latin America.*

Inter-American Development Bank (IDB), 1300 New York Avenue, NW, Washington, DC 20577, (202) 623-1000, Fax: (202) 623-3096, www.iadb.org; *The Politics of Policies: Economic and Social Progress in Latin America - 2006 Report.*

M.E. Sharpe, 80 Business Park Drive, Armonk, NY 10504, (800) 541-6563, Fax: (914) 273-2106, www.mesharpe.com; *The Illustrated Book of World Rankings.*

Organisation for Economic Cooperation and Development (OECD), 2 rue Andre Pascal, F-75775 Paris Cedex 16, France, (Telephone in U.S. (202) 785-6323), (Fax in U.S. (202) 785-0350), www.oecd.org; *World Energy Outlook 2007.*

Organization of American States (OAS), 17th Street Constitution Avenue NW, Washington, DC 20006, (202) 458-3000, www.oas.org; *The OAS in Transition: 1994-2004.*

Palgrave Macmillan Ltd., Houndmills, Basingstoke, Hampshire, RG21 6XS, England, (Telephone in U.S. (888) 330-8477), (Fax in U.S. (800) 672-2054), www.palgrave.com; *The Statesman's Yearbook 2008.*

PennWell Corporation, 1421 South Sheridan Road, Tulsa, OK 74112, (918) 835-3161, www.pennwell.com; *International Petroleum Encyclopedia 2007* and *Oil Gas Journal Latinoamericana.*

U.S. Department of Energy (DOE), Energy Information Administration (EIA), 1000 Independence Avenue, SW, Washington, DC 20585, (202) 586-8800, www.eia.doe.gov; *International Energy Annual 2004* and *International Energy Outlook 2006.*

United Nations Conference on Trade and Development (UNCTAD), DC2-1120, United Nations, New York, NY 10017, (212) 963-0027, www.unctad.org; *UNCTAD Commodity Yearbook.*

United Nations Food and Agricultural Organization (FAO), Viale delle Terme di Caracalla, 00100 Rome, Italy, (Dial from U.S. (202) 653-2400), (Fax from U.S. (202) 653 5760), www.fao.org; *The State of Food and Agriculture (SOFA) 2006.*

United Nations Statistics Division, New York, NY 10017, (800) 253-9646, Fax: (212) 963-4116, http://unstats.un.org; *Statistical Yearbook.*

BRAZIL - PHOSPHATES PRODUCTION

See BRAZIL - MINERAL INDUSTRIES

BRAZIL - PLASTICS INDUSTRY AND TRADE

United Nations Statistics Division, New York, NY 10017, (800) 253-9646, Fax: (212) 963-4116, http://unstats.un.org; *Statistical Yearbook.*

BRAZIL - POLITICAL SCIENCE

Brazilian Statistical and Geographic Institute (Instituto Brasileiro de Geografia e Estatistica (IBGE)), Rua General Canabarro, 706 - Maracana, Rio de Janeiro, RJ 20271-201, Brazil, www.ibge.gov.br/english/default.php; *Profile of Brazilian Municipalities - Public Administration.*

Central Intelligence Agency, Office of Public Affairs, Washington, DC 20505, (703) 482-0623, Fax: (703) 482-1739, www.cia.gov; *The World Factbook.*

Inter-American Development Bank (IDB), 1300 New York Avenue, NW, Washington, DC 20577, (202) 623-1000, Fax: (202) 623-3096, www.iadb.org; *The Politics of Policies: Economic and Social Progress in Latin America - 2006 Report.*

International Monetary Fund (IMF), 700 Nineteenth Street, NW, Washington, DC 20431, (202) 623-7000, Fax: (202) 623-4661, www.imf.org; *Government Finance Statistics Yearbook (2008 Edition).*

Taylor and Francis Group, An Informa Business, 2 Park Square, Milton Park, Abingdon, Oxford OX14 4RN, United Kingdom, (Dial from U.S. (212) 216-7800), (Fax from U.S. (212) 564-7854), www.tandf.co.uk; *The Europa World Year Book.*

UCLA Latin American Institute, 10343 Bunche Hall, Box 951447, Los Angeles, CA 90095-1447, (310) 825-4571, Fax: (310) 206-6859, www.international.ucla.edu/lac; *Statistical Abstract of Latin America.*

United Nations Statistics Division, New York, NY 10017, (800) 253-9646, Fax: (212) 963-4116, http://unstats.un.org; *Human Development Report 2006* and *Statistical Yearbook.*

The World Bank, 1818 H Street, NW, Washington, DC 20433, (202) 473-1000, Fax: (202) 477-6391, www.worldbank.org; *World Development Indicators (WDI) 2008* and *World Development Report 2008.*

BRAZIL - POPULATION

Central Intelligence Agency, Office of Public Affairs, Washington, DC 20505, (703) 482-0623, Fax: (703) 482-1739, www.cia.gov; *The World Factbook.*

Economist Intelligence Unit, 111 West 57th Street, New York, NY 10019, (212) 554-0600, Fax: (212) 586-1181, www.eiu.com; *Brazil Country Report* and *Business Latin America.*

Euromonitor International, Inc., 224 S. Michigan Avenue, Suite 1500, Chicago, IL 60604, (312) 922-1115, Fax: (312) 922-1157, www.euromonitor.com; *International Marketing Data and Statistics 2008.*

Federal Statistical Office Germany, D-65180 Wiesbaden, Germany, www.destatis.de; *Brazil 2006.*

Inter-American Development Bank (IDB), 1300 New York Avenue, NW, Washington, DC 20577, (202) 623-1000, Fax: (202) 623-3096, www.iadb.org; *The Politics of Policies: Economic and Social Progress in Latin America - 2006 Report.*

International Labour Office, I.L.O. Publications, 4 route des Morillons, CH-1211 Geneva 22, Switzerland, (Telephone in U.S. (202) 653-7652), (Fax in U.S. (202) 653-7687), www.ilo.org; *Yearbook of Labour Statistics 2006.*

M.E. Sharpe, 80 Business Park Drive, Armonk, NY 10504, (800) 541-6563, Fax: (914) 273-2106, www.mesharpe.com; *The Illustrated Book of World Rankings.*

Organization of American States (OAS), 17th Street Constitution Avenue NW, Washington, DC 20006, (202) 458-3000, www.oas.org; *The OAS in Transition: 1994-2004.*

Palgrave Macmillan Ltd., Houndmills, Basingstoke, Hampshire, RG21 6XS, England, (Telephone in U.S. (888) 330-8477), (Fax in U.S. (800) 672-2054), www.palgrave.com; *The Statesman's Yearbook 2008.*

Taylor and Francis Group, An Informa Business, 2 Park Square, Milton Park, Abingdon, Oxford OX14 4RN, United Kingdom, (Dial from U.S. (212) 216-7800), (Fax from U.S. (212) 564-7854), www.tandf.co.uk; *The Europa World Year Book.*

U.S. Department of State (DOS), 2201 C Street NW, Washington, DC 20520, (202) 647-4000, www.state.gov; *World Military Expenditures and Arms Transfers (WMEAT).*

UCLA Latin American Institute, 10343 Bunche Hall, Box 951447, Los Angeles, CA 90095-1447, (310) 825-4571, Fax: (310) 206-6859, www.international.ucla.edu/lac; *Statistical Abstract of Latin America.*

UNESCO Institute for Statistics, C.P. 6128 Succursale Centre-Ville, Montreal, Quebec, H3C 3J7 Canada, (Dial from U.S. (514) 343-6880), (Fax from U.S. (514) 343 6882), www.uis.unesco.org; *Statistical Tables.*

United Nations Food and Agricultural Organization (FAO), Viale delle Terme di Caracalla, 00100 Rome, Italy, (Dial from U.S. (202) 653-2400), (Fax from U.S. (202) 653 5760), www.fao.org; *FAO Production Yearbook 2002.*

United Nations Statistics Division, New York, NY 10017, (800) 253-9646, Fax: (212) 963-4116, http://unstats.un.org; *Demographic Yearbook; Statistical Yearbook; Statistical Yearbook for Latin America and the Caribbean 2004;* and *World Statistics Pocketbook.*

The World Bank, 1818 H Street, NW, Washington, DC 20433, (202) 473-1000, Fax: (202) 477-6391, www.worldbank.org; *Brazil; The World Bank Atlas 2003-2004;* and *World Development Report 2008.*

World Health Organization (WHO), Avenue Appia 20, 1211 Geneve 27, Switzerland, (Telephone in U.S. (212) 331-9081), www.who.int; *World Health Report 2006.*

BRAZIL - POPULATION DENSITY

Central Intelligence Agency, Office of Public Affairs, Washington, DC 20505, (703) 482-0623, Fax: (703) 482-1739, www.cia.gov; *The World Factbook.*

Euromonitor International, Inc., 224 S. Michigan Avenue, Suite 1500, Chicago, IL 60604, (312) 922-1115, Fax: (312) 922-1157, www.euromonitor.com; *International Marketing Data and Statistics 2008* and *The World Economic Factbook 2008.*

Federal Statistical Office Germany, D-65180 Wiesbaden, Germany, www.destatis.de; *Brazil 2006.*

Inter-American Development Bank (IDB), 1300 New York Avenue, NW, Washington, DC 20577, (202) 623-1000, Fax: (202) 623-3096, www.iadb.org; *The Politics of Policies: Economic and Social Progress in Latin America - 2006 Report.*

M.E. Sharpe, 80 Business Park Drive, Armonk, NY 10504, (800) 541-6563, Fax: (914) 273-2106, www.mesharpe.com; *The Illustrated Book of World Rankings.*

Palgrave Macmillan Ltd., Houndmills, Basingstoke, Hampshire, RG21 6XS, England, (Telephone in U.S. (888) 330-8477), (Fax in U.S. (800) 672-2054), www.palgrave.com; *The Statesman's Yearbook 2008.*

Taylor and Francis Group, An Informa Business, 2 Park Square, Milton Park, Abingdon, Oxford OX14 4RN, United Kingdom, (Dial from U.S. (212) 216-7800), (Fax from U.S. (212) 564-7854), www.tandf.co.uk; *The Europa World Year Book.*

United Nations Food and Agricultural Organization (FAO), Viale delle Terme di Caracalla, 00100 Rome, Italy, (Dial from U.S. (202) 653-2400), (Fax from U.S. (202) 653 5760), www.fao.org; *The State of Food and Agriculture (SOFA) 2006.*

United Nations Statistics Division, New York, NY 10017, (800) 253-9646, Fax: (212) 963-4116, http://unstats.un.org; *Statistical Yearbook.*

The World Bank, 1818 H Street, NW, Washington, DC 20433, (202) 473-1000, Fax: (202) 477-6391, www.worldbank.org; *Brazil* and *World Development Report 2008.*

BRAZIL - POSTAL SERVICE

M.E. Sharpe, 80 Business Park Drive, Armonk, NY 10504, (800) 541-6563, Fax: (914) 273-2106, www.mesharpe.com; *The Illustrated Book of World Rankings.*

Palgrave Macmillan Ltd., Houndmills, Basingstoke, Hampshire, RG21 6XS, England, (Telephone in U.S. (888) 330-8477), (Fax in U.S. (800) 672-2054), www.palgrave.com; *The Statesman's Yearbook 2008.*

United Nations Statistics Division, New York, NY 10017, (800) 253-9646, Fax: (212) 963-4116, http://unstats.un.org; *Statistical Yearbook.*

BRAZIL - POWER RESOURCES

Economist Intelligence Unit, 111 West 57th Street, New York, NY 10019, (212) 554-0600, Fax: (212) 586-1181, www.eiu.com; *Business Latin America.*

Euromonitor International, Inc., 224 S. Michigan Avenue, Suite 1500, Chicago, IL 60604, (312) 922-1115, Fax: (312) 922-1157, www.euromonitor.com; *International Marketing Data and Statistics 2008; The World Economic Factbook 2008;* and *World Marketing Data and Statistics.*

M.E. Sharpe, 80 Business Park Drive, Armonk, NY 10504, (800) 541-6563, Fax: (914) 273-2106, www.mesharpe.com; *The Illustrated Book of World Rankings.*

Organisation for Economic Cooperation and Development (OECD), 2 rue Andre Pascal, F-75775 Paris Cedex 16, France, (Telephone in U.S. (202) 785-6323), (Fax in U.S. (202) 785-0350), www.oecd.org; *World Energy Outlook 2007.*

Palgrave Macmillan Ltd., Houndmills, Basingstoke, Hampshire, RG21 6XS, England, (Telephone in U.S. (888) 330-8477), (Fax in U.S. (800) 672-2054), www.palgrave.com; *The Statesman's Yearbook 2008.*

Platts, 2 Penn Plaza, 25th Floor, New York, NY 10121-2298, (212) 904-3070, www.platts.com; *Energy Economist.*

U.S. Department of Energy (DOE), Energy Information Administration (EIA), 1000 Independence Avenue, SW, Washington, DC 20585, (202) 586-8800, www.eia.doe.gov; *International Energy Annual 2004* and *International Energy Outlook 2006.*

UCLA Latin American Institute, 10343 Bunche Hall, Box 951447, Los Angeles, CA 90095-1447, (310) 825-4571, Fax: (310) 206-6859, www.international.ucla.edu/lac; *Statistical Abstract of Latin America.*

United Nations Food and Agricultural Organization (FAO), Viale delle Terme di Caracalla, 00100 Rome, Italy, (Dial from U.S. (202) 653-2400), (Fax from U.S. (202) 653 5760), www.fao.org; *The State of Food and Agriculture (SOFA) 2006.*

United Nations Statistics Division, New York, NY 10017, (800) 253-9646, Fax: (212) 963-4116, http://unstats.un.org; *Energy Statistics Yearbook 2003; Human Development Report 2006; Statistical Yearbook for Latin America and the Caribbean 2004;* and *World Statistics Pocketbook.*

The World Bank, 1818 H Street, NW, Washington, DC 20433, (202) 473-1000, Fax: (202) 477-6391, www.worldbank.org; *The World Bank Atlas 2003-2004* and *World Development Report 2008.*

BRAZIL - PRICES

Economist Intelligence Unit, 111 West 57th Street, New York, NY 10019, (212) 554-0600, Fax: (212) 586-1181, www.eiu.com; *Business Latin America.*

Euromonitor International, Inc., 224 S. Michigan Avenue, Suite 1500, Chicago, IL 60604, (312) 922-1115, Fax: (312) 922-1157, www.euromonitor.com; *World Marketing Data and Statistics.*

Federal Statistical Office Germany, D-65180 Wiesbaden, Germany, www.destatis.de; *Brazil 2006.*

International Labour Office, I.L.O. Publications, 4 route des Morillons, CH-1211 Geneva 22, Switzerland, (Telephone in U.S. (202) 653-7652), (Fax in U.S. (202) 653-7687), www.ilo.org; *Yearbook of Labour Statistics 2006.*

International Monetary Fund (IMF), 700 Nineteenth Street, NW, Washington, DC 20431, (202) 623-7000, Fax: (202) 623-4661, www.imf.org; *International Financial Statistics Yearbook 2007.*

M.E. Sharpe, 80 Business Park Drive, Armonk, NY 10504, (800) 541-6563, Fax: (914) 273-2106, www.mesharpe.com; *The Illustrated Book of World Rankings.*

Organization of American States (OAS), 17th Street Constitution Avenue NW, Washington, DC 20006, (202) 458-3000, www.oas.org; *The OAS in Transition: 1994-2004.*

Taylor and Francis Group, An Informa Business, 2 Park Square, Milton Park, Abingdon, Oxford OX14 4RN, United Kingdom, (Dial from U.S. (212) 216-7800), (Fax from U.S. (212) 564-7854), www.tandf.co.uk; *The Europa World Year Book.*

UCLA Latin American Institute, 10343 Bunche Hall, Box 951447, Los Angeles, CA 90095-1447, (310) 825-4571, Fax: (310) 206-6859, www.international.ucla.edu/lac; *Statistical Abstract of Latin America.*

United Nations Food and Agricultural Organization (FAO), Viale delle Terme di Caracalla, 00100 Rome, Italy, (Dial from U.S. (202) 653-2400), (Fax from U.S. (202) 653 5760), www.fao.org; *FAO Production Yearbook 2002* and *The State of Food and Agriculture (SOFA) 2006.*

United Nations Statistics Division, New York, NY 10017, (800) 253-9646, Fax: (212) 963-4116, http://unstats.un.org; *Statistical Yearbook for Latin America and the Caribbean 2004.*

The World Bank, 1818 H Street, NW, Washington, DC 20433, (202) 473-1000, Fax: (202) 477-6391, www.worldbank.org; *Brazil.*

World Bureau of Metal Statistics (WBMS), 27a High Street, Ware, Hertfordshire, SG12 9BA, United Kingdom, www.world-bureau.com; *World Flow Charts* and *World Metal Statistics.*

BRAZIL - PROFESSIONS

UCLA Latin American Institute, 10343 Bunche Hall, Box 951447, Los Angeles, CA 90095-1447, (310) 825-4571, Fax: (310) 206-6859, www.international.ucla.edu/lac; *Statistical Abstract of Latin America.*

United Nations Statistics Division, New York, NY 10017, (800) 253-9646, Fax: (212) 963-4116, http://unstats.un.org; *Statistical Yearbook.*

BRAZIL - PUBLIC HEALTH

Economist Intelligence Unit, 111 West 57th Street, New York, NY 10019, (212) 554-0600, Fax: (212) 586-1181, www.eiu.com; *Business Latin America.*

Euromonitor International, Inc., 224 S. Michigan Avenue, Suite 1500, Chicago, IL 60604, (312) 922-1115, Fax: (312) 922-1157, www.euromonitor.com; *World Health Databook 2007/2008* and *World Marketing Data and Statistics.*

Federal Statistical Office Germany, D-65180 Wiesbaden, Germany, www.destatis.de; *Brazil 2006.*

International Monetary Fund (IMF), 700 Nineteenth Street, NW, Washington, DC 20431, (202) 623-7000, Fax: (202) 623-4661, www.imf.org; *Government Finance Statistics Yearbook (2008 Edition).*

M.E. Sharpe, 80 Business Park Drive, Armonk, NY 10504, (800) 541-6563, Fax: (914) 273-2106, www.mesharpe.com; *The Illustrated Book of World Rankings.*

Palgrave Macmillan Ltd., Houndmills, Basingstoke, Hampshire, RG21 6XS, England, (Telephone in U.S. (888) 330-8477), (Fax in U.S. (800) 672-2054), www.palgrave.com; *The Statesman's Yearbook 2008.*

UCLA Latin American Institute, 10343 Bunche Hall, Box 951447, Los Angeles, CA 90095-1447, (310) 825-4571, Fax: (310) 206-6859, www.international.ucla.edu/lac; *Statistical Abstract of Latin America.*

UNICEF, 3 United Nations Plaza, New York, NY 10017, (800) 253-9646, Fax: (212) 887-7465, www.unicef.org; *The State of the World's Children 2008.*

United Nations Statistics Division, New York, NY 10017, (800) 253-9646, Fax: (212) 963-4116, http://unstats.un.org; *Human Development Report 2006* and *Statistical Yearbook.*

The World Bank, 1818 H Street, NW, Washington, DC 20433, (202) 473-1000, Fax: (202) 477-6391, www.worldbank.org; *Brazil* and *World Development Report 2008.*

World Health Organization (WHO), Avenue Appia 20, 1211 Geneve 27, Switzerland, (Telephone in U.S. (212) 331-9081), www.who.int; The WHO Global Atlas of Infectious Diseases and *World Health Report 2006.*

BRAZIL - PUBLIC UTILITIES

UCLA Latin American Institute, 10343 Bunche Hall, Box 951447, Los Angeles, CA 90095-1447, (310) 825-4571, Fax: (310) 206-6859, www.international.ucla.edu/lac; *Statistical Abstract of Latin America.*

BRAZIL - PUBLISHERS AND PUBLISHING

United Nations Statistics Division, New York, NY 10017, (800) 253-9646, Fax: (212) 963-4116, http://unstats.un.org; *Statistical Yearbook.*

BRAZIL - RADIO - RECEIVERS AND RECEPTION

United Nations Statistics Division, New York, NY 10017, (800) 253-9646, Fax: (212) 963-4116, http://unstats.un.org; *Statistical Yearbook.*

BRAZIL - RAILROADS

Economist Intelligence Unit, 111 West 57th Street, New York, NY 10019, (212) 554-0600, Fax: (212) 586-1181, www.eiu.com; *Business Latin America.*

Jane's Information Group, 110 North Royal Street, Suite 200, Alexandria, VA 22314, (703) 683-3700, Fax: (800) 836-0297, www.janes.com; *Jane's World Railways.*

Palgrave Macmillan Ltd., Houndmills, Basingstoke, Hampshire, RG21 6XS, England, (Telephone in U.S. (888) 330-8477), (Fax in U.S. (800) 672-2054), www.palgrave.com; *The Statesman's Yearbook 2008.*

Taylor and Francis Group, An Informa Business, 2 Park Square, Milton Park, Abingdon, Oxford OX14 4RN, United Kingdom, (Dial from U.S. (212) 216-7800), (Fax from U.S. (212) 564-7854), www.tandf.co.uk; *The Europa World Year Book.*

United Nations Statistics Division, New York, NY 10017, (800) 253-9646, Fax: (212) 963-4116, http://unstats.un.org; *Statistical Yearbook.*

BRAZIL - RANCHING

UCLA Latin American Institute, 10343 Bunche Hall, Box 951447, Los Angeles, CA 90095-1447, (310) 825-4571, Fax: (310) 206-6859, www.international.ucla.edu/lac; *Statistical Abstract of Latin America.*

BRAZIL - RELIGION

Central Intelligence Agency, Office of Public Affairs, Washington, DC 20505, (703) 482-0623, Fax: (703) 482-1739, www.cia.gov; *The World Factbook.*

M.E. Sharpe, 80 Business Park Drive, Armonk, NY 10504, (800) 541-6563, Fax: (914) 273-2106, www.mesharpe.com; *The Illustrated Book of World Rankings.*

Palgrave Macmillan Ltd., Houndmills, Basingstoke, Hampshire, RG21 6XS, England, (Telephone in U.S. (888) 330-8477), (Fax in U.S. (800) 672-2054), www.palgrave.com; *The Statesman's Yearbook 2008.*

UCLA Latin American Institute, 10343 Bunche Hall, Box 951447, Los Angeles, CA 90095-1447, (310) 825-4571, Fax: (310) 206-6859, www.international.ucla.edu/lac; *Statistical Abstract of Latin America.*

BRAZIL - RENT CHARGES

International Labour Office, I.L.O. Publications, 4 route des Morillons, CH-1211 Geneva 22, Switzerland, (Telephone in U.S. (202) 653-7652), (Fax in U.S. (202) 653-7687), www.ilo.org; *Yearbook of Labour Statistics 2006.*

BRAZIL - RESERVES (ACCOUNTING)

Economist Intelligence Unit, 111 West 57th Street, New York, NY 10019, (212) 554-0600, Fax: (212) 586-1181, www.eiu.com; *Business Latin America.*

Euromonitor International, Inc., 224 S. Michigan Avenue, Suite 1500, Chicago, IL 60604, (312) 922-1115, Fax: (312) 922-1157, www.euromonitor.com; *International Marketing Data and Statistics 2008.*

Inter-American Development Bank (IDB), 1300 New York Avenue, NW, Washington, DC 20577, (202) 623-1000, Fax: (202) 623-3096, www.iadb.org; *The Politics of Policies: Economic and Social Progress in Latin America - 2006 Report.*

Organization of American States (OAS), 17th Street Constitution Avenue NW, Washington, DC 20006, (202) 458-3000, www.oas.org; *The OAS in Transition: 1994-2004.*

The World Bank, 1818 H Street, NW, Washington, DC 20433, (202) 473-1000, Fax: (202) 477-6391, www.worldbank.org; *World Development Indicators (WDI) 2008.*

BRAZIL - RETAIL TRADE

Euromonitor International, Inc., 224 S. Michigan Avenue, Suite 1500, Chicago, IL 60604, (312) 922-1115, Fax: (312) 922-1157, www.euromonitor.com; *Retail Trade International 2007* and *World Marketing Data and Statistics.*

Inter-American Development Bank (IDB), 1300 New York Avenue, NW, Washington, DC 20577, (202) 623-1000, Fax: (202) 623-3096, www.iadb.org; *The Politics of Policies: Economic and Social Progress in Latin America - 2006 Report.*

United Nations Statistics Division, New York, NY 10017, (800) 253-9646, Fax: (212) 963-4116, http://unstats.un.org; *Statistical Yearbook.*

BRAZIL - RICE PRODUCTION

See BRAZIL - CROPS

BRAZIL - ROADS

Central Intelligence Agency, Office of Public Affairs, Washington, DC 20505, (703) 482-0623, Fax: (703) 482-1739, www.cia.gov; *The World Factbook.*

Economist Intelligence Unit, 111 West 57th Street, New York, NY 10019, (212) 554-0600, Fax: (212) 586-1181, www.eiu.com; *Business Latin America.*

International Road Federation (IFR), Madison Place, 500 Montgomery Street, 5th Floor, Alexandria, VA 22314, (703) 535-1001, Fax: (703) 535-1007, www.irfnet.org; *World Road Statistics 2006.*

Palgrave Macmillan Ltd., Houndmills, Basingstoke, Hampshire, RG21 6XS, England, (Telephone in U.S. (888) 330-8477), (Fax in U.S. (800) 672-2054), www.palgrave.com; *The Statesman's Yearbook 2008.*

BRAZIL - RUBBER INDUSTRY AND TRADE

International Rubber Study Group (IRSG), 1st Floor, Heron House, 109/115 Wembley Hill Road, Wembley, Middlesex HA9 8DA, United Kingdom, www.rubberstudy.com; *Rubber Statistical Bulletin; Summary of World Rubber Statistics 2005; World Rubber Statistics Handbook (Volume 6, 1975-2001);* and *World Rubber Statistics Historic Handbook.*

M.E. Sharpe, 80 Business Park Drive, Armonk, NY 10504, (800) 541-6563, Fax: (914) 273-2106, www.mesharpe.com; *The Illustrated Book of World Rankings.*

United Nations Statistics Division, New York, NY 10017, (800) 253-9646, Fax: (212) 963-4116, http://unstats.un.org; *Statistical Yearbook.*

BRAZIL - SALT PRODUCTION

See BRAZIL - MINERAL INDUSTRIES

BRAZIL - SHEEP

See BRAZIL - LIVESTOCK

BRAZIL - SHIPPING

Lloyd's Register - Fairplay, 8410 N.W. 53rd Terrace, Suite 207, Miami FL 33166, (305) 718-9929, Fax: (305) 718-9663, www.lrfairplay.com; *Register of Ships 2007-2008; World Casualty Statistics 2007; World Fleet Statistics 2006; World Marine Propulsion Report 2006-2010; World Shipbuilding Statistics 2007;* and The World Shipping Encyclopaedia.

Taylor and Francis Group, An Informa Business, 2 Park Square, Milton Park, Abingdon, Oxford OX14 4RN, United Kingdom, (Dial from U.S. (212) 216-7800), (Fax from U.S. (212) 564-7854), www.tandf.co.uk; *The Europa World Year Book.*

U.S. Department of Transportation (DOT), Maritime Administration (MARAD), West Building, Southeast Federal Center, 1200 New Jersey Avenue, SE, Washington, DC 20590, (800) 99-MARAD, www.marad.dot.gov; *World Merchant Fleet 2005.*

United Nations Statistics Division, New York, NY 10017, (800) 253-9646, Fax: (212) 963-4116, http://unstats.un.org; *Statistical Yearbook.*

BRAZIL - SILVER PRODUCTION

See BRAZIL - MINERAL INDUSTRIES

BRAZIL - SOCIAL ECOLOGY

M.E. Sharpe, 80 Business Park Drive, Armonk, NY 10504, (800) 541-6563, Fax: (914) 273-2106, www.mesharpe.com; *The Illustrated Book of World Rankings.*

UCLA Latin American Institute, 10343 Bunche Hall, Box 951447, Los Angeles, CA 90095-1447, (310) 825-4571, Fax: (310) 206-6859, www.international.ucla.edu/lac; *Statistical Abstract of Latin America.*

United Nations Statistics Division, New York, NY 10017, (800) 253-9646, Fax: (212) 963-4116, http://unstats.un.org; *World Statistics Pocketbook.*

BRAZIL - SOCIAL SECURITY

Inter-American Development Bank (IDB), 1300 New York Avenue, NW, Washington, DC 20577, (202) 623-1000, Fax: (202) 623-3096, www.iadb.org; *The Politics of Policies: Economic and Social Progress in Latin America - 2006 Report.*

International Monetary Fund (IMF), 700 Nineteenth Street, NW, Washington, DC 20431, (202) 623-7000, Fax: (202) 623-4661, www.imf.org; *Government Finance Statistics Yearbook (2008 Edition).*

United Nations Statistics Division, New York, NY 10017, (800) 253-9646, Fax: (212) 963-4116, http://unstats.un.org; *National Accounts Statistics: Compendium of Income Distribution Statistics.*

BRAZIL - SOYBEAN PRODUCTION

See BRAZIL - CROPS

BRAZIL - STEEL PRODUCTION

See BRAZIL - MINERAL INDUSTRIES

BRAZIL - SUGAR PRODUCTION

See BRAZIL - CROPS

BRAZIL - SULPHUR PRODUCTION

See BRAZIL - MINERAL INDUSTRIES

BRAZIL - TAXATION

Inter-American Development Bank (IDB), 1300 New York Avenue, NW, Washington, DC 20577, (202) 623-1000, Fax: (202) 623-3096, www.iadb.org; *The Politics of Policies: Economic and Social Progress in Latin America - 2006 Report.*

International Monetary Fund (IMF), 700 Nineteenth Street, NW, Washington, DC 20431, (202) 623-7000, Fax: (202) 623-4661, www.imf.org; *Government Finance Statistics Yearbook (2008 Edition).*

International Road Federation (IFR), Madison Place, 500 Montgomery Street, 5th Floor, Alexandria, VA 22314, (703) 535-1001, Fax: (703) 535-1007, www.irfnet.org; *World Road Statistics 2006.*

Taylor and Francis Group, An Informa Business, 2 Park Square, Milton Park, Abingdon, Oxford OX14 4RN, United Kingdom, (Dial from U.S. (212) 216-7800), (Fax from U.S. (212) 564-7854), www.tandf.co.uk; *The Europa World Year Book.*

United Nations Statistics Division, New York, NY 10017, (800) 253-9646, Fax: (212) 963-4116, http://unstats.un.org; *Statistical Yearbook for Latin America and the Caribbean 2004.*

The World Bank, 1818 H Street, NW, Washington, DC 20433, (202) 473-1000, Fax: (202) 477-6391, www.worldbank.org; *World Development Indicators (WDI) 2008.*

BRAZIL - TEA PRODUCTION

See BRAZIL - CROPS

BRAZIL - TELEPHONE

Economist Intelligence Unit, 111 West 57th Street, New York, NY 10019, (212) 554-0600, Fax: (212) 586-1181, www.eiu.com; *Business Latin America.*

International Telecommunication Union (ITU), Place des Nations, 1211 Geneva 20, Switzerland, www.itu.int; World Telecommunication Indicators Database.

Palgrave Macmillan Ltd., Houndmills, Basingstoke, Hampshire, RG21 6XS, England, (Telephone in U.S. (888) 330-8477), (Fax in U.S. (800) 672-2054), www.palgrave.com; *The Statesman's Yearbook 2008.*

Taylor and Francis Group, An Informa Business, 2 Park Square, Milton Park, Abingdon, Oxford OX14 4RN, United Kingdom, (Dial from U.S. (212) 216-7800), (Fax from U.S. (212) 564-7854), www.tandf.co.uk; *The Europa World Year Book.*

United Nations Statistics Division, New York, NY 10017, (800) 253-9646, Fax: (212) 963-4116, http://unstats.un.org; *Statistical Yearbook* and *World Statistics Pocketbook.*

BRAZIL - TELEVISION - RECEIVERS AND RECEPTION

United Nations Statistics Division, New York, NY 10017, (800) 253-9646, Fax: (212) 963-4116, http://unstats.un.org; *Statistical Yearbook.*

BRAZIL - TEXTILE INDUSTRY

Euromonitor International, Inc., 224 S. Michigan Avenue, Suite 1500, Chicago, IL 60604, (312) 922-1115, Fax: (312) 922-1157, www.euromonitor.com; *World Marketing Data and Statistics.*

M.E. Sharpe, 80 Business Park Drive, Armonk, NY 10504, (800) 541-6563, Fax: (914) 273-2106, www.mesharpe.com; *The Illustrated Book of World Rankings.*

Palgrave Macmillan Ltd., Houndmills, Basingstoke, Hampshire, RG21 6XS, England, (Telephone in U.S. (888) 330-8477), (Fax in U.S. (800) 672-2054), www.palgrave.com; *The Statesman's Yearbook 2008.*

United Nations Conference on Trade and Development (UNCTAD), DC2-1120, United Nations, New York, NY 10017, (212) 963-0027, www.unctad.org; *UNCTAD Commodity Yearbook.*

United Nations Statistics Division, New York, NY 10017, (800) 253-9646, Fax: (212) 963-4116, http://unstats.un.org; *Statistical Yearbook.*

BRAZIL - THEATER

UNESCO Institute for Statistics, C.P. 6128 Succursale Centre-Ville, Montreal, Quebec, H3C 3J7 Canada, (Dial from U.S. (514) 343-6880), (Fax from U.S. (514) 343 6882), www.uis.unesco.org; *Statistical Tables.*

BRAZIL - TIN PRODUCTION

See BRAZIL - MINERAL INDUSTRIES

BRAZIL - TIRE INDUSTRY

United Nations Statistics Division, New York, NY 10017, (800) 253-9646, Fax: (212) 963-4116, http://unstats.un.org; *Statistical Yearbook.*

BRAZIL - TOBACCO INDUSTRY

Foreign Agricultural Service (FAS), U.S. Department of Agriculture (USDA), 1400 Independence Avenue, SW, Washington, DC 20250, (202) 720-3935, www.fas.usda.gov; *Tobacco: World Markets and Trade.*

M.E. Sharpe, 80 Business Park Drive, Armonk, NY 10504, (800) 541-6563, Fax: (914) 273-2106, www.mesharpe.com; *The Illustrated Book of World Rankings.*

United Nations Statistics Division, New York, NY 10017, (800) 253-9646, Fax: (212) 963-4116, http://unstats.un.org; *Statistical Yearbook.*

BRAZIL - TOURISM

Economist Intelligence Unit, 111 West 57th Street, New York, NY 10019, (212) 554-0600, Fax: (212) 586-1181, www.eiu.com; *Business Latin America.*

Euromonitor International, Inc., 224 S. Michigan Avenue, Suite 1500, Chicago, IL 60604, (312) 922-1115, Fax: (312) 922-1157, www.euromonitor.com; *World Marketing Data and Statistics.*

Federal Statistical Office Germany, D-65180 Wiesbaden, Germany, www.destatis.de; *Brazil 2006.*

M.E. Sharpe, 80 Business Park Drive, Armonk, NY 10504, (800) 541-6563, Fax: (914) 273-2106, www.mesharpe.com; *The Illustrated Book of World Rankings.*

Palgrave Macmillan Ltd., Houndmills, Basingstoke, Hampshire, RG21 6XS, England, (Telephone in U.S. (888) 330-8477), (Fax in U.S. (800) 672-2054), www.palgrave.com; *The Statesman's Yearbook 2008.*

Taylor and Francis Group, An Informa Business, 2 Park Square, Milton Park, Abingdon, Oxford OX14 4RN, United Kingdom, (Dial from U.S. (212) 216-7800), (Fax from U.S. (212) 564-7854), www.tandf.co.uk; *The Europa World Year Book.*

UCLA Latin American Institute, 10343 Bunche Hall, Box 951447, Los Angeles, CA 90095-1447, (310) 825-4571, Fax: (310) 206-6859, www.international.ucla.edu/lac; *Statistical Abstract of Latin America.*

United Nations Statistics Division, New York, NY 10017, (800) 253-9646, Fax: (212) 963-4116, http://unstats.un.org; *Statistical Yearbook* and *Statistical Yearbook for Latin America and the Caribbean 2004.*

United Nations World Tourism Organization (UNWTO), Capitan Haya 42, 28020 Madrid, Spain, www.world-tourism.org; *Yearbook of Tourism Statistics.*

The World Bank, 1818 H Street, NW, Washington, DC 20433, (202) 473-1000, Fax: (202) 477-6391, www.worldbank.org; *Brazil.*

BRAZIL - TRADE

See BRAZIL - INTERNATIONAL TRADE

BRAZIL - TRANSPORTATION

Central Intelligence Agency, Office of Public Affairs, Washington, DC 20505, (703) 482-0623, Fax: (703) 482-1739, www.cia.gov; *The World Factbook.*

Economist Intelligence Unit, 111 West 57th Street, New York, NY 10019, (212) 554-0600, Fax: (212) 586-1181, www.eiu.com; *Business Latin America.*

Euromonitor International, Inc., 224 S. Michigan Avenue, Suite 1500, Chicago, IL 60604, (312) 922-1115, Fax: (312) 922-1157, www.euromonitor.com; *International Marketing Data and Statistics 2008* and *World Marketing Data and Statistics.*

Federal Statistical Office Germany, D-65180 Wiesbaden, Germany, www.destatis.de; *Brazil 2006.*

Inter-American Development Bank (IDB), 1300 New York Avenue, NW, Washington, DC 20577, (202) 623-1000, Fax: (202) 623-3096, www.iadb.org; *The Politics of Policies: Economic and Social Progress in Latin America - 2006 Report.*

M.E. Sharpe, 80 Business Park Drive, Armonk, NY 10504, (800) 541-6563, Fax: (914) 273-2106, www.mesharpe.com; *The Illustrated Book of World Rankings.*

Palgrave Macmillan Ltd., Houndmills, Basingstoke, Hampshire, RG21 6XS, England, (Telephone in U.S. (888) 330-8477), (Fax in U.S. (800) 672-2054), www.palgrave.com; *The Statesman's Yearbook 2008.*

Taylor and Francis Group, An Informa Business, 2 Park Square, Milton Park, Abingdon, Oxford OX14 4RN, United Kingdom, (Dial from U.S. (212) 216-7800), (Fax from U.S. (212) 564-7854), www.tandf.co.uk; *The Europa World Year Book.*

UCLA Latin American Institute, 10343 Bunche Hall, Box 951447, Los Angeles, CA 90095-1447, (310) 825-4571, Fax: (310) 206-6859, www.international.ucla.edu/lac; *Statistical Abstract of Latin America.*

United Nations Statistics Division, New York, NY 10017, (800) 253-9646, Fax: (212) 963-4116, http://unstats.un.org; *Statistical Yearbook for Latin America and the Caribbean 2004.*

The World Bank, 1818 H Street, NW, Washington, DC 20433, (202) 473-1000, Fax: (202) 477-6391, www.worldbank.org; *Brazil.*

BRAZIL - TURKEYS

See BRAZIL - LIVESTOCK

BRAZIL - UNEMPLOYMENT

Central Intelligence Agency, Office of Public Affairs, Washington, DC 20505, (703) 482-0623, Fax: (703) 482-1739, www.cia.gov; *The World Factbook.*

Economist Intelligence Unit, 111 West 57th Street, New York, NY 10019, (212) 554-0600, Fax: (212) 586-1181, www.eiu.com; *Business Latin America.*

Euromonitor International, Inc., 224 S. Michigan Avenue, Suite 1500, Chicago, IL 60604, (312) 922-1115, Fax: (312) 922-1157, www.euromonitor.com; *International Marketing Data and Statistics 2008.*

Federal Statistical Office Germany, D-65180 Wiesbaden, Germany, www.destatis.de; *Brazil 2006.*

International Labour Office, I.L.O. Publications, 4 route des Morillons, CH-1211 Geneva 22, Switzerland, (Telephone in U.S. (202) 653-7652), (Fax in U.S. (202) 653-7687), www.ilo.org; *Yearbook of Labour Statistics 2006.*

Organisation for Economic Cooperation and Development (OECD), 2 rue Andre Pascal, F-75775 Paris Cedex 16, France, (Telephone in U.S. (202) 785-6323), (Fax in U.S. (202) 785-0350), www.oecd.org; *OECD Economic Survey - Brazil 2006.*

UCLA Latin American Institute, 10343 Bunche Hall, Box 951447, Los Angeles, CA 90095-1447, (310) 825-4571, Fax: (310) 206-6859, www.international.ucla.edu/lac; *Statistical Abstract of Latin America.*

United Nations Statistics Division, New York, NY 10017, (800) 253-9646, Fax: (212) 963-4116, http://unstats.un.org; *Statistical Yearbook.*

BRAZIL - URANIUM PRODUCTION AND CONSUMPTION

See BRAZIL - MINERAL INDUSTRIES

BRAZIL - VITAL STATISTICS

Euromonitor International, Inc., 224 S. Michigan Avenue, Suite 1500, Chicago, IL 60604, (312) 922-1115, Fax: (312) 922-1157, www.euromonitor.com; *International Marketing Data and Statistics 2008.*

Palgrave Macmillan Ltd., Houndmills, Basingstoke, Hampshire, RG21 6XS, England, (Telephone in U.S. (888) 330-8477), (Fax in U.S. (800) 672-2054), www.palgrave.com; *The Statesman's Yearbook 2008.*

United Nations Statistics Division, New York, NY 10017, (800) 253-9646, Fax: (212) 963-4116, http://unstats.un.org; *Statistical Yearbook.*

World Health Organization (WHO), Avenue Appia 20, 1211 Geneve 27, Switzerland, (Telephone in U.S. (212) 331-9081), www.who.int; *World Health Report 2006.*

BRAZIL - WAGES

Federal Statistical Office Germany, D-65180 Wiesbaden, Germany, www.destatis.de; *Brazil 2006.*

International Labour Office, I.L.O. Publications, 4 route des Morillons, CH-1211 Geneva 22, Switzerland, (Telephone in U.S. (202) 653-7652), (Fax in U.S. (202) 653-7687), www.ilo.org; *Yearbook of Labour Statistics 2006.*

Organization of American States (OAS), 17th Street Constitution Avenue NW, Washington, DC 20006, (202) 458-3000, www.oas.org; *The OAS in Transition: 1994-2004.*

Taylor and Francis Group, An Informa Business, 2 Park Square, Milton Park, Abingdon, Oxford OX14 4RN, United Kingdom, (Dial from U.S. (212) 216-7800), (Fax from U.S. (212) 564-7854), www.tandf.co.uk; *The Europa World Year Book.*

UCLA Latin American Institute, 10343 Bunche Hall, Box 951447, Los Angeles, CA 90095-1447, (310) 825-4571, Fax: (310) 206-6859, www.international.ucla.edu/lac; *Statistical Abstract of Latin America.*

United Nations Statistics Division, New York, NY 10017, (800) 253-9646, Fax: (212) 963-4116, http://unstats.un.org; *Statistical Yearbook.*

The World Bank, 1818 H Street, NW, Washington, DC 20433, (202) 473-1000, Fax: (202) 477-6391, www.worldbank.org; *Brazil.*

BRAZIL - WALNUT PRODUCTION

See BRAZIL - CROPS

BRAZIL - WEATHER

See BRAZIL - CLIMATE

BRAZIL - WELFARE STATE

Inter-American Development Bank (IDB), 1300 New York Avenue, NW, Washington, DC 20577, (202) 623-1000, Fax: (202) 623-3096, www.iadb.org; *The Politics of Policies: Economic and Social Progress in Latin America - 2006 Report.*

International Monetary Fund (IMF), 700 Nineteenth Street, NW, Washington, DC 20431, (202) 623-7000, Fax: (202) 623-4661, www.imf.org; *Government Finance Statistics Yearbook (2008 Edition).*

BRAZIL - WHALES

See BRAZIL - FISHERIES

BRAZIL - WHEAT PRODUCTION

See BRAZIL - CROPS

BRAZIL - WHOLESALE PRICE INDEXES

Inter-American Development Bank (IDB), 1300 New York Avenue, NW, Washington, DC 20577, (202) 623-1000, Fax: (202) 623-3096, www.iadb.org; *The Politics of Policies: Economic and Social Progress in Latin America - 2006 Report.*

International Monetary Fund (IMF), 700 Nineteenth Street, NW, Washington, DC 20431, (202) 623-7000, Fax: (202) 623-4661, www.imf.org; *International Financial Statistics Yearbook 2007.*

Organization of American States (OAS), 17th Street Constitution Avenue NW, Washington, DC 20006, (202) 458-3000, www.oas.org; *The OAS in Transition: 1994-2004.*

United Nations Statistics Division, New York, NY 10017, (800) 253-9646, Fax: (212) 963-4116, http://unstats.un.org; *Statistical Yearbook.*

BRAZIL - WHOLESALE TRADE

Inter-American Development Bank (IDB), 1300 New York Avenue, NW, Washington, DC 20577, (202) 623-1000, Fax: (202) 623-3096, www.iadb.org; *The Politics of Policies: Economic and Social Progress in Latin America - 2006 Report.*

United Nations Statistics Division, New York, NY 10017, (800) 253-9646, Fax: (212) 963-4116, http://unstats.un.org; *Statistical Yearbook.*

BRAZIL - WINE AND WINE MAKING

M.E. Sharpe, 80 Business Park Drive, Armonk, NY 10504, (800) 541-6563, Fax: (914) 273-2106, www.mesharpe.com; *The Illustrated Book of World Rankings.*

United Nations Statistics Division, New York, NY 10017, (800) 253-9646, Fax: (212) 963-4116, http://unstats.un.org; *Statistical Yearbook.*

BRAZIL - WOOD AND WOOD PULP

See BRAZIL - FORESTS AND FORESTRY

BRAZIL - WOOL PRODUCTION

See BRAZIL - TEXTILE INDUSTRY

BRAZIL - YARN PRODUCTION

See BRAZIL - TEXTILE INDUSTRY

BRAZIL - ZINC AND ZINC ORE

See BRAZIL - MINERAL INDUSTRIES

BRAZIL - ZOOS

UNESCO Institute for Statistics, C.P. 6128 Succursale Centre-Ville, Montreal, Quebec, H3C 3J7 Canada, (Dial from U.S. (514) 343-6880), (Fax from U.S. (514) 343 6882), www.uis.unesco.org; *Statistical Tables.*

BREAD

U.S. Bureau of Labor Statistics (BLS), Postal Square Building, 2 Massachusetts Avenue, NE, Washington, DC 20212-0001, (202) 691-5200, Fax: (202) 691-6325, www.bls.gov; *Consumer Price Index Detailed Report* and *Monthly Labor Review (MLR).*

BREAST - CANCER

American Cancer Society, 1599 Clifton Road, NE, Atlanta, GA 30329-4250, (404) 320-3333, www.cancer.org; *Breast Cancer Facts and Figures 2007-2008* and *Cancer Facts and Figures 2008.*

National Cancer Institute (NCI), National Institutes of Health (NIH), Public Inquiries Office, 6116 Executive Boulevard, Room 3036A, Bethesda, MD 20892-8322, (800) 422-6237, www.cancer.gov; *2006-2007 Annual Report to the Nation; Assessing Progress, Advancing Change: 2005-2006 Annual President's Cancer Panel; Atlas of Cancer Mortality in the United States, 1950-94; Cancer Epidemiology in Older Adolescents and Young Adults 15 to 29 Years of Age, Including SEER Incidence and Survival: 1975-2000; Cancer Research Across Borders: Second Report 2001-2002;* and *SEER Cancer Statistics Review, 1975-2005.*

BRIDGE INVENTORY

U.S. Department of Transportation (DOT), Federal Highway Administration (FHA), 1200 New Jersey Avenue, SE, Washington, DC 20590, (202) 366-0660, www.fhwa.dot.gov; unpublished data.British Columbia

BC Stats, Box 9410 Stn Prov Govt, Victoria, BC, V8V 9V1, Canada, (Dial from U.S. (250) 387-0327), www.bcstats.gov.bc.ca; BC STATS Database. Subject coverage: Business and industry, census data, economic statistics, labor, population, mapping and geography.

British Columbia Vital Statistics Agency, PO Box 9657 STN PROV GOVT, Victoria BC V8W 9P3, Canada, (Dial from U.S. (250) 952-2681), (Fax from U.S. (250) 952-2527), www.vs.gov.bc.ca; *Annual Report 2006; Health Status Registry Report, 2005; Quarterly Digest;* and *Regional Analysis of Health Statistics for Status Indians in British Columbia, 1992-2002.*

BRITISH HONDURAS

See BELIZE

BRITISH INDIAN OCEAN TERRITORY - AGRICULTURE

United Nations Food and Agricultural Organization (FAO), Viale delle Terme di Caracalla, 00100 Rome, Italy, (Dial from U.S. (202) 653-2400), (Fax from U.S. (202) 653 5760), www.fao.org; AQUASTAT; *FAO Production Yearbook 2002; FAO Trade Yearbook;* and *The State of Food and Agriculture (SOFA) 2006.*

The World Bank, 1818 H Street, NW, Washington, DC 20433, (202) 473-1000, Fax: (202) 477-6391, www.worldbank.org; *Africa Live Database (LDB)* and *African Development Indicators (ADI) 2007.*

BRITISH INDIAN OCEAN TERRITORY - AIRPORTS

Central Intelligence Agency, Office of Public Affairs, Washington, DC 20505, (703) 482-0623, Fax: (703) 482-1739, www.cia.gov; *The World Factbook.*

BRITISH INDIAN OCEAN TERRITORY - ARMED FORCES

Central Intelligence Agency, Office of Public Affairs, Washington, DC 20505, (703) 482-0623, Fax: (703) 482-1739, www.cia.gov; *The World Factbook.*

BRITISH INDIAN OCEAN TERRITORY - BROADCASTING

Central Intelligence Agency, Office of Public Affairs, Washington, DC 20505, (703) 482-0623, Fax: (703) 482-1739, www.cia.gov; *The World Factbook.*

BRITISH INDIAN OCEAN TERRITORY - BUDGET

Central Intelligence Agency, Office of Public Affairs, Washington, DC 20505, (703) 482-0623, Fax: (703) 482-1739, www.cia.gov; *The World Factbook.*

BRITISH INDIAN OCEAN TERRITORY - CHILDBIRTH - STATISTICS

Central Intelligence Agency, Office of Public Affairs, Washington, DC 20505, (703) 482-0623, Fax: (703) 482-1739, www.cia.gov; *The World Factbook.*

United Nations Statistics Division, New York, NY 10017, (800) 253-9646, Fax: (212) 963-4116, http://unstats.un.org; *Demographic Yearbook.*

BRITISH INDIAN OCEAN TERRITORY - COMMODITY EXCHANGES

United Nations Food and Agricultural Organization (FAO), Viale delle Terme di Caracalla, 00100 Rome, Italy, (Dial from U.S. (202) 653-2400), (Fax from U.S. (202) 653 5760), www.fao.org; *The State of Food and Agriculture (SOFA) 2006.*

BRITISH INDIAN OCEAN TERRITORY - CORN INDUSTRY

See BRITISH INDIAN OCEAN TERRITORY - CROPS

BRITISH INDIAN OCEAN TERRITORY - CROPS

United Nations Food and Agricultural Organization (FAO), Viale delle Terme di Caracalla, 00100 Rome, Italy, (Dial from U.S. (202) 653-2400), (Fax from U.S. (202) 653 5760), www.fao.org; *The State of Food and Agriculture (SOFA) 2006.*

BRITISH INDIAN OCEAN TERRITORY - DAIRY PROCESSING

United Nations Food and Agricultural Organization (FAO), Viale delle Terme di Caracalla, 00100 Rome, Italy, (Dial from U.S. (202) 653-2400), (Fax from U.S. (202) 653 5760), www.fao.org; *The State of Food and Agriculture (SOFA) 2006.*

BRITISH INDIAN OCEAN TERRITORY - DIVORCE

United Nations Statistics Division, New York, NY 10017, (800) 253-9646, Fax: (212) 963-4116, http://unstats.un.org; *Demographic Yearbook.*

BRITISH INDIAN OCEAN TERRITORY - ECONOMIC CONDITIONS

African Development Bank Group, Rue Joseph Anoma, 01 BP 1387 Abidjan 01, Cote d'Ivoire, www.afdb.org; *The African Statistical Journal; Gender, Poverty and Environmental Indicators on African Countries 2007;* and *Selected Statistics on African Countries 2007.*

Central Intelligence Agency, Office of Public Affairs, Washington, DC 20505, (703) 482-0623, Fax: (703) 482-1739, www.cia.gov; *The World Factbook.*

Economist Intelligence Unit, 111 West 57th Street, New York, NY 10019, (212) 554-0600, Fax: (212) 586-1181, www.eiu.com; *Business Africa.*

The World Bank, 1818 H Street, NW, Washington, DC 20433, (202) 473-1000, Fax: (202) 477-6391, www.worldbank.org; *Africa Household Survey Databank; Africa Live Database (LDB); Africa Standardized Files and Indicators;* and *African Development Indicators (ADI) 2007.*

BRITISH INDIAN OCEAN TERRITORY - EXPORTS

Central Intelligence Agency, Office of Public Affairs, Washington, DC 20505, (703) 482-0623, Fax: (703) 482-1739, www.cia.gov; *The World Factbook.*

United Nations Food and Agricultural Organization (FAO), Viale delle Terme di Caracalla, 00100 Rome, Italy, (Dial from U.S. (202) 653-2400), (Fax from U.S. (202) 653 5760), www.fao.org; *The State of Food and Agriculture (SOFA) 2006.*

BRITISH INDIAN OCEAN TERRITORY - FERTILITY, HUMAN

Central Intelligence Agency, Office of Public Affairs, Washington, DC 20505, (703) 482-0623, Fax: (703) 482-1739, www.cia.gov; *The World Factbook.*

BRITISH INDIAN OCEAN TERRITORY - FERTILIZER INDUSTRY

United Nations Food and Agricultural Organization (FAO), Viale delle Terme di Caracalla, 00100 Rome, Italy, (Dial from U.S. (202) 653-2400), (Fax from U.S. (202) 653 5760), www.fao.org; *The State of Food and Agriculture (SOFA) 2006.*

BRITISH INDIAN OCEAN TERRITORY - FETAL MORTALITY

See BRITISH INDIAN OCEAN TERRITORY - MORTALITY

BRITISH INDIAN OCEAN TERRITORY - FISHERIES

United Nations Food and Agricultural Organization (FAO), Viale delle Terme di Caracalla, 00100 Rome, Italy, (Dial from U.S. (202) 653-2400), (Fax from U.S. (202) 653 5760), www.fao.org; *FAO Yearbook of Fishery Statistics;* Fishery Databases; FISHSTAT Database. Subjects covered include: Aquaculture production, capture production, fishery commodities; and *The State of Food and Agriculture (SOFA) 2006.*

BRITISH INDIAN OCEAN TERRITORY - FOOD

United Nations Food and Agricultural Organization (FAO), Viale delle Terme di Caracalla, 00100 Rome, Italy, (Dial from U.S. (202) 653-2400), (Fax from U.S. (202) 653 5760), www.fao.org; *FAO Production Yearbook 2002* and *The State of Food and Agriculture (SOFA) 2006.*

BRITISH INDIAN OCEAN TERRITORY - FOREIGN EXCHANGE RATES

Central Intelligence Agency, Office of Public Affairs, Washington, DC 20505, (703) 482-0623, Fax: (703) 482-1739, www.cia.gov; *The World Factbook.*

BRITISH INDIAN OCEAN TERRITORY - FORESTS AND FORESTRY

United Nations Food and Agricultural Organization (FAO), Viale delle Terme di Caracalla, 00100 Rome, Italy, (Dial from U.S. (202) 653-2400), (Fax from U.S. (202) 653 5760), www.fao.org; *The State of Food and Agriculture (SOFA) 2006.*

BRITISH INDIAN OCEAN TERRITORY - IMPORTS

Central Intelligence Agency, Office of Public Affairs, Washington, DC 20505, (703) 482-0623, Fax: (703) 482-1739, www.cia.gov; *The World Factbook.*

United Nations Food and Agricultural Organization (FAO), Viale delle Terme di Caracalla, 00100 Rome, Italy, (Dial from U.S. (202) 653-2400), (Fax from U.S. (202) 653 5760), www.fao.org; *The State of Food and Agriculture (SOFA) 2006.*

BRITISH INDIAN OCEAN TERRITORY - INDUSTRIES

Central Intelligence Agency, Office of Public Affairs, Washington, DC 20505, (703) 482-0623, Fax: (703) 482-1739, www.cia.gov; *The World Factbook.*

BRITISH INDIAN OCEAN TERRITORY - INFANT AND MATERNAL MORTALITY

See BRITISH INDIAN OCEAN TERRITORY - MORTALITY

BRITISH INDIAN OCEAN TERRITORY - INTERNATIONAL TRADE

United Nations Food and Agricultural Organization (FAO), Viale delle Terme di Caracalla, 00100 Rome, Italy, (Dial from U.S. (202) 653-2400), (Fax from U.S. (202) 653 5760), www.fao.org; *FAO Trade Yearbook* and *The State of Food and Agriculture (SOFA) 2006.*

World Trade Organization (WTO), Centre William Rappard, Rue de Lausanne 154, CH-1211 Geneva 21, Switzerland, www.wto.org; *International Trade Statistics 2006.*

BRITISH INDIAN OCEAN TERRITORY - LABOR

Central Intelligence Agency, Office of Public Affairs, Washington, DC 20505, (703) 482-0623, Fax: (703) 482-1739, www.cia.gov; *The World Factbook.*

United Nations Food and Agricultural Organization (FAO), Viale delle Terme di Caracalla, 00100 Rome, Italy, (Dial from U.S. (202) 653-2400), (Fax from U.S. (202) 653 5760), www.fao.org; *The State of Food and Agriculture (SOFA) 2006.*

BRITISH INDIAN OCEAN TERRITORY - LAND USE

Central Intelligence Agency, Office of Public Affairs, Washington, DC 20505, (703) 482-0623, Fax: (703) 482-1739, www.cia.gov; *The World Factbook.*

United Nations Food and Agricultural Organization (FAO), Viale delle Terme di Caracalla, 00100 Rome, Italy, (Dial from U.S. (202) 653-2400), (Fax from U.S. (202) 653 5760), www.fao.org; *FAO Production Yearbook 2002.*

BRITISH INDIAN OCEAN TERRITORY - LIFE EXPECTANCY

Central Intelligence Agency, Office of Public Affairs, Washington, DC 20505, (703) 482-0623, Fax: (703) 482-1739, www.cia.gov; *The World Factbook.*

BRITISH INDIAN OCEAN TERRITORY - LIVESTOCK

United Nations Food and Agricultural Organization (FAO), Viale delle Terme di Caracalla, 00100 Rome, Italy, (Dial from U.S. (202) 653-2400), (Fax from U.S. (202) 653 5760), www.fao.org; *FAO Production Yearbook 2002* and *The State of Food and Agriculture (SOFA) 2006.*

BRITISH INDIAN OCEAN TERRITORY - MARRIAGE

United Nations Statistics Division, New York, NY 10017, (800) 253-9646, Fax: (212) 963-4116, http://unstats.un.org; *Demographic Yearbook.*

BRITISH INDIAN OCEAN TERRITORY - MEAT PRODUCTION

See BRITISH INDIAN OCEAN TERRITORY - LIVESTOCK

BRITISH INDIAN OCEAN TERRITORY - MORTALITY

Central Intelligence Agency, Office of Public Affairs, Washington, DC 20505, (703) 482-0623, Fax: (703) 482-1739, www.cia.gov; *The World Factbook.*

United Nations Statistics Division, New York, NY 10017, (800) 253-9646, Fax: (212) 963-4116, http://unstats.un.org; *Demographic Yearbook.*

BRITISH INDIAN OCEAN TERRITORY - NUTRITION

United Nations Food and Agricultural Organization (FAO), Viale delle Terme di Caracalla, 00100 Rome, Italy, (Dial from U.S. (202) 653-2400), (Fax from U.S. (202) 653 5760), www.fao.org; *The State of Food and Agriculture (SOFA) 2006.*

BRITISH INDIAN OCEAN TERRITORY - PESTICIDES

United Nations Food and Agricultural Organization (FAO), Viale delle Terme di Caracalla, 00100 Rome, Italy, (Dial from U.S. (202) 653-2400), (Fax from U.S. (202) 653 5760), www.fao.org; *The State of Food and Agriculture (SOFA) 2006.*

BRITISH INDIAN OCEAN TERRITORY - PETROLEUM INDUSTRY AND TRADE

PennWell Corporation, 1421 South Sheridan Road, Tulsa, OK 74112, (918) 835-3161, www.pennwell.com; *International Petroleum Encyclopedia 2007.*

United Nations Food and Agricultural Organization (FAO), Viale delle Terme di Caracalla, 00100 Rome, Italy, (Dial from U.S. (202) 653-2400), (Fax from

U.S. (202) 653 5760), www.fao.org; *The State of Food and Agriculture (SOFA) 2006.*

BRITISH INDIAN OCEAN TERRITORY - POLITICAL SCIENCE

Central Intelligence Agency, Office of Public Affairs, Washington, DC 20505, (703) 482-0623, Fax: (703) 482-1739, www.cia.gov; *The World Factbook.*

BRITISH INDIAN OCEAN TERRITORY - POPULATION

African Development Bank Group, Rue Joseph Anoma, 01 BP 1387 Abidjan 01, Cote d'Ivoire, www.afdb.org; *The African Statistical Journal; Gender, Poverty and Environmental Indicators on African Countries 2007;* and *Selected Statistics on African Countries 2007.*

Central Intelligence Agency, Office of Public Affairs, Washington, DC 20505, (703) 482-0623, Fax: (703) 482-1739, www.cia.gov; *The World Factbook.*

United Nations Food and Agricultural Organization (FAO), Viale delle Terme di Caracalla, 00100 Rome, Italy, (Dial from U.S. (202) 653-2400), (Fax from U.S. (202) 653 5760), www.fao.org; *FAO Production Yearbook 2002.*

United Nations Statistics Division, New York, NY 10017, (800) 253-9646, Fax: (212) 963-4116, http://unstats.un.org; *Demographic Yearbook* and *Statistical Yearbook.*

World Health Organization (WHO), Avenue Appia 20, 1211 Geneve 27, Switzerland, (Telephone in U.S. (212) 331-9081), www.who.int; *World Health Report 2006.*

BRITISH INDIAN OCEAN TERRITORY - POPULATION DENSITY

Central Intelligence Agency, Office of Public Affairs, Washington, DC 20505, (703) 482-0623, Fax: (703) 482-1739, www.cia.gov; *The World Factbook.*

United Nations Food and Agricultural Organization (FAO), Viale delle Terme di Caracalla, 00100 Rome, Italy, (Dial from U.S. (202) 653-2400), (Fax from U.S. (202) 653 5760), www.fao.org; *The State of Food and Agriculture (SOFA) 2006.*

United Nations Statistics Division, New York, NY 10017, (800) 253-9646, Fax: (212) 963-4116, http://unstats.un.org; *Statistical Yearbook.*

BRITISH INDIAN OCEAN TERRITORY - POWER RESOURCES

United Nations Food and Agricultural Organization (FAO), Viale delle Terme di Caracalla, 00100 Rome, Italy, (Dial from U.S. (202) 653-2400), (Fax from U.S. (202) 653 5760), www.fao.org; *The State of Food and Agriculture (SOFA) 2006.*

BRITISH INDIAN OCEAN TERRITORY - PRICES

United Nations Food and Agricultural Organization (FAO), Viale delle Terme di Caracalla, 00100 Rome, Italy, (Dial from U.S. (202) 653-2400), (Fax from U.S. (202) 653 5760), www.fao.org; *FAO Production Yearbook 2002* and *The State of Food and Agriculture (SOFA) 2006.*

BRITISH INDIAN OCEAN TERRITORY - RELIGION

Central Intelligence Agency, Office of Public Affairs, Washington, DC 20505, (703) 482-0623, Fax: (703) 482-1739, www.cia.gov; *The World Factbook.*

BRITISH INDIAN OCEAN TERRITORY - ROADS

Central Intelligence Agency, Office of Public Affairs, Washington, DC 20505, (703) 482-0623, Fax: (703) 482-1739, www.cia.gov; *The World Factbook.*

BRITISH INDIAN OCEAN TERRITORY - TELEPHONE

Central Intelligence Agency, Office of Public Affairs, Washington, DC 20505, (703) 482-0623, Fax: (703) 482-1739, www.cia.gov; *The World Factbook.*

BRITISH INDIAN OCEAN TERRITORY - TRADE

See BRITISH INDIAN OCEAN TERRITORY - INTERNATIONAL TRADE

BRITISH INDIAN OCEAN TERRITORY - TRANSPORTATION

Central Intelligence Agency, Office of Public Affairs, Washington, DC 20505, (703) 482-0623, Fax: (703) 482-1739, www.cia.gov; *The World Factbook.*

The World Bank, 1818 H Street, NW, Washington, DC 20433, (202) 473-1000, Fax: (202) 477-6391, www.worldbank.org; *Africa Live Database (LDB).*

BRITISH INDIAN OCEAN TERRITORY - UNEMPLOYMENT

Central Intelligence Agency, Office of Public Affairs, Washington, DC 20505, (703) 482-0623, Fax: (703) 482-1739, www.cia.gov; *The World Factbook.*

BRITISH INDIAN OCEAN TERRITORY - VITAL STATISTICS

World Health Organization (WHO), Avenue Appia 20, 1211 Geneve 27, Switzerland, (Telephone in U.S. (212) 331-9081), www.who.int; *World Health Report 2006.*

BRITISH VIRGIN ISLANDS - AGRICULTURAL MACHINERY

United Nations Statistics Division, New York, NY 10017, (800) 253-9646, Fax: (212) 963-4116, http://unstats.un.org; *Statistical Yearbook.*

BRITISH VIRGIN ISLANDS - AGRICULTURE

Economist Intelligence Unit, 111 West 57th Street, New York, NY 10019, (212) 554-0600, Fax: (212) 586-1181, www.eiu.com; *Virgin Islands (British) Country Report.*

Euromonitor International, Inc., 224 S. Michigan Avenue, Suite 1500, Chicago, IL 60604, (312) 922-1115, Fax: (312) 922-1157, www.euromonitor.com; *World Marketing Data and Statistics.*

Palgrave Macmillan Ltd., Houndmills, Basingstoke, Hampshire, RG21 6XS, England, (Telephone in U.S. (888) 330-8477), (Fax in U.S. (800) 672-2054), www.palgrave.com; *The Statesman's Yearbook 2008.*

Taylor and Francis Group, An Informa Business, 2 Park Square, Milton Park, Abingdon, Oxford OX14 4RN, United Kingdom, (Dial from U.S. (212) 216-7800), (Fax from U.S. (212) 564-7854), www.tandf.co.uk; *The Europa World Year Book.*

United Nations Conference on Trade and Development (UNCTAD), DC2-1120, United Nations, New York, NY 10017, (212) 963-0027, www.unctad.org; *UNCTAD Commodity Yearbook.*

United Nations Food and Agricultural Organization (FAO), Viale delle Terme di Caracalla, 00100 Rome, Italy, (Dial from U.S. (202) 653-2400), (Fax from U.S. (202) 653 5760), www.fao.org; AQUASTAT; *FAO Production Yearbook 2002; FAO Trade Yearbook;* and *The State of Food and Agriculture (SOFA) 2006.*

United Nations Statistics Division, New York, NY 10017, (800) 253-9646, Fax: (212) 963-4116, http://unstats.un.org; *Statistical Yearbook.*

BRITISH VIRGIN ISLANDS - AIRLINES

International Civil Aviation Organization (ICAO), External Relations and Public Information Office (EPO), 999 University Street, Montreal, Quebec H3C 5H7, Canada, (Dial from U.S. (514) 954-8219), (Fax from U.S. (514) 954-6077), www.icao.int; *Civil Aviation Statistics of the World.*

Palgrave Macmillan Ltd., Houndmills, Basingstoke, Hampshire, RG21 6XS, England, (Telephone in U.S. (888) 330-8477), (Fax in U.S. (800) 672-2054), www.palgrave.com; *The Statesman's Yearbook 2008.*

Taylor and Francis Group, An Informa Business, 2 Park Square, Milton Park, Abingdon, Oxford OX14 4RN, United Kingdom, (Dial from U.S. (212) 216-7800), (Fax from U.S. (212) 564-7854), www.tandf.co.uk; *The Europa World Year Book.*

BRITISH VIRGIN ISLANDS - AIRPORTS

Central Intelligence Agency, Office of Public Affairs, Washington, DC 20505, (703) 482-0623, Fax: (703) 482-1739, www.cia.gov; *The World Factbook.*

BRITISH VIRGIN ISLANDS - ARMED FORCES

Central Intelligence Agency, Office of Public Affairs, Washington, DC 20505, (703) 482-0623, Fax: (703) 482-1739, www.cia.gov; *The World Factbook.*

Euromonitor International, Inc., 224 S. Michigan Avenue, Suite 1500, Chicago, IL 60604, (312) 922-1115, Fax: (312) 922-1157, www.euromonitor.com; *World Marketing Data and Statistics.*

BRITISH VIRGIN ISLANDS - BANKS AND BANKING

Euromonitor International, Inc., 224 S. Michigan Avenue, Suite 1500, Chicago, IL 60604, (312) 922-1115, Fax: (312) 922-1157, www.euromonitor.com; *World Marketing Data and Statistics.*

Palgrave Macmillan Ltd., Houndmills, Basingstoke, Hampshire, RG21 6XS, England, (Telephone in U.S. (888) 330-8477), (Fax in U.S. (800) 672-2054), www.palgrave.com; *The Statesman's Yearbook 2008.*

BRITISH VIRGIN ISLANDS - BROADCASTING

Central Intelligence Agency, Office of Public Affairs, Washington, DC 20505, (703) 482-0623, Fax: (703) 482-1739, www.cia.gov; *The World Factbook.*

Euromonitor International, Inc., 224 S. Michigan Avenue, Suite 1500, Chicago, IL 60604, (312) 922-1115, Fax: (312) 922-1157, www.euromonitor.com; *World Marketing Data and Statistics.*

Palgrave Macmillan Ltd., Houndmills, Basingstoke, Hampshire, RG21 6XS, England, (Telephone in U.S. (888) 330-8477), (Fax in U.S. (800) 672-2054), www.palgrave.com; *The Statesman's Yearbook 2008.*

UNESCO Institute for Statistics, C.P. 6128 Succursale Centre-Ville, Montreal, Quebec, H3C 3J7 Canada, (Dial from U.S. (514) 343-6880), (Fax from U.S. (514) 343 6882), www.uis.unesco.org; *Statistical Tables.*

WRTH Publications Limited, PO Box 290, Oxford OX2 7FT, UK, www.wrth.com; *World Radio TV Handbook 2007.*

BRITISH VIRGIN ISLANDS - BUDGET

Central Intelligence Agency, Office of Public Affairs, Washington, DC 20505, (703) 482-0623, Fax: (703) 482-1739, www.cia.gov; *The World Factbook.*

BRITISH VIRGIN ISLANDS - CATTLE

See BRITISH VIRGIN ISLANDS - LIVESTOCK

BRITISH VIRGIN ISLANDS - CHILDBIRTH - STATISTICS

Central Intelligence Agency, Office of Public Affairs, Washington, DC 20505, (703) 482-0623, Fax: (703) 482-1739, www.cia.gov; *The World Factbook.*

Euromonitor International, Inc., 224 S. Michigan Avenue, Suite 1500, Chicago, IL 60604, (312) 922-1115, Fax: (312) 922-1157, www.euromonitor.com; *International Marketing Data and Statistics 2008* and *The World Economic Factbook 2008.*

Taylor and Francis Group, An Informa Business, 2 Park Square, Milton Park, Abingdon, Oxford OX14 4RN, United Kingdom, (Dial from U.S. (212) 216-7800), (Fax from U.S. (212) 564-7854), www.tandf.co.uk; *The Europa World Year Book.*

United Nations Statistics Division, New York, NY 10017, (800) 253-9646, Fax: (212) 963-4116, http://unstats.un.org; *Demographic Yearbook* and *Statistical Yearbook.*

BRITISH VIRGIN ISLANDS - CLIMATE

Palgrave Macmillan Ltd., Houndmills, Basingstoke, Hampshire, RG21 6XS, England, (Telephone in U.S. (888) 330-8477), (Fax in U.S. (800) 672-2054), www.palgrave.com; *The Statesman's Yearbook 2008.*

BRITISH VIRGIN ISLANDS - COMMERCE

Palgrave Macmillan Ltd., Houndmills, Basingstoke, Hampshire, RG21 6XS, England, (Telephone in U.S. (888) 330-8477), (Fax in U.S. (800) 672-2054), www.palgrave.com; *The Statesman's Yearbook 2008.*

BRITISH VIRGIN ISLANDS - COMMODITY EXCHANGES

United Nations Food and Agricultural Organization (FAO), Viale delle Terme di Caracalla, 00100 Rome, Italy, (Dial from U.S. (202) 653-2400), (Fax from U.S. (202) 653 5760), www.fao.org; *The State of Food and Agriculture (SOFA) 2006.*

BRITISH VIRGIN ISLANDS - CONSTRUCTION INDUSTRY

Palgrave Macmillan Ltd., Houndmills, Basingstoke, Hampshire, RG21 6XS, England, (Telephone in U.S. (888) 330-8477), (Fax in U.S. (800) 672-2054), www.palgrave.com; *The Statesman's Yearbook 2008.*

BRITISH VIRGIN ISLANDS - CONSUMER PRICE INDEXES

Taylor and Francis Group, An Informa Business, 2 Park Square, Milton Park, Abingdon, Oxford OX14 4RN, United Kingdom, (Dial from U.S. (212) 216-7800), (Fax from U.S. (212) 564-7854), www.tandf.co.uk; *The Europa World Year Book.*

United Nations Statistics Division, New York, NY 10017, (800) 253-9646, Fax: (212) 963-4116, http://unstats.un.org; *Statistical Yearbook.*

BRITISH VIRGIN ISLANDS - CORN INDUSTRY

See BRITISH VIRGIN ISLANDS - CROPS

BRITISH VIRGIN ISLANDS - CROPS

Palgrave Macmillan Ltd., Houndmills, Basingstoke, Hampshire, RG21 6XS, England, (Telephone in U.S. (888) 330-8477), (Fax in U.S. (800) 672-2054), www.palgrave.com; *The Statesman's Yearbook 2008.*

United Nations Conference on Trade and Development (UNCTAD), DC2-1120, United Nations, New York, NY 10017, (212) 963-0027, www.unctad.org; *UNCTAD Commodity Yearbook.*

United Nations Food and Agricultural Organization (FAO), Viale delle Terme di Caracalla, 00100 Rome, Italy, (Dial from U.S. (202) 653-2400), (Fax from U.S. (202) 653 5760), www.fao.org; *The State of Food and Agriculture (SOFA) 2006.*

BRITISH VIRGIN ISLANDS - CUSTOMS ADMINISTRATION

Palgrave Macmillan Ltd., Houndmills, Basingstoke, Hampshire, RG21 6XS, England, (Telephone in U.S. (888) 330-8477), (Fax in U.S. (800) 672-2054), www.palgrave.com; *The Statesman's Yearbook 2008.*

BRITISH VIRGIN ISLANDS - DAIRY PROCESSING

United Nations Food and Agricultural Organization (FAO), Viale delle Terme di Caracalla, 00100 Rome, Italy, (Dial from U.S. (202) 653-2400), (Fax from U.S. (202) 653 5760), www.fao.org; *The State of Food and Agriculture (SOFA) 2006.*

BRITISH VIRGIN ISLANDS - DEATH RATES

See BRITISH VIRGIN ISLANDS - MORTALITY

BRITISH VIRGIN ISLANDS - DEMOGRAPHY

Euromonitor International, Inc., 224 S. Michigan Avenue, Suite 1500, Chicago, IL 60604, (312) 922-1115, Fax: (312) 922-1157, www.euromonitor.com; *International Marketing Data and Statistics 2008; The World Economic Factbook 2008;* and *World Marketing Data and Statistics.*

BRITISH VIRGIN ISLANDS - DISPOSABLE INCOME

United Nations Statistics Division, New York, NY 10017, (800) 253-9646, Fax: (212) 963-4116, http://unstats.un.org; *National Accounts Statistics: Compendium of Income Distribution Statistics.*

BRITISH VIRGIN ISLANDS - DIVORCE

United Nations Statistics Division, New York, NY 10017, (800) 253-9646, Fax: (212) 963-4116, http://unstats.un.org; *Demographic Yearbook* and *Statistical Yearbook.*

BRITISH VIRGIN ISLANDS - ECONOMIC CONDITIONS

Central Intelligence Agency, Office of Public Affairs, Washington, DC 20505, (703) 482-0623, Fax: (703) 482-1739, www.cia.gov; *The World Factbook.*

Economist Intelligence Unit, 111 West 57th Street, New York, NY 10019, (212) 554-0600, Fax: (212) 586-1181, www.eiu.com; *Virgin Islands (British) Country Report.*

Euromonitor International, Inc., 224 S. Michigan Avenue, Suite 1500, Chicago, IL 60604, (312) 922-1115, Fax: (312) 922-1157, www.euromonitor.com; *The World Economic Factbook 2008.*

Palgrave Macmillan Ltd., Houndmills, Basingstoke, Hampshire, RG21 6XS, England, (Telephone in U.S. (888) 330-8477), (Fax in U.S. (800) 672-2054), www.palgrave.com; *The Statesman's Yearbook 2008.*

Taylor and Francis Group, An Informa Business, 2 Park Square, Milton Park, Abingdon, Oxford OX14 4RN, United Kingdom, (Dial from U.S. (212) 216-7800), (Fax from U.S. (212) 564-7854), www.tandf.co.uk; *The Europa World Year Book.*

BRITISH VIRGIN ISLANDS - EDUCATION

Euromonitor International, Inc., 224 S. Michigan Avenue, Suite 1500, Chicago, IL 60604, (312) 922-1115, Fax: (312) 922-1157, www.euromonitor.com; *International Marketing Data and Statistics 2008* and *World Marketing Data and Statistics.*

Palgrave Macmillan Ltd., Houndmills, Basingstoke, Hampshire, RG21 6XS, England, (Telephone in U.S. (888) 330-8477), (Fax in U.S. (800) 672-2054), www.palgrave.com; *The Statesman's Yearbook 2008.*

Taylor and Francis Group, An Informa Business, 2 Park Square, Milton Park, Abingdon, Oxford OX14 4RN, United Kingdom, (Dial from U.S. (212) 216-7800), (Fax from U.S. (212) 564-7854), www.tandf.co.uk; *The Europa World Year Book.*

UNESCO Institute for Statistics, C.P. 6128 Succursale Centre-Ville, Montreal, Quebec, H3C 3J7 Canada, (Dial from U.S. (514) 343-6880), (Fax from U.S. (514) 343 6882), www.uis.unesco.org; *Statistical Tables.*

BRITISH VIRGIN ISLANDS - ELECTRICITY

Palgrave Macmillan Ltd., Houndmills, Basingstoke, Hampshire, RG21 6XS, England, (Telephone in U.S. (888) 330-8477), (Fax in U.S. (800) 672-2054), www.palgrave.com; *The Statesman's Yearbook 2008.*

BRITISH VIRGIN ISLANDS - EMPLOYMENT

Euromonitor International, Inc., 224 S. Michigan Avenue, Suite 1500, Chicago, IL 60604, (312) 922-1115, Fax: (312) 922-1157, www.euromonitor.com; *International Marketing Data and Statistics 2008.*

International Labour Office, I.L.O. Publications, 4 route des Morillons, CH-1211 Geneva 22, Switzerland, (Telephone in U.S. (202) 653-7652), (Fax in U.S. (202) 653-7687), www.ilo.org; *Yearbook of Labour Statistics 2006.*

BRITISH VIRGIN ISLANDS - ENVIRONMENTAL CONDITIONS

DSI Data Service Information, Xantener Strasse 51a, D-47495 Rheinberg, Germany, www.dsidata.com; *Campus Solution.*

Economist Intelligence Unit, 111 West 57th Street, New York, NY 10019, (212) 554-0600, Fax: (212) 586-1181, www.eiu.com; *Virgin Islands (British) Country Report.*

BRITISH VIRGIN ISLANDS - EXPORTS

Central Intelligence Agency, Office of Public Affairs, Washington, DC 20505, (703) 482-0623, Fax: (703) 482-1739, www.cia.gov; *The World Factbook.*

Economist Intelligence Unit, 111 West 57th Street, New York, NY 10019, (212) 554-0600, Fax: (212) 586-1181, www.eiu.com; *Virgin Islands (British) Country Report.*

Euromonitor International, Inc., 224 S. Michigan Avenue, Suite 1500, Chicago, IL 60604, (312) 922-1115, Fax: (312) 922-1157, www.euromonitor.com; *International Marketing Data and Statistics 2008.*

Palgrave Macmillan Ltd., Houndmills, Basingstoke, Hampshire, RG21 6XS, England, (Telephone in U.S. (888) 330-8477), (Fax in U.S. (800) 672-2054), www.palgrave.com; *The Statesman's Yearbook 2008.*

Taylor and Francis Group, An Informa Business, 2 Park Square, Milton Park, Abingdon, Oxford OX14 4RN, United Kingdom, (Dial from U.S. (212) 216-7800), (Fax from U.S. (212) 564-7854), www.tandf.co.uk; *The Europa World Year Book.*

United Nations Food and Agricultural Organization (FAO), Viale delle Terme di Caracalla, 00100 Rome, Italy, (Dial from U.S. (202) 653-2400), (Fax from U.S. (202) 653 5760), www.fao.org; *The State of Food and Agriculture (SOFA) 2006.*

BRITISH VIRGIN ISLANDS - FERTILITY, HUMAN

Central Intelligence Agency, Office of Public Affairs, Washington, DC 20505, (703) 482-0623, Fax: (703) 482-1739, www.cia.gov; *The World Factbook.*

BRITISH VIRGIN ISLANDS - FERTILIZER INDUSTRY

United Nations Food and Agricultural Organization (FAO), Viale delle Terme di Caracalla, 00100 Rome, Italy, (Dial from U.S. (202) 653-2400), (Fax from U.S. (202) 653 5760), www.fao.org; *The State of Food and Agriculture (SOFA) 2006.*

BRITISH VIRGIN ISLANDS - FETAL MORTALITY

See BRITISH VIRGIN ISLANDS - MORTALITY

BRITISH VIRGIN ISLANDS - FINANCE

United Nations Statistics Division, New York, NY 10017, (800) 253-9646, Fax: (212) 963-4116, http://unstats.un.org; *Demographic Yearbook; National Accounts Statistics: Compendium of Income Distribution Statistics;* and *Statistical Yearbook.*

BRITISH VIRGIN ISLANDS - FINANCE, PUBLIC

Economist Intelligence Unit, 111 West 57th Street, New York, NY 10019, (212) 554-0600, Fax: (212) 586-1181, www.eiu.com; *Virgin Islands (British) Country Report.*

Palgrave Macmillan Ltd., Houndmills, Basingstoke, Hampshire, RG21 6XS, England, (Telephone in U.S. (888) 330-8477), (Fax in U.S. (800) 672-2054), www.palgrave.com; *The Statesman's Yearbook 2008.*

Taylor and Francis Group, An Informa Business, 2 Park Square, Milton Park, Abingdon, Oxford OX14 4RN, United Kingdom, (Dial from U.S. (212) 216-7800), (Fax from U.S. (212) 564-7854), www.tandf.co.uk; *The Europa World Year Book.*

BRITISH VIRGIN ISLANDS - FISHERIES

Palgrave Macmillan Ltd., Houndmills, Basingstoke, Hampshire, RG21 6XS, England, (Telephone in U.S. (888) 330-8477), (Fax in U.S. (800) 672-2054), www.palgrave.com; *The Statesman's Yearbook 2008.*

Taylor and Francis Group, An Informa Business, 2 Park Square, Milton Park, Abingdon, Oxford OX14 4RN, United Kingdom, (Dial from U.S. (212) 216-

7800), (Fax from U.S. (212) 564-7854), www.tandf.co.uk; *The Europa World Year Book.*

United Nations Conference on Trade and Development (UNCTAD), DC2-1120, United Nations, New York, NY 10017, (212) 963-0027, www.unctad.org; *UNCTAD Commodity Yearbook.*

United Nations Food and Agricultural Organization (FAO), Viale delle Terme di Caracalla, 00100 Rome, Italy, (Dial from U.S. (202) 653-2400), (Fax from U.S. (202) 653 5760), www.fao.org; *FAO Yearbook of Fishery Statistics;* Fishery Databases; FISHSTAT Database. Subjects covered include: Aquaculture production, capture production, fishery commodities; and *The State of Food and Agriculture (SOFA) 2006.*

BRITISH VIRGIN ISLANDS - FOOD

United Nations Conference on Trade and Development (UNCTAD), DC2-1120, United Nations, New York, NY 10017, (212) 963-0027, www.unctad.org; *UNCTAD Commodity Yearbook.*

United Nations Food and Agricultural Organization (FAO), Viale delle Terme di Caracalla, 00100 Rome, Italy, (Dial from U.S. (202) 653-2400), (Fax from U.S. (202) 653 5760), www.fao.org; *FAO Production Yearbook 2002* and *The State of Food and Agriculture (SOFA) 2006.*

BRITISH VIRGIN ISLANDS - FOREIGN EXCHANGE RATES

Central Intelligence Agency, Office of Public Affairs, Washington, DC 20505, (703) 482-0623, Fax: (703) 482-1739, www.cia.gov; *The World Factbook.*

Euromonitor International, Inc., 224 S. Michigan Avenue, Suite 1500, Chicago, IL 60604, (312) 922-1115, Fax: (312) 922-1157, www.euromonitor.com; *International Marketing Data and Statistics 2008* and *The World Economic Factbook 2008.*

Taylor and Francis Group, An Informa Business, 2 Park Square, Milton Park, Abingdon, Oxford OX14 4RN, United Kingdom, (Dial from U.S. (212) 216-7800), (Fax from U.S. (212) 564-7854), www.tandf.co.uk; *The Europa World Year Book.*

BRITISH VIRGIN ISLANDS - FORESTS AND FORESTRY

United Nations Conference on Trade and Development (UNCTAD), DC2-1120, United Nations, New York, NY 10017, (212) 963-0027, www.unctad.org; *UNCTAD Commodity Yearbook.*

United Nations Food and Agricultural Organization (FAO), Viale delle Terme di Caracalla, 00100 Rome, Italy, (Dial from U.S. (202) 653-2400), (Fax from U.S. (202) 653 5760), www.fao.org; *The State of Food and Agriculture (SOFA) 2006.*

United Nations Statistics Division, New York, NY 10017, (800) 253-9646, Fax: (212) 963-4116, http://unstats.un.org; *Statistical Yearbook.*

BRITISH VIRGIN ISLANDS - GROSS DOMESTIC PRODUCT

Economist Intelligence Unit, 111 West 57th Street, New York, NY 10019, (212) 554-0600, Fax: (212) 586-1181, www.eiu.com; *Virgin Islands (British) Country Report.*

Euromonitor International, Inc., 224 S. Michigan Avenue, Suite 1500, Chicago, IL 60604, (312) 922-1115, Fax: (312) 922-1157, www.euromonitor.com; *International Marketing Data and Statistics 2008* and *The World Economic Factbook 2008.*

Taylor and Francis Group, An Informa Business, 2 Park Square, Milton Park, Abingdon, Oxford OX14 4RN, United Kingdom, (Dial from U.S. (212) 216-7800), (Fax from U.S. (212) 564-7854), www.tandf.co.uk; *The Europa World Year Book.*

United Nations Statistics Division, New York, NY 10017, (800) 253-9646, Fax: (212) 963-4116, http://unstats.un.org; *National Accounts Statistics: Compendium of Income Distribution Statistics* and *Statistical Yearbook.*

BRITISH VIRGIN ISLANDS - GROSS NATIONAL PRODUCT

Palgrave Macmillan Ltd., Houndmills, Basingstoke, Hampshire, RG21 6XS, England, (Telephone in U.S. (888) 330-8477), (Fax in U.S. (800) 672-2054), www.palgrave.com; *The Statesman's Yearbook 2008.*

BRITISH VIRGIN ISLANDS - HIDES AND SKINS INDUSTRY

United Nations Food and Agricultural Organization (FAO), Viale delle Terme di Caracalla, 00100 Rome, Italy, (Dial from U.S. (202) 653-2400), (Fax from U.S. (202) 653 5760), www.fao.org; *FAO Production Yearbook 2002.*

BRITISH VIRGIN ISLANDS - HOUSING

Euromonitor International, Inc., 224 S. Michigan Avenue, Suite 1500, Chicago, IL 60604, (312) 922-1115, Fax: (312) 922-1157, www.euromonitor.com; *World Marketing Data and Statistics.*

BRITISH VIRGIN ISLANDS - ILLITERATE PERSONS

Euromonitor International, Inc., 224 S. Michigan Avenue, Suite 1500, Chicago, IL 60604, (312) 922-1115, Fax: (312) 922-1157, www.euromonitor.com; *The World Economic Factbook 2008.*

UNESCO Institute for Statistics, C.P. 6128 Succursale Centre-Ville, Montreal, Quebec, H3C 3J7 Canada, (Dial from U.S. (514) 343-6880), (Fax from U.S. (514) 343 6882), www.uis.unesco.org; *Statistical Tables.*

BRITISH VIRGIN ISLANDS - IMPORTS

Central Intelligence Agency, Office of Public Affairs, Washington, DC 20505, (703) 482-0623, Fax: (703) 482-1739, www.cia.gov; *The World Factbook.*

Economist Intelligence Unit, 111 West 57th Street, New York, NY 10019, (212) 554-0600, Fax: (212) 586-1181, www.eiu.com; *Virgin Islands (British) Country Report.*

Euromonitor International, Inc., 224 S. Michigan Avenue, Suite 1500, Chicago, IL 60604, (312) 922-1115, Fax: (312) 922-1157, www.euromonitor.com; *International Marketing Data and Statistics 2008* and *The World Economic Factbook 2008.*

Palgrave Macmillan Ltd., Houndmills, Basingstoke, Hampshire, RG21 6XS, England, (Telephone in U.S. (888) 330-8477), (Fax in U.S. (800) 672-2054), www.palgrave.com; *The Statesman's Yearbook 2008.*

Taylor and Francis Group, An Informa Business, 2 Park Square, Milton Park, Abingdon, Oxford OX14 4RN, United Kingdom, (Dial from U.S. (212) 216-7800), (Fax from U.S. (212) 564-7854), www.tandf.co.uk; *The Europa World Year Book.*

United Nations Food and Agricultural Organization (FAO), Viale delle Terme di Caracalla, 00100 Rome, Italy, (Dial from U.S. (202) 653-2400), (Fax from U.S. (202) 653 5760), www.fao.org; *The State of Food and Agriculture (SOFA) 2006.*

BRITISH VIRGIN ISLANDS - INDUSTRIES

Central Intelligence Agency, Office of Public Affairs, Washington, DC 20505, (703) 482-0623, Fax: (703) 482-1739, www.cia.gov; *The World Factbook.*

Economist Intelligence Unit, 111 West 57th Street, New York, NY 10019, (212) 554-0600, Fax: (212) 586-1181, www.eiu.com; *Virgin Islands (British) Country Report.*

Euromonitor International, Inc., 224 S. Michigan Avenue, Suite 1500, Chicago, IL 60604, (312) 922-1115, Fax: (312) 922-1157, www.euromonitor.com; *The World Economic Factbook 2008* and *World Marketing Data and Statistics.*

International Labour Office, I.L.O. Publications, 4 route des Morillons, CH-1211 Geneva 22, Switzerland, (Telephone in U.S. (202) 653-7652), (Fax in U.S. (202) 653-7687), www.ilo.org; *Yearbook of Labour Statistics 2006.*

Palgrave Macmillan Ltd., Houndmills, Basingstoke, Hampshire, RG21 6XS, England, (Telephone in U.S. (888) 330-8477), (Fax in U.S. (800) 672-2054), www.palgrave.com; *The Statesman's Yearbook 2008.*

Taylor and Francis Group, An Informa Business, 2 Park Square, Milton Park, Abingdon, Oxford OX14 4RN, United Kingdom, (Dial from U.S. (212) 216-7800), (Fax from U.S. (212) 564-7854), www.tandf.co.uk; *The Europa World Year Book.*

BRITISH VIRGIN ISLANDS - INFANT AND MATERNAL MORTALITY

See BRITISH VIRGIN ISLANDS - MORTALITY

BRITISH VIRGIN ISLANDS - INTERNATIONAL TRADE

Economist Intelligence Unit, 111 West 57th Street, New York, NY 10019, (212) 554-0600, Fax: (212) 586-1181, www.eiu.com; *Virgin Islands (British) Country Report.*

Euromonitor International, Inc., 224 S. Michigan Avenue, Suite 1500, Chicago, IL 60604, (312) 922-1115, Fax: (312) 922-1157, www.euromonitor.com; *The World Economic Factbook 2008* and *World Marketing Data and Statistics.*

Palgrave Macmillan Ltd., Houndmills, Basingstoke, Hampshire, RG21 6XS, England, (Telephone in U.S. (888) 330-8477), (Fax in U.S. (800) 672-2054), www.palgrave.com; *The Statesman's Yearbook 2008.*

Taylor and Francis Group, An Informa Business, 2 Park Square, Milton Park, Abingdon, Oxford OX14 4RN, United Kingdom, (Dial from U.S. (212) 216-7800), (Fax from U.S. (212) 564-7854), www.tandf.co.uk; *The Europa World Year Book.*

United Nations Conference on Trade and Development (UNCTAD), DC2-1120, United Nations, New York, NY 10017, (212) 963-0027, www.unctad.org; *UNCTAD Commodity Yearbook.*

United Nations Food and Agricultural Organization (FAO), Viale delle Terme di Caracalla, 00100 Rome, Italy, (Dial from U.S. (202) 653-2400), (Fax from U.S. (202) 653 5760), www.fao.org; *FAO Trade Yearbook* and *The State of Food and Agriculture (SOFA) 2006.*

United Nations Statistics Division, New York, NY 10017, (800) 253-9646, Fax: (212) 963-4116, http://unstats.un.org; *International Trade Statistics Yearbook.*

World Trade Organization (WTO), Centre William Rappard, Rue de Lausanne 154, CH-1211 Geneva 21, Switzerland, www.wto.org; *International Trade Statistics 2006.*

BRITISH VIRGIN ISLANDS - LABOR

Central Intelligence Agency, Office of Public Affairs, Washington, DC 20505, (703) 482-0623, Fax: (703) 482-1739, www.cia.gov; *The World Factbook.*

Euromonitor International, Inc., 224 S. Michigan Avenue, Suite 1500, Chicago, IL 60604, (312) 922-1115, Fax: (312) 922-1157, www.euromonitor.com; *International Marketing Data and Statistics 2008* and *World Marketing Data and Statistics.*

International Labour Office, I.L.O. Publications, 4 route des Morillons, CH-1211 Geneva 22, Switzerland, (Telephone in U.S. (202) 653-7652), (Fax in U.S. (202) 653-7687), www.ilo.org; *Yearbook of Labour Statistics 2006.*

Taylor and Francis Group, An Informa Business, 2 Park Square, Milton Park, Abingdon, Oxford OX14 4RN, United Kingdom, (Dial from U.S. (212) 216-7800), (Fax from U.S. (212) 564-7854), www.tandf.co.uk; *The Europa World Year Book.*

United Nations Food and Agricultural Organization (FAO), Viale delle Terme di Caracalla, 00100 Rome, Italy, (Dial from U.S. (202) 653-2400), (Fax from U.S. (202) 653 5760), www.fao.org; *The State of Food and Agriculture (SOFA) 2006.*

BRITISH VIRGIN ISLANDS - LAND USE

Central Intelligence Agency, Office of Public Affairs, Washington, DC 20505, (703) 482-0623, Fax: (703) 482-1739, www.cia.gov; *The World Factbook.*

Euromonitor International, Inc., 224 S. Michigan Avenue, Suite 1500, Chicago, IL 60604, (312) 922-1115, Fax: (312) 922-1157, www.euromonitor.com; *International Marketing Data and Statistics 2008.*

United Nations Food and Agricultural Organization (FAO), Viale delle Terme di Caracalla, 00100 Rome, Italy, (Dial from U.S. (202) 653-2400), (Fax from U.S. (202) 653 5760), www.fao.org; *FAO Production Yearbook 2002.*

BRITISH VIRGIN ISLANDS - LIBRARIES

UNESCO Institute for Statistics, C.P. 6128 Succursale Centre-Ville, Montreal, Quebec, H3C 3J7 Canada, (Dial from U.S. (514) 343-6880), (Fax from U.S. (514) 343 6882), www.uis.unesco.org; *Statistical Tables.*

BRITISH VIRGIN ISLANDS - LIFE EXPECTANCY

Central Intelligence Agency, Office of Public Affairs, Washington, DC 20505, (703) 482-0623, Fax: (703) 482-1739, www.cia.gov; *The World Factbook.*

Euromonitor International, Inc., 224 S. Michigan Avenue, Suite 1500, Chicago, IL 60604, (312) 922-1115, Fax: (312) 922-1157, www.euromonitor.com; *The World Economic Factbook 2008.*

BRITISH VIRGIN ISLANDS - LITERACY

Euromonitor International, Inc., 224 S. Michigan Avenue, Suite 1500, Chicago, IL 60604, (312) 922-1115, Fax: (312) 922-1157, www.euromonitor.com; *World Marketing Data and Statistics.*

BRITISH VIRGIN ISLANDS - LIVESTOCK

Palgrave Macmillan Ltd., Houndmills, Basingstoke, Hampshire, RG21 6XS, England, (Telephone in U.S. (888) 330-8477), (Fax in U.S. (800) 672-2054), www.palgrave.com; *The Statesman's Yearbook 2008.*

United Nations Conference on Trade and Development (UNCTAD), DC2-1120, United Nations, New York, NY 10017, (212) 963-0027, www.unctad.org; *UNCTAD Commodity Yearbook.*

United Nations Food and Agricultural Organization (FAO), Viale delle Terme di Caracalla, 00100 Rome, Italy, (Dial from U.S. (202) 653-2400), (Fax from U.S. (202) 653 5760), www.fao.org; *FAO Production Yearbook 2002* and *The State of Food and Agriculture (SOFA) 2006.*

United Nations Statistics Division, New York, NY 10017, (800) 253-9646, Fax: (212) 963-4116, http://unstats.un.org; *Statistical Yearbook.*

BRITISH VIRGIN ISLANDS - MARRIAGE

Taylor and Francis Group, An Informa Business, 2 Park Square, Milton Park, Abingdon, Oxford OX14 4RN, United Kingdom, (Dial from U.S. (212) 216-7800), (Fax from U.S. (212) 564-7854), www.tandf.co.uk; *The Europa World Year Book.*

United Nations Statistics Division, New York, NY 10017, (800) 253-9646, Fax: (212) 963-4116, http://unstats.un.org; *Demographic Yearbook* and *Statistical Yearbook.*

BRITISH VIRGIN ISLANDS - MEAT PRODUCTION

See BRITISH VIRGIN ISLANDS - LIVESTOCK

BRITISH VIRGIN ISLANDS - MINERAL INDUSTRIES

United Nations Conference on Trade and Development (UNCTAD), DC2-1120, United Nations, New York, NY 10017, (212) 963-0027, www.unctad.org; *UNCTAD Commodity Yearbook.*

BRITISH VIRGIN ISLANDS - MONEY SUPPLY

Economist Intelligence Unit, 111 West 57th Street, New York, NY 10019, (212) 554-0600, Fax: (212) 586-1181, www.eiu.com; *Virgin Islands (British) Country Report.*

BRITISH VIRGIN ISLANDS - MORTALITY

Central Intelligence Agency, Office of Public Affairs, Washington, DC 20505, (703) 482-0623, Fax: (703) 482-1739, www.cia.gov; *The World Factbook.*

Euromonitor International, Inc., 224 S. Michigan Avenue, Suite 1500, Chicago, IL 60604, (312) 922-1115, Fax: (312) 922-1157, www.euromonitor.com; *International Marketing Data and Statistics 2008* and *The World Economic Factbook 2008.*

Taylor and Francis Group, An Informa Business, 2 Park Square, Milton Park, Abingdon, Oxford OX14 4RN, United Kingdom, (Dial from U.S. (212) 216-7800), (Fax from U.S. (212) 564-7854), www.tandf.co.uk; *The Europa World Year Book.*

United Nations Statistics Division, New York, NY 10017, (800) 253-9646, Fax: (212) 963-4116, http://unstats.un.org; *Demographic Yearbook* and *Statistical Yearbook.*

World Health Organization (WHO), Avenue Appia 20, 1211 Geneve 27, Switzerland, (Telephone in U.S. (212) 331-9081), www.who.int; *World Health Report 2006.*

BRITISH VIRGIN ISLANDS - MOTION PICTURES

United Nations Statistics Division, New York, NY 10017, (800) 253-9646, Fax: (212) 963-4116, http://unstats.un.org; *Statistical Yearbook.*

BRITISH VIRGIN ISLANDS - MOTOR VEHICLES

Taylor and Francis Group, An Informa Business, 2 Park Square, Milton Park, Abingdon, Oxford OX14 4RN, United Kingdom, (Dial from U.S. (212) 216-7800), (Fax from U.S. (212) 564-7854), www.tandf.co.uk; *The Europa World Year Book.*

United Nations Statistics Division, New York, NY 10017, (800) 253-9646, Fax: (212) 963-4116, http://unstats.un.org; *Statistical Yearbook.*

BRITISH VIRGIN ISLANDS - MUSEUMS

UNESCO Institute for Statistics, C.P. 6128 Succursale Centre-Ville, Montreal, Quebec, H3C 3J7 Canada, (Dial from U.S. (514) 343-6880), (Fax from U.S. (514) 343 6882), www.uis.unesco.org; *Statistical Tables.*

BRITISH VIRGIN ISLANDS - NUTRITION

United Nations Food and Agricultural Organization (FAO), Viale delle Terme di Caracalla, 00100 Rome, Italy, (Dial from U.S. (202) 653-2400), (Fax from U.S. (202) 653 5760), www.fao.org; *The State of Food and Agriculture (SOFA) 2006.*

BRITISH VIRGIN ISLANDS - PERIODICALS

UNESCO Institute for Statistics, C.P. 6128 Succursale Centre-Ville, Montreal, Quebec, H3C 3J7 Canada, (Dial from U.S. (514) 343-6880), (Fax from U.S. (514) 343 6882), www.uis.unesco.org; *Statistical Tables.*

BRITISH VIRGIN ISLANDS - PESTICIDES

United Nations Food and Agricultural Organization (FAO), Viale delle Terme di Caracalla, 00100 Rome, Italy, (Dial from U.S. (202) 653-2400), (Fax from U.S. (202) 653 5760), www.fao.org; *The State of Food and Agriculture (SOFA) 2006.*

BRITISH VIRGIN ISLANDS - PETROLEUM INDUSTRY AND TRADE

PennWell Corporation, 1421 South Sheridan Road, Tulsa, OK 74112, (918) 835-3161, www.pennwell.com; *International Petroleum Encyclopedia 2007.*

United Nations Conference on Trade and Development (UNCTAD), DC2-1120, United Nations, New York, NY 10017, (212) 963-0027, www.unctad.org; *UNCTAD Commodity Yearbook.*

United Nations Food and Agricultural Organization (FAO), Viale delle Terme di Caracalla, 00100 Rome, Italy, (Dial from U.S. (202) 653-2400), (Fax from U.S. (202) 653 5760), www.fao.org; *The State of Food and Agriculture (SOFA) 2006.*

BRITISH VIRGIN ISLANDS - POLITICAL SCIENCE

Central Intelligence Agency, Office of Public Affairs, Washington, DC 20505, (703) 482-0623, Fax: (703) 482-1739, www.cia.gov; *The World Factbook.*

Palgrave Macmillan Ltd., Houndmills, Basingstoke, Hampshire, RG21 6XS, England, (Telephone in U.S. (888) 330-8477), (Fax in U.S. (800) 672-2054), www.palgrave.com; *The Statesman's Yearbook 2008.*

Taylor and Francis Group, An Informa Business, 2 Park Square, Milton Park, Abingdon, Oxford OX14 4RN, United Kingdom, (Dial from U.S. (212) 216-7800), (Fax from U.S. (212) 564-7854), www.tandf.co.uk; *The Europa World Year Book.*

United Nations Statistics Division, New York, NY 10017, (800) 253-9646, Fax: (212) 963-4116, http://unstats.un.org; *National Accounts Statistics: Compendium of Income Distribution Statistics.*

BRITISH VIRGIN ISLANDS - POPULATION

Caribbean Epidemiology Centre (CAREC), 16-18 Jamaica Boulevard, Federation Park, PO Box 164, Port of Spain, Republic of Trinidad and Tobago, (Dial from U.S. (868) 622-4261), (Fax from U.S. (868) 622-2792), www.carec.org; *Population Data.*

Central Intelligence Agency, Office of Public Affairs, Washington, DC 20505, (703) 482-0623, Fax: (703) 482-1739, www.cia.gov; *The World Factbook.*

Economist Intelligence Unit, 111 West 57th Street, New York, NY 10019, (212) 554-0600, Fax: (212) 586-1181, www.eiu.com; *Virgin Islands (British) Country Report.*

Euromonitor International, Inc., 224 S. Michigan Avenue, Suite 1500, Chicago, IL 60604, (312) 922-1115, Fax: (312) 922-1157, www.euromonitor.com; *International Marketing Data and Statistics 2008* and *The World Economic Factbook 2008.*

International Labour Office, I.L.O. Publications, 4 route des Morillons, CH-1211 Geneva 22, Switzerland, (Telephone in U.S. (202) 653-7652), (Fax in U.S. (202) 653-7687), www.ilo.org; *Yearbook of Labour Statistics 2006.*

Palgrave Macmillan Ltd., Houndmills, Basingstoke, Hampshire, RG21 6XS, England, (Telephone in U.S. (888) 330-8477), (Fax in U.S. (800) 672-2054), www.palgrave.com; *The Statesman's Yearbook 2008.*

Taylor and Francis Group, An Informa Business, 2 Park Square, Milton Park, Abingdon, Oxford OX14 4RN, United Kingdom, (Dial from U.S. (212) 216-7800), (Fax from U.S. (212) 564-7854), www.tandf.co.uk; *The Europa World Year Book.*

United Nations Food and Agricultural Organization (FAO), Viale delle Terme di Caracalla, 00100 Rome, Italy, (Dial from U.S. (202) 653-2400), (Fax from U.S. (202) 653 5760), www.fao.org; *FAO Production Yearbook 2002.*

United Nations Statistics Division, New York, NY 10017, (800) 253-9646, Fax: (212) 963-4116, http://unstats.un.org; *Demographic Yearbook* and *Statistical Yearbook.*

World Health Organization (WHO), Avenue Appia 20, 1211 Geneve 27, Switzerland, (Telephone in U.S. (212) 331-9081), www.who.int; *World Health Report 2006.*

BRITISH VIRGIN ISLANDS - POPULATION DENSITY

Central Intelligence Agency, Office of Public Affairs, Washington, DC 20505, (703) 482-0623, Fax: (703) 482-1739, www.cia.gov; *The World Factbook.*

Euromonitor International, Inc., 224 S. Michigan Avenue, Suite 1500, Chicago, IL 60604, (312) 922-1115, Fax: (312) 922-1157, www.euromonitor.com; *The World Economic Factbook 2008.*

Palgrave Macmillan Ltd., Houndmills, Basingstoke, Hampshire, RG21 6XS, England, (Telephone in U.S. (888) 330-8477), (Fax in U.S. (800) 672-2054), www.palgrave.com; *The Statesman's Yearbook 2008.*

Taylor and Francis Group, An Informa Business, 2 Park Square, Milton Park, Abingdon, Oxford OX14 4RN, United Kingdom, (Dial from U.S. (212) 216-7800), (Fax from U.S. (212) 564-7854), www.tandf.co.uk; *The Europa World Year Book.*

United Nations Food and Agricultural Organization (FAO), Viale delle Terme di Caracalla, 00100 Rome, Italy, (Dial from U.S. (202) 653-2400), (Fax from U.S. (202) 653 5760), www.fao.org; *The State of Food and Agriculture (SOFA) 2006.*

United Nations Statistics Division, New York, NY 10017, (800) 253-9646, Fax: (212) 963-4116, http://unstats.un.org; *Statistical Yearbook.*

BRITISH VIRGIN ISLANDS - POWER RESOURCES

Euromonitor International, Inc., 224 S. Michigan Avenue, Suite 1500, Chicago, IL 60604, (312) 922-1115, Fax: (312) 922-1157, www.euromonitor.com; *International Marketing Data and Statistics 2008; The World Economic Factbook 2008;* and *World Marketing Data and Statistics.*

Platts, 2 Penn Plaza, 25th Floor, New York, NY 10121-2298, (212) 904-3070, www.platts.com; *Energy Economist.*

United Nations Food and Agricultural Organization (FAO), Viale delle Terme di Caracalla, 00100 Rome, Italy, (Dial from U.S. (202) 653-2400), (Fax from U.S. (202) 653 5760), www.fao.org; *The State of Food and Agriculture (SOFA) 2006.*

United Nations Statistics Division, New York, NY 10017, (800) 253-9646, Fax: (212) 963-4116, http://unstats.un.org; *Energy Statistics Yearbook 2003.*

BRITISH VIRGIN ISLANDS - PRICES

Euromonitor International, Inc., 224 S. Michigan Avenue, Suite 1500, Chicago, IL 60604, (312) 922-1115, Fax: (312) 922-1157, www.euromonitor.com; *World Marketing Data and Statistics.*

International Labour Office, I.L.O. Publications, 4 route des Morillons, CH-1211 Geneva 22, Switzerland, (Telephone in U.S. (202) 653-7652), (Fax in U.S. (202) 653-7687), www.ilo.org; *Yearbook of Labour Statistics 2006.*

United Nations Food and Agricultural Organization (FAO), Viale delle Terme di Caracalla, 00100 Rome, Italy, (Dial from U.S. (202) 653-2400), (Fax from U.S. (202) 653 5760), www.fao.org; *FAO Production Yearbook 2002* and *The State of Food and Agriculture (SOFA) 2006.*

BRITISH VIRGIN ISLANDS - PUBLIC HEALTH

Euromonitor International, Inc., 224 S. Michigan Avenue, Suite 1500, Chicago, IL 60604, (312) 922-1115, Fax: (312) 922-1157, www.euromonitor.com; *World Marketing Data and Statistics.*

Palgrave Macmillan Ltd., Houndmills, Basingstoke, Hampshire, RG21 6XS, England, (Telephone in U.S. (888) 330-8477), (Fax in U.S. (800) 672-2054), www.palgrave.com; *The Statesman's Yearbook 2008.*

United Nations Statistics Division, New York, NY 10017, (800) 253-9646, Fax: (212) 963-4116, http://unstats.un.org; *Statistical Yearbook.*

World Health Organization (WHO), Avenue Appia 20, 1211 Geneve 27, Switzerland, (Telephone in U.S. (212) 331-9081), www.who.int; *World Health Report 2006.*

BRITISH VIRGIN ISLANDS - RADIO BROADCASTING

Palgrave Macmillan Ltd., Houndmills, Basingstoke, Hampshire, RG21 6XS, England, (Telephone in U.S. (888) 330-8477), (Fax in U.S. (800) 672-2054), www.palgrave.com; *The Statesman's Yearbook 2008.*

BRITISH VIRGIN ISLANDS - RELIGION

Central Intelligence Agency, Office of Public Affairs, Washington, DC 20505, (703) 482-0623, Fax: (703) 482-1739, www.cia.gov; *The World Factbook.*

Palgrave Macmillan Ltd., Houndmills, Basingstoke, Hampshire, RG21 6XS, England, (Telephone in U.S. (888) 330-8477), (Fax in U.S. (800) 672-2054), www.palgrave.com; *The Statesman's Yearbook 2008.*

BRITISH VIRGIN ISLANDS - RENT CHARGES

International Labour Office, I.L.O. Publications, 4 route des Morillons, CH-1211 Geneva 22, Switzerland, (Telephone in U.S. (202) 653-7652), (Fax in U.S. (202) 653-7687), www.ilo.org; *Yearbook of Labour Statistics 2006.*

BRITISH VIRGIN ISLANDS - RETAIL TRADE

Euromonitor International, Inc., 224 S. Michigan Avenue, Suite 1500, Chicago, IL 60604, (312) 922-1115, Fax: (312) 922-1157, www.euromonitor.com; *World Marketing Data and Statistics.*

BRITISH VIRGIN ISLANDS - ROADS

Central Intelligence Agency, Office of Public Affairs, Washington, DC 20505, (703) 482-0623, Fax: (703) 482-1739, www.cia.gov; *The World Factbook.*

Palgrave Macmillan Ltd., Houndmills, Basingstoke, Hampshire, RG21 6XS, England, (Telephone in U.S. (888) 330-8477), (Fax in U.S. (800) 672-2054), www.palgrave.com; *The Statesman's Yearbook 2008.*

BRITISH VIRGIN ISLANDS - SHIPPING

Palgrave Macmillan Ltd., Houndmills, Basingstoke, Hampshire, RG21 6XS, England, (Telephone in U.S. (888) 330-8477), (Fax in U.S. (800) 672-2054), www.palgrave.com; *The Statesman's Yearbook 2008.*

Taylor and Francis Group, An Informa Business, 2 Park Square, Milton Park, Abingdon, Oxford OX14 4RN, United Kingdom, (Dial from U.S. (212) 216-7800), (Fax from U.S. (212) 564-7854), www.tandf.co.uk; *The Europa World Year Book.*

United Nations Statistics Division, New York, NY 10017, (800) 253-9646, Fax: (212) 963-4116, http://unstats.un.org; *Statistical Yearbook.*

BRITISH VIRGIN ISLANDS - SOCIAL SECURITY

United Nations Statistics Division, New York, NY 10017, (800) 253-9646, Fax: (212) 963-4116, http://unstats.un.org; *National Accounts Statistics: Compendium of Income Distribution Statistics.*

BRITISH VIRGIN ISLANDS - TELEPHONE

International Telecommunication Union (ITU), Place des Nations, 1211 Geneva 20, Switzerland, www.itu.int; World Telecommunication Indicators Database.

Palgrave Macmillan Ltd., Houndmills, Basingstoke, Hampshire, RG21 6XS, England, (Telephone in U.S. (888) 330-8477), (Fax in U.S. (800) 672-2054), www.palgrave.com; *The Statesman's Yearbook 2008.*

Taylor and Francis Group, An Informa Business, 2 Park Square, Milton Park, Abingdon, Oxford OX14 4RN, United Kingdom, (Dial from U.S. (212) 216-7800), (Fax from U.S. (212) 564-7854), www.tandf.co.uk; *The Europa World Year Book.*

United Nations Statistics Division, New York, NY 10017, (800) 253-9646, Fax: (212) 963-4116, http://unstats.un.org; *Statistical Yearbook.*

BRITISH VIRGIN ISLANDS - TEXTILE INDUSTRY

United Nations Conference on Trade and Development (UNCTAD), DC2-1120, United Nations, New York, NY 10017, (212) 963-0027, www.unctad.org; *UNCTAD Commodity Yearbook.*

BRITISH VIRGIN ISLANDS - THEATER

UNESCO Institute for Statistics, C.P. 6128 Succursale Centre-Ville, Montreal, Quebec, H3C 3J7 Canada, (Dial from U.S. (514) 343-6880), (Fax from U.S. (514) 343 6882), www.uis.unesco.org; *Statistical Tables.*

BRITISH VIRGIN ISLANDS - TOURISM

Euromonitor International, Inc., 224 S. Michigan Avenue, Suite 1500, Chicago, IL 60604, (312) 922-1115, Fax: (312) 922-1157, www.euromonitor.com; *The World Economic Factbook 2008* and *World Marketing Data and Statistics.*

Palgrave Macmillan Ltd., Houndmills, Basingstoke, Hampshire, RG21 6XS, England, (Telephone in U.S. (888) 330-8477), (Fax in U.S. (800) 672-2054), www.palgrave.com; *The Statesman's Yearbook 2008.*

Taylor and Francis Group, An Informa Business, 2 Park Square, Milton Park, Abingdon, Oxford OX14 4RN, United Kingdom, (Dial from U.S. (212) 216-7800), (Fax from U.S. (212) 564-7854), www.tandf.co.uk; *The Europa World Year Book.*

BRITISH VIRGIN ISLANDS - TRADE

See BRITISH VIRGIN ISLANDS - INTERNATIONAL TRADE

BRITISH VIRGIN ISLANDS - TRANSPORTATION

Central Intelligence Agency, Office of Public Affairs, Washington, DC 20505, (703) 482-0623, Fax: (703) 482-1739, www.cia.gov; *The World Factbook.*

Euromonitor International, Inc., 224 S. Michigan Avenue, Suite 1500, Chicago, IL 60604, (312) 922-1115, Fax: (312) 922-1157, www.euromonitor.com; *International Marketing Data and Statistics 2008* and *World Marketing Data and Statistics.*

Palgrave Macmillan Ltd., Houndmills, Basingstoke, Hampshire, RG21 6XS, England, (Telephone in U.S. (888) 330-8477), (Fax in U.S. (800) 672-2054), www.palgrave.com; *The Statesman's Yearbook 2008.*

Taylor and Francis Group, An Informa Business, 2 Park Square, Milton Park, Abingdon, Oxford OX14 4RN, United Kingdom, (Dial from U.S. (212) 216-7800), (Fax from U.S. (212) 564-7854), www.tandf.co.uk; *The Europa World Year Book.*

BRITISH VIRGIN ISLANDS - UNEMPLOYMENT

Central Intelligence Agency, Office of Public Affairs, Washington, DC 20505, (703) 482-0623, Fax: (703) 482-1739, www.cia.gov; *The World Factbook.*

International Labour Office, I.L.O. Publications, 4 route des Morillons, CH-1211 Geneva 22, Switzerland, (Telephone in U.S. (202) 653-7652), (Fax in U.S. (202) 653-7687), www.ilo.org; *Yearbook of Labour Statistics 2006.*

BRITISH VIRGIN ISLANDS - WAGES

International Labour Office, I.L.O. Publications, 4 route des Morillons, CH-1211 Geneva 22, Switzerland, (Telephone in U.S. (202) 653-7652), (Fax in U.S. (202) 653-7687), www.ilo.org; *Yearbook of Labour Statistics 2006.*

BROADCASTING AND TELECOMMUNICATIONS INDUSTRY

Federal Communications Commission (FCC), Media Bureau (MB), 445 12th Street, SW, Washington, DC 20554, (202) 418-1500, Fax: (866) 418-0232, www.fcc.gov/mb; Media Bureau Databases: Broadcast and cable information.

Federal Communications Commission (FCC), Wireless Telecommunications Bureau (WTB), 445 12th Street, SW, Washington, DC 20554, (202) 418-1500, Fax: (866) 418-0232, http://wireless.fcc.gov; *Commercial Mobile Radio Services (CMRS) Competition Reports.*

Federal Communications Commission (FCC), Wireline Competition Bureau (WCB), 445 12th Street, SW, Washington, DC 20554, (202) 418-1500, Fax: (202) 418-2825, www.fcc.gov/wcb; *Analyses and Data on the Telecommunications Industry* and *Trends in the International Telecommunications Industry, September 2005.*

International Telecommunication Union (ITU), Place des Nations, 1211 Geneva 20, Switzerland, www.itu.int; *African Telecommunication/ICT Indicators 2008: At a Crossroads; Trends in Telecommunication Reform 2007: The Road to Next-Generation Networks (NGN); World Telecommunication/ICT*

Indicators Database on CD-ROM; World Telecommunication/ICT Indicators Database Online; and *Yearbook of Statistics - Telecommunication Services (Chronological Time Series 1997-2006).*

International Telecommunication Union (ITU), Place des Nations, 1211 Geneva 20, Switzerland, www.itu.int; *Asia-Pacific Telecommunication Indicators.*

International Telecommunication Union (ITU), Place des Nations, 1211 Geneva 20, Switzerland, www.itu.int; *African Telecommunication/ICT Indicators 2008: At a Crossroads; Trends in Telecommunication Reform 2007: The Road to Next-Generation Networks (NGN); World Telecommunication/ICT Indicators Database on CD-ROM; World Telecommunication/ICT Indicators Database Online;* and *Yearbook of Statistics - Telecommunication Services (Chronological Time Series 1997-2006).*

Lithuanian Department of Statistics (Statistics Lithuania), Gedimino av. 29, LT-01500 Vilnius, Lithuania, www.stat.gov.lt/en; *Transport and Communications 2006.*

U.S. Census Bureau, Service Sector Statistics Division, 4700 Silver Hill Road, Washington DC 20233-0001, (301) 763-3030, www.census.gov/svsd/www/economic.html; *2004 Service Annual Survey: Information Sector Services.*

BROADCASTING AND TELECOMMUNICATIONS INDUSTRY - EARNINGS

U.S. Census Bureau, Center for Economic Studies, 4600 Silver Hill Road, Washington DC 20233, (301) 457-1235, www.ces.census.gov; *2002 Economic Census, Information.*

U.S. Census Bureau, Company Statistics Division, 4700 Silver Hill Road, Washington DC 20233-0001, (301) 763-3030, www.census.gov/csd/; *County Business Patterns 2004.*

BROADCASTING AND TELECOMMUNICATIONS INDUSTRY - EMPLOYEES

U.S. Census Bureau, Center for Economic Studies, 4600 Silver Hill Road, Washington DC 20233, (301) 457-1235, www.ces.census.gov; *2002 Economic Census, Information.*

U.S. Census Bureau, Company Statistics Division, 4700 Silver Hill Road, Washington DC 20233-0001, (301) 763-3030, www.census.gov/csd/; *County Business Patterns 2004.*

BROADCASTING AND TELECOMMUNICATIONS INDUSTRY - ESTABLISHMENTS

U.S. Census Bureau, Center for Economic Studies, 4600 Silver Hill Road, Washington DC 20233, (301) 457-1235, www.ces.census.gov; *2002 Economic Census, Information.*

U.S. Census Bureau, Company Statistics Division, 4700 Silver Hill Road, Washington DC 20233-0001, (301) 763-3030, www.census.gov/csd/; *County Business Patterns 2004.*

BROADCASTING AND TELECOMMUNICATIONS INDUSTRY - FINANCES

U.S. Census Bureau, Center for Economic Studies, 4600 Silver Hill Road, Washington DC 20233, (301) 457-1235, www.ces.census.gov; *2002 Economic Census, Information.*

U.S. Census Bureau, Service Sector Statistics Division, 4700 Silver Hill Road, Washington DC 20233-0001, (301) 763-3030, www.census.gov/svsd/www/economic.html; *2004 Service Annual Survey.*

BROADCASTING AND TELECOMMUNICATIONS INDUSTRY - RECEIPTS, REVENUE

U.S. Census Bureau, Center for Economic Studies, 4600 Silver Hill Road, Washington DC 20233, (301) 457-1235, www.ces.census.gov; *2002 Economic Census, Information.*

U.S. Census Bureau, Service Sector Statistics Division, 4700 Silver Hill Road, Washington DC 20233-0001, (301) 763-3030, www.census.gov/svsd/www/economic.html; *2004 Service Annual Survey.*

BROADCASTING AND TELECOMMUNICATIONS INDUSTRY - WORLD

Federal Communications Commission (FCC), International Bureau (IB), 445 12th Street, SW, Washington, DC 20554, (202) 418-1500, Fax: (866) 418-0232, www.fcc.gov/ib; *Annual Circuit Status Report; Annual International Telecommunications Data;* and *International Traffic Data.*

International Telecommunication Union (ITU), Place des Nations, 1211 Geneva 20, Switzerland, www.itu.int; *Asia-Pacific Telecommunication Indicators.*

BROADWAY AND OFF-BROADWAY SHOWS

The League of American Theatres and Producers, Inc., 226 West 47th Street, New York, NY 10036, (212) 764-1122, Fax: (212) 944-2136, www.livebroadway.com; unpublished data.

BROCCOLI

Economic Research Service (ERS), U.S. Department of Agriculture (USDA), 1800 M Street, NW, Washington, DC 20036-5831, (202) 694-5050, Fax: (202) 694-5689, www.ers.usda.gov; *Agricultural Outlook; Agricultural Statistics;* and *Food CPI, Prices, and Expenditures.*

National Agricultural Statistics Service (NASS), U.S. Department of Agriculture (USDA), 1400 Independence Avenue, SW, Washington, DC 20250, (800) 727-9540, Fax: (202) 690-2090, www.nass.usda.gov; *Vegetables: 2004 Annual Summary.*

BROILERS

Economic Research Service (ERS), U.S. Department of Agriculture (USDA), 1800 M Street, NW, Washington, DC 20036-5831, (202) 694-5050, Fax: (202) 694-5689, www.ers.usda.gov; *Agricultural Outlook; Agricultural Statistics;* and *Food CPI, Prices, and Expenditures.*

National Agricultural Statistics Service (NASS), U.S. Department of Agriculture (USDA), 1400 Independence Avenue, SW, Washington, DC 20250, (800) 727-9540, Fax: (202) 690-2090, www.nass.usda.gov; *Poultry - Production and Value: 2006 Summary.*

BROMINE

U.S. Department of the Interior (DOI), U.S. Geological Survey (USGS), Office of Minerals Information, 12201 Sunrise Valley Drive, Reston, VA 20192, Mr. Kenneth A. Beckman, (703) 648-4916, Fax: (703) 648-4995, http://minerals.usgs.gov/minerals; *Mineral Commodity Summaries.*

BRONCHITIS, EMPHYSEMA, ETC

Bernan Essential Government Publications, 4611-F Assembly Drive, Lanham MD, 20706-4391, (301) 459-2255, Fax: (800) 865-3450, www.bernan.com; *Vital Statistics of the United States: Births, Life Expectancy, Deaths, and Selected Health Data.*

National Center for Health Statistics (NCHS), Centers for Disease Control and Prevention (CDC), U.S. Department of Health and Human Services (HHS), 3311 Toledo Road, Hyattsville, MD 20782, (866) 232-4636, www.cdc.gov/nchs; *Faststats A to Z; National Vital Statistics Reports (NVSR); Vital Statistics of the United States (VSUS);* and unpublished data.

BRUNEI - NATIONAL STATISTICAL OFFICE

Department of Economic Planning and Development, Prime Minister's Office, Istana Nurul Iman, Bandar Seri Begawan BA 1000, Brunei, www.depd.gov.bn; National Data Center.

BRUNEI - AGRICULTURAL MACHINERY

United Nations Statistics Division, New York, NY 10017, (800) 253-9646, Fax: (212) 963-4116, http://unstats.un.org; *Statistical Yearbook.*

BRUNEI - AGRICULTURE

Economist Intelligence Unit, 111 West 57th Street, New York, NY 10019, (212) 554-0600, Fax: (212) 586-1181, www.eiu.com; *Brunei Country Report.*

Euromonitor International, Inc., 224 S. Michigan Avenue, Suite 1500, Chicago, IL 60604, (312) 922-1115, Fax: (312) 922-1157, www.euromonitor.com; *World Marketing Data and Statistics.*

Palgrave Macmillan Ltd., Houndmills, Basingstoke, Hampshire, RG21 6XS, England, (Telephone in U.S. (888) 330-8477), (Fax in U.S. (800) 672-2054), www.palgrave.com; *The Statesman's Yearbook 2008.*

Taylor and Francis Group, An Informa Business, 2 Park Square, Milton Park, Abingdon, Oxford OX14 4RN, United Kingdom, (Dial from U.S. (212) 216-7800), (Fax from U.S. (212) 564-7854), www.tandf.co.uk; *The Europa World Year Book.*

United Nations Conference on Trade and Development (UNCTAD), DC2-1120, United Nations, New York, NY 10017, (212) 963-0027, www.unctad.org; *UNCTAD Commodity Yearbook.*

United Nations Food and Agricultural Organization (FAO), Viale delle Terme di Caracalla, 00100 Rome, Italy, (Dial from U.S. (202) 653-2400), (Fax from U.S. (202) 653 5760), www.fao.org; AQUASTAT; *FAO Production Yearbook 2002; FAO Trade Yearbook;* and *The State of Food and Agriculture (SOFA) 2006.*

United Nations Statistics Division, New York, NY 10017, (800) 253-9646, Fax: (212) 963-4116, http://unstats.un.org; *Asia-Pacific in Figures 2004; Statistical Yearbook;* and *Statistical Yearbook for Asia and the Pacific 2004.*

The World Bank, 1818 H Street, NW, Washington, DC 20433, (202) 473-1000, Fax: (202) 477-6391, www.worldbank.org; *Brunei Darussalam.*

BRUNEI - AIRLINES

Economist Intelligence Unit, 111 West 57th Street, New York, NY 10019, (212) 554-0600, Fax: (212) 586-1181, www.eiu.com; *Business Asia.*

Palgrave Macmillan Ltd., Houndmills, Basingstoke, Hampshire, RG21 6XS, England, (Telephone in U.S. (888) 330-8477), (Fax in U.S. (800) 672-2054), www.palgrave.com; *The Statesman's Yearbook 2008.*

Taylor and Francis Group, An Informa Business, 2 Park Square, Milton Park, Abingdon, Oxford OX14 4RN, United Kingdom, (Dial from U.S. (212) 216-7800), (Fax from U.S. (212) 564-7854), www.tandf.co.uk; *The Europa World Year Book.*

BRUNEI - AIRPORTS

Central Intelligence Agency, Office of Public Affairs, Washington, DC 20505, (703) 482-0623, Fax: (703) 482-1739, www.cia.gov; *The World Factbook.*

BRUNEI - ARMED FORCES

Central Intelligence Agency, Office of Public Affairs, Washington, DC 20505, (703) 482-0623, Fax: (703) 482-1739, www.cia.gov; *The World Factbook.*

Economist Intelligence Unit, 111 West 57th Street, New York, NY 10019, (212) 554-0600, Fax: (212) 586-1181, www.eiu.com; *Business Asia.*

Euromonitor International, Inc., 224 S. Michigan Avenue, Suite 1500, Chicago, IL 60604, (312) 922-1115, Fax: (312) 922-1157, www.euromonitor.com; *World Marketing Data and Statistics.*

International Institute for Strategic Studies (IISS), Arundel House, 13-15 Arundel Street, Temple Place, London WC2R 3DX, England, www.iiss.org; *The Military Balance 2007.*

Palgrave Macmillan Ltd., Houndmills, Basingstoke, Hampshire, RG21 6XS, England, (Telephone in U.S. (888) 330-8477), (Fax in U.S. (800) 672-2054), www.palgrave.com; *The Statesman's Yearbook 2008.*

United Nations Statistics Division, New York, NY 10017, (800) 253-9646, Fax: (212) 963-4116, http://unstats.un.org; *Human Development Report 2006.*

BRUNEI - BALANCE OF PAYMENTS

The World Bank, 1818 H Street, NW, Washington, DC 20433, (202) 473-1000, Fax: (202) 477-6391, www.worldbank.org; *Brunei Darussalam.*

BRUNEI - BANKS AND BANKING

Euromonitor International, Inc., 224 S. Michigan Avenue, Suite 1500, Chicago, IL 60604, (312) 922-1115, Fax: (312) 922-1157, www.euromonitor.com; *World Marketing Data and Statistics.*

Palgrave Macmillan Ltd., Houndmills, Basingstoke, Hampshire, RG21 6XS, England, (Telephone in U.S. (888) 330-8477), (Fax in U.S. (800) 672-2054), www.palgrave.com; *The Statesman's Yearbook 2008.*

BRUNEI - BROADCASTING

Central Intelligence Agency, Office of Public Affairs, Washington, DC 20505, (703) 482-0623, Fax: (703) 482-1739, www.cia.gov; *The World Factbook.*

Economist Intelligence Unit, 111 West 57th Street, New York, NY 10019, (212) 554-0600, Fax: (212) 586-1181, www.eiu.com; *Business Asia.*

Euromonitor International, Inc., 224 S. Michigan Avenue, Suite 1500, Chicago, IL 60604, (312) 922-1115, Fax: (312) 922-1157, www.euromonitor.com; *World Marketing Data and Statistics.*

Palgrave Macmillan Ltd., Houndmills, Basingstoke, Hampshire, RG21 6XS, England, (Telephone in U.S. (888) 330-8477), (Fax in U.S. (800) 672-2054), www.palgrave.com; *The Statesman's Yearbook 2008.*

UNESCO Institute for Statistics, C.P. 6128 Succursale Centre-Ville, Montreal, Quebec, H3C 3J7 Canada, (Dial from U.S. (514) 343-6880), (Fax from U.S. (514) 343 6882), www.uis.unesco.org; *Statistical Tables.*

WRTH Publications Limited, PO Box 290, Oxford OX2 7FT, UK, www.wrth.com; *World Radio TV Handbook 2007.*

BRUNEI - BUDGET

Central Intelligence Agency, Office of Public Affairs, Washington, DC 20505, (703) 482-0623, Fax: (703) 482-1739, www.cia.gov; *The World Factbook.*

BRUNEI - BUSINESS

United Nations Statistics Division, New York, NY 10017, (800) 253-9646, Fax: (212) 963-4116, http://unstats.un.org; *Statistical Yearbook for Asia and the Pacific 2004.*

BRUNEI - CATTLE

See BRUNEI - LIVESTOCK

BRUNEI - CHILDBIRTH - STATISTICS

Central Intelligence Agency, Office of Public Affairs, Washington, DC 20505, (703) 482-0623, Fax: (703) 482-1739, www.cia.gov; *The World Factbook.*

Economist Intelligence Unit, 111 West 57th Street, New York, NY 10019, (212) 554-0600, Fax: (212) 586-1181, www.eiu.com; *Business Asia.*

Euromonitor International, Inc., 224 S. Michigan Avenue, Suite 1500, Chicago, IL 60604, (312) 922-1115, Fax: (312) 922-1157, www.euromonitor.com; *The World Economic Factbook 2008.*

Palgrave Macmillan Ltd., Houndmills, Basingstoke, Hampshire, RG21 6XS, England, (Telephone in U.S. (888) 330-8477), (Fax in U.S. (800) 672-2054), www.palgrave.com; *The Statesman's Yearbook 2008.*

Taylor and Francis Group, An Informa Business, 2 Park Square, Milton Park, Abingdon, Oxford OX14 4RN, United Kingdom, (Dial from U.S. (212) 216-7800), (Fax from U.S. (212) 564-7854), www.tandf.co.uk; *The Europa World Year Book.*

United Nations Statistics Division, New York, NY 10017, (800) 253-9646, Fax: (212) 963-4116, http://unstats.un.org; *Asia-Pacific in Figures 2004; Demographic Yearbook;* and *Statistical Yearbook.*

World Health Organization (WHO), Avenue Appia 20, 1211 Geneve 27, Switzerland, (Telephone in U.S. (212) 331-9081), www.who.int; *World Health Report 2006.*

BRUNEI - CLIMATE

Palgrave Macmillan Ltd., Houndmills, Basingstoke, Hampshire, RG21 6XS, England, (Telephone in U.S. (888) 330-8477), (Fax in U.S. (800) 672-2054), www.palgrave.com; *The Statesman's Yearbook 2008.*

BRUNEI - COAL PRODUCTION

See BRUNEI - MINERAL INDUSTRIES

BRUNEI - COMMERCE

Palgrave Macmillan Ltd., Houndmills, Basingstoke, Hampshire, RG21 6XS, England, (Telephone in U.S. (888) 330-8477), (Fax in U.S. (800) 672-2054), www.palgrave.com; *The Statesman's Yearbook 2008.*

BRUNEI - COMMODITY EXCHANGES

Commodity Research Bureau, 330 South Wells Street, Suite 612, Chicago, IL 60606-7110, (800) 621-5271, Fax: (312) 939-4135, www.crbtrader.com; *2006 CRB Commodity Yearbook and CD.*

International Monetary Fund (IMF), 700 Nineteenth Street, NW, Washington, DC 20431, (202) 623-7000, Fax: (202) 623-4661, www.imf.org; *IMF Primary Commodity Prices.*

United Nations Food and Agricultural Organization (FAO), Viale delle Terme di Caracalla, 00100 Rome, Italy, (Dial from U.S. (202) 653-2400), (Fax from U.S. (202) 653 5760), www.fao.org; *The State of Food and Agriculture (SOFA) 2006.*

BRUNEI - CONSUMER PRICE INDEXES

Taylor and Francis Group, An Informa Business, 2 Park Square, Milton Park, Abingdon, Oxford OX14 4RN, United Kingdom, (Dial from U.S. (212) 216-7800), (Fax from U.S. (212) 564-7854), www.tandf.co.uk; *The Europa World Year Book.*

United Nations Statistics Division, New York, NY 10017, (800) 253-9646, Fax: (212) 963-4116, http://unstats.un.org; *Statistical Yearbook.*

The World Bank, 1818 H Street, NW, Washington, DC 20433, (202) 473-1000, Fax: (202) 477-6391, www.worldbank.org; *Brunei Darussalam.*

BRUNEI - CORN INDUSTRY

See BRUNEI - CROPS

BRUNEI - CRIME

International Criminal Police Organization (INTERPOL), General Secretariat, 200 quai Charles de Gaulle, 69006 Lyon, France, www.interpol.int; *International Crime Statistics.*

Yale University Press, PO Box 209040, New Haven, CT 06520-9040, (203) 432-0960, Fax: (203) 432-0948, http://yalepress.yale.edu/yupbooks; *Violence and Crime in Cross-National Perspective.*

BRUNEI - CROPS

Palgrave Macmillan Ltd., Houndmills, Basingstoke, Hampshire, RG21 6XS, England, (Telephone in U.S. (888) 330-8477), (Fax in U.S. (800) 672-2054), www.palgrave.com; *The Statesman's Yearbook 2008.*

Taylor and Francis Group, An Informa Business, 2 Park Square, Milton Park, Abingdon, Oxford OX14 4RN, United Kingdom, (Dial from U.S. (212) 216-7800), (Fax from U.S. (212) 564-7854), www.tandf.co.uk; *The Europa World Year Book.*

United Nations Conference on Trade and Development (UNCTAD), DC2-1120, United Nations, New York, NY 10017, (212) 963-0027, www.unctad.org; *UNCTAD Commodity Yearbook.*

United Nations Food and Agricultural Organization (FAO), Viale delle Terme di Caracalla, 00100 Rome, Italy, (Dial from U.S. (202) 653-2400), (Fax from U.S. (202) 653 5760), www.fao.org; *The State of Food and Agriculture (SOFA) 2006.*

United Nations Statistics Division, New York, NY 10017, (800) 253-9646, Fax: (212) 963-4116, http://unstats.un.org; *Statistical Yearbook.*

BRUNEI - CUSTOMS ADMINISTRATION

Palgrave Macmillan Ltd., Houndmills, Basingstoke, Hampshire, RG21 6XS, England, (Telephone in U.S. (888) 330-8477), (Fax in U.S. (800) 672-2054), www.palgrave.com; *The Statesman's Yearbook 2008.*

BRUNEI - DAIRY PROCESSING

United Nations Food and Agricultural Organization (FAO), Viale delle Terme di Caracalla, 00100 Rome, Italy, (Dial from U.S. (202) 653-2400), (Fax from U.S. (202) 653 5760), www.fao.org; *The State of Food and Agriculture (SOFA) 2006.*

BRUNEI - DEATH RATES

See BRUNEI - MORTALITY

BRUNEI - DEBTS, EXTERNAL

Palgrave Macmillan Ltd., Houndmills, Basingstoke, Hampshire, RG21 6XS, England, (Telephone in U.S. (888) 330-8477), (Fax in U.S. (800) 672-2054), www.palgrave.com; *The Statesman's Yearbook 2008.*

The World Bank, 1818 H Street, NW, Washington, DC 20433, (202) 473-1000, Fax: (202) 477-6391, www.worldbank.org; *Global Development Finance 2007.*

Worldinformation.com, 2 Market Street, Saffron Walden, Essex CB10 1HZ, United Kingdom, www.worldinformation.com; The World of Information (www.worldinformation.com).

BRUNEI - DEMOGRAPHY

Economist Intelligence Unit, 111 West 57th Street, New York, NY 10019, (212) 554-0600, Fax: (212) 586-1181, www.eiu.com; *Business Asia.*

Euromonitor International, Inc., 224 S. Michigan Avenue, Suite 1500, Chicago, IL 60604, (312) 922-1115, Fax: (312) 922-1157, www.euromonitor.com; *International Marketing Data and Statistics 2008; The World Economic Factbook 2008;* and *World Marketing Data and Statistics.*

United Nations Statistics Division, New York, NY 10017, (800) 253-9646, Fax: (212) 963-4116, http://unstats.un.org; *Asia-Pacific in Figures 2004* and *Human Development Report 2006.*

The World Bank, 1818 H Street, NW, Washington, DC 20433, (202) 473-1000, Fax: (202) 477-6391, www.worldbank.org; *Brunei Darussalam.*

BRUNEI - DISPOSABLE INCOME

United Nations Statistics Division, New York, NY 10017, (800) 253-9646, Fax: (212) 963-4116, http://unstats.un.org; *National Accounts Statistics: Compendium of Income Distribution Statistics* and *Statistical Yearbook.*

BRUNEI - DIVORCE

United Nations Statistics Division, New York, NY 10017, (800) 253-9646, Fax: (212) 963-4116, http://unstats.un.org; *Demographic Yearbook* and *Statistical Yearbook.*

BRUNEI - ECONOMIC ASSISTANCE

United Nations Statistics Division, New York, NY 10017, (800) 253-9646, Fax: (212) 963-4116, http://unstats.un.org; *Statistical Yearbook.*

BRUNEI - ECONOMIC CONDITIONS

Center for International Business Education Research (CIBER), Columbia Business School and School of International and Public Affairs, Uris Hall, Room 212, 3022 Broadway, New York, NY 10027-6902, Mr. Joshua Safier, (212) 854-4750, Fax: (212) 222-9821, www.columbia.edu/cu/ciber/; Datastream International.

Central Intelligence Agency, Office of Public Affairs, Washington, DC 20505, (703) 482-0623, Fax: (703) 482-1739, www.cia.gov; *The World Factbook.*

DSI Data Service Information, Xantener Strasse 51a, D-47495 Rheinberg, Germany, www.dsidata.com; *Campus Solution.*

Dun and Bradstreet (DB) Corporation, 103 JFK Parkway, Short Hills, NJ 07078, (973) 921-5500, www.dnb.com; *Country Report.*

Economist Intelligence Unit, 111 West 57th Street, New York, NY 10019, (212) 554-0600, Fax: (212) 586-1181, www.eiu.com; *Brunei Country Report.*

Euromonitor International, Inc., 224 S. Michigan Avenue, Suite 1500, Chicago, IL 60604, (312) 922-1115, Fax: (312) 922-1157, www.euromonitor.com; *The World Economic Factbook 2008* and *World Marketing Data and Statistics.*

International Monetary Fund (IMF), 700 Nineteenth Street, NW, Washington, DC 20431, (202) 623-7000, Fax: (202) 623-4661, www.imf.org; *World Economic Outlook Reports.*

Palgrave Macmillan Ltd., Houndmills, Basingstoke, Hampshire, RG21 6XS, England, (Telephone in U.S. (888) 330-8477), (Fax in U.S. (800) 672-2054), www.palgrave.com; *The Statesman's Yearbook 2008.*

Taylor and Francis Group, An Informa Business, 2 Park Square, Milton Park, Abingdon, Oxford OX14 4RN, United Kingdom, (Dial from U.S. (212) 216-7800), (Fax from U.S. (212) 564-7854), www.tandf.co.uk; *The Europa World Year Book.*

United Nations Statistics Division, New York, NY 10017, (800) 253-9646, Fax: (212) 963-4116, http://unstats.un.org; *World Statistics Pocketbook.*

The World Bank, 1818 H Street, NW, Washington, DC 20433, (202) 473-1000, Fax: (202) 477-6391, www.worldbank.org; *Brunei Darussalam; Global Economic Monitor (GEM); Global Economic Prospects 2008;* and *The World Bank Atlas 2003-2004.*

BRUNEI - EDUCATION

Economist Intelligence Unit, 111 West 57th Street, New York, NY 10019, (212) 554-0600, Fax: (212) 586-1181, www.eiu.com; *Business Asia.*

Euromonitor International, Inc., 224 S. Michigan Avenue, Suite 1500, Chicago, IL 60604, (312) 922-1115, Fax: (312) 922-1157, www.euromonitor.com; *International Marketing Data and Statistics 2008* and *World Marketing Data and Statistics.*

Palgrave Macmillan Ltd., Houndmills, Basingstoke, Hampshire, RG21 6XS, England, (Telephone in U.S. (888) 330-8477), (Fax in U.S. (800) 672-2054), www.palgrave.com; *The Statesman's Yearbook 2008.*

Taylor and Francis Group, An Informa Business, 2 Park Square, Milton Park, Abingdon, Oxford OX14 4RN, United Kingdom, (Dial from U.S. (212) 216-7800), (Fax from U.S. (212) 564-7854), www.tandf.co.uk; *The Europa World Year Book.*

UNESCO Institute for Statistics, C.P. 6128 Succursale Centre-Ville, Montreal, Quebec, H3C 3J7 Canada, (Dial from U.S. (514) 343-6880), (Fax from U.S. (514) 343 6882), www.uis.unesco.org; *Statistical Tables.*

United Nations Statistics Division, New York, NY 10017, (800) 253-9646, Fax: (212) 963-4116, http://unstats.un.org; *Asia-Pacific in Figures 2004; Human Development Report 2006;* and *Statistical Yearbook for Asia and the Pacific 2004.*

The World Bank, 1818 H Street, NW, Washington, DC 20433, (202) 473-1000, Fax: (202) 477-6391, www.worldbank.org; *Brunei Darussalam.*

BRUNEI - ELECTRICITY

Organisation for Economic Cooperation and Development (OECD), 2 rue Andre Pascal, F-75775 Paris Cedex 16, France, (Telephone in U.S. (202) 785-6323), (Fax in U.S. (202) 785-0350), www.oecd.org; *World Energy Outlook 2007.*

Palgrave Macmillan Ltd., Houndmills, Basingstoke, Hampshire, RG21 6XS, England, (Telephone in U.S. (888) 330-8477), (Fax in U.S. (800) 672-2054), www.palgrave.com; *The Statesman's Yearbook 2008.*

U.S. Department of Energy (DOE), Energy Information Administration (EIA), 1000 Independence Avenue, SW, Washington, DC 20585, (202) 586-8800, www.eia.doe.gov; *International Energy Annual 2004* and *International Energy Outlook 2006.*

United Nations Statistics Division, New York, NY 10017, (800) 253-9646, Fax: (212) 963-4116, http://unstats.un.org; *Human Development Report 2006* and *Statistical Yearbook.*

BRUNEI - EMPLOYMENT

Euromonitor International, Inc., 224 S. Michigan Avenue, Suite 1500, Chicago, IL 60604, (312) 922-1115, Fax: (312) 922-1157, www.euromonitor.com; *International Marketing Data and Statistics 2008.*

International Labour Office, I.L.O. Publications, 4 route des Morillons, CH-1211 Geneva 22, Switzerland, (Telephone in U.S. (202) 653-7652), (Fax in U.S. (202) 653-7687), www.ilo.org; *Yearbook of Labour Statistics 2006.*

United Nations Statistics Division, New York, NY 10017, (800) 253-9646, Fax: (212) 963-4116, http://unstats.un.org; *Asia-Pacific in Figures 2004* and *Statistical Yearbook.*

The World Bank, 1818 H Street, NW, Washington, DC 20433, (202) 473-1000, Fax: (202) 477-6391, www.worldbank.org; *Brunei Darussalam.*

BRUNEI - ENVIRONMENTAL CONDITIONS

DSI Data Service Information, Xantener Strasse 51a, D-47495 Rheinberg, Germany, www.dsidata.com; *Campus Solution* and *DSI's Global Environmental Database.*

Economist Intelligence Unit, 111 West 57th Street, New York, NY 10019, (212) 554-0600, Fax: (212) 586-1181, www.eiu.com; *Brunei Country Report.*

United Nations Statistics Division, New York, NY 10017, (800) 253-9646, Fax: (212) 963-4116, http://unstats.un.org; *World Statistics Pocketbook.*

BRUNEI - EXPORTS

Central Intelligence Agency, Office of Public Affairs, Washington, DC 20505, (703) 482-0623, Fax: (703) 482-1739, www.cia.gov; *The World Factbook.*

Economist Intelligence Unit, 111 West 57th Street, New York, NY 10019, (212) 554-0600, Fax: (212) 586-1181, www.eiu.com; *Brunei Country Report.*

Euromonitor International, Inc., 224 S. Michigan Avenue, Suite 1500, Chicago, IL 60604, (312) 922-1115, Fax: (312) 922-1157, www.euromonitor.com; *International Marketing Data and Statistics 2008* and *The World Economic Factbook 2008.*

International Monetary Fund (IMF), 700 Nineteenth Street, NW, Washington, DC 20431, (202) 623-7000, Fax: (202) 623-4661, www.imf.org; *Direction of Trade Statistics Yearbook 2007.*

Palgrave Macmillan Ltd., Houndmills, Basingstoke, Hampshire, RG21 6XS, England, (Telephone in U.S. (888) 330-8477), (Fax in U.S. (800) 672-2054), www.palgrave.com; *The Statesman's Yearbook 2008.*

Taylor and Francis Group, An Informa Business, 2 Park Square, Milton Park, Abingdon, Oxford OX14 4RN, United Kingdom, (Dial from U.S. (212) 216-7800), (Fax from U.S. (212) 564-7854), www.tandf.co.uk; *The Europa World Year Book.*

United Nations Food and Agricultural Organization (FAO), Viale delle Terme di Caracalla, 00100 Rome, Italy, (Dial from U.S. (202) 653-2400), (Fax from U.S. (202) 653 5760), www.fao.org; *The State of Food and Agriculture (SOFA) 2006.*

United Nations Statistics Division, New York, NY 10017, (800) 253-9646, Fax: (212) 963-4116, http://unstats.un.org; *Foreign Trade Statistics of Asia and the Pacific 1996-2000; Statistical Yearbook;* and *Statistical Yearbook for Asia and the Pacific 2004.*

Worldinformation.com, 2 Market Street, Saffron Walden, Essex CB10 1HZ, United Kingdom, www.worldinformation.com; The World of Information (www.worldinformation.com).

BRUNEI - FERTILITY, HUMAN

Central Intelligence Agency, Office of Public Affairs, Washington, DC 20505, (703) 482-0623, Fax: (703) 482-1739, www.cia.gov; *The World Factbook.*

United Nations Statistics Division, New York, NY 10017, (800) 253-9646, Fax: (212) 963-4116, http://unstats.un.org; *Human Development Report 2006.*

The World Bank, 1818 H Street, NW, Washington, DC 20433, (202) 473-1000, Fax: (202) 477-6391, www.worldbank.org; *The World Bank Atlas 2003-2004.*

BRUNEI - FERTILIZER INDUSTRY

United Nations Food and Agricultural Organization (FAO), Viale delle Terme di Caracalla, 00100 Rome, Italy, (Dial from U.S. (202) 653-2400), (Fax from U.S. (202) 653 5760), www.fao.org; *The State of Food and Agriculture (SOFA) 2006.*

BRUNEI - FETAL MORTALITY

See BRUNEI - MORTALITY

BRUNEI - FILM

See BRUNEI - MOTION PICTURES

BRUNEI - FINANCE

United Nations Statistics Division, New York, NY 10017, (800) 253-9646, Fax: (212) 963-4116, http://unstats.un.org; *Asia-Pacific in Figures 2004; Statistical Yearbook;* and *Statistical Yearbook for Asia and the Pacific 2004.*

The World Bank, 1818 H Street, NW, Washington, DC 20433, (202) 473-1000, Fax: (202) 477-6391, www.worldbank.org; *Brunei Darussalam.*

BRUNEI - FINANCE, PUBLIC

Bernan Essential Government Publications, 4611-F Assembly Drive, Lanham MD, 20706-4391, (301) 459-2255, Fax: (800) 865-3450, www.bernan.com; *National Accounts Statistics.*

Economist Intelligence Unit, 111 West 57th Street, New York, NY 10019, (212) 554-0600, Fax: (212) 586-1181, www.eiu.com; *Brunei Country Report.*

International Monetary Fund (IMF), 700 Nineteenth Street, NW, Washington, DC 20431, (202) 623-7000, Fax: (202) 623-4661, www.imf.org; *International Financial Statistics* and *International Financial Statistics Online Service.*

Palgrave Macmillan Ltd., Houndmills, Basingstoke, Hampshire, RG21 6XS, England, (Telephone in U.S. (888) 330-8477), (Fax in U.S. (800) 672-2054), www.palgrave.com; *The Statesman's Yearbook 2008.*

Taylor and Francis Group, An Informa Business, 2 Park Square, Milton Park, Abingdon, Oxford OX14 4RN, United Kingdom, (Dial from U.S. (212) 216-7800), (Fax from U.S. (212) 564-7854), www.tandf.co.uk; *The Europa World Year Book.*

United Nations Statistics Division, New York, NY 10017, (800) 253-9646, Fax: (212) 963-4116, http://unstats.un.org; *Statistical Yearbook for Asia and the Pacific 2004.*

The World Bank, 1818 H Street, NW, Washington, DC 20433, (202) 473-1000, Fax: (202) 477-6391, www.worldbank.org; *Brunei Darussalam.*

BRUNEI - FISHERIES

Palgrave Macmillan Ltd., Houndmills, Basingstoke, Hampshire, RG21 6XS, England, (Telephone in U.S. (888) 330-8477), (Fax in U.S. (800) 672-2054), www.palgrave.com; *The Statesman's Yearbook 2008.*

Taylor and Francis Group, An Informa Business, 2 Park Square, Milton Park, Abingdon, Oxford OX14 4RN, United Kingdom, (Dial from U.S. (212) 216-7800), (Fax from U.S. (212) 564-7854), www.tandf.co.uk; *The Europa World Year Book.*

United Nations Conference on Trade and Development (UNCTAD), DC2-1120, United Nations, New York, NY 10017, (212) 963-0027, www.unctad.org; *UNCTAD Commodity Yearbook.*

United Nations Food and Agricultural Organization (FAO), Viale delle Terme di Caracalla, 00100 Rome, Italy, (Dial from U.S. (202) 653-2400), (Fax from U.S. (202) 653 5760), www.fao.org; *FAO Yearbook of Fishery Statistics;* Fishery Databases; FISHSTAT Database. Subjects covered include: Aquaculture production, capture production, fishery commodities; and *The State of Food and Agriculture (SOFA) 2006.*

United Nations Statistics Division, New York, NY 10017, (800) 253-9646, Fax: (212) 963-4116, http://unstats.un.org; *Statistical Yearbook.*

The World Bank, 1818 H Street, NW, Washington, DC 20433, (202) 473-1000, Fax: (202) 477-6391, www.worldbank.org; *Brunei Darussalam.*

BRUNEI - FOOD

United Nations Conference on Trade and Development (UNCTAD), DC2-1120, United Nations, New York, NY 10017, (212) 963-0027, www.unctad.org; *UNCTAD Commodity Yearbook.*

United Nations Food and Agricultural Organization (FAO), Viale delle Terme di Caracalla, 00100 Rome, Italy, (Dial from U.S. (202) 653-2400), (Fax from U.S. (202) 653 5760), www.fao.org; *FAO Production Yearbook 2002* and *The State of Food and Agriculture (SOFA) 2006.*

United Nations Statistics Division, New York, NY 10017, (800) 253-9646, Fax: (212) 963-4116, http://unstats.un.org; *Human Development Report 2006* and *Statistical Yearbook for Asia and the Pacific 2004.*

BRUNEI - FOREIGN EXCHANGE RATES

Central Intelligence Agency, Office of Public Affairs, Washington, DC 20505, (703) 482-0623, Fax: (703) 482-1739, www.cia.gov; *The World Factbook.*

Economist Intelligence Unit, 111 West 57th Street, New York, NY 10019, (212) 554-0600, Fax: (212) 586-1181, www.eiu.com; *Business Asia.*

Euromonitor International, Inc., 224 S. Michigan Avenue, Suite 1500, Chicago, IL 60604, (312) 922-1115, Fax: (312) 922-1157, www.euromonitor.com; *International Marketing Data and Statistics 2008* and *The World Economic Factbook 2008.*

Taylor and Francis Group, An Informa Business, 2 Park Square, Milton Park, Abingdon, Oxford OX14 4RN, United Kingdom, (Dial from U.S. (212) 216-7800), (Fax from U.S. (212) 564-7854), www.tandf.co.uk; *The Europa World Year Book.*

United Nations Statistics Division, New York, NY 10017, (800) 253-9646, Fax: (212) 963-4116, http://unstats.un.org; *World Statistics Pocketbook.*

Worldinformation.com, 2 Market Street, Saffron Walden, Essex CB10 1HZ, United Kingdom, www.worldinformation.com; The World of Information (www.worldinformation.com).

BRUNEI - FORESTS AND FORESTRY

Economist Intelligence Unit, 111 West 57th Street, New York, NY 10019, (212) 554-0600, Fax: (212) 586-1181, www.eiu.com; *Business Asia.*

Palgrave Macmillan Ltd., Houndmills, Basingstoke, Hampshire, RG21 6XS, England, (Telephone in U.S. (888) 330-8477), (Fax in U.S. (800) 672-2054), www.palgrave.com; *The Statesman's Yearbook 2008.*

Taylor and Francis Group, An Informa Business, 2 Park Square, Milton Park, Abingdon, Oxford OX14 4RN, United Kingdom, (Dial from U.S. (212) 216-7800), (Fax from U.S. (212) 564-7854), www.tandf.co.uk; *The Europa World Year Book.*

UNESCO Institute for Statistics, C.P. 6128 Succursale Centre-Ville, Montreal, Quebec, H3C 3J7 Canada, (Dial from U.S. (514) 343-6880), (Fax from U.S. (514) 343 6882), www.uis.unesco.org; *Statistical Tables.*

United Nations Conference on Trade and Development (UNCTAD), DC2-1120, United Nations, New York, NY 10017, (212) 963-0027, www.unctad.org; *UNCTAD Commodity Yearbook.*

United Nations Food and Agricultural Organization (FAO), Viale delle Terme di Caracalla, 00100 Rome, Italy, (Dial from U.S. (202) 653-2400), (Fax from U.S. (202) 653 5760), www.fao.org; *FAO Yearbook of Forest Products* and *The State of Food and Agriculture (SOFA) 2006.*

United Nations Statistics Division, New York, NY 10017, (800) 253-9646, Fax: (212) 963-4116, http://unstats.un.org; *Statistical Yearbook.*

The World Bank, 1818 H Street, NW, Washington, DC 20433, (202) 473-1000, Fax: (202) 477-6391, www.worldbank.org; *Brunei Darussalam.*

BRUNEI - GAS PRODUCTION

See BRUNEI - MINERAL INDUSTRIES

BRUNEI - GEOGRAPHIC INFORMATION SYSTEMS

The World Bank, 1818 H Street, NW, Washington, DC 20433, (202) 473-1000, Fax: (202) 477-6391, www.worldbank.org; *Brunei Darussalam.*

BRUNEI - GROSS DOMESTIC PRODUCT

Economist Intelligence Unit, 111 West 57th Street, New York, NY 10019, (212) 554-0600, Fax: (212) 586-1181, www.eiu.com; *Brunei Country Report* and *Business Asia.*

Euromonitor International, Inc., 224 S. Michigan Avenue, Suite 1500, Chicago, IL 60604, (312) 922-1115, Fax: (312) 922-1157, www.euromonitor.com; *International Marketing Data and Statistics 2008* and *The World Economic Factbook 2008.*

Taylor and Francis Group, An Informa Business, 2 Park Square, Milton Park, Abingdon, Oxford OX14 4RN, United Kingdom, (Dial from U.S. (212) 216-7800), (Fax from U.S. (212) 564-7854), www.tandf.co.uk; *The Europa World Year Book.*

United Nations Statistics Division, New York, NY 10017, (800) 253-9646, Fax: (212) 963-4116, http://unstats.un.org; *Human Development Report 2006; National Accounts Statistics: Compendium of Income Distribution Statistics;* and *Statistical Yearbook.*

BRUNEI - GROSS NATIONAL PRODUCT

Palgrave Macmillan Ltd., Houndmills, Basingstoke, Hampshire, RG21 6XS, England, (Telephone in U.S. (888) 330-8477), (Fax in U.S. (800) 672-2054), www.palgrave.com; *The Statesman's Yearbook 2008.*

The World Bank, 1818 H Street, NW, Washington, DC 20433, (202) 473-1000, Fax: (202) 477-6391, www.worldbank.org; *The World Bank Atlas 2003-2004.*

Worldinformation.com, 2 Market Street, Saffron Walden, Essex CB10 1HZ, United Kingdom, www.worldinformation.com; The World of Information (www.worldinformation.com).

BRUNEI - HIDES AND SKINS INDUSTRY

United Nations Food and Agricultural Organization (FAO), Viale delle Terme di Caracalla, 00100 Rome, Italy, (Dial from U.S. (202) 653-2400), (Fax from U.S. (202) 653 5760), www.fao.org; *FAO Production Yearbook 2002.*

BRUNEI - HOUSING

Euromonitor International, Inc., 224 S. Michigan Avenue, Suite 1500, Chicago, IL 60604, (312) 922-1115, Fax: (312) 922-1157, www.euromonitor.com; *World Marketing Data and Statistics.*

BRUNEI - ILLITERATE PERSONS

Euromonitor International, Inc., 224 S. Michigan Avenue, Suite 1500, Chicago, IL 60604, (312) 922-1115, Fax: (312) 922-1157, www.euromonitor.com; *The World Economic Factbook 2008.*

UNESCO Institute for Statistics, C.P. 6128 Succursale Centre-Ville, Montreal, Quebec, H3C 3J7 Canada, (Dial from U.S. (514) 343-6880), (Fax from U.S. (514) 343 6882), www.uis.unesco.org; *Statistical Tables.*

United Nations Statistics Division, New York, NY 10017, (800) 253-9646, Fax: (212) 963-4116, http://unstats.un.org; *Asia-Pacific in Figures 2004* and *Human Development Report 2006.*

BRUNEI - IMPORTS

Central Intelligence Agency, Office of Public Affairs, Washington, DC 20505, (703) 482-0623, Fax: (703) 482-1739, www.cia.gov; *The World Factbook.*

Economist Intelligence Unit, 111 West 57th Street, New York, NY 10019, (212) 554-0600, Fax: (212) 586-1181, www.eiu.com; *Brunei Country Report.*

Euromonitor International, Inc., 224 S. Michigan Avenue, Suite 1500, Chicago, IL 60604, (312) 922-1115, Fax: (312) 922-1157, www.euromonitor.com; *International Marketing Data and Statistics 2008* and *The World Economic Factbook 2008.*

International Monetary Fund (IMF), 700 Nineteenth Street, NW, Washington, DC 20431, (202) 623-7000, Fax: (202) 623-4661, www.imf.org; *Direction of Trade Statistics Yearbook 2007.*

Palgrave Macmillan Ltd., Houndmills, Basingstoke, Hampshire, RG21 6XS, England, (Telephone in U.S. (888) 330-8477), (Fax in U.S. (800) 672-2054), www.palgrave.com; *The Statesman's Yearbook 2008.*

Taylor and Francis Group, An Informa Business, 2 Park Square, Milton Park, Abingdon, Oxford OX14 4RN, United Kingdom, (Dial from U.S. (212) 216-7800), (Fax from U.S. (212) 564-7854), www.tandf.co.uk; *The Europa World Year Book.*

United Nations Food and Agricultural Organization (FAO), Viale delle Terme di Caracalla, 00100 Rome, Italy, (Dial from U.S. (202) 653-2400), (Fax from U.S. (202) 653 5760), www.fao.org; *The State of Food and Agriculture (SOFA) 2006.*

United Nations Statistics Division, New York, NY 10017, (800) 253-9646, Fax: (212) 963-4116, http://unstats.un.org; *Foreign Trade Statistics of Asia and the Pacific 1996-2000.*

Worldinformation.com, 2 Market Street, Saffron Walden, Essex CB10 1HZ, United Kingdom, www.worldinformation.com; The World of Information (www.worldinformation.com).

BRUNEI - INDUSTRIES

Central Intelligence Agency, Office of Public Affairs, Washington, DC 20505, (703) 482-0623, Fax: (703) 482-1739, www.cia.gov; *The World Factbook.*

Economist Intelligence Unit, 111 West 57th Street, New York, NY 10019, (212) 554-0600, Fax: (212) 586-1181, www.eiu.com; *Brunei Country Report.*

Euromonitor International, Inc., 224 S. Michigan Avenue, Suite 1500, Chicago, IL 60604, (312) 922-1115, Fax: (312) 922-1157, www.euromonitor.com; *The World Economic Factbook 2008* and *World Marketing Data and Statistics.*

International Labour Office, I.L.O. Publications, 4 route des Morillons, CH-1211 Geneva 22, Switzerland, (Telephone in U.S. (202) 653-7652), (Fax in U.S. (202) 653-7687), www.ilo.org; *Yearbook of Labour Statistics 2006.*

Palgrave Macmillan Ltd., Houndmills, Basingstoke, Hampshire, RG21 6XS, England, (Telephone in U.S. (888) 330-8477), (Fax in U.S. (800) 672-2054), www.palgrave.com; *The Statesman's Yearbook 2008.*

Taylor and Francis Group, An Informa Business, 2 Park Square, Milton Park, Abingdon, Oxford OX14 4RN, United Kingdom, (Dial from U.S. (212) 216-7800), (Fax from U.S. (212) 564-7854), www.tandf.co.uk; *The Europa World Year Book.*

United Nations Industrial Development Organization (UNIDO), 1 United Nations Plaza, New York, NY 10017, (212) 963 6890, Fax: (212) 963-7904, http://unido.org; Industrial Statistics Database 2008 (INDSTAT) and *The International Yearbook of Industrial Statistics 2008.*

United Nations Statistics Division, New York, NY 10017, (800) 253-9646, Fax: (212) 963-4116, http://unstats.un.org; *Asia-Pacific in Figures 2004* and *Statistical Yearbook for Asia and the Pacific 2004.*

The World Bank, 1818 H Street, NW, Washington, DC 20433, (202) 473-1000, Fax: (202) 477-6391, www.worldbank.org; *Brunei Darussalam.*

BRUNEI - INFANT AND MATERNAL MORTALITY

See BRUNEI - MORTALITY

BRUNEI - INTERNATIONAL TRADE

Economist Intelligence Unit, 111 West 57th Street, New York, NY 10019, (212) 554-0600, Fax: (212) 586-1181, www.eiu.com; *Brunei Country Report* and *Business Asia.*

Euromonitor International, Inc., 224 S. Michigan Avenue, Suite 1500, Chicago, IL 60604, (312) 922-1115, Fax: (312) 922-1157, www.euromonitor.com; *The World Economic Factbook 2008* and *World Marketing Data and Statistics.*

Organisation for Economic Cooperation and Development (OECD), 2 rue Andre Pascal, F-75775 Paris Cedex 16, France, (Telephone in U.S. (202) 785-6323), (Fax in U.S. (202) 785-0350), www.oecd.org; *International Trade by Commodity Statistics (ITCS).*

Palgrave Macmillan Ltd., Houndmills, Basingstoke, Hampshire, RG21 6XS, England, (Telephone in U.S. (888) 330-8477), (Fax in U.S. (800) 672-2054), www.palgrave.com; *The Statesman's Yearbook 2008.*

Taylor and Francis Group, An Informa Business, 2 Park Square, Milton Park, Abingdon, Oxford OX14 4RN, United Kingdom, (Dial from U.S. (212) 216-7800), (Fax from U.S. (212) 564-7854), www.tandf.co.uk; *The Europa World Year Book.*

United Nations Conference on Trade and Development (UNCTAD), DC2-1120, United Nations, New York, NY 10017, (212) 963-0027, www.unctad.org; *UNCTAD Commodity Yearbook.*

United Nations Food and Agricultural Organization (FAO), Viale delle Terme di Caracalla, 00100 Rome, Italy, (Dial from U.S. (202) 653-2400), (Fax from U.S. (202) 653 5760), www.fao.org; *FAO Trade Yearbook* and *The State of Food and Agriculture (SOFA) 2006.*

United Nations Statistics Division, New York, NY 10017, (800) 253-9646, Fax: (212) 963-4116, http://unstats.un.org; *Asia-Pacific in Figures 2004; International Trade Statistics Yearbook;* and *Statistical Yearbook.*

The World Bank, 1818 H Street, NW, Washington, DC 20433, (202) 473-1000, Fax: (202) 477-6391, www.worldbank.org; *Brunei Darussalam.*

World Trade Organization (WTO), Centre William Rappard, Rue de Lausanne 154, CH-1211 Geneva 21, Switzerland, www.wto.org; *International Trade Statistics 2006.*

BRUNEI - INTERNET USERS

International Telecommunication Union (ITU), Place des Nations, 1211 Geneva 20, Switzerland, www.itu.int; *World Telecommunication/ICT Indicators Database on CD-ROM; World Telecommunication/ICT Indicators Database Online;* and *Yearbook of Statistics - Telecommunication Services (Chronological Time Series 1997-2006).*

The World Bank, 1818 H Street, NW, Washington, DC 20433, (202) 473-1000, Fax: (202) 477-6391, www.worldbank.org; *Brunei Darussalam.*

BRUNEI - LABOR

Central Intelligence Agency, Office of Public Affairs, Washington, DC 20505, (703) 482-0623, Fax: (703) 482-1739, www.cia.gov; *The World Factbook.*

Economist Intelligence Unit, 111 West 57th Street, New York, NY 10019, (212) 554-0600, Fax: (212) 586-1181, www.eiu.com; *Business Asia.*

Euromonitor International, Inc., 224 S. Michigan Avenue, Suite 1500, Chicago, IL 60604, (312) 922-1115, Fax: (312) 922-1157, www.euromonitor.com; *International Marketing Data and Statistics 2008* and *World Marketing Data and Statistics.*

International Labour Office, I.L.O. Publications, 4 route des Morillons, CH-1211 Geneva 22, Switzerland, (Telephone in U.S. (202) 653-7652), (Fax in U.S. (202) 653-7687), www.ilo.org; *Yearbook of Labour Statistics 2006.*

Palgrave Macmillan Ltd., Houndmills, Basingstoke, Hampshire, RG21 6XS, England, (Telephone in U.S. (888) 330-8477), (Fax in U.S. (800) 672-2054), www.palgrave.com; *The Statesman's Yearbook 2008.*

Taylor and Francis Group, An Informa Business, 2 Park Square, Milton Park, Abingdon, Oxford OX14 4RN, United Kingdom, (Dial from U.S. (212) 216-7800), (Fax from U.S. (212) 564-7854), www.tandf.co.uk; *The Europa World Year Book.*

United Nations Food and Agricultural Organization (FAO), Viale delle Terme di Caracalla, 00100 Rome, Italy, (Dial from U.S. (202) 653-2400), (Fax from U.S. (202) 653 5760), www.fao.org; *The State of Food and Agriculture (SOFA) 2006.*

United Nations Statistics Division, New York, NY 10017, (800) 253-9646, Fax: (212) 963-4116, http://unstats.un.org; *Human Development Report 2006.*

The World Bank, 1818 H Street, NW, Washington, DC 20433, (202) 473-1000, Fax: (202) 477-6391, www.worldbank.org; *The World Bank Atlas 2003-2004.*

BRUNEI - LAND USE

Central Intelligence Agency, Office of Public Affairs, Washington, DC 20505, (703) 482-0623, Fax: (703) 482-1739, www.cia.gov; *The World Factbook.*

Euromonitor International, Inc., 224 S. Michigan Avenue, Suite 1500, Chicago, IL 60604, (312) 922-1115, Fax: (312) 922-1157, www.euromonitor.com; *International Marketing Data and Statistics 2008.*

United Nations Food and Agricultural Organization (FAO), Viale delle Terme di Caracalla, 00100 Rome, Italy, (Dial from U.S. (202) 653-2400), (Fax from U.S. (202) 653 5760), www.fao.org; *FAO Production Yearbook 2002.*

BRUNEI - LIBRARIES

UNESCO Institute for Statistics, C.P. 6128 Succursale Centre-Ville, Montreal, Quebec, H3C 3J7 Canada, (Dial from U.S. (514) 343-6880), (Fax from U.S. (514) 343 6882), www.uis.unesco.org; *Statistical Tables.*

BRUNEI - LIFE EXPECTANCY

Central Intelligence Agency, Office of Public Affairs, Washington, DC 20505, (703) 482-0623, Fax: (703) 482-1739, www.cia.gov; *The World Factbook.*

Economist Intelligence Unit, 111 West 57th Street, New York, NY 10019, (212) 554-0600, Fax: (212) 586-1181, www.eiu.com; *Business Asia.*

Euromonitor International, Inc., 224 S. Michigan Avenue, Suite 1500, Chicago, IL 60604, (312) 922-1115, Fax: (312) 922-1157, www.euromonitor.com; *The World Economic Factbook 2008.*

Palgrave Macmillan Ltd., Houndmills, Basingstoke, Hampshire, RG21 6XS, England, (Telephone in U.S. (888) 330-8477), (Fax in U.S. (800) 672-2054), www.palgrave.com; *The Statesman's Yearbook 2008.*

United Nations Statistics Division, New York, NY 10017, (800) 253-9646, Fax: (212) 963-4116, http://unstats.un.org; *Asia-Pacific in Figures 2004; Human Development Report 2006;* and *World Statistics Pocketbook.*

The World Bank, 1818 H Street, NW, Washington, DC 20433, (202) 473-1000, Fax: (202) 477-6391, www.worldbank.org; *The World Bank Atlas 2003-2004.*

BRUNEI - LITERACY

Euromonitor International, Inc., 224 S. Michigan Avenue, Suite 1500, Chicago, IL 60604, (312) 922-1115, Fax: (312) 922-1157, www.euromonitor.com; *World Marketing Data and Statistics.*

BRUNEI - LIVESTOCK

Palgrave Macmillan Ltd., Houndmills, Basingstoke, Hampshire, RG21 6XS, England, (Telephone in U.S. (888) 330-8477), (Fax in U.S. (800) 672-2054), www.palgrave.com; *The Statesman's Yearbook 2008.*

Taylor and Francis Group, An Informa Business, 2 Park Square, Milton Park, Abingdon, Oxford OX14 4RN, United Kingdom, (Dial from U.S. (212) 216-7800), (Fax from U.S. (212) 564-7854), www.tandf.co.uk; *The Europa World Year Book.*

United Nations Conference on Trade and Development (UNCTAD), DC2-1120, United Nations, New York, NY 10017, (212) 963-0027, www.unctad.org; *UNCTAD Commodity Yearbook.*

United Nations Food and Agricultural Organization (FAO), Viale delle Terme di Caracalla, 00100 Rome, Italy, (Dial from U.S. (202) 653-2400), (Fax from U.S. (202) 653 5760), www.fao.org; *FAO Production Yearbook 2002* and *The State of Food and Agriculture (SOFA) 2006.*

United Nations Statistics Division, New York, NY 10017, (800) 253-9646, Fax: (212) 963-4116, http://unstats.un.org; *Statistical Yearbook.*

BRUNEI - MANPOWER

United Nations Statistics Division, New York, NY 10017, (800) 253-9646, Fax: (212) 963-4116, http://unstats.un.org; *Statistical Yearbook for Asia and the Pacific 2004.*

BRUNEI - MANUFACTURES

United Nations Statistics Division, New York, NY 10017, (800) 253-9646, Fax: (212) 963-4116, http://unstats.un.org; *Statistical Yearbook.*

BRUNEI - MARRIAGE

Taylor and Francis Group, An Informa Business, 2 Park Square, Milton Park, Abingdon, Oxford OX14 4RN, United Kingdom, (Dial from U.S. (212) 216-7800), (Fax from U.S. (212) 564-7854), www.tandf.co.uk; *The Europa World Year Book.*

United Nations Statistics Division, New York, NY 10017, (800) 253-9646, Fax: (212) 963-4116, http://unstats.un.org; *Demographic Yearbook* and *Statistical Yearbook.*

BRUNEI - MEAT PRODUCTION

See BRUNEI - LIVESTOCK

BRUNEI - MINERAL INDUSTRIES

Organisation for Economic Cooperation and Development (OECD), 2 rue Andre Pascal, F-75775 Paris Cedex 16, France, (Telephone in U.S. (202) 785-6323), (Fax in U.S. (202) 785-0350), www.oecd.org; *World Energy Outlook 2007.*

Palgrave Macmillan Ltd., Houndmills, Basingstoke, Hampshire, RG21 6XS, England, (Telephone in U.S. (888) 330-8477), (Fax in U.S. (800) 672-2054), www.palgrave.com; *The Statesman's Yearbook 2008.*

Taylor and Francis Group, An Informa Business, 2 Park Square, Milton Park, Abingdon, Oxford OX14 4RN, United Kingdom, (Dial from U.S. (212) 216-7800), (Fax from U.S. (212) 564-7854), www.tandf.co.uk; *The Europa World Year Book.*

United Nations Conference on Trade and Development (UNCTAD), DC2-1120, United Nations, New York, NY 10017, (212) 963-0027, www.unctad.org; *UNCTAD Commodity Yearbook.*

United Nations Statistics Division, New York, NY 10017, (800) 253-9646, Fax: (212) 963-4116, http://unstats.un.org; *Statistical Yearbook.*

BRUNEI - MONEY SUPPLY

Economist Intelligence Unit, 111 West 57th Street, New York, NY 10019, (212) 554-0600, Fax: (212) 586-1181, www.eiu.com; *Brunei Country Report.*

The World Bank, 1818 H Street, NW, Washington, DC 20433, (202) 473-1000, Fax: (202) 477-6391, www.worldbank.org; *Brunei Darussalam.*

BRUNEI - MORTALITY

Central Intelligence Agency, Office of Public Affairs, Washington, DC 20505, (703) 482-0623, Fax: (703) 482-1739, www.cia.gov; *The World Factbook.*

Euromonitor International, Inc., 224 S. Michigan Avenue, Suite 1500, Chicago, IL 60604, (312) 922-1115, Fax: (312) 922-1157, www.euromonitor.com; *International Marketing Data and Statistics 2008* and *The World Economic Factbook 2008.*

Palgrave Macmillan Ltd., Houndmills, Basingstoke, Hampshire, RG21 6XS, England, (Telephone in U.S. (888) 330-8477), (Fax in U.S. (800) 672-2054), www.palgrave.com; *The Statesman's Yearbook 2008.*

Taylor and Francis Group, An Informa Business, 2 Park Square, Milton Park, Abingdon, Oxford OX14 4RN, United Kingdom, (Dial from U.S. (212) 216-

7800), (Fax from U.S. (212) 564-7854), www.tandf.co.uk; *The Europa World Year Book.*

United Nations Statistics Division, New York, NY 10017, (800) 253-9646, Fax: (212) 963-4116, http://unstats.un.org; *Asia-Pacific in Figures 2004; Demographic Yearbook; Human Development Report 2006; Statistical Yearbook;* and *World Statistics Pocketbook.*

The World Bank, 1818 H Street, NW, Washington, DC 20433, (202) 473-1000, Fax: (202) 477-6391, www.worldbank.org; *The World Bank Atlas 2003-2004.*

World Health Organization (WHO), Avenue Appia 20, 1211 Geneve 27, Switzerland, (Telephone in U.S. (212) 331-9081), www.who.int; The WHO Global Atlas of Infectious Diseases and *World Health Report 2006.*

BRUNEI - MOTION PICTURES

UNESCO Institute for Statistics, C.P. 6128 Succursale Centre-Ville, Montreal, Quebec, H3C 3J7 Canada, (Dial from U.S. (514) 343-6880), (Fax from U.S. (514) 343 6882), www.uis.unesco.org; *Statistical Tables.*

United Nations Statistics Division, New York, NY 10017, (800) 253-9646, Fax: (212) 963-4116, http://unstats.un.org; *Statistical Yearbook.*

BRUNEI - MOTOR VEHICLES

Taylor and Francis Group, An Informa Business, 2 Park Square, Milton Park, Abingdon, Oxford OX14 4RN, United Kingdom, (Dial from U.S. (212) 216-7800), (Fax from U.S. (212) 564-7854), www.tandf.co.uk; *The Europa World Year Book.*

United Nations Statistics Division, New York, NY 10017, (800) 253-9646, Fax: (212) 963-4116, http://unstats.un.org; *Statistical Yearbook.*

BRUNEI - MUSEUMS

UNESCO Institute for Statistics, C.P. 6128 Succursale Centre-Ville, Montreal, Quebec, H3C 3J7 Canada, (Dial from U.S. (514) 343-6880), (Fax from U.S. (514) 343 6882), www.uis.unesco.org; *Statistical Tables.*

BRUNEI - NATURAL GAS PRODUCTION

See BRUNEI - MINERAL INDUSTRIES

BRUNEI - NUTRITION

United Nations Food and Agricultural Organization (FAO), Viale delle Terme di Caracalla, 00100 Rome, Italy, (Dial from U.S. (202) 653-2400), (Fax from U.S. (202) 653 5760), www.fao.org; *The State of Food and Agriculture (SOFA) 2006.*

BRUNEI - PAPER

See BRUNEI - FORESTS AND FORESTRY

BRUNEI - PERIODICALS

UNESCO Institute for Statistics, C.P. 6128 Succursale Centre-Ville, Montreal, Quebec, H3C 3J7 Canada, (Dial from U.S. (514) 343-6880), (Fax from U.S. (514) 343 6882), www.uis.unesco.org; *Statistical Tables.*

BRUNEI - PESTICIDES

United Nations Food and Agricultural Organization (FAO), Viale delle Terme di Caracalla, 00100 Rome, Italy, (Dial from U.S. (202) 653-2400), (Fax from U.S. (202) 653 5760), www.fao.org; *The State of Food and Agriculture (SOFA) 2006.*

BRUNEI - PETROLEUM INDUSTRY AND TRADE

Organisation for Economic Cooperation and Development (OECD), 2 rue Andre Pascal, F-75775 Paris Cedex 16, France, (Telephone in U.S. (202) 785-6323), (Fax in U.S. (202) 785-0350), www.oecd.org; *World Energy Outlook 2007.*

Palgrave Macmillan Ltd., Houndmills, Basingstoke, Hampshire, RG21 6XS, England, (Telephone in U.S. (888) 330-8477), (Fax in U.S. (800) 672-2054), www.palgrave.com; *The Statesman's Yearbook 2008.*

PennWell Corporation, 1421 South Sheridan Road, Tulsa, OK 74112, (918) 835-3161, www.pennwell.com; *International Petroleum Encyclopedia 2007.*

U.S. Department of Energy (DOE), Energy Information Administration (EIA), 1000 Independence Avenue, SW, Washington, DC 20585, (202) 586-8800, www.eia.doe.gov; *International Energy Annual 2004* and *International Energy Outlook 2006.*

United Nations Conference on Trade and Development (UNCTAD), DC2-1120, United Nations, New York, NY 10017, (212) 963-0027, www.unctad.org; *UNCTAD Commodity Yearbook.*

United Nations Food and Agricultural Organization (FAO), Viale delle Terme di Caracalla, 00100 Rome, Italy, (Dial from U.S. (202) 653-2400), (Fax from U.S. (202) 653 5760), www.fao.org; *The State of Food and Agriculture (SOFA) 2006.*

United Nations Statistics Division, New York, NY 10017, (800) 253-9646, Fax: (212) 963-4116, http://unstats.un.org; *Statistical Yearbook.*

BRUNEI - POLITICAL SCIENCE

Central Intelligence Agency, Office of Public Affairs, Washington, DC 20505, (703) 482-0623, Fax: (703) 482-1739, www.cia.gov; *The World Factbook.*

Palgrave Macmillan Ltd., Houndmills, Basingstoke, Hampshire, RG21 6XS, England, (Telephone in U.S. (888) 330-8477), (Fax in U.S. (800) 672-2054), www.palgrave.com; *The Statesman's Yearbook 2008.*

Taylor and Francis Group, An Informa Business, 2 Park Square, Milton Park, Abingdon, Oxford OX14 4RN, United Kingdom, (Dial from U.S. (212) 216-7800), (Fax from U.S. (212) 564-7854), www.tandf.co.uk; *The Europa World Year Book.*

United Nations Statistics Division, New York, NY 10017, (800) 253-9646, Fax: (212) 963-4116, http://unstats.un.org; *Asia-Pacific in Figures 2004* and *National Accounts Statistics: Compendium of Income Distribution Statistics.*

BRUNEI - POPULATION

Central Intelligence Agency, Office of Public Affairs, Washington, DC 20505, (703) 482-0623, Fax: (703) 482-1739, www.cia.gov; *The World Factbook.*

Economist Intelligence Unit, 111 West 57th Street, New York, NY 10019, (212) 554-0600, Fax: (212) 586-1181, www.eiu.com; *Brunei Country Report* and *Business Asia.*

Euromonitor International, Inc., 224 S. Michigan Avenue, Suite 1500, Chicago, IL 60604, (312) 922-1115, Fax: (312) 922-1157, www.euromonitor.com; *International Marketing Data and Statistics 2008* and *The World Economic Factbook 2008.*

International Labour Office, I.L.O. Publications, 4 route des Morillons, CH-1211 Geneva 22, Switzerland, (Telephone in U.S. (202) 653-7652), (Fax in U.S. (202) 653-7687), www.ilo.org; *Yearbook of Labour Statistics 2006.*

Palgrave Macmillan Ltd., Houndmills, Basingstoke, Hampshire, RG21 6XS, England, (Telephone in U.S. (888) 330-8477), (Fax in U.S. (800) 672-2054), www.palgrave.com; *The Statesman's Yearbook 2008.*

Taylor and Francis Group, An Informa Business, 2 Park Square, Milton Park, Abingdon, Oxford OX14 4RN, United Kingdom, (Dial from U.S. (212) 216-7800), (Fax from U.S. (212) 564-7854), www.tandf.co.uk; *The Europa World Year Book.*

UNESCO Institute for Statistics, C.P. 6128 Succursale Centre-Ville, Montreal, Quebec, H3C 3J7 Canada, (Dial from U.S. (514) 343-6880), (Fax from U.S. (514) 343 6882), www.uis.unesco.org; *Statistical Tables.*

United Nations Food and Agricultural Organization (FAO), Viale delle Terme di Caracalla, 00100 Rome, Italy, (Dial from U.S. (202) 653-2400), (Fax from U.S. (202) 653 5760), www.fao.org; *FAO Production Yearbook 2002.*

United Nations Statistics Division, New York, NY 10017, (800) 253-9646, Fax: (212) 963-4116, http://unstats.un.org; *Asia-Pacific in Figures 2004; Demographic Yearbook; Human Development Report 2006; Statistical Yearbook;* and *Statistical Yearbook for Asia and the Pacific 2004.*

The World Bank, 1818 H Street, NW, Washington, DC 20433, (202) 473-1000, Fax: (202) 477-6391, www.worldbank.org; *Brunei Darussalam* and *The World Bank Atlas 2003-2004.*

World Health Organization (WHO), Avenue Appia 20, 1211 Geneve 27, Switzerland, (Telephone in U.S. (212) 331-9081), www.who.int; *World Health Report 2006.*

Worldinformation.com, 2 Market Street, Saffron Walden, Essex CB10 1HZ, United Kingdom, www.worldinformation.com; The World of Information (www.worldinformation.com).

BRUNEI - POPULATION DENSITY

Central Intelligence Agency, Office of Public Affairs, Washington, DC 20505, (703) 482-0623, Fax: (703) 482-1739, www.cia.gov; *The World Factbook.*

Euromonitor International, Inc., 224 S. Michigan Avenue, Suite 1500, Chicago, IL 60604, (312) 922-1115, Fax: (312) 922-1157, www.euromonitor.com; *The World Economic Factbook 2008.*

Palgrave Macmillan Ltd., Houndmills, Basingstoke, Hampshire, RG21 6XS, England, (Telephone in U.S. (888) 330-8477), (Fax in U.S. (800) 672-2054), www.palgrave.com; *The Statesman's Yearbook 2008.*

Taylor and Francis Group, An Informa Business, 2 Park Square, Milton Park, Abingdon, Oxford OX14 4RN, United Kingdom, (Dial from U.S. (212) 216-7800), (Fax from U.S. (212) 564-7854), www.tandf.co.uk; *The Europa World Year Book.*

United Nations Food and Agricultural Organization (FAO), Viale delle Terme di Caracalla, 00100 Rome, Italy, (Dial from U.S. (202) 653-2400), (Fax from U.S. (202) 653 5760), www.fao.org; *The State of Food and Agriculture (SOFA) 2006.*

United Nations Statistics Division, New York, NY 10017, (800) 253-9646, Fax: (212) 963-4116, http://unstats.un.org; *Statistical Yearbook.*

The World Bank, 1818 H Street, NW, Washington, DC 20433, (202) 473-1000, Fax: (202) 477-6391, www.worldbank.org; *Brunei Darussalam.*

BRUNEI - POSTAL SERVICE

Palgrave Macmillan Ltd., Houndmills, Basingstoke, Hampshire, RG21 6XS, England, (Telephone in U.S. (888) 330-8477), (Fax in U.S. (800) 672-2054), www.palgrave.com; *The Statesman's Yearbook 2008.*

United Nations Statistics Division, New York, NY 10017, (800) 253-9646, Fax: (212) 963-4116, http://unstats.un.org; *Statistical Yearbook.*

BRUNEI - POWER RESOURCES

Euromonitor International, Inc., 224 S. Michigan Avenue, Suite 1500, Chicago, IL 60604, (312) 922-1115, Fax: (312) 922-1157, www.euromonitor.com; *International Marketing Data and Statistics 2008; The World Economic Factbook 2008;* and *World Marketing Data and Statistics.*

Organisation for Economic Cooperation and Development (OECD), 2 rue Andre Pascal, F-75775 Paris Cedex 16, France, (Telephone in U.S. (202) 785-6323), (Fax in U.S. (202) 785-0350), www.oecd.org; *World Energy Outlook 2007.*

Palgrave Macmillan Ltd., Houndmills, Basingstoke, Hampshire, RG21 6XS, England, (Telephone in U.S. (888) 330-8477), (Fax in U.S. (800) 672-2054), www.palgrave.com; *The Statesman's Yearbook 2008.*

Platts, 2 Penn Plaza, 25th Floor, New York, NY 10121-2298, (212) 904-3070, www.platts.com; *Energy Economist.*

U.S. Department of Energy (DOE), Energy Information Administration (EIA), 1000 Independence Avenue, SW, Washington, DC 20585, (202) 586-8800, www.eia.doe.gov; *International Energy Annual 2004* and *International Energy Outlook 2006.*

United Nations Food and Agricultural Organization (FAO), Viale delle Terme di Caracalla, 00100 Rome,

Italy, (Dial from U.S. (202) 653-2400), (Fax from U.S. (202) 653 5760), www.fao.org; *The State of Food and Agriculture (SOFA) 2006.*

United Nations Statistics Division, New York, NY 10017, (800) 253-9646, Fax: (212) 963-4116, http://unstats.un.org; *Asia-Pacific in Figures 2004; Energy Statistics Yearbook 2003; Human Development Report 2006; Statistical Yearbook for Asia and the Pacific 2004;* and *World Statistics Pocketbook.*

The World Bank, 1818 H Street, NW, Washington, DC 20433, (202) 473-1000, Fax: (202) 477-6391, www.worldbank.org; *The World Bank Atlas 2003-2004.*

BRUNEI - PRICES

Euromonitor International, Inc., 224 S. Michigan Avenue, Suite 1500, Chicago, IL 60604, (312) 922-1115, Fax: (312) 922-1157, www.euromonitor.com; *World Marketing Data and Statistics.*

International Labour Office, I.L.O. Publications, 4 route des Morillons, CH-1211 Geneva 22, Switzerland, (Telephone in U.S. (202) 653-7652), (Fax in U.S. (202) 653-7687), www.ilo.org; *Yearbook of Labour Statistics 2006.*

United Nations Food and Agricultural Organization (FAO), Viale delle Terme di Caracalla, 00100 Rome, Italy, (Dial from U.S. (202) 653-2400), (Fax from U.S. (202) 653 5760), www.fao.org; *FAO Production Yearbook 2002* and *The State of Food and Agriculture (SOFA) 2006.*

The World Bank, 1818 H Street, NW, Washington, DC 20433, (202) 473-1000, Fax: (202) 477-6391, www.worldbank.org; *Brunei Darussalam.*

BRUNEI - PROFESSIONS

UNESCO Institute for Statistics, C.P. 6128 Succursale Centre-Ville, Montreal, Quebec, H3C 3J7 Canada, (Dial from U.S. (514) 343-6880), (Fax from U.S. (514) 343 6882), www.uis.unesco.org; *Statistical Tables.*

United Nations Statistics Division, New York, NY 10017, (800) 253-9646, Fax: (212) 963-4116, http://unstats.un.org; *Statistical Yearbook.*

BRUNEI - PUBLIC HEALTH

Economist Intelligence Unit, 111 West 57th Street, New York, NY 10019, (212) 554-0600, Fax: (212) 586-1181, www.eiu.com; *Business Asia.*

Euromonitor International, Inc., 224 S. Michigan Avenue, Suite 1500, Chicago, IL 60604, (312) 922-1115, Fax: (312) 922-1157, www.euromonitor.com; *World Marketing Data and Statistics.*

Palgrave Macmillan Ltd., Houndmills, Basingstoke, Hampshire, RG21 6XS, England, (Telephone in U.S. (888) 330-8477), (Fax in U.S. (800) 672-2054), www.palgrave.com; *The Statesman's Yearbook 2008.*

United Nations Statistics Division, New York, NY 10017, (800) 253-9646, Fax: (212) 963-4116, http://unstats.un.org; *Asia-Pacific in Figures 2004; Human Development Report 2006;* and *Statistical Yearbook.*

The World Bank, 1818 H Street, NW, Washington, DC 20433, (202) 473-1000, Fax: (202) 477-6391, www.worldbank.org; *Brunei Darussalam.*

World Health Organization (WHO), Avenue Appia 20, 1211 Geneve 27, Switzerland, (Telephone in U.S. (212) 331-9081), www.who.int; The WHO Global Atlas of Infectious Diseases and *World Health Report 2006.*

BRUNEI - PUBLISHERS AND PUBLISHING

Taylor and Francis Group, An Informa Business, 2 Park Square, Milton Park, Abingdon, Oxford OX14 4RN, United Kingdom, (Dial from U.S. (212) 216-7800), (Fax from U.S. (212) 564-7854), www.tandf.co.uk; *The Europa World Year Book.*

UNESCO Institute for Statistics, C.P. 6128 Succursale Centre-Ville, Montreal, Quebec, H3C 3J7 Canada, (Dial from U.S. (514) 343-6880), (Fax from U.S. (514) 343 6882), www.uis.unesco.org; *Statistical Tables.*

BRUNEI - RADIO BROADCASTING

Palgrave Macmillan Ltd., Houndmills, Basingstoke, Hampshire, RG21 6XS, England, (Telephone in U.S. (888) 330-8477), (Fax in U.S. (800) 672-2054), www.palgrave.com; *The Statesman's Yearbook 2008.*

BRUNEI - RELIGION

Central Intelligence Agency, Office of Public Affairs, Washington, DC 20505, (703) 482-0623, Fax: (703) 482-1739, www.cia.gov; *The World Factbook.*

Palgrave Macmillan Ltd., Houndmills, Basingstoke, Hampshire, RG21 6XS, England, (Telephone in U.S. (888) 330-8477), (Fax in U.S. (800) 672-2054), www.palgrave.com; *The Statesman's Yearbook 2008.*

BRUNEI - RENT CHARGES

International Labour Office, I.L.O. Publications, 4 route des Morillons, CH-1211 Geneva 22, Switzerland, (Telephone in U.S. (202) 653-7652), (Fax in U.S. (202) 653-7687), www.ilo.org; *Yearbook of Labour Statistics 2006.*

BRUNEI - RETAIL TRADE

Euromonitor International, Inc., 224 S. Michigan Avenue, Suite 1500, Chicago, IL 60604, (312) 922-1115, Fax: (312) 922-1157, www.euromonitor.com; *World Marketing Data and Statistics.*

BRUNEI - RICE PRODUCTION

See BRUNEI - CROPS

BRUNEI - ROADS

Central Intelligence Agency, Office of Public Affairs, Washington, DC 20505, (703) 482-0623, Fax: (703) 482-1739, www.cia.gov; *The World Factbook.*

Economist Intelligence Unit, 111 West 57th Street, New York, NY 10019, (212) 554-0600, Fax: (212) 586-1181, www.eiu.com; *Business Asia.*

Palgrave Macmillan Ltd., Houndmills, Basingstoke, Hampshire, RG21 6XS, England, (Telephone in U.S. (888) 330-8477), (Fax in U.S. (800) 672-2054), www.palgrave.com; *The Statesman's Yearbook 2008.*

BRUNEI - SHIPPING

Taylor and Francis Group, An Informa Business, 2 Park Square, Milton Park, Abingdon, Oxford OX14 4RN, United Kingdom, (Dial from U.S. (212) 216-7800), (Fax from U.S. (212) 564-7854), www.tandf.co.uk; *The Europa World Year Book.*

United Nations Statistics Division, New York, NY 10017, (800) 253-9646, Fax: (212) 963-4116, http://unstats.un.org; *Statistical Yearbook.*

BRUNEI - SOCIAL ECOLOGY

United Nations Statistics Division, New York, NY 10017, (800) 253-9646, Fax: (212) 963-4116, http://unstats.un.org; *World Statistics Pocketbook.*

BRUNEI - SOCIAL SECURITY

United Nations Statistics Division, New York, NY 10017, (800) 253-9646, Fax: (212) 963-4116, http://unstats.un.org; *National Accounts Statistics: Compendium of Income Distribution Statistics.*

BRUNEI - TELEPHONE

Economist Intelligence Unit, 111 West 57th Street, New York, NY 10019, (212) 554-0600, Fax: (212) 586-1181, www.eiu.com; *Business Asia.*

International Telecommunication Union (ITU), Place des Nations, 1211 Geneva 20, Switzerland, www.itu.int; World Telecommunication Indicators Database.

Taylor and Francis Group, An Informa Business, 2 Park Square, Milton Park, Abingdon, Oxford OX14 4RN, United Kingdom, (Dial from U.S. (212) 216-7800), (Fax from U.S. (212) 564-7854), www.tandf.co.uk; *The Europa World Year Book.*

United Nations Statistics Division, New York, NY 10017, (800) 253-9646, Fax: (212) 963-4116, http://unstats.un.org; *World Statistics Pocketbook.*

BRUNEI - TEXTILE INDUSTRY

United Nations Conference on Trade and Development (UNCTAD), DC2-1120, United Nations, New York, NY 10017, (212) 963-0027, www.unctad.org; *UNCTAD Commodity Yearbook.*

BRUNEI - THEATER

UNESCO Institute for Statistics, C.P. 6128 Succursale Centre-Ville, Montreal, Quebec, H3C 3J7 Canada, (Dial from U.S. (514) 343-6880), (Fax from U.S. (514) 343 6882), www.uis.unesco.org; *Statistical Tables.*

BRUNEI - TOURISM

Euromonitor International, Inc., 224 S. Michigan Avenue, Suite 1500, Chicago, IL 60604, (312) 922-1115, Fax: (312) 922-1157, www.euromonitor.com; *The World Economic Factbook 2008* and *World Marketing Data and Statistics.*

Palgrave Macmillan Ltd., Houndmills, Basingstoke, Hampshire, RG21 6XS, England, (Telephone in U.S. (888) 330-8477), (Fax in U.S. (800) 672-2054), www.palgrave.com; *The Statesman's Yearbook 2008.*

Taylor and Francis Group, An Informa Business, 2 Park Square, Milton Park, Abingdon, Oxford OX14 4RN, United Kingdom, (Dial from U.S. (212) 216-7800), (Fax from U.S. (212) 564-7854), www.tandf.co.uk; *The Europa World Year Book.*

United Nations World Tourism Organization (UNWTO), Capitan Haya 42, 28020 Madrid, Spain, www.world-tourism.org; *Yearbook of Tourism Statistics.*

The World Bank, 1818 H Street, NW, Washington, DC 20433, (202) 473-1000, Fax: (202) 477-6391, www.worldbank.org; *Brunei Darussalam.*

BRUNEI - TRADE

See BRUNEI - INTERNATIONAL TRADE

BRUNEI - TRANSPORTATION

Central Intelligence Agency, Office of Public Affairs, Washington, DC 20505, (703) 482-0623, Fax: (703) 482-1739, www.cia.gov; *The World Factbook.*

Economist Intelligence Unit, 111 West 57th Street, New York, NY 10019, (212) 554-0600, Fax: (212) 586-1181, www.eiu.com; *Business Asia.*

Euromonitor International, Inc., 224 S. Michigan Avenue, Suite 1500, Chicago, IL 60604, (312) 922-1115, Fax: (312) 922-1157, www.euromonitor.com; *International Marketing Data and Statistics 2008* and *World Marketing Data and Statistics.*

Taylor and Francis Group, An Informa Business, 2 Park Square, Milton Park, Abingdon, Oxford OX14 4RN, United Kingdom, (Dial from U.S. (212) 216-7800), (Fax from U.S. (212) 564-7854), www.tandf.co.uk; *The Europa World Year Book.*

United Nations Statistics Division, New York, NY 10017, (800) 253-9646, Fax: (212) 963-4116, http://unstats.un.org; *Human Development Report 2006* and *Statistical Yearbook for Asia and the Pacific 2004.*

The World Bank, 1818 H Street, NW, Washington, DC 20433, (202) 473-1000, Fax: (202) 477-6391, www.worldbank.org; *Brunei Darussalam.*

BRUNEI - UNEMPLOYMENT

Central Intelligence Agency, Office of Public Affairs, Washington, DC 20505, (703) 482-0623, Fax: (703) 482-1739, www.cia.gov; *The World Factbook.*

International Labour Office, I.L.O. Publications, 4 route des Morillons, CH-1211 Geneva 22, Switzerland, (Telephone in U.S. (202) 653-7652), (Fax in U.S. (202) 653-7687), www.ilo.org; *Yearbook of Labour Statistics 2006.*

United Nations Statistics Division, New York, NY 10017, (800) 253-9646, Fax: (212) 963-4116, http://unstats.un.org; *Statistical Yearbook.*

BRUNEI - VITAL STATISTICS

Palgrave Macmillan Ltd., Houndmills, Basingstoke, Hampshire, RG21 6XS, England, (Telephone in U.S.

(888) 330-8477), (Fax in U.S. (800) 672-2054), www.palgrave.com; *The Statesman's Yearbook 2008.*

United Nations Statistics Division, New York, NY 10017, (800) 253-9646, Fax: (212) 963-4116, http://unstats.un.org; *Statistical Yearbook.*

World Health Organization (WHO), Avenue Appia 20, 1211 Geneve 27, Switzerland, (Telephone in U.S. (212) 331-9081), www.who.int; *World Health Report 2006.*

BRUNEI - WAGES

International Labour Office, I.L.O. Publications, 4 route des Morillons, CH-1211 Geneva 22, Switzerland, (Telephone in U.S. (202) 653-7652), (Fax in U.S. (202) 653-7687), www.ilo.org; *Yearbook of Labour Statistics 2006.*

United Nations Statistics Division, New York, NY 10017, (800) 253-9646, Fax: (212) 963-4116, http://unstats.un.org; *Statistical Yearbook* and *Statistical Yearbook for Asia and the Pacific 2004.*

The World Bank, 1818 H Street, NW, Washington, DC 20433, (202) 473-1000, Fax: (202) 477-6391, www.worldbank.org; *Brunei Darussalam.*

BRUNEI - ZOOS

UNESCO Institute for Statistics, C.P. 6128 Succursale Centre-Ville, Montreal, Quebec, H3C 3J7 Canada, (Dial from U.S. (514) 343-6880), (Fax from U.S. (514) 343 6882), www.uis.unesco.org; *Statistical Tables.*

BUDDHIST POPULATION

See RELIGION

BUDGET, FEDERAL - OUTLAYS

The Office of Management and Budget (OMB), 725 17th Street, NW, Washington, DC 20503, (202) 395-3080, Fax: (202) 395-3888, www.whitehouse.gov/omb; *Budget of the United States Government, Federal Year 2009* and *Historical Tables.*

BUDGET, FEDERAL - RECEIPTS

The Office of Management and Budget (OMB), 725 17th Street, NW, Washington, DC 20503, (202) 395-3080, Fax: (202) 395-3888, www.whitehouse.gov/omb; *Historical Tables.*

BUDGET, FEDERAL - REVENUE LOSSES (TAX EXPENDITURES)

The Office of Management and Budget (OMB), 725 17th Street, NW, Washington, DC 20503, (202) 395-3080, Fax: (202) 395-3888, www.whitehouse.gov/omb; *Budget of the United States Government, Federal Year 2009.*

BUDGET, FEDERAL - TAX EXPENDITURES

The Office of Management and Budget (OMB), 725 17th Street, NW, Washington, DC 20503, (202) 395-3080, Fax: (202) 395-3888, www.whitehouse.gov/omb; *Budget of the United States Government, Federal Year 2009.*

BUDGET, FEDERAL - TAXES

The Office of Management and Budget (OMB), 725 17th Street, NW, Washington, DC 20503, (202) 395-3080, Fax: (202) 395-3888, www.whitehouse.gov/omb; *Budget of the United States Government, Federal Year 2009* and *Historical Tables.*

BUDGET, FEDERAL - TRUST FUNDS

The Office of Management and Budget (OMB), 725 17th Street, NW, Washington, DC 20503, (202) 395-3080, Fax: (202) 395-3888, www.whitehouse.gov/omb; *Analytical Perspectives, Budget of the United States Government, Fiscal Year 2009* and *Budget of the United States Government, Federal Year 2009.*

BUILDING CONTRACTORS, GENERAL - EARNINGS

U.S. Bureau of Labor Statistics (BLS), Postal Square Building, 2 Massachusetts Avenue, NE, Washington, DC 20212-0001, (202) 691-5200, Fax: (202) 691-6325, www.bls.gov; *Current Employment Statistics Survey (CES)* and *Employment and Earnings (EE).*

U.S. Census Bureau, Center for Economic Studies, 4600 Silver Hill Road, Washington DC 20233, (301) 457-1235, www.ces.census.gov; *2002 Economic Census, Construction.*

U.S. Census Bureau, Company Statistics Division, 4700 Silver Hill Road, Washington DC 20233-0001, (301) 763-3030, www.census.gov/csd/; *County Business Patterns 2004.*

BUILDING CONTRACTORS, GENERAL - EMPLOYEES

U.S. Bureau of Labor Statistics (BLS), Postal Square Building, 2 Massachusetts Avenue, NE, Washington, DC 20212-0001, (202) 691-5200, Fax: (202) 691-6325, www.bls.gov; *Current Employment Statistics Survey (CES)* and *Employment and Earnings (EE).*

U.S. Census Bureau, Center for Economic Studies, 4600 Silver Hill Road, Washington DC 20233, (301) 457-1235, www.ces.census.gov; *2002 Economic Census, Construction.*

U.S. Census Bureau, Company Statistics Division, 4700 Silver Hill Road, Washington DC 20233-0001, (301) 763-3030, www.census.gov/csd/; *County Business Patterns 2004.*

BUILDING CONTRACTORS, GENERAL - ESTABLISHMENTS

U.S. Census Bureau, Center for Economic Studies, 4600 Silver Hill Road, Washington DC 20233, (301) 457-1235, www.ces.census.gov; *2002 Economic Census, Construction.*

U.S. Census Bureau, Company Statistics Division, 4700 Silver Hill Road, Washington DC 20233-0001, (301) 763-3030, www.census.gov/csd/; *County Business Patterns 2004.*

BUILDING CONTRACTORS, GENERAL - INDUSTRIAL SAFETY

U.S. Bureau of Labor Statistics (BLS), Postal Square Building, 2 Massachusetts Avenue, NE, Washington, DC 20212-0001, (202) 691-5200, Fax: (202) 691-6325, www.bls.gov; *Injuries, Illnesses, and Fatalities (IIF).*

BUILDING CONTRACTORS, GENERAL - VALUE OF WORK

U.S. Census Bureau, Center for Economic Studies, 4600 Silver Hill Road, Washington DC 20233, (301) 457-1235, www.ces.census.gov; *2002 Economic Census, Construction.*

BUILDING MATERIALS AND GARDEN SUPPLIES, RETAIL STORES

Office of Trade and Industry Information (OTII), Manufacturing and Services, International Trade Administration, U.S. Department of Commerce, 1401 Constitution Ave, NW, Washington, DC 20230, (800) USA TRAD(E), http://trade.gov/index.asp; *TradeStats Express.*

U.S. Census Bureau, Center for Economic Studies, 4600 Silver Hill Road, Washington DC 20233, (301) 457-1235, www.ces.census.gov; *2002 Economic Census, Retail Trade* and *2002 Economic Census, Wholesale Trade.*

U.S. Census Bureau, Company Statistics Division, 4700 Silver Hill Road, Washington DC 20233-0001, (301) 763-3030, www.census.gov/csd/; *County Business Patterns 2004.*

BUILDING MATERIALS AND GARDEN SUPPLIES, RETAIL STORES - EARNINGS

Office of Trade and Industry Information (OTII), Manufacturing and Services, International Trade Administration, U.S. Department of Commerce, 1401 Constitution Ave, NW, Washington, DC 20230, (800) USA TRAD(E), http://trade.gov/index.asp; *TradeStats Express.*

U.S. Census Bureau, Center for Economic Studies, 4600 Silver Hill Road, Washington DC 20233, (301) 457-1235, www.ces.census.gov; *2002 Economic Census, Retail Trade* and *2002 Economic Census, Wholesale Trade.*

U.S. Census Bureau, Company Statistics Division, 4700 Silver Hill Road, Washington DC 20233-0001, (301) 763-3030, www.census.gov/csd/; *County Business Patterns 2004.*

BUILDING MATERIALS AND GARDEN SUPPLIES, RETAIL STORES - EMPLOYEES

U.S. Census Bureau, Center for Economic Studies, 4600 Silver Hill Road, Washington DC 20233, (301) 457-1235, www.ces.census.gov; *2002 Economic Census, Retail Trade* and *2002 Economic Census, Wholesale Trade.*

U.S. Census Bureau, Company Statistics Division, 4700 Silver Hill Road, Washington DC 20233-0001, (301) 763-3030, www.census.gov/csd/; *County Business Patterns 2004.*

BUILDING MATERIALS AND GARDEN SUPPLIES, RETAIL STORES - INVENTORIES

Office of Trade and Industry Information (OTII), Manufacturing and Services, International Trade Administration, U.S. Department of Commerce, 1401 Constitution Ave, NW, Washington, DC 20230, (800) USA TRAD(E), http://trade.gov/index.asp; *TradeStats Express.*

U.S. Census Bureau, 4700 Silver Hill Road, Washington DC 20233-0001, (301) 763-3030, www.census.gov; unpublished data.

U.S. Census Bureau, Center for Economic Studies, 4600 Silver Hill Road, Washington DC 20233, (301) 457-1235, www.ces.census.gov; *2002 Economic Census, Retail Trade* and *2002 Economic Census, Wholesale Trade.*

U.S. Census Bureau, Company Statistics Division, 4700 Silver Hill Road, Washington DC 20233-0001, (301) 763-3030, www.census.gov/csd/; *Current Business Reports.*

BUILDING MATERIALS AND GARDEN SUPPLIES, RETAIL STORES - NONEMPLOYERS

U.S. Census Bureau, 4700 Silver Hill Road, Washington DC 20233-0001, (301) 763-3030, www.census.gov; *2002 Economic Census, Nonemployer Statistics.*

BUILDING MATERIALS AND GARDEN SUPPLIES, RETAIL STORES - PRODUCTIVITY

U.S. Bureau of Labor Statistics (BLS), Postal Square Building, 2 Massachusetts Avenue, NE, Washington, DC 20212-0001, (202) 691-5200, Fax: (202) 691-6325, www.bls.gov; *Industry Productivity and Costs.*

BUILDING MATERIALS AND GARDEN SUPPLIES, RETAIL STORES - PURCHASES

Office of Trade and Industry Information (OTII), Manufacturing and Services, International Trade Administration, U.S. Department of Commerce, 1401 Constitution Ave, NW, Washington, DC 20230, (800) USA TRAD(E), http://trade.gov/index.asp; *TradeStats Express.*

U.S. Census Bureau, 4700 Silver Hill Road, Washington DC 20233-0001, (301) 763-3030, www.census.gov; unpublished data.

U.S. Census Bureau, Center for Economic Studies, 4600 Silver Hill Road, Washington DC 20233, (301) 457-1235, www.ces.census.gov; *2002 Economic Census, Retail Trade* and *2002 Economic Census, Wholesale Trade.*

U.S. Census Bureau, Company Statistics Division, 4700 Silver Hill Road, Washington DC 20233-0001, (301) 763-3030, www.census.gov/csd/; *Current Business Reports.*

BUILDING MATERIALS AND GARDEN SUPPLIES, RETAIL STORES - SALES

Claritas, 5375 Mira Sorrento Place, Suite 400, San Diego, CA 92121, (800) 866-6520, Fax: (858) 550-5800, www.claritas.com; *Consumer Buying Power.*

Office of Trade and Industry Information (OTII), Manufacturing and Services, International Trade Administration, U.S. Department of Commerce, 1401 Constitution Ave, NW, Washington, DC 20230, (800) USA TRAD(E), http://trade.gov/index.asp; *TradeStats Express.*

U.S. Census Bureau, 4700 Silver Hill Road, Washington DC 20233-0001, (301) 763-3030, www.census.gov; unpublished data.

U.S. Census Bureau, Center for Economic Studies, 4600 Silver Hill Road, Washington DC 20233, (301) 457-1235, www.ces.census.gov; *2002 Economic Census, Retail Trade* and *2002 Economic Census, Wholesale Trade.*

U.S. Census Bureau, Company Statistics Division, 4700 Silver Hill Road, Washington DC 20233-0001, (301) 763-3030, www.census.gov/csd/; *Current Business Reports.*

BUILDING PERMITS

See CONSTRUCTION INDUSTRY - BUILDING PERMITS - VALUE

BUILDINGS

See also CONSTRUCTION INDUSTRY

McGraw-Hill Construction, Dodge Analytics, 1221 Avenue of The Americas, Manhattan, NY 10020, (800) 393-6343, http://dodge.construction.com/analytics; *Green Building SmartMarket Report 2006.*

BUILDINGS - CONSTRUCTION VALUE

U.S. Census Bureau, Manufacturing and Construction Division, 4600 Silver Hill Road, Washington DC 20233, (301) 763-4673, www.census.gov/mcd; *Current Construction Reports* and *Value of New Construction Put in Place.*

BUILDINGS - CORRECTIONAL FACILITIES

U.S. Department of Justice (DOJ), Bureau of Justice Statistics, 810 Seventh Street, NW, Washington, DC 20531, (202) 307-0765, www.ojp.usdoj.gov/bjs/; *Census of State and Federal Correctional Facilities* and *Jails in Indian Country, 2003.*

BUILDINGS - FEDERAL

General Services Administration (GSA), 1800 F Street, NW, Washington, DC 20405, (202) 708-5082, www.gsa.gov; *Federal Real Property Profile 2004 (FRPP).*

BUILDINGS - FIRE AND PROPERTY LOSS

National Fire Protection Association (NFPA), One Batterymarch Park, Quincy, MA 02169-7471, (617) 770-3000, Fax: (617) 770-0700, www.nfpa.org; *Fire statistics.*

BUILDINGS - FLOOR SPACE

General Services Administration (GSA), 1800 F Street, NW, Washington, DC 20405, (202) 708-5082, www.gsa.gov; *Federal Real Property Profile 2004 (FRPP).*

BUILDINGS - OFFICE VACANCY RATE

ONCOR International, 1 Campus Drive, Parsippany, NJ 07054, (973) 407-6363, Fax: (973) 407-4666, www.oncorintl.com; *North American Office Market Report.*

Society of Industrial and Office Realtors, 1201 New York Avenue, NW, Suite 350, Washington, DC 20005-6126, (202) 449-8200, Fax: (202) 216-9325, www.sior.com; *Comparative Statistics of Industrial and Office Real Estate Markets 2005.*

BULGARIA - NATIONAL STATISTICAL OFFICE

National Statistical Insitute (NSI), 2, P. Volov Street, 1038 Sofia, Bulgaria, www.nsi.bg; National Data Center.

BULGARIA - PRIMARY STATISTICS SOURCES

Eurostat, Batiment Jean Monnet, Rue Alcide de Gasperi, L-2920 Luxembourg, http://epp.eurostat.ec.europa.eu; *Pocketbook on Candidate and Potential Candidate Countries.*

National Statistical Insitute (NSI), 2, P. Volov Street, 1038 Sofia, Bulgaria, www.nsi.bg; *Statistical Reference Book 2008; Statistical Yearbook of the Republic of Bulgaria 2006;* and *Statistics Journal 2007.*

BULGARIA - ABORTION

United Nations Statistics Division, New York, NY 10017, (800) 253-9646, Fax: (212) 963-4116, http://unstats.un.org; *Trends in Europe and North America: The Statistical Yearbook of the ECE 2005.*

BULGARIA - AGRICULTURAL MACHINERY

United Nations Statistics Division, New York, NY 10017, (800) 253-9646, Fax: (212) 963-4116, http://unstats.un.org; *Statistical Yearbook.*

BULGARIA - AGRICULTURE

Economist Intelligence Unit, 111 West 57th Street, New York, NY 10019, (212) 554-0600, Fax: (212) 586-1181, www.eiu.com; *Bulgaria Country Report.*

Euromonitor International, Inc., 224 S. Michigan Avenue, Suite 1500, Chicago, IL 60604, (312) 922-1115, Fax: (312) 922-1157, www.euromonitor.com; *World Marketing Data and Statistics.*

Eurostat, Batiment Jean Monnet, Rue Alcide de Gasperi, L-2920 Luxembourg, http://epp.eurostat.ec.europa.eu; *EU Agricultural Prices in 2007.*

M.E. Sharpe, 80 Business Park Drive, Armonk, NY 10504, (800) 541-6563, Fax: (914) 273-2106, www.mesharpe.com; *The Illustrated Book of World Rankings.*

Palgrave Macmillan Ltd., Houndmills, Basingstoke, Hampshire, RG21 6XS, England, (Telephone in U.S. (888) 330-8477), (Fax in U.S. (800) 672-2054), www.palgrave.com; *The Statesman's Yearbook 2008.*

Taylor and Francis Group, An Informa Business, 2 Park Square, Milton Park, Abingdon, Oxford OX14 4RN, United Kingdom, (Dial from U.S. (212) 216-7800), (Fax from U.S. (212) 564-7854), www.tandf.co.uk; *The Europa World Year Book.*

United Nations Conference on Trade and Development (UNCTAD), DC2-1120, United Nations, New York, NY 10017, (212) 963-0027, www.unctad.org; *UNCTAD Commodity Yearbook.*

United Nations Food and Agricultural Organization (FAO), Viale delle Terme di Caracalla, 00100 Rome, Italy, (Dial from U.S. (202) 653-2400), (Fax from U.S. (202) 653 5760), www.fao.org; AQUASTAT; *FAO Production Yearbook 2002; FAO Trade Yearbook;* and *The State of Food and Agriculture (SOFA) 2006.*

United Nations Statistics Division, New York, NY 10017, (800) 253-9646, Fax: (212) 963-4116, http://unstats.un.org; *Statistical Yearbook.*

The World Bank, 1818 H Street, NW, Washington, DC 20433, (202) 473-1000, Fax: (202) 477-6391, www.worldbank.org; *Bulgaria.*

BULGARIA - AIRLINES

Eurostat, Batiment Jean Monnet, Rue Alcide de Gasperi, L-2920 Luxembourg, http://epp.eurostat.ec.europa.eu; *Regional Passenger and Freight Air Transport in Europe in 2006.*

M.E. Sharpe, 80 Business Park Drive, Armonk, NY 10504, (800) 541-6563, Fax: (914) 273-2106, www.mesharpe.com; *The Illustrated Book of World Rankings.*

Palgrave Macmillan Ltd., Houndmills, Basingstoke, Hampshire, RG21 6XS, England, (Telephone in U.S. (888) 330-8477), (Fax in U.S. (800) 672-2054), www.palgrave.com; *The Statesman's Yearbook 2008.*

Taylor and Francis Group, An Informa Business, 2 Park Square, Milton Park, Abingdon, Oxford OX14 4RN, United Kingdom, (Dial from U.S. (212) 216-7800), (Fax from U.S. (212) 564-7854), www.tandf.co.uk; *The Europa World Year Book.*

United Nations Statistics Division, New York, NY 10017, (800) 253-9646, Fax: (212) 963-4116, http://unstats.un.org; *Statistical Yearbook.*

BULGARIA - AIRPORTS

Central Intelligence Agency, Office of Public Affairs, Washington, DC 20505, (703) 482-0623, Fax: (703) 482-1739, www.cia.gov; *The World Factbook.*

BULGARIA - ALMOND PRODUCTION

See BULGARIA - CROPS

BULGARIA - ALUMINUM PRODUCTION

See BULGARIA - MINERAL INDUSTRIES

BULGARIA - ARMED FORCES

Central Intelligence Agency, Office of Public Affairs, Washington, DC 20505, (703) 482-0623, Fax: (703) 482-1739, www.cia.gov; *The World Factbook.*

Euromonitor International, Inc., 224 S. Michigan Avenue, Suite 1500, Chicago, IL 60604, (312) 922-1115, Fax: (312) 922-1157, www.euromonitor.com; *World Marketing Data and Statistics.*

International Institute for Strategic Studies (IISS), Arundel House, 13-15 Arundel Street, Temple Place, London WC2R 3DX, England, www.iiss.org; *The Military Balance 2007.*

Palgrave Macmillan Ltd., Houndmills, Basingstoke, Hampshire, RG21 6XS, England, (Telephone in U.S. (888) 330-8477), (Fax in U.S. (800) 672-2054), www.palgrave.com; *The Statesman's Yearbook 2008.*

United Nations Statistics Division, New York, NY 10017, (800) 253-9646, Fax: (212) 963-4116, http://unstats.un.org; *Human Development Report 2006.*

BULGARIA - AUTOMOBILE INDUSTRY AND TRADE

United Nations Statistics Division, New York, NY 10017, (800) 253-9646, Fax: (212) 963-4116, http://unstats.un.org; *Statistical Yearbook.*

BULGARIA - BALANCE OF PAYMENTS

United Nations Conference on Trade and Development (UNCTAD), DC2-1120, United Nations, New York, NY 10017, (212) 963-0027, www.unctad.org; *Handbook of Statistics 2005.*

The World Bank, 1818 H Street, NW, Washington, DC 20433, (202) 473-1000, Fax: (202) 477-6391, www.worldbank.org; *Bulgaria* and *World Development Report 2008.*

BULGARIA - BANKS AND BANKING

Euromonitor International, Inc., 224 S. Michigan Avenue, Suite 1500, Chicago, IL 60604, (312) 922-1115, Fax: (312) 922-1157, www.euromonitor.com; *World Marketing Data and Statistics.*

European Union, Delegation of the European Commission to the United States, 2300 M Street, NW, Washington, DC 20037, (202) 862-9500, Fax: (202) 429-1766, www.eurunion.org; *The EU Economy, 2007 Review: Moving Europe's Productivity Frontier.*

M.E. Sharpe, 80 Business Park Drive, Armonk, NY 10504, (800) 541-6563, Fax: (914) 273-2106, www.mesharpe.com; *The Illustrated Book of World Rankings.*

Palgrave Macmillan Ltd., Houndmills, Basingstoke, Hampshire, RG21 6XS, England, (Telephone in U.S. (888) 330-8477), (Fax in U.S. (800) 672-2054), www.palgrave.com; *The Statesman's Yearbook 2008.*

BULGARIA - BARLEY PRODUCTION

See BULGARIA - CROPS

BULGARIA - BEVERAGE INDUSTRY

M.E. Sharpe, 80 Business Park Drive, Armonk, NY 10504, (800) 541-6563, Fax: (914) 273-2106, www.mesharpe.com; *The Illustrated Book of World Rankings.*

United Nations Statistics Division, New York, NY 10017, (800) 253-9646, Fax: (212) 963-4116, http://unstats.un.org; *Statistical Yearbook.*

BULGARIA - BROADCASTING

Central Intelligence Agency, Office of Public Affairs, Washington, DC 20505, (703) 482-0623, Fax: (703) 482-1739, www.cia.gov; *The World Factbook.*

Euromonitor International, Inc., 224 S. Michigan Avenue, Suite 1500, Chicago, IL 60604, (312) 922-1115, Fax: (312) 922-1157, www.euromonitor.com; *World Marketing Data and Statistics.*

M.E. Sharpe, 80 Business Park Drive, Armonk, NY 10504, (800) 541-6563, Fax: (914) 273-2106, www.mesharpe.com; *The Illustrated Book of World Rankings.*

Palgrave Macmillan Ltd., Houndmills, Basingstoke, Hampshire, RG21 6XS, England, (Telephone in U.S. (888) 330-8477), (Fax in U.S. (800) 672-2054), www.palgrave.com; *The Statesman's Yearbook 2008.*

United Nations Statistics Division, New York, NY 10017, (800) 253-9646, Fax: (212) 963-4116, http://unstats.un.org; *Trends in Europe and North America: The Statistical Yearbook of the ECE 2005.*

WRTH Publications Limited, PO Box 290, Oxford OX2 7FT, UK, www.wrth.com; *World Radio TV Handbook 2007.*

BULGARIA - BUDGET

Central Intelligence Agency, Office of Public Affairs, Washington, DC 20505, (703) 482-0623, Fax: (703) 482-1739, www.cia.gov; *The World Factbook.*

Eurostat, Batiment Jean Monnet, Rue Alcide de Gasperi, L-2920 Luxembourg, http://epp.eurostat.ec.europa.eu; *Government Budgets.*

BULGARIA - BUSINESS

Economist Intelligence Unit, 111 West 57th Street, New York, NY 10019, (212) 554-0600, Fax: (212) 586-1181, www.eiu.com; *Business Eastern Europe.*

United Nations Statistics Division, New York, NY 10017, (800) 253-9646, Fax: (212) 963-4116, http://unstats.un.org; *Statistical Yearbook.*

BULGARIA - CATTLE

See BULGARIA - LIVESTOCK

BULGARIA - CHICK PEA PRODUCTION

See BULGARIA - CROPS

BULGARIA - CHILDBIRTH - STATISTICS

Central Intelligence Agency, Office of Public Affairs, Washington, DC 20505, (703) 482-0623, Fax: (703) 482-1739, www.cia.gov; *The World Factbook.*

Euromonitor International, Inc., 224 S. Michigan Avenue, Suite 1500, Chicago, IL 60604, (312) 922-1115, Fax: (312) 922-1157, www.euromonitor.com; *The World Economic Factbook 2008.*

M.E. Sharpe, 80 Business Park Drive, Armonk, NY 10504, (800) 541-6563, Fax: (914) 273-2106, www.mesharpe.com; *The Illustrated Book of World Rankings.*

Palgrave Macmillan Ltd., Houndmills, Basingstoke, Hampshire, RG21 6XS, England, (Telephone in U.S. (888) 330-8477), (Fax in U.S. (800) 672-2054), www.palgrave.com; *The Statesman's Yearbook 2008.*

Taylor and Francis Group, An Informa Business, 2 Park Square, Milton Park, Abingdon, Oxford OX14 4RN, United Kingdom, (Dial from U.S. (212) 216-7800), (Fax from U.S. (212) 564-7854), www.tandf.co.uk; *The Europa World Year Book.*

United Nations Statistics Division, New York, NY 10017, (800) 253-9646, Fax: (212) 963-4116, http://unstats.un.org; *Demographic Yearbook* and *Statistical Yearbook.*

World Health Organization (WHO), Avenue Appia 20, 1211 Geneve 27, Switzerland, (Telephone in U.S. (212) 331-9081), www.who.int; *World Health Report 2006.*

BULGARIA - CLIMATE

M.E. Sharpe, 80 Business Park Drive, Armonk, NY 10504, (800) 541-6563, Fax: (914) 273-2106, www.mesharpe.com; *The Illustrated Book of World Rankings.*

Palgrave Macmillan Ltd., Houndmills, Basingstoke, Hampshire, RG21 6XS, England, (Telephone in U.S. (888) 330-8477), (Fax in U.S. (800) 672-2054), www.palgrave.com; *The Statesman's Yearbook 2008.*

BULGARIA - COAL PRODUCTION

See BULGARIA - MINERAL INDUSTRIES

BULGARIA - COFFEE

See BULGARIA - CROPS

BULGARIA - COMMERCE

Palgrave Macmillan Ltd., Houndmills, Basingstoke, Hampshire, RG21 6XS, England, (Telephone in U.S. (888) 330-8477), (Fax in U.S. (800) 672-2054), www.palgrave.com; *The Statesman's Yearbook 2008.*

BULGARIA - COMMODITY EXCHANGES

Commodity Research Bureau, 330 South Wells Street, Suite 612, Chicago, IL 60606-7110, (800) 621-5271, Fax: (312) 939-4135, www.crbtrader.com; *2006 CRB Commodity Yearbook and CD.*

International Lead and Zinc Study Group (ILZSG), Rua Almirante Barroso 38, 5th Floor, Lisbon 1000 - 013, Portugal, www.ilzsg.org; Interactive Statistical Database.

International Monetary Fund (IMF), 700 Nineteenth Street, NW, Washington, DC 20431, (202) 623-7000, Fax: (202) 623-4661, www.imf.org; *IMF Primary Commodity Prices.*

United Nations Food and Agricultural Organization (FAO), Viale delle Terme di Caracalla, 00100 Rome, Italy, (Dial from U.S. (202) 653-2400), (Fax from U.S. (202) 653 5760), www.fao.org; *The State of Food and Agriculture (SOFA) 2006.*

BULGARIA - COMMUNICATION AND TRAFFIC

United Nations Statistics Division, New York, NY 10017, (800) 253-9646, Fax: (212) 963-4116, http://unstats.un.org; *Statistical Yearbook.*

BULGARIA - CONSTRUCTION INDUSTRY

M.E. Sharpe, 80 Business Park Drive, Armonk, NY 10504, (800) 541-6563, Fax: (914) 273-2106, www.mesharpe.com; *The Illustrated Book of World Rankings.*

Palgrave Macmillan Ltd., Houndmills, Basingstoke, Hampshire, RG21 6XS, England, (Telephone in U.S. (888) 330-8477), (Fax in U.S. (800) 672-2054), www.palgrave.com; *The Statesman's Yearbook 2008.*

United Nations Statistics Division, New York, NY 10017, (800) 253-9646, Fax: (212) 963-4116, http://unstats.un.org; *Statistical Yearbook.*

BULGARIA - CONSUMER PRICE INDEXES

Taylor and Francis Group, An Informa Business, 2 Park Square, Milton Park, Abingdon, Oxford OX14 4RN, United Kingdom, (Dial from U.S. (212) 216-7800), (Fax from U.S. (212) 564-7854), www.tandf.co.uk; *The Europa World Year Book.*

United Nations Statistics Division, New York, NY 10017, (800) 253-9646, Fax: (212) 963-4116, http://unstats.un.org; *Statistical Yearbook* and *Trends in Europe and North America: The Statistical Yearbook of the ECE 2005.*

The World Bank, 1818 H Street, NW, Washington, DC 20433, (202) 473-1000, Fax: (202) 477-6391, www.worldbank.org; *Bulgaria.*

BULGARIA - CONSUMPTION (ECONOMICS)

International Lead and Zinc Study Group (ILZSG), Rua Almirante Barroso 38, 5th Floor, Lisbon 1000 - 013, Portugal, www.ilzsg.org; Interactive Statistical Database.

The World Bank, 1818 H Street, NW, Washington, DC 20433, (202) 473-1000, Fax: (202) 477-6391, www.worldbank.org; *World Development Report 2008.*

BULGARIA - COPPER INDUSTRY AND TRADE

See BULGARIA - MINERAL INDUSTRIES

BULGARIA - CORN INDUSTRY

See BULGARIA - CROPS

BULGARIA - COTTON

See BULGARIA - CROPS

BULGARIA - CRIME

Eurostat, Batiment Jean Monnet, Rue Alcide de Gasperi, L-2920 Luxembourg, http://epp.eurostat.ec.europa.eu; *Crime and Criminal Justice; General Government Expenditure and Revenue in the EU, 2006;* and *Study on Crime Victimisation.*

U.S. Department of Justice (DOJ), Bureau of Justice Statistics, 810 Seventh Street, NW, Washington, DC 20531, (202) 307-0765, www.ojp.usdoj.gov/bjs/; *The World Factbook of Criminal Justice Systems.*

United Nations Statistics Division, New York, NY 10017, (800) 253-9646, Fax: (212) 963-4116, http://unstats.un.org; *Trends in Europe and North America: The Statistical Yearbook of the ECE 2005.*

Yale University Press, PO Box 209040, New Haven, CT 06520-9040, (203) 432-0960, Fax: (203) 432-0948, http://yalepress.yale.edu/yupbooks; *Violence and Crime in Cross-National Perspective.*

BULGARIA - CROPS

Euromonitor International, Inc., 224 S. Michigan Avenue, Suite 1500, Chicago, IL 60604, (312) 922-1115, Fax: (312) 922-1157, www.euromonitor.com; *European Marketing Data and Statistics 2008.*

M.E. Sharpe, 80 Business Park Drive, Armonk, NY 10504, (800) 541-6563, Fax: (914) 273-2106, www.mesharpe.com; *The Illustrated Book of World Rankings.*

Palgrave Macmillan Ltd., Houndmills, Basingstoke, Hampshire, RG21 6XS, England, (Telephone in U.S. (888) 330-8477), (Fax in U.S. (800) 672-2054), www.palgrave.com; *The Statesman's Yearbook 2008.*

Taylor and Francis Group, An Informa Business, 2 Park Square, Milton Park, Abingdon, Oxford OX14 4RN, United Kingdom, (Dial from U.S. (212) 216-7800), (Fax from U.S. (212) 564-7854), www.tandf.co.uk; *The Europa World Year Book.*

United Nations Conference on Trade and Development (UNCTAD), DC2-1120, United Nations, New York, NY 10017, (212) 963-0027, www.unctad.org; *UNCTAD Commodity Yearbook.*

United Nations Food and Agricultural Organization (FAO), Viale delle Terme di Caracalla, 00100 Rome, Italy, (Dial from U.S. (202) 653-2400), (Fax from U.S. (202) 653 5760), www.fao.org; *The State of Food and Agriculture (SOFA) 2006.*

BULGARIA - CUSTOMS ADMINISTRATION

Palgrave Macmillan Ltd., Houndmills, Basingstoke, Hampshire, RG21 6XS, England, (Telephone in U.S.

(888) 330-8477), (Fax in U.S. (800) 672-2054), www.palgrave.com; *The Statesman's Yearbook 2008.*

BULGARIA - DAIRY PROCESSING

M.E. Sharpe, 80 Business Park Drive, Armonk, NY 10504, (800) 541-6563, Fax: (914) 273-2106, www.mesharpe.com; *The Illustrated Book of World Rankings.*

Palgrave Macmillan Ltd., Houndmills, Basingstoke, Hampshire, RG21 6XS, England, (Telephone in U.S. (888) 330-8477), (Fax in U.S. (800) 672-2054), www.palgrave.com; *The Statesman's Yearbook 2008.*

Taylor and Francis Group, An Informa Business, 2 Park Square, Milton Park, Abingdon, Oxford OX14 4RN, United Kingdom, (Dial from U.S. (212) 216-7800), (Fax from U.S. (212) 564-7854), www.tandf.co.uk; *The Europa World Year Book.*

United Nations Food and Agricultural Organization (FAO), Viale delle Terme di Caracalla, 00100 Rome, Italy, (Dial from U.S. (202) 653-2400), (Fax from U.S. (202) 653 5760), www.fao.org; *FAO Production Yearbook 2002* and *The State of Food and Agriculture (SOFA) 2006.*

United Nations Statistics Division, New York, NY 10017, (800) 253-9646, Fax: (212) 963-4116, http://unstats.un.org; *Statistical Yearbook.*

BULGARIA - DEATH RATES

See BULGARIA - MORTALITY

BULGARIA - DEBTS, EXTERNAL

Palgrave Macmillan Ltd., Houndmills, Basingstoke, Hampshire, RG21 6XS, England, (Telephone in U.S. (888) 330-8477), (Fax in U.S. (800) 672-2054), www.palgrave.com; *The Statesman's Yearbook 2008.*

The World Bank, 1818 H Street, NW, Washington, DC 20433, (202) 473-1000, Fax: (202) 477-6391, www.worldbank.org; *Global Development Finance 2007* and *World Development Report 2008.*

BULGARIA - DEMOGRAPHY

Euromonitor International, Inc., 224 S. Michigan Avenue, Suite 1500, Chicago, IL 60604, (312) 922-1115, Fax: (312) 922-1157, www.euromonitor.com; *World Marketing Data and Statistics.*

Eurostat, Batiment Jean Monnet, Rue Alcide de Gasperi, L-2920 Luxembourg, http://epp.eurostat.ec.europa.eu; *Demographic Outlook - National Reports on the Demographic Developments in 2006.*

M.E. Sharpe, 80 Business Park Drive, Armonk, NY 10504, (800) 541-6563, Fax: (914) 273-2106, www.mesharpe.com; *The Illustrated Book of World Rankings.*

National Statistical Insitute (NSI), 2, P. Volov Street, 1038 Sofia, Bulgaria, www.nsi.bg; *Bulgaria 2006: Social-Economic Development* and *Population and Demographic Processes 2006.*

United Nations Statistics Division, New York, NY 10017, (800) 253-9646, Fax: (212) 963-4116, http://unstats.un.org; *Human Development Report 2006.*

The World Bank, 1818 H Street, NW, Washington, DC 20433, (202) 473-1000, Fax: (202) 477-6391, www.worldbank.org; *Bulgaria.*

BULGARIA - DIAMONDS

See BULGARIA - MINERAL INDUSTRIES

BULGARIA - DISPOSABLE INCOME

M.E. Sharpe, 80 Business Park Drive, Armonk, NY 10504, (800) 541-6563, Fax: (914) 273-2106, www.mesharpe.com; *The Illustrated Book of World Rankings.*

United Nations Statistics Division, New York, NY 10017, (800) 253-9646, Fax: (212) 963-4116, http://unstats.un.org; *National Accounts Statistics: Compendium of Income Distribution Statistics* and *Statistical Yearbook.*

BULGARIA - DIVORCE

M.E. Sharpe, 80 Business Park Drive, Armonk, NY 10504, (800) 541-6563, Fax: (914) 273-2106, www.mesharpe.com; *The Illustrated Book of World Rankings.*

United Nations Statistics Division, New York, NY 10017, (800) 253-9646, Fax: (212) 963-4116, http://unstats.un.org; *Demographic Yearbook; Statistical Yearbook;* and *Trends in Europe and North America: The Statistical Yearbook of the ECE 2005.*

BULGARIA - ECONOMIC ASSISTANCE

United Nations Statistics Division, New York, NY 10017, (800) 253-9646, Fax: (212) 963-4116, http://unstats.un.org; *Statistical Yearbook.*

BULGARIA - ECONOMIC CONDITIONS

Center for International Business Education Research (CIBER), Columbia Business School and School of International and Public Affairs, Uris Hall, Room 212, 3022 Broadway, New York, NY 10027-6902, Mr. Joshua Safier, (212) 854-4750, Fax: (212) 222-9821, www.columbia.edu/cu/ciber/; Datastream International.

Central Intelligence Agency, Office of Public Affairs, Washington, DC 20505, (703) 482-0623, Fax: (703) 482-1739, www.cia.gov; *The World Factbook.*

DSI Data Service Information, Xantener Strasse 51a, D-47495 Rheinberg, Germany, www.dsidata.com; *Campus Solution.*

Dun and Bradstreet (DB) Corporation, 103 JFK Parkway, Short Hills, NJ 07078, (973) 921-5500, www.dnb.com; *Country Report.*

Economist Intelligence Unit, 111 West 57th Street, New York, NY 10019, (212) 554-0600, Fax: (212) 586-1181, www.eiu.com; *Bulgaria Country Report.*

Euromonitor International, Inc., 224 S. Michigan Avenue, Suite 1500, Chicago, IL 60604, (312) 922-1115, Fax: (312) 922-1157, www.euromonitor.com; *European Marketing Data and Statistics 2008; The World Economic Factbook 2008;* and *World Marketing Data and Statistics.*

European Union, Delegation of the European Commission to the United States, 2300 M Street, NW, Washington, DC 20037, (202) 862-9500, Fax: (202) 429-1766, www.eurunion.org; *The EU Economy, 2007 Review: Moving Europe's Productivity Frontier.*

Eurostat, Batiment Jean Monnet, Rue Alcide de Gasperi, L-2920 Luxembourg, http://epp.eurostat.ec.europa.eu; *Consumers in Europe - Facts and Figures on Services of General Interest* and *EU Economic Data Pocketbook.*

Federal Statistical Office Germany, D-65180 Wiesbaden, Germany, www.destatis.de; *Bulgaria 2006.*

International Monetary Fund (IMF), 700 Nineteenth Street, NW, Washington, DC 20431, (202) 623-7000, Fax: (202) 623-4661, www.imf.org; *World Economic Outlook Reports.*

M.E. Sharpe, 80 Business Park Drive, Armonk, NY 10504, (800) 541-6563, Fax: (914) 273-2106, www.mesharpe.com; *The Illustrated Book of World Rankings.*

National Statistical Insitute (NSI), 2, P. Volov Street, 1038 Sofia, Bulgaria, www.nsi.bg; *Bulgaria - The Challenges of Poverty* and *Bulgaria 2006: Social-Economic Development.*

Palgrave Macmillan Ltd., Houndmills, Basingstoke, Hampshire, RG21 6XS, England, (Telephone in U.S. (888) 330-8477), (Fax in U.S. (800) 672-2054), www.palgrave.com; *The Statesman's Yearbook 2008.*

Taylor and Francis Group, An Informa Business, 2 Park Square, Milton Park, Abingdon, Oxford OX14 4RN, United Kingdom, (Dial from U.S. (212) 216-7800), (Fax from U.S. (212) 564-7854), www.tandf.co.uk; *The Europa World Year Book.*

United Nations Statistics Division, New York, NY 10017, (800) 253-9646, Fax: (212) 963-4116, http://unstats.un.org; *World Statistics Pocketbook.*

The World Bank, 1818 H Street, NW, Washington, DC 20433, (202) 473-1000, Fax: (202) 477-6391, www.worldbank.org; *Bulgaria; Global Economic Monitor (GEM); Global Economic Prospects 2008; The World Bank Atlas 2003-2004;* and *World Development Report 2008.*

BULGARIA - EDUCATION

Euromonitor International, Inc., 224 S. Michigan Avenue, Suite 1500, Chicago, IL 60604, (312) 922-1115, Fax: (312) 922-1157, www.euromonitor.com; *European Marketing Data and Statistics 2008* and *World Marketing Data and Statistics.*

European Union, Delegation of the European Commission to the United States, 2300 M Street, NW, Washington, DC 20037, (202) 862-9500, Fax: (202) 429-1766, www.eurunion.org; *Education across Europe 2003.*

Eurostat, Batiment Jean Monnet, Rue Alcide de Gasperi, L-2920 Luxembourg, http://epp.eurostat.ec.europa.eu; *Education, Science and Culture Statistics.*

M.E. Sharpe, 80 Business Park Drive, Armonk, NY 10504, (800) 541-6563, Fax: (914) 273-2106, www.mesharpe.com; *The Illustrated Book of World Rankings.*

National Statistical Insitute (NSI), 2, P. Volov Street, 1038 Sofia, Bulgaria, www.nsi.bg; *Education in the Republic of Bulgaria 2007.*

Palgrave Macmillan Ltd., Houndmills, Basingstoke, Hampshire, RG21 6XS, England, (Telephone in U.S. (888) 330-8477), (Fax in U.S. (800) 672-2054), www.palgrave.com; *The Statesman's Yearbook 2008.*

Taylor and Francis Group, An Informa Business, 2 Park Square, Milton Park, Abingdon, Oxford OX14 4RN, United Kingdom, (Dial from U.S. (212) 216-7800), (Fax from U.S. (212) 564-7854), www.tandf.co.uk; *The Europa World Year Book.*

UNESCO Institute for Statistics, C.P. 6128 Succursale Centre-Ville, Montreal, Quebec, H3C 3J7 Canada, (Dial from U.S. (514) 343-6880), (Fax from U.S. (514) 343 6882), www.uis.unesco.org; *Statistical Tables.*

United Nations Statistics Division, New York, NY 10017, (800) 253-9646, Fax: (212) 963-4116, http://unstats.un.org; *Human Development Report 2006* and *Trends in Europe and North America: The Statistical Yearbook of the ECE 2005.*

The World Bank, 1818 H Street, NW, Washington, DC 20433, (202) 473-1000, Fax: (202) 477-6391, www.worldbank.org; *Bulgaria* and *World Development Report 2008.*

BULGARIA - EGGPLANT PRODUCTION

See BULGARIA - CROPS

BULGARIA - ELECTRICITY

Eurostat, Batiment Jean Monnet, Rue Alcide de Gasperi, L-2920 Luxembourg, http://epp.eurostat.ec.europa.eu; *Energy - Monthly Statistics* and *Panorama of Energy - 2007 Edition.*

M.E. Sharpe, 80 Business Park Drive, Armonk, NY 10504, (800) 541-6563, Fax: (914) 273-2106, www.mesharpe.com; *The Illustrated Book of World Rankings.*

Organisation for Economic Cooperation and Development (OECD), 2 rue Andre Pascal, F-75775 Paris Cedex 16, France, (Telephone in U.S. (202) 785-6323), (Fax in U.S. (202) 785-0350), www.oecd.org; *World Energy Outlook 2007.*

Palgrave Macmillan Ltd., Houndmills, Basingstoke, Hampshire, RG21 6XS, England, (Telephone in U.S. (888) 330-8477), (Fax in U.S. (800) 672-2054), www.palgrave.com; *The Statesman's Yearbook 2008.*

Platts, 2 Penn Plaza, 25th Floor, New York, NY 10121-2298, (212) 904-3070, www.platts.com; *EU Energy* and *European Electricity Review 2004.*

U.S. Department of Energy (DOE), Energy Information Administration (EIA), 1000 Independence Avenue, SW, Washington, DC 20585, (202) 586-8800, www.eia.doe.gov; *International Energy Annual 2004* and *International Energy Outlook 2006.*

United Nations Statistics Division, New York, NY 10017, (800) 253-9646, Fax: (212) 963-4116, http://unstats.un.org; *Human Development Report 2006; Statistical Yearbook;* and *Trends in Europe and North America: The Statistical Yearbook of the ECE 2005.*

BULGARIA - EMPLOYMENT

Euromonitor International, Inc., 224 S. Michigan Avenue, Suite 1500, Chicago, IL 60604, (312) 922-1115, Fax: (312) 922-1157, www.euromonitor.com; *European Marketing Data and Statistics 2008.*

International Labour Office, I.L.O. Publications, 4 route des Morillons, CH-1211 Geneva 22, Switzerland, (Telephone in U.S. (202) 653-7652), (Fax in U.S. (202) 653-7687), www.ilo.org; *Yearbook of Labour Statistics 2006.*

M.E. Sharpe, 80 Business Park Drive, Armonk, NY 10504, (800) 541-6563, Fax: (914) 273-2106, www.mesharpe.com; *The Illustrated Book of World Rankings.*

United Nations Statistics Division, New York, NY 10017, (800) 253-9646, Fax: (212) 963-4116, http://unstats.un.org; *Statistical Yearbook* and *Trends in Europe and North America: The Statistical Yearbook of the ECE 2005.*

The World Bank, 1818 H Street, NW, Washington, DC 20433, (202) 473-1000, Fax: (202) 477-6391, www.worldbank.org; *Bulgaria.*

BULGARIA - ENERGY INDUSTRIES

Enerdata, 10 Rue Royale, 75008 Paris, France, www.enerdata.fr; *Global Energy Market Data.*

Eurostat, Batiment Jean Monnet, Rue Alcide de Gasperi, L-2920 Luxembourg, http://epp.eurostat.ec.europa.eu; *Energy - Monthly Statistics* and *Panorama of Energy - 2007 Edition.*

Platts, 2 Penn Plaza, 25th Floor, New York, NY 10121-2298, (212) 904-3070, www.platts.com; *Energy in East Europe; EU Energy;* and *European Power Daily.*

United Nations Statistics Division, New York, NY 10017, (800) 253-9646, Fax: (212) 963-4116, http://unstats.un.org; *Statistical Yearbook.*

BULGARIA - ENVIRONMENTAL CONDITIONS

Center for Research on the Epidemiology of Disasters (CRED), Universite Catholique de Louvain, Ecole de Sante Publique, 30.94 Clos Chapelle-aux-Champs, 1200 Brussels, Belgium, www.cred.be; *Three Decades of Floods in Europe: A Preliminary Analysis of EMDAT Data.*

DSI Data Service Information, Xantener Strasse 51a, D-47495 Rheinberg, Germany, www.dsidata.com; *Campus Solution* and *DSI's Global Environmental Database.*

Economist Intelligence Unit, 111 West 57th Street, New York, NY 10019, (212) 554-0600, Fax: (212) 586-1181, www.eiu.com; *Bulgaria Country Report.*

Eurostat, Batiment Jean Monnet, Rue Alcide de Gasperi, L-2920 Luxembourg, http://epp.eurostat.ec.europa.eu; *Environmental Protection Expenditure in Europe.*

Federal Statistical Office Germany, D-65180 Wiesbaden, Germany, www.destatis.de; *Bulgaria 2006.*

United Nations Statistics Division, New York, NY 10017, (800) 253-9646, Fax: (212) 963-4116, http://unstats.un.org; *Trends in Europe and North America: The Statistical Yearbook of the ECE 2005* and *World Statistics Pocketbook.*

BULGARIA - EXPENDITURES, PUBLIC

Eurostat, Batiment Jean Monnet, Rue Alcide de Gasperi, L-2920 Luxembourg, http://epp.eurostat.ec.europa.eu; *European Social Statistics - Social Protection Expenditure and Receipts - Data 1997-2005.*

BULGARIA - EXPORTS

Central Intelligence Agency, Office of Public Affairs, Washington, DC 20505, (703) 482-0623, Fax: (703) 482-1739, www.cia.gov; *The World Factbook.*

Economist Intelligence Unit, 111 West 57th Street, New York, NY 10019, (212) 554-0600, Fax: (212) 586-1181, www.eiu.com; *Bulgaria Country Report.*

Euromonitor International, Inc., 224 S. Michigan Avenue, Suite 1500, Chicago, IL 60604, (312) 922-1115, Fax: (312) 922-1157, www.euromonitor.com; *The World Economic Factbook 2008.*

International Lead and Zinc Study Group (ILZSG), Rua Almirante Barroso 38, 5th Floor, Lisbon 1000 - 013, Portugal, www.ilzsg.org; Interactive Statistical Database.

International Monetary Fund (IMF), 700 Nineteenth Street, NW, Washington, DC 20431, (202) 623-7000, Fax: (202) 623-4661, www.imf.org; *Direction of Trade Statistics Yearbook 2007.*

Palgrave Macmillan Ltd., Houndmills, Basingstoke, Hampshire, RG21 6XS, England, (Telephone in U.S. (888) 330-8477), (Fax in U.S. (800) 672-2054), www.palgrave.com; *The Statesman's Yearbook 2008.*

Taylor and Francis Group, An Informa Business, 2 Park Square, Milton Park, Abingdon, Oxford OX14 4RN, United Kingdom, (Dial from U.S. (212) 216-7800), (Fax from U.S. (212) 564-7854), www.tandf.co.uk; *The Europa World Year Book.*

United Nations Conference on Trade and Development (UNCTAD), DC2-1120, United Nations, New York, NY 10017, (212) 963-0027, www.unctad.org; *Handbook of Statistics 2005.*

United Nations Food and Agricultural Organization (FAO), Viale delle Terme di Caracalla, 00100 Rome, Italy, (Dial from U.S. (202) 653-2400), (Fax from U.S. (202) 653 5760), www.fao.org; *The State of Food and Agriculture (SOFA) 2006.*

United Nations Statistics Division, New York, NY 10017, (800) 253-9646, Fax: (212) 963-4116, http://unstats.un.org; *Trends in Europe and North America: The Statistical Yearbook of the ECE 2005.*

The World Bank, 1818 H Street, NW, Washington, DC 20433, (202) 473-1000, Fax: (202) 477-6391, www.worldbank.org; *World Development Report 2008.*

BULGARIA - FERTILITY, HUMAN

Central Intelligence Agency, Office of Public Affairs, Washington, DC 20505, (703) 482-0623, Fax: (703) 482-1739, www.cia.gov; *The World Factbook.*

M.E. Sharpe, 80 Business Park Drive, Armonk, NY 10504, (800) 541-6563, Fax: (914) 273-2106, www.mesharpe.com; *The Illustrated Book of World Rankings.*

United Nations Statistics Division, New York, NY 10017, (800) 253-9646, Fax: (212) 963-4116, http://unstats.un.org; *Human Development Report 2006* and *Trends in Europe and North America: The Statistical Yearbook of the ECE 2005.*

The World Bank, 1818 H Street, NW, Washington, DC 20433, (202) 473-1000, Fax: (202) 477-6391, www.worldbank.org; *The World Bank Atlas 2003-2004* and *World Development Report 2008.*

BULGARIA - FERTILIZER INDUSTRY

United Nations Food and Agricultural Organization (FAO), Viale delle Terme di Caracalla, 00100 Rome, Italy, (Dial from U.S. (202) 653-2400), (Fax from U.S. (202) 653 5760), www.fao.org; *FAO Fertilizer Yearbook* and *The State of Food and Agriculture (SOFA) 2006.*

United Nations Statistics Division, New York, NY 10017, (800) 253-9646, Fax: (212) 963-4116, http://unstats.un.org; *Statistical Yearbook.*

BULGARIA - FETAL MORTALITY

See BULGARIA - MORTALITY

BULGARIA - FILM

See BULGARIA - MOTION PICTURES

BULGARIA - FINANCE

Taylor and Francis Group, An Informa Business, 2 Park Square, Milton Park, Abingdon, Oxford OX14 4RN, United Kingdom, (Dial from U.S. (212) 216-7800), (Fax from U.S. (212) 564-7854), www.tandf.co.uk; *The Europa World Year Book.*

United Nations Statistics Division, New York, NY 10017, (800) 253-9646, Fax: (212) 963-4116, http://unstats.un.org; *National Accounts Statistics: Compendium of Income Distribution Statistics* and *Statistical Yearbook.*

The World Bank, 1818 H Street, NW, Washington, DC 20433, (202) 473-1000, Fax: (202) 477-6391, www.worldbank.org; *Bulgaria.*

BULGARIA - FINANCE, PUBLIC

Bernan Essential Government Publications, 4611-F Assembly Drive, Lanham MD, 20706-4391, (301) 459-2255, Fax: (800) 865-3450, www.bernan.com; *National Accounts Statistics.*

Economist Intelligence Unit, 111 West 57th Street, New York, NY 10019, (212) 554-0600, Fax: (212) 586-1181, www.eiu.com; *Bulgaria Country Report.*

International Monetary Fund (IMF), 700 Nineteenth Street, NW, Washington, DC 20431, (202) 623-7000, Fax: (202) 623-4661, www.imf.org; *International Financial Statistics; International Financial Statistics Online Service;* and *International Financial Statistics Yearbook 2007.*

M.E. Sharpe, 80 Business Park Drive, Armonk, NY 10504, (800) 541-6563, Fax: (914) 273-2106, www.mesharpe.com; *The Illustrated Book of World Rankings.*

Palgrave Macmillan Ltd., Houndmills, Basingstoke, Hampshire, RG21 6XS, England, (Telephone in U.S. (888) 330-8477), (Fax in U.S. (800) 672-2054), www.palgrave.com; *The Statesman's Yearbook 2008.*

Taylor and Francis Group, An Informa Business, 2 Park Square, Milton Park, Abingdon, Oxford OX14 4RN, United Kingdom, (Dial from U.S. (212) 216-7800), (Fax from U.S. (212) 564-7854), www.tandf.co.uk; *The Europa World Year Book.*

The World Bank, 1818 H Street, NW, Washington, DC 20433, (202) 473-1000, Fax: (202) 477-6391, www.worldbank.org; *Bulgaria.*

BULGARIA - FISHERIES

Euromonitor International, Inc., 224 S. Michigan Avenue, Suite 1500, Chicago, IL 60604, (312) 922-1115, Fax: (312) 922-1157, www.euromonitor.com; *European Marketing Data and Statistics 2008.*

M.E. Sharpe, 80 Business Park Drive, Armonk, NY 10504, (800) 541-6563, Fax: (914) 273-2106, www.mesharpe.com; *The Illustrated Book of World Rankings.*

Taylor and Francis Group, An Informa Business, 2 Park Square, Milton Park, Abingdon, Oxford OX14 4RN, United Kingdom, (Dial from U.S. (212) 216-7800), (Fax from U.S. (212) 564-7854), www.tandf.co.uk; *The Europa World Year Book.*

United Nations Conference on Trade and Development (UNCTAD), DC2-1120, United Nations, New York, NY 10017, (212) 963-0027, www.unctad.org; *UNCTAD Commodity Yearbook.*

United Nations Food and Agricultural Organization (FAO), Viale delle Terme di Caracalla, 00100 Rome, Italy, (Dial from U.S. (202) 653-2400), (Fax from U.S. (202) 653 5760), www.fao.org; *FAO Yearbook of Fishery Statistics;* Fishery Databases; FISHSTAT Database. Subjects covered include: Aquaculture production, capture production, fishery commodities; and *The State of Food and Agriculture (SOFA) 2006.*

United Nations Statistics Division, New York, NY 10017, (800) 253-9646, Fax: (212) 963-4116, http://unstats.un.org; *Statistical Yearbook.*

The World Bank, 1818 H Street, NW, Washington, DC 20433, (202) 473-1000, Fax: (202) 477-6391, www.worldbank.org; *Bulgaria.*

BULGARIA - FLOUR INDUSTRY

United Nations Statistics Division, New York, NY 10017, (800) 253-9646, Fax: (212) 963-4116, http://unstats.un.org; *Statistical Yearbook.*

BULGARIA - FOOD

Euromonitor International, Inc., 224 S. Michigan Avenue, Suite 1500, Chicago, IL 60604, (312) 922-

1115, Fax: (312) 922-1157, www.euromonitor.com; *Retail Trade International 2007.*

United Nations Conference on Trade and Development (UNCTAD), DC2-1120, United Nations, New York, NY 10017, (212) 963-0027, www.unctad.org; *UNCTAD Commodity Yearbook.*

United Nations Food and Agricultural Organization (FAO), Viale delle Terme di Caracalla, 00100 Rome, Italy, (Dial from U.S. (202) 653-2400), (Fax from U.S. (202) 653 5760), www.fao.org; *FAO Production Yearbook 2002* and *The State of Food and Agriculture (SOFA) 2006.*

United Nations Statistics Division, New York, NY 10017, (800) 253-9646, Fax: (212) 963-4116, http://unstats.un.org; *Human Development Report 2006.*

BULGARIA - FOREIGN EXCHANGE RATES

Central Intelligence Agency, Office of Public Affairs, Washington, DC 20505, (703) 482-0623, Fax: (703) 482-1739, www.cia.gov; *The World Factbook.*

Euromonitor International, Inc., 224 S. Michigan Avenue, Suite 1500, Chicago, IL 60604, (312) 922-1115, Fax: (312) 922-1157, www.euromonitor.com; *The World Economic Factbook 2008.*

Taylor and Francis Group, An Informa Business, 2 Park Square, Milton Park, Abingdon, Oxford OX14 4RN, United Kingdom, (Dial from U.S. (212) 216-7800), (Fax from U.S. (212) 564-7854), www.tandf.co.uk; *The Europa World Year Book.*

United Nations Statistics Division, New York, NY 10017, (800) 253-9646, Fax: (212) 963-4116, http://unstats.un.org; *Statistical Yearbook; Trends in Europe and North America: The Statistical Yearbook of the ECE 2005;* and *World Statistics Pocketbook.*

BULGARIA - FORESTS AND FORESTRY

Euromonitor International, Inc., 224 S. Michigan Avenue, Suite 1500, Chicago, IL 60604, (312) 922-1115, Fax: (312) 922-1157, www.euromonitor.com; *European Marketing Data and Statistics 2008.*

M.E. Sharpe, 80 Business Park Drive, Armonk, NY 10504, (800) 541-6563, Fax: (914) 273-2106, www.mesharpe.com; *The Illustrated Book of World Rankings.*

Palgrave Macmillan Ltd., Houndmills, Basingstoke, Hampshire, RG21 6XS, England, (Telephone in U.S. (888) 330-8477), (Fax in U.S. (800) 672-2054), www.palgrave.com; *The Statesman's Yearbook 2008.*

Taylor and Francis Group, An Informa Business, 2 Park Square, Milton Park, Abingdon, Oxford OX14 4RN, United Kingdom, (Dial from U.S. (212) 216-7800), (Fax from U.S. (212) 564-7854), www.tandf.co.uk; *The Europa World Year Book.*

UNESCO Institute for Statistics, C.P. 6128 Succursale Centre-Ville, Montreal, Quebec, H3C 3J7 Canada, (Dial from U.S. (514) 343-6880), (Fax from U.S. (514) 343 6882), www.uis.unesco.org; *Statistical Tables.*

United Nations Conference on Trade and Development (UNCTAD), DC2-1120, United Nations, New York, NY 10017, (212) 963-0027, www.unctad.org; *UNCTAD Commodity Yearbook.*

United Nations Food and Agricultural Organization (FAO), Viale delle Terme di Caracalla, 00100 Rome, Italy, (Dial from U.S. (202) 653-2400), (Fax from U.S. (202) 653 5760), www.fao.org; *FAO Yearbook of Forest Products* and *The State of Food and Agriculture (SOFA) 2006.*

United Nations Statistics Division, New York, NY 10017, (800) 253-9646, Fax: (212) 963-4116, http://unstats.un.org; *Statistical Yearbook* and *Trends in Europe and North America: The Statistical Yearbook of the ECE 2005.*

The World Bank, 1818 H Street, NW, Washington, DC 20433, (202) 473-1000, Fax: (202) 477-6391, www.worldbank.org; *Bulgaria* and *World Development Report 2008.*

BULGARIA - GAS PRODUCTION

See BULGARIA - MINERAL INDUSTRIES

BULGARIA - GEOGRAPHIC INFORMATION SYSTEMS

M.E. Sharpe, 80 Business Park Drive, Armonk, NY 10504, (800) 541-6563, Fax: (914) 273-2106, www.mesharpe.com; *The Illustrated Book of World Rankings.*

The World Bank, 1818 H Street, NW, Washington, DC 20433, (202) 473-1000, Fax: (202) 477-6391, www.worldbank.org; *Bulgaria.*

BULGARIA - GOLD PRODUCTION

See BULGARIA - MINERAL INDUSTRIES

BULGARIA - GREEN PEPPER AND CHILIE PRODUCTION

See BULGARIA - CROPS

BULGARIA - GROSS DOMESTIC PRODUCT

Economist Intelligence Unit, 111 West 57th Street, New York, NY 10019, (212) 554-0600, Fax: (212) 586-1181, www.eiu.com; *Bulgaria Country Report.*

Euromonitor International, Inc., 224 S. Michigan Avenue, Suite 1500, Chicago, IL 60604, (312) 922-1115, Fax: (312) 922-1157, www.euromonitor.com; *The World Economic Factbook 2008.*

M.E. Sharpe, 80 Business Park Drive, Armonk, NY 10504, (800) 541-6563, Fax: (914) 273-2106, www.mesharpe.com; *The Illustrated Book of World Rankings.*

United Nations Statistics Division, New York, NY 10017, (800) 253-9646, Fax: (212) 963-4116, http://unstats.un.org; *Human Development Report 2006; National Accounts Statistics: Compendium of Income Distribution Statistics; Statistical Yearbook;* and *Trends in Europe and North America: The Statistical Yearbook of the ECE 2005.*

The World Bank, 1818 H Street, NW, Washington, DC 20433, (202) 473-1000, Fax: (202) 477-6391, www.worldbank.org; *World Development Report 2008.*

BULGARIA - GROSS NATIONAL PRODUCT

European Union, Delegation of the European Commission to the United States, 2300 M Street, NW, Washington, DC 20037, (202) 862-9500, Fax: (202) 429-1766, www.eurunion.org; *The EU Economy, 2007 Review: Moving Europe's Productivity Frontier.*

M.E. Sharpe, 80 Business Park Drive, Armonk, NY 10504, (800) 541-6563, Fax: (914) 273-2106, www.mesharpe.com; *The Illustrated Book of World Rankings.*

Palgrave Macmillan Ltd., Houndmills, Basingstoke, Hampshire, RG21 6XS, England, (Telephone in U.S. (888) 330-8477), (Fax in U.S. (800) 672-2054), www.palgrave.com; *The Statesman's Yearbook 2008.*

United Nations Statistics Division, New York, NY 10017, (800) 253-9646, Fax: (212) 963-4116, http://unstats.un.org; *Statistical Yearbook.*

The World Bank, 1818 H Street, NW, Washington, DC 20433, (202) 473-1000, Fax: (202) 477-6391, www.worldbank.org; *The World Bank Atlas 2003-2004* and *World Development Report 2008.*

BULGARIA - HAZELNUT PRODUCTION

See BULGARIA - CROPS

BULGARIA - HEMP FIBRE PRODUCTION

See BULGARIA - TEXTILE INDUSTRY

BULGARIA - HIDES AND SKINS INDUSTRY

United Nations Food and Agricultural Organization (FAO), Viale delle Terme di Caracalla, 00100 Rome, Italy, (Dial from U.S. (202) 653-2400), (Fax from U.S. (202) 653 5760), www.fao.org; *FAO Production Yearbook 2002.*

BULGARIA - HOPS PRODUCTION

See BULGARIA - CROPS

BULGARIA - HOUSING

Euromonitor International, Inc., 224 S. Michigan Avenue, Suite 1500, Chicago, IL 60604, (312) 922-1115, Fax: (312) 922-1157, www.euromonitor.com; *World Marketing Data and Statistics.*

M.E. Sharpe, 80 Business Park Drive, Armonk, NY 10504, (800) 541-6563, Fax: (914) 273-2106, www.mesharpe.com; *The Illustrated Book of World Rankings.*

United Nations Statistics Division, New York, NY 10017, (800) 253-9646, Fax: (212) 963-4116, http://unstats.un.org; *Trends in Europe and North America: The Statistical Yearbook of the ECE 2005.*

BULGARIA - ILLITERATE PERSONS

Euromonitor International, Inc., 224 S. Michigan Avenue, Suite 1500, Chicago, IL 60604, (312) 922-1115, Fax: (312) 922-1157, www.euromonitor.com; *The World Economic Factbook 2008.*

UNESCO Institute for Statistics, C.P. 6128 Succursale Centre-Ville, Montreal, Quebec, H3C 3J7 Canada, (Dial from U.S. (514) 343-6880), (Fax from U.S. (514) 343 6882), www.uis.unesco.org; *Statistical Tables.*

United Nations Statistics Division, New York, NY 10017, (800) 253-9646, Fax: (212) 963-4116, http://unstats.un.org; *Human Development Report 2006.*

BULGARIA - IMPORTS

Central Intelligence Agency, Office of Public Affairs, Washington, DC 20505, (703) 482-0623, Fax: (703) 482-1739, www.cia.gov; *The World Factbook.*

Economist Intelligence Unit, 111 West 57th Street, New York, NY 10019, (212) 554-0600, Fax: (212) 586-1181, www.eiu.com; *Bulgaria Country Report.*

Euromonitor International, Inc., 224 S. Michigan Avenue, Suite 1500, Chicago, IL 60604, (312) 922-1115, Fax: (312) 922-1157, www.euromonitor.com; *The World Economic Factbook 2008.*

International Lead and Zinc Study Group (ILZSG), Rua Almirante Barroso 38, 5th Floor, Lisbon 1000 - 013, Portugal, www.ilzsg.org; Interactive Statistical Database.

International Monetary Fund (IMF), 700 Nineteenth Street, NW, Washington, DC 20431, (202) 623-7000, Fax: (202) 623-4661, www.imf.org; *Direction of Trade Statistics Yearbook 2007.*

Palgrave Macmillan Ltd., Houndmills, Basingstoke, Hampshire, RG21 6XS, England, (Telephone in U.S. (888) 330-8477), (Fax in U.S. (800) 672-2054), www.palgrave.com; *The Statesman's Yearbook 2008.*

Taylor and Francis Group, An Informa Business, 2 Park Square, Milton Park, Abingdon, Oxford OX14 4RN, United Kingdom, (Dial from U.S. (212) 216-7800), (Fax from U.S. (212) 564-7854), www.tandf.co.uk; *The Europa World Year Book.*

United Nations Conference on Trade and Development (UNCTAD), DC2-1120, United Nations, New York, NY 10017, (212) 963-0027, www.unctad.org; *Handbook of Statistics 2005.*

United Nations Food and Agricultural Organization (FAO), Viale delle Terme di Caracalla, 00100 Rome, Italy, (Dial from U.S. (202) 653-2400), (Fax from U.S. (202) 653 5760), www.fao.org; *The State of Food and Agriculture (SOFA) 2006.*

United Nations Statistics Division, New York, NY 10017, (800) 253-9646, Fax: (212) 963-4116, http://unstats.un.org; *Trends in Europe and North America: The Statistical Yearbook of the ECE 2005.*

The World Bank, 1818 H Street, NW, Washington, DC 20433, (202) 473-1000, Fax: (202) 477-6391, www.worldbank.org; *World Development Report 2008.*

BULGARIA - INDUSTRIAL METALS PRODUCTION

See BULGARIA - MINERAL INDUSTRIES

BULGARIA - INDUSTRIAL PRODUCTIVITY

International Lead and Zinc Study Group (ILZSG), Rua Almirante Barroso 38, 5th Floor, Lisbon 1000 - 013, Portugal, www.ilzsg.org; Interactive Statistical Database.

M.E. Sharpe, 80 Business Park Drive, Armonk, NY 10504, (800) 541-6563, Fax: (914) 273-2106, www.mesharpe.com; *The Illustrated Book of World Rankings.*

BULGARIA - INDUSTRIAL PROPERTY

United Nations Statistics Division, New York, NY 10017, (800) 253-9646, Fax: (212) 963-4116, http://unstats.un.org; *Statistical Yearbook.*

World Intellectual Property Organization (WIPO), PO Box 18, CH-1211 Geneva 20, Switzerland, www.wipo.int; *Industrial Property Statistics* and *Industrial Property Statistics Online Directory.*

BULGARIA - INDUSTRIES

Central Intelligence Agency, Office of Public Affairs, Washington, DC 20505, (703) 482-0623, Fax: (703) 482-1739, www.cia.gov; *The World Factbook.*

Economist Intelligence Unit, 111 West 57th Street, New York, NY 10019, (212) 554-0600, Fax: (212) 586-1181, www.eiu.com; *Bulgaria Country Report.*

Euromonitor International, Inc., 224 S. Michigan Avenue, Suite 1500, Chicago, IL 60604, (312) 922-1115, Fax: (312) 922-1157, www.euromonitor.com; *The World Economic Factbook 2008* and *World Marketing Data and Statistics.*

International Labour Office, I.L.O. Publications, 4 route des Morillons, CH-1211 Geneva 22, Switzerland, (Telephone in U.S. (202) 653-7652), (Fax in U.S. (202) 653-7687), www.ilo.org; *Yearbook of Labour Statistics 2006.*

M.E. Sharpe, 80 Business Park Drive, Armonk, NY 10504, (800) 541-6563, Fax: (914) 273-2106, www.mesharpe.com; *The Illustrated Book of World Rankings.*

Organisation for Economic Cooperation and Development (OECD), 2 rue Andre Pascal, F-75775 Paris Cedex 16, France, (Telephone in U.S. (202) 785-6323), (Fax in U.S. (202) 785-0350), www.oecd.org; *A New World Map in Textiles and Clothing: Adjusting to Change.*

Palgrave Macmillan Ltd., Houndmills, Basingstoke, Hampshire, RG21 6XS, England, (Telephone in U.S. (888) 330-8477), (Fax in U.S. (800) 672-2054), www.palgrave.com; *The Statesman's Yearbook 2008.*

Taylor and Francis Group, An Informa Business, 2 Park Square, Milton Park, Abingdon, Oxford OX14 4RN, United Kingdom, (Dial from U.S. (212) 216-7800), (Fax from U.S. (212) 564-7854), www.tandf.co.uk; *The Europa World Year Book.*

United Nations Conference on Trade and Development (UNCTAD), DC2-1120, United Nations, New York, NY 10017, (212) 963-0027, www.unctad.org; *UNCTAD Commodity Yearbook.*

United Nations Food and Agricultural Organization (FAO), Viale delle Terme di Caracalla, 00100 Rome, Italy, (Dial from U.S. (202) 653-2400), (Fax from U.S. (202) 653 5760), www.fao.org; *The State of Food and Agriculture (SOFA) 2006.*

United Nations Industrial Development Organization (UNIDO), 1 United Nations Plaza, New York, NY 10017, (212) 963 6890, Fax: (212) 963-7904, http://unido.org; Industrial Statistics Database 2008 (INDSTAT) and *The International Yearbook of Industrial Statistics 2008.*

United Nations Statistics Division, New York, NY 10017, (800) 253-9646, Fax: (212) 963-4116, http://unstats.un.org; *2004 Industrial Commodity Statistics Yearbook; Statistical Yearbook;* and *Trends in Europe and North America: The Statistical Yearbook of the ECE 2005.*

The World Bank, 1818 H Street, NW, Washington, DC 20433, (202) 473-1000, Fax: (202) 477-6391, www.worldbank.org; *Bulgaria.*

World Intellectual Property Organization (WIPO), PO Box 18, CH-1211 Geneva 20, Switzerland, www.wipo.int; *Industrial Property Statistics* and *Industrial Property Statistics Online Directory.*

BULGARIA - INFANT AND MATERNAL MORTALITY

See BULGARIA - MORTALITY

BULGARIA - INORGANIC ACIDS

United Nations Statistics Division, New York, NY 10017, (800) 253-9646, Fax: (212) 963-4116, http://unstats.un.org; *Statistical Yearbook.*

BULGARIA - INTERNATIONAL TRADE

Economist Intelligence Unit, 111 West 57th Street, New York, NY 10019, (212) 554-0600, Fax: (212) 586-1181, www.eiu.com; *Bulgaria Country Report.*

Euromonitor International, Inc., 224 S. Michigan Avenue, Suite 1500, Chicago, IL 60604, (312) 922-1115, Fax: (312) 922-1157, www.euromonitor.com; *European Marketing Data and Statistics 2008; The World Economic Factbook 2008;* and *World Marketing Data and Statistics.*

Eurostat, Batiment Jean Monnet, Rue Alcide de Gasperi, L-2920 Luxembourg, http://epp.eurostat.ec.europa.eu; Intra- and Extra-EU Trade.

M.E. Sharpe, 80 Business Park Drive, Armonk, NY 10504, (800) 541-6563, Fax: (914) 273-2106, www.mesharpe.com; *The Illustrated Book of World Rankings.*

Palgrave Macmillan Ltd., Houndmills, Basingstoke, Hampshire, RG21 6XS, England, (Telephone in U.S. (888) 330-8477), (Fax in U.S. (800) 672-2054), www.palgrave.com; *The Statesman's Yearbook 2008.*

Taylor and Francis Group, An Informa Business, 2 Park Square, Milton Park, Abingdon, Oxford OX14 4RN, United Kingdom, (Dial from U.S. (212) 216-7800), (Fax from U.S. (212) 564-7854), www.tandf.co.uk; *The Europa World Year Book.*

United Nations Conference on Trade and Development (UNCTAD), DC2-1120, United Nations, New York, NY 10017, (212) 963-0027, www.unctad.org; *UNCTAD Commodity Yearbook.*

United Nations Food and Agricultural Organization (FAO), Viale delle Terme di Caracalla, 00100 Rome, Italy, (Dial from U.S. (202) 653-2400), (Fax from U.S. (202) 653 5760), www.fao.org; *FAO Trade Yearbook* and *The State of Food and Agriculture (SOFA) 2006.*

United Nations Statistics Division, New York, NY 10017, (800) 253-9646, Fax: (212) 963-4116, http://unstats.un.org; *International Trade Statistics Yearbook* and *Statistical Yearbook.*

The World Bank, 1818 H Street, NW, Washington, DC 20433, (202) 473-1000, Fax: (202) 477-6391, www.worldbank.org; *Bulgaria* and *World Development Report 2008.*

World Trade Organization (WTO), Centre William Rappard, Rue de Lausanne 154, CH-1211 Geneva 21, Switzerland, www.wto.org; *International Trade Statistics 2006.*

BULGARIA - INTERNET USERS

Eurostat, Batiment Jean Monnet, Rue Alcide de Gasperi, L-2920 Luxembourg, http://epp.eurostat.ec.europa.eu; *Internet Usage by Enterprises 2007.*

International Telecommunication Union (ITU), Place des Nations, 1211 Geneva 20, Switzerland, www.itu.int; *World Telecommunication/ICT Indicators Database on CD-ROM; World Telecommunication/ICT Indicators Database Online;* and *Yearbook of Statistics - Telecommunication Services (Chronological Time Series 1997-2006).*

The World Bank, 1818 H Street, NW, Washington, DC 20433, (202) 473-1000, Fax: (202) 477-6391, www.worldbank.org; *Bulgaria.*

BULGARIA - IRON AND IRON ORE PRODUCTION

See BULGARIA - MINERAL INDUSTRIES

BULGARIA - LABOR

Central Intelligence Agency, Office of Public Affairs, Washington, DC 20505, (703) 482-0623, Fax: (703) 482-1739, www.cia.gov; *The World Factbook.*

Euromonitor International, Inc., 224 S. Michigan Avenue, Suite 1500, Chicago, IL 60604, (312) 922-1115, Fax: (312) 922-1157, www.euromonitor.com; *World Marketing Data and Statistics.*

Federal Statistical Office Germany, D-65180 Wiesbaden, Germany, www.destatis.de; *Bulgaria 2006.*

International Labour Office, I.L.O. Publications, 4 route des Morillons, CH-1211 Geneva 22, Switzerland, (Telephone in U.S. (202) 653-7652), (Fax in U.S. (202) 653-7687), www.ilo.org; *Yearbook of Labour Statistics 2006.*

M.E. Sharpe, 80 Business Park Drive, Armonk, NY 10504, (800) 541-6563, Fax: (914) 273-2106, www.mesharpe.com; *The Illustrated Book of World Rankings.*

Palgrave Macmillan Ltd., Houndmills, Basingstoke, Hampshire, RG21 6XS, England, (Telephone in U.S. (888) 330-8477), (Fax in U.S. (800) 672-2054), www.palgrave.com; *The Statesman's Yearbook 2008.*

Taylor and Francis Group, An Informa Business, 2 Park Square, Milton Park, Abingdon, Oxford OX14 4RN, United Kingdom, (Dial from U.S. (212) 216-7800), (Fax from U.S. (212) 564-7854), www.tandf.co.uk; *The Europa World Year Book.*

United Nations Food and Agricultural Organization (FAO), Viale delle Terme di Caracalla, 00100 Rome, Italy, (Dial from U.S. (202) 653-2400), (Fax from U.S. (202) 653 5760), www.fao.org; *The State of Food and Agriculture (SOFA) 2006.*

United Nations Statistics Division, New York, NY 10017, (800) 253-9646, Fax: (212) 963-4116, http://unstats.un.org; *Human Development Report 2006.*

The World Bank, 1818 H Street, NW, Washington, DC 20433, (202) 473-1000, Fax: (202) 477-6391, www.worldbank.org; *The World Bank Atlas 2003-2004* and *World Development Report 2008.*

BULGARIA - LAND USE

Central Intelligence Agency, Office of Public Affairs, Washington, DC 20505, (703) 482-0623, Fax: (703) 482-1739, www.cia.gov; *The World Factbook.*

Euromonitor International, Inc., 224 S. Michigan Avenue, Suite 1500, Chicago, IL 60604, (312) 922-1115, Fax: (312) 922-1157, www.euromonitor.com; *European Marketing Data and Statistics 2008.*

United Nations Food and Agricultural Organization (FAO), Viale delle Terme di Caracalla, 00100 Rome, Italy, (Dial from U.S. (202) 653-2400), (Fax from U.S. (202) 653 5760), www.fao.org; *FAO Production Yearbook 2002.*

The World Bank, 1818 H Street, NW, Washington, DC 20433, (202) 473-1000, Fax: (202) 477-6391, www.worldbank.org; *World Development Report 2008.*

BULGARIA - LIBRARIES

Euromonitor International, Inc., 224 S. Michigan Avenue, Suite 1500, Chicago, IL 60604, (312) 922-1115, Fax: (312) 922-1157, www.euromonitor.com; *European Marketing Data and Statistics 2008.*

M.E. Sharpe, 80 Business Park Drive, Armonk, NY 10504, (800) 541-6563, Fax: (914) 273-2106, www.mesharpe.com; *The Illustrated Book of World Rankings.*

UNESCO Institute for Statistics, C.P. 6128 Succursale Centre-Ville, Montreal, Quebec, H3C 3J7 Canada, (Dial from U.S. (514) 343-6880), (Fax from U.S. (514) 343 6882), www.uis.unesco.org; *Statistical Tables.*

United Nations Statistics Division, New York, NY 10017, (800) 253-9646, Fax: (212) 963-4116, http://unstats.un.org; *Trends in Europe and North America: The Statistical Yearbook of the ECE 2005.*

BULGARIA - LIFE EXPECTANCY

Central Intelligence Agency, Office of Public Affairs, Washington, DC 20505, (703) 482-0623, Fax: (703) 482-1739, www.cia.gov; *The World Factbook.*

Euromonitor International, Inc., 224 S. Michigan Avenue, Suite 1500, Chicago, IL 60604, (312) 922-1115, Fax: (312) 922-1157, www.euromonitor.com; *The World Economic Factbook 2008.*

Palgrave Macmillan Ltd., Houndmills, Basingstoke, Hampshire, RG21 6XS, England, (Telephone in U.S. (888) 330-8477), (Fax in U.S. (800) 672-2054), www.palgrave.com; *The Statesman's Yearbook 2008.*

United Nations Statistics Division, New York, NY 10017, (800) 253-9646, Fax: (212) 963-4116, http://unstats.un.org; *Human Development Report 2006; Trends in Europe and North America: The Statistical Yearbook of the ECE 2005;* and *World Statistics Pocketbook.*

The World Bank, 1818 H Street, NW, Washington, DC 20433, (202) 473-1000, Fax: (202) 477-6391, www.worldbank.org; *The World Bank Atlas 2003-2004* and *World Development Report 2008.*

BULGARIA - LITERACY

Euromonitor International, Inc., 224 S. Michigan Avenue, Suite 1500, Chicago, IL 60604, (312) 922-1115, Fax: (312) 922-1157, www.euromonitor.com; *World Marketing Data and Statistics.*

BULGARIA - LIVESTOCK

Euromonitor International, Inc., 224 S. Michigan Avenue, Suite 1500, Chicago, IL 60604, (312) 922-1115, Fax: (312) 922-1157, www.euromonitor.com; *European Marketing Data and Statistics 2008.*

M.E. Sharpe, 80 Business Park Drive, Armonk, NY 10504, (800) 541-6563, Fax: (914) 273-2106, www.mesharpe.com; *The Illustrated Book of World Rankings.*

Palgrave Macmillan Ltd., Houndmills, Basingstoke, Hampshire, RG21 6XS, England, (Telephone in U.S. (888) 330-8477), (Fax in U.S. (800) 672-2054), www.palgrave.com; *The Statesman's Yearbook 2008.*

Taylor and Francis Group, An Informa Business, 2 Park Square, Milton Park, Abingdon, Oxford OX14 4RN, United Kingdom, (Dial from U.S. (212) 216-7800), (Fax from U.S. (212) 564-7854), www.tandf.co.uk; *The Europa World Year Book.*

United Nations Conference on Trade and Development (UNCTAD), DC2-1120, United Nations, New York, NY 10017, (212) 963-0027, www.unctad.org; *UNCTAD Commodity Yearbook.*

United Nations Food and Agricultural Organization (FAO), Viale delle Terme di Caracalla, 00100 Rome, Italy, (Dial from U.S. (202) 653-2400), (Fax from U.S. (202) 653 5760), www.fao.org; *FAO Production Yearbook 2002* and *The State of Food and Agriculture (SOFA) 2006.*

United Nations Statistics Division, New York, NY 10017, (800) 253-9646, Fax: (212) 963-4116, http://unstats.un.org; *Statistical Yearbook.*

BULGARIA - MANUFACTURES

M.E. Sharpe, 80 Business Park Drive, Armonk, NY 10504, (800) 541-6563, Fax: (914) 273-2106, www.mesharpe.com; *The Illustrated Book of World Rankings.*

United Nations Statistics Division, New York, NY 10017, (800) 253-9646, Fax: (212) 963-4116, http://unstats.un.org; *Statistical Yearbook.*

BULGARIA - MARRIAGE

M.E. Sharpe, 80 Business Park Drive, Armonk, NY 10504, (800) 541-6563, Fax: (914) 273-2106, www.mesharpe.com; *The Illustrated Book of World Rankings.*

Taylor and Francis Group, An Informa Business, 2 Park Square, Milton Park, Abingdon, Oxford OX14 4RN, United Kingdom, (Dial from U.S. (212) 216-7800), (Fax from U.S. (212) 564-7854), www.tandf.co.uk; *The Europa World Year Book.*

United Nations Statistics Division, New York, NY 10017, (800) 253-9646, Fax: (212) 963-4116, http://unstats.un.org; *Demographic Yearbook; Statistical Yearbook;* and *Trends in Europe and North America: The Statistical Yearbook of the ECE 2005.*

BULGARIA - MEAT PRODUCTION

See BULGARIA - LIVESTOCK

BULGARIA - MILK PRODUCTION

See BULGARIA - DAIRY PROCESSING

BULGARIA - MINERAL INDUSTRIES

Commodity Research Bureau, 330 South Wells Street, Suite 612, Chicago, IL 60606-7110, (800) 621-5271, Fax: (312) 939-4135, www.crbtrader.com; *2006 CRB Commodity Yearbook and CD.*

Eurostat, Batiment Jean Monnet, Rue Alcide de Gasperi, L-2920 Luxembourg, http://epp.eurostat.ec.europa.eu; *Energy - Monthly Statistics* and *Panorama of Energy - 2007 Edition.*

International Lead and Zinc Study Group (ILZSG), Rua Almirante Barroso 38, 5th Floor, Lisbon 1000 - 013, Portugal, www.ilzsg.org; Interactive Statistical Database.

M.E. Sharpe, 80 Business Park Drive, Armonk, NY 10504, (800) 541-6563, Fax: (914) 273-2106, www.mesharpe.com; *The Illustrated Book of World Rankings.*

Organisation for Economic Cooperation and Development (OECD), 2 rue Andre Pascal, F-75775 Paris Cedex 16, France, (Telephone in U.S. (202) 785-6323), (Fax in U.S. (202) 785-0350), www.oecd.org; *World Energy Outlook 2007.*

Palgrave Macmillan Ltd., Houndmills, Basingstoke, Hampshire, RG21 6XS, England, (Telephone in U.S. (888) 330-8477), (Fax in U.S. (800) 672-2054), www.palgrave.com; *The Statesman's Yearbook 2008.*

Platts, 2 Penn Plaza, 25th Floor, New York, NY 10121-2298, (212) 904-3070, www.platts.com; *Energy in East Europe* and *EU Energy.*

Taylor and Francis Group, An Informa Business, 2 Park Square, Milton Park, Abingdon, Oxford OX14 4RN, United Kingdom, (Dial from U.S. (212) 216-7800), (Fax from U.S. (212) 564-7854), www.tandf.co.uk; *The Europa World Year Book.*

United Nations Conference on Trade and Development (UNCTAD), DC2-1120, United Nations, New York, NY 10017, (212) 963-0027, www.unctad.org; *UNCTAD Commodity Yearbook.*

United Nations Statistics Division, New York, NY 10017, (800) 253-9646, Fax: (212) 963-4116, http://unstats.un.org; *Statistical Yearbook.*

BULGARIA - MONEY EXCHANGE RATES

See BULGARIA - FOREIGN EXCHANGE RATES

BULGARIA - MONEY SUPPLY

Economist Intelligence Unit, 111 West 57th Street, New York, NY 10019, (212) 554-0600, Fax: (212) 586-1181, www.eiu.com; *Bulgaria Country Report.*

The World Bank, 1818 H Street, NW, Washington, DC 20433, (202) 473-1000, Fax: (202) 477-6391, www.worldbank.org; *Bulgaria.*

BULGARIA - MORTALITY

Central Intelligence Agency, Office of Public Affairs, Washington, DC 20505, (703) 482-0623, Fax: (703) 482-1739, www.cia.gov; *The World Factbook.*

Euromonitor International, Inc., 224 S. Michigan Avenue, Suite 1500, Chicago, IL 60604, (312) 922-1115, Fax: (312) 922-1157, www.euromonitor.com; *The World Economic Factbook 2008.*

Palgrave Macmillan Ltd., Houndmills, Basingstoke, Hampshire, RG21 6XS, England, (Telephone in U.S. (888) 330-8477), (Fax in U.S. (800) 672-2054), www.palgrave.com; *The Statesman's Yearbook 2008.*

Taylor and Francis Group, An Informa Business, 2 Park Square, Milton Park, Abingdon, Oxford OX14 4RN, United Kingdom, (Dial from U.S. (212) 216-7800), (Fax from U.S. (212) 564-7854), www.tandf.co.uk; *The Europa World Year Book.*

UNICEF, 3 United Nations Plaza, New York, NY 10017, (800) 253-9646, Fax: (212) 887-7465, www.unicef.org; *The State of the World's Children 2008.*

United Nations Statistics Division, New York, NY 10017, (800) 253-9646, Fax: (212) 963-4116, http://unstats.un.org; *Demographic Yearbook; Human Development Report 2006; Statistical Yearbook; Trends in Europe and North America: The Statistical Yearbook of the ECE 2005;* and *World Statistics Pocketbook.*

The World Bank, 1818 H Street, NW, Washington, DC 20433, (202) 473-1000, Fax: (202) 477-6391, www.worldbank.org; *The World Bank Atlas 2003-2004* and *World Development Report 2008.*

World Health Organization (WHO), Avenue Appia 20, 1211 Geneve 27, Switzerland, (Telephone in U.S. (212) 331-9081), www.who.int; The WHO Global Atlas of Infectious Diseases and *World Health Report 2006.*

BULGARIA - MOTION PICTURES

Palgrave Macmillan Ltd., Houndmills, Basingstoke, Hampshire, RG21 6XS, England, (Telephone in U.S. (888) 330-8477), (Fax in U.S. (800) 672-2054), www.palgrave.com; *The Statesman's Yearbook 2008.*

UNESCO Institute for Statistics, C.P. 6128 Succursale Centre-Ville, Montreal, Quebec, H3C 3J7 Canada, (Dial from U.S. (514) 343-6880), (Fax from U.S. (514) 343 6882), www.uis.unesco.org; *Statistical Tables.*

United Nations Statistics Division, New York, NY 10017, (800) 253-9646, Fax: (212) 963-4116, http://unstats.un.org; *Statistical Yearbook.*

BULGARIA - MOTOR VEHICLES

International Road Federation (IFR), Madison Place, 500 Montgomery Street, 5th Floor, Alexandria, VA 22314, (703) 535-1001, Fax: (703) 535-1007, www.irfnet.org; *World Road Statistics 2006.*

BULGARIA - MUSEUMS

M.E. Sharpe, 80 Business Park Drive, Armonk, NY 10504, (800) 541-6563, Fax: (914) 273-2106, www.mesharpe.com; *The Illustrated Book of World Rankings.*

UNESCO Institute for Statistics, C.P. 6128 Succursale Centre-Ville, Montreal, Quebec, H3C 3J7 Canada, (Dial from U.S. (514) 343-6880), (Fax from U.S. (514) 343 6882), www.uis.unesco.org; *Statistical Tables.*

BULGARIA - NATIONAL INCOME

United Nations Statistics Division, New York, NY 10017, (800) 253-9646, Fax: (212) 963-4116, http://unstats.un.org; *Statistical Yearbook.*

BULGARIA - NATURAL GAS PRODUCTION

See BULGARIA - MINERAL INDUSTRIES

BULGARIA - NUTRITION

United Nations Food and Agricultural Organization (FAO), Viale delle Terme di Caracalla, 00100 Rome, Italy, (Dial from U.S. (202) 653-2400), (Fax from U.S. (202) 653 5760), www.fao.org; *The State of Food and Agriculture (SOFA) 2006.*

BULGARIA - OATS PRODUCTION

See BULGARIA - CROPS

BULGARIA - OLDER PEOPLE

M.E. Sharpe, 80 Business Park Drive, Armonk, NY 10504, (800) 541-6563, Fax: (914) 273-2106, www.mesharpe.com; *The Illustrated Book of World Rankings.*

BULGARIA - PAPER

See BULGARIA - FORESTS AND FORESTRY

BULGARIA - PEANUT PRODUCTION

See BULGARIA - CROPS

BULGARIA - PERIODICALS

UNESCO Institute for Statistics, C.P. 6128 Succursale Centre-Ville, Montreal, Quebec, H3C 3J7 Canada, (Dial from U.S. (514) 343-6880), (Fax from U.S. (514) 343 6882), www.uis.unesco.org; *Statistical Tables.*

BULGARIA - PESTICIDES

United Nations Food and Agricultural Organization (FAO), Viale delle Terme di Caracalla, 00100 Rome, Italy, (Dial from U.S. (202) 653-2400), (Fax from U.S. (202) 653 5760), www.fao.org; *The State of Food and Agriculture (SOFA) 2006.*

BULGARIA - PETROLEUM INDUSTRY AND TRADE

Euromonitor International, Inc., 224 S. Michigan Avenue, Suite 1500, Chicago, IL 60604, (312) 922-1115, Fax: (312) 922-1157, www.euromonitor.com; *European Marketing Data and Statistics 2008.*

M.E. Sharpe, 80 Business Park Drive, Armonk, NY 10504, (800) 541-6563, Fax: (914) 273-2106, www.mesharpe.com; *The Illustrated Book of World Rankings.*

Organisation for Economic Cooperation and Development (OECD), 2 rue Andre Pascal, F-75775 Paris Cedex 16, France, (Telephone in U.S. (202) 785-6323), (Fax in U.S. (202) 785-0350), www.oecd.org; *World Energy Outlook 2007.*

Palgrave Macmillan Ltd., Houndmills, Basingstoke, Hampshire, RG21 6XS, England, (Telephone in U.S. (888) 330-8477), (Fax in U.S. (800) 672-2054), www.palgrave.com; *The Statesman's Yearbook 2008.*

PennWell Corporation, 1421 South Sheridan Road, Tulsa, OK 74112, (918) 835-3161, www.pennwell.com; *International Petroleum Encyclopedia 2007.*

U.S. Department of Energy (DOE), Energy Information Administration (EIA), 1000 Independence Avenue, SW, Washington, DC 20585, (202) 586-8800, www.eia.doe.gov; *International Energy Annual 2004* and *International Energy Outlook 2006.*

United Nations Conference on Trade and Development (UNCTAD), DC2-1120, United Nations, New York, NY 10017, (212) 963-0027, www.unctad.org; *UNCTAD Commodity Yearbook.*

United Nations Food and Agricultural Organization (FAO), Viale delle Terme di Caracalla, 00100 Rome, Italy, (Dial from U.S. (202) 653-2400), (Fax from U.S. (202) 653 5760), www.fao.org; *The State of Food and Agriculture (SOFA) 2006.*

United Nations Statistics Division, New York, NY 10017, (800) 253-9646, Fax: (212) 963-4116, http://unstats.un.org; *Statistical Yearbook* and *Trends in Europe and North America: The Statistical Yearbook of the ECE 2005.*

BULGARIA - PLASTICS INDUSTRY AND TRADE

United Nations Statistics Division, New York, NY 10017, (800) 253-9646, Fax: (212) 963-4116, http://unstats.un.org; *Statistical Yearbook.*

BULGARIA - POLITICAL SCIENCE

Central Intelligence Agency, Office of Public Affairs, Washington, DC 20505, (703) 482-0623, Fax: (703) 482-1739, www.cia.gov; *The World Factbook.*

Palgrave Macmillan Ltd., Houndmills, Basingstoke, Hampshire, RG21 6XS, England, (Telephone in U.S. (888) 330-8477), (Fax in U.S. (800) 672-2054), www.palgrave.com; *The Statesman's Yearbook 2008.*

Taylor and Francis Group, An Informa Business, 2 Park Square, Milton Park, Abingdon, Oxford OX14 4RN, United Kingdom, (Dial from U.S. (212) 216-7800), (Fax from U.S. (212) 564-7854), www.tandf.co.uk; *The Europa World Year Book.*

United Nations Statistics Division, New York, NY 10017, (800) 253-9646, Fax: (212) 963-4116, http://unstats.un.org; *National Accounts Statistics: Compendium of Income Distribution Statistics* and *Statistical Yearbook.*

The World Bank, 1818 H Street, NW, Washington, DC 20433, (202) 473-1000, Fax: (202) 477-6391, www.worldbank.org; *World Development Report 2008.*

BULGARIA - POPULATION

Central Intelligence Agency, Office of Public Affairs, Washington, DC 20505, (703) 482-0623, Fax: (703) 482-1739, www.cia.gov; *The World Factbook.*

Economist Intelligence Unit, 111 West 57th Street, New York, NY 10019, (212) 554-0600, Fax: (212) 586-1181, www.eiu.com; *Bulgaria Country Report.*

Euromonitor International, Inc., 224 S. Michigan Avenue, Suite 1500, Chicago, IL 60604, (312) 922-1115, Fax: (312) 922-1157, www.euromonitor.com; *European Marketing Data and Statistics 2008* and *The World Economic Factbook 2008.*

Eurostat, Batiment Jean Monnet, Rue Alcide de Gasperi, L-2920 Luxembourg, http://epp.eurostat.ec.europa.eu; *The Life of Women and Men in Europe - A Statistical Portrait.*

Federal Statistical Office Germany, D-65180 Wiesbaden, Germany, www.destatis.de; *Bulgaria 2006.*

International Labour Office, I.L.O. Publications, 4 route des Morillons, CH-1211 Geneva 22, Switzerland, (Telephone in U.S. (202) 653-7652), (Fax in U.S. (202) 653-7687), www.ilo.org; *Yearbook of Labour Statistics 2006.*

M.E. Sharpe, 80 Business Park Drive, Armonk, NY 10504, (800) 541-6563, Fax: (914) 273-2106, www.mesharpe.com; *The Illustrated Book of World Rankings.*

National Statistical Insitute (NSI), 2, P. Volov Street, 1038 Sofia, Bulgaria, www.nsi.bg; *Bulgaria 2006: Social-Economic Development* and *Population and Demographic Processes 2006.*

Palgrave Macmillan Ltd., Houndmills, Basingstoke, Hampshire, RG21 6XS, England, (Telephone in U.S. (888) 330-8477), (Fax in U.S. (800) 672-2054), www.palgrave.com; *The Statesman's Yearbook 2008.*

Taylor and Francis Group, An Informa Business, 2 Park Square, Milton Park, Abingdon, Oxford OX14 4RN, United Kingdom, (Dial from U.S. (212) 216-7800), (Fax from U.S. (212) 564-7854), www.tandf.co.uk; *The Europa World Year Book.*

UNESCO Institute for Statistics, C.P. 6128 Succursale Centre-Ville, Montreal, Quebec, H3C 3J7 Canada, (Dial from U.S. (514) 343-6880), (Fax from U.S. (514) 343 6882), www.uis.unesco.org; *Statistical Tables.*

United Nations Food and Agricultural Organization (FAO), Viale delle Terme di Caracalla, 00100 Rome, Italy, (Dial from U.S. (202) 653-2400), (Fax from U.S. (202) 653 5760), www.fao.org; *FAO Production Yearbook 2002.*

United Nations Statistics Division, New York, NY 10017, (800) 253-9646, Fax: (212) 963-4116, http://unstats.un.org; *Demographic Yearbook; Human Development Report 2006; Statistical Yearbook; Trends in Europe and North America: The Statistical Yearbook of the ECE 2005;* and *World Statistics Pocketbook.*

The World Bank, 1818 H Street, NW, Washington, DC 20433, (202) 473-1000, Fax: (202) 477-6391, www.worldbank.org; *Bulgaria; The World Bank Atlas 2003-2004;* and *World Development Report 2008.*

World Health Organization (WHO), Avenue Appia 20, 1211 Geneve 27, Switzerland, (Telephone in U.S. (212) 331-9081), www.who.int; *World Health Report 2006.*

BULGARIA - POPULATION DENSITY

Central Intelligence Agency, Office of Public Affairs, Washington, DC 20505, (703) 482-0623, Fax: (703) 482-1739, www.cia.gov; *The World Factbook.*

Euromonitor International, Inc., 224 S. Michigan Avenue, Suite 1500, Chicago, IL 60604, (312) 922-1115, Fax: (312) 922-1157, www.euromonitor.com; *The World Economic Factbook 2008.*

M.E. Sharpe, 80 Business Park Drive, Armonk, NY 10504, (800) 541-6563, Fax: (914) 273-2106, www.mesharpe.com; *The Illustrated Book of World Rankings.*

Palgrave Macmillan Ltd., Houndmills, Basingstoke, Hampshire, RG21 6XS, England, (Telephone in U.S. (888) 330-8477), (Fax in U.S. (800) 672-2054), www.palgrave.com; *The Statesman's Yearbook 2008.*

Taylor and Francis Group, An Informa Business, 2 Park Square, Milton Park, Abingdon, Oxford OX14 4RN, United Kingdom, (Dial from U.S. (212) 216-7800), (Fax from U.S. (212) 564-7854), www.tandf.co.uk; *The Europa World Year Book.*

United Nations Food and Agricultural Organization (FAO), Viale delle Terme di Caracalla, 00100 Rome, Italy, (Dial from U.S. (202) 653-2400), (Fax from U.S. (202) 653 5760), www.fao.org; *The State of Food and Agriculture (SOFA) 2006.*

United Nations Statistics Division, New York, NY 10017, (800) 253-9646, Fax: (212) 963-4116, http://unstats.un.org; *Statistical Yearbook* and *Trends in Europe and North America: The Statistical Yearbook of the ECE 2005.*

The World Bank, 1818 H Street, NW, Washington, DC 20433, (202) 473-1000, Fax: (202) 477-6391, www.worldbank.org; *Bulgaria* and *World Development Report 2008.*

BULGARIA - POSTAL SERVICE

M.E. Sharpe, 80 Business Park Drive, Armonk, NY 10504, (800) 541-6563, Fax: (914) 273-2106, www.mesharpe.com; *The Illustrated Book of World Rankings.*

Palgrave Macmillan Ltd., Houndmills, Basingstoke, Hampshire, RG21 6XS, England, (Telephone in U.S. (888) 330-8477), (Fax in U.S. (800) 672-2054), www.palgrave.com; *The Statesman's Yearbook 2008.*

United Nations Statistics Division, New York, NY 10017, (800) 253-9646, Fax: (212) 963-4116, http://unstats.un.org; *Trends in Europe and North America: The Statistical Yearbook of the ECE 2005.*

BULGARIA - POULTRY

See BULGARIA - LIVESTOCK

BULGARIA - POWER RESOURCES

Euromonitor International, Inc., 224 S. Michigan Avenue, Suite 1500, Chicago, IL 60604, (312) 922-1115, Fax: (312) 922-1157, www.euromonitor.com; *European Marketing Data and Statistics 2008; The World Economic Factbook 2008;* and *World Marketing Data and Statistics.*

M.E. Sharpe, 80 Business Park Drive, Armonk, NY 10504, (800) 541-6563, Fax: (914) 273-2106, www.mesharpe.com; *The Illustrated Book of World Rankings.*

Organisation for Economic Cooperation and Development (OECD), 2 rue Andre Pascal, F-75775 Paris Cedex 16, France, (Telephone in U.S. (202) 785-6323), (Fax in U.S. (202) 785-0350), www.oecd.org; *World Energy Outlook 2007.*

Palgrave Macmillan Ltd., Houndmills, Basingstoke, Hampshire, RG21 6XS, England, (Telephone in U.S. (888) 330-8477), (Fax in U.S. (800) 672-2054), www.palgrave.com; *The Statesman's Yearbook 2008.*

Platts, 2 Penn Plaza, 25th Floor, New York, NY 10121-2298, (212) 904-3070, www.platts.com; *Energy Economist* and *European Power Daily.*

U.S. Department of Energy (DOE), Energy Information Administration (EIA), 1000 Independence Avenue, SW, Washington, DC 20585, (202) 586-8800, www.eia.doe.gov; *International Energy Annual 2004* and *International Energy Outlook 2006.*

United Nations Food and Agricultural Organization (FAO), Viale delle Terme di Caracalla, 00100 Rome, Italy, (Dial from U.S. (202) 653-2400), (Fax from U.S. (202) 653 5760), www.fao.org; *The State of Food and Agriculture (SOFA) 2006.*

United Nations Statistics Division, New York, NY 10017, (800) 253-9646, Fax: (212) 963-4116, http://unstats.un.org; *Energy Statistics Yearbook 2003; Human Development Report 2006; Statistical Yearbook; Trends in Europe and North America: The Statistical Yearbook of the ECE 2005;* and *World Statistics Pocketbook.*

The World Bank, 1818 H Street, NW, Washington, DC 20433, (202) 473-1000, Fax: (202) 477-6391, www.worldbank.org; *The World Bank Atlas 2003-2004* and *World Development Report 2008.*

BULGARIA - PRICES

Euromonitor International, Inc., 224 S. Michigan Avenue, Suite 1500, Chicago, IL 60604, (312) 922-1115, Fax: (312) 922-1157, www.euromonitor.com; *European Marketing Data and Statistics 2008* and *World Marketing Data and Statistics.*

International Labour Office, I.L.O. Publications, 4 route des Morillons, CH-1211 Geneva 22, Switzerland, (Telephone in U.S. (202) 653-7652), (Fax in U.S. (202) 653-7687), www.ilo.org; *Yearbook of Labour Statistics 2006.*

International Lead and Zinc Study Group (ILZSG), Rua Almirante Barroso 38, 5th Floor, Lisbon 1000 - 013, Portugal, www.ilzsg.org; Interactive Statistical Database.

M.E. Sharpe, 80 Business Park Drive, Armonk, NY 10504, (800) 541-6563, Fax: (914) 273-2106, www.mesharpe.com; *The Illustrated Book of World Rankings.*

United Nations Food and Agricultural Organization (FAO), Viale delle Terme di Caracalla, 00100 Rome, Italy, (Dial from U.S. (202) 653-2400), (Fax from U.S. (202) 653 5760), www.fao.org; *FAO Production Yearbook 2002* and *The State of Food and Agriculture (SOFA) 2006.*

The World Bank, 1818 H Street, NW, Washington, DC 20433, (202) 473-1000, Fax: (202) 477-6391, www.worldbank.org; *Bulgaria.*

BULGARIA - PROFESSIONS

United Nations Statistics Division, New York, NY 10017, (800) 253-9646, Fax: (212) 963-4116, http://unstats.un.org; *Statistical Yearbook.*

BULGARIA - PUBLIC HEALTH

Euromonitor International, Inc., 224 S. Michigan Avenue, Suite 1500, Chicago, IL 60604, (312) 922-1115, Fax: (312) 922-1157, www.euromonitor.com; *World Health Databook 2007/2008* and *World Marketing Data and Statistics.*

Health and Consumer Protection Directorate-General, European Commission, B-1049 Brussels, Belgium, http://ec.europa.eu/dgs/health_consumer/index_en.htm; *Injuries in the European Union: Statistics Summary 2002-2004.*

M.E. Sharpe, 80 Business Park Drive, Armonk, NY 10504, (800) 541-6563, Fax: (914) 273-2106, www.mesharpe.com; *The Illustrated Book of World Rankings.*

Palgrave Macmillan Ltd., Houndmills, Basingstoke, Hampshire, RG21 6XS, England, (Telephone in U.S. (888) 330-8477), (Fax in U.S. (800) 672-2054), www.palgrave.com; *The Statesman's Yearbook 2008.*

Robert Koch Institute, Nordufer 20, D 13353 Berlin, Germany, www.rki.de; *EUVAC-NET Report: Pertussis-Surveillance 1998-2002.*

UNICEF, 3 United Nations Plaza, New York, NY 10017, (800) 253-9646, Fax: (212) 887-7465, www.unicef.org; *The State of the World's Children 2008.*

United Nations Statistics Division, New York, NY 10017, (800) 253-9646, Fax: (212) 963-4116, http://unstats.un.org; *Human Development Report 2006; Statistical Yearbook;* and *Trends in Europe and North America: The Statistical Yearbook of the ECE 2005.*

The World Bank, 1818 H Street, NW, Washington, DC 20433, (202) 473-1000, Fax: (202) 477-6391, www.worldbank.org; *Bulgaria* and *World Development Report 2008.*

World Health Organization (WHO), Avenue Appia 20, 1211 Geneve 27, Switzerland, (Telephone in U.S. (212) 331-9081), www.who.int; The WHO Global Atlas of Infectious Diseases and *World Health Report 2006.*

BULGARIA - PUBLISHERS AND PUBLISHING

Palgrave Macmillan Ltd., Houndmills, Basingstoke, Hampshire, RG21 6XS, England, (Telephone in U.S. (888) 330-8477), (Fax in U.S. (800) 672-2054), www.palgrave.com; *The Statesman's Yearbook 2008.*

Taylor and Francis Group, An Informa Business, 2 Park Square, Milton Park, Abingdon, Oxford OX14 4RN, United Kingdom, (Dial from U.S. (212) 216-7800), (Fax from U.S. (212) 564-7854), www.tandf.co.uk; *The Europa World Year Book.*

UNESCO Institute for Statistics, C.P. 6128 Succursale Centre-Ville, Montreal, Quebec, H3C 3J7 Canada, (Dial from U.S. (514) 343-6880), (Fax from U.S. (514) 343 6882), www.uis.unesco.org; *Statistical Tables.*

United Nations Statistics Division, New York, NY 10017, (800) 253-9646, Fax: (212) 963-4116, http://unstats.un.org; *Trends in Europe and North America: The Statistical Yearbook of the ECE 2005.*

BULGARIA - RADIO - RECEIVERS AND RECEPTION

Palgrave Macmillan Ltd., Houndmills, Basingstoke, Hampshire, RG21 6XS, England, (Telephone in U.S. (888) 330-8477), (Fax in U.S. (800) 672-2054), www.palgrave.com; *The Statesman's Yearbook 2008.*

United Nations Statistics Division, New York, NY 10017, (800) 253-9646, Fax: (212) 963-4116, http://unstats.un.org; *Statistical Yearbook.*

BULGARIA - RAILROADS

Euromonitor International, Inc., 224 S. Michigan Avenue, Suite 1500, Chicago, IL 60604, (312) 922-1115, Fax: (312) 922-1157, www.euromonitor.com; *European Marketing Data and Statistics 2008.*

Jane's Information Group, 110 North Royal Street, Suite 200, Alexandria, VA 22314, (703) 683-3700, Fax: (800) 836-0297, www.janes.com; *Jane's World Railways.*

Palgrave Macmillan Ltd., Houndmills, Basingstoke, Hampshire, RG21 6XS, England, (Telephone in U.S. (888) 330-8477), (Fax in U.S. (800) 672-2054), www.palgrave.com; *The Statesman's Yearbook 2008.*

Taylor and Francis Group, An Informa Business, 2 Park Square, Milton Park, Abingdon, Oxford OX14 4RN, United Kingdom, (Dial from U.S. (212) 216-7800), (Fax from U.S. (212) 564-7854), www.tandf.co.uk; *The Europa World Year Book.*

United Nations Statistics Division, New York, NY 10017, (800) 253-9646, Fax: (212) 963-4116, http://unstats.un.org; *Annual Bulletin of Transport Statistics for Europe and North America 2004; Statistical Yearbook;* and *Trends in Europe and North America: The Statistical Yearbook of the ECE 2005.*

BULGARIA - RELIGION

Central Intelligence Agency, Office of Public Affairs, Washington, DC 20505, (703) 482-0623, Fax: (703) 482-1739, www.cia.gov; *The World Factbook.*

M.E. Sharpe, 80 Business Park Drive, Armonk, NY 10504, (800) 541-6563, Fax: (914) 273-2106, www.mesharpe.com; *The Illustrated Book of World Rankings.*

Palgrave Macmillan Ltd., Houndmills, Basingstoke, Hampshire, RG21 6XS, England, (Telephone in U.S. (888) 330-8477), (Fax in U.S. (800) 672-2054), www.palgrave.com; *The Statesman's Yearbook 2008.*

BULGARIA - RETAIL TRADE

Euromonitor International, Inc., 224 S. Michigan Avenue, Suite 1500, Chicago, IL 60604, (312) 922-1115, Fax: (312) 922-1157, www.euromonitor.com; *Retail Trade International 2007* and *World Marketing Data and Statistics.*

United Nations Statistics Division, New York, NY 10017, (800) 253-9646, Fax: (212) 963-4116, http://unstats.un.org; *Statistical Yearbook.*

BULGARIA - RICE PRODUCTION

See BULGARIA - CROPS

BULGARIA - ROADS

Central Intelligence Agency, Office of Public Affairs, Washington, DC 20505, (703) 482-0623, Fax: (703) 482-1739, www.cia.gov; *The World Factbook.*

International Road Federation (IFR), Madison Place, 500 Montgomery Street, 5th Floor, Alexandria, VA 22314, (703) 535-1001, Fax: (703) 535-1007, www.irfnet.org; *World Road Statistics 2006.*

Palgrave Macmillan Ltd., Houndmills, Basingstoke, Hampshire, RG21 6XS, England, (Telephone in U.S. (888) 330-8477), (Fax in U.S. (800) 672-2054), www.palgrave.com; *The Statesman's Yearbook 2008.*

United Nations Statistics Division, New York, NY 10017, (800) 253-9646, Fax: (212) 963-4116, http://unstats.un.org; *Annual Bulletin of Transport Statistics for Europe and North America 2004* and *Trends in Europe and North America: The Statistical Yearbook of the ECE 2005.*

BULGARIA - RUBBER INDUSTRY AND TRADE

International Rubber Study Group (IRSG), 1st Floor, Heron House, 109/115 Wembley Hill Road, Wembley, Middlesex HA9 8DA, United Kingdom, www.rubberstudy.com; *Rubber Statistical Bulletin; Summary of World Rubber Statistics 2005; World Rubber Statistics Handbook (Volume 6, 1975-2001);* and *World Rubber Statistics Historic Handbook.*

M.E. Sharpe, 80 Business Park Drive, Armonk, NY 10504, (800) 541-6563, Fax: (914) 273-2106, www.mesharpe.com; *The Illustrated Book of World Rankings.*

United Nations Statistics Division, New York, NY 10017, (800) 253-9646, Fax: (212) 963-4116, http://unstats.un.org; *Statistical Yearbook.*

BULGARIA - SALT PRODUCTION

See BULGARIA - MINERAL INDUSTRIES

BULGARIA - SHEEP

See BULGARIA - LIVESTOCK

BULGARIA - SHIPPING

Lloyd's Register - Fairplay, 8410 N.W. 53rd Terrace, Suite 207, Miami FL 33166, (305) 718-9929, Fax: (305) 718-9663, www.lrfairplay.com; *Register of Ships 2007-2008; World Casualty Statistics 2007; World Fleet Statistics 2006; World Marine Propulsion Report 2006-2010; World Shipbuilding Statistics 2007;* and The World Shipping Encyclopaedia.

Palgrave Macmillan Ltd., Houndmills, Basingstoke, Hampshire, RG21 6XS, England, (Telephone in U.S. (888) 330-8477), (Fax in U.S. (800) 672-2054), www.palgrave.com; *The Statesman's Yearbook 2008.*

Taylor and Francis Group, An Informa Business, 2 Park Square, Milton Park, Abingdon, Oxford OX14 4RN, United Kingdom, (Dial from U.S. (212) 216-7800), (Fax from U.S. (212) 564-7854), www.tandf.co.uk; *The Europa World Year Book.*

U.S. Department of Transportation (DOT), Maritime Administration (MARAD), West Building, Southeast Federal Center, 1200 New Jersey Avenue, SE, Washington, DC 20590, (800) 99-MARAD, www.marad.dot.gov; *World Merchant Fleet 2005.*

United Nations Statistics Division, New York, NY 10017, (800) 253-9646, Fax: (212) 963-4116, http://unstats.un.org; *Annual Bulletin of Transport Statistics for Europe and North America 2004* and *Statistical Yearbook.*

BULGARIA - SILVER PRODUCTION

See BULGARIA - MINERAL INDUSTRIES

BULGARIA - SOCIAL ECOLOGY

M.E. Sharpe, 80 Business Park Drive, Armonk, NY 10504, (800) 541-6563, Fax: (914) 273-2106, www.mesharpe.com; *The Illustrated Book of World Rankings.*

United Nations Statistics Division, New York, NY 10017, (800) 253-9646, Fax: (212) 963-4116, http://unstats.un.org; *World Statistics Pocketbook.*

BULGARIA - SOCIAL SECURITY

Palgrave Macmillan Ltd., Houndmills, Basingstoke, Hampshire, RG21 6XS, England, (Telephone in U.S. (888) 330-8477), (Fax in U.S. (800) 672-2054), www.palgrave.com; *The Statesman's Yearbook 2008.*

United Nations Statistics Division, New York, NY 10017, (800) 253-9646, Fax: (212) 963-4116, http://unstats.un.org; *National Accounts Statistics: Compendium of Income Distribution Statistics.*

BULGARIA - SOYBEAN PRODUCTION

See BULGARIA - CROPS

BULGARIA - STEEL PRODUCTION

See BULGARIA - MINERAL INDUSTRIES

BULGARIA - SUGAR PRODUCTION

See BULGARIA - CROPS

BULGARIA - SULPHUR PRODUCTION

See BULGARIA - MINERAL INDUSTRIES

BULGARIA - TAXATION

International Road Federation (IFR), Madison Place, 500 Montgomery Street, 5th Floor, Alexandria, VA 22314, (703) 535-1001, Fax: (703) 535-1007, www.irfnet.org; *World Road Statistics 2006.*

Palgrave Macmillan Ltd., Houndmills, Basingstoke, Hampshire, RG21 6XS, England, (Telephone in U.S. (888) 330-8477), (Fax in U.S. (800) 672-2054), www.palgrave.com; *The Statesman's Yearbook 2008.*

Taylor and Francis Group, An Informa Business, 2 Park Square, Milton Park, Abingdon, Oxford OX14 4RN, United Kingdom, (Dial from U.S. (212) 216-7800), (Fax from U.S. (212) 564-7854), www.tandf.co.uk; *The Europa World Year Book.*

BULGARIA - TELEPHONE

International Telecommunication Union (ITU), Place des Nations, 1211 Geneva 20, Switzerland, www.itu.int; World Telecommunication Indicators Database.

Palgrave Macmillan Ltd., Houndmills, Basingstoke, Hampshire, RG21 6XS, England, (Telephone in U.S. (888) 330-8477), (Fax in U.S. (800) 672-2054), www.palgrave.com; *The Statesman's Yearbook 2008.*

Taylor and Francis Group, An Informa Business, 2 Park Square, Milton Park, Abingdon, Oxford OX14 4RN, United Kingdom, (Dial from U.S. (212) 216-7800), (Fax from U.S. (212) 564-7854), www.tandf.co.uk; *The Europa World Year Book.*

United Nations Statistics Division, New York, NY 10017, (800) 253-9646, Fax: (212) 963-4116, http://unstats.un.org; *Statistical Yearbook; Trends in Europe and North America: The Statistical Yearbook of the ECE 2005;* and *World Statistics Pocketbook.*

BULGARIA - TELEVISION - RECEIVERS AND RECEPTION

United Nations Statistics Division, New York, NY 10017, (800) 253-9646, Fax: (212) 963-4116, http://unstats.un.org; *Statistical Yearbook.*

BULGARIA - THEATER

UNESCO Institute for Statistics, C.P. 6128 Succursale Centre-Ville, Montreal, Quebec, H3C 3J7 Canada, (Dial from U.S. (514) 343-6880), (Fax from U.S. (514) 343 6882), www.uis.unesco.org; *Statistical Tables.*

BULGARIA - TIN PRODUCTION

See BULGARIA - MINERAL INDUSTRIES

BULGARIA - TIRE INDUSTRY

United Nations Statistics Division, New York, NY 10017, (800) 253-9646, Fax: (212) 963-4116, http://unstats.un.org; *Statistical Yearbook.*

BULGARIA - TOBACCO INDUSTRY

Euromonitor International, Inc., 224 S. Michigan Avenue, Suite 1500, Chicago, IL 60604, (312) 922-1115, Fax: (312) 922-1157, www.euromonitor.com; *European Marketing Data and Statistics 2008.*

Foreign Agricultural Service (FAS), U.S. Department of Agriculture (USDA), 1400 Independence Avenue, SW, Washington, DC 20250, (202) 720-3935, www.fas.usda.gov; *Tobacco: World Markets and Trade.*

M.E. Sharpe, 80 Business Park Drive, Armonk, NY 10504, (800) 541-6563, Fax: (914) 273-2106, www.mesharpe.com; *The Illustrated Book of World Rankings.*

United Nations Statistics Division, New York, NY 10017, (800) 253-9646, Fax: (212) 963-4116, http://unstats.un.org; *Statistical Yearbook.*

BULGARIA - TOURISM

Euromonitor International, Inc., 224 S. Michigan Avenue, Suite 1500, Chicago, IL 60604, (312) 922-1115, Fax: (312) 922-1157, www.euromonitor.com; *European Marketing Data and Statistics 2008; The World Economic Factbook 2008;* and *World Marketing Data and Statistics.*

M.E. Sharpe, 80 Business Park Drive, Armonk, NY 10504, (800) 541-6563, Fax: (914) 273-2106, www.mesharpe.com; *The Illustrated Book of World Rankings.*

Palgrave Macmillan Ltd., Houndmills, Basingstoke, Hampshire, RG21 6XS, England, (Telephone in U.S. (888) 330-8477), (Fax in U.S. (800) 672-2054), www.palgrave.com; *The Statesman's Yearbook 2008.*

Taylor and Francis Group, An Informa Business, 2 Park Square, Milton Park, Abingdon, Oxford OX14 4RN, United Kingdom, (Dial from U.S. (212) 216-7800), (Fax from U.S. (212) 564-7854), www.tandf.co.uk; *The Europa World Year Book.*

United Nations Statistics Division, New York, NY 10017, (800) 253-9646, Fax: (212) 963-4116, http://unstats.un.org; *Statistical Yearbook* and *Trends in Europe and North America: The Statistical Yearbook of the ECE 2005.*

United Nations World Tourism Organization (UNWTO), Capitan Haya 42, 28020 Madrid, Spain, www.world-tourism.org; *Yearbook of Tourism Statistics.*

The World Bank, 1818 H Street, NW, Washington, DC 20433, (202) 473-1000, Fax: (202) 477-6391, www.worldbank.org; *Bulgaria.*

BULGARIA - TRADE

See BULGARIA - INTERNATIONAL TRADE

BULGARIA - TRANSPORTATION

Central Intelligence Agency, Office of Public Affairs, Washington, DC 20505, (703) 482-0623, Fax: (703) 482-1739, www.cia.gov; *The World Factbook.*

Euromonitor International, Inc., 224 S. Michigan Avenue, Suite 1500, Chicago, IL 60604, (312) 922-1115, Fax: (312) 922-1157, www.euromonitor.com; *World Marketing Data and Statistics.*

Eurostat, Batiment Jean Monnet, Rue Alcide de Gasperi, L-2920 Luxembourg, http://epp.eurostat.ec.europa.eu; *Regional Passenger and Freight Air Transport in Europe in 2006* and *Regional Road and Rail Transport Networks.*

M.E. Sharpe, 80 Business Park Drive, Armonk, NY 10504, (800) 541-6563, Fax: (914) 273-2106, www.mesharpe.com; *The Illustrated Book of World Rankings.*

Palgrave Macmillan Ltd., Houndmills, Basingstoke, Hampshire, RG21 6XS, England, (Telephone in U.S. (888) 330-8477), (Fax in U.S. (800) 672-2054), www.palgrave.com; *The Statesman's Yearbook 2008.*

Taylor and Francis Group, An Informa Business, 2 Park Square, Milton Park, Abingdon, Oxford OX14 4RN, United Kingdom, (Dial from U.S. (212) 216-7800), (Fax from U.S. (212) 564-7854), www.tandf.co.uk; *The Europa World Year Book.*

United Nations Statistics Division, New York, NY 10017, (800) 253-9646, Fax: (212) 963-4116, http://unstats.un.org; *Human Development Report 2006* and *Trends in Europe and North America: The Statistical Yearbook of the ECE 2005.*

The World Bank, 1818 H Street, NW, Washington, DC 20433, (202) 473-1000, Fax: (202) 477-6391, www.worldbank.org; *Bulgaria.*

BULGARIA - TURKEYS

See BULGARIA - LIVESTOCK

BULGARIA - UNEMPLOYMENT

Central Intelligence Agency, Office of Public Affairs, Washington, DC 20505, (703) 482-0623, Fax: (703) 482-1739, www.cia.gov; *The World Factbook.*

Euromonitor International, Inc., 224 S. Michigan Avenue, Suite 1500, Chicago, IL 60604, (312) 922-1115, Fax: (312) 922-1157, www.euromonitor.com; *European Marketing Data and Statistics 2008.*

International Labour Office, I.L.O. Publications, 4 route des Morillons, CH-1211 Geneva 22, Switzerland, (Telephone in U.S. (202) 653-7652), (Fax in U.S. (202) 653-7687), www.ilo.org; *Yearbook of Labour Statistics 2006.*

Palgrave Macmillan Ltd., Houndmills, Basingstoke, Hampshire, RG21 6XS, England, (Telephone in U.S. (888) 330-8477), (Fax in U.S. (800) 672-2054), www.palgrave.com; *The Statesman's Yearbook 2008.*

United Nations Statistics Division, New York, NY 10017, (800) 253-9646, Fax: (212) 963-4116, http://unstats.un.org; *Trends in Europe and North America: The Statistical Yearbook of the ECE 2005.*

BULGARIA - VITAL STATISTICS

National Statistical Insitute (NSI), 2, P. Volov Street, 1038 Sofia, Bulgaria, www.nsi.bg; *Bulgaria 2006: Social-Economic Development* and *Population and Demographic Processes 2006.*

Palgrave Macmillan Ltd., Houndmills, Basingstoke, Hampshire, RG21 6XS, England, (Telephone in U.S. (888) 330-8477), (Fax in U.S. (800) 672-2054), www.palgrave.com; *The Statesman's Yearbook 2008.*

United Nations Statistics Division, New York, NY 10017, (800) 253-9646, Fax: (212) 963-4116, http://unstats.un.org; *Statistical Yearbook.*

World Health Organization (WHO), Avenue Appia 20, 1211 Geneve 27, Switzerland, (Telephone in U.S. (212) 331-9081), www.who.int; *World Health Report 2006.*

BULGARIA - WAGES

Euromonitor International, Inc., 224 S. Michigan Avenue, Suite 1500, Chicago, IL 60604, (312) 922-1115, Fax: (312) 922-1157, www.euromonitor.com; *European Marketing Data and Statistics 2008.*

International Labour Office, I.L.O. Publications, 4 route des Morillons, CH-1211 Geneva 22, Switzerland, (Telephone in U.S. (202) 653-7652), (Fax in U.S. (202) 653-7687), www.ilo.org; *Yearbook of Labour Statistics 2006.*

United Nations Statistics Division, New York, NY 10017, (800) 253-9646, Fax: (212) 963-4116, http://unstats.un.org; *Statistical Yearbook.*

The World Bank, 1818 H Street, NW, Washington, DC 20433, (202) 473-1000, Fax: (202) 477-6391, www.worldbank.org; *Bulgaria.*

BULGARIA - WALNUT PRODUCTION

See BULGARIA - CROPS

BULGARIA - WATERWAYS

United Nations Statistics Division, New York, NY 10017, (800) 253-9646, Fax: (212) 963-4116, http://

unstats.un.org; *Annual Bulletin of Transport Statistics for Europe and North America 2004.*

BULGARIA - WEATHER

See BULGARIA - CLIMATE

BULGARIA - WELFARE STATE

Palgrave Macmillan Ltd., Houndmills, Basingstoke, Hampshire, RG21 6XS, England, (Telephone in U.S. (888) 330-8477), (Fax in U.S. (800) 672-2054), www.palgrave.com; *The Statesman's Yearbook 2008.*

BULGARIA - WHEAT PRODUCTION

See BULGARIA - CROPS

BULGARIA - WINE PRODUCTION

See BULGARIA - BEVERAGE INDUSTRY

BULGARIA - WOOD AND WOOD PULP

See BULGARIA - FORESTS AND FORESTRY

BULGARIA - WOOL PRODUCTION

See BULGARIA - TEXTILE INDUSTRY

BULGARIA - YARN PRODUCTION

See BULGARIA - TEXTILE INDUSTRY

BULGARIA - ZINC AND ZINC ORE

See BULGARIA - MINERAL INDUSTRIES

BURGLARY

Federal Bureau of Investigation (FBI), J. Edgar Hoover Building, 935 Pennsylvania Avenue, NW, Washington, DC 20535-0001, (202) 324-3000, www.fbi.gov; *Crime in the United States (CIUS) 2007 (Preliminary).*

Justice Research and Statistics Association (JRSA), 777 N. Capitol Street, NE, Suite 801, Washington, DC 20002, (202) 842-9330, Fax: (202) 842-9329, www.jrsa.org; *Crime and Justice Atlas 2001.*

U.S. Department of Justice (DOJ), Bureau of Justice Statistics, 810 Seventh Street, NW, Washington, DC 20531, (202) 307-0765, www.ojp.usdoj.gov/bjs/; *Criminal Victimization, 2005.*

BURKINA FASO - PRIMARY STATISTICS SOURCES

Institut National de la Statistique et de la Demographie (INSD), Ministere de l'Economie et du Developpement, 555, Boulevard de l'Independance 01, BP 374 Ouagadougou 01, Burkina Faso, www.insd.bf; *Annuaire Statistique du Burkina Faso.*

BURKINA FASO - AGRICULTURAL MACHINERY

United Nations Statistics Division, New York, NY 10017, (800) 253-9646, Fax: (212) 963-4116, http://unstats.un.org; *Statistical Yearbook.*

BURKINA FASO - AGRICULTURE

Economist Intelligence Unit, 111 West 57th Street, New York, NY 10019, (212) 554-0600, Fax: (212) 586-1181, www.eiu.com; *Burkina Faso Country Report.*

Euromonitor International, Inc., 224 S. Michigan Avenue, Suite 1500, Chicago, IL 60604, (312) 922-1115, Fax: (312) 922-1157, www.euromonitor.com; *International Marketing Data and Statistics 2008* and *World Marketing Data and Statistics.*

International Food Policy Research Institute (IFPRI), 2033 K Street, NW, Washington, D.C., 2006, (202) 862-5600, www.ifpri.org; *Burkina Faso PNDSA II Impact Analysis Baseline Survey, 2002-2003.*

Palgrave Macmillan Ltd., Houndmills, Basingstoke, Hampshire, RG21 6XS, England, (Telephone in U.S. (888) 330-8477), (Fax in U.S. (800) 672-2054), www.palgrave.com; *The Statesman's Yearbook 2008.*

Taylor and Francis Group, An Informa Business, 2 Park Square, Milton Park, Abingdon, Oxford OX14 4RN, United Kingdom, (Dial from U.S. (212) 216-7800), (Fax from U.S. (212) 564-7854), www.tandf.co.uk; *The Europa World Year Book.*

United Nations Conference on Trade and Development (UNCTAD), DC2-1120, United Nations, New York, NY 10017, (212) 963-0027, www.unctad.org; *UNCTAD Commodity Yearbook.*

United Nations Economic Commission for Africa (ECA), PO Box 3001, Addis Ababa, Ethiopia, (Telephone in U.S. (212) 963-4957), www.uneca.org; *African Statistical Yearbook 2006.*

United Nations Food and Agricultural Organization (FAO), Viale delle Terme di Caracalla, 00100 Rome, Italy, (Dial from U.S. (202) 653-2400), (Fax from U.S. (202) 653 5760), www.fao.org; AQUASTAT; *FAO Trade Yearbook;* and *The State of Food and Agriculture (SOFA) 2006.*

United Nations Statistics Division, New York, NY 10017, (800) 253-9646, Fax: (212) 963-4116, http://unstats.un.org; *Statistical Yearbook* and *Survey of Economic and Social Conditions in Africa 2005.*

The World Bank, 1818 H Street, NW, Washington, DC 20433, (202) 473-1000, Fax: (202) 477-6391, www.worldbank.org; *Africa Live Database (LDB); African Development Indicators (ADI) 2007; Burkina Faso;* and *World Development Indicators (WDI) 2008.*

BURKINA FASO - AIRLINES

Palgrave Macmillan Ltd., Houndmills, Basingstoke, Hampshire, RG21 6XS, England, (Telephone in U.S. (888) 330-8477), (Fax in U.S. (800) 672-2054), www.palgrave.com; *The Statesman's Yearbook 2008.*

Taylor and Francis Group, An Informa Business, 2 Park Square, Milton Park, Abingdon, Oxford OX14 4RN, United Kingdom, (Dial from U.S. (212) 216-7800), (Fax from U.S. (212) 564-7854), www.tandf.co.uk; *The Europa World Year Book.*

United Nations Economic Commission for Africa (ECA), PO Box 3001, Addis Ababa, Ethiopia, (Telephone in U.S. (212) 963-4957), www.uneca.org; *African Statistical Yearbook 2006.*

United Nations Statistics Division, New York, NY 10017, (800) 253-9646, Fax: (212) 963-4116, http://unstats.un.org; *Statistical Yearbook.*

BURKINA FASO - AIRPORTS

Central Intelligence Agency, Office of Public Affairs, Washington, DC 20505, (703) 482-0623, Fax: (703) 482-1739, www.cia.gov; *The World Factbook.*

BURKINA FASO - ARMED FORCES

Central Intelligence Agency, Office of Public Affairs, Washington, DC 20505, (703) 482-0623, Fax: (703) 482-1739, www.cia.gov; *The World Factbook.*

Euromonitor International, Inc., 224 S. Michigan Avenue, Suite 1500, Chicago, IL 60604, (312) 922-1115, Fax: (312) 922-1157, www.euromonitor.com; *World Marketing Data and Statistics.*

International Institute for Strategic Studies (IISS), Arundel House, 13-15 Arundel Street, Temple Place, London WC2R 3DX, England, www.iiss.org; *The Military Balance 2007.*

International Monetary Fund (IMF), 700 Nineteenth Street, NW, Washington, DC 20431, (202) 623-7000, Fax: (202) 623-4661, www.imf.org; *Government Finance Statistics Yearbook (2008 Edition).*

Palgrave Macmillan Ltd., Houndmills, Basingstoke, Hampshire, RG21 6XS, England, (Telephone in U.S. (888) 330-8477), (Fax in U.S. (800) 672-2054), www.palgrave.com; *The Statesman's Yearbook 2008.*

U.S. Department of State (DOS), 2201 C Street NW, Washington, DC 20520, (202) 647-4000, www.state.gov; *World Military Expenditures and Arms Transfers (WMEAT).*

United Nations Statistics Division, New York, NY 10017, (800) 253-9646, Fax: (212) 963-4116, http://unstats.un.org; *Human Development Report 2006.*

BURKINA FASO - BALANCE OF PAYMENTS

African Development Bank Group, Rue Joseph Anoma, 01 BP 1387 Abidjan 01, Cote d'Ivoire, www.afdb.org; *Statistics Pocketbook 2008.*

International Monetary Fund (IMF), 700 Nineteenth Street, NW, Washington, DC 20431, (202) 623-7000, Fax: (202) 623-4661, www.imf.org; *Balance of Payments Statistics Newsletter* and *Balance of Payments Statistics Yearbook 2007.*

Taylor and Francis Group, An Informa Business, 2 Park Square, Milton Park, Abingdon, Oxford OX14 4RN, United Kingdom, (Dial from U.S. (212) 216-7800), (Fax from U.S. (212) 564-7854), www.tandf.co.uk; *The Europa World Year Book.*

United Nations Conference on Trade and Development (UNCTAD), DC2-1120, United Nations, New York, NY 10017, (212) 963-0027, www.unctad.org; *Handbook of Statistics 2005.*

United Nations Economic Commission for Africa (ECA), PO Box 3001, Addis Ababa, Ethiopia, (Telephone in U.S. (212) 963-4957), www.uneca.org; *African Statistical Yearbook 2006.*

The World Bank, 1818 H Street, NW, Washington, DC 20433, (202) 473-1000, Fax: (202) 477-6391, www.worldbank.org; *Burkina Faso; World Development Indicators (WDI) 2008;* and *World Development Report 2008.*

BURKINA FASO - BANKS AND BANKING

Euromonitor International, Inc., 224 S. Michigan Avenue, Suite 1500, Chicago, IL 60604, (312) 922-1115, Fax: (312) 922-1157, www.euromonitor.com; *World Marketing Data and Statistics.*

International Monetary Fund (IMF), 700 Nineteenth Street, NW, Washington, DC 20431, (202) 623-7000, Fax: (202) 623-4661, www.imf.org; *International Financial Statistics Yearbook 2007.*

Palgrave Macmillan Ltd., Houndmills, Basingstoke, Hampshire, RG21 6XS, England, (Telephone in U.S. (888) 330-8477), (Fax in U.S. (800) 672-2054), www.palgrave.com; *The Statesman's Yearbook 2008.*

Taylor and Francis Group, An Informa Business, 2 Park Square, Milton Park, Abingdon, Oxford OX14 4RN, United Kingdom, (Dial from U.S. (212) 216-7800), (Fax from U.S. (212) 564-7854), www.tandf.co.uk; *The Europa World Year Book.*

United Nations Economic Commission for Africa (ECA), PO Box 3001, Addis Ababa, Ethiopia, (Telephone in U.S. (212) 963-4957), www.uneca.org; *African Statistical Yearbook 2006.*

United Nations Statistics Division, New York, NY 10017, (800) 253-9646, Fax: (212) 963-4116, http://unstats.un.org; *Statistical Yearbook.*

BURKINA FASO - BEVERAGE INDUSTRY

United Nations Statistics Division, New York, NY 10017, (800) 253-9646, Fax: (212) 963-4116, http://unstats.un.org; *Statistical Yearbook.*

BURKINA FASO - BROADCASTING

Central Intelligence Agency, Office of Public Affairs, Washington, DC 20505, (703) 482-0623, Fax: (703) 482-1739, www.cia.gov; *The World Factbook.*

Euromonitor International, Inc., 224 S. Michigan Avenue, Suite 1500, Chicago, IL 60604, (312) 922-1115, Fax: (312) 922-1157, www.euromonitor.com; *World Marketing Data and Statistics.*

Palgrave Macmillan Ltd., Houndmills, Basingstoke, Hampshire, RG21 6XS, England, (Telephone in U.S. (888) 330-8477), (Fax in U.S. (800) 672-2054), www.palgrave.com; *The Statesman's Yearbook 2008.*

UNESCO Institute for Statistics, C.P. 6128 Succursale Centre-Ville, Montreal, Quebec, H3C 3J7 Canada, (Dial from U.S. (514) 343-6880), (Fax from U.S. (514) 343 6882), www.uis.unesco.org; *Statistical Tables.*

WRTH Publications Limited, PO Box 290, Oxford OX2 7FT, UK, www.wrth.com; *World Radio TV Handbook 2007.*

BURKINA FASO - BUDGET

Central Intelligence Agency, Office of Public Affairs, Washington, DC 20505, (703) 482-0623, Fax: (703) 482-1739, www.cia.gov; *The World Factbook.*

BURKINA FASO - CAPITAL LEVY

International Monetary Fund (IMF), 700 Nineteenth Street, NW, Washington, DC 20431, (202) 623-7000, Fax: (202) 623-4661, www.imf.org; *Government Finance Statistics Yearbook (2008 Edition).*

BURKINA FASO - CATTLE

See BURKINA FASO - LIVESTOCK

BURKINA FASO - CHICKENS

See BURKINA FASO - LIVESTOCK

BURKINA FASO - CHILDBIRTH - STATISTICS

Central Intelligence Agency, Office of Public Affairs, Washington, DC 20505, (703) 482-0623, Fax: (703) 482-1739, www.cia.gov; *The World Factbook.*

Euromonitor International, Inc., 224 S. Michigan Avenue, Suite 1500, Chicago, IL 60604, (312) 922-1115, Fax: (312) 922-1157, www.euromonitor.com; *International Marketing Data and Statistics 2008* and *The World Economic Factbook 2008.*

Palgrave Macmillan Ltd., Houndmills, Basingstoke, Hampshire, RG21 6XS, England, (Telephone in U.S. (888) 330-8477), (Fax in U.S. (800) 672-2054), www.palgrave.com; *The Statesman's Yearbook 2008.*

Taylor and Francis Group, An Informa Business, 2 Park Square, Milton Park, Abingdon, Oxford OX14 4RN, United Kingdom, (Dial from U.S. (212) 216-7800), (Fax from U.S. (212) 564-7854), www.tandf.co.uk; *The Europa World Year Book.*

United Nations Statistics Division, New York, NY 10017, (800) 253-9646, Fax: (212) 963-4116, http://unstats.un.org; *Demographic Yearbook; Statistical Yearbook;* and *Survey of Economic and Social Conditions in Africa 2005.*

The World Bank, 1818 H Street, NW, Washington, DC 20433, (202) 473-1000, Fax: (202) 477-6391, www.worldbank.org; *World Development Indicators (WDI) 2008.*

BURKINA FASO - CLIMATE

International Institute for Environment and Development (IIED), 3 Endsleigh Street, London, England, WC1H 0DD, United Kingdom, www.iied.org; *Environment Urbanization* and *Haramata - Bulletin of the Drylands.*

Palgrave Macmillan Ltd., Houndmills, Basingstoke, Hampshire, RG21 6XS, England, (Telephone in U.S. (888) 330-8477), (Fax in U.S. (800) 672-2054), www.palgrave.com; *The Statesman's Yearbook 2008.*

BURKINA FASO - COAL PRODUCTION

See BURKINA FASO - MINERAL INDUSTRIES

BURKINA FASO - COMMERCE

Palgrave Macmillan Ltd., Houndmills, Basingstoke, Hampshire, RG21 6XS, England, (Telephone in U.S. (888) 330-8477), (Fax in U.S. (800) 672-2054), www.palgrave.com; *The Statesman's Yearbook 2008.*

BURKINA FASO - COMMODITY EXCHANGES

Commodity Research Bureau, 330 South Wells Street, Suite 612, Chicago, IL 60606-7110, (800) 621-5271, Fax: (312) 939-4135, www.crbtrader.com; *2006 CRB Commodity Yearbook and CD.*

International Monetary Fund (IMF), 700 Nineteenth Street, NW, Washington, DC 20431, (202) 623-7000, Fax: (202) 623-4661, www.imf.org; *IMF Primary Commodity Prices.*

United Nations Food and Agricultural Organization (FAO), Viale delle Terme di Caracalla, 00100 Rome, Italy, (Dial from U.S. (202) 653-2400), (Fax from U.S. (202) 653 5760), www.fao.org; *The State of Food and Agriculture (SOFA) 2006.*

BURKINA FASO - COMMUNICATION AND TRAFFIC

United Nations Statistics Division, New York, NY 10017, (800) 253-9646, Fax: (212) 963-4116, http://unstats.un.org; *Statistical Yearbook.*

BURKINA FASO - CONSTRUCTION INDUSTRY

United Nations Economic Commission for Africa (ECA), PO Box 3001, Addis Ababa, Ethiopia, (Telephone in U.S. (212) 963-4957), www.uneca.org; *African Statistical Yearbook 2006.*

BURKINA FASO - CONSUMER PRICE INDEXES

Taylor and Francis Group, An Informa Business, 2 Park Square, Milton Park, Abingdon, Oxford OX14 4RN, United Kingdom, (Dial from U.S. (212) 216-7800), (Fax from U.S. (212) 564-7854), www.tandf.co.uk; *The Europa World Year Book.*

United Nations Economic Commission for Africa (ECA), PO Box 3001, Addis Ababa, Ethiopia, (Telephone in U.S. (212) 963-4957), www.uneca.org; *African Statistical Yearbook 2006.*

United Nations Statistics Division, New York, NY 10017, (800) 253-9646, Fax: (212) 963-4116, http://unstats.un.org; *Survey of Economic and Social Conditions in Africa 2005.*

The World Bank, 1818 H Street, NW, Washington, DC 20433, (202) 473-1000, Fax: (202) 477-6391, www.worldbank.org; *Burkina Faso.*

BURKINA FASO - CONSUMPTION (ECONOMICS)

African Development Bank Group, Rue Joseph Anoma, 01 BP 1387 Abidjan 01, Cote d'Ivoire, www.afdb.org; *Statistics Pocketbook 2008.*

United Nations Statistics Division, New York, NY 10017, (800) 253-9646, Fax: (212) 963-4116, http://unstats.un.org; *Survey of Economic and Social Conditions in Africa 2005.*

The World Bank, 1818 H Street, NW, Washington, DC 20433, (202) 473-1000, Fax: (202) 477-6391, www.worldbank.org; *World Development Report 2008.*

BURKINA FASO - CORN INDUSTRY

See BURKINA FASO - CROPS

BURKINA FASO - COTTON

See BURKINA FASO - CROPS

BURKINA FASO - CROPS

International Monetary Fund (IMF), 700 Nineteenth Street, NW, Washington, DC 20431, (202) 623-7000, Fax: (202) 623-4661, www.imf.org; *International Financial Statistics Yearbook 2007.*

Palgrave Macmillan Ltd., Houndmills, Basingstoke, Hampshire, RG21 6XS, England, (Telephone in U.S. (888) 330-8477), (Fax in U.S. (800) 672-2054), www.palgrave.com; *The Statesman's Yearbook 2008.*

Taylor and Francis Group, An Informa Business, 2 Park Square, Milton Park, Abingdon, Oxford OX14 4RN, United Kingdom, (Dial from U.S. (212) 216-7800), (Fax from U.S. (212) 564-7854), www.tandf.co.uk; *The Europa World Year Book.*

United Nations Conference on Trade and Development (UNCTAD), DC2-1120, United Nations, New York, NY 10017, (212) 963-0027, www.unctad.org; *UNCTAD Commodity Yearbook.*

United Nations Economic Commission for Africa (ECA), PO Box 3001, Addis Ababa, Ethiopia, (Telephone in U.S. (212) 963-4957), www.uneca.org; *African Statistical Yearbook 2006.*

United Nations Food and Agricultural Organization (FAO), Viale delle Terme di Caracalla, 00100 Rome, Italy, (Dial from U.S. (202) 653-2400), (Fax from U.S. (202) 653 5760), www.fao.org; *The State of Food and Agriculture (SOFA) 2006.*

United Nations Statistics Division, New York, NY 10017, (800) 253-9646, Fax: (212) 963-4116, http://unstats.un.org; *Statistical Yearbook.*

BURKINA FASO - CUSTOMS ADMINISTRATION

International Monetary Fund (IMF), 700 Nineteenth Street, NW, Washington, DC 20431, (202) 623-7000, Fax: (202) 623-4661, www.imf.org; *Government Finance Statistics Yearbook (2008 Edition).*

BURKINA FASO - DAIRY PROCESSING

Palgrave Macmillan Ltd., Houndmills, Basingstoke, Hampshire, RG21 6XS, England, (Telephone in U.S. (888) 330-8477), (Fax in U.S. (800) 672-2054), www.palgrave.com; *The Statesman's Yearbook 2008.*

Taylor and Francis Group, An Informa Business, 2 Park Square, Milton Park, Abingdon, Oxford OX14 4RN, United Kingdom, (Dial from U.S. (212) 216-7800), (Fax from U.S. (212) 564-7854), www.tandf.co.uk; *The Europa World Year Book.*

United Nations Food and Agricultural Organization (FAO), Viale delle Terme di Caracalla, 00100 Rome, Italy, (Dial from U.S. (202) 653-2400), (Fax from U.S. (202) 653 5760), www.fao.org; *The State of Food and Agriculture (SOFA) 2006.*

United Nations Statistics Division, New York, NY 10017, (800) 253-9646, Fax: (212) 963-4116, http://unstats.un.org; *Statistical Yearbook.*

BURKINA FASO - DEATH RATES

See BURKINA FASO - MORTALITY

BURKINA FASO - DEBTS, EXTERNAL

African Development Bank Group, Rue Joseph Anoma, 01 BP 1387 Abidjan 01, Cote d'Ivoire, www.afdb.org; *Statistics Pocketbook 2008.*

Palgrave Macmillan Ltd., Houndmills, Basingstoke, Hampshire, RG21 6XS, England, (Telephone in U.S. (888) 330-8477), (Fax in U.S. (800) 672-2054), www.palgrave.com; *The Statesman's Yearbook 2008.*

United Nations Statistics Division, New York, NY 10017, (800) 253-9646, Fax: (212) 963-4116, http://unstats.un.org; *Survey of Economic and Social Conditions in Africa 2005.*

The World Bank, 1818 H Street, NW, Washington, DC 20433, (202) 473-1000, Fax: (202) 477-6391, www.worldbank.org; *Africa Live Database (LDB); African Development Indicators (ADI) 2007; Global Development Finance 2007; World Development Indicators (WDI) 2008;* and *World Development Report 2008.*

BURKINA FASO - DEFENSE EXPENDITURES

See BURKINA FASO - ARMED FORCES

BURKINA FASO - DEMOGRAPHY

Euromonitor International, Inc., 224 S. Michigan Avenue, Suite 1500, Chicago, IL 60604, (312) 922-1115, Fax: (312) 922-1157, www.euromonitor.com; *International Marketing Data and Statistics 2008; The World Economic Factbook 2008;* and *World Marketing Data and Statistics.*

United Nations Statistics Division, New York, NY 10017, (800) 253-9646, Fax: (212) 963-4116, http://unstats.un.org; *Human Development Report 2006* and *Survey of Economic and Social Conditions in Africa 2005.*

The World Bank, 1818 H Street, NW, Washington, DC 20433, (202) 473-1000, Fax: (202) 477-6391, www.worldbank.org; *Burkina Faso.*

BURKINA FASO - DISPOSABLE INCOME

United Nations Statistics Division, New York, NY 10017, (800) 253-9646, Fax: (212) 963-4116, http://unstats.un.org; *National Accounts Statistics: Compendium of Income Distribution Statistics* and *Statistical Yearbook.*

BURKINA FASO - DIVORCE

United Nations Statistics Division, New York, NY 10017, (800) 253-9646, Fax: (212) 963-4116, http://unstats.un.org; *Demographic Yearbook.*

BURKINA FASO - ECONOMIC ASSISTANCE

International Food Policy Research Institute (IFPRI), 2033 K Street, NW, Washington, D.C., 2006, (202) 862-5600, www.ifpri.org; *Burkina Faso PNDSA II Impact Analysis Baseline Survey, 2002-2003.*

United Nations Statistics Division, New York, NY 10017, (800) 253-9646, Fax: (212) 963-4116, http://unstats.un.org; *Statistical Yearbook.*

BURKINA FASO - ECONOMIC CONDITIONS

African Development Bank Group, Rue Joseph Anoma, 01 BP 1387 Abidjan 01, Cote d'Ivoire, www.afdb.org; *The African Statistical Journal; Gender, Poverty and Environmental Indicators on African Countries 2007; Selected Statistics on African Countries 2007;* and *Statistics Pocketbook 2008.*

Center for International Business Education Research (CIBER), Columbia Business School and School of International and Public Affairs, Uris Hall, Room 212, 3022 Broadway, New York, NY 10027-6902, Mr. Joshua Safier, (212) 854-4750, Fax: (212) 222-9821, www.columbia.edu/cu/ciber/; Datastream International.

Central Intelligence Agency, Office of Public Affairs, Washington, DC 20505, (703) 482-0623, Fax: (703) 482-1739, www.cia.gov; *The World Factbook.*

DSI Data Service Information, Xantener Strasse 51a, D-47495 Rheinberg, Germany, www.dsidata.com; *Campus Solution.*

Dun and Bradstreet (DB) Corporation, 103 JFK Parkway, Short Hills, NJ 07078, (973) 921-5500, www.dnb.com; *Country Report.*

Economist Intelligence Unit, 111 West 57th Street, New York, NY 10019, (212) 554-0600, Fax: (212) 586-1181, www.eiu.com; *Burkina Faso Country Report* and *Business Africa.*

Euromonitor International, Inc., 224 S. Michigan Avenue, Suite 1500, Chicago, IL 60604, (312) 922-1115, Fax: (312) 922-1157, www.euromonitor.com; *International Marketing Data and Statistics 2008; The World Economic Factbook 2008;* and *World Marketing Data and Statistics.*

International Food Policy Research Institute (IFPRI), 2033 K Street, NW, Washington, D.C., 2006, (202) 862-5600, www.ifpri.org; *Burkina Faso PNDSA II Impact Analysis Baseline Survey, 2002-2003.*

International Monetary Fund (IMF), 700 Nineteenth Street, NW, Washington, DC 20431, (202) 623-7000, Fax: (202) 623-4661, www.imf.org; *World Economic Outlook Reports.*

Palgrave Macmillan Ltd., Houndmills, Basingstoke, Hampshire, RG21 6XS, England, (Telephone in U.S. (888) 330-8477), (Fax in U.S. (800) 672-2054), www.palgrave.com; *The Statesman's Yearbook 2008.*

Taylor and Francis Group, An Informa Business, 2 Park Square, Milton Park, Abingdon, Oxford OX14 4RN, United Kingdom, (Dial from U.S. (212) 216-7800), (Fax from U.S. (212) 564-7854), www.tandf.co.uk; *The Europa World Year Book.*

United Nations Statistics Division, New York, NY 10017, (800) 253-9646, Fax: (212) 963-4116, http://unstats.un.org; *Compendium of Intra-African and Related Foreign Trade Statistics 2003* and *World Statistics Pocketbook.*

The World Bank, 1818 H Street, NW, Washington, DC 20433, (202) 473-1000, Fax: (202) 477-6391, www.worldbank.org; *Africa Household Survey Databank; Africa Live Database (LDB); Africa Standardized Files and Indicators; African Development Indicators (ADI) 2007; Burkina Faso; Global Economic Monitor (GEM); Global Economic Prospects 2008; The World Bank Atlas 2003-2004;* and *World Development Report 2008.*

BURKINA FASO - EDUCATION

African Development Bank Group, Rue Joseph Anoma, 01 BP 1387 Abidjan 01, Cote d'Ivoire, www.afdb.org; *Statistics Pocketbook 2008.*

Euromonitor International, Inc., 224 S. Michigan Avenue, Suite 1500, Chicago, IL 60604, (312) 922-1115, Fax: (312) 922-1157, www.euromonitor.com; *International Marketing Data and Statistics 2008* and *World Marketing Data and Statistics.*

International Monetary Fund (IMF), 700 Nineteenth Street, NW, Washington, DC 20431, (202) 623-7000, Fax: (202) 623-4661, www.imf.org; *Government Finance Statistics Yearbook (2008 Edition).*

Palgrave Macmillan Ltd., Houndmills, Basingstoke, Hampshire, RG21 6XS, England, (Telephone in U.S. (888) 330-8477), (Fax in U.S. (800) 672-2054), www.palgrave.com; *The Statesman's Yearbook 2008.*

Taylor and Francis Group, An Informa Business, 2 Park Square, Milton Park, Abingdon, Oxford OX14 4RN, United Kingdom, (Dial from U.S. (212) 216-7800), (Fax from U.S. (212) 564-7854), www.tandf.co.uk; *The Europa World Year Book.*

UNESCO Institute for Statistics, C.P. 6128 Succursale Centre-Ville, Montreal, Quebec, H3C 3J7 Canada, (Dial from U.S. (514) 343-6880), (Fax from U.S. (514) 343 6882), www.uis.unesco.org; *Statistical Tables.*

United Nations Economic Commission for Africa (ECA), PO Box 3001, Addis Ababa, Ethiopia, (Telephone in U.S. (212) 963-4957), www.uneca.org; *African Statistical Yearbook 2006.*

United Nations Statistics Division, New York, NY 10017, (800) 253-9646, Fax: (212) 963-4116, http://unstats.un.org; *Human Development Report 2006* and *Survey of Economic and Social Conditions in Africa 2005.*

The World Bank, 1818 H Street, NW, Washington, DC 20433, (202) 473-1000, Fax: (202) 477-6391, www.worldbank.org; *Burkina Faso; World Development Indicators (WDI) 2008;* and *World Development Report 2008.*

BURKINA FASO - ELECTRICITY

Palgrave Macmillan Ltd., Houndmills, Basingstoke, Hampshire, RG21 6XS, England, (Telephone in U.S. (888) 330-8477), (Fax in U.S. (800) 672-2054), www.palgrave.com; *The Statesman's Yearbook 2008.*

United Nations Economic Commission for Africa (ECA), PO Box 3001, Addis Ababa, Ethiopia, (Telephone in U.S. (212) 963-4957), www.uneca.org; *African Statistical Yearbook 2006.*

United Nations Statistics Division, New York, NY 10017, (800) 253-9646, Fax: (212) 963-4116, http://unstats.un.org; *Human Development Report 2006; Statistical Yearbook;* and *Survey of Economic and Social Conditions in Africa 2005.*

BURKINA FASO - EMPLOYMENT

Euromonitor International, Inc., 224 S. Michigan Avenue, Suite 1500, Chicago, IL 60604, (312) 922-1115, Fax: (312) 922-1157, www.euromonitor.com; *International Marketing Data and Statistics 2008.*

International Labour Office, I.L.O. Publications, 4 route des Morillons, CH-1211 Geneva 22, Switzerland, (Telephone in U.S. (202) 653-7652), (Fax in U.S. (202) 653-7687), www.ilo.org; *Yearbook of Labour Statistics 2006.*

United Nations Economic Commission for Africa (ECA), PO Box 3001, Addis Ababa, Ethiopia, (Telephone in U.S. (212) 963-4957), www.uneca.org; *African Statistical Yearbook 2006.*

United Nations Statistics Division, New York, NY 10017, (800) 253-9646, Fax: (212) 963-4116, http://unstats.un.org; *Statistical Yearbook* and *Survey of Economic and Social Conditions in Africa 2005.*

The World Bank, 1818 H Street, NW, Washington, DC 20433, (202) 473-1000, Fax: (202) 477-6391, www.worldbank.org; *Burkina Faso.*

BURKINA FASO - ENVIRONMENTAL CONDITIONS

DSI Data Service Information, Xantener Strasse 51a, D-47495 Rheinberg, Germany, www.dsidata.com; *Campus Solution* and *DSI's Global Environmental Database.*

Economist Intelligence Unit, 111 West 57th Street, New York, NY 10019, (212) 554-0600, Fax: (212) 586-1181, www.eiu.com; *Burkina Faso Country Report.*

International Institute for Environment and Development (IIED), 3 Endsleigh Street, London, England, WC1H 0DD, United Kingdom, www.iied.org; *Environment Urbanization* and *Haramata - Bulletin of the Drylands.*

United Nations Statistics Division, New York, NY 10017, (800) 253-9646, Fax: (212) 963-4116, http://unstats.un.org; *World Statistics Pocketbook.*

BURKINA FASO - EXPORTS

African Development Bank Group, Rue Joseph Anoma, 01 BP 1387 Abidjan 01, Cote d'Ivoire, www.afdb.org; *Statistics Pocketbook 2008.*

Central Intelligence Agency, Office of Public Affairs, Washington, DC 20505, (703) 482-0623, Fax: (703) 482-1739, www.cia.gov; *The World Factbook.*

Economist Intelligence Unit, 111 West 57th Street, New York, NY 10019, (212) 554-0600, Fax: (212) 586-1181, www.eiu.com; *Burkina Faso Country Report.*

Euromonitor International, Inc., 224 S. Michigan Avenue, Suite 1500, Chicago, IL 60604, (312) 922-1115, Fax: (312) 922-1157, www.euromonitor.com; *International Marketing Data and Statistics 2008* and *The World Economic Factbook 2008.*

International Monetary Fund (IMF), 700 Nineteenth Street, NW, Washington, DC 20431, (202) 623-7000, Fax: (202) 623-4661, www.imf.org; *Direction of Trade Statistics Yearbook 2007; Government Finance Statistics Yearbook (2008 Edition);* and *International Financial Statistics Yearbook 2007.*

Palgrave Macmillan Ltd., Houndmills, Basingstoke, Hampshire, RG21 6XS, England, (Telephone in U.S. (888) 330-8477), (Fax in U.S. (800) 672-2054), www.palgrave.com; *The Statesman's Yearbook 2008.*

Taylor and Francis Group, An Informa Business, 2 Park Square, Milton Park, Abingdon, Oxford OX14 4RN, United Kingdom, (Dial from U.S. (212) 216-7800), (Fax from U.S. (212) 564-7854), www.tandf.co.uk; *The Europa World Year Book.*

United Nations Conference on Trade and Development (UNCTAD), DC2-1120, United Nations, New York, NY 10017, (212) 963-0027, www.unctad.org; *Handbook of Statistics 2005.*

United Nations Economic Commission for Africa (ECA), PO Box 3001, Addis Ababa, Ethiopia, (Telephone in U.S. (212) 963-4957), www.uneca.org; *African Statistical Yearbook 2006.*

United Nations Food and Agricultural Organization (FAO), Viale delle Terme di Caracalla, 00100 Rome, Italy, (Dial from U.S. (202) 653-2400), (Fax from U.S. (202) 653 5760), www.fao.org; *The State of Food and Agriculture (SOFA) 2006.*

United Nations Statistics Division, New York, NY 10017, (800) 253-9646, Fax: (212) 963-4116, http://unstats.un.org; *Compendium of Intra-African and Related Foreign Trade Statistics 2003* and *Survey of Economic and Social Conditions in Africa 2005.*

The World Bank, 1818 H Street, NW, Washington, DC 20433, (202) 473-1000, Fax: (202) 477-6391, www.worldbank.org; *World Development Indicators (WDI) 2008* and *World Development Report 2008.*

BURKINA FASO - FEMALE WORKING POPULATION

See BURKINA FASO - EMPLOYMENT

BURKINA FASO - FERTILITY, HUMAN

Central Intelligence Agency, Office of Public Affairs, Washington, DC 20505, (703) 482-0623, Fax: (703) 482-1739, www.cia.gov; *The World Factbook.*

United Nations Statistics Division, New York, NY 10017, (800) 253-9646, Fax: (212) 963-4116, http://unstats.un.org; *Human Development Report 2006* and *Survey of Economic and Social Conditions in Africa 2005.*

The World Bank, 1818 H Street, NW, Washington, DC 20433, (202) 473-1000, Fax: (202) 477-6391, www.worldbank.org; *The World Bank Atlas 2003-2004; World Development Indicators (WDI) 2008;* and *World Development Report 2008.*

BURKINA FASO - FERTILIZER INDUSTRY

United Nations Food and Agricultural Organization (FAO), Viale delle Terme di Caracalla, 00100 Rome, Italy, (Dial from U.S. (202) 653-2400), (Fax from U.S. (202) 653 5760), www.fao.org; *FAO Fertilizer Yearbook* and *The State of Food and Agriculture (SOFA) 2006.*

United Nations Statistics Division, New York, NY 10017, (800) 253-9646, Fax: (212) 963-4116, http://unstats.un.org; *Statistical Yearbook.*

BURKINA FASO - FETAL DEATH

United Nations Statistics Division, New York, NY 10017, (800) 253-9646, Fax: (212) 963-4116, http://unstats.un.org; *Demographic Yearbook.*

BURKINA FASO - FINANCE

Taylor and Francis Group, An Informa Business, 2 Park Square, Milton Park, Abingdon, Oxford OX14 4RN, United Kingdom, (Dial from U.S. (212) 216-7800), (Fax from U.S. (212) 564-7854), www.tandf.co.uk; *The Europa World Year Book.*

United Nations Economic Commission for Africa (ECA), PO Box 3001, Addis Ababa, Ethiopia, (Telephone in U.S. (212) 963-4957), www.uneca.org; *African Statistical Yearbook 2006.*

United Nations Statistics Division, New York, NY 10017, (800) 253-9646, Fax: (212) 963-4116, http://unstats.un.org; *National Accounts Statistics: Compendium of Income Distribution Statistics* and *Statistical Yearbook.*

The World Bank, 1818 H Street, NW, Washington, DC 20433, (202) 473-1000, Fax: (202) 477-6391, www.worldbank.org; *Burkina Faso.*

BURKINA FASO - FINANCE, PUBLIC

African Development Bank Group, Rue Joseph Anoma, 01 BP 1387 Abidjan 01, Cote d'Ivoire, www.afdb.org; *Statistics Pocketbook 2008.*

Bernan Essential Government Publications, 4611-F Assembly Drive, Lanham MD, 20706-4391, (301) 459-2255, Fax: (800) 865-3450, www.bernan.com; *National Accounts Statistics.*

Economist Intelligence Unit, 111 West 57th Street, New York, NY 10019, (212) 554-0600, Fax: (212) 586-1181, www.eiu.com; *Burkina Faso Country Report.*

International Monetary Fund (IMF), 700 Nineteenth Street, NW, Washington, DC 20431, (202) 623-7000, Fax: (202) 623-4661, www.imf.org; *International Financial Statistics* and *International Financial Statistics Online Service.*

Palgrave Macmillan Ltd., Houndmills, Basingstoke, Hampshire, RG21 6XS, England, (Telephone in U.S. (888) 330-8477), (Fax in U.S. (800) 672-2054), www.palgrave.com; *The Statesman's Yearbook 2008.*

Taylor and Francis Group, An Informa Business, 2 Park Square, Milton Park, Abingdon, Oxford OX14 4RN, United Kingdom, (Dial from U.S. (212) 216-7800), (Fax from U.S. (212) 564-7854), www.tandf.co.uk; *The Europa World Year Book.*

United Nations Economic Commission for Africa (ECA), PO Box 3001, Addis Ababa, Ethiopia, (Telephone in U.S. (212) 963-4957), www.uneca.org; *African Statistical Yearbook 2006.*

The World Bank, 1818 H Street, NW, Washington, DC 20433, (202) 473-1000, Fax: (202) 477-6391, www.worldbank.org; *Burkina Faso.*

BURKINA FASO - FISHERIES

Palgrave Macmillan Ltd., Houndmills, Basingstoke, Hampshire, RG21 6XS, England, (Telephone in U.S. (888) 330-8477), (Fax in U.S. (800) 672-2054), www.palgrave.com; *The Statesman's Yearbook 2008.*

Taylor and Francis Group, An Informa Business, 2 Park Square, Milton Park, Abingdon, Oxford OX14 4RN, United Kingdom, (Dial from U.S. (212) 216-7800), (Fax from U.S. (212) 564-7854), www.tandf.co.uk; *The Europa World Year Book.*

United Nations Conference on Trade and Development (UNCTAD), DC2-1120, United Nations, New York, NY 10017, (212) 963-0027, www.unctad.org; *UNCTAD Commodity Yearbook.*

United Nations Economic Commission for Africa (ECA), PO Box 3001, Addis Ababa, Ethiopia, (Telephone in U.S. (212) 963-4957), www.uneca.org; *African Statistical Yearbook 2006.*

United Nations Food and Agricultural Organization (FAO), Viale delle Terme di Caracalla, 00100 Rome, Italy, (Dial from U.S. (202) 653-2400), (Fax from U.S. (202) 653 5760), www.fao.org; *FAO Yearbook of Fishery Statistics;* Fishery Databases; FISHSTAT Database. Subjects covered include: Aquaculture production, capture production, fishery commodities; and *The State of Food and Agriculture (SOFA) 2006.*

United Nations Statistics Division, New York, NY 10017, (800) 253-9646, Fax: (212) 963-4116, http://unstats.un.org; *Statistical Yearbook* and *Survey of Economic and Social Conditions in Africa 2005.*

The World Bank, 1818 H Street, NW, Washington, DC 20433, (202) 473-1000, Fax: (202) 477-6391, www.worldbank.org; *Burkina Faso.*

BURKINA FASO - FOOD

African Development Bank Group, Rue Joseph Anoma, 01 BP 1387 Abidjan 01, Cote d'Ivoire, www.afdb.org; *Statistics Pocketbook 2008.*

United Nations Conference on Trade and Development (UNCTAD), DC2-1120, United Nations, New York, NY 10017, (212) 963-0027, www.unctad.org; *UNCTAD Commodity Yearbook.*

United Nations Food and Agricultural Organization (FAO), Viale delle Terme di Caracalla, 00100 Rome, Italy, (Dial from U.S. (202) 653-2400), (Fax from U.S. (202) 653 5760), www.fao.org; *FAO Production Yearbook 2002* and *The State of Food and Agriculture (SOFA) 2006.*

United Nations Statistics Division, New York, NY 10017, (800) 253-9646, Fax: (212) 963-4116, http://unstats.un.org; *Human Development Report 2006.*

BURKINA FASO - FOREIGN EXCHANGE RATES

African Development Bank Group, Rue Joseph Anoma, 01 BP 1387 Abidjan 01, Cote d'Ivoire, www.afdb.org; *Statistics Pocketbook 2008.*

Central Intelligence Agency, Office of Public Affairs, Washington, DC 20505, (703) 482-0623, Fax: (703) 482-1739, www.cia.gov; *The World Factbook.*

Euromonitor International, Inc., 224 S. Michigan Avenue, Suite 1500, Chicago, IL 60604, (312) 922-1115, Fax: (312) 922-1157, www.euromonitor.com; *International Marketing Data and Statistics 2008* and *The World Economic Factbook 2008.*

International Monetary Fund (IMF), 700 Nineteenth Street, NW, Washington, DC 20431, (202) 623-7000, Fax: (202) 623-4661, www.imf.org; *International Financial Statistics Yearbook 2007.*

Taylor and Francis Group, An Informa Business, 2 Park Square, Milton Park, Abingdon, Oxford OX14 4RN, United Kingdom, (Dial from U.S. (212) 216-7800), (Fax from U.S. (212) 564-7854), www.tandf.co.uk; *The Europa World Year Book.*

United Nations Statistics Division, New York, NY 10017, (800) 253-9646, Fax: (212) 963-4116, http://unstats.un.org; *Compendium of Intra-African and Related Foreign Trade Statistics 2003; Statistical Yearbook;* and *World Statistics Pocketbook.*

BURKINA FASO - FORESTS AND FORESTRY

Organisation for Economic Cooperation and Development (OECD), 2 rue Andre Pascal, F-75775 Paris Cedex 16, France, (Telephone in U.S. (202) 785-6323), (Fax in U.S. (202) 785-0350), www.oecd.org; *Indicators of Industrial Activity.*

Palgrave Macmillan Ltd., Houndmills, Basingstoke, Hampshire, RG21 6XS, England, (Telephone in U.S. (888) 330-8477), (Fax in U.S. (800) 672-2054), www.palgrave.com; *The Statesman's Yearbook 2008.*

Taylor and Francis Group, An Informa Business, 2 Park Square, Milton Park, Abingdon, Oxford OX14 4RN, United Kingdom, (Dial from U.S. (212) 216-7800), (Fax from U.S. (212) 564-7854), www.tandf.co.uk; *The Europa World Year Book.*

United Nations Conference on Trade and Development (UNCTAD), DC2-1120, United Nations, New York, NY 10017, (212) 963-0027, www.unctad.org; *UNCTAD Commodity Yearbook.*

United Nations Economic Commission for Africa (ECA), PO Box 3001, Addis Ababa, Ethiopia, (Telephone in U.S. (212) 963-4957), www.uneca.org; *African Statistical Yearbook 2006.*

United Nations Food and Agricultural Organization (FAO), Viale delle Terme di Caracalla, 00100 Rome, Italy, (Dial from U.S. (202) 653-2400), (Fax from U.S. (202) 653 5760), www.fao.org; *FAO Yearbook of Forest Products* and *The State of Food and Agriculture (SOFA) 2006.*

The World Bank, 1818 H Street, NW, Washington, DC 20433, (202) 473-1000, Fax: (202) 477-6391, www.worldbank.org; *Burkina Faso* and *World Development Report 2008.*

BURKINA FASO - GEOGRAPHIC INFORMATION SYSTEMS

The World Bank, 1818 H Street, NW, Washington, DC 20433, (202) 473-1000, Fax: (202) 477-6391, www.worldbank.org; *Burkina Faso.*

BURKINA FASO - GOLD INDUSTRY

International Monetary Fund (IMF), 700 Nineteenth Street, NW, Washington, DC 20431, (202) 623-7000, Fax: (202) 623-4661, www.imf.org; *International Financial Statistics Yearbook 2007.*

United Nations Statistics Division, New York, NY 10017, (800) 253-9646, Fax: (212) 963-4116, http://unstats.un.org; *Statistical Yearbook.*

The World Bank, 1818 H Street, NW, Washington, DC 20433, (202) 473-1000, Fax: (202) 477-6391, www.worldbank.org; *World Development Indicators (WDI) 2008.*

BURKINA FASO - GRANTS-IN-AID

International Monetary Fund (IMF), 700 Nineteenth Street, NW, Washington, DC 20431, (202) 623-7000, Fax: (202) 623-4661, www.imf.org; *Government Finance Statistics Yearbook (2008 Edition).*

BURKINA FASO - GROSS DOMESTIC PRODUCT

African Development Bank Group, Rue Joseph Anoma, 01 BP 1387 Abidjan 01, Cote d'Ivoire, www.afdb.org; *Statistics Pocketbook 2008.*

Economist Intelligence Unit, 111 West 57th Street, New York, NY 10019, (212) 554-0600, Fax: (212) 586-1181, www.eiu.com; *Burkina Faso Country Report.*

Euromonitor International, Inc., 224 S. Michigan Avenue, Suite 1500, Chicago, IL 60604, (312) 922-1115, Fax: (312) 922-1157, www.euromonitor.com; *International Marketing Data and Statistics 2008* and *The World Economic Factbook 2008.*

Taylor and Francis Group, An Informa Business, 2 Park Square, Milton Park, Abingdon, Oxford OX14 4RN, United Kingdom, (Dial from U.S. (212) 216-7800), (Fax from U.S. (212) 564-7854), www.tandf.co.uk; *The Europa World Year Book.*

United Nations Economic Commission for Africa (ECA), PO Box 3001, Addis Ababa, Ethiopia, (Telephone in U.S. (212) 963-4957), www.uneca.org; *African Statistical Yearbook 2006.*

United Nations Statistics Division, New York, NY 10017, (800) 253-9646, Fax: (212) 963-4116, http://

unstats.un.org; *Human Development Report 2006; National Accounts Statistics: Compendium of Income Distribution Statistics; Statistical Yearbook;* and *Survey of Economic and Social Conditions in Africa 2005.*

The World Bank, 1818 H Street, NW, Washington, DC 20433, (202) 473-1000, Fax: (202) 477-6391, www.worldbank.org; *World Development Indicators (WDI) 2008* and *World Development Report 2008.*

BURKINA FASO - GROSS NATIONAL PRODUCT

Euromonitor International, Inc., 224 S. Michigan Avenue, Suite 1500, Chicago, IL 60604, (312) 922-1115, Fax: (312) 922-1157, www.euromonitor.com; *International Marketing Data and Statistics 2008.*

Palgrave Macmillan Ltd., Houndmills, Basingstoke, Hampshire, RG21 6XS, England, (Telephone in U.S. (888) 330-8477), (Fax in U.S. (800) 672-2054), www.palgrave.com; *The Statesman's Yearbook 2008.*

Taylor and Francis Group, An Informa Business, 2 Park Square, Milton Park, Abingdon, Oxford OX14 4RN, United Kingdom, (Dial from U.S. (212) 216-7800), (Fax from U.S. (212) 564-7854), www.tandf.co.uk; *The Europa World Year Book.*

U.S. Department of State (DOS), 2201 C Street NW, Washington, DC 20520, (202) 647-4000, www.state.gov; *World Military Expenditures and Arms Transfers (WMEAT).*

The World Bank, 1818 H Street, NW, Washington, DC 20433, (202) 473-1000, Fax: (202) 477-6391, www.worldbank.org; *The World Bank Atlas 2003-2004; World Development Indicators (WDI) 2008;* and *World Development Report 2008.*

BURKINA FASO - HIDES AND SKINS INDUSTRY

United Nations Food and Agricultural Organization (FAO), Viale delle Terme di Caracalla, 00100 Rome, Italy, (Dial from U.S. (202) 653-2400), (Fax from U.S. (202) 653 5760), www.fao.org; *FAO Production Yearbook 2002.*

BURKINA FASO - HOUSING

Euromonitor International, Inc., 224 S. Michigan Avenue, Suite 1500, Chicago, IL 60604, (312) 922-1115, Fax: (312) 922-1157, www.euromonitor.com; *World Marketing Data and Statistics.*

International Monetary Fund (IMF), 700 Nineteenth Street, NW, Washington, DC 20431, (202) 623-7000, Fax: (202) 623-4661, www.imf.org; *Government Finance Statistics Yearbook (2008 Edition).*

BURKINA FASO - ILLITERATE PERSONS

Euromonitor International, Inc., 224 S. Michigan Avenue, Suite 1500, Chicago, IL 60604, (312) 922-1115, Fax: (312) 922-1157, www.euromonitor.com; *The World Economic Factbook 2008.*

UNESCO Institute for Statistics, C.P. 6128 Succursale Centre-Ville, Montreal, Quebec, H3C 3J7 Canada, (Dial from U.S. (514) 343-6880), (Fax from U.S. (514) 343 6882), www.uis.unesco.org; *Statistical Tables.*

United Nations Statistics Division, New York, NY 10017, (800) 253-9646, Fax: (212) 963-4116, http://unstats.un.org; *Human Development Report 2006.*

BURKINA FASO - IMPORTS

Central Intelligence Agency, Office of Public Affairs, Washington, DC 20505, (703) 482-0623, Fax: (703) 482-1739, www.cia.gov; *The World Factbook.*

Economist Intelligence Unit, 111 West 57th Street, New York, NY 10019, (212) 554-0600, Fax: (212) 586-1181, www.eiu.com; *Burkina Faso Country Report.*

Euromonitor International, Inc., 224 S. Michigan Avenue, Suite 1500, Chicago, IL 60604, (312) 922-1115, Fax: (312) 922-1157, www.euromonitor.com; *International Marketing Data and Statistics 2008* and *The World Economic Factbook 2008.*

International Monetary Fund (IMF), 700 Nineteenth Street, NW, Washington, DC 20431, (202) 623-7000, Fax: (202) 623-4661, www.imf.org; *Direction of Trade Statistics Yearbook 2007; Government Finance Statistics Yearbook (2008 Edition);* and *International Financial Statistics Yearbook 2007.*

Palgrave Macmillan Ltd., Houndmills, Basingstoke, Hampshire, RG21 6XS, England, (Telephone in U.S. (888) 330-8477), (Fax in U.S. (800) 672-2054), www.palgrave.com; *The Statesman's Yearbook 2008.*

Taylor and Francis Group, An Informa Business, 2 Park Square, Milton Park, Abingdon, Oxford OX14 4RN, United Kingdom, (Dial from U.S. (212) 216-7800), (Fax from U.S. (212) 564-7854), www.tandf.co.uk; *The Europa World Year Book.*

United Nations Conference on Trade and Development (UNCTAD), DC2-1120, United Nations, New York, NY 10017, (212) 963-0027, www.unctad.org; *Handbook of Statistics 2005.*

United Nations Economic Commission for Africa (ECA), PO Box 3001, Addis Ababa, Ethiopia, (Telephone in U.S. (212) 963-4957), www.uneca.org; *African Statistical Yearbook 2006.*

United Nations Food and Agricultural Organization (FAO), Viale delle Terme di Caracalla, 00100 Rome, Italy, (Dial from U.S. (202) 653-2400), (Fax from U.S. (202) 653 5760), www.fao.org; *The State of Food and Agriculture (SOFA) 2006.*

United Nations Statistics Division, New York, NY 10017, (800) 253-9646, Fax: (212) 963-4116, http://unstats.un.org; *Compendium of Intra-African and Related Foreign Trade Statistics 2003* and *Survey of Economic and Social Conditions in Africa 2005.*

The World Bank, 1818 H Street, NW, Washington, DC 20433, (202) 473-1000, Fax: (202) 477-6391, www.worldbank.org; *World Development Indicators (WDI) 2008* and *World Development Report 2008.*

BURKINA FASO - INCOME TAXES

See BURKINA FASO - TAXATION

BURKINA FASO - INDUSTRIAL PRODUCTIVITY

Euromonitor International, Inc., 224 S. Michigan Avenue, Suite 1500, Chicago, IL 60604, (312) 922-1115, Fax: (312) 922-1157, www.euromonitor.com; *International Marketing Data and Statistics 2008.*

BURKINA FASO - INDUSTRIES

Central Intelligence Agency, Office of Public Affairs, Washington, DC 20505, (703) 482-0623, Fax: (703) 482-1739, www.cia.gov; *The World Factbook.*

Economist Intelligence Unit, 111 West 57th Street, New York, NY 10019, (212) 554-0600, Fax: (212) 586-1181, www.eiu.com; *Burkina Faso Country Report.*

Euromonitor International, Inc., 224 S. Michigan Avenue, Suite 1500, Chicago, IL 60604, (312) 922-1115, Fax: (312) 922-1157, www.euromonitor.com; *International Marketing Data and Statistics 2008; The World Economic Factbook 2008;* and *World Marketing Data and Statistics.*

International Labour Office, I.L.O. Publications, 4 route des Morillons, CH-1211 Geneva 22, Switzerland, (Telephone in U.S. (202) 653-7652), (Fax in U.S. (202) 653-7687), www.ilo.org; *Yearbook of Labour Statistics 2006.*

Palgrave Macmillan Ltd., Houndmills, Basingstoke, Hampshire, RG21 6XS, England, (Telephone in U.S. (888) 330-8477), (Fax in U.S. (800) 672-2054), www.palgrave.com; *The Statesman's Yearbook 2008.*

Taylor and Francis Group, An Informa Business, 2 Park Square, Milton Park, Abingdon, Oxford OX14 4RN, United Kingdom, (Dial from U.S. (212) 216-7800), (Fax from U.S. (212) 564-7854), www.tandf.co.uk; *The Europa World Year Book.*

United Nations Economic Commission for Africa (ECA), PO Box 3001, Addis Ababa, Ethiopia, (Telephone in U.S. (212) 963-4957), www.uneca.org; *African Statistical Yearbook 2006.*

United Nations Industrial Development Organization (UNIDO), 1 United Nations Plaza, New York, NY 10017, (212) 963 6890, Fax: (212) 963-7904, http://unido.org; Industrial Statistics Database 2008 (INDSTAT) and *The International Yearbook of Industrial Statistics 2008.*

United Nations Statistics Division, New York, NY 10017, (800) 253-9646, Fax: (212) 963-4116, http://unstats.un.org; *2004 Industrial Commodity Statistics Yearbook* and *Survey of Economic and Social Conditions in Africa 2005.*

The World Bank, 1818 H Street, NW, Washington, DC 20433, (202) 473-1000, Fax: (202) 477-6391, www.worldbank.org; *Burkina Faso* and *World Development Indicators (WDI) 2008.*

BURKINA FASO - INFANT AND MATERNAL MORTALITY

See BURKINA FASO - MORTALITY

BURKINA FASO - INTERNATIONAL LIQUIDITY

International Monetary Fund (IMF), 700 Nineteenth Street, NW, Washington, DC 20431, (202) 623-7000, Fax: (202) 623-4661, www.imf.org; *International Financial Statistics Yearbook 2007.*

BURKINA FASO - INTERNATIONAL TRADE

African Development Bank Group, Rue Joseph Anoma, 01 BP 1387 Abidjan 01, Cote d'Ivoire, www.afdb.org; *Statistics Pocketbook 2008.*

Economist Intelligence Unit, 111 West 57th Street, New York, NY 10019, (212) 554-0600, Fax: (212) 586-1181, www.eiu.com; *Burkina Faso Country Report.*

Euromonitor International, Inc., 224 S. Michigan Avenue, Suite 1500, Chicago, IL 60604, (312) 922-1115, Fax: (312) 922-1157, www.euromonitor.com; *International Marketing Data and Statistics 2008; The World Economic Factbook 2008;* and *World Marketing Data and Statistics.*

Palgrave Macmillan Ltd., Houndmills, Basingstoke, Hampshire, RG21 6XS, England, (Telephone in U.S. (888) 330-8477), (Fax in U.S. (800) 672-2054), www.palgrave.com; *The Statesman's Yearbook 2008.*

Taylor and Francis Group, An Informa Business, 2 Park Square, Milton Park, Abingdon, Oxford OX14 4RN, United Kingdom, (Dial from U.S. (212) 216-7800), (Fax from U.S. (212) 564-7854), www.tandf.co.uk; *The Europa World Year Book.*

United Nations Conference on Trade and Development (UNCTAD), DC2-1120, United Nations, New York, NY 10017, (212) 963-0027, www.unctad.org; *UNCTAD Commodity Yearbook.*

United Nations Economic Commission for Africa (ECA), PO Box 3001, Addis Ababa, Ethiopia, (Telephone in U.S. (212) 963-4957), www.uneca.org; *African Statistical Yearbook 2006.*

United Nations Food and Agricultural Organization (FAO), Viale delle Terme di Caracalla, 00100 Rome, Italy, (Dial from U.S. (202) 653-2400), (Fax from U.S. (202) 653 5760), www.fao.org; *FAO Trade Yearbook* and *The State of Food and Agriculture (SOFA) 2006.*

United Nations Statistics Division, New York, NY 10017, (800) 253-9646, Fax: (212) 963-4116, http://unstats.un.org; *Compendium of Intra-African and Related Foreign Trade Statistics 2003; International Trade Statistics Yearbook;* and *Statistical Yearbook.*

The World Bank, 1818 H Street, NW, Washington, DC 20433, (202) 473-1000, Fax: (202) 477-6391, www.worldbank.org; *Burkina Faso; World Development Indicators (WDI) 2008;* and *World Development Report 2008.*

World Trade Organization (WTO), Centre William Rappard, Rue de Lausanne 154, CH-1211 Geneva 21, Switzerland, www.wto.org; *International Trade Statistics 2006.*

BURKINA FASO - INTERNET USERS

International Telecommunication Union (ITU), Place des Nations, 1211 Geneva 20, Switzerland, www.

itu.int; *World Telecommunication/ICT Indicators Database on CD-ROM; World Telecommunication/ ICT Indicators Database Online;* and *Yearbook of Statistics - Telecommunication Services (Chronological Time Series 1997-2006).*

The World Bank, 1818 H Street, NW, Washington, DC 20433, (202) 473-1000, Fax: (202) 477-6391, www.worldbank.org; *Burkina Faso.*

BURKINA FASO - IRRIGATION

Euromonitor International, Inc., 224 S. Michigan Avenue, Suite 1500, Chicago, IL 60604, (312) 922-1115, Fax: (312) 922-1157, www.euromonitor.com; *International Marketing Data and Statistics 2008.*

BURKINA FASO - LABOR

African Development Bank Group, Rue Joseph Anoma, 01 BP 1387 Abidjan 01, Cote d'Ivoire, www.afdb.org; *Statistics Pocketbook 2008.*

Central Intelligence Agency, Office of Public Affairs, Washington, DC 20505, (703) 482-0623, Fax: (703) 482-1739, www.cia.gov; *The World Factbook.*

Euromonitor International, Inc., 224 S. Michigan Avenue, Suite 1500, Chicago, IL 60604, (312) 922-1115, Fax: (312) 922-1157, www.euromonitor.com; *International Marketing Data and Statistics 2008* and *World Marketing Data and Statistics.*

International Labour Office, I.L.O. Publications, 4 route des Morillons, CH-1211 Geneva 22, Switzerland, (Telephone in U.S. (202) 653-7652), (Fax in U.S. (202) 653-7687), www.ilo.org; *Yearbook of Labour Statistics 2006.*

Palgrave Macmillan Ltd., Houndmills, Basingstoke, Hampshire, RG21 6XS, England, (Telephone in U.S. (888) 330-8477), (Fax in U.S. (800) 672-2054), www.palgrave.com; *The Statesman's Yearbook 2008.*

United Nations Food and Agricultural Organization (FAO), Viale delle Terme di Caracalla, 00100 Rome, Italy, (Dial from U.S. (202) 653-2400), (Fax from U.S. (202) 653 5760), www.fao.org; *The State of Food and Agriculture (SOFA) 2006.*

United Nations Statistics Division, New York, NY 10017, (800) 253-9646, Fax: (212) 963-4116, http://unstats.un.org; *Human Development Report 2006.*

The World Bank, 1818 H Street, NW, Washington, DC 20433, (202) 473-1000, Fax: (202) 477-6391, www.worldbank.org; *The World Bank Atlas 2003-2004; World Development Indicators (WDI) 2008;* and *World Development Report 2008.*

BURKINA FASO - LAND USE

Central Intelligence Agency, Office of Public Affairs, Washington, DC 20505, (703) 482-0623, Fax: (703) 482-1739, www.cia.gov; *The World Factbook.*

Euromonitor International, Inc., 224 S. Michigan Avenue, Suite 1500, Chicago, IL 60604, (312) 922-1115, Fax: (312) 922-1157, www.euromonitor.com; *International Marketing Data and Statistics 2008.*

United Nations Food and Agricultural Organization (FAO), Viale delle Terme di Caracalla, 00100 Rome, Italy, (Dial from U.S. (202) 653-2400), (Fax from U.S. (202) 653 5760), www.fao.org; *FAO Production Yearbook 2002.*

The World Bank, 1818 H Street, NW, Washington, DC 20433, (202) 473-1000, Fax: (202) 477-6391, www.worldbank.org; *World Development Report 2008.*

BURKINA FASO - LIBRARIES

UNESCO Institute for Statistics, C.P. 6128 Succursale Centre-Ville, Montreal, Quebec, H3C 3J7 Canada, (Dial from U.S. (514) 343-6880), (Fax from U.S. (514) 343 6882), www.uis.unesco.org; *Statistical Tables.*

BURKINA FASO - LICENSES

International Monetary Fund (IMF), 700 Nineteenth Street, NW, Washington, DC 20431, (202) 623-7000, Fax: (202) 623-4661, www.imf.org; *Government Finance Statistics Yearbook (2008 Edition).*

BURKINA FASO - LIFE EXPECTANCY

African Development Bank Group, Rue Joseph Anoma, 01 BP 1387 Abidjan 01, Cote d'Ivoire, www.afdb.org; *Statistics Pocketbook 2008.*

Central Intelligence Agency, Office of Public Affairs, Washington, DC 20505, (703) 482-0623, Fax: (703) 482-1739, www.cia.gov; *The World Factbook.*

Euromonitor International, Inc., 224 S. Michigan Avenue, Suite 1500, Chicago, IL 60604, (312) 922-1115, Fax: (312) 922-1157, www.euromonitor.com; *The World Economic Factbook 2008.*

Palgrave Macmillan Ltd., Houndmills, Basingstoke, Hampshire, RG21 6XS, England, (Telephone in U.S. (888) 330-8477), (Fax in U.S. (800) 672-2054), www.palgrave.com; *The Statesman's Yearbook 2008.*

United Nations Statistics Division, New York, NY 10017, (800) 253-9646, Fax: (212) 963-4116, http://unstats.un.org; *Human Development Report 2006* and *World Statistics Pocketbook.*

The World Bank, 1818 H Street, NW, Washington, DC 20433, (202) 473-1000, Fax: (202) 477-6391, www.worldbank.org; *The World Bank Atlas 2003-2004* and *World Development Report 2008.*

BURKINA FASO - LITERACY

Euromonitor International, Inc., 224 S. Michigan Avenue, Suite 1500, Chicago, IL 60604, (312) 922-1115, Fax: (312) 922-1157, www.euromonitor.com; *World Marketing Data and Statistics.*

United Nations Statistics Division, New York, NY 10017, (800) 253-9646, Fax: (212) 963-4116, http://unstats.un.org; *Survey of Economic and Social Conditions in Africa 2005.*

BURKINA FASO - LIVESTOCK

Euromonitor International, Inc., 224 S. Michigan Avenue, Suite 1500, Chicago, IL 60604, (312) 922-1115, Fax: (312) 922-1157, www.euromonitor.com; *International Marketing Data and Statistics 2008.*

Palgrave Macmillan Ltd., Houndmills, Basingstoke, Hampshire, RG21 6XS, England, (Telephone in U.S. (888) 330-8477), (Fax in U.S. (800) 672-2054), www.palgrave.com; *The Statesman's Yearbook 2008.*

Taylor and Francis Group, An Informa Business, 2 Park Square, Milton Park, Abingdon, Oxford OX14 4RN, United Kingdom, (Dial from U.S. (212) 216-7800), (Fax from U.S. (212) 564-7854), www.tandf.co.uk; *The Europa World Year Book.*

United Nations Conference on Trade and Development (UNCTAD), DC2-1120, United Nations, New York, NY 10017, (212) 963-0027, www.unctad.org; *UNCTAD Commodity Yearbook.*

United Nations Economic Commission for Africa (ECA), PO Box 3001, Addis Ababa, Ethiopia, (Telephone in U.S. (212) 963-4957), www.uneca.org; *African Statistical Yearbook 2006.*

United Nations Food and Agricultural Organization (FAO), Viale delle Terme di Caracalla, 00100 Rome, Italy, (Dial from U.S. (202) 653-2400), (Fax from U.S. (202) 653 5760), www.fao.org; *FAO Production Yearbook 2002* and *The State of Food and Agriculture (SOFA) 2006.*

United Nations Statistics Division, New York, NY 10017, (800) 253-9646, Fax: (212) 963-4116, http://unstats.un.org; *Statistical Yearbook* and *Survey of Economic and Social Conditions in Africa 2005.*

BURKINA FASO - LOCAL TAXATION

Euromonitor International, Inc., 224 S. Michigan Avenue, Suite 1500, Chicago, IL 60604, (312) 922-1115, Fax: (312) 922-1157, www.euromonitor.com; *International Marketing Data and Statistics 2008.*

BURKINA FASO - MANUFACTURES

United Nations Economic Commission for Africa (ECA), PO Box 3001, Addis Ababa, Ethiopia, (Telephone in U.S. (212) 963-4957), www.uneca.org; *African Statistical Yearbook 2006.*

United Nations Statistics Division, New York, NY 10017, (800) 253-9646, Fax: (212) 963-4116, http://unstats.un.org; *Statistical Yearbook* and *Survey of Economic and Social Conditions in Africa 2005.*

The World Bank, 1818 H Street, NW, Washington, DC 20433, (202) 473-1000, Fax: (202) 477-6391, www.worldbank.org; *World Development Indicators (WDI) 2008.*

BURKINA FASO - MARRIAGE

United Nations Statistics Division, New York, NY 10017, (800) 253-9646, Fax: (212) 963-4116, http://unstats.un.org; *Demographic Yearbook.*

BURKINA FASO - MEAT PRODUCTION

See BURKINA FASO - LIVESTOCK

BURKINA FASO - MILK PRODUCTION

See BURKINA FASO - DAIRY PROCESSING

BURKINA FASO - MINERAL INDUSTRIES

Palgrave Macmillan Ltd., Houndmills, Basingstoke, Hampshire, RG21 6XS, England, (Telephone in U.S. (888) 330-8477), (Fax in U.S. (800) 672-2054), www.palgrave.com; *The Statesman's Yearbook 2008.*

United Nations Conference on Trade and Development (UNCTAD), DC2-1120, United Nations, New York, NY 10017, (212) 963-0027, www.unctad.org; *UNCTAD Commodity Yearbook.*

United Nations Economic Commission for Africa (ECA), PO Box 3001, Addis Ababa, Ethiopia, (Telephone in U.S. (212) 963-4957), www.uneca.org; *African Statistical Yearbook 2006.*

BURKINA FASO - MONEY SUPPLY

African Development Bank Group, Rue Joseph Anoma, 01 BP 1387 Abidjan 01, Cote d'Ivoire, www.afdb.org; *Statistics Pocketbook 2008.*

Economist Intelligence Unit, 111 West 57th Street, New York, NY 10019, (212) 554-0600, Fax: (212) 586-1181, www.eiu.com; *Burkina Faso Country Report.*

Euromonitor International, Inc., 224 S. Michigan Avenue, Suite 1500, Chicago, IL 60604, (312) 922-1115, Fax: (312) 922-1157, www.euromonitor.com; *International Marketing Data and Statistics 2008.*

Taylor and Francis Group, An Informa Business, 2 Park Square, Milton Park, Abingdon, Oxford OX14 4RN, United Kingdom, (Dial from U.S. (212) 216-7800), (Fax from U.S. (212) 564-7854), www.tandf.co.uk; *The Europa World Year Book.*

United Nations Statistics Division, New York, NY 10017, (800) 253-9646, Fax: (212) 963-4116, http://unstats.un.org; *Statistical Yearbook.*

The World Bank, 1818 H Street, NW, Washington, DC 20433, (202) 473-1000, Fax: (202) 477-6391, www.worldbank.org; *Burkina Faso* and *World Development Indicators (WDI) 2008.*

BURKINA FASO - MORTALITY

Central Intelligence Agency, Office of Public Affairs, Washington, DC 20505, (703) 482-0623, Fax: (703) 482-1739, www.cia.gov; *The World Factbook.*

Euromonitor International, Inc., 224 S. Michigan Avenue, Suite 1500, Chicago, IL 60604, (312) 922-1115, Fax: (312) 922-1157, www.euromonitor.com; *International Marketing Data and Statistics 2008* and *The World Economic Factbook 2008.*

Palgrave Macmillan Ltd., Houndmills, Basingstoke, Hampshire, RG21 6XS, England, (Telephone in U.S. (888) 330-8477), (Fax in U.S. (800) 672-2054), www.palgrave.com; *The Statesman's Yearbook 2008.*

Taylor and Francis Group, An Informa Business, 2 Park Square, Milton Park, Abingdon, Oxford OX14 4RN, United Kingdom, (Dial from U.S. (212) 216-7800), (Fax from U.S. (212) 564-7854), www.tandf.co.uk; *The Europa World Year Book.*

UNICEF, 3 United Nations Plaza, New York, NY 10017, (800) 253-9646, Fax: (212) 887-7465, www.unicef.org; *The State of the World's Children 2008.*

United Nations Statistics Division, New York, NY 10017, (800) 253-9646, Fax: (212) 963-4116, http://

unstats.un.org; *Demographic Yearbook; Human Development Report 2006; Statistical Yearbook; Survey of Economic and Social Conditions in Africa 2005;* and *World Statistics Pocketbook.*

The World Bank, 1818 H Street, NW, Washington, DC 20433, (202) 473-1000, Fax: (202) 477-6391, www.worldbank.org; *The World Bank Atlas 2003-2004; World Development Indicators (WDI) 2008;* and *World Development Report 2008.*

World Health Organization (WHO), Avenue Appia 20, 1211 Geneve 27, Switzerland, (Telephone in U.S. (212) 331-9081), www.who.int; The WHO Global Atlas of Infectious Diseases and *World Health Report 2006.*

BURKINA FASO - MOTION PICTURES

Palgrave Macmillan Ltd., Houndmills, Basingstoke, Hampshire, RG21 6XS, England, (Telephone in U.S. (888) 330-8477), (Fax in U.S. (800) 672-2054), www.palgrave.com; *The Statesman's Yearbook 2008.*

BURKINA FASO - MOTOR VEHICLES

International Road Federation (IFR), Madison Place, 500 Montgomery Street, 5th Floor, Alexandria, VA 22314, (703) 535-1001, Fax: (703) 535-1007, www.irfnet.org; *World Road Statistics 2006.*

Taylor and Francis Group, An Informa Business, 2 Park Square, Milton Park, Abingdon, Oxford OX14 4RN, United Kingdom, (Dial from U.S. (212) 216-7800), (Fax from U.S. (212) 564-7854), www.tandf.co.uk; *The Europa World Year Book.*

United Nations Statistics Division, New York, NY 10017, (800) 253-9646, Fax: (212) 963-4116, http://unstats.un.org; *Statistical Yearbook* and *Survey of Economic and Social Conditions in Africa 2005.*

BURKINA FASO - NUTRITION

African Development Bank Group, Rue Joseph Anoma, 01 BP 1387 Abidjan 01, Cote d'Ivoire, www.afdb.org; *Statistics Pocketbook 2008.*

United Nations Food and Agricultural Organization (FAO), Viale delle Terme di Caracalla, 00100 Rome, Italy, (Dial from U.S. (202) 653-2400), (Fax from U.S. (202) 653 5760), www.fao.org; *The State of Food and Agriculture (SOFA) 2006.*

BURKINA FASO - PERIODICALS

UNESCO Institute for Statistics, C.P. 6128 Succursale Centre-Ville, Montreal, Quebec, H3C 3J7 Canada, (Dial from U.S. (514) 343-6880), (Fax from U.S. (514) 343 6882), www.uis.unesco.org; *Statistical Tables.*

BURKINA FASO - PESTICIDES

United Nations Food and Agricultural Organization (FAO), Viale delle Terme di Caracalla, 00100 Rome, Italy, (Dial from U.S. (202) 653-2400), (Fax from U.S. (202) 653 5760), www.fao.org; *The State of Food and Agriculture (SOFA) 2006.*

BURKINA FASO - PETROLEUM INDUSTRY AND TRADE

PennWell Corporation, 1421 South Sheridan Road, Tulsa, OK 74112, (918) 835-3161, www.pennwell.com; *International Petroleum Encyclopedia 2007.*

United Nations Conference on Trade and Development (UNCTAD), DC2-1120, United Nations, New York, NY 10017, (212) 963-0027, www.unctad.org; *UNCTAD Commodity Yearbook.*

United Nations Food and Agricultural Organization (FAO), Viale delle Terme di Caracalla, 00100 Rome, Italy, (Dial from U.S. (202) 653-2400), (Fax from U.S. (202) 653 5760), www.fao.org; *The State of Food and Agriculture (SOFA) 2006.*

BURKINA FASO - POLITICAL SCIENCE

Central Intelligence Agency, Office of Public Affairs, Washington, DC 20505, (703) 482-0623, Fax: (703) 482-1739, www.cia.gov; *The World Factbook.*

International Monetary Fund (IMF), 700 Nineteenth Street, NW, Washington, DC 20431, (202) 623-7000, Fax: (202) 623-4661, www.imf.org; *Government Finance Statistics Yearbook (2008 Edition).*

Palgrave Macmillan Ltd., Houndmills, Basingstoke, Hampshire, RG21 6XS, England, (Telephone in U.S. (888) 330-8477), (Fax in U.S. (800) 672-2054), www.palgrave.com; *The Statesman's Yearbook 2008.*

Taylor and Francis Group, An Informa Business, 2 Park Square, Milton Park, Abingdon, Oxford OX14 4RN, United Kingdom, (Dial from U.S. (212) 216-7800), (Fax from U.S. (212) 564-7854), www.tandf.co.uk; *The Europa World Year Book.*

United Nations Statistics Division, New York, NY 10017, (800) 253-9646, Fax: (212) 963-4116, http://unstats.un.org; *National Accounts Statistics: Compendium of Income Distribution Statistics* and *Survey of Economic and Social Conditions in Africa 2005.*

The World Bank, 1818 H Street, NW, Washington, DC 20433, (202) 473-1000, Fax: (202) 477-6391, www.worldbank.org; *World Development Indicators (WDI) 2008* and *World Development Report 2008.*

BURKINA FASO - POPULATION

African Development Bank Group, Rue Joseph Anoma, 01 BP 1387 Abidjan 01, Cote d'Ivoire, www.afdb.org; *The African Statistical Journal; Gender, Poverty and Environmental Indicators on African Countries 2007; Selected Statistics on African Countries 2007;* and *Statistics Pocketbook 2008.*

Central Intelligence Agency, Office of Public Affairs, Washington, DC 20505, (703) 482-0623, Fax: (703) 482-1739, www.cia.gov; *The World Factbook.*

Economist Intelligence Unit, 111 West 57th Street, New York, NY 10019, (212) 554-0600, Fax: (212) 586-1181, www.eiu.com; *Burkina Faso Country Report.*

Euromonitor International, Inc., 224 S. Michigan Avenue, Suite 1500, Chicago, IL 60604, (312) 922-1115, Fax: (312) 922-1157, www.euromonitor.com; *International Marketing Data and Statistics 2008* and *The World Economic Factbook 2008.*

Eurostat, Batiment Jean Monnet, Rue Alcide de Gasperi, L-2920 Luxembourg, http://epp.eurostat.ec.europa.eu; *Demographic Indicators - Population by Age-Classes.*

International Labour Office, I.L.O. Publications, 4 route des Morillons, CH-1211 Geneva 22, Switzerland, (Telephone in U.S. (202) 653-7652), (Fax in U.S. (202) 653-7687), www.ilo.org; *Yearbook of Labour Statistics 2006.*

Palgrave Macmillan Ltd., Houndmills, Basingstoke, Hampshire, RG21 6XS, England, (Telephone in U.S. (888) 330-8477), (Fax in U.S. (800) 672-2054), www.palgrave.com; *The Statesman's Yearbook 2008.*

Taylor and Francis Group, An Informa Business, 2 Park Square, Milton Park, Abingdon, Oxford OX14 4RN, United Kingdom, (Dial from U.S. (212) 216-7800), (Fax from U.S. (212) 564-7854), www.tandf.co.uk; *The Europa World Year Book.*

U.S. Department of State (DOS), 2201 C Street NW, Washington, DC 20520, (202) 647-4000, www.state.gov; *World Military Expenditures and Arms Transfers (WMEAT).*

UNESCO Institute for Statistics, C.P. 6128 Succursale Centre-Ville, Montreal, Quebec, H3C 3J7 Canada, (Dial from U.S. (514) 343-6880), (Fax from U.S. (514) 343 6882), www.uis.unesco.org; *Statistical Tables.*

United Nations Food and Agricultural Organization (FAO), Viale delle Terme di Caracalla, 00100 Rome, Italy, (Dial from U.S. (202) 653-2400), (Fax from U.S. (202) 653 5760), www.fao.org; *FAO Production Yearbook 2002.*

United Nations Statistics Division, New York, NY 10017, (800) 253-9646, Fax: (212) 963-4116, http://unstats.un.org; *Demographic Yearbook; Human Development Report 2006; Statistical Yearbook; Survey of Economic and Social Conditions in Africa 2005;* and *World Statistics Pocketbook.*

The World Bank, 1818 H Street, NW, Washington, DC 20433, (202) 473-1000, Fax: (202) 477-6391, www.worldbank.org; *Burkina Faso; The World Bank Atlas 2003-2004;* and *World Development Report 2008.*

World Health Organization (WHO), Avenue Appia 20, 1211 Geneve 27, Switzerland, (Telephone in U.S. (212) 331-9081), www.who.int; *World Health Report 2006.*

BURKINA FASO - POPULATION DENSITY

African Development Bank Group, Rue Joseph Anoma, 01 BP 1387 Abidjan 01, Cote d'Ivoire, www.afdb.org; *Statistics Pocketbook 2008.*

Central Intelligence Agency, Office of Public Affairs, Washington, DC 20505, (703) 482-0623, Fax: (703) 482-1739, www.cia.gov; *The World Factbook.*

Euromonitor International, Inc., 224 S. Michigan Avenue, Suite 1500, Chicago, IL 60604, (312) 922-1115, Fax: (312) 922-1157, www.euromonitor.com; *International Marketing Data and Statistics 2008* and *The World Economic Factbook 2008.*

Palgrave Macmillan Ltd., Houndmills, Basingstoke, Hampshire, RG21 6XS, England, (Telephone in U.S. (888) 330-8477), (Fax in U.S. (800) 672-2054), www.palgrave.com; *The Statesman's Yearbook 2008.*

Taylor and Francis Group, An Informa Business, 2 Park Square, Milton Park, Abingdon, Oxford OX14 4RN, United Kingdom, (Dial from U.S. (212) 216-7800), (Fax from U.S. (212) 564-7854), www.tandf.co.uk; *The Europa World Year Book.*

UNESCO Institute for Statistics, C.P. 6128 Succursale Centre-Ville, Montreal, Quebec, H3C 3J7 Canada, (Dial from U.S. (514) 343-6880), (Fax from U.S. (514) 343 6882), www.uis.unesco.org; *Statistical Tables.*

United Nations Food and Agricultural Organization (FAO), Viale delle Terme di Caracalla, 00100 Rome, Italy, (Dial from U.S. (202) 653-2400), (Fax from U.S. (202) 653 5760), www.fao.org; *The State of Food and Agriculture (SOFA) 2006.*

United Nations Statistics Division, New York, NY 10017, (800) 253-9646, Fax: (212) 963-4116, http://unstats.un.org; *Statistical Yearbook* and *Survey of Economic and Social Conditions in Africa 2005.*

The World Bank, 1818 H Street, NW, Washington, DC 20433, (202) 473-1000, Fax: (202) 477-6391, www.worldbank.org; *Burkina Faso* and *World Development Report 2008.*

BURKINA FASO - POSTAL SERVICE

Palgrave Macmillan Ltd., Houndmills, Basingstoke, Hampshire, RG21 6XS, England, (Telephone in U.S. (888) 330-8477), (Fax in U.S. (800) 672-2054), www.palgrave.com; *The Statesman's Yearbook 2008.*

United Nations Statistics Division, New York, NY 10017, (800) 253-9646, Fax: (212) 963-4116, http://unstats.un.org; *Statistical Yearbook.*

BURKINA FASO - POWER RESOURCES

Euromonitor International, Inc., 224 S. Michigan Avenue, Suite 1500, Chicago, IL 60604, (312) 922-1115, Fax: (312) 922-1157, www.euromonitor.com; *International Marketing Data and Statistics 2008; The World Economic Factbook 2008;* and *World Marketing Data and Statistics.*

Palgrave Macmillan Ltd., Houndmills, Basingstoke, Hampshire, RG21 6XS, England, (Telephone in U.S. (888) 330-8477), (Fax in U.S. (800) 672-2054), www.palgrave.com; *The Statesman's Yearbook 2008.*

Platts, 2 Penn Plaza, 25th Floor, New York, NY 10121-2298, (212) 904-3070, www.platts.com; *Energy Economist.*

United Nations Economic Commission for Africa (ECA), PO Box 3001, Addis Ababa, Ethiopia, (Telephone in U.S. (212) 963-4957), www.uneca.org; *African Statistical Yearbook 2006.*

United Nations Food and Agricultural Organization (FAO), Viale delle Terme di Caracalla, 00100 Rome, Italy, (Dial from U.S. (202) 653-2400), (Fax from U.S. (202) 653 5760), www.fao.org; *The State of Food and Agriculture (SOFA) 2006.*

United Nations Statistics Division, New York, NY 10017, (800) 253-9646, Fax: (212) 963-4116, http://unstats.un.org; *Energy Statistics Yearbook 2003; Human Development Report 2006; Statistical Yearbook;* and *World Statistics Pocketbook.*

The World Bank, 1818 H Street, NW, Washington, DC 20433, (202) 473-1000, Fax: (202) 477-6391, www.worldbank.org; *The World Bank Atlas 2003-2004* and *World Development Report 2008.*

BURKINA FASO - PRICES

Euromonitor International, Inc., 224 S. Michigan Avenue, Suite 1500, Chicago, IL 60604, (312) 922-1115, Fax: (312) 922-1157, www.euromonitor.com; *World Marketing Data and Statistics.*

International Labour Office, I.L.O. Publications, 4 route des Morillons, CH-1211 Geneva 22, Switzerland, (Telephone in U.S. (202) 653-7652), (Fax in U.S. (202) 653-7687), www.ilo.org; *Yearbook of Labour Statistics 2006.*

International Monetary Fund (IMF), 700 Nineteenth Street, NW, Washington, DC 20431, (202) 623-7000, Fax: (202) 623-4661, www.imf.org; *International Financial Statistics Yearbook 2007.*

United Nations Economic Commission for Africa (ECA), PO Box 3001, Addis Ababa, Ethiopia, (Telephone in U.S. (212) 963-4957), www.uneca.org; *African Statistical Yearbook 2006.*

United Nations Food and Agricultural Organization (FAO), Viale delle Terme di Caracalla, 00100 Rome, Italy, (Dial from U.S. (202) 653-2400), (Fax from U.S. (202) 653 5760), www.fao.org; *FAO Production Yearbook 2002* and *The State of Food and Agriculture (SOFA) 2006.*

The World Bank, 1818 H Street, NW, Washington, DC 20433, (202) 473-1000, Fax: (202) 477-6391, www.worldbank.org; *Burkina Faso.*

BURKINA FASO - PROFESSIONS

UNESCO Institute for Statistics, C.P. 6128 Succursale Centre-Ville, Montreal, Quebec, H3C 3J7 Canada, (Dial from U.S. (514) 343-6880), (Fax from U.S. (514) 343 6882), www.uis.unesco.org; *Statistical Tables.*

United Nations Statistics Division, New York, NY 10017, (800) 253-9646, Fax: (212) 963-4116, http://unstats.un.org; *Statistical Yearbook.*

BURKINA FASO - PUBLIC HEALTH

African Development Bank Group, Rue Joseph Anoma, 01 BP 1387 Abidjan 01, Cote d'Ivoire, www.afdb.org; *Statistics Pocketbook 2008.*

Euromonitor International, Inc., 224 S. Michigan Avenue, Suite 1500, Chicago, IL 60604, (312) 922-1115, Fax: (312) 922-1157, www.euromonitor.com; *World Marketing Data and Statistics.*

International Monetary Fund (IMF), 700 Nineteenth Street, NW, Washington, DC 20431, (202) 623-7000, Fax: (202) 623-4661, www.imf.org; *Government Finance Statistics Yearbook (2008 Edition).*

Palgrave Macmillan Ltd., Houndmills, Basingstoke, Hampshire, RG21 6XS, England, (Telephone in U.S. (888) 330-8477), (Fax in U.S. (800) 672-2054), www.palgrave.com; *The Statesman's Yearbook 2008.*

UNICEF, 3 United Nations Plaza, New York, NY 10017, (800) 253-9646, Fax: (212) 887-7465, www.unicef.org; *The State of the World's Children 2008.*

United Nations Economic Commission for Africa (ECA), PO Box 3001, Addis Ababa, Ethiopia, (Telephone in U.S. (212) 963-4957), www.uneca.org; *African Statistical Yearbook 2006.*

United Nations Statistics Division, New York, NY 10017, (800) 253-9646, Fax: (212) 963-4116, http://unstats.un.org; *Human Development Report 2006* and *Statistical Yearbook.*

The World Bank, 1818 H Street, NW, Washington, DC 20433, (202) 473-1000, Fax: (202) 477-6391, www.worldbank.org; *Burkina Faso* and *World Development Report 2008.*

World Health Organization (WHO), Avenue Appia 20, 1211 Geneve 27, Switzerland, (Telephone in U.S. (212) 331-9081), www.who.int; The WHO Global Atlas of Infectious Diseases and *World Health Report 2006.*

BURKINA FASO - PUBLISHERS AND PUBLISHING

Taylor and Francis Group, An Informa Business, 2 Park Square, Milton Park, Abingdon, Oxford OX14 4RN, United Kingdom, (Dial from U.S. (212) 216-7800), (Fax from U.S. (212) 564-7854), www.tandf.co.uk; *The Europa World Year Book.*

BURKINA FASO - RADIO BROADCASTING

Palgrave Macmillan Ltd., Houndmills, Basingstoke, Hampshire, RG21 6XS, England, (Telephone in U.S. (888) 330-8477), (Fax in U.S. (800) 672-2054), www.palgrave.com; *The Statesman's Yearbook 2008.*

BURKINA FASO - RAILROADS

Jane's Information Group, 110 North Royal Street, Suite 200, Alexandria, VA 22314, (703) 683-3700, Fax: (800) 836-0297, www.janes.com; *Jane's World Railways.*

Palgrave Macmillan Ltd., Houndmills, Basingstoke, Hampshire, RG21 6XS, England, (Telephone in U.S. (888) 330-8477), (Fax in U.S. (800) 672-2054), www.palgrave.com; *The Statesman's Yearbook 2008.*

Taylor and Francis Group, An Informa Business, 2 Park Square, Milton Park, Abingdon, Oxford OX14 4RN, United Kingdom, (Dial from U.S. (212) 216-7800), (Fax from U.S. (212) 564-7854), www.tandf.co.uk; *The Europa World Year Book.*

United Nations Economic Commission for Africa (ECA), PO Box 3001, Addis Ababa, Ethiopia, (Telephone in U.S. (212) 963-4957), www.uneca.org; *African Statistical Yearbook 2006.*

United Nations Statistics Division, New York, NY 10017, (800) 253-9646, Fax: (212) 963-4116, http://unstats.un.org; *Statistical Yearbook* and *Survey of Economic and Social Conditions in Africa 2005.*

BURKINA FASO - RELIGION

Central Intelligence Agency, Office of Public Affairs, Washington, DC 20505, (703) 482-0623, Fax: (703) 482-1739, www.cia.gov; *The World Factbook.*

BURKINA FASO - RESERVES (ACCOUNTING)

African Development Bank Group, Rue Joseph Anoma, 01 BP 1387 Abidjan 01, Cote d'Ivoire, www.afdb.org; *Statistics Pocketbook 2008.*

Euromonitor International, Inc., 224 S. Michigan Avenue, Suite 1500, Chicago, IL 60604, (312) 922-1115, Fax: (312) 922-1157, www.euromonitor.com; *International Marketing Data and Statistics 2008.*

United Nations Statistics Division, New York, NY 10017, (800) 253-9646, Fax: (212) 963-4116, http://unstats.un.org; *Statistical Yearbook.*

The World Bank, 1818 H Street, NW, Washington, DC 20433, (202) 473-1000, Fax: (202) 477-6391, www.worldbank.org; *World Development Indicators (WDI) 2008.*

BURKINA FASO - RETAIL TRADE

Euromonitor International, Inc., 224 S. Michigan Avenue, Suite 1500, Chicago, IL 60604, (312) 922-1115, Fax: (312) 922-1157, www.euromonitor.com; *World Marketing Data and Statistics.*

BURKINA FASO - RICE PRODUCTION

See BURKINA FASO - CROPS

BURKINA FASO - ROADS

Central Intelligence Agency, Office of Public Affairs, Washington, DC 20505, (703) 482-0623, Fax: (703) 482-1739, www.cia.gov; *The World Factbook.*

International Road Federation (IFR), Madison Place, 500 Montgomery Street, 5th Floor, Alexandria, VA 22314, (703) 535-1001, Fax: (703) 535-1007, www.irfnet.org; *World Road Statistics 2006.*

Palgrave Macmillan Ltd., Houndmills, Basingstoke, Hampshire, RG21 6XS, England, (Telephone in U.S. (888) 330-8477), (Fax in U.S. (800) 672-2054), www.palgrave.com; *The Statesman's Yearbook 2008.*

United Nations Economic Commission for Africa (ECA), PO Box 3001, Addis Ababa, Ethiopia, (Telephone in U.S. (212) 963-4957), www.uneca.org; *African Statistical Yearbook 2006.*

United Nations Statistics Division, New York, NY 10017, (800) 253-9646, Fax: (212) 963-4116, http://unstats.un.org; *Survey of Economic and Social Conditions in Africa 2005.*

BURKINA FASO - SAVING AND INVESTMENT

International Monetary Fund (IMF), 700 Nineteenth Street, NW, Washington, DC 20431, (202) 623-7000, Fax: (202) 623-4661, www.imf.org; *International Financial Statistics Yearbook 2007.*

BURKINA FASO - SHEEP

See BURKINA FASO - LIVESTOCK

BURKINA FASO - SHIPPING

United Nations Economic Commission for Africa (ECA), PO Box 3001, Addis Ababa, Ethiopia, (Telephone in U.S. (212) 963-4957), www.uneca.org; *African Statistical Yearbook 2006.*

BURKINA FASO - SOCIAL ECOLOGY

United Nations Statistics Division, New York, NY 10017, (800) 253-9646, Fax: (212) 963-4116, http://unstats.un.org; *World Statistics Pocketbook.*

BURKINA FASO - SOCIAL SECURITY

International Monetary Fund (IMF), 700 Nineteenth Street, NW, Washington, DC 20431, (202) 623-7000, Fax: (202) 623-4661, www.imf.org; *Government Finance Statistics Yearbook (2008 Edition).*

United Nations Statistics Division, New York, NY 10017, (800) 253-9646, Fax: (212) 963-4116, http://unstats.un.org; *National Accounts Statistics: Compendium of Income Distribution Statistics.*

BURKINA FASO - SUGAR PRODUCTION

See BURKINA FASO - CROPS

BURKINA FASO - TAXATION

International Monetary Fund (IMF), 700 Nineteenth Street, NW, Washington, DC 20431, (202) 623-7000, Fax: (202) 623-4661, www.imf.org; *Government Finance Statistics Yearbook (2008 Edition).*

International Road Federation (IFR), Madison Place, 500 Montgomery Street, 5th Floor, Alexandria, VA 22314, (703) 535-1001, Fax: (703) 535-1007, www.irfnet.org; *World Road Statistics 2006.*

Taylor and Francis Group, An Informa Business, 2 Park Square, Milton Park, Abingdon, Oxford OX14 4RN, United Kingdom, (Dial from U.S. (212) 216-7800), (Fax from U.S. (212) 564-7854), www.tandf.co.uk; *The Europa World Year Book.*

The World Bank, 1818 H Street, NW, Washington, DC 20433, (202) 473-1000, Fax: (202) 477-6391, www.worldbank.org; *World Development Indicators (WDI) 2008.*

BURKINA FASO - TELEPHONE

International Telecommunication Union (ITU), Place des Nations, 1211 Geneva 20, Switzerland, www.itu.int; World Telecommunication Indicators Database.

Taylor and Francis Group, An Informa Business, 2 Park Square, Milton Park, Abingdon, Oxford OX14 4RN, United Kingdom, (Dial from U.S. (212) 216-7800), (Fax from U.S. (212) 564-7854), www.tandf.co.uk; *The Europa World Year Book.*

United Nations Statistics Division, New York, NY 10017, (800) 253-9646, Fax: (212) 963-4116, http://unstats.un.org; *Statistical Yearbook* and *World Statistics Pocketbook.*

BURKINA FASO - TEXTILE INDUSTRY

Palgrave Macmillan Ltd., Houndmills, Basingstoke, Hampshire, RG21 6XS, England, (Telephone in U.S. (888) 330-8477), (Fax in U.S. (800) 672-2054), www.palgrave.com; *The Statesman's Yearbook 2008.*

United Nations Conference on Trade and Development (UNCTAD), DC2-1120, United Nations, New York, NY 10017, (212) 963-0027, www.unctad.org; *UNCTAD Commodity Yearbook.*

United Nations Food and Agricultural Organization (FAO), Viale delle Terme di Caracalla, 00100 Rome, Italy, (Dial from U.S. (202) 653-2400), (Fax from U.S. (202) 653 5760), www.fao.org; *The State of Food and Agriculture (SOFA) 2006.*

United Nations Statistics Division, New York, NY 10017, (800) 253-9646, Fax: (212) 963-4116, http://unstats.un.org; *Statistical Yearbook.*

BURKINA FASO - TOBACCO INDUSTRY

Foreign Agricultural Service (FAS), U.S. Department of Agriculture (USDA), 1400 Independence Avenue, SW, Washington, DC 20250, (202) 720-3935, www.fas.usda.gov; *Tobacco: World Markets and Trade.*

M.E. Sharpe, 80 Business Park Drive, Armonk, NY 10504, (800) 541-6563, Fax: (914) 273-2106, www.mesharpe.com; *The Illustrated Book of World Rankings.*

United Nations Statistics Division, New York, NY 10017, (800) 253-9646, Fax: (212) 963-4116, http://unstats.un.org; *Statistical Yearbook.*

BURKINA FASO - TOURISM

Euromonitor International, Inc., 224 S. Michigan Avenue, Suite 1500, Chicago, IL 60604, (312) 922-1115, Fax: (312) 922-1157, www.euromonitor.com; *World Marketing Data and Statistics.*

Palgrave Macmillan Ltd., Houndmills, Basingstoke, Hampshire, RG21 6XS, England, (Telephone in U.S. (888) 330-8477), (Fax in U.S. (800) 672-2054), www.palgrave.com; *The Statesman's Yearbook 2008.*

Taylor and Francis Group, An Informa Business, 2 Park Square, Milton Park, Abingdon, Oxford OX14 4RN, United Kingdom, (Dial from U.S. (212) 216-7800), (Fax from U.S. (212) 564-7854), www.tandf.co.uk; *The Europa World Year Book.*

United Nations Economic Commission for Africa (ECA), PO Box 3001, Addis Ababa, Ethiopia, (Telephone in U.S. (212) 963-4957), www.uneca.org; *African Statistical Yearbook 2006.*

United Nations Statistics Division, New York, NY 10017, (800) 253-9646, Fax: (212) 963-4116, http://unstats.un.org; *Statistical Yearbook.*

United Nations World Tourism Organization (UNWTO), Capitan Haya 42, 28020 Madrid, Spain, www.world-tourism.org; *Yearbook of Tourism Statistics.*

The World Bank, 1818 H Street, NW, Washington, DC 20433, (202) 473-1000, Fax: (202) 477-6391, www.worldbank.org; *Burkina Faso.*

BURKINA FASO - TRADE

See BURKINA FASO - INTERNATIONAL TRADE

BURKINA FASO - TRANSPORTATION

Euromonitor International, Inc., 224 S. Michigan Avenue, Suite 1500, Chicago, IL 60604, (312) 922-1115, Fax: (312) 922-1157, www.euromonitor.com; *International Marketing Data and Statistics 2008* and *World Marketing Data and Statistics.*

Palgrave Macmillan Ltd., Houndmills, Basingstoke, Hampshire, RG21 6XS, England, (Telephone in U.S. (888) 330-8477), (Fax in U.S. (800) 672-2054), www.palgrave.com; *The Statesman's Yearbook 2008.*

Taylor and Francis Group, An Informa Business, 2 Park Square, Milton Park, Abingdon, Oxford OX14 4RN, United Kingdom, (Dial from U.S. (212) 216-7800), (Fax from U.S. (212) 564-7854), www.tandf.co.uk; *The Europa World Year Book.*

United Nations Economic Commission for Africa (ECA), PO Box 3001, Addis Ababa, Ethiopia, (Telephone in U.S. (212) 963-4957), www.uneca.org; *African Statistical Yearbook 2006.*

United Nations Statistics Division, New York, NY 10017, (800) 253-9646, Fax: (212) 963-4116, http://unstats.un.org; *Human Development Report 2006.*

The World Bank, 1818 H Street, NW, Washington, DC 20433, (202) 473-1000, Fax: (202) 477-6391, www.worldbank.org; *Africa Live Database (LDB)* and *Burkina Faso.*

BURKINA FASO - UNEMPLOYMENT

Central Intelligence Agency, Office of Public Affairs, Washington, DC 20505, (703) 482-0623, Fax: (703) 482-1739, www.cia.gov; *The World Factbook.*

Euromonitor International, Inc., 224 S. Michigan Avenue, Suite 1500, Chicago, IL 60604, (312) 922-1115, Fax: (312) 922-1157, www.euromonitor.com; *International Marketing Data and Statistics 2008.*

International Labour Office, I.L.O. Publications, 4 route des Morillons, CH-1211 Geneva 22, Switzerland, (Telephone in U.S. (202) 653-7652), (Fax in U.S. (202) 653-7687), www.ilo.org; *Yearbook of Labour Statistics 2006.*

United Nations Statistics Division, New York, NY 10017, (800) 253-9646, Fax: (212) 963-4116, http://unstats.un.org; *Statistical Yearbook.*

BURKINA FASO - VITAL STATISTICS

Euromonitor International, Inc., 224 S. Michigan Avenue, Suite 1500, Chicago, IL 60604, (312) 922-1115, Fax: (312) 922-1157, www.euromonitor.com; *International Marketing Data and Statistics 2008.*

Palgrave Macmillan Ltd., Houndmills, Basingstoke, Hampshire, RG21 6XS, England, (Telephone in U.S. (888) 330-8477), (Fax in U.S. (800) 672-2054), www.palgrave.com; *The Statesman's Yearbook 2008.*

World Health Organization (WHO), Avenue Appia 20, 1211 Geneve 27, Switzerland, (Telephone in U.S. (212) 331-9081), www.who.int; *World Health Report 2006.*

BURKINA FASO - WAGES

International Labour Office, I.L.O. Publications, 4 route des Morillons, CH-1211 Geneva 22, Switzerland, (Telephone in U.S. (202) 653-7652), (Fax in U.S. (202) 653-7687), www.ilo.org; *Yearbook of Labour Statistics 2006.*

United Nations Statistics Division, New York, NY 10017, (800) 253-9646, Fax: (212) 963-4116, http://unstats.un.org; *Statistical Yearbook.*

The World Bank, 1818 H Street, NW, Washington, DC 20433, (202) 473-1000, Fax: (202) 477-6391, www.worldbank.org; *Burkina Faso.*

BURKINA FASO - WELFARE STATE

International Monetary Fund (IMF), 700 Nineteenth Street, NW, Washington, DC 20431, (202) 623-7000, Fax: (202) 623-4661, www.imf.org; *Government Finance Statistics Yearbook (2008 Edition).*

BURKINA FASO - YARN PRODUCTION

See BURKINA FASO - TEXTILE INDUSTRY

BURMA - NATIONAL STATISTICAL OFFICE

Central Statistical Organization (CSO), Ministry of National Planning and Economic Development, Building 32, Nay Pyi Taw, Myanmar, www.csostat.gov.mm; National Data Center.

BURMA - PRIMARY STATISTICS SOURCES

Central Statistical Organization (CSO), Ministry of National Planning and Economic Development, Building 32, Nay Pyi Taw, Myanmar, www.csostat.gov.mm; *Statistical Yearbook 2005.*

BURMA - AGRICULTURAL MACHINERY

United Nations Statistics Division, New York, NY 10017, (800) 253-9646, Fax: (212) 963-4116, http://unstats.un.org; *Statistical Yearbook.*

BURMA - AGRICULTURE

Asian Development Bank (ADB), PO Box 789, 0980 Manila, Philippines, www.adb.org; *Key Indicators of Developing Asian and Pacific Countries 2006.*

Economist Intelligence Unit, 111 West 57th Street, New York, NY 10019, (212) 554-0600, Fax: (212) 586-1181, www.eiu.com; *Myanmar (Burma) Country Report.*

Euromonitor International, Inc., 224 S. Michigan Avenue, Suite 1500, Chicago, IL 60604, (312) 922-1115, Fax: (312) 922-1157, www.euromonitor.com; *International Marketing Data and Statistics 2008* and *World Marketing Data and Statistics.*

M.E. Sharpe, 80 Business Park Drive, Armonk, NY 10504, (800) 541-6563, Fax: (914) 273-2106, www.mesharpe.com; *The Illustrated Book of World Rankings.*

Palgrave Macmillan Ltd., Houndmills, Basingstoke, Hampshire, RG21 6XS, England, (Telephone in U.S. (888) 330-8477), (Fax in U.S. (800) 672-2054), www.palgrave.com; *The Statesman's Yearbook 2008.*

Taylor and Francis Group, An Informa Business, 2 Park Square, Milton Park, Abingdon, Oxford OX14 4RN, United Kingdom, (Dial from U.S. (212) 216-7800), (Fax from U.S. (212) 564-7854), www.tandf.co.uk; *The Europa World Year Book.*

United Nations Conference on Trade and Development (UNCTAD), DC2-1120, United Nations, New York, NY 10017, (212) 963-0027, www.unctad.org; *UNCTAD Commodity Yearbook.*

United Nations Food and Agricultural Organization (FAO), Viale delle Terme di Caracalla, 00100 Rome, Italy, (Dial from U.S. (202) 653-2400), (Fax from U.S. (202) 653 5760), www.fao.org; AQUASTAT; *FAO Production Yearbook 2002; FAO Trade Yearbook;* and *The State of Food and Agriculture (SOFA) 2006.*

United Nations Statistics Division, New York, NY 10017, (800) 253-9646, Fax: (212) 963-4116, http://unstats.un.org; *Asia-Pacific in Figures 2004* and *Statistical Yearbook.*

The World Bank, 1818 H Street, NW, Washington, DC 20433, (202) 473-1000, Fax: (202) 477-6391, www.worldbank.org; *Myanmar.*

BURMA - AIRLINES

Economist Intelligence Unit, 111 West 57th Street, New York, NY 10019, (212) 554-0600, Fax: (212) 586-1181, www.eiu.com; *Business Asia.*

International Civil Aviation Organization (ICAO), External Relations and Public Information Office (EPO), 999 University Street, Montreal, Quebec H3C 5H7, Canada, (Dial from U.S. (514) 954-8219), (Fax from U.S. (514) 954-6077), www.icao.int; *Civil Aviation Statistics of the World.*

M.E. Sharpe, 80 Business Park Drive, Armonk, NY 10504, (800) 541-6563, Fax: (914) 273-2106, www.mesharpe.com; *The Illustrated Book of World Rankings.*

Palgrave Macmillan Ltd., Houndmills, Basingstoke, Hampshire, RG21 6XS, England, (Telephone in U.S. (888) 330-8477), (Fax in U.S. (800) 672-2054), www.palgrave.com; *The Statesman's Yearbook 2008.*

Taylor and Francis Group, An Informa Business, 2 Park Square, Milton Park, Abingdon, Oxford OX14 4RN, United Kingdom, (Dial from U.S. (212) 216-7800), (Fax from U.S. (212) 564-7854), www.tandf.co.uk; *The Europa World Year Book.*

United Nations Statistics Division, New York, NY 10017, (800) 253-9646, Fax: (212) 963-4116, http://unstats.un.org; *Statistical Yearbook.*

BURMA - AIRPORTS

Central Intelligence Agency, Office of Public Affairs, Washington, DC 20505, (703) 482-0623, Fax: (703) 482-1739, www.cia.gov; *The World Factbook.*

BURMA - ALUMINUM PRODUCTION

See BURMA - MINERAL INDUSTRIES

BURMA - ARMED FORCES

Central Intelligence Agency, Office of Public Affairs, Washington, DC 20505, (703) 482-0623, Fax: (703) 482-1739, www.cia.gov; *The World Factbook.*

Economist Intelligence Unit, 111 West 57th Street, New York, NY 10019, (212) 554-0600, Fax: (212) 586-1181, www.eiu.com; *Business Asia.*

Euromonitor International, Inc., 224 S. Michigan Avenue, Suite 1500, Chicago, IL 60604, (312) 922-1115, Fax: (312) 922-1157, www.euromonitor.com; *World Marketing Data and Statistics.*

International Institute for Strategic Studies (IISS), Arundel House, 13-15 Arundel Street, Temple Place, London WC2R 3DX, England, www.iiss.org; *The Military Balance 2007.*

Palgrave Macmillan Ltd., Houndmills, Basingstoke, Hampshire, RG21 6XS, England, (Telephone in U.S. (888) 330-8477), (Fax in U.S. (800) 672-2054), www.palgrave.com; *The Statesman's Yearbook 2008.*

U.S. Department of State (DOS), 2201 C Street NW, Washington, DC 20520, (202) 647-4000, www.state.gov; *World Military Expenditures and Arms Transfers (WMEAT).*

United Nations Statistics Division, New York, NY 10017, (800) 253-9646, Fax: (212) 963-4116, http://unstats.un.org; *Human Development Report 2006.*

BURMA - AUTOMOBILE INDUSTRY AND TRADE

United Nations Statistics Division, New York, NY 10017, (800) 253-9646, Fax: (212) 963-4116, http://unstats.un.org; *Statistical Yearbook.*

BURMA - BALANCE OF PAYMENTS

International Monetary Fund (IMF), 700 Nineteenth Street, NW, Washington, DC 20431, (202) 623-7000, Fax: (202) 623-4661, www.imf.org; *International Financial Statistics Yearbook 2007.*

Taylor and Francis Group, An Informa Business, 2 Park Square, Milton Park, Abingdon, Oxford OX14 4RN, United Kingdom, (Dial from U.S. (212) 216-7800), (Fax from U.S. (212) 564-7854), www.tandf.co.uk; *The Europa World Year Book.*

United Nations Conference on Trade and Development (UNCTAD), DC2-1120, United Nations, New York, NY 10017, (212) 963-0027, www.unctad.org; *Handbook of Statistics 2005.*

The World Bank, 1818 H Street, NW, Washington, DC 20433, (202) 473-1000, Fax: (202) 477-6391, www.worldbank.org; *Myanmar* and *World Development Report 2008.*

BURMA - BANKS AND BANKING

Asian Development Bank (ADB), PO Box 789, 0980 Manila, Philippines, www.adb.org; *Key Indicators of Developing Asian and Pacific Countries 2006.*

Euromonitor International, Inc., 224 S. Michigan Avenue, Suite 1500, Chicago, IL 60604, (312) 922-1115, Fax: (312) 922-1157, www.euromonitor.com; *World Marketing Data and Statistics.*

International Monetary Fund (IMF), 700 Nineteenth Street, NW, Washington, DC 20431, (202) 623-7000, Fax: (202) 623-4661, www.imf.org; *International Financial Statistics Yearbook 2007.*

M.E. Sharpe, 80 Business Park Drive, Armonk, NY 10504, (800) 541-6563, Fax: (914) 273-2106, www.mesharpe.com; *The Illustrated Book of World Rankings.*

Palgrave Macmillan Ltd., Houndmills, Basingstoke, Hampshire, RG21 6XS, England, (Telephone in U.S. (888) 330-8477), (Fax in U.S. (800) 672-2054), www.palgrave.com; *The Statesman's Yearbook 2008.*

Taylor and Francis Group, An Informa Business, 2 Park Square, Milton Park, Abingdon, Oxford OX14 4RN, United Kingdom, (Dial from U.S. (212) 216-7800), (Fax from U.S. (212) 564-7854), www.tandf.co.uk; *The Europa World Year Book.*

BURMA - BARLEY PRODUCTION

See BURMA - CROPS

BURMA - BEVERAGE INDUSTRY

M.E. Sharpe, 80 Business Park Drive, Armonk, NY 10504, (800) 541-6563, Fax: (914) 273-2106, www.mesharpe.com; *The Illustrated Book of World Rankings.*

United Nations Statistics Division, New York, NY 10017, (800) 253-9646, Fax: (212) 963-4116, http://unstats.un.org; *Statistical Yearbook.*

BURMA - BONDS

Asian Development Bank (ADB), PO Box 789, 0980 Manila, Philippines, www.adb.org; *Key Indicators of Developing Asian and Pacific Countries 2006.*

BURMA - BROADCASTING

Central Intelligence Agency, Office of Public Affairs, Washington, DC 20505, (703) 482-0623, Fax: (703) 482-1739, www.cia.gov; *The World Factbook.*

Economist Intelligence Unit, 111 West 57th Street, New York, NY 10019, (212) 554-0600, Fax: (212) 586-1181, www.eiu.com; *Business Asia.*

Euromonitor International, Inc., 224 S. Michigan Avenue, Suite 1500, Chicago, IL 60604, (312) 922-1115, Fax: (312) 922-1157, www.euromonitor.com; *World Marketing Data and Statistics.*

M.E. Sharpe, 80 Business Park Drive, Armonk, NY 10504, (800) 541-6563, Fax: (914) 273-2106, www.mesharpe.com; *The Illustrated Book of World Rankings.*

Palgrave Macmillan Ltd., Houndmills, Basingstoke, Hampshire, RG21 6XS, England, (Telephone in U.S. (888) 330-8477), (Fax in U.S. (800) 672-2054), www.palgrave.com; *The Statesman's Yearbook 2008.*

WRTH Publications Limited, PO Box 290, Oxford OX2 7FT, UK, www.wrth.com; *World Radio TV Handbook 2007.*

BURMA - BUDGET

Central Intelligence Agency, Office of Public Affairs, Washington, DC 20505, (703) 482-0623, Fax: (703) 482-1739, www.cia.gov; *The World Factbook.*

BURMA - BUSINESS

United Nations Statistics Division, New York, NY 10017, (800) 253-9646, Fax: (212) 963-4116, http://unstats.un.org; *Statistical Yearbook for Asia and the Pacific 2004.*

BURMA - CAPITAL INVESTMENTS

Asian Development Bank (ADB), PO Box 789, 0980 Manila, Philippines, www.adb.org; *Key Indicators of Developing Asian and Pacific Countries 2006.*

BURMA - CAPITAL LEVY

Asian Development Bank (ADB), PO Box 789, 0980 Manila, Philippines, www.adb.org; *Key Indicators of Developing Asian and Pacific Countries 2006.*

BURMA - CATTLE

See BURMA - LIVESTOCK

BURMA - CHICK PEA PRODUCTION

See BURMA - CROPS

BURMA - CHICKENS

See BURMA - LIVESTOCK

BURMA - CHILDBIRTH - STATISTICS

Central Intelligence Agency, Office of Public Affairs, Washington, DC 20505, (703) 482-0623, Fax: (703) 482-1739, www.cia.gov; *The World Factbook.*

Economist Intelligence Unit, 111 West 57th Street, New York, NY 10019, (212) 554-0600, Fax: (212) 586-1181, www.eiu.com; *Business Asia.*

Euromonitor International, Inc., 224 S. Michigan Avenue, Suite 1500, Chicago, IL 60604, (312) 922-1115, Fax: (312) 922-1157, www.euromonitor.com; *International Marketing Data and Statistics 2008* and *The World Economic Factbook 2008.*

M.E. Sharpe, 80 Business Park Drive, Armonk, NY 10504, (800) 541-6563, Fax: (914) 273-2106, www.mesharpe.com; *The Illustrated Book of World Rankings.*

Palgrave Macmillan Ltd., Houndmills, Basingstoke, Hampshire, RG21 6XS, England, (Telephone in U.S. (888) 330-8477), (Fax in U.S. (800) 672-2054), www.palgrave.com; *The Statesman's Yearbook 2008.*

Taylor and Francis Group, An Informa Business, 2 Park Square, Milton Park, Abingdon, Oxford OX14 4RN, United Kingdom, (Dial from U.S. (212) 216-7800), (Fax from U.S. (212) 564-7854), www.tandf.co.uk; *The Europa World Year Book.*

United Nations Statistics Division, New York, NY 10017, (800) 253-9646, Fax: (212) 963-4116, http://unstats.un.org; *Asia-Pacific in Figures 2004; Demographic Yearbook;* and *Statistical Yearbook.*

BURMA - CLIMATE

International Institute for Environment and Development (IIED), 3 Endsleigh Street, London, England, WC1H 0DD, United Kingdom, www.iied.org; *Environment Urbanization.*

M.E. Sharpe, 80 Business Park Drive, Armonk, NY 10504, (800) 541-6563, Fax: (914) 273-2106, www.mesharpe.com; *The Illustrated Book of World Rankings.*

Palgrave Macmillan Ltd., Houndmills, Basingstoke, Hampshire, RG21 6XS, England, (Telephone in U.S. (888) 330-8477), (Fax in U.S. (800) 672-2054), www.palgrave.com; *The Statesman's Yearbook 2008.*

BURMA - COAL PRODUCTION

See BURMA - MINERAL INDUSTRIES

BURMA - COFFEE

See BURMA - CROPS

BURMA - COMMERCE

Palgrave Macmillan Ltd., Houndmills, Basingstoke, Hampshire, RG21 6XS, England, (Telephone in U.S. (888) 330-8477), (Fax in U.S. (800) 672-2054), www.palgrave.com; *The Statesman's Yearbook 2008.*

BURMA - COMMODITY EXCHANGES

Commodity Research Bureau, 330 South Wells Street, Suite 612, Chicago, IL 60606-7110, (800) 621-5271, Fax: (312) 939-4135, www.crbtrader.com; *2006 CRB Commodity Yearbook and CD.*

International Monetary Fund (IMF), 700 Nineteenth Street, NW, Washington, DC 20431, (202) 623-7000, Fax: (202) 623-4661, www.imf.org; *IMF Primary Commodity Prices.*

United Nations Food and Agricultural Organization (FAO), Viale delle Terme di Caracalla, 00100 Rome, Italy, (Dial from U.S. (202) 653-2400), (Fax from U.S. (202) 653 5760), www.fao.org; *The State of Food and Agriculture (SOFA) 2006.*

BURMA - COMMUNICATION AND TRAFFIC

United Nations Statistics Division, New York, NY 10017, (800) 253-9646, Fax: (212) 963-4116, http://unstats.un.org; *Statistical Yearbook.*

BURMA - CONSTRUCTION INDUSTRY

M.E. Sharpe, 80 Business Park Drive, Armonk, NY 10504, (800) 541-6563, Fax: (914) 273-2106, www.mesharpe.com; *The Illustrated Book of World Rankings.*

United Nations Statistics Division, New York, NY 10017, (800) 253-9646, Fax: (212) 963-4116, http://unstats.un.org; *Statistical Yearbook.*

BURMA - CONSUMER PRICE INDEXES

Asian Development Bank (ADB), PO Box 789, 0980 Manila, Philippines, www.adb.org; *Key Indicators of Developing Asian and Pacific Countries 2006.*

Taylor and Francis Group, An Informa Business, 2 Park Square, Milton Park, Abingdon, Oxford OX14 4RN, United Kingdom, (Dial from U.S. (212) 216-7800), (Fax from U.S. (212) 564-7854), www.tandf.co.uk; *The Europa World Year Book.*

United Nations Statistics Division, New York, NY 10017, (800) 253-9646, Fax: (212) 963-4116, http://unstats.un.org; *Statistical Yearbook.*

The World Bank, 1818 H Street, NW, Washington, DC 20433, (202) 473-1000, Fax: (202) 477-6391, www.worldbank.org; *Myanmar.*

BURMA - CONSUMPTION (ECONOMICS)

The World Bank, 1818 H Street, NW, Washington, DC 20433, (202) 473-1000, Fax: (202) 477-6391, www.worldbank.org; *World Development Report 2008.*

BURMA - COPPER INDUSTRY AND TRADE

See BURMA - MINERAL INDUSTRIES

BURMA - CORN INDUSTRY

See BURMA - CROPS

BURMA - COST AND STANDARD OF LIVING

Asian Development Bank (ADB), PO Box 789, 0980 Manila, Philippines, www.adb.org; *Key Indicators of Developing Asian and Pacific Countries 2006.*

International Labour Office, I.L.O. Publications, 4 route des Morillons, CH-1211 Geneva 22, Switzerland, (Telephone in U.S. (202) 653-7652), (Fax in U.S. (202) 653-7687), www.ilo.org; *Yearbook of Labour Statistics 2006.*

International Monetary Fund (IMF), 700 Nineteenth Street, NW, Washington, DC 20431, (202) 623-7000, Fax: (202) 623-4661, www.imf.org; *International Financial Statistics Yearbook 2007.*

M.E. Sharpe, 80 Business Park Drive, Armonk, NY 10504, (800) 541-6563, Fax: (914) 273-2106, www.mesharpe.com; *The Illustrated Book of World Rankings.*

United Nations Food and Agricultural Organization (FAO), Viale delle Terme di Caracalla, 00100 Rome, Italy, (Dial from U.S. (202) 653-2400), (Fax from U.S. (202) 653 5760), www.fao.org; *FAO Production Yearbook 2002* and *The State of Food and Agriculture (SOFA) 2006.*

The World Bank, 1818 H Street, NW, Washington, DC 20433, (202) 473-1000, Fax: (202) 477-6391, www.worldbank.org; *Myanmar.*

BURMA - COTTON

See BURMA - CROPS

BURMA - CRIME

International Criminal Police Organization (INTERPOL), General Secretariat, 200 quai Charles de Gaulle, 69006 Lyon, France, www.interpol.int; *International Crime Statistics.*

Yale University Press, PO Box 209040, New Haven, CT 06520-9040, (203) 432-0960, Fax: (203) 432-0948, http://yalepress.yale.edu/yupbooks; *Violence and Crime in Cross-National Perspective.*

BURMA - CROPS

Asian Development Bank (ADB), PO Box 789, 0980 Manila, Philippines, www.adb.org; *Key Indicators of Developing Asian and Pacific Countries 2006.*

International Monetary Fund (IMF), 700 Nineteenth Street, NW, Washington, DC 20431, (202) 623-7000, Fax: (202) 623-4661, www.imf.org; *International Financial Statistics Yearbook 2007.*

M.E. Sharpe, 80 Business Park Drive, Armonk, NY 10504, (800) 541-6563, Fax: (914) 273-2106, www.mesharpe.com; *The Illustrated Book of World Rankings.*

Palgrave Macmillan Ltd., Houndmills, Basingstoke, Hampshire, RG21 6XS, England, (Telephone in U.S. (888) 330-8477), (Fax in U.S. (800) 672-2054), www.palgrave.com; *The Statesman's Yearbook 2008.*

Taylor and Francis Group, An Informa Business, 2 Park Square, Milton Park, Abingdon, Oxford OX14 4RN, United Kingdom, (Dial from U.S. (212) 216-7800), (Fax from U.S. (212) 564-7854), www.tandf.co.uk; *The Europa World Year Book.*

United Nations Conference on Trade and Development (UNCTAD), DC2-1120, United Nations, New York, NY 10017, (212) 963-0027, www.unctad.org; *UNCTAD Commodity Yearbook.*

United Nations Food and Agricultural Organization (FAO), Viale delle Terme di Caracalla, 00100 Rome, Italy, (Dial from U.S. (202) 653-2400), (Fax from U.S. (202) 653 5760), www.fao.org; *FAO Production Yearbook 2002* and *The State of Food and Agriculture (SOFA) 2006.*

United Nations Statistics Division, New York, NY 10017, (800) 253-9646, Fax: (212) 963-4116, http://unstats.un.org; *Statistical Yearbook.*

BURMA - CUSTOMS ADMINISTRATION

Palgrave Macmillan Ltd., Houndmills, Basingstoke, Hampshire, RG21 6XS, England, (Telephone in U.S. (888) 330-8477), (Fax in U.S. (800) 672-2054), www.palgrave.com; *The Statesman's Yearbook 2008.*

BURMA - DAIRY PROCESSING

M.E. Sharpe, 80 Business Park Drive, Armonk, NY 10504, (800) 541-6563, Fax: (914) 273-2106, www.mesharpe.com; *The Illustrated Book of World Rankings.*

Palgrave Macmillan Ltd., Houndmills, Basingstoke, Hampshire, RG21 6XS, England, (Telephone in U.S. (888) 330-8477), (Fax in U.S. (800) 672-2054), www.palgrave.com; *The Statesman's Yearbook 2008.*

Taylor and Francis Group, An Informa Business, 2 Park Square, Milton Park, Abingdon, Oxford OX14 4RN, United Kingdom, (Dial from U.S. (212) 216-7800), (Fax from U.S. (212) 564-7854), www.tandf.co.uk; *The Europa World Year Book.*

United Nations Food and Agricultural Organization (FAO), Viale delle Terme di Caracalla, 00100 Rome, Italy, (Dial from U.S. (202) 653-2400), (Fax from U.S. (202) 653 5760), www.fao.org; *FAO Production Yearbook 2002* and *The State of Food and Agriculture (SOFA) 2006.*

United Nations Statistics Division, New York, NY 10017, (800) 253-9646, Fax: (212) 963-4116, http://unstats.un.org; *Statistical Yearbook.*

BURMA - DEATH RATES

See BURMA - MORTALITY

BURMA - DEBTS, EXTERNAL

Asian Development Bank (ADB), PO Box 789, 0980 Manila, Philippines, www.adb.org; *Key Indicators of Developing Asian and Pacific Countries 2006.*

Palgrave Macmillan Ltd., Houndmills, Basingstoke, Hampshire, RG21 6XS, England, (Telephone in U.S. (888) 330-8477), (Fax in U.S. (800) 672-2054), www.palgrave.com; *The Statesman's Yearbook 2008.*

The World Bank, 1818 H Street, NW, Washington, DC 20433, (202) 473-1000, Fax: (202) 477-6391, www.worldbank.org; *Global Development Finance 2007* and *World Development Report 2008.*

Worldinformation.com, 2 Market Street, Saffron Walden, Essex CB10 1HZ, United Kingdom, www.worldinformation.com; The World of Information (www.worldinformation.com).

BURMA - DEFENSE EXPENDITURES

See BURMA - ARMED FORCES

BURMA - DEMOGRAPHY

Economist Intelligence Unit, 111 West 57th Street, New York, NY 10019, (212) 554-0600, Fax: (212) 586-1181, www.eiu.com; *Business Asia.*

Euromonitor International, Inc., 224 S. Michigan Avenue, Suite 1500, Chicago, IL 60604, (312) 922-1115, Fax: (312) 922-1157, www.euromonitor.com; *International Marketing Data and Statistics 2008; The World Economic Factbook 2008;* and *World Marketing Data and Statistics.*

M.E. Sharpe, 80 Business Park Drive, Armonk, NY 10504, (800) 541-6563, Fax: (914) 273-2106, www.mesharpe.com; *The Illustrated Book of World Rankings.*

United Nations Statistics Division, New York, NY 10017, (800) 253-9646, Fax: (212) 963-4116, http://unstats.un.org; *Asia-Pacific in Figures 2004* and *Human Development Report 2006.*

The World Bank, 1818 H Street, NW, Washington, DC 20433, (202) 473-1000, Fax: (202) 477-6391, www.worldbank.org; *Myanmar.*

BURMA - DIAMONDS

See BURMA - MINERAL INDUSTRIES

BURMA - DISPOSABLE INCOME

M.E. Sharpe, 80 Business Park Drive, Armonk, NY 10504, (800) 541-6563, Fax: (914) 273-2106, www.mesharpe.com; *The Illustrated Book of World Rankings.*

United Nations Statistics Division, New York, NY 10017, (800) 253-9646, Fax: (212) 963-4116, http://unstats.un.org; *National Accounts Statistics: Compendium of Income Distribution Statistics* and *Statistical Yearbook.*

BURMA - DIVORCE

M.E. Sharpe, 80 Business Park Drive, Armonk, NY 10504, (800) 541-6563, Fax: (914) 273-2106, www.mesharpe.com; *The Illustrated Book of World Rankings.*

United Nations Statistics Division, New York, NY 10017, (800) 253-9646, Fax: (212) 963-4116, http://unstats.un.org; *Demographic Yearbook.*

BURMA - ECONOMIC ASSISTANCE

Asian Development Bank (ADB), PO Box 789, 0980 Manila, Philippines, www.adb.org; *Key Indicators of Developing Asian and Pacific Countries 2006.*

United Nations Statistics Division, New York, NY 10017, (800) 253-9646, Fax: (212) 963-4116, http://unstats.un.org; *Statistical Yearbook.*

BURMA - ECONOMIC CONDITIONS

Asian Development Bank (ADB), PO Box 789, 0980 Manila, Philippines, www.adb.org; *Key Indicators of Developing Asian and Pacific Countries 2006.*

Center for International Business Education Research (CIBER), Columbia Business School and School of International and Public Affairs, Uris Hall, Room 212, 3022 Broadway, New York, NY 10027-6902, Mr. Joshua Safier, (212) 854-4750, Fax: (212) 222-9821, www.columbia.edu/cu/ciber/; Datastream International.

Central Intelligence Agency, Office of Public Affairs, Washington, DC 20505, (703) 482-0623, Fax: (703) 482-1739, www.cia.gov; *The World Factbook.*

Central Statistical Organization (CSO), Ministry of National Planning and Economic Development, Building 32, Nay Pyi Taw, Myanmar, www.csostat.gov.mm; *Selected Monthly Economic Indicators (December 2007).*

DSI Data Service Information, Xantener Strasse 51a, D-47495 Rheinberg, Germany, www.dsidata.com; *Campus Solution.*

Dun and Bradstreet (DB) Corporation, 103 JFK Parkway, Short Hills, NJ 07078, (973) 921-5500, www.dnb.com; *Country Report.*

Economist Intelligence Unit, 111 West 57th Street, New York, NY 10019, (212) 554-0600, Fax: (212) 586-1181, www.eiu.com; *Myanmar (Burma) Country Report.*

Euromonitor International, Inc., 224 S. Michigan Avenue, Suite 1500, Chicago, IL 60604, (312) 922-1115, Fax: (312) 922-1157, www.euromonitor.com;

International Marketing Data and Statistics 2008; The World Economic Factbook 2008; and *World Marketing Data and Statistics.*

International Monetary Fund (IMF), 700 Nineteenth Street, NW, Washington, DC 20431, (202) 623-7000, Fax: (202) 623-4661, www.imf.org; *World Economic Outlook Reports.*

M.E. Sharpe, 80 Business Park Drive, Armonk, NY 10504, (800) 541-6563, Fax: (914) 273-2106, www.mesharpe.com; *The Illustrated Book of World Rankings.*

Nomura Research Institute (NRI), 2 World Financial Center, Building B, 19th Fl., New York, NY 10281-1198, (212) 667-1670, www.nri.co.jp/english; *Asian Economic Outlook 2003-2004.*

Palgrave Macmillan Ltd., Houndmills, Basingstoke, Hampshire, RG21 6XS, England, (Telephone in U.S. (888) 330-8477), (Fax in U.S. (800) 672-2054), www.palgrave.com; *The Statesman's Yearbook 2008.*

Taylor and Francis Group, An Informa Business, 2 Park Square, Milton Park, Abingdon, Oxford OX14 4RN, United Kingdom, (Dial from U.S. (212) 216-7800), (Fax from U.S. (212) 564-7854), www.tandf.co.uk; *The Europa World Year Book.*

United Nations Statistics Division, New York, NY 10017, (800) 253-9646, Fax: (212) 963-4116, http://unstats.un.org; *World Statistics Pocketbook.*

The World Bank, 1818 H Street, NW, Washington, DC 20433, (202) 473-1000, Fax: (202) 477-6391, www.worldbank.org; *Global Economic Monitor (GEM); Global Economic Prospects 2008; Myanmar; The World Bank Atlas 2003-2004;* and *World Development Report 2008.*

BURMA - EDUCATION

Economist Intelligence Unit, 111 West 57th Street, New York, NY 10019, (212) 554-0600, Fax: (212) 586-1181, www.eiu.com; *Business Asia.*

Euromonitor International, Inc., 224 S. Michigan Avenue, Suite 1500, Chicago, IL 60604, (312) 922-1115, Fax: (312) 922-1157, www.euromonitor.com; *International Marketing Data and Statistics 2008.*

M.E. Sharpe, 80 Business Park Drive, Armonk, NY 10504, (800) 541-6563, Fax: (914) 273-2106, www.mesharpe.com; *The Illustrated Book of World Rankings.*

Palgrave Macmillan Ltd., Houndmills, Basingstoke, Hampshire, RG21 6XS, England, (Telephone in U.S. (888) 330-8477), (Fax in U.S. (800) 672-2054), www.palgrave.com; *The Statesman's Yearbook 2008.*

Taylor and Francis Group, An Informa Business, 2 Park Square, Milton Park, Abingdon, Oxford OX14 4RN, United Kingdom, (Dial from U.S. (212) 216-7800), (Fax from U.S. (212) 564-7854), www.tandf.co.uk; *The Europa World Year Book.*

UNESCO Institute for Statistics, C.P. 6128 Succursale Centre-Ville, Montreal, Quebec, H3C 3J7 Canada, (Dial from U.S. (514) 343-6880), (Fax from U.S. (514) 343 6882), www.uis.unesco.org; *Statistical Tables.*

United Nations Statistics Division, New York, NY 10017, (800) 253-9646, Fax: (212) 963-4116, http://unstats.un.org; *Asia-Pacific in Figures 2004; Human Development Report 2006;* and *Statistical Yearbook for Asia and the Pacific 2004.*

The World Bank, 1818 H Street, NW, Washington, DC 20433, (202) 473-1000, Fax: (202) 477-6391, www.worldbank.org; *Myanmar* and *World Development Report 2008.*

BURMA - ELECTRICITY

Asian Development Bank (ADB), PO Box 789, 0980 Manila, Philippines, www.adb.org; *Key Indicators of Developing Asian and Pacific Countries 2006.*

Central Intelligence Agency, Office of Public Affairs, Washington, DC 20505, (703) 482-0623, Fax: (703) 482-1739, www.cia.gov; *The World Factbook.*

M.E. Sharpe, 80 Business Park Drive, Armonk, NY 10504, (800) 541-6563, Fax: (914) 273-2106, www.mesharpe.com; *The Illustrated Book of World Rankings.*

Organisation for Economic Cooperation and Development (OECD), 2 rue Andre Pascal, F-75775 Paris Cedex 16, France, (Telephone in U.S. (202) 785-6323), (Fax in U.S. (202) 785-0350), www.oecd.org; *World Energy Outlook 2007.*

Palgrave Macmillan Ltd., Houndmills, Basingstoke, Hampshire, RG21 6XS, England, (Telephone in U.S. (888) 330-8477), (Fax in U.S. (800) 672-2054), www.palgrave.com; *The Statesman's Yearbook 2008.*

U.S. Department of Energy (DOE), Energy Information Administration (EIA), 1000 Independence Avenue, SW, Washington, DC 20585, (202) 586-8800, www.eia.doe.gov; *International Energy Annual 2004* and *International Energy Outlook 2006.*

United Nations Statistics Division, New York, NY 10017, (800) 253-9646, Fax: (212) 963-4116, http://unstats.un.org; *Electric Power in Asia and the Pacific 2001 and 2002; Human Development Report 2006;* and *Statistical Yearbook.*

BURMA - EMPLOYMENT

Euromonitor International, Inc., 224 S. Michigan Avenue, Suite 1500, Chicago, IL 60604, (312) 922-1115, Fax: (312) 922-1157, www.euromonitor.com; *International Marketing Data and Statistics 2008.*

International Labour Office, I.L.O. Publications, 4 route des Morillons, CH-1211 Geneva 22, Switzerland, (Telephone in U.S. (202) 653-7652), (Fax in U.S. (202) 653-7687), www.ilo.org; *Yearbook of Labour Statistics 2006.*

M.E. Sharpe, 80 Business Park Drive, Armonk, NY 10504, (800) 541-6563, Fax: (914) 273-2106, www.mesharpe.com; *The Illustrated Book of World Rankings.*

United Nations Statistics Division, New York, NY 10017, (800) 253-9646, Fax: (212) 963-4116, http://unstats.un.org; *Asia-Pacific in Figures 2004* and *Statistical Yearbook.*

The World Bank, 1818 H Street, NW, Washington, DC 20433, (202) 473-1000, Fax: (202) 477-6391, www.worldbank.org; *Myanmar.*

BURMA - ENERGY INDUSTRIES

Enerdata, 10 Rue Royale, 75008 Paris, France, www.enerdata.fr; *Global Energy Market Data.*

Euromonitor International, Inc., 224 S. Michigan Avenue, Suite 1500, Chicago, IL 60604, (312) 922-1115, Fax: (312) 922-1157, www.euromonitor.com; *International Marketing Data and Statistics 2008; The World Economic Factbook 2008;* and *World Marketing Data and Statistics.*

M.E. Sharpe, 80 Business Park Drive, Armonk, NY 10504, (800) 541-6563, Fax: (914) 273-2106, www.mesharpe.com; *The Illustrated Book of World Rankings.*

Organisation for Economic Cooperation and Development (OECD), 2 rue Andre Pascal, F-75775 Paris Cedex 16, France, (Telephone in U.S. (202) 785-6323), (Fax in U.S. (202) 785-0350), www.oecd.org; *World Energy Outlook 2007.*

Palgrave Macmillan Ltd., Houndmills, Basingstoke, Hampshire, RG21 6XS, England, (Telephone in U.S. (888) 330-8477), (Fax in U.S. (800) 672-2054), www.palgrave.com; *The Statesman's Yearbook 2008.*

Platts, 2 Penn Plaza, 25th Floor, New York, NY 10121-2298, (212) 904-3070, www.platts.com; *Energy Economist.*

U.S. Department of Energy (DOE), Energy Information Administration (EIA), 1000 Independence Avenue, SW, Washington, DC 20585, (202) 586-8800, www.eia.doe.gov; *International Energy Annual 2004* and *International Energy Outlook 2006.*

United Nations Statistics Division, New York, NY 10017, (800) 253-9646, Fax: (212) 963-4116, http://unstats.un.org; *Asia-Pacific in Figures 2004; Electric Power in Asia and the Pacific 2001 and 2002; Energy Statistics Yearbook 2003; Human Development Report 2006; Statistical Yearbook; Statistical Yearbook for Asia and the Pacific 2004;* and *World Statistics Pocketbook.*

The World Bank, 1818 H Street, NW, Washington, DC 20433, (202) 473-1000, Fax: (202) 477-6391, www.worldbank.org; *The World Bank Atlas 2003-2004* and *World Development Report 2008.*

BURMA - ENVIRONMENTAL CONDITIONS

DSI Data Service Information, Xantener Strasse 51a, D-47495 Rheinberg, Germany, www.dsidata.com; *Campus Solution* and *DSI's Global Environmental Database.*

Economist Intelligence Unit, 111 West 57th Street, New York, NY 10019, (212) 554-0600, Fax: (212) 586-1181, www.eiu.com; *Myanmar (Burma) Country Report.*

International Institute for Environment and Development (IIED), 3 Endsleigh Street, London, England, WC1H 0DD, United Kingdom, www.iied.org; *Environment Urbanization.*

United Nations Statistics Division, New York, NY 10017, (800) 253-9646, Fax: (212) 963-4116, http://unstats.un.org; *World Statistics Pocketbook.*

BURMA - EXPORTS

Asian Development Bank (ADB), PO Box 789, 0980 Manila, Philippines, www.adb.org; *Key Indicators of Developing Asian and Pacific Countries 2006.*

Central Intelligence Agency, Office of Public Affairs, Washington, DC 20505, (703) 482-0623, Fax: (703) 482-1739, www.cia.gov; *The World Factbook.*

Economist Intelligence Unit, 111 West 57th Street, New York, NY 10019, (212) 554-0600, Fax: (212) 586-1181, www.eiu.com; *Myanmar (Burma) Country Report.*

Euromonitor International, Inc., 224 S. Michigan Avenue, Suite 1500, Chicago, IL 60604, (312) 922-1115, Fax: (312) 922-1157, www.euromonitor.com; *International Marketing Data and Statistics 2008* and *The World Economic Factbook 2008.*

International Monetary Fund (IMF), 700 Nineteenth Street, NW, Washington, DC 20431, (202) 623-7000, Fax: (202) 623-4661, www.imf.org; *Direction of Trade Statistics Yearbook 2007* and *International Financial Statistics Yearbook 2007.*

Palgrave Macmillan Ltd., Houndmills, Basingstoke, Hampshire, RG21 6XS, England, (Telephone in U.S. (888) 330-8477), (Fax in U.S. (800) 672-2054), www.palgrave.com; *The Statesman's Yearbook 2008.*

Taylor and Francis Group, An Informa Business, 2 Park Square, Milton Park, Abingdon, Oxford OX14 4RN, United Kingdom, (Dial from U.S. (212) 216-7800), (Fax from U.S. (212) 564-7854), www.tandf.co.uk; *The Europa World Year Book.*

United Nations Conference on Trade and Development (UNCTAD), DC2-1120, United Nations, New York, NY 10017, (212) 963-0027, www.unctad.org; *Handbook of Statistics 2005.*

United Nations Food and Agricultural Organization (FAO), Viale delle Terme di Caracalla, 00100 Rome, Italy, (Dial from U.S. (202) 653-2400), (Fax from U.S. (202) 653 5760), www.fao.org; *The State of Food and Agriculture (SOFA) 2006.*

The World Bank, 1818 H Street, NW, Washington, DC 20433, (202) 473-1000, Fax: (202) 477-6391, www.worldbank.org; *World Development Report 2008.*

Worldinformation.com, 2 Market Street, Saffron Walden, Essex CB10 1HZ, United Kingdom, www.worldinformation.com; The World of Information (www.worldinformation.com).

BURMA - FEMALE WORKING POPULATION

See BURMA - EMPLOYMENT

BURMA - FERTILITY, HUMAN

Central Intelligence Agency, Office of Public Affairs, Washington, DC 20505, (703) 482-0623, Fax: (703) 482-1739, www.cia.gov; *The World Factbook.*

M.E. Sharpe, 80 Business Park Drive, Armonk, NY 10504, (800) 541-6563, Fax: (914) 273-2106, www.mesharpe.com; *The Illustrated Book of World Rankings.*

United Nations Statistics Division, New York, NY 10017, (800) 253-9646, Fax: (212) 963-4116, http://unstats.un.org; *Human Development Report 2006.*

The World Bank, 1818 H Street, NW, Washington, DC 20433, (202) 473-1000, Fax: (202) 477-6391, www.worldbank.org; *The World Bank Atlas 2003-2004* and *World Development Report 2008.*

BURMA - FERTILIZER INDUSTRY

United Nations Food and Agricultural Organization (FAO), Viale delle Terme di Caracalla, 00100 Rome, Italy, (Dial from U.S. (202) 653-2400), (Fax from U.S. (202) 653 5760), www.fao.org; *The State of Food and Agriculture (SOFA) 2006.*

United Nations Statistics Division, New York, NY 10017, (800) 253-9646, Fax: (212) 963-4116, http://unstats.un.org; *Statistical Yearbook.*

BURMA - FETAL MORTALITY

See BURMA - MORTALITY

BURMA - FINANCE

Economist Intelligence Unit, 111 West 57th Street, New York, NY 10019, (212) 554-0600, Fax: (212) 586-1181, www.eiu.com; *Myanmar (Burma) Country Report.*

International Monetary Fund (IMF), 700 Nineteenth Street, NW, Washington, DC 20431, (202) 623-7000, Fax: (202) 623-4661, www.imf.org; *International Financial Statistics Yearbook 2007.*

M.E. Sharpe, 80 Business Park Drive, Armonk, NY 10504, (800) 541-6563, Fax: (914) 273-2106, www.mesharpe.com; *The Illustrated Book of World Rankings.*

Palgrave Macmillan Ltd., Houndmills, Basingstoke, Hampshire, RG21 6XS, England, (Telephone in U.S. (888) 330-8477), (Fax in U.S. (800) 672-2054), www.palgrave.com; *The Statesman's Yearbook 2008.*

Taylor and Francis Group, An Informa Business, 2 Park Square, Milton Park, Abingdon, Oxford OX14 4RN, United Kingdom, (Dial from U.S. (212) 216-7800), (Fax from U.S. (212) 564-7854), www.tandf.co.uk; *The Europa World Year Book.*

United Nations Statistics Division, New York, NY 10017, (800) 253-9646, Fax: (212) 963-4116, http://unstats.un.org; *Asia-Pacific in Figures 2004; National Accounts Statistics: Compendium of Income Distribution Statistics; Statistical Yearbook;* and *Statistical Yearbook for Asia and the Pacific 2004.*

The World Bank, 1818 H Street, NW, Washington, DC 20433, (202) 473-1000, Fax: (202) 477-6391, www.worldbank.org; *Myanmar.*

BURMA - FISHERIES

M.E. Sharpe, 80 Business Park Drive, Armonk, NY 10504, (800) 541-6563, Fax: (914) 273-2106, www.mesharpe.com; *The Illustrated Book of World Rankings.*

Palgrave Macmillan Ltd., Houndmills, Basingstoke, Hampshire, RG21 6XS, England, (Telephone in U.S. (888) 330-8477), (Fax in U.S. (800) 672-2054), www.palgrave.com; *The Statesman's Yearbook 2008.*

Taylor and Francis Group, An Informa Business, 2 Park Square, Milton Park, Abingdon, Oxford OX14 4RN, United Kingdom, (Dial from U.S. (212) 216-7800), (Fax from U.S. (212) 564-7854), www.tandf.co.uk; *The Europa World Year Book.*

United Nations Conference on Trade and Development (UNCTAD), DC2-1120, United Nations, New York, NY 10017, (212) 963-0027, www.unctad.org; *UNCTAD Commodity Yearbook.*

United Nations Food and Agricultural Organization (FAO), Viale delle Terme di Caracalla, 00100 Rome, Italy, (Dial from U.S. (202) 653-2400), (Fax from U.S. (202) 653 5760), www.fao.org; *FAO Yearbook of Fishery Statistics;* Fishery Databases; FISHSTAT Database. Subjects covered include: Aquaculture production, capture production, fishery commodities; and *The State of Food and Agriculture (SOFA) 2006.*

United Nations Statistics Division, New York, NY 10017, (800) 253-9646, Fax: (212) 963-4116, http://unstats.un.org; *Statistical Yearbook.*

The World Bank, 1818 H Street, NW, Washington, DC 20433, (202) 473-1000, Fax: (202) 477-6391, www.worldbank.org; *Myanmar.*

BURMA - FLOUR INDUSTRY

United Nations Statistics Division, New York, NY 10017, (800) 253-9646, Fax: (212) 963-4116, http://unstats.un.org; *Statistical Yearbook.*

BURMA - FOOD

United Nations Conference on Trade and Development (UNCTAD), DC2-1120, United Nations, New York, NY 10017, (212) 963-0027, www.unctad.org; *UNCTAD Commodity Yearbook.*

United Nations Food and Agricultural Organization (FAO), Viale delle Terme di Caracalla, 00100 Rome, Italy, (Dial from U.S. (202) 653-2400), (Fax from U.S. (202) 653 5760), www.fao.org; *FAO Production Yearbook 2002* and *The State of Food and Agriculture (SOFA) 2006.*

United Nations Statistics Division, New York, NY 10017, (800) 253-9646, Fax: (212) 963-4116, http://unstats.un.org; *Human Development Report 2006* and *Statistical Yearbook for Asia and the Pacific 2004.*

BURMA - FOREIGN EXCHANGE RATES

Asian Development Bank (ADB), PO Box 789, 0980 Manila, Philippines, www.adb.org; *Key Indicators of Developing Asian and Pacific Countries 2006.*

Central Intelligence Agency, Office of Public Affairs, Washington, DC 20505, (703) 482-0623, Fax: (703) 482-1739, www.cia.gov; *The World Factbook.*

Economist Intelligence Unit, 111 West 57th Street, New York, NY 10019, (212) 554-0600, Fax: (212) 586-1181, www.eiu.com; *Business Asia.*

Euromonitor International, Inc., 224 S. Michigan Avenue, Suite 1500, Chicago, IL 60604, (312) 922-1115, Fax: (312) 922-1157, www.euromonitor.com; *International Marketing Data and Statistics 2008* and *The World Economic Factbook 2008.*

International Civil Aviation Organization (ICAO), External Relations and Public Information Office (EPO), 999 University Street, Montreal, Quebec H3C 5H7, Canada, (Dial from U.S. (514) 954-8219), (Fax from U.S. (514) 954-6077), www.icao.int; *Civil Aviation Statistics of the World.*

International Monetary Fund (IMF), 700 Nineteenth Street, NW, Washington, DC 20431, (202) 623-7000, Fax: (202) 623-4661, www.imf.org; *International Financial Statistics Yearbook 2007.*

Taylor and Francis Group, An Informa Business, 2 Park Square, Milton Park, Abingdon, Oxford OX14 4RN, United Kingdom, (Dial from U.S. (212) 216-7800), (Fax from U.S. (212) 564-7854), www.tandf.co.uk; *The Europa World Year Book.*

United Nations Statistics Division, New York, NY 10017, (800) 253-9646, Fax: (212) 963-4116, http://unstats.un.org; *Statistical Yearbook* and *World Statistics Pocketbook.*

Worldinformation.com, 2 Market Street, Saffron Walden, Essex CB10 1HZ, United Kingdom, www.worldinformation.com; The World of Information (www.worldinformation.com).

BURMA - FORESTS AND FORESTRY

Economist Intelligence Unit, 111 West 57th Street, New York, NY 10019, (212) 554-0600, Fax: (212) 586-1181, www.eiu.com; *Business Asia.*

M.E. Sharpe, 80 Business Park Drive, Armonk, NY 10504, (800) 541-6563, Fax: (914) 273-2106, www.mesharpe.com; *The Illustrated Book of World Rankings.*

Palgrave Macmillan Ltd., Houndmills, Basingstoke, Hampshire, RG21 6XS, England, (Telephone in U.S. (888) 330-8477), (Fax in U.S. (800) 672-2054), www.palgrave.com; *The Statesman's Yearbook 2008.*

Taylor and Francis Group, An Informa Business, 2 Park Square, Milton Park, Abingdon, Oxford OX14 4RN, United Kingdom, (Dial from U.S. (212) 216-7800), (Fax from U.S. (212) 564-7854), www.tandf.co.uk; *The Europa World Year Book.*

UNESCO Institute for Statistics, C.P. 6128 Succursale Centre-Ville, Montreal, Quebec, H3C 3J7 Canada, (Dial from U.S. (514) 343-6880), (Fax from U.S. (514) 343 6882), www.uis.unesco.org; *Statistical Tables.*

United Nations Food and Agricultural Organization (FAO), Viale delle Terme di Caracalla, 00100 Rome, Italy, (Dial from U.S. (202) 653-2400), (Fax from U.S. (202) 653 5760), www.fao.org; *FAO Yearbook of Forest Products* and *The State of Food and Agriculture (SOFA) 2006.*

United Nations Statistics Division, New York, NY 10017, (800) 253-9646, Fax: (212) 963-4116, http://unstats.un.org; *Statistical Yearbook.*

The World Bank, 1818 H Street, NW, Washington, DC 20433, (202) 473-1000, Fax: (202) 477-6391, www.worldbank.org; *Myanmar* and *World Development Report 2008.*

BURMA - GAS PRODUCTION

See BURMA - MINERAL INDUSTRIES

BURMA - GEOGRAPHIC INFORMATION SYSTEMS

M.E. Sharpe, 80 Business Park Drive, Armonk, NY 10504, (800) 541-6563, Fax: (914) 273-2106, www.mesharpe.com; *The Illustrated Book of World Rankings.*

The World Bank, 1818 H Street, NW, Washington, DC 20433, (202) 473-1000, Fax: (202) 477-6391, www.worldbank.org; *Myanmar.*

BURMA - GOLD INDUSTRY

International Monetary Fund (IMF), 700 Nineteenth Street, NW, Washington, DC 20431, (202) 623-7000, Fax: (202) 623-4661, www.imf.org; *International Financial Statistics Yearbook 2007.*

United Nations Statistics Division, New York, NY 10017, (800) 253-9646, Fax: (212) 963-4116, http://unstats.un.org; *Statistical Yearbook.*

BURMA - GOLD PRODUCTION

See BURMA - MINERAL INDUSTRIES

BURMA - GRAIN TRADE

United Nations Food and Agricultural Organization (FAO), Viale delle Terme di Caracalla, 00100 Rome, Italy, (Dial from U.S. (202) 653-2400), (Fax from U.S. (202) 653 5760), www.fao.org; *The State of Food and Agriculture (SOFA) 2006.*

BURMA - GROSS DOMESTIC PRODUCT

Asian Development Bank (ADB), PO Box 789, 0980 Manila, Philippines, www.adb.org; *Key Indicators of Developing Asian and Pacific Countries 2006.*

Economist Intelligence Unit, 111 West 57th Street, New York, NY 10019, (212) 554-0600, Fax: (212) 586-1181, www.eiu.com; *Business Asia* and *Myanmar (Burma) Country Report.*

Euromonitor International, Inc., 224 S. Michigan Avenue, Suite 1500, Chicago, IL 60604, (312) 922-1115, Fax: (312) 922-1157, www.euromonitor.com; *International Marketing Data and Statistics 2008* and *The World Economic Factbook 2008.*

M.E. Sharpe, 80 Business Park Drive, Armonk, NY 10504, (800) 541-6563, Fax: (914) 273-2106, www.mesharpe.com; *The Illustrated Book of World Rankings.*

Taylor and Francis Group, An Informa Business, 2 Park Square, Milton Park, Abingdon, Oxford OX14 4RN, United Kingdom, (Dial from U.S. (212) 216-7800), (Fax from U.S. (212) 564-7854), www.tandf.co.uk; *The Europa World Year Book.*

United Nations Statistics Division, New York, NY 10017, (800) 253-9646, Fax: (212) 963-4116, http://

unstats.un.org; *Human Development Report 2006; National Accounts Statistics: Compendium of Income Distribution Statistics;* and *Statistical Yearbook.*

The World Bank, 1818 H Street, NW, Washington, DC 20433, (202) 473-1000, Fax: (202) 477-6391, www.worldbank.org; *World Development Report 2008.*

BURMA - GROSS NATIONAL PRODUCT

Asian Development Bank (ADB), PO Box 789, 0980 Manila, Philippines, www.adb.org; *Key Indicators of Developing Asian and Pacific Countries 2006.*

Euromonitor International, Inc., 224 S. Michigan Avenue, Suite 1500, Chicago, IL 60604, (312) 922-1115, Fax: (312) 922-1157, www.euromonitor.com; *International Marketing Data and Statistics 2008.*

M.E. Sharpe, 80 Business Park Drive, Armonk, NY 10504, (800) 541-6563, Fax: (914) 273-2106, www.mesharpe.com; *The Illustrated Book of World Rankings.*

U.S. Department of State (DOS), 2201 C Street NW, Washington, DC 20520, (202) 647-4000, www.state.gov; *World Military Expenditures and Arms Transfers (WMEAT).*

United Nations Statistics Division, New York, NY 10017, (800) 253-9646, Fax: (212) 963-4116, http://unstats.un.org; *Statistical Yearbook.*

The World Bank, 1818 H Street, NW, Washington, DC 20433, (202) 473-1000, Fax: (202) 477-6391, www.worldbank.org; *The World Bank Atlas 2003-2004* and *World Development Report 2008.*

Worldinformation.com, 2 Market Street, Saffron Walden, Essex CB10 1HZ, United Kingdom, www.worldinformation.com; The World of Information (www.worldinformation.com).

BURMA - HIDES AND SKINS INDUSTRY

United Nations Food and Agricultural Organization (FAO), Viale delle Terme di Caracalla, 00100 Rome, Italy, (Dial from U.S. (202) 653-2400), (Fax from U.S. (202) 653 5760), www.fao.org; *FAO Production Yearbook 2002.*

BURMA - HOUSING

Euromonitor International, Inc., 224 S. Michigan Avenue, Suite 1500, Chicago, IL 60604, (312) 922-1115, Fax: (312) 922-1157, www.euromonitor.com; *World Marketing Data and Statistics.*

M.E. Sharpe, 80 Business Park Drive, Armonk, NY 10504, (800) 541-6563, Fax: (914) 273-2106, www.mesharpe.com; *The Illustrated Book of World Rankings.*

BURMA - ILLITERATE PERSONS

Euromonitor International, Inc., 224 S. Michigan Avenue, Suite 1500, Chicago, IL 60604, (312) 922-1115, Fax: (312) 922-1157, www.euromonitor.com; *The World Economic Factbook 2008.*

UNESCO Institute for Statistics, C.P. 6128 Succursale Centre-Ville, Montreal, Quebec, H3C 3J7 Canada, (Dial from U.S. (514) 343-6880), (Fax from U.S. (514) 343 6882), www.uis.unesco.org; *Statistical Tables.*

United Nations Statistics Division, New York, NY 10017, (800) 253-9646, Fax: (212) 963-4116, http://unstats.un.org; *Asia-Pacific in Figures 2004* and *Human Development Report 2006.*

BURMA - IMPORTS

Asian Development Bank (ADB), PO Box 789, 0980 Manila, Philippines, www.adb.org; *Key Indicators of Developing Asian and Pacific Countries 2006.*

Central Intelligence Agency, Office of Public Affairs, Washington, DC 20505, (703) 482-0623, Fax: (703) 482-1739, www.cia.gov; *The World Factbook.*

Economist Intelligence Unit, 111 West 57th Street, New York, NY 10019, (212) 554-0600, Fax: (212) 586-1181, www.eiu.com; *Myanmar (Burma) Country Report.*

Euromonitor International, Inc., 224 S. Michigan Avenue, Suite 1500, Chicago, IL 60604, (312) 922-1115, Fax: (312) 922-1157, www.euromonitor.com; *International Marketing Data and Statistics 2008* and *The World Economic Factbook 2008.*

International Monetary Fund (IMF), 700 Nineteenth Street, NW, Washington, DC 20431, (202) 623-7000, Fax: (202) 623-4661, www.imf.org; *Direction of Trade Statistics Yearbook 2007* and *International Financial Statistics Yearbook 2007.*

Palgrave Macmillan Ltd., Houndmills, Basingstoke, Hampshire, RG21 6XS, England, (Telephone in U.S. (888) 330-8477), (Fax in U.S. (800) 672-2054), www.palgrave.com; *The Statesman's Yearbook 2008.*

Taylor and Francis Group, An Informa Business, 2 Park Square, Milton Park, Abingdon, Oxford OX14 4RN, United Kingdom, (Dial from U.S. (212) 216-7800), (Fax from U.S. (212) 564-7854), www.tandf.co.uk; *The Europa World Year Book.*

United Nations Conference on Trade and Development (UNCTAD), DC2-1120, United Nations, New York, NY 10017, (212) 963-0027, www.unctad.org; *Handbook of Statistics 2005.*

United Nations Food and Agricultural Organization (FAO), Viale delle Terme di Caracalla, 00100 Rome, Italy, (Dial from U.S. (202) 653-2400), (Fax from U.S. (202) 653 5760), www.fao.org; *The State of Food and Agriculture (SOFA) 2006.*

The World Bank, 1818 H Street, NW, Washington, DC 20433, (202) 473-1000, Fax: (202) 477-6391, www.worldbank.org; *World Development Report 2008.*

Worldinformation.com, 2 Market Street, Saffron Walden, Essex CB10 1HZ, United Kingdom, www.worldinformation.com; The World of Information (www.worldinformation.com).

BURMA - INDUSTRIAL METALS PRODUCTION

See BURMA - MINERAL INDUSTRIES

BURMA - INDUSTRIAL PRODUCTIVITY

Euromonitor International, Inc., 224 S. Michigan Avenue, Suite 1500, Chicago, IL 60604, (312) 922-1115, Fax: (312) 922-1157, www.euromonitor.com; *International Marketing Data and Statistics 2008.*

M.E. Sharpe, 80 Business Park Drive, Armonk, NY 10504, (800) 541-6563, Fax: (914) 273-2106, www.mesharpe.com; *The Illustrated Book of World Rankings.*

BURMA - INDUSTRIES

Central Intelligence Agency, Office of Public Affairs, Washington, DC 20505, (703) 482-0623, Fax: (703) 482-1739, www.cia.gov; *The World Factbook.*

Economist Intelligence Unit, 111 West 57th Street, New York, NY 10019, (212) 554-0600, Fax: (212) 586-1181, www.eiu.com; *Myanmar (Burma) Country Report.*

Euromonitor International, Inc., 224 S. Michigan Avenue, Suite 1500, Chicago, IL 60604, (312) 922-1115, Fax: (312) 922-1157, www.euromonitor.com; *International Marketing Data and Statistics 2008; The World Economic Factbook 2008;* and *World Marketing Data and Statistics.*

International Labour Office, I.L.O. Publications, 4 route des Morillons, CH-1211 Geneva 22, Switzerland, (Telephone in U.S. (202) 653-7652), (Fax in U.S. (202) 653-7687), www.ilo.org; *Yearbook of Labour Statistics 2006.*

M.E. Sharpe, 80 Business Park Drive, Armonk, NY 10504, (800) 541-6563, Fax: (914) 273-2106, www.mesharpe.com; *The Illustrated Book of World Rankings.*

Taylor and Francis Group, An Informa Business, 2 Park Square, Milton Park, Abingdon, Oxford OX14 4RN, United Kingdom, (Dial from U.S. (212) 216-7800), (Fax from U.S. (212) 564-7854), www.tandf.co.uk; *The Europa World Year Book.*

United Nations Industrial Development Organization (UNIDO), 1 United Nations Plaza, New York, NY 10017, (212) 963 6890, Fax: (212) 963-7904, http://unido.org; Industrial Statistics Database 2008 (INDSTAT) and *The International Yearbook of Industrial Statistics 2008.*

United Nations Statistics Division, New York, NY 10017, (800) 253-9646, Fax: (212) 963-4116, http://unstats.un.org; *Asia-Pacific in Figures 2004* and *Statistical Yearbook for Asia and the Pacific 2004.*

The World Bank, 1818 H Street, NW, Washington, DC 20433, (202) 473-1000, Fax: (202) 477-6391, www.worldbank.org; *Myanmar.*

BURMA - INFANT AND MATERNAL MORTALITY

See BURMA - MORTALITY

BURMA - INTERNATIONAL FINANCE

Asian Development Bank (ADB), PO Box 789, 0980 Manila, Philippines, www.adb.org; *Key Indicators of Developing Asian and Pacific Countries 2006.*

BURMA - INTERNATIONAL LIQUIDITY

International Monetary Fund (IMF), 700 Nineteenth Street, NW, Washington, DC 20431, (202) 623-7000, Fax: (202) 623-4661, www.imf.org; *International Financial Statistics Yearbook 2007.*

BURMA - INTERNATIONAL STATISTICS

Asian Development Bank (ADB), PO Box 789, 0980 Manila, Philippines, www.adb.org; *Key Indicators of Developing Asian and Pacific Countries 2006.*

BURMA - INTERNATIONAL TRADE

Asian Development Bank (ADB), PO Box 789, 0980 Manila, Philippines, www.adb.org; *Key Indicators of Developing Asian and Pacific Countries 2006.*

Economist Intelligence Unit, 111 West 57th Street, New York, NY 10019, (212) 554-0600, Fax: (212) 586-1181, www.eiu.com; *Business Asia* and *Myanmar (Burma) Country Report.*

Euromonitor International, Inc., 224 S. Michigan Avenue, Suite 1500, Chicago, IL 60604, (312) 922-1115, Fax: (312) 922-1157, www.euromonitor.com; *International Marketing Data and Statistics 2008; The World Economic Factbook 2008;* and *World Marketing Data and Statistics.*

M.E. Sharpe, 80 Business Park Drive, Armonk, NY 10504, (800) 541-6563, Fax: (914) 273-2106, www.mesharpe.com; *The Illustrated Book of World Rankings.*

Organisation for Economic Cooperation and Development (OECD), 2 rue Andre Pascal, F-75775 Paris Cedex 16, France, (Telephone in U.S. (202) 785-6323), (Fax in U.S. (202) 785-0350), www.oecd.org; *International Trade by Commodity Statistics (ITCS).*

Palgrave Macmillan Ltd., Houndmills, Basingstoke, Hampshire, RG21 6XS, England, (Telephone in U.S. (888) 330-8477), (Fax in U.S. (800) 672-2054), www.palgrave.com; *The Statesman's Yearbook 2008.*

Taylor and Francis Group, An Informa Business, 2 Park Square, Milton Park, Abingdon, Oxford OX14 4RN, United Kingdom, (Dial from U.S. (212) 216-7800), (Fax from U.S. (212) 564-7854), www.tandf.co.uk; *The Europa World Year Book.*

United Nations Conference on Trade and Development (UNCTAD), DC2-1120, United Nations, New York, NY 10017, (212) 963-0027, www.unctad.org; *UNCTAD Commodity Yearbook.*

United Nations Food and Agricultural Organization (FAO), Viale delle Terme di Caracalla, 00100 Rome, Italy, (Dial from U.S. (202) 653-2400), (Fax from U.S. (202) 653 5760), www.fao.org; *FAO Trade Yearbook* and *The State of Food and Agriculture (SOFA) 2006.*

United Nations Statistics Division, New York, NY 10017, (800) 253-9646, Fax: (212) 963-4116, http://unstats.un.org; *Asia-Pacific in Figures 2004; International Trade Statistics Yearbook; Statistical Yearbook;* and *Statistical Yearbook for Asia and the Pacific 2004.*

The World Bank, 1818 H Street, NW, Washington, DC 20433, (202) 473-1000, Fax: (202) 477-6391, www.worldbank.org; *Myanmar* and *World Development Report 2008.*

World Trade Organization (WTO), Centre William Rappard, Rue de Lausanne 154, CH-1211 Geneva 21, Switzerland, www.wto.org; *International Trade Statistics 2006.*

BURMA - INTERNET USERS

International Telecommunication Union (ITU), Place des Nations, 1211 Geneva 20, Switzerland, www.itu.int; *World Telecommunication/ICT Indicators Database on CD-ROM; World Telecommunication/ICT Indicators Database Online;* and *Yearbook of Statistics - Telecommunication Services (Chronological Time Series 1997-2006).*

BURMA - INVESTMENTS

International Monetary Fund (IMF), 700 Nineteenth Street, NW, Washington, DC 20431, (202) 623-7000, Fax: (202) 623-4661, www.imf.org; *International Financial Statistics Yearbook 2007.*

BURMA - IRON AND IRON ORE PRODUCTION

See BURMA - MINERAL INDUSTRIES

BURMA - IRRIGATION

Euromonitor International, Inc., 224 S. Michigan Avenue, Suite 1500, Chicago, IL 60604, (312) 922-1115, Fax: (312) 922-1157, www.euromonitor.com; *International Marketing Data and Statistics 2008.*

BURMA - JUTE PRODUCTION

See BURMA - CROPS

BURMA - LABOR

Central Intelligence Agency, Office of Public Affairs, Washington, DC 20505, (703) 482-0623, Fax: (703) 482-1739, www.cia.gov; *The World Factbook.*

Economist Intelligence Unit, 111 West 57th Street, New York, NY 10019, (212) 554-0600, Fax: (212) 586-1181, www.eiu.com; *Business Asia.*

Euromonitor International, Inc., 224 S. Michigan Avenue, Suite 1500, Chicago, IL 60604, (312) 922-1115, Fax: (312) 922-1157, www.euromonitor.com; *International Marketing Data and Statistics 2008* and *World Marketing Data and Statistics.*

International Labour Office, I.L.O. Publications, 4 route des Morillons, CH-1211 Geneva 22, Switzerland, (Telephone in U.S. (202) 653-7652), (Fax in U.S. (202) 653-7687), www.ilo.org; *Yearbook of Labour Statistics 2006.*

M.E. Sharpe, 80 Business Park Drive, Armonk, NY 10504, (800) 541-6563, Fax: (914) 273-2106, www.mesharpe.com; *The Illustrated Book of World Rankings.*

Palgrave Macmillan Ltd., Houndmills, Basingstoke, Hampshire, RG21 6XS, England, (Telephone in U.S. (888) 330-8477), (Fax in U.S. (800) 672-2054), www.palgrave.com; *The Statesman's Yearbook 2008.*

Taylor and Francis Group, An Informa Business, 2 Park Square, Milton Park, Abingdon, Oxford OX14 4RN, United Kingdom, (Dial from U.S. (212) 216-7800), (Fax from U.S. (212) 564-7854), www.tandf.co.uk; *The Europa World Year Book.*

United Nations Food and Agricultural Organization (FAO), Viale delle Terme di Caracalla, 00100 Rome, Italy, (Dial from U.S. (202) 653-2400), (Fax from U.S. (202) 653 5760), www.fao.org; *The State of Food and Agriculture (SOFA) 2006.*

United Nations Statistics Division, New York, NY 10017, (800) 253-9646, Fax: (212) 963-4116, http://unstats.un.org; *Human Development Report 2006.*

The World Bank, 1818 H Street, NW, Washington, DC 20433, (202) 473-1000, Fax: (202) 477-6391, www.worldbank.org; *The World Bank Atlas 2003-2004* and *World Development Report 2008.*

BURMA - LAND USE

Central Intelligence Agency, Office of Public Affairs, Washington, DC 20505, (703) 482-0623, Fax: (703) 482-1739, www.cia.gov; *The World Factbook.*

Euromonitor International, Inc., 224 S. Michigan Avenue, Suite 1500, Chicago, IL 60604, (312) 922-1115, Fax: (312) 922-1157, www.euromonitor.com; *International Marketing Data and Statistics 2008.*

United Nations Food and Agricultural Organization (FAO), Viale delle Terme di Caracalla, 00100 Rome, Italy, (Dial from U.S. (202) 653-2400), (Fax from U.S. (202) 653 5760), www.fao.org; *FAO Production Yearbook 2002.*

The World Bank, 1818 H Street, NW, Washington, DC 20433, (202) 473-1000, Fax: (202) 477-6391, www.worldbank.org; *World Development Report 2008.*

BURMA - LIBRARIES

M.E. Sharpe, 80 Business Park Drive, Armonk, NY 10504, (800) 541-6563, Fax: (914) 273-2106, www.mesharpe.com; *The Illustrated Book of World Rankings.*

BURMA - LIFE EXPECTANCY

Central Intelligence Agency, Office of Public Affairs, Washington, DC 20505, (703) 482-0623, Fax: (703) 482-1739, www.cia.gov; *The World Factbook.*

Economist Intelligence Unit, 111 West 57th Street, New York, NY 10019, (212) 554-0600, Fax: (212) 586-1181, www.eiu.com; *Business Asia.*

Euromonitor International, Inc., 224 S. Michigan Avenue, Suite 1500, Chicago, IL 60604, (312) 922-1115, Fax: (312) 922-1157, www.euromonitor.com; *The World Economic Factbook 2008.*

Palgrave Macmillan Ltd., Houndmills, Basingstoke, Hampshire, RG21 6XS, England, (Telephone in U.S. (888) 330-8477), (Fax in U.S. (800) 672-2054), www.palgrave.com; *The Statesman's Yearbook 2008.*

United Nations Statistics Division, New York, NY 10017, (800) 253-9646, Fax: (212) 963-4116, http://unstats.un.org; *Asia-Pacific in Figures 2004; Human Development Report 2006;* and *World Statistics Pocketbook.*

The World Bank, 1818 H Street, NW, Washington, DC 20433, (202) 473-1000, Fax: (202) 477-6391, www.worldbank.org; *The World Bank Atlas 2003-2004* and *World Development Report 2008.*

BURMA - LITERACY

Euromonitor International, Inc., 224 S. Michigan Avenue, Suite 1500, Chicago, IL 60604, (312) 922-1115, Fax: (312) 922-1157, www.euromonitor.com; *World Marketing Data and Statistics.*

BURMA - LIVESTOCK

Euromonitor International, Inc., 224 S. Michigan Avenue, Suite 1500, Chicago, IL 60604, (312) 922-1115, Fax: (312) 922-1157, www.euromonitor.com; *International Marketing Data and Statistics 2008.*

M.E. Sharpe, 80 Business Park Drive, Armonk, NY 10504, (800) 541-6563, Fax: (914) 273-2106, www.mesharpe.com; *The Illustrated Book of World Rankings.*

Taylor and Francis Group, An Informa Business, 2 Park Square, Milton Park, Abingdon, Oxford OX14 4RN, United Kingdom, (Dial from U.S. (212) 216-7800), (Fax from U.S. (212) 564-7854), www.tandf.co.uk; *The Europa World Year Book.*

United Nations Conference on Trade and Development (UNCTAD), DC2-1120, United Nations, New York, NY 10017, (212) 963-0027, www.unctad.org; *UNCTAD Commodity Yearbook.*

United Nations Food and Agricultural Organization (FAO), Viale delle Terme di Caracalla, 00100 Rome, Italy, (Dial from U.S. (202) 653-2400), (Fax from U.S. (202) 653 5760), www.fao.org; *FAO Production Yearbook 2002* and *The State of Food and Agriculture (SOFA) 2006.*

United Nations Statistics Division, New York, NY 10017, (800) 253-9646, Fax: (212) 963-4116, http://unstats.un.org; *Statistical Yearbook.*

BURMA - LOCAL TAXATION

Euromonitor International, Inc., 224 S. Michigan Avenue, Suite 1500, Chicago, IL 60604, (312) 922-1115, Fax: (312) 922-1157, www.euromonitor.com; *International Marketing Data and Statistics 2008.*

BURMA - MANPOWER

United Nations Statistics Division, New York, NY 10017, (800) 253-9646, Fax: (212) 963-4116, http://unstats.un.org; *Statistical Yearbook for Asia and the Pacific 2004.*

BURMA - MANUFACTURES

Asian Development Bank (ADB), PO Box 789, 0980 Manila, Philippines, www.adb.org; *Key Indicators of Developing Asian and Pacific Countries 2006.*

M.E. Sharpe, 80 Business Park Drive, Armonk, NY 10504, (800) 541-6563, Fax: (914) 273-2106, www.mesharpe.com; *The Illustrated Book of World Rankings.*

United Nations Statistics Division, New York, NY 10017, (800) 253-9646, Fax: (212) 963-4116, http://unstats.un.org; *Statistical Yearbook.*

BURMA - MARRIAGE

M.E. Sharpe, 80 Business Park Drive, Armonk, NY 10504, (800) 541-6563, Fax: (914) 273-2106, www.mesharpe.com; *The Illustrated Book of World Rankings.*

United Nations Statistics Division, New York, NY 10017, (800) 253-9646, Fax: (212) 963-4116, http://unstats.un.org; *Demographic Yearbook.*

BURMA - MEAT PRODUCTION

See BURMA - LIVESTOCK

BURMA - MEDICAL CARE

United Nations Statistics Division, New York, NY 10017, (800) 253-9646, Fax: (212) 963-4116, http://unstats.un.org; *Statistical Yearbook.*

The World Bank, 1818 H Street, NW, Washington, DC 20433, (202) 473-1000, Fax: (202) 477-6391, www.worldbank.org; *Myanmar.*

BURMA - MILK PRODUCTION

See BURMA - DAIRY PROCESSING

BURMA - MINERAL INDUSTRIES

Asian Development Bank (ADB), PO Box 789, 0980 Manila, Philippines, www.adb.org; *Key Indicators of Developing Asian and Pacific Countries 2006.*

M.E. Sharpe, 80 Business Park Drive, Armonk, NY 10504, (800) 541-6563, Fax: (914) 273-2106, www.mesharpe.com; *The Illustrated Book of World Rankings.*

Organisation for Economic Cooperation and Development (OECD), 2 rue Andre Pascal, F-75775 Paris Cedex 16, France, (Telephone in U.S. (202) 785-6323), (Fax in U.S. (202) 785-0350), www.oecd.org; *World Energy Outlook 2007.*

Palgrave Macmillan Ltd., Houndmills, Basingstoke, Hampshire, RG21 6XS, England, (Telephone in U.S. (888) 330-8477), (Fax in U.S. (800) 672-2054), www.palgrave.com; *The Statesman's Yearbook 2008.*

Taylor and Francis Group, An Informa Business, 2 Park Square, Milton Park, Abingdon, Oxford OX14 4RN, United Kingdom, (Dial from U.S. (212) 216-7800), (Fax from U.S. (212) 564-7854), www.tandf.co.uk; *The Europa World Year Book.*

United Nations Conference on Trade and Development (UNCTAD), DC2-1120, United Nations, New York, NY 10017, (212) 963-0027, www.unctad.org; *UNCTAD Commodity Yearbook.*

United Nations Statistics Division, New York, NY 10017, (800) 253-9646, Fax: (212) 963-4116, http://unstats.un.org; *Statistical Yearbook.*

BURMA - MONEY EXCHANGE RATES

See BURMA - FOREIGN EXCHANGE RATES

BURMA - MONEY SUPPLY

Asian Development Bank (ADB), PO Box 789, 0980 Manila, Philippines, www.adb.org; *Key Indicators of Developing Asian and Pacific Countries 2006.*

Economist Intelligence Unit, 111 West 57th Street, New York, NY 10019, (212) 554-0600, Fax: (212) 586-1181, www.eiu.com; *Myanmar (Burma) Country Report.*

Euromonitor International, Inc., 224 S. Michigan Avenue, Suite 1500, Chicago, IL 60604, (312) 922-1115, Fax: (312) 922-1157, www.euromonitor.com; *International Marketing Data and Statistics 2008.*

International Monetary Fund (IMF), 700 Nineteenth Street, NW, Washington, DC 20431, (202) 623-7000, Fax: (202) 623-4661, www.imf.org; *International Financial Statistics Yearbook 2007.*

Taylor and Francis Group, An Informa Business, 2 Park Square, Milton Park, Abingdon, Oxford OX14 4RN, United Kingdom, (Dial from U.S. (212) 216-7800), (Fax from U.S. (212) 564-7854), www.tandf.co.uk; *The Europa World Year Book.*

United Nations Statistics Division, New York, NY 10017, (800) 253-9646, Fax: (212) 963-4116, http://unstats.un.org; *Statistical Yearbook.*

The World Bank, 1818 H Street, NW, Washington, DC 20433, (202) 473-1000, Fax: (202) 477-6391, www.worldbank.org; *Myanmar.*

BURMA - MORTALITY

Central Intelligence Agency, Office of Public Affairs, Washington, DC 20505, (703) 482-0623, Fax: (703) 482-1739, www.cia.gov; *The World Factbook.*

Euromonitor International, Inc., 224 S. Michigan Avenue, Suite 1500, Chicago, IL 60604, (312) 922-1115, Fax: (312) 922-1157, www.euromonitor.com; *International Marketing Data and Statistics 2008* and *The World Economic Factbook 2008.*

Palgrave Macmillan Ltd., Houndmills, Basingstoke, Hampshire, RG21 6XS, England, (Telephone in U.S. (888) 330-8477), (Fax in U.S. (800) 672-2054), www.palgrave.com; *The Statesman's Yearbook 2008.*

Taylor and Francis Group, An Informa Business, 2 Park Square, Milton Park, Abingdon, Oxford OX14 4RN, United Kingdom, (Dial from U.S. (212) 216-7800), (Fax from U.S. (212) 564-7854), www.tandf.co.uk; *The Europa World Year Book.*

UNICEF, 3 United Nations Plaza, New York, NY 10017, (800) 253-9646, Fax: (212) 887-7465, www.unicef.org; *The State of the World's Children 2008.*

United Nations Statistics Division, New York, NY 10017, (800) 253-9646, Fax: (212) 963-4116, http://unstats.un.org; *Asia-Pacific in Figures 2004; Demographic Yearbook; Human Development Report 2006; Statistical Yearbook;* and *World Statistics Pocketbook.*

The World Bank, 1818 H Street, NW, Washington, DC 20433, (202) 473-1000, Fax: (202) 477-6391, www.worldbank.org; *The World Bank Atlas 2003-2004* and *World Development Report 2008.*

World Health Organization (WHO), Avenue Appia 20, 1211 Geneve 27, Switzerland, (Telephone in U.S. (212) 331-9081), www.who.int; The WHO Global Atlas of Infectious Diseases and *World Health Report 2006.*

BURMA - MOTION PICTURES

UNESCO Institute for Statistics, C.P. 6128 Succursale Centre-Ville, Montreal, Quebec, H3C 3J7 Canada, (Dial from U.S. (514) 343-6880), (Fax from U.S. (514) 343 6882), www.uis.unesco.org; *Statistical Tables.*

United Nations Statistics Division, New York, NY 10017, (800) 253-9646, Fax: (212) 963-4116, http://unstats.un.org; *Statistical Yearbook.*

BURMA - MOTOR VEHICLES

International Road Federation (IFR), Madison Place, 500 Montgomery Street, 5th Floor, Alexandria, VA 22314, (703) 535-1001, Fax: (703) 535-1007, www.irfnet.org; *World Road Statistics 2006.*

United Nations Statistics Division, New York, NY 10017, (800) 253-9646, Fax: (212) 963-4116, http://unstats.un.org; *Statistical Yearbook.*

BURMA - MUSEUMS

M.E. Sharpe, 80 Business Park Drive, Armonk, NY 10504, (800) 541-6563, Fax: (914) 273-2106, www.mesharpe.com; *The Illustrated Book of World Rankings.*

UNESCO Institute for Statistics, C.P. 6128 Succursale Centre-Ville, Montreal, Quebec, H3C 3J7 Canada, (Dial from U.S. (514) 343-6880), (Fax from U.S. (514) 343 6882), www.uis.unesco.org; *Statistical Tables.*

BURMA - NATURAL GAS PRODUCTION

See BURMA - MINERAL INDUSTRIES

BURMA - NICKEL AND NICKEL ORE

See BURMA - MINERAL INDUSTRIES

BURMA - NUTRITION

Asian Development Bank (ADB), PO Box 789, 0980 Manila, Philippines, www.adb.org; *Key Indicators of Developing Asian and Pacific Countries 2006.*

United Nations Food and Agricultural Organization (FAO), Viale delle Terme di Caracalla, 00100 Rome, Italy, (Dial from U.S. (202) 653-2400), (Fax from U.S. (202) 653 5760), www.fao.org; *The State of Food and Agriculture (SOFA) 2006.*

BURMA - OIL INDUSTRY

International Monetary Fund (IMF), 700 Nineteenth Street, NW, Washington, DC 20431, (202) 623-7000, Fax: (202) 623-4661, www.imf.org; *International Financial Statistics Yearbook 2007.*

BURMA - OLDER PEOPLE

M.E. Sharpe, 80 Business Park Drive, Armonk, NY 10504, (800) 541-6563, Fax: (914) 273-2106, www.mesharpe.com; *The Illustrated Book of World Rankings.*

BURMA - PAPER

See BURMA - FORESTS AND FORESTRY

BURMA - PEANUT PRODUCTION

See BURMA - CROPS

BURMA - PERIODICALS

UNESCO Institute for Statistics, C.P. 6128 Succursale Centre-Ville, Montreal, Quebec, H3C 3J7 Canada, (Dial from U.S. (514) 343-6880), (Fax from U.S. (514) 343 6882), www.uis.unesco.org; *Statistical Tables.*

BURMA - PESTICIDES

United Nations Food and Agricultural Organization (FAO), Viale delle Terme di Caracalla, 00100 Rome, Italy, (Dial from U.S. (202) 653-2400), (Fax from U.S. (202) 653 5760), www.fao.org; *The State of Food and Agriculture (SOFA) 2006.*

BURMA - PETROLEUM INDUSTRY AND TRADE

Asian Development Bank (ADB), PO Box 789, 0980 Manila, Philippines, www.adb.org; *Key Indicators of Developing Asian and Pacific Countries 2006.*

M.E. Sharpe, 80 Business Park Drive, Armonk, NY 10504, (800) 541-6563, Fax: (914) 273-2106, www.mesharpe.com; *The Illustrated Book of World Rankings.*

Organisation for Economic Cooperation and Development (OECD), 2 rue Andre Pascal, F-75775 Paris Cedex 16, France, (Telephone in U.S. (202) 785-6323), (Fax in U.S. (202) 785-0350), www.oecd.org; *World Energy Outlook 2007.*

Palgrave Macmillan Ltd., Houndmills, Basingstoke, Hampshire, RG21 6XS, England, (Telephone in U.S. (888) 330-8477), (Fax in U.S. (800) 672-2054), www.palgrave.com; *The Statesman's Yearbook 2008.*

PennWell Corporation, 1421 South Sheridan Road, Tulsa, OK 74112, (918) 835-3161, www.pennwell.com; *International Petroleum Encyclopedia 2007.*

U.S. Department of Energy (DOE), Energy Information Administration (EIA), 1000 Independence Avenue, SW, Washington, DC 20585, (202) 586-8800, www.eia.doe.gov; *International Energy Annual 2004* and *International Energy Outlook 2006.*

United Nations Conference on Trade and Development (UNCTAD), DC2-1120, United Nations, New York, NY 10017, (212) 963-0027, www.unctad.org; *UNCTAD Commodity Yearbook.*

United Nations Food and Agricultural Organization (FAO), Viale delle Terme di Caracalla, 00100 Rome, Italy, (Dial from U.S. (202) 653-2400), (Fax from U.S. (202) 653 5760), www.fao.org; *The State of Food and Agriculture (SOFA) 2006.*

United Nations Statistics Division, New York, NY 10017, (800) 253-9646, Fax: (212) 963-4116, http://unstats.un.org; *Statistical Yearbook.*

BURMA - POLITICAL SCIENCE

Asian Development Bank (ADB), PO Box 789, 0980 Manila, Philippines, www.adb.org; *Key Indicators of Developing Asian and Pacific Countries 2006.*

Central Intelligence Agency, Office of Public Affairs, Washington, DC 20505, (703) 482-0623, Fax: (703) 482-1739, www.cia.gov; *The World Factbook.*

International Monetary Fund (IMF), 700 Nineteenth Street, NW, Washington, DC 20431, (202) 623-7000, Fax: (202) 623-4661, www.imf.org; *International Financial Statistics Yearbook 2007.*

Palgrave Macmillan Ltd., Houndmills, Basingstoke, Hampshire, RG21 6XS, England, (Telephone in U.S. (888) 330-8477), (Fax in U.S. (800) 672-2054), www.palgrave.com; *The Statesman's Yearbook 2008.*

Taylor and Francis Group, An Informa Business, 2 Park Square, Milton Park, Abingdon, Oxford OX14 4RN, United Kingdom, (Dial from U.S. (212) 216-7800), (Fax from U.S. (212) 564-7854), www.tandf.co.uk; *The Europa World Year Book.*

United Nations Statistics Division, New York, NY 10017, (800) 253-9646, Fax: (212) 963-4116, http://unstats.un.org; *Asia-Pacific in Figures 2004; National Accounts Statistics: Compendium of Income Distribution Statistics;* and *Statistical Yearbook.*

The World Bank, 1818 H Street, NW, Washington, DC 20433, (202) 473-1000, Fax: (202) 477-6391, www.worldbank.org; *World Development Report 2008.*

BURMA - POPULATION

Asian Development Bank (ADB), PO Box 789, 0980 Manila, Philippines, www.adb.org; *Key Indicators of Developing Asian and Pacific Countries 2006.*

Central Intelligence Agency, Office of Public Affairs, Washington, DC 20505, (703) 482-0623, Fax: (703) 482-1739, www.cia.gov; *The World Factbook.*

Economist Intelligence Unit, 111 West 57th Street, New York, NY 10019, (212) 554-0600, Fax: (212) 586-1181, www.eiu.com; *Business Asia* and *Myanmar (Burma) Country Report.*

Euromonitor International, Inc., 224 S. Michigan Avenue, Suite 1500, Chicago, IL 60604, (312) 922-1115, Fax: (312) 922-1157, www.euromonitor.com; *International Marketing Data and Statistics 2008* and *The World Economic Factbook 2008.*

International Labour Office, I.L.O. Publications, 4 route des Morillons, CH-1211 Geneva 22, Switzerland, (Telephone in U.S. (202) 653-7652), (Fax in U.S. (202) 653-7687), www.ilo.org; *Yearbook of Labour Statistics 2006.*

M.E. Sharpe, 80 Business Park Drive, Armonk, NY 10504, (800) 541-6563, Fax: (914) 273-2106, www.mesharpe.com; *The Illustrated Book of World Rankings.*

Palgrave Macmillan Ltd., Houndmills, Basingstoke, Hampshire, RG21 6XS, England, (Telephone in U.S. (888) 330-8477), (Fax in U.S. (800) 672-2054), www.palgrave.com; *The Statesman's Yearbook 2008.*

Taylor and Francis Group, An Informa Business, 2 Park Square, Milton Park, Abingdon, Oxford OX14 4RN, United Kingdom, (Dial from U.S. (212) 216-

7800), (Fax from U.S. (212) 564-7854), www.tandf.co.uk; *The Europa World Year Book.*

U.S. Department of State (DOS), 2201 C Street NW, Washington, DC 20520, (202) 647-4000, www.state.gov; *World Military Expenditures and Arms Transfers (WMEAT).*

UNESCO Institute for Statistics, C.P. 6128 Succursale Centre-Ville, Montreal, Quebec, H3C 3J7 Canada, (Dial from U.S. (514) 343-6880), (Fax from U.S. (514) 343 6882), www.uis.unesco.org; *Statistical Tables.*

United Nations Food and Agricultural Organization (FAO), Viale delle Terme di Caracalla, 00100 Rome, Italy, (Dial from U.S. (202) 653-2400), (Fax from U.S. (202) 653 5760), www.fao.org; *FAO Production Yearbook 2002.*

United Nations Statistics Division, New York, NY 10017, (800) 253-9646, Fax: (212) 963-4116, http://unstats.un.org; *Asia-Pacific in Figures 2004; Demographic Yearbook; Human Development Report 2006; Statistical Yearbook; Statistical Yearbook for Asia and the Pacific 2004;* and *World Statistics Pocketbook.*

The World Bank, 1818 H Street, NW, Washington, DC 20433, (202) 473-1000, Fax: (202) 477-6391, www.worldbank.org; *Myanmar; The World Bank Atlas 2003-2004;* and *World Development Report 2008.*

World Health Organization (WHO), Avenue Appia 20, 1211 Geneve 27, Switzerland, (Telephone in U.S. (212) 331-9081), www.who.int; *World Health Report 2006.*

Worldinformation.com, 2 Market Street, Saffron Walden, Essex CB10 1HZ, United Kingdom, www.worldinformation.com; The World of Information (www.worldinformation.com).

BURMA - POPULATION DENSITY

Central Intelligence Agency, Office of Public Affairs, Washington, DC 20505, (703) 482-0623, Fax: (703) 482-1739, www.cia.gov; *The World Factbook.*

Euromonitor International, Inc., 224 S. Michigan Avenue, Suite 1500, Chicago, IL 60604, (312) 922-1115, Fax: (312) 922-1157, www.euromonitor.com; *International Marketing Data and Statistics 2008* and *The World Economic Factbook 2008.*

M.E. Sharpe, 80 Business Park Drive, Armonk, NY 10504, (800) 541-6563, Fax: (914) 273-2106, www.mesharpe.com; *The Illustrated Book of World Rankings.*

Palgrave Macmillan Ltd., Houndmills, Basingstoke, Hampshire, RG21 6XS, England, (Telephone in U.S. (888) 330-8477), (Fax in U.S. (800) 672-2054), www.palgrave.com; *The Statesman's Yearbook 2008.*

Taylor and Francis Group, An Informa Business, 2 Park Square, Milton Park, Abingdon, Oxford OX14 4RN, United Kingdom, (Dial from U.S. (212) 216-7800), (Fax from U.S. (212) 564-7854), www.tandf.co.uk; *The Europa World Year Book.*

United Nations Food and Agricultural Organization (FAO), Viale delle Terme di Caracalla, 00100 Rome, Italy, (Dial from U.S. (202) 653-2400), (Fax from U.S. (202) 653 5760), www.fao.org; *The State of Food and Agriculture (SOFA) 2006.*

United Nations Statistics Division, New York, NY 10017, (800) 253-9646, Fax: (212) 963-4116, http://unstats.un.org; *Statistical Yearbook.*

The World Bank, 1818 H Street, NW, Washington, DC 20433, (202) 473-1000, Fax: (202) 477-6391, www.worldbank.org; *Myanmar* and *World Development Report 2008.*

BURMA - POSTAL SERVICE

M.E. Sharpe, 80 Business Park Drive, Armonk, NY 10504, (800) 541-6563, Fax: (914) 273-2106, www.mesharpe.com; *The Illustrated Book of World Rankings.*

Palgrave Macmillan Ltd., Houndmills, Basingstoke, Hampshire, RG21 6XS, England, (Telephone in U.S. (888) 330-8477), (Fax in U.S. (800) 672-2054), www.palgrave.com; *The Statesman's Yearbook 2008.*

United Nations Statistics Division, New York, NY 10017, (800) 253-9646, Fax: (212) 963-4116, http://unstats.un.org; *Statistical Yearbook.*

BURMA - PRICES

Euromonitor International, Inc., 224 S. Michigan Avenue, Suite 1500, Chicago, IL 60604, (312) 922-1115, Fax: (312) 922-1157, www.euromonitor.com; *World Marketing Data and Statistics.*

International Labour Office, I.L.O. Publications, 4 route des Morillons, CH-1211 Geneva 22, Switzerland, (Telephone in U.S. (202) 653-7652), (Fax in U.S. (202) 653-7687), www.ilo.org; *Yearbook of Labour Statistics 2006.*

International Monetary Fund (IMF), 700 Nineteenth Street, NW, Washington, DC 20431, (202) 623-7000, Fax: (202) 623-4661, www.imf.org; *International Financial Statistics Yearbook 2007.*

The World Bank, 1818 H Street, NW, Washington, DC 20433, (202) 473-1000, Fax: (202) 477-6391, www.worldbank.org; *Myanmar.*

BURMA - PROFESSIONS

United Nations Statistics Division, New York, NY 10017, (800) 253-9646, Fax: (212) 963-4116, http://unstats.un.org; *Statistical Yearbook.*

BURMA - PUBLIC HEALTH

Economist Intelligence Unit, 111 West 57th Street, New York, NY 10019, (212) 554-0600, Fax: (212) 586-1181, www.eiu.com; *Business Asia.*

Euromonitor International, Inc., 224 S. Michigan Avenue, Suite 1500, Chicago, IL 60604, (312) 922-1115, Fax: (312) 922-1157, www.euromonitor.com; *World Marketing Data and Statistics.*

M.E. Sharpe, 80 Business Park Drive, Armonk, NY 10504, (800) 541-6563, Fax: (914) 273-2106, www.mesharpe.com; *The Illustrated Book of World Rankings.*

Palgrave Macmillan Ltd., Houndmills, Basingstoke, Hampshire, RG21 6XS, England, (Telephone in U.S. (888) 330-8477), (Fax in U.S. (800) 672-2054), www.palgrave.com; *The Statesman's Yearbook 2008.*

UNICEF, 3 United Nations Plaza, New York, NY 10017, (800) 253-9646, Fax: (212) 887-7465, www.unicef.org; *The State of the World's Children 2008.*

United Nations Statistics Division, New York, NY 10017, (800) 253-9646, Fax: (212) 963-4116, http://unstats.un.org; *Asia-Pacific in Figures 2004; Human Development Report 2006;* and *Statistical Yearbook.*

The World Bank, 1818 H Street, NW, Washington, DC 20433, (202) 473-1000, Fax: (202) 477-6391, www.worldbank.org; *Myanmar* and *World Development Report 2008.*

World Health Organization (WHO), Avenue Appia 20, 1211 Geneve 27, Switzerland, (Telephone in U.S. (212) 331-9081), www.who.int; The WHO Global Atlas of Infectious Diseases and *World Health Report 2006.*

BURMA - PUBLIC UTILITIES

United Nations Statistics Division, New York, NY 10017, (800) 253-9646, Fax: (212) 963-4116, http://unstats.un.org; *Electric Power in Asia and the Pacific 2001 and 2002.*

BURMA - RADIO - RECEIVERS AND RECEPTION

Palgrave Macmillan Ltd., Houndmills, Basingstoke, Hampshire, RG21 6XS, England, (Telephone in U.S. (888) 330-8477), (Fax in U.S. (800) 672-2054), www.palgrave.com; *The Statesman's Yearbook 2008.*

BURMA - RADIO BROADCASTING

United Nations Statistics Division, New York, NY 10017, (800) 253-9646, Fax: (212) 963-4116, http://unstats.un.org; *Statistical Yearbook.*

BURMA - RAILROADS

Palgrave Macmillan Ltd., Houndmills, Basingstoke, Hampshire, RG21 6XS, England, (Telephone in U.S. (888) 330-8477), (Fax in U.S. (800) 672-2054), www.palgrave.com; *The Statesman's Yearbook 2008.*

Taylor and Francis Group, An Informa Business, 2 Park Square, Milton Park, Abingdon, Oxford OX14 4RN, United Kingdom, (Dial from U.S. (212) 216-7800), (Fax from U.S. (212) 564-7854), www.tandf.co.uk; *The Europa World Year Book.*

United Nations Statistics Division, New York, NY 10017, (800) 253-9646, Fax: (212) 963-4116, http://unstats.un.org; *Statistical Yearbook.*

BURMA - RELIGION

Central Intelligence Agency, Office of Public Affairs, Washington, DC 20505, (703) 482-0623, Fax: (703) 482-1739, www.cia.gov; *The World Factbook.*

M.E. Sharpe, 80 Business Park Drive, Armonk, NY 10504, (800) 541-6563, Fax: (914) 273-2106, www.mesharpe.com; *The Illustrated Book of World Rankings.*

Palgrave Macmillan Ltd., Houndmills, Basingstoke, Hampshire, RG21 6XS, England, (Telephone in U.S. (888) 330-8477), (Fax in U.S. (800) 672-2054), www.palgrave.com; *The Statesman's Yearbook 2008.*

BURMA - RENT CHARGES

International Labour Office, I.L.O. Publications, 4 route des Morillons, CH-1211 Geneva 22, Switzerland, (Telephone in U.S. (202) 653-7652), (Fax in U.S. (202) 653-7687), www.ilo.org; *Yearbook of Labour Statistics 2006.*

BURMA - RESERVES (ACCOUNTING)

Asian Development Bank (ADB), PO Box 789, 0980 Manila, Philippines, www.adb.org; *Key Indicators of Developing Asian and Pacific Countries 2006.*

Euromonitor International, Inc., 224 S. Michigan Avenue, Suite 1500, Chicago, IL 60604, (312) 922-1115, Fax: (312) 922-1157, www.euromonitor.com; *International Marketing Data and Statistics 2008.*

United Nations Statistics Division, New York, NY 10017, (800) 253-9646, Fax: (212) 963-4116, http://unstats.un.org; *Statistical Yearbook.*

BURMA - RETAIL TRADE

Euromonitor International, Inc., 224 S. Michigan Avenue, Suite 1500, Chicago, IL 60604, (312) 922-1115, Fax: (312) 922-1157, www.euromonitor.com; *World Marketing Data and Statistics.*

BURMA - RICE PRODUCTION

See BURMA - CROPS

BURMA - ROADS

Central Intelligence Agency, Office of Public Affairs, Washington, DC 20505, (703) 482-0623, Fax: (703) 482-1739, www.cia.gov; *The World Factbook.*

Economist Intelligence Unit, 111 West 57th Street, New York, NY 10019, (212) 554-0600, Fax: (212) 586-1181, www.eiu.com; *Business Asia.*

International Road Federation (IFR), Madison Place, 500 Montgomery Street, 5th Floor, Alexandria, VA 22314, (703) 535-1001, Fax: (703) 535-1007, www.irfnet.org; *World Road Statistics 2006.*

Palgrave Macmillan Ltd., Houndmills, Basingstoke, Hampshire, RG21 6XS, England, (Telephone in U.S. (888) 330-8477), (Fax in U.S. (800) 672-2054), www.palgrave.com; *The Statesman's Yearbook 2008.*

BURMA - RUBBER INDUSTRY AND TRADE

International Rubber Study Group (IRSG), 1st Floor, Heron House, 109/115 Wembley Hill Road, Wembley, Middlesex HA9 8DA, United Kingdom, www.rubberstudy.com; *Rubber Statistical Bulletin; Summary of World Rubber Statistics 2005; World Rubber Statistics Handbook (Volume 6, 1975-2001);* and *World Rubber Statistics Historic Handbook.*

M.E. Sharpe, 80 Business Park Drive, Armonk, NY 10504, (800) 541-6563, Fax: (914) 273-2106, www.mesharpe.com; *The Illustrated Book of World Rankings.*

United Nations Statistics Division, New York, NY 10017, (800) 253-9646, Fax: (212) 963-4116, http://unstats.un.org; *Statistical Yearbook.*

BURMA - SALT PRODUCTION

See BURMA - MINERAL INDUSTRIES

BURMA - SHEEP

See BURMA - LIVESTOCK

BURMA - SHIPPING

Lloyd's Register - Fairplay, 8410 N.W. 53rd Terrace, Suite 207, Miami FL 33166, (305) 718-9929, Fax: (305) 718-9663, www.lrfairplay.com; *Register of Ships 2007-2008; World Casualty Statistics 2007; World Fleet Statistics 2006; World Marine Propulsion Report 2006-2010; World Shipbuilding Statistics 2007;* and The World Shipping Encyclopaedia.

Palgrave Macmillan Ltd., Houndmills, Basingstoke, Hampshire, RG21 6XS, England, (Telephone in U.S. (888) 330-8477), (Fax in U.S. (800) 672-2054), www.palgrave.com; *The Statesman's Yearbook 2008.*

Taylor and Francis Group, An Informa Business, 2 Park Square, Milton Park, Abingdon, Oxford OX14 4RN, United Kingdom, (Dial from U.S. (212) 216-7800), (Fax from U.S. (212) 564-7854), www.tandf.co.uk; *The Europa World Year Book.*

U.S. Department of Transportation (DOT), Maritime Administration (MARAD), West Building, Southeast Federal Center, 1200 New Jersey Avenue, SE, Washington, DC 20590, (800) 99-MARAD, www.marad.dot.gov; *World Merchant Fleet 2005.*

United Nations Statistics Division, New York, NY 10017, (800) 253-9646, Fax: (212) 963-4116, http://unstats.un.org; *Statistical Yearbook.*

BURMA - SILVER PRODUCTION

See BURMA - MINERAL INDUSTRIES

BURMA - SOCIAL SECURITY

Asian Development Bank (ADB), PO Box 789, 0980 Manila, Philippines, www.adb.org; *Key Indicators of Developing Asian and Pacific Countries 2006.*

M.E. Sharpe, 80 Business Park Drive, Armonk, NY 10504, (800) 541-6563, Fax: (914) 273-2106, www.mesharpe.com; *The Illustrated Book of World Rankings.*

United Nations Statistics Division, New York, NY 10017, (800) 253-9646, Fax: (212) 963-4116, http://unstats.un.org; *National Accounts Statistics: Compendium of Income Distribution Statistics.*

BURMA - SOYBEAN PRODUCTION

See BURMA - CROPS

BURMA - STEEL PRODUCTION

See BURMA - MINERAL INDUSTRIES

BURMA - SUGAR PRODUCTION

See BURMA - CROPS

BURMA - TAXATION

International Road Federation (IFR), Madison Place, 500 Montgomery Street, 5th Floor, Alexandria, VA 22314, (703) 535-1001, Fax: (703) 535-1007, www.irfnet.org; *World Road Statistics 2006.*

Taylor and Francis Group, An Informa Business, 2 Park Square, Milton Park, Abingdon, Oxford OX14 4RN, United Kingdom, (Dial from U.S. (212) 216-7800), (Fax from U.S. (212) 564-7854), www.tandf.co.uk; *The Europa World Year Book.*

BURMA - TEAK

International Monetary Fund (IMF), 700 Nineteenth Street, NW, Washington, DC 20431, (202) 623-7000, Fax: (202) 623-4661, www.imf.org; *International Financial Statistics Yearbook 2007.*

BURMA - TELEPHONE

Economist Intelligence Unit, 111 West 57th Street, New York, NY 10019, (212) 554-0600, Fax: (212) 586-1181, www.eiu.com; *Business Asia.*

International Telecommunication Union (ITU), Place des Nations, 1211 Geneva 20, Switzerland, www.itu.int; World Telecommunication Indicators Database.

Palgrave Macmillan Ltd., Houndmills, Basingstoke, Hampshire, RG21 6XS, England, (Telephone in U.S. (888) 330-8477), (Fax in U.S. (800) 672-2054), www.palgrave.com; *The Statesman's Yearbook 2008.*

Taylor and Francis Group, An Informa Business, 2 Park Square, Milton Park, Abingdon, Oxford OX14 4RN, United Kingdom, (Dial from U.S. (212) 216-7800), (Fax from U.S. (212) 564-7854), www.tandf.co.uk; *The Europa World Year Book.*

United Nations Statistics Division, New York, NY 10017, (800) 253-9646, Fax: (212) 963-4116, http://unstats.un.org; *Statistical Yearbook* and *World Statistics Pocketbook.*

BURMA - TEXTILE INDUSTRY

M.E. Sharpe, 80 Business Park Drive, Armonk, NY 10504, (800) 541-6563, Fax: (914) 273-2106, www.mesharpe.com; *The Illustrated Book of World Rankings.*

United Nations Conference on Trade and Development (UNCTAD), DC2-1120, United Nations, New York, NY 10017, (212) 963-0027, www.unctad.org; *UNCTAD Commodity Yearbook.*

United Nations Statistics Division, New York, NY 10017, (800) 253-9646, Fax: (212) 963-4116, http://unstats.un.org; *Statistical Yearbook.*

BURMA - TIN PRODUCTION

See BURMA - MINERAL INDUSTRIES

BURMA - TOBACCO INDUSTRY

Foreign Agricultural Service (FAS), U.S. Department of Agriculture (USDA), 1400 Independence Avenue, SW, Washington, DC 20250, (202) 720-3935, www.fas.usda.gov; *Tobacco: World Markets and Trade.*

M.E. Sharpe, 80 Business Park Drive, Armonk, NY 10504, (800) 541-6563, Fax: (914) 273-2106, www.mesharpe.com; *The Illustrated Book of World Rankings.*

United Nations Statistics Division, New York, NY 10017, (800) 253-9646, Fax: (212) 963-4116, http://unstats.un.org; *Statistical Yearbook.*

BURMA - TOURISM

Euromonitor International, Inc., 224 S. Michigan Avenue, Suite 1500, Chicago, IL 60604, (312) 922-1115, Fax: (312) 922-1157, www.euromonitor.com; *The World Economic Factbook 2008* and *World Marketing Data and Statistics.*

M.E. Sharpe, 80 Business Park Drive, Armonk, NY 10504, (800) 541-6563, Fax: (914) 273-2106, www.mesharpe.com; *The Illustrated Book of World Rankings.*

Palgrave Macmillan Ltd., Houndmills, Basingstoke, Hampshire, RG21 6XS, England, (Telephone in U.S. (888) 330-8477), (Fax in U.S. (800) 672-2054), www.palgrave.com; *The Statesman's Yearbook 2008.*

Taylor and Francis Group, An Informa Business, 2 Park Square, Milton Park, Abingdon, Oxford OX14 4RN, United Kingdom, (Dial from U.S. (212) 216-7800), (Fax from U.S. (212) 564-7854), www.tandf.co.uk; *The Europa World Year Book.*

The World Bank, 1818 H Street, NW, Washington, DC 20433, (202) 473-1000, Fax: (202) 477-6391, www.worldbank.org; *Myanmar.*

BURMA - TRADE

See BURMA - INTERNATIONAL TRADE

BURMA - TRANSPORTATION

Central Intelligence Agency, Office of Public Affairs, Washington, DC 20505, (703) 482-0623, Fax: (703) 482-1739, www.cia.gov; *The World Factbook.*

Economist Intelligence Unit, 111 West 57th Street, New York, NY 10019, (212) 554-0600, Fax: (212) 586-1181, www.eiu.com; *Business Asia.*

Euromonitor International, Inc., 224 S. Michigan Avenue, Suite 1500, Chicago, IL 60604, (312) 922-1115, Fax: (312) 922-1157, www.euromonitor.com; *International Marketing Data and Statistics 2008* and *World Marketing Data and Statistics.*

M.E. Sharpe, 80 Business Park Drive, Armonk, NY 10504, (800) 541-6563, Fax: (914) 273-2106, www.mesharpe.com; *The Illustrated Book of World Rankings.*

Palgrave Macmillan Ltd., Houndmills, Basingstoke, Hampshire, RG21 6XS, England, (Telephone in U.S. (888) 330-8477), (Fax in U.S. (800) 672-2054), www.palgrave.com; *The Statesman's Yearbook 2008.*

Taylor and Francis Group, An Informa Business, 2 Park Square, Milton Park, Abingdon, Oxford OX14 4RN, United Kingdom, (Dial from U.S. (212) 216-7800), (Fax from U.S. (212) 564-7854), www.tandf.co.uk; *The Europa World Year Book.*

United Nations Statistics Division, New York, NY 10017, (800) 253-9646, Fax: (212) 963-4116, http://unstats.un.org; *Human Development Report 2006* and *Statistical Yearbook for Asia and the Pacific 2004.*

The World Bank, 1818 H Street, NW, Washington, DC 20433, (202) 473-1000, Fax: (202) 477-6391, www.worldbank.org; *Myanmar.*

BURMA - TUNGSTEN

United Nations Statistics Division, New York, NY 10017, (800) 253-9646, Fax: (212) 963-4116, http://unstats.un.org; *Statistical Yearbook.*

BURMA - TURKEYS

See BURMA - LIVESTOCK

BURMA - UNEMPLOYMENT

Central Intelligence Agency, Office of Public Affairs, Washington, DC 20505, (703) 482-0623, Fax: (703) 482-1739, www.cia.gov; *The World Factbook.*

Euromonitor International, Inc., 224 S. Michigan Avenue, Suite 1500, Chicago, IL 60604, (312) 922-1115, Fax: (312) 922-1157, www.euromonitor.com; *International Marketing Data and Statistics 2008.*

International Labour Office, I.L.O. Publications, 4 route des Morillons, CH-1211 Geneva 22, Switzerland, (Telephone in U.S. (202) 653-7652), (Fax in U.S. (202) 653-7687), www.ilo.org; *Yearbook of Labour Statistics 2006.*

United Nations Statistics Division, New York, NY 10017, (800) 253-9646, Fax: (212) 963-4116, http://unstats.un.org; *Statistical Yearbook.*

BURMA - VITAL STATISTICS

Euromonitor International, Inc., 224 S. Michigan Avenue, Suite 1500, Chicago, IL 60604, (312) 922-1115, Fax: (312) 922-1157, www.euromonitor.com; *International Marketing Data and Statistics 2008.*

Palgrave Macmillan Ltd., Houndmills, Basingstoke, Hampshire, RG21 6XS, England, (Telephone in U.S. (888) 330-8477), (Fax in U.S. (800) 672-2054), www.palgrave.com; *The Statesman's Yearbook 2008.*

United Nations Statistics Division, New York, NY 10017, (800) 253-9646, Fax: (212) 963-4116, http://unstats.un.org; *Statistical Yearbook.*

World Health Organization (WHO), Avenue Appia 20, 1211 Geneve 27, Switzerland, (Telephone in U.S. (212) 331-9081), www.who.int; *World Health Report 2006.*

BURMA - WAGES

International Labour Office, I.L.O. Publications, 4 route des Morillons, CH-1211 Geneva 22, Switzerland, (Telephone in U.S. (202) 653-7652), (Fax in U.S. (202) 653-7687), www.ilo.org; *Yearbook of Labour Statistics 2006.*

United Nations Statistics Division, New York, NY 10017, (800) 253-9646, Fax: (212) 963-4116, http://unstats.un.org; *Statistical Yearbook for Asia and the Pacific 2004.*

The World Bank, 1818 H Street, NW, Washington, DC 20433, (202) 473-1000, Fax: (202) 477-6391, www.worldbank.org; *Myanmar.*

BURMA - WEATHER

See BURMA - CLIMATE

BURMA - WHEAT PRODUCTION

See BURMA - CROPS

BURMA - WHOLESALE PRICE INDEXES

Asian Development Bank (ADB), PO Box 789, 0980 Manila, Philippines, www.adb.org; *Key Indicators of Developing Asian and Pacific Countries 2006.*

BURUNDI - PRIMARY STATISTICS SOURCES

Institut de Statistiques et des Etudes Economiques du Burundi (ISTEEBU), BP 1156, Bujumbura, Burundi; *Annuaire Statistique* (Statistical Yearbook) and *Bulletin Statistique* (Statistical Bulletin).

BURUNDI - AGRICULTURAL MACHINERY

United Nations Statistics Division, New York, NY 10017, (800) 253-9646, Fax: (212) 963-4116, http://unstats.un.org; *Statistical Yearbook.*

BURUNDI - AGRICULTURE

Economist Intelligence Unit, 111 West 57th Street, New York, NY 10019, (212) 554-0600, Fax: (212) 586-1181, www.eiu.com; *Burundi Country Report.*

Euromonitor International, Inc., 224 S. Michigan Avenue, Suite 1500, Chicago, IL 60604, (312) 922-1115, Fax: (312) 922-1157, www.euromonitor.com; *International Marketing Data and Statistics 2008* and *World Marketing Data and Statistics.*

Palgrave Macmillan Ltd., Houndmills, Basingstoke, Hampshire, RG21 6XS, England, (Telephone in U.S. (888) 330-8477), (Fax in U.S. (800) 672-2054), www.palgrave.com; *The Statesman's Yearbook 2008.*

Taylor and Francis Group, An Informa Business, 2 Park Square, Milton Park, Abingdon, Oxford OX14 4RN, United Kingdom, (Dial from U.S. (212) 216-7800), (Fax from U.S. (212) 564-7854), www.tandf.co.uk; *The Europa World Year Book.*

United Nations Conference on Trade and Development (UNCTAD), DC2-1120, United Nations, New York, NY 10017, (212) 963-0027, www.unctad.org; *UNCTAD Commodity Yearbook.*

United Nations Economic Commission for Africa (ECA), PO Box 3001, Addis Ababa, Ethiopia, (Telephone in U.S. (212) 963-4957), www.uneca.org; *African Statistical Yearbook 2006.*

United Nations Food and Agricultural Organization (FAO), Viale delle Terme di Caracalla, 00100 Rome, Italy, (Dial from U.S. (202) 653-2400), (Fax from U.S. (202) 653 5760), www.fao.org; AQUASTAT; *FAO Production Yearbook 2002; FAO Trade Yearbook;* and *The State of Food and Agriculture (SOFA) 2006.*

United Nations Statistics Division, New York, NY 10017, (800) 253-9646, Fax: (212) 963-4116, http://unstats.un.org; *Statistical Yearbook* and *Survey of Economic and Social Conditions in Africa 2005.*

The World Bank, 1818 H Street, NW, Washington, DC 20433, (202) 473-1000, Fax: (202) 477-6391, www.worldbank.org; *Burundi.*

BURUNDI - AIRLINES

Palgrave Macmillan Ltd., Houndmills, Basingstoke, Hampshire, RG21 6XS, England, (Telephone in U.S. (888) 330-8477), (Fax in U.S. (800) 672-2054), www.palgrave.com; *The Statesman's Yearbook 2008.*

Taylor and Francis Group, An Informa Business, 2 Park Square, Milton Park, Abingdon, Oxford OX14 4RN, United Kingdom, (Dial from U.S. (212) 216-7800), (Fax from U.S. (212) 564-7854), www.tandf.co.uk; *The Europa World Year Book.*

United Nations Economic Commission for Africa (ECA), PO Box 3001, Addis Ababa, Ethiopia, (Telephone in U.S. (212) 963-4957), www.uneca.org; *African Statistical Yearbook 2006.*

BURUNDI - AIRPORTS

Central Intelligence Agency, Office of Public Affairs, Washington, DC 20505, (703) 482-0623, Fax: (703) 482-1739, www.cia.gov; *The World Factbook.*

BURUNDI - ARMED FORCES

Central Intelligence Agency, Office of Public Affairs, Washington, DC 20505, (703) 482-0623, Fax: (703) 482-1739, www.cia.gov; *The World Factbook.*

Euromonitor International, Inc., 224 S. Michigan Avenue, Suite 1500, Chicago, IL 60604, (312) 922-1115, Fax: (312) 922-1157, www.euromonitor.com; *World Marketing Data and Statistics.*

International Institute for Strategic Studies (IISS), Arundel House, 13-15 Arundel Street, Temple Place, London WC2R 3DX, England, www.iiss.org; *The Military Balance 2007.*

Palgrave Macmillan Ltd., Houndmills, Basingstoke, Hampshire, RG21 6XS, England, (Telephone in U.S. (888) 330-8477), (Fax in U.S. (800) 672-2054), www.palgrave.com; *The Statesman's Yearbook 2008.*

U.S. Department of State (DOS), 2201 C Street NW, Washington, DC 20520, (202) 647-4000, www.state.gov; *World Military Expenditures and Arms Transfers (WMEAT).*

United Nations Statistics Division, New York, NY 10017, (800) 253-9646, Fax: (212) 963-4116, http://unstats.un.org; *Human Development Report 2006.*

BURUNDI - BALANCE OF PAYMENTS

African Development Bank Group, Rue Joseph Anoma, 01 BP 1387 Abidjan 01, Cote d'Ivoire, www.afdb.org; *Statistics Pocketbook 2008.*

Taylor and Francis Group, An Informa Business, 2 Park Square, Milton Park, Abingdon, Oxford OX14 4RN, United Kingdom, (Dial from U.S. (212) 216-7800), (Fax from U.S. (212) 564-7854), www.tandf.co.uk; *The Europa World Year Book.*

United Nations Conference on Trade and Development (UNCTAD), DC2-1120, United Nations, New York, NY 10017, (212) 963-0027, www.unctad.org; *Handbook of Statistics 2005.*

United Nations Economic Commission for Africa (ECA), PO Box 3001, Addis Ababa, Ethiopia, (Telephone in U.S. (212) 963-4957), www.uneca.org; *African Statistical Yearbook 2006.*

The World Bank, 1818 H Street, NW, Washington, DC 20433, (202) 473-1000, Fax: (202) 477-6391, www.worldbank.org; *Burundi* and *World Development Report 2008.*

BURUNDI - BANKS AND BANKING

Euromonitor International, Inc., 224 S. Michigan Avenue, Suite 1500, Chicago, IL 60604, (312) 922-1115, Fax: (312) 922-1157, www.euromonitor.com; *World Marketing Data and Statistics.*

International Monetary Fund (IMF), 700 Nineteenth Street, NW, Washington, DC 20431, (202) 623-7000, Fax: (202) 623-4661, www.imf.org; *International Financial Statistics Yearbook 2007.*

Palgrave Macmillan Ltd., Houndmills, Basingstoke, Hampshire, RG21 6XS, England, (Telephone in U.S. (888) 330-8477), (Fax in U.S. (800) 672-2054), www.palgrave.com; *The Statesman's Yearbook 2008.*

Taylor and Francis Group, An Informa Business, 2 Park Square, Milton Park, Abingdon, Oxford OX14 4RN, United Kingdom, (Dial from U.S. (212) 216-7800), (Fax from U.S. (212) 564-7854), www.tandf.co.uk; *The Europa World Year Book.*

BURUNDI - BEVERAGE INDUSTRY

United Nations Statistics Division, New York, NY 10017, (800) 253-9646, Fax: (212) 963-4116, http://unstats.un.org; *Statistical Yearbook.*

BURUNDI - BROADCASTING

Central Intelligence Agency, Office of Public Affairs, Washington, DC 20505, (703) 482-0623, Fax: (703) 482-1739, www.cia.gov; *The World Factbook.*

Euromonitor International, Inc., 224 S. Michigan Avenue, Suite 1500, Chicago, IL 60604, (312) 922-1115, Fax: (312) 922-1157, www.euromonitor.com; *World Marketing Data and Statistics.*

Palgrave Macmillan Ltd., Houndmills, Basingstoke, Hampshire, RG21 6XS, England, (Telephone in U.S. (888) 330-8477), (Fax in U.S. (800) 672-2054), www.palgrave.com; *The Statesman's Yearbook 2008.*

WRTH Publications Limited, PO Box 290, Oxford OX2 7FT, UK, www.wrth.com; *World Radio TV Handbook 2007.*

BURUNDI - BUDGET

Central Intelligence Agency, Office of Public Affairs, Washington, DC 20505, (703) 482-0623, Fax: (703) 482-1739, www.cia.gov; *The World Factbook.*

BURUNDI - CATTLE

See BURUNDI - LIVESTOCK

BURUNDI - CHICKENS

See BURUNDI - LIVESTOCK

BURUNDI - CHILDBIRTH - STATISTICS

Central Intelligence Agency, Office of Public Affairs, Washington, DC 20505, (703) 482-0623, Fax: (703) 482-1739, www.cia.gov; *The World Factbook.*

Euromonitor International, Inc., 224 S. Michigan Avenue, Suite 1500, Chicago, IL 60604, (312) 922-1115, Fax: (312) 922-1157, www.euromonitor.com; *International Marketing Data and Statistics 2008* and *The World Economic Factbook 2008.*

Taylor and Francis Group, An Informa Business, 2 Park Square, Milton Park, Abingdon, Oxford OX14 4RN, United Kingdom, (Dial from U.S. (212) 216-7800), (Fax from U.S. (212) 564-7854), www.tandf.co.uk; *The Europa World Year Book.*

United Nations Statistics Division, New York, NY 10017, (800) 253-9646, Fax: (212) 963-4116, http://unstats.un.org; *Demographic Yearbook; Statistical Yearbook;* and *Survey of Economic and Social Conditions in Africa 2005.*

BURUNDI - CLIMATE

International Institute for Environment and Development (IIED), 3 Endsleigh Street, London, England, WC1H 0DD, United Kingdom, www.iied.org; *Environment Urbanization* and *Haramata - Bulletin of the Drylands.*

Palgrave Macmillan Ltd., Houndmills, Basingstoke, Hampshire, RG21 6XS, England, (Telephone in U.S. (888) 330-8477), (Fax in U.S. (800) 672-2054), www.palgrave.com; *The Statesman's Yearbook 2008.*

BURUNDI - COAL PRODUCTION

See BURUNDI - MINERAL INDUSTRIES

BURUNDI - COFFEE

See BURUNDI - CROPS

BURUNDI - COMMERCE

Palgrave Macmillan Ltd., Houndmills, Basingstoke, Hampshire, RG21 6XS, England, (Telephone in U.S. (888) 330-8477), (Fax in U.S. (800) 672-2054), www.palgrave.com; *The Statesman's Yearbook 2008.*

BURUNDI - COMMODITY EXCHANGES

Commodity Research Bureau, 330 South Wells Street, Suite 612, Chicago, IL 60606-7110, (800) 621-5271, Fax: (312) 939-4135, www.crbtrader.com; *2006 CRB Commodity Yearbook and CD.*

International Monetary Fund (IMF), 700 Nineteenth Street, NW, Washington, DC 20431, (202) 623-7000, Fax: (202) 623-4661, www.imf.org; *IMF Primary Commodity Prices.*

United Nations Food and Agricultural Organization (FAO), Viale delle Terme di Caracalla, 00100 Rome, Italy, (Dial from U.S. (202) 653-2400), (Fax from U.S. (202) 653 5760), www.fao.org; *The State of Food and Agriculture (SOFA) 2006.*

BURUNDI - CONSTRUCTION INDUSTRY

United Nations Economic Commission for Africa (ECA), PO Box 3001, Addis Ababa, Ethiopia, (Telephone in U.S. (212) 963-4957), www.uneca.org; *African Statistical Yearbook 2006.*

BURUNDI - CONSUMER PRICE INDEXES

Taylor and Francis Group, An Informa Business, 2 Park Square, Milton Park, Abingdon, Oxford OX14 4RN, United Kingdom, (Dial from U.S. (212) 216-7800), (Fax from U.S. (212) 564-7854), www.tandf.co.uk; *The Europa World Year Book.*

United Nations Economic Commission for Africa (ECA), PO Box 3001, Addis Ababa, Ethiopia, (Telephone in U.S. (212) 963-4957), www.uneca.org; *African Statistical Yearbook 2006.*

United Nations Statistics Division, New York, NY 10017, (800) 253-9646, Fax: (212) 963-4116, http://unstats.un.org; *Statistical Yearbook* and *Survey of Economic and Social Conditions in Africa 2005.*

The World Bank, 1818 H Street, NW, Washington, DC 20433, (202) 473-1000, Fax: (202) 477-6391, www.worldbank.org; *Burundi.*

BURUNDI - CONSUMPTION (ECONOMICS)

African Development Bank Group, Rue Joseph Anoma, 01 BP 1387 Abidjan 01, Cote d'Ivoire, www.afdb.org; *Statistics Pocketbook 2008.*

United Nations Statistics Division, New York, NY 10017, (800) 253-9646, Fax: (212) 963-4116, http://unstats.un.org; *Survey of Economic and Social Conditions in Africa 2005.*

The World Bank, 1818 H Street, NW, Washington, DC 20433, (202) 473-1000, Fax: (202) 477-6391, www.worldbank.org; *World Development Report 2008.*

BURUNDI - CORN INDUSTRY

United Nations Food and Agricultural Organization (FAO), Viale delle Terme di Caracalla, 00100 Rome, Italy, (Dial from U.S. (202) 653-2400), (Fax from U.S. (202) 653 5760), www.fao.org; *The State of Food and Agriculture (SOFA) 2006.*

United Nations Statistics Division, New York, NY 10017, (800) 253-9646, Fax: (212) 963-4116, http://unstats.un.org; *Statistical Yearbook.*

BURUNDI - COTTON

See BURUNDI - CROPS

BURUNDI - CRIME

International Criminal Police Organization (INTERPOL), General Secretariat, 200 quai Charles de Gaulle, 69006 Lyon, France, www.interpol.int; *International Crime Statistics.*

BURUNDI - CROPS

International Monetary Fund (IMF), 700 Nineteenth Street, NW, Washington, DC 20431, (202) 623-7000, Fax: (202) 623-4661, www.imf.org; *International Financial Statistics Yearbook 2007.*

Palgrave Macmillan Ltd., Houndmills, Basingstoke, Hampshire, RG21 6XS, England, (Telephone in U.S. (888) 330-8477), (Fax in U.S. (800) 672-2054), www.palgrave.com; *The Statesman's Yearbook 2008.*

Taylor and Francis Group, An Informa Business, 2 Park Square, Milton Park, Abingdon, Oxford OX14 4RN, United Kingdom, (Dial from U.S. (212) 216-7800), (Fax from U.S. (212) 564-7854), www.tandf.co.uk; *The Europa World Year Book.*

United Nations Conference on Trade and Development (UNCTAD), DC2-1120, United Nations, New York, NY 10017, (212) 963-0027, www.unctad.org; *UNCTAD Commodity Yearbook.*

United Nations Economic Commission for Africa (ECA), PO Box 3001, Addis Ababa, Ethiopia, (Telephone in U.S. (212) 963-4957), www.uneca.org; *African Statistical Yearbook 2006.*

United Nations Food and Agricultural Organization (FAO), Viale delle Terme di Caracalla, 00100 Rome, Italy, (Dial from U.S. (202) 653-2400), (Fax from U.S. (202) 653 5760), www.fao.org; *The State of Food and Agriculture (SOFA) 2006.*

United Nations Statistics Division, New York, NY 10017, (800) 253-9646, Fax: (212) 963-4116, http://unstats.un.org; *Statistical Yearbook.*

BURUNDI - DAIRY PROCESSING

Palgrave Macmillan Ltd., Houndmills, Basingstoke, Hampshire, RG21 6XS, England, (Telephone in U.S. (888) 330-8477), (Fax in U.S. (800) 672-2054), www.palgrave.com; *The Statesman's Yearbook 2008.*

Taylor and Francis Group, An Informa Business, 2 Park Square, Milton Park, Abingdon, Oxford OX14 4RN, United Kingdom, (Dial from U.S. (212) 216-7800), (Fax from U.S. (212) 564-7854), www.tandf.co.uk; *The Europa World Year Book.*

United Nations Food and Agricultural Organization (FAO), Viale delle Terme di Caracalla, 00100 Rome, Italy, (Dial from U.S. (202) 653-2400), (Fax from U.S. (202) 653 5760), www.fao.org; *FAO Production Yearbook 2002* and *The State of Food and Agriculture (SOFA) 2006.*

United Nations Statistics Division, New York, NY 10017, (800) 253-9646, Fax: (212) 963-4116, http://unstats.un.org; *Statistical Yearbook.*

BURUNDI - DEATH RATES

See BURUNDI - MORTALITY

BURUNDI - DEBTS, EXTERNAL

African Development Bank Group, Rue Joseph Anoma, 01 BP 1387 Abidjan 01, Cote d'Ivoire, www.afdb.org; *Statistics Pocketbook 2008.*

Palgrave Macmillan Ltd., Houndmills, Basingstoke, Hampshire, RG21 6XS, England, (Telephone in U.S. (888) 330-8477), (Fax in U.S. (800) 672-2054), www.palgrave.com; *The Statesman's Yearbook 2008.*

United Nations Statistics Division, New York, NY 10017, (800) 253-9646, Fax: (212) 963-4116, http://unstats.un.org; *Survey of Economic and Social Conditions in Africa 2005.*

The World Bank, 1818 H Street, NW, Washington, DC 20433, (202) 473-1000, Fax: (202) 477-6391, www.worldbank.org; *Global Development Finance 2007* and *World Development Report 2008.*

BURUNDI - DEFENSE EXPENDITURES

See BURUNDI - ARMED FORCES

BURUNDI - DEMOGRAPHY

Euromonitor International, Inc., 224 S. Michigan Avenue, Suite 1500, Chicago, IL 60604, (312) 922-1115, Fax: (312) 922-1157, www.euromonitor.com; *International Marketing Data and Statistics 2008; The World Economic Factbook 2008;* and *World Marketing Data and Statistics.*

United Nations Statistics Division, New York, NY 10017, (800) 253-9646, Fax: (212) 963-4116, http://unstats.un.org; *Human Development Report 2006* and *Survey of Economic and Social Conditions in Africa 2005.*

The World Bank, 1818 H Street, NW, Washington, DC 20433, (202) 473-1000, Fax: (202) 477-6391, www.worldbank.org; *Burundi.*

BURUNDI - DISPOSABLE INCOME

United Nations Statistics Division, New York, NY 10017, (800) 253-9646, Fax: (212) 963-4116, http://unstats.un.org; *National Accounts Statistics: Compendium of Income Distribution Statistics* and *Statistical Yearbook.*

BURUNDI - DIVORCE

United Nations Statistics Division, New York, NY 10017, (800) 253-9646, Fax: (212) 963-4116, http://unstats.un.org; *Demographic Yearbook.*

BURUNDI - ECONOMIC ASSISTANCE

United Nations Statistics Division, New York, NY 10017, (800) 253-9646, Fax: (212) 963-4116, http://unstats.un.org; *Statistical Yearbook.*

BURUNDI - ECONOMIC CONDITIONS

African Development Bank Group, Rue Joseph Anoma, 01 BP 1387 Abidjan 01, Cote d'Ivoire, www.afdb.org; *Statistics Pocketbook 2008.*

Center for International Business Education Research (CIBER), Columbia Business School and School of International and Public Affairs, Uris Hall, Room 212, 3022 Broadway, New York, NY 10027-6902, Mr. Joshua Safier, (212) 854-4750, Fax: (212) 222-9821, www.columbia.edu/cu/ciber/; Datastream International.

Central Intelligence Agency, Office of Public Affairs, Washington, DC 20505, (703) 482-0623, Fax: (703) 482-1739, www.cia.gov; *The World Factbook.*

DSI Data Service Information, Xantener Strasse 51a, D-47495 Rheinberg, Germany, www.dsidata.com; *Campus Solution.*

Dun and Bradstreet (DB) Corporation, 103 JFK Parkway, Short Hills, NJ 07078, (973) 921-5500, www.dnb.com; *Country Report.*

Economist Intelligence Unit, 111 West 57th Street, New York, NY 10019, (212) 554-0600, Fax: (212) 586-1181, www.eiu.com; *Burundi Country Report.*

Euromonitor International, Inc., 224 S. Michigan Avenue, Suite 1500, Chicago, IL 60604, (312) 922-1115, Fax: (312) 922-1157, www.euromonitor.com; *International Marketing Data and Statistics 2008; The World Economic Factbook 2008;* and *World Marketing Data and Statistics.*

International Monetary Fund (IMF), 700 Nineteenth Street, NW, Washington, DC 20431, (202) 623-7000, Fax: (202) 623-4661, www.imf.org; *World Economic Outlook Reports.*

Palgrave Macmillan Ltd., Houndmills, Basingstoke, Hampshire, RG21 6XS, England, (Telephone in U.S. (888) 330-8477), (Fax in U.S. (800) 672-2054), www.palgrave.com; *The Statesman's Yearbook 2008.*

Taylor and Francis Group, An Informa Business, 2 Park Square, Milton Park, Abingdon, Oxford OX14 4RN, United Kingdom, (Dial from U.S. (212) 216-7800), (Fax from U.S. (212) 564-7854), www.tandf.co.uk; *The Europa World Year Book.*

United Nations Statistics Division, New York, NY 10017, (800) 253-9646, Fax: (212) 963-4116, http://unstats.un.org; *Compendium of Intra-African and Related Foreign Trade Statistics 2003* and *World Statistics Pocketbook.*

The World Bank, 1818 H Street, NW, Washington, DC 20433, (202) 473-1000, Fax: (202) 477-6391, www.worldbank.org; *Burundi; Global Economic Monitor (GEM); Global Economic Prospects 2008; The World Bank Atlas 2003-2004;* and *World Development Report 2008.*

BURUNDI - EDUCATION

African Development Bank Group, Rue Joseph Anoma, 01 BP 1387 Abidjan 01, Cote d'Ivoire, www.afdb.org; *Statistics Pocketbook 2008.*

Euromonitor International, Inc., 224 S. Michigan Avenue, Suite 1500, Chicago, IL 60604, (312) 922-1115, Fax: (312) 922-1157, www.euromonitor.com; *International Marketing Data and Statistics 2008* and *World Marketing Data and Statistics.*

Palgrave Macmillan Ltd., Houndmills, Basingstoke, Hampshire, RG21 6XS, England, (Telephone in U.S. (888) 330-8477), (Fax in U.S. (800) 672-2054), www.palgrave.com; *The Statesman's Yearbook 2008.*

Taylor and Francis Group, An Informa Business, 2 Park Square, Milton Park, Abingdon, Oxford OX14 4RN, United Kingdom, (Dial from U.S. (212) 216-

7800), (Fax from U.S. (212) 564-7854), www.tandf.co.uk; *The Europa World Year Book.*

UNESCO Institute for Statistics, C.P. 6128 Succursale Centre-Ville, Montreal, Quebec, H3C 3J7 Canada, (Dial from U.S. (514) 343-6880), (Fax from U.S. (514) 343 6882), www.uis.unesco.org; *Statistical Tables.*

United Nations Economic Commission for Africa (ECA), PO Box 3001, Addis Ababa, Ethiopia, (Telephone in U.S. (212) 963-4957), www.uneca.org; *African Statistical Yearbook 2006.*

United Nations Statistics Division, New York, NY 10017, (800) 253-9646, Fax: (212) 963-4116, http://unstats.un.org; *Human Development Report 2006* and *Survey of Economic and Social Conditions in Africa 2005.*

The World Bank, 1818 H Street, NW, Washington, DC 20433, (202) 473-1000, Fax: (202) 477-6391, www.worldbank.org; *Burundi* and *World Development Report 2008.*

BURUNDI - ELECTRICITY

Palgrave Macmillan Ltd., Houndmills, Basingstoke, Hampshire, RG21 6XS, England, (Telephone in U.S. (888) 330-8477), (Fax in U.S. (800) 672-2054), www.palgrave.com; *The Statesman's Yearbook 2008.*

United Nations Economic Commission for Africa (ECA), PO Box 3001, Addis Ababa, Ethiopia, (Telephone in U.S. (212) 963-4957), www.uneca.org; *African Statistical Yearbook 2006.*

United Nations Statistics Division, New York, NY 10017, (800) 253-9646, Fax: (212) 963-4116, http://unstats.un.org; *Human Development Report 2006* and *Survey of Economic and Social Conditions in Africa 2005.*

BURUNDI - EMPLOYMENT

Euromonitor International, Inc., 224 S. Michigan Avenue, Suite 1500, Chicago, IL 60604, (312) 922-1115, Fax: (312) 922-1157, www.euromonitor.com; *International Marketing Data and Statistics 2008.*

International Labour Office, I.L.O. Publications, 4 route des Morillons, CH-1211 Geneva 22, Switzerland, (Telephone in U.S. (202) 653-7652), (Fax in U.S. (202) 653-7687), www.ilo.org; *Yearbook of Labour Statistics 2006.*

United Nations Economic Commission for Africa (ECA), PO Box 3001, Addis Ababa, Ethiopia, (Telephone in U.S. (212) 963-4957), www.uneca.org; *African Statistical Yearbook 2006.*

United Nations Statistics Division, New York, NY 10017, (800) 253-9646, Fax: (212) 963-4116, http://unstats.un.org; *Statistical Yearbook* and *Survey of Economic and Social Conditions in Africa 2005.*

The World Bank, 1818 H Street, NW, Washington, DC 20433, (202) 473-1000, Fax: (202) 477-6391, www.worldbank.org; *Burundi.*

BURUNDI - ENVIRONMENTAL CONDITIONS

DSI Data Service Information, Xantener Strasse 51a, D-47495 Rheinberg, Germany, www.dsidata.com; *Campus Solution* and *DSI's Global Environmental Database.*

Economist Intelligence Unit, 111 West 57th Street, New York, NY 10019, (212) 554-0600, Fax: (212) 586-1181, www.eiu.com; *Burundi Country Report.*

International Institute for Environment and Development (IIED), 3 Endsleigh Street, London, England, WC1H 0DD, United Kingdom, www.iied.org; *Environment Urbanization* and *Haramata - Bulletin of the Drylands.*

United Nations Statistics Division, New York, NY 10017, (800) 253-9646, Fax: (212) 963-4116, http://unstats.un.org; *World Statistics Pocketbook.*

BURUNDI - EXPORTS

African Development Bank Group, Rue Joseph Anoma, 01 BP 1387 Abidjan 01, Cote d'Ivoire, www.afdb.org; *Statistics Pocketbook 2008.*

Central Intelligence Agency, Office of Public Affairs, Washington, DC 20505, (703) 482-0623, Fax: (703) 482-1739, www.cia.gov; *The World Factbook.*

Economist Intelligence Unit, 111 West 57th Street, New York, NY 10019, (212) 554-0600, Fax: (212) 586-1181, www.eiu.com; *Burundi Country Report.*

Euromonitor International, Inc., 224 S. Michigan Avenue, Suite 1500, Chicago, IL 60604, (312) 922-1115, Fax: (312) 922-1157, www.euromonitor.com; *International Marketing Data and Statistics 2008* and *The World Economic Factbook 2008.*

International Monetary Fund (IMF), 700 Nineteenth Street, NW, Washington, DC 20431, (202) 623-7000, Fax: (202) 623-4661, www.imf.org; *Direction of Trade Statistics Yearbook 2007* and *International Financial Statistics Yearbook 2007.*

Palgrave Macmillan Ltd., Houndmills, Basingstoke, Hampshire, RG21 6XS, England, (Telephone in U.S. (888) 330-8477), (Fax in U.S. (800) 672-2054), www.palgrave.com; *The Statesman's Yearbook 2008.*

Taylor and Francis Group, An Informa Business, 2 Park Square, Milton Park, Abingdon, Oxford OX14 4RN, United Kingdom, (Dial from U.S. (212) 216-7800), (Fax from U.S. (212) 564-7854), www.tandf.co.uk; *The Europa World Year Book.*

United Nations Conference on Trade and Development (UNCTAD), DC2-1120, United Nations, New York, NY 10017, (212) 963-0027, www.unctad.org; *Handbook of Statistics 2005.*

United Nations Economic Commission for Africa (ECA), PO Box 3001, Addis Ababa, Ethiopia, (Telephone in U.S. (212) 963-4957), www.uneca.org; *African Statistical Yearbook 2006.*

United Nations Food and Agricultural Organization (FAO), Viale delle Terme di Caracalla, 00100 Rome, Italy, (Dial from U.S. (202) 653-2400), (Fax from U.S. (202) 653 5760), www.fao.org; *The State of Food and Agriculture (SOFA) 2006.*

United Nations Statistics Division, New York, NY 10017, (800) 253-9646, Fax: (212) 963-4116, http://unstats.un.org; *Compendium of Intra-African and Related Foreign Trade Statistics 2003* and *Survey of Economic and Social Conditions in Africa 2005.*

The World Bank, 1818 H Street, NW, Washington, DC 20433, (202) 473-1000, Fax: (202) 477-6391, www.worldbank.org; *World Development Report 2008.*

BURUNDI - FEMALE WORKING POPULATION

See BURUNDI - EMPLOYMENT

BURUNDI - FERTILITY, HUMAN

Central Intelligence Agency, Office of Public Affairs, Washington, DC 20505, (703) 482-0623, Fax: (703) 482-1739, www.cia.gov; *The World Factbook.*

United Nations Statistics Division, New York, NY 10017, (800) 253-9646, Fax: (212) 963-4116, http://unstats.un.org; *Human Development Report 2006* and *Survey of Economic and Social Conditions in Africa 2005.*

The World Bank, 1818 H Street, NW, Washington, DC 20433, (202) 473-1000, Fax: (202) 477-6391, www.worldbank.org; *The World Bank Atlas 2003-2004* and *World Development Report 2008.*

BURUNDI - FERTILIZER INDUSTRY

United Nations Food and Agricultural Organization (FAO), Viale delle Terme di Caracalla, 00100 Rome, Italy, (Dial from U.S. (202) 653-2400), (Fax from U.S. (202) 653 5760), www.fao.org; *The State of Food and Agriculture (SOFA) 2006.*

United Nations Statistics Division, New York, NY 10017, (800) 253-9646, Fax: (212) 963-4116, http://unstats.un.org; *Statistical Yearbook.*

BURUNDI - FETAL MORTALITY

See BURUNDI - MORTALITY

BURUNDI - FINANCE

Taylor and Francis Group, An Informa Business, 2 Park Square, Milton Park, Abingdon, Oxford OX14 4RN, United Kingdom, (Dial from U.S. (212) 216-7800), (Fax from U.S. (212) 564-7854), www.tandf.co.uk; *The Europa World Year Book.*

United Nations Economic Commission for Africa (ECA), PO Box 3001, Addis Ababa, Ethiopia, (Telephone in U.S. (212) 963-4957), www.uneca.org; *African Statistical Yearbook 2006.*

United Nations Statistics Division, New York, NY 10017, (800) 253-9646, Fax: (212) 963-4116, http://unstats.un.org; *National Accounts Statistics: Compendium of Income Distribution Statistics* and *Statistical Yearbook.*

The World Bank, 1818 H Street, NW, Washington, DC 20433, (202) 473-1000, Fax: (202) 477-6391, www.worldbank.org; *Burundi.*

BURUNDI - FINANCE, PUBLIC

African Development Bank Group, Rue Joseph Anoma, 01 BP 1387 Abidjan 01, Cote d'Ivoire, www.afdb.org; *Statistics Pocketbook 2008.*

Bernan Essential Government Publications, 4611-F Assembly Drive, Lanham MD, 20706-4391, (301) 459-2255, Fax: (800) 865-3450, www.bernan.com; *National Accounts Statistics.*

Economist Intelligence Unit, 111 West 57th Street, New York, NY 10019, (212) 554-0600, Fax: (212) 586-1181, www.eiu.com; *Burundi Country Report.*

International Monetary Fund (IMF), 700 Nineteenth Street, NW, Washington, DC 20431, (202) 623-7000, Fax: (202) 623-4661, www.imf.org; *International Financial Statistics* and *International Financial Statistics Online Service.*

Palgrave Macmillan Ltd., Houndmills, Basingstoke, Hampshire, RG21 6XS, England, (Telephone in U.S. (888) 330-8477), (Fax in U.S. (800) 672-2054), www.palgrave.com; *The Statesman's Yearbook 2008.*

Taylor and Francis Group, An Informa Business, 2 Park Square, Milton Park, Abingdon, Oxford OX14 4RN, United Kingdom, (Dial from U.S. (212) 216-7800), (Fax from U.S. (212) 564-7854), www.tandf.co.uk; *The Europa World Year Book.*

United Nations Economic Commission for Africa (ECA), PO Box 3001, Addis Ababa, Ethiopia, (Telephone in U.S. (212) 963-4957), www.uneca.org; *African Statistical Yearbook 2006.*

The World Bank, 1818 H Street, NW, Washington, DC 20433, (202) 473-1000, Fax: (202) 477-6391, www.worldbank.org; *Burundi.*

BURUNDI - FISHERIES

Palgrave Macmillan Ltd., Houndmills, Basingstoke, Hampshire, RG21 6XS, England, (Telephone in U.S. (888) 330-8477), (Fax in U.S. (800) 672-2054), www.palgrave.com; *The Statesman's Yearbook 2008.*

Taylor and Francis Group, An Informa Business, 2 Park Square, Milton Park, Abingdon, Oxford OX14 4RN, United Kingdom, (Dial from U.S. (212) 216-7800), (Fax from U.S. (212) 564-7854), www.tandf.co.uk; *The Europa World Year Book.*

United Nations Conference on Trade and Development (UNCTAD), DC2-1120, United Nations, New York, NY 10017, (212) 963-0027, www.unctad.org; *UNCTAD Commodity Yearbook.*

United Nations Economic Commission for Africa (ECA), PO Box 3001, Addis Ababa, Ethiopia, (Telephone in U.S. (212) 963-4957), www.uneca.org; *African Statistical Yearbook 2006.*

United Nations Food and Agricultural Organization (FAO), Viale delle Terme di Caracalla, 00100 Rome, Italy, (Dial from U.S. (202) 653-2400), (Fax from U.S. (202) 653 5760), www.fao.org; *FAO Yearbook of Fishery Statistics;* Fishery Databases; FISHSTAT Database. Subjects covered include: Aquaculture production, capture production, fishery commodities; and *The State of Food and Agriculture (SOFA) 2006.*

United Nations Statistics Division, New York, NY 10017, (800) 253-9646, Fax: (212) 963-4116, http://unstats.un.org; *Statistical Yearbook* and *Survey of Economic and Social Conditions in Africa 2005.*

The World Bank, 1818 H Street, NW, Washington, DC 20433, (202) 473-1000, Fax: (202) 477-6391, www.worldbank.org; *Burundi.*

BURUNDI - FOOD

African Development Bank Group, Rue Joseph Anoma, 01 BP 1387 Abidjan 01, Cote d'Ivoire, www.afdb.org; *Statistics Pocketbook 2008.*

United Nations Conference on Trade and Development (UNCTAD), DC2-1120, United Nations, New York, NY 10017, (212) 963-0027, www.unctad.org; *UNCTAD Commodity Yearbook.*

United Nations Food and Agricultural Organization (FAO), Viale delle Terme di Caracalla, 00100 Rome, Italy, (Dial from U.S. (202) 653-2400), (Fax from U.S. (202) 653 5760), www.fao.org; *FAO Production Yearbook 2002* and *The State of Food and Agriculture (SOFA) 2006.*

United Nations Statistics Division, New York, NY 10017, (800) 253-9646, Fax: (212) 963-4116, http://unstats.un.org; *Human Development Report 2006.*

BURUNDI - FOREIGN EXCHANGE RATES

African Development Bank Group, Rue Joseph Anoma, 01 BP 1387 Abidjan 01, Cote d'Ivoire, www.afdb.org; *Statistics Pocketbook 2008.*

Central Intelligence Agency, Office of Public Affairs, Washington, DC 20505, (703) 482-0623, Fax: (703) 482-1739, www.cia.gov; *The World Factbook.*

Euromonitor International, Inc., 224 S. Michigan Avenue, Suite 1500, Chicago, IL 60604, (312) 922-1115, Fax: (312) 922-1157, www.euromonitor.com; *International Marketing Data and Statistics 2008* and *The World Economic Factbook 2008.*

International Monetary Fund (IMF), 700 Nineteenth Street, NW, Washington, DC 20431, (202) 623-7000, Fax: (202) 623-4661, www.imf.org; *International Financial Statistics Yearbook 2007.*

Taylor and Francis Group, An Informa Business, 2 Park Square, Milton Park, Abingdon, Oxford OX14 4RN, United Kingdom, (Dial from U.S. (212) 216-7800), (Fax from U.S. (212) 564-7854), www.tandf.co.uk; *The Europa World Year Book.*

United Nations Statistics Division, New York, NY 10017, (800) 253-9646, Fax: (212) 963-4116, http://unstats.un.org; *Compendium of Intra-African and Related Foreign Trade Statistics 2003; Statistical Yearbook;* and *World Statistics Pocketbook.*

BURUNDI - FORESTS AND FORESTRY

Palgrave Macmillan Ltd., Houndmills, Basingstoke, Hampshire, RG21 6XS, England, (Telephone in U.S. (888) 330-8477), (Fax in U.S. (800) 672-2054), www.palgrave.com; *The Statesman's Yearbook 2008.*

Taylor and Francis Group, An Informa Business, 2 Park Square, Milton Park, Abingdon, Oxford OX14 4RN, United Kingdom, (Dial from U.S. (212) 216-7800), (Fax from U.S. (212) 564-7854), www.tandf.co.uk; *The Europa World Year Book.*

UNESCO Institute for Statistics, C.P. 6128 Succursale Centre-Ville, Montreal, Quebec, H3C 3J7 Canada, (Dial from U.S. (514) 343-6880), (Fax from U.S. (514) 343 6882), www.uis.unesco.org; *Statistical Tables.*

United Nations Conference on Trade and Development (UNCTAD), DC2-1120, United Nations, New York, NY 10017, (212) 963-0027, www.unctad.org; *UNCTAD Commodity Yearbook.*

United Nations Economic Commission for Africa (ECA), PO Box 3001, Addis Ababa, Ethiopia, (Telephone in U.S. (212) 963-4957), www.uneca.org; *African Statistical Yearbook 2006.*

United Nations Food and Agricultural Organization (FAO), Viale delle Terme di Caracalla, 00100 Rome, Italy, (Dial from U.S. (202) 653-2400), (Fax from U.S. (202) 653 5760), www.fao.org; *FAO Yearbook of Forest Products* and *The State of Food and Agriculture (SOFA) 2006.*

United Nations Statistics Division, New York, NY 10017, (800) 253-9646, Fax: (212) 963-4116, http://unstats.un.org; *Statistical Yearbook.*

The World Bank, 1818 H Street, NW, Washington, DC 20433, (202) 473-1000, Fax: (202) 477-6391, www.worldbank.org; *Burundi* and *World Development Report 2008.*

BURUNDI - GEOGRAPHIC INFORMATION SYSTEMS

The World Bank, 1818 H Street, NW, Washington, DC 20433, (202) 473-1000, Fax: (202) 477-6391, www.worldbank.org; *Burundi.*

BURUNDI - GOLD INDUSTRY

International Monetary Fund (IMF), 700 Nineteenth Street, NW, Washington, DC 20431, (202) 623-7000, Fax: (202) 623-4661, www.imf.org; *International Financial Statistics Yearbook 2007.*

United Nations Statistics Division, New York, NY 10017, (800) 253-9646, Fax: (212) 963-4116, http://unstats.un.org; *Statistical Yearbook.*

BURUNDI - GROSS DOMESTIC PRODUCT

African Development Bank Group, Rue Joseph Anoma, 01 BP 1387 Abidjan 01, Cote d'Ivoire, www.afdb.org; *Statistics Pocketbook 2008.*

Economist Intelligence Unit, 111 West 57th Street, New York, NY 10019, (212) 554-0600, Fax: (212) 586-1181, www.eiu.com; *Burundi Country Report.*

Euromonitor International, Inc., 224 S. Michigan Avenue, Suite 1500, Chicago, IL 60604, (312) 922-1115, Fax: (312) 922-1157, www.euromonitor.com; *International Marketing Data and Statistics 2008* and *The World Economic Factbook 2008.*

Palgrave Macmillan Ltd., Houndmills, Basingstoke, Hampshire, RG21 6XS, England, (Telephone in U.S. (888) 330-8477), (Fax in U.S. (800) 672-2054), www.palgrave.com; *The Statesman's Yearbook 2008.*

Taylor and Francis Group, An Informa Business, 2 Park Square, Milton Park, Abingdon, Oxford OX14 4RN, United Kingdom, (Dial from U.S. (212) 216-7800), (Fax from U.S. (212) 564-7854), www.tandf.co.uk; *The Europa World Year Book.*

United Nations Economic Commission for Africa (ECA), PO Box 3001, Addis Ababa, Ethiopia, (Telephone in U.S. (212) 963-4957), www.uneca.org; *African Statistical Yearbook 2006.*

United Nations Statistics Division, New York, NY 10017, (800) 253-9646, Fax: (212) 963-4116, http://unstats.un.org; *Human Development Report 2006; National Accounts Statistics: Compendium of Income Distribution Statistics; Statistical Yearbook;* and *Survey of Economic and Social Conditions in Africa 2005.*

The World Bank, 1818 H Street, NW, Washington, DC 20433, (202) 473-1000, Fax: (202) 477-6391, www.worldbank.org; *World Development Report 2008.*

BURUNDI - GROSS NATIONAL PRODUCT

Euromonitor International, Inc., 224 S. Michigan Avenue, Suite 1500, Chicago, IL 60604, (312) 922-1115, Fax: (312) 922-1157, www.euromonitor.com; *International Marketing Data and Statistics 2008.*

U.S. Department of State (DOS), 2201 C Street NW, Washington, DC 20520, (202) 647-4000, www.state.gov; *World Military Expenditures and Arms Transfers (WMEAT).*

The World Bank, 1818 H Street, NW, Washington, DC 20433, (202) 473-1000, Fax: (202) 477-6391, www.worldbank.org; *The World Bank Atlas 2003-2004* and *World Development Report 2008.*

BURUNDI - HIDES AND SKINS INDUSTRY

United Nations Food and Agricultural Organization (FAO), Viale delle Terme di Caracalla, 00100 Rome, Italy, (Dial from U.S. (202) 653-2400), (Fax from U.S. (202) 653 5760), www.fao.org; *FAO Production Yearbook 2002.*

BURUNDI - HOUSING

Euromonitor International, Inc., 224 S. Michigan Avenue, Suite 1500, Chicago, IL 60604, (312) 922-1115, Fax: (312) 922-1157, www.euromonitor.com; *World Marketing Data and Statistics.*

BURUNDI - ILLITERATE PERSONS

Euromonitor International, Inc., 224 S. Michigan Avenue, Suite 1500, Chicago, IL 60604, (312) 922-1115, Fax: (312) 922-1157, www.euromonitor.com; *The World Economic Factbook 2008.*

UNESCO Institute for Statistics, C.P. 6128 Succursale Centre-Ville, Montreal, Quebec, H3C 3J7 Canada, (Dial from U.S. (514) 343-6880), (Fax from U.S. (514) 343 6882), www.uis.unesco.org; *Statistical Tables.*

United Nations Statistics Division, New York, NY 10017, (800) 253-9646, Fax: (212) 963-4116, http://unstats.un.org; *Human Development Report 2006.*

BURUNDI - IMPORTS

Central Intelligence Agency, Office of Public Affairs, Washington, DC 20505, (703) 482-0623, Fax: (703) 482-1739, www.cia.gov; *The World Factbook.*

Economist Intelligence Unit, 111 West 57th Street, New York, NY 10019, (212) 554-0600, Fax: (212) 586-1181, www.eiu.com; *Burundi Country Report.*

Euromonitor International, Inc., 224 S. Michigan Avenue, Suite 1500, Chicago, IL 60604, (312) 922-1115, Fax: (312) 922-1157, www.euromonitor.com; *International Marketing Data and Statistics 2008* and *The World Economic Factbook 2008.*

International Monetary Fund (IMF), 700 Nineteenth Street, NW, Washington, DC 20431, (202) 623-7000, Fax: (202) 623-4661, www.imf.org; *Direction of Trade Statistics Yearbook 2007* and *International Financial Statistics Yearbook 2007.*

Palgrave Macmillan Ltd., Houndmills, Basingstoke, Hampshire, RG21 6XS, England, (Telephone in U.S. (888) 330-8477), (Fax in U.S. (800) 672-2054), www.palgrave.com; *The Statesman's Yearbook 2008.*

Taylor and Francis Group, An Informa Business, 2 Park Square, Milton Park, Abingdon, Oxford OX14 4RN, United Kingdom, (Dial from U.S. (212) 216-7800), (Fax from U.S. (212) 564-7854), www.tandf.co.uk; *The Europa World Year Book.*

United Nations Conference on Trade and Development (UNCTAD), DC2-1120, United Nations, New York, NY 10017, (212) 963-0027, www.unctad.org; *Handbook of Statistics 2005.*

United Nations Economic Commission for Africa (ECA), PO Box 3001, Addis Ababa, Ethiopia, (Telephone in U.S. (212) 963-4957), www.uneca.org; *African Statistical Yearbook 2006.*

United Nations Food and Agricultural Organization (FAO), Viale delle Terme di Caracalla, 00100 Rome, Italy, (Dial from U.S. (202) 653-2400), (Fax from U.S. (202) 653 5760), www.fao.org; *The State of Food and Agriculture (SOFA) 2006.*

United Nations Statistics Division, New York, NY 10017, (800) 253-9646, Fax: (212) 963-4116, http://unstats.un.org; *Compendium of Intra-African and Related Foreign Trade Statistics 2003* and *Survey of Economic and Social Conditions in Africa 2005.*

The World Bank, 1818 H Street, NW, Washington, DC 20433, (202) 473-1000, Fax: (202) 477-6391, www.worldbank.org; *World Development Report 2008.*

BURUNDI - INDUSTRIAL PRODUCTIVITY

Euromonitor International, Inc., 224 S. Michigan Avenue, Suite 1500, Chicago, IL 60604, (312) 922-1115, Fax: (312) 922-1157, www.euromonitor.com; *International Marketing Data and Statistics 2008.*

BURUNDI - INDUSTRIAL PROPERTY

U.S. Department of State (DOS), 2201 C Street NW, Washington, DC 20520, (202) 647-4000, www.state.gov; *World Military Expenditures and Arms Transfers (WMEAT).*

United Nations Statistics Division, New York, NY 10017, (800) 253-9646, Fax: (212) 963-4116, http://unstats.un.org; *Statistical Yearbook.*

BURUNDI - INDUSTRIES

Central Intelligence Agency, Office of Public Affairs, Washington, DC 20505, (703) 482-0623, Fax: (703) 482-1739, www.cia.gov; *The World Factbook.*

Economist Intelligence Unit, 111 West 57th Street, New York, NY 10019, (212) 554-0600, Fax: (212) 586-1181, www.eiu.com; *Burundi Country Report.*

Euromonitor International, Inc., 224 S. Michigan Avenue, Suite 1500, Chicago, IL 60604, (312) 922-1115, Fax: (312) 922-1157, www.euromonitor.com; *International Marketing Data and Statistics 2008; The World Economic Factbook 2008;* and *World Marketing Data and Statistics.*

International Labour Office, I.L.O. Publications, 4 route des Morillons, CH-1211 Geneva 22, Switzerland, (Telephone in U.S. (202) 653-7652), (Fax in U.S. (202) 653-7687), www.ilo.org; *Yearbook of Labour Statistics 2006.*

Palgrave Macmillan Ltd., Houndmills, Basingstoke, Hampshire, RG21 6XS, England, (Telephone in U.S. (888) 330-8477), (Fax in U.S. (800) 672-2054), www.palgrave.com; *The Statesman's Yearbook 2008.*

Taylor and Francis Group, An Informa Business, 2 Park Square, Milton Park, Abingdon, Oxford OX14 4RN, United Kingdom, (Dial from U.S. (212) 216-7800), (Fax from U.S. (212) 564-7854), www.tandf.co.uk; *The Europa World Year Book.*

United Nations Economic Commission for Africa (ECA), PO Box 3001, Addis Ababa, Ethiopia, (Telephone in U.S. (212) 963-4957), www.uneca.org; *African Statistical Yearbook 2006.*

United Nations Industrial Development Organization (UNIDO), 1 United Nations Plaza, New York, NY 10017, (212) 963 6890, Fax: (212) 963-7904, http://unido.org; Industrial Statistics Database 2008 (INDSTAT) and *The International Yearbook of Industrial Statistics 2008.*

United Nations Statistics Division, New York, NY 10017, (800) 253-9646, Fax: (212) 963-4116, http://unstats.un.org; *Statistical Yearbook* and *Survey of Economic and Social Conditions in Africa 2005.*

The World Bank, 1818 H Street, NW, Washington, DC 20433, (202) 473-1000, Fax: (202) 477-6391, www.worldbank.org; *Burundi.*

World Intellectual Property Organization (WIPO), PO Box 18, CH-1211 Geneva 20, Switzerland, www.wipo.int; *Industrial Property Statistics* and *Industrial Property Statistics Online Directory.*

BURUNDI - INFANT AND MATERNAL MORTALITY

See BURUNDI - MORTALITY

BURUNDI - INTERNATIONAL LIQUIDITY

International Monetary Fund (IMF), 700 Nineteenth Street, NW, Washington, DC 20431, (202) 623-7000, Fax: (202) 623-4661, www.imf.org; *International Financial Statistics Yearbook 2007.*

BURUNDI - INTERNATIONAL TRADE

African Development Bank Group, Rue Joseph Anoma, 01 BP 1387 Abidjan 01, Cote d'Ivoire, www.afdb.org; *Statistics Pocketbook 2008.*

Economist Intelligence Unit, 111 West 57th Street, New York, NY 10019, (212) 554-0600, Fax: (212) 586-1181, www.eiu.com; *Burundi Country Report.*

Euromonitor International, Inc., 224 S. Michigan Avenue, Suite 1500, Chicago, IL 60604, (312) 922-1115, Fax: (312) 922-1157, www.euromonitor.com; *International Marketing Data and Statistics 2008; The World Economic Factbook 2008;* and *World Marketing Data and Statistics.*

Organisation for Economic Cooperation and Development (OECD), 2 rue Andre Pascal, F-75775 Paris Cedex 16, France, (Telephone in U.S. (202) 785-6323), (Fax in U.S. (202) 785-0350), www.oecd.org; *International Trade by Commodity Statistics (ITCS).*

Palgrave Macmillan Ltd., Houndmills, Basingstoke, Hampshire, RG21 6XS, England, (Telephone in U.S. (888) 330-8477), (Fax in U.S. (800) 672-2054), www.palgrave.com; *The Statesman's Yearbook 2008.*

Taylor and Francis Group, An Informa Business, 2 Park Square, Milton Park, Abingdon, Oxford OX14 4RN, United Kingdom, (Dial from U.S. (212) 216-7800), (Fax from U.S. (212) 564-7854), www.tandf.co.uk; *The Europa World Year Book.*

United Nations Conference on Trade and Development (UNCTAD), DC2-1120, United Nations, New York, NY 10017, (212) 963-0027, www.unctad.org; *UNCTAD Commodity Yearbook.*

United Nations Economic Commission for Africa (ECA), PO Box 3001, Addis Ababa, Ethiopia, (Telephone in U.S. (212) 963-4957), www.uneca.org; *African Statistical Yearbook 2006.*

United Nations Food and Agricultural Organization (FAO), Viale delle Terme di Caracalla, 00100 Rome, Italy, (Dial from U.S. (202) 653-2400), (Fax from U.S. (202) 653 5760), www.fao.org; *FAO Trade Yearbook* and *The State of Food and Agriculture (SOFA) 2006.*

United Nations Statistics Division, New York, NY 10017, (800) 253-9646, Fax: (212) 963-4116, http://unstats.un.org; *Compendium of Intra-African and Related Foreign Trade Statistics 2003; International Trade Statistics Yearbook;* and *Statistical Yearbook.*

The World Bank, 1818 H Street, NW, Washington, DC 20433, (202) 473-1000, Fax: (202) 477-6391, www.worldbank.org; *Burundi* and *World Development Report 2008.*

World Trade Organization (WTO), Centre William Rappard, Rue de Lausanne 154, CH-1211 Geneva 21, Switzerland, www.wto.org; *International Trade Statistics 2006.*

BURUNDI - INTERNET USERS

International Telecommunication Union (ITU), Place des Nations, 1211 Geneva 20, Switzerland, www.itu.int; *World Telecommunication/ICT Indicators Database on CD-ROM; World Telecommunication/ICT Indicators Database Online;* and *Yearbook of Statistics - Telecommunication Services (Chronological Time Series 1997-2006).*

The World Bank, 1818 H Street, NW, Washington, DC 20433, (202) 473-1000, Fax: (202) 477-6391, www.worldbank.org; *Burundi.*

BURUNDI - IRRIGATION

Euromonitor International, Inc., 224 S. Michigan Avenue, Suite 1500, Chicago, IL 60604, (312) 922-1115, Fax: (312) 922-1157, www.euromonitor.com; *International Marketing Data and Statistics 2008.*

BURUNDI - LABOR

African Development Bank Group, Rue Joseph Anoma, 01 BP 1387 Abidjan 01, Cote d'Ivoire, www.afdb.org; *Statistics Pocketbook 2008.*

Central Intelligence Agency, Office of Public Affairs, Washington, DC 20505, (703) 482-0623, Fax: (703) 482-1739, www.cia.gov; *The World Factbook.*

Euromonitor International, Inc., 224 S. Michigan Avenue, Suite 1500, Chicago, IL 60604, (312) 922-1115, Fax: (312) 922-1157, www.euromonitor.com; *International Marketing Data and Statistics 2008* and *World Marketing Data and Statistics.*

International Labour Office, I.L.O. Publications, 4 route des Morillons, CH-1211 Geneva 22, Switzerland, (Telephone in U.S. (202) 653-7652), (Fax in U.S. (202) 653-7687), www.ilo.org; *Yearbook of Labour Statistics 2006.*

Palgrave Macmillan Ltd., Houndmills, Basingstoke, Hampshire, RG21 6XS, England, (Telephone in U.S. (888) 330-8477), (Fax in U.S. (800) 672-2054), www.palgrave.com; *The Statesman's Yearbook 2008.*

Taylor and Francis Group, An Informa Business, 2 Park Square, Milton Park, Abingdon, Oxford OX14 4RN, United Kingdom, (Dial from U.S. (212) 216-7800), (Fax from U.S. (212) 564-7854), www.tandf.co.uk; *The Europa World Year Book.*

United Nations Food and Agricultural Organization (FAO), Viale delle Terme di Caracalla, 00100 Rome, Italy, (Dial from U.S. (202) 653-2400), (Fax from U.S. (202) 653 5760), www.fao.org; *The State of Food and Agriculture (SOFA) 2006.*

United Nations Statistics Division, New York, NY 10017, (800) 253-9646, Fax: (212) 963-4116, http://unstats.un.org; *Human Development Report 2006.*

The World Bank, 1818 H Street, NW, Washington, DC 20433, (202) 473-1000, Fax: (202) 477-6391, www.worldbank.org; *The World Bank Atlas 2003-2004* and *World Development Report 2008.*

BURUNDI - LAND USE

Central Intelligence Agency, Office of Public Affairs, Washington, DC 20505, (703) 482-0623, Fax: (703) 482-1739, www.cia.gov; *The World Factbook.*

Euromonitor International, Inc., 224 S. Michigan Avenue, Suite 1500, Chicago, IL 60604, (312) 922-1115, Fax: (312) 922-1157, www.euromonitor.com; *International Marketing Data and Statistics 2008.*

United Nations Food and Agricultural Organization (FAO), Viale delle Terme di Caracalla, 00100 Rome, Italy, (Dial from U.S. (202) 653-2400), (Fax from U.S. (202) 653 5760), www.fao.org; *FAO Production Yearbook 2002.*

The World Bank, 1818 H Street, NW, Washington, DC 20433, (202) 473-1000, Fax: (202) 477-6391, www.worldbank.org; *World Development Report 2008.*

BURUNDI - LIBRARIES

UNESCO Institute for Statistics, C.P. 6128 Succursale Centre-Ville, Montreal, Quebec, H3C 3J7 Canada, (Dial from U.S. (514) 343-6880), (Fax from U.S. (514) 343 6882), www.uis.unesco.org; *Statistical Tables.*

BURUNDI - LIFE EXPECTANCY

African Development Bank Group, Rue Joseph Anoma, 01 BP 1387 Abidjan 01, Cote d'Ivoire, www.afdb.org; *Statistics Pocketbook 2008.*

Central Intelligence Agency, Office of Public Affairs, Washington, DC 20505, (703) 482-0623, Fax: (703) 482-1739, www.cia.gov; *The World Factbook.*

Euromonitor International, Inc., 224 S. Michigan Avenue, Suite 1500, Chicago, IL 60604, (312) 922-1115, Fax: (312) 922-1157, www.euromonitor.com; *The World Economic Factbook 2008.*

United Nations Statistics Division, New York, NY 10017, (800) 253-9646, Fax: (212) 963-4116, http://unstats.un.org; *Human Development Report 2006* and *World Statistics Pocketbook.*

The World Bank, 1818 H Street, NW, Washington, DC 20433, (202) 473-1000, Fax: (202) 477-6391, www.worldbank.org; *The World Bank Atlas 2003-2004* and *World Development Report 2008.*

BURUNDI - LITERACY

Euromonitor International, Inc., 224 S. Michigan Avenue, Suite 1500, Chicago, IL 60604, (312) 922-1115, Fax: (312) 922-1157, www.euromonitor.com; *World Marketing Data and Statistics.*

United Nations Statistics Division, New York, NY 10017, (800) 253-9646, Fax: (212) 963-4116, http://unstats.un.org; *Survey of Economic and Social Conditions in Africa 2005.*

BURUNDI - LIVESTOCK

Euromonitor International, Inc., 224 S. Michigan Avenue, Suite 1500, Chicago, IL 60604, (312) 922-1115, Fax: (312) 922-1157, www.euromonitor.com; *International Marketing Data and Statistics 2008.*

Taylor and Francis Group, An Informa Business, 2 Park Square, Milton Park, Abingdon, Oxford OX14 4RN, United Kingdom, (Dial from U.S. (212) 216-7800), (Fax from U.S. (212) 564-7854), www.tandf.co.uk; *The Europa World Year Book.*

United Nations Conference on Trade and Development (UNCTAD), DC2-1120, United Nations, New York, NY 10017, (212) 963-0027, www.unctad.org; *UNCTAD Commodity Yearbook.*

United Nations Economic Commission for Africa (ECA), PO Box 3001, Addis Ababa, Ethiopia,

(Telephone in U.S. (212) 963-4957), www.uneca.org; *African Statistical Yearbook 2006.*

United Nations Food and Agricultural Organization (FAO), Viale delle Terme di Caracalla, 00100 Rome, Italy, (Dial from U.S. (202) 653-2400), (Fax from U.S. (202) 653 5760), www.fao.org; *FAO Production Yearbook 2002* and *The State of Food and Agriculture (SOFA) 2006.*

United Nations Statistics Division, New York, NY 10017, (800) 253-9646, Fax: (212) 963-4116, http://unstats.un.org; *Statistical Yearbook* and *Survey of Economic and Social Conditions in Africa 2005.*

BURUNDI - LOCAL TAXATION

Euromonitor International, Inc., 224 S. Michigan Avenue, Suite 1500, Chicago, IL 60604, (312) 922-1115, Fax: (312) 922-1157, www.euromonitor.com; *International Marketing Data and Statistics 2008.*

BURUNDI - MANUFACTURES

United Nations Economic Commission for Africa (ECA), PO Box 3001, Addis Ababa, Ethiopia, (Telephone in U.S. (212) 963-4957), www.uneca.org; *African Statistical Yearbook 2006.*

United Nations Statistics Division, New York, NY 10017, (800) 253-9646, Fax: (212) 963-4116, http://unstats.un.org; *Statistical Yearbook* and *Survey of Economic and Social Conditions in Africa 2005.*

BURUNDI - MARRIAGE

United Nations Statistics Division, New York, NY 10017, (800) 253-9646, Fax: (212) 963-4116, http://unstats.un.org; *Demographic Yearbook.*

BURUNDI - MEAT PRODUCTION

See BURUNDI - LIVESTOCK

BURUNDI - MILK PRODUCTION

See BURUNDI - DAIRY PROCESSING

BURUNDI - MINERAL INDUSTRIES

Palgrave Macmillan Ltd., Houndmills, Basingstoke, Hampshire, RG21 6XS, England, (Telephone in U.S. (888) 330-8477), (Fax in U.S. (800) 672-2054), www.palgrave.com; *The Statesman's Yearbook 2008.*

Taylor and Francis Group, An Informa Business, 2 Park Square, Milton Park, Abingdon, Oxford OX14 4RN, United Kingdom, (Dial from U.S. (212) 216-7800), (Fax from U.S. (212) 564-7854), www.tandf.co.uk; *The Europa World Year Book.*

United Nations Conference on Trade and Development (UNCTAD), DC2-1120, United Nations, New York, NY 10017, (212) 963-0027, www.unctad.org; *UNCTAD Commodity Yearbook.*

United Nations Economic Commission for Africa (ECA), PO Box 3001, Addis Ababa, Ethiopia, (Telephone in U.S. (212) 963-4957), www.uneca.org; *African Statistical Yearbook 2006.*

BURUNDI - MONEY EXCHANGE RATES

See BURUNDI - FOREIGN EXCHANGE RATES

BURUNDI - MONEY SUPPLY

African Development Bank Group, Rue Joseph Anoma, 01 BP 1387 Abidjan 01, Cote d'Ivoire, www.afdb.org; *Statistics Pocketbook 2008.*

Economist Intelligence Unit, 111 West 57th Street, New York, NY 10019, (212) 554-0600, Fax: (212) 586-1181, www.eiu.com; *Burundi Country Report.*

Euromonitor International, Inc., 224 S. Michigan Avenue, Suite 1500, Chicago, IL 60604, (312) 922-1115, Fax: (312) 922-1157, www.euromonitor.com; *International Marketing Data and Statistics 2008.*

International Monetary Fund (IMF), 700 Nineteenth Street, NW, Washington, DC 20431, (202) 623-7000, Fax: (202) 623-4661, www.imf.org; *International Financial Statistics Yearbook 2007.*

Taylor and Francis Group, An Informa Business, 2 Park Square, Milton Park, Abingdon, Oxford OX14 4RN, United Kingdom, (Dial from U.S. (212) 216-7800), (Fax from U.S. (212) 564-7854), www.tandf.co.uk; *The Europa World Year Book.*

United Nations Statistics Division, New York, NY 10017, (800) 253-9646, Fax: (212) 963-4116, http://unstats.un.org; *Statistical Yearbook.*

The World Bank, 1818 H Street, NW, Washington, DC 20433, (202) 473-1000, Fax: (202) 477-6391, www.worldbank.org; *Burundi.*

BURUNDI - MORTALITY

Central Intelligence Agency, Office of Public Affairs, Washington, DC 20505, (703) 482-0623, Fax: (703) 482-1739, www.cia.gov; *The World Factbook.*

Euromonitor International, Inc., 224 S. Michigan Avenue, Suite 1500, Chicago, IL 60604, (312) 922-1115, Fax: (312) 922-1157, www.euromonitor.com; *International Marketing Data and Statistics 2008* and *The World Economic Factbook 2008.*

Taylor and Francis Group, An Informa Business, 2 Park Square, Milton Park, Abingdon, Oxford OX14 4RN, United Kingdom, (Dial from U.S. (212) 216-7800), (Fax from U.S. (212) 564-7854), www.tandf.co.uk; *The Europa World Year Book.*

UNICEF, 3 United Nations Plaza, New York, NY 10017, (800) 253-9646, Fax: (212) 887-7465, www.unicef.org; *The State of the World's Children 2008.*

United Nations Statistics Division, New York, NY 10017, (800) 253-9646, Fax: (212) 963-4116, http://unstats.un.org; *Demographic Yearbook; Human Development Report 2006; Statistical Yearbook; Survey of Economic and Social Conditions in Africa 2005;* and *World Statistics Pocketbook.*

The World Bank, 1818 H Street, NW, Washington, DC 20433, (202) 473-1000, Fax: (202) 477-6391, www.worldbank.org; *The World Bank Atlas 2003-2004* and *World Development Report 2008.*

World Health Organization (WHO), Avenue Appia 20, 1211 Geneve 27, Switzerland, (Telephone in U.S. (212) 331-9081), www.who.int; The WHO Global Atlas of Infectious Diseases.

BURUNDI - MOTION PICTURES

Palgrave Macmillan Ltd., Houndmills, Basingstoke, Hampshire, RG21 6XS, England, (Telephone in U.S. (888) 330-8477), (Fax in U.S. (800) 672-2054), www.palgrave.com; *The Statesman's Yearbook 2008.*

United Nations Statistics Division, New York, NY 10017, (800) 253-9646, Fax: (212) 963-4116, http://unstats.un.org; *Statistical Yearbook.*

BURUNDI - MOTOR VEHICLES

Taylor and Francis Group, An Informa Business, 2 Park Square, Milton Park, Abingdon, Oxford OX14 4RN, United Kingdom, (Dial from U.S. (212) 216-7800), (Fax from U.S. (212) 564-7854), www.tandf.co.uk; *The Europa World Year Book.*

United Nations Statistics Division, New York, NY 10017, (800) 253-9646, Fax: (212) 963-4116, http://unstats.un.org; *Statistical Yearbook* and *Survey of Economic and Social Conditions in Africa 2005.*

BURUNDI - MUSEUMS

UNESCO Institute for Statistics, C.P. 6128 Succursale Centre-Ville, Montreal, Quebec, H3C 3J7 Canada, (Dial from U.S. (514) 343-6880), (Fax from U.S. (514) 343 6882), www.uis.unesco.org; *Statistical Tables.*

BURUNDI - NUTRITION

African Development Bank Group, Rue Joseph Anoma, 01 BP 1387 Abidjan 01, Cote d'Ivoire, www.afdb.org; *Statistics Pocketbook 2008.*

United Nations Food and Agricultural Organization (FAO), Viale delle Terme di Caracalla, 00100 Rome, Italy, (Dial from U.S. (202) 653-2400), (Fax from U.S. (202) 653 5760), www.fao.org; *The State of Food and Agriculture (SOFA) 2006.*

BURUNDI - PERIODICALS

UNESCO Institute for Statistics, C.P. 6128 Succursale Centre-Ville, Montreal, Quebec, H3C 3J7 Canada, (Dial from U.S. (514) 343-6880), (Fax from U.S. (514) 343 6882), www.uis.unesco.org; *Statistical Tables.*

BURUNDI - PESTICIDES

United Nations Food and Agricultural Organization (FAO), Viale delle Terme di Caracalla, 00100 Rome, Italy, (Dial from U.S. (202) 653-2400), (Fax from U.S. (202) 653 5760), www.fao.org; *The State of Food and Agriculture (SOFA) 2006.*

BURUNDI - PETROLEUM INDUSTRY AND TRADE

PennWell Corporation, 1421 South Sheridan Road, Tulsa, OK 74112, (918) 835-3161, www.pennwell.com; *International Petroleum Encyclopedia 2007.*

United Nations Conference on Trade and Development (UNCTAD), DC2-1120, United Nations, New York, NY 10017, (212) 963-0027, www.unctad.org; *UNCTAD Commodity Yearbook.*

United Nations Food and Agricultural Organization (FAO), Viale delle Terme di Caracalla, 00100 Rome, Italy, (Dial from U.S. (202) 653-2400), (Fax from U.S. (202) 653 5760), www.fao.org; *The State of Food and Agriculture (SOFA) 2006.*

BURUNDI - POLITICAL SCIENCE

Central Intelligence Agency, Office of Public Affairs, Washington, DC 20505, (703) 482-0623, Fax: (703) 482-1739, www.cia.gov; *The World Factbook.*

International Monetary Fund (IMF), 700 Nineteenth Street, NW, Washington, DC 20431, (202) 623-7000, Fax: (202) 623-4661, www.imf.org; *International Financial Statistics Yearbook 2007.*

Palgrave Macmillan Ltd., Houndmills, Basingstoke, Hampshire, RG21 6XS, England, (Telephone in U.S. (888) 330-8477), (Fax in U.S. (800) 672-2054), www.palgrave.com; *The Statesman's Yearbook 2008.*

Taylor and Francis Group, An Informa Business, 2 Park Square, Milton Park, Abingdon, Oxford OX14 4RN, United Kingdom, (Dial from U.S. (212) 216-7800), (Fax from U.S. (212) 564-7854), www.tandf.co.uk; *The Europa World Year Book.*

United Nations Statistics Division, New York, NY 10017, (800) 253-9646, Fax: (212) 963-4116, http://unstats.un.org; *National Accounts Statistics: Compendium of Income Distribution Statistics* and *Survey of Economic and Social Conditions in Africa 2005.*

The World Bank, 1818 H Street, NW, Washington, DC 20433, (202) 473-1000, Fax: (202) 477-6391, www.worldbank.org; *World Development Report 2008.*

BURUNDI - POPULATION

African Development Bank Group, Rue Joseph Anoma, 01 BP 1387 Abidjan 01, Cote d'Ivoire, www.afdb.org; *Statistics Pocketbook 2008.*

Central Intelligence Agency, Office of Public Affairs, Washington, DC 20505, (703) 482-0623, Fax: (703) 482-1739, www.cia.gov; *The World Factbook.*

Economist Intelligence Unit, 111 West 57th Street, New York, NY 10019, (212) 554-0600, Fax: (212) 586-1181, www.eiu.com; *Burundi Country Report.*

Euromonitor International, Inc., 224 S. Michigan Avenue, Suite 1500, Chicago, IL 60604, (312) 922-1115, Fax: (312) 922-1157, www.euromonitor.com; *International Marketing Data and Statistics 2008* and *The World Economic Factbook 2008.*

Eurostat, Batiment Jean Monnet, Rue Alcide de Gasperi, L-2920 Luxembourg, http://epp.eurostat.ec.europa.eu; *Demographic Indicators - Population by Age-Classes.*

International Labour Office, I.L.O. Publications, 4 route des Morillons, CH-1211 Geneva 22, Switzerland, (Telephone in U.S. (202) 653-7652), (Fax in U.S. (202) 653-7687), www.ilo.org; *Yearbook of Labour Statistics 2006.*

Palgrave Macmillan Ltd., Houndmills, Basingstoke, Hampshire, RG21 6XS, England, (Telephone in U.S. (888) 330-8477), (Fax in U.S. (800) 672-2054), www.palgrave.com; *The Statesman's Yearbook 2008.*

Taylor and Francis Group, An Informa Business, 2 Park Square, Milton Park, Abingdon, Oxford OX14 4RN, United Kingdom, (Dial from U.S. (212) 216-7800), (Fax from U.S. (212) 564-7854), www.tandf.co.uk; *The Europa World Year Book.*

U.S. Department of State (DOS), 2201 C Street NW, Washington, DC 20520, (202) 647-4000, www.state.gov; *World Military Expenditures and Arms Transfers (WMEAT).*

United Nations Food and Agricultural Organization (FAO), Viale delle Terme di Caracalla, 00100 Rome, Italy, (Dial from U.S. (202) 653-2400), (Fax from U.S. (202) 653 5760), www.fao.org; *FAO Production Yearbook 2002.*

United Nations Statistics Division, New York, NY 10017, (800) 253-9646, Fax: (212) 963-4116, http://unstats.un.org; *Demographic Yearbook; Human Development Report 2006; Statistical Yearbook; Survey of Economic and Social Conditions in Africa 2005;* and *World Statistics Pocketbook.*

The World Bank, 1818 H Street, NW, Washington, DC 20433, (202) 473-1000, Fax: (202) 477-6391, www.worldbank.org; *Burundi; The World Bank Atlas 2003-2004;* and *World Development Report 2008.*

World Health Organization (WHO), Avenue Appia 20, 1211 Geneve 27, Switzerland, (Telephone in U.S. (212) 331-9081), www.who.int; *World Health Report 2006.*

BURUNDI - POPULATION DENSITY

African Development Bank Group, Rue Joseph Anoma, 01 BP 1387 Abidjan 01, Cote d'Ivoire, www.afdb.org; *Statistics Pocketbook 2008.*

Central Intelligence Agency, Office of Public Affairs, Washington, DC 20505, (703) 482-0623, Fax: (703) 482-1739, www.cia.gov; *The World Factbook.*

Euromonitor International, Inc., 224 S. Michigan Avenue, Suite 1500, Chicago, IL 60604, (312) 922-1115, Fax: (312) 922-1157, www.euromonitor.com; *International Marketing Data and Statistics 2008* and *The World Economic Factbook 2008.*

Palgrave Macmillan Ltd., Houndmills, Basingstoke, Hampshire, RG21 6XS, England, (Telephone in U.S. (888) 330-8477), (Fax in U.S. (800) 672-2054), www.palgrave.com; *The Statesman's Yearbook 2008.*

Taylor and Francis Group, An Informa Business, 2 Park Square, Milton Park, Abingdon, Oxford OX14 4RN, United Kingdom, (Dial from U.S. (212) 216-7800), (Fax from U.S. (212) 564-7854), www.tandf.co.uk; *The Europa World Year Book.*

United Nations Food and Agricultural Organization (FAO), Viale delle Terme di Caracalla, 00100 Rome, Italy, (Dial from U.S. (202) 653-2400), (Fax from U.S. (202) 653 5760), www.fao.org; *The State of Food and Agriculture (SOFA) 2006.*

United Nations Statistics Division, New York, NY 10017, (800) 253-9646, Fax: (212) 963-4116, http://unstats.un.org; *Statistical Yearbook* and *Survey of Economic and Social Conditions in Africa 2005.*

The World Bank, 1818 H Street, NW, Washington, DC 20433, (202) 473-1000, Fax: (202) 477-6391, www.worldbank.org; *Burundi* and *World Development Report 2008.*

BURUNDI - POSTAL SERVICE

Palgrave Macmillan Ltd., Houndmills, Basingstoke, Hampshire, RG21 6XS, England, (Telephone in U.S. (888) 330-8477), (Fax in U.S. (800) 672-2054), www.palgrave.com; *The Statesman's Yearbook 2008.*

United Nations Statistics Division, New York, NY 10017, (800) 253-9646, Fax: (212) 963-4116, http://unstats.un.org; *Statistical Yearbook.*

BURUNDI - POWER RESOURCES

Euromonitor International, Inc., 224 S. Michigan Avenue, Suite 1500, Chicago, IL 60604, (312) 922-1115, Fax: (312) 922-1157, www.euromonitor.com; *International Marketing Data and Statistics 2008* and *The World Economic Factbook 2008.*

Palgrave Macmillan Ltd., Houndmills, Basingstoke, Hampshire, RG21 6XS, England, (Telephone in U.S. (888) 330-8477), (Fax in U.S. (800) 672-2054), www.palgrave.com; *The Statesman's Yearbook 2008.*

Platts, 2 Penn Plaza, 25th Floor, New York, NY 10121-2298, (212) 904-3070, www.platts.com; *Energy Economist.*

United Nations Economic Commission for Africa (ECA), PO Box 3001, Addis Ababa, Ethiopia, (Telephone in U.S. (212) 963-4957), www.uneca.org; *African Statistical Yearbook 2006.*

United Nations Food and Agricultural Organization (FAO), Viale delle Terme di Caracalla, 00100 Rome, Italy, (Dial from U.S. (202) 653-2400), (Fax from U.S. (202) 653 5760), www.fao.org; *The State of Food and Agriculture (SOFA) 2006.*

United Nations Statistics Division, New York, NY 10017, (800) 253-9646, Fax: (212) 963-4116, http://unstats.un.org; *Energy Statistics Yearbook 2003; Human Development Report 2006; Statistical Yearbook;* and *World Statistics Pocketbook.*

The World Bank, 1818 H Street, NW, Washington, DC 20433, (202) 473-1000, Fax: (202) 477-6391, www.worldbank.org; *The World Bank Atlas 2003-2004* and *World Development Report 2008.*

BURUNDI - PRICES

Euromonitor International, Inc., 224 S. Michigan Avenue, Suite 1500, Chicago, IL 60604, (312) 922-1115, Fax: (312) 922-1157, www.euromonitor.com; *World Marketing Data and Statistics.*

International Labour Office, I.L.O. Publications, 4 route des Morillons, CH-1211 Geneva 22, Switzerland, (Telephone in U.S. (202) 653-7652), (Fax in U.S. (202) 653-7687), www.ilo.org; *Yearbook of Labour Statistics 2006.*

International Monetary Fund (IMF), 700 Nineteenth Street, NW, Washington, DC 20431, (202) 623-7000, Fax: (202) 623-4661, www.imf.org; *International Financial Statistics Yearbook 2007.*

United Nations Economic Commission for Africa (ECA), PO Box 3001, Addis Ababa, Ethiopia, (Telephone in U.S. (212) 963-4957), www.uneca.org; *African Statistical Yearbook 2006.*

United Nations Food and Agricultural Organization (FAO), Viale delle Terme di Caracalla, 00100 Rome, Italy, (Dial from U.S. (202) 653-2400), (Fax from U.S. (202) 653 5760), www.fao.org; *FAO Production Yearbook 2002* and *The State of Food and Agriculture (SOFA) 2006.*

The World Bank, 1818 H Street, NW, Washington, DC 20433, (202) 473-1000, Fax: (202) 477-6391, www.worldbank.org; *Burundi.*

BURUNDI - PUBLIC HEALTH

African Development Bank Group, Rue Joseph Anoma, 01 BP 1387 Abidjan 01, Cote d'Ivoire, www.afdb.org; *Statistics Pocketbook 2008.*

Euromonitor International, Inc., 224 S. Michigan Avenue, Suite 1500, Chicago, IL 60604, (312) 922-1115, Fax: (312) 922-1157, www.euromonitor.com; *World Marketing Data and Statistics.*

Palgrave Macmillan Ltd., Houndmills, Basingstoke, Hampshire, RG21 6XS, England, (Telephone in U.S. (888) 330-8477), (Fax in U.S. (800) 672-2054), www.palgrave.com; *The Statesman's Yearbook 2008.*

UNICEF, 3 United Nations Plaza, New York, NY 10017, (800) 253-9646, Fax: (212) 887-7465, www.unicef.org; *The State of the World's Children 2008.*

United Nations Economic Commission for Africa (ECA), PO Box 3001, Addis Ababa, Ethiopia, (Telephone in U.S. (212) 963-4957), www.uneca.org; *African Statistical Yearbook 2006.*

United Nations Statistics Division, New York, NY 10017, (800) 253-9646, Fax: (212) 963-4116, http://unstats.un.org; *Human Development Report 2006* and *Statistical Yearbook.*

The World Bank, 1818 H Street, NW, Washington, DC 20433, (202) 473-1000, Fax: (202) 477-6391, www.worldbank.org; *Burundi* and *World Development Report 2008.*

World Health Organization (WHO), Avenue Appia 20, 1211 Geneve 27, Switzerland, (Telephone in U.S. (212) 331-9081), www.who.int; The WHO Global Atlas of Infectious Diseases.

BURUNDI - RADIO BROADCASTING

Palgrave Macmillan Ltd., Houndmills, Basingstoke, Hampshire, RG21 6XS, England, (Telephone in U.S. (888) 330-8477), (Fax in U.S. (800) 672-2054), www.palgrave.com; *The Statesman's Yearbook 2008.*

BURUNDI - RAILROADS

United Nations Economic Commission for Africa (ECA), PO Box 3001, Addis Ababa, Ethiopia, (Telephone in U.S. (212) 963-4957), www.uneca.org; *African Statistical Yearbook 2006.*

BURUNDI - RELIGION

Central Intelligence Agency, Office of Public Affairs, Washington, DC 20505, (703) 482-0623, Fax: (703) 482-1739, www.cia.gov; *The World Factbook.*

Palgrave Macmillan Ltd., Houndmills, Basingstoke, Hampshire, RG21 6XS, England, (Telephone in U.S. (888) 330-8477), (Fax in U.S. (800) 672-2054), www.palgrave.com; *The Statesman's Yearbook 2008.*

BURUNDI - RENT CHARGES

International Labour Office, I.L.O. Publications, 4 route des Morillons, CH-1211 Geneva 22, Switzerland, (Telephone in U.S. (202) 653-7652), (Fax in U.S. (202) 653-7687), www.ilo.org; *Yearbook of Labour Statistics 2006.*

BURUNDI - RESERVES (ACCOUNTING)

African Development Bank Group, Rue Joseph Anoma, 01 BP 1387 Abidjan 01, Cote d'Ivoire, www.afdb.org; *Statistics Pocketbook 2008.*

Euromonitor International, Inc., 224 S. Michigan Avenue, Suite 1500, Chicago, IL 60604, (312) 922-1115, Fax: (312) 922-1157, www.euromonitor.com; *International Marketing Data and Statistics 2008.*

United Nations Statistics Division, New York, NY 10017, (800) 253-9646, Fax: (212) 963-4116, http://unstats.un.org; *Statistical Yearbook.*

BURUNDI - RETAIL TRADE

Euromonitor International, Inc., 224 S. Michigan Avenue, Suite 1500, Chicago, IL 60604, (312) 922-1115, Fax: (312) 922-1157, www.euromonitor.com; *World Marketing Data and Statistics.*

BURUNDI - RICE PRODUCTION

See BURUNDI - CROPS

BURUNDI - ROADS

Central Intelligence Agency, Office of Public Affairs, Washington, DC 20505, (703) 482-0623, Fax: (703) 482-1739, www.cia.gov; *The World Factbook.*

Palgrave Macmillan Ltd., Houndmills, Basingstoke, Hampshire, RG21 6XS, England, (Telephone in U.S. (888) 330-8477), (Fax in U.S. (800) 672-2054), www.palgrave.com; *The Statesman's Yearbook 2008.*

United Nations Economic Commission for Africa (ECA), PO Box 3001, Addis Ababa, Ethiopia, (Telephone in U.S. (212) 963-4957), www.uneca.org; *African Statistical Yearbook 2006.*

United Nations Statistics Division, New York, NY 10017, (800) 253-9646, Fax: (212) 963-4116, http://unstats.un.org; *Survey of Economic and Social Conditions in Africa 2005.*

BURUNDI - SHEEP

See BURUNDI - LIVESTOCK

BURUNDI - SHIPPING

Palgrave Macmillan Ltd., Houndmills, Basingstoke, Hampshire, RG21 6XS, England, (Telephone in U.S. (888) 330-8477), (Fax in U.S. (800) 672-2054), www.palgrave.com; *The Statesman's Yearbook 2008.*

United Nations Economic Commission for Africa (ECA), PO Box 3001, Addis Ababa, Ethiopia, (Telephone in U.S. (212) 963-4957), www.uneca.org; *African Statistical Yearbook 2006.*

BURUNDI - SOCIAL ECOLOGY

United Nations Statistics Division, New York, NY 10017, (800) 253-9646, Fax: (212) 963-4116, http://unstats.un.org; *World Statistics Pocketbook.*

BURUNDI - SOCIAL SECURITY

Palgrave Macmillan Ltd., Houndmills, Basingstoke, Hampshire, RG21 6XS, England, (Telephone in U.S. (888) 330-8477), (Fax in U.S. (800) 672-2054), www.palgrave.com; *The Statesman's Yearbook 2008.*

United Nations Statistics Division, New York, NY 10017, (800) 253-9646, Fax: (212) 963-4116, http://unstats.un.org; *National Accounts Statistics: Compendium of Income Distribution Statistics.*

BURUNDI - TAXATION

Taylor and Francis Group, An Informa Business, 2 Park Square, Milton Park, Abingdon, Oxford OX14 4RN, United Kingdom, (Dial from U.S. (212) 216-7800), (Fax from U.S. (212) 564-7854), www.tandf.co.uk; *The Europa World Year Book.*

BURUNDI - TEA PRODUCTION

See BURUNDI - CROPS

BURUNDI - TELEPHONE

International Telecommunication Union (ITU), Place des Nations, 1211 Geneva 20, Switzerland, www.itu.int; World Telecommunication Indicators Database.

Palgrave Macmillan Ltd., Houndmills, Basingstoke, Hampshire, RG21 6XS, England, (Telephone in U.S. (888) 330-8477), (Fax in U.S. (800) 672-2054), www.palgrave.com; *The Statesman's Yearbook 2008.*

Taylor and Francis Group, An Informa Business, 2 Park Square, Milton Park, Abingdon, Oxford OX14 4RN, United Kingdom, (Dial from U.S. (212) 216-7800), (Fax from U.S. (212) 564-7854), www.tandf.co.uk; *The Europa World Year Book.*

United Nations Statistics Division, New York, NY 10017, (800) 253-9646, Fax: (212) 963-4116, http://unstats.un.org; *Statistical Yearbook* and *World Statistics Pocketbook.*

BURUNDI - TEXTILE INDUSTRY

Palgrave Macmillan Ltd., Houndmills, Basingstoke, Hampshire, RG21 6XS, England, (Telephone in U.S. (888) 330-8477), (Fax in U.S. (800) 672-2054), www.palgrave.com; *The Statesman's Yearbook 2008.*

United Nations Conference on Trade and Development (UNCTAD), DC2-1120, United Nations, New York, NY 10017, (212) 963-0027, www.unctad.org; *UNCTAD Commodity Yearbook.*

BURUNDI - THEATER

UNESCO Institute for Statistics, C.P. 6128 Succursale Centre-Ville, Montreal, Quebec, H3C 3J7 Canada, (Dial from U.S. (514) 343-6880), (Fax from U.S. (514) 343 6882), www.uis.unesco.org; *Statistical Tables.*

BURUNDI - TIN PRODUCTION

See BURUNDI - MINERAL INDUSTRIES

BURUNDI - TOBACCO INDUSTRY

Foreign Agricultural Service (FAS), U.S. Department of Agriculture (USDA), 1400 Independence Avenue, SW, Washington, DC 20250, (202) 720-3935, www.fas.usda.gov; *Tobacco: World Markets and Trade.*

United Nations Statistics Division, New York, NY 10017, (800) 253-9646, Fax: (212) 963-4116, http://unstats.un.org; *Statistical Yearbook.*

BURUNDI - TOURISM

Euromonitor International, Inc., 224 S. Michigan Avenue, Suite 1500, Chicago, IL 60604, (312) 922-1115, Fax: (312) 922-1157, www.euromonitor.com; *The World Economic Factbook 2008* and *World Marketing Data and Statistics.*

Palgrave Macmillan Ltd., Houndmills, Basingstoke, Hampshire, RG21 6XS, England, (Telephone in U.S. (888) 330-8477), (Fax in U.S. (800) 672-2054), www.palgrave.com; *The Statesman's Yearbook 2008.*

Taylor and Francis Group, An Informa Business, 2 Park Square, Milton Park, Abingdon, Oxford OX14 4RN, United Kingdom, (Dial from U.S. (212) 216-7800), (Fax from U.S. (212) 564-7854), www.tandf.co.uk; *The Europa World Year Book.*

United Nations Economic Commission for Africa (ECA), PO Box 3001, Addis Ababa, Ethiopia, (Telephone in U.S. (212) 963-4957), www.uneca.org; *African Statistical Yearbook 2006.*

United Nations Statistics Division, New York, NY 10017, (800) 253-9646, Fax: (212) 963-4116, http://unstats.un.org; *Statistical Yearbook.*

United Nations World Tourism Organization (UNWTO), Capitan Haya 42, 28020 Madrid, Spain, www.world-tourism.org; *Yearbook of Tourism Statistics.*

The World Bank, 1818 H Street, NW, Washington, DC 20433, (202) 473-1000, Fax: (202) 477-6391, www.worldbank.org; *Burundi.*

BURUNDI - TRADE

See BURUNDI - INTERNATIONAL TRADE

BURUNDI - TRANSPORTATION

Central Intelligence Agency, Office of Public Affairs, Washington, DC 20505, (703) 482-0623, Fax: (703) 482-1739, www.cia.gov; *The World Factbook.*

Euromonitor International, Inc., 224 S. Michigan Avenue, Suite 1500, Chicago, IL 60604, (312) 922-1115, Fax: (312) 922-1157, www.euromonitor.com; *International Marketing Data and Statistics 2008* and *World Marketing Data and Statistics.*

Palgrave Macmillan Ltd., Houndmills, Basingstoke, Hampshire, RG21 6XS, England, (Telephone in U.S. (888) 330-8477), (Fax in U.S. (800) 672-2054), www.palgrave.com; *The Statesman's Yearbook 2008.*

Taylor and Francis Group, An Informa Business, 2 Park Square, Milton Park, Abingdon, Oxford OX14 4RN, United Kingdom, (Dial from U.S. (212) 216-7800), (Fax from U.S. (212) 564-7854), www.tandf.co.uk; *The Europa World Year Book.*

United Nations Economic Commission for Africa (ECA), PO Box 3001, Addis Ababa, Ethiopia, (Telephone in U.S. (212) 963-4957), www.uneca.org; *African Statistical Yearbook 2006.*

United Nations Statistics Division, New York, NY 10017, (800) 253-9646, Fax: (212) 963-4116, http://unstats.un.org; *Human Development Report 2006.*

The World Bank, 1818 H Street, NW, Washington, DC 20433, (202) 473-1000, Fax: (202) 477-6391, www.worldbank.org; *Burundi.*

BURUNDI - UNEMPLOYMENT

Central Intelligence Agency, Office of Public Affairs, Washington, DC 20505, (703) 482-0623, Fax: (703) 482-1739, www.cia.gov; *The World Factbook.*

Euromonitor International, Inc., 224 S. Michigan Avenue, Suite 1500, Chicago, IL 60604, (312) 922-1115, Fax: (312) 922-1157, www.euromonitor.com; *International Marketing Data and Statistics 2008.*

International Labour Office, I.L.O. Publications, 4 route des Morillons, CH-1211 Geneva 22, Switzerland, (Telephone in U.S. (202) 653-7652), (Fax in U.S. (202) 653-7687), www.ilo.org; *Yearbook of Labour Statistics 2006.*

BURUNDI - VITAL STATISTICS

Euromonitor International, Inc., 224 S. Michigan Avenue, Suite 1500, Chicago, IL 60604, (312) 922-1115, Fax: (312) 922-1157, www.euromonitor.com; *International Marketing Data and Statistics 2008.*

United Nations Statistics Division, New York, NY 10017, (800) 253-9646, Fax: (212) 963-4116, http://unstats.un.org; *Statistical Yearbook.*

World Health Organization (WHO), Avenue Appia 20, 1211 Geneve 27, Switzerland, (Telephone in U.S. (212) 331-9081), www.who.int; *World Health Report 2006.*

BURUNDI - WAGES

International Labour Office, I.L.O. Publications, 4 route des Morillons, CH-1211 Geneva 22, Switzerland, (Telephone in U.S. (202) 653-7652), (Fax in U.S. (202) 653-7687), www.ilo.org; *Yearbook of Labour Statistics 2006.*

United Nations Statistics Division, New York, NY 10017, (800) 253-9646, Fax: (212) 963-4116, http://unstats.un.org; *Statistical Yearbook.*

The World Bank, 1818 H Street, NW, Washington, DC 20433, (202) 473-1000, Fax: (202) 477-6391, www.worldbank.org; *Burundi.*

BURUNDI - WHEAT PRODUCTION

See BURUNDI - CROPS

BUSES AND BUS TRANSPORTATION

See also PASSENGER TRANSIT INDUSTRY

National Center for Statistics and Analysis (NCSA) of the National Highway Traffic Safety Administration, West Building, 1200 New Jersey Avenue, S.E., Washington, DC 20590, (202) 366-1503, Fax: (202) 366-7078, www.nhtsa.gov; *Traffic Safety Fact Sheets, 2006 Data - School Transportation-Related Crashes.*

National Transportation Safety Board (NTSB), 490 L'Enfant Plaza, SW, Washington, DC 20594, (202) 314-6000, www.ntsb.gov; *Transportation Safety Databases.*

U.S. Department of Transportation (DOT), Research and Innovative Technology Administration (RITA), Bureau of Transportation Statistics (BTS), 1200 New Jersey Avenue, SE, Washington, DC 20590, (800) 853-1351, www.bts.gov; *TranStats.*

BUSES AND BUS TRANSPORTATION - FINANCES

American Bus Association (ABA), 700 13th Street, NW, Suite 575, Washington, DC 20005-5923, (202) 842-1645, Fax: (202) 842-0850, www.buses.org; unpublished data.

U.S. Department of Transportation (DOT), Research and Innovative Technology Administration (RITA), Bureau of Transportation Statistics (BTS), 1200 New Jersey Avenue, SE, Washington, DC 20590, (800) 853-1351, www.bts.gov; *Motor Carrier Financial and Operating Information Program.*

BUSES AND BUS TRANSPORTATION - FOREIGN COUNTRIES

U.S. Department of Transportation (DOT), Federal Highway Administration (FHA), 1200 New Jersey Avenue, SE, Washington, DC 20590, (202) 366-0660, www.fhwa.dot.gov; *Highway Statistics 2006.*

BUSES AND BUS TRANSPORTATION - PASSENGER TRAFFIC AND OUTLAYS

American Bus Association (ABA), 700 13th Street, NW, Suite 575, Washington, DC 20005-5923, (202) 842-1645, Fax: (202) 842-0850, www.buses.org; unpublished data.

Eno Transportation Foundation, 1634 I Street, NW, Suite 500, Washington, DC 20006, (202) 879-4700, Fax: (202) 879-4719, www.enotrans.com; *Transportation in America.*

BUSINESS ENTERPRISE

Banque de France, 48 rue Croix des Petits champs, 75001 Paris, France, www.banque-france.fr/home.htm; *Monthly Business Survey Overview.*

Bernan Essential Government Publications, 4611-F Assembly Drive, Lanham MD, 20706-4391, (301) 459-2255, Fax: (800) 865-3450, www.bernan.com; *Business Statistics of the United States: Patterns of Economic Change* .

The Brookings Institution, 1775 Massachusetts Avenue, NW, Washington, DC 20036, (202) 797-6000, Fax: (202) 797-6004, www.brook.edu; *Downtown Detroit In Focus: A Profile of Market Opportunity; The Economic Potential of American Cities;* and *Finding Exurbia: America's Fast-Growing Communities at the Metropolitan Fringe.*

Dun and Bradstreet (DB) Corporation, 103 JFK Parkway, Short Hills, NJ 07078, (973) 921-5500, www.dnb.com; *The Industry Report.*

Economic and Policy Analysis Research Center (EPARC), University of Missouri-Columbia, 10 Professional Building, Columbia, MO 65211, (573) 882-4805, Fax: (573) 882-5563, http://econ.missouri.edu/eparc; *Effect of Wal-Mart Stores on Economic Environment of Rural Communities.*

Economist Intelligence Unit, 111 West 57th Street, New York, NY 10019, (212) 554-0600, Fax: (212) 586-1181, www.eiu.com; *Business Eastern Europe.*

Edison Electric Institute (EEI), 701 Pennsylvania Avenue, NW, Washington, DC 20004-2696, (202) 508-5000, www.eei.org; *Profiles and Rankings Data Tables - May 2007.*

Environmental Business International, Inc., 4452 Park Boulevard, Suite 306, San Diego, CA 92116, (619) 295-7685, Fax: (619) 295-5743, www.ebiusa.com; *Environmental Business Journal (EBJ) 2006; Environmental Market Reports;* and *U.S. and Global Environmental Market Data.*

Forbes, Inc., 60 Fifth Avenue, New York, NY 10011, (212) 366-8900, www.forbes.com; *America's Best Big Companies* and *The 200 Best Small Companies.*

National Technical Information Service (NTIS), U.S. Department of Commerce (DOC), 5285 Port Royal Road, Springfield, VA 22161, (703) 605-6000, www.ntis.gov; unpublished data.

Thomson Financial, 195 Broadway, New York, NY 10007, (646) 822-2000, www.thomson.com; *Acquisitions Monthly.*

U.S. Census Bureau, 4700 Silver Hill Road, Washington DC 20233-0001, (301) 763-3030, www.census.gov; *2002 Economic Census, Nonemployer Statistics.*

U.S. Census Bureau, Center for Economic Studies, 4600 Silver Hill Road, Washington DC 20233, (301) 457-1235, www.ces.census.gov; *The Dynamics of Plant-Level Productivity in U.S. Manufacturing* and *2002 Economic Census, Geographic Area Series.*

U.S. Census Bureau, Company Statistics Division, 4700 Silver Hill Road, Washington DC 20233-0001, (301) 763-3030, www.census.gov/csd/; *County Business Patterns 2004* and *Information and Communication Technology (ICT) Survey.*

U.S. Department of Commerce (DOC), Economics and Statistics Administration (ESA), 1401 Constitution Avenue, NW, Washington, DC 20230, (800) 782-8872, www.esa.doc.gov; *Main Street in the Digital Age: How Small and Medium-sized Businesses Are Using the Tools of the New Economy.*

BUSINESS ENTERPRISE - AMERICAN INDIAN AND ALAKSA NATIVE OWNED BUSINESS

U.S. Census Bureau, Company Statistics Division, 4700 Silver Hill Road, Washington DC 20233-0001, (301) 763-3030, www.census.gov/csd/; *2002 Survey of Business Owners (SBO)* and *Survey of Minority-Owned Business Enterprises.*

BUSINESS ENTERPRISE - ASIAN AND PACIFIC ISLANDER POPULATION

U.S. Census Bureau, Company Statistics Division, 4700 Silver Hill Road, Washington DC 20233-0001, (301) 763-3030, www.census.gov/csd/; *Survey of Minority-Owned Business Enterprises.*

BUSINESS ENTERPRISE - BANKRUPTCIES FILED

Office of Public Affairs, Administrative Office of the United States Courts, Washington, DC 20544, (202) 502-2600, www.uscourts.gov; *Statistical Tables for the Federal Judiciary* and unpublished data.

BUSINESS ENTERPRISE - BLACK-OWNED BUSINESS

U.S. Census Bureau, Company Statistics Division, 4700 Silver Hill Road, Washington DC 20233-0001, (301) 763-3030, www.census.gov/csd/; *2002 Survey of Business Owners (SBO)* and *Survey of Minority-Owned Business Enterprises.*

BUSINESS ENTERPRISE - CAPITAL, FIXED BY INDUSTRY

Bureau of Economic Analysis (BEA), U.S. Department of Commerce (DOC), 1441 L Street NW, Washington, DC 20230, (202) 606-9900, www.bea.gov; *Survey of Current Business (SCB).*

BUSINESS ENTERPRISE - CORPORATIONS - PHILANTHROPY

The Giving Institute, 4700 W. Lake Ave, Glenview, IL 60025, (800) 462-2372, Fax: (866) 607-0913, www.aafrc.org; *Giving USA 2006.*

BUSINESS ENTERPRISE - CORPORATIONS - PROFITS AND SALES

Standard and Poor's Corporation, 55 Water Street, New York, NY 10041, (212) 438-1000, www.standardandpoors.com; *Compustat Global; Compustat North America;* and *Market Insight.*

U.S. Department of the Treasury (DOT), Internal Revenue Service (IRS), Statistics of Income Division (SIS), PO Box 2608, Washington, DC, 20013-2608, (202) 874-0410, Fax: (202) 874-0964, www.irs.ustreas.gov; *Statistics of Income Bulletin.*

BUSINESS ENTERPRISE - CORPORATIONS, PARTNERSHIPS, AND PROPRIETORSHIPS

U.S. Department of the Treasury (DOT), Internal Revenue Service (IRS), Statistics of Income Division (SIS), PO Box 2608, Washington, DC, 20013-2608, (202) 874-0410, Fax: (202) 874-0964, www.irs.ustreas.gov; *Statistics of Income Bulletin;* unpublished data; and various fact sheets.

BUSINESS ENTERPRISE - CYCLES

National Bureau of Economic Research, Inc. (NBER), 1050 Massachusetts Avenue, Cambridge, MA 02138-5398, (617) 868-3900, Fax: (617) 868-2742, www.nber.org; *Business Cycle Expansions and Contractions.*

BUSINESS ENTERPRISE - DIVESTITURES

Thomson Financial, 195 Broadway, New York, NY 10007, (646) 822-2000, www.thomson.com; Thomson Research.

BUSINESS ENTERPRISE - ECONOMIC INDICATORS

The Brookings Institution, 1775 Massachusetts Avenue, NW, Washington, DC 20036, (202) 797-6000, Fax: (202) 797-6004, www.brook.edu; *The Economic Potential of American Cities* and *Finding Exurbia: America's Fast-Growing Communities at the Metropolitan Fringe.*

The Conference Board, 845 Third Avenue, New York, NY 10022-6679, (212) 759-0900, Fax: (212) 980-7014, www.conference-board.org; *Business Cycle Indicators.*

Dun and Bradstreet (DB) Corporation, 103 JFK Parkway, Short Hills, NJ 07078, (973) 921-5500, www.dnb.com; *The Industry Report.*

Economic and Business Research, Eller College of Management, The University of Arizona, PO Box 210108, Tucson, AZ 85721-0108, (520) 621-2155, Fax: (520) 621-2150, http://ebr.eller.arizona.edu/; *Outlook 2007/2008.*

RAND Corporation, 1776 Main Street, PO Box 2138, Santa Monica, CA 90407-2138, (310) 393-0411, www.rand.org; *High-Technology Manufacturing and U.S. Competitiveness.*

Standard and Poor's Corporation, 55 Water Street, New York, NY 10041, (212) 438-1000, www.standardandpoors.com; *Compustat Global; Compustat North America;* and *Market Insight.*

Thomson Financial, 195 Broadway, New York, NY 10007, (646) 822-2000, www.thomson.com; *Acquisitions Monthly.*

Tourism Intelligence International, An der Wolfskuhle 48, 33619 Bielefeld, Germany, www.tourism-intelligence.com; *Successful Hotel Resorts - Lessons from the Leaders; Tourism Industry Intelligence;* and *Tourism, Technology and Competitive Strategies.*

U.S. Census Bureau, Center for Economic Studies, 4600 Silver Hill Road, Washington DC 20233, (301) 457-1235, www.ces.census.gov; *The Dynamics of Plant-Level Productivity in U.S. Manufacturing; 2002 Economic Census, Finance and Insurance; 2002 Economic Census, Management of Company and Enterprises; The Impact of Hurricanes Katrina, Rita and Wilma on Business Establishments: A GIS Approach;* and *Volatility and Dispersion in Business Growth Rates: Publicly Traded Versus Privately Held Firms.*

U.S. Department of Commerce (DOC), Economics and Statistics Administration (ESA), 1401 Constitution Avenue, NW, Washington, DC 20230, (800) 782-8872, www.esa.doc.gov; *Main Street in the Digital Age: How Small and Medium-sized Businesses Are Using the Tools of the New Economy.*

BUSINESS ENTERPRISE - EMPLOYEES

Bureau of Economic Analysis (BEA), U.S. Department of Commerce (DOC), 1441 L Street NW, Washington, DC 20230, (202) 606-9900, www.bea.gov; *Survey of Current Business (SCB).*

U.S. Bureau of Labor Statistics (BLS), Postal Square Building, 2 Massachusetts Avenue, NE, Washington, DC 20212-0001, (202) 691-5200, Fax: (202) 691-6325, www.bls.gov; *Employee Benefits in Medium and Large Private Establishments; Employee Benefits in Small Private Industry Establishments;* and *Employer Costs for Employee Compensation.*

U.S. Census Bureau, Company Statistics Division, 4700 Silver Hill Road, Washington DC 20233-0001, (301) 763-3030, www.census.gov/csd/; *County Business Patterns 2004* and *Statistics of U.S. Businesses (SUSB).*

BUSINESS ENTERPRISE - EXPENDITURES

U.S. Bureau of Labor Statistics (BLS), Postal Square Building, 2 Massachusetts Avenue, NE, Washington, DC 20212-0001, (202) 691-5200, Fax: (202) 691-6325, www.bls.gov; *Employee Benefits in Medium and Large Private Establishments* and *Employer Costs for Employee Compensation.*

U.S. Census Bureau, Company Statistics Division, 4700 Silver Hill Road, Washington DC 20233-0001, (301) 763-3030, www.census.gov/csd/; *Annual Capital Expenditures Survey (ACES); 2002 Business Expenses Survey (BES);* and *Statistics of U.S. Businesses (SUSB).*

BUSINESS ENTERPRISE - EXPENDITURES - RESEARCH AND DEVELOPMENT

National Science Foundation, Division of Science Resources Statistics (SRS), 4201 Wilson Boulevard, Arlington, VA 22230, (703) 292-8780, Fax: (703) 292-9092, www.nsf.gov; *National Patterns of Research and Development Resources: 2006 Data Update.*

BUSINESS ENTERPRISE - FAILURES AND STARTS

Small Business Administration (SBA), 409 3rd Street, SW, Washington, DC 20024-3212, (202) 205-6533, Fax: (202) 206-6928, www.sba.gov; *Small Business Economic Indicators.*

BUSINESS ENTERPRISE - FINANCES

Association of American Railroads (AAR), 50 F Street, NW, Washington, DC 20001-1564, (202) 639-2100, www.aar.org; *Railroad Revenues, Expenses and Income.*

Board of Governors of the Federal Reserve System, Constitution Avenue, NW, Washington, DC 20551, (202) 452-3000, www.federalreserve.gov; *Flow of Funds Accounts of the United States.*

Bureau of Economic Analysis (BEA), U.S. Department of Commerce (DOC), 1441 L Street NW, Washington, DC 20230, (202) 606-9900, www.bea.gov; *2007 Annual Revision of the National Income and Product Accounts (NIPA)* and *Survey of Current Business (SCB).*

Dun and Bradstreet (DB) Corporation, 103 JFK Parkway, Short Hills, NJ 07078, (973) 921-5500, www.dnb.com; *The Industry Report.*

Economic and Policy Analysis Research Center (EPARC), University of Missouri-Columbia, 10 Professional Building, Columbia, MO 65211, (573) 882-4805, Fax: (573) 882-5563, http://econ.missouri.edu/eparc; *Certified Capital Companies and State Economic Development.*

Standard and Poor's Corporation, 55 Water Street, New York, NY 10041, (212) 438-1000, www.standardandpoors.com; *Compustat Global; Compustat North America;* and *Market Insight.*

U.S. Bureau of Labor Statistics (BLS), Postal Square Building, 2 Massachusetts Avenue, NE, Washington, DC 20212-0001, (202) 691-5200, Fax: (202) 691-6325, www.bls.gov; *Employee Benefits in Medium and Large Private Establishments* and *Employer Costs for Employee Compensation.*

U.S. Census Bureau, Center for Economic Studies, 4600 Silver Hill Road, Washington DC 20233, (301) 457-1235, www.ces.census.gov; *2002 Economic Census, Finance and Insurance; The Impact of Hurricanes Katrina, Rita and Wilma on Business Establishments: A GIS Approach;* and *Volatility and Dispersion in Business Growth Rates: Publicly Traded Versus Privately Held Firms.*

U.S. Census Bureau, Company Statistics Division, 4700 Silver Hill Road, Washington DC 20233-0001, (301) 763-3030, www.census.gov/csd/; *Annual Capital Expenditures Survey (ACES); Quarterly Financial Report (QFR), U.S. Manufacturing, Mining, and Trade Corporations;* and *Statistics of U.S. Businesses (SUSB).*

U.S. Census Bureau, Manufacturing and Construction Division, 4600 Silver Hill Road, Washington DC 20233, (301) 763-4673, www.census.gov/mcd; *Quarterly Financial Report for Manufacturing, Mining and Trade Corporations.*

U.S. Department of Commerce (DOC), Economics and Statistics Administration (ESA), 1401 Constitution Avenue, NW, Washington, DC 20230, (800) 782-8872, www.esa.doc.gov; *Main Street in the Digital Age: How Small and Medium-sized Businesses Are Using the Tools of the New Economy.*

U.S. Department of the Treasury (DOT), Internal Revenue Service (IRS), Statistics of Income Division (SIS), PO Box 2608, Washington, DC, 20013-2608, (202) 874-0410, Fax: (202) 874-0964, www.irs.ustreas.gov; *Statistics of Income Bulletin* and *Statistics of Income Bulletin, Partnership Returns.*

BUSINESS ENTERPRISE - FLOW OF FUNDS

Board of Governors of the Federal Reserve System, Constitution Avenue, NW, Washington, DC 20551, (202) 452-3000, www.federalreserve.gov; *Flow of Funds Accounts of the United States.*

U.S. Census Bureau, Center for Economic Studies, 4600 Silver Hill Road, Washington DC 20233, (301) 457-1235, www.ces.census.gov; *Cementing Relationships: Vertical Integration, Foreclosure, Productivity, and Prices* and *Volatility and Dispersion in Business Growth Rates: Publicly Traded Versus Privately Held Firms.*

U.S. Census Bureau, Company Statistics Division, 4700 Silver Hill Road, Washington DC 20233-0001, (301) 763-3030, www.census.gov/csd/; *Annual Capital Expenditures Survey (ACES)* and *Statistics of U.S. Businesses (SUSB).*

BUSINESS ENTERPRISE - FOREIGN INVESTMENT IN THE UNITED STATES

Bureau of Economic Analysis (BEA), U.S. Department of Commerce (DOC), 1441 L Street NW, Washington, DC 20230, (202) 606-9900, www.bea.gov; *Foreign Direct Investment in the United States (FDIUS); Survey of Current Business (SCB);* and *U.S. Direct Investment Abroad (USDIA).*

BUSINESS ENTERPRISE - HISPANIC-OWNED BUSINESSES

U.S. Census Bureau, Company Statistics Division, 4700 Silver Hill Road, Washington DC 20233-0001, (301) 763-3030, www.census.gov/csd/; *2002 Survey of Business Owners (SBO)* and *Survey of Minority-Owned Business Enterprises.*

BUSINESS ENTERPRISE - LEADING INDICATORS

The Conference Board, 845 Third Avenue, New York, NY 10022-6679, (212) 759-0900, Fax: (212) 980-7014, www.conference-board.org; *Business Cycle Indicators.*

Standard and Poor's Corporation, 55 Water Street, New York, NY 10041, (212) 438-1000, www.standardandpoors.com; *Compustat Global; Compustat North America;* and *Market Insight.*

Tourism Intelligence International, An der Wolfskuhle 48, 33619 Bielefeld, Germany, www.tourism-intelligence.com; *Tourism Industry Intelligence* and *Tourism, Technology and Competitive Strategies.*

BUSINESS ENTERPRISE - LEVERAGED BUY-OUTS

Thomson Financial, 195 Broadway, New York, NY 10007, (646) 822-2000, www.thomson.com; Thomson Research.

BUSINESS ENTERPRISE - LOANS TO MINORITY-OPERATED SMALL BUSINESSES

Small Business Administration (SBA), 409 3rd Street, SW, Washington, DC 20024-3212, (202) 205-6533, Fax: (202) 206-6928, www.sba.gov; *The Small Business Economy: A Report to the President 2007* and unpublished data.

BUSINESS ENTERPRISE - MERGERS AND ACQUISITIONS

Thomson Financial, 195 Broadway, New York, NY 10007, (646) 822-2000, www.thomson.com; *Acquisitions Monthly* and Thomson Research.

BUSINESS ENTERPRISE - MINORITY-OWNED BUSINESSES

U.S. Census Bureau, 4700 Silver Hill Road, Washington DC 20233-0001, (301) 763-3030, www.census.gov; *State and County QuickFacts.*

BUSINESS ENTERPRISE - MULTINATIONAL COMPANIES

Bureau of Economic Analysis (BEA), U.S. Department of Commerce (DOC), 1441 L Street NW, Washington, DC 20230, (202) 606-9900, www.bea.gov; *Survey of Current Business (SCB).*

BUSINESS ENTERPRISE - PATENTS

U.S. Patent and Trademark Office (USPTO), PO Box 1450, Alexandria, VA 22313-1450, (571) 272-1000, www.uspto.gov; *2007 Performance and Accountability Report; Patenting Trends Calendar Year 2003;* and *Trilateral Statistics Report.*

BUSINESS ENTERPRISE - PAYROLL

U.S. Census Bureau, Company Statistics Division, 4700 Silver Hill Road, Washington DC 20233-0001, (301) 763-3030, www.census.gov/csd/; *County Business Patterns 2004* and *Statistics of U.S. Businesses (SUSB).*

BUSINESS ENTERPRISE - PROFITS

Bureau of Economic Analysis (BEA), U.S. Department of Commerce (DOC), 1441 L Street NW, Washington, DC 20230, (202) 606-9900, www.bea.gov; *2007 Annual Revision of the National Income and Product Accounts (NIPA)* and *Survey of Current Business (SCB).*

Tourism Intelligence International, An der Wolfskuhle 48, 33619 Bielefeld, Germany, www.tourism-intelligence.com; *Successful Hotel Resorts - Lessons from the Leaders* and *Tourism Industry Intelligence.*

U.S. Census Bureau, Manufacturing and Construction Division, 4600 Silver Hill Road, Washington DC 20233, (301) 763-4673, www.census.gov/mcd; *Quarterly Financial Report for Manufacturing, Mining and Trade Corporations.*

BUSINESS ENTERPRISE - SALES, SHIPMENTS AND RECEIPTS

RAND Corporation, 1776 Main Street, PO Box 2138, Santa Monica, CA 90407-2138, (310) 393-0411, www.rand.org; *High-Technology Manufacturing and U.S. Competitiveness.*

Standard and Poor's Corporation, 55 Water Street, New York, NY 10041, (212) 438-1000, www.standardandpoors.com; *Compustat Global; Compustat North America;* and *Market Insight.*

U.S. Census Bureau, 4700 Silver Hill Road, Washington DC 20233-0001, (301) 763-3030, www.census.gov; *State and County QuickFacts.*

U.S. Census Bureau, Center for Economic Studies, 4600 Silver Hill Road, Washington DC 20233, (301) 457-1235, www.ces.census.gov; *Cementing Relationships: Vertical Integration, Foreclosure, Productivity, and Prices* and *Volatility and Dispersion in Business Growth Rates: Publicly Traded Versus Privately Held Firms.*

U.S. Census Bureau, Manufacturing and Construction Division, 4600 Silver Hill Road, Washington DC 20233, (301) 763-4673, www.census.gov/mcd; *Quarterly Financial Report for Manufacturing, Mining and Trade Corporations.*

BUSINESS ENTERPRISE - SMALL BUSINESS

Dun and Bradstreet (DB) Corporation, 103 JFK Parkway, Short Hills, NJ 07078, (973) 921-5500, www.dnb.com; *The Industry Report.*

Forbes, Inc., 60 Fifth Avenue, New York, NY 10011, (212) 366-8900, www.forbes.com; *The 200 Best Small Companies.*

Small Business Administration (SBA), 409 3rd Street, SW, Washington, DC 20024-3212, (202) 205-6533, Fax: (202) 206-6928, www.sba.gov; *Self-Employed Business Ownership Rates in the United States: 1979-2003; The Small Business Economy: A Report to the President 2007;* and unpublished data.

U.S. Department of Commerce (DOC), Economics and Statistics Administration (ESA), 1401 Constitution Avenue, NW, Washington, DC 20230, (800) 782-8872, www.esa.doc.gov; *Main Street in the Digital Age: How Small and Medium-sized Businesses Are Using the Tools of the New Economy.*

BUSINESS ENTERPRISE - VENTURE CAPITAL

Thomson Financial, 195 Broadway, New York, NY 10007, (646) 822-2000, www.thomson.com; *Venture Capital Journal.*

U.S. Census Bureau, Company Statistics Division, 4700 Silver Hill Road, Washington DC 20233-0001, (301) 763-3030, www.census.gov/csd/; *Annual Capital Expenditures Survey (ACES).*

BUSINESS ENTERPRISE - WOMEN-OWNED BUSINESSES

U.S. Census Bureau, 4700 Silver Hill Road, Washington DC 20233-0001, (301) 763-3030, www.census.gov; *State and County QuickFacts.*

U.S. Census Bureau, Company Statistics Division, 4700 Silver Hill Road, Washington DC 20233-0001, (301) 763-3030, www.census.gov/csd/; *2002 Survey of Business Owners (SBO)* and *Survey of Minority-Owned Business Enterprises.*

BUSINESS MANAGEMENT

U.S. Census Bureau, Center for Economic Studies, 4600 Silver Hill Road, Washington DC 20233, (301) 457-1235, www.ces.census.gov; *2002 Economic Census, Management of Company and Enterprises.*

BUSINESS MANAGEMENT - DEGREES CONFERRED

National Center for Education Statistics (NCES), 1990 K Street, NW, Washington, DC 20006, (202) 502-7300, http://nces.ed.gov; *Digest of Education Statistics 2007.*

BUSINESS MANAGEMENT - DEGREES CONFERRED - SALARY OFFERS

National Association of Colleges and Employers (NACE), 62 Highland Avenue, Bethlehem, PA 18017, (800) 544-5272, Fax: (610) 868-0208, www.naceweb.org; *Salary Survey.*

BUSINESS SERVICES - CAPITAL

Bureau of Economic Analysis (BEA), U.S. Department of Commerce (DOC), 1441 L Street NW, Washington, DC 20230, (202) 606-9900, www.bea.gov; *Survey of Current Business (SCB).*

Economic and Policy Analysis Research Center (EPARC), University of Missouri-Columbia, 10 Professional Building, Columbia, MO 65211, (573) 882-4805, Fax: (573) 882-5563, http://econ.missouri.edu/eparc; *Certified Capital Companies and State Economic Development.*

BUSINESS SERVICES - EARNINGS

U.S. Bureau of Labor Statistics (BLS), Postal Square Building, 2 Massachusetts Avenue, NE, Washington, DC 20212-0001, (202) 691-5200, Fax: (202) 691-6325, www.bls.gov; *Current Employment Statistics Survey (CES)* and *Employment and Earnings (EE).*

BUSINESS SERVICES - EMPLOYEES

U.S. Bureau of Labor Statistics (BLS), Postal Square Building, 2 Massachusetts Avenue, NE, Washington, DC 20212-0001, (202) 691-5200, Fax: (202) 691-6325, www.bls.gov; *Current Employment Statistics Survey (CES); Employment and Earnings (EE); Monthly Labor Review (MLR);* and unpublished data.

BUSINESS SERVICES - GROSS DOMESTIC PRODUCT

Bureau of Economic Analysis (BEA), U.S. Department of Commerce (DOC), 1441 L Street NW, Washington, DC 20230, (202) 606-9900, www.bea.gov; *Survey of Current Business (SCB).*

Fiber Economics Bureau (FEB), 1530 Wilson Boulevard, Suite 690, Arlington VA 22209, (703) 875-0676, Fax: (703) 875-0675, www.fibereconomics.com; *Manufactured Fiber Handbook.*

BUSINESS SERVICES - INDUSTRIAL SAFETY

U.S. Bureau of Labor Statistics (BLS), Postal Square Building, 2 Massachusetts Avenue, NE, Washington, DC 20212-0001, (202) 691-5200, Fax: (202) 691-6325, www.bls.gov; *Injuries, Illnesses, and Fatalities (IIF).*

BUSINESS SERVICES - MERGERS AND ACQUISITIONS

Thomson Financial, 195 Broadway, New York, NY 10007, (646) 822-2000, www.thomson.com; *Acquisitions Monthly* and Thomson Research.

BUSINESS SERVICES - MULTINATIONAL COMPANIES

Bureau of Economic Analysis (BEA), U.S. Department of Commerce (DOC), 1441 L Street NW, Washington, DC 20230, (202) 606-9900, www.bea.gov; *Survey of Current Business (SCB).*

BUSINESS SERVICES - RECEIPTS

U.S. Census Bureau, 4700 Silver Hill Road, Washington DC 20233-0001, (301) 763-3030, www.census.gov; unpublished data.

U.S. Census Bureau, Center for Economic Studies, 4600 Silver Hill Road, Washington DC 20233, (301) 457-1235, www.ces.census.gov; *2002 Economic Census, Professional, Scientific and Technical Services.*

U.S. Census Bureau, Company Statistics Division, 4700 Silver Hill Road, Washington DC 20233-0001, (301) 763-3030, www.census.gov/csd/; *County Business Patterns 2004* and *Current Business Reports.*

BUTTER

Economic Research Service (ERS), U.S. Department of Agriculture (USDA), 1800 M Street, NW, Washington, DC 20036-5831, (202) 694-5050, Fax: (202) 694-5689, www.ers.usda.gov; *Agricultural Outlook* and *Food CPI, Prices, and Expenditures.*

National Agricultural Statistics Service (NASS), U.S. Department of Agriculture (USDA), 1400 Independence Avenue, SW, Washington, DC 20250, (800) 727-9540, Fax: (202) 690-2090, www.nass.usda.gov; *Dairy Products* and *Milk Cows and Milk Production.*

BUTTERFISH

National Marine Fisheries Service (NMFS), National Oceanic and Atmospheric Administration (NOAA), Office of Constituent Services, 1315 East West Highway, 9th Floor, Silver Spring, MD 20910, (301) 713-2379, Fax: (301) 713-2385, www.nmfs.noaa.gov; *Fisheries of the United States - 2006.* STATISTICS SOURCES, Thirty-second Edition - 2009STATISTICS SOURCES, Thirty-second Edition - 2009

CABBAGE

Economic Research Service (ERS), U.S. Department of Agriculture (USDA), 1800 M Street, NW, Washington, DC 20036-5831, (202) 694-5050, Fax: (202) 694-5689, www.ers.usda.gov; *Agricultural Statistics.*

National Agricultural Statistics Service (NASS), U.S. Department of Agriculture (USDA), 1400 Independence Avenue, SW, Washington, DC 20250, (800) 727-9540, Fax: (202) 690-2090, www.nass.usda.gov; *Vegetables: 2004 Annual Summary.*

CABLE TELEVISION

See SUBSCRIPTION TELEVISION

CADMIUM

U.S. Department of the Interior (DOI), U.S. Geological Survey (USGS), Office of Minerals Information, 12201 Sunrise Valley Drive, Reston, VA 20192, Mr. Kenneth A. Beckman, (703) 648-4916, Fax: (703) 648-4995, http://minerals.usgs.gov/minerals; *Mineral Commodity Summaries* and *Minerals Yearbook.*

CAFETERIAS

See FOOD SERVICE AND DRINKING PLACES

CALCIUM - DIETARY

Center for Nutrition Policy and Promotion (CNPP), U.S. Department of Agriculture (USDA), 3101 Park Center Drive, 10th Floor, Alexandria, VA 22302-1594, (703) 305-7600, Fax: (703) 305-3300, www.usda.gov/cnpp; *Nutrient Content of the U.S. Food Supply Summary Report 2005.*

Economic Research Service (ERS), U.S. Department of Agriculture (USDA), 1800 M Street, NW, Washington, DC 20036-5831, (202) 694-5050, Fax: (202) 694-5689, www.ers.usda.gov; *Food CPI, Prices, and Expenditures.*

CALCIUM CHLORIDE

U.S. Department of the Interior (DOI), U.S. Geological Survey (USGS), Office of Minerals Information, 12201 Sunrise Valley Drive, Reston, VA 20192, Mr. Kenneth A. Beckman, (703) 648-4916, Fax: (703) 648-4995, http://minerals.usgs.gov/minerals; *Mineral Commodity Summaries* and *Minerals Yearbook.*

CALIFORNIA

See also - STATE DATA (FOR INDIVIDUAL STATES)

The Annie E. Casey Foundation, 701 Saint Paul Street, Baltimore, MD 21202, (410) 547-6600, Fax: (410) 547-3610, www.aecf.org; *Of, By, And For the Community: The Story of PUENTE Learning Center.*

National Center for Children in Poverty (NCCP), 215 W. 125th Street, 3rd Floor, New York, NY 10027, (646) 284-9600, Fax: (646) 284-9623, www.nccp.org; *The Changing Face of Child Poverty in California.*

Public/Private Ventures (P/PV), 2000 Market Street, Suite 600, Philadelphia, PA 19103, (215) 557-4400, Fax: (215) 557 4469, www.ppv.org; *After-School Pursuits: An Examination of Outcomes in the San Francisco Beacon Initiative; Beacons In Brief; Launching Literacy in After-School Programs: Early Lessons from the CORAL Initiative; A Portrait of Preteens in Santa Clara and San Mateo Counties: What We Know About 9- to 13-Year Olds;* and *Promoting Emotional and Behavioral Health in Preteens: Benchmarks of Success and Challenges Among Programs in Santa Clara and San Mateo Counties.*

RAND Corporation, 1776 Main Street, PO Box 2138, Santa Monica, CA 90407-2138, (310) 393-0411, www.rand.org; *Hospital Competition, Managed Care, and Mortality After Hospitalization for Medical Conditions in California* and RAND California: An Online Source for California and U.S. Statistics.

CALIFORNIA - STATE DATA CENTERS

Association of Bay Area Governments (ABAG), 101 Eighth Street, Oakland CA 94607, (510) 464-7900, Fax: (510) 433-5557, www.abag.ca.gov; State Data Center.

Demographic Research Unit of the California Department of Finance, 915 L Street, Sacramento, CA 95814, (916) 445-3878, www.dof.ca.gov/html/Demograp/druhpar.htm; State Data Center.

Sacramento Area Council of Governments (SACOG), 1415 L Street, Suite 300, Sacramento, CA 95814, (916) 321-9000, Fax: (916) 321-9551, www.sacog.org; State Data Center.

San Diego Association of Governments (SANDAG), 401 B Street, Suite 800, San Diego, CA 92101, Ms. Kristen Rohanna, (619) 699-6918, Fax: (619) 699-1905, www.sandag.cog.ca.us; State Data Center.

Southern California Association of Governments (SCAG), 818 West 7th Street, 12th Floor (Main Office), Los Angeles, CA 90017, Mr. Javier Minjares, Information Services, (213) 236-1893, Fax: (213) 236-1825, www.scag.ca.gov; State Data Center.

UC DATA, Survey Research Center, 2538 Channing Way #5100, Berkeley, CA 94720-5100, (510) 642-6571, Fax: (510) 643-8292, http://ucdata.berkeley.edu; State Data Center.

CALIFORNIA - PRIMARY STATISTICS SOURCES

California Department of Finance, 915 L Street, Sacramento, CA 95814, (916) 445-3878, www.dof.ca.gov; *California Statistical Abstract 2004.*

RAND Corporation, 1776 Main Street, PO Box 2138, Santa Monica, CA 90407-2138, (310) 393-0411, www.rand.org; RAND California: An Online Source for California and U.S. Statistics.

CALISTHENICS

National Sporting Goods Association (NSGA), 1601 Feehanville Drive, Suite 300, Mount Prospect, IL 60056, (847) 296-6742, Fax: (847) 391-9827, www.nsga.org; *2006 Sports Participation.*

CALVES

Economic Research Service (ERS), U.S. Department of Agriculture (USDA), 1800 M Street, NW, Washington, DC 20036-5831, (202) 694-5050, Fax: (202) 694-5689, www.ers.usda.gov; *Food CPI, Prices, and Expenditures.*

National Agricultural Statistics Service (NASS), U.S. Department of Agriculture (USDA), 1400 Independence Avenue, SW, Washington, DC 20250, (800) 727-9540, Fax: (202) 690-2090, www.nass.usda.gov; *Cattle: Final Estimates, 1999-2003; Livestock Slaughter;* and *Meat Animals Production, Disposition, and Income.*

CAMBODIA - NATIONAL STATISTICAL OFFICE

National Institute of Statistics (NIS), Ministry of Planning, Preah Monivong Boulevard, Sankat Boeung Keng Kang 1, Phnom Penh, Cambodia, www.nis.gov.kh; National Data Center.

CAMBODIA - PRIMARY STATISTICS SOURCES

National Institute of Statistics (NIS), Ministry of Planning, Preah Monivong Boulevard, Sankat Boeung Keng Kang 1, Phnom Penh, Cambodia, www.nis.gov.kh; *Cambodia Inter-Censal Population Survey 2004* and *General Population Census of Cambodia 1998.*

CAMBODIA - DATABASES

National Institute of Statistics (NIS), Ministry of Planning, Preah Monivong Boulevard, Sankat Boeung Keng Kang 1, Phnom Penh, Cambodia, www.nis.gov.kh; *2005 Cambodia's Socio-economic Indicator Database (CamInfo 2005).*

CAMBODIA - AGRICULTURAL MACHINERY

United Nations Statistics Division, New York, NY 10017, (800) 253-9646, Fax: (212) 963-4116, http://unstats.un.org; *Statistical Yearbook.*

CAMBODIA - AGRICULTURE

Economist Intelligence Unit, 111 West 57th Street, New York, NY 10019, (212) 554-0600, Fax: (212) 586-1181, www.eiu.com; *Cambodia Country Report.*

Euromonitor International, Inc., 224 S. Michigan Avenue, Suite 1500, Chicago, IL 60604, (312) 922-

1115, Fax: (312) 922-1157, www.euromonitor.com; *International Marketing Data and Statistics 2008* and *World Marketing Data and Statistics.*

Palgrave Macmillan Ltd., Houndmills, Basingstoke, Hampshire, RG21 6XS, England, (Telephone in U.S. (888) 330-8477), (Fax in U.S. (800) 672-2054), www.palgrave.com; *The Statesman's Yearbook 2008.*

Taylor and Francis Group, An Informa Business, 2 Park Square, Milton Park, Abingdon, Oxford OX14 4RN, United Kingdom, (Dial from U.S. (212) 216-7800), (Fax from U.S. (212) 564-7854), www.tandf.co.uk; *The Europa World Year Book.*

United Nations Conference on Trade and Development (UNCTAD), DC2-1120, United Nations, New York, NY 10017, (212) 963-0027, www.unctad.org; *UNCTAD Commodity Yearbook.*

United Nations Food and Agricultural Organization (FAO), Viale delle Terme di Caracalla, 00100 Rome, Italy, (Dial from U.S. (202) 653-2400), (Fax from U.S. (202) 653 5760), www.fao.org; AQUASTAT and *The State of Food and Agriculture (SOFA) 2006.*

United Nations Statistics Division, New York, NY 10017, (800) 253-9646, Fax: (212) 963-4116, http://unstats.un.org; *Asia-Pacific in Figures 2004; Statistical Yearbook;* and *Statistical Yearbook for Asia and the Pacific 2004.*

The World Bank, 1818 H Street, NW, Washington, DC 20433, (202) 473-1000, Fax: (202) 477-6391, www.worldbank.org; *Cambodia.*

CAMBODIA - AIRLINES

Economist Intelligence Unit, 111 West 57th Street, New York, NY 10019, (212) 554-0600, Fax: (212) 586-1181, www.eiu.com; *Business Asia.*

Palgrave Macmillan Ltd., Houndmills, Basingstoke, Hampshire, RG21 6XS, England, (Telephone in U.S. (888) 330-8477), (Fax in U.S. (800) 672-2054), www.palgrave.com; *The Statesman's Yearbook 2008.*

Taylor and Francis Group, An Informa Business, 2 Park Square, Milton Park, Abingdon, Oxford OX14 4RN, United Kingdom, (Dial from U.S. (212) 216-7800), (Fax from U.S. (212) 564-7854), www.tandf.co.uk; *The Europa World Year Book.*

United Nations Statistics Division, New York, NY 10017, (800) 253-9646, Fax: (212) 963-4116, http://unstats.un.org; *Statistical Yearbook.*

CAMBODIA - AIRPORTS

Central Intelligence Agency, Office of Public Affairs, Washington, DC 20505, (703) 482-0623, Fax: (703) 482-1739, www.cia.gov; *The World Factbook.*

CAMBODIA - ARMED FORCES

Central Intelligence Agency, Office of Public Affairs, Washington, DC 20505, (703) 482-0623, Fax: (703) 482-1739, www.cia.gov; *The World Factbook.*

Economist Intelligence Unit, 111 West 57th Street, New York, NY 10019, (212) 554-0600, Fax: (212) 586-1181, www.eiu.com; *Business Asia.*

Euromonitor International, Inc., 224 S. Michigan Avenue, Suite 1500, Chicago, IL 60604, (312) 922-1115, Fax: (312) 922-1157, www.euromonitor.com; *World Marketing Data and Statistics.*

International Institute for Strategic Studies (IISS), Arundel House, 13-15 Arundel Street, Temple Place, London WC2R 3DX, England, www.iiss.org; *The Military Balance 2007.*

Palgrave Macmillan Ltd., Houndmills, Basingstoke, Hampshire, RG21 6XS, England, (Telephone in U.S. (888) 330-8477), (Fax in U.S. (800) 672-2054), www.palgrave.com; *The Statesman's Yearbook 2008.*

U.S. Department of State (DOS), 2201 C Street NW, Washington, DC 20520, (202) 647-4000, www.state.gov; *World Military Expenditures and Arms Transfers (WMEAT).*

United Nations Statistics Division, New York, NY 10017, (800) 253-9646, Fax: (212) 963-4116, http://unstats.un.org; *Human Development Report 2006.*

CAMBODIA - BALANCE OF PAYMENTS

United Nations Conference on Trade and Development (UNCTAD), DC2-1120, United Nations, New York, NY 10017, (212) 963-0027, www.unctad.org; *Handbook of Statistics 2005.*

The World Bank, 1818 H Street, NW, Washington, DC 20433, (202) 473-1000, Fax: (202) 477-6391, www.worldbank.org; *Cambodia.*

CAMBODIA - BANKS AND BANKING

Euromonitor International, Inc., 224 S. Michigan Avenue, Suite 1500, Chicago, IL 60604, (312) 922-1115, Fax: (312) 922-1157, www.euromonitor.com; *World Marketing Data and Statistics.*

Palgrave Macmillan Ltd., Houndmills, Basingstoke, Hampshire, RG21 6XS, England, (Telephone in U.S. (888) 330-8477), (Fax in U.S. (800) 672-2054), www.palgrave.com; *The Statesman's Yearbook 2008.*

CAMBODIA - BEVERAGE INDUSTRY

United Nations Statistics Division, New York, NY 10017, (800) 253-9646, Fax: (212) 963-4116, http://unstats.un.org; *Statistical Yearbook.*

CAMBODIA - BROADCASTING

Central Intelligence Agency, Office of Public Affairs, Washington, DC 20505, (703) 482-0623, Fax: (703) 482-1739, www.cia.gov; *The World Factbook.*

Euromonitor International, Inc., 224 S. Michigan Avenue, Suite 1500, Chicago, IL 60604, (312) 922-1115, Fax: (312) 922-1157, www.euromonitor.com; *World Marketing Data and Statistics.*

Palgrave Macmillan Ltd., Houndmills, Basingstoke, Hampshire, RG21 6XS, England, (Telephone in U.S. (888) 330-8477), (Fax in U.S. (800) 672-2054), www.palgrave.com; *The Statesman's Yearbook 2008.*

WRTH Publications Limited, PO Box 290, Oxford OX2 7FT, UK, www.wrth.com; *World Radio TV Handbook 2007.*

CAMBODIA - BUDGET

Central Intelligence Agency, Office of Public Affairs, Washington, DC 20505, (703) 482-0623, Fax: (703) 482-1739, www.cia.gov; *The World Factbook.*

CAMBODIA - BUSINESS

United Nations Statistics Division, New York, NY 10017, (800) 253-9646, Fax: (212) 963-4116, http://unstats.un.org; *Statistical Yearbook for Asia and the Pacific 2004.*

CAMBODIA - CATTLE

See CAMBODIA - LIVESTOCK

CAMBODIA - CHICKENS

See CAMBODIA - LIVESTOCK

CAMBODIA - CHILDBIRTH - STATISTICS

Central Intelligence Agency, Office of Public Affairs, Washington, DC 20505, (703) 482-0623, Fax: (703) 482-1739, www.cia.gov; *The World Factbook.*

Economist Intelligence Unit, 111 West 57th Street, New York, NY 10019, (212) 554-0600, Fax: (212) 586-1181, www.eiu.com; *Business Asia.*

Euromonitor International, Inc., 224 S. Michigan Avenue, Suite 1500, Chicago, IL 60604, (312) 922-1115, Fax: (312) 922-1157, www.euromonitor.com; *International Marketing Data and Statistics 2008* and *The World Economic Factbook 2008.*

Taylor and Francis Group, An Informa Business, 2 Park Square, Milton Park, Abingdon, Oxford OX14 4RN, United Kingdom, (Dial from U.S. (212) 216-7800), (Fax from U.S. (212) 564-7854), www.tandf.co.uk; *The Europa World Year Book.*

United Nations Statistics Division, New York, NY 10017, (800) 253-9646, Fax: (212) 963-4116, http://unstats.un.org; *Asia-Pacific in Figures 2004; Demographic Yearbook;* and *Statistical Yearbook.*

CAMBODIA - CLIMATE

International Institute for Environment and Development (IIED), 3 Endsleigh Street, London, England, WC1H 0DD, United Kingdom, www.iied.org; *Environment Urbanization.*

Palgrave Macmillan Ltd., Houndmills, Basingstoke, Hampshire, RG21 6XS, England, (Telephone in U.S. (888) 330-8477), (Fax in U.S. (800) 672-2054), www.palgrave.com; *The Statesman's Yearbook 2008.*

CAMBODIA - COAL PRODUCTION

See CAMBODIA - MINERAL INDUSTRIES

CAMBODIA - COMMERCE

Palgrave Macmillan Ltd., Houndmills, Basingstoke, Hampshire, RG21 6XS, England, (Telephone in U.S. (888) 330-8477), (Fax in U.S. (800) 672-2054), www.palgrave.com; *The Statesman's Yearbook 2008.*

CAMBODIA - COMMODITY EXCHANGES

Commodity Research Bureau, 330 South Wells Street, Suite 612, Chicago, IL 60606-7110, (800) 621-5271, Fax: (312) 939-4135, www.crbtrader.com; *2006 CRB Commodity Yearbook and CD.*

International Monetary Fund (IMF), 700 Nineteenth Street, NW, Washington, DC 20431, (202) 623-7000, Fax: (202) 623-4661, www.imf.org; *IMF Primary Commodity Prices.*

United Nations Food and Agricultural Organization (FAO), Viale delle Terme di Caracalla, 00100 Rome, Italy, (Dial from U.S. (202) 653-2400), (Fax from U.S. (202) 653 5760), www.fao.org; *The State of Food and Agriculture (SOFA) 2006.*

CAMBODIA - CONSUMER PRICE INDEXES

United Nations Statistics Division, New York, NY 10017, (800) 253-9646, Fax: (212) 963-4116, http://unstats.un.org; *Statistical Yearbook.*

The World Bank, 1818 H Street, NW, Washington, DC 20433, (202) 473-1000, Fax: (202) 477-6391, www.worldbank.org; *Cambodia.*

CAMBODIA - CORN INDUSTRY

See CAMBODIA - CROPS

CAMBODIA - COTTON

See CAMBODIA - CROPS

CAMBODIA - CROPS

Palgrave Macmillan Ltd., Houndmills, Basingstoke, Hampshire, RG21 6XS, England, (Telephone in U.S. (888) 330-8477), (Fax in U.S. (800) 672-2054), www.palgrave.com; *The Statesman's Yearbook 2008.*

Taylor and Francis Group, An Informa Business, 2 Park Square, Milton Park, Abingdon, Oxford OX14 4RN, United Kingdom, (Dial from U.S. (212) 216-7800), (Fax from U.S. (212) 564-7854), www.tandf.co.uk; *The Europa World Year Book.*

United Nations Conference on Trade and Development (UNCTAD), DC2-1120, United Nations, New York, NY 10017, (212) 963-0027, www.unctad.org; *UNCTAD Commodity Yearbook.*

United Nations Food and Agricultural Organization (FAO), Viale delle Terme di Caracalla, 00100 Rome, Italy, (Dial from U.S. (202) 653-2400), (Fax from U.S. (202) 653 5760), www.fao.org; *FAO Production Yearbook 2002* and *The State of Food and Agriculture (SOFA) 2006.*

United Nations Statistics Division, New York, NY 10017, (800) 253-9646, Fax: (212) 963-4116, http://unstats.un.org; *Statistical Yearbook.*

CAMBODIA - DAIRY PROCESSING

Palgrave Macmillan Ltd., Houndmills, Basingstoke, Hampshire, RG21 6XS, England, (Telephone in U.S. (888) 330-8477), (Fax in U.S. (800) 672-2054), www.palgrave.com; *The Statesman's Yearbook 2008.*

Taylor and Francis Group, An Informa Business, 2 Park Square, Milton Park, Abingdon, Oxford OX14 4RN, United Kingdom, (Dial from U.S. (212) 216-7800), (Fax from U.S. (212) 564-7854), www.tandf.co.uk; *The Europa World Year Book.*

United Nations Food and Agricultural Organization (FAO), Viale delle Terme di Caracalla, 00100 Rome, Italy, (Dial from U.S. (202) 653-2400), (Fax from U.S. (202) 653 5760), www.fao.org; *The State of Food and Agriculture (SOFA) 2006.*

United Nations Statistics Division, New York, NY 10017, (800) 253-9646, Fax: (212) 963-4116, http://unstats.un.org; *Statistical Yearbook.*

CAMBODIA - DEATH RATES

See CAMBODIA - MORTALITY

CAMBODIA - DEBTS, EXTERNAL

The World Bank, 1818 H Street, NW, Washington, DC 20433, (202) 473-1000, Fax: (202) 477-6391, www.worldbank.org; *Global Development Finance 2007.*

Worldinformation.com, 2 Market Street, Saffron Walden, Essex CB10 1HZ, United Kingdom, www.worldinformation.com; The World of Information (www.worldinformation.com).

CAMBODIA - DEFENSE EXPENDITURES

See CAMBODIA - ARMED FORCES

CAMBODIA - DEMOGRAPHY

Economist Intelligence Unit, 111 West 57th Street, New York, NY 10019, (212) 554-0600, Fax: (212) 586-1181, www.eiu.com; *Business Asia.*

Euromonitor International, Inc., 224 S. Michigan Avenue, Suite 1500, Chicago, IL 60604, (312) 922-1115, Fax: (312) 922-1157, www.euromonitor.com; *International Marketing Data and Statistics 2008; The World Economic Factbook 2008;* and *World Marketing Data and Statistics.*

National Institute of Statistics (NIS), Ministry of Planning, Preah Monivong Boulevard, Sankat Boeung Keng Kang 1, Phnom Penh, Cambodia, www.nis.gov.kh; *Cambodia Demographic and Health Survey 2000.*

United Nations Statistics Division, New York, NY 10017, (800) 253-9646, Fax: (212) 963-4116, http://unstats.un.org; *Asia-Pacific in Figures 2004* and *Human Development Report 2006.*

The World Bank, 1818 H Street, NW, Washington, DC 20433, (202) 473-1000, Fax: (202) 477-6391, www.worldbank.org; *Cambodia.*

CAMBODIA - DISPOSABLE INCOME

United Nations Statistics Division, New York, NY 10017, (800) 253-9646, Fax: (212) 963-4116, http://unstats.un.org; *Statistical Yearbook.*

CAMBODIA - DIVORCE

United Nations Statistics Division, New York, NY 10017, (800) 253-9646, Fax: (212) 963-4116, http://unstats.un.org; *Demographic Yearbook.*

CAMBODIA - ECONOMIC ASSISTANCE

United Nations Statistics Division, New York, NY 10017, (800) 253-9646, Fax: (212) 963-4116, http://unstats.un.org; *Statistical Yearbook.*

CAMBODIA - ECONOMIC CONDITIONS

Center for International Business Education Research (CIBER), Columbia Business School and School of International and Public Affairs, Uris Hall, Room 212, 3022 Broadway, New York, NY 10027-6902, Mr. Joshua Safier, (212) 854-4750, Fax: (212) 222-9821, www.columbia.edu/cu/ciber/; Datastream International.

Central Intelligence Agency, Office of Public Affairs, Washington, DC 20505, (703) 482-0623, Fax: (703) 482-1739, www.cia.gov; *The World Factbook.*

DSI Data Service Information, Xantener Strasse 51a, D-47495 Rheinberg, Germany, www.dsidata.com; *Campus Solution.*

Dun and Bradstreet (DB) Corporation, 103 JFK Parkway, Short Hills, NJ 07078, (973) 921-5500, www.dnb.com; *Country Report.*

Economist Intelligence Unit, 111 West 57th Street, New York, NY 10019, (212) 554-0600, Fax: (212) 586-1181, www.eiu.com; *Cambodia Country Report.*

Euromonitor International, Inc., 224 S. Michigan Avenue, Suite 1500, Chicago, IL 60604, (312) 922-1115, Fax: (312) 922-1157, www.euromonitor.com; *International Marketing Data and Statistics 2008; The World Economic Factbook 2008;* and *World Marketing Data and Statistics.*

International Monetary Fund (IMF), 700 Nineteenth Street, NW, Washington, DC 20431, (202) 623-7000, Fax: (202) 623-4661, www.imf.org; *World Economic Outlook Reports.*

National Institute of Statistics (NIS), Ministry of Planning, Preah Monivong Boulevard, Sankat Boeung Keng Kang 1, Phnom Penh, Cambodia, www.nis.gov.kh; *2005 Cambodia's Socio-economic Indicator Database (CamInfo 2005).*

Nomura Research Institute (NRI), 2 World Financial Center, Building B, 19th Fl., New York, NY 10281-1198, (212) 667-1670, www.nri.co.jp/english; *Asian Economic Outlook 2003-2004.*

Palgrave Macmillan Ltd., Houndmills, Basingstoke, Hampshire, RG21 6XS, England, (Telephone in U.S. (888) 330-8477), (Fax in U.S. (800) 672-2054), www.palgrave.com; *The Statesman's Yearbook 2008.*

Taylor and Francis Group, An Informa Business, 2 Park Square, Milton Park, Abingdon, Oxford OX14 4RN, United Kingdom, (Dial from U.S. (212) 216-7800), (Fax from U.S. (212) 564-7854), www.tandf.co.uk; *The Europa World Year Book.*

United Nations Statistics Division, New York, NY 10017, (800) 253-9646, Fax: (212) 963-4116, http://unstats.un.org; *World Statistics Pocketbook.*

The World Bank, 1818 H Street, NW, Washington, DC 20433, (202) 473-1000, Fax: (202) 477-6391, www.worldbank.org; *Cambodia; Global Economic Monitor (GEM); Global Economic Prospects 2008;* and *The World Bank Atlas 2003-2004.*

CAMBODIA - EDUCATION

Economist Intelligence Unit, 111 West 57th Street, New York, NY 10019, (212) 554-0600, Fax: (212) 586-1181, www.eiu.com; *Business Asia.*

Euromonitor International, Inc., 224 S. Michigan Avenue, Suite 1500, Chicago, IL 60604, (312) 922-1115, Fax: (312) 922-1157, www.euromonitor.com; *International Marketing Data and Statistics 2008* and *World Marketing Data and Statistics.*

Palgrave Macmillan Ltd., Houndmills, Basingstoke, Hampshire, RG21 6XS, England, (Telephone in U.S. (888) 330-8477), (Fax in U.S. (800) 672-2054), www.palgrave.com; *The Statesman's Yearbook 2008.*

Taylor and Francis Group, An Informa Business, 2 Park Square, Milton Park, Abingdon, Oxford OX14 4RN, United Kingdom, (Dial from U.S. (212) 216-7800), (Fax from U.S. (212) 564-7854), www.tandf.co.uk; *The Europa World Year Book.*

United Nations Statistics Division, New York, NY 10017, (800) 253-9646, Fax: (212) 963-4116, http://unstats.un.org; *Asia-Pacific in Figures 2004; Human Development Report 2006;* and *Statistical Yearbook for Asia and the Pacific 2004.*

The World Bank, 1818 H Street, NW, Washington, DC 20433, (202) 473-1000, Fax: (202) 477-6391, www.worldbank.org; *Cambodia.*

CAMBODIA - ELECTRICITY

Central Intelligence Agency, Office of Public Affairs, Washington, DC 20505, (703) 482-0623, Fax: (703) 482-1739, www.cia.gov; *The World Factbook.*

United Nations Statistics Division, New York, NY 10017, (800) 253-9646, Fax: (212) 963-4116, http://unstats.un.org; *Human Development Report 2006* and *Statistical Yearbook.*

CAMBODIA - EMPLOYMENT

Euromonitor International, Inc., 224 S. Michigan Avenue, Suite 1500, Chicago, IL 60604, (312) 922-1115, Fax: (312) 922-1157, www.euromonitor.com; *International Marketing Data and Statistics 2008.*

National Institute of Statistics (NIS), Ministry of Planning, Preah Monivong Boulevard, Sankat Boeung Keng Kang 1, Phnom Penh, Cambodia, www.nis.gov.kh; *Cambodia Child Labor Survey 2001* and *Child Domestic Worker Survey Phnom Penh 2003.*

United Nations Statistics Division, New York, NY 10017, (800) 253-9646, Fax: (212) 963-4116, http://unstats.un.org; *Asia-Pacific in Figures 2004.*

The World Bank, 1818 H Street, NW, Washington, DC 20433, (202) 473-1000, Fax: (202) 477-6391, www.worldbank.org; *Cambodia.*

CAMBODIA - ENVIRONMENTAL CONDITIONS

DSI Data Service Information, Xantener Strasse 51a, D-47495 Rheinberg, Germany, www.dsidata.com; *Campus Solution* and *DSI's Global Environmental Database.*

Economist Intelligence Unit, 111 West 57th Street, New York, NY 10019, (212) 554-0600, Fax: (212) 586-1181, www.eiu.com; *Cambodia Country Report.*

International Institute for Environment and Development (IIED), 3 Endsleigh Street, London, England, WC1H 0DD, United Kingdom, www.iied.org; *Environment Urbanization.*

United Nations Statistics Division, New York, NY 10017, (800) 253-9646, Fax: (212) 963-4116, http://unstats.un.org; *World Statistics Pocketbook.*

CAMBODIA - EXPORTS

Central Intelligence Agency, Office of Public Affairs, Washington, DC 20505, (703) 482-0623, Fax: (703) 482-1739, www.cia.gov; *The World Factbook.*

Economist Intelligence Unit, 111 West 57th Street, New York, NY 10019, (212) 554-0600, Fax: (212) 586-1181, www.eiu.com; *Cambodia Country Report.*

Euromonitor International, Inc., 224 S. Michigan Avenue, Suite 1500, Chicago, IL 60604, (312) 922-1115, Fax: (312) 922-1157, www.euromonitor.com; *International Marketing Data and Statistics 2008* and *The World Economic Factbook 2008.*

International Monetary Fund (IMF), 700 Nineteenth Street, NW, Washington, DC 20431, (202) 623-7000, Fax: (202) 623-4661, www.imf.org; *Direction of Trade Statistics Yearbook 2007.*

Palgrave Macmillan Ltd., Houndmills, Basingstoke, Hampshire, RG21 6XS, England, (Telephone in U.S. (888) 330-8477), (Fax in U.S. (800) 672-2054), www.palgrave.com; *The Statesman's Yearbook 2008.*

Taylor and Francis Group, An Informa Business, 2 Park Square, Milton Park, Abingdon, Oxford OX14 4RN, United Kingdom, (Dial from U.S. (212) 216-7800), (Fax from U.S. (212) 564-7854), www.tandf.co.uk; *The Europa World Year Book.*

United Nations Conference on Trade and Development (UNCTAD), DC2-1120, United Nations, New York, NY 10017, (212) 963-0027, www.unctad.org; *Handbook of Statistics 2005.*

United Nations Food and Agricultural Organization (FAO), Viale delle Terme di Caracalla, 00100 Rome, Italy, (Dial from U.S. (202) 653-2400), (Fax from U.S. (202) 653 5760), www.fao.org; *The State of Food and Agriculture (SOFA) 2006.*

Worldinformation.com, 2 Market Street, Saffron Walden, Essex CB10 1HZ, United Kingdom, www.worldinformation.com; The World of Information (www.worldinformation.com).

CAMBODIA - FEMALE WORKING POPULATION

See CAMBODIA - EMPLOYMENT

CAMBODIA - FERTILITY, HUMAN

Central Intelligence Agency, Office of Public Affairs, Washington, DC 20505, (703) 482-0623, Fax: (703) 482-1739, www.cia.gov; *The World Factbook.*

United Nations Statistics Division, New York, NY 10017, (800) 253-9646, Fax: (212) 963-4116, http://unstats.un.org; *Human Development Report 2006.*

The World Bank, 1818 H Street, NW, Washington, DC 20433, (202) 473-1000, Fax: (202) 477-6391, www.worldbank.org; *The World Bank Atlas 2003-2004.*

CAMBODIA - FERTILIZER INDUSTRY

United Nations Food and Agricultural Organization (FAO), Viale delle Terme di Caracalla, 00100 Rome, Italy, (Dial from U.S. (202) 653-2400), (Fax from U.S. (202) 653 5760), www.fao.org; *The State of Food and Agriculture (SOFA) 2006.*

United Nations Statistics Division, New York, NY 10017, (800) 253-9646, Fax: (212) 963-4116, http://unstats.un.org; *Statistical Yearbook.*

CAMBODIA - FETAL MORTALITY

See CAMBODIA - MORTALITY

CAMBODIA - FINANCE

United Nations Statistics Division, New York, NY 10017, (800) 253-9646, Fax: (212) 963-4116, http://unstats.un.org; *Asia-Pacific in Figures 2004; National Accounts Statistics: Compendium of Income Distribution Statistics; Statistical Yearbook;* and *Statistical Yearbook for Asia and the Pacific 2004.*

The World Bank, 1818 H Street, NW, Washington, DC 20433, (202) 473-1000, Fax: (202) 477-6391, www.worldbank.org; *Cambodia.*

CAMBODIA - FINANCE, PUBLIC

Bernan Essential Government Publications, 4611-F Assembly Drive, Lanham MD, 20706-4391, (301) 459-2255, Fax: (800) 865-3450, www.bernan.com; *National Accounts Statistics.*

Economist Intelligence Unit, 111 West 57th Street, New York, NY 10019, (212) 554-0600, Fax: (212) 586-1181, www.eiu.com; *Cambodia Country Report.*

International Monetary Fund (IMF), 700 Nineteenth Street, NW, Washington, DC 20431, (202) 623-7000, Fax: (202) 623-4661, www.imf.org; *International Financial Statistics* and *International Financial Statistics Online Service.*

Palgrave Macmillan Ltd., Houndmills, Basingstoke, Hampshire, RG21 6XS, England, (Telephone in U.S. (888) 330-8477), (Fax in U.S. (800) 672-2054), www.palgrave.com; *The Statesman's Yearbook 2008.*

Taylor and Francis Group, An Informa Business, 2 Park Square, Milton Park, Abingdon, Oxford OX14 4RN, United Kingdom, (Dial from U.S. (212) 216-7800), (Fax from U.S. (212) 564-7854), www.tandf.co.uk; *The Europa World Year Book.*

United Nations Statistics Division, New York, NY 10017, (800) 253-9646, Fax: (212) 963-4116, http://unstats.un.org; *Statistical Yearbook for Asia and the Pacific 2004.*

The World Bank, 1818 H Street, NW, Washington, DC 20433, (202) 473-1000, Fax: (202) 477-6391, www.worldbank.org; *Cambodia.*

CAMBODIA - FISHERIES

Palgrave Macmillan Ltd., Houndmills, Basingstoke, Hampshire, RG21 6XS, England, (Telephone in U.S. (888) 330-8477), (Fax in U.S. (800) 672-2054), www.palgrave.com; *The Statesman's Yearbook 2008.*

Taylor and Francis Group, An Informa Business, 2 Park Square, Milton Park, Abingdon, Oxford OX14 4RN, United Kingdom, (Dial from U.S. (212) 216-7800), (Fax from U.S. (212) 564-7854), www.tandf.co.uk; *The Europa World Year Book.*

United Nations Conference on Trade and Development (UNCTAD), DC2-1120, United Nations, New York, NY 10017, (212) 963-0027, www.unctad.org; *UNCTAD Commodity Yearbook.*

United Nations Food and Agricultural Organization (FAO), Viale delle Terme di Caracalla, 00100 Rome, Italy, (Dial from U.S. (202) 653-2400), (Fax from U.S. (202) 653 5760), www.fao.org; *The State of Food and Agriculture (SOFA) 2006.*

United Nations Statistics Division, New York, NY 10017, (800) 253-9646, Fax: (212) 963-4116, http://unstats.un.org; *Statistical Yearbook.*

The World Bank, 1818 H Street, NW, Washington, DC 20433, (202) 473-1000, Fax: (202) 477-6391, www.worldbank.org; *Cambodia.*

CAMBODIA - FOOD

United Nations Conference on Trade and Development (UNCTAD), DC2-1120, United Nations, New York, NY 10017, (212) 963-0027, www.unctad.org; *UNCTAD Commodity Yearbook.*

United Nations Food and Agricultural Organization (FAO), Viale delle Terme di Caracalla, 00100 Rome, Italy, (Dial from U.S. (202) 653-2400), (Fax from U.S. (202) 653 5760), www.fao.org; *The State of Food and Agriculture (SOFA) 2006.*

United Nations Statistics Division, New York, NY 10017, (800) 253-9646, Fax: (212) 963-4116, http://unstats.un.org; *Human Development Report 2006* and *Statistical Yearbook for Asia and the Pacific 2004.*

CAMBODIA - FOREIGN EXCHANGE RATES

Central Intelligence Agency, Office of Public Affairs, Washington, DC 20505, (703) 482-0623, Fax: (703) 482-1739, www.cia.gov; *The World Factbook.*

Economist Intelligence Unit, 111 West 57th Street, New York, NY 10019, (212) 554-0600, Fax: (212) 586-1181, www.eiu.com; *Business Asia.*

Euromonitor International, Inc., 224 S. Michigan Avenue, Suite 1500, Chicago, IL 60604, (312) 922-1115, Fax: (312) 922-1157, www.euromonitor.com; *International Marketing Data and Statistics 2008* and *The World Economic Factbook 2008.*

Taylor and Francis Group, An Informa Business, 2 Park Square, Milton Park, Abingdon, Oxford OX14 4RN, United Kingdom, (Dial from U.S. (212) 216-7800), (Fax from U.S. (212) 564-7854), www.tandf.co.uk; *The Europa World Year Book.*

United Nations Statistics Division, New York, NY 10017, (800) 253-9646, Fax: (212) 963-4116, http://unstats.un.org; *Statistical Yearbook* and *World Statistics Pocketbook.*

Worldinformation.com, 2 Market Street, Saffron Walden, Essex CB10 1HZ, United Kingdom, www.worldinformation.com; The World of Information (www.worldinformation.com).

CAMBODIA - FORESTS AND FORESTRY

Economist Intelligence Unit, 111 West 57th Street, New York, NY 10019, (212) 554-0600, Fax: (212) 586-1181, www.eiu.com; *Business Asia.*

Palgrave Macmillan Ltd., Houndmills, Basingstoke, Hampshire, RG21 6XS, England, (Telephone in U.S. (888) 330-8477), (Fax in U.S. (800) 672-2054), www.palgrave.com; *The Statesman's Yearbook 2008.*

Taylor and Francis Group, An Informa Business, 2 Park Square, Milton Park, Abingdon, Oxford OX14 4RN, United Kingdom, (Dial from U.S. (212) 216-7800), (Fax from U.S. (212) 564-7854), www.tandf.co.uk; *The Europa World Year Book.*

UNESCO Institute for Statistics, C.P. 6128 Succursale Centre-Ville, Montreal, Quebec, H3C 3J7 Canada, (Dial from U.S. (514) 343-6880), (Fax from U.S. (514) 343 6882), www.uis.unesco.org; *Statistical Tables.*

United Nations Conference on Trade and Development (UNCTAD), DC2-1120, United Nations, New York, NY 10017, (212) 963-0027, www.unctad.org; *UNCTAD Commodity Yearbook.*

United Nations Food and Agricultural Organization (FAO), Viale delle Terme di Caracalla, 00100 Rome, Italy, (Dial from U.S. (202) 653-2400), (Fax from U.S. (202) 653 5760), www.fao.org; *FAO Yearbook of Forest Products* and *The State of Food and Agriculture (SOFA) 2006.*

United Nations Statistics Division, New York, NY 10017, (800) 253-9646, Fax: (212) 963-4116, http://unstats.un.org; *Statistical Yearbook.*

The World Bank, 1818 H Street, NW, Washington, DC 20433, (202) 473-1000, Fax: (202) 477-6391, www.worldbank.org; *Cambodia.*

CAMBODIA - GROSS DOMESTIC PRODUCT

Economist Intelligence Unit, 111 West 57th Street, New York, NY 10019, (212) 554-0600, Fax: (212) 586-1181, www.eiu.com; *Business Asia* and *Cambodia Country Report.*

Euromonitor International, Inc., 224 S. Michigan Avenue, Suite 1500, Chicago, IL 60604, (312) 922-1115, Fax: (312) 922-1157, www.euromonitor.com; *International Marketing Data and Statistics 2008* and *The World Economic Factbook 2008.*

United Nations Statistics Division, New York, NY 10017, (800) 253-9646, Fax: (212) 963-4116, http://unstats.un.org; *Human Development Report 2006* and *Statistical Yearbook.*

CAMBODIA - GROSS NATIONAL PRODUCT

Euromonitor International, Inc., 224 S. Michigan Avenue, Suite 1500, Chicago, IL 60604, (312) 922-1115, Fax: (312) 922-1157, www.euromonitor.com; *International Marketing Data and Statistics 2008.*

Palgrave Macmillan Ltd., Houndmills, Basingstoke, Hampshire, RG21 6XS, England, (Telephone in U.S. (888) 330-8477), (Fax in U.S. (800) 672-2054), www.palgrave.com; *The Statesman's Yearbook 2008.*

U.S. Department of State (DOS), 2201 C Street NW, Washington, DC 20520, (202) 647-4000, www.state.gov; *World Military Expenditures and Arms Transfers (WMEAT).*

United Nations Statistics Division, New York, NY 10017, (800) 253-9646, Fax: (212) 963-4116, http://unstats.un.org; *Statistical Yearbook.*

The World Bank, 1818 H Street, NW, Washington, DC 20433, (202) 473-1000, Fax: (202) 477-6391, www.worldbank.org; *The World Bank Atlas 2003-2004.*

Worldinformation.com, 2 Market Street, Saffron Walden, Essex CB10 1HZ, United Kingdom, www.worldinformation.com; The World of Information (www.worldinformation.com).

CAMBODIA - HIDES AND SKINS INDUSTRY

United Nations Food and Agricultural Organization (FAO), Viale delle Terme di Caracalla, 00100 Rome, Italy, (Dial from U.S. (202) 653-2400), (Fax from U.S. (202) 653 5760), www.fao.org; *FAO Production Yearbook 2002.*

CAMBODIA - HOUSING

Euromonitor International, Inc., 224 S. Michigan Avenue, Suite 1500, Chicago, IL 60604, (312) 922-1115, Fax: (312) 922-1157, www.euromonitor.com; *World Marketing Data and Statistics.*

CAMBODIA - ILLITERATE PERSONS

Euromonitor International, Inc., 224 S. Michigan Avenue, Suite 1500, Chicago, IL 60604, (312) 922-1115, Fax: (312) 922-1157, www.euromonitor.com; *The World Economic Factbook 2008.*

UNESCO Institute for Statistics, C.P. 6128 Succursale Centre-Ville, Montreal, Quebec, H3C 3J7 Canada, (Dial from U.S. (514) 343-6880), (Fax from U.S. (514) 343 6882), www.uis.unesco.org; *Statistical Tables.*

United Nations Statistics Division, New York, NY 10017, (800) 253-9646, Fax: (212) 963-4116, http://unstats.un.org; *Asia-Pacific in Figures 2004* and *Human Development Report 2006.*

CAMBODIA - IMPORTS

Central Intelligence Agency, Office of Public Affairs, Washington, DC 20505, (703) 482-0623, Fax: (703) 482-1739, www.cia.gov; *The World Factbook.*

Economist Intelligence Unit, 111 West 57th Street, New York, NY 10019, (212) 554-0600, Fax: (212) 586-1181, www.eiu.com; *Cambodia Country Report.*

Euromonitor International, Inc., 224 S. Michigan Avenue, Suite 1500, Chicago, IL 60604, (312) 922-1115, Fax: (312) 922-1157, www.euromonitor.com; *International Marketing Data and Statistics 2008* and *The World Economic Factbook 2008.*

International Monetary Fund (IMF), 700 Nineteenth Street, NW, Washington, DC 20431, (202) 623-7000, Fax: (202) 623-4661, www.imf.org; *Direction of Trade Statistics Yearbook 2007.*

Palgrave Macmillan Ltd., Houndmills, Basingstoke, Hampshire, RG21 6XS, England, (Telephone in U.S. (888) 330-8477), (Fax in U.S. (800) 672-2054), www.palgrave.com; *The Statesman's Yearbook 2008.*

Taylor and Francis Group, An Informa Business, 2 Park Square, Milton Park, Abingdon, Oxford OX14 4RN, United Kingdom, (Dial from U.S. (212) 216-7800), (Fax from U.S. (212) 564-7854), www.tandf.co.uk; *The Europa World Year Book.*

United Nations Conference on Trade and Development (UNCTAD), DC2-1120, United Nations, New York, NY 10017, (212) 963-0027, www.unctad.org; *Handbook of Statistics 2005.*

United Nations Food and Agricultural Organization (FAO), Viale delle Terme di Caracalla, 00100 Rome, Italy, (Dial from U.S. (202) 653-2400), (Fax from U.S. (202) 653 5760), www.fao.org; *The State of Food and Agriculture (SOFA) 2006.*

Worldinformation.com, 2 Market Street, Saffron Walden, Essex CB10 1HZ, United Kingdom, www.worldinformation.com; The World of Information (www.worldinformation.com).

CAMBODIA - INDUSTRIAL PRODUCTIVITY

Euromonitor International, Inc., 224 S. Michigan Avenue, Suite 1500, Chicago, IL 60604, (312) 922-1115, Fax: (312) 922-1157, www.euromonitor.com; *International Marketing Data and Statistics 2008.*

CAMBODIA - INDUSTRIAL PROPERTY

United Nations Statistics Division, New York, NY 10017, (800) 253-9646, Fax: (212) 963-4116, http://unstats.un.org; *Statistical Yearbook.*

CAMBODIA - INDUSTRIES

Central Intelligence Agency, Office of Public Affairs, Washington, DC 20505, (703) 482-0623, Fax: (703) 482-1739, www.cia.gov; *The World Factbook.*

Economist Intelligence Unit, 111 West 57th Street, New York, NY 10019, (212) 554-0600, Fax: (212) 586-1181, www.eiu.com; *Cambodia Country Report.*

Euromonitor International, Inc., 224 S. Michigan Avenue, Suite 1500, Chicago, IL 60604, (312) 922-1115, Fax: (312) 922-1157, www.euromonitor.com; *International Marketing Data and Statistics 2008; The World Economic Factbook 2008;* and *World Marketing Data and Statistics.*

Palgrave Macmillan Ltd., Houndmills, Basingstoke, Hampshire, RG21 6XS, England, (Telephone in U.S. (888) 330-8477), (Fax in U.S. (800) 672-2054), www.palgrave.com; *The Statesman's Yearbook 2008.*

Taylor and Francis Group, An Informa Business, 2 Park Square, Milton Park, Abingdon, Oxford OX14 4RN, United Kingdom, (Dial from U.S. (212) 216-7800), (Fax from U.S. (212) 564-7854), www.tandf.co.uk; *The Europa World Year Book.*

United Nations Industrial Development Organization (UNIDO), 1 United Nations Plaza, New York, NY 10017, (212) 963 6890, Fax: (212) 963-7904, http://unido.org; Industrial Statistics Database 2008 (INDSTAT) and *The International Yearbook of Industrial Statistics 2008.*

United Nations Statistics Division, New York, NY 10017, (800) 253-9646, Fax: (212) 963-4116, http://unstats.un.org; *Asia-Pacific in Figures 2004* and *Statistical Yearbook for Asia and the Pacific 2004.*

The World Bank, 1818 H Street, NW, Washington, DC 20433, (202) 473-1000, Fax: (202) 477-6391, www.worldbank.org; *Cambodia.*

CAMBODIA - INFANT AND MATERNAL MORTALITY

See CAMBODIA - MORTALITY

CAMBODIA - INTERNATIONAL TRADE

Economist Intelligence Unit, 111 West 57th Street, New York, NY 10019, (212) 554-0600, Fax: (212) 586-1181, www.eiu.com; *Business Asia* and *Cambodia Country Report.*

Euromonitor International, Inc., 224 S. Michigan Avenue, Suite 1500, Chicago, IL 60604, (312) 922-1115, Fax: (312) 922-1157, www.euromonitor.com; *International Marketing Data and Statistics 2008; The World Economic Factbook 2008;* and *World Marketing Data and Statistics.*

Palgrave Macmillan Ltd., Houndmills, Basingstoke, Hampshire, RG21 6XS, England, (Telephone in U.S. (888) 330-8477), (Fax in U.S. (800) 672-2054), www.palgrave.com; *The Statesman's Yearbook 2008.*

Taylor and Francis Group, An Informa Business, 2 Park Square, Milton Park, Abingdon, Oxford OX14 4RN, United Kingdom, (Dial from U.S. (212) 216-7800), (Fax from U.S. (212) 564-7854), www.tandf.co.uk; *The Europa World Year Book.*

United Nations Conference on Trade and Development (UNCTAD), DC2-1120, United Nations, New York, NY 10017, (212) 963-0027, www.unctad.org; *UNCTAD Commodity Yearbook.*

United Nations Food and Agricultural Organization (FAO), Viale delle Terme di Caracalla, 00100 Rome, Italy, (Dial from U.S. (202) 653-2400), (Fax from U.S. (202) 653 5760), www.fao.org; *The State of Food and Agriculture (SOFA) 2006.*

United Nations Statistics Division, New York, NY 10017, (800) 253-9646, Fax: (212) 963-4116, http://unstats.un.org; *Asia-Pacific in Figures 2004; International Trade Statistics Yearbook; Statistical Yearbook;* and *Statistical Yearbook for Asia and the Pacific 2004.*

The World Bank, 1818 H Street, NW, Washington, DC 20433, (202) 473-1000, Fax: (202) 477-6391, www.worldbank.org; *Cambodia.*

World Trade Organization (WTO), Centre William Rappard, Rue de Lausanne 154, CH-1211 Geneva 21, Switzerland, www.wto.org; *International Trade Statistics 2006.*

CAMBODIA - INTERNET USERS

International Telecommunication Union (ITU), Place des Nations, 1211 Geneva 20, Switzerland, www.itu.int; *World Telecommunication/ICT Indicators Database on CD-ROM; World Telecommunication/ICT Indicators Database Online;* and *Yearbook of Statistics - Telecommunication Services (Chronological Time Series 1997-2006).*

The World Bank, 1818 H Street, NW, Washington, DC 20433, (202) 473-1000, Fax: (202) 477-6391, www.worldbank.org; *Cambodia.*

CAMBODIA - IRRIGATION

Euromonitor International, Inc., 224 S. Michigan Avenue, Suite 1500, Chicago, IL 60604, (312) 922-1115, Fax: (312) 922-1157, www.euromonitor.com; *International Marketing Data and Statistics 2008.*

CAMBODIA - JUTE PRODUCTION

See CAMBODIA - CROPS

CAMBODIA - LABOR

Central Intelligence Agency, Office of Public Affairs, Washington, DC 20505, (703) 482-0623, Fax: (703) 482-1739, www.cia.gov; *The World Factbook.*

Economist Intelligence Unit, 111 West 57th Street, New York, NY 10019, (212) 554-0600, Fax: (212) 586-1181, www.eiu.com; *Business Asia.*

Euromonitor International, Inc., 224 S. Michigan Avenue, Suite 1500, Chicago, IL 60604, (312) 922-1115, Fax: (312) 922-1157, www.euromonitor.com; *International Marketing Data and Statistics 2008* and *World Marketing Data and Statistics.*

National Institute of Statistics (NIS), Ministry of Planning, Preah Monivong Boulevard, Sankat Boeung Keng Kang 1, Phnom Penh, Cambodia, www.nis.gov.kh; *Cambodia Child Labor Survey 2001* and *Child Domestic Worker Survey Phnom Penh 2003.*

Palgrave Macmillan Ltd., Houndmills, Basingstoke, Hampshire, RG21 6XS, England, (Telephone in U.S. (888) 330-8477), (Fax in U.S. (800) 672-2054), www.palgrave.com; *The Statesman's Yearbook 2008.*

United Nations Food and Agricultural Organization (FAO), Viale delle Terme di Caracalla, 00100 Rome, Italy, (Dial from U.S. (202) 653-2400), (Fax from U.S. (202) 653 5760), www.fao.org; *The State of Food and Agriculture (SOFA) 2006.*

United Nations Statistics Division, New York, NY 10017, (800) 253-9646, Fax: (212) 963-4116, http://unstats.un.org; *Human Development Report 2006.*

The World Bank, 1818 H Street, NW, Washington, DC 20433, (202) 473-1000, Fax: (202) 477-6391, www.worldbank.org; *The World Bank Atlas 2003-2004.*

CAMBODIA - LAND USE

Central Intelligence Agency, Office of Public Affairs, Washington, DC 20505, (703) 482-0623, Fax: (703) 482-1739, www.cia.gov; *The World Factbook.*

Euromonitor International, Inc., 224 S. Michigan Avenue, Suite 1500, Chicago, IL 60604, (312) 922-1115, Fax: (312) 922-1157, www.euromonitor.com; *International Marketing Data and Statistics 2008.*

CAMBODIA - LIFE EXPECTANCY

Central Intelligence Agency, Office of Public Affairs, Washington, DC 20505, (703) 482-0623, Fax: (703) 482-1739, www.cia.gov; *The World Factbook.*

Economist Intelligence Unit, 111 West 57th Street, New York, NY 10019, (212) 554-0600, Fax: (212) 586-1181, www.eiu.com; *Business Asia.*

Euromonitor International, Inc., 224 S. Michigan Avenue, Suite 1500, Chicago, IL 60604, (312) 922-1115, Fax: (312) 922-1157, www.euromonitor.com; *The World Economic Factbook 2008.*

Palgrave Macmillan Ltd., Houndmills, Basingstoke, Hampshire, RG21 6XS, England, (Telephone in U.S. (888) 330-8477), (Fax in U.S. (800) 672-2054), www.palgrave.com; *The Statesman's Yearbook 2008.*

United Nations Statistics Division, New York, NY 10017, (800) 253-9646, Fax: (212) 963-4116, http://unstats.un.org; *Asia-Pacific in Figures 2004; Human Development Report 2006;* and *World Statistics Pocketbook.*

The World Bank, 1818 H Street, NW, Washington, DC 20433, (202) 473-1000, Fax: (202) 477-6391, www.worldbank.org; *The World Bank Atlas 2003-2004.*

CAMBODIA - LITERACY

Euromonitor International, Inc., 224 S. Michigan Avenue, Suite 1500, Chicago, IL 60604, (312) 922-1115, Fax: (312) 922-1157, www.euromonitor.com; *World Marketing Data and Statistics.*

CAMBODIA - LIVESTOCK

Euromonitor International, Inc., 224 S. Michigan Avenue, Suite 1500, Chicago, IL 60604, (312) 922-1115, Fax: (312) 922-1157, www.euromonitor.com; *International Marketing Data and Statistics 2008.*

Palgrave Macmillan Ltd., Houndmills, Basingstoke, Hampshire, RG21 6XS, England, (Telephone in U.S. (888) 330-8477), (Fax in U.S. (800) 672-2054), www.palgrave.com; *The Statesman's Yearbook 2008.*

Taylor and Francis Group, An Informa Business, 2 Park Square, Milton Park, Abingdon, Oxford OX14 4RN, United Kingdom, (Dial from U.S. (212) 216-7800), (Fax from U.S. (212) 564-7854), www.tandf.co.uk; *The Europa World Year Book.*

United Nations Conference on Trade and Development (UNCTAD), DC2-1120, United Nations, New York, NY 10017, (212) 963-0027, www.unctad.org; *UNCTAD Commodity Yearbook.*

United Nations Food and Agricultural Organization (FAO), Viale delle Terme di Caracalla, 00100 Rome, Italy, (Dial from U.S. (202) 653-2400), (Fax from U.S. (202) 653 5760), www.fao.org; *FAO Production Yearbook 2002* and *The State of Food and Agriculture (SOFA) 2006*.

United Nations Statistics Division, New York, NY 10017, (800) 253-9646, Fax: (212) 963-4116, http://unstats.un.org; *Statistical Yearbook*.

CAMBODIA - LOCAL TAXATION

Euromonitor International, Inc., 224 S. Michigan Avenue, Suite 1500, Chicago, IL 60604, (312) 922-1115, Fax: (312) 922-1157, www.euromonitor.com; *International Marketing Data and Statistics 2008*.

CAMBODIA - MANPOWER

United Nations Statistics Division, New York, NY 10017, (800) 253-9646, Fax: (212) 963-4116, http://unstats.un.org; *Statistical Yearbook for Asia and the Pacific 2004*.

CAMBODIA - MARRIAGE

United Nations Statistics Division, New York, NY 10017, (800) 253-9646, Fax: (212) 963-4116, http://unstats.un.org; *Demographic Yearbook*.

CAMBODIA - MEAT PRODUCTION

See CAMBODIA - LIVESTOCK

CAMBODIA - MINERAL INDUSTRIES

Palgrave Macmillan Ltd., Houndmills, Basingstoke, Hampshire, RG21 6XS, England, (Telephone in U.S. (888) 330-8477), (Fax in U.S. (800) 672-2054), www.palgrave.com; *The Statesman's Yearbook 2008*.

Taylor and Francis Group, An Informa Business, 2 Park Square, Milton Park, Abingdon, Oxford OX14 4RN, United Kingdom, (Dial from U.S. (212) 216-7800), (Fax from U.S. (212) 564-7854), www.tandf.co.uk; *The Europa World Year Book*.

United Nations Conference on Trade and Development (UNCTAD), DC2-1120, United Nations, New York, NY 10017, (212) 963-0027, www.unctad.org; *UNCTAD Commodity Yearbook*.

United Nations Statistics Division, New York, NY 10017, (800) 253-9646, Fax: (212) 963-4116, http://unstats.un.org; *Statistical Yearbook*.

The World Bank, 1818 H Street, NW, Washington, DC 20433, (202) 473-1000, Fax: (202) 477-6391, www.worldbank.org; *Cambodia*.

CAMBODIA - MONEY EXCHANGE RATES

See CAMBODIA - FOREIGN EXCHANGE RATES

CAMBODIA - MONEY SUPPLY

Economist Intelligence Unit, 111 West 57th Street, New York, NY 10019, (212) 554-0600, Fax: (212) 586-1181, www.eiu.com; *Cambodia Country Report*.

Euromonitor International, Inc., 224 S. Michigan Avenue, Suite 1500, Chicago, IL 60604, (312) 922-1115, Fax: (312) 922-1157, www.euromonitor.com; *International Marketing Data and Statistics 2008*.

The World Bank, 1818 H Street, NW, Washington, DC 20433, (202) 473-1000, Fax: (202) 477-6391, www.worldbank.org; *Cambodia*.

CAMBODIA - MORTALITY

Central Intelligence Agency, Office of Public Affairs, Washington, DC 20505, (703) 482-0623, Fax: (703) 482-1739, www.cia.gov; *The World Factbook*.

Economist Intelligence Unit, 111 West 57th Street, New York, NY 10019, (212) 554-0600, Fax: (212) 586-1181, www.eiu.com; *Business Asia*.

Euromonitor International, Inc., 224 S. Michigan Avenue, Suite 1500, Chicago, IL 60604, (312) 922-1115, Fax: (312) 922-1157, www.euromonitor.com; *International Marketing Data and Statistics 2008* and *The World Economic Factbook 2008*.

Taylor and Francis Group, An Informa Business, 2 Park Square, Milton Park, Abingdon, Oxford OX14 4RN, United Kingdom, (Dial from U.S. (212) 216-7800), (Fax from U.S. (212) 564-7854), www.tandf.co.uk; *The Europa World Year Book*.

UNICEF, 3 United Nations Plaza, New York, NY 10017, (800) 253-9646, Fax: (212) 887-7465, www.unicef.org; *The State of the World's Children 2008*.

United Nations Statistics Division, New York, NY 10017, (800) 253-9646, Fax: (212) 963-4116, http://unstats.un.org; *Asia-Pacific in Figures 2004; Demographic Yearbook; Human Development Report 2006; Statistical Yearbook;* and *World Statistics Pocketbook*.

The World Bank, 1818 H Street, NW, Washington, DC 20433, (202) 473-1000, Fax: (202) 477-6391, www.worldbank.org; *The World Bank Atlas 2003-2004*.

World Health Organization (WHO), Avenue Appia 20, 1211 Geneve 27, Switzerland, (Telephone in U.S. (212) 331-9081), www.who.int; The WHO Global Atlas of Infectious Diseases.

CAMBODIA - MOTOR VEHICLES

Taylor and Francis Group, An Informa Business, 2 Park Square, Milton Park, Abingdon, Oxford OX14 4RN, United Kingdom, (Dial from U.S. (212) 216-7800), (Fax from U.S. (212) 564-7854), www.tandf.co.uk; *The Europa World Year Book*.

United Nations Statistics Division, New York, NY 10017, (800) 253-9646, Fax: (212) 963-4116, http://unstats.un.org; *Statistical Yearbook*.

CAMBODIA - NUTRITION

United Nations Food and Agricultural Organization (FAO), Viale delle Terme di Caracalla, 00100 Rome, Italy, (Dial from U.S. (202) 653-2400), (Fax from U.S. (202) 653 5760), www.fao.org; *The State of Food and Agriculture (SOFA) 2006*.

CAMBODIA - PAPER

See CAMBODIA - FORESTS AND FORESTRY

CAMBODIA - PESTICIDES

United Nations Food and Agricultural Organization (FAO), Viale delle Terme di Caracalla, 00100 Rome, Italy, (Dial from U.S. (202) 653-2400), (Fax from U.S. (202) 653 5760), www.fao.org; *The State of Food and Agriculture (SOFA) 2006*.

CAMBODIA - PETROLEUM INDUSTRY AND TRADE

Palgrave Macmillan Ltd., Houndmills, Basingstoke, Hampshire, RG21 6XS, England, (Telephone in U.S. (888) 330-8477), (Fax in U.S. (800) 672-2054), www.palgrave.com; *The Statesman's Yearbook 2008*.

PennWell Corporation, 1421 South Sheridan Road, Tulsa, OK 74112, (918) 835-3161, www.pennwell.com; *International Petroleum Encyclopedia 2007*.

United Nations Conference on Trade and Development (UNCTAD), DC2-1120, United Nations, New York, NY 10017, (212) 963-0027, www.unctad.org; *UNCTAD Commodity Yearbook*.

United Nations Food and Agricultural Organization (FAO), Viale delle Terme di Caracalla, 00100 Rome, Italy, (Dial from U.S. (202) 653-2400), (Fax from U.S. (202) 653 5760), www.fao.org; *The State of Food and Agriculture (SOFA) 2006*.

United Nations Statistics Division, New York, NY 10017, (800) 253-9646, Fax: (212) 963-4116, http://unstats.un.org; *Statistical Yearbook*.

CAMBODIA - POLITICAL SCIENCE

Central Intelligence Agency, Office of Public Affairs, Washington, DC 20505, (703) 482-0623, Fax: (703) 482-1739, www.cia.gov; *The World Factbook*.

Palgrave Macmillan Ltd., Houndmills, Basingstoke, Hampshire, RG21 6XS, England, (Telephone in U.S. (888) 330-8477), (Fax in U.S. (800) 672-2054), www.palgrave.com; *The Statesman's Yearbook 2008*.

United Nations Statistics Division, New York, NY 10017, (800) 253-9646, Fax: (212) 963-4116, http://unstats.un.org; *Asia-Pacific in Figures 2004*.

CAMBODIA - POPULATION

Central Intelligence Agency, Office of Public Affairs, Washington, DC 20505, (703) 482-0623, Fax: (703) 482-1739, www.cia.gov; *The World Factbook*.

Economist Intelligence Unit, 111 West 57th Street, New York, NY 10019, (212) 554-0600, Fax: (212) 586-1181, www.eiu.com; *Business Asia* and *Cambodia Country Report*.

Euromonitor International, Inc., 224 S. Michigan Avenue, Suite 1500, Chicago, IL 60604, (312) 922-1115, Fax: (312) 922-1157, www.euromonitor.com; *International Marketing Data and Statistics 2008* and *The World Economic Factbook 2008*.

National Institute of Statistics (NIS), Ministry of Planning, Preah Monivong Boulevard, Sankat Boeung Keng Kang 1, Phnom Penh, Cambodia, www.nis.gov.kh; *Cambodia Inter-Censal Population Survey 2004*.

Palgrave Macmillan Ltd., Houndmills, Basingstoke, Hampshire, RG21 6XS, England, (Telephone in U.S. (888) 330-8477), (Fax in U.S. (800) 672-2054), www.palgrave.com; *The Statesman's Yearbook 2008*.

Taylor and Francis Group, An Informa Business, 2 Park Square, Milton Park, Abingdon, Oxford OX14 4RN, United Kingdom, (Dial from U.S. (212) 216-7800), (Fax from U.S. (212) 564-7854), www.tandf.co.uk; *The Europa World Year Book*.

U.S. Department of State (DOS), 2201 C Street NW, Washington, DC 20520, (202) 647-4000, www.state.gov; *World Military Expenditures and Arms Transfers (WMEAT)*.

United Nations Statistics Division, New York, NY 10017, (800) 253-9646, Fax: (212) 963-4116, http://unstats.un.org; *Asia-Pacific in Figures 2004; Demographic Yearbook; Human Development Report 2006; Statistical Yearbook; Statistical Yearbook for Asia and the Pacific 2004;* and *World Statistics Pocketbook*.

The World Bank, 1818 H Street, NW, Washington, DC 20433, (202) 473-1000, Fax: (202) 477-6391, www.worldbank.org; *Cambodia* and *The World Bank Atlas 2003-2004*.

World Health Organization (WHO), Avenue Appia 20, 1211 Geneve 27, Switzerland, (Telephone in U.S. (212) 331-9081), www.who.int; *World Health Report 2006*.

Worldinformation.com, 2 Market Street, Saffron Walden, Essex CB10 1HZ, United Kingdom, www.worldinformation.com; The World of Information (www.worldinformation.com).

CAMBODIA - POPULATION DENSITY

Central Intelligence Agency, Office of Public Affairs, Washington, DC 20505, (703) 482-0623, Fax: (703) 482-1739, www.cia.gov; *The World Factbook*.

Euromonitor International, Inc., 224 S. Michigan Avenue, Suite 1500, Chicago, IL 60604, (312) 922-1115, Fax: (312) 922-1157, www.euromonitor.com; *International Marketing Data and Statistics 2008* and *The World Economic Factbook 2008*.

Palgrave Macmillan Ltd., Houndmills, Basingstoke, Hampshire, RG21 6XS, England, (Telephone in U.S. (888) 330-8477), (Fax in U.S. (800) 672-2054), www.palgrave.com; *The Statesman's Yearbook 2008*.

Taylor and Francis Group, An Informa Business, 2 Park Square, Milton Park, Abingdon, Oxford OX14 4RN, United Kingdom, (Dial from U.S. (212) 216-7800), (Fax from U.S. (212) 564-7854), www.tandf.co.uk; *The Europa World Year Book*.

United Nations Food and Agricultural Organization (FAO), Viale delle Terme di Caracalla, 00100 Rome, Italy, (Dial from U.S. (202) 653-2400), (Fax from U.S. (202) 653 5760), www.fao.org; *The State of Food and Agriculture (SOFA) 2006*.

United Nations Statistics Division, New York, NY 10017, (800) 253-9646, Fax: (212) 963-4116, http://unstats.un.org; *Statistical Yearbook*.

The World Bank, 1818 H Street, NW, Washington, DC 20433, (202) 473-1000, Fax: (202) 477-6391, www.worldbank.org; *Cambodia.*

CAMBODIA - POSTAL SERVICE

United Nations Statistics Division, New York, NY 10017, (800) 253-9646, Fax: (212) 963-4116, http://unstats.un.org; *Statistical Yearbook.*

CAMBODIA - POULTRY

See CAMBODIA - LIVESTOCK

CAMBODIA - POWER RESOURCES

Euromonitor International, Inc., 224 S. Michigan Avenue, Suite 1500, Chicago, IL 60604, (312) 922-1115, Fax: (312) 922-1157, www.euromonitor.com; *International Marketing Data and Statistics 2008; The World Economic Factbook 2008;* and *World Marketing Data and Statistics.*

Platts, 2 Penn Plaza, 25th Floor, New York, NY 10121-2298, (212) 904-3070, www.platts.com; *Energy Economist.*

United Nations Food and Agricultural Organization (FAO), Viale delle Terme di Caracalla, 00100 Rome, Italy, (Dial from U.S. (202) 653-2400), (Fax from U.S. (202) 653 5760), www.fao.org; *The State of Food and Agriculture (SOFA) 2006.*

United Nations Statistics Division, New York, NY 10017, (800) 253-9646, Fax: (212) 963-4116, http://unstats.un.org; *Asia-Pacific in Figures 2004; Energy Statistics Yearbook 2003; Human Development Report 2006; Statistical Yearbook;* and *World Statistics Pocketbook.*

The World Bank, 1818 H Street, NW, Washington, DC 20433, (202) 473-1000, Fax: (202) 477-6391, www.worldbank.org; *The World Bank Atlas 2003-2004.*

CAMBODIA - PRICES

Euromonitor International, Inc., 224 S. Michigan Avenue, Suite 1500, Chicago, IL 60604, (312) 922-1115, Fax: (312) 922-1157, www.euromonitor.com; *World Marketing Data and Statistics.*

United Nations Food and Agricultural Organization (FAO), Viale delle Terme di Caracalla, 00100 Rome, Italy, (Dial from U.S. (202) 653-2400), (Fax from U.S. (202) 653 5760), www.fao.org; *The State of Food and Agriculture (SOFA) 2006.*

The World Bank, 1818 H Street, NW, Washington, DC 20433, (202) 473-1000, Fax: (202) 477-6391, www.worldbank.org; *Cambodia.*

CAMBODIA - PUBLIC HEALTH

Economist Intelligence Unit, 111 West 57th Street, New York, NY 10019, (212) 554-0600, Fax: (212) 586-1181, www.eiu.com; *Business Asia.*

Euromonitor International, Inc., 224 S. Michigan Avenue, Suite 1500, Chicago, IL 60604, (312) 922-1115, Fax: (312) 922-1157, www.euromonitor.com; *World Marketing Data and Statistics.*

National Institute of Statistics (NIS), Ministry of Planning, Preah Monivong Boulevard, Sankat Boeung Keng Kang 1, Phnom Penh, Cambodia, www.nis.gov.kh; *Cambodia Demographic and Health Survey 2000.*

Palgrave Macmillan Ltd., Houndmills, Basingstoke, Hampshire, RG21 6XS, England, (Telephone in U.S. (888) 330-8477), (Fax in U.S. (800) 672-2054), www.palgrave.com; *The Statesman's Yearbook 2008.*

UNICEF, 3 United Nations Plaza, New York, NY 10017, (800) 253-9646, Fax: (212) 887-7465, www.unicef.org; *The State of the World's Children 2008.*

United Nations Statistics Division, New York, NY 10017, (800) 253-9646, Fax: (212) 963-4116, http://unstats.un.org; *Asia-Pacific in Figures 2004; Human Development Report 2006;* and *Statistical Yearbook.*

The World Bank, 1818 H Street, NW, Washington, DC 20433, (202) 473-1000, Fax: (202) 477-6391, www.worldbank.org; *Cambodia.*

World Health Organization (WHO), Avenue Appia 20, 1211 Geneve 27, Switzerland, (Telephone in U.S. (212) 331-9081), www.who.int; The WHO Global Atlas of Infectious Diseases.

CAMBODIA - RADIO BROADCASTING

Economist Intelligence Unit, 111 West 57th Street, New York, NY 10019, (212) 554-0600, Fax: (212) 586-1181, www.eiu.com; *Business Asia.*

Palgrave Macmillan Ltd., Houndmills, Basingstoke, Hampshire, RG21 6XS, England, (Telephone in U.S. (888) 330-8477), (Fax in U.S. (800) 672-2054), www.palgrave.com; *The Statesman's Yearbook 2008.*

CAMBODIA - RAILROADS

Jane's Information Group, 110 North Royal Street, Suite 200, Alexandria, VA 22314, (703) 683-3700, Fax: (800) 836-0297, www.janes.com; *Jane's World Railways.*

Palgrave Macmillan Ltd., Houndmills, Basingstoke, Hampshire, RG21 6XS, England, (Telephone in U.S. (888) 330-8477), (Fax in U.S. (800) 672-2054), www.palgrave.com; *The Statesman's Yearbook 2008.*

Taylor and Francis Group, An Informa Business, 2 Park Square, Milton Park, Abingdon, Oxford OX14 4RN, United Kingdom, (Dial from U.S. (212) 216-7800), (Fax from U.S. (212) 564-7854), www.tandf.co.uk; *The Europa World Year Book.*

United Nations Statistics Division, New York, NY 10017, (800) 253-9646, Fax: (212) 963-4116, http://unstats.un.org; *Statistical Yearbook.*

CAMBODIA - RELIGION

Central Intelligence Agency, Office of Public Affairs, Washington, DC 20505, (703) 482-0623, Fax: (703) 482-1739, www.cia.gov; *The World Factbook.*

Palgrave Macmillan Ltd., Houndmills, Basingstoke, Hampshire, RG21 6XS, England, (Telephone in U.S. (888) 330-8477), (Fax in U.S. (800) 672-2054), www.palgrave.com; *The Statesman's Yearbook 2008.*

CAMBODIA - RESERVES (ACCOUNTING)

Euromonitor International, Inc., 224 S. Michigan Avenue, Suite 1500, Chicago, IL 60604, (312) 922-1115, Fax: (312) 922-1157, www.euromonitor.com; *International Marketing Data and Statistics 2008.*

CAMBODIA - RETAIL TRADE

Euromonitor International, Inc., 224 S. Michigan Avenue, Suite 1500, Chicago, IL 60604, (312) 922-1115, Fax: (312) 922-1157, www.euromonitor.com; *World Marketing Data and Statistics.*

CAMBODIA - RICE PRODUCTION

See CAMBODIA - CROPS

CAMBODIA - ROADS

Central Intelligence Agency, Office of Public Affairs, Washington, DC 20505, (703) 482-0623, Fax: (703) 482-1739, www.cia.gov; *The World Factbook.*

Economist Intelligence Unit, 111 West 57th Street, New York, NY 10019, (212) 554-0600, Fax: (212) 586-1181, www.eiu.com; *Business Asia.*

Palgrave Macmillan Ltd., Houndmills, Basingstoke, Hampshire, RG21 6XS, England, (Telephone in U.S. (888) 330-8477), (Fax in U.S. (800) 672-2054), www.palgrave.com; *The Statesman's Yearbook 2008.*

CAMBODIA - RUBBER INDUSTRY AND TRADE

International Rubber Study Group (IRSG), 1st Floor, Heron House, 109/115 Wembley Hill Road, Wembley, Middlesex HA9 8DA, United Kingdom, www.rubberstudy.com; *Rubber Statistical Bulletin; Summary of World Rubber Statistics 2005; World Rubber Statistics Handbook (Volume 6, 1975-2001);* and *World Rubber Statistics Historic Handbook.*

United Nations Statistics Division, New York, NY 10017, (800) 253-9646, Fax: (212) 963-4116, http://unstats.un.org; *Statistical Yearbook.*

CAMBODIA - SALT PRODUCTION

See CAMBODIA - MINERAL INDUSTRIES

CAMBODIA - SHEEP

See CAMBODIA - LIVESTOCK

CAMBODIA - SHIPPING

Palgrave Macmillan Ltd., Houndmills, Basingstoke, Hampshire, RG21 6XS, England, (Telephone in U.S. (888) 330-8477), (Fax in U.S. (800) 672-2054), www.palgrave.com; *The Statesman's Yearbook 2008.*

Taylor and Francis Group, An Informa Business, 2 Park Square, Milton Park, Abingdon, Oxford OX14 4RN, United Kingdom, (Dial from U.S. (212) 216-7800), (Fax from U.S. (212) 564-7854), www.tandf.co.uk; *The Europa World Year Book.*

United Nations Statistics Division, New York, NY 10017, (800) 253-9646, Fax: (212) 963-4116, http://unstats.un.org; *Statistical Yearbook.*

CAMBODIA - SOCIAL ECOLOGY

United Nations Statistics Division, New York, NY 10017, (800) 253-9646, Fax: (212) 963-4116, http://unstats.un.org; *World Statistics Pocketbook.*

CAMBODIA - SOCIAL SECURITY

Palgrave Macmillan Ltd., Houndmills, Basingstoke, Hampshire, RG21 6XS, England, (Telephone in U.S. (888) 330-8477), (Fax in U.S. (800) 672-2054), www.palgrave.com; *The Statesman's Yearbook 2008.*

CAMBODIA - SOYBEAN PRODUCTION

See CAMBODIA - CROPS

CAMBODIA - STEEL PRODUCTION

See CAMBODIA - MINERAL INDUSTRIES

CAMBODIA - TELEPHONE

Economist Intelligence Unit, 111 West 57th Street, New York, NY 10019, (212) 554-0600, Fax: (212) 586-1181, www.eiu.com; *Business Asia.*

Palgrave Macmillan Ltd., Houndmills, Basingstoke, Hampshire, RG21 6XS, England, (Telephone in U.S. (888) 330-8477), (Fax in U.S. (800) 672-2054), www.palgrave.com; *The Statesman's Yearbook 2008.*

United Nations Statistics Division, New York, NY 10017, (800) 253-9646, Fax: (212) 963-4116, http://unstats.un.org; *Statistical Yearbook* and *World Statistics Pocketbook.*

CAMBODIA - TELEVISION BROADCASTING

Economist Intelligence Unit, 111 West 57th Street, New York, NY 10019, (212) 554-0600, Fax: (212) 586-1181, www.eiu.com; *Business Asia.*

CAMBODIA - TEXTILE FABRICS

United Nations Statistics Division, New York, NY 10017, (800) 253-9646, Fax: (212) 963-4116, http://unstats.un.org; *Statistical Yearbook.*

CAMBODIA - TEXTILE INDUSTRY

United Nations Conference on Trade and Development (UNCTAD), DC2-1120, United Nations, New York, NY 10017, (212) 963-0027, www.unctad.org; *UNCTAD Commodity Yearbook.*

CAMBODIA - TOBACCO INDUSTRY

Foreign Agricultural Service (FAS), U.S. Department of Agriculture (USDA), 1400 Independence Avenue, SW, Washington, DC 20250, (202) 720-3935, www.fas.usda.gov; *Tobacco: World Markets and Trade.*

United Nations Statistics Division, New York, NY 10017, (800) 253-9646, Fax: (212) 963-4116, http://unstats.un.org; *Statistical Yearbook.*

CAMBODIA - TOURISM

Euromonitor International, Inc., 224 S. Michigan Avenue, Suite 1500, Chicago, IL 60604, (312) 922-

1115, Fax: (312) 922-1157, www.euromonitor.com; *The World Economic Factbook 2008* and *World Marketing Data and Statistics.*

The World Bank, 1818 H Street, NW, Washington, DC 20433, (202) 473-1000, Fax: (202) 477-6391, www.worldbank.org; *Cambodia.*

CAMBODIA - TRADE

See CAMBODIA - INTERNATIONAL TRADE

CAMBODIA - TRANSPORTATION

Central Intelligence Agency, Office of Public Affairs, Washington, DC 20505, (703) 482-0623, Fax: (703) 482-1739, www.cia.gov; *The World Factbook.*

Economist Intelligence Unit, 111 West 57th Street, New York, NY 10019, (212) 554-0600, Fax: (212) 586-1181, www.eiu.com; *Business Asia.*

Euromonitor International, Inc., 224 S. Michigan Avenue, Suite 1500, Chicago, IL 60604, (312) 922-1115, Fax: (312) 922-1157, www.euromonitor.com; *International Marketing Data and Statistics 2008* and *World Marketing Data and Statistics.*

Taylor and Francis Group, An Informa Business, 2 Park Square, Milton Park, Abingdon, Oxford OX14 4RN, United Kingdom, (Dial from U.S. (212) 216-7800), (Fax from U.S. (212) 564-7854), www.tandf.co.uk; *The Europa World Year Book.*

United Nations Statistics Division, New York, NY 10017, (800) 253-9646, Fax: (212) 963-4116, http://unstats.un.org; *Human Development Report 2006* and *Statistical Yearbook for Asia and the Pacific 2004.*

The World Bank, 1818 H Street, NW, Washington, DC 20433, (202) 473-1000, Fax: (202) 477-6391, www.worldbank.org; *Cambodia.*

CAMBODIA - UNEMPLOYMENT

Central Intelligence Agency, Office of Public Affairs, Washington, DC 20505, (703) 482-0623, Fax: (703) 482-1739, www.cia.gov; *The World Factbook.*

Euromonitor International, Inc., 224 S. Michigan Avenue, Suite 1500, Chicago, IL 60604, (312) 922-1115, Fax: (312) 922-1157, www.euromonitor.com; *International Marketing Data and Statistics 2008.*

United Nations Statistics Division, New York, NY 10017, (800) 253-9646, Fax: (212) 963-4116, http://unstats.un.org; *Statistical Yearbook for Asia and the Pacific 2004.*

The World Bank, 1818 H Street, NW, Washington, DC 20433, (202) 473-1000, Fax: (202) 477-6391, www.worldbank.org; *Cambodia.*

CAMBODIA - VITAL STATISTICS

Euromonitor International, Inc., 224 S. Michigan Avenue, Suite 1500, Chicago, IL 60604, (312) 922-1115, Fax: (312) 922-1157, www.euromonitor.com; *International Marketing Data and Statistics 2008.*

National Institute of Statistics (NIS), Ministry of Planning, Preah Monivong Boulevard, Sankat Boeung Keng Kang 1, Phnom Penh, Cambodia, www.nis.gov.kh; *Cambodia Demographic and Health Survey 2000; Cambodia Inter-Censal Population Survey 2004;* and *2005 Cambodia's Socio-economic Indicator Database (CamInfo 2005).*

United Nations Statistics Division, New York, NY 10017, (800) 253-9646, Fax: (212) 963-4116, http://unstats.un.org; *Statistical Yearbook.*

World Health Organization (WHO), Avenue Appia 20, 1211 Geneve 27, Switzerland, (Telephone in U.S. (212) 331-9081), www.who.int; *World Health Report 2006.*

CAMBODIA - WAGES

United Nations Statistics Division, New York, NY 10017, (800) 253-9646, Fax: (212) 963-4116, http://unstats.un.org; *Statistical Yearbook for Asia and the Pacific 2004.*

The World Bank, 1818 H Street, NW, Washington, DC 20433, (202) 473-1000, Fax: (202) 477-6391, www.worldbank.org; *Cambodia.*

CAMBODIAN POPULATION

U.S. Census Bureau, Demographic Surveys Division, 4700 Silver Hill Road, Washington DC 20233-0001, (301) 763-3030, www.census.gov; *Census 2000: Demographic Profiles.*

CAMEROON - NATIONAL STATISTICAL OFFICE

Institut National de la Statistique (National Institute of Statistics), BP 134 Yaounde, Cameroon, www.statistics-cameroon.org; National Data Center.

CAMEROON - PRIMARY STATISTICS SOURCES

Institut National de la Statistique (National Institute of Statistics), BP 134 Yaounde, Cameroon, www.statistics-cameroon.org; *Annuaire statistique du Cameroun 2006* and *Cameroon in Figures 2006.*

CAMEROON - AGRICULTURAL MACHINERY

United Nations Statistics Division, New York, NY 10017, (800) 253-9646, Fax: (212) 963-4116, http://unstats.un.org; *Statistical Yearbook.*

CAMEROON - AGRICULTURE

Economist Intelligence Unit, 111 West 57th Street, New York, NY 10019, (212) 554-0600, Fax: (212) 586-1181, www.eiu.com; *Cameroon Country Report.*

Euromonitor International, Inc., 224 S. Michigan Avenue, Suite 1500, Chicago, IL 60604, (312) 922-1115, Fax: (312) 922-1157, www.euromonitor.com; *International Marketing Data and Statistics 2008* and *World Marketing Data and Statistics.*

M.E. Sharpe, 80 Business Park Drive, Armonk, NY 10504, (800) 541-6563, Fax: (914) 273-2106, www.mesharpe.com; *The Illustrated Book of World Rankings.*

Palgrave Macmillan Ltd., Houndmills, Basingstoke, Hampshire, RG21 6XS, England, (Telephone in U.S. (888) 330-8477), (Fax in U.S. (800) 672-2054), www.palgrave.com; *The Statesman's Yearbook 2008.*

Taylor and Francis Group, An Informa Business, 2 Park Square, Milton Park, Abingdon, Oxford OX14 4RN, United Kingdom, (Dial from U.S. (212) 216-7800), (Fax from U.S. (212) 564-7854), www.tandf.co.uk; *The Europa World Year Book.*

United Nations Conference on Trade and Development (UNCTAD), DC2-1120, United Nations, New York, NY 10017, (212) 963-0027, www.unctad.org; *UNCTAD Commodity Yearbook.*

United Nations Economic Commission for Africa (ECA), PO Box 3001, Addis Ababa, Ethiopia, (Telephone in U.S. (212) 963-4957), www.uneca.org; *African Statistical Yearbook 2006.*

United Nations Food and Agricultural Organization (FAO), Viale delle Terme di Caracalla, 00100 Rome, Italy, (Dial from U.S. (202) 653-2400), (Fax from U.S. (202) 653 5760), www.fao.org; AQUASTAT; *FAO Production Yearbook 2002; FAO Trade Yearbook;* and *The State of Food and Agriculture (SOFA) 2006.*

United Nations Statistics Division, New York, NY 10017, (800) 253-9646, Fax: (212) 963-4116, http://unstats.un.org; *Statistical Yearbook* and *Survey of Economic and Social Conditions in Africa 2005.*

The World Bank, 1818 H Street, NW, Washington, DC 20433, (202) 473-1000, Fax: (202) 477-6391, www.worldbank.org; *Africa Live Database (LDB); African Development Indicators (ADI) 2007; Cameroon;* and *The World Bank Atlas 2003-2004.*

CAMEROON - AIRLINES

International Civil Aviation Organization (ICAO), External Relations and Public Information Office (EPO), 999 University Street, Montreal, Quebec H3C 5H7, Canada, (Dial from U.S. (514) 954-8219), (Fax from U.S. (514) 954-6077), www.icao.int; *Civil Aviation Statistics of the World.*

M.E. Sharpe, 80 Business Park Drive, Armonk, NY 10504, (800) 541-6563, Fax: (914) 273-2106, www.mesharpe.com; *The Illustrated Book of World Rankings.*

Palgrave Macmillan Ltd., Houndmills, Basingstoke, Hampshire, RG21 6XS, England, (Telephone in U.S. (888) 330-8477), (Fax in U.S. (800) 672-2054), www.palgrave.com; *The Statesman's Yearbook 2008.*

Taylor and Francis Group, An Informa Business, 2 Park Square, Milton Park, Abingdon, Oxford OX14 4RN, United Kingdom, (Dial from U.S. (212) 216-7800), (Fax from U.S. (212) 564-7854), www.tandf.co.uk; *The Europa World Year Book.*

United Nations Economic Commission for Africa (ECA), PO Box 3001, Addis Ababa, Ethiopia, (Telephone in U.S. (212) 963-4957), www.uneca.org; *African Statistical Yearbook 2006.*

United Nations Statistics Division, New York, NY 10017, (800) 253-9646, Fax: (212) 963-4116, http://unstats.un.org; *Statistical Yearbook.*

CAMEROON - AIRPORTS

Central Intelligence Agency, Office of Public Affairs, Washington, DC 20505, (703) 482-0623, Fax: (703) 482-1739, www.cia.gov; *The World Factbook.*

CAMEROON - ALUMINUM PRODUCTION

See CAMEROON - MINERAL INDUSTRIES

CAMEROON - ARMED FORCES

Central Intelligence Agency, Office of Public Affairs, Washington, DC 20505, (703) 482-0623, Fax: (703) 482-1739, www.cia.gov; *The World Factbook.*

Euromonitor International, Inc., 224 S. Michigan Avenue, Suite 1500, Chicago, IL 60604, (312) 922-1115, Fax: (312) 922-1157, www.euromonitor.com; *World Marketing Data and Statistics.*

International Institute for Strategic Studies (IISS), Arundel House, 13-15 Arundel Street, Temple Place, London WC2R 3DX, England, www.iiss.org; *The Military Balance 2007.*

International Monetary Fund (IMF), 700 Nineteenth Street, NW, Washington, DC 20431, (202) 623-7000, Fax: (202) 623-4661, www.imf.org; *Government Finance Statistics Yearbook (2008 Edition).*

Palgrave Macmillan Ltd., Houndmills, Basingstoke, Hampshire, RG21 6XS, England, (Telephone in U.S. (888) 330-8477), (Fax in U.S. (800) 672-2054), www.palgrave.com; *The Statesman's Yearbook 2008.*

U.S. Department of State (DOS), 2201 C Street NW, Washington, DC 20520, (202) 647-4000, www.state.gov; *World Military Expenditures and Arms Transfers (WMEAT).*

United Nations Statistics Division, New York, NY 10017, (800) 253-9646, Fax: (212) 963-4116, http://unstats.un.org; *Human Development Report 2006.*

CAMEROON - BALANCE OF PAYMENTS

African Development Bank Group, Rue Joseph Anoma, 01 BP 1387 Abidjan 01, Cote d'Ivoire, www.afdb.org; *Statistics Pocketbook 2008.*

Taylor and Francis Group, An Informa Business, 2 Park Square, Milton Park, Abingdon, Oxford OX14 4RN, United Kingdom, (Dial from U.S. (212) 216-7800), (Fax from U.S. (212) 564-7854), www.tandf.co.uk; *The Europa World Year Book.*

United Nations Conference on Trade and Development (UNCTAD), DC2-1120, United Nations, New York, NY 10017, (212) 963-0027, www.unctad.org; *Handbook of Statistics 2005.*

United Nations Economic Commission for Africa (ECA), PO Box 3001, Addis Ababa, Ethiopia, (Telephone in U.S. (212) 963-4957), www.uneca.org; *African Statistical Yearbook 2006.*

The World Bank, 1818 H Street, NW, Washington, DC 20433, (202) 473-1000, Fax: (202) 477-6391, www.worldbank.org; *Camaroon* and *The World Bank Atlas 2003-2004.*

CAMEROON - BANKS AND BANKING

Euromonitor International, Inc., 224 S. Michigan Avenue, Suite 1500, Chicago, IL 60604, (312) 922-1115, Fax: (312) 922-1157, www.euromonitor.com; *World Marketing Data and Statistics.*

International Monetary Fund (IMF), 700 Nineteenth Street, NW, Washington, DC 20431, (202) 623-7000, Fax: (202) 623-4661, www.imf.org; *Government Finance Statistics Yearbook (2008 Edition)* and *International Financial Statistics Yearbook 2007.*

M.E. Sharpe, 80 Business Park Drive, Armonk, NY 10504, (800) 541-6563, Fax: (914) 273-2106, www.mesharpe.com; *The Illustrated Book of World Rankings.*

Palgrave Macmillan Ltd., Houndmills, Basingstoke, Hampshire, RG21 6XS, England, (Telephone in U.S. (888) 330-8477), (Fax in U.S. (800) 672-2054), www.palgrave.com; *The Statesman's Yearbook 2008.*

Taylor and Francis Group, An Informa Business, 2 Park Square, Milton Park, Abingdon, Oxford OX14 4RN, United Kingdom, (Dial from U.S. (212) 216-7800), (Fax from U.S. (212) 564-7854), www.tandf.co.uk; *The Europa World Year Book.*

United Nations Economic Commission for Africa (ECA), PO Box 3001, Addis Ababa, Ethiopia, (Telephone in U.S. (212) 963-4957), www.uneca.org; *African Statistical Yearbook 2006.*

CAMEROON - BARLEY PRODUCTION

See CAMEROON - CROPS

CAMEROON - BEVERAGE INDUSTRY

M.E. Sharpe, 80 Business Park Drive, Armonk, NY 10504, (800) 541-6563, Fax: (914) 273-2106, www.mesharpe.com; *The Illustrated Book of World Rankings.*

United Nations Statistics Division, New York, NY 10017, (800) 253-9646, Fax: (212) 963-4116, http://unstats.un.org; *Statistical Yearbook.*

CAMEROON - BONDS

International Monetary Fund (IMF), 700 Nineteenth Street, NW, Washington, DC 20431, (202) 623-7000, Fax: (202) 623-4661, www.imf.org; *Government Finance Statistics Yearbook (2008 Edition).*

CAMEROON - BROADCASTING

Central Intelligence Agency, Office of Public Affairs, Washington, DC 20505, (703) 482-0623, Fax: (703) 482-1739, www.cia.gov; *The World Factbook.*

Euromonitor International, Inc., 224 S. Michigan Avenue, Suite 1500, Chicago, IL 60604, (312) 922-1115, Fax: (312) 922-1157, www.euromonitor.com; *World Marketing Data and Statistics.*

M.E. Sharpe, 80 Business Park Drive, Armonk, NY 10504, (800) 541-6563, Fax: (914) 273-2106, www.mesharpe.com; *The Illustrated Book of World Rankings.*

Palgrave Macmillan Ltd., Houndmills, Basingstoke, Hampshire, RG21 6XS, England, (Telephone in U.S. (888) 330-8477), (Fax in U.S. (800) 672-2054), www.palgrave.com; *The Statesman's Yearbook 2008.*

WRTH Publications Limited, PO Box 290, Oxford OX2 7FT, UK, www.wrth.com; *World Radio TV Handbook 2007.*

CAMEROON - BUDGET

Central Intelligence Agency, Office of Public Affairs, Washington, DC 20505, (703) 482-0623, Fax: (703) 482-1739, www.cia.gov; *The World Factbook.*

CAMEROON - CACAO

See CAMEROON - CROPS

CAMEROON - CAPITAL LEVY

International Monetary Fund (IMF), 700 Nineteenth Street, NW, Washington, DC 20431, (202) 623-7000, Fax: (202) 623-4661, www.imf.org; *Government Finance Statistics Yearbook (2008 Edition).*

CAMEROON - CATTLE

See CAMEROON - LIVESTOCK

CAMEROON - CHICKENS

See CAMEROON - LIVESTOCK

CAMEROON - CHILDBIRTH - STATISTICS

Central Intelligence Agency, Office of Public Affairs, Washington, DC 20505, (703) 482-0623, Fax: (703) 482-1739, www.cia.gov; *The World Factbook.*

Euromonitor International, Inc., 224 S. Michigan Avenue, Suite 1500, Chicago, IL 60604, (312) 922-1115, Fax: (312) 922-1157, www.euromonitor.com; *International Marketing Data and Statistics 2008* and *The World Economic Factbook 2008.*

M.E. Sharpe, 80 Business Park Drive, Armonk, NY 10504, (800) 541-6563, Fax: (914) 273-2106, www.mesharpe.com; *The Illustrated Book of World Rankings.*

Palgrave Macmillan Ltd., Houndmills, Basingstoke, Hampshire, RG21 6XS, England, (Telephone in U.S. (888) 330-8477), (Fax in U.S. (800) 672-2054), www.palgrave.com; *The Statesman's Yearbook 2008.*

Taylor and Francis Group, An Informa Business, 2 Park Square, Milton Park, Abingdon, Oxford OX14 4RN, United Kingdom, (Dial from U.S. (212) 216-7800), (Fax from U.S. (212) 564-7854), www.tandf.co.uk; *The Europa World Year Book.*

United Nations Statistics Division, New York, NY 10017, (800) 253-9646, Fax: (212) 963-4116, http://unstats.un.org; *Demographic Yearbook; Statistical Yearbook;* and *Survey of Economic and Social Conditions in Africa 2005.*

The World Bank, 1818 H Street, NW, Washington, DC 20433, (202) 473-1000, Fax: (202) 477-6391, www.worldbank.org; *The World Bank Atlas 2003-2004.*

CAMEROON - CLIMATE

International Institute for Environment and Development (IIED), 3 Endsleigh Street, London, England, WC1H 0DD, United Kingdom, www.iied.org; *Environment Urbanization* and *Haramata - Bulletin of the Drylands.*

M.E. Sharpe, 80 Business Park Drive, Armonk, NY 10504, (800) 541-6563, Fax: (914) 273-2106, www.mesharpe.com; *The Illustrated Book of World Rankings.*

Palgrave Macmillan Ltd., Houndmills, Basingstoke, Hampshire, RG21 6XS, England, (Telephone in U.S. (888) 330-8477), (Fax in U.S. (800) 672-2054), www.palgrave.com; *The Statesman's Yearbook 2008.*

CAMEROON - COAL PRODUCTION

See CAMEROON - MINERAL INDUSTRIES

CAMEROON - COCOA PRODUCTION

See CAMEROON - CROPS

CAMEROON - COFFEE

See CAMEROON - CROPS

CAMEROON - COMMERCE

Palgrave Macmillan Ltd., Houndmills, Basingstoke, Hampshire, RG21 6XS, England, (Telephone in U.S. (888) 330-8477), (Fax in U.S. (800) 672-2054), www.palgrave.com; *The Statesman's Yearbook 2008.*

CAMEROON - COMMODITY EXCHANGES

Commodity Research Bureau, 330 South Wells Street, Suite 612, Chicago, IL 60606-7110, (800) 621-5271, Fax: (312) 939-4135, www.crbtrader.com; *2006 CRB Commodity Yearbook and CD.*

International Monetary Fund (IMF), 700 Nineteenth Street, NW, Washington, DC 20431, (202) 623-7000, Fax: (202) 623-4661, www.imf.org; *IMF Primary Commodity Prices.*

United Nations Food and Agricultural Organization (FAO), Viale delle Terme di Caracalla, 00100 Rome, Italy, (Dial from U.S. (202) 653-2400), (Fax from U.S. (202) 653 5760), www.fao.org; *The State of Food and Agriculture (SOFA) 2006.*

CAMEROON - COMMUNICATION AND TRAFFIC

United Nations Statistics Division, New York, NY 10017, (800) 253-9646, Fax: (212) 963-4116, http://unstats.un.org; *Statistical Yearbook.*

CAMEROON - CONSTRUCTION INDUSTRY

M.E. Sharpe, 80 Business Park Drive, Armonk, NY 10504, (800) 541-6563, Fax: (914) 273-2106, www.mesharpe.com; *The Illustrated Book of World Rankings.*

United Nations Economic Commission for Africa (ECA), PO Box 3001, Addis Ababa, Ethiopia, (Telephone in U.S. (212) 963-4957), www.uneca.org; *African Statistical Yearbook 2006.*

United Nations Statistics Division, New York, NY 10017, (800) 253-9646, Fax: (212) 963-4116, http://unstats.un.org; *Statistical Yearbook.*

CAMEROON - CONSUMER PRICE INDEXES

Taylor and Francis Group, An Informa Business, 2 Park Square, Milton Park, Abingdon, Oxford OX14 4RN, United Kingdom, (Dial from U.S. (212) 216-7800), (Fax from U.S. (212) 564-7854), www.tandf.co.uk; *The Europa World Year Book.*

United Nations Economic Commission for Africa (ECA), PO Box 3001, Addis Ababa, Ethiopia, (Telephone in U.S. (212) 963-4957), www.uneca.org; *African Statistical Yearbook 2006.*

United Nations Statistics Division, New York, NY 10017, (800) 253-9646, Fax: (212) 963-4116, http://unstats.un.org; *Statistical Yearbook* and *Survey of Economic and Social Conditions in Africa 2005.*

The World Bank, 1818 H Street, NW, Washington, DC 20433, (202) 473-1000, Fax: (202) 477-6391, www.worldbank.org; *Camaroon.*

CAMEROON - CONSUMPTION (ECONOMICS)

African Development Bank Group, Rue Joseph Anoma, 01 BP 1387 Abidjan 01, Cote d'Ivoire, www.afdb.org; *Statistics Pocketbook 2008.*

United Nations Statistics Division, New York, NY 10017, (800) 253-9646, Fax: (212) 963-4116, http://unstats.un.org; *Survey of Economic and Social Conditions in Africa 2005.*

The World Bank, 1818 H Street, NW, Washington, DC 20433, (202) 473-1000, Fax: (202) 477-6391, www.worldbank.org; *The World Bank Atlas 2003-2004.*

CAMEROON - COPPER INDUSTRY AND TRADE

See CAMEROON - MINERAL INDUSTRIES

CAMEROON - CORN INDUSTRY

See CAMEROON - CROPS

CAMEROON - COTTON

See CAMEROON - CROPS

CAMEROON - CRIME

Yale University Press, PO Box 209040, New Haven, CT 06520-9040, (203) 432-0960, Fax: (203) 432-0948, http://yalepress.yale.edu/yupbooks; *Violence and Crime in Cross-National Perspective.*

CAMEROON - CROPS

International Monetary Fund (IMF), 700 Nineteenth Street, NW, Washington, DC 20431, (202) 623-7000, Fax: (202) 623-4661, www.imf.org; *International Financial Statistics Yearbook 2007.*

M.E. Sharpe, 80 Business Park Drive, Armonk, NY 10504, (800) 541-6563, Fax: (914) 273-2106, www.mesharpe.com; *The Illustrated Book of World Rankings.*

Palgrave Macmillan Ltd., Houndmills, Basingstoke, Hampshire, RG21 6XS, England, (Telephone in U.S. (888) 330-8477), (Fax in U.S. (800) 672-2054), www.palgrave.com; *The Statesman's Yearbook 2008.*

Taylor and Francis Group, An Informa Business, 2 Park Square, Milton Park, Abingdon, Oxford OX14 4RN, United Kingdom, (Dial from U.S. (212) 216-7800), (Fax from U.S. (212) 564-7854), www.tandf.co.uk; *The Europa World Year Book.*

United Nations Conference on Trade and Development (UNCTAD), DC2-1120, United Nations, New York, NY 10017, (212) 963-0027, www.unctad.org; *UNCTAD Commodity Yearbook.*

United Nations Economic Commission for Africa (ECA), PO Box 3001, Addis Ababa, Ethiopia, (Telephone in U.S. (212) 963-4957), www.uneca.org; *African Statistical Yearbook 2006.*

United Nations Food and Agricultural Organization (FAO), Viale delle Terme di Caracalla, 00100 Rome, Italy, (Dial from U.S. (202) 653-2400), (Fax from U.S. (202) 653 5760), www.fao.org; *The State of Food and Agriculture (SOFA) 2006.*

United Nations Statistics Division, New York, NY 10017, (800) 253-9646, Fax: (212) 963-4116, http://unstats.un.org; *Statistical Yearbook.*

CAMEROON - CUSTOMS ADMINISTRATION

International Monetary Fund (IMF), 700 Nineteenth Street, NW, Washington, DC 20431, (202) 623-7000, Fax: (202) 623-4661, www.imf.org; *Government Finance Statistics Yearbook (2008 Edition).*

Palgrave Macmillan Ltd., Houndmills, Basingstoke, Hampshire, RG21 6XS, England, (Telephone in U.S. (888) 330-8477), (Fax in U.S. (800) 672-2054), www.palgrave.com; *The Statesman's Yearbook 2008.*

CAMEROON - DAIRY PROCESSING

M.E. Sharpe, 80 Business Park Drive, Armonk, NY 10504, (800) 541-6563, Fax: (914) 273-2106, www.mesharpe.com; *The Illustrated Book of World Rankings.*

Palgrave Macmillan Ltd., Houndmills, Basingstoke, Hampshire, RG21 6XS, England, (Telephone in U.S. (888) 330-8477), (Fax in U.S. (800) 672-2054), www.palgrave.com; *The Statesman's Yearbook 2008.*

Taylor and Francis Group, An Informa Business, 2 Park Square, Milton Park, Abingdon, Oxford OX14 4RN, United Kingdom, (Dial from U.S. (212) 216-7800), (Fax from U.S. (212) 564-7854), www.tandf.co.uk; *The Europa World Year Book.*

United Nations Food and Agricultural Organization (FAO), Viale delle Terme di Caracalla, 00100 Rome, Italy, (Dial from U.S. (202) 653-2400), (Fax from U.S. (202) 653 5760), www.fao.org; *The State of Food and Agriculture (SOFA) 2006.*

United Nations Statistics Division, New York, NY 10017, (800) 253-9646, Fax: (212) 963-4116, http://unstats.un.org; *Statistical Yearbook.*

CAMEROON - DEATH RATES

See CAMEROON - MORTALITY

CAMEROON - DEBTS, EXTERNAL

African Development Bank Group, Rue Joseph Anoma, 01 BP 1387 Abidjan 01, Cote d'Ivoire, www.afdb.org; *Statistics Pocketbook 2008.*

International Monetary Fund (IMF), 700 Nineteenth Street, NW, Washington, DC 20431, (202) 623-7000, Fax: (202) 623-4661, www.imf.org; *Government Finance Statistics Yearbook (2008 Edition).*

Palgrave Macmillan Ltd., Houndmills, Basingstoke, Hampshire, RG21 6XS, England, (Telephone in U.S. (888) 330-8477), (Fax in U.S. (800) 672-2054), www.palgrave.com; *The Statesman's Yearbook 2008.*

United Nations Statistics Division, New York, NY 10017, (800) 253-9646, Fax: (212) 963-4116, http://unstats.un.org; *Survey of Economic and Social Conditions in Africa 2005.*

The World Bank, 1818 H Street, NW, Washington, DC 20433, (202) 473-1000, Fax: (202) 477-6391, www.worldbank.org; *Africa Live Database (LDB); African Development Indicators (ADI) 2007; Global Development Finance 2007; World Development Indicators (WDI) 2008;* and *World Development Report 2008.*

CAMEROON - DEFENSE EXPENDITURES

See CAMEROON - ARMED FORCES

CAMEROON - DEMOGRAPHY

Euromonitor International, Inc., 224 S. Michigan Avenue, Suite 1500, Chicago, IL 60604, (312) 922-1115, Fax: (312) 922-1157, www.euromonitor.com; *International Marketing Data and Statistics 2008; The World Economic Factbook 2008;* and *World Marketing Data and Statistics.*

M.E. Sharpe, 80 Business Park Drive, Armonk, NY 10504, (800) 541-6563, Fax: (914) 273-2106, www.mesharpe.com; *The Illustrated Book of World Rankings.*

United Nations Statistics Division, New York, NY 10017, (800) 253-9646, Fax: (212) 963-4116, http://unstats.un.org; *Human Development Report 2006* and *Survey of Economic and Social Conditions in Africa 2005.*

The World Bank, 1818 H Street, NW, Washington, DC 20433, (202) 473-1000, Fax: (202) 477-6391, www.worldbank.org; *Camaroon.*

CAMEROON - DIAMONDS

See CAMEROON - MINERAL INDUSTRIES

CAMEROON - DISPOSABLE INCOME

M.E. Sharpe, 80 Business Park Drive, Armonk, NY 10504, (800) 541-6563, Fax: (914) 273-2106, www.mesharpe.com; *The Illustrated Book of World Rankings.*

United Nations Statistics Division, New York, NY 10017, (800) 253-9646, Fax: (212) 963-4116, http://unstats.un.org; *National Accounts Statistics: Compendium of Income Distribution Statistics* and *Statistical Yearbook.*

CAMEROON - DIVORCE

M.E. Sharpe, 80 Business Park Drive, Armonk, NY 10504, (800) 541-6563, Fax: (914) 273-2106, www.mesharpe.com; *The Illustrated Book of World Rankings.*

United Nations Statistics Division, New York, NY 10017, (800) 253-9646, Fax: (212) 963-4116, http://unstats.un.org; *Demographic Yearbook.*

CAMEROON - ECONOMIC ASSISTANCE

United Nations Statistics Division, New York, NY 10017, (800) 253-9646, Fax: (212) 963-4116, http://unstats.un.org; *Statistical Yearbook.*

CAMEROON - ECONOMIC CONDITIONS

African Development Bank Group, Rue Joseph Anoma, 01 BP 1387 Abidjan 01, Cote d'Ivoire, www.afdb.org; *The African Statistical Journal; Gender, Poverty and Environmental Indicators on African Countries 2007; Selected Statistics on African Countries 2007;* and *Statistics Pocketbook 2008.*

Center for International Business Education Research (CIBER), Columbia Business School and School of International and Public Affairs, Uris Hall, Room 212, 3022 Broadway, New York, NY 10027-6902, Mr. Joshua Safier, (212) 854-4750, Fax: (212) 222-9821, www.columbia.edu/cu/ciber/; Datastream International.

Central Intelligence Agency, Office of Public Affairs, Washington, DC 20505, (703) 482-0623, Fax: (703) 482-1739, www.cia.gov; *The World Factbook.*

DSI Data Service Information, Xantener Strasse 51a, D-47495 Rheinberg, Germany, www.dsidata.com; *Campus Solution.*

Dun and Bradstreet (DB) Corporation, 103 JFK Parkway, Short Hills, NJ 07078, (973) 921-5500, www.dnb.com; *Country Report.*

Economist Intelligence Unit, 111 West 57th Street, New York, NY 10019, (212) 554-0600, Fax: (212) 586-1181, www.eiu.com; *Business Africa* and *Cameroon Country Report.*

Euromonitor International, Inc., 224 S. Michigan Avenue, Suite 1500, Chicago, IL 60604, (312) 922-1115, Fax: (312) 922-1157, www.euromonitor.com; *International Marketing Data and Statistics 2008; The World Economic Factbook 2008;* and *World Marketing Data and Statistics.*

International Monetary Fund (IMF), 700 Nineteenth Street, NW, Washington, DC 20431, (202) 623-7000, Fax: (202) 623-4661, www.imf.org; *World Economic Outlook Reports.*

M.E. Sharpe, 80 Business Park Drive, Armonk, NY 10504, (800) 541-6563, Fax: (914) 273-2106, www.mesharpe.com; *The Illustrated Book of World Rankings.*

Palgrave Macmillan Ltd., Houndmills, Basingstoke, Hampshire, RG21 6XS, England, (Telephone in U.S. (888) 330-8477), (Fax in U.S. (800) 672-2054), www.palgrave.com; *The Statesman's Yearbook 2008.*

Taylor and Francis Group, An Informa Business, 2 Park Square, Milton Park, Abingdon, Oxford OX14 4RN, United Kingdom, (Dial from U.S. (212) 216-7800), (Fax from U.S. (212) 564-7854), www.tandf.co.uk; *The Europa World Year Book.*

United Nations Statistics Division, New York, NY 10017, (800) 253-9646, Fax: (212) 963-4116, http://unstats.un.org; *Compendium of Intra-African and Related Foreign Trade Statistics 2003* and *World Statistics Pocketbook.*

The World Bank, 1818 H Street, NW, Washington, DC 20433, (202) 473-1000, Fax: (202) 477-6391, www.worldbank.org; *Africa Household Survey Databank; Africa Live Database (LDB); Africa Standardized Files and Indicators; African Development Indicators (ADI) 2007; Camaroon; Global Economic Monitor (GEM); Global Economic Prospects 2008; The World Bank Atlas 2003-2004;* and *World Development Report 2008.*

CAMEROON - EDUCATION

African Development Bank Group, Rue Joseph Anoma, 01 BP 1387 Abidjan 01, Cote d'Ivoire, www.afdb.org; *Statistics Pocketbook 2008.*

Euromonitor International, Inc., 224 S. Michigan Avenue, Suite 1500, Chicago, IL 60604, (312) 922-1115, Fax: (312) 922-1157, www.euromonitor.com; *International Marketing Data and Statistics 2008* and *World Marketing Data and Statistics.*

International Monetary Fund (IMF), 700 Nineteenth Street, NW, Washington, DC 20431, (202) 623-7000, Fax: (202) 623-4661, www.imf.org; *Government Finance Statistics Yearbook (2008 Edition).*

M.E. Sharpe, 80 Business Park Drive, Armonk, NY 10504, (800) 541-6563, Fax: (914) 273-2106, www.mesharpe.com; *The Illustrated Book of World Rankings.*

Palgrave Macmillan Ltd., Houndmills, Basingstoke, Hampshire, RG21 6XS, England, (Telephone in U.S. (888) 330-8477), (Fax in U.S. (800) 672-2054), www.palgrave.com; *The Statesman's Yearbook 2008.*

Taylor and Francis Group, An Informa Business, 2 Park Square, Milton Park, Abingdon, Oxford OX14 4RN, United Kingdom, (Dial from U.S. (212) 216-7800), (Fax from U.S. (212) 564-7854), www.tandf.co.uk; *The Europa World Year Book.*

UNESCO Institute for Statistics, C.P. 6128 Succursale Centre-Ville, Montreal, Quebec, H3C 3J7 Canada, (Dial from U.S. (514) 343-6880), (Fax from U.S. (514) 343 6882), www.uis.unesco.org; *Statistical Tables.*

United Nations Economic Commission for Africa (ECA), PO Box 3001, Addis Ababa, Ethiopia, (Telephone in U.S. (212) 963-4957), www.uneca.org; *African Statistical Yearbook 2006.*

United Nations Statistics Division, New York, NY 10017, (800) 253-9646, Fax: (212) 963-4116, http://

unstats.un.org; *Human Development Report 2006* and *Survey of Economic and Social Conditions in Africa 2005.*

The World Bank, 1818 H Street, NW, Washington, DC 20433, (202) 473-1000, Fax: (202) 477-6391, www.worldbank.org; *Camaroon; World Development Indicators (WDI) 2008;* and *World Development Report 2008.*

CAMEROON - ELECTRICITY

M.E. Sharpe, 80 Business Park Drive, Armonk, NY 10504, (800) 541-6563, Fax: (914) 273-2106, www.mesharpe.com; *The Illustrated Book of World Rankings.*

Organisation for Economic Cooperation and Development (OECD), 2 rue Andre Pascal, F-75775 Paris Cedex 16, France, (Telephone in U.S. (202) 785-6323), (Fax in U.S. (202) 785-0350), www.oecd.org; *World Energy Outlook 2007.*

Palgrave Macmillan Ltd., Houndmills, Basingstoke, Hampshire, RG21 6XS, England, (Telephone in U.S. (888) 330-8477), (Fax in U.S. (800) 672-2054), www.palgrave.com; *The Statesman's Yearbook 2008.*

U.S. Department of Energy (DOE), Energy Information Administration (EIA), 1000 Independence Avenue, SW, Washington, DC 20585, (202) 586-8800, www.eia.doe.gov; *International Energy Annual 2004* and *International Energy Outlook 2006.*

United Nations Economic Commission for Africa (ECA), PO Box 3001, Addis Ababa, Ethiopia, (Telephone in U.S. (212) 963-4957), www.uneca.org; *African Statistical Yearbook 2006.*

United Nations Statistics Division, New York, NY 10017, (800) 253-9646, Fax: (212) 963-4116, http://unstats.un.org; *Human Development Report 2006; Statistical Yearbook;* and *Survey of Economic and Social Conditions in Africa 2005.*

CAMEROON - EMPLOYMENT

Euromonitor International, Inc., 224 S. Michigan Avenue, Suite 1500, Chicago, IL 60604, (312) 922-1115, Fax: (312) 922-1157, www.euromonitor.com; *International Marketing Data and Statistics 2008.*

International Labour Office, I.L.O. Publications, 4 route des Morillons, CH-1211 Geneva 22, Switzerland, (Telephone in U.S. (202) 653-7652), (Fax in U.S. (202) 653-7687), www.ilo.org; *Yearbook of Labour Statistics 2006.*

M.E. Sharpe, 80 Business Park Drive, Armonk, NY 10504, (800) 541-6563, Fax: (914) 273-2106, www.mesharpe.com; *The Illustrated Book of World Rankings.*

United Nations Economic Commission for Africa (ECA), PO Box 3001, Addis Ababa, Ethiopia, (Telephone in U.S. (212) 963-4957), www.uneca.org; *African Statistical Yearbook 2006.*

United Nations Statistics Division, New York, NY 10017, (800) 253-9646, Fax: (212) 963-4116, http://unstats.un.org; *Statistical Yearbook* and *Survey of Economic and Social Conditions in Africa 2005.*

The World Bank, 1818 H Street, NW, Washington, DC 20433, (202) 473-1000, Fax: (202) 477-6391, www.worldbank.org; *Camaroon.*

CAMEROON - ENVIRONMENTAL CONDITIONS

DSI Data Service Information, Xantener Strasse 51a, D-47495 Rheinberg, Germany, www.dsidata.com; *Campus Solution* and *DSI's Global Environmental Database.*

Economist Intelligence Unit, 111 West 57th Street, New York, NY 10019, (212) 554-0600, Fax: (212) 586-1181, www.eiu.com; *Cameroon Country Report.*

International Institute for Environment and Development (IIED), 3 Endsleigh Street, London, England, WC1H 0DD, United Kingdom, www.iied.org; *Environment Urbanization* and *Haramata - Bulletin of the Drylands.*

United Nations Statistics Division, New York, NY 10017, (800) 253-9646, Fax: (212) 963-4116, http://unstats.un.org; *World Statistics Pocketbook.*

CAMEROON - EXPORTS

African Development Bank Group, Rue Joseph Anoma, 01 BP 1387 Abidjan 01, Cote d'Ivoire, www.afdb.org; *Statistics Pocketbook 2008.*

Central Intelligence Agency, Office of Public Affairs, Washington, DC 20505, (703) 482-0623, Fax: (703) 482-1739, www.cia.gov; *The World Factbook.*

Economist Intelligence Unit, 111 West 57th Street, New York, NY 10019, (212) 554-0600, Fax: (212) 586-1181, www.eiu.com; *Cameroon Country Report.*

Euromonitor International, Inc., 224 S. Michigan Avenue, Suite 1500, Chicago, IL 60604, (312) 922-1115, Fax: (312) 922-1157, www.euromonitor.com; *International Marketing Data and Statistics 2008* and *The World Economic Factbook 2008.*

International Monetary Fund (IMF), 700 Nineteenth Street, NW, Washington, DC 20431, (202) 623-7000, Fax: (202) 623-4661, www.imf.org; *Direction of Trade Statistics Yearbook 2007; Government Finance Statistics Yearbook (2008 Edition);* and *International Financial Statistics Yearbook 2007.*

Palgrave Macmillan Ltd., Houndmills, Basingstoke, Hampshire, RG21 6XS, England, (Telephone in U.S. (888) 330-8477), (Fax in U.S. (800) 672-2054), www.palgrave.com; *The Statesman's Yearbook 2008.*

Taylor and Francis Group, An Informa Business, 2 Park Square, Milton Park, Abingdon, Oxford OX14 4RN, United Kingdom, (Dial from U.S. (212) 216-7800), (Fax from U.S. (212) 564-7854), www.tandf.co.uk; *The Europa World Year Book.*

United Nations Conference on Trade and Development (UNCTAD), DC2-1120, United Nations, New York, NY 10017, (212) 963-0027, www.unctad.org; *Handbook of Statistics 2005.*

United Nations Economic Commission for Africa (ECA), PO Box 3001, Addis Ababa, Ethiopia, (Telephone in U.S. (212) 963-4957), www.uneca.org; *African Statistical Yearbook 2006.*

United Nations Food and Agricultural Organization (FAO), Viale delle Terme di Caracalla, 00100 Rome, Italy, (Dial from U.S. (202) 653-2400), (Fax from U.S. (202) 653 5760), www.fao.org; *The State of Food and Agriculture (SOFA) 2006.*

United Nations Statistics Division, New York, NY 10017, (800) 253-9646, Fax: (212) 963-4116, http://unstats.un.org; *Compendium of Intra-African and Related Foreign Trade Statistics 2003* and *Survey of Economic and Social Conditions in Africa 2005.*

The World Bank, 1818 H Street, NW, Washington, DC 20433, (202) 473-1000, Fax: (202) 477-6391, www.worldbank.org; *World Development Indicators (WDI) 2008* and *World Development Report 2008.*

CAMEROON - FEMALE WORKING POPULATION

See CAMEROON - EMPLOYMENT

CAMEROON - FERTILITY, HUMAN

Central Intelligence Agency, Office of Public Affairs, Washington, DC 20505, (703) 482-0623, Fax: (703) 482-1739, www.cia.gov; *The World Factbook.*

M.E. Sharpe, 80 Business Park Drive, Armonk, NY 10504, (800) 541-6563, Fax: (914) 273-2106, www.mesharpe.com; *The Illustrated Book of World Rankings.*

United Nations Statistics Division, New York, NY 10017, (800) 253-9646, Fax: (212) 963-4116, http://unstats.un.org; *Human Development Report 2006* and *Survey of Economic and Social Conditions in Africa 2005.*

The World Bank, 1818 H Street, NW, Washington, DC 20433, (202) 473-1000, Fax: (202) 477-6391, www.worldbank.org; *The World Bank Atlas 2003-2004; World Development Indicators (WDI) 2008;* and *World Development Report 2008.*

CAMEROON - FERTILIZER INDUSTRY

United Nations Food and Agricultural Organization (FAO), Viale delle Terme di Caracalla, 00100 Rome, Italy, (Dial from U.S. (202) 653-2400), (Fax from U.S. (202) 653 5760), www.fao.org; *FAO Fertilizer Yearbook* and *The State of Food and Agriculture (SOFA) 2006.*

United Nations Statistics Division, New York, NY 10017, (800) 253-9646, Fax: (212) 963-4116, http://unstats.un.org; *Statistical Yearbook.*

CAMEROON - FETAL MORTALITY

See CAMEROON - MORTALITY

CAMEROON - FILM

See CAMEROON - MOTION PICTURES

CAMEROON - FINANCE

Taylor and Francis Group, An Informa Business, 2 Park Square, Milton Park, Abingdon, Oxford OX14 4RN, United Kingdom, (Dial from U.S. (212) 216-7800), (Fax from U.S. (212) 564-7854), www.tandf.co.uk; *The Europa World Year Book.*

United Nations Economic Commission for Africa (ECA), PO Box 3001, Addis Ababa, Ethiopia, (Telephone in U.S. (212) 963-4957), www.uneca.org; *African Statistical Yearbook 2006.*

United Nations Statistics Division, New York, NY 10017, (800) 253-9646, Fax: (212) 963-4116, http://unstats.un.org; *National Accounts Statistics: Compendium of Income Distribution Statistics* and *Statistical Yearbook.*

The World Bank, 1818 H Street, NW, Washington, DC 20433, (202) 473-1000, Fax: (202) 477-6391, www.worldbank.org; *Camaroon.*

CAMEROON - FINANCE, PUBLIC

African Development Bank Group, Rue Joseph Anoma, 01 BP 1387 Abidjan 01, Cote d'Ivoire, www.afdb.org; *Statistics Pocketbook 2008.*

Bernan Essential Government Publications, 4611-F Assembly Drive, Lanham MD, 20706-4391, (301) 459-2255, Fax: (800) 865-3450, www.bernan.com; *National Accounts Statistics.*

Economist Intelligence Unit, 111 West 57th Street, New York, NY 10019, (212) 554-0600, Fax: (212) 586-1181, www.eiu.com; *Cameroon Country Report.*

International Monetary Fund (IMF), 700 Nineteenth Street, NW, Washington, DC 20431, (202) 623-7000, Fax: (202) 623-4661, www.imf.org; *Government Finance Statistics Yearbook (2008 Edition); International Financial Statistics; International Financial Statistics Online Service;* and *International Financial Statistics Yearbook 2007.*

M.E. Sharpe, 80 Business Park Drive, Armonk, NY 10504, (800) 541-6563, Fax: (914) 273-2106, www.mesharpe.com; *The Illustrated Book of World Rankings.*

Palgrave Macmillan Ltd., Houndmills, Basingstoke, Hampshire, RG21 6XS, England, (Telephone in U.S. (888) 330-8477), (Fax in U.S. (800) 672-2054), www.palgrave.com; *The Statesman's Yearbook 2008.*

Taylor and Francis Group, An Informa Business, 2 Park Square, Milton Park, Abingdon, Oxford OX14 4RN, United Kingdom, (Dial from U.S. (212) 216-7800), (Fax from U.S. (212) 564-7854), www.tandf.co.uk; *The Europa World Year Book.*

United Nations Economic Commission for Africa (ECA), PO Box 3001, Addis Ababa, Ethiopia, (Telephone in U.S. (212) 963-4957), www.uneca.org; *African Statistical Yearbook 2006.*

The World Bank, 1818 H Street, NW, Washington, DC 20433, (202) 473-1000, Fax: (202) 477-6391, www.worldbank.org; *Camaroon.*

CAMEROON - FISHERIES

M.E. Sharpe, 80 Business Park Drive, Armonk, NY 10504, (800) 541-6563, Fax: (914) 273-2106, www.mesharpe.com; *The Illustrated Book of World Rankings.*

Palgrave Macmillan Ltd., Houndmills, Basingstoke, Hampshire, RG21 6XS, England, (Telephone in U.S. (888) 330-8477), (Fax in U.S. (800) 672-2054), www.palgrave.com; *The Statesman's Yearbook 2008.*

Taylor and Francis Group, An Informa Business, 2 Park Square, Milton Park, Abingdon, Oxford OX14 4RN, United Kingdom, (Dial from U.S. (212) 216-7800), (Fax from U.S. (212) 564-7854), www.tandf.co.uk; *The Europa World Year Book.*

United Nations Conference on Trade and Development (UNCTAD), DC2-1120, United Nations, New York, NY 10017, (212) 963-0027, www.unctad.org; *UNCTAD Commodity Yearbook.*

United Nations Economic Commission for Africa (ECA), PO Box 3001, Addis Ababa, Ethiopia, (Telephone in U.S. (212) 963-4957), www.uneca.org; *African Statistical Yearbook 2006.*

United Nations Food and Agricultural Organization (FAO), Viale delle Terme di Caracalla, 00100 Rome, Italy, (Dial from U.S. (202) 653-2400), (Fax from U.S. (202) 653 5760), www.fao.org; *FAO Yearbook of Fishery Statistics;* Fishery Databases; FISHSTAT Database. Subjects covered include: Aquaculture production, capture production, fishery commodities; and *The State of Food and Agriculture (SOFA) 2006.*

United Nations Statistics Division, New York, NY 10017, (800) 253-9646, Fax: (212) 963-4116, http://unstats.un.org; *Statistical Yearbook* and *Survey of Economic and Social Conditions in Africa 2005.*

The World Bank, 1818 H Street, NW, Washington, DC 20433, (202) 473-1000, Fax: (202) 477-6391, www.worldbank.org; *Camaroon.*

CAMEROON - FLOUR INDUSTRY

United Nations Statistics Division, New York, NY 10017, (800) 253-9646, Fax: (212) 963-4116, http://unstats.un.org; *Statistical Yearbook.*

CAMEROON - FOOD

African Development Bank Group, Rue Joseph Anoma, 01 BP 1387 Abidjan 01, Cote d'Ivoire, www.afdb.org; *Statistics Pocketbook 2008.*

United Nations Conference on Trade and Development (UNCTAD), DC2-1120, United Nations, New York, NY 10017, (212) 963-0027, www.unctad.org; *UNCTAD Commodity Yearbook.*

United Nations Food and Agricultural Organization (FAO), Viale delle Terme di Caracalla, 00100 Rome, Italy, (Dial from U.S. (202) 653-2400), (Fax from U.S. (202) 653 5760), www.fao.org; *FAO Production Yearbook 2002* and *The State of Food and Agriculture (SOFA) 2006.*

United Nations Statistics Division, New York, NY 10017, (800) 253-9646, Fax: (212) 963-4116, http://unstats.un.org; *Human Development Report 2006.*

CAMEROON - FOREIGN EXCHANGE RATES

African Development Bank Group, Rue Joseph Anoma, 01 BP 1387 Abidjan 01, Cote d'Ivoire, www.afdb.org; *Statistics Pocketbook 2008.*

Central Intelligence Agency, Office of Public Affairs, Washington, DC 20505, (703) 482-0623, Fax: (703) 482-1739, www.cia.gov; *The World Factbook.*

Euromonitor International, Inc., 224 S. Michigan Avenue, Suite 1500, Chicago, IL 60604, (312) 922-1115, Fax: (312) 922-1157, www.euromonitor.com; *International Marketing Data and Statistics 2008* and *The World Economic Factbook 2008.*

International Civil Aviation Organization (ICAO), External Relations and Public Information Office (EPO), 999 University Street, Montreal, Quebec H3C 5H7, Canada, (Dial from U.S. (514) 954-8219), (Fax from U.S. (514) 954-6077), www.icao.int; *Civil Aviation Statistics of the World.*

International Monetary Fund (IMF), 700 Nineteenth Street, NW, Washington, DC 20431, (202) 623-7000, Fax: (202) 623-4661, www.imf.org; *International Financial Statistics Yearbook 2007.*

Taylor and Francis Group, An Informa Business, 2 Park Square, Milton Park, Abingdon, Oxford OX14 4RN, United Kingdom, (Dial from U.S. (212) 216-7800), (Fax from U.S. (212) 564-7854), www.tandf.co.uk; *The Europa World Year Book.*

United Nations Statistics Division, New York, NY 10017, (800) 253-9646, Fax: (212) 963-4116, http://unstats.un.org; *Compendium of Intra-African and Related Foreign Trade Statistics 2003* and *World Statistics Pocketbook.*

CAMEROON - FORESTS AND FORESTRY

International Monetary Fund (IMF), 700 Nineteenth Street, NW, Washington, DC 20431, (202) 623-7000, Fax: (202) 623-4661, www.imf.org; *International Financial Statistics Yearbook 2007.*

M.E. Sharpe, 80 Business Park Drive, Armonk, NY 10504, (800) 541-6563, Fax: (914) 273-2106, www.mesharpe.com; *The Illustrated Book of World Rankings.*

Palgrave Macmillan Ltd., Houndmills, Basingstoke, Hampshire, RG21 6XS, England, (Telephone in U.S. (888) 330-8477), (Fax in U.S. (800) 672-2054), www.palgrave.com; *The Statesman's Yearbook 2008.*

Taylor and Francis Group, An Informa Business, 2 Park Square, Milton Park, Abingdon, Oxford OX14 4RN, United Kingdom, (Dial from U.S. (212) 216-7800), (Fax from U.S. (212) 564-7854), www.tandf.co.uk; *The Europa World Year Book.*

UNESCO Institute for Statistics, C.P. 6128 Succursale Centre-Ville, Montreal, Quebec, H3C 3J7 Canada, (Dial from U.S. (514) 343-6880), (Fax from U.S. (514) 343 6882), www.uis.unesco.org; *Statistical Tables.*

United Nations Conference on Trade and Development (UNCTAD), DC2-1120, United Nations, New York, NY 10017, (212) 963-0027, www.unctad.org; *UNCTAD Commodity Yearbook.*

United Nations Economic Commission for Africa (ECA), PO Box 3001, Addis Ababa, Ethiopia, (Telephone in U.S. (212) 963-4957), www.uneca.org; *African Statistical Yearbook 2006.*

United Nations Food and Agricultural Organization (FAO), Viale delle Terme di Caracalla, 00100 Rome, Italy, (Dial from U.S. (202) 653-2400), (Fax from U.S. (202) 653 5760), www.fao.org; *FAO Yearbook of Forest Products* and *The State of Food and Agriculture (SOFA) 2006.*

United Nations Statistics Division, New York, NY 10017, (800) 253-9646, Fax: (212) 963-4116, http://unstats.un.org; *Statistical Yearbook.*

The World Bank, 1818 H Street, NW, Washington, DC 20433, (202) 473-1000, Fax: (202) 477-6391, www.worldbank.org; *Camaroon* and *World Development Report 2008.*

CAMEROON - GAS PRODUCTION

See CAMEROON - MINERAL INDUSTRIES

CAMEROON - GEOGRAPHIC INFORMATION SYSTEMS

M.E. Sharpe, 80 Business Park Drive, Armonk, NY 10504, (800) 541-6563, Fax: (914) 273-2106, www.mesharpe.com; *The Illustrated Book of World Rankings.*

The World Bank, 1818 H Street, NW, Washington, DC 20433, (202) 473-1000, Fax: (202) 477-6391, www.worldbank.org; *Camaroon.*

CAMEROON - GOLD INDUSTRY

International Monetary Fund (IMF), 700 Nineteenth Street, NW, Washington, DC 20431, (202) 623-7000, Fax: (202) 623-4661, www.imf.org; *International Financial Statistics Yearbook 2007.*

The World Bank, 1818 H Street, NW, Washington, DC 20433, (202) 473-1000, Fax: (202) 477-6391, www.worldbank.org; *World Development Indicators (WDI) 2008.*

CAMEROON - GOLD PRODUCTION

See CAMEROON - MINERAL INDUSTRIES

CAMEROON - GRANTS-IN-AID

International Monetary Fund (IMF), 700 Nineteenth Street, NW, Washington, DC 20431, (202) 623-7000, Fax: (202) 623-4661, www.imf.org; *Government Finance Statistics Yearbook (2008 Edition).*

CAMEROON - GROSS DOMESTIC PRODUCT

African Development Bank Group, Rue Joseph Anoma, 01 BP 1387 Abidjan 01, Cote d'Ivoire, www.afdb.org; *Statistics Pocketbook 2008.*

Economist Intelligence Unit, 111 West 57th Street, New York, NY 10019, (212) 554-0600, Fax: (212) 586-1181, www.eiu.com; *Cameroon Country Report.*

Euromonitor International, Inc., 224 S. Michigan Avenue, Suite 1500, Chicago, IL 60604, (312) 922-1115, Fax: (312) 922-1157, www.euromonitor.com; *International Marketing Data and Statistics 2008* and *The World Economic Factbook 2008.*

International Monetary Fund (IMF), 700 Nineteenth Street, NW, Washington, DC 20431, (202) 623-7000, Fax: (202) 623-4661, www.imf.org; *International Financial Statistics Yearbook 2007.*

M.E. Sharpe, 80 Business Park Drive, Armonk, NY 10504, (800) 541-6563, Fax: (914) 273-2106, www.mesharpe.com; *The Illustrated Book of World Rankings.*

Taylor and Francis Group, An Informa Business, 2 Park Square, Milton Park, Abingdon, Oxford OX14 4RN, United Kingdom, (Dial from U.S. (212) 216-7800), (Fax from U.S. (212) 564-7854), www.tandf.co.uk; *The Europa World Year Book.*

United Nations Economic Commission for Africa (ECA), PO Box 3001, Addis Ababa, Ethiopia, (Telephone in U.S. (212) 963-4957), www.uneca.org; *African Statistical Yearbook 2006.*

United Nations Statistics Division, New York, NY 10017, (800) 253-9646, Fax: (212) 963-4116, http://unstats.un.org; *Human Development Report 2006; National Accounts Statistics: Compendium of Income Distribution Statistics; Statistical Yearbook;* and *Survey of Economic and Social Conditions in Africa 2005.*

The World Bank, 1818 H Street, NW, Washington, DC 20433, (202) 473-1000, Fax: (202) 477-6391, www.worldbank.org; *World Development Indicators (WDI) 2008* and *World Development Report 2008.*

CAMEROON - GROSS NATIONAL PRODUCT

Euromonitor International, Inc., 224 S. Michigan Avenue, Suite 1500, Chicago, IL 60604, (312) 922-1115, Fax: (312) 922-1157, www.euromonitor.com; *International Marketing Data and Statistics 2008.*

M.E. Sharpe, 80 Business Park Drive, Armonk, NY 10504, (800) 541-6563, Fax: (914) 273-2106, www.mesharpe.com; *The Illustrated Book of World Rankings.*

Palgrave Macmillan Ltd., Houndmills, Basingstoke, Hampshire, RG21 6XS, England, (Telephone in U.S. (888) 330-8477), (Fax in U.S. (800) 672-2054), www.palgrave.com; *The Statesman's Yearbook 2008.*

Taylor and Francis Group, An Informa Business, 2 Park Square, Milton Park, Abingdon, Oxford OX14 4RN, United Kingdom, (Dial from U.S. (212) 216-7800), (Fax from U.S. (212) 564-7854), www.tandf.co.uk; *The Europa World Year Book.*

U.S. Department of State (DOS), 2201 C Street NW, Washington, DC 20520, (202) 647-4000, www.state.gov; *World Military Expenditures and Arms Transfers (WMEAT).*

United Nations Statistics Division, New York, NY 10017, (800) 253-9646, Fax: (212) 963-4116, http://unstats.un.org; *Statistical Yearbook.*

The World Bank, 1818 H Street, NW, Washington, DC 20433, (202) 473-1000, Fax: (202) 477-6391, www.worldbank.org; *The World Bank Atlas 2003-2004; World Development Indicators (WDI) 2008;* and *World Development Report 2008.*

CAMEROON - HIDES AND SKINS INDUSTRY

United Nations Food and Agricultural Organization (FAO), Viale delle Terme di Caracalla, 00100 Rome,

Italy, (Dial from U.S. (202) 653-2400), (Fax from U.S. (202) 653 5760), www.fao.org; *FAO Production Yearbook 2002.*

CAMEROON - HOUSING

Euromonitor International, Inc., 224 S. Michigan Avenue, Suite 1500, Chicago, IL 60604, (312) 922-1115, Fax: (312) 922-1157, www.euromonitor.com; *World Marketing Data and Statistics.*

M.E. Sharpe, 80 Business Park Drive, Armonk, NY 10504, (800) 541-6563, Fax: (914) 273-2106, www.mesharpe.com; *The Illustrated Book of World Rankings.*

United Nations Statistics Division, New York, NY 10017, (800) 253-9646, Fax: (212) 963-4116, http://unstats.un.org; *Statistical Yearbook.*

CAMEROON - ILLITERATE PERSONS

Euromonitor International, Inc., 224 S. Michigan Avenue, Suite 1500, Chicago, IL 60604, (312) 922-1115, Fax: (312) 922-1157, www.euromonitor.com; *The World Economic Factbook 2008.*

Palgrave Macmillan Ltd., Houndmills, Basingstoke, Hampshire, RG21 6XS, England, (Telephone in U.S. (888) 330-8477), (Fax in U.S. (800) 672-2054), www.palgrave.com; *The Statesman's Yearbook 2008.*

UNESCO Institute for Statistics, C.P. 6128 Succursale Centre-Ville, Montreal, Quebec, H3C 3J7 Canada, (Dial from U.S. (514) 343-6880), (Fax from U.S. (514) 343 6882), www.uis.unesco.org; *Statistical Tables.*

United Nations Statistics Division, New York, NY 10017, (800) 253-9646, Fax: (212) 963-4116, http://unstats.un.org; *Human Development Report 2006.*

CAMEROON - IMPORTS

Central Intelligence Agency, Office of Public Affairs, Washington, DC 20505, (703) 482-0623, Fax: (703) 482-1739, www.cia.gov; *The World Factbook.*

Economist Intelligence Unit, 111 West 57th Street, New York, NY 10019, (212) 554-0600, Fax: (212) 586-1181, www.eiu.com; *Cameroon Country Report.*

Euromonitor International, Inc., 224 S. Michigan Avenue, Suite 1500, Chicago, IL 60604, (312) 922-1115, Fax: (312) 922-1157, www.euromonitor.com; *International Marketing Data and Statistics 2008* and *The World Economic Factbook 2008.*

International Monetary Fund (IMF), 700 Nineteenth Street, NW, Washington, DC 20431, (202) 623-7000, Fax: (202) 623-4661, www.imf.org; *Direction of Trade Statistics Yearbook 2007* and *Government Finance Statistics Yearbook (2008 Edition).*

Palgrave Macmillan Ltd., Houndmills, Basingstoke, Hampshire, RG21 6XS, England, (Telephone in U.S. (888) 330-8477), (Fax in U.S. (800) 672-2054), www.palgrave.com; *The Statesman's Yearbook 2008.*

Taylor and Francis Group, An Informa Business, 2 Park Square, Milton Park, Abingdon, Oxford OX14 4RN, United Kingdom, (Dial from U.S. (212) 216-7800), (Fax from U.S. (212) 564-7854), www.tandf.co.uk; *The Europa World Year Book.*

United Nations Conference on Trade and Development (UNCTAD), DC2-1120, United Nations, New York, NY 10017, (212) 963-0027, www.unctad.org; *Handbook of Statistics 2005.*

United Nations Economic Commission for Africa (ECA), PO Box 3001, Addis Ababa, Ethiopia, (Telephone in U.S. (212) 963-4957), www.uneca.org; *African Statistical Yearbook 2006.*

United Nations Food and Agricultural Organization (FAO), Viale delle Terme di Caracalla, 00100 Rome, Italy, (Dial from U.S. (202) 653-2400), (Fax from U.S. (202) 653 5760), www.fao.org; *The State of Food and Agriculture (SOFA) 2006.*

United Nations Statistics Division, New York, NY 10017, (800) 253-9646, Fax: (212) 963-4116, http://unstats.un.org; *Compendium of Intra-African and Related Foreign Trade Statistics 2003* and *Survey of Economic and Social Conditions in Africa 2005.*

The World Bank, 1818 H Street, NW, Washington, DC 20433, (202) 473-1000, Fax: (202) 477-6391, www.worldbank.org; *World Development Indicators (WDI) 2008* and *World Development Report 2008.*

CAMEROON - INCOME TAXES

See CAMEROON - TAXATION

CAMEROON - INDUSTRIAL METALS PRODUCTION

See CAMEROON - MINERAL INDUSTRIES

CAMEROON - INDUSTRIAL PRODUCTIVITY

Euromonitor International, Inc., 224 S. Michigan Avenue, Suite 1500, Chicago, IL 60604, (312) 922-1115, Fax: (312) 922-1157, www.euromonitor.com; *International Marketing Data and Statistics 2008.*

M.E. Sharpe, 80 Business Park Drive, Armonk, NY 10504, (800) 541-6563, Fax: (914) 273-2106, www.mesharpe.com; *The Illustrated Book of World Rankings.*

CAMEROON - INDUSTRIES

Central Intelligence Agency, Office of Public Affairs, Washington, DC 20505, (703) 482-0623, Fax: (703) 482-1739, www.cia.gov; *The World Factbook.*

Economist Intelligence Unit, 111 West 57th Street, New York, NY 10019, (212) 554-0600, Fax: (212) 586-1181, www.eiu.com; *Cameroon Country Report.*

Euromonitor International, Inc., 224 S. Michigan Avenue, Suite 1500, Chicago, IL 60604, (312) 922-1115, Fax: (312) 922-1157, www.euromonitor.com; *International Marketing Data and Statistics 2008; The World Economic Factbook 2008;* and *World Marketing Data and Statistics.*

International Labour Office, I.L.O. Publications, 4 route des Morillons, CH-1211 Geneva 22, Switzerland, (Telephone in U.S. (202) 653-7652), (Fax in U.S. (202) 653-7687), www.ilo.org; *Yearbook of Labour Statistics 2006.*

M.E. Sharpe, 80 Business Park Drive, Armonk, NY 10504, (800) 541-6563, Fax: (914) 273-2106, www.mesharpe.com; *The Illustrated Book of World Rankings.*

Taylor and Francis Group, An Informa Business, 2 Park Square, Milton Park, Abingdon, Oxford OX14 4RN, United Kingdom, (Dial from U.S. (212) 216-7800), (Fax from U.S. (212) 564-7854), www.tandf.co.uk; *The Europa World Year Book.*

United Nations Economic Commission for Africa (ECA), PO Box 3001, Addis Ababa, Ethiopia, (Telephone in U.S. (212) 963-4957), www.uneca.org; *African Statistical Yearbook 2006.*

United Nations Industrial Development Organization (UNIDO), 1 United Nations Plaza, New York, NY 10017, (212) 963 6890, Fax: (212) 963-7904, http://unido.org; Industrial Statistics Database 2008 (INDSTAT) and *The International Yearbook of Industrial Statistics 2008.*

United Nations Statistics Division, New York, NY 10017, (800) 253-9646, Fax: (212) 963-4116, http://unstats.un.org; *Survey of Economic and Social Conditions in Africa 2005.*

The World Bank, 1818 H Street, NW, Washington, DC 20433, (202) 473-1000, Fax: (202) 477-6391, www.worldbank.org; *Camaroon* and *World Development Indicators (WDI) 2008.*

CAMEROON - INTERNATIONAL LIQUIDITY

International Monetary Fund (IMF), 700 Nineteenth Street, NW, Washington, DC 20431, (202) 623-7000, Fax: (202) 623-4661, www.imf.org; *International Financial Statistics Yearbook 2007.*

CAMEROON - INTERNATIONAL TRADE

African Development Bank Group, Rue Joseph Anoma, 01 BP 1387 Abidjan 01, Cote d'Ivoire, www.afdb.org; *Statistics Pocketbook 2008.*

Economist Intelligence Unit, 111 West 57th Street, New York, NY 10019, (212) 554-0600, Fax: (212) 586-1181, www.eiu.com; *Cameroon Country Report.*

Euromonitor International, Inc., 224 S. Michigan Avenue, Suite 1500, Chicago, IL 60604, (312) 922-1115, Fax: (312) 922-1157, www.euromonitor.com; *International Marketing Data and Statistics 2008; The World Economic Factbook 2008;* and *World Marketing Data and Statistics.*

M.E. Sharpe, 80 Business Park Drive, Armonk, NY 10504, (800) 541-6563, Fax: (914) 273-2106, www.mesharpe.com; *The Illustrated Book of World Rankings.*

Organisation for Economic Cooperation and Development (OECD), 2 rue Andre Pascal, F-75775 Paris Cedex 16, France, (Telephone in U.S. (202) 785-6323), (Fax in U.S. (202) 785-0350), www.oecd.org; *OECD Economic Outlook 2008.*

Palgrave Macmillan Ltd., Houndmills, Basingstoke, Hampshire, RG21 6XS, England, (Telephone in U.S. (888) 330-8477), (Fax in U.S. (800) 672-2054), www.palgrave.com; *The Statesman's Yearbook 2008.*

Taylor and Francis Group, An Informa Business, 2 Park Square, Milton Park, Abingdon, Oxford OX14 4RN, United Kingdom, (Dial from U.S. (212) 216-7800), (Fax from U.S. (212) 564-7854), www.tandf.co.uk; *The Europa World Year Book.*

United Nations Conference on Trade and Development (UNCTAD), DC2-1120, United Nations, New York, NY 10017, (212) 963-0027, www.unctad.org; *UNCTAD Commodity Yearbook.*

United Nations Economic Commission for Africa (ECA), PO Box 3001, Addis Ababa, Ethiopia, (Telephone in U.S. (212) 963-4957), www.uneca.org; *African Statistical Yearbook 2006.*

United Nations Food and Agricultural Organization (FAO), Viale delle Terme di Caracalla, 00100 Rome, Italy, (Dial from U.S. (202) 653-2400), (Fax from U.S. (202) 653 5760), www.fao.org; *FAO Trade Yearbook* and *The State of Food and Agriculture (SOFA) 2006.*

United Nations Statistics Division, New York, NY 10017, (800) 253-9646, Fax: (212) 963-4116, http://unstats.un.org; *Compendium of Intra-African and Related Foreign Trade Statistics 2003; International Trade Statistics Yearbook;* and *Statistical Yearbook.*

The World Bank, 1818 H Street, NW, Washington, DC 20433, (202) 473-1000, Fax: (202) 477-6391, www.worldbank.org; *Camaroon; World Development Indicators (WDI) 2008;* and *World Development Report 2008.*

World Trade Organization (WTO), Centre William Rappard, Rue de Lausanne 154, CH-1211 Geneva 21, Switzerland, www.wto.org; *International Trade Statistics 2006.*

CAMEROON - INTERNET USERS

International Telecommunication Union (ITU), Place des Nations, 1211 Geneva 20, Switzerland, www.itu.int; *World Telecommunication/ICT Indicators Database on CD-ROM; World Telecommunication/ICT Indicators Database Online;* and *Yearbook of Statistics - Telecommunication Services (Chronological Time Series 1997-2006).*

The World Bank, 1818 H Street, NW, Washington, DC 20433, (202) 473-1000, Fax: (202) 477-6391, www.worldbank.org; *Camaroon.*

CAMEROON - IRON AND IRON ORE PRODUCTION

See CAMEROON - MINERAL INDUSTRIES

CAMEROON - IRRIGATION

Euromonitor International, Inc., 224 S. Michigan Avenue, Suite 1500, Chicago, IL 60604, (312) 922-1115, Fax: (312) 922-1157, www.euromonitor.com; *International Marketing Data and Statistics 2008.*

CAMEROON - LABOR

African Development Bank Group, Rue Joseph Anoma, 01 BP 1387 Abidjan 01, Cote d'Ivoire, www.afdb.org; *Statistics Pocketbook 2008.*

Central Intelligence Agency, Office of Public Affairs, Washington, DC 20505, (703) 482-0623, Fax: (703) 482-1739, www.cia.gov; *The World Factbook.*

Euromonitor International, Inc., 224 S. Michigan Avenue, Suite 1500, Chicago, IL 60604, (312) 922-1115, Fax: (312) 922-1157, www.euromonitor.com; *International Marketing Data and Statistics 2008* and *World Marketing Data and Statistics.*

International Labour Office, I.L.O. Publications, 4 route des Morillons, CH-1211 Geneva 22, Switzerland, (Telephone in U.S. (202) 653-7652), (Fax in U.S. (202) 653-7687), www.ilo.org; *Yearbook of Labour Statistics 2006.*

M.E. Sharpe, 80 Business Park Drive, Armonk, NY 10504, (800) 541-6563, Fax: (914) 273-2106, www.mesharpe.com; *The Illustrated Book of World Rankings.*

Palgrave Macmillan Ltd., Houndmills, Basingstoke, Hampshire, RG21 6XS, England, (Telephone in U.S. (888) 330-8477), (Fax in U.S. (800) 672-2054), www.palgrave.com; *The Statesman's Yearbook 2008.*

Taylor and Francis Group, An Informa Business, 2 Park Square, Milton Park, Abingdon, Oxford OX14 4RN, United Kingdom, (Dial from U.S. (212) 216-7800), (Fax from U.S. (212) 564-7854), www.tandf.co.uk; *The Europa World Year Book.*

United Nations Food and Agricultural Organization (FAO), Viale delle Terme di Caracalla, 00100 Rome, Italy, (Dial from U.S. (202) 653-2400), (Fax from U.S. (202) 653 5760), www.fao.org; *The State of Food and Agriculture (SOFA) 2006.*

United Nations Statistics Division, New York, NY 10017, (800) 253-9646, Fax: (212) 963-4116, http://unstats.un.org; *Human Development Report 2006.*

The World Bank, 1818 H Street, NW, Washington, DC 20433, (202) 473-1000, Fax: (202) 477-6391, www.worldbank.org; *The World Bank Atlas 2003-2004; World Development Indicators (WDI) 2008;* and *World Development Report 2008.*

CAMEROON - LAND USE

Central Intelligence Agency, Office of Public Affairs, Washington, DC 20505, (703) 482-0623, Fax: (703) 482-1739, www.cia.gov; *The World Factbook.*

Euromonitor International, Inc., 224 S. Michigan Avenue, Suite 1500, Chicago, IL 60604, (312) 922-1115, Fax: (312) 922-1157, www.euromonitor.com; *International Marketing Data and Statistics 2008.*

United Nations Food and Agricultural Organization (FAO), Viale delle Terme di Caracalla, 00100 Rome, Italy, (Dial from U.S. (202) 653-2400), (Fax from U.S. (202) 653 5760), www.fao.org; *FAO Production Yearbook 2002.*

The World Bank, 1818 H Street, NW, Washington, DC 20433, (202) 473-1000, Fax: (202) 477-6391, www.worldbank.org; *World Development Report 2008.*

CAMEROON - LIBRARIES

M.E. Sharpe, 80 Business Park Drive, Armonk, NY 10504, (800) 541-6563, Fax: (914) 273-2106, www.mesharpe.com; *The Illustrated Book of World Rankings.*

CAMEROON - LICENSES

International Monetary Fund (IMF), 700 Nineteenth Street, NW, Washington, DC 20431, (202) 623-7000, Fax: (202) 623-4661, www.imf.org; *Government Finance Statistics Yearbook (2008 Edition).*

CAMEROON - LIFE EXPECTANCY

African Development Bank Group, Rue Joseph Anoma, 01 BP 1387 Abidjan 01, Cote d'Ivoire, www.afdb.org; *Statistics Pocketbook 2008.*

Central Intelligence Agency, Office of Public Affairs, Washington, DC 20505, (703) 482-0623, Fax: (703) 482-1739, www.cia.gov; *The World Factbook.*

Euromonitor International, Inc., 224 S. Michigan Avenue, Suite 1500, Chicago, IL 60604, (312) 922-1115, Fax: (312) 922-1157, www.euromonitor.com; *The World Economic Factbook 2008.*

United Nations Statistics Division, New York, NY 10017, (800) 253-9646, Fax: (212) 963-4116, http://unstats.un.org; *Human Development Report 2006* and *World Statistics Pocketbook.*

The World Bank, 1818 H Street, NW, Washington, DC 20433, (202) 473-1000, Fax: (202) 477-6391, www.worldbank.org; *The World Bank Atlas 2003-2004* and *World Development Report 2008.*

CAMEROON - LITERACY

Euromonitor International, Inc., 224 S. Michigan Avenue, Suite 1500, Chicago, IL 60604, (312) 922-1115, Fax: (312) 922-1157, www.euromonitor.com; *World Marketing Data and Statistics.*

United Nations Statistics Division, New York, NY 10017, (800) 253-9646, Fax: (212) 963-4116, http://unstats.un.org; *Survey of Economic and Social Conditions in Africa 2005.*

CAMEROON - LIVESTOCK

Euromonitor International, Inc., 224 S. Michigan Avenue, Suite 1500, Chicago, IL 60604, (312) 922-1115, Fax: (312) 922-1157, www.euromonitor.com; *International Marketing Data and Statistics 2008.*

M.E. Sharpe, 80 Business Park Drive, Armonk, NY 10504, (800) 541-6563, Fax: (914) 273-2106, www.mesharpe.com; *The Illustrated Book of World Rankings.*

Palgrave Macmillan Ltd., Houndmills, Basingstoke, Hampshire, RG21 6XS, England, (Telephone in U.S. (888) 330-8477), (Fax in U.S. (800) 672-2054), www.palgrave.com; *The Statesman's Yearbook 2008.*

Taylor and Francis Group, An Informa Business, 2 Park Square, Milton Park, Abingdon, Oxford OX14 4RN, United Kingdom, (Dial from U.S. (212) 216-7800), (Fax from U.S. (212) 564-7854), www.tandf.co.uk; *The Europa World Year Book.*

United Nations Conference on Trade and Development (UNCTAD), DC2-1120, United Nations, New York, NY 10017, (212) 963-0027, www.unctad.org; *UNCTAD Commodity Yearbook.*

United Nations Economic Commission for Africa (ECA), PO Box 3001, Addis Ababa, Ethiopia, (Telephone in U.S. (212) 963-4957), www.uneca.org; *African Statistical Yearbook 2006.*

United Nations Food and Agricultural Organization (FAO), Viale delle Terme di Caracalla, 00100 Rome, Italy, (Dial from U.S. (202) 653-2400), (Fax from U.S. (202) 653 5760), www.fao.org; *FAO Production Yearbook 2002* and *The State of Food and Agriculture (SOFA) 2006.*

United Nations Statistics Division, New York, NY 10017, (800) 253-9646, Fax: (212) 963-4116, http://unstats.un.org; *Statistical Yearbook* and *Survey of Economic and Social Conditions in Africa 2005.*

CAMEROON - LOCAL TAXATION

Euromonitor International, Inc., 224 S. Michigan Avenue, Suite 1500, Chicago, IL 60604, (312) 922-1115, Fax: (312) 922-1157, www.euromonitor.com; *International Marketing Data and Statistics 2008.*

CAMEROON - MANUFACTURES

M.E. Sharpe, 80 Business Park Drive, Armonk, NY 10504, (800) 541-6563, Fax: (914) 273-2106, www.mesharpe.com; *The Illustrated Book of World Rankings.*

United Nations Economic Commission for Africa (ECA), PO Box 3001, Addis Ababa, Ethiopia, (Telephone in U.S. (212) 963-4957), www.uneca.org; *African Statistical Yearbook 2006.*

United Nations Statistics Division, New York, NY 10017, (800) 253-9646, Fax: (212) 963-4116, http://unstats.un.org; *Statistical Yearbook* and *Survey of Economic and Social Conditions in Africa 2005.*

The World Bank, 1818 H Street, NW, Washington, DC 20433, (202) 473-1000, Fax: (202) 477-6391, www.worldbank.org; *World Development Indicators (WDI) 2008.*

CAMEROON - MARRIAGE

M.E. Sharpe, 80 Business Park Drive, Armonk, NY 10504, (800) 541-6563, Fax: (914) 273-2106, www.mesharpe.com; *The Illustrated Book of World Rankings.*

United Nations Statistics Division, New York, NY 10017, (800) 253-9646, Fax: (212) 963-4116, http://unstats.un.org; *Demographic Yearbook.*

CAMEROON - MATERNAL AND INFANT WELFARE

United Nations Statistics Division, New York, NY 10017, (800) 253-9646, Fax: (212) 963-4116, http://unstats.un.org; *Demographic Yearbook; Statistical Yearbook;* and *Survey of Economic and Social Conditions in Africa 2005.*

The World Bank, 1818 H Street, NW, Washington, DC 20433, (202) 473-1000, Fax: (202) 477-6391, www.worldbank.org; *World Development Indicators (WDI) 2008.*

CAMEROON - MEAT PRODUCTION

See CAMEROON - LIVESTOCK

CAMEROON - MEDICAL CARE, COST OF

International Monetary Fund (IMF), 700 Nineteenth Street, NW, Washington, DC 20431, (202) 623-7000, Fax: (202) 623-4661, www.imf.org; *Government Finance Statistics Yearbook (2008 Edition).*

CAMEROON - MILK PRODUCTION

See CAMEROON - DAIRY PROCESSING

CAMEROON - MINERAL INDUSTRIES

Commodity Research Bureau, 330 South Wells Street, Suite 612, Chicago, IL 60606-7110, (800) 621-5271, Fax: (312) 939-4135, www.crbtrader.com; *2006 CRB Commodity Yearbook and CD.*

M.E. Sharpe, 80 Business Park Drive, Armonk, NY 10504, (800) 541-6563, Fax: (914) 273-2106, www.mesharpe.com; *The Illustrated Book of World Rankings.*

Organisation for Economic Cooperation and Development (OECD), 2 rue Andre Pascal, F-75775 Paris Cedex 16, France, (Telephone in U.S. (202) 785-6323), (Fax in U.S. (202) 785-0350), www.oecd.org; *World Energy Outlook 2007.*

Palgrave Macmillan Ltd., Houndmills, Basingstoke, Hampshire, RG21 6XS, England, (Telephone in U.S. (888) 330-8477), (Fax in U.S. (800) 672-2054), www.palgrave.com; *The Statesman's Yearbook 2008.*

Taylor and Francis Group, An Informa Business, 2 Park Square, Milton Park, Abingdon, Oxford OX14 4RN, United Kingdom, (Dial from U.S. (212) 216-7800), (Fax from U.S. (212) 564-7854), www.tandf.co.uk; *The Europa World Year Book.*

United Nations Conference on Trade and Development (UNCTAD), DC2-1120, United Nations, New York, NY 10017, (212) 963-0027, www.unctad.org; *UNCTAD Commodity Yearbook.*

United Nations Economic Commission for Africa (ECA), PO Box 3001, Addis Ababa, Ethiopia, (Telephone in U.S. (212) 963-4957), www.uneca.org; *African Statistical Yearbook 2006.*

United Nations Statistics Division, New York, NY 10017, (800) 253-9646, Fax: (212) 963-4116, http://unstats.un.org; *Statistical Yearbook.*

CAMEROON - MONEY EXCHANGE RATES

See CAMEROON - FOREIGN EXCHANGE RATES

CAMEROON - MONEY SUPPLY

African Development Bank Group, Rue Joseph Anoma, 01 BP 1387 Abidjan 01, Cote d'Ivoire, www.afdb.org; *Statistics Pocketbook 2008.*

Economist Intelligence Unit, 111 West 57th Street, New York, NY 10019, (212) 554-0600, Fax: (212) 586-1181, www.eiu.com; *Cameroon Country Report.*

Euromonitor International, Inc., 224 S. Michigan Avenue, Suite 1500, Chicago, IL 60604, (312) 922-1115, Fax: (312) 922-1157, www.euromonitor.com; *International Marketing Data and Statistics 2008.*

International Monetary Fund (IMF), 700 Nineteenth Street, NW, Washington, DC 20431, (202) 623-

7000, Fax: (202) 623-4661, www.imf.org; *International Financial Statistics Yearbook 2007.*

Taylor and Francis Group, An Informa Business, 2 Park Square, Milton Park, Abingdon, Oxford OX14 4RN, United Kingdom, (Dial from U.S. (212) 216-7800), (Fax from U.S. (212) 564-7854), www.tandf.co.uk; *The Europa World Year Book.*

The World Bank, 1818 H Street, NW, Washington, DC 20433, (202) 473-1000, Fax: (202) 477-6391, www.worldbank.org; *Camaroon* and *World Development Indicators (WDI) 2008.*

CAMEROON - MORTALITY

Central Intelligence Agency, Office of Public Affairs, Washington, DC 20505, (703) 482-0623, Fax: (703) 482-1739, www.cia.gov; *The World Factbook.*

Euromonitor International, Inc., 224 S. Michigan Avenue, Suite 1500, Chicago, IL 60604, (312) 922-1115, Fax: (312) 922-1157, www.euromonitor.com; *International Marketing Data and Statistics 2008* and *The World Economic Factbook 2008.*

Palgrave Macmillan Ltd., Houndmills, Basingstoke, Hampshire, RG21 6XS, England, (Telephone in U.S. (888) 330-8477), (Fax in U.S. (800) 672-2054), www.palgrave.com; *The Statesman's Yearbook 2008.*

Taylor and Francis Group, An Informa Business, 2 Park Square, Milton Park, Abingdon, Oxford OX14 4RN, United Kingdom, (Dial from U.S. (212) 216-7800), (Fax from U.S. (212) 564-7854), www.tandf.co.uk; *The Europa World Year Book.*

UNICEF, 3 United Nations Plaza, New York, NY 10017, (800) 253-9646, Fax: (212) 887-7465, www.unicef.org; *The State of the World's Children 2008.*

United Nations Statistics Division, New York, NY 10017, (800) 253-9646, Fax: (212) 963-4116, http://unstats.un.org; *Demographic Yearbook; Human Development Report 2006; Statistical Yearbook; Survey of Economic and Social Conditions in Africa 2005;* and *World Statistics Pocketbook.*

The World Bank, 1818 H Street, NW, Washington, DC 20433, (202) 473-1000, Fax: (202) 477-6391, www.worldbank.org; *The World Bank Atlas 2003-2004* and *World Development Report 2008.*

World Health Organization (WHO), Avenue Appia 20, 1211 Geneve 27, Switzerland, (Telephone in U.S. (212) 331-9081), www.who.int; The WHO Global Atlas of Infectious Diseases.

CAMEROON - MOTION PICTURES

Palgrave Macmillan Ltd., Houndmills, Basingstoke, Hampshire, RG21 6XS, England, (Telephone in U.S. (888) 330-8477), (Fax in U.S. (800) 672-2054), www.palgrave.com; *The Statesman's Yearbook 2008.*

UNESCO Institute for Statistics, C.P. 6128 Succursale Centre-Ville, Montreal, Quebec, H3C 3J7 Canada, (Dial from U.S. (514) 343-6880), (Fax from U.S. (514) 343 6882), www.uis.unesco.org; *Statistical Tables.*

United Nations Statistics Division, New York, NY 10017, (800) 253-9646, Fax: (212) 963-4116, http://unstats.un.org; *Statistical Yearbook.*

CAMEROON - MOTOR VEHICLES

International Road Federation (IFR), Madison Place, 500 Montgomery Street, 5th Floor, Alexandria, VA 22314, (703) 535-1001, Fax: (703) 535-1007, www.irfnet.org; *World Road Statistics 2006.*

Taylor and Francis Group, An Informa Business, 2 Park Square, Milton Park, Abingdon, Oxford OX14 4RN, United Kingdom, (Dial from U.S. (212) 216-7800), (Fax from U.S. (212) 564-7854), www.tandf.co.uk; *The Europa World Year Book.*

United Nations Statistics Division, New York, NY 10017, (800) 253-9646, Fax: (212) 963-4116, http://unstats.un.org; *Statistical Yearbook* and *Survey of Economic and Social Conditions in Africa 2005.*

CAMEROON - MUSEUMS

M.E. Sharpe, 80 Business Park Drive, Armonk, NY 10504, (800) 541-6563, Fax: (914) 273-2106, www.mesharpe.com; *The Illustrated Book of World Rankings.*

UNESCO Institute for Statistics, C.P. 6128 Succursale Centre-Ville, Montreal, Quebec, H3C 3J7 Canada, (Dial from U.S. (514) 343-6880), (Fax from U.S. (514) 343 6882), www.uis.unesco.org; *Statistical Tables.*

CAMEROON - NATURAL GAS PRODUCTION

See CAMEROON - MINERAL INDUSTRIES

CAMEROON - NUTRITION

African Development Bank Group, Rue Joseph Anoma, 01 BP 1387 Abidjan 01, Cote d'Ivoire, www.afdb.org; *Statistics Pocketbook 2008.*

United Nations Food and Agricultural Organization (FAO), Viale delle Terme di Caracalla, 00100 Rome, Italy, (Dial from U.S. (202) 653-2400), (Fax from U.S. (202) 653 5760), www.fao.org; *The State of Food and Agriculture (SOFA) 2006.*

CAMEROON - OLDER PEOPLE

M.E. Sharpe, 80 Business Park Drive, Armonk, NY 10504, (800) 541-6563, Fax: (914) 273-2106, www.mesharpe.com; *The Illustrated Book of World Rankings.*

CAMEROON - PALM OIL PRODUCTION

See CAMEROON - CROPS

CAMEROON - PAPER MANUFACTURING

UNESCO Institute for Statistics, C.P. 6128 Succursale Centre-Ville, Montreal, Quebec, H3C 3J7 Canada, (Dial from U.S. (514) 343-6880), (Fax from U.S. (514) 343 6882), www.uis.unesco.org; *Statistical Tables.*

CAMEROON - PEANUT PRODUCTION

See CAMEROON - CROPS

CAMEROON - PERIODICALS

UNESCO Institute for Statistics, C.P. 6128 Succursale Centre-Ville, Montreal, Quebec, H3C 3J7 Canada, (Dial from U.S. (514) 343-6880), (Fax from U.S. (514) 343 6882), www.uis.unesco.org; *Statistical Tables.*

CAMEROON - PESTICIDES

United Nations Food and Agricultural Organization (FAO), Viale delle Terme di Caracalla, 00100 Rome, Italy, (Dial from U.S. (202) 653-2400), (Fax from U.S. (202) 653 5760), www.fao.org; *The State of Food and Agriculture (SOFA) 2006.*

CAMEROON - PETROLEUM INDUSTRY AND TRADE

M.E. Sharpe, 80 Business Park Drive, Armonk, NY 10504, (800) 541-6563, Fax: (914) 273-2106, www.mesharpe.com; *The Illustrated Book of World Rankings.*

Organisation for Economic Cooperation and Development (OECD), 2 rue Andre Pascal, F-75775 Paris Cedex 16, France, (Telephone in U.S. (202) 785-6323), (Fax in U.S. (202) 785-0350), www.oecd.org; *World Energy Outlook 2007.*

Palgrave Macmillan Ltd., Houndmills, Basingstoke, Hampshire, RG21 6XS, England, (Telephone in U.S. (888) 330-8477), (Fax in U.S. (800) 672-2054), www.palgrave.com; *The Statesman's Yearbook 2008.*

PennWell Corporation, 1421 South Sheridan Road, Tulsa, OK 74112, (918) 835-3161, www.pennwell.com; *International Petroleum Encyclopedia 2007.*

U.S. Department of Energy (DOE), Energy Information Administration (EIA), 1000 Independence Avenue, SW, Washington, DC 20585, (202) 586-8800, www.eia.doe.gov; *International Energy Annual 2004* and *International Energy Outlook 2006.*

United Nations Conference on Trade and Development (UNCTAD), DC2-1120, United Nations, New York, NY 10017, (212) 963-0027, www.unctad.org; *UNCTAD Commodity Yearbook.*

United Nations Food and Agricultural Organization (FAO), Viale delle Terme di Caracalla, 00100 Rome, Italy, (Dial from U.S. (202) 653-2400), (Fax from U.S. (202) 653 5760), www.fao.org; *The State of Food and Agriculture (SOFA) 2006.*

CAMEROON - POLITICAL SCIENCE

Central Intelligence Agency, Office of Public Affairs, Washington, DC 20505, (703) 482-0623, Fax: (703) 482-1739, www.cia.gov; *The World Factbook.*

International Monetary Fund (IMF), 700 Nineteenth Street, NW, Washington, DC 20431, (202) 623-7000, Fax: (202) 623-4661, www.imf.org; *Government Finance Statistics Yearbook (2008 Edition)* and *International Financial Statistics Yearbook 2007.*

Palgrave Macmillan Ltd., Houndmills, Basingstoke, Hampshire, RG21 6XS, England, (Telephone in U.S. (888) 330-8477), (Fax in U.S. (800) 672-2054), www.palgrave.com; *The Statesman's Yearbook 2008.*

Taylor and Francis Group, An Informa Business, 2 Park Square, Milton Park, Abingdon, Oxford OX14 4RN, United Kingdom, (Dial from U.S. (212) 216-7800), (Fax from U.S. (212) 564-7854), www.tandf.co.uk; *The Europa World Year Book.*

United Nations Statistics Division, New York, NY 10017, (800) 253-9646, Fax: (212) 963-4116, http://unstats.un.org; *National Accounts Statistics: Compendium of Income Distribution Statistics* and *Survey of Economic and Social Conditions in Africa 2005.*

The World Bank, 1818 H Street, NW, Washington, DC 20433, (202) 473-1000, Fax: (202) 477-6391, www.worldbank.org; *World Development Indicators (WDI) 2008* and *World Development Report 2008.*

CAMEROON - POPULATION

African Development Bank Group, Rue Joseph Anoma, 01 BP 1387 Abidjan 01, Cote d'Ivoire, www.afdb.org; *The African Statistical Journal; Gender, Poverty and Environmental Indicators on African Countries 2007; Selected Statistics on African Countries 2007;* and *Statistics Pocketbook 2008.*

Central Intelligence Agency, Office of Public Affairs, Washington, DC 20505, (703) 482-0623, Fax: (703) 482-1739, www.cia.gov; *The World Factbook.*

Economist Intelligence Unit, 111 West 57th Street, New York, NY 10019, (212) 554-0600, Fax: (212) 586-1181, www.eiu.com; *Cameroon Country Report.*

Euromonitor International, Inc., 224 S. Michigan Avenue, Suite 1500, Chicago, IL 60604, (312) 922-1115, Fax: (312) 922-1157, www.euromonitor.com; *International Marketing Data and Statistics 2008* and *The World Economic Factbook 2008.*

Eurostat, Batiment Jean Monnet, Rue Alcide de Gasperi, L-2920 Luxembourg, http://epp.eurostat.ec.europa.eu; *Demographic Indicators - Population by Age-Classes.*

International Labour Office, I.L.O. Publications, 4 route des Morillons, CH-1211 Geneva 22, Switzerland, (Telephone in U.S. (202) 653-7652), (Fax in U.S. (202) 653-7687), www.ilo.org; *Yearbook of Labour Statistics 2006.*

M.E. Sharpe, 80 Business Park Drive, Armonk, NY 10504, (800) 541-6563, Fax: (914) 273-2106, www.mesharpe.com; *The Illustrated Book of World Rankings.*

Palgrave Macmillan Ltd., Houndmills, Basingstoke, Hampshire, RG21 6XS, England, (Telephone in U.S. (888) 330-8477), (Fax in U.S. (800) 672-2054), www.palgrave.com; *The Statesman's Yearbook 2008.*

Taylor and Francis Group, An Informa Business, 2 Park Square, Milton Park, Abingdon, Oxford OX14 4RN, United Kingdom, (Dial from U.S. (212) 216-7800), (Fax from U.S. (212) 564-7854), www.tandf.co.uk; *The Europa World Year Book.*

U.S. Department of State (DOS), 2201 C Street NW, Washington, DC 20520, (202) 647-4000, www.state.gov; *World Military Expenditures and Arms Transfers (WMEAT).*

UNESCO Institute for Statistics, C.P. 6128 Succursale Centre-Ville, Montreal, Quebec, H3C 3J7

Canada, (Dial from U.S. (514) 343-6880), (Fax from U.S. (514) 343 6882), www.uis.unesco.org; *Statistical Tables.*

United Nations Food and Agricultural Organization (FAO), Viale delle Terme di Caracalla, 00100 Rome, Italy, (Dial from U.S. (202) 653-2400), (Fax from U.S. (202) 653 5760), www.fao.org; *FAO Production Yearbook 2002.*

United Nations Statistics Division, New York, NY 10017, (800) 253-9646, Fax: (212) 963-4116, http://unstats.un.org; *Human Development Report 2006; Statistical Yearbook; Survey of Economic and Social Conditions in Africa 2005;* and *World Statistics Pocketbook.*

The World Bank, 1818 H Street, NW, Washington, DC 20433, (202) 473-1000, Fax: (202) 477-6391, www.worldbank.org; *Camaroon; The World Bank Atlas 2003-2004;* and *World Development Report 2008.*

CAMEROON - POPULATION DENSITY

African Development Bank Group, Rue Joseph Anoma, 01 BP 1387 Abidjan 01, Cote d'Ivoire, www.afdb.org; *Statistics Pocketbook 2008.*

Central Intelligence Agency, Office of Public Affairs, Washington, DC 20505, (703) 482-0623, Fax: (703) 482-1739, www.cia.gov; *The World Factbook.*

Euromonitor International, Inc., 224 S. Michigan Avenue, Suite 1500, Chicago, IL 60604, (312) 922-1115, Fax: (312) 922-1157, www.euromonitor.com; *International Marketing Data and Statistics 2008* and *The World Economic Factbook 2008.*

M.E. Sharpe, 80 Business Park Drive, Armonk, NY 10504, (800) 541-6563, Fax: (914) 273-2106, www.mesharpe.com; *The Illustrated Book of World Rankings.*

Palgrave Macmillan Ltd., Houndmills, Basingstoke, Hampshire, RG21 6XS, England, (Telephone in U.S. (888) 330-8477), (Fax in U.S. (800) 672-2054), www.palgrave.com; *The Statesman's Yearbook 2008.*

Taylor and Francis Group, An Informa Business, 2 Park Square, Milton Park, Abingdon, Oxford OX14 4RN, United Kingdom, (Dial from U.S. (212) 216-7800), (Fax from U.S. (212) 564-7854), www.tandf.co.uk; *The Europa World Year Book.*

UNESCO Institute for Statistics, C.P. 6128 Succursale Centre-Ville, Montreal, Quebec, H3C 3J7 Canada, (Dial from U.S. (514) 343-6880), (Fax from U.S. (514) 343 6882), www.uis.unesco.org; *Statistical Tables.*

United Nations Food and Agricultural Organization (FAO), Viale delle Terme di Caracalla, 00100 Rome, Italy, (Dial from U.S. (202) 653-2400), (Fax from U.S. (202) 653 5760), www.fao.org; *The State of Food and Agriculture (SOFA) 2006.*

United Nations Statistics Division, New York, NY 10017, (800) 253-9646, Fax: (212) 963-4116, http://unstats.un.org; *Statistical Yearbook* and *Survey of Economic and Social Conditions in Africa 2005.*

The World Bank, 1818 H Street, NW, Washington, DC 20433, (202) 473-1000, Fax: (202) 477-6391, www.worldbank.org; *Camaroon* and *The World Bank Atlas 2003-2004.*

CAMEROON - POSTAL SERVICE

M.E. Sharpe, 80 Business Park Drive, Armonk, NY 10504, (800) 541-6563, Fax: (914) 273-2106, www.mesharpe.com; *The Illustrated Book of World Rankings.*

United Nations Statistics Division, New York, NY 10017, (800) 253-9646, Fax: (212) 963-4116, http://unstats.un.org; *Statistical Yearbook.*

CAMEROON - POWER RESOURCES

Euromonitor International, Inc., 224 S. Michigan Avenue, Suite 1500, Chicago, IL 60604, (312) 922-1115, Fax: (312) 922-1157, www.euromonitor.com; *International Marketing Data and Statistics 2008; The World Economic Factbook 2008;* and *World Marketing Data and Statistics.*

M.E. Sharpe, 80 Business Park Drive, Armonk, NY 10504, (800) 541-6563, Fax: (914) 273-2106, www.mesharpe.com; *The Illustrated Book of World Rankings.*

Organisation for Economic Cooperation and Development (OECD), 2 rue Andre Pascal, F-75775 Paris Cedex 16, France, (Telephone in U.S. (202) 785-6323), (Fax in U.S. (202) 785-0350), www.oecd.org; *World Energy Outlook 2007.*

Palgrave Macmillan Ltd., Houndmills, Basingstoke, Hampshire, RG21 6XS, England, (Telephone in U.S. (888) 330-8477), (Fax in U.S. (800) 672-2054), www.palgrave.com; *The Statesman's Yearbook 2008.*

U.S. Department of Energy (DOE), Energy Information Administration (EIA), 1000 Independence Avenue, SW, Washington, DC 20585, (202) 586-8800, www.eia.doe.gov; *International Energy Annual 2004* and *International Energy Outlook 2006.*

United Nations Economic Commission for Africa (ECA), PO Box 3001, Addis Ababa, Ethiopia, (Telephone in U.S. (212) 963-4957), www.uneca.org; *African Statistical Yearbook 2006.*

United Nations Food and Agricultural Organization (FAO), Viale delle Terme di Caracalla, 00100 Rome, Italy, (Dial from U.S. (202) 653-2400), (Fax from U.S. (202) 653 5760), www.fao.org; *The State of Food and Agriculture (SOFA) 2006.*

United Nations Statistics Division, New York, NY 10017, (800) 253-9646, Fax: (212) 963-4116, http://unstats.un.org; *Human Development Report 2006; Statistical Yearbook;* and *World Statistics Pocketbook.*

The World Bank, 1818 H Street, NW, Washington, DC 20433, (202) 473-1000, Fax: (202) 477-6391, www.worldbank.org; *The World Bank Atlas 2003-2004* and *World Development Report 2008.*

CAMEROON - PRICES

Euromonitor International, Inc., 224 S. Michigan Avenue, Suite 1500, Chicago, IL 60604, (312) 922-1115, Fax: (312) 922-1157, www.euromonitor.com; *World Marketing Data and Statistics.*

International Labour Office, I.L.O. Publications, 4 route des Morillons, CH-1211 Geneva 22, Switzerland, (Telephone in U.S. (202) 653-7652), (Fax in U.S. (202) 653-7687), www.ilo.org; *Yearbook of Labour Statistics 2006.*

International Monetary Fund (IMF), 700 Nineteenth Street, NW, Washington, DC 20431, (202) 623-7000, Fax: (202) 623-4661, www.imf.org; *International Financial Statistics Yearbook 2007.*

M.E. Sharpe, 80 Business Park Drive, Armonk, NY 10504, (800) 541-6563, Fax: (914) 273-2106, www.mesharpe.com; *The Illustrated Book of World Rankings.*

United Nations Economic Commission for Africa (ECA), PO Box 3001, Addis Ababa, Ethiopia, (Telephone in U.S. (212) 963-4957), www.uneca.org; *African Statistical Yearbook 2006.*

United Nations Food and Agricultural Organization (FAO), Viale delle Terme di Caracalla, 00100 Rome, Italy, (Dial from U.S. (202) 653-2400), (Fax from U.S. (202) 653 5760), www.fao.org; *FAO Production Yearbook 2002* and *The State of Food and Agriculture (SOFA) 2006.*

The World Bank, 1818 H Street, NW, Washington, DC 20433, (202) 473-1000, Fax: (202) 477-6391, www.worldbank.org; *Camaroon.*

CAMEROON - PROFESSIONS

UNESCO Institute for Statistics, C.P. 6128 Succursale Centre-Ville, Montreal, Quebec, H3C 3J7 Canada, (Dial from U.S. (514) 343-6880), (Fax from U.S. (514) 343 6882), www.uis.unesco.org; *Statistical Tables.*

United Nations Statistics Division, New York, NY 10017, (800) 253-9646, Fax: (212) 963-4116, http://unstats.un.org; *Statistical Yearbook.*

CAMEROON - PUBLIC HEALTH

African Development Bank Group, Rue Joseph Anoma, 01 BP 1387 Abidjan 01, Cote d'Ivoire, www.afdb.org; *Statistics Pocketbook 2008.*

Euromonitor International, Inc., 224 S. Michigan Avenue, Suite 1500, Chicago, IL 60604, (312) 922-1115, Fax: (312) 922-1157, www.euromonitor.com; *World Marketing Data and Statistics.*

M.E. Sharpe, 80 Business Park Drive, Armonk, NY 10504, (800) 541-6563, Fax: (914) 273-2106, www.mesharpe.com; *The Illustrated Book of World Rankings.*

Palgrave Macmillan Ltd., Houndmills, Basingstoke, Hampshire, RG21 6XS, England, (Telephone in U.S. (888) 330-8477), (Fax in U.S. (800) 672-2054), www.palgrave.com; *The Statesman's Yearbook 2008.*

UNICEF, 3 United Nations Plaza, New York, NY 10017, (800) 253-9646, Fax: (212) 887-7465, www.unicef.org; *The State of the World's Children 2008.*

United Nations Economic Commission for Africa (ECA), PO Box 3001, Addis Ababa, Ethiopia, (Telephone in U.S. (212) 963-4957), www.uneca.org; *African Statistical Yearbook 2006.*

United Nations Statistics Division, New York, NY 10017, (800) 253-9646, Fax: (212) 963-4116, http://unstats.un.org; *Human Development Report 2006* and *Statistical Yearbook.*

The World Bank, 1818 H Street, NW, Washington, DC 20433, (202) 473-1000, Fax: (202) 477-6391, www.worldbank.org; *Camaroon* and *World Development Report 2008.*

World Health Organization (WHO), Avenue Appia 20, 1211 Geneve 27, Switzerland, (Telephone in U.S. (212) 331-9081), www.who.int; The WHO Global Atlas of Infectious Diseases.

CAMEROON - PUBLISHERS AND PUBLISHING

UNESCO Institute for Statistics, C.P. 6128 Succursale Centre-Ville, Montreal, Quebec, H3C 3J7 Canada, (Dial from U.S. (514) 343-6880), (Fax from U.S. (514) 343 6882), www.uis.unesco.org; *Statistical Tables.*

CAMEROON - RADIO - RECEIVERS AND RECEPTION

Palgrave Macmillan Ltd., Houndmills, Basingstoke, Hampshire, RG21 6XS, England, (Telephone in U.S. (888) 330-8477), (Fax in U.S. (800) 672-2054), www.palgrave.com; *The Statesman's Yearbook 2008.*

United Nations Statistics Division, New York, NY 10017, (800) 253-9646, Fax: (212) 963-4116, http://unstats.un.org; *Statistical Yearbook.*

CAMEROON - RAILROADS

Jane's Information Group, 110 North Royal Street, Suite 200, Alexandria, VA 22314, (703) 683-3700, Fax: (800) 836-0297, www.janes.com; *Jane's World Railways.*

Palgrave Macmillan Ltd., Houndmills, Basingstoke, Hampshire, RG21 6XS, England, (Telephone in U.S. (888) 330-8477), (Fax in U.S. (800) 672-2054), www.palgrave.com; *The Statesman's Yearbook 2008.*

Taylor and Francis Group, An Informa Business, 2 Park Square, Milton Park, Abingdon, Oxford OX14 4RN, United Kingdom, (Dial from U.S. (212) 216-7800), (Fax from U.S. (212) 564-7854), www.tandf.co.uk; *The Europa World Year Book.*

United Nations Economic Commission for Africa (ECA), PO Box 3001, Addis Ababa, Ethiopia, (Telephone in U.S. (212) 963-4957), www.uneca.org; *African Statistical Yearbook 2006.*

United Nations Statistics Division, New York, NY 10017, (800) 253-9646, Fax: (212) 963-4116, http://unstats.un.org; *Statistical Yearbook* and *Survey of Economic and Social Conditions in Africa 2005.*

CAMEROON - RELIGION

Central Intelligence Agency, Office of Public Affairs, Washington, DC 20505, (703) 482-0623, Fax: (703) 482-1739, www.cia.gov; *The World Factbook.*

M.E. Sharpe, 80 Business Park Drive, Armonk, NY 10504, (800) 541-6563, Fax: (914) 273-2106, www.mesharpe.com; *The Illustrated Book of World Rankings.*

Palgrave Macmillan Ltd., Houndmills, Basingstoke, Hampshire, RG21 6XS, England, (Telephone in U.S. (888) 330-8477), (Fax in U.S. (800) 672-2054), www.palgrave.com; *The Statesman's Yearbook 2008.*

CAMEROON - RENT CHARGES

International Labour Office, I.L.O. Publications, 4 route des Morillons, CH-1211 Geneva 22, Switzerland, (Telephone in U.S. (202) 653-7652), (Fax in U.S. (202) 653-7687), www.ilo.org; *Yearbook of Labour Statistics 2006.*

CAMEROON - RESERVES (ACCOUNTING)

African Development Bank Group, Rue Joseph Anoma, 01 BP 1387 Abidjan 01, Cote d'Ivoire, www.afdb.org; *Statistics Pocketbook 2008.*

Euromonitor International, Inc., 224 S. Michigan Avenue, Suite 1500, Chicago, IL 60604, (312) 922-1115, Fax: (312) 922-1157, www.euromonitor.com; *International Marketing Data and Statistics 2008.*

The World Bank, 1818 H Street, NW, Washington, DC 20433, (202) 473-1000, Fax: (202) 477-6391, www.worldbank.org; *World Development Indicators (WDI) 2008.*

CAMEROON - RETAIL TRADE

Euromonitor International, Inc., 224 S. Michigan Avenue, Suite 1500, Chicago, IL 60604, (312) 922-1115, Fax: (312) 922-1157, www.euromonitor.com; *World Marketing Data and Statistics.*

CAMEROON - RICE PRODUCTION

See CAMEROON - CROPS

CAMEROON - ROADS

Central Intelligence Agency, Office of Public Affairs, Washington, DC 20505, (703) 482-0623, Fax: (703) 482-1739, www.cia.gov; *The World Factbook.*

International Road Federation (IFR), Madison Place, 500 Montgomery Street, 5th Floor, Alexandria, VA 22314, (703) 535-1001, Fax: (703) 535-1007, www.irfnet.org; *World Road Statistics 2006.*

Palgrave Macmillan Ltd., Houndmills, Basingstoke, Hampshire, RG21 6XS, England, (Telephone in U.S. (888) 330-8477), (Fax in U.S. (800) 672-2054), www.palgrave.com; *The Statesman's Yearbook 2008.*

United Nations Economic Commission for Africa (ECA), PO Box 3001, Addis Ababa, Ethiopia, (Telephone in U.S. (212) 963-4957), www.uneca.org; *African Statistical Yearbook 2006.*

United Nations Statistics Division, New York, NY 10017, (800) 253-9646, Fax: (212) 963-4116, http://unstats.un.org; *Survey of Economic and Social Conditions in Africa 2005.*

CAMEROON - RUBBER INDUSTRY AND TRADE

International Rubber Study Group (IRSG), 1st Floor, Heron House, 109/115 Wembley Hill Road, Wembley, Middlesex HA9 8DA, United Kingdom, www.rubberstudy.com; *Rubber Statistical Bulletin; Summary of World Rubber Statistics 2005; World Rubber Statistics Handbook (Volume 6, 1975-2001);* and *World Rubber Statistics Historic Handbook.*

M.E. Sharpe, 80 Business Park Drive, Armonk, NY 10504, (800) 541-6563, Fax: (914) 273-2106, www.mesharpe.com; *The Illustrated Book of World Rankings.*

United Nations Statistics Division, New York, NY 10017, (800) 253-9646, Fax: (212) 963-4116, http://unstats.un.org; *Statistical Yearbook.*

CAMEROON - SHEEP

See CAMEROON - LIVESTOCK

CAMEROON - SHIPPING

Palgrave Macmillan Ltd., Houndmills, Basingstoke, Hampshire, RG21 6XS, England, (Telephone in U.S. (888) 330-8477), (Fax in U.S. (800) 672-2054), www.palgrave.com; *The Statesman's Yearbook 2008.*

Taylor and Francis Group, An Informa Business, 2 Park Square, Milton Park, Abingdon, Oxford OX14 4RN, United Kingdom, (Dial from U.S. (212) 216-7800), (Fax from U.S. (212) 564-7854), www.tandf.co.uk; *The Europa World Year Book.*

U.S. Department of Transportation (DOT), Maritime Administration (MARAD), West Building, Southeast Federal Center, 1200 New Jersey Avenue, SE, Washington, DC 20590, (800) 99-MARAD, www.marad.dot.gov; *World Merchant Fleet 2005.*

United Nations Economic Commission for Africa (ECA), PO Box 3001, Addis Ababa, Ethiopia, (Telephone in U.S. (212) 963-4957), www.uneca.org; *African Statistical Yearbook 2006.*

United Nations Statistics Division, New York, NY 10017, (800) 253-9646, Fax: (212) 963-4116, http://unstats.un.org; *Statistical Yearbook.*

CAMEROON - SILVER PRODUCTION

See CAMEROON - MINERAL INDUSTRIES

CAMEROON - SOCIAL ECOLOGY

M.E. Sharpe, 80 Business Park Drive, Armonk, NY 10504, (800) 541-6563, Fax: (914) 273-2106, www.mesharpe.com; *The Illustrated Book of World Rankings.*

United Nations Statistics Division, New York, NY 10017, (800) 253-9646, Fax: (212) 963-4116, http://unstats.un.org; *World Statistics Pocketbook.*

CAMEROON - SOCIAL SECURITY

International Monetary Fund (IMF), 700 Nineteenth Street, NW, Washington, DC 20431, (202) 623-7000, Fax: (202) 623-4661, www.imf.org; *Government Finance Statistics Yearbook (2008 Edition).*

United Nations Statistics Division, New York, NY 10017, (800) 253-9646, Fax: (212) 963-4116, http://unstats.un.org; *National Accounts Statistics: Compendium of Income Distribution Statistics.*

CAMEROON - STEEL PRODUCTION

See CAMEROON - MINERAL INDUSTRIES

CAMEROON - SUGAR PRODUCTION

See CAMEROON - CROPS

CAMEROON - TAXATION

International Monetary Fund (IMF), 700 Nineteenth Street, NW, Washington, DC 20431, (202) 623-7000, Fax: (202) 623-4661, www.imf.org; *Government Finance Statistics Yearbook (2008 Edition).*

International Road Federation (IFR), Madison Place, 500 Montgomery Street, 5th Floor, Alexandria, VA 22314, (703) 535-1001, Fax: (703) 535-1007, www.irfnet.org; *World Road Statistics 2006.*

Taylor and Francis Group, An Informa Business, 2 Park Square, Milton Park, Abingdon, Oxford OX14 4RN, United Kingdom, (Dial from U.S. (212) 216-7800), (Fax from U.S. (212) 564-7854), www.tandf.co.uk; *The Europa World Year Book.*

The World Bank, 1818 H Street, NW, Washington, DC 20433, (202) 473-1000, Fax: (202) 477-6391, www.worldbank.org; *World Development Indicators (WDI) 2008.*

CAMEROON - TEA PRODUCTION

See CAMEROON - CROPS

CAMEROON - TELEPHONE

International Telecommunication Union (ITU), Place des Nations, 1211 Geneva 20, Switzerland, www.itu.int; World Telecommunication Indicators Database.

Palgrave Macmillan Ltd., Houndmills, Basingstoke, Hampshire, RG21 6XS, England, (Telephone in U.S. (888) 330-8477), (Fax in U.S. (800) 672-2054), www.palgrave.com; *The Statesman's Yearbook 2008.*

Taylor and Francis Group, An Informa Business, 2 Park Square, Milton Park, Abingdon, Oxford OX14 4RN, United Kingdom, (Dial from U.S. (212) 216-7800), (Fax from U.S. (212) 564-7854), www.tandf.co.uk; *The Europa World Year Book.*

United Nations Statistics Division, New York, NY 10017, (800) 253-9646, Fax: (212) 963-4116, http://unstats.un.org; *World Statistics Pocketbook.*

CAMEROON - TEXTILE INDUSTRY

M.E. Sharpe, 80 Business Park Drive, Armonk, NY 10504, (800) 541-6563, Fax: (914) 273-2106, www.mesharpe.com; *The Illustrated Book of World Rankings.*

United Nations Conference on Trade and Development (UNCTAD), DC2-1120, United Nations, New York, NY 10017, (212) 963-0027, www.unctad.org; *UNCTAD Commodity Yearbook.*

CAMEROON - THEATER

UNESCO Institute for Statistics, C.P. 6128 Succursale Centre-Ville, Montreal, Quebec, H3C 3J7 Canada, (Dial from U.S. (514) 343-6880), (Fax from U.S. (514) 343 6882), www.uis.unesco.org; *Statistical Tables.*

CAMEROON - TIN PRODUCTION

See CAMEROON - MINERAL INDUSTRIES

CAMEROON - TOBACCO INDUSTRY

Foreign Agricultural Service (FAS), U.S. Department of Agriculture (USDA), 1400 Independence Avenue, SW, Washington, DC 20250, (202) 720-3935, www.fas.usda.gov; *Tobacco: World Markets and Trade.*

M.E. Sharpe, 80 Business Park Drive, Armonk, NY 10504, (800) 541-6563, Fax: (914) 273-2106, www.mesharpe.com; *The Illustrated Book of World Rankings.*

United Nations Statistics Division, New York, NY 10017, (800) 253-9646, Fax: (212) 963-4116, http://unstats.un.org; *Statistical Yearbook.*

CAMEROON - TOURISM

Euromonitor International, Inc., 224 S. Michigan Avenue, Suite 1500, Chicago, IL 60604, (312) 922-1115, Fax: (312) 922-1157, www.euromonitor.com; *The World Economic Factbook 2008* and *World Marketing Data and Statistics.*

M.E. Sharpe, 80 Business Park Drive, Armonk, NY 10504, (800) 541-6563, Fax: (914) 273-2106, www.mesharpe.com; *The Illustrated Book of World Rankings.*

Palgrave Macmillan Ltd., Houndmills, Basingstoke, Hampshire, RG21 6XS, England, (Telephone in U.S. (888) 330-8477), (Fax in U.S. (800) 672-2054), www.palgrave.com; *The Statesman's Yearbook 2008.*

Taylor and Francis Group, An Informa Business, 2 Park Square, Milton Park, Abingdon, Oxford OX14 4RN, United Kingdom, (Dial from U.S. (212) 216-7800), (Fax from U.S. (212) 564-7854), www.tandf.co.uk; *The Europa World Year Book.*

United Nations Economic Commission for Africa (ECA), PO Box 3001, Addis Ababa, Ethiopia, (Telephone in U.S. (212) 963-4957), www.uneca.org; *African Statistical Yearbook 2006.*

United Nations Statistics Division, New York, NY 10017, (800) 253-9646, Fax: (212) 963-4116, http://unstats.un.org; *Statistical Yearbook.*

The World Bank, 1818 H Street, NW, Washington, DC 20433, (202) 473-1000, Fax: (202) 477-6391, www.worldbank.org; *Camaroon.*

CAMEROON - TRADE

See CAMEROON - INTERNATIONAL TRADE

CAMEROON - TRANSPORTATION

Central Intelligence Agency, Office of Public Affairs, Washington, DC 20505, (703) 482-0623, Fax: (703) 482-1739, www.cia.gov; *The World Factbook.*

Euromonitor International, Inc., 224 S. Michigan Avenue, Suite 1500, Chicago, IL 60604, (312) 922-1115, Fax: (312) 922-1157, www.euromonitor.com; *International Marketing Data and Statistics 2008* and *World Marketing Data and Statistics.*

M.E. Sharpe, 80 Business Park Drive, Armonk, NY 10504, (800) 541-6563, Fax: (914) 273-2106, www.mesharpe.com; *The Illustrated Book of World Rankings.*

Palgrave Macmillan Ltd., Houndmills, Basingstoke, Hampshire, RG21 6XS, England, (Telephone in U.S. (888) 330-8477), (Fax in U.S. (800) 672-2054), www.palgrave.com; *The Statesman's Yearbook 2008.*

Taylor and Francis Group, An Informa Business, 2 Park Square, Milton Park, Abingdon, Oxford OX14 4RN, United Kingdom, (Dial from U.S. (212) 216-7800), (Fax from U.S. (212) 564-7854), www.tandf.co.uk; *The Europa World Year Book.*

United Nations Economic Commission for Africa (ECA), PO Box 3001, Addis Ababa, Ethiopia, (Telephone in U.S. (212) 963-4957), www.uneca.org; *African Statistical Yearbook 2006.*

United Nations Statistics Division, New York, NY 10017, (800) 253-9646, Fax: (212) 963-4116, http://unstats.un.org; *Human Development Report 2006.*

The World Bank, 1818 H Street, NW, Washington, DC 20433, (202) 473-1000, Fax: (202) 477-6391, www.worldbank.org; *Africa Live Database (LDB); African Development Indicators (ADI) 2007;* and *Camaroon.*

CAMEROON - TRAVEL COSTS

International Monetary Fund (IMF), 700 Nineteenth Street, NW, Washington, DC 20431, (202) 623-7000, Fax: (202) 623-4661, www.imf.org; *Government Finance Statistics Yearbook (2008 Edition).*

CAMEROON - UNEMPLOYMENT

Central Intelligence Agency, Office of Public Affairs, Washington, DC 20505, (703) 482-0623, Fax: (703) 482-1739, www.cia.gov; *The World Factbook.*

Euromonitor International, Inc., 224 S. Michigan Avenue, Suite 1500, Chicago, IL 60604, (312) 922-1115, Fax: (312) 922-1157, www.euromonitor.com; *International Marketing Data and Statistics 2008.*

International Labour Office, I.L.O. Publications, 4 route des Morillons, CH-1211 Geneva 22, Switzerland, (Telephone in U.S. (202) 653-7652), (Fax in U.S. (202) 653-7687), www.ilo.org; *Yearbook of Labour Statistics 2006.*

United Nations Statistics Division, New York, NY 10017, (800) 253-9646, Fax: (212) 963-4116, http://unstats.un.org; *Statistical Yearbook.*

CAMEROON - VITAL STATISTICS

Euromonitor International, Inc., 224 S. Michigan Avenue, Suite 1500, Chicago, IL 60604, (312) 922-1115, Fax: (312) 922-1157, www.euromonitor.com; *International Marketing Data and Statistics 2008.*

Palgrave Macmillan Ltd., Houndmills, Basingstoke, Hampshire, RG21 6XS, England, (Telephone in U.S. (888) 330-8477), (Fax in U.S. (800) 672-2054), www.palgrave.com; *The Statesman's Yearbook 2008.*

United Nations Statistics Division, New York, NY 10017, (800) 253-9646, Fax: (212) 963-4116, http://unstats.un.org; *Statistical Yearbook.*

CAMEROON - WAGES

International Labour Office, I.L.O. Publications, 4 route des Morillons, CH-1211 Geneva 22, Switzerland, (Telephone in U.S. (202) 653-7652), (Fax in U.S. (202) 653-7687), www.ilo.org; *Yearbook of Labour Statistics 2006.*

The World Bank, 1818 H Street, NW, Washington, DC 20433, (202) 473-1000, Fax: (202) 477-6391, www.worldbank.org; *Camaroon.*

CAMEROON - WEATHER

See CAMEROON - CLIMATE

CAMEROON - WHEAT PRODUCTION

See CAMEROON - CROPS

CAMEROON - WINE PRODUCTION

See CAMEROON - BEVERAGE INDUSTRY

CAMEROON - WOOD AND WOOD PULP

See CAMEROON - FORESTS AND FORESTRY

CAMEROON - WOOL PRODUCTION

See CAMEROON - TEXTILE INDUSTRY

CAMPAIGNS - FUND RAISING

Congressional Quarterly, Inc., 1255 22nd Street, NW, Washington, DC 20037, (202) 419-8500, www.cq.com; *CQ's Politics in America 2006: The 109th Congress.*

Federal Election Commission (FEC), 999 E Street, NW, Washington, DC 20463, (800) 424-9530, www.fec.gov; *Annual Report 2006; Combined Federal/State Disclosure and Election Directory 2008;* and unpublished data.

CAMPING, ETC

National Sporting Goods Association (NSGA), 1601 Feehanville Drive, Suite 300, Mount Prospect, IL 60056, (847) 296-6742, Fax: (847) 391-9827, www.nsga.org; *2006 Sports Participation* and *Ten-Year History of Selected Sports Participation, 1996-2006.*

CANADA - NATIONAL STATISTICAL OFFICE

Statistics Canada, 100 Tunney's Pasture Driveway, Ottawa, Ontario K1A 0T6, (Dial from U.S. (800) 263-1136), (Fax from U.S. (877) 287-4369), www.statcan.ca; National Data Center.

CANADA - PRIMARY STATISTICS SOURCES

British Columbia Vital Statistics Agency, PO Box 9657 STN PROV GOVT, Victoria BC V8W 9P3, Canada, (Dial from U.S. (250) 952-2681), (Fax from U.S. (250) 952-2527), www.vs.gov.bc.ca; *Quarterly Digest.*

Economics and Statistics Division, Nova Scotia Department of Finance, 1723 Hollis Street, PO Box 187, Halifax, Nova Scotia B3J 2N3, Canada, (Dial from U.S. (902) 424-2740), (Fax from U.S. (902) 424-0714), www.gov.ns.ca/finance/statistics/agency; *DailyStats; Nova Scotia Statistical Review 2007;* and *Statistical Review 2007.*

Northwest Territories Bureau of Statistics, Government of the Northwest Territories, PO Box 1320, Yellowknife, NWT, Canada X1A 2L9, (867) 873-7147, www.stats.gov.nt.ca; *Statistics Quarterly.*

Statistics Canada, 100 Tunney's Pasture Driveway, Ottawa, Ontario K1A 0T6, (Dial from U.S. (800) 263-1136), (Fax from U.S. (877) 287-4369), www.statcan.ca; *Canada Year Book 2007; Historical Statistics of Canada;* and *Infomat, a Weekly Review.*

CANADA - DATABASES

Alberta Economic Development (AED), 6th Floor, Commerce Place, 10155 - 102 Street, Edmonton, AB T5J 4L6, Canada, (Dial from U.S. (780) 415-1319), www.alberta-canada.com/statpub/; *Facts on Alberta.*

BC Stats, Box 9410 Stn Prov Govt, Victoria, BC, V8V 9V1, Canada, (Dial from U.S. (250) 387-0327), www.bcstats.gov.bc.ca; BC STATS Database. Subject coverage: Business and industry, census data, economic statistics, labor, population, mapping and geography.

The Conference Board of Canada, 255 Smyth Road, Ottawa, ON K1H 8M7, Canada, (Dial from U.S. (866) 711-2262), (Fax from U.S. (613) 526-4857), www.conferenceboard.ca; Canadian Forecast Database. Five-year or 20 year forecasts for nine sectors of the national economy. More than 540 indicators are available; Metropolitan Forecast Database. Five-year forecasts for 25 Canadian census metropolitan areas (CMA). More than 100 indicators for each CMA; and Provincial Forecast Database. Five-year or 20 year forecasts for all 10 provinces. More than 1,500 indicators are available.

Information and Documentation Centre, Institute de la statistique du Quebec, 200 Chemin Sainte-Foy, 3rd Floor, Quebec City, Quebec G1R 5T4, Canada, (Dial from U.S. (418) 691-2401), (Fax from U.S. (418) 643-4129), www.stat.gouv.qc.ca; *Databank of Official Statistics on Quebec.*

Statistics Canada, 100 Tunney's Pasture Driveway, Ottawa, Ontario K1A 0T6, (Dial from U.S. (800) 263-1136), (Fax from U.S. (877) 287-4369), www.statcan.ca; CANSIM (Canadian Socio-Economic Information Management System).

CANADA - ABORTION

United Nations Statistics Division, New York, NY 10017, (800) 253-9646, Fax: (212) 963-4116, http://unstats.un.org; *Trends in Europe and North America: The Statistical Yearbook of the ECE 2005.*

CANADA - AGRICULTURAL MACHINERY

United Nations Statistics Division, New York, NY 10017, (800) 253-9646, Fax: (212) 963-4116, http://unstats.un.org; *Statistical Yearbook.*

CANADA - AGRICULTURE

Economist Intelligence Unit, 111 West 57th Street, New York, NY 10019, (212) 554-0600, Fax: (212) 586-1181, www.eiu.com; *Canada Country Report.*

Euromonitor International, Inc., 224 S. Michigan Avenue, Suite 1500, Chicago, IL 60604, (312) 922-1115, Fax: (312) 922-1157, www.euromonitor.com; *International Marketing Data and Statistics 2008* and *World Marketing Data and Statistics.*

M.E. Sharpe, 80 Business Park Drive, Armonk, NY 10504, (800) 541-6563, Fax: (914) 273-2106, www.mesharpe.com; *The Illustrated Book of World Rankings.*

Organisation for Economic Cooperation and Development (OECD), 2 rue Andre Pascal, F-75775 Paris Cedex 16, France, (Telephone in U.S. (202) 785-6323), (Fax in U.S. (202) 785-0350), www.oecd.org; *Indicators of Industrial Activity; 2005 OECD Agricultural Outlook Tables, 1970-2014; OECD Agricultural Outlook: 2007-2016; OECD Economic Survey - Canada 2008;* and STructural ANalysis (STAN) database.

Palgrave Macmillan Ltd., Houndmills, Basingstoke, Hampshire, RG21 6XS, England, (Telephone in U.S. (888) 330-8477), (Fax in U.S. (800) 672-2054), www.palgrave.com; *The Statesman's Yearbook 2008.*

Statistics Canada, 100 Tunney's Pasture Driveway, Ottawa, Ontario K1A 0T6, (Dial from U.S. (800) 263-1136), (Fax from U.S. (877) 287-4369), www.statcan.ca; *Net Farm Income - Agriculture Economic Statistics.*

Taylor and Francis Group, An Informa Business, 2 Park Square, Milton Park, Abingdon, Oxford OX14 4RN, United Kingdom, (Dial from U.S. (212) 216-7800), (Fax from U.S. (212) 564-7854), www.tandf.co.uk; *The Europa World Year Book.*

United Nations Conference on Trade and Development (UNCTAD), DC2-1120, United Nations, New York, NY 10017, (212) 963-0027, www.unctad.org; *UNCTAD Commodity Yearbook.*

United Nations Food and Agricultural Organization (FAO), Viale delle Terme di Caracalla, 00100 Rome, Italy, (Dial from U.S. (202) 653-2400), (Fax from U.S. (202) 653 5760), www.fao.org; AQUASTAT; *FAO Production Yearbook 2002; FAO Trade Yearbook;* and *The State of Food and Agriculture (SOFA) 2006.*

United Nations Statistics Division, New York, NY 10017, (800) 253-9646, Fax: (212) 963-4116, http://unstats.un.org; *Statistical Yearbook.*

The World Bank, 1818 H Street, NW, Washington, DC 20433, (202) 473-1000, Fax: (202) 477-6391, www.worldbank.org; *Canada* and *World Development Indicators (WDI) 2008.*

CANADA - AIRLINES

International Civil Aviation Organization (ICAO), External Relations and Public Information Office (EPO), 999 University Street, Montreal, Quebec H3C 5H7, Canada, (Dial from U.S. (514) 954-8219), (Fax from U.S. (514) 954-6077), www.icao.int; *Civil Aviation Statistics of the World.*

M.E. Sharpe, 80 Business Park Drive, Armonk, NY 10504, (800) 541-6563, Fax: (914) 273-2106, www.mesharpe.com; *The Illustrated Book of World Rankings.*

Organisation for Economic Cooperation and Development (OECD), 2 rue Andre Pascal, F-75775 Paris Cedex 16, France, (Telephone in U.S. (202) 785-6323), (Fax in U.S. (202) 785-0350), www.oecd.org; *Household, Tourism, Travel: Trends, Environmental Impacts and Policy Responses.*

Palgrave Macmillan Ltd., Houndmills, Basingstoke, Hampshire, RG21 6XS, England, (Telephone in U.S. (888) 330-8477), (Fax in U.S. (800) 672-2054), www.palgrave.com; *The Statesman's Yearbook 2008.*

Taylor and Francis Group, An Informa Business, 2 Park Square, Milton Park, Abingdon, Oxford OX14 4RN, United Kingdom, (Dial from U.S. (212) 216-7800), (Fax from U.S. (212) 564-7854), www.tandf.co.uk; *The Europa World Year Book.*

United Nations Statistics Division, New York, NY 10017, (800) 253-9646, Fax: (212) 963-4116, http://unstats.un.org; *Statistical Yearbook.*

CANADA - AIRPORTS

Central Intelligence Agency, Office of Public Affairs, Washington, DC 20505, (703) 482-0623, Fax: (703) 482-1739, www.cia.gov; *The World Factbook.*

CANADA - ALUMINUM PRODUCTION

See CANADA - MINERAL INDUSTRIES

CANADA - ANIMAL FEEDING

Organisation for Economic Cooperation and Development (OECD), 2 rue Andre Pascal, F-75775 Paris Cedex 16, France, (Telephone in U.S. (202) 785-6323), (Fax in U.S. (202) 785-0350), www.oecd.org; *International Trade by Commodity Statistics (ITCS).*

United Nations Statistics Division, New York, NY 10017, (800) 253-9646, Fax: (212) 963-4116, http://unstats.un.org; *Statistical Yearbook.*

CANADA - APPLE PRODUCTION

See CANADA - CROPS

CANADA - ARMED FORCES

Central Intelligence Agency, Office of Public Affairs, Washington, DC 20505, (703) 482-0623, Fax: (703) 482-1739, www.cia.gov; *The World Factbook.*

Euromonitor International, Inc., 224 S. Michigan Avenue, Suite 1500, Chicago, IL 60604, (312) 922-1115, Fax: (312) 922-1157, www.euromonitor.com; *World Marketing Data and Statistics.*

International Institute for Strategic Studies (IISS), Arundel House, 13-15 Arundel Street, Temple Place, London WC2R 3DX, England, www.iiss.org; *The Military Balance 2007.*

International Monetary Fund (IMF), 700 Nineteenth Street, NW, Washington, DC 20431, (202) 623-7000, Fax: (202) 623-4661, www.imf.org; *Government Finance Statistics Yearbook (2008 Edition).*

Palgrave Macmillan Ltd., Houndmills, Basingstoke, Hampshire, RG21 6XS, England, (Telephone in U.S. (888) 330-8477), (Fax in U.S. (800) 672-2054), www.palgrave.com; *The Statesman's Yearbook 2008.*

U.S. Department of State (DOS), 2201 C Street NW, Washington, DC 20520, (202) 647-4000, www.state.gov; *World Military Expenditures and Arms Transfers (WMEAT).*

United Nations Statistics Division, New York, NY 10017, (800) 253-9646, Fax: (212) 963-4116, http://unstats.un.org; *Human Development Report 2006.*

CANADA - AUTOMOBILE INDUSTRY AND TRADE

Organisation for Economic Cooperation and Development (OECD), 2 rue Andre Pascal, F-75775 Paris Cedex 16, France, (Telephone in U.S. (202) 785-6323), (Fax in U.S. (202) 785-0350), www.oecd.org; *Indicators of Industrial Activity* and *International Trade by Commodity Statistics (ITCS).*

Taylor and Francis Group, An Informa Business, 2 Park Square, Milton Park, Abingdon, Oxford OX14 4RN, United Kingdom, (Dial from U.S. (212) 216-7800), (Fax from U.S. (212) 564-7854), www.tandf.co.uk; *The Europa World Year Book.*

United Nations Statistics Division, New York, NY 10017, (800) 253-9646, Fax: (212) 963-4116, http://unstats.un.org; *Statistical Yearbook.*

CANADA - BALANCE OF PAYMENTS

International Monetary Fund (IMF), 700 Nineteenth Street, NW, Washington, DC 20431, (202) 623-7000, Fax: (202) 623-4661, www.imf.org; *Balance of Payments Statistics Newsletter; Balance of Payments Statistics Yearbook 2007;* and *International Financial Statistics Yearbook 2007.*

Organisation for Economic Cooperation and Development (OECD), 2 rue Andre Pascal, F-75775 Paris Cedex 16, France, (Telephone in U.S. (202) 785-6323), (Fax in U.S. (202) 785-0350), www.oecd.org; *Geographical Distribution of Financial Flows to Aid Recipients 2002-2006; OECD Economic Outlook 2008; OECD Economic Survey - Canada 2008;* and *OECD Main Economic Indicators (MEI).*

Taylor and Francis Group, An Informa Business, 2 Park Square, Milton Park, Abingdon, Oxford OX14 4RN, United Kingdom, (Dial from U.S. (212) 216-7800), (Fax from U.S. (212) 564-7854), www.tandf.co.uk; *The Europa World Year Book.*

United Nations Conference on Trade and Development (UNCTAD), DC2-1120, United Nations, New York, NY 10017, (212) 963-0027, www.unctad.org; *Handbook of Statistics 2005.*

The World Bank, 1818 H Street, NW, Washington, DC 20433, (202) 473-1000, Fax: (202) 477-6391, www.worldbank.org; *Canada; World Development Indicators (WDI) 2008;* and *World Development Report 2008.*

CANADA - BANKS AND BANKING

Euromonitor International, Inc., 224 S. Michigan Avenue, Suite 1500, Chicago, IL 60604, (312) 922-1115, Fax: (312) 922-1157, www.euromonitor.com; *World Marketing Data and Statistics.*

International Monetary Fund (IMF), 700 Nineteenth Street, NW, Washington, DC 20431, (202) 623-7000, Fax: (202) 623-4661, www.imf.org; *International Financial Statistics Yearbook 2007.*

M.E. Sharpe, 80 Business Park Drive, Armonk, NY 10504, (800) 541-6563, Fax: (914) 273-2106, www.mesharpe.com; *The Illustrated Book of World Rankings.*

Organisation for Economic Cooperation and Development (OECD), 2 rue Andre Pascal, F-75775 Paris Cedex 16, France, (Telephone in U.S. (202) 785-6323), (Fax in U.S. (202) 785-0350), www.oecd.org; *Financial Market Trends: OECD Periodical; OECD Economic Outlook 2008;* and *OECD Economic Survey - Canada 2008.*

Palgrave Macmillan Ltd., Houndmills, Basingstoke, Hampshire, RG21 6XS, England, (Telephone in U.S. (888) 330-8477), (Fax in U.S. (800) 672-2054), www.palgrave.com; *The Statesman's Yearbook 2008.*

Taylor and Francis Group, An Informa Business, 2 Park Square, Milton Park, Abingdon, Oxford OX14 4RN, United Kingdom, (Dial from U.S. (212) 216-7800), (Fax from U.S. (212) 564-7854), www.tandf.co.uk; *The Europa World Year Book.*

United Nations Statistics Division, New York, NY 10017, (800) 253-9646, Fax: (212) 963-4116, http://unstats.un.org; *Statistical Yearbook.*

CANADA - BARLEY PRODUCTION

See CANADA - CROPS

CANADA - BEVERAGE INDUSTRY

M.E. Sharpe, 80 Business Park Drive, Armonk, NY 10504, (800) 541-6563, Fax: (914) 273-2106, www.mesharpe.com; *The Illustrated Book of World Rankings.*

Organisation for Economic Cooperation and Development (OECD), 2 rue Andre Pascal, F-75775 Paris Cedex 16, France, (Telephone in U.S. (202) 785-6323), (Fax in U.S. (202) 785-0350), www.oecd.org; *Indicators of Industrial Activity.*

United Nations Food and Agricultural Organization (FAO), Viale delle Terme di Caracalla, 00100 Rome, Italy, (Dial from U.S. (202) 653-2400), (Fax from U.S. (202) 653 5760), www.fao.org; *The State of Food and Agriculture (SOFA) 2006.*

United Nations Statistics Division, New York, NY 10017, (800) 253-9646, Fax: (212) 963-4116, http://unstats.un.org; *Statistical Yearbook.*

CANADA - BONDS

International Monetary Fund (IMF), 700 Nineteenth Street, NW, Washington, DC 20431, (202) 623-7000, Fax: (202) 623-4661, www.imf.org; *Government Finance Statistics Yearbook (2008 Edition).*

Organisation for Economic Cooperation and Development (OECD), 2 rue Andre Pascal, F-75775 Paris Cedex 16, France, (Telephone in U.S. (202) 785-6323), (Fax in U.S. (202) 785-0350), www.oecd.org; *Financial Market Trends: OECD Periodical.*

United Nations Statistics Division, New York, NY 10017, (800) 253-9646, Fax: (212) 963-4116, http://unstats.un.org; *Statistical Yearbook.*

CANADA - BROADCASTING

Central Intelligence Agency, Office of Public Affairs, Washington, DC 20505, (703) 482-0623, Fax: (703) 482-1739, www.cia.gov; *The World Factbook.*

Euromonitor International, Inc., 224 S. Michigan Avenue, Suite 1500, Chicago, IL 60604, (312) 922-1115, Fax: (312) 922-1157, www.euromonitor.com; *World Marketing Data and Statistics.*

M.E. Sharpe, 80 Business Park Drive, Armonk, NY 10504, (800) 541-6563, Fax: (914) 273-2106, www.mesharpe.com; *The Illustrated Book of World Rankings.*

Palgrave Macmillan Ltd., Houndmills, Basingstoke, Hampshire, RG21 6XS, England, (Telephone in U.S. (888) 330-8477), (Fax in U.S. (800) 672-2054), www.palgrave.com; *The Statesman's Yearbook 2008.*

UNESCO Institute for Statistics, C.P. 6128 Succursale Centre-Ville, Montreal, Quebec, H3C 3J7 Canada, (Dial from U.S. (514) 343-6880), (Fax from U.S. (514) 343 6882), www.uis.unesco.org; *Statistical Tables.*

United Nations Statistics Division, New York, NY 10017, (800) 253-9646, Fax: (212) 963-4116, http://unstats.un.org; *Trends in Europe and North America: The Statistical Yearbook of the ECE 2005.*

WRTH Publications Limited, PO Box 290, Oxford OX2 7FT, UK, www.wrth.com; *World Radio TV Handbook 2007.*

CANADA - BUDGET

Central Intelligence Agency, Office of Public Affairs, Washington, DC 20505, (703) 482-0623, Fax: (703) 482-1739, www.cia.gov; *The World Factbook.*

CANADA - BUSINESS

Economics and Statistics Division, Nova Scotia Department of Finance, 1723 Hollis Street, PO Box 187, Halifax, Nova Scotia B3J 2N3, Canada, (Dial from U.S. (902) 424-2740), (Fax from U.S. (902) 424-0714), www.gov.ns.ca/finance/statistics/agency; *Nova Scotia Business Statistics 2008.*

Organisation for Economic Cooperation and Development (OECD), 2 rue Andre Pascal, F-75775 Paris

Cedex 16, France, (Telephone in U.S. (202) 785-6323), (Fax in U.S. (202) 785-0350), www.oecd.org; *OECD Main Economic Indicators (MEI).*

Standard and Poor's Corporation, 55 Water Street, New York, NY 10041, (212) 438-1000, www.standardandpoors.com; *Compustat Global* and *Compustat North America.*

Statistics Canada, 100 Tunney's Pasture Driveway, Ottawa, Ontario K1A 0T6, (Dial from U.S. (800) 263-1136), (Fax from U.S. (877) 287-4369), www.statcan.ca; *Greenhouse Gas Reduction Technologies: Industry Expenditures and Business Opportunities.*

CANADA - CADMIUM PRODUCTION

See CANADA - MINERAL INDUSTRIES

CANADA - CAPITAL INVESTMENTS

Organisation for Economic Cooperation and Development (OECD), 2 rue Andre Pascal, F-75775 Paris Cedex 16, France, (Telephone in U.S. (202) 785-6323), (Fax in U.S. (202) 785-0350), www.oecd.org; *Financial Market Trends: OECD Periodical* and *OECD Economic Outlook 2008.*

CANADA - CAPITAL LEVY

International Monetary Fund (IMF), 700 Nineteenth Street, NW, Washington, DC 20431, (202) 623-7000, Fax: (202) 623-4661, www.imf.org; *Government Finance Statistics Yearbook (2008 Edition).*

Organisation for Economic Cooperation and Development (OECD), 2 rue Andre Pascal, F-75775 Paris Cedex 16, France, (Telephone in U.S. (202) 785-6323), (Fax in U.S. (202) 785-0350), www.oecd.org; *Financial Market Trends: OECD Periodical* and *OECD Economic Outlook 2008.*

CANADA - CATTLE

See CANADA - LIVESTOCK

CANADA - CHICKENS

See CANADA - LIVESTOCK

CANADA - CHILDBIRTH - STATISTICS

Central Intelligence Agency, Office of Public Affairs, Washington, DC 20505, (703) 482-0623, Fax: (703) 482-1739, www.cia.gov; *The World Factbook.*

Euromonitor International, Inc., 224 S. Michigan Avenue, Suite 1500, Chicago, IL 60604, (312) 922-1115, Fax: (312) 922-1157, www.euromonitor.com; *International Marketing Data and Statistics 2008* and *The World Economic Factbook 2008.*

M.E. Sharpe, 80 Business Park Drive, Armonk, NY 10504, (800) 541-6563, Fax: (914) 273-2106, www.mesharpe.com; *The Illustrated Book of World Rankings.*

Palgrave Macmillan Ltd., Houndmills, Basingstoke, Hampshire, RG21 6XS, England, (Telephone in U.S. (888) 330-8477), (Fax in U.S. (800) 672-2054), www.palgrave.com; *The Statesman's Yearbook 2008.*

Taylor and Francis Group, An Informa Business, 2 Park Square, Milton Park, Abingdon, Oxford OX14 4RN, United Kingdom, (Dial from U.S. (212) 216-7800), (Fax from U.S. (212) 564-7854), www.tandf.co.uk; *The Europa World Year Book.*

United Nations Statistics Division, New York, NY 10017, (800) 253-9646, Fax: (212) 963-4116, http://unstats.un.org; *Demographic Yearbook* and *Statistical Yearbook.*

The World Bank, 1818 H Street, NW, Washington, DC 20433, (202) 473-1000, Fax: (202) 477-6391, www.worldbank.org; *World Development Indicators (WDI) 2008.*

World Health Organization (WHO), Avenue Appia 20, 1211 Geneve 27, Switzerland, (Telephone in U.S. (212) 331-9081), www.who.int; *World Health Report 2006.*

CANADA - CHILDREN

Information and Documentation Centre, Institute de la statistique du Quebec, 200 Chemin Sainte-Foy, 3rd Floor, Quebec City, Quebec G1R 5T4, Canada, (Dial from U.S. (418) 691-2401), (Fax from U.S. (418) 643-4129), www.stat.gouv.qc.ca; *Disciplining Children in Quebec: Parenting Norms and Practices in 2004* and *Longitudinal Study of Child Development in Quebec.*

Royal Canadian Mounted Police (RCMP), 1200 Vanier Parkway, Ottawa, ON K1A 0R2, Canada, (613) 993-7267, www.rcmp-grc.gc.ca; *The Direct and Indirect Impacts of Organized Crime on Youth, as Offenders and Victims.*

CANADA - CLIMATE

M.E. Sharpe, 80 Business Park Drive, Armonk, NY 10504, (800) 541-6563, Fax: (914) 273-2106, www.mesharpe.com; *The Illustrated Book of World Rankings.*

Palgrave Macmillan Ltd., Houndmills, Basingstoke, Hampshire, RG21 6XS, England, (Telephone in U.S. (888) 330-8477), (Fax in U.S. (800) 672-2054), www.palgrave.com; *The Statesman's Yearbook 2008.*

CANADA - CLOTHING EXPORTS AND IMPORTS

See CANADA - TEXTILE INDUSTRY

CANADA - COAL PRODUCTION

See CANADA - MINERAL INDUSTRIES

CANADA - COBALT PRODUCTION

See CANADA - MINERAL INDUSTRIES

CANADA - COFFEE

See CANADA - CROPS

CANADA - COFFEE INDUSTRY

United Nations Statistics Division, New York, NY 10017, (800) 253-9646, Fax: (212) 963-4116, http://unstats.un.org; *Statistical Yearbook.*

CANADA - COMMERCE

Palgrave Macmillan Ltd., Houndmills, Basingstoke, Hampshire, RG21 6XS, England, (Telephone in U.S. (888) 330-8477), (Fax in U.S. (800) 672-2054), www.palgrave.com; *The Statesman's Yearbook 2008.*

CANADA - COMMODITY EXCHANGES

Commodity Research Bureau, 330 South Wells Street, Suite 612, Chicago, IL 60606-7110, (800) 621-5271, Fax: (312) 939-4135, www.crbtrader.com; *2006 CRB Commodity Yearbook and CD.*

International Lead and Zinc Study Group (ILZSG), Rua Almirante Barroso 38, 5th Floor, Lisbon 1000 - 013, Portugal, www.ilzsg.org; Interactive Statistical Database.

International Monetary Fund (IMF), 700 Nineteenth Street, NW, Washington, DC 20431, (202) 623-7000, Fax: (202) 623-4661, www.imf.org; *IMF Primary Commodity Prices.*

United Nations Food and Agricultural Organization (FAO), Viale delle Terme di Caracalla, 00100 Rome, Italy, (Dial from U.S. (202) 653-2400), (Fax from U.S. (202) 653 5760), www.fao.org; *The State of Food and Agriculture (SOFA) 2006.*

United Nations Statistics Division, New York, NY 10017, (800) 253-9646, Fax: (212) 963-4116, http://unstats.un.org; *Statistical Yearbook.*

World Bureau of Metal Statistics (WBMS), 27a High Street, Ware, Hertfordshire, SG12 9BA, United Kingdom, www.world-bureau.com; *Annual Stainless Steel Statistics; World Flow Charts; World Metal Statistics; World Nickel Statistics;* and *World Tin Statistics.*

CANADA - COMMUNICATION AND TRAFFIC

United Nations Statistics Division, New York, NY 10017, (800) 253-9646, Fax: (212) 963-4116, http://unstats.un.org; *Statistical Yearbook.*

CANADA - CONSTRUCTION INDUSTRY

M.E. Sharpe, 80 Business Park Drive, Armonk, NY 10504, (800) 541-6563, Fax: (914) 273-2106, www.mesharpe.com; *The Illustrated Book of World Rankings.*

Organisation for Economic Cooperation and Development (OECD), 2 rue Andre Pascal, F-75775 Paris Cedex 16, France, (Telephone in U.S. (202) 785-6323), (Fax in U.S. (202) 785-0350), www.oecd.org; *Iron and Steel Industry in 2004 (2006 Edition); OECD Economic Survey - Canada 2008; OECD Main Economic Indicators (MEI);* and STructural ANalysis (STAN) database.

Palgrave Macmillan Ltd., Houndmills, Basingstoke, Hampshire, RG21 6XS, England, (Telephone in U.S. (888) 330-8477), (Fax in U.S. (800) 672-2054), www.palgrave.com; *The Statesman's Yearbook 2008.*

United Nations Statistics Division, New York, NY 10017, (800) 253-9646, Fax: (212) 963-4116, http://unstats.un.org; *Statistical Yearbook.*

CANADA - CONSUMER PRICE INDEXES

Organisation for Economic Cooperation and Development (OECD), 2 rue Andre Pascal, F-75775 Paris Cedex 16, France, (Telephone in U.S. (202) 785-6323), (Fax in U.S. (202) 785-0350), www.oecd.org; *OECD Economic Outlook 2008.*

Taylor and Francis Group, An Informa Business, 2 Park Square, Milton Park, Abingdon, Oxford OX14 4RN, United Kingdom, (Dial from U.S. (212) 216-7800), (Fax from U.S. (212) 564-7854), www.tandf.co.uk; *The Europa World Year Book.*

United Nations Statistics Division, New York, NY 10017, (800) 253-9646, Fax: (212) 963-4116, http://unstats.un.org; *Statistical Yearbook* and *Trends in Europe and North America: The Statistical Yearbook of the ECE 2005.*

The World Bank, 1818 H Street, NW, Washington, DC 20433, (202) 473-1000, Fax: (202) 477-6391, www.worldbank.org; *Canada.*

CANADA - CONSUMPTION (ECONOMICS)

International Iron and Steel Institute (IISI), Rue Colonel Bourg 120, B-1140 Brussels, Belgium, www.worldsteel.org; *Steel Statistical Yearbook 2006.*

International Lead and Zinc Study Group (ILZSG), Rua Almirante Barroso 38, 5th Floor, Lisbon 1000 - 013, Portugal, www.ilzsg.org; Interactive Statistical Database.

International Monetary Fund (IMF), 700 Nineteenth Street, NW, Washington, DC 20431, (202) 623-7000, Fax: (202) 623-4661, www.imf.org; *International Financial Statistics Yearbook 2007.*

Organisation for Economic Cooperation and Development (OECD), 2 rue Andre Pascal, F-75775 Paris Cedex 16, France, (Telephone in U.S. (202) 785-6323), (Fax in U.S. (202) 785-0350), www.oecd.org; *Environmental Impacts of Foreign Direct Investment in the Mining Sector in the Newly Independent States (NIS); Iron and Steel Industry in 2004 (2006 Edition); A New World Map in Textiles and Clothing: Adjusting to Change; 2005 OECD Agricultural Outlook Tables, 1970-2014; Revenue Statistics 1965-2006 - 2007 Edition;* and *Towards Sustainable Household Consumption?: Trends and Policies in OECD Countries.*

Technical Association of the Pulp and Paper Industry (TAPPI), 15 Technology Parkway South, Norcross, GA 30092, (770) 446-1400, Fax: (770) 446-6947, www.tappi.org; *TAPPI Annual Report.*

The World Bank, 1818 H Street, NW, Washington, DC 20433, (202) 473-1000, Fax: (202) 477-6391, www.worldbank.org; *World Development Report 2008.*

CANADA - COPPER INDUSTRY AND TRADE

See CANADA - MINERAL INDUSTRIES

CANADA - CORN INDUSTRY

See CANADA - CROPS

CANADA - COST AND STANDARD OF LIVING

International Monetary Fund (IMF), 700 Nineteenth Street, NW, Washington, DC 20431, (202) 623-7000, Fax: (202) 623-4661, www.imf.org; *Government Finance Statistics Yearbook (2008 Edition).*

CANADA - COTTON

See CANADA - CROPS

CANADA - CRIME

International Criminal Police Organization (INTERPOL), General Secretariat, 200 quai Charles de Gaulle, 69006 Lyon, France, www.interpol.int; *International Crime Statistics.*

Royal Canadian Mounted Police (RCMP), 1200 Vanier Parkway, Ottawa, ON K1A 0R2, Canada, (613) 993-7267, www.rcmp-grc.gc.ca; *The Direct and Indirect Impacts of Organized Crime on Youth, as Offenders and Victims* and *Drug Situation in Canada - 2004.*

U.S. Department of Justice (DOJ), Bureau of Justice Statistics, 810 Seventh Street, NW, Washington, DC 20531, (202) 307-0765, www.ojp.usdoj.gov/bjs/; *Cross-National Studies in Crime and Justice* and *The World Factbook of Criminal Justice Systems.*

United Nations Statistics Division, New York, NY 10017, (800) 253-9646, Fax: (212) 963-4116, http://unstats.un.org; *Trends in Europe and North America: The Statistical Yearbook of the ECE 2005.*

Yale University Press, PO Box 209040, New Haven, CT 06520-9040, (203) 432-0960, Fax: (203) 432-0948, http://yalepress.yale.edu/yupbooks; *Violence and Crime in Cross-National Perspective.*

CANADA - CROPS

International Monetary Fund (IMF), 700 Nineteenth Street, NW, Washington, DC 20431, (202) 623-7000, Fax: (202) 623-4661, www.imf.org; *International Financial Statistics Yearbook 2007.*

M.E. Sharpe, 80 Business Park Drive, Armonk, NY 10504, (800) 541-6563, Fax: (914) 273-2106, www.mesharpe.com; *The Illustrated Book of World Rankings.*

Organisation for Economic Cooperation and Development (OECD), 2 rue Andre Pascal, F-75775 Paris Cedex 16, France, (Telephone in U.S. (202) 785-6323), (Fax in U.S. (202) 785-0350), www.oecd.org; *International Trade by Commodity Statistics (ITCS)* and *2005 OECD Agricultural Outlook Tables, 1970-2014.*

Palgrave Macmillan Ltd., Houndmills, Basingstoke, Hampshire, RG21 6XS, England, (Telephone in U.S. (888) 330-8477), (Fax in U.S. (800) 672-2054), www.palgrave.com; *The Statesman's Yearbook 2008.*

Statistics Canada, 100 Tunney's Pasture Driveway, Ottawa, Ontario K1A 0T6, (Dial from U.S. (800) 263-1136), (Fax from U.S. (877) 287-4369), www.statcan.ca; *Net Farm Income - Agriculture Economic Statistics.*

Taylor and Francis Group, An Informa Business, 2 Park Square, Milton Park, Abingdon, Oxford OX14 4RN, United Kingdom, (Dial from U.S. (212) 216-7800), (Fax from U.S. (212) 564-7854), www.tandf.co.uk; *The Europa World Year Book.*

United Nations Conference on Trade and Development (UNCTAD), DC2-1120, United Nations, New York, NY 10017, (212) 963-0027, www.unctad.org; *UNCTAD Commodity Yearbook.*

United Nations Food and Agricultural Organization (FAO), Viale delle Terme di Caracalla, 00100 Rome, Italy, (Dial from U.S. (202) 653-2400), (Fax from U.S. (202) 653 5760), www.fao.org; *FAO Production Yearbook 2002* and *The State of Food and Agriculture (SOFA) 2006.*

United Nations Statistics Division, New York, NY 10017, (800) 253-9646, Fax: (212) 963-4116, http://unstats.un.org; *Statistical Yearbook.*

CANADA - CUSTOMS ADMINISTRATION

International Monetary Fund (IMF), 700 Nineteenth Street, NW, Washington, DC 20431, (202) 623-7000, Fax: (202) 623-4661, www.imf.org; *Government Finance Statistics Yearbook (2008 Edition).*

Organisation for Economic Cooperation and Development (OECD), 2 rue Andre Pascal, F-75775 Paris Cedex 16, France, (Telephone in U.S. (202) 785-6323), (Fax in U.S. (202) 785-0350), www.oecd.org; *Environmental Impacts of Foreign Direct Investment in the Mining Sector in the Newly Independent States (NIS).*

Palgrave Macmillan Ltd., Houndmills, Basingstoke, Hampshire, RG21 6XS, England, (Telephone in U.S. (888) 330-8477), (Fax in U.S. (800) 672-2054), www.palgrave.com; *The Statesman's Yearbook 2008.*

CANADA - DAIRY PROCESSING

M.E. Sharpe, 80 Business Park Drive, Armonk, NY 10504, (800) 541-6563, Fax: (914) 273-2106, www.mesharpe.com; *The Illustrated Book of World Rankings.*

Organisation for Economic Cooperation and Development (OECD), 2 rue Andre Pascal, F-75775 Paris Cedex 16, France, (Telephone in U.S. (202) 785-6323), (Fax in U.S. (202) 785-0350), www.oecd.org; *2005 OECD Agricultural Outlook Tables, 1970-2014.*

Palgrave Macmillan Ltd., Houndmills, Basingstoke, Hampshire, RG21 6XS, England, (Telephone in U.S. (888) 330-8477), (Fax in U.S. (800) 672-2054), www.palgrave.com; *The Statesman's Yearbook 2008.*

Taylor and Francis Group, An Informa Business, 2 Park Square, Milton Park, Abingdon, Oxford OX14 4RN, United Kingdom, (Dial from U.S. (212) 216-7800), (Fax from U.S. (212) 564-7854), www.tandf.co.uk; *The Europa World Year Book.*

United Nations Food and Agricultural Organization (FAO), Viale delle Terme di Caracalla, 00100 Rome, Italy, (Dial from U.S. (202) 653-2400), (Fax from U.S. (202) 653 5760), www.fao.org; *FAO Production Yearbook 2002* and *The State of Food and Agriculture (SOFA) 2006.*

United Nations Statistics Division, New York, NY 10017, (800) 253-9646, Fax: (212) 963-4116, http://unstats.un.org; *Statistical Yearbook.*

CANADA - DEATH RATES

See CANADA - MORTALITY

CANADA - DEBTS, EXTERNAL

International Monetary Fund (IMF), 700 Nineteenth Street, NW, Washington, DC 20431, (202) 623-7000, Fax: (202) 623-4661, www.imf.org; *Government Finance Statistics Yearbook (2008 Edition).*

Organisation for Economic Cooperation and Development (OECD), 2 rue Andre Pascal, F-75775 Paris Cedex 16, France, (Telephone in U.S. (202) 785-6323), (Fax in U.S. (202) 785-0350), www.oecd.org; *Financial Market Trends: OECD Periodical; Geographical Distribution of Financial Flows to Aid Recipients 2002-2006;* and *OECD Economic Outlook 2008.*

Palgrave Macmillan Ltd., Houndmills, Basingstoke, Hampshire, RG21 6XS, England, (Telephone in U.S. (888) 330-8477), (Fax in U.S. (800) 672-2054), www.palgrave.com; *The Statesman's Yearbook 2008.*

The World Bank, 1818 H Street, NW, Washington, DC 20433, (202) 473-1000, Fax: (202) 477-6391, www.worldbank.org; *Global Development Finance 2007; World Development Indicators (WDI) 2008;* and *World Development Report 2008.*

CANADA - DEFENSE EXPENDITURES

See CANADA - ARMED FORCES

CANADA - DEMOGRAPHY

Euromonitor International, Inc., 224 S. Michigan Avenue, Suite 1500, Chicago, IL 60604, (312) 922-1115, Fax: (312) 922-1157, www.euromonitor.com; *International Marketing Data and Statistics 2008; The World Economic Factbook 2008;* and *World Marketing Data and Statistics.*

M.E. Sharpe, 80 Business Park Drive, Armonk, NY 10504, (800) 541-6563, Fax: (914) 273-2106, www.mesharpe.com; *The Illustrated Book of World Rankings.*

United Nations Statistics Division, New York, NY 10017, (800) 253-9646, Fax: (212) 963-4116, http://unstats.un.org; *Human Development Report 2006.*

The World Bank, 1818 H Street, NW, Washington, DC 20433, (202) 473-1000, Fax: (202) 477-6391, www.worldbank.org; *Canada.*

CANADA - DIAMONDS

See CANADA - MINERAL INDUSTRIES

CANADA - DISPOSABLE INCOME

M.E. Sharpe, 80 Business Park Drive, Armonk, NY 10504, (800) 541-6563, Fax: (914) 273-2106, www.mesharpe.com; *The Illustrated Book of World Rankings.*

Organisation for Economic Cooperation and Development (OECD), 2 rue Andre Pascal, F-75775 Paris Cedex 16, France, (Telephone in U.S. (202) 785-6323), (Fax in U.S. (202) 785-0350), www.oecd.org; *OECD Economic Outlook 2008.*

United Nations Statistics Division, New York, NY 10017, (800) 253-9646, Fax: (212) 963-4116, http://unstats.un.org; *National Accounts Statistics: Compendium of Income Distribution Statistics* and *Statistical Yearbook.*

CANADA - DIVORCE

M.E. Sharpe, 80 Business Park Drive, Armonk, NY 10504, (800) 541-6563, Fax: (914) 273-2106, www.mesharpe.com; *The Illustrated Book of World Rankings.*

United Nations Statistics Division, New York, NY 10017, (800) 253-9646, Fax: (212) 963-4116, http://unstats.un.org; *Demographic Yearbook; Statistical Yearbook;* and *Trends in Europe and North America: The Statistical Yearbook of the ECE 2005.*

CANADA - ECONOMIC ASSISTANCE

Organisation for Economic Cooperation and Development (OECD), 2 rue Andre Pascal, F-75775 Paris Cedex 16, France, (Telephone in U.S. (202) 785-6323), (Fax in U.S. (202) 785-0350), www.oecd.org; *Geographical Distribution of Financial Flows to Aid Recipients 2002-2006.*

United Nations Statistics Division, New York, NY 10017, (800) 253-9646, Fax: (212) 963-4116, http://unstats.un.org; *Statistical Yearbook.*

CANADA - ECONOMIC CONDITIONS

Center for International Business Education Research (CIBER), Columbia Business School and School of International and Public Affairs, Uris Hall, Room 212, 3022 Broadway, New York, NY 10027-6902, Mr. Joshua Safier, (212) 854-4750, Fax: (212) 222-9821, www.columbia.edu/cu/ciber/; Datastream International.

Central Intelligence Agency, Office of Public Affairs, Washington, DC 20505, (703) 482-0623, Fax: (703) 482-1739, www.cia.gov; *The World Factbook.*

DSI Data Service Information, Xantener Strasse 51a, D-47495 Rheinberg, Germany, www.dsidata.com; *Campus Solution.*

Dun and Bradstreet (DB) Corporation, 103 JFK Parkway, Short Hills, NJ 07078, (973) 921-5500, www.dnb.com; *Country Report.*

Economics and Statistics Division, Nova Scotia Department of Finance, 1723 Hollis Street, PO Box 187, Halifax, Nova Scotia B3J 2N3, Canada, (Dial from U.S. (902) 424-2740), (Fax from U.S. (902) 424-0714), www.gov.ns.ca/finance/statistics/agency; *Nova Scotia Economic Overview 2007.*

Economics, Statistics Fiscal Analysis Division, Department of Provincial Treasury, PO Box 2000, Charlottetown, Prince Edward Island C1A 7N8, Canada, (Dial from U.S. (902) 368-4050), (Fax from U.S. (902) 368-6575), www.gov.pe.ca/pt/index.php3; *A First Look at the 2001 Census of Population; 2006 Progress Report on the PEI Economy;* and *Tourism Indicators: 2007 Annual Review.*

Economist Intelligence Unit, 111 West 57th Street, New York, NY 10019, (212) 554-0600, Fax: (212) 586-1181, www.eiu.com; *Canada Country Report.*

Euromonitor International, Inc., 224 S. Michigan Avenue, Suite 1500, Chicago, IL 60604, (312) 922-1115, Fax: (312) 922-1157, www.euromonitor.com; *International Marketing Data and Statistics 2008; The World Economic Factbook 2008;* and *World Marketing Data and Statistics.*

International Monetary Fund (IMF), 700 Nineteenth Street, NW, Washington, DC 20431, (202) 623-7000, Fax: (202) 623-4661, www.imf.org; *World Economic Outlook Reports.*

M.E. Sharpe, 80 Business Park Drive, Armonk, NY 10504, (800) 541-6563, Fax: (914) 273-2106, www.mesharpe.com; *The Illustrated Book of World Rankings.*

Newfoundland Labrador Statistics Agency, Economics and Statistics Branch, Government of Newfoundland and Labrador, Department of Finance, PO Box 8700, St. John's, NL A1B 4J6, Canada, (Dial from U.S. (709) 729-2913), (Fax from U.S. (709) 729-5149), www.stats.gov.nl.ca/Statistics; *The Economy 2006.*

Northwest Territories Bureau of Statistics, Government of the Northwest Territories, PO Box 1320, Yellowknife, NWT, Canada X1A 2L9, (867) 873-7147, www.stats.gov.nt.ca; *2006 NWT Socio-Economic Scan.*

Organisation for Economic Cooperation and Development (OECD), 2 rue Andre Pascal, F-75775 Paris Cedex 16, France, (Telephone in U.S. (202) 785-6323), (Fax in U.S. (202) 785-0350), www.oecd.org; *Geographical Distribution of Financial Flows to Aid Recipients 2002-2006; ICT Sector Data and Metadata by Country; Labour Force Statistics: 1986-2005, 2007 Edition; OECD Composite Leading Indicators (CLIs), Updated September 2007; OECD Economic Outlook 2008; OECD Economic Survey - Canada 2008; OECD Employment Outlook 2007; OECD in Figures 2007;* and *OECD Main Economic Indicators (MEI).*

Palgrave Macmillan Ltd., Houndmills, Basingstoke, Hampshire, RG21 6XS, England, (Telephone in U.S. (888) 330-8477), (Fax in U.S. (800) 672-2054), www.palgrave.com; *The Statesman's Yearbook 2008.*

Saskatchewan Bureau of Statistics (SBS), 9th Floor, 2350 Albert Street, Regina, Saskatchewan S4P 4A6, Canada, (Dial from U.S. (306) 787-6327), (Fax from U.S. (306) 787-6311), www.stats.gov.sk.ca; *2006 Economic Review.*

Standard and Poor's Corporation, 55 Water Street, New York, NY 10041, (212) 438-1000, www.standardandpoors.com; *Compustat Global* and *Compustat North America.*

Taylor and Francis Group, An Informa Business, 2 Park Square, Milton Park, Abingdon, Oxford OX14 4RN, United Kingdom, (Dial from U.S. (212) 216-7800), (Fax from U.S. (212) 564-7854), www.tandf.co.uk; *The Europa World Year Book.*

United Nations Statistics Division, New York, NY 10017, (800) 253-9646, Fax: (212) 963-4116, http://unstats.un.org; *World Statistics Pocketbook.*

The World Bank, 1818 H Street, NW, Washington, DC 20433, (202) 473-1000, Fax: (202) 477-6391, www.worldbank.org; *Canada; Global Economic Monitor (GEM); Global Economic Prospects 2008; The World Bank Atlas 2003-2004;* and *World Development Report 2008.*

CANADA - ECONOMICS - SOCIOLOGICAL ASPECTS

Organisation for Economic Cooperation and Development (OECD), 2 rue Andre Pascal, F-75775 Paris Cedex 16, France, (Telephone in U.S. (202) 785-6323), (Fax in U.S. (202) 785-0350), www.oecd.org; *OECD Economic Outlook 2008.*

CANADA - EDUCATION

Euromonitor International, Inc., 224 S. Michigan Avenue, Suite 1500, Chicago, IL 60604, (312) 922-1115, Fax: (312) 922-1157, www.euromonitor.com; *International Marketing Data and Statistics 2008* and *World Marketing Data and Statistics.*

International Monetary Fund (IMF), 700 Nineteenth Street, NW, Washington, DC 20431, (202) 623-7000, Fax: (202) 623-4661, www.imf.org; *Government Finance Statistics Yearbook (2008 Edition).*

M.E. Sharpe, 80 Business Park Drive, Armonk, NY 10504, (800) 541-6563, Fax: (914) 273-2106, www.mesharpe.com; *The Illustrated Book of World Rankings.*

Organisation for Economic Cooperation and Development (OECD), 2 rue Andre Pascal, F-75775 Paris Cedex 16, France, (Telephone in U.S. (202) 785-6323), (Fax in U.S. (202) 785-0350), www.oecd.org; *Education at a Glance* (2007 Edition).

Palgrave Macmillan Ltd., Houndmills, Basingstoke, Hampshire, RG21 6XS, England, (Telephone in U.S. (888) 330-8477), (Fax in U.S. (800) 672-2054), www.palgrave.com; *The Statesman's Yearbook 2008.*

Taylor and Francis Group, An Informa Business, 2 Park Square, Milton Park, Abingdon, Oxford OX14 4RN, United Kingdom, (Dial from U.S. (212) 216-7800), (Fax from U.S. (212) 564-7854), www.tandf.co.uk; *The Europa World Year Book.*

UNESCO Institute for Statistics, C.P. 6128 Succursale Centre-Ville, Montreal, Quebec, H3C 3J7 Canada, (Dial from U.S. (514) 343-6880), (Fax from U.S. (514) 343 6882), www.uis.unesco.org; *Statistical Tables.*

United Nations Statistics Division, New York, NY 10017, (800) 253-9646, Fax: (212) 963-4116, http://unstats.un.org; *Human Development Report 2006* and *Trends in Europe and North America: The Statistical Yearbook of the ECE 2005.*

The World Bank, 1818 H Street, NW, Washington, DC 20433, (202) 473-1000, Fax: (202) 477-6391, www.worldbank.org; *Canada; World Development Indicators (WDI) 2008;* and *World Development Report 2008.*

CANADA - ELECTRICITY

M.E. Sharpe, 80 Business Park Drive, Armonk, NY 10504, (800) 541-6563, Fax: (914) 273-2106, www.mesharpe.com; *The Illustrated Book of World Rankings.*

Organisation for Economic Cooperation and Development (OECD), 2 rue Andre Pascal, F-75775 Paris Cedex 16, France, (Telephone in U.S. (202) 785-6323), (Fax in U.S. (202) 785-0350), www.oecd.org; *Coal Information: 2007 Edition; Energy Statistics of OECD Countries* (2007 Edition); *Indicators of Industrial Activity;* STructural ANalysis (STAN) database; and *World Energy Outlook 2007.*

Palgrave Macmillan Ltd., Houndmills, Basingstoke, Hampshire, RG21 6XS, England, (Telephone in U.S. (888) 330-8477), (Fax in U.S. (800) 672-2054), www.palgrave.com; *The Statesman's Yearbook 2008.*

Platts, 2 Penn Plaza, 25th Floor, New York, NY 10121-2298, (212) 904-3070, www.platts.com; *Emissions Daily.*

U.S. Department of Energy (DOE), Energy Information Administration (EIA), 1000 Independence Avenue, SW, Washington, DC 20585, (202) 586-8800, www.eia.doe.gov; *International Energy Annual 2004* and *International Energy Outlook 2006.*

United Nations Statistics Division, New York, NY 10017, (800) 253-9646, Fax: (212) 963-4116, http://unstats.un.org; *Human Development Report 2006; Statistical Yearbook;* and *Trends in Europe and North America: The Statistical Yearbook of the ECE 2005.*

CANADA - EMPLOYMENT

Bernan Essential Government Publications, 4611-F Assembly Drive, Lanham MD, 20706-4391, (301) 459-2255, Fax: (800) 865-3450, www.bernan.com; *OECD Factbook 2006.*

Economics and Statistics Division, Nova Scotia Department of Finance, 1723 Hollis Street, PO Box 187, Halifax, Nova Scotia B3J 2N3, Canada, (Dial from U.S. (902) 424-2740), (Fax from U.S. (902) 424-0714), www.gov.ns.ca/finance/statistics/agency; *Nova Scotia Economic Overview 2007.*

Euromonitor International, Inc., 224 S. Michigan Avenue, Suite 1500, Chicago, IL 60604, (312) 922-1115, Fax: (312) 922-1157, www.euromonitor.com; *International Marketing Data and Statistics 2008.*

International Labour Office, I.L.O. Publications, 4 route des Morillons, CH-1211 Geneva 22, Switzerland, (Telephone in U.S. (202) 653-7652), (Fax in U.S. (202) 653-7687), www.ilo.org; *Yearbook of Labour Statistics 2006.*

M.E. Sharpe, 80 Business Park Drive, Armonk, NY 10504, (800) 541-6563, Fax: (914) 273-2106, www.mesharpe.com; *The Illustrated Book of World Rankings.*

Organisation for Economic Cooperation and Development (OECD), 2 rue Andre Pascal, F-75775 Paris Cedex 16, France, (Telephone in U.S. (202) 785-6323), (Fax in U.S. (202) 785-0350), www.oecd.org; *ICT Sector Data and Metadata by Country; Iron and Steel Industry in 2004 (2006 Edition); Labour Force Statistics: 1986-2005, 2007 Edition; A New World Map in Textiles and Clothing: Adjusting to Change; OECD Composite Leading Indicators (CLIs), Updated September 2007; OECD Economic Outlook 2008; OECD Economic Survey - Canada 2008; OECD Employment Outlook 2007;* and *OECD in Figures 2007.*

Statistics Canada, 100 Tunney's Pasture Driveway, Ottawa, Ontario K1A 0T6, (Dial from U.S. (800) 263-1136), (Fax from U.S. (877) 287-4369), www.statcan.ca; *Measuring Employment in the Environment Industry.*

United Nations Statistics Division, New York, NY 10017, (800) 253-9646, Fax: (212) 963-4116, http://unstats.un.org; *Statistical Yearbook* and *Trends in Europe and North America: The Statistical Yearbook of the ECE 2005.*

The World Bank, 1818 H Street, NW, Washington, DC 20433, (202) 473-1000, Fax: (202) 477-6391, www.worldbank.org; *Canada.*

CANADA - ENERGY INDUSTRIES

Enerdata, 10 Rue Royale, 75008 Paris, France, www.enerdata.fr; *Global Energy Market Data.*

International Energy Agency (IEA), 9, rue de la Federation, 75739 Paris Cedex 15, France, www.iea.org; *Key World Energy Statistics 2007.*

Organisation for Economic Cooperation and Development (OECD), 2 rue Andre Pascal, F-75775 Paris Cedex 16, France, (Telephone in U.S. (202) 785-6323), (Fax in U.S. (202) 785-0350), www.oecd.org; *Towards Sustainable Household Consumption?: Trends and Policies in OECD Countries.*

Platts, 2 Penn Plaza, 25th Floor, New York, NY 10121-2298, (212) 904-3070, www.platts.com; *Emissions Daily.*

United Nations Statistics Division, New York, NY 10017, (800) 253-9646, Fax: (212) 963-4116, http://unstats.un.org; *Statistical Yearbook.*

CANADA - ENVIRONMENTAL CONDITIONS

DSI Data Service Information, Xantener Strasse 51a, D-47495 Rheinberg, Germany, www.dsidata.com; *Campus Solution* and *DSI's Global Environmental Database.*

Economist Intelligence Unit, 111 West 57th Street, New York, NY 10019, (212) 554-0600, Fax: (212) 586-1181, www.eiu.com; *Canada Country Report.*

Organisation for Economic Cooperation and Development (OECD), 2 rue Andre Pascal, F-75775 Paris Cedex 16, France, (Telephone in U.S. (202) 785-6323), (Fax in U.S. (202) 785-0350), www.oecd.org; *Key Environmental Indicators 2004.*

Platts, 2 Penn Plaza, 25th Floor, New York, NY 10121-2298, (212) 904-3070, www.platts.com; *Emissions Daily.*

United Nations Statistics Division, New York, NY 10017, (800) 253-9646, Fax: (212) 963-4116, http://unstats.un.org; *Trends in Europe and North America: The Statistical Yearbook of the ECE 2005* and *World Statistics Pocketbook.*

CANADA - ENVIRONMENTAL INDUSTRY

Statistics Canada, 100 Tunney's Pasture Driveway, Ottawa, Ontario K1A 0T6, (Dial from U.S. (800) 263-1136), (Fax from U.S. (877) 287-4369), www.statcan.ca; *Greenhouse Gas Reduction Technologies: Industry Expenditures and Business Opportunities* and *Measuring Employment in the Environment Industry.*

CANADA - EXPENDITURES, PUBLIC

Organisation for Economic Cooperation and Development (OECD), 2 rue Andre Pascal, F-75775 Paris Cedex 16, France, (Telephone in U.S. (202) 785-6323), (Fax in U.S. (202) 785-0350), www.oecd.org; *Revenue Statistics 1965-2006 - 2007 Edition.*

CANADA - EXPORTS

Central Intelligence Agency, Office of Public Affairs, Washington, DC 20505, (703) 482-0623, Fax: (703) 482-1739, www.cia.gov; *The World Factbook.*

Economist Intelligence Unit, 111 West 57th Street, New York, NY 10019, (212) 554-0600, Fax: (212) 586-1181, www.eiu.com; *Canada Country Report.*

Euromonitor International, Inc., 224 S. Michigan Avenue, Suite 1500, Chicago, IL 60604, (312) 922-1115, Fax: (312) 922-1157, www.euromonitor.com; *International Marketing Data and Statistics 2008* and *The World Economic Factbook 2008.*

International Iron and Steel Institute (IISI), Rue Colonel Bourg 120, B-1140 Brussels, Belgium, www.worldsteel.org; *Steel Statistical Yearbook 2006.*

International Lead and Zinc Study Group (ILZSG), Rua Almirante Barroso 38, 5th Floor, Lisbon 1000 - 013, Portugal, www.ilzsg.org; Interactive Statistical Database.

International Monetary Fund (IMF), 700 Nineteenth Street, NW, Washington, DC 20431, (202) 623-7000, Fax: (202) 623-4661, www.imf.org; *Direction of Trade Statistics Yearbook 2007; Government Finance Statistics Yearbook (2008 Edition);* and *International Financial Statistics Yearbook 2007.*

Organisation for Economic Cooperation and Development (OECD), 2 rue Andre Pascal, F-75775 Paris Cedex 16, France, (Telephone in U.S. (202) 785-6323), (Fax in U.S. (202) 785-0350), www.oecd.org; *Geographical Distribution of Financial Flows to Aid Recipients 2002-2006; International Trade by Commodity Statistics (ITCS); Iron and Steel Industry in 2004 (2006 Edition); 2005 OECD Agricultural Outlook Tables, 1970-2014; OECD Economic Outlook 2008; OECD Economic Survey - Canada 2008; Review of Fisheries in OECD Countries: Country Statistics 2001 to 2003 - 2005 Edition;* and STRuctural ANalysis (STAN) database.

Palgrave Macmillan Ltd., Houndmills, Basingstoke, Hampshire, RG21 6XS, England, (Telephone in U.S. (888) 330-8477), (Fax in U.S. (800) 672-2054), www.palgrave.com; *The Statesman's Yearbook 2008.*

Taylor and Francis Group, An Informa Business, 2 Park Square, Milton Park, Abingdon, Oxford OX14 4RN, United Kingdom, (Dial from U.S. (212) 216-7800), (Fax from U.S. (212) 564-7854), www.tandf.co.uk; *The Europa World Year Book.*

Technical Association of the Pulp and Paper Industry (TAPPI), 15 Technology Parkway South, Norcross, GA 30092, (770) 446-1400, Fax: (770) 446-6947, www.tappi.org; *TAPPI Annual Report.*

United Nations Conference on Trade and Development (UNCTAD), DC2-1120, United Nations, New York, NY 10017, (212) 963-0027, www.unctad.org; *Handbook of Statistics 2005.*

United Nations Food and Agricultural Organization (FAO), Viale delle Terme di Caracalla, 00100 Rome, Italy, (Dial from U.S. (202) 653-2400), (Fax from U.S. (202) 653 5760), www.fao.org; *The State of Food and Agriculture (SOFA) 2006.*

United Nations Statistics Division, New York, NY 10017, (800) 253-9646, Fax: (212) 963-4116, http://unstats.un.org; *Trends in Europe and North America: The Statistical Yearbook of the ECE 2005.*

The World Bank, 1818 H Street, NW, Washington, DC 20433, (202) 473-1000, Fax: (202) 477-6391, www.worldbank.org; *World Development Indicators (WDI) 2008* and *World Development Report 2008.*

CANADA - FEMALE WORKING POPULATION

See CANADA - EMPLOYMENT

CANADA - FERTILITY, HUMAN

Central Intelligence Agency, Office of Public Affairs, Washington, DC 20505, (703) 482-0623, Fax: (703) 482-1739, www.cia.gov; *The World Factbook.*

M.E. Sharpe, 80 Business Park Drive, Armonk, NY 10504, (800) 541-6563, Fax: (914) 273-2106, www.mesharpe.com; *The Illustrated Book of World Rankings.*

United Nations Statistics Division, New York, NY 10017, (800) 253-9646, Fax: (212) 963-4116, http://unstats.un.org; *Human Development Report 2006* and *Trends in Europe and North America: The Statistical Yearbook of the ECE 2005.*

The World Bank, 1818 H Street, NW, Washington, DC 20433, (202) 473-1000, Fax: (202) 477-6391, www.worldbank.org; *The World Bank Atlas 2003-2004; World Development Indicators (WDI) 2008;* and *World Development Report 2008.*

CANADA - FERTILIZER INDUSTRY

Organisation for Economic Cooperation and Development (OECD), 2 rue Andre Pascal, F-75775 Paris Cedex 16, France, (Telephone in U.S. (202) 785-6323), (Fax in U.S. (202) 785-0350), www.oecd.org; *International Trade by Commodity Statistics (ITCS)* and *2005 OECD Agricultural Outlook Tables, 1970-2014.*

United Nations Food and Agricultural Organization (FAO), Viale delle Terme di Caracalla, 00100 Rome, Italy, (Dial from U.S. (202) 653-2400), (Fax from U.S. (202) 653 5760), www.fao.org; *FAO Fertilizer Yearbook* and *The State of Food and Agriculture (SOFA) 2006.*

United Nations Statistics Division, New York, NY 10017, (800) 253-9646, Fax: (212) 963-4116, http://unstats.un.org; *Statistical Yearbook.*

CANADA - FETAL MORTALITY

See CANADA - MORTALITY

CANADA - FILM

See CANADA - MOTION PICTURES

CANADA - FINANCE

International Monetary Fund (IMF), 700 Nineteenth Street, NW, Washington, DC 20431, (202) 623-7000, Fax: (202) 623-4661, www.imf.org; *International Financial Statistics Yearbook 2007.*

Organisation for Economic Cooperation and Development (OECD), 2 rue Andre Pascal, F-75775 Paris Cedex 16, France, (Telephone in U.S. (202) 785-6323), (Fax in U.S. (202) 785-0350), www.oecd.org; *OECD Economic Outlook 2008.*

Taylor and Francis Group, An Informa Business, 2 Park Square, Milton Park, Abingdon, Oxford OX14 4RN, United Kingdom, (Dial from U.S. (212) 216-7800), (Fax from U.S. (212) 564-7854), www.tandf.co.uk; *The Europa World Year Book.*

United Nations Statistics Division, New York, NY 10017, (800) 253-9646, Fax: (212) 963-4116, http://unstats.un.org; *National Accounts Statistics: Compendium of Income Distribution Statistics* and *Statistical Yearbook.*

The World Bank, 1818 H Street, NW, Washington, DC 20433, (202) 473-1000, Fax: (202) 477-6391, www.worldbank.org; *Canada.*

CANADA - FINANCE, PUBLIC

Bernan Essential Government Publications, 4611-F Assembly Drive, Lanham MD, 20706-4391, (301) 459-2255, Fax: (800) 865-3450, www.bernan.com; *National Accounts Statistics.*

Economist Intelligence Unit, 111 West 57th Street, New York, NY 10019, (212) 554-0600, Fax: (212) 586-1181, www.eiu.com; *Canada Country Report.*

International Monetary Fund (IMF), 700 Nineteenth Street, NW, Washington, DC 20431, (202) 623-7000, Fax: (202) 623-4661, www.imf.org; *Government Finance Statistics Yearbook (2008 Edition); International Financial Statistics; International Financial Statistics Online Service;* and *International Financial Statistics Yearbook 2007.*

M.E. Sharpe, 80 Business Park Drive, Armonk, NY 10504, (800) 541-6563, Fax: (914) 273-2106, www.mesharpe.com; *The Illustrated Book of World Rankings.*

Organisation for Economic Cooperation and Development (OECD), 2 rue Andre Pascal, F-75775 Paris Cedex 16, France, (Telephone in U.S. (202) 785-6323), (Fax in U.S. (202) 785-0350), www.oecd.org; *Financial Market Trends: OECD Periodical; Geographical Distribution of Financial Flows to Aid Recipients 2002-2006; OECD Economic Outlook 2008;* and *Revenue Statistics 1965-2006 - 2007 Edition.*

Palgrave Macmillan Ltd., Houndmills, Basingstoke, Hampshire, RG21 6XS, England, (Telephone in U.S. (888) 330-8477), (Fax in U.S. (800) 672-2054), www.palgrave.com; *The Statesman's Yearbook 2008.*

Taylor and Francis Group, An Informa Business, 2 Park Square, Milton Park, Abingdon, Oxford OX14 4RN, United Kingdom, (Dial from U.S. (212) 216-7800), (Fax from U.S. (212) 564-7854), www.tandf.co.uk; *The Europa World Year Book.*

The World Bank, 1818 H Street, NW, Washington, DC 20433, (202) 473-1000, Fax: (202) 477-6391, www.worldbank.org; *Canada.*

CANADA - FISHERIES

M.E. Sharpe, 80 Business Park Drive, Armonk, NY 10504, (800) 541-6563, Fax: (914) 273-2106, www.mesharpe.com; *The Illustrated Book of World Rankings.*

Organisation for Economic Cooperation and Development (OECD), 2 rue Andre Pascal, F-75775 Paris Cedex 16, France, (Telephone in U.S. (202) 785-6323), (Fax in U.S. (202) 785-0350), www.oecd.org; *International Trade by Commodity Statistics (ITCS); Review of Fisheries in OECD Countries: Country Statistics 2001 to 2003 - 2005 Edition;* and STRuctural ANalysis (STAN) database.

Palgrave Macmillan Ltd., Houndmills, Basingstoke, Hampshire, RG21 6XS, England, (Telephone in U.S. (888) 330-8477), (Fax in U.S. (800) 672-2054), www.palgrave.com; *The Statesman's Yearbook 2008.*

Taylor and Francis Group, An Informa Business, 2 Park Square, Milton Park, Abingdon, Oxford OX14 4RN, United Kingdom, (Dial from U.S. (212) 216-7800), (Fax from U.S. (212) 564-7854), www.tandf.co.uk; *The Europa World Year Book.*

United Nations Conference on Trade and Development (UNCTAD), DC2-1120, United Nations, New York, NY 10017, (212) 963-0027, www.unctad.org; *UNCTAD Commodity Yearbook.*

United Nations Food and Agricultural Organization (FAO), Viale delle Terme di Caracalla, 00100 Rome, Italy, (Dial from U.S. (202) 653-2400), (Fax from U.S. (202) 653 5760), www.fao.org; *FAO Yearbook of Fishery Statistics;* Fishery Databases; FISHSTAT Database. Subjects covered include: Aquaculture production, capture production, fishery commodities; and *The State of Food and Agriculture (SOFA) 2006.*

United Nations Statistics Division, New York, NY 10017, (800) 253-9646, Fax: (212) 963-4116, http://unstats.un.org; *Statistical Yearbook.*

The World Bank, 1818 H Street, NW, Washington, DC 20433, (202) 473-1000, Fax: (202) 477-6391, www.worldbank.org; *Canada.*

CANADA - FLOUR INDUSTRY

United Nations Statistics Division, New York, NY 10017, (800) 253-9646, Fax: (212) 963-4116, http://unstats.un.org; *Statistical Yearbook.*

CANADA - FOOD

Euromonitor International, Inc., 224 S. Michigan Avenue, Suite 1500, Chicago, IL 60604, (312) 922-1115, Fax: (312) 922-1157, www.euromonitor.com; *Retail Trade International 2007.*

Organisation for Economic Cooperation and Development (OECD), 2 rue Andre Pascal, F-75775 Paris Cedex 16, France, (Telephone in U.S. (202) 785-6323), (Fax in U.S. (202) 785-0350), www.oecd.org; *International Trade by Commodity Statistics (ITCS)* and *Towards Sustainable Household Consumption?: Trends and Policies in OECD Countries.*

United Nations Conference on Trade and Development (UNCTAD), DC2-1120, United Nations, New York, NY 10017, (212) 963-0027, www.unctad.org; *UNCTAD Commodity Yearbook.*

United Nations Food and Agricultural Organization (FAO), Viale delle Terme di Caracalla, 00100 Rome, Italy, (Dial from U.S. (202) 653-2400), (Fax from U.S. (202) 653 5760), www.fao.org; *The State of Food and Agriculture (SOFA) 2006.*

United Nations Statistics Division, New York, NY 10017, (800) 253-9646, Fax: (212) 963-4116, http://unstats.un.org; *Human Development Report 2006.*

CANADA - FOOTWEAR

Organisation for Economic Cooperation and Development (OECD), 2 rue Andre Pascal, F-75775 Paris Cedex 16, France, (Telephone in U.S. (202) 785-6323), (Fax in U.S. (202) 785-0350), www.oecd.org; *Indicators of Industrial Activity.*

CANADA - FOREIGN EXCHANGE RATES

Central Intelligence Agency, Office of Public Affairs, Washington, DC 20505, (703) 482-0623, Fax: (703) 482-1739, www.cia.gov; *The World Factbook.*

Euromonitor International, Inc., 224 S. Michigan Avenue, Suite 1500, Chicago, IL 60604, (312) 922-1115, Fax: (312) 922-1157, www.euromonitor.com; *International Marketing Data and Statistics 2008* and *The World Economic Factbook 2008.*

International Civil Aviation Organization (ICAO), External Relations and Public Information Office (EPO), 999 University Street, Montreal, Quebec H3C 5H7, Canada, (Dial from U.S. (514) 954-8219), (Fax from U.S. (514) 954-6077), www.icao.int; *Civil Aviation Statistics of the World.*

International Monetary Fund (IMF), 700 Nineteenth Street, NW, Washington, DC 20431, (202) 623-7000, Fax: (202) 623-4661, www.imf.org; *International Financial Statistics Yearbook 2007.*

Organisation for Economic Cooperation and Development (OECD), 2 rue Andre Pascal, F-75775 Paris Cedex 16, France, (Telephone in U.S. (202) 785-6323), (Fax in U.S. (202) 785-0350), www.oecd.org; *Financial Market Trends: OECD Periodical; Household, Tourism, Travel: Trends, Environmental Impacts and Policy Responses; OECD Economic Outlook 2008;* and *Revenue Statistics 1965-2006 - 2007 Edition.*

Taylor and Francis Group, An Informa Business, 2 Park Square, Milton Park, Abingdon, Oxford OX14 4RN, United Kingdom, (Dial from U.S. (212) 216-7800), (Fax from U.S. (212) 564-7854), www.tandf.co.uk; *The Europa World Year Book.*

United Nations Statistics Division, New York, NY 10017, (800) 253-9646, Fax: (212) 963-4116, http://unstats.un.org; *Statistical Yearbook; Trends in Europe and North America: The Statistical Yearbook of the ECE 2005;* and *World Statistics Pocketbook.*

CANADA - FORESTS AND FORESTRY

American Forest Paper Association (AFPA), 1111 Nineteenth Street, NW, Suite 800, Washington, DC 20036, (800) 878-8878, www.afandpa.org; *2007 Annual Statistics of Paper, Paperboard, and Wood Pulp.*

International Monetary Fund (IMF), 700 Nineteenth Street, NW, Washington, DC 20431, (202) 623-7000, Fax: (202) 623-4661, www.imf.org; *International Financial Statistics Yearbook 2007.*

M.E. Sharpe, 80 Business Park Drive, Armonk, NY 10504, (800) 541-6563, Fax: (914) 273-2106, www.mesharpe.com; *The Illustrated Book of World Rankings.*

Organisation for Economic Cooperation and Development (OECD), 2 rue Andre Pascal, F-75775 Paris Cedex 16, France, (Telephone in U.S. (202) 785-6323), (Fax in U.S. (202) 785-0350), www.oecd.org; *Indicators of Industrial Activity; International Trade by Commodity Statistics (ITCS);* and STructural ANalysis (STAN) database.

Palgrave Macmillan Ltd., Houndmills, Basingstoke, Hampshire, RG21 6XS, England, (Telephone in U.S. (888) 330-8477), (Fax in U.S. (800) 672-2054), www.palgrave.com; *The Statesman's Yearbook 2008.*

Taylor and Francis Group, An Informa Business, 2 Park Square, Milton Park, Abingdon, Oxford OX14 4RN, United Kingdom, (Dial from U.S. (212) 216-7800), (Fax from U.S. (212) 564-7854), www.tandf.co.uk; *The Europa World Year Book.*

Technical Association of the Pulp and Paper Industry (TAPPI), 15 Technology Parkway South, Norcross, GA 30092, (770) 446-1400, Fax: (770) 446-6947, www.tappi.org; *TAPPI Annual Report.*

United Nations Conference on Trade and Development (UNCTAD), DC2-1120, United Nations, New York, NY 10017, (212) 963-0027, www.unctad.org; *UNCTAD Commodity Yearbook.*

United Nations Food and Agricultural Organization (FAO), Viale delle Terme di Caracalla, 00100 Rome, Italy, (Dial from U.S. (202) 653-2400), (Fax from U.S. (202) 653 5760), www.fao.org; *FAO Yearbook of Forest Products* and *The State of Food and Agriculture (SOFA) 2006.*

United Nations Statistics Division, New York, NY 10017, (800) 253-9646, Fax: (212) 963-4116, http://unstats.un.org; *Statistical Yearbook* and *Trends in Europe and North America: The Statistical Yearbook of the ECE 2005.*

The World Bank, 1818 H Street, NW, Washington, DC 20433, (202) 473-1000, Fax: (202) 477-6391, www.worldbank.org; *Canada* and *World Development Report 2008.*

CANADA - FRUIT PRODUCTION

See CANADA - CROPS

CANADA - GAS PRODUCTION

See CANADA - MINERAL INDUSTRIES

CANADA - GEOGRAPHIC INFORMATION SYSTEMS

M.E. Sharpe, 80 Business Park Drive, Armonk, NY 10504, (800) 541-6563, Fax: (914) 273-2106, www.mesharpe.com; *The Illustrated Book of World Rankings.*

The World Bank, 1818 H Street, NW, Washington, DC 20433, (202) 473-1000, Fax: (202) 477-6391, www.worldbank.org; *Canada.*

CANADA - GLASS AND GLASS PRODUCTS

See CANADA - MINERAL INDUSTRIES

CANADA - GOLD INDUSTRY

International Monetary Fund (IMF), 700 Nineteenth Street, NW, Washington, DC 20431, (202) 623-7000, Fax: (202) 623-4661, www.imf.org; *International Financial Statistics Yearbook 2007.*

United Nations Statistics Division, New York, NY 10017, (800) 253-9646, Fax: (212) 963-4116, http://unstats.un.org; *Statistical Yearbook.*

The World Bank, 1818 H Street, NW, Washington, DC 20433, (202) 473-1000, Fax: (202) 477-6391, www.worldbank.org; *World Development Indicators (WDI) 2008.*

CANADA - GOLD PRODUCTION

See CANADA - MINERAL INDUSTRIES

CANADA - GRANTS-IN-AID

Canadian International Development Agency (CIDA), 200 Promenade du Portage, Gatineau, Quebec K1A 0G4, Canada, (Dial from U.S. (819) 997-5006), (Fax from U.S. (819) 953-6088), www.acdi-cida.gc.ca/index-e.htm; *Statistical Report on Official Development Assistance - Fiscal Year 2003-2004.*

International Monetary Fund (IMF), 700 Nineteenth Street, NW, Washington, DC 20431, (202) 623-7000, Fax: (202) 623-4661, www.imf.org; *Government Finance Statistics Yearbook (2008 Edition).*

Organisation for Economic Cooperation and Development (OECD), 2 rue Andre Pascal, F-75775 Paris Cedex 16, France, (Telephone in U.S. (202) 785-6323), (Fax in U.S. (202) 785-0350), www.oecd.org; *Geographical Distribution of Financial Flows to Aid Recipients 2002-2006.*

CANADA - GREEN PEPPER AND CHILIE PRODUCTION

See CANADA - CROPS

CANADA - GROSS DOMESTIC PRODUCT

Economics and Statistics Division, Nova Scotia Department of Finance, 1723 Hollis Street, PO Box 187, Halifax, Nova Scotia B3J 2N3, Canada, (Dial from U.S. (902) 424-2740), (Fax from U.S. (902) 424-0714), www.gov.ns.ca/finance/statistics/agency; *Nova Scotia Economic Overview 2007.*

Economist Intelligence Unit, 111 West 57th Street, New York, NY 10019, (212) 554-0600, Fax: (212) 586-1181, www.eiu.com; *Canada Country Report.*

Euromonitor International, Inc., 224 S. Michigan Avenue, Suite 1500, Chicago, IL 60604, (312) 922-1115, Fax: (312) 922-1157, www.euromonitor.com; *International Marketing Data and Statistics 2008* and *The World Economic Factbook 2008.*

International Monetary Fund (IMF), 700 Nineteenth Street, NW, Washington, DC 20431, (202) 623-7000, Fax: (202) 623-4661, www.imf.org; *International Financial Statistics Yearbook 2007.*

M.E. Sharpe, 80 Business Park Drive, Armonk, NY 10504, (800) 541-6563, Fax: (914) 273-2106, www.mesharpe.com; *The Illustrated Book of World Rankings.*

Organisation for Economic Cooperation and Development (OECD), 2 rue Andre Pascal, F-75775 Paris Cedex 16, France, (Telephone in U.S. (202) 785-6323), (Fax in U.S. (202) 785-0350), www.oecd.org; *Comparison of Gross Domestic Product (GDP) for OECD Countries; Geographical Distribution of Financial Flows to Aid Recipients 2002-2006; OECD Economic Outlook 2008; OECD Main Economic Indicators (MEI);* and *Revenue Statistics 1965-2006 - 2007 Edition.*

Taylor and Francis Group, An Informa Business, 2 Park Square, Milton Park, Abingdon, Oxford OX14 4RN, United Kingdom, (Dial from U.S. (212) 216-7800), (Fax from U.S. (212) 564-7854), www.tandf.co.uk; *The Europa World Year Book.*

United Nations Statistics Division, New York, NY 10017, (800) 253-9646, Fax: (212) 963-4116, http://unstats.un.org; *Human Development Report 2006; National Accounts Statistics: Compendium of Income Distribution Statistics; Statistical Yearbook;* and *Trends in Europe and North America: The Statistical Yearbook of the ECE 2005.*

The World Bank, 1818 H Street, NW, Washington, DC 20433, (202) 473-1000, Fax: (202) 477-6391, www.worldbank.org; *World Development Indicators (WDI) 2008* and *World Development Report 2008.*

CANADA - GROSS NATIONAL PRODUCT

Euromonitor International, Inc., 224 S. Michigan Avenue, Suite 1500, Chicago, IL 60604, (312) 922-1115, Fax: (312) 922-1157, www.euromonitor.com; *International Marketing Data and Statistics 2008.*

M.E. Sharpe, 80 Business Park Drive, Armonk, NY 10504, (800) 541-6563, Fax: (914) 273-2106, www.mesharpe.com; *The Illustrated Book of World Rankings.*

Organisation for Economic Cooperation and Development (OECD), 2 rue Andre Pascal, F-75775 Paris Cedex 16, France, (Telephone in U.S. (202) 785-6323), (Fax in U.S. (202) 785-0350), www.oecd.org; *Geographical Distribution of Financial Flows to Aid Recipients 2002-2006; OECD Composite Leading Indicators (CLIs), Updated September 2007; OECD Economic Outlook 2008;* and *OECD Main Economic Indicators (MEI).*

Palgrave Macmillan Ltd., Houndmills, Basingstoke, Hampshire, RG21 6XS, England, (Telephone in U.S. (888) 330-8477), (Fax in U.S. (800) 672-2054), www.palgrave.com; *The Statesman's Yearbook 2008.*

Taylor and Francis Group, An Informa Business, 2 Park Square, Milton Park, Abingdon, Oxford OX14 4RN, United Kingdom, (Dial from U.S. (212) 216-7800), (Fax from U.S. (212) 564-7854), www.tandf.co.uk; *The Europa World Year Book.*

U.S. Department of State (DOS), 2201 C Street NW, Washington, DC 20520, (202) 647-4000, www.state.gov; *World Military Expenditures and Arms Transfers (WMEAT).*

United Nations Statistics Division, New York, NY 10017, (800) 253-9646, Fax: (212) 963-4116, http://unstats.un.org; *Statistical Yearbook.*

The World Bank, 1818 H Street, NW, Washington, DC 20433, (202) 473-1000, Fax: (202) 477-6391, www.worldbank.org; *The World Bank Atlas 2003-2004; World Development Indicators (WDI) 2008;* and *World Development Report 2008.*

CANADA - HIDES AND SKINS INDUSTRY

Organisation for Economic Cooperation and Development (OECD), 2 rue Andre Pascal, F-75775 Paris Cedex 16, France, (Telephone in U.S. (202) 785-6323), (Fax in U.S. (202) 785-0350), www.oecd.org; *Indicators of Industrial Activity* and *International Trade by Commodity Statistics (ITCS).*

United Nations Food and Agricultural Organization (FAO), Viale delle Terme di Caracalla, 00100 Rome, Italy, (Dial from U.S. (202) 653-2400), (Fax from U.S. (202) 653 5760), www.fao.org; *FAO Production Yearbook 2002.*

CANADA - HOUSING

Euromonitor International, Inc., 224 S. Michigan Avenue, Suite 1500, Chicago, IL 60604, (312) 922-1115, Fax: (312) 922-1157, www.euromonitor.com; *World Marketing Data and Statistics.*

M.E. Sharpe, 80 Business Park Drive, Armonk, NY 10504, (800) 541-6563, Fax: (914) 273-2106, www.mesharpe.com; *The Illustrated Book of World Rankings.*

United Nations Statistics Division, New York, NY 10017, (800) 253-9646, Fax: (212) 963-4116, http://unstats.un.org; *Statistical Yearbook* and *Trends in Europe and North America: The Statistical Yearbook of the ECE 2005.*

CANADA - HOUSING - FINANCE

Organisation for Economic Cooperation and Development (OECD), 2 rue Andre Pascal, F-75775 Paris Cedex 16, France, (Telephone in U.S. (202) 785-6323), (Fax in U.S. (202) 785-0350), www.oecd.org; *OECD Main Economic Indicators (MEI).*

CANADA - HOUSING CONSTRUCTION

See CANADA - CONSTRUCTION INDUSTRY

CANADA - ILLITERATE PERSONS

Euromonitor International, Inc., 224 S. Michigan Avenue, Suite 1500, Chicago, IL 60604, (312) 922-1115, Fax: (312) 922-1157, www.euromonitor.com; *The World Economic Factbook 2008.*

Palgrave Macmillan Ltd., Houndmills, Basingstoke, Hampshire, RG21 6XS, England, (Telephone in U.S. (888) 330-8477), (Fax in U.S. (800) 672-2054), www.palgrave.com; *The Statesman's Yearbook 2008.*

United Nations Statistics Division, New York, NY 10017, (800) 253-9646, Fax: (212) 963-4116, http://unstats.un.org; *Human Development Report 2006.*

CANADA - IMPORTS

Central Intelligence Agency, Office of Public Affairs, Washington, DC 20505, (703) 482-0623, Fax: (703) 482-1739, www.cia.gov; *The World Factbook.*

Economist Intelligence Unit, 111 West 57th Street, New York, NY 10019, (212) 554-0600, Fax: (212) 586-1181, www.eiu.com; *Canada Country Report.*

Euromonitor International, Inc., 224 S. Michigan Avenue, Suite 1500, Chicago, IL 60604, (312) 922-1115, Fax: (312) 922-1157, www.euromonitor.com; *International Marketing Data and Statistics 2008* and *The World Economic Factbook 2008.*

International Iron and Steel Institute (IISI), Rue Colonel Bourg 120, B-1140 Brussels, Belgium, www.worldsteel.org; *Steel Statistical Yearbook 2006.*

International Lead and Zinc Study Group (ILZSG), Rua Almirante Barroso 38, 5th Floor, Lisbon 1000 - 013, Portugal, www.ilzsg.org; Interactive Statistical Database.

International Monetary Fund (IMF), 700 Nineteenth Street, NW, Washington, DC 20431, (202) 623-7000, Fax: (202) 623-4661, www.imf.org; *Direction of Trade Statistics Yearbook 2007; Government Finance Statistics Yearbook (2008 Edition);* and *International Financial Statistics Yearbook 2007.*

Organisation for Economic Cooperation and Development (OECD), 2 rue Andre Pascal, F-75775 Paris Cedex 16, France, (Telephone in U.S. (202) 785-6323), (Fax in U.S. (202) 785-0350), www.oecd.org; *Iron and Steel Industry in 2004 (2006 Edition); 2005 OECD Agricultural Outlook Tables, 1970-2014; OECD Economic Outlook 2008; OECD Economic Survey - Canada 2008; Review of Fisheries in OECD Countries: Country Statistics 2001 to 2003 - 2005 Edition;* and STructural ANalysis (STAN) database.

Palgrave Macmillan Ltd., Houndmills, Basingstoke, Hampshire, RG21 6XS, England, (Telephone in U.S. (888) 330-8477), (Fax in U.S. (800) 672-2054), www.palgrave.com; *The Statesman's Yearbook 2008.*

Taylor and Francis Group, An Informa Business, 2 Park Square, Milton Park, Abingdon, Oxford OX14 4RN, United Kingdom, (Dial from U.S. (212) 216-7800), (Fax from U.S. (212) 564-7854), www.tandf.co.uk; *The Europa World Year Book.*

Technical Association of the Pulp and Paper Industry (TAPPI), 15 Technology Parkway South, Norcross, GA 30092, (770) 446-1400, Fax: (770) 446-6947, www.tappi.org; *TAPPI Annual Report.*

United Nations Conference on Trade and Development (UNCTAD), DC2-1120, United Nations, New York, NY 10017, (212) 963-0027, www.unctad.org; *Handbook of Statistics 2005.*

United Nations Food and Agricultural Organization (FAO), Viale delle Terme di Caracalla, 00100 Rome, Italy, (Dial from U.S. (202) 653-2400), (Fax from U.S. (202) 653 5760), www.fao.org; *The State of Food and Agriculture (SOFA) 2006.*

United Nations Statistics Division, New York, NY 10017, (800) 253-9646, Fax: (212) 963-4116, http://unstats.un.org; *Trends in Europe and North America: The Statistical Yearbook of the ECE 2005.*

The World Bank, 1818 H Street, NW, Washington, DC 20433, (202) 473-1000, Fax: (202) 477-6391, www.worldbank.org; *World Development Indicators (WDI) 2008* and *World Development Report 2008.*

CANADA - INCOME TAXES

See CANADA - TAXATION

CANADA - INDUSTRIAL METALS PRODUCTION

See CANADA - MINERAL INDUSTRIES

CANADA - INDUSTRIAL PRODUCTIVITY

Euromonitor International, Inc., 224 S. Michigan Avenue, Suite 1500, Chicago, IL 60604, (312) 922-1115, Fax: (312) 922-1157, www.euromonitor.com; *International Marketing Data and Statistics 2008.*

International Iron and Steel Institute (IISI), Rue Colonel Bourg 120, B-1140 Brussels, Belgium, www.worldsteel.org; *Steel Statistical Yearbook 2006.*

International Lead and Zinc Study Group (ILZSG), Rua Almirante Barroso 38, 5th Floor, Lisbon 1000 - 013, Portugal, www.ilzsg.org; Interactive Statistical Database.

M.E. Sharpe, 80 Business Park Drive, Armonk, NY 10504, (800) 541-6563, Fax: (914) 273-2106, www.mesharpe.com; *The Illustrated Book of World Rankings.*

Organisation for Economic Cooperation and Development (OECD), 2 rue Andre Pascal, F-75775 Paris Cedex 16, France, (Telephone in U.S. (202) 785-6323), (Fax in U.S. (202) 785-0350), www.oecd.org; *Environmental Impacts of Foreign Direct Investment in the Mining Sector in the Newly Independent States (NIS); Indicators of Industrial Activity; Iron and Steel Industry in 2004 (2006 Edition); A New World Map in Textiles and Clothing: Adjusting to Change; 2005 OECD Agricultural Outlook Tables, 1970-2014; OECD Economic Outlook 2008; OECD Main Economic Indicators (MEI);* and STructural ANalysis (STAN) database.

Technical Association of the Pulp and Paper Industry (TAPPI), 15 Technology Parkway South, Norcross, GA 30092, (770) 446-1400, Fax: (770) 446-6947, www.tappi.org; *TAPPI Annual Report.*

CANADA - INDUSTRIAL PROPERTY

United Nations Statistics Division, New York, NY 10017, (800) 253-9646, Fax: (212) 963-4116, http://unstats.un.org; *Statistical Yearbook.*

World Intellectual Property Organization (WIPO), PO Box 18, CH-1211 Geneva 20, Switzerland, www.wipo.int; *Industrial Property Statistics* and *Industrial Property Statistics Online Directory.*

CANADA - INDUSTRIES

Central Intelligence Agency, Office of Public Affairs, Washington, DC 20505, (703) 482-0623, Fax: (703) 482-1739, www.cia.gov; *The World Factbook.*

Economist Intelligence Unit, 111 West 57th Street, New York, NY 10019, (212) 554-0600, Fax: (212) 586-1181, www.eiu.com; *Canada Country Report.*

Euromonitor International, Inc., 224 S. Michigan Avenue, Suite 1500, Chicago, IL 60604, (312) 922-1115, Fax: (312) 922-1157, www.euromonitor.com; *International Marketing Data and Statistics 2008; The World Economic Factbook 2008;* and *World Marketing Data and Statistics.*

International Labour Office, I.L.O. Publications, 4 route des Morillons, CH-1211 Geneva 22, Switzerland, (Telephone in U.S. (202) 653-7652), (Fax in U.S. (202) 653-7687), www.ilo.org; *Yearbook of Labour Statistics 2006.*

M.E. Sharpe, 80 Business Park Drive, Armonk, NY 10504, (800) 541-6563, Fax: (914) 273-2106, www.mesharpe.com; *The Illustrated Book of World Rankings.*

Organisation for Economic Cooperation and Development (OECD), 2 rue Andre Pascal, F-75775 Paris Cedex 16, France, (Telephone in U.S. (202) 785-6323), (Fax in U.S. (202) 785-0350), www.oecd.org; *Indicators of Industrial Activity; Key Environmental Indicators 2004; OECD Economic Outlook 2008;* and STructural ANalysis (STAN) database.

Palgrave Macmillan Ltd., Houndmills, Basingstoke, Hampshire, RG21 6XS, England, (Telephone in U.S. (888) 330-8477), (Fax in U.S. (800) 672-2054), www.palgrave.com; *The Statesman's Yearbook 2008.*

Statistics Canada, 100 Tunney's Pasture Driveway, Ottawa, Ontario K1A 0T6, (Dial from U.S. (800) 263-1136), (Fax from U.S. (877) 287-4369), www.statcan.ca; *Greenhouse Gas Reduction Technologies: Industry Expenditures and Business Opportunities* and *Measuring Employment in the Environment Industry.*

Taylor and Francis Group, An Informa Business, 2 Park Square, Milton Park, Abingdon, Oxford OX14 4RN, United Kingdom, (Dial from U.S. (212) 216-

7800), (Fax from U.S. (212) 564-7854), www.tandf.co.uk; *The Europa World Year Book.*

United Nations Industrial Development Organization (UNIDO), 1 United Nations Plaza, New York, NY 10017, (212) 963 6890, Fax: (212) 963-7904, http://unido.org; Industrial Statistics Database 2008 (INDSTAT) and *The International Yearbook of Industrial Statistics 2008.*

United Nations Statistics Division, New York, NY 10017, (800) 253-9646, Fax: (212) 963-4116, http://unstats.un.org; *2004 Industrial Commodity Statistics Yearbook* and *Trends in Europe and North America: The Statistical Yearbook of the ECE 2005.*

The World Bank, 1818 H Street, NW, Washington, DC 20433, (202) 473-1000, Fax: (202) 477-6391, www.worldbank.org; *Canada* and *World Development Indicators (WDI) 2008.*

World Intellectual Property Organization (WIPO), PO Box 18, CH-1211 Geneva 20, Switzerland, www.wipo.int; *Industrial Property Statistics* and *Industrial Property Statistics Online Directory.*

CANADA - INFANT AND MATERNAL MORTALITY

See CANADA - MORTALITY

CANADA - INORGANIC ACIDS

United Nations Statistics Division, New York, NY 10017, (800) 253-9646, Fax: (212) 963-4116, http://unstats.un.org; *Statistical Yearbook.*

CANADA - INTEREST RATES

Organisation for Economic Cooperation and Development (OECD), 2 rue Andre Pascal, F-75775 Paris Cedex 16, France, (Telephone in U.S. (202) 785-6323), (Fax in U.S. (202) 785-0350), www.oecd.org; *Financial Market Trends: OECD Periodical; OECD Economic Outlook 2008;* and *OECD Main Economic Indicators (MEI).*

United Nations Statistics Division, New York, NY 10017, (800) 253-9646, Fax: (212) 963-4116, http://unstats.un.org; *Statistical Yearbook.*

CANADA - INTERNAL REVENUE

Organisation for Economic Cooperation and Development (OECD), 2 rue Andre Pascal, F-75775 Paris Cedex 16, France, (Telephone in U.S. (202) 785-6323), (Fax in U.S. (202) 785-0350), www.oecd.org; *Revenue Statistics 1965-2006 - 2007 Edition.*

CANADA - INTERNATIONAL FINANCE

International Finance Corporation (IFC), 2121 Pennsylvania Avenue, NW, Washington, DC 20433 USA, (202) 473-1000, Fax: (202) 974-4384, www.ifc.org; *Annual Report 2007.*

Organisation for Economic Cooperation and Development (OECD), 2 rue Andre Pascal, F-75775 Paris Cedex 16, France, (Telephone in U.S. (202) 785-6323), (Fax in U.S. (202) 785-0350), www.oecd.org; *Financial Market Trends: OECD Periodical; OECD Economic Outlook 2008;* and *OECD Main Economic Indicators (MEI).*

CANADA - INTERNATIONAL LIQUIDITY

International Monetary Fund (IMF), 700 Nineteenth Street, NW, Washington, DC 20431, (202) 623-7000, Fax: (202) 623-4661, www.imf.org; *International Financial Statistics Yearbook 2007.*

Organisation for Economic Cooperation and Development (OECD), 2 rue Andre Pascal, F-75775 Paris Cedex 16, France, (Telephone in U.S. (202) 785-6323), (Fax in U.S. (202) 785-0350), www.oecd.org; *Financial Market Trends: OECD Periodical* and *OECD Economic Outlook 2008.*

CANADA - INTERNATIONAL STATISTICS

Organisation for Economic Cooperation and Development (OECD), 2 rue Andre Pascal, F-75775 Paris Cedex 16, France, (Telephone in U.S. (202) 785-6323), (Fax in U.S. (202) 785-0350), www.oecd.org; *Financial Market Trends: OECD Periodical* and *Household, Tourism, Travel: Trends, Environmental Impacts and Policy Responses.*

CANADA - INTERNATIONAL TRADE

Bernan Essential Government Publications, 4611-F Assembly Drive, Lanham MD, 20706-4391, (301) 459-2255, Fax: (800) 865-3450, www.bernan.com; *OECD Factbook 2006.*

Economist Intelligence Unit, 111 West 57th Street, New York, NY 10019, (212) 554-0600, Fax: (212) 586-1181, www.eiu.com; *Canada Country Report.*

Euromonitor International, Inc., 224 S. Michigan Avenue, Suite 1500, Chicago, IL 60604, (312) 922-1115, Fax: (312) 922-1157, www.euromonitor.com; *International Marketing Data and Statistics 2008; The World Economic Factbook 2008;* and *World Marketing Data and Statistics.*

International Iron and Steel Institute (IISI), Rue Colonel Bourg 120, B-1140 Brussels, Belgium, www.worldsteel.org; *Steel Statistical Yearbook 2006.*

M.E. Sharpe, 80 Business Park Drive, Armonk, NY 10504, (800) 541-6563, Fax: (914) 273-2106, www.mesharpe.com; *The Illustrated Book of World Rankings.*

Organisation for Economic Cooperation and Development (OECD), 2 rue Andre Pascal, F-75775 Paris Cedex 16, France, (Telephone in U.S. (202) 785-6323), (Fax in U.S. (202) 785-0350), www.oecd.org; *International Trade by Commodity Statistics (ITCS); 2005 OECD Agricultural Outlook Tables, 1970-2014; OECD Economic Outlook 2008; OECD Economic Survey - Canada 2008; OECD in Figures 2007; OECD Main Economic Indicators (MEI);* and *Statistics on Ship Production, Exports and Orders in 2004.*

Palgrave Macmillan Ltd., Houndmills, Basingstoke, Hampshire, RG21 6XS, England, (Telephone in U.S. (888) 330-8477), (Fax in U.S. (800) 672-2054), www.palgrave.com; *The Statesman's Yearbook 2008.*

Taylor and Francis Group, An Informa Business, 2 Park Square, Milton Park, Abingdon, Oxford OX14 4RN, United Kingdom, (Dial from U.S. (212) 216-7800), (Fax from U.S. (212) 564-7854), www.tandf.co.uk; *The Europa World Year Book.*

United Nations Conference on Trade and Development (UNCTAD), DC2-1120, United Nations, New York, NY 10017, (212) 963-0027, www.unctad.org; *UNCTAD Commodity Yearbook.*

United Nations Food and Agricultural Organization (FAO), Viale delle Terme di Caracalla, 00100 Rome, Italy, (Dial from U.S. (202) 653-2400), (Fax from U.S. (202) 653 5760), www.fao.org; *FAO Trade Yearbook* and *The State of Food and Agriculture (SOFA) 2006.*

United Nations Statistics Division, New York, NY 10017, (800) 253-9646, Fax: (212) 963-4116, http://unstats.un.org; *International Trade Statistics Yearbook* and *Statistical Yearbook.*

The World Bank, 1818 H Street, NW, Washington, DC 20433, (202) 473-1000, Fax: (202) 477-6391, www.worldbank.org; *Canada; World Development Indicators (WDI) 2008;* and *World Development Report 2008.*

World Bureau of Metal Statistics (WBMS), 27a High Street, Ware, Hertfordshire, SG12 9BA, United Kingdom, www.world-bureau.com; *World Flow Charts* and *World Metal Statistics.*

World Trade Organization (WTO), Centre William Rappard, Rue de Lausanne 154, CH-1211 Geneva 21, Switzerland, www.wto.org; *International Trade Statistics 2006.*

CANADA - INTERNET USERS

International Telecommunication Union (ITU), Place des Nations, 1211 Geneva 20, Switzerland, www.itu.int; *World Telecommunication/ICT Indicators Database on CD-ROM; World Telecommunication/ICT Indicators Database Online;* and *Yearbook of Statistics - Telecommunication Services (Chronological Time Series 1997-2006).*

The World Bank, 1818 H Street, NW, Washington, DC 20433, (202) 473-1000, Fax: (202) 477-6391, www.worldbank.org; *Canada.*

CANADA - INVESTMENTS

International Monetary Fund (IMF), 700 Nineteenth Street, NW, Washington, DC 20431, (202) 623-7000, Fax: (202) 623-4661, www.imf.org; *International Financial Statistics Yearbook 2007.*

Organisation for Economic Cooperation and Development (OECD), 2 rue Andre Pascal, F-75775 Paris Cedex 16, France, (Telephone in U.S. (202) 785-6323), (Fax in U.S. (202) 785-0350), www.oecd.org; *Financial Market Trends: OECD Periodical; Iron and Steel Industry in 2004 (2006 Edition); A New World Map in Textiles and Clothing: Adjusting to Change; OECD Economic Outlook 2008;* and STructural ANalysis (STAN) database.

Standard and Poor's Corporation, 55 Water Street, New York, NY 10041, (212) 438-1000, www.standardandpoors.com; *Compustat Global* and *Compustat North America.*

CANADA - IRON AND IRON ORE PRODUCTION

See CANADA - MINERAL INDUSTRIES

CANADA - IRRIGATION

Euromonitor International, Inc., 224 S. Michigan Avenue, Suite 1500, Chicago, IL 60604, (312) 922-1115, Fax: (312) 922-1157, www.euromonitor.com; *International Marketing Data and Statistics 2008.*

CANADA - LABOR

Central Intelligence Agency, Office of Public Affairs, Washington, DC 20505, (703) 482-0623, Fax: (703) 482-1739, www.cia.gov; *The World Factbook.*

Euromonitor International, Inc., 224 S. Michigan Avenue, Suite 1500, Chicago, IL 60604, (312) 922-1115, Fax: (312) 922-1157, www.euromonitor.com; *International Marketing Data and Statistics 2008* and *World Marketing Data and Statistics.*

International Labour Office, I.L.O. Publications, 4 route des Morillons, CH-1211 Geneva 22, Switzerland, (Telephone in U.S. (202) 653-7652), (Fax in U.S. (202) 653-7687), www.ilo.org; *Yearbook of Labour Statistics 2006.*

M.E. Sharpe, 80 Business Park Drive, Armonk, NY 10504, (800) 541-6563, Fax: (914) 273-2106, www.mesharpe.com; *The Illustrated Book of World Rankings.*

Organisation for Economic Cooperation and Development (OECD), 2 rue Andre Pascal, F-75775 Paris Cedex 16, France, (Telephone in U.S. (202) 785-6323), (Fax in U.S. (202) 785-0350), www.oecd.org; *Iron and Steel Industry in 2004 (2006 Edition); A New World Map in Textiles and Clothing: Adjusting to Change; OECD Economic Outlook 2008; OECD Economic Survey - Canada 2008; OECD Employment Outlook 2007; OECD Main Economic Indicators (MEI);* and *Statistics on Ship Production, Exports and Orders in 2004.*

Palgrave Macmillan Ltd., Houndmills, Basingstoke, Hampshire, RG21 6XS, England, (Telephone in U.S. (888) 330-8477), (Fax in U.S. (800) 672-2054), www.palgrave.com; *The Statesman's Yearbook 2008.*

Statistics Canada, 100 Tunney's Pasture Driveway, Ottawa, Ontario K1A 0T6, (Dial from U.S. (800) 263-1136), (Fax from U.S. (877) 287-4369), www.statcan.ca; *Measuring Employment in the Environment Industry.*

Taylor and Francis Group, An Informa Business, 2 Park Square, Milton Park, Abingdon, Oxford OX14 4RN, United Kingdom, (Dial from U.S. (212) 216-7800), (Fax from U.S. (212) 564-7854), www.tandf.co.uk; *The Europa World Year Book.*

United Nations Food and Agricultural Organization (FAO), Viale delle Terme di Caracalla, 00100 Rome, Italy, (Dial from U.S. (202) 653-2400), (Fax from U.S. (202) 653 5760), www.fao.org; *The State of Food and Agriculture (SOFA) 2006.*

United Nations Statistics Division, New York, NY 10017, (800) 253-9646, Fax: (212) 963-4116, http://unstats.un.org; *Human Development Report 2006.*

The World Bank, 1818 H Street, NW, Washington, DC 20433, (202) 473-1000, Fax: (202) 477-6391,

www.worldbank.org; *The World Bank Atlas 2003-2004; World Development Indicators (WDI) 2008;* and *World Development Report 2008.*

CANADA - LAND USE

Central Intelligence Agency, Office of Public Affairs, Washington, DC 20505, (703) 482-0623, Fax: (703) 482-1739, www.cia.gov; *The World Factbook.*

Euromonitor International, Inc., 224 S. Michigan Avenue, Suite 1500, Chicago, IL 60604, (312) 922-1115, Fax: (312) 922-1157, www.euromonitor.com; *International Marketing Data and Statistics 2008.*

United Nations Food and Agricultural Organization (FAO), Viale delle Terme di Caracalla, 00100 Rome, Italy, (Dial from U.S. (202) 653-2400), (Fax from U.S. (202) 653 5760), www.fao.org; *FAO Production Yearbook 2002.*

The World Bank, 1818 H Street, NW, Washington, DC 20433, (202) 473-1000, Fax: (202) 477-6391, www.worldbank.org; *World Development Report 2008.*

CANADA - LEATHER INDUSTRY AND TRADE

Organisation for Economic Cooperation and Development (OECD), 2 rue Andre Pascal, F-75775 Paris Cedex 16, France, (Telephone in U.S. (202) 785-6323), (Fax in U.S. (202) 785-0350), www.oecd.org; *Indicators of Industrial Activity.*

CANADA - LIBRARIES

M.E. Sharpe, 80 Business Park Drive, Armonk, NY 10504, (800) 541-6563, Fax: (914) 273-2106, www.mesharpe.com; *The Illustrated Book of World Rankings.*

UNESCO Institute for Statistics, C.P. 6128 Succursale Centre-Ville, Montreal, Quebec, H3C 3J7 Canada, (Dial from U.S. (514) 343-6880), (Fax from U.S. (514) 343 6882), www.uis.unesco.org; *Statistical Tables.*

United Nations Statistics Division, New York, NY 10017, (800) 253-9646, Fax: (212) 963-4116, http://unstats.un.org; *Trends in Europe and North America: The Statistical Yearbook of the ECE 2005.*

CANADA - LIFE EXPECTANCY

Central Intelligence Agency, Office of Public Affairs, Washington, DC 20505, (703) 482-0623, Fax: (703) 482-1739, www.cia.gov; *The World Factbook.*

Euromonitor International, Inc., 224 S. Michigan Avenue, Suite 1500, Chicago, IL 60604, (312) 922-1115, Fax: (312) 922-1157, www.euromonitor.com; *The World Economic Factbook 2008.*

Organisation for Economic Cooperation and Development (OECD), 2 rue Andre Pascal, F-75775 Paris Cedex 16, France, (Telephone in U.S. (202) 785-6323), (Fax in U.S. (202) 785-0350), www.oecd.org; *OECD Economic Outlook 2008.*

United Nations Statistics Division, New York, NY 10017, (800) 253-9646, Fax: (212) 963-4116, http://unstats.un.org; *Human Development Report 2006; Trends in Europe and North America: The Statistical Yearbook of the ECE 2005;* and *World Statistics Pocketbook.*

The World Bank, 1818 H Street, NW, Washington, DC 20433, (202) 473-1000, Fax: (202) 477-6391, www.worldbank.org; *The World Bank Atlas 2003-2004* and *World Development Report 2008.*

CANADA - LITERACY

Euromonitor International, Inc., 224 S. Michigan Avenue, Suite 1500, Chicago, IL 60604, (312) 922-1115, Fax: (312) 922-1157, www.euromonitor.com; *World Marketing Data and Statistics.*

CANADA - LIVESTOCK

Euromonitor International, Inc., 224 S. Michigan Avenue, Suite 1500, Chicago, IL 60604, (312) 922-1115, Fax: (312) 922-1157, www.euromonitor.com; *International Marketing Data and Statistics 2008.*

M.E. Sharpe, 80 Business Park Drive, Armonk, NY 10504, (800) 541-6563, Fax: (914) 273-2106, www.mesharpe.com; *The Illustrated Book of World Rankings.*

Organisation for Economic Cooperation and Development (OECD), 2 rue Andre Pascal, F-75775 Paris Cedex 16, France, (Telephone in U.S. (202) 785-6323), (Fax in U.S. (202) 785-0350), www.oecd.org; *2005 OECD Agricultural Outlook Tables, 1970-2014.*

Palgrave Macmillan Ltd., Houndmills, Basingstoke, Hampshire, RG21 6XS, England, (Telephone in U.S. (888) 330-8477), (Fax in U.S. (800) 672-2054), www.palgrave.com; *The Statesman's Yearbook 2008.*

Taylor and Francis Group, An Informa Business, 2 Park Square, Milton Park, Abingdon, Oxford OX14 4RN, United Kingdom, (Dial from U.S. (212) 216-7800), (Fax from U.S. (212) 564-7854), www.tandf.co.uk; *The Europa World Year Book.*

United Nations Conference on Trade and Development (UNCTAD), DC2-1120, United Nations, New York, NY 10017, (212) 963-0027, www.unctad.org; *UNCTAD Commodity Yearbook.*

United Nations Food and Agricultural Organization (FAO), Viale delle Terme di Caracalla, 00100 Rome, Italy, (Dial from U.S. (202) 653-2400), (Fax from U.S. (202) 653 5760), www.fao.org; *FAO Production Yearbook 2002* and *The State of Food and Agriculture (SOFA) 2006.*

United Nations Statistics Division, New York, NY 10017, (800) 253-9646, Fax: (212) 963-4116, http://unstats.un.org; *Statistical Yearbook.*

CANADA - LOCAL TAXATION

Euromonitor International, Inc., 224 S. Michigan Avenue, Suite 1500, Chicago, IL 60604, (312) 922-1115, Fax: (312) 922-1157, www.euromonitor.com; *International Marketing Data and Statistics 2008.*

CANADA - MACHINERY

Organisation for Economic Cooperation and Development (OECD), 2 rue Andre Pascal, F-75775 Paris Cedex 16, France, (Telephone in U.S. (202) 785-6323), (Fax in U.S. (202) 785-0350), www.oecd.org; *Indicators of Industrial Activity.*

CANADA - MAGNESIUM PRODUCTION AND CONSUMPTION

See CANADA - MINERAL INDUSTRIES

CANADA - MANUFACTURES

M.E. Sharpe, 80 Business Park Drive, Armonk, NY 10504, (800) 541-6563, Fax: (914) 273-2106, www.mesharpe.com; *The Illustrated Book of World Rankings.*

Organisation for Economic Cooperation and Development (OECD), 2 rue Andre Pascal, F-75775 Paris Cedex 16, France, (Telephone in U.S. (202) 785-6323), (Fax in U.S. (202) 785-0350), www.oecd.org; *Indicators of Industrial Activity; International Trade by Commodity Statistics (ITCS); OECD Economic Survey - Canada 2008; OECD Main Economic Indicators (MEI);* and STructural ANalysis (STAN) database.

United Nations Statistics Division, New York, NY 10017, (800) 253-9646, Fax: (212) 963-4116, http://unstats.un.org; *Statistical Yearbook.*

The World Bank, 1818 H Street, NW, Washington, DC 20433, (202) 473-1000, Fax: (202) 477-6391, www.worldbank.org; *World Development Indicators (WDI) 2008.*

CANADA - MARRIAGE

M.E. Sharpe, 80 Business Park Drive, Armonk, NY 10504, (800) 541-6563, Fax: (914) 273-2106, www.mesharpe.com; *The Illustrated Book of World Rankings.*

Taylor and Francis Group, An Informa Business, 2 Park Square, Milton Park, Abingdon, Oxford OX14 4RN, United Kingdom, (Dial from U.S. (212) 216-7800), (Fax from U.S. (212) 564-7854), www.tandf.co.uk; *The Europa World Year Book.*

United Nations Statistics Division, New York, NY 10017, (800) 253-9646, Fax: (212) 963-4116, http://unstats.un.org; *Demographic Yearbook* and *Trends in Europe and North America: The Statistical Yearbook of the ECE 2005.*

CANADA - MEAT PRODUCTION

See CANADA - LIVESTOCK

CANADA - MERCURY PRODUCTION

See CANADA - MINERAL INDUSTRIES

CANADA - MILK PRODUCTION

See CANADA - DAIRY PROCESSING

CANADA - MINERAL INDUSTRIES

Commodity Research Bureau, 330 South Wells Street, Suite 612, Chicago, IL 60606-7110, (800) 621-5271, Fax: (312) 939-4135, www.crbtrader.com; *2006 CRB Commodity Yearbook and CD.*

International Energy Agency (IEA), 9, rue de la Federation, 75739 Paris Cedex 15, France, www.iea.org; *Key World Energy Statistics 2007.*

International Iron and Steel Institute (IISI), Rue Colonel Bourg 120, B-1140 Brussels, Belgium, www.worldsteel.org; *Steel Statistical Yearbook 2006.*

International Lead and Zinc Study Group (ILZSG), Rua Almirante Barroso 38, 5th Floor, Lisbon 1000 - 013, Portugal, www.ilzsg.org; Interactive Statistical Database.

International Monetary Fund (IMF), 700 Nineteenth Street, NW, Washington, DC 20431, (202) 623-7000, Fax: (202) 623-4661, www.imf.org; *International Financial Statistics Yearbook 2007.*

M.E. Sharpe, 80 Business Park Drive, Armonk, NY 10504, (800) 541-6563, Fax: (914) 273-2106, www.mesharpe.com; *The Illustrated Book of World Rankings.*

Organisation for Economic Cooperation and Development (OECD), 2 rue Andre Pascal, F-75775 Paris Cedex 16, France, (Telephone in U.S. (202) 785-6323), (Fax in U.S. (202) 785-0350), www.oecd.org; *Coal Information: 2007 Edition; Energy Statistics of OECD Countries* (2007 Edition); *Environmental Impacts of Foreign Direct Investment in the Mining Sector in the Newly Independent States (NIS); Indicators of Industrial Activity; International Trade by Commodity Statistics (ITCS); Iron and Steel Industry in 2004 (2006 Edition);* STructural ANalysis (STAN) database; and *World Energy Outlook 2007.*

Palgrave Macmillan Ltd., Houndmills, Basingstoke, Hampshire, RG21 6XS, England, (Telephone in U.S. (888) 330-8477), (Fax in U.S. (800) 672-2054), www.palgrave.com; *The Statesman's Yearbook 2008.*

Taylor and Francis Group, An Informa Business, 2 Park Square, Milton Park, Abingdon, Oxford OX14 4RN, United Kingdom, (Dial from U.S. (212) 216-7800), (Fax from U.S. (212) 564-7854), www.tandf.co.uk; *The Europa World Year Book.*

United Nations Conference on Trade and Development (UNCTAD), DC2-1120, United Nations, New York, NY 10017, (212) 963-0027, www.unctad.org; *UNCTAD Commodity Yearbook.*

United Nations Statistics Division, New York, NY 10017, (800) 253-9646, Fax: (212) 963-4116, http://unstats.un.org; *Statistical Yearbook.*

World Bureau of Metal Statistics (WBMS), 27a High Street, Ware, Hertfordshire, SG12 9BA, United Kingdom, www.world-bureau.com; *Annual Stainless Steel Statistics; World Flow Charts; World Metal Statistics; World Nickel Statistics;* and *World Tin Statistics.*

CANADA - MONEY EXCHANGE RATES

See CANADA - FOREIGN EXCHANGE RATES

CANADA - MONEY SUPPLY

Economist Intelligence Unit, 111 West 57th Street, New York, NY 10019, (212) 554-0600, Fax: (212) 586-1181, www.eiu.com; *Canada Country Report.*

Euromonitor International, Inc., 224 S. Michigan Avenue, Suite 1500, Chicago, IL 60604, (312) 922-1115, Fax: (312) 922-1157, www.euromonitor.com; *International Marketing Data and Statistics 2008.*

International Monetary Fund (IMF), 700 Nineteenth Street, NW, Washington, DC 20431, (202) 623-7000, Fax: (202) 623-4661, www.imf.org; *International Financial Statistics Yearbook 2007.*

Organisation for Economic Cooperation and Development (OECD), 2 rue Andre Pascal, F-75775 Paris Cedex 16, France, (Telephone in U.S. (202) 785-6323), (Fax in U.S. (202) 785-0350), www.oecd.org; *OECD Economic Outlook 2008.*

United Nations Statistics Division, New York, NY 10017, (800) 253-9646, Fax: (212) 963-4116, http://unstats.un.org; *Statistical Yearbook.*

The World Bank, 1818 H Street, NW, Washington, DC 20433, (202) 473-1000, Fax: (202) 477-6391, www.worldbank.org; *Canada* and *World Development Indicators (WDI) 2008.*

CANADA - MONUMENTS AND HISTORIC SITES

UNESCO Institute for Statistics, C.P. 6128 Succursale Centre-Ville, Montreal, Quebec, H3C 3J7 Canada, (Dial from U.S. (514) 343-6880), (Fax from U.S. (514) 343 6882), www.uis.unesco.org; *Statistical Tables.*

CANADA - MORTALITY

Central Intelligence Agency, Office of Public Affairs, Washington, DC 20505, (703) 482-0623, Fax: (703) 482-1739, www.cia.gov; *The World Factbook.*

Euromonitor International, Inc., 224 S. Michigan Avenue, Suite 1500, Chicago, IL 60604, (312) 922-1115, Fax: (312) 922-1157, www.euromonitor.com; *International Marketing Data and Statistics 2008* and *The World Economic Factbook 2008.*

Palgrave Macmillan Ltd., Houndmills, Basingstoke, Hampshire, RG21 6XS, England, (Telephone in U.S. (888) 330-8477), (Fax in U.S. (800) 672-2054), www.palgrave.com; *The Statesman's Yearbook 2008.*

Taylor and Francis Group, An Informa Business, 2 Park Square, Milton Park, Abingdon, Oxford OX14 4RN, United Kingdom, (Dial from U.S. (212) 216-7800), (Fax from U.S. (212) 564-7854), www.tandf.co.uk; *The Europa World Year Book.*

UNICEF, 3 United Nations Plaza, New York, NY 10017, (800) 253-9646, Fax: (212) 887-7465, www.unicef.org; *The State of the World's Children 2008.*

United Nations Statistics Division, New York, NY 10017, (800) 253-9646, Fax: (212) 963-4116, http://unstats.un.org; *Demographic Yearbook; Human Development Report 2006; Statistical Yearbook; Trends in Europe and North America: The Statistical Yearbook of the ECE 2005;* and *World Statistics Pocketbook.*

The World Bank, 1818 H Street, NW, Washington, DC 20433, (202) 473-1000, Fax: (202) 477-6391, www.worldbank.org; *The World Bank Atlas 2003-2004; World Development Indicators (WDI) 2008;* and *World Development Report 2008.*

World Health Organization (WHO), Avenue Appia 20, 1211 Geneve 27, Switzerland, (Telephone in U.S. (212) 331-9081), www.who.int; The WHO Global Atlas of Infectious Diseases and *World Health Report 2006.*

CANADA - MOTION PICTURES

Palgrave Macmillan Ltd., Houndmills, Basingstoke, Hampshire, RG21 6XS, England, (Telephone in U.S. (888) 330-8477), (Fax in U.S. (800) 672-2054), www.palgrave.com; *The Statesman's Yearbook 2008.*

UNESCO Institute for Statistics, C.P. 6128 Succursale Centre-Ville, Montreal, Quebec, H3C 3J7 Canada, (Dial from U.S. (514) 343-6880), (Fax from U.S. (514) 343 6882), www.uis.unesco.org; *Statistical Tables.*

United Nations Statistics Division, New York, NY 10017, (800) 253-9646, Fax: (212) 963-4116, http://unstats.un.org; *Statistical Yearbook.*

CANADA - MOTOR VEHICLES

International Road Federation (IFR), Madison Place, 500 Montgomery Street, 5th Floor, Alexandria, VA 22314, (703) 535-1001, Fax: (703) 535-1007, www.irfnet.org; *World Road Statistics 2006.*

United Nations Statistics Division, New York, NY 10017, (800) 253-9646, Fax: (212) 963-4116, http://unstats.un.org; *Statistical Yearbook.*

CANADA - MUSEUMS

M.E. Sharpe, 80 Business Park Drive, Armonk, NY 10504, (800) 541-6563, Fax: (914) 273-2106, www.mesharpe.com; *The Illustrated Book of World Rankings.*

UNESCO Institute for Statistics, C.P. 6128 Succursale Centre-Ville, Montreal, Quebec, H3C 3J7 Canada, (Dial from U.S. (514) 343-6880), (Fax from U.S. (514) 343 6882), www.uis.unesco.org; *Statistical Tables.*

CANADA - NATIONAL INCOME

United Nations Statistics Division, New York, NY 10017, (800) 253-9646, Fax: (212) 963-4116, http://unstats.un.org; *Statistical Yearbook.*

CANADA - NATURAL GAS PRODUCTION

See CANADA - MINERAL INDUSTRIES

CANADA - NICKEL AND NICKEL ORE

See CANADA - MINERAL INDUSTRIES

CANADA - NUTRITION

United Nations Food and Agricultural Organization (FAO), Viale delle Terme di Caracalla, 00100 Rome, Italy, (Dial from U.S. (202) 653-2400), (Fax from U.S. (202) 653 5760), www.fao.org; *The State of Food and Agriculture (SOFA) 2006.*

CANADA - OATS PRODUCTION

See CANADA - CROPS

CANADA - OILSEED PLANTS

Organisation for Economic Cooperation and Development (OECD), 2 rue Andre Pascal, F-75775 Paris Cedex 16, France, (Telephone in U.S. (202) 785-6323), (Fax in U.S. (202) 785-0350), www.oecd.org; *International Trade by Commodity Statistics (ITCS).*

CANADA - OLDER PEOPLE

M.E. Sharpe, 80 Business Park Drive, Armonk, NY 10504, (800) 541-6563, Fax: (914) 273-2106, www.mesharpe.com; *The Illustrated Book of World Rankings.*

CANADA - PAPER

See CANADA - FORESTS AND FORESTRY

CANADA - PEANUT PRODUCTION

See CANADA - CROPS

CANADA - PERIODICALS

UNESCO Institute for Statistics, C.P. 6128 Succursale Centre-Ville, Montreal, Quebec, H3C 3J7 Canada, (Dial from U.S. (514) 343-6880), (Fax from U.S. (514) 343 6882), www.uis.unesco.org; *Statistical Tables.*

CANADA - PESTICIDES

United Nations Food and Agricultural Organization (FAO), Viale delle Terme di Caracalla, 00100 Rome, Italy, (Dial from U.S. (202) 653-2400), (Fax from U.S. (202) 653 5760), www.fao.org; *The State of Food and Agriculture (SOFA) 2006.*

CANADA - PETROLEUM INDUSTRY AND TRADE

International Energy Agency (IEA), 9, rue de la Federation, 75739 Paris Cedex 15, France, www.iea.org; *Key World Energy Statistics 2007.*

International Monetary Fund (IMF), 700 Nineteenth Street, NW, Washington, DC 20431, (202) 623-7000, Fax: (202) 623-4661, www.imf.org; *International Financial Statistics Yearbook 2007.*

M.E. Sharpe, 80 Business Park Drive, Armonk, NY 10504, (800) 541-6563, Fax: (914) 273-2106, www.mesharpe.com; *The Illustrated Book of World Rankings.*

Organisation for Economic Cooperation and Development (OECD), 2 rue Andre Pascal, F-75775 Paris Cedex 16, France, (Telephone in U.S. (202) 785-6323), (Fax in U.S. (202) 785-0350), www.oecd.org; *Energy Statistics of OECD Countries* (2007 Edition); *Indicators of Industrial Activity; International Trade by Commodity Statistics (ITCS); Oil Information 2006 Edition;* and *World Energy Outlook 2007.*

Palgrave Macmillan Ltd., Houndmills, Basingstoke, Hampshire, RG21 6XS, England, (Telephone in U.S. (888) 330-8477), (Fax in U.S. (800) 672-2054), www.palgrave.com; *The Statesman's Yearbook 2008.*

PennWell Corporation, 1421 South Sheridan Road, Tulsa, OK 74112, (918) 835-3161, www.pennwell.com; *International Petroleum Encyclopedia 2007.*

U.S. Department of Energy (DOE), Energy Information Administration (EIA), 1000 Independence Avenue, SW, Washington, DC 20585, (202) 586-8800, www.eia.doe.gov; *International Energy Annual 2004* and *International Energy Outlook 2006.*

United Nations Conference on Trade and Development (UNCTAD), DC2-1120, United Nations, New York, NY 10017, (212) 963-0027, www.unctad.org; *UNCTAD Commodity Yearbook.*

United Nations Food and Agricultural Organization (FAO), Viale delle Terme di Caracalla, 00100 Rome, Italy, (Dial from U.S. (202) 653-2400), (Fax from U.S. (202) 653 5760), www.fao.org; *The State of Food and Agriculture (SOFA) 2006.*

United Nations Statistics Division, New York, NY 10017, (800) 253-9646, Fax: (212) 963-4116, http://unstats.un.org; *Statistical Yearbook* and *Trends in Europe and North America: The Statistical Yearbook of the ECE 2005.*

CANADA - PHOSPHATES PRODUCTION

See CANADA - MINERAL INDUSTRIES

CANADA - PIPELINES

United Nations Statistics Division, New York, NY 10017, (800) 253-9646, Fax: (212) 963-4116, http://unstats.un.org; *Annual Bulletin of Transport Statistics for Europe and North America 2004.*

CANADA - PLASTICS INDUSTRY AND TRADE

Organisation for Economic Cooperation and Development (OECD), 2 rue Andre Pascal, F-75775 Paris Cedex 16, France, (Telephone in U.S. (202) 785-6323), (Fax in U.S. (202) 785-0350), www.oecd.org; *International Trade by Commodity Statistics (ITCS).*

United Nations Statistics Division, New York, NY 10017, (800) 253-9646, Fax: (212) 963-4116, http://unstats.un.org; *Statistical Yearbook.*

CANADA - PLATINUM PRODUCTION

See CANADA - MINERAL INDUSTRIES

CANADA - POLITICAL SCIENCE

Central Intelligence Agency, Office of Public Affairs, Washington, DC 20505, (703) 482-0623, Fax: (703) 482-1739, www.cia.gov; *The World Factbook.*

International Monetary Fund (IMF), 700 Nineteenth Street, NW, Washington, DC 20431, (202) 623-7000, Fax: (202) 623-4661, www.imf.org; *Government Finance Statistics Yearbook (2008 Edition)* and *International Financial Statistics Yearbook 2007.*

Organisation for Economic Cooperation and Development (OECD), 2 rue Andre Pascal, F-75775 Paris Cedex 16, France, (Telephone in U.S. (202) 785-6323), (Fax in U.S. (202) 785-0350), www.oecd.org; *OECD Economic Outlook 2008* and *Revenue Statistics 1965-2006 - 2007 Edition.*

Palgrave Macmillan Ltd., Houndmills, Basingstoke, Hampshire, RG21 6XS, England, (Telephone in U.S. (888) 330-8477), (Fax in U.S. (800) 672-2054), www.palgrave.com; *The Statesman's Yearbook 2008.*

Taylor and Francis Group, An Informa Business, 2 Park Square, Milton Park, Abingdon, Oxford OX14 4RN, United Kingdom, (Dial from U.S. (212) 216-7800), (Fax from U.S. (212) 564-7854), www.tandf.co.uk; *The Europa World Year Book.*

United Nations Statistics Division, New York, NY 10017, (800) 253-9646, Fax: (212) 963-4116, http://unstats.un.org; *National Accounts Statistics: Compendium of Income Distribution Statistics* and *Statistical Yearbook.*

The World Bank, 1818 H Street, NW, Washington, DC 20433, (202) 473-1000, Fax: (202) 477-6391, www.worldbank.org; *World Development Indicators (WDI) 2008* and *World Development Report 2008.*

CANADA - POPULATION

Central Intelligence Agency, Office of Public Affairs, Washington, DC 20505, (703) 482-0623, Fax: (703) 482-1739, www.cia.gov; *The World Factbook.*

Economics, Statistics Fiscal Analysis Division, Department of Provincial Treasury, PO Box 2000, Charlottetown, Prince Edward Island C1A 7N8, Canada, (Dial from U.S. (902) 368-4050), (Fax from U.S. (902) 368-6575), www.gov.pe.ca/pt/index.php3; *A First Look at the 2001 Census of Population* and *Women in Prince Edward Island: A Statistical Review.*

Economist Intelligence Unit, 111 West 57th Street, New York, NY 10019, (212) 554-0600, Fax: (212) 586-1181, www.eiu.com; *Canada Country Report.*

Euromonitor International, Inc., 224 S. Michigan Avenue, Suite 1500, Chicago, IL 60604, (312) 922-1115, Fax: (312) 922-1157, www.euromonitor.com; *International Marketing Data and Statistics 2008* and *The World Economic Factbook 2008.*

International Labour Office, I.L.O. Publications, 4 route des Morillons, CH-1211 Géneva 22, Switzerland, (Telephone in U.S. (202) 653-7652), (Fax in U.S. (202) 653-7687), www.ilo.org; *Yearbook of Labour Statistics 2006.*

M.E. Sharpe, 80 Business Park Drive, Armonk, NY 10504, (800) 541-6563, Fax: (914) 273-2106, www.mesharpe.com; *The Illustrated Book of World Rankings.*

Northwest Territories Bureau of Statistics, Government of the Northwest Territories, PO Box 1320, Yellowknife, NWT, Canada X1A 2L9, (867) 873-7147, www.stats.gov.nt.ca; *Northwest Territories 2007 ... by the numbers; NWT Community Profiles; NWT Social Indicators; 2006 NWT Socio-Economic Scan; Quarterly Territorial Population Estimates; Summary of NWT Community Statistics - 2007; Summary of NWT Community Statistics - 2007;* and *Vital Statistics.*

Organisation for Economic Cooperation and Development (OECD), 2 rue Andre Pascal, F-75775 Paris Cedex 16, France, (Telephone in U.S. (202) 785-6323), (Fax in U.S. (202) 785-0350), www.oecd.org; *Labour Force Statistics: 1986-2005, 2007 Edition.*

Palgrave Macmillan Ltd., Houndmills, Basingstoke, Hampshire, RG21 6XS, England, (Telephone in U.S. (888) 330-8477), (Fax in U.S. (800) 672-2054), www.palgrave.com; *The Statesman's Yearbook 2008.*

Taylor and Francis Group, An Informa Business, 2 Park Square, Milton Park, Abingdon, Oxford OX14 4RN, United Kingdom, (Dial from U.S. (212) 216-7800), (Fax from U.S. (212) 564-7854), www.tandf.co.uk; *The Europa World Year Book.*

U.S. Department of State (DOS), 2201 C Street NW, Washington, DC 20520, (202) 647-4000, www.state.gov; *World Military Expenditures and Arms Transfers (WMEAT).*

UNESCO Institute for Statistics, C.P. 6128 Succursale Centre-Ville, Montreal, Quebec, H3C 3J7 Canada, (Dial from U.S. (514) 343-6880), (Fax from U.S. (514) 343 6882), www.uis.unesco.org; *Statistical Tables.*

United Nations Food and Agricultural Organization (FAO), Viale delle Terme di Caracalla, 00100 Rome, Italy, (Dial from U.S. (202) 653-2400), (Fax from U.S. (202) 653 5760), www.fao.org; *FAO Production Yearbook 2002.*

United Nations Statistics Division, New York, NY 10017, (800) 253-9646, Fax: (212) 963-4116, http://unstats.un.org; *Demographic Yearbook; Human Development Report 2006; Statistical Yearbook; Trends in Europe and North America: The Statistical Yearbook of the ECE 2005;* and *World Statistics Pocketbook.*

The World Bank, 1818 H Street, NW, Washington, DC 20433, (202) 473-1000, Fax: (202) 477-6391, www.worldbank.org; *Canada; The World Bank Atlas 2003-2004;* and *World Development Report 2008.*

World Health Organization (WHO), Avenue Appia 20, 1211 Geneve 27, Switzerland, (Telephone in U.S. (212) 331-9081), www.who.int; *World Health Report 2006.*

CANADA - POPULATION DENSITY

Central Intelligence Agency, Office of Public Affairs, Washington, DC 20505, (703) 482-0623, Fax: (703) 482-1739, www.cia.gov; *The World Factbook.*

Euromonitor International, Inc., 224 S. Michigan Avenue, Suite 1500, Chicago, IL 60604, (312) 922-1115, Fax: (312) 922-1157, www.euromonitor.com; *International Marketing Data and Statistics 2008* and *The World Economic Factbook 2008.*

M.E. Sharpe, 80 Business Park Drive, Armonk, NY 10504, (800) 541-6563, Fax: (914) 273-2106, www.mesharpe.com; *The Illustrated Book of World Rankings.*

Palgrave Macmillan Ltd., Houndmills, Basingstoke, Hampshire, RG21 6XS, England, (Telephone in U.S. (888) 330-8477), (Fax in U.S. (800) 672-2054), www.palgrave.com; *The Statesman's Yearbook 2008.*

Taylor and Francis Group, An Informa Business, 2 Park Square, Milton Park, Abingdon, Oxford OX14 4RN, United Kingdom, (Dial from U.S. (212) 216-7800), (Fax from U.S. (212) 564-7854), www.tandf.co.uk; *The Europa World Year Book.*

UNESCO Institute for Statistics, C.P. 6128 Succursale Centre-Ville, Montreal, Quebec, H3C 3J7 Canada, (Dial from U.S. (514) 343-6880), (Fax from U.S. (514) 343 6882), www.uis.unesco.org; *Statistical Tables.*

United Nations Food and Agricultural Organization (FAO), Viale delle Terme di Caracalla, 00100 Rome, Italy, (Dial from U.S. (202) 653-2400), (Fax from U.S. (202) 653 5760), www.fao.org; *The State of Food and Agriculture (SOFA) 2006.*

United Nations Statistics Division, New York, NY 10017, (800) 253-9646, Fax: (212) 963-4116, http://unstats.un.org; *Statistical Yearbook* and *Trends in Europe and North America: The Statistical Yearbook of the ECE 2005.*

The World Bank, 1818 H Street, NW, Washington, DC 20433, (202) 473-1000, Fax: (202) 477-6391, www.worldbank.org; *Canada* and *World Development Report 2008.*

CANADA - POSTAL SERVICE

M.E. Sharpe, 80 Business Park Drive, Armonk, NY 10504, (800) 541-6563, Fax: (914) 273-2106, www.mesharpe.com; *The Illustrated Book of World Rankings.*

Palgrave Macmillan Ltd., Houndmills, Basingstoke, Hampshire, RG21 6XS, England, (Telephone in U.S. (888) 330-8477), (Fax in U.S. (800) 672-2054), www.palgrave.com; *The Statesman's Yearbook 2008.*

United Nations Statistics Division, New York, NY 10017, (800) 253-9646, Fax: (212) 963-4116, http://unstats.un.org; *Statistical Yearbook* and *Trends in Europe and North America: The Statistical Yearbook of the ECE 2005.*

CANADA - POWER RESOURCES

Euromonitor International, Inc., 224 S. Michigan Avenue, Suite 1500, Chicago, IL 60604, (312) 922-1115, Fax: (312) 922-1157, www.euromonitor.com; *International Marketing Data and Statistics 2008; The World Economic Factbook 2008;* and *World Marketing Data and Statistics.*

M.E. Sharpe, 80 Business Park Drive, Armonk, NY 10504, (800) 541-6563, Fax: (914) 273-2106, www.mesharpe.com; *The Illustrated Book of World Rankings.*

Organisation for Economic Cooperation and Development (OECD), 2 rue Andre Pascal, F-75775 Paris Cedex 16, France, (Telephone in U.S. (202) 785-6323), (Fax in U.S. (202) 785-0350), www.oecd.org; *Coal Information: 2007 Edition; Energy Statistics of OECD Countries* (2007 Edition); *Key Environmental Indicators 2004; Oil Information 2006 Edition;* and *World Energy Outlook 2007.*

Palgrave Macmillan Ltd., Houndmills, Basingstoke, Hampshire, RG21 6XS, England, (Telephone in U.S. (888) 330-8477), (Fax in U.S. (800) 672-2054), www.palgrave.com; *The Statesman's Yearbook 2008.*

Platts, 2 Penn Plaza, 25th Floor, New York, NY 10121-2298, (212) 904-3070, www.platts.com; *Emissions Daily* and *Energy Economist.*

U.S. Department of Energy (DOE), Energy Information Administration (EIA), 1000 Independence Avenue, SW, Washington, DC 20585, (202) 586-8800, www.eia.doe.gov; *International Energy Annual 2004* and *International Energy Outlook 2006.*

United Nations Statistics Division, New York, NY 10017, (800) 253-9646, Fax: (212) 963-4116, http://unstats.un.org; *Energy Statistics Yearbook 2003; Human Development Report 2006; Statistical Yearbook; Trends in Europe and North America: The Statistical Yearbook of the ECE 2005;* and *World Statistics Pocketbook.*

The World Bank, 1818 H Street, NW, Washington, DC 20433, (202) 473-1000, Fax: (202) 477-6391, www.worldbank.org; *The World Bank Atlas 2003-2004* and *World Development Report 2008.*

CANADA - PRICES

Euromonitor International, Inc., 224 S. Michigan Avenue, Suite 1500, Chicago, IL 60604, (312) 922-1115, Fax: (312) 922-1157, www.euromonitor.com; *World Marketing Data and Statistics.*

International Labour Office, I.L.O. Publications, 4 route des Morillons, CH-1211 Geneva 22, Switzerland, (Telephone in U.S. (202) 653-7652), (Fax in U.S. (202) 653-7687), www.ilo.org; *Yearbook of Labour Statistics 2006.*

International Lead and Zinc Study Group (ILZSG), Rua Almirante Barroso 38, 5th Floor, Lisbon 1000 - 013, Portugal, www.ilzsg.org; Interactive Statistical Database.

International Monetary Fund (IMF), 700 Nineteenth Street, NW, Washington, DC 20431, (202) 623-7000, Fax: (202) 623-4661, www.imf.org; *International Financial Statistics Yearbook 2007.*

M.E. Sharpe, 80 Business Park Drive, Armonk, NY 10504, (800) 541-6563, Fax: (914) 273-2106, www.mesharpe.com; *The Illustrated Book of World Rankings.*

Organisation for Economic Cooperation and Development (OECD), 2 rue Andre Pascal, F-75775 Paris Cedex 16, France, (Telephone in U.S. (202) 785-6323), (Fax in U.S. (202) 785-0350), www.oecd.org; *Indicators of Industrial Activity; Iron and Steel Industry in 2004 (2006 Edition); OECD Economic Outlook 2008;* and *OECD Main Economic Indicators (MEI).*

Technical Association of the Pulp and Paper Industry (TAPPI), 15 Technology Parkway South, Norcross, GA 30092, (770) 446-1400, Fax: (770) 446-6947, www.tappi.org; *TAPPI Annual Report.*

United Nations Food and Agricultural Organization (FAO), Viale delle Terme di Caracalla, 00100 Rome, Italy, (Dial from U.S. (202) 653-2400), (Fax from U.S. (202) 653 5760), www.fao.org; *FAO Production Yearbook 2002* and *The State of Food and Agriculture (SOFA) 2006.*

The World Bank, 1818 H Street, NW, Washington, DC 20433, (202) 473-1000, Fax: (202) 477-6391, www.worldbank.org; *Canada.*

World Bureau of Metal Statistics (WBMS), 27a High Street, Ware, Hertfordshire, SG12 9BA, United Kingdom, www.world-bureau.com; *World Flow Charts* and *World Metal Statistics.*

CANADA - PROFESSIONS

United Nations Statistics Division, New York, NY 10017, (800) 253-9646, Fax: (212) 963-4116, http://unstats.un.org; *Statistical Yearbook.*

CANADA - PROPERTY TAX

International Monetary Fund (IMF), 700 Nineteenth Street, NW, Washington, DC 20431, (202) 623-7000, Fax: (202) 623-4661, www.imf.org; *Government Finance Statistics Yearbook (2008 Edition).*

Organisation for Economic Cooperation and Development (OECD), 2 rue Andre Pascal, F-75775 Paris Cedex 16, France, (Telephone in U.S. (202) 785-6323), (Fax in U.S. (202) 785-0350), www.oecd.org; *Revenue Statistics 1965-2006 - 2007 Edition.*

CANADA - PUBLIC HEALTH

British Columbia Vital Statistics Agency, PO Box 9657 STN PROV GOVT, Victoria BC V8W 9P3, Canada, (Dial from U.S. (250) 952-2681), (Fax from U.S. (250) 952-2527), www.vs.gov.bc.ca; *Health Status Registry Report, 2005* and *Regional Analysis of Health Statistics for Status Indians in British Columbia, 1992-2002.*

Euromonitor International, Inc., 224 S. Michigan Avenue, Suite 1500, Chicago, IL 60604, (312) 922-1115, Fax: (312) 922-1157, www.euromonitor.com; *World Health Databook 2007/2008* and *World Marketing Data and Statistics.*

European Centre for Disease Prevention and Control (ECDC), 171 83 Stockholm, Sweden, www.ecdc.europa.eu; *Emergence of Clostridium Difficile-Associated Disease in Canada, the United States of America and Europe.*

International Monetary Fund (IMF), 700 Nineteenth Street, NW, Washington, DC 20431, (202) 623-7000, Fax: (202) 623-4661, www.imf.org; *Government Finance Statistics Yearbook (2008 Edition).*

M.E. Sharpe, 80 Business Park Drive, Armonk, NY 10504, (800) 541-6563, Fax: (914) 273-2106, www.mesharpe.com; *The Illustrated Book of World Rankings.*

Organisation for Economic Cooperation and Development (OECD), 2 rue Andre Pascal, F-75775 Paris Cedex 16, France, (Telephone in U.S. (202) 785-6323), (Fax in U.S. (202) 785-0350), www.oecd.org; *Health at a Glance 2007 - OECD Indicators.*

Palgrave Macmillan Ltd., Houndmills, Basingstoke, Hampshire, RG21 6XS, England, (Telephone in U.S. (888) 330-8477), (Fax in U.S. (800) 672-2054), www.palgrave.com; *The Statesman's Yearbook 2008.*

UNICEF, 3 United Nations Plaza, New York, NY 10017, (800) 253-9646, Fax: (212) 887-7465, www.unicef.org; *The State of the World's Children 2008.*

United Nations Statistics Division, New York, NY 10017, (800) 253-9646, Fax: (212) 963-4116, http://unstats.un.org; *Human Development Report 2006; Statistical Yearbook;* and *Trends in Europe and North America: The Statistical Yearbook of the ECE 2005.*

The World Bank, 1818 H Street, NW, Washington, DC 20433, (202) 473-1000, Fax: (202) 477-6391, www.worldbank.org; *Canada* and *World Development Report 2008.*

World Health Organization (WHO), Avenue Appia 20, 1211 Geneve 27, Switzerland, (Telephone in U.S. (212) 331-9081), www.who.int; The WHO Global Atlas of Infectious Diseases and *World Health Report 2006.*

CANADA - PUBLISHERS AND PUBLISHING

Organisation for Economic Cooperation and Development (OECD), 2 rue Andre Pascal, F-75775 Paris Cedex 16, France, (Telephone in U.S. (202) 785-6323), (Fax in U.S. (202) 785-0350), www.oecd.org; *Indicators of Industrial Activity.*

Palgrave Macmillan Ltd., Houndmills, Basingstoke, Hampshire, RG21 6XS, England, (Telephone in U.S. (888) 330-8477), (Fax in U.S. (800) 672-2054), www.palgrave.com; *The Statesman's Yearbook 2008.*

UNESCO Institute for Statistics, C.P. 6128 Succursale Centre-Ville, Montreal, Quebec, H3C 3J7 Canada, (Dial from U.S. (514) 343-6880), (Fax from U.S. (514) 343 6882), www.uis.unesco.org; *Statistical Tables.*

United Nations Statistics Division, New York, NY 10017, (800) 253-9646, Fax: (212) 963-4116, http://unstats.un.org; *Trends in Europe and North America: The Statistical Yearbook of the ECE 2005.*

CANADA - RADIO - RECEIVERS AND RECEPTION

Palgrave Macmillan Ltd., Houndmills, Basingstoke, Hampshire, RG21 6XS, England, (Telephone in U.S. (888) 330-8477), (Fax in U.S. (800) 672-2054), www.palgrave.com; *The Statesman's Yearbook 2008.*

United Nations Statistics Division, New York, NY 10017, (800) 253-9646, Fax: (212) 963-4116, http://unstats.un.org; *Statistical Yearbook.*

CANADA - RAILROADS

Association of American Railroads (AAR), 50 F Street, NW, Washington, DC 20001-1564, (202) 639-2100, www.aar.org; *Railroad Equipment Report 2006.*

Jane's Information Group, 110 North Royal Street, Suite 200, Alexandria, VA 22314, (703) 683-3700, Fax: (800) 836-0297, www.janes.com; *Jane's World Railways.*

Palgrave Macmillan Ltd., Houndmills, Basingstoke, Hampshire, RG21 6XS, England, (Telephone in U.S. (888) 330-8477), (Fax in U.S. (800) 672-2054), www.palgrave.com; *The Statesman's Yearbook 2008.*

Taylor and Francis Group, An Informa Business, 2 Park Square, Milton Park, Abingdon, Oxford OX14 4RN, United Kingdom, (Dial from U.S. (212) 216-7800), (Fax from U.S. (212) 564-7854), www.tandf.co.uk; *The Europa World Year Book.*

United Nations Statistics Division, New York, NY 10017, (800) 253-9646, Fax: (212) 963-4116, http://unstats.un.org; *Annual Bulletin of Transport Statistics for Europe and North America 2004; Statistical Yearbook;* and *Trends in Europe and North America: The Statistical Yearbook of the ECE 2005.*

CANADA - RELIGION

Central Intelligence Agency, Office of Public Affairs, Washington, DC 20505, (703) 482-0623, Fax: (703) 482-1739, www.cia.gov; *The World Factbook.*

M.E. Sharpe, 80 Business Park Drive, Armonk, NY 10504, (800) 541-6563, Fax: (914) 273-2106, www.mesharpe.com; *The Illustrated Book of World Rankings.*

Palgrave Macmillan Ltd., Houndmills, Basingstoke, Hampshire, RG21 6XS, England, (Telephone in U.S. (888) 330-8477), (Fax in U.S. (800) 672-2054), www.palgrave.com; *The Statesman's Yearbook 2008.*

CANADA - RESERVES (ACCOUNTING)

Euromonitor International, Inc., 224 S. Michigan Avenue, Suite 1500, Chicago, IL 60604, (312) 922-1115, Fax: (312) 922-1157, www.euromonitor.com; *International Marketing Data and Statistics 2008.*

Organisation for Economic Cooperation and Development (OECD), 2 rue Andre Pascal, F-75775 Paris Cedex 16, France, (Telephone in U.S. (202) 785-6323), (Fax in U.S. (202) 785-0350), www.oecd.org; *Financial Market Trends: OECD Periodical* and *OECD Economic Outlook 2008.*

The World Bank, 1818 H Street, NW, Washington, DC 20433, (202) 473-1000, Fax: (202) 477-6391, www.worldbank.org; *World Development Indicators (WDI) 2008.*

CANADA - RETAIL TRADE

Euromonitor International, Inc., 224 S. Michigan Avenue, Suite 1500, Chicago, IL 60604, (312) 922-1115, Fax: (312) 922-1157, www.euromonitor.com; *World Marketing Data and Statistics.*

United Nations Statistics Division, New York, NY 10017, (800) 253-9646, Fax: (212) 963-4116, http://unstats.un.org; *Statistical Yearbook.*

CANADA - RICE PRODUCTION

See CANADA - CROPS

CANADA - ROADS

Central Intelligence Agency, Office of Public Affairs, Washington, DC 20505, (703) 482-0623, Fax: (703) 482-1739, www.cia.gov; *The World Factbook.*

International Road Federation (IFR), Madison Place, 500 Montgomery Street, 5th Floor, Alexandria, VA 22314, (703) 535-1001, Fax: (703) 535-1007, www.irfnet.org; *World Road Statistics 2006.*

Palgrave Macmillan Ltd., Houndmills, Basingstoke, Hampshire, RG21 6XS, England, (Telephone in U.S. (888) 330-8477), (Fax in U.S. (800) 672-2054), www.palgrave.com; *The Statesman's Yearbook 2008.*

United Nations Statistics Division, New York, NY 10017, (800) 253-9646, Fax: (212) 963-4116, http://unstats.un.org; *Annual Bulletin of Transport Statistics for Europe and North America 2004* and *Trends in Europe and North America: The Statistical Yearbook of the ECE 2005.*

CANADA - RUBBER INDUSTRY AND TRADE

International Rubber Study Group (IRSG), 1st Floor, Heron House, 109/115 Wembley Hill Road, Wembley, Middlesex HA9 8DA, United Kingdom, www.rubberstudy.com; *Rubber Statistical Bulletin; Summary of World Rubber Statistics 2005; World Rubber Statistics Handbook (Volume 6, 1975-2001);* and *World Rubber Statistics Historic Handbook.*

M.E. Sharpe, 80 Business Park Drive, Armonk, NY 10504, (800) 541-6563, Fax: (914) 273-2106, www.mesharpe.com; *The Illustrated Book of World Rankings.*

Organisation for Economic Cooperation and Development (OECD), 2 rue Andre Pascal, F-75775 Paris Cedex 16, France, (Telephone in U.S. (202) 785-6323), (Fax in U.S. (202) 785-0350), www.oecd.org; *International Trade by Commodity Statistics (ITCS).*

United Nations Statistics Division, New York, NY 10017, (800) 253-9646, Fax: (212) 963-4116, http://unstats.un.org; *Statistical Yearbook.*

CANADA - RYE PRODUCTION

See CANADA - CROPS

CANADA - SALT PRODUCTION

See CANADA - MINERAL INDUSTRIES

CANADA - SHEEP

See CANADA - LIVESTOCK

CANADA - SHIPBUILDING

Organisation for Economic Cooperation and Development (OECD), 2 rue Andre Pascal, F-75775 Paris Cedex 16, France, (Telephone in U.S. (202) 785-6323), (Fax in U.S. (202) 785-0350), www.oecd.org; *Indicators of Industrial Activity.*

CANADA - SHIPPING

Lloyd's Register - Fairplay, 8410 N.W. 53rd Terrace, Suite 207, Miami FL 33166, (305) 718-9929, Fax: (305) 718-9663, www.lrfairplay.com; *Register of Ships 2007-2008; World Casualty Statistics 2007; World Fleet Statistics 2006; World Marine Propulsion Report 2006-2010; World Shipbuilding Statistics 2007;* and The World Shipping Encyclopaedia.

Organisation for Economic Cooperation and Development (OECD), 2 rue Andre Pascal, F-75775 Paris Cedex 16, France, (Telephone in U.S. (202) 785-

6323), (Fax in U.S. (202) 785-0350), www.oecd.org; *Statistics on Ship Production, Exports and Orders in 2004.*

Palgrave Macmillan Ltd., Houndmills, Basingstoke, Hampshire, RG21 6XS, England, (Telephone in U.S. (888) 330-8477), (Fax in U.S. (800) 672-2054), www.palgrave.com; *The Statesman's Yearbook 2008.*

Taylor and Francis Group, An Informa Business, 2 Park Square, Milton Park, Abingdon, Oxford OX14 4RN, United Kingdom, (Dial from U.S. (212) 216-7800), (Fax from U.S. (212) 564-7854), www.tandf.co.uk; *The Europa World Year Book.*

U.S. Department of Transportation (DOT), Maritime Administration (MARAD), West Building, Southeast Federal Center, 1200 New Jersey Avenue, SE, Washington, DC 20590, (800) 99-MARAD, www.marad.dot.gov; *World Merchant Fleet 2005.*

United Nations Statistics Division, New York, NY 10017, (800) 253-9646, Fax: (212) 963-4116, http://unstats.un.org; *Statistical Yearbook.*

CANADA - SILVER PRODUCTION

See CANADA - MINERAL INDUSTRIES

CANADA - SOCIAL ECOLOGY

M.E. Sharpe, 80 Business Park Drive, Armonk, NY 10504, (800) 541-6563, Fax: (914) 273-2106, www.mesharpe.com; *The Illustrated Book of World Rankings.*

United Nations Statistics Division, New York, NY 10017, (800) 253-9646, Fax: (212) 963-4116, http://unstats.un.org; *World Statistics Pocketbook.*

CANADA - SOCIAL SECURITY

International Monetary Fund (IMF), 700 Nineteenth Street, NW, Washington, DC 20431, (202) 623-7000, Fax: (202) 623-4661, www.imf.org; *Government Finance Statistics Yearbook (2008 Edition).*

Organisation for Economic Cooperation and Development (OECD), 2 rue Andre Pascal, F-75775 Paris Cedex 16, France, (Telephone in U.S. (202) 785-6323), (Fax in U.S. (202) 785-0350), www.oecd.org; *Revenue Statistics 1965-2006 - 2007 Edition.*

Palgrave Macmillan Ltd., Houndmills, Basingstoke, Hampshire, RG21 6XS, England, (Telephone in U.S. (888) 330-8477), (Fax in U.S. (800) 672-2054), www.palgrave.com; *The Statesman's Yearbook 2008.*

United Nations Statistics Division, New York, NY 10017, (800) 253-9646, Fax: (212) 963-4116, http://unstats.un.org; *National Accounts Statistics: Compendium of Income Distribution Statistics.*

CANADA - SOYBEAN PRODUCTION

See CANADA - CROPS

CANADA - STEEL PRODUCTION

See CANADA - MINERAL INDUSTRIES

CANADA - SUGAR PRODUCTION

See CANADA - CROPS

CANADA - SULPHUR PRODUCTION

See CANADA - MINERAL INDUSTRIES

CANADA - TAXATION

International Monetary Fund (IMF), 700 Nineteenth Street, NW, Washington, DC 20431, (202) 623-7000, Fax: (202) 623-4661, www.imf.org; *Government Finance Statistics Yearbook (2008 Edition).*

International Road Federation (IFR), Madison Place, 500 Montgomery Street, 5th Floor, Alexandria, VA 22314, (703) 535-1001, Fax: (703) 535-1007, www.irfnet.org; *World Road Statistics 2006.*

Organisation for Economic Cooperation and Development (OECD), 2 rue Andre Pascal, F-75775 Paris Cedex 16, France, (Telephone in U.S. (202) 785-6323), (Fax in U.S. (202) 785-0350), www.oecd.org; *Revenue Statistics 1965-2006 - 2007 Edition.*

Palgrave Macmillan Ltd., Houndmills, Basingstoke, Hampshire, RG21 6XS, England, (Telephone in U.S. (888) 330-8477), (Fax in U.S. (800) 672-2054), www.palgrave.com; *The Statesman's Yearbook 2008.*

Taylor and Francis Group, An Informa Business, 2 Park Square, Milton Park, Abingdon, Oxford OX14 4RN, United Kingdom, (Dial from U.S. (212) 216-7800), (Fax from U.S. (212) 564-7854), www.tandf.co.uk; *The Europa World Year Book.*

The World Bank, 1818 H Street, NW, Washington, DC 20433, (202) 473-1000, Fax: (202) 477-6391, www.worldbank.org; *World Development Indicators (WDI) 2008.*

CANADA - TELEPHONE

Central Intelligence Agency, Office of Public Affairs, Washington, DC 20505, (703) 482-0623, Fax: (703) 482-1739, www.cia.gov; *The World Factbook.*

International Telecommunication Union (ITU), Place des Nations, 1211 Geneva 20, Switzerland, www.itu.int; World Telecommunication Indicators Database.

Palgrave Macmillan Ltd., Houndmills, Basingstoke, Hampshire, RG21 6XS, England, (Telephone in U.S. (888) 330-8477), (Fax in U.S. (800) 672-2054), www.palgrave.com; *The Statesman's Yearbook 2008.*

Taylor and Francis Group, An Informa Business, 2 Park Square, Milton Park, Abingdon, Oxford OX14 4RN, United Kingdom, (Dial from U.S. (212) 216-7800), (Fax from U.S. (212) 564-7854), www.tandf.co.uk; *The Europa World Year Book.*

United Nations Statistics Division, New York, NY 10017, (800) 253-9646, Fax: (212) 963-4116, http://unstats.un.org; *Statistical Yearbook; Trends in Europe and North America: The Statistical Yearbook of the ECE 2005;* and *World Statistics Pocketbook.*

CANADA - TELEVISION - RECEIVERS AND RECEPTION

United Nations Statistics Division, New York, NY 10017, (800) 253-9646, Fax: (212) 963-4116, http://unstats.un.org; *Statistical Yearbook.*

CANADA - TEXTILE INDUSTRY

Euromonitor International, Inc., 224 S. Michigan Avenue, Suite 1500, Chicago, IL 60604, (312) 922-1115, Fax: (312) 922-1157, www.euromonitor.com; *World Marketing Data and Statistics.*

M.E. Sharpe, 80 Business Park Drive, Armonk, NY 10504, (800) 541-6563, Fax: (914) 273-2106, www.mesharpe.com; *The Illustrated Book of World Rankings.*

Organisation for Economic Cooperation and Development (OECD), 2 rue Andre Pascal, F-75775 Paris Cedex 16, France, (Telephone in U.S. (202) 785-6323), (Fax in U.S. (202) 785-0350), www.oecd.org; *Indicators of Industrial Activity; International Trade by Commodity Statistics (ITCS); A New World Map in Textiles and Clothing: Adjusting to Change; 2005 OECD Agricultural Outlook Tables, 1970-2014;* and STructural ANalysis (STAN) database.

Palgrave Macmillan Ltd., Houndmills, Basingstoke, Hampshire, RG21 6XS, England, (Telephone in U.S. (888) 330-8477), (Fax in U.S. (800) 672-2054), www.palgrave.com; *The Statesman's Yearbook 2008.*

United Nations Statistics Division, New York, NY 10017, (800) 253-9646, Fax: (212) 963-4116, http://unstats.un.org; *Statistical Yearbook.*

CANADA - THEATER

UNESCO Institute for Statistics, C.P. 6128 Succursale Centre-Ville, Montreal, Quebec, H3C 3J7 Canada, (Dial from U.S. (514) 343-6880), (Fax from U.S. (514) 343 6882), www.uis.unesco.org; *Statistical Tables.*

CANADA - TIN PRODUCTION

See CANADA - MINERAL INDUSTRIES

CANADA - TIRE INDUSTRY

United Nations Statistics Division, New York, NY 10017, (800) 253-9646, Fax: (212) 963-4116, http://unstats.un.org; *Statistical Yearbook.*

CANADA - TOBACCO INDUSTRY

Foreign Agricultural Service (FAS), U.S. Department of Agriculture (USDA), 1400 Independence Avenue, SW, Washington, DC 20250, (202) 720-3935, www.fas.usda.gov; *Tobacco: World Markets and Trade.*

M.E. Sharpe, 80 Business Park Drive, Armonk, NY 10504, (800) 541-6563, Fax: (914) 273-2106, www.mesharpe.com; *The Illustrated Book of World Rankings.*

Organisation for Economic Cooperation and Development (OECD), 2 rue Andre Pascal, F-75775 Paris Cedex 16, France, (Telephone in U.S. (202) 785-6323), (Fax in U.S. (202) 785-0350), www.oecd.org; *Indicators of Industrial Activity; International Trade by Commodity Statistics (ITCS);* and STructural ANalysis (STAN) database.

United Nations Statistics Division, New York, NY 10017, (800) 253-9646, Fax: (212) 963-4116, http://unstats.un.org; *Statistical Yearbook.*

CANADA - TOURISM

Economics, Statistics Fiscal Analysis Division, Department of Provincial Treasury, PO Box 2000, Charlottetown, Prince Edward Island C1A 7N8, Canada, (Dial from U.S. (902) 368-4050), (Fax from U.S. (902) 368-6575), www.gov.pe.ca/pt/index.php3; *Tourism Indicators: 2007 Annual Review.*

Euromonitor International, Inc., 224 S. Michigan Avenue, Suite 1500, Chicago, IL 60604, (312) 922-1115, Fax: (312) 922-1157, www.euromonitor.com; *The World Economic Factbook 2008* and *World Marketing Data and Statistics.*

M.E. Sharpe, 80 Business Park Drive, Armonk, NY 10504, (800) 541-6563, Fax: (914) 273-2106, www.mesharpe.com; *The Illustrated Book of World Rankings.*

Organisation for Economic Cooperation and Development (OECD), 2 rue Andre Pascal, F-75775 Paris Cedex 16, France, (Telephone in U.S. (202) 785-6323), (Fax in U.S. (202) 785-0350), www.oecd.org; *Household, Tourism, Travel: Trends, Environmental Impacts and Policy Responses.*

Taylor and Francis Group, An Informa Business, 2 Park Square, Milton Park, Abingdon, Oxford OX14 4RN, United Kingdom, (Dial from U.S. (212) 216-7800), (Fax from U.S. (212) 564-7854), www.tandf.co.uk; *The Europa World Year Book.*

United Nations Statistics Division, New York, NY 10017, (800) 253-9646, Fax: (212) 963-4116, http://unstats.un.org; *Statistical Yearbook* and *Trends in Europe and North America: The Statistical Yearbook of the ECE 2005.*

United Nations World Tourism Organization (UNWTO), Capitan Haya 42, 28020 Madrid, Spain, www.world-tourism.org; *The Canadian Ecotourism Market; Tourism Market Trends 2004 - Americas;* and *Yearbook of Tourism Statistics.*

The World Bank, 1818 H Street, NW, Washington, DC 20433, (202) 473-1000, Fax: (202) 477-6391, www.worldbank.org; *Canada.*

CANADA - TRADE

See CANADA - INTERNATIONAL TRADE

CANADA - TRANSPORTATION

Central Intelligence Agency, Office of Public Affairs, Washington, DC 20505, (703) 482-0623, Fax: (703) 482-1739, www.cia.gov; *The World Factbook.*

Euromonitor International, Inc., 224 S. Michigan Avenue, Suite 1500, Chicago, IL 60604, (312) 922-1115, Fax: (312) 922-1157, www.euromonitor.com; *International Marketing Data and Statistics 2008* and *World Marketing Data and Statistics.*

M.E. Sharpe, 80 Business Park Drive, Armonk, NY 10504, (800) 541-6563, Fax: (914) 273-2106, www.mesharpe.com; *The Illustrated Book of World Rankings.*

Palgrave Macmillan Ltd., Houndmills, Basingstoke, Hampshire, RG21 6XS, England, (Telephone in U.S. (888) 330-8477), (Fax in U.S. (800) 672-2054), www.palgrave.com; *The Statesman's Yearbook 2008.*

Taylor and Francis Group, An Informa Business, 2 Park Square, Milton Park, Abingdon, Oxford OX14 4RN, United Kingdom, (Dial from U.S. (212) 216-7800), (Fax from U.S. (212) 564-7854), www.tandf.co.uk; *The Europa World Year Book.*

United Nations Statistics Division, New York, NY 10017, (800) 253-9646, Fax: (212) 963-4116, http://unstats.un.org; *Human Development Report 2006* and *Trends in Europe and North America: The Statistical Yearbook of the ECE 2005.*

The World Bank, 1818 H Street, NW, Washington, DC 20433, (202) 473-1000, Fax: (202) 477-6391, www.worldbank.org; *Canada.*

CANADA - TURKEYS

See CANADA - LIVESTOCK

CANADA - UNEMPLOYMENT

Central Intelligence Agency, Office of Public Affairs, Washington, DC 20505, (703) 482-0623, Fax: (703) 482-1739, www.cia.gov; *The World Factbook.*

Euromonitor International, Inc., 224 S. Michigan Avenue, Suite 1500, Chicago, IL 60604, (312) 922-1115, Fax: (312) 922-1157, www.euromonitor.com; *International Marketing Data and Statistics 2008.*

International Labour Office, I.L.O. Publications, 4 route des Morillons, CH-1211 Geneva 22, Switzerland, (Telephone in U.S. (202) 653-7652), (Fax in U.S. (202) 653-7687), www.ilo.org; *Yearbook of Labour Statistics 2006.*

Organisation for Economic Cooperation and Development (OECD), 2 rue Andre Pascal, F-75775 Paris Cedex 16, France, (Telephone in U.S. (202) 785-6323), (Fax in U.S. (202) 785-0350), www.oecd.org; *Labour Force Statistics: 1986-2005, 2007 Edition; OECD Composite Leading Indicators (CLIs), Updated September 2007; OECD Economic Outlook 2008;* and *OECD Employment Outlook 2007.*

Palgrave Macmillan Ltd., Houndmills, Basingstoke, Hampshire, RG21 6XS, England, (Telephone in U.S. (888) 330-8477), (Fax in U.S. (800) 672-2054), www.palgrave.com; *The Statesman's Yearbook 2008.*

United Nations Statistics Division, New York, NY 10017, (800) 253-9646, Fax: (212) 963-4116, http://unstats.un.org; *Statistical Yearbook* and *Trends in Europe and North America: The Statistical Yearbook of the ECE 2005.*

CANADA - URANIUM PRODUCTION AND CONSUMPTION

See CANADA - MINERAL INDUSTRIES

CANADA - VITAL STATISTICS

Euromonitor International, Inc., 224 S. Michigan Avenue, Suite 1500, Chicago, IL 60604, (312) 922-1115, Fax: (312) 922-1157, www.euromonitor.com; *International Marketing Data and Statistics 2008.*

Northwest Territories Bureau of Statistics, Government of the Northwest Territories, PO Box 1320, Yellowknife, NWT, Canada X1A 2L9, (867) 873-7147, www.stats.gov.nt.ca; *Northwest Territories 2007 ... by the numbers; NWT Community Profiles; NWT Social Indicators; 2006 NWT Socio-Economic Scan; Quarterly Territorial Population Estimates; Summary of NWT Community Statistics - 2007; Summary of NWT Community Statistics - 2007;* and *Vital Statistics.*

Palgrave Macmillan Ltd., Houndmills, Basingstoke, Hampshire, RG21 6XS, England, (Telephone in U.S. (888) 330-8477), (Fax in U.S. (800) 672-2054), www.palgrave.com; *The Statesman's Yearbook 2008.*

United Nations Statistics Division, New York, NY 10017, (800) 253-9646, Fax: (212) 963-4116, http://unstats.un.org; *Statistical Yearbook.*

The Vital Statistics Agency, 254 Portage Avenue, Winnipeg, MB R3C 0B6, Canada, (Dial from U.S. (204) 945-3701), (Fax from U.S. (204) 948-3128), http://web2.gov.mb.ca/cca/vital/; Vital Statistics Database.

World Health Organization (WHO), Avenue Appia 20, 1211 Geneve 27, Switzerland, (Telephone in U.S. (212) 331-9081), www.who.int; *World Health Report 2006.*

CANADA - WAGES

International Labour Office, I.L.O. Publications, 4 route des Morillons, CH-1211 Geneva 22, Switzerland, (Telephone in U.S. (202) 653-7652), (Fax in U.S. (202) 653-7687), www.ilo.org; *Yearbook of Labour Statistics 2006.*

Organisation for Economic Cooperation and Development (OECD), 2 rue Andre Pascal, F-75775 Paris Cedex 16, France, (Telephone in U.S. (202) 785-6323), (Fax in U.S. (202) 785-0350), www.oecd.org; *ICT Sector Data and Metadata by Country; OECD Economic Outlook 2008; OECD Main Economic Indicators (MEI);* and STructural ANalysis (STAN) database.

United Nations Statistics Division, New York, NY 10017, (800) 253-9646, Fax: (212) 963-4116, http://unstats.un.org; *Statistical Yearbook.*

The World Bank, 1818 H Street, NW, Washington, DC 20433, (202) 473-1000, Fax: (202) 477-6391, www.worldbank.org; *Canada.*

CANADA - WEATHER

See CANADA - CLIMATE

CANADA - WELFARE STATE

Palgrave Macmillan Ltd., Houndmills, Basingstoke, Hampshire, RG21 6XS, England, (Telephone in U.S. (888) 330-8477), (Fax in U.S. (800) 672-2054), www.palgrave.com; *The Statesman's Yearbook 2008.*

CANADA - WHALES

See CANADA - FISHERIES

CANADA - WHEAT PRODUCTION

See CANADA - CROPS

CANADA - WHOLESALE PRICE INDEXES

United Nations Statistics Division, New York, NY 10017, (800) 253-9646, Fax: (212) 963-4116, http://unstats.un.org; *Statistical Yearbook.*

CANADA - WHOLESALE TRADE

United Nations Statistics Division, New York, NY 10017, (800) 253-9646, Fax: (212) 963-4116, http://unstats.un.org; *Statistical Yearbook.*

CANADA - WINE PRODUCTION

See CANADA - BEVERAGE INDUSTRY

CANADA - WOOD AND WOOD PULP

See CANADA - FORESTS AND FORESTRY

CANADA - WOOD PRODUCTS

Organisation for Economic Cooperation and Development (OECD), 2 rue Andre Pascal, F-75775 Paris Cedex 16, France, (Telephone in U.S. (202) 785-6323), (Fax in U.S. (202) 785-0350), www.oecd.org; *International Trade by Commodity Statistics (ITCS)* and STructural ANalysis (STAN) database.

CANADA - WOOL PRODUCTION

See CANADA - TEXTILE INDUSTRY

CANADA - YARN PRODUCTION

See CANADA - TEXTILE INDUSTRY

CANADA - ZINC AND ZINC ORE

See CANADA - MINERAL INDUSTRIES

CANADA - ZOOS

UNESCO Institute for Statistics, C.P. 6128 Succursale Centre-Ville, Montreal, Quebec, H3C 3J7 Canada, (Dial from U.S. (514) 343-6880), (Fax from U.S. (514) 343 6882), www.uis.unesco.org; *Statistical Tables.*

CANCER (MALIGNANCIES)

American Cancer Society, 1599 Clifton Road, NE, Atlanta, GA 30329-4250, (404) 320-3333, www.cancer.org; *Breast Cancer Facts and Figures 2007-2008; Cancer Facts and Figures 2008;* and *Cancer Facts and Figures for African Americans 2007-2008.*

Bernan Essential Government Publications, 4611-F Assembly Drive, Lanham MD, 20706-4391, (301) 459-2255, Fax: (800) 865-3450, www.bernan.com; *Vital Statistics of the United States: Births, Life Expectancy, Deaths, and Selected Health Data.*

National Cancer Institute (NCI), National Institutes of Health (NIH), Public Inquiries Office, 6116 Executive Boulevard, Room 3036A, Bethesda, MD 20892-8322, (800) 422-6237, www.cancer.gov; *2006-2007 Annual Report to the Nation; Assessing Progress, Advancing Change: 2005-2006 Annual President's Cancer Panel; Atlas of Cancer Mortality in the United States, 1950-94; Cancer Epidemiology in Older Adolescents and Young Adults 15 to 29 Years of Age, Including SEER Incidence and Survival: 1975-2000; Cancer Research Across Borders: Second Report 2001-2002; Decades of Progress 1983 to 2003 Community Clinical Oncology Program; Fighting Cancer in Indian Country: The Yakama Nation and Pacific Northwest Tribes President's Cancer Panel Annual Report 2002; Pancreatic Cancer: An Agenda for Action: Report of the Pancreatic Cancer Progress Review Group, February 2001; Report of the Brain Tumor Progress Review Group, November 2000; Report of the Gynecologic Cancers Progress Review Group, November 2001; Report of the Leukemia, Lymphoma, and Myeloma Progress Review Group, May 2001; Report of the Lung Cancer Progress Review Group, August 2001; Report of the Sarcoma Progress Review Group, A Roadmap for Sarcoma Research, January 2004;* and *SEER Cancer Statistics Review, 1975-2005.*

National Center for Chronic Disease Prevention and Health Promotion (NCCDPHP), Centers for Disease Control and Prevention (CDC), 4770 Buford Hwy, NE, MS K-40, Atlanta, GA 30341-3717, (404) 639-3311, www.cdc.gov/nccdphp; *Racial and Ethnic Approaches to Community Health (REACH 2010): Addressing Disparities in Health.*

National Center for Health Statistics (NCHS), Centers for Disease Control and Prevention (CDC), U.S. Department of Health and Human Services (HHS), 3311 Toledo Road, Hyattsville, MD 20782, (866) 232-4636, www.cdc.gov/nchs; *Faststats A to Z; Health, United States, 2006, with Chartbook on Trends in the Health of Americans with Special Feature on Pain; National Vital Statistics Reports (NVSR); Vital Statistics of the United States (VSUS);* and unpublished data.

CANCER (MALIGNANCIES) - DEATHS

American Cancer Society, 1599 Clifton Road, NE, Atlanta, GA 30329-4250, (404) 320-3333, www.cancer.org; *Cancer Facts and Figures 2008.*

Bernan Essential Government Publications, 4611-F Assembly Drive, Lanham MD, 20706-4391, (301) 459-2255, Fax: (800) 865-3450, www.bernan.com; *Vital Statistics of the United States: Births, Life Expectancy, Deaths, and Selected Health Data.*

National Cancer Institute (NCI), National Institutes of Health (NIH), Public Inquiries Office, 6116 Executive Boulevard, Room 3036A, Bethesda, MD 20892-8322, (800) 422-6237, www.cancer.gov; *2006-2007 Annual Report to the Nation; Assessing Progress, Advancing Change: 2005-2006 Annual President's Cancer Panel; Atlas of Cancer Mortality in the United States, 1950-94; Cancer Epidemiology in Older Adolescents and Young Adults 15 to 29 Years of Age, Including SEER Incidence and Survival: 1975-2000; Decades of Progress 1983 to 2003 Community Clinical Oncology Program; Fighting Cancer in Indian Country: The Yakama Nation and Pacific Northwest Tribes President's Cancer Panel Annual Report 2002; Pancreatic Cancer: An Agenda for Action: Report of the Pancreatic Cancer Progress Review Group, February 2001; Report of the Brain Tumor Progress Review Group, November 2000; Report of the Gynecologic Cancers Progress Review Group, November 2001; Report of the Leukemia, Lymphoma, and Myeloma Progress Review Group, May 2001; Report of the Lung Cancer Progress Review Group, August 2001; Report of the Sarcoma*

Progress Review Group, A Roadmap for Sarcoma Research, January 2004; and *SEER Cancer Statistics Review, 1975-2005.*

National Center for Health Statistics (NCHS), Centers for Disease Control and Prevention (CDC), U.S. Department of Health and Human Services (HHS), 3311 Toledo Road, Hyattsville, MD 20782, (866) 232-4636, www.cdc.gov/nchs; *National Vital Statistics Reports (NVSR); Vital Statistics of the United States (VSUS);* and unpublished data.

CANTALOUPE

Centers for Medicare and Medicaid Services (CMS), U.S. Department of Health and Human Services (HHS), 7500 Security Boulevard, Baltimore, MD 21244-1850, (410) 786-3000, http://cms.hhs.gov; *CMS Facts Figures.*

CAPACITY UTILIZATION INDEX

Board of Governors of the Federal Reserve System, Constitution Avenue, NW, Washington, DC 20551, (202) 452-3000, www.federalreserve.gov; *Industrial Production and Capacity Utilization.*

CAPE VERDE - NATIONAL STATISTICAL OFFICE

Instituto Nacional de Estatistica (INE), C.P. 116, Praia, Cape Verde, www.ine.cv; National Data Center.

CAPE VERDE - PRIMARY STATISTICS SOURCES

Instituto Nacional de Estatistica (INE), C.P. 116, Praia, Cape Verde, www.ine.cv; *Dados do CENSO 2000.*

CAPE VERDE - AGRICULTURAL MACHINERY

United Nations Statistics Division, New York, NY 10017, (800) 253-9646, Fax: (212) 963-4116, http://unstats.un.org; *Statistical Yearbook.*

CAPE VERDE - AGRICULTURE

Economist Intelligence Unit, 111 West 57th Street, New York, NY 10019, (212) 554-0600, Fax: (212) 586-1181, www.eiu.com; *Cape Verde Country Report.*

Euromonitor International, Inc., 224 S. Michigan Avenue, Suite 1500, Chicago, IL 60604, (312) 922-1115, Fax: (312) 922-1157, www.euromonitor.com; *World Marketing Data and Statistics.*

Palgrave Macmillan Ltd., Houndmills, Basingstoke, Hampshire, RG21 6XS, England, (Telephone in U.S. (888) 330-8477), (Fax in U.S. (800) 672-2054), www.palgrave.com; *The Statesman's Yearbook 2008.*

Taylor and Francis Group, An Informa Business, 2 Park Square, Milton Park, Abingdon, Oxford OX14 4RN, United Kingdom, (Dial from U.S. (212) 216-7800), (Fax from U.S. (212) 564-7854), www.tandf.co.uk; *The Europa World Year Book.*

United Nations Conference on Trade and Development (UNCTAD), DC2-1120, United Nations, New York, NY 10017, (212) 963-0027, www.unctad.org; *UNCTAD Commodity Yearbook.*

United Nations Economic Commission for Africa (ECA), PO Box 3001, Addis Ababa, Ethiopia, (Telephone in U.S. (212) 963-4957), www.uneca.org; *African Statistical Yearbook 2006.*

United Nations Food and Agricultural Organization (FAO), Viale delle Terme di Caracalla, 00100 Rome, Italy, (Dial from U.S. (202) 653-2400), (Fax from U.S. (202) 653 5760), www.fao.org; AQUASTAT; *FAO Production Yearbook 2002; FAO Trade Yearbook;* and *The State of Food and Agriculture (SOFA) 2006.*

United Nations Statistics Division, New York, NY 10017, (800) 253-9646, Fax: (212) 963-4116, http://unstats.un.org; *Statistical Yearbook* and *Survey of Economic and Social Conditions in Africa 2005.*

The World Bank, 1818 H Street, NW, Washington, DC 20433, (202) 473-1000, Fax: (202) 477-6391, www.worldbank.org; *Africa Live Database (LDB); African Development Indicators (ADI) 2007; Cape Verde;* and *World Development Indicators (WDI) 2008.*

CAPE VERDE - AIRLINES

Palgrave Macmillan Ltd., Houndmills, Basingstoke, Hampshire, RG21 6XS, England, (Telephone in U.S. (888) 330-8477), (Fax in U.S. (800) 672-2054), www.palgrave.com; *The Statesman's Yearbook 2008.*

Taylor and Francis Group, An Informa Business, 2 Park Square, Milton Park, Abingdon, Oxford OX14 4RN, United Kingdom, (Dial from U.S. (212) 216-7800), (Fax from U.S. (212) 564-7854), www.tandf.co.uk; *The Europa World Year Book.*

United Nations Economic Commission for Africa (ECA), PO Box 3001, Addis Ababa, Ethiopia, (Telephone in U.S. (212) 963-4957), www.uneca.org; *African Statistical Yearbook 2006.*

CAPE VERDE - AIRPORTS

Central Intelligence Agency, Office of Public Affairs, Washington, DC 20505, (703) 482-0623, Fax: (703) 482-1739, www.cia.gov; *The World Factbook.*

CAPE VERDE - ARMED FORCES

Central Intelligence Agency, Office of Public Affairs, Washington, DC 20505, (703) 482-0623, Fax: (703) 482-1739, www.cia.gov; *The World Factbook.*

Euromonitor International, Inc., 224 S. Michigan Avenue, Suite 1500, Chicago, IL 60604, (312) 922-1115, Fax: (312) 922-1157, www.euromonitor.com; *World Marketing Data and Statistics.*

International Institute for Strategic Studies (IISS), Arundel House, 13-15 Arundel Street, Temple Place, London WC2R 3DX, England, www.iiss.org; *The Military Balance 2007.*

Palgrave Macmillan Ltd., Houndmills, Basingstoke, Hampshire, RG21 6XS, England, (Telephone in U.S. (888) 330-8477), (Fax in U.S. (800) 672-2054), www.palgrave.com; *The Statesman's Yearbook 2008.*

U.S. Department of State (DOS), 2201 C Street NW, Washington, DC 20520, (202) 647-4000, www.state.gov; *World Military Expenditures and Arms Transfers (WMEAT).*

United Nations Statistics Division, New York, NY 10017, (800) 253-9646, Fax: (212) 963-4116, http://unstats.un.org; *Human Development Report 2006.*

CAPE VERDE - BALANCE OF PAYMENTS

African Development Bank Group, Rue Joseph Anoma, 01 BP 1387 Abidjan 01, Cote d'Ivoire, www.afdb.org; *Statistics Pocketbook 2008.*

Taylor and Francis Group, An Informa Business, 2 Park Square, Milton Park, Abingdon, Oxford OX14 4RN, United Kingdom, (Dial from U.S. (212) 216-7800), (Fax from U.S. (212) 564-7854), www.tandf.co.uk; *The Europa World Year Book.*

United Nations Conference on Trade and Development (UNCTAD), DC2-1120, United Nations, New York, NY 10017, (212) 963-0027, www.unctad.org; *Handbook of Statistics 2005.*

United Nations Economic Commission for Africa (ECA), PO Box 3001, Addis Ababa, Ethiopia, (Telephone in U.S. (212) 963-4957), www.uneca.org; *African Statistical Yearbook 2006.*

The World Bank, 1818 H Street, NW, Washington, DC 20433, (202) 473-1000, Fax: (202) 477-6391, www.worldbank.org; *Cape Verde* and *World Development Indicators (WDI) 2008.*

CAPE VERDE - BANKS AND BANKING

Euromonitor International, Inc., 224 S. Michigan Avenue, Suite 1500, Chicago, IL 60604, (312) 922-1115, Fax: (312) 922-1157, www.euromonitor.com; *World Marketing Data and Statistics.*

Palgrave Macmillan Ltd., Houndmills, Basingstoke, Hampshire, RG21 6XS, England, (Telephone in U.S. (888) 330-8477), (Fax in U.S. (800) 672-2054), www.palgrave.com; *The Statesman's Yearbook 2008.*

Taylor and Francis Group, An Informa Business, 2 Park Square, Milton Park, Abingdon, Oxford OX14 4RN, United Kingdom, (Dial from U.S. (212) 216-7800), (Fax from U.S. (212) 564-7854), www.tandf.co.uk; *The Europa World Year Book.*

United Nations Economic Commission for Africa (ECA), PO Box 3001, Addis Ababa, Ethiopia, (Telephone in U.S. (212) 963-4957), www.uneca.org; *African Statistical Yearbook 2006.*

CAPE VERDE - BROADCASTING

Central Intelligence Agency, Office of Public Affairs, Washington, DC 20505, (703) 482-0623, Fax: (703) 482-1739, www.cia.gov; *The World Factbook.*

Euromonitor International, Inc., 224 S. Michigan Avenue, Suite 1500, Chicago, IL 60604, (312) 922-1115, Fax: (312) 922-1157, www.euromonitor.com; *World Marketing Data and Statistics.*

Palgrave Macmillan Ltd., Houndmills, Basingstoke, Hampshire, RG21 6XS, England, (Telephone in U.S. (888) 330-8477), (Fax in U.S. (800) 672-2054), www.palgrave.com; *The Statesman's Yearbook 2008.*

WRTH Publications Limited, PO Box 290, Oxford OX2 7FT, UK, www.wrth.com; *World Radio TV Handbook 2007.*

CAPE VERDE - BUDGET

Central Intelligence Agency, Office of Public Affairs, Washington, DC 20505, (703) 482-0623, Fax: (703) 482-1739, www.cia.gov; *The World Factbook.*

CAPE VERDE - CATTLE

See CAPE VERDE - LIVESTOCK

CAPE VERDE - CHILDBIRTH - STATISTICS

Central Intelligence Agency, Office of Public Affairs, Washington, DC 20505, (703) 482-0623, Fax: (703) 482-1739, www.cia.gov; *The World Factbook.*

Euromonitor International, Inc., 224 S. Michigan Avenue, Suite 1500, Chicago, IL 60604, (312) 922-1115, Fax: (312) 922-1157, www.euromonitor.com; *International Marketing Data and Statistics 2008* and *The World Economic Factbook 2008.*

Palgrave Macmillan Ltd., Houndmills, Basingstoke, Hampshire, RG21 6XS, England, (Telephone in U.S. (888) 330-8477), (Fax in U.S. (800) 672-2054), www.palgrave.com; *The Statesman's Yearbook 2008.*

Taylor and Francis Group, An Informa Business, 2 Park Square, Milton Park, Abingdon, Oxford OX14 4RN, United Kingdom, (Dial from U.S. (212) 216-7800), (Fax from U.S. (212) 564-7854), www.tandf.co.uk; *The Europa World Year Book.*

United Nations Statistics Division, New York, NY 10017, (800) 253-9646, Fax: (212) 963-4116, http://unstats.un.org; *Demographic Yearbook; Statistical Yearbook;* and *Survey of Economic and Social Conditions in Africa 2005.*

The World Bank, 1818 H Street, NW, Washington, DC 20433, (202) 473-1000, Fax: (202) 477-6391, www.worldbank.org; *World Development Indicators (WDI) 2008.*

World Health Organization (WHO), Avenue Appia 20, 1211 Geneve 27, Switzerland, (Telephone in U.S. (212) 331-9081), www.who.int; *World Health Report 2006.*

CAPE VERDE - CLIMATE

International Institute for Environment and Development (IIED), 3 Endsleigh Street, London, England, WC1H 0DD, United Kingdom, www.iied.org; *Environment Urbanization* and *Haramata - Bulletin of the Drylands.*

Palgrave Macmillan Ltd., Houndmills, Basingstoke, Hampshire, RG21 6XS, England, (Telephone in U.S.

(888) 330-8477), (Fax in U.S. (800) 672-2054), www.palgrave.com; *The Statesman's Yearbook 2008.*

CAPE VERDE - COAL PRODUCTION

See CAPE VERDE - MINERAL INDUSTRIES

CAPE VERDE - COMMERCE

Palgrave Macmillan Ltd., Houndmills, Basingstoke, Hampshire, RG21 6XS, England, (Telephone in U.S. (888) 330-8477), (Fax in U.S. (800) 672-2054), www.palgrave.com; *The Statesman's Yearbook 2008.*

CAPE VERDE - COMMODITY EXCHANGES

Commodity Research Bureau, 330 South Wells Street, Suite 612, Chicago, IL 60606-7110, (800) 621-5271, Fax: (312) 939-4135, www.crbtrader.com; *2006 CRB Commodity Yearbook and CD.*

International Monetary Fund (IMF), 700 Nineteenth Street, NW, Washington, DC 20431, (202) 623-7000, Fax: (202) 623-4661, www.imf.org; *IMF Primary Commodity Prices.*

United Nations Food and Agricultural Organization (FAO), Viale delle Terme di Caracalla, 00100 Rome, Italy, (Dial from U.S. (202) 653-2400), (Fax from U.S. (202) 653 5760), www.fao.org; *The State of Food and Agriculture (SOFA) 2006.*

CAPE VERDE - COMMUNICATION AND TRAFFIC

United Nations Statistics Division, New York, NY 10017, (800) 253-9646, Fax: (212) 963-4116, http://unstats.un.org; *Statistical Yearbook.*

CAPE VERDE - CONSTRUCTION INDUSTRY

United Nations Economic Commission for Africa (ECA), PO Box 3001, Addis Ababa, Ethiopia, (Telephone in U.S. (212) 963-4957), www.uneca.org; *African Statistical Yearbook 2006.*

United Nations Statistics Division, New York, NY 10017, (800) 253-9646, Fax: (212) 963-4116, http://unstats.un.org; *Statistical Yearbook.*

CAPE VERDE - CONSUMER PRICE INDEXES

Taylor and Francis Group, An Informa Business, 2 Park Square, Milton Park, Abingdon, Oxford OX14 4RN, United Kingdom, (Dial from U.S. (212) 216-7800), (Fax from U.S. (212) 564-7854), www.tandf.co.uk; *The Europa World Year Book.*

United Nations Statistics Division, New York, NY 10017, (800) 253-9646, Fax: (212) 963-4116, http://unstats.un.org; *Statistical Yearbook* and *Survey of Economic and Social Conditions in Africa 2005.*

The World Bank, 1818 H Street, NW, Washington, DC 20433, (202) 473-1000, Fax: (202) 477-6391, www.worldbank.org; *Cape Verde.*

CAPE VERDE - CONSUMPTION (ECONOMICS)

African Development Bank Group, Rue Joseph Anoma, 01 BP 1387 Abidjan 01, Cote d'Ivoire, www.afdb.org; *Statistics Pocketbook 2008.*

United Nations Statistics Division, New York, NY 10017, (800) 253-9646, Fax: (212) 963-4116, http://unstats.un.org; *Survey of Economic and Social Conditions in Africa 2005.*

CAPE VERDE - CORN INDUSTRY

See CAPE VERDE - CROPS

CAPE VERDE - CROPS

Palgrave Macmillan Ltd., Houndmills, Basingstoke, Hampshire, RG21 6XS, England, (Telephone in U.S. (888) 330-8477), (Fax in U.S. (800) 672-2054), www.palgrave.com; *The Statesman's Yearbook 2008.*

Taylor and Francis Group, An Informa Business, 2 Park Square, Milton Park, Abingdon, Oxford OX14 4RN, United Kingdom, (Dial from U.S. (212) 216-7800), (Fax from U.S. (212) 564-7854), www.tandf.co.uk; *The Europa World Year Book.*

United Nations Conference on Trade and Development (UNCTAD), DC2-1120, United Nations, New York, NY 10017, (212) 963-0027, www.unctad.org; *UNCTAD Commodity Yearbook.*

United Nations Economic Commission for Africa (ECA), PO Box 3001, Addis Ababa, Ethiopia, (Telephone in U.S. (212) 963-4957), www.uneca.org; *African Statistical Yearbook 2006.*

United Nations Food and Agricultural Organization (FAO), Viale delle Terme di Caracalla, 00100 Rome, Italy, (Dial from U.S. (202) 653-2400), (Fax from U.S. (202) 653 5760), www.fao.org; *The State of Food and Agriculture (SOFA) 2006.*

United Nations Statistics Division, New York, NY 10017, (800) 253-9646, Fax: (212) 963-4116, http://unstats.un.org; *Statistical Yearbook.*

CAPE VERDE - DAIRY PROCESSING

Palgrave Macmillan Ltd., Houndmills, Basingstoke, Hampshire, RG21 6XS, England, (Telephone in U.S. (888) 330-8477), (Fax in U.S. (800) 672-2054), www.palgrave.com; *The Statesman's Yearbook 2008.*

United Nations Food and Agricultural Organization (FAO), Viale delle Terme di Caracalla, 00100 Rome, Italy, (Dial from U.S. (202) 653-2400), (Fax from U.S. (202) 653 5760), www.fao.org; *The State of Food and Agriculture (SOFA) 2006.*

CAPE VERDE - DEATH RATES

See CAPE VERDE - MORTALITY

CAPE VERDE - DEBTS, EXTERNAL

African Development Bank Group, Rue Joseph Anoma, 01 BP 1387 Abidjan 01, Cote d'Ivoire, www.afdb.org; *Statistics Pocketbook 2008.*

M.E. Sharpe, 80 Business Park Drive, Armonk, NY 10504, (800) 541-6563, Fax: (914) 273-2106, www.mesharpe.com; *The Illustrated Book of World Rankings.*

United Nations Statistics Division, New York, NY 10017, (800) 253-9646, Fax: (212) 963-4116, http://unstats.un.org; *Survey of Economic and Social Conditions in Africa 2005.*

The World Bank, 1818 H Street, NW, Washington, DC 20433, (202) 473-1000, Fax: (202) 477-6391, www.worldbank.org; *Africa Live Database (LDB); African Development Indicators (ADI) 2007;* and *Global Development Finance 2007.*

CAPE VERDE - DEFENSE EXPENDITURES

See CAPE VERDE - ARMED FORCES

CAPE VERDE - DEMOGRAPHY

Euromonitor International, Inc., 224 S. Michigan Avenue, Suite 1500, Chicago, IL 60604, (312) 922-1115, Fax: (312) 922-1157, www.euromonitor.com; *International Marketing Data and Statistics 2008; The World Economic Factbook 2008;* and *World Marketing Data and Statistics.*

United Nations Statistics Division, New York, NY 10017, (800) 253-9646, Fax: (212) 963-4116, http://unstats.un.org; *Human Development Report 2006* and *Survey of Economic and Social Conditions in Africa 2005.*

The World Bank, 1818 H Street, NW, Washington, DC 20433, (202) 473-1000, Fax: (202) 477-6391, www.worldbank.org; *Cape Verde.*

CAPE VERDE - DISPOSABLE INCOME

United Nations Statistics Division, New York, NY 10017, (800) 253-9646, Fax: (212) 963-4116, http://unstats.un.org; *National Accounts Statistics: Compendium of Income Distribution Statistics.*

CAPE VERDE - DIVORCE

United Nations Statistics Division, New York, NY 10017, (800) 253-9646, Fax: (212) 963-4116, http://unstats.un.org; *Demographic Yearbook.*

CAPE VERDE - ECONOMIC ASSISTANCE

United Nations Statistics Division, New York, NY 10017, (800) 253-9646, Fax: (212) 963-4116, http://unstats.un.org; *Statistical Yearbook.*

CAPE VERDE - ECONOMIC CONDITIONS

African Development Bank Group, Rue Joseph Anoma, 01 BP 1387 Abidjan 01, Cote d'Ivoire, www.afdb.org; *The African Statistical Journal; Gender, Poverty and Environmental Indicators on African Countries 2007; Selected Statistics on African Countries 2007;* and *Statistics Pocketbook 2008.*

Center for International Business Education Research (CIBER), Columbia Business School and School of International and Public Affairs, Uris Hall, Room 212, 3022 Broadway, New York, NY 10027-6902, Mr. Joshua Safier, (212) 854-4750, Fax: (212) 222-9821, www.columbia.edu/cu/ciber/; Datastream International.

Central Intelligence Agency, Office of Public Affairs, Washington, DC 20505, (703) 482-0623, Fax: (703) 482-1739, www.cia.gov; *The World Factbook.*

DSI Data Service Information, Xantener Strasse 51a, D-47495 Rheinberg, Germany, www.dsidata.com; *Campus Solution.*

Dun and Bradstreet (DB) Corporation, 103 JFK Parkway, Short Hills, NJ 07078, (973) 921-5500, www.dnb.com; *Country Report.*

Economist Intelligence Unit, 111 West 57th Street, New York, NY 10019, (212) 554-0600, Fax: (212) 586-1181, www.eiu.com; *Business Africa* and *Cape Verde Country Report.*

Euromonitor International, Inc., 224 S. Michigan Avenue, Suite 1500, Chicago, IL 60604, (312) 922-1115, Fax: (312) 922-1157, www.euromonitor.com; *The World Economic Factbook 2008* and *World Marketing Data and Statistics.*

International Monetary Fund (IMF), 700 Nineteenth Street, NW, Washington, DC 20431, (202) 623-7000, Fax: (202) 623-4661, www.imf.org; *World Economic Outlook Reports.*

Palgrave Macmillan Ltd., Houndmills, Basingstoke, Hampshire, RG21 6XS, England, (Telephone in U.S. (888) 330-8477), (Fax in U.S. (800) 672-2054), www.palgrave.com; *The Statesman's Yearbook 2008.*

Taylor and Francis Group, An Informa Business, 2 Park Square, Milton Park, Abingdon, Oxford OX14 4RN, United Kingdom, (Dial from U.S. (212) 216-7800), (Fax from U.S. (212) 564-7854), www.tandf.co.uk; *The Europa World Year Book.*

United Nations Statistics Division, New York, NY 10017, (800) 253-9646, Fax: (212) 963-4116, http://unstats.un.org; *Compendium of Intra-African and Related Foreign Trade Statistics 2003* and *World Statistics Pocketbook.*

The World Bank, 1818 H Street, NW, Washington, DC 20433, (202) 473-1000, Fax: (202) 477-6391, www.worldbank.org; *Africa Household Survey Databank; Africa Live Database (LDB); Africa Standardized Files and Indicators; African Development Indicators (ADI) 2007; Cape Verde; Global Economic Monitor (GEM); Global Economic Prospects 2008;* and *The World Bank Atlas 2003-2004.*

CAPE VERDE - EDUCATION

African Development Bank Group, Rue Joseph Anoma, 01 BP 1387 Abidjan 01, Cote d'Ivoire, www.afdb.org; *Statistics Pocketbook 2008.*

Euromonitor International, Inc., 224 S. Michigan Avenue, Suite 1500, Chicago, IL 60604, (312) 922-1115, Fax: (312) 922-1157, www.euromonitor.com; *International Marketing Data and Statistics 2008* and *World Marketing Data and Statistics.*

Palgrave Macmillan Ltd., Houndmills, Basingstoke, Hampshire, RG21 6XS, England, (Telephone in U.S. (888) 330-8477), (Fax in U.S. (800) 672-2054), www.palgrave.com; *The Statesman's Yearbook 2008.*

Taylor and Francis Group, An Informa Business, 2 Park Square, Milton Park, Abingdon, Oxford OX14 4RN, United Kingdom, (Dial from U.S. (212) 216-

7800), (Fax from U.S. (212) 564-7854), www.tandf.co.uk; *The Europa World Year Book.*

UNESCO Institute for Statistics, C.P. 6128 Succursale Centre-Ville, Montreal, Quebec, H3C 3J7 Canada, (Dial from U.S. (514) 343-6880), (Fax from U.S. (514) 343 6882), www.uis.unesco.org; *Statistical Tables.*

United Nations Economic Commission for Africa (ECA), PO Box 3001, Addis Ababa, Ethiopia, (Telephone in U.S. (212) 963-4957), www.uneca.org; *African Statistical Yearbook 2006.*

United Nations Statistics Division, New York, NY 10017, (800) 253-9646, Fax: (212) 963-4116, http://unstats.un.org; *Human Development Report 2006* and *Survey of Economic and Social Conditions in Africa 2005.*

The World Bank, 1818 H Street, NW, Washington, DC 20433, (202) 473-1000, Fax: (202) 477-6391, www.worldbank.org; *Cape Verde* and *World Development Indicators (WDI) 2008.*

CAPE VERDE - ELECTRICITY

Palgrave Macmillan Ltd., Houndmills, Basingstoke, Hampshire, RG21 6XS, England, (Telephone in U.S. (888) 330-8477), (Fax in U.S. (800) 672-2054), www.palgrave.com; *The Statesman's Yearbook 2008.*

United Nations Economic Commission for Africa (ECA), PO Box 3001, Addis Ababa, Ethiopia, (Telephone in U.S. (212) 963-4957), www.uneca.org; *African Statistical Yearbook 2006.*

United Nations Statistics Division, New York, NY 10017, (800) 253-9646, Fax: (212) 963-4116, http://unstats.un.org; *Human Development Report 2006* and *Survey of Economic and Social Conditions in Africa 2005.*

CAPE VERDE - EMPLOYMENT

Euromonitor International, Inc., 224 S. Michigan Avenue, Suite 1500, Chicago, IL 60604, (312) 922-1115, Fax: (312) 922-1157, www.euromonitor.com; *International Marketing Data and Statistics 2008.*

International Labour Office, I.L.O. Publications, 4 route des Morillons, CH-1211 Geneva 22, Switzerland, (Telephone in U.S. (202) 653-7652), (Fax in U.S. (202) 653-7687), www.ilo.org; *Yearbook of Labour Statistics 2006.*

United Nations Economic Commission for Africa (ECA), PO Box 3001, Addis Ababa, Ethiopia, (Telephone in U.S. (212) 963-4957), www.uneca.org; *African Statistical Yearbook 2006.*

United Nations Statistics Division, New York, NY 10017, (800) 253-9646, Fax: (212) 963-4116, http://unstats.un.org; *Survey of Economic and Social Conditions in Africa 2005.*

The World Bank, 1818 H Street, NW, Washington, DC 20433, (202) 473-1000, Fax: (202) 477-6391, www.worldbank.org; *Cape Verde.*

CAPE VERDE - ENVIRONMENTAL CONDITIONS

DSI Data Service Information, Xantener Strasse 51a, D-47495 Rheinberg, Germany, www.dsidata.com; *Campus Solution* and *DSI's Global Environmental Database.*

Economist Intelligence Unit, 111 West 57th Street, New York, NY 10019, (212) 554-0600, Fax: (212) 586-1181, www.eiu.com; *Cape Verde Country Report.*

International Institute for Environment and Development (IIED), 3 Endsleigh Street, London, England, WC1H 0DD, United Kingdom, www.iied.org; *Environment Urbanization* and *Haramata - Bulletin of the Drylands.*

United Nations Statistics Division, New York, NY 10017, (800) 253-9646, Fax: (212) 963-4116, http://unstats.un.org; *World Statistics Pocketbook.*

CAPE VERDE - EXPORTS

African Development Bank Group, Rue Joseph Anoma, 01 BP 1387 Abidjan 01, Cote d'Ivoire, www.afdb.org; *Statistics Pocketbook 2008.*

Central Intelligence Agency, Office of Public Affairs, Washington, DC 20505, (703) 482-0623, Fax: (703) 482-1739, www.cia.gov; *The World Factbook.*

Economist Intelligence Unit, 111 West 57th Street, New York, NY 10019, (212) 554-0600, Fax: (212) 586-1181, www.eiu.com; *Cape Verde Country Report.*

Euromonitor International, Inc., 224 S. Michigan Avenue, Suite 1500, Chicago, IL 60604, (312) 922-1115, Fax: (312) 922-1157, www.euromonitor.com; *International Marketing Data and Statistics 2008* and *The World Economic Factbook 2008.*

International Monetary Fund (IMF), 700 Nineteenth Street, NW, Washington, DC 20431, (202) 623-7000, Fax: (202) 623-4661, www.imf.org; *Direction of Trade Statistics Yearbook 2007.*

Palgrave Macmillan Ltd., Houndmills, Basingstoke, Hampshire, RG21 6XS, England, (Telephone in U.S. (888) 330-8477), (Fax in U.S. (800) 672-2054), www.palgrave.com; *The Statesman's Yearbook 2008.*

Taylor and Francis Group, An Informa Business, 2 Park Square, Milton Park, Abingdon, Oxford OX14 4RN, United Kingdom, (Dial from U.S. (212) 216-7800), (Fax from U.S. (212) 564-7854), www.tandf.co.uk; *The Europa World Year Book.*

United Nations Conference on Trade and Development (UNCTAD), DC2-1120, United Nations, New York, NY 10017, (212) 963-0027, www.unctad.org; *Handbook of Statistics 2005.*

United Nations Economic Commission for Africa (ECA), PO Box 3001, Addis Ababa, Ethiopia, (Telephone in U.S. (212) 963-4957), www.uneca.org; *African Statistical Yearbook 2006.*

United Nations Food and Agricultural Organization (FAO), Viale delle Terme di Caracalla, 00100 Rome, Italy, (Dial from U.S. (202) 653-2400), (Fax from U.S. (202) 653 5760), www.fao.org; *The State of Food and Agriculture (SOFA) 2006.*

United Nations Statistics Division, New York, NY 10017, (800) 253-9646, Fax: (212) 963-4116, http://unstats.un.org; *Compendium of Intra-African and Related Foreign Trade Statistics 2003* and *Survey of Economic and Social Conditions in Africa 2005.*

The World Bank, 1818 H Street, NW, Washington, DC 20433, (202) 473-1000, Fax: (202) 477-6391, www.worldbank.org; *World Development Indicators (WDI) 2008.*

CAPE VERDE - FERTILITY, HUMAN

Central Intelligence Agency, Office of Public Affairs, Washington, DC 20505, (703) 482-0623, Fax: (703) 482-1739, www.cia.gov; *The World Factbook.*

United Nations Statistics Division, New York, NY 10017, (800) 253-9646, Fax: (212) 963-4116, http://unstats.un.org; *Human Development Report 2006* and *Survey of Economic and Social Conditions in Africa 2005.*

The World Bank, 1818 H Street, NW, Washington, DC 20433, (202) 473-1000, Fax: (202) 477-6391, www.worldbank.org; *The World Bank Atlas 2003-2004* and *World Development Indicators (WDI) 2008.*

CAPE VERDE - FERTILIZER INDUSTRY

United Nations Food and Agricultural Organization (FAO), Viale delle Terme di Caracalla, 00100 Rome, Italy, (Dial from U.S. (202) 653-2400), (Fax from U.S. (202) 653 5760), www.fao.org; *The State of Food and Agriculture (SOFA) 2006.*

CAPE VERDE - FETAL MORTALITY

See CAPE VERDE - MORTALITY

CAPE VERDE - FINANCE

United Nations Economic Commission for Africa (ECA), PO Box 3001, Addis Ababa, Ethiopia, (Telephone in U.S. (212) 963-4957), www.uneca.org; *African Statistical Yearbook 2006.*

The World Bank, 1818 H Street, NW, Washington, DC 20433, (202) 473-1000, Fax: (202) 477-6391, www.worldbank.org; *Cape Verde.*

CAPE VERDE - FINANCE, PUBLIC

African Development Bank Group, Rue Joseph Anoma, 01 BP 1387 Abidjan 01, Cote d'Ivoire, www.afdb.org; *Statistics Pocketbook 2008.*

Bernan Essential Government Publications, 4611-F Assembly Drive, Lanham MD, 20706-4391, (301) 459-2255, Fax: (800) 865-3450, www.bernan.com; *National Accounts Statistics.*

Economist Intelligence Unit, 111 West 57th Street, New York, NY 10019, (212) 554-0600, Fax: (212) 586-1181, www.eiu.com; *Cape Verde Country Report.*

International Monetary Fund (IMF), 700 Nineteenth Street, NW, Washington, DC 20431, (202) 623-7000, Fax: (202) 623-4661, www.imf.org; *International Financial Statistics* and *International Financial Statistics Online Service.*

Palgrave Macmillan Ltd., Houndmills, Basingstoke, Hampshire, RG21 6XS, England, (Telephone in U.S. (888) 330-8477), (Fax in U.S. (800) 672-2054), www.palgrave.com; *The Statesman's Yearbook 2008.*

Taylor and Francis Group, An Informa Business, 2 Park Square, Milton Park, Abingdon, Oxford OX14 4RN, United Kingdom, (Dial from U.S. (212) 216-7800), (Fax from U.S. (212) 564-7854), www.tandf.co.uk; *The Europa World Year Book.*

United Nations Economic Commission for Africa (ECA), PO Box 3001, Addis Ababa, Ethiopia, (Telephone in U.S. (212) 963-4957), www.uneca.org; *African Statistical Yearbook 2006.*

The World Bank, 1818 H Street, NW, Washington, DC 20433, (202) 473-1000, Fax: (202) 477-6391, www.worldbank.org; *Cape Verde.*

CAPE VERDE - FISHERIES

Palgrave Macmillan Ltd., Houndmills, Basingstoke, Hampshire, RG21 6XS, England, (Telephone in U.S. (888) 330-8477), (Fax in U.S. (800) 672-2054), www.palgrave.com; *The Statesman's Yearbook 2008.*

Taylor and Francis Group, An Informa Business, 2 Park Square, Milton Park, Abingdon, Oxford OX14 4RN, United Kingdom, (Dial from U.S. (212) 216-7800), (Fax from U.S. (212) 564-7854), www.tandf.co.uk; *The Europa World Year Book.*

United Nations Conference on Trade and Development (UNCTAD), DC2-1120, United Nations, New York, NY 10017, (212) 963-0027, www.unctad.org; *UNCTAD Commodity Yearbook.*

United Nations Economic Commission for Africa (ECA), PO Box 3001, Addis Ababa, Ethiopia, (Telephone in U.S. (212) 963-4957), www.uneca.org; *African Statistical Yearbook 2006.*

United Nations Food and Agricultural Organization (FAO), Viale delle Terme di Caracalla, 00100 Rome, Italy, (Dial from U.S. (202) 653-2400), (Fax from U.S. (202) 653 5760), www.fao.org; *FAO Yearbook of Fishery Statistics;* Fishery Databases; FISHSTAT Database. Subjects covered include: Aquaculture production, capture production, fishery commodities; and *The State of Food and Agriculture (SOFA) 2006.*

United Nations Statistics Division, New York, NY 10017, (800) 253-9646, Fax: (212) 963-4116, http://unstats.un.org; *Statistical Yearbook* and *Survey of Economic and Social Conditions in Africa 2005.*

The World Bank, 1818 H Street, NW, Washington, DC 20433, (202) 473-1000, Fax: (202) 477-6391, www.worldbank.org; *Cape Verde.*

CAPE VERDE - FOOD

African Development Bank Group, Rue Joseph Anoma, 01 BP 1387 Abidjan 01, Cote d'Ivoire, www.afdb.org; *Statistics Pocketbook 2008.*

United Nations Conference on Trade and Development (UNCTAD), DC2-1120, United Nations, New York, NY 10017, (212) 963-0027, www.unctad.org; *UNCTAD Commodity Yearbook.*

United Nations Food and Agricultural Organization (FAO), Viale delle Terme di Caracalla, 00100 Rome, Italy, (Dial from U.S. (202) 653-2400), (Fax from

U.S. (202) 653 5760), www.fao.org; *FAO Production Yearbook 2002* and *The State of Food and Agriculture (SOFA) 2006.*

United Nations Statistics Division, New York, NY 10017, (800) 253-9646, Fax: (212) 963-4116, http://unstats.un.org; *Human Development Report 2006.*

CAPE VERDE - FOREIGN EXCHANGE RATES

African Development Bank Group, Rue Joseph Anoma, 01 BP 1387 Abidjan 01, Cote d'Ivoire, www.afdb.org; *Statistics Pocketbook 2008.*

Central Intelligence Agency, Office of Public Affairs, Washington, DC 20505, (703) 482-0623, Fax: (703) 482-1739, www.cia.gov; *The World Factbook.*

Euromonitor International, Inc., 224 S. Michigan Avenue, Suite 1500, Chicago, IL 60604, (312) 922-1115, Fax: (312) 922-1157, www.euromonitor.com; *International Marketing Data and Statistics 2008* and *The World Economic Factbook 2008.*

Taylor and Francis Group, An Informa Business, 2 Park Square, Milton Park, Abingdon, Oxford OX14 4RN, United Kingdom, (Dial from U.S. (212) 216-7800), (Fax from U.S. (212) 564-7854), www.tandf.co.uk; *The Europa World Year Book.*

United Nations Statistics Division, New York, NY 10017, (800) 253-9646, Fax: (212) 963-4116, http://unstats.un.org; *Compendium of Intra-African and Related Foreign Trade Statistics 2003; Statistical Yearbook;* and *World Statistics Pocketbook.*

CAPE VERDE - FORESTS AND FORESTRY

United Nations Conference on Trade and Development (UNCTAD), DC2-1120, United Nations, New York, NY 10017, (212) 963-0027, www.unctad.org; *UNCTAD Commodity Yearbook.*

United Nations Economic Commission for Africa (ECA), PO Box 3001, Addis Ababa, Ethiopia, (Telephone in U.S. (212) 963-4957), www.uneca.org; *African Statistical Yearbook 2006.*

United Nations Food and Agricultural Organization (FAO), Viale delle Terme di Caracalla, 00100 Rome, Italy, (Dial from U.S. (202) 653-2400), (Fax from U.S. (202) 653 5760), www.fao.org; *FAO Yearbook of Forest Products* and *The State of Food and Agriculture (SOFA) 2006.*

The World Bank, 1818 H Street, NW, Washington, DC 20433, (202) 473-1000, Fax: (202) 477-6391, www.worldbank.org; *Cape Verde.*

CAPE VERDE - GEOGRAPHIC INFORMATION SYSTEMS

The World Bank, 1818 H Street, NW, Washington, DC 20433, (202) 473-1000, Fax: (202) 477-6391, www.worldbank.org; *Cape Verde.*

CAPE VERDE - GOLD INDUSTRY

The World Bank, 1818 H Street, NW, Washington, DC 20433, (202) 473-1000, Fax: (202) 477-6391, www.worldbank.org; *World Development Indicators (WDI) 2008.*

CAPE VERDE - GROSS DOMESTIC PRODUCT

African Development Bank Group, Rue Joseph Anoma, 01 BP 1387 Abidjan 01, Cote d'Ivoire, www.afdb.org; *Statistics Pocketbook 2008.*

Economist Intelligence Unit, 111 West 57th Street, New York, NY 10019, (212) 554-0600, Fax: (212) 586-1181, www.eiu.com; *Cape Verde Country Report.*

Euromonitor International, Inc., 224 S. Michigan Avenue, Suite 1500, Chicago, IL 60604, (312) 922-1115, Fax: (312) 922-1157, www.euromonitor.com; *International Marketing Data and Statistics 2008* and *The World Economic Factbook 2008.*

Taylor and Francis Group, An Informa Business, 2 Park Square, Milton Park, Abingdon, Oxford OX14 4RN, United Kingdom, (Dial from U.S. (212) 216-7800), (Fax from U.S. (212) 564-7854), www.tandf.co.uk; *The Europa World Year Book.*

United Nations Economic Commission for Africa (ECA), PO Box 3001, Addis Ababa, Ethiopia, (Telephone in U.S. (212) 963-4957), www.uneca.org; *African Statistical Yearbook 2006.*

United Nations Statistics Division, New York, NY 10017, (800) 253-9646, Fax: (212) 963-4116, http://unstats.un.org; *Human Development Report 2006; National Accounts Statistics: Compendium of Income Distribution Statistics;* and *Survey of Economic and Social Conditions in Africa 2005.*

The World Bank, 1818 H Street, NW, Washington, DC 20433, (202) 473-1000, Fax: (202) 477-6391, www.worldbank.org; *World Development Indicators (WDI) 2008.*

CAPE VERDE - GROSS NATIONAL PRODUCT

Palgrave Macmillan Ltd., Houndmills, Basingstoke, Hampshire, RG21 6XS, England, (Telephone in U.S. (888) 330-8477), (Fax in U.S. (800) 672-2054), www.palgrave.com; *The Statesman's Yearbook 2008.*

U.S. Department of State (DOS), 2201 C Street NW, Washington, DC 20520, (202) 647-4000, www.state.gov; *World Military Expenditures and Arms Transfers (WMEAT).*

The World Bank, 1818 H Street, NW, Washington, DC 20433, (202) 473-1000, Fax: (202) 477-6391, www.worldbank.org; *The World Bank Atlas 2003-2004* and *World Development Indicators (WDI) 2008.*

CAPE VERDE - HIDES AND SKINS INDUSTRY

United Nations Food and Agricultural Organization (FAO), Viale delle Terme di Caracalla, 00100 Rome, Italy, (Dial from U.S. (202) 653-2400), (Fax from U.S. (202) 653 5760), www.fao.org; *FAO Production Yearbook 2002.*

CAPE VERDE - HOUSING

Euromonitor International, Inc., 224 S. Michigan Avenue, Suite 1500, Chicago, IL 60604, (312) 922-1115, Fax: (312) 922-1157, www.euromonitor.com; *World Marketing Data and Statistics.*

CAPE VERDE - ILLITERATE PERSONS

Euromonitor International, Inc., 224 S. Michigan Avenue, Suite 1500, Chicago, IL 60604, (312) 922-1115, Fax: (312) 922-1157, www.euromonitor.com; *The World Economic Factbook 2008.*

UNESCO Institute for Statistics, C.P. 6128 Succursale Centre-Ville, Montreal, Quebec, H3C 3J7 Canada, (Dial from U.S. (514) 343-6880), (Fax from U.S. (514) 343 6882), www.uis.unesco.org; *Statistical Tables.*

United Nations Statistics Division, New York, NY 10017, (800) 253-9646, Fax: (212) 963-4116, http://unstats.un.org; *Human Development Report 2006.*

CAPE VERDE - IMPORTS

Central Intelligence Agency, Office of Public Affairs, Washington, DC 20505, (703) 482-0623, Fax: (703) 482-1739, www.cia.gov; *The World Factbook.*

Economist Intelligence Unit, 111 West 57th Street, New York, NY 10019, (212) 554-0600, Fax: (212) 586-1181, www.eiu.com; *Cape Verde Country Report.*

Euromonitor International, Inc., 224 S. Michigan Avenue, Suite 1500, Chicago, IL 60604, (312) 922-1115, Fax: (312) 922-1157, www.euromonitor.com; *International Marketing Data and Statistics 2008* and *The World Economic Factbook 2008.*

International Monetary Fund (IMF), 700 Nineteenth Street, NW, Washington, DC 20431, (202) 623-7000, Fax: (202) 623-4661, www.imf.org; *Direction of Trade Statistics Yearbook 2007.*

Palgrave Macmillan Ltd., Houndmills, Basingstoke, Hampshire, RG21 6XS, England, (Telephone in U.S. (888) 330-8477), (Fax in U.S. (800) 672-2054), www.palgrave.com; *The Statesman's Yearbook 2008.*

Taylor and Francis Group, An Informa Business, 2 Park Square, Milton Park, Abingdon, Oxford OX14 4RN, United Kingdom, (Dial from U.S. (212) 216-7800), (Fax from U.S. (212) 564-7854), www.tandf.co.uk; *The Europa World Year Book.*

United Nations Conference on Trade and Development (UNCTAD), DC2-1120, United Nations, New York, NY 10017, (212) 963-0027, www.unctad.org; *Handbook of Statistics 2005.*

United Nations Economic Commission for Africa (ECA), PO Box 3001, Addis Ababa, Ethiopia, (Telephone in U.S. (212) 963-4957), www.uneca.org; *African Statistical Yearbook 2006.*

United Nations Food and Agricultural Organization (FAO), Viale delle Terme di Caracalla, 00100 Rome, Italy, (Dial from U.S. (202) 653-2400), (Fax from U.S. (202) 653 5760), www.fao.org; *The State of Food and Agriculture (SOFA) 2006.*

United Nations Statistics Division, New York, NY 10017, (800) 253-9646, Fax: (212) 963-4116, http://unstats.un.org; *Compendium of Intra-African and Related Foreign Trade Statistics 2003* and *Survey of Economic and Social Conditions in Africa 2005.*

The World Bank, 1818 H Street, NW, Washington, DC 20433, (202) 473-1000, Fax: (202) 477-6391, www.worldbank.org; *World Development Indicators (WDI) 2008.*

CAPE VERDE - INDUSTRIES

Central Intelligence Agency, Office of Public Affairs, Washington, DC 20505, (703) 482-0623, Fax: (703) 482-1739, www.cia.gov; *The World Factbook.*

Economist Intelligence Unit, 111 West 57th Street, New York, NY 10019, (212) 554-0600, Fax: (212) 586-1181, www.eiu.com; *Cape Verde Country Report.*

Euromonitor International, Inc., 224 S. Michigan Avenue, Suite 1500, Chicago, IL 60604, (312) 922-1115, Fax: (312) 922-1157, www.euromonitor.com; *The World Economic Factbook 2008* and *World Marketing Data and Statistics.*

International Labour Office, I.L.O. Publications, 4 route des Morillons, CH-1211 Geneva 22, Switzerland, (Telephone in U.S. (202) 653-7652), (Fax in U.S. (202) 653-7687), www.ilo.org; *Yearbook of Labour Statistics 2006.*

Palgrave Macmillan Ltd., Houndmills, Basingstoke, Hampshire, RG21 6XS, England, (Telephone in U.S. (888) 330-8477), (Fax in U.S. (800) 672-2054), www.palgrave.com; *The Statesman's Yearbook 2008.*

Taylor and Francis Group, An Informa Business, 2 Park Square, Milton Park, Abingdon, Oxford OX14 4RN, United Kingdom, (Dial from U.S. (212) 216-7800), (Fax from U.S. (212) 564-7854), www.tandf.co.uk; *The Europa World Year Book.*

United Nations Economic Commission for Africa (ECA), PO Box 3001, Addis Ababa, Ethiopia, (Telephone in U.S. (212) 963-4957), www.uneca.org; *African Statistical Yearbook 2006.*

United Nations Industrial Development Organization (UNIDO), 1 United Nations Plaza, New York, NY 10017, (212) 963 6890, Fax: (212) 963-7904, http://unido.org; Industrial Statistics Database 2008 (INDSTAT) and *The International Yearbook of Industrial Statistics 2008.*

United Nations Statistics Division, New York, NY 10017, (800) 253-9646, Fax: (212) 963-4116, http://unstats.un.org; *Survey of Economic and Social Conditions in Africa 2005.*

The World Bank, 1818 H Street, NW, Washington, DC 20433, (202) 473-1000, Fax: (202) 477-6391, www.worldbank.org; *Cape Verde* and *World Development Indicators (WDI) 2008.*

CAPE VERDE - INFANT AND MATERNAL MORTALITY

See CAPE VERDE - MORTALITY

CAPE VERDE - INTERNATIONAL TRADE

African Development Bank Group, Rue Joseph Anoma, 01 BP 1387 Abidjan 01, Cote d'Ivoire, www.afdb.org; *Statistics Pocketbook 2008.*

Economist Intelligence Unit, 111 West 57th Street, New York, NY 10019, (212) 554-0600, Fax: (212) 586-1181, www.eiu.com; *Cape Verde Country Report.*

Euromonitor International, Inc., 224 S. Michigan Avenue, Suite 1500, Chicago, IL 60604, (312) 922-1115, Fax: (312) 922-1157, www.euromonitor.com; *The World Economic Factbook 2008* and *World Marketing Data and Statistics.*

Organisation for Economic Cooperation and Development (OECD), 2 rue Andre Pascal, F-75775 Paris Cedex 16, France, (Telephone in U.S. (202) 785-6323), (Fax in U.S. (202) 785-0350), www.oecd.org; *International Trade by Commodity Statistics (ITCS).*

Palgrave Macmillan Ltd., Houndmills, Basingstoke, Hampshire, RG21 6XS, England, (Telephone in U.S. (888) 330-8477), (Fax in U.S. (800) 672-2054), www.palgrave.com; *The Statesman's Yearbook 2008.*

Taylor and Francis Group, An Informa Business, 2 Park Square, Milton Park, Abingdon, Oxford OX14 4RN, United Kingdom, (Dial from U.S. (212) 216-7800), (Fax from U.S. (212) 564-7854), www.tandf.co.uk; *The Europa World Year Book.*

United Nations Conference on Trade and Development (UNCTAD), DC2-1120, United Nations, New York, NY 10017, (212) 963-0027, www.unctad.org; *UNCTAD Commodity Yearbook.*

United Nations Economic Commission for Africa (ECA), PO Box 3001, Addis Ababa, Ethiopia, (Telephone in U.S. (212) 963-4957), www.uneca.org; *African Statistical Yearbook 2006.*

United Nations Food and Agricultural Organization (FAO), Viale delle Terme di Caracalla, 00100 Rome, Italy, (Dial from U.S. (202) 653-2400), (Fax from U.S. (202) 653 5760), www.fao.org; *FAO Trade Yearbook* and *The State of Food and Agriculture (SOFA) 2006.*

United Nations Statistics Division, New York, NY 10017, (800) 253-9646, Fax: (212) 963-4116, http://unstats.un.org; *Compendium of Intra-African and Related Foreign Trade Statistics 2003; International Trade Statistics Yearbook;* and *Statistical Yearbook.*

The World Bank, 1818 H Street, NW, Washington, DC 20433, (202) 473-1000, Fax: (202) 477-6391, www.worldbank.org; *Cape Verde* and *World Development Indicators (WDI) 2008.*

World Trade Organization (WTO), Centre William Rappard, Rue de Lausanne 154, CH-1211 Geneva 21, Switzerland, www.wto.org; *International Trade Statistics 2006.*

CAPE VERDE - INTERNET USERS

International Telecommunication Union (ITU), Place des Nations, 1211 Geneva 20, Switzerland, www.itu.int; *World Telecommunication/ICT Indicators Database on CD-ROM; World Telecommunication/ICT Indicators Database Online;* and *Yearbook of Statistics - Telecommunication Services (Chronological Time Series 1997-2006).*

The World Bank, 1818 H Street, NW, Washington, DC 20433, (202) 473-1000, Fax: (202) 477-6391, www.worldbank.org; *Cape Verde.*

CAPE VERDE - LABOR

African Development Bank Group, Rue Joseph Anoma, 01 BP 1387 Abidjan 01, Cote d'Ivoire, www.afdb.org; *Statistics Pocketbook 2008.*

Central Intelligence Agency, Office of Public Affairs, Washington, DC 20505, (703) 482-0623, Fax: (703) 482-1739, www.cia.gov; *The World Factbook.*

Euromonitor International, Inc., 224 S. Michigan Avenue, Suite 1500, Chicago, IL 60604, (312) 922-1115, Fax: (312) 922-1157, www.euromonitor.com; *International Marketing Data and Statistics 2008* and *World Marketing Data and Statistics.*

International Labour Office, I.L.O. Publications, 4 route des Morillons, CH-1211 Geneva 22, Switzerland, (Telephone in U.S. (202) 653-7652), (Fax in U.S. (202) 653-7687), www.ilo.org; *Yearbook of Labour Statistics 2006.*

Palgrave Macmillan Ltd., Houndmills, Basingstoke, Hampshire, RG21 6XS, England, (Telephone in U.S. (888) 330-8477), (Fax in U.S. (800) 672-2054), www.palgrave.com; *The Statesman's Yearbook 2008.*

Taylor and Francis Group, An Informa Business, 2 Park Square, Milton Park, Abingdon, Oxford OX14 4RN, United Kingdom, (Dial from U.S. (212) 216-7800), (Fax from U.S. (212) 564-7854), www.tandf.co.uk; *The Europa World Year Book.*

United Nations Food and Agricultural Organization (FAO), Viale delle Terme di Caracalla, 00100 Rome, Italy, (Dial from U.S. (202) 653-2400), (Fax from U.S. (202) 653 5760), www.fao.org; *The State of Food and Agriculture (SOFA) 2006.*

United Nations Statistics Division, New York, NY 10017, (800) 253-9646, Fax: (212) 963-4116, http://unstats.un.org; *Human Development Report 2006.*

The World Bank, 1818 H Street, NW, Washington, DC 20433, (202) 473-1000, Fax: (202) 477-6391, www.worldbank.org; *The World Bank Atlas 2003-2004* and *World Development Indicators (WDI) 2008.*

CAPE VERDE - LAND USE

Central Intelligence Agency, Office of Public Affairs, Washington, DC 20505, (703) 482-0623, Fax: (703) 482-1739, www.cia.gov; *The World Factbook.*

Euromonitor International, Inc., 224 S. Michigan Avenue, Suite 1500, Chicago, IL 60604, (312) 922-1115, Fax: (312) 922-1157, www.euromonitor.com; *International Marketing Data and Statistics 2008.*

United Nations Food and Agricultural Organization (FAO), Viale delle Terme di Caracalla, 00100 Rome, Italy, (Dial from U.S. (202) 653-2400), (Fax from U.S. (202) 653 5760), www.fao.org; *FAO Production Yearbook 2002.*

CAPE VERDE - LIFE EXPECTANCY

African Development Bank Group, Rue Joseph Anoma, 01 BP 1387 Abidjan 01, Cote d'Ivoire, www.afdb.org; *Statistics Pocketbook 2008.*

Central Intelligence Agency, Office of Public Affairs, Washington, DC 20505, (703) 482-0623, Fax: (703) 482-1739, www.cia.gov; *The World Factbook.*

Euromonitor International, Inc., 224 S. Michigan Avenue, Suite 1500, Chicago, IL 60604, (312) 922-1115, Fax: (312) 922-1157, www.euromonitor.com; *The World Economic Factbook 2008.*

Palgrave Macmillan Ltd., Houndmills, Basingstoke, Hampshire, RG21 6XS, England, (Telephone in U.S. (888) 330-8477), (Fax in U.S. (800) 672-2054), www.palgrave.com; *The Statesman's Yearbook 2008.*

United Nations Statistics Division, New York, NY 10017, (800) 253-9646, Fax: (212) 963-4116, http://unstats.un.org; *Human Development Report 2006* and *World Statistics Pocketbook.*

The World Bank, 1818 H Street, NW, Washington, DC 20433, (202) 473-1000, Fax: (202) 477-6391, www.worldbank.org; *The World Bank Atlas 2003-2004.*

CAPE VERDE - LITERACY

Euromonitor International, Inc., 224 S. Michigan Avenue, Suite 1500, Chicago, IL 60604, (312) 922-1115, Fax: (312) 922-1157, www.euromonitor.com; *World Marketing Data and Statistics.*

United Nations Statistics Division, New York, NY 10017, (800) 253-9646, Fax: (212) 963-4116, http://unstats.un.org; *Survey of Economic and Social Conditions in Africa 2005.*

CAPE VERDE - LIVESTOCK

Palgrave Macmillan Ltd., Houndmills, Basingstoke, Hampshire, RG21 6XS, England, (Telephone in U.S. (888) 330-8477), (Fax in U.S. (800) 672-2054), www.palgrave.com; *The Statesman's Yearbook 2008.*

Taylor and Francis Group, An Informa Business, 2 Park Square, Milton Park, Abingdon, Oxford OX14 4RN, United Kingdom, (Dial from U.S. (212) 216-7800), (Fax from U.S. (212) 564-7854), www.tandf.co.uk; *The Europa World Year Book.*

United Nations Conference on Trade and Development (UNCTAD), DC2-1120, United Nations, New York, NY 10017, (212) 963-0027, www.unctad.org; *UNCTAD Commodity Yearbook.*

United Nations Economic Commission for Africa (ECA), PO Box 3001, Addis Ababa, Ethiopia, (Telephone in U.S. (212) 963-4957), www.uneca.org; *African Statistical Yearbook 2006.*

United Nations Food and Agricultural Organization (FAO), Viale delle Terme di Caracalla, 00100 Rome, Italy, (Dial from U.S. (202) 653-2400), (Fax from U.S. (202) 653 5760), www.fao.org; *FAO Production Yearbook 2002* and *The State of Food and Agriculture (SOFA) 2006.*

United Nations Statistics Division, New York, NY 10017, (800) 253-9646, Fax: (212) 963-4116, http://unstats.un.org; *Statistical Yearbook* and *Survey of Economic and Social Conditions in Africa 2005.*

CAPE VERDE - MANUFACTURES

United Nations Economic Commission for Africa (ECA), PO Box 3001, Addis Ababa, Ethiopia, (Telephone in U.S. (212) 963-4957), www.uneca.org; *African Statistical Yearbook 2006.*

United Nations Statistics Division, New York, NY 10017, (800) 253-9646, Fax: (212) 963-4116, http://unstats.un.org; *Survey of Economic and Social Conditions in Africa 2005.*

The World Bank, 1818 H Street, NW, Washington, DC 20433, (202) 473-1000, Fax: (202) 477-6391, www.worldbank.org; *World Development Indicators (WDI) 2008.*

CAPE VERDE - MARRIAGE

United Nations Statistics Division, New York, NY 10017, (800) 253-9646, Fax: (212) 963-4116, http://unstats.un.org; *Demographic Yearbook* and *Statistical Yearbook.*

CAPE VERDE - MEAT PRODUCTION

See CAPE VERDE - LIVESTOCK

CAPE VERDE - MINERAL INDUSTRIES

Palgrave Macmillan Ltd., Houndmills, Basingstoke, Hampshire, RG21 6XS, England, (Telephone in U.S. (888) 330-8477), (Fax in U.S. (800) 672-2054), www.palgrave.com; *The Statesman's Yearbook 2008.*

Taylor and Francis Group, An Informa Business, 2 Park Square, Milton Park, Abingdon, Oxford OX14 4RN, United Kingdom, (Dial from U.S. (212) 216-7800), (Fax from U.S. (212) 564-7854), www.tandf.co.uk; *The Europa World Year Book.*

United Nations Conference on Trade and Development (UNCTAD), DC2-1120, United Nations, New York, NY 10017, (212) 963-0027, www.unctad.org; *UNCTAD Commodity Yearbook.*

United Nations Economic Commission for Africa (ECA), PO Box 3001, Addis Ababa, Ethiopia, (Telephone in U.S. (212) 963-4957), www.uneca.org; *African Statistical Yearbook 2006.*

United Nations Statistics Division, New York, NY 10017, (800) 253-9646, Fax: (212) 963-4116, http://unstats.un.org; *Statistical Yearbook.*

CAPE VERDE - MONEY EXCHANGE RATES

See CAPE VERDE - FOREIGN EXCHANGE RATES

CAPE VERDE - MONEY SUPPLY

African Development Bank Group, Rue Joseph Anoma, 01 BP 1387 Abidjan 01, Cote d'Ivoire, www.afdb.org; *Statistics Pocketbook 2008.*

Economist Intelligence Unit, 111 West 57th Street, New York, NY 10019, (212) 554-0600, Fax: (212) 586-1181, www.eiu.com; *Cape Verde Country Report.*

Taylor and Francis Group, An Informa Business, 2 Park Square, Milton Park, Abingdon, Oxford OX14 4RN, United Kingdom, (Dial from U.S. (212) 216-7800), (Fax from U.S. (212) 564-7854), www.tandf.co.uk; *The Europa World Year Book.*

The World Bank, 1818 H Street, NW, Washington, DC 20433, (202) 473-1000, Fax: (202) 477-6391, www.worldbank.org; *Cape Verde* and *World Development Indicators (WDI) 2008.*

CAPE VERDE - MORTALITY

Central Intelligence Agency, Office of Public Affairs, Washington, DC 20505, (703) 482-0623, Fax: (703) 482-1739, www.cia.gov; *The World Factbook.*

Euromonitor International, Inc., 224 S. Michigan Avenue, Suite 1500, Chicago, IL 60604, (312) 922-1115, Fax: (312) 922-1157, www.euromonitor.com; *International Marketing Data and Statistics 2008* and *The World Economic Factbook 2008.*

Palgrave Macmillan Ltd., Houndmills, Basingstoke, Hampshire, RG21 6XS, England, (Telephone in U.S. (888) 330-8477), (Fax in U.S. (800) 672-2054), www.palgrave.com; *The Statesman's Yearbook 2008.*

Taylor and Francis Group, An Informa Business, 2 Park Square, Milton Park, Abingdon, Oxford OX14 4RN, United Kingdom, (Dial from U.S. (212) 216-7800), (Fax from U.S. (212) 564-7854), www.tandf.co.uk; *The Europa World Year Book.*

United Nations Statistics Division, New York, NY 10017, (800) 253-9646, Fax: (212) 963-4116, http://unstats.un.org; *Demographic Yearbook; Human Development Report 2006; Statistical Yearbook; Survey of Economic and Social Conditions in Africa 2005;* and *World Statistics Pocketbook.*

The World Bank, 1818 H Street, NW, Washington, DC 20433, (202) 473-1000, Fax: (202) 477-6391, www.worldbank.org; *The World Bank Atlas 2003-2004* and *World Development Indicators (WDI) 2008.*

World Health Organization (WHO), Avenue Appia 20, 1211 Geneve 27, Switzerland, (Telephone in U.S. (212) 331-9081), www.who.int; The WHO Global Atlas of Infectious Diseases and *World Health Report 2006.*

CAPE VERDE - MOTION PICTURES

United Nations Statistics Division, New York, NY 10017, (800) 253-9646, Fax: (212) 963-4116, http://unstats.un.org; *Statistical Yearbook.*

CAPE VERDE - MOTOR VEHICLES

Taylor and Francis Group, An Informa Business, 2 Park Square, Milton Park, Abingdon, Oxford OX14 4RN, United Kingdom, (Dial from U.S. (212) 216-7800), (Fax from U.S. (212) 564-7854), www.tandf.co.uk; *The Europa World Year Book.*

United Nations Statistics Division, New York, NY 10017, (800) 253-9646, Fax: (212) 963-4116, http://unstats.un.org; *Statistical Yearbook* and *Survey of Economic and Social Conditions in Africa 2005.*

CAPE VERDE - NUTRITION

African Development Bank Group, Rue Joseph Anoma, 01 BP 1387 Abidjan 01, Cote d'Ivoire, www.afdb.org; *Statistics Pocketbook 2008.*

United Nations Food and Agricultural Organization (FAO), Viale delle Terme di Caracalla, 00100 Rome, Italy, (Dial from U.S. (202) 653-2400), (Fax from U.S. (202) 653 5760), www.fao.org; *The State of Food and Agriculture (SOFA) 2006.*

CAPE VERDE - PESTICIDES

United Nations Food and Agricultural Organization (FAO), Viale delle Terme di Caracalla, 00100 Rome, Italy, (Dial from U.S. (202) 653-2400), (Fax from U.S. (202) 653 5760), www.fao.org; *The State of Food and Agriculture (SOFA) 2006.*

CAPE VERDE - PETROLEUM INDUSTRY AND TRADE

PennWell Corporation, 1421 South Sheridan Road, Tulsa, OK 74112, (918) 835-3161, www.pennwell.com; *International Petroleum Encyclopedia 2007.*

United Nations Conference on Trade and Development (UNCTAD), DC2-1120, United Nations, New York, NY 10017, (212) 963-0027, www.unctad.org; *UNCTAD Commodity Yearbook.*

United Nations Food and Agricultural Organization (FAO), Viale delle Terme di Caracalla, 00100 Rome, Italy, (Dial from U.S. (202) 653-2400), (Fax from U.S. (202) 653 5760), www.fao.org; *The State of Food and Agriculture (SOFA) 2006.*

CAPE VERDE - POLITICAL SCIENCE

Central Intelligence Agency, Office of Public Affairs, Washington, DC 20505, (703) 482-0623, Fax: (703) 482-1739, www.cia.gov; *The World Factbook.*

Palgrave Macmillan Ltd., Houndmills, Basingstoke, Hampshire, RG21 6XS, England, (Telephone in U.S. (888) 330-8477), (Fax in U.S. (800) 672-2054), www.palgrave.com; *The Statesman's Yearbook 2008.*

Taylor and Francis Group, An Informa Business, 2 Park Square, Milton Park, Abingdon, Oxford OX14 4RN, United Kingdom, (Dial from U.S. (212) 216-7800), (Fax from U.S. (212) 564-7854), www.tandf.co.uk; *The Europa World Year Book.*

United Nations Statistics Division, New York, NY 10017, (800) 253-9646, Fax: (212) 963-4116, http://unstats.un.org; *National Accounts Statistics: Compendium of Income Distribution Statistics* and *Survey of Economic and Social Conditions in Africa 2005.*

The World Bank, 1818 H Street, NW, Washington, DC 20433, (202) 473-1000, Fax: (202) 477-6391, www.worldbank.org; *World Development Indicators (WDI) 2008.*

CAPE VERDE - POPULATION

African Development Bank Group, Rue Joseph Anoma, 01 BP 1387 Abidjan 01, Cote d'Ivoire, www.afdb.org; *The African Statistical Journal; Gender, Poverty and Environmental Indicators on African Countries 2007; Selected Statistics on African Countries 2007;* and *Statistics Pocketbook 2008.*

Central Intelligence Agency, Office of Public Affairs, Washington, DC 20505, (703) 482-0623, Fax: (703) 482-1739, www.cia.gov; *The World Factbook.*

Economist Intelligence Unit, 111 West 57th Street, New York, NY 10019, (212) 554-0600, Fax: (212) 586-1181, www.eiu.com; *Cape Verde Country Report.*

Euromonitor International, Inc., 224 S. Michigan Avenue, Suite 1500, Chicago, IL 60604, (312) 922-1115, Fax: (312) 922-1157, www.euromonitor.com; *International Marketing Data and Statistics 2008* and *The World Economic Factbook 2008.*

Eurostat, Batiment Jean Monnet, Rue Alcide de Gasperi, L-2920 Luxembourg, http://epp.eurostat.ec.europa.eu; *Demographic Indicators - Population by Age-Classes.*

International Labour Office, I.L.O. Publications, 4 route des Morillons, CH-1211 Geneva 22, Switzerland, (Telephone in U.S. (202) 653-7652), (Fax in U.S. (202) 653-7687), www.ilo.org; *Yearbook of Labour Statistics 2006.*

Palgrave Macmillan Ltd., Houndmills, Basingstoke, Hampshire, RG21 6XS, England, (Telephone in U.S. (888) 330-8477), (Fax in U.S. (800) 672-2054), www.palgrave.com; *The Statesman's Yearbook 2008.*

Taylor and Francis Group, An Informa Business, 2 Park Square, Milton Park, Abingdon, Oxford OX14 4RN, United Kingdom, (Dial from U.S. (212) 216-7800), (Fax from U.S. (212) 564-7854), www.tandf.co.uk; *The Europa World Year Book.*

U.S. Department of State (DOS), 2201 C Street NW, Washington, DC 20520, (202) 647-4000, www.state.gov; *World Military Expenditures and Arms Transfers (WMEAT).*

UNESCO Institute for Statistics, C.P. 6128 Succursale Centre-Ville, Montreal, Quebec, H3C 3J7 Canada, (Dial from U.S. (514) 343-6880), (Fax from U.S. (514) 343 6882), www.uis.unesco.org; *Statistical Tables.*

United Nations Food and Agricultural Organization (FAO), Viale delle Terme di Caracalla, 00100 Rome, Italy, (Dial from U.S. (202) 653-2400), (Fax from U.S. (202) 653 5760), www.fao.org; *FAO Production Yearbook 2002.*

United Nations Statistics Division, New York, NY 10017, (800) 253-9646, Fax: (212) 963-4116, http://unstats.un.org; *Demographic Yearbook; Human Development Report 2006; Statistical Yearbook; Survey of Economic and Social Conditions in Africa 2005;* and *World Statistics Pocketbook.*

The World Bank, 1818 H Street, NW, Washington, DC 20433, (202) 473-1000, Fax: (202) 477-6391, www.worldbank.org; *Cape Verde* and *The World Bank Atlas 2003-2004.*

World Health Organization (WHO), Avenue Appia 20, 1211 Geneve 27, Switzerland, (Telephone in U.S. (212) 331-9081), www.who.int; *World Health Report 2006.*

CAPE VERDE - POPULATION DENSITY

African Development Bank Group, Rue Joseph Anoma, 01 BP 1387 Abidjan 01, Cote d'Ivoire, www.afdb.org; *Statistics Pocketbook 2008.*

Central Intelligence Agency, Office of Public Affairs, Washington, DC 20505, (703) 482-0623, Fax: (703) 482-1739, www.cia.gov; *The World Factbook.*

Euromonitor International, Inc., 224 S. Michigan Avenue, Suite 1500, Chicago, IL 60604, (312) 922-1115, Fax: (312) 922-1157, www.euromonitor.com; *The World Economic Factbook 2008.*

Palgrave Macmillan Ltd., Houndmills, Basingstoke, Hampshire, RG21 6XS, England, (Telephone in U.S. (888) 330-8477), (Fax in U.S. (800) 672-2054), www.palgrave.com; *The Statesman's Yearbook 2008.*

Taylor and Francis Group, An Informa Business, 2 Park Square, Milton Park, Abingdon, Oxford OX14 4RN, United Kingdom, (Dial from U.S. (212) 216-7800), (Fax from U.S. (212) 564-7854), www.tandf.co.uk; *The Europa World Year Book.*

UNESCO Institute for Statistics, C.P. 6128 Succursale Centre-Ville, Montreal, Quebec, H3C 3J7 Canada, (Dial from U.S. (514) 343-6880), (Fax from U.S. (514) 343 6882), www.uis.unesco.org; *Statistical Tables.*

United Nations Food and Agricultural Organization (FAO), Viale delle Terme di Caracalla, 00100 Rome, Italy, (Dial from U.S. (202) 653-2400), (Fax from U.S. (202) 653 5760), www.fao.org; *The State of Food and Agriculture (SOFA) 2006.*

United Nations Statistics Division, New York, NY 10017, (800) 253-9646, Fax: (212) 963-4116, http://unstats.un.org; *Statistical Yearbook* and *Survey of Economic and Social Conditions in Africa 2005.*

The World Bank, 1818 H Street, NW, Washington, DC 20433, (202) 473-1000, Fax: (202) 477-6391, www.worldbank.org; *Cape Verde.*

CAPE VERDE - POSTAL SERVICE

United Nations Statistics Division, New York, NY 10017, (800) 253-9646, Fax: (212) 963-4116, http://unstats.un.org; *Statistical Yearbook.*

CAPE VERDE - POWER RESOURCES

Euromonitor International, Inc., 224 S. Michigan Avenue, Suite 1500, Chicago, IL 60604, (312) 922-1115, Fax: (312) 922-1157, www.euromonitor.com; *International Marketing Data and Statistics 2008; The World Economic Factbook 2008;* and *World Marketing Data and Statistics.*

Platts, 2 Penn Plaza, 25th Floor, New York, NY 10121-2298, (212) 904-3070, www.platts.com; *Energy Economist.*

United Nations Economic Commission for Africa (ECA), PO Box 3001, Addis Ababa, Ethiopia, (Telephone in U.S. (212) 963-4957), www.uneca.org; *African Statistical Yearbook 2006.*

United Nations Food and Agricultural Organization (FAO), Viale delle Terme di Caracalla, 00100 Rome, Italy, (Dial from U.S. (202) 653-2400), (Fax from U.S. (202) 653 5760), www.fao.org; *The State of Food and Agriculture (SOFA) 2006.*

United Nations Statistics Division, New York, NY 10017, (800) 253-9646, Fax: (212) 963-4116, http://unstats.un.org; *Energy Statistics Yearbook 2003; Human Development Report 2006;* and *World Statistics Pocketbook.*

The World Bank, 1818 H Street, NW, Washington, DC 20433, (202) 473-1000, Fax: (202) 477-6391, www.worldbank.org; *The World Bank Atlas 2003-2004.*

CAPE VERDE - PRICES

Euromonitor International, Inc., 224 S. Michigan Avenue, Suite 1500, Chicago, IL 60604, (312) 922-1115, Fax: (312) 922-1157, www.euromonitor.com; *World Marketing Data and Statistics.*

International Labour Office, I.L.O. Publications, 4 route des Morillons, CH-1211 Geneva 22, Switzerland, (Telephone in U.S. (202) 653-7652), (Fax in U.S. (202) 653-7687), www.ilo.org; *Yearbook of Labour Statistics 2006.*

United Nations Food and Agricultural Organization (FAO), Viale delle Terme di Caracalla, 00100 Rome, Italy, (Dial from U.S. (202) 653-2400), (Fax from U.S. (202) 653 5760), www.fao.org; *FAO Production Yearbook 2002* and *The State of Food and Agriculture (SOFA) 2006.*

The World Bank, 1818 H Street, NW, Washington, DC 20433, (202) 473-1000, Fax: (202) 477-6391, www.worldbank.org; *Cape Verde.*

CAPE VERDE - PUBLIC HEALTH

African Development Bank Group, Rue Joseph Anoma, 01 BP 1387 Abidjan 01, Cote d'Ivoire, www.afdb.org; *Statistics Pocketbook 2008.*

Euromonitor International, Inc., 224 S. Michigan Avenue, Suite 1500, Chicago, IL 60604, (312) 922-1115, Fax: (312) 922-1157, www.euromonitor.com; *World Marketing Data and Statistics.*

Palgrave Macmillan Ltd., Houndmills, Basingstoke, Hampshire, RG21 6XS, England, (Telephone in U.S. (888) 330-8477), (Fax in U.S. (800) 672-2054), www.palgrave.com; *The Statesman's Yearbook 2008.*

United Nations Economic Commission for Africa (ECA), PO Box 3001, Addis Ababa, Ethiopia, (Telephone in U.S. (212) 963-4957), www.uneca.org; *African Statistical Yearbook 2006.*

United Nations Statistics Division, New York, NY 10017, (800) 253-9646, Fax: (212) 963-4116, http://unstats.un.org; *Human Development Report 2006* and *Statistical Yearbook.*

The World Bank, 1818 H Street, NW, Washington, DC 20433, (202) 473-1000, Fax: (202) 477-6391, www.worldbank.org; *Cape Verde.*

World Health Organization (WHO), Avenue Appia 20, 1211 Geneve 27, Switzerland, (Telephone in U.S. (212) 331-9081), www.who.int; The WHO Global Atlas of Infectious Diseases and *World Health Report 2006.*

CAPE VERDE - PUBLISHERS AND PUBLISHING

Taylor and Francis Group, An Informa Business, 2 Park Square, Milton Park, Abingdon, Oxford OX14 4RN, United Kingdom, (Dial from U.S. (212) 216-7800), (Fax from U.S. (212) 564-7854), www.tandf.co.uk; *The Europa World Year Book.*

CAPE VERDE - RADIO BROADCASTING

Palgrave Macmillan Ltd., Houndmills, Basingstoke, Hampshire, RG21 6XS, England, (Telephone in U.S. (888) 330-8477), (Fax in U.S. (800) 672-2054), www.palgrave.com; *The Statesman's Yearbook 2008.*

CAPE VERDE - RAILROADS

United Nations Economic Commission for Africa (ECA), PO Box 3001, Addis Ababa, Ethiopia, (Telephone in U.S. (212) 963-4957), www.uneca.org; *African Statistical Yearbook 2006.*

CAPE VERDE - RELIGION

Central Intelligence Agency, Office of Public Affairs, Washington, DC 20505, (703) 482-0623, Fax: (703) 482-1739, www.cia.gov; *The World Factbook.*

Palgrave Macmillan Ltd., Houndmills, Basingstoke, Hampshire, RG21 6XS, England, (Telephone in U.S. (888) 330-8477), (Fax in U.S. (800) 672-2054), www.palgrave.com; *The Statesman's Yearbook 2008.*

CAPE VERDE - RESERVES (ACCOUNTING)

African Development Bank Group, Rue Joseph Anoma, 01 BP 1387 Abidjan 01, Cote d'Ivoire, www.afdb.org; *Statistics Pocketbook 2008.*

The World Bank, 1818 H Street, NW, Washington, DC 20433, (202) 473-1000, Fax: (202) 477-6391, www.worldbank.org; *World Development Indicators (WDI) 2008.*

CAPE VERDE - RETAIL TRADE

Euromonitor International, Inc., 224 S. Michigan Avenue, Suite 1500, Chicago, IL 60604, (312) 922-1115, Fax: (312) 922-1157, www.euromonitor.com; *World Marketing Data and Statistics.*

CAPE VERDE - ROADS

Central Intelligence Agency, Office of Public Affairs, Washington, DC 20505, (703) 482-0623, Fax: (703) 482-1739, www.cia.gov; *The World Factbook.*

Palgrave Macmillan Ltd., Houndmills, Basingstoke, Hampshire, RG21 6XS, England, (Telephone in U.S. (888) 330-8477), (Fax in U.S. (800) 672-2054), www.palgrave.com; *The Statesman's Yearbook 2008.*

United Nations Economic Commission for Africa (ECA), PO Box 3001, Addis Ababa, Ethiopia, (Telephone in U.S. (212) 963-4957), www.uneca.org; *African Statistical Yearbook 2006.*

United Nations Statistics Division, New York, NY 10017, (800) 253-9646, Fax: (212) 963-4116, http://unstats.un.org; *Survey of Economic and Social Conditions in Africa 2005.*

CAPE VERDE - SALT PRODUCTION

See CAPE VERDE - MINERAL INDUSTRIES

CAPE VERDE - SHEEP

See CAPE VERDE - LIVESTOCK

CAPE VERDE - SHIPPING

Palgrave Macmillan Ltd., Houndmills, Basingstoke, Hampshire, RG21 6XS, England, (Telephone in U.S. (888) 330-8477), (Fax in U.S. (800) 672-2054), www.palgrave.com; *The Statesman's Yearbook 2008.*

Taylor and Francis Group, An Informa Business, 2 Park Square, Milton Park, Abingdon, Oxford OX14 4RN, United Kingdom, (Dial from U.S. (212) 216-7800), (Fax from U.S. (212) 564-7854), www.tandf.co.uk; *The Europa World Year Book.*

United Nations Economic Commission for Africa (ECA), PO Box 3001, Addis Ababa, Ethiopia, (Telephone in U.S. (212) 963-4957), www.uneca.org; *African Statistical Yearbook 2006.*

United Nations Statistics Division, New York, NY 10017, (800) 253-9646, Fax: (212) 963-4116, http://unstats.un.org; *Statistical Yearbook.*

CAPE VERDE - SOCIAL ECOLOGY

United Nations Statistics Division, New York, NY 10017, (800) 253-9646, Fax: (212) 963-4116, http://unstats.un.org; *World Statistics Pocketbook.*

CAPE VERDE - SOCIAL SECURITY

Palgrave Macmillan Ltd., Houndmills, Basingstoke, Hampshire, RG21 6XS, England, (Telephone in U.S. (888) 330-8477), (Fax in U.S. (800) 672-2054), www.palgrave.com; *The Statesman's Yearbook 2008.*

United Nations Statistics Division, New York, NY 10017, (800) 253-9646, Fax: (212) 963-4116, http://unstats.un.org; *National Accounts Statistics: Compendium of Income Distribution Statistics.*

CAPE VERDE - TAXATION

The World Bank, 1818 H Street, NW, Washington, DC 20433, (202) 473-1000, Fax: (202) 477-6391, www.worldbank.org; *World Development Indicators (WDI) 2008.*

CAPE VERDE - TELEPHONE

International Telecommunication Union (ITU), Place des Nations, 1211 Geneva 20, Switzerland, www.itu.int; World Telecommunication Indicators Database.

Palgrave Macmillan Ltd., Houndmills, Basingstoke, Hampshire, RG21 6XS, England, (Telephone in U.S. (888) 330-8477), (Fax in U.S. (800) 672-2054), www.palgrave.com; *The Statesman's Yearbook 2008.*

Taylor and Francis Group, An Informa Business, 2 Park Square, Milton Park, Abingdon, Oxford OX14 4RN, United Kingdom, (Dial from U.S. (212) 216-7800), (Fax from U.S. (212) 564-7854), www.tandf.co.uk; *The Europa World Year Book.*

United Nations Statistics Division, New York, NY 10017, (800) 253-9646, Fax: (212) 963-4116, http://unstats.un.org; *Statistical Yearbook* and *World Statistics Pocketbook.*

CAPE VERDE - TEXTILE INDUSTRY

Palgrave Macmillan Ltd., Houndmills, Basingstoke, Hampshire, RG21 6XS, England, (Telephone in U.S. (888) 330-8477), (Fax in U.S. (800) 672-2054), www.palgrave.com; *The Statesman's Yearbook 2008.*

United Nations Conference on Trade and Development (UNCTAD), DC2-1120, United Nations, New York, NY 10017, (212) 963-0027, www.unctad.org; *UNCTAD Commodity Yearbook.*

CAPE VERDE - TOBACCO INDUSTRY

Foreign Agricultural Service (FAS), U.S. Department of Agriculture (USDA), 1400 Independence Avenue, SW, Washington, DC 20250, (202) 720-3935, www.fas.usda.gov; *Tobacco: World Markets and Trade.*

United Nations Statistics Division, New York, NY 10017, (800) 253-9646, Fax: (212) 963-4116, http://unstats.un.org; *Statistical Yearbook.*

CAPE VERDE - TOURISM

Euromonitor International, Inc., 224 S. Michigan Avenue, Suite 1500, Chicago, IL 60604, (312) 922-1115, Fax: (312) 922-1157, www.euromonitor.com; *The World Economic Factbook 2008* and *World Marketing Data and Statistics.*

United Nations Economic Commission for Africa (ECA), PO Box 3001, Addis Ababa, Ethiopia, (Telephone in U.S. (212) 963-4957), www.uneca.org; *African Statistical Yearbook 2006.*

The World Bank, 1818 H Street, NW, Washington, DC 20433, (202) 473-1000, Fax: (202) 477-6391, www.worldbank.org; *Cape Verde.*

CAPE VERDE - TRADE

See CAPE VERDE - INTERNATIONAL TRADE

CAPE VERDE - TRANSPORTATION

Central Intelligence Agency, Office of Public Affairs, Washington, DC 20505, (703) 482-0623, Fax: (703) 482-1739, www.cia.gov; *The World Factbook.*

Euromonitor International, Inc., 224 S. Michigan Avenue, Suite 1500, Chicago, IL 60604, (312) 922-1115, Fax: (312) 922-1157, www.euromonitor.com; *International Marketing Data and Statistics 2008* and *World Marketing Data and Statistics.*

Palgrave Macmillan Ltd., Houndmills, Basingstoke, Hampshire, RG21 6XS, England, (Telephone in U.S. (888) 330-8477), (Fax in U.S. (800) 672-2054), www.palgrave.com; *The Statesman's Yearbook 2008.*

Taylor and Francis Group, An Informa Business, 2 Park Square, Milton Park, Abingdon, Oxford OX14 4RN, United Kingdom, (Dial from U.S. (212) 216-7800), (Fax from U.S. (212) 564-7854), www.tandf.co.uk; *The Europa World Year Book.*

United Nations Economic Commission for Africa (ECA), PO Box 3001, Addis Ababa, Ethiopia, (Telephone in U.S. (212) 963-4957), www.uneca.org; *African Statistical Yearbook 2006.*

United Nations Statistics Division, New York, NY 10017, (800) 253-9646, Fax: (212) 963-4116, http://unstats.un.org; *Human Development Report 2006.*

The World Bank, 1818 H Street, NW, Washington, DC 20433, (202) 473-1000, Fax: (202) 477-6391, www.worldbank.org; *Africa Live Database (LDB)* and *Cape Verde*.

CAPE VERDE - UNEMPLOYMENT

Central Intelligence Agency, Office of Public Affairs, Washington, DC 20505, (703) 482-0623, Fax: (703) 482-1739, www.cia.gov; *The World Factbook*.

International Labour Office, I.L.O. Publications, 4 route des Morillons, CH-1211 Geneva 22, Switzerland, (Telephone in U.S. (202) 653-7652), (Fax in U.S. (202) 653-7687), www.ilo.org; *Yearbook of Labour Statistics 2006*.

CAPE VERDE - VITAL STATISTICS

Palgrave Macmillan Ltd., Houndmills, Basingstoke, Hampshire, RG21 6XS, England, (Telephone in U.S. (888) 330-8477), (Fax in U.S. (800) 672-2054), www.palgrave.com; *The Statesman's Yearbook 2008*.

United Nations Statistics Division, New York, NY 10017, (800) 253-9646, Fax: (212) 963-4116, http://unstats.un.org; *Statistical Yearbook*.

World Health Organization (WHO), Avenue Appia 20, 1211 Geneve 27, Switzerland, (Telephone in U.S. (212) 331-9081), www.who.int; *World Health Report 2006*.

CAPE VERDE - WAGES

International Labour Office, I.L.O. Publications, 4 route des Morillons, CH-1211 Geneva 22, Switzerland, (Telephone in U.S. (202) 653-7652), (Fax in U.S. (202) 653-7687), www.ilo.org; *Yearbook of Labour Statistics 2006*.

The World Bank, 1818 H Street, NW, Washington, DC 20433, (202) 473-1000, Fax: (202) 477-6391, www.worldbank.org; *Cape Verde*.

CAPITAL

See also Individual industries

International Monetary Fund (IMF), 700 Nineteenth Street, NW, Washington, DC 20431, (202) 623-7000, Fax: (202) 623-4661, www.imf.org; *GFSR Market Update* and *Global Financial Stability Report (April 2008 Edition)*.

Thomson Financial, 195 Broadway, New York, NY 10007, (646) 822-2000, www.thomson.com; *International Financing Review (IFR)* and *Thomson Financial News*.

CAPITAL - BANKS AND BANKING

Federal Deposit Insurance Corporation (FDIC), 550 Seventeenth Street, NW, Washington, DC 20429-0002, (877) 275-3342, www.fdic.gov; *Quarterly Banking Profile (QBP)* and *State Banking Performance Summary*.

CAPITAL - EXPENDITURES

U.S. Census Bureau, Company Statistics Division, 4700 Silver Hill Road, Washington DC 20233-0001, (301) 763-3030, www.census.gov/csd/; *Annual Capital Expenditures Survey (ACES)*.

CAPITAL - NEW SECURITY ISSUES

Board of Governors of the Federal Reserve System, Constitution Avenue, NW, Washington, DC 20551, (202) 452-3000, www.federalreserve.gov; *Federal Reserve Bulletin*.

CAPITAL - RESIDENTIAL

Bureau of Economic Analysis (BEA), U.S. Department of Commerce (DOC), 1441 L Street NW, Washington, DC 20230, (202) 606-9900, www.bea.gov; National Income and Product Accounts (NIPA) Tables (web app) and *Survey of Current Business (SCB)*.

CAPITAL - STOCKS - COMMODITY MARKET PRICE INDEXES

Bureau of Economic Analysis (BEA), U.S. Department of Commerce (DOC), 1441 L Street NW, Washington, DC 20230, (202) 606-9900, www.bea.gov; *Survey of Current Business (SCB)* and unpublished data.

U.S. Census Bureau, Manufacturing and Construction Division, 4600 Silver Hill Road, Washington DC 20233, (301) 763-4673, www.census.gov/mcd; *Current Industrial Reports*.

CAPITAL - UTILITIES

American Gas Association, 400 North Capitol Street, NW, Washington, DC 20001-1535, (202) 824-7000, www.aga.org; *Gas Facts*.

Edison Electric Institute (EEI), 701 Pennsylvania Avenue, NW, Washington, DC 20004-2696, (202) 508-5000, www.eei.org; *Historical Statistics of the Electric Utility Industry through 1992*.

Federal Communications Commission (FCC), Wireline Competition Bureau (WCB), 445 12th Street, SW, Washington, DC 20554, (202) 418-1500, Fax: (202) 418-2825, www.fcc.gov/wcb; *Statistics of Communications Common Carriers 2005/2006*.

U.S. Department of Energy (DOE), Energy Information Administration (EIA), 1000 Independence Avenue, SW, Washington, DC 20585, (202) 586-8800, www.eia.doe.gov; *Electric Power Annual*.

CAPITAL EQUIPMENT - PRODUCER PRICE INDEXES

U.S. Bureau of Labor Statistics (BLS), Postal Square Building, 2 Massachusetts Avenue, NE, Washington, DC 20212-0001, (202) 691-5200, Fax: (202) 691-6325, www.bls.gov; *Producer Price Indexes (PPI)*.

CAPITAL PUNISHMENT

Death Penalty Information Center, 1101 Vermont Avenue, NW, Suite 701, Washington, DC 20005, (202) 289-2275, www.deathpenaltyinfo.org; *Blind Justice: Juries Deciding Life and Death with Only Half the Truth; A Crisis of Confidence: Americans' Doubts About the Death Penalty; The Death Penalty in 2005: Death Sentences Reach Record Lows as Country Turns to Life Without Parole; The Death Penalty in 2006: Use of the Death Penalty Declines in 2006; The Death Penalty in 2007: Execution Chambers Silent as Supreme Court Considers Next Step; The Death Penalty in Black and White: Who Lives, Who Dies, Who Decides; Innocence and the Crisis in the American Death Penalty;* and *International Perspectives on the Death Penalty: A Costly Isolation for the U.S.*

U.S. Department of Justice (DOJ), Bureau of Justice Statistics, 810 Seventh Street, NW, Washington, DC 20531, (202) 307-0765, www.ojp.usdoj.gov/bjs/; *Capital Punishment, 2004*.

CARBON DIOXIDE EMISSIONS

Intergovernmental Panel on Climate Change (IPCC), www.ipcc.ch; *Carbon Dioxide Capture and Storage; Climate Change 2007: Working Group II Report - Impacts, Adaptation and Vulnerability; The Regional Impacts of Climate Change: An Assessment of Vulnerability;* and *Safeguarding the Ozone Layer and the Global Climate System: Issues Related to Hydrofluorocarbons and Perfluorocarbons*.

Platts, 2 Penn Plaza, 25th Floor, New York, NY 10121-2298, (212) 904-3070, www.platts.com; *Emissions Daily* and *European Power Daily*.

Population Reference Bureau, 1875 Connecticut Avenue, NW, Suite 520, Washington, DC, 20009-5728, (800) 877-9881, Fax: (202) 328-3937, www.prb.org; *Making the Link: Population, Health, Environment*.

U.S. Department of Energy (DOE), Energy Information Administration (EIA), 1000 Independence Avenue, SW, Washington, DC 20585, (202) 586-8800, www.eia.doe.gov; *Emissions of Greenhouse Gases in the United States 2005; International Energy Annual 2004; International Energy Outlook 2006;* and *International Energy Outlook 2006*.

U.S. Environmental Protection Agency (EPA) National Center for Environmental Research (NCER), Ariel Rios Building, 1200 Pennsylvania Avenue, NW, Washington, D.C. 20460, http://es.epa.gov/ncer; *Combustion Emissions from Hazardous Waste Incinerators, Boilers and Industrial Furnaces, and Municipal Solid Waste Incinerators - Results from Five STAR Grants and Research Needs*.

United Nations Environment Programme (UNEP), PO Box 30552, Nairobi, Kenya, www.unep.org; *Climate Action*.

CARDIAC CATHERIZATION

National Center for Health Statistics (NCHS), Centers for Disease Control and Prevention (CDC), U.S. Department of Health and Human Services (HHS), 3311 Toledo Road, Hyattsville, MD 20782, (866) 232-4636, www.cdc.gov/nchs; unpublished data.

CARDIOVASCULAR DISEASE

See HEART DISEASE

CARIBBEAN AREA

Caribbean Epidemiology Centre (CAREC), 16-18 Jamaica Boulevard, Federation Park, PO Box 164, Port of Spain, Republic of Trinidad and Tobago, (Dial from U.S. (868) 622-4261), (Fax from U.S. (868) 622-2792), www.carec.org; *20 Years of the HIV/AIDS Epidemic in the Caribbean;* AIDS Statistics; and *Population Data*.

Economic Commission for Latin America and the Caribbean (ECLAC), Av. Dag Hammarskjold 3477, Vitacura, Santiago, Chile, www.eclac.cl/estadisticas/default.asp?idioma=IN; *Statistical Yearbook for Latin America and the Caribbean, 2005*.

CARJACKING

U.S. Department of Justice (DOJ), Bureau of Justice Statistics, 810 Seventh Street, NW, Washington, DC 20531, (202) 307-0765, www.ojp.usdoj.gov/bjs/; *Carjacking, 1993-2002*.

CARPETS AND RUGS

U.S. Census Bureau, Manufacturing and Construction Division, 4600 Silver Hill Road, Washington DC 20233, (301) 763-4673, www.census.gov/mcd; *Current Industrial Reports* and *Current Industrial Reports, Manufacturing Profiles*.

CARROTS

Economic Research Service (ERS), U.S. Department of Agriculture (USDA), 1800 M Street, NW, Washington, DC 20036-5831, (202) 694-5050, Fax: (202) 694-5689, www.ers.usda.gov; *Agricultural Income and Finance Outlook; Agricultural Outlook; Agricultural Statistics;* and *Food CPI, Prices, and Expenditures*.

National Agricultural Statistics Service (NASS), U.S. Department of Agriculture (USDA), 1400 Independence Avenue, SW, Washington, DC 20250, (800) 727-9540, Fax: (202) 690-2090, www.nass.usda.gov; *Vegetables: 2004 Annual Summary*.

CARS

See AUTOMOBILES

CASSETTES

Recording Industry Association of America (RIAA), 10th Floor, 1025 F Street, NW, Washington, DC 20004, (202) 775-0101, www.riaa.com; *2007 U.S. Manufacturers' Unit Shipments and Value Chart*.

CASUALTIES - MILITARY CONFLICT

U.S. Department of Defense (DOD), Statistical Information Analysis Division (SIAD), The Pentagon, Washington, DC 20301, (703) 545-6700, http://siadapp.dior.whs.mil/; unpublished data.

CASUALTY INSURANCE

Insurance Information Institute (III), 110 William Street, New York, NY 10038, (212) 346-5500, www.iii.org; *Insurance Fact Book 2007*.

CAT OWNERSHIP

American Veterinary Medical Association (AVMA), 1931 North Meacham Road, Suite 100, Schaumburg, IL 60173, (847) 925-8070, Fax: (847) 925-1329, www.avma.org; *U.S. Pet Ownership and Demographics Sourcebook.*

CAT SCAN

National Center for Health Statistics (NCHS), Centers for Disease Control and Prevention (CDC), U.S. Department of Health and Human Services (HHS), 3311 Toledo Road, Hyattsville, MD 20782, (866) 232-4636, www.cdc.gov/nchs; unpublished data.

CATALOG AND MAIL SALES

Office of Trade and Industry Information (OTII), Manufacturing and Services, International Trade Administration, U.S. Department of Commerce, 1401 Constitution Ave, NW, Washington, DC 20230, (800) USA TRAD(E), http://trade.gov/index.asp; *TradeStats Express.*

U.S. Census Bureau, 4700 Silver Hill Road, Washington DC 20233-0001, (301) 763-3030, www.census.gov; unpublished data.

U.S. Census Bureau, Center for Economic Studies, 4600 Silver Hill Road, Washington DC 20233, (301) 457-1235, www.ces.census.gov; *2002 Economic Census, Retail Trade* and *2002 Economic Census, Wholesale Trade.*

U.S. Census Bureau, Company Statistics Division, 4700 Silver Hill Road, Washington DC 20233-0001, (301) 763-3030, www.census.gov/csd/; *Current Business Reports.*

CATFISH

National Agricultural Statistics Service (NASS), U.S. Department of Agriculture (USDA), 1400 Independence Avenue, SW, Washington, DC 20250, (800) 727-9540, Fax: (202) 690-2090, www.nass.usda.gov; *Catfish Processing* and *Catfish Production.*

CATHOLIC POPULATION

See RELIGION

CATTLE - FARM MARKETINGS, SALES

Economic Research Service (ERS), U.S. Department of Agriculture (USDA), 1800 M Street, NW, Washington, DC 20036-5831, (202) 694-5050, Fax: (202) 694-5689, www.ers.usda.gov; *Agricultural Resource Management Study (ARMS).*

CATTLE - IMPORTS

Economic Research Service (ERS), U.S. Department of Agriculture (USDA), 1800 M Street, NW, Washington, DC 20036-5831, (202) 694-5050, Fax: (202) 694-5689, www.ers.usda.gov; *Foreign Agricultural Trade of the United States (FATUS)* and *U.S. Agricultural Trade Update: 2006.*

CATTLE - NUMBER ON FARMS

Economic Research Service (ERS), U.S. Department of Agriculture (USDA), 1800 M Street, NW, Washington, DC 20036-5831, (202) 694-5050, Fax: (202) 694-5689, www.ers.usda.gov; *Agricultural Statistics.*

National Agricultural Statistics Service (NASS), U.S. Department of Agriculture (USDA), 1400 Independence Avenue, SW, Washington, DC 20250, (800) 727-9540, Fax: (202) 690-2090, www.nass.usda.gov; *2006 Agricultural Statistics; Cattle: Final Estimates, 1999-2003; Meat Animals Production, Disposition, and Income;* and *Milk Cows and Milk Production.*

CATTLE - ORGANIC

Economic Research Service (ERS), U.S. Department of Agriculture (USDA), 1800 M Street, NW, Washington, DC 20036-5831, (202) 694-5050, Fax: (202) 694-5689, www.ers.usda.gov; *Organic Production.*

CATTLE - PRICES

Economic Research Service (ERS), U.S. Department of Agriculture (USDA), 1800 M Street, NW, Washington, DC 20036-5831, (202) 694-5050, Fax: (202) 694-5689, www.ers.usda.gov; *Agricultural Statistics.*

National Agricultural Statistics Service (NASS), U.S. Department of Agriculture (USDA), 1400 Independence Avenue, SW, Washington, DC 20250, (800) 727-9540, Fax: (202) 690-2090, www.nass.usda.gov; *Cattle: Final Estimates, 1999-2003* and *Meat Animals Production, Disposition, and Income.*

CATTLE - PRODUCTION

Economic Research Service (ERS), U.S. Department of Agriculture (USDA), 1800 M Street, NW, Washington, DC 20036-5831, (202) 694-5050, Fax: (202) 694-5689, www.ers.usda.gov; *Agricultural Statistics.*

National Agricultural Statistics Service (NASS), U.S. Department of Agriculture (USDA), 1400 Independence Avenue, SW, Washington, DC 20250, (800) 727-9540, Fax: (202) 690-2090, www.nass.usda.gov; *2006 Agricultural Statistics* and *Meat Animals Production, Disposition, and Income.*

CATTLE - SLAUGHTER

National Agricultural Statistics Service (NASS), U.S. Department of Agriculture (USDA), 1400 Independence Avenue, SW, Washington, DC 20250, (800) 727-9540, Fax: (202) 690-2090, www.nass.usda.gov; *Livestock Slaughter* and *Meat Animals Production, Disposition, and Income.*

CATTLE - VALUE ON FARMS

Economic Research Service (ERS), U.S. Department of Agriculture (USDA), 1800 M Street, NW, Washington, DC 20036-5831, (202) 694-5050, Fax: (202) 694-5689, www.ers.usda.gov; *Agricultural Statistics.*

National Agricultural Statistics Service (NASS), U.S. Department of Agriculture (USDA), 1400 Independence Avenue, SW, Washington, DC 20250, (800) 727-9540, Fax: (202) 690-2090, www.nass.usda.gov; *Meat Animals Production, Disposition, and Income.*

CAULIFLOWER

Economic Research Service (ERS), U.S. Department of Agriculture (USDA), 1800 M Street, NW, Washington, DC 20036-5831, (202) 694-5050, Fax: (202) 694-5689, www.ers.usda.gov; *Agricultural Outlook; Agricultural Statistics;* and *Food CPI, Prices, and Expenditures.*

National Agricultural Statistics Service (NASS), U.S. Department of Agriculture (USDA), 1400 Independence Avenue, SW, Washington, DC 20250, (800) 727-9540, Fax: (202) 690-2090, www.nass.usda.gov; *Vegetables: 2004 Annual Summary.*

CAYMAN ISLANDS - NATIONAL STATISTICAL OFFICE

Economics Statistics Office, Government Administration Building, Grand Cayman, Cayman Islands BWI, (Dial from U.S. (345) 949-0940), (Fax from U.S. (345) 949-8782), www.eso.ky; National Data Center.

CAYMAN ISLANDS - PRIMARY STATISTICS SOURCES

Economics Statistics Office, Government Administration Building, Grand Cayman, Cayman Islands BWI, (Dial from U.S. (345) 949-0940), (Fax from U.S. (345) 949-8782), www.eso.ky; *2004 Compendium of Statistics.*

CAYMAN ISLANDS - AGRICULTURE

Economist Intelligence Unit, 111 West 57th Street, New York, NY 10019, (212) 554-0600, Fax: (212) 586-1181, www.eiu.com; *Cayman Islands Country Report.*

Euromonitor International, Inc., 224 S. Michigan Avenue, Suite 1500, Chicago, IL 60604, (312) 922-1115, Fax: (312) 922-1157, www.euromonitor.com; *World Marketing Data and Statistics.*

Taylor and Francis Group, An Informa Business, 2 Park Square, Milton Park, Abingdon, Oxford OX14 4RN, United Kingdom, (Dial from U.S. (212) 216-7800), (Fax from U.S. (212) 564-7854), www.tandf.co.uk; *The Europa World Year Book.*

United Nations Conference on Trade and Development (UNCTAD), DC2-1120, United Nations, New York, NY 10017, (212) 963-0027, www.unctad.org; *UNCTAD Commodity Yearbook.*

United Nations Food and Agricultural Organization (FAO), Viale delle Terme di Caracalla, 00100 Rome, Italy, (Dial from U.S. (202) 653-2400), (Fax from U.S. (202) 653 5760), www.fao.org; AQUASTAT; *FAO Production Yearbook 2002; FAO Trade Yearbook;* and *The State of Food and Agriculture (SOFA) 2006.*

CAYMAN ISLANDS - AIRLINES

Palgrave Macmillan Ltd., Houndmills, Basingstoke, Hampshire, RG21 6XS, England, (Telephone in U.S. (888) 330-8477), (Fax in U.S. (800) 672-2054), www.palgrave.com; *The Statesman's Yearbook 2008.*

CAYMAN ISLANDS - AIRPORTS

Central Intelligence Agency, Office of Public Affairs, Washington, DC 20505, (703) 482-0623, Fax: (703) 482-1739, www.cia.gov; *The World Factbook.*

CAYMAN ISLANDS - ARMED FORCES

Central Intelligence Agency, Office of Public Affairs, Washington, DC 20505, (703) 482-0623, Fax: (703) 482-1739, www.cia.gov; *The World Factbook.*

Euromonitor International, Inc., 224 S. Michigan Avenue, Suite 1500, Chicago, IL 60604, (312) 922-1115, Fax: (312) 922-1157, www.euromonitor.com; *World Marketing Data and Statistics.*

CAYMAN ISLANDS - BANKS AND BANKING

Euromonitor International, Inc., 224 S. Michigan Avenue, Suite 1500, Chicago, IL 60604, (312) 922-1115, Fax: (312) 922-1157, www.euromonitor.com; *World Marketing Data and Statistics.*

Palgrave Macmillan Ltd., Houndmills, Basingstoke, Hampshire, RG21 6XS, England, (Telephone in U.S. (888) 330-8477), (Fax in U.S. (800) 672-2054), www.palgrave.com; *The Statesman's Yearbook 2008.*

CAYMAN ISLANDS - BROADCASTING

Central Intelligence Agency, Office of Public Affairs, Washington, DC 20505, (703) 482-0623, Fax: (703) 482-1739, www.cia.gov; *The World Factbook.*

Euromonitor International, Inc., 224 S. Michigan Avenue, Suite 1500, Chicago, IL 60604, (312) 922-1115, Fax: (312) 922-1157, www.euromonitor.com; *World Marketing Data and Statistics.*

Palgrave Macmillan Ltd., Houndmills, Basingstoke, Hampshire, RG21 6XS, England, (Telephone in U.S. (888) 330-8477), (Fax in U.S. (800) 672-2054), www.palgrave.com; *The Statesman's Yearbook 2008.*

UNESCO Institute for Statistics, C.P. 6128 Succursale Centre-Ville, Montreal, Quebec, H3C 3J7 Canada, (Dial from U.S. (514) 343-6880), (Fax from U.S. (514) 343 6882), www.uis.unesco.org; *Statistical Tables.*

WRTH Publications Limited, PO Box 290, Oxford OX2 7FT, UK, www.wrth.com; *World Radio TV Handbook 2007.*

CAYMAN ISLANDS - BUDGET

Central Intelligence Agency, Office of Public Affairs, Washington, DC 20505, (703) 482-0623, Fax: (703) 482-1739, www.cia.gov; *The World Factbook.*

CAYMAN ISLANDS - CHILDBIRTH - STATISTICS

Central Intelligence Agency, Office of Public Affairs, Washington, DC 20505, (703) 482-0623, Fax: (703) 482-1739, www.cia.gov; *The World Factbook.*

Euromonitor International, Inc., 224 S. Michigan Avenue, Suite 1500, Chicago, IL 60604, (312) 922-1115, Fax: (312) 922-1157, www.euromonitor.com; *International Marketing Data and Statistics 2008* and *The World Economic Factbook 2008.*

Taylor and Francis Group, An Informa Business, 2 Park Square, Milton Park, Abingdon, Oxford OX14 4RN, United Kingdom, (Dial from U.S. (212) 216-7800), (Fax from U.S. (212) 564-7854), www.tandf.co.uk; *The Europa World Year Book.*

United Nations Statistics Division, New York, NY 10017, (800) 253-9646, Fax: (212) 963-4116, http://unstats.un.org; *Demographic Yearbook* and *Statistical Yearbook.*

CAYMAN ISLANDS - CLIMATE

Palgrave Macmillan Ltd., Houndmills, Basingstoke, Hampshire, RG21 6XS, England, (Telephone in U.S. (888) 330-8477), (Fax in U.S. (800) 672-2054), www.palgrave.com; *The Statesman's Yearbook 2008.*

CAYMAN ISLANDS - COAL PRODUCTION

See CAYMAN ISLANDS - MINERAL INDUSTRIES

CAYMAN ISLANDS - COMMERCE

Palgrave Macmillan Ltd., Houndmills, Basingstoke, Hampshire, RG21 6XS, England, (Telephone in U.S. (888) 330-8477), (Fax in U.S. (800) 672-2054), www.palgrave.com; *The Statesman's Yearbook 2008.*

CAYMAN ISLANDS - COMMODITY EXCHANGES

United Nations Food and Agricultural Organization (FAO), Viale delle Terme di Caracalla, 00100 Rome, Italy, (Dial from U.S. (202) 653-2400), (Fax from U.S. (202) 653 5760), www.fao.org; *The State of Food and Agriculture (SOFA) 2006.*

CAYMAN ISLANDS - CONSUMER PRICE INDEXES

Taylor and Francis Group, An Informa Business, 2 Park Square, Milton Park, Abingdon, Oxford OX14 4RN, United Kingdom, (Dial from U.S. (212) 216-7800), (Fax from U.S. (212) 564-7854), www.tandf.co.uk; *The Europa World Year Book.*

CAYMAN ISLANDS - CORN INDUSTRY

See CAYMAN ISLANDS - CROPS

CAYMAN ISLANDS - CROPS

United Nations Conference on Trade and Development (UNCTAD), DC2-1120, United Nations, New York, NY 10017, (212) 963-0027, www.unctad.org; *UNCTAD Commodity Yearbook.*

United Nations Food and Agricultural Organization (FAO), Viale delle Terme di Caracalla, 00100 Rome, Italy, (Dial from U.S. (202) 653-2400), (Fax from U.S. (202) 653 5760), www.fao.org; *The State of Food and Agriculture (SOFA) 2006.*

CAYMAN ISLANDS - DAIRY PROCESSING

United Nations Food and Agricultural Organization (FAO), Viale delle Terme di Caracalla, 00100 Rome, Italy, (Dial from U.S. (202) 653-2400), (Fax from U.S. (202) 653 5760), www.fao.org; *The State of Food and Agriculture (SOFA) 2006.*

CAYMAN ISLANDS - DEATH RATES

See CAYMAN ISLANDS - MORTALITY

CAYMAN ISLANDS - DEMOGRAPHY

Euromonitor International, Inc., 224 S. Michigan Avenue, Suite 1500, Chicago, IL 60604, (312) 922-1115, Fax: (312) 922-1157, www.euromonitor.com; *International Marketing Data and Statistics 2008; The World Economic Factbook 2008;* and *World Marketing Data and Statistics.*

CAYMAN ISLANDS - DISPOSABLE INCOME

United Nations Statistics Division, New York, NY 10017, (800) 253-9646, Fax: (212) 963-4116, http://unstats.un.org; *National Accounts Statistics: Compendium of Income Distribution Statistics.*

CAYMAN ISLANDS - DIVORCE

United Nations Statistics Division, New York, NY 10017, (800) 253-9646, Fax: (212) 963-4116, http://unstats.un.org; *Demographic Yearbook* and *Statistical Yearbook.*

CAYMAN ISLANDS - ECONOMIC CONDITIONS

Central Intelligence Agency, Office of Public Affairs, Washington, DC 20505, (703) 482-0623, Fax: (703) 482-1739, www.cia.gov; *The World Factbook.*

Economist Intelligence Unit, 111 West 57th Street, New York, NY 10019, (212) 554-0600, Fax: (212) 586-1181, www.eiu.com; *Cayman Islands Country Report.*

Euromonitor International, Inc., 224 S. Michigan Avenue, Suite 1500, Chicago, IL 60604, (312) 922-1115, Fax: (312) 922-1157, www.euromonitor.com; *The World Economic Factbook 2008* and *World Marketing Data and Statistics.*

Palgrave Macmillan Ltd., Houndmills, Basingstoke, Hampshire, RG21 6XS, England, (Telephone in U.S. (888) 330-8477), (Fax in U.S. (800) 672-2054), www.palgrave.com; *The Statesman's Yearbook 2008.*

CAYMAN ISLANDS - EDUCATION

Euromonitor International, Inc., 224 S. Michigan Avenue, Suite 1500, Chicago, IL 60604, (312) 922-1115, Fax: (312) 922-1157, www.euromonitor.com; *International Marketing Data and Statistics 2008* and *World Marketing Data and Statistics.*

Palgrave Macmillan Ltd., Houndmills, Basingstoke, Hampshire, RG21 6XS, England, (Telephone in U.S. (888) 330-8477), (Fax in U.S. (800) 672-2054), www.palgrave.com; *The Statesman's Yearbook 2008.*

Taylor and Francis Group, An Informa Business, 2 Park Square, Milton Park, Abingdon, Oxford OX14 4RN, United Kingdom, (Dial from U.S. (212) 216-7800), (Fax from U.S. (212) 564-7854), www.tandf.co.uk; *The Europa World Year Book.*

UNESCO Institute for Statistics, C.P. 6128 Succursale Centre-Ville, Montreal, Quebec, H3C 3J7 Canada, (Dial from U.S. (514) 343-6880), (Fax from U.S. (514) 343 6882), www.uis.unesco.org; *Statistical Tables.*

CAYMAN ISLANDS - ELECTRICITY

Palgrave Macmillan Ltd., Houndmills, Basingstoke, Hampshire, RG21 6XS, England, (Telephone in U.S. (888) 330-8477), (Fax in U.S. (800) 672-2054), www.palgrave.com; *The Statesman's Yearbook 2008.*

United Nations Statistics Division, New York, NY 10017, (800) 253-9646, Fax: (212) 963-4116, http://unstats.un.org; *Statistical Yearbook.*

CAYMAN ISLANDS - EMPLOYMENT

Euromonitor International, Inc., 224 S. Michigan Avenue, Suite 1500, Chicago, IL 60604, (312) 922-1115, Fax: (312) 922-1157, www.euromonitor.com; *International Marketing Data and Statistics 2008.*

CAYMAN ISLANDS - ENVIRONMENTAL CONDITIONS

DSI Data Service Information, Xantener Strasse 51a, D-47495 Rheinberg, Germany, www.dsidata.com; *Campus Solution.*

Economist Intelligence Unit, 111 West 57th Street, New York, NY 10019, (212) 554-0600, Fax: (212) 586-1181, www.eiu.com; *Cayman Islands Country Report.*

CAYMAN ISLANDS - EXPORTS

Central Intelligence Agency, Office of Public Affairs, Washington, DC 20505, (703) 482-0623, Fax: (703) 482-1739, www.cia.gov; *The World Factbook.*

Economist Intelligence Unit, 111 West 57th Street, New York, NY 10019, (212) 554-0600, Fax: (212) 586-1181, www.eiu.com; *Cayman Islands Country Report.*

Euromonitor International, Inc., 224 S. Michigan Avenue, Suite 1500, Chicago, IL 60604, (312) 922-1115, Fax: (312) 922-1157, www.euromonitor.com; *International Marketing Data and Statistics 2008* and *The World Economic Factbook 2008.*

Palgrave Macmillan Ltd., Houndmills, Basingstoke, Hampshire, RG21 6XS, England, (Telephone in U.S. (888) 330-8477), (Fax in U.S. (800) 672-2054), www.palgrave.com; *The Statesman's Yearbook 2008.*

Taylor and Francis Group, An Informa Business, 2 Park Square, Milton Park, Abingdon, Oxford OX14 4RN, United Kingdom, (Dial from U.S. (212) 216-7800), (Fax from U.S. (212) 564-7854), www.tandf.co.uk; *The Europa World Year Book.*

United Nations Food and Agricultural Organization (FAO), Viale delle Terme di Caracalla, 00100 Rome, Italy, (Dial from U.S. (202) 653-2400), (Fax from U.S. (202) 653 5760), www.fao.org; *The State of Food and Agriculture (SOFA) 2006.*

CAYMAN ISLANDS - FERTILITY, HUMAN

Central Intelligence Agency, Office of Public Affairs, Washington, DC 20505, (703) 482-0623, Fax: (703) 482-1739, www.cia.gov; *The World Factbook.*

CAYMAN ISLANDS - FERTILIZER INDUSTRY

United Nations Food and Agricultural Organization (FAO), Viale delle Terme di Caracalla, 00100 Rome, Italy, (Dial from U.S. (202) 653-2400), (Fax from U.S. (202) 653 5760), www.fao.org; *The State of Food and Agriculture (SOFA) 2006.*

CAYMAN ISLANDS - FETAL MORTALITY

See CAYMAN ISLANDS - MORTALITY

CAYMAN ISLANDS - FINANCE, PUBLIC

Economist Intelligence Unit, 111 West 57th Street, New York, NY 10019, (212) 554-0600, Fax: (212) 586-1181, www.eiu.com; *Cayman Islands Country Report.*

Palgrave Macmillan Ltd., Houndmills, Basingstoke, Hampshire, RG21 6XS, England, (Telephone in U.S. (888) 330-8477), (Fax in U.S. (800) 672-2054), www.palgrave.com; *The Statesman's Yearbook 2008.*

Taylor and Francis Group, An Informa Business, 2 Park Square, Milton Park, Abingdon, Oxford OX14 4RN, United Kingdom, (Dial from U.S. (212) 216-7800), (Fax from U.S. (212) 564-7854), www.tandf.co.uk; *The Europa World Year Book.*

CAYMAN ISLANDS - FISHERIES

Taylor and Francis Group, An Informa Business, 2 Park Square, Milton Park, Abingdon, Oxford OX14 4RN, United Kingdom, (Dial from U.S. (212) 216-7800), (Fax from U.S. (212) 564-7854), www.tandf.co.uk; *The Europa World Year Book.*

United Nations Conference on Trade and Development (UNCTAD), DC2-1120, United Nations, New York, NY 10017, (212) 963-0027, www.unctad.org; *UNCTAD Commodity Yearbook.*

United Nations Food and Agricultural Organization (FAO), Viale delle Terme di Caracalla, 00100 Rome, Italy, (Dial from U.S. (202) 653-2400), (Fax from U.S. (202) 653 5760), www.fao.org; *FAO Yearbook of Fishery Statistics;* Fishery Databases; FISHSTAT Database. Subjects covered include: Aquaculture production, capture production, fishery commodities; and *The State of Food and Agriculture (SOFA) 2006.*

CAYMAN ISLANDS - FOOD

United Nations Conference on Trade and Development (UNCTAD), DC2-1120, United Nations, New York, NY 10017, (212) 963-0027, www.unctad.org; *UNCTAD Commodity Yearbook.*

United Nations Food and Agricultural Organization (FAO), Viale delle Terme di Caracalla, 00100 Rome, Italy, (Dial from U.S. (202) 653-2400), (Fax from U.S. (202) 653 5760), www.fao.org; *FAO Production Yearbook 2002* and *The State of Food and Agriculture (SOFA) 2006.*

CAYMAN ISLANDS - FOREIGN EXCHANGE RATES

Central Intelligence Agency, Office of Public Affairs, Washington, DC 20505, (703) 482-0623, Fax: (703) 482-1739, www.cia.gov; *The World Factbook.*

Euromonitor International, Inc., 224 S. Michigan Avenue, Suite 1500, Chicago, IL 60604, (312) 922-1115, Fax: (312) 922-1157, www.euromonitor.com; *International Marketing Data and Statistics 2008* and *The World Economic Factbook 2008.*

Taylor and Francis Group, An Informa Business, 2 Park Square, Milton Park, Abingdon, Oxford OX14 4RN, United Kingdom, (Dial from U.S. (212) 216-7800), (Fax from U.S. (212) 564-7854), www.tandf.co.uk; *The Europa World Year Book.*

CAYMAN ISLANDS - FORESTS AND FORESTRY

United Nations Conference on Trade and Development (UNCTAD), DC2-1120, United Nations, New York, NY 10017, (212) 963-0027, www.unctad.org; *UNCTAD Commodity Yearbook.*

United Nations Food and Agricultural Organization (FAO), Viale delle Terme di Caracalla, 00100 Rome, Italy, (Dial from U.S. (202) 653-2400), (Fax from U.S. (202) 653 5760), www.fao.org; *The State of Food and Agriculture (SOFA) 2006.*

United Nations Statistics Division, New York, NY 10017, (800) 253-9646, Fax: (212) 963-4116, http://unstats.un.org; *Statistical Yearbook.*

CAYMAN ISLANDS - GROSS DOMESTIC PRODUCT

Economist Intelligence Unit, 111 West 57th Street, New York, NY 10019, (212) 554-0600, Fax: (212) 586-1181, www.eiu.com; *Cayman Islands Country Report.*

Euromonitor International, Inc., 224 S. Michigan Avenue, Suite 1500, Chicago, IL 60604, (312) 922-1115, Fax: (312) 922-1157, www.euromonitor.com; *International Marketing Data and Statistics 2008* and *The World Economic Factbook 2008.*

Taylor and Francis Group, An Informa Business, 2 Park Square, Milton Park, Abingdon, Oxford OX14 4RN, United Kingdom, (Dial from U.S. (212) 216-7800), (Fax from U.S. (212) 564-7854), www.tandf.co.uk; *The Europa World Year Book.*

United Nations Statistics Division, New York, NY 10017, (800) 253-9646, Fax: (212) 963-4116, http://unstats.un.org; *National Accounts Statistics: Compendium of Income Distribution Statistics.*

CAYMAN ISLANDS - GROSS NATIONAL PRODUCT

Palgrave Macmillan Ltd., Houndmills, Basingstoke, Hampshire, RG21 6XS, England, (Telephone in U.S. (888) 330-8477), (Fax in U.S. (800) 672-2054), www.palgrave.com; *The Statesman's Yearbook 2008.*

CAYMAN ISLANDS - HOUSING

Euromonitor International, Inc., 224 S. Michigan Avenue, Suite 1500, Chicago, IL 60604, (312) 922-1115, Fax: (312) 922-1157, www.euromonitor.com; *World Marketing Data and Statistics.*

CAYMAN ISLANDS - ILLITERATE PERSONS

Euromonitor International, Inc., 224 S. Michigan Avenue, Suite 1500, Chicago, IL 60604, (312) 922-1115, Fax: (312) 922-1157, www.euromonitor.com; *The World Economic Factbook 2008.*

UNESCO Institute for Statistics, C.P. 6128 Succursale Centre-Ville, Montreal, Quebec, H3C 3J7 Canada, (Dial from U.S. (514) 343-6880), (Fax from U.S. (514) 343 6882), www.uis.unesco.org; *Statistical Tables.*

CAYMAN ISLANDS - IMPORTS

Central Intelligence Agency, Office of Public Affairs, Washington, DC 20505, (703) 482-0623, Fax: (703) 482-1739, www.cia.gov; *The World Factbook.*

Economist Intelligence Unit, 111 West 57th Street, New York, NY 10019, (212) 554-0600, Fax: (212) 586-1181, www.eiu.com; *Cayman Islands Country Report.*

Euromonitor International, Inc., 224 S. Michigan Avenue, Suite 1500, Chicago, IL 60604, (312) 922-1115, Fax: (312) 922-1157, www.euromonitor.com; *International Marketing Data and Statistics 2008* and *The World Economic Factbook 2008.*

Palgrave Macmillan Ltd., Houndmills, Basingstoke, Hampshire, RG21 6XS, England, (Telephone in U.S. (888) 330-8477), (Fax in U.S. (800) 672-2054), www.palgrave.com; *The Statesman's Yearbook 2008.*

Taylor and Francis Group, An Informa Business, 2 Park Square, Milton Park, Abingdon, Oxford OX14 4RN, United Kingdom, (Dial from U.S. (212) 216-7800), (Fax from U.S. (212) 564-7854), www.tandf.co.uk; *The Europa World Year Book.*

United Nations Food and Agricultural Organization (FAO), Viale delle Terme di Caracalla, 00100 Rome, Italy, (Dial from U.S. (202) 653-2400), (Fax from U.S. (202) 653 5760), www.fao.org; *The State of Food and Agriculture (SOFA) 2006.*

CAYMAN ISLANDS - INDUSTRIES

Central Intelligence Agency, Office of Public Affairs, Washington, DC 20505, (703) 482-0623, Fax: (703) 482-1739, www.cia.gov; *The World Factbook.*

Economist Intelligence Unit, 111 West 57th Street, New York, NY 10019, (212) 554-0600, Fax: (212) 586-1181, www.eiu.com; *Cayman Islands Country Report.*

Euromonitor International, Inc., 224 S. Michigan Avenue, Suite 1500, Chicago, IL 60604, (312) 922-1115, Fax: (312) 922-1157, www.euromonitor.com; *The World Economic Factbook 2008* and *World Marketing Data and Statistics.*

Palgrave Macmillan Ltd., Houndmills, Basingstoke, Hampshire, RG21 6XS, England, (Telephone in U.S. (888) 330-8477), (Fax in U.S. (800) 672-2054), www.palgrave.com; *The Statesman's Yearbook 2008.*

Taylor and Francis Group, An Informa Business, 2 Park Square, Milton Park, Abingdon, Oxford OX14 4RN, United Kingdom, (Dial from U.S. (212) 216-7800), (Fax from U.S. (212) 564-7854), www.tandf.co.uk; *The Europa World Year Book.*

CAYMAN ISLANDS - INFANT AND MATERNAL MORTALITY

See CAYMAN ISLANDS - MORTALITY

CAYMAN ISLANDS - INTERNATIONAL TRADE

Economist Intelligence Unit, 111 West 57th Street, New York, NY 10019, (212) 554-0600, Fax: (212) 586-1181, www.eiu.com; *Cayman Islands Country Report.*

Euromonitor International, Inc., 224 S. Michigan Avenue, Suite 1500, Chicago, IL 60604, (312) 922-1115, Fax: (312) 922-1157, www.euromonitor.com; *The World Economic Factbook 2008* and *World Marketing Data and Statistics.*

Organisation for Economic Cooperation and Development (OECD), 2 rue Andre Pascal, F-75775 Paris Cedex 16, France, (Telephone in U.S. (202) 785-6323), (Fax in U.S. (202) 785-0350), www.oecd.org; *International Trade by Commodity Statistics (ITCS).*

Palgrave Macmillan Ltd., Houndmills, Basingstoke, Hampshire, RG21 6XS, England, (Telephone in U.S. (888) 330-8477), (Fax in U.S. (800) 672-2054), www.palgrave.com; *The Statesman's Yearbook 2008.*

United Nations Conference on Trade and Development (UNCTAD), DC2-1120, United Nations, New York, NY 10017, (212) 963-0027, www.unctad.org; *UNCTAD Commodity Yearbook.*

United Nations Food and Agricultural Organization (FAO), Viale delle Terme di Caracalla, 00100 Rome, Italy, (Dial from U.S. (202) 653-2400), (Fax from U.S. (202) 653 5760), www.fao.org; *FAO Trade Yearbook* and *The State of Food and Agriculture (SOFA) 2006.*

World Trade Organization (WTO), Centre William Rappard, Rue de Lausanne 154, CH-1211 Geneva 21, Switzerland, www.wto.org; *International Trade Statistics 2006.*

CAYMAN ISLANDS - LABOR

Central Intelligence Agency, Office of Public Affairs, Washington, DC 20505, (703) 482-0623, Fax: (703) 482-1739, www.cia.gov; *The World Factbook.*

Euromonitor International, Inc., 224 S. Michigan Avenue, Suite 1500, Chicago, IL 60604, (312) 922-1115, Fax: (312) 922-1157, www.euromonitor.com; *International Marketing Data and Statistics 2008* and *World Marketing Data and Statistics.*

Taylor and Francis Group, An Informa Business, 2 Park Square, Milton Park, Abingdon, Oxford OX14 4RN, United Kingdom, (Dial from U.S. (212) 216-7800), (Fax from U.S. (212) 564-7854), www.tandf.co.uk; *The Europa World Year Book.*

United Nations Food and Agricultural Organization (FAO), Viale delle Terme di Caracalla, 00100 Rome, Italy, (Dial from U.S. (202) 653-2400), (Fax from U.S. (202) 653 5760), www.fao.org; *The State of Food and Agriculture (SOFA) 2006.*

CAYMAN ISLANDS - LAND USE

Central Intelligence Agency, Office of Public Affairs, Washington, DC 20505, (703) 482-0623, Fax: (703) 482-1739, www.cia.gov; *The World Factbook.*

Euromonitor International, Inc., 224 S. Michigan Avenue, Suite 1500, Chicago, IL 60604, (312) 922-1115, Fax: (312) 922-1157, www.euromonitor.com; *International Marketing Data and Statistics 2008.*

United Nations Food and Agricultural Organization (FAO), Viale delle Terme di Caracalla, 00100 Rome, Italy, (Dial from U.S. (202) 653-2400), (Fax from U.S. (202) 653 5760), www.fao.org; *FAO Production Yearbook 2002.*

CAYMAN ISLANDS - LIFE EXPECTANCY

Central Intelligence Agency, Office of Public Affairs, Washington, DC 20505, (703) 482-0623, Fax: (703) 482-1739, www.cia.gov; *The World Factbook.*

Euromonitor International, Inc., 224 S. Michigan Avenue, Suite 1500, Chicago, IL 60604, (312) 922-1115, Fax: (312) 922-1157, www.euromonitor.com; *The World Economic Factbook 2008.*

CAYMAN ISLANDS - LITERACY

Euromonitor International, Inc., 224 S. Michigan Avenue, Suite 1500, Chicago, IL 60604, (312) 922-1115, Fax: (312) 922-1157, www.euromonitor.com; *World Marketing Data and Statistics.*

CAYMAN ISLANDS - LIVESTOCK

Taylor and Francis Group, An Informa Business, 2 Park Square, Milton Park, Abingdon, Oxford OX14 4RN, United Kingdom, (Dial from U.S. (212) 216-7800), (Fax from U.S. (212) 564-7854), www.tandf.co.uk; *The Europa World Year Book.*

United Nations Conference on Trade and Development (UNCTAD), DC2-1120, United Nations, New York, NY 10017, (212) 963-0027, www.unctad.org; *UNCTAD Commodity Yearbook.*

United Nations Food and Agricultural Organization (FAO), Viale delle Terme di Caracalla, 00100 Rome, Italy, (Dial from U.S. (202) 653-2400), (Fax from U.S. (202) 653 5760), www.fao.org; *FAO Production Yearbook 2002* and *The State of Food and Agriculture (SOFA) 2006.*

CAYMAN ISLANDS - MARRIAGE

Taylor and Francis Group, An Informa Business, 2 Park Square, Milton Park, Abingdon, Oxford OX14 4RN, United Kingdom, (Dial from U.S. (212) 216-7800), (Fax from U.S. (212) 564-7854), www.tandf.co.uk; *The Europa World Year Book.*

United Nations Statistics Division, New York, NY 10017, (800) 253-9646, Fax: (212) 963-4116, http://unstats.un.org; *Demographic Yearbook* and *Statistical Yearbook.*

CAYMAN ISLANDS - MEAT PRODUCTION

See CAYMAN ISLANDS - LIVESTOCK

CAYMAN ISLANDS - MINERAL INDUSTRIES

United Nations Conference on Trade and Development (UNCTAD), DC2-1120, United Nations, New York, NY 10017, (212) 963-0027, www.unctad.org; *UNCTAD Commodity Yearbook.*

United Nations Statistics Division, New York, NY 10017, (800) 253-9646, Fax: (212) 963-4116, http://unstats.un.org; *Statistical Yearbook.*

CAYMAN ISLANDS - MONEY SUPPLY

Economist Intelligence Unit, 111 West 57th Street, New York, NY 10019, (212) 554-0600, Fax: (212) 586-1181, www.eiu.com; *Cayman Islands Country Report.*

CAYMAN ISLANDS - MORTALITY

Central Intelligence Agency, Office of Public Affairs, Washington, DC 20505, (703) 482-0623, Fax: (703) 482-1739, www.cia.gov; *The World Factbook.*

Euromonitor International, Inc., 224 S. Michigan Avenue, Suite 1500, Chicago, IL 60604, (312) 922-1115, Fax: (312) 922-1157, www.euromonitor.com; *International Marketing Data and Statistics 2008* and *The World Economic Factbook 2008.*

Taylor and Francis Group, An Informa Business, 2 Park Square, Milton Park, Abingdon, Oxford OX14 4RN, United Kingdom, (Dial from U.S. (212) 216-7800), (Fax from U.S. (212) 564-7854), www.tandf.co.uk; *The Europa World Year Book.*

United Nations Statistics Division, New York, NY 10017, (800) 253-9646, Fax: (212) 963-4116, http://unstats.un.org; *Demographic Yearbook* and *Statistical Yearbook.*

World Health Organization (WHO), Avenue Appia 20, 1211 Geneve 27, Switzerland, (Telephone in U.S. (212) 331-9081), www.who.int; *World Health Report 2006.*

CAYMAN ISLANDS - MOTION PICTURES

United Nations Statistics Division, New York, NY 10017, (800) 253-9646, Fax: (212) 963-4116, http://unstats.un.org; *Statistical Yearbook.*

CAYMAN ISLANDS - MOTOR VEHICLES

Taylor and Francis Group, An Informa Business, 2 Park Square, Milton Park, Abingdon, Oxford OX14 4RN, United Kingdom, (Dial from U.S. (212) 216-7800), (Fax from U.S. (212) 564-7854), www.tandf.co.uk; *The Europa World Year Book.*

CAYMAN ISLANDS - NUTRITION

United Nations Food and Agricultural Organization (FAO), Viale delle Terme di Caracalla, 00100 Rome, Italy, (Dial from U.S. (202) 653-2400), (Fax from U.S. (202) 653 5760), www.fao.org; *The State of Food and Agriculture (SOFA) 2006.*

CAYMAN ISLANDS - PERIODICALS

UNESCO Institute for Statistics, C.P. 6128 Succursale Centre-Ville, Montreal, Quebec, H3C 3J7 Canada, (Dial from U.S. (514) 343-6880), (Fax from U.S. (514) 343 6882), www.uis.unesco.org; *Statistical Tables.*

CAYMAN ISLANDS - PESTICIDES

United Nations Food and Agricultural Organization (FAO), Viale delle Terme di Caracalla, 00100 Rome, Italy, (Dial from U.S. (202) 653-2400), (Fax from U.S. (202) 653 5760), www.fao.org; *The State of Food and Agriculture (SOFA) 2006.*

CAYMAN ISLANDS - PETROLEUM INDUSTRY AND TRADE

PennWell Corporation, 1421 South Sheridan Road, Tulsa, OK 74112, (918) 835-3161, www.pennwell.com; *International Petroleum Encyclopedia 2007.*

United Nations Conference on Trade and Development (UNCTAD), DC2-1120, United Nations, New York, NY 10017, (212) 963-0027, www.unctad.org; *UNCTAD Commodity Yearbook.*

United Nations Food and Agricultural Organization (FAO), Viale delle Terme di Caracalla, 00100 Rome, Italy, (Dial from U.S. (202) 653-2400), (Fax from U.S. (202) 653 5760), www.fao.org; *The State of Food and Agriculture (SOFA) 2006.*

CAYMAN ISLANDS - POLITICAL SCIENCE

Central Intelligence Agency, Office of Public Affairs, Washington, DC 20505, (703) 482-0623, Fax: (703) 482-1739, www.cia.gov; *The World Factbook.*

Palgrave Macmillan Ltd., Houndmills, Basingstoke, Hampshire, RG21 6XS, England, (Telephone in U.S. (888) 330-8477), (Fax in U.S. (800) 672-2054), www.palgrave.com; *The Statesman's Yearbook 2008.*

Taylor and Francis Group, An Informa Business, 2 Park Square, Milton Park, Abingdon, Oxford OX14 4RN, United Kingdom, (Dial from U.S. (212) 216-7800), (Fax from U.S. (212) 564-7854), www.tandf.co.uk; *The Europa World Year Book.*

United Nations Statistics Division, New York, NY 10017, (800) 253-9646, Fax: (212) 963-4116, http://unstats.un.org; *National Accounts Statistics: Compendium of Income Distribution Statistics.*

CAYMAN ISLANDS - POPULATION

Caribbean Epidemiology Centre (CAREC), 16-18 Jamaica Boulevard, Federation Park, PO Box 164, Port of Spain, Republic of Trinidad and Tobago, (Dial from U.S. (868) 622-4261), (Fax from U.S. (868) 622-2792), www.carec.org; *Population Data.*

Central Intelligence Agency, Office of Public Affairs, Washington, DC 20505, (703) 482-0623, Fax: (703) 482-1739, www.cia.gov; *The World Factbook.*

Economist Intelligence Unit, 111 West 57th Street, New York, NY 10019, (212) 554-0600, Fax: (212) 586-1181, www.eiu.com; *Cayman Islands Country Report.*

Euromonitor International, Inc., 224 S. Michigan Avenue, Suite 1500, Chicago, IL 60604, (312) 922-1115, Fax: (312) 922-1157, www.euromonitor.com; *International Marketing Data and Statistics 2008* and *The World Economic Factbook 2008.*

Eurostat, Batiment Jean Monnet, Rue Alcide de Gasperi, L-2920 Luxembourg, http://epp.eurostat.ec.europa.eu; *Demographic Indicators - Population by Age-Classes.*

Palgrave Macmillan Ltd., Houndmills, Basingstoke, Hampshire, RG21 6XS, England, (Telephone in U.S. (888) 330-8477), (Fax in U.S. (800) 672-2054), www.palgrave.com; *The Statesman's Yearbook 2008.*

Taylor and Francis Group, An Informa Business, 2 Park Square, Milton Park, Abingdon, Oxford OX14 4RN, United Kingdom, (Dial from U.S. (212) 216-7800), (Fax from U.S. (212) 564-7854), www.tandf.co.uk; *The Europa World Year Book.*

UNESCO Institute for Statistics, C.P. 6128 Succursale Centre-Ville, Montreal, Quebec, H3C 3J7 Canada, (Dial from U.S. (514) 343-6880), (Fax from U.S. (514) 343 6882), www.uis.unesco.org; *Statistical Tables.*

United Nations Food and Agricultural Organization (FAO), Viale delle Terme di Caracalla, 00100 Rome, Italy, (Dial from U.S. (202) 653-2400), (Fax from U.S. (202) 653 5760), www.fao.org; *FAO Production Yearbook 2002.*

United Nations Statistics Division, New York, NY 10017, (800) 253-9646, Fax: (212) 963-4116, http://unstats.un.org; *Demographic Yearbook* and *Statistical Yearbook.*

World Health Organization (WHO), Avenue Appia 20, 1211 Geneve 27, Switzerland, (Telephone in U.S. (212) 331-9081), www.who.int; *World Health Report 2006.*

CAYMAN ISLANDS - POPULATION DENSITY

Central Intelligence Agency, Office of Public Affairs, Washington, DC 20505, (703) 482-0623, Fax: (703) 482-1739, www.cia.gov; *The World Factbook.*

Euromonitor International, Inc., 224 S. Michigan Avenue, Suite 1500, Chicago, IL 60604, (312) 922-1115, Fax: (312) 922-1157, www.euromonitor.com; *The World Economic Factbook 2008.*

Palgrave Macmillan Ltd., Houndmills, Basingstoke, Hampshire, RG21 6XS, England, (Telephone in U.S. (888) 330-8477), (Fax in U.S. (800) 672-2054), www.palgrave.com; *The Statesman's Yearbook 2008.*

Taylor and Francis Group, An Informa Business, 2 Park Square, Milton Park, Abingdon, Oxford OX14 4RN, United Kingdom, (Dial from U.S. (212) 216-7800), (Fax from U.S. (212) 564-7854), www.tandf.co.uk; *The Europa World Year Book.*

UNESCO Institute for Statistics, C.P. 6128 Succursale Centre-Ville, Montreal, Quebec, H3C 3J7 Canada, (Dial from U.S. (514) 343-6880), (Fax from U.S. (514) 343 6882), www.uis.unesco.org; *Statistical Tables.*

United Nations Food and Agricultural Organization (FAO), Viale delle Terme di Caracalla, 00100 Rome, Italy, (Dial from U.S. (202) 653-2400), (Fax from U.S. (202) 653 5760), www.fao.org; *The State of Food and Agriculture (SOFA) 2006.*

United Nations Statistics Division, New York, NY 10017, (800) 253-9646, Fax: (212) 963-4116, http://unstats.un.org; *Statistical Yearbook.*

CAYMAN ISLANDS - POSTAL SERVICE

United Nations Statistics Division, New York, NY 10017, (800) 253-9646, Fax: (212) 963-4116, http://unstats.un.org; *Statistical Yearbook.*

CAYMAN ISLANDS - POWER RESOURCES

Euromonitor International, Inc., 224 S. Michigan Avenue, Suite 1500, Chicago, IL 60604, (312) 922-1115, Fax: (312) 922-1157, www.euromonitor.com; *International Marketing Data and Statistics 2008; The World Economic Factbook 2008;* and *World Marketing Data and Statistics.*

Platts, 2 Penn Plaza, 25th Floor, New York, NY 10121-2298, (212) 904-3070, www.platts.com; *Energy Economist.*

United Nations Food and Agricultural Organization (FAO), Viale delle Terme di Caracalla, 00100 Rome, Italy, (Dial from U.S. (202) 653-2400), (Fax from U.S. (202) 653 5760), www.fao.org; *The State of Food and Agriculture (SOFA) 2006.*

United Nations Statistics Division, New York, NY 10017, (800) 253-9646, Fax: (212) 963-4116, http://unstats.un.org; *Energy Statistics Yearbook 2003.*

CAYMAN ISLANDS - PRICES

Euromonitor International, Inc., 224 S. Michigan Avenue, Suite 1500, Chicago, IL 60604, (312) 922-1115, Fax: (312) 922-1157, www.euromonitor.com; *World Marketing Data and Statistics.*

United Nations Food and Agricultural Organization (FAO), Viale delle Terme di Caracalla, 00100 Rome, Italy, (Dial from U.S. (202) 653-2400), (Fax from U.S. (202) 653 5760), www.fao.org; *FAO Production Yearbook 2002* and *The State of Food and Agriculture (SOFA) 2006.*

CAYMAN ISLANDS - PROFESSIONS

United Nations Statistics Division, New York, NY 10017, (800) 253-9646, Fax: (212) 963-4116, http://unstats.un.org; *Statistical Yearbook.*

CAYMAN ISLANDS - PUBLIC HEALTH

Euromonitor International, Inc., 224 S. Michigan Avenue, Suite 1500, Chicago, IL 60604, (312) 922-1115, Fax: (312) 922-1157, www.euromonitor.com; *World Marketing Data and Statistics.*

Palgrave Macmillan Ltd., Houndmills, Basingstoke, Hampshire, RG21 6XS, England, (Telephone in U.S.

(888) 330-8477), (Fax in U.S. (800) 672-2054), www.palgrave.com; *The Statesman's Yearbook 2008.*

United Nations Statistics Division, New York, NY 10017, (800) 253-9646, Fax: (212) 963-4116, http://unstats.un.org; *Statistical Yearbook.*

World Health Organization (WHO), Avenue Appia 20, 1211 Geneve 27, Switzerland, (Telephone in U.S. (212) 331-9081), www.who.int; *World Health Report 2006.*

CAYMAN ISLANDS - RADIO BROADCASTING

Palgrave Macmillan Ltd., Houndmills, Basingstoke, Hampshire, RG21 6XS, England, (Telephone in U.S. (888) 330-8477), (Fax in U.S. (800) 672-2054), www.palgrave.com; *The Statesman's Yearbook 2008.*

CAYMAN ISLANDS - RELIGION

Central Intelligence Agency, Office of Public Affairs, Washington, DC 20505, (703) 482-0623, Fax: (703) 482-1739, www.cia.gov; *The World Factbook.*

Palgrave Macmillan Ltd., Houndmills, Basingstoke, Hampshire, RG21 6XS, England, (Telephone in U.S. (888) 330-8477), (Fax in U.S. (800) 672-2054), www.palgrave.com; *The Statesman's Yearbook 2008.*

CAYMAN ISLANDS - RETAIL TRADE

Euromonitor International, Inc., 224 S. Michigan Avenue, Suite 1500, Chicago, IL 60604, (312) 922-1115, Fax: (312) 922-1157, www.euromonitor.com; *World Marketing Data and Statistics.*

CAYMAN ISLANDS - ROADS

Central Intelligence Agency, Office of Public Affairs, Washington, DC 20505, (703) 482-0623, Fax: (703) 482-1739, www.cia.gov; *The World Factbook.*

Palgrave Macmillan Ltd., Houndmills, Basingstoke, Hampshire, RG21 6XS, England, (Telephone in U.S. (888) 330-8477), (Fax in U.S. (800) 672-2054), www.palgrave.com; *The Statesman's Yearbook 2008.*

CAYMAN ISLANDS - SHIPPING

Palgrave Macmillan Ltd., Houndmills, Basingstoke, Hampshire, RG21 6XS, England, (Telephone in U.S. (888) 330-8477), (Fax in U.S. (800) 672-2054), www.palgrave.com; *The Statesman's Yearbook 2008.*

Taylor and Francis Group, An Informa Business, 2 Park Square, Milton Park, Abingdon, Oxford OX14 4RN, United Kingdom, (Dial from U.S. (212) 216-7800), (Fax from U.S. (212) 564-7854), www.tandf.co.uk; *The Europa World Year Book.*

United Nations Statistics Division, New York, NY 10017, (800) 253-9646, Fax: (212) 963-4116, http://unstats.un.org; *Statistical Yearbook.*

CAYMAN ISLANDS - SOCIAL SECURITY

United Nations Statistics Division, New York, NY 10017, (800) 253-9646, Fax: (212) 963-4116, http://unstats.un.org; *National Accounts Statistics: Compendium of Income Distribution Statistics.*

CAYMAN ISLANDS - TAXATION

Taylor and Francis Group, An Informa Business, 2 Park Square, Milton Park, Abingdon, Oxford OX14 4RN, United Kingdom, (Dial from U.S. (212) 216-7800), (Fax from U.S. (212) 564-7854), www.tandf.co.uk; *The Europa World Year Book.*

CAYMAN ISLANDS - TELEPHONE

International Telecommunication Union (ITU), Place des Nations, 1211 Geneva 20, Switzerland, www.itu.int; World Telecommunication Indicators Database.

Palgrave Macmillan Ltd., Houndmills, Basingstoke, Hampshire, RG21 6XS, England, (Telephone in U.S. (888) 330-8477), (Fax in U.S. (800) 672-2054), www.palgrave.com; *The Statesman's Yearbook 2008.*

Taylor and Francis Group, An Informa Business, 2 Park Square, Milton Park, Abingdon, Oxford OX14 4RN, United Kingdom, (Dial from U.S. (212) 216-7800), (Fax from U.S. (212) 564-7854), www.tandf.co.uk; *The Europa World Year Book.*

United Nations Statistics Division, New York, NY 10017, (800) 253-9646, Fax: (212) 963-4116, http://unstats.un.org; *Statistical Yearbook.*

CAYMAN ISLANDS - TEXTILE INDUSTRY

Palgrave Macmillan Ltd., Houndmills, Basingstoke, Hampshire, RG21 6XS, England, (Telephone in U.S. (888) 330-8477), (Fax in U.S. (800) 672-2054), www.palgrave.com; *The Statesman's Yearbook 2008.*

United Nations Conference on Trade and Development (UNCTAD), DC2-1120, United Nations, New York, NY 10017, (212) 963-0027, www.unctad.org; *UNCTAD Commodity Yearbook.*

CAYMAN ISLANDS - TOURISM

Euromonitor International, Inc., 224 S. Michigan Avenue, Suite 1500, Chicago, IL 60604, (312) 922-1115, Fax: (312) 922-1157, www.euromonitor.com; *The World Economic Factbook 2008* and *World Marketing Data and Statistics.*

Palgrave Macmillan Ltd., Houndmills, Basingstoke, Hampshire, RG21 6XS, England, (Telephone in U.S. (888) 330-8477), (Fax in U.S. (800) 672-2054), www.palgrave.com; *The Statesman's Yearbook 2008.*

Taylor and Francis Group, An Informa Business, 2 Park Square, Milton Park, Abingdon, Oxford OX14 4RN, United Kingdom, (Dial from U.S. (212) 216-7800), (Fax from U.S. (212) 564-7854), www.tandf.co.uk; *The Europa World Year Book.*

United Nations Statistics Division, New York, NY 10017, (800) 253-9646, Fax: (212) 963-4116, http://unstats.un.org; *Statistical Yearbook.*

United Nations World Tourism Organization (UNWTO), Capitan Haya 42, 28020 Madrid, Spain, www.world-tourism.org; *Yearbook of Tourism Statistics.*

CAYMAN ISLANDS - TRADE

See CAYMAN ISLANDS - INTERNATIONAL TRADE

CAYMAN ISLANDS - TRANSPORTATION

Central Intelligence Agency, Office of Public Affairs, Washington, DC 20505, (703) 482-0623, Fax: (703) 482-1739, www.cia.gov; *The World Factbook.*

Euromonitor International, Inc., 224 S. Michigan Avenue, Suite 1500, Chicago, IL 60604, (312) 922-1115, Fax: (312) 922-1157, www.euromonitor.com; *International Marketing Data and Statistics 2008* and *World Marketing Data and Statistics.*

Palgrave Macmillan Ltd., Houndmills, Basingstoke, Hampshire, RG21 6XS, England, (Telephone in U.S. (888) 330-8477), (Fax in U.S. (800) 672-2054), www.palgrave.com; *The Statesman's Yearbook 2008.*

Taylor and Francis Group, An Informa Business, 2 Park Square, Milton Park, Abingdon, Oxford OX14 4RN, United Kingdom, (Dial from U.S. (212) 216-7800), (Fax from U.S. (212) 564-7854), www.tandf.co.uk; *The Europa World Year Book.*

CAYMAN ISLANDS - UNEMPLOYMENT

Central Intelligence Agency, Office of Public Affairs, Washington, DC 20505, (703) 482-0623, Fax: (703) 482-1739, www.cia.gov; *The World Factbook.*

CAYMAN ISLANDS - VITAL STATISTICS

Palgrave Macmillan Ltd., Houndmills, Basingstoke, Hampshire, RG21 6XS, England, (Telephone in U.S. (888) 330-8477), (Fax in U.S. (800) 672-2054), www.palgrave.com; *The Statesman's Yearbook 2008.*

United Nations Statistics Division, New York, NY 10017, (800) 253-9646, Fax: (212) 963-4116, http://unstats.un.org; *Statistical Yearbook.*

World Health Organization (WHO), Avenue Appia 20, 1211 Geneve 27, Switzerland, (Telephone in U.S. (212) 331-9081), www.who.int; *World Health Report 2006.*

CD-ROMS IN SCHOOLS

Quality Education Data (QED), 1050 17th Street, Suite 1100, Denver, Colorado 80265, (800) 525-5811, Fax: (303) 209-9444, www.qeddata.com; *Market Overview: State Counts.*

CELERY

Economic Research Service (ERS), U.S. Department of Agriculture (USDA), 1800 M Street, NW, Washington, DC 20036-5831, (202) 694-5050, Fax: (202) 694-5689, www.ers.usda.gov; *Agricultural Outlook; Agricultural Statistics;* and *Food CPI, Prices, and Expenditures.*

National Agricultural Statistics Service (NASS), U.S. Department of Agriculture (USDA), 1400 Independence Avenue, SW, Washington, DC 20250, (800) 727-9540, Fax: (202) 690-2090, www.nass.usda.gov; *Vegetables: 2004 Annual Summary.*

CELLULAR TELEPHONES

National Center for Statistics and Analysis (NCSA) of the National Highway Traffic Safety Administration, West Building, 1200 New Jersey Avenue, S.E., Washington, DC 20590, (202) 366-1503, Fax: (202) 366-7078, www.nhtsa.gov; *Cell Phone Use on the Roads in 2002.*

CELLULAR TELEPHONES

See TELEPHONE CARRIERS

CEMENT - CONSUMPTION

U.S. Department of the Interior (DOI), U.S. Geological Survey (USGS), Office of Minerals Information, 12201 Sunrise Valley Drive, Reston, VA 20192, Mr. Kenneth A. Beckman, (703) 648-4916, Fax: (703) 648-4995, http://minerals.usgs.gov/minerals; *Mineral Commodity Summaries* and *Minerals Yearbook.*

CEMENT - EMPLOYMENT

U.S. Department of the Interior (DOI), U.S. Geological Survey (USGS), Office of Minerals Information, 12201 Sunrise Valley Drive, Reston, VA 20192, Mr. Kenneth A. Beckman, (703) 648-4916, Fax: (703) 648-4995, http://minerals.usgs.gov/minerals; *Mineral Commodity Summaries.*

CEMENT - INTERNATIONAL TRADE

U.S. Department of the Interior (DOI), U.S. Geological Survey (USGS), Office of Minerals Information, 12201 Sunrise Valley Drive, Reston, VA 20192, Mr. Kenneth A. Beckman, (703) 648-4916, Fax: (703) 648-4995, http://minerals.usgs.gov/minerals; *Mineral Commodity Summaries.*

CEMENT - PRICE INDEXES

U.S. Bureau of Labor Statistics (BLS), Postal Square Building, 2 Massachusetts Avenue, NE, Washington, DC 20212-0001, (202) 691-5200, Fax: (202) 691-6325, www.bls.gov; *Producer Price Indexes (PPI).*

CEMENT - PRICES

U.S. Department of the Interior (DOI), U.S. Geological Survey (USGS), Office of Minerals Information, 12201 Sunrise Valley Drive, Reston, VA 20192, Mr. Kenneth A. Beckman, (703) 648-4916, Fax: (703) 648-4995, http://minerals.usgs.gov/minerals; *Mineral Commodity Summaries.*

CEMENT - PRODUCTION AND VALUE

U.S. Census Bureau, Center for Economic Studies, 4600 Silver Hill Road, Washington DC 20233, (301) 457-1235, www.ces.census.gov; *Cementing Relationships: Vertical Integration, Foreclosure, Productivity, and Prices.*

U.S. Department of the Interior (DOI), U.S. Geological Survey (USGS), Office of Minerals Information, 12201 Sunrise Valley Drive, Reston, VA 20192, Mr. Kenneth A. Beckman, (703) 648-4916, Fax: (703) 648-4995, http://minerals.usgs.gov/minerals; *Mineral Commodity Summaries* and *Minerals Yearbook.*

CEMENT - WORLD PRODUCTION

U.S. Department of the Interior (DOI), U.S. Geological Survey (USGS), Office of Minerals Information,

12201 Sunrise Valley Drive, Reston, VA 20192, Mr. Kenneth A. Beckman, (703) 648-4916, Fax: (703) 648-4995, http://minerals.usgs.gov/minerals; *Mineral Commodity Summaries* and *Minerals Yearbook*.

CENTRAL AFRICAN REPUBLIC - NATIONAL STATISTICAL OFFICE

Direction Generale des Statistiques, des Etudes Economiques et Sociales, BP 696 Bangui, Central African Republic, www.stat-centrafrique.com; National Data Center.

CENTRAL AFRICAN REPUBLIC - PRIMARY STATISTICS SOURCES

Direction Generale des Statistiques, des Etudes Economiques et Sociales, BP 696 Bangui, Central African Republic, www.stat-centrafrique.com; *Annuaire statistique* (Statistical Yearbook) and *Bulletin Trimestriel de Statistique* (Quarterly Bulletin of Statistics).

CENTRAL AFRICAN REPUBLIC - AGRICULTURAL MACHINERY

United Nations Statistics Division, New York, NY 10017, (800) 253-9646, Fax: (212) 963-4116, http://unstats.un.org; *Statistical Yearbook*.

CENTRAL AFRICAN REPUBLIC - AGRICULTURE

Economist Intelligence Unit, 111 West 57th Street, New York, NY 10019, (212) 554-0600, Fax: (212) 586-1181, www.eiu.com; *Central African Republic Country Report*.

Euromonitor International, Inc., 224 S. Michigan Avenue, Suite 1500, Chicago, IL 60604, (312) 922-1115, Fax: (312) 922-1157, www.euromonitor.com; *World Marketing Data and Statistics*.

M.E. Sharpe, 80 Business Park Drive, Armonk, NY 10504, (800) 541-6563, Fax: (914) 273-2106, www.mesharpe.com; *The Illustrated Book of World Rankings*.

Palgrave Macmillan Ltd., Houndmills, Basingstoke, Hampshire, RG21 6XS, England, (Telephone in U.S. (888) 330-8477), (Fax in U.S. (800) 672-2054), www.palgrave.com; *The Statesman's Yearbook 2008*.

Taylor and Francis Group, An Informa Business, 2 Park Square, Milton Park, Abingdon, Oxford OX14 4RN, United Kingdom, (Dial from U.S. (212) 216-7800), (Fax from U.S. (212) 564-7854), www.tandf.co.uk; *The Europa World Year Book*.

United Nations Conference on Trade and Development (UNCTAD), DC2-1120, United Nations, New York, NY 10017, (212) 963-0027, www.unctad.org; *UNCTAD Commodity Yearbook*.

United Nations Economic Commission for Africa (ECA), PO Box 3001, Addis Ababa, Ethiopia, (Telephone in U.S. (212) 963-4957), www.uneca.org; *African Statistical Yearbook 2006*.

United Nations Food and Agricultural Organization (FAO), Viale delle Terme di Caracalla, 00100 Rome, Italy, (Dial from U.S. (202) 653-2400), (Fax from U.S. (202) 653 5760), www.fao.org; AQUASTAT; *FAO Production Yearbook 2002; FAO Trade Yearbook;* and *The State of Food and Agriculture (SOFA) 2006*.

United Nations Statistics Division, New York, NY 10017, (800) 253-9646, Fax: (212) 963-4116, http://unstats.un.org; *Statistical Yearbook* and *Survey of Economic and Social Conditions in Africa 2005*.

The World Bank, 1818 H Street, NW, Washington, DC 20433, (202) 473-1000, Fax: (202) 477-6391, www.worldbank.org; *Africa Live Database (LDB); African Development Indicators (ADI) 2007; Central African Republic;* and *World Development Indicators (WDI) 2008*.

WRTH Publications Limited, PO Box 290, Oxford OX2 7FT, UK, www.wrth.com; *World Radio TV Handbook 2007*.

CENTRAL AFRICAN REPUBLIC - AIRLINES

M.E. Sharpe, 80 Business Park Drive, Armonk, NY 10504, (800) 541-6563, Fax: (914) 273-2106, www.mesharpe.com; *The Illustrated Book of World Rankings*.

Palgrave Macmillan Ltd., Houndmills, Basingstoke, Hampshire, RG21 6XS, England, (Telephone in U.S. (888) 330-8477), (Fax in U.S. (800) 672-2054), www.palgrave.com; *The Statesman's Yearbook 2008*.

Taylor and Francis Group, An Informa Business, 2 Park Square, Milton Park, Abingdon, Oxford OX14 4RN, United Kingdom, (Dial from U.S. (212) 216-7800), (Fax from U.S. (212) 564-7854), www.tandf.co.uk; *The Europa World Year Book*.

United Nations Economic Commission for Africa (ECA), PO Box 3001, Addis Ababa, Ethiopia, (Telephone in U.S. (212) 963-4957), www.uneca.org; *African Statistical Yearbook 2006*.

United Nations Statistics Division, New York, NY 10017, (800) 253-9646, Fax: (212) 963-4116, http://unstats.un.org; *Statistical Yearbook*.

CENTRAL AFRICAN REPUBLIC - AIRPORTS

Central Intelligence Agency, Office of Public Affairs, Washington, DC 20505, (703) 482-0623, Fax: (703) 482-1739, www.cia.gov; *The World Factbook*.

CENTRAL AFRICAN REPUBLIC - ALUMINUM PRODUCTION

See CENTRAL AFRICAN REPUBLIC - MINERAL INDUSTRIES

CENTRAL AFRICAN REPUBLIC - ARMED FORCES

Central Intelligence Agency, Office of Public Affairs, Washington, DC 20505, (703) 482-0623, Fax: (703) 482-1739, www.cia.gov; *The World Factbook*.

Euromonitor International, Inc., 224 S. Michigan Avenue, Suite 1500, Chicago, IL 60604, (312) 922-1115, Fax: (312) 922-1157, www.euromonitor.com; *World Marketing Data and Statistics*.

International Institute for Strategic Studies (IISS), Arundel House, 13-15 Arundel Street, Temple Place, London WC2R 3DX, England, www.iiss.org; *The Military Balance 2007*.

Palgrave Macmillan Ltd., Houndmills, Basingstoke, Hampshire, RG21 6XS, England, (Telephone in U.S. (888) 330-8477), (Fax in U.S. (800) 672-2054), www.palgrave.com; *The Statesman's Yearbook 2008*.

U.S. Department of State (DOS), 2201 C Street NW, Washington, DC 20520, (202) 647-4000, www.state.gov; *World Military Expenditures and Arms Transfers (WMEAT)*.

United Nations Statistics Division, New York, NY 10017, (800) 253-9646, Fax: (212) 963-4116, http://unstats.un.org; *Human Development Report 2006*.

CENTRAL AFRICAN REPUBLIC - BALANCE OF PAYMENTS

African Development Bank Group, Rue Joseph Anoma, 01 BP 1387 Abidjan 01, Cote d'Ivoire, www.afdb.org; *Statistics Pocketbook 2008*.

International Monetary Fund (IMF), 700 Nineteenth Street, NW, Washington, DC 20431, (202) 623-7000, Fax: (202) 623-4661, www.imf.org; *Balance of Payments Statistics Newsletter* and *Balance of Payments Statistics Yearbook 2007*.

Taylor and Francis Group, An Informa Business, 2 Park Square, Milton Park, Abingdon, Oxford OX14 4RN, United Kingdom, (Dial from U.S. (212) 216-7800), (Fax from U.S. (212) 564-7854), www.tandf.co.uk; *The Europa World Year Book*.

United Nations Conference on Trade and Development (UNCTAD), DC2-1120, United Nations, New York, NY 10017, (212) 963-0027, www.unctad.org; *Handbook of Statistics 2005*.

United Nations Economic Commission for Africa (ECA), PO Box 3001, Addis Ababa, Ethiopia, (Telephone in U.S. (212) 963-4957), www.uneca.org; *African Statistical Yearbook 2006*.

The World Bank, 1818 H Street, NW, Washington, DC 20433, (202) 473-1000, Fax: (202) 477-6391, www.worldbank.org; *Central African Republic; World Development Indicators (WDI) 2008;* and *World Development Report 2008*.

CENTRAL AFRICAN REPUBLIC - BANKS AND BANKING

Euromonitor International, Inc., 224 S. Michigan Avenue, Suite 1500, Chicago, IL 60604, (312) 922-1115, Fax: (312) 922-1157, www.euromonitor.com; *World Marketing Data and Statistics*.

International Monetary Fund (IMF), 700 Nineteenth Street, NW, Washington, DC 20431, (202) 623-7000, Fax: (202) 623-4661, www.imf.org; *International Financial Statistics Yearbook 2007*.

M.E. Sharpe, 80 Business Park Drive, Armonk, NY 10504, (800) 541-6563, Fax: (914) 273-2106, www.mesharpe.com; *The Illustrated Book of World Rankings*.

Palgrave Macmillan Ltd., Houndmills, Basingstoke, Hampshire, RG21 6XS, England, (Telephone in U.S. (888) 330-8477), (Fax in U.S. (800) 672-2054), www.palgrave.com; *The Statesman's Yearbook 2008*.

Taylor and Francis Group, An Informa Business, 2 Park Square, Milton Park, Abingdon, Oxford OX14 4RN, United Kingdom, (Dial from U.S. (212) 216-7800), (Fax from U.S. (212) 564-7854), www.tandf.co.uk; *The Europa World Year Book*.

United Nations Economic Commission for Africa (ECA), PO Box 3001, Addis Ababa, Ethiopia, (Telephone in U.S. (212) 963-4957), www.uneca.org; *African Statistical Yearbook 2006*.

CENTRAL AFRICAN REPUBLIC - BARLEY PRODUCTION

See CENTRAL AFRICAN REPUBLIC - CROPS

CENTRAL AFRICAN REPUBLIC - BEVERAGE INDUSTRY

M.E. Sharpe, 80 Business Park Drive, Armonk, NY 10504, (800) 541-6563, Fax: (914) 273-2106, www.mesharpe.com; *The Illustrated Book of World Rankings*.

United Nations Statistics Division, New York, NY 10017, (800) 253-9646, Fax: (212) 963-4116, http://unstats.un.org; *Statistical Yearbook*.

CENTRAL AFRICAN REPUBLIC - BROADCASTING

Central Intelligence Agency, Office of Public Affairs, Washington, DC 20505, (703) 482-0623, Fax: (703) 482-1739, www.cia.gov; *The World Factbook*.

Euromonitor International, Inc., 224 S. Michigan Avenue, Suite 1500, Chicago, IL 60604, (312) 922-1115, Fax: (312) 922-1157, www.euromonitor.com; *World Marketing Data and Statistics*.

M.E. Sharpe, 80 Business Park Drive, Armonk, NY 10504, (800) 541-6563, Fax: (914) 273-2106, www.mesharpe.com; *The Illustrated Book of World Rankings*.

Palgrave Macmillan Ltd., Houndmills, Basingstoke, Hampshire, RG21 6XS, England, (Telephone in U.S. (888) 330-8477), (Fax in U.S. (800) 672-2054), www.palgrave.com; *The Statesman's Yearbook 2008*.

CENTRAL AFRICAN REPUBLIC - BUDGET

Central Intelligence Agency, Office of Public Affairs, Washington, DC 20505, (703) 482-0623, Fax: (703) 482-1739, www.cia.gov; *The World Factbook*.

CENTRAL AFRICAN REPUBLIC - CATTLE

See CENTRAL AFRICAN REPUBLIC - LIVESTOCK

CENTRAL AFRICAN REPUBLIC - CHICKENS

See CENTRAL AFRICAN REPUBLIC - LIVESTOCK

CENTRAL AFRICAN REPUBLIC - CHILDBIRTH - STATISTICS

Central Intelligence Agency, Office of Public Affairs, Washington, DC 20505, (703) 482-0623, Fax: (703) 482-1739, www.cia.gov; *The World Factbook.*

Euromonitor International, Inc., 224 S. Michigan Avenue, Suite 1500, Chicago, IL 60604, (312) 922-1115, Fax: (312) 922-1157, www.euromonitor.com; *International Marketing Data and Statistics 2008* and *The World Economic Factbook 2008.*

M.E. Sharpe, 80 Business Park Drive, Armonk, NY 10504, (800) 541-6563, Fax: (914) 273-2106, www.mesharpe.com; *The Illustrated Book of World Rankings.*

Taylor and Francis Group, An Informa Business, 2 Park Square, Milton Park, Abingdon, Oxford OX14 4RN, United Kingdom, (Dial from U.S. (212) 216-7800), (Fax from U.S. (212) 564-7854), www.tandf.co.uk; *The Europa World Year Book.*

United Nations Statistics Division, New York, NY 10017, (800) 253-9646, Fax: (212) 963-4116, http://unstats.un.org; *Demographic Yearbook; Statistical Yearbook;* and *Survey of Economic and Social Conditions in Africa 2005.*

The World Bank, 1818 H Street, NW, Washington, DC 20433, (202) 473-1000, Fax: (202) 477-6391, www.worldbank.org; *World Development Indicators (WDI) 2008.*

CENTRAL AFRICAN REPUBLIC - CLIMATE

International Institute for Environment and Development (IIED), 3 Endsleigh Street, London, England, WC1H 0DD, United Kingdom, www.iied.org; *Environment Urbanization* and *Haramata - Bulletin of the Drylands.*

M.E. Sharpe, 80 Business Park Drive, Armonk, NY 10504, (800) 541-6563, Fax: (914) 273-2106, www.mesharpe.com; *The Illustrated Book of World Rankings.*

Palgrave Macmillan Ltd., Houndmills, Basingstoke, Hampshire, RG21 6XS, England, (Telephone in U.S. (888) 330-8477), (Fax in U.S. (800) 672-2054), www.palgrave.com; *The Statesman's Yearbook 2008.*

CENTRAL AFRICAN REPUBLIC - COAL PRODUCTION

See CENTRAL AFRICAN REPUBLIC - MINERAL INDUSTRIES

CENTRAL AFRICAN REPUBLIC - COCOA PRODUCTION

See CENTRAL AFRICAN REPUBLIC - CROPS

CENTRAL AFRICAN REPUBLIC - COFFEE

See CENTRAL AFRICAN REPUBLIC - CROPS

CENTRAL AFRICAN REPUBLIC - COMMERCE

Palgrave Macmillan Ltd., Houndmills, Basingstoke, Hampshire, RG21 6XS, England, (Telephone in U.S. (888) 330-8477), (Fax in U.S. (800) 672-2054), www.palgrave.com; *The Statesman's Yearbook 2008.*

CENTRAL AFRICAN REPUBLIC - COMMODITY EXCHANGES

Commodity Research Bureau, 330 South Wells Street, Suite 612, Chicago, IL 60606-7110, (800) 621-5271, Fax: (312) 939-4135, www.crbtrader.com; *2006 CRB Commodity Yearbook and CD.*

International Monetary Fund (IMF), 700 Nineteenth Street, NW, Washington, DC 20431, (202) 623-7000, Fax: (202) 623-4661, www.imf.org; *IMF Primary Commodity Prices.*

United Nations Food and Agricultural Organization (FAO), Viale delle Terme di Caracalla, 00100 Rome, Italy, (Dial from U.S. (202) 653-2400), (Fax from U.S. (202) 653 5760), www.fao.org; *The State of Food and Agriculture (SOFA) 2006.*

CENTRAL AFRICAN REPUBLIC - COMMUNICATION AND TRAFFIC

United Nations Statistics Division, New York, NY 10017, (800) 253-9646, Fax: (212) 963-4116, http://unstats.un.org; *Statistical Yearbook.*

CENTRAL AFRICAN REPUBLIC - CONSTRUCTION INDUSTRY

M.E. Sharpe, 80 Business Park Drive, Armonk, NY 10504, (800) 541-6563, Fax: (914) 273-2106, www.mesharpe.com; *The Illustrated Book of World Rankings.*

United Nations Economic Commission for Africa (ECA), PO Box 3001, Addis Ababa, Ethiopia, (Telephone in U.S. (212) 963-4957), www.uneca.org; *African Statistical Yearbook 2006.*

CENTRAL AFRICAN REPUBLIC - CONSUMER PRICE INDEXES

Taylor and Francis Group, An Informa Business, 2 Park Square, Milton Park, Abingdon, Oxford OX14 4RN, United Kingdom, (Dial from U.S. (212) 216-7800), (Fax from U.S. (212) 564-7854), www.tandf.co.uk; *The Europa World Year Book.*

United Nations Economic Commission for Africa (ECA), PO Box 3001, Addis Ababa, Ethiopia, (Telephone in U.S. (212) 963-4957), www.uneca.org; *African Statistical Yearbook 2006.*

United Nations Statistics Division, New York, NY 10017, (800) 253-9646, Fax: (212) 963-4116, http://unstats.un.org; *Statistical Yearbook* and *Survey of Economic and Social Conditions in Africa 2005.*

The World Bank, 1818 H Street, NW, Washington, DC 20433, (202) 473-1000, Fax: (202) 477-6391, www.worldbank.org; *Central African Republic.*

CENTRAL AFRICAN REPUBLIC - CONSUMPTION (ECONOMICS)

African Development Bank Group, Rue Joseph Anoma, 01 BP 1387 Abidjan 01, Cote d'Ivoire, www.afdb.org; *Statistics Pocketbook 2008.*

United Nations Statistics Division, New York, NY 10017, (800) 253-9646, Fax: (212) 963-4116, http://unstats.un.org; *Survey of Economic and Social Conditions in Africa 2005.*

The World Bank, 1818 H Street, NW, Washington, DC 20433, (202) 473-1000, Fax: (202) 477-6391, www.worldbank.org; *World Development Report 2008.*

CENTRAL AFRICAN REPUBLIC - COPPER INDUSTRY AND TRADE

See CENTRAL AFRICAN REPUBLIC - MINERAL INDUSTRIES

CENTRAL AFRICAN REPUBLIC - CORN INDUSTRY

See CENTRAL AFRICAN REPUBLIC - CROPS

CENTRAL AFRICAN REPUBLIC - COTTON

See CENTRAL AFRICAN REPUBLIC - CROPS

CENTRAL AFRICAN REPUBLIC - CRIME

International Criminal Police Organization (INTERPOL), General Secretariat, 200 quai Charles de Gaulle, 69006 Lyon, France, www.interpol.int; *International Crime Statistics.*

Yale University Press, PO Box 209040, New Haven, CT 06520-9040, (203) 432-0960, Fax: (203) 432-0948, http://yalepress.yale.edu/yupbooks; *Violence and Crime in Cross-National Perspective.*

CENTRAL AFRICAN REPUBLIC - CROPS

M.E. Sharpe, 80 Business Park Drive, Armonk, NY 10504, (800) 541-6563, Fax: (914) 273-2106, www.mesharpe.com; *The Illustrated Book of World Rankings.*

Palgrave Macmillan Ltd., Houndmills, Basingstoke, Hampshire, RG21 6XS, England, (Telephone in U.S. (888) 330-8477), (Fax in U.S. (800) 672-2054), www.palgrave.com; *The Statesman's Yearbook 2008.*

Taylor and Francis Group, An Informa Business, 2 Park Square, Milton Park, Abingdon, Oxford OX14 4RN, United Kingdom, (Dial from U.S. (212) 216-7800), (Fax from U.S. (212) 564-7854), www.tandf.co.uk; *The Europa World Year Book.*

United Nations Conference on Trade and Development (UNCTAD), DC2-1120, United Nations, New York, NY 10017, (212) 963-0027, www.unctad.org; *UNCTAD Commodity Yearbook.*

United Nations Economic Commission for Africa (ECA), PO Box 3001, Addis Ababa, Ethiopia, (Telephone in U.S. (212) 963-4957), www.uneca.org; *African Statistical Yearbook 2006.*

United Nations Food and Agricultural Organization (FAO), Viale delle Terme di Caracalla, 00100 Rome, Italy, (Dial from U.S. (202) 653-2400), (Fax from U.S. (202) 653 5760), www.fao.org; *FAO Production Yearbook 2002* and *The State of Food and Agriculture (SOFA) 2006.*

United Nations Statistics Division, New York, NY 10017, (800) 253-9646, Fax: (212) 963-4116, http://unstats.un.org; *Statistical Yearbook.*

CENTRAL AFRICAN REPUBLIC - DAIRY PROCESSING

M.E. Sharpe, 80 Business Park Drive, Armonk, NY 10504, (800) 541-6563, Fax: (914) 273-2106, www.mesharpe.com; *The Illustrated Book of World Rankings.*

Palgrave Macmillan Ltd., Houndmills, Basingstoke, Hampshire, RG21 6XS, England, (Telephone in U.S. (888) 330-8477), (Fax in U.S. (800) 672-2054), www.palgrave.com; *The Statesman's Yearbook 2008.*

Taylor and Francis Group, An Informa Business, 2 Park Square, Milton Park, Abingdon, Oxford OX14 4RN, United Kingdom, (Dial from U.S. (212) 216-7800), (Fax from U.S. (212) 564-7854), www.tandf.co.uk; *The Europa World Year Book.*

United Nations Food and Agricultural Organization (FAO), Viale delle Terme di Caracalla, 00100 Rome, Italy, (Dial from U.S. (202) 653-2400), (Fax from U.S. (202) 653 5760), www.fao.org; *The State of Food and Agriculture (SOFA) 2006.*

CENTRAL AFRICAN REPUBLIC - DEATH RATES

See CENTRAL AFRICAN REPUBLIC - MORTALITY

CENTRAL AFRICAN REPUBLIC - DEBTS, EXTERNAL

African Development Bank Group, Rue Joseph Anoma, 01 BP 1387 Abidjan 01, Cote d'Ivoire, www.afdb.org; *Statistics Pocketbook 2008.*

United Nations Statistics Division, New York, NY 10017, (800) 253-9646, Fax: (212) 963-4116, http://unstats.un.org; *Survey of Economic and Social Conditions in Africa 2005.*

The World Bank, 1818 H Street, NW, Washington, DC 20433, (202) 473-1000, Fax: (202) 477-6391, www.worldbank.org; *Africa Live Database (LDB); African Development Indicators (ADI) 2007; Global Development Finance 2007; World Development Indicators (WDI) 2008;* and *World Development Report 2008.*

CENTRAL AFRICAN REPUBLIC - DEFENSE EXPENDITURES

See CENTRAL AFRICAN REPUBLIC - ARMED FORCES

CENTRAL AFRICAN REPUBLIC - DEMOGRAPHY

Euromonitor International, Inc., 224 S. Michigan Avenue, Suite 1500, Chicago, IL 60604, (312) 922-1115, Fax: (312) 922-1157, www.euromonitor.com; *International Marketing Data and Statistics 2008; The World Economic Factbook 2008;* and *World Marketing Data and Statistics.*

M.E. Sharpe, 80 Business Park Drive, Armonk, NY 10504, (800) 541-6563, Fax: (914) 273-2106, www.mesharpe.com; *The Illustrated Book of World Rankings.*

United Nations Statistics Division, New York, NY 10017, (800) 253-9646, Fax: (212) 963-4116, http://unstats.un.org; *Human Development Report 2006* and *Survey of Economic and Social Conditions in Africa 2005.*

The World Bank, 1818 H Street, NW, Washington, DC 20433, (202) 473-1000, Fax: (202) 477-6391, www.worldbank.org; *Central African Republic.*

CENTRAL AFRICAN REPUBLIC - DIAMONDS

See CENTRAL AFRICAN REPUBLIC - MINERAL INDUSTRIES

CENTRAL AFRICAN REPUBLIC - DISPOSABLE INCOME

M.E. Sharpe, 80 Business Park Drive, Armonk, NY 10504, (800) 541-6563, Fax: (914) 273-2106, www.mesharpe.com; *The Illustrated Book of World Rankings.*

United Nations Statistics Division, New York, NY 10017, (800) 253-9646, Fax: (212) 963-4116, http://unstats.un.org; *National Accounts Statistics: Compendium of Income Distribution Statistics* and *Statistical Yearbook.*

CENTRAL AFRICAN REPUBLIC - DIVORCE

M.E. Sharpe, 80 Business Park Drive, Armonk, NY 10504, (800) 541-6563, Fax: (914) 273-2106, www.mesharpe.com; *The Illustrated Book of World Rankings.*

United Nations Statistics Division, New York, NY 10017, (800) 253-9646, Fax: (212) 963-4116, http://unstats.un.org; *Demographic Yearbook.*

CENTRAL AFRICAN REPUBLIC - ECONOMIC ASSISTANCE

United Nations Statistics Division, New York, NY 10017, (800) 253-9646, Fax: (212) 963-4116, http://unstats.un.org; *Statistical Yearbook.*

CENTRAL AFRICAN REPUBLIC - ECONOMIC CONDITIONS

African Development Bank Group, Rue Joseph Anoma, 01 BP 1387 Abidjan 01, Cote d'Ivoire, www.afdb.org; *The African Statistical Journal; Gender, Poverty and Environmental Indicators on African Countries 2007; Selected Statistics on African Countries 2007;* and *Statistics Pocketbook 2008.*

Center for International Business Education Research (CIBER), Columbia Business School and School of International and Public Affairs, Uris Hall, Room 212, 3022 Broadway, New York, NY 10027-6902, Mr. Joshua Safier, (212) 854-4750, Fax: (212) 222-9821, www.columbia.edu/cu/ciber/; Datastream International.

Central Intelligence Agency, Office of Public Affairs, Washington, DC 20505, (703) 482-0623, Fax: (703) 482-1739, www.cia.gov; *The World Factbook.*

DSI Data Service Information, Xantener Strasse 51a, D-47495 Rheinberg, Germany, www.dsidata.com; *Campus Solution.*

Dun and Bradstreet (DB) Corporation, 103 JFK Parkway, Short Hills, NJ 07078, (973) 921-5500, www.dnb.com; *Country Report.*

Economist Intelligence Unit, 111 West 57th Street, New York, NY 10019, (212) 554-0600, Fax: (212) 586-1181, www.eiu.com; *Business Africa* and *Central African Republic Country Report.*

Euromonitor International, Inc., 224 S. Michigan Avenue, Suite 1500, Chicago, IL 60604, (312) 922-1115, Fax: (312) 922-1157, www.euromonitor.com; *The World Economic Factbook 2008* and *World Marketing Data and Statistics.*

International Monetary Fund (IMF), 700 Nineteenth Street, NW, Washington, DC 20431, (202) 623-7000, Fax: (202) 623-4661, www.imf.org; *World Economic Outlook Reports.*

M.E. Sharpe, 80 Business Park Drive, Armonk, NY 10504, (800) 541-6563, Fax: (914) 273-2106, www.mesharpe.com; *The Illustrated Book of World Rankings.*

Palgrave Macmillan Ltd., Houndmills, Basingstoke, Hampshire, RG21 6XS, England, (Telephone in U.S. (888) 330-8477), (Fax in U.S. (800) 672-2054), www.palgrave.com; *The Statesman's Yearbook 2008.*

Taylor and Francis Group, An Informa Business, 2 Park Square, Milton Park, Abingdon, Oxford OX14 4RN, United Kingdom, (Dial from U.S. (212) 216-7800), (Fax from U.S. (212) 564-7854), www.tandf.co.uk; *The Europa World Year Book.*

United Nations Statistics Division, New York, NY 10017, (800) 253-9646, Fax: (212) 963-4116, http://unstats.un.org; *Compendium of Intra-African and Related Foreign Trade Statistics 2003* and *World Statistics Pocketbook.*

The World Bank, 1818 H Street, NW, Washington, DC 20433, (202) 473-1000, Fax: (202) 477-6391, www.worldbank.org; *Africa Household Survey Databank; Africa Live Database (LDB); Africa Standardized Files and Indicators; African Development Indicators (ADI) 2007; Central African Republic; Global Economic Monitor (GEM); Global Economic Prospects 2008; The World Bank Atlas 2003-2004;* and *World Development Report 2008.*

CENTRAL AFRICAN REPUBLIC - EDUCATION

African Development Bank Group, Rue Joseph Anoma, 01 BP 1387 Abidjan 01, Cote d'Ivoire, www.afdb.org; *Statistics Pocketbook 2008.*

Euromonitor International, Inc., 224 S. Michigan Avenue, Suite 1500, Chicago, IL 60604, (312) 922-1115, Fax: (312) 922-1157, www.euromonitor.com; *International Marketing Data and Statistics 2008* and *World Marketing Data and Statistics.*

M.E. Sharpe, 80 Business Park Drive, Armonk, NY 10504, (800) 541-6563, Fax: (914) 273-2106, www.mesharpe.com; *The Illustrated Book of World Rankings.*

Palgrave Macmillan Ltd., Houndmills, Basingstoke, Hampshire, RG21 6XS, England, (Telephone in U.S. (888) 330-8477), (Fax in U.S. (800) 672-2054), www.palgrave.com; *The Statesman's Yearbook 2008.*

Taylor and Francis Group, An Informa Business, 2 Park Square, Milton Park, Abingdon, Oxford OX14 4RN, United Kingdom, (Dial from U.S. (212) 216-7800), (Fax from U.S. (212) 564-7854), www.tandf.co.uk; *The Europa World Year Book.*

UNESCO Institute for Statistics, C.P. 6128 Succursale Centre-Ville, Montreal, Quebec, H3C 3J7 Canada, (Dial from U.S. (514) 343-6880), (Fax from U.S. (514) 343 6882), www.uis.unesco.org; *Statistical Tables.*

United Nations Economic Commission for Africa (ECA), PO Box 3001, Addis Ababa, Ethiopia, (Telephone in U.S. (212) 963-4957), www.uneca.org; *African Statistical Yearbook 2006.*

United Nations Statistics Division, New York, NY 10017, (800) 253-9646, Fax: (212) 963-4116, http://unstats.un.org; *Human Development Report 2006* and *Survey of Economic and Social Conditions in Africa 2005.*

The World Bank, 1818 H Street, NW, Washington, DC 20433, (202) 473-1000, Fax: (202) 477-6391, www.worldbank.org; *Central African Republic; World Development Indicators (WDI) 2008;* and *World Development Report 2008.*

CENTRAL AFRICAN REPUBLIC - ELECTRICITY

M.E. Sharpe, 80 Business Park Drive, Armonk, NY 10504, (800) 541-6563, Fax: (914) 273-2106, www.mesharpe.com; *The Illustrated Book of World Rankings.*

Palgrave Macmillan Ltd., Houndmills, Basingstoke, Hampshire, RG21 6XS, England, (Telephone in U.S. (888) 330-8477), (Fax in U.S. (800) 672-2054), www.palgrave.com; *The Statesman's Yearbook 2008.*

United Nations Economic Commission for Africa (ECA), PO Box 3001, Addis Ababa, Ethiopia, (Telephone in U.S. (212) 963-4957), www.uneca.org; *African Statistical Yearbook 2006.*

United Nations Statistics Division, New York, NY 10017, (800) 253-9646, Fax: (212) 963-4116, http://unstats.un.org; *Human Development Report 2006; Statistical Yearbook;* and *Survey of Economic and Social Conditions in Africa 2005.*

CENTRAL AFRICAN REPUBLIC - EMPLOYMENT

Euromonitor International, Inc., 224 S. Michigan Avenue, Suite 1500, Chicago, IL 60604, (312) 922-1115, Fax: (312) 922-1157, www.euromonitor.com; *International Marketing Data and Statistics 2008.*

International Labour Office, I.L.O. Publications, 4 route des Morillons, CH-1211 Geneva 22, Switzerland, (Telephone in U.S. (202) 653-7652), (Fax in U.S. (202) 653-7687), www.ilo.org; *Yearbook of Labour Statistics 2006.*

M.E. Sharpe, 80 Business Park Drive, Armonk, NY 10504, (800) 541-6563, Fax: (914) 273-2106, www.mesharpe.com; *The Illustrated Book of World Rankings.*

United Nations Economic Commission for Africa (ECA), PO Box 3001, Addis Ababa, Ethiopia, (Telephone in U.S. (212) 963-4957), www.uneca.org; *African Statistical Yearbook 2006.*

United Nations Statistics Division, New York, NY 10017, (800) 253-9646, Fax: (212) 963-4116, http://unstats.un.org; *Statistical Yearbook* and *Survey of Economic and Social Conditions in Africa 2005.*

The World Bank, 1818 H Street, NW, Washington, DC 20433, (202) 473-1000, Fax: (202) 477-6391, www.worldbank.org; *Central African Republic.*

CENTRAL AFRICAN REPUBLIC - ENVIRONMENTAL CONDITIONS

DSI Data Service Information, Xantener Strasse 51a, D-47495 Rheinberg, Germany, www.dsidata.com; *Campus Solution* and *DSI's Global Environmental Database.*

Economist Intelligence Unit, 111 West 57th Street, New York, NY 10019, (212) 554-0600, Fax: (212) 586-1181, www.eiu.com; *Central African Republic Country Report.*

International Institute for Environment and Development (IIED), 3 Endsleigh Street, London, England, WC1H 0DD, United Kingdom, www.iied.org; *Environment Urbanization* and *Haramata - Bulletin of the Drylands.*

United Nations Statistics Division, New York, NY 10017, (800) 253-9646, Fax: (212) 963-4116, http://unstats.un.org; *World Statistics Pocketbook.*

CENTRAL AFRICAN REPUBLIC - EXPORTS

African Development Bank Group, Rue Joseph Anoma, 01 BP 1387 Abidjan 01, Cote d'Ivoire, www.afdb.org; *Statistics Pocketbook 2008.*

Central Intelligence Agency, Office of Public Affairs, Washington, DC 20505, (703) 482-0623, Fax: (703) 482-1739, www.cia.gov; *The World Factbook.*

Economist Intelligence Unit, 111 West 57th Street, New York, NY 10019, (212) 554-0600, Fax: (212) 586-1181, www.eiu.com; *Central African Republic Country Report.*

Euromonitor International, Inc., 224 S. Michigan Avenue, Suite 1500, Chicago, IL 60604, (312) 922-1115, Fax: (312) 922-1157, www.euromonitor.com; *International Marketing Data and Statistics 2008* and *The World Economic Factbook 2008.*

International Monetary Fund (IMF), 700 Nineteenth Street, NW, Washington, DC 20431, (202) 623-7000, Fax: (202) 623-4661, www.imf.org; *Direction of Trade Statistics Yearbook 2007.*

Palgrave Macmillan Ltd., Houndmills, Basingstoke, Hampshire, RG21 6XS, England, (Telephone in U.S.

(888) 330-8477), (Fax in U.S. (800) 672-2054), www.palgrave.com; *The Statesman's Yearbook 2008.*

Taylor and Francis Group, An Informa Business, 2 Park Square, Milton Park, Abingdon, Oxford OX14 4RN, United Kingdom, (Dial from U.S. (212) 216-7800), (Fax from U.S. (212) 564-7854), www.tandf.co.uk; *The Europa World Year Book.*

United Nations Conference on Trade and Development (UNCTAD), DC2-1120, United Nations, New York, NY 10017, (212) 963-0027, www.unctad.org; *Handbook of Statistics 2005.*

United Nations Economic Commission for Africa (ECA), PO Box 3001, Addis Ababa, Ethiopia, (Telephone in U.S. (212) 963-4957), www.uneca.org; *African Statistical Yearbook 2006.*

United Nations Food and Agricultural Organization (FAO), Viale delle Terme di Caracalla, 00100 Rome, Italy, (Dial from U.S. (202) 653-2400), (Fax from U.S. (202) 653 5760), www.fao.org; *The State of Food and Agriculture (SOFA) 2006.*

United Nations Statistics Division, New York, NY 10017, (800) 253-9646, Fax: (212) 963-4116, http://unstats.un.org; *Compendium of Intra-African and Related Foreign Trade Statistics 2003* and *Survey of Economic and Social Conditions in Africa 2005.*

The World Bank, 1818 H Street, NW, Washington, DC 20433, (202) 473-1000, Fax: (202) 477-6391, www.worldbank.org; *World Development Indicators (WDI) 2008* and *World Development Report 2008.*

CENTRAL AFRICAN REPUBLIC - FERTILITY, HUMAN

Central Intelligence Agency, Office of Public Affairs, Washington, DC 20505, (703) 482-0623, Fax: (703) 482-1739, www.cia.gov; *The World Factbook.*

M.E. Sharpe, 80 Business Park Drive, Armonk, NY 10504, (800) 541-6563, Fax: (914) 273-2106, www.mesharpe.com; *The Illustrated Book of World Rankings.*

United Nations Statistics Division, New York, NY 10017, (800) 253-9646, Fax: (212) 963-4116, http://unstats.un.org; *Human Development Report 2006* and *Survey of Economic and Social Conditions in Africa 2005.*

The World Bank, 1818 H Street, NW, Washington, DC 20433, (202) 473-1000, Fax: (202) 477-6391, www.worldbank.org; *The World Bank Atlas 2003-2004; World Development Indicators (WDI) 2008;* and *World Development Report 2008.*

CENTRAL AFRICAN REPUBLIC - FERTILIZER INDUSTRY

United Nations Food and Agricultural Organization (FAO), Viale delle Terme di Caracalla, 00100 Rome, Italy, (Dial from U.S. (202) 653-2400), (Fax from U.S. (202) 653 5760), www.fao.org; *FAO Fertilizer Yearbook* and *The State of Food and Agriculture (SOFA) 2006.*

United Nations Statistics Division, New York, NY 10017, (800) 253-9646, Fax: (212) 963-4116, http://unstats.un.org; *Statistical Yearbook.*

CENTRAL AFRICAN REPUBLIC - FETAL MORTALITY

See CENTRAL AFRICAN REPUBLIC - MORTALITY

CENTRAL AFRICAN REPUBLIC - FINANCE

Taylor and Francis Group, An Informa Business, 2 Park Square, Milton Park, Abingdon, Oxford OX14 4RN, United Kingdom, (Dial from U.S. (212) 216-7800), (Fax from U.S. (212) 564-7854), www.tandf.co.uk; *The Europa World Year Book.*

United Nations Economic Commission for Africa (ECA), PO Box 3001, Addis Ababa, Ethiopia, (Telephone in U.S. (212) 963-4957), www.uneca.org; *African Statistical Yearbook 2006.*

United Nations Statistics Division, New York, NY 10017, (800) 253-9646, Fax: (212) 963-4116, http://unstats.un.org; *National Accounts Statistics: Compendium of Income Distribution Statistics* and *Statistical Yearbook.*

The World Bank, 1818 H Street, NW, Washington, DC 20433, (202) 473-1000, Fax: (202) 477-6391, www.worldbank.org; *Central African Republic.*

CENTRAL AFRICAN REPUBLIC - FINANCE, PUBLIC

African Development Bank Group, Rue Joseph Anoma, 01 BP 1387 Abidjan 01, Cote d'Ivoire, www.afdb.org; *Statistics Pocketbook 2008.*

Bernan Essential Government Publications, 4611-F Assembly Drive, Lanham MD, 20706-4391, (301) 459-2255, Fax: (800) 865-3450, www.bernan.com; *National Accounts Statistics.*

Economist Intelligence Unit, 111 West 57th Street, New York, NY 10019, (212) 554-0600, Fax: (212) 586-1181, www.eiu.com; *Central African Republic Country Report.*

International Monetary Fund (IMF), 700 Nineteenth Street, NW, Washington, DC 20431, (202) 623-7000, Fax: (202) 623-4661, www.imf.org; *International Financial Statistics; International Financial Statistics Online Service;* and *International Financial Statistics Yearbook 2007.*

M.E. Sharpe, 80 Business Park Drive, Armonk, NY 10504, (800) 541-6563, Fax: (914) 273-2106, www.mesharpe.com; *The Illustrated Book of World Rankings.*

Taylor and Francis Group, An Informa Business, 2 Park Square, Milton Park, Abingdon, Oxford OX14 4RN, United Kingdom, (Dial from U.S. (212) 216-7800), (Fax from U.S. (212) 564-7854), www.tandf.co.uk; *The Europa World Year Book.*

United Nations Economic Commission for Africa (ECA), PO Box 3001, Addis Ababa, Ethiopia, (Telephone in U.S. (212) 963-4957), www.uneca.org; *African Statistical Yearbook 2006.*

The World Bank, 1818 H Street, NW, Washington, DC 20433, (202) 473-1000, Fax: (202) 477-6391, www.worldbank.org; *Central African Republic.*

CENTRAL AFRICAN REPUBLIC - FISHERIES

M.E. Sharpe, 80 Business Park Drive, Armonk, NY 10504, (800) 541-6563, Fax: (914) 273-2106, www.mesharpe.com; *The Illustrated Book of World Rankings.*

Palgrave Macmillan Ltd., Houndmills, Basingstoke, Hampshire, RG21 6XS, England, (Telephone in U.S. (888) 330-8477), (Fax in U.S. (800) 672-2054), www.palgrave.com; *The Statesman's Yearbook 2008.*

Taylor and Francis Group, An Informa Business, 2 Park Square, Milton Park, Abingdon, Oxford OX14 4RN, United Kingdom, (Dial from U.S. (212) 216-7800), (Fax from U.S. (212) 564-7854), www.tandf.co.uk; *The Europa World Year Book.*

United Nations Conference on Trade and Development (UNCTAD), DC2-1120, United Nations, New York, NY 10017, (212) 963-0027, www.unctad.org; *UNCTAD Commodity Yearbook.*

United Nations Economic Commission for Africa (ECA), PO Box 3001, Addis Ababa, Ethiopia, (Telephone in U.S. (212) 963-4957), www.uneca.org; *African Statistical Yearbook 2006.*

United Nations Food and Agricultural Organization (FAO), Viale delle Terme di Caracalla, 00100 Rome, Italy, (Dial from U.S. (202) 653-2400), (Fax from U.S. (202) 653 5760), www.fao.org; *FAO Yearbook of Fishery Statistics;* Fishery Databases; FISHSTAT Database. Subjects covered include: Aquaculture production, capture production, fishery commodities; and *The State of Food and Agriculture (SOFA) 2006.*

United Nations Statistics Division, New York, NY 10017, (800) 253-9646, Fax: (212) 963-4116, http://unstats.un.org; *Statistical Yearbook* and *Survey of Economic and Social Conditions in Africa 2005.*

The World Bank, 1818 H Street, NW, Washington, DC 20433, (202) 473-1000, Fax: (202) 477-6391, www.worldbank.org; *Central African Republic.*

CENTRAL AFRICAN REPUBLIC - FLOUR INDUSTRY

United Nations Statistics Division, New York, NY 10017, (800) 253-9646, Fax: (212) 963-4116, http://unstats.un.org; *Statistical Yearbook.*

CENTRAL AFRICAN REPUBLIC - FOOD

African Development Bank Group, Rue Joseph Anoma, 01 BP 1387 Abidjan 01, Cote d'Ivoire, www.afdb.org; *Statistics Pocketbook 2008.*

United Nations Conference on Trade and Development (UNCTAD), DC2-1120, United Nations, New York, NY 10017, (212) 963-0027, www.unctad.org; *UNCTAD Commodity Yearbook.*

United Nations Food and Agricultural Organization (FAO), Viale delle Terme di Caracalla, 00100 Rome, Italy, (Dial from U.S. (202) 653-2400), (Fax from U.S. (202) 653 5760), www.fao.org; *FAO Production Yearbook 2002* and *The State of Food and Agriculture (SOFA) 2006.*

United Nations Statistics Division, New York, NY 10017, (800) 253-9646, Fax: (212) 963-4116, http://unstats.un.org; *Human Development Report 2006.*

CENTRAL AFRICAN REPUBLIC - FOREIGN EXCHANGE RATES

African Development Bank Group, Rue Joseph Anoma, 01 BP 1387 Abidjan 01, Cote d'Ivoire, www.afdb.org; *Statistics Pocketbook 2008.*

Central Intelligence Agency, Office of Public Affairs, Washington, DC 20505, (703) 482-0623, Fax: (703) 482-1739, www.cia.gov; *The World Factbook.*

Euromonitor International, Inc., 224 S. Michigan Avenue, Suite 1500, Chicago, IL 60604, (312) 922-1115, Fax: (312) 922-1157, www.euromonitor.com; *International Marketing Data and Statistics 2008* and *The World Economic Factbook 2008.*

International Monetary Fund (IMF), 700 Nineteenth Street, NW, Washington, DC 20431, (202) 623-7000, Fax: (202) 623-4661, www.imf.org; *International Financial Statistics Yearbook 2007.*

Taylor and Francis Group, An Informa Business, 2 Park Square, Milton Park, Abingdon, Oxford OX14 4RN, United Kingdom, (Dial from U.S. (212) 216-7800), (Fax from U.S. (212) 564-7854), www.tandf.co.uk; *The Europa World Year Book.*

United Nations Statistics Division, New York, NY 10017, (800) 253-9646, Fax: (212) 963-4116, http://unstats.un.org; *Compendium of Intra-African and Related Foreign Trade Statistics 2003; Statistical Yearbook;* and *World Statistics Pocketbook.*

CENTRAL AFRICAN REPUBLIC - FORESTS AND FORESTRY

M.E. Sharpe, 80 Business Park Drive, Armonk, NY 10504, (800) 541-6563, Fax: (914) 273-2106, www.mesharpe.com; *The Illustrated Book of World Rankings.*

Palgrave Macmillan Ltd., Houndmills, Basingstoke, Hampshire, RG21 6XS, England, (Telephone in U.S. (888) 330-8477), (Fax in U.S. (800) 672-2054), www.palgrave.com; *The Statesman's Yearbook 2008.*

Taylor and Francis Group, An Informa Business, 2 Park Square, Milton Park, Abingdon, Oxford OX14 4RN, United Kingdom, (Dial from U.S. (212) 216-7800), (Fax from U.S. (212) 564-7854), www.tandf.co.uk; *The Europa World Year Book.*

UNESCO Institute for Statistics, C.P. 6128 Succursale Centre-Ville, Montreal, Quebec, H3C 3J7 Canada, (Dial from U.S. (514) 343-6880), (Fax from U.S. (514) 343 6882), www.uis.unesco.org; *Statistical Tables.*

United Nations Conference on Trade and Development (UNCTAD), DC2-1120, United Nations, New York, NY 10017, (212) 963-0027, www.unctad.org; *UNCTAD Commodity Yearbook.*

United Nations Economic Commission for Africa (ECA), PO Box 3001, Addis Ababa, Ethiopia, (Telephone in U.S. (212) 963-4957), www.uneca.org; *African Statistical Yearbook 2006.*

United Nations Food and Agricultural Organization (FAO), Viale delle Terme di Caracalla, 00100 Rome, Italy, (Dial from U.S. (202) 653-2400), (Fax from U.S. (202) 653 5760), www.fao.org; *FAO Yearbook of Forest Products* and *The State of Food and Agriculture (SOFA) 2006.*

United Nations Statistics Division, New York, NY 10017, (800) 253-9646, Fax: (212) 963-4116, http://unstats.un.org; *Statistical Yearbook.*

The World Bank, 1818 H Street, NW, Washington, DC 20433, (202) 473-1000, Fax: (202) 477-6391, www.worldbank.org; *Central African Republic* and *World Development Report 2008.*

CENTRAL AFRICAN REPUBLIC - GAS INDUSTRY

M.E. Sharpe, 80 Business Park Drive, Armonk, NY 10504, (800) 541-6563, Fax: (914) 273-2106, www.mesharpe.com; *The Illustrated Book of World Rankings.*

CENTRAL AFRICAN REPUBLIC - GEOGRAPHIC INFORMATION SYSTEMS

M.E. Sharpe, 80 Business Park Drive, Armonk, NY 10504, (800) 541-6563, Fax: (914) 273-2106, www.mesharpe.com; *The Illustrated Book of World Rankings.*

The World Bank, 1818 H Street, NW, Washington, DC 20433, (202) 473-1000, Fax: (202) 477-6391, www.worldbank.org; *Central African Republic.*

CENTRAL AFRICAN REPUBLIC - GOLD INDUSTRY

International Monetary Fund (IMF), 700 Nineteenth Street, NW, Washington, DC 20431, (202) 623-7000, Fax: (202) 623-4661, www.imf.org; *International Financial Statistics Yearbook 2007.*

United Nations Statistics Division, New York, NY 10017, (800) 253-9646, Fax: (212) 963-4116, http://unstats.un.org; *Statistical Yearbook.*

The World Bank, 1818 H Street, NW, Washington, DC 20433, (202) 473-1000, Fax: (202) 477-6391, www.worldbank.org; *World Development Indicators (WDI) 2008.*

CENTRAL AFRICAN REPUBLIC - GOLD PRODUCTION

See CENTRAL AFRICAN REPUBLIC - MINERAL INDUSTRIES

CENTRAL AFRICAN REPUBLIC - GROSS DOMESTIC PRODUCT

African Development Bank Group, Rue Joseph Anoma, 01 BP 1387 Abidjan 01, Cote d'Ivoire, www.afdb.org; *Statistics Pocketbook 2008.*

Economist Intelligence Unit, 111 West 57th Street, New York, NY 10019, (212) 554-0600, Fax: (212) 586-1181, www.eiu.com; *Central African Republic Country Report.*

Euromonitor International, Inc., 224 S. Michigan Avenue, Suite 1500, Chicago, IL 60604, (312) 922-1115, Fax: (312) 922-1157, www.euromonitor.com; *International Marketing Data and Statistics 2008* and *The World Economic Factbook 2008.*

M.E. Sharpe, 80 Business Park Drive, Armonk, NY 10504, (800) 541-6563, Fax: (914) 273-2106, www.mesharpe.com; *The Illustrated Book of World Rankings.*

Taylor and Francis Group, An Informa Business, 2 Park Square, Milton Park, Abingdon, Oxford OX14 4RN, United Kingdom, (Dial from U.S. (212) 216-7800), (Fax from U.S. (212) 564-7854), www.tandf.co.uk; *The Europa World Year Book.*

United Nations Economic Commission for Africa (ECA), PO Box 3001, Addis Ababa, Ethiopia, (Telephone in U.S. (212) 963-4957), www.uneca.org; *African Statistical Yearbook 2006.*

United Nations Statistics Division, New York, NY 10017, (800) 253-9646, Fax: (212) 963-4116, http://unstats.un.org; *Human Development Report 2006; National Accounts Statistics: Compendium of Income Distribution Statistics; Statistical Yearbook;* and *Survey of Economic and Social Conditions in Africa 2005.*

The World Bank, 1818 H Street, NW, Washington, DC 20433, (202) 473-1000, Fax: (202) 477-6391, www.worldbank.org; *World Development Indicators (WDI) 2008* and *World Development Report 2008.*

CENTRAL AFRICAN REPUBLIC - GROSS NATIONAL PRODUCT

M.E. Sharpe, 80 Business Park Drive, Armonk, NY 10504, (800) 541-6563, Fax: (914) 273-2106, www.mesharpe.com; *The Illustrated Book of World Rankings.*

Palgrave Macmillan Ltd., Houndmills, Basingstoke, Hampshire, RG21 6XS, England, (Telephone in U.S. (888) 330-8477), (Fax in U.S. (800) 672-2054), www.palgrave.com; *The Statesman's Yearbook 2008.*

U.S. Department of State (DOS), 2201 C Street NW, Washington, DC 20520, (202) 647-4000, www.state.gov; *World Military Expenditures and Arms Transfers (WMEAT).*

The World Bank, 1818 H Street, NW, Washington, DC 20433, (202) 473-1000, Fax: (202) 477-6391, www.worldbank.org; *The World Bank Atlas 2003-2004; World Development Indicators (WDI) 2008;* and *World Development Report 2008.*

CENTRAL AFRICAN REPUBLIC - HIDES AND SKINS INDUSTRY

United Nations Food and Agricultural Organization (FAO), Viale delle Terme di Caracalla, 00100 Rome, Italy, (Dial from U.S. (202) 653-2400), (Fax from U.S. (202) 653 5760), www.fao.org; *FAO Production Yearbook 2002.*

CENTRAL AFRICAN REPUBLIC - HOUSING

Euromonitor International, Inc., 224 S. Michigan Avenue, Suite 1500, Chicago, IL 60604, (312) 922-1115, Fax: (312) 922-1157, www.euromonitor.com; *World Marketing Data and Statistics.*

M.E. Sharpe, 80 Business Park Drive, Armonk, NY 10504, (800) 541-6563, Fax: (914) 273-2106, www.mesharpe.com; *The Illustrated Book of World Rankings.*

CENTRAL AFRICAN REPUBLIC - ILLITERATE PERSONS

Euromonitor International, Inc., 224 S. Michigan Avenue, Suite 1500, Chicago, IL 60604, (312) 922-1115, Fax: (312) 922-1157, www.euromonitor.com; *The World Economic Factbook 2008.*

UNESCO Institute for Statistics, C.P. 6128 Succursale Centre-Ville, Montreal, Quebec, H3C 3J7 Canada, (Dial from U.S. (514) 343-6880), (Fax from U.S. (514) 343 6882), www.uis.unesco.org; *Statistical Tables.*

United Nations Statistics Division, New York, NY 10017, (800) 253-9646, Fax: (212) 963-4116, http://unstats.un.org; *Human Development Report 2006.*

CENTRAL AFRICAN REPUBLIC - IMPORTS

Central Intelligence Agency, Office of Public Affairs, Washington, DC 20505, (703) 482-0623, Fax: (703) 482-1739, www.cia.gov; *The World Factbook.*

Economist Intelligence Unit, 111 West 57th Street, New York, NY 10019, (212) 554-0600, Fax: (212) 586-1181, www.eiu.com; *Central African Republic Country Report.*

Euromonitor International, Inc., 224 S. Michigan Avenue, Suite 1500, Chicago, IL 60604, (312) 922-1115, Fax: (312) 922-1157, www.euromonitor.com; *International Marketing Data and Statistics 2008* and *The World Economic Factbook 2008.*

International Monetary Fund (IMF), 700 Nineteenth Street, NW, Washington, DC 20431, (202) 623-7000, Fax: (202) 623-4661, www.imf.org; *Direction of Trade Statistics Yearbook 2007.*

Palgrave Macmillan Ltd., Houndmills, Basingstoke, Hampshire, RG21 6XS, England, (Telephone in U.S. (888) 330-8477), (Fax in U.S. (800) 672-2054), www.palgrave.com; *The Statesman's Yearbook 2008.*

Taylor and Francis Group, An Informa Business, 2 Park Square, Milton Park, Abingdon, Oxford OX14 4RN, United Kingdom, (Dial from U.S. (212) 216-7800), (Fax from U.S. (212) 564-7854), www.tandf.co.uk; *The Europa World Year Book.*

United Nations Conference on Trade and Development (UNCTAD), DC2-1120, United Nations, New York, NY 10017, (212) 963-0027, www.unctad.org; *Handbook of Statistics 2005.*

United Nations Economic Commission for Africa (ECA), PO Box 3001, Addis Ababa, Ethiopia, (Telephone in U.S. (212) 963-4957), www.uneca.org; *African Statistical Yearbook 2006.*

United Nations Food and Agricultural Organization (FAO), Viale delle Terme di Caracalla, 00100 Rome, Italy, (Dial from U.S. (202) 653-2400), (Fax from U.S. (202) 653 5760), www.fao.org; *The State of Food and Agriculture (SOFA) 2006.*

United Nations Statistics Division, New York, NY 10017, (800) 253-9646, Fax: (212) 963-4116, http://unstats.un.org; *Compendium of Intra-African and Related Foreign Trade Statistics 2003* and *Survey of Economic and Social Conditions in Africa 2005.*

The World Bank, 1818 H Street, NW, Washington, DC 20433, (202) 473-1000, Fax: (202) 477-6391, www.worldbank.org; *World Development Indicators (WDI) 2008* and *World Development Report 2008.*

CENTRAL AFRICAN REPUBLIC - INDUSTRIAL PRODUCTIVITY

M.E. Sharpe, 80 Business Park Drive, Armonk, NY 10504, (800) 541-6563, Fax: (914) 273-2106, www.mesharpe.com; *The Illustrated Book of World Rankings.*

CENTRAL AFRICAN REPUBLIC - INDUSTRIES

Central Intelligence Agency, Office of Public Affairs, Washington, DC 20505, (703) 482-0623, Fax: (703) 482-1739, www.cia.gov; *The World Factbook.*

Economist Intelligence Unit, 111 West 57th Street, New York, NY 10019, (212) 554-0600, Fax: (212) 586-1181, www.eiu.com; *Central African Republic Country Report.*

Euromonitor International, Inc., 224 S. Michigan Avenue, Suite 1500, Chicago, IL 60604, (312) 922-1115, Fax: (312) 922-1157, www.euromonitor.com; *The World Economic Factbook 2008* and *World Marketing Data and Statistics.*

International Labour Office, I.L.O. Publications, 4 route des Morillons, CH-1211 Geneva 22, Switzerland, (Telephone in U.S. (202) 653-7652), (Fax in U.S. (202) 653-7687), www.ilo.org; *Yearbook of Labour Statistics 2006.*

M.E. Sharpe, 80 Business Park Drive, Armonk, NY 10504, (800) 541-6563, Fax: (914) 273-2106, www.mesharpe.com; *The Illustrated Book of World Rankings.*

Palgrave Macmillan Ltd., Houndmills, Basingstoke, Hampshire, RG21 6XS, England, (Telephone in U.S. (888) 330-8477), (Fax in U.S. (800) 672-2054), www.palgrave.com; *The Statesman's Yearbook 2008.*

Taylor and Francis Group, An Informa Business, 2 Park Square, Milton Park, Abingdon, Oxford OX14 4RN, United Kingdom, (Dial from U.S. (212) 216-7800), (Fax from U.S. (212) 564-7854), www.tandf.co.uk; *The Europa World Year Book.*

United Nations Economic Commission for Africa (ECA), PO Box 3001, Addis Ababa, Ethiopia, (Telephone in U.S. (212) 963-4957), www.uneca.org; *African Statistical Yearbook 2006.*

United Nations Industrial Development Organization (UNIDO), 1 United Nations Plaza, New York, NY 10017, (212) 963 6890, Fax: (212) 963-7904, http://unido.org; Industrial Statistics Database 2008 (INDSTAT) and *The International Yearbook of Industrial Statistics 2008.*

United Nations Statistics Division, New York, NY 10017, (800) 253-9646, Fax: (212) 963-4116, http://unstats.un.org; *2004 Industrial Commodity Statistics Yearbook* and *Survey of Economic and Social Conditions in Africa 2005*.

The World Bank, 1818 H Street, NW, Washington, DC 20433, (202) 473-1000, Fax: (202) 477-6391, www.worldbank.org; *Central African Republic* and *World Development Indicators (WDI) 2008*.

CENTRAL AFRICAN REPUBLIC - INFANT AND MATERNAL MORTALITY

See CENTRAL AFRICAN REPUBLIC - MORTALITY

CENTRAL AFRICAN REPUBLIC - INTERNATIONAL LIQUIDITY

International Monetary Fund (IMF), 700 Nineteenth Street, NW, Washington, DC 20431, (202) 623-7000, Fax: (202) 623-4661, www.imf.org; *International Financial Statistics Yearbook 2007*.

CENTRAL AFRICAN REPUBLIC - INTERNATIONAL TRADE

African Development Bank Group, Rue Joseph Anoma, 01 BP 1387 Abidjan 01, Cote d'Ivoire, www.afdb.org; *Statistics Pocketbook 2008*.

Economist Intelligence Unit, 111 West 57th Street, New York, NY 10019, (212) 554-0600, Fax: (212) 586-1181, www.eiu.com; *Central African Republic Country Report*.

Euromonitor International, Inc., 224 S. Michigan Avenue, Suite 1500, Chicago, IL 60604, (312) 922-1115, Fax: (312) 922-1157, www.euromonitor.com; *The World Economic Factbook 2008* and *World Marketing Data and Statistics*.

M.E. Sharpe, 80 Business Park Drive, Armonk, NY 10504, (800) 541-6563, Fax: (914) 273-2106, www.mesharpe.com; *The Illustrated Book of World Rankings*.

Organisation for Economic Cooperation and Development (OECD), 2 rue Andre Pascal, F-75775 Paris Cedex 16, France, (Telephone in U.S. (202) 785-6323), (Fax in U.S. (202) 785-0350), www.oecd.org; *International Trade by Commodity Statistics (ITCS)*.

Palgrave Macmillan Ltd., Houndmills, Basingstoke, Hampshire, RG21 6XS, England, (Telephone in U.S. (888) 330-8477), (Fax in U.S. (800) 672-2054), www.palgrave.com; *The Statesman's Yearbook 2008*.

Taylor and Francis Group, An Informa Business, 2 Park Square, Milton Park, Abingdon, Oxford OX14 4RN, United Kingdom, (Dial from U.S. (212) 216-7800), (Fax from U.S. (212) 564-7854), www.tandf.co.uk; *The Europa World Year Book*.

United Nations Conference on Trade and Development (UNCTAD), DC2-1120, United Nations, New York, NY 10017, (212) 963-0027, www.unctad.org; *UNCTAD Commodity Yearbook*.

United Nations Economic Commission for Africa (ECA), PO Box 3001, Addis Ababa, Ethiopia, (Telephone in U.S. (212) 963-4957), www.uneca.org; *African Statistical Yearbook 2006*.

United Nations Food and Agricultural Organization (FAO), Viale delle Terme di Caracalla, 00100 Rome, Italy, (Dial from U.S. (202) 653-2400), (Fax from U.S. (202) 653 5760), www.fao.org; *FAO Trade Yearbook* and *The State of Food and Agriculture (SOFA) 2006*.

United Nations Statistics Division, New York, NY 10017, (800) 253-9646, Fax: (212) 963-4116, http://unstats.un.org; *Compendium of Intra-African and Related Foreign Trade Statistics 2003* and *Statistical Yearbook*.

The World Bank, 1818 H Street, NW, Washington, DC 20433, (202) 473-1000, Fax: (202) 477-6391, www.worldbank.org; *Central African Republic; World Development Indicators (WDI) 2008;* and *World Development Report 2008*.

World Trade Organization (WTO), Centre William Rappard, Rue de Lausanne 154, CH-1211 Geneva 21, Switzerland, www.wto.org; *International Trade Statistics 2006*.

CENTRAL AFRICAN REPUBLIC - INTERNET USERS

International Telecommunication Union (ITU), Place des Nations, 1211 Geneva 20, Switzerland, www.itu.int; *World Telecommunication/ICT Indicators Database on CD-ROM; World Telecommunication/ICT Indicators Database Online;* and *Yearbook of Statistics - Telecommunication Services (Chronological Time Series 1997-2006)*.

The World Bank, 1818 H Street, NW, Washington, DC 20433, (202) 473-1000, Fax: (202) 477-6391, www.worldbank.org; *Central African Republic*.

CENTRAL AFRICAN REPUBLIC - IRON AND IRON ORE PRODUCTION

See CENTRAL AFRICAN REPUBLIC - MINERAL INDUSTRIES

CENTRAL AFRICAN REPUBLIC - LABOR

African Development Bank Group, Rue Joseph Anoma, 01 BP 1387 Abidjan 01, Cote d'Ivoire, www.afdb.org; *Statistics Pocketbook 2008*.

Central Intelligence Agency, Office of Public Affairs, Washington, DC 20505, (703) 482-0623, Fax: (703) 482-1739, www.cia.gov; *The World Factbook*.

Euromonitor International, Inc., 224 S. Michigan Avenue, Suite 1500, Chicago, IL 60604, (312) 922-1115, Fax: (312) 922-1157, www.euromonitor.com; *International Marketing Data and Statistics 2008* and *World Marketing Data and Statistics*.

International Labour Office, I.L.O. Publications, 4 route des Morillons, CH-1211 Geneva 22, Switzerland, (Telephone in U.S. (202) 653-7652), (Fax in U.S. (202) 653-7687), www.ilo.org; *Yearbook of Labour Statistics 2006*.

M.E. Sharpe, 80 Business Park Drive, Armonk, NY 10504, (800) 541-6563, Fax: (914) 273-2106, www.mesharpe.com; *The Illustrated Book of World Rankings*.

Palgrave Macmillan Ltd., Houndmills, Basingstoke, Hampshire, RG21 6XS, England, (Telephone in U.S. (888) 330-8477), (Fax in U.S. (800) 672-2054), www.palgrave.com; *The Statesman's Yearbook 2008*.

United Nations Food and Agricultural Organization (FAO), Viale delle Terme di Caracalla, 00100 Rome, Italy, (Dial from U.S. (202) 653-2400), (Fax from U.S. (202) 653 5760), www.fao.org; *The State of Food and Agriculture (SOFA) 2006*.

United Nations Statistics Division, New York, NY 10017, (800) 253-9646, Fax: (212) 963-4116, http://unstats.un.org; *Human Development Report 2006*.

The World Bank, 1818 H Street, NW, Washington, DC 20433, (202) 473-1000, Fax: (202) 477-6391, www.worldbank.org; *The World Bank Atlas 2003-2004; World Development Indicators (WDI) 2008;* and *World Development Report 2008*.

CENTRAL AFRICAN REPUBLIC - LAND USE

Central Intelligence Agency, Office of Public Affairs, Washington, DC 20505, (703) 482-0623, Fax: (703) 482-1739, www.cia.gov; *The World Factbook*.

Euromonitor International, Inc., 224 S. Michigan Avenue, Suite 1500, Chicago, IL 60604, (312) 922-1115, Fax: (312) 922-1157, www.euromonitor.com; *International Marketing Data and Statistics 2008*.

United Nations Food and Agricultural Organization (FAO), Viale delle Terme di Caracalla, 00100 Rome, Italy, (Dial from U.S. (202) 653-2400), (Fax from U.S. (202) 653 5760), www.fao.org; *FAO Production Yearbook 2002*.

The World Bank, 1818 H Street, NW, Washington, DC 20433, (202) 473-1000, Fax: (202) 477-6391, www.worldbank.org; *World Development Report 2008*.

CENTRAL AFRICAN REPUBLIC - LIBRARIES

M.E. Sharpe, 80 Business Park Drive, Armonk, NY 10504, (800) 541-6563, Fax: (914) 273-2106, www.mesharpe.com; *The Illustrated Book of World Rankings*.

CENTRAL AFRICAN REPUBLIC - LIFE EXPECTANCY

African Development Bank Group, Rue Joseph Anoma, 01 BP 1387 Abidjan 01, Cote d'Ivoire, www.afdb.org; *Statistics Pocketbook 2008*.

Central Intelligence Agency, Office of Public Affairs, Washington, DC 20505, (703) 482-0623, Fax: (703) 482-1739, www.cia.gov; *The World Factbook*.

Euromonitor International, Inc., 224 S. Michigan Avenue, Suite 1500, Chicago, IL 60604, (312) 922-1115, Fax: (312) 922-1157, www.euromonitor.com; *The World Economic Factbook 2008*.

Palgrave Macmillan Ltd., Houndmills, Basingstoke, Hampshire, RG21 6XS, England, (Telephone in U.S. (888) 330-8477), (Fax in U.S. (800) 672-2054), www.palgrave.com; *The Statesman's Yearbook 2008*.

United Nations Statistics Division, New York, NY 10017, (800) 253-9646, Fax: (212) 963-4116, http://unstats.un.org; *Human Development Report 2006* and *World Statistics Pocketbook*.

The World Bank, 1818 H Street, NW, Washington, DC 20433, (202) 473-1000, Fax: (202) 477-6391, www.worldbank.org; *The World Bank Atlas 2003-2004* and *World Development Report 2008*.

CENTRAL AFRICAN REPUBLIC - LITERACY

Euromonitor International, Inc., 224 S. Michigan Avenue, Suite 1500, Chicago, IL 60604, (312) 922-1115, Fax: (312) 922-1157, www.euromonitor.com; *World Marketing Data and Statistics*.

United Nations Statistics Division, New York, NY 10017, (800) 253-9646, Fax: (212) 963-4116, http://unstats.un.org; *Survey of Economic and Social Conditions in Africa 2005*.

CENTRAL AFRICAN REPUBLIC - LIVESTOCK

M.E. Sharpe, 80 Business Park Drive, Armonk, NY 10504, (800) 541-6563, Fax: (914) 273-2106, www.mesharpe.com; *The Illustrated Book of World Rankings*.

Palgrave Macmillan Ltd., Houndmills, Basingstoke, Hampshire, RG21 6XS, England, (Telephone in U.S. (888) 330-8477), (Fax in U.S. (800) 672-2054), www.palgrave.com; *The Statesman's Yearbook 2008*.

Taylor and Francis Group, An Informa Business, 2 Park Square, Milton Park, Abingdon, Oxford OX14 4RN, United Kingdom, (Dial from U.S. (212) 216-7800), (Fax from U.S. (212) 564-7854), www.tandf.co.uk; *The Europa World Year Book*.

United Nations Conference on Trade and Development (UNCTAD), DC2-1120, United Nations, New York, NY 10017, (212) 963-0027, www.unctad.org; *UNCTAD Commodity Yearbook*.

United Nations Economic Commission for Africa (ECA), PO Box 3001, Addis Ababa, Ethiopia, (Telephone in U.S. (212) 963-4957), www.uneca.org; *African Statistical Yearbook 2006*.

United Nations Food and Agricultural Organization (FAO), Viale delle Terme di Caracalla, 00100 Rome, Italy, (Dial from U.S. (202) 653-2400), (Fax from U.S. (202) 653 5760), www.fao.org; *FAO Production Yearbook 2002* and *The State of Food and Agriculture (SOFA) 2006*.

United Nations Statistics Division, New York, NY 10017, (800) 253-9646, Fax: (212) 963-4116, http://unstats.un.org; *Statistical Yearbook* and *Survey of Economic and Social Conditions in Africa 2005*.

CENTRAL AFRICAN REPUBLIC - MANUFACTURES

M.E. Sharpe, 80 Business Park Drive, Armonk, NY 10504, (800) 541-6563, Fax: (914) 273-2106, www.mesharpe.com; *The Illustrated Book of World Rankings*.

United Nations Economic Commission for Africa (ECA), PO Box 3001, Addis Ababa, Ethiopia, (Telephone in U.S. (212) 963-4957), www.uneca.org; *African Statistical Yearbook 2006*.

United Nations Statistics Division, New York, NY 10017, (800) 253-9646, Fax: (212) 963-4116, http://unstats.un.org; *Statistical Yearbook* and *Survey of Economic and Social Conditions in Africa 2005*.

The World Bank, 1818 H Street, NW, Washington, DC 20433, (202) 473-1000, Fax: (202) 477-6391, www.worldbank.org; *World Development Indicators (WDI) 2008*.

CENTRAL AFRICAN REPUBLIC - MARRIAGE

M.E. Sharpe, 80 Business Park Drive, Armonk, NY 10504, (800) 541-6563, Fax: (914) 273-2106, www.mesharpe.com; *The Illustrated Book of World Rankings*.

Taylor and Francis Group, An Informa Business, 2 Park Square, Milton Park, Abingdon, Oxford OX14 4RN, United Kingdom, (Dial from U.S. (212) 216-7800), (Fax from U.S. (212) 564-7854), www.tandf.co.uk; *The Europa World Year Book*.

United Nations Statistics Division, New York, NY 10017, (800) 253-9646, Fax: (212) 963-4116, http://unstats.un.org; *Demographic Yearbook*.

CENTRAL AFRICAN REPUBLIC - MEAT PRODUCTION

See CENTRAL AFRICAN REPUBLIC - LIVESTOCK

CENTRAL AFRICAN REPUBLIC - MILK PRODUCTION

See CENTRAL AFRICAN REPUBLIC - DAIRY PROCESSING

CENTRAL AFRICAN REPUBLIC - MINERAL INDUSTRIES

M.E. Sharpe, 80 Business Park Drive, Armonk, NY 10504, (800) 541-6563, Fax: (914) 273-2106, www.mesharpe.com; *The Illustrated Book of World Rankings*.

Palgrave Macmillan Ltd., Houndmills, Basingstoke, Hampshire, RG21 6XS, England, (Telephone in U.S. (888) 330-8477), (Fax in U.S. (800) 672-2054), www.palgrave.com; *The Statesman's Yearbook 2008*.

Taylor and Francis Group, An Informa Business, 2 Park Square, Milton Park, Abingdon, Oxford OX14 4RN, United Kingdom, (Dial from U.S. (212) 216-7800), (Fax from U.S. (212) 564-7854), www.tandf.co.uk; *The Europa World Year Book*.

United Nations Conference on Trade and Development (UNCTAD), DC2-1120, United Nations, New York, NY 10017, (212) 963-0027, www.unctad.org; *UNCTAD Commodity Yearbook*.

United Nations Economic Commission for Africa (ECA), PO Box 3001, Addis Ababa, Ethiopia, (Telephone in U.S. (212) 963-4957), www.uneca.org; *African Statistical Yearbook 2006*.

United Nations Statistics Division, New York, NY 10017, (800) 253-9646, Fax: (212) 963-4116, http://unstats.un.org; *Statistical Yearbook*.

CENTRAL AFRICAN REPUBLIC - MONEY EXCHANGE RATES

See CENTRAL AFRICAN REPUBLIC - FOREIGN EXCHANGE RATES

CENTRAL AFRICAN REPUBLIC - MONEY SUPPLY

African Development Bank Group, Rue Joseph Anoma, 01 BP 1387 Abidjan 01, Cote d'Ivoire, www.afdb.org; *Statistics Pocketbook 2008*.

Economist Intelligence Unit, 111 West 57th Street, New York, NY 10019, (212) 554-0600, Fax: (212) 586-1181, www.eiu.com; *Central African Republic Country Report*.

International Monetary Fund (IMF), 700 Nineteenth Street, NW, Washington, DC 20431, (202) 623-7000, Fax: (202) 623-4661, www.imf.org; *International Financial Statistics Yearbook 2007*.

Taylor and Francis Group, An Informa Business, 2 Park Square, Milton Park, Abingdon, Oxford OX14 4RN, United Kingdom, (Dial from U.S. (212) 216-7800), (Fax from U.S. (212) 564-7854), www.tandf.co.uk; *The Europa World Year Book*.

United Nations Statistics Division, New York, NY 10017, (800) 253-9646, Fax: (212) 963-4116, http://unstats.un.org; *Statistical Yearbook*.

The World Bank, 1818 H Street, NW, Washington, DC 20433, (202) 473-1000, Fax: (202) 477-6391, www.worldbank.org; *Central African Republic* and *World Development Indicators (WDI) 2008*.

CENTRAL AFRICAN REPUBLIC - MONUMENTS AND HISTORIC SITES

UNESCO Institute for Statistics, C.P. 6128 Succursale Centre-Ville, Montreal, Quebec, H3C 3J7 Canada, (Dial from U.S. (514) 343-6880), (Fax from U.S. (514) 343 6882), www.uis.unesco.org; *Statistical Tables*.

CENTRAL AFRICAN REPUBLIC - MORTALITY

Central Intelligence Agency, Office of Public Affairs, Washington, DC 20505, (703) 482-0623, Fax: (703) 482-1739, www.cia.gov; *The World Factbook*.

Euromonitor International, Inc., 224 S. Michigan Avenue, Suite 1500, Chicago, IL 60604, (312) 922-1115, Fax: (312) 922-1157, www.euromonitor.com; *International Marketing Data and Statistics 2008* and *The World Economic Factbook 2008*.

Taylor and Francis Group, An Informa Business, 2 Park Square, Milton Park, Abingdon, Oxford OX14 4RN, United Kingdom, (Dial from U.S. (212) 216-7800), (Fax from U.S. (212) 564-7854), www.tandf.co.uk; *The Europa World Year Book*.

UNICEF, 3 United Nations Plaza, New York, NY 10017, (800) 253-9646, Fax: (212) 887-7465, www.unicef.org; *The State of the World's Children 2008*.

United Nations Statistics Division, New York, NY 10017, (800) 253-9646, Fax: (212) 963-4116, http://unstats.un.org; *Demographic Yearbook; Human Development Report 2006; Statistical Yearbook; Survey of Economic and Social Conditions in Africa 2005;* and *World Statistics Pocketbook*.

The World Bank, 1818 H Street, NW, Washington, DC 20433, (202) 473-1000, Fax: (202) 477-6391, www.worldbank.org; *The World Bank Atlas 2003-2004; World Development Indicators (WDI) 2008;* and *World Development Report 2008*.

World Health Organization (WHO), Avenue Appia 20, 1211 Geneve 27, Switzerland, (Telephone in U.S. (212) 331-9081), www.who.int; The WHO Global Atlas of Infectious Diseases and *World Health Report 2006*.

CENTRAL AFRICAN REPUBLIC - MOTION PICTURES

Palgrave Macmillan Ltd., Houndmills, Basingstoke, Hampshire, RG21 6XS, England, (Telephone in U.S. (888) 330-8477), (Fax in U.S. (800) 672-2054), www.palgrave.com; *The Statesman's Yearbook 2008*.

CENTRAL AFRICAN REPUBLIC - MOTOR VEHICLES

International Road Federation (IFR), Madison Place, 500 Montgomery Street, 5th Floor, Alexandria, VA 22314, (703) 535-1001, Fax: (703) 535-1007, www.irfnet.org; *World Road Statistics 2006*.

Taylor and Francis Group, An Informa Business, 2 Park Square, Milton Park, Abingdon, Oxford OX14 4RN, United Kingdom, (Dial from U.S. (212) 216-7800), (Fax from U.S. (212) 564-7854), www.tandf.co.uk; *The Europa World Year Book*.

United Nations Statistics Division, New York, NY 10017, (800) 253-9646, Fax: (212) 963-4116, http://unstats.un.org; *Statistical Yearbook* and *Survey of Economic and Social Conditions in Africa 2005*.

CENTRAL AFRICAN REPUBLIC - MUSEUMS

M.E. Sharpe, 80 Business Park Drive, Armonk, NY 10504, (800) 541-6563, Fax: (914) 273-2106, www.mesharpe.com; *The Illustrated Book of World Rankings*.

UNESCO Institute for Statistics, C.P. 6128 Succursale Centre-Ville, Montreal, Quebec, H3C 3J7 Canada, (Dial from U.S. (514) 343-6880), (Fax from U.S. (514) 343 6882), www.uis.unesco.org; *Statistical Tables*.

CENTRAL AFRICAN REPUBLIC - NATIONAL INCOME

United Nations Statistics Division, New York, NY 10017, (800) 253-9646, Fax: (212) 963-4116, http://unstats.un.org; *Statistical Yearbook*.

CENTRAL AFRICAN REPUBLIC - NATURAL GAS PRODUCTION

See CENTRAL AFRICAN REPUBLIC - MINERAL INDUSTRIES

CENTRAL AFRICAN REPUBLIC - NUTRITION

African Development Bank Group, Rue Joseph Anoma, 01 BP 1387 Abidjan 01, Cote d'Ivoire, www.afdb.org; *Statistics Pocketbook 2008*.

United Nations Food and Agricultural Organization (FAO), Viale delle Terme di Caracalla, 00100 Rome, Italy, (Dial from U.S. (202) 653-2400), (Fax from U.S. (202) 653 5760), www.fao.org; *The State of Food and Agriculture (SOFA) 2006*.

CENTRAL AFRICAN REPUBLIC - OLDER PEOPLE

M.E. Sharpe, 80 Business Park Drive, Armonk, NY 10504, (800) 541-6563, Fax: (914) 273-2106, www.mesharpe.com; *The Illustrated Book of World Rankings*.

CENTRAL AFRICAN REPUBLIC - PALM OIL PRODUCTION

See CENTRAL AFRICAN REPUBLIC - CROPS

CENTRAL AFRICAN REPUBLIC - PAPER

See CENTRAL AFRICAN REPUBLIC - FORESTS AND FORESTRY

CENTRAL AFRICAN REPUBLIC - PEANUT PRODUCTION

See CENTRAL AFRICAN REPUBLIC - CROPS

CENTRAL AFRICAN REPUBLIC - PERIODICALS

UNESCO Institute for Statistics, C.P. 6128 Succursale Centre-Ville, Montreal, Quebec, H3C 3J7 Canada, (Dial from U.S. (514) 343-6880), (Fax from U.S. (514) 343 6882), www.uis.unesco.org; *Statistical Tables*.

CENTRAL AFRICAN REPUBLIC - PESTICIDES

United Nations Food and Agricultural Organization (FAO), Viale delle Terme di Caracalla, 00100 Rome, Italy, (Dial from U.S. (202) 653-2400), (Fax from U.S. (202) 653 5760), www.fao.org; *The State of Food and Agriculture (SOFA) 2006*.

CENTRAL AFRICAN REPUBLIC - PETROLEUM INDUSTRY AND TRADE

M.E. Sharpe, 80 Business Park Drive, Armonk, NY 10504, (800) 541-6563, Fax: (914) 273-2106, www.mesharpe.com; *The Illustrated Book of World Rankings*.

PennWell Corporation, 1421 South Sheridan Road, Tulsa, OK 74112, (918) 835-3161, www.pennwell.com; *International Petroleum Encyclopedia 2007*.

United Nations Conference on Trade and Development (UNCTAD), DC2-1120, United Nations, New York, NY 10017, (212) 963-0027, www.unctad.org; *UNCTAD Commodity Yearbook*.

United Nations Food and Agricultural Organization (FAO), Viale delle Terme di Caracalla, 00100 Rome, Italy, (Dial from U.S. (202) 653-2400), (Fax from U.S. (202) 653 5760), www.fao.org; *The State of Food and Agriculture (SOFA) 2006*.

CENTRAL AFRICAN REPUBLIC - POLITICAL SCIENCE

Central Intelligence Agency, Office of Public Affairs, Washington, DC 20505, (703) 482-0623, Fax: (703) 482-1739, www.cia.gov; *The World Factbook.*

International Monetary Fund (IMF), 700 Nineteenth Street, NW, Washington, DC 20431, (202) 623-7000, Fax: (202) 623-4661, www.imf.org; *International Financial Statistics Yearbook 2007.*

Palgrave Macmillan Ltd., Houndmills, Basingstoke, Hampshire, RG21 6XS, England, (Telephone in U.S. (888) 330-8477), (Fax in U.S. (800) 672-2054), www.palgrave.com; *The Statesman's Yearbook 2008.*

Taylor and Francis Group, An Informa Business, 2 Park Square, Milton Park, Abingdon, Oxford OX14 4RN, United Kingdom, (Dial from U.S. (212) 216-7800), (Fax from U.S. (212) 564-7854), www.tandf.co.uk; *The Europa World Year Book.*

United Nations Statistics Division, New York, NY 10017, (800) 253-9646, Fax: (212) 963-4116, http://unstats.un.org; *National Accounts Statistics: Compendium of Income Distribution Statistics* and *Survey of Economic and Social Conditions in Africa 2005.*

The World Bank, 1818 H Street, NW, Washington, DC 20433, (202) 473-1000, Fax: (202) 477-6391, www.worldbank.org; *World Development Indicators (WDI) 2008* and *World Development Report 2008.*

CENTRAL AFRICAN REPUBLIC - POPULATION

African Development Bank Group, Rue Joseph Anoma, 01 BP 1387 Abidjan 01, Cote d'Ivoire, www.afdb.org; *The African Statistical Journal; Gender, Poverty and Environmental Indicators on African Countries 2007; Selected Statistics on African Countries 2007;* and *Statistics Pocketbook 2008.*

Central Intelligence Agency, Office of Public Affairs, Washington, DC 20505, (703) 482-0623, Fax: (703) 482-1739, www.cia.gov; *The World Factbook.*

Economist Intelligence Unit, 111 West 57th Street, New York, NY 10019, (212) 554-0600, Fax: (212) 586-1181, www.eiu.com; *Central African Republic Country Report.*

Euromonitor International, Inc., 224 S. Michigan Avenue, Suite 1500, Chicago, IL 60604, (312) 922-1115, Fax: (312) 922-1157, www.euromonitor.com; *International Marketing Data and Statistics 2008* and *The World Economic Factbook 2008.*

Eurostat, Batiment Jean Monnet, Rue Alcide de Gasperi, L-2920 Luxembourg, http://epp.eurostat.ec.europa.eu; *Demographic Indicators - Population by Age-Classes.*

International Labour Office, I.L.O. Publications, 4 route des Morillons, CH-1211 Geneva 22, Switzerland, (Telephone in U.S. (202) 653-7652), (Fax in U.S. (202) 653-7687), www.ilo.org; *Yearbook of Labour Statistics 2006.*

M.E. Sharpe, 80 Business Park Drive, Armonk, NY 10504, (800) 541-6563, Fax: (914) 273-2106, www.mesharpe.com; *The Illustrated Book of World Rankings.*

Palgrave Macmillan Ltd., Houndmills, Basingstoke, Hampshire, RG21 6XS, England, (Telephone in U.S. (888) 330-8477), (Fax in U.S. (800) 672-2054), www.palgrave.com; *The Statesman's Yearbook 2008.*

Taylor and Francis Group, An Informa Business, 2 Park Square, Milton Park, Abingdon, Oxford OX14 4RN, United Kingdom, (Dial from U.S. (212) 216-7800), (Fax from U.S. (212) 564-7854), www.tandf.co.uk; *The Europa World Year Book.*

U.S. Department of State (DOS), 2201 C Street NW, Washington, DC 20520, (202) 647-4000, www.state.gov; *World Military Expenditures and Arms Transfers (WMEAT).*

UNESCO Institute for Statistics, C.P. 6128 Succursale Centre-Ville, Montreal, Quebec, H3C 3J7 Canada, (Dial from U.S. (514) 343-6880), (Fax from U.S. (514) 343 6882), www.uis.unesco.org; *Statistical Tables.*

United Nations Food and Agricultural Organization (FAO), Viale delle Terme di Caracalla, 00100 Rome, Italy, (Dial from U.S. (202) 653-2400), (Fax from U.S. (202) 653 5760), www.fao.org; *FAO Production Yearbook 2002.*

United Nations Statistics Division, New York, NY 10017, (800) 253-9646, Fax: (212) 963-4116, http://unstats.un.org; *Demographic Yearbook; Human Development Report 2006; Statistical Yearbook; Survey of Economic and Social Conditions in Africa 2005;* and *World Statistics Pocketbook.*

The World Bank, 1818 H Street, NW, Washington, DC 20433, (202) 473-1000, Fax: (202) 477-6391, www.worldbank.org; *Central African Republic; The World Bank Atlas 2003-2004;* and *World Development Report 2008.*

World Health Organization (WHO), Avenue Appia 20, 1211 Geneve 27, Switzerland, (Telephone in U.S. (212) 331-9081), www.who.int; *World Health Report 2006.*

CENTRAL AFRICAN REPUBLIC - POPULATION DENSITY

African Development Bank Group, Rue Joseph Anoma, 01 BP 1387 Abidjan 01, Cote d'Ivoire, www.afdb.org; *Statistics Pocketbook 2008.*

Central Intelligence Agency, Office of Public Affairs, Washington, DC 20505, (703) 482-0623, Fax: (703) 482-1739, www.cia.gov; *The World Factbook.*

Euromonitor International, Inc., 224 S. Michigan Avenue, Suite 1500, Chicago, IL 60604, (312) 922-1115, Fax: (312) 922-1157, www.euromonitor.com; *The World Economic Factbook 2008.*

M.E. Sharpe, 80 Business Park Drive, Armonk, NY 10504, (800) 541-6563, Fax: (914) 273-2106, www.mesharpe.com; *The Illustrated Book of World Rankings.*

Palgrave Macmillan Ltd., Houndmills, Basingstoke, Hampshire, RG21 6XS, England, (Telephone in U.S. (888) 330-8477), (Fax in U.S. (800) 672-2054), www.palgrave.com; *The Statesman's Yearbook 2008.*

Taylor and Francis Group, An Informa Business, 2 Park Square, Milton Park, Abingdon, Oxford OX14 4RN, United Kingdom, (Dial from U.S. (212) 216-7800), (Fax from U.S. (212) 564-7854), www.tandf.co.uk; *The Europa World Year Book.*

UNESCO Institute for Statistics, C.P. 6128 Succursale Centre-Ville, Montreal, Quebec, H3C 3J7 Canada, (Dial from U.S. (514) 343-6880), (Fax from U.S. (514) 343 6882), www.uis.unesco.org; *Statistical Tables.*

United Nations Food and Agricultural Organization (FAO), Viale delle Terme di Caracalla, 00100 Rome, Italy, (Dial from U.S. (202) 653-2400), (Fax from U.S. (202) 653 5760), www.fao.org; *The State of Food and Agriculture (SOFA) 2006.*

United Nations Statistics Division, New York, NY 10017, (800) 253-9646, Fax: (212) 963-4116, http://unstats.un.org; *Statistical Yearbook* and *Survey of Economic and Social Conditions in Africa 2005.*

The World Bank, 1818 H Street, NW, Washington, DC 20433, (202) 473-1000, Fax: (202) 477-6391, www.worldbank.org; *Central African Republic* and *World Development Report 2008.*

CENTRAL AFRICAN REPUBLIC - POSTAL SERVICE

M.E. Sharpe, 80 Business Park Drive, Armonk, NY 10504, (800) 541-6563, Fax: (914) 273-2106, www.mesharpe.com; *The Illustrated Book of World Rankings.*

United Nations Statistics Division, New York, NY 10017, (800) 253-9646, Fax: (212) 963-4116, http://unstats.un.org; *Statistical Yearbook.*

CENTRAL AFRICAN REPUBLIC - POWER RESOURCES

Euromonitor International, Inc., 224 S. Michigan Avenue, Suite 1500, Chicago, IL 60604, (312) 922-1115, Fax: (312) 922-1157, www.euromonitor.com; *International Marketing Data and Statistics 2008; The World Economic Factbook 2008;* and *World Marketing Data and Statistics.*

M.E. Sharpe, 80 Business Park Drive, Armonk, NY 10504, (800) 541-6563, Fax: (914) 273-2106, www.mesharpe.com; *The Illustrated Book of World Rankings.*

Palgrave Macmillan Ltd., Houndmills, Basingstoke, Hampshire, RG21 6XS, England, (Telephone in U.S. (888) 330-8477), (Fax in U.S. (800) 672-2054), www.palgrave.com; *The Statesman's Yearbook 2008.*

Platts, 2 Penn Plaza, 25th Floor, New York, NY 10121-2298, (212) 904-3070, www.platts.com; *Energy Economist.*

United Nations Economic Commission for Africa (ECA), PO Box 3001, Addis Ababa, Ethiopia, (Telephone in U.S. (212) 963-4957), www.uneca.org; *African Statistical Yearbook 2006.*

United Nations Food and Agricultural Organization (FAO), Viale delle Terme di Caracalla, 00100 Rome, Italy, (Dial from U.S. (202) 653-2400), (Fax from U.S. (202) 653 5760), www.fao.org; *The State of Food and Agriculture (SOFA) 2006.*

United Nations Statistics Division, New York, NY 10017, (800) 253-9646, Fax: (212) 963-4116, http://unstats.un.org; *Energy Statistics Yearbook 2003; Human Development Report 2006; Statistical Yearbook;* and *World Statistics Pocketbook.*

The World Bank, 1818 H Street, NW, Washington, DC 20433, (202) 473-1000, Fax: (202) 477-6391, www.worldbank.org; *The World Bank Atlas 2003-2004* and *World Development Report 2008.*

CENTRAL AFRICAN REPUBLIC - PRICES

Euromonitor International, Inc., 224 S. Michigan Avenue, Suite 1500, Chicago, IL 60604, (312) 922-1115, Fax: (312) 922-1157, www.euromonitor.com; *World Marketing Data and Statistics.*

International Labour Office, I.L.O. Publications, 4 route des Morillons, CH-1211 Geneva 22, Switzerland, (Telephone in U.S. (202) 653-7652), (Fax in U.S. (202) 653-7687), www.ilo.org; *Yearbook of Labour Statistics 2006.*

International Monetary Fund (IMF), 700 Nineteenth Street, NW, Washington, DC 20431, (202) 623-7000, Fax: (202) 623-4661, www.imf.org; *International Financial Statistics Yearbook 2007.*

M.E. Sharpe, 80 Business Park Drive, Armonk, NY 10504, (800) 541-6563, Fax: (914) 273-2106, www.mesharpe.com; *The Illustrated Book of World Rankings.*

United Nations Economic Commission for Africa (ECA), PO Box 3001, Addis Ababa, Ethiopia, (Telephone in U.S. (212) 963-4957), www.uneca.org; *African Statistical Yearbook 2006.*

United Nations Food and Agricultural Organization (FAO), Viale delle Terme di Caracalla, 00100 Rome, Italy, (Dial from U.S. (202) 653-2400), (Fax from U.S. (202) 653 5760), www.fao.org; *FAO Production Yearbook 2002* and *The State of Food and Agriculture (SOFA) 2006.*

The World Bank, 1818 H Street, NW, Washington, DC 20433, (202) 473-1000, Fax: (202) 477-6391, www.worldbank.org; *Central African Republic.*

CENTRAL AFRICAN REPUBLIC - PROFESSIONS

UNESCO Institute for Statistics, C.P. 6128 Succursale Centre-Ville, Montreal, Quebec, H3C 3J7 Canada, (Dial from U.S. (514) 343-6880), (Fax from U.S. (514) 343 6882), www.uis.unesco.org; *Statistical Tables.*

CENTRAL AFRICAN REPUBLIC - PUBLIC HEALTH

African Development Bank Group, Rue Joseph Anoma, 01 BP 1387 Abidjan 01, Cote d'Ivoire, www.afdb.org; *Statistics Pocketbook 2008.*

Euromonitor International, Inc., 224 S. Michigan Avenue, Suite 1500, Chicago, IL 60604, (312) 922-1115, Fax: (312) 922-1157, www.euromonitor.com; *World Marketing Data and Statistics.*

M.E. Sharpe, 80 Business Park Drive, Armonk, NY 10504, (800) 541-6563, Fax: (914) 273-2106, www.mesharpe.com; *The Illustrated Book of World Rankings.*

Palgrave Macmillan Ltd., Houndmills, Basingstoke, Hampshire, RG21 6XS, England, (Telephone in U.S. (888) 330-8477), (Fax in U.S. (800) 672-2054), www.palgrave.com; *The Statesman's Yearbook 2008.*

UNICEF, 3 United Nations Plaza, New York, NY 10017, (800) 253-9646, Fax: (212) 887-7465, www.unicef.org; *The State of the World's Children 2008.*

United Nations Economic Commission for Africa (ECA), PO Box 3001, Addis Ababa, Ethiopia, (Telephone in U.S. (212) 963-4957), www.uneca.org; *African Statistical Yearbook 2006.*

United Nations Statistics Division, New York, NY 10017, (800) 253-9646, Fax: (212) 963-4116, http://unstats.un.org; *Human Development Report 2006* and *Statistical Yearbook.*

The World Bank, 1818 H Street, NW, Washington, DC 20433, (202) 473-1000, Fax: (202) 477-6391, www.worldbank.org; *Central African Republic* and *World Development Report 2008.*

World Health Organization (WHO), Avenue Appia 20, 1211 Geneve 27, Switzerland, (Telephone in U.S. (212) 331-9081), www.who.int; The WHO Global Atlas of Infectious Diseases and *World Health Report 2006.*

CENTRAL AFRICAN REPUBLIC - RADIO - RECEIVERS AND RECEPTION

Palgrave Macmillan Ltd., Houndmills, Basingstoke, Hampshire, RG21 6XS, England, (Telephone in U.S. (888) 330-8477), (Fax in U.S. (800) 672-2054), www.palgrave.com; *The Statesman's Yearbook 2008.*

United Nations Statistics Division, New York, NY 10017, (800) 253-9646, Fax: (212) 963-4116, http://unstats.un.org; *Statistical Yearbook.*

CENTRAL AFRICAN REPUBLIC - RAILROADS

United Nations Economic Commission for Africa (ECA), PO Box 3001, Addis Ababa, Ethiopia, (Telephone in U.S. (212) 963-4957), www.uneca.org; *African Statistical Yearbook 2006.*

CENTRAL AFRICAN REPUBLIC - RELIGION

Central Intelligence Agency, Office of Public Affairs, Washington, DC 20505, (703) 482-0623, Fax: (703) 482-1739, www.cia.gov; *The World Factbook.*

M.E. Sharpe, 80 Business Park Drive, Armonk, NY 10504, (800) 541-6563, Fax: (914) 273-2106, www.mesharpe.com; *The Illustrated Book of World Rankings.*

Palgrave Macmillan Ltd., Houndmills, Basingstoke, Hampshire, RG21 6XS, England, (Telephone in U.S. (888) 330-8477), (Fax in U.S. (800) 672-2054), www.palgrave.com; *The Statesman's Yearbook 2008.*

CENTRAL AFRICAN REPUBLIC - RESERVES (ACCOUNTING)

African Development Bank Group, Rue Joseph Anoma, 01 BP 1387 Abidjan 01, Cote d'Ivoire, www.afdb.org; *Statistics Pocketbook 2008.*

The World Bank, 1818 H Street, NW, Washington, DC 20433, (202) 473-1000, Fax: (202) 477-6391, www.worldbank.org; *World Development Indicators (WDI) 2008.*

CENTRAL AFRICAN REPUBLIC - RETAIL TRADE

Euromonitor International, Inc., 224 S. Michigan Avenue, Suite 1500, Chicago, IL 60604, (312) 922-1115, Fax: (312) 922-1157, www.euromonitor.com; *World Marketing Data and Statistics.*

CENTRAL AFRICAN REPUBLIC - RICE PRODUCTION

See CENTRAL AFRICAN REPUBLIC - CROPS

CENTRAL AFRICAN REPUBLIC - ROADS

Central Intelligence Agency, Office of Public Affairs, Washington, DC 20505, (703) 482-0623, Fax: (703) 482-1739, www.cia.gov; *The World Factbook.*

International Road Federation (IFR), Madison Place, 500 Montgomery Street, 5th Floor, Alexandria, VA 22314, (703) 535-1001, Fax: (703) 535-1007, www.irfnet.org; *World Road Statistics 2006.*

Palgrave Macmillan Ltd., Houndmills, Basingstoke, Hampshire, RG21 6XS, England, (Telephone in U.S. (888) 330-8477), (Fax in U.S. (800) 672-2054), www.palgrave.com; *The Statesman's Yearbook 2008.*

United Nations Economic Commission for Africa (ECA), PO Box 3001, Addis Ababa, Ethiopia, (Telephone in U.S. (212) 963-4957), www.uneca.org; *African Statistical Yearbook 2006.*

United Nations Statistics Division, New York, NY 10017, (800) 253-9646, Fax: (212) 963-4116, http://unstats.un.org; *Survey of Economic and Social Conditions in Africa 2005.*

CENTRAL AFRICAN REPUBLIC - RUBBER INDUSTRY AND TRADE

International Rubber Study Group (IRSG), 1st Floor, Heron House, 109/115 Wembley Hill Road, Wembley, Middlesex HA9 8DA, United Kingdom, www.rubberstudy.com; *Rubber Statistical Bulletin; Summary of World Rubber Statistics 2005; World Rubber Statistics Handbook (Volume 6, 1975-2001);* and *World Rubber Statistics Historic Handbook.*

M.E. Sharpe, 80 Business Park Drive, Armonk, NY 10504, (800) 541-6563, Fax: (914) 273-2106, www.mesharpe.com; *The Illustrated Book of World Rankings.*

United Nations Statistics Division, New York, NY 10017, (800) 253-9646, Fax: (212) 963-4116, http://unstats.un.org; *Statistical Yearbook.*

CENTRAL AFRICAN REPUBLIC - SHEEP

See CENTRAL AFRICAN REPUBLIC - LIVESTOCK

CENTRAL AFRICAN REPUBLIC - SHIPPING

Palgrave Macmillan Ltd., Houndmills, Basingstoke, Hampshire, RG21 6XS, England, (Telephone in U.S. (888) 330-8477), (Fax in U.S. (800) 672-2054), www.palgrave.com; *The Statesman's Yearbook 2008.*

Taylor and Francis Group, An Informa Business, 2 Park Square, Milton Park, Abingdon, Oxford OX14 4RN, United Kingdom, (Dial from U.S. (212) 216-7800), (Fax from U.S. (212) 564-7854), www.tandf.co.uk; *The Europa World Year Book.*

United Nations Economic Commission for Africa (ECA), PO Box 3001, Addis Ababa, Ethiopia, (Telephone in U.S. (212) 963-4957), www.uneca.org; *African Statistical Yearbook 2006.*

CENTRAL AFRICAN REPUBLIC - SILVER PRODUCTION

See CENTRAL AFRICAN REPUBLIC - MINERAL INDUSTRIES

CENTRAL AFRICAN REPUBLIC - SOCIAL ECOLOGY

M.E. Sharpe, 80 Business Park Drive, Armonk, NY 10504, (800) 541-6563, Fax: (914) 273-2106, www.mesharpe.com; *The Illustrated Book of World Rankings.*

United Nations Statistics Division, New York, NY 10017, (800) 253-9646, Fax: (212) 963-4116, http://unstats.un.org; *World Statistics Pocketbook.*

CENTRAL AFRICAN REPUBLIC - SOCIAL SECURITY

United Nations Statistics Division, New York, NY 10017, (800) 253-9646, Fax: (212) 963-4116, http://unstats.un.org; *National Accounts Statistics: Compendium of Income Distribution Statistics.*

CENTRAL AFRICAN REPUBLIC - STEEL PRODUCTION

See CENTRAL AFRICAN REPUBLIC - MINERAL INDUSTRIES

CENTRAL AFRICAN REPUBLIC - SUGAR PRODUCTION

See CENTRAL AFRICAN REPUBLIC - CROPS

CENTRAL AFRICAN REPUBLIC - TAXATION

International Road Federation (IFR), Madison Place, 500 Montgomery Street, 5th Floor, Alexandria, VA 22314, (703) 535-1001, Fax: (703) 535-1007, www.irfnet.org; *World Road Statistics 2006.*

The World Bank, 1818 H Street, NW, Washington, DC 20433, (202) 473-1000, Fax: (202) 477-6391, www.worldbank.org; *World Development Indicators (WDI) 2008.*

CENTRAL AFRICAN REPUBLIC - TELEPHONE

International Telecommunication Union (ITU), Place des Nations, 1211 Geneva 20, Switzerland, www.itu.int; World Telecommunication Indicators Database.

Palgrave Macmillan Ltd., Houndmills, Basingstoke, Hampshire, RG21 6XS, England, (Telephone in U.S. (888) 330-8477), (Fax in U.S. (800) 672-2054), www.palgrave.com; *The Statesman's Yearbook 2008.*

Taylor and Francis Group, An Informa Business, 2 Park Square, Milton Park, Abingdon, Oxford OX14 4RN, United Kingdom, (Dial from U.S. (212) 216-7800), (Fax from U.S. (212) 564-7854), www.tandf.co.uk; *The Europa World Year Book.*

United Nations Statistics Division, New York, NY 10017, (800) 253-9646, Fax: (212) 963-4116, http://unstats.un.org; *World Statistics Pocketbook.*

CENTRAL AFRICAN REPUBLIC - TEXTILE INDUSTRY

M.E. Sharpe, 80 Business Park Drive, Armonk, NY 10504, (800) 541-6563, Fax: (914) 273-2106, www.mesharpe.com; *The Illustrated Book of World Rankings.*

Palgrave Macmillan Ltd., Houndmills, Basingstoke, Hampshire, RG21 6XS, England, (Telephone in U.S. (888) 330-8477), (Fax in U.S. (800) 672-2054), www.palgrave.com; *The Statesman's Yearbook 2008.*

United Nations Conference on Trade and Development (UNCTAD), DC2-1120, United Nations, New York, NY 10017, (212) 963-0027, www.unctad.org; *UNCTAD Commodity Yearbook.*

United Nations Statistics Division, New York, NY 10017, (800) 253-9646, Fax: (212) 963-4116, http://unstats.un.org; *Statistical Yearbook.*

CENTRAL AFRICAN REPUBLIC - TOBACCO INDUSTRY

Foreign Agricultural Service (FAS), U.S. Department of Agriculture (USDA), 1400 Independence Avenue, SW, Washington, DC 20250, (202) 720-3935, www.fas.usda.gov; *Tobacco: World Markets and Trade.*

M.E. Sharpe, 80 Business Park Drive, Armonk, NY 10504, (800) 541-6563, Fax: (914) 273-2106, www.mesharpe.com; *The Illustrated Book of World Rankings.*

United Nations Statistics Division, New York, NY 10017, (800) 253-9646, Fax: (212) 963-4116, http://unstats.un.org; *Statistical Yearbook.*

CENTRAL AFRICAN REPUBLIC - TOURISM

Euromonitor International, Inc., 224 S. Michigan Avenue, Suite 1500, Chicago, IL 60604, (312) 922-1115, Fax: (312) 922-1157, www.euromonitor.com; *The World Economic Factbook 2008* and *World Marketing Data and Statistics.*

M.E. Sharpe, 80 Business Park Drive, Armonk, NY 10504, (800) 541-6563, Fax: (914) 273-2106, www.mesharpe.com; *The Illustrated Book of World Rankings.*

Taylor and Francis Group, An Informa Business, 2 Park Square, Milton Park, Abingdon, Oxford OX14 4RN, United Kingdom, (Dial from U.S. (212) 216-

7800), (Fax from U.S. (212) 564-7854), www.tandf.co.uk; *The Europa World Year Book.*

United Nations Economic Commission for Africa (ECA), PO Box 3001, Addis Ababa, Ethiopia, (Telephone in U.S. (212) 963-4957), www.uneca.org; *African Statistical Yearbook 2006.*

United Nations Statistics Division, New York, NY 10017, (800) 253-9646, Fax: (212) 963-4116, http://unstats.un.org; *Statistical Yearbook.*

The World Bank, 1818 H Street, NW, Washington, DC 20433, (202) 473-1000, Fax: (202) 477-6391, www.worldbank.org; *Central African Republic.*

CENTRAL AFRICAN REPUBLIC - TRADE

See CENTRAL AFRICAN REPUBLIC - INTERNATIONAL TRADE

CENTRAL AFRICAN REPUBLIC - TRANSPORTATION

Central Intelligence Agency, Office of Public Affairs, Washington, DC 20505, (703) 482-0623, Fax: (703) 482-1739, www.cia.gov; *The World Factbook.*

Euromonitor International, Inc., 224 S. Michigan Avenue, Suite 1500, Chicago, IL 60604, (312) 922-1115, Fax: (312) 922-1157, www.euromonitor.com; *International Marketing Data and Statistics 2008* and *World Marketing Data and Statistics.*

M.E. Sharpe, 80 Business Park Drive, Armonk, NY 10504, (800) 541-6563, Fax: (914) 273-2106, www.mesharpe.com; *The Illustrated Book of World Rankings.*

Palgrave Macmillan Ltd., Houndmills, Basingstoke, Hampshire, RG21 6XS, England, (Telephone in U.S. (888) 330-8477), (Fax in U.S. (800) 672-2054), www.palgrave.com; *The Statesman's Yearbook 2008.*

Taylor and Francis Group, An Informa Business, 2 Park Square, Milton Park, Abingdon, Oxford OX14 4RN, United Kingdom, (Dial from U.S. (212) 216-7800), (Fax from U.S. (212) 564-7854), www.tandf.co.uk; *The Europa World Year Book.*

United Nations Economic Commission for Africa (ECA), PO Box 3001, Addis Ababa, Ethiopia, (Telephone in U.S. (212) 963-4957), www.uneca.org; *African Statistical Yearbook 2006.*

United Nations Statistics Division, New York, NY 10017, (800) 253-9646, Fax: (212) 963-4116, http://unstats.un.org; *Human Development Report 2006.*

The World Bank, 1818 H Street, NW, Washington, DC 20433, (202) 473-1000, Fax: (202) 477-6391, www.worldbank.org; *Africa Live Database (LDB)* and *Central African Republic.*

CENTRAL AFRICAN REPUBLIC - UNEMPLOYMENT

Central Intelligence Agency, Office of Public Affairs, Washington, DC 20505, (703) 482-0623, Fax: (703) 482-1739, www.cia.gov; *The World Factbook.*

International Labour Office, I.L.O. Publications, 4 route des Morillons, CH-1211 Geneva 22, Switzerland, (Telephone in U.S. (202) 653-7652), (Fax in U.S. (202) 653-7687), www.ilo.org; *Yearbook of Labour Statistics 2006.*

United Nations Statistics Division, New York, NY 10017, (800) 253-9646, Fax: (212) 963-4116, http://unstats.un.org; *Statistical Yearbook.*

CENTRAL AFRICAN REPUBLIC - URANIUM PRODUCTION AND CONSUMPTION

See CENTRAL AFRICAN REPUBLIC - MINERAL INDUSTRIES

CENTRAL AFRICAN REPUBLIC - VITAL STATISTICS

United Nations Statistics Division, New York, NY 10017, (800) 253-9646, Fax: (212) 963-4116, http://unstats.un.org; *Statistical Yearbook.*

World Health Organization (WHO), Avenue Appia 20, 1211 Geneve 27, Switzerland, (Telephone in U.S. (212) 331-9081), www.who.int; *World Health Report 2006.*

CENTRAL AFRICAN REPUBLIC - WAGES

International Labour Office, I.L.O. Publications, 4 route des Morillons, CH-1211 Geneva 22, Switzerland, (Telephone in U.S. (202) 653-7652), (Fax in U.S. (202) 653-7687), www.ilo.org; *Yearbook of Labour Statistics 2006.*

The World Bank, 1818 H Street, NW, Washington, DC 20433, (202) 473-1000, Fax: (202) 477-6391, www.worldbank.org; *Central African Republic.*

CENTRAL AFRICAN REPUBLIC - WEATHER

See CENTRAL AFRICAN REPUBLIC - CLIMATE

CENTRAL AFRICAN REPUBLIC - WHEAT PRODUCTION

See CENTRAL AFRICAN REPUBLIC - CROPS

CENTRAL AFRICAN REPUBLIC - WHOLESALE PRICE INDEXES

International Monetary Fund (IMF), 700 Nineteenth Street, NW, Washington, DC 20431, (202) 623-7000, Fax: (202) 623-4661, www.imf.org; *International Financial Statistics Yearbook 2007.*

United Nations Statistics Division, New York, NY 10017, (800) 253-9646, Fax: (212) 963-4116, http://unstats.un.org; *Statistical Yearbook.*

CENTRAL AFRICAN REPUBLIC - WINE PRODUCTION

See CENTRAL AFRICAN REPUBLIC - BEVERAGE INDUSTRY

CENTRAL AFRICAN REPUBLIC - WOOL PRODUCTION

See CENTRAL AFRICAN REPUBLIC - TEXTILE INDUSTRY

CENTRAL AMERICA

International Trade Administration (ITA), U.S. Department of Commerce (DOC), 1401 Constitution Avenue, NW, Washington, DC 20230, (800) USA-TRAD(E), Fax: (202) 482-4473, www.ita.doc.gov; *CAFTA-DR: A State Export Overview, 2000-2004.*

U.S. Department of Labor (DOL), Bureau of International Labor Affairs (ILAB), Frances Perkins Building, Room C-4325, 200 Constitution Avenue, NW, Washington, DC 20210, (202) 693-4770, Fax: (202) 693-4780, www.dol.gov/ilab; *Labor Rights Report.*

United Nations World Tourism Organization (UNWTO), Capitan Haya 42, 28020 Madrid, Spain, www.world-tourism.org; *Tourism Market Trends 2004 - Americas.*

CENTRAL AND SOUTH AMERICAN POPULATION (HISPANIC ORIGIN)

Bernan Essential Government Publications, 4611-F Assembly Drive, Lanham MD, 20706-4391, (301) 459-2255, Fax: (800) 865-3450, www.bernan.com; *Vital Statistics of the United States: Births, Life Expectancy, Deaths, and Selected Health Data.*

National Center for Health Statistics (NCHS), Centers for Disease Control and Prevention (CDC), U.S. Department of Health and Human Services (HHS), 3311 Toledo Road, Hyattsville, MD 20782, (866) 232-4636, www.cdc.gov/nchs; *National Vital Statistics Reports (NVSR); Vital Statistics of the United States (VSUS);* and unpublished data.

U.S. Census Bureau, Population Division, 4700 Silver Hill Road, Washington DC 20233-0001, (301) 763-3030, www.census.gov/population/www/; *Current Population Reports.*

CEREAL AND BAKERY PRODUCTS

Progressive Grocer, 770 Broadway, New York, NY 10003, (866) 890-8541, www.progressivegrocer.com; *Progressive Grocer 2006 Bakery Study.*

CEREAL AND BAKERY PRODUCTS - EXPENDITURES - PRICES

Economic Research Service (ERS), U.S. Department of Agriculture (USDA), 1800 M Street, NW, Washington, DC 20036-5831, (202) 694-5050, Fax: (202) 694-5689, www.ers.usda.gov; *Agricultural Statistics* and *Food CPI, Prices, and Expenditures.*

U.S. Bureau of Labor Statistics (BLS), Postal Square Building, 2 Massachusetts Avenue, NE, Washington, DC 20212-0001, (202) 691-5200, Fax: (202) 691-6325, www.bls.gov; *Consumer Expenditures in 2006; Consumer Price Index Detailed Report; Monthly Labor Review (MLR);* and unpublished data.

CEREAL AND BAKERY PRODUCTS - INTERNATIONAL TRADE

U.S. Census Bureau, Foreign Trade Division, 4700 Silver Hill Road, Washington DC 20233-0001, (301) 763-3030, www.census.gov/foreign-trade/www/; *U.S. International Trade in Goods and Services.*

CEREBROVASCULAR DISEASES

National Center for Chronic Disease Prevention and Health Promotion (NCCDPHP), Centers for Disease Control and Prevention (CDC), 4770 Buford Hwy, NE, MS K-40, Atlanta, GA 30341-3717, (404) 639-3311, www.cdc.gov/nccdphp; *The Atlas of Heart Disease and Stroke.*

CEREBROVASCULAR DISEASES - DEATHS

Bernan Essential Government Publications, 4611-F Assembly Drive, Lanham MD, 20706-4391, (301) 459-2255, Fax: (800) 865-3450, www.bernan.com; *Vital Statistics of the United States: Births, Life Expectancy, Deaths, and Selected Health Data.*

National Center for Health Statistics (NCHS), Centers for Disease Control and Prevention (CDC), U.S. Department of Health and Human Services (HHS), 3311 Toledo Road, Hyattsville, MD 20782, (866) 232-4636, www.cdc.gov/nchs; *National Vital Statistics Reports (NVSR); Vital Statistics of the United States (VSUS);* and unpublished data.

CERTIFICATES OF DEPOSIT

Board of Governors of the Federal Reserve System, Constitution Avenue, NW, Washington, DC 20551, (202) 452-3000, www.federalreserve.gov; *Federal Reserve Bulletin* and unpublished data.

CERVICAL CANCER

American Cancer Society, 1599 Clifton Road, NE, Atlanta, GA 30329-4250, (404) 320-3333, www.cancer.org; *Cancer Facts and Figures 2008.*

National Cancer Institute (NCI), National Institutes of Health (NIH), Public Inquiries Office, 6116 Executive Boulevard, Room 3036A, Bethesda, MD 20892-8322, (800) 422-6237, www.cancer.gov; *2006-2007 Annual Report to the Nation; Assessing Progress, Advancing Change: 2005-2006 Annual President's Cancer Panel;* and *SEER Cancer Statistics Review, 1975-2005.*

CESAREAN SECTION DELIVERIES

National Center for Health Statistics (NCHS), Centers for Disease Control and Prevention (CDC), U.S. Department of Health and Human Services (HHS), 3311 Toledo Road, Hyattsville, MD 20782, (866) 232-4636, www.cdc.gov/nchs; *Faststats A to Z; Vital Statistics of the United States (VSUS);* and unpublished data.

CESIUM

U.S. Department of the Interior (DOI), U.S. Geological Survey (USGS), Office of Minerals Information, 12201 Sunrise Valley Drive, Reston, VA 20192, Mr. Kenneth A. Beckman, (703) 648-4916, Fax: (703) 648-4995, http://minerals.usgs.gov/minerals; *Mineral Commodity Summaries.*

CFC (CHLOROFLUROCARBON) GASES

U.S. Department of Energy (DOE), Energy Information Administration (EIA), 1000 Independence Avenue, SW, Washington, DC 20585, (202) 586-8800, www.eia.doe.gov; *Emissions of Greenhouse Gases in the United States 2005.*

CHAD - NATIONAL STATISTICAL OFFICE

Institut National de la Statistique, des Etudes Economiques et Demographiques, Ministere du Plan, du Developpement et de la Cooperation, Boite Postale 453, N'Djamena, Chad, www.inseed-tchad.org; National Data Center.

CHAD - PRIMARY STATISTICS SOURCES

Institut National de la Statistique, des Etudes Economiques et Demographiques, Ministere du Plan, du Developpement et de la Cooperation, Boite Postale 453, N'Djamena, Chad, www.inseed-tchad.org; *Deuxieme Enquete Demographique et de Sante Tchad EDST-II 2004.*

CHAD - AGRICULTURAL MACHINERY

United Nations Statistics Division, New York, NY 10017, (800) 253-9646, Fax: (212) 963-4116, http://unstats.un.org; *Statistical Yearbook.*

CHAD - AGRICULTURE

Economist Intelligence Unit, 111 West 57th Street, New York, NY 10019, (212) 554-0600, Fax: (212) 586-1181, www.eiu.com; *Chad Country Report.*

Euromonitor International, Inc., 224 S. Michigan Avenue, Suite 1500, Chicago, IL 60604, (312) 922-1115, Fax: (312) 922-1157, www.euromonitor.com; *International Marketing Data and Statistics 2008* and *World Marketing Data and Statistics.*

M.E. Sharpe, 80 Business Park Drive, Armonk, NY 10504, (800) 541-6563, Fax: (914) 273-2106, www.mesharpe.com; *The Illustrated Book of World Rankings.*

Palgrave Macmillan Ltd., Houndmills, Basingstoke, Hampshire, RG21 6XS, England, (Telephone in U.S. (888) 330-8477), (Fax in U.S. (800) 672-2054), www.palgrave.com; *The Statesman's Yearbook 2008.*

Taylor and Francis Group, An Informa Business, 2 Park Square, Milton Park, Abingdon, Oxford OX14 4RN, United Kingdom, (Dial from U.S. (212) 216-7800), (Fax from U.S. (212) 564-7854), www.tandf.co.uk; *The Europa World Year Book.*

United Nations Conference on Trade and Development (UNCTAD), DC2-1120, United Nations, New York, NY 10017, (212) 963-0027, www.unctad.org; *UNCTAD Commodity Yearbook.*

United Nations Economic Commission for Africa (ECA), PO Box 3001, Addis Ababa, Ethiopia, (Telephone in U.S. (212) 963-4957), www.uneca.org; *African Statistical Yearbook 2006.*

United Nations Food and Agricultural Organization (FAO), Viale delle Terme di Caracalla, 00100 Rome, Italy, (Dial from U.S. (202) 653-2400), (Fax from U.S. (202) 653 5760), www.fao.org; *AQUASTAT; FAO Production Yearbook 2002; FAO Trade Yearbook;* and *The State of Food and Agriculture (SOFA) 2006.*

United Nations Statistics Division, New York, NY 10017, (800) 253-9646, Fax: (212) 963-4116, http://unstats.un.org; *Statistical Yearbook* and *Survey of Economic and Social Conditions in Africa 2005.*

The World Bank, 1818 H Street, NW, Washington, DC 20433, (202) 473-1000, Fax: (202) 477-6391, www.worldbank.org; *Africa Live Database (LDB); African Development Indicators (ADI) 2007; Chad;* and *World Development Indicators (WDI) 2008.*

WRTH Publications Limited, PO Box 290, Oxford OX2 7FT, UK, www.wrth.com; *World Radio TV Handbook 2007.*

CHAD - AIRLINES

M.E. Sharpe, 80 Business Park Drive, Armonk, NY 10504, (800) 541-6563, Fax: (914) 273-2106, www.mesharpe.com; *The Illustrated Book of World Rankings.*

Palgrave Macmillan Ltd., Houndmills, Basingstoke, Hampshire, RG21 6XS, England, (Telephone in U.S. (888) 330-8477), (Fax in U.S. (800) 672-2054), www.palgrave.com; *The Statesman's Yearbook 2008.*

Taylor and Francis Group, An Informa Business, 2 Park Square, Milton Park, Abingdon, Oxford OX14 4RN, United Kingdom, (Dial from U.S. (212) 216-7800), (Fax from U.S. (212) 564-7854), www.tandf.co.uk; *The Europa World Year Book.*

United Nations Economic Commission for Africa (ECA), PO Box 3001, Addis Ababa, Ethiopia, (Telephone in U.S. (212) 963-4957), www.uneca.org; *African Statistical Yearbook 2006.*

United Nations Statistics Division, New York, NY 10017, (800) 253-9646, Fax: (212) 963-4116, http://unstats.un.org; *Statistical Yearbook.*

CHAD - AIRPORTS

Central Intelligence Agency, Office of Public Affairs, Washington, DC 20505, (703) 482-0623, Fax: (703) 482-1739, www.cia.gov; *The World Factbook.*

CHAD - ALUMINUM PRODUCTION

See CHAD - MINERAL INDUSTRIES

CHAD - ARMED FORCES

Central Intelligence Agency, Office of Public Affairs, Washington, DC 20505, (703) 482-0623, Fax: (703) 482-1739, www.cia.gov; *The World Factbook.*

Euromonitor International, Inc., 224 S. Michigan Avenue, Suite 1500, Chicago, IL 60604, (312) 922-1115, Fax: (312) 922-1157, www.euromonitor.com; *World Marketing Data and Statistics.*

International Institute for Strategic Studies (IISS), Arundel House, 13-15 Arundel Street, Temple Place, London WC2R 3DX, England, www.iiss.org; *The Military Balance 2007.*

International Monetary Fund (IMF), 700 Nineteenth Street, NW, Washington, DC 20431, (202) 623-7000, Fax: (202) 623-4661, www.imf.org; *Government Finance Statistics Yearbook (2008 Edition).*

Palgrave Macmillan Ltd., Houndmills, Basingstoke, Hampshire, RG21 6XS, England, (Telephone in U.S. (888) 330-8477), (Fax in U.S. (800) 672-2054), www.palgrave.com; *The Statesman's Yearbook 2008.*

U.S. Department of State (DOS), 2201 C Street NW, Washington, DC 20520, (202) 647-4000, www.state.gov; *World Military Expenditures and Arms Transfers (WMEAT).*

United Nations Statistics Division, New York, NY 10017, (800) 253-9646, Fax: (212) 963-4116, http://unstats.un.org; *Human Development Report 2006.*

CHAD - BALANCE OF PAYMENTS

African Development Bank Group, Rue Joseph Anoma, 01 BP 1387 Abidjan 01, Cote d'Ivoire, www.afdb.org; *Statistics Pocketbook 2008.*

International Monetary Fund (IMF), 700 Nineteenth Street, NW, Washington, DC 20431, (202) 623-7000, Fax: (202) 623-4661, www.imf.org; *Balance of Payments Statistics Newsletter* and *Balance of Payments Statistics Yearbook 2007.*

Taylor and Francis Group, An Informa Business, 2 Park Square, Milton Park, Abingdon, Oxford OX14 4RN, United Kingdom, (Dial from U.S. (212) 216-7800), (Fax from U.S. (212) 564-7854), www.tandf.co.uk; *The Europa World Year Book.*

United Nations Conference on Trade and Development (UNCTAD), DC2-1120, United Nations, New York, NY 10017, (212) 963-0027, www.unctad.org; *Handbook of Statistics 2005.*

United Nations Economic Commission for Africa (ECA), PO Box 3001, Addis Ababa, Ethiopia, (Telephone in U.S. (212) 963-4957), www.uneca.org; *African Statistical Yearbook 2006.*

The World Bank, 1818 H Street, NW, Washington, DC 20433, (202) 473-1000, Fax: (202) 477-6391, www.worldbank.org; *Chad; World Development Indicators (WDI) 2008;* and *World Development Report 2008.*

CHAD - BANKS AND BANKING

Euromonitor International, Inc., 224 S. Michigan Avenue, Suite 1500, Chicago, IL 60604, (312) 922-1115, Fax: (312) 922-1157, www.euromonitor.com; *World Marketing Data and Statistics.*

International Monetary Fund (IMF), 700 Nineteenth Street, NW, Washington, DC 20431, (202) 623-7000, Fax: (202) 623-4661, www.imf.org; *Government Finance Statistics Yearbook (2008 Edition)* and *International Financial Statistics Yearbook 2007.*

M.E. Sharpe, 80 Business Park Drive, Armonk, NY 10504, (800) 541-6563, Fax: (914) 273-2106, www.mesharpe.com; *The Illustrated Book of World Rankings.*

Palgrave Macmillan Ltd., Houndmills, Basingstoke, Hampshire, RG21 6XS, England, (Telephone in U.S. (888) 330-8477), (Fax in U.S. (800) 672-2054), www.palgrave.com; *The Statesman's Yearbook 2008.*

Taylor and Francis Group, An Informa Business, 2 Park Square, Milton Park, Abingdon, Oxford OX14 4RN, United Kingdom, (Dial from U.S. (212) 216-7800), (Fax from U.S. (212) 564-7854), www.tandf.co.uk; *The Europa World Year Book.*

United Nations Economic Commission for Africa (ECA), PO Box 3001, Addis Ababa, Ethiopia, (Telephone in U.S. (212) 963-4957), www.uneca.org; *African Statistical Yearbook 2006.*

CHAD - BARLEY PRODUCTION

See CHAD - CROPS

CHAD - BEVERAGE INDUSTRY

M.E. Sharpe, 80 Business Park Drive, Armonk, NY 10504, (800) 541-6563, Fax: (914) 273-2106, www.mesharpe.com; *The Illustrated Book of World Rankings.*

United Nations Statistics Division, New York, NY 10017, (800) 253-9646, Fax: (212) 963-4116, http://unstats.un.org; *Statistical Yearbook.*

CHAD - BONDS

International Monetary Fund (IMF), 700 Nineteenth Street, NW, Washington, DC 20431, (202) 623-7000, Fax: (202) 623-4661, www.imf.org; *Government Finance Statistics Yearbook (2008 Edition).*

CHAD - BROADCASTING

Central Intelligence Agency, Office of Public Affairs, Washington, DC 20505, (703) 482-0623, Fax: (703) 482-1739, www.cia.gov; *The World Factbook.*

Euromonitor International, Inc., 224 S. Michigan Avenue, Suite 1500, Chicago, IL 60604, (312) 922-1115, Fax: (312) 922-1157, www.euromonitor.com; *World Marketing Data and Statistics.*

M.E. Sharpe, 80 Business Park Drive, Armonk, NY 10504, (800) 541-6563, Fax: (914) 273-2106, www.mesharpe.com; *The Illustrated Book of World Rankings.*

Palgrave Macmillan Ltd., Houndmills, Basingstoke, Hampshire, RG21 6XS, England, (Telephone in U.S. (888) 330-8477), (Fax in U.S. (800) 672-2054), www.palgrave.com; *The Statesman's Yearbook 2008.*

CHAD - BUDGET

Central Intelligence Agency, Office of Public Affairs, Washington, DC 20505, (703) 482-0623, Fax: (703) 482-1739, www.cia.gov; *The World Factbook.*

CHAD - CAPITAL LEVY

International Monetary Fund (IMF), 700 Nineteenth Street, NW, Washington, DC 20431, (202) 623-7000, Fax: (202) 623-4661, www.imf.org; *Government Finance Statistics Yearbook (2008 Edition).*

CHAD - CATTLE

See CHAD - LIVESTOCK

CHAD - CHICKENS

See CHAD - LIVESTOCK

CHAD - CHILDBIRTH - STATISTICS

Central Intelligence Agency, Office of Public Affairs, Washington, DC 20505, (703) 482-0623, Fax: (703) 482-1739, www.cia.gov; *The World Factbook.*

Euromonitor International, Inc., 224 S. Michigan Avenue, Suite 1500, Chicago, IL 60604, (312) 922-1115, Fax: (312) 922-1157, www.euromonitor.com; *International Marketing Data and Statistics 2008* and *The World Economic Factbook 2008.*

M.E. Sharpe, 80 Business Park Drive, Armonk, NY 10504, (800) 541-6563, Fax: (914) 273-2106, www.mesharpe.com; *The Illustrated Book of World Rankings.*

Taylor and Francis Group, An Informa Business, 2 Park Square, Milton Park, Abingdon, Oxford OX14 4RN, United Kingdom, (Dial from U.S. (212) 216-7800), (Fax from U.S. (212) 564-7854), www.tandf.co.uk; *The Europa World Year Book.*

United Nations Statistics Division, New York, NY 10017, (800) 253-9646, Fax: (212) 963-4116, http://unstats.un.org; *Demographic Yearbook; Statistical Yearbook;* and *Survey of Economic and Social Conditions in Africa 2005.*

The World Bank, 1818 H Street, NW, Washington, DC 20433, (202) 473-1000, Fax: (202) 477-6391, www.worldbank.org; *World Development Indicators (WDI) 2008.*

CHAD - CLIMATE

International Institute for Environment and Development (IIED), 3 Endsleigh Street, London, England, WC1H 0DD, United Kingdom, www.iied.org; *Environment Urbanization* and *Haramata - Bulletin of the Drylands.*

M.E. Sharpe, 80 Business Park Drive, Armonk, NY 10504, (800) 541-6563, Fax: (914) 273-2106, www.mesharpe.com; *The Illustrated Book of World Rankings.*

Palgrave Macmillan Ltd., Houndmills, Basingstoke, Hampshire, RG21 6XS, England, (Telephone in U.S. (888) 330-8477), (Fax in U.S. (800) 672-2054), www.palgrave.com; *The Statesman's Yearbook 2008.*

CHAD - COAL PRODUCTION

See CHAD - MINERAL INDUSTRIES

CHAD - COFFEE

See CHAD - CROPS

CHAD - COMMERCE

Palgrave Macmillan Ltd., Houndmills, Basingstoke, Hampshire, RG21 6XS, England, (Telephone in U.S. (888) 330-8477), (Fax in U.S. (800) 672-2054), www.palgrave.com; *The Statesman's Yearbook 2008.*

CHAD - COMMODITY EXCHANGES

Commodity Research Bureau, 330 South Wells Street, Suite 612, Chicago, IL 60606-7110, (800) 621-5271, Fax: (312) 939-4135, www.crbtrader.com; *2006 CRB Commodity Yearbook and CD.*

International Monetary Fund (IMF), 700 Nineteenth Street, NW, Washington, DC 20431, (202) 623-7000, Fax: (202) 623-4661, www.imf.org; *IMF Primary Commodity Prices.*

United Nations Food and Agricultural Organization (FAO), Viale delle Terme di Caracalla, 00100 Rome, Italy, (Dial from U.S. (202) 653-2400), (Fax from U.S. (202) 653 5760), www.fao.org; *The State of Food and Agriculture (SOFA) 2006.*

CHAD - COMMUNICATION AND TRAFFIC

United Nations Statistics Division, New York, NY 10017, (800) 253-9646, Fax: (212) 963-4116, http://unstats.un.org; *Statistical Yearbook.*

CHAD - CONSTRUCTION INDUSTRY

M.E. Sharpe, 80 Business Park Drive, Armonk, NY 10504, (800) 541-6563, Fax: (914) 273-2106, www.mesharpe.com; *The Illustrated Book of World Rankings.*

United Nations Economic Commission for Africa (ECA), PO Box 3001, Addis Ababa, Ethiopia, (Telephone in U.S. (212) 963-4957), www.uneca.org; *African Statistical Yearbook 2006.*

CHAD - CONSUMER PRICE INDEXES

Taylor and Francis Group, An Informa Business, 2 Park Square, Milton Park, Abingdon, Oxford OX14 4RN, United Kingdom, (Dial from U.S. (212) 216-7800), (Fax from U.S. (212) 564-7854), www.tandf.co.uk; *The Europa World Year Book.*

United Nations Economic Commission for Africa (ECA), PO Box 3001, Addis Ababa, Ethiopia, (Telephone in U.S. (212) 963-4957), www.uneca.org; *African Statistical Yearbook 2006.*

United Nations Statistics Division, New York, NY 10017, (800) 253-9646, Fax: (212) 963-4116, http://unstats.un.org; *Statistical Yearbook* and *Survey of Economic and Social Conditions in Africa 2005.*

CHAD - CONSUMPTION (ECONOMICS)

African Development Bank Group, Rue Joseph Anoma, 01 BP 1387 Abidjan 01, Cote d'Ivoire, www.afdb.org; *Statistics Pocketbook 2008.*

United Nations Statistics Division, New York, NY 10017, (800) 253-9646, Fax: (212) 963-4116, http://unstats.un.org; *Survey of Economic and Social Conditions in Africa 2005.*

The World Bank, 1818 H Street, NW, Washington, DC 20433, (202) 473-1000, Fax: (202) 477-6391, www.worldbank.org; *World Development Report 2008.*

CHAD - COPPER INDUSTRY AND TRADE

See CHAD - MINERAL INDUSTRIES

CHAD - CORN INDUSTRY

See CHAD - CROPS

CHAD - COST AND STANDARD OF LIVING

International Monetary Fund (IMF), 700 Nineteenth Street, NW, Washington, DC 20431, (202) 623-7000, Fax: (202) 623-4661, www.imf.org; *Government Finance Statistics Yearbook (2008 Edition).*

CHAD - COTTON

See CHAD - CROPS

CHAD - CRIME

Yale University Press, PO Box 209040, New Haven, CT 06520-9040, (203) 432-0960, Fax: (203) 432-0948, http://yalepress.yale.edu/yupbooks; *Violence and Crime in Cross-National Perspective.*

CHAD - CROPS

International Monetary Fund (IMF), 700 Nineteenth Street, NW, Washington, DC 20431, (202) 623-7000, Fax: (202) 623-4661, www.imf.org; *International Financial Statistics Yearbook 2007.*

M.E. Sharpe, 80 Business Park Drive, Armonk, NY 10504, (800) 541-6563, Fax: (914) 273-2106, www.mesharpe.com; *The Illustrated Book of World Rankings.*

Palgrave Macmillan Ltd., Houndmills, Basingstoke, Hampshire, RG21 6XS, England, (Telephone in U.S. (888) 330-8477), (Fax in U.S. (800) 672-2054), www.palgrave.com; *The Statesman's Yearbook 2008.*

Taylor and Francis Group, An Informa Business, 2 Park Square, Milton Park, Abingdon, Oxford OX14 4RN, United Kingdom, (Dial from U.S. (212) 216-7800), (Fax from U.S. (212) 564-7854), www.tandf.co.uk; *The Europa World Year Book.*

United Nations Conference on Trade and Development (UNCTAD), DC2-1120, United Nations, New York, NY 10017, (212) 963-0027, www.unctad.org; *UNCTAD Commodity Yearbook.*

United Nations Economic Commission for Africa (ECA), PO Box 3001, Addis Ababa, Ethiopia, (Telephone in U.S. (212) 963-4957), www.uneca.org; *African Statistical Yearbook 2006.*

United Nations Food and Agricultural Organization (FAO), Viale delle Terme di Caracalla, 00100 Rome, Italy, (Dial from U.S. (202) 653-2400), (Fax from U.S. (202) 653 5760), www.fao.org; *FAO Production Yearbook 2002* and *The State of Food and Agriculture (SOFA) 2006.*

United Nations Statistics Division, New York, NY 10017, (800) 253-9646, Fax: (212) 963-4116, http://unstats.un.org; *Statistical Yearbook.*

CHAD - CUSTOMS ADMINISTRATION

International Monetary Fund (IMF), 700 Nineteenth Street, NW, Washington, DC 20431, (202) 623-7000, Fax: (202) 623-4661, www.imf.org; *Government Finance Statistics Yearbook (2008 Edition).*

Palgrave Macmillan Ltd., Houndmills, Basingstoke, Hampshire, RG21 6XS, England, (Telephone in U.S. (888) 330-8477), (Fax in U.S. (800) 672-2054), www.palgrave.com; *The Statesman's Yearbook 2008.*

CHAD - DAIRY PROCESSING

M.E. Sharpe, 80 Business Park Drive, Armonk, NY 10504, (800) 541-6563, Fax: (914) 273-2106, www.mesharpe.com; *The Illustrated Book of World Rankings.*

Palgrave Macmillan Ltd., Houndmills, Basingstoke, Hampshire, RG21 6XS, England, (Telephone in U.S. (888) 330-8477), (Fax in U.S. (800) 672-2054), www.palgrave.com; *The Statesman's Yearbook 2008.*

Taylor and Francis Group, An Informa Business, 2 Park Square, Milton Park, Abingdon, Oxford OX14 4RN, United Kingdom, (Dial from U.S. (212) 216-7800), (Fax from U.S. (212) 564-7854), www.tandf.co.uk; *The Europa World Year Book.*

United Nations Food and Agricultural Organization (FAO), Viale delle Terme di Caracalla, 00100 Rome, Italy, (Dial from U.S. (202) 653-2400), (Fax from U.S. (202) 653 5760), www.fao.org; *The State of Food and Agriculture (SOFA) 2006.*

United Nations Statistics Division, New York, NY 10017, (800) 253-9646, Fax: (212) 963-4116, http://unstats.un.org; *Statistical Yearbook.*

CHAD - DEATH RATES

See CHAD - MORTALITY

CHAD - DEBTS, EXTERNAL

African Development Bank Group, Rue Joseph Anoma, 01 BP 1387 Abidjan 01, Cote d'Ivoire, www.afdb.org; *Statistics Pocketbook 2008.*

International Monetary Fund (IMF), 700 Nineteenth Street, NW, Washington, DC 20431, (202) 623-7000, Fax: (202) 623-4661, www.imf.org; *Government Finance Statistics Yearbook (2008 Edition).*

United Nations Statistics Division, New York, NY 10017, (800) 253-9646, Fax: (212) 963-4116, http://unstats.un.org; *Survey of Economic and Social Conditions in Africa 2005.*

The World Bank, 1818 H Street, NW, Washington, DC 20433, (202) 473-1000, Fax: (202) 477-6391, www.worldbank.org; *Africa Live Database (LDB); African Development Indicators (ADI) 2007; Global Development Finance 2007; World Development Indicators (WDI) 2008;* and *World Development Report 2008.*

CHAD - DEFENSE EXPENDITURES

See CHAD - ARMED FORCES

CHAD - DEMOGRAPHY

Euromonitor International, Inc., 224 S. Michigan Avenue, Suite 1500, Chicago, IL 60604, (312) 922-1115, Fax: (312) 922-1157, www.euromonitor.com; *International Marketing Data and Statistics 2008; The World Economic Factbook 2008;* and *World Marketing Data and Statistics.*

M.E. Sharpe, 80 Business Park Drive, Armonk, NY 10504, (800) 541-6563, Fax: (914) 273-2106, www.mesharpe.com; *The Illustrated Book of World Rankings.*

United Nations Statistics Division, New York, NY 10017, (800) 253-9646, Fax: (212) 963-4116, http://

unstats.un.org; *Human Development Report 2006* and *Survey of Economic and Social Conditions in Africa 2005.*

The World Bank, 1818 H Street, NW, Washington, DC 20433, (202) 473-1000, Fax: (202) 477-6391, www.worldbank.org; *Chad.*

CHAD - DIAMONDS

See CHAD - MINERAL INDUSTRIES

CHAD - DISPOSABLE INCOME

M.E. Sharpe, 80 Business Park Drive, Armonk, NY 10504, (800) 541-6563, Fax: (914) 273-2106, www.mesharpe.com; *The Illustrated Book of World Rankings.*

United Nations Statistics Division, New York, NY 10017, (800) 253-9646, Fax: (212) 963-4116, http://unstats.un.org; *National Accounts Statistics: Compendium of Income Distribution Statistics* and *Statistical Yearbook.*

CHAD - DIVORCE

M.E. Sharpe, 80 Business Park Drive, Armonk, NY 10504, (800) 541-6563, Fax: (914) 273-2106, www.mesharpe.com; *The Illustrated Book of World Rankings.*

United Nations Statistics Division, New York, NY 10017, (800) 253-9646, Fax: (212) 963-4116, http://unstats.un.org; *Demographic Yearbook.*

CHAD - ECONOMIC ASSISTANCE

United Nations Statistics Division, New York, NY 10017, (800) 253-9646, Fax: (212) 963-4116, http://unstats.un.org; *Statistical Yearbook.*

CHAD - ECONOMIC CONDITIONS

African Development Bank Group, Rue Joseph Anoma, 01 BP 1387 Abidjan 01, Cote d'Ivoire, www.afdb.org; *The African Statistical Journal; Gender, Poverty and Environmental Indicators on African Countries 2007; Selected Statistics on African Countries 2007;* and *Statistics Pocketbook 2008.*

Center for International Business Education Research (CIBER), Columbia Business School and School of International and Public Affairs, Uris Hall, Room 212, 3022 Broadway, New York, NY 10027-6902, Mr. Joshua Safier, (212) 854-4750, Fax: (212) 222-9821, www.columbia.edu/cu/ciber/; Datastream International.

Central Intelligence Agency, Office of Public Affairs, Washington, DC 20505, (703) 482-0623, Fax: (703) 482-1739, www.cia.gov; *The World Factbook.*

DSI Data Service Information, Xantener Strasse 51a, D-47495 Rheinberg, Germany, www.dsidata.com; *Campus Solution.*

Dun and Bradstreet (DB) Corporation, 103 JFK Parkway, Short Hills, NJ 07078, (973) 921-5500, www.dnb.com; *Country Report.*

Economist Intelligence Unit, 111 West 57th Street, New York, NY 10019, (212) 554-0600, Fax: (212) 586-1181, www.eiu.com; *Business Africa* and *Chad Country Report.*

Euromonitor International, Inc., 224 S. Michigan Avenue, Suite 1500, Chicago, IL 60604, (312) 922-1115, Fax: (312) 922-1157, www.euromonitor.com; *International Marketing Data and Statistics 2008; The World Economic Factbook 2008;* and *World Marketing Data and Statistics.*

International Monetary Fund (IMF), 700 Nineteenth Street, NW, Washington, DC 20431, (202) 623-7000, Fax: (202) 623-4661, www.imf.org; *World Economic Outlook Reports.*

M.E. Sharpe, 80 Business Park Drive, Armonk, NY 10504, (800) 541-6563, Fax: (914) 273-2106, www.mesharpe.com; *The Illustrated Book of World Rankings.*

Palgrave Macmillan Ltd., Houndmills, Basingstoke, Hampshire, RG21 6XS, England, (Telephone in U.S. (888) 330-8477), (Fax in U.S. (800) 672-2054), www.palgrave.com; *The Statesman's Yearbook 2008.*

Taylor and Francis Group, An Informa Business, 2 Park Square, Milton Park, Abingdon, Oxford OX14 4RN, United Kingdom, (Dial from U.S. (212) 216-7800), (Fax from U.S. (212) 564-7854), www.tandf.co.uk; *The Europa World Year Book.*

United Nations Statistics Division, New York, NY 10017, (800) 253-9646, Fax: (212) 963-4116, http://unstats.un.org; *Compendium of Intra-African and Related Foreign Trade Statistics 2003* and *World Statistics Pocketbook.*

The World Bank, 1818 H Street, NW, Washington, DC 20433, (202) 473-1000, Fax: (202) 477-6391, www.worldbank.org; *Africa Household Survey Databank; Africa Live Database (LDB); Africa Standardized Files and Indicators; African Development Indicators (ADI) 2007; Chad; Global Economic Monitor (GEM); Global Economic Prospects 2008; The World Bank Atlas 2003-2004;* and *World Development Report 2008.*

CHAD - EDUCATION

African Development Bank Group, Rue Joseph Anoma, 01 BP 1387 Abidjan 01, Cote d'Ivoire, www.afdb.org; *Statistics Pocketbook 2008.*

Euromonitor International, Inc., 224 S. Michigan Avenue, Suite 1500, Chicago, IL 60604, (312) 922-1115, Fax: (312) 922-1157, www.euromonitor.com; *International Marketing Data and Statistics 2008* and *World Marketing Data and Statistics.*

International Monetary Fund (IMF), 700 Nineteenth Street, NW, Washington, DC 20431, (202) 623-7000, Fax: (202) 623-4661, www.imf.org; *Government Finance Statistics Yearbook (2008 Edition).*

M.E. Sharpe, 80 Business Park Drive, Armonk, NY 10504, (800) 541-6563, Fax: (914) 273-2106, www.mesharpe.com; *The Illustrated Book of World Rankings.*

Palgrave Macmillan Ltd., Houndmills, Basingstoke, Hampshire, RG21 6XS, England, (Telephone in U.S. (888) 330-8477), (Fax in U.S. (800) 672-2054), www.palgrave.com; *The Statesman's Yearbook 2008.*

Taylor and Francis Group, An Informa Business, 2 Park Square, Milton Park, Abingdon, Oxford OX14 4RN, United Kingdom, (Dial from U.S. (212) 216-7800), (Fax from U.S. (212) 564-7854), www.tandf.co.uk; *The Europa World Year Book.*

UNESCO Institute for Statistics, C.P. 6128 Succursale Centre-Ville, Montreal, Quebec, H3C 3J7 Canada, (Dial from U.S. (514) 343-6880), (Fax from U.S. (514) 343 6882), www.uis.unesco.org; *Statistical Tables.*

United Nations Economic Commission for Africa (ECA), PO Box 3001, Addis Ababa, Ethiopia, (Telephone in U.S. (212) 963-4957), www.uneca.org; *African Statistical Yearbook 2006.*

United Nations Statistics Division, New York, NY 10017, (800) 253-9646, Fax: (212) 963-4116, http://unstats.un.org; *Human Development Report 2006* and *Survey of Economic and Social Conditions in Africa 2005.*

The World Bank, 1818 H Street, NW, Washington, DC 20433, (202) 473-1000, Fax: (202) 477-6391, www.worldbank.org; *Chad; World Development Indicators (WDI) 2008;* and *World Development Report 2008.*

CHAD - ELECTRICITY

M.E. Sharpe, 80 Business Park Drive, Armonk, NY 10504, (800) 541-6563, Fax: (914) 273-2106, www.mesharpe.com; *The Illustrated Book of World Rankings.*

Palgrave Macmillan Ltd., Houndmills, Basingstoke, Hampshire, RG21 6XS, England, (Telephone in U.S. (888) 330-8477), (Fax in U.S. (800) 672-2054), www.palgrave.com; *The Statesman's Yearbook 2008.*

United Nations Economic Commission for Africa (ECA), PO Box 3001, Addis Ababa, Ethiopia, (Telephone in U.S. (212) 963-4957), www.uneca.org; *African Statistical Yearbook 2006.*

United Nations Statistics Division, New York, NY 10017, (800) 253-9646, Fax: (212) 963-4116, http://unstats.un.org; *Human Development Report 2006; Statistical Yearbook;* and *Survey of Economic and Social Conditions in Africa 2005.*

CHAD - EMPLOYMENT

Euromonitor International, Inc., 224 S. Michigan Avenue, Suite 1500, Chicago, IL 60604, (312) 922-1115, Fax: (312) 922-1157, www.euromonitor.com; *International Marketing Data and Statistics 2008.*

International Labour Office, I.L.O. Publications, 4 route des Morillons, CH-1211 Geneva 22, Switzerland, (Telephone in U.S. (202) 653-7652), (Fax in U.S. (202) 653-7687), www.ilo.org; *Yearbook of Labour Statistics 2006.*

M.E. Sharpe, 80 Business Park Drive, Armonk, NY 10504, (800) 541-6563, Fax: (914) 273-2106, www.mesharpe.com; *The Illustrated Book of World Rankings.*

United Nations Economic Commission for Africa (ECA), PO Box 3001, Addis Ababa, Ethiopia, (Telephone in U.S. (212) 963-4957), www.uneca.org; *African Statistical Yearbook 2006.*

United Nations Statistics Division, New York, NY 10017, (800) 253-9646, Fax: (212) 963-4116, http://unstats.un.org; *Survey of Economic and Social Conditions in Africa 2005.*

The World Bank, 1818 H Street, NW, Washington, DC 20433, (202) 473-1000, Fax: (202) 477-6391, www.worldbank.org; *Chad.*

CHAD - ENVIRONMENTAL CONDITIONS

DSI Data Service Information, Xantener Strasse 51a, D-47495 Rheinberg, Germany, www.dsidata.com; *Campus Solution* and *DSI's Global Environmental Database.*

Economist Intelligence Unit, 111 West 57th Street, New York, NY 10019, (212) 554-0600, Fax: (212) 586-1181, www.eiu.com; *Chad Country Report.*

International Institute for Environment and Development (IIED), 3 Endsleigh Street, London, England, WC1H 0DD, United Kingdom, www.iied.org; *Environment Urbanization* and *Haramata - Bulletin of the Drylands.*

United Nations Statistics Division, New York, NY 10017, (800) 253-9646, Fax: (212) 963-4116, http://unstats.un.org; *World Statistics Pocketbook.*

CHAD - EXPORTS

African Development Bank Group, Rue Joseph Anoma, 01 BP 1387 Abidjan 01, Cote d'Ivoire, www.afdb.org; *Statistics Pocketbook 2008.*

Central Intelligence Agency, Office of Public Affairs, Washington, DC 20505, (703) 482-0623, Fax: (703) 482-1739, www.cia.gov; *The World Factbook.*

Economist Intelligence Unit, 111 West 57th Street, New York, NY 10019, (212) 554-0600, Fax: (212) 586-1181, www.eiu.com; *Chad Country Report.*

Euromonitor International, Inc., 224 S. Michigan Avenue, Suite 1500, Chicago, IL 60604, (312) 922-1115, Fax: (312) 922-1157, www.euromonitor.com; *International Marketing Data and Statistics 2008* and *The World Economic Factbook 2008.*

International Monetary Fund (IMF), 700 Nineteenth Street, NW, Washington, DC 20431, (202) 623-7000, Fax: (202) 623-4661, www.imf.org; *Direction of Trade Statistics Yearbook 2007; Government Finance Statistics Yearbook (2008 Edition);* and *International Financial Statistics Yearbook 2007.*

Palgrave Macmillan Ltd., Houndmills, Basingstoke, Hampshire, RG21 6XS, England, (Telephone in U.S. (888) 330-8477), (Fax in U.S. (800) 672-2054), www.palgrave.com; *The Statesman's Yearbook 2008.*

Taylor and Francis Group, An Informa Business, 2 Park Square, Milton Park, Abingdon, Oxford OX14 4RN, United Kingdom, (Dial from U.S. (212) 216-7800), (Fax from U.S. (212) 564-7854), www.tandf.co.uk; *The Europa World Year Book.*

United Nations Conference on Trade and Development (UNCTAD), DC2-1120, United Nations, New York, NY 10017, (212) 963-0027, www.unctad.org; *Handbook of Statistics 2005.*

United Nations Economic Commission for Africa (ECA), PO Box 3001, Addis Ababa, Ethiopia, (Telephone in U.S. (212) 963-4957), www.uneca.org; *African Statistical Yearbook 2006.*

United Nations Food and Agricultural Organization (FAO), Viale delle Terme di Caracalla, 00100 Rome, Italy, (Dial from U.S. (202) 653-2400), (Fax from U.S. (202) 653 5760), www.fao.org; *The State of Food and Agriculture (SOFA) 2006.*

United Nations Statistics Division, New York, NY 10017, (800) 253-9646, Fax: (212) 963-4116, http://unstats.un.org; *Compendium of Intra-African and Related Foreign Trade Statistics 2003* and *Survey of Economic and Social Conditions in Africa 2005.*

The World Bank, 1818 H Street, NW, Washington, DC 20433, (202) 473-1000, Fax: (202) 477-6391, www.worldbank.org; *World Development Indicators (WDI) 2008* and *World Development Report 2008.*

CHAD - FEMALE WORKING POPULATION

See CHAD - EMPLOYMENT

CHAD - FERTILITY, HUMAN

Central Intelligence Agency, Office of Public Affairs, Washington, DC 20505, (703) 482-0623, Fax: (703) 482-1739, www.cia.gov; *The World Factbook.*

M.E. Sharpe, 80 Business Park Drive, Armonk, NY 10504, (800) 541-6563, Fax: (914) 273-2106, www.mesharpe.com; *The Illustrated Book of World Rankings.*

United Nations Statistics Division, New York, NY 10017, (800) 253-9646, Fax: (212) 963-4116, http://unstats.un.org; *Human Development Report 2006* and *Survey of Economic and Social Conditions in Africa 2005.*

The World Bank, 1818 H Street, NW, Washington, DC 20433, (202) 473-1000, Fax: (202) 477-6391, www.worldbank.org; *The World Bank Atlas 2003-2004; World Development Indicators (WDI) 2008;* and *World Development Report 2008.*

CHAD - FERTILIZER INDUSTRY

United Nations Food and Agricultural Organization (FAO), Viale delle Terme di Caracalla, 00100 Rome, Italy, (Dial from U.S. (202) 653-2400), (Fax from U.S. (202) 653 5760), www.fao.org; *FAO Fertilizer Yearbook* and *The State of Food and Agriculture (SOFA) 2006.*

United Nations Statistics Division, New York, NY 10017, (800) 253-9646, Fax: (212) 963-4116, http://unstats.un.org; *Statistical Yearbook.*

CHAD - FETAL MORTALITY

See CHAD - MORTALITY

CHAD - FINANCE

Taylor and Francis Group, An Informa Business, 2 Park Square, Milton Park, Abingdon, Oxford OX14 4RN, United Kingdom, (Dial from U.S. (212) 216-7800), (Fax from U.S. (212) 564-7854), www.tandf.co.uk; *The Europa World Year Book.*

United Nations Economic Commission for Africa (ECA), PO Box 3001, Addis Ababa, Ethiopia, (Telephone in U.S. (212) 963-4957), www.uneca.org; *African Statistical Yearbook 2006.*

United Nations Statistics Division, New York, NY 10017, (800) 253-9646, Fax: (212) 963-4116, http://unstats.un.org; *National Accounts Statistics: Compendium of Income Distribution Statistics* and *Statistical Yearbook.*

The World Bank, 1818 H Street, NW, Washington, DC 20433, (202) 473-1000, Fax: (202) 477-6391, www.worldbank.org; *Chad.*

CHAD - FINANCE, PUBLIC

African Development Bank Group, Rue Joseph Anoma, 01 BP 1387 Abidjan 01, Cote d'Ivoire, www.afdb.org; *Statistics Pocketbook 2008.*

Bernan Essential Government Publications, 4611-F Assembly Drive, Lanham MD, 20706-4391, (301) 459-2255, Fax: (800) 865-3450, www.bernan.com; *National Accounts Statistics.*

Economist Intelligence Unit, 111 West 57th Street, New York, NY 10019, (212) 554-0600, Fax: (212) 586-1181, www.eiu.com; *Chad Country Report.*

International Monetary Fund (IMF), 700 Nineteenth Street, NW, Washington, DC 20431, (202) 623-7000, Fax: (202) 623-4661, www.imf.org; *Government Finance Statistics Yearbook (2008 Edition); International Financial Statistics; International Financial Statistics Online Service;* and *International Financial Statistics Yearbook 2007.*

M.E. Sharpe, 80 Business Park Drive, Armonk, NY 10504, (800) 541-6563, Fax: (914) 273-2106, www.mesharpe.com; *The Illustrated Book of World Rankings.*

Palgrave Macmillan Ltd., Houndmills, Basingstoke, Hampshire, RG21 6XS, England, (Telephone in U.S. (888) 330-8477), (Fax in U.S. (800) 672-2054), www.palgrave.com; *The Statesman's Yearbook 2008.*

Taylor and Francis Group, An Informa Business, 2 Park Square, Milton Park, Abingdon, Oxford OX14 4RN, United Kingdom, (Dial from U.S. (212) 216-7800), (Fax from U.S. (212) 564-7854), www.tandf.co.uk; *The Europa World Year Book.*

United Nations Economic Commission for Africa (ECA), PO Box 3001, Addis Ababa, Ethiopia, (Telephone in U.S. (212) 963-4957), www.uneca.org; *African Statistical Yearbook 2006.*

The World Bank, 1818 H Street, NW, Washington, DC 20433, (202) 473-1000, Fax: (202) 477-6391, www.worldbank.org; *Chad.*

CHAD - FISHERIES

M.E. Sharpe, 80 Business Park Drive, Armonk, NY 10504, (800) 541-6563, Fax: (914) 273-2106, www.mesharpe.com; *The Illustrated Book of World Rankings.*

Palgrave Macmillan Ltd., Houndmills, Basingstoke, Hampshire, RG21 6XS, England, (Telephone in U.S. (888) 330-8477), (Fax in U.S. (800) 672-2054), www.palgrave.com; *The Statesman's Yearbook 2008.*

Taylor and Francis Group, An Informa Business, 2 Park Square, Milton Park, Abingdon, Oxford OX14 4RN, United Kingdom, (Dial from U.S. (212) 216-7800), (Fax from U.S. (212) 564-7854), www.tandf.co.uk; *The Europa World Year Book.*

United Nations Conference on Trade and Development (UNCTAD), DC2-1120, United Nations, New York, NY 10017, (212) 963-0027, www.unctad.org; *UNCTAD Commodity Yearbook.*

United Nations Economic Commission for Africa (ECA), PO Box 3001, Addis Ababa, Ethiopia, (Telephone in U.S. (212) 963-4957), www.uneca.org; *African Statistical Yearbook 2006.*

United Nations Food and Agricultural Organization (FAO), Viale delle Terme di Caracalla, 00100 Rome, Italy, (Dial from U.S. (202) 653-2400), (Fax from U.S. (202) 653 5760), www.fao.org; *FAO Yearbook of Fishery Statistics;* Fishery Databases; FISHSTAT Database. Subjects covered include: Aquaculture production, capture production, fishery commodities; and *The State of Food and Agriculture (SOFA) 2006.*

United Nations Statistics Division, New York, NY 10017, (800) 253-9646, Fax: (212) 963-4116, http://unstats.un.org; *Statistical Yearbook* and *Survey of Economic and Social Conditions in Africa 2005.*

The World Bank, 1818 H Street, NW, Washington, DC 20433, (202) 473-1000, Fax: (202) 477-6391, www.worldbank.org; *Chad.*

CHAD - FLOUR INDUSTRY

United Nations Statistics Division, New York, NY 10017, (800) 253-9646, Fax: (212) 963-4116, http://unstats.un.org; *Statistical Yearbook.*

CHAD - FOOD

African Development Bank Group, Rue Joseph Anoma, 01 BP 1387 Abidjan 01, Cote d'Ivoire, www.afdb.org; *Statistics Pocketbook 2008.*

United Nations Conference on Trade and Development (UNCTAD), DC2-1120, United Nations, New York, NY 10017, (212) 963-0027, www.unctad.org; *UNCTAD Commodity Yearbook.*

United Nations Food and Agricultural Organization (FAO), Viale delle Terme di Caracalla, 00100 Rome, Italy, (Dial from U.S. (202) 653-2400), (Fax from U.S. (202) 653 5760), www.fao.org; *FAO Production Yearbook 2002* and *The State of Food and Agriculture (SOFA) 2006.*

United Nations Statistics Division, New York, NY 10017, (800) 253-9646, Fax: (212) 963-4116, http://unstats.un.org; *Human Development Report 2006.*

CHAD - FOREIGN EXCHANGE RATES

African Development Bank Group, Rue Joseph Anoma, 01 BP 1387 Abidjan 01, Cote d'Ivoire, www.afdb.org; *Statistics Pocketbook 2008.*

Central Intelligence Agency, Office of Public Affairs, Washington, DC 20505, (703) 482-0623, Fax: (703) 482-1739, www.cia.gov; *The World Factbook.*

Euromonitor International, Inc., 224 S. Michigan Avenue, Suite 1500, Chicago, IL 60604, (312) 922-1115, Fax: (312) 922-1157, www.euromonitor.com; *International Marketing Data and Statistics 2008* and *The World Economic Factbook 2008.*

International Monetary Fund (IMF), 700 Nineteenth Street, NW, Washington, DC 20431, (202) 623-7000, Fax: (202) 623-4661, www.imf.org; *International Financial Statistics Yearbook 2007.*

Taylor and Francis Group, An Informa Business, 2 Park Square, Milton Park, Abingdon, Oxford OX14 4RN, United Kingdom, (Dial from U.S. (212) 216-7800), (Fax from U.S. (212) 564-7854), www.tandf.co.uk; *The Europa World Year Book.*

United Nations Statistics Division, New York, NY 10017, (800) 253-9646, Fax: (212) 963-4116, http://unstats.un.org; *Compendium of Intra-African and Related Foreign Trade Statistics 2003; Statistical Yearbook;* and *World Statistics Pocketbook.*

CHAD - FORESTS AND FORESTRY

M.E. Sharpe, 80 Business Park Drive, Armonk, NY 10504, (800) 541-6563, Fax: (914) 273-2106, www.mesharpe.com; *The Illustrated Book of World Rankings.*

Taylor and Francis Group, An Informa Business, 2 Park Square, Milton Park, Abingdon, Oxford OX14 4RN, United Kingdom, (Dial from U.S. (212) 216-7800), (Fax from U.S. (212) 564-7854), www.tandf.co.uk; *The Europa World Year Book.*

United Nations Conference on Trade and Development (UNCTAD), DC2-1120, United Nations, New York, NY 10017, (212) 963-0027, www.unctad.org; *UNCTAD Commodity Yearbook.*

United Nations Economic Commission for Africa (ECA), PO Box 3001, Addis Ababa, Ethiopia, (Telephone in U.S. (212) 963-4957), www.uneca.org; *African Statistical Yearbook 2006.*

United Nations Food and Agricultural Organization (FAO), Viale delle Terme di Caracalla, 00100 Rome, Italy, (Dial from U.S. (202) 653-2400), (Fax from U.S. (202) 653 5760), www.fao.org; *FAO Yearbook of Forest Products* and *The State of Food and Agriculture (SOFA) 2006.*

United Nations Statistics Division, New York, NY 10017, (800) 253-9646, Fax: (212) 963-4116, http://unstats.un.org; *Demographic Yearbook.*

The World Bank, 1818 H Street, NW, Washington, DC 20433, (202) 473-1000, Fax: (202) 477-6391, www.worldbank.org; *Chad* and *World Development Report 2008.*

CHAD - GAS INDUSTRY

M.E. Sharpe, 80 Business Park Drive, Armonk, NY 10504, (800) 541-6563, Fax: (914) 273-2106, www.mesharpe.com; *The Illustrated Book of World Rankings.*

CHAD - GEOGRAPHIC INFORMATION SYSTEMS

M.E. Sharpe, 80 Business Park Drive, Armonk, NY 10504, (800) 541-6563, Fax: (914) 273-2106, www.mesharpe.com; *The Illustrated Book of World Rankings.*

CHAD - GOLD INDUSTRY

International Monetary Fund (IMF), 700 Nineteenth Street, NW, Washington, DC 20431, (202) 623-7000, Fax: (202) 623-4661, www.imf.org; *International Financial Statistics Yearbook 2007.*

United Nations Statistics Division, New York, NY 10017, (800) 253-9646, Fax: (212) 963-4116, http://unstats.un.org; *Statistical Yearbook.*

The World Bank, 1818 H Street, NW, Washington, DC 20433, (202) 473-1000, Fax: (202) 477-6391, www.worldbank.org; *World Development Indicators (WDI) 2008.*

CHAD - GOLD PRODUCTION

See CHAD - MINERAL INDUSTRIES

CHAD - GRANTS-IN-AID

International Monetary Fund (IMF), 700 Nineteenth Street, NW, Washington, DC 20431, (202) 623-7000, Fax: (202) 623-4661, www.imf.org; *Government Finance Statistics Yearbook (2008 Edition).*

CHAD - GROSS DOMESTIC PRODUCT

African Development Bank Group, Rue Joseph Anoma, 01 BP 1387 Abidjan 01, Cote d'Ivoire, www.afdb.org; *Statistics Pocketbook 2008.*

Economist Intelligence Unit, 111 West 57th Street, New York, NY 10019, (212) 554-0600, Fax: (212) 586-1181, www.eiu.com; *Chad Country Report.*

Euromonitor International, Inc., 224 S. Michigan Avenue, Suite 1500, Chicago, IL 60604, (312) 922-1115, Fax: (312) 922-1157, www.euromonitor.com; *International Marketing Data and Statistics 2008* and *The World Economic Factbook 2008.*

M.E. Sharpe, 80 Business Park Drive, Armonk, NY 10504, (800) 541-6563, Fax: (914) 273-2106, www.mesharpe.com; *The Illustrated Book of World Rankings.*

Taylor and Francis Group, An Informa Business, 2 Park Square, Milton Park, Abingdon, Oxford OX14 4RN, United Kingdom, (Dial from U.S. (212) 216-7800), (Fax from U.S. (212) 564-7854), www.tandf.co.uk; *The Europa World Year Book.*

United Nations Economic Commission for Africa (ECA), PO Box 3001, Addis Ababa, Ethiopia, (Telephone in U.S. (212) 963-4957), www.uneca.org; *African Statistical Yearbook 2006.*

United Nations Statistics Division, New York, NY 10017, (800) 253-9646, Fax: (212) 963-4116, http://unstats.un.org; *Human Development Report 2006; National Accounts Statistics: Compendium of Income Distribution Statistics; Statistical Yearbook;* and *Survey of Economic and Social Conditions in Africa 2005.*

The World Bank, 1818 H Street, NW, Washington, DC 20433, (202) 473-1000, Fax: (202) 477-6391, www.worldbank.org; *World Development Indicators (WDI) 2008* and *World Development Report 2008.*

CHAD - GROSS NATIONAL PRODUCT

Euromonitor International, Inc., 224 S. Michigan Avenue, Suite 1500, Chicago, IL 60604, (312) 922-1115, Fax: (312) 922-1157, www.euromonitor.com; *International Marketing Data and Statistics 2008.*

M.E. Sharpe, 80 Business Park Drive, Armonk, NY 10504, (800) 541-6563, Fax: (914) 273-2106, www.mesharpe.com; *The Illustrated Book of World Rankings.*

Palgrave Macmillan Ltd., Houndmills, Basingstoke, Hampshire, RG21 6XS, England, (Telephone in U.S. (888) 330-8477), (Fax in U.S. (800) 672-2054), www.palgrave.com; *The Statesman's Yearbook 2008.*

U.S. Department of State (DOS), 2201 C Street NW, Washington, DC 20520, (202) 647-4000, www.state.gov; *World Military Expenditures and Arms Transfers (WMEAT).*

United Nations Statistics Division, New York, NY 10017, (800) 253-9646, Fax: (212) 963-4116, http://unstats.un.org; *Statistical Yearbook.*

The World Bank, 1818 H Street, NW, Washington, DC 20433, (202) 473-1000, Fax: (202) 477-6391, www.worldbank.org; *The World Bank Atlas 2003-2004; World Development Indicators (WDI) 2008;* and *World Development Report 2008.*

CHAD - HIDES AND SKINS INDUSTRY

United Nations Food and Agricultural Organization (FAO), Viale delle Terme di Caracalla, 00100 Rome, Italy, (Dial from U.S. (202) 653-2400), (Fax from U.S. (202) 653 5760), www.fao.org; *FAO Production Yearbook 2002.*

CHAD - HOUSING

Euromonitor International, Inc., 224 S. Michigan Avenue, Suite 1500, Chicago, IL 60604, (312) 922-1115, Fax: (312) 922-1157, www.euromonitor.com; *World Marketing Data and Statistics.*

M.E. Sharpe, 80 Business Park Drive, Armonk, NY 10504, (800) 541-6563, Fax: (914) 273-2106, www.mesharpe.com; *The Illustrated Book of World Rankings.*

CHAD - ILLITERATE PERSONS

Euromonitor International, Inc., 224 S. Michigan Avenue, Suite 1500, Chicago, IL 60604, (312) 922-1115, Fax: (312) 922-1157, www.euromonitor.com; *The World Economic Factbook 2008.*

UNESCO Institute for Statistics, C.P. 6128 Succursale Centre-Ville, Montreal, Quebec, H3C 3J7 Canada, (Dial from U.S. (514) 343-6880), (Fax from U.S. (514) 343 6882), www.uis.unesco.org; *Statistical Tables.*

United Nations Statistics Division, New York, NY 10017, (800) 253-9646, Fax: (212) 963-4116, http://unstats.un.org; *Human Development Report 2006.*

CHAD - IMPORTS

Central Intelligence Agency, Office of Public Affairs, Washington, DC 20505, (703) 482-0623, Fax: (703) 482-1739, www.cia.gov; *The World Factbook.*

Economist Intelligence Unit, 111 West 57th Street, New York, NY 10019, (212) 554-0600, Fax: (212) 586-1181, www.eiu.com; *Chad Country Report.*

Euromonitor International, Inc., 224 S. Michigan Avenue, Suite 1500, Chicago, IL 60604, (312) 922-1115, Fax: (312) 922-1157, www.euromonitor.com; *International Marketing Data and Statistics 2008* and *The World Economic Factbook 2008.*

International Monetary Fund (IMF), 700 Nineteenth Street, NW, Washington, DC 20431, (202) 623-7000, Fax: (202) 623-4661, www.imf.org; *Direction of Trade Statistics Yearbook 2007; Government Finance Statistics Yearbook (2008 Edition);* and *International Financial Statistics Yearbook 2007.*

Palgrave Macmillan Ltd., Houndmills, Basingstoke, Hampshire, RG21 6XS, England, (Telephone in U.S. (888) 330-8477), (Fax in U.S. (800) 672-2054), www.palgrave.com; *The Statesman's Yearbook 2008.*

Taylor and Francis Group, An Informa Business, 2 Park Square, Milton Park, Abingdon, Oxford OX14 4RN, United Kingdom, (Dial from U.S. (212) 216-7800), (Fax from U.S. (212) 564-7854), www.tandf.co.uk; *The Europa World Year Book.*

United Nations Conference on Trade and Development (UNCTAD), DC2-1120, United Nations, New York, NY 10017, (212) 963-0027, www.unctad.org; *Handbook of Statistics 2005.*

United Nations Economic Commission for Africa (ECA), PO Box 3001, Addis Ababa, Ethiopia, (Telephone in U.S. (212) 963-4957), www.uneca.org; *African Statistical Yearbook 2006.*

United Nations Food and Agricultural Organization (FAO), Viale delle Terme di Caracalla, 00100 Rome, Italy, (Dial from U.S. (202) 653-2400), (Fax from U.S. (202) 653 5760), www.fao.org; *The State of Food and Agriculture (SOFA) 2006.*

United Nations Statistics Division, New York, NY 10017, (800) 253-9646, Fax: (212) 963-4116, http://unstats.un.org; *Compendium of Intra-African and Related Foreign Trade Statistics 2003* and *Survey of Economic and Social Conditions in Africa 2005.*

The World Bank, 1818 H Street, NW, Washington, DC 20433, (202) 473-1000, Fax: (202) 477-6391, www.worldbank.org; *World Development Indicators (WDI) 2008* and *World Development Report 2008.*

CHAD - INCOME TAXES

See CHAD - TAXATION

CHAD - INDUSTRIAL PRODUCTIVITY

Euromonitor International, Inc., 224 S. Michigan Avenue, Suite 1500, Chicago, IL 60604, (312) 922-1115, Fax: (312) 922-1157, www.euromonitor.com; *International Marketing Data and Statistics 2008.*

M.E. Sharpe, 80 Business Park Drive, Armonk, NY 10504, (800) 541-6563, Fax: (914) 273-2106, www.mesharpe.com; *The Illustrated Book of World Rankings.*

CHAD - INDUSTRIES

Central Intelligence Agency, Office of Public Affairs, Washington, DC 20505, (703) 482-0623, Fax: (703) 482-1739, www.cia.gov; *The World Factbook.*

Economist Intelligence Unit, 111 West 57th Street, New York, NY 10019, (212) 554-0600, Fax: (212) 586-1181, www.eiu.com; *Chad Country Report.*

Euromonitor International, Inc., 224 S. Michigan Avenue, Suite 1500, Chicago, IL 60604, (312) 922-1115, Fax: (312) 922-1157, www.euromonitor.com; *International Marketing Data and Statistics 2008; The World Economic Factbook 2008;* and *World Marketing Data and Statistics.*

International Labour Office, I.L.O. Publications, 4 route des Morillons, CH-1211 Geneva 22, Switzerland, (Telephone in U.S. (202) 653-7652), (Fax in U.S. (202) 653-7687), www.ilo.org; *Yearbook of Labour Statistics 2006.*

M.E. Sharpe, 80 Business Park Drive, Armonk, NY 10504, (800) 541-6563, Fax: (914) 273-2106, www.mesharpe.com; *The Illustrated Book of World Rankings.*

Palgrave Macmillan Ltd., Houndmills, Basingstoke, Hampshire, RG21 6XS, England, (Telephone in U.S. (888) 330-8477), (Fax in U.S. (800) 672-2054), www.palgrave.com; *The Statesman's Yearbook 2008.*

Taylor and Francis Group, An Informa Business, 2 Park Square, Milton Park, Abingdon, Oxford OX14 4RN, United Kingdom, (Dial from U.S. (212) 216-7800), (Fax from U.S. (212) 564-7854), www.tandf.co.uk; *The Europa World Year Book.*

United Nations Economic Commission for Africa (ECA), PO Box 3001, Addis Ababa, Ethiopia, (Telephone in U.S. (212) 963-4957), www.uneca.org; *African Statistical Yearbook 2006.*

United Nations Industrial Development Organization (UNIDO), 1 United Nations Plaza, New York, NY 10017, (212) 963 6890, Fax: (212) 963-7904, http://unido.org; Industrial Statistics Database 2008 (INDSTAT) and *The International Yearbook of Industrial Statistics 2008.*

United Nations Statistics Division, New York, NY 10017, (800) 253-9646, Fax: (212) 963-4116, http://unstats.un.org; *Survey of Economic and Social Conditions in Africa 2005.*

The World Bank, 1818 H Street, NW, Washington, DC 20433, (202) 473-1000, Fax: (202) 477-6391, www.worldbank.org; *Chad* and *World Development Indicators (WDI) 2008.*

CHAD - INFANT AND MATERNAL MORTALITY

See CHAD - MORTALITY

CHAD - INTERNATIONAL LIQUIDITY

International Monetary Fund (IMF), 700 Nineteenth Street, NW, Washington, DC 20431, (202) 623-7000, Fax: (202) 623-4661, www.imf.org; *International Financial Statistics Yearbook 2007.*

CHAD - INTERNATIONAL TRADE

African Development Bank Group, Rue Joseph Anoma, 01 BP 1387 Abidjan 01, Cote d'Ivoire, www.afdb.org; *Statistics Pocketbook 2008.*

Economist Intelligence Unit, 111 West 57th Street, New York, NY 10019, (212) 554-0600, Fax: (212) 586-1181, www.eiu.com; *Chad Country Report.*

Euromonitor International, Inc., 224 S. Michigan Avenue, Suite 1500, Chicago, IL 60604, (312) 922-1115, Fax: (312) 922-1157, www.euromonitor.com; *International Marketing Data and Statistics 2008; The World Economic Factbook 2008;* and *World Marketing Data and Statistics.*

M.E. Sharpe, 80 Business Park Drive, Armonk, NY 10504, (800) 541-6563, Fax: (914) 273-2106, www.mesharpe.com; *The Illustrated Book of World Rankings.*

Organisation for Economic Cooperation and Development (OECD), 2 rue Andre Pascal, F-75775 Paris Cedex 16, France, (Telephone in U.S. (202) 785-6323), (Fax in U.S. (202) 785-0350), www.oecd.org; *International Trade by Commodity Statistics (ITCS).*

Palgrave Macmillan Ltd., Houndmills, Basingstoke, Hampshire, RG21 6XS, England, (Telephone in U.S. (888) 330-8477), (Fax in U.S. (800) 672-2054), www.palgrave.com; *The Statesman's Yearbook 2008.*

Taylor and Francis Group, An Informa Business, 2 Park Square, Milton Park, Abingdon, Oxford OX14 4RN, United Kingdom, (Dial from U.S. (212) 216-7800), (Fax from U.S. (212) 564-7854), www.tandf.co.uk; *The Europa World Year Book.*

United Nations Conference on Trade and Development (UNCTAD), DC2-1120, United Nations, New York, NY 10017, (212) 963-0027, www.unctad.org; *UNCTAD Commodity Yearbook.*

United Nations Economic Commission for Africa (ECA), PO Box 3001, Addis Ababa, Ethiopia, (Telephone in U.S. (212) 963-4957), www.uneca.org; *African Statistical Yearbook 2006.*

United Nations Food and Agricultural Organization (FAO), Viale delle Terme di Caracalla, 00100 Rome, Italy, (Dial from U.S. (202) 653-2400), (Fax from U.S. (202) 653 5760), www.fao.org; *FAO Trade Yearbook* and *The State of Food and Agriculture (SOFA) 2006.*

United Nations Statistics Division, New York, NY 10017, (800) 253-9646, Fax: (212) 963-4116, http://unstats.un.org; *Compendium of Intra-African and Related Foreign Trade Statistics 2003; International Trade Statistics Yearbook;* and *Statistical Yearbook.*

The World Bank, 1818 H Street, NW, Washington, DC 20433, (202) 473-1000, Fax: (202) 477-6391, www.worldbank.org; *Chad; World Development Indicators (WDI) 2008;* and *World Development Report 2008.*

World Trade Organization (WTO), Centre William Rappard, Rue de Lausanne 154, CH-1211 Geneva 21, Switzerland, www.wto.org; *International Trade Statistics 2006.*

CHAD - INTERNET USERS

International Telecommunication Union (ITU), Place des Nations, 1211 Geneva 20, Switzerland, www.itu.int; *World Telecommunication/ICT Indicators Database on CD-ROM; World Telecommunication/ICT Indicators Database Online;* and *Yearbook of Statistics - Telecommunication Services (Chronological Time Series 1997-2006).*

The World Bank, 1818 H Street, NW, Washington, DC 20433, (202) 473-1000, Fax: (202) 477-6391, www.worldbank.org; *Chad.*

CHAD - IRON AND IRON ORE PRODUCTION

See CHAD - MINERAL INDUSTRIES

CHAD - IRRIGATION

Euromonitor International, Inc., 224 S. Michigan Avenue, Suite 1500, Chicago, IL 60604, (312) 922-1115, Fax: (312) 922-1157, www.euromonitor.com; *International Marketing Data and Statistics 2008.*

CHAD - LABOR

African Development Bank Group, Rue Joseph Anoma, 01 BP 1387 Abidjan 01, Cote d'Ivoire, www.afdb.org; *Statistics Pocketbook 2008.*

Central Intelligence Agency, Office of Public Affairs, Washington, DC 20505, (703) 482-0623, Fax: (703) 482-1739, www.cia.gov; *The World Factbook.*

Euromonitor International, Inc., 224 S. Michigan Avenue, Suite 1500, Chicago, IL 60604, (312) 922-1115, Fax: (312) 922-1157, www.euromonitor.com; *International Marketing Data and Statistics 2008* and *World Marketing Data and Statistics.*

International Labour Office, I.L.O. Publications, 4 route des Morillons, CH-1211 Geneva 22, Switzerland, (Telephone in U.S. (202) 653-7652), (Fax in U.S. (202) 653-7687), www.ilo.org; *Yearbook of Labour Statistics 2006.*

M.E. Sharpe, 80 Business Park Drive, Armonk, NY 10504, (800) 541-6563, Fax: (914) 273-2106, www.mesharpe.com; *The Illustrated Book of World Rankings.*

Palgrave Macmillan Ltd., Houndmills, Basingstoke, Hampshire, RG21 6XS, England, (Telephone in U.S. (888) 330-8477), (Fax in U.S. (800) 672-2054), www.palgrave.com; *The Statesman's Yearbook 2008.*

United Nations Food and Agricultural Organization (FAO), Viale delle Terme di Caracalla, 00100 Rome, Italy, (Dial from U.S. (202) 653-2400), (Fax from U.S. (202) 653 5760), www.fao.org; *The State of Food and Agriculture (SOFA) 2006.*

United Nations Statistics Division, New York, NY 10017, (800) 253-9646, Fax: (212) 963-4116, http://unstats.un.org; *Human Development Report 2006.*

The World Bank, 1818 H Street, NW, Washington, DC 20433, (202) 473-1000, Fax: (202) 477-6391, www.worldbank.org; *The World Bank Atlas 2003-2004; World Development Indicators (WDI) 2008;* and *World Development Report 2008.*

CHAD - LAND USE

Central Intelligence Agency, Office of Public Affairs, Washington, DC 20505, (703) 482-0623, Fax: (703) 482-1739, www.cia.gov; *The World Factbook.*

Euromonitor International, Inc., 224 S. Michigan Avenue, Suite 1500, Chicago, IL 60604, (312) 922-1115, Fax: (312) 922-1157, www.euromonitor.com; *International Marketing Data and Statistics 2008.*

United Nations Food and Agricultural Organization (FAO), Viale delle Terme di Caracalla, 00100 Rome, Italy, (Dial from U.S. (202) 653-2400), (Fax from U.S. (202) 653 5760), www.fao.org; *FAO Production Yearbook 2002.*

The World Bank, 1818 H Street, NW, Washington, DC 20433, (202) 473-1000, Fax: (202) 477-6391, www.worldbank.org; *World Development Report 2008.*

CHAD - LIBRARIES

M.E. Sharpe, 80 Business Park Drive, Armonk, NY 10504, (800) 541-6563, Fax: (914) 273-2106, www.mesharpe.com; *The Illustrated Book of World Rankings.*

CHAD - LICENSES

International Monetary Fund (IMF), 700 Nineteenth Street, NW, Washington, DC 20431, (202) 623-7000, Fax: (202) 623-4661, www.imf.org; *Government Finance Statistics Yearbook (2008 Edition).*

CHAD - LIFE EXPECTANCY

African Development Bank Group, Rue Joseph Anoma, 01 BP 1387 Abidjan 01, Cote d'Ivoire, www.afdb.org; *Statistics Pocketbook 2008.*

Central Intelligence Agency, Office of Public Affairs, Washington, DC 20505, (703) 482-0623, Fax: (703) 482-1739, www.cia.gov; *The World Factbook.*

Euromonitor International, Inc., 224 S. Michigan Avenue, Suite 1500, Chicago, IL 60604, (312) 922-1115, Fax: (312) 922-1157, www.euromonitor.com; *The World Economic Factbook 2008.*

United Nations Statistics Division, New York, NY 10017, (800) 253-9646, Fax: (212) 963-4116, http://unstats.un.org; *Human Development Report 2006* and *World Statistics Pocketbook.*

The World Bank, 1818 H Street, NW, Washington, DC 20433, (202) 473-1000, Fax: (202) 477-6391, www.worldbank.org; *The World Bank Atlas 2003-2004* and *World Development Report 2008.*

CHAD - LITERACY

Euromonitor International, Inc., 224 S. Michigan Avenue, Suite 1500, Chicago, IL 60604, (312) 922-1115, Fax: (312) 922-1157, www.euromonitor.com; *World Marketing Data and Statistics.*

United Nations Statistics Division, New York, NY 10017, (800) 253-9646, Fax: (212) 963-4116, http://unstats.un.org; *Survey of Economic and Social Conditions in Africa 2005.*

CHAD - LIVESTOCK

Euromonitor International, Inc., 224 S. Michigan Avenue, Suite 1500, Chicago, IL 60604, (312) 922-1115, Fax: (312) 922-1157, www.euromonitor.com; *International Marketing Data and Statistics 2008.*

M.E. Sharpe, 80 Business Park Drive, Armonk, NY 10504, (800) 541-6563, Fax: (914) 273-2106, www.mesharpe.com; *The Illustrated Book of World Rankings.*

Palgrave Macmillan Ltd., Houndmills, Basingstoke, Hampshire, RG21 6XS, England, (Telephone in U.S. (888) 330-8477), (Fax in U.S. (800) 672-2054), www.palgrave.com; *The Statesman's Yearbook 2008.*

Taylor and Francis Group, An Informa Business, 2 Park Square, Milton Park, Abingdon, Oxford OX14 4RN, United Kingdom, (Dial from U.S. (212) 216-7800), (Fax from U.S. (212) 564-7854), www.tandf.co.uk; *The Europa World Year Book.*

United Nations Conference on Trade and Development (UNCTAD), DC2-1120, United Nations, New York, NY 10017, (212) 963-0027, www.unctad.org; *UNCTAD Commodity Yearbook.*

United Nations Economic Commission for Africa (ECA), PO Box 3001, Addis Ababa, Ethiopia, (Telephone in U.S. (212) 963-4957), www.uneca.org; *African Statistical Yearbook 2006.*

United Nations Food and Agricultural Organization (FAO), Viale delle Terme di Caracalla, 00100 Rome, Italy, (Dial from U.S. (202) 653-2400), (Fax from U.S. (202) 653 5760), www.fao.org; *FAO Production Yearbook 2002* and *The State of Food and Agriculture (SOFA) 2006.*

United Nations Statistics Division, New York, NY 10017, (800) 253-9646, Fax: (212) 963-4116, http://unstats.un.org; *Statistical Yearbook* and *Survey of Economic and Social Conditions in Africa 2005.*

CHAD - LOCAL TAXATION

Euromonitor International, Inc., 224 S. Michigan Avenue, Suite 1500, Chicago, IL 60604, (312) 922-1115, Fax: (312) 922-1157, www.euromonitor.com; *International Marketing Data and Statistics 2008.*

CHAD - MANUFACTURES

M.E. Sharpe, 80 Business Park Drive, Armonk, NY 10504, (800) 541-6563, Fax: (914) 273-2106, www.mesharpe.com; *The Illustrated Book of World Rankings.*

United Nations Economic Commission for Africa (ECA), PO Box 3001, Addis Ababa, Ethiopia, (Telephone in U.S. (212) 963-4957), www.uneca.org; *African Statistical Yearbook 2006.*

United Nations Statistics Division, New York, NY 10017, (800) 253-9646, Fax: (212) 963-4116, http://unstats.un.org; *Survey of Economic and Social Conditions in Africa 2005.*

The World Bank, 1818 H Street, NW, Washington, DC 20433, (202) 473-1000, Fax: (202) 477-6391, www.worldbank.org; *World Development Indicators (WDI) 2008.*

CHAD - MARRIAGE

M.E. Sharpe, 80 Business Park Drive, Armonk, NY 10504, (800) 541-6563, Fax: (914) 273-2106, www.mesharpe.com; *The Illustrated Book of World Rankings.*

United Nations Statistics Division, New York, NY 10017, (800) 253-9646, Fax: (212) 963-4116, http://unstats.un.org; *Demographic Yearbook.*

CHAD - MEAT PRODUCTION

See CHAD - LIVESTOCK

CHAD - MEDICAL CARE, COST OF

International Monetary Fund (IMF), 700 Nineteenth Street, NW, Washington, DC 20431, (202) 623-7000, Fax: (202) 623-4661, www.imf.org; *Government Finance Statistics Yearbook (2008 Edition).*

CHAD - MILK PRODUCTION

See CHAD - DAIRY PROCESSING

CHAD - MINERAL INDUSTRIES

M.E. Sharpe, 80 Business Park Drive, Armonk, NY 10504, (800) 541-6563, Fax: (914) 273-2106, www.mesharpe.com; *The Illustrated Book of World Rankings.*

Palgrave Macmillan Ltd., Houndmills, Basingstoke, Hampshire, RG21 6XS, England, (Telephone in U.S. (888) 330-8477), (Fax in U.S. (800) 672-2054), www.palgrave.com; *The Statesman's Yearbook 2008.*

United Nations Conference on Trade and Development (UNCTAD), DC2-1120, United Nations, New York, NY 10017, (212) 963-0027, www.unctad.org; *UNCTAD Commodity Yearbook.*

United Nations Economic Commission for Africa (ECA), PO Box 3001, Addis Ababa, Ethiopia, (Telephone in U.S. (212) 963-4957), www.uneca.org; *African Statistical Yearbook 2006.*

The World Bank, 1818 H Street, NW, Washington, DC 20433, (202) 473-1000, Fax: (202) 477-6391, www.worldbank.org; *Chad.*

CHAD - MONEY EXCHANGE RATES

See CHAD - FOREIGN EXCHANGE RATES

CHAD - MONEY SUPPLY

African Development Bank Group, Rue Joseph Anoma, 01 BP 1387 Abidjan 01, Cote d'Ivoire, www.afdb.org; *Statistics Pocketbook 2008.*

Economist Intelligence Unit, 111 West 57th Street, New York, NY 10019, (212) 554-0600, Fax: (212) 586-1181, www.eiu.com; *Chad Country Report.*

International Monetary Fund (IMF), 700 Nineteenth Street, NW, Washington, DC 20431, (202) 623-7000, Fax: (202) 623-4661, www.imf.org; *International Financial Statistics Yearbook 2007.*

Taylor and Francis Group, An Informa Business, 2 Park Square, Milton Park, Abingdon, Oxford OX14 4RN, United Kingdom, (Dial from U.S. (212) 216-7800), (Fax from U.S. (212) 564-7854), www.tandf.co.uk; *The Europa World Year Book.*

United Nations Statistics Division, New York, NY 10017, (800) 253-9646, Fax: (212) 963-4116, http://unstats.un.org; *Statistical Yearbook.*

The World Bank, 1818 H Street, NW, Washington, DC 20433, (202) 473-1000, Fax: (202) 477-6391, www.worldbank.org; *Chad* and *World Development Indicators (WDI) 2008.*

CHAD - MORTALITY

Central Intelligence Agency, Office of Public Affairs, Washington, DC 20505, (703) 482-0623, Fax: (703) 482-1739, www.cia.gov; *The World Factbook.*

Euromonitor International, Inc., 224 S. Michigan Avenue, Suite 1500, Chicago, IL 60604, (312) 922-1115, Fax: (312) 922-1157, www.euromonitor.com; *International Marketing Data and Statistics 2008* and *The World Economic Factbook 2008.*

Taylor and Francis Group, An Informa Business, 2 Park Square, Milton Park, Abingdon, Oxford OX14 4RN, United Kingdom, (Dial from U.S. (212) 216-7800), (Fax from U.S. (212) 564-7854), www.tandf.co.uk; *The Europa World Year Book.*

United Nations Statistics Division, New York, NY 10017, (800) 253-9646, Fax: (212) 963-4116, http://unstats.un.org; *Demographic Yearbook; Human Development Report 2006; Statistical Yearbook; Survey of Economic and Social Conditions in Africa 2005;* and *World Statistics Pocketbook.*

The World Bank, 1818 H Street, NW, Washington, DC 20433, (202) 473-1000, Fax: (202) 477-6391, www.worldbank.org; *The World Bank Atlas 2003-2004; World Development Indicators (WDI) 2008;* and *World Development Report 2008.*

World Health Organization (WHO), Avenue Appia 20, 1211 Geneve 27, Switzerland, (Telephone in U.S. (212) 331-9081), www.who.int; The WHO Global Atlas of Infectious Diseases and *World Health Report 2006.*

CHAD - MOTOR VEHICLES

International Road Federation (IFR), Madison Place, 500 Montgomery Street, 5th Floor, Alexandria, VA 22314, (703) 535-1001, Fax: (703) 535-1007, www.irfnet.org; *World Road Statistics 2006.*

Taylor and Francis Group, An Informa Business, 2 Park Square, Milton Park, Abingdon, Oxford OX14 4RN, United Kingdom, (Dial from U.S. (212) 216-7800), (Fax from U.S. (212) 564-7854), www.tandf.co.uk; *The Europa World Year Book.*

United Nations Statistics Division, New York, NY 10017, (800) 253-9646, Fax: (212) 963-4116, http://unstats.un.org; *Statistical Yearbook* and *Survey of Economic and Social Conditions in Africa 2005.*

CHAD - MUSEUMS

M.E. Sharpe, 80 Business Park Drive, Armonk, NY 10504, (800) 541-6563, Fax: (914) 273-2106, www.mesharpe.com; *The Illustrated Book of World Rankings.*

UNESCO Institute for Statistics, C.P. 6128 Succursale Centre-Ville, Montreal, Quebec, H3C 3J7 Canada, (Dial from U.S. (514) 343-6880), (Fax from U.S. (514) 343 6882), www.uis.unesco.org; *Statistical Tables.*

CHAD - NATURAL GAS PRODUCTION

See CHAD - MINERAL INDUSTRIES

CHAD - NUTRITION

African Development Bank Group, Rue Joseph Anoma, 01 BP 1387 Abidjan 01, Cote d'Ivoire, www.afdb.org; *Statistics Pocketbook 2008.*

United Nations Food and Agricultural Organization (FAO), Viale delle Terme di Caracalla, 00100 Rome, Italy, (Dial from U.S. (202) 653-2400), (Fax from U.S. (202) 653 5760), www.fao.org; *The State of Food and Agriculture (SOFA) 2006.*

CHAD - OLDER PEOPLE

M.E. Sharpe, 80 Business Park Drive, Armonk, NY 10504, (800) 541-6563, Fax: (914) 273-2106, www.mesharpe.com; *The Illustrated Book of World Rankings.*

CHAD - PAPER

See CHAD - FORESTS AND FORESTRY

CHAD - PAPER PRODUCTS INDUSTRY

UNESCO Institute for Statistics, C.P. 6128 Succursale Centre-Ville, Montreal, Quebec, H3C 3J7 Canada, (Dial from U.S. (514) 343-6880), (Fax from U.S. (514) 343 6882), www.uis.unesco.org; *Statistical Tables.*

CHAD - PEANUT PRODUCTION

See CHAD - CROPS

CHAD - PESTICIDES

United Nations Food and Agricultural Organization (FAO), Viale delle Terme di Caracalla, 00100 Rome, Italy, (Dial from U.S. (202) 653-2400), (Fax from U.S. (202) 653 5760), www.fao.org; *The State of Food and Agriculture (SOFA) 2006.*

CHAD - PETROLEUM INDUSTRY AND TRADE

M.E. Sharpe, 80 Business Park Drive, Armonk, NY 10504, (800) 541-6563, Fax: (914) 273-2106, www.mesharpe.com; *The Illustrated Book of World Rankings.*

PennWell Corporation, 1421 South Sheridan Road, Tulsa, OK 74112, (918) 835-3161, www.pennwell.com; *International Petroleum Encyclopedia 2007.*

United Nations Conference on Trade and Development (UNCTAD), DC2-1120, United Nations, New York, NY 10017, (212) 963-0027, www.unctad.org; *UNCTAD Commodity Yearbook.*

United Nations Food and Agricultural Organization (FAO), Viale delle Terme di Caracalla, 00100 Rome, Italy, (Dial from U.S. (202) 653-2400), (Fax from U.S. (202) 653 5760), www.fao.org; *The State of Food and Agriculture (SOFA) 2006.*

CHAD - POLITICAL SCIENCE

Central Intelligence Agency, Office of Public Affairs, Washington, DC 20505, (703) 482-0623, Fax: (703) 482-1739, www.cia.gov; *The World Factbook.*

International Monetary Fund (IMF), 700 Nineteenth Street, NW, Washington, DC 20431, (202) 623-7000, Fax: (202) 623-4661, www.imf.org; *Government Finance Statistics Yearbook (2008 Edition)* and *International Financial Statistics Yearbook 2007.*

Palgrave Macmillan Ltd., Houndmills, Basingstoke, Hampshire, RG21 6XS, England, (Telephone in U.S. (888) 330-8477), (Fax in U.S. (800) 672-2054), www.palgrave.com; *The Statesman's Yearbook 2008.*

Taylor and Francis Group, An Informa Business, 2 Park Square, Milton Park, Abingdon, Oxford OX14 4RN, United Kingdom, (Dial from U.S. (212) 216-7800), (Fax from U.S. (212) 564-7854), www.tandf.co.uk; *The Europa World Year Book.*

United Nations Statistics Division, New York, NY 10017, (800) 253-9646, Fax: (212) 963-4116, http://unstats.un.org; *National Accounts Statistics: Compendium of Income Distribution Statistics* and *Survey of Economic and Social Conditions in Africa 2005.*

The World Bank, 1818 H Street, NW, Washington, DC 20433, (202) 473-1000, Fax: (202) 477-6391, www.worldbank.org; *World Development Indicators (WDI) 2008* and *World Development Report 2008.*

CHAD - POPULATION

African Development Bank Group, Rue Joseph Anoma, 01 BP 1387 Abidjan 01, Cote d'Ivoire, www.afdb.org; *The African Statistical Journal; Gender, Poverty and Environmental Indicators on African Countries 2007; Selected Statistics on African Countries 2007;* and *Statistics Pocketbook 2008.*

Central Intelligence Agency, Office of Public Affairs, Washington, DC 20505, (703) 482-0623, Fax: (703) 482-1739, www.cia.gov; *The World Factbook.*

Economist Intelligence Unit, 111 West 57th Street, New York, NY 10019, (212) 554-0600, Fax: (212) 586-1181, www.eiu.com; *Chad Country Report.*

Euromonitor International, Inc., 224 S. Michigan Avenue, Suite 1500, Chicago, IL 60604, (312) 922-1115, Fax: (312) 922-1157, www.euromonitor.com; *International Marketing Data and Statistics 2008* and *The World Economic Factbook 2008.*

Eurostat, Batiment Jean Monnet, Rue Alcide de Gasperi, L-2920 Luxembourg, http://epp.eurostat.ec.europa.eu; *Demographic Indicators - Population by Age-Classes.*

International Labour Office, I.L.O. Publications, 4 route des Morillons, CH-1211 Geneva 22, Switzerland, (Telephone in U.S. (202) 653-7652), (Fax in U.S. (202) 653-7687), www.ilo.org; *Yearbook of Labour Statistics 2006.*

M.E. Sharpe, 80 Business Park Drive, Armonk, NY 10504, (800) 541-6563, Fax: (914) 273-2106, www.mesharpe.com; *The Illustrated Book of World Rankings.*

Palgrave Macmillan Ltd., Houndmills, Basingstoke, Hampshire, RG21 6XS, England, (Telephone in U.S. (888) 330-8477), (Fax in U.S. (800) 672-2054), www.palgrave.com; *The Statesman's Yearbook 2008.*

Taylor and Francis Group, An Informa Business, 2 Park Square, Milton Park, Abingdon, Oxford OX14 4RN, United Kingdom, (Dial from U.S. (212) 216-7800), (Fax from U.S. (212) 564-7854), www.tandf.co.uk; *The Europa World Year Book.*

U.S. Department of State (DOS), 2201 C Street NW, Washington, DC 20520, (202) 647-4000, www.state.gov; *World Military Expenditures and Arms Transfers (WMEAT).*

UNESCO Institute for Statistics, C.P. 6128 Succursale Centre-Ville, Montreal, Quebec, H3C 3J7 Canada, (Dial from U.S. (514) 343-6880), (Fax from U.S. (514) 343 6882), www.uis.unesco.org; *Statistical Tables.*

United Nations Food and Agricultural Organization (FAO), Viale delle Terme di Caracalla, 00100 Rome, Italy, (Dial from U.S. (202) 653-2400), (Fax from U.S. (202) 653 5760), www.fao.org; *FAO Production Yearbook 2002.*

United Nations Statistics Division, New York, NY 10017, (800) 253-9646, Fax: (212) 963-4116, http://unstats.un.org; *Demographic Yearbook; Human Development Report 2006; Statistical Yearbook; Survey of Economic and Social Conditions in Africa 2005;* and *World Statistics Pocketbook.*

The World Bank, 1818 H Street, NW, Washington, DC 20433, (202) 473-1000, Fax: (202) 477-6391, www.worldbank.org; *Chad; The World Bank Atlas 2003-2004;* and *World Development Report 2008.*

World Health Organization (WHO), Avenue Appia 20, 1211 Geneve 27, Switzerland, (Telephone in U.S. (212) 331-9081), www.who.int; *World Health Report 2006.*

CHAD - POPULATION DENSITY

African Development Bank Group, Rue Joseph Anoma, 01 BP 1387 Abidjan 01, Cote d'Ivoire, www.afdb.org; *Statistics Pocketbook 2008.*

Central Intelligence Agency, Office of Public Affairs, Washington, DC 20505, (703) 482-0623, Fax: (703) 482-1739, www.cia.gov; *The World Factbook.*

Euromonitor International, Inc., 224 S. Michigan Avenue, Suite 1500, Chicago, IL 60604, (312) 922-1115, Fax: (312) 922-1157, www.euromonitor.com; *International Marketing Data and Statistics 2008* and *The World Economic Factbook 2008.*

M.E. Sharpe, 80 Business Park Drive, Armonk, NY 10504, (800) 541-6563, Fax: (914) 273-2106, www.mesharpe.com; *The Illustrated Book of World Rankings.*

Palgrave Macmillan Ltd., Houndmills, Basingstoke, Hampshire, RG21 6XS, England, (Telephone in U.S. (888) 330-8477), (Fax in U.S. (800) 672-2054), www.palgrave.com; *The Statesman's Yearbook 2008.*

Taylor and Francis Group, An Informa Business, 2 Park Square, Milton Park, Abingdon, Oxford OX14 4RN, United Kingdom, (Dial from U.S. (212) 216-7800), (Fax from U.S. (212) 564-7854), www.tandf.co.uk; *The Europa World Year Book.*

UNESCO Institute for Statistics, C.P. 6128 Succursale Centre-Ville, Montreal, Quebec, H3C 3J7 Canada, (Dial from U.S. (514) 343-6880), (Fax from U.S. (514) 343 6882), www.uis.unesco.org; *Statistical Tables.*

United Nations Food and Agricultural Organization (FAO), Viale delle Terme di Caracalla, 00100 Rome, Italy, (Dial from U.S. (202) 653-2400), (Fax from U.S. (202) 653 5760), www.fao.org; *The State of Food and Agriculture (SOFA) 2006.*

United Nations Statistics Division, New York, NY 10017, (800) 253-9646, Fax: (212) 963-4116, http://unstats.un.org; *Statistical Yearbook* and *Survey of Economic and Social Conditions in Africa 2005.*

The World Bank, 1818 H Street, NW, Washington, DC 20433, (202) 473-1000, Fax: (202) 477-6391, www.worldbank.org; *Chad* and *World Development Report 2008.*

CHAD - POSTAL SERVICE

M.E. Sharpe, 80 Business Park Drive, Armonk, NY 10504, (800) 541-6563, Fax: (914) 273-2106, www.mesharpe.com; *The Illustrated Book of World Rankings.*

United Nations Statistics Division, New York, NY 10017, (800) 253-9646, Fax: (212) 963-4116, http://unstats.un.org; *Statistical Yearbook.*

CHAD - POWER RESOURCES

Euromonitor International, Inc., 224 S. Michigan Avenue, Suite 1500, Chicago, IL 60604, (312) 922-1115, Fax: (312) 922-1157, www.euromonitor.com; *International Marketing Data and Statistics 2008; The World Economic Factbook 2008;* and *World Marketing Data and Statistics.*

M.E. Sharpe, 80 Business Park Drive, Armonk, NY 10504, (800) 541-6563, Fax: (914) 273-2106, www.mesharpe.com; *The Illustrated Book of World Rankings.*

Palgrave Macmillan Ltd., Houndmills, Basingstoke, Hampshire, RG21 6XS, England, (Telephone in U.S. (888) 330-8477), (Fax in U.S. (800) 672-2054), www.palgrave.com; *The Statesman's Yearbook 2008.*

Platts, 2 Penn Plaza, 25th Floor, New York, NY 10121-2298, (212) 904-3070, www.platts.com; *Energy Economist.*

United Nations Economic Commission for Africa (ECA), PO Box 3001, Addis Ababa, Ethiopia, (Telephone in U.S. (212) 963-4957), www.uneca.org; *African Statistical Yearbook 2006.*

United Nations Food and Agricultural Organization (FAO), Viale delle Terme di Caracalla, 00100 Rome, Italy, (Dial from U.S. (202) 653-2400), (Fax from U.S. (202) 653 5760), www.fao.org; *The State of Food and Agriculture (SOFA) 2006.*

United Nations Statistics Division, New York, NY 10017, (800) 253-9646, Fax: (212) 963-4116, http://unstats.un.org; *Energy Statistics Yearbook 2003; Human Development Report 2006;* and *World Statistics Pocketbook.*

The World Bank, 1818 H Street, NW, Washington, DC 20433, (202) 473-1000, Fax: (202) 477-6391, www.worldbank.org; *The World Bank Atlas 2003-2004* and *World Development Report 2008.*

CHAD - PRICES

Euromonitor International, Inc., 224 S. Michigan Avenue, Suite 1500, Chicago, IL 60604, (312) 922-1115, Fax: (312) 922-1157, www.euromonitor.com; *World Marketing Data and Statistics.*

International Labour Office, I.L.O. Publications, 4 route des Morillons, CH-1211 Geneva 22, Switzerland, (Telephone in U.S. (202) 653-7652), (Fax in U.S. (202) 653-7687), www.ilo.org; *Yearbook of Labour Statistics 2006.*

International Monetary Fund (IMF), 700 Nineteenth Street, NW, Washington, DC 20431, (202) 623-7000, Fax: (202) 623-4661, www.imf.org; *International Financial Statistics Yearbook 2007.*

M.E. Sharpe, 80 Business Park Drive, Armonk, NY 10504, (800) 541-6563, Fax: (914) 273-2106, www.mesharpe.com; *The Illustrated Book of World Rankings.*

United Nations Economic Commission for Africa (ECA), PO Box 3001, Addis Ababa, Ethiopia, (Telephone in U.S. (212) 963-4957), www.uneca.org; *African Statistical Yearbook 2006.*

United Nations Food and Agricultural Organization (FAO), Viale delle Terme di Caracalla, 00100 Rome, Italy, (Dial from U.S. (202) 653-2400), (Fax from U.S. (202) 653 5760), www.fao.org; *FAO Production Yearbook 2002* and *The State of Food and Agriculture (SOFA) 2006.*

The World Bank, 1818 H Street, NW, Washington, DC 20433, (202) 473-1000, Fax: (202) 477-6391, www.worldbank.org; *Chad.*

CHAD - PROFESSIONS

UNESCO Institute for Statistics, C.P. 6128 Succursale Centre-Ville, Montreal, Quebec, H3C 3J7 Canada, (Dial from U.S. (514) 343-6880), (Fax from U.S. (514) 343 6882), www.uis.unesco.org; *Statistical Tables.*

United Nations Statistics Division, New York, NY 10017, (800) 253-9646, Fax: (212) 963-4116, http://unstats.un.org; *Statistical Yearbook.*

CHAD - PROPERTY TAX

International Monetary Fund (IMF), 700 Nineteenth Street, NW, Washington, DC 20431, (202) 623-7000, Fax: (202) 623-4661, www.imf.org; *Government Finance Statistics Yearbook (2008 Edition).*

CHAD - PUBLIC HEALTH

African Development Bank Group, Rue Joseph Anoma, 01 BP 1387 Abidjan 01, Cote d'Ivoire, www.afdb.org; *Statistics Pocketbook 2008.*

Euromonitor International, Inc., 224 S. Michigan Avenue, Suite 1500, Chicago, IL 60604, (312) 922-1115, Fax: (312) 922-1157, www.euromonitor.com; *World Marketing Data and Statistics.*

M.E. Sharpe, 80 Business Park Drive, Armonk, NY 10504, (800) 541-6563, Fax: (914) 273-2106, www.mesharpe.com; *The Illustrated Book of World Rankings.*

Palgrave Macmillan Ltd., Houndmills, Basingstoke, Hampshire, RG21 6XS, England, (Telephone in U.S. (888) 330-8477), (Fax in U.S. (800) 672-2054), www.palgrave.com; *The Statesman's Yearbook 2008.*

UNICEF, 3 United Nations Plaza, New York, NY 10017, (800) 253-9646, Fax: (212) 887-7465, www.unicef.org; *The State of the World's Children 2008.*

United Nations Economic Commission for Africa (ECA), PO Box 3001, Addis Ababa, Ethiopia, (Telephone in U.S. (212) 963-4957), www.uneca.org; *African Statistical Yearbook 2006.*

United Nations Statistics Division, New York, NY 10017, (800) 253-9646, Fax: (212) 963-4116, http://unstats.un.org; *Statistical Yearbook.*

The World Bank, 1818 H Street, NW, Washington, DC 20433, (202) 473-1000, Fax: (202) 477-6391, www.worldbank.org; *Chad* and *World Development Report 2008.*

World Health Organization (WHO), Avenue Appia 20, 1211 Geneve 27, Switzerland, (Telephone in U.S. (212) 331-9081), www.who.int; The WHO Global Atlas of Infectious Diseases and *World Health Report 2006.*

CHAD - RADIO BROADCASTING

Palgrave Macmillan Ltd., Houndmills, Basingstoke, Hampshire, RG21 6XS, England, (Telephone in U.S. (888) 330-8477), (Fax in U.S. (800) 672-2054), www.palgrave.com; *The Statesman's Yearbook 2008.*

CHAD - RAILROADS

United Nations Economic Commission for Africa (ECA), PO Box 3001, Addis Ababa, Ethiopia, (Telephone in U.S. (212) 963-4957), www.uneca.org; *African Statistical Yearbook 2006.*

CHAD - RELIGION

Central Intelligence Agency, Office of Public Affairs, Washington, DC 20505, (703) 482-0623, Fax: (703) 482-1739, www.cia.gov; *The World Factbook.*

M.E. Sharpe, 80 Business Park Drive, Armonk, NY 10504, (800) 541-6563, Fax: (914) 273-2106, www.mesharpe.com; *The Illustrated Book of World Rankings.*

Palgrave Macmillan Ltd., Houndmills, Basingstoke, Hampshire, RG21 6XS, England, (Telephone in U.S. (888) 330-8477), (Fax in U.S. (800) 672-2054), www.palgrave.com; *The Statesman's Yearbook 2008.*

CHAD - RESERVES (ACCOUNTING)

African Development Bank Group, Rue Joseph Anoma, 01 BP 1387 Abidjan 01, Cote d'Ivoire, www.afdb.org; *Statistics Pocketbook 2008.*

Euromonitor International, Inc., 224 S. Michigan Avenue, Suite 1500, Chicago, IL 60604, (312) 922-1115, Fax: (312) 922-1157, www.euromonitor.com; *International Marketing Data and Statistics 2008.*

The World Bank, 1818 H Street, NW, Washington, DC 20433, (202) 473-1000, Fax: (202) 477-6391, www.worldbank.org; *World Development Indicators (WDI) 2008.*

CHAD - RETAIL TRADE

Euromonitor International, Inc., 224 S. Michigan Avenue, Suite 1500, Chicago, IL 60604, (312) 922-1115, Fax: (312) 922-1157, www.euromonitor.com; *World Marketing Data and Statistics.*

CHAD - RICE PRODUCTION

See CHAD - CROPS

CHAD - ROADS

Central Intelligence Agency, Office of Public Affairs, Washington, DC 20505, (703) 482-0623, Fax: (703) 482-1739, www.cia.gov; *The World Factbook.*

International Road Federation (IFR), Madison Place, 500 Montgomery Street, 5th Floor, Alexandria, VA 22314, (703) 535-1001, Fax: (703) 535-1007, www.irfnet.org; *World Road Statistics 2006.*

Palgrave Macmillan Ltd., Houndmills, Basingstoke, Hampshire, RG21 6XS, England, (Telephone in U.S. (888) 330-8477), (Fax in U.S. (800) 672-2054), www.palgrave.com; *The Statesman's Yearbook 2008.*

United Nations Economic Commission for Africa (ECA), PO Box 3001, Addis Ababa, Ethiopia, (Telephone in U.S. (212) 963-4957), www.uneca.org; *African Statistical Yearbook 2006.*

United Nations Statistics Division, New York, NY 10017, (800) 253-9646, Fax: (212) 963-4116, http://unstats.un.org; *Survey of Economic and Social Conditions in Africa 2005.*

CHAD - RUBBER INDUSTRY AND TRADE

International Rubber Study Group (IRSG), 1st Floor, Heron House, 109/115 Wembley Hill Road, Wembley, Middlesex HA9 8DA, United Kingdom, www.rubberstudy.com; *Rubber Statistical Bulletin; Summary of World Rubber Statistics 2005; World Rubber Statistics Handbook (Volume 6, 1975-2001);* and *World Rubber Statistics Historic Handbook.*

M.E. Sharpe, 80 Business Park Drive, Armonk, NY 10504, (800) 541-6563, Fax: (914) 273-2106, www.mesharpe.com; *The Illustrated Book of World Rankings.*

CHAD - SHEEP

See CHAD - LIVESTOCK

CHAD - SHIPPING

United Nations Economic Commission for Africa (ECA), PO Box 3001, Addis Ababa, Ethiopia, (Telephone in U.S. (212) 963-4957), www.uneca.org; *African Statistical Yearbook 2006.*

CHAD - SILVER PRODUCTION

See CHAD - MINERAL INDUSTRIES

CHAD - SOCIAL ECOLOGY

M.E. Sharpe, 80 Business Park Drive, Armonk, NY 10504, (800) 541-6563, Fax: (914) 273-2106, www.mesharpe.com; *The Illustrated Book of World Rankings.*

United Nations Statistics Division, New York, NY 10017, (800) 253-9646, Fax: (212) 963-4116, http://unstats.un.org; *World Statistics Pocketbook.*

CHAD - SOCIAL SECURITY

International Monetary Fund (IMF), 700 Nineteenth Street, NW, Washington, DC 20431, (202) 623-7000, Fax: (202) 623-4661, www.imf.org; *Government Finance Statistics Yearbook (2008 Edition).*

United Nations Statistics Division, New York, NY 10017, (800) 253-9646, Fax: (212) 963-4116, http://unstats.un.org; *National Accounts Statistics: Compendium of Income Distribution Statistics.*

CHAD - STEEL PRODUCTION

See CHAD - MINERAL INDUSTRIES

CHAD - SUGAR PRODUCTION

See CHAD - CROPS

CHAD - TAXATION

International Monetary Fund (IMF), 700 Nineteenth Street, NW, Washington, DC 20431, (202) 623-7000, Fax: (202) 623-4661, www.imf.org; *Government Finance Statistics Yearbook (2008 Edition).*

International Road Federation (IFR), Madison Place, 500 Montgomery Street, 5th Floor, Alexandria, VA 22314, (703) 535-1001, Fax: (703) 535-1007, www.irfnet.org; *World Road Statistics 2006.*

Palgrave Macmillan Ltd., Houndmills, Basingstoke, Hampshire, RG21 6XS, England, (Telephone in U.S. (888) 330-8477), (Fax in U.S. (800) 672-2054), www.palgrave.com; *The Statesman's Yearbook 2008.*

Taylor and Francis Group, An Informa Business, 2 Park Square, Milton Park, Abingdon, Oxford OX14 4RN, United Kingdom, (Dial from U.S. (212) 216-7800), (Fax from U.S. (212) 564-7854), www.tandf.co.uk; *The Europa World Year Book.*

The World Bank, 1818 H Street, NW, Washington, DC 20433, (202) 473-1000, Fax: (202) 477-6391, www.worldbank.org; *World Development Indicators (WDI) 2008.*

CHAD - TELEPHONE

International Telecommunication Union (ITU), Place des Nations, 1211 Geneva 20, Switzerland, www.itu.int; World Telecommunication Indicators Database.

Palgrave Macmillan Ltd., Houndmills, Basingstoke, Hampshire, RG21 6XS, England, (Telephone in U.S. (888) 330-8477), (Fax in U.S. (800) 672-2054), www.palgrave.com; *The Statesman's Yearbook 2008.*

Taylor and Francis Group, An Informa Business, 2 Park Square, Milton Park, Abingdon, Oxford OX14 4RN, United Kingdom, (Dial from U.S. (212) 216-7800), (Fax from U.S. (212) 564-7854), www.tandf.co.uk; *The Europa World Year Book.*

United Nations Statistics Division, New York, NY 10017, (800) 253-9646, Fax: (212) 963-4116, http://unstats.un.org; *Statistical Yearbook* and *World Statistics Pocketbook.*

CHAD - TEXTILE INDUSTRY

M.E. Sharpe, 80 Business Park Drive, Armonk, NY 10504, (800) 541-6563, Fax: (914) 273-2106, www.mesharpe.com; *The Illustrated Book of World Rankings.*

United Nations Conference on Trade and Development (UNCTAD), DC2-1120, United Nations, New York, NY 10017, (212) 963-0027, www.unctad.org; *UNCTAD Commodity Yearbook.*

United Nations Statistics Division, New York, NY 10017, (800) 253-9646, Fax: (212) 963-4116, http://unstats.un.org; *Statistical Yearbook.*

CHAD - THEATER

UNESCO Institute for Statistics, C.P. 6128 Succursale Centre-Ville, Montreal, Quebec, H3C 3J7 Canada, (Dial from U.S. (514) 343-6880), (Fax from U.S. (514) 343 6882), www.uis.unesco.org; *Statistical Tables.*

CHAD - TOBACCO INDUSTRY

Foreign Agricultural Service (FAS), U.S. Department of Agriculture (USDA), 1400 Independence Avenue, SW, Washington, DC 20250, (202) 720-3935, www.fas.usda.gov; *Tobacco: World Markets and Trade.*

M.E. Sharpe, 80 Business Park Drive, Armonk, NY 10504, (800) 541-6563, Fax: (914) 273-2106, www.mesharpe.com; *The Illustrated Book of World Rankings.*

United Nations Statistics Division, New York, NY 10017, (800) 253-9646, Fax: (212) 963-4116, http://unstats.un.org; *Statistical Yearbook.*

CHAD - TOURISM

Euromonitor International, Inc., 224 S. Michigan Avenue, Suite 1500, Chicago, IL 60604, (312) 922-1115, Fax: (312) 922-1157, www.euromonitor.com; *The World Economic Factbook 2008* and *World Marketing Data and Statistics.*

M.E. Sharpe, 80 Business Park Drive, Armonk, NY 10504, (800) 541-6563, Fax: (914) 273-2106, www.mesharpe.com; *The Illustrated Book of World Rankings.*

Taylor and Francis Group, An Informa Business, 2 Park Square, Milton Park, Abingdon, Oxford OX14 4RN, United Kingdom, (Dial from U.S. (212) 216-7800), (Fax from U.S. (212) 564-7854), www.tandf.co.uk; *The Europa World Year Book.*

United Nations Economic Commission for Africa (ECA), PO Box 3001, Addis Ababa, Ethiopia, (Telephone in U.S. (212) 963-4957), www.uneca.org; *African Statistical Yearbook 2006.*

United Nations Statistics Division, New York, NY 10017, (800) 253-9646, Fax: (212) 963-4116, http://unstats.un.org; *Statistical Yearbook.*

United Nations World Tourism Organization (UNWTO), Capitan Haya 42, 28020 Madrid, Spain, www.world-tourism.org; *Yearbook of Tourism Statistics.*

The World Bank, 1818 H Street, NW, Washington, DC 20433, (202) 473-1000, Fax: (202) 477-6391, www.worldbank.org; *Chad.*

CHAD - TRADE

See CHAD - INTERNATIONAL TRADE

CHAD - TRANSPORTATION

Central Intelligence Agency, Office of Public Affairs, Washington, DC 20505, (703) 482-0623, Fax: (703) 482-1739, www.cia.gov; *The World Factbook.*

Euromonitor International, Inc., 224 S. Michigan Avenue, Suite 1500, Chicago, IL 60604, (312) 922-1115, Fax: (312) 922-1157, www.euromonitor.com; *International Marketing Data and Statistics 2008* and *World Marketing Data and Statistics.*

M.E. Sharpe, 80 Business Park Drive, Armonk, NY 10504, (800) 541-6563, Fax: (914) 273-2106, www.mesharpe.com; *The Illustrated Book of World Rankings.*

Palgrave Macmillan Ltd., Houndmills, Basingstoke, Hampshire, RG21 6XS, England, (Telephone in U.S. (888) 330-8477), (Fax in U.S. (800) 672-2054), www.palgrave.com; *The Statesman's Yearbook 2008.*

Taylor and Francis Group, An Informa Business, 2 Park Square, Milton Park, Abingdon, Oxford OX14 4RN, United Kingdom, (Dial from U.S. (212) 216-7800), (Fax from U.S. (212) 564-7854), www.tandf.co.uk; *The Europa World Year Book.*

United Nations Economic Commission for Africa (ECA), PO Box 3001, Addis Ababa, Ethiopia, (Telephone in U.S. (212) 963-4957), www.uneca.org; *African Statistical Yearbook 2006.*

United Nations Statistics Division, New York, NY 10017, (800) 253-9646, Fax: (212) 963-4116, http://unstats.un.org; *Human Development Report 2006.*

The World Bank, 1818 H Street, NW, Washington, DC 20433, (202) 473-1000, Fax: (202) 477-6391, www.worldbank.org; *Africa Live Database (LDB)* and *Chad.*

CHAD - UNEMPLOYMENT

Central Intelligence Agency, Office of Public Affairs, Washington, DC 20505, (703) 482-0623, Fax: (703) 482-1739, www.cia.gov; *The World Factbook.*

Euromonitor International, Inc., 224 S. Michigan Avenue, Suite 1500, Chicago, IL 60604, (312) 922-1115, Fax: (312) 922-1157, www.euromonitor.com; *International Marketing Data and Statistics 2008.*

International Labour Office, I.L.O. Publications, 4 route des Morillons, CH-1211 Geneva 22, Switzerland, (Telephone in U.S. (202) 653-7652), (Fax in U.S. (202) 653-7687), www.ilo.org; *Yearbook of Labour Statistics 2006.*

The World Bank, 1818 H Street, NW, Washington, DC 20433, (202) 473-1000, Fax: (202) 477-6391, www.worldbank.org; *Chad.*

CHAD - VITAL STATISTICS

Euromonitor International, Inc., 224 S. Michigan Avenue, Suite 1500, Chicago, IL 60604, (312) 922-1115, Fax: (312) 922-1157, www.euromonitor.com; *International Marketing Data and Statistics 2008.*

United Nations Statistics Division, New York, NY 10017, (800) 253-9646, Fax: (212) 963-4116, http://unstats.un.org; *Statistical Yearbook.*

World Health Organization (WHO), Avenue Appia 20, 1211 Geneve 27, Switzerland, (Telephone in U.S. (212) 331-9081), www.who.int; *World Health Report 2006.*

CHAD - WAGES

International Labour Office, I.L.O. Publications, 4 route des Morillons, CH-1211 Geneva 22, Switzerland, (Telephone in U.S. (202) 653-7652), (Fax in U.S. (202) 653-7687), www.ilo.org; *Yearbook of Labour Statistics 2006.*

The World Bank, 1818 H Street, NW, Washington, DC 20433, (202) 473-1000, Fax: (202) 477-6391, www.worldbank.org; *Chad.*

CHAD - WEATHER

See CHAD - CLIMATE

CHAD - WELFARE STATE

International Monetary Fund (IMF), 700 Nineteenth Street, NW, Washington, DC 20431, (202) 623-7000, Fax: (202) 623-4661, www.imf.org; *Government Finance Statistics Yearbook (2008 Edition).*

CHAD - WHEAT PRODUCTION

See CHAD - CROPS

CHAD - WINE PRODUCTION

See CHAD - BEVERAGE INDUSTRY

CHAD - WOOL PRODUCTION

See CHAD - TEXTILE INDUSTRY

CHAMBERS OF COMMERCE

Thomson Gale, 27500 Drake Road, Farmington Hills, MI 48331, (248) 699-4253, www.galegroup.com; *Encyclopedia of Associations.*

CHARITABLE CONTRIBUTIONS

See also PHILANTHROPY

The Foundation Center, 79 Fifth Avenue, New York, NY 10003-3076, (212) 620-4230, Fax: (212) 807-3677, www.fdncenter.org; *FC Stats - Grantmaker; FC Stats - Grants;* and *Top Funders: Top 100 U.S. Foundations by Asset Size.*

The Giving Institute, 4700 W. Lake Ave, Glenview, IL 60025, (800) 462-2372, Fax: (866) 607-0913, www.aafrc.org; *Giving USA 2006.*

Hartford Institute for Religion Research, Hartford Seminary, 77 Sherman Street, Hartford, CT 06105-2260, (860) 509-9543, Fax: (860) 509-9551, http://hirr.hartsem.edu; *Faith Based Social Services/Charitable Choice.*

Independent Sector, 1200 Eighteenth Street, NW, Suite 200, Washington, DC 20036, (202) 467-6100, Fax: (202) 467-6101, www.independentsector.org; *Giving and Volunteering in the United States 2001.*

U.S. Department of the Treasury (DOT), Internal Revenue Service (IRS), Statistics of Income Division (SIS), PO Box 2608, Washington, DC, 20013-2608, (202) 874-0410, Fax: (202) 874-0964, www.irs.ustreas.gov; *Statistics of Income Bulletin* and *Statistics of Income Bulletin, Individual Income Tax Returns.*

The Wallace Foundation, 5 Penn Plaza, 7th Floor, New York, NY 10001, (212) 251-9700, www.wallacefoundation.org; *Knowledge Center.*

CHARTER SCHOOLS

US Charter Schools, www.uscharterschools.org; *Charter Achievement Among Low-Income Students; State of the Charter School Movement 2005: Trends, Issues, and Indicators;* and *A Straightforward Comparison of Charter Schools and Regular Public Schools in the United States.*

U.S. Department of Education (ED), Office of Innovation and Improvement (OII), 400 Maryland Avenue, SW, Washington, DC 20202, (202) 205-4500, www.ed.gov/oii; *Evaluation of the Public Charter Schools Program (PCSP)* and *Public Charter Schools Program.*

CHECKING ACCOUNTS

Board of Governors of the Federal Reserve System, Constitution Avenue, NW, Washington, DC 20551, (202) 452-3000, www.federalreserve.gov; *Annual Report to the Congress on Retail Fees and Services of Depository Institutions; Federal Reserve Bulletin;* and unpublished data.

Center for Nutrition Policy and Promotion (CNPP), U.S. Department of Agriculture (USDA), 3101 Park Center Drive, 10th Floor, Alexandria, VA 22302-1594, (703) 305-7600, Fax: (703) 305-3300, www.usda.gov/cnpp; *Nutrient Content of the U.S. Food Supply Summary Report 2005.*

The Nilson Report, 1110 Eugenia Place, Suite 100, Carpinteria, CA 93013-9921, (805) 684-8800, Fax: (805) 684-8825, www.nilsonreport.com; *The Nilson Report.*

CHEESE

See also DAIRY PRODUCTS

Economic Research Service (ERS), U.S. Department of Agriculture (USDA), 1800 M Street, NW, Washington, DC 20036-5831, (202) 694-5050, Fax: (202) 694-5689, www.ers.usda.gov; *Agricultural Outlook* and *Food CPI, Prices, and Expenditures.*

Foreign Agricultural Service (FAS), U.S. Department of Agriculture (USDA), 1400 Independence Avenue, SW, Washington, DC 20250, (202) 720-3935, www.fas.usda.gov; Production, Supply and Distribution Online (PSD) Online.

National Agricultural Statistics Service (NASS), U.S. Department of Agriculture (USDA), 1400 Independence Avenue, SW, Washington, DC 20250, (800) 727-9540, Fax: (202) 690-2090, www.nass.usda.gov; *Dairy Products* and *Milk Cows and Milk Production.*

U.S. Bureau of Labor Statistics (BLS), Postal Square Building, 2 Massachusetts Avenue, NE, Washington, DC 20212-0001, (202) 691-5200, Fax: (202) 691-6325, www.bls.gov; *Consumer Price Index Detailed Report* and *Monthly Labor Review (MLR).*

CHEFS

American Personal Chef Association, 4572 Delaware Street, San Diego, CA 92116, (800) 644-8389, www.personalchef.com; unpublished data.

CHEMICAL PRODUCTS

Health Protection Agency, 7th Floor, Holborn Gate, 330 High Holborn, London WC1V 7PP, United Kingdom, www.hpa.org.uk; *Chemical Incidents in England and Wales 2005.*

U.S. Census Bureau, Foreign Trade Division, 4700 Silver Hill Road, Washington DC 20233-0001, (301) 763-3030, www.census.gov/foreign-trade/www/; *U.S. International Trade in Goods and Services.*

CHEMICAL PRODUCTS - PRODUCER PRICE INDEXES

U.S. Bureau of Labor Statistics (BLS), Postal Square Building, 2 Massachusetts Avenue, NE, Washington, DC 20212-0001, (202) 691-5200, Fax: (202) 691-6325, www.bls.gov; *Consumer Price Index Detailed Report* and *Monthly Labor Review (MLR).*

CHEMICAL PRODUCTS - PRODUCTION

U.S. Census Bureau, Manufacturing and Construction Division, 4600 Silver Hill Road, Washington DC 20233, (301) 763-4673, www.census.gov/mcd; *Current Industrial Reports.*

CHEMICAL PRODUCTS - TOXIC CHEMICAL RELEASES

International Tanker Owners Pollution Federation (ITOPF), ITOPF Ltd, 1 Oliver's Yard, 55 City Road, London, EC1Y 1HQ, United Kingdom, www.itopf.com; *ITOPF Handbook.*

U.S. Environmental Protection Agency (EPA), Ariel Rios Building, 1200 Pennsylvania Avenue, NW, Washington, DC 20460, (202) 272-0167, www.epa.gov; Toxics Release Inventory (TRI) Database.

CHEMICALS MANUFACTURING - EARNINGS

U.S. Bureau of Labor Statistics (BLS), Postal Square Building, 2 Massachusetts Avenue, NE, Washington, DC 20212-0001, (202) 691-5200, Fax: (202) 691-6325, www.bls.gov; *Current Employment Statistics Survey (CES)* and *Employment and Earnings (EE).*

U.S. Census Bureau, Company Statistics Division, 4700 Silver Hill Road, Washington DC 20233-0001, (301) 763-3030, www.census.gov/csd/; *County Business Patterns 2004.*

U.S. Census Bureau, Manufacturing and Construction Division, 4600 Silver Hill Road, Washington DC 20233, (301) 763-4673, www.census.gov/mcd; *Annual Survey of Manufactures, Statistics for Industry Groups and Industries.*

CHEMICALS MANUFACTURING - ELECTRONIC COMMERCE

U.S. Census Bureau, 4700 Silver Hill Road, Washington DC 20233-0001, (301) 763-3030, www.census.gov; *E-Stats - Measuring the Electronic Economy.*

CHEMICALS MANUFACTURING - EMPLOYEES

Bureau of Economic Analysis (BEA), U.S. Department of Commerce (DOC), 1441 L Street NW, Washington, DC 20230, (202) 606-9900, www.bea.gov; *Survey of Current Business (SCB).*

U.S. Bureau of Labor Statistics (BLS), Postal Square Building, 2 Massachusetts Avenue, NE, Washington, DC 20212-0001, (202) 691-5200, Fax: (202) 691-6325, www.bls.gov; *Current Employment Statistics Survey (CES)* and *Employment and Earnings (EE).*

U.S. Census Bureau, Company Statistics Division, 4700 Silver Hill Road, Washington DC 20233-0001, (301) 763-3030, www.census.gov/csd/; *County Business Patterns 2004.*

U.S. Census Bureau, Manufacturing and Construction Division, 4600 Silver Hill Road, Washington DC 20233, (301) 763-4673, www.census.gov/mcd; *Annual Survey of Manufactures, Statistics for Industry Groups and Industries.*

CHEMICALS MANUFACTURING - ENERGY CONSUMPTION

U.S. Department of Energy (DOE), Energy Information Administration (EIA), 1000 Independence Avenue, SW, Washington, DC 20585, (202) 586-8800, www.eia.doe.gov; *Manufacturing Energy Consumption Survey (MECS) 2002.*

CHEMICALS MANUFACTURING - GROSS DOMESTIC PRODUCT

Bureau of Economic Analysis (BEA), U.S. Department of Commerce (DOC), 1441 L Street NW,

Washington, DC 20230, (202) 606-9900, www.bea.gov; *Survey of Current Business (SCB).*

CHEMICALS MANUFACTURING - INDUSTRIAL SAFETY

Health Protection Agency, 7th Floor, Holborn Gate, 330 High Holborn, London WC1V 7PP, United Kingdom, www.hpa.org.uk; *Chemical Incidents in England and Wales 2005.*

U.S. Bureau of Labor Statistics (BLS), Postal Square Building, 2 Massachusetts Avenue, NE, Washington, DC 20212-0001, (202) 691-5200, Fax: (202) 691-6325, www.bls.gov; *Injuries, Illnesses, and Fatalities (IIF).*

CHEMICALS MANUFACTURING - INTERNATIONAL TRADE

Bureau of Statistics, Directorate-General of Budget, Accounting and Statistics, Executive Yuan, Republic of China, Number 1, Section 1, Jhongsiao East Road, Taipei City 100, Taiwan (R.O.C.), http://eng.dgbas.gov.tw/mp.asp?mp=2; *Statistical Yearbook of the Republic of China.*

International Trade Administration (ITA), U.S. Department of Commerce (DOC), 1401 Constitution Avenue, NW, Washington, DC 20230, (800) USA-TRAD(E), Fax: (202) 482-4473, www.ita.doc.gov; unpublished data.

U.S. Census Bureau, 4700 Silver Hill Road, Washington DC 20233-0001, (301) 763-3030, www.census.gov; unpublished data.

U.S. Census Bureau, Foreign Trade Division, 4700 Silver Hill Road, Washington DC 20233-0001, (301) 763-3030, www.census.gov/foreign-trade/www/; *U.S. International Trade in Goods and Services.*

CHEMICALS MANUFACTURING - INVENTORIES

U.S. Census Bureau, Manufacturing and Construction Division, 4600 Silver Hill Road, Washington DC 20233, (301) 763-4673, www.census.gov/mcd; *Current Industrial Reports* and *Manufacturers Shipments, Inventories and Orders.*

CHEMICALS MANUFACTURING - MERGERS AND ACQUISITIONS

Thomson Financial, 195 Broadway, New York, NY 10007, (646) 822-2000, www.thomson.com; Thomson Research.

CHEMICALS MANUFACTURING - MULTINATIONAL COMPANIES

Bureau of Economic Analysis (BEA), U.S. Department of Commerce (DOC), 1441 L Street NW, Washington, DC 20230, (202) 606-9900, www.bea.gov; *Survey of Current Business (SCB).*

CHEMICALS MANUFACTURING - PATENTS

U.S. Patent and Trademark Office (USPTO), PO Box 1450, Alexandria, VA 22313-1450, (571) 272-1000, www.uspto.gov; *Patenting Trends Calendar Year 2003.*

CHEMICALS MANUFACTURING - PRODUCTIVITY

U.S. Bureau of Labor Statistics (BLS), Postal Square Building, 2 Massachusetts Avenue, NE, Washington, DC 20212-0001, (202) 691-5200, Fax: (202) 691-6325, www.bls.gov; *Industry Productivity and Costs.*

CHEMICALS MANUFACTURING - PROFITS

Bureau of Economic Analysis (BEA), U.S. Department of Commerce (DOC), 1441 L Street NW, Washington, DC 20230, (202) 606-9900, www.bea.gov; *2007 Annual Revision of the National Income and Product Accounts (NIPA)* and *Survey of Current Business (SCB).*

U.S. Census Bureau, Manufacturing and Construction Division, 4600 Silver Hill Road, Washington DC 20233, (301) 763-4673, www.census.gov/mcd; *Quarterly Financial Report for Manufacturing, Mining and Trade Corporations.*

CHEMICALS MANUFACTURING - RESEARCH AND DEVELOPMENT

National Science Foundation, Division of Science Resources Statistics (SRS), 4201 Wilson Boulevard, Arlington, VA 22230, (703) 292-8780, Fax: (703) 292-9092, www.nsf.gov; *Research and Development in Industry: 2003.*

CHEMICALS MANUFACTURING - SHIPMENTS

Association of American Railroads (AAR), 50 F Street, NW, Washington, DC 20001-1564, (202) 639-2100, www.aar.org; *Rail Transportation of Chemicals.*

International Tanker Owners Pollution Federation (ITOPF), ITOPF Ltd, 1 Oliver's Yard, 55 City Road, London, EC1Y 1HQ, United Kingdom, www.itopf.com; *ITOPF Handbook.*

U.S. Census Bureau, Manufacturing and Construction Division, 4600 Silver Hill Road, Washington DC 20233, (301) 763-4673, www.census.gov/mcd; *Manufacturers Shipments, Inventories and Orders.*

CHEMICALS MANUFACTURING - TOXIC CHEMICAL RELEASES

Health Protection Agency, 7th Floor, Holborn Gate, 330 High Holborn, London WC1V 7PP, United Kingdom, www.hpa.org.uk; *Chemical Incidents in England and Wales 2005.*

U.S. Environmental Protection Agency (EPA), Ariel Rios Building, 1200 Pennsylvania Avenue, NW, Washington, DC 20460, (202) 272-0167, www.epa.gov; Toxics Release Inventory (TRI) Database.

CHEMISTRY

See also PHYSICAL SCIENCES

CHEMISTRY - EMPLOYMENT

U.S. Bureau of Labor Statistics (BLS), Postal Square Building, 2 Massachusetts Avenue, NE, Washington, DC 20212-0001, (202) 691-5200, Fax: (202) 691-6325, www.bls.gov; *Employment and Earnings (EE)* and unpublished data.

CHEMISTRY - NOBEL PRIZE LAUREATES

National Science Foundation, Division of Science Resources Statistics (SRS), 4201 Wilson Boulevard, Arlington, VA 22230, (703) 292-8780, Fax: (703) 292-9092, www.nsf.gov; unpublished data.

CHEMISTRY - SALARY OFFERS

National Association of Colleges and Employers (NACE), 62 Highland Avenue, Bethlehem, PA 18017, (800) 544-5272, Fax: (610) 868-0208, www.naceweb.org; *Salary Survey.*

CHERRIES

National Agricultural Statistics Service (NASS), U.S. Department of Agriculture (USDA), 1400 Independence Avenue, SW, Washington, DC 20250, (800) 727-9540, Fax: (202) 690-2090, www.nass.usda.gov; *Noncitrus Fruits and Nuts: Final Estimates 1998-2003.*

CHESS

Unites States Chess Federation (USCF), PO Box 3967, Crossville, TN 38557, (931) 787-1234, Fax: (931) 787-1200, www.uschess.org; *Chess and Cognitive Development* and unpublished data.

CHICKEN POX

Centers for Disease Control and Prevention (CDC), U.S. Department of Health and Human Services (HHS), 1600 Clifton Road, Atlanta, GA 30333, (800) 311-3435, www.cdc.gov; *Morbidity and Mortality Weekly Report (MMWR)* and *Summary of Notifiable Diseases, United States, 2006.*

CHICKENS

See LIVESTOCK AND LIVESTOCK PRODUCTS

CHILD ABUSE

Administration for Children and Families (ACF), U.S. Department of Health and Human Services (HHS), 370 L'Enfant Promenade, SW, Washington, DC 20447, (202) 401-2337, www.acf.hhs.gov; *Child Maltreatment 2006.*

Child Welfare Information Gateway, Children's Bureau/ACYF, 1250 Maryland Avenue, SW, Eighth Floor, Washington, DC 20024, (800) 394-3366, Fax: (703) 385-3206, www.childwelfare.gov; *Alternative Responses to Child Maltreatment: Findings from NCANDS.*

Inter-American Commission of Women (CIM), Organization of American States (OAS), 17th Street and Constitution Avenue, NW, Washington, D.C. 20006, (202) 458-3000, www.oas.org/CIM/english/About.htm; *Trafficking in Women and Children: Research Findings and Follow-Up.*

National Center for Juvenile Justice (NCJJ), 3700 South Water Street, Suite 200, Pittsburgh, PA 15203, (412) 227-6950, Fax: (412) 227-6955, http://ncjj.servehttp.com/NCJJWebsite/main.htm; *Jury Trial in Abuse, Neglect, Dependency Cases.*

U.S. Department of Justice (DOJ), Bureau of Justice Statistics, 810 Seventh Street, NW, Washington, DC 20531, (202) 307-0765, www.ojp.usdoj.gov/bjs/; *Family Violence Statistics: Including Statistics on Strangers and Acquaintances* and *Federal Criminal Case Processing, 2002: With trends 1982-2002, Reconciled Data.*

CHILD CARE

The Children's Foundation, 725 Fifteenth Street, NW, Suite 505, Washington, DC 20005-2109, (202) 347-3300, Fax: (202) 347-3382; *2005 Child Care Center Licensing Study* and *The National Directory of Family Child Care Associations, Support Groups and Support Agencies.*

National Center for Children in Poverty (NCCP), 215 W. 125th Street, 3rd Floor, New York, NY 10027, (646) 284-9600, Fax: (646) 284-9623, www.nccp.org; *Research-to-Policy Connections.*

National Center for Education Statistics (NCES), 1990 K Street, NW, Washington, DC 20006, (202) 502-7300, http://nces.ed.gov; *Digest of Education Statistics 2007.*

U.S. Bureau of Labor Statistics (BLS), Postal Square Building, 2 Massachusetts Avenue, NE, Washington, DC 20212-0001, (202) 691-5200, Fax: (202) 691-6325, www.bls.gov; *Consumer Price Index Detailed Report* and *Monthly Labor Review (MLR).*

U.S. Census Bureau, Housing and Household Economics Statistics Division, 4700 Silver Hill Road, Washington DC 20233-0001, (301) 763-3030, www.census.gov/hhes/www; *2006 American Community Survey (ACS)* and *American Housing Survey (AHS).*

CHILD CARE - EXPENDITURES FOR

Center for Nutrition Policy and Promotion (CNPP), U.S. Department of Agriculture (USDA), 3101 Park Center Drive, 10th Floor, Alexandria, VA 22302-1594, (703) 305-7600, Fax: (703) 305-3300, www.usda.gov/cnpp; *Expenditures on Children by Families: 2007 Annual Reportaa.*

National Center for Children in Poverty (NCCP), 215 W. 125th Street, 3rd Floor, New York, NY 10027, (646) 284-9600, Fax: (646) 284-9623, www.nccp.org; *Parent Employment and the Use of Child Care Subsidies* and *Predictors of Child Care Subsidy Use.*

CHILD DAY CARE SERVICES

U.S. Census Bureau, 4700 Silver Hill Road, Washington DC 20233-0001, (301) 763-3030, www.census.gov; *2002 Economic Census, Nonemployer Statistics.*

U.S. Census Bureau, Service Sector Statistics Division, 4700 Silver Hill Road, Washington DC 20233-

0001, (301) 763-3030, www.census.gov/svsd/www/economic.html; *2004 Service Annual Survey: Health Care and Social Assistance.*

CHILD DAY CARE SERVICES - EARNINGS

U.S. Census Bureau, 4700 Silver Hill Road, Washington DC 20233-0001, (301) 763-3030, www.census.gov; *2002 Economic Census, Nonemployer Statistics.*

U.S. Census Bureau, Service Sector Statistics Division, 4700 Silver Hill Road, Washington DC 20233-0001, (301) 763-3030, www.census.gov/svsd/www/economic.html; *2004 Service Annual Survey: Health Care and Social Assistance.*

CHILD DAY CARE SERVICES - EMPLOYEES

U.S. Bureau of Labor Statistics (BLS), Postal Square Building, 2 Massachusetts Avenue, NE, Washington, DC 20212-0001, (202) 691-5200, Fax: (202) 691-6325, www.bls.gov; *Monthly Labor Review (MLR).*

U.S. Census Bureau, 4700 Silver Hill Road, Washington DC 20233-0001, (301) 763-3030, www.census.gov; *2002 Economic Census, Nonemployer Statistics.*

U.S. Census Bureau, Service Sector Statistics Division, 4700 Silver Hill Road, Washington DC 20233-0001, (301) 763-3030, www.census.gov/svsd/www/economic.html; *2004 Service Annual Survey: Health Care and Social Assistance.*

CHILD DAY CARE SERVICES - FINANCES

U.S. Census Bureau, 4700 Silver Hill Road, Washington DC 20233-0001, (301) 763-3030, www.census.gov; *2002 Economic Census, Nonemployer Statistics.*

U.S. Census Bureau, Service Sector Statistics Division, 4700 Silver Hill Road, Washington DC 20233-0001, (301) 763-3030, www.census.gov/svsd/www/economic.html; *2004 Service Annual Survey: Health Care and Social Assistance.*

CHILD LABOR

National Institute of Statistics (NIS), Ministry of Planning, Preah Monivong Boulevard, Sankat Boeung Keng Kang 1, Phnom Penh, Cambodia, www.nis.gov.kh; *Cambodia Child Labor Survey 2001* and *Child Domestic Worker Survey Phnom Penh 2003.*

U.S. Department of Labor (DOL), Bureau of International Labor Affairs (ILAB), Frances Perkins Building, Room C-4325, 200 Constitution Avenue, NW, Washington, DC 20210, (202) 693-4770, Fax: (202) 693-4780, www.dol.gov/ilab; *The Department of Labor's 2005 Findings on the Worst Forms of Child Labor.*

CHILD SUPPORT

Administration for Children and Families (ACF), Office of Child Support Enforcement (OCSE), U.S. Department of Health and Human Services (HHS), 4th Floor, Aerospace Building, 370 L'Enfant Promenade, SW, Washington, DC 20201, (202) 401-9373, www.acf.dhhs.gov/programs/cse; *Child Support Enforcement FY 2007 Preliminary Data Report.*

U.S. Census Bureau, 4700 Silver Hill Road, Washington DC 20233-0001, (301) 763-3030, www.census.gov; unpublished data.

U.S. Census Bureau, Population Division, 4700 Silver Hill Road, Washington DC 20233-0001, (301) 763-3030, www.census.gov/population/www/; *Current Population Reports.*

CHILDBIRTH

Alan Guttmacher Institute, 125 Maiden Lane, 7th Floor, New York, NY 10038, (212) 248-1111, Fax: (212) 248-1951, www.agi-usa.org; *U.S. Teenage Pregnancy Statistics: Overall Trends, Trends by Race and Ethnicity and State-by-State Information* and *U.S. Teenage Pregnancy Statistics: Overall Trends, Trends by Race and Ethnicity and State-by-State Information.*

Bernan Essential Government Publications, 4611-F Assembly Drive, Lanham MD, 20706-4391, (301) 459-2255, Fax: (800) 865-3450, www.bernan.com; *Vital Statistics of the United States: Births, Life Expectancy, Deaths, and Selected Health Data.*

National Center for Chronic Disease Prevention and Health Promotion (NCCDPHP), Centers for Disease Control and Prevention (CDC), 4770 Buford Hwy, NE, MS K-40, Atlanta, GA 30341-3717, (404) 639-3311, www.cdc.gov/nccdphp; *2005 Assisted Reproductive Technology Success Rates.*

National Center for Health Statistics (NCHS), Centers for Disease Control and Prevention (CDC), U.S. Department of Health and Human Services (HHS), 3311 Toledo Road, Hyattsville, MD 20782, (866) 232-4636, www.cdc.gov/nchs; *Faststats A to Z; National Vital Statistics Reports (NVSR); Vital Statistics of the United States (VSUS);* and unpublished data.

Population Reference Bureau, 1875 Connecticut Avenue, NW, Suite 520, Washington, DC, 20009-5728, (800) 877-9881, Fax: (202) 328-3937, www.prb.org; *Family Planning Worldwide.*

U.S. Census Bureau, Population Division, 4700 Silver Hill Road, Washington DC 20233-0001, (301) 763-3030, www.census.gov/population/www/; *Current Population Reports.*

CHILDBIRTH - AMERICAN INDIAN, ESKIMO, AND ALEUT POPULATION

Bernan Essential Government Publications, 4611-F Assembly Drive, Lanham MD, 20706-4391, (301) 459-2255, Fax: (800) 865-3450, www.bernan.com; *Vital Statistics of the United States: Births, Life Expectancy, Deaths, and Selected Health Data.*

National Center for Health Statistics (NCHS), Centers for Disease Control and Prevention (CDC), U.S. Department of Health and Human Services (HHS), 3311 Toledo Road, Hyattsville, MD 20782, (866) 232-4636, www.cdc.gov/nchs; *National Vital Statistics Reports (NVSR); Vital Statistics of the United States (VSUS);* and unpublished data.

CHILDBIRTH - ASIAN AND PACIFIC ISLANDER POPULATION

Bernan Essential Government Publications, 4611-F Assembly Drive, Lanham MD, 20706-4391, (301) 459-2255, Fax: (800) 865-3450, www.bernan.com; *Vital Statistics of the United States: Births, Life Expectancy, Deaths, and Selected Health Data.*

National Center for Health Statistics (NCHS), Centers for Disease Control and Prevention (CDC), U.S. Department of Health and Human Services (HHS), 3311 Toledo Road, Hyattsville, MD 20782, (866) 232-4636, www.cdc.gov/nchs; *National Vital Statistics Reports (NVSR); Vital Statistics of the United States (VSUS);* and unpublished data.

CHILDBIRTH - BIRTH WEIGHT

Bernan Essential Government Publications, 4611-F Assembly Drive, Lanham MD, 20706-4391, (301) 459-2255, Fax: (800) 865-3450, www.bernan.com; *Vital Statistics of the United States: Births, Life Expectancy, Deaths, and Selected Health Data.*

National Center for Health Statistics (NCHS), Centers for Disease Control and Prevention (CDC), U.S. Department of Health and Human Services (HHS), 3311 Toledo Road, Hyattsville, MD 20782, (866) 232-4636, www.cdc.gov/nchs; *National Vital Statistics Reports (NVSR); Vital Statistics of the United States (VSUS);* and unpublished data.

CHILDBIRTH - BIRTHS TO MOTHERS WHO SMOKED

Bernan Essential Government Publications, 4611-F Assembly Drive, Lanham MD, 20706-4391, (301) 459-2255, Fax: (800) 865-3450, www.bernan.com; *Vital Statistics of the United States: Births, Life Expectancy, Deaths, and Selected Health Data.*

National Center for Health Statistics (NCHS), Centers for Disease Control and Prevention (CDC), U.S. Department of Health and Human Services (HHS), 3311 Toledo Road, Hyattsville, MD 20782, (866) 232-4636, www.cdc.gov/nchs; *National Vital Statistics Reports (NVSR).*

CHILDBIRTH - BIRTHS TO SINGLE OR UNMARRIED WOMEN

Alan Guttmacher Institute, 125 Maiden Lane, 7th Floor, New York, NY 10038, (212) 248-1111, Fax: (212) 248-1951, www.agi-usa.org; *U.S. Teenage Pregnancy Statistics: Overall Trends, Trends by Race and Ethnicity and State-by-State Information* and *U.S. Teenage Pregnancy Statistics: Overall Trends, Trends by Race and Ethnicity and State-by-State Information.*

Bernan Essential Government Publications, 4611-F Assembly Drive, Lanham MD, 20706-4391, (301) 459-2255, Fax: (800) 865-3450, www.bernan.com; *Vital Statistics of the United States: Births, Life Expectancy, Deaths, and Selected Health Data.*

National Center for Health Statistics (NCHS), Centers for Disease Control and Prevention (CDC), U.S. Department of Health and Human Services (HHS), 3311 Toledo Road, Hyattsville, MD 20782, (866) 232-4636, www.cdc.gov/nchs; *National Vital Statistics Reports (NVSR); Vital Statistics of the United States (VSUS);* and unpublished data.

U.S. Census Bureau, Population Division, 4700 Silver Hill Road, Washington DC 20233-0001, (301) 763-3030, www.census.gov/population/www/; *Current Population Reports.*

CHILDBIRTH - BIRTHS TO TEENAGE MOTHERS

Alan Guttmacher Institute, 125 Maiden Lane, 7th Floor, New York, NY 10038, (212) 248-1111, Fax: (212) 248-1951, www.agi-usa.org; *State-by-State Teenage Pregnancy Statistics* (2004, special report); *U.S. Teenage Pregnancy Statistics: Overall Trends, Trends by Race and Ethnicity and State-by-State Information;* and *U.S. Teenage Pregnancy Statistics: Overall Trends, Trends by Race and Ethnicity and State-by-State Information.*

Bernan Essential Government Publications, 4611-F Assembly Drive, Lanham MD, 20706-4391, (301) 459-2255, Fax: (800) 865-3450, www.bernan.com; *Vital Statistics of the United States: Births, Life Expectancy, Deaths, and Selected Health Data.*

National Center for Health Statistics (NCHS), Centers for Disease Control and Prevention (CDC), U.S. Department of Health and Human Services (HHS), 3311 Toledo Road, Hyattsville, MD 20782, (866) 232-4636, www.cdc.gov/nchs; *National Vital Statistics Reports (NVSR); Vital Statistics of the United States (VSUS);* and unpublished data.

CHILDBIRTH - BLACK POPULATION

Alan Guttmacher Institute, 125 Maiden Lane, 7th Floor, New York, NY 10038, (212) 248-1111, Fax: (212) 248-1951, www.agi-usa.org; *U.S. Teenage Pregnancy Statistics: Overall Trends, Trends by Race and Ethnicity and State-by-State Information* and *U.S. Teenage Pregnancy Statistics: Overall Trends, Trends by Race and Ethnicity and State-by-State Information.*

Bernan Essential Government Publications, 4611-F Assembly Drive, Lanham MD, 20706-4391, (301) 459-2255, Fax: (800) 865-3450, www.bernan.com; *Vital Statistics of the United States: Births, Life Expectancy, Deaths, and Selected Health Data.*

National Center for Health Statistics (NCHS), Centers for Disease Control and Prevention (CDC), U.S. Department of Health and Human Services (HHS), 3311 Toledo Road, Hyattsville, MD 20782, (866) 232-4636, www.cdc.gov/nchs; *National Vital Statistics Reports (NVSR); Vital Statistics of the United States (VSUS);* and unpublished data.

U.S. Census Bureau, 4700 Silver Hill Road, Washington DC 20233-0001, (301) 763-3030, www.census.gov; unpublished data.

U.S. Census Bureau, Population Division, 4700 Silver Hill Road, Washington DC 20233-0001, (301) 763-3030, www.census.gov/population/www/; *Current Population Reports.*

CHILDBIRTH - CESAREAN SECTION DELIVERIES

National Center for Health Statistics (NCHS), Centers for Disease Control and Prevention (CDC), U.S. Department of Health and Human Services (HHS), 3311 Toledo Road, Hyattsville, MD 20782, (866) 232-4636, www.cdc.gov/nchs; unpublished data.

CHILDBIRTH - CHARACTERISTICS OF MOTHER

Alan Guttmacher Institute, 125 Maiden Lane, 7th Floor, New York, NY 10038, (212) 248-1111, Fax: (212) 248-1951, www.agi-usa.org; *U.S. Teenage Pregnancy Statistics: Overall Trends, Trends by Race and Ethnicity and State-by-State Information* and *U.S. Teenage Pregnancy Statistics: Overall Trends, Trends by Race and Ethnicity and State-by-State Information.*

Bernan Essential Government Publications, 4611-F Assembly Drive, Lanham MD, 20706-4391, (301) 459-2255, Fax: (800) 865-3450, www.bernan.com; *Vital Statistics of the United States: Births, Life Expectancy, Deaths, and Selected Health Data.*

National Center for Health Statistics (NCHS), Centers for Disease Control and Prevention (CDC), U.S. Department of Health and Human Services (HHS), 3311 Toledo Road, Hyattsville, MD 20782, (866) 232-4636, www.cdc.gov/nchs; *National Vital Statistics Reports (NVSR); Vital Statistics of the United States (VSUS);* and unpublished data.

CHILDBIRTH - DELIVERY PROCEDURES

National Center for Health Statistics (NCHS), Centers for Disease Control and Prevention (CDC), U.S. Department of Health and Human Services (HHS), 3311 Toledo Road, Hyattsville, MD 20782, (866) 232-4636, www.cdc.gov/nchs; unpublished data.

CHILDBIRTH - EDUCATIONAL ATTAINMENT OF MOTHER

Alan Guttmacher Institute, 125 Maiden Lane, 7th Floor, New York, NY 10038, (212) 248-1111, Fax: (212) 248-1951, www.agi-usa.org; *U.S. Teenage Pregnancy Statistics: Overall Trends, Trends by Race and Ethnicity and State-by-State Information* and *U.S. Teenage Pregnancy Statistics: Overall Trends, Trends by Race and Ethnicity and State-by-State Information.*

Bernan Essential Government Publications, 4611-F Assembly Drive, Lanham MD, 20706-4391, (301) 459-2255, Fax: (800) 865-3450, www.bernan.com; *Vital Statistics of the United States: Births, Life Expectancy, Deaths, and Selected Health Data.*

National Center for Health Statistics (NCHS), Centers for Disease Control and Prevention (CDC), U.S. Department of Health and Human Services (HHS), 3311 Toledo Road, Hyattsville, MD 20782, (866) 232-4636, www.cdc.gov/nchs; *National Vital Statistics Reports (NVSR).*

CHILDBIRTH - FIRST BIRTHS

U.S. Census Bureau, 4700 Silver Hill Road, Washington DC 20233-0001, (301) 763-3030, www.census.gov; unpublished data.

U.S. Census Bureau, Population Division, 4700 Silver Hill Road, Washington DC 20233-0001, (301) 763-3030, www.census.gov/population/www/; *Current Population Reports.*

CHILDBIRTH - FOREIGN COUNTRIES

Population Reference Bureau, 1875 Connecticut Avenue, NW, Suite 520, Washington, DC, 20009-5728, (800) 877-9881, Fax: (202) 328-3937, www.prb.org; *Family Planning Worldwide.*

RAND Corporation, 1776 Main Street, PO Box 2138, Santa Monica, CA 90407-2138, (310) 393-0411, www.rand.org; *The Provision of Neonatal Services: Data for International Comparisons.*

U.S. Census Bureau, Population Division, 4700 Silver Hill Road, Washington DC 20233-0001, (301) 763-3030, www.census.gov/population/www/; International Data Base (IDB).

CHILDBIRTH - HISPANIC POPULATION

Alan Guttmacher Institute, 125 Maiden Lane, 7th Floor, New York, NY 10038, (212) 248-1111, Fax: (212) 248-1951, www.agi-usa.org; *U.S. Teenage Pregnancy Statistics: Overall Trends, Trends by Race and Ethnicity and State-by-State Information* and *U.S. Teenage Pregnancy Statistics: Overall Trends, Trends by Race and Ethnicity and State-by-State Information.*

Bernan Essential Government Publications, 4611-F Assembly Drive, Lanham MD, 20706-4391, (301) 459-2255, Fax: (800) 865-3450, www.bernan.com; *Vital Statistics of the United States: Births, Life Expectancy, Deaths, and Selected Health Data.*

National Center for Health Statistics (NCHS), Centers for Disease Control and Prevention (CDC), U.S. Department of Health and Human Services (HHS), 3311 Toledo Road, Hyattsville, MD 20782, (866) 232-4636, www.cdc.gov/nchs; *National Vital Statistics Reports (NVSR); Vital Statistics of the United States (VSUS);* and unpublished data.

CHILDBIRTH - LOW BIRTH WEIGHT BY SMOKING STATUS

Bernan Essential Government Publications, 4611-F Assembly Drive, Lanham MD, 20706-4391, (301) 459-2255, Fax: (800) 865-3450, www.bernan.com; *Vital Statistics of the United States: Births, Life Expectancy, Deaths, and Selected Health Data.*

National Center for Health Statistics (NCHS), Centers for Disease Control and Prevention (CDC), U.S. Department of Health and Human Services (HHS), 3311 Toledo Road, Hyattsville, MD 20782, (866) 232-4636, www.cdc.gov/nchs; *National Vital Statistics Reports (NVSR).*

CHILDBIRTH - OUTLYING AREAS OF THE UNITED STATES

National Center for Health Statistics (NCHS), Centers for Disease Control and Prevention (CDC), U.S. Department of Health and Human Services (HHS), 3311 Toledo Road, Hyattsville, MD 20782, (866) 232-4636, www.cdc.gov/nchs; *Vital Statistics of the United States (VSUS).*

CHILDBIRTH - PRENATAL CARE

Bernan Essential Government Publications, 4611-F Assembly Drive, Lanham MD, 20706-4391, (301) 459-2255, Fax: (800) 865-3450, www.bernan.com; *Vital Statistics of the United States: Births, Life Expectancy, Deaths, and Selected Health Data.*

National Center for Health Statistics (NCHS), Centers for Disease Control and Prevention (CDC), U.S. Department of Health and Human Services (HHS), 3311 Toledo Road, Hyattsville, MD 20782, (866) 232-4636, www.cdc.gov/nchs; *National Vital Statistics Reports (NVSR); Vital Statistics of the United States (VSUS);* and unpublished data.

RAND Corporation, 1776 Main Street, PO Box 2138, Santa Monica, CA 90407-2138, (310) 393-0411, www.rand.org; *The Provision of Neonatal Services: Data for International Comparisons.*

CHILDBIRTH - RACE

Alan Guttmacher Institute, 125 Maiden Lane, 7th Floor, New York, NY 10038, (212) 248-1111, Fax: (212) 248-1951, www.agi-usa.org; *U.S. Teenage Pregnancy Statistics: Overall Trends, Trends by Race and Ethnicity and State-by-State Information* and *U.S. Teenage Pregnancy Statistics: Overall Trends, Trends by Race and Ethnicity and State-by-State Information.*

Bernan Essential Government Publications, 4611-F Assembly Drive, Lanham MD, 20706-4391, (301) 459-2255, Fax: (800) 865-3450, www.bernan.com; *Vital Statistics of the United States: Births, Life Expectancy, Deaths, and Selected Health Data.*

National Center for Health Statistics (NCHS), Centers for Disease Control and Prevention (CDC), U.S. Department of Health and Human Services (HHS), 3311 Toledo Road, Hyattsville, MD 20782, (866) 232-4636, www.cdc.gov/nchs; *National Vital Statistics Reports (NVSR); Vital Statistics of the United States (VSUS);* and unpublished data.

U.S. Census Bureau, Population Division, 4700 Silver Hill Road, Washington DC 20233-0001, (301) 763-3030, www.census.gov/population/www/; *Current Population Reports.*

CHILDREN

See also POPULATION and VITAL STATISTICS

The Annie E. Casey Foundation, 701 Saint Paul Street, Baltimore, MD 21202, (410) 547-6600, Fax: (410) 547-3610, www.aecf.org; *Children at Risk: State Trends 1990-2000; City and Rural KIDS COUNT Data Book; KIDS COUNT; Rural KIDS COUNT Pocket Guide; Undercounted, Underserved: Immigrant and Refugee Families in the Child Welfare System; Update: Latest Findings in Children's Mental Health;* and *Vermont Communities Count: Using Results to Strengthen Services for Families and Children.*

Federal Interagency Forum on Child and Family Statistics, 2070 Chain Bridge Road, Suite 450, Vienna, VA 22182-2536, (888) ASK-HRSA, www.childstats.gov; *America's Children: Key National Indicators of Well-Being 2006.*

Information and Documentation Centre, Institute de la statistique du Quebec, 200 Chemin Sainte-Foy, 3rd Floor, Quebec City, Quebec G1R 5T4, Canada, (Dial from U.S. (418) 691-2401), (Fax from U.S. (418) 643-4129), www.stat.gouv.qc.ca; *Longitudinal Study of Child Development in Quebec.*

National Center for Statistics and Analysis (NCSA) of the National Highway Traffic Safety Administration, West Building, 1200 New Jersey Avenue, S.E., Washington, DC 20590, (202) 366-1503, Fax: (202) 366-7078, www.nhtsa.gov; *Child Passenger Fatalities and Injuries, Based on Restraint Use, Vehicle Type, Seat Position, and Number of Vehicles in the Crash; Traffic Safety Fact Sheets, 2006 Data - Children;* and *Traffic Safety Fact Sheets, 2006 Data - School Transportation-Related Crashes.*

NeighborhoodInfo DC, c/o The Urban Institute, 2100 M Street, NW, Washington, DC 20037, (202) 261-5760, Fax: (202) 872-9322, www.neighborhoodinfodc.org; *Every Kid Counts in the District of Columbia: Twelfth Annual Fact Book, 2005.*

Public/Private Ventures (P/PV), 2000 Market Street, Suite 600, Philadelphia, PA 19103, (215) 557-4400, Fax: (215) 557 4469, www.ppv.org; *After-School Pursuits: An Examination of Outcomes in the San Francisco Beacon Initiative; Beyond Safe Havens: A Synthesis of 20 Years of Research on the Boys Girls Clubs, Full Report;* and *A Portrait of Preteens in Santa Clara and San Mateo Counties: What We Know About 9- to 13-Year Olds.*

U.S. Census Bureau, 4700 Silver Hill Road, Washington DC 20233-0001, (301) 763-3030, www.census.gov; American FactFinder (web app); *County and City Data Book 2007;* and *State and County QuickFacts.*

U.S. Department of Health and Human Services, Health Resources and Services Administration, Maternal and Child Health Bureau, Parklawn Building Room 18-05, 5600 Fishers Lane, Rockville, Maryland 20857, (301) 443-2170, http://mchb.hrsa.gov; *Data Summaries for Title V Expenditures and Individuals Served* and *Title V: A Snapshot of Maternal and Child Health.*

U.S. Department of Justice (DOJ), National Institute of Justice (NIJ), 810 Seventh Street, NW, Washington, DC 20531, (202) 307-2942, Fax: (202) 616-0275, www.ojp.usdoj.gov/nij/; *Does Parental Incarceration Increase a Child's Risk for Foster Care Placement?*

U.S. Environmental Protection Agency (EPA) National Center for Environmental Research (NCER), Ariel Rios Building, 1200 Pennsylvania Avenue, NW, Washington, D.C. 20460, http://es.epa.gov/ncer; *A Decade of Children's Environmental Health Research: Highlights from EPA's Science to Achieve Results Program.*

United Way of Massachusetts Bay, 51 Sleeper Street, Boston, MA 02210, (617) 624-8000, www.uwmb.org; *Faith and Action: Improving the Lives of At-Risk Youth.*

CHILDREN - ACTIVITY LIMITATION

National Center for Health Statistics (NCHS), Centers for Disease Control and Prevention (CDC), U.S. Department of Health and Human Services (HHS), 3311 Toledo Road, Hyattsville, MD 20782, (866) 232-4636, www.cdc.gov/nchs; *Health, United States, 2006, with Chartbook on Trends in the Health of Americans with Special Feature on Pain.*

CHILDREN - AGE AND/OR SEX

U.S. Census Bureau, 4700 Silver Hill Road, Washington DC 20233-0001, (301) 763-3030, www.census.gov; unpublished data.

U.S. Census Bureau, Population Division, 4700 Silver Hill Road, Washington DC 20233-0001, (301) 763-3030, www.census.gov/population/www/; *Current Population Reports.*

CHILDREN - AIDS

Centers for Disease Control and Prevention (CDC), U.S. Department of Health and Human Services (HHS), 1600 Clifton Road, Atlanta, GA 30333, (800) 311-3435, www.cdc.gov; *HIV/AIDS Surveillance Report* and unpublished data.

CHILDREN - ALCOHOL USE

Substance Abuse and Mental Health Services Administration (SAMHSA), 1 Choke Cherry Road, Rockville, MD 20857, (240) 777-1311, www.oas.samhsa.gov; *National Survey of Substance Abuse Treatment Services (N-SSATS)* and *National Survey on Drug Use Health (NSDUH).*

CHILDREN - CHILD ABUSE

Administration for Children and Families (ACF), Office of Planning, Research Evaluation (OPRE), U.S. Department of Health and Human Services (HHS), 370 L'Enfant Promenade, SW, Washington, DC 20201, (202) 401-9200, www.acf.hhs.gov/programs/opre; *National Survey of Child and Adolescent Well-Being (NSCAW), 1997-2010.*

Australian Institute of Health and Welfare (AIHW), GPO Box 570, Canberra ACT 2601, Australia, www.aihw.gov.au; *Child Protection Australia 2006-07.*

Child Welfare Information Gateway, Children's Bureau/ACYF, 1250 Maryland Avenue, SW, Eighth Floor, Washington, DC 20024, (800) 394-3366, Fax: (703) 385-3206, www.childwelfare.gov; *Alternative Responses to Child Maltreatment: Findings from NCANDS.*

National Center for Juvenile Justice (NCJJ), 3700 South Water Street, Suite 200, Pittsburgh, PA 15203, (412) 227-6950, Fax: (412) 227-6955, http://ncjj.servehttp.com/NCJJWebsite/main.htm; *Jury Trial in Abuse, Neglect, Dependency Cases.*

U.S. Department of Justice (DOJ), Bureau of Justice Statistics, 810 Seventh Street, NW, Washington, DC 20531, (202) 307-0765, www.ojp.usdoj.gov/bjs/; *Family Violence Statistics: Including Statistics on Strangers and Acquaintances; Federal Criminal Case Processing, 2002: With trends 1982-2002, Reconciled Data;* and *Sexual Assault of Young Children as Reported to Law Enforcement: Victim, Incident, and Offender Characteristics.*

U.S. Department of Justice (DOJ), National Institute of Justice (NIJ), 810 Seventh Street, NW, Washington, DC 20531, (202) 307-2942, Fax: (202) 616-0275, www.ojp.usdoj.gov/nij/; *Youth Victimization: Prevalence and Implications* .

CHILDREN - CHILD CASE WORKERS

Australian Institute of Health and Welfare (AIHW), GPO Box 570, Canberra ACT 2601, Australia, www.aihw.gov.au; *Child Protection Australia 2006-07.*

U.S. Bureau of Labor Statistics (BLS), Postal Square Building, 2 Massachusetts Avenue, NE, Washington, DC 20212-0001, (202) 691-5200, Fax: (202) 691-6325, www.bls.gov; *Monthly Labor Review (MLR).*

CHILDREN - CHILD DAY CARE

The Children's Foundation, 725 Fifteenth Street, NW, Suite 505, Washington, DC 20005-2109, (202) 347-3300, Fax: (202) 347-3382; *2005 Child Care Center Licensing Study* and *The National Directory of Family Child Care Associations, Support Groups and Support Agencies.*

National Center for Children in Poverty (NCCP), 215 W. 125th Street, 3rd Floor, New York, NY 10027, (646) 284-9600, Fax: (646) 284-9623, www.nccp.org; *Parent Employment and the Use of Child Care Subsidies; Predictors of Child Care Subsidy Use;* and *Research-to-Policy Connections.*

National Center for Education Statistics (NCES), 1990 K Street, NW, Washington, DC 20006, (202) 502-7300, http://nces.ed.gov; *Digest of Education Statistics 2007.*

U.S. Bureau of Labor Statistics (BLS), Postal Square Building, 2 Massachusetts Avenue, NE, Washington, DC 20212-0001, (202) 691-5200, Fax: (202) 691-6325, www.bls.gov; *Consumer Price Index Detailed Report* and *Monthly Labor Review (MLR).*

CHILDREN - CHILD SUPPORT

Administration for Children and Families (ACF), Office of Child Support Enforcement (OCSE), U.S. Department of Health and Human Services (HHS), 4th Floor, Aerospace Building, 370 L'Enfant Promenade, SW, Washington, DC 20201, (202) 401-9373, www.acf.dhhs.gov/programs/cse; *Child Support Enforcement FY 2007 Preliminary Data Report.*

National Center for Children in Poverty (NCCP), 215 W. 125th Street, 3rd Floor, New York, NY 10027, (646) 284-9600, Fax: (646) 284-9623, www.nccp.org; *Parent Employment and the Use of Child Care Subsidies* and *Predictors of Child Care Subsidy Use.*

U.S. Census Bureau, 4700 Silver Hill Road, Washington DC 20233-0001, (301) 763-3030, www.census.gov; unpublished data.

U.S. Census Bureau, Population Division, 4700 Silver Hill Road, Washington DC 20233-0001, (301) 763-3030, www.census.gov/population/www/; *Current Population Reports.*

CHILDREN - CIGARETTE SMOKING

Robert Wood Johnson Foundation, PO Box 2316, College Road East and Route 1, Princeton, NJ 08543, (877) 843-7953, www.rwjf.org; *A Broken Promise to Our Children: The 1998 State Tobacco Settlement Six Years Later.*

Substance Abuse and Mental Health Services Administration (SAMHSA), 1 Choke Cherry Road, Rockville, MD 20857, (240) 777-1311, www.oas.samhsa.gov; *National Survey on Drug Use Health (NSDUH).*

CHILDREN - COLLEGE ENROLLMENT

National Center for Education Statistics (NCES), 1990 K Street, NW, Washington, DC 20006, (202) 502-7300, http://nces.ed.gov; *Digest of Education Statistics 2007.*

CHILDREN - COMMUNITY SERVICE

National Center for Education Statistics (NCES), 1990 K Street, NW, Washington, DC 20006, (202) 502-7300, http://nces.ed.gov; various fact sheets.

CHILDREN - COMPUTER USE

Market Data Retrieval (MDR), 6 Armstrong Road, Shelton, CT 06484, (800) 333-8802, www.schooldata.com; *The K-12 Technology Review 2005.*

Mediamark Research, Inc., 75 Ninth Avenue, 5th Floor, New York, NY 10011, (212) 884-9200, Fax: (212) 884-9339, www.mediamark.com; *The American Kids Study.*

National Center for Education Statistics (NCES), 1990 K Street, NW, Washington, DC 20006, (202) 502-7300, http://nces.ed.gov; *Digest of Education Statistics 2007* and *Internet Access in U.S. Public Schools and Classrooms: 1994-2005.*

National Telecommunications and Information Administration (NTIA), U.S. Department of Commerce (DOC), 1401 Constitution Avenue, NW, Washington, DC 20230, (202) 482-7002, www.ntia.doc.gov; *A Nation Online: Entering the Broadband Age.*

CHILDREN - CONGENITAL ABNORMALITIES

National Center for Health Statistics (NCHS), Centers for Disease Control and Prevention (CDC), U.S. Department of Health and Human Services (HHS), 3311 Toledo Road, Hyattsville, MD 20782, (866) 232-4636, www.cdc.gov/nchs; *Health, United States, 2006, with Chartbook on Trends in the Health of Americans with Special Feature on Pain.*

CHILDREN - COST OF RAISING

Center for Nutrition Policy and Promotion (CNPP), U.S. Department of Agriculture (USDA), 3101 Park Center Drive, 10th Floor, Alexandria, VA 22302-1594, (703) 305-7600, Fax: (703) 305-3300, www.usda.gov/cnpp; *Expenditures on Children by Families: 2007 Annual Reportaa* and *The Healthy Eating Index.*

National Center for Children in Poverty (NCCP), 215 W. 125th Street, 3rd Floor, New York, NY 10027, (646) 284-9600, Fax: (646) 284-9623, www.nccp.org; *Parent Employment and the Use of Child Care Subsidies* and *Predictors of Child Care Subsidy Use.*

CHILDREN - CRIMINAL STATISTICS

Royal Canadian Mounted Police (RCMP), 1200 Vanier Parkway, Ottawa, ON K1A 0R2, Canada, (613) 993-7267, www.rcmp-grc.gc.ca; *The Direct and Indirect Impacts of Organized Crime on Youth, as Offenders and Victims.*

U.S. Department of Justice (DOJ), Bureau of Justice Statistics, 810 Seventh Street, NW, Washington, DC 20531, (202) 307-0765, www.ojp.usdoj.gov/bjs/; *Crime and the Nation's Households, 2004; Criminal Victimization, 2005; Incarcerated Parents and Their Children;* and *Sexual Assault of Young Children as Reported to Law Enforcement: Victim, Incident, and Offender Characteristics.*

U.S. Department of Justice (DOJ), National Institute of Justice (NIJ), 810 Seventh Street, NW, Washington, DC 20531, (202) 307-2942, Fax: (202) 616-0275, www.ojp.usdoj.gov/nij/; *Youth Victimization: Prevalence and Implications* .

CHILDREN - DEATHS AND DEATH RATES

Bernan Essential Government Publications, 4611-F Assembly Drive, Lanham MD, 20706-4391, (301) 459-2255, Fax: (800) 865-3450, www.bernan.com; *Vital Statistics of the United States: Births, Life Expectancy, Deaths, and Selected Health Data.*

Centers for Disease Control and Prevention (CDC), U.S. Department of Health and Human Services (HHS), 1600 Clifton Road, Atlanta, GA 30333, (800) 311-3435, www.cdc.gov; *HIV/AIDS Surveillance Report* and unpublished data.

Child Welfare League of America (CWLA), 440 First Street, NW, Third Floor, Washington, DC 20001-2085, (202) 638-2952, Fax: (202) 638-4004, www.cwla.org; *Mortality Trends Among U.S. Children and Youth.*

Kids and Cars, 2913 West 113th Street, Leawood, KS 66211, (913) 327-0013, www.kidsandcars.org; www.kidsandcars.org.

National Center for Health Statistics (NCHS), Centers for Disease Control and Prevention (CDC), U.S. Department of Health and Human Services (HHS), 3311 Toledo Road, Hyattsville, MD 20782, (866) 232-4636, www.cdc.gov/nchs; *National Vital Statistics Reports (NVSR); Vital Statistics of the United States (VSUS);* and unpublished data.

National Center for Statistics and Analysis (NCSA) of the National Highway Traffic Safety Administration, West Building, 1200 New Jersey Avenue, S.E., Washington, DC 20590, (202) 366-1503, Fax: (202) 366-7078, www.nhtsa.gov; *Child Passenger Fatalities and Injuries, Based on Restraint Use, Vehicle Type, Seat Position, and Number of Vehicles in the Crash; Traffic Safety Fact Sheets, 2006 Data - Children;* and *Traffic Safety Fact Sheets, 2006 Data - School Transportation-Related Crashes.*

CHILDREN - DISABILITY STATUS

National Center for Education Statistics (NCES), 1990 K Street, NW, Washington, DC 20006, (202) 502-7300, http://nces.ed.gov; Data Analysis System (DAS).

CHILDREN - DRUG USE

Center for Substance Abuse Research (CESAR), 4321 Hartwick Road, Suite 501, College Park, MD 20740, (301) 405-9770, Fax: (301) 403-8342, www.cesar.umd.edu; *DEWS Investigates: Identifying Maryland Public School Students Who Have Tried Multiple Drugs.*

Substance Abuse and Mental Health Services Administration (SAMHSA), 1 Choke Cherry Road, Rockville, MD 20857, (240) 777-1311, www.oas.samhsa.gov; *National Survey on Drug Use Health (NSDUH).*

CHILDREN - EDUCATION

The Annie E. Casey Foundation, 701 Saint Paul Street, Baltimore, MD 21202, (410) 547-6600, Fax: (410) 547-3610, www.aecf.org; *Improving School Readiness Outcomes* and *Maryland's Early Care and Education Committee Progress Report.*

Public/Private Ventures (P/PV), 2000 Market Street, Suite 600, Philadelphia, PA 19103, (215) 557-4400, Fax: (215) 557 4469, www.ppv.org; *Promoting Emotional and Behavioral Health in Preteens: Benchmarks of Success and Challenges Among Programs in Santa Clara and San Mateo Counties.*

United Way of Massachusetts Bay, 51 Sleeper Street, Boston, MA 02210, (617) 624-8000, www.uwmb.org; *Faith and Action: Improving the Lives of At-Risk Youth.*

CHILDREN - FAMILIES WITH

The Annie E. Casey Foundation, 701 Saint Paul Street, Baltimore, MD 21202, (410) 547-6600, Fax: (410) 547-3610, www.aecf.org; *Children at Risk: State Trends 1990-2000; City and Rural KIDS COUNT Data Book; KIDS COUNT; Of, By, And For the Community: The Story of PUENTE Learning Center; Rural KIDS COUNT Pocket Guide;* and *Vermont Communities Count: Using Results to Strengthen Services for Families and Children.*

National Center for Children in Poverty (NCCP), 215 W. 125th Street, 3rd Floor, New York, NY 10027, (646) 284-9600, Fax: (646) 284-9623, www.nccp.org; *Promoting the Emotional Well-Being of Children and Families; Research-to-Policy Connections;* and *Social Security Resources.*

National Center for Juvenile Justice (NCJJ), 3700 South Water Street, Suite 200, Pittsburgh, PA 15203, (412) 227-6950, Fax: (412) 227-6955, http://ncjj.servehttp.com/NCJJWebsite/main.htm; *Jury Trial in Termination of Parental Rights (2005 Update).*

U.S. Census Bureau, 4700 Silver Hill Road, Washington DC 20233-0001, (301) 763-3030, www.census.gov; unpublished data.

U.S. Census Bureau, Population Division, 4700 Silver Hill Road, Washington DC 20233-0001, (301) 763-3030, www.census.gov/population/www/; *Current Population Reports.*

U.S. Department of Health and Human Services, Health Resources and Services Administration, Maternal and Child Health Bureau, Parklawn Building Room 18-05, 5600 Fishers Lane, Rockville, Maryland 20857, (301) 443-2170, http://mchb.hrsa.gov; *Data Summaries for Title V Expenditures and Individuals Served* and *Title V: A Snapshot of Maternal and Child Health.*

U.S. Department of Justice (DOJ), Bureau of Justice Statistics, 810 Seventh Street, NW, Washington, DC 20531, (202) 307-0765, www.ojp.usdoj.gov/bjs/; *Incarcerated Parents and Their Children.*

U.S. Department of Justice (DOJ), National Institute of Justice (NIJ), 810 Seventh Street, NW, Washington, DC 20531, (202) 307-2942, Fax: (202) 616-0275, www.ojp.usdoj.gov/nij/; *Does Parental Incarceration Increase a Child's Risk for Foster Care Placement?* and *Youth Victimization: Prevalence and Implications* .

CHILDREN - FOOD INSECURITY

Economic Research Service (ERS), U.S. Department of Agriculture (USDA), 1800 M Street, NW, Washington, DC 20036-5831, (202) 694-5050, Fax: (202) 694-5689, www.ers.usda.gov; *Food Assistance and Nutrition Research Program, Final Report: Fiscal 2007 Activities; The Food Assistance Landscape: Federal Year 2007 Annual Report; Household Food Security in the United States, 2006;* and *Summer Food Service Program Map Machine.*

NeighborhoodInfo DC, c/o The Urban Institute, 2100 M Street, NW, Washington, DC 20037, (202) 261-5760, Fax: (202) 872-9322, www.neighborhoodinfodc.org; *Measuring Need for Youth Services in D.C.: Comparing Poverty and TANF Data.*

CHILDREN - FOOD STAMP PROGRAM

Food and Nutrition Service (FNS), U.S. Department of Agriculture (USDA), 3101 Park Center Drive, Alexandria, VA 22302, (703) 305-2062, www.fns.usda.gov/fns; *Characteristics of Food Stamp Households: Fiscal Year 2005; WIC Participant and Program Characteristics 2006;* and *WIC Program Coverage: How Many Eligible Individuals Participated in the Special Supplemental Nutrition Program for Women, Infants, and Children (WIC): 1994 to 2003?*

NeighborhoodInfo DC, c/o The Urban Institute, 2100 M Street, NW, Washington, DC 20037, (202) 261-5760, Fax: (202) 872-9322, www.neighborhoodinfodc.org; *Measuring Need for Youth Services in D.C.: Comparing Poverty and TANF Data.*

CHILDREN - FOREIGN BORN POPULATION

National Center for Children in Poverty (NCCP), 215 W. 125th Street, 3rd Floor, New York, NY 10027, (646) 284-9600, Fax: (646) 284-9623, www.nccp.org; *Children in Low-Income Immigrant Families* and *Children of Immigrants: A Statistical Profile.*

U.S. Census Bureau, Population Division, 4700 Silver Hill Road, Washington DC 20233-0001, (301) 763-3030, www.census.gov/population/www/; *Foreign-Born Population in the U.S. 2003.*

CHILDREN - FRACTURES

National Center for Health Statistics (NCHS), Centers for Disease Control and Prevention (CDC), U.S. Department of Health and Human Services (HHS), 3311 Toledo Road, Hyattsville, MD 20782, (866) 232-4636, www.cdc.gov/nchs; *Health, United States, 2006, with Chartbook on Trends in the Health of Americans with Special Feature on Pain.*

CHILDREN - GROUP QUARTERS POPULATION

Population Reference Bureau, 1875 Connecticut Avenue, NW, Suite 520, Washington, DC, 20009-5728, (800) 877-9881, Fax: (202) 328-3937, www.prb.org; *The American People Series.*

U.S. Census Bureau, Housing and Household Economics Statistics Division, 4700 Silver Hill Road, Washington DC 20233-0001, (301) 763-3030, www.census.gov/hhes/www; *Census 2000 Summary File 1.*

U.S. Census Bureau, Population Division, 4700 Silver Hill Road, Washington DC 20233-0001, (301) 763-3030, www.census.gov/population/www/; *Census 2000 Profiles of General Demographic Characteristics.*

CHILDREN - HEAD START PROGRAM

Administration for Children and Families (ACF), Office of Planning, Research Evaluation (OPRE), U.S. Department of Health and Human Services (HHS), 370 L'Enfant Promenade, SW, Washington, DC 20201, (202) 401-9200, www.acf.hhs.gov/programs/opre; *ACF Annual Performance Plans and Reports, 2000-2008* and *Head Start Impact Study and Follow-up, 2000-2009.*

CHILDREN - HEALTH INSURANCE COVERAGE

Australian Institute of Health and Welfare (AIHW), GPO Box 570, Canberra ACT 2601, Australia, www.aihw.gov.au; *Key National Indicators of Children's Health, Development and Wellbeing: Indicator Framework of 'A Picture of Australia's Children 2009'.*

Federal Interagency Forum on Child and Family Statistics, 2070 Chain Bridge Road, Suite 450, Vienna, VA 22182-2536, (888) ASK-HRSA, www.childstats.gov; *America's Children: Key National Indicators of Well-Being 2006.*

Indian Health Service (IHS), U.S. Department of Health and Human Services, The Reyes Building, 801 Thompson Avenue, Suite 400, Rockville, MD 20852-1627, (301) 443-1180, www.ihs.gov; *Indian Health Focus - Youth.*

National Center for Children in Poverty (NCCP), 215 W. 125th Street, 3rd Floor, New York, NY 10027, (646) 284-9600, Fax: (646) 284-9623, www.nccp.org; *Unclaimed Children Revisited.*

U.S. Census Bureau, 4700 Silver Hill Road, Washington DC 20233-0001, (301) 763-3030, www.census.gov; unpublished data.

U.S. Census Bureau, Housing and Household Economics Statistics Division, 4700 Silver Hill Road, Washington DC 20233-0001, (301) 763-3030, www.census.gov/hhes/www; *Health Insurance Coverage Status and Type of Coverage by Selected Characteristics for All People in Poverty Universe.*

U.S. Census Bureau, Population Division, 4700 Silver Hill Road, Washington DC 20233-0001, (301) 763-3030, www.census.gov/population/www/; *Current Population Reports.*

U.S. Department of Health and Human Services, Health Resources and Services Administration, Maternal and Child Health Bureau, Parklawn Building Room 18-05, 5600 Fishers Lane, Rockville, Maryland 20857, (301) 443-2170, http://mchb.hrsa.gov; *Data Summaries for Title V Expenditures and Individuals Served* and *Title V: A Snapshot of Maternal and Child Health.*

CHILDREN - HIGH SCHOOL DROPOUTS

U.S. Census Bureau, 4700 Silver Hill Road, Washington DC 20233-0001, (301) 763-3030, www.census.gov; unpublished data.

U.S. Census Bureau, Population Division, 4700 Silver Hill Road, Washington DC 20233-0001, (301) 763-3030, www.census.gov/population/www/; *Current Population Reports.*

CHILDREN - HIGH SCHOOL GRADUATES

National Center for Education Statistics (NCES), 1990 K Street, NW, Washington, DC 20006, (202) 502-7300, http://nces.ed.gov; *Digest of Education Statistics 2007.*

National Education Association (NEA), 1201 Sixteenth Street, NW, Washington, DC 20036-3290, (202) 833-4000, Fax: (202) 822-7974, www.nea.org; *Education Statistics: Rankings and Estimates 2006-2007.*

CHILDREN - HISPANIC ORIGIN POPULATION

U.S. Census Bureau, Population Division, 4700 Silver Hill Road, Washington DC 20233-0001, (301) 763-3030, www.census.gov/population/www/; *The Hispanic Population in the United States.*

CHILDREN - HOMESCHOOLED

National Center for Education Statistics (NCES), 1990 K Street, NW, Washington, DC 20006, (202)

502-7300, http://nces.ed.gov; *1.1 Million Homeschooled Students in the United States in 2003* and *Homeschooling in the United States: 2003.*

CHILDREN - HOSPITAL UTILIZATION

Australian Institute of Health and Welfare (AIHW), GPO Box 570, Canberra ACT 2601, Australia, www.aihw.gov.au; *Key National Indicators of Children's Health, Development and Wellbeing: Indicator Framework of 'A Picture of Australia's Children 2009'.*

National Center for Health Statistics (NCHS), Centers for Disease Control and Prevention (CDC), U.S. Department of Health and Human Services (HHS), 3311 Toledo Road, Hyattsville, MD 20782, (866) 232-4636, www.cdc.gov/nchs; *Faststats A to Z* and *Health, United States, 2006, with Chartbook on Trends in the Health of Americans with Special Feature on Pain.*

CHILDREN - HUNGER

Economic Research Service (ERS), U.S. Department of Agriculture (USDA), 1800 M Street, NW, Washington, DC 20036-5831, (202) 694-5050, Fax: (202) 694-5689, www.ers.usda.gov; *Food Assistance and Nutrition Research Program, Final Report: Fiscal 2007 Activities; The Food Assistance Landscape: Federal Year 2007 Annual Report;* and *Summer Food Service Program Map Machine.*

Federal Interagency Forum on Child and Family Statistics, 2070 Chain Bridge Road, Suite 450, Vienna, VA 22182-2536, (888) ASK-HRSA, www.childstats.gov; *America's Children: Key National Indicators of Well-Being 2006.*

CHILDREN - IMMIGRANTS

The Annie E. Casey Foundation, 701 Saint Paul Street, Baltimore, MD 21202, (410) 547-6600, Fax: (410) 547-3610, www.aecf.org; *Undercounted, Underserved: Immigrant and Refugee Families in the Child Welfare System.*

National Center for Children in Poverty (NCCP), 215 W. 125th Street, 3rd Floor, New York, NY 10027, (646) 284-9600, Fax: (646) 284-9623, www.nccp.org; *Children in Low-Income Immigrant Families* and *Children of Immigrants: A Statistical Profile.*

U.S. Citizenship and Immigration Services (USCIS), Washington District Office, 2675 Prosperity Avenue, Fairfax, VA 22031, (800) 375-5283, http://uscis.gov; *2005 Yearbook of Immigration Statistics.*

U.S. Department of Homeland Security (DHS), Office of Immigration Statistics, Washington, DC 20528, (202) 282-8000, www.dhs.gov; *Characteristics of Diversity Legal Permanent Residents: 2004* and *Estimates of the Legal Permanent Resident Population and Population Eligible to Naturalize in 2004.*

United Nations High Commissioner for Refugees (UNHCR), Case Postale 2500, CH-1211 Geneve 2 Depot, Switzerland, www.unhcr.org; *Unaccompanied and Separated Children Seeking Asylum, 2001-2003.*

CHILDREN - IMMUNIZATION AGAINST DISEASES

Centers for Disease Control and Prevention (CDC), U.S. Department of Health and Human Services (HHS), 1600 Clifton Road, Atlanta, GA 30333, (800) 311-3435, www.cdc.gov; *Morbidity and Mortality Weekly Report (MMWR).*

European Centre for Disease Prevention and Control (ECDC), 171 83 Stockholm, Sweden, www.ecdc.europa.eu; *Infant and Children Seasonal Immunisation Against Influenza on a Routine Basis During Inter-pandemic Period; Sudden Deaths and Influenza Vaccinations in Israel - ECDC Interim Risk Assessment;* and *Vaccines and Immunisation - VI news.*

Indian Health Service (IHS), U.S. Department of Health and Human Services, The Reyes Building, 801 Thompson Avenue, Suite 400, Rockville, MD 20852-1627, (301) 443-1180, www.ihs.gov; *Indian Health Focus - Youth.*

CHILDREN - INCOME - FAMILIES WITH CHILDREN

The Annie E. Casey Foundation, 701 Saint Paul Street, Baltimore, MD 21202, (410) 547-6600, Fax: (410) 547-3610, www.aecf.org; *Children at Risk: State Trends 1990-2000; KIDS COUNT;* and *Rural KIDS COUNT Pocket Guide.*

Federal Interagency Forum on Child and Family Statistics, 2070 Chain Bridge Road, Suite 450, Vienna, VA 22182-2536, (888) ASK-HRSA, www.childstats.gov; *America's Children: Key National Indicators of Well-Being 2006.*

National Center for Children in Poverty (NCCP), 215 W. 125th Street, 3rd Floor, New York, NY 10027, (646) 284-9600, Fax: (646) 284-9623, www.nccp.org; *Basic Facts About Low-Income Children; Child Poverty in 21st Century America; Low-Income Children in the United States: National and State Trend Data, 1996-2006; Parent Employment and the Use of Child Care Subsidies; Predictors of Child Care Subsidy Use;* and *Social Security Resources.*

Population Reference Bureau, 1875 Connecticut Avenue, NW, Suite 520, Washington, DC, 20009-5728, (800) 877-9881, Fax: (202) 328-3937, www.prb.org; *Child Poverty in Rural America* and *Strengthening Rural Families: America's Rural Children.*

U.S. Census Bureau, Population Division, 4700 Silver Hill Road, Washington DC 20233-0001, (301) 763-3030, www.census.gov/population/www/; *Current Population Reports.*

CHILDREN - INJURIES

Australian Institute of Health and Welfare (AIHW), GPO Box 570, Canberra ACT 2601, Australia, www.aihw.gov.au; *Key National Indicators of Children's Health, Development and Wellbeing: Indicator Framework of 'A Picture of Australia's Children 2009'.*

Kids and Cars, 2913 West 113th Street, Leawood, KS 66211, (913) 327-0013, www.kidsandcars.org; www.kidsandcars.org.

National Center for Health Statistics (NCHS), Centers for Disease Control and Prevention (CDC), U.S. Department of Health and Human Services (HHS), 3311 Toledo Road, Hyattsville, MD 20782, (866) 232-4636, www.cdc.gov/nchs; *Faststats A to Z.*

National Center for Statistics and Analysis (NCSA) of the National Highway Traffic Safety Administration, West Building, 1200 New Jersey Avenue, S.E., Washington, DC 20590, (202) 366-1503, Fax: (202) 366-7078, www.nhtsa.gov; *Child Passenger Fatalities and Injuries, Based on Restraint Use, Vehicle Type, Seat Position, and Number of Vehicles in the Crash.*

CHILDREN - INTERNET ACCESS

Mediamark Research, Inc., 75 Ninth Avenue, 5th Floor, New York, NY 10011, (212) 884-9200, Fax: (212) 884-9339, www.mediamark.com; *The American Kids Study.*

National Telecommunications and Information Administration (NTIA), U.S. Department of Commerce (DOC), 1401 Constitution Avenue, NW, Washington, DC 20230, (202) 482-7002, www.ntia.doc.gov; *A Nation Online: Entering the Broadband Age.*

U.S. Census Bureau, Population Division, 4700 Silver Hill Road, Washington DC 20233-0001, (301) 763-3030, www.census.gov/population/www/; *Current Population Reports.*

CHILDREN - JUVENILE DELINQUENCY

National Center for Juvenile Justice (NCJJ), 3700 South Water Street, Suite 200, Pittsburgh, PA 15203, (412) 227-6950, Fax: (412) 227-6955, http://ncjj.servehttp.com/NCJJWebsite/main.htm; *Detention and Delinquency Cases 1990-1999 (2003); Good News: Measuring Juvenile Court Outcomes at Case Closing, 2003 (2003); How Does the Juvenile Justice System Measure Up? Applying Performance Measures in Five Jurisdictions (2006); Juvenile Arrests 2003 (2005); Juvenile Court Statistics 2000 (2004); Juvenile Offenders and Victims: 2006 National Report; Juveniles in Corrections (2004);* and *Person Offenses in Juvenile Court, 1990-1999 (2003).*

National Criminal Justice Reference Service (NCJRS), PO Box 6000, Rockville, MD 20849-6000, (800) 851-3420, Fax: (301) 519-5212, www.ncjrs.org; *Delaware Juvenile Recidivism 1994-2005 Juvenile Level III, IV and V Recidivism Study.*

Office of Juvenile Justice and Delinquency Prevention (OJJDP), 810 Seventh Street, NW, Washington, DC 20531, (202) 307-5911, www.ojjdp.ncjrs.org; *Statistical Briefing Book (SBB).*

Public/Private Ventures (P/PV), 2000 Market Street, Suite 600, Philadelphia, PA 19103, (215) 557-4400, Fax: (215) 557 4469, www.ppv.org; *Serving High-Risk Youth: Lessons from Research and Programming.*

Royal Canadian Mounted Police (RCMP), 1200 Vanier Parkway, Ottawa, ON K1A 0R2, Canada, (613) 993-7267, www.rcmp-grc.gc.ca; *The Direct and Indirect Impacts of Organized Crime on Youth, as Offenders and Victims.*

U.S. Department of Justice (DOJ), Bureau of Justice Statistics, 810 Seventh Street, NW, Washington, DC 20531, (202) 307-0765, www.ojp.usdoj.gov/bjs/; *Juvenile Victimization and Offending, 1993-2003.*

U.S. Department of Justice (DOJ), National Institute of Justice (NIJ), 810 Seventh Street, NW, Washington, DC 20531, (202) 307-2942, Fax: (202) 616-0275, www.ojp.usdoj.gov/nij/; *Co-Offending and Patterns of Juvenile Crime.*

United Way of Massachusetts Bay, 51 Sleeper Street, Boston, MA 02210, (617) 624-8000, www.uwmb.org; *Faith and Action: Improving the Lives of At-Risk Youth.*

The Urban Institute, 2100 M Street, N.W., Washington, DC 20037, (202) 833-7200, www.urban.org; *Juvenile Crime in Washington, D.C.; The Rise and Fall of American Youth Violence: 1980 to 2000;* and *Youth Crime Drop.*

CHILDREN - LABOR FORCE (16 TO 19 YEARS OLD) - EMPLOYED

U.S. Bureau of Labor Statistics (BLS), Postal Square Building, 2 Massachusetts Avenue, NE, Washington, DC 20212-0001, (202) 691-5200, Fax: (202) 691-6325, www.bls.gov; *Current Population Survey (CPS); Employment and Earnings (EE);* and unpublished data.

CHILDREN - LABOR FORCE (16 TO 19 YEARS OLD) - EMPLOYMENT STATUS

U.S. Bureau of Labor Statistics (BLS), Postal Square Building, 2 Massachusetts Avenue, NE, Washington, DC 20212-0001, (202) 691-5200, Fax: (202) 691-6325, www.bls.gov; *Current Population Survey (CPS); Monthly Labor Review (MLR);* and unpublished data.

CHILDREN - LABOR FORCE (16 TO 19 YEARS OLD) - MINIMUM WAGE WORKERS

U.S. Bureau of Labor Statistics (BLS), Postal Square Building, 2 Massachusetts Avenue, NE, Washington, DC 20212-0001, (202) 691-5200, Fax: (202) 691-6325, www.bls.gov; *Employment and Earnings (EE).*

CHILDREN - LABOR FORCE (16 TO 19 YEARS OLD) - PARTICIPATION RATES

U.S. Bureau of Labor Statistics (BLS), Postal Square Building, 2 Massachusetts Avenue, NE, Washington, DC 20212-0001, (202) 691-5200, Fax: (202) 691-6325, www.bls.gov; *Monthly Labor Review (MLR)* and unpublished data.

CHILDREN - LABOR FORCE (16 TO 19 YEARS OLD) - SEX

U.S. Bureau of Labor Statistics (BLS), Postal Square Building, 2 Massachusetts Avenue, NE,

Washington, DC 20212-0001, (202) 691-5200, Fax: (202) 691-6325, www.bls.gov; *Current Population Survey (CPS); Employment and Earnings (EE); Monthly Labor Review (MLR);* and unpublished data.

CHILDREN - LABOR FORCE (16 TO 19 YEARS OLD) - UNEMPLOYED

U.S. Bureau of Labor Statistics (BLS), Postal Square Building, 2 Massachusetts Avenue, NE, Washington, DC 20212-0001, (202) 691-5200, Fax: (202) 691-6325, www.bls.gov; *Employment and Earnings (EE)* and unpublished data.

CHILDREN - LABOR FORCE MULTIPLE JOB HOLDERS

U.S. Bureau of Labor Statistics (BLS), Postal Square Building, 2 Massachusetts Avenue, NE, Washington, DC 20212-0001, (202) 691-5200, Fax: (202) 691-6325, www.bls.gov; *Employment and Earnings (EE).*

CHILDREN - LITERACY

National Center for Education Statistics (NCES), 1990 K Street, NW, Washington, DC 20006, (202) 502-7300, http://nces.ed.gov; *Home Literacy Activities and Signs of Children's Emerging Literacy* and various fact sheets.

Public/Private Ventures (P/PV), 2000 Market Street, Suite 600, Philadelphia, PA 19103, (215) 557-4400, Fax: (215) 557 4469, www.ppv.org; *Launching Literacy in After-School Programs: Early Lessons from the CORAL Initiative.*

CHILDREN - MENTAL HEALTH

The Annie E. Casey Foundation, 701 Saint Paul Street, Baltimore, MD 21202, (410) 547-6600, Fax: (410) 547-3610, www.aecf.org; *Update: Latest Findings in Children's Mental Health.*

Australian Institute of Health and Welfare (AIHW), GPO Box 570, Canberra ACT 2601, Australia, www.aihw.gov.au; *Key National Indicators of Children's Health, Development and Wellbeing: Indicator Framework of 'A Picture of Australia's Children 2009'.*

Federal Interagency Forum on Child and Family Statistics, 2070 Chain Bridge Road, Suite 450, Vienna, VA 22182-2536, (888) ASK-HRSA, www.childstats.gov; *America's Children: Key National Indicators of Well-Being 2006.*

National Center for Children in Poverty (NCCP), 215 W. 125th Street, 3rd Floor, New York, NY 10027, (646) 284-9600, Fax: (646) 284-9623, www.nccp.org; *Promoting the Emotional Well-Being of Children and Families* and *Unclaimed Children Revisited.*

National Center for Health Statistics (NCHS), Centers for Disease Control and Prevention (CDC), U.S. Department of Health and Human Services (HHS), 3311 Toledo Road, Hyattsville, MD 20782, (866) 232-4636, www.cdc.gov/nchs; *NCHS Survey Measures Catalog: Child and Adolescent Mental Health.*

United Way of Massachusetts Bay, 51 Sleeper Street, Boston, MA 02210, (617) 624-8000, www.uwmb.org; *Faith and Action: Improving the Lives of At-Risk Youth.*

CHILDREN - MOBILITY STATUS

U.S. Census Bureau, Population Division, 4700 Silver Hill Road, Washington DC 20233-0001, (301) 763-3030, www.census.gov/population/www/; *Current Population Reports.*

CHILDREN - MOTHERS IN LABOR FORCE - BY AGE OF CHILDREN

U.S. Bureau of Labor Statistics (BLS), Postal Square Building, 2 Massachusetts Avenue, NE, Washington, DC 20212-0001, (202) 691-5200, Fax: (202) 691-6325, www.bls.gov; *Current Population Survey (CPS); Employment and Earnings (EE);* and unpublished data.

CHILDREN - MUSIC PURCHASES

Mediamark Research, Inc., 75 Ninth Avenue, 5th Floor, New York, NY 10011, (212) 884-9200, Fax: (212) 884-9339, www.mediamark.com; *The American Kids Study.*

Recording Industry Association of America (RIAA), 10th Floor, 1025 F Street, NW, Washington, DC 20004, (202) 775-0101, www.riaa.com; *The 2007 Annual Consumer Profile Chart.*

CHILDREN - OVERWEIGHT

Robert Wood Johnson Foundation, PO Box 2316, College Road East and Route 1, Princeton, NJ 08543, (877) 843-7953, www.rwjf.org; *Tracking Progress: The Third Annual Arkansas Assessment.*

CHILDREN - PARENTAL INVOLVEMENT

Information and Documentation Centre, Institute de la statistique du Quebec, 200 Chemin Sainte-Foy, 3rd Floor, Quebec City, Quebec G1R 5T4, Canada, (Dial from U.S. (418) 691-2401), (Fax from U.S. (418) 643-4129), www.stat.gouv.qc.ca; *Disciplining Children in Quebec: Parenting Norms and Practices in 2004.*

Mediamark Research, Inc., 75 Ninth Avenue, 5th Floor, New York, NY 10011, (212) 884-9200, Fax: (212) 884-9339, www.mediamark.com; *The American Kids Study.*

National Center for Education Statistics (NCES), 1990 K Street, NW, Washington, DC 20006, (202) 502-7300, http://nces.ed.gov; *The National Household Education Surveys Program (NHES).*

National Center for Juvenile Justice (NCJJ), 3700 South Water Street, Suite 200, Pittsburgh, PA 15203, (412) 227-6950, Fax: (412) 227-6955, http://ncjj.servehttp.com/NCJJWebsite/main.htm; *Jury Trial in Termination of Parental Rights (2005 Update).*

Policy Research Bureau, 2a Tabernacle Street, London EC2A 4LU, United Kingdom, www.prb.org.uk; *Parenting in Poor Environments: Stress, Support and Coping. A Summary of Key Messages for Policy and Practice from a Major National Study.*

U.S. Department of Justice (DOJ), National Institute of Justice (NIJ), 810 Seventh Street, NW, Washington, DC 20531, (202) 307-2942, Fax: (202) 616-0275, www.ojp.usdoj.gov/nij/; *Does Parental Incarceration Increase a Child's Risk for Foster Care Placement?*

CHILDREN - PHYSICIAN VISITS

Australian Institute of Health and Welfare (AIHW), GPO Box 570, Canberra ACT 2601, Australia, www.aihw.gov.au; *Key National Indicators of Children's Health, Development and Wellbeing: Indicator Framework of 'A Picture of Australia's Children 2009'.*

National Center for Health Statistics (NCHS), Centers for Disease Control and Prevention (CDC), U.S. Department of Health and Human Services (HHS), 3311 Toledo Road, Hyattsville, MD 20782, (866) 232-4636, www.cdc.gov/nchs; *Faststats A to Z* and *Health, United States, 2006, with Chartbook on Trends in the Health of Americans with Special Feature on Pain.*

CHILDREN - PNEUMONIA

National Center for Health Statistics (NCHS), Centers for Disease Control and Prevention (CDC), U.S. Department of Health and Human Services (HHS), 3311 Toledo Road, Hyattsville, MD 20782, (866) 232-4636, www.cdc.gov/nchs; *Health, United States, 2006, with Chartbook on Trends in the Health of Americans with Special Feature on Pain.*

CHILDREN - POVERTY

The Annie E. Casey Foundation, 701 Saint Paul Street, Baltimore, MD 21202, (410) 547-6600, Fax: (410) 547-3610, www.aecf.org; *Beyond the Boundaries: Low-Income Residents, Faith-Based Organizations and Neighborhood Coalition Building; Change that Abides: A Retrospective Look at Five Community and Family Stengthening Projects and Their Enduring Results; Children at Risk: State Trends 1990-2000; City and Rural KIDS COUNT Data Book; The High Cost of Being Poor: What It Takes for Low-Income Families to Get By and Get Ahead in Rural America; KIDS COUNT; Rural KIDS COUNT Pocket Guide; Undercounted, Underserved: Immigrant and Refugee Families in the Child Welfare System;* and *Vermont Communities Count: Using Results to Strengthen Services for Families and Children.*

Economic Research Service (ERS), U.S. Department of Agriculture (USDA), 1800 M Street, NW, Washington, DC 20036-5831, (202) 694-5050, Fax: (202) 694-5689, www.ers.usda.gov; *Summer Food Service Program Map Machine.*

Federal Interagency Forum on Child and Family Statistics, 2070 Chain Bridge Road, Suite 450, Vienna, VA 22182-2536, (888) ASK-HRSA, www.childstats.gov; *America's Children: Key National Indicators of Well-Being 2006.*

National Center for Children in Poverty (NCCP), 215 W. 125th Street, 3rd Floor, New York, NY 10027, (646) 284-9600, Fax: (646) 284-9623, www.nccp.org; *2007 Annual Report; Basic Facts About Low-Income Children; The Changing Demographics of Low-Income Families and Their Children; The Changing Face of Child Poverty in California; Child Poverty in 21st Century America; Child Poverty in States Hit by Hurricane Katrina; Children in Low-Income Immigrant Families; Children of Immigrants: A Statistical Profile; Early Childhood Poverty: A Statistical Profile; Geography of Low-Income Families and Children; Living at the Edge; Low-Income Children in the United States: National and State Trend Data, 1996-2006; Unclaimed Children Revisited;* and *Welfare Research Perspectives.*

NeighborhoodInfo DC, c/o The Urban Institute, 2100 M Street, NW, Washington, DC 20037, (202) 261-5760, Fax: (202) 872-9322, www.neighborhoodinfodc.org; *Every Kid Counts in the District of Columbia: Twelfth Annual Fact Book, 2005; The Financial Structure and Fiscal Health of Nonprofit Child and Youth Providers in the Washington, D.C. Metropolitan Region; Measuring Need for Youth Services in D.C.: Comparing Poverty and TANF Data;* and *Vital Signs: Indicators of the Nonprofit Safety Net for Children in the Washington, D.C., Region.*

Population Reference Bureau, 1875 Connecticut Avenue, NW, Suite 520, Washington, DC, 20009-5728, (800) 877-9881, Fax: (202) 328-3937, www.prb.org; *Child Poverty in Rural America* and *Strengthening Rural Families: America's Rural Children.*

U.S. Census Bureau, 4700 Silver Hill Road, Washington DC 20233-0001, (301) 763-3030, www.census.gov; unpublished data.

U.S. Census Bureau, Housing and Household Economics Statistics Division, 4700 Silver Hill Road, Washington DC 20233-0001, (301) 763-3030, www.census.gov/hhes/www; *Historical Poverty Tables.*

U.S. Census Bureau, Population Division, 4700 Silver Hill Road, Washington DC 20233-0001, (301) 763-3030, www.census.gov/population/www/; *Current Population Reports.*

CHILDREN - PROJECTIONS

U.S. Census Bureau, 4700 Silver Hill Road, Washington DC 20233-0001, (301) 763-3030, www.census.gov; unpublished data.

U.S. Census Bureau, Population Division, 4700 Silver Hill Road, Washington DC 20233-0001, (301) 763-3030, www.census.gov/population/www/; *Current Population Reports.*

CHILDREN - RESPIRATORY INFECTION

National Center for Health Statistics (NCHS), Centers for Disease Control and Prevention (CDC), U.S. Department of Health and Human Services (HHS), 3311 Toledo Road, Hyattsville, MD 20782, (866) 232-4636, www.cdc.gov/nchs; *Health, United States, 2006, with Chartbook on Trends in the Health of Americans with Special Feature on Pain.*

CHILDREN - SCHOOL CRIMES

National Center for Education Statistics (NCES), 1990 K Street, NW, Washington, DC 20006, (202) 502-7300, http://nces.ed.gov; *Indicators of School Crime and Safety: 2007.*

CHILDREN - SCHOOL ENROLLMENT

Market Data Retrieval (MDR), 6 Armstrong Road, Shelton, CT 06484, (800) 333-8802, www.school-data.com; *MDR's Enrollment Comparison Report, 2007-2008.*

National Center for Education Statistics (NCES), 1990 K Street, NW, Washington, DC 20006, (202) 502-7300, http://nces.ed.gov; *Digest of Education Statistics 2007; Projections of Education Statistics to 2016;* and unpublished data.

U.S. Census Bureau, 4700 Silver Hill Road, Washington DC 20233-0001, (301) 763-3030, www.census.gov; unpublished data.

U.S. Census Bureau, Population Division, 4700 Silver Hill Road, Washington DC 20233-0001, (301) 763-3030, www.census.gov/population/www/; *Current Population Reports.*

CHILDREN - SCHOOL ENROLLMENT - PREPRIMARY SCHOOL ENROLLMENT

National Center for Children in Poverty (NCCP), 215 W. 125th Street, 3rd Floor, New York, NY 10027, (646) 284-9600, Fax: (646) 284-9623, www.nccp.org; *Research-to-Policy Connections.*

U.S. Census Bureau, Population Division, 4700 Silver Hill Road, Washington DC 20233-0001, (301) 763-3030, www.census.gov/population/www/; *Current Population Reports.*

CHILDREN - SCHOOL ENROLLMENT - PROJECTIONS

National Center for Education Statistics (NCES), 1990 K Street, NW, Washington, DC 20006, (202) 502-7300, http://nces.ed.gov; *Digest of Education Statistics 2007* and *Projections of Education Statistics to 2016.*

CHILDREN - SCHOOL READINESS

The Annie E. Casey Foundation, 701 Saint Paul Street, Baltimore, MD 21202, (410) 547-6600, Fax: (410) 547-3610, www.aecf.org; *Improving School Readiness Outcomes* and *Maryland's Early Care and Education Committee Progress Report.*

National Center for Education Statistics (NCES), 1990 K Street, NW, Washington, DC 20006, (202) 502-7300, http://nces.ed.gov; *Home Literacy Activities and Signs of Children's Emerging Literacy.*

CHILDREN - SOCIAL ORGANIZATIONS

Public/Private Ventures (P/PV), 2000 Market Street, Suite 600, Philadelphia, PA 19103, (215) 557-4400, Fax: (215) 557 4469, www.ppv.org; *Beyond Safe Havens: A Synthesis of 20 Years of Research on the Boys Girls Clubs, Full Report.*

CHILDREN - SOCIAL SECURITY BENEFICIARIES AND PAYMENTS

National Center for Children in Poverty (NCCP), 215 W. 125th Street, 3rd Floor, New York, NY 10027, (646) 284-9600, Fax: (646) 284-9623, www.nccp.org; *Social Security Resources.*

Social Security Administration (SSA), Office of Public Inquiries, Windsor Park Building, 6401 Security Boulevard, Baltimore, MD 21235, (800) 772-1213, www.ssa.gov; *Annual Statistical Supplement, 2007* and unpublished data.

CHILDREN - SOCIAL WELFARE PROGRAMS

The Annie E. Casey Foundation, 701 Saint Paul Street, Baltimore, MD 21202, (410) 547-6600, Fax: (410) 547-3610, www.aecf.org; *Undercounted, Underserved: Immigrant and Refugee Families in the Child Welfare System.*

Economic Research Service (ERS), U.S. Department of Agriculture (USDA), 1800 M Street, NW, Washington, DC 20036-5831, (202) 694-5050, Fax: (202) 694-5689, www.ers.usda.gov; *Summer Food Service Program Map Machine.*

Federal Interagency Forum on Child and Family Statistics, 2070 Chain Bridge Road, Suite 450, Vienna, VA 22182-2536, (888) ASK-HRSA, www.childstats.gov; *America's Children: Key National Indicators of Well-Being 2006.*

National Center for Children in Poverty (NCCP), 215 W. 125th Street, 3rd Floor, New York, NY 10027, (646) 284-9600, Fax: (646) 284-9623, www.nccp.org; *Basic Facts About Low-Income Children; Child Poverty in 21st Century America; Children in Low-Income Immigrant Families; Children of Immigrants: A Statistical Profile; Living at the Edge; Low-Income Children in the United States: National and State Trend Data, 1996-2006; Parent Employment and the Use of Child Care Subsidies; Predictors of Child Care Subsidy Use; Promoting the Emotional Well-Being of Children and Families; Unclaimed Children Revisited;* and *Welfare Research Perspectives.*

NeighborhoodInfo DC, c/o The Urban Institute, 2100 M Street, NW, Washington, DC 20037, (202) 261-5760, Fax: (202) 872-9322, www.neighborhoodinfodc.org; *Every Kid Counts in the District of Columbia: Twelfth Annual Fact Book, 2005; The Financial Structure and Fiscal Health of Nonprofit Child and Youth Providers in the Washington, D.C. Metropolitan Region;* and *Measuring Need for Youth Services in D.C.: Comparing Poverty and TANF Data.*

Population Reference Bureau, 1875 Connecticut Avenue, NW, Suite 520, Washington, DC, 20009-5728, (800) 877-9881, Fax: (202) 328-3937, www.prb.org; *Child Poverty in Rural America* and *Strengthening Rural Families: America's Rural Children.*

U.S. Library of Congress (LOC), Congressional Research Service (CRS), The Library of Congress, 101 Independence Avenue, SE, Washington, DC 20540-7500, (202) 707-5700, www.loc.gov/crsinfo; *Cash and Non-cash Benefits for Persons With Limited Income: Eligibility Rules, Recipient and Expenditure Data.*

CHILDREN - SUICIDES

Bernan Essential Government Publications, 4611-F Assembly Drive, Lanham MD, 20706-4391, (301) 459-2255, Fax: (800) 865-3450, www.bernan.com; *Vital Statistics of the United States: Births, Life Expectancy, Deaths, and Selected Health Data.*

National Center for Health Statistics (NCHS), Centers for Disease Control and Prevention (CDC), U.S. Department of Health and Human Services (HHS), 3311 Toledo Road, Hyattsville, MD 20782, (866) 232-4636, www.cdc.gov/nchs; *National Vital Statistics Reports (NVSR)* and *Vital Statistics of the United States (VSUS).*

CHILE - NATIONAL STATISTICAL OFFICE

Instituto Nacional de Estadisticas (INE), Paseo Bulnes 418, Santiago de Chile, www.ine.cl; National Data Center.

CHILE - PRIMARY STATISTICS SOURCES

Instituto Nacional de Estadisticas (INE), Paseo Bulnes 418, Santiago de Chile, www.ine.cl; *Compendio Estadistico 2005.*

CHILE - AGRICULTURAL MACHINERY

Economist Intelligence Unit, 111 West 57th Street, New York, NY 10019, (212) 554-0600, Fax: (212) 586-1181, www.eiu.com; *Business Latin America.*

United Nations Statistics Division, New York, NY 10017, (800) 253-9646, Fax: (212) 963-4116, http://unstats.un.org; *Statistical Yearbook.*

CHILE - AGRICULTURE

Economist Intelligence Unit, 111 West 57th Street, New York, NY 10019, (212) 554-0600, Fax: (212) 586-1181, www.eiu.com; *Business Latin America* and *Chile Country Report.*

Euromonitor International, Inc., 224 S. Michigan Avenue, Suite 1500, Chicago, IL 60604, (312) 922-1115, Fax: (312) 922-1157, www.euromonitor.com; *International Marketing Data and Statistics 2008* and *World Marketing Data and Statistics.*

Inter-American Development Bank (IDB), 1300 New York Avenue, NW, Washington, DC 20577, (202) 623-1000, Fax: (202) 623-3096, www.iadb.org; *The Politics of Policies: Economic and Social Progress in Latin America - 2006 Report.*

M.E. Sharpe, 80 Business Park Drive, Armonk, NY 10504, (800) 541-6563, Fax: (914) 273-2106, www.mesharpe.com; *The Illustrated Book of World Rankings.*

Organisation for Economic Cooperation and Development (OECD), 2 rue Andre Pascal, F-75775 Paris Cedex 16, France, (Telephone in U.S. (202) 785-6323), (Fax in U.S. (202) 785-0350), www.oecd.org; *OECD Economic Survey - Chile 2007.*

Palgrave Macmillan Ltd., Houndmills, Basingstoke, Hampshire, RG21 6XS, England, (Telephone in U.S. (888) 330-8477), (Fax in U.S. (800) 672-2054), www.palgrave.com; *The Statesman's Yearbook 2008.*

Taylor and Francis Group, An Informa Business, 2 Park Square, Milton Park, Abingdon, Oxford OX14 4RN, United Kingdom, (Dial from U.S. (212) 216-7800), (Fax from U.S. (212) 564-7854), www.tandf.co.uk; *The Europa World Year Book.*

UCLA Latin American Institute, 10343 Bunche Hall, Box 951447, Los Angeles, CA 90095-1447, (310) 825-4571, Fax: (310) 206-6859, www.international.ucla.edu/lac; *Statistical Abstract of Latin America.*

United Nations Conference on Trade and Development (UNCTAD), DC2-1120, United Nations, New York, NY 10017, (212) 963-0027, www.unctad.org; *UNCTAD Commodity Yearbook.*

United Nations Food and Agricultural Organization (FAO), Viale delle Terme di Caracalla, 00100 Rome, Italy, (Dial from U.S. (202) 653-2400), (Fax from U.S. (202) 653 5760), www.fao.org; AQUASTAT; *FAO Production Yearbook 2002; FAO Trade Yearbook;* and *The State of Food and Agriculture (SOFA) 2006.*

United Nations Statistics Division, New York, NY 10017, (800) 253-9646, Fax: (212) 963-4116, http://unstats.un.org; *Statistical Yearbook* and *Statistical Yearbook for Latin America and the Caribbean 2004.*

The World Bank, 1818 H Street, NW, Washington, DC 20433, (202) 473-1000, Fax: (202) 477-6391, www.worldbank.org; *Chile* and *World Development Indicators (WDI) 2008.*

CHILE - AIRLINES

Economist Intelligence Unit, 111 West 57th Street, New York, NY 10019, (212) 554-0600, Fax: (212) 586-1181, www.eiu.com; *Business Latin America.*

International Civil Aviation Organization (ICAO), External Relations and Public Information Office (EPO), 999 University Street, Montreal, Quebec H3C 5H7, Canada, (Dial from U.S. (514) 954-8219), (Fax from U.S. (514) 954-6077), www.icao.int; *Civil Aviation Statistics of the World.*

M.E. Sharpe, 80 Business Park Drive, Armonk, NY 10504, (800) 541-6563, Fax: (914) 273-2106, www.mesharpe.com; *The Illustrated Book of World Rankings.*

Palgrave Macmillan Ltd., Houndmills, Basingstoke, Hampshire, RG21 6XS, England, (Telephone in U.S. (888) 330-8477), (Fax in U.S. (800) 672-2054), www.palgrave.com; *The Statesman's Yearbook 2008.*

Taylor and Francis Group, An Informa Business, 2 Park Square, Milton Park, Abingdon, Oxford OX14 4RN, United Kingdom, (Dial from U.S. (212) 216-7800), (Fax from U.S. (212) 564-7854), www.tandf.co.uk; *The Europa World Year Book.*

United Nations Statistics Division, New York, NY 10017, (800) 253-9646, Fax: (212) 963-4116, http://unstats.un.org; *Statistical Yearbook.*

CHILE - AIRPORTS

Central Intelligence Agency, Office of Public Affairs, Washington, DC 20505, (703) 482-0623, Fax: (703) 482-1739, www.cia.gov; *The World Factbook.*

CHILE - ALUMINUM PRODUCTION

See CHILE - MINERAL INDUSTRIES

CHILE - ANIMAL FEEDING

United Nations Statistics Division, New York, NY 10017, (800) 253-9646, Fax: (212) 963-4116, http://unstats.un.org; *Statistical Yearbook.*

CHILE - AREA

Economist Intelligence Unit, 111 West 57th Street, New York, NY 10019, (212) 554-0600, Fax: (212) 586-1181, www.eiu.com; *Business Latin America.*

CHILE - ARMED FORCES

Central Intelligence Agency, Office of Public Affairs, Washington, DC 20505, (703) 482-0623, Fax: (703) 482-1739, www.cia.gov; *The World Factbook.*

Economist Intelligence Unit, 111 West 57th Street, New York, NY 10019, (212) 554-0600, Fax: (212) 586-1181, www.eiu.com; *Business Latin America.*

Euromonitor International, Inc., 224 S. Michigan Avenue, Suite 1500, Chicago, IL 60604, (312) 922-1115, Fax: (312) 922-1157, www.euromonitor.com; *World Marketing Data and Statistics.*

International Institute for Strategic Studies (IISS), Arundel House, 13-15 Arundel Street, Temple Place, London WC2R 3DX, England, www.iiss.org; *The Military Balance 2007.*

International Monetary Fund (IMF), 700 Nineteenth Street, NW, Washington, DC 20431, (202) 623-7000, Fax: (202) 623-4661, www.imf.org; *Government Finance Statistics Yearbook (2008 Edition).*

Palgrave Macmillan Ltd., Houndmills, Basingstoke, Hampshire, RG21 6XS, England, (Telephone in U.S. (888) 330-8477), (Fax in U.S. (800) 672-2054), www.palgrave.com; *The Statesman's Yearbook 2008.*

U.S. Department of State (DOS), 2201 C Street NW, Washington, DC 20520, (202) 647-4000, www.state.gov; *World Military Expenditures and Arms Transfers (WMEAT).*

UCLA Latin American Institute, 10343 Bunche Hall, Box 951447, Los Angeles, CA 90095-1447, (310) 825-4571, Fax: (310) 206-6859, www.international.ucla.edu/lac; *Statistical Abstract of Latin America.*

United Nations Statistics Division, New York, NY 10017, (800) 253-9646, Fax: (212) 963-4116, http://unstats.un.org; *Human Development Report 2006.*

CHILE - ARTICHOKE PRODUCTION

See CHILE - CROPS

CHILE - BALANCE OF PAYMENTS

Economist Intelligence Unit, 111 West 57th Street, New York, NY 10019, (212) 554-0600, Fax: (212) 586-1181, www.eiu.com; *Business Latin America.*

Inter-American Development Bank (IDB), 1300 New York Avenue, NW, Washington, DC 20577, (202) 623-1000, Fax: (202) 623-3096, www.iadb.org; *The Politics of Policies: Economic and Social Progress in Latin America - 2006 Report.*

International Monetary Fund (IMF), 700 Nineteenth Street, NW, Washington, DC 20431, (202) 623-7000, Fax: (202) 623-4661, www.imf.org; *Balance of Payments Statistics Newsletter* and *Balance of Payments Statistics Yearbook 2007.*

Organisation for Economic Cooperation and Development (OECD), 2 rue Andre Pascal, F-75775 Paris Cedex 16, France, (Telephone in U.S. (202) 785-6323), (Fax in U.S. (202) 785-0350), www.oecd.org; *OECD Economic Survey - Chile 2007.*

Organization of American States (OAS), 17th Street Constitution Avenue NW, Washington, DC 20006, (202) 458-3000, www.oas.org; *The OAS in Transition: 1994-2004.*

Taylor and Francis Group, An Informa Business, 2 Park Square, Milton Park, Abingdon, Oxford OX14 4RN, United Kingdom, (Dial from U.S. (212) 216-7800), (Fax from U.S. (212) 564-7854), www.tandf.co.uk; *The Europa World Year Book.*

UCLA Latin American Institute, 10343 Bunche Hall, Box 951447, Los Angeles, CA 90095-1447, (310) 825-4571, Fax: (310) 206-6859, www.international.ucla.edu/lac; *Statistical Abstract of Latin America.*

United Nations Conference on Trade and Development (UNCTAD), DC2-1120, United Nations, New York, NY 10017, (212) 963-0027, www.unctad.org; *Handbook of Statistics 2005.*

United Nations Statistics Division, New York, NY 10017, (800) 253-9646, Fax: (212) 963-4116, http://unstats.un.org; *Economic Survey of Latin America and the Caribbean 2004-2005* and *Statistical Yearbook for Latin America and the Caribbean 2004.*

The World Bank, 1818 H Street, NW, Washington, DC 20433, (202) 473-1000, Fax: (202) 477-6391, www.worldbank.org; *Chile; World Development Indicators (WDI) 2008;* and *World Development Report 2008.*

CHILE - BANKS AND BANKING

Euromonitor International, Inc., 224 S. Michigan Avenue, Suite 1500, Chicago, IL 60604, (312) 922-1115, Fax: (312) 922-1157, www.euromonitor.com; *World Marketing Data and Statistics.*

Inter-American Development Bank (IDB), 1300 New York Avenue, NW, Washington, DC 20577, (202) 623-1000, Fax: (202) 623-3096, www.iadb.org; *The Politics of Policies: Economic and Social Progress in Latin America - 2006 Report.*

International Monetary Fund (IMF), 700 Nineteenth Street, NW, Washington, DC 20431, (202) 623-7000, Fax: (202) 623-4661, www.imf.org; *Government Finance Statistics Yearbook (2008 Edition)* and *International Financial Statistics Yearbook 2007.*

M.E. Sharpe, 80 Business Park Drive, Armonk, NY 10504, (800) 541-6563, Fax: (914) 273-2106, www.mesharpe.com; *The Illustrated Book of World Rankings.*

Organisation for Economic Cooperation and Development (OECD), 2 rue Andre Pascal, F-75775 Paris Cedex 16, France, (Telephone in U.S. (202) 785-6323), (Fax in U.S. (202) 785-0350), www.oecd.org; *OECD Economic Survey - Chile 2007.*

Palgrave Macmillan Ltd., Houndmills, Basingstoke, Hampshire, RG21 6XS, England, (Telephone in U.S. (888) 330-8477), (Fax in U.S. (800) 672-2054), www.palgrave.com; *The Statesman's Yearbook 2008.*

Taylor and Francis Group, An Informa Business, 2 Park Square, Milton Park, Abingdon, Oxford OX14 4RN, United Kingdom, (Dial from U.S. (212) 216-7800), (Fax from U.S. (212) 564-7854), www.tandf.co.uk; *The Europa World Year Book.*

United Nations Statistics Division, New York, NY 10017, (800) 253-9646, Fax: (212) 963-4116, http://unstats.un.org; *Statistical Yearbook for Latin America and the Caribbean 2004.*

CHILE - BARLEY PRODUCTION

See CHILE - CROPS

CHILE - BEVERAGE INDUSTRY

M.E. Sharpe, 80 Business Park Drive, Armonk, NY 10504, (800) 541-6563, Fax: (914) 273-2106, www.mesharpe.com; *The Illustrated Book of World Rankings.*

United Nations Statistics Division, New York, NY 10017, (800) 253-9646, Fax: (212) 963-4116, http://unstats.un.org; *Statistical Yearbook.*

CHILE - BIRTH CONTROL

UCLA Latin American Institute, 10343 Bunche Hall, Box 951447, Los Angeles, CA 90095-1447, (310) 825-4571, Fax: (310) 206-6859, www.international.ucla.edu/lac; *Statistical Abstract of Latin America.*

CHILE - BONDS

Inter-American Development Bank (IDB), 1300 New York Avenue, NW, Washington, DC 20577, (202) 623-1000, Fax: (202) 623-3096, www.iadb.org; *The Politics of Policies: Economic and Social Progress in Latin America - 2006 Report.*

International Monetary Fund (IMF), 700 Nineteenth Street, NW, Washington, DC 20431, (202) 623-7000, Fax: (202) 623-4661, www.imf.org; *Government Finance Statistics Yearbook (2008 Edition).*

CHILE - BROADCASTING

Central Intelligence Agency, Office of Public Affairs, Washington, DC 20505, (703) 482-0623, Fax: (703) 482-1739, www.cia.gov; *The World Factbook.*

Euromonitor International, Inc., 224 S. Michigan Avenue, Suite 1500, Chicago, IL 60604, (312) 922-1115, Fax: (312) 922-1157, www.euromonitor.com; *World Marketing Data and Statistics.*

M.E. Sharpe, 80 Business Park Drive, Armonk, NY 10504, (800) 541-6563, Fax: (914) 273-2106, www.mesharpe.com; *The Illustrated Book of World Rankings.*

Palgrave Macmillan Ltd., Houndmills, Basingstoke, Hampshire, RG21 6XS, England, (Telephone in U.S. (888) 330-8477), (Fax in U.S. (800) 672-2054), www.palgrave.com; *The Statesman's Yearbook 2008.*

WRTH Publications Limited, PO Box 290, Oxford OX2 7FT, UK, www.wrth.com; *World Radio TV Handbook 2007.*

CHILE - BUDGET

Central Intelligence Agency, Office of Public Affairs, Washington, DC 20505, (703) 482-0623, Fax: (703) 482-1739, www.cia.gov; *The World Factbook.*

CHILE - BUSINESS

Inter-American Development Bank (IDB), 1300 New York Avenue, NW, Washington, DC 20577, (202) 623-1000, Fax: (202) 623-3096, www.iadb.org; *The Politics of Policies: Economic and Social Progress in Latin America - 2006 Report.*

CHILE - CADMIUM PRODUCTION

See CHILE - MINERAL INDUSTRIES

CHILE - CAPITAL INVESTMENTS

Inter-American Development Bank (IDB), 1300 New York Avenue, NW, Washington, DC 20577, (202) 623-1000, Fax: (202) 623-3096, www.iadb.org; *The Politics of Policies: Economic and Social Progress in Latin America - 2006 Report.*

CHILE - CAPITAL LEVY

Inter-American Development Bank (IDB), 1300 New York Avenue, NW, Washington, DC 20577, (202) 623-1000, Fax: (202) 623-3096, www.iadb.org; *The Politics of Policies: Economic and Social Progress in Latin America - 2006 Report.*

International Monetary Fund (IMF), 700 Nineteenth Street, NW, Washington, DC 20431, (202) 623-7000, Fax: (202) 623-4661, www.imf.org; *Government Finance Statistics Yearbook (2008 Edition).*

CHILE - CATTLE

See CHILE - LIVESTOCK

CHILE - CHICK PEA PRODUCTION

See CHILE - CROPS

CHILE - CHICKENS

See CHILE - LIVESTOCK

CHILE - CHILDBIRTH - STATISTICS

Central Intelligence Agency, Office of Public Affairs, Washington, DC 20505, (703) 482-0623, Fax: (703) 482-1739, www.cia.gov; *The World Factbook.*

Euromonitor International, Inc., 224 S. Michigan Avenue, Suite 1500, Chicago, IL 60604, (312) 922-1115, Fax: (312) 922-1157, www.euromonitor.com; *International Marketing Data and Statistics 2008* and *The World Economic Factbook 2008.*

M.E. Sharpe, 80 Business Park Drive, Armonk, NY 10504, (800) 541-6563, Fax: (914) 273-2106, www.mesharpe.com; *The Illustrated Book of World Rankings.*

Palgrave Macmillan Ltd., Houndmills, Basingstoke, Hampshire, RG21 6XS, England, (Telephone in U.S. (888) 330-8477), (Fax in U.S. (800) 672-2054), www.palgrave.com; *The Statesman's Yearbook 2008.*

Taylor and Francis Group, An Informa Business, 2 Park Square, Milton Park, Abingdon, Oxford OX14 4RN, United Kingdom, (Dial from U.S. (212) 216-7800), (Fax from U.S. (212) 564-7854), www.tandf.co.uk; *The Europa World Year Book.*

United Nations Statistics Division, New York, NY 10017, (800) 253-9646, Fax: (212) 963-4116, http://unstats.un.org; *Demographic Yearbook; Statistical Yearbook;* and *Statistical Yearbook for Latin America and the Caribbean 2004.*

The World Bank, 1818 H Street, NW, Washington, DC 20433, (202) 473-1000, Fax: (202) 477-6391, www.worldbank.org; *World Development Indicators (WDI) 2008.*

World Health Organization (WHO), Avenue Appia 20, 1211 Geneve 27, Switzerland, (Telephone in U.S. (212) 331-9081), www.who.int; *World Health Report 2006.*

CHILE - CLIMATE

M.E. Sharpe, 80 Business Park Drive, Armonk, NY 10504, (800) 541-6563, Fax: (914) 273-2106, www.mesharpe.com; *The Illustrated Book of World Rankings.*

Palgrave Macmillan Ltd., Houndmills, Basingstoke, Hampshire, RG21 6XS, England, (Telephone in U.S. (888) 330-8477), (Fax in U.S. (800) 672-2054), www.palgrave.com; *The Statesman's Yearbook 2008.*

CHILE - COAL PRODUCTION

See CHILE - MINERAL INDUSTRIES

CHILE - COFFEE

See CHILE - CROPS

CHILE - COMMERCE

Palgrave Macmillan Ltd., Houndmills, Basingstoke, Hampshire, RG21 6XS, England, (Telephone in U.S. (888) 330-8477), (Fax in U.S. (800) 672-2054), www.palgrave.com; *The Statesman's Yearbook 2008.*

CHILE - COMMODITY EXCHANGES

Commodity Research Bureau, 330 South Wells Street, Suite 612, Chicago, IL 60606-7110, (800) 621-5271, Fax: (312) 939-4135, www.crbtrader.com; *2006 CRB Commodity Yearbook and CD.*

International Monetary Fund (IMF), 700 Nineteenth Street, NW, Washington, DC 20431, (202) 623-7000, Fax: (202) 623-4661, www.imf.org; *IMF Primary Commodity Prices.*

United Nations Food and Agricultural Organization (FAO), Viale delle Terme di Caracalla, 00100 Rome, Italy, (Dial from U.S. (202) 653-2400), (Fax from U.S. (202) 653 5760), www.fao.org; *The State of Food and Agriculture (SOFA) 2006.*

United Nations Statistics Division, New York, NY 10017, (800) 253-9646, Fax: (212) 963-4116, http://unstats.un.org; *Statistical Yearbook.*

World Bureau of Metal Statistics (WBMS), 27a High Street, Ware, Hertfordshire, SG12 9BA, United Kingdom, www.world-bureau.com; *Annual Stainless Steel Statistics; World Flow Charts; World Metal Statistics; World Nickel Statistics;* and *World Tin Statistics.*

CHILE - COMMUNICATION AND TRAFFIC

United Nations Statistics Division, New York, NY 10017, (800) 253-9646, Fax: (212) 963-4116, http://unstats.un.org; *Statistical Yearbook.*

CHILE - CONSTRUCTION INDUSTRY

Economist Intelligence Unit, 111 West 57th Street, New York, NY 10019, (212) 554-0600, Fax: (212) 586-1181, www.eiu.com; *Business Latin America.*

Inter-American Development Bank (IDB), 1300 New York Avenue, NW, Washington, DC 20577, (202) 623-1000, Fax: (202) 623-3096, www.iadb.org; *The Politics of Policies: Economic and Social Progress in Latin America - 2006 Report.*

M.E. Sharpe, 80 Business Park Drive, Armonk, NY 10504, (800) 541-6563, Fax: (914) 273-2106, www.mesharpe.com; *The Illustrated Book of World Rankings.*

Organisation for Economic Cooperation and Development (OECD), 2 rue Andre Pascal, F-75775 Paris Cedex 16, France, (Telephone in U.S. (202) 785-6323), (Fax in U.S. (202) 785-0350), www.oecd.org; *OECD Economic Survey - Chile 2007.*

Organization of American States (OAS), 17th Street Constitution Avenue NW, Washington, DC 20006, (202) 458-3000, www.oas.org; *The OAS in Transition: 1994-2004.*

Palgrave Macmillan Ltd., Houndmills, Basingstoke, Hampshire, RG21 6XS, England, (Telephone in U.S. (888) 330-8477), (Fax in U.S. (800) 672-2054), www.palgrave.com; *The Statesman's Yearbook 2008.*

UCLA Latin American Institute, 10343 Bunche Hall, Box 951447, Los Angeles, CA 90095-1447, (310) 825-4571, Fax: (310) 206-6859, www.international.ucla.edu/lac; *Statistical Abstract of Latin America.*

United Nations Statistics Division, New York, NY 10017, (800) 253-9646, Fax: (212) 963-4116, http://unstats.un.org; *Statistical Yearbook.*

CHILE - CONSUMER COOPERATIVES

UCLA Latin American Institute, 10343 Bunche Hall, Box 951447, Los Angeles, CA 90095-1447, (310) 825-4571, Fax: (310) 206-6859, www.international.ucla.edu/lac; *Statistical Abstract of Latin America.*

CHILE - CONSUMER PRICE INDEXES

Taylor and Francis Group, An Informa Business, 2 Park Square, Milton Park, Abingdon, Oxford OX14 4RN, United Kingdom, (Dial from U.S. (212) 216-7800), (Fax from U.S. (212) 564-7854), www.tandf.co.uk; *The Europa World Year Book.*

United Nations Statistics Division, New York, NY 10017, (800) 253-9646, Fax: (212) 963-4116, http://unstats.un.org; *Statistical Yearbook.*

The World Bank, 1818 H Street, NW, Washington, DC 20433, (202) 473-1000, Fax: (202) 477-6391, www.worldbank.org; *Chile.*

CHILE - CONSUMPTION (ECONOMICS)

Economist Intelligence Unit, 111 West 57th Street, New York, NY 10019, (212) 554-0600, Fax: (212) 586-1181, www.eiu.com; *Business Latin America.*

Inter-American Development Bank (IDB), 1300 New York Avenue, NW, Washington, DC 20577, (202) 623-1000, Fax: (202) 623-3096, www.iadb.org; *The Politics of Policies: Economic and Social Progress in Latin America - 2006 Report.*

United Nations Statistics Division, New York, NY 10017, (800) 253-9646, Fax: (212) 963-4116, http://unstats.un.org; *Statistical Yearbook for Latin America and the Caribbean 2004.*

The World Bank, 1818 H Street, NW, Washington, DC 20433, (202) 473-1000, Fax: (202) 477-6391, www.worldbank.org; *World Development Report 2008.*

CHILE - COPPER INDUSTRY AND TRADE

See CHILE - MINERAL INDUSTRIES

CHILE - CORN INDUSTRY

See CHILE - CROPS

CHILE - COST AND STANDARD OF LIVING

International Monetary Fund (IMF), 700 Nineteenth Street, NW, Washington, DC 20431, (202) 623-7000, Fax: (202) 623-4661, www.imf.org; *Government Finance Statistics Yearbook (2008 Edition).*

CHILE - COTTON

See CHILE - CROPS

CHILE - CRIME

International Criminal Police Organization (INTERPOL), General Secretariat, 200 quai Charles de Gaulle, 69006 Lyon, France, www.interpol.int; *International Crime Statistics.*

U.S. Department of Justice (DOJ), National Institute of Justice (NIJ), 810 Seventh Street, NW, Washington, DC 20531, (202) 307-2942, Fax: (202) 616-0275, www.ojp.usdoj.gov/nij/; *I-ADAM in Eight Countries: Approaches and Challenges.*

Yale University Press, PO Box 209040, New Haven, CT 06520-9040, (203) 432-0960, Fax: (203) 432-0948, http://yalepress.yale.edu/yupbooks; *Violence and Crime in Cross-National Perspective.*

CHILE - CROPS

Economist Intelligence Unit, 111 West 57th Street, New York, NY 10019, (212) 554-0600, Fax: (212) 586-1181, www.eiu.com; *Business Latin America.*

M.E. Sharpe, 80 Business Park Drive, Armonk, NY 10504, (800) 541-6563, Fax: (914) 273-2106, www.mesharpe.com; *The Illustrated Book of World Rankings.*

Palgrave Macmillan Ltd., Houndmills, Basingstoke, Hampshire, RG21 6XS, England, (Telephone in U.S. (888) 330-8477), (Fax in U.S. (800) 672-2054), www.palgrave.com; *The Statesman's Yearbook 2008.*

Taylor and Francis Group, An Informa Business, 2 Park Square, Milton Park, Abingdon, Oxford OX14 4RN, United Kingdom, (Dial from U.S. (212) 216-7800), (Fax from U.S. (212) 564-7854), www.tandf.co.uk; *The Europa World Year Book.*

United Nations Conference on Trade and Development (UNCTAD), DC2-1120, United Nations, New York, NY 10017, (212) 963-0027, www.unctad.org; *UNCTAD Commodity Yearbook.*

United Nations Food and Agricultural Organization (FAO), Viale delle Terme di Caracalla, 00100 Rome, Italy, (Dial from U.S. (202) 653-2400), (Fax from U.S. (202) 653 5760), www.fao.org; *FAO Production Yearbook 2002* and *The State of Food and Agriculture (SOFA) 2006.*

United Nations Statistics Division, New York, NY 10017, (800) 253-9646, Fax: (212) 963-4116, http://unstats.un.org; *Statistical Yearbook.*

CHILE - CUSTOMS ADMINISTRATION

Inter-American Development Bank (IDB), 1300 New York Avenue, NW, Washington, DC 20577, (202) 623-1000, Fax: (202) 623-3096, www.iadb.org; *The Politics of Policies: Economic and Social Progress in Latin America - 2006 Report.*

International Monetary Fund (IMF), 700 Nineteenth Street, NW, Washington, DC 20431, (202) 623-7000, Fax: (202) 623-4661, www.imf.org; *Government Finance Statistics Yearbook (2008 Edition).*

Palgrave Macmillan Ltd., Houndmills, Basingstoke, Hampshire, RG21 6XS, England, (Telephone in U.S. (888) 330-8477), (Fax in U.S. (800) 672-2054), www.palgrave.com; *The Statesman's Yearbook 2008.*

CHILE - DAIRY PROCESSING

M.E. Sharpe, 80 Business Park Drive, Armonk, NY 10504, (800) 541-6563, Fax: (914) 273-2106, www.mesharpe.com; *The Illustrated Book of World Rankings.*

Palgrave Macmillan Ltd., Houndmills, Basingstoke, Hampshire, RG21 6XS, England, (Telephone in U.S. (888) 330-8477), (Fax in U.S. (800) 672-2054), www.palgrave.com; *The Statesman's Yearbook 2008.*

United Nations Food and Agricultural Organization (FAO), Viale delle Terme di Caracalla, 00100 Rome, Italy, (Dial from U.S. (202) 653-2400), (Fax from U.S. (202) 653 5760), www.fao.org; *The State of Food and Agriculture (SOFA) 2006.*

United Nations Statistics Division, New York, NY 10017, (800) 253-9646, Fax: (212) 963-4116, http://unstats.un.org; *Statistical Yearbook.*

CHILE - DEATH RATES

See CHILE - MORTALITY

CHILE - DEBT

Economist Intelligence Unit, 111 West 57th Street, New York, NY 10019, (212) 554-0600, Fax: (212) 586-1181, www.eiu.com; *Business Latin America.*

The World Bank, 1818 H Street, NW, Washington, DC 20433, (202) 473-1000, Fax: (202) 477-6391, www.worldbank.org; *Global Development Finance 2007.*

CHILE - DEBTS, EXTERNAL

Economist Intelligence Unit, 111 West 57th Street, New York, NY 10019, (212) 554-0600, Fax: (212) 586-1181, www.eiu.com; *Business Latin America.*

Inter-American Development Bank (IDB), 1300 New York Avenue, NW, Washington, DC 20577, (202) 623-1000, Fax: (202) 623-3096, www.iadb.org; *The Politics of Policies: Economic and Social Progress in Latin America - 2006 Report.*

International Monetary Fund (IMF), 700 Nineteenth Street, NW, Washington, DC 20431, (202) 623-7000, Fax: (202) 623-4661, www.imf.org; *Government Finance Statistics Yearbook (2008 Edition).*

Palgrave Macmillan Ltd., Houndmills, Basingstoke, Hampshire, RG21 6XS, England, (Telephone in U.S. (888) 330-8477), (Fax in U.S. (800) 672-2054), www.palgrave.com; *The Statesman's Yearbook 2008.*

United Nations Statistics Division, New York, NY 10017, (800) 253-9646, Fax: (212) 963-4116, http://unstats.un.org; *Economic Survey of Latin America and the Caribbean 2004-2005* and *Statistical Yearbook for Latin America and the Caribbean 2004.*

The World Bank, 1818 H Street, NW, Washington, DC 20433, (202) 473-1000, Fax: (202) 477-6391, www.worldbank.org; *Global Development Finance 2007; World Development Indicators (WDI) 2008;* and *World Development Report 2008.*

CHILE - DEFENSE EXPENDITURES

See CHILE - ARMED FORCES

CHILE - DEMOGRAPHY

Euromonitor International, Inc., 224 S. Michigan Avenue, Suite 1500, Chicago, IL 60604, (312) 922-1115, Fax: (312) 922-1157, www.euromonitor.com; *International Marketing Data and Statistics 2008; The World Economic Factbook 2008;* and *World Marketing Data and Statistics.*

M.E. Sharpe, 80 Business Park Drive, Armonk, NY 10504, (800) 541-6563, Fax: (914) 273-2106, www.mesharpe.com; *The Illustrated Book of World Rankings.*

United Nations Statistics Division, New York, NY 10017, (800) 253-9646, Fax: (212) 963-4116, http://unstats.un.org; *Human Development Report 2006.*

The World Bank, 1818 H Street, NW, Washington, DC 20433, (202) 473-1000, Fax: (202) 477-6391, www.worldbank.org; *Chile.*

CHILE - DIAMONDS

See CHILE - MINERAL INDUSTRIES

CHILE - DISPOSABLE INCOME

Inter-American Development Bank (IDB), 1300 New York Avenue, NW, Washington, DC 20577, (202) 623-1000, Fax: (202) 623-3096, www.iadb.org; *The Politics of Policies: Economic and Social Progress in Latin America - 2006 Report.*

M.E. Sharpe, 80 Business Park Drive, Armonk, NY 10504, (800) 541-6563, Fax: (914) 273-2106, www.mesharpe.com; *The Illustrated Book of World Rankings.*

United Nations Statistics Division, New York, NY 10017, (800) 253-9646, Fax: (212) 963-4116, http://unstats.un.org; *National Accounts Statistics: Compendium of Income Distribution Statistics* and *Statistical Yearbook for Latin America and the Caribbean 2004.*

CHILE - DIVORCE

M.E. Sharpe, 80 Business Park Drive, Armonk, NY 10504, (800) 541-6563, Fax: (914) 273-2106, www.mesharpe.com; *The Illustrated Book of World Rankings.*

United Nations Statistics Division, New York, NY 10017, (800) 253-9646, Fax: (212) 963-4116, http://unstats.un.org; *Demographic Yearbook* and *Statistical Yearbook.*

CHILE - ECONOMIC ASSISTANCE

Inter-American Development Bank (IDB), 1300 New York Avenue, NW, Washington, DC 20577, (202) 623-1000, Fax: (202) 623-3096, www.iadb.org; *The Politics of Policies: Economic and Social Progress in Latin America - 2006 Report.*

United Nations Statistics Division, New York, NY 10017, (800) 253-9646, Fax: (212) 963-4116, http://unstats.un.org; *Statistical Yearbook.*

CHILE - ECONOMIC CONDITIONS

Center for International Business Education Research (CIBER), Columbia Business School and School of International and Public Affairs, Uris Hall, Room 212, 3022 Broadway, New York, NY 10027-6902, Mr. Joshua Safier, (212) 854-4750, Fax: (212) 222-9821, www.columbia.edu/cu/ciber/; Datastream International.

Central Intelligence Agency, Office of Public Affairs, Washington, DC 20505, (703) 482-0623, Fax: (703) 482-1739, www.cia.gov; *The World Factbook.*

DSI Data Service Information, Xantener Strasse 51a, D-47495 Rheinberg, Germany, www.dsidata.com; *Campus Solution.*

Dun and Bradstreet (DB) Corporation, 103 JFK Parkway, Short Hills, NJ 07078, (973) 921-5500, www.dnb.com; *Country Report.*

Economist Intelligence Unit, 111 West 57th Street, New York, NY 10019, (212) 554-0600, Fax: (212) 586-1181, www.eiu.com; *Chile Country Report.*

Euromonitor International, Inc., 224 S. Michigan Avenue, Suite 1500, Chicago, IL 60604, (312) 922-1115, Fax: (312) 922-1157, www.euromonitor.com; *International Marketing Data and Statistics 2008; The World Economic Factbook 2008;* and *World Marketing Data and Statistics.*

Inter-American Development Bank (IDB), 1300 New York Avenue, NW, Washington, DC 20577, (202) 623-1000, Fax: (202) 623-3096, www.iadb.org; *The Politics of Policies: Economic and Social Progress in Latin America - 2006 Report.*

International Monetary Fund (IMF), 700 Nineteenth Street, NW, Washington, DC 20431, (202) 623-7000, Fax: (202) 623-4661, www.imf.org; *World Economic Outlook Reports.*

M.E. Sharpe, 80 Business Park Drive, Armonk, NY 10504, (800) 541-6563, Fax: (914) 273-2106, www.mesharpe.com; *The Illustrated Book of World Rankings.*

Organisation for Economic Cooperation and Development (OECD), 2 rue Andre Pascal, F-75775 Paris Cedex 16, France, (Telephone in U.S. (202) 785-6323), (Fax in U.S. (202) 785-0350), www.oecd.org; *OECD Economic Survey - Chile 2007.*

Organization of American States (OAS), 17th Street Constitution Avenue NW, Washington, DC 20006, (202) 458-3000, www.oas.org; *The OAS in Transition: 1994-2004.*

Palgrave Macmillan Ltd., Houndmills, Basingstoke, Hampshire, RG21 6XS, England, (Telephone in U.S. (888) 330-8477), (Fax in U.S. (800) 672-2054), www.palgrave.com; *The Statesman's Yearbook 2008.*

Taylor and Francis Group, An Informa Business, 2 Park Square, Milton Park, Abingdon, Oxford OX14 4RN, United Kingdom, (Dial from U.S. (212) 216-7800), (Fax from U.S. (212) 564-7854), www.tandf.co.uk; *The Europa World Year Book.*

UCLA Latin American Institute, 10343 Bunche Hall, Box 951447, Los Angeles, CA 90095-1447, (310) 825-4571, Fax: (310) 206-6859, www.international.ucla.edu/lac; *Statistical Abstract of Latin America.*

United Nations Statistics Division, New York, NY 10017, (800) 253-9646, Fax: (212) 963-4116, http://unstats.un.org; *Economic Survey of Latin America and the Caribbean 2004-2005* and *World Statistics Pocketbook.*

The World Bank, 1818 H Street, NW, Washington, DC 20433, (202) 473-1000, Fax: (202) 477-6391, www.worldbank.org; *Chile; Global Economic Monitor (GEM); Global Economic Prospects 2008; The World Bank Atlas 2003-2004;* and *World Development Report 2008.*

CHILE - ECONOMICS - SOCIOLOGICAL ASPECTS

Inter-American Development Bank (IDB), 1300 New York Avenue, NW, Washington, DC 20577, (202) 623-1000, Fax: (202) 623-3096, www.iadb.org; *The Politics of Policies: Economic and Social Progress in Latin America - 2006 Report.*

UCLA Latin American Institute, 10343 Bunche Hall, Box 951447, Los Angeles, CA 90095-1447, (310) 825-4571, Fax: (310) 206-6859, www.international.ucla.edu/lac; *Statistical Abstract of Latin America.*

CHILE - EDUCATION

Economist Intelligence Unit, 111 West 57th Street, New York, NY 10019, (212) 554-0600, Fax: (212) 586-1181, www.eiu.com; *Business Latin America.*

Euromonitor International, Inc., 224 S. Michigan Avenue, Suite 1500, Chicago, IL 60604, (312) 922-1115, Fax: (312) 922-1157, www.euromonitor.com; *International Marketing Data and Statistics 2008* and *World Marketing Data and Statistics.*

International Monetary Fund (IMF), 700 Nineteenth Street, NW, Washington, DC 20431, (202) 623-7000, Fax: (202) 623-4661, www.imf.org; *Government Finance Statistics Yearbook (2008 Edition).*

M.E. Sharpe, 80 Business Park Drive, Armonk, NY 10504, (800) 541-6563, Fax: (914) 273-2106, www.mesharpe.com; *The Illustrated Book of World Rankings.*

Palgrave Macmillan Ltd., Houndmills, Basingstoke, Hampshire, RG21 6XS, England, (Telephone in U.S. (888) 330-8477), (Fax in U.S. (800) 672-2054), www.palgrave.com; *The Statesman's Yearbook 2008.*

Taylor and Francis Group, An Informa Business, 2 Park Square, Milton Park, Abingdon, Oxford OX14 4RN, United Kingdom, (Dial from U.S. (212) 216-7800), (Fax from U.S. (212) 564-7854), www.tandf.co.uk; *The Europa World Year Book.*

UCLA Latin American Institute, 10343 Bunche Hall, Box 951447, Los Angeles, CA 90095-1447, (310) 825-4571, Fax: (310) 206-6859, www.international.ucla.edu/lac; *Statistical Abstract of Latin America.*

UNESCO Institute for Statistics, C.P. 6128 Succursale Centre-Ville, Montreal, Quebec, H3C 3J7 Canada, (Dial from U.S. (514) 343-6880), (Fax from U.S. (514) 343 6882), www.uis.unesco.org; *Statistical Tables.*

United Nations Statistics Division, New York, NY 10017, (800) 253-9646, Fax: (212) 963-4116, http://unstats.un.org; *Human Development Report 2006* and *Statistical Yearbook for Latin America and the Caribbean 2004.*

The World Bank, 1818 H Street, NW, Washington, DC 20433, (202) 473-1000, Fax: (202) 477-6391, www.worldbank.org; *Chile; World Development Indicators (WDI) 2008;* and *World Development Report 2008.*

CHILE - ELECTRICITY

Economist Intelligence Unit, 111 West 57th Street, New York, NY 10019, (212) 554-0600, Fax: (212) 586-1181, www.eiu.com; *Business Latin America.*

Inter-American Development Bank (IDB), 1300 New York Avenue, NW, Washington, DC 20577, (202) 623-1000, Fax: (202) 623-3096, www.iadb.org; *The Politics of Policies: Economic and Social Progress in Latin America - 2006 Report.*

M.E. Sharpe, 80 Business Park Drive, Armonk, NY 10504, (800) 541-6563, Fax: (914) 273-2106, www.mesharpe.com; *The Illustrated Book of World Rankings.*

Organisation for Economic Cooperation and Development (OECD), 2 rue Andre Pascal, F-75775 Paris Cedex 16, France, (Telephone in U.S. (202) 785-

6323), (Fax in U.S. (202) 785-0350), www.oecd.org; *World Energy Outlook 2007.*

Organization of American States (OAS), 17th Street Constitution Avenue NW, Washington, DC 20006, (202) 458-3000, www.oas.org; *The OAS in Transition: 1994-2004.*

Palgrave Macmillan Ltd., Houndmills, Basingstoke, Hampshire, RG21 6XS, England, (Telephone in U.S. (888) 330-8477), (Fax in U.S. (800) 672-2054), www.palgrave.com; *The Statesman's Yearbook 2008.*

U.S. Department of Energy (DOE), Energy Information Administration (EIA), 1000 Independence Avenue, SW, Washington, DC 20585, (202) 586-8800, www.eia.doe.gov; *International Energy Annual 2004* and *International Energy Outlook 2006.*

United Nations Statistics Division, New York, NY 10017, (800) 253-9646, Fax: (212) 963-4116, http://unstats.un.org; *Human Development Report 2006* and *Statistical Yearbook.*

CHILE - EMIGRATION AND IMMIGRATION

UCLA Latin American Institute, 10343 Bunche Hall, Box 951447, Los Angeles, CA 90095-1447, (310) 825-4571, Fax: (310) 206-6859, www.international.ucla.edu/lac; *Statistical Abstract of Latin America.*

CHILE - EMPLOYMENT

Euromonitor International, Inc., 224 S. Michigan Avenue, Suite 1500, Chicago, IL 60604, (312) 922-1115, Fax: (312) 922-1157, www.euromonitor.com; *International Marketing Data and Statistics 2008.*

International Labour Office, I.L.O. Publications, 4 route des Morillons, CH-1211 Geneva 22, Switzerland, (Telephone in U.S. (202) 653-7652), (Fax in U.S. (202) 653-7687), www.ilo.org; *Yearbook of Labour Statistics 2006.*

M.E. Sharpe, 80 Business Park Drive, Armonk, NY 10504, (800) 541-6563, Fax: (914) 273-2106, www.mesharpe.com; *The Illustrated Book of World Rankings.*

Organisation for Economic Cooperation and Development (OECD), 2 rue Andre Pascal, F-75775 Paris Cedex 16, France, (Telephone in U.S. (202) 785-6323), (Fax in U.S. (202) 785-0350), www.oecd.org; *OECD Economic Survey - Chile 2007.*

Organization of American States (OAS), 17th Street Constitution Avenue NW, Washington, DC 20006, (202) 458-3000, www.oas.org; *The OAS in Transition: 1994-2004.*

UCLA Latin American Institute, 10343 Bunche Hall, Box 951447, Los Angeles, CA 90095-1447, (310) 825-4571, Fax: (310) 206-6859, www.international.ucla.edu/lac; *Statistical Abstract of Latin America.*

United Nations Statistics Division, New York, NY 10017, (800) 253-9646, Fax: (212) 963-4116, http://unstats.un.org; *Statistical Yearbook for Latin America and the Caribbean 2004.*

The World Bank, 1818 H Street, NW, Washington, DC 20433, (202) 473-1000, Fax: (202) 477-6391, www.worldbank.org; *Chile.*

CHILE - ENVIRONMENTAL CONDITIONS

DSI Data Service Information, Xantener Strasse 51a, D-47495 Rheinberg, Germany, www.dsidata.com; *Campus Solution* and *DSI's Global Environmental Database.*

Economist Intelligence Unit, 111 West 57th Street, New York, NY 10019, (212) 554-0600, Fax: (212) 586-1181, www.eiu.com; *Chile Country Report.*

United Nations Statistics Division, New York, NY 10017, (800) 253-9646, Fax: (212) 963-4116, http://unstats.un.org; *World Statistics Pocketbook.*

CHILE - EXPENDITURES, PUBLIC

Inter-American Development Bank (IDB), 1300 New York Avenue, NW, Washington, DC 20577, (202) 623-1000, Fax: (202) 623-3096, www.iadb.org; *The Politics of Policies: Economic and Social Progress in Latin America - 2006 Report.*

Organization of American States (OAS), 17th Street Constitution Avenue NW, Washington, DC 20006, (202) 458-3000, www.oas.org; *The OAS in Transition: 1994-2004.*

United Nations Statistics Division, New York, NY 10017, (800) 253-9646, Fax: (212) 963-4116, http://unstats.un.org; *Statistical Yearbook for Latin America and the Caribbean 2004.*

CHILE - EXPORTS

Central Intelligence Agency, Office of Public Affairs, Washington, DC 20505, (703) 482-0623, Fax: (703) 482-1739, www.cia.gov; *The World Factbook.*

Economist Intelligence Unit, 111 West 57th Street, New York, NY 10019, (212) 554-0600, Fax: (212) 586-1181, www.eiu.com; *Business Latin America* and *Chile Country Report.*

Euromonitor International, Inc., 224 S. Michigan Avenue, Suite 1500, Chicago, IL 60604, (312) 922-1115, Fax: (312) 922-1157, www.euromonitor.com; *International Marketing Data and Statistics 2008* and *The World Economic Factbook 2008.*

Inter-American Development Bank (IDB), 1300 New York Avenue, NW, Washington, DC 20577, (202) 623-1000, Fax: (202) 623-3096, www.iadb.org; *The Politics of Policies: Economic and Social Progress in Latin America - 2006 Report.*

International Monetary Fund (IMF), 700 Nineteenth Street, NW, Washington, DC 20431, (202) 623-7000, Fax: (202) 623-4661, www.imf.org; *Direction of Trade Statistics Yearbook 2007* and *International Financial Statistics Yearbook 2007.*

Organisation for Economic Cooperation and Development (OECD), 2 rue Andre Pascal, F-75775 Paris Cedex 16, France, (Telephone in U.S. (202) 785-6323), (Fax in U.S. (202) 785-0350), www.oecd.org; *OECD Economic Survey - Chile 2007.*

Organization of American States (OAS), 17th Street Constitution Avenue NW, Washington, DC 20006, (202) 458-3000, www.oas.org; *The OAS in Transition: 1994-2004.*

Palgrave Macmillan Ltd., Houndmills, Basingstoke, Hampshire, RG21 6XS, England, (Telephone in U.S. (888) 330-8477), (Fax in U.S. (800) 672-2054), www.palgrave.com; *The Statesman's Yearbook 2008.*

Taylor and Francis Group, An Informa Business, 2 Park Square, Milton Park, Abingdon, Oxford OX14 4RN, United Kingdom, (Dial from U.S. (212) 216-7800), (Fax from U.S. (212) 564-7854), www.tandf.co.uk; *The Europa World Year Book.*

United Nations Conference on Trade and Development (UNCTAD), DC2-1120, United Nations, New York, NY 10017, (212) 963-0027, www.unctad.org; *Handbook of Statistics 2005.*

United Nations Food and Agricultural Organization (FAO), Viale delle Terme di Caracalla, 00100 Rome, Italy, (Dial from U.S. (202) 653-2400), (Fax from U.S. (202) 653 5760), www.fao.org; *The State of Food and Agriculture (SOFA) 2006.*

United Nations Statistics Division, New York, NY 10017, (800) 253-9646, Fax: (212) 963-4116, http://unstats.un.org; *Statistical Yearbook for Latin America and the Caribbean 2004.*

The World Bank, 1818 H Street, NW, Washington, DC 20433, (202) 473-1000, Fax: (202) 477-6391, www.worldbank.org; *World Development Indicators (WDI) 2008* and *World Development Report 2008.*

CHILE - FEMALE WORKING POPULATION

See CHILE - EMPLOYMENT

CHILE - FERTILITY, HUMAN

Central Intelligence Agency, Office of Public Affairs, Washington, DC 20505, (703) 482-0623, Fax: (703) 482-1739, www.cia.gov; *The World Factbook.*

M.E. Sharpe, 80 Business Park Drive, Armonk, NY 10504, (800) 541-6563, Fax: (914) 273-2106, www.mesharpe.com; *The Illustrated Book of World Rankings.*

United Nations Statistics Division, New York, NY 10017, (800) 253-9646, Fax: (212) 963-4116, http://unstats.un.org; *Human Development Report 2006.*

The World Bank, 1818 H Street, NW, Washington, DC 20433, (202) 473-1000, Fax: (202) 477-6391, www.worldbank.org; *The World Bank Atlas 2003-2004; World Development Indicators (WDI) 2008;* and *World Development Report 2008.*

CHILE - FERTILIZER INDUSTRY

Economist Intelligence Unit, 111 West 57th Street, New York, NY 10019, (212) 554-0600, Fax: (212) 586-1181, www.eiu.com; *Business Latin America.*

United Nations Food and Agricultural Organization (FAO), Viale delle Terme di Caracalla, 00100 Rome, Italy, (Dial from U.S. (202) 653-2400), (Fax from U.S. (202) 653 5760), www.fao.org; *FAO Fertilizer Yearbook* and *The State of Food and Agriculture (SOFA) 2006.*

United Nations Statistics Division, New York, NY 10017, (800) 253-9646, Fax: (212) 963-4116, http://unstats.un.org; *Statistical Yearbook.*

CHILE - FETAL MORTALITY

See CHILE - MORTALITY

CHILE - FINANCE

Inter-American Development Bank (IDB), 1300 New York Avenue, NW, Washington, DC 20577, (202) 623-1000, Fax: (202) 623-3096, www.iadb.org; *The Politics of Policies: Economic and Social Progress in Latin America - 2006 Report.*

Organization of American States (OAS), 17th Street Constitution Avenue NW, Washington, DC 20006, (202) 458-3000, www.oas.org; *The OAS in Transition: 1994-2004.*

Taylor and Francis Group, An Informa Business, 2 Park Square, Milton Park, Abingdon, Oxford OX14 4RN, United Kingdom, (Dial from U.S. (212) 216-7800), (Fax from U.S. (212) 564-7854), www.tandf.co.uk; *The Europa World Year Book.*

UCLA Latin American Institute, 10343 Bunche Hall, Box 951447, Los Angeles, CA 90095-1447, (310) 825-4571, Fax: (310) 206-6859, www.international.ucla.edu/lac; *Statistical Abstract of Latin America.*

United Nations Statistics Division, New York, NY 10017, (800) 253-9646, Fax: (212) 963-4116, http://unstats.un.org; *National Accounts Statistics: Compendium of Income Distribution Statistics* and *Statistical Yearbook.*

The World Bank, 1818 H Street, NW, Washington, DC 20433, (202) 473-1000, Fax: (202) 477-6391, www.worldbank.org; *Chile.*

CHILE - FINANCE, PUBLIC

Bernan Essential Government Publications, 4611-F Assembly Drive, Lanham MD, 20706-4391, (301) 459-2255, Fax: (800) 865-3450, www.bernan.com; *National Accounts Statistics.*

Economist Intelligence Unit, 111 West 57th Street, New York, NY 10019, (212) 554-0600, Fax: (212) 586-1181, www.eiu.com; *Chile Country Report.*

Inter-American Development Bank (IDB), 1300 New York Avenue, NW, Washington, DC 20577, (202) 623-1000, Fax: (202) 623-3096, www.iadb.org; *The Politics of Policies: Economic and Social Progress in Latin America - 2006 Report.*

International Monetary Fund (IMF), 700 Nineteenth Street, NW, Washington, DC 20431, (202) 623-7000, Fax: (202) 623-4661, www.imf.org; *Government Finance Statistics Yearbook (2008 Edition); International Financial Statistics; International Financial Statistics Online Service;* and *International Financial Statistics Yearbook 2007.*

M.E. Sharpe, 80 Business Park Drive, Armonk, NY 10504, (800) 541-6563, Fax: (914) 273-2106, www.mesharpe.com; *The Illustrated Book of World Rankings.*

Organization of American States (OAS), 17th Street Constitution Avenue NW, Washington, DC 20006, (202) 458-3000, www.oas.org; *The OAS in Transition: 1994-2004.*

Palgrave Macmillan Ltd., Houndmills, Basingstoke, Hampshire, RG21 6XS, England, (Telephone in U.S. (888) 330-8477), (Fax in U.S. (800) 672-2054), www.palgrave.com; *The Statesman's Yearbook 2008.*

Taylor and Francis Group, An Informa Business, 2 Park Square, Milton Park, Abingdon, Oxford OX14 4RN, United Kingdom, (Dial from U.S. (212) 216-7800), (Fax from U.S. (212) 564-7854), www.tandf.co.uk; *The Europa World Year Book.*

UCLA Latin American Institute, 10343 Bunche Hall, Box 951447, Los Angeles, CA 90095-1447, (310) 825-4571, Fax: (310) 206-6859, www.international.ucla.edu/lac; *Statistical Abstract of Latin America.*

The World Bank, 1818 H Street, NW, Washington, DC 20433, (202) 473-1000, Fax: (202) 477-6391, www.worldbank.org; *Chile.*

CHILE - FISHERIES

Inter-American Development Bank (IDB), 1300 New York Avenue, NW, Washington, DC 20577, (202) 623-1000, Fax: (202) 623-3096, www.iadb.org; *The Politics of Policies: Economic and Social Progress in Latin America - 2006 Report.*

M.E. Sharpe, 80 Business Park Drive, Armonk, NY 10504, (800) 541-6563, Fax: (914) 273-2106, www.mesharpe.com; *The Illustrated Book of World Rankings.*

Palgrave Macmillan Ltd., Houndmills, Basingstoke, Hampshire, RG21 6XS, England, (Telephone in U.S. (888) 330-8477), (Fax in U.S. (800) 672-2054), www.palgrave.com; *The Statesman's Yearbook 2008.*

Taylor and Francis Group, An Informa Business, 2 Park Square, Milton Park, Abingdon, Oxford OX14 4RN, United Kingdom, (Dial from U.S. (212) 216-7800), (Fax from U.S. (212) 564-7854), www.tandf.co.uk; *The Europa World Year Book.*

UCLA Latin American Institute, 10343 Bunche Hall, Box 951447, Los Angeles, CA 90095-1447, (310) 825-4571, Fax: (310) 206-6859, www.international.ucla.edu/lac; *Statistical Abstract of Latin America.*

United Nations Conference on Trade and Development (UNCTAD), DC2-1120, United Nations, New York, NY 10017, (212) 963-0027, www.unctad.org; *UNCTAD Commodity Yearbook.*

United Nations Food and Agricultural Organization (FAO), Viale delle Terme di Caracalla, 00100 Rome, Italy, (Dial from U.S. (202) 653-2400), (Fax from U.S. (202) 653 5760), www.fao.org; *FAO Yearbook of Fishery Statistics;* Fishery Databases; FISHSTAT Database. Subjects covered include: Aquaculture production, capture production, fishery commodities; and *The State of Food and Agriculture (SOFA) 2006.*

United Nations Statistics Division, New York, NY 10017, (800) 253-9646, Fax: (212) 963-4116, http://unstats.un.org; *Statistical Yearbook.*

The World Bank, 1818 H Street, NW, Washington, DC 20433, (202) 473-1000, Fax: (202) 477-6391, www.worldbank.org; *Chile.*

CHILE - FLOUR INDUSTRY

United Nations Statistics Division, New York, NY 10017, (800) 253-9646, Fax: (212) 963-4116, http://unstats.un.org; *Statistical Yearbook.*

CHILE - FOOD

Euromonitor International, Inc., 224 S. Michigan Avenue, Suite 1500, Chicago, IL 60604, (312) 922-1115, Fax: (312) 922-1157, www.euromonitor.com; *Retail Trade International 2007.*

United Nations Conference on Trade and Development (UNCTAD), DC2-1120, United Nations, New York, NY 10017, (212) 963-0027, www.unctad.org; *UNCTAD Commodity Yearbook.*

United Nations Food and Agricultural Organization (FAO), Viale delle Terme di Caracalla, 00100 Rome, Italy, (Dial from U.S. (202) 653-2400), (Fax from U.S. (202) 653 5760), www.fao.org; *FAO Production Yearbook 2002* and *The State of Food and Agriculture (SOFA) 2006.*

United Nations Statistics Division, New York, NY 10017, (800) 253-9646, Fax: (212) 963-4116, http://unstats.un.org; *Human Development Report 2006.*

CHILE - FOREIGN EXCHANGE RATES

Central Intelligence Agency, Office of Public Affairs, Washington, DC 20505, (703) 482-0623, Fax: (703) 482-1739, www.cia.gov; *The World Factbook.*

Euromonitor International, Inc., 224 S. Michigan Avenue, Suite 1500, Chicago, IL 60604, (312) 922-1115, Fax: (312) 922-1157, www.euromonitor.com; *International Marketing Data and Statistics 2008* and *The World Economic Factbook 2008.*

Inter-American Development Bank (IDB), 1300 New York Avenue, NW, Washington, DC 20577, (202) 623-1000, Fax: (202) 623-3096, www.iadb.org; *The Politics of Policies: Economic and Social Progress in Latin America - 2006 Report.*

International Civil Aviation Organization (ICAO), External Relations and Public Information Office (EPO), 999 University Street, Montreal, Quebec H3C 5H7, Canada, (Dial from U.S. (514) 954-8219), (Fax from U.S. (514) 954-6077), www.icao.int; *Civil Aviation Statistics of the World.*

International Monetary Fund (IMF), 700 Nineteenth Street, NW, Washington, DC 20431, (202) 623-7000, Fax: (202) 623-4661, www.imf.org; *International Financial Statistics Yearbook 2007.*

Organization of American States (OAS), 17th Street Constitution Avenue NW, Washington, DC 20006, (202) 458-3000, www.oas.org; *The OAS in Transition: 1994-2004.*

Taylor and Francis Group, An Informa Business, 2 Park Square, Milton Park, Abingdon, Oxford OX14 4RN, United Kingdom, (Dial from U.S. (212) 216-7800), (Fax from U.S. (212) 564-7854), www.tandf.co.uk; *The Europa World Year Book.*

UCLA Latin American Institute, 10343 Bunche Hall, Box 951447, Los Angeles, CA 90095-1447, (310) 825-4571, Fax: (310) 206-6859, www.international.ucla.edu/lac; *Statistical Abstract of Latin America.*

United Nations Statistics Division, New York, NY 10017, (800) 253-9646, Fax: (212) 963-4116, http://unstats.un.org; *Statistical Yearbook* and *World Statistics Pocketbook.*

CHILE - FORESTS AND FORESTRY

American Forest Paper Association (AFPA), 1111 Nineteenth Street, NW, Suite 800, Washington, DC 20036, (800) 878-8878, www.afandpa.org; *2007 Annual Statistics of Paper, Paperboard, and Wood Pulp.*

Economist Intelligence Unit, 111 West 57th Street, New York, NY 10019, (212) 554-0600, Fax: (212) 586-1181, www.eiu.com; *Business Latin America.*

Inter-American Development Bank (IDB), 1300 New York Avenue, NW, Washington, DC 20577, (202) 623-1000, Fax: (202) 623-3096, www.iadb.org; *The Politics of Policies: Economic and Social Progress in Latin America - 2006 Report.*

M.E. Sharpe, 80 Business Park Drive, Armonk, NY 10504, (800) 541-6563, Fax: (914) 273-2106, www.mesharpe.com; *The Illustrated Book of World Rankings.*

Palgrave Macmillan Ltd., Houndmills, Basingstoke, Hampshire, RG21 6XS, England, (Telephone in U.S. (888) 330-8477), (Fax in U.S. (800) 672-2054), www.palgrave.com; *The Statesman's Yearbook 2008.*

Taylor and Francis Group, An Informa Business, 2 Park Square, Milton Park, Abingdon, Oxford OX14 4RN, United Kingdom, (Dial from U.S. (212) 216-7800), (Fax from U.S. (212) 564-7854), www.tandf.co.uk; *The Europa World Year Book.*

UCLA Latin American Institute, 10343 Bunche Hall, Box 951447, Los Angeles, CA 90095-1447, (310) 825-4571, Fax: (310) 206-6859, www.international.ucla.edu/lac; *Statistical Abstract of Latin America.*

UNESCO Institute for Statistics, C.P. 6128 Succursale Centre-Ville, Montreal, Quebec, H3C 3J7 Canada, (Dial from U.S. (514) 343-6880), (Fax from U.S. (514) 343 6882), www.uis.unesco.org; *Statistical Tables.*

United Nations Conference on Trade and Development (UNCTAD), DC2-1120, United Nations, New York, NY 10017, (212) 963-0027, www.unctad.org; *UNCTAD Commodity Yearbook.*

United Nations Food and Agricultural Organization (FAO), Viale delle Terme di Caracalla, 00100 Rome, Italy, (Dial from U.S. (202) 653-2400), (Fax from U.S. (202) 653 5760), www.fao.org; *FAO Yearbook of Forest Products* and *The State of Food and Agriculture (SOFA) 2006.*

United Nations Statistics Division, New York, NY 10017, (800) 253-9646, Fax: (212) 963-4116, http://unstats.un.org; *Statistical Yearbook.*

The World Bank, 1818 H Street, NW, Washington, DC 20433, (202) 473-1000, Fax: (202) 477-6391, www.worldbank.org; *Chile* and *World Development Report 2008.*

CHILE - GAS PRODUCTION

See CHILE - MINERAL INDUSTRIES

CHILE - GEOGRAPHIC INFORMATION SYSTEMS

M.E. Sharpe, 80 Business Park Drive, Armonk, NY 10504, (800) 541-6563, Fax: (914) 273-2106, www.mesharpe.com; *The Illustrated Book of World Rankings.*

UCLA Latin American Institute, 10343 Bunche Hall, Box 951447, Los Angeles, CA 90095-1447, (310) 825-4571, Fax: (310) 206-6859, www.international.ucla.edu/lac; *Statistical Abstract of Latin America.*

The World Bank, 1818 H Street, NW, Washington, DC 20433, (202) 473-1000, Fax: (202) 477-6391, www.worldbank.org; *Chile.*

CHILE - GOLD INDUSTRY

Economist Intelligence Unit, 111 West 57th Street, New York, NY 10019, (212) 554-0600, Fax: (212) 586-1181, www.eiu.com; *Business Latin America.*

International Monetary Fund (IMF), 700 Nineteenth Street, NW, Washington, DC 20431, (202) 623-7000, Fax: (202) 623-4661, www.imf.org; *International Financial Statistics Yearbook 2007.*

United Nations Statistics Division, New York, NY 10017, (800) 253-9646, Fax: (212) 963-4116, http://unstats.un.org; *Statistical Yearbook.*

The World Bank, 1818 H Street, NW, Washington, DC 20433, (202) 473-1000, Fax: (202) 477-6391, www.worldbank.org; *World Development Indicators (WDI) 2008.*

CHILE - GOLD PRODUCTION

See CHILE - MINERAL INDUSTRIES

CHILE - GRANTS-IN-AID

International Monetary Fund (IMF), 700 Nineteenth Street, NW, Washington, DC 20431, (202) 623-7000, Fax: (202) 623-4661, www.imf.org; *Government Finance Statistics Yearbook (2008 Edition).*

CHILE - GREEN PEPPER AND CHILIE PRODUCTION

See CHILE - CROPS

CHILE - GROSS DOMESTIC PRODUCT

Economist Intelligence Unit, 111 West 57th Street, New York, NY 10019, (212) 554-0600, Fax: (212) 586-1181, www.eiu.com; *Business Latin America* and *Chile Country Report.*

Euromonitor International, Inc., 224 S. Michigan Avenue, Suite 1500, Chicago, IL 60604, (312) 922-1115, Fax: (312) 922-1157, www.euromonitor.com; *International Marketing Data and Statistics 2008* and *The World Economic Factbook 2008.*

Inter-American Development Bank (IDB), 1300 New York Avenue, NW, Washington, DC 20577, (202)

623-1000, Fax: (202) 623-3096, www.iadb.org; *The Politics of Policies: Economic and Social Progress in Latin America - 2006 Report.*

M.E. Sharpe, 80 Business Park Drive, Armonk, NY 10504, (800) 541-6563, Fax: (914) 273-2106, www.mesharpe.com; *The Illustrated Book of World Rankings.*

Organization of American States (OAS), 17th Street Constitution Avenue NW, Washington, DC 20006, (202) 458-3000, www.oas.org; *The OAS in Transition: 1994-2004.*

Taylor and Francis Group, An Informa Business, 2 Park Square, Milton Park, Abingdon, Oxford OX14 4RN, United Kingdom, (Dial from U.S. (212) 216-7800), (Fax from U.S. (212) 564-7854), www.tandf.co.uk; *The Europa World Year Book.*

UCLA Latin American Institute, 10343 Bunche Hall, Box 951447, Los Angeles, CA 90095-1447, (310) 825-4571, Fax: (310) 206-6859, www.international.ucla.edu/lac; *Statistical Abstract of Latin America.*

United Nations Statistics Division, New York, NY 10017, (800) 253-9646, Fax: (212) 963-4116, http://unstats.un.org; *Human Development Report 2006; National Accounts Statistics: Compendium of Income Distribution Statistics; Statistical Yearbook;* and *Statistical Yearbook for Latin America and the Caribbean 2004.*

The World Bank, 1818 H Street, NW, Washington, DC 20433, (202) 473-1000, Fax: (202) 477-6391, www.worldbank.org; *World Development Indicators (WDI) 2008* and *World Development Report 2008.*

CHILE - GROSS NATIONAL PRODUCT

Euromonitor International, Inc., 224 S. Michigan Avenue, Suite 1500, Chicago, IL 60604, (312) 922-1115, Fax: (312) 922-1157, www.euromonitor.com; *International Marketing Data and Statistics 2008.*

Inter-American Development Bank (IDB), 1300 New York Avenue, NW, Washington, DC 20577, (202) 623-1000, Fax: (202) 623-3096, www.iadb.org; *The Politics of Policies: Economic and Social Progress in Latin America - 2006 Report.*

M.E. Sharpe, 80 Business Park Drive, Armonk, NY 10504, (800) 541-6563, Fax: (914) 273-2106, www.mesharpe.com; *The Illustrated Book of World Rankings.*

Palgrave Macmillan Ltd., Houndmills, Basingstoke, Hampshire, RG21 6XS, England, (Telephone in U.S. (888) 330-8477), (Fax in U.S. (800) 672-2054), www.palgrave.com; *The Statesman's Yearbook 2008.*

U.S. Department of State (DOS), 2201 C Street NW, Washington, DC 20520, (202) 647-4000, www.state.gov; *World Military Expenditures and Arms Transfers (WMEAT).*

United Nations Statistics Division, New York, NY 10017, (800) 253-9646, Fax: (212) 963-4116, http://unstats.un.org; *Statistical Yearbook.*

The World Bank, 1818 H Street, NW, Washington, DC 20433, (202) 473-1000, Fax: (202) 477-6391, www.worldbank.org; *The World Bank Atlas 2003-2004; World Development Indicators (WDI) 2008;* and *World Development Report 2008.*

CHILE - HIDES AND SKINS INDUSTRY

United Nations Food and Agricultural Organization (FAO), Viale delle Terme di Caracalla, 00100 Rome, Italy, (Dial from U.S. (202) 653-2400), (Fax from U.S. (202) 653 5760), www.fao.org; *FAO Production Yearbook 2002.*

CHILE - HOUSING

Euromonitor International, Inc., 224 S. Michigan Avenue, Suite 1500, Chicago, IL 60604, (312) 922-1115, Fax: (312) 922-1157, www.euromonitor.com; *World Marketing Data and Statistics.*

M.E. Sharpe, 80 Business Park Drive, Armonk, NY 10504, (800) 541-6563, Fax: (914) 273-2106, www.mesharpe.com; *The Illustrated Book of World Rankings.*

UCLA Latin American Institute, 10343 Bunche Hall, Box 951447, Los Angeles, CA 90095-1447, (310) 825-4571, Fax: (310) 206-6859, www.international.ucla.edu/lac; *Statistical Abstract of Latin America.*

United Nations Statistics Division, New York, NY 10017, (800) 253-9646, Fax: (212) 963-4116, http://unstats.un.org; *Statistical Yearbook for Latin America and the Caribbean 2004.*

CHILE - ILLITERATE PERSONS

Central Intelligence Agency, Office of Public Affairs, Washington, DC 20505, (703) 482-0623, Fax: (703) 482-1739, www.cia.gov; *The World Factbook.*

Economist Intelligence Unit, 111 West 57th Street, New York, NY 10019, (212) 554-0600, Fax: (212) 586-1181, www.eiu.com; *Business Latin America.*

Euromonitor International, Inc., 224 S. Michigan Avenue, Suite 1500, Chicago, IL 60604, (312) 922-1115, Fax: (312) 922-1157, www.euromonitor.com; *The World Economic Factbook 2008.*

Palgrave Macmillan Ltd., Houndmills, Basingstoke, Hampshire, RG21 6XS, England, (Telephone in U.S. (888) 330-8477), (Fax in U.S. (800) 672-2054), www.palgrave.com; *The Statesman's Yearbook 2008.*

UNESCO Institute for Statistics, C.P. 6128 Succursale Centre-Ville, Montreal, Quebec, H3C 3J7 Canada, (Dial from U.S. (514) 343-6880), (Fax from U.S. (514) 343 6882), www.uis.unesco.org; *Statistical Tables.*

United Nations Statistics Division, New York, NY 10017, (800) 253-9646, Fax: (212) 963-4116, http://unstats.un.org; *Human Development Report 2006* and *Statistical Yearbook for Latin America and the Caribbean 2004.*

CHILE - IMPORTS

Central Intelligence Agency, Office of Public Affairs, Washington, DC 20505, (703) 482-0623, Fax: (703) 482-1739, www.cia.gov; *The World Factbook.*

Economist Intelligence Unit, 111 West 57th Street, New York, NY 10019, (212) 554-0600, Fax: (212) 586-1181, www.eiu.com; *Business Latin America* and *Chile Country Report.*

Euromonitor International, Inc., 224 S. Michigan Avenue, Suite 1500, Chicago, IL 60604, (312) 922-1115, Fax: (312) 922-1157, www.euromonitor.com; *International Marketing Data and Statistics 2008* and *The World Economic Factbook 2008.*

Inter-American Development Bank (IDB), 1300 New York Avenue, NW, Washington, DC 20577, (202) 623-1000, Fax: (202) 623-3096, www.iadb.org; *The Politics of Policies: Economic and Social Progress in Latin America - 2006 Report.*

International Monetary Fund (IMF), 700 Nineteenth Street, NW, Washington, DC 20431, (202) 623-7000, Fax: (202) 623-4661, www.imf.org; *Direction of Trade Statistics Yearbook 2007; Government Finance Statistics Yearbook (2008 Edition);* and *International Financial Statistics Yearbook 2007.*

Organisation for Economic Cooperation and Development (OECD), 2 rue Andre Pascal, F-75775 Paris Cedex 16, France, (Telephone in U.S. (202) 785-6323), (Fax in U.S. (202) 785-0350), www.oecd.org; *OECD Economic Survey - Chile 2007.*

Organization of American States (OAS), 17th Street Constitution Avenue NW, Washington, DC 20006, (202) 458-3000, www.oas.org; *The OAS in Transition: 1994-2004.*

Palgrave Macmillan Ltd., Houndmills, Basingstoke, Hampshire, RG21 6XS, England, (Telephone in U.S. (888) 330-8477), (Fax in U.S. (800) 672-2054), www.palgrave.com; *The Statesman's Yearbook 2008.*

Taylor and Francis Group, An Informa Business, 2 Park Square, Milton Park, Abingdon, Oxford OX14 4RN, United Kingdom, (Dial from U.S. (212) 216-7800), (Fax from U.S. (212) 564-7854), www.tandf.co.uk; *The Europa World Year Book.*

United Nations Conference on Trade and Development (UNCTAD), DC2-1120, United Nations, New York, NY 10017, (212) 963-0027, www.unctad.org; *Handbook of Statistics 2005.*

United Nations Food and Agricultural Organization (FAO), Viale delle Terme di Caracalla, 00100 Rome, Italy, (Dial from U.S. (202) 653-2400), (Fax from U.S. (202) 653 5760), www.fao.org; *The State of Food and Agriculture (SOFA) 2006.*

United Nations Statistics Division, New York, NY 10017, (800) 253-9646, Fax: (212) 963-4116, http://unstats.un.org; *Statistical Yearbook for Latin America and the Caribbean 2004.*

The World Bank, 1818 H Street, NW, Washington, DC 20433, (202) 473-1000, Fax: (202) 477-6391, www.worldbank.org; *World Development Indicators (WDI) 2008* and *World Development Report 2008.*

CHILE - INCOME DISTRIBUTION

UCLA Latin American Institute, 10343 Bunche Hall, Box 951447, Los Angeles, CA 90095-1447, (310) 825-4571, Fax: (310) 206-6859, www.international.ucla.edu/lac; *Statistical Abstract of Latin America.*

United Nations Statistics Division, New York, NY 10017, (800) 253-9646, Fax: (212) 963-4116, http://unstats.un.org; *Statistical Yearbook for Latin America and the Caribbean 2004.*

CHILE - INCOME TAXES

See CHILE - TAXATION

CHILE - INDUSTRIAL METALS PRODUCTION

See CHILE - MINERAL INDUSTRIES

CHILE - INDUSTRIAL PRODUCTIVITY

Euromonitor International, Inc., 224 S. Michigan Avenue, Suite 1500, Chicago, IL 60604, (312) 922-1115, Fax: (312) 922-1157, www.euromonitor.com; *International Marketing Data and Statistics 2008.*

M.E. Sharpe, 80 Business Park Drive, Armonk, NY 10504, (800) 541-6563, Fax: (914) 273-2106, www.mesharpe.com; *The Illustrated Book of World Rankings.*

CHILE - INDUSTRIAL PROPERTY

Organisation for Economic Cooperation and Development (OECD), 2 rue Andre Pascal, F-75775 Paris Cedex 16, France, (Telephone in U.S. (202) 785-6323), (Fax in U.S. (202) 785-0350), www.oecd.org; *World Energy Outlook 2007.*

United Nations Statistics Division, New York, NY 10017, (800) 253-9646, Fax: (212) 963-4116, http://unstats.un.org; *Statistical Yearbook.*

World Intellectual Property Organization (WIPO), PO Box 18, CH-1211 Geneva 20, Switzerland, www.wipo.int; *Industrial Property Statistics* and *Industrial Property Statistics Online Directory.*

CHILE - INDUSTRIES

Central Intelligence Agency, Office of Public Affairs, Washington, DC 20505, (703) 482-0623, Fax: (703) 482-1739, www.cia.gov; *The World Factbook.*

Economist Intelligence Unit, 111 West 57th Street, New York, NY 10019, (212) 554-0600, Fax: (212) 586-1181, www.eiu.com; *Chile Country Report.*

Euromonitor International, Inc., 224 S. Michigan Avenue, Suite 1500, Chicago, IL 60604, (312) 922-1115, Fax: (312) 922-1157, www.euromonitor.com; *The World Economic Factbook 2008* and *World Marketing Data and Statistics.*

M.E. Sharpe, 80 Business Park Drive, Armonk, NY 10504, (800) 541-6563, Fax: (914) 273-2106, www.mesharpe.com; *The Illustrated Book of World Rankings.*

Organisation for Economic Cooperation and Development (OECD), 2 rue Andre Pascal, F-75775 Paris Cedex 16, France, (Telephone in U.S. (202) 785-6323), (Fax in U.S. (202) 785-0350), www.oecd.org; *World Energy Outlook 2007.*

Palgrave Macmillan Ltd., Houndmills, Basingstoke, Hampshire, RG21 6XS, England, (Telephone in U.S. (888) 330-8477), (Fax in U.S. (800) 672-2054), www.palgrave.com; *The Statesman's Yearbook 2008.*

Taylor and Francis Group, An Informa Business, 2 Park Square, Milton Park, Abingdon, Oxford OX14

4RN, United Kingdom, (Dial from U.S. (212) 216-7800), (Fax from U.S. (212) 564-7854), www.tandf.co.uk; *The Europa World Year Book.*

UCLA Latin American Institute, 10343 Bunche Hall, Box 951447, Los Angeles, CA 90095-1447, (310) 825-4571, Fax: (310) 206-6859, www.international.ucla.edu/lac; *Statistical Abstract of Latin America.*

United Nations Industrial Development Organization (UNIDO), 1 United Nations Plaza, New York, NY 10017, (212) 963 6890, Fax: (212) 963-7904, http://unido.org; Industrial Statistics Database 2008 (INDSTAT) and *The International Yearbook of Industrial Statistics 2008.*

United Nations Statistics Division, New York, NY 10017, (800) 253-9646, Fax: (212) 963-4116, http://unstats.un.org; *Economic Survey of Latin America and the Caribbean 2004-2005; 2004 Industrial Commodity Statistics Yearbook;* and *Statistical Yearbook.*

The World Bank, 1818 H Street, NW, Washington, DC 20433, (202) 473-1000, Fax: (202) 477-6391, www.worldbank.org; *Chile* and *World Development Indicators (WDI) 2008.*

CHILE - INFANT AND MATERNAL MORTALITY

See CHILE - MORTALITY

CHILE - INFLATION (FINANCE)

United Nations Statistics Division, New York, NY 10017, (800) 253-9646, Fax: (212) 963-4116, http://unstats.un.org; *Economic Survey of Latin America and the Caribbean 2004-2005.*

CHILE - INORGANIC ACIDS

United Nations Statistics Division, New York, NY 10017, (800) 253-9646, Fax: (212) 963-4116, http://unstats.un.org; *Statistical Yearbook.*

CHILE - INTEREST RATES

Inter-American Development Bank (IDB), 1300 New York Avenue, NW, Washington, DC 20577, (202) 623-1000, Fax: (202) 623-3096, www.iadb.org; *The Politics of Policies: Economic and Social Progress in Latin America - 2006 Report.*

CHILE - INTERNAL REVENUE

Inter-American Development Bank (IDB), 1300 New York Avenue, NW, Washington, DC 20577, (202) 623-1000, Fax: (202) 623-3096, www.iadb.org; *The Politics of Policies: Economic and Social Progress in Latin America - 2006 Report.*

Organization of American States (OAS), 17th Street Constitution Avenue NW, Washington, DC 20006, (202) 458-3000, www.oas.org; *The OAS in Transition: 1994-2004.*

CHILE - INTERNATIONAL FINANCE

Inter-American Development Bank (IDB), 1300 New York Avenue, NW, Washington, DC 20577, (202) 623-1000, Fax: (202) 623-3096, www.iadb.org; *The Politics of Policies: Economic and Social Progress in Latin America - 2006 Report.*

UCLA Latin American Institute, 10343 Bunche Hall, Box 951447, Los Angeles, CA 90095-1447, (310) 825-4571, Fax: (310) 206-6859, www.international.ucla.edu/lac; *Statistical Abstract of Latin America.*

United Nations Statistics Division, New York, NY 10017, (800) 253-9646, Fax: (212) 963-4116, http://unstats.un.org; *Statistical Yearbook for Latin America and the Caribbean 2004.*

CHILE - INTERNATIONAL LIQUIDITY

Inter-American Development Bank (IDB), 1300 New York Avenue, NW, Washington, DC 20577, (202) 623-1000, Fax: (202) 623-3096, www.iadb.org; *The Politics of Policies: Economic and Social Progress in Latin America - 2006 Report.*

International Monetary Fund (IMF), 700 Nineteenth Street, NW, Washington, DC 20431, (202) 623-7000, Fax: (202) 623-4661, www.imf.org; *International Financial Statistics Yearbook 2007.*

CHILE - INTERNATIONAL STATISTICS

Inter-American Development Bank (IDB), 1300 New York Avenue, NW, Washington, DC 20577, (202) 623-1000, Fax: (202) 623-3096, www.iadb.org; *The Politics of Policies: Economic and Social Progress in Latin America - 2006 Report.*

UCLA Latin American Institute, 10343 Bunche Hall, Box 951447, Los Angeles, CA 90095-1447, (310) 825-4571, Fax: (310) 206-6859, www.international.ucla.edu/lac; *Statistical Abstract of Latin America.*

CHILE - INTERNATIONAL TRADE

Economist Intelligence Unit, 111 West 57th Street, New York, NY 10019, (212) 554-0600, Fax: (212) 586-1181, www.eiu.com; *Business Latin America* and *Chile Country Report.*

Euromonitor International, Inc., 224 S. Michigan Avenue, Suite 1500, Chicago, IL 60604, (312) 922-1115, Fax: (312) 922-1157, www.euromonitor.com; *The World Economic Factbook 2008* and *World Marketing Data and Statistics.*

Inter-American Development Bank (IDB), 1300 New York Avenue, NW, Washington, DC 20577, (202) 623-1000, Fax: (202) 623-3096, www.iadb.org; *The Politics of Policies: Economic and Social Progress in Latin America - 2006 Report.*

International Monetary Fund (IMF), 700 Nineteenth Street, NW, Washington, DC 20431, (202) 623-7000, Fax: (202) 623-4661, www.imf.org; *International Financial Statistics Yearbook 2007.*

M.E. Sharpe, 80 Business Park Drive, Armonk, NY 10504, (800) 541-6563, Fax: (914) 273-2106, www.mesharpe.com; *The Illustrated Book of World Rankings.*

Organisation for Economic Cooperation and Development (OECD), 2 rue Andre Pascal, F-75775 Paris Cedex 16, France, (Telephone in U.S. (202) 785-6323), (Fax in U.S. (202) 785-0350), www.oecd.org; *International Trade by Commodity Statistics (ITCS)* and *OECD Economic Survey - Chile 2007.*

Palgrave Macmillan Ltd., Houndmills, Basingstoke, Hampshire, RG21 6XS, England, (Telephone in U.S. (888) 330-8477), (Fax in U.S. (800) 672-2054), www.palgrave.com; *The Statesman's Yearbook 2008.*

Taylor and Francis Group, An Informa Business, 2 Park Square, Milton Park, Abingdon, Oxford OX14 4RN, United Kingdom, (Dial from U.S. (212) 216-7800), (Fax from U.S. (212) 564-7854), www.tandf.co.uk; *The Europa World Year Book.*

UCLA Latin American Institute, 10343 Bunche Hall, Box 951447, Los Angeles, CA 90095-1447, (310) 825-4571, Fax: (310) 206-6859, www.international.ucla.edu/lac; *Statistical Abstract of Latin America.*

United Nations Conference on Trade and Development (UNCTAD), DC2-1120, United Nations, New York, NY 10017, (212) 963-0027, www.unctad.org; *UNCTAD Commodity Yearbook.*

United Nations Food and Agricultural Organization (FAO), Viale delle Terme di Caracalla, 00100 Rome, Italy, (Dial from U.S. (202) 653-2400), (Fax from U.S. (202) 653 5760), www.fao.org; *FAO Production Yearbook 2002; FAO Trade Yearbook;* and *The State of Food and Agriculture (SOFA) 2006.*

United Nations Statistics Division, New York, NY 10017, (800) 253-9646, Fax: (212) 963-4116, http://unstats.un.org; *Economic Survey of Latin America and the Caribbean 2004-2005; International Trade Statistics Yearbook; Statistical Yearbook;* and *Statistical Yearbook for Latin America and the Caribbean 2004.*

The World Bank, 1818 H Street, NW, Washington, DC 20433, (202) 473-1000, Fax: (202) 477-6391, www.worldbank.org; *Chile; World Development Indicators (WDI) 2008;* and *World Development Report 2008.*

World Bureau of Metal Statistics (WBMS), 27a High Street, Ware, Hertfordshire, SG12 9BA, United Kingdom, www.world-bureau.com; *World Flow Charts* and *World Metal Statistics.*

World Trade Organization (WTO), Centre William Rappard, Rue de Lausanne 154, CH-1211 Geneva 21, Switzerland, www.wto.org; *International Trade Statistics 2006.*

CHILE - INTERNET USERS

International Telecommunication Union (ITU), Place des Nations, 1211 Geneva 20, Switzerland, www.itu.int; *World Telecommunication/ICT Indicators Database on CD-ROM; World Telecommunication/ICT Indicators Database Online;* and *Yearbook of Statistics - Telecommunication Services (Chronological Time Series 1997-2006).*

The World Bank, 1818 H Street, NW, Washington, DC 20433, (202) 473-1000, Fax: (202) 477-6391, www.worldbank.org; *Chile.*

CHILE - INVESTMENTS

Inter-American Development Bank (IDB), 1300 New York Avenue, NW, Washington, DC 20577, (202) 623-1000, Fax: (202) 623-3096, www.iadb.org; *The Politics of Policies: Economic and Social Progress in Latin America - 2006 Report.*

United Nations Statistics Division, New York, NY 10017, (800) 253-9646, Fax: (212) 963-4116, http://unstats.un.org; *Statistical Yearbook for Latin America and the Caribbean 2004.*

CHILE - INVESTMENTS, FOREIGN

Economist Intelligence Unit, 111 West 57th Street, New York, NY 10019, (212) 554-0600, Fax: (212) 586-1181, www.eiu.com; *Business Latin America.*

CHILE - IRON AND IRON ORE PRODUCTION

See CHILE - MINERAL INDUSTRIES

CHILE - IRRIGATION

Euromonitor International, Inc., 224 S. Michigan Avenue, Suite 1500, Chicago, IL 60604, (312) 922-1115, Fax: (312) 922-1157, www.euromonitor.com; *International Marketing Data and Statistics 2008.*

Inter-American Development Bank (IDB), 1300 New York Avenue, NW, Washington, DC 20577, (202) 623-1000, Fax: (202) 623-3096, www.iadb.org; *The Politics of Policies: Economic and Social Progress in Latin America - 2006 Report.*

CHILE - LABOR

Central Intelligence Agency, Office of Public Affairs, Washington, DC 20505, (703) 482-0623, Fax: (703) 482-1739, www.cia.gov; *The World Factbook.*

Economist Intelligence Unit, 111 West 57th Street, New York, NY 10019, (212) 554-0600, Fax: (212) 586-1181, www.eiu.com; *Business Latin America.*

Euromonitor International, Inc., 224 S. Michigan Avenue, Suite 1500, Chicago, IL 60604, (312) 922-1115, Fax: (312) 922-1157, www.euromonitor.com; *International Marketing Data and Statistics 2008* and *World Marketing Data and Statistics.*

International Labour Office, I.L.O. Publications, 4 route des Morillons, CH-1211 Geneva 22, Switzerland, (Telephone in U.S. (202) 653-7652), (Fax in U.S. (202) 653-7687), www.ilo.org; *Yearbook of Labour Statistics 2006.*

M.E. Sharpe, 80 Business Park Drive, Armonk, NY 10504, (800) 541-6563, Fax: (914) 273-2106, www.mesharpe.com; *The Illustrated Book of World Rankings.*

Organisation for Economic Cooperation and Development (OECD), 2 rue Andre Pascal, F-75775 Paris Cedex 16, France, (Telephone in U.S. (202) 785-6323), (Fax in U.S. (202) 785-0350), www.oecd.org; *OECD Economic Survey - Chile 2007.*

Palgrave Macmillan Ltd., Houndmills, Basingstoke, Hampshire, RG21 6XS, England, (Telephone in U.S. (888) 330-8477), (Fax in U.S. (800) 672-2054), www.palgrave.com; *The Statesman's Yearbook 2008.*

Taylor and Francis Group, An Informa Business, 2 Park Square, Milton Park, Abingdon, Oxford OX14

4RN, United Kingdom, (Dial from U.S. (212) 216-7800), (Fax from U.S. (212) 564-7854), www.tandf.co.uk; *The Europa World Year Book.*

U.S. Department of Labor (DOL), Bureau of International Labor Affairs (ILAB), Frances Perkins Building, Room C-4325, 200 Constitution Avenue, NW, Washington, DC 20210, (202) 693-4770, Fax: (202) 693-4780, www.dol.gov/ilab; *Labor Rights Report.*

United Nations Food and Agricultural Organization (FAO), Viale delle Terme di Caracalla, 00100 Rome, Italy, (Dial from U.S. (202) 653-2400), (Fax from U.S. (202) 653 5760), www.fao.org; *The State of Food and Agriculture (SOFA) 2006.*

United Nations Statistics Division, New York, NY 10017, (800) 253-9646, Fax: (212) 963-4116, http://unstats.un.org; *Human Development Report 2006.*

The World Bank, 1818 H Street, NW, Washington, DC 20433, (202) 473-1000, Fax: (202) 477-6391, www.worldbank.org; *The World Bank Atlas 2003-2004; World Development Indicators (WDI) 2008;* and *World Development Report 2008.*

CHILE - LAND USE

Central Intelligence Agency, Office of Public Affairs, Washington, DC 20505, (703) 482-0623, Fax: (703) 482-1739, www.cia.gov; *The World Factbook.*

Euromonitor International, Inc., 224 S. Michigan Avenue, Suite 1500, Chicago, IL 60604, (312) 922-1115, Fax: (312) 922-1157, www.euromonitor.com; *International Marketing Data and Statistics 2008.*

Inter-American Development Bank (IDB), 1300 New York Avenue, NW, Washington, DC 20577, (202) 623-1000, Fax: (202) 623-3096, www.iadb.org; *The Politics of Policies: Economic and Social Progress in Latin America - 2006 Report.*

United Nations Food and Agricultural Organization (FAO), Viale delle Terme di Caracalla, 00100 Rome, Italy, (Dial from U.S. (202) 653-2400), (Fax from U.S. (202) 653 5760), www.fao.org; *FAO Production Yearbook 2002.*

The World Bank, 1818 H Street, NW, Washington, DC 20433, (202) 473-1000, Fax: (202) 477-6391, www.worldbank.org; *World Development Report 2008.*

CHILE - LIBRARIES

M.E. Sharpe, 80 Business Park Drive, Armonk, NY 10504, (800) 541-6563, Fax: (914) 273-2106, www.mesharpe.com; *The Illustrated Book of World Rankings.*

UNESCO Institute for Statistics, C.P. 6128 Succursale Centre-Ville, Montreal, Quebec, H3C 3J7 Canada, (Dial from U.S. (514) 343-6880), (Fax from U.S. (514) 343 6882), www.uis.unesco.org; *Statistical Tables.*

CHILE - LIFE EXPECTANCY

Central Intelligence Agency, Office of Public Affairs, Washington, DC 20505, (703) 482-0623, Fax: (703) 482-1739, www.cia.gov; *The World Factbook.*

Economist Intelligence Unit, 111 West 57th Street, New York, NY 10019, (212) 554-0600, Fax: (212) 586-1181, www.eiu.com; *Business Latin America.*

Euromonitor International, Inc., 224 S. Michigan Avenue, Suite 1500, Chicago, IL 60604, (312) 922-1115, Fax: (312) 922-1157, www.euromonitor.com; *The World Economic Factbook 2008.*

Palgrave Macmillan Ltd., Houndmills, Basingstoke, Hampshire, RG21 6XS, England, (Telephone in U.S. (888) 330-8477), (Fax in U.S. (800) 672-2054), www.palgrave.com; *The Statesman's Yearbook 2008.*

United Nations Statistics Division, New York, NY 10017, (800) 253-9646, Fax: (212) 963-4116, http://unstats.un.org; *Human Development Report 2006; Statistical Yearbook for Latin America and the Caribbean 2004;* and *World Statistics Pocketbook.*

The World Bank, 1818 H Street, NW, Washington, DC 20433, (202) 473-1000, Fax: (202) 477-6391, www.worldbank.org; *The World Bank Atlas 2003-2004* and *World Development Report 2008.*

CHILE - LITERACY

Euromonitor International, Inc., 224 S. Michigan Avenue, Suite 1500, Chicago, IL 60604, (312) 922-1115, Fax: (312) 922-1157, www.euromonitor.com; *World Marketing Data and Statistics.*

CHILE - LIVESTOCK

M.E. Sharpe, 80 Business Park Drive, Armonk, NY 10504, (800) 541-6563, Fax: (914) 273-2106, www.mesharpe.com; *The Illustrated Book of World Rankings.*

Palgrave Macmillan Ltd., Houndmills, Basingstoke, Hampshire, RG21 6XS, England, (Telephone in U.S. (888) 330-8477), (Fax in U.S. (800) 672-2054), www.palgrave.com; *The Statesman's Yearbook 2008.*

Taylor and Francis Group, An Informa Business, 2 Park Square, Milton Park, Abingdon, Oxford OX14 4RN, United Kingdom, (Dial from U.S. (212) 216-7800), (Fax from U.S. (212) 564-7854), www.tandf.co.uk; *The Europa World Year Book.*

United Nations Conference on Trade and Development (UNCTAD), DC2-1120, United Nations, New York, NY 10017, (212) 963-0027, www.unctad.org; *UNCTAD Commodity Yearbook.*

United Nations Food and Agricultural Organization (FAO), Viale delle Terme di Caracalla, 00100 Rome, Italy, (Dial from U.S. (202) 653-2400), (Fax from U.S. (202) 653 5760), www.fao.org; *FAO Production Yearbook 2002* and *The State of Food and Agriculture (SOFA) 2006.*

United Nations Statistics Division, New York, NY 10017, (800) 253-9646, Fax: (212) 963-4116, http://unstats.un.org; *Statistical Yearbook.*

CHILE - LOCAL TAXATION

Euromonitor International, Inc., 224 S. Michigan Avenue, Suite 1500, Chicago, IL 60604, (312) 922-1115, Fax: (312) 922-1157, www.euromonitor.com; *International Marketing Data and Statistics 2008.*

Inter-American Development Bank (IDB), 1300 New York Avenue, NW, Washington, DC 20577, (202) 623-1000, Fax: (202) 623-3096, www.iadb.org; *The Politics of Policies: Economic and Social Progress in Latin America - 2006 Report.*

CHILE - MANUFACTURES

Economist Intelligence Unit, 111 West 57th Street, New York, NY 10019, (212) 554-0600, Fax: (212) 586-1181, www.eiu.com; *Business Latin America.*

Inter-American Development Bank (IDB), 1300 New York Avenue, NW, Washington, DC 20577, (202) 623-1000, Fax: (202) 623-3096, www.iadb.org; *The Politics of Policies: Economic and Social Progress in Latin America - 2006 Report.*

International Monetary Fund (IMF), 700 Nineteenth Street, NW, Washington, DC 20431, (202) 623-7000, Fax: (202) 623-4661, www.imf.org; *International Financial Statistics Yearbook 2007.*

M.E. Sharpe, 80 Business Park Drive, Armonk, NY 10504, (800) 541-6563, Fax: (914) 273-2106, www.mesharpe.com; *The Illustrated Book of World Rankings.*

Organisation for Economic Cooperation and Development (OECD), 2 rue Andre Pascal, F-75775 Paris Cedex 16, France, (Telephone in U.S. (202) 785-6323), (Fax in U.S. (202) 785-0350), www.oecd.org; *OECD Economic Survey - Chile 2007.*

Organization of American States (OAS), 17th Street Constitution Avenue NW, Washington, DC 20006, (202) 458-3000, www.oas.org; *The OAS in Transition: 1994-2004.*

United Nations Statistics Division, New York, NY 10017, (800) 253-9646, Fax: (212) 963-4116, http://unstats.un.org; *Statistical Yearbook* and *Statistical Yearbook for Latin America and the Caribbean 2004.*

The World Bank, 1818 H Street, NW, Washington, DC 20433, (202) 473-1000, Fax: (202) 477-6391, www.worldbank.org; *World Development Indicators (WDI) 2008.*

CHILE - MARRIAGE

M.E. Sharpe, 80 Business Park Drive, Armonk, NY 10504, (800) 541-6563, Fax: (914) 273-2106, www.mesharpe.com; *The Illustrated Book of World Rankings.*

Taylor and Francis Group, An Informa Business, 2 Park Square, Milton Park, Abingdon, Oxford OX14 4RN, United Kingdom, (Dial from U.S. (212) 216-7800), (Fax from U.S. (212) 564-7854), www.tandf.co.uk; *The Europa World Year Book.*

United Nations Statistics Division, New York, NY 10017, (800) 253-9646, Fax: (212) 963-4116, http://unstats.un.org; *Demographic Yearbook* and *Statistical Yearbook.*

CHILE - MEAT PRODUCTION

See CHILE - LIVESTOCK

CHILE - MEDICAL CARE, COST OF

International Monetary Fund (IMF), 700 Nineteenth Street, NW, Washington, DC 20431, (202) 623-7000, Fax: (202) 623-4661, www.imf.org; *Government Finance Statistics Yearbook (2008 Edition).*

United Nations Statistics Division, New York, NY 10017, (800) 253-9646, Fax: (212) 963-4116, http://unstats.un.org; *Statistical Yearbook for Latin America and the Caribbean 2004.*

CHILE - MEDICAL PERSONNEL

UCLA Latin American Institute, 10343 Bunche Hall, Box 951447, Los Angeles, CA 90095-1447, (310) 825-4571, Fax: (310) 206-6859, www.international.ucla.edu/lac; *Statistical Abstract of Latin America.*

CHILE - MERCURY PRODUCTION

See CHILE - MINERAL INDUSTRIES

CHILE - MILK PRODUCTION

See CHILE - DAIRY PROCESSING

CHILE - MINERAL INDUSTRIES

Commodity Research Bureau, 330 South Wells Street, Suite 612, Chicago, IL 60606-7110, (800) 621-5271, Fax: (312) 939-4135, www.crbtrader.com; *2006 CRB Commodity Yearbook and CD.*

Economist Intelligence Unit, 111 West 57th Street, New York, NY 10019, (212) 554-0600, Fax: (212) 586-1181, www.eiu.com; *Business Latin America.*

Inter-American Development Bank (IDB), 1300 New York Avenue, NW, Washington, DC 20577, (202) 623-1000, Fax: (202) 623-3096, www.iadb.org; *The Politics of Policies: Economic and Social Progress in Latin America - 2006 Report.*

International Monetary Fund (IMF), 700 Nineteenth Street, NW, Washington, DC 20431, (202) 623-7000, Fax: (202) 623-4661, www.imf.org; *International Financial Statistics Yearbook 2007.*

Organisation for Economic Cooperation and Development (OECD), 2 rue Andre Pascal, F-75775 Paris Cedex 16, France, (Telephone in U.S. (202) 785-6323), (Fax in U.S. (202) 785-0350), www.oecd.org; *OECD Economic Survey - Chile 2007* and *World Energy Outlook 2007.*

Organization of American States (OAS), 17th Street Constitution Avenue NW, Washington, DC 20006, (202) 458-3000, www.oas.org; *The OAS in Transition: 1994-2004.*

Palgrave Macmillan Ltd., Houndmills, Basingstoke, Hampshire, RG21 6XS, England, (Telephone in U.S. (888) 330-8477), (Fax in U.S. (800) 672-2054), www.palgrave.com; *The Statesman's Yearbook 2008.*

PennWell Corporation, 1421 South Sheridan Road, Tulsa, OK 74112, (918) 835-3161, www.pennwell.com; *Oil Gas Journal Latinoamericana.*

Taylor and Francis Group, An Informa Business, 2 Park Square, Milton Park, Abingdon, Oxford OX14 4RN, United Kingdom, (Dial from U.S. (212) 216-7800), (Fax from U.S. (212) 564-7854), www.tandf.co.uk; *The Europa World Year Book.*

UCLA Latin American Institute, 10343 Bunche Hall, Box 951447, Los Angeles, CA 90095-1447, (310) 825-4571, Fax: (310) 206-6859, www.international.ucla.edu/lac; *Statistical Abstract of Latin America.*

United Nations Conference on Trade and Development (UNCTAD), DC2-1120, United Nations, New York, NY 10017, (212) 963-0027, www.unctad.org; *UNCTAD Commodity Yearbook.*

United Nations Statistics Division, New York, NY 10017, (800) 253-9646, Fax: (212) 963-4116, http://unstats.un.org; *Statistical Yearbook* and *Statistical Yearbook for Latin America and the Caribbean 2004.*

World Bureau of Metal Statistics (WBMS), 27a High Street, Ware, Hertfordshire, SG12 9BA, United Kingdom, www.world-bureau.com; *Annual Stainless Steel Statistics; World Flow Charts; World Metal Statistics; World Nickel Statistics;* and *World Tin Statistics.*

CHILE - MONEY EXCHANGE RATES

See CHILE - FOREIGN EXCHANGE RATES

CHILE - MONEY SUPPLY

Economist Intelligence Unit, 111 West 57th Street, New York, NY 10019, (212) 554-0600, Fax: (212) 586-1181, www.eiu.com; *Chile Country Report.*

Euromonitor International, Inc., 224 S. Michigan Avenue, Suite 1500, Chicago, IL 60604, (312) 922-1115, Fax: (312) 922-1157, www.euromonitor.com; *International Marketing Data and Statistics 2008.*

Inter-American Development Bank (IDB), 1300 New York Avenue, NW, Washington, DC 20577, (202) 623-1000, Fax: (202) 623-3096, www.iadb.org; *The Politics of Policies: Economic and Social Progress in Latin America - 2006 Report.*

International Monetary Fund (IMF), 700 Nineteenth Street, NW, Washington, DC 20431, (202) 623-7000, Fax: (202) 623-4661, www.imf.org; *International Financial Statistics Yearbook 2007.*

Organisation for Economic Cooperation and Development (OECD), 2 rue Andre Pascal, F-75775 Paris Cedex 16, France, (Telephone in U.S. (202) 785-6323), (Fax in U.S. (202) 785-0350), www.oecd.org; *OECD Economic Survey - Chile 2007.*

Taylor and Francis Group, An Informa Business, 2 Park Square, Milton Park, Abingdon, Oxford OX14 4RN, United Kingdom, (Dial from U.S. (212) 216-7800), (Fax from U.S. (212) 564-7854), www.tandf.co.uk; *The Europa World Year Book.*

UCLA Latin American Institute, 10343 Bunche Hall, Box 951447, Los Angeles, CA 90095-1447, (310) 825-4571, Fax: (310) 206-6859, www.international.ucla.edu/lac; *Statistical Abstract of Latin America.*

United Nations Statistics Division, New York, NY 10017, (800) 253-9646, Fax: (212) 963-4116, http://unstats.un.org; *Statistical Yearbook.*

The World Bank, 1818 H Street, NW, Washington, DC 20433, (202) 473-1000, Fax: (202) 477-6391, www.worldbank.org; *Chile* and *World Development Indicators (WDI) 2008.*

CHILE - MORTALITY

Central Intelligence Agency, Office of Public Affairs, Washington, DC 20505, (703) 482-0623, Fax: (703) 482-1739, www.cia.gov; *The World Factbook.*

Economist Intelligence Unit, 111 West 57th Street, New York, NY 10019, (212) 554-0600, Fax: (212) 586-1181, www.eiu.com; *Business Latin America.*

Euromonitor International, Inc., 224 S. Michigan Avenue, Suite 1500, Chicago, IL 60604, (312) 922-1115, Fax: (312) 922-1157, www.euromonitor.com; *International Marketing Data and Statistics 2008* and *The World Economic Factbook 2008.*

Palgrave Macmillan Ltd., Houndmills, Basingstoke, Hampshire, RG21 6XS, England, (Telephone in U.S. (888) 330-8477), (Fax in U.S. (800) 672-2054), www.palgrave.com; *The Statesman's Yearbook 2008.*

Taylor and Francis Group, An Informa Business, 2 Park Square, Milton Park, Abingdon, Oxford OX14 4RN, United Kingdom, (Dial from U.S. (212) 216-7800), (Fax from U.S. (212) 564-7854), www.tandf.co.uk; *The Europa World Year Book.*

UNICEF, 3 United Nations Plaza; New York, NY 10017, (800) 253-9646, Fax: (212) 887-7465, www.unicef.org; *The State of the World's Children 2008.*

United Nations Statistics Division, New York, NY 10017, (800) 253-9646, Fax: (212) 963-4116, http://unstats.un.org; *Demographic Yearbook; Human Development Report 2006; Statistical Yearbook; Statistical Yearbook for Latin America and the Caribbean 2004;* and *World Statistics Pocketbook.*

The World Bank, 1818 H Street, NW, Washington, DC 20433, (202) 473-1000, Fax: (202) 477-6391, www.worldbank.org; *The World Bank Atlas 2003-2004; World Development Indicators (WDI) 2008;* and *World Development Report 2008.*

World Health Organization (WHO), Avenue Appia 20, 1211 Geneve 27, Switzerland, (Telephone in U.S. (212) 331-9081), www.who.int; *The WHO Global Atlas of Infectious Diseases* and *World Health Report 2006.*

CHILE - MOTION PICTURES

Palgrave Macmillan Ltd., Houndmills, Basingstoke, Hampshire, RG21 6XS, England, (Telephone in U.S. (888) 330-8477), (Fax in U.S. (800) 672-2054), www.palgrave.com; *The Statesman's Yearbook 2008.*

United Nations Statistics Division, New York, NY 10017, (800) 253-9646, Fax: (212) 963-4116, http://unstats.un.org; *Statistical Yearbook.*

CHILE - MOTOR VEHICLES

Economist Intelligence Unit, 111 West 57th Street, New York, NY 10019, (212) 554-0600, Fax: (212) 586-1181, www.eiu.com; *Business Latin America.*

International Road Federation (IFR), Madison Place, 500 Montgomery Street, 5th Floor, Alexandria, VA 22314, (703) 535-1001, Fax: (703) 535-1007, www.irfnet.org; *World Road Statistics 2006.*

Taylor and Francis Group, An Informa Business, 2 Park Square, Milton Park, Abingdon, Oxford OX14 4RN, United Kingdom, (Dial from U.S. (212) 216-7800), (Fax from U.S. (212) 564-7854), www.tandf.co.uk; *The Europa World Year Book.*

United Nations Statistics Division, New York, NY 10017, (800) 253-9646, Fax: (212) 963-4116, http://unstats.un.org; *Statistical Yearbook.*

CHILE - MUSEUMS

M.E. Sharpe, 80 Business Park Drive, Armonk, NY 10504, (800) 541-6563, Fax: (914) 273-2106, www.mesharpe.com; *The Illustrated Book of World Rankings.*

UNESCO Institute for Statistics, C.P. 6128 Succursale Centre-Ville, Montreal, Quebec, H3C 3J7 Canada, (Dial from U.S. (514) 343-6880), (Fax from U.S. (514) 343 6882), www.uis.unesco.org; *Statistical Tables.*

CHILE - NATURAL GAS PRODUCTION

See CHILE - MINERAL INDUSTRIES

CHILE - NICKEL AND NICKEL ORE

See CHILE - MINERAL INDUSTRIES

CHILE - NUTRITION

United Nations Food and Agricultural Organization (FAO), Viale delle Terme di Caracalla, 00100 Rome, Italy, (Dial from U.S. (202) 653-2400), (Fax from U.S. (202) 653 5760), www.fao.org; *The State of Food and Agriculture (SOFA) 2006.*

United Nations Statistics Division, New York, NY 10017, (800) 253-9646, Fax: (212) 963-4116, http://unstats.un.org; *Statistical Yearbook for Latin America and the Caribbean 2004.*

CHILE - OATS PRODUCTION

See CHILE - CROPS

CHILE - OLDER PEOPLE

M.E. Sharpe, 80 Business Park Drive, Armonk, NY 10504, (800) 541-6563, Fax: (914) 273-2106, www.mesharpe.com; *The Illustrated Book of World Rankings.*

CHILE - PAPER

See CHILE - FORESTS AND FORESTRY

CHILE - PEANUT PRODUCTION

See CHILE - CROPS

CHILE - PERIODICALS

UNESCO Institute for Statistics, C.P. 6128 Succursale Centre-Ville, Montreal, Quebec, H3C 3J7 Canada, (Dial from U.S. (514) 343-6880), (Fax from U.S. (514) 343 6882), www.uis.unesco.org; *Statistical Tables.*

CHILE - PESTICIDES

United Nations Food and Agricultural Organization (FAO), Viale delle Terme di Caracalla, 00100 Rome, Italy, (Dial from U.S. (202) 653-2400), (Fax from U.S. (202) 653 5760), www.fao.org; *The State of Food and Agriculture (SOFA) 2006.*

CHILE - PETROLEUM INDUSTRY AND TRADE

Economist Intelligence Unit, 111 West 57th Street, New York, NY 10019, (212) 554-0600, Fax: (212) 586-1181, www.eiu.com; *Business Latin America.*

Inter-American Development Bank (IDB), 1300 New York Avenue, NW, Washington, DC 20577, (202) 623-1000, Fax: (202) 623-3096, www.iadb.org; *The Politics of Policies: Economic and Social Progress in Latin America - 2006 Report.*

M.E. Sharpe, 80 Business Park Drive, Armonk, NY 10504, (800) 541-6563, Fax: (914) 273-2106, www.mesharpe.com; *The Illustrated Book of World Rankings.*

Organisation for Economic Cooperation and Development (OECD), 2 rue Andre Pascal, F-75775 Paris Cedex 16, France, (Telephone in U.S. (202) 785-6323), (Fax in U.S. (202) 785-0350), www.oecd.org; *World Energy Outlook 2007.*

Palgrave Macmillan Ltd., Houndmills, Basingstoke, Hampshire, RG21 6XS, England, (Telephone in U.S. (888) 330-8477), (Fax in U.S. (800) 672-2054), www.palgrave.com; *The Statesman's Yearbook 2008.*

PennWell Corporation, 1421 South Sheridan Road, Tulsa, OK 74112, (918) 835-3161, www.pennwell.com; *International Petroleum Encyclopedia 2007.*

U.S. Department of Energy (DOE), Energy Information Administration (EIA), 1000 Independence Avenue, SW, Washington, DC 20585, (202) 586-8800, www.eia.doe.gov; *International Energy Annual 2004* and *International Energy Outlook 2006.*

United Nations Conference on Trade and Development (UNCTAD), DC2-1120, United Nations, New York, NY 10017, (212) 963-0027, www.unctad.org; *UNCTAD Commodity Yearbook.*

United Nations Food and Agricultural Organization (FAO), Viale delle Terme di Caracalla, 00100 Rome, Italy, (Dial from U.S. (202) 653-2400), (Fax from U.S. (202) 653 5760), www.fao.org; *The State of Food and Agriculture (SOFA) 2006.*

United Nations Statistics Division, New York, NY 10017, (800) 253-9646, Fax: (212) 963-4116, http://unstats.un.org; *Statistical Yearbook.*

CHILE - PLASTICS INDUSTRY AND TRADE

United Nations Statistics Division, New York, NY 10017, (800) 253-9646, Fax: (212) 963-4116, http://unstats.un.org; *Statistical Yearbook.*

CHILE - POLITICAL SCIENCE

Central Intelligence Agency, Office of Public Affairs, Washington, DC 20505, (703) 482-0623, Fax: (703) 482-1739, www.cia.gov; *The World Factbook.*

Inter-American Development Bank (IDB), 1300 New York Avenue, NW, Washington, DC 20577, (202) 623-1000, Fax: (202) 623-3096, www.iadb.org; *The Politics of Policies: Economic and Social Progress in Latin America - 2006 Report.*

International Monetary Fund (IMF), 700 Nineteenth Street, NW, Washington, DC 20431, (202) 623-7000, Fax: (202) 623-4661, www.imf.org; *Government Finance Statistics Yearbook (2008 Edition).*

Palgrave Macmillan Ltd., Houndmills, Basingstoke, Hampshire, RG21 6XS, England, (Telephone in U.S. (888) 330-8477), (Fax in U.S. (800) 672-2054), www.palgrave.com; *The Statesman's Yearbook 2008.*

Taylor and Francis Group, An Informa Business, 2 Park Square, Milton Park, Abingdon, Oxford OX14 4RN, United Kingdom, (Dial from U.S. (212) 216-7800), (Fax from U.S. (212) 564-7854), www.tandf.co.uk; *The Europa World Year Book.*

UCLA Latin American Institute, 10343 Bunche Hall, Box 951447, Los Angeles, CA 90095-1447, (310) 825-4571, Fax: (310) 206-6859, www.international.ucla.edu/lac; *Statistical Abstract of Latin America.*

United Nations Statistics Division, New York, NY 10017, (800) 253-9646, Fax: (212) 963-4116, http://unstats.un.org; *National Accounts Statistics: Compendium of Income Distribution Statistics* and *Statistical Yearbook.*

The World Bank, 1818 H Street, NW, Washington, DC 20433, (202) 473-1000, Fax: (202) 477-6391, www.worldbank.org; *World Development Indicators (WDI) 2008* and *World Development Report 2008.*

CHILE - POPULATION

Central Intelligence Agency, Office of Public Affairs, Washington, DC 20505, (703) 482-0623, Fax: (703) 482-1739, www.cia.gov; *The World Factbook.*

Economist Intelligence Unit, 111 West 57th Street, New York, NY 10019, (212) 554-0600, Fax: (212) 586-1181, www.eiu.com; *Business Latin America* and *Chile Country Report.*

Euromonitor International, Inc., 224 S. Michigan Avenue, Suite 1500, Chicago, IL 60604, (312) 922-1115, Fax: (312) 922-1157, www.euromonitor.com; *International Marketing Data and Statistics 2008* and *The World Economic Factbook 2008.*

Inter-American Development Bank (IDB), 1300 New York Avenue, NW, Washington, DC 20577, (202) 623-1000, Fax: (202) 623-3096, www.iadb.org; *The Politics of Policies: Economic and Social Progress in Latin America - 2006 Report.*

International Labour Office, I.L.O. Publications, 4 route des Morillons, CH-1211 Geneva 22, Switzerland, (Telephone in U.S. (202) 653-7652), (Fax in U.S. (202) 653-7687), www.ilo.org; *Yearbook of Labour Statistics 2006.*

M.E. Sharpe, 80 Business Park Drive, Armonk, NY 10504, (800) 541-6563, Fax: (914) 273-2106, www.mesharpe.com; *The Illustrated Book of World Rankings.*

Organization of American States (OAS), 17th Street Constitution Avenue NW, Washington, DC 20006, (202) 458-3000, www.oas.org; *The OAS in Transition: 1994-2004.*

Palgrave Macmillan Ltd., Houndmills, Basingstoke, Hampshire, RG21 6XS, England, (Telephone in U.S. (888) 330-8477), (Fax in U.S. (800) 672-2054), www.palgrave.com; *The Statesman's Yearbook 2008.*

Taylor and Francis Group, An Informa Business, 2 Park Square, Milton Park, Abingdon, Oxford OX14 4RN, United Kingdom, (Dial from U.S. (212) 216-7800), (Fax from U.S. (212) 564-7854), www.tandf.co.uk; *The Europa World Year Book.*

U.S. Department of State (DOS), 2201 C Street NW, Washington, DC 20520, (202) 647-4000, www.state.gov; *World Military Expenditures and Arms Transfers (WMEAT).*

UCLA Latin American Institute, 10343 Bunche Hall, Box 951447, Los Angeles, CA 90095-1447, (310) 825-4571, Fax: (310) 206-6859, www.international.ucla.edu/lac; *Statistical Abstract of Latin America.*

UNESCO Institute for Statistics, C.P. 6128 Succursale Centre-Ville, Montreal, Quebec, H3C 3J7 Canada, (Dial from U.S. (514) 343-6880), (Fax from U.S. (514) 343 6882), www.uis.unesco.org; *Statistical Tables.*

United Nations Food and Agricultural Organization (FAO), Viale delle Terme di Caracalla, 00100 Rome, Italy, (Dial from U.S. (202) 653-2400), (Fax from U.S. (202) 653 5760), www.fao.org; *FAO Production Yearbook 2002.*

United Nations Statistics Division, New York, NY 10017, (800) 253-9646, Fax: (212) 963-4116, http://unstats.un.org; *Demographic Yearbook; Human Development Report 2006; Statistical Yearbook; Statistical Yearbook for Latin America and the Caribbean 2004;* and *World Statistics Pocketbook.*

The World Bank, 1818 H Street, NW, Washington, DC 20433, (202) 473-1000, Fax: (202) 477-6391, www.worldbank.org; *Chile; The World Bank Atlas 2003-2004;* and *World Development Report 2008.*

World Health Organization (WHO), Avenue Appia 20, 1211 Geneve 27, Switzerland, (Telephone in U.S. (212) 331-9081), www.who.int; *World Health Report 2006.*

CHILE - POPULATION DENSITY

Central Intelligence Agency, Office of Public Affairs, Washington, DC 20505, (703) 482-0623, Fax: (703) 482-1739, www.cia.gov; *The World Factbook.*

Euromonitor International, Inc., 224 S. Michigan Avenue, Suite 1500, Chicago, IL 60604, (312) 922-1115, Fax: (312) 922-1157, www.euromonitor.com; *International Marketing Data and Statistics 2008* and *The World Economic Factbook 2008.*

Inter-American Development Bank (IDB), 1300 New York Avenue, NW, Washington, DC 20577, (202) 623-1000, Fax: (202) 623-3096, www.iadb.org; *The Politics of Policies: Economic and Social Progress in Latin America - 2006 Report.*

M.E. Sharpe, 80 Business Park Drive, Armonk, NY 10504, (800) 541-6563, Fax: (914) 273-2106, www.mesharpe.com; *The Illustrated Book of World Rankings.*

Palgrave Macmillan Ltd., Houndmills, Basingstoke, Hampshire, RG21 6XS, England, (Telephone in U.S. (888) 330-8477), (Fax in U.S. (800) 672-2054), www.palgrave.com; *The Statesman's Yearbook 2008.*

Taylor and Francis Group, An Informa Business, 2 Park Square, Milton Park, Abingdon, Oxford OX14 4RN, United Kingdom, (Dial from U.S. (212) 216-7800), (Fax from U.S. (212) 564-7854), www.tandf.co.uk; *The Europa World Year Book.*

UNESCO Institute for Statistics, C.P. 6128 Succursale Centre-Ville, Montreal, Quebec, H3C 3J7 Canada, (Dial from U.S. (514) 343-6880), (Fax from U.S. (514) 343 6882), www.uis.unesco.org; *Statistical Tables.*

United Nations Food and Agricultural Organization (FAO), Viale delle Terme di Caracalla, 00100 Rome, Italy, (Dial from U.S. (202) 653-2400), (Fax from U.S. (202) 653 5760), www.fao.org; *The State of Food and Agriculture (SOFA) 2006.*

United Nations Statistics Division, New York, NY 10017, (800) 253-9646, Fax: (212) 963-4116, http://unstats.un.org; *Statistical Yearbook.*

The World Bank, 1818 H Street, NW, Washington, DC 20433, (202) 473-1000, Fax: (202) 477-6391, www.worldbank.org; *Chile* and *World Development Report 2008.*

CHILE - POSTAL SERVICE

M.E. Sharpe, 80 Business Park Drive, Armonk, NY 10504, (800) 541-6563, Fax: (914) 273-2106, www.mesharpe.com; *The Illustrated Book of World Rankings.*

Palgrave Macmillan Ltd., Houndmills, Basingstoke, Hampshire, RG21 6XS, England, (Telephone in U.S. (888) 330-8477), (Fax in U.S. (800) 672-2054), www.palgrave.com; *The Statesman's Yearbook 2008.*

United Nations Statistics Division, New York, NY 10017, (800) 253-9646, Fax: (212) 963-4116, http://unstats.un.org; *Statistical Yearbook.*

CHILE - POWER RESOURCES

Economist Intelligence Unit, 111 West 57th Street, New York, NY 10019, (212) 554-0600, Fax: (212) 586-1181, www.eiu.com; *Business Latin America.*

Euromonitor International, Inc., 224 S. Michigan Avenue, Suite 1500, Chicago, IL 60604, (312) 922-1115, Fax: (312) 922-1157, www.euromonitor.com; *International Marketing Data and Statistics 2008; The World Economic Factbook 2008;* and *World Marketing Data and Statistics.*

M.E. Sharpe, 80 Business Park Drive, Armonk, NY 10504, (800) 541-6563, Fax: (914) 273-2106, www.mesharpe.com; *The Illustrated Book of World Rankings.*

Organisation for Economic Cooperation and Development (OECD), 2 rue Andre Pascal, F-75775 Paris Cedex 16, France, (Telephone in U.S. (202) 785-6323), (Fax in U.S. (202) 785-0350), www.oecd.org; *World Energy Outlook 2007.*

Palgrave Macmillan Ltd., Houndmills, Basingstoke, Hampshire, RG21 6XS, England, (Telephone in U.S. (888) 330-8477), (Fax in U.S. (800) 672-2054), www.palgrave.com; *The Statesman's Yearbook 2008.*

Platts, 2 Penn Plaza, 25th Floor, New York, NY 10121-2298, (212) 904-3070, www.platts.com; *Energy Economist.*

U.S. Department of Energy (DOE), Energy Information Administration (EIA), 1000 Independence Avenue, SW, Washington, DC 20585, (202) 586-8800, www.eia.doe.gov; *International Energy Annual 2004* and *International Energy Outlook 2006.*

UCLA Latin American Institute, 10343 Bunche Hall, Box 951447, Los Angeles, CA 90095-1447, (310) 825-4571, Fax: (310) 206-6859, www.international.ucla.edu/lac; *Statistical Abstract of Latin America.*

United Nations Food and Agricultural Organization (FAO), Viale delle Terme di Caracalla, 00100 Rome, Italy, (Dial from U.S. (202) 653-2400), (Fax from U.S. (202) 653 5760), www.fao.org; *The State of Food and Agriculture (SOFA) 2006.*

United Nations Statistics Division, New York, NY 10017, (800) 253-9646, Fax: (212) 963-4116, http://unstats.un.org; *Energy Statistics Yearbook 2003; Human Development Report 2006; Statistical Yearbook for Latin America and the Caribbean 2004;* and *World Statistics Pocketbook.*

The World Bank, 1818 H Street, NW, Washington, DC 20433, (202) 473-1000, Fax: (202) 477-6391, www.worldbank.org; *The World Bank Atlas 2003-2004* and *World Development Report 2008.*

CHILE - PRICES

Economist Intelligence Unit, 111 West 57th Street, New York, NY 10019, (212) 554-0600, Fax: (212) 586-1181, www.eiu.com; *Business Latin America.*

Euromonitor International, Inc., 224 S. Michigan Avenue, Suite 1500, Chicago, IL 60604, (312) 922-1115, Fax: (312) 922-1157, www.euromonitor.com; *World Marketing Data and Statistics.*

International Labour Office, I.L.O. Publications, 4 route des Morillons, CH-1211 Geneva 22, Switzerland, (Telephone in U.S. (202) 653-7652), (Fax in U.S. (202) 653-7687), www.ilo.org; *Yearbook of Labour Statistics 2006.*

International Monetary Fund (IMF), 700 Nineteenth Street, NW, Washington, DC 20431, (202) 623-7000, Fax: (202) 623-4661, www.imf.org; *International Financial Statistics Yearbook 2007.*

M.E. Sharpe, 80 Business Park Drive, Armonk, NY 10504, (800) 541-6563, Fax: (914) 273-2106, www.mesharpe.com; *The Illustrated Book of World Rankings.*

Organization of American States (OAS), 17th Street Constitution Avenue NW, Washington, DC 20006, (202) 458-3000, www.oas.org; *The OAS in Transition: 1994-2004.*

UCLA Latin American Institute, 10343 Bunche Hall, Box 951447, Los Angeles, CA 90095-1447, (310) 825-4571, Fax: (310) 206-6859, www.international.ucla.edu/lac; *Statistical Abstract of Latin America.*

United Nations Food and Agricultural Organization (FAO), Viale delle Terme di Caracalla, 00100 Rome, Italy, (Dial from U.S. (202) 653-2400), (Fax from U.S. (202) 653 5760), www.fao.org; *FAO Production Yearbook 2002* and *The State of Food and Agriculture (SOFA) 2006.*

United Nations Statistics Division, New York, NY 10017, (800) 253-9646, Fax: (212) 963-4116, http://unstats.un.org; *Statistical Yearbook for Latin America and the Caribbean 2004.*

The World Bank, 1818 H Street, NW, Washington, DC 20433, (202) 473-1000, Fax: (202) 477-6391, www.worldbank.org; *Chile.*

World Bureau of Metal Statistics (WBMS), 27a High Street, Ware, Hertfordshire, SG12 9BA, United Kingdom, www.world-bureau.com; *World Flow Charts* and *World Metal Statistics.*

CHILE - PROFESSIONS

UCLA Latin American Institute, 10343 Bunche Hall, Box 951447, Los Angeles, CA 90095-1447, (310) 825-4571, Fax: (310) 206-6859, www.international.ucla.edu/lac; *Statistical Abstract of Latin America.*

United Nations Statistics Division, New York, NY 10017, (800) 253-9646, Fax: (212) 963-4116, http://unstats.un.org; *Statistical Yearbook.*

CHILE - PUBLIC HEALTH

Economist Intelligence Unit, 111 West 57th Street, New York, NY 10019, (212) 554-0600, Fax: (212) 586-1181, www.eiu.com; *Business Latin America.*

Euromonitor International, Inc., 224 S. Michigan Avenue, Suite 1500, Chicago, IL 60604, (312) 922-1115, Fax: (312) 922-1157, www.euromonitor.com; *World Health Databook 2007/2008* and *World Marketing Data and Statistics.*

M.E. Sharpe, 80 Business Park Drive, Armonk, NY 10504, (800) 541-6563, Fax: (914) 273-2106, www.mesharpe.com; *The Illustrated Book of World Rankings.*

Palgrave Macmillan Ltd., Houndmills, Basingstoke, Hampshire, RG21 6XS, England, (Telephone in U.S. (888) 330-8477), (Fax in U.S. (800) 672-2054), www.palgrave.com; *The Statesman's Yearbook 2008.*

UCLA Latin American Institute, 10343 Bunche Hall, Box 951447, Los Angeles, CA 90095-1447, (310) 825-4571, Fax: (310) 206-6859, www.international.ucla.edu/lac; *Statistical Abstract of Latin America.*

UNICEF, 3 United Nations Plaza, New York, NY 10017, (800) 253-9646, Fax: (212) 887-7465, www.unicef.org; *The State of the World's Children 2008.*

United Nations Statistics Division, New York, NY 10017, (800) 253-9646, Fax: (212) 963-4116, http://unstats.un.org; *Human Development Report 2006* and *Statistical Yearbook.*

The World Bank, 1818 H Street, NW, Washington, DC 20433, (202) 473-1000, Fax: (202) 477-6391, www.worldbank.org; *Chile* and *World Development Report 2008.*

World Health Organization (WHO), Avenue Appia 20, 1211 Geneve 27, Switzerland, (Telephone in U.S. (212) 331-9081), www.who.int; The WHO Global Atlas of Infectious Diseases and *World Health Report 2006.*

CHILE - PUBLIC UTILITIES

UCLA Latin American Institute, 10343 Bunche Hall, Box 951447, Los Angeles, CA 90095-1447, (310) 825-4571, Fax: (310) 206-6859, www.international.ucla.edu/lac; *Statistical Abstract of Latin America.*

CHILE - PUBLISHERS AND PUBLISHING

Taylor and Francis Group, An Informa Business, 2 Park Square, Milton Park, Abingdon, Oxford OX14 4RN, United Kingdom, (Dial from U.S. (212) 216-7800), (Fax from U.S. (212) 564-7854), www.tandf.co.uk; *The Europa World Year Book.*

UNESCO Institute for Statistics, C.P. 6128 Succursale Centre-Ville, Montreal, Quebec, H3C 3J7 Canada, (Dial from U.S. (514) 343-6880), (Fax from U.S. (514) 343 6882), www.uis.unesco.org; *Statistical Tables.*

CHILE - RADIO - RECEIVERS AND RECEPTION

Palgrave Macmillan Ltd., Houndmills, Basingstoke, Hampshire, RG21 6XS, England, (Telephone in U.S. (888) 330-8477), (Fax in U.S. (800) 672-2054), www.palgrave.com; *The Statesman's Yearbook 2008.*

United Nations Statistics Division, New York, NY 10017, (800) 253-9646, Fax: (212) 963-4116, http://unstats.un.org; *Statistical Yearbook.*

CHILE - RAILROADS

Economist Intelligence Unit, 111 West 57th Street, New York, NY 10019, (212) 554-0600, Fax: (212) 586-1181, www.eiu.com; *Business Latin America.*

Jane's Information Group, 110 North Royal Street, Suite 200, Alexandria, VA 22314, (703) 683-3700, Fax: (800) 836-0297, www.janes.com; *Jane's World Railways.*

Palgrave Macmillan Ltd., Houndmills, Basingstoke, Hampshire, RG21 6XS, England, (Telephone in U.S. (888) 330-8477), (Fax in U.S. (800) 672-2054), www.palgrave.com; *The Statesman's Yearbook 2008.*

Taylor and Francis Group, An Informa Business, 2 Park Square, Milton Park, Abingdon, Oxford OX14 4RN, United Kingdom, (Dial from U.S. (212) 216-7800), (Fax from U.S. (212) 564-7854), www.tandf.co.uk; *The Europa World Year Book.*

United Nations Statistics Division, New York, NY 10017, (800) 253-9646, Fax: (212) 963-4116, http://unstats.un.org; *Statistical Yearbook.*

CHILE - RELIGION

Central Intelligence Agency, Office of Public Affairs, Washington, DC 20505, (703) 482-0623, Fax: (703) 482-1739, www.cia.gov; *The World Factbook.*

M.E. Sharpe, 80 Business Park Drive, Armonk, NY 10504, (800) 541-6563, Fax: (914) 273-2106, www.mesharpe.com; *The Illustrated Book of World Rankings.*

Palgrave Macmillan Ltd., Houndmills, Basingstoke, Hampshire, RG21 6XS, England, (Telephone in U.S. (888) 330-8477), (Fax in U.S. (800) 672-2054), www.palgrave.com; *The Statesman's Yearbook 2008.*

UCLA Latin American Institute, 10343 Bunche Hall, Box 951447, Los Angeles, CA 90095-1447, (310) 825-4571, Fax: (310) 206-6859, www.international.ucla.edu/lac; *Statistical Abstract of Latin America.*

CHILE - RENT CHARGES

International Labour Office, I.L.O. Publications, 4 route des Morillons, CH-1211 Geneva 22, Switzerland, (Telephone in U.S. (202) 653-7652), (Fax in U.S. (202) 653-7687), www.ilo.org; *Yearbook of Labour Statistics 2006.*

CHILE - RESERVES (ACCOUNTING)

Economist Intelligence Unit, 111 West 57th Street, New York, NY 10019, (212) 554-0600, Fax: (212) 586-1181, www.eiu.com; *Business Latin America.*

Euromonitor International, Inc., 224 S. Michigan Avenue, Suite 1500, Chicago, IL 60604, (312) 922-1115, Fax: (312) 922-1157, www.euromonitor.com; *International Marketing Data and Statistics 2008.*

Inter-American Development Bank (IDB), 1300 New York Avenue, NW, Washington, DC 20577, (202) 623-1000, Fax: (202) 623-3096, www.iadb.org; *The Politics of Policies: Economic and Social Progress in Latin America - 2006 Report.*

Organization of American States (OAS), 17th Street Constitution Avenue NW, Washington, DC 20006, (202) 458-3000, www.oas.org; *The OAS in Transition: 1994-2004.*

The World Bank, 1818 H Street, NW, Washington, DC 20433, (202) 473-1000, Fax: (202) 477-6391, www.worldbank.org; *World Development Indicators (WDI) 2008.*

CHILE - RETAIL TRADE

Euromonitor International, Inc., 224 S. Michigan Avenue, Suite 1500, Chicago, IL 60604, (312) 922-1115, Fax: (312) 922-1157, www.euromonitor.com; *Retail Trade International 2007* and *World Marketing Data and Statistics.*

Inter-American Development Bank (IDB), 1300 New York Avenue, NW, Washington, DC 20577, (202) 623-1000, Fax: (202) 623-3096, www.iadb.org; *The Politics of Policies: Economic and Social Progress in Latin America - 2006 Report.*

CHILE - RICE PRODUCTION

See CHILE - CROPS

CHILE - ROADS

Central Intelligence Agency, Office of Public Affairs, Washington, DC 20505, (703) 482-0623, Fax: (703) 482-1739, www.cia.gov; *The World Factbook.*

Economist Intelligence Unit, 111 West 57th Street, New York, NY 10019, (212) 554-0600, Fax: (212) 586-1181, www.eiu.com; *Business Latin America.*

International Road Federation (IFR), Madison Place, 500 Montgomery Street, 5th Floor, Alexandria, VA 22314, (703) 535-1001, Fax: (703) 535-1007, www.irfnet.org; *World Road Statistics 2006.*

Palgrave Macmillan Ltd., Houndmills, Basingstoke, Hampshire, RG21 6XS, England, (Telephone in U.S. (888) 330-8477), (Fax in U.S. (800) 672-2054), www.palgrave.com; *The Statesman's Yearbook 2008.*

CHILE - RUBBER INDUSTRY AND TRADE

International Rubber Study Group (IRSG), 1st Floor, Heron House, 109/115 Wembley Hill Road, Wembley, Middlesex HA9 8DA, United Kingdom, www.rubberstudy.com; *Rubber Statistical Bulletin; Summary of World Rubber Statistics 2005; World Rubber Statistics Handbook (Volume 6, 1975-2001);* and *World Rubber Statistics Historic Handbook.*

M.E. Sharpe, 80 Business Park Drive, Armonk, NY 10504, (800) 541-6563, Fax: (914) 273-2106, www.mesharpe.com; *The Illustrated Book of World Rankings.*

CHILE - SALT PRODUCTION

See CHILE - MINERAL INDUSTRIES

CHILE - SHEEP

See CHILE - LIVESTOCK

CHILE - SHIPPING

Lloyd's Register - Fairplay, 8410 N.W. 53rd Terrace, Suite 207, Miami FL 33166, (305) 718-9929, Fax: (305) 718-9663, www.lrfairplay.com; *Register of Ships 2007-2008; World Casualty Statistics 2007; World Fleet Statistics 2006; World Marine Propulsion Report 2006-2010; World Shipbuilding Statistics 2007;* and The World Shipping Encyclopaedia.

Palgrave Macmillan Ltd., Houndmills, Basingstoke, Hampshire, RG21 6XS, England, (Telephone in U.S. (888) 330-8477), (Fax in U.S. (800) 672-2054), www.palgrave.com; *The Statesman's Yearbook 2008.*

Taylor and Francis Group, An Informa Business, 2 Park Square, Milton Park, Abingdon, Oxford OX14 4RN, United Kingdom, (Dial from U.S. (212) 216-7800), (Fax from U.S. (212) 564-7854), www.tandf.co.uk; *The Europa World Year Book.*

U.S. Department of Transportation (DOT), Maritime Administration (MARAD), West Building, Southeast Federal Center, 1200 New Jersey Avenue, SE, Washington, DC 20590, (800) 99-MARAD, www.marad.dot.gov; *World Merchant Fleet 2005.*

United Nations Statistics Division, New York, NY 10017, (800) 253-9646, Fax: (212) 963-4116, http://unstats.un.org; *Statistical Yearbook.*

CHILE - SILVER PRODUCTION

See CHILE - MINERAL INDUSTRIES

CHILE - SOCIAL ECOLOGY

M.E. Sharpe, 80 Business Park Drive, Armonk, NY 10504, (800) 541-6563, Fax: (914) 273-2106, www.mesharpe.com; *The Illustrated Book of World Rankings.*

UCLA Latin American Institute, 10343 Bunche Hall, Box 951447, Los Angeles, CA 90095-1447, (310) 825-4571, Fax: (310) 206-6859, www.international.ucla.edu/lac; *Statistical Abstract of Latin America.*

United Nations Statistics Division, New York, NY 10017, (800) 253-9646, Fax: (212) 963-4116, http://unstats.un.org; *World Statistics Pocketbook.*

CHILE - SOCIAL SECURITY

Inter-American Development Bank (IDB), 1300 New York Avenue, NW, Washington, DC 20577, (202) 623-1000, Fax: (202) 623-3096, www.iadb.org; *The Politics of Policies: Economic and Social Progress in Latin America - 2006 Report.*

International Civil Aviation Organization (ICAO), External Relations and Public Information Office (EPO), 999 University Street, Montreal, Quebec H3C 5H7, Canada, (Dial from U.S. (514) 954-8219), (Fax from U.S. (514) 954-6077), www.icao.int; *Civil Aviation Statistics of the World.*

Palgrave Macmillan Ltd., Houndmills, Basingstoke, Hampshire, RG21 6XS, England, (Telephone in U.S. (888) 330-8477), (Fax in U.S. (800) 672-2054), www.palgrave.com; *The Statesman's Yearbook 2008.*

United Nations Statistics Division, New York, NY 10017, (800) 253-9646, Fax: (212) 963-4116, http://unstats.un.org; *National Accounts Statistics: Compendium of Income Distribution Statistics.*

CHILE - SOYBEAN PRODUCTION

See CHILE - CROPS

CHILE - STEEL PRODUCTION

See CHILE - MINERAL INDUSTRIES

CHILE - SUGAR PRODUCTION

See CHILE - CROPS

CHILE - SULPHUR PRODUCTION

See CHILE - MINERAL INDUSTRIES

CHILE - TAXATION

Inter-American Development Bank (IDB), 1300 New York Avenue, NW, Washington, DC 20577, (202) 623-1000, Fax: (202) 623-3096, www.iadb.org; *The Politics of Policies: Economic and Social Progress in Latin America - 2006 Report.*

International Monetary Fund (IMF), 700 Nineteenth Street, NW, Washington, DC 20431, (202) 623-7000, Fax: (202) 623-4661, www.imf.org; *Government Finance Statistics Yearbook (2008 Edition).*

International Road Federation (IFR), Madison Place, 500 Montgomery Street, 5th Floor, Alexandria, VA 22314, (703) 535-1001, Fax: (703) 535-1007, www.irfnet.org; *World Road Statistics 2006.*

Taylor and Francis Group, An Informa Business, 2 Park Square, Milton Park, Abingdon, Oxford OX14 4RN, United Kingdom, (Dial from U.S. (212) 216-7800), (Fax from U.S. (212) 564-7854), www.tandf.co.uk; *The Europa World Year Book.*

United Nations Statistics Division, New York, NY 10017, (800) 253-9646, Fax: (212) 963-4116, http://unstats.un.org; *Statistical Yearbook for Latin America and the Caribbean 2004.*

The World Bank, 1818 H Street, NW, Washington, DC 20433, (202) 473-1000, Fax: (202) 477-6391, www.worldbank.org; *World Development Indicators (WDI) 2008.*

CHILE - TEA PRODUCTION

See CHILE - CROPS

CHILE - TELEPHONE

Economist Intelligence Unit, 111 West 57th Street, New York, NY 10019, (212) 554-0600, Fax: (212) 586-1181, www.eiu.com; *Business Latin America.*

International Telecommunication Union (ITU), Place des Nations, 1211 Geneva 20, Switzerland, www.itu.int; World Telecommunication Indicators Database.

Palgrave Macmillan Ltd., Houndmills, Basingstoke, Hampshire, RG21 6XS, England, (Telephone in U.S. (888) 330-8477), (Fax in U.S. (800) 672-2054), www.palgrave.com; *The Statesman's Yearbook 2008.*

Taylor and Francis Group, An Informa Business, 2 Park Square, Milton Park, Abingdon, Oxford OX14 4RN, United Kingdom, (Dial from U.S. (212) 216-7800), (Fax from U.S. (212) 564-7854), www.tandf.co.uk; *The Europa World Year Book.*

United Nations Statistics Division, New York, NY 10017, (800) 253-9646, Fax: (212) 963-4116, http://unstats.un.org; *Statistical Yearbook* and *World Statistics Pocketbook.*

CHILE - TELEVISION - RECEIVERS AND RECEPTION

United Nations Statistics Division, New York, NY 10017, (800) 253-9646, Fax: (212) 963-4116, http://unstats.un.org; *Statistical Yearbook.*

CHILE - TEXTILE INDUSTRY

Euromonitor International, Inc., 224 S. Michigan Avenue, Suite 1500, Chicago, IL 60604, (312) 922-1115, Fax: (312) 922-1157, www.euromonitor.com; *Retail Trade International 2007.*

M.E. Sharpe, 80 Business Park Drive, Armonk, NY 10504, (800) 541-6563, Fax: (914) 273-2106, www.mesharpe.com; *The Illustrated Book of World Rankings.*

United Nations Food and Agricultural Organization (FAO), Viale delle Terme di Caracalla, 00100 Rome, Italy, (Dial from U.S. (202) 653-2400), (Fax from U.S. (202) 653 5760), www.fao.org; *FAO Production Yearbook 2002.*

United Nations Statistics Division, New York, NY 10017, (800) 253-9646, Fax: (212) 963-4116, http://unstats.un.org; *Statistical Yearbook.*

CHILE - THEATER

UNESCO Institute for Statistics, C.P. 6128 Succursale Centre-Ville, Montreal, Quebec, H3C 3J7 Canada, (Dial from U.S. (514) 343-6880), (Fax from U.S. (514) 343 6882), www.uis.unesco.org; *Statistical Tables.*

CHILE - TIN PRODUCTION

See CHILE - MINERAL INDUSTRIES

CHILE - TIRE INDUSTRY

United Nations Statistics Division, New York, NY 10017, (800) 253-9646, Fax: (212) 963-4116, http://unstats.un.org; *Statistical Yearbook.*

CHILE - TOBACCO INDUSTRY

Foreign Agricultural Service (FAS), U.S. Department of Agriculture (USDA), 1400 Independence Avenue, SW, Washington, DC 20250, (202) 720-3935, www.fas.usda.gov; *Tobacco: World Markets and Trade.*

M.E. Sharpe, 80 Business Park Drive, Armonk, NY 10504, (800) 541-6563, Fax: (914) 273-2106, www.mesharpe.com; *The Illustrated Book of World Rankings.*

United Nations Statistics Division, New York, NY 10017, (800) 253-9646, Fax: (212) 963-4116, http://unstats.un.org; *Statistical Yearbook.*

CHILE - TOURISM

Economist Intelligence Unit, 111 West 57th Street, New York, NY 10019, (212) 554-0600, Fax: (212) 586-1181, www.eiu.com; *Business Latin America.*

Euromonitor International, Inc., 224 S. Michigan Avenue, Suite 1500, Chicago, IL 60604, (312) 922-1115, Fax: (312) 922-1157, www.euromonitor.com; *The World Economic Factbook 2008* and *World Marketing Data and Statistics.*

M.E. Sharpe, 80 Business Park Drive, Armonk, NY 10504, (800) 541-6563, Fax: (914) 273-2106, www.mesharpe.com; *The Illustrated Book of World Rankings.*

Palgrave Macmillan Ltd., Houndmills, Basingstoke, Hampshire, RG21 6XS, England, (Telephone in U.S. (888) 330-8477), (Fax in U.S. (800) 672-2054), www.palgrave.com; *The Statesman's Yearbook 2008.*

Taylor and Francis Group, An Informa Business, 2 Park Square, Milton Park, Abingdon, Oxford OX14 4RN, United Kingdom, (Dial from U.S. (212) 216-7800), (Fax from U.S. (212) 564-7854), www.tandf.co.uk; *The Europa World Year Book.*

UCLA Latin American Institute, 10343 Bunche Hall, Box 951447, Los Angeles, CA 90095-1447, (310) 825-4571, Fax: (310) 206-6859, www.international.ucla.edu/lac; *Statistical Abstract of Latin America.*

United Nations Statistics Division, New York, NY 10017, (800) 253-9646, Fax: (212) 963-4116, http://unstats.un.org; *Statistical Yearbook* and *Statistical Yearbook for Latin America and the Caribbean 2004.*

United Nations World Tourism Organization (UNWTO), Capitan Haya 42, 28020 Madrid, Spain, www.world-tourism.org; *Yearbook of Tourism Statistics.*

The World Bank, 1818 H Street, NW, Washington, DC 20433, (202) 473-1000, Fax: (202) 477-6391, www.worldbank.org; *Chile.*

CHILE - TRADE

See CHILE - INTERNATIONAL TRADE

CHILE - TRANSPORTATION

Central Intelligence Agency, Office of Public Affairs, Washington, DC 20505, (703) 482-0623, Fax: (703) 482-1739, www.cia.gov; *The World Factbook.*

Economist Intelligence Unit, 111 West 57th Street, New York, NY 10019, (212) 554-0600, Fax: (212) 586-1181, www.eiu.com; *Business Asia.*

Euromonitor International, Inc., 224 S. Michigan Avenue, Suite 1500, Chicago, IL 60604, (312) 922-1115, Fax: (312) 922-1157, www.euromonitor.com; *International Marketing Data and Statistics 2008* and *World Marketing Data and Statistics.*

Inter-American Development Bank (IDB), 1300 New York Avenue, NW, Washington, DC 20577, (202) 623-1000, Fax: (202) 623-3096, www.iadb.org; *The Politics of Policies: Economic and Social Progress in Latin America - 2006 Report.*

M.E. Sharpe, 80 Business Park Drive, Armonk, NY 10504, (800) 541-6563, Fax: (914) 273-2106, www.mesharpe.com; *The Illustrated Book of World Rankings.*

Palgrave Macmillan Ltd., Houndmills, Basingstoke, Hampshire, RG21 6XS, England, (Telephone in U.S. (888) 330-8477), (Fax in U.S. (800) 672-2054), www.palgrave.com; *The Statesman's Yearbook 2008.*

Taylor and Francis Group, An Informa Business, 2 Park Square, Milton Park, Abingdon, Oxford OX14 4RN, United Kingdom, (Dial from U.S. (212) 216-7800), (Fax from U.S. (212) 564-7854), www.tandf.co.uk; *The Europa World Year Book.*

UCLA Latin American Institute, 10343 Bunche Hall, Box 951447, Los Angeles, CA 90095-1447, (310) 825-4571, Fax: (310) 206-6859, www.international.ucla.edu/lac; *Statistical Abstract of Latin America.*

United Nations Statistics Division, New York, NY 10017, (800) 253-9646, Fax: (212) 963-4116, http://unstats.un.org; *Human Development Report 2006* and *Statistical Yearbook for Latin America and the Caribbean 2004.*

The World Bank, 1818 H Street, NW, Washington, DC 20433, (202) 473-1000, Fax: (202) 477-6391, www.worldbank.org; *Chile.*

CHILE - UNEMPLOYMENT

Central Intelligence Agency, Office of Public Affairs, Washington, DC 20505, (703) 482-0623, Fax: (703) 482-1739, www.cia.gov; *The World Factbook.*

Economist Intelligence Unit, 111 West 57th Street, New York, NY 10019, (212) 554-0600, Fax: (212) 586-1181, www.eiu.com; *Business Asia.*

Euromonitor International, Inc., 224 S. Michigan Avenue, Suite 1500, Chicago, IL 60604, (312) 922-1115, Fax: (312) 922-1157, www.euromonitor.com; *International Marketing Data and Statistics 2008.*

International Labour Office, I.L.O. Publications, 4 route des Morillons, CH-1211 Geneva 22, Switzerland, (Telephone in U.S. (202) 653-7652), (Fax in U.S. (202) 653-7687), www.ilo.org; *Yearbook of Labour Statistics 2006.*

Organisation for Economic Cooperation and Development (OECD), 2 rue Andre Pascal, F-75775 Paris Cedex 16, France, (Telephone in U.S. (202) 785-6323), (Fax in U.S. (202) 785-0350), www.oecd.org; *OECD Economic Survey - Chile 2007.*

Organization of American States (OAS), 17th Street Constitution Avenue NW, Washington, DC 20006, (202) 458-3000, www.oas.org; *The OAS in Transition: 1994-2004.*

Palgrave Macmillan Ltd., Houndmills, Basingstoke, Hampshire, RG21 6XS, England, (Telephone in U.S. (888) 330-8477), (Fax in U.S. (800) 672-2054), www.palgrave.com; *The Statesman's Yearbook 2008.*

UCLA Latin American Institute, 10343 Bunche Hall, Box 951447, Los Angeles, CA 90095-1447, (310) 825-4571, Fax: (310) 206-6859, www.international.ucla.edu/lac; *Statistical Abstract of Latin America.*

United Nations Statistics Division, New York, NY 10017, (800) 253-9646, Fax: (212) 963-4116, http://unstats.un.org; *Statistical Yearbook.*

CHILE - VITAL STATISTICS

Euromonitor International, Inc., 224 S. Michigan Avenue, Suite 1500, Chicago, IL 60604, (312) 922-1115, Fax: (312) 922-1157, www.euromonitor.com; *International Marketing Data and Statistics 2008.*

Palgrave Macmillan Ltd., Houndmills, Basingstoke, Hampshire, RG21 6XS, England, (Telephone in U.S. (888) 330-8477), (Fax in U.S. (800) 672-2054), www.palgrave.com; *The Statesman's Yearbook 2008.*

United Nations Statistics Division, New York, NY 10017, (800) 253-9646, Fax: (212) 963-4116, http://unstats.un.org; *Statistical Yearbook.*

World Health Organization (WHO), Avenue Appia 20, 1211 Geneve 27, Switzerland, (Telephone in U.S. (212) 331-9081), www.who.int; *World Health Report 2006.*

CHILE - WAGES

International Labour Office, I.L.O. Publications, 4 route des Morillons, CH-1211 Geneva 22, Switzerland, (Telephone in U.S. (202) 653-7652), (Fax in U.S. (202) 653-7687), www.ilo.org; *Yearbook of Labour Statistics 2006.*

Organization of American States (OAS), 17th Street Constitution Avenue NW, Washington, DC 20006, (202) 458-3000, www.oas.org; *The OAS in Transition: 1994-2004.*

UCLA Latin American Institute, 10343 Bunche Hall, Box 951447, Los Angeles, CA 90095-1447, (310) 825-4571, Fax: (310) 206-6859, www.international.ucla.edu/lac; *Statistical Abstract of Latin America.*

United Nations Statistics Division, New York, NY 10017, (800) 253-9646, Fax: (212) 963-4116, http://unstats.un.org; *Statistical Yearbook.*

The World Bank, 1818 H Street, NW, Washington, DC 20433, (202) 473-1000, Fax: (202) 477-6391, www.worldbank.org; *Chile.*

CHILE - WELFARE STATE

Inter-American Development Bank (IDB), 1300 New York Avenue, NW, Washington, DC 20577, (202) 623-1000, Fax: (202) 623-3096, www.iadb.org; *The Politics of Policies: Economic and Social Progress in Latin America - 2006 Report.*

International Monetary Fund (IMF), 700 Nineteenth Street, NW, Washington, DC 20431, (202) 623-7000, Fax: (202) 623-4661, www.imf.org; *Government Finance Statistics Yearbook (2008 Edition).*

CHILE - WHALES

See CHILE - FISHERIES

CHILE - WHEAT PRODUCTION

See CHILE - CROPS

CHILE - WHOLESALE PRICE INDEXES

Inter-American Development Bank (IDB), 1300 New York Avenue, NW, Washington, DC 20577, (202) 623-1000, Fax: (202) 623-3096, www.iadb.org; *The Politics of Policies: Economic and Social Progress in Latin America - 2006 Report.*

Organization of American States (OAS), 17th Street Constitution Avenue NW, Washington, DC 20006, (202) 458-3000, www.oas.org; *The OAS in Transition: 1994-2004.*

United Nations Statistics Division, New York, NY 10017, (800) 253-9646, Fax: (212) 963-4116, http://unstats.un.org; *Statistical Yearbook.*

CHILE - WHOLESALE TRADE

Inter-American Development Bank (IDB), 1300 New York Avenue, NW, Washington, DC 20577, (202) 623-1000, Fax: (202) 623-3096, www.iadb.org; *The Politics of Policies: Economic and Social Progress in Latin America - 2006 Report.*

United Nations Statistics Division, New York, NY 10017, (800) 253-9646, Fax: (212) 963-4116, http://unstats.un.org; *Statistical Yearbook.*

CHILE - WINE PRODUCTION

See CHILE - BEVERAGE INDUSTRY

CHILE - WOOD AND WOOD PULP

See CHILE - FORESTS AND FORESTRY

CHILE - WOOL PRODUCTION

See CHILE - TEXTILE INDUSTRY

CHILE - YARN PRODUCTION

See CHILE - TEXTILE INDUSTRY

CHILE - ZINC AND ZINC ORE

See CHILE - MINERAL INDUSTRIES

CHINA - NATIONAL STATISTICAL OFFICE

National Bureau of Statistics of China (NBS), No. 57, Yuetan Nanjie, Sanlihe, Xicheng District, Beijing 100826, China, www.stats.gov.cn/english; National Data Center.

CHINA - PRIMARY STATISTICS SOURCES

Academic International Press, PO Box 1111, Gulf Breeze, FL 32562-1111, Fax: (850) 934-0953, www.ai-press.com; *China Facts and Figures Annual.*

Japan Center for Economic Research (JCER), Nikkei Kayabacho Building, Nihombashi Kayabacho, 2-6-1, Chuo-ku, Tokyo 103-0025, Japan, www.jcer.or.jp/eng; *China Research Report.*

National Bureau of Statistics of China (NBS), No. 57, Yuetan Nanjie, Sanlihe, Xicheng District, Beijing 100826, China, www.stats.gov.cn/english; *China Statistical Yearbook 2007.*

The World Bank, 1818 H Street, NW, Washington, DC 20433, (202) 473-1000, Fax: (202) 477-6391, www.worldbank.org; *Macao, China.*

CHINA - AGRICULTURAL MACHINERY

Academic International Press, PO Box 1111, Gulf Breeze, FL 32562-1111, Fax: (850) 934-0953, www.ai-press.com; *China Facts and Figures Annual.*

National Bureau of Statistics of China (NBS), No. 57, Yuetan Nanjie, Sanlihe, Xicheng District, Beijing 100826, China, www.stats.gov.cn/english; *China Statistical Yearbook 2007* and *Monthly Statistical Data.*

United Nations Statistics Division, New York, NY 10017, (800) 253-9646, Fax: (212) 963-4116, http://unstats.un.org; *Statistical Yearbook.*

CHINA - AGRICULTURE

Academic International Press, PO Box 1111, Gulf Breeze, FL 32562-1111, Fax: (850) 934-0953, www.ai-press.com; *China Facts and Figures Annual.*

Asian Development Bank (ADB), PO Box 789, 0980 Manila, Philippines, www.adb.org; *Key Indicators of Developing Asian and Pacific Countries 2006.*

Economist Intelligence Unit, 111 West 57th Street, New York, NY 10019, (212) 554-0600, Fax: (212) 586-1181, www.eiu.com; *Business China* and *China Country Report.*

Euromonitor International, Inc., 224 S. Michigan Avenue, Suite 1500, Chicago, IL 60604, (312) 922-1115, Fax: (312) 922-1157, www.euromonitor.com; *International Marketing Data and Statistics 2008* and *World Marketing Data and Statistics.*

Federal Statistical Office Germany, D-65180 Wiesbaden, Germany, www.destatis.de; *China 2004.*

Japan Center for Economic Research (JCER), Nikkei Kayabacho Building, Nihombashi Kayabacho, 2-6-1, Chuo-ku, Tokyo 103-0025, Japan, www.jcer.or.jp/eng; *China Research Report.*

M.E. Sharpe, 80 Business Park Drive, Armonk, NY 10504, (800) 541-6563, Fax: (914) 273-2106, www.mesharpe.com; *The Illustrated Book of World Rankings.*

National Bureau of Statistics of China (NBS), No. 57, Yuetan Nanjie, Sanlihe, Xicheng District, Beijing 100826, China, www.stats.gov.cn/english; *China Statistical Yearbook 2007* and *Monthly Statistical Data.*

Palgrave Macmillan Ltd., Houndmills, Basingstoke, Hampshire, RG21 6XS, England, (Telephone in U.S. (888) 330-8477), (Fax in U.S. (800) 672-2054), www.palgrave.com; *The Statesman's Yearbook 2008.*

Taylor and Francis Group, An Informa Business, 2 Park Square, Milton Park, Abingdon, Oxford OX14 4RN, United Kingdom, (Dial from U.S. (212) 216-7800), (Fax from U.S. (212) 564-7854), www.tandf.co.uk; *The Europa World Year Book.*

United Nations Conference on Trade and Development (UNCTAD), DC2-1120, United Nations, New York, NY 10017, (212) 963-0027, www.unctad.org; *UNCTAD Commodity Yearbook.*

United Nations Food and Agricultural Organization (FAO), Viale delle Terme di Caracalla, 00100 Rome, Italy, (Dial from U.S. (202) 653-2400), (Fax from U.S. (202) 653 5760), www.fao.org; AQUASTAT; *FAO Production Yearbook 2002; FAO Trade Yearbook;* and *The State of Food and Agriculture (SOFA) 2006.*

United Nations Statistics Division, New York, NY 10017, (800) 253-9646, Fax: (212) 963-4116, http://unstats.un.org; *Asia-Pacific in Figures 2004; Statistical Yearbook;* and *Statistical Yearbook for Asia and the Pacific 2004.*

The World Bank, 1818 H Street, NW, Washington, DC 20433, (202) 473-1000, Fax: (202) 477-6391, www.worldbank.org; *World Development Indicators (WDI) 2008.*

CHINA - AIRLINES

Economist Intelligence Unit, 111 West 57th Street, New York, NY 10019, (212) 554-0600, Fax: (212) 586-1181, www.eiu.com; *Business Asia* and *Business China.*

M.E. Sharpe, 80 Business Park Drive, Armonk, NY 10504, (800) 541-6563, Fax: (914) 273-2106, www.mesharpe.com; *The Illustrated Book of World Rankings.*

Palgrave Macmillan Ltd., Houndmills, Basingstoke, Hampshire, RG21 6XS, England, (Telephone in U.S.

(888) 330-8477), (Fax in U.S. (800) 672-2054), www.palgrave.com; *The Statesman's Yearbook 2008*.

Taylor and Francis Group, An Informa Business, 2 Park Square, Milton Park, Abingdon, Oxford OX14 4RN, United Kingdom, (Dial from U.S. (212) 216-7800), (Fax from U.S. (212) 564-7854), www.tandf.co.uk; *The Europa World Year Book*.

CHINA - AIRPORTS

Central Intelligence Agency, Office of Public Affairs, Washington, DC 20505, (703) 482-0623, Fax: (703) 482-1739, www.cia.gov; *The World Factbook*.

CHINA - ALUMINUM PRODUCTION

See CHINA - MINERAL INDUSTRIES

CHINA - ARMED FORCES

Central Intelligence Agency, Office of Public Affairs, Washington, DC 20505, (703) 482-0623, Fax: (703) 482-1739, www.cia.gov; *The World Factbook*.

Economist Intelligence Unit, 111 West 57th Street, New York, NY 10019, (212) 554-0600, Fax: (212) 586-1181, www.eiu.com; *Business Asia*.

Euromonitor International, Inc., 224 S. Michigan Avenue, Suite 1500, Chicago, IL 60604, (312) 922-1115, Fax: (312) 922-1157, www.euromonitor.com; *World Marketing Data and Statistics*.

International Institute for Strategic Studies (IISS), Arundel House, 13-15 Arundel Street, Temple Place, London WC2R 3DX, England, www.iiss.org; *The Military Balance 2007*.

Palgrave Macmillan Ltd., Houndmills, Basingstoke, Hampshire, RG21 6XS, England, (Telephone in U.S. (888) 330-8477), (Fax in U.S. (800) 672-2054), www.palgrave.com; *The Statesman's Yearbook 2008*.

U.S. Department of State (DOS), 2201 C Street NW, Washington, DC 20520, (202) 647-4000, www.state.gov; *World Military Expenditures and Arms Transfers (WMEAT)*.

United Nations Statistics Division, New York, NY 10017, (800) 253-9646, Fax: (212) 963-4116, http://unstats.un.org; *Human Development Report 2006*.

CHINA - AUTOMOBILE INDUSTRY AND TRADE

Academic International Press, PO Box 1111, Gulf Breeze, FL 32562-1111, Fax: (850) 934-0953, www.ai-press.com; *China Facts and Figures Annual*.

Economist Intelligence Unit, 111 West 57th Street, New York, NY 10019, (212) 554-0600, Fax: (212) 586-1181, www.eiu.com; *Business China*.

Japan Center for Economic Research (JCER), Nikkei Kayabacho Building, Nihombashi Kayabacho, 2-6-1, Chuo-ku, Tokyo 103-0025, Japan, www.jcer.or.jp/eng; *China Research Report*.

National Bureau of Statistics of China (NBS), No. 57, Yuetan Nanjie, Sanlihe, Xicheng District, Beijing 100826, China, www.stats.gov.cn/english; *China Statistical Yearbook 2007*.

CHINA - BALANCE OF PAYMENTS

Academic International Press, PO Box 1111, Gulf Breeze, FL 32562-1111, Fax: (850) 934-0953, www.ai-press.com; *China Facts and Figures Annual*.

International Monetary Fund (IMF), 700 Nineteenth Street, NW, Washington, DC 20431, (202) 623-7000, Fax: (202) 623-4661, www.imf.org; *Balance of Payments Statistics Newsletter* and *Balance of Payments Statistics Yearbook 2007*.

Japan Center for Economic Research (JCER), Nikkei Kayabacho Building, Nihombashi Kayabacho, 2-6-1, Chuo-ku, Tokyo 103-0025, Japan, www.jcer.or.jp/eng; *China Research Report*.

National Bureau of Statistics of China (NBS), No. 57, Yuetan Nanjie, Sanlihe, Xicheng District, Beijing 100826, China, www.stats.gov.cn/english; *China Statistical Yearbook 2007; Monthly Statistical Data;* and *National Accounts*.

Taylor and Francis Group, An Informa Business, 2 Park Square, Milton Park, Abingdon, Oxford OX14 4RN, United Kingdom, (Dial from U.S. (212) 216-7800), (Fax from U.S. (212) 564-7854), www.tandf.co.uk; *The Europa World Year Book*.

United Nations Conference on Trade and Development (UNCTAD), DC2-1120, United Nations, New York, NY 10017, (212) 963-0027, www.unctad.org; *Handbook of Statistics 2005*.

The World Bank, 1818 H Street, NW, Washington, DC 20433, (202) 473-1000, Fax: (202) 477-6391, www.worldbank.org; *World Development Indicators (WDI) 2008* and *World Development Report 2008*.

CHINA - BANKS AND BANKING

Academic International Press, PO Box 1111, Gulf Breeze, FL 32562-1111, Fax: (850) 934-0953, www.ai-press.com; *China Facts and Figures Annual*.

Asian Development Bank (ADB), PO Box 789, 0980 Manila, Philippines, www.adb.org; *Key Indicators of Developing Asian and Pacific Countries 2006*.

Economist Intelligence Unit, 111 West 57th Street, New York, NY 10019, (212) 554-0600, Fax: (212) 586-1181, www.eiu.com; *Business China*.

Euromonitor International, Inc., 224 S. Michigan Avenue, Suite 1500, Chicago, IL 60604, (312) 922-1115, Fax: (312) 922-1157, www.euromonitor.com; *World Marketing Data and Statistics*.

Japan Center for Economic Research (JCER), Nikkei Kayabacho Building, Nihombashi Kayabacho, 2-6-1, Chuo-ku, Tokyo 103-0025, Japan, www.jcer.or.jp/eng; *China Research Report*.

M.E. Sharpe, 80 Business Park Drive, Armonk, NY 10504, (800) 541-6563, Fax: (914) 273-2106, www.mesharpe.com; *The Illustrated Book of World Rankings*.

National Bureau of Statistics of China (NBS), No. 57, Yuetan Nanjie, Sanlihe, Xicheng District, Beijing 100826, China, www.stats.gov.cn/english; *Banking and Insurance* and *China Statistical Yearbook 2007*.

Palgrave Macmillan Ltd., Houndmills, Basingstoke, Hampshire, RG21 6XS, England, (Telephone in U.S. (888) 330-8477), (Fax in U.S. (800) 672-2054), www.palgrave.com; *The Statesman's Yearbook 2008*.

Taylor and Francis Group, An Informa Business, 2 Park Square, Milton Park, Abingdon, Oxford OX14 4RN, United Kingdom, (Dial from U.S. (212) 216-7800), (Fax from U.S. (212) 564-7854), www.tandf.co.uk; *The Europa World Year Book*.

CHINA - BARLEY PRODUCTION

See CHINA - CROPS

CHINA - BEVERAGE INDUSTRY

Academic International Press, PO Box 1111, Gulf Breeze, FL 32562-1111, Fax: (850) 934-0953, www.ai-press.com; *China Facts and Figures Annual*.

Japan Center for Economic Research (JCER), Nikkei Kayabacho Building, Nihombashi Kayabacho, 2-6-1, Chuo-ku, Tokyo 103-0025, Japan, www.jcer.or.jp/eng; *China Research Report*.

M.E. Sharpe, 80 Business Park Drive, Armonk, NY 10504, (800) 541-6563, Fax: (914) 273-2106, www.mesharpe.com; *The Illustrated Book of World Rankings*.

National Bureau of Statistics of China (NBS), No. 57, Yuetan Nanjie, Sanlihe, Xicheng District, Beijing 100826, China, www.stats.gov.cn/english; *China Statistical Yearbook 2007*.

United Nations Statistics Division, New York, NY 10017, (800) 253-9646, Fax: (212) 963-4116, http://unstats.un.org; *Statistical Yearbook*.

CHINA - BONDS

Asian Development Bank (ADB), PO Box 789, 0980 Manila, Philippines, www.adb.org; *Key Indicators of Developing Asian and Pacific Countries 2006*.

CHINA - BROADCASTING

Central Intelligence Agency, Office of Public Affairs, Washington, DC 20505, (703) 482-0623, Fax: (703) 482-1739, www.cia.gov; *The World Factbook*.

Economist Intelligence Unit, 111 West 57th Street, New York, NY 10019, (212) 554-0600, Fax: (212) 586-1181, www.eiu.com; *Business Asia*.

Euromonitor International, Inc., 224 S. Michigan Avenue, Suite 1500, Chicago, IL 60604, (312) 922-1115, Fax: (312) 922-1157, www.euromonitor.com; *World Marketing Data and Statistics*.

M.E. Sharpe, 80 Business Park Drive, Armonk, NY 10504, (800) 541-6563, Fax: (914) 273-2106, www.mesharpe.com; *The Illustrated Book of World Rankings*.

Palgrave Macmillan Ltd., Houndmills, Basingstoke, Hampshire, RG21 6XS, England, (Telephone in U.S. (888) 330-8477), (Fax in U.S. (800) 672-2054), www.palgrave.com; *The Statesman's Yearbook 2008*.

WRTH Publications Limited, PO Box 290, Oxford OX2 7FT, UK, www.wrth.com; *World Radio TV Handbook 2007*.

CHINA - BUDGET

Central Intelligence Agency, Office of Public Affairs, Washington, DC 20505, (703) 482-0623, Fax: (703) 482-1739, www.cia.gov; *The World Factbook*.

National Bureau of Statistics of China (NBS), No. 57, Yuetan Nanjie, Sanlihe, Xicheng District, Beijing 100826, China, www.stats.gov.cn/english; *Government Finance* and *National Accounts*.

CHINA - BUSINESS

Academic International Press, PO Box 1111, Gulf Breeze, FL 32562-1111, Fax: (850) 934-0953, www.ai-press.com; *China Facts and Figures Annual*.

Japan Center for Economic Research (JCER), Nikkei Kayabacho Building, Nihombashi Kayabacho, 2-6-1, Chuo-ku, Tokyo 103-0025, Japan, www.jcer.or.jp/eng; *China Research Report*.

National Bureau of Statistics of China (NBS), No. 57, Yuetan Nanjie, Sanlihe, Xicheng District, Beijing 100826, China, www.stats.gov.cn/english; *China Statistical Yearbook 2007* and *Monthly Statistical Data*.

United Nations Statistics Division, New York, NY 10017, (800) 253-9646, Fax: (212) 963-4116, http://unstats.un.org; *Statistical Yearbook for Asia and the Pacific 2004*.

CHINA - CAPITAL INVESTMENTS

Academic International Press, PO Box 1111, Gulf Breeze, FL 32562-1111, Fax: (850) 934-0953, www.ai-press.com; *China Facts and Figures Annual*.

Asian Development Bank (ADB), PO Box 789, 0980 Manila, Philippines, www.adb.org; *Key Indicators of Developing Asian and Pacific Countries 2006*.

Economist Intelligence Unit, 111 West 57th Street, New York, NY 10019, (212) 554-0600, Fax: (212) 586-1181, www.eiu.com; *Business China*.

Japan Center for Economic Research (JCER), Nikkei Kayabacho Building, Nihombashi Kayabacho, 2-6-1, Chuo-ku, Tokyo 103-0025, Japan, www.jcer.or.jp/eng; *China Research Report*.

National Bureau of Statistics of China (NBS), No. 57, Yuetan Nanjie, Sanlihe, Xicheng District, Beijing 100826, China, www.stats.gov.cn/english; *China Statistical Yearbook 2007*.

CHINA - CAPITAL LEVY

Academic International Press, PO Box 1111, Gulf Breeze, FL 32562-1111, Fax: (850) 934-0953, www.ai-press.com; *China Facts and Figures Annual*.

Asian Development Bank (ADB), PO Box 789, 0980 Manila, Philippines, www.adb.org; *Key Indicators of Developing Asian and Pacific Countries 2006*.

Japan Center for Economic Research (JCER), Nikkei Kayabacho Building, Nihombashi Kayabacho, 2-6-1, Chuo-ku, Tokyo 103-0025, Japan, www.jcer.or.jp/eng; *China Research Report*.

National Bureau of Statistics of China (NBS), No. 57, Yuetan Nanjie, Sanlihe, Xicheng District, Beijing 100826, China, www.stats.gov.cn/english; *China Statistical Yearbook 2007*.

CHINA - CATTLE

See CHINA - LIVESTOCK

CHINA - CHESTNUT PRODUCTION

See CHINA - CROPS

CHINA - CHICKENS

See CHINA - LIVESTOCK

CHINA - CHILDBIRTH - STATISTICS

Academic International Press, PO Box 1111, Gulf Breeze, FL 32562-1111, Fax: (850) 934-0953, www.ai-press.com; *China Facts and Figures Annual.*

Central Intelligence Agency, Office of Public Affairs, Washington, DC 20505, (703) 482-0623, Fax: (703) 482-1739, www.cia.gov; *The World Factbook.*

Economist Intelligence Unit, 111 West 57th Street, New York, NY 10019, (212) 554-0600, Fax: (212) 586-1181, www.eiu.com; *Business Asia* and *Business China.*

Euromonitor International, Inc., 224 S. Michigan Avenue, Suite 1500, Chicago, IL 60604, (312) 922-1115, Fax: (312) 922-1157, www.euromonitor.com; *International Marketing Data and Statistics 2008* and *The World Economic Factbook 2008.*

M.E. Sharpe, 80 Business Park Drive, Armonk, NY 10504, (800) 541-6563, Fax: (914) 273-2106, www.mesharpe.com; *The Illustrated Book of World Rankings.*

National Bureau of Statistics of China (NBS), No. 57, Yuetan Nanjie, Sanlihe, Xicheng District, Beijing 100826, China, www.stats.gov.cn/english; *China Statistical Yearbook 2007* and *Monthly Statistical Data.*

Palgrave Macmillan Ltd., Houndmills, Basingstoke, Hampshire, RG21 6XS, England, (Telephone in U.S. (888) 330-8477), (Fax in U.S. (800) 672-2054), www.palgrave.com; *The Statesman's Yearbook 2008.*

Taylor and Francis Group, An Informa Business, 2 Park Square, Milton Park, Abingdon, Oxford OX14 4RN, United Kingdom, (Dial from U.S. (212) 216-7800), (Fax from U.S. (212) 564-7854), www.tandf.co.uk; *The Europa World Year Book.*

United Nations Statistics Division, New York, NY 10017, (800) 253-9646, Fax: (212) 963-4116, http://unstats.un.org; *Asia-Pacific in Figures 2004; Demographic Yearbook;* and *Statistical Yearbook.*

The World Bank, 1818 H Street, NW, Washington, DC 20433, (202) 473-1000, Fax: (202) 477-6391, www.worldbank.org; *World Development Indicators (WDI) 2008.*

World Health Organization (WHO), Avenue Appia 20, 1211 Geneve 27, Switzerland, (Telephone in U.S. (212) 331-9081), www.who.int; *World Health Report 2006.*

CHINA - CLIMATE

International Institute for Environment and Development (IIED), 3 Endsleigh Street, London, England, WC1H 0DD, United Kingdom, www.iied.org; *Environment Urbanization.*

M.E. Sharpe, 80 Business Park Drive, Armonk, NY 10504, (800) 541-6563, Fax: (914) 273-2106, www.mesharpe.com; *The Illustrated Book of World Rankings.*

Palgrave Macmillan Ltd., Houndmills, Basingstoke, Hampshire, RG21 6XS, England, (Telephone in U.S. (888) 330-8477), (Fax in U.S. (800) 672-2054), www.palgrave.com; *The Statesman's Yearbook 2008.*

CHINA - CLOTHING EXPORTS AND IMPORTS

See CHINA - TEXTILE INDUSTRY

CHINA - COAL PRODUCTION

See CHINA - MINERAL INDUSTRIES

CHINA - COFFEE

See CHINA - CROPS

CHINA - COMMERCE

National Bureau of Statistics of China (NBS), No. 57, Yuetan Nanjie, Sanlihe, Xicheng District, Beijing 100826, China, www.stats.gov.cn/english; *National Accounts.*

Palgrave Macmillan Ltd., Houndmills, Basingstoke, Hampshire, RG21 6XS, England, (Telephone in U.S. (888) 330-8477), (Fax in U.S. (800) 672-2054), www.palgrave.com; *The Statesman's Yearbook 2008.*

CHINA - COMMODITY EXCHANGES

Academic International Press, PO Box 1111, Gulf Breeze, FL 32562-1111, Fax: (850) 934-0953, www.ai-press.com; *China Facts and Figures Annual.*

Commodity Research Bureau, 330 South Wells Street, Suite 612, Chicago, IL 60606-7110, (800) 621-5271, Fax: (312) 939-4135, www.crbtrader.com; *2006 CRB Commodity Yearbook and CD.*

International Monetary Fund (IMF), 700 Nineteenth Street, NW, Washington, DC 20431, (202) 623-7000, Fax: (202) 623-4661, www.imf.org; *IMF Primary Commodity Prices.*

Japan Center for Economic Research (JCER), Nikkei Kayabacho Building, Nihombashi Kayabacho, 2-6-1, Chuo-ku, Tokyo 103-0025, Japan, www.jcer.or.jp/eng; *China Research Report.*

National Bureau of Statistics of China (NBS), No. 57, Yuetan Nanjie, Sanlihe, Xicheng District, Beijing 100826, China, www.stats.gov.cn/english; *China Statistical Yearbook 2007* and *Monthly Statistical Data.*

United Nations Food and Agricultural Organization (FAO), Viale delle Terme di Caracalla, 00100 Rome, Italy, (Dial from U.S. (202) 653-2400), (Fax from U.S. (202) 653 5760), www.fao.org; *The State of Food and Agriculture (SOFA) 2006.*

CHINA - CONSTRUCTION INDUSTRY

Academic International Press, PO Box 1111, Gulf Breeze, FL 32562-1111, Fax: (850) 934-0953, www.ai-press.com; *China Facts and Figures Annual.*

Economist Intelligence Unit, 111 West 57th Street, New York, NY 10019, (212) 554-0600, Fax: (212) 586-1181, www.eiu.com; *Business China.*

Japan Center for Economic Research (JCER), Nikkei Kayabacho Building, Nihombashi Kayabacho, 2-6-1, Chuo-ku, Tokyo 103-0025, Japan, www.jcer.or.jp/eng; *China Research Report.*

M.E. Sharpe, 80 Business Park Drive, Armonk, NY 10504, (800) 541-6563, Fax: (914) 273-2106, www.mesharpe.com; *The Illustrated Book of World Rankings.*

National Bureau of Statistics of China (NBS), No. 57, Yuetan Nanjie, Sanlihe, Xicheng District, Beijing 100826, China, www.stats.gov.cn/english; *China Statistical Yearbook 2007.*

Palgrave Macmillan Ltd., Houndmills, Basingstoke, Hampshire, RG21 6XS, England, (Telephone in U.S. (888) 330-8477), (Fax in U.S. (800) 672-2054), www.palgrave.com; *The Statesman's Yearbook 2008.*

CHINA - CONSUMER GOODS

Economist Intelligence Unit, 111 West 57th Street, New York, NY 10019, (212) 554-0600, Fax: (212) 586-1181, www.eiu.com; *Business China.*

CHINA - CONSUMER PRICE INDEXES

Asian Development Bank (ADB), PO Box 789, 0980 Manila, Philippines, www.adb.org; *Key Indicators of Developing Asian and Pacific Countries 2006.*

National Bureau of Statistics of China (NBS), No. 57, Yuetan Nanjie, Sanlihe, Xicheng District, Beijing 100826, China, www.stats.gov.cn/english; *Price Indices.*

Taylor and Francis Group, An Informa Business, 2 Park Square, Milton Park, Abingdon, Oxford OX14 4RN, United Kingdom, (Dial from U.S. (212) 216-7800), (Fax from U.S. (212) 564-7854), www.tandf.co.uk; *The Europa World Year Book.*

CHINA - CONSUMPTION (ECONOMICS)

Economist Intelligence Unit, 111 West 57th Street, New York, NY 10019, (212) 554-0600, Fax: (212) 586-1181, www.eiu.com; *Business China.*

The World Bank, 1818 H Street, NW, Washington, DC 20433, (202) 473-1000, Fax: (202) 477-6391, www.worldbank.org; *World Development Report 2008.*

CHINA - COPPER INDUSTRY AND TRADE

See CHINA - MINERAL INDUSTRIES

CHINA - CORN INDUSTRY

See CHINA - CROPS

CHINA - COTTON

See CHINA - CROPS

CHINA - CRIME

Academic International Press, PO Box 1111, Gulf Breeze, FL 32562-1111, Fax: (850) 934-0953, www.ai-press.com; *China Facts and Figures Annual.*

International Criminal Police Organization (INTERPOL), General Secretariat, 200 quai Charles de Gaulle, 69006 Lyon, France, www.interpol.int; *International Crime Statistics.*

National Bureau of Statistics of China (NBS), No. 57, Yuetan Nanjie, Sanlihe, Xicheng District, Beijing 100826, China, www.stats.gov.cn/english; *China Statistical Yearbook 2007.*

U.S. Department of Justice (DOJ), Bureau of Justice Statistics, 810 Seventh Street, NW, Washington, DC 20531, (202) 307-0765, www.ojp.usdoj.gov/bjs/; *The World Factbook of Criminal Justice Systems.*

Yale University Press, PO Box 209040, New Haven, CT 06520-9040, (203) 432-0960, Fax: (203) 432-0948, http://yalepress.yale.edu/yupbooks; *Violence and Crime in Cross-National Perspective.*

CHINA - CROPS

Academic International Press, PO Box 1111, Gulf Breeze, FL 32562-1111, Fax: (850) 934-0953, www.ai-press.com; *China Facts and Figures Annual.*

Asian Development Bank (ADB), PO Box 789, 0980 Manila, Philippines, www.adb.org; *Key Indicators of Developing Asian and Pacific Countries 2006.*

Economist Intelligence Unit, 111 West 57th Street, New York, NY 10019, (212) 554-0600, Fax: (212) 586-1181, www.eiu.com; *Business China.*

Japan Center for Economic Research (JCER), Nikkei Kayabacho Building, Nihombashi Kayabacho, 2-6-1, Chuo-ku, Tokyo 103-0025, Japan, www.jcer.or.jp/eng; *China Research Report.*

M.E. Sharpe, 80 Business Park Drive, Armonk, NY 10504, (800) 541-6563, Fax: (914) 273-2106, www.mesharpe.com; *The Illustrated Book of World Rankings.*

National Bureau of Statistics of China (NBS), No. 57, Yuetan Nanjie, Sanlihe, Xicheng District, Beijing 100826, China, www.stats.gov.cn/english; *China Statistical Yearbook 2007* and *Monthly Statistical Data.*

Palgrave Macmillan Ltd., Houndmills, Basingstoke, Hampshire, RG21 6XS, England, (Telephone in U.S. (888) 330-8477), (Fax in U.S. (800) 672-2054), www.palgrave.com; *The Statesman's Yearbook 2008.*

Taylor and Francis Group, An Informa Business, 2 Park Square, Milton Park, Abingdon, Oxford OX14 4RN, United Kingdom, (Dial from U.S. (212) 216-7800), (Fax from U.S. (212) 564-7854), www.tandf.co.uk; *The Europa World Year Book.*

United Nations Conference on Trade and Development (UNCTAD), DC2-1120, United Nations, New York, NY 10017, (212) 963-0027, www.unctad.org; *UNCTAD Commodity Yearbook.*

United Nations Food and Agricultural Organization (FAO), Viale delle Terme di Caracalla, 00100 Rome, Italy, (Dial from U.S. (202) 653-2400), (Fax from

U.S. (202) 653 5760), www.fao.org; *The State of Food and Agriculture (SOFA) 2006.*

United Nations Statistics Division, New York, NY 10017, (800) 253-9646, Fax: (212) 963-4116, http://unstats.un.org; *Statistical Yearbook.*

CHINA - CUSTOMS ADMINISTRATION

Palgrave Macmillan Ltd., Houndmills, Basingstoke, Hampshire, RG21 6XS, England, (Telephone in U.S. (888) 330-8477), (Fax in U.S. (800) 672-2054), www.palgrave.com; *The Statesman's Yearbook 2008.*

CHINA - DAIRY PROCESSING

Academic International Press, PO Box 1111, Gulf Breeze, FL 32562-1111, Fax: (850) 934-0953, www.ai-press.com; *China Facts and Figures Annual.*

Economist Intelligence Unit, 111 West 57th Street, New York, NY 10019, (212) 554-0600, Fax: (212) 586-1181, www.eiu.com; *Business China.*

Japan Center for Economic Research (JCER), Nikkei Kayabacho Building, Nihombashi Kayabacho, 2-6-1, Chuo-ku, Tokyo 103-0025, Japan, www.jcer.or.jp/eng; *China Research Report.*

M.E. Sharpe, 80 Business Park Drive, Armonk, NY 10504, (800) 541-6563, Fax: (914) 273-2106, www.mesharpe.com; *The Illustrated Book of World Rankings.*

National Bureau of Statistics of China (NBS), No. 57, Yuetan Nanjie, Sanlihe, Xicheng District, Beijing 100826, China, www.stats.gov.cn/english; *China Statistical Yearbook 2007* and *Monthly Statistical Data.*

Palgrave Macmillan Ltd., Houndmills, Basingstoke, Hampshire, RG21 6XS, England, (Telephone in U.S. (888) 330-8477), (Fax in U.S. (800) 672-2054), www.palgrave.com; *The Statesman's Yearbook 2008.*

Taylor and Francis Group, An Informa Business, 2 Park Square, Milton Park, Abingdon, Oxford OX14 4RN, United Kingdom, (Dial from U.S. (212) 216-7800), (Fax from U.S. (212) 564-7854), www.tandf.co.uk; *The Europa World Year Book.*

United Nations Food and Agricultural Organization (FAO), Viale delle Terme di Caracalla, 00100 Rome, Italy, (Dial from U.S. (202) 653-2400), (Fax from U.S. (202) 653 5760), www.fao.org; *FAO Production Yearbook 2002* and *The State of Food and Agriculture (SOFA) 2006.*

United Nations Statistics Division, New York, NY 10017, (800) 253-9646, Fax: (212) 963-4116, http://unstats.un.org; *Statistical Yearbook.*

CHINA - DEATH RATES

See CHINA - MORTALITY

CHINA - DEBTS, EXTERNAL

Asian Development Bank (ADB), PO Box 789, 0980 Manila, Philippines, www.adb.org; *Key Indicators of Developing Asian and Pacific Countries 2006.*

National Bureau of Statistics of China (NBS), No. 57, Yuetan Nanjie, Sanlihe, Xicheng District, Beijing 100826, China, www.stats.gov.cn/english; *Government Finance* and *National Accounts.*

Palgrave Macmillan Ltd., Houndmills, Basingstoke, Hampshire, RG21 6XS, England, (Telephone in U.S. (888) 330-8477), (Fax in U.S. (800) 672-2054), www.palgrave.com; *The Statesman's Yearbook 2008.*

The World Bank, 1818 H Street, NW, Washington, DC 20433, (202) 473-1000, Fax: (202) 477-6391, www.worldbank.org; *Global Development Finance 2007; World Development Indicators (WDI) 2008;* and *World Development Report 2008.*

Worldinformation.com, 2 Market Street, Saffron Walden, Essex CB10 1HZ, United Kingdom, www.worldinformation.com; The World of Information (www.worldinformation.com).

CHINA - DEFENSE EXPENDITURES

See CHINA - ARMED FORCES

CHINA - DEMOGRAPHY

Economist Intelligence Unit, 111 West 57th Street, New York, NY 10019, (212) 554-0600, Fax: (212) 586-1181, www.eiu.com; *Business Asia.*

Euromonitor International, Inc., 224 S. Michigan Avenue, Suite 1500, Chicago, IL 60604, (312) 922-1115, Fax: (312) 922-1157, www.euromonitor.com; *International Marketing Data and Statistics 2008; The World Economic Factbook 2008;* and *World Marketing Data and Statistics.*

M.E. Sharpe, 80 Business Park Drive, Armonk, NY 10504, (800) 541-6563, Fax: (914) 273-2106, www.mesharpe.com; *The Illustrated Book of World Rankings.*

United Nations Statistics Division, New York, NY 10017, (800) 253-9646, Fax: (212) 963-4116, http://unstats.un.org; *Asia-Pacific in Figures 2004* and *Human Development Report 2006.*

CHINA - DIAMONDS

See CHINA - MINERAL INDUSTRIES

CHINA - DISPOSABLE INCOME

M.E. Sharpe, 80 Business Park Drive, Armonk, NY 10504, (800) 541-6563, Fax: (914) 273-2106, www.mesharpe.com; *The Illustrated Book of World Rankings.*

United Nations Statistics Division, New York, NY 10017, (800) 253-9646, Fax: (212) 963-4116, http://unstats.un.org; *National Accounts Statistics: Compendium of Income Distribution Statistics.*

CHINA - DIVORCE

Academic International Press, PO Box 1111, Gulf Breeze, FL 32562-1111, Fax: (850) 934-0953, www.ai-press.com; *China Facts and Figures Annual.*

M.E. Sharpe, 80 Business Park Drive, Armonk, NY 10504, (800) 541-6563, Fax: (914) 273-2106, www.mesharpe.com; *The Illustrated Book of World Rankings.*

National Bureau of Statistics of China (NBS), No. 57, Yuetan Nanjie, Sanlihe, Xicheng District, Beijing 100826, China, www.stats.gov.cn/english; *China Statistical Yearbook 2007.*

United Nations Statistics Division, New York, NY 10017, (800) 253-9646, Fax: (212) 963-4116, http://unstats.un.org; *Demographic Yearbook.*

CHINA - ECONOMIC ASSISTANCE

Academic International Press, PO Box 1111, Gulf Breeze, FL 32562-1111, Fax: (850) 934-0953, www.ai-press.com; *China Facts and Figures Annual.*

Asian Development Bank (ADB), PO Box 789, 0980 Manila, Philippines, www.adb.org; *Key Indicators of Developing Asian and Pacific Countries 2006.*

International Organization for Migration (IOM), 17, Route des Morillons, CH-1211 Geneva 19, Switzerland, www.iom.int; *Migration and Poverty Alleviation in China.*

Japan Center for Economic Research (JCER), Nikkei Kayabacho Building, Nihombashi Kayabacho, 2-6-1, Chuo-ku, Tokyo 103-0025, Japan, www.jcer.or.jp/eng; *China Research Report.*

National Bureau of Statistics of China (NBS), No. 57, Yuetan Nanjie, Sanlihe, Xicheng District, Beijing 100826, China, www.stats.gov.cn/english; *China Statistical Yearbook 2007.*

United Nations Statistics Division, New York, NY 10017, (800) 253-9646, Fax: (212) 963-4116, http://unstats.un.org; *Statistical Yearbook.*

CHINA - ECONOMIC CONDITIONS

Academic International Press, PO Box 1111, Gulf Breeze, FL 32562-1111, Fax: (850) 934-0953, www.ai-press.com; *China Facts and Figures Annual.*

Asian Development Bank (ADB), PO Box 789, 0980 Manila, Philippines, www.adb.org; *Key Indicators of Developing Asian and Pacific Countries 2006.*

Center for International Business Education Research (CIBER), Columbia Business School and School of International and Public Affairs, Uris Hall, Room 212, 3022 Broadway, New York, NY 10027-6902, Mr. Joshua Safier, (212) 854-4750, Fax: (212) 222-9821, www.columbia.edu/cu/ciber/; Datastream International.

Central Intelligence Agency, Office of Public Affairs, Washington, DC 20505, (703) 482-0623, Fax: (703) 482-1739, www.cia.gov; *The World Factbook.*

DSI Data Service Information, Xantener Strasse 51a, D-47495 Rheinberg, Germany, www.dsidata.com; *Campus Solution.*

Dun and Bradstreet (DB) Corporation, 103 JFK Parkway, Short Hills, NJ 07078, (973) 921-5500, www.dnb.com; *Country Report.*

Economist Intelligence Unit, 111 West 57th Street, New York, NY 10019, (212) 554-0600, Fax: (212) 586-1181, www.eiu.com; *Business China* and *China Country Report.*

Euromonitor International, Inc., 224 S. Michigan Avenue, Suite 1500, Chicago, IL 60604, (312) 922-1115, Fax: (312) 922-1157, www.euromonitor.com; *International Marketing Data and Statistics 2008; The World Economic Factbook 2008;* and *World Marketing Data and Statistics.*

Federal Statistical Office Germany, D-65180 Wiesbaden, Germany, www.destatis.de; *China 2004.*

International Monetary Fund (IMF), 700 Nineteenth Street, NW, Washington, DC 20431, (202) 623-7000, Fax: (202) 623-4661, www.imf.org; *World Economic Outlook Reports.*

Japan Center for Economic Research (JCER), Nikkei Kayabacho Building, Nihombashi Kayabacho, 2-6-1, Chuo-ku, Tokyo 103-0025, Japan, www.jcer.or.jp/eng; *Asia Research Report* and *China Research Report.*

M.E. Sharpe, 80 Business Park Drive, Armonk, NY 10504, (800) 541-6563, Fax: (914) 273-2106, www.mesharpe.com; *The Illustrated Book of World Rankings.*

National Bureau of Statistics of China (NBS), No. 57, Yuetan Nanjie, Sanlihe, Xicheng District, Beijing 100826, China, www.stats.gov.cn/english; *Banking and Insurance; China Statistical Yearbook 2007; Investment of Fixed Assets; Monthly Statistical Data;* and *Price Indices.*

Nomura Research Institute (NRI), 2 World Financial Center, Building B, 19th Fl., New York, NY 10281-1198, (212) 667-1670, www.nri.co.jp/english; *Asian Economic Outlook 2003-2004.*

Palgrave Macmillan Ltd., Houndmills, Basingstoke, Hampshire, RG21 6XS, England, (Telephone in U.S. (888) 330-8477), (Fax in U.S. (800) 672-2054), www.palgrave.com; *The Statesman's Yearbook 2008.*

Taylor and Francis Group, An Informa Business, 2 Park Square, Milton Park, Abingdon, Oxford OX14 4RN, United Kingdom, (Dial from U.S. (212) 216-7800), (Fax from U.S. (212) 564-7854), www.tandf.co.uk; *The Europa World Year Book.*

United Nations Statistics Division, New York, NY 10017, (800) 253-9646, Fax: (212) 963-4116, http://unstats.un.org; *World Statistics Pocketbook.*

The World Bank, 1818 H Street, NW, Washington, DC 20433, (202) 473-1000, Fax: (202) 477-6391, www.worldbank.org; *Global Economic Monitor (GEM); Global Economic Prospects 2008; The World Bank Atlas 2003-2004;* and *World Development Report 2008.*

CHINA - EDUCATION

Academic International Press, PO Box 1111, Gulf Breeze, FL 32562-1111, Fax: (850) 934-0953, www.ai-press.com; *China Facts and Figures Annual.*

Economist Intelligence Unit, 111 West 57th Street, New York, NY 10019, (212) 554-0600, Fax: (212) 586-1181, www.eiu.com; *Business Asia* and *Business China.*

Euromonitor International, Inc., 224 S. Michigan Avenue, Suite 1500, Chicago, IL 60604, (312) 922-

1115, Fax: (312) 922-1157, www.euromonitor.com; *International Marketing Data and Statistics 2008* and *World Marketing Data and Statistics.*

M.E. Sharpe, 80 Business Park Drive, Armonk, NY 10504, (800) 541-6563, Fax: (914) 273-2106, www.mesharpe.com; *The Illustrated Book of World Rankings.*

National Bureau of Statistics of China (NBS), No. 57, Yuetan Nanjie, Sanlihe, Xicheng District, Beijing 100826, China, www.stats.gov.cn/english; *China Statistical Yearbook 2007* and *Monthly Statistical Data.*

Palgrave Macmillan Ltd., Houndmills, Basingstoke, Hampshire, RG21 6XS, England, (Telephone in U.S. (888) 330-8477), (Fax in U.S. (800) 672-2054), www.palgrave.com; *The Statesman's Yearbook 2008.*

Taylor and Francis Group, An Informa Business, 2 Park Square, Milton Park, Abingdon, Oxford OX14 4RN, United Kingdom, (Dial from U.S. (212) 216-7800), (Fax from U.S. (212) 564-7854), www.tandf.co.uk; *The Europa World Year Book.*

UNESCO Institute for Statistics, C.P. 6128 Succursale Centre-Ville, Montreal, Quebec, H3C 3J7 Canada, (Dial from U.S. (514) 343-6880), (Fax from U.S. (514) 343 6882), www.uis.unesco.org; *Statistical Tables.*

United Nations Statistics Division, New York, NY 10017, (800) 253-9646, Fax: (212) 963-4116, http://unstats.un.org; *Asia-Pacific in Figures 2004; Human Development Report 2006;* and *Statistical Yearbook for Asia and the Pacific 2004.*

The World Bank, 1818 H Street, NW, Washington, DC 20433, (202) 473-1000, Fax: (202) 477-6391, www.worldbank.org; *World Development Indicators (WDI) 2008* and *World Development Report 2008.*

CHINA - EGGPLANT PRODUCTION

See CHINA - CROPS

CHINA - ELECTRICITY

Academic International Press, PO Box 1111, Gulf Breeze, FL 32562-1111, Fax: (850) 934-0953, www.ai-press.com; *China Facts and Figures Annual.*

Asian Development Bank (ADB), PO Box 789, 0980 Manila, Philippines, www.adb.org; *Key Indicators of Developing Asian and Pacific Countries 2006.*

M.E. Sharpe, 80 Business Park Drive, Armonk, NY 10504, (800) 541-6563, Fax: (914) 273-2106, www.mesharpe.com; *The Illustrated Book of World Rankings.*

National Bureau of Statistics of China (NBS), No. 57, Yuetan Nanjie, Sanlihe, Xicheng District, Beijing 100826, China, www.stats.gov.cn/english; *China Statistical Yearbook 2007.*

Organisation for Economic Cooperation and Development (OECD), 2 rue Andre Pascal, F-75775 Paris Cedex 16, France, (Telephone in U.S. (202) 785-6323), (Fax in U.S. (202) 785-0350), www.oecd.org; *World Energy Outlook 2007.*

Palgrave Macmillan Ltd., Houndmills, Basingstoke, Hampshire, RG21 6XS, England, (Telephone in U.S. (888) 330-8477), (Fax in U.S. (800) 672-2054), www.palgrave.com; *The Statesman's Yearbook 2008.*

Platts, 2 Penn Plaza, 25th Floor, New York, NY 10121-2298, (212) 904-3070, www.platts.com; *Asian Electricity Outlook 2006* and *Emissions Daily.*

U.S. Department of Energy (DOE), Energy Information Administration (EIA), 1000 Independence Avenue, SW, Washington, DC 20585, (202) 586-8800, www.eia.doe.gov; *International Energy Annual 2004* and *International Energy Outlook 2006.*

United Nations Statistics Division, New York, NY 10017, (800) 253-9646, Fax: (212) 963-4116, http://unstats.un.org; *Electric Power in Asia and the Pacific 2001 and 2002; Human Development Report 2006;* and *Statistical Yearbook.*

The World Bank, 1818 H Street, NW, Washington, DC 20433, (202) 473-1000, Fax: (202) 477-6391, www.worldbank.org; *World Development Indicators (WDI) 2008.*

CHINA - ELECTRONIC INDUSTRIES

Economist Intelligence Unit, 111 West 57th Street, New York, NY 10019, (212) 554-0600, Fax: (212) 586-1181, www.eiu.com; *Business China.*

CHINA - EMIGRATION AND IMMIGRATION

International Organization for Migration (IOM), 17, Route des Morillons, CH-1211 Geneva 19, Switzerland, www.iom.int; *Domestic Migrant Remittances in China: Distribution, Channels and Livelihoods* and *Migration and Poverty Alleviation in China.*

CHINA - EMPLOYMENT

Academic International Press, PO Box 1111, Gulf Breeze, FL 32562-1111, Fax: (850) 934-0953, www.ai-press.com; *China Facts and Figures Annual.*

Euromonitor International, Inc., 224 S. Michigan Avenue, Suite 1500, Chicago, IL 60604, (312) 922-1115, Fax: (312) 922-1157, www.euromonitor.com; *International Marketing Data and Statistics 2008.*

Japan Center for Economic Research (JCER), Nikkei Kayabacho Building, Nihombashi Kayabacho, 2-6-1, Chuo-ku, Tokyo 103-0025, Japan, www.jcer.or.jp/eng; *China Research Report.*

M.E. Sharpe, 80 Business Park Drive, Armonk, NY 10504, (800) 541-6563, Fax: (914) 273-2106, www.mesharpe.com; *The Illustrated Book of World Rankings.*

National Bureau of Statistics of China (NBS), No. 57, Yuetan Nanjie, Sanlihe, Xicheng District, Beijing 100826, China, www.stats.gov.cn/english; *China Statistical Yearbook 2007* and *Monthly Statistical Data.*

United Nations Statistics Division, New York, NY 10017, (800) 253-9646, Fax: (212) 963-4116, http://unstats.un.org; *Asia-Pacific in Figures 2004.*

The World Bank, 1818 H Street, NW, Washington, DC 20433, (202) 473-1000, Fax: (202) 477-6391, www.worldbank.org; *World Development Indicators (WDI) 2008.*

CHINA - ENERGY INDUSTRIES

Academic International Press, PO Box 1111, Gulf Breeze, FL 32562-1111, Fax: (850) 934-0953, www.ai-press.com; *China Facts and Figures Annual.*

Economist Intelligence Unit, 111 West 57th Street, New York, NY 10019, (212) 554-0600, Fax: (212) 586-1181, www.eiu.com; *Business China.*

Enerdata, 10 Rue Royale, 75008 Paris, France, www.enerdata.fr; *Global Energy Market Data.*

Japan Center for Economic Research (JCER), Nikkei Kayabacho Building, Nihombashi Kayabacho, 2-6-1, Chuo-ku, Tokyo 103-0025, Japan, www.jcer.or.jp/eng; *China Research Report.*

National Bureau of Statistics of China (NBS), No. 57, Yuetan Nanjie, Sanlihe, Xicheng District, Beijing 100826, China, www.stats.gov.cn/english; *China Statistical Yearbook 2007.*

Platts, 2 Penn Plaza, 25th Floor, New York, NY 10121-2298, (212) 904-3070, www.platts.com; *Asian Electricity Outlook 2006* and *Emissions Daily.*

United Nations Statistics Division, New York, NY 10017, (800) 253-9646, Fax: (212) 963-4116, http://unstats.un.org; *Electric Power in Asia and the Pacific 2001 and 2002.*

CHINA - ENVIRONMENTAL CONDITIONS

DSI Data Service Information, Xantener Strasse 51a, D-47495 Rheinberg, Germany, www.dsidata.com; *Campus Solution* and *DSI's Global Environmental Database.*

Economist Intelligence Unit, 111 West 57th Street, New York, NY 10019, (212) 554-0600, Fax: (212) 586-1181, www.eiu.com; *China Country Report.*

Federal Statistical Office Germany, D-65180 Wiesbaden, Germany, www.destatis.de; *China 2004.*

International Institute for Environment and Development (IIED), 3 Endsleigh Street, London, England, WC1H 0DD, United Kingdom, www.iied.org; *Environment Urbanization* and *Up in Smoke? Asia and the Pacific.*

Platts, 2 Penn Plaza, 25th Floor, New York, NY 10121-2298, (212) 904-3070, www.platts.com; *Emissions Daily.*

United Nations Statistics Division, New York, NY 10017, (800) 253-9646, Fax: (212) 963-4116, http://unstats.un.org; *World Statistics Pocketbook.*

CHINA - EXPORTS

Academic International Press, PO Box 1111, Gulf Breeze, FL 32562-1111, Fax: (850) 934-0953, www.ai-press.com; *China Facts and Figures Annual.*

Asian Development Bank (ADB), PO Box 789, 0980 Manila, Philippines, www.adb.org; *Key Indicators of Developing Asian and Pacific Countries 2006.*

Central Intelligence Agency, Office of Public Affairs, Washington, DC 20505, (703) 482-0623, Fax: (703) 482-1739, www.cia.gov; *The World Factbook.*

Economist Intelligence Unit, 111 West 57th Street, New York, NY 10019, (212) 554-0600, Fax: (212) 586-1181, www.eiu.com; *Business China* and *China Country Report.*

Euromonitor International, Inc., 224 S. Michigan Avenue, Suite 1500, Chicago, IL 60604, (312) 922-1115, Fax: (312) 922-1157, www.euromonitor.com; *International Marketing Data and Statistics 2008* and *The World Economic Factbook 2008.*

Federal Statistical Office Germany, D-65180 Wiesbaden, Germany, www.destatis.de; *China 2004.*

International Monetary Fund (IMF), 700 Nineteenth Street, NW, Washington, DC 20431, (202) 623-7000, Fax: (202) 623-4661, www.imf.org; *Direction of Trade Statistics Yearbook 2007* and *International Financial Statistics Yearbook 2007.*

Japan Center for Economic Research (JCER), Nikkei Kayabacho Building, Nihombashi Kayabacho, 2-6-1, Chuo-ku, Tokyo 103-0025, Japan, www.jcer.or.jp/eng; *China Research Report.*

National Bureau of Statistics of China (NBS), No. 57, Yuetan Nanjie, Sanlihe, Xicheng District, Beijing 100826, China, www.stats.gov.cn/english; *China Statistical Yearbook 2007; Monthly Statistical Data;* and *National Accounts.*

Palgrave Macmillan Ltd., Houndmills, Basingstoke, Hampshire, RG21 6XS, England, (Telephone in U.S. (888) 330-8477), (Fax in U.S. (800) 672-2054), www.palgrave.com; *The Statesman's Yearbook 2008.*

Taylor and Francis Group, An Informa Business, 2 Park Square, Milton Park, Abingdon, Oxford OX14 4RN, United Kingdom, (Dial from U.S. (212) 216-7800), (Fax from U.S. (212) 564-7854), www.tandf.co.uk; *The Europa World Year Book.*

United Nations Conference on Trade and Development (UNCTAD), DC2-1120, United Nations, New York, NY 10017, (212) 963-0027, www.unctad.org; *Handbook of Statistics 2005.*

United Nations Food and Agricultural Organization (FAO), Viale delle Terme di Caracalla, 00100 Rome, Italy, (Dial from U.S. (202) 653-2400), (Fax from U.S. (202) 653 5760), www.fao.org; *The State of Food and Agriculture (SOFA) 2006.*

The World Bank, 1818 H Street, NW, Washington, DC 20433, (202) 473-1000, Fax: (202) 477-6391, www.worldbank.org; *World Development Indicators (WDI) 2008* and *World Development Report 2008.*

Worldinformation.com, 2 Market Street, Saffron Walden, Essex CB10 1HZ, United Kingdom, www.worldinformation.com; The World of Information (www.worldinformation.com).

CHINA - FEMALE WORKING POPULATION

See CHINA - EMPLOYMENT

CHINA - FERTILITY, HUMAN

Central Intelligence Agency, Office of Public Affairs, Washington, DC 20505, (703) 482-0623, Fax: (703) 482-1739, www.cia.gov; *The World Factbook.*

M.E. Sharpe, 80 Business Park Drive, Armonk, NY 10504, (800) 541-6563, Fax: (914) 273-2106, www.mesharpe.com; *The Illustrated Book of World Rankings.*

United Nations Statistics Division, New York, NY 10017, (800) 253-9646, Fax: (212) 963-4116, http://unstats.un.org; *Human Development Report 2006.*

The World Bank, 1818 H Street, NW, Washington, DC 20433, (202) 473-1000, Fax: (202) 477-6391, www.worldbank.org; *The World Bank Atlas 2003-2004; World Development Indicators (WDI) 2008;* and *World Development Report 2008.*

CHINA - FERTILIZER INDUSTRY

Academic International Press, PO Box 1111, Gulf Breeze, FL 32562-1111, Fax: (850) 934-0953, www.ai-press.com; *China Facts and Figures Annual.*

Economist Intelligence Unit, 111 West 57th Street, New York, NY 10019, (212) 554-0600, Fax: (212) 586-1181, www.eiu.com; *Business China.*

Japan Center for Economic Research (JCER), Nikkei Kayabacho Building, Nihombashi Kayabacho, 2-6-1, Chuo-ku, Tokyo 103-0025, Japan, www.jcer.or.jp/eng; *China Research Report.*

National Bureau of Statistics of China (NBS), No. 57, Yuetan Nanjie, Sanlihe, Xicheng District, Beijing 100826, China, www.stats.gov.cn/english; *China Statistical Yearbook 2007* and *Monthly Statistical Data.*

United Nations Food and Agricultural Organization (FAO), Viale delle Terme di Caracalla, 00100 Rome, Italy, (Dial from U.S. (202) 653-2400), (Fax from U.S. (202) 653 5760), www.fao.org; *FAO Fertilizer Yearbook* and *The State of Food and Agriculture (SOFA) 2006.*

United Nations Statistics Division, New York, NY 10017, (800) 253-9646, Fax: (212) 963-4116, http://unstats.un.org; *Statistical Yearbook.*

CHINA - FETAL DEATH

Academic International Press, PO Box 1111, Gulf Breeze, FL 32562-1111, Fax: (850) 934-0953, www.ai-press.com; *China Facts and Figures Annual.*

Japan Center for Economic Research (JCER), Nikkei Kayabacho Building, Nihombashi Kayabacho, 2-6-1, Chuo-ku, Tokyo 103-0025, Japan, www.jcer.or.jp/eng; *China Research Report.*

National Bureau of Statistics of China (NBS), No. 57, Yuetan Nanjie, Sanlihe, Xicheng District, Beijing 100826, China, www.stats.gov.cn/english; *China Statistical Yearbook 2007.*

United Nations Statistics Division, New York, NY 10017, (800) 253-9646, Fax: (212) 963-4116, http://unstats.un.org; *Demographic Yearbook.*

CHINA - FINANCE

Academic International Press, PO Box 1111, Gulf Breeze, FL 32562-1111, Fax: (850) 934-0953, www.ai-press.com; *China Facts and Figures Annual.*

International Monetary Fund (IMF), 700 Nineteenth Street, NW, Washington, DC 20431, (202) 623-7000, Fax: (202) 623-4661, www.imf.org; *International Financial Statistics Yearbook 2007.*

Japan Center for Economic Research (JCER), Nikkei Kayabacho Building, Nihombashi Kayabacho, 2-6-1, Chuo-ku, Tokyo 103-0025, Japan, www.jcer.or.jp/eng; *China Research Report.*

National Bureau of Statistics of China (NBS), No. 57, Yuetan Nanjie, Sanlihe, Xicheng District, Beijing 100826, China, www.stats.gov.cn/english; *Banking and Insurance; China Statistical Yearbook 2007;* and *Investment of Fixed Assets.*

Taylor and Francis Group, An Informa Business, 2 Park Square, Milton Park, Abingdon, Oxford OX14 4RN, United Kingdom, (Dial from U.S. (212) 216-7800), (Fax from U.S. (212) 564-7854), www.tandf.co.uk; *The Europa World Year Book.*

United Nations Statistics Division, New York, NY 10017, (800) 253-9646, Fax: (212) 963-4116, http://unstats.un.org; *Asia-Pacific in Figures 2004* and *Statistical Yearbook for Asia and the Pacific 2004.*

CHINA - FINANCE, PUBLIC

Academic International Press, PO Box 1111, Gulf Breeze, FL 32562-1111, Fax: (850) 934-0953, www.ai-press.com; *China Facts and Figures Annual.*

Asian Development Bank (ADB), PO Box 789, 0980 Manila, Philippines, www.adb.org; *Key Indicators of Developing Asian and Pacific Countries 2006.*

Bernan Essential Government Publications, 4611-F Assembly Drive, Lanham MD, 20706-4391, (301) 459-2255, Fax: (800) 865-3450, www.bernan.com; *National Accounts Statistics.*

Economist Intelligence Unit, 111 West 57th Street, New York, NY 10019, (212) 554-0600, Fax: (212) 586-1181, www.eiu.com; *Business China* and *China Country Report.*

Federal Statistical Office Germany, D-65180 Wiesbaden, Germany, www.destatis.de; *China 2004.*

International Monetary Fund (IMF), 700 Nineteenth Street, NW, Washington, DC 20431, (202) 623-7000, Fax: (202) 623-4661, www.imf.org; *International Financial Statistics; International Financial Statistics Online Service;* and *International Financial Statistics Yearbook 2007.*

Japan Center for Economic Research (JCER), Nikkei Kayabacho Building, Nihombashi Kayabacho, 2-6-1, Chuo-ku, Tokyo 103-0025, Japan, www.jcer.or.jp/eng; *China Research Report.*

M.E. Sharpe, 80 Business Park Drive, Armonk, NY 10504, (800) 541-6563, Fax: (914) 273-2106, www.mesharpe.com; *The Illustrated Book of World Rankings.*

National Bureau of Statistics of China (NBS), No. 57, Yuetan Nanjie, Sanlihe, Xicheng District, Beijing 100826, China, www.stats.gov.cn/english; *China Statistical Yearbook 2007; Government Finance; Monthly Statistical Data;* and *National Accounts.*

Palgrave Macmillan Ltd., Houndmills, Basingstoke, Hampshire, RG21 6XS, England, (Telephone in U.S. (888) 330-8477), (Fax in U.S. (800) 672-2054), www.palgrave.com; *The Statesman's Yearbook 2008.*

Taylor and Francis Group, An Informa Business, 2 Park Square, Milton Park, Abingdon, Oxford OX14 4RN, United Kingdom, (Dial from U.S. (212) 216-7800), (Fax from U.S. (212) 564-7854), www.tandf.co.uk; *The Europa World Year Book.*

United Nations Statistics Division, New York, NY 10017, (800) 253-9646, Fax: (212) 963-4116, http://unstats.un.org; *Statistical Yearbook for Asia and the Pacific 2004.*

CHINA - FISHERIES

Academic International Press, PO Box 1111, Gulf Breeze, FL 32562-1111, Fax: (850) 934-0953, www.ai-press.com; *China Facts and Figures Annual.*

Economist Intelligence Unit, 111 West 57th Street, New York, NY 10019, (212) 554-0600, Fax: (212) 586-1181, www.eiu.com; *Business China.*

Japan Center for Economic Research (JCER), Nikkei Kayabacho Building, Nihombashi Kayabacho, 2-6-1, Chuo-ku, Tokyo 103-0025, Japan, www.jcer.or.jp/eng; *China Research Report.*

M.E. Sharpe, 80 Business Park Drive, Armonk, NY 10504, (800) 541-6563, Fax: (914) 273-2106, www.mesharpe.com; *The Illustrated Book of World Rankings.*

National Bureau of Statistics of China (NBS), No. 57, Yuetan Nanjie, Sanlihe, Xicheng District, Beijing 100826, China, www.stats.gov.cn/english; *China Statistical Yearbook 2007* and *Monthly Statistical Data.*

Palgrave Macmillan Ltd., Houndmills, Basingstoke, Hampshire, RG21 6XS, England, (Telephone in U.S. (888) 330-8477), (Fax in U.S. (800) 672-2054), www.palgrave.com; *The Statesman's Yearbook 2008.*

Taylor and Francis Group, An Informa Business, 2 Park Square, Milton Park, Abingdon, Oxford OX14 4RN, United Kingdom, (Dial from U.S. (212) 216-7800), (Fax from U.S. (212) 564-7854), www.tandf.co.uk; *The Europa World Year Book.*

United Nations Conference on Trade and Development (UNCTAD), DC2-1120, United Nations, New York, NY 10017, (212) 963-0027, www.unctad.org; *UNCTAD Commodity Yearbook.*

United Nations Food and Agricultural Organization (FAO), Viale delle Terme di Caracalla, 00100 Rome, Italy, (Dial from U.S. (202) 653-2400), (Fax from U.S. (202) 653 5760), www.fao.org; *FAO Yearbook of Fishery Statistics;* Fishery Databases; FISHSTAT Database. Subjects covered include: Aquaculture production, capture production, fishery commodities; and *The State of Food and Agriculture (SOFA) 2006.*

United Nations Statistics Division, New York, NY 10017, (800) 253-9646, Fax: (212) 963-4116, http://unstats.un.org; *Statistical Yearbook.*

CHINA - FOOD

Academic International Press, PO Box 1111, Gulf Breeze, FL 32562-1111, Fax: (850) 934-0953, www.ai-press.com; *China Facts and Figures Annual.*

Euromonitor International, Inc., 224 S. Michigan Avenue, Suite 1500, Chicago, IL 60604, (312) 922-1115, Fax: (312) 922-1157, www.euromonitor.com; *Retail Trade International 2007.*

Japan Center for Economic Research (JCER), Nikkei Kayabacho Building, Nihombashi Kayabacho, 2-6-1, Chuo-ku, Tokyo 103-0025, Japan, www.jcer.or.jp/eng; *China Research Report.*

National Bureau of Statistics of China (NBS), No. 57, Yuetan Nanjie, Sanlihe, Xicheng District, Beijing 100826, China, www.stats.gov.cn/english; *China Statistical Yearbook 2007* and *Monthly Statistical Data.*

United Nations Conference on Trade and Development (UNCTAD), DC2-1120, United Nations, New York, NY 10017, (212) 963-0027, www.unctad.org; *UNCTAD Commodity Yearbook.*

United Nations Food and Agricultural Organization (FAO), Viale delle Terme di Caracalla, 00100 Rome, Italy, (Dial from U.S. (202) 653-2400), (Fax from U.S. (202) 653 5760), www.fao.org; *FAO Production Yearbook 2002* and *The State of Food and Agriculture (SOFA) 2006.*

United Nations Statistics Division, New York, NY 10017, (800) 253-9646, Fax: (212) 963-4116, http://unstats.un.org; *Human Development Report 2006* and *Statistical Yearbook for Asia and the Pacific 2004.*

CHINA - FOREIGN EXCHANGE RATES

Academic International Press, PO Box 1111, Gulf Breeze, FL 32562-1111, Fax: (850) 934-0953, www.ai-press.com; *China Facts and Figures Annual.*

Asian Development Bank (ADB), PO Box 789, 0980 Manila, Philippines, www.adb.org; *Key Indicators of Developing Asian and Pacific Countries 2006.*

Central Intelligence Agency, Office of Public Affairs, Washington, DC 20505, (703) 482-0623, Fax: (703) 482-1739, www.cia.gov; *The World Factbook.*

Economist Intelligence Unit, 111 West 57th Street, New York, NY 10019, (212) 554-0600, Fax: (212) 586-1181, www.eiu.com; *Business Asia.*

Euromonitor International, Inc., 224 S. Michigan Avenue, Suite 1500, Chicago, IL 60604, (312) 922-1115, Fax: (312) 922-1157, www.euromonitor.com; *International Marketing Data and Statistics 2008* and *The World Economic Factbook 2008.*

International Monetary Fund (IMF), 700 Nineteenth Street, NW, Washington, DC 20431, (202) 623-7000, Fax: (202) 623-4661, www.imf.org; *International Financial Statistics Yearbook 2007.*

Japan Center for Economic Research (JCER), Nikkei Kayabacho Building, Nihombashi Kayabacho, 2-6-1, Chuo-ku, Tokyo 103-0025, Japan, www.jcer.or.jp/eng; *China Research Report.*

National Bureau of Statistics of China (NBS), No. 57, Yuetan Nanjie, Sanlihe, Xicheng District, Beijing 100826, China, www.stats.gov.cn/english; *China Statistical Yearbook 2007* and *Monthly Statistical Data.*

Taylor and Francis Group, An Informa Business, 2 Park Square, Milton Park, Abingdon, Oxford OX14 4RN, United Kingdom, (Dial from U.S. (212) 216-7800), (Fax from U.S. (212) 564-7854), www.tandf.co.uk; *The Europa World Year Book.*

United Nations Statistics Division, New York, NY 10017, (800) 253-9646, Fax: (212) 963-4116, http://unstats.un.org; *Statistical Yearbook* and *World Statistics Pocketbook.*

Worldinformation.com, 2 Market Street, Saffron Walden, Essex CB10 1HZ, United Kingdom, www.worldinformation.com; The World of Information (www.worldinformation.com).

CHINA - FORESTS AND FORESTRY

Academic International Press, PO Box 1111, Gulf Breeze, FL 32562-1111, Fax: (850) 934-0953, www.ai-press.com; *China Facts and Figures Annual.*

American Forest Paper Association (AFPA), 1111 Nineteenth Street, NW, Suite 800, Washington, DC 20036, (800) 878-8878, www.afandpa.org; *2007 Annual Statistics of Paper, Paperboard, and Wood Pulp.*

Economist Intelligence Unit, 111 West 57th Street, New York, NY 10019, (212) 554-0600, Fax: (212) 586-1181, www.eiu.com; *Business China.*

Japan Center for Economic Research (JCER), Nikkei Kayabacho Building, Nihombashi Kayabacho, 2-6-1, Chuo-ku, Tokyo 103-0025, Japan, www.jcer.or.jp/eng; *China Research Report.*

M.E. Sharpe, 80 Business Park Drive, Armonk, NY 10504, (800) 541-6563, Fax: (914) 273-2106, www.mesharpe.com; *The Illustrated Book of World Rankings.*

National Bureau of Statistics of China (NBS), No. 57, Yuetan Nanjie, Sanlihe, Xicheng District, Beijing 100826, China, www.stats.gov.cn/english; *China Statistical Yearbook 2007* and *Monthly Statistical Data.*

Palgrave Macmillan Ltd., Houndmills, Basingstoke, Hampshire, RG21 6XS, England, (Telephone in U.S. (888) 330-8477), (Fax in U.S. (800) 672-2054), www.palgrave.com; *The Statesman's Yearbook 2008.*

Taylor and Francis Group, An Informa Business, 2 Park Square, Milton Park, Abingdon, Oxford OX14 4RN, United Kingdom, (Dial from U.S. (212) 216-7800), (Fax from U.S. (212) 564-7854), www.tandf.co.uk; *The Europa World Year Book.*

UNESCO Institute for Statistics, C.P. 6128 Succursale Centre-Ville, Montreal, Quebec, H3C 3J7 Canada, (Dial from U.S. (514) 343-6880), (Fax from U.S. (514) 343 6882), www.uis.unesco.org; *Statistical Tables.*

United Nations Conference on Trade and Development (UNCTAD), DC2-1120, United Nations, New York, NY 10017, (212) 963-0027, www.unctad.org; *UNCTAD Commodity Yearbook.*

United Nations Food and Agricultural Organization (FAO), Viale delle Terme di Caracalla, 00100 Rome, Italy, (Dial from U.S. (202) 653-2400), (Fax from U.S. (202) 653 5760), www.fao.org; *FAO Yearbook of Forest Products* and *The State of Food and Agriculture (SOFA) 2006.*

The World Bank, 1818 H Street, NW, Washington, DC 20433, (202) 473-1000, Fax: (202) 477-6391, www.worldbank.org; *World Development Report 2008.*

CHINA - FRUIT PRODUCTION

See CHINA - CROPS

CHINA - GAS PRODUCTION

See CHINA - MINERAL INDUSTRIES

CHINA - GEOGRAPHIC INFORMATION SYSTEMS

M.E. Sharpe, 80 Business Park Drive, Armonk, NY 10504, (800) 541-6563, Fax: (914) 273-2106, www.mesharpe.com; *The Illustrated Book of World Rankings.*

CHINA - GOLD INDUSTRY

Academic International Press, PO Box 1111, Gulf Breeze, FL 32562-1111, Fax: (850) 934-0953, www.ai-press.com; *China Facts and Figures Annual.*

International Monetary Fund (IMF), 700 Nineteenth Street, NW, Washington, DC 20431, (202) 623-7000, Fax: (202) 623-4661, www.imf.org; *International Financial Statistics Yearbook 2007.*

Japan Center for Economic Research (JCER), Nikkei Kayabacho Building, Nihombashi Kayabacho, 2-6-1, Chuo-ku, Tokyo 103-0025, Japan, www.jcer.or.jp/eng; *China Research Report.*

National Bureau of Statistics of China (NBS), No. 57, Yuetan Nanjie, Sanlihe, Xicheng District, Beijing 100826, China, www.stats.gov.cn/english; *China Statistical Yearbook 2007.*

The World Bank, 1818 H Street, NW, Washington, DC 20433, (202) 473-1000, Fax: (202) 477-6391, www.worldbank.org; *World Development Indicators (WDI) 2008.*

CHINA - GOLD PRODUCTION

See CHINA - MINERAL INDUSTRIES

CHINA - GREEN PEPPER AND CHILIE PRODUCTION

See CHINA - CROPS

CHINA - GROSS DOMESTIC PRODUCT

Asian Development Bank (ADB), PO Box 789, 0980 Manila, Philippines, www.adb.org; *Key Indicators of Developing Asian and Pacific Countries 2006.*

Economist Intelligence Unit, 111 West 57th Street, New York, NY 10019, (212) 554-0600, Fax: (212) 586-1181, www.eiu.com; *Business Asia; Business China;* and *China Country Report.*

Euromonitor International, Inc., 224 S. Michigan Avenue, Suite 1500, Chicago, IL 60604, (312) 922-1115, Fax: (312) 922-1157, www.euromonitor.com; *International Marketing Data and Statistics 2008* and *The World Economic Factbook 2008.*

Federal Statistical Office Germany, D-65180 Wiesbaden, Germany, www.destatis.de; *China 2004.*

M.E. Sharpe, 80 Business Park Drive, Armonk, NY 10504, (800) 541-6563, Fax: (914) 273-2106, www.mesharpe.com; *The Illustrated Book of World Rankings.*

National Bureau of Statistics of China (NBS), No. 57, Yuetan Nanjie, Sanlihe, Xicheng District, Beijing 100826, China, www.stats.gov.cn/english; *National Accounts.*

United Nations Statistics Division, New York, NY 10017, (800) 253-9646, Fax: (212) 963-4116, http://unstats.un.org; *Human Development Report 2006* and *National Accounts Statistics: Compendium of Income Distribution Statistics.*

The World Bank, 1818 H Street, NW, Washington, DC 20433, (202) 473-1000, Fax: (202) 477-6391, www.worldbank.org; *World Development Indicators (WDI) 2008* and *World Development Report 2008.*

CHINA - GROSS NATIONAL PRODUCT

Academic International Press, PO Box 1111, Gulf Breeze, FL 32562-1111, Fax: (850) 934-0953, www.ai-press.com; *China Facts and Figures Annual.*

Asian Development Bank (ADB), PO Box 789, 0980 Manila, Philippines, www.adb.org; *Key Indicators of Developing Asian and Pacific Countries 2006.*

Economist Intelligence Unit, 111 West 57th Street, New York, NY 10019, (212) 554-0600, Fax: (212) 586-1181, www.eiu.com; *Business China.*

Euromonitor International, Inc., 224 S. Michigan Avenue, Suite 1500, Chicago, IL 60604, (312) 922-1115, Fax: (312) 922-1157, www.euromonitor.com; *International Marketing Data and Statistics 2008.*

Japan Center for Economic Research (JCER), Nikkei Kayabacho Building, Nihombashi Kayabacho, 2-6-1, Chuo-ku, Tokyo 103-0025, Japan, www.jcer.or.jp/eng; *China Research Report.*

M.E. Sharpe, 80 Business Park Drive, Armonk, NY 10504, (800) 541-6563, Fax: (914) 273-2106, www.mesharpe.com; *The Illustrated Book of World Rankings.*

National Bureau of Statistics of China (NBS), No. 57, Yuetan Nanjie, Sanlihe, Xicheng District, Beijing 100826, China, www.stats.gov.cn/english; *China Statistical Yearbook 2007* and *National Accounts.*

Palgrave Macmillan Ltd., Houndmills, Basingstoke, Hampshire, RG21 6XS, England, (Telephone in U.S. (888) 330-8477), (Fax in U.S. (800) 672-2054), www.palgrave.com; *The Statesman's Yearbook 2008.*

U.S. Department of State (DOS), 2201 C Street NW, Washington, DC 20520, (202) 647-4000, www.state.gov; *World Military Expenditures and Arms Transfers (WMEAT).*

The World Bank, 1818 H Street, NW, Washington, DC 20433, (202) 473-1000, Fax: (202) 477-6391, www.worldbank.org; *The World Bank Atlas 2003-2004; World Development Indicators (WDI) 2008;* and *World Development Report 2008.*

Worldinformation.com, 2 Market Street, Saffron Walden, Essex CB10 1HZ, United Kingdom, www.worldinformation.com; The World of Information (www.worldinformation.com).

CHINA - HEMP FIBRE PRODUCTION

See CHINA - TEXTILE INDUSTRY

CHINA - HIDES AND SKINS INDUSTRY

Academic International Press, PO Box 1111, Gulf Breeze, FL 32562-1111, Fax: (850) 934-0953, www.ai-press.com; *China Facts and Figures Annual.*

Japan Center for Economic Research (JCER), Nikkei Kayabacho Building, Nihombashi Kayabacho, 2-6-1, Chuo-ku, Tokyo 103-0025, Japan, www.jcer.or.jp/eng; *China Research Report.*

National Bureau of Statistics of China (NBS), No. 57, Yuetan Nanjie, Sanlihe, Xicheng District, Beijing 100826, China, www.stats.gov.cn/english; *China Statistical Yearbook 2007* and *Monthly Statistical Data.*

United Nations Food and Agricultural Organization (FAO), Viale delle Terme di Caracalla, 00100 Rome, Italy, (Dial from U.S. (202) 653-2400), (Fax from U.S. (202) 653 5760), www.fao.org; *FAO Production Yearbook 2002.*

CHINA - HONEY TRADE

Academic International Press, PO Box 1111, Gulf Breeze, FL 32562-1111, Fax: (850) 934-0953, www.ai-press.com; *China Facts and Figures Annual.*

Japan Center for Economic Research (JCER), Nikkei Kayabacho Building, Nihombashi Kayabacho, 2-6-1, Chuo-ku, Tokyo 103-0025, Japan, www.jcer.or.jp/eng; *China Research Report.*

National Bureau of Statistics of China (NBS), No. 57, Yuetan Nanjie, Sanlihe, Xicheng District, Beijing 100826, China, www.stats.gov.cn/english; *China Statistical Yearbook 2007* and *Monthly Statistical Data.*

CHINA - HOUSING

Academic International Press, PO Box 1111, Gulf Breeze, FL 32562-1111, Fax: (850) 934-0953, www.ai-press.com; *China Facts and Figures Annual.*

Economist Intelligence Unit, 111 West 57th Street, New York, NY 10019, (212) 554-0600, Fax: (212) 586-1181, www.eiu.com; *Business China.*

Euromonitor International, Inc., 224 S. Michigan Avenue, Suite 1500, Chicago, IL 60604, (312) 922-1115, Fax: (312) 922-1157, www.euromonitor.com; *World Marketing Data and Statistics.*

Japan Center for Economic Research (JCER), Nikkei Kayabacho Building, Nihombashi Kayabacho, 2-6-1, Chuo-ku, Tokyo 103-0025, Japan, www.jcer.or.jp/eng; *China Research Report.*

M.E. Sharpe, 80 Business Park Drive, Armonk, NY 10504, (800) 541-6563, Fax: (914) 273-2106, www.mesharpe.com; *The Illustrated Book of World Rankings.*

National Bureau of Statistics of China (NBS), No. 57, Yuetan Nanjie, Sanlihe, Xicheng District, Beijing 100826, China, www.stats.gov.cn/english; *China Statistical Yearbook 2007* and *Monthly Statistical Data.*

CHINA - ILLITERATE PERSONS

Economist Intelligence Unit, 111 West 57th Street, New York, NY 10019, (212) 554-0600, Fax: (212) 586-1181, www.eiu.com; *Business China.*

Euromonitor International, Inc., 224 S. Michigan Avenue, Suite 1500, Chicago, IL 60604, (312) 922-1115, Fax: (312) 922-1157, www.euromonitor.com; *The World Economic Factbook 2008.*

Palgrave Macmillan Ltd., Houndmills, Basingstoke, Hampshire, RG21 6XS, England, (Telephone in U.S. (888) 330-8477), (Fax in U.S. (800) 672-2054), www.palgrave.com; *The Statesman's Yearbook 2008.*

United Nations Statistics Division, New York, NY 10017, (800) 253-9646, Fax: (212) 963-4116, http://unstats.un.org; *Asia-Pacific in Figures 2004* and *Human Development Report 2006.*

CHINA - IMPORTS

Academic International Press, PO Box 1111, Gulf Breeze, FL 32562-1111, Fax: (850) 934-0953, www.ai-press.com; *China Facts and Figures Annual.*

Asian Development Bank (ADB), PO Box 789, 0980 Manila, Philippines, www.adb.org; *Key Indicators of Developing Asian and Pacific Countries 2006.*

Central Intelligence Agency, Office of Public Affairs, Washington, DC 20505, (703) 482-0623, Fax: (703) 482-1739, www.cia.gov; *The World Factbook.*

Economist Intelligence Unit, 111 West 57th Street, New York, NY 10019, (212) 554-0600, Fax: (212) 586-1181, www.eiu.com; *Business China* and *China Country Report.*

Euromonitor International, Inc., 224 S. Michigan Avenue, Suite 1500, Chicago, IL 60604, (312) 922-1115, Fax: (312) 922-1157, www.euromonitor.com; *International Marketing Data and Statistics 2008; The World Economic Factbook 2008;* and *World Marketing Data and Statistics.*

Federal Statistical Office Germany, D-65180 Wiesbaden, Germany, www.destatis.de; *China 2004.*

International Monetary Fund (IMF), 700 Nineteenth Street, NW, Washington, DC 20431, (202) 623-7000, Fax: (202) 623-4661, www.imf.org; *Direction of Trade Statistics Yearbook 2007* and *International Financial Statistics Yearbook 2007.*

Japan Center for Economic Research (JCER), Nikkei Kayabacho Building, Nihombashi Kayabacho, 2-6-1, Chuo-ku, Tokyo 103-0025, Japan, www.jcer.or.jp/eng; *China Research Report.*

National Bureau of Statistics of China (NBS), No. 57, Yuetan Nanjie, Sanlihe, Xicheng District, Beijing 100826, China, www.stats.gov.cn/english; *China Statistical Yearbook 2007; Monthly Statistical Data;* and *National Accounts.*

Palgrave Macmillan Ltd., Houndmills, Basingstoke, Hampshire, RG21 6XS, England, (Telephone in U.S. (888) 330-8477), (Fax in U.S. (800) 672-2054), www.palgrave.com; *The Statesman's Yearbook 2008.*

Taylor and Francis Group, An Informa Business, 2 Park Square, Milton Park, Abingdon, Oxford OX14 4RN, United Kingdom, (Dial from U.S. (212) 216-7800), (Fax from U.S. (212) 564-7854), www.tandf.co.uk; *The Europa World Year Book.*

United Nations Food and Agricultural Organization (FAO), Viale delle Terme di Caracalla, 00100 Rome, Italy, (Dial from U.S. (202) 653-2400), (Fax from U.S. (202) 653 5760), www.fao.org; *The State of Food and Agriculture (SOFA) 2006.*

The World Bank, 1818 H Street, NW, Washington, DC 20433, (202) 473-1000, Fax: (202) 477-6391, www.worldbank.org; *World Development Indicators (WDI) 2008* and *World Development Report 2008.*

Worldinformation.com, 2 Market Street, Saffron Walden, Essex CB10 1HZ, United Kingdom, www.worldinformation.com; The World of Information (www.worldinformation.com).

CHINA - INDUSTRIAL METALS PRODUCTION

See CHINA - MINERAL INDUSTRIES

CHINA - INDUSTRIAL PRODUCTIVITY

Academic International Press, PO Box 1111, Gulf Breeze, FL 32562-1111, Fax: (850) 934-0953, www.ai-press.com; *China Facts and Figures Annual.*

Euromonitor International, Inc., 224 S. Michigan Avenue, Suite 1500, Chicago, IL 60604, (312) 922-1115, Fax: (312) 922-1157, www.euromonitor.com; *International Marketing Data and Statistics 2008.*

Japan Center for Economic Research (JCER), Nikkei Kayabacho Building, Nihombashi Kayabacho, 2-6-1, Chuo-ku, Tokyo 103-0025, Japan, www.jcer.or.jp/eng; *China Research Report.*

M.E. Sharpe, 80 Business Park Drive, Armonk, NY 10504, (800) 541-6563, Fax: (914) 273-2106, www.mesharpe.com; *The Illustrated Book of World Rankings.*

National Bureau of Statistics of China (NBS), No. 57, Yuetan Nanjie, Sanlihe, Xicheng District, Beijing 100826, China, www.stats.gov.cn/english; *China Statistical Yearbook 2007* and *Monthly Statistical Data.*

CHINA - INDUSTRIAL PROPERTY

World Intellectual Property Organization (WIPO), PO Box 18, CH-1211 Geneva 20, Switzerland, www.wipo.int; *Industrial Property Statistics* and *Industrial Property Statistics Online Directory.*

CHINA - INDUSTRIES

Academic International Press, PO Box 1111, Gulf Breeze, FL 32562-1111, Fax: (850) 934-0953, www.ai-press.com; *China Facts and Figures Annual.*

Central Intelligence Agency, Office of Public Affairs, Washington, DC 20505, (703) 482-0623, Fax: (703) 482-1739, www.cia.gov; *The World Factbook.*

Economist Intelligence Unit, 111 West 57th Street, New York, NY 10019, (212) 554-0600, Fax: (212) 586-1181, www.eiu.com; *Business China* and *China Country Report.*

Euromonitor International, Inc., 224 S. Michigan Avenue, Suite 1500, Chicago, IL 60604, (312) 922-1115, Fax: (312) 922-1157, www.euromonitor.com; *The World Economic Factbook 2008* and *World Marketing Data and Statistics.*

Japan Center for Economic Research (JCER), Nikkei Kayabacho Building, Nihombashi Kayabacho, 2-6-1, Chuo-ku, Tokyo 103-0025, Japan, www.jcer.or.jp/eng; *China Research Report.*

M.E. Sharpe, 80 Business Park Drive, Armonk, NY 10504, (800) 541-6563, Fax: (914) 273-2106, www.mesharpe.com; *The Illustrated Book of World Rankings.*

National Bureau of Statistics of China (NBS), No. 57, Yuetan Nanjie, Sanlihe, Xicheng District, Beijing 100826, China, www.stats.gov.cn/english; *China Statistical Yearbook 2007.*

Palgrave Macmillan Ltd., Houndmills, Basingstoke, Hampshire, RG21 6XS, England, (Telephone in U.S. (888) 330-8477), (Fax in U.S. (800) 672-2054), www.palgrave.com; *The Statesman's Yearbook 2008.*

Taylor and Francis Group, An Informa Business, 2 Park Square, Milton Park, Abingdon, Oxford OX14 4RN, United Kingdom, (Dial from U.S. (212) 216-7800), (Fax from U.S. (212) 564-7854), www.tandf.co.uk; *The Europa World Year Book.*

United Nations Industrial Development Organization (UNIDO), 1 United Nations Plaza, New York, NY 10017, (212) 963 6890, Fax: (212) 963-7904, http://unido.org; Industrial Statistics Database 2008 (INDSTAT) and *The International Yearbook of Industrial Statistics 2008.*

United Nations Statistics Division, New York, NY 10017, (800) 253-9646, Fax: (212) 963-4116, http://unstats.un.org; *Asia-Pacific in Figures 2004* and *Statistical Yearbook for Asia and the Pacific 2004.*

The World Bank, 1818 H Street, NW, Washington, DC 20433, (202) 473-1000, Fax: (202) 477-6391, www.worldbank.org; *World Development Indicators (WDI) 2008.*

World Intellectual Property Organization (WIPO), PO Box 18, CH-1211 Geneva 20, Switzerland, www.wipo.int; *Industrial Property Statistics* and *Industrial Property Statistics Online Directory.*

CHINA - INFANT AND MATERNAL MORTALITY

See CHINA - MORTALITY

CHINA - INTERNATIONAL FINANCE

Asian Development Bank (ADB), PO Box 789, 0980 Manila, Philippines, www.adb.org; *Key Indicators of Developing Asian and Pacific Countries 2006.*

CHINA - INTERNATIONAL LIQUIDITY

International Monetary Fund (IMF), 700 Nineteenth Street, NW, Washington, DC 20431, (202) 623-7000, Fax: (202) 623-4661, www.imf.org; *International Financial Statistics Yearbook 2007.*

CHINA - INTERNATIONAL STATISTICS

Asian Development Bank (ADB), PO Box 789, 0980 Manila, Philippines, www.adb.org; *Key Indicators of Developing Asian and Pacific Countries 2006.*

CHINA - INTERNATIONAL TRADE

Academic International Press, PO Box 1111, Gulf Breeze, FL 32562-1111, Fax: (850) 934-0953, www.ai-press.com; *China Facts and Figures Annual.*

Asian Development Bank (ADB), PO Box 789, 0980 Manila, Philippines, www.adb.org; *Key Indicators of Developing Asian and Pacific Countries 2006.*

Economist Intelligence Unit, 111 West 57th Street, New York, NY 10019, (212) 554-0600, Fax: (212) 586-1181, www.eiu.com; *Business Asia; Business China;* and *China Country Report.*

Euromonitor International, Inc., 224 S. Michigan Avenue, Suite 1500, Chicago, IL 60604, (312) 922-1115, Fax: (312) 922-1157, www.euromonitor.com; *International Marketing Data and Statistics 2008; The World Economic Factbook 2008;* and *World Marketing Data and Statistics.*

Federal Statistical Office Germany, D-65180 Wiesbaden, Germany, www.destatis.de; *China 2004.*

Japan Center for Economic Research (JCER), Nikkei Kayabacho Building, Nihombashi Kayabacho, 2-6-1, Chuo-ku, Tokyo 103-0025, Japan, www.jcer.or.jp/eng; *China Research Report.*

M.E. Sharpe, 80 Business Park Drive, Armonk, NY 10504, (800) 541-6563, Fax: (914) 273-2106, www.mesharpe.com; *The Illustrated Book of World Rankings.*

National Bureau of Statistics of China (NBS), No. 57, Yuetan Nanjie, Sanlihe, Xicheng District, Beijing 100826, China, www.stats.gov.cn/english; *China Statistical Yearbook 2007; Monthly Statistical Data;* and *National Accounts.*

Organisation for Economic Cooperation and Development (OECD), 2 rue Andre Pascal, F-75775 Paris Cedex 16, France, (Telephone in U.S. (202) 785-6323), (Fax in U.S. (202) 785-0350), www.oecd.org; *International Trade by Commodity Statistics (ITCS).*

Palgrave Macmillan Ltd., Houndmills, Basingstoke, Hampshire, RG21 6XS, England, (Telephone in U.S. (888) 330-8477), (Fax in U.S. (800) 672-2054), www.palgrave.com; *The Statesman's Yearbook 2008.*

Taylor and Francis Group, An Informa Business, 2 Park Square, Milton Park, Abingdon, Oxford OX14 4RN, United Kingdom, (Dial from U.S. (212) 216-7800), (Fax from U.S. (212) 564-7854), www.tandf.co.uk; *The Europa World Year Book.*

U.S. Library of Congress (LOC), Congressional Research Service (CRS), The Library of Congress, 101 Independence Avenue, SE, Washington, DC 20540-7500, (202) 707-5700, www.loc.gov/crsinfo; *What's the Difference? Comparing U.S. and Chinese Trade Data.*

United Nations Conference on Trade and Development (UNCTAD), DC2-1120, United Nations, New York, NY 10017, (212) 963-0027, www.unctad.org; *UNCTAD Commodity Yearbook.*

United Nations Food and Agricultural Organization (FAO), Viale delle Terme di Caracalla, 00100 Rome, Italy, (Dial from U.S. (202) 653-2400), (Fax from U.S. (202) 653 5760), www.fao.org; *FAO Trade Yearbook* and *The State of Food and Agriculture (SOFA) 2006.*

United Nations Statistics Division, New York, NY 10017, (800) 253-9646, Fax: (212) 963-4116, http://unstats.un.org; *Asia-Pacific in Figures 2004; Statistical Yearbook;* and *Statistical Yearbook for Asia and the Pacific 2004.*

The World Bank, 1818 H Street, NW, Washington, DC 20433, (202) 473-1000, Fax: (202) 477-6391, www.worldbank.org; *World Development Indicators (WDI) 2008* and *World Development Report 2008.*

World Trade Organization (WTO), Centre William Rappard, Rue de Lausanne 154, CH-1211 Geneva 21, Switzerland, www.wto.org; *International Trade Statistics 2006.*

CHINA - INTERNET USERS

Federal Statistical Office Germany, D-65180 Wiesbaden, Germany, www.destatis.de; *China 2004.*

International Telecommunication Union (ITU), Place des Nations, 1211 Geneva 20, Switzerland, www.itu.int; *World Telecommunication/ICT Indicators Database on CD-ROM; World Telecommunication/ICT Indicators Database Online;* and *Yearbook of Statistics - Telecommunication Services (Chronological Time Series 1997-2006).*

CHINA - INVESTMENTS

National Bureau of Statistics of China (NBS), No. 57, Yuetan Nanjie, Sanlihe, Xicheng District, Beijing 100826, China, www.stats.gov.cn/english; *Investment of Fixed Assets.*

CHINA - IRON AND IRON ORE PRODUCTION

See CHINA - MINERAL INDUSTRIES

CHINA - IRRIGATION

Euromonitor International, Inc., 224 S. Michigan Avenue, Suite 1500, Chicago, IL 60604, (312) 922-1115, Fax: (312) 922-1157, www.euromonitor.com; *International Marketing Data and Statistics 2008.*

National Bureau of Statistics of China (NBS), No. 57, Yuetan Nanjie, Sanlihe, Xicheng District, Beijing 100826, China, www.stats.gov.cn/english; *Monthly Statistical Data.*

CHINA - JUTE PRODUCTION

See CHINA - CROPS

CHINA - LABOR

Academic International Press, PO Box 1111, Gulf Breeze, FL 32562-1111, Fax: (850) 934-0953, www.ai-press.com; *China Facts and Figures Annual.*

Central Intelligence Agency, Office of Public Affairs, Washington, DC 20505, (703) 482-0623, Fax: (703) 482-1739, www.cia.gov; *The World Factbook.*

Economist Intelligence Unit, 111 West 57th Street, New York, NY 10019, (212) 554-0600, Fax: (212) 586-1181, www.eiu.com; *Business Asia* and *Business China.*

Euromonitor International, Inc., 224 S. Michigan Avenue, Suite 1500, Chicago, IL 60604, (312) 922-1115, Fax: (312) 922-1157, www.euromonitor.com; *International Marketing Data and Statistics 2008* and *World Marketing Data and Statistics.*

Federal Statistical Office Germany, D-65180 Wiesbaden, Germany, www.destatis.de; *China 2004.*

Japan Center for Economic Research (JCER), Nikkei Kayabacho Building, Nihombashi Kayabacho, 2-6-1, Chuo-ku, Tokyo 103-0025, Japan, www.jcer.or.jp/eng; *China Research Report.*

M.E. Sharpe, 80 Business Park Drive, Armonk, NY 10504, (800) 541-6563, Fax: (914) 273-2106, www.mesharpe.com; *The Illustrated Book of World Rankings.*

National Bureau of Statistics of China (NBS), No. 57, Yuetan Nanjie, Sanlihe, Xicheng District, Beijing 100826, China, www.stats.gov.cn/english; *China Statistical Yearbook 2007* and *Monthly Statistical Data.*

Palgrave Macmillan Ltd., Houndmills, Basingstoke, Hampshire, RG21 6XS, England, (Telephone in U.S. (888) 330-8477), (Fax in U.S. (800) 672-2054), www.palgrave.com; *The Statesman's Yearbook 2008.*

United Nations Food and Agricultural Organization (FAO), Viale delle Terme di Caracalla, 00100 Rome, Italy, (Dial from U.S. (202) 653-2400), (Fax from U.S. (202) 653 5760), www.fao.org; *The State of Food and Agriculture (SOFA) 2006.*

United Nations Statistics Division, New York, NY 10017, (800) 253-9646, Fax: (212) 963-4116, http://unstats.un.org; *Human Development Report 2006.*

The World Bank, 1818 H Street, NW, Washington, DC 20433, (202) 473-1000, Fax: (202) 477-6391, www.worldbank.org; *The World Bank Atlas 2003-2004; World Development Indicators (WDI) 2008;* and *World Development Report 2008.*

CHINA - LAND USE

Academic International Press, PO Box 1111, Gulf Breeze, FL 32562-1111, Fax: (850) 934-0953, www.ai-press.com; *China Facts and Figures Annual.*

Central Intelligence Agency, Office of Public Affairs, Washington, DC 20505, (703) 482-0623, Fax: (703) 482-1739, www.cia.gov; *The World Factbook.*

Euromonitor International, Inc., 224 S. Michigan Avenue, Suite 1500, Chicago, IL 60604, (312) 922-1115, Fax: (312) 922-1157, www.euromonitor.com; *International Marketing Data and Statistics 2008.*

Japan Center for Economic Research (JCER), Nikkei Kayabacho Building, Nihombashi Kayabacho, 2-6-1, Chuo-ku, Tokyo 103-0025, Japan, www.jcer.or.jp/eng; *China Research Report.*

National Bureau of Statistics of China (NBS), No. 57, Yuetan Nanjie, Sanlihe, Xicheng District, Beijing 100826, China, www.stats.gov.cn/english; *China Statistical Yearbook 2007* and *Monthly Statistical Data.*

United Nations Food and Agricultural Organization (FAO), Viale delle Terme di Caracalla, 00100 Rome, Italy, (Dial from U.S. (202) 653-2400), (Fax from U.S. (202) 653 5760), www.fao.org; *FAO Production Yearbook 2002.*

The World Bank, 1818 H Street, NW, Washington, DC 20433, (202) 473-1000, Fax: (202) 477-6391, www.worldbank.org; *World Development Report 2008.*

CHINA - LIBRARIES

M.E. Sharpe, 80 Business Park Drive, Armonk, NY 10504, (800) 541-6563, Fax: (914) 273-2106, www.mesharpe.com; *The Illustrated Book of World Rankings.*

CHINA - LIFE EXPECTANCY

Central Intelligence Agency, Office of Public Affairs, Washington, DC 20505, (703) 482-0623, Fax: (703) 482-1739, www.cia.gov; *The World Factbook.*

Economist Intelligence Unit, 111 West 57th Street, New York, NY 10019, (212) 554-0600, Fax: (212) 586-1181, www.eiu.com; *Business Asia* and *Business China.*

Euromonitor International, Inc., 224 S. Michigan Avenue, Suite 1500, Chicago, IL 60604, (312) 922-1115, Fax: (312) 922-1157, www.euromonitor.com; *The World Economic Factbook 2008.*

Palgrave Macmillan Ltd., Houndmills, Basingstoke, Hampshire, RG21 6XS, England, (Telephone in U.S. (888) 330-8477), (Fax in U.S. (800) 672-2054), www.palgrave.com; *The Statesman's Yearbook 2008.*

United Nations Statistics Division, New York, NY 10017, (800) 253-9646, Fax: (212) 963-4116, http://unstats.un.org; *Asia-Pacific in Figures 2004; Human Development Report 2006;* and *World Statistics Pocketbook.*

The World Bank, 1818 H Street, NW, Washington, DC 20433, (202) 473-1000, Fax: (202) 477-6391, www.worldbank.org; *The World Bank Atlas 2003-2004* and *World Development Report 2008.*

CHINA - LITERACY

Euromonitor International, Inc., 224 S. Michigan Avenue, Suite 1500, Chicago, IL 60604, (312) 922-1115, Fax: (312) 922-1157, www.euromonitor.com; *World Marketing Data and Statistics.*

CHINA - LIVESTOCK

Academic International Press, PO Box 1111, Gulf Breeze, FL 32562-1111, Fax: (850) 934-0953, www.ai-press.com; *China Facts and Figures Annual.*

Economist Intelligence Unit, 111 West 57th Street, New York, NY 10019, (212) 554-0600, Fax: (212) 586-1181, www.eiu.com; *Business China.*

Japan Center for Economic Research (JCER), Nikkei Kayabacho Building, Nihombashi Kayabacho, 2-6-1, Chuo-ku, Tokyo 103-0025, Japan, www.jcer.or.jp/eng; *China Research Report.*

M.E. Sharpe, 80 Business Park Drive, Armonk, NY 10504, (800) 541-6563, Fax: (914) 273-2106, www.mesharpe.com; *The Illustrated Book of World Rankings.*

National Bureau of Statistics of China (NBS), No. 57, Yuetan Nanjie, Sanlihe, Xicheng District, Beijing 100826, China, www.stats.gov.cn/english; *China Statistical Yearbook 2007* and *Monthly Statistical Data.*

Palgrave Macmillan Ltd., Houndmills, Basingstoke, Hampshire, RG21 6XS, England, (Telephone in U.S. (888) 330-8477), (Fax in U.S. (800) 672-2054), www.palgrave.com; *The Statesman's Yearbook 2008.*

Taylor and Francis Group, An Informa Business, 2 Park Square, Milton Park, Abingdon, Oxford OX14 4RN, United Kingdom, (Dial from U.S. (212) 216-7800), (Fax from U.S. (212) 564-7854), www.tandf.co.uk; *The Europa World Year Book.*

United Nations Conference on Trade and Development (UNCTAD), DC2-1120, United Nations, New York, NY 10017, (212) 963-0027, www.unctad.org; *UNCTAD Commodity Yearbook.*

United Nations Food and Agricultural Organization (FAO), Viale delle Terme di Caracalla, 00100 Rome, Italy, (Dial from U.S. (202) 653-2400), (Fax from U.S. (202) 653 5760), www.fao.org; *FAO Production Yearbook 2002* and *The State of Food and Agriculture (SOFA) 2006.*

United Nations Statistics Division, New York, NY 10017, (800) 253-9646, Fax: (212) 963-4116, http://unstats.un.org; *Statistical Yearbook.*

CHINA - LOCAL TAXATION

Euromonitor International, Inc., 224 S. Michigan Avenue, Suite 1500, Chicago, IL 60604, (312) 922-1115, Fax: (312) 922-1157, www.euromonitor.com; *International Marketing Data and Statistics 2008.*

CHINA - MAGNESIUM PRODUCTION AND CONSUMPTION

See CHINA - MINERAL INDUSTRIES

CHINA - MANPOWER

Academic International Press, PO Box 1111, Gulf Breeze, FL 32562-1111, Fax: (850) 934-0953, www.ai-press.com; *China Facts and Figures Annual.*

Japan Center for Economic Research (JCER), Nikkei Kayabacho Building, Nihombashi Kayabacho, 2-6-1, Chuo-ku, Tokyo 103-0025, Japan, www.jcer.or.jp/eng; *China Research Report.*

National Bureau of Statistics of China (NBS), No. 57, Yuetan Nanjie, Sanlihe, Xicheng District, Beijing 100826, China, www.stats.gov.cn/english; *China Statistical Yearbook 2007* and *Monthly Statistical Data.*

United Nations Statistics Division, New York, NY 10017, (800) 253-9646, Fax: (212) 963-4116, http://unstats.un.org; *Statistical Yearbook for Asia and the Pacific 2004.*

CHINA - MANUFACTURES

Academic International Press, PO Box 1111, Gulf Breeze, FL 32562-1111, Fax: (850) 934-0953, www.ai-press.com; *China Facts and Figures Annual.*

Asian Development Bank (ADB), PO Box 789, 0980 Manila, Philippines, www.adb.org; *Key Indicators of Developing Asian and Pacific Countries 2006.*

Japan Center for Economic Research (JCER), Nikkei Kayabacho Building, Nihombashi Kayabacho, 2-6-1, Chuo-ku, Tokyo 103-0025, Japan, www.jcer.or.jp/eng; *China Research Report.*

M.E. Sharpe, 80 Business Park Drive, Armonk, NY 10504, (800) 541-6563, Fax: (914) 273-2106, www.mesharpe.com; *The Illustrated Book of World Rankings.*

National Bureau of Statistics of China (NBS), No. 57, Yuetan Nanjie, Sanlihe, Xicheng District, Beijing 100826, China, www.stats.gov.cn/english; *China Statistical Yearbook 2007* and *Monthly Statistical Data.*

The World Bank, 1818 H Street, NW, Washington, DC 20433, (202) 473-1000, Fax: (202) 477-6391, www.worldbank.org; *World Development Indicators (WDI) 2008.*

CHINA - MARRIAGE

Academic International Press, PO Box 1111, Gulf Breeze, FL 32562-1111, Fax: (850) 934-0953, www.ai-press.com; *China Facts and Figures Annual.*

M.E. Sharpe, 80 Business Park Drive, Armonk, NY 10504, (800) 541-6563, Fax: (914) 273-2106, www.mesharpe.com; *The Illustrated Book of World Rankings.*

National Bureau of Statistics of China (NBS), No. 57, Yuetan Nanjie, Sanlihe, Xicheng District, Beijing 100826, China, www.stats.gov.cn/english; *China Statistical Yearbook 2007.*

United Nations Statistics Division, New York, NY 10017, (800) 253-9646, Fax: (212) 963-4116, http://unstats.un.org; *Demographic Yearbook.*

CHINA - MEAT PRODUCTION

See CHINA - LIVESTOCK

CHINA - MERCURY PRODUCTION

See CHINA - MINERAL INDUSTRIES

CHINA - MILK PRODUCTION

See CHINA - DAIRY PROCESSING

CHINA - MINERAL INDUSTRIES

Academic International Press, PO Box 1111, Gulf Breeze, FL 32562-1111, Fax: (850) 934-0953, www.ai-press.com; *China Facts and Figures Annual.*

Asian Development Bank (ADB), PO Box 789, 0980 Manila, Philippines, www.adb.org; *Key Indicators of Developing Asian and Pacific Countries 2006.*

Commodity Research Bureau, 330 South Wells Street, Suite 612, Chicago, IL 60606-7110, (800) 621-5271, Fax: (312) 939-4135, www.crbtrader.com; *2006 CRB Commodity Yearbook and CD.*

Economist Intelligence Unit, 111 West 57th Street, New York, NY 10019, (212) 554-0600, Fax: (212) 586-1181, www.eiu.com; *Business China.*

Japan Center for Economic Research (JCER), Nikkei Kayabacho Building, Nihombashi Kayabacho, 2-6-1, Chuo-ku, Tokyo 103-0025, Japan, www.jcer.or.jp/eng; *China Research Report.*

M.E. Sharpe, 80 Business Park Drive, Armonk, NY 10504, (800) 541-6563, Fax: (914) 273-2106, www.mesharpe.com; *The Illustrated Book of World Rankings.*

National Bureau of Statistics of China (NBS), No. 57, Yuetan Nanjie, Sanlihe, Xicheng District, Beijing 100826, China, www.stats.gov.cn/english; *China Statistical Yearbook 2007.*

Organisation for Economic Cooperation and Development (OECD), 2 rue Andre Pascal, F-75775 Paris Cedex 16, France, (Telephone in U.S. (202) 785-6323), (Fax in U.S. (202) 785-0350), www.oecd.org; *World Energy Outlook 2007.*

Palgrave Macmillan Ltd., Houndmills, Basingstoke, Hampshire, RG21 6XS, England, (Telephone in U.S. (888) 330-8477), (Fax in U.S. (800) 672-2054), www.palgrave.com; *The Statesman's Yearbook 2008.*

Taylor and Francis Group, An Informa Business, 2 Park Square, Milton Park, Abingdon, Oxford OX14 4RN, United Kingdom, (Dial from U.S. (212) 216-7800), (Fax from U.S. (212) 564-7854), www.tandf.co.uk; *The Europa World Year Book.*

United Nations Conference on Trade and Development (UNCTAD), DC2-1120, United Nations, New York, NY 10017, (212) 963-0027, www.unctad.org; *UNCTAD Commodity Yearbook.*

United Nations Statistics Division, New York, NY 10017, (800) 253-9646, Fax: (212) 963-4116, http://unstats.un.org; *Statistical Yearbook.*

CHINA - MONEY EXCHANGE RATES

See CHINA - FOREIGN EXCHANGE RATES

CHINA - MONEY SUPPLY

Academic International Press, PO Box 1111, Gulf Breeze, FL 32562-1111, Fax: (850) 934-0953, www.ai-press.com; *China Facts and Figures Annual.*

Asian Development Bank (ADB), PO Box 789, 0980 Manila, Philippines, www.adb.org; *Key Indicators of Developing Asian and Pacific Countries 2006.*

Economist Intelligence Unit, 111 West 57th Street, New York, NY 10019, (212) 554-0600, Fax: (212) 586-1181, www.eiu.com; *China Country Report.*

Euromonitor International, Inc., 224 S. Michigan Avenue, Suite 1500, Chicago, IL 60604, (312) 922-1115, Fax: (312) 922-1157, www.euromonitor.com; *International Marketing Data and Statistics 2008.*

Federal Statistical Office Germany, D-65180 Wiesbaden, Germany, www.destatis.de; *China 2004.*

International Monetary Fund (IMF), 700 Nineteenth Street, NW, Washington, DC 20431, (202) 623-7000, Fax: (202) 623-4661, www.imf.org; *International Financial Statistics Yearbook 2007.*

Japan Center for Economic Research (JCER), Nikkei Kayabacho Building, Nihombashi Kayabacho, 2-6-1, Chuo-ku, Tokyo 103-0025, Japan, www.jcer.or.jp/eng; *China Research Report.*

National Bureau of Statistics of China (NBS), No. 57, Yuetan Nanjie, Sanlihe, Xicheng District, Beijing 100826, China, www.stats.gov.cn/english; *China Statistical Yearbook 2007.*

Taylor and Francis Group, An Informa Business, 2 Park Square, Milton Park, Abingdon, Oxford OX14 4RN, United Kingdom, (Dial from U.S. (212) 216-7800), (Fax from U.S. (212) 564-7854), www.tandf.co.uk; *The Europa World Year Book.*

The World Bank, 1818 H Street, NW, Washington, DC 20433, (202) 473-1000, Fax: (202) 477-6391, www.worldbank.org; *World Development Indicators (WDI) 2008.*

CHINA - MORTALITY

Academic International Press, PO Box 1111, Gulf Breeze, FL 32562-1111, Fax: (850) 934-0953, www.ai-press.com; *China Facts and Figures Annual.*

Central Intelligence Agency, Office of Public Affairs, Washington, DC 20505, (703) 482-0623, Fax: (703) 482-1739, www.cia.gov; *The World Factbook.*

Economist Intelligence Unit, 111 West 57th Street, New York, NY 10019, (212) 554-0600, Fax: (212) 586-1181, www.eiu.com; *Business China.*

Euromonitor International, Inc., 224 S. Michigan Avenue, Suite 1500, Chicago, IL 60604, (312) 922-1115, Fax: (312) 922-1157, www.euromonitor.com; *International Marketing Data and Statistics 2008* and *The World Economic Factbook 2008.*

National Bureau of Statistics of China (NBS), No. 57, Yuetan Nanjie, Sanlihe, Xicheng District, Beijing 100826, China, www.stats.gov.cn/english; *China Statistical Yearbook 2007* and *Monthly Statistical Data.*

Palgrave Macmillan Ltd., Houndmills, Basingstoke, Hampshire, RG21 6XS, England, (Telephone in U.S. (888) 330-8477), (Fax in U.S. (800) 672-2054), www.palgrave.com; *The Statesman's Yearbook 2008.*

UNICEF, 3 United Nations Plaza, New York, NY 10017, (800) 253-9646, Fax: (212) 887-7465, www.unicef.org; *The State of the World's Children 2008.*

United Nations Statistics Division, New York, NY 10017, (800) 253-9646, Fax: (212) 963-4116, http://unstats.un.org; *Asia-Pacific in Figures 2004; Demographic Yearbook; Human Development Report 2006; Statistical Yearbook;* and *World Statistics Pocketbook.*

The World Bank, 1818 H Street, NW, Washington, DC 20433, (202) 473-1000, Fax: (202) 477-6391, www.worldbank.org; *The World Bank Atlas 2003-2004; World Development Indicators (WDI) 2008;* and *World Development Report 2008.*

World Health Organization (WHO), Avenue Appia 20, 1211 Geneve 27, Switzerland, (Telephone in U.S. (212) 331-9081), www.who.int; The WHO Global Atlas of Infectious Diseases and *World Health Report 2006.*

CHINA - MOTION PICTURES

Palgrave Macmillan Ltd., Houndmills, Basingstoke, Hampshire, RG21 6XS, England, (Telephone in U.S. (888) 330-8477), (Fax in U.S. (800) 672-2054), www.palgrave.com; *The Statesman's Yearbook 2008.*

CHINA - MUSEUMS

M.E. Sharpe, 80 Business Park Drive, Armonk, NY 10504, (800) 541-6563, Fax: (914) 273-2106, www.mesharpe.com; *The Illustrated Book of World Rankings.*

CHINA - NATURAL GAS PRODUCTION

See CHINA - MINERAL INDUSTRIES

CHINA - NUTRITION

Asian Development Bank (ADB), PO Box 789, 0980 Manila, Philippines, www.adb.org; *Key Indicators of Developing Asian and Pacific Countries 2006.*

United Nations Food and Agricultural Organization (FAO), Viale delle Terme di Caracalla, 00100 Rome, Italy, (Dial from U.S. (202) 653-2400), (Fax from U.S. (202) 653 5760), www.fao.org; *The State of Food and Agriculture (SOFA) 2006.*

CHINA - OATS PRODUCTION

See CHINA - CROPS

CHINA - OLDER PEOPLE

M.E. Sharpe, 80 Business Park Drive, Armonk, NY 10504, (800) 541-6563, Fax: (914) 273-2106, www.mesharpe.com; *The Illustrated Book of World Rankings.*

CHINA - PALM OIL PRODUCTION

See CHINA - CROPS

CHINA - PAPER

See CHINA - FORESTS AND FORESTRY

CHINA - PEANUT PRODUCTION

See CHINA - CROPS

CHINA - PERIODICALS

Academic International Press, PO Box 1111, Gulf Breeze, FL 32562-1111, Fax: (850) 934-0953, www.ai-press.com; *China Facts and Figures Annual.*

National Bureau of Statistics of China (NBS), No. 57, Yuetan Nanjie, Sanlihe, Xicheng District, Beijing 100826, China, www.stats.gov.cn/english; *China Statistical Yearbook 2007.*

CHINA - PESTICIDES

Economist Intelligence Unit, 111 West 57th Street, New York, NY 10019, (212) 554-0600, Fax: (212) 586-1181, www.eiu.com; *Business China.*

United Nations Food and Agricultural Organization (FAO), Viale delle Terme di Caracalla, 00100 Rome, Italy, (Dial from U.S. (202) 653-2400), (Fax from U.S. (202) 653 5760), www.fao.org; *The State of Food and Agriculture (SOFA) 2006.*

CHINA - PETROLEUM INDUSTRY AND TRADE

Academic International Press, PO Box 1111, Gulf Breeze, FL 32562-1111, Fax: (850) 934-0953, www.ai-press.com; *China Facts and Figures Annual.*

Asian Development Bank (ADB), PO Box 789, 0980 Manila, Philippines, www.adb.org; *Key Indicators of Developing Asian and Pacific Countries 2006.*

Economist Intelligence Unit, 111 West 57th Street, New York, NY 10019, (212) 554-0600, Fax: (212) 586-1181, www.eiu.com; *Business China.*

Japan Center for Economic Research (JCER), Nikkei Kayabacho Building, Nihombashi Kayabacho, 2-6-1, Chuo-ku, Tokyo 103-0025, Japan, www.jcer.or.jp/eng; *China Research Report.*

M.E. Sharpe, 80 Business Park Drive, Armonk, NY 10504, (800) 541-6563, Fax: (914) 273-2106, www.mesharpe.com; *The Illustrated Book of World Rankings.*

National Bureau of Statistics of China (NBS), No. 57, Yuetan Nanjie, Sanlihe, Xicheng District, Beijing 100826, China, www.stats.gov.cn/english; *China Statistical Yearbook 2007.*

Organisation for Economic Cooperation and Development (OECD), 2 rue Andre Pascal, F-75775 Paris Cedex 16, France, (Telephone in U.S. (202) 785-6323), (Fax in U.S. (202) 785-0350), www.oecd.org; *World Energy Outlook 2007.*

Palgrave Macmillan Ltd., Houndmills, Basingstoke, Hampshire, RG21 6XS, England, (Telephone in U.S. (888) 330-8477), (Fax in U.S. (800) 672-2054), www.palgrave.com; *The Statesman's Yearbook 2008.*

PennWell Corporation, 1421 South Sheridan Road, Tulsa, OK 74112, (918) 835-3161, www.pennwell.com; *International Petroleum Encyclopedia 2007.*

U.S. Department of Energy (DOE), Energy Information Administration (EIA), 1000 Independence Avenue, SW, Washington, DC 20585, (202) 586-8800, www.eia.doe.gov; *International Energy Annual 2004* and *International Energy Outlook 2006.*

United Nations Conference on Trade and Development (UNCTAD), DC2-1120, United Nations, New York, NY 10017, (212) 963-0027, www.unctad.org; *UNCTAD Commodity Yearbook.*

United Nations Food and Agricultural Organization (FAO), Viale delle Terme di Caracalla, 00100 Rome, Italy, (Dial from U.S. (202) 653-2400), (Fax from U.S. (202) 653 5760), www.fao.org; *The State of Food and Agriculture (SOFA) 2006.*

United Nations Statistics Division, New York, NY 10017, (800) 253-9646, Fax: (212) 963-4116, http://unstats.un.org; *Statistical Yearbook.*

CHINA - PHOSPHATES PRODUCTION

See CHINA - MINERAL INDUSTRIES

CHINA - PLASTICS INDUSTRY AND TRADE

Academic International Press, PO Box 1111, Gulf Breeze, FL 32562-1111, Fax: (850) 934-0953, www.ai-press.com; *China Facts and Figures Annual.*

Economist Intelligence Unit, 111 West 57th Street, New York, NY 10019, (212) 554-0600, Fax: (212) 586-1181, www.eiu.com; *Business China.*

Japan Center for Economic Research (JCER), Nikkei Kayabacho Building, Nihombashi Kayabacho, 2-6-1, Chuo-ku, Tokyo 103-0025, Japan, www.jcer.or.jp/eng; *China Research Report.*

National Bureau of Statistics of China (NBS), No. 57, Yuetan Nanjie, Sanlihe, Xicheng District, Beijing 100826, China, www.stats.gov.cn/english; *China Statistical Yearbook 2007.*

CHINA - POLITICAL SCIENCE

Asian Development Bank (ADB), PO Box 789, 0980 Manila, Philippines, www.adb.org; *Key Indicators of Developing Asian and Pacific Countries 2006.*

Central Intelligence Agency, Office of Public Affairs, Washington, DC 20505, (703) 482-0623, Fax: (703) 482-1739, www.cia.gov; *The World Factbook.*

Economist Intelligence Unit, 111 West 57th Street, New York, NY 10019, (212) 554-0600, Fax: (212) 586-1181, www.eiu.com; *Business China.*

International Monetary Fund (IMF), 700 Nineteenth Street, NW, Washington, DC 20431, (202) 623-7000, Fax: (202) 623-4661, www.imf.org; *International Financial Statistics Yearbook 2007.*

Palgrave Macmillan Ltd., Houndmills, Basingstoke, Hampshire, RG21 6XS, England, (Telephone in U.S. (888) 330-8477), (Fax in U.S. (800) 672-2054), www.palgrave.com; *The Statesman's Yearbook 2008.*

Taylor and Francis Group, An Informa Business, 2 Park Square, Milton Park, Abingdon, Oxford OX14 4RN, United Kingdom, (Dial from U.S. (212) 216-7800), (Fax from U.S. (212) 564-7854), www.tandf.co.uk; *The Europa World Year Book.*

United Nations Statistics Division, New York, NY 10017, (800) 253-9646, Fax: (212) 963-4116, http://unstats.un.org; *Asia-Pacific in Figures 2004* and *National Accounts Statistics: Compendium of Income Distribution Statistics.*

The World Bank, 1818 H Street, NW, Washington, DC 20433, (202) 473-1000, Fax: (202) 477-6391, www.worldbank.org; *World Development Indicators (WDI) 2008* and *World Development Report 2008.*

CHINA - POLLUTION

Economist Intelligence Unit, 111 West 57th Street, New York, NY 10019, (212) 554-0600, Fax: (212) 586-1181, www.eiu.com; *Business China.*

CHINA - POPULATION

Academic International Press, PO Box 1111, Gulf Breeze, FL 32562-1111, Fax: (850) 934-0953, www.ai-press.com; *China Facts and Figures Annual.*

Asian Development Bank (ADB), PO Box 789, 0980 Manila, Philippines, www.adb.org; *Key Indicators of Developing Asian and Pacific Countries 2006.*

Central Intelligence Agency, Office of Public Affairs, Washington, DC 20505, (703) 482-0623, Fax: (703) 482-1739, www.cia.gov; *The World Factbook.*

Economist Intelligence Unit, 111 West 57th Street, New York, NY 10019, (212) 554-0600, Fax: (212) 586-1181, www.eiu.com; *Business Asia; Business China;* and *China Country Report.*

Euromonitor International, Inc., 224 S. Michigan Avenue, Suite 1500, Chicago, IL 60604, (312) 922-1115, Fax: (312) 922-1157, www.euromonitor.com; *International Marketing Data and Statistics 2008* and *The World Economic Factbook 2008.*

Federal Statistical Office Germany, D-65180 Wiesbaden, Germany, www.destatis.de; *China 2004.*

International Organization for Migration (IOM), 17, Route des Morillons, CH-1211 Geneva 19, Switzerland, www.iom.int; *Domestic Migrant Remittances in China: Distribution, Channels and Livelihoods* and *Migration and Poverty Alleviation in China.*

Japan Center for Economic Research (JCER), Nikkei Kayabacho Building, Nihombashi Kayabacho, 2-6-1, Chuo-ku, Tokyo 103-0025, Japan, www.jcer.or.jp/eng; *China Research Report.*

M.E. Sharpe, 80 Business Park Drive, Armonk, NY 10504, (800) 541-6563, Fax: (914) 273-2106, www.mesharpe.com; *The Illustrated Book of World Rankings.*

National Bureau of Statistics of China (NBS), No. 57, Yuetan Nanjie, Sanlihe, Xicheng District, Beijing 100826, China, www.stats.gov.cn/english; *China Statistical Yearbook 2007; Monthly Statistical Data;* and *Women and Men in China: Facts and Figures.*

Palgrave Macmillan Ltd., Houndmills, Basingstoke, Hampshire, RG21 6XS, England, (Telephone in U.S. (888) 330-8477), (Fax in U.S. (800) 672-2054), www.palgrave.com; *The Statesman's Yearbook 2008.*

Taylor and Francis Group, An Informa Business, 2 Park Square, Milton Park, Abingdon, Oxford OX14 4RN, United Kingdom, (Dial from U.S. (212) 216-7800), (Fax from U.S. (212) 564-7854), www.tandf.co.uk; *The Europa World Year Book.*

U.S. Department of State (DOS), 2201 C Street NW, Washington, DC 20520, (202) 647-4000, www.state.gov; *World Military Expenditures and Arms Transfers (WMEAT).*

UNESCO Institute for Statistics, C.P. 6128 Succursale Centre-Ville, Montreal, Quebec, H3C 3J7 Canada, (Dial from U.S. (514) 343-6880), (Fax from U.S. (514) 343 6882), www.uis.unesco.org; *Statistical Tables.*

United Nations Food and Agricultural Organization (FAO), Viale delle Terme di Caracalla, 00100 Rome, Italy, (Dial from U.S. (202) 653-2400), (Fax from U.S. (202) 653 5760), www.fao.org; *FAO Production Yearbook 2002.*

United Nations Statistics Division, New York, NY 10017, (800) 253-9646, Fax: (212) 963-4116, http://unstats.un.org; *Asia-Pacific in Figures 2004; Demographic Yearbook; Human Development Report 2006; Statistical Yearbook; Statistical Yearbook for Asia and the Pacific 2004;* and *World Statistics Pocketbook.*

The World Bank, 1818 H Street, NW, Washington, DC 20433, (202) 473-1000, Fax: (202) 477-6391, www.worldbank.org; *The World Bank Atlas 2003-2004* and *World Development Report 2008.*

World Health Organization (WHO), Avenue Appia 20, 1211 Geneve 27, Switzerland, (Telephone in U.S. (212) 331-9081), www.who.int; *World Health Report 2006.*

Worldinformation.com, 2 Market Street, Saffron Walden, Essex CB10 1HZ, United Kingdom, www.worldinformation.com; The World of Information (www.worldinformation.com).

CHINA - POPULATION DENSITY

Academic International Press, PO Box 1111, Gulf Breeze, FL 32562-1111, Fax: (850) 934-0953, www.ai-press.com; *China Facts and Figures Annual.*

Central Intelligence Agency, Office of Public Affairs, Washington, DC 20505, (703) 482-0623, Fax: (703) 482-1739, www.cia.gov; *The World Factbook.*

Economist Intelligence Unit, 111 West 57th Street, New York, NY 10019, (212) 554-0600, Fax: (212) 586-1181, www.eiu.com; *Business China.*

Euromonitor International, Inc., 224 S. Michigan Avenue, Suite 1500, Chicago, IL 60604, (312) 922-1115, Fax: (312) 922-1157, www.euromonitor.com; *International Marketing Data and Statistics 2008* and *The World Economic Factbook 2008.*

M.E. Sharpe, 80 Business Park Drive, Armonk, NY 10504, (800) 541-6563, Fax: (914) 273-2106, www.mesharpe.com; *The Illustrated Book of World Rankings.*

National Bureau of Statistics of China (NBS), No. 57, Yuetan Nanjie, Sanlihe, Xicheng District, Beijing 100826, China, www.stats.gov.cn/english; *China Statistical Yearbook 2007* and *Monthly Statistical Data.*

Palgrave Macmillan Ltd., Houndmills, Basingstoke, Hampshire, RG21 6XS, England, (Telephone in U.S. (888) 330-8477), (Fax in U.S. (800) 672-2054), www.palgrave.com; *The Statesman's Yearbook 2008.*

Taylor and Francis Group, An Informa Business, 2 Park Square, Milton Park, Abingdon, Oxford OX14 4RN, United Kingdom, (Dial from U.S. (212) 216-7800), (Fax from U.S. (212) 564-7854), www.tandf.co.uk; *The Europa World Year Book.*

UNESCO Institute for Statistics, C.P. 6128 Succursale Centre-Ville, Montreal, Quebec, H3C 3J7 Canada, (Dial from U.S. (514) 343-6880), (Fax from U.S. (514) 343 6882), www.uis.unesco.org; *Statistical Tables.*

United Nations Food and Agricultural Organization (FAO), Viale delle Terme di Caracalla, 00100 Rome, Italy, (Dial from U.S. (202) 653-2400), (Fax from U.S. (202) 653 5760), www.fao.org; *The State of Food and Agriculture (SOFA) 2006.*

United Nations Statistics Division, New York, NY 10017, (800) 253-9646, Fax: (212) 963-4116, http://unstats.un.org; *Statistical Yearbook.*

The World Bank, 1818 H Street, NW, Washington, DC 20433, (202) 473-1000, Fax: (202) 477-6391, www.worldbank.org; *World Development Report 2008.*

CHINA - POSTAL SERVICE

Academic International Press, PO Box 1111, Gulf Breeze, FL 32562-1111, Fax: (850) 934-0953, www.ai-press.com; *China Facts and Figures Annual.*

M.E. Sharpe, 80 Business Park Drive, Armonk, NY 10504, (800) 541-6563, Fax: (914) 273-2106, www.mesharpe.com; *The Illustrated Book of World Rankings.*

National Bureau of Statistics of China (NBS), No. 57, Yuetan Nanjie, Sanlihe, Xicheng District, Beijing 100826, China, www.stats.gov.cn/english; *China Statistical Yearbook 2007.*

Palgrave Macmillan Ltd., Houndmills, Basingstoke, Hampshire, RG21 6XS, England, (Telephone in U.S. (888) 330-8477), (Fax in U.S. (800) 672-2054), www.palgrave.com; *The Statesman's Yearbook 2008.*

CHINA - POWER RESOURCES

Academic International Press, PO Box 1111, Gulf Breeze, FL 32562-1111, Fax: (850) 934-0953, www.ai-press.com; *China Facts and Figures Annual.*

Euromonitor International, Inc., 224 S. Michigan Avenue, Suite 1500, Chicago, IL 60604, (312) 922-1115, Fax: (312) 922-1157, www.euromonitor.com; *International Marketing Data and Statistics 2008* and *The World Economic Factbook 2008.*

Japan Center for Economic Research (JCER), Nikkei Kayabacho Building, Nihombashi Kayabacho, 2-6-1, Chuo-ku, Tokyo 103-0025, Japan, www.jcer.or.jp/eng; *China Research Report.*

M.E. Sharpe, 80 Business Park Drive, Armonk, NY 10504, (800) 541-6563, Fax: (914) 273-2106, www.mesharpe.com; *The Illustrated Book of World Rankings.*

National Bureau of Statistics of China (NBS), No. 57, Yuetan Nanjie, Sanlihe, Xicheng District, Beijing 100826, China, www.stats.gov.cn/english; *China Statistical Yearbook 2007.*

Organisation for Economic Cooperation and Development (OECD), 2 rue Andre Pascal, F-75775 Paris Cedex 16, France, (Telephone in U.S. (202) 785-6323), (Fax in U.S. (202) 785-0350), www.oecd.org; *World Energy Outlook 2007.*

Palgrave Macmillan Ltd., Houndmills, Basingstoke, Hampshire, RG21 6XS, England, (Telephone in U.S. (888) 330-8477), (Fax in U.S. (800) 672-2054), www.palgrave.com; *The Statesman's Yearbook 2008.*

Platts, 2 Penn Plaza, 25th Floor, New York, NY 10121-2298, (212) 904-3070, www.platts.com; *Asian Electricity Outlook 2006* and *Emissions Daily.*

U.S. Department of Energy (DOE), Energy Information Administration (EIA), 1000 Independence Avenue, SW, Washington, DC 20585, (202) 586-8800, www.eia.doe.gov; *International Energy Annual 2004* and *International Energy Outlook 2006.*

United Nations Statistics Division, New York, NY 10017, (800) 253-9646, Fax: (212) 963-4116, http://unstats.un.org; *Asia-Pacific in Figures 2004; Human Development Report 2006; Statistical Yearbook;* and *World Statistics Pocketbook.*

The World Bank, 1818 H Street, NW, Washington, DC 20433, (202) 473-1000, Fax: (202) 477-6391, www.worldbank.org; *The World Bank Atlas 2003-2004* and *World Development Report 2008.*

CHINA - PRICES

Academic International Press, PO Box 1111, Gulf Breeze, FL 32562-1111, Fax: (850) 934-0953, www.ai-press.com; *China Facts and Figures Annual.*

Asian Development Bank (ADB), PO Box 789, 0980 Manila, Philippines, www.adb.org; *Key Indicators of Developing Asian and Pacific Countries 2006.*

Euromonitor International, Inc., 224 S. Michigan Avenue, Suite 1500, Chicago, IL 60604, (312) 922-1115, Fax: (312) 922-1157, www.euromonitor.com; *World Marketing Data and Statistics.*

International Monetary Fund (IMF), 700 Nineteenth Street, NW, Washington, DC 20431, (202) 623-7000, Fax: (202) 623-4661, www.imf.org; *International Financial Statistics Yearbook 2007.*

Japan Center for Economic Research (JCER), Nikkei Kayabacho Building, Nihombashi Kayabacho, 2-6-1, Chuo-ku, Tokyo 103-0025, Japan, www.jcer.or.jp/eng; *China Research Report.*

M.E. Sharpe, 80 Business Park Drive, Armonk, NY 10504, (800) 541-6563, Fax: (914) 273-2106, www.mesharpe.com; *The Illustrated Book of World Rankings.*

National Bureau of Statistics of China (NBS), No. 57, Yuetan Nanjie, Sanlihe, Xicheng District, Beijing 100826, China, www.stats.gov.cn/english; *China Statistical Yearbook 2007; Monthly Statistical Data;* and *Price Indices.*

United Nations Food and Agricultural Organization (FAO), Viale delle Terme di Caracalla, 00100 Rome, Italy, (Dial from U.S. (202) 653-2400), (Fax from U.S. (202) 653 5760), www.fao.org; *FAO Production Yearbook 2002* and *The State of Food and Agriculture (SOFA) 2006.*

CHINA - PUBLIC HEALTH

Academic International Press, PO Box 1111, Gulf Breeze, FL 32562-1111, Fax: (850) 934-0953, www.ai-press.com; *China Facts and Figures Annual.*

Economist Intelligence Unit, 111 West 57th Street, New York, NY 10019, (212) 554-0600, Fax: (212) 586-1181, www.eiu.com; *Business Asia* and *Business China.*

Euromonitor International, Inc., 224 S. Michigan Avenue, Suite 1500, Chicago, IL 60604, (312) 922-1115, Fax: (312) 922-1157, www.euromonitor.com; *World Health Databook 2007/2008* and *World Marketing Data and Statistics.*

M.E. Sharpe, 80 Business Park Drive, Armonk, NY 10504, (800) 541-6563, Fax: (914) 273-2106, www.mesharpe.com; *The Illustrated Book of World Rankings.*

National Bureau of Statistics of China (NBS), No. 57, Yuetan Nanjie, Sanlihe, Xicheng District, Beijing 100826, China, www.stats.gov.cn/english; *China Statistical Yearbook 2007* and *Monthly Statistical Data.*

Palgrave Macmillan Ltd., Houndmills, Basingstoke, Hampshire, RG21 6XS, England, (Telephone in U.S. (888) 330-8477), (Fax in U.S. (800) 672-2054), www.palgrave.com; *The Statesman's Yearbook 2008.*

UNICEF, 3 United Nations Plaza, New York, NY 10017, (800) 253-9646, Fax: (212) 887-7465, www.unicef.org; *The State of the World's Children 2008.*

United Nations Statistics Division, New York, NY 10017, (800) 253-9646, Fax: (212) 963-4116, http://unstats.un.org; *Asia-Pacific in Figures 2004; Human Development Report 2006;* and *Statistical Yearbook.*

The World Bank, 1818 H Street, NW, Washington, DC 20433, (202) 473-1000, Fax: (202) 477-6391, www.worldbank.org; *World Development Report 2008.*

World Health Organization (WHO), Avenue Appia 20, 1211 Geneve 27, Switzerland, (Telephone in U.S. (212) 331-9081), www.who.int; The WHO Global Atlas of Infectious Diseases and *World Health Report 2006.*

CHINA - PUBLIC UTILITIES

Academic International Press, PO Box 1111, Gulf Breeze, FL 32562-1111, Fax: (850) 934-0953, www.ai-press.com; *China Facts and Figures Annual.*

Japan Center for Economic Research (JCER), Nikkei Kayabacho Building, Nihombashi Kayabacho, 2-6-1, Chuo-ku, Tokyo 103-0025, Japan, www.jcer.or.jp/eng; *China Research Report.*

National Bureau of Statistics of China (NBS), No. 57, Yuetan Nanjie, Sanlihe, Xicheng District, Beijing 100826, China, www.stats.gov.cn/english; *China Statistical Yearbook 2007.*

United Nations Statistics Division, New York, NY 10017, (800) 253-9646, Fax: (212) 963-4116, http://unstats.un.org; *Electric Power in Asia and the Pacific 2001 and 2002.*

CHINA - PUBLISHERS AND PUBLISHING

Academic International Press, PO Box 1111, Gulf Breeze, FL 32562-1111, Fax: (850) 934-0953, www.ai-press.com; *China Facts and Figures Annual.*

Japan Center for Economic Research (JCER), Nikkei Kayabacho Building, Nihombashi Kayabacho, 2-6-1, Chuo-ku, Tokyo 103-0025, Japan, www.jcer.or.jp/eng; *China Research Report.*

National Bureau of Statistics of China (NBS), No. 57, Yuetan Nanjie, Sanlihe, Xicheng District, Beijing 100826, China, www.stats.gov.cn/english; *China Statistical Yearbook 2007.*

Palgrave Macmillan Ltd., Houndmills, Basingstoke, Hampshire, RG21 6XS, England, (Telephone in U.S. (888) 330-8477), (Fax in U.S. (800) 672-2054), www.palgrave.com; *The Statesman's Yearbook 2008.*

Taylor and Francis Group, An Informa Business, 2 Park Square, Milton Park, Abingdon, Oxford OX14 4RN, United Kingdom, (Dial from U.S. (212) 216-7800), (Fax from U.S. (212) 564-7854), www.tandf.co.uk; *The Europa World Year Book.*

UNESCO Institute for Statistics, C.P. 6128 Succursale Centre-Ville, Montreal, Quebec, H3C 3J7 Canada, (Dial from U.S. (514) 343-6880), (Fax from U.S. (514) 343 6882), www.uis.unesco.org; *Statistical Tables.*

CHINA - RADIO BROADCASTING

Palgrave Macmillan Ltd., Houndmills, Basingstoke, Hampshire, RG21 6XS, England, (Telephone in U.S. (888) 330-8477), (Fax in U.S. (800) 672-2054), www.palgrave.com; *The Statesman's Yearbook 2008.*

CHINA - RAILROADS

Academic International Press, PO Box 1111, Gulf Breeze, FL 32562-1111, Fax: (850) 934-0953, www.ai-press.com; *China Facts and Figures Annual.*

Economist Intelligence Unit, 111 West 57th Street, New York, NY 10019, (212) 554-0600, Fax: (212) 586-1181, www.eiu.com; *Business China.*

Jane's Information Group, 110 North Royal Street, Suite 200, Alexandria, VA 22314, (703) 683-3700, Fax: (800) 836-0297, www.janes.com; *Jane's World Railways.*

Japan Center for Economic Research (JCER), Nikkei Kayabacho Building, Nihombashi Kayabacho, 2-6-1, Chuo-ku, Tokyo 103-0025, Japan, www.jcer.or.jp/eng; *China Research Report.*

National Bureau of Statistics of China (NBS), No. 57, Yuetan Nanjie, Sanlihe, Xicheng District, Beijing 100826, China, www.stats.gov.cn/english; *China Statistical Yearbook 2007.*

Palgrave Macmillan Ltd., Houndmills, Basingstoke, Hampshire, RG21 6XS, England, (Telephone in U.S. (888) 330-8477), (Fax in U.S. (800) 672-2054), www.palgrave.com; *The Statesman's Yearbook 2008.*

Taylor and Francis Group, An Informa Business, 2 Park Square, Milton Park, Abingdon, Oxford OX14 4RN, United Kingdom, (Dial from U.S. (212) 216-7800), (Fax from U.S. (212) 564-7854), www.tandf.co.uk; *The Europa World Year Book.*

United Nations Statistics Division, New York, NY 10017, (800) 253-9646, Fax: (212) 963-4116, http://unstats.un.org; *Statistical Yearbook.*

CHINA - RELIGION

Central Intelligence Agency, Office of Public Affairs, Washington, DC 20505, (703) 482-0623, Fax: (703) 482-1739, www.cia.gov; *The World Factbook*.

M.E. Sharpe, 80 Business Park Drive, Armonk, NY 10504, (800) 541-6563, Fax: (914) 273-2106, www.mesharpe.com; *The Illustrated Book of World Rankings*.

Palgrave Macmillan Ltd., Houndmills, Basingstoke, Hampshire, RG21 6XS, England, (Telephone in U.S. (888) 330-8477), (Fax in U.S. (800) 672-2054), www.palgrave.com; *The Statesman's Yearbook 2008*.

CHINA - RESERVES (ACCOUNTING)

Academic International Press, PO Box 1111, Gulf Breeze, FL 32562-1111, Fax: (850) 934-0953, www.ai-press.com; *China Facts and Figures Annual*.

Asian Development Bank (ADB), PO Box 789, 0980 Manila, Philippines, www.adb.org; *Key Indicators of Developing Asian and Pacific Countries 2006*.

Euromonitor International, Inc., 224 S. Michigan Avenue, Suite 1500, Chicago, IL 60604, (312) 922-1115, Fax: (312) 922-1157, www.euromonitor.com; *International Marketing Data and Statistics 2008*.

Japan Center for Economic Research (JCER), Nikkei Kayabacho Building, Nihombashi Kayabacho, 2-6-1, Chuo-ku, Tokyo 103-0025, Japan, www.jcer.or.jp/eng; *China Research Report*.

National Bureau of Statistics of China (NBS), No. 57, Yuetan Nanjie, Sanlihe, Xicheng District, Beijing 100826, China, www.stats.gov.cn/english; *China Statistical Yearbook 2007*.

The World Bank, 1818 H Street, NW, Washington, DC 20433, (202) 473-1000, Fax: (202) 477-6391, www.worldbank.org; *World Development Indicators (WDI) 2008*.

CHINA - RETAIL TRADE

Academic International Press, PO Box 1111, Gulf Breeze, FL 32562-1111, Fax: (850) 934-0953, www.ai-press.com; *China Facts and Figures Annual*.

Economist Intelligence Unit, 111 West 57th Street, New York, NY 10019, (212) 554-0600, Fax: (212) 586-1181, www.eiu.com; *Business China*.

Euromonitor International, Inc., 224 S. Michigan Avenue, Suite 1500, Chicago, IL 60604, (312) 922-1115, Fax: (312) 922-1157, www.euromonitor.com; *Retail Trade International 2007* and *World Marketing Data and Statistics*.

Japan Center for Economic Research (JCER), Nikkei Kayabacho Building, Nihombashi Kayabacho, 2-6-1, Chuo-ku, Tokyo 103-0025, Japan, www.jcer.or.jp/eng; *China Research Report*.

National Bureau of Statistics of China (NBS), No. 57, Yuetan Nanjie, Sanlihe, Xicheng District, Beijing 100826, China, www.stats.gov.cn/english; *China Statistical Yearbook 2007* and *Monthly Statistical Data*.

CHINA - RICE PRODUCTION

See CHINA - CROPS

CHINA - ROADS

Central Intelligence Agency, Office of Public Affairs, Washington, DC 20505, (703) 482-0623, Fax: (703) 482-1739, www.cia.gov; *The World Factbook*.

Economist Intelligence Unit, 111 West 57th Street, New York, NY 10019, (212) 554-0600, Fax: (212) 586-1181, www.eiu.com; *Business Asia* and *Business China*.

Palgrave Macmillan Ltd., Houndmills, Basingstoke, Hampshire, RG21 6XS, England, (Telephone in U.S. (888) 330-8477), (Fax in U.S. (800) 672-2054), www.palgrave.com; *The Statesman's Yearbook 2008*.

CHINA - RUBBER INDUSTRY AND TRADE

Academic International Press, PO Box 1111, Gulf Breeze, FL 32562-1111, Fax: (850) 934-0953, www.ai-press.com; *China Facts and Figures Annual*.

International Rubber Study Group (IRSG), 1st Floor, Heron House, 109/115 Wembley Hill Road, Wembley, Middlesex HA9 8DA, United Kingdom, www.rubberstudy.com; *Rubber Statistical Bulletin; Summary of World Rubber Statistics 2005; World Rubber Statistics Handbook (Volume 6, 1975-2001);* and *World Rubber Statistics Historic Handbook*.

Japan Center for Economic Research (JCER), Nikkei Kayabacho Building, Nihombashi Kayabacho, 2-6-1, Chuo-ku, Tokyo 103-0025, Japan, www.jcer.or.jp/eng; *China Research Report*.

M.E. Sharpe, 80 Business Park Drive, Armonk, NY 10504, (800) 541-6563, Fax: (914) 273-2106, www.mesharpe.com; *The Illustrated Book of World Rankings*.

National Bureau of Statistics of China (NBS), No. 57, Yuetan Nanjie, Sanlihe, Xicheng District, Beijing 100826, China, www.stats.gov.cn/english; *China Statistical Yearbook 2007* and *Monthly Statistical Data*.

United Nations Statistics Division, New York, NY 10017, (800) 253-9646, Fax: (212) 963-4116, http://unstats.un.org; *Statistical Yearbook*.

CHINA - SALT PRODUCTION

See CHINA - MINERAL INDUSTRIES

CHINA - SHEEP

See CHINA - LIVESTOCK

CHINA - SHIPPING

Academic International Press, PO Box 1111, Gulf Breeze, FL 32562-1111, Fax: (850) 934-0953, www.ai-press.com; *China Facts and Figures Annual*.

Japan Center for Economic Research (JCER), Nikkei Kayabacho Building, Nihombashi Kayabacho, 2-6-1, Chuo-ku, Tokyo 103-0025, Japan, www.jcer.or.jp/eng; *China Research Report*.

Lloyd's Register - Fairplay, 8410 N.W. 53rd Terrace, Suite 207, Miami FL 33166, (305) 718-9929, Fax: (305) 718-9663, www.lrfairplay.com; *Register of Ships 2007-2008; World Casualty Statistics 2007; World Fleet Statistics 2006; World Marine Propulsion Report 2006-2010; World Shipbuilding Statistics 2007;* and The World Shipping Encyclopaedia.

National Bureau of Statistics of China (NBS), No. 57, Yuetan Nanjie, Sanlihe, Xicheng District, Beijing 100826, China, www.stats.gov.cn/english; *China Statistical Yearbook 2007*.

Palgrave Macmillan Ltd., Houndmills, Basingstoke, Hampshire, RG21 6XS, England, (Telephone in U.S. (888) 330-8477), (Fax in U.S. (800) 672-2054), www.palgrave.com; *The Statesman's Yearbook 2008*.

Taylor and Francis Group, An Informa Business, 2 Park Square, Milton Park, Abingdon, Oxford OX14 4RN, United Kingdom, (Dial from U.S. (212) 216-7800), (Fax from U.S. (212) 564-7854), www.tandf.co.uk; *The Europa World Year Book*.

U.S. Department of Transportation (DOT), Maritime Administration (MARAD), West Building, Southeast Federal Center, 1200 New Jersey Avenue, SE, Washington, DC 20590, (800) 99-MARAD, www.marad.dot.gov; *World Merchant Fleet 2005*.

United Nations Statistics Division, New York, NY 10017, (800) 253-9646, Fax: (212) 963-4116, http://unstats.un.org; *Statistical Yearbook*.

CHINA - SILVER PRODUCTION

See CHINA - MINERAL INDUSTRIES

CHINA - SOCIAL ECOLOGY

Academic International Press, PO Box 1111, Gulf Breeze, FL 32562-1111, Fax: (850) 934-0953, www.ai-press.com; *China Facts and Figures Annual*.

Asian Development Bank (ADB), PO Box 789, 0980 Manila, Philippines, www.adb.org; *Key Indicators of Developing Asian and Pacific Countries 2006*.

Japan Center for Economic Research (JCER), Nikkei Kayabacho Building, Nihombashi Kayabacho, 2-6-1, Chuo-ku, Tokyo 103-0025, Japan, www.jcer.or.jp/eng; *China Research Report*.

National Bureau of Statistics of China (NBS), No. 57, Yuetan Nanjie, Sanlihe, Xicheng District, Beijing 100826, China, www.stats.gov.cn/english; *China Statistical Yearbook 2007*.

United Nations Statistics Division, New York, NY 10017, (800) 253-9646, Fax: (212) 963-4116, http://unstats.un.org; *World Statistics Pocketbook*.

CHINA - SOCIAL SECURITY

Palgrave Macmillan Ltd., Houndmills, Basingstoke, Hampshire, RG21 6XS, England, (Telephone in U.S. (888) 330-8477), (Fax in U.S. (800) 672-2054), www.palgrave.com; *The Statesman's Yearbook 2008*.

United Nations Statistics Division, New York, NY 10017, (800) 253-9646, Fax: (212) 963-4116, http://unstats.un.org; *National Accounts Statistics: Compendium of Income Distribution Statistics*.

CHINA - SOYBEAN PRODUCTION

See CHINA - CROPS

CHINA - STEEL PRODUCTION

See CHINA - MINERAL INDUSTRIES

CHINA - SUGAR PRODUCTION

See CHINA - CROPS

CHINA - SULPHUR PRODUCTION

See CHINA - MINERAL INDUSTRIES

CHINA - TAXATION

Economist Intelligence Unit, 111 West 57th Street, New York, NY 10019, (212) 554-0600, Fax: (212) 586-1181, www.eiu.com; *Business China*.

Palgrave Macmillan Ltd., Houndmills, Basingstoke, Hampshire, RG21 6XS, England, (Telephone in U.S. (888) 330-8477), (Fax in U.S. (800) 672-2054), www.palgrave.com; *The Statesman's Yearbook 2008*.

Taylor and Francis Group, An Informa Business, 2 Park Square, Milton Park, Abingdon, Oxford OX14 4RN, United Kingdom, (Dial from U.S. (212) 216-7800), (Fax from U.S. (212) 564-7854), www.tandf.co.uk; *The Europa World Year Book*.

The World Bank, 1818 H Street, NW, Washington, DC 20433, (202) 473-1000, Fax: (202) 477-6391, www.worldbank.org; *World Development Indicators (WDI) 2008*.

CHINA - TEA PRODUCTION

See CHINA - CROPS

CHINA - TELEPHONE

Economist Intelligence Unit, 111 West 57th Street, New York, NY 10019, (212) 554-0600, Fax: (212) 586-1181, www.eiu.com; *Business Asia* and *Business China*.

International Telecommunication Union (ITU), Place des Nations, 1211 Geneva 20, Switzerland, www.itu.int; World Telecommunication Indicators Database.

Palgrave Macmillan Ltd., Houndmills, Basingstoke, Hampshire, RG21 6XS, England, (Telephone in U.S. (888) 330-8477), (Fax in U.S. (800) 672-2054), www.palgrave.com; *The Statesman's Yearbook 2008*.

United Nations Statistics Division, New York, NY 10017, (800) 253-9646, Fax: (212) 963-4116, http://unstats.un.org; *World Statistics Pocketbook*.

CHINA - TEXTILE INDUSTRY

Academic International Press, PO Box 1111, Gulf Breeze, FL 32562-1111, Fax: (850) 934-0953, www.ai-press.com; *China Facts and Figures Annual*.

Economist Intelligence Unit, 111 West 57th Street, New York, NY 10019, (212) 554-0600, Fax: (212) 586-1181, www.eiu.com; *Business China*.

Euromonitor International, Inc., 224 S. Michigan Avenue, Suite 1500, Chicago, IL 60604, (312) 922-1115, Fax: (312) 922-1157, www.euromonitor.com; *Retail Trade International 2007.*

Japan Center for Economic Research (JCER), Nikkei Kayabacho Building, Nihombashi Kayabacho, 2-6-1, Chuo-ku, Tokyo 103-0025, Japan, www.jcer.or.jp/eng; *China Research Report.*

M.E. Sharpe, 80 Business Park Drive, Armonk, NY 10504, (800) 541-6563, Fax: (914) 273-2106, www.mesharpe.com; *The Illustrated Book of World Rankings.*

National Bureau of Statistics of China (NBS), No. 57, Yuetan Nanjie, Sanlihe, Xicheng District, Beijing 100826, China, www.stats.gov.cn/english; *China Statistical Yearbook 2007* and *Monthly Statistical Data.*

Palgrave Macmillan Ltd., Houndmills, Basingstoke, Hampshire, RG21 6XS, England, (Telephone in U.S. (888) 330-8477), (Fax in U.S. (800) 672-2054), www.palgrave.com; *The Statesman's Yearbook 2008.*

United Nations Conference on Trade and Development (UNCTAD), DC2-1120, United Nations, New York, NY 10017, (212) 963-0027, www.unctad.org; *UNCTAD Commodity Yearbook.*

United Nations Food and Agricultural Organization (FAO), Viale delle Terme di Caracalla, 00100 Rome, Italy, (Dial from U.S. (202) 653-2400), (Fax from U.S. (202) 653 5760), www.fao.org; *FAO Production Yearbook 2002.*

United Nations Statistics Division, New York, NY 10017, (800) 253-9646, Fax: (212) 963-4116, http://unstats.un.org; *Statistical Yearbook.*

CHINA - TOBACCO INDUSTRY

Academic International Press, PO Box 1111, Gulf Breeze, FL 32562-1111, Fax: (850) 934-0953, www.ai-press.com; *China Facts and Figures Annual.*

Economist Intelligence Unit, 111 West 57th Street, New York, NY 10019, (212) 554-0600, Fax: (212) 586-1181, www.eiu.com; *Business China.*

Foreign Agricultural Service (FAS), U.S. Department of Agriculture (USDA), 1400 Independence Avenue, SW, Washington, DC 20250, (202) 720-3935, www.fas.usda.gov; *Tobacco: World Markets and Trade.*

Japan Center for Economic Research (JCER), Nikkei Kayabacho Building, Nihombashi Kayabacho, 2-6-1, Chuo-ku, Tokyo 103-0025, Japan, www.jcer.or.jp/eng; *China Research Report.*

M.E. Sharpe, 80 Business Park Drive, Armonk, NY 10504, (800) 541-6563, Fax: (914) 273-2106, www.mesharpe.com; *The Illustrated Book of World Rankings.*

National Bureau of Statistics of China (NBS), No. 57, Yuetan Nanjie, Sanlihe, Xicheng District, Beijing 100826, China, www.stats.gov.cn/english; *China Statistical Yearbook 2007* and *Monthly Statistical Data.*

United Nations Statistics Division, New York, NY 10017, (800) 253-9646, Fax: (212) 963-4116, http://unstats.un.org; *Statistical Yearbook.*

CHINA - TOURISM

Academic International Press, PO Box 1111, Gulf Breeze, FL 32562-1111, Fax: (850) 934-0953, www.ai-press.com; *China Facts and Figures Annual.*

Economist Intelligence Unit, 111 West 57th Street, New York, NY 10019, (212) 554-0600, Fax: (212) 586-1181, www.eiu.com; *Business China.*

Euromonitor International, Inc., 224 S. Michigan Avenue, Suite 1500, Chicago, IL 60604, (312) 922-1115, Fax: (312) 922-1157, www.euromonitor.com; *The World Economic Factbook 2008* and *World Marketing Data and Statistics.*

Japan Center for Economic Research (JCER), Nikkei Kayabacho Building, Nihombashi Kayabacho, 2-6-1, Chuo-ku, Tokyo 103-0025, Japan, www.jcer.or.jp/eng; *China Research Report.*

M.E. Sharpe, 80 Business Park Drive, Armonk, NY 10504, (800) 541-6563, Fax: (914) 273-2106, www.mesharpe.com; *The Illustrated Book of World Rankings.*

National Bureau of Statistics of China (NBS), No. 57, Yuetan Nanjie, Sanlihe, Xicheng District, Beijing 100826, China, www.stats.gov.cn/english; *China Statistical Yearbook 2007; Monthly Statistical Data;* and *Tourism.*

Palgrave Macmillan Ltd., Houndmills, Basingstoke, Hampshire, RG21 6XS, England, (Telephone in U.S. (888) 330-8477), (Fax in U.S. (800) 672-2054), www.palgrave.com; *The Statesman's Yearbook 2008.*

Taylor and Francis Group, An Informa Business, 2 Park Square, Milton Park, Abingdon, Oxford OX14 4RN, United Kingdom, (Dial from U.S. (212) 216-7800), (Fax from U.S. (212) 564-7854), www.tandf.co.uk; *The Europa World Year Book.*

United Nations World Tourism Organization (UNWTO), Capitan Haya 42, 28020 Madrid, Spain, www.world-tourism.org; *Yearbook of Tourism Statistics.*

CHINA - TRADE

See CHINA - INTERNATIONAL TRADE

CHINA - TRANSPORTATION

Academic International Press, PO Box 1111, Gulf Breeze, FL 32562-1111, Fax: (850) 934-0953, www.ai-press.com; *China Facts and Figures Annual.*

Central Intelligence Agency, Office of Public Affairs, Washington, DC 20505, (703) 482-0623, Fax: (703) 482-1739, www.cia.gov; *The World Factbook.*

Economist Intelligence Unit, 111 West 57th Street, New York, NY 10019, (212) 554-0600, Fax: (212) 586-1181, www.eiu.com; *Business Asia* and *Business China.*

Euromonitor International, Inc., 224 S. Michigan Avenue, Suite 1500, Chicago, IL 60604, (312) 922-1115, Fax: (312) 922-1157, www.euromonitor.com; *International Marketing Data and Statistics 2008* and *World Marketing Data and Statistics.*

Japan Center for Economic Research (JCER), Nikkei Kayabacho Building, Nihombashi Kayabacho, 2-6-1, Chuo-ku, Tokyo 103-0025, Japan, www.jcer.or.jp/eng; *China Research Report.*

M.E. Sharpe, 80 Business Park Drive, Armonk, NY 10504, (800) 541-6563, Fax: (914) 273-2106, www.mesharpe.com; *The Illustrated Book of World Rankings.*

National Bureau of Statistics of China (NBS), No. 57, Yuetan Nanjie, Sanlihe, Xicheng District, Beijing 100826, China, www.stats.gov.cn/english; *China Statistical Yearbook 2007* and *Monthly Statistical Data.*

Palgrave Macmillan Ltd., Houndmills, Basingstoke, Hampshire, RG21 6XS, England, (Telephone in U.S. (888) 330-8477), (Fax in U.S. (800) 672-2054), www.palgrave.com; *The Statesman's Yearbook 2008.*

Taylor and Francis Group, An Informa Business, 2 Park Square, Milton Park, Abingdon, Oxford OX14 4RN, United Kingdom, (Dial from U.S. (212) 216-7800), (Fax from U.S. (212) 564-7854), www.tandf.co.uk; *The Europa World Year Book.*

United Nations Statistics Division, New York, NY 10017, (800) 253-9646, Fax: (212) 963-4116, http://unstats.un.org; *Human Development Report 2006* and *Statistical Yearbook for Asia and the Pacific 2004.*

CHINA - TURKEYS

See CHINA - LIVESTOCK

CHINA - UNEMPLOYMENT

Academic International Press, PO Box 1111, Gulf Breeze, FL 32562-1111, Fax: (850) 934-0953, www.ai-press.com; *China Facts and Figures Annual.*

Central Intelligence Agency, Office of Public Affairs, Washington, DC 20505, (703) 482-0623, Fax: (703) 482-1739, www.cia.gov; *The World Factbook.*

Euromonitor International, Inc., 224 S. Michigan Avenue, Suite 1500, Chicago, IL 60604, (312) 922-1115, Fax: (312) 922-1157, www.euromonitor.com; *International Marketing Data and Statistics 2008.*

Japan Center for Economic Research (JCER), Nikkei Kayabacho Building, Nihombashi Kayabacho, 2-6-1, Chuo-ku, Tokyo 103-0025, Japan, www.jcer.or.jp/eng; *China Research Report.*

National Bureau of Statistics of China (NBS), No. 57, Yuetan Nanjie, Sanlihe, Xicheng District, Beijing 100826, China, www.stats.gov.cn/english; *China Statistical Yearbook 2007.*

Palgrave Macmillan Ltd., Houndmills, Basingstoke, Hampshire, RG21 6XS, England, (Telephone in U.S. (888) 330-8477), (Fax in U.S. (800) 672-2054), www.palgrave.com; *The Statesman's Yearbook 2008.*

CHINA - VITAL STATISTICS

Academic International Press, PO Box 1111, Gulf Breeze, FL 32562-1111, Fax: (850) 934-0953, www.ai-press.com; *China Facts and Figures Annual.*

Euromonitor International, Inc., 224 S. Michigan Avenue, Suite 1500, Chicago, IL 60604, (312) 922-1115, Fax: (312) 922-1157, www.euromonitor.com; *International Marketing Data and Statistics 2008.*

International Organization for Migration (IOM), 17, Route des Morillons, CH-1211 Geneva 19, Switzerland, www.iom.int; *Domestic Migrant Remittances in China: Distribution, Channels and Livelihoods* and *Migration and Poverty Alleviation in China.*

Japan Center for Economic Research (JCER), Nikkei Kayabacho Building, Nihombashi Kayabacho, 2-6-1, Chuo-ku, Tokyo 103-0025, Japan, www.jcer.or.jp/eng; *China Research Report.*

National Bureau of Statistics of China (NBS), No. 57, Yuetan Nanjie, Sanlihe, Xicheng District, Beijing 100826, China, www.stats.gov.cn/english; *China Statistical Yearbook 2007; Monthly Statistical Data;* and *Women and Men in China: Facts and Figures.*

Palgrave Macmillan Ltd., Houndmills, Basingstoke, Hampshire, RG21 6XS, England, (Telephone in U.S. (888) 330-8477), (Fax in U.S. (800) 672-2054), www.palgrave.com; *The Statesman's Yearbook 2008.*

United Nations Statistics Division, New York, NY 10017, (800) 253-9646, Fax: (212) 963-4116, http://unstats.un.org; *Statistical Yearbook.*

World Health Organization (WHO), Avenue Appia 20, 1211 Geneve 27, Switzerland, (Telephone in U.S. (212) 331-9081), www.who.int; *World Health Report 2006.*

CHINA - WAGES

Academic International Press, PO Box 1111, Gulf Breeze, FL 32562-1111, Fax: (850) 934-0953, www.ai-press.com; *China Facts and Figures Annual.*

Economist Intelligence Unit, 111 West 57th Street, New York, NY 10019, (212) 554-0600, Fax: (212) 586-1181, www.eiu.com; *Business China.*

Japan Center for Economic Research (JCER), Nikkei Kayabacho Building, Nihombashi Kayabacho, 2-6-1, Chuo-ku, Tokyo 103-0025, Japan, www.jcer.or.jp/eng; *China Research Report.*

National Bureau of Statistics of China (NBS), No. 57, Yuetan Nanjie, Sanlihe, Xicheng District, Beijing 100826, China, www.stats.gov.cn/english; *China Statistical Yearbook 2007* and *Monthly Statistical Data.*

United Nations Statistics Division, New York, NY 10017, (800) 253-9646, Fax: (212) 963-4116, http://unstats.un.org; *Statistical Yearbook for Asia and the Pacific 2004.*

CHINA - WALNUT PRODUCTION

See CHINA - CROPS

CHINA - WEATHER

See CHINA - CLIMATE

CHINA - WELFARE STATE

Palgrave Macmillan Ltd., Houndmills, Basingstoke, Hampshire, RG21 6XS, England, (Telephone in U.S.

(888) 330-8477), (Fax in U.S. (800) 672-2054), www.palgrave.com; *The Statesman's Yearbook 2008.*

CHINA - WHEAT PRODUCTION

See CHINA - CROPS

CHINA - WHOLESALE PRICE INDEXES

Asian Development Bank (ADB), PO Box 789, 0980 Manila, Philippines, www.adb.org; *Key Indicators of Developing Asian and Pacific Countries 2006.*

International Monetary Fund (IMF), 700 Nineteenth Street, NW, Washington, DC 20431, (202) 623-7000, Fax: (202) 623-4661, www.imf.org; *Government Finance Statistics Yearbook (2008 Edition).*

National Bureau of Statistics of China (NBS), No. 57, Yuetan Nanjie, Sanlihe, Xicheng District, Beijing 100826, China, www.stats.gov.cn/english; *Monthly Statistical Data.*

CHINA - WHOLESALE TRADE

National Bureau of Statistics of China (NBS), No. 57, Yuetan Nanjie, Sanlihe, Xicheng District, Beijing 100826, China, www.stats.gov.cn/english; *Monthly Statistical Data.*

CHINA - WINE PRODUCTION

See CHINA - BEVERAGE INDUSTRY

CHINA - WOOD AND WOOD PULP

See CHINA - FORESTS AND FORESTRY

CHINA - WOOL PRODUCTION

See CHINA - TEXTILE INDUSTRY

CHINA - YARN PRODUCTION

See CHINA - TEXTILE INDUSTRY

CHINA - ZINC AND ZINC ORE

See CHINA - MINERAL INDUSTRIES

CHINA, REPUBLIC OF (TAIWAN)

See TAIWAN

CHINESE POPULATION

U.S. Census Bureau, Demographic Surveys Division, 4700 Silver Hill Road, Washington DC 20233-0001, (301) 763-3030, www.census.gov; *Census 2000: Demographic Profiles.*

CHIROPRACTOR'S OFFICES

U.S. Census Bureau, 4700 Silver Hill Road, Washington DC 20233-0001, (301) 763-3030, www.census.gov; *2002 Economic Census, Nonemployer Statistics.*

U.S. Census Bureau, Service Sector Statistics Division, 4700 Silver Hill Road, Washington DC 20233-0001, (301) 763-3030, www.census.gov/svsd/www/economic.html; *2004 Service Annual Survey: Health Care and Social Assistance.*

CHLOROFLUROCARBON GASES

U.S. Department of Energy (DOE), Energy Information Administration (EIA), 1000 Independence Avenue, SW, Washington, DC 20585, (202) 586-8800, www.eia.doe.gov; *Emissions of Greenhouse Gases in the United States 2005.*

CHLOROFLUROCARBONS (CFCs)

U.S. Department of Energy (DOE), Energy Information Administration (EIA), 1000 Independence Avenue, SW, Washington, DC 20585, (202) 586-8800, www.eia.doe.gov; *Emissions of Greenhouse Gases in the United States 2005.*

CHOCOLATE

See COCOA

CHOLELITHIASIS - DEATHS

Bernan Essential Government Publications, 4611-F Assembly Drive, Lanham MD, 20706-4391, (301) 459-2255, Fax: (800) 865-3450, www.bernan.com; *Vital Statistics of the United States: Births, Life Expectancy, Deaths, and Selected Health Data.*

National Center for Health Statistics (NCHS), Centers for Disease Control and Prevention (CDC), U.S. Department of Health and Human Services (HHS), 3311 Toledo Road, Hyattsville, MD 20782, (866) 232-4636, www.cdc.gov/nchs; *National Vital Statistics Reports (NVSR)* and *Vital Statistics of the United States (VSUS).*

CHOLERA

Centers for Disease Control and Prevention (CDC), U.S. Department of Health and Human Services (HHS), 1600 Clifton Road, Atlanta, GA 30333, (800) 311-3435, www.cdc.gov; *Morbidity and Mortality Weekly Report (MMWR)* and *Summary of Notifiable Diseases, United States, 2006.*

CHOLESTEROL

Center for Nutrition Policy and Promotion (CNPP), U.S. Department of Agriculture (USDA), 3101 Park Center Drive, 10th Floor, Alexandria, VA 22302-1594, (703) 305-7600, Fax: (703) 305-3300, www.usda.gov/cnpp; *Nutrient Content of the U.S. Food Supply Summary Report 2005.*

National Center for Health Statistics (NCHS), Centers for Disease Control and Prevention (CDC), U.S. Department of Health and Human Services (HHS), 3311 Toledo Road, Hyattsville, MD 20782, (866) 232-4636, www.cdc.gov/nchs; *Faststats A to Z.*

CHRISTIAN POPULATION

See RELIGION

CHRISTMAS ISLAND - AGRICULTURE

United Nations Conference on Trade and Development (UNCTAD), DC2-1120, United Nations, New York, NY 10017, (212) 963-0027, www.unctad.org; *UNCTAD Commodity Yearbook.*

United Nations Food and Agricultural Organization (FAO), Viale delle Terme di Caracalla, 00100 Rome, Italy, (Dial from U.S. (202) 653-2400), (Fax from U.S. (202) 653 5760), www.fao.org; AQUASTAT; *FAO Production Yearbook 2002; FAO Trade Yearbook;* and *The State of Food and Agriculture (SOFA) 2006.*

CHRISTMAS ISLAND - AIRLINES

Palgrave Macmillan Ltd., Houndmills, Basingstoke, Hampshire, RG21 6XS, England, (Telephone in U.S. (888) 330-8477), (Fax in U.S. (800) 672-2054), www.palgrave.com; *The Statesman's Yearbook 2008.*

CHRISTMAS ISLAND - AIRPORTS

Central Intelligence Agency, Office of Public Affairs, Washington, DC 20505, (703) 482-0623, Fax: (703) 482-1739, www.cia.gov; *The World Factbook.*

CHRISTMAS ISLAND - ARMED FORCES

Central Intelligence Agency, Office of Public Affairs, Washington, DC 20505, (703) 482-0623, Fax: (703) 482-1739, www.cia.gov; *The World Factbook.*

CHRISTMAS ISLAND - BROADCASTING

Central Intelligence Agency, Office of Public Affairs, Washington, DC 20505, (703) 482-0623, Fax: (703) 482-1739, www.cia.gov; *The World Factbook.*

WRTH Publications Limited, PO Box 290, Oxford OX2 7FT, UK, www.wrth.com; *World Radio TV Handbook 2007.*

CHRISTMAS ISLAND - BUDGET

Central Intelligence Agency, Office of Public Affairs, Washington, DC 20505, (703) 482-0623, Fax: (703) 482-1739, www.cia.gov; *The World Factbook.*

CHRISTMAS ISLAND - CHILDBIRTH - STATISTICS

Central Intelligence Agency, Office of Public Affairs, Washington, DC 20505, (703) 482-0623, Fax: (703) 482-1739, www.cia.gov; *The World Factbook.*

Taylor and Francis Group, An Informa Business, 2 Park Square, Milton Park, Abingdon, Oxford OX14 4RN, United Kingdom, (Dial from U.S. (212) 216-7800), (Fax from U.S. (212) 564-7854), www.tandf.co.uk; *The Europa World Year Book.*

United Nations Statistics Division, New York, NY 10017, (800) 253-9646, Fax: (212) 963-4116, http://unstats.un.org; *Demographic Yearbook* and *Statistical Yearbook.*

World Health Organization (WHO), Avenue Appia 20, 1211 Geneve 27, Switzerland, (Telephone in U.S. (212) 331-9081), www.who.int; *World Health Report 2006.*

CHRISTMAS ISLAND - CLIMATE

Palgrave Macmillan Ltd., Houndmills, Basingstoke, Hampshire, RG21 6XS, England, (Telephone in U.S. (888) 330-8477), (Fax in U.S. (800) 672-2054), www.palgrave.com; *The Statesman's Yearbook 2008.*

CHRISTMAS ISLAND - COMMODITY EXCHANGES

United Nations Food and Agricultural Organization (FAO), Viale delle Terme di Caracalla, 00100 Rome, Italy, (Dial from U.S. (202) 653-2400), (Fax from U.S. (202) 653 5760), www.fao.org; *The State of Food and Agriculture (SOFA) 2006.*

CHRISTMAS ISLAND - CORN INDUSTRY

See CHRISTMAS ISLAND - CROPS

CHRISTMAS ISLAND - CROPS

United Nations Conference on Trade and Development (UNCTAD), DC2-1120, United Nations, New York, NY 10017, (212) 963-0027, www.unctad.org; *UNCTAD Commodity Yearbook.*

United Nations Food and Agricultural Organization (FAO), Viale delle Terme di Caracalla, 00100 Rome, Italy, (Dial from U.S. (202) 653-2400), (Fax from U.S. (202) 653 5760), www.fao.org; *The State of Food and Agriculture (SOFA) 2006.*

CHRISTMAS ISLAND - DAIRY PROCESSING

United Nations Food and Agricultural Organization (FAO), Viale delle Terme di Caracalla, 00100 Rome, Italy, (Dial from U.S. (202) 653-2400), (Fax from U.S. (202) 653 5760), www.fao.org; *The State of Food and Agriculture (SOFA) 2006.*

CHRISTMAS ISLAND - DEATH RATES

See CHRISTMAS ISLAND - MORTALITY

CHRISTMAS ISLAND - DIVORCE

United Nations Statistics Division, New York, NY 10017, (800) 253-9646, Fax: (212) 963-4116, http://unstats.un.org; *Statistical Yearbook.*

CHRISTMAS ISLAND - ECONOMIC CONDITIONS

Central Intelligence Agency, Office of Public Affairs, Washington, DC 20505, (703) 482-0623, Fax: (703) 482-1739, www.cia.gov; *The World Factbook.*

CHRISTMAS ISLAND - EDUCATION

Palgrave Macmillan Ltd., Houndmills, Basingstoke, Hampshire, RG21 6XS, England, (Telephone in U.S. (888) 330-8477), (Fax in U.S. (800) 672-2054), www.palgrave.com; *The Statesman's Yearbook 2008.*

CHRISTMAS ISLAND - ELECTRICITY

Palgrave Macmillan Ltd., Houndmills, Basingstoke, Hampshire, RG21 6XS, England, (Telephone in U.S. (888) 330-8477), (Fax in U.S. (800) 672-2054), www.palgrave.com; *The Statesman's Yearbook 2008.*

CHRISTMAS ISLAND - EXPORTS

Central Intelligence Agency, Office of Public Affairs, Washington, DC 20505, (703) 482-0623, Fax: (703) 482-1739, www.cia.gov; *The World Factbook.*

Palgrave Macmillan Ltd., Houndmills, Basingstoke, Hampshire, RG21 6XS, England, (Telephone in U.S. (888) 330-8477), (Fax in U.S. (800) 672-2054), www.palgrave.com; *The Statesman's Yearbook 2008.*

Taylor and Francis Group, An Informa Business, 2 Park Square, Milton Park, Abingdon, Oxford OX14 4RN, United Kingdom, (Dial from U.S. (212) 216-7800), (Fax from U.S. (212) 564-7854), www.tandf.co.uk; *The Europa World Year Book.*

United Nations Food and Agricultural Organization (FAO), Viale delle Terme di Caracalla, 00100 Rome, Italy, (Dial from U.S. (202) 653-2400), (Fax from U.S. (202) 653 5760), www.fao.org; *The State of Food and Agriculture (SOFA) 2006.*

CHRISTMAS ISLAND - FERTILITY, HUMAN

Central Intelligence Agency, Office of Public Affairs, Washington, DC 20505, (703) 482-0623, Fax: (703) 482-1739, www.cia.gov; *The World Factbook.*

CHRISTMAS ISLAND - FERTILIZER INDUSTRY

United Nations Food and Agricultural Organization (FAO), Viale delle Terme di Caracalla, 00100 Rome, Italy, (Dial from U.S. (202) 653-2400), (Fax from U.S. (202) 653 5760), www.fao.org; *The State of Food and Agriculture (SOFA) 2006.*

CHRISTMAS ISLAND - FETAL MORTALITY

See CHRISTMAS ISLAND - MORTALITY

CHRISTMAS ISLAND - FINANCE, PUBLIC

Taylor and Francis Group, An Informa Business, 2 Park Square, Milton Park, Abingdon, Oxford OX14 4RN, United Kingdom, (Dial from U.S. (212) 216-7800), (Fax from U.S. (212) 564-7854), www.tandf.co.uk; *The Europa World Year Book.*

CHRISTMAS ISLAND - FISHERIES

United Nations Conference on Trade and Development (UNCTAD), DC2-1120, United Nations, New York, NY 10017, (212) 963-0027, www.unctad.org; *UNCTAD Commodity Yearbook.*

United Nations Food and Agricultural Organization (FAO), Viale delle Terme di Caracalla, 00100 Rome, Italy, (Dial from U.S. (202) 653-2400), (Fax from U.S. (202) 653 5760), www.fao.org; *FAO Yearbook of Fishery Statistics;* Fishery Databases; FISHSTAT Database. Subjects covered include: Aquaculture production, capture production, fishery commodities; and *The State of Food and Agriculture (SOFA) 2006.*

CHRISTMAS ISLAND - FOOD

United Nations Conference on Trade and Development (UNCTAD), DC2-1120, United Nations, New York, NY 10017, (212) 963-0027, www.unctad.org; *UNCTAD Commodity Yearbook.*

United Nations Food and Agricultural Organization (FAO), Viale delle Terme di Caracalla, 00100 Rome, Italy, (Dial from U.S. (202) 653-2400), (Fax from U.S. (202) 653 5760), www.fao.org; *FAO Production Yearbook 2002* and *The State of Food and Agriculture (SOFA) 2006.*

CHRISTMAS ISLAND - FOREIGN EXCHANGE RATES

Central Intelligence Agency, Office of Public Affairs, Washington, DC 20505, (703) 482-0623, Fax: (703) 482-1739, www.cia.gov; *The World Factbook.*

Taylor and Francis Group, An Informa Business, 2 Park Square, Milton Park, Abingdon, Oxford OX14 4RN, United Kingdom, (Dial from U.S. (212) 216-7800), (Fax from U.S. (212) 564-7854), www.tandf.co.uk; *The Europa World Year Book.*

CHRISTMAS ISLAND - FORESTS AND FORESTRY

United Nations Conference on Trade and Development (UNCTAD), DC2-1120, United Nations, New York, NY 10017, (212) 963-0027, www.unctad.org; *UNCTAD Commodity Yearbook.*

United Nations Food and Agricultural Organization (FAO), Viale delle Terme di Caracalla, 00100 Rome, Italy, (Dial from U.S. (202) 653-2400), (Fax from U.S. (202) 653 5760), www.fao.org; *The State of Food and Agriculture (SOFA) 2006.*

CHRISTMAS ISLAND - IMPORTS

Central Intelligence Agency, Office of Public Affairs, Washington, DC 20505, (703) 482-0623, Fax: (703) 482-1739, www.cia.gov; *The World Factbook.*

Taylor and Francis Group, An Informa Business, 2 Park Square, Milton Park, Abingdon, Oxford OX14 4RN, United Kingdom, (Dial from U.S. (212) 216-7800), (Fax from U.S. (212) 564-7854), www.tandf.co.uk; *The Europa World Year Book.*

United Nations Food and Agricultural Organization (FAO), Viale delle Terme di Caracalla, 00100 Rome, Italy, (Dial from U.S. (202) 653-2400), (Fax from U.S. (202) 653 5760), www.fao.org; *The State of Food and Agriculture (SOFA) 2006.*

CHRISTMAS ISLAND - INDUSTRIES

Central Intelligence Agency, Office of Public Affairs, Washington, DC 20505, (703) 482-0623, Fax: (703) 482-1739, www.cia.gov; *The World Factbook.*

Palgrave Macmillan Ltd., Houndmills, Basingstoke, Hampshire, RG21 6XS, England, (Telephone in U.S. (888) 330-8477), (Fax in U.S. (800) 672-2054), www.palgrave.com; *The Statesman's Yearbook 2008.*

CHRISTMAS ISLAND - INTERNATIONAL TRADE

Organisation for Economic Cooperation and Development (OECD), 2 rue Andre Pascal, F-75775 Paris Cedex 16, France, (Telephone in U.S. (202) 785-6323), (Fax in U.S. (202) 785-0350), www.oecd.org; *International Trade by Commodity Statistics (ITCS).*

Taylor and Francis Group, An Informa Business, 2 Park Square, Milton Park, Abingdon, Oxford OX14 4RN, United Kingdom, (Dial from U.S. (212) 216-7800), (Fax from U.S. (212) 564-7854), www.tandf.co.uk; *The Europa World Year Book.*

United Nations Conference on Trade and Development (UNCTAD), DC2-1120, United Nations, New York, NY 10017, (212) 963-0027, www.unctad.org; *UNCTAD Commodity Yearbook.*

United Nations Food and Agricultural Organization (FAO), Viale delle Terme di Caracalla, 00100 Rome, Italy, (Dial from U.S. (202) 653-2400), (Fax from U.S. (202) 653 5760), www.fao.org; *FAO Trade Yearbook* and *The State of Food and Agriculture (SOFA) 2006.*

World Trade Organization (WTO), Centre William Rappard, Rue de Lausanne 154, CH-1211 Geneva 21, Switzerland, www.wto.org; *International Trade Statistics 2006.*

CHRISTMAS ISLAND - LABOR

Central Intelligence Agency, Office of Public Affairs, Washington, DC 20505, (703) 482-0623, Fax: (703) 482-1739, www.cia.gov; *The World Factbook.*

United Nations Food and Agricultural Organization (FAO), Viale delle Terme di Caracalla, 00100 Rome, Italy, (Dial from U.S. (202) 653-2400), (Fax from U.S. (202) 653 5760), www.fao.org; *The State of Food and Agriculture (SOFA) 2006.*

CHRISTMAS ISLAND - LAND USE

Central Intelligence Agency, Office of Public Affairs, Washington, DC 20505, (703) 482-0623, Fax: (703) 482-1739, www.cia.gov; *The World Factbook.*

United Nations Food and Agricultural Organization (FAO), Viale delle Terme di Caracalla, 00100 Rome, Italy, (Dial from U.S. (202) 653-2400), (Fax from U.S. (202) 653 5760), www.fao.org; *FAO Production Yearbook 2002.*

CHRISTMAS ISLAND - LIFE EXPECTANCY

Central Intelligence Agency, Office of Public Affairs, Washington, DC 20505, (703) 482-0623, Fax: (703) 482-1739, www.cia.gov; *The World Factbook.*

CHRISTMAS ISLAND - LIVESTOCK

United Nations Conference on Trade and Development (UNCTAD), DC2-1120, United Nations, New York, NY 10017, (212) 963-0027, www.unctad.org; *UNCTAD Commodity Yearbook.*

United Nations Food and Agricultural Organization (FAO), Viale delle Terme di Caracalla, 00100 Rome, Italy, (Dial from U.S. (202) 653-2400), (Fax from U.S. (202) 653 5760), www.fao.org; *FAO Production Yearbook 2002* and *The State of Food and Agriculture (SOFA) 2006.*

CHRISTMAS ISLAND - MARRIAGE

United Nations Statistics Division, New York, NY 10017, (800) 253-9646, Fax: (212) 963-4116, http://unstats.un.org; *Demographic Yearbook* and *Statistical Yearbook.*

CHRISTMAS ISLAND - MEAT PRODUCTION

See CHRISTMAS ISLAND - LIVESTOCK

CHRISTMAS ISLAND - MINERAL INDUSTRIES

Palgrave Macmillan Ltd., Houndmills, Basingstoke, Hampshire, RG21 6XS, England, (Telephone in U.S. (888) 330-8477), (Fax in U.S. (800) 672-2054), www.palgrave.com; *The Statesman's Yearbook 2008.*

Taylor and Francis Group, An Informa Business, 2 Park Square, Milton Park, Abingdon, Oxford OX14 4RN, United Kingdom, (Dial from U.S. (212) 216-7800), (Fax from U.S. (212) 564-7854), www.tandf.co.uk; *The Europa World Year Book.*

United Nations Conference on Trade and Development (UNCTAD), DC2-1120, United Nations, New York, NY 10017, (212) 963-0027, www.unctad.org; *UNCTAD Commodity Yearbook.*

CHRISTMAS ISLAND - MORTALITY

Central Intelligence Agency, Office of Public Affairs, Washington, DC 20505, (703) 482-0623, Fax: (703) 482-1739, www.cia.gov; *The World Factbook.*

Taylor and Francis Group, An Informa Business, 2 Park Square, Milton Park, Abingdon, Oxford OX14 4RN, United Kingdom, (Dial from U.S. (212) 216-7800), (Fax from U.S. (212) 564-7854), www.tandf.co.uk; *The Europa World Year Book.*

United Nations Statistics Division, New York, NY 10017, (800) 253-9646, Fax: (212) 963-4116, http://unstats.un.org; *Demographic Yearbook* and *Statistical Yearbook.*

World Health Organization (WHO), Avenue Appia 20, 1211 Geneve 27, Switzerland, (Telephone in U.S. (212) 331-9081), www.who.int; *World Health Report 2006.*

CHRISTMAS ISLAND - NUTRITION

United Nations Food and Agricultural Organization (FAO), Viale delle Terme di Caracalla, 00100 Rome, Italy, (Dial from U.S. (202) 653-2400), (Fax from U.S. (202) 653 5760), www.fao.org; *The State of Food and Agriculture (SOFA) 2006.*

CHRISTMAS ISLAND - PESTICIDES

United Nations Food and Agricultural Organization (FAO), Viale delle Terme di Caracalla, 00100 Rome, Italy, (Dial from U.S. (202) 653-2400), (Fax from U.S. (202) 653 5760), www.fao.org; *The State of Food and Agriculture (SOFA) 2006.*

CHRISTMAS ISLAND - PETROLEUM INDUSTRY AND TRADE

PennWell Corporation, 1421 South Sheridan Road, Tulsa, OK 74112, (918) 835-3161, www.pennwell.com; *International Petroleum Encyclopedia 2007.*

United Nations Conference on Trade and Development (UNCTAD), DC2-1120, United Nations, New York, NY 10017, (212) 963-0027, www.unctad.org; *UNCTAD Commodity Yearbook.*

United Nations Food and Agricultural Organization (FAO), Viale delle Terme di Caracalla, 00100 Rome, Italy, (Dial from U.S. (202) 653-2400), (Fax from U.S. (202) 653 5760), www.fao.org; *The State of Food and Agriculture (SOFA) 2006.*

CHRISTMAS ISLAND - POLITICAL SCIENCE

Central Intelligence Agency, Office of Public Affairs, Washington, DC 20505, (703) 482-0623, Fax: (703) 482-1739, www.cia.gov; *The World Factbook.*

Palgrave Macmillan Ltd., Houndmills, Basingstoke, Hampshire, RG21 6XS, England, (Telephone in U.S. (888) 330-8477), (Fax in U.S. (800) 672-2054), www.palgrave.com; *The Statesman's Yearbook 2008.*

CHRISTMAS ISLAND - POPULATION

Central Intelligence Agency, Office of Public Affairs, Washington, DC 20505, (703) 482-0623, Fax: (703) 482-1739, www.cia.gov; *The World Factbook.*

Palgrave Macmillan Ltd., Houndmills, Basingstoke, Hampshire, RG21 6XS, England, (Telephone in U.S. (888) 330-8477), (Fax in U.S. (800) 672-2054), www.palgrave.com; *The Statesman's Yearbook 2008.*

Taylor and Francis Group, An Informa Business, 2 Park Square, Milton Park, Abingdon, Oxford OX14 4RN, United Kingdom, (Dial from U.S. (212) 216-7800), (Fax from U.S. (212) 564-7854), www.tandf.co.uk; *The Europa World Year Book.*

UNESCO Institute for Statistics, C.P. 6128 Succursale Centre-Ville, Montreal, Quebec, H3C 3J7 Canada, (Dial from U.S. (514) 343-6880), (Fax from U.S. (514) 343 6882), www.uis.unesco.org; *Statistical Tables.*

United Nations Food and Agricultural Organization (FAO), Viale delle Terme di Caracalla, 00100 Rome, Italy, (Dial from U.S. (202) 653-2400), (Fax from U.S. (202) 653 5760), www.fao.org; *FAO Production Yearbook 2002.*

United Nations Statistics Division, New York, NY 10017, (800) 253-9646, Fax: (212) 963-4116, http://unstats.un.org; *Demographic Yearbook* and *Statistical Yearbook.*

World Health Organization (WHO), Avenue Appia 20, 1211 Geneve 27, Switzerland, (Telephone in U.S. (212) 331-9081), www.who.int; *World Health Report 2006.*

CHRISTMAS ISLAND - POPULATION DENSITY

Central Intelligence Agency, Office of Public Affairs, Washington, DC 20505, (703) 482-0623, Fax: (703) 482-1739, www.cia.gov; *The World Factbook.*

Taylor and Francis Group, An Informa Business, 2 Park Square, Milton Park, Abingdon, Oxford OX14 4RN, United Kingdom, (Dial from U.S. (212) 216-7800), (Fax from U.S. (212) 564-7854), www.tandf.co.uk; *The Europa World Year Book.*

UNESCO Institute for Statistics, C.P. 6128 Succursale Centre-Ville, Montreal, Quebec, H3C 3J7 Canada, (Dial from U.S. (514) 343-6880), (Fax from U.S. (514) 343 6882), www.uis.unesco.org; *Statistical Tables.*

United Nations Food and Agricultural Organization (FAO), Viale delle Terme di Caracalla, 00100 Rome, Italy, (Dial from U.S. (202) 653-2400), (Fax from U.S. (202) 653 5760), www.fao.org; *The State of Food and Agriculture (SOFA) 2006.*

United Nations Statistics Division, New York, NY 10017, (800) 253-9646, Fax: (212) 963-4116, http://unstats.un.org; *Statistical Yearbook.*

CHRISTMAS ISLAND - POWER RESOURCES

United Nations Food and Agricultural Organization (FAO), Viale delle Terme di Caracalla, 00100 Rome, Italy, (Dial from U.S. (202) 653-2400), (Fax from U.S. (202) 653 5760), www.fao.org; *The State of Food and Agriculture (SOFA) 2006.*

United Nations Statistics Division, New York, NY 10017, (800) 253-9646, Fax: (212) 963-4116, http://unstats.un.org; *Statistical Yearbook.*

CHRISTMAS ISLAND - PRICES

United Nations Food and Agricultural Organization (FAO), Viale delle Terme di Caracalla, 00100 Rome, Italy, (Dial from U.S. (202) 653-2400), (Fax from U.S. (202) 653 5760), www.fao.org; *FAO Production Yearbook 2002* and *The State of Food and Agriculture (SOFA) 2006.*

CHRISTMAS ISLAND - PUBLIC HEALTH

Palgrave Macmillan Ltd., Houndmills, Basingstoke, Hampshire, RG21 6XS, England, (Telephone in U.S. (888) 330-8477), (Fax in U.S. (800) 672-2054), www.palgrave.com; *The Statesman's Yearbook 2008.*

CHRISTMAS ISLAND - RADIO BROADCASTING

Palgrave Macmillan Ltd., Houndmills, Basingstoke, Hampshire, RG21 6XS, England, (Telephone in U.S. (888) 330-8477), (Fax in U.S. (800) 672-2054), www.palgrave.com; *The Statesman's Yearbook 2008.*

CHRISTMAS ISLAND - RELIGION

Central Intelligence Agency, Office of Public Affairs, Washington, DC 20505, (703) 482-0623, Fax: (703) 482-1739, www.cia.gov; *The World Factbook.*

Palgrave Macmillan Ltd., Houndmills, Basingstoke, Hampshire, RG21 6XS, England, (Telephone in U.S. (888) 330-8477), (Fax in U.S. (800) 672-2054), www.palgrave.com; *The Statesman's Yearbook 2008.*

CHRISTMAS ISLAND - ROADS

Central Intelligence Agency, Office of Public Affairs, Washington, DC 20505, (703) 482-0623, Fax: (703) 482-1739, www.cia.gov; *The World Factbook.*

Palgrave Macmillan Ltd., Houndmills, Basingstoke, Hampshire, RG21 6XS, England, (Telephone in U.S. (888) 330-8477), (Fax in U.S. (800) 672-2054), www.palgrave.com; *The Statesman's Yearbook 2008.*

CHRISTMAS ISLAND - SHIPPING

Taylor and Francis Group, An Informa Business, 2 Park Square, Milton Park, Abingdon, Oxford OX14 4RN, United Kingdom, (Dial from U.S. (212) 216-7800), (Fax from U.S. (212) 564-7854), www.tandf.co.uk; *The Europa World Year Book.*

United Nations Statistics Division, New York, NY 10017, (800) 253-9646, Fax: (212) 963-4116, http://unstats.un.org; *Statistical Yearbook.*

CHRISTMAS ISLAND - TELEPHONE

International Telecommunication Union (ITU), Place des Nations, 1211 Geneva 20, Switzerland, www.itu.int; World Telecommunication Indicators Database.

CHRISTMAS ISLAND - TEXTILE INDUSTRY

United Nations Conference on Trade and Development (UNCTAD), DC2-1120, United Nations, New York, NY 10017, (212) 963-0027, www.unctad.org; *UNCTAD Commodity Yearbook.*

CHRISTMAS ISLAND - TOURISM

Palgrave Macmillan Ltd., Houndmills, Basingstoke, Hampshire, RG21 6XS, England, (Telephone in U.S. (888) 330-8477), (Fax in U.S. (800) 672-2054), www.palgrave.com; *The Statesman's Yearbook 2008.*

CHRISTMAS ISLAND - TRADE

See CHRISTMAS ISLAND - INTERNATIONAL TRADE

CHRISTMAS ISLAND - TRANSPORTATION

Central Intelligence Agency, Office of Public Affairs, Washington, DC 20505, (703) 482-0623, Fax: (703) 482-1739, www.cia.gov; *The World Factbook.*

Palgrave Macmillan Ltd., Houndmills, Basingstoke, Hampshire, RG21 6XS, England, (Telephone in U.S. (888) 330-8477), (Fax in U.S. (800) 672-2054), www.palgrave.com; *The Statesman's Yearbook 2008.*

Taylor and Francis Group, An Informa Business, 2 Park Square, Milton Park, Abingdon, Oxford OX14 4RN, United Kingdom, (Dial from U.S. (212) 216-7800), (Fax from U.S. (212) 564-7854), www.tandf.co.uk; *The Europa World Year Book.*

CHRISTMAS ISLAND - UNEMPLOYMENT

Central Intelligence Agency, Office of Public Affairs, Washington, DC 20505, (703) 482-0623, Fax: (703) 482-1739, www.cia.gov; *The World Factbook.*

CHRISTMAS ISLAND - VITAL STATISTICS

United Nations Statistics Division, New York, NY 10017, (800) 253-9646, Fax: (212) 963-4116, http://unstats.un.org; *Statistical Yearbook.*

World Health Organization (WHO), Avenue Appia 20, 1211 Geneve 27, Switzerland, (Telephone in U.S. (212) 331-9081), www.who.int; *World Health Report 2006.*

CHROMITE

U.S. Department of the Interior (DOI), U.S. Geological Survey (USGS), Office of Minerals Information, 12201 Sunrise Valley Drive, Reston, VA 20192, Mr. Kenneth A. Beckman, (703) 648-4916, Fax: (703) 648-4995, http://minerals.usgs.gov/minerals; *Mineral Commodity Summaries* and *Minerals Yearbook.*

CHROMIUM

U.S. Census Bureau, Foreign Trade Division, 4700 Silver Hill Road, Washington DC 20233-0001, (301) 763-3030, www.census.gov/foreign-trade/www/; *U.S. International Trade in Goods and Services.*

U.S. Department of Defense (DOD), Defense Logistics Agency (DLA), 8725 John J. Kingman Road, Fort Belvoir, VA 22060, (703) 767-6666, www.dla.mil; *Stockpile Report to the Congress 2002.*

U.S. Department of the Interior (DOI), U.S. Geological Survey (USGS), Office of Minerals Information, 12201 Sunrise Valley Drive, Reston, VA 20192, Mr. Kenneth A. Beckman, (703) 648-4916, Fax: (703) 648-4995, http://minerals.usgs.gov/minerals; *Mineral Commodity Summaries.*

CHRONIC DISEASES

Australian Institute of Health and Welfare (AIHW), GPO Box 570, Canberra ACT 2601, Australia, www.aihw.gov.au; *Indicators for Chronic Diseases and Their Determinants 2008.*

National Center for Chronic Disease Prevention and Health Promotion (NCCDPHP), Centers for Disease Control and Prevention (CDC), 4770 Buford Hwy, NE, MS K-40, Atlanta, GA 30341-3717, (404) 639-3311, www.cdc.gov/nccdphp; *Actual Causes of Death in the United States; The Burden of Chronic Disease and the Future of Public Health; The Burden of Chronic Diseases and Their Risk Factors: National and State Perspectives 2004; Chronic Disease Prevention Databases;* and *Chronic Diseases: The Leading Causes of Death.*

CHURCHES

The Annie E. Casey Foundation, 701 Saint Paul Street, Baltimore, MD 21202, (410) 547-6600, Fax: (410) 547-3610, www.aecf.org; *Beyond the Boundaries: Low-Income Residents, Faith-Based Organizations and Neighborhood Coalition Building* and *Faith Matters: Race/Ethnicity, Religion, and Substance Abuse.*

Hartford Institute for Religion Research, Hartford Seminary, 77 Sherman Street, Hartford, CT 06105-2260, (860) 509-9543, Fax: (860) 509-9551, http://hirr.hartsem.edu; *Faith Based Social Services/Charitable Choice.*

United Way of Massachusetts Bay, 51 Sleeper Street, Boston, MA 02210, (617) 624-8000, www.uwmb.org; *Faith and Action: Improving the Lives of At-Risk Youth.*

CHURCHES - CONSTRUCTION VALUE

McGraw-Hill Construction, Dodge Analytics, 1221 Avenue of The Americas, Manhattan, NY 10020, (800) 393-6343, http://dodge.construction.com/analytics; *Construction Outlook 2008.*

U.S. Census Bureau, Manufacturing and Construction Division, 4600 Silver Hill Road, Washington DC 20233, (301) 763-4673, www.census.gov/mcd; *Current Construction Reports.*

CHURCHES - GRANTS, FOUNDATIONS

The Foundation Center, 79 Fifth Avenue, New York, NY 10003-3076, (212) 620-4230, Fax: (212) 807-3677, www.fdncenter.org; *FC Stats - Grantmaker; FC Stats - Grants; Foundation Giving Trends (2008 Edition);* and *Top Funders: Top 100 U.S. Foundations by Asset Size.*

CHURCHES - NUMBER AND MEMBERSHIP

Hartford Institute for Religion Research, Hartford Seminary, 77 Sherman Street, Hartford, CT 06105-2260, (860) 509-9543, Fax: (860) 509-9551, http://hirr.hartsem.edu; *Church Growth and Decline.*

CHURCHES - VOLUNTEERS

Hartford Institute for Religion Research, Hartford Seminary, 77 Sherman Street, Hartford, CT 06105-2260, (860) 509-9543, Fax: (860) 509-9551, http://hirr.hartsem.edu; *Faith Based Social Services/Charitable Choice.*

Independent Sector, 1200 Eighteenth Street, NW, Suite 200, Washington, DC 20036, (202) 467-6100, Fax: (202) 467-6101, www.independentsector.org; *Giving and Volunteering in the United States 2001.*

CIGAR USAGE

Substance Abuse and Mental Health Services Administration (SAMHSA), 1 Choke Cherry Road, Rockville, MD 20857, (240) 777-1311, www.oas.samhsa.gov; *National Survey on Drug Use Health (NSDUH).*

CIGARETTES

See also TOBACCO INDUSTRY

Robert Wood Johnson Foundation, PO Box 2316, College Road East and Route 1, Princeton, NJ 08543, (877) 843-7953, www.rwjf.org; *A Broken Promise to Our Children: The 1998 State Tobacco Settlement Six Years Later.*

CIGARETTES - ADVERTISING

Magazine Publishers of America (MPA), 810 Seventh Avenue, 24th Floor, New York, NY 10019, (212) 872-3700, www.magazine.org; *The Media Research Index.*

CIGARETTES - INTERNATIONAL TRADE

U.S. Census Bureau, Foreign Trade Division, 4700 Silver Hill Road, Washington DC 20233-0001, (301) 763-3030, www.census.gov/foreign-trade/www/; *U.S. International Trade in Goods and Services.*

CIGARETTES - PRODUCTION

Economic Research Service (ERS), U.S. Department of Agriculture (USDA), 1800 M Street, NW, Washington, DC 20036-5831, (202) 694-5050, Fax: (202) 694-5689, www.ers.usda.gov; *Tobacco Outlook 2006.*

CIGARETTES - SMOKERS AND USE

Centers for Disease Control and Prevention (CDC), U.S. Department of Health and Human Services (HHS), 1600 Clifton Road, Atlanta, GA 30333, (800) 311-3435, www.cdc.gov; *Morbidity and Mortality Weekly Report (MMWR).*

National Center for Health Statistics (NCHS), Centers for Disease Control and Prevention (CDC), U.S. Department of Health and Human Services (HHS), 3311 Toledo Road, Hyattsville, MD 20782, (866) 232-4636, www.cdc.gov/nchs; *Health, United States, 2006, with Chartbook on Trends in the Health of Americans with Special Feature on Pain.*

Substance Abuse and Mental Health Services Administration (SAMHSA), 1 Choke Cherry Road, Rockville, MD 20857, (240) 777-1311, www.oas.samhsa.gov; *National Survey on Drug Use Health (NSDUH).*

CIRCUIT BOARDS

Electronic Industries Alliance (EIA), 2500 Wilson Boulevard, Arlington, VA 22201, (703) 907-7500, www.eia.org; unpublished data.

U.S. Census Bureau, Manufacturing and Construction Division, 4600 Silver Hill Road, Washington DC 20233, (301) 763-4673, www.census.gov/mcd; *Current Industrial Reports.*

CIRCULATION OF NEWSPAPERS AND PERIODICALS

Audit Bureau of Circulations (ABC), 900 N. Meacham Road, Schaumburg, IL 60173-4968, (847) 605-0909, www.accessabc.com; Database: Subject coverage includes audit reports, publishers' statements, and other reports.

Editor and Publisher, 770 Broadway, New York, NY 10003-9595, (800) 336-4380, Fax: (646) 654-5370, www.editorandpublisher.com; *Editor and Publisher International Year Book, 2006.*

Thomson Gale, 27500 Drake Road, Farmington Hills, MI 48331, (248) 699-4253, www.galegroup.com; *Gale Directory of Publications and Broadcast Media.*

CIRCULATION OF NEWSPAPERS AND PERIODICALS - FOREIGN COUNTRIES

Audit Bureau of Circulations (ABC), 900 N. Meacham Road, Schaumburg, IL 60173-4968, (847) 605-0909, www.accessabc.com; Database: Subject coverage includes audit reports, publishers' statements, and other reports.

UNESCO Institute for Statistics, C.P. 6128 Succursale Centre-Ville, Montreal, Quebec, H3C 3J7 Canada, (Dial from U.S. (514) 343-6880), (Fax from U.S. (514) 343 6882), www.uis.unesco.org; *Statistical Tables.*

CIRRHOSIS OF THE LIVER

National Center for Health Statistics (NCHS), Centers for Disease Control and Prevention (CDC), U.S. Department of Health and Human Services (HHS), 3311 Toledo Road, Hyattsville, MD 20782, (866) 232-4636, www.cdc.gov/nchs; *Faststats A to Z.*

CIRRHOSIS OF THE LIVER - DEATHS

Bernan Essential Government Publications, 4611-F Assembly Drive, Lanham MD, 20706-4391, (301) 459-2255, Fax: (800) 865-3450, www.bernan.com; *Vital Statistics of the United States: Births, Life Expectancy, Deaths, and Selected Health Data.*

National Center for Health Statistics (NCHS), Centers for Disease Control and Prevention (CDC), U.S. Department of Health and Human Services (HHS), 3311 Toledo Road, Hyattsville, MD 20782, (866) 232-4636, www.cdc.gov/nchs; *National Vital Statistics Reports (NVSR); Vital Statistics of the United States (VSUS);* and unpublished data.

CITIES

The Annie E. Casey Foundation, 701 Saint Paul Street, Baltimore, MD 21202, (410) 547-6600, Fax: (410) 547-3610, www.aecf.org; *City and Rural KIDS COUNT Data Book* and *Making Connections to Improve Education: A Snapshot of School-Based Education Investments in Seven Making Connections Sites.*

The Brookings Institution, 1775 Massachusetts Avenue, NW, Washington, DC 20036, (202) 797-6000, Fax: (202) 797-6004, www.brook.edu; *Downtown Detroit In Focus: A Profile of Market Opportunity; The Economic Potential of American Cities; Finding Exurbia: America's Fast-Growing Communities at the Metropolitan Fringe; From 'There' to 'Here': Refugee Resettlement in Metropolitan America; The State of American Cities;* and *Two Steps Back: City and Suburban Poverty Trends 1999-2005.*

National Center for Statistics and Analysis (NCSA) of the National Highway Traffic Safety Administration, West Building, 1200 New Jersey Avenue, S.E., Washington, DC 20590, (202) 366-1503, Fax: (202) 366-7078, www.nhtsa.gov; *Traffic Safety Fact Sheets, 2006 Data - Rural/Urban Comparison.*

State of Connecticut, Department of Economic and Community Development (DECD), 505 Hudson Street, Hartford, CT 06106-7107, (860) 270-8000, www.ct.gov/ecd/; *Connecticut Town Profiles.*

U.S. Census Bureau, Governments Division, 4600 Silver Hill Road, Washington DC 20233, (800) 242-2184, www.census.gov/govs/www; *2002 Census of Governments, Government Organization.*

CITIES - AMERICAN INDIAN POPULATION

DataPlace by KnowledgePlex, c/o Fannie Mae Foundation, 4000 Wisconsin Avenue, N.W., North Tower, Suite One, Washington, DC 20016-2804, www.dataplace.org; *Database. Subject coverage: Community, regional and national housing and demographic data.*

Population Reference Bureau, 1875 Connecticut Avenue, NW, Suite 520, Washington, DC, 20009-5728, (800) 877-9881, Fax: (202) 328-3937, www.prb.org; *The American People Series.*

U.S. Census Bureau, 4700 Silver Hill Road, Washington DC 20233-0001, (301) 763-3030, www.census.gov; American FactFinder (web app); *County and City Data Book 2007; LandView 6;* and *State and County QuickFacts.*

U.S. Census Bureau, Population Division, 4700 Silver Hill Road, Washington DC 20233-0001, (301) 763-3030, www.census.gov/population/www/; *Census 2000 Profiles of General Demographic Characteristics.*

CITIES - AREA

U.S. Census Bureau, 4700 Silver Hill Road, Washington DC 20233-0001, (301) 763-3030, www.census.gov; *LandView 6.*

CITIES - ASIAN POPULATION

DataPlace by KnowledgePlex, c/o Fannie Mae Foundation, 4000 Wisconsin Avenue, N.W., North Tower, Suite One, Washington, DC 20016-2804, www.dataplace.org; *Database. Subject coverage: Community, regional and national housing and demographic data.*

Population Reference Bureau, 1875 Connecticut Avenue, NW, Suite 520, Washington, DC, 20009-5728, (800) 877-9881, Fax: (202) 328-3937, www.prb.org; *The American People Series.*

U.S. Census Bureau, 4700 Silver Hill Road, Washington DC 20233-0001, (301) 763-3030, www.census.gov; American FactFinder (web app); *County and City Data Book 2007; LandView 6;* and *State and County QuickFacts.*

U.S. Census Bureau, Population Division, 4700 Silver Hill Road, Washington DC 20233-0001, (301) 763-3030, www.census.gov/population/www/; *Census 2000 Profiles of General Demographic Characteristics.*

CITIES - BLACK POPULATION

DataPlace by KnowledgePlex, c/o Fannie Mae Foundation, 4000 Wisconsin Avenue, N.W., North Tower, Suite One, Washington, DC 20016-2804, www.dataplace.org; *Database. Subject coverage: Community, regional and national housing and demographic data.*

Population Reference Bureau, 1875 Connecticut Avenue, NW, Suite 520, Washington, DC, 20009-5728, (800) 877-9881, Fax: (202) 328-3937, www.prb.org; *The American People Series.*

U.S. Census Bureau, 4700 Silver Hill Road, Washington DC 20233-0001, (301) 763-3030, www.census.gov; American FactFinder (web app); *County and City Data Book 2007; LandView 6;* and *State and County QuickFacts.*

U.S. Census Bureau, Population Division, 4700 Silver Hill Road, Washington DC 20233-0001, (301) 763-3030, www.census.gov/population/www/; *Census 2000 Profiles of General Demographic Characteristics.*

CITIES - CLIMATE

National Climatic Data Center (NCDC), National Oceanic and Atmospheric Administration (NOAA), Federal Building, 151 Patton Avenue, Asheville, NC 28801-5001, (828) 271-4800, Fax: (828) 271-4876, www.ncdc.noaa.gov; Climatological Data (CD) and *Comparative Climatic Data, 2005.*

CITIES - CLIMATE - FOREIGN COUNTRIES

National Climatic Data Center (NCDC), National Oceanic and Atmospheric Administration (NOAA), Federal Building, 151 Patton Avenue, Asheville, NC 28801-5001, (828) 271-4800, Fax: (828) 271-4876, www.ncdc.noaa.gov; *Climates of the World.*

CITIES - COMMUTING TO WORK

Eno Transportation Foundation, 1634 I Street, NW, Suite 500, Washington, DC 20006, (202) 879-4700, Fax: (202) 879-4719, www.enotrans.com; *Commuting in America II.*

Population Reference Bureau, 1875 Connecticut Avenue, NW, Suite 520, Washington, DC, 20009-5728, (800) 877-9881, Fax: (202) 328-3937, www.prb.org; *The American People Series.*

U.S. Census Bureau, 4700 Silver Hill Road, Washington DC 20233-0001, (301) 763-3030, www.census.gov; American FactFinder (web app); American FactFinder (web app); *State and County QuickFacts;* and *State and County QuickFacts.*

U.S. Census Bureau, Population Division, 4700 Silver Hill Road, Washington DC 20233-0001, (301) 763-3030, www.census.gov/population/www/; *Census 2000 Profiles of General Demographic Characteristics.*

CITIES - CRIME

The Brookings Institution, 1775 Massachusetts Avenue, NW, Washington, DC 20036, (202) 797-6000, Fax: (202) 797-6004, www.brook.edu; *The State of American Cities.*

Federal Bureau of Investigation (FBI), J. Edgar Hoover Building, 935 Pennsylvania Avenue, NW, Washington, DC 20535-0001, (202) 324-3000, www.fbi.gov; *Crime in the United States (CIUS) 2007 (Preliminary).*

Justice Research and Statistics Association (JRSA), 777 N. Capitol Street, NE, Suite 801, Washington, DC 20002, (202) 842-9330, Fax: (202) 842-9329, www.jrsa.org; *An Analysis of Variables Affecting the Clearance of Homicides: A Multistate Study* and *Crime and Justice Atlas 2001.*

RAND Corporation, 1776 Main Street, PO Box 2138, Santa Monica, CA 90407-2138, (310) 393-0411, www.rand.org; *Police-Community Relations in Cincinnati.*

U.S. Department of Justice (DOJ), Bureau of Justice Statistics, 810 Seventh Street, NW, Washington, DC 20531, (202) 307-0765, www.ojp.usdoj.gov/bjs/; *Felony Defendants in Large Urban Counties, 2002; Homicide Trends in the United States: 2002 Update; Police Departments in Large Cities, 1990-2000; Punitive Damage Awards in Large Counties, 2001;* and *Violence by Gang Members, 1993-2003.*

U.S. Department of Justice (DOJ), National Institute of Justice (NIJ), 810 Seventh Street, NW, Washington, DC 20531, (202) 307-2942, Fax: (202) 616-0275, www.ojp.usdoj.gov/nij/; *Community Policing and "The New Immigrants": Latinos in Chicago; Fighting Crime with COPS Citizens; Responding to Gangs: Evaluation and Research;* and *Taking Stock: Community Policing in Chicago.*

CITIES - DEBT

U.S. Census Bureau, Governments Division, 4600 Silver Hill Road, Washington DC 20233, (800) 242-2184, www.census.gov/govs/www; *2002 Census of Governments, Government Finances.*

CITIES - DISABILITY POPULATION

Population Reference Bureau, 1875 Connecticut Avenue, NW, Suite 520, Washington, DC, 20009-5728, (800) 877-9881, Fax: (202) 328-3937, www.prb.org; *The American People Series.*

U.S. Census Bureau, 4700 Silver Hill Road, Washington DC 20233-0001, (301) 763-3030, www.census.gov; American FactFinder (web app); *County and City Data Book 2007;* and *State and County QuickFacts.*

U.S. Census Bureau, Population Division, 4700 Silver Hill Road, Washington DC 20233-0001, (301) 763-3030, www.census.gov/population/www/; *Census 2000 Profiles of General Demographic Characteristics.*

CITIES - DRUG USE

U.S. Department of Justice (DOJ), National Institute of Justice (NIJ), 810 Seventh Street, NW, Washington, DC 20531, (202) 307-2942, Fax: (202) 616-0275, www.ojp.usdoj.gov/nij/; *Annual Report.*

CITIES - ECONOMIC INDICATORS

The Brookings Institution, 1775 Massachusetts Avenue, NW, Washington, DC 20036, (202) 797-6000, Fax: (202) 797-6004, www.brook.edu; *Downtown Detroit In Focus: A Profile of Market Opportunity; The Economic Potential of American Cities; Finding Exurbia: America's Fast-Growing Communities at the Metropolitan Fringe; The State of American Cities;* and *Two Steps Back: City and Suburban Poverty Trends 1999-2005.*

CITIES - EMPLOYEES, EARNINGS, PAYROLLS

U.S. Census Bureau, Governments Division, 4600 Silver Hill Road, Washington DC 20233, (800) 242-2184, www.census.gov/govs/www; *2002 Census of Governments, Public Employment and Payroll.*

U.S. Department of Labor (DOL), Bureau of Labor Statistics (BLS), Postal Square Building, 2 Massachusetts Avenue, NE, Washington, DC 20212-0001, (202) 691-5200, Fax: (202) 691-6325, www.bls.gov; *Wages by Area and Occupation.*

CITIES - FINANCES OF CITY GOVERNMENTS

U.S. Census Bureau, Governments Division, 4600 Silver Hill Road, Washington DC 20233, (800) 242-2184, www.census.gov/govs/www; *2002 Census of Governments, Government Finances.*

CITIES - HAWAIIAN POPULATION

Population Reference Bureau, 1875 Connecticut Avenue, NW, Suite 520, Washington, DC, 20009-5728, (800) 877-9881, Fax: (202) 328-3937, www.prb.org; *The American People Series.*

U.S. Census Bureau, 4700 Silver Hill Road, Washington DC 20233-0001, (301) 763-3030, www.census.gov; American FactFinder (web app); *County and City Data Book 2007; LandView 6;* and *State and County QuickFacts.*

U.S. Census Bureau, Population Division, 4700 Silver Hill Road, Washington DC 20233-0001, (301) 763-3030, www.census.gov/population/www/; *Census 2000 Profiles of General Demographic Characteristics.*

CITIES - HISPANIC POPULATION

DataPlace by KnowledgePlex, c/o Fannie Mae Foundation, 4000 Wisconsin Avenue, N.W., North Tower, Suite One, Washington, DC 20016-2804, www.dataplace.org; *Database. Subject coverage: Community, regional and national housing and demographic data.*

Population Reference Bureau, 1875 Connecticut Avenue, NW, Suite 520, Washington, DC, 20009-5728, (800) 877-9881, Fax: (202) 328-3937, www.prb.org; *The American People Series.*

U.S. Census Bureau, 4700 Silver Hill Road, Washington DC 20233-0001, (301) 763-3030, www.census.gov; American FactFinder (web app); *County and City Data Book 2007; LandView 6;* and *State and County QuickFacts.*

U.S. Census Bureau, Population Division, 4700 Silver Hill Road, Washington DC 20233-0001, (301) 763-3030, www.census.gov/population/www/; *Census 2000 Profiles of General Demographic Characteristics.*

U.S. Department of Justice (DOJ), National Institute of Justice (NIJ), 810 Seventh Street, NW, Washington, DC 20531, (202) 307-2942, Fax: (202) 616-0275, www.ojp.usdoj.gov/nij/; *Community Policing and "The New Immigrants": Latinos in Chicago.*

CITIES - HOUSEHOLDS

The Brookings Institution, 1775 Massachusetts Avenue, NW, Washington, DC 20036, (202) 797-6000, Fax: (202) 797-6004, www.brook.edu; *The State of American Cities* and *Two Steps Back: City and Suburban Poverty Trends 1999-2005.*

DataPlace by KnowledgePlex, c/o Fannie Mae Foundation, 4000 Wisconsin Avenue, N.W., North Tower, Suite One, Washington, DC 20016-2804, www.dataplace.org; *Database. Subject coverage: Community, regional and national housing and demographic data.*

Population Reference Bureau, 1875 Connecticut Avenue, NW, Suite 520, Washington, DC, 20009-5728, (800) 877-9881, Fax: (202) 328-3937, www.prb.org; *The American People Series.*

State of Connecticut, Department of Economic and Community Development (DECD), 505 Hudson Street, Hartford, CT 06106-7107, (860) 270-8000, www.ct.gov/ecd/; *Connecticut Town Profiles.*

U.S. Census Bureau, 4700 Silver Hill Road, Washington DC 20233-0001, (301) 763-3030, www.census.gov; American FactFinder (web app); *County and City Data Book 2007; LandView 6;* and *State and County QuickFacts.*

U.S. Census Bureau, Housing and Household Economics Statistics Division, 4700 Silver Hill Road, Washington DC 20233-0001, (301) 763-3030, www.census.gov/hhes/www; *Housing Characteristics: 2000.*

U.S. Census Bureau, Population Division, 4700 Silver Hill Road, Washington DC 20233-0001, (301) 763-3030, www.census.gov/population/www/; *Census 2000 Profiles of General Demographic Characteristics.*

CITIES - HOUSING

The Brookings Institution, 1775 Massachusetts Avenue, NW, Washington, DC 20036, (202) 797-6000, Fax: (202) 797-6004, www.brook.edu; *The State of American Cities* and *Two Steps Back: City and Suburban Poverty Trends 1999-2005.*

DataPlace by KnowledgePlex, c/o Fannie Mae Foundation, 4000 Wisconsin Avenue, N.W., North Tower, Suite One, Washington, DC 20016-2804, www.dataplace.org; *Database. Subject coverage: Community, regional and national housing and demographic data.*

NeighborhoodInfo DC, c/o The Urban Institute, 2100 M Street, NW, Washington, DC 20037, (202) 261-5760, Fax: (202) 872-9322, www.neighborhoodinfodc.org; *District of Columbia Housing Monitor.*

Population Reference Bureau, 1875 Connecticut Avenue, NW, Suite 520, Washington, DC, 20009-5728, (800) 877-9881, Fax: (202) 328-3937, www.prb.org; *The American People Series.*

U.S. Census Bureau, 4700 Silver Hill Road, Washington DC 20233-0001, (301) 763-3030, www.census.gov; American FactFinder (web app); *County and City Data Book 2007; County and City Data Book 2007; LandView 6;* and *State and County QuickFacts.*

U.S. Census Bureau, Housing and Household Economics Statistics Division, 4700 Silver Hill Road, Washington DC 20233-0001, (301) 763-3030, www.census.gov/hhes/www; *Housing Characteristics: 2000.*

U.S. Census Bureau, Population Division, 4700 Silver Hill Road, Washington DC 20233-0001, (301) 763-3030, www.census.gov/population/www/; *Census 2000 Profiles of General Demographic Characteristics.*

CITIES - LANGUAGE SPOKEN AT HOME

Population Reference Bureau, 1875 Connecticut Avenue, NW, Suite 520, Washington, DC, 20009-5728, (800) 877-9881, Fax: (202) 328-3937, www.prb.org; *The American People Series.*

U.S. Census Bureau, 4700 Silver Hill Road, Washington DC 20233-0001, (301) 763-3030, www.census.gov; American FactFinder (web app); *County and City Data Book 2007;* and *State and County QuickFacts.*

U.S. Census Bureau, Population Division, 4700 Silver Hill Road, Washington DC 20233-0001, (301) 763-3030, www.census.gov/population/www/; *Census 2000 Profiles of General Demographic Characteristics.*

CITIES - OFFICE VACANCY RATES

ONCOR International, 1 Campus Drive, Parsippany, NJ 07054, (973) 407-6363, Fax: (973) 407-4666, www.oncorintl.com; *North American Office Market Report.*

CITIES - OFFICIALS ELECTED

Joint Center for Political and Economic Studies, 1090 Vermont Avenue, NW, Suite 1100, Washington, DC 20005-4928, (202) 789-3500, Fax: (202) 789-6390, www.jointcenter.org; *Black Elected Officials: A Statistical Summary.*

CITIES - POPULATION

The Annie E. Casey Foundation, 701 Saint Paul Street, Baltimore, MD 21202, (410) 547-6600, Fax: (410) 547-3610, www.aecf.org; *City and Rural KIDS COUNT Data Book.*

The Brookings Institution, 1775 Massachusetts Avenue, NW, Washington, DC 20036, (202) 797-6000, Fax: (202) 797-6004, www.brook.edu; *From 'There' to 'Here': Refugee Resettlement in Metropolitan America; The State of American Cities;* and *Two Steps Back: City and Suburban Poverty Trends 1999-2005.*

DataPlace by KnowledgePlex, c/o Fannie Mae Foundation, 4000 Wisconsin Avenue, N.W., North Tower, Suite One, Washington, DC 20016-2804, www.dataplace.org; *Database. Subject coverage: Community, regional and national housing and demographic data.*

National Center for Statistics and Analysis (NCSA) of the National Highway Traffic Safety Administration, West Building, 1200 New Jersey Avenue, S.E., Washington, DC 20590, (202) 366-1503, Fax: (202) 366-7078, www.nhtsa.gov; *Traffic Safety Fact Sheets, 2006 Data - Rural/Urban Comparison.*

NeighborhoodInfo DC, c/o The Urban Institute, 2100 M Street, NW, Washington, DC 20037, (202) 261-5760, Fax: (202) 872-9322, www.neighborhoodinfodc.org; *Every Kid Counts in the District of Columbia: Twelfth Annual Fact Book, 2005; The Financial Structure and Fiscal Health of Nonprofit Child and Youth Providers in the Washington, D.C. Metropolitan Region; Insurance and Uninsurance in the District of Columbia: Starting with the Numbers; Measuring Need for Youth Services in D.C.: Comparing Poverty and TANF Data;* and *Vital Signs: Indicators of the Nonprofit Safety Net for Children in the Washington, D.C., Region.*

Population Reference Bureau, 1875 Connecticut Avenue, NW, Suite 520, Washington, DC, 20009-5728, (800) 877-9881, Fax: (202) 328-3937, www.prb.org; *The American People Series.*

RAND Corporation, 1776 Main Street, PO Box 2138, Santa Monica, CA 90407-2138, (310) 393-0411, www.rand.org; *Police-Community Relations in Cincinnati.*

State of Connecticut, Department of Economic and Community Development (DECD), 505 Hudson Street, Hartford, CT 06106-7107, (860) 270-8000, www.ct.gov/ecd/; *Connecticut Town Profiles.*

U.S. Census Bureau, 4700 Silver Hill Road, Washington DC 20233-0001, (301) 763-3030, www.census.gov; American FactFinder (web app); *County and City Data Book 2007;* and *State and County QuickFacts.*

U.S. Census Bureau, Housing and Household Economics Statistics Division, 4700 Silver Hill Road, Washington DC 20233-0001, (301) 763-3030, www.census.gov/hhes/www; *Housing Characteristics: 2000.*

U.S. Census Bureau, Population Division, 4700 Silver Hill Road, Washington DC 20233-0001, (301) 763-3030, www.census.gov/population/www/; *Census 2000 Profiles of General Demographic Characteristics.*

CITIES - PROPERTY TAX RATES

District of Columbia Government, Office of Revenue Analysis, John A. Wilson Building, 1350 Pennsylvania Avenue, NW, Washington, DC 20004, (202) 727-1000, www.dc.gov; *Tax Rates and Tax Burdens in the District of Columbia - A Nationwide Comparison 2005.*

CITIES - SCHOOLS

Council of the Great City Schools (CGCS), 1301 Pennsylvania Avenue, NW, Suite 702, Washington DC, 20004, (202) 393-2427, www.cgcs.org; *Critical Trends in Urban Education: Fifth Biennial Survey of America's Great City Schools; Foundations for Success: Case Studies of How Urban School Systems Improve Student Achievement;* and *Urban Indicator: Urban School Superintendents - Characteristics, Tenure, and Salary.*

CITIES - TAXES PAID - BY FAMILY INCOME LEVEL

District of Columbia Government, Office of Revenue Analysis, John A. Wilson Building, 1350 Pennsylvania Avenue, NW, Washington, DC 20004, (202) 727-1000, www.dc.gov; *Tax Rates and Tax Burdens in the District of Columbia - A Nationwide Comparison 2005.*

CITRUS FRUITS - CONSUMPTION

Economic Research Service (ERS), U.S. Department of Agriculture (USDA), 1800 M Street, NW, Washington, DC 20036-5831, (202) 694-5050, Fax: (202) 694-5689, www.ers.usda.gov; *Agricultural Outlook* and *Food CPI, Prices, and Expenditures.*

CITRUS FRUITS - INTERNATIONAL TRADE

Economic Research Service (ERS), U.S. Department of Agriculture (USDA), 1800 M Street, NW, Washington, DC 20036-5831, (202) 694-5050, Fax: (202) 694-5689, www.ers.usda.gov; *Food CPI, Prices, and Expenditures* and *Fruit and Tree Nuts Outlook.*

CITRUS FRUITS - PESTICIDES

Foreign Agricultural Service (FAS), U.S. Department of Agriculture (USDA), 1400 Independence Avenue, SW, Washington, DC 20250, (202) 720-3935, www.fas.usda.gov; Production, Supply and Distribution Online (PSD) Online.

CITRUS FRUITS - PRODUCTION

Economic Research Service (ERS), U.S. Department of Agriculture (USDA), 1800 M Street, NW, Washington, DC 20036-5831, (202) 694-5050, Fax: (202) 694-5689, www.ers.usda.gov; *Food CPI, Prices, and Expenditures* and *Fruit and Tree Nuts Outlook.*

National Agricultural Statistics Service (NASS), U.S. Department of Agriculture (USDA), 1400 Independence Avenue, SW, Washington, DC 20250, (800) 727-9540, Fax: (202) 690-2090, www.nass.usda.gov; *Citrus Fruits* and *Cold Storage.*

CIVIL AVIATION

See AERONAUTICS, COMMERCIAL

CIVIL CASES - U.S. DISTRICT COURTS

Justice Research and Statistics Association (JRSA), 777 N. Capitol Street, NE, Suite 801, Washington, DC 20002, (202) 842-9330, Fax: (202) 842-9329, www.jrsa.org; *Directory of Justice Issues in the States* and InfoBase of State Activities and Research (ISAR).

Office of Public Affairs, Administrative Office of the United States Courts, Washington, DC 20544, (202) 502-2600, www.uscourts.gov; *Statistical Tables for the Federal Judiciary.*

U.S. Department of Justice (DOJ), Bureau of Justice Statistics, 810 Seventh Street, NW, Washington, DC 20531, (202) 307-0765, www.ojp.usdoj.gov/bjs/; *Appeals from General Civil Trials in 46 Large Counties, 2001-2005; Civil Rights Complaints in U.S. District Courts, 2000; Civil Trial Cases and Verdicts in Large Counties, 2001; Intellectual Property Theft, 2002; Medical Malpractice Trials and Verdicts in Large Counties, 2001;* and *Punitive Damage Awards in Large Counties, 2001.*

CIVIL SERVICE EMPLOYEES

See GOVERNMENT

CLAMS

National Marine Fisheries Service (NMFS), National Oceanic and Atmospheric Administration (NOAA), Office of Constituent Services, 1315 East West Highway, 9th Floor, Silver Spring, MD 20910, (301) 713-2379, Fax: (301) 713-2385, www.nmfs.noaa.gov; *Fisheries of the United States - 2006.*

CLAY CONSTRUCTION PRODUCTS

U.S. Census Bureau, Manufacturing and Construction Division, 4600 Silver Hill Road, Washington DC 20233, (301) 763-4673, www.census.gov/mcd; *Current Industrial Reports, Manufacturing Profiles.*

CLERGYMEN

National Council of the Churches of Christ in the USA, 475 Riverside Drive, Suite 880, New York, NY 10115, (212) 870-2227, Fax: (212) 870-2030, www.ncccusa.org; *2007 Yearbook of American and Canadian Churches.*

CLERGYMEN - EMPLOYMENT

U.S. Bureau of Labor Statistics (BLS), Postal Square Building, 2 Massachusetts Avenue, NE, Washington, DC 20212-0001, (202) 691-5200, Fax: (202) 691-6325, www.bls.gov; *Employment and Earnings (EE)* and unpublished data.

CLIMATE

Environmental Defense Fund, 257 Park Avenue South, New York, NY 10010, (800) 684-3322, www.edf.org; *Cars and Climate Change: How Automakers Stack Up* and unpublished data.

Intergovernmental Panel on Climate Change (IPCC), www.ipcc.ch; *Carbon Dioxide Capture and Storage; Climate Change 2007: Working Group II Report - Impacts, Adaptation and Vulnerability; The Regional Impacts of Climate Change: An Assessment of Vulnerability;* and *Safeguarding the Ozone Layer and the Global Climate System: Issues Related to Hydrofluorocarbons and Perfluorocarbons.*

International Food Policy Research Institute (IFPRI), 2033 K Street, NW, Washington, D.C., 2006, (202) 862-5600, www.ifpri.org; *Food Prices, Biofuels, and Climate Change.*

International Institute for Environment and Development (IIED), 3 Endsleigh Street, London, England, WC1H 0DD, United Kingdom, www.iied.org; *The*

Economic Impact of Climate Change in Namibia: How Climate Change Will Affect the Contribution of Namibia's Natural Resources to Its Economy and *Tiempo: A Bulletin on Climate Change and Development.*

National Oceanic and Atmospheric Administration (NOAA), 1401 Constitution Avenue, NW, Room 6217, Washington, DC 20230, (202) 482-6090, Fax: (202) 482-3154, www.noaa.gov; *U.S. Climate at a Glance.*

National Oceanographic Data Center (NOCD), National Oceanic and Atmospheric Administration (NOAA), SSMC3, 4th Floor, 1315 East-West Highway, Silver Spring, MD 20910-3282, (301) 713-3277, Fax: (301) 713-3302, www.nodc.noaa.gov; *Heat Content 2004* and *Warming of the World Ocean, 1955-2003.*

Statistics Indonesia (Badan Pusat Statistik (BPS)), Jl. Dr. Sutomo 6-8, Jakarta 10710, Indonesia, www.bps.go.id; *Environmental Statistical of Indonesia 2005.*

United Nations Environment Programme (UNEP), PO Box 30552, Nairobi, Kenya, www.unep.org; *Climate Action; One Planet, Many People: Atlas of Our Changing Environment; Our Planet Magazine; Planet in Peril: Atlas of Current Threats to People and the Environment;* The UNEP Year Book 2008; *World Atlas of Biodiversity: Earth's Living Resources in the 21st Century;* and *World Atlas of Desertification.*

World Meteorological Organization (WMO), 7bis, avenue de la Paix, Case postale No. 2300, CH-1211 Geneva 2, Switzerland, www.wmo.ch; *Climate Change and Desertification; Climate Information for Adaptation and Development Needs ; MeteoWorld; State of the Climate in 2005; WMO Bulletin;* and *World Climate News.*

World Resources Institute (WRI), 10 G Street, NE, Suite 800 Washington, DC 20002, (202) 729-7600, www.wri.org; *Charting the Midwest: An Inventory and Analysis of Greenhouse Gas Emissions in America's Heartland* and *Painting the Global Picture of Tree Cover Change: Tree Cover Loss in the Humid Tropics.*

CLIMATE - SELECTED CITIES

Environmental Defense Fund, 257 Park Avenue South, New York, NY 10010, (800) 684-3322, www.edf.org; *All Choked Up: Heavy Traffic, Dirty Air and the Risk to New Yorkers.*

National Climatic Data Center (NCDC), National Oceanic and Atmospheric Administration (NOAA), Federal Building, 151 Patton Avenue, Asheville, NC 28801-5001, (828) 271-4800, Fax: (828) 271-4876, www.ncdc.noaa.gov; Climatological Data (CD) and *Comparative Climatic Data, 2005.*

CLIMATE - SELECTED CITIES - PRECIPITATION

National Climatic Data Center (NCDC), National Oceanic and Atmospheric Administration (NOAA), Federal Building, 151 Patton Avenue, Asheville, NC 28801-5001, (828) 271-4800, Fax: (828) 271-4876, www.ncdc.noaa.gov; Climatological Data (CD) and *Comparative Climatic Data, 2005.*

CLIMATE - SELECTED CITIES - TEMPERATURE

National Climatic Data Center (NCDC), National Oceanic and Atmospheric Administration (NOAA), Federal Building, 151 Patton Avenue, Asheville, NC 28801-5001, (828) 271-4800, Fax: (828) 271-4876, www.ncdc.noaa.gov; Climatological Data (CD) and *Comparative Climatic Data, 2005.*

CLOCKS AND WATCHES

U.S. Census Bureau, Foreign Trade Division, 4700 Silver Hill Road, Washington DC 20233-0001, (301) 763-3030, www.census.gov/foreign-trade/www/; *U.S. International Trade in Goods and Services.*

CLOTHING AND ACCESSORY STORES - RETAIL - CONSUMER PRICE INDEXES

The NPD Group, Port Washington, 900 West Shore Road, Port Washington, NY 11050, (866) 444-1411, www.npd.com; *Market Research for the Apparel and Footwear Industries.*

U.S. Department of Labor (DOL), Bureau of Labor Statistics (BLS), Postal Square Building, 2 Massachusetts Avenue, NE, Washington, DC 20212-0001, (202) 691-5200, Fax: (202) 691-6325, www.bls.gov; *Consumer Price Indexes (CPI).*

CLOTHING AND ACCESSORY STORES - RETAIL - EARNINGS

The NPD Group, Port Washington, 900 West Shore Road, Port Washington, NY 11050, (866) 444-1411, www.npd.com; *Market Research for the Apparel and Footwear Industries.*

Office of Trade and Industry Information (OTII), Manufacturing and Services, International Trade Administration, U.S. Department of Commerce, 1401 Constitution Ave, NW, Washington, DC 20230, (800) USA TRAD(E), http://trade.gov/index.asp; *TradeStats Express.*

U.S. Bureau of Labor Statistics (BLS), Postal Square Building, 2 Massachusetts Avenue, NE, Washington, DC 20212-0001, (202) 691-5200, Fax: (202) 691-6325, www.bls.gov; *Current Employment Statistics Survey (CES)* and *Employment and Earnings (EE).*

U.S. Census Bureau, Center for Economic Studies, 4600 Silver Hill Road, Washington DC 20233, (301) 457-1235, www.ces.census.gov; *2002 Economic Census, Retail Trade* and *2002 Economic Census, Wholesale Trade.*

U.S. Census Bureau, Company Statistics Division, 4700 Silver Hill Road, Washington DC 20233-0001, (301) 763-3030, www.census.gov/csd/; *County Business Patterns 2004.*

CLOTHING AND ACCESSORY STORES - RETAIL - ELECTRONIC COMMERCE

U.S. Census Bureau, 4700 Silver Hill Road, Washington DC 20233-0001, (301) 763-3030, www.census.gov; *2006 E-Commerce Multi-Sector Report* and *E-Stats - Measuring the Electronic Economy.*

CLOTHING AND ACCESSORY STORES - RETAIL - EMPLOYEES

U.S. Bureau of Labor Statistics (BLS), Postal Square Building, 2 Massachusetts Avenue, NE, Washington, DC 20212-0001, (202) 691-5200, Fax: (202) 691-6325, www.bls.gov; *Current Employment Statistics Survey (CES)* and *Employment and Earnings (EE).*

U.S. Census Bureau, Center for Economic Studies, 4600 Silver Hill Road, Washington DC 20233, (301) 457-1235, www.ces.census.gov; *2002 Economic Census, Retail Trade* and *2002 Economic Census, Wholesale Trade.*

U.S. Census Bureau, Company Statistics Division, 4700 Silver Hill Road, Washington DC 20233-0001, (301) 763-3030, www.census.gov/csd/; *County Business Patterns 2004.*

CLOTHING AND ACCESSORY STORES - RETAIL - ESTABLISHMENTS

Office of Trade and Industry Information (OTII), Manufacturing and Services, International Trade Administration, U.S. Department of Commerce, 1401 Constitution Ave, NW, Washington, DC 20230, (800) USA TRAD(E), http://trade.gov/index.asp; *TradeStats Express.*

U.S. Census Bureau, 4700 Silver Hill Road, Washington DC 20233-0001, (301) 763-3030, www.census.gov; *2002 Economic Census, Nonemployer Statistics.*

U.S. Census Bureau, Center for Economic Studies, 4600 Silver Hill Road, Washington DC 20233, (301) 457-1235, www.ces.census.gov; *2002 Economic Census, Retail Trade* and *2002 Economic Census, Wholesale Trade.*

U.S. Census Bureau, Company Statistics Division, 4700 Silver Hill Road, Washington DC 20233-0001, (301) 763-3030, www.census.gov/csd/; *County Business Patterns 2004.*

CLOTHING AND ACCESSORY STORES - RETAIL - INVENTORIES

Office of Trade and Industry Information (OTII), Manufacturing and Services, International Trade Administration, U.S. Department of Commerce, 1401 Constitution Ave, NW, Washington, DC 20230, (800) USA TRAD(E), http://trade.gov/index.asp; *TradeStats Express.*

U.S. Census Bureau, Center for Economic Studies, 4600 Silver Hill Road, Washington DC 20233, (301) 457-1235, www.ces.census.gov; *2002 Economic Census, Retail Trade* and *2002 Economic Census, Wholesale Trade.*

U.S. Census Bureau, Company Statistics Division, 4700 Silver Hill Road, Washington DC 20233-0001, (301) 763-3030, www.census.gov/csd/; *Current Business Reports.*

CLOTHING AND ACCESSORY STORES - RETAIL - NONEMPLOYERS

U.S. Census Bureau, 4700 Silver Hill Road, Washington DC 20233-0001, (301) 763-3030, www.census.gov; *2002 Economic Census, Nonemployer Statistics.*

CLOTHING AND ACCESSORY STORES - RETAIL - PRODUCTIVITY

U.S. Bureau of Labor Statistics (BLS), Postal Square Building, 2 Massachusetts Avenue, NE, Washington, DC 20212-0001, (202) 691-5200, Fax: (202) 691-6325, www.bls.gov; *Industry Productivity and Costs.*

CLOTHING AND ACCESSORY STORES - RETAIL - PURCHASES

Office of Trade and Industry Information (OTII), Manufacturing and Services, International Trade Administration, U.S. Department of Commerce, 1401 Constitution Ave, NW, Washington, DC 20230, (800) USA TRAD(E), http://trade.gov/index.asp; *TradeStats Express.*

U.S. Census Bureau, Center for Economic Studies, 4600 Silver Hill Road, Washington DC 20233, (301) 457-1235, www.ces.census.gov; *2002 Economic Census, Retail Trade* and *2002 Economic Census, Wholesale Trade.*

U.S. Census Bureau, Company Statistics Division, 4700 Silver Hill Road, Washington DC 20233-0001, (301) 763-3030, www.census.gov/csd/; *Current Business Reports.*

CLOTHING AND ACCESSORY STORES - RETAIL - SALES

Claritas, 5375 Mira Sorrento Place, Suite 400, San Diego, CA 92121, (800) 866-6520, Fax: (858) 550-5800, www.claritas.com; *Consumer Buying Power.*

The NPD Group, Port Washington, 900 West Shore Road, Port Washington, NY 11050, (866) 444-1411, www.npd.com; *Market Research for the Apparel and Footwear Industries.*

Office of Trade and Industry Information (OTII), Manufacturing and Services, International Trade Administration, U.S. Department of Commerce, 1401 Constitution Ave, NW, Washington, DC 20230, (800) USA TRAD(E), http://trade.gov/index.asp; *TradeStats Express.*

U.S. Census Bureau, 4700 Silver Hill Road, Washington DC 20233-0001, (301) 763-3030, www.census.gov; *2002 Economic Census, Nonemployer Statistics.*

U.S. Census Bureau, Center for Economic Studies, 4600 Silver Hill Road, Washington DC 20233, (301) 457-1235, www.ces.census.gov; *2002 Economic Census, Retail Trade* and *2002 Economic Census, Wholesale Trade.*

U.S. Census Bureau, Company Statistics Division, 4700 Silver Hill Road, Washington DC 20233-0001, (301) 763-3030, www.census.gov/csd/; *Current Business Reports.*

COAL

See also PETROLEUM INDUSTRY AND TRADE

Platts, 2 Penn Plaza, 25th Floor, New York, NY 10121-2298, (212) 904-3070, www.platts.com; *Energy in East Europe.*

U.S. Library of Congress (LOC), Congressional Research Service (CRS), The Library of Congress, 101 Independence Avenue, SE, Washington, DC 20540-7500, (202) 707-5700, www.loc.gov/crsinfo; *Energy: Selected Facts and Numbers.*

COAL - CAR LOADINGS

Association of American Railroads (AAR), 50 F Street, NW, Washington, DC 20001-1564, (202) 639-2100, www.aar.org; *Freight Commodity Statistics; Freight Loss and Damage;* and *Weekly Railroad Traffic.*

COAL - CONSUMPTION

U.S. Department of Energy (DOE), Energy Information Administration (EIA), 1000 Independence Avenue, SW, Washington, DC 20585, (202) 586-8800, www.eia.doe.gov; *Annual Energy Outlook 2006; Annual Energy Review 2005; Monthly Energy Review (MER);* and *State Energy Data Report.*

COAL - CONSUMPTION - ELECTRIC UTILITIES

Edison Electric Institute (EEI), 701 Pennsylvania Avenue, NW, Washington, DC 20004-2696, (202) 508-5000, www.eei.org; *Historical Statistics of the Electric Utility Industry through 1992.*

U.S. Department of Energy (DOE), Energy Information Administration (EIA), 1000 Independence Avenue, SW, Washington, DC 20585, (202) 586-8800, www.eia.doe.gov; *Annual Energy Review 2005; Electric Power Annual; Electric Power Monthly (EPM); Inventory of Electric Utility Power Plants in the United States 2000;* and unpublished data.

COAL - EXPENDITURES

U.S. Department of Energy (DOE), Energy Information Administration (EIA), 1000 Independence Avenue, SW, Washington, DC 20585, (202) 586-8800, www.eia.doe.gov; *State Energy Data 2003 Price and Expenditure Data.*

COAL - INTERNATIONAL TRADE

U.S. Census Bureau, Foreign Trade Division, 4700 Silver Hill Road, Washington DC 20233-0001, (301) 763-3030, www.census.gov/foreign-trade/www/; *U.S. International Trade in Goods and Services.*

U.S. Department of Energy (DOE), Energy Information Administration (EIA), 1000 Independence Avenue, SW, Washington, DC 20585, (202) 586-8800, www.eia.doe.gov; *Annual Coal Report 2005; Annual Energy Outlook 2006; Annual Energy Review 2005; Monthly Energy Review (MER);* and unpublished data.

COAL - PRICES

U.S. Department of Energy (DOE), Energy Information Administration (EIA), 1000 Independence Avenue, SW, Washington, DC 20585, (202) 586-8800, www.eia.doe.gov; *Annual Energy Review 2005* and *Monthly Energy Review (MER).*

COAL - PRODUCTION

International Energy Agency (IEA), 9, rue de la Federation, 75739 Paris Cedex 15, France, www.iea.org; *Key World Energy Statistics 2007.*

U.S. Department of Energy (DOE), Energy Information Administration (EIA), 1000 Independence Avenue, SW, Washington, DC 20585, (202) 586-8800, www.eia.doe.gov; *Annual Coal Report 2005; Annual Energy Outlook 2006; Annual Energy Review 2005; Monthly Energy Review (MER);* and unpublished data.

COAL - PRODUCTION - WORLD

International Energy Agency (IEA), 9, rue de la Federation, 75739 Paris Cedex 15, France, www.iea.org; *Key World Energy Statistics 2007.*

Platts, 2 Penn Plaza, 25th Floor, New York, NY 10121-2298, (212) 904-3070, www.platts.com; *Energy in East Europe.*

U.S. Department of Energy (DOE), Energy Information Administration (EIA), 1000 Independence Avenue, SW, Washington, DC 20585, (202) 586-8800, www.eia.doe.gov; *Annual Energy Review 2005; International Energy Annual 2004;* and *International Energy Outlook 2006.*

U.S. Department of the Interior (DOI), U.S. Geological Survey (USGS), Office of Minerals Information, 12201 Sunrise Valley Drive, Reston, VA 20192, Mr. Kenneth A. Beckman, (703) 648-4916, Fax: (703) 648-4995, http://minerals.usgs.gov/minerals; *Mineral Commodity Summaries* and *Minerals Yearbook.*

COAL - RESERVES

U.S. Department of Energy (DOE), Energy Information Administration (EIA), 1000 Independence Avenue, SW, Washington, DC 20585, (202) 586-8800, www.eia.doe.gov; *Annual Coal Report 2005.*

COAL MINING INDUSTRY - CAPITAL

U.S. Census Bureau, Center for Economic Studies, 4600 Silver Hill Road, Washington DC 20233, (301) 457-1235, www.ces.census.gov; *2002 Economic Census, Mining.*

COAL MINING INDUSTRY - EARNINGS

U.S. Bureau of Labor Statistics (BLS), Postal Square Building, 2 Massachusetts Avenue, NE, Washington, DC 20212-0001, (202) 691-5200, Fax: (202) 691-6325, www.bls.gov; *Current Employment Statistics Survey (CES)* and *Employment and Earnings (EE).*

COAL MINING INDUSTRY - EMPLOYMENT

U.S. Bureau of Labor Statistics (BLS), Postal Square Building, 2 Massachusetts Avenue, NE, Washington, DC 20212-0001, (202) 691-5200, Fax: (202) 691-6325, www.bls.gov; *Current Employment Statistics Survey (CES)* and *Employment and Earnings (EE).*

U.S. Department of Energy (DOE), Energy Information Administration (EIA), 1000 Independence Avenue, SW, Washington, DC 20585, (202) 586-8800, www.eia.doe.gov; *Annual Coal Report 2005; Annual Energy Review 2005;* and unpublished data.

COAL MINING INDUSTRY - ESTABLISHMENTS

U.S. Census Bureau, Center for Economic Studies, 4600 Silver Hill Road, Washington DC 20233, (301) 457-1235, www.ces.census.gov; *2002 Economic Census, Mining.*

COAL MINING INDUSTRY - INDUSTRIAL SAFETY

U.S. Bureau of Labor Statistics (BLS), Postal Square Building, 2 Massachusetts Avenue, NE, Washington, DC 20212-0001, (202) 691-5200, Fax: (202) 691-6325, www.bls.gov; *Injuries, Illnesses, and Fatalities (IIF).*

U.S. Department of Labor (DOL), Mine Safety and Health Administration (MSHA), 1100 Wilson Boulevard, 21st Floor, Arlington, VA 22209-3939, (202) 693-9400, Fax: (202) 693-9401, www.msha.gov; *Mine Injury and Worktime Quarterly Statistics; Mine Safety and Health at a Glance;* and *Statistics Single Source Page.*

COAL MINING INDUSTRY - MINES

U.S. Department of Energy (DOE), Energy Information Administration (EIA), 1000 Independence Avenue, SW, Washington, DC 20585, (202) 586-8800, www.eia.doe.gov; *Annual Coal Report 2005; Annual Energy Review 2005; International Energy Outlook 2006;* and unpublished data.

COAL MINING INDUSTRY - OUTPUT

Board of Governors of the Federal Reserve System, Constitution Avenue, NW, Washington, DC 20551, (202) 452-3000, www.federalreserve.gov; *Federal Reserve Bulletin* and *Industrial Production and Capacity Utilization.*

International Energy Agency (IEA), 9, rue de la Federation, 75739 Paris Cedex 15, France, www.iea.org; *Key World Energy Statistics 2007.*

U.S. Department of Energy (DOE), Energy Information Administration (EIA), 1000 Independence Avenue, SW, Washington, DC 20585, (202) 586-8800, www.eia.doe.gov; *Monthly Energy Review (MER)* and *State Energy Data Report.*

U.S. Library of Congress (LOC), Congressional Research Service (CRS), The Library of Congress, 101 Independence Avenue, SE, Washington, DC 20540-7500, (202) 707-5700, www.loc.gov/crsinfo; *Energy: Selected Facts and Numbers.*

COAL MINING INDUSTRY - PRODUCTIVITY

U.S. Bureau of Labor Statistics (BLS), Postal Square Building, 2 Massachusetts Avenue, NE, Washington, DC 20212-0001, (202) 691-5200, Fax: (202) 691-6325, www.bls.gov; *Industry Productivity and Costs.*

U.S. Department of Energy (DOE), Energy Information Administration (EIA), 1000 Independence Avenue, SW, Washington, DC 20585, (202) 586-8800, www.eia.doe.gov; *Annual Coal Report 2005* and *Annual Energy Review 2005.*

COAL MINING INDUSTRY - SHIPMENTS

Association of American Railroads (AAR), 50 F Street, NW, Washington, DC 20001-1564, (202) 639-2100, www.aar.org; *Rail Transportation of Coal.*

U.S. Census Bureau, Center for Economic Studies, 4600 Silver Hill Road, Washington DC 20233, (301) 457-1235, www.ces.census.gov; *2002 Economic Census, Mining.*

COAL MINING INDUSTRY - VALUE ADDED

U.S. Census Bureau, Center for Economic Studies, 4600 Silver Hill Road, Washington DC 20233, (301) 457-1235, www.ces.census.gov; *2002 Economic Census, Mining.*

COAST GUARD PERSONNEL

U.S. Coast Guard (USCG), U.S. Department of Homeland Security (DHS), Coast Guard Headquarters, Commandant, U.S. Coast Guard, 2100 Second Street, SW, Washington, DC 20593, (202) 267-1587, www.uscg.mil; *Fiscal Year 2004 Coast Guard Report: FY2003 Performance Report and FY2005 Budget in Brief.*

U.S. Library of Congress (LOC), Congressional Research Service (CRS), The Library of Congress, 101 Independence Avenue, SE, Washington, DC 20540-7500, (202) 707-5700, www.loc.gov/crsinfo; *Homeland Security: Coast Guard Operations - Background and Issues for Congress* and *Port and Maritime Security: Background and Issues for Congress.*

COASTAL POPULATION

U.S. Census Bureau, 4700 Silver Hill Road, Washington DC 20233-0001, (301) 763-3030, www.census.gov; unpublished data.

United Nations Environment Programme (UNEP), PO Box 30552, Nairobi, Kenya, www.unep.org; *Eastern African Atlas of Coastal Resources.*

World Resources Institute (WRI), 10 G Street, NE, Suite 800 Washington, DC 20002, (202) 729-7600, www.wri.org; *Eutrophication and Hypoxia in Coastal Areas: A Global Assessment of the State of Knowledge.*

COBALT

U.S. Census Bureau, Foreign Trade Division, 4700 Silver Hill Road, Washington DC 20233-0001, (301) 763-3030, www.census.gov/foreign-trade/www/; *U.S. International Trade in Goods and Services.*

U.S. Department of Defense (DOD), Defense Logistics Agency (DLA), 8725 John J. Kingman Road, Fort Belvoir, VA 22060, (703) 767-6666, www.dla.mil; *Stockpile Report to the Congress 2002.*

U.S. Department of the Interior (DOI), U.S. Geological Survey (USGS), Office of Minerals Information, 12201 Sunrise Valley Drive, Reston, VA 20192, Mr. Kenneth A. Beckman, (703) 648-4916, Fax: (703) 648-4995, http://minerals.usgs.gov/minerals; *Mineral Commodity Summaries.*

World Bureau of Metal Statistics (WBMS), 27a High Street, Ware, Hertfordshire, SG12 9BA, United Kingdom, www.world-bureau.com; *Annual Cobalt Statistics.*

COCAINE - ARRESTS

Federal Bureau of Investigation (FBI), J. Edgar Hoover Building, 935 Pennsylvania Avenue, NW, Washington, DC 20535-0001, (202) 324-3000, www.fbi.gov; *Crime in the United States (CIUS) 2007 (Preliminary).*

Justice Research and Statistics Association (JRSA), 777 N. Capitol Street, NE, Suite 801, Washington, DC 20002, (202) 842-9330, Fax: (202) 842-9329, www.jrsa.org; *Crime and Justice Atlas 2001.*

Substance Abuse and Mental Health Services Administration (SAMHSA), 1 Choke Cherry Road, Rockville, MD 20857, (240) 777-1311, www.oas.samhsa.gov; *National Survey on Drug Use Health (NSDUH).*

U.S. Department of Justice (DOJ), Bureau of Justice Statistics, 810 Seventh Street, NW, Washington, DC 20531, (202) 307-0765, www.ojp.usdoj.gov/bjs/; *Drugs Crime Facts.*

U.S. Department of Justice (DOJ), Drug Enforcement Administration (DEA), 2401 Jefferson Davis Highway, Alexandria, VA 22301, (202) 307-1000, www.usdoj.gov/dea; *State Factsheets.*

U.S. Department of Justice (DOJ), National Institute of Justice (NIJ), 810 Seventh Street, NW, Washington, DC 20531, (202) 307-2942, Fax: (202) 616-0275, www.ojp.usdoj.gov/nij/; *ADAM Preliminary 2000 Findings on Drug Use Drug Markets: Adult Male Arrestees; Drug Courts: The Second Decade;* and *I-ADAM in Eight Countries: Approaches and Challenges.*

COCOA

Economic Research Service (ERS), U.S. Department of Agriculture (USDA), 1800 M Street, NW, Washington, DC 20036-5831, (202) 694-5050, Fax: (202) 694-5689, www.ers.usda.gov; *Agricultural Outlook; Food CPI, Prices, and Expenditures;* and *Foreign Agricultural Trade of the United States (FATUS).*

COCOS (KEELING) ISLANDS - ABORTION

United Nations Statistics Division, New York, NY 10017, (800) 253-9646, Fax: (212) 963-4116, http://unstats.un.org; *Demographic Yearbook.*

COCOS (KEELING) ISLANDS - AGRICULTURE

Taylor and Francis Group, An Informa Business, 2 Park Square, Milton Park, Abingdon, Oxford OX14 4RN, United Kingdom, (Dial from U.S. (212) 216-7800), (Fax from U.S. (212) 564-7854), www.tandf.co.uk; *The Europa World Year Book.*

United Nations Food and Agricultural Organization (FAO), Viale delle Terme di Caracalla, 00100 Rome, Italy, (Dial from U.S. (202) 653-2400), (Fax from U.S. (202) 653 5760), www.fao.org; AQUASTAT; *FAO Production Yearbook 2002; FAO Trade Yearbook;* and *The State of Food and Agriculture (SOFA) 2006.*

COCOS (KEELING) ISLANDS - AIRLINES

Palgrave Macmillan Ltd., Houndmills, Basingstoke, Hampshire, RG21 6XS, England, (Telephone in U.S. (888) 330-8477), (Fax in U.S. (800) 672-2054), www.palgrave.com; *The Statesman's Yearbook 2008.*

COCOS (KEELING) ISLANDS - AIRPORTS

Central Intelligence Agency, Office of Public Affairs, Washington, DC 20505, (703) 482-0623, Fax: (703) 482-1739, www.cia.gov; *The World Factbook.*

COCOS (KEELING) ISLANDS - ARMED FORCES

Central Intelligence Agency, Office of Public Affairs, Washington, DC 20505, (703) 482-0623, Fax: (703) 482-1739, www.cia.gov; *The World Factbook.*

COCOS (KEELING) ISLANDS - BROADCASTING

Central Intelligence Agency, Office of Public Affairs, Washington, DC 20505, (703) 482-0623, Fax: (703) 482-1739, www.cia.gov; *The World Factbook.*

WRTH Publications Limited, PO Box 290, Oxford OX2 7FT, UK, www.wrth.com; *World Radio TV Handbook 2007.*

COCOS (KEELING) ISLANDS - BUDGET

Central Intelligence Agency, Office of Public Affairs, Washington, DC 20505, (703) 482-0623, Fax: (703) 482-1739, www.cia.gov; *The World Factbook.*

COCOS (KEELING) ISLANDS - CHILDBIRTH - STATISTICS

Central Intelligence Agency, Office of Public Affairs, Washington, DC 20505, (703) 482-0623, Fax: (703) 482-1739, www.cia.gov; *The World Factbook.*

Taylor and Francis Group, An Informa Business, 2 Park Square, Milton Park, Abingdon, Oxford OX14 4RN, United Kingdom, (Dial from U.S. (212) 216-7800), (Fax from U.S. (212) 564-7854), www.tandf.co.uk; *The Europa World Year Book.*

United Nations Statistics Division, New York, NY 10017, (800) 253-9646, Fax: (212) 963-4116, http://unstats.un.org; *Demographic Yearbook* and *Statistical Yearbook.*

World Health Organization (WHO), Avenue Appia 20, 1211 Geneve 27, Switzerland, (Telephone in U.S. (212) 331-9081), www.who.int; *World Health Report 2006.*

COCOS (KEELING) ISLANDS - CLIMATE

Palgrave Macmillan Ltd., Houndmills, Basingstoke, Hampshire, RG21 6XS, England, (Telephone in U.S. (888) 330-8477), (Fax in U.S. (800) 672-2054), www.palgrave.com; *The Statesman's Yearbook 2008.*

COCOS (KEELING) ISLANDS - COMMODITY EXCHANGES

United Nations Food and Agricultural Organization (FAO), Viale delle Terme di Caracalla, 00100 Rome, Italy, (Dial from U.S. (202) 653-2400), (Fax from U.S. (202) 653 5760), www.fao.org; *The State of Food and Agriculture (SOFA) 2006.*

COCOS (KEELING) ISLANDS - CORN INDUSTRY

See COCOS (KEELING) ISLANDS - CROPS

COCOS (KEELING) ISLANDS - CROPS

Taylor and Francis Group, An Informa Business, 2 Park Square, Milton Park, Abingdon, Oxford OX14 4RN, United Kingdom, (Dial from U.S. (212) 216-7800), (Fax from U.S. (212) 564-7854), www.tandf.co.uk; *The Europa World Year Book.*

United Nations Food and Agricultural Organization (FAO), Viale delle Terme di Caracalla, 00100 Rome, Italy, (Dial from U.S. (202) 653-2400), (Fax from U.S. (202) 653 5760), www.fao.org; *The State of Food and Agriculture (SOFA) 2006.*

COCOS (KEELING) ISLANDS - DAIRY PROCESSING

United Nations Food and Agricultural Organization (FAO), Viale delle Terme di Caracalla, 00100 Rome, Italy, (Dial from U.S. (202) 653-2400), (Fax from U.S. (202) 653 5760), www.fao.org; *The State of Food and Agriculture (SOFA) 2006.*

COCOS (KEELING) ISLANDS - DEATH RATES

See COCOS (KEELING) ISLANDS - MORTALITY

COCOS (KEELING) ISLANDS - DIVORCE

United Nations Statistics Division, New York, NY 10017, (800) 253-9646, Fax: (212) 963-4116, http://unstats.un.org; *Demographic Yearbook.*

COCOS (KEELING) ISLANDS - ECONOMIC CONDITIONS

Central Intelligence Agency, Office of Public Affairs, Washington, DC 20505, (703) 482-0623, Fax: (703) 482-1739, www.cia.gov; *The World Factbook.*

COCOS (KEELING) ISLANDS - EDUCATION

Palgrave Macmillan Ltd., Houndmills, Basingstoke, Hampshire, RG21 6XS, England, (Telephone in U.S. (888) 330-8477), (Fax in U.S. (800) 672-2054), www.palgrave.com; *The Statesman's Yearbook 2008.*

COCOS (KEELING) ISLANDS - ELECTRICITY

Palgrave Macmillan Ltd., Houndmills, Basingstoke, Hampshire, RG21 6XS, England, (Telephone in U.S. (888) 330-8477), (Fax in U.S. (800) 672-2054), www.palgrave.com; *The Statesman's Yearbook 2008.*

COCOS (KEELING) ISLANDS - EXPORTS

Central Intelligence Agency, Office of Public Affairs, Washington, DC 20505, (703) 482-0623, Fax: (703) 482-1739, www.cia.gov; *The World Factbook.*

Taylor and Francis Group, An Informa Business, 2 Park Square, Milton Park, Abingdon, Oxford OX14 4RN, United Kingdom, (Dial from U.S. (212) 216-7800), (Fax from U.S. (212) 564-7854), www.tandf.co.uk; *The Europa World Year Book.*

United Nations Food and Agricultural Organization (FAO), Viale delle Terme di Caracalla, 00100 Rome, Italy, (Dial from U.S. (202) 653-2400), (Fax from U.S. (202) 653 5760), www.fao.org; *The State of Food and Agriculture (SOFA) 2006.*

COCOS (KEELING) ISLANDS - FERTILITY, HUMAN

Central Intelligence Agency, Office of Public Affairs, Washington, DC 20505, (703) 482-0623, Fax: (703) 482-1739, www.cia.gov; *The World Factbook.*

COCOS (KEELING) ISLANDS - FERTILIZER INDUSTRY

United Nations Food and Agricultural Organization (FAO), Viale delle Terme di Caracalla, 00100 Rome, Italy, (Dial from U.S. (202) 653-2400), (Fax from U.S. (202) 653 5760), www.fao.org; *The State of Food and Agriculture (SOFA) 2006.*

COCOS (KEELING) ISLANDS - FETAL MORTALITY

See COCOS (KEELING) ISLANDS - MORTALITY

COCOS (KEELING) ISLANDS - FINANCE, PUBLIC

Taylor and Francis Group, An Informa Business, 2 Park Square, Milton Park, Abingdon, Oxford OX14 4RN, United Kingdom, (Dial from U.S. (212) 216-7800), (Fax from U.S. (212) 564-7854), www.tandf.co.uk; *The Europa World Year Book.*

COCOS (KEELING) ISLANDS - FISHERIES

United Nations Food and Agricultural Organization (FAO), Viale delle Terme di Caracalla, 00100 Rome, Italy, (Dial from U.S. (202) 653-2400), (Fax from U.S. (202) 653 5760), www.fao.org; *FAO Yearbook of Fishery Statistics;* Fishery Databases; FISHSTAT Database. Subjects covered include: Aquaculture production, capture production, fishery commodities; and *The State of Food and Agriculture (SOFA) 2006.*

COCOS (KEELING) ISLANDS - FOOD

United Nations Food and Agricultural Organization (FAO), Viale delle Terme di Caracalla, 00100 Rome, Italy, (Dial from U.S. (202) 653-2400), (Fax from U.S. (202) 653 5760), www.fao.org; *FAO Production Yearbook 2002* and *The State of Food and Agriculture (SOFA) 2006.*

COCOS (KEELING) ISLANDS - FOREIGN EXCHANGE RATES

Central Intelligence Agency, Office of Public Affairs, Washington, DC 20505, (703) 482-0623, Fax: (703) 482-1739, www.cia.gov; *The World Factbook.*

Taylor and Francis Group, An Informa Business, 2 Park Square, Milton Park, Abingdon, Oxford OX14 4RN, United Kingdom, (Dial from U.S. (212) 216-7800), (Fax from U.S. (212) 564-7854), www.tandf.co.uk; *The Europa World Year Book.*

COCOS (KEELING) ISLANDS - FORESTS AND FORESTRY

United Nations Food and Agricultural Organization (FAO), Viale delle Terme di Caracalla, 00100 Rome, Italy, (Dial from U.S. (202) 653-2400), (Fax from U.S. (202) 653 5760), www.fao.org; *The State of Food and Agriculture (SOFA) 2006.*

COCOS (KEELING) ISLANDS - IMPORTS

Central Intelligence Agency, Office of Public Affairs, Washington, DC 20505, (703) 482-0623, Fax: (703) 482-1739, www.cia.gov; *The World Factbook.*

Taylor and Francis Group, An Informa Business, 2 Park Square, Milton Park, Abingdon, Oxford OX14 4RN, United Kingdom, (Dial from U.S. (212) 216-7800), (Fax from U.S. (212) 564-7854), www.tandf.co.uk; *The Europa World Year Book.*

United Nations Food and Agricultural Organization (FAO), Viale delle Terme di Caracalla, 00100 Rome, Italy, (Dial from U.S. (202) 653-2400), (Fax from U.S. (202) 653 5760), www.fao.org; *The State of Food and Agriculture (SOFA) 2006.*

COCOS (KEELING) ISLANDS - INDUSTRIES

Central Intelligence Agency, Office of Public Affairs, Washington, DC 20505, (703) 482-0623, Fax: (703) 482-1739, www.cia.gov; *The World Factbook.*

COCOS (KEELING) ISLANDS - INFANT AND MATERNAL MORTALITY

See COCOS (KEELING) ISLANDS - MORTALITY

COCOS (KEELING) ISLANDS - INTERNATIONAL TRADE

Organisation for Economic Cooperation and Development (OECD), 2 rue Andre Pascal, F-75775 Paris Cedex 16, France, (Telephone in U.S. (202) 785-6323), (Fax in U.S. (202) 785-0350), www.oecd.org; *International Trade by Commodity Statistics (ITCS).*

Taylor and Francis Group, An Informa Business, 2 Park Square, Milton Park, Abingdon, Oxford OX14 4RN, United Kingdom, (Dial from U.S. (212) 216-7800), (Fax from U.S. (212) 564-7854), www.tandf.co.uk; *The Europa World Year Book.*

United Nations Food and Agricultural Organization (FAO), Viale delle Terme di Caracalla, 00100 Rome, Italy, (Dial from U.S. (202) 653-2400), (Fax from U.S. (202) 653 5760), www.fao.org; *FAO Trade Yearbook* and *The State of Food and Agriculture (SOFA) 2006.*

World Trade Organization (WTO), Centre William Rappard, Rue de Lausanne 154, CH-1211 Geneva 21, Switzerland, www.wto.org; *International Trade Statistics 2006.*

COCOS (KEELING) ISLANDS - LABOR

Central Intelligence Agency, Office of Public Affairs, Washington, DC 20505, (703) 482-0623, Fax: (703) 482-1739, www.cia.gov; *The World Factbook.*

United Nations Food and Agricultural Organization (FAO), Viale delle Terme di Caracalla, 00100 Rome, Italy, (Dial from U.S. (202) 653-2400), (Fax from U.S. (202) 653 5760), www.fao.org; *The State of Food and Agriculture (SOFA) 2006.*

COCOS (KEELING) ISLANDS - LAND USE

Central Intelligence Agency, Office of Public Affairs, Washington, DC 20505, (703) 482-0623, Fax: (703) 482-1739, www.cia.gov; *The World Factbook.*

United Nations Food and Agricultural Organization (FAO), Viale delle Terme di Caracalla, 00100 Rome, Italy, (Dial from U.S. (202) 653-2400), (Fax from U.S. (202) 653 5760), www.fao.org; *FAO Production Yearbook 2002.*

COCOS (KEELING) ISLANDS - LIFE EXPECTANCY

Central Intelligence Agency, Office of Public Affairs, Washington, DC 20505, (703) 482-0623, Fax: (703) 482-1739, www.cia.gov; *The World Factbook.*

COCOS (KEELING) ISLANDS - LIVESTOCK

United Nations Food and Agricultural Organization (FAO), Viale delle Terme di Caracalla, 00100 Rome, Italy, (Dial from U.S. (202) 653-2400), (Fax from U.S. (202) 653 5760), www.fao.org; *FAO Production Yearbook 2002* and *The State of Food and Agriculture (SOFA) 2006.*

COCOS (KEELING) ISLANDS - MARRIAGE

United Nations Statistics Division, New York, NY 10017, (800) 253-9646, Fax: (212) 963-4116, http://unstats.un.org; *Demographic Yearbook* and *Statistical Yearbook.*

COCOS (KEELING) ISLANDS - MEAT PRODUCTION

See COCOS (KEELING) ISLANDS - LIVESTOCK

COCOS (KEELING) ISLANDS - MORTALITY

Central Intelligence Agency, Office of Public Affairs, Washington, DC 20505, (703) 482-0623, Fax: (703) 482-1739, www.cia.gov; *The World Factbook.*

Taylor and Francis Group, An Informa Business, 2 Park Square, Milton Park, Abingdon, Oxford OX14 4RN, United Kingdom, (Dial from U.S. (212) 216-7800), (Fax from U.S. (212) 564-7854), www.tandf.co.uk; *The Europa World Year Book.*

United Nations Statistics Division, New York, NY 10017, (800) 253-9646, Fax: (212) 963-4116, http://unstats.un.org; *Demographic Yearbook.*

World Health Organization (WHO), Avenue Appia 20, 1211 Geneve 27, Switzerland, (Telephone in U.S. (212) 331-9081), www.who.int; *World Health Report 2006.*

COCOS (KEELING) ISLANDS - NUTRITION

United Nations Food and Agricultural Organization (FAO), Viale delle Terme di Caracalla, 00100 Rome, Italy, (Dial from U.S. (202) 653-2400), (Fax from U.S. (202) 653 5760), www.fao.org; *The State of Food and Agriculture (SOFA) 2006.*

COCOS (KEELING) ISLANDS - PESTICIDES

United Nations Food and Agricultural Organization (FAO), Viale delle Terme di Caracalla, 00100 Rome, Italy, (Dial from U.S. (202) 653-2400), (Fax from U.S. (202) 653 5760), www.fao.org; *The State of Food and Agriculture (SOFA) 2006.*

COCOS (KEELING) ISLANDS - PETROLEUM INDUSTRY AND TRADE

PennWell Corporation, 1421 South Sheridan Road, Tulsa, OK 74112, (918) 835-3161, www.pennwell.com; *International Petroleum Encyclopedia 2007.*

United Nations Food and Agricultural Organization (FAO), Viale delle Terme di Caracalla, 00100 Rome, Italy, (Dial from U.S. (202) 653-2400), (Fax from U.S. (202) 653 5760), www.fao.org; *The State of Food and Agriculture (SOFA) 2006.*

COCOS (KEELING) ISLANDS - POLITICAL SCIENCE

Central Intelligence Agency, Office of Public Affairs, Washington, DC 20505, (703) 482-0623, Fax: (703) 482-1739, www.cia.gov; *The World Factbook.*

COCOS (KEELING) ISLANDS - POPULATION

Central Intelligence Agency, Office of Public Affairs, Washington, DC 20505, (703) 482-0623, Fax: (703) 482-1739, www.cia.gov; *The World Factbook.*

Palgrave Macmillan Ltd., Houndmills, Basingstoke, Hampshire, RG21 6XS, England, (Telephone in U.S. (888) 330-8477), (Fax in U.S. (800) 672-2054), www.palgrave.com; *The Statesman's Yearbook 2008.*

Taylor and Francis Group, An Informa Business, 2 Park Square, Milton Park, Abingdon, Oxford OX14 4RN, United Kingdom, (Dial from U.S. (212) 216-7800), (Fax from U.S. (212) 564-7854), www.tandf.co.uk; *The Europa World Year Book.*

UNESCO Institute for Statistics, C.P. 6128 Succursale Centre-Ville, Montreal, Quebec, H3C 3J7 Canada, (Dial from U.S. (514) 343-6880), (Fax from U.S. (514) 343 6882), www.uis.unesco.org; *Statistical Tables.*

United Nations Food and Agricultural Organization (FAO), Viale delle Terme di Caracalla, 00100 Rome, Italy, (Dial from U.S. (202) 653-2400), (Fax from U.S. (202) 653 5760), www.fao.org; *FAO Production Yearbook 2002.*

United Nations Statistics Division, New York, NY 10017, (800) 253-9646, Fax: (212) 963-4116, http://unstats.un.org; *Demographic Yearbook* and *Statistical Yearbook.*

World Health Organization (WHO), Avenue Appia 20, 1211 Geneve 27, Switzerland, (Telephone in U.S. (212) 331-9081), www.who.int; *World Health Report 2006.*

COCOS (KEELING) ISLANDS - POPULATION DENSITY

Central Intelligence Agency, Office of Public Affairs, Washington, DC 20505, (703) 482-0623, Fax: (703) 482-1739, www.cia.gov; *The World Factbook.*

Taylor and Francis Group, An Informa Business, 2 Park Square, Milton Park, Abingdon, Oxford OX14 4RN, United Kingdom, (Dial from U.S. (212) 216-7800), (Fax from U.S. (212) 564-7854), www.tandf.co.uk; *The Europa World Year Book.*

United Nations Food and Agricultural Organization (FAO), Viale delle Terme di Caracalla, 00100 Rome, Italy, (Dial from U.S. (202) 653-2400), (Fax from U.S. (202) 653 5760), www.fao.org; *The State of Food and Agriculture (SOFA) 2006.*

United Nations Statistics Division, New York, NY 10017, (800) 253-9646, Fax: (212) 963-4116, http://unstats.un.org; *Statistical Yearbook.*

COCOS (KEELING) ISLANDS - POSTAL SERVICE

Palgrave Macmillan Ltd., Houndmills, Basingstoke, Hampshire, RG21 6XS, England, (Telephone in U.S. (888) 330-8477), (Fax in U.S. (800) 672-2054), www.palgrave.com; *The Statesman's Yearbook 2008.*

COCOS (KEELING) ISLANDS - POWER RESOURCES

United Nations Food and Agricultural Organization (FAO), Viale delle Terme di Caracalla, 00100 Rome, Italy, (Dial from U.S. (202) 653-2400), (Fax from U.S. (202) 653 5760), www.fao.org; *The State of Food and Agriculture (SOFA) 2006.*

COCOS (KEELING) ISLANDS - PRICES

United Nations Food and Agricultural Organization (FAO), Viale delle Terme di Caracalla, 00100 Rome, Italy, (Dial from U.S. (202) 653-2400), (Fax from

U.S. (202) 653 5760), www.fao.org; *FAO Production Yearbook 2002* and *The State of Food and Agriculture (SOFA) 2006*.

COCOS (KEELING) ISLANDS - PUBLIC HEALTH

Palgrave Macmillan Ltd., Houndmills, Basingstoke, Hampshire, RG21 6XS, England, (Telephone in U.S. (888) 330-8477), (Fax in U.S. (800) 672-2054), www.palgrave.com; *The Statesman's Yearbook 2008*.

COCOS (KEELING) ISLANDS - RADIO BROADCASTING

Palgrave Macmillan Ltd., Houndmills, Basingstoke, Hampshire, RG21 6XS, England, (Telephone in U.S. (888) 330-8477), (Fax in U.S. (800) 672-2054), www.palgrave.com; *The Statesman's Yearbook 2008*.

COCOS (KEELING) ISLANDS - RELIGION

Central Intelligence Agency, Office of Public Affairs, Washington, DC 20505, (703) 482-0623, Fax: (703) 482-1739, www.cia.gov; *The World Factbook*.

Palgrave Macmillan Ltd., Houndmills, Basingstoke, Hampshire, RG21 6XS, England, (Telephone in U.S. (888) 330-8477), (Fax in U.S. (800) 672-2054), www.palgrave.com; *The Statesman's Yearbook 2008*.

COCOS (KEELING) ISLANDS - ROADS

Central Intelligence Agency, Office of Public Affairs, Washington, DC 20505, (703) 482-0623, Fax: (703) 482-1739, www.cia.gov; *The World Factbook*.

Palgrave Macmillan Ltd., Houndmills, Basingstoke, Hampshire, RG21 6XS, England, (Telephone in U.S. (888) 330-8477), (Fax in U.S. (800) 672-2054), www.palgrave.com; *The Statesman's Yearbook 2008*.

COCOS (KEELING) ISLANDS - TELEPHONE

International Telecommunication Union (ITU), Place des Nations, 1211 Geneva 20, Switzerland, www.itu.int; World Telecommunication Indicators Database.

Palgrave Macmillan Ltd., Houndmills, Basingstoke, Hampshire, RG21 6XS, England, (Telephone in U.S. (888) 330-8477), (Fax in U.S. (800) 672-2054), www.palgrave.com; *The Statesman's Yearbook 2008*.

COCOS (KEELING) ISLANDS - TRADE

See COCOS (KEELING) ISLANDS - INTERNATIONAL TRADE

COCOS (KEELING) ISLANDS - TRANSPORTATION

Central Intelligence Agency, Office of Public Affairs, Washington, DC 20505, (703) 482-0623, Fax: (703) 482-1739, www.cia.gov; *The World Factbook*.

Palgrave Macmillan Ltd., Houndmills, Basingstoke, Hampshire, RG21 6XS, England, (Telephone in U.S. (888) 330-8477), (Fax in U.S. (800) 672-2054), www.palgrave.com; *The Statesman's Yearbook 2008*.

COCOS (KEELING) ISLANDS - UNEMPLOYMENT

Central Intelligence Agency, Office of Public Affairs, Washington, DC 20505, (703) 482-0623, Fax: (703) 482-1739, www.cia.gov; *The World Factbook*.

COCOS (KEELING) ISLANDS - VITAL STATISTICS

United Nations Statistics Division, New York, NY 10017, (800) 253-9646, Fax: (212) 963-4116, http://unstats.un.org; *Statistical Yearbook*.

World Health Organization (WHO), Avenue Appia 20, 1211 Geneve 27, Switzerland, (Telephone in U.S. (212) 331-9081), www.who.int; *World Health Report 2006*.

COD

National Marine Fisheries Service (NMFS), National Oceanic and Atmospheric Administration (NOAA), Office of Constituent Services, 1315 East West Highway, 9th Floor, Silver Spring, MD 20910, (301) 713-2379, Fax: (301) 713-2385, www.nmfs.noaa.gov; *Fisheries of the United States - 2006*.

COFFEE - CONSUMPTION

Economic Research Service (ERS), U.S. Department of Agriculture (USDA), 1800 M Street, NW, Washington, DC 20036-5831, (202) 694-5050, Fax: (202) 694-5689, www.ers.usda.gov; *Agricultural Outlook* and *Food CPI, Prices, and Expenditures*.

COFFEE - INTERNATIONAL TRADE

Economic Research Service (ERS), U.S. Department of Agriculture (USDA), 1800 M Street, NW, Washington, DC 20036-5831, (202) 694-5050, Fax: (202) 694-5689, www.ers.usda.gov; *Foreign Agricultural Trade of the United States (FATUS)* and *U.S. Agricultural Trade Update: 2006*.

U.S. Census Bureau, Foreign Trade Division, 4700 Silver Hill Road, Washington DC 20233-0001, (301) 763-3030, www.census.gov/foreign-trade/www/; *U.S. International Trade in Goods and Services*.

COFFEE - PRICE INDEXES

U.S. Bureau of Labor Statistics (BLS), Postal Square Building, 2 Massachusetts Avenue, NE, Washington, DC 20212-0001, (202) 691-5200, Fax: (202) 691-6325, www.bls.gov; *Consumer Price Index Detailed Report* and *Monthly Labor Review (MLR)*.

COFFEE - PRICES

U.S. Bureau of Labor Statistics (BLS), Postal Square Building, 2 Massachusetts Avenue, NE, Washington, DC 20212-0001, (202) 691-5200, Fax: (202) 691-6325, www.bls.gov; *Consumer Price Index Detailed Report* and *Monthly Labor Review (MLR)*.

COFFEE - WORLD PRODUCTION

United Nations Statistics Division, New York, NY 10017, (800) 253-9646, Fax: (212) 963-4116, http://unstats.un.org; *Monthly Bulletin of Statistics*.

COGENERATION OF ELECTRICITY

Edison Electric Institute (EEI), 701 Pennsylvania Avenue, NW, Washington, DC 20004-2696, (202) 508-5000, www.eei.org; *Historical Statistics of the Electric Utility Industry through 1992*.

U.S. Department of Energy (DOE), Energy Information Administration (EIA), 1000 Independence Avenue, SW, Washington, DC 20585, (202) 586-8800, www.eia.doe.gov; *Electric Power Annual* and *Inventory of Nonutility Electric Power Plants in the United States*.

COKE - CAR LOADING AND FREIGHT CARRIED

Association of American Railroads (AAR), 50 F Street, NW, Washington, DC 20001-1564, (202) 639-2100, www.aar.org; *Weekly Railroad Traffic*.

COLLEGE STUDENTS

Center for Substance Abuse Research (CESAR), 4321 Hartwick Road, Suite 501, College Park, MD 20740, (301) 405-9770, Fax: (301) 403-8342, www.cesar.umd.edu; *College Students' Perceptions of Non-Medical Use of Prescription Stimulants by Their Peers: Findings From the April 2005 Administration of the Student Drug Research (SDR) Survey* and *DEWS Investigates: Perceptions of Prescription Stimulant Misuse Among College Students at High and Low Risk of Drug Use*.

Higher Education Research Institute (HERI), University of California, Los Angeles, 3005 Moore Hall/Box 951521, Los Angeles, CA 90095-1521, (310) 825-1925, Fax: (310) 206-2228, www.gseis.ucla.edu/heri/index.php; *American Freshman: National Norms for 2006; How Service Learning Affects Students;* and *The 2007 Your First College Year (YFCY) Survey*.

Institute of International Education (IIE), 809 United Nations Plaza, New York, NY 10017-3580, (212) 883-8200, Fax: (212) 984-5452, www.iie.org; *International Student Enrollment Survey: Survey Report Fall 2007* and *Open Doors 1948-2004: CD-ROM*.

Public/Private Ventures (P/PV), 2000 Market Street, Suite 600, Philadelphia, PA 19103, (215) 557-4400, Fax: (215) 557 4469, www.ppv.org; *College Students as Mentors for At-Risk Youth: A Study of Six Campus Partners in Learning Programs*.

U.S. Department of Justice (DOJ), Bureau of Justice Statistics, 810 Seventh Street, NW, Washington, DC 20531, (202) 307-0765, www.ojp.usdoj.gov/bjs/; *Sexual Victimization of College Women* and *Violent Victimization of College Students, 1995-2002*.

U.S. Department of Justice (DOJ), Office of Community Oriented Policing Services (COPS), 1100 Vermont Avenue, NW, Washington, DC 20530, (202) 307-1480, www.cops.usdoj.gov; *Acquaintance Rape of College Students*.

COLLEGE TUITION

Investment Company Institute (ICI), 1401 H Street, NW, Suite 1200, Washington, DC 20005-2040, (202) 326-5800, www.ici.org; *Profile of Households Saving for College*.

National Center for Education Statistics (NCES), 1990 K Street, NW, Washington, DC 20006, (202) 502-7300, http://nces.ed.gov; *Digest of Education Statistics 2007*.

COLLEGE TUITION - PRICE INDEXES

U.S. Bureau of Labor Statistics (BLS), Postal Square Building, 2 Massachusetts Avenue, NE, Washington, DC 20212-0001, (202) 691-5200, Fax: (202) 691-6325, www.bls.gov; *Consumer Price Index Detailed Report* and *Monthly Labor Review (MLR)*.

COLLEGES AND UNIVERSITIES

See EDUCATION - HIGHER EDUCATION INSTITUTIONS

COLOMBIA - NATIONAL STATISTICAL OFFICE

Departamento Administrativo Nacional de Estadisticas (DANE), A.A 80043 Zona Postal 611, Bogota D.C., Colombia, www.dane.gov.co; National Data Center.

COLOMBIA - PRIMARY STATISTICS SOURCES

Departamento Administrativo Nacional de Estadisticas (DANE), A.A 80043 Zona Postal 611, Bogota D.C., Colombia, www.dane.gov.co; *Censo General 2005* (General Census 2005) and *Estadisticas Vitales* (Vital Statistics).

COLOMBIA - AGRICULTURAL MACHINERY

Economist Intelligence Unit, 111 West 57th Street, New York, NY 10019, (212) 554-0600, Fax: (212) 586-1181, www.eiu.com; *Business Latin America*.

United Nations Statistics Division, New York, NY 10017, (800) 253-9646, Fax: (212) 963-4116, http://unstats.un.org; *Statistical Yearbook*.

COLOMBIA - AGRICULTURE

Economist Intelligence Unit, 111 West 57th Street, New York, NY 10019, (212) 554-0600, Fax: (212) 586-1181, www.eiu.com; *Business Latin America* and *Colombia Country Report*.

Euromonitor International, Inc., 224 S. Michigan Avenue, Suite 1500, Chicago, IL 60604, (312) 922-1115, Fax: (312) 922-1157, www.euromonitor.com; *International Marketing Data and Statistics 2008* and *World Marketing Data and Statistics*.

Inter-American Development Bank (IDB), 1300 New York Avenue, NW, Washington, DC 20577, (202)

623-1000, Fax: (202) 623-3096, www.iadb.org; *The Politics of Policies: Economic and Social Progress in Latin America - 2006 Report.*

M.E. Sharpe, 80 Business Park Drive, Armonk, NY 10504, (800) 541-6563, Fax: (914) 273-2106, www.mesharpe.com; *The Illustrated Book of World Rankings.*

Palgrave Macmillan Ltd., Houndmills, Basingstoke, Hampshire, RG21 6XS, England, (Telephone in U.S. (888) 330-8477), (Fax in U.S. (800) 672-2054), www.palgrave.com; *The Statesman's Yearbook 2008.*

Taylor and Francis Group, An Informa Business, 2 Park Square, Milton Park, Abingdon, Oxford OX14 4RN, United Kingdom, (Dial from U.S. (212) 216-7800), (Fax from U.S. (212) 564-7854), www.tandf.co.uk; *The Europa World Year Book.*

UCLA Latin American Institute, 10343 Bunche Hall, Box 951447, Los Angeles, CA 90095-1447, (310) 825-4571, Fax: (310) 206-6859, www.international.ucla.edu/lac; *Statistical Abstract of Latin America.*

United Nations Conference on Trade and Development (UNCTAD), DC2-1120, United Nations, New York, NY 10017, (212) 963-0027, www.unctad.org; *UNCTAD Commodity Yearbook.*

United Nations Food and Agricultural Organization (FAO), Viale delle Terme di Caracalla, 00100 Rome, Italy, (Dial from U.S. (202) 653-2400), (Fax from U.S. (202) 653 5760), www.fao.org; AQUASTAT; *FAO Production Yearbook 2002; FAO Trade Yearbook;* and *The State of Food and Agriculture (SOFA) 2006.*

United Nations Statistics Division, New York, NY 10017, (800) 253-9646, Fax: (212) 963-4116, http://unstats.un.org; *Statistical Yearbook* and *Statistical Yearbook for Latin America and the Caribbean 2004.*

The World Bank, 1818 H Street, NW, Washington, DC 20433, (202) 473-1000, Fax: (202) 477-6391, www.worldbank.org; *Colombia.*

COLOMBIA - AIRLINES

Economist Intelligence Unit, 111 West 57th Street, New York, NY 10019, (212) 554-0600, Fax: (212) 586-1181, www.eiu.com; *Business Latin America.*

International Civil Aviation Organization (ICAO), External Relations and Public Information Office (EPO), 999 University Street, Montreal, Quebec H3C 5H7, Canada, (Dial from U.S. (514) 954-8219), (Fax from U.S. (514) 954-6077), www.icao.int; *Civil Aviation Statistics of the World.*

M.E. Sharpe, 80 Business Park Drive, Armonk, NY 10504, (800) 541-6563, Fax: (914) 273-2106, www.mesharpe.com; *The Illustrated Book of World Rankings.*

Palgrave Macmillan Ltd., Houndmills, Basingstoke, Hampshire, RG21 6XS, England, (Telephone in U.S. (888) 330-8477), (Fax in U.S. (800) 672-2054), www.palgrave.com; *The Statesman's Yearbook 2008.*

Taylor and Francis Group, An Informa Business, 2 Park Square, Milton Park, Abingdon, Oxford OX14 4RN, United Kingdom, (Dial from U.S. (212) 216-7800), (Fax from U.S. (212) 564-7854), www.tandf.co.uk; *The Europa World Year Book.*

United Nations Statistics Division, New York, NY 10017, (800) 253-9646, Fax: (212) 963-4116, http://unstats.un.org; *Statistical Yearbook.*

COLOMBIA - AIRPORTS

Central Intelligence Agency, Office of Public Affairs, Washington, DC 20505, (703) 482-0623, Fax: (703) 482-1739, www.cia.gov; *The World Factbook.*

COLOMBIA - ALUMINUM PRODUCTION

See COLOMBIA - MINERAL INDUSTRIES

COLOMBIA - AREA

Economist Intelligence Unit, 111 West 57th Street, New York, NY 10019, (212) 554-0600, Fax: (212) 586-1181, www.eiu.com; *Business Latin America.*

COLOMBIA - ARMED FORCES

Central Intelligence Agency, Office of Public Affairs, Washington, DC 20505, (703) 482-0623, Fax: (703) 482-1739, www.cia.gov; *The World Factbook.*

Economist Intelligence Unit, 111 West 57th Street, New York, NY 10019, (212) 554-0600, Fax: (212) 586-1181, www.eiu.com; *Business Latin America.*

Euromonitor International, Inc., 224 S. Michigan Avenue, Suite 1500, Chicago, IL 60604, (312) 922-1115, Fax: (312) 922-1157, www.euromonitor.com; *World Marketing Data and Statistics.*

International Institute for Strategic Studies (IISS), Arundel House, 13-15 Arundel Street, Temple Place, London WC2R 3DX, England, www.iiss.org; *The Military Balance 2007.*

Palgrave Macmillan Ltd., Houndmills, Basingstoke, Hampshire, RG21 6XS, England, (Telephone in U.S. (888) 330-8477), (Fax in U.S. (800) 672-2054), www.palgrave.com; *The Statesman's Yearbook 2008.*

U.S. Department of State (DOS), 2201 C Street NW, Washington, DC 20520, (202) 647-4000, www.state.gov; *World Military Expenditures and Arms Transfers (WMEAT).*

UCLA Latin American Institute, 10343 Bunche Hall, Box 951447, Los Angeles, CA 90095-1447, (310) 825-4571, Fax: (310) 206-6859, www.international.ucla.edu/lac; *Statistical Abstract of Latin America.*

United Nations Statistics Division, New York, NY 10017, (800) 253-9646, Fax: (212) 963-4116, http://unstats.un.org; *Human Development Report 2006.*

COLOMBIA - AUTOMOBILE INDUSTRY AND TRADE

United Nations Statistics Division, New York, NY 10017, (800) 253-9646, Fax: (212) 963-4116, http://unstats.un.org; *Statistical Yearbook.*

COLOMBIA - BALANCE OF PAYMENTS

Inter-American Development Bank (IDB), 1300 New York Avenue, NW, Washington, DC 20577, (202) 623-1000, Fax: (202) 623-3096, www.iadb.org; *The Politics of Policies: Economic and Social Progress in Latin America - 2006 Report.*

International Monetary Fund (IMF), 700 Nineteenth Street, NW, Washington, DC 20431, (202) 623-7000, Fax: (202) 623-4661, www.imf.org; *Balance of Payments Statistics Newsletter* and *Balance of Payments Statistics Yearbook 2007.*

Organization of American States (OAS), 17th Street Constitution Avenue NW, Washington, DC 20006, (202) 458-3000, www.oas.org; *The OAS in Transition: 1994-2004.*

Taylor and Francis Group, An Informa Business, 2 Park Square, Milton Park, Abingdon, Oxford OX14 4RN, United Kingdom, (Dial from U.S. (212) 216-7800), (Fax from U.S. (212) 564-7854), www.tandf.co.uk; *The Europa World Year Book.*

UCLA Latin American Institute, 10343 Bunche Hall, Box 951447, Los Angeles, CA 90095-1447, (310) 825-4571, Fax: (310) 206-6859, www.international.ucla.edu/lac; *Statistical Abstract of Latin America.*

United Nations Conference on Trade and Development (UNCTAD), DC2-1120, United Nations, New York, NY 10017, (212) 963-0027, www.unctad.org; *Handbook of Statistics 2005.*

United Nations Statistics Division, New York, NY 10017, (800) 253-9646, Fax: (212) 963-4116, http://unstats.un.org; *Economic Survey of Latin America and the Caribbean 2004-2005* and *Statistical Yearbook for Latin America and the Caribbean 2004.*

The World Bank, 1818 H Street, NW, Washington, DC 20433, (202) 473-1000, Fax: (202) 477-6391, www.worldbank.org; *Colombia* and *World Development Report 2008.*

COLOMBIA - BANKS AND BANKING

Euromonitor International, Inc., 224 S. Michigan Avenue, Suite 1500, Chicago, IL 60604, (312) 922-1115, Fax: (312) 922-1157, www.euromonitor.com; *World Marketing Data and Statistics.*

Inter-American Development Bank (IDB), 1300 New York Avenue, NW, Washington, DC 20577, (202) 623-1000, Fax: (202) 623-3096, www.iadb.org; *The Politics of Policies: Economic and Social Progress in Latin America - 2006 Report.*

International Monetary Fund (IMF), 700 Nineteenth Street, NW, Washington, DC 20431, (202) 623-7000, Fax: (202) 623-4661, www.imf.org; *International Financial Statistics Yearbook 2007.*

M.E. Sharpe, 80 Business Park Drive, Armonk, NY 10504, (800) 541-6563, Fax: (914) 273-2106, www.mesharpe.com; *The Illustrated Book of World Rankings.*

Palgrave Macmillan Ltd., Houndmills, Basingstoke, Hampshire, RG21 6XS, England, (Telephone in U.S. (888) 330-8477), (Fax in U.S. (800) 672-2054), www.palgrave.com; *The Statesman's Yearbook 2008.*

Taylor and Francis Group, An Informa Business, 2 Park Square, Milton Park, Abingdon, Oxford OX14 4RN, United Kingdom, (Dial from U.S. (212) 216-7800), (Fax from U.S. (212) 564-7854), www.tandf.co.uk; *The Europa World Year Book.*

United Nations Statistics Division, New York, NY 10017, (800) 253-9646, Fax: (212) 963-4116, http://unstats.un.org; *Statistical Yearbook* and *Statistical Yearbook for Latin America and the Caribbean 2004.*

COLOMBIA - BARLEY PRODUCTION

See COLOMBIA - CROPS

COLOMBIA - BEVERAGE INDUSTRY

M.E. Sharpe, 80 Business Park Drive, Armonk, NY 10504, (800) 541-6563, Fax: (914) 273-2106, www.mesharpe.com; *The Illustrated Book of World Rankings.*

United Nations Statistics Division, New York, NY 10017, (800) 253-9646, Fax: (212) 963-4116, http://unstats.un.org; *Statistical Yearbook.*

COLOMBIA - BIRTH CONTROL

UCLA Latin American Institute, 10343 Bunche Hall, Box 951447, Los Angeles, CA 90095-1447, (310) 825-4571, Fax: (310) 206-6859, www.international.ucla.edu/lac; *Statistical Abstract of Latin America.*

COLOMBIA - BONDS

Inter-American Development Bank (IDB), 1300 New York Avenue, NW, Washington, DC 20577, (202) 623-1000, Fax: (202) 623-3096, www.iadb.org; *The Politics of Policies: Economic and Social Progress in Latin America - 2006 Report.*

COLOMBIA - BROADCASTING

Central Intelligence Agency, Office of Public Affairs, Washington, DC 20505, (703) 482-0623, Fax: (703) 482-1739, www.cia.gov; *The World Factbook.*

Euromonitor International, Inc., 224 S. Michigan Avenue, Suite 1500, Chicago, IL 60604, (312) 922-1115, Fax: (312) 922-1157, www.euromonitor.com; *World Marketing Data and Statistics.*

M.E. Sharpe, 80 Business Park Drive, Armonk, NY 10504, (800) 541-6563, Fax: (914) 273-2106, www.mesharpe.com; *The Illustrated Book of World Rankings.*

Palgrave Macmillan Ltd., Houndmills, Basingstoke, Hampshire, RG21 6XS, England, (Telephone in U.S. (888) 330-8477), (Fax in U.S. (800) 672-2054), www.palgrave.com; *The Statesman's Yearbook 2008.*

UNESCO Institute for Statistics, C.P. 6128 Succursale Centre-Ville, Montreal, Quebec, H3C 3J7 Canada, (Dial from U.S. (514) 343-6880), (Fax from U.S. (514) 343 6882), www.uis.unesco.org; *Statistical Tables.*

WRTH Publications Limited, PO Box 290, Oxford OX2 7FT, UK, www.wrth.com; *World Radio TV Handbook 2007.*

COLOMBIA - BUDGET

Central Intelligence Agency, Office of Public Affairs, Washington, DC 20505, (703) 482-0623, Fax: (703) 482-1739, www.cia.gov; *The World Factbook.*

COLOMBIA - BUSINESS

Inter-American Development Bank (IDB), 1300 New York Avenue, NW, Washington, DC 20577, (202) 623-1000, Fax: (202) 623-3096, www.iadb.org; *The Politics of Policies: Economic and Social Progress in Latin America - 2006 Report.*

COLOMBIA - CAPITAL INVESTMENTS

Inter-American Development Bank (IDB), 1300 New York Avenue, NW, Washington, DC 20577, (202) 623-1000, Fax: (202) 623-3096, www.iadb.org; *The Politics of Policies: Economic and Social Progress in Latin America - 2006 Report.*

COLOMBIA - CAPITAL LEVY

Inter-American Development Bank (IDB), 1300 New York Avenue, NW, Washington, DC 20577, (202) 623-1000, Fax: (202) 623-3096, www.iadb.org; *The Politics of Policies: Economic and Social Progress in Latin America - 2006 Report.*

International Monetary Fund (IMF), 700 Nineteenth Street, NW, Washington, DC 20431, (202) 623-7000, Fax: (202) 623-4661, www.imf.org; *Government Finance Statistics Yearbook (2008 Edition).*

COLOMBIA - CATTLE

See COLOMBIA - LIVESTOCK

COLOMBIA - CHICK PEA PRODUCTION

See COLOMBIA - CROPS

COLOMBIA - CHICKENS

See COLOMBIA - LIVESTOCK

COLOMBIA - CHILDBIRTH - STATISTICS

Central Intelligence Agency, Office of Public Affairs, Washington, DC 20505, (703) 482-0623, Fax: (703) 482-1739, www.cia.gov; *The World Factbook.*

Euromonitor International, Inc., 224 S. Michigan Avenue, Suite 1500, Chicago, IL 60604, (312) 922-1115, Fax: (312) 922-1157, www.euromonitor.com; *The World Economic Factbook 2008.*

M.E. Sharpe, 80 Business Park Drive, Armonk, NY 10504, (800) 541-6563, Fax: (914) 273-2106, www.mesharpe.com; *The Illustrated Book of World Rankings.*

Taylor and Francis Group, An Informa Business, 2 Park Square, Milton Park, Abingdon, Oxford OX14 4RN, United Kingdom, (Dial from U.S. (212) 216-7800), (Fax from U.S. (212) 564-7854), www.tandf.co.uk; *The Europa World Year Book.*

United Nations Statistics Division, New York, NY 10017, (800) 253-9646, Fax: (212) 963-4116, http://unstats.un.org; *Demographic Yearbook; Statistical Yearbook;* and *Statistical Yearbook for Latin America and the Caribbean 2004.*

World Health Organization (WHO), Avenue Appia 20, 1211 Geneve 27, Switzerland, (Telephone in U.S. (212) 331-9081), www.who.int; *World Health Report 2006.*

COLOMBIA - CLIMATE

M.E. Sharpe, 80 Business Park Drive, Armonk, NY 10504, (800) 541-6563, Fax: (914) 273-2106, www.mesharpe.com; *The Illustrated Book of World Rankings.*

Palgrave Macmillan Ltd., Houndmills, Basingstoke, Hampshire, RG21 6XS, England, (Telephone in U.S. (888) 330-8477), (Fax in U.S. (800) 672-2054), www.palgrave.com; *The Statesman's Yearbook 2008.*

COLOMBIA - COAL PRODUCTION

See COLOMBIA - MINERAL INDUSTRIES

COLOMBIA - COCOA PRODUCTION

See COLOMBIA - CROPS

COLOMBIA - COFFEE

See COLOMBIA - CROPS

COLOMBIA - COMMERCE

Palgrave Macmillan Ltd., Houndmills, Basingstoke, Hampshire, RG21 6XS, England, (Telephone in U.S. (888) 330-8477), (Fax in U.S. (800) 672-2054), www.palgrave.com; *The Statesman's Yearbook 2008.*

COLOMBIA - COMMODITY EXCHANGES

Commodity Research Bureau, 330 South Wells Street, Suite 612, Chicago, IL 60606-7110, (800) 621-5271, Fax: (312) 939-4135, www.crbtrader.com; *2006 CRB Commodity Yearbook and CD.*

International Monetary Fund (IMF), 700 Nineteenth Street, NW, Washington, DC 20431, (202) 623-7000, Fax: (202) 623-4661, www.imf.org; *IMF Primary Commodity Prices.*

United Nations Food and Agricultural Organization (FAO), Viale delle Terme di Caracalla, 00100 Rome, Italy, (Dial from U.S. (202) 653-2400), (Fax from U.S. (202) 653 5760), www.fao.org; *The State of Food and Agriculture (SOFA) 2006.*

United Nations Statistics Division, New York, NY 10017, (800) 253-9646, Fax: (212) 963-4116, http://unstats.un.org; *Statistical Yearbook.*

COLOMBIA - COMMUNICATION AND TRAFFIC

United Nations Statistics Division, New York, NY 10017, (800) 253-9646, Fax: (212) 963-4116, http://unstats.un.org; *Statistical Yearbook.*

COLOMBIA - CONSTRUCTION INDUSTRY

Economist Intelligence Unit, 111 West 57th Street, New York, NY 10019, (212) 554-0600, Fax: (212) 586-1181, www.eiu.com; *Business Latin America.*

Inter-American Development Bank (IDB), 1300 New York Avenue, NW, Washington, DC 20577, (202) 623-1000, Fax: (202) 623-3096, www.iadb.org; *The Politics of Policies: Economic and Social Progress in Latin America - 2006 Report.*

M.E. Sharpe, 80 Business Park Drive, Armonk, NY 10504, (800) 541-6563, Fax: (914) 273-2106, www.mesharpe.com; *The Illustrated Book of World Rankings.*

UCLA Latin American Institute, 10343 Bunche Hall, Box 951447, Los Angeles, CA 90095-1447, (310) 825-4571, Fax: (310) 206-6859, www.international.ucla.edu/lac; *Statistical Abstract of Latin America.*

United Nations Statistics Division, New York, NY 10017, (800) 253-9646, Fax: (212) 963-4116, http://unstats.un.org; *Statistical Yearbook.*

COLOMBIA - CONSUMER COOPERATIVES

UCLA Latin American Institute, 10343 Bunche Hall, Box 951447, Los Angeles, CA 90095-1447, (310) 825-4571, Fax: (310) 206-6859, www.international.ucla.edu/lac; *Statistical Abstract of Latin America.*

COLOMBIA - CONSUMER PRICE INDEXES

Economist Intelligence Unit, 111 West 57th Street, New York, NY 10019, (212) 554-0600, Fax: (212) 586-1181, www.eiu.com; *Business Latin America.*

Taylor and Francis Group, An Informa Business, 2 Park Square, Milton Park, Abingdon, Oxford OX14 4RN, United Kingdom, (Dial from U.S. (212) 216-7800), (Fax from U.S. (212) 564-7854), www.tandf.co.uk; *The Europa World Year Book.*

United Nations Statistics Division, New York, NY 10017, (800) 253-9646, Fax: (212) 963-4116, http://unstats.un.org; *Statistical Yearbook.*

The World Bank, 1818 H Street, NW, Washington, DC 20433, (202) 473-1000, Fax: (202) 477-6391, www.worldbank.org; *Colombia.*

COLOMBIA - CONSUMPTION (ECONOMICS)

Economist Intelligence Unit, 111 West 57th Street, New York, NY 10019, (212) 554-0600, Fax: (212) 586-1181, www.eiu.com; *Business Latin America.*

Inter-American Development Bank (IDB), 1300 New York Avenue, NW, Washington, DC 20577, (202) 623-1000, Fax: (202) 623-3096, www.iadb.org; *The Politics of Policies: Economic and Social Progress in Latin America - 2006 Report.*

United Nations Statistics Division, New York, NY 10017, (800) 253-9646, Fax: (212) 963-4116, http://unstats.un.org; *Statistical Yearbook for Latin America and the Caribbean 2004.*

The World Bank, 1818 H Street, NW, Washington, DC 20433, (202) 473-1000, Fax: (202) 477-6391, www.worldbank.org; *World Development Report 2008.*

COLOMBIA - COPPER INDUSTRY AND TRADE

See COLOMBIA - MINERAL INDUSTRIES

COLOMBIA - CORN INDUSTRY

See COLOMBIA - CROPS

COLOMBIA - COTTON

See COLOMBIA - CROPS

COLOMBIA - CRIME

U.S. Department of Justice (DOJ), Bureau of Justice Statistics, 810 Seventh Street, NW, Washington, DC 20531, (202) 307-0765, www.ojp.usdoj.gov/bjs/; *The World Factbook of Criminal Justice Systems.*

Yale University Press, PO Box 209040, New Haven, CT 06520-9040, (203) 432-0960, Fax: (203) 432-0948, http://yalepress.yale.edu/yupbooks; *Violence and Crime in Cross-National Perspective.*

COLOMBIA - CROPS

Economist Intelligence Unit, 111 West 57th Street, New York, NY 10019, (212) 554-0600, Fax: (212) 586-1181, www.eiu.com; *Business Latin America.*

International Monetary Fund (IMF), 700 Nineteenth Street, NW, Washington, DC 20431, (202) 623-7000, Fax: (202) 623-4661, www.imf.org; *International Financial Statistics Yearbook 2007.*

M.E. Sharpe, 80 Business Park Drive, Armonk, NY 10504, (800) 541-6563, Fax: (914) 273-2106, www.mesharpe.com; *The Illustrated Book of World Rankings.*

Organization of American States (OAS), 17th Street Constitution Avenue NW, Washington, DC 20006, (202) 458-3000, www.oas.org; *The OAS in Transition: 1994-2004.*

Palgrave Macmillan Ltd., Houndmills, Basingstoke, Hampshire, RG21 6XS, England, (Telephone in U.S. (888) 330-8477), (Fax in U.S. (800) 672-2054), www.palgrave.com; *The Statesman's Yearbook 2008.*

Taylor and Francis Group, An Informa Business, 2 Park Square, Milton Park, Abingdon, Oxford OX14 4RN, United Kingdom, (Dial from U.S. (212) 216-7800), (Fax from U.S. (212) 564-7854), www.tandf.co.uk; *The Europa World Year Book.*

United Nations Conference on Trade and Development (UNCTAD), DC2-1120, United Nations, New York, NY 10017, (212) 963-0027, www.unctad.org; *UNCTAD Commodity Yearbook.*

United Nations Food and Agricultural Organization (FAO), Viale delle Terme di Caracalla, 00100 Rome, Italy, (Dial from U.S. (202) 653-2400), (Fax from U.S. (202) 653 5760), www.fao.org; *FAO Production Yearbook 2002* and *The State of Food and Agriculture (SOFA) 2006.*

United Nations Statistics Division, New York, NY 10017, (800) 253-9646, Fax: (212) 963-4116, http://unstats.un.org; *Statistical Yearbook.*

COLOMBIA - CUSTOMS ADMINISTRATION

Inter-American Development Bank (IDB), 1300 New York Avenue, NW, Washington, DC 20577, (202) 623-1000, Fax: (202) 623-3096, www.iadb.org; *The Politics of Policies: Economic and Social Progress in Latin America - 2006 Report.*

International Monetary Fund (IMF), 700 Nineteenth Street, NW, Washington, DC 20431, (202) 623-7000, Fax: (202) 623-4661, www.imf.org; *Government Finance Statistics Yearbook (2008 Edition).*

Palgrave Macmillan Ltd., Houndmills, Basingstoke, Hampshire, RG21 6XS, England, (Telephone in U.S. (888) 330-8477), (Fax in U.S. (800) 672-2054), www.palgrave.com; *The Statesman's Yearbook 2008.*

COLOMBIA - DAIRY PROCESSING

M.E. Sharpe, 80 Business Park Drive, Armonk, NY 10504, (800) 541-6563, Fax: (914) 273-2106, www.mesharpe.com; *The Illustrated Book of World Rankings.*

Palgrave Macmillan Ltd., Houndmills, Basingstoke, Hampshire, RG21 6XS, England, (Telephone in U.S. (888) 330-8477), (Fax in U.S. (800) 672-2054), www.palgrave.com; *The Statesman's Yearbook 2008.*

Taylor and Francis Group, An Informa Business, 2 Park Square, Milton Park, Abingdon, Oxford OX14 4RN, United Kingdom, (Dial from U.S. (212) 216-7800), (Fax from U.S. (212) 564-7854), www.tandf.co.uk; *The Europa World Year Book.*

United Nations Food and Agricultural Organization (FAO), Viale delle Terme di Caracalla, 00100 Rome, Italy, (Dial from U.S. (202) 653-2400), (Fax from U.S. (202) 653 5760), www.fao.org; *The State of Food and Agriculture (SOFA) 2006.*

United Nations Statistics Division, New York, NY 10017, (800) 253-9646, Fax: (212) 963-4116, http://unstats.un.org; *Statistical Yearbook.*

COLOMBIA - DEATH RATES

See COLOMBIA - MORTALITY

COLOMBIA - DEBT

Economist Intelligence Unit, 111 West 57th Street, New York, NY 10019, (212) 554-0600, Fax: (212) 586-1181, www.eiu.com; *Business Latin America.*

The World Bank, 1818 H Street, NW, Washington, DC 20433, (202) 473-1000, Fax: (202) 477-6391, www.worldbank.org; *Global Development Finance 2007.*

COLOMBIA - DEBTS, EXTERNAL

Economist Intelligence Unit, 111 West 57th Street, New York, NY 10019, (212) 554-0600, Fax: (212) 586-1181, www.eiu.com; *Business Latin America.*

Inter-American Development Bank (IDB), 1300 New York Avenue, NW, Washington, DC 20577, (202) 623-1000, Fax: (202) 623-3096, www.iadb.org; *The Politics of Policies: Economic and Social Progress in Latin America - 2006 Report.*

Palgrave Macmillan Ltd., Houndmills, Basingstoke, Hampshire, RG21 6XS, England, (Telephone in U.S. (888) 330-8477), (Fax in U.S. (800) 672-2054), www.palgrave.com; *The Statesman's Yearbook 2008.*

United Nations Statistics Division, New York, NY 10017, (800) 253-9646, Fax: (212) 963-4116, http://unstats.un.org; *Economic Survey of Latin America and the Caribbean 2004-2005* and *Statistical Yearbook for Latin America and the Caribbean 2004.*

The World Bank, 1818 H Street, NW, Washington, DC 20433, (202) 473-1000, Fax: (202) 477-6391, www.worldbank.org; *Global Development Finance 2007* and *World Development Report 2008.*

COLOMBIA - DEFENSE EXPENDITURES

See COLOMBIA - ARMED FORCES

COLOMBIA - DEMOGRAPHY

Euromonitor International, Inc., 224 S. Michigan Avenue, Suite 1500, Chicago, IL 60604, (312) 922-1115, Fax: (312) 922-1157, www.euromonitor.com; *International Marketing Data and Statistics 2008; The World Economic Factbook 2008;* and *World Marketing Data and Statistics.*

M.E. Sharpe, 80 Business Park Drive, Armonk, NY 10504, (800) 541-6563, Fax: (914) 273-2106, www.mesharpe.com; *The Illustrated Book of World Rankings.*

United Nations Statistics Division, New York, NY 10017, (800) 253-9646, Fax: (212) 963-4116, http://unstats.un.org; *Human Development Report 2006.*

The World Bank, 1818 H Street, NW, Washington, DC 20433, (202) 473-1000, Fax: (202) 477-6391, www.worldbank.org; *Colombia.*

COLOMBIA - DIAMONDS

See COLOMBIA - MINERAL INDUSTRIES

COLOMBIA - DISPOSABLE INCOME

Inter-American Development Bank (IDB), 1300 New York Avenue, NW, Washington, DC 20577, (202) 623-1000, Fax: (202) 623-3096, www.iadb.org; *The Politics of Policies: Economic and Social Progress in Latin America - 2006 Report.*

M.E. Sharpe, 80 Business Park Drive, Armonk, NY 10504, (800) 541-6563, Fax: (914) 273-2106, www.mesharpe.com; *The Illustrated Book of World Rankings.*

United Nations Statistics Division, New York, NY 10017, (800) 253-9646, Fax: (212) 963-4116, http://unstats.un.org; *National Accounts Statistics: Compendium of Income Distribution Statistics; Statistical Yearbook;* and *Statistical Yearbook for Latin America and the Caribbean 2004.*

COLOMBIA - DIVORCE

M.E. Sharpe, 80 Business Park Drive, Armonk, NY 10504, (800) 541-6563, Fax: (914) 273-2106, www.mesharpe.com; *The Illustrated Book of World Rankings.*

United Nations Statistics Division, New York, NY 10017, (800) 253-9646, Fax: (212) 963-4116, http://unstats.un.org; *Demographic Yearbook* and *Statistical Yearbook.*

COLOMBIA - ECONOMIC ASSISTANCE

Inter-American Development Bank (IDB), 1300 New York Avenue, NW, Washington, DC 20577, (202) 623-1000, Fax: (202) 623-3096, www.iadb.org; *The Politics of Policies: Economic and Social Progress in Latin America - 2006 Report.*

United Nations Statistics Division, New York, NY 10017, (800) 253-9646, Fax: (212) 963-4116, http://unstats.un.org; *Statistical Yearbook.*

COLOMBIA - ECONOMIC CONDITIONS

Center for International Business Education Research (CIBER), Columbia Business School and School of International and Public Affairs, Uris Hall, Room 212, 3022 Broadway, New York, NY 10027-6902, Mr. Joshua Safier, (212) 854-4750, Fax: (212) 222-9821, www.columbia.edu/cu/ciber/; Datastream International.

Central Intelligence Agency, Office of Public Affairs, Washington, DC 20505, (703) 482-0623, Fax: (703) 482-1739, www.cia.gov; *The World Factbook.*

DSI Data Service Information, Xantener Strasse 51a, D-47495 Rheinberg, Germany, www.dsidata.com; *Campus Solution.*

Dun and Bradstreet (DB) Corporation, 103 JFK Parkway, Short Hills, NJ 07078, (973) 921-5500, www.dnb.com; *Country Report.*

Economist Intelligence Unit, 111 West 57th Street, New York, NY 10019, (212) 554-0600, Fax: (212) 586-1181, www.eiu.com; *Colombia Country Report.*

Euromonitor International, Inc., 224 S. Michigan Avenue, Suite 1500, Chicago, IL 60604, (312) 922-1115, Fax: (312) 922-1157, www.euromonitor.com; *International Marketing Data and Statistics 2008; The World Economic Factbook 2008;* and *World Marketing Data and Statistics.*

Inter-American Development Bank (IDB), 1300 New York Avenue, NW, Washington, DC 20577, (202) 623-1000, Fax: (202) 623-3096, www.iadb.org; *The Politics of Policies: Economic and Social Progress in Latin America - 2006 Report.*

International Monetary Fund (IMF), 700 Nineteenth Street, NW, Washington, DC 20431, (202) 623-7000, Fax: (202) 623-4661, www.imf.org; *World Economic Outlook Reports.*

M.E. Sharpe, 80 Business Park Drive, Armonk, NY 10504, (800) 541-6563, Fax: (914) 273-2106, www.mesharpe.com; *The Illustrated Book of World Rankings.*

Organization of American States (OAS), 17th Street Constitution Avenue NW, Washington, DC 20006, (202) 458-3000, www.oas.org; *The OAS in Transition: 1994-2004.*

Palgrave Macmillan Ltd., Houndmills, Basingstoke, Hampshire, RG21 6XS, England, (Telephone in U.S. (888) 330-8477), (Fax in U.S. (800) 672-2054), www.palgrave.com; *The Statesman's Yearbook 2008.*

Taylor and Francis Group, An Informa Business, 2 Park Square, Milton Park, Abingdon, Oxford OX14 4RN, United Kingdom, (Dial from U.S. (212) 216-7800), (Fax from U.S. (212) 564-7854), www.tandf.co.uk; *The Europa World Year Book.*

UCLA Latin American Institute, 10343 Bunche Hall, Box 951447, Los Angeles, CA 90095-1447, (310) 825-4571, Fax: (310) 206-6859, www.international.ucla.edu/lac; *Statistical Abstract of Latin America.*

United Nations Statistics Division, New York, NY 10017, (800) 253-9646, Fax: (212) 963-4116, http://unstats.un.org; *Economic Survey of Latin America and the Caribbean 2004-2005* and *World Statistics Pocketbook.*

The World Bank, 1818 H Street, NW, Washington, DC 20433, (202) 473-1000, Fax: (202) 477-6391, www.worldbank.org; *Colombia; Global Economic Monitor (GEM); Global Economic Prospects 2008; The World Bank Atlas 2003-2004;* and *World Development Report 2008.*

COLOMBIA - ECONOMICS - SOCIOLOGICAL ASPECTS

Inter-American Development Bank (IDB), 1300 New York Avenue, NW, Washington, DC 20577, (202) 623-1000, Fax: (202) 623-3096, www.iadb.org; *The Politics of Policies: Economic and Social Progress in Latin America - 2006 Report.*

UCLA Latin American Institute, 10343 Bunche Hall, Box 951447, Los Angeles, CA 90095-1447, (310) 825-4571, Fax: (310) 206-6859, www.international.ucla.edu/lac; *Statistical Abstract of Latin America.*

COLOMBIA - EDUCATION

Economist Intelligence Unit, 111 West 57th Street, New York, NY 10019, (212) 554-0600, Fax: (212) 586-1181, www.eiu.com; *Business Latin America.*

Euromonitor International, Inc., 224 S. Michigan Avenue, Suite 1500, Chicago, IL 60604, (312) 922-1115, Fax: (312) 922-1157, www.euromonitor.com; *International Marketing Data and Statistics 2008* and *World Marketing Data and Statistics.*

M.E. Sharpe, 80 Business Park Drive, Armonk, NY 10504, (800) 541-6563, Fax: (914) 273-2106, www.mesharpe.com; *The Illustrated Book of World Rankings.*

Palgrave Macmillan Ltd., Houndmills, Basingstoke, Hampshire, RG21 6XS, England, (Telephone in U.S. (888) 330-8477), (Fax in U.S. (800) 672-2054), www.palgrave.com; *The Statesman's Yearbook 2008.*

Taylor and Francis Group, An Informa Business, 2 Park Square, Milton Park, Abingdon, Oxford OX14 4RN, United Kingdom, (Dial from U.S. (212) 216-7800), (Fax from U.S. (212) 564-7854), www.tandf.co.uk; *The Europa World Year Book.*

UCLA Latin American Institute, 10343 Bunche Hall, Box 951447, Los Angeles, CA 90095-1447, (310) 825-4571, Fax: (310) 206-6859, www.international.ucla.edu/lac; *Statistical Abstract of Latin America.*

UNESCO Institute for Statistics, C.P. 6128 Succursale Centre-Ville, Montreal, Quebec, H3C 3J7 Canada, (Dial from U.S. (514) 343-6880), (Fax from U.S. (514) 343 6882), www.uis.unesco.org; *Statistical Tables.*

United Nations Statistics Division, New York, NY 10017, (800) 253-9646, Fax: (212) 963-4116, http://

unstats.un.org; *Human Development Report 2006* and *Statistical Yearbook for Latin America and the Caribbean 2004.*

The World Bank, 1818 H Street, NW, Washington, DC 20433, (202) 473-1000, Fax: (202) 477-6391, www.worldbank.org; *Colombia* and *World Development Report 2008.*

COLOMBIA - ELECTRICITY

Economist Intelligence Unit, 111 West 57th Street, New York, NY 10019, (212) 554-0600, Fax: (212) 586-1181, www.eiu.com; *Business Latin America.*

Inter-American Development Bank (IDB), 1300 New York Avenue, NW, Washington, DC 20577, (202) 623-1000, Fax: (202) 623-3096, www.iadb.org; *The Politics of Policies: Economic and Social Progress in Latin America - 2006 Report.*

M.E. Sharpe, 80 Business Park Drive, Armonk, NY 10504, (800) 541-6563, Fax: (914) 273-2106, www.mesharpe.com; *The Illustrated Book of World Rankings.*

Organisation for Economic Cooperation and Development (OECD), 2 rue Andre Pascal, F-75775 Paris Cedex 16, France, (Telephone in U.S. (202) 785-6323), (Fax in U.S. (202) 785-0350), www.oecd.org; *World Energy Outlook 2007.*

Palgrave Macmillan Ltd., Houndmills, Basingstoke, Hampshire, RG21 6XS, England, (Telephone in U.S. (888) 330-8477), (Fax in U.S. (800) 672-2054), www.palgrave.com; *The Statesman's Yearbook 2008.*

U.S. Department of Energy (DOE), Energy Information Administration (EIA), 1000 Independence Avenue, SW, Washington, DC 20585, (202) 586-8800, www.eia.doe.gov; *International Energy Annual 2004* and *International Energy Outlook 2006.*

United Nations Statistics Division, New York, NY 10017, (800) 253-9646, Fax: (212) 963-4116, http://unstats.un.org; *Human Development Report 2006* and *Statistical Yearbook.*

COLOMBIA - EMIGRATION AND IMMIGRATION

UCLA Latin American Institute, 10343 Bunche Hall, Box 951447, Los Angeles, CA 90095-1447, (310) 825-4571, Fax: (310) 206-6859, www.international.ucla.edu/lac; *Statistical Abstract of Latin America.*

COLOMBIA - EMPLOYMENT

Euromonitor International, Inc., 224 S. Michigan Avenue, Suite 1500, Chicago, IL 60604, (312) 922-1115, Fax: (312) 922-1157, www.euromonitor.com; *International Marketing Data and Statistics 2008.*

International Labour Office, I.L.O. Publications, 4 route des Morillons, CH-1211 Geneva 22, Switzerland, (Telephone in U.S. (202) 653-7652), (Fax in U.S. (202) 653-7687), www.ilo.org; *Yearbook of Labour Statistics 2006.*

M.E. Sharpe, 80 Business Park Drive, Armonk, NY 10504, (800) 541-6563, Fax: (914) 273-2106, www.mesharpe.com; *The Illustrated Book of World Rankings.*

Organization of American States (OAS), 17th Street Constitution Avenue NW, Washington, DC 20006, (202) 458-3000, www.oas.org; *The OAS in Transition: 1994-2004.*

UCLA Latin American Institute, 10343 Bunche Hall, Box 951447, Los Angeles, CA 90095-1447, (310) 825-4571, Fax: (310) 206-6859, www.international.ucla.edu/lac; *Statistical Abstract of Latin America.*

United Nations Statistics Division, New York, NY 10017, (800) 253-9646, Fax: (212) 963-4116, http://unstats.un.org; *Statistical Yearbook for Latin America and the Caribbean 2004.*

The World Bank, 1818 H Street, NW, Washington, DC 20433, (202) 473-1000, Fax: (202) 477-6391, www.worldbank.org; *Colombia.*

COLOMBIA - ENVIRONMENTAL CONDITIONS

DSI Data Service Information, Xantener Strasse 51a, D-47495 Rheinberg, Germany, www.dsidata.com; *Campus Solution* and *DSI's Global Environmental Database.*

Economist Intelligence Unit, 111 West 57th Street, New York, NY 10019, (212) 554-0600, Fax: (212) 586-1181, www.eiu.com; *Colombia Country Report.*

United Nations Statistics Division, New York, NY 10017, (800) 253-9646, Fax: (212) 963-4116, http://unstats.un.org; *World Statistics Pocketbook.*

COLOMBIA - EXCISE TAX

Inter-American Development Bank (IDB), 1300 New York Avenue, NW, Washington, DC 20577, (202) 623-1000, Fax: (202) 623-3096, www.iadb.org; *The Politics of Policies: Economic and Social Progress in Latin America - 2006 Report.*

International Monetary Fund (IMF), 700 Nineteenth Street, NW, Washington, DC 20431, (202) 623-7000, Fax: (202) 623-4661, www.imf.org; *Government Finance Statistics Yearbook (2008 Edition).*

COLOMBIA - EXPENDITURES, PUBLIC

Inter-American Development Bank (IDB), 1300 New York Avenue, NW, Washington, DC 20577, (202) 623-1000, Fax: (202) 623-3096, www.iadb.org; *The Politics of Policies: Economic and Social Progress in Latin America - 2006 Report.*

Organization of American States (OAS), 17th Street Constitution Avenue NW, Washington, DC 20006, (202) 458-3000, www.oas.org; *The OAS in Transition: 1994-2004.*

United Nations Statistics Division, New York, NY 10017, (800) 253-9646, Fax: (212) 963-4116, http://unstats.un.org; *Statistical Yearbook for Latin America and the Caribbean 2004.*

COLOMBIA - EXPORTS

Central Intelligence Agency, Office of Public Affairs, Washington, DC 20505, (703) 482-0623, Fax: (703) 482-1739, www.cia.gov; *The World Factbook.*

Economist Intelligence Unit, 111 West 57th Street, New York, NY 10019, (212) 554-0600, Fax: (212) 586-1181, www.eiu.com; *Business Latin America* and *Colombia Country Report.*

Euromonitor International, Inc., 224 S. Michigan Avenue, Suite 1500, Chicago, IL 60604, (312) 922-1115, Fax: (312) 922-1157, www.euromonitor.com; *International Marketing Data and Statistics 2008* and *The World Economic Factbook 2008.*

Inter-American Development Bank (IDB), 1300 New York Avenue, NW, Washington, DC 20577, (202) 623-1000, Fax: (202) 623-3096, www.iadb.org; *The Politics of Policies: Economic and Social Progress in Latin America - 2006 Report.*

International Monetary Fund (IMF), 700 Nineteenth Street, NW, Washington, DC 20431, (202) 623-7000, Fax: (202) 623-4661, www.imf.org; *Direction of Trade Statistics Yearbook 2007* and *International Financial Statistics Yearbook 2007.*

Organization of American States (OAS), 17th Street Constitution Avenue NW, Washington, DC 20006, (202) 458-3000, www.oas.org; *The OAS in Transition: 1994-2004.*

Palgrave Macmillan Ltd., Houndmills, Basingstoke, Hampshire, RG21 6XS, England, (Telephone in U.S. (888) 330-8477), (Fax in U.S. (800) 672-2054), www.palgrave.com; *The Statesman's Yearbook 2008.*

Taylor and Francis Group, An Informa Business, 2 Park Square, Milton Park, Abingdon, Oxford OX14 4RN, United Kingdom, (Dial from U.S. (212) 216-7800), (Fax from U.S. (212) 564-7854), www.tandf.co.uk; *The Europa World Year Book.*

United Nations Food and Agricultural Organization (FAO), Viale delle Terme di Caracalla, 00100 Rome, Italy, (Dial from U.S. (202) 653-2400), (Fax from U.S. (202) 653 5760), www.fao.org; *The State of Food and Agriculture (SOFA) 2006.*

United Nations Statistics Division, New York, NY 10017, (800) 253-9646, Fax: (212) 963-4116, http://unstats.un.org; *Statistical Yearbook for Latin America and the Caribbean 2004.*

The World Bank, 1818 H Street, NW, Washington, DC 20433, (202) 473-1000, Fax: (202) 477-6391, www.worldbank.org; *World Development Report 2008.*

COLOMBIA - FEMALE WORKING POPULATION

See COLOMBIA - EMPLOYMENT

COLOMBIA - FERTILITY, HUMAN

Central Intelligence Agency, Office of Public Affairs, Washington, DC 20505, (703) 482-0623, Fax: (703) 482-1739, www.cia.gov; *The World Factbook.*

M.E. Sharpe, 80 Business Park Drive, Armonk, NY 10504, (800) 541-6563, Fax: (914) 273-2106, www.mesharpe.com; *The Illustrated Book of World Rankings.*

United Nations Statistics Division, New York, NY 10017, (800) 253-9646, Fax: (212) 963-4116, http://unstats.un.org; *Human Development Report 2006.*

The World Bank, 1818 H Street, NW, Washington, DC 20433, (202) 473-1000, Fax: (202) 477-6391, www.worldbank.org; *The World Bank Atlas 2003-2004* and *World Development Report 2008.*

COLOMBIA - FERTILIZER INDUSTRY

Economist Intelligence Unit, 111 West 57th Street, New York, NY 10019, (212) 554-0600, Fax: (212) 586-1181, www.eiu.com; *Business Latin America.*

United Nations Food and Agricultural Organization (FAO), Viale delle Terme di Caracalla, 00100 Rome, Italy, (Dial from U.S. (202) 653-2400), (Fax from U.S. (202) 653 5760), www.fao.org; *FAO Fertilizer Yearbook* and *The State of Food and Agriculture (SOFA) 2006.*

United Nations Statistics Division, New York, NY 10017, (800) 253-9646, Fax: (212) 963-4116, http://unstats.un.org; *Statistical Yearbook.*

COLOMBIA - FETAL MORTALITY

See COLOMBIA - MORTALITY

COLOMBIA - FILM

See COLOMBIA - MOTION PICTURES

COLOMBIA - FINANCE

Inter-American Development Bank (IDB), 1300 New York Avenue, NW, Washington, DC 20577, (202) 623-1000, Fax: (202) 623-3096, www.iadb.org; *The Politics of Policies: Economic and Social Progress in Latin America - 2006 Report.*

Organization of American States (OAS), 17th Street Constitution Avenue NW, Washington, DC 20006, (202) 458-3000, www.oas.org; *The OAS in Transition: 1994-2004.*

Taylor and Francis Group, An Informa Business, 2 Park Square, Milton Park, Abingdon, Oxford OX14 4RN, United Kingdom, (Dial from U.S. (212) 216-7800), (Fax from U.S. (212) 564-7854), www.tandf.co.uk; *The Europa World Year Book.*

UCLA Latin American Institute, 10343 Bunche Hall, Box 951447, Los Angeles, CA 90095-1447, (310) 825-4571, Fax: (310) 206-6859, www.international.ucla.edu/lac; *Statistical Abstract of Latin America.*

United Nations Statistics Division, New York, NY 10017, (800) 253-9646, Fax: (212) 963-4116, http://unstats.un.org; *National Accounts Statistics: Compendium of Income Distribution Statistics* and *Statistical Yearbook.*

The World Bank, 1818 H Street, NW, Washington, DC 20433, (202) 473-1000, Fax: (202) 477-6391, www.worldbank.org; *Colombia.*

COLOMBIA - FINANCE, PUBLIC

Bernan Essential Government Publications, 4611-F Assembly Drive, Lanham MD, 20706-4391, (301)

459-2255, Fax: (800) 865-3450, www.bernan.com; *National Accounts Statistics.*

Economist Intelligence Unit, 111 West 57th Street, New York, NY 10019, (212) 554-0600, Fax: (212) 586-1181, www.eiu.com; *Colombia Country Report.*

Inter-American Development Bank (IDB), 1300 New York Avenue, NW, Washington, DC 20577, (202) 623-1000, Fax: (202) 623-3096, www.iadb.org; *The Politics of Policies: Economic and Social Progress in Latin America - 2006 Report.*

International Monetary Fund (IMF), 700 Nineteenth Street, NW, Washington, DC 20431, (202) 623-7000, Fax: (202) 623-4661, www.imf.org; *International Financial Statistics; International Financial Statistics Online Service;* and *International Financial Statistics Yearbook 2007.*

M.E. Sharpe, 80 Business Park Drive, Armonk, NY 10504, (800) 541-6563, Fax: (914) 273-2106, www.mesharpe.com; *The Illustrated Book of World Rankings.*

Organization of American States (OAS), 17th Street Constitution Avenue NW, Washington, DC 20006, (202) 458-3000, www.oas.org; *The OAS in Transition: 1994-2004.*

Palgrave Macmillan Ltd., Houndmills, Basingstoke, Hampshire, RG21 6XS, England, (Telephone in U.S. (888) 330-8477), (Fax in U.S. (800) 672-2054), www.palgrave.com; *The Statesman's Yearbook 2008.*

Taylor and Francis Group, An Informa Business, 2 Park Square, Milton Park, Abingdon, Oxford OX14 4RN, United Kingdom, (Dial from U.S. (212) 216-7800), (Fax from U.S. (212) 564-7854), www.tandf.co.uk; *The Europa World Year Book.*

UCLA Latin American Institute, 10343 Bunche Hall, Box 951447, Los Angeles, CA 90095-1447, (310) 825-4571, Fax: (310) 206-6859, www.international.ucla.edu/lac; *Statistical Abstract of Latin America.*

The World Bank, 1818 H Street, NW, Washington, DC 20433, (202) 473-1000, Fax: (202) 477-6391, www.worldbank.org; *Colombia.*

COLOMBIA - FISHERIES

Inter-American Development Bank (IDB), 1300 New York Avenue, NW, Washington, DC 20577, (202) 623-1000, Fax: (202) 623-3096, www.iadb.org; *The Politics of Policies: Economic and Social Progress in Latin America - 2006 Report.*

M.E. Sharpe, 80 Business Park Drive, Armonk, NY 10504, (800) 541-6563, Fax: (914) 273-2106, www.mesharpe.com; *The Illustrated Book of World Rankings.*

Palgrave Macmillan Ltd., Houndmills, Basingstoke, Hampshire, RG21 6XS, England, (Telephone in U.S. (888) 330-8477), (Fax in U.S. (800) 672-2054), www.palgrave.com; *The Statesman's Yearbook 2008.*

Taylor and Francis Group, An Informa Business, 2 Park Square, Milton Park, Abingdon, Oxford OX14 4RN, United Kingdom, (Dial from U.S. (212) 216-7800), (Fax from U.S. (212) 564-7854), www.tandf.co.uk; *The Europa World Year Book.*

UCLA Latin American Institute, 10343 Bunche Hall, Box 951447, Los Angeles, CA 90095-1447, (310) 825-4571, Fax: (310) 206-6859, www.international.ucla.edu/lac; *Statistical Abstract of Latin America.*

United Nations Conference on Trade and Development (UNCTAD), DC2-1120, United Nations, New York, NY 10017, (212) 963-0027, www.unctad.org; *UNCTAD Commodity Yearbook.*

United Nations Food and Agricultural Organization (FAO), Viale delle Terme di Caracalla, 00100 Rome, Italy, (Dial from U.S. (202) 653-2400), (Fax from U.S. (202) 653 5760), www.fao.org; *FAO Yearbook of Fishery Statistics;* Fishery Databases; FISHSTAT Database. Subjects covered include: Aquaculture production, capture production, fishery commodities; and *The State of Food and Agriculture (SOFA) 2006.*

United Nations Statistics Division, New York, NY 10017, (800) 253-9646, Fax: (212) 963-4116, http://unstats.un.org; *Statistical Yearbook* and *Survey of Economic and Social Conditions in Africa 2005.*

The World Bank, 1818 H Street, NW, Washington, DC 20433, (202) 473-1000, Fax: (202) 477-6391, www.worldbank.org; *Colombia.*

COLOMBIA - FLOUR INDUSTRY

United Nations Statistics Division, New York, NY 10017, (800) 253-9646, Fax: (212) 963-4116, http://unstats.un.org; *Statistical Yearbook.*

COLOMBIA - FOOD

Euromonitor International, Inc., 224 S. Michigan Avenue, Suite 1500, Chicago, IL 60604, (312) 922-1115, Fax: (312) 922-1157, www.euromonitor.com; *Retail Trade International 2007.*

United Nations Conference on Trade and Development (UNCTAD), DC2-1120, United Nations, New York, NY 10017, (212) 963-0027, www.unctad.org; *UNCTAD Commodity Yearbook.*

United Nations Food and Agricultural Organization (FAO), Viale delle Terme di Caracalla, 00100 Rome, Italy, (Dial from U.S. (202) 653-2400), (Fax from U.S. (202) 653 5760), www.fao.org; *FAO Production Yearbook 2002* and *The State of Food and Agriculture (SOFA) 2006.*

United Nations Statistics Division, New York, NY 10017, (800) 253-9646, Fax: (212) 963-4116, http://unstats.un.org; *Human Development Report 2006.*

COLOMBIA - FOREIGN EXCHANGE RATES

Central Intelligence Agency, Office of Public Affairs, Washington, DC 20505, (703) 482-0623, Fax: (703) 482-1739, www.cia.gov; *The World Factbook.*

Euromonitor International, Inc., 224 S. Michigan Avenue, Suite 1500, Chicago, IL 60604, (312) 922-1115, Fax: (312) 922-1157, www.euromonitor.com; *International Marketing Data and Statistics 2008* and *The World Economic Factbook 2008.*

Inter-American Development Bank (IDB), 1300 New York Avenue, NW, Washington, DC 20577, (202) 623-1000, Fax: (202) 623-3096, www.iadb.org; *The Politics of Policies: Economic and Social Progress in Latin America - 2006 Report.*

International Civil Aviation Organization (ICAO), External Relations and Public Information Office (EPO), 999 University Street, Montreal, Quebec H3C 5H7, Canada, (Dial from U.S. (514) 954-8219), (Fax from U.S. (514) 954-6077), www.icao.int; *Civil Aviation Statistics of the World.*

International Monetary Fund (IMF), 700 Nineteenth Street, NW, Washington, DC 20431, (202) 623-7000, Fax: (202) 623-4661, www.imf.org; *International Financial Statistics Yearbook 2007.*

Organization of American States (OAS), 17th Street Constitution Avenue NW, Washington, DC 20006, (202) 458-3000, www.oas.org; *The OAS in Transition: 1994-2004.*

Taylor and Francis Group, An Informa Business, 2 Park Square, Milton Park, Abingdon, Oxford OX14 4RN, United Kingdom, (Dial from U.S. (212) 216-7800), (Fax from U.S. (212) 564-7854), www.tandf.co.uk; *The Europa World Year Book.*

UCLA Latin American Institute, 10343 Bunche Hall, Box 951447, Los Angeles, CA 90095-1447, (310) 825-4571, Fax: (310) 206-6859, www.international.ucla.edu/lac; *Statistical Abstract of Latin America.*

United Nations Statistics Division, New York, NY 10017, (800) 253-9646, Fax: (212) 963-4116, http://unstats.un.org; *Statistical Yearbook* and *World Statistics Pocketbook.*

COLOMBIA - FORESTS AND FORESTRY

American Forest Paper Association (AFPA), 1111 Nineteenth Street, NW, Suite 800, Washington, DC 20036, (800) 878-8878, www.afandpa.org; *2007 Annual Statistics of Paper, Paperboard, and Wood Pulp.*

Economist Intelligence Unit, 111 West 57th Street, New York, NY 10019, (212) 554-0600, Fax: (212) 586-1181, www.eiu.com; *Business Latin America.*

Inter-American Development Bank (IDB), 1300 New York Avenue, NW, Washington, DC 20577, (202) 623-1000, Fax: (202) 623-3096, www.iadb.org; *The Politics of Policies: Economic and Social Progress in Latin America - 2006 Report.*

M.E. Sharpe, 80 Business Park Drive, Armonk, NY 10504, (800) 541-6563, Fax: (914) 273-2106, www.mesharpe.com; *The Illustrated Book of World Rankings.*

Taylor and Francis Group, An Informa Business, 2 Park Square, Milton Park, Abingdon, Oxford OX14 4RN, United Kingdom, (Dial from U.S. (212) 216-7800), (Fax from U.S. (212) 564-7854), www.tandf.co.uk; *The Europa World Year Book.*

UCLA Latin American Institute, 10343 Bunche Hall, Box 951447, Los Angeles, CA 90095-1447, (310) 825-4571, Fax: (310) 206-6859, www.international.ucla.edu/lac; *Statistical Abstract of Latin America.*

UNESCO Institute for Statistics, C.P. 6128 Succursale Centre-Ville, Montreal, Quebec, H3C 3J7 Canada, (Dial from U.S. (514) 343-6880), (Fax from U.S. (514) 343 6882), www.uis.unesco.org; *Statistical Tables.*

United Nations Conference on Trade and Development (UNCTAD), DC2-1120, United Nations, New York, NY 10017, (212) 963-0027, www.unctad.org; *UNCTAD Commodity Yearbook.*

United Nations Food and Agricultural Organization (FAO), Viale delle Terme di Caracalla, 00100 Rome, Italy, (Dial from U.S. (202) 653-2400), (Fax from U.S. (202) 653 5760), www.fao.org; *FAO Yearbook of Forest Products* and *The State of Food and Agriculture (SOFA) 2006.*

United Nations Statistics Division, New York, NY 10017, (800) 253-9646, Fax: (212) 963-4116, http://unstats.un.org; *Statistical Yearbook.*

The World Bank, 1818 H Street, NW, Washington, DC 20433, (202) 473-1000, Fax: (202) 477-6391, www.worldbank.org; *Colombia* and *World Development Report 2008.*

COLOMBIA - GAS PRODUCTION

See COLOMBIA - MINERAL INDUSTRIES

COLOMBIA - GEOGRAPHIC INFORMATION SYSTEMS

M.E. Sharpe, 80 Business Park Drive, Armonk, NY 10504, (800) 541-6563, Fax: (914) 273-2106, www.mesharpe.com; *The Illustrated Book of World Rankings.*

UCLA Latin American Institute, 10343 Bunche Hall, Box 951447, Los Angeles, CA 90095-1447, (310) 825-4571, Fax: (310) 206-6859, www.international.ucla.edu/lac; *Statistical Abstract of Latin America.*

The World Bank, 1818 H Street, NW, Washington, DC 20433, (202) 473-1000, Fax: (202) 477-6391, www.worldbank.org; *Colombia.*

COLOMBIA - GOLD INDUSTRY

Economist Intelligence Unit, 111 West 57th Street, New York, NY 10019, (212) 554-0600, Fax: (212) 586-1181, www.eiu.com; *Business Latin America.*

International Monetary Fund (IMF), 700 Nineteenth Street, NW, Washington, DC 20431, (202) 623-7000, Fax: (202) 623-4661, www.imf.org; *International Financial Statistics Yearbook 2007.*

United Nations Statistics Division, New York, NY 10017, (800) 253-9646, Fax: (212) 963-4116, http://unstats.un.org; *Statistical Yearbook.*

COLOMBIA - GOLD PRODUCTION

See COLOMBIA - MINERAL INDUSTRIES

COLOMBIA - GRANTS-IN-AID

International Monetary Fund (IMF), 700 Nineteenth Street, NW, Washington, DC 20431, (202) 623-7000, Fax: (202) 623-4661, www.imf.org; *Government Finance Statistics Yearbook (2008 Edition).*

COLOMBIA - GREEN PEPPER AND CHILIE PRODUCTION

See COLOMBIA - CROPS

COLOMBIA - GROSS DOMESTIC PRODUCT

Economist Intelligence Unit, 111 West 57th Street, New York, NY 10019, (212) 554-0600, Fax: (212) 586-1181, www.eiu.com; *Business Latin America* and *Colombia Country Report*.

Euromonitor International, Inc., 224 S. Michigan Avenue, Suite 1500, Chicago, IL 60604, (312) 922-1115, Fax: (312) 922-1157, www.euromonitor.com; *International Marketing Data and Statistics 2008* and *The World Economic Factbook 2008*.

Inter-American Development Bank (IDB), 1300 New York Avenue, NW, Washington, DC 20577, (202) 623-1000, Fax: (202) 623-3096, www.iadb.org; *The Politics of Policies: Economic and Social Progress in Latin America - 2006 Report*.

M.E. Sharpe, 80 Business Park Drive, Armonk, NY 10504, (800) 541-6563, Fax: (914) 273-2106, www.mesharpe.com; *The Illustrated Book of World Rankings*.

Organization of American States (OAS), 17th Street Constitution Avenue NW, Washington, DC 20006, (202) 458-3000, www.oas.org; *The OAS in Transition: 1994-2004*.

Taylor and Francis Group, An Informa Business, 2 Park Square, Milton Park, Abingdon, Oxford OX14 4RN, United Kingdom, (Dial from U.S. (212) 216-7800), (Fax from U.S. (212) 564-7854), www.tandf.co.uk; *The Europa World Year Book*.

UCLA Latin American Institute, 10343 Bunche Hall, Box 951447, Los Angeles, CA 90095-1447, (310) 825-4571, Fax: (310) 206-6859, www.international.ucla.edu/lac; *Statistical Abstract of Latin America*.

United Nations Statistics Division, New York, NY 10017, (800) 253-9646, Fax: (212) 963-4116, http://unstats.un.org; *Human Development Report 2006; National Accounts Statistics: Compendium of Income Distribution Statistics; Statistical Yearbook;* and *Statistical Yearbook for Latin America and the Caribbean 2004*.

The World Bank, 1818 H Street, NW, Washington, DC 20433, (202) 473-1000, Fax: (202) 477-6391, www.worldbank.org; *World Development Report 2008*.

COLOMBIA - GROSS NATIONAL PRODUCT

Euromonitor International, Inc., 224 S. Michigan Avenue, Suite 1500, Chicago, IL 60604, (312) 922-1115, Fax: (312) 922-1157, www.euromonitor.com; *International Marketing Data and Statistics 2008*.

Inter-American Development Bank (IDB), 1300 New York Avenue, NW, Washington, DC 20577, (202) 623-1000, Fax: (202) 623-3096, www.iadb.org; *The Politics of Policies: Economic and Social Progress in Latin America - 2006 Report*.

M.E. Sharpe, 80 Business Park Drive, Armonk, NY 10504, (800) 541-6563, Fax: (914) 273-2106, www.mesharpe.com; *The Illustrated Book of World Rankings*.

Palgrave Macmillan Ltd., Houndmills, Basingstoke, Hampshire, RG21 6XS, England, (Telephone in U.S. (888) 330-8477), (Fax in U.S. (800) 672-2054), www.palgrave.com; *The Statesman's Yearbook 2008*.

U.S. Department of State (DOS), 2201 C Street NW, Washington, DC 20520, (202) 647-4000, www.state.gov; *World Military Expenditures and Arms Transfers (WMEAT)*.

United Nations Statistics Division, New York, NY 10017, (800) 253-9646, Fax: (212) 963-4116, http://unstats.un.org; *Statistical Yearbook*.

The World Bank, 1818 H Street, NW, Washington, DC 20433, (202) 473-1000, Fax: (202) 477-6391, www.worldbank.org; *The World Bank Atlas 2003-2004* and *World Development Report 2008*.

COLOMBIA - HIDES AND SKINS INDUSTRY

United Nations Food and Agricultural Organization (FAO), Viale delle Terme di Caracalla, 00100 Rome, Italy, (Dial from U.S. (202) 653-2400), (Fax from U.S. (202) 653 5760), www.fao.org; *FAO Production Yearbook 2002*.

COLOMBIA - HOUSING

Euromonitor International, Inc., 224 S. Michigan Avenue, Suite 1500, Chicago, IL 60604, (312) 922-1115, Fax: (312) 922-1157, www.euromonitor.com; *World Marketing Data and Statistics*.

M.E. Sharpe, 80 Business Park Drive, Armonk, NY 10504, (800) 541-6563, Fax: (914) 273-2106, www.mesharpe.com; *The Illustrated Book of World Rankings*.

UCLA Latin American Institute, 10343 Bunche Hall, Box 951447, Los Angeles, CA 90095-1447, (310) 825-4571, Fax: (310) 206-6859, www.international.ucla.edu/lac; *Statistical Abstract of Latin America*.

United Nations Statistics Division, New York, NY 10017, (800) 253-9646, Fax: (212) 963-4116, http://unstats.un.org; *Statistical Yearbook for Latin America and the Caribbean 2004*.

COLOMBIA - ILLITERATE PERSONS

Economist Intelligence Unit, 111 West 57th Street, New York, NY 10019, (212) 554-0600, Fax: (212) 586-1181, www.eiu.com; *Business Latin America*.

Euromonitor International, Inc., 224 S. Michigan Avenue, Suite 1500, Chicago, IL 60604, (312) 922-1115, Fax: (312) 922-1157, www.euromonitor.com; *The World Economic Factbook 2008*.

UNESCO Institute for Statistics, C.P. 6128 Succursale Centre-Ville, Montreal, Quebec, H3C 3J7 Canada, (Dial from U.S. (514) 343-6880), (Fax from U.S. (514) 343 6882), www.uis.unesco.org; *Statistical Tables*.

United Nations Statistics Division, New York, NY 10017, (800) 253-9646, Fax: (212) 963-4116, http://unstats.un.org; *Human Development Report 2006* and *Statistical Yearbook for Latin America and the Caribbean 2004*.

COLOMBIA - IMPORTS

Central Intelligence Agency, Office of Public Affairs, Washington, DC 20505, (703) 482-0623, Fax: (703) 482-1739, www.cia.gov; *The World Factbook*.

Economist Intelligence Unit, 111 West 57th Street, New York, NY 10019, (212) 554-0600, Fax: (212) 586-1181, www.eiu.com; *Business Latin America* and *Colombia Country Report*.

Euromonitor International, Inc., 224 S. Michigan Avenue, Suite 1500, Chicago, IL 60604, (312) 922-1115, Fax: (312) 922-1157, www.euromonitor.com; *International Marketing Data and Statistics 2008* and *The World Economic Factbook 2008*.

Inter-American Development Bank (IDB), 1300 New York Avenue, NW, Washington, DC 20577, (202) 623-1000, Fax: (202) 623-3096, www.iadb.org; *The Politics of Policies: Economic and Social Progress in Latin America - 2006 Report*.

International Monetary Fund (IMF), 700 Nineteenth Street, NW, Washington, DC 20431, (202) 623-7000, Fax: (202) 623-4661, www.imf.org; *Direction of Trade Statistics Yearbook 2007* and *International Financial Statistics Yearbook 2007*.

Organization of American States (OAS), 17th Street Constitution Avenue NW, Washington, DC 20006, (202) 458-3000, www.oas.org; *The OAS in Transition: 1994-2004*.

Palgrave Macmillan Ltd., Houndmills, Basingstoke, Hampshire, RG21 6XS, England, (Telephone in U.S. (888) 330-8477), (Fax in U.S. (800) 672-2054), www.palgrave.com; *The Statesman's Yearbook 2008*.

Taylor and Francis Group, An Informa Business, 2 Park Square, Milton Park, Abingdon, Oxford OX14 4RN, United Kingdom, (Dial from U.S. (212) 216-7800), (Fax from U.S. (212) 564-7854), www.tandf.co.uk; *The Europa World Year Book*.

United Nations Food and Agricultural Organization (FAO), Viale delle Terme di Caracalla, 00100 Rome, Italy, (Dial from U.S. (202) 653-2400), (Fax from U.S. (202) 653 5760), www.fao.org; *The State of Food and Agriculture (SOFA) 2006*.

United Nations Statistics Division, New York, NY 10017, (800) 253-9646, Fax: (212) 963-4116, http://unstats.un.org; *Statistical Yearbook for Latin America and the Caribbean 2004*.

The World Bank, 1818 H Street, NW, Washington, DC 20433, (202) 473-1000, Fax: (202) 477-6391, www.worldbank.org; *World Development Report 2008*.

COLOMBIA - INCOME DISTRIBUTION

UCLA Latin American Institute, 10343 Bunche Hall, Box 951447, Los Angeles, CA 90095-1447, (310) 825-4571, Fax: (310) 206-6859, www.international.ucla.edu/lac; *Statistical Abstract of Latin America*.

United Nations Statistics Division, New York, NY 10017, (800) 253-9646, Fax: (212) 963-4116, http://unstats.un.org; *Statistical Yearbook for Latin America and the Caribbean 2004*.

COLOMBIA - INCOME TAX

Inter-American Development Bank (IDB), 1300 New York Avenue, NW, Washington, DC 20577, (202) 623-1000, Fax: (202) 623-3096, www.iadb.org; *The Politics of Policies: Economic and Social Progress in Latin America - 2006 Report*.

International Monetary Fund (IMF), 700 Nineteenth Street, NW, Washington, DC 20431, (202) 623-7000, Fax: (202) 623-4661, www.imf.org; *Government Finance Statistics Yearbook (2008 Edition)*.

COLOMBIA - INDUSTRIAL METALS PRODUCTIONS

See COLOMBIA - MINERAL INDUSTRIES

COLOMBIA - INDUSTRIAL PRODUCTIVITY

Euromonitor International, Inc., 224 S. Michigan Avenue, Suite 1500, Chicago, IL 60604, (312) 922-1115, Fax: (312) 922-1157, www.euromonitor.com; *International Marketing Data and Statistics 2008*.

M.E. Sharpe, 80 Business Park Drive, Armonk, NY 10504, (800) 541-6563, Fax: (914) 273-2106, www.mesharpe.com; *The Illustrated Book of World Rankings*.

COLOMBIA - INDUSTRIAL PROPERTY

United Nations Statistics Division, New York, NY 10017, (800) 253-9646, Fax: (212) 963-4116, http://unstats.un.org; *Statistical Yearbook*.

World Intellectual Property Organization (WIPO), PO Box 18, CH-1211 Geneva 20, Switzerland, www.wipo.int; *Industrial Property Statistics* and *Industrial Property Statistics Online Directory*.

COLOMBIA - INDUSTRIES

Central Intelligence Agency, Office of Public Affairs, Washington, DC 20505, (703) 482-0623, Fax: (703) 482-1739, www.cia.gov; *The World Factbook*.

Economist Intelligence Unit, 111 West 57th Street, New York, NY 10019, (212) 554-0600, Fax: (212) 586-1181, www.eiu.com; *Colombia Country Report*.

Euromonitor International, Inc., 224 S. Michigan Avenue, Suite 1500, Chicago, IL 60604, (312) 922-1115, Fax: (312) 922-1157, www.euromonitor.com; *The World Economic Factbook 2008* and *World Marketing Data and Statistics*.

International Labour Office, I.L.O. Publications, 4 route des Morillons, CH-1211 Geneva 22, Switzerland, (Telephone in U.S. (202) 653-7652), (Fax in U.S. (202) 653-7687), www.ilo.org; *Yearbook of Labour Statistics 2006*.

M.E. Sharpe, 80 Business Park Drive, Armonk, NY 10504, (800) 541-6563, Fax: (914) 273-2106, www.mesharpe.com; *The Illustrated Book of World Rankings*.

Palgrave Macmillan Ltd., Houndmills, Basingstoke, Hampshire, RG21 6XS, England, (Telephone in U.S.

(888) 330-8477), (Fax in U.S. (800) 672-2054), www.palgrave.com; *The Statesman's Yearbook 2008.*

Taylor and Francis Group, An Informa Business, 2 Park Square, Milton Park, Abingdon, Oxford OX14 4RN, United Kingdom, (Dial from U.S. (212) 216-7800), (Fax from U.S. (212) 564-7854), www.tandf.co.uk; *The Europa World Year Book.*

UCLA Latin American Institute, 10343 Bunche Hall, Box 951447, Los Angeles, CA 90095-1447, (310) 825-4571, Fax: (310) 206-6859, www.international.ucla.edu/lac; *Statistical Abstract of Latin America.*

United Nations Industrial Development Organization (UNIDO), 1 United Nations Plaza, New York, NY 10017, (212) 963 6890, Fax: (212) 963-7904, http://unido.org; Industrial Statistics Database 2008 (INDSTAT) and *The International Yearbook of Industrial Statistics 2008.*

United Nations Statistics Division, New York, NY 10017, (800) 253-9646, Fax: (212) 963-4116, http://unstats.un.org; *Economic Survey of Latin America and the Caribbean 2004-2005; 2004 Industrial Commodity Statistics Yearbook;* and *Statistical Yearbook.*

The World Bank, 1818 H Street, NW, Washington, DC 20433, (202) 473-1000, Fax: (202) 477-6391, www.worldbank.org; *Colombia.*

World Intellectual Property Organization (WIPO), PO Box 18, CH-1211 Geneva 20, Switzerland, www.wipo.int; *Industrial Property Statistics* and *Industrial Property Statistics Online Directory.*

COLOMBIA - INFANT AND MATERNAL MORTALITY

See COLOMBIA - MORTALITY

COLOMBIA - INFLATION (FINANCE)

United Nations Statistics Division, New York, NY 10017, (800) 253-9646, Fax: (212) 963-4116, http://unstats.un.org; *Economic Survey of Latin America and the Caribbean 2004-2005.*

COLOMBIA - INORGANIC ACIDS

United Nations Statistics Division, New York, NY 10017, (800) 253-9646, Fax: (212) 963-4116, http://unstats.un.org; *Statistical Yearbook.*

COLOMBIA - INTEREST RATES

Inter-American Development Bank (IDB), 1300 New York Avenue, NW, Washington, DC 20577, (202) 623-1000, Fax: (202) 623-3096, www.iadb.org; *The Politics of Policies: Economic and Social Progress in Latin America - 2006 Report.*

Organization of American States (OAS), 17th Street Constitution Avenue NW, Washington, DC 20006, (202) 458-3000, www.oas.org; *The OAS in Transition: 1994-2004.*

COLOMBIA - INTERNAL REVENUE

Inter-American Development Bank (IDB), 1300 New York Avenue, NW, Washington, DC 20577, (202) 623-1000, Fax: (202) 623-3096, www.iadb.org; *The Politics of Policies: Economic and Social Progress in Latin America - 2006 Report.*

Organization of American States (OAS), 17th Street Constitution Avenue NW, Washington, DC 20006, (202) 458-3000, www.oas.org; *The OAS in Transition: 1994-2004.*

COLOMBIA - INTERNATIONAL FINANCE

Inter-American Development Bank (IDB), 1300 New York Avenue, NW, Washington, DC 20577, (202) 623-1000, Fax: (202) 623-3096, www.iadb.org; *The Politics of Policies: Economic and Social Progress in Latin America - 2006 Report.*

UCLA Latin American Institute, 10343 Bunche Hall, Box 951447, Los Angeles, CA 90095-1447, (310) 825-4571, Fax: (310) 206-6859, www.international.ucla.edu/lac; *Statistical Abstract of Latin America.*

United Nations Statistics Division, New York, NY 10017, (800) 253-9646, Fax: (212) 963-4116, http://unstats.un.org; *Statistical Yearbook for Latin America and the Caribbean 2004.*

COLOMBIA - INTERNATIONAL LIQUIDITY

Inter-American Development Bank (IDB), 1300 New York Avenue, NW, Washington, DC 20577, (202) 623-1000, Fax: (202) 623-3096, www.iadb.org; *The Politics of Policies: Economic and Social Progress in Latin America - 2006 Report.*

International Monetary Fund (IMF), 700 Nineteenth Street, NW, Washington, DC 20431, (202) 623-7000, Fax: (202) 623-4661, www.imf.org; *International Financial Statistics Yearbook 2007.*

COLOMBIA - INTERNATIONAL STATISTICS

Inter-American Development Bank (IDB), 1300 New York Avenue, NW, Washington, DC 20577, (202) 623-1000, Fax: (202) 623-3096, www.iadb.org; *The Politics of Policies: Economic and Social Progress in Latin America - 2006 Report.*

UCLA Latin American Institute, 10343 Bunche Hall, Box 951447, Los Angeles, CA 90095-1447, (310) 825-4571, Fax: (310) 206-6859, www.international.ucla.edu/lac; *Statistical Abstract of Latin America.*

COLOMBIA - INTERNATIONAL TRADE

Economist Intelligence Unit, 111 West 57th Street, New York, NY 10019, (212) 554-0600, Fax: (212) 586-1181, www.eiu.com; *Business Latin America* and *Colombia Country Report.*

Euromonitor International, Inc., 224 S. Michigan Avenue, Suite 1500, Chicago, IL 60604, (312) 922-1115, Fax: (312) 922-1157, www.euromonitor.com; *International Marketing Data and Statistics 2008; The World Economic Factbook 2008;* and *World Marketing Data and Statistics.*

Inter-American Development Bank (IDB), 1300 New York Avenue, NW, Washington, DC 20577, (202) 623-1000, Fax: (202) 623-3096, www.iadb.org; *The Politics of Policies: Economic and Social Progress in Latin America - 2006 Report.*

International Monetary Fund (IMF), 700 Nineteenth Street, NW, Washington, DC 20431, (202) 623-7000, Fax: (202) 623-4661, www.imf.org; *International Financial Statistics Yearbook 2007.*

M.E. Sharpe, 80 Business Park Drive, Armonk, NY 10504, (800) 541-6563, Fax: (914) 273-2106, www.mesharpe.com; *The Illustrated Book of World Rankings.*

Organisation for Economic Cooperation and Development (OECD), 2 rue Andre Pascal, F-75775 Paris Cedex 16, France, (Telephone in U.S. (202) 785-6323), (Fax in U.S. (202) 785-0350), www.oecd.org; *International Trade by Commodity Statistics (ITCS).*

Palgrave Macmillan Ltd., Houndmills, Basingstoke, Hampshire, RG21 6XS, England, (Telephone in U.S. (888) 330-8477), (Fax in U.S. (800) 672-2054), www.palgrave.com; *The Statesman's Yearbook 2008.*

Taylor and Francis Group, An Informa Business, 2 Park Square, Milton Park, Abingdon, Oxford OX14 4RN, United Kingdom, (Dial from U.S. (212) 216-7800), (Fax from U.S. (212) 564-7854), www.tandf.co.uk; *The Europa World Year Book.*

UCLA Latin American Institute, 10343 Bunche Hall, Box 951447, Los Angeles, CA 90095-1447, (310) 825-4571, Fax: (310) 206-6859, www.international.ucla.edu/lac; *Statistical Abstract of Latin America.*

United Nations Conference on Trade and Development (UNCTAD), DC2-1120, United Nations, New York, NY 10017, (212) 963-0027, www.unctad.org; *UNCTAD Commodity Yearbook.*

United Nations Food and Agricultural Organization (FAO), Viale delle Terme di Caracalla, 00100 Rome, Italy, (Dial from U.S. (202) 653-2400), (Fax from U.S. (202) 653 5760), www.fao.org; *FAO Trade Yearbook* and *The State of Food and Agriculture (SOFA) 2006.*

United Nations Statistics Division, New York, NY 10017, (800) 253-9646, Fax: (212) 963-4116, http://unstats.un.org; *Economic Survey of Latin America and the Caribbean 2004-2005; International Trade Statistics Yearbook; Statistical Yearbook;* and *Statistical Yearbook for Latin America and the Caribbean 2004.*

The World Bank, 1818 H Street, NW, Washington, DC 20433, (202) 473-1000, Fax: (202) 477-6391, www.worldbank.org; *Colombia* and *World Development Report 2008.*

World Trade Organization (WTO), Centre William Rappard, Rue de Lausanne 154, CH-1211 Geneva 21, Switzerland, www.wto.org; *International Trade Statistics 2006.*

COLOMBIA - INTERNET USERS

International Telecommunication Union (ITU), Place des Nations, 1211 Geneva 20, Switzerland, www.itu.int; *World Telecommunication/ICT Indicators Database on CD-ROM; World Telecommunication/ICT Indicators Database Online;* and *Yearbook of Statistics - Telecommunication Services (Chronological Time Series 1997-2006).*

The World Bank, 1818 H Street, NW, Washington, DC 20433, (202) 473-1000, Fax: (202) 477-6391, www.worldbank.org; *Colombia.*

COLOMBIA - INVESTMENTS

Inter-American Development Bank (IDB), 1300 New York Avenue, NW, Washington, DC 20577, (202) 623-1000, Fax: (202) 623-3096, www.iadb.org; *The Politics of Policies: Economic and Social Progress in Latin America - 2006 Report.*

United Nations Statistics Division, New York, NY 10017, (800) 253-9646, Fax: (212) 963-4116, http://unstats.un.org; *Statistical Yearbook for Latin America and the Caribbean 2004.*

COLOMBIA - INVESTMENTS, FOREIGN

Economist Intelligence Unit, 111 West 57th Street, New York, NY 10019, (212) 554-0600, Fax: (212) 586-1181, www.eiu.com; *Business Latin America.*

COLOMBIA - IRON AND IRON ORE PRODUCTION

See COLOMBIA - MINERAL INDUSTRIES

COLOMBIA - IRRIGATION

Euromonitor International, Inc., 224 S. Michigan Avenue, Suite 1500, Chicago, IL 60604, (312) 922-1115, Fax: (312) 922-1157, www.euromonitor.com; *International Marketing Data and Statistics 2008.*

Inter-American Development Bank (IDB), 1300 New York Avenue, NW, Washington, DC 20577, (202) 623-1000, Fax: (202) 623-3096, www.iadb.org; *The Politics of Policies: Economic and Social Progress in Latin America - 2006 Report.*

COLOMBIA - LABOR

Central Intelligence Agency, Office of Public Affairs, Washington, DC 20505, (703) 482-0623, Fax: (703) 482-1739, www.cia.gov; *The World Factbook.*

Economist Intelligence Unit, 111 West 57th Street, New York, NY 10019, (212) 554-0600, Fax: (212) 586-1181, www.eiu.com; *Business Latin America.*

Euromonitor International, Inc., 224 S. Michigan Avenue, Suite 1500, Chicago, IL 60604, (312) 922-1115, Fax: (312) 922-1157, www.euromonitor.com; *International Marketing Data and Statistics 2008* and *World Marketing Data and Statistics.*

International Labour Office, I.L.O. Publications, 4 route des Morillons, CH-1211 Geneva 22, Switzerland, (Telephone in U.S. (202) 653-7652), (Fax in U.S. (202) 653-7687), www.ilo.org; *Yearbook of Labour Statistics 2006.*

M.E. Sharpe, 80 Business Park Drive, Armonk, NY 10504, (800) 541-6563, Fax: (914) 273-2106, www.mesharpe.com; *The Illustrated Book of World Rankings.*

Palgrave Macmillan Ltd., Houndmills, Basingstoke, Hampshire, RG21 6XS, England, (Telephone in U.S. (888) 330-8477), (Fax in U.S. (800) 672-2054), www.palgrave.com; *The Statesman's Yearbook 2008.*

Taylor and Francis Group, An Informa Business, 2 Park Square, Milton Park, Abingdon, Oxford OX14 4RN, United Kingdom, (Dial from U.S. (212) 216-

7800), (Fax from U.S. (212) 564-7854), www.tandf.co.uk; *The Europa World Year Book.*

United Nations Food and Agricultural Organization (FAO), Viale delle Terme di Caracalla, 00100 Rome, Italy, (Dial from U.S. (202) 653-2400), (Fax from U.S. (202) 653 5760), www.fao.org; *The State of Food and Agriculture (SOFA) 2006.*

United Nations Statistics Division, New York, NY 10017, (800) 253-9646, Fax: (212) 963-4116, http://unstats.un.org; *Human Development Report 2006.*

The World Bank, 1818 H Street, NW, Washington, DC 20433, (202) 473-1000, Fax: (202) 477-6391, www.worldbank.org; *The World Bank Atlas 2003-2004* and *World Development Report 2008.*

COLOMBIA - LAND USE

Central Intelligence Agency, Office of Public Affairs, Washington, DC 20505, (703) 482-0623, Fax: (703) 482-1739, www.cia.gov; *The World Factbook.*

Euromonitor International, Inc., 224 S. Michigan Avenue, Suite 1500, Chicago, IL 60604, (312) 922-1115, Fax: (312) 922-1157, www.euromonitor.com; *International Marketing Data and Statistics 2008.*

Inter-American Development Bank (IDB), 1300 New York Avenue, NW, Washington, DC 20577, (202) 623-1000, Fax: (202) 623-3096, www.iadb.org; *The Politics of Policies: Economic and Social Progress in Latin America - 2006 Report.*

United Nations Food and Agricultural Organization (FAO), Viale delle Terme di Caracalla, 00100 Rome, Italy, (Dial from U.S. (202) 653-2400), (Fax from U.S. (202) 653 5760), www.fao.org; *FAO Production Yearbook 2002.*

The World Bank, 1818 H Street, NW, Washington, DC 20433, (202) 473-1000, Fax: (202) 477-6391, www.worldbank.org; *World Development Report 2008.*

COLOMBIA - LIBRARIES

M.E. Sharpe, 80 Business Park Drive, Armonk, NY 10504, (800) 541-6563, Fax: (914) 273-2106, www.mesharpe.com; *The Illustrated Book of World Rankings.*

UNESCO Institute for Statistics, C.P. 6128 Succursale Centre-Ville, Montreal, Quebec, H3C 3J7 Canada, (Dial from U.S. (514) 343-6880), (Fax from U.S. (514) 343 6882), www.uis.unesco.org; *Statistical Tables.*

COLOMBIA - LIFE EXPECTANCY

Central Intelligence Agency, Office of Public Affairs, Washington, DC 20505, (703) 482-0623, Fax: (703) 482-1739, www.cia.gov; *The World Factbook.*

Economist Intelligence Unit, 111 West 57th Street, New York, NY 10019, (212) 554-0600, Fax: (212) 586-1181, www.eiu.com; *Business Latin America.*

Euromonitor International, Inc., 224 S. Michigan Avenue, Suite 1500, Chicago, IL 60604, (312) 922-1115, Fax: (312) 922-1157, www.euromonitor.com; *The World Economic Factbook 2008.*

United Nations Statistics Division, New York, NY 10017, (800) 253-9646, Fax: (212) 963-4116, http://unstats.un.org; *Human Development Report 2006; Statistical Yearbook for Latin America and the Caribbean 2004;* and *World Statistics Pocketbook.*

The World Bank, 1818 H Street, NW, Washington, DC 20433, (202) 473-1000, Fax: (202) 477-6391, www.worldbank.org; *The World Bank Atlas 2003-2004* and *World Development Report 2008.*

COLOMBIA - LITERACY

Euromonitor International, Inc., 224 S. Michigan Avenue, Suite 1500, Chicago, IL 60604, (312) 922-1115, Fax: (312) 922-1157, www.euromonitor.com; *World Marketing Data and Statistics.*

COLOMBIA - LIVESTOCK

Euromonitor International, Inc., 224 S. Michigan Avenue, Suite 1500, Chicago, IL 60604, (312) 922-1115, Fax: (312) 922-1157, www.euromonitor.com; *International Marketing Data and Statistics 2008.*

M.E. Sharpe, 80 Business Park Drive, Armonk, NY 10504, (800) 541-6563, Fax: (914) 273-2106, www.mesharpe.com; *The Illustrated Book of World Rankings.*

Palgrave Macmillan Ltd., Houndmills, Basingstoke, Hampshire, RG21 6XS, England, (Telephone in U.S. (888) 330-8477), (Fax in U.S. (800) 672-2054), www.palgrave.com; *The Statesman's Yearbook 2008.*

Taylor and Francis Group, An Informa Business, 2 Park Square, Milton Park, Abingdon, Oxford OX14 4RN, United Kingdom, (Dial from U.S. (212) 216-7800), (Fax from U.S. (212) 564-7854), www.tandf.co.uk; *The Europa World Year Book.*

United Nations Conference on Trade and Development (UNCTAD), DC2-1120, United Nations, New York, NY 10017, (212) 963-0027, www.unctad.org; *UNCTAD Commodity Yearbook.*

United Nations Food and Agricultural Organization (FAO), Viale delle Terme di Caracalla, 00100 Rome, Italy, (Dial from U.S. (202) 653-2400), (Fax from U.S. (202) 653 5760), www.fao.org; *FAO Production Yearbook 2002* and *The State of Food and Agriculture (SOFA) 2006.*

United Nations Statistics Division, New York, NY 10017, (800) 253-9646, Fax: (212) 963-4116, http://unstats.un.org; *Statistical Yearbook* and *Survey of Economic and Social Conditions in Africa 2005.*

COLOMBIA - LOCAL TAXATION

Euromonitor International, Inc., 224 S. Michigan Avenue, Suite 1500, Chicago, IL 60604, (312) 922-1115, Fax: (312) 922-1157, www.euromonitor.com; *International Marketing Data and Statistics 2008.*

Inter-American Development Bank (IDB), 1300 New York Avenue, NW, Washington, DC 20577, (202) 623-1000, Fax: (202) 623-3096, www.iadb.org; *The Politics of Policies: Economic and Social Progress in Latin America - 2006 Report.*

COLOMBIA - MANUFACTURES

Economist Intelligence Unit, 111 West 57th Street, New York, NY 10019, (212) 554-0600, Fax: (212) 586-1181, www.eiu.com; *Business Latin America.*

Inter-American Development Bank (IDB), 1300 New York Avenue, NW, Washington, DC 20577, (202) 623-1000, Fax: (202) 623-3096, www.iadb.org; *The Politics of Policies: Economic and Social Progress in Latin America - 2006 Report.*

M.E. Sharpe, 80 Business Park Drive, Armonk, NY 10504, (800) 541-6563, Fax: (914) 273-2106, www.mesharpe.com; *The Illustrated Book of World Rankings.*

United Nations Statistics Division, New York, NY 10017, (800) 253-9646, Fax: (212) 963-4116, http://unstats.un.org; *Statistical Yearbook* and *Statistical Yearbook for Latin America and the Caribbean 2004.*

COLOMBIA - MARRIAGE

M.E. Sharpe, 80 Business Park Drive, Armonk, NY 10504, (800) 541-6563, Fax: (914) 273-2106, www.mesharpe.com; *The Illustrated Book of World Rankings.*

Taylor and Francis Group, An Informa Business, 2 Park Square, Milton Park, Abingdon, Oxford OX14 4RN, United Kingdom, (Dial from U.S. (212) 216-7800), (Fax from U.S. (212) 564-7854), www.tandf.co.uk; *The Europa World Year Book.*

United Nations Statistics Division, New York, NY 10017, (800) 253-9646, Fax: (212) 963-4116, http://unstats.un.org; *Demographic Yearbook* and *Statistical Yearbook.*

COLOMBIA - MEAT PRODUCTION

See COLOMBIA - LIVESTOCK

COLOMBIA - MEDICAL CARE, COST OF

United Nations Statistics Division, New York, NY 10017, (800) 253-9646, Fax: (212) 963-4116, http://unstats.un.org; *Statistical Yearbook for Latin America and the Caribbean 2004.*

COLOMBIA - MEDICAL PERSONNEL

UCLA Latin American Institute, 10343 Bunche Hall, Box 951447, Los Angeles, CA 90095-1447, (310) 825-4571, Fax: (310) 206-6859, www.international.ucla.edu/lac; *Statistical Abstract of Latin America.*

COLOMBIA - MERCURY PRODUCTION

See COLOMBIA - MINERAL INDUSTRIES

COLOMBIA - MILK PRODUCTION

See COLOMBIA - DAIRY PROCESSING

COLOMBIA - MINERAL INDUSTRIES

Commodity Research Bureau, 330 South Wells Street, Suite 612, Chicago, IL 60606-7110, (800) 621-5271, Fax: (312) 939-4135, www.crbtrader.com; *2006 CRB Commodity Yearbook and CD.*

Economist Intelligence Unit, 111 West 57th Street, New York, NY 10019, (212) 554-0600, Fax: (212) 586-1181, www.eiu.com; *Business Latin America.*

Inter-American Development Bank (IDB), 1300 New York Avenue, NW, Washington, DC 20577, (202) 623-1000, Fax: (202) 623-3096, www.iadb.org; *The Politics of Policies: Economic and Social Progress in Latin America - 2006 Report.*

M.E. Sharpe, 80 Business Park Drive, Armonk, NY 10504, (800) 541-6563, Fax: (914) 273-2106, www.mesharpe.com; *The Illustrated Book of World Rankings.*

Organisation for Economic Cooperation and Development (OECD), 2 rue Andre Pascal, F-75775 Paris Cedex 16, France, (Telephone in U.S. (202) 785-6323), (Fax in U.S. (202) 785-0350), www.oecd.org; *World Energy Outlook 2007.*

Palgrave Macmillan Ltd., Houndmills, Basingstoke, Hampshire, RG21 6XS, England, (Telephone in U.S. (888) 330-8477), (Fax in U.S. (800) 672-2054), www.palgrave.com; *The Statesman's Yearbook 2008.*

Taylor and Francis Group, An Informa Business, 2 Park Square, Milton Park, Abingdon, Oxford OX14 4RN, United Kingdom, (Dial from U.S. (212) 216-7800), (Fax from U.S. (212) 564-7854), www.tandf.co.uk; *The Europa World Year Book.*

UCLA Latin American Institute, 10343 Bunche Hall, Box 951447, Los Angeles, CA 90095-1447, (310) 825-4571, Fax: (310) 206-6859, www.international.ucla.edu/lac; *Statistical Abstract of Latin America.*

United Nations Conference on Trade and Development (UNCTAD), DC2-1120, United Nations, New York, NY 10017, (212) 963-0027, www.unctad.org; *UNCTAD Commodity Yearbook.*

United Nations Statistics Division, New York, NY 10017, (800) 253-9646, Fax: (212) 963-4116, http://unstats.un.org; *Statistical Yearbook.*

COLOMBIA - MONEY EXCHANGE RATES

See COLOMBIA - FOREIGN EXCHANGE RATES

COLOMBIA - MONEY SUPPLY

Economist Intelligence Unit, 111 West 57th Street, New York, NY 10019, (212) 554-0600, Fax: (212) 586-1181, www.eiu.com; *Colombia Country Report.*

Euromonitor International, Inc., 224 S. Michigan Avenue, Suite 1500, Chicago, IL 60604, (312) 922-1115, Fax: (312) 922-1157, www.euromonitor.com; *International Marketing Data and Statistics 2008.*

Inter-American Development Bank (IDB), 1300 New York Avenue, NW, Washington, DC 20577, (202) 623-1000, Fax: (202) 623-3096, www.iadb.org; *The Politics of Policies: Economic and Social Progress in Latin America - 2006 Report.*

International Monetary Fund (IMF), 700 Nineteenth Street, NW, Washington, DC 20431, (202) 623-7000, Fax: (202) 623-4661, www.imf.org; *International Financial Statistics Yearbook 2007.*

Taylor and Francis Group, An Informa Business, 2 Park Square, Milton Park, Abingdon, Oxford OX14

4RN, United Kingdom, (Dial from U.S. (212) 216-7800), (Fax from U.S. (212) 564-7854), www.tandf.co.uk; *The Europa World Year Book.*

UCLA Latin American Institute, 10343 Bunche Hall, Box 951447, Los Angeles, CA 90095-1447, (310) 825-4571, Fax: (310) 206-6859, www.international.ucla.edu/lac; *Statistical Abstract of Latin America.*

United Nations Statistics Division, New York, NY 10017, (800) 253-9646, Fax: (212) 963-4116, http://unstats.un.org; *Statistical Yearbook.*

The World Bank, 1818 H Street, NW, Washington, DC 20433, (202) 473-1000, Fax: (202) 477-6391, www.worldbank.org; *Colombia.*

COLOMBIA - MONUMENTS AND HISTORIC SITES

UNESCO Institute for Statistics, C.P. 6128 Succursale Centre-Ville, Montreal, Quebec, H3C 3J7 Canada, (Dial from U.S. (514) 343-6880), (Fax from U.S. (514) 343 6882), www.uis.unesco.org; *Statistical Tables.*

COLOMBIA - MORTALITY

Central Intelligence Agency, Office of Public Affairs, Washington, DC 20505, (703) 482-0623, Fax: (703) 482-1739, www.cia.gov; *The World Factbook.*

Economist Intelligence Unit, 111 West 57th Street, New York, NY 10019, (212) 554-0600, Fax: (212) 586-1181, www.eiu.com; *Business Latin America.*

Euromonitor International, Inc., 224 S. Michigan Avenue, Suite 1500, Chicago, IL 60604, (312) 922-1115, Fax: (312) 922-1157, www.euromonitor.com; *International Marketing Data and Statistics 2008* and *The World Economic Factbook 2008.*

Taylor and Francis Group, An Informa Business, 2 Park Square, Milton Park, Abingdon, Oxford OX14 4RN, United Kingdom, (Dial from U.S. (212) 216-7800), (Fax from U.S. (212) 564-7854), www.tandf.co.uk; *The Europa World Year Book.*

UNICEF, 3 United Nations Plaza, New York, NY 10017, (800) 253-9646, Fax: (212) 887-7465, www.unicef.org; *The State of the World's Children 2008.*

United Nations Statistics Division, New York, NY 10017, (800) 253-9646, Fax: (212) 963-4116, http://unstats.un.org; *Demographic Yearbook; Human Development Report 2006; Statistical Yearbook; Statistical Yearbook for Latin America and the Caribbean 2004;* and *World Statistics Pocketbook.*

The World Bank, 1818 H Street, NW, Washington, DC 20433, (202) 473-1000, Fax: (202) 477-6391, www.worldbank.org; *The World Bank Atlas 2003-2004* and *World Development Report 2008.*

World Health Organization (WHO), Avenue Appia 20, 1211 Geneve 27, Switzerland, (Telephone in U.S. (212) 331-9081), www.who.int; The WHO Global Atlas of Infectious Diseases and *World Health Report 2006.*

COLOMBIA - MOTION PICTURES

Palgrave Macmillan Ltd., Houndmills, Basingstoke, Hampshire, RG21 6XS, England, (Telephone in U.S. (888) 330-8477), (Fax in U.S. (800) 672-2054), www.palgrave.com; *The Statesman's Yearbook 2008.*

UNESCO Institute for Statistics, C.P. 6128 Succursale Centre-Ville, Montreal, Quebec, H3C 3J7 Canada, (Dial from U.S. (514) 343-6880), (Fax from U.S. (514) 343 6882), www.uis.unesco.org; *Statistical Tables.*

United Nations Statistics Division, New York, NY 10017, (800) 253-9646, Fax: (212) 963-4116, http://unstats.un.org; *Statistical Yearbook.*

COLOMBIA - MOTOR VEHICLES

Economist Intelligence Unit, 111 West 57th Street, New York, NY 10019, (212) 554-0600, Fax: (212) 586-1181, www.eiu.com; *Business Latin America.*

International Road Federation (IFR), Madison Place, 500 Montgomery Street, 5th Floor, Alexandria, VA 22314, (703) 535-1001, Fax: (703) 535-1007, www.irfnet.org; *World Road Statistics 2006.*

Taylor and Francis Group, An Informa Business, 2 Park Square, Milton Park, Abingdon, Oxford OX14 4RN, United Kingdom, (Dial from U.S. (212) 216-7800), (Fax from U.S. (212) 564-7854), www.tandf.co.uk; *The Europa World Year Book.*

United Nations Statistics Division, New York, NY 10017, (800) 253-9646, Fax: (212) 963-4116, http://unstats.un.org; *Statistical Yearbook.*

COLOMBIA - MUSEUMS

M.E. Sharpe, 80 Business Park Drive, Armonk, NY 10504, (800) 541-6563, Fax: (914) 273-2106, www.mesharpe.com; *The Illustrated Book of World Rankings.*

UNESCO Institute for Statistics, C.P. 6128 Succursale Centre-Ville, Montreal, Quebec, H3C 3J7 Canada, (Dial from U.S. (514) 343-6880), (Fax from U.S. (514) 343 6882), www.uis.unesco.org; *Statistical Tables.*

COLOMBIA - NATURAL GAS PRODUCTION

See COLOMBIA - MINERAL INDUSTRIES

COLOMBIA - NUTRITION

United Nations Food and Agricultural Organization (FAO), Viale delle Terme di Caracalla, 00100 Rome, Italy, (Dial from U.S. (202) 653-2400), (Fax from U.S. (202) 653 5760), www.fao.org; *The State of Food and Agriculture (SOFA) 2006.*

United Nations Statistics Division, New York, NY 10017, (800) 253-9646, Fax: (212) 963-4116, http://unstats.un.org; *Statistical Yearbook for Latin America and the Caribbean 2004.*

COLOMBIA - OIL INDUSTRIES

International Monetary Fund (IMF), 700 Nineteenth Street, NW, Washington, DC 20431, (202) 623-7000, Fax: (202) 623-4661, www.imf.org; *International Financial Statistics Yearbook 2007.*

PennWell Corporation, 1421 South Sheridan Road, Tulsa, OK 74112, (918) 835-3161, www.pennwell.com; *Oil Gas Journal Latinoamericana.*

COLOMBIA - OLDER PEOPLE

M.E. Sharpe, 80 Business Park Drive, Armonk, NY 10504, (800) 541-6563, Fax: (914) 273-2106, www.mesharpe.com; *The Illustrated Book of World Rankings.*

COLOMBIA - PALM OIL PRODUCTION

See COLOMBIA - CROPS

COLOMBIA - PAPER

See COLOMBIA - FORESTS AND FORESTRY

COLOMBIA - PEANUT PRODUCTION

See COLOMBIA - CROPS

COLOMBIA - PERIODICALS

UNESCO Institute for Statistics, C.P. 6128 Succursale Centre-Ville, Montreal, Quebec, H3C 3J7 Canada, (Dial from U.S. (514) 343-6880), (Fax from U.S. (514) 343 6882), www.uis.unesco.org; *Statistical Tables.*

COLOMBIA - PESTICIDES

United Nations Food and Agricultural Organization (FAO), Viale delle Terme di Caracalla, 00100 Rome, Italy, (Dial from U.S. (202) 653-2400), (Fax from U.S. (202) 653 5760), www.fao.org; *The State of Food and Agriculture (SOFA) 2006.*

COLOMBIA - PETROLEUM INDUSTRY AND TRADE

Economist Intelligence Unit, 111 West 57th Street, New York, NY 10019, (212) 554-0600, Fax: (212) 586-1181, www.eiu.com; *Business Latin America.*

Inter-American Development Bank (IDB), 1300 New York Avenue, NW, Washington, DC 20577, (202) 623-1000, Fax: (202) 623-3096, www.iadb.org; *The Politics of Policies: Economic and Social Progress in Latin America - 2006 Report.*

International Monetary Fund (IMF), 700 Nineteenth Street, NW, Washington, DC 20431, (202) 623-7000, Fax: (202) 623-4661, www.imf.org; *International Financial Statistics Yearbook 2007.*

M.E. Sharpe, 80 Business Park Drive, Armonk, NY 10504, (800) 541-6563, Fax: (914) 273-2106, www.mesharpe.com; *The Illustrated Book of World Rankings.*

Organisation for Economic Cooperation and Development (OECD), 2 rue Andre Pascal, F-75775 Paris Cedex 16, France, (Telephone in U.S. (202) 785-6323), (Fax in U.S. (202) 785-0350), www.oecd.org; *World Energy Outlook 2007.*

Organization of American States (OAS), 17th Street Constitution Avenue NW, Washington, DC 20006, (202) 458-3000, www.oas.org; *The OAS in Transition: 1994-2004.*

PennWell Corporation, 1421 South Sheridan Road, Tulsa, OK 74112, (918) 835-3161, www.pennwell.com; *International Petroleum Encyclopedia 2007* and *Oil Gas Journal Latinoamericana.*

U.S. Department of Energy (DOE), Energy Information Administration (EIA), 1000 Independence Avenue, SW, Washington, DC 20585, (202) 586-8800, www.eia.doe.gov; *International Energy Annual 2004* and *International Energy Outlook 2006.*

United Nations Conference on Trade and Development (UNCTAD), DC2-1120, United Nations, New York, NY 10017, (212) 963-0027, www.unctad.org; *UNCTAD Commodity Yearbook.*

United Nations Food and Agricultural Organization (FAO), Viale delle Terme di Caracalla, 00100 Rome, Italy, (Dial from U.S. (202) 653-2400), (Fax from U.S. (202) 653 5760), www.fao.org; *The State of Food and Agriculture (SOFA) 2006.*

United Nations Statistics Division, New York, NY 10017, (800) 253-9646, Fax: (212) 963-4116, http://unstats.un.org; *Statistical Yearbook.*

COLOMBIA - PHOSPHATES PRODUCTION

See COLOMBIA - MINERAL INDUSTRIES

COLOMBIA - PLASTICS INDUSTRY AND TRADE

United Nations Statistics Division, New York, NY 10017, (800) 253-9646, Fax: (212) 963-4116, http://unstats.un.org; *Statistical Yearbook.*

COLOMBIA - PLATINUM PRODUCTION

See COLOMBIA - MINERAL INDUSTRIES

COLOMBIA - POLITICAL SCIENCE

Central Intelligence Agency, Office of Public Affairs, Washington, DC 20505, (703) 482-0623, Fax: (703) 482-1739, www.cia.gov; *The World Factbook.*

Inter-American Development Bank (IDB), 1300 New York Avenue, NW, Washington, DC 20577, (202) 623-1000, Fax: (202) 623-3096, www.iadb.org; *The Politics of Policies: Economic and Social Progress in Latin America - 2006 Report.*

International Monetary Fund (IMF), 700 Nineteenth Street, NW, Washington, DC 20431, (202) 623-7000, Fax: (202) 623-4661, www.imf.org; *International Financial Statistics Yearbook 2007.*

Palgrave Macmillan Ltd., Houndmills, Basingstoke, Hampshire, RG21 6XS, England, (Telephone in U.S. (888) 330-8477), (Fax in U.S. (800) 672-2054), www.palgrave.com; *The Statesman's Yearbook 2008.*

Taylor and Francis Group, An Informa Business, 2 Park Square, Milton Park, Abingdon, Oxford OX14 4RN, United Kingdom, (Dial from U.S. (212) 216-7800), (Fax from U.S. (212) 564-7854), www.tandf.co.uk; *The Europa World Year Book.*

UCLA Latin American Institute, 10343 Bunche Hall, Box 951447, Los Angeles, CA 90095-1447, (310)

825-4571, Fax: (310) 206-6859, www.international.ucla.edu/lac; *Statistical Abstract of Latin America.*

United Nations Statistics Division, New York, NY 10017, (800) 253-9646, Fax: (212) 963-4116, http://unstats.un.org; *National Accounts Statistics: Compendium of Income Distribution Statistics* and *Statistical Yearbook.*

The World Bank, 1818 H Street, NW, Washington, DC 20433, (202) 473-1000, Fax: (202) 477-6391, www.worldbank.org; *World Development Report 2008.*

COLOMBIA - POPULATION

Central Intelligence Agency, Office of Public Affairs, Washington, DC 20505, (703) 482-0623, Fax: (703) 482-1739, www.cia.gov; *The World Factbook.*

Economist Intelligence Unit, 111 West 57th Street, New York, NY 10019, (212) 554-0600, Fax: (212) 586-1181, www.eiu.com; *Business Latin America* and *Colombia Country Report.*

Euromonitor International, Inc., 224 S. Michigan Avenue, Suite 1500, Chicago, IL 60604, (312) 922-1115, Fax: (312) 922-1157, www.euromonitor.com; *International Marketing Data and Statistics 2008* and *The World Economic Factbook 2008.*

Inter-American Development Bank (IDB), 1300 New York Avenue, NW, Washington, DC 20577, (202) 623-1000, Fax: (202) 623-3096, www.iadb.org; *The Politics of Policies: Economic and Social Progress in Latin America - 2006 Report.*

International Labour Office, I.L.O. Publications, 4 route des Morillons, CH-1211 Geneva 22, Switzerland, (Telephone in U.S. (202) 653-7652), (Fax in U.S. (202) 653-7687), www.ilo.org; *Yearbook of Labour Statistics 2006.*

M.E. Sharpe, 80 Business Park Drive, Armonk, NY 10504, (800) 541-6563, Fax: (914) 273-2106, www.mesharpe.com; *The Illustrated Book of World Rankings.*

Organization of American States (OAS), 17th Street Constitution Avenue NW, Washington, DC 20006, (202) 458-3000, www.oas.org; *The OAS in Transition: 1994-2004.*

Palgrave Macmillan Ltd., Houndmills, Basingstoke, Hampshire, RG21 6XS, England, (Telephone in U.S. (888) 330-8477), (Fax in U.S. (800) 672-2054), www.palgrave.com; *The Statesman's Yearbook 2008.*

Taylor and Francis Group, An Informa Business, 2 Park Square, Milton Park, Abingdon, Oxford OX14 4RN, United Kingdom, (Dial from U.S. (212) 216-7800), (Fax from U.S. (212) 564-7854), www.tandf.co.uk; *The Europa World Year Book.*

U.S. Department of State (DOS), 2201 C Street NW, Washington, DC 20520, (202) 647-4000, www.state.gov; *World Military Expenditures and Arms Transfers (WMEAT).*

UCLA Latin American Institute, 10343 Bunche Hall, Box 951447, Los Angeles, CA 90095-1447, (310) 825-4571, Fax: (310) 206-6859, www.international.ucla.edu/lac; *Statistical Abstract of Latin America.*

UNESCO Institute for Statistics, C.P. 6128 Succursale Centre-Ville, Montreal, Quebec, H3C 3J7 Canada, (Dial from U.S. (514) 343-6880), (Fax from U.S. (514) 343 6882), www.uis.unesco.org; *Statistical Tables.*

United Nations Food and Agricultural Organization (FAO), Viale delle Terme di Caracalla, 00100 Rome, Italy, (Dial from U.S. (202) 653-2400), (Fax from U.S. (202) 653 5760), www.fao.org; *FAO Production Yearbook 2002.*

United Nations Statistics Division, New York, NY 10017, (800) 253-9646, Fax: (212) 963-4116, http://unstats.un.org; *Demographic Yearbook; Human Development Report 2006; Statistical Yearbook; Statistical Yearbook for Latin America and the Caribbean 2004;* and *World Statistics Pocketbook.*

The World Bank, 1818 H Street, NW, Washington, DC 20433, (202) 473-1000, Fax: (202) 477-6391, www.worldbank.org; *Colombia; The World Bank Atlas 2003-2004;* and *World Development Report 2008.*

World Health Organization (WHO), Avenue Appia 20, 1211 Geneve 27, Switzerland, (Telephone in U.S. (212) 331-9081), www.who.int; *World Health Report 2006.*

COLOMBIA - POPULATION DENSITY

Central Intelligence Agency, Office of Public Affairs, Washington, DC 20505, (703) 482-0623, Fax: (703) 482-1739, www.cia.gov; *The World Factbook.*

Euromonitor International, Inc., 224 S. Michigan Avenue, Suite 1500, Chicago, IL 60604, (312) 922-1115, Fax: (312) 922-1157, www.euromonitor.com; *International Marketing Data and Statistics 2008* and *The World Economic Factbook 2008.*

Inter-American Development Bank (IDB), 1300 New York Avenue, NW, Washington, DC 20577, (202) 623-1000, Fax: (202) 623-3096, www.iadb.org; *The Politics of Policies: Economic and Social Progress in Latin America - 2006 Report.*

M.E. Sharpe, 80 Business Park Drive, Armonk, NY 10504, (800) 541-6563, Fax: (914) 273-2106, www.mesharpe.com; *The Illustrated Book of World Rankings.*

Palgrave Macmillan Ltd., Houndmills, Basingstoke, Hampshire, RG21 6XS, England, (Telephone in U.S. (888) 330-8477), (Fax in U.S. (800) 672-2054), www.palgrave.com; *The Statesman's Yearbook 2008.*

Taylor and Francis Group, An Informa Business, 2 Park Square, Milton Park, Abingdon, Oxford OX14 4RN, United Kingdom, (Dial from U.S. (212) 216-7800), (Fax from U.S. (212) 564-7854), www.tandf.co.uk; *The Europa World Year Book.*

UNESCO Institute for Statistics, C.P. 6128 Succursale Centre-Ville, Montreal, Quebec, H3C 3J7 Canada, (Dial from U.S. (514) 343-6880), (Fax from U.S. (514) 343 6882), www.uis.unesco.org; *Statistical Tables.*

United Nations Food and Agricultural Organization (FAO), Viale delle Terme di Caracalla, 00100 Rome, Italy, (Dial from U.S. (202) 653-2400), (Fax from U.S. (202) 653 5760), www.fao.org; *The State of Food and Agriculture (SOFA) 2006.*

United Nations Statistics Division, New York, NY 10017, (800) 253-9646, Fax: (212) 963-4116, http://unstats.un.org; *Statistical Yearbook.*

The World Bank, 1818 H Street, NW, Washington, DC 20433, (202) 473-1000, Fax: (202) 477-6391, www.worldbank.org; *Colombia* and *World Development Report 2008.*

COLOMBIA - POSTAL SERVICE

M.E. Sharpe, 80 Business Park Drive, Armonk, NY 10504, (800) 541-6563, Fax: (914) 273-2106, www.mesharpe.com; *The Illustrated Book of World Rankings.*

United Nations Statistics Division, New York, NY 10017, (800) 253-9646, Fax: (212) 963-4116, http://unstats.un.org; *Statistical Yearbook.*

COLOMBIA - POWER RESOURCES

Economist Intelligence Unit, 111 West 57th Street, New York, NY 10019, (212) 554-0600, Fax: (212) 586-1181, www.eiu.com; *Business Latin America.*

Euromonitor International, Inc., 224 S. Michigan Avenue, Suite 1500, Chicago, IL 60604, (312) 922-1115, Fax: (312) 922-1157, www.euromonitor.com; *International Marketing Data and Statistics 2008; The World Economic Factbook 2008;* and *World Marketing Data and Statistics.*

M.E. Sharpe, 80 Business Park Drive, Armonk, NY 10504, (800) 541-6563, Fax: (914) 273-2106, www.mesharpe.com; *The Illustrated Book of World Rankings.*

Organisation for Economic Cooperation and Development (OECD), 2 rue Andre Pascal, F-75775 Paris Cedex 16, France, (Telephone in U.S. (202) 785-6323), (Fax in U.S. (202) 785-0350), www.oecd.org; *World Energy Outlook 2007.*

Palgrave Macmillan Ltd., Houndmills, Basingstoke, Hampshire, RG21 6XS, England, (Telephone in U.S. (888) 330-8477), (Fax in U.S. (800) 672-2054), www.palgrave.com; *The Statesman's Yearbook 2008.*

Platts, 2 Penn Plaza, 25th Floor, New York, NY 10121-2298, (212) 904-3070, www.platts.com; *Energy Economist.*

U.S. Department of Energy (DOE), Energy Information Administration (EIA), 1000 Independence Avenue, SW, Washington, DC 20585, (202) 586-8800, www.eia.doe.gov; *International Energy Annual 2004* and *International Energy Outlook 2006.*

UCLA Latin American Institute, 10343 Bunche Hall, Box 951447, Los Angeles, CA 90095-1447, (310) 825-4571, Fax: (310) 206-6859, www.international.ucla.edu/lac; *Statistical Abstract of Latin America.*

United Nations Food and Agricultural Organization (FAO), Viale delle Terme di Caracalla, 00100 Rome, Italy, (Dial from U.S. (202) 653-2400), (Fax from U.S. (202) 653 5760), www.fao.org; *The State of Food and Agriculture (SOFA) 2006.*

United Nations Statistics Division, New York, NY 10017, (800) 253-9646, Fax: (212) 963-4116, http://unstats.un.org; *Energy Statistics Yearbook 2003; Human Development Report 2006; Statistical Yearbook; Statistical Yearbook for Latin America and the Caribbean 2004;* and *World Statistics Pocketbook.*

The World Bank, 1818 H Street, NW, Washington, DC 20433, (202) 473-1000, Fax: (202) 477-6391, www.worldbank.org; *The World Bank Atlas 2003-2004* and *World Development Report 2008.*

COLOMBIA - PRICES

Euromonitor International, Inc., 224 S. Michigan Avenue, Suite 1500, Chicago, IL 60604, (312) 922-1115, Fax: (312) 922-1157, www.euromonitor.com; *World Marketing Data and Statistics.*

International Labour Office, I.L.O. Publications, 4 route des Morillons, CH-1211 Geneva 22, Switzerland, (Telephone in U.S. (202) 653-7652), (Fax in U.S. (202) 653-7687), www.ilo.org; *Yearbook of Labour Statistics 2006.*

International Monetary Fund (IMF), 700 Nineteenth Street, NW, Washington, DC 20431, (202) 623-7000, Fax: (202) 623-4661, www.imf.org; *International Financial Statistics Yearbook 2007.*

M.E. Sharpe, 80 Business Park Drive, Armonk, NY 10504, (800) 541-6563, Fax: (914) 273-2106, www.mesharpe.com; *The Illustrated Book of World Rankings.*

Organization of American States (OAS), 17th Street Constitution Avenue NW, Washington, DC 20006, (202) 458-3000, www.oas.org; *The OAS in Transition: 1994-2004.*

UCLA Latin American Institute, 10343 Bunche Hall, Box 951447, Los Angeles, CA 90095-1447, (310) 825-4571, Fax: (310) 206-6859, www.international.ucla.edu/lac; *Statistical Abstract of Latin America.*

United Nations Food and Agricultural Organization (FAO), Viale delle Terme di Caracalla, 00100 Rome, Italy, (Dial from U.S. (202) 653-2400), (Fax from U.S. (202) 653 5760), www.fao.org; *FAO Production Yearbook 2002* and *The State of Food and Agriculture (SOFA) 2006.*

United Nations Statistics Division, New York, NY 10017, (800) 253-9646, Fax: (212) 963-4116, http://unstats.un.org; *Economic Survey of Latin America and the Caribbean 2004-2005* and *Statistical Yearbook for Latin America and the Caribbean 2004.*

The World Bank, 1818 H Street, NW, Washington, DC 20433, (202) 473-1000, Fax: (202) 477-6391, www.worldbank.org; *Colombia.*

COLOMBIA - PROFESSIONS

UCLA Latin American Institute, 10343 Bunche Hall, Box 951447, Los Angeles, CA 90095-1447, (310) 825-4571, Fax: (310) 206-6859, www.international.ucla.edu/lac; *Statistical Abstract of Latin America.*

United Nations Statistics Division, New York, NY 10017, (800) 253-9646, Fax: (212) 963-4116, http://unstats.un.org; *Statistical Yearbook.*

COLOMBIA - PUBLIC HEALTH

Economist Intelligence Unit, 111 West 57th Street, New York, NY 10019, (212) 554-0600, Fax: (212) 586-1181, www.eiu.com; *Business Latin America.*

Euromonitor International, Inc., 224 S. Michigan Avenue, Suite 1500, Chicago, IL 60604, (312) 922-1115, Fax: (312) 922-1157, www.euromonitor.com; *World Health Databook 2007/2008* and *World Marketing Data and Statistics.*

M.E. Sharpe, 80 Business Park Drive, Armonk, NY 10504, (800) 541-6563, Fax: (914) 273-2106, www.mesharpe.com; *The Illustrated Book of World Rankings.*

Palgrave Macmillan Ltd., Houndmills, Basingstoke, Hampshire, RG21 6XS, England, (Telephone in U.S. (888) 330-8477), (Fax in U.S. (800) 672-2054), www.palgrave.com; *The Statesman's Yearbook 2008.*

UCLA Latin American Institute, 10343 Bunche Hall, Box 951447, Los Angeles, CA 90095-1447, (310) 825-4571, Fax: (310) 206-6859, www.international.ucla.edu/lac; *Statistical Abstract of Latin America.*

UNICEF, 3 United Nations Plaza, New York, NY 10017, (800) 253-9646, Fax: (212) 887-7465, www.unicef.org; *The State of the World's Children 2008.*

United Nations Statistics Division, New York, NY 10017, (800) 253-9646, Fax: (212) 963-4116, http://unstats.un.org; *Human Development Report 2006* and *Statistical Yearbook.*

The World Bank, 1818 H Street, NW, Washington, DC 20433, (202) 473-1000, Fax: (202) 477-6391, www.worldbank.org; *Colombia* and *World Development Report 2008.*

World Health Organization (WHO), Avenue Appia 20, 1211 Geneve 27, Switzerland, (Telephone in U.S. (212) 331-9081), www.who.int; The WHO Global Atlas of Infectious Diseases and *World Health Report 2006.*

COLOMBIA - PUBLIC UTILITIES

UCLA Latin American Institute, 10343 Bunche Hall, Box 951447, Los Angeles, CA 90095-1447, (310) 825-4571, Fax: (310) 206-6859, www.international.ucla.edu/lac; *Statistical Abstract of Latin America.*

COLOMBIA - PUBLISHERS AND PUBLISHING

Taylor and Francis Group, An Informa Business, 2 Park Square, Milton Park, Abingdon, Oxford OX14 4RN, United Kingdom, (Dial from U.S. (212) 216-7800), (Fax from U.S. (212) 564-7854), www.tandf.co.uk; *The Europa World Year Book.*

UNESCO Institute for Statistics, C.P. 6128 Succursale Centre-Ville, Montreal, Quebec, H3C 3J7 Canada, (Dial from U.S. (514) 343-6880), (Fax from U.S. (514) 343 6882), www.uis.unesco.org; *Statistical Tables.*

COLOMBIA - RADIO - RECEIVERS AND RECEPTION

Palgrave Macmillan Ltd., Houndmills, Basingstoke, Hampshire, RG21 6XS, England, (Telephone in U.S. (888) 330-8477), (Fax in U.S. (800) 672-2054), www.palgrave.com; *The Statesman's Yearbook 2008.*

United Nations Statistics Division, New York, NY 10017, (800) 253-9646, Fax: (212) 963-4116, http://unstats.un.org; *Statistical Yearbook.*

COLOMBIA - RAILROADS

Economist Intelligence Unit, 111 West 57th Street, New York, NY 10019, (212) 554-0600, Fax: (212) 586-1181, www.eiu.com; *Business Latin America.*

Jane's Information Group, 110 North Royal Street, Suite 200, Alexandria, VA 22314, (703) 683-3700, Fax: (800) 836-0297, www.janes.com; *Jane's World Railways.*

Palgrave Macmillan Ltd., Houndmills, Basingstoke, Hampshire, RG21 6XS, England, (Telephone in U.S. (888) 330-8477), (Fax in U.S. (800) 672-2054), www.palgrave.com; *The Statesman's Yearbook 2008.*

Taylor and Francis Group, An Informa Business, 2 Park Square, Milton Park, Abingdon, Oxford OX14 4RN, United Kingdom, (Dial from U.S. (212) 216-7800), (Fax from U.S. (212) 564-7854), www.tandf.co.uk; *The Europa World Year Book.*

United Nations Statistics Division, New York, NY 10017, (800) 253-9646, Fax: (212) 963-4116, http://unstats.un.org; *Statistical Yearbook.*

COLOMBIA - RELIGION

Central Intelligence Agency, Office of Public Affairs, Washington, DC 20505, (703) 482-0623, Fax: (703) 482-1739, www.cia.gov; *The World Factbook.*

M.E. Sharpe, 80 Business Park Drive, Armonk, NY 10504, (800) 541-6563, Fax: (914) 273-2106, www.mesharpe.com; *The Illustrated Book of World Rankings.*

Palgrave Macmillan Ltd., Houndmills, Basingstoke, Hampshire, RG21 6XS, England, (Telephone in U.S. (888) 330-8477), (Fax in U.S. (800) 672-2054), www.palgrave.com; *The Statesman's Yearbook 2008.*

UCLA Latin American Institute, 10343 Bunche Hall, Box 951447, Los Angeles, CA 90095-1447, (310) 825-4571, Fax: (310) 206-6859, www.international.ucla.edu/lac; *Statistical Abstract of Latin America.*

COLOMBIA - RENT CHARGES

International Labour Office, I.L.O. Publications, 4 route des Morillons, CH-1211 Geneva 22, Switzerland, (Telephone in U.S. (202) 653-7652), (Fax in U.S. (202) 653-7687), www.ilo.org; *Yearbook of Labour Statistics 2006.*

COLOMBIA - RESERVES (ACCOUNTING)

Economist Intelligence Unit, 111 West 57th Street, New York, NY 10019, (212) 554-0600, Fax: (212) 586-1181, www.eiu.com; *Business Latin America.*

Euromonitor International, Inc., 224 S. Michigan Avenue, Suite 1500, Chicago, IL 60604, (312) 922-1115, Fax: (312) 922-1157, www.euromonitor.com; *International Marketing Data and Statistics 2008.*

Inter-American Development Bank (IDB), 1300 New York Avenue, NW, Washington, DC 20577, (202) 623-1000, Fax: (202) 623-3096, www.iadb.org; *The Politics of Policies: Economic and Social Progress in Latin America - 2006 Report.*

Organization of American States (OAS), 17th Street Constitution Avenue NW, Washington, DC 20006, (202) 458-3000, www.oas.org; *The OAS in Transition: 1994-2004.*

COLOMBIA - RETAIL TRADE

Euromonitor International, Inc., 224 S. Michigan Avenue, Suite 1500, Chicago, IL 60604, (312) 922-1115, Fax: (312) 922-1157, www.euromonitor.com; *World Marketing Data and Statistics.*

Inter-American Development Bank (IDB), 1300 New York Avenue, NW, Washington, DC 20577, (202) 623-1000, Fax: (202) 623-3096, www.iadb.org; *The Politics of Policies: Economic and Social Progress in Latin America - 2006 Report.*

United Nations Statistics Division, New York, NY 10017, (800) 253-9646, Fax: (212) 963-4116, http://unstats.un.org; *Statistical Yearbook.*

COLOMBIA - RICE PRODUCTION

See COLOMBIA - CROPS

COLOMBIA - ROADS

Central Intelligence Agency, Office of Public Affairs, Washington, DC 20505, (703) 482-0623, Fax: (703) 482-1739, www.cia.gov; *The World Factbook.*

Economist Intelligence Unit, 111 West 57th Street, New York, NY 10019, (212) 554-0600, Fax: (212) 586-1181, www.eiu.com; *Business Latin America.*

International Road Federation (IFR), Madison Place, 500 Montgomery Street, 5th Floor, Alexandria, VA 22314, (703) 535-1001, Fax: (703) 535-1007, www.irfnet.org; *World Road Statistics 2006.*

Palgrave Macmillan Ltd., Houndmills, Basingstoke, Hampshire, RG21 6XS, England, (Telephone in U.S. (888) 330-8477), (Fax in U.S. (800) 672-2054), www.palgrave.com; *The Statesman's Yearbook 2008.*

COLOMBIA - RUBBER INDUSTRY AND TRADE

International Rubber Study Group (IRSG), 1st Floor, Heron House, 109/115 Wembley Hill Road, Wembley, Middlesex HA9 8DA, United Kingdom, www.rubberstudy.com; *Rubber Statistical Bulletin; Summary of World Rubber Statistics 2005; World Rubber Statistics Handbook (Volume 6, 1975-2001);* and *World Rubber Statistics Historic Handbook.*

M.E. Sharpe, 80 Business Park Drive, Armonk, NY 10504, (800) 541-6563, Fax: (914) 273-2106, www.mesharpe.com; *The Illustrated Book of World Rankings.*

COLOMBIA - SALT PRODUCTION

See COLOMBIA - MINERAL INDUSTRIES

COLOMBIA - SHEEP

See COLOMBIA - LIVESTOCK

COLOMBIA - SHIPPING

Lloyd's Register - Fairplay, 8410 N.W. 53rd Terrace, Suite 207, Miami FL 33166, (305) 718-9929, Fax: (305) 718-9663, www.lrfairplay.com; *Register of Ships 2007-2008; World Casualty Statistics 2007; World Fleet Statistics 2006; World Marine Propulsion Report 2006-2010; World Shipbuilding Statistics 2007;* and The World Shipping Encyclopaedia.

Palgrave Macmillan Ltd., Houndmills, Basingstoke, Hampshire, RG21 6XS, England, (Telephone in U.S. (888) 330-8477), (Fax in U.S. (800) 672-2054), www.palgrave.com; *The Statesman's Yearbook 2008.*

Taylor and Francis Group, An Informa Business, 2 Park Square, Milton Park, Abingdon, Oxford OX14 4RN, United Kingdom, (Dial from U.S. (212) 216-7800), (Fax from U.S. (212) 564-7854), www.tandf.co.uk; *The Europa World Year Book.*

U.S. Department of Transportation (DOT), Maritime Administration (MARAD), West Building, Southeast Federal Center, 1200 New Jersey Avenue, SE, Washington, DC 20590, (800) 99-MARAD, www.marad.dot.gov; *World Merchant Fleet 2005.*

United Nations Statistics Division, New York, NY 10017, (800) 253-9646, Fax: (212) 963-4116, http://unstats.un.org; *Statistical Yearbook.*

COLOMBIA - SILVER PRODUCTION

See COLOMBIA - MINERAL INDUSTRIES

COLOMBIA - SOCIAL ECOLOGY

M.E. Sharpe, 80 Business Park Drive, Armonk, NY 10504, (800) 541-6563, Fax: (914) 273-2106, www.mesharpe.com; *The Illustrated Book of World Rankings.*

UCLA Latin American Institute, 10343 Bunche Hall, Box 951447, Los Angeles, CA 90095-1447, (310) 825-4571, Fax: (310) 206-6859, www.international.ucla.edu/lac; *Statistical Abstract of Latin America.*

United Nations Statistics Division, New York, NY 10017, (800) 253-9646, Fax: (212) 963-4116, http://unstats.un.org; *World Statistics Pocketbook.*

COLOMBIA - SOCIAL SECURITY

Inter-American Development Bank (IDB), 1300 New York Avenue, NW, Washington, DC 20577, (202) 623-1000, Fax: (202) 623-3096, www.iadb.org; *The Politics of Policies: Economic and Social Progress in Latin America - 2006 Report.*

United Nations Statistics Division, New York, NY 10017, (800) 253-9646, Fax: (212) 963-4116, http://unstats.un.org; *National Accounts Statistics: Compendium of Income Distribution Statistics.*

COLOMBIA - SOYBEAN PRODUCTION

See COLOMBIA - CROPS

COLOMBIA - STEEL PRODUCTION

See COLOMBIA - MINERAL INDUSTRIES

COLOMBIA - SUGAR PRODUCTION

See COLOMBIA - CROPS

COLOMBIA - SULPHUR PRODUCTION

See COLOMBIA - MINERAL INDUSTRIES

COLOMBIA - TAXATION

Inter-American Development Bank (IDB), 1300 New York Avenue, NW, Washington, DC 20577, (202) 623-1000, Fax: (202) 623-3096, www.iadb.org; *The Politics of Policies: Economic and Social Progress in Latin America - 2006 Report.*

International Monetary Fund (IMF), 700 Nineteenth Street, NW, Washington, DC 20431, (202) 623-7000, Fax: (202) 623-4661, www.imf.org; *Government Finance Statistics Yearbook (2008 Edition).*

International Road Federation (IFR), Madison Place, 500 Montgomery Street, 5th Floor, Alexandria, VA 22314, (703) 535-1001, Fax: (703) 535-1007, www.irfnet.org; *World Road Statistics 2006.*

Taylor and Francis Group, An Informa Business, 2 Park Square, Milton Park, Abingdon, Oxford OX14 4RN, United Kingdom, (Dial from U.S. (212) 216-7800), (Fax from U.S. (212) 564-7854), www.tandf.co.uk; *The Europa World Year Book.*

United Nations Statistics Division, New York, NY 10017, (800) 253-9646, Fax: (212) 963-4116, http://unstats.un.org; *Statistical Yearbook for Latin America and the Caribbean 2004.*

COLOMBIA - TELEPHONE

Central Intelligence Agency, Office of Public Affairs, Washington, DC 20505, (703) 482-0623, Fax: (703) 482-1739, www.cia.gov; *The World Factbook.*

Economist Intelligence Unit, 111 West 57th Street, New York, NY 10019, (212) 554-0600, Fax: (212) 586-1181, www.eiu.com; *Business Latin America.*

International Telecommunication Union (ITU), Place des Nations, 1211 Geneva 20, Switzerland, www.itu.int; World Telecommunication Indicators Database.

Palgrave Macmillan Ltd., Houndmills, Basingstoke, Hampshire, RG21 6XS, England, (Telephone in U.S. (888) 330-8477), (Fax in U.S. (800) 672-2054), www.palgrave.com; *The Statesman's Yearbook 2008.*

Taylor and Francis Group, An Informa Business, 2 Park Square, Milton Park, Abingdon, Oxford OX14 4RN, United Kingdom, (Dial from U.S. (212) 216-7800), (Fax from U.S. (212) 564-7854), www.tandf.co.uk; *The Europa World Year Book.*

United Nations Statistics Division, New York, NY 10017, (800) 253-9646, Fax: (212) 963-4116, http://unstats.un.org; *Statistical Yearbook* and *World Statistics Pocketbook.*

COLOMBIA - TELEVISION - RECEIVERS AND RECEPTION

United Nations Statistics Division, New York, NY 10017, (800) 253-9646, Fax: (212) 963-4116, http://unstats.un.org; *Statistical Yearbook.*

COLOMBIA - TEXTILE INDUSTRY

Euromonitor International, Inc., 224 S. Michigan Avenue, Suite 1500, Chicago, IL 60604, (312) 922-1115, Fax: (312) 922-1157, www.euromonitor.com; *Retail Trade International 2007.*

M.E. Sharpe, 80 Business Park Drive, Armonk, NY 10504, (800) 541-6563, Fax: (914) 273-2106, www.mesharpe.com; *The Illustrated Book of World Rankings.*

United Nations Conference on Trade and Development (UNCTAD), DC2-1120, United Nations, New York, NY 10017, (212) 963-0027, www.unctad.org; *UNCTAD Commodity Yearbook.*

United Nations Statistics Division, New York, NY 10017, (800) 253-9646, Fax: (212) 963-4116, http://unstats.un.org; *Statistical Yearbook.*

COLOMBIA - THEATER

UNESCO Institute for Statistics, C.P. 6128 Succursale Centre-Ville, Montreal, Quebec, H3C 3J7 Canada, (Dial from U.S. (514) 343-6880), (Fax from U.S. (514) 343 6882), www.uis.unesco.org; *Statistical Tables.*

COLOMBIA - TIN PRODUCTION

See COLOMBIA - MINERAL INDUSTRIES

COLOMBIA - TIRE INDUSTRY

United Nations Statistics Division, New York, NY 10017, (800) 253-9646, Fax: (212) 963-4116, http://unstats.un.org; *Statistical Yearbook.*

COLOMBIA - TOBACCO INDUSTRY

Foreign Agricultural Service (FAS), U.S. Department of Agriculture (USDA), 1400 Independence Avenue, SW, Washington, DC 20250, (202) 720-3935, www.fas.usda.gov; *Tobacco: World Markets and Trade.*

M.E. Sharpe, 80 Business Park Drive, Armonk, NY 10504, (800) 541-6563, Fax: (914) 273-2106, www.mesharpe.com; *The Illustrated Book of World Rankings.*

United Nations Statistics Division, New York, NY 10017, (800) 253-9646, Fax: (212) 963-4116, http://unstats.un.org; *Statistical Yearbook.*

COLOMBIA - TOURISM

Economist Intelligence Unit, 111 West 57th Street, New York, NY 10019, (212) 554-0600, Fax: (212) 586-1181, www.eiu.com; *Business Latin America.*

Euromonitor International, Inc., 224 S. Michigan Avenue, Suite 1500, Chicago, IL 60604, (312) 922-1115, Fax: (312) 922-1157, www.euromonitor.com; *The World Economic Factbook 2008* and *World Marketing Data and Statistics.*

M.E. Sharpe, 80 Business Park Drive, Armonk, NY 10504, (800) 541-6563, Fax: (914) 273-2106, www.mesharpe.com; *The Illustrated Book of World Rankings.*

Palgrave Macmillan Ltd., Houndmills, Basingstoke, Hampshire, RG21 6XS, England, (Telephone in U.S. (888) 330-8477), (Fax in U.S. (800) 672-2054), www.palgrave.com; *The Statesman's Yearbook 2008.*

Taylor and Francis Group, An Informa Business, 2 Park Square, Milton Park, Abingdon, Oxford OX14 4RN, United Kingdom, (Dial from U.S. (212) 216-7800), (Fax from U.S. (212) 564-7854), www.tandf.co.uk; *The Europa World Year Book.*

UCLA Latin American Institute, 10343 Bunche Hall, Box 951447, Los Angeles, CA 90095-1447, (310) 825-4571, Fax: (310) 206-6859, www.international.ucla.edu/lac; *Statistical Abstract of Latin America.*

United Nations Statistics Division, New York, NY 10017, (800) 253-9646, Fax: (212) 963-4116, http://unstats.un.org; *Statistical Yearbook* and *Statistical Yearbook for Latin America and the Caribbean 2004.*

United Nations World Tourism Organization (UNWTO), Capitan Haya 42, 28020 Madrid, Spain, www.world-tourism.org; *Yearbook of Tourism Statistics.*

The World Bank, 1818 H Street, NW, Washington, DC 20433, (202) 473-1000, Fax: (202) 477-6391, www.worldbank.org; *Colombia.*

COLOMBIA - TRADE

See COLOMBIA - INTERNATIONAL TRADE

COLOMBIA - TRANSPORTATION

Central Intelligence Agency, Office of Public Affairs, Washington, DC 20505, (703) 482-0623, Fax: (703) 482-1739, www.cia.gov; *The World Factbook.*

Economist Intelligence Unit, 111 West 57th Street, New York, NY 10019, (212) 554-0600, Fax: (212) 586-1181, www.eiu.com; *Business Latin America.*

Euromonitor International, Inc., 224 S. Michigan Avenue, Suite 1500, Chicago, IL 60604, (312) 922-1115, Fax: (312) 922-1157, www.euromonitor.com; *International Marketing Data and Statistics 2008* and *World Marketing Data and Statistics.*

Inter-American Development Bank (IDB), 1300 New York Avenue, NW, Washington, DC 20577, (202) 623-1000, Fax: (202) 623-3096, www.iadb.org; *The Politics of Policies: Economic and Social Progress in Latin America - 2006 Report.*

M.E. Sharpe, 80 Business Park Drive, Armonk, NY 10504, (800) 541-6563, Fax: (914) 273-2106, www.mesharpe.com; *The Illustrated Book of World Rankings.*

Palgrave Macmillan Ltd., Houndmills, Basingstoke, Hampshire, RG21 6XS, England, (Telephone in U.S. (888) 330-8477), (Fax in U.S. (800) 672-2054), www.palgrave.com; *The Statesman's Yearbook 2008.*

Taylor and Francis Group, An Informa Business, 2 Park Square, Milton Park, Abingdon, Oxford OX14 4RN, United Kingdom, (Dial from U.S. (212) 216-7800), (Fax from U.S. (212) 564-7854), www.tandf.co.uk; *The Europa World Year Book.*

UCLA Latin American Institute, 10343 Bunche Hall, Box 951447, Los Angeles, CA 90095-1447, (310) 825-4571, Fax: (310) 206-6859, www.international.ucla.edu/lac; *Statistical Abstract of Latin America.*

United Nations Statistics Division, New York, NY 10017, (800) 253-9646, Fax: (212) 963-4116, http://unstats.un.org; *Human Development Report 2006* and *Statistical Yearbook for Latin America and the Caribbean 2004.*

The World Bank, 1818 H Street, NW, Washington, DC 20433, (202) 473-1000, Fax: (202) 477-6391, www.worldbank.org; *Colombia.*

COLOMBIA - UNEMPLOYMENT

Central Intelligence Agency, Office of Public Affairs, Washington, DC 20505, (703) 482-0623, Fax: (703) 482-1739, www.cia.gov; *The World Factbook.*

Economist Intelligence Unit, 111 West 57th Street, New York, NY 10019, (212) 554-0600, Fax: (212) 586-1181, www.eiu.com; *Business Latin America.*

Euromonitor International, Inc., 224 S. Michigan Avenue, Suite 1500, Chicago, IL 60604, (312) 922-1115, Fax: (312) 922-1157, www.euromonitor.com; *International Marketing Data and Statistics 2008.*

International Labour Office, I.L.O. Publications, 4 route des Morillons, CH-1211 Geneva 22, Switzerland, (Telephone in U.S. (202) 653-7652), (Fax in U.S. (202) 653-7687), www.ilo.org; *Yearbook of Labour Statistics 2006.*

UCLA Latin American Institute, 10343 Bunche Hall, Box 951447, Los Angeles, CA 90095-1447, (310) 825-4571, Fax: (310) 206-6859, www.international.ucla.edu/lac; *Statistical Abstract of Latin America.*

United Nations Statistics Division, New York, NY 10017, (800) 253-9646, Fax: (212) 963-4116, http://unstats.un.org; *Statistical Yearbook.*

COLOMBIA - VITAL STATISTICS

Euromonitor International, Inc., 224 S. Michigan Avenue, Suite 1500, Chicago, IL 60604, (312) 922-1115, Fax: (312) 922-1157, www.euromonitor.com; *International Marketing Data and Statistics 2008.*

Palgrave Macmillan Ltd., Houndmills, Basingstoke, Hampshire, RG21 6XS, England, (Telephone in U.S. (888) 330-8477), (Fax in U.S. (800) 672-2054), www.palgrave.com; *The Statesman's Yearbook 2008.*

United Nations Statistics Division, New York, NY 10017, (800) 253-9646, Fax: (212) 963-4116, http://unstats.un.org; *Statistical Yearbook.*

World Health Organization (WHO), Avenue Appia 20, 1211 Geneve 27, Switzerland, (Telephone in U.S. (212) 331-9081), www.who.int; *World Health Report 2006.*

COLOMBIA - WAGES

International Labour Office, I.L.O. Publications, 4 route des Morillons, CH-1211 Geneva 22, Switzerland, (Telephone in U.S. (202) 653-7652), (Fax in U.S. (202) 653-7687), www.ilo.org; *Yearbook of Labour Statistics 2006.*

Organization of American States (OAS), 17th Street Constitution Avenue NW, Washington, DC 20006, (202) 458-3000, www.oas.org; *The OAS in Transition: 1994-2004.*

UCLA Latin American Institute, 10343 Bunche Hall, Box 951447, Los Angeles, CA 90095-1447, (310) 825-4571, Fax: (310) 206-6859, www.international.ucla.edu/lac; *Statistical Abstract of Latin America.*

United Nations Statistics Division, New York, NY 10017, (800) 253-9646, Fax: (212) 963-4116, http://unstats.un.org; *Statistical Yearbook.*

The World Bank, 1818 H Street, NW, Washington, DC 20433, (202) 473-1000, Fax: (202) 477-6391, www.worldbank.org; *Colombia.*

COLOMBIA - WEATHER

See COLOMBIA - CLIMATE

COLOMBIA - WELFARE STATE

Inter-American Development Bank (IDB), 1300 New York Avenue, NW, Washington, DC 20577, (202) 623-1000, Fax: (202) 623-3096, www.iadb.org; *The Politics of Policies: Economic and Social Progress in Latin America - 2006 Report.*

COLOMBIA - WHEAT PRODUCTION

See COLOMBIA - CROPS

COLOMBIA - WHOLESALE PRICE INDEXES

Inter-American Development Bank (IDB), 1300 New York Avenue, NW, Washington, DC 20577, (202) 623-1000, Fax: (202) 623-3096, www.iadb.org; *The Politics of Policies: Economic and Social Progress in Latin America - 2006 Report.*

International Monetary Fund (IMF), 700 Nineteenth Street, NW, Washington, DC 20431, (202) 623-7000, Fax: (202) 623-4661, www.imf.org; *International Financial Statistics Yearbook 2007.*

Organization of American States (OAS), 17th Street Constitution Avenue NW, Washington, DC 20006, (202) 458-3000, www.oas.org; *The OAS in Transition: 1994-2004.*

United Nations Statistics Division, New York, NY 10017, (800) 253-9646, Fax: (212) 963-4116, http://unstats.un.org; *Statistical Yearbook.*

COLOMBIA - WHOLESALE TRADE

Inter-American Development Bank (IDB), 1300 New York Avenue, NW, Washington, DC 20577, (202) 623-1000, Fax: (202) 623-3096, www.iadb.org; *The Politics of Policies: Economic and Social Progress in Latin America - 2006 Report.*

United Nations Statistics Division, New York, NY 10017, (800) 253-9646, Fax: (212) 963-4116, http://unstats.un.org; *Statistical Yearbook.*

COLOMBIA - WINE PRODUCTION

See COLOMBIA - BEVERAGE INDUSTRY

COLOMBIA - WOOD AND WOOD PULP

See COLOMBIA - FORESTS AND FORESTRY

COLOMBIA - WOOL PRODUCTION

See COLOMBIA - TEXTILE INDUSTRY

COLOMBIA - YARN PRODUCTION

See COLOMBIA - TEXTILE INDUSTRY

COLOMBIA - ZINC AND ZINC ORE

See COLOMBIA - MINERAL INDUSTRIES

COLOMBIA - ZOOS

UNESCO Institute for Statistics, C.P. 6128 Succursale Centre-Ville, Montreal, Quebec, H3C 3J7 Canada, (Dial from U.S. (514) 343-6880), (Fax from U.S. (514) 343 6882), www.uis.unesco.org; *Statistical Tables.*

COLORADO

See also - STATE DATA (FOR INDIVIDUAL STATES)

COLORADO - STATE DATA CENTERS

Business Research Division (BRD), University of Colorado at Boulder, 420 UCB, Boulder, CO 80309-0420, Mr. Richard Wobbekind, Director, (303) 492-1147, Fax: (303) 492-3620, http://leeds.colorado.edu/brd; State Data Center.

Colorado Demography Office, 1313 Sherman Street, Room 521, Denver, CO 80203, (303) 866-4147, Fax: (303) 866-2660, http://dola.colorado.gov/demog/demog.cfm; State Data Center.

Colorado State University Libraries, Documents Processing, 1019 Campus Delivery, Fort Collins, CO 80523-1019, (970) 491-1879, http://lib.colostate.edu/acq/docindex.html; State Data Center.

Department of Agricultural and Resource Economics (DARE), College of Agricultural Sciences, Clark B-320, Colorado State University, Fort Collins, CO 80523, (970) 491-6325, Fax: (970) 491-2067, http://dare.agsci.colostate.edu; *Fact Sheets.*

COLORADO - PRIMARY STATISTICS SOURCES

Government Publications Library, University of Colorado at Boulder, University Libraries, 184 UCB, 1720 Pleasant Street, University of Colorado, Boulder, CO 80309-0184, (303) 492-8834, Fax: (303) 492-1881, http://ucblibraries.colorado.edu/govpubs; *Colorado by the Numbers (CBN).*

COLUMBIUM - TANTALUM

U.S. Department of the Interior (DOI), U.S. Geological Survey (USGS), Office of Minerals Information, 12201 Sunrise Valley Drive, Reston, VA 20192, Mr. Kenneth A. Beckman, (703) 648-4916, Fax: (703) 648-4995, http://minerals.usgs.gov/minerals; *Mineral Commodity Summaries* and *Minerals Yearbook.*

COMMERCE - DOMESTIC

U.S. Census Bureau, 4700 Silver Hill Road, Washington DC 20233-0001, (301) 763-3030, www.census.gov; *2006 E-Commerce Multi-Sector Report.*

COMMERCE - DOMESTIC - BY RAIL

Association of American Railroads (AAR), 50 F Street, NW, Washington, DC 20001-1564, (202) 639-2100, www.aar.org; *Weekly Railroad Traffic.*

COMMERCE - DOMESTIC - BY WATER

Waterborne Commerce Statistics Center (WCSC), Navigation Data Center (NDC), U.S. Army Corps of Engineers, PO Box 61280, New Orleans, LA 70161-1280, (504) 862-1426, www.iwr.usace.army.mil/ndc/wcsc/wcsc.htm; *Internal U.S. Waterway Monthly Tonnage Indicators; 2006 Waterborne Commerce of the United States (WCUS);* and *2006 Waterborne Container Traffic for U.S. Ports and all 50 States and U.S. Territories.*

COMMERCE - FOREIGN

See INTERNATIONAL TRADE

COMMERCE AND HOUSING CREDIT

The Office of Management and Budget (OMB), 725 17th Street, NW, Washington, DC 20503, (202) 395-3080, Fax: (202) 395-3888, www.whitehouse.gov/omb; *Historical Tables.*

COMMERCIAL BUILDINGS - CONSTRUCTION VALUE

McGraw-Hill Construction, Dodge Analytics, 1221 Avenue of The Americas, Manhattan, NY 10020, (800) 393-6343, http://dodge.construction.com/analytics; *Construction Outlook 2008.*

U.S. Census Bureau, Manufacturing and Construction Division, 4600 Silver Hill Road, Washington DC 20233, (301) 763-4673, www.census.gov/mcd; *Current Construction Reports.*

COMMERCIAL BUILDINGS - COST OF CONSTRUCTION

U.S. Census Bureau, Manufacturing and Construction Division, 4600 Silver Hill Road, Washington DC 20233, (301) 763-4673, www.census.gov/mcd; *Census of Construction Industries.*

COMMERCIAL BUILDINGS - CRIMINAL STATISTICS

U.S. Department of Justice (DOJ), Bureau of Justice Statistics, 810 Seventh Street, NW, Washington, DC 20531, (202) 307-0765, www.ojp.usdoj.gov/bjs/; *Criminal Victimization, 2005.*

COMMERCIAL BUILDINGS - ENERGY CHARACTERISTICS

McGraw-Hill Construction, Dodge Analytics, 1221 Avenue of The Americas, Manhattan, NY 10020, (800) 393-6343, http://dodge.construction.com/analytics; *Green Building SmartMarket Report 2006.*

U.S. Department of Energy (DOE), Energy Information Administration (EIA), 1000 Independence Avenue, SW, Washington, DC 20585, (202) 586-8800, www.eia.doe.gov; *Commercial Buildings Energy Consumption Survey (CBECS).*

COMMERCIAL BUILDINGS - FLOOR SPACE

McGraw-Hill Construction, Dodge Analytics, 1221 Avenue of The Americas, Manhattan, NY 10020, (800) 393-6343, http://dodge.construction.com/analytics; *Construction Outlook 2008.*

U.S. Department of Energy (DOE), Energy Information Administration (EIA), 1000 Independence Avenue, SW, Washington, DC 20585, (202) 586-8800, www.eia.doe.gov; *Commercial Buildings Energy Consumption Survey (CBECS).*

COMMERCIAL BUILDINGS - INVENTORIES

U.S. Department of Energy (DOE), Energy Information Administration (EIA), 1000 Independence Avenue, SW, Washington, DC 20585, (202) 586-8800, www.eia.doe.gov; *Commercial Buildings Energy Consumption Survey (CBECS).*

COMMERCIAL BUILDINGS - VACANCY RATES

ONCOR International, 1 Campus Drive, Parsippany, NJ 07054, (973) 407-6363, Fax: (973) 407-4666, www.oncorintl.com; *North American Office Market Report.*

Society of Industrial and Office Realtors, 1201 New York Avenue, NW, Suite 350, Washington, DC 20005-6126, (202) 449-8200, Fax: (202) 216-9325, www.sior.com; *Comparative Statistics of Industrial and Office Real Estate Markets 2005.*

COMMERCIAL PAPER

American Forest Paper Association (AFPA), 1111 Nineteenth Street, NW, Suite 800, Washington, DC 20036, (800) 878-8878, www.afandpa.org; *2007 Annual Statistics of Paper, Paperboard, and Wood Pulp* and *U.S. Recovered Paperstock Export/Import Monthly Report (PR2).*

Board of Governors of the Federal Reserve System, Constitution Avenue, NW, Washington, DC 20551, (202) 452-3000, www.federalreserve.gov; *Federal Reserve Bulletin.*

COMMODITIES

See Individual commodities

COMMODITY FLOW

Commodity Research Bureau, 330 South Wells Street, Suite 612, Chicago, IL 60606-7110, (800) 621-5271, Fax: (312) 939-4135, www.crbtrader.com; *2006 CRB Commodity Yearbook and CD.*

Lithuanian Department of Statistics (Statistics Lithuania), Gedimino av. 29, LT-01500 Vilnius, Lithuania, www.stat.gov.lt/en; *Production of Commodities 2000-2006.*

U.S. Census Bureau, Center for Economic Studies, 4600 Silver Hill Road, Washington DC 20233, (301)

457-1235, www.ces.census.gov; *2002 Economic Census, Transportation and Warehousing.*

U.S. Department of Transportation (DOT), Research and Innovative Technology Administration (RITA), Bureau of Transportation Statistics (BTS), 1200 New Jersey Avenue, SE, Washington, DC 20590, (800) 853-1351, www.bts.gov; *2007 Commodity Flow Survey (CFS).*

COMMUNICABLE DISEASES

Centers for Disease Control and Prevention (CDC), U.S. Department of Health and Human Services (HHS), 1600 Clifton Road, Atlanta, GA 30333, (800) 311-3435, www.cdc.gov; *Morbidity and Mortality Weekly Report (MMWR)* and *Summary of Notifiable Diseases, United States, 2006.*

EpiNorth, c/o Norwegian Institute of Public Health, PO Box 4404 Nydalen, N-0430 Oslo, Norway, www.epinorth.org; www.epinorth.org.

European Centre for Disease Prevention and Control (ECDC), 171 83 Stockholm, Sweden, www.ecdc.europa.eu; *The First European Communicable Disease Epidemiological Report; Infant and Children Seasonal Immunisation Against Influenza on a Routine Basis During Inter-pandemic Period; Sudden Deaths and Influenza Vaccinations in Israel - ECDC Interim Risk Assessment;* and *Vaccines and Immunisation - VI news.*

Health Protection Agency, 7th Floor, Holborn Gate, 330 High Holborn, London WC1V 7PP, United Kingdom, www.hpa.org.uk; *Communicable Disease in London 2002-05; Indications of Public Health in the English Regions: Sexual Health (November 2006); Migrant Health: Infectious Diseases in Non-UK Born Populations in England, Wales and Northern Ireland (A Baseline Report - 2006); Surveillance of Healthcare Associated Infections Report 2007;* and *Testing Times - HIV and other Sexually Transmitted Infections in the United Kingdom: 2007.*

World Health Organization (WHO), Avenue Appia 20, 1211 Geneve 27, Switzerland, (Telephone in U.S. (212) 331-9081), www.who.int; The WHO Global Atlas of Infectious Diseases.

COMMUNICATIONS - DEGREES CONFERRED

National Center for Education Statistics (NCES), 1990 K Street, NW, Washington, DC 20006, (202) 502-7300, http://nces.ed.gov; *Digest of Education Statistics 2007.*

COMMUNICATIONS EQUIPMENT - MANUFACTURING - EARNINGS

U.S. Bureau of Labor Statistics (BLS), Postal Square Building, 2 Massachusetts Avenue, NE, Washington, DC 20212-0001, (202) 691-5200, Fax: (202) 691-6325, www.bls.gov; *Current Employment Statistics Survey (CES)* and *Employment and Earnings (EE).*

U.S. Census Bureau, Manufacturing and Construction Division, 4600 Silver Hill Road, Washington DC 20233, (301) 763-4673, www.census.gov/mcd; *Annual Survey of Manufactures (ASM)* and *Census of Manufactures.*

COMMUNICATIONS EQUIPMENT - MANUFACTURING - EMPLOYEES

U.S. Bureau of Labor Statistics (BLS), Postal Square Building, 2 Massachusetts Avenue, NE, Washington, DC 20212-0001, (202) 691-5200, Fax: (202) 691-6325, www.bls.gov; *Current Employment Statistics Survey (CES)* and *Employment and Earnings (EE).*

U.S. Census Bureau, Manufacturing and Construction Division, 4600 Silver Hill Road, Washington DC 20233, (301) 763-4673, www.census.gov/mcd; *Annual Survey of Manufactures (ASM)* and *Census of Manufactures.*

COMMUNICATIONS EQUIPMENT - MANUFACTURING - ESTABLISHMENTS

U.S. Census Bureau, Manufacturing and Construction Division, 4600 Silver Hill Road, Washington DC 20233, (301) 763-4673, www.census.gov/mcd; *Annual Survey of Manufactures (ASM)* and *Census of Manufactures.*

COMMUNICATIONS EQUIPMENT - MANUFACTURING - INVENTORIES

U.S. Census Bureau, Manufacturing and Construction Division, 4600 Silver Hill Road, Washington DC 20233, (301) 763-4673, www.census.gov/mcd; *Current Industrial Reports* and *Manufacturers Shipments, Inventories and Orders.*

COMMUNICATIONS EQUIPMENT - MANUFACTURING - MERGERS AND ACQUISITIONS

Thomson Financial, 195 Broadway, New York, NY 10007, (646) 822-2000, www.thomson.com; Thomson Research.

COMMUNICATIONS EQUIPMENT - MANUFACTURING - PRODUCTIVITY

U.S. Bureau of Labor Statistics (BLS), Postal Square Building, 2 Massachusetts Avenue, NE, Washington, DC 20212-0001, (202) 691-5200, Fax: (202) 691-6325, www.bls.gov; *Industry Productivity and Costs.*

COMMUNICATIONS EQUIPMENT - MANUFACTURING - SHIPMENTS

U.S. Census Bureau, Manufacturing and Construction Division, 4600 Silver Hill Road, Washington DC 20233, (301) 763-4673, www.census.gov/mcd; *Annual Survey of Manufactures (ASM); Census of Manufactures; Current Industrial Reports;* and *Manufacturers Shipments, Inventories and Orders.*

COMMUNICATIONS INDUSTRY

See INFORMATION INDUSTRY; TELECOMMUNICATIONS INDUSTRY

COMMUNITY CARE FACILITIES FOR THE ELDERLY - INDUSTRY

U.S. Census Bureau, 4700 Silver Hill Road, Washington DC 20233-0001, (301) 763-3030, www.census.gov; *2002 Economic Census, Nonemployer Statistics.*

U.S. Census Bureau, Service Sector Statistics Division, 4700 Silver Hill Road, Washington DC 20233-0001, (301) 763-3030, www.census.gov/svsd/www/economic.html; *2004 Service Annual Survey: Health Care and Social Assistance.*

COMMUNITY DEVELOPMENT - FEDERAL OUTLAYS

The Office of Management and Budget (OMB), 725 17th Street, NW, Washington, DC 20503, (202) 395-3080, Fax: (202) 395-3888, www.whitehouse.gov/omb; *Historical Tables.*

COMMUNITY FOOD, HOUSING SERVICES

U.S. Census Bureau, 4700 Silver Hill Road, Washington DC 20233-0001, (301) 763-3030, www.census.gov; *2002 Economic Census, Nonemployer Statistics.*

U.S. Census Bureau, Service Sector Statistics Division, 4700 Silver Hill Road, Washington DC 20233-0001, (301) 763-3030, www.census.gov/svsd/www/economic.html; *2004 Service Annual Survey: Health Care and Social Assistance.*

COMMUNITY SERVICE

The Annie E. Casey Foundation, 701 Saint Paul Street, Baltimore, MD 21202, (410) 547-6600, Fax: (410) 547-3610, www.aecf.org; *Beyond the Boundaries: Low-Income Residents, Faith-Based Organizations and Neighborhood Coalition Building; Change that Abides: A Retrospective Look at Five Community and Family Stengthening Projects and Their Enduring Results;* and *Change that Abides: A Retrospective Look at Five Community and Family Stengthening Projects and Their Enduring Results.*

COMMUNITY SERVICE - STUDENTS

Higher Education Research Institute (HERI), University of California, Los Angeles, 3005 Moore Hall/Box 951521, Los Angeles, CA 90095-1521, (310) 825-1925, Fax: (310) 206-2228, www.gseis.ucla.edu/heri/index.php; *How Service Learning Affects Students.*

National Center for Education Statistics (NCES), 1990 K Street, NW, Washington, DC 20006, (202) 502-7300, http://nces.ed.gov; various fact sheets.

COMMUTING TO WORK

Eno Transportation Foundation, 1634 I Street, NW, Suite 500, Washington, DC 20006, (202) 879-4700, Fax: (202) 879-4719, www.enotrans.com; *Commuting in America II.*

Population Reference Bureau, 1875 Connecticut Avenue, NW, Suite 520, Washington, DC, 20009-5728, (800) 877-9881, Fax: (202) 328-3937, www.prb.org; *The American People Series.*

U.S. Census Bureau, 4700 Silver Hill Road, Washington DC 20233-0001, (301) 763-3030, www.census.gov; American FactFinder (web app); *County and City Data Book 2007;* and *State and County QuickFacts.*

U.S. Census Bureau, Demographic Surveys Division, 4700 Silver Hill Road, Washington DC 20233-0001, (301) 763-3030, www.census.gov; *Demographic Profiles: 100-percent and Sample Data.*

U.S. Census Bureau, Population Division, 4700 Silver Hill Road, Washington DC 20233-0001, (301) 763-3030, www.census.gov/population/www/; *Census 2000 Profiles of General Demographic Characteristics.*

COMOROS - NATIONAL STATISTICAL OFFICE

Direction de la Statistique, BP 131, Moroni, Comoros; National Data Center.

COMOROS - AGRICULTURE

Economist Intelligence Unit, 111 West 57th Street, New York, NY 10019, (212) 554-0600, Fax: (212) 586-1181, www.eiu.com; *Comoros Country Report.*

Euromonitor International, Inc., 224 S. Michigan Avenue, Suite 1500, Chicago, IL 60604, (312) 922-1115, Fax: (312) 922-1157, www.euromonitor.com; *World Marketing Data and Statistics.*

Palgrave Macmillan Ltd., Houndmills, Basingstoke, Hampshire, RG21 6XS, England, (Telephone in U.S. (888) 330-8477), (Fax in U.S. (800) 672-2054), www.palgrave.com; *The Statesman's Yearbook 2008.*

Taylor and Francis Group, An Informa Business, 2 Park Square, Milton Park, Abingdon, Oxford OX14 4RN, United Kingdom, (Dial from U.S. (212) 216-7800), (Fax from U.S. (212) 564-7854), www.tandf.co.uk; *The Europa World Year Book.*

United Nations Conference on Trade and Development (UNCTAD), DC2-1120, United Nations, New York, NY 10017, (212) 963-0027, www.unctad.org; *UNCTAD Commodity Yearbook.*

United Nations Economic Commission for Africa (ECA), PO Box 3001, Addis Ababa, Ethiopia, (Telephone in U.S. (212) 963-4957), www.uneca.org; *African Statistical Yearbook 2006.*

United Nations Food and Agricultural Organization (FAO), Viale delle Terme di Caracalla, 00100 Rome, Italy, (Dial from U.S. (202) 653-2400), (Fax from U.S. (202) 653 5760), www.fao.org; AQUASTAT; *FAO Production Yearbook 2002; FAO Trade Yearbook;* and *The State of Food and Agriculture (SOFA) 2006.*

United Nations Statistics Division, New York, NY 10017, (800) 253-9646, Fax: (212) 963-4116, http://unstats.un.org; *Survey of Economic and Social Conditions in Africa 2005.*

The World Bank, 1818 H Street, NW, Washington, DC 20433, (202) 473-1000, Fax: (202) 477-6391,

www.worldbank.org; *Africa Live Database (LDB); African Development Indicators (ADI) 2007;* and *Comoros.*

COMOROS - AIRLINES

Palgrave Macmillan Ltd., Houndmills, Basingstoke, Hampshire, RG21 6XS, England, (Telephone in U.S. (888) 330-8477), (Fax in U.S. (800) 672-2054), www.palgrave.com; *The Statesman's Yearbook 2008.*

Taylor and Francis Group, An Informa Business, 2 Park Square, Milton Park, Abingdon, Oxford OX14 4RN, United Kingdom, (Dial from U.S. (212) 216-7800), (Fax from U.S. (212) 564-7854), www.tandf.co.uk; *The Europa World Year Book.*

United Nations Economic Commission for Africa (ECA), PO Box 3001, Addis Ababa, Ethiopia, (Telephone in U.S. (212) 963-4957), www.uneca.org; *African Statistical Yearbook 2006.*

COMOROS - AIRPORTS

Central Intelligence Agency, Office of Public Affairs, Washington, DC 20505, (703) 482-0623, Fax: (703) 482-1739, www.cia.gov; *The World Factbook.*

COMOROS - ARMED FORCES

Central Intelligence Agency, Office of Public Affairs, Washington, DC 20505, (703) 482-0623, Fax: (703) 482-1739, www.cia.gov; *The World Factbook.*

Euromonitor International, Inc., 224 S. Michigan Avenue, Suite 1500, Chicago, IL 60604, (312) 922-1115, Fax: (312) 922-1157, www.euromonitor.com; *World Marketing Data and Statistics.*

Palgrave Macmillan Ltd., Houndmills, Basingstoke, Hampshire, RG21 6XS, England, (Telephone in U.S. (888) 330-8477), (Fax in U.S. (800) 672-2054), www.palgrave.com; *The Statesman's Yearbook 2008.*

United Nations Statistics Division, New York, NY 10017, (800) 253-9646, Fax: (212) 963-4116, http://unstats.un.org; *Human Development Report 2006.*

COMOROS - BALANCE OF PAYMENTS

African Development Bank Group, Rue Joseph Anoma, 01 BP 1387 Abidjan 01, Cote d'Ivoire, www.afdb.org; *Statistics Pocketbook 2008.*

Taylor and Francis Group, An Informa Business, 2 Park Square, Milton Park, Abingdon, Oxford OX14 4RN, United Kingdom, (Dial from U.S. (212) 216-7800), (Fax from U.S. (212) 564-7854), www.tandf.co.uk; *The Europa World Year Book.*

United Nations Conference on Trade and Development (UNCTAD), DC2-1120, United Nations, New York, NY 10017, (212) 963-0027, www.unctad.org; *Handbook of Statistics 2005.*

United Nations Economic Commission for Africa (ECA), PO Box 3001, Addis Ababa, Ethiopia, (Telephone in U.S. (212) 963-4957), www.uneca.org; *African Statistical Yearbook 2006.*

The World Bank, 1818 H Street, NW, Washington, DC 20433, (202) 473-1000, Fax: (202) 477-6391, www.worldbank.org; *Comoros.*

COMOROS - BANKS AND BANKING

Euromonitor International, Inc., 224 S. Michigan Avenue, Suite 1500, Chicago, IL 60604, (312) 922-1115, Fax: (312) 922-1157, www.euromonitor.com; *World Marketing Data and Statistics.*

Palgrave Macmillan Ltd., Houndmills, Basingstoke, Hampshire, RG21 6XS, England, (Telephone in U.S. (888) 330-8477), (Fax in U.S. (800) 672-2054), www.palgrave.com; *The Statesman's Yearbook 2008.*

Taylor and Francis Group, An Informa Business, 2 Park Square, Milton Park, Abingdon, Oxford OX14 4RN, United Kingdom, (Dial from U.S. (212) 216-7800), (Fax from U.S. (212) 564-7854), www.tandf.co.uk; *The Europa World Year Book.*

United Nations Economic Commission for Africa (ECA), PO Box 3001, Addis Ababa, Ethiopia, (Telephone in U.S. (212) 963-4957), www.uneca.org; *African Statistical Yearbook 2006.*

COMOROS - BROADCASTING

Central Intelligence Agency, Office of Public Affairs, Washington, DC 20505, (703) 482-0623, Fax: (703) 482-1739, www.cia.gov; *The World Factbook.*

Euromonitor International, Inc., 224 S. Michigan Avenue, Suite 1500, Chicago, IL 60604, (312) 922-1115, Fax: (312) 922-1157, www.euromonitor.com; *World Marketing Data and Statistics.*

Palgrave Macmillan Ltd., Houndmills, Basingstoke, Hampshire, RG21 6XS, England, (Telephone in U.S. (888) 330-8477), (Fax in U.S. (800) 672-2054), www.palgrave.com; *The Statesman's Yearbook 2008.*

WRTH Publications Limited, PO Box 290, Oxford OX2 7FT, UK, www.wrth.com; *World Radio TV Handbook 2007.*

COMOROS - BUDGET

Central Intelligence Agency, Office of Public Affairs, Washington, DC 20505, (703) 482-0623, Fax: (703) 482-1739, www.cia.gov; *The World Factbook.*

COMOROS - CATTLE

See COMOROS - LIVESTOCK

COMOROS - CHILDBIRTH - STATISTICS

Central Intelligence Agency, Office of Public Affairs, Washington, DC 20505, (703) 482-0623, Fax: (703) 482-1739, www.cia.gov; *The World Factbook.*

Euromonitor International, Inc., 224 S. Michigan Avenue, Suite 1500, Chicago, IL 60604, (312) 922-1115, Fax: (312) 922-1157, www.euromonitor.com; *International Marketing Data and Statistics 2008* and *The World Economic Factbook 2008.*

Palgrave Macmillan Ltd., Houndmills, Basingstoke, Hampshire, RG21 6XS, England, (Telephone in U.S. (888) 330-8477), (Fax in U.S. (800) 672-2054), www.palgrave.com; *The Statesman's Yearbook 2008.*

Taylor and Francis Group, An Informa Business, 2 Park Square, Milton Park, Abingdon, Oxford OX14 4RN, United Kingdom, (Dial from U.S. (212) 216-7800), (Fax from U.S. (212) 564-7854), www.tandf.co.uk; *The Europa World Year Book.*

United Nations Statistics Division, New York, NY 10017, (800) 253-9646, Fax: (212) 963-4116, http://unstats.un.org; *Demographic Yearbook; Statistical Yearbook;* and *Survey of Economic and Social Conditions in Africa 2005.*

COMOROS - CLIMATE

International Institute for Environment and Development (IIED), 3 Endsleigh Street, London, England, WC1H 0DD, United Kingdom, www.iied.org; *Environment Urbanization* and *Haramata - Bulletin of the Drylands.*

Palgrave Macmillan Ltd., Houndmills, Basingstoke, Hampshire, RG21 6XS, England, (Telephone in U.S. (888) 330-8477), (Fax in U.S. (800) 672-2054), www.palgrave.com; *The Statesman's Yearbook 2008.*

COMOROS - COAL PRODUCTION

See COMOROS - MINERAL INDUSTRIES

COMOROS - COCOA PRODUCTION

See COMOROS - CROPS

COMOROS - COMMERCE

Palgrave Macmillan Ltd., Houndmills, Basingstoke, Hampshire, RG21 6XS, England, (Telephone in U.S. (888) 330-8477), (Fax in U.S. (800) 672-2054), www.palgrave.com; *The Statesman's Yearbook 2008.*

COMOROS - COMMODITY EXCHANGES

United Nations Food and Agricultural Organization (FAO), Viale delle Terme di Caracalla, 00100 Rome, Italy, (Dial from U.S. (202) 653-2400), (Fax from U.S. (202) 653 5760), www.fao.org; *The State of Food and Agriculture (SOFA) 2006.*

COMOROS - CONSTRUCTION INDUSTRY

United Nations Economic Commission for Africa (ECA), PO Box 3001, Addis Ababa, Ethiopia, (Telephone in U.S. (212) 963-4957), www.uneca.org; *African Statistical Yearbook 2006.*

COMOROS - CONSUMER PRICE INDEXES

United Nations Statistics Division, New York, NY 10017, (800) 253-9646, Fax: (212) 963-4116, http://unstats.un.org; *Survey of Economic and Social Conditions in Africa 2005.*

The World Bank, 1818 H Street, NW, Washington, DC 20433, (202) 473-1000, Fax: (202) 477-6391, www.worldbank.org; *Comoros.*

COMOROS - CONSUMPTION (ECONOMICS)

African Development Bank Group, Rue Joseph Anoma, 01 BP 1387 Abidjan 01, Cote d'Ivoire, www.afdb.org; *Statistics Pocketbook 2008.*

United Nations Statistics Division, New York, NY 10017, (800) 253-9646, Fax: (212) 963-4116, http://unstats.un.org; *Survey of Economic and Social Conditions in Africa 2005.*

COMOROS - CORN INDUSTRY

See COMOROS - CROPS

COMOROS - CROPS

Palgrave Macmillan Ltd., Houndmills, Basingstoke, Hampshire, RG21 6XS, England, (Telephone in U.S. (888) 330-8477), (Fax in U.S. (800) 672-2054), www.palgrave.com; *The Statesman's Yearbook 2008.*

Taylor and Francis Group, An Informa Business, 2 Park Square, Milton Park, Abingdon, Oxford OX14 4RN, United Kingdom, (Dial from U.S. (212) 216-7800), (Fax from U.S. (212) 564-7854), www.tandf.co.uk; *The Europa World Year Book.*

United Nations Conference on Trade and Development (UNCTAD), DC2-1120, United Nations, New York, NY 10017, (212) 963-0027, www.unctad.org; *UNCTAD Commodity Yearbook.*

United Nations Economic Commission for Africa (ECA), PO Box 3001, Addis Ababa, Ethiopia, (Telephone in U.S. (212) 963-4957), www.uneca.org; *African Statistical Yearbook 2006.*

United Nations Food and Agricultural Organization (FAO), Viale delle Terme di Caracalla, 00100 Rome, Italy, (Dial from U.S. (202) 653-2400), (Fax from U.S. (202) 653 5760), www.fao.org; *FAO Production Yearbook 2002* and *The State of Food and Agriculture (SOFA) 2006.*

United Nations Statistics Division, New York, NY 10017, (800) 253-9646, Fax: (212) 963-4116, http://unstats.un.org; *Statistical Yearbook.*

COMOROS - DAIRY PROCESSING

Palgrave Macmillan Ltd., Houndmills, Basingstoke, Hampshire, RG21 6XS, England, (Telephone in U.S. (888) 330-8477), (Fax in U.S. (800) 672-2054), www.palgrave.com; *The Statesman's Yearbook 2008.*

Taylor and Francis Group, An Informa Business, 2 Park Square, Milton Park, Abingdon, Oxford OX14 4RN, United Kingdom, (Dial from U.S. (212) 216-7800), (Fax from U.S. (212) 564-7854), www.tandf.co.uk; *The Europa World Year Book.*

United Nations Food and Agricultural Organization (FAO), Viale delle Terme di Caracalla, 00100 Rome, Italy, (Dial from U.S. (202) 653-2400), (Fax from U.S. (202) 653 5760), www.fao.org; *The State of Food and Agriculture (SOFA) 2006.*

COMOROS - DEATH RATES

See COMOROS - MORTALITY

COMOROS - DEBTS, EXTERNAL

African Development Bank Group, Rue Joseph Anoma, 01 BP 1387 Abidjan 01, Cote d'Ivoire, www.afdb.org; *Statistics Pocketbook 2008.*

United Nations Statistics Division, New York, NY 10017, (800) 253-9646, Fax: (212) 963-4116, http://unstats.un.org; *Survey of Economic and Social Conditions in Africa 2005.*

The World Bank, 1818 H Street, NW, Washington, DC 20433, (202) 473-1000, Fax: (202) 477-6391, www.worldbank.org; *Africa Live Database (LDB)* and *African Development Indicators (ADI) 2007.*

COMOROS - DEMOGRAPHY

Euromonitor International, Inc., 224 S. Michigan Avenue, Suite 1500, Chicago, IL 60604, (312) 922-1115, Fax: (312) 922-1157, www.euromonitor.com; *International Marketing Data and Statistics 2008; The World Economic Factbook 2008;* and *World Marketing Data and Statistics.*

United Nations Statistics Division, New York, NY 10017, (800) 253-9646, Fax: (212) 963-4116, http://unstats.un.org; *Human Development Report 2006* and *Survey of Economic and Social Conditions in Africa 2005.*

The World Bank, 1818 H Street, NW, Washington, DC 20433, (202) 473-1000, Fax: (202) 477-6391, www.worldbank.org; *Comoros.*

COMOROS - DISPOSABLE INCOME

United Nations Statistics Division, New York, NY 10017, (800) 253-9646, Fax: (212) 963-4116, http://unstats.un.org; *Statistical Yearbook.*

COMOROS - DIVORCE

United Nations Statistics Division, New York, NY 10017, (800) 253-9646, Fax: (212) 963-4116, http://unstats.un.org; *Demographic Yearbook* and *Statistical Yearbook.*

COMOROS - ECONOMIC ASSISTANCE

United Nations Statistics Division, New York, NY 10017, (800) 253-9646, Fax: (212) 963-4116, http://unstats.un.org; *Statistical Yearbook.*

COMOROS - ECONOMIC CONDITIONS

African Development Bank Group, Rue Joseph Anoma, 01 BP 1387 Abidjan 01, Cote d'Ivoire, www.afdb.org; *The African Statistical Journal; Gender, Poverty and Environmental Indicators on African Countries 2007; Selected Statistics on African Countries 2007;* and *Statistics Pocketbook 2008.*

Central Intelligence Agency, Office of Public Affairs, Washington, DC 20505, (703) 482-0623, Fax: (703) 482-1739, www.cia.gov; *The World Factbook.*

Economist Intelligence Unit, 111 West 57th Street, New York, NY 10019, (212) 554-0600, Fax: (212) 586-1181, www.eiu.com; *Business Africa* and *Comoros Country Report.*

Euromonitor International, Inc., 224 S. Michigan Avenue, Suite 1500, Chicago, IL 60604, (312) 922-1115, Fax: (312) 922-1157, www.euromonitor.com; *The World Economic Factbook 2008* and *World Marketing Data and Statistics.*

Taylor and Francis Group, An Informa Business, 2 Park Square, Milton Park, Abingdon, Oxford OX14 4RN, United Kingdom, (Dial from U.S. (212) 216-7800), (Fax from U.S. (212) 564-7854), www.tandf.co.uk; *The Europa World Year Book.*

United Nations Statistics Division, New York, NY 10017, (800) 253-9646, Fax: (212) 963-4116, http://unstats.un.org; *World Statistics Pocketbook.*

The World Bank, 1818 H Street, NW, Washington, DC 20433, (202) 473-1000, Fax: (202) 477-6391, www.worldbank.org; *Africa Household Survey Databank; Africa Live Database (LDB); Africa Standardized Files and Indicators; African Development Indicators (ADI) 2007; Comoros;* and *The World Bank Atlas 2003-2004.*

COMOROS - EDUCATION

African Development Bank Group, Rue Joseph Anoma, 01 BP 1387 Abidjan 01, Cote d'Ivoire, www.afdb.org; *Statistics Pocketbook 2008.*

Euromonitor International, Inc., 224 S. Michigan Avenue, Suite 1500, Chicago, IL 60604, (312) 922-1115, Fax: (312) 922-1157, www.euromonitor.com; *International Marketing Data and Statistics 2008* and *World Marketing Data and Statistics.*

Palgrave Macmillan Ltd., Houndmills, Basingstoke, Hampshire, RG21 6XS, England, (Telephone in U.S. (888) 330-8477), (Fax in U.S. (800) 672-2054), www.palgrave.com; *The Statesman's Yearbook 2008.*

Taylor and Francis Group, An Informa Business, 2 Park Square, Milton Park, Abingdon, Oxford OX14 4RN, United Kingdom, (Dial from U.S. (212) 216-7800), (Fax from U.S. (212) 564-7854), www.tandf.co.uk; *The Europa World Year Book.*

United Nations Economic Commission for Africa (ECA), PO Box 3001, Addis Ababa, Ethiopia, (Telephone in U.S. (212) 963-4957), www.uneca.org; *African Statistical Yearbook 2006.*

United Nations Statistics Division, New York, NY 10017, (800) 253-9646, Fax: (212) 963-4116, http://unstats.un.org; *Human Development Report 2006* and *Survey of Economic and Social Conditions in Africa 2005.*

The World Bank, 1818 H Street, NW, Washington, DC 20433, (202) 473-1000, Fax: (202) 477-6391, www.worldbank.org; *Comoros.*

COMOROS - ELECTRICITY

United Nations Economic Commission for Africa (ECA), PO Box 3001, Addis Ababa, Ethiopia, (Telephone in U.S. (212) 963-4957), www.uneca.org; *African Statistical Yearbook 2006.*

United Nations Statistics Division, New York, NY 10017, (800) 253-9646, Fax: (212) 963-4116, http://unstats.un.org; *Human Development Report 2006* and *Survey of Economic and Social Conditions in Africa 2005.*

COMOROS - EMPLOYMENT

Euromonitor International, Inc., 224 S. Michigan Avenue, Suite 1500, Chicago, IL 60604, (312) 922-1115, Fax: (312) 922-1157, www.euromonitor.com; *International Marketing Data and Statistics 2008.*

United Nations Economic Commission for Africa (ECA), PO Box 3001, Addis Ababa, Ethiopia, (Telephone in U.S. (212) 963-4957), www.uneca.org; *African Statistical Yearbook 2006.*

United Nations Statistics Division, New York, NY 10017, (800) 253-9646, Fax: (212) 963-4116, http://unstats.un.org; *Survey of Economic and Social Conditions in Africa 2005.*

The World Bank, 1818 H Street, NW, Washington, DC 20433, (202) 473-1000, Fax: (202) 477-6391, www.worldbank.org; *Comoros.*

COMOROS - ENVIRONMENTAL CONDITIONS

DSI Data Service Information, Xantener Strasse 51a, D-47495 Rheinberg, Germany, www.dsidata.com; *Campus Solution.*

Economist Intelligence Unit, 111 West 57th Street, New York, NY 10019, (212) 554-0600, Fax: (212) 586-1181, www.eiu.com; *Comoros Country Report.*

International Institute for Environment and Development (IIED), 3 Endsleigh Street, London, England, WC1H 0DD, United Kingdom, www.iied.org; *Environment Urbanization* and *Haramata - Bulletin of the Drylands.*

United Nations Statistics Division, New York, NY 10017, (800) 253-9646, Fax: (212) 963-4116, http://unstats.un.org; *World Statistics Pocketbook.*

COMOROS - EXPORTS

African Development Bank Group, Rue Joseph Anoma, 01 BP 1387 Abidjan 01, Cote d'Ivoire, www.afdb.org; *Statistics Pocketbook 2008.*

Central Intelligence Agency, Office of Public Affairs, Washington, DC 20505, (703) 482-0623, Fax: (703) 482-1739, www.cia.gov; *The World Factbook.*

Economist Intelligence Unit, 111 West 57th Street, New York, NY 10019, (212) 554-0600, Fax: (212) 586-1181, www.eiu.com; *Comoros Country Report.*

Euromonitor International, Inc., 224 S. Michigan Avenue, Suite 1500, Chicago, IL 60604, (312) 922-1115, Fax: (312) 922-1157, www.euromonitor.com; *International Marketing Data and Statistics 2008* and *The World Economic Factbook 2008.*

International Monetary Fund (IMF), 700 Nineteenth Street, NW, Washington, DC 20431, (202) 623-7000, Fax: (202) 623-4661, www.imf.org; *Direction of Trade Statistics Yearbook 2007.*

Palgrave Macmillan Ltd., Houndmills, Basingstoke, Hampshire, RG21 6XS, England, (Telephone in U.S. (888) 330-8477), (Fax in U.S. (800) 672-2054), www.palgrave.com; *The Statesman's Yearbook 2008.*

Taylor and Francis Group, An Informa Business, 2 Park Square, Milton Park, Abingdon, Oxford OX14 4RN, United Kingdom, (Dial from U.S. (212) 216-7800), (Fax from U.S. (212) 564-7854), www.tandf.co.uk; *The Europa World Year Book.*

United Nations Conference on Trade and Development (UNCTAD), DC2-1120, United Nations, New York, NY 10017, (212) 963-0027, www.unctad.org; *Handbook of Statistics 2005.*

United Nations Economic Commission for Africa (ECA), PO Box 3001, Addis Ababa, Ethiopia, (Telephone in U.S. (212) 963-4957), www.uneca.org; *African Statistical Yearbook 2006.*

United Nations Food and Agricultural Organization (FAO), Viale delle Terme di Caracalla, 00100 Rome, Italy, (Dial from U.S. (202) 653-2400), (Fax from U.S. (202) 653 5760), www.fao.org; *The State of Food and Agriculture (SOFA) 2006.*

United Nations Statistics Division, New York, NY 10017, (800) 253-9646, Fax: (212) 963-4116, http://unstats.un.org; *Survey of Economic and Social Conditions in Africa 2005.*

COMOROS - FERTILITY, HUMAN

Central Intelligence Agency, Office of Public Affairs, Washington, DC 20505, (703) 482-0623, Fax: (703) 482-1739, www.cia.gov; *The World Factbook.*

United Nations Statistics Division, New York, NY 10017, (800) 253-9646, Fax: (212) 963-4116, http://unstats.un.org; *Human Development Report 2006* and *Survey of Economic and Social Conditions in Africa 2005.*

The World Bank, 1818 H Street, NW, Washington, DC 20433, (202) 473-1000, Fax: (202) 477-6391, www.worldbank.org; *The World Bank Atlas 2003-2004.*

COMOROS - FERTILIZER INDUSTRY

United Nations Food and Agricultural Organization (FAO), Viale delle Terme di Caracalla, 00100 Rome, Italy, (Dial from U.S. (202) 653-2400), (Fax from U.S. (202) 653 5760), www.fao.org; *The State of Food and Agriculture (SOFA) 2006.*

COMOROS - FETAL MORTALITY

See COMOROS - MORTALITY

COMOROS - FINANCE

United Nations Economic Commission for Africa (ECA), PO Box 3001, Addis Ababa, Ethiopia, (Telephone in U.S. (212) 963-4957), www.uneca.org; *African Statistical Yearbook 2006.*

United Nations Statistics Division, New York, NY 10017, (800) 253-9646, Fax: (212) 963-4116, http://unstats.un.org; *Statistical Yearbook.*

The World Bank, 1818 H Street, NW, Washington, DC 20433, (202) 473-1000, Fax: (202) 477-6391, www.worldbank.org; *Comoros.*

COMOROS - FINANCE, PUBLIC

African Development Bank Group, Rue Joseph Anoma, 01 BP 1387 Abidjan 01, Cote d'Ivoire, www.afdb.org; *Statistics Pocketbook 2008.*

Economist Intelligence Unit, 111 West 57th Street, New York, NY 10019, (212) 554-0600, Fax: (212) 586-1181, www.eiu.com; *Comoros Country Report.*

Palgrave Macmillan Ltd., Houndmills, Basingstoke, Hampshire, RG21 6XS, England, (Telephone in U.S.

(888) 330-8477), (Fax in U.S. (800) 672-2054), www.palgrave.com; *The Statesman's Yearbook 2008.*

Taylor and Francis Group, An Informa Business, 2 Park Square, Milton Park, Abingdon, Oxford OX14 4RN, United Kingdom, (Dial from U.S. (212) 216-7800), (Fax from U.S. (212) 564-7854), www.tandf.co.uk; *The Europa World Year Book.*

United Nations Economic Commission for Africa (ECA), PO Box 3001, Addis Ababa, Ethiopia, (Telephone in U.S. (212) 963-4957), www.uneca.org; *African Statistical Yearbook 2006.*

The World Bank, 1818 H Street, NW, Washington, DC 20433, (202) 473-1000, Fax: (202) 477-6391, www.worldbank.org; *Comoros.*

COMOROS - FISHERIES

Taylor and Francis Group, An Informa Business, 2 Park Square, Milton Park, Abingdon, Oxford OX14 4RN, United Kingdom, (Dial from U.S. (212) 216-7800), (Fax from U.S. (212) 564-7854), www.tandf.co.uk; *The Europa World Year Book.*

United Nations Conference on Trade and Development (UNCTAD), DC2-1120, United Nations, New York, NY 10017, (212) 963-0027, www.unctad.org; *UNCTAD Commodity Yearbook.*

United Nations Economic Commission for Africa (ECA), PO Box 3001, Addis Ababa, Ethiopia, (Telephone in U.S. (212) 963-4957), www.uneca.org; *African Statistical Yearbook 2006.*

United Nations Food and Agricultural Organization (FAO), Viale delle Terme di Caracalla, 00100 Rome, Italy, (Dial from U.S. (202) 653-2400), (Fax from U.S. (202) 653 5760), www.fao.org; *FAO Yearbook of Fishery Statistics;* Fishery Databases; FISHSTAT Database. Subjects covered include: Aquaculture production, capture production, fishery commodities; and *The State of Food and Agriculture (SOFA) 2006.*

United Nations Statistics Division, New York, NY 10017, (800) 253-9646, Fax: (212) 963-4116, http://unstats.un.org; *Statistical Yearbook* and *Survey of Economic and Social Conditions in Africa 2005.*

The World Bank, 1818 H Street, NW, Washington, DC 20433, (202) 473-1000, Fax: (202) 477-6391, www.worldbank.org; *Comoros.*

COMOROS - FOOD

African Development Bank Group, Rue Joseph Anoma, 01 BP 1387 Abidjan 01, Cote d'Ivoire, www.afdb.org; *Statistics Pocketbook 2008.*

United Nations Conference on Trade and Development (UNCTAD), DC2-1120, United Nations, New York, NY 10017, (212) 963-0027, www.unctad.org; *UNCTAD Commodity Yearbook.*

United Nations Food and Agricultural Organization (FAO), Viale delle Terme di Caracalla, 00100 Rome, Italy, (Dial from U.S. (202) 653-2400), (Fax from U.S. (202) 653 5760), www.fao.org; *FAO Production Yearbook 2002* and *The State of Food and Agriculture (SOFA) 2006.*

United Nations Statistics Division, New York, NY 10017, (800) 253-9646, Fax: (212) 963-4116, http://unstats.un.org; *Human Development Report 2006.*

COMOROS - FOREIGN EXCHANGE RATES

African Development Bank Group, Rue Joseph Anoma, 01 BP 1387 Abidjan 01, Cote d'Ivoire, www.afdb.org; *Statistics Pocketbook 2008.*

Central Intelligence Agency, Office of Public Affairs, Washington, DC 20505, (703) 482-0623, Fax: (703) 482-1739, www.cia.gov; *The World Factbook.*

Euromonitor International, Inc., 224 S. Michigan Avenue, Suite 1500, Chicago, IL 60604, (312) 922-1115, Fax: (312) 922-1157, www.euromonitor.com; *International Marketing Data and Statistics 2008* and *The World Economic Factbook 2008.*

Taylor and Francis Group, An Informa Business, 2 Park Square, Milton Park, Abingdon, Oxford OX14 4RN, United Kingdom, (Dial from U.S. (212) 216-7800), (Fax from U.S. (212) 564-7854), www.tandf.co.uk; *The Europa World Year Book.*

United Nations Statistics Division, New York, NY 10017, (800) 253-9646, Fax: (212) 963-4116, http://unstats.un.org; *Statistical Yearbook* and *World Statistics Pocketbook.*

COMOROS - FORESTS AND FORESTRY

Palgrave Macmillan Ltd., Houndmills, Basingstoke, Hampshire, RG21 6XS, England, (Telephone in U.S. (888) 330-8477), (Fax in U.S. (800) 672-2054), www.palgrave.com; *The Statesman's Yearbook 2008.*

United Nations Conference on Trade and Development (UNCTAD), DC2-1120, United Nations, New York, NY 10017, (212) 963-0027, www.unctad.org; *UNCTAD Commodity Yearbook.*

United Nations Economic Commission for Africa (ECA), PO Box 3001, Addis Ababa, Ethiopia, (Telephone in U.S. (212) 963-4957), www.uneca.org; *African Statistical Yearbook 2006.*

United Nations Food and Agricultural Organization (FAO), Viale delle Terme di Caracalla, 00100 Rome, Italy, (Dial from U.S. (202) 653-2400), (Fax from U.S. (202) 653 5760), www.fao.org; *The State of Food and Agriculture (SOFA) 2006.*

The World Bank, 1818 H Street, NW, Washington, DC 20433, (202) 473-1000, Fax: (202) 477-6391, www.worldbank.org; *Comoros.*

COMOROS - GROSS DOMESTIC PRODUCT

African Development Bank Group, Rue Joseph Anoma, 01 BP 1387 Abidjan 01, Cote d'Ivoire, www.afdb.org; *Statistics Pocketbook 2008.*

Economist Intelligence Unit, 111 West 57th Street, New York, NY 10019, (212) 554-0600, Fax: (212) 586-1181, www.eiu.com; *Comoros Country Report.*

Euromonitor International, Inc., 224 S. Michigan Avenue, Suite 1500, Chicago, IL 60604, (312) 922-1115, Fax: (312) 922-1157, www.euromonitor.com; *International Marketing Data and Statistics 2008* and *The World Economic Factbook 2008.*

Taylor and Francis Group, An Informa Business, 2 Park Square, Milton Park, Abingdon, Oxford OX14 4RN, United Kingdom, (Dial from U.S. (212) 216-7800), (Fax from U.S. (212) 564-7854), www.tandf.co.uk; *The Europa World Year Book.*

United Nations Economic Commission for Africa (ECA), PO Box 3001, Addis Ababa, Ethiopia, (Telephone in U.S. (212) 963-4957), www.uneca.org; *African Statistical Yearbook 2006.*

United Nations Statistics Division, New York, NY 10017, (800) 253-9646, Fax: (212) 963-4116, http://unstats.un.org; *Human Development Report 2006; Statistical Yearbook;* and *Survey of Economic and Social Conditions in Africa 2005.*

COMOROS - GROSS NATIONAL PRODUCT

Palgrave Macmillan Ltd., Houndmills, Basingstoke, Hampshire, RG21 6XS, England, (Telephone in U.S. (888) 330-8477), (Fax in U.S. (800) 672-2054), www.palgrave.com; *The Statesman's Yearbook 2008.*

The World Bank, 1818 H Street, NW, Washington, DC 20433, (202) 473-1000, Fax: (202) 477-6391, www.worldbank.org; *The World Bank Atlas 2003-2004.*

COMOROS - HIDES AND SKINS INDUSTRY

United Nations Food and Agricultural Organization (FAO), Viale delle Terme di Caracalla, 00100 Rome, Italy, (Dial from U.S. (202) 653-2400), (Fax from U.S. (202) 653 5760), www.fao.org; *FAO Production Yearbook 2002.*

COMOROS - HOUSING

Euromonitor International, Inc., 224 S. Michigan Avenue, Suite 1500, Chicago, IL 60604, (312) 922-1115, Fax: (312) 922-1157, www.euromonitor.com; *World Marketing Data and Statistics.*

COMOROS - ILLITERATE PERSONS

Euromonitor International, Inc., 224 S. Michigan Avenue, Suite 1500, Chicago, IL 60604, (312) 922-1115, Fax: (312) 922-1157, www.euromonitor.com; *The World Economic Factbook 2008.*

UNESCO Institute for Statistics, C.P. 6128 Succursale Centre-Ville, Montreal, Quebec, H3C 3J7 Canada, (Dial from U.S. (514) 343-6880), (Fax from U.S. (514) 343 6882), www.uis.unesco.org; *Statistical Tables.*

United Nations Statistics Division, New York, NY 10017, (800) 253-9646, Fax: (212) 963-4116, http://unstats.un.org; *Human Development Report 2006.*

COMOROS - IMPORTS

Central Intelligence Agency, Office of Public Affairs, Washington, DC 20505, (703) 482-0623, Fax: (703) 482-1739, www.cia.gov; *The World Factbook.*

Economist Intelligence Unit, 111 West 57th Street, New York, NY 10019, (212) 554-0600, Fax: (212) 586-1181, www.eiu.com; *Comoros Country Report.*

Euromonitor International, Inc., 224 S. Michigan Avenue, Suite 1500, Chicago, IL 60604, (312) 922-1115, Fax: (312) 922-1157, www.euromonitor.com; *International Marketing Data and Statistics 2008* and *The World Economic Factbook 2008.*

International Monetary Fund (IMF), 700 Nineteenth Street, NW, Washington, DC 20431, (202) 623-7000, Fax: (202) 623-4661, www.imf.org; *Direction of Trade Statistics Yearbook 2007.*

Palgrave Macmillan Ltd., Houndmills, Basingstoke, Hampshire, RG21 6XS, England, (Telephone in U.S. (888) 330-8477), (Fax in U.S. (800) 672-2054), www.palgrave.com; *The Statesman's Yearbook 2008.*

Taylor and Francis Group, An Informa Business, 2 Park Square, Milton Park, Abingdon, Oxford OX14 4RN, United Kingdom, (Dial from U.S. (212) 216-7800), (Fax from U.S. (212) 564-7854), www.tandf.co.uk; *The Europa World Year Book.*

United Nations Conference on Trade and Development (UNCTAD), DC2-1120, United Nations, New York, NY 10017, (212) 963-0027, www.unctad.org; *Handbook of Statistics 2005.*

United Nations Economic Commission for Africa (ECA), PO Box 3001, Addis Ababa, Ethiopia, (Telephone in U.S. (212) 963-4957), www.uneca.org; *African Statistical Yearbook 2006.*

United Nations Food and Agricultural Organization (FAO), Viale delle Terme di Caracalla, 00100 Rome, Italy, (Dial from U.S. (202) 653-2400), (Fax from U.S. (202) 653 5760), www.fao.org; *The State of Food and Agriculture (SOFA) 2006.*

United Nations Statistics Division, New York, NY 10017, (800) 253-9646, Fax: (212) 963-4116, http://unstats.un.org; *Survey of Economic and Social Conditions in Africa 2005.*

COMOROS - INDUSTRIES

Central Intelligence Agency, Office of Public Affairs, Washington, DC 20505, (703) 482-0623, Fax: (703) 482-1739, www.cia.gov; *The World Factbook.*

Economist Intelligence Unit, 111 West 57th Street, New York, NY 10019, (212) 554-0600, Fax: (212) 586-1181, www.eiu.com; *Comoros Country Report.*

Euromonitor International, Inc., 224 S. Michigan Avenue, Suite 1500, Chicago, IL 60604, (312) 922-1115, Fax: (312) 922-1157, www.euromonitor.com; *The World Economic Factbook 2008* and *World Marketing Data and Statistics.*

Palgrave Macmillan Ltd., Houndmills, Basingstoke, Hampshire, RG21 6XS, England, (Telephone in U.S. (888) 330-8477), (Fax in U.S. (800) 672-2054), www.palgrave.com; *The Statesman's Yearbook 2008.*

Taylor and Francis Group, An Informa Business, 2 Park Square, Milton Park, Abingdon, Oxford OX14 4RN, United Kingdom, (Dial from U.S. (212) 216-7800), (Fax from U.S. (212) 564-7854), www.tandf.co.uk; *The Europa World Year Book.*

United Nations Economic Commission for Africa (ECA), PO Box 3001, Addis Ababa, Ethiopia,

(Telephone in U.S. (212) 963-4957), www.uneca. org; *African Statistical Yearbook 2006.*

United Nations Statistics Division, New York, NY 10017, (800) 253-9646, Fax: (212) 963-4116, http:// unstats.un.org; *Survey of Economic and Social Conditions in Africa 2005.*

The World Bank, 1818 H Street, NW, Washington, DC 20433, (202) 473-1000, Fax: (202) 477-6391, www.worldbank.org; *Comoros.*

COMOROS - INFANT AND MATERNAL MORTALITY

See COMOROS - MORTALITY

COMOROS - INTERNATIONAL TRADE

African Development Bank Group, Rue Joseph Anoma, 01 BP 1387 Abidjan 01, Cote d'Ivoire, www. afdb.org; *Statistics Pocketbook 2008.*

Economist Intelligence Unit, 111 West 57th Street, New York, NY 10019, (212) 554-0600, Fax: (212) 586-1181, www.eiu.com; *Comoros Country Report.*

Euromonitor International, Inc., 224 S. Michigan Avenue, Suite 1500, Chicago, IL 60604, (312) 922-1115, Fax: (312) 922-1157, www.euromonitor.com; *The World Economic Factbook 2008* and *World Marketing Data and Statistics.*

Organisation for Economic Cooperation and Development (OECD), 2 rue Andre Pascal, F-75775 Paris Cedex 16, France, (Telephone in U.S. (202) 785-6323), (Fax in U.S. (202) 785-0350), www.oecd.org; *International Trade by Commodity Statistics (ITCS).*

Palgrave Macmillan Ltd., Houndmills, Basingstoke, Hampshire, RG21 6XS, England, (Telephone in U.S. (888) 330-8477), (Fax in U.S. (800) 672-2054), www.palgrave.com; *The Statesman's Yearbook 2008.*

Taylor and Francis Group, An Informa Business, 2 Park Square, Milton Park, Abingdon, Oxford OX14 4RN, United Kingdom, (Dial from U.S. (212) 216-7800), (Fax from U.S. (212) 564-7854), www.tandf. co.uk; *The Europa World Year Book.*

United Nations Conference on Trade and Development (UNCTAD), DC2-1120, United Nations, New York, NY 10017, (212) 963-0027, www.unctad.org; *UNCTAD Commodity Yearbook.*

United Nations Economic Commission for Africa (ECA), PO Box 3001, Addis Ababa, Ethiopia, (Telephone in U.S. (212) 963-4957), www.uneca. org; *African Statistical Yearbook 2006.*

United Nations Food and Agricultural Organization (FAO), Viale delle Terme di Caracalla, 00100 Rome, Italy, (Dial from U.S. (202) 653-2400), (Fax from U.S. (202) 653 5760), www.fao.org; *FAO Trade Yearbook* and *The State of Food and Agriculture (SOFA) 2006.*

United Nations Statistics Division, New York, NY 10017, (800) 253-9646, Fax: (212) 963-4116, http:// unstats.un.org; *International Trade Statistics Yearbook.*

The World Bank, 1818 H Street, NW, Washington, DC 20433, (202) 473-1000, Fax: (202) 477-6391, www.worldbank.org; *Comoros.*

World Trade Organization (WTO), Centre William Rappard, Rue de Lausanne 154, CH-1211 Geneva 21, Switzerland, www.wto.org; *International Trade Statistics 2006.*

COMOROS - LABOR

African Development Bank Group, Rue Joseph Anoma, 01 BP 1387 Abidjan 01, Cote d'Ivoire, www. afdb.org; *Statistics Pocketbook 2008.*

Central Intelligence Agency, Office of Public Affairs, Washington, DC 20505, (703) 482-0623, Fax: (703) 482-1739, www.cia.gov; *The World Factbook.*

Euromonitor International, Inc., 224 S. Michigan Avenue, Suite 1500, Chicago, IL 60604, (312) 922-1115, Fax: (312) 922-1157, www.euromonitor.com; *International Marketing Data and Statistics 2008* and *World Marketing Data and Statistics.*

United Nations Food and Agricultural Organization (FAO), Viale delle Terme di Caracalla, 00100 Rome, Italy, (Dial from U.S. (202) 653-2400), (Fax from U.S. (202) 653 5760), www.fao.org; *The State of Food and Agriculture (SOFA) 2006.*

United Nations Statistics Division, New York, NY 10017, (800) 253-9646, Fax: (212) 963-4116, http:// unstats.un.org; *Human Development Report 2006.*

The World Bank, 1818 H Street, NW, Washington, DC 20433, (202) 473-1000, Fax: (202) 477-6391, www.worldbank.org; *The World Bank Atlas 2003-2004.*

COMOROS - LAND USE

Central Intelligence Agency, Office of Public Affairs, Washington, DC 20505, (703) 482-0623, Fax: (703) 482-1739, www.cia.gov; *The World Factbook.*

Euromonitor International, Inc., 224 S. Michigan Avenue, Suite 1500, Chicago, IL 60604, (312) 922-1115, Fax: (312) 922-1157, www.euromonitor.com; *International Marketing Data and Statistics 2008.*

United Nations Food and Agricultural Organization (FAO), Viale delle Terme di Caracalla, 00100 Rome, Italy, (Dial from U.S. (202) 653-2400), (Fax from U.S. (202) 653 5760), www.fao.org; *FAO Production Yearbook 2002.*

COMOROS - LIBRARIES

UNESCO Institute for Statistics, C.P. 6128 Succursale Centre-Ville, Montreal, Quebec, H3C 3J7 Canada, (Dial from U.S. (514) 343-6880), (Fax from U.S. (514) 343 6882), www.uis.unesco.org; *Statistical Tables.*

COMOROS - LIFE EXPECTANCY

African Development Bank Group, Rue Joseph Anoma, 01 BP 1387 Abidjan 01, Cote d'Ivoire, www. afdb.org; *Statistics Pocketbook 2008.*

Central Intelligence Agency, Office of Public Affairs, Washington, DC 20505, (703) 482-0623, Fax: (703) 482-1739, www.cia.gov; *The World Factbook.*

Euromonitor International, Inc., 224 S. Michigan Avenue, Suite 1500, Chicago, IL 60604, (312) 922-1115, Fax: (312) 922-1157, www.euromonitor.com; *The World Economic Factbook 2008.*

Palgrave Macmillan Ltd., Houndmills, Basingstoke, Hampshire, RG21 6XS, England, (Telephone in U.S. (888) 330-8477), (Fax in U.S. (800) 672-2054), www.palgrave.com; *The Statesman's Yearbook 2008.*

United Nations Statistics Division, New York, NY 10017, (800) 253-9646, Fax: (212) 963-4116, http:// unstats.un.org; *Human Development Report 2006* and *World Statistics Pocketbook.*

The World Bank, 1818 H Street, NW, Washington, DC 20433, (202) 473-1000, Fax: (202) 477-6391, www.worldbank.org; *The World Bank Atlas 2003-2004.*

COMOROS - LITERACY

Euromonitor International, Inc., 224 S. Michigan Avenue, Suite 1500, Chicago, IL 60604, (312) 922-1115, Fax: (312) 922-1157, www.euromonitor.com; *World Marketing Data and Statistics.*

United Nations Statistics Division, New York, NY 10017, (800) 253-9646, Fax: (212) 963-4116, http:// unstats.un.org; *Survey of Economic and Social Conditions in Africa 2005.*

COMOROS - LIVESTOCK

Palgrave Macmillan Ltd., Houndmills, Basingstoke, Hampshire, RG21 6XS, England, (Telephone in U.S. (888) 330-8477), (Fax in U.S. (800) 672-2054), www.palgrave.com; *The Statesman's Yearbook 2008.*

Taylor and Francis Group, An Informa Business, 2 Park Square, Milton Park, Abingdon, Oxford OX14 4RN, United Kingdom, (Dial from U.S. (212) 216-7800), (Fax from U.S. (212) 564-7854), www.tandf. co.uk; *The Europa World Year Book.*

United Nations Conference on Trade and Development (UNCTAD), DC2-1120, United Nations, New York, NY 10017, (212) 963-0027, www.unctad.org; *UNCTAD Commodity Yearbook.*

United Nations Economic Commission for Africa (ECA), PO Box 3001, Addis Ababa, Ethiopia, (Telephone in U.S. (212) 963-4957), www.uneca. org; *African Statistical Yearbook 2006.*

United Nations Food and Agricultural Organization (FAO), Viale delle Terme di Caracalla, 00100 Rome, Italy, (Dial from U.S. (202) 653-2400), (Fax from U.S. (202) 653 5760), www.fao.org; *FAO Production Yearbook 2002* and *The State of Food and Agriculture (SOFA) 2006.*

United Nations Statistics Division, New York, NY 10017, (800) 253-9646, Fax: (212) 963-4116, http:// unstats.un.org; *Statistical Yearbook* and *Survey of Economic and Social Conditions in Africa 2005.*

COMOROS - MANUFACTURES

United Nations Economic Commission for Africa (ECA), PO Box 3001, Addis Ababa, Ethiopia, (Telephone in U.S. (212) 963-4957), www.uneca. org; *African Statistical Yearbook 2006.*

United Nations Statistics Division, New York, NY 10017, (800) 253-9646, Fax: (212) 963-4116, http:// unstats.un.org; *Survey of Economic and Social Conditions in Africa 2005.*

COMOROS - MARRIAGE

United Nations Statistics Division, New York, NY 10017, (800) 253-9646, Fax: (212) 963-4116, http:// unstats.un.org; *Demographic Yearbook* and *Statistical Yearbook.*

COMOROS - MEAT PRODUCTION

See COMOROS - LIVESTOCK

COMOROS - MINERAL INDUSTRIES

United Nations Conference on Trade and Development (UNCTAD), DC2-1120, United Nations, New York, NY 10017, (212) 963-0027, www.unctad.org; *UNCTAD Commodity Yearbook.*

United Nations Economic Commission for Africa (ECA), PO Box 3001, Addis Ababa, Ethiopia, (Telephone in U.S. (212) 963-4957), www.uneca. org; *African Statistical Yearbook 2006.*

The World Bank, 1818 H Street, NW, Washington, DC 20433, (202) 473-1000, Fax: (202) 477-6391, www.worldbank.org; *Comoros.*

COMOROS - MONEY EXCHANGE RATES

See COMOROS - FOREIGN EXCHANGE RATES

COMOROS - MONEY SUPPLY

African Development Bank Group, Rue Joseph Anoma, 01 BP 1387 Abidjan 01, Cote d'Ivoire, www. afdb.org; *Statistics Pocketbook 2008.*

Economist Intelligence Unit, 111 West 57th Street, New York, NY 10019, (212) 554-0600, Fax: (212) 586-1181, www.eiu.com; *Comoros Country Report.*

The World Bank, 1818 H Street, NW, Washington, DC 20433, (202) 473-1000, Fax: (202) 477-6391, www.worldbank.org; *Comoros.*

COMOROS - MORTALITY

Central Intelligence Agency, Office of Public Affairs, Washington, DC 20505, (703) 482-0623, Fax: (703) 482-1739, www.cia.gov; *The World Factbook.*

Euromonitor International, Inc., 224 S. Michigan Avenue, Suite 1500, Chicago, IL 60604, (312) 922-1115, Fax: (312) 922-1157, www.euromonitor.com; *International Marketing Data and Statistics 2008* and *The World Economic Factbook 2008.*

Palgrave Macmillan Ltd., Houndmills, Basingstoke, Hampshire, RG21 6XS, England, (Telephone in U.S. (888) 330-8477), (Fax in U.S. (800) 672-2054), www.palgrave.com; *The Statesman's Yearbook 2008.*

Taylor and Francis Group, An Informa Business, 2 Park Square, Milton Park, Abingdon, Oxford OX14 4RN, United Kingdom, (Dial from U.S. (212) 216-7800), (Fax from U.S. (212) 564-7854), www.tandf. co.uk; *The Europa World Year Book.*

United Nations Statistics Division, New York, NY 10017, (800) 253-9646, Fax: (212) 963-4116, http://unstats.un.org; *Human Development Report 2006; Statistical Yearbook; Survey of Economic and Social Conditions in Africa 2005;* and *World Statistics Pocketbook.*

The World Bank, 1818 H Street, NW, Washington, DC 20433, (202) 473-1000, Fax: (202) 477-6391, www.worldbank.org; *The World Bank Atlas 2003-2004.*

COMOROS - MOTION PICTURES

United Nations Statistics Division, New York, NY 10017, (800) 253-9646, Fax: (212) 963-4116, http://unstats.un.org; *Statistical Yearbook.*

COMOROS - MOTOR VEHICLES

Taylor and Francis Group, An Informa Business, 2 Park Square, Milton Park, Abingdon, Oxford OX14 4RN, United Kingdom, (Dial from U.S. (212) 216-7800), (Fax from U.S. (212) 564-7854), www.tandf.co.uk; *The Europa World Year Book.*

United Nations Statistics Division, New York, NY 10017, (800) 253-9646, Fax: (212) 963-4116, http://unstats.un.org; *Survey of Economic and Social Conditions in Africa 2005.*

COMOROS - NUTRITION

African Development Bank Group, Rue Joseph Anoma, 01 BP 1387 Abidjan 01, Cote d'Ivoire, www.afdb.org; *Statistics Pocketbook 2008.*

United Nations Food and Agricultural Organization (FAO), Viale delle Terme di Caracalla, 00100 Rome, Italy, (Dial from U.S. (202) 653-2400), (Fax from U.S. (202) 653 5760), www.fao.org; *The State of Food and Agriculture (SOFA) 2006.*

COMOROS - PESTICIDES

United Nations Food and Agricultural Organization (FAO), Viale delle Terme di Caracalla, 00100 Rome, Italy, (Dial from U.S. (202) 653-2400), (Fax from U.S. (202) 653 5760), www.fao.org; *The State of Food and Agriculture (SOFA) 2006.*

COMOROS - PETROLEUM INDUSTRY AND TRADE

PennWell Corporation, 1421 South Sheridan Road, Tulsa, OK 74112, (918) 835-3161, www.pennwell.com; *International Petroleum Encyclopedia 2007.*

United Nations Conference on Trade and Development (UNCTAD), DC2-1120, United Nations, New York, NY 10017, (212) 963-0027, www.unctad.org; *UNCTAD Commodity Yearbook.*

United Nations Food and Agricultural Organization (FAO), Viale delle Terme di Caracalla, 00100 Rome, Italy, (Dial from U.S. (202) 653-2400), (Fax from U.S. (202) 653 5760), www.fao.org; *The State of Food and Agriculture (SOFA) 2006.*

COMOROS - POLITICAL SCIENCE

Central Intelligence Agency, Office of Public Affairs, Washington, DC 20505, (703) 482-0623, Fax: (703) 482-1739, www.cia.gov; *The World Factbook.*

Palgrave Macmillan Ltd., Houndmills, Basingstoke, Hampshire, RG21 6XS, England, (Telephone in U.S. (888) 330-8477), (Fax in U.S. (800) 672-2054), www.palgrave.com; *The Statesman's Yearbook 2008.*

Taylor and Francis Group, An Informa Business, 2 Park Square, Milton Park, Abingdon, Oxford OX14 4RN, United Kingdom, (Dial from U.S. (212) 216-7800), (Fax from U.S. (212) 564-7854), www.tandf.co.uk; *The Europa World Year Book.*

United Nations Statistics Division, New York, NY 10017, (800) 253-9646, Fax: (212) 963-4116, http://unstats.un.org; *Survey of Economic and Social Conditions in Africa 2005.*

COMOROS - POPULATION

African Development Bank Group, Rue Joseph Anoma, 01 BP 1387 Abidjan 01, Cote d'Ivoire, www.afdb.org; *The African Statistical Journal; Gender, Poverty and Environmental Indicators on African Countries 2007; Selected Statistics on African Countries 2007;* and *Statistics Pocketbook 2008.*

Central Intelligence Agency, Office of Public Affairs, Washington, DC 20505, (703) 482-0623, Fax: (703) 482-1739, www.cia.gov; *The World Factbook.*

Economist Intelligence Unit, 111 West 57th Street, New York, NY 10019, (212) 554-0600, Fax: (212) 586-1181, www.eiu.com; *Comoros Country Report.*

Euromonitor International, Inc., 224 S. Michigan Avenue, Suite 1500, Chicago, IL 60604, (312) 922-1115, Fax: (312) 922-1157, www.euromonitor.com; *International Marketing Data and Statistics 2008* and *The World Economic Factbook 2008.*

Eurostat, Batiment Jean Monnet, Rue Alcide de Gasperi, L-2920 Luxembourg, http://epp.eurostat.ec.europa.eu; *Demographic Indicators - Population by Age-Classes.*

Palgrave Macmillan Ltd., Houndmills, Basingstoke, Hampshire, RG21 6XS, England, (Telephone in U.S. (888) 330-8477), (Fax in U.S. (800) 672-2054), www.palgrave.com; *The Statesman's Yearbook 2008.*

Taylor and Francis Group, An Informa Business, 2 Park Square, Milton Park, Abingdon, Oxford OX14 4RN, United Kingdom, (Dial from U.S. (212) 216-7800), (Fax from U.S. (212) 564-7854), www.tandf.co.uk; *The Europa World Year Book.*

UNESCO Institute for Statistics, C.P. 6128 Succursale Centre-Ville, Montreal, Quebec, H3C 3J7 Canada, (Dial from U.S. (514) 343-6880), (Fax from U.S. (514) 343 6882), www.uis.unesco.org; *Statistical Tables.*

United Nations Food and Agricultural Organization (FAO), Viale delle Terme di Caracalla, 00100 Rome, Italy, (Dial from U.S. (202) 653-2400), (Fax from U.S. (202) 653 5760), www.fao.org; *FAO Production Yearbook 2002.*

United Nations Statistics Division, New York, NY 10017, (800) 253-9646, Fax: (212) 963-4116, http://unstats.un.org; *Demographic Yearbook; Human Development Report 2006; Statistical Yearbook; Survey of Economic and Social Conditions in Africa 2005;* and *World Statistics Pocketbook.*

The World Bank, 1818 H Street, NW, Washington, DC 20433, (202) 473-1000, Fax: (202) 477-6391, www.worldbank.org; *Comoros* and *The World Bank Atlas 2003-2004.*

World Health Organization (WHO), Avenue Appia 20, 1211 Geneve 27, Switzerland, (Telephone in U.S. (212) 331-9081), www.who.int; *World Health Report 2006.*

COMOROS - POPULATION DENSITY

African Development Bank Group, Rue Joseph Anoma, 01 BP 1387 Abidjan 01, Cote d'Ivoire, www.afdb.org; *Statistics Pocketbook 2008.*

Central Intelligence Agency, Office of Public Affairs, Washington, DC 20505, (703) 482-0623, Fax: (703) 482-1739, www.cia.gov; *The World Factbook.*

Euromonitor International, Inc., 224 S. Michigan Avenue, Suite 1500, Chicago, IL 60604, (312) 922-1115, Fax: (312) 922-1157, www.euromonitor.com; *The World Economic Factbook 2008.*

Palgrave Macmillan Ltd., Houndmills, Basingstoke, Hampshire, RG21 6XS, England, (Telephone in U.S. (888) 330-8477), (Fax in U.S. (800) 672-2054), www.palgrave.com; *The Statesman's Yearbook 2008.*

Taylor and Francis Group, An Informa Business, 2 Park Square, Milton Park, Abingdon, Oxford OX14 4RN, United Kingdom, (Dial from U.S. (212) 216-7800), (Fax from U.S. (212) 564-7854), www.tandf.co.uk; *The Europa World Year Book.*

UNESCO Institute for Statistics, C.P. 6128 Succursale Centre-Ville, Montreal, Quebec, H3C 3J7 Canada, (Dial from U.S. (514) 343-6880), (Fax from U.S. (514) 343 6882), www.uis.unesco.org; *Statistical Tables.*

United Nations Food and Agricultural Organization (FAO), Viale delle Terme di Caracalla, 00100 Rome, Italy, (Dial from U.S. (202) 653-2400), (Fax from U.S. (202) 653 5760), www.fao.org; *The State of Food and Agriculture (SOFA) 2006.*

United Nations Statistics Division, New York, NY 10017, (800) 253-9646, Fax: (212) 963-4116, http://unstats.un.org; *Statistical Yearbook* and *Survey of Economic and Social Conditions in Africa 2005.*

The World Bank, 1818 H Street, NW, Washington, DC 20433, (202) 473-1000, Fax: (202) 477-6391, www.worldbank.org; *Comoros.*

COMOROS - POSTAL SERVICE

United Nations Statistics Division, New York, NY 10017, (800) 253-9646, Fax: (212) 963-4116, http://unstats.un.org; *Statistical Yearbook.*

COMOROS - POWER RESOURCES

Euromonitor International, Inc., 224 S. Michigan Avenue, Suite 1500, Chicago, IL 60604, (312) 922-1115, Fax: (312) 922-1157, www.euromonitor.com; *International Marketing Data and Statistics 2008; The World Economic Factbook 2008;* and *World Marketing Data and Statistics.*

Platts, 2 Penn Plaza, 25th Floor, New York, NY 10121-2298, (212) 904-3070, www.platts.com; *Energy Economist.*

United Nations Economic Commission for Africa (ECA), PO Box 3001, Addis Ababa, Ethiopia, (Telephone in U.S. (212) 963-4957), www.uneca.org; *African Statistical Yearbook 2006.*

United Nations Food and Agricultural Organization (FAO), Viale delle Terme di Caracalla, 00100 Rome, Italy, (Dial from U.S. (202) 653-2400), (Fax from U.S. (202) 653 5760), www.fao.org; *The State of Food and Agriculture (SOFA) 2006.*

United Nations Statistics Division, New York, NY 10017, (800) 253-9646, Fax: (212) 963-4116, http://unstats.un.org; *Energy Statistics Yearbook 2003; Human Development Report 2006; Statistical Yearbook;* and *World Statistics Pocketbook.*

The World Bank, 1818 H Street, NW, Washington, DC 20433, (202) 473-1000, Fax: (202) 477-6391, www.worldbank.org; *The World Bank Atlas 2003-2004.*

COMOROS - PRICES

Euromonitor International, Inc., 224 S. Michigan Avenue, Suite 1500, Chicago, IL 60604, (312) 922-1115, Fax: (312) 922-1157, www.euromonitor.com; *World Marketing Data and Statistics.*

United Nations Economic Commission for Africa (ECA), PO Box 3001, Addis Ababa, Ethiopia, (Telephone in U.S. (212) 963-4957), www.uneca.org; *African Statistical Yearbook 2006.*

United Nations Food and Agricultural Organization (FAO), Viale delle Terme di Caracalla, 00100 Rome, Italy, (Dial from U.S. (202) 653-2400), (Fax from U.S. (202) 653 5760), www.fao.org; *FAO Production Yearbook 2002* and *The State of Food and Agriculture (SOFA) 2006.*

The World Bank, 1818 H Street, NW, Washington, DC 20433, (202) 473-1000, Fax: (202) 477-6391, www.worldbank.org; *Comoros.*

COMOROS - PUBLIC HEALTH

African Development Bank Group, Rue Joseph Anoma, 01 BP 1387 Abidjan 01, Cote d'Ivoire, www.afdb.org; *Statistics Pocketbook 2008.*

Euromonitor International, Inc., 224 S. Michigan Avenue, Suite 1500, Chicago, IL 60604, (312) 922-1115, Fax: (312) 922-1157, www.euromonitor.com; *World Marketing Data and Statistics.*

Palgrave Macmillan Ltd., Houndmills, Basingstoke, Hampshire, RG21 6XS, England, (Telephone in U.S. (888) 330-8477), (Fax in U.S. (800) 672-2054), www.palgrave.com; *The Statesman's Yearbook 2008.*

United Nations Economic Commission for Africa (ECA), PO Box 3001, Addis Ababa, Ethiopia, (Telephone in U.S. (212) 963-4957), www.uneca.org; *African Statistical Yearbook 2006.*

United Nations Statistics Division, New York, NY 10017, (800) 253-9646, Fax: (212) 963-4116, http://unstats.un.org; *Human Development Report 2006* and *Statistical Yearbook.*

The World Bank, 1818 H Street, NW, Washington, DC 20433, (202) 473-1000, Fax: (202) 477-6391, www.worldbank.org; *Comoros.*

COMOROS - RADIO BROADCASTING

Palgrave Macmillan Ltd., Houndmills, Basingstoke, Hampshire, RG21 6XS, England, (Telephone in U.S. (888) 330-8477), (Fax in U.S. (800) 672-2054), www.palgrave.com; *The Statesman's Yearbook 2008.*

COMOROS - RAILROADS

United Nations Economic Commission for Africa (ECA), PO Box 3001, Addis Ababa, Ethiopia, (Telephone in U.S. (212) 963-4957), www.uneca.org; *African Statistical Yearbook 2006.*

COMOROS - RELIGION

Central Intelligence Agency, Office of Public Affairs, Washington, DC 20505, (703) 482-0623, Fax: (703) 482-1739, www.cia.gov; *The World Factbook.*

Palgrave Macmillan Ltd., Houndmills, Basingstoke, Hampshire, RG21 6XS, England, (Telephone in U.S. (888) 330-8477), (Fax in U.S. (800) 672-2054), www.palgrave.com; *The Statesman's Yearbook 2008.*

COMOROS - RESERVES (ACCOUNTING)

African Development Bank Group, Rue Joseph Anoma, 01 BP 1387 Abidjan 01, Cote d'Ivoire, www.afdb.org; *Statistics Pocketbook 2008.*

COMOROS - RETAIL TRADE

Euromonitor International, Inc., 224 S. Michigan Avenue, Suite 1500, Chicago, IL 60604, (312) 922-1115, Fax: (312) 922-1157, www.euromonitor.com; *World Marketing Data and Statistics.*

COMOROS - RICE PRODUCTION

See COMOROS - CROPS.

COMOROS - ROADS

Central Intelligence Agency, Office of Public Affairs, Washington, DC 20505, (703) 482-0623, Fax: (703) 482-1739, www.cia.gov; *The World Factbook.*

Palgrave Macmillan Ltd., Houndmills, Basingstoke, Hampshire, RG21 6XS, England, (Telephone in U.S. (888) 330-8477), (Fax in U.S. (800) 672-2054), www.palgrave.com; *The Statesman's Yearbook 2008.*

United Nations Economic Commission for Africa (ECA), PO Box 3001, Addis Ababa, Ethiopia, (Telephone in U.S. (212) 963-4957), www.uneca.org; *African Statistical Yearbook 2006.*

United Nations Statistics Division, New York, NY 10017, (800) 253-9646, Fax: (212) 963-4116, http://unstats.un.org; *Survey of Economic and Social Conditions in Africa 2005.*

COMOROS - SHEEP

See COMOROS - LIVESTOCK

COMOROS - SHIPPING

Lloyd's Register - Fairplay, 8410 N.W. 53rd Terrace, Suite 207, Miami FL 33166, (305) 718-9929, Fax: (305) 718-9663, www.lrfairplay.com; *Register of Ships 2007-2008; World Casualty Statistics 2007; World Fleet Statistics 2006; World Marine Propulsion Report 2006-2010; World Shipbuilding Statistics 2007;* and The World Shipping Encyclopaedia.

Taylor and Francis Group, An Informa Business, 2 Park Square, Milton Park, Abingdon, Oxford OX14 4RN, United Kingdom, (Dial from U.S. (212) 216-7800), (Fax from U.S. (212) 564-7854), www.tandf.co.uk; *The Europa World Year Book.*

United Nations Economic Commission for Africa (ECA), PO Box 3001, Addis Ababa, Ethiopia, (Telephone in U.S. (212) 963-4957), www.uneca.org; *African Statistical Yearbook 2006.*

United Nations Statistics Division, New York, NY 10017, (800) 253-9646, Fax: (212) 963-4116, http://unstats.un.org; *Statistical Yearbook.*

COMOROS - SOCIAL ECOLOGY

United Nations Statistics Division, New York, NY 10017, (800) 253-9646, Fax: (212) 963-4116, http://unstats.un.org; *World Statistics Pocketbook.*

COMOROS - TAXATION

Taylor and Francis Group, An Informa Business, 2 Park Square, Milton Park, Abingdon, Oxford OX14 4RN, United Kingdom, (Dial from U.S. (212) 216-7800), (Fax from U.S. (212) 564-7854), www.tandf.co.uk; *The Europa World Year Book.*

COMOROS - TELEPHONE

International Telecommunication Union (ITU), Place des Nations, 1211 Geneva 20, Switzerland, www.itu.int; World Telecommunication Indicators Database.

Palgrave Macmillan Ltd., Houndmills, Basingstoke, Hampshire, RG21 6XS, England, (Telephone in U.S. (888) 330-8477), (Fax in U.S. (800) 672-2054), www.palgrave.com; *The Statesman's Yearbook 2008.*

Taylor and Francis Group, An Informa Business, 2 Park Square, Milton Park, Abingdon, Oxford OX14 4RN, United Kingdom, (Dial from U.S. (212) 216-7800), (Fax from U.S. (212) 564-7854), www.tandf.co.uk; *The Europa World Year Book.*

United Nations Statistics Division, New York, NY 10017, (800) 253-9646, Fax: (212) 963-4116, http://unstats.un.org; *Statistical Yearbook* and *World Statistics Pocketbook.*

COMOROS - TEXTILE INDUSTRY

United Nations Conference on Trade and Development (UNCTAD), DC2-1120, United Nations, New York, NY 10017, (212) 963-0027, www.unctad.org; *UNCTAD Commodity Yearbook.*

COMOROS - TOURISM

Euromonitor International, Inc., 224 S. Michigan Avenue, Suite 1500, Chicago, IL 60604, (312) 922-1115, Fax: (312) 922-1157, www.euromonitor.com; *The World Economic Factbook 2008* and *World Marketing Data and Statistics.*

United Nations Economic Commission for Africa (ECA), PO Box 3001, Addis Ababa, Ethiopia, (Telephone in U.S. (212) 963-4957), www.uneca.org; *African Statistical Yearbook 2006.*

United Nations World Tourism Organization (UNWTO), Capitan Haya 42, 28020 Madrid, Spain, www.world-tourism.org; *Yearbook of Tourism Statistics.*

The World Bank, 1818 H Street, NW, Washington, DC 20433, (202) 473-1000, Fax: (202) 477-6391, www.worldbank.org; *Comoros.*

COMOROS - TRADE

See COMOROS - INTERNATIONAL TRADE

COMOROS - TRANSPORTATION

Central Intelligence Agency, Office of Public Affairs, Washington, DC 20505, (703) 482-0623, Fax: (703) 482-1739, www.cia.gov; *The World Factbook.*

Euromonitor International, Inc., 224 S. Michigan Avenue, Suite 1500, Chicago, IL 60604, (312) 922-1115, Fax: (312) 922-1157, www.euromonitor.com; *International Marketing Data and Statistics 2008* and *World Marketing Data and Statistics.*

Palgrave Macmillan Ltd., Houndmills, Basingstoke, Hampshire, RG21 6XS, England, (Telephone in U.S. (888) 330-8477), (Fax in U.S. (800) 672-2054), www.palgrave.com; *The Statesman's Yearbook 2008.*

Taylor and Francis Group, An Informa Business, 2 Park Square, Milton Park, Abingdon, Oxford OX14 4RN, United Kingdom, (Dial from U.S. (212) 216-7800), (Fax from U.S. (212) 564-7854), www.tandf.co.uk; *The Europa World Year Book.*

United Nations Economic Commission for Africa (ECA), PO Box 3001, Addis Ababa, Ethiopia, (Telephone in U.S. (212) 963-4957), www.uneca.org; *African Statistical Yearbook 2006.*

United Nations Statistics Division, New York, NY 10017, (800) 253-9646, Fax: (212) 963-4116, http://unstats.un.org; *Human Development Report 2006.*

The World Bank, 1818 H Street, NW, Washington, DC 20433, (202) 473-1000, Fax: (202) 477-6391, www.worldbank.org; *Africa Live Database (LDB)* and *Comoros.*

COMOROS - UNEMPLOYMENT

Central Intelligence Agency, Office of Public Affairs, Washington, DC 20505, (703) 482-0623, Fax: (703) 482-1739, www.cia.gov; *The World Factbook.*

The World Bank, 1818 H Street, NW, Washington, DC 20433, (202) 473-1000, Fax: (202) 477-6391, www.worldbank.org; *Comoros.*

COMOROS - VITAL STATISTICS

Palgrave Macmillan Ltd., Houndmills, Basingstoke, Hampshire, RG21 6XS, England, (Telephone in U.S. (888) 330-8477), (Fax in U.S. (800) 672-2054), www.palgrave.com; *The Statesman's Yearbook 2008.*

United Nations Statistics Division, New York, NY 10017, (800) 253-9646, Fax: (212) 963-4116, http://unstats.un.org; *Statistical Yearbook.*

World Health Organization (WHO), Avenue Appia 20, 1211 Geneve 27, Switzerland, (Telephone in U.S. (212) 331-9081), www.who.int; *World Health Report 2006.*

COMOROS - WAGES

The World Bank, 1818 H Street, NW, Washington, DC 20433, (202) 473-1000, Fax: (202) 477-6391, www.worldbank.org; *Comoros.*

COMPACT DISCS (CD-ROM)

Electronic Industries Alliance (EIA), 2500 Wilson Boulevard, Arlington, VA 22201, (703) 907-7500, www.eia.org; unpublished data.

Mediamark Research, Inc., 75 Ninth Avenue, 5th Floor, New York, NY 10011, (212) 884-9200, Fax: (212) 884-9339, www.mediamark.com; *The American Kids Study.*

U.S. Census Bureau, Center for Economic Studies, 4600 Silver Hill Road, Washington DC 20233, (301) 457-1235, www.ces.census.gov; *2002 Economic Census, Information.*

COMPUTER - ADVERTISING EXPENDITURES

Magazine Publishers of America (MPA), 810 Seventh Avenue, 24th Floor, New York, NY 10019, (212) 872-3700, www.magazine.org; unpublished data.

The NPD Group, Port Washington, 900 West Shore Road, Port Washington, NY 11050, (866) 444-1411, www.npd.com; *Market Research for the Consumer Technology Industry.*

COMPUTER - INTERNATIONAL TRADE

The NPD Group, Port Washington, 900 West Shore Road, Port Washington, NY 11050, (866) 444-1411, www.npd.com; *Market Research for the Consumer Technology Industry.*

U.S. Census Bureau, Foreign Trade Division, 4700 Silver Hill Road, Washington DC 20233-0001, (301) 763-3030, www.census.gov/foreign-trade/www/; *U.S. International Trade in Goods and Services.*

COMPUTER - SALES

Gartner, Inc., 56 Top Gallant Road, Stamford, CT 06904-7700, (203) 964 0096, www.gartner.com; Gartner Dataquest and unpublished data.

The NPD Group, Port Washington, 900 West Shore Road, Port Washington, NY 11050, (866) 444-1411, www.npd.com; *Market Research for the Consumer Technology Industry; Market Research for the Film, Music, PC Games, Video Games, and Video Industries;* and *Wireless.*

U.S. Department of Commerce (DOC), Economics and Statistics Administration (ESA), 1401 Constitution Avenue, NW, Washington, DC 20230, (800) 782-8872, www.esa.doc.gov; *Falling Through the Net: Toward Digital Inclusion.*

COMPUTER - USE

Linux Counter Project, http://counter.li.org; *Reports from the Linux Counter.*

Market Data Retrieval (MDR), 6 Armstrong Road, Shelton, CT 06484, (800) 333-8802, www.schooldata.com; *The College Technology Review 2006* and *The K-12 Technology Review 2005.*

Mediamark Research, Inc., 75 Ninth Avenue, 5th Floor, New York, NY 10011, (212) 884-9200, Fax: (212) 884-9339, www.mediamark.com; MRI+.

National Center for Education Statistics (NCES), 1990 K Street, NW, Washington, DC 20006, (202) 502-7300, http://nces.ed.gov; *Digest of Education Statistics 2007.*

Organisation for Economic Cooperation and Development (OECD), 2 rue Andre Pascal, F-75775 Paris Cedex 16, France, (Telephone in U.S. (202) 785-6323), (Fax in U.S. (202) 785-0350), www.oecd.org; *OECD Information Technology Outlook 2006.*

U.S. Department of Commerce (DOC), Economics and Statistics Administration (ESA), 1401 Constitution Avenue, NW, Washington, DC 20230, (800) 782-8872, www.esa.doc.gov; *Falling Through the Net: Toward Digital Inclusion; Main Street in the Digital Age: How Small and Medium-sized Businesses Are Using the Tools of the New Economy;* and *A Nation Online.*

COMPUTER CRIMES

Federal Bureau of Investigation (FBI), J. Edgar Hoover Building, 935 Pennsylvania Avenue, NW, Washington, DC 20535-0001, (202) 324-3000, www.fbi.gov; *Crime in the United States (CIUS) 2007 (Preliminary).*

Justice Research and Statistics Association (JRSA), 777 N. Capitol Street, NE, Suite 801, Washington, DC 20002, (202) 842-9330, Fax: (202) 842-9329, www.jrsa.org; *Crime and Justice Atlas 2001.*

U.S. Department of Justice (DOJ), Bureau of Justice Statistics, 810 Seventh Street, NW, Washington, DC 20531, (202) 307-0765, www.ojp.usdoj.gov/bjs/; *Cybercrime against Businesses: Pilot Test Results, 2001 Computer Security Survey* and *Identity Theft, 2004.*

U.S. Government Accountablity Office (GAO), 441 G Street, NW, Washington, DC 20548, (202) 512-3000, www.gao.gov; *Identity Theft: Greater Awareness and Use of Existing Data Are Needed.*

U.S. Library of Congress (LOC), Congressional Research Service (CRS), The Library of Congress, 101 Independence Avenue, SE, Washington, DC 20540-7500, (202) 707-5700, www.loc.gov/crsinfo; *The Economic Impact of Cyber-Attacks.*

COMPUTER GAMES

The NPD Group, Port Washington, 900 West Shore Road, Port Washington, NY 11050, (866) 444-1411, www.npd.com; *Market Research for the Film, Music, PC Games, Video Games, and Video Industries.*

COMPUTER PROGRAMMING AND DATA PROCESSING SERVICES - EARNINGS

U.S. Bureau of Labor Statistics (BLS), Postal Square Building, 2 Massachusetts Avenue, NE, Washington, DC 20212-0001, (202) 691-5200, Fax: (202) 691-6325, www.bls.gov; *Current Employment Statistics Survey (CES)* and *Employment and Earnings (EE).*

U.S. Census Bureau, Service Sector Statistics Division, 4700 Silver Hill Road, Washington DC 20233-0001, (301) 763-3030, www.census.gov/svsd/www/economic.html; *2004 Service Annual Survey.*

U.S. Department of Commerce (DOC), Economics and Statistics Administration (ESA), 1401 Constitution Avenue, NW, Washington, DC 20230, (800) 782-8872, www.esa.doc.gov; *The Digital Economy 2003.*

COMPUTER PROGRAMMING AND DATA PROCESSING SERVICES - EMPLOYEES

U.S. Bureau of Labor Statistics (BLS), Postal Square Building, 2 Massachusetts Avenue, NE, Washington, DC 20212-0001, (202) 691-5200, Fax: (202) 691-6325, www.bls.gov; *Current Employment Statistics Survey (CES)* and *Employment and Earnings (EE).*

U.S. Census Bureau, Service Sector Statistics Division, 4700 Silver Hill Road, Washington DC 20233-0001, (301) 763-3030, www.census.gov/svsd/www/economic.html; *2004 Service Annual Survey.*

U.S. Department of Commerce (DOC), Economics and Statistics Administration (ESA), 1401 Constitution Avenue, NW, Washington, DC 20230, (800) 782-8872, www.esa.doc.gov; *The Digital Economy 2003.*

COMPUTER PROGRAMMING AND DATA PROCESSING SERVICES - GROSS DOMESTIC PRODUCT

U.S. Department of Commerce (DOC), Economics and Statistics Administration (ESA), 1401 Constitution Avenue, NW, Washington, DC 20230, (800) 782-8872, www.esa.doc.gov; *The Digital Economy 2003.*

COMPUTER SPECIALISTS - DEGREES CONFERRED

National Center for Education Statistics (NCES), 1990 K Street, NW, Washington, DC 20006, (202) 502-7300, http://nces.ed.gov; *Digest of Education Statistics 2007.*

National Science Foundation, Division of Science Resources Statistics (SRS), 4201 Wilson Boulevard, Arlington, VA 22230, (703) 292-8780, Fax: (703) 292-9092, www.nsf.gov; *National Survey of Recent College Graduates: 2006; Selected Data on Science and Engineering Doctorate Awards;* and unpublished data.

COMPUTER SPECIALISTS - LABOR FORCE

U.S. Bureau of Labor Statistics (BLS), Postal Square Building, 2 Massachusetts Avenue, NE, Washington, DC 20212-0001, (202) 691-5200, Fax: (202) 691-6325, www.bls.gov; *Monthly Labor Review (MLR).*

COMPUTER SPECIALISTS - LABOR FORCE - SALARY OFFERS

National Association of Colleges and Employers (NACE), 62 Highland Avenue, Bethlehem, PA 18017, (800) 544-5272, Fax: (610) 868-0208, www.naceweb.org; *Salary Survey.*

COMPUTER USE

Market Data Retrieval (MDR), 6 Armstrong Road, Shelton, CT 06484, (800) 333-8802, www.schooldata.com; *The K-12 Technology Review 2005.*

National Center for Education Statistics (NCES), 1990 K Street, NW, Washington, DC 20006, (202) 502-7300, http://nces.ed.gov; *Digest of Education Statistics 2007.*

National Education Association (NEA), 1201 Sixteenth Street, NW, Washington, DC 20036-3290, (202) 833-4000, Fax: (202) 822-7974, www.nea.org; *Status of the American Public School Teacher, 2000-2001.*

Quality Education Data (QED), 1050 17th Street, Suite 1100, Denver, Colorado 80265, (800) 525-5811, Fax: (303) 209-9444, www.qeddata.com; *Market Overview: State Counts.*

COMPUTERS AND ELECTRONIC EQUIPMENT, MANUFACTURING

U.S. Census Bureau, Company Statistics Division, 4700 Silver Hill Road, Washington DC 20233-0001, (301) 763-3030, www.census.gov/csd/; *County Business Patterns 2004.*

COMPUTERS AND ELECTRONIC EQUIPMENT, MANUFACTURING - EARNINGS

U.S. Bureau of Labor Statistics (BLS), Postal Square Building, 2 Massachusetts Avenue, NE, Washington, DC 20212-0001, (202) 691-5200, Fax: (202) 691-6325, www.bls.gov; *Employment and Earnings (EE).*

U.S. Census Bureau, Manufacturing and Construction Division, 4600 Silver Hill Road, Washington DC 20233, (301) 763-4673, www.census.gov/mcd; *Annual Survey of Manufactures (ASM)* and *Census of Manufactures.*

U.S. Department of Commerce (DOC), Economics and Statistics Administration (ESA), 1401 Constitution Avenue, NW, Washington, DC 20230, (800) 782-8872, www.esa.doc.gov; *The Digital Economy 2003.*

COMPUTERS AND ELECTRONIC EQUIPMENT, MANUFACTURING - ELECTRONIC COMMERCE

U.S. Census Bureau, 4700 Silver Hill Road, Washington DC 20233-0001, (301) 763-3030, www.census.gov; *E-Stats - Measuring the Electronic Economy.*

COMPUTERS AND ELECTRONIC EQUIPMENT, MANUFACTURING - EMPLOYEES

U.S. Bureau of Labor Statistics (BLS), Postal Square Building, 2 Massachusetts Avenue, NE, Washington, DC 20212-0001, (202) 691-5200, Fax: (202) 691-6325, www.bls.gov; *Current Employment Statistics Survey (CES); Employment and Earnings (EE);* and *Monthly Labor Review (MLR).*

U.S. Census Bureau, Manufacturing and Construction Division, 4600 Silver Hill Road, Washington DC 20233, (301) 763-4673, www.census.gov/mcd; *Annual Survey of Manufactures (ASM)* and *Census of Manufactures.*

U.S. Department of Commerce (DOC), Economics and Statistics Administration (ESA), 1401 Constitution Avenue, NW, Washington, DC 20230, (800) 782-8872, www.esa.doc.gov; *The Digital Economy 2003.*

COMPUTERS AND ELECTRONIC EQUIPMENT, MANUFACTURING - GROSS DOMESTIC PRODUCT

U.S. Department of Commerce (DOC), Economics and Statistics Administration (ESA), 1401 Constitution Avenue, NW, Washington, DC 20230, (800) 782-8872, www.esa.doc.gov; *The Digital Economy 2003.*

COMPUTERS AND ELECTRONIC EQUIPMENT, MANUFACTURING - INVENTORIES

U.S. Census Bureau, Manufacturing and Construction Division, 4600 Silver Hill Road, Washington DC 20233, (301) 763-4673, www.census.gov/mcd; *Current Industrial Reports* and *Manufacturers Shipments, Inventories and Orders.*

COMPUTERS AND ELECTRONIC EQUIPMENT, MANUFACTURING - MERGERS AND ACQUISITIONS

Thomson Financial, 195 Broadway, New York, NY 10007, (646) 822-2000, www.thomson.com; Thomson Research.

COMPUTERS AND ELECTRONIC EQUIPMENT, MANUFACTURING - MULTINATIONAL COMPANIES

Bureau of Economic Analysis (BEA), U.S. Department of Commerce (DOC), 1441 L Street NW, Washington, DC 20230, (202) 606-9900, www.bea.gov; *Survey of Current Business (SCB).*

COMPUTERS AND ELECTRONIC EQUIPMENT, MANUFACTURING - SALES

Consumer Electronics Association (CEA), 2500 Wilson Boulevard, Arlington, VA 22201-3834, (703) 907-7600, Fax: (703) 907 7675, www.ce.org; *Digital America 2006.*

COMPUTERS AND ELECTRONIC EQUIPMENT, MANUFACTURING - SHIPMENTS

Electronic Industries Alliance (EIA), 2500 Wilson Boulevard, Arlington, VA 22201, (703) 907-7500, www.eia.org; unpublished data.

U.S. Census Bureau, Foreign Trade Division, 4700 Silver Hill Road, Washington DC 20233-0001, (301) 763-3030, www.census.gov/foreign-trade/www/; *U.S. International Trade in Goods and Services.*

U.S. Census Bureau, Manufacturing and Construction Division, 4600 Silver Hill Road, Washington DC 20233, (301) 763-4673, www.census.gov/mcd; *Annual Survey of Manufactures (ASM); Census of Manufactures;* and *Current Industrial Reports, Manufacturing Profiles.*

CONCERTS - SYMPHONY ORCHESTRAS

American Symphony Orchestra League, 33 West 60th Street, 5th Floor, New York, NY 10023-7905, (212) 262-5161, Fax: (212) 262-5198, www.symphony.org; *2005-2006 Orchestra Repertoire Report.*

CONDENSED AND EVAPORATED MILK

Economic Research Service (ERS), U.S. Department of Agriculture (USDA), 1800 M Street, NW, Washington, DC 20036-5831, (202) 694-5050, Fax: (202) 694-5689, www.ers.usda.gov; *Agricultural Outlook* and *Food CPI, Prices, and Expenditures.*

National Agricultural Statistics Service (NASS), U.S. Department of Agriculture (USDA), 1400 Independence Avenue, SW, Washington, DC 20250, (800) 727-9540, Fax: (202) 690-2090, www.nass.usda.gov; *Dairy Products* and *Milk Cows and Milk Production.*

CONDOMINIUMS

U.S. Census Bureau, Manufacturing and Construction Division, 4600 Silver Hill Road, Washington DC 20233, (301) 763-4673, www.census.gov/mcd; *Current Construction Reports.*

CONGO - PRIMARY STATISTICS SOURCES

Centre National de la Statistique et des Etudes Economiques, Immeuble du Plan, Rond point du Centre Culturel Francais (CCF), B.P. 2031 Brazzaville, Congo, www.cnsee.org; *Annuaire Statistique du Congo 2004* (Statistical Yearbook of Congo 2004).

CONGO - ALUMINUM PRODUCTION

See CONGO, REPUBLIC OF THE - MINERAL INDUSTRIES

CONGO - BARLEY PRODUCTION

See CONGO, REPUBLIC OF THE - CROPS

CONGO - CATTLE

See CONGO, REPUBLIC OF THE - LIVESTOCK

CONGO - CHICKENS

See CONGO, REPUBLIC OF THE - LIVESTOCK

CONGO - COAL PRODUCTION

See CONGO, REPUBLIC OF THE - MINERAL INDUSTRIES

CONGO - COCOA PRODUCTION

See CONGO, REPUBLIC OF THE - CROPS

CONGO - COFFEE

See CONGO, REPUBLIC OF THE - CROPS

CONGO - COPPER INDUSTRY AND TRADE

See CONGO, REPUBLIC OF THE - MINERAL INDUSTRIES

CONGO - CORN INDUSTRY

See CONGO, REPUBLIC OF THE - CROPS

CONGO - COTTON

See CONGO, REPUBLIC OF THE - CROPS

CONGO - DEATH RATES

See CONGO, REPUBLIC OF THE - MORTALITY

CONGO - DEFENSE EXPENDITURES

See CONGO, REPUBLIC OF THE - ARMED FORCES

CONGO - DIAMONDS

See CONGO, REPUBLIC OF THE - MINERAL INDUSTRIES

CONGO - FETAL MORTALITY

See CONGO, REPUBLIC OF THE - MORTALITY

CONGO - GAS PRODUCTION

See CONGO, REPUBLIC OF THE - MINERAL INDUSTRIES

CONGO - GOLD PRODUCTION

See CONGO, REPUBLIC OF THE - MINERAL INDUSTRIES

CONGO - INCOME TAXES

See CONGO, REPUBLIC OF THE - TAXATION

CONGO - INFANT AND MATERNAL MORTALITY

See CONGO, REPUBLIC OF THE - MORTALITY

CONGO - IRON AND IRON ORE PRODUCTION

See CONGO, REPUBLIC OF THE - MINERAL INDUSTRIES

CONGO - MEAT PRODUCTION

See CONGO, REPUBLIC OF THE - LIVESTOCK

CONGO - MILK PRODUCTION

See CONGO, REPUBLIC OF THE - DAIRY PROCESSING

CONGO - MONEY EXCHANGE RATES

See CONGO, REPUBLIC OF THE - FOREIGN EXCHANGE RATES

CONGO - NATURAL GAS PRODUCTION

See CONGO, REPUBLIC OF THE - MINERAL INDUSTRIES

CONGO - PALM OIL PRODUCTION

See CONGO, REPUBLIC OF THE - CROPS

CONGO - PAPER

See CONGO, REPUBLIC OF THE - FORESTS AND FORESTRY

CONGO - PEANUT PRODUCTION

See CONGO, REPUBLIC OF THE - CROPS

CONGO - RICE PRODUCTION

See CONGO, REPUBLIC OF THE - CROPS

CONGO - SHEEP

See CONGO, REPUBLIC OF THE - LIVESTOCK

CONGO - SILVER PRODUCTION

See CONGO, REPUBLIC OF THE - MINERAL INDUSTRIES

CONGO - STEEL PRODUCTION

See CONGO, REPUBLIC OF THE - MINERAL INDUSTRIES

CONGO - SUGAR PRODUCTION

See CONGO, REPUBLIC OF THE - CROPS

CONGO - TIN PRODUCTION

See CONGO, REPUBLIC OF THE - MINERAL INDUSTRIES

CONGO - TRADE

See CONGO, REPUBLIC OF THE - INTERNATIONAL TRADE

CONGO - WEATHER

See CONGO, REPUBLIC OF THE - CLIMATE

CONGO - WHEAT PRODUCTION

See CONGO, REPUBLIC OF THE - CROPS

CONGO - WINE PRODUCTION

See CONGO, REPUBLIC OF THE - BEVERAGE INDUSTRY

CONGO - WOOD AND WOOD PULP

See CONGO, REPUBLIC OF THE - FORESTS AND FORESTRY

CONGO - WOOL PRODUCTION

See CONGO, REPUBLIC OF THE - TEXTILE INDUSTRY

CONGO - ZINC AND ZINC ORE

See CONGO, REPUBLIC OF THE - MINERAL INDUSTRIES

CONGO, DEMOCRATIC REPUBLIC OF THE - NATIONAL STATISTICAL OFFICE

Centre National de la Statistique et des Etudes Economiques, Immeuble du Plan, Rond point du Centre Culturel Francais (CCF), B.P. 2031 Brazzaville, Congo, www.cnsee.org; National Data Center.

CONGO, DEMOCRATIC REPUBLIC OF THE - AGRICULTURAL MACHINERY

United Nations Statistics Division, New York, NY 10017, (800) 253-9646, Fax: (212) 963-4116, http://unstats.un.org; *Statistical Yearbook.*

CONGO, DEMOCRATIC REPUBLIC OF THE - AGRICULTURE

Economist Intelligence Unit, 111 West 57th Street, New York, NY 10019, (212) 554-0600, Fax: (212) 586-1181, www.eiu.com; *Congo (Democratic Republic) Country Report.*

Euromonitor International, Inc., 224 S. Michigan Avenue, Suite 1500, Chicago, IL 60604, (312) 922-1115, Fax: (312) 922-1157, www.euromonitor.com; *International Marketing Data and Statistics 2008.*

M.E. Sharpe, 80 Business Park Drive, Armonk, NY 10504, (800) 541-6563, Fax: (914) 273-2106, www.mesharpe.com; *The Illustrated Book of World Rankings.*

Palgrave Macmillan Ltd., Houndmills, Basingstoke, Hampshire, RG21 6XS, England, (Telephone in U.S. (888) 330-8477), (Fax in U.S. (800) 672-2054), www.palgrave.com; *The Statesman's Yearbook 2008.*

Taylor and Francis Group, An Informa Business, 2 Park Square, Milton Park, Abingdon, Oxford OX14 4RN, United Kingdom, (Dial from U.S. (212) 216-7800), (Fax from U.S. (212) 564-7854), www.tandf.co.uk; *The Europa World Year Book.*

United Nations Conference on Trade and Development (UNCTAD), DC2-1120, United Nations, New York, NY 10017, (212) 963-0027, www.unctad.org; *UNCTAD Commodity Yearbook.*

United Nations Economic Commission for Africa (ECA), PO Box 3001, Addis Ababa, Ethiopia, (Telephone in U.S. (212) 963-4957), www.uneca.org; *African Statistical Yearbook 2006.*

United Nations Food and Agricultural Organization (FAO), Viale delle Terme di Caracalla, 00100 Rome, Italy, (Dial from U.S. (202) 653-2400), (Fax from U.S. (202) 653 5760), www.fao.org; AQUASTAT; *FAO Production Yearbook 2002; FAO Trade Yearbook;* and *The State of Food and Agriculture (SOFA) 2006.*

United Nations Statistics Division, New York, NY 10017, (800) 253-9646, Fax: (212) 963-4116, http://unstats.un.org; *Statistical Yearbook* and *Survey of Economic and Social Conditions in Africa 2005.*

The World Bank, 1818 H Street, NW, Washington, DC 20433, (202) 473-1000, Fax: (202) 477-6391, www.worldbank.org; *Africa Live Database (LDB); African Development Indicators (ADI) 2007; Congo, The Democratic Republic of the;* and *World Development Indicators (WDI) 2008.*

CONGO, DEMOCRATIC REPUBLIC OF THE - AIRLINES

M.E. Sharpe, 80 Business Park Drive, Armonk, NY 10504, (800) 541-6563, Fax: (914) 273-2106, www.mesharpe.com; *The Illustrated Book of World Rankings.*

Palgrave Macmillan Ltd., Houndmills, Basingstoke, Hampshire, RG21 6XS, England, (Telephone in U.S. (888) 330-8477), (Fax in U.S. (800) 672-2054), www.palgrave.com; *The Statesman's Yearbook 2008.*

Taylor and Francis Group, An Informa Business, 2 Park Square, Milton Park, Abingdon, Oxford OX14 4RN, United Kingdom, (Dial from U.S. (212) 216-7800), (Fax from U.S. (212) 564-7854), www.tandf.co.uk; *The Europa World Year Book.*

United Nations Economic Commission for Africa (ECA), PO Box 3001, Addis Ababa, Ethiopia, (Telephone in U.S. (212) 963-4957), www.uneca.org; *African Statistical Yearbook 2006.*

United Nations Statistics Division, New York, NY 10017, (800) 253-9646, Fax: (212) 963-4116, http://unstats.un.org; *Statistical Yearbook.*

CONGO, DEMOCRATIC REPUBLIC OF THE - AIRPORTS

Central Intelligence Agency, Office of Public Affairs, Washington, DC 20505, (703) 482-0623, Fax: (703) 482-1739, www.cia.gov; *The World Factbook.*

CONGO, DEMOCRATIC REPUBLIC OF THE - ARMED FORCES

Central Intelligence Agency, Office of Public Affairs, Washington, DC 20505, (703) 482-0623, Fax: (703) 482-1739, www.cia.gov; *The World Factbook.*

International Institute for Strategic Studies (IISS), Arundel House, 13-15 Arundel Street, Temple Place, London WC2R 3DX, England, www.iiss.org; *The Military Balance 2007.*

Palgrave Macmillan Ltd., Houndmills, Basingstoke, Hampshire, RG21 6XS, England, (Telephone in U.S. (888) 330-8477), (Fax in U.S. (800) 672-2054), www.palgrave.com; *The Statesman's Yearbook 2008.*

U.S. Department of State (DOS), 2201 C Street NW, Washington, DC 20520, (202) 647-4000, www.state.gov; *World Military Expenditures and Arms Transfers (WMEAT).*

United Nations Statistics Division, New York, NY 10017, (800) 253-9646, Fax: (212) 963-4116, http://unstats.un.org; *Human Development Report 2006.*

CONGO, DEMOCRATIC REPUBLIC OF THE - AUTOMOBILE INDUSTRY AND TRADE

Taylor and Francis Group, An Informa Business, 2 Park Square, Milton Park, Abingdon, Oxford OX14 4RN, United Kingdom, (Dial from U.S. (212) 216-7800), (Fax from U.S. (212) 564-7854), www.tandf.co.uk; *The Europa World Year Book.*

United Nations Statistics Division, New York, NY 10017, (800) 253-9646, Fax: (212) 963-4116, http://unstats.un.org; *Statistical Yearbook.*

CONGO, DEMOCRATIC REPUBLIC OF THE - BALANCE OF PAYMENTS

African Development Bank Group, Rue Joseph Anoma, 01 BP 1387 Abidjan 01, Cote d'Ivoire, www.afdb.org; *Statistics Pocketbook 2008.*

International Monetary Fund (IMF), 700 Nineteenth Street, NW, Washington, DC 20431, (202) 623-7000, Fax: (202) 623-4661, www.imf.org; *Balance of Payments Statistics Newsletter; Balance of Payments Statistics Yearbook 2007;* and *International Financial Statistics Yearbook 2007.*

Palgrave Macmillan Ltd., Houndmills, Basingstoke, Hampshire, RG21 6XS, England, (Telephone in U.S. (888) 330-8477), (Fax in U.S. (800) 672-2054), www.palgrave.com; *The Statesman's Yearbook 2008.*

Taylor and Francis Group, An Informa Business, 2 Park Square, Milton Park, Abingdon, Oxford OX14 4RN, United Kingdom, (Dial from U.S. (212) 216-7800), (Fax from U.S. (212) 564-7854), www.tandf.co.uk; *The Europa World Year Book.*

United Nations Conference on Trade and Development (UNCTAD), DC2-1120, United Nations, New York, NY 10017, (212) 963-0027, www.unctad.org; *Handbook of Statistics 2005.*

United Nations Economic Commission for Africa (ECA), PO Box 3001, Addis Ababa, Ethiopia, (Telephone in U.S. (212) 963-4957), www.uneca.org; *African Statistical Yearbook 2006.*

The World Bank, 1818 H Street, NW, Washington, DC 20433, (202) 473-1000, Fax: (202) 477-6391, www.worldbank.org; *Congo, The Democratic Republic of the* and *World Development Indicators (WDI) 2008.*

CONGO, DEMOCRATIC REPUBLIC OF THE - BANKS AND BANKING

International Monetary Fund (IMF), 700 Nineteenth Street, NW, Washington, DC 20431, (202) 623-7000, Fax: (202) 623-4661, www.imf.org; *Government Finance Statistics Yearbook (2008 Edition)* and *International Financial Statistics Yearbook 2007.*

M.E. Sharpe, 80 Business Park Drive, Armonk, NY 10504, (800) 541-6563, Fax: (914) 273-2106, www.mesharpe.com; *The Illustrated Book of World Rankings.*

Taylor and Francis Group, An Informa Business, 2 Park Square, Milton Park, Abingdon, Oxford OX14 4RN, United Kingdom, (Dial from U.S. (212) 216-7800), (Fax from U.S. (212) 564-7854), www.tandf.co.uk; *The Europa World Year Book.*

CONGO, DEMOCRATIC REPUBLIC OF THE - BARLEY PRODUCTION

See CONGO, DEMOCRATIC REPUBLIC OF THE - CROPS

CONGO, DEMOCRATIC REPUBLIC OF THE - BEVERAGE INDUSTRY

M.E. Sharpe, 80 Business Park Drive, Armonk, NY 10504, (800) 541-6563, Fax: (914) 273-2106, www.mesharpe.com; *The Illustrated Book of World Rankings.*

United Nations Statistics Division, New York, NY 10017, (800) 253-9646, Fax: (212) 963-4116, http://unstats.un.org; *Statistical Yearbook.*

CONGO, DEMOCRATIC REPUBLIC OF THE - BONDS

International Monetary Fund (IMF), 700 Nineteenth Street, NW, Washington, DC 20431, (202) 623-7000, Fax: (202) 623-4661, www.imf.org; *Government Finance Statistics Yearbook (2008 Edition).*

CONGO, DEMOCRATIC REPUBLIC OF THE - BROADCASTING

Central Intelligence Agency, Office of Public Affairs, Washington, DC 20505, (703) 482-0623, Fax: (703) 482-1739, www.cia.gov; *The World Factbook.*

M.E. Sharpe, 80 Business Park Drive, Armonk, NY 10504, (800) 541-6563, Fax: (914) 273-2106, www.mesharpe.com; *The Illustrated Book of World Rankings.*

Palgrave Macmillan Ltd., Houndmills, Basingstoke, Hampshire, RG21 6XS, England, (Telephone in U.S. (888) 330-8477), (Fax in U.S. (800) 672-2054), www.palgrave.com; *The Statesman's Yearbook 2008.*

WRTH Publications Limited, PO Box 290, Oxford OX2 7FT, UK, www.wrth.com; *World Radio TV Handbook 2007.*

CONGO, DEMOCRATIC REPUBLIC OF THE - BUDGET

Central Intelligence Agency, Office of Public Affairs, Washington, DC 20505, (703) 482-0623, Fax: (703) 482-1739, www.cia.gov; *The World Factbook.*

CONGO, DEMOCRATIC REPUBLIC OF THE - CATTLE

See CONGO, DEMOCRATIC REPUBLIC OF THE - LIVESTOCK

CONGO, DEMOCRATIC REPUBLIC OF THE - CHICKENS

See CONGO, DEMOCRATIC REPUBLIC OF THE - LIVESTOCK

CONGO, DEMOCRATIC REPUBLIC OF THE - CHILDBIRTH - STATISTICS

Central Intelligence Agency, Office of Public Affairs, Washington, DC 20505, (703) 482-0623, Fax: (703) 482-1739, www.cia.gov; *The World Factbook.*

Euromonitor International, Inc., 224 S. Michigan Avenue, Suite 1500, Chicago, IL 60604, (312) 922-1115, Fax: (312) 922-1157, www.euromonitor.com; *International Marketing Data and Statistics 2008* and *The World Economic Factbook 2008.*

M.E. Sharpe, 80 Business Park Drive, Armonk, NY 10504, (800) 541-6563, Fax: (914) 273-2106, www.mesharpe.com; *The Illustrated Book of World Rankings.*

Taylor and Francis Group, An Informa Business, 2 Park Square, Milton Park, Abingdon, Oxford OX14 4RN, United Kingdom, (Dial from U.S. (212) 216-7800), (Fax from U.S. (212) 564-7854), www.tandf.co.uk; *The Europa World Year Book.*

United Nations Statistics Division, New York, NY 10017, (800) 253-9646, Fax: (212) 963-4116, http://unstats.un.org; *Demographic Yearbook; Statistical Yearbook;* and *Survey of Economic and Social Conditions in Africa 2005.*

The World Bank, 1818 H Street, NW, Washington, DC 20433, (202) 473-1000, Fax: (202) 477-6391, www.worldbank.org; *World Development Indicators (WDI) 2008.*

CONGO, DEMOCRATIC REPUBLIC OF THE - CLIMATE

International Institute for Environment and Development (IIED), 3 Endsleigh Street, London, England, WC1H 0DD, United Kingdom, www.iied.org; *Environment Urbanization* and *Haramata - Bulletin of the Drylands.*

M.E. Sharpe, 80 Business Park Drive, Armonk, NY 10504, (800) 541-6563, Fax: (914) 273-2106, www.mesharpe.com; *The Illustrated Book of World Rankings.*

Palgrave Macmillan Ltd., Houndmills, Basingstoke, Hampshire, RG21 6XS, England, (Telephone in U.S. (888) 330-8477), (Fax in U.S. (800) 672-2054), www.palgrave.com; *The Statesman's Yearbook 2008.*

CONGO, DEMOCRATIC REPUBLIC OF THE - COAL PRODUCTION

See CONGO, DEMOCRATIC REPUBLIC OF THE - MINERAL INDUSTRIES

CONGO, DEMOCRATIC REPUBLIC OF THE - COCOA PRODUCTION

See CONGO, DEMOCRATIC REPUBLIC OF THE - CROPS

CONGO, DEMOCRATIC REPUBLIC OF THE - COMMERCE

Palgrave Macmillan Ltd., Houndmills, Basingstoke, Hampshire, RG21 6XS, England, (Telephone in U.S.

(888) 330-8477), (Fax in U.S. (800) 672-2054), www.palgrave.com; *The Statesman's Yearbook 2008.*

CONGO, DEMOCRATIC REPUBLIC OF THE - COMMODITY EXCHANGES

Commodity Research Bureau, 330 South Wells Street, Suite 612, Chicago, IL 60606-7110, (800) 621-5271, Fax: (312) 939-4135, www.crbtrader.com; *2006 CRB Commodity Yearbook and CD.*

International Monetary Fund (IMF), 700 Nineteenth Street, NW, Washington, DC 20431, (202) 623-7000, Fax: (202) 623-4661, www.imf.org; *IMF Primary Commodity Prices.*

United Nations Food and Agricultural Organization (FAO), Viale delle Terme di Caracalla, 00100 Rome, Italy, (Dial from U.S. (202) 653-2400), (Fax from U.S. (202) 653 5760), www.fao.org; *The State of Food and Agriculture (SOFA) 2006.*

World Bureau of Metal Statistics (WBMS), 27a High Street, Ware, Hertfordshire, SG12 9BA, United Kingdom, www.world-bureau.com; *Annual Stainless Steel Statistics; World Flow Charts; World Metal Statistics; World Nickel Statistics;* and *World Tin Statistics.*

CONGO, DEMOCRATIC REPUBLIC OF THE - COMMUNICATION AND TRAFFIC

United Nations Statistics Division, New York, NY 10017, (800) 253-9646, Fax: (212) 963-4116, http://unstats.un.org; *Statistical Yearbook.*

CONGO, DEMOCRATIC REPUBLIC OF THE - CONSTRUCTION INDUSTRY

M.E. Sharpe, 80 Business Park Drive, Armonk, NY 10504, (800) 541-6563, Fax: (914) 273-2106, www.mesharpe.com; *The Illustrated Book of World Rankings.*

United Nations Economic Commission for Africa (ECA), PO Box 3001, Addis Ababa, Ethiopia, (Telephone in U.S. (212) 963-4957), www.uneca.org; *African Statistical Yearbook 2006.*

United Nations Statistics Division, New York, NY 10017, (800) 253-9646, Fax: (212) 963-4116, http://unstats.un.org; *Statistical Yearbook.*

CONGO, DEMOCRATIC REPUBLIC OF THE - CONSUMER PRICE INDEXES

Taylor and Francis Group, An Informa Business, 2 Park Square, Milton Park, Abingdon, Oxford OX14 4RN, United Kingdom, (Dial from U.S. (212) 216-7800), (Fax from U.S. (212) 564-7854), www.tandf.co.uk; *The Europa World Year Book.*

United Nations Economic Commission for Africa (ECA), PO Box 3001, Addis Ababa, Ethiopia, (Telephone in U.S. (212) 963-4957), www.uneca.org; *African Statistical Yearbook 2006.*

United Nations Statistics Division, New York, NY 10017, (800) 253-9646, Fax: (212) 963-4116, http://unstats.un.org; *Statistical Yearbook* and *Survey of Economic and Social Conditions in Africa 2005.*

The World Bank, 1818 H Street, NW, Washington, DC 20433, (202) 473-1000, Fax: (202) 477-6391, www.worldbank.org; *Congo, The Democratic Republic of the.*

CONGO, DEMOCRATIC REPUBLIC OF THE - CONSUMPTION (ECONOMICS)

African Development Bank Group, Rue Joseph Anoma, 01 BP 1387 Abidjan 01, Cote d'Ivoire, www.afdb.org; *Statistics Pocketbook 2008.*

International Monetary Fund (IMF), 700 Nineteenth Street, NW, Washington, DC 20431, (202) 623-7000, Fax: (202) 623-4661, www.imf.org; *International Financial Statistics Yearbook 2007.*

United Nations Statistics Division, New York, NY 10017, (800) 253-9646, Fax: (212) 963-4116, http://unstats.un.org; *Survey of Economic and Social Conditions in Africa 2005.*

CONGO, DEMOCRATIC REPUBLIC OF THE - CORN INDUSTRY

See CONGO, DEMOCRATIC REPUBLIC OF THE - CROPS

CONGO, DEMOCRATIC REPUBLIC OF THE - COTTON

See CONGO, DEMOCRATIC REPUBLIC OF THE - CROPS

CONGO, DEMOCRATIC REPUBLIC OF THE - CROPS

International Monetary Fund (IMF), 700 Nineteenth Street, NW, Washington, DC 20431, (202) 623-7000, Fax: (202) 623-4661, www.imf.org; *Government Finance Statistics Yearbook (2008 Edition).*

M.E. Sharpe, 80 Business Park Drive, Armonk, NY 10504, (800) 541-6563, Fax: (914) 273-2106, www.mesharpe.com; *The Illustrated Book of World Rankings.*

Palgrave Macmillan Ltd., Houndmills, Basingstoke, Hampshire, RG21 6XS, England, (Telephone in U.S. (888) 330-8477), (Fax in U.S. (800) 672-2054), www.palgrave.com; *The Statesman's Yearbook 2008.*

Taylor and Francis Group, An Informa Business, 2 Park Square, Milton Park, Abingdon, Oxford OX14 4RN, United Kingdom, (Dial from U.S. (212) 216-7800), (Fax from U.S. (212) 564-7854), www.tandf.co.uk; *The Europa World Year Book.*

United Nations Conference on Trade and Development (UNCTAD), DC2-1120, United Nations, New York, NY 10017, (212) 963-0027, www.unctad.org; *UNCTAD Commodity Yearbook.*

United Nations Economic Commission for Africa (ECA), PO Box 3001, Addis Ababa, Ethiopia, (Telephone in U.S. (212) 963-4957), www.uneca.org; *African Statistical Yearbook 2006.*

United Nations Statistics Division, New York, NY 10017, (800) 253-9646, Fax: (212) 963-4116, http://unstats.un.org; *Statistical Yearbook.*

CONGO, DEMOCRATIC REPUBLIC OF THE - CUSTOMS ADMINISTRATION

International Monetary Fund (IMF), 700 Nineteenth Street, NW, Washington, DC 20431, (202) 623-7000, Fax: (202) 623-4661, www.imf.org; *Government Finance Statistics Yearbook (2008 Edition).*

Palgrave Macmillan Ltd., Houndmills, Basingstoke, Hampshire, RG21 6XS, England, (Telephone in U.S. (888) 330-8477), (Fax in U.S. (800) 672-2054), www.palgrave.com; *The Statesman's Yearbook 2008.*

CONGO, DEMOCRATIC REPUBLIC OF THE - DAIRY PROCESSING

M.E. Sharpe, 80 Business Park Drive, Armonk, NY 10504, (800) 541-6563, Fax: (914) 273-2106, www.mesharpe.com; *The Illustrated Book of World Rankings.*

Palgrave Macmillan Ltd., Houndmills, Basingstoke, Hampshire, RG21 6XS, England, (Telephone in U.S. (888) 330-8477), (Fax in U.S. (800) 672-2054), www.palgrave.com; *The Statesman's Yearbook 2008.*

Taylor and Francis Group, An Informa Business, 2 Park Square, Milton Park, Abingdon, Oxford OX14 4RN, United Kingdom, (Dial from U.S. (212) 216-7800), (Fax from U.S. (212) 564-7854), www.tandf.co.uk; *The Europa World Year Book.*

United Nations Food and Agricultural Organization (FAO), Viale delle Terme di Caracalla, 00100 Rome, Italy, (Dial from U.S. (202) 653-2400), (Fax from U.S. (202) 653 5760), www.fao.org; *The State of Food and Agriculture (SOFA) 2006.*

United Nations Statistics Division, New York, NY 10017, (800) 253-9646, Fax: (212) 963-4116, http://unstats.un.org; *Statistical Yearbook.*

CONGO, DEMOCRATIC REPUBLIC OF THE - DEATH RATES

See CONGO, DEMOCRATIC REPUBLIC OF THE - MORTALITY

CONGO, DEMOCRATIC REPUBLIC OF THE - DEBTS, EXTERNAL

African Development Bank Group, Rue Joseph Anoma, 01 BP 1387 Abidjan 01, Cote d'Ivoire, www.afdb.org; *Statistics Pocketbook 2008.*

International Monetary Fund (IMF), 700 Nineteenth Street, NW, Washington, DC 20431, (202) 623-7000, Fax: (202) 623-4661, www.imf.org; *Government Finance Statistics Yearbook (2008 Edition).*

United Nations Statistics Division, New York, NY 10017, (800) 253-9646, Fax: (212) 963-4116, http://unstats.un.org; *Survey of Economic and Social Conditions in Africa 2005.*

The World Bank, 1818 H Street, NW, Washington, DC 20433, (202) 473-1000, Fax: (202) 477-6391, www.worldbank.org; *Africa Live Database (LDB); African Development Indicators (ADI) 2007; Global Development Finance 2007;* and *World Development Indicators (WDI) 2008.*

CONGO, DEMOCRATIC REPUBLIC OF THE - DEFENSE EXPENDITURES

See CONGO, DEMOCRATIC REPUBLIC OF THE - ARMED FORCES

CONGO, DEMOCRATIC REPUBLIC OF THE - DEMOGRAPHY

Euromonitor International, Inc., 224 S. Michigan Avenue, Suite 1500, Chicago, IL 60604, (312) 922-1115, Fax: (312) 922-1157, www.euromonitor.com; *International Marketing Data and Statistics 2008* and *The World Economic Factbook 2008.*

M.E. Sharpe, 80 Business Park Drive, Armonk, NY 10504, (800) 541-6563, Fax: (914) 273-2106, www.mesharpe.com; *The Illustrated Book of World Rankings.*

United Nations Statistics Division, New York, NY 10017, (800) 253-9646, Fax: (212) 963-4116, http://unstats.un.org; *Human Development Report 2006* and *Survey of Economic and Social Conditions in Africa 2005.*

The World Bank, 1818 H Street, NW, Washington, DC 20433, (202) 473-1000, Fax: (202) 477-6391, www.worldbank.org; *Congo, The Democratic Republic of the.*

CONGO, DEMOCRATIC REPUBLIC OF THE - DIAMONDS

See CONGO, DEMOCRATIC REPUBLIC OF THE - MINERAL INDUSTRIES

CONGO, DEMOCRATIC REPUBLIC OF THE - DISPOSABLE INCOME

African Development Bank Group, Rue Joseph Anoma, 01 BP 1387 Abidjan 01, Cote d'Ivoire, www.afdb.org; *Statistics Pocketbook 2008.*

M.E. Sharpe, 80 Business Park Drive, Armonk, NY 10504, (800) 541-6563, Fax: (914) 273-2106, www.mesharpe.com; *The Illustrated Book of World Rankings.*

United Nations Statistics Division, New York, NY 10017, (800) 253-9646, Fax: (212) 963-4116, http://unstats.un.org; *National Accounts Statistics: Compendium of Income Distribution Statistics* and *Statistical Yearbook.*

CONGO, DEMOCRATIC REPUBLIC OF THE - DIVORCE

M.E. Sharpe, 80 Business Park Drive, Armonk, NY 10504, (800) 541-6563, Fax: (914) 273-2106, www.mesharpe.com; *The Illustrated Book of World Rankings.*

United Nations Statistics Division, New York, NY 10017, (800) 253-9646, Fax: (212) 963-4116, http://unstats.un.org; *Demographic Yearbook.*

CONGO, DEMOCRATIC REPUBLIC OF THE - ECONOMIC ASSISTANCE

United Nations Statistics Division, New York, NY 10017, (800) 253-9646, Fax: (212) 963-4116, http://unstats.un.org; *Statistical Yearbook.*

CONGO, DEMOCRATIC REPUBLIC OF THE - ECONOMIC CONDITIONS

African Development Bank Group, Rue Joseph Anoma, 01 BP 1387 Abidjan 01, Cote d'Ivoire, www.

afdb.org; *The African Statistical Journal; Gender, Poverty and Environmental Indicators on African Countries 2007; Selected Statistics on African Countries 2007;* and *Statistics Pocketbook 2008.*

Center for International Business Education Research (CIBER), Columbia Business School and School of International and Public Affairs, Uris Hall, Room 212, 3022 Broadway, New York, NY 10027-6902, Mr. Joshua Safier, (212) 854-4750, Fax: (212) 222-9821, www.columbia.edu/cu/ciber/; Datastream International.

Central Intelligence Agency, Office of Public Affairs, Washington, DC 20505, (703) 482-0623, Fax: (703) 482-1739, www.cia.gov; *The World Factbook.*

DSI Data Service Information, Xantener Strasse 51a, D-47495 Rheinberg, Germany, www.dsidata.com; *Campus Solution.*

Dun and Bradstreet (DB) Corporation, 103 JFK Parkway, Short Hills, NJ 07078, (973) 921-5500, www.dnb.com; *Country Report.*

Economist Intelligence Unit, 111 West 57th Street, New York, NY 10019, (212) 554-0600, Fax: (212) 586-1181, www.eiu.com; *Business Africa* and *Congo (Democratic Republic) Country Report.*

Euromonitor International, Inc., 224 S. Michigan Avenue, Suite 1500, Chicago, IL 60604, (312) 922-1115, Fax: (312) 922-1157, www.euromonitor.com; *International Marketing Data and Statistics 2008.*

International Monetary Fund (IMF), 700 Nineteenth Street, NW, Washington, DC 20431, (202) 623-7000, Fax: (202) 623-4661, www.imf.org; *World Economic Outlook Reports.*

M.E. Sharpe, 80 Business Park Drive, Armonk, NY 10504, (800) 541-6563, Fax: (914) 273-2106, www.mesharpe.com; *The Illustrated Book of World Rankings.*

Palgrave Macmillan Ltd., Houndmills, Basingstoke, Hampshire, RG21 6XS, England, (Telephone in U.S. (888) 330-8477), (Fax in U.S. (800) 672-2054), www.palgrave.com; *The Statesman's Yearbook 2008.*

Taylor and Francis Group, An Informa Business, 2 Park Square, Milton Park, Abingdon, Oxford OX14 4RN, United Kingdom, (Dial from U.S. (212) 216-7800), (Fax from U.S. (212) 564-7854), www.tandf.co.uk; *The Europa World Year Book.*

United Nations Statistics Division, New York, NY 10017, (800) 253-9646, Fax: (212) 963-4116, http://unstats.un.org; *Compendium of Intra-African and Related Foreign Trade Statistics 2003.*

The World Bank, 1818 H Street, NW, Washington, DC 20433, (202) 473-1000, Fax: (202) 477-6391, www.worldbank.org; *Africa Household Survey Databank; Africa Live Database (LDB); Africa Standardized Files and Indicators; African Development Indicators (ADI) 2007; Congo, The Democratic Republic of the; Global Economic Monitor (GEM); Global Economic Prospects 2008;* and *The World Bank Atlas 2003-2004.*

CONGO, DEMOCRATIC REPUBLIC OF THE - EDUCATION

African Development Bank Group, Rue Joseph Anoma, 01 BP 1387 Abidjan 01, Cote d'Ivoire, www.afdb.org; *Statistics Pocketbook 2008.*

Euromonitor International, Inc., 224 S. Michigan Avenue, Suite 1500, Chicago, IL 60604, (312) 922-1115, Fax: (312) 922-1157, www.euromonitor.com; *International Marketing Data and Statistics 2008.*

M.E. Sharpe, 80 Business Park Drive, Armonk, NY 10504, (800) 541-6563, Fax: (914) 273-2106, www.mesharpe.com; *The Illustrated Book of World Rankings.*

Palgrave Macmillan Ltd., Houndmills, Basingstoke, Hampshire, RG21 6XS, England, (Telephone in U.S. (888) 330-8477), (Fax in U.S. (800) 672-2054), www.palgrave.com; *The Statesman's Yearbook 2008.*

Taylor and Francis Group, An Informa Business, 2 Park Square, Milton Park, Abingdon, Oxford OX14 4RN, United Kingdom, (Dial from U.S. (212) 216-7800), (Fax from U.S. (212) 564-7854), www.tandf.co.uk; *The Europa World Year Book.*

UNESCO Institute for Statistics, C.P. 6128 Succursale Centre-Ville, Montreal, Quebec, H3C 3J7 Canada, (Dial from U.S. (514) 343-6880), (Fax from U.S. (514) 343 6882), www.uis.unesco.org; *Statistical Tables.*

United Nations Economic Commission for Africa (ECA), PO Box 3001, Addis Ababa, Ethiopia, (Telephone in U.S. (212) 963-4957), www.uneca.org; *African Statistical Yearbook 2006.*

United Nations Statistics Division, New York, NY 10017, (800) 253-9646, Fax: (212) 963-4116, http://unstats.un.org; *Human Development Report 2006* and *Survey of Economic and Social Conditions in Africa 2005.*

The World Bank, 1818 H Street, NW, Washington, DC 20433, (202) 473-1000, Fax: (202) 477-6391, www.worldbank.org; *Congo, The Democratic Republic of the* and *World Development Indicators (WDI) 2008.*

CONGO, DEMOCRATIC REPUBLIC OF THE - ELECTRICITY

M.E. Sharpe, 80 Business Park Drive, Armonk, NY 10504, (800) 541-6563, Fax: (914) 273-2106, www.mesharpe.com; *The Illustrated Book of World Rankings.*

Organisation for Economic Cooperation and Development (OECD), 2 rue Andre Pascal, F-75775 Paris Cedex 16, France, (Telephone in U.S. (202) 785-6323), (Fax in U.S. (202) 785-0350), www.oecd.org; *World Energy Outlook 2007.*

Palgrave Macmillan Ltd., Houndmills, Basingstoke, Hampshire, RG21 6XS, England, (Telephone in U.S. (888) 330-8477), (Fax in U.S. (800) 672-2054), www.palgrave.com; *The Statesman's Yearbook 2008.*

U.S. Department of Energy (DOE), Energy Information Administration (EIA), 1000 Independence Avenue, SW, Washington, DC 20585, (202) 586-8800, www.eia.doe.gov; *International Energy Annual 2004* and *International Energy Outlook 2006.*

United Nations Economic Commission for Africa (ECA), PO Box 3001, Addis Ababa, Ethiopia, (Telephone in U.S. (212) 963-4957), www.uneca.org; *African Statistical Yearbook 2006.*

United Nations Statistics Division, New York, NY 10017, (800) 253-9646, Fax: (212) 963-4116, http://unstats.un.org; *Human Development Report 2006; Statistical Yearbook;* and *Survey of Economic and Social Conditions in Africa 2005.*

CONGO, DEMOCRATIC REPUBLIC OF THE - EMPLOYMENT

Euromonitor International, Inc., 224 S. Michigan Avenue, Suite 1500, Chicago, IL 60604, (312) 922-1115, Fax: (312) 922-1157, www.euromonitor.com; *International Marketing Data and Statistics 2008.*

International Labour Office, I.L.O. Publications, 4 route des Morillons, CH-1211 Geneva 22, Switzerland, (Telephone in U.S. (202) 653-7652), (Fax in U.S. (202) 653-7687), www.ilo.org; *Yearbook of Labour Statistics 2006.*

M.E. Sharpe, 80 Business Park Drive, Armonk, NY 10504, (800) 541-6563, Fax: (914) 273-2106, www.mesharpe.com; *The Illustrated Book of World Rankings.*

United Nations Economic Commission for Africa (ECA), PO Box 3001, Addis Ababa, Ethiopia, (Telephone in U.S. (212) 963-4957), www.uneca.org; *African Statistical Yearbook 2006.*

United Nations Statistics Division, New York, NY 10017, (800) 253-9646, Fax: (212) 963-4116, http://unstats.un.org; *Statistical Yearbook* and *Survey of Economic and Social Conditions in Africa 2005.*

The World Bank, 1818 H Street, NW, Washington, DC 20433, (202) 473-1000, Fax: (202) 477-6391, www.worldbank.org; *Congo, The Democratic Republic of the.*

CONGO, DEMOCRATIC REPUBLIC OF THE - ENERGY INDUSTRIES

Enerdata, 10 Rue Royale, 75008 Paris, France, www.enerdata.fr; *Global Energy Market Data.*

United Nations Statistics Division, New York, NY 10017, (800) 253-9646, Fax: (212) 963-4116, http://unstats.un.org; *Statistical Yearbook.*

CONGO, DEMOCRATIC REPUBLIC OF THE - ENVIRONMENTAL CONDITIONS

DSI Data Service Information, Xantener Strasse 51a, D-47495 Rheinberg, Germany, www.dsidata.com; *Campus Solution* and *DSI's Global Environmental Database.*

Economist Intelligence Unit, 111 West 57th Street, New York, NY 10019, (212) 554-0600, Fax: (212) 586-1181, www.eiu.com; *Congo (Democratic Republic) Country Report.*

International Institute for Environment and Development (IIED), 3 Endsleigh Street, London, England, WC1H 0DD, United Kingdom, www.iied.org; *Environment Urbanization* and *Haramata - Bulletin of the Drylands.*

CONGO, DEMOCRATIC REPUBLIC OF THE - EXPORTS

African Development Bank Group, Rue Joseph Anoma, 01 BP 1387 Abidjan 01, Cote d'Ivoire, www.afdb.org; *Statistics Pocketbook 2008.*

Central Intelligence Agency, Office of Public Affairs, Washington, DC 20505, (703) 482-0623, Fax: (703) 482-1739, www.cia.gov; *The World Factbook.*

Economist Intelligence Unit, 111 West 57th Street, New York, NY 10019, (212) 554-0600, Fax: (212) 586-1181, www.eiu.com; *Congo (Democratic Republic) Country Report.*

Euromonitor International, Inc., 224 S. Michigan Avenue, Suite 1500, Chicago, IL 60604, (312) 922-1115, Fax: (312) 922-1157, www.euromonitor.com; *International Marketing Data and Statistics 2008* and *The World Economic Factbook 2008.*

International Monetary Fund (IMF), 700 Nineteenth Street, NW, Washington, DC 20431, (202) 623-7000, Fax: (202) 623-4661, www.imf.org; *Direction of Trade Statistics Yearbook 2007; Government Finance Statistics Yearbook (2008 Edition);* and *International Financial Statistics Yearbook 2007.*

Palgrave Macmillan Ltd., Houndmills, Basingstoke, Hampshire, RG21 6XS, England, (Telephone in U.S. (888) 330-8477), (Fax in U.S. (800) 672-2054), www.palgrave.com; *The Statesman's Yearbook 2008.*

Taylor and Francis Group, An Informa Business, 2 Park Square, Milton Park, Abingdon, Oxford OX14 4RN, United Kingdom, (Dial from U.S. (212) 216-7800), (Fax from U.S. (212) 564-7854), www.tandf.co.uk; *The Europa World Year Book.*

United Nations Conference on Trade and Development (UNCTAD), DC2-1120, United Nations, New York, NY 10017, (212) 963-0027, www.unctad.org; *Handbook of Statistics 2005.*

United Nations Economic Commission for Africa (ECA), PO Box 3001, Addis Ababa, Ethiopia, (Telephone in U.S. (212) 963-4957), www.uneca.org; *African Statistical Yearbook 2006.*

United Nations Food and Agricultural Organization (FAO), Viale delle Terme di Caracalla, 00100 Rome, Italy, (Dial from U.S. (202) 653-2400), (Fax from U.S. (202) 653 5760), www.fao.org; *The State of Food and Agriculture (SOFA) 2006.*

United Nations Statistics Division, New York, NY 10017, (800) 253-9646, Fax: (212) 963-4116, http://unstats.un.org; *Compendium of Intra-African and Related Foreign Trade Statistics 2003* and *Survey of Economic and Social Conditions in Africa 2005.*

The World Bank, 1818 H Street, NW, Washington, DC 20433, (202) 473-1000, Fax: (202) 477-6391, www.worldbank.org; *World Development Indicators (WDI) 2008.*

CONGO, DEMOCRATIC REPUBLIC OF THE - FEMALE WORKING POPULATION

See CONGO, DEMOCRATIC REPUBLIC OF THE - EMPLOYMENT

CONGO, DEMOCRATIC REPUBLIC OF THE - FERTILITY, HUMAN

Central Intelligence Agency, Office of Public Affairs, Washington, DC 20505, (703) 482-0623, Fax: (703) 482-1739, www.cia.gov; *The World Factbook.*

M.E. Sharpe, 80 Business Park Drive, Armonk, NY 10504, (800) 541-6563, Fax: (914) 273-2106, www.mesharpe.com; *The Illustrated Book of World Rankings.*

United Nations Statistics Division, New York, NY 10017, (800) 253-9646, Fax: (212) 963-4116, http://unstats.un.org; *Human Development Report 2006* and *Survey of Economic and Social Conditions in Africa 2005.*

The World Bank, 1818 H Street, NW, Washington, DC 20433, (202) 473-1000, Fax: (202) 477-6391, www.worldbank.org; *The World Bank Atlas 2003-2004* and *World Development Indicators (WDI) 2008.*

CONGO, DEMOCRATIC REPUBLIC OF THE - FERTILIZER INDUSTRY

United Nations Food and Agricultural Organization (FAO), Viale delle Terme di Caracalla, 00100 Rome, Italy, (Dial from U.S. (202) 653-2400), (Fax from U.S. (202) 653 5760), www.fao.org; *The State of Food and Agriculture (SOFA) 2006.*

United Nations Statistics Division, New York, NY 10017, (800) 253-9646, Fax: (212) 963-4116, http://unstats.un.org; *Statistical Yearbook.*

CONGO, DEMOCRATIC REPUBLIC OF THE - FETAL MORTALITY

See CONGO, DEMOCRATIC REPUBLIC OF THE - MORTALITY

CONGO, DEMOCRATIC REPUBLIC OF THE - FINANCE

International Monetary Fund (IMF), 700 Nineteenth Street, NW, Washington, DC 20431, (202) 623-7000, Fax: (202) 623-4661, www.imf.org; *International Financial Statistics Yearbook 2007.*

Taylor and Francis Group, An Informa Business, 2 Park Square, Milton Park, Abingdon, Oxford OX14 4RN, United Kingdom, (Dial from U.S. (212) 216-7800), (Fax from U.S. (212) 564-7854), www.tandf.co.uk; *The Europa World Year Book.*

United Nations Economic Commission for Africa (ECA), PO Box 3001, Addis Ababa, Ethiopia, (Telephone in U.S. (212) 963-4957), www.uneca.org; *African Statistical Yearbook 2006.*

United Nations Statistics Division, New York, NY 10017, (800) 253-9646, Fax: (212) 963-4116, http://unstats.un.org; *National Accounts Statistics: Compendium of Income Distribution Statistics* and *Statistical Yearbook.*

The World Bank, 1818 H Street, NW, Washington, DC 20433, (202) 473-1000, Fax: (202) 477-6391, www.worldbank.org; *Congo, The Democratic Republic of the.*

CONGO, DEMOCRATIC REPUBLIC OF THE - FINANCE, PUBLIC

African Development Bank Group, Rue Joseph Anoma, 01 BP 1387 Abidjan 01, Cote d'Ivoire, www.afdb.org; *Statistics Pocketbook 2008.*

Bernan Essential Government Publications, 4611-F Assembly Drive, Lanham MD, 20706-4391, (301) 459-2255, Fax: (800) 865-3450, www.bernan.com; *National Accounts Statistics.*

Economist Intelligence Unit, 111 West 57th Street, New York, NY 10019, (212) 554-0600, Fax: (212) 586-1181, www.eiu.com; *Congo (Democratic Republic) Country Report.*

International Monetary Fund (IMF), 700 Nineteenth Street, NW, Washington, DC 20431, (202) 623-7000, Fax: (202) 623-4661, www.imf.org; *Government Finance Statistics Yearbook (2008 Edition); International Financial Statistics; International Financial Statistics Online Service;* and *International Financial Statistics Yearbook 2007.*

M.E. Sharpe, 80 Business Park Drive, Armonk, NY 10504, (800) 541-6563, Fax: (914) 273-2106, www.mesharpe.com; *The Illustrated Book of World Rankings.*

Palgrave Macmillan Ltd., Houndmills, Basingstoke, Hampshire, RG21 6XS, England, (Telephone in U.S. (888) 330-8477), (Fax in U.S. (800) 672-2054), www.palgrave.com; *The Statesman's Yearbook 2008.*

Taylor and Francis Group, An Informa Business, 2 Park Square, Milton Park, Abingdon, Oxford OX14 4RN, United Kingdom, (Dial from U.S. (212) 216-7800), (Fax from U.S. (212) 564-7854), www.tandf.co.uk; *The Europa World Year Book.*

United Nations Economic Commission for Africa (ECA), PO Box 3001, Addis Ababa, Ethiopia, (Telephone in U.S. (212) 963-4957), www.uneca.org; *African Statistical Yearbook 2006.*

The World Bank, 1818 H Street, NW, Washington, DC 20433, (202) 473-1000, Fax: (202) 477-6391, www.worldbank.org; *Congo, The Democratic Republic of the.*

CONGO, DEMOCRATIC REPUBLIC OF THE - FISHERIES

M.E. Sharpe, 80 Business Park Drive, Armonk, NY 10504, (800) 541-6563, Fax: (914) 273-2106, www.mesharpe.com; *The Illustrated Book of World Rankings.*

Palgrave Macmillan Ltd., Houndmills, Basingstoke, Hampshire, RG21 6XS, England, (Telephone in U.S. (888) 330-8477), (Fax in U.S. (800) 672-2054), www.palgrave.com; *The Statesman's Yearbook 2008.*

Taylor and Francis Group, An Informa Business, 2 Park Square, Milton Park, Abingdon, Oxford OX14 4RN, United Kingdom, (Dial from U.S. (212) 216-7800), (Fax from U.S. (212) 564-7854), www.tandf.co.uk; *The Europa World Year Book.*

United Nations Conference on Trade and Development (UNCTAD), DC2-1120, United Nations, New York, NY 10017, (212) 963-0027, www.unctad.org; *UNCTAD Commodity Yearbook.*

United Nations Economic Commission for Africa (ECA), PO Box 3001, Addis Ababa, Ethiopia, (Telephone in U.S. (212) 963-4957), www.uneca.org; *African Statistical Yearbook 2006.*

United Nations Food and Agricultural Organization (FAO), Viale delle Terme di Caracalla, 00100 Rome, Italy, (Dial from U.S. (202) 653-2400), (Fax from U.S. (202) 653 5760), www.fao.org; *FAO Yearbook of Fishery Statistics;* Fishery Databases; FISHSTAT Database. Subjects covered include: Aquaculture production, capture production, fishery commodities; and *The State of Food and Agriculture (SOFA) 2006.*

United Nations Statistics Division, New York, NY 10017, (800) 253-9646, Fax: (212) 963-4116, http://unstats.un.org; *Statistical Yearbook* and *Survey of Economic and Social Conditions in Africa 2005.*

The World Bank, 1818 H Street, NW, Washington, DC 20433, (202) 473-1000, Fax: (202) 477-6391, www.worldbank.org; *Congo, The Democratic Republic of the.*

CONGO, DEMOCRATIC REPUBLIC OF THE - FOOD

African Development Bank Group, Rue Joseph Anoma, 01 BP 1387 Abidjan 01, Cote d'Ivoire, www.afdb.org; *Statistics Pocketbook 2008.*

United Nations Conference on Trade and Development (UNCTAD), DC2-1120, United Nations, New York, NY 10017, (212) 963-0027, www.unctad.org; *UNCTAD Commodity Yearbook.*

United Nations Food and Agricultural Organization (FAO), Viale delle Terme di Caracalla, 00100 Rome, Italy, (Dial from U.S. (202) 653-2400), (Fax from U.S. (202) 653 5760), www.fao.org; *The State of Food and Agriculture (SOFA) 2006.*

United Nations Statistics Division, New York, NY 10017, (800) 253-9646, Fax: (212) 963-4116, http://unstats.un.org; *Human Development Report 2006.*

CONGO, DEMOCRATIC REPUBLIC OF THE - FOREIGN EXCHANGE RATES

African Development Bank Group, Rue Joseph Anoma, 01 BP 1387 Abidjan 01, Cote d'Ivoire, www.afdb.org; *Statistics Pocketbook 2008.*

Central Intelligence Agency, Office of Public Affairs, Washington, DC 20505, (703) 482-0623, Fax: (703) 482-1739, www.cia.gov; *The World Factbook.*

Euromonitor International, Inc., 224 S. Michigan Avenue, Suite 1500, Chicago, IL 60604, (312) 922-1115, Fax: (312) 922-1157, www.euromonitor.com; *International Marketing Data and Statistics 2008* and *The World Economic Factbook 2008.*

International Monetary Fund (IMF), 700 Nineteenth Street, NW, Washington, DC 20431, (202) 623-7000, Fax: (202) 623-4661, www.imf.org; *International Financial Statistics Yearbook 2007.*

Taylor and Francis Group, An Informa Business, 2 Park Square, Milton Park, Abingdon, Oxford OX14 4RN, United Kingdom, (Dial from U.S. (212) 216-7800), (Fax from U.S. (212) 564-7854), www.tandf.co.uk; *The Europa World Year Book.*

United Nations Statistics Division, New York, NY 10017, (800) 253-9646, Fax: (212) 963-4116, http://unstats.un.org; *Compendium of Intra-African and Related Foreign Trade Statistics 2003* and *Statistical Yearbook.*

CONGO, DEMOCRATIC REPUBLIC OF THE - FORESTS AND FORESTRY

M.E. Sharpe, 80 Business Park Drive, Armonk, NY 10504, (800) 541-6563, Fax: (914) 273-2106, www.mesharpe.com; *The Illustrated Book of World Rankings.*

Palgrave Macmillan Ltd., Houndmills, Basingstoke, Hampshire, RG21 6XS, England, (Telephone in U.S. (888) 330-8477), (Fax in U.S. (800) 672-2054), www.palgrave.com; *The Statesman's Yearbook 2008.*

Taylor and Francis Group, An Informa Business, 2 Park Square, Milton Park, Abingdon, Oxford OX14 4RN, United Kingdom, (Dial from U.S. (212) 216-7800), (Fax from U.S. (212) 564-7854), www.tandf.co.uk; *The Europa World Year Book.*

UNESCO Institute for Statistics, C.P. 6128 Succursale Centre-Ville, Montreal, Quebec, H3C 3J7 Canada, (Dial from U.S. (514) 343-6880), (Fax from U.S. (514) 343 6882), www.uis.unesco.org; *Statistical Tables.*

United Nations Conference on Trade and Development (UNCTAD), DC2-1120, United Nations, New York, NY 10017, (212) 963-0027, www.unctad.org; *UNCTAD Commodity Yearbook.*

United Nations Economic Commission for Africa (ECA), PO Box 3001, Addis Ababa, Ethiopia, (Telephone in U.S. (212) 963-4957), www.uneca.org; *African Statistical Yearbook 2006.*

United Nations Food and Agricultural Organization (FAO), Viale delle Terme di Caracalla, 00100 Rome, Italy, (Dial from U.S. (202) 653-2400), (Fax from U.S. (202) 653 5760), www.fao.org; *FAO Yearbook of Forest Products* and *The State of Food and Agriculture (SOFA) 2006.*

United Nations Statistics Division, New York, NY 10017, (800) 253-9646, Fax: (212) 963-4116, http://unstats.un.org; *Statistical Yearbook.*

The World Bank, 1818 H Street, NW, Washington, DC 20433, (202) 473-1000, Fax: (202) 477-6391, www.worldbank.org; *Congo, The Democratic Republic of the.*

CONGO, DEMOCRATIC REPUBLIC OF THE - GAS PRODUCTION

See CONGO, DEMOCRATIC REPUBLIC OF THE - MINERAL INDUSTRIES

CONGO, DEMOCRATIC REPUBLIC OF THE - GEOGRAPHIC INFORMATION SYSTEMS

M.E. Sharpe, 80 Business Park Drive, Armonk, NY 10504, (800) 541-6563, Fax: (914) 273-2106, www.mesharpe.com; *The Illustrated Book of World Rankings.*

CONGO, DEMOCRATIC REPUBLIC OF THE - GOLD INDUSTRY

International Monetary Fund (IMF), 700 Nineteenth Street, NW, Washington, DC 20431, (202) 623-7000, Fax: (202) 623-4661, www.imf.org; *International Financial Statistics Yearbook 2007.*

United Nations Statistics Division, New York, NY 10017, (800) 253-9646, Fax: (212) 963-4116, http://unstats.un.org; *Statistical Yearbook.*

The World Bank, 1818 H Street, NW, Washington, DC 20433, (202) 473-1000, Fax: (202) 477-6391, www.worldbank.org; *World Development Indicators (WDI) 2008.*

CONGO, DEMOCRATIC REPUBLIC OF THE - GOLD PRODUCTION

See CONGO, DEMOCRATIC REPUBLIC OF THE - MINERAL INDUSTRIES

CONGO, DEMOCRATIC REPUBLIC OF THE - GRANTS-IN-AID

International Monetary Fund (IMF), 700 Nineteenth Street, NW, Washington, DC 20431, (202) 623-7000, Fax: (202) 623-4661, www.imf.org; *Government Finance Statistics Yearbook (2008 Edition).*

CONGO, DEMOCRATIC REPUBLIC OF THE - GROSS DOMESTIC PRODUCT

African Development Bank Group, Rue Joseph Anoma, 01 BP 1387 Abidjan 01, Cote d'Ivoire, www.afdb.org; *Statistics Pocketbook 2008.*

Economist Intelligence Unit, 111 West 57th Street, New York, NY 10019, (212) 554-0600, Fax: (212) 586-1181, www.eiu.com; *Congo (Democratic Republic) Country Report.*

Euromonitor International, Inc., 224 S. Michigan Avenue, Suite 1500, Chicago, IL 60604, (312) 922-1115, Fax: (312) 922-1157, www.euromonitor.com; *International Marketing Data and Statistics 2008* and *The World Economic Factbook 2008.*

International Monetary Fund (IMF), 700 Nineteenth Street, NW, Washington, DC 20431, (202) 623-7000, Fax: (202) 623-4661, www.imf.org; *International Financial Statistics Yearbook 2007.*

M.E. Sharpe, 80 Business Park Drive, Armonk, NY 10504, (800) 541-6563, Fax: (914) 273-2106, www.mesharpe.com; *The Illustrated Book of World Rankings.*

Taylor and Francis Group, An Informa Business, 2 Park Square, Milton Park, Abingdon, Oxford OX14 4RN, United Kingdom, (Dial from U.S. (212) 216-7800), (Fax from U.S. (212) 564-7854), www.tandf.co.uk; *The Europa World Year Book.*

United Nations Economic Commission for Africa (ECA), PO Box 3001, Addis Ababa, Ethiopia, (Telephone in U.S. (212) 963-4957), www.uneca.org; *African Statistical Yearbook 2006.*

United Nations Statistics Division, New York, NY 10017, (800) 253-9646, Fax: (212) 963-4116, http://unstats.un.org; *Human Development Report 2006; National Accounts Statistics: Compendium of Income Distribution Statistics; Statistical Yearbook;* and *Survey of Economic and Social Conditions in Africa 2005.*

The World Bank, 1818 H Street, NW, Washington, DC 20433, (202) 473-1000, Fax: (202) 477-6391, www.worldbank.org; *World Development Indicators (WDI) 2008.*

CONGO, DEMOCRATIC REPUBLIC OF THE - GROSS NATIONAL PRODUCT

Euromonitor International, Inc., 224 S. Michigan Avenue, Suite 1500, Chicago, IL 60604, (312) 922-1115, Fax: (312) 922-1157, www.euromonitor.com; *International Marketing Data and Statistics 2008.*

M.E. Sharpe, 80 Business Park Drive, Armonk, NY 10504, (800) 541-6563, Fax: (914) 273-2106, www.mesharpe.com; *The Illustrated Book of World Rankings.*

Palgrave Macmillan Ltd., Houndmills, Basingstoke, Hampshire, RG21 6XS, England, (Telephone in U.S. (888) 330-8477), (Fax in U.S. (800) 672-2054), www.palgrave.com; *The Statesman's Yearbook 2008.*

U.S. Department of State (DOS), 2201 C Street NW, Washington, DC 20520, (202) 647-4000, www.state.gov; *World Military Expenditures and Arms Transfers (WMEAT).*

United Nations Statistics Division, New York, NY 10017, (800) 253-9646, Fax: (212) 963-4116, http://unstats.un.org; *Statistical Yearbook.*

The World Bank, 1818 H Street, NW, Washington, DC 20433, (202) 473-1000, Fax: (202) 477-6391, www.worldbank.org; *The World Bank Atlas 2003-2004* and *World Development Indicators (WDI) 2008.*

CONGO, DEMOCRATIC REPUBLIC OF THE - HOUSING

M.E. Sharpe, 80 Business Park Drive, Armonk, NY 10504, (800) 541-6563, Fax: (914) 273-2106, www.mesharpe.com; *The Illustrated Book of World Rankings.*

CONGO, DEMOCRATIC REPUBLIC OF THE - ILLITERATE PERSONS

Euromonitor International, Inc., 224 S. Michigan Avenue, Suite 1500, Chicago, IL 60604, (312) 922-1115, Fax: (312) 922-1157, www.euromonitor.com; *The World Economic Factbook 2008.*

Palgrave Macmillan Ltd., Houndmills, Basingstoke, Hampshire, RG21 6XS, England, (Telephone in U.S. (888) 330-8477), (Fax in U.S. (800) 672-2054), www.palgrave.com; *The Statesman's Yearbook 2008.*

UNESCO Institute for Statistics, C.P. 6128 Succursale Centre-Ville, Montreal, Quebec, H3C 3J7 Canada, (Dial from U.S. (514) 343-6880), (Fax from U.S. (514) 343 6882), www.uis.unesco.org; *Statistical Tables.*

United Nations Statistics Division, New York, NY 10017, (800) 253-9646, Fax: (212) 963-4116, http://unstats.un.org; *Human Development Report 2006.*

CONGO, DEMOCRATIC REPUBLIC OF THE - IMPORTS

Central Intelligence Agency, Office of Public Affairs, Washington, DC 20505, (703) 482-0623, Fax: (703) 482-1739, www.cia.gov; *The World Factbook.*

Economist Intelligence Unit, 111 West 57th Street, New York, NY 10019, (212) 554-0600, Fax: (212) 586-1181, www.eiu.com; *Congo (Democratic Republic) Country Report.*

Euromonitor International, Inc., 224 S. Michigan Avenue, Suite 1500, Chicago, IL 60604, (312) 922-1115, Fax: (312) 922-1157, www.euromonitor.com; *International Marketing Data and Statistics 2008; The World Economic Factbook 2008;* and *World Marketing Data and Statistics.*

International Monetary Fund (IMF), 700 Nineteenth Street, NW, Washington, DC 20431, (202) 623-7000, Fax: (202) 623-4661, www.imf.org; *Direction of Trade Statistics Yearbook 2007* and *International Financial Statistics Yearbook 2007.*

Palgrave Macmillan Ltd., Houndmills, Basingstoke, Hampshire, RG21 6XS, England, (Telephone in U.S. (888) 330-8477), (Fax in U.S. (800) 672-2054), www.palgrave.com; *The Statesman's Yearbook 2008.*

Taylor and Francis Group, An Informa Business, 2 Park Square, Milton Park, Abingdon, Oxford OX14 4RN, United Kingdom, (Dial from U.S. (212) 216-7800), (Fax from U.S. (212) 564-7854), www.tandf.co.uk; *The Europa World Year Book.*

United Nations Economic Commission for Africa (ECA), PO Box 3001, Addis Ababa, Ethiopia, (Telephone in U.S. (212) 963-4957), www.uneca.org; *African Statistical Yearbook 2006.*

United Nations Food and Agricultural Organization (FAO), Viale delle Terme di Caracalla, 00100 Rome, Italy, (Dial from U.S. (202) 653-2400), (Fax from U.S. (202) 653 5760), www.fao.org; *The State of Food and Agriculture (SOFA) 2006.*

United Nations Statistics Division, New York, NY 10017, (800) 253-9646, Fax: (212) 963-4116, http://unstats.un.org; *Compendium of Intra-African and Related Foreign Trade Statistics 2003* and *Survey of Economic and Social Conditions in Africa 2005.*

The World Bank, 1818 H Street, NW, Washington, DC 20433, (202) 473-1000, Fax: (202) 477-6391, www.worldbank.org; *World Development Indicators (WDI) 2008.*

CONGO, DEMOCRATIC REPUBLIC OF THE - INCOME TAXES

See CONGO, DEMOCRATIC REPUBLIC OF THE - TAXATION

CONGO, DEMOCRATIC REPUBLIC OF THE - INDUSTRIAL METALS PRODUCTION

See CONGO, DEMOCRATIC REPUBLIC OF THE - MINERAL INDUSTRIES

CONGO, DEMOCRATIC REPUBLIC OF THE - INDUSTRIAL PRODUCTIVITY

Euromonitor International, Inc., 224 S. Michigan Avenue, Suite 1500, Chicago, IL 60604, (312) 922-1115, Fax: (312) 922-1157, www.euromonitor.com; *International Marketing Data and Statistics 2008.*

M.E. Sharpe, 80 Business Park Drive, Armonk, NY 10504, (800) 541-6563, Fax: (914) 273-2106, www.mesharpe.com; *The Illustrated Book of World Rankings.*

CONGO, DEMOCRATIC REPUBLIC OF THE - INDUSTRIAL PROPERTY

United Nations Statistics Division, New York, NY 10017, (800) 253-9646, Fax: (212) 963-4116, http://unstats.un.org; *Statistical Yearbook.*

CONGO, DEMOCRATIC REPUBLIC OF THE - INDUSTRIES

Central Intelligence Agency, Office of Public Affairs, Washington, DC 20505, (703) 482-0623, Fax: (703) 482-1739, www.cia.gov; *The World Factbook.*

Economist Intelligence Unit, 111 West 57th Street, New York, NY 10019, (212) 554-0600, Fax: (212) 586-1181, www.eiu.com; *Congo (Democratic Republic) Country Report.*

Euromonitor International, Inc., 224 S. Michigan Avenue, Suite 1500, Chicago, IL 60604, (312) 922-1115, Fax: (312) 922-1157, www.euromonitor.com; *International Marketing Data and Statistics 2008* and *The World Economic Factbook 2008.*

International Labour Office, I.L.O. Publications, 4 route des Morillons, CH-1211 Geneva 22, Switzerland, (Telephone in U.S. (202) 653-7652), (Fax in U.S. (202) 653-7687), www.ilo.org; *Yearbook of Labour Statistics 2006.*

M.E. Sharpe, 80 Business Park Drive, Armonk, NY 10504, (800) 541-6563, Fax: (914) 273-2106, www.mesharpe.com; *The Illustrated Book of World Rankings.*

Palgrave Macmillan Ltd., Houndmills, Basingstoke, Hampshire, RG21 6XS, England, (Telephone in U.S. (888) 330-8477), (Fax in U.S. (800) 672-2054), www.palgrave.com; *The Statesman's Yearbook 2008.*

Taylor and Francis Group, An Informa Business, 2 Park Square, Milton Park, Abingdon, Oxford OX14 4RN, United Kingdom, (Dial from U.S. (212) 216-7800), (Fax from U.S. (212) 564-7854), www.tandf.co.uk; *The Europa World Year Book.*

United Nations Industrial Development Organization (UNIDO), 1 United Nations Plaza, New York, NY 10017, (212) 963 6890, Fax: (212) 963-7904, http://unido.org; Industrial Statistics Database 2008 (INDSTAT) and *The International Yearbook of Industrial Statistics 2008.*

United Nations Statistics Division, New York, NY 10017, (800) 253-9646, Fax: (212) 963-4116, http://unstats.un.org; *Survey of Economic and Social Conditions in Africa 2005.*

The World Bank, 1818 H Street, NW, Washington, DC 20433, (202) 473-1000, Fax: (202) 477-6391,

www.worldbank.org; *Congo, The Democratic Republic of the* and *World Development Indicators (WDI) 2008.*

CONGO, DEMOCRATIC REPUBLIC OF THE - INFANT AND MATERNAL MORTALITY

See CONGO, DEMOCRATIC REPUBLIC OF THE - MORTALITY

CONGO, DEMOCRATIC REPUBLIC OF THE - INTERNATIONAL LIQUIDITY

International Monetary Fund (IMF), 700 Nineteenth Street, NW, Washington, DC 20431, (202) 623-7000, Fax: (202) 623-4661, www.imf.org; *International Financial Statistics Yearbook 2007.*

CONGO, DEMOCRATIC REPUBLIC OF THE - INTERNATIONAL TRADE

African Development Bank Group, Rue Joseph Anoma, 01 BP 1387 Abidjan 01, Cote d'Ivoire, www.afdb.org; *Statistics Pocketbook 2008.*

Economist Intelligence Unit, 111 West 57th Street, New York, NY 10019, (212) 554-0600, Fax: (212) 586-1181, www.eiu.com; *Congo (Democratic Republic) Country Report.*

Euromonitor International, Inc., 224 S. Michigan Avenue, Suite 1500, Chicago, IL 60604, (312) 922-1115, Fax: (312) 922-1157, www.euromonitor.com; *International Marketing Data and Statistics 2008* and *The World Economic Factbook 2008.*

International Monetary Fund (IMF), 700 Nineteenth Street, NW, Washington, DC 20431, (202) 623-7000, Fax: (202) 623-4661, www.imf.org; *International Financial Statistics Yearbook 2007.*

M.E. Sharpe, 80 Business Park Drive, Armonk, NY 10504, (800) 541-6563, Fax: (914) 273-2106, www.mesharpe.com; *The Illustrated Book of World Rankings.*

Palgrave Macmillan Ltd., Houndmills, Basingstoke, Hampshire, RG21 6XS, England, (Telephone in U.S. (888) 330-8477), (Fax in U.S. (800) 672-2054), www.palgrave.com; *The Statesman's Yearbook 2008.*

Taylor and Francis Group, An Informa Business, 2 Park Square, Milton Park, Abingdon, Oxford OX14 4RN, United Kingdom, (Dial from U.S. (212) 216-7800), (Fax from U.S. (212) 564-7854), www.tandf.co.uk; *The Europa World Year Book.*

United Nations Conference on Trade and Development (UNCTAD), DC2-1120, United Nations, New York, NY 10017, (212) 963-0027, www.unctad.org; *UNCTAD Commodity Yearbook.*

United Nations Economic Commission for Africa (ECA), PO Box 3001, Addis Ababa, Ethiopia, (Telephone in U.S. (212) 963-4957), www.uneca.org; *African Statistical Yearbook 2006.*

United Nations Food and Agricultural Organization (FAO), Viale delle Terme di Caracalla, 00100 Rome, Italy, (Dial from U.S. (202) 653-2400), (Fax from U.S. (202) 653 5760), www.fao.org; *The State of Food and Agriculture (SOFA) 2006.*

United Nations Statistics Division, New York, NY 10017, (800) 253-9646, Fax: (212) 963-4116, http://unstats.un.org; *Compendium of Intra-African and Related Foreign Trade Statistics 2003; International Trade Statistics Yearbook;* and *Statistical Yearbook.*

The World Bank, 1818 H Street, NW, Washington, DC 20433, (202) 473-1000, Fax: (202) 477-6391, www.worldbank.org; *Congo, The Democratic Republic of the* and *World Development Indicators (WDI) 2008.*

World Bureau of Metal Statistics (WBMS), 27a High Street, Ware, Hertfordshire, SG12 9BA, United Kingdom, www.world-bureau.com; *World Flow Charts* and *World Metal Statistics.*

World Trade Organization (WTO), Centre William Rappard, Rue de Lausanne 154, CH-1211 Geneva 21, Switzerland, www.wto.org; *International Trade Statistics 2006.*

CONGO, DEMOCRATIC REPUBLIC OF THE - INTERNET USERS

International Telecommunication Union (ITU), Place des Nations, 1211 Geneva 20, Switzerland, www.itu.int; *World Telecommunication/ICT Indicators Database on CD-ROM; World Telecommunication/ICT Indicators Database Online;* and *Yearbook of Statistics - Telecommunication Services (Chronological Time Series 1997-2006).*

The World Bank, 1818 H Street, NW, Washington, DC 20433, (202) 473-1000, Fax: (202) 477-6391, www.worldbank.org; *Congo, The Democratic Republic of the.*

CONGO, DEMOCRATIC REPUBLIC OF THE - INVESTMENTS

International Monetary Fund (IMF), 700 Nineteenth Street, NW, Washington, DC 20431, (202) 623-7000, Fax: (202) 623-4661, www.imf.org; *International Financial Statistics Yearbook 2007.*

CONGO, DEMOCRATIC REPUBLIC OF THE - IRRIGATION

Euromonitor International, Inc., 224 S. Michigan Avenue, Suite 1500, Chicago, IL 60604, (312) 922-1115, Fax: (312) 922-1157, www.euromonitor.com; *International Marketing Data and Statistics 2008.*

CONGO, DEMOCRATIC REPUBLIC OF THE - LABOR

African Development Bank Group, Rue Joseph Anoma, 01 BP 1387 Abidjan 01, Cote d'Ivoire, www.afdb.org; *Statistics Pocketbook 2008.*

Central Intelligence Agency, Office of Public Affairs, Washington, DC 20505, (703) 482-0623, Fax: (703) 482-1739, www.cia.gov; *The World Factbook.*

Euromonitor International, Inc., 224 S. Michigan Avenue, Suite 1500, Chicago, IL 60604, (312) 922-1115, Fax: (312) 922-1157, www.euromonitor.com; *International Marketing Data and Statistics 2008.*

International Labour Office, I.L.O. Publications, 4 route des Morillons, CH-1211 Geneva 22, Switzerland, (Telephone in U.S. (202) 653-7652), (Fax in U.S. (202) 653-7687), www.ilo.org; *Yearbook of Labour Statistics 2006.*

M.E. Sharpe, 80 Business Park Drive, Armonk, NY 10504, (800) 541-6563, Fax: (914) 273-2106, www.mesharpe.com; *The Illustrated Book of World Rankings.*

Palgrave Macmillan Ltd., Houndmills, Basingstoke, Hampshire, RG21 6XS, England, (Telephone in U.S. (888) 330-8477), (Fax in U.S. (800) 672-2054), www.palgrave.com; *The Statesman's Yearbook 2008.*

United Nations Food and Agricultural Organization (FAO), Viale delle Terme di Caracalla, 00100 Rome, Italy, (Dial from U.S. (202) 653-2400), (Fax from U.S. (202) 653 5760), www.fao.org; *The State of Food and Agriculture (SOFA) 2006.*

United Nations Statistics Division, New York, NY 10017, (800) 253-9646, Fax: (212) 963-4116, http://unstats.un.org; *Human Development Report 2006.*

The World Bank, 1818 H Street, NW, Washington, DC 20433, (202) 473-1000, Fax: (202) 477-6391, www.worldbank.org; *The World Bank Atlas 2003-2004* and *World Development Indicators (WDI) 2008.*

CONGO, DEMOCRATIC REPUBLIC OF THE - LAND USE

Central Intelligence Agency, Office of Public Affairs, Washington, DC 20505, (703) 482-0623, Fax: (703) 482-1739, www.cia.gov; *The World Factbook.*

Euromonitor International, Inc., 224 S. Michigan Avenue, Suite 1500, Chicago, IL 60604, (312) 922-1115, Fax: (312) 922-1157, www.euromonitor.com; *International Marketing Data and Statistics 2008.*

CONGO, DEMOCRATIC REPUBLIC OF THE - LIBRARIES

M.E. Sharpe, 80 Business Park Drive, Armonk, NY 10504, (800) 541-6563, Fax: (914) 273-2106, www.mesharpe.com; *The Illustrated Book of World Rankings.*

UNESCO Institute for Statistics, C.P. 6128 Succursale Centre-Ville, Montreal, Quebec, H3C 3J7 Canada, (Dial from U.S. (514) 343-6880), (Fax from U.S. (514) 343 6882), www.uis.unesco.org; *Statistical Tables.*

CONGO, DEMOCRATIC REPUBLIC OF THE - LICENSES

International Monetary Fund (IMF), 700 Nineteenth Street, NW, Washington, DC 20431, (202) 623-7000, Fax: (202) 623-4661, www.imf.org; *Government Finance Statistics Yearbook (2008 Edition).*

CONGO, DEMOCRATIC REPUBLIC OF THE - LIFE EXPECTANCY

African Development Bank Group, Rue Joseph Anoma, 01 BP 1387 Abidjan 01, Cote d'Ivoire, www.afdb.org; *Statistics Pocketbook 2008.*

Central Intelligence Agency, Office of Public Affairs, Washington, DC 20505, (703) 482-0623, Fax: (703) 482-1739, www.cia.gov; *The World Factbook.*

Euromonitor International, Inc., 224 S. Michigan Avenue, Suite 1500, Chicago, IL 60604, (312) 922-1115, Fax: (312) 922-1157, www.euromonitor.com; *The World Economic Factbook 2008.*

United Nations Statistics Division, New York, NY 10017, (800) 253-9646, Fax: (212) 963-4116, http://unstats.un.org; *Human Development Report 2006.*

The World Bank, 1818 H Street, NW, Washington, DC 20433, (202) 473-1000, Fax: (202) 477-6391, www.worldbank.org; *The World Bank Atlas 2003-2004.*

CONGO, DEMOCRATIC REPUBLIC OF THE - LITERACY

United Nations Statistics Division, New York, NY 10017, (800) 253-9646, Fax: (212) 963-4116, http://unstats.un.org; *Survey of Economic and Social Conditions in Africa 2005.*

CONGO, DEMOCRATIC REPUBLIC OF THE - LIVESTOCK

Euromonitor International, Inc., 224 S. Michigan Avenue, Suite 1500, Chicago, IL 60604, (312) 922-1115, Fax: (312) 922-1157, www.euromonitor.com; *International Marketing Data and Statistics 2008.*

M.E. Sharpe, 80 Business Park Drive, Armonk, NY 10504, (800) 541-6563, Fax: (914) 273-2106, www.mesharpe.com; *The Illustrated Book of World Rankings.*

Palgrave Macmillan Ltd., Houndmills, Basingstoke, Hampshire, RG21 6XS, England, (Telephone in U.S. (888) 330-8477), (Fax in U.S. (800) 672-2054), www.palgrave.com; *The Statesman's Yearbook 2008.*

Taylor and Francis Group, An Informa Business, 2 Park Square, Milton Park, Abingdon, Oxford OX14 4RN, United Kingdom, (Dial from U.S. (212) 216-7800), (Fax from U.S. (212) 564-7854), www.tandf.co.uk; *The Europa World Year Book.*

United Nations Conference on Trade and Development (UNCTAD), DC2-1120, United Nations, New York, NY 10017, (212) 963-0027, www.unctad.org; *UNCTAD Commodity Yearbook.*

United Nations Economic Commission for Africa (ECA), PO Box 3001, Addis Ababa, Ethiopia, (Telephone in U.S. (212) 963-4957), www.uneca.org; *African Statistical Yearbook 2006.*

United Nations Food and Agricultural Organization (FAO), Viale delle Terme di Caracalla, 00100 Rome, Italy, (Dial from U.S. (202) 653-2400), (Fax from U.S. (202) 653 5760), www.fao.org; *The State of Food and Agriculture (SOFA) 2006.*

United Nations Statistics Division, New York, NY 10017, (800) 253-9646, Fax: (212) 963-4116, http://unstats.un.org; *Statistical Yearbook* and *Survey of Economic and Social Conditions in Africa 2005.*

CONGO, DEMOCRATIC REPUBLIC OF THE - LOCAL TAXATION

Euromonitor International, Inc., 224 S. Michigan Avenue, Suite 1500, Chicago, IL 60604, (312) 922-

1115, Fax: (312) 922-1157, www.euromonitor.com; *International Marketing Data and Statistics 2008.*

CONGO, DEMOCRATIC REPUBLIC OF THE - MANUFACTURES

M.E. Sharpe, 80 Business Park Drive, Armonk, NY 10504, (800) 541-6563, Fax: (914) 273-2106, www.mesharpe.com; *The Illustrated Book of World Rankings.*

United Nations Economic Commission for Africa (ECA), PO Box 3001, Addis Ababa, Ethiopia, (Telephone in U.S. (212) 963-4957), www.uneca.org; *African Statistical Yearbook 2006.*

United Nations Statistics Division, New York, NY 10017, (800) 253-9646, Fax: (212) 963-4116, http://unstats.un.org; *Statistical Yearbook* and *Survey of Economic and Social Conditions in Africa 2005.*

The World Bank, 1818 H Street, NW, Washington, DC 20433, (202) 473-1000, Fax: (202) 477-6391, www.worldbank.org; *World Development Indicators (WDI) 2008.*

CONGO, DEMOCRATIC REPUBLIC OF THE - MARRIAGE

M.E. Sharpe, 80 Business Park Drive, Armonk, NY 10504, (800) 541-6563, Fax: (914) 273-2106, www.mesharpe.com; *The Illustrated Book of World Rankings.*

United Nations Statistics Division, New York, NY 10017, (800) 253-9646, Fax: (212) 963-4116, http://unstats.un.org; *Demographic Yearbook.*

CONGO, DEMOCRATIC REPUBLIC OF THE - MILK PRODUCTION

See CONGO, DEMOCRATIC REPUBLIC OF THE - DAIRY PROCESSING

CONGO, DEMOCRATIC REPUBLIC OF THE - MINERAL INDUSTRIES

Commodity Research Bureau, 330 South Wells Street, Suite 612, Chicago, IL 60606-7110, (800) 621-5271, Fax: (312) 939-4135, www.crbtrader.com; *2006 CRB Commodity Yearbook and CD.*

International Monetary Fund (IMF), 700 Nineteenth Street, NW, Washington, DC 20431, (202) 623-7000, Fax: (202) 623-4661, www.imf.org; *International Financial Statistics Yearbook 2007.*

M.E. Sharpe, 80 Business Park Drive, Armonk, NY 10504, (800) 541-6563, Fax: (914) 273-2106, www.mesharpe.com; *The Illustrated Book of World Rankings.*

Organisation for Economic Cooperation and Development (OECD), 2 rue Andre Pascal, F-75775 Paris Cedex 16, France, (Telephone in U.S. (202) 785-6323), (Fax in U.S. (202) 785-0350), www.oecd.org; *World Energy Outlook 2007.*

Palgrave Macmillan Ltd., Houndmills, Basingstoke, Hampshire, RG21 6XS, England, (Telephone in U.S. (888) 330-8477), (Fax in U.S. (800) 672-2054), www.palgrave.com; *The Statesman's Yearbook 2008.*

Taylor and Francis Group, An Informa Business, 2 Park Square, Milton Park, Abingdon, Oxford OX14 4RN, United Kingdom, (Dial from U.S. (212) 216-7800), (Fax from U.S. (212) 564-7854), www.tandf.co.uk; *The Europa World Year Book.*

United Nations Conference on Trade and Development (UNCTAD), DC2-1120, United Nations, New York, NY 10017, (212) 963-0027, www.unctad.org; *UNCTAD Commodity Yearbook.*

United Nations Economic Commission for Africa (ECA), PO Box 3001, Addis Ababa, Ethiopia, (Telephone in U.S. (212) 963-4957), www.uneca.org; *African Statistical Yearbook 2006.*

United Nations Statistics Division, New York, NY 10017, (800) 253-9646, Fax: (212) 963-4116, http://unstats.un.org; *Statistical Yearbook.*

The World Bank, 1818 H Street, NW, Washington, DC 20433, (202) 473-1000, Fax: (202) 477-6391, www.worldbank.org; *Congo, The Democratic Republic of the.*

World Bureau of Metal Statistics (WBMS), 27a High Street, Ware, Hertfordshire, SG12 9BA, United Kingdom, www.world-bureau.com; *Annual Stainless Steel Statistics; World Flow Charts; World Metal Statistics; World Nickel Statistics;* and *World Tin Statistics.*

CONGO, DEMOCRATIC REPUBLIC OF THE - MONEY SUPPLY

African Development Bank Group, Rue Joseph Anoma, 01 BP 1387 Abidjan 01, Cote d'Ivoire, www.afdb.org; *Statistics Pocketbook 2008.*

Economist Intelligence Unit, 111 West 57th Street, New York, NY 10019, (212) 554-0600, Fax: (212) 586-1181, www.eiu.com; *Congo (Democratic Republic) Country Report.*

Euromonitor International, Inc., 224 S. Michigan Avenue, Suite 1500, Chicago, IL 60604, (312) 922-1115, Fax: (312) 922-1157, www.euromonitor.com; *International Marketing Data and Statistics 2008.*

International Monetary Fund (IMF), 700 Nineteenth Street, NW, Washington, DC 20431, (202) 623-7000, Fax: (202) 623-4661, www.imf.org; *International Financial Statistics Yearbook 2007.*

Taylor and Francis Group, An Informa Business, 2 Park Square, Milton Park, Abingdon, Oxford OX14 4RN, United Kingdom, (Dial from U.S. (212) 216-7800), (Fax from U.S. (212) 564-7854), www.tandf.co.uk; *The Europa World Year Book.*

United Nations Statistics Division, New York, NY 10017, (800) 253-9646, Fax: (212) 963-4116, http://unstats.un.org; *Statistical Yearbook.*

The World Bank, 1818 H Street, NW, Washington, DC 20433, (202) 473-1000, Fax: (202) 477-6391, www.worldbank.org; *Congo, The Democratic Republic of the* and *World Development Indicators (WDI) 2008.*

CONGO, DEMOCRATIC REPUBLIC OF THE - MORTALITY

Central Intelligence Agency, Office of Public Affairs, Washington, DC 20505, (703) 482-0623, Fax: (703) 482-1739, www.cia.gov; *The World Factbook.*

Euromonitor International, Inc., 224 S. Michigan Avenue, Suite 1500, Chicago, IL 60604, (312) 922-1115, Fax: (312) 922-1157, www.euromonitor.com; *International Marketing Data and Statistics 2008* and *The World Economic Factbook 2008.*

Taylor and Francis Group, An Informa Business, 2 Park Square, Milton Park, Abingdon, Oxford OX14 4RN, United Kingdom, (Dial from U.S. (212) 216-7800), (Fax from U.S. (212) 564-7854), www.tandf.co.uk; *The Europa World Year Book.*

UNICEF, 3 United Nations Plaza, New York, NY 10017, (800) 253-9646, Fax: (212) 887-7465, www.unicef.org; *The State of the World's Children 2008.*

United Nations Statistics Division, New York, NY 10017, (800) 253-9646, Fax: (212) 963-4116, http://unstats.un.org; *Demographic Yearbook; Human Development Report 2006; Statistical Yearbook;* and *Survey of Economic and Social Conditions in Africa 2005.*

The World Bank, 1818 H Street, NW, Washington, DC 20433, (202) 473-1000, Fax: (202) 477-6391, www.worldbank.org; *The World Bank Atlas 2003-2004* and *World Development Indicators (WDI) 2008.*

World Health Organization (WHO), Avenue Appia 20, 1211 Geneve 27, Switzerland, (Telephone in U.S. (212) 331-9081), www.who.int; The WHO Global Atlas of Infectious Diseases.

CONGO, DEMOCRATIC REPUBLIC OF THE - MOTION PICTURES

United Nations Statistics Division, New York, NY 10017, (800) 253-9646, Fax: (212) 963-4116, http://unstats.un.org; *Statistical Yearbook.*

CONGO, DEMOCRATIC REPUBLIC OF THE - MOTOR VEHICLES

International Road Federation (IFR), Madison Place, 500 Montgomery Street, 5th Floor, Alexandria, VA 22314, (703) 535-1001, Fax: (703) 535-1007, www.irfnet.org; *World Road Statistics 2006.*

United Nations Statistics Division, New York, NY 10017, (800) 253-9646, Fax: (212) 963-4116, http://unstats.un.org; *Statistical Yearbook* and *Survey of Economic and Social Conditions in Africa 2005.*

CONGO, DEMOCRATIC REPUBLIC OF THE - MUSEUMS

M.E. Sharpe, 80 Business Park Drive, Armonk, NY 10504, (800) 541-6563, Fax: (914) 273-2106, www.mesharpe.com; *The Illustrated Book of World Rankings.*

UNESCO Institute for Statistics, C.P. 6128 Succursale Centre-Ville, Montreal, Quebec, H3C 3J7 Canada, (Dial from U.S. (514) 343-6880), (Fax from U.S. (514) 343 6882), www.uis.unesco.org; *Statistical Tables.*

CONGO, DEMOCRATIC REPUBLIC OF THE - NATURAL GAS PRODUCTION

See CONGO, DEMOCRATIC REPUBLIC OF THE - MINERAL INDUSTRIES

CONGO, DEMOCRATIC REPUBLIC OF THE - NUTRITION

African Development Bank Group, Rue Joseph Anoma, 01 BP 1387 Abidjan 01, Cote d'Ivoire, www.afdb.org; *Statistics Pocketbook 2008.*

United Nations Food and Agricultural Organization (FAO), Viale delle Terme di Caracalla, 00100 Rome, Italy, (Dial from U.S. (202) 653-2400), (Fax from U.S. (202) 653 5760), www.fao.org; *The State of Food and Agriculture (SOFA) 2006.*

CONGO, DEMOCRATIC REPUBLIC OF THE - OATS PRODUCTION

See CONGO, DEMOCRATIC REPUBLIC OF THE - CROPS

CONGO, DEMOCRATIC REPUBLIC OF THE - OLDER PEOPLE

M.E. Sharpe, 80 Business Park Drive, Armonk, NY 10504, (800) 541-6563, Fax: (914) 273-2106, www.mesharpe.com; *The Illustrated Book of World Rankings.*

CONGO, DEMOCRATIC REPUBLIC OF THE - PAPER

See CONGO, DEMOCRATIC REPUBLIC OF THE - FORESTS AND FORESTRY

CONGO, DEMOCRATIC REPUBLIC OF THE - PEANUT PRODUCTION

See CONGO, DEMOCRATIC REPUBLIC OF THE - CROPS

CONGO, DEMOCRATIC REPUBLIC OF THE - PESTICIDES

United Nations Food and Agricultural Organization (FAO), Viale delle Terme di Caracalla, 00100 Rome, Italy, (Dial from U.S. (202) 653-2400), (Fax from U.S. (202) 653 5760), www.fao.org; *The State of Food and Agriculture (SOFA) 2006.*

CONGO, DEMOCRATIC REPUBLIC OF THE - PETROLEUM INDUSTRY AND TRADE

M.E. Sharpe, 80 Business Park Drive, Armonk, NY 10504, (800) 541-6563, Fax: (914) 273-2106, www.mesharpe.com; *The Illustrated Book of World Rankings.*

Organisation for Economic Cooperation and Development (OECD), 2 rue Andre Pascal, F-75775 Paris Cedex 16, France, (Telephone in U.S. (202) 785-6323), (Fax in U.S. (202) 785-0350), www.oecd.org; *World Energy Outlook 2007.*

Palgrave Macmillan Ltd., Houndmills, Basingstoke, Hampshire, RG21 6XS, England, (Telephone in U.S. (888) 330-8477), (Fax in U.S. (800) 672-2054), www.palgrave.com; *The Statesman's Yearbook 2008.*

PennWell Corporation, 1421 South Sheridan Road, Tulsa, OK 74112, (918) 835-3161, www.pennwell.com; *International Petroleum Encyclopedia 2007.*

U.S. Department of Energy (DOE), Energy Information Administration (EIA), 1000 Independence Avenue, SW, Washington, DC 20585, (202) 586-8800, www.eia.doe.gov; *International Energy Annual 2004* and *International Energy Outlook 2006.*

United Nations Conference on Trade and Development (UNCTAD), DC2-1120, United Nations, New York, NY 10017, (212) 963-0027, www.unctad.org; *UNCTAD Commodity Yearbook.*

United Nations Food and Agricultural Organization (FAO), Viale delle Terme di Caracalla, 00100 Rome, Italy, (Dial from U.S. (202) 653-2400), (Fax from U.S. (202) 653 5760), www.fao.org; *The State of Food and Agriculture (SOFA) 2006.*

United Nations Statistics Division, New York, NY 10017, (800) 253-9646, Fax: (212) 963-4116, http://unstats.un.org; *Statistical Yearbook.*

CONGO, DEMOCRATIC REPUBLIC OF THE - POLITICAL SCIENCE

Central Intelligence Agency, Office of Public Affairs, Washington, DC 20505, (703) 482-0623, Fax: (703) 482-1739, www.cia.gov; *The World Factbook.*

International Monetary Fund (IMF), 700 Nineteenth Street, NW, Washington, DC 20431, (202) 623-7000, Fax: (202) 623-4661, www.imf.org; *Government Finance Statistics Yearbook (2008 Edition)* and *International Financial Statistics Yearbook 2007.*

Palgrave Macmillan Ltd., Houndmills, Basingstoke, Hampshire, RG21 6XS, England, (Telephone in U.S. (888) 330-8477), (Fax in U.S. (800) 672-2054), www.palgrave.com; *The Statesman's Yearbook 2008.*

Taylor and Francis Group, An Informa Business, 2 Park Square, Milton Park, Abingdon, Oxford OX14 4RN, United Kingdom, (Dial from U.S. (212) 216-7800), (Fax from U.S. (212) 564-7854), www.tandf.co.uk; *The Europa World Year Book.*

United Nations Statistics Division, New York, NY 10017, (800) 253-9646, Fax: (212) 963-4116, http://unstats.un.org; *National Accounts Statistics: Compendium of Income Distribution Statistics; Statistical Yearbook;* and *Survey of Economic and Social Conditions in Africa 2005.*

The World Bank, 1818 H Street, NW, Washington, DC 20433, (202) 473-1000, Fax: (202) 477-6391, www.worldbank.org; *World Development Indicators (WDI) 2008.*

CONGO, DEMOCRATIC REPUBLIC OF THE - POPULATION

African Development Bank Group, Rue Joseph Anoma, 01 BP 1387 Abidjan 01, Cote d'Ivoire, www.afdb.org; *The African Statistical Journal; Gender, Poverty and Environmental Indicators on African Countries 2007; Selected Statistics on African Countries 2007;* and *Statistics Pocketbook 2008.*

Central Intelligence Agency, Office of Public Affairs, Washington, DC 20505, (703) 482-0623, Fax: (703) 482-1739, www.cia.gov; *The World Factbook.*

Economist Intelligence Unit, 111 West 57th Street, New York, NY 10019, (212) 554-0600, Fax: (212) 586-1181, www.eiu.com; *Congo (Democratic Republic) Country Report.*

Euromonitor International, Inc., 224 S. Michigan Avenue, Suite 1500, Chicago, IL 60604, (312) 922-1115, Fax: (312) 922-1157, www.euromonitor.com; *International Marketing Data and Statistics 2008* and *The World Economic Factbook 2008.*

Eurostat, Batiment Jean Monnet, Rue Alcide de Gasperi, L-2920 Luxembourg, http://epp.eurostat.ec.europa.eu; *Demographic Indicators - Population by Age-Classes.*

International Labour Office, I.L.O. Publications, 4 route des Morillons, CH-1211 Geneva 22, Switzerland, (Telephone in U.S. (202) 653-7652), (Fax in U.S. (202) 653-7687), www.ilo.org; *Yearbook of Labour Statistics 2006.*

M.E. Sharpe, 80 Business Park Drive, Armonk, NY 10504, (800) 541-6563, Fax: (914) 273-2106, www.mesharpe.com; *The Illustrated Book of World Rankings.*

Palgrave Macmillan Ltd., Houndmills, Basingstoke, Hampshire, RG21 6XS, England, (Telephone in U.S. (888) 330-8477), (Fax in U.S. (800) 672-2054), www.palgrave.com; *The Statesman's Yearbook 2008.*

Taylor and Francis Group, An Informa Business, 2 Park Square, Milton Park, Abingdon, Oxford OX14 4RN, United Kingdom, (Dial from U.S. (212) 216-7800), (Fax from U.S. (212) 564-7854), www.tandf.co.uk; *The Europa World Year Book.*

U.S. Department of State (DOS), 2201 C Street NW, Washington, DC 20520, (202) 647-4000, www.state.gov; *World Military Expenditures and Arms Transfers (WMEAT).*

UNESCO Institute for Statistics, C.P. 6128 Succursale Centre-Ville, Montreal, Quebec, H3C 3J7 Canada, (Dial from U.S. (514) 343-6880), (Fax from U.S. (514) 343 6882), www.uis.unesco.org; *Statistical Tables.*

United Nations Statistics Division, New York, NY 10017, (800) 253-9646, Fax: (212) 963-4116, http://unstats.un.org; *Demographic Yearbook; Human Development Report 2006; Statistical Yearbook;* and *Survey of Economic and Social Conditions in Africa 2005.*

The World Bank, 1818 H Street, NW, Washington, DC 20433, (202) 473-1000, Fax: (202) 477-6391, www.worldbank.org; *Congo, The Democratic Republic of the* and *The World Bank Atlas 2003-2004.*

World Health Organization (WHO), Avenue Appia 20, 1211 Geneve 27, Switzerland, (Telephone in U.S. (212) 331-9081), www.who.int; *World Health Report 2006.*

CONGO, DEMOCRATIC REPUBLIC OF THE - POPULATION DENSITY

African Development Bank Group, Rue Joseph Anoma, 01 BP 1387 Abidjan 01, Cote d'Ivoire, www.afdb.org; *Statistics Pocketbook 2008.*

Central Intelligence Agency, Office of Public Affairs, Washington, DC 20505, (703) 482-0623, Fax: (703) 482-1739, www.cia.gov; *The World Factbook.*

Euromonitor International, Inc., 224 S. Michigan Avenue, Suite 1500, Chicago, IL 60604, (312) 922-1115, Fax: (312) 922-1157, www.euromonitor.com; *International Marketing Data and Statistics 2008* and *The World Economic Factbook 2008.*

M.E. Sharpe, 80 Business Park Drive, Armonk, NY 10504, (800) 541-6563, Fax: (914) 273-2106, www.mesharpe.com; *The Illustrated Book of World Rankings.*

Palgrave Macmillan Ltd., Houndmills, Basingstoke, Hampshire, RG21 6XS, England, (Telephone in U.S. (888) 330-8477), (Fax in U.S. (800) 672-2054), www.palgrave.com; *The Statesman's Yearbook 2008.*

Taylor and Francis Group, An Informa Business, 2 Park Square, Milton Park, Abingdon, Oxford OX14 4RN, United Kingdom, (Dial from U.S. (212) 216-7800), (Fax from U.S. (212) 564-7854), www.tandf.co.uk; *The Europa World Year Book.*

UNESCO Institute for Statistics, C.P. 6128 Succursale Centre-Ville, Montreal, Quebec, H3C 3J7 Canada, (Dial from U.S. (514) 343-6880), (Fax from U.S. (514) 343 6882), www.uis.unesco.org; *Statistical Tables.*

United Nations Food and Agricultural Organization (FAO), Viale delle Terme di Caracalla, 00100 Rome, Italy, (Dial from U.S. (202) 653-2400), (Fax from U.S. (202) 653 5760), www.fao.org; *The State of Food and Agriculture (SOFA) 2006.*

United Nations Statistics Division, New York, NY 10017, (800) 253-9646, Fax: (212) 963-4116, http://unstats.un.org; *Statistical Yearbook* and *Survey of Economic and Social Conditions in Africa 2005.*

The World Bank, 1818 H Street, NW, Washington, DC 20433, (202) 473-1000, Fax: (202) 477-6391, www.worldbank.org; *Congo, The Democratic Republic of the.*

CONGO, DEMOCRATIC REPUBLIC OF THE - POSTAL SERVICE

M.E. Sharpe, 80 Business Park Drive, Armonk, NY 10504, (800) 541-6563, Fax: (914) 273-2106, www.mesharpe.com; *The Illustrated Book of World Rankings.*

Palgrave Macmillan Ltd., Houndmills, Basingstoke, Hampshire, RG21 6XS, England, (Telephone in U.S. (888) 330-8477), (Fax in U.S. (800) 672-2054), www.palgrave.com; *The Statesman's Yearbook 2008.*

United Nations Statistics Division, New York, NY 10017, (800) 253-9646, Fax: (212) 963-4116, http://unstats.un.org; *Statistical Yearbook.*

CONGO, DEMOCRATIC REPUBLIC OF THE - POWER RESOURCES

Euromonitor International, Inc., 224 S. Michigan Avenue, Suite 1500, Chicago, IL 60604, (312) 922-1115, Fax: (312) 922-1157, www.euromonitor.com; *International Marketing Data and Statistics 2008* and *The World Economic Factbook 2008.*

M.E. Sharpe, 80 Business Park Drive, Armonk, NY 10504, (800) 541-6563, Fax: (914) 273-2106, www.mesharpe.com; *The Illustrated Book of World Rankings.*

Organisation for Economic Cooperation and Development (OECD), 2 rue Andre Pascal, F-75775 Paris Cedex 16, France, (Telephone in U.S. (202) 785-6323), (Fax in U.S. (202) 785-0350), www.oecd.org; *World Energy Outlook 2007.*

Palgrave Macmillan Ltd., Houndmills, Basingstoke, Hampshire, RG21 6XS, England, (Telephone in U.S. (888) 330-8477), (Fax in U.S. (800) 672-2054), www.palgrave.com; *The Statesman's Yearbook 2008.*

Platts, 2 Penn Plaza, 25th Floor, New York, NY 10121-2298, (212) 904-3070, www.platts.com; *Energy Economist.*

U.S. Department of Energy (DOE), Energy Information Administration (EIA), 1000 Independence Avenue, SW, Washington, DC 20585, (202) 586-8800, www.eia.doe.gov; *International Energy Annual 2004* and *International Energy Outlook 2006.*

United Nations Economic Commission for Africa (ECA), PO Box 3001, Addis Ababa, Ethiopia, (Telephone in U.S. (212) 963-4957), www.uneca.org; *African Statistical Yearbook 2006.*

United Nations Food and Agricultural Organization (FAO), Viale delle Terme di Caracalla, 00100 Rome, Italy, (Dial from U.S. (202) 653-2400), (Fax from U.S. (202) 653 5760), www.fao.org; *The State of Food and Agriculture (SOFA) 2006.*

United Nations Statistics Division, New York, NY 10017, (800) 253-9646, Fax: (212) 963-4116, http://unstats.un.org; *Energy Statistics Yearbook 2003; Human Development Report 2006;* and *Statistical Yearbook.*

The World Bank, 1818 H Street, NW, Washington, DC 20433, (202) 473-1000, Fax: (202) 477-6391, www.worldbank.org; *The World Bank Atlas 2003-2004.*

CONGO, DEMOCRATIC REPUBLIC OF THE - PRICES

International Labour Office, I.L.O. Publications, 4 route des Morillons, CH-1211 Geneva 22, Switzerland, (Telephone in U.S. (202) 653-7652), (Fax in U.S. (202) 653-7687), www.ilo.org; *Yearbook of Labour Statistics 2006.*

International Monetary Fund (IMF), 700 Nineteenth Street, NW, Washington, DC 20431, (202) 623-7000, Fax: (202) 623-4661, www.imf.org; *International Financial Statistics Yearbook 2007.*

M.E. Sharpe, 80 Business Park Drive, Armonk, NY 10504, (800) 541-6563, Fax: (914) 273-2106, www.mesharpe.com; *The Illustrated Book of World Rankings.*

United Nations Economic Commission for Africa (ECA), PO Box 3001, Addis Ababa, Ethiopia, (Telephone in U.S. (212) 963-4957), www.uneca.org; *African Statistical Yearbook 2006.*

United Nations Food and Agricultural Organization (FAO), Viale delle Terme di Caracalla, 00100 Rome, Italy, (Dial from U.S. (202) 653-2400), (Fax from U.S. (202) 653 5760), www.fao.org; *The State of Food and Agriculture (SOFA) 2006.*

The World Bank, 1818 H Street, NW, Washington, DC 20433, (202) 473-1000, Fax: (202) 477-6391, www.worldbank.org; *Congo, The Democratic Republic of the.*

World Bureau of Metal Statistics (WBMS), 27a High Street, Ware, Hertfordshire, SG12 9BA, United Kingdom, www.world-bureau.com; *World Flow Charts* and *World Metal Statistics.*

CONGO, DEMOCRATIC REPUBLIC OF THE - PUBLIC HEALTH

African Development Bank Group, Rue Joseph Anoma, 01 BP 1387 Abidjan 01, Cote d'Ivoire, www.afdb.org; *Statistics Pocketbook 2008.*

M.E. Sharpe, 80 Business Park Drive, Armonk, NY 10504, (800) 541-6563, Fax: (914) 273-2106, www.mesharpe.com; *The Illustrated Book of World Rankings.*

Palgrave Macmillan Ltd., Houndmills, Basingstoke, Hampshire, RG21 6XS, England, (Telephone in U.S. (888) 330-8477), (Fax in U.S. (800) 672-2054), www.palgrave.com; *The Statesman's Yearbook 2008.*

UNICEF, 3 United Nations Plaza, New York, NY 10017, (800) 253-9646, Fax: (212) 887-7465, www.unicef.org; *The State of the World's Children 2008.*

United Nations Economic Commission for Africa (ECA), PO Box 3001, Addis Ababa, Ethiopia, (Telephone in U.S. (212) 963-4957), www.uneca.org; *African Statistical Yearbook 2006.*

United Nations Statistics Division, New York, NY 10017, (800) 253-9646, Fax: (212) 963-4116, http://unstats.un.org; *Statistical Yearbook.*

The World Bank, 1818 H Street, NW, Washington, DC 20433, (202) 473-1000, Fax: (202) 477-6391, www.worldbank.org; *Congo, The Democratic Republic of the.*

World Health Organization (WHO), Avenue Appia 20, 1211 Geneve 27, Switzerland, (Telephone in U.S. (212) 331-9081), www.who.int; The WHO Global Atlas of Infectious Diseases and *World Health Report 2006.*

CONGO, DEMOCRATIC REPUBLIC OF THE - PUBLISHERS AND PUBLISHING

UNESCO Institute for Statistics, C.P. 6128 Succursale Centre-Ville, Montreal, Quebec, H3C 3J7 Canada, (Dial from U.S. (514) 343-6880), (Fax from U.S. (514) 343 6882), www.uis.unesco.org; *Statistical Tables.*

CONGO, DEMOCRATIC REPUBLIC OF THE - RADIO - RECEIVERS AND RECEPTION

United Nations Statistics Division, New York, NY 10017, (800) 253-9646, Fax: (212) 963-4116, http://unstats.un.org; *Statistical Yearbook.*

CONGO, DEMOCRATIC REPUBLIC OF THE - RADIO BROADCASTING

Palgrave Macmillan Ltd., Houndmills, Basingstoke, Hampshire, RG21 6XS, England, (Telephone in U.S. (888) 330-8477), (Fax in U.S. (800) 672-2054), www.palgrave.com; *The Statesman's Yearbook 2008.*

CONGO, DEMOCRATIC REPUBLIC OF THE - RAILROADS

Jane's Information Group, 110 North Royal Street, Suite 200, Alexandria, VA 22314, (703) 683-3700, Fax: (800) 836-0297, www.janes.com; *Jane's World Railways.*

Palgrave Macmillan Ltd., Houndmills, Basingstoke, Hampshire, RG21 6XS, England, (Telephone in U.S. (888) 330-8477), (Fax in U.S. (800) 672-2054), www.palgrave.com; *The Statesman's Yearbook 2008.*

Taylor and Francis Group, An Informa Business, 2 Park Square, Milton Park, Abingdon, Oxford OX14 4RN, United Kingdom, (Dial from U.S. (212) 216-7800), (Fax from U.S. (212) 564-7854), www.tandf.co.uk; *The Europa World Year Book.*

United Nations Economic Commission for Africa (ECA), PO Box 3001, Addis Ababa, Ethiopia, (Telephone in U.S. (212) 963-4957), www.uneca.org; *African Statistical Yearbook 2006.*

United Nations Statistics Division, New York, NY 10017, (800) 253-9646, Fax: (212) 963-4116, http://unstats.un.org; *Statistical Yearbook* and *Survey of Economic and Social Conditions in Africa 2005.*

CONGO, DEMOCRATIC REPUBLIC OF THE - RELIGION

Central Intelligence Agency, Office of Public Affairs, Washington, DC 20505, (703) 482-0623, Fax: (703) 482-1739, www.cia.gov; *The World Factbook.*

M.E. Sharpe, 80 Business Park Drive, Armonk, NY 10504, (800) 541-6563, Fax: (914) 273-2106, www.mesharpe.com; *The Illustrated Book of World Rankings.*

Palgrave Macmillan Ltd., Houndmills, Basingstoke, Hampshire, RG21 6XS, England, (Telephone in U.S. (888) 330-8477), (Fax in U.S. (800) 672-2054), www.palgrave.com; *The Statesman's Yearbook 2008.*

CONGO, DEMOCRATIC REPUBLIC OF THE - RENT CHARGES

International Labour Office, I.L.O. Publications, 4 route des Morillons, CH-1211 Geneva 22, Switzerland, (Telephone in U.S. (202) 653-7652), (Fax in U.S. (202) 653-7687), www.ilo.org; *Yearbook of Labour Statistics 2006.*

CONGO, DEMOCRATIC REPUBLIC OF THE - RESERVES (ACCOUNTING)

African Development Bank Group, Rue Joseph Anoma, 01 BP 1387 Abidjan 01, Cote d'Ivoire, www.afdb.org; *Statistics Pocketbook 2008.*

Euromonitor International, Inc., 224 S. Michigan Avenue, Suite 1500, Chicago, IL 60604, (312) 922-1115, Fax: (312) 922-1157, www.euromonitor.com; *International Marketing Data and Statistics 2008.*

United Nations Statistics Division, New York, NY 10017, (800) 253-9646, Fax: (212) 963-4116, http://unstats.un.org; *Statistical Yearbook.*

The World Bank, 1818 H Street, NW, Washington, DC 20433, (202) 473-1000, Fax: (202) 477-6391, www.worldbank.org; *World Development Indicators (WDI) 2008.*

CONGO, DEMOCRATIC REPUBLIC OF THE - RICE PRODUCTION

See CONGO, DEMOCRATIC REPUBLIC OF THE - CROPS

CONGO, DEMOCRATIC REPUBLIC OF THE - ROADS

Central Intelligence Agency, Office of Public Affairs, Washington, DC 20505, (703) 482-0623, Fax: (703) 482-1739, www.cia.gov; *The World Factbook.*

International Road Federation (IFR), Madison Place, 500 Montgomery Street, 5th Floor, Alexandria, VA 22314, (703) 535-1001, Fax: (703) 535-1007, www.irfnet.org; *World Road Statistics 2006.*

Palgrave Macmillan Ltd., Houndmills, Basingstoke, Hampshire, RG21 6XS, England, (Telephone in U.S. (888) 330-8477), (Fax in U.S. (800) 672-2054), www.palgrave.com; *The Statesman's Yearbook 2008.*

United Nations Economic Commission for Africa (ECA), PO Box 3001, Addis Ababa, Ethiopia, (Telephone in U.S. (212) 963-4957), www.uneca.org; *African Statistical Yearbook 2006.*

United Nations Statistics Division, New York, NY 10017, (800) 253-9646, Fax: (212) 963-4116, http://unstats.un.org; *Survey of Economic and Social Conditions in Africa 2005.*

CONGO, DEMOCRATIC REPUBLIC OF THE - RUBBER INDUSTRY AND TRADE

International Rubber Study Group (IRSG), 1st Floor, Heron House, 109/115 Wembley Hill Road, Wembley, Middlesex HA9 8DA, United Kingdom, www.rubberstudy.com; *Rubber Statistical Bulletin; Summary of World Rubber Statistics 2005; World Rubber Statistics Handbook (Volume 6, 1975-2001);* and *World Rubber Statistics Historic Handbook.*

M.E. Sharpe, 80 Business Park Drive, Armonk, NY 10504, (800) 541-6563, Fax: (914) 273-2106, www.mesharpe.com; *The Illustrated Book of World Rankings.*

United Nations Statistics Division, New York, NY 10017, (800) 253-9646, Fax: (212) 963-4116, http://unstats.un.org; *Statistical Yearbook.*

CONGO, DEMOCRATIC REPUBLIC OF THE - SHEEP

See CONGO, DEMOCRATIC REPUBLIC OF THE - LIVESTOCK

CONGO, DEMOCRATIC REPUBLIC OF THE - SHIPPING

Palgrave Macmillan Ltd., Houndmills, Basingstoke, Hampshire, RG21 6XS, England, (Telephone in U.S. (888) 330-8477), (Fax in U.S. (800) 672-2054), www.palgrave.com; *The Statesman's Yearbook 2008.*

Taylor and Francis Group, An Informa Business, 2 Park Square, Milton Park, Abingdon, Oxford OX14 4RN, United Kingdom, (Dial from U.S. (212) 216-7800), (Fax from U.S. (212) 564-7854), www.tandf.co.uk; *The Europa World Year Book.*

U.S. Department of Transportation (DOT), Maritime Administration (MARAD), West Building, Southeast Federal Center, 1200 New Jersey Avenue, SE, Washington, DC 20590, (800) 99-MARAD, www.marad.dot.gov; *World Merchant Fleet 2005.*

United Nations Economic Commission for Africa (ECA), PO Box 3001, Addis Ababa, Ethiopia, (Telephone in U.S. (212) 963-4957), www.uneca.org; *African Statistical Yearbook 2006.*

United Nations Statistics Division, New York, NY 10017, (800) 253-9646, Fax: (212) 963-4116, http://unstats.un.org; *Statistical Yearbook.*

CONGO, DEMOCRATIC REPUBLIC OF THE - SOCIAL ECOLOGY

M.E. Sharpe, 80 Business Park Drive, Armonk, NY 10504, (800) 541-6563, Fax: (914) 273-2106, www.mesharpe.com; *The Illustrated Book of World Rankings.*

CONGO, DEMOCRATIC REPUBLIC OF THE - SOCIAL SECURITY

United Nations Statistics Division, New York, NY 10017, (800) 253-9646, Fax: (212) 963-4116, http://unstats.un.org; *National Accounts Statistics: Compendium of Income Distribution Statistics.*

CONGO, DEMOCRATIC REPUBLIC OF THE - SOYBEAN PRODUCTION

See CONGO, DEMOCRATIC REPUBLIC OF THE - CROPS

CONGO, DEMOCRATIC REPUBLIC OF THE - STEEL PRODUCTION

See CONGO, DEMOCRATIC REPUBLIC OF THE - MINERAL INDUSTRIES

CONGO, DEMOCRATIC REPUBLIC OF THE - SUGAR PRODUCTION

See CONGO, DEMOCRATIC REPUBLIC OF THE - CROPS

CONGO, DEMOCRATIC REPUBLIC OF THE - SULPHUR PRODUCTION

See CONGO, DEMOCRATIC REPUBLIC OF THE - MINERAL INDUSTRIES

CONGO, DEMOCRATIC REPUBLIC OF THE - TAXATION

International Monetary Fund (IMF), 700 Nineteenth Street, NW, Washington, DC 20431, (202) 623-

7000, Fax: (202) 623-4661, www.imf.org; *Government Finance Statistics Yearbook (2008 Edition).*

International Road Federation (IFR), Madison Place, 500 Montgomery Street, 5th Floor, Alexandria, VA 22314, (703) 535-1001, Fax: (703) 535-1007, www.irfnet.org; *World Road Statistics 2006.*

Taylor and Francis Group, An Informa Business, 2 Park Square, Milton Park, Abingdon, Oxford OX14 4RN, United Kingdom, (Dial from U.S. (212) 216-7800), (Fax from U.S. (212) 564-7854), www.tandf.co.uk; *The Europa World Year Book.*

The World Bank, 1818 H Street, NW, Washington, DC 20433, (202) 473-1000, Fax: (202) 477-6391, www.worldbank.org; *World Development Indicators (WDI) 2008.*

CONGO, DEMOCRATIC REPUBLIC OF THE - TEA PRODUCTION

See CONGO, DEMOCRATIC REPUBLIC OF THE - CROPS

CONGO, DEMOCRATIC REPUBLIC OF THE - TELEPHONE

International Telecommunication Union (ITU), Place des Nations, 1211 Geneva 20, Switzerland, www.itu.int; World Telecommunication Indicators Database.

Palgrave Macmillan Ltd., Houndmills, Basingstoke, Hampshire, RG21 6XS, England, (Telephone in U.S. (888) 330-8477), (Fax in U.S. (800) 672-2054), www.palgrave.com; *The Statesman's Yearbook 2008.*

Taylor and Francis Group, An Informa Business, 2 Park Square, Milton Park, Abingdon, Oxford OX14 4RN, United Kingdom, (Dial from U.S. (212) 216-7800), (Fax from U.S. (212) 564-7854), www.tandf.co.uk; *The Europa World Year Book.*

United Nations Statistics Division, New York, NY 10017, (800) 253-9646, Fax: (212) 963-4116, http://unstats.un.org; *Statistical Yearbook.*

CONGO, DEMOCRATIC REPUBLIC OF THE - TEXTILE INDUSTRY

M.E. Sharpe, 80 Business Park Drive, Armonk, NY 10504, (800) 541-6563, Fax: (914) 273-2106, www.mesharpe.com; *The Illustrated Book of World Rankings.*

Palgrave Macmillan Ltd., Houndmills, Basingstoke, Hampshire, RG21 6XS, England, (Telephone in U.S. (888) 330-8477), (Fax in U.S. (800) 672-2054), www.palgrave.com; *The Statesman's Yearbook 2008.*

United Nations Conference on Trade and Development (UNCTAD), DC2-1120, United Nations, New York, NY 10017, (212) 963-0027, www.unctad.org; *UNCTAD Commodity Yearbook.*

United Nations Statistics Division, New York, NY 10017, (800) 253-9646, Fax: (212) 963-4116, http://unstats.un.org; *Statistical Yearbook.*

CONGO, DEMOCRATIC REPUBLIC OF THE - THEATER

UNESCO Institute for Statistics, C.P. 6128 Succursale Centre-Ville, Montreal, Quebec, H3C 3J7 Canada, (Dial from U.S. (514) 343-6880), (Fax from U.S. (514) 343 6882), www.uis.unesco.org; *Statistical Tables.*

CONGO, DEMOCRATIC REPUBLIC OF THE - TIN PRODUCTION

See CONGO, DEMOCRATIC REPUBLIC OF THE - MINERAL INDUSTRIES

CONGO, DEMOCRATIC REPUBLIC OF THE - TOBACCO INDUSTRY

Foreign Agricultural Service (FAS), U.S. Department of Agriculture (USDA), 1400 Independence Avenue, SW, Washington, DC 20250, (202) 720-3935, www.fas.usda.gov; *Tobacco: World Markets and Trade.*

M.E. Sharpe, 80 Business Park Drive, Armonk, NY 10504, (800) 541-6563, Fax: (914) 273-2106, www.mesharpe.com; *The Illustrated Book of World Rankings.*

United Nations Statistics Division, New York, NY 10017, (800) 253-9646, Fax: (212) 963-4116, http://unstats.un.org; *Statistical Yearbook.*

CONGO, DEMOCRATIC REPUBLIC OF THE - TOURISM

Euromonitor International, Inc., 224 S. Michigan Avenue, Suite 1500, Chicago, IL 60604, (312) 922-1115, Fax: (312) 922-1157, www.euromonitor.com; *The World Economic Factbook 2008.*

M.E. Sharpe, 80 Business Park Drive, Armonk, NY 10504, (800) 541-6563, Fax: (914) 273-2106, www.mesharpe.com; *The Illustrated Book of World Rankings.*

Palgrave Macmillan Ltd., Houndmills, Basingstoke, Hampshire, RG21 6XS, England, (Telephone in U.S. (888) 330-8477), (Fax in U.S. (800) 672-2054), www.palgrave.com; *The Statesman's Yearbook 2008.*

Taylor and Francis Group, An Informa Business, 2 Park Square, Milton Park, Abingdon, Oxford OX14 4RN, United Kingdom, (Dial from U.S. (212) 216-7800), (Fax from U.S. (212) 564-7854), www.tandf.co.uk; *The Europa World Year Book.*

United Nations Economic Commission for Africa (ECA), PO Box 3001, Addis Ababa, Ethiopia, (Telephone in U.S. (212) 963-4957), www.uneca.org; *African Statistical Yearbook 2006.*

United Nations Statistics Division, New York, NY 10017, (800) 253-9646, Fax: (212) 963-4116, http://unstats.un.org; *Statistical Yearbook.*

United Nations World Tourism Organization (UNWTO), Capitan Haya 42, 28020 Madrid, Spain, www.world-tourism.org; *Yearbook of Tourism Statistics.*

The World Bank, 1818 H Street, NW, Washington, DC 20433, (202) 473-1000, Fax: (202) 477-6391, www.worldbank.org; *Congo, The Democratic Republic of the.*

CONGO, DEMOCRATIC REPUBLIC OF THE - TRADE

See CONGO, DEMOCRATIC REPUBLIC OF THE - INTERNATIONAL TRADE

CONGO, DEMOCRATIC REPUBLIC OF THE - TRANSPORTATION

Central Intelligence Agency, Office of Public Affairs, Washington, DC 20505, (703) 482-0623, Fax: (703) 482-1739, www.cia.gov; *The World Factbook.*

Euromonitor International, Inc., 224 S. Michigan Avenue, Suite 1500, Chicago, IL 60604, (312) 922-1115, Fax: (312) 922-1157, www.euromonitor.com; *International Marketing Data and Statistics 2008.*

M.E. Sharpe, 80 Business Park Drive, Armonk, NY 10504, (800) 541-6563, Fax: (914) 273-2106, www.mesharpe.com; *The Illustrated Book of World Rankings.*

Palgrave Macmillan Ltd., Houndmills, Basingstoke, Hampshire, RG21 6XS, England, (Telephone in U.S. (888) 330-8477), (Fax in U.S. (800) 672-2054), www.palgrave.com; *The Statesman's Yearbook 2008.*

Taylor and Francis Group, An Informa Business, 2 Park Square, Milton Park, Abingdon, Oxford OX14 4RN, United Kingdom, (Dial from U.S. (212) 216-7800), (Fax from U.S. (212) 564-7854), www.tandf.co.uk; *The Europa World Year Book.*

United Nations Economic Commission for Africa (ECA), PO Box 3001, Addis Ababa, Ethiopia, (Telephone in U.S. (212) 963-4957), www.uneca.org; *African Statistical Yearbook 2006.*

United Nations Statistics Division, New York, NY 10017, (800) 253-9646, Fax: (212) 963-4116, http://unstats.un.org; *Human Development Report 2006.*

The World Bank, 1818 H Street, NW, Washington, DC 20433, (202) 473-1000, Fax: (202) 477-6391, www.worldbank.org; *Africa Live Database (LDB)* and *Congo, The Democratic Republic of the.*

CONGO, DEMOCRATIC REPUBLIC OF THE - UNEMPLOYMENT

Central Intelligence Agency, Office of Public Affairs, Washington, DC 20505, (703) 482-0623, Fax: (703) 482-1739, www.cia.gov; *The World Factbook.*

Euromonitor International, Inc., 224 S. Michigan Avenue, Suite 1500, Chicago, IL 60604, (312) 922-1115, Fax: (312) 922-1157, www.euromonitor.com; *International Marketing Data and Statistics 2008.*

International Labour Office, I.L.O. Publications, 4 route des Morillons, CH-1211 Geneva 22, Switzerland, (Telephone in U.S. (202) 653-7652), (Fax in U.S. (202) 653-7687), www.ilo.org; *Yearbook of Labour Statistics 2006.*

The World Bank, 1818 H Street, NW, Washington, DC 20433, (202) 473-1000, Fax: (202) 477-6391, www.worldbank.org; *Congo, The Democratic Republic of the.*

CONGO, DEMOCRATIC REPUBLIC OF THE - VITAL STATISTICS

Euromonitor International, Inc., 224 S. Michigan Avenue, Suite 1500, Chicago, IL 60604, (312) 922-1115, Fax: (312) 922-1157, www.euromonitor.com; *International Marketing Data and Statistics 2008.*

United Nations Statistics Division, New York, NY 10017, (800) 253-9646, Fax: (212) 963-4116, http://unstats.un.org; *Statistical Yearbook.*

World Health Organization (WHO), Avenue Appia 20, 1211 Geneve 27, Switzerland, (Telephone in U.S. (212) 331-9081), www.who.int; *World Health Report 2006.*

CONGO, DEMOCRATIC REPUBLIC OF THE - WAGES

International Labour Office, I.L.O. Publications, 4 route des Morillons, CH-1211 Geneva 22, Switzerland, (Telephone in U.S. (202) 653-7652), (Fax in U.S. (202) 653-7687), www.ilo.org; *Yearbook of Labour Statistics 2006.*

The World Bank, 1818 H Street, NW, Washington, DC 20433, (202) 473-1000, Fax: (202) 477-6391, www.worldbank.org; *Congo, The Democratic Republic of the.*

CONGO, DEMOCRATIC REPUBLIC OF THE - WEATHER

See CONGO, DEMOCRATIC REPUBLIC OF THE - CLIMATE

CONGO, DEMOCRATIC REPUBLIC OF THE - WHEAT PRODUCTION

See CONGO, DEMOCRATIC REPUBLIC OF THE - CROPS

CONGO, DEMOCRATIC REPUBLIC OF THE - WINE PRODUCTION

See CONGO, DEMOCRATIC REPUBLIC OF THE - BEVERAGE INDUSTRY

CONGO, DEMOCRATIC REPUBLIC OF THE - WOOL PRODUCTION

See CONGO, DEMOCRATIC REPUBLIC OF THE - TEXTILE INDUSTRY

CONGO, REPUBLIC OF THE - NATIONAL STATISTICAL OFFICE

Centre National de la Statistique et des Etudes Economiques (CNSEE), BP 2031, Brazzaville, Congo, www.cnsee.org; National Data Center.

CONGO, REPUBLIC OF THE - PRIMARY STATISTICS SOURCES

Centre National de la Statistique et des Etudes Economiques (CNSEE), BP 2031, Brazzaville,

Congo, www.cnsee.org; *Annuaire statistique du Congo 2000-2004* (Statistical Yearbook 2000-2004).

CONGO, REPUBLIC OF THE - AGRICULTURAL MACHINERY

United Nations Statistics Division, New York, NY 10017, (800) 253-9646, Fax: (212) 963-4116, http://unstats.un.org; *Statistical Yearbook.*

CONGO, REPUBLIC OF THE - AGRICULTURE

Economist Intelligence Unit, 111 West 57th Street, New York, NY 10019, (212) 554-0600, Fax: (212) 586-1181, www.eiu.com; *Congo (Brazzaville) Country Report.*

Euromonitor International, Inc., 224 S. Michigan Avenue, Suite 1500, Chicago, IL 60604, (312) 922-1115, Fax: (312) 922-1157, www.euromonitor.com; *World Marketing Data and Statistics.*

M.E. Sharpe, 80 Business Park Drive, Armonk, NY 10504, (800) 541-6563, Fax: (914) 273-2106, www.mesharpe.com; *The Illustrated Book of World Rankings.*

Palgrave Macmillan Ltd., Houndmills, Basingstoke, Hampshire, RG21 6XS, England, (Telephone in U.S. (888) 330-8477), (Fax in U.S. (800) 672-2054), www.palgrave.com; *The Statesman's Yearbook 2008.*

Taylor and Francis Group, An Informa Business, 2 Park Square, Milton Park, Abingdon, Oxford OX14 4RN, United Kingdom, (Dial from U.S. (212) 216-7800), (Fax from U.S. (212) 564-7854), www.tandf.co.uk; *The Europa World Year Book.*

United Nations Conference on Trade and Development (UNCTAD), DC2-1120, United Nations, New York, NY 10017, (212) 963-0027, www.unctad.org; *UNCTAD Commodity Yearbook.*

United Nations Economic Commission for Africa (ECA), PO Box 3001, Addis Ababa, Ethiopia, (Telephone in U.S. (212) 963-4957), www.uneca.org; *African Statistical Yearbook 2006.*

United Nations Food and Agricultural Organization (FAO), Viale delle Terme di Caracalla, 00100 Rome, Italy, (Dial from U.S. (202) 653-2400), (Fax from U.S. (202) 653 5760), www.fao.org; AQUASTAT; *FAO Production Yearbook 2002; FAO Trade Yearbook;* and *The State of Food and Agriculture (SOFA) 2006.*

United Nations Statistics Division, New York, NY 10017, (800) 253-9646, Fax: (212) 963-4116, http://unstats.un.org; *Statistical Yearbook* and *Survey of Economic and Social Conditions in Africa 2005.*

The World Bank, 1818 H Street, NW, Washington, DC 20433, (202) 473-1000, Fax: (202) 477-6391, www.worldbank.org; *Africa Live Database (LDB); African Development Indicators (ADI) 2007; Congo, Democratic Republic of;* and *World Development Indicators (WDI) 2008.*

CONGO, REPUBLIC OF THE - AIRLINES

M.E. Sharpe, 80 Business Park Drive, Armonk, NY 10504, (800) 541-6563, Fax: (914) 273-2106, www.mesharpe.com; *The Illustrated Book of World Rankings.*

Palgrave Macmillan Ltd., Houndmills, Basingstoke, Hampshire, RG21 6XS, England, (Telephone in U.S. (888) 330-8477), (Fax in U.S. (800) 672-2054), www.palgrave.com; *The Statesman's Yearbook 2008.*

Taylor and Francis Group, An Informa Business, 2 Park Square, Milton Park, Abingdon, Oxford OX14 4RN, United Kingdom, (Dial from U.S. (212) 216-7800), (Fax from U.S. (212) 564-7854), www.tandf.co.uk; *The Europa World Year Book.*

United Nations Economic Commission for Africa (ECA), PO Box 3001, Addis Ababa, Ethiopia, (Telephone in U.S. (212) 963-4957), www.uneca.org; *African Statistical Yearbook 2006.*

United Nations Statistics Division, New York, NY 10017, (800) 253-9646, Fax: (212) 963-4116, http://unstats.un.org; *Statistical Yearbook.*

CONGO, REPUBLIC OF THE - AIRPORTS

Central Intelligence Agency, Office of Public Affairs, Washington, DC 20505, (703) 482-0623, Fax: (703) 482-1739, www.cia.gov; *The World Factbook.*

CONGO, REPUBLIC OF THE - ARMED FORCES

Central Intelligence Agency, Office of Public Affairs, Washington, DC 20505, (703) 482-0623, Fax: (703) 482-1739, www.cia.gov; *The World Factbook.*

Euromonitor International, Inc., 224 S. Michigan Avenue, Suite 1500, Chicago, IL 60604, (312) 922-1115, Fax: (312) 922-1157, www.euromonitor.com; *World Marketing Data and Statistics.*

International Institute for Strategic Studies (IISS), Arundel House, 13-15 Arundel Street, Temple Place, London WC2R 3DX, England, www.iiss.org; *The Military Balance 2007.*

International Monetary Fund (IMF), 700 Nineteenth Street, NW, Washington, DC 20431, (202) 623-7000, Fax: (202) 623-4661, www.imf.org; *Government Finance Statistics Yearbook (2008 Edition).*

Palgrave Macmillan Ltd., Houndmills, Basingstoke, Hampshire, RG21 6XS, England, (Telephone in U.S. (888) 330-8477), (Fax in U.S. (800) 672-2054), www.palgrave.com; *The Statesman's Yearbook 2008.*

U.S. Department of State (DOS), 2201 C Street NW, Washington, DC 20520, (202) 647-4000, www.state.gov; *World Military Expenditures and Arms Transfers (WMEAT).*

United Nations Statistics Division, New York, NY 10017, (800) 253-9646, Fax: (212) 963-4116, http://unstats.un.org; *Human Development Report 2006.*

CONGO, REPUBLIC OF THE - BALANCE OF PAYMENTS

African Development Bank Group, Rue Joseph Anoma, 01 BP 1387 Abidjan 01, Cote d'Ivoire, www.afdb.org; *Statistics Pocketbook 2008.*

International Monetary Fund (IMF), 700 Nineteenth Street, NW, Washington, DC 20431, (202) 623-7000, Fax: (202) 623-4661, www.imf.org; *Balance of Payments Statistics Newsletter* and *Balance of Payments Statistics Yearbook 2007.*

Taylor and Francis Group, An Informa Business, 2 Park Square, Milton Park, Abingdon, Oxford OX14 4RN, United Kingdom, (Dial from U.S. (212) 216-7800), (Fax from U.S. (212) 564-7854), www.tandf.co.uk; *The Europa World Year Book.*

United Nations Conference on Trade and Development (UNCTAD), DC2-1120, United Nations, New York, NY 10017, (212) 963-0027, www.unctad.org; *Handbook of Statistics 2005.*

United Nations Economic Commission for Africa (ECA), PO Box 3001, Addis Ababa, Ethiopia, (Telephone in U.S. (212) 963-4957), www.uneca.org; *African Statistical Yearbook 2006.*

The World Bank, 1818 H Street, NW, Washington, DC 20433, (202) 473-1000, Fax: (202) 477-6391, www.worldbank.org; *Congo, Democratic Republic of; World Development Indicators (WDI) 2008;* and *World Development Report 2008.*

CONGO, REPUBLIC OF THE - BANKS AND BANKING

Euromonitor International, Inc., 224 S. Michigan Avenue, Suite 1500, Chicago, IL 60604, (312) 922-1115, Fax: (312) 922-1157, www.euromonitor.com; *World Marketing Data and Statistics.*

International Monetary Fund (IMF), 700 Nineteenth Street, NW, Washington, DC 20431, (202) 623-7000, Fax: (202) 623-4661, www.imf.org; *International Financial Statistics Yearbook 2007.*

M.E. Sharpe, 80 Business Park Drive, Armonk, NY 10504, (800) 541-6563, Fax: (914) 273-2106, www.mesharpe.com; *The Illustrated Book of World Rankings.*

Palgrave Macmillan Ltd., Houndmills, Basingstoke, Hampshire, RG21 6XS, England, (Telephone in U.S. (888) 330-8477), (Fax in U.S. (800) 672-2054), www.palgrave.com; *The Statesman's Yearbook 2008.*

Taylor and Francis Group, An Informa Business, 2 Park Square, Milton Park, Abingdon, Oxford OX14 4RN, United Kingdom, (Dial from U.S. (212) 216-7800), (Fax from U.S. (212) 564-7854), www.tandf.co.uk; *The Europa World Year Book.*

United Nations Economic Commission for Africa (ECA), PO Box 3001, Addis Ababa, Ethiopia, (Telephone in U.S. (212) 963-4957), www.uneca.org; *African Statistical Yearbook 2006.*

CONGO, REPUBLIC OF THE - BEVERAGE INDUSTRY

M.E. Sharpe, 80 Business Park Drive, Armonk, NY 10504, (800) 541-6563, Fax: (914) 273-2106, www.mesharpe.com; *The Illustrated Book of World Rankings.*

United Nations Statistics Division, New York, NY 10017, (800) 253-9646, Fax: (212) 963-4116, http://unstats.un.org; *Statistical Yearbook.*

CONGO, REPUBLIC OF THE - BROADCASTING

Central Intelligence Agency, Office of Public Affairs, Washington, DC 20505, (703) 482-0623, Fax: (703) 482-1739, www.cia.gov; *The World Factbook.*

Euromonitor International, Inc., 224 S. Michigan Avenue, Suite 1500, Chicago, IL 60604, (312) 922-1115, Fax: (312) 922-1157, www.euromonitor.com; *World Marketing Data and Statistics.*

M.E. Sharpe, 80 Business Park Drive, Armonk, NY 10504, (800) 541-6563, Fax: (914) 273-2106, www.mesharpe.com; *The Illustrated Book of World Rankings.*

Palgrave Macmillan Ltd., Houndmills, Basingstoke, Hampshire, RG21 6XS, England, (Telephone in U.S. (888) 330-8477), (Fax in U.S. (800) 672-2054), www.palgrave.com; *The Statesman's Yearbook 2008.*

WRTH Publications Limited, PO Box 290, Oxford OX2 7FT, UK, www.wrth.com; *World Radio TV Handbook 2007.*

CONGO, REPUBLIC OF THE - BUDGET

Central Intelligence Agency, Office of Public Affairs, Washington, DC 20505, (703) 482-0623, Fax: (703) 482-1739, www.cia.gov; *The World Factbook.*

CONGO, REPUBLIC OF THE - CAPITAL LEVY

International Monetary Fund (IMF), 700 Nineteenth Street, NW, Washington, DC 20431, (202) 623-7000, Fax: (202) 623-4661, www.imf.org; *Government Finance Statistics Yearbook (2008 Edition).*

CONGO, REPUBLIC OF THE - CHILDBIRTH - STATISTICS

Central Intelligence Agency, Office of Public Affairs, Washington, DC 20505, (703) 482-0623, Fax: (703) 482-1739, www.cia.gov; *The World Factbook.*

Euromonitor International, Inc., 224 S. Michigan Avenue, Suite 1500, Chicago, IL 60604, (312) 922-1115, Fax: (312) 922-1157, www.euromonitor.com; *International Marketing Data and Statistics 2008* and *The World Economic Factbook 2008.*

M.E. Sharpe, 80 Business Park Drive, Armonk, NY 10504, (800) 541-6563, Fax: (914) 273-2106, www.mesharpe.com; *The Illustrated Book of World Rankings.*

Taylor and Francis Group, An Informa Business, 2 Park Square, Milton Park, Abingdon, Oxford OX14 4RN, United Kingdom, (Dial from U.S. (212) 216-7800), (Fax from U.S. (212) 564-7854), www.tandf.co.uk; *The Europa World Year Book.*

United Nations Statistics Division, New York, NY 10017, (800) 253-9646, Fax: (212) 963-4116, http://unstats.un.org; *Demographic Yearbook; Statistical Yearbook;* and *Survey of Economic and Social Conditions in Africa 2005.*

The World Bank, 1818 H Street, NW, Washington, DC 20433, (202) 473-1000, Fax: (202) 477-6391, www.worldbank.org; *World Development Indicators (WDI) 2008.*

CONGO, REPUBLIC OF THE - CLIMATE

M.E. Sharpe, 80 Business Park Drive, Armonk, NY 10504, (800) 541-6563, Fax: (914) 273-2106, www.mesharpe.com; *The Illustrated Book of World Rankings.*

Palgrave Macmillan Ltd., Houndmills, Basingstoke, Hampshire, RG21 6XS, England, (Telephone in U.S. (888) 330-8477), (Fax in U.S. (800) 672-2054), www.palgrave.com; *The Statesman's Yearbook 2008.*

CONGO, REPUBLIC OF THE - COMMERCE

Palgrave Macmillan Ltd., Houndmills, Basingstoke, Hampshire, RG21 6XS, England, (Telephone in U.S. (888) 330-8477), (Fax in U.S. (800) 672-2054), www.palgrave.com; *The Statesman's Yearbook 2008.*

CONGO, REPUBLIC OF THE - COMMODITY EXCHANGES

Commodity Research Bureau, 330 South Wells Street, Suite 612, Chicago, IL 60606-7110, (800) 621-5271, Fax: (312) 939-4135, www.crbtrader.com; *2006 CRB Commodity Yearbook and CD.*

International Monetary Fund (IMF), 700 Nineteenth Street, NW, Washington, DC 20431, (202) 623-7000, Fax: (202) 623-4661, www.imf.org; *IMF Primary Commodity Prices.*

United Nations Food and Agricultural Organization (FAO), Viale delle Terme di Caracalla, 00100 Rome, Italy, (Dial from U.S. (202) 653-2400), (Fax from U.S. (202) 653 5760), www.fao.org; *The State of Food and Agriculture (SOFA) 2006.*

CONGO, REPUBLIC OF THE - COMMUNICATION AND TRAFFIC

United Nations Statistics Division, New York, NY 10017, (800) 253-9646, Fax: (212) 963-4116, http://unstats.un.org; *Statistical Yearbook.*

CONGO, REPUBLIC OF THE - CONSTRUCTION INDUSTRY

M.E. Sharpe, 80 Business Park Drive, Armonk, NY 10504, (800) 541-6563, Fax: (914) 273-2106, www.mesharpe.com; *The Illustrated Book of World Rankings.*

United Nations Economic Commission for Africa (ECA), PO Box 3001, Addis Ababa, Ethiopia, (Telephone in U.S. (212) 963-4957), www.uneca.org; *African Statistical Yearbook 2006.*

CONGO, REPUBLIC OF THE - CONSUMER PRICE INDEXES

Taylor and Francis Group, An Informa Business, 2 Park Square, Milton Park, Abingdon, Oxford OX14 4RN, United Kingdom, (Dial from U.S. (212) 216-7800), (Fax from U.S. (212) 564-7854), www.tandf.co.uk; *The Europa World Year Book.*

United Nations Economic Commission for Africa (ECA), PO Box 3001, Addis Ababa, Ethiopia, (Telephone in U.S. (212) 963-4957), www.uneca.org; *African Statistical Yearbook 2006.*

United Nations Statistics Division, New York, NY 10017, (800) 253-9646, Fax: (212) 963-4116, http://unstats.un.org; *Statistical Yearbook* and *Survey of Economic and Social Conditions in Africa 2005.*

The World Bank, 1818 H Street, NW, Washington, DC 20433, (202) 473-1000, Fax: (202) 477-6391, www.worldbank.org; *Congo, Democratic Republic of.*

CONGO, REPUBLIC OF THE - CONSUMPTION (ECONOMICS)

African Development Bank Group, Rue Joseph Anoma, 01 BP 1387 Abidjan 01, Cote d'Ivoire, www.afdb.org; *Statistics Pocketbook 2008.*

United Nations Statistics Division, New York, NY 10017, (800) 253-9646, Fax: (212) 963-4116, http://unstats.un.org; *Survey of Economic and Social Conditions in Africa 2005.*

The World Bank, 1818 H Street, NW, Washington, DC 20433, (202) 473-1000, Fax: (202) 477-6391, www.worldbank.org; *World Development Report 2008.*

CONGO, REPUBLIC OF THE - COST AND STANDARD OF LIVING

International Monetary Fund (IMF), 700 Nineteenth Street, NW, Washington, DC 20431, (202) 623-7000, Fax: (202) 623-4661, www.imf.org; *Government Finance Statistics Yearbook (2008 Edition).*

CONGO, REPUBLIC OF THE - CRIME

Yale University Press, PO Box 209040, New Haven, CT 06520-9040, (203) 432-0960, Fax: (203) 432-0948, http://yalepress.yale.edu/yupbooks; *Violence and Crime in Cross-National Perspective.*

CONGO, REPUBLIC OF THE - CROPS

M.E. Sharpe, 80 Business Park Drive, Armonk, NY 10504, (800) 541-6563, Fax: (914) 273-2106, www.mesharpe.com; *The Illustrated Book of World Rankings.*

Palgrave Macmillan Ltd., Houndmills, Basingstoke, Hampshire, RG21 6XS, England, (Telephone in U.S. (888) 330-8477), (Fax in U.S. (800) 672-2054), www.palgrave.com; *The Statesman's Yearbook 2008.*

Taylor and Francis Group, An Informa Business, 2 Park Square, Milton Park, Abingdon, Oxford OX14 4RN, United Kingdom, (Dial from U.S. (212) 216-7800), (Fax from U.S. (212) 564-7854), www.tandf.co.uk; *The Europa World Year Book.*

United Nations Conference on Trade and Development (UNCTAD), DC2-1120, United Nations, New York, NY 10017, (212) 963-0027, www.unctad.org; *UNCTAD Commodity Yearbook.*

United Nations Economic Commission for Africa (ECA), PO Box 3001, Addis Ababa, Ethiopia, (Telephone in U.S. (212) 963-4957), www.uneca.org; *African Statistical Yearbook 2006.*

United Nations Food and Agricultural Organization (FAO), Viale delle Terme di Caracalla, 00100 Rome, Italy, (Dial from U.S. (202) 653-2400), (Fax from U.S. (202) 653 5760), www.fao.org; *The State of Food and Agriculture (SOFA) 2006.*

United Nations Statistics Division, New York, NY 10017, (800) 253-9646, Fax: (212) 963-4116, http://unstats.un.org; *Statistical Yearbook.*

CONGO, REPUBLIC OF THE - CUSTOMS ADMINISTRATION

International Monetary Fund (IMF), 700 Nineteenth Street, NW, Washington, DC 20431, (202) 623-7000, Fax: (202) 623-4661, www.imf.org; *Government Finance Statistics Yearbook (2008 Edition).*

CONGO, REPUBLIC OF THE - DAIRY PROCESSING

M.E. Sharpe, 80 Business Park Drive, Armonk, NY 10504, (800) 541-6563, Fax: (914) 273-2106, www.mesharpe.com; *The Illustrated Book of World Rankings.*

Palgrave Macmillan Ltd., Houndmills, Basingstoke, Hampshire, RG21 6XS, England, (Telephone in U.S. (888) 330-8477), (Fax in U.S. (800) 672-2054), www.palgrave.com; *The Statesman's Yearbook 2008.*

Taylor and Francis Group, An Informa Business, 2 Park Square, Milton Park, Abingdon, Oxford OX14 4RN, United Kingdom, (Dial from U.S. (212) 216-7800), (Fax from U.S. (212) 564-7854), www.tandf.co.uk; *The Europa World Year Book.*

United Nations Food and Agricultural Organization (FAO), Viale delle Terme di Caracalla, 00100 Rome, Italy, (Dial from U.S. (202) 653-2400), (Fax from U.S. (202) 653 5760), www.fao.org; *The State of Food and Agriculture (SOFA) 2006.*

CONGO, REPUBLIC OF THE - DEBTS, EXTERNAL

African Development Bank Group, Rue Joseph Anoma, 01 BP 1387 Abidjan 01, Cote d'Ivoire, www.afdb.org; *Statistics Pocketbook 2008.*

Palgrave Macmillan Ltd., Houndmills, Basingstoke, Hampshire, RG21 6XS, England, (Telephone in U.S. (888) 330-8477), (Fax in U.S. (800) 672-2054), www.palgrave.com; *The Statesman's Yearbook 2008.*

United Nations Statistics Division, New York, NY 10017, (800) 253-9646, Fax: (212) 963-4116, http://unstats.un.org; *Survey of Economic and Social Conditions in Africa 2005.*

The World Bank, 1818 H Street, NW, Washington, DC 20433, (202) 473-1000, Fax: (202) 477-6391, www.worldbank.org; *Africa Live Database (LDB); African Development Indicators (ADI) 2007; Global Development Finance 2007; World Development Indicators (WDI) 2008;* and *World Development Report 2008.*

CONGO, REPUBLIC OF THE - DEMOGRAPHY

Euromonitor International, Inc., 224 S. Michigan Avenue, Suite 1500, Chicago, IL 60604, (312) 922-1115, Fax: (312) 922-1157, www.euromonitor.com; *International Marketing Data and Statistics 2008; The World Economic Factbook 2008;* and *World Marketing Data and Statistics.*

M.E. Sharpe, 80 Business Park Drive, Armonk, NY 10504, (800) 541-6563, Fax: (914) 273-2106, www.mesharpe.com; *The Illustrated Book of World Rankings.*

United Nations Statistics Division, New York, NY 10017, (800) 253-9646, Fax: (212) 963-4116, http://unstats.un.org; *Human Development Report 2006* and *Survey of Economic and Social Conditions in Africa 2005.*

The World Bank, 1818 H Street, NW, Washington, DC 20433, (202) 473-1000, Fax: (202) 477-6391, www.worldbank.org; *Congo, Democratic Republic of.*

CONGO, REPUBLIC OF THE - DISPOSABLE INCOME

M.E. Sharpe, 80 Business Park Drive, Armonk, NY 10504, (800) 541-6563, Fax: (914) 273-2106, www.mesharpe.com; *The Illustrated Book of World Rankings.*

United Nations Statistics Division, New York, NY 10017, (800) 253-9646, Fax: (212) 963-4116, http://unstats.un.org; *National Accounts Statistics: Compendium of Income Distribution Statistics* and *Statistical Yearbook.*

CONGO, REPUBLIC OF THE - DIVORCE

M.E. Sharpe, 80 Business Park Drive, Armonk, NY 10504, (800) 541-6563, Fax: (914) 273-2106, www.mesharpe.com; *The Illustrated Book of World Rankings.*

United Nations Statistics Division, New York, NY 10017, (800) 253-9646, Fax: (212) 963-4116, http://unstats.un.org; *Demographic Yearbook* and *Statistical Yearbook.*

CONGO, REPUBLIC OF THE - ECONOMIC ASSISTANCE

United Nations Statistics Division, New York, NY 10017, (800) 253-9646, Fax: (212) 963-4116, http://unstats.un.org; *Statistical Yearbook.*

CONGO, REPUBLIC OF THE - ECONOMIC CONDITIONS

African Development Bank Group, Rue Joseph Anoma, 01 BP 1387 Abidjan 01, Cote d'Ivoire, www.afdb.org; *The African Statistical Journal; Gender, Poverty and Environmental Indicators on African Countries 2007; Selected Statistics on African Countries 2007;* and *Statistics Pocketbook 2008.*

Center for International Business Education Research (CIBER), Columbia Business School and School of International and Public Affairs, Uris Hall, Room 212, 3022 Broadway, New York, NY 10027-6902, Mr. Joshua Safier, (212) 854-4750, Fax: (212) 222-9821, www.columbia.edu/cu/ciber/; Datastream International.

Central Intelligence Agency, Office of Public Affairs, Washington, DC 20505, (703) 482-0623, Fax: (703) 482-1739, www.cia.gov; *The World Factbook.*

DSI Data Service Information, Xantener Strasse 51a, D-47495 Rheinberg, Germany, www.dsidata.com; *Campus Solution.*

Dun and Bradstreet (DB) Corporation, 103 JFK Parkway, Short Hills, NJ 07078, (973) 921-5500, www.dnb.com; *Country Report.*

Economist Intelligence Unit, 111 West 57th Street, New York, NY 10019, (212) 554-0600, Fax: (212) 586-1181, www.eiu.com; *Business Africa* and *Congo (Brazzaville) Country Report.*

Euromonitor International, Inc., 224 S. Michigan Avenue, Suite 1500, Chicago, IL 60604, (312) 922-1115, Fax: (312) 922-1157, www.euromonitor.com; *The World Economic Factbook 2008* and *World Marketing Data and Statistics.*

International Monetary Fund (IMF), 700 Nineteenth Street, NW, Washington, DC 20431, (202) 623-7000, Fax: (202) 623-4661, www.imf.org; *World Economic Outlook Reports.*

M.E. Sharpe, 80 Business Park Drive, Armonk, NY 10504, (800) 541-6563, Fax: (914) 273-2106, www.mesharpe.com; *The Illustrated Book of World Rankings.*

Palgrave Macmillan Ltd., Houndmills, Basingstoke, Hampshire, RG21 6XS, England, (Telephone in U.S. (888) 330-8477), (Fax in U.S. (800) 672-2054), www.palgrave.com; *The Statesman's Yearbook 2008.*

Taylor and Francis Group, An Informa Business, 2 Park Square, Milton Park, Abingdon, Oxford OX14 4RN, United Kingdom, (Dial from U.S. (212) 216-7800), (Fax from U.S. (212) 564-7854), www.tandf.co.uk; *The Europa World Year Book.*

United Nations Statistics Division, New York, NY 10017, (800) 253-9646, Fax: (212) 963-4116, http://unstats.un.org; *Compendium of Intra-African and Related Foreign Trade Statistics 2003* and *World Statistics Pocketbook.*

The World Bank, 1818 H Street, NW, Washington, DC 20433, (202) 473-1000, Fax: (202) 477-6391, www.worldbank.org; *Africa Household Survey Databank; Africa Live Database (LDB); Africa Standardized Files and Indicators; African Development Indicators (ADI) 2007; Congo, Democratic Republic of; Global Economic Monitor (GEM); Global Economic Prospects 2008; The World Bank Atlas 2003-2004;* and *World Development Report 2008.*

CONGO, REPUBLIC OF THE - EDUCATION

African Development Bank Group, Rue Joseph Anoma, 01 BP 1387 Abidjan 01, Cote d'Ivoire, www.afdb.org; *Statistics Pocketbook 2008.*

Euromonitor International, Inc., 224 S. Michigan Avenue, Suite 1500, Chicago, IL 60604, (312) 922-1115, Fax: (312) 922-1157, www.euromonitor.com; *International Marketing Data and Statistics 2008* and *World Marketing Data and Statistics.*

International Monetary Fund (IMF), 700 Nineteenth Street, NW, Washington, DC 20431, (202) 623-7000, Fax: (202) 623-4661, www.imf.org; *Government Finance Statistics Yearbook (2008 Edition).*

M.E. Sharpe, 80 Business Park Drive, Armonk, NY 10504, (800) 541-6563, Fax: (914) 273-2106, www.mesharpe.com; *The Illustrated Book of World Rankings.*

Palgrave Macmillan Ltd., Houndmills, Basingstoke, Hampshire, RG21 6XS, England, (Telephone in U.S. (888) 330-8477), (Fax in U.S. (800) 672-2054), www.palgrave.com; *The Statesman's Yearbook 2008.*

Taylor and Francis Group, An Informa Business, 2 Park Square, Milton Park, Abingdon, Oxford OX14 4RN, United Kingdom, (Dial from U.S. (212) 216-7800), (Fax from U.S. (212) 564-7854), www.tandf.co.uk; *The Europa World Year Book.*

UNESCO Institute for Statistics, C.P. 6128 Succursale Centre-Ville, Montreal, Quebec, H3C 3J7 Canada, (Dial from U.S. (514) 343-6880), (Fax from U.S. (514) 343 6882), www.uis.unesco.org; *Statistical Tables.*

United Nations Economic Commission for Africa (ECA), PO Box 3001, Addis Ababa, Ethiopia, (Telephone in U.S. (212) 963-4957), www.uneca.org; *African Statistical Yearbook 2006.*

United Nations Statistics Division, New York, NY 10017, (800) 253-9646, Fax: (212) 963-4116, http://unstats.un.org; *Human Development Report 2006* and *Survey of Economic and Social Conditions in Africa 2005.*

The World Bank, 1818 H Street, NW, Washington, DC 20433, (202) 473-1000, Fax: (202) 477-6391, www.worldbank.org; *Congo, Democratic Republic of; World Development Indicators (WDI) 2008;* and *World Development Report 2008.*

CONGO, REPUBLIC OF THE - ELECTRICITY

M.E. Sharpe, 80 Business Park Drive, Armonk, NY 10504, (800) 541-6563, Fax: (914) 273-2106, www.mesharpe.com; *The Illustrated Book of World Rankings.*

Organisation for Economic Cooperation and Development (OECD), 2 rue Andre Pascal, F-75775 Paris Cedex 16, France, (Telephone in U.S. (202) 785-6323), (Fax in U.S. (202) 785-0350), www.oecd.org; *World Energy Outlook 2007.*

Palgrave Macmillan Ltd., Houndmills, Basingstoke, Hampshire, RG21 6XS, England, (Telephone in U.S. (888) 330-8477), (Fax in U.S. (800) 672-2054), www.palgrave.com; *The Statesman's Yearbook 2008.*

U.S. Department of Energy (DOE), Energy Information Administration (EIA), 1000 Independence Avenue, SW, Washington, DC 20585, (202) 586-8800, www.eia.doe.gov; *International Energy Annual 2004* and *International Energy Outlook 2006.*

United Nations Economic Commission for Africa (ECA), PO Box 3001, Addis Ababa, Ethiopia, (Telephone in U.S. (212) 963-4957), www.uneca.org; *African Statistical Yearbook 2006.*

United Nations Statistics Division, New York, NY 10017, (800) 253-9646, Fax: (212) 963-4116, http://unstats.un.org; *Human Development Report 2006; Statistical Yearbook;* and *Survey of Economic and Social Conditions in Africa 2005.*

CONGO, REPUBLIC OF THE - EMPLOYMENT

Euromonitor International, Inc., 224 S. Michigan Avenue, Suite 1500, Chicago, IL 60604, (312) 922-1115, Fax: (312) 922-1157, www.euromonitor.com; *International Marketing Data and Statistics 2008.*

International Labour Office, I.L.O. Publications, 4 route des Morillons, CH-1211 Geneva 22, Switzerland, (Telephone in U.S. (202) 653-7652), (Fax in U.S. (202) 653-7687), www.ilo.org; *Yearbook of Labour Statistics 2006.*

M.E. Sharpe, 80 Business Park Drive, Armonk, NY 10504, (800) 541-6563, Fax: (914) 273-2106, www.mesharpe.com; *The Illustrated Book of World Rankings.*

United Nations Economic Commission for Africa (ECA), PO Box 3001, Addis Ababa, Ethiopia, (Telephone in U.S. (212) 963-4957), www.uneca.org; *African Statistical Yearbook 2006.*

United Nations Statistics Division, New York, NY 10017, (800) 253-9646, Fax: (212) 963-4116, http://unstats.un.org; *Statistical Yearbook* and *Survey of Economic and Social Conditions in Africa 2005.*

The World Bank, 1818 H Street, NW, Washington, DC 20433, (202) 473-1000, Fax: (202) 477-6391, www.worldbank.org; *Congo, Democratic Republic of.*

CONGO, REPUBLIC OF THE - ENVIRONMENTAL CONDITIONS

DSI Data Service Information, Xantener Strasse 51a, D-47495 Rheinberg, Germany, www.dsidata.com; *Campus Solution* and *DSI's Global Environmental Database.*

Economist Intelligence Unit, 111 West 57th Street, New York, NY 10019, (212) 554-0600, Fax: (212) 586-1181, www.eiu.com; *Congo (Brazzaville) Country Report.*

United Nations Statistics Division, New York, NY 10017, (800) 253-9646, Fax: (212) 963-4116, http://unstats.un.org; *World Statistics Pocketbook.*

CONGO, REPUBLIC OF THE - EXPORTS

African Development Bank Group, Rue Joseph Anoma, 01 BP 1387 Abidjan 01, Cote d'Ivoire, www.afdb.org; *Statistics Pocketbook 2008.*

Central Intelligence Agency, Office of Public Affairs, Washington, DC 20505, (703) 482-0623, Fax: (703) 482-1739, www.cia.gov; *The World Factbook.*

Economist Intelligence Unit, 111 West 57th Street, New York, NY 10019, (212) 554-0600, Fax: (212) 586-1181, www.eiu.com; *Congo (Brazzaville) Country Report.*

Euromonitor International, Inc., 224 S. Michigan Avenue, Suite 1500, Chicago, IL 60604, (312) 922-1115, Fax: (312) 922-1157, www.euromonitor.com; *International Marketing Data and Statistics 2008* and *The World Economic Factbook 2008.*

International Monetary Fund (IMF), 700 Nineteenth Street, NW, Washington, DC 20431, (202) 623-7000, Fax: (202) 623-4661, www.imf.org; *Direction of Trade Statistics Yearbook 2007; Government Finance Statistics Yearbook (2008 Edition);* and *International Financial Statistics Yearbook 2007.*

Palgrave Macmillan Ltd., Houndmills, Basingstoke, Hampshire, RG21 6XS, England, (Telephone in U.S. (888) 330-8477), (Fax in U.S. (800) 672-2054), www.palgrave.com; *The Statesman's Yearbook 2008.*

Taylor and Francis Group, An Informa Business, 2 Park Square, Milton Park, Abingdon, Oxford OX14 4RN, United Kingdom, (Dial from U.S. (212) 216-7800), (Fax from U.S. (212) 564-7854), www.tandf.co.uk; *The Europa World Year Book.*

United Nations Conference on Trade and Development (UNCTAD), DC2-1120, United Nations, New York, NY 10017, (212) 963-0027, www.unctad.org; *Handbook of Statistics 2005.*

United Nations Economic Commission for Africa (ECA), PO Box 3001, Addis Ababa, Ethiopia, (Telephone in U.S. (212) 963-4957), www.uneca.org; *African Statistical Yearbook 2006.*

United Nations Food and Agricultural Organization (FAO), Viale delle Terme di Caracalla, 00100 Rome, Italy, (Dial from U.S. (202) 653-2400), (Fax from U.S. (202) 653 5760), www.fao.org; *The State of Food and Agriculture (SOFA) 2006.*

United Nations Statistics Division, New York, NY 10017, (800) 253-9646, Fax: (212) 963-4116, http://unstats.un.org; *Compendium of Intra-African and Related Foreign Trade Statistics 2003* and *Survey of Economic and Social Conditions in Africa 2005.*

The World Bank, 1818 H Street, NW, Washington, DC 20433, (202) 473-1000, Fax: (202) 477-6391, www.worldbank.org; *World Development Indicators (WDI) 2008* and *World Development Report 2008.*

CONGO, REPUBLIC OF THE - FERTILITY, HUMAN

Central Intelligence Agency, Office of Public Affairs, Washington, DC 20505, (703) 482-0623, Fax: (703) 482-1739, www.cia.gov; *The World Factbook.*

M.E. Sharpe, 80 Business Park Drive, Armonk, NY 10504, (800) 541-6563, Fax: (914) 273-2106, www.mesharpe.com; *The Illustrated Book of World Rankings.*

United Nations Statistics Division, New York, NY 10017, (800) 253-9646, Fax: (212) 963-4116, http://unstats.un.org; *Human Development Report 2006* and *Survey of Economic and Social Conditions in Africa 2005.*

The World Bank, 1818 H Street, NW, Washington, DC 20433, (202) 473-1000, Fax: (202) 477-6391, www.worldbank.org; *The World Bank Atlas 2003-2004; World Development Indicators (WDI) 2008;* and *World Development Report 2008.*

CONGO, REPUBLIC OF THE - FERTILIZER INDUSTRY

United Nations Food and Agricultural Organization (FAO), Viale delle Terme di Caracalla, 00100 Rome, Italy, (Dial from U.S. (202) 653-2400), (Fax from

U.S. (202) 653 5760), www.fao.org; *FAO Fertilizer Yearbook* and *The State of Food and Agriculture (SOFA) 2006.*

United Nations Statistics Division, New York, NY 10017, (800) 253-9646, Fax: (212) 963-4116, http://unstats.un.org; *Statistical Yearbook.*

CONGO, REPUBLIC OF THE - FINANCE

Taylor and Francis Group, An Informa Business, 2 Park Square, Milton Park, Abingdon, Oxford OX14 4RN, United Kingdom, (Dial from U.S. (212) 216-7800), (Fax from U.S. (212) 564-7854), www.tandf.co.uk; *The Europa World Year Book.*

United Nations Economic Commission for Africa (ECA), PO Box 3001, Addis Ababa, Ethiopia, (Telephone in U.S. (212) 963-4957), www.uneca.org; *African Statistical Yearbook 2006.*

United Nations Statistics Division, New York, NY 10017, (800) 253-9646, Fax: (212) 963-4116, http://unstats.un.org; *National Accounts Statistics: Compendium of Income Distribution Statistics* and *Statistical Yearbook.*

The World Bank, 1818 H Street, NW, Washington, DC 20433, (202) 473-1000, Fax: (202) 477-6391, www.worldbank.org; *Congo, Democratic Republic of.*

CONGO, REPUBLIC OF THE - FINANCE, PUBLIC

African Development Bank Group, Rue Joseph Anoma, 01 BP 1387 Abidjan 01, Cote d'Ivoire, www.afdb.org; *Statistics Pocketbook 2008.*

Bernan Essential Government Publications, 4611-F Assembly Drive, Lanham MD, 20706-4391, (301) 459-2255, Fax: (800) 865-3450, www.bernan.com; *National Accounts Statistics.*

Economist Intelligence Unit, 111 West 57th Street, New York, NY 10019, (212) 554-0600, Fax: (212) 586-1181, www.eiu.com; *Congo (Brazzaville) Country Report.*

International Monetary Fund (IMF), 700 Nineteenth Street, NW, Washington, DC 20431, (202) 623-7000, Fax: (202) 623-4661, www.imf.org; *International Financial Statistics; International Financial Statistics Online Service;* and *International Financial Statistics Yearbook 2007.*

M.E. Sharpe, 80 Business Park Drive, Armonk, NY 10504, (800) 541-6563, Fax: (914) 273-2106, www.mesharpe.com; *The Illustrated Book of World Rankings.*

Palgrave Macmillan Ltd., Houndmills, Basingstoke, Hampshire, RG21 6XS, England, (Telephone in U.S. (888) 330-8477), (Fax in U.S. (800) 672-2054), www.palgrave.com; *The Statesman's Yearbook 2008.*

Taylor and Francis Group, An Informa Business, 2 Park Square, Milton Park, Abingdon, Oxford OX14 4RN, United Kingdom, (Dial from U.S. (212) 216-7800), (Fax from U.S. (212) 564-7854), www.tandf.co.uk; *The Europa World Year Book.*

United Nations Economic Commission for Africa (ECA), PO Box 3001, Addis Ababa, Ethiopia, (Telephone in U.S. (212) 963-4957), www.uneca.org; *African Statistical Yearbook 2006.*

The World Bank, 1818 H Street, NW, Washington, DC 20433, (202) 473-1000, Fax: (202) 477-6391, www.worldbank.org; *Congo, Democratic Republic of.*

CONGO, REPUBLIC OF THE - FISHERIES

M.E. Sharpe, 80 Business Park Drive, Armonk, NY 10504, (800) 541-6563, Fax: (914) 273-2106, www.mesharpe.com; *The Illustrated Book of World Rankings.*

Palgrave Macmillan Ltd., Houndmills, Basingstoke, Hampshire, RG21 6XS, England, (Telephone in U.S. (888) 330-8477), (Fax in U.S. (800) 672-2054), www.palgrave.com; *The Statesman's Yearbook 2008.*

Taylor and Francis Group, An Informa Business, 2 Park Square, Milton Park, Abingdon, Oxford OX14 4RN, United Kingdom, (Dial from U.S. (212) 216-7800), (Fax from U.S. (212) 564-7854), www.tandf.co.uk; *The Europa World Year Book.*

United Nations Conference on Trade and Development (UNCTAD), DC2-1120, United Nations, New York, NY 10017, (212) 963-0027, www.unctad.org; *UNCTAD Commodity Yearbook.*

United Nations Economic Commission for Africa (ECA), PO Box 3001, Addis Ababa, Ethiopia, (Telephone in U.S. (212) 963-4957), www.uneca.org; *African Statistical Yearbook 2006.*

United Nations Food and Agricultural Organization (FAO), Viale delle Terme di Caracalla, 00100 Rome, Italy, (Dial from U.S. (202) 653-2400), (Fax from U.S. (202) 653 5760), www.fao.org; *FAO Yearbook of Fishery Statistics;* Fishery Databases; FISHSTAT Database. Subjects covered include: Aquaculture production, capture production, fishery commodities; and *The State of Food and Agriculture (SOFA) 2006.*

United Nations Statistics Division, New York, NY 10017, (800) 253-9646, Fax: (212) 963-4116, http://unstats.un.org; *Statistical Yearbook* and *Survey of Economic and Social Conditions in Africa 2005.*

The World Bank, 1818 H Street, NW, Washington, DC 20433, (202) 473-1000, Fax: (202) 477-6391, www.worldbank.org; *Congo, Democratic Republic of.*

CONGO, REPUBLIC OF THE - FLOUR INDUSTRY

United Nations Statistics Division, New York, NY 10017, (800) 253-9646, Fax: (212) 963-4116, http://unstats.un.org; *Statistical Yearbook.*

CONGO, REPUBLIC OF THE - FOOD

African Development Bank Group, Rue Joseph Anoma, 01 BP 1387 Abidjan 01, Cote d'Ivoire, www.afdb.org; *Statistics Pocketbook 2008.*

United Nations Conference on Trade and Development (UNCTAD), DC2-1120, United Nations, New York, NY 10017, (212) 963-0027, www.unctad.org; *UNCTAD Commodity Yearbook.*

United Nations Food and Agricultural Organization (FAO), Viale delle Terme di Caracalla, 00100 Rome, Italy, (Dial from U.S. (202) 653-2400), (Fax from U.S. (202) 653 5760), www.fao.org; *FAO Production Yearbook 2002* and *The State of Food and Agriculture (SOFA) 2006.*

United Nations Statistics Division, New York, NY 10017, (800) 253-9646, Fax: (212) 963-4116, http://unstats.un.org; *Human Development Report 2006.*

CONGO, REPUBLIC OF THE - FOREIGN EXCHANGE RATES

African Development Bank Group, Rue Joseph Anoma, 01 BP 1387 Abidjan 01, Cote d'Ivoire, www.afdb.org; *Statistics Pocketbook 2008.*

Central Intelligence Agency, Office of Public Affairs, Washington, DC 20505, (703) 482-0623, Fax: (703) 482-1739, www.cia.gov; *The World Factbook.*

Euromonitor International, Inc., 224 S. Michigan Avenue, Suite 1500, Chicago, IL 60604, (312) 922-1115, Fax: (312) 922-1157, www.euromonitor.com; *International Marketing Data and Statistics 2008* and *The World Economic Factbook 2008.*

International Monetary Fund (IMF), 700 Nineteenth Street, NW, Washington, DC 20431, (202) 623-7000, Fax: (202) 623-4661, www.imf.org; *International Financial Statistics Yearbook 2007.*

Taylor and Francis Group, An Informa Business, 2 Park Square, Milton Park, Abingdon, Oxford OX14 4RN, United Kingdom, (Dial from U.S. (212) 216-7800), (Fax from U.S. (212) 564-7854), www.tandf.co.uk; *The Europa World Year Book.*

United Nations Statistics Division, New York, NY 10017, (800) 253-9646, Fax: (212) 963-4116, http://unstats.un.org; *Compendium of Intra-African and Related Foreign Trade Statistics 2003; Statistical Yearbook;* and *World Statistics Pocketbook.*

CONGO, REPUBLIC OF THE - FORESTS AND FORESTRY

International Monetary Fund (IMF), 700 Nineteenth Street, NW, Washington, DC 20431, (202) 623-7000, Fax: (202) 623-4661, www.imf.org; *International Financial Statistics Yearbook 2007.*

M.E. Sharpe, 80 Business Park Drive, Armonk, NY 10504, (800) 541-6563, Fax: (914) 273-2106, www.mesharpe.com; *The Illustrated Book of World Rankings.*

Palgrave Macmillan Ltd., Houndmills, Basingstoke, Hampshire, RG21 6XS, England, (Telephone in U.S. (888) 330-8477), (Fax in U.S. (800) 672-2054), www.palgrave.com; *The Statesman's Yearbook 2008.*

Taylor and Francis Group, An Informa Business, 2 Park Square, Milton Park, Abingdon, Oxford OX14 4RN, United Kingdom, (Dial from U.S. (212) 216-7800), (Fax from U.S. (212) 564-7854), www.tandf.co.uk; *The Europa World Year Book.*

UNESCO Institute for Statistics, C.P. 6128 Succursale Centre-Ville, Montreal, Quebec, H3C 3J7 Canada, (Dial from U.S. (514) 343-6880), (Fax from U.S. (514) 343 6882), www.uis.unesco.org; *Statistical Tables.*

United Nations Conference on Trade and Development (UNCTAD), DC2-1120, United Nations, New York, NY 10017, (212) 963-0027, www.unctad.org; *UNCTAD Commodity Yearbook.*

United Nations Economic Commission for Africa (ECA), PO Box 3001, Addis Ababa, Ethiopia, (Telephone in U.S. (212) 963-4957), www.uneca.org; *African Statistical Yearbook 2006.*

United Nations Food and Agricultural Organization (FAO), Viale delle Terme di Caracalla, 00100 Rome, Italy, (Dial from U.S. (202) 653-2400), (Fax from U.S. (202) 653 5760), www.fao.org; *FAO Yearbook of Forest Products* and *The State of Food and Agriculture (SOFA) 2006.*

The World Bank, 1818 H Street, NW, Washington, DC 20433, (202) 473-1000, Fax: (202) 477-6391, www.worldbank.org; *Congo, Democratic Republic of* and *World Development Report 2008.*

CONGO, REPUBLIC OF THE - GEOGRAPHIC INFORMATION SYSTEMS

M.E. Sharpe, 80 Business Park Drive, Armonk, NY 10504, (800) 541-6563, Fax: (914) 273-2106, www.mesharpe.com; *The Illustrated Book of World Rankings.*

The World Bank, 1818 H Street, NW, Washington, DC 20433, (202) 473-1000, Fax: (202) 477-6391, www.worldbank.org; *Congo, Democratic Republic of.*

CONGO, REPUBLIC OF THE - GOLD INDUSTRY

International Monetary Fund (IMF), 700 Nineteenth Street, NW, Washington, DC 20431, (202) 623-7000, Fax: (202) 623-4661, www.imf.org; *International Financial Statistics Yearbook 2007.*

United Nations Statistics Division, New York, NY 10017, (800) 253-9646, Fax: (212) 963-4116, http://unstats.un.org; *Statistical Yearbook.*

The World Bank, 1818 H Street, NW, Washington, DC 20433, (202) 473-1000, Fax: (202) 477-6391, www.worldbank.org; *World Development Indicators (WDI) 2008.*

CONGO, REPUBLIC OF THE - GRANTS-IN-AID

International Monetary Fund (IMF), 700 Nineteenth Street, NW, Washington, DC 20431, (202) 623-7000, Fax: (202) 623-4661, www.imf.org; *Government Finance Statistics Yearbook (2008 Edition).*

CONGO, REPUBLIC OF THE - GROSS DOMESTIC PRODUCT

African Development Bank Group, Rue Joseph Anoma, 01 BP 1387 Abidjan 01, Cote d'Ivoire, www.afdb.org; *Statistics Pocketbook 2008.*

Economist Intelligence Unit, 111 West 57th Street, New York, NY 10019, (212) 554-0600, Fax: (212) 586-1181, www.eiu.com; *Congo (Brazzaville) Country Report.*

Euromonitor International, Inc., 224 S. Michigan Avenue, Suite 1500, Chicago, IL 60604, (312) 922-1115, Fax: (312) 922-1157, www.euromonitor.com; *International Marketing Data and Statistics 2008* and *The World Economic Factbook 2008.*

M.E. Sharpe, 80 Business Park Drive, Armonk, NY 10504, (800) 541-6563, Fax: (914) 273-2106, www.mesharpe.com; *The Illustrated Book of World Rankings.*

Taylor and Francis Group, An Informa Business, 2 Park Square, Milton Park, Abingdon, Oxford OX14 4RN, United Kingdom, (Dial from U.S. (212) 216-7800), (Fax from U.S. (212) 564-7854), www.tandf.co.uk; *The Europa World Year Book.*

United Nations Economic Commission for Africa (ECA), PO Box 3001, Addis Ababa, Ethiopia, (Telephone in U.S. (212) 963-4957), www.uneca.org; *African Statistical Yearbook 2006.*

United Nations Statistics Division, New York, NY 10017, (800) 253-9646, Fax: (212) 963-4116, http://unstats.un.org; *Human Development Report 2006; National Accounts Statistics: Compendium of Income Distribution Statistics; Statistical Yearbook;* and *Survey of Economic and Social Conditions in Africa 2005.*

The World Bank, 1818 H Street, NW, Washington, DC 20433, (202) 473-1000, Fax: (202) 477-6391, www.worldbank.org; *World Development Indicators (WDI) 2008* and *World Development Report 2008.*

CONGO, REPUBLIC OF THE - GROSS NATIONAL PRODUCT

M.E. Sharpe, 80 Business Park Drive, Armonk, NY 10504, (800) 541-6563, Fax: (914) 273-2106, www.mesharpe.com; *The Illustrated Book of World Rankings.*

Palgrave Macmillan Ltd., Houndmills, Basingstoke, Hampshire, RG21 6XS, England, (Telephone in U.S. (888) 330-8477), (Fax in U.S. (800) 672-2054), www.palgrave.com; *The Statesman's Yearbook 2008.*

Taylor and Francis Group, An Informa Business, 2 Park Square, Milton Park, Abingdon, Oxford OX14 4RN, United Kingdom, (Dial from U.S. (212) 216-7800), (Fax from U.S. (212) 564-7854), www.tandf.co.uk; *The Europa World Year Book.*

U.S. Department of State (DOS), 2201 C Street NW, Washington, DC 20520, (202) 647-4000, www.state.gov; *World Military Expenditures and Arms Transfers (WMEAT).*

The World Bank, 1818 H Street, NW, Washington, DC 20433, (202) 473-1000, Fax: (202) 477-6391, www.worldbank.org; *The World Bank Atlas 2003-2004; World Development Indicators (WDI) 2008;* and *World Development Report 2008.*

CONGO, REPUBLIC OF THE - HIDES AND SKINS INDUSTRY

United Nations Food and Agricultural Organization (FAO), Viale delle Terme di Caracalla, 00100 Rome, Italy, (Dial from U.S. (202) 653-2400), (Fax from U.S. (202) 653 5760), www.fao.org; *FAO Production Yearbook 2002.*

CONGO, REPUBLIC OF THE - HOUSING

Euromonitor International, Inc., 224 S. Michigan Avenue, Suite 1500, Chicago, IL 60604, (312) 922-1115, Fax: (312) 922-1157, www.euromonitor.com; *World Marketing Data and Statistics.*

M.E. Sharpe, 80 Business Park Drive, Armonk, NY 10504, (800) 541-6563, Fax: (914) 273-2106, www.mesharpe.com; *The Illustrated Book of World Rankings.*

United Nations Statistics Division, New York, NY 10017, (800) 253-9646, Fax: (212) 963-4116, http://unstats.un.org; *Statistical Yearbook.*

CONGO, REPUBLIC OF THE - ILLITERATE PERSONS

Euromonitor International, Inc., 224 S. Michigan Avenue, Suite 1500, Chicago, IL 60604, (312) 922-1115, Fax: (312) 922-1157, www.euromonitor.com; *The World Economic Factbook 2008.*

Palgrave Macmillan Ltd., Houndmills, Basingstoke, Hampshire, RG21 6XS, England, (Telephone in U.S. (888) 330-8477), (Fax in U.S. (800) 672-2054), www.palgrave.com; *The Statesman's Yearbook 2008.*

UNESCO Institute for Statistics, C.P. 6128 Succursale Centre-Ville, Montreal, Quebec, H3C 3J7 Canada, (Dial from U.S. (514) 343-6880), (Fax from U.S. (514) 343 6882), www.uis.unesco.org; *Statistical Tables.*

United Nations Statistics Division, New York, NY 10017, (800) 253-9646, Fax: (212) 963-4116, http://unstats.un.org; *Human Development Report 2006.*

CONGO, REPUBLIC OF THE - IMPORTS

Central Intelligence Agency, Office of Public Affairs, Washington, DC 20505, (703) 482-0623, Fax: (703) 482-1739, www.cia.gov; *The World Factbook.*

Economist Intelligence Unit, 111 West 57th Street, New York, NY 10019, (212) 554-0600, Fax: (212) 586-1181, www.eiu.com; *Congo (Brazzaville) Country Report.*

Euromonitor International, Inc., 224 S. Michigan Avenue, Suite 1500, Chicago, IL 60604, (312) 922-1115, Fax: (312) 922-1157, www.euromonitor.com; *International Marketing Data and Statistics 2008; The World Economic Factbook 2008;* and *World Marketing Data and Statistics.*

International Monetary Fund (IMF), 700 Nineteenth Street, NW, Washington, DC 20431, (202) 623-7000, Fax: (202) 623-4661, www.imf.org; *Direction of Trade Statistics Yearbook 2007; Government Finance Statistics Yearbook (2008 Edition);* and *International Financial Statistics Yearbook 2007.*

Palgrave Macmillan Ltd., Houndmills, Basingstoke, Hampshire, RG21 6XS, England, (Telephone in U.S. (888) 330-8477), (Fax in U.S. (800) 672-2054), www.palgrave.com; *The Statesman's Yearbook 2008.*

Taylor and Francis Group, An Informa Business, 2 Park Square, Milton Park, Abingdon, Oxford OX14 4RN, United Kingdom, (Dial from U.S. (212) 216-7800), (Fax from U.S. (212) 564-7854), www.tandf.co.uk; *The Europa World Year Book.*

United Nations Economic Commission for Africa (ECA), PO Box 3001, Addis Ababa, Ethiopia, (Telephone in U.S. (212) 963-4957), www.uneca.org; *African Statistical Yearbook 2006.*

United Nations Food and Agricultural Organization (FAO), Viale delle Terme di Caracalla, 00100 Rome, Italy, (Dial from U.S. (202) 653-2400), (Fax from U.S. (202) 653 5760), www.fao.org; *The State of Food and Agriculture (SOFA) 2006.*

United Nations Statistics Division, New York, NY 10017, (800) 253-9646, Fax: (212) 963-4116, http://unstats.un.org; *Compendium of Intra-African and Related Foreign Trade Statistics 2003* and *Survey of Economic and Social Conditions in Africa 2005.*

The World Bank, 1818 H Street, NW, Washington, DC 20433, (202) 473-1000, Fax: (202) 477-6391, www.worldbank.org; *World Development Indicators (WDI) 2008* and *World Development Report 2008.*

CONGO, REPUBLIC OF THE - INDUSTRIAL PRODUCTIVITY

M.E. Sharpe, 80 Business Park Drive, Armonk, NY 10504, (800) 541-6563, Fax: (914) 273-2106, www.mesharpe.com; *The Illustrated Book of World Rankings.*

CONGO, REPUBLIC OF THE - INDUSTRIES

Central Intelligence Agency, Office of Public Affairs, Washington, DC 20505, (703) 482-0623, Fax: (703) 482-1739, www.cia.gov; *The World Factbook.*

Economist Intelligence Unit, 111 West 57th Street, New York, NY 10019, (212) 554-0600, Fax: (212) 586-1181, www.eiu.com; *Congo (Brazzaville) Country Report.*

Euromonitor International, Inc., 224 S. Michigan Avenue, Suite 1500, Chicago, IL 60604, (312) 922-1115, Fax: (312) 922-1157, www.euromonitor.com; *The World Economic Factbook 2008* and *World Marketing Data and Statistics.*

International Labour Office, I.L.O. Publications, 4 route des Morillons, CH-1211 Geneva 22, Switzerland, (Telephone in U.S. (202) 653-7652), (Fax in U.S. (202) 653-7687), www.ilo.org; *Yearbook of Labour Statistics 2006.*

M.E. Sharpe, 80 Business Park Drive, Armonk, NY 10504, (800) 541-6563, Fax: (914) 273-2106, www.mesharpe.com; *The Illustrated Book of World Rankings.*

Palgrave Macmillan Ltd., Houndmills, Basingstoke, Hampshire, RG21 6XS, England, (Telephone in U.S. (888) 330-8477), (Fax in U.S. (800) 672-2054), www.palgrave.com; *The Statesman's Yearbook 2008.*

Taylor and Francis Group, An Informa Business, 2 Park Square, Milton Park, Abingdon, Oxford OX14 4RN, United Kingdom, (Dial from U.S. (212) 216-7800), (Fax from U.S. (212) 564-7854), www.tandf.co.uk; *The Europa World Year Book.*

United Nations Economic Commission for Africa (ECA), PO Box 3001, Addis Ababa, Ethiopia, (Telephone in U.S. (212) 963-4957), www.uneca.org; *African Statistical Yearbook 2006.*

United Nations Industrial Development Organization (UNIDO), 1 United Nations Plaza, New York, NY 10017, (212) 963 6890, Fax: (212) 963-7904, http://unido.org; Industrial Statistics Database 2008 (INDSTAT) and *The International Yearbook of Industrial Statistics 2008.*

United Nations Statistics Division, New York, NY 10017, (800) 253-9646, Fax: (212) 963-4116, http://unstats.un.org; *Survey of Economic and Social Conditions in Africa 2005.*

The World Bank, 1818 H Street, NW, Washington, DC 20433, (202) 473-1000, Fax: (202) 477-6391, www.worldbank.org; *Congo, Democratic Republic of* and *World Development Indicators (WDI) 2008.*

CONGO, REPUBLIC OF THE - INTERNATIONAL LIQUIDITY

International Monetary Fund (IMF), 700 Nineteenth Street, NW, Washington, DC 20431, (202) 623-7000, Fax: (202) 623-4661, www.imf.org; *International Financial Statistics Yearbook 2007.*

CONGO, REPUBLIC OF THE - INTERNATIONAL TRADE

African Development Bank Group, Rue Joseph Anoma, 01 BP 1387 Abidjan 01, Cote d'Ivoire, www.afdb.org; *Statistics Pocketbook 2008.*

Economist Intelligence Unit, 111 West 57th Street, New York, NY 10019, (212) 554-0600, Fax: (212) 586-1181, www.eiu.com; *Congo (Brazzaville) Country Report.*

Euromonitor International, Inc., 224 S. Michigan Avenue, Suite 1500, Chicago, IL 60604, (312) 922-1115, Fax: (312) 922-1157, www.euromonitor.com; *The World Economic Factbook 2008* and *World Marketing Data and Statistics.*

M.E. Sharpe, 80 Business Park Drive, Armonk, NY 10504, (800) 541-6563, Fax: (914) 273-2106, www.mesharpe.com; *The Illustrated Book of World Rankings.*

Organisation for Economic Cooperation and Development (OECD), 2 rue Andre Pascal, F-75775 Paris Cedex 16, France, (Telephone in U.S. (202) 785-6323), (Fax in U.S. (202) 785-0350), www.oecd.org; *International Trade by Commodity Statistics (ITCS).*

Palgrave Macmillan Ltd., Houndmills, Basingstoke, Hampshire, RG21 6XS, England, (Telephone in U.S. (888) 330-8477), (Fax in U.S. (800) 672-2054), www.palgrave.com; *The Statesman's Yearbook 2008.*

Taylor and Francis Group, An Informa Business, 2 Park Square, Milton Park, Abingdon, Oxford OX14 4RN, United Kingdom, (Dial from U.S. (212) 216-7800), (Fax from U.S. (212) 564-7854), www.tandf.co.uk; *The Europa World Year Book.*

United Nations Conference on Trade and Development (UNCTAD), DC2-1120, United Nations, New York, NY 10017, (212) 963-0027, www.unctad.org; *UNCTAD Commodity Yearbook.*

United Nations Economic Commission for Africa (ECA), PO Box 3001, Addis Ababa, Ethiopia, (Telephone in U.S. (212) 963-4957), www.uneca.org; *African Statistical Yearbook 2006.*

United Nations Food and Agricultural Organization (FAO), Viale delle Terme di Caracalla, 00100 Rome, Italy, (Dial from U.S. (202) 653-2400), (Fax from U.S. (202) 653 5760), www.fao.org; *FAO Trade Yearbook* and *The State of Food and Agriculture (SOFA) 2006.*

United Nations Statistics Division, New York, NY 10017, (800) 253-9646, Fax: (212) 963-4116, http://unstats.un.org; *Compendium of Intra-African and Related Foreign Trade Statistics 2003; International Trade Statistics Yearbook;* and *Statistical Yearbook.*

The World Bank, 1818 H Street, NW, Washington, DC 20433, (202) 473-1000, Fax: (202) 477-6391, www.worldbank.org; *Congo, Democratic Republic of; World Development Indicators (WDI) 2008;* and *World Development Report 2008.*

World Trade Organization (WTO), Centre William Rappard, Rue de Lausanne 154, CH-1211 Geneva 21, Switzerland, www.wto.org; *International Trade Statistics 2006.*

CONGO, REPUBLIC OF THE - INTERNET USERS

International Telecommunication Union (ITU), Place des Nations, 1211 Geneva 20, Switzerland, www.itu.int; *World Telecommunication/ICT Indicators Database on CD-ROM; World Telecommunication/ICT Indicators Database Online;* and *Yearbook of Statistics - Telecommunication Services (Chronological Time Series 1997-2006).*

The World Bank, 1818 H Street, NW, Washington, DC 20433, (202) 473-1000, Fax: (202) 477-6391, www.worldbank.org; *Congo, Democratic Republic of.*

CONGO, REPUBLIC OF THE - LABOR

African Development Bank Group, Rue Joseph Anoma, 01 BP 1387 Abidjan 01, Cote d'Ivoire, www.afdb.org; *Statistics Pocketbook 2008.*

Central Intelligence Agency, Office of Public Affairs, Washington, DC 20505, (703) 482-0623, Fax: (703) 482-1739, www.cia.gov; *The World Factbook.*

Euromonitor International, Inc., 224 S. Michigan Avenue, Suite 1500, Chicago, IL 60604, (312) 922-1115, Fax: (312) 922-1157, www.euromonitor.com; *International Marketing Data and Statistics 2008* and *World Marketing Data and Statistics.*

International Labour Office, I.L.O. Publications, 4 route des Morillons, CH-1211 Geneva 22, Switzerland, (Telephone in U.S. (202) 653-7652), (Fax in U.S. (202) 653-7687), www.ilo.org; *Yearbook of Labour Statistics 2006.*

M.E. Sharpe, 80 Business Park Drive, Armonk, NY 10504, (800) 541-6563, Fax: (914) 273-2106, www.mesharpe.com; *The Illustrated Book of World Rankings.*

Palgrave Macmillan Ltd., Houndmills, Basingstoke, Hampshire, RG21 6XS, England, (Telephone in U.S. (888) 330-8477), (Fax in U.S. (800) 672-2054), www.palgrave.com; *The Statesman's Yearbook 2008.*

United Nations Food and Agricultural Organization (FAO), Viale delle Terme di Caracalla, 00100 Rome, Italy, (Dial from U.S. (202) 653-2400), (Fax from U.S. (202) 653 5760), www.fao.org; *The State of Food and Agriculture (SOFA) 2006.*

United Nations Statistics Division, New York, NY 10017, (800) 253-9646, Fax: (212) 963-4116, http://unstats.un.org; *Human Development Report 2006.*

The World Bank, 1818 H Street, NW, Washington, DC 20433, (202) 473-1000, Fax: (202) 477-6391, www.worldbank.org; *The World Bank Atlas 2003-2004; World Development Indicators (WDI) 2008;* and *World Development Report 2008.*

CONGO, REPUBLIC OF THE - LAND USE

Central Intelligence Agency, Office of Public Affairs, Washington, DC 20505, (703) 482-0623, Fax: (703) 482-1739, www.cia.gov; *The World Factbook.*

Euromonitor International, Inc., 224 S. Michigan Avenue, Suite 1500, Chicago, IL 60604, (312) 922-1115, Fax: (312) 922-1157, www.euromonitor.com; *International Marketing Data and Statistics 2008.*

United Nations Food and Agricultural Organization (FAO), Viale delle Terme di Caracalla, 00100 Rome, Italy, (Dial from U.S. (202) 653-2400), (Fax from U.S. (202) 653 5760), www.fao.org; *FAO Production Yearbook 2002.*

The World Bank, 1818 H Street, NW, Washington, DC 20433, (202) 473-1000, Fax: (202) 477-6391, www.worldbank.org; *World Development Report 2008.*

CONGO, REPUBLIC OF THE - LIBRARIES

M.E. Sharpe, 80 Business Park Drive, Armonk, NY 10504, (800) 541-6563, Fax: (914) 273-2106, www.mesharpe.com; *The Illustrated Book of World Rankings.*

CONGO, REPUBLIC OF THE - LICENSES

International Monetary Fund (IMF), 700 Nineteenth Street, NW, Washington, DC 20431, (202) 623-7000, Fax: (202) 623-4661, www.imf.org; *Government Finance Statistics Yearbook (2008 Edition).*

CONGO, REPUBLIC OF THE - LIFE EXPECTANCY

African Development Bank Group, Rue Joseph Anoma, 01 BP 1387 Abidjan 01, Cote d'Ivoire, www.afdb.org; *Statistics Pocketbook 2008.*

Central Intelligence Agency, Office of Public Affairs, Washington, DC 20505, (703) 482-0623, Fax: (703) 482-1739, www.cia.gov; *The World Factbook.*

Euromonitor International, Inc., 224 S. Michigan Avenue, Suite 1500, Chicago, IL 60604, (312) 922-1115, Fax: (312) 922-1157, www.euromonitor.com; *The World Economic Factbook 2008.*

United Nations Statistics Division, New York, NY 10017, (800) 253-9646, Fax: (212) 963-4116, http://unstats.un.org; *Human Development Report 2006* and *World Statistics Pocketbook.*

The World Bank, 1818 H Street, NW, Washington, DC 20433, (202) 473-1000, Fax: (202) 477-6391, www.worldbank.org; *The World Bank Atlas 2003-2004* and *World Development Report 2008.*

CONGO, REPUBLIC OF THE - LITERACY

Euromonitor International, Inc., 224 S. Michigan Avenue, Suite 1500, Chicago, IL 60604, (312) 922-1115, Fax: (312) 922-1157, www.euromonitor.com; *World Marketing Data and Statistics.*

United Nations Statistics Division, New York, NY 10017, (800) 253-9646, Fax: (212) 963-4116, http://unstats.un.org; *Survey of Economic and Social Conditions in Africa 2005.*

CONGO, REPUBLIC OF THE - LIVESTOCK

M.E. Sharpe, 80 Business Park Drive, Armonk, NY 10504, (800) 541-6563, Fax: (914) 273-2106, www.mesharpe.com; *The Illustrated Book of World Rankings.*

Palgrave Macmillan Ltd., Houndmills, Basingstoke, Hampshire, RG21 6XS, England, (Telephone in U.S. (888) 330-8477), (Fax in U.S. (800) 672-2054), www.palgrave.com; *The Statesman's Yearbook 2008.*

Taylor and Francis Group, An Informa Business, 2 Park Square, Milton Park, Abingdon, Oxford OX14 4RN, United Kingdom, (Dial from U.S. (212) 216-7800), (Fax from U.S. (212) 564-7854), www.tandf.co.uk; *The Europa World Year Book.*

United Nations Conference on Trade and Development (UNCTAD), DC2-1120, United Nations, New York, NY 10017, (212) 963-0027, www.unctad.org; *UNCTAD Commodity Yearbook.*

United Nations Economic Commission for Africa (ECA), PO Box 3001, Addis Ababa, Ethiopia, (Telephone in U.S. (212) 963-4957), www.uneca.org; *African Statistical Yearbook 2006.*

United Nations Food and Agricultural Organization (FAO), Viale delle Terme di Caracalla, 00100 Rome, Italy, (Dial from U.S. (202) 653-2400), (Fax from U.S. (202) 653 5760), www.fao.org; *FAO Production Yearbook 2002* and *The State of Food and Agriculture (SOFA) 2006.*

United Nations Statistics Division, New York, NY 10017, (800) 253-9646, Fax: (212) 963-4116, http://unstats.un.org; *Statistical Yearbook* and *Survey of Economic and Social Conditions in Africa 2005.*

CONGO, REPUBLIC OF THE - MANUFACTURES

M.E. Sharpe, 80 Business Park Drive, Armonk, NY 10504, (800) 541-6563, Fax: (914) 273-2106, www.mesharpe.com; *The Illustrated Book of World Rankings.*

United Nations Economic Commission for Africa (ECA), PO Box 3001, Addis Ababa, Ethiopia, (Telephone in U.S. (212) 963-4957), www.uneca.org; *African Statistical Yearbook 2006.*

United Nations Statistics Division, New York, NY 10017, (800) 253-9646, Fax: (212) 963-4116, http://unstats.un.org; *Statistical Yearbook* and *Survey of Economic and Social Conditions in Africa 2005.*

The World Bank, 1818 H Street, NW, Washington, DC 20433, (202) 473-1000, Fax: (202) 477-6391, www.worldbank.org; *World Development Indicators (WDI) 2008.*

CONGO, REPUBLIC OF THE - MARRIAGE

M.E. Sharpe, 80 Business Park Drive, Armonk, NY 10504, (800) 541-6563, Fax: (914) 273-2106, www.mesharpe.com; *The Illustrated Book of World Rankings.*

United Nations Statistics Division, New York, NY 10017, (800) 253-9646, Fax: (212) 963-4116, http://unstats.un.org; *Demographic Yearbook* and *Statistical Yearbook.*

CONGO, REPUBLIC OF THE - MINERAL INDUSTRIES

M.E. Sharpe, 80 Business Park Drive, Armonk, NY 10504, (800) 541-6563, Fax: (914) 273-2106, www.mesharpe.com; *The Illustrated Book of World Rankings.*

Organisation for Economic Cooperation and Development (OECD), 2 rue Andre Pascal, F-75775 Paris Cedex 16, France, (Telephone in U.S. (202) 785-6323), (Fax in U.S. (202) 785-0350), www.oecd.org; *World Energy Outlook 2007.*

Palgrave Macmillan Ltd., Houndmills, Basingstoke, Hampshire, RG21 6XS, England, (Telephone in U.S. (888) 330-8477), (Fax in U.S. (800) 672-2054), www.palgrave.com; *The Statesman's Yearbook 2008.*

Taylor and Francis Group, An Informa Business, 2 Park Square, Milton Park, Abingdon, Oxford OX14 4RN, United Kingdom, (Dial from U.S. (212) 216-7800), (Fax from U.S. (212) 564-7854), www.tandf.co.uk; *The Europa World Year Book.*

United Nations Conference on Trade and Development (UNCTAD), DC2-1120, United Nations, New York, NY 10017, (212) 963-0027, www.unctad.org; *UNCTAD Commodity Yearbook.*

United Nations Economic Commission for Africa (ECA), PO Box 3001, Addis Ababa, Ethiopia, (Telephone in U.S. (212) 963-4957), www.uneca.org; *African Statistical Yearbook 2006.*

United Nations Statistics Division, New York, NY 10017, (800) 253-9646, Fax: (212) 963-4116, http://unstats.un.org; *Statistical Yearbook.*

CONGO, REPUBLIC OF THE - MONEY SUPPLY

African Development Bank Group, Rue Joseph Anoma, 01 BP 1387 Abidjan 01, Cote d'Ivoire, www.afdb.org; *Statistics Pocketbook 2008.*

Economist Intelligence Unit, 111 West 57th Street, New York, NY 10019, (212) 554-0600, Fax: (212) 586-1181, www.eiu.com; *Congo (Brazzaville) Country Report.*

International Monetary Fund (IMF), 700 Nineteenth Street, NW, Washington, DC 20431, (202) 623-7000, Fax: (202) 623-4661, www.imf.org; *International Financial Statistics Yearbook 2007.*

Taylor and Francis Group, An Informa Business, 2 Park Square, Milton Park, Abingdon, Oxford OX14 4RN, United Kingdom, (Dial from U.S. (212) 216-7800), (Fax from U.S. (212) 564-7854), www.tandf.co.uk; *The Europa World Year Book.*

United Nations Statistics Division, New York, NY 10017, (800) 253-9646, Fax: (212) 963-4116, http://unstats.un.org; *Statistical Yearbook.*

The World Bank, 1818 H Street, NW, Washington, DC 20433, (202) 473-1000, Fax: (202) 477-6391, www.worldbank.org; *Congo, Democratic Republic of* and *World Development Indicators (WDI) 2008.*

CONGO, REPUBLIC OF THE - MORTALITY

Central Intelligence Agency, Office of Public Affairs, Washington, DC 20505, (703) 482-0623, Fax: (703) 482-1739, www.cia.gov; *The World Factbook.*

Euromonitor International, Inc., 224 S. Michigan Avenue, Suite 1500, Chicago, IL 60604, (312) 922-1115, Fax: (312) 922-1157, www.euromonitor.com; *International Marketing Data and Statistics 2008* and *The World Economic Factbook 2008.*

Taylor and Francis Group, An Informa Business, 2 Park Square, Milton Park, Abingdon, Oxford OX14 4RN, United Kingdom, (Dial from U.S. (212) 216-7800), (Fax from U.S. (212) 564-7854), www.tandf.co.uk; *The Europa World Year Book.*

UNICEF, 3 United Nations Plaza, New York, NY 10017, (800) 253-9646, Fax: (212) 887-7465, www.unicef.org; *The State of the World's Children 2008.*

United Nations Statistics Division, New York, NY 10017, (800) 253-9646, Fax: (212) 963-4116, http://unstats.un.org; *Demographic Yearbook; Human Development Report 2006; Statistical Yearbook; Survey of Economic and Social Conditions in Africa 2005;* and *World Statistics Pocketbook.*

The World Bank, 1818 H Street, NW, Washington, DC 20433, (202) 473-1000, Fax: (202) 477-6391, www.worldbank.org; *The World Bank Atlas 2003-2004; World Development Indicators (WDI) 2008;* and *World Development Report 2008.*

World Health Organization (WHO), Avenue Appia 20, 1211 Geneve 27, Switzerland, (Telephone in U.S. (212) 331-9081), www.who.int; *The WHO Global Atlas of Infectious Diseases* and *World Health Report 2006.*

CONGO, REPUBLIC OF THE - MOTION PICTURES

United Nations Statistics Division, New York, NY 10017, (800) 253-9646, Fax: (212) 963-4116, http://unstats.un.org; *Statistical Yearbook.*

CONGO, REPUBLIC OF THE - MOTOR VEHICLES

International Road Federation (IFR), Madison Place, 500 Montgomery Street, 5th Floor, Alexandria, VA 22314, (703) 535-1001, Fax: (703) 535-1007, www.irfnet.org; *World Road Statistics 2006.*

Taylor and Francis Group, An Informa Business, 2 Park Square, Milton Park, Abingdon, Oxford OX14 4RN, United Kingdom, (Dial from U.S. (212) 216-7800), (Fax from U.S. (212) 564-7854), www.tandf.co.uk; *The Europa World Year Book.*

United Nations Statistics Division, New York, NY 10017, (800) 253-9646, Fax: (212) 963-4116, http://unstats.un.org; *Statistical Yearbook* and *Survey of Economic and Social Conditions in Africa 2005.*

CONGO, REPUBLIC OF THE - MUSEUMS

M.E. Sharpe, 80 Business Park Drive, Armonk, NY 10504, (800) 541-6563, Fax: (914) 273-2106, www.mesharpe.com; *The Illustrated Book of World Rankings.*

UNESCO Institute for Statistics, C.P. 6128 Succursale Centre-Ville, Montreal, Quebec, H3C 3J7 Canada, (Dial from U.S. (514) 343-6880), (Fax from U.S. (514) 343 6882), www.uis.unesco.org; *Statistical Tables.*

CONGO, REPUBLIC OF THE - NUTRITION

African Development Bank Group, Rue Joseph Anoma, 01 BP 1387 Abidjan 01, Cote d'Ivoire, www.afdb.org; *Statistics Pocketbook 2008.*

United Nations Food and Agricultural Organization (FAO), Viale delle Terme di Caracalla, 00100 Rome, Italy, (Dial from U.S. (202) 653-2400), (Fax from U.S. (202) 653 5760), www.fao.org; *The State of Food and Agriculture (SOFA) 2006.*

CONGO, REPUBLIC OF THE - OLDER PEOPLE

M.E. Sharpe, 80 Business Park Drive, Armonk, NY 10504, (800) 541-6563, Fax: (914) 273-2106, www.mesharpe.com; *The Illustrated Book of World Rankings.*

CONGO, REPUBLIC OF THE - PERIODICALS

UNESCO Institute for Statistics, C.P. 6128 Succursale Centre-Ville, Montreal, Quebec, H3C 3J7 Canada, (Dial from U.S. (514) 343-6880), (Fax from U.S. (514) 343 6882), www.uis.unesco.org; *Statistical Tables.*

CONGO, REPUBLIC OF THE - PESTICIDES

United Nations Food and Agricultural Organization (FAO), Viale delle Terme di Caracalla, 00100 Rome, Italy, (Dial from U.S. (202) 653-2400), (Fax from U.S. (202) 653 5760), www.fao.org; *The State of Food and Agriculture (SOFA) 2006.*

CONGO, REPUBLIC OF THE - PETROLEUM INDUSTRY AND TRADE

International Monetary Fund (IMF), 700 Nineteenth Street, NW, Washington, DC 20431, (202) 623-7000, Fax: (202) 623-4661, www.imf.org; *International Financial Statistics Yearbook 2007.*

M.E. Sharpe, 80 Business Park Drive, Armonk, NY 10504, (800) 541-6563, Fax: (914) 273-2106, www.mesharpe.com; *The Illustrated Book of World Rankings.*

Organisation for Economic Cooperation and Development (OECD), 2 rue Andre Pascal, F-75775 Paris Cedex 16, France, (Telephone in U.S. (202) 785-6323), (Fax in U.S. (202) 785-0350), www.oecd.org; *World Energy Outlook 2007.*

PennWell Corporation, 1421 South Sheridan Road, Tulsa, OK 74112, (918) 835-3161, www.pennwell.com; *International Petroleum Encyclopedia 2007.*

U.S. Department of Energy (DOE), Energy Information Administration (EIA), 1000 Independence Avenue, SW, Washington, DC 20585, (202) 586-8800, www.eia.doe.gov; *International Energy Annual 2004* and *International Energy Outlook 2006.*

United Nations Conference on Trade and Development (UNCTAD), DC2-1120, United Nations, New York, NY 10017, (212) 963-0027, www.unctad.org; *UNCTAD Commodity Yearbook.*

United Nations Food and Agricultural Organization (FAO), Viale delle Terme di Caracalla, 00100 Rome, Italy, (Dial from U.S. (202) 653-2400), (Fax from U.S. (202) 653 5760), www.fao.org; *The State of Food and Agriculture (SOFA) 2006.*

United Nations Statistics Division, New York, NY 10017, (800) 253-9646, Fax: (212) 963-4116, http://unstats.un.org; *Statistical Yearbook.*

CONGO, REPUBLIC OF THE - POLITICAL SCIENCE

Central Intelligence Agency, Office of Public Affairs, Washington, DC 20505, (703) 482-0623, Fax: (703) 482-1739, www.cia.gov; *The World Factbook.*

International Monetary Fund (IMF), 700 Nineteenth Street, NW, Washington, DC 20431, (202) 623-7000, Fax: (202) 623-4661, www.imf.org; *Government Finance Statistics Yearbook (2008 Edition)* and *International Financial Statistics Yearbook 2007.*

Palgrave Macmillan Ltd., Houndmills, Basingstoke, Hampshire, RG21 6XS, England, (Telephone in U.S. (888) 330-8477), (Fax in U.S. (800) 672-2054), www.palgrave.com; *The Statesman's Yearbook 2008.*

Taylor and Francis Group, An Informa Business, 2 Park Square, Milton Park, Abingdon, Oxford OX14 4RN, United Kingdom, (Dial from U.S. (212) 216-7800), (Fax from U.S. (212) 564-7854), www.tandf.co.uk; *The Europa World Year Book.*

United Nations Statistics Division, New York, NY 10017, (800) 253-9646, Fax: (212) 963-4116, http://unstats.un.org; *National Accounts Statistics: Compendium of Income Distribution Statistics* and *Survey of Economic and Social Conditions in Africa 2005.*

The World Bank, 1818 H Street, NW, Washington, DC 20433, (202) 473-1000, Fax: (202) 477-6391, www.worldbank.org; *World Development Indicators (WDI) 2008* and *World Development Report 2008.*

CONGO, REPUBLIC OF THE - POPULATION

African Development Bank Group, Rue Joseph Anoma, 01 BP 1387 Abidjan 01, Cote d'Ivoire, www.afdb.org; *The African Statistical Journal; Gender, Poverty and Environmental Indicators on African Countries 2007; Selected Statistics on African Countries 2007;* and *Statistics Pocketbook 2008.*

Central Intelligence Agency, Office of Public Affairs, Washington, DC 20505, (703) 482-0623, Fax: (703) 482-1739, www.cia.gov; *The World Factbook.*

Economist Intelligence Unit, 111 West 57th Street, New York, NY 10019, (212) 554-0600, Fax: (212) 586-1181, www.eiu.com; *Congo (Brazzaville) Country Report.*

Euromonitor International, Inc., 224 S. Michigan Avenue, Suite 1500, Chicago, IL 60604, (312) 922-1115, Fax: (312) 922-1157, www.euromonitor.com; *International Marketing Data and Statistics 2008* and *The World Economic Factbook 2008.*

Eurostat, Batiment Jean Monnet, Rue Alcide de Gasperi, L-2920 Luxembourg, http://epp.eurostat.ec.europa.eu; *Demographic Indicators - Population by Age-Classes.*

International Labour Office, I.L.O. Publications, 4 route des Morillons, CH-1211 Geneva 22, Switzerland, (Telephone in U.S. (202) 653-7652), (Fax in U.S. (202) 653-7687), www.ilo.org; *Yearbook of Labour Statistics 2006.*

M.E. Sharpe, 80 Business Park Drive, Armonk, NY 10504, (800) 541-6563, Fax: (914) 273-2106, www.mesharpe.com; *The Illustrated Book of World Rankings.*

Palgrave Macmillan Ltd., Houndmills, Basingstoke, Hampshire, RG21 6XS, England, (Telephone in U.S. (888) 330-8477), (Fax in U.S. (800) 672-2054), www.palgrave.com; *The Statesman's Yearbook 2008.*

Taylor and Francis Group, An Informa Business, 2 Park Square, Milton Park, Abingdon, Oxford OX14 4RN, United Kingdom, (Dial from U.S. (212) 216-7800), (Fax from U.S. (212) 564-7854), www.tandf.co.uk; *The Europa World Year Book.*

U.S. Department of State (DOS), 2201 C Street NW, Washington, DC 20520, (202) 647-4000, www.state.gov; *World Military Expenditures and Arms Transfers (WMEAT).*

UNESCO Institute for Statistics, C.P. 6128 Succursale Centre-Ville, Montreal, Quebec, H3C 3J7 Canada, (Dial from U.S. (514) 343-6880), (Fax from U.S. (514) 343 6882), www.uis.unesco.org; *Statistical Tables.*

United Nations Food and Agricultural Organization (FAO), Viale delle Terme di Caracalla, 00100 Rome, Italy, (Dial from U.S. (202) 653-2400), (Fax from U.S. (202) 653 5760), www.fao.org; *FAO Production Yearbook 2002.*

United Nations Statistics Division, New York, NY 10017, (800) 253-9646, Fax: (212) 963-4116, http://unstats.un.org; *Demographic Yearbook; Human Development Report 2006; Statistical Yearbook; Survey of Economic and Social Conditions in Africa 2005;* and *World Statistics Pocketbook.*

The World Bank, 1818 H Street, NW, Washington, DC 20433, (202) 473-1000, Fax: (202) 477-6391, www.worldbank.org; *Congo, Democratic Republic of; The World Bank Atlas 2003-2004;* and *World Development Report 2008.*

World Health Organization (WHO), Avenue Appia 20, 1211 Geneve 27, Switzerland, (Telephone in U.S. (212) 331-9081), www.who.int; *World Health Report 2006.*

CONGO, REPUBLIC OF THE - POPULATION DENSITY

African Development Bank Group, Rue Joseph Anoma, 01 BP 1387 Abidjan 01, Cote d'Ivoire, www.afdb.org; *Statistics Pocketbook 2008.*

Central Intelligence Agency, Office of Public Affairs, Washington, DC 20505, (703) 482-0623, Fax: (703) 482-1739, www.cia.gov; *The World Factbook.*

Euromonitor International, Inc., 224 S. Michigan Avenue, Suite 1500, Chicago, IL 60604, (312) 922-1115, Fax: (312) 922-1157, www.euromonitor.com; *The World Economic Factbook 2008.*

M.E. Sharpe, 80 Business Park Drive, Armonk, NY 10504, (800) 541-6563, Fax: (914) 273-2106, www.mesharpe.com; *The Illustrated Book of World Rankings.*

Palgrave Macmillan Ltd., Houndmills, Basingstoke, Hampshire, RG21 6XS, England, (Telephone in U.S. (888) 330-8477), (Fax in U.S. (800) 672-2054), www.palgrave.com; *The Statesman's Yearbook 2008.*

Taylor and Francis Group, An Informa Business, 2 Park Square, Milton Park, Abingdon, Oxford OX14 4RN, United Kingdom, (Dial from U.S. (212) 216-7800), (Fax from U.S. (212) 564-7854), www.tandf.co.uk; *The Europa World Year Book.*

UNESCO Institute for Statistics, C.P. 6128 Succursale Centre-Ville, Montreal, Quebec, H3C 3J7 Canada, (Dial from U.S. (514) 343-6880), (Fax from U.S. (514) 343 6882), www.uis.unesco.org; *Statistical Tables.*

United Nations Food and Agricultural Organization (FAO), Viale delle Terme di Caracalla, 00100 Rome, Italy, (Dial from U.S. (202) 653-2400), (Fax from U.S. (202) 653 5760), www.fao.org; *The State of Food and Agriculture (SOFA) 2006.*

United Nations Statistics Division, New York, NY 10017, (800) 253-9646, Fax: (212) 963-4116, http://unstats.un.org; *Statistical Yearbook* and *Survey of Economic and Social Conditions in Africa 2005.*

The World Bank, 1818 H Street, NW, Washington, DC 20433, (202) 473-1000, Fax: (202) 477-6391, www.worldbank.org; *Congo, Democratic Republic of* and *World Development Report 2008.*

CONGO, REPUBLIC OF THE - POSTAL SERVICE

M.E. Sharpe, 80 Business Park Drive, Armonk, NY 10504, (800) 541-6563, Fax: (914) 273-2106, www.mesharpe.com; *The Illustrated Book of World Rankings.*

United Nations Statistics Division, New York, NY 10017, (800) 253-9646, Fax: (212) 963-4116, http://unstats.un.org; *Statistical Yearbook.*

CONGO, REPUBLIC OF THE - POWER RESOURCES

Euromonitor International, Inc., 224 S. Michigan Avenue, Suite 1500, Chicago, IL 60604, (312) 922-1115, Fax: (312) 922-1157, www.euromonitor.com; *International Marketing Data and Statistics 2008; The World Economic Factbook 2008;* and *World Marketing Data and Statistics.*

M.E. Sharpe, 80 Business Park Drive, Armonk, NY 10504, (800) 541-6563, Fax: (914) 273-2106, www.mesharpe.com; *The Illustrated Book of World Rankings.*

Organisation for Economic Cooperation and Development (OECD), 2 rue Andre Pascal, F-75775 Paris Cedex 16, France, (Telephone in U.S. (202) 785-6323), (Fax in U.S. (202) 785-0350), www.oecd.org; *World Energy Outlook 2007.*

Palgrave Macmillan Ltd., Houndmills, Basingstoke, Hampshire, RG21 6XS, England, (Telephone in U.S. (888) 330-8477), (Fax in U.S. (800) 672-2054), www.palgrave.com; *The Statesman's Yearbook 2008.*

Platts, 2 Penn Plaza, 25th Floor, New York, NY 10121-2298, (212) 904-3070, www.platts.com; *Energy Economist.*

U.S. Department of Energy (DOE), Energy Information Administration (EIA), 1000 Independence Avenue, SW, Washington, DC 20585, (202) 586-8800, www.eia.doe.gov; *International Energy Annual 2004* and *International Energy Outlook 2006.*

United Nations Economic Commission for Africa (ECA), PO Box 3001, Addis Ababa, Ethiopia, (Telephone in U.S. (212) 963-4957), www.uneca.org; *African Statistical Yearbook 2006.*

United Nations Food and Agricultural Organization (FAO), Viale delle Terme di Caracalla, 00100 Rome, Italy, (Dial from U.S. (202) 653-2400), (Fax from U.S. (202) 653 5760), www.fao.org; *The State of Food and Agriculture (SOFA) 2006.*

United Nations Statistics Division, New York, NY 10017, (800) 253-9646, Fax: (212) 963-4116, http://unstats.un.org; *Energy Statistics Yearbook 2003; Human Development Report 2006; Statistical Yearbook;* and *World Statistics Pocketbook.*

The World Bank, 1818 H Street, NW, Washington, DC 20433, (202) 473-1000, Fax: (202) 477-6391, www.worldbank.org; *The World Bank Atlas 2003-2004* and *World Development Report 2008.*

CONGO, REPUBLIC OF THE - PRICES

Euromonitor International, Inc., 224 S. Michigan Avenue, Suite 1500, Chicago, IL 60604, (312) 922-1115, Fax: (312) 922-1157, www.euromonitor.com; *World Marketing Data and Statistics.*

International Labour Office, I.L.O. Publications, 4 route des Morillons, CH-1211 Geneva 22, Switzerland, (Telephone in U.S. (202) 653-7652), (Fax in U.S. (202) 653-7687), www.ilo.org; *Yearbook of Labour Statistics 2006.*

International Monetary Fund (IMF), 700 Nineteenth Street, NW, Washington, DC 20431, (202) 623-7000, Fax: (202) 623-4661, www.imf.org; *International Financial Statistics Yearbook 2007.*

M.E. Sharpe, 80 Business Park Drive, Armonk, NY 10504, (800) 541-6563, Fax: (914) 273-2106, www.mesharpe.com; *The Illustrated Book of World Rankings.*

United Nations Economic Commission for Africa (ECA), PO Box 3001, Addis Ababa, Ethiopia, (Telephone in U.S. (212) 963-4957), www.uneca.org; *African Statistical Yearbook 2006.*

United Nations Food and Agricultural Organization (FAO), Viale delle Terme di Caracalla, 00100 Rome, Italy, (Dial from U.S. (202) 653-2400), (Fax from U.S. (202) 653 5760), www.fao.org; *FAO Production Yearbook 2002* and *The State of Food and Agriculture (SOFA) 2006.*

The World Bank, 1818 H Street, NW, Washington, DC 20433, (202) 473-1000, Fax: (202) 477-6391, www.worldbank.org; *Congo, Democratic Republic of.*

CONGO, REPUBLIC OF THE - PROFESSIONS

UNESCO Institute for Statistics, C.P. 6128 Succursale Centre-Ville, Montreal, Quebec, H3C 3J7 Canada, (Dial from U.S. (514) 343-6880), (Fax from U.S. (514) 343 6882), www.uis.unesco.org; *Statistical Tables.*

CONGO, REPUBLIC OF THE - PUBLIC HEALTH

African Development Bank Group, Rue Joseph Anoma, 01 BP 1387 Abidjan 01, Cote d'Ivoire, www.afdb.org; *Statistics Pocketbook 2008.*

International Monetary Fund (IMF), 700 Nineteenth Street, NW, Washington, DC 20431, (202) 623-7000, Fax: (202) 623-4661, www.imf.org; *Government Finance Statistics Yearbook (2008 Edition).*

M.E. Sharpe, 80 Business Park Drive, Armonk, NY 10504, (800) 541-6563, Fax: (914) 273-2106, www.mesharpe.com; *The Illustrated Book of World Rankings.*

Palgrave Macmillan Ltd., Houndmills, Basingstoke, Hampshire, RG21 6XS, England, (Telephone in U.S. (888) 330-8477), (Fax in U.S. (800) 672-2054), www.palgrave.com; *The Statesman's Yearbook 2008.*

UNICEF, 3 United Nations Plaza, New York, NY 10017, (800) 253-9646, Fax: (212) 887-7465, www.unicef.org; *The State of the World's Children 2008.*

United Nations Economic Commission for Africa (ECA), PO Box 3001, Addis Ababa, Ethiopia, (Telephone in U.S. (212) 963-4957), www.uneca.org; *African Statistical Yearbook 2006.*

United Nations Statistics Division, New York, NY 10017, (800) 253-9646, Fax: (212) 963-4116, http://unstats.un.org; *Human Development Report 2006* and *Statistical Yearbook.*

The World Bank, 1818 H Street, NW, Washington, DC 20433, (202) 473-1000, Fax: (202) 477-6391, www.worldbank.org; *Congo, Democratic Republic of* and *World Development Report 2008.*

World Health Organization (WHO), Avenue Appia 20, 1211 Geneve 27, Switzerland, (Telephone in U.S. (212) 331-9081), www.who.int; The WHO Global Atlas of Infectious Diseases and *World Health Report 2006.*

CONGO, REPUBLIC OF THE - PUBLISHERS AND PUBLISHING

UNESCO Institute for Statistics, C.P. 6128 Succursale Centre-Ville, Montreal, Quebec, H3C 3J7 Canada, (Dial from U.S. (514) 343-6880), (Fax from U.S. (514) 343 6882), www.uis.unesco.org; *Statistical Tables.*

CONGO, REPUBLIC OF THE - RADIO BROADCASTING

Palgrave Macmillan Ltd., Houndmills, Basingstoke, Hampshire, RG21 6XS, England, (Telephone in U.S. (888) 330-8477), (Fax in U.S. (800) 672-2054), www.palgrave.com; *The Statesman's Yearbook 2008.*

CONGO, REPUBLIC OF THE - RAILROADS

Jane's Information Group, 110 North Royal Street, Suite 200, Alexandria, VA 22314, (703) 683-3700, Fax: (800) 836-0297, www.janes.com; *Jane's World Railways.*

Palgrave Macmillan Ltd., Houndmills, Basingstoke, Hampshire, RG21 6XS, England, (Telephone in U.S. (888) 330-8477), (Fax in U.S. (800) 672-2054), www.palgrave.com; *The Statesman's Yearbook 2008.*

Taylor and Francis Group, An Informa Business, 2 Park Square, Milton Park, Abingdon, Oxford OX14 4RN, United Kingdom, (Dial from U.S. (212) 216-7800), (Fax from U.S. (212) 564-7854), www.tandf.co.uk; *The Europa World Year Book.*

United Nations Economic Commission for Africa (ECA), PO Box 3001, Addis Ababa, Ethiopia, (Telephone in U.S. (212) 963-4957), www.uneca.org; *African Statistical Yearbook 2006.*

United Nations Statistics Division, New York, NY 10017, (800) 253-9646, Fax: (212) 963-4116, http://unstats.un.org; *Statistical Yearbook* and *Survey of Economic and Social Conditions in Africa 2005.*

CONGO, REPUBLIC OF THE - RELIGION

Central Intelligence Agency, Office of Public Affairs, Washington, DC 20505, (703) 482-0623, Fax: (703) 482-1739, www.cia.gov; *The World Factbook.*

M.E. Sharpe, 80 Business Park Drive, Armonk, NY 10504, (800) 541-6563, Fax: (914) 273-2106, www.mesharpe.com; *The Illustrated Book of World Rankings.*

Palgrave Macmillan Ltd., Houndmills, Basingstoke, Hampshire, RG21 6XS, England, (Telephone in U.S. (888) 330-8477), (Fax in U.S. (800) 672-2054), www.palgrave.com; *The Statesman's Yearbook 2008.*

CONGO, REPUBLIC OF THE - RESERVES (ACCOUNTING)

African Development Bank Group, Rue Joseph Anoma, 01 BP 1387 Abidjan 01, Cote d'Ivoire, www.afdb.org; *Statistics Pocketbook 2008.*

The World Bank, 1818 H Street, NW, Washington, DC 20433, (202) 473-1000, Fax: (202) 477-6391, www.worldbank.org; *World Development Indicators (WDI) 2008.*

CONGO, REPUBLIC OF THE - RETAIL TRADE

Euromonitor International, Inc., 224 S. Michigan Avenue, Suite 1500, Chicago, IL 60604, (312) 922-1115, Fax: (312) 922-1157, www.euromonitor.com; *World Marketing Data and Statistics.*

CONGO, REPUBLIC OF THE - ROADS

Central Intelligence Agency, Office of Public Affairs, Washington, DC 20505, (703) 482-0623, Fax: (703) 482-1739, www.cia.gov; *The World Factbook.*

International Road Federation (IFR), Madison Place, 500 Montgomery Street, 5th Floor, Alexandria, VA 22314, (703) 535-1001, Fax: (703) 535-1007, www.irfnet.org; *World Road Statistics 2006.*

Palgrave Macmillan Ltd., Houndmills, Basingstoke, Hampshire, RG21 6XS, England, (Telephone in U.S. (888) 330-8477), (Fax in U.S. (800) 672-2054), www.palgrave.com; *The Statesman's Yearbook 2008.*

United Nations Economic Commission for Africa (ECA), PO Box 3001, Addis Ababa, Ethiopia, (Telephone in U.S. (212) 963-4957), www.uneca.org; *African Statistical Yearbook 2006.*

United Nations Statistics Division, New York, NY 10017, (800) 253-9646, Fax: (212) 963-4116, http://unstats.un.org; *Survey of Economic and Social Conditions in Africa 2005.*

CONGO, REPUBLIC OF THE - RUBBER INDUSTRY AND TRADE

International Rubber Study Group (IRSG), 1st Floor, Heron House, 109/115 Wembley Hill Road, Wembley, Middlesex HA9 8DA, United Kingdom, www.rubberstudy.com; *Rubber Statistical Bulletin; Summary of World Rubber Statistics 2005; World Rubber Statistics Handbook (Volume 6, 1975-2001);* and *World Rubber Statistics Historic Handbook.*

M.E. Sharpe, 80 Business Park Drive, Armonk, NY 10504, (800) 541-6563, Fax: (914) 273-2106, www.mesharpe.com; *The Illustrated Book of World Rankings.*

CONGO, REPUBLIC OF THE - SHIPPING

Lloyd's Register - Fairplay, 8410 N.W. 53rd Terrace, Suite 207, Miami FL 33166, (305) 718-9929, Fax: (305) 718-9663, www.lrfairplay.com; *Register of Ships 2007-2008; World Casualty Statistics 2007; World Fleet Statistics 2006; World Marine Propulsion Report 2006-2010; World Shipbuilding Statistics 2007;* and The World Shipping Encyclopaedia.

Palgrave Macmillan Ltd., Houndmills, Basingstoke, Hampshire, RG21 6XS, England, (Telephone in U.S. (888) 330-8477), (Fax in U.S. (800) 672-2054), www.palgrave.com; *The Statesman's Yearbook 2008.*

Taylor and Francis Group, An Informa Business, 2 Park Square, Milton Park, Abingdon, Oxford OX14 4RN, United Kingdom, (Dial from U.S. (212) 216-7800), (Fax from U.S. (212) 564-7854), www.tandf.co.uk; *The Europa World Year Book.*

United Nations Economic Commission for Africa (ECA), PO Box 3001, Addis Ababa, Ethiopia, (Telephone in U.S. (212) 963-4957), www.uneca.org; *African Statistical Yearbook 2006.*

United Nations Statistics Division, New York, NY 10017, (800) 253-9646, Fax: (212) 963-4116, http://unstats.un.org; *Statistical Yearbook.*

CONGO, REPUBLIC OF THE - SOCIAL ECOLOGY

International Monetary Fund (IMF), 700 Nineteenth Street, NW, Washington, DC 20431, (202) 623-7000, Fax: (202) 623-4661, www.imf.org; *Government Finance Statistics Yearbook (2008 Edition).*

M.E. Sharpe, 80 Business Park Drive, Armonk, NY 10504, (800) 541-6563, Fax: (914) 273-2106, www.mesharpe.com; *The Illustrated Book of World Rankings.*

United Nations Statistics Division, New York, NY 10017, (800) 253-9646, Fax: (212) 963-4116, http://unstats.un.org; *World Statistics Pocketbook.*

CONGO, REPUBLIC OF THE - SOCIAL SECURITY

United Nations Statistics Division, New York, NY 10017, (800) 253-9646, Fax: (212) 963-4116, http://unstats.un.org; *National Accounts Statistics: Compendium of Income Distribution Statistics.*

CONGO, REPUBLIC OF THE - TAXATION

International Monetary Fund (IMF), 700 Nineteenth Street, NW, Washington, DC 20431, (202) 623-7000, Fax: (202) 623-4661, www.imf.org; *Government Finance Statistics Yearbook (2008 Edition).*

International Road Federation (IFR), Madison Place, 500 Montgomery Street, 5th Floor, Alexandria, VA 22314, (703) 535-1001, Fax: (703) 535-1007, www.irfnet.org; *World Road Statistics 2006.*

The World Bank, 1818 H Street, NW, Washington, DC 20433, (202) 473-1000, Fax: (202) 477-6391, www.worldbank.org; *World Development Indicators (WDI) 2008.*

CONGO, REPUBLIC OF THE - TELEPHONE

International Telecommunication Union (ITU), Place des Nations, 1211 Geneva 20, Switzerland, www.itu.int; World Telecommunication Indicators Database.

Palgrave Macmillan Ltd., Houndmills, Basingstoke, Hampshire, RG21 6XS, England, (Telephone in U.S. (888) 330-8477), (Fax in U.S. (800) 672-2054), www.palgrave.com; *The Statesman's Yearbook 2008.*

Taylor and Francis Group, An Informa Business, 2 Park Square, Milton Park, Abingdon, Oxford OX14 4RN, United Kingdom, (Dial from U.S. (212) 216-7800), (Fax from U.S. (212) 564-7854), www.tandf.co.uk; *The Europa World Year Book.*

United Nations Statistics Division, New York, NY 10017, (800) 253-9646, Fax: (212) 963-4116, http://unstats.un.org; *Statistical Yearbook* and *World Statistics Pocketbook.*

CONGO, REPUBLIC OF THE - TEXTILE INDUSTRY

M.E. Sharpe, 80 Business Park Drive, Armonk, NY 10504, (800) 541-6563, Fax: (914) 273-2106, www.mesharpe.com; *The Illustrated Book of World Rankings.*

Palgrave Macmillan Ltd., Houndmills, Basingstoke, Hampshire, RG21 6XS, England, (Telephone in U.S. (888) 330-8477), (Fax in U.S. (800) 672-2054), www.palgrave.com; *The Statesman's Yearbook 2008.*

United Nations Conference on Trade and Development (UNCTAD), DC2-1120, United Nations, New York, NY 10017, (212) 963-0027, www.unctad.org; *UNCTAD Commodity Yearbook.*

CONGO, REPUBLIC OF THE - THEATER

UNESCO Institute for Statistics, C.P. 6128 Succursale Centre-Ville, Montreal, Quebec, H3C 3J7 Canada, (Dial from U.S. (514) 343-6880), (Fax from U.S. (514) 343 6882), www.uis.unesco.org; *Statistical Tables.*

CONGO, REPUBLIC OF THE - TOBACCO INDUSTRY

Foreign Agricultural Service (FAS), U.S. Department of Agriculture (USDA), 1400 Independence Avenue, SW, Washington, DC 20250, (202) 720-3935, www.fas.usda.gov; *Tobacco: World Markets and Trade.*

M.E. Sharpe, 80 Business Park Drive, Armonk, NY 10504, (800) 541-6563, Fax: (914) 273-2106, www.mesharpe.com; *The Illustrated Book of World Rankings.*

United Nations Statistics Division, New York, NY 10017, (800) 253-9646, Fax: (212) 963-4116, http://unstats.un.org; *Statistical Yearbook.*

CONGO, REPUBLIC OF THE - TOURISM

Euromonitor International, Inc., 224 S. Michigan Avenue, Suite 1500, Chicago, IL 60604, (312) 922-1115, Fax: (312) 922-1157, www.euromonitor.com; *The World Economic Factbook 2008* and *World Marketing Data and Statistics.*

M.E. Sharpe, 80 Business Park Drive, Armonk, NY 10504, (800) 541-6563, Fax: (914) 273-2106, www.mesharpe.com; *The Illustrated Book of World Rankings.*

Palgrave Macmillan Ltd., Houndmills, Basingstoke, Hampshire, RG21 6XS, England, (Telephone in U.S. (888) 330-8477), (Fax in U.S. (800) 672-2054), www.palgrave.com; *The Statesman's Yearbook 2008.*

Taylor and Francis Group, An Informa Business, 2 Park Square, Milton Park, Abingdon, Oxford OX14 4RN, United Kingdom, (Dial from U.S. (212) 216-7800), (Fax from U.S. (212) 564-7854), www.tandf.co.uk; *The Europa World Year Book.*

United Nations Economic Commission for Africa (ECA), PO Box 3001, Addis Ababa, Ethiopia, (Telephone in U.S. (212) 963-4957), www.uneca.org; *African Statistical Yearbook 2006.*

United Nations Statistics Division, New York, NY 10017, (800) 253-9646, Fax: (212) 963-4116, http://unstats.un.org; *Statistical Yearbook.*

United Nations World Tourism Organization (UNWTO), Capitan Haya 42, 28020 Madrid, Spain, www.world-tourism.org; *Yearbook of Tourism Statistics.*

The World Bank, 1818 H Street, NW, Washington, DC 20433, (202) 473-1000, Fax: (202) 477-6391, www.worldbank.org; *Congo, Democratic Republic of.*

CONGO, REPUBLIC OF THE - TRANSPORTATION

Central Intelligence Agency, Office of Public Affairs, Washington, DC 20505, (703) 482-0623, Fax: (703) 482-1739, www.cia.gov; *The World Factbook.*

Euromonitor International, Inc., 224 S. Michigan Avenue, Suite 1500, Chicago, IL 60604, (312) 922-1115, Fax: (312) 922-1157, www.euromonitor.com; *International Marketing Data and Statistics 2008* and *World Marketing Data and Statistics.*

M.E. Sharpe, 80 Business Park Drive, Armonk, NY 10504, (800) 541-6563, Fax: (914) 273-2106, www.mesharpe.com; *The Illustrated Book of World Rankings.*

Palgrave Macmillan Ltd., Houndmills, Basingstoke, Hampshire, RG21 6XS, England, (Telephone in U.S. (888) 330-8477), (Fax in U.S. (800) 672-2054), www.palgrave.com; *The Statesman's Yearbook 2008.*

Taylor and Francis Group, An Informa Business, 2 Park Square, Milton Park, Abingdon, Oxford OX14 4RN, United Kingdom, (Dial from U.S. (212) 216-7800), (Fax from U.S. (212) 564-7854), www.tandf.co.uk; *The Europa World Year Book.*

United Nations Economic Commission for Africa (ECA), PO Box 3001, Addis Ababa, Ethiopia, (Telephone in U.S. (212) 963-4957), www.uneca.org; *African Statistical Yearbook 2006.*

United Nations Statistics Division, New York, NY 10017, (800) 253-9646, Fax: (212) 963-4116, http://unstats.un.org; *Human Development Report 2006.*

The World Bank, 1818 H Street, NW, Washington, DC 20433, (202) 473-1000, Fax: (202) 477-6391, www.worldbank.org; *Africa Live Database (LDB)* and *Congo, Democratic Republic of.*

CONGO, REPUBLIC OF THE - UNEMPLOYMENT

Central Intelligence Agency, Office of Public Affairs, Washington, DC 20505, (703) 482-0623, Fax: (703) 482-1739, www.cia.gov; *The World Factbook.*

International Labour Office, I.L.O. Publications, 4 route des Morillons, CH-1211 Geneva 22, Switzerland, (Telephone in U.S. (202) 653-7652), (Fax in U.S. (202) 653-7687), www.ilo.org; *Yearbook of Labour Statistics 2006.*

CONGO, REPUBLIC OF THE - VITAL STATISTICS

Palgrave Macmillan Ltd., Houndmills, Basingstoke, Hampshire, RG21 6XS, England, (Telephone in U.S. (888) 330-8477), (Fax in U.S. (800) 672-2054), www.palgrave.com; *The Statesman's Yearbook 2008.*

United Nations Statistics Division, New York, NY 10017, (800) 253-9646, Fax: (212) 963-4116, http://unstats.un.org; *Statistical Yearbook.*

World Health Organization (WHO), Avenue Appia 20, 1211 Geneve 27, Switzerland, (Telephone in U.S. (212) 331-9081), www.who.int; *World Health Report 2006.*

CONGO, REPUBLIC OF THE - WAGES

International Labour Office, I.L.O. Publications, 4 route des Morillons, CH-1211 Geneva 22, Switzerland, (Telephone in U.S. (202) 653-7652), (Fax in U.S. (202) 653-7687), www.ilo.org; *Yearbook of Labour Statistics 2006.*

United Nations Statistics Division, New York, NY 10017, (800) 253-9646, Fax: (212) 963-4116, http://unstats.un.org; *Statistical Yearbook.*

The World Bank, 1818 H Street, NW, Washington, DC 20433, (202) 473-1000, Fax: (202) 477-6391, www.worldbank.org; *Congo, Democratic Republic of.*

CONGO, REPUBLIC OF THE - WELFARE STATE

International Monetary Fund (IMF), 700 Nineteenth Street, NW, Washington, DC 20431, (202) 623-7000, Fax: (202) 623-4661, www.imf.org; *Government Finance Statistics Yearbook (2008 Edition).*

CONGO, REPUBLIC OF THE - WHOLESALE PRICE INDEXES

International Monetary Fund (IMF), 700 Nineteenth Street, NW, Washington, DC 20431, (202) 623-7000, Fax: (202) 623-4661, www.imf.org; *International Financial Statistics Yearbook 2007.*

United Nations Statistics Division, New York, NY 10017, (800) 253-9646, Fax: (212) 963-4116, http://unstats.un.org; *Statistical Yearbook.*

CONGRESS, UNITED STATES

Congressional Quarterly, Inc., 1255 22nd Street, NW, Washington, DC 20037, (202) 419-8500, www.cq.com; *CQ Voting and Elections Collection* and *CQ's Politics in America 2006: The 109th Congress.*

U.S. Government Printing Office (GPO), Office of Congressional Publishing Services (OCPS), 732 North Capitol Street NW, Washington, DC 20401, (202) 512-0224, www.gpo.gov/customerservices/cps.htm; *Congressional Directory.*

U.S. Library of Congress (LOC), Congressional Research Service (CRS), The Library of Congress, 101 Independence Avenue, SE, Washington, DC 20540-7500, (202) 707-5700, www.loc.gov/crsinfo; *FY2006 Appropriations for State and Local Homeland Security; Homeland Security Department: FY2006 Appropriations; Party Leaders in the United States Congress, 1789-2007; Speed of Presidential and Senate Actions on Supreme Court Nominations, 1900-2005;* and *State and Local Homeland Security: Unresolved Issues for the 109th Congress.*

CONGRESS, UNITED STATES - ASIAN, PACIFIC ISLANDER MEMBERS

U.S. Government Printing Office (GPO), Office of Congressional Publishing Services (OCPS), 732 North Capitol Street NW, Washington, DC 20401, (202) 512-0224, www.gpo.gov/customerservices/cps.htm; *Congressional Directory.*

CONGRESS, UNITED STATES - BILLS, ACTS, RESOLUTIONS

U.S. Department of Education (ED), Office of Postsecondary Education (OPE), 1990 K Street, NW, Washington, DC 20006, (202) 502-7750, www.ed.gov/ope; *Meeting the Highly Qualified Teachers Challenge: The Secretary's Third Annual Report on Teacher Quality.*

U.S. Department of Education (ED), Office of Special Education and Rehabilitative Services (OSERS), 400 Maryland Ave., SW, Washington, DC 20202-7100, (202) 245-7468, www.ed.gov/osers; *Twenty-Seventh Annual Report to Congress on the Implementation of the Individuals with Disabilities Education Act.*

U.S. Government Printing Office (GPO), Office of Congressional Publishing Services (OCPS), 732 North Capitol Street NW, Washington, DC 20401, (202) 512-0224, www.gpo.gov/customerservices/cps.htm; *Calendars of the U.S. House of Representatives and History of Legislation; Congressional Record;* and *Senate Calendar of Business.*

U.S. Library of Congress (LOC), Congressional Research Service (CRS), The Library of Congress, 101 Independence Avenue, SE, Washington, DC 20540-7500, (202) 707-5700, www.loc.gov/crsinfo; *Presidential Vetoes, 1789-Present: A Summary Overview.*

CONGRESS, UNITED STATES - BLACK MEMBERS

Joint Center for Political and Economic Studies, 1090 Vermont Avenue, NW, Suite 1100, Washington, DC 20005-4928, (202) 789-3500, Fax: (202) 789-6390, www.jointcenter.org; *Black Elected Officials: A Statistical Summary.*

U.S. Government Printing Office (GPO), Office of Congressional Publishing Services (OCPS), 732 North Capitol Street NW, Washington, DC 20401, (202) 512-0224, www.gpo.gov/customerservices/cps.htm; *Congressional Directory.*

CONGRESS, UNITED STATES - CAMPAIGN FINANCES

Federal Election Commission (FEC), 999 E Street, NW, Washington, DC 20463, (800) 424-9530, www.fec.gov; *Annual Report 2006; Combined Federal/State Disclosure and Election Directory 2008;* and unpublished data.

CONGRESS, UNITED STATES - COMPOSITION

U.S. Government Printing Office (GPO), Office of Congressional Publishing Services (OCPS), 732 North Capitol Street NW, Washington, DC 20401, (202) 512-0224, www.gpo.gov/customerservices/cps.htm; *Congressional Directory* and unpublished data.

CONGRESS, UNITED STATES - CONGRESSIONAL DISTRICTS - CANDIDATES, VOTES CAST

Congressional Quarterly, Inc., 1255 22nd Street, NW, Washington, DC 20037, (202) 419-8500, www.cq.com; *America Votes 27: Election Returns by State, 2005-2006* and *Statistical History of the American Electorate.*

CONGRESS, UNITED STATES - FINANCES

U.S. Library of Congress (LOC), Congressional Research Service (CRS), The Library of Congress, 101 Independence Avenue, SE, Washington, DC 20540-7500, (202) 707-5700, www.loc.gov/crsinfo; *The Low-Income Home Energy Assistance Program (LIHEAP): Program and Funding Issues.*

CONGRESS, UNITED STATES - HISPANIC MEMBERS

National Association of Latino Elected and Appointed Officials (NALEO) Educational Fund, 1122 West Washington Blvd., 3rd Floor, Los Angeles CA 90015, (213) 747-7606, Fax: (213) 747-7664, www.naleo.org; *2006 National Directory of Latino Elected Officials.*

U.S. Government Printing Office (GPO), Office of Congressional Publishing Services (OCPS), 732 North Capitol Street NW, Washington, DC 20401, (202) 512-0224, www.gpo.gov/customerservices/cps.htm; *Congressional Directory.*

CONGRESS, UNITED STATES - PUBLIC CONFIDENCE

Independent Sector, 1200 Eighteenth Street, NW, Suite 200, Washington, DC 20036, (202) 467-6100, Fax: (202) 467-6101, www.independentsector.org; *Giving and Volunteering in the United States 2001.*

CONGRESS, UNITED STATES - REPRESENTATIVES - VOTE CAST

Congressional Quarterly, Inc., 1255 22nd Street, NW, Washington, DC 20037, (202) 419-8500, www.cq.com; *America Votes 27: Election Returns by State, 2005-2006; Congressional Quarterly Weekly Report; CQ Congress Collection;* and *Statistical History of the American Electorate.*

U.S. Census Bureau, Population Division, 4700 Silver Hill Road, Washington DC 20233-0001, (301) 763-3030, www.census.gov/population/www/; *Current Population Reports.*

CONGRESS, UNITED STATES - SENATORS - VOTE CAST

Congressional Quarterly, Inc., 1255 22nd Street, NW, Washington, DC 20037, (202) 419-8500, www.cq.com; *America Votes 27: Election Returns by State, 2005-2006* and *Statistical History of the American Electorate.*

CONGRESS, UNITED STATES - SENIORITY

U.S. Government Printing Office (GPO), Office of Congressional Publishing Services (OCPS), 732 North Capitol Street NW, Washington, DC 20401, (202) 512-0224, www.gpo.gov/customerservices/cps.htm; *Congressional Directory.*

CONGRESS, UNITED STATES - TIME IN SESSION

U.S. Government Printing Office (GPO), Office of Congressional Publishing Services (OCPS), 732 North Capitol Street NW, Washington, DC 20401, (202) 512-0224, www.gpo.gov/customerservices/cps.htm; *Calendars of the U.S. House of Representatives and History of Legislation* and *Congressional Record.*

CONGRESS, UNITED STATES - WOMEN MEMBERS

U.S. Government Printing Office (GPO), Office of Congressional Publishing Services (OCPS), 732 North Capitol Street NW, Washington, DC 20401, (202) 512-0224, www.gpo.gov/customerservices/cps.htm; *Congressional Directory.*

CONNECTICUT

See also - STATE DATA (FOR INDIVIDUAL STATES)

State of Connecticut, Department of Economic and Community Development (DECD), 505 Hudson Street, Hartford, CT 06106-7107, (860) 270-8000, www.ct.gov/ecd/; *The Contribution of Bradley International Airport to Connecticut's Economy; The Contribution of the Groton Naval Sub Base and the Electric Boat Company to the Economies of Con-*

necticut and Southeastern Connecticut; DECD Economic and Community Development Investment Performance and Economic Impact Report Federal Year 2002-2003; The Economic Impact of a Cruise Ship Visit on Connecticut's Economy; The Economic Impact of Avian Influenza on Connecticut's Egg Industry; Housing a Region in Transition - An Analysis of Housing Needs in Southeastern Connecticut 2000-2005; State of Connecticut Analysis of Impediments to Fair Housing Choice Update; and *Tenant Demography Report and Survey Tables.*

CONNECTICUT - STATE DATA CENTERS

Capitol Region Council of Governments (CRCOG), 241 Main Street, Hartford, CT 06106-5310, (860) 522-2217, Fax: (860) 724-1274, www.crcog.org; State Data Center.

Connecticut State Library, 231 Capitol Avenue, Hartford, CT 06106, (860) 757-6500, www.cslib.org; State Data Center.

Department of Economic and Community Development (DECD), State of Connecticut, 505 Hudson Street, Hartford, CT 06106-7107, (860) 270-8000, www.ct.gov/ecd/site/; State Data Center.

Office of Policy and Management (OPM), 450 Capitol Avenue, Hartford, CT 06106-1379, (860) 418-6200, Fax: (860) 418-6487, www.opm.state.ct.us/pdpd3/data/sdc.htm; State Data Center.

CONNECTICUT - PRIMARY STATISTICS SOURCES

State of Connecticut, Department of Economic and Community Development (DECD), 505 Hudson Street, Hartford, CT 06106-7107, (860) 270-8000, www.ct.gov/ecd/; *Connecticut Economic Digest; Connecticut Market Data;* and *Connecticut Town Profiles.*

CONSTRUCTION INDUSTRY

Building Societies Association (BSA), 6th Floor, York House, 23 Kingsway, London WC2B 6UJ, United Kingdom, www.bsa.org.uk; *Statistics.*

McGraw-Hill Construction, Dodge Analytics, 1221 Avenue of The Americas, Manhattan, NY 10020, (800) 393-6343, http://dodge.construction.com/analytics; *Green Building SmartMarket Report 2006.*

NeighborhoodInfo DC, c/o The Urban Institute, 2100 M Street, NW, Washington, DC 20037, (202) 261-5760, Fax: (202) 872-9322, www.neighborhoodinfodc.org; *District of Columbia Housing Monitor.*

State of Hawaii Department of Business, Economic Development Tourism (DBEDT), Research and Economic Analysis Division (READ), PO Box 2359 Honolulu, HI 96804, (808) 586-2423, Fax: (808) 587-2790, www.hawaii.gov/dbedt/info/economic/census; *Construction and Hawaii's Economy.*

U.S. Bureau of Labor Statistics (BLS), Postal Square Building, 2 Massachusetts Avenue, NE, Washington, DC 20212-0001, (202) 691-5200, Fax: (202) 691-6325, www.bls.gov; *Industries at a Glance.*

U.S. Census Bureau, Center for Economic Studies, 4600 Silver Hill Road, Washington DC 20233, (301) 457-1235, www.ces.census.gov; *Cementing Relationships: Vertical Integration, Foreclosure, Productivity, and Prices;* Economic Census (web app); and *2002 Economic Census of Puerto Rico and the Island Areas.*

U.S. Census Bureau, Company Statistics Division, 4700 Silver Hill Road, Washington DC 20233-0001, (301) 763-3030, www.census.gov/csd/; *County Business Patterns 2004* and *Statistics of U.S. Businesses (SUSB).*

U.S. Census Bureau, Manufacturing and Construction Division, 4600 Silver Hill Road, Washington DC 20233, (301) 763-4673, www.census.gov/mcd; *Census of Construction Industries.*

United Nations Statistics Division, New York, NY 10017, (800) 253-9646, Fax: (212) 963-4116, http://unstats.un.org; United Nations Common Database (UNCDB).

CONSTRUCTION INDUSTRY - BUILDING AUTHORIZED

U.S. Census Bureau, Manufacturing and Construction Division, 4600 Silver Hill Road, Washington DC 20233, (301) 763-4673, www.census.gov/mcd; Building Permits and *Current Construction Reports.*

CONSTRUCTION INDUSTRY - BUILDING PERMITS - VALUE

U.S. Census Bureau, Manufacturing and Construction Division, 4600 Silver Hill Road, Washington DC 20233, (301) 763-4673, www.census.gov/mcd; Building Permits and *Current Construction Reports.*

CONSTRUCTION INDUSTRY - CAPITAL

Bureau of Economic Analysis (BEA), U.S. Department of Commerce (DOC), 1441 L Street NW, Washington, DC 20230, (202) 606-9900, www.bea.gov; *Survey of Current Business (SCB).*

U.S. Census Bureau, Center for Economic Studies, 4600 Silver Hill Road, Washington DC 20233, (301) 457-1235, www.ces.census.gov; *2002 Economic Census, Construction.*

CONSTRUCTION INDUSTRY - CONSTRUCTION CONTRACTS

McGraw-Hill Construction, Dodge Analytics, 1221 Avenue of The Americas, Manhattan, NY 10020, (800) 393-6343, http://dodge.construction.com/analytics; *Construction Outlook 2008.*

CONSTRUCTION INDUSTRY - COST

U.S. Census Bureau, Center for Economic Studies, 4600 Silver Hill Road, Washington DC 20233, (301) 457-1235, www.ces.census.gov; *2002 Economic Census, Construction.*

U.S. Census Bureau, Manufacturing and Construction Division, 4600 Silver Hill Road, Washington DC 20233, (301) 763-4673, www.census.gov/mcd; *Census of Construction Industries.*

CONSTRUCTION INDUSTRY - EARNINGS

Bureau of Economic Analysis (BEA), U.S. Department of Commerce (DOC), 1441 L Street NW, Washington, DC 20230, (202) 606-9900, www.bea.gov; *2007 Annual Revision of the National Income and Product Accounts (NIPA)* and *Survey of Current Business (SCB).*

U.S. Bureau of Labor Statistics (BLS), Postal Square Building, 2 Massachusetts Avenue, NE, Washington, DC 20212-0001, (202) 691-5200, Fax: (202) 691-6325, www.bls.gov; *Current Employment Statistics Survey (CES)* and *Employment and Earnings (EE).*

U.S. Census Bureau, Center for Economic Studies, 4600 Silver Hill Road, Washington DC 20233, (301) 457-1235, www.ces.census.gov; *2002 Economic Census of Puerto Rico and the Island Areas* and *2002 Economic Census, Construction.*

U.S. Census Bureau, Company Statistics Division, 4700 Silver Hill Road, Washington DC 20233-0001, (301) 763-3030, www.census.gov/csd/; *County Business Patterns 2004* and *Statistics of U.S. Businesses (SUSB).*

U.S. Census Bureau, Manufacturing and Construction Division, 4600 Silver Hill Road, Washington DC 20233, (301) 763-4673, www.census.gov/mcd; *Census of Construction Industries.*

CONSTRUCTION INDUSTRY - EMPLOYEES

U.S. Bureau of Labor Statistics (BLS), Postal Square Building, 2 Massachusetts Avenue, NE, Washington, DC 20212-0001, (202) 691-5200, Fax: (202) 691-6325, www.bls.gov; *Current Employment Statistics Survey (CES); Employment and Earnings (EE); Monthly Labor Review (MLR);* and unpublished data.

U.S. Census Bureau, Center for Economic Studies, 4600 Silver Hill Road, Washington DC 20233, (301) 457-1235, www.ces.census.gov; *2002 Economic Census of Puerto Rico and the Island Areas.*

U.S. Census Bureau, Company Statistics Division, 4700 Silver Hill Road, Washington DC 20233-0001, (301) 763-3030, www.census.gov/csd/; *County Business Patterns 2004* and *Statistics of U.S. Businesses (SUSB).*

U.S. Census Bureau, Manufacturing and Construction Division, 4600 Silver Hill Road, Washington DC 20233, (301) 763-4673, www.census.gov/mcd; *Census of Construction Industries.*

CONSTRUCTION INDUSTRY - FINANCES

Financial Services Authority (FSA), 25 The North Colonnade, Canary Wharf, London E14 5HS, United Kingdom, www.fsa.gov.uk; *Building Society Statistics 2006.*

U.S. Census Bureau, Center for Economic Studies, 4600 Silver Hill Road, Washington DC 20233, (301) 457-1235, www.ces.census.gov; *2002 Economic Census, Construction.*

U.S. Department of the Treasury (DOT), Internal Revenue Service (IRS), Statistics of Income Division (SIS), PO Box 2608, Washington, DC, 20013-2608, (202) 874-0410, Fax: (202) 874-0964, www.irs.ustreas.gov; *Statistics of Income Bulletin; Statistics of Income Bulletin, Corporation Income Tax Returns;* and *Statistics of Income Bulletin, Partnership Returns.*

CONSTRUCTION INDUSTRY - GROSS DOMESTIC PRODUCT

Bureau of Economic Analysis (BEA), U.S. Department of Commerce (DOC), 1441 L Street NW, Washington, DC 20230, (202) 606-9900, www.bea.gov; *Survey of Current Business (SCB).*

CONSTRUCTION INDUSTRY - INDUSTRIAL SAFETY

National Safety Council (NSC), 1121 Spring Lake Drive, Itasca, IL 60143-3201, (630) 285-1121, www.nsc.org; *Injury Facts.*

U.S. Bureau of Labor Statistics (BLS), Postal Square Building, 2 Massachusetts Avenue, NE, Washington, DC 20212-0001, (202) 691-5200, Fax: (202) 691-6325, www.bls.gov; *Injuries, Illnesses, and Fatalities (IIF).*

CONSTRUCTION INDUSTRY - MERGERS AND ACQUISITIONS

Thomson Financial, 195 Broadway, New York, NY 10007, (646) 822-2000, www.thomson.com; Thomson Research.

CONSTRUCTION INDUSTRY - MINORITY-OWNED BUSINESSES

U.S. Census Bureau, Company Statistics Division, 4700 Silver Hill Road, Washington DC 20233-0001, (301) 763-3030, www.census.gov/csd/; *Survey of Minority-Owned Business Enterprises.*

CONSTRUCTION INDUSTRY - NONEMPLOYER

U.S. Census Bureau, 4700 Silver Hill Road, Washington DC 20233-0001, (301) 763-3030, www.census.gov; *2002 Economic Census, Nonemployer Statistics.*

CONSTRUCTION INDUSTRY - PRODUCER PRICE INDEXES

U.S. Bureau of Labor Statistics (BLS), Postal Square Building, 2 Massachusetts Avenue, NE, Washington, DC 20212-0001, (202) 691-5200, Fax: (202) 691-6325, www.bls.gov; *Producer Price Indexes (PPI).*

CONSTRUCTION INDUSTRY - PROFITS

Bureau of Economic Analysis (BEA), U.S. Department of Commerce (DOC), 1441 L Street NW, Washington, DC 20230, (202) 606-9900, www.bea.

gov; *2007 Annual Revision of the National Income and Product Accounts (NIPA)* and *Survey of Current Business (SCB).*

Forbes, Inc., 60 Fifth Avenue, New York, NY 10011, (212) 366-8900, www.forbes.com; *America's Largest Private Companies.*

U.S. Census Bureau, Center for Economic Studies, 4600 Silver Hill Road, Washington DC 20233, (301) 457-1235, www.ces.census.gov; *2002 Economic Census, Construction.*

U.S. Department of the Treasury (DOT), Internal Revenue Service (IRS), Statistics of Income Division (SIS), PO Box 2608, Washington, DC, 20013-2608, (202) 874-0410, Fax: (202) 874-0964, www.irs.ustreas.gov; *Statistics of Income Bulletin; Statistics of Income Bulletin, Corporation Income Tax Returns;* unpublished data; and various fact sheets.

CONSTRUCTION INDUSTRY - RESIDENTIAL

HUD USER, PO Box 23268, Washington, DC 20026-3268, (800) 245-2691, Fax: (202) 708-9981, www.huduser.org; *Comprehensive Market Analysis Reports* and *U.S. Housing Market Conditions.*

National Association of Home Builders (NAHB), 1201 15th Street, NW, Washington, DC 20005, (202) 266-8200, Fax: (202) 266-8400, www.nahb.com; HousingEconomics.com.

U.S. Census Bureau, 4700 Silver Hill Road, Washington DC 20233-0001, (301) 763-3030, www.census.gov; unpublished data.

U.S. Census Bureau, Manufacturing and Construction Division, 4600 Silver Hill Road, Washington DC 20233, (301) 763-4673, www.census.gov/mcd; Building Permits and *Current Construction Reports.*

CONSTRUCTION INDUSTRY - SHIPMENTS, RECEIPTS

Forbes, Inc., 60 Fifth Avenue, New York, NY 10011, (212) 366-8900, www.forbes.com; *America's Largest Private Companies.*

U.S. Census Bureau, Center for Economic Studies, 4600 Silver Hill Road, Washington DC 20233, (301) 457-1235, www.ces.census.gov; *2002 Economic Census, Construction.*

U.S. Census Bureau, Manufacturing and Construction Division, 4600 Silver Hill Road, Washington DC 20233, (301) 763-4673, www.census.gov/mcd; *Census of Construction Industries.*

U.S. Department of the Treasury (DOT), Internal Revenue Service (IRS), Statistics of Income Division (SIS), PO Box 2608, Washington, DC, 20013-2608, (202) 874-0410, Fax: (202) 874-0964, www.irs.ustreas.gov; *Statistics of Income Bulletin* and unpublished data.

CONSTRUCTION INDUSTRY - UNIONS

U.S. Bureau of Labor Statistics (BLS), Postal Square Building, 2 Massachusetts Avenue, NE, Washington, DC 20212-0001, (202) 691-5200, Fax: (202) 691-6325, www.bls.gov; *Employment and Earnings (EE).*

CONSTRUCTION INDUSTRY - VALUE, WORK

U.S. Census Bureau, Manufacturing and Construction Division, 4600 Silver Hill Road, Washington DC 20233, (301) 763-4673, www.census.gov/mcd; *Census of Construction Industries* and *Current Construction Reports.*

CONSTRUCTION INDUSTRY - WOMEN-OWNED BUSINESSES

U.S. Census Bureau, Company Statistics Division, 4700 Silver Hill Road, Washington DC 20233-0001, (301) 763-3030, www.census.gov/csd/; *Survey of Women-Owned Businesses.*

CONSTRUCTION MACHINERY - MANUFACTURING - EARNINGS

U.S. Bureau of Labor Statistics (BLS), Postal Square Building, 2 Massachusetts Avenue, NE, Washington, DC 20212-0001, (202) 691-5200, Fax: (202) 691-6325, www.bls.gov; *Current Employment Statistics Survey (CES)* and *Employment and Earnings (EE).*

U.S. Census Bureau, Manufacturing and Construction Division, 4600 Silver Hill Road, Washington DC 20233, (301) 763-4673, www.census.gov/mcd; *Annual Survey of Manufactures (ASM)* and *Census of Manufactures.*

CONSTRUCTION MACHINERY - MANUFACTURING - EMPLOYEES

U.S. Bureau of Labor Statistics (BLS), Postal Square Building, 2 Massachusetts Avenue, NE, Washington, DC 20212-0001, (202) 691-5200, Fax: (202) 691-6325, www.bls.gov; *Current Employment Statistics Survey (CES)* and *Employment and Earnings (EE).*

U.S. Census Bureau, Manufacturing and Construction Division, 4600 Silver Hill Road, Washington DC 20233, (301) 763-4673, www.census.gov/mcd; *Annual Survey of Manufactures (ASM)* and *Census of Manufactures.*

CONSTRUCTION MACHINERY - MANUFACTURING - SHIPMENTS

U.S. Census Bureau, Manufacturing and Construction Division, 4600 Silver Hill Road, Washington DC 20233, (301) 763-4673, www.census.gov/mcd; *Annual Survey of Manufactures (ASM); Census of Manufactures; Current Industrial Reports; Current Industrial Reports, Manufacturing Profiles;* and *Manufacturers Shipments, Inventories and Orders.*

CONSTRUCTION MATERIALS

See BUILDING MATERIALS AND GARDEN SUPPLIES

CONSUMER - CONSUMER GOODS - PRODUCER PRICES

The NPD Group, Port Washington, 900 West Shore Road, Port Washington, NY 11050, (866) 444-1411, www.npd.com; *Market Research for the Apparel and Footwear Industries; Market Research for the Appliances, Home Improvement, Home Textiles, and Housewares Industries; Market Research for the Automotive Aftermarket; Market Research for the Beauty Industry; Market Research for the Consumer Technology Industry; Market Research for the Film, Music, PC Games, Video Games, and Video Industries;* Market Research for the Food and Beverage Industries; *Market Research for the Foodservice Industry;* and *Market Research for the Toy Industry.*

U.S. Bureau of Labor Statistics (BLS), Postal Square Building, 2 Massachusetts Avenue, NE, Washington, DC 20212-0001, (202) 691-5200, Fax: (202) 691-6325, www.bls.gov; *Producer Price Indexes (PPI).*

CONSUMER - CONSUMER INQUIRIES

Federal Communications Commission (FCC), Consumer and Governmental Affairs Bureau (CGB), 445 12th Street, SW, Washington, DC 20554, (202) 418-1500, Fax: (866) 418-0232, www.fcc.gov/cgb; *Quarterly Inquiries and Complaints Reports.*

CONSUMER - CREDIT

Board of Governors of the Federal Reserve System, Constitution Avenue, NW, Washington, DC 20551, (202) 452-3000, www.federalreserve.gov; *Federal Reserve Bulletin; Flow of Funds Accounts of the United States; Statistical Digest;* and unpublished data.

CONSUMER - CREDIT - DELINQUENCY RATES

Federal Financial Institutions Examination Council (FFIEC), 3501 Fairfax Drive, Room D8073A, Arlington, VA 22226, (202) 872-7500, www.ffiec.gov; *Uniform Bank Performance Report (UBPR).*

CONSUMER - ELECTRONICS

Consumer Electronics Association (CEA), 2500 Wilson Boulevard, Arlington, VA 22201-3834, (703) 907-7600, Fax: (703) 907 7675, www.ce.org; *Digital America 2006.*

Electronic Industries Alliance (EIA), 2500 Wilson Boulevard, Arlington, VA 22201, (703) 907-7500, www.eia.org; unpublished data.

Mediamark Research, Inc., 75 Ninth Avenue, 5th Floor, New York, NY 10011, (212) 884-9200, Fax: (212) 884-9339, www.mediamark.com; *The American Kids Study.*

CONSUMER - EXPENDITURES

Department of Statistics (DOS), PO Box 2015, Amman 11181, Jordan, www.dos.gov.jo; *Household Income and Expenditure Survey.*

Eurostat, Batiment Jean Monnet, Rue Alcide de Gasperi, L-2920 Luxembourg, http://epp.eurostat.ec.europa.eu; *Consumers in Europe - Facts and Figures on Services of General Interest.*

JupiterResearch, 233 Broadway, Suite 1005, New York, NY 10279, USA, (212) 857-0700, Fax: (212) 857-0701, www.jupiterresearch.com; *Primary Consumer Research.*

Mediamark Research, Inc., 75 Ninth Avenue, 5th Floor, New York, NY 10011, (212) 884-9200, Fax: (212) 884-9339, www.mediamark.com; *The American Kids Study.*

The NPD Group, Port Washington, 900 West Shore Road, Port Washington, NY 11050, (866) 444-1411, www.npd.com; *Market Research for the Apparel and Footwear Industries; Market Research for the Appliances, Home Improvement, Home Textiles, and Housewares Industries; Market Research for the Automotive Aftermarket; Market Research for the Beauty Industry; Market Research for the Consumer Technology Industry; Market Research for the Film, Music, PC Games, Video Games, and Video Industries;* Market Research for the Food and Beverage Industries; *Market Research for the Foodservice Industry; Market Research for the Toy Industry; Wireless;* and *Wireless.*

Progressive Grocer, 770 Broadway, New York, NY 10003, (866) 890-8541, www.progressivegrocer.com; *2006 Consumer Expenditures Study; Marketing to American Latinos, Part I;* and *Marketing to American Latinos, Part II.*

Recreation Vehicle Industry Association (RVIA), 1896 Preston White Drive, Reston, VA 20191, (703) 620-6003, Fax: (703) 620-5071, www.rvia.org; *The RV Consumer: A Demographic Profile 2005 Survey.*

Selig Center for Economic Growth, Terry College of Business, University of Georgia, Athens, GA 30602-6269, Mr. Jeffrey M. Humphreys, Director, (706) 425-2962, www.selig.uga.edu; *The Multicultural Economy: Minority Buying Power in 2006.*

U.S. Bureau of Labor Statistics (BLS), Postal Square Building, 2 Massachusetts Avenue, NE, Washington, DC 20212-0001, (202) 691-5200, Fax: (202) 691-6325, www.bls.gov; *Consumer Expenditures in 2006.*

CONSUMER - EXPENDITURES - BOOKS

Book Industry Study Group (BISG), 370 Lexington Avenue, Suite 900, New York, NY 10017, (646) 336-7141, Fax: (646) 336-6214, www.bisg.org; *The African-American Book Buyers Study; Book Industry Trends 2007;* and *Used-Book Sales.*

LISU, Holywell Park, Loughborough University, Leicestershire, LE11 3TU, United Kingdom, www.lboro.ac.uk/departments/dis/lisu; *Average Prices of British and USA Academic Books.*

CONSUMER - EXPENDITURES - COMMUNICATIONS

Veronis Suhler Stevenson Partners LLC, 350 Park Avenue, New York, NY 10022, (212) 935-4990, Fax: (212) 381-8168, www.vss.com; Communications Industry Report.

CONSUMER - EXPENDITURES - ENTERTAINMENT

U.S. Bureau of Labor Statistics (BLS), Postal Square Building, 2 Massachusetts Avenue, NE, Washington, DC 20212-0001, (202) 691-5200, Fax: (202) 691-6325, www.bls.gov; *Consumer Expenditures in 2006.*

CONSUMER - EXPENDITURES - FOOD

Economic Research Service (ERS), U.S. Department of Agriculture (USDA), 1800 M Street, NW, Washington, DC 20036-5831, (202) 694-5050, Fax: (202) 694-5689, www.ers.usda.gov; *Agricultural Statistics; Amber Waves: The Economics of Food, Farming, Natural Resources, and Rural America;* and *Food CPI, Prices, and Expenditures.*

National Agricultural Statistics Service (NASS), U.S. Department of Agriculture (USDA), 1400 Independence Avenue, SW, Washington, DC 20250, (800) 727-9540, Fax: (202) 690-2090, www.nass.usda.gov; *2006 Agricultural Statistics.*

Progressive Grocer, 770 Broadway, New York, NY 10003, (866) 890-8541, www.progressivegrocer.com; *2006 Consumer Expenditures Study; Marketing to American Latinos, Part I; Marketing to American Latinos, Part II; Progressive Grocer 2006 Bakery Study;* and *Progressive Grocer's 75th Annual Report of the Grocery Industry.*

U.S. Bureau of Labor Statistics (BLS), Postal Square Building, 2 Massachusetts Avenue, NE, Washington, DC 20212-0001, (202) 691-5200, Fax: (202) 691-6325, www.bls.gov; *Consumer Expenditures in 2006.*

CONSUMER - EXPENDITURES - HOUSING

U.S. Bureau of Labor Statistics (BLS), Postal Square Building, 2 Massachusetts Avenue, NE, Washington, DC 20212-0001, (202) 691-5200, Fax: (202) 691-6325, www.bls.gov; *Consumer Expenditures in 2006.*

CONSUMER - EXPENDITURES - MEDICAL CARE

Centers for Medicare and Medicaid Services (CMS), U.S. Department of Health and Human Services (HHS), 7500 Security Boulevard, Baltimore, MD 21244-1850, (410) 786-3000, http://cms.hhs.gov; *Health Care Financing Review.*

U.S. Bureau of Labor Statistics (BLS), Postal Square Building, 2 Massachusetts Avenue, NE, Washington, DC 20212-0001, (202) 691-5200, Fax: (202) 691-6325, www.bls.gov; *Consumer Expenditures in 2006.*

CONSUMER - EXPENDITURES - METROPOLITAN AREAS

U.S. Bureau of Labor Statistics (BLS), Postal Square Building, 2 Massachusetts Avenue, NE, Washington, DC 20212-0001, (202) 691-5200, Fax: (202) 691-6325, www.bls.gov; *Consumer Expenditures in 2006.*

CONSUMER - EXPENDITURES - READING MATERIALS

Book Industry Study Group (BISG), 370 Lexington Avenue, Suite 900, New York, NY 10017, (646) 336-7141, Fax: (646) 336-6214, www.bisg.org; *Consumer Research Study on Book Purchasing.*

LISU, Holywell Park, Loughborough University, Leicestershire, LE11 3TU, United Kingdom, www.lboro.ac.uk/departments/dis/lisu; *Average Prices of British and USA Academic Books.*

U.S. Bureau of Labor Statistics (BLS), Postal Square Building, 2 Massachusetts Avenue, NE, Washington, DC 20212-0001, (202) 691-5200, Fax: (202) 691-6325, www.bls.gov; *Consumer Expenditures in 2006.*

CONSUMER - EXPENDITURES - SPORTING GOODS

National Sporting Goods Association (NSGA), 1601 Feehanville Drive, Suite 300, Mount Prospect, IL 60056, (847) 296-6742, Fax: (847) 391-9827, www.nsga.org; *Ten-Year History of Selected Sports Participation, 1996-2006.*

CONSUMER BEHAVIOR

Eurostat, Batiment Jean Monnet, Rue Alcide de Gasperi, L-2920 Luxembourg, http://epp.eurostat.ec.europa.eu; *Consumers in Europe - Facts and Figures on Services of General Interest.*

Mediamark Research, Inc., 75 Ninth Avenue, 5th Floor, New York, NY 10011, (212) 884-9200, Fax: (212) 884-9339, www.mediamark.com; *The American Kids Study.*

The NPD Group, Port Washington, 900 West Shore Road, Port Washington, NY 11050, (866) 444-1411, www.npd.com; *Market Research for the Apparel and Footwear Industries; Market Research for the Appliances, Home Improvement, Home Textiles, and Housewares Industries; Market Research for the Automotive Aftermarket; Market Research for the Beauty Industry; Market Research for the Consumer Technology Industry; Market Research for the Film, Music, PC Games, Video Games, and Video Industries;* Market Research for the Food and Beverage Industries; *Market Research for the Foodservice Industry;* and *Market Research for the Toy Industry.*

Progressive Grocer, 770 Broadway, New York, NY 10003, (866) 890-8541, www.progressivegrocer.com; *Marketing to American Latinos, Part I* and *Marketing to American Latinos, Part II.*

Selig Center for Economic Growth, Terry College of Business, University of Georgia, Athens, GA 30602-6269, Mr. Jeffrey M. Humphreys, Director, (706) 425-2962, www.selig.uga.edu; *The Multicultural Economy: Minority Buying Power in 2006.*

CONSUMER COMPLAINTS

Federal Communications Commission (FCC), Consumer and Governmental Affairs Bureau (CGB), 445 12th Street, SW, Washington, DC 20554, (202) 418-1500, Fax: (866) 418-0232, www.fcc.gov/cgb; *Quarterly Inquiries and Complaints Reports.*

CONSUMER COMPLAINTS AGAINST AIRLINES

U.S. Department of Transportation (DOT), Office of Aviation Enforcement and Proceedings (OAEP), 1200 New Jersey Ave, SE, Washington, DC 20590, (202) 366-4000, http://airconsumer.ost.dot.gov; *Air Travel Consumer Report 2008.*

CONSUMER PAYMENT SYSTEMS

The Nilson Report, 1110 Eugenia Place, Suite 100, Carpinteria, CA 93013-9921, (805) 684-8800, Fax: (805) 684-8825, www.nilsonreport.com; *The Nilson Report.*

CONSUMER PRICE INDEXES

Bureau of Economic Analysis (BEA), U.S. Department of Commerce (DOC), 1441 L Street NW, Washington, DC 20230, (202) 606-9900, www.bea.gov; *Survey of Current Business (SCB).*

JupiterResearch, 233 Broadway, Suite 1005, New York, NY 10279, USA, (212) 857-0700, Fax: (212) 857-0701, www.jupiterresearch.com; *Primary Consumer Research.*

U.S. Bureau of Labor Statistics (BLS), Postal Square Building, 2 Massachusetts Avenue, NE, Washington, DC 20212-0001, (202) 691-5200, Fax: (202) 691-6325, www.bls.gov; *Consumer Price Index Detailed Report* and *Monthly Labor Review (MLR).*

U.S. Department of Labor (DOL), Bureau of Labor Statistics (BLS), Postal Square Building, 2 Massachusetts Avenue, NE, Washington, DC 20212-0001, (202) 691-5200, Fax: (202) 691-6325, www.bls.gov; *Consumer Price Indexes (CPI).*

U.S. Library of Congress (LOC), Congressional Research Service (CRS), The Library of Congress, 101 Independence Avenue, SE, Washington, DC 20540-7500, (202) 707-5700, www.loc.gov/crsinfo; *Social Security: The Cost-of-Living Adjustment in January 2003.*

CONSUMER PRICE INDEXES - BY COMMODITY GROUPS

U.S. Bureau of Labor Statistics (BLS), Postal Square Building, 2 Massachusetts Avenue, NE, Washington, DC 20212-0001, (202) 691-5200, Fax: (202) 691-6325, www.bls.gov; *Consumer Price Index Detailed Report* and *Monthly Labor Review (MLR).*

CONSUMER PRICE INDEXES - FOREIGN COUNTRIES

International Monetary Fund (IMF), 700 Nineteenth Street, NW, Washington, DC 20431, (202) 623-7000, Fax: (202) 623-4661, www.imf.org; *International Financial Statistics Yearbook 2007.*

Organisation for Economic Cooperation and Development (OECD), 2 rue Andre Pascal, F-75775 Paris Cedex 16, France, (Telephone in U.S. (202) 785-6323), (Fax in U.S. (202) 785-0350), www.oecd.org; *OECD Main Economic Indicators (MEI).*

CONSUMER PRICE INDEXES - MEDICAL CARE

U.S. Bureau of Labor Statistics (BLS), Postal Square Building, 2 Massachusetts Avenue, NE, Washington, DC 20212-0001, (202) 691-5200, Fax: (202) 691-6325, www.bls.gov; *Consumer Price Index Detailed Report* and *Monthly Labor Review (MLR).*

CONSUMER PRICE INDEXES - PURCHASING POWER OF THE DOLLAR

Bureau of Economic Analysis (BEA), U.S. Department of Commerce (DOC), 1441 L Street NW, Washington, DC 20230, (202) 606-9900, www.bea.gov; *Survey of Current Business (SCB).*

CONSUMER PRICE INDEXES - YEAR TO YEAR CHANGES

U.S. Bureau of Labor Statistics (BLS), Postal Square Building, 2 Massachusetts Avenue, NE, Washington, DC 20212-0001, (202) 691-5200, Fax: (202) 691-6325, www.bls.gov; *Industry Productivity and Costs* and *Monthly Labor Review (MLR).*

CONSUMPTION

See Individual commodities

CONTRACEPTIVE USE

Alan Guttmacher Institute, 125 Maiden Lane, 7th Floor, New York, NY 10038, (212) 248-1111, Fax: (212) 248-1951, www.agi-usa.org; *Contraceptive Needs and Services, 2001-2006* and *Public Funding for Contraceptive, Sterilization and Abortion Services, FY 1980-2001.*

National Center for Health Statistics (NCHS), Centers for Disease Control and Prevention (CDC), U.S. Department of Health and Human Services (HHS), 3311 Toledo Road, Hyattsville, MD 20782, (866) 232-4636, www.cdc.gov/nchs; *Faststats A to Z.*

Population Reference Bureau, 1875 Connecticut Avenue, NW, Suite 520, Washington, DC, 20009-5728, (800) 877-9881, Fax: (202) 328-3937, www.prb.org; *Family Planning Worldwide.*

CONVENIENCE STORES

Economic Research Service (ERS), U.S. Department of Agriculture (USDA), 1800 M Street, NW, Washington, DC 20036-5831, (202) 694-5050, Fax: (202) 694-5689, www.ers.usda.gov; *Food Marketing and Price Spreads.*

Progressive Grocer, 770 Broadway, New York, NY 10003, (866) 890-8541, www.progressivegrocer.com; *The VNU Retail Index.*

COOK ISLANDS - NATIONAL STATISTICAL OFFICE

Statistics Office, PO Box 41, Avarua, Rarotonga, Cook Islands, www.stats.gov.ck; National Data Center.

COOK ISLANDS - PRIMARY STATISTICS SOURCES

Statistics Office, PO Box 41, Avarua, Rarotonga, Cook Islands, www.stats.gov.ck; *Annual Statistical Bulletin 2004.*

COOK ISLANDS - AGRICULTURAL MACHINERY

United Nations Statistics Division, New York, NY 10017, (800) 253-9646, Fax: (212) 963-4116, http://unstats.un.org; *Statistical Yearbook*.

COOK ISLANDS - AGRICULTURE

Asian Development Bank (ADB), PO Box 789, 0980 Manila, Philippines, www.adb.org; *Key Indicators of Developing Asian and Pacific Countries 2006*.

Palgrave Macmillan Ltd., Houndmills, Basingstoke, Hampshire, RG21 6XS, England, (Telephone in U.S. (888) 330-8477), (Fax in U.S. (800) 672-2054), www.palgrave.com; *The Statesman's Yearbook 2008*.

Taylor and Francis Group, An Informa Business, 2 Park Square, Milton Park, Abingdon, Oxford OX14 4RN, United Kingdom, (Dial from U.S. (212) 216-7800), (Fax from U.S. (212) 564-7854), www.tandf.co.uk; *The Europa World Year Book*.

United Nations Conference on Trade and Development (UNCTAD), DC2-1120, United Nations, New York, NY 10017, (212) 963-0027, www.unctad.org; *UNCTAD Commodity Yearbook*.

United Nations Food and Agricultural Organization (FAO), Viale delle Terme di Caracalla, 00100 Rome, Italy, (Dial from U.S. (202) 653-2400), (Fax from U.S. (202) 653 5760), www.fao.org; AQUASTAT; *FAO Production Yearbook 2002; FAO Trade Yearbook;* and *The State of Food and Agriculture (SOFA) 2006*.

United Nations Statistics Division, New York, NY 10017, (800) 253-9646, Fax: (212) 963-4116, http://unstats.un.org; *Asia-Pacific in Figures 2004; Statistical Yearbook;* and *Statistical Yearbook for Asia and the Pacific 2004*.

COOK ISLANDS - AIRLINES

Palgrave Macmillan Ltd., Houndmills, Basingstoke, Hampshire, RG21 6XS, England, (Telephone in U.S. (888) 330-8477), (Fax in U.S. (800) 672-2054), www.palgrave.com; *The Statesman's Yearbook 2008*.

Taylor and Francis Group, An Informa Business, 2 Park Square, Milton Park, Abingdon, Oxford OX14 4RN, United Kingdom, (Dial from U.S. (212) 216-7800), (Fax from U.S. (212) 564-7854), www.tandf.co.uk; *The Europa World Year Book*.

COOK ISLANDS - AIRPORTS

Central Intelligence Agency, Office of Public Affairs, Washington, DC 20505, (703) 482-0623, Fax: (703) 482-1739, www.cia.gov; *The World Factbook*.

COOK ISLANDS - ARMED FORCES

Central Intelligence Agency, Office of Public Affairs, Washington, DC 20505, (703) 482-0623, Fax: (703) 482-1739, www.cia.gov; *The World Factbook*.

COOK ISLANDS - BANKS AND BANKING

Asian Development Bank (ADB), PO Box 789, 0980 Manila, Philippines, www.adb.org; *Key Indicators of Developing Asian and Pacific Countries 2006*.

Palgrave Macmillan Ltd., Houndmills, Basingstoke, Hampshire, RG21 6XS, England, (Telephone in U.S. (888) 330-8477), (Fax in U.S. (800) 672-2054), www.palgrave.com; *The Statesman's Yearbook 2008*.

COOK ISLANDS - BONDS

Asian Development Bank (ADB), PO Box 789, 0980 Manila, Philippines, www.adb.org; *Key Indicators of Developing Asian and Pacific Countries 2006*.

COOK ISLANDS - BROADCASTING

Central Intelligence Agency, Office of Public Affairs, Washington, DC 20505, (703) 482-0623, Fax: (703) 482-1739, www.cia.gov; *The World Factbook*.

Palgrave Macmillan Ltd., Houndmills, Basingstoke, Hampshire, RG21 6XS, England, (Telephone in U.S. (888) 330-8477), (Fax in U.S. (800) 672-2054), www.palgrave.com; *The Statesman's Yearbook 2008*.

UNESCO Institute for Statistics, C.P. 6128 Succursale Centre-Ville, Montreal, Quebec, H3C 3J7 Canada, (Dial from U.S. (514) 343-6880), (Fax from U.S. (514) 343 6882), www.uis.unesco.org; *Statistical Tables*.

WRTH Publications Limited, PO Box 290, Oxford OX2 7FT, UK, www.wrth.com; *World Radio TV Handbook 2007*.

COOK ISLANDS - BUDGET

Central Intelligence Agency, Office of Public Affairs, Washington, DC 20505, (703) 482-0623, Fax: (703) 482-1739, www.cia.gov; *The World Factbook*.

COOK ISLANDS - BUSINESS

United Nations Statistics Division, New York, NY 10017, (800) 253-9646, Fax: (212) 963-4116, http://unstats.un.org; *Statistical Yearbook for Asia and the Pacific 2004*.

COOK ISLANDS - CAPITAL INVESTMENTS

Asian Development Bank (ADB), PO Box 789, 0980 Manila, Philippines, www.adb.org; *Key Indicators of Developing Asian and Pacific Countries 2006*.

COOK ISLANDS - CAPITAL LEVY

Asian Development Bank (ADB), PO Box 789, 0980 Manila, Philippines, www.adb.org; *Key Indicators of Developing Asian and Pacific Countries 2006*.

COOK ISLANDS - CATTLE

See COOK ISLANDS - LIVESTOCK

COOK ISLANDS - CHILDBIRTH - STATISTICS

Central Intelligence Agency, Office of Public Affairs, Washington, DC 20505, (703) 482-0623, Fax: (703) 482-1739, www.cia.gov; *The World Factbook*.

Palgrave Macmillan Ltd., Houndmills, Basingstoke, Hampshire, RG21 6XS, England, (Telephone in U.S. (888) 330-8477), (Fax in U.S. (800) 672-2054), www.palgrave.com; *The Statesman's Yearbook 2008*.

Taylor and Francis Group, An Informa Business, 2 Park Square, Milton Park, Abingdon, Oxford OX14 4RN, United Kingdom, (Dial from U.S. (212) 216-7800), (Fax from U.S. (212) 564-7854), www.tandf.co.uk; *The Europa World Year Book*.

United Nations Statistics Division, New York, NY 10017, (800) 253-9646, Fax: (212) 963-4116, http://unstats.un.org; *Asia-Pacific in Figures 2004; Demographic Yearbook;* and *Statistical Yearbook*.

World Health Organization (WHO), Avenue Appia 20, 1211 Geneve 27, Switzerland, (Telephone in U.S. (212) 331-9081), www.who.int; *World Health Report 2006*.

COOK ISLANDS - CLOTHING EXPORTS AND IMPORTS

See COOK ISLANDS - TEXTILE INDUSTRY

COOK ISLANDS - COAL PRODUCTION

See COOK ISLANDS - MINERAL INDUSTRIES

COOK ISLANDS - COMMERCE

Palgrave Macmillan Ltd., Houndmills, Basingstoke, Hampshire, RG21 6XS, England, (Telephone in U.S. (888) 330-8477), (Fax in U.S. (800) 672-2054), www.palgrave.com; *The Statesman's Yearbook 2008*.

COOK ISLANDS - COMMODITY EXCHANGES

United Nations Food and Agricultural Organization (FAO), Viale delle Terme di Caracalla, 00100 Rome, Italy, (Dial from U.S. (202) 653-2400), (Fax from U.S. (202) 653 5760), www.fao.org; *The State of Food and Agriculture (SOFA) 2006*.

COOK ISLANDS - CONSUMER PRICE INDEXES

Asian Development Bank (ADB), PO Box 789, 0980 Manila, Philippines, www.adb.org; *Key Indicators of Developing Asian and Pacific Countries 2006*.

Taylor and Francis Group, An Informa Business, 2 Park Square, Milton Park, Abingdon, Oxford OX14 4RN, United Kingdom, (Dial from U.S. (212) 216-7800), (Fax from U.S. (212) 564-7854), www.tandf.co.uk; *The Europa World Year Book*.

United Nations Statistics Division, New York, NY 10017, (800) 253-9646, Fax: (212) 963-4116, http://unstats.un.org; *Statistical Yearbook*.

COOK ISLANDS - CONSUMPTION (ECONOMICS)

Secretariat of the Pacific Community (SPC), BP D5, 98848 Noumea Cedex, New Caledonia, www.spc.int/corp; *Selected Pacific Economies - a Statistical Summary (SPESS)*.

COOK ISLANDS - CORN INDUSTRY

See COOK ISLANDS - CROPS

COOK ISLANDS - COST AND STANDARD OF LIVING

Secretariat of the Pacific Community (SPC), BP D5, 98848 Noumea Cedex, New Caledonia, www.spc.int/corp; *Selected Pacific Economies - a Statistical Summary (SPESS)*.

COOK ISLANDS - CROPS

Asian Development Bank (ADB), PO Box 789, 0980 Manila, Philippines, www.adb.org; *Key Indicators of Developing Asian and Pacific Countries 2006*.

Palgrave Macmillan Ltd., Houndmills, Basingstoke, Hampshire, RG21 6XS, England, (Telephone in U.S. (888) 330-8477), (Fax in U.S. (800) 672-2054), www.palgrave.com; *The Statesman's Yearbook 2008*.

Taylor and Francis Group, An Informa Business, 2 Park Square, Milton Park, Abingdon, Oxford OX14 4RN, United Kingdom, (Dial from U.S. (212) 216-7800), (Fax from U.S. (212) 564-7854), www.tandf.co.uk; *The Europa World Year Book*.

United Nations Conference on Trade and Development (UNCTAD), DC2-1120, United Nations, New York, NY 10017, (212) 963-0027, www.unctad.org; *UNCTAD Commodity Yearbook*.

United Nations Food and Agricultural Organization (FAO), Viale delle Terme di Caracalla, 00100 Rome, Italy, (Dial from U.S. (202) 653-2400), (Fax from U.S. (202) 653 5760), www.fao.org; *The State of Food and Agriculture (SOFA) 2006*.

COOK ISLANDS - DAIRY PROCESSING

M.E. Sharpe, 80 Business Park Drive, Armonk, NY 10504, (800) 541-6563, Fax: (914) 273-2106, www.mesharpe.com; *The Illustrated Book of World Rankings*.

United Nations Food and Agricultural Organization (FAO), Viale delle Terme di Caracalla, 00100 Rome, Italy, (Dial from U.S. (202) 653-2400), (Fax from U.S. (202) 653 5760), www.fao.org; *The State of Food and Agriculture (SOFA) 2006*.

COOK ISLANDS - DEATH RATES

See COOK ISLANDS - MORTALITY

COOK ISLANDS - DEBTS, EXTERNAL

Asian Development Bank (ADB), PO Box 789, 0980 Manila, Philippines, www.adb.org; *Key Indicators of Developing Asian and Pacific Countries 2006*.

Worldinformation.com, 2 Market Street, Saffron Walden, Essex CB10 1HZ, United Kingdom, www.worldinformation.com; The World of Information (www.worldinformation.com).

COOK ISLANDS - DEMOGRAPHY

United Nations Statistics Division, New York, NY 10017, (800) 253-9646, Fax: (212) 963-4116, http://unstats.un.org; *Asia-Pacific in Figures 2004*.

COOK ISLANDS - DISPOSABLE INCOME

United Nations Statistics Division, New York, NY 10017, (800) 253-9646, Fax: (212) 963-4116, http://

unstats.un.org; *National Accounts Statistics: Compendium of Income Distribution Statistics* and *Statistical Yearbook*.

COOK ISLANDS - DIVORCE

United Nations Statistics Division, New York, NY 10017, (800) 253-9646, Fax: (212) 963-4116, http://unstats.un.org; *Demographic Yearbook* and *Statistical Yearbook*.

COOK ISLANDS - ECONOMIC ASSISTANCE

Asian Development Bank (ADB), PO Box 789, 0980 Manila, Philippines, www.adb.org; *Key Indicators of Developing Asian and Pacific Countries 2006*.

United Nations Statistics Division, New York, NY 10017, (800) 253-9646, Fax: (212) 963-4116, http://unstats.un.org; *Statistical Yearbook*.

COOK ISLANDS - ECONOMIC CONDITIONS

Asian Development Bank (ADB), PO Box 789, 0980 Manila, Philippines, www.adb.org; *Key Indicators of Developing Asian and Pacific Countries 2006*.

Central Intelligence Agency, Office of Public Affairs, Washington, DC 20505, (703) 482-0623, Fax: (703) 482-1739, www.cia.gov; *The World Factbook*.

Palgrave Macmillan Ltd., Houndmills, Basingstoke, Hampshire, RG21 6XS, England, (Telephone in U.S. (888) 330-8477), (Fax in U.S. (800) 672-2054), www.palgrave.com; *The Statesman's Yearbook 2008*.

Secretariat of the Pacific Community (SPC), BP D5, 98848 Noumea Cedex, New Caledonia, www.spc.int/corp; PRISM (Pacific Regional Information System).

United Nations Statistics Division, New York, NY 10017, (800) 253-9646, Fax: (212) 963-4116, http://unstats.un.org; *World Statistics Pocketbook*.

COOK ISLANDS - EDUCATION

Palgrave Macmillan Ltd., Houndmills, Basingstoke, Hampshire, RG21 6XS, England, (Telephone in U.S. (888) 330-8477), (Fax in U.S. (800) 672-2054), www.palgrave.com; *The Statesman's Yearbook 2008*.

Taylor and Francis Group, An Informa Business, 2 Park Square, Milton Park, Abingdon, Oxford OX14 4RN, United Kingdom, (Dial from U.S. (212) 216-7800), (Fax from U.S. (212) 564-7854), www.tandf.co.uk; *The Europa World Year Book*.

UNESCO Institute for Statistics, C.P. 6128 Succursale Centre-Ville, Montreal, Quebec, H3C 3J7 Canada, (Dial from U.S. (514) 343-6880), (Fax from U.S. (514) 343 6882), www.uis.unesco.org; *Statistical Tables*.

United Nations Statistics Division, New York, NY 10017, (800) 253-9646, Fax: (212) 963-4116, http://unstats.un.org; *Asia-Pacific in Figures 2004* and *Statistical Yearbook for Asia and the Pacific 2004*.

COOK ISLANDS - ELECTRICITY

Asian Development Bank (ADB), PO Box 789, 0980 Manila, Philippines, www.adb.org; *Key Indicators of Developing Asian and Pacific Countries 2006*.

Palgrave Macmillan Ltd., Houndmills, Basingstoke, Hampshire, RG21 6XS, England, (Telephone in U.S. (888) 330-8477), (Fax in U.S. (800) 672-2054), www.palgrave.com; *The Statesman's Yearbook 2008*.

United Nations Statistics Division, New York, NY 10017, (800) 253-9646, Fax: (212) 963-4116, http://unstats.un.org; *Electric Power in Asia and the Pacific 2001 and 2002*.

COOK ISLANDS - EMPLOYMENT

International Labour Office, I.L.O. Publications, 4 route des Morillons, CH-1211 Geneva 22, Switzerland, (Telephone in U.S. (202) 653-7652), (Fax in U.S. (202) 653-7687), www.ilo.org; *Yearbook of Labour Statistics 2006*.

United Nations Statistics Division, New York, NY 10017, (800) 253-9646, Fax: (212) 963-4116, http://unstats.un.org; *Asia-Pacific in Figures 2004*.

COOK ISLANDS - ENERGY INDUSTRIES

United Nations Statistics Division, New York, NY 10017, (800) 253-9646, Fax: (212) 963-4116, http://unstats.un.org; *Electric Power in Asia and the Pacific 2001 and 2002*.

COOK ISLANDS - ENVIRONMENTAL CONDITIONS

DSI Data Service Information, Xantener Strasse 51a, D-47495 Rheinberg, Germany, www.dsidata.com; *Campus Solution*.

United Nations Statistics Division, New York, NY 10017, (800) 253-9646, Fax: (212) 963-4116, http://unstats.un.org; *World Statistics Pocketbook*.

COOK ISLANDS - EXPORTS

Asian Development Bank (ADB), PO Box 789, 0980 Manila, Philippines, www.adb.org; *Key Indicators of Developing Asian and Pacific Countries 2006*.

Central Intelligence Agency, Office of Public Affairs, Washington, DC 20505, (703) 482-0623, Fax: (703) 482-1739, www.cia.gov; *The World Factbook*.

Palgrave Macmillan Ltd., Houndmills, Basingstoke, Hampshire, RG21 6XS, England, (Telephone in U.S. (888) 330-8477), (Fax in U.S. (800) 672-2054), www.palgrave.com; *The Statesman's Yearbook 2008*.

Secretariat of the Pacific Community (SPC), BP D5, 98848 Noumea Cedex, New Caledonia, www.spc.int/corp; *Selected Pacific Economies - a Statistical Summary (SPESS)*.

Taylor and Francis Group, An Informa Business, 2 Park Square, Milton Park, Abingdon, Oxford OX14 4RN, United Kingdom, (Dial from U.S. (212) 216-7800), (Fax from U.S. (212) 564-7854), www.tandf.co.uk; *The Europa World Year Book*.

United Nations Food and Agricultural Organization (FAO), Viale delle Terme di Caracalla, 00100 Rome, Italy, (Dial from U.S. (202) 653-2400), (Fax from U.S. (202) 653 5760), www.fao.org; *The State of Food and Agriculture (SOFA) 2006*.

Worldinformation.com, 2 Market Street, Saffron Walden, Essex CB10 1HZ, United Kingdom, www.worldinformation.com; The World of Information (www.worldinformation.com).

COOK ISLANDS - FERTILITY, HUMAN

Central Intelligence Agency, Office of Public Affairs, Washington, DC 20505, (703) 482-0623, Fax: (703) 482-1739, www.cia.gov; *The World Factbook*.

COOK ISLANDS - FERTILIZER INDUSTRY

United Nations Food and Agricultural Organization (FAO), Viale delle Terme di Caracalla, 00100 Rome, Italy, (Dial from U.S. (202) 653-2400), (Fax from U.S. (202) 653 5760), www.fao.org; *The State of Food and Agriculture (SOFA) 2006*.

COOK ISLANDS - FETAL MORTALITY

See COOK ISLANDS - MORTALITY

COOK ISLANDS - FINANCE

United Nations Statistics Division, New York, NY 10017, (800) 253-9646, Fax: (212) 963-4116, http://unstats.un.org; *Asia-Pacific in Figures 2004; National Accounts Statistics: Compendium of Income Distribution Statistics; Statistical Yearbook;* and *Statistical Yearbook for Asia and the Pacific 2004*.

COOK ISLANDS - FINANCE, PUBLIC

Asian Development Bank (ADB), PO Box 789, 0980 Manila, Philippines, www.adb.org; *Key Indicators of Developing Asian and Pacific Countries 2006*.

Palgrave Macmillan Ltd., Houndmills, Basingstoke, Hampshire, RG21 6XS, England, (Telephone in U.S. (888) 330-8477), (Fax in U.S. (800) 672-2054), www.palgrave.com; *The Statesman's Yearbook 2008*.

Taylor and Francis Group, An Informa Business, 2 Park Square, Milton Park, Abingdon, Oxford OX14 4RN, United Kingdom, (Dial from U.S. (212) 216-7800), (Fax from U.S. (212) 564-7854), www.tandf.co.uk; *The Europa World Year Book*.

United Nations Statistics Division, New York, NY 10017, (800) 253-9646, Fax: (212) 963-4116, http://unstats.un.org; *Statistical Yearbook for Asia and the Pacific 2004*.

COOK ISLANDS - FISHERIES

Palgrave Macmillan Ltd., Houndmills, Basingstoke, Hampshire, RG21 6XS, England, (Telephone in U.S. (888) 330-8477), (Fax in U.S. (800) 672-2054), www.palgrave.com; *The Statesman's Yearbook 2008*.

Taylor and Francis Group, An Informa Business, 2 Park Square, Milton Park, Abingdon, Oxford OX14 4RN, United Kingdom, (Dial from U.S. (212) 216-7800), (Fax from U.S. (212) 564-7854), www.tandf.co.uk; *The Europa World Year Book*.

United Nations Conference on Trade and Development (UNCTAD), DC2-1120, United Nations, New York, NY 10017, (212) 963-0027, www.unctad.org; *UNCTAD Commodity Yearbook*.

United Nations Food and Agricultural Organization (FAO), Viale delle Terme di Caracalla, 00100 Rome, Italy, (Dial from U.S. (202) 653-2400), (Fax from U.S. (202) 653 5760), www.fao.org; *FAO Yearbook of Fishery Statistics;* Fishery Databases; FISHSTAT Database. Subjects covered include: Aquaculture production, capture production, fishery commodities; and *The State of Food and Agriculture (SOFA) 2006*.

United Nations Statistics Division, New York, NY 10017, (800) 253-9646, Fax: (212) 963-4116, http://unstats.un.org; *Statistical Yearbook*.

COOK ISLANDS - FOOD

Secretariat of the Pacific Community (SPC), BP D5, 98848 Noumea Cedex, New Caledonia, www.spc.int/corp; *Selected Pacific Economies - a Statistical Summary (SPESS)*.

United Nations Conference on Trade and Development (UNCTAD), DC2-1120, United Nations, New York, NY 10017, (212) 963-0027, www.unctad.org; *UNCTAD Commodity Yearbook*.

United Nations Food and Agricultural Organization (FAO), Viale delle Terme di Caracalla, 00100 Rome, Italy, (Dial from U.S. (202) 653-2400), (Fax from U.S. (202) 653 5760), www.fao.org; *FAO Production Yearbook 2002* and *The State of Food and Agriculture (SOFA) 2006*.

United Nations Statistics Division, New York, NY 10017, (800) 253-9646, Fax: (212) 963-4116, http://unstats.un.org; *Statistical Yearbook for Asia and the Pacific 2004*.

COOK ISLANDS - FOREIGN EXCHANGE RATES

Asian Development Bank (ADB), PO Box 789, 0980 Manila, Philippines, www.adb.org; *Key Indicators of Developing Asian and Pacific Countries 2006*.

Central Intelligence Agency, Office of Public Affairs, Washington, DC 20505, (703) 482-0623, Fax: (703) 482-1739, www.cia.gov; *The World Factbook*.

Taylor and Francis Group, An Informa Business, 2 Park Square, Milton Park, Abingdon, Oxford OX14 4RN, United Kingdom, (Dial from U.S. (212) 216-7800), (Fax from U.S. (212) 564-7854), www.tandf.co.uk; *The Europa World Year Book*.

United Nations Statistics Division, New York, NY 10017, (800) 253-9646, Fax: (212) 963-4116, http://unstats.un.org; *World Statistics Pocketbook*.

Worldinformation.com, 2 Market Street, Saffron Walden, Essex CB10 1HZ, United Kingdom, www.worldinformation.com; The World of Information (www.worldinformation.com).

COOK ISLANDS - FORESTS AND FORESTRY

UNESCO Institute for Statistics, C.P. 6128 Succursale Centre-Ville, Montreal, Quebec, H3C 3J7 Canada, (Dial from U.S. (514) 343-6880), (Fax from U.S. (514) 343 6882), www.uis.unesco.org; *Statistical Tables*.

United Nations Conference on Trade and Development (UNCTAD), DC2-1120, United Nations, New York, NY 10017, (212) 963-0027, www.unctad.org; *UNCTAD Commodity Yearbook.*

United Nations Food and Agricultural Organization (FAO), Viale delle Terme di Caracalla, 00100 Rome, Italy, (Dial from U.S. (202) 653-2400), (Fax from U.S. (202) 653 5760), www.fao.org; *The State of Food and Agriculture (SOFA) 2006.*

United Nations Statistics Division, New York, NY 10017, (800) 253-9646, Fax: (212) 963-4116, http://unstats.un.org; *Statistical Yearbook.*

COOK ISLANDS - GROSS DOMESTIC PRODUCT

Asian Development Bank (ADB), PO Box 789, 0980 Manila, Philippines, www.adb.org; *Key Indicators of Developing Asian and Pacific Countries 2006.*

Taylor and Francis Group, An Informa Business, 2 Park Square, Milton Park, Abingdon, Oxford OX14 4RN, United Kingdom, (Dial from U.S. (212) 216-7800), (Fax from U.S. (212) 564-7854), www.tandf.co.uk; *The Europa World Year Book.*

United Nations Statistics Division, New York, NY 10017, (800) 253-9646, Fax: (212) 963-4116, http://unstats.un.org; *National Accounts Statistics: Compendium of Income Distribution Statistics* and *Statistical Yearbook.*

COOK ISLANDS - GROSS NATIONAL PRODUCT

Asian Development Bank (ADB), PO Box 789, 0980 Manila, Philippines, www.adb.org; *Key Indicators of Developing Asian and Pacific Countries 2006.*

United Nations Statistics Division, New York, NY 10017, (800) 253-9646, Fax: (212) 963-4116, http://unstats.un.org; *Statistical Yearbook.*

Worldinformation.com, 2 Market Street, Saffron Walden, Essex CB10 1HZ, United Kingdom, www.worldinformation.com; The World of Information (www.worldinformation.com).

COOK ISLANDS - HIDES AND SKINS INDUSTRY

United Nations Food and Agricultural Organization (FAO), Viale delle Terme di Caracalla, 00100 Rome, Italy, (Dial from U.S. (202) 653-2400), (Fax from U.S. (202) 653 5760), www.fao.org; *FAO Production Yearbook 2002.*

COOK ISLANDS - HOUSING

Secretariat of the Pacific Community (SPC), BP D5, 98848 Noumea Cedex, New Caledonia, www.spc.int/corp; *Selected Pacific Economies - a Statistical Summary (SPESS).*

United Nations Statistics Division, New York, NY 10017, (800) 253-9646, Fax: (212) 963-4116, http://unstats.un.org; *Statistical Yearbook.*

COOK ISLANDS - ILLITERATE PERSONS

UNESCO Institute for Statistics, C.P. 6128 Succursale Centre-Ville, Montreal, Quebec, H3C 3J7 Canada, (Dial from U.S. (514) 343-6880), (Fax from U.S. (514) 343 6882), www.uis.unesco.org; *Statistical Tables.*

United Nations Statistics Division, New York, NY 10017, (800) 253-9646, Fax: (212) 963-4116, http://unstats.un.org; *Asia-Pacific in Figures 2004.*

COOK ISLANDS - IMPORTS

Asian Development Bank (ADB), PO Box 789, 0980 Manila, Philippines, www.adb.org; *Key Indicators of Developing Asian and Pacific Countries 2006.*

Central Intelligence Agency, Office of Public Affairs, Washington, DC 20505, (703) 482-0623, Fax: (703) 482-1739, www.cia.gov; *The World Factbook.*

Palgrave Macmillan Ltd., Houndmills, Basingstoke, Hampshire, RG21 6XS, England, (Telephone in U.S. (888) 330-8477), (Fax in U.S. (800) 672-2054), www.palgrave.com; *The Statesman's Yearbook 2008.*

Secretariat of the Pacific Community (SPC), BP D5, 98848 Noumea Cedex, New Caledonia, www.spc.int/corp; *Selected Pacific Economies - a Statistical Summary (SPESS).*

Taylor and Francis Group, An Informa Business, 2 Park Square, Milton Park, Abingdon, Oxford OX14 4RN, United Kingdom, (Dial from U.S. (212) 216-7800), (Fax from U.S. (212) 564-7854), www.tandf.co.uk; *The Europa World Year Book.*

United Nations Food and Agricultural Organization (FAO), Viale delle Terme di Caracalla, 00100 Rome, Italy, (Dial from U.S. (202) 653-2400), (Fax from U.S. (202) 653 5760), www.fao.org; *The State of Food and Agriculture (SOFA) 2006.*

Worldinformation.com, 2 Market Street, Saffron Walden, Essex CB10 1HZ, United Kingdom, www.worldinformation.com; The World of Information (www.worldinformation.com).

COOK ISLANDS - INDUSTRIES

Central Intelligence Agency, Office of Public Affairs, Washington, DC 20505, (703) 482-0623, Fax: (703) 482-1739, www.cia.gov; *The World Factbook.*

International Labour Office, I.L.O. Publications, 4 route des Morillons, CH-1211 Geneva 22, Switzerland, (Telephone in U.S. (202) 653-7652), (Fax in U.S. (202) 653-7687), www.ilo.org; *Yearbook of Labour Statistics 2006.*

Palgrave Macmillan Ltd., Houndmills, Basingstoke, Hampshire, RG21 6XS, England, (Telephone in U.S. (888) 330-8477), (Fax in U.S. (800) 672-2054), www.palgrave.com; *The Statesman's Yearbook 2008.*

United Nations Statistics Division, New York, NY 10017, (800) 253-9646, Fax: (212) 963-4116, http://unstats.un.org; *Asia-Pacific in Figures 2004* and *Statistical Yearbook for Asia and the Pacific 2004.*

COOK ISLANDS - INFANT AND MATERNAL MORTALITY

See COOK ISLANDS - MORTALITY

COOK ISLANDS - INTERNATIONAL FINANCE

Asian Development Bank (ADB), PO Box 789, 0980 Manila, Philippines, www.adb.org; *Key Indicators of Developing Asian and Pacific Countries 2006.*

COOK ISLANDS - INTERNATIONAL STATISTICS

Asian Development Bank (ADB), PO Box 789, 0980 Manila, Philippines, www.adb.org; *Key Indicators of Developing Asian and Pacific Countries 2006.*

COOK ISLANDS - INTERNATIONAL TRADE

Asian Development Bank (ADB), PO Box 789, 0980 Manila, Philippines, www.adb.org; *Key Indicators of Developing Asian and Pacific Countries 2006.*

Organisation for Economic Cooperation and Development (OECD), 2 rue Andre Pascal, F-75775 Paris Cedex 16, France, (Telephone in U.S. (202) 785-6323), (Fax in U.S. (202) 785-0350), www.oecd.org; *International Trade by Commodity Statistics (ITCS).*

Palgrave Macmillan Ltd., Houndmills, Basingstoke, Hampshire, RG21 6XS, England, (Telephone in U.S. (888) 330-8477), (Fax in U.S. (800) 672-2054), www.palgrave.com; *The Statesman's Yearbook 2008.*

Secretariat of the Pacific Community (SPC), BP D5, 98848 Noumea Cedex, New Caledonia, www.spc.int/corp; *Selected Pacific Economies - a Statistical Summary (SPESS).*

Taylor and Francis Group, An Informa Business, 2 Park Square, Milton Park, Abingdon, Oxford OX14 4RN, United Kingdom, (Dial from U.S. (212) 216-7800), (Fax from U.S. (212) 564-7854), www.tandf.co.uk; *The Europa World Year Book.*

United Nations Conference on Trade and Development (UNCTAD), DC2-1120, United Nations, New York, NY 10017, (212) 963-0027, www.unctad.org; *UNCTAD Commodity Yearbook.*

United Nations Food and Agricultural Organization (FAO), Viale delle Terme di Caracalla, 00100 Rome, Italy, (Dial from U.S. (202) 653-2400), (Fax from U.S. (202) 653 5760), www.fao.org; *FAO Trade Yearbook* and *The State of Food and Agriculture (SOFA) 2006.*

United Nations Statistics Division, New York, NY 10017, (800) 253-9646, Fax: (212) 963-4116, http://unstats.un.org; *Asia-Pacific in Figures 2004; International Trade Statistics Yearbook; Statistical Yearbook;* and *Statistical Yearbook for Asia and the Pacific 2004.*

World Trade Organization (WTO), Centre William Rappard, Rue de Lausanne 154, CH-1211 Geneva 21, Switzerland, www.wto.org; *International Trade Statistics 2006.*

COOK ISLANDS - LABOR

Central Intelligence Agency, Office of Public Affairs, Washington, DC 20505, (703) 482-0623, Fax: (703) 482-1739, www.cia.gov; *The World Factbook.*

International Labour Office, I.L.O. Publications, 4 route des Morillons, CH-1211 Geneva 22, Switzerland, (Telephone in U.S. (202) 653-7652), (Fax in U.S. (202) 653-7687), www.ilo.org; *Yearbook of Labour Statistics 2006.*

Palgrave Macmillan Ltd., Houndmills, Basingstoke, Hampshire, RG21 6XS, England, (Telephone in U.S. (888) 330-8477), (Fax in U.S. (800) 672-2054), www.palgrave.com; *The Statesman's Yearbook 2008.*

United Nations Food and Agricultural Organization (FAO), Viale delle Terme di Caracalla, 00100 Rome, Italy, (Dial from U.S. (202) 653-2400), (Fax from U.S. (202) 653 5760), www.fao.org; *The State of Food and Agriculture (SOFA) 2006.*

COOK ISLANDS - LAND USE

Central Intelligence Agency, Office of Public Affairs, Washington, DC 20505, (703) 482-0623, Fax: (703) 482-1739, www.cia.gov; *The World Factbook.*

United Nations Food and Agricultural Organization (FAO), Viale delle Terme di Caracalla, 00100 Rome, Italy, (Dial from U.S. (202) 653-2400), (Fax from U.S. (202) 653 5760), www.fao.org; *FAO Production Yearbook 2002.*

COOK ISLANDS - LIBRARIES

UNESCO Institute for Statistics, C.P. 6128 Succursale Centre-Ville, Montreal, Quebec, H3C 3J7 Canada, (Dial from U.S. (514) 343-6880), (Fax from U.S. (514) 343 6882), www.uis.unesco.org; *Statistical Tables.*

COOK ISLANDS - LIFE EXPECTANCY

Central Intelligence Agency, Office of Public Affairs, Washington, DC 20505, (703) 482-0623, Fax: (703) 482-1739, www.cia.gov; *The World Factbook.*

United Nations Statistics Division, New York, NY 10017, (800) 253-9646, Fax: (212) 963-4116, http://unstats.un.org; *Asia-Pacific in Figures 2004* and *World Statistics Pocketbook.*

COOK ISLANDS - LIVESTOCK

Palgrave Macmillan Ltd., Houndmills, Basingstoke, Hampshire, RG21 6XS, England, (Telephone in U.S. (888) 330-8477), (Fax in U.S. (800) 672-2054), www.palgrave.com; *The Statesman's Yearbook 2008.*

Taylor and Francis Group, An Informa Business, 2 Park Square, Milton Park, Abingdon, Oxford OX14 4RN, United Kingdom, (Dial from U.S. (212) 216-7800), (Fax from U.S. (212) 564-7854), www.tandf.co.uk; *The Europa World Year Book.*

United Nations Conference on Trade and Development (UNCTAD), DC2-1120, United Nations, New York, NY 10017, (212) 963-0027, www.unctad.org; *UNCTAD Commodity Yearbook.*

United Nations Food and Agricultural Organization (FAO), Viale delle Terme di Caracalla, 00100 Rome, Italy, (Dial from U.S. (202) 653-2400), (Fax from U.S. (202) 653 5760), www.fao.org; *FAO Production Yearbook 2002* and *The State of Food and Agriculture (SOFA) 2006.*

United Nations Statistics Division, New York, NY 10017, (800) 253-9646, Fax: (212) 963-4116, http://unstats.un.org; *Statistical Yearbook.*

COOK ISLANDS - MANPOWER

United Nations Statistics Division, New York, NY 10017, (800) 253-9646, Fax: (212) 963-4116, http://unstats.un.org; *Statistical Yearbook for Asia and the Pacific 2004.*

COOK ISLANDS - MANUFACTURES

Asian Development Bank (ADB), PO Box 789, 0980 Manila, Philippines, www.adb.org; *Key Indicators of Developing Asian and Pacific Countries 2006.*

COOK ISLANDS - MARRIAGE

Taylor and Francis Group, An Informa Business, 2 Park Square, Milton Park, Abingdon, Oxford OX14 4RN, United Kingdom, (Dial from U.S. (212) 216-7800), (Fax from U.S. (212) 564-7854), www.tandf.co.uk; *The Europa World Year Book.*

United Nations Statistics Division, New York, NY 10017, (800) 253-9646, Fax: (212) 963-4116, http://unstats.un.org; *Demographic Yearbook* and *Statistical Yearbook.*

COOK ISLANDS - MINERAL INDUSTRIES

Asian Development Bank (ADB), PO Box 789, 0980 Manila, Philippines, www.adb.org; *Key Indicators of Developing Asian and Pacific Countries 2006.*

United Nations Conference on Trade and Development (UNCTAD), DC2-1120, United Nations, New York, NY 10017, (212) 963-0027, www.unctad.org; *UNCTAD Commodity Yearbook.*

COOK ISLANDS - MONEY SUPPLY

Asian Development Bank (ADB), PO Box 789, 0980 Manila, Philippines, www.adb.org; *Key Indicators of Developing Asian and Pacific Countries 2006.*

COOK ISLANDS - MORTALITY

Central Intelligence Agency, Office of Public Affairs, Washington, DC 20505, (703) 482-0623, Fax: (703) 482-1739, www.cia.gov; *The World Factbook.*

Palgrave Macmillan Ltd., Houndmills, Basingstoke, Hampshire, RG21 6XS, England, (Telephone in U.S. (888) 330-8477), (Fax in U.S. (800) 672-2054), www.palgrave.com; *The Statesman's Yearbook 2008.*

United Nations Statistics Division, New York, NY 10017, (800) 253-9646, Fax: (212) 963-4116, http://unstats.un.org; *Asia-Pacific in Figures 2004; Demographic Yearbook; Statistical Yearbook;* and *World Statistics Pocketbook.*

World Health Organization (WHO), Avenue Appia 20, 1211 Geneve 27, Switzerland, (Telephone in U.S. (212) 331-9081), www.who.int; *World Health Report 2006.*

COOK ISLANDS - MOTOR VEHICLES

Taylor and Francis Group, An Informa Business, 2 Park Square, Milton Park, Abingdon, Oxford OX14 4RN, United Kingdom, (Dial from U.S. (212) 216-7800), (Fax from U.S. (212) 564-7854), www.tandf.co.uk; *The Europa World Year Book.*

COOK ISLANDS - MUSEUMS

UNESCO Institute for Statistics, C.P. 6128 Succursale Centre-Ville, Montreal, Quebec, H3C 3J7 Canada, (Dial from U.S. (514) 343-6880), (Fax from U.S. (514) 343 6882), www.uis.unesco.org; *Statistical Tables.*

COOK ISLANDS - NUTRITION

Asian Development Bank (ADB), PO Box 789, 0980 Manila, Philippines, www.adb.org; *Key Indicators of Developing Asian and Pacific Countries 2006.*

United Nations Food and Agricultural Organization (FAO), Viale delle Terme di Caracalla, 00100 Rome, Italy, (Dial from U.S. (202) 653-2400), (Fax from U.S. (202) 653 5760), www.fao.org; *The State of Food and Agriculture (SOFA) 2006.*

COOK ISLANDS - PESTICIDES

United Nations Food and Agricultural Organization (FAO), Viale delle Terme di Caracalla, 00100 Rome, Italy, (Dial from U.S. (202) 653-2400), (Fax from U.S. (202) 653 5760), www.fao.org; *The State of Food and Agriculture (SOFA) 2006.*

COOK ISLANDS - PETROLEUM INDUSTRY AND TRADE

Asian Development Bank (ADB), PO Box 789, 0980 Manila, Philippines, www.adb.org; *Key Indicators of Developing Asian and Pacific Countries 2006.*

PennWell Corporation, 1421 South Sheridan Road, Tulsa, OK 74112, (918) 835-3161, www.pennwell.com; *International Petroleum Encyclopedia 2007.*

United Nations Conference on Trade and Development (UNCTAD), DC2-1120, United Nations, New York, NY 10017, (212) 963-0027, www.unctad.org; *UNCTAD Commodity Yearbook.*

United Nations Food and Agricultural Organization (FAO), Viale delle Terme di Caracalla, 00100 Rome, Italy, (Dial from U.S. (202) 653-2400), (Fax from U.S. (202) 653 5760), www.fao.org; *The State of Food and Agriculture (SOFA) 2006.*

COOK ISLANDS - POLITICAL SCIENCE

Asian Development Bank (ADB), PO Box 789, 0980 Manila, Philippines, www.adb.org; *Key Indicators of Developing Asian and Pacific Countries 2006.*

Central Intelligence Agency, Office of Public Affairs, Washington, DC 20505, (703) 482-0623, Fax: (703) 482-1739, www.cia.gov; *The World Factbook.*

Palgrave Macmillan Ltd., Houndmills, Basingstoke, Hampshire, RG21 6XS, England, (Telephone in U.S. (888) 330-8477), (Fax in U.S. (800) 672-2054), www.palgrave.com; *The Statesman's Yearbook 2008.*

Taylor and Francis Group, An Informa Business, 2 Park Square, Milton Park, Abingdon, Oxford OX14 4RN, United Kingdom, (Dial from U.S. (212) 216-7800), (Fax from U.S. (212) 564-7854), www.tandf.co.uk; *The Europa World Year Book.*

United Nations Statistics Division, New York, NY 10017, (800) 253-9646, Fax: (212) 963-4116, http://unstats.un.org; *Asia-Pacific in Figures 2004* and *National Accounts Statistics: Compendium of Income Distribution Statistics.*

COOK ISLANDS - POPULATION

Asian Development Bank (ADB), PO Box 789, 0980 Manila, Philippines, www.adb.org; *Key Indicators of Developing Asian and Pacific Countries 2006.*

Central Intelligence Agency, Office of Public Affairs, Washington, DC 20505, (703) 482-0623, Fax: (703) 482-1739, www.cia.gov; *The World Factbook.*

International Labour Office, I.L.O. Publications, 4 route des Morillons, CH-1211 Geneva 22, Switzerland, (Telephone in U.S. (202) 653-7652), (Fax in U.S. (202) 653-7687), www.ilo.org; *Yearbook of Labour Statistics 2006.*

Palgrave Macmillan Ltd., Houndmills, Basingstoke, Hampshire, RG21 6XS, England, (Telephone in U.S. (888) 330-8477), (Fax in U.S. (800) 672-2054), www.palgrave.com; *The Statesman's Yearbook 2008.*

Taylor and Francis Group, An Informa Business, 2 Park Square, Milton Park, Abingdon, Oxford OX14 4RN, United Kingdom, (Dial from U.S. (212) 216-7800), (Fax from U.S. (212) 564-7854), www.tandf.co.uk; *The Europa World Year Book.*

UNESCO Institute for Statistics, C.P. 6128 Succursale Centre-Ville, Montreal, Quebec, H3C 3J7 Canada, (Dial from U.S. (514) 343-6880), (Fax from U.S. (514) 343 6882), www.uis.unesco.org; *Statistical Tables.*

United Nations Food and Agricultural Organization (FAO), Viale delle Terme di Caracalla, 00100 Rome, Italy, (Dial from U.S. (202) 653-2400), (Fax from U.S. (202) 653 5760), www.fao.org; *FAO Production Yearbook 2002.*

United Nations Statistics Division, New York, NY 10017, (800) 253-9646, Fax: (212) 963-4116, http://unstats.un.org; *Asia-Pacific in Figures 2004; Demographic Yearbook; Statistical Yearbook; Statistical Yearbook for Asia and the Pacific 2004;* and *World Statistics Pocketbook.*

World Health Organization (WHO), Avenue Appia 20, 1211 Geneve 27, Switzerland, (Telephone in U.S. (212) 331-9081), www.who.int; *World Health Report 2006.*

Worldinformation.com, 2 Market Street, Saffron Walden, Essex CB10 1HZ, United Kingdom, www.worldinformation.com; The World of Information (www.worldinformation.com).

COOK ISLANDS - POPULATION DENSITY

Central Intelligence Agency, Office of Public Affairs, Washington, DC 20505, (703) 482-0623, Fax: (703) 482-1739, www.cia.gov; *The World Factbook.*

Palgrave Macmillan Ltd., Houndmills, Basingstoke, Hampshire, RG21 6XS, England, (Telephone in U.S. (888) 330-8477), (Fax in U.S. (800) 672-2054), www.palgrave.com; *The Statesman's Yearbook 2008.*

Taylor and Francis Group, An Informa Business, 2 Park Square, Milton Park, Abingdon, Oxford OX14 4RN, United Kingdom, (Dial from U.S. (212) 216-7800), (Fax from U.S. (212) 564-7854), www.tandf.co.uk; *The Europa World Year Book.*

UNESCO Institute for Statistics, C.P. 6128 Succursale Centre-Ville, Montreal, Quebec, H3C 3J7 Canada, (Dial from U.S. (514) 343-6880), (Fax from U.S. (514) 343 6882), www.uis.unesco.org; *Statistical Tables.*

United Nations Food and Agricultural Organization (FAO), Viale delle Terme di Caracalla, 00100 Rome, Italy, (Dial from U.S. (202) 653-2400), (Fax from U.S. (202) 653 5760), www.fao.org; *The State of Food and Agriculture (SOFA) 2006.*

United Nations Statistics Division, New York, NY 10017, (800) 253-9646, Fax: (212) 963-4116, http://unstats.un.org; *Statistical Yearbook.*

COOK ISLANDS - POWER RESOURCES

Palgrave Macmillan Ltd., Houndmills, Basingstoke, Hampshire, RG21 6XS, England, (Telephone in U.S. (888) 330-8477), (Fax in U.S. (800) 672-2054), www.palgrave.com; *The Statesman's Yearbook 2008.*

Platts, 2 Penn Plaza, 25th Floor, New York, NY 10121-2298, (212) 904-3070, www.platts.com; *Energy Economist.*

United Nations Food and Agricultural Organization (FAO), Viale delle Terme di Caracalla, 00100 Rome, Italy, (Dial from U.S. (202) 653-2400), (Fax from U.S. (202) 653 5760), www.fao.org; *The State of Food and Agriculture (SOFA) 2006.*

United Nations Statistics Division, New York, NY 10017, (800) 253-9646, Fax: (212) 963-4116, http://unstats.un.org; *Asia-Pacific in Figures 2004; Energy Statistics Yearbook 2003; Statistical Yearbook; Statistical Yearbook for Asia and the Pacific 2004;* and *World Statistics Pocketbook.*

COOK ISLANDS - PRICES

Asian Development Bank (ADB), PO Box 789, 0980 Manila, Philippines, www.adb.org; *Key Indicators of Developing Asian and Pacific Countries 2006.*

International Labour Office, I.L.O. Publications, 4 route des Morillons, CH-1211 Geneva 22, Switzerland, (Telephone in U.S. (202) 653-7652), (Fax in U.S. (202) 653-7687), www.ilo.org; *Yearbook of Labour Statistics 2006.*

Secretariat of the Pacific Community (SPC), BP D5, 98848 Noumea Cedex, New Caledonia, www.spc.int/corp; *Selected Pacific Economies - a Statistical Summary (SPESS).*

United Nations Food and Agricultural Organization (FAO), Viale delle Terme di Caracalla, 00100 Rome, Italy, (Dial from U.S. (202) 653-2400), (Fax from U.S. (202) 653 5760), www.fao.org; *FAO Production Yearbook 2002* and *The State of Food and Agriculture (SOFA) 2006.*

COOK ISLANDS - PROFESSIONS

United Nations Statistics Division, New York, NY 10017, (800) 253-9646, Fax: (212) 963-4116, http://unstats.un.org; *Statistical Yearbook.*

COOK ISLANDS - PUBLIC HEALTH

Palgrave Macmillan Ltd., Houndmills, Basingstoke, Hampshire, RG21 6XS, England, (Telephone in U.S. (888) 330-8477), (Fax in U.S. (800) 672-2054), www.palgrave.com; *The Statesman's Yearbook 2008.*

Secretariat of the Pacific Community (SPC), BP D5, 98848 Noumea Cedex, New Caledonia, www.spc.int/corp; *Selected Pacific Economies - a Statistical Summary (SPESS).*

United Nations Statistics Division, New York, NY 10017, (800) 253-9646, Fax: (212) 963-4116, http://unstats.un.org; *Asia-Pacific in Figures 2004* and *Statistical Yearbook.*

World Health Organization (WHO), Avenue Appia 20, 1211 Geneve 27, Switzerland, (Telephone in U.S. (212) 331-9081), www.who.int; *World Health Report 2006.*

COOK ISLANDS - PUBLIC UTILITIES

United Nations Statistics Division, New York, NY 10017, (800) 253-9646, Fax: (212) 963-4116, http://unstats.un.org; *Electric Power in Asia and the Pacific 2001 and 2002.*

COOK ISLANDS - RADIO BROADCASTING

Palgrave Macmillan Ltd., Houndmills, Basingstoke, Hampshire, RG21 6XS, England, (Telephone in U.S. (888) 330-8477), (Fax in U.S. (800) 672-2054), www.palgrave.com; *The Statesman's Yearbook 2008.*

COOK ISLANDS - RELIGION

Central Intelligence Agency, Office of Public Affairs, Washington, DC 20505, (703) 482-0623, Fax: (703) 482-1739, www.cia.gov; *The World Factbook.*

Palgrave Macmillan Ltd., Houndmills, Basingstoke, Hampshire, RG21 6XS, England, (Telephone in U.S. (888) 330-8477), (Fax in U.S. (800) 672-2054), www.palgrave.com; *The Statesman's Yearbook 2008.*

COOK ISLANDS - RENT CHARGES

International Labour Office, I.L.O. Publications, 4 route des Morillons, CH-1211 Geneva 22, Switzerland, (Telephone in U.S. (202) 653-7652), (Fax in U.S. (202) 653-7687), www.ilo.org; *Yearbook of Labour Statistics 2006.*

COOK ISLANDS - RESERVES (ACCOUNTING)

Asian Development Bank (ADB), PO Box 789, 0980 Manila, Philippines, www.adb.org; *Key Indicators of Developing Asian and Pacific Countries 2006.*

COOK ISLANDS - RICE PRODUCTION

See COOK ISLANDS - CROPS

COOK ISLANDS - ROADS

Central Intelligence Agency, Office of Public Affairs, Washington, DC 20505, (703) 482-0623, Fax: (703) 482-1739, www.cia.gov; *The World Factbook.*

Palgrave Macmillan Ltd., Houndmills, Basingstoke, Hampshire, RG21 6XS, England, (Telephone in U.S. (888) 330-8477), (Fax in U.S. (800) 672-2054), www.palgrave.com; *The Statesman's Yearbook 2008.*

COOK ISLANDS - SHIPPING

Palgrave Macmillan Ltd., Houndmills, Basingstoke, Hampshire, RG21 6XS, England, (Telephone in U.S. (888) 330-8477), (Fax in U.S. (800) 672-2054), www.palgrave.com; *The Statesman's Yearbook 2008.*

Taylor and Francis Group, An Informa Business, 2 Park Square, Milton Park, Abingdon, Oxford OX14 4RN, United Kingdom, (Dial from U.S. (212) 216-7800), (Fax from U.S. (212) 564-7854), www.tandf.co.uk; *The Europa World Year Book.*

United Nations Statistics Division, New York, NY 10017, (800) 253-9646, Fax: (212) 963-4116, http://unstats.un.org; *Statistical Yearbook.*

COOK ISLANDS - SOCIAL ECOLOGY

Asian Development Bank (ADB), PO Box 789, 0980 Manila, Philippines, www.adb.org; *Key Indicators of Developing Asian and Pacific Countries 2006.*

United Nations Statistics Division, New York, NY 10017, (800) 253-9646, Fax: (212) 963-4116, http://unstats.un.org; *World Statistics Pocketbook.*

COOK ISLANDS - SOCIAL SECURITY

United Nations Statistics Division, New York, NY 10017, (800) 253-9646, Fax: (212) 963-4116, http://unstats.un.org; *National Accounts Statistics: Compendium of Income Distribution Statistics.*

COOK ISLANDS - TAXATION

Inter-American Development Bank (IDB), 1300 New York Avenue, NW, Washington, DC 20577, (202) 623-1000, Fax: (202) 623-3096, www.iadb.org; *The Politics of Policies: Economic and Social Progress in Latin America - 2006 Report.*

International Monetary Fund (IMF), 700 Nineteenth Street, NW, Washington, DC 20431, (202) 623-7000, Fax: (202) 623-4661, www.imf.org; *Government Finance Statistics Yearbook (2008 Edition).*

Palgrave Macmillan Ltd., Houndmills, Basingstoke, Hampshire, RG21 6XS, England, (Telephone in U.S. (888) 330-8477), (Fax in U.S. (800) 672-2054), www.palgrave.com; *The Statesman's Yearbook 2008.*

Taylor and Francis Group, An Informa Business, 2 Park Square, Milton Park, Abingdon, Oxford OX14 4RN, United Kingdom, (Dial from U.S. (212) 216-7800), (Fax from U.S. (212) 564-7854), www.tandf.co.uk; *The Europa World Year Book.*

COOK ISLANDS - TELEPHONE

International Telecommunication Union (ITU), Place des Nations, 1211 Geneva 20, Switzerland, www.itu.int; World Telecommunication Indicators Database.

Palgrave Macmillan Ltd., Houndmills, Basingstoke, Hampshire, RG21 6XS, England, (Telephone in U.S. (888) 330-8477), (Fax in U.S. (800) 672-2054), www.palgrave.com; *The Statesman's Yearbook 2008.*

Taylor and Francis Group, An Informa Business, 2 Park Square, Milton Park, Abingdon, Oxford OX14 4RN, United Kingdom, (Dial from U.S. (212) 216-7800), (Fax from U.S. (212) 564-7854), www.tandf.co.uk; *The Europa World Year Book.*

United Nations Statistics Division, New York, NY 10017, (800) 253-9646, Fax: (212) 963-4116, http://unstats.un.org; *World Statistics Pocketbook.*

COOK ISLANDS - TEXTILE INDUSTRY

Palgrave Macmillan Ltd., Houndmills, Basingstoke, Hampshire, RG21 6XS, England, (Telephone in U.S. (888) 330-8477), (Fax in U.S. (800) 672-2054), www.palgrave.com; *The Statesman's Yearbook 2008.*

Secretariat of the Pacific Community (SPC), BP D5, 98848 Noumea Cedex, New Caledonia, www.spc.int/corp; *Selected Pacific Economies - a Statistical Summary (SPESS).*

United Nations Conference on Trade and Development (UNCTAD), DC2-1120, United Nations, New York, NY 10017, (212) 963-0027, www.unctad.org; *UNCTAD Commodity Yearbook.*

COOK ISLANDS - TOBACCO INDUSTRY

Foreign Agricultural Service (FAS), U.S. Department of Agriculture (USDA), 1400 Independence Avenue, SW, Washington, DC 20250, (202) 720-3935, www.fas.usda.gov; *Tobacco: World Markets and Trade.*

Secretariat of the Pacific Community (SPC), BP D5, 98848 Noumea Cedex, New Caledonia, www.spc.int/corp; *Selected Pacific Economies - a Statistical Summary (SPESS).*

COOK ISLANDS - TOURISM

Taylor and Francis Group, An Informa Business, 2 Park Square, Milton Park, Abingdon, Oxford OX14 4RN, United Kingdom, (Dial from U.S. (212) 216-7800), (Fax from U.S. (212) 564-7854), www.tandf.co.uk; *The Europa World Year Book.*

United Nations Statistics Division, New York, NY 10017, (800) 253-9646, Fax: (212) 963-4116, http://unstats.un.org; *Statistical Yearbook.*

United Nations World Tourism Organization (UNWTO), Capitan Haya 42, 28020 Madrid, Spain, www.world-tourism.org; *Yearbook of Tourism Statistics.*

COOK ISLANDS - TRADE

See COOK ISLANDS - INTERNATIONAL TRADE

COOK ISLANDS - TRANSPORTATION

Central Intelligence Agency, Office of Public Affairs, Washington, DC 20505, (703) 482-0623, Fax: (703) 482-1739, www.cia.gov; *The World Factbook.*

Palgrave Macmillan Ltd., Houndmills, Basingstoke, Hampshire, RG21 6XS, England, (Telephone in U.S. (888) 330-8477), (Fax in U.S. (800) 672-2054), www.palgrave.com; *The Statesman's Yearbook 2008.*

Secretariat of the Pacific Community (SPC), BP D5, 98848 Noumea Cedex, New Caledonia, www.spc.int/corp; *Selected Pacific Economies - a Statistical Summary (SPESS).*

Taylor and Francis Group, An Informa Business, 2 Park Square, Milton Park, Abingdon, Oxford OX14 4RN, United Kingdom, (Dial from U.S. (212) 216-7800), (Fax from U.S. (212) 564-7854), www.tandf.co.uk; *The Europa World Year Book.*

United Nations Statistics Division, New York, NY 10017, (800) 253-9646, Fax: (212) 963-4116, http://unstats.un.org; *Statistical Yearbook for Asia and the Pacific 2004.*

COOK ISLANDS - UNEMPLOYMENT

Central Intelligence Agency, Office of Public Affairs, Washington, DC 20505, (703) 482-0623, Fax: (703) 482-1739, www.cia.gov; *The World Factbook.*

International Labour Office, I.L.O. Publications, 4 route des Morillons, CH-1211 Geneva 22, Switzerland, (Telephone in U.S. (202) 653-7652), (Fax in U.S. (202) 653-7687), www.ilo.org; *Yearbook of Labour Statistics 2006.*

COOK ISLANDS - VITAL STATISTICS

Palgrave Macmillan Ltd., Houndmills, Basingstoke, Hampshire, RG21 6XS, England, (Telephone in U.S. (888) 330-8477), (Fax in U.S. (800) 672-2054), www.palgrave.com; *The Statesman's Yearbook 2008.*

World Health Organization (WHO), Avenue Appia 20, 1211 Geneve 27, Switzerland, (Telephone in U.S. (212) 331-9081), www.who.int; *World Health Report 2006.*

COOK ISLANDS - WAGES

International Labour Office, I.L.O. Publications, 4 route des Morillons, CH-1211 Geneva 22, Switzerland, (Telephone in U.S. (202) 653-7652), (Fax in U.S. (202) 653-7687), www.ilo.org; *Yearbook of Labour Statistics 2006.*

United Nations Statistics Division, New York, NY 10017, (800) 253-9646, Fax: (212) 963-4116, http://unstats.un.org; *Statistical Yearbook for Asia and the Pacific 2004.*

COOK ISLANDS - WHOLESALE PRICE INDEXES

Asian Development Bank (ADB), PO Box 789, 0980 Manila, Philippines, www.adb.org; *Key Indicators of Developing Asian and Pacific Countries 2006.*

COOKIES

U.S. Bureau of Labor Statistics (BLS), Postal Square Building, 2 Massachusetts Avenue, NE, Washington, DC 20212-0001, (202) 691-5200, Fax: (202) 691-6325, www.bls.gov; *Consumer Price Index Detailed Report* and *Monthly Labor Review (MLR).*

COOKING OILS CONSUMPTION

Economic Research Service (ERS), U.S. Department of Agriculture (USDA), 1800 M Street, NW, Washington, DC 20036-5831, (202) 694-5050, Fax: (202) 694-5689, www.ers.usda.gov; *Agricultural Outlook* and *Food CPI, Prices, and Expenditures.*

COPPER - CONSUMPTION

U.S. Department of the Interior (DOI), U.S. Geological Survey (USGS), Office of Minerals Information, 12201 Sunrise Valley Drive, Reston, VA 20192, Mr. Kenneth A. Beckman, (703) 648-4916, Fax: (703) 648-4995, http://minerals.usgs.gov/minerals; *Mineral Commodity Summaries.*

COPPER - INTERNATIONAL TRADE

U.S. Department of the Interior (DOI), U.S. Geological Survey (USGS), Office of Minerals Information, 12201 Sunrise Valley Drive, Reston, VA 20192, Mr. Kenneth A. Beckman, (703) 648-4916, Fax: (703) 648-4995, http://minerals.usgs.gov/minerals; *Mineral Commodity Summaries.*

COPPER - PRICES

U.S. Department of the Interior (DOI), U.S. Geological Survey (USGS), Office of Minerals Information, 12201 Sunrise Valley Drive, Reston, VA 20192, Mr. Kenneth A. Beckman, (703) 648-4916, Fax: (703) 648-4995, http://minerals.usgs.gov/minerals; *Mineral Commodity Summaries.*

COPPER - PRODUCTION - WORLD

U.S. Department of the Interior (DOI), U.S. Geological Survey (USGS), Office of Minerals Information, 12201 Sunrise Valley Drive, Reston, VA 20192, Mr. Kenneth A. Beckman, (703) 648-4916, Fax: (703) 648-4995, http://minerals.usgs.gov/minerals; *Mineral Commodity Summaries.*

COPPER - PRODUCTION AND VALUE

U.S. Department of the Interior (DOI), U.S. Geological Survey (USGS), Office of Minerals Information, 12201 Sunrise Valley Drive, Reston, VA 20192, Mr. Kenneth A. Beckman, (703) 648-4916, Fax: (703) 648-4995, http://minerals.usgs.gov/minerals; *Metal Industry Indicators (MII)* and *Mineral Commodity Summaries.*

COPYRIGHTS

LISU, Holywell Park, Loughborough University, Leicestershire, LE11 3TU, United Kingdom, www.lboro.ac.uk/departments/dis/lisu; *Clearing the Way: Copyright Clearance in UK Libraries* and *The Cost of Copyright Compliance in Further and Higher Education Institutions.*

U.S. Department of Justice (DOJ), Bureau of Justice Statistics, 810 Seventh Street, NW, Washington, DC 20531, (202) 307-0765, www.ojp.usdoj.gov/bjs/; *Intellectual Property Theft, 2002.*

COPYRIGHTS - REGISTRATION

U.S. Copyright Office, 101 Independence Ave. SE, Washington, DC 20559-6000, (202) 707-3000, www.copyright.gov; *Annual Report of the Register of Copyrights 2006.*

CORN - ACREAGE

National Agricultural Statistics Service (NASS), U.S. Department of Agriculture (USDA), 1400 Independence Avenue, SW, Washington, DC 20250, (800) 727-9540, Fax: (202) 690-2090, www.nass.usda.gov; *Crop Production* and *Crop Values 2007 Summary.*

World Resources Institute (WRI), 10 G Street, NE, Suite 800 Washington, DC 20002, (202) 729-7600, www.wri.org; *Thirst for Corn: What 2007 Plantings Could Mean for the Environment.*

CORN - ACREAGE - GENETICALLY MODIFIED SEED PLANTINGS

National Agricultural Statistics Service (NASS), U.S. Department of Agriculture (USDA), 1400 Independence Avenue, SW, Washington, DC 20250, (800) 727-9540, Fax: (202) 690-2090, www.nass.usda.gov; *Acreage.*

CORN - ACREAGE - ORGANIC

Economic Research Service (ERS), U.S. Department of Agriculture (USDA), 1800 M Street, NW, Washington, DC 20036-5831, (202) 694-5050, Fax: (202) 694-5689, www.ers.usda.gov; *Organic Production.*

CORN - CONSUMPTION

Economic Research Service (ERS), U.S. Department of Agriculture (USDA), 1800 M Street, NW, Washington, DC 20036-5831, (202) 694-5050, Fax: (202) 694-5689, www.ers.usda.gov; *Agricultural Outlook* and *Food CPI, Prices, and Expenditures.*

CORN - INTERNATIONAL TRADE

Economic Research Service (ERS), U.S. Department of Agriculture (USDA), 1800 M Street, NW, Washington, DC 20036-5831, (202) 694-5050, Fax: (202) 694-5689, www.ers.usda.gov; *Agricultural Statistics* and *Foreign Agricultural Trade of the United States (FATUS).*

Foreign Agricultural Service (FAS), U.S. Department of Agriculture (USDA), 1400 Independence Avenue, SW, Washington, DC 20250, (202) 720-3935, www.fas.usda.gov; Foreign Agricultural Service's U.S. Trade Internet System and Production, Supply and Distribution Online (PSD) Online.

U.S. Census Bureau, Foreign Trade Division, 4700 Silver Hill Road, Washington DC 20233-0001, (301) 763-3030, www.census.gov/foreign-trade/www/; *U.S. International Trade in Goods and Services.*

CORN - PESTICIDES

Foreign Agricultural Service (FAS), U.S. Department of Agriculture (USDA), 1400 Independence Avenue, SW, Washington, DC 20250, (202) 720-3935, www.fas.usda.gov; Production, Supply and Distribution Online (PSD) Online.

CORN - PRICES

National Agricultural Statistics Service (NASS), U.S. Department of Agriculture (USDA), 1400 Independence Avenue, SW, Washington, DC 20250, (800) 727-9540, Fax: (202) 690-2090, www.nass.usda.gov; *Crop Production* and *Crop Values 2007 Summary.*

CORN - PRODUCTION

Economic Research Service (ERS), U.S. Department of Agriculture (USDA), 1800 M Street, NW, Washington, DC 20036-5831, (202) 694-5050, Fax: (202) 694-5689, www.ers.usda.gov; *Agricultural Outlook; Agricultural Statistics; Feed Yearbook: Report;* and *World Agricultural Supply and Demand Estimates (WASDE): 2008.*

Foreign Agricultural Service (FAS), U.S. Department of Agriculture (USDA), 1400 Independence Avenue, SW, Washington, DC 20250, (202) 720-3935, www.fas.usda.gov; Foreign Agricultural Service's U.S. Trade Internet System.

National Agricultural Statistics Service (NASS), U.S. Department of Agriculture (USDA), 1400 Independence Avenue, SW, Washington, DC 20250, (800) 727-9540, Fax: (202) 690-2090, www.nass.usda.gov; *Crop Production; Crop Values 2007 Summary; Grain Stocks;* and *Vegetables: 2004 Annual Summary.*

World Resources Institute (WRI), 10 G Street, NE, Suite 800 Washington, DC 20002, (202) 729-7600, www.wri.org; *Thirst for Corn: What 2007 Plantings Could Mean for the Environment.*

CORN - PRODUCTION - WORLD

Economic Research Service (ERS), U.S. Department of Agriculture (USDA), 1800 M Street, NW, Washington, DC 20036-5831, (202) 694-5050, Fax: (202) 694-5689, www.ers.usda.gov; *Agricultural Outlook.*

Foreign Agricultural Service (FAS), U.S. Department of Agriculture (USDA), 1400 Independence Avenue, SW, Washington, DC 20250, (202) 720-3935, www.fas.usda.gov; Foreign Agricultural Service's U.S. Trade Internet System and Production, Supply and Distribution Online (PSD) Online.

CORN - SUPPLY AND DISAPPEARANCE

Economic Research Service (ERS), U.S. Department of Agriculture (USDA), 1800 M Street, NW, Washington, DC 20036-5831, (202) 694-5050, Fax: (202) 694-5689, www.ers.usda.gov; *Agricultural Outlook; Agricultural Statistics; Feed Yearbook: Report;* and *World Agricultural Supply and Demand Estimates (WASDE): 2008.*

World Resources Institute (WRI), 10 G Street, NE, Suite 800 Washington, DC 20002, (202) 729-7600, www.wri.org; *Thirst for Corn: What 2007 Plantings Could Mean for the Environment.*

CORONARY PROCEDURES

National Center for Health Statistics (NCHS), Centers for Disease Control and Prevention (CDC), U.S. Department of Health and Human Services (HHS), 3311 Toledo Road, Hyattsville, MD 20782, (866) 232-4636, www.cdc.gov/nchs; unpublished data.

CORPORATE BUSINESS SECTOR

Board of Governors of the Federal Reserve System, Constitution Avenue, NW, Washington, DC 20551, (202) 452-3000, www.federalreserve.gov; *Flow of Funds Accounts of the United States.*

Organisation for Economic Cooperation and Development (OECD), 2 rue Andre Pascal, F-75775 Paris Cedex 16, France, (Telephone in U.S. (202) 785-6323), (Fax in U.S. (202) 785-0350), www.oecd.org; *OECD Science, Technology and Industry Outlook 2006.*

CORPORATE BUSINESS SECTOR - POLITICAL ACTION COMMITTEES (PACS)

Federal Election Commission (FEC), 999 E Street, NW, Washington, DC 20463, (800) 424-9530, www.fec.gov; *Annual Report 2006; Combined Federal/State Disclosure and Election Directory 2008;* and press releases.

CORPORATIONS - CAPITAL

Economic and Policy Analysis Research Center (EPARC), University of Missouri-Columbia, 10 Professional Building, Columbia, MO 65211, (573) 882-4805, Fax: (573) 882-5563, http://econ.missouri.edu/eparc; *Certified Capital Companies and State Economic Development.*

U.S. Department of the Treasury (DOT), Internal Revenue Service (IRS), Statistics of Income Division (SIS), PO Box 2608, Washington, DC, 20013-2608, (202) 874-0410, Fax: (202) 874-0964, www.irs.ustreas.gov; *Statistics of Income Bulletin, Corporation Income Tax Returns.*

CORPORATIONS - DIVIDEND PAYMENTS

Bureau of Economic Analysis (BEA), U.S. Department of Commerce (DOC), 1441 L Street NW, Washington, DC 20230, (202) 606-9900, www.bea.gov; *2007 Annual Revision of the National Income and Product Accounts (NIPA)* and *Survey of Current Business (SCB).*

CORPORATIONS - FINANCES

Board of Governors of the Federal Reserve System, Constitution Avenue, NW, Washington, DC 20551, (202) 452-3000, www.federalreserve.gov; *Flow of Funds Accounts of the United States.*

Department of Employment and Economic Development, Minnesota Trade Office, 1st National Bank Building, Suite E200, 332 Minnesota Street, St. Paul, MN 55101-1351, (651) 297-4222, Fax: (651) 296-3555, http://www.exportminnesota.com/mtomap.htm; *Industry Reports and Fact Sheets.*

Economic and Policy Analysis Research Center (EPARC), University of Missouri-Columbia, 10

Professional Building, Columbia, MO 65211, (573) 882-4805, Fax: (573) 882-5563, http://econ.missouri.edu/eparc; *Effect of Wal-Mart Stores on Economic Environment of Rural Communities.*

European Central Bank (ECB), Postfach 160319, D-60066 Frankfurt am Main, Germany, www.ecb.int; *Monetary Financial Institutions (MFI) Interest Rate Statistics (MIR).*

Securities and Exchange Commission (SEC), 100 F Street, NE, Washington, DC 20549, (202) 942-8088, www.sec.gov; Electronic Data Gathering, Analysis, and Retrieval (EDGAR) System.

Standard and Poor's Corporation, 55 Water Street, New York, NY 10041, (212) 438-1000, www.standardandpoors.com; *KENNYBASE: Comprehensive On-line Fixed Income Database* and *Market Insight.*

U.S. Bureau of Labor Statistics (BLS), Postal Square Building, 2 Massachusetts Avenue, NE, Washington, DC 20212-0001, (202) 691-5200, Fax: (202) 691-6325, www.bls.gov; *Employee Benefits in Medium and Large Private Establishments* and *Employer Costs for Employee Compensation.*

U.S. Census Bureau, Center for Economic Studies, 4600 Silver Hill Road, Washington DC 20233, (301) 457-1235, www.ces.census.gov; *2002 Economic Census, Management of Company and Enterprises.*

U.S. Census Bureau, Company Statistics Division, 4700 Silver Hill Road, Washington DC 20233-0001, (301) 763-3030, www.census.gov/csd/; *Quarterly Financial Report (QFR), U.S. Manufacturing, Mining, and Trade Corporations.*

U.S. Department of the Treasury (DOT), Internal Revenue Service (IRS), Statistics of Income Division (SIS), PO Box 2608, Washington, DC, 20013-2608, (202) 874-0410, Fax: (202) 874-0964, www.irs.ustreas.gov; *Statistics of Income Bulletin; Statistics of Income Bulletin, Corporation Income Tax Returns;* unpublished data; and various fact sheets.

CORPORATIONS - MANUFACTURING

U.S. Census Bureau, Manufacturing and Construction Division, 4600 Silver Hill Road, Washington DC 20233, (301) 763-4673, www.census.gov/mcd; *Quarterly Financial Report for Manufacturing, Mining and Trade Corporations.*

CORPORATIONS - NONFINANCIAL

Board of Governors of the Federal Reserve System, Constitution Avenue, NW, Washington, DC 20551, (202) 452-3000, www.federalreserve.gov; *Flow of Funds Accounts of the United States.*

CORPORATIONS - PHILANTHROPY

The Giving Institute, 4700 W. Lake Ave, Glenview, IL 60025, (800) 462-2372, Fax: (866) 607-0913, www.aafrc.org; *Giving USA 2006.*

CORPORATIONS - PROFITS

Bureau of Economic Analysis (BEA), U.S. Department of Commerce (DOC), 1441 L Street NW, Washington, DC 20230, (202) 606-9900, www.bea.gov; *2007 Annual Revision of the National Income and Product Accounts (NIPA)* and *Survey of Current Business (SCB).*

Executive Office of the President, Council of Economic Advisors, The White House, 1600 Pennsylvania Avenue NW, Washington, DC 20500, (202) 456-1414, www.whitehouse.gov/cea; *2007 Economic Report of the President.*

Forbes, Inc., 60 Fifth Avenue, New York, NY 10011, (212) 366-8900, www.forbes.com; *America's Largest Private Companies.*

Standard and Poor's Corporation, 55 Water Street, New York, NY 10041, (212) 438-1000, www.standardandpoors.com; *Market Insight.*

U.S. Census Bureau, Manufacturing and Construction Division, 4600 Silver Hill Road, Washington DC 20233, (301) 763-4673, www.census.gov/mcd; *Quarterly Financial Report for Manufacturing, Mining and Trade Corporations.*

U.S. Department of the Treasury (DOT), Internal Revenue Service (IRS), Statistics of Income Division (SIS), PO Box 2608, Washington, DC, 20013-2608, (202) 874-0410, Fax: (202) 874-0964, www.irs.ustreas.gov; *Statistics of Income Bulletin* and *Statistics of Income Bulletin, Corporation Income Tax Returns.*

CORPORATIONS - PUBLIC CONFIDENCE

Independent Sector, 1200 Eighteenth Street, NW, Suite 200, Washington, DC 20036, (202) 467-6100, Fax: (202) 467-6101, www.independentsector.org; *Giving and Volunteering in the United States 2001.*

CORPORATIONS - RECEIPTS

U.S. Department of Commerce (DOC), Economics and Statistics Administration (ESA), 1401 Constitution Avenue, NW, Washington, DC 20230, (800) 782-8872, www.esa.doc.gov; *Impact of Increased Natural Gas Prices on U.S. Economy and Industries: Report to Congress.*

U.S. Department of the Treasury (DOT), Internal Revenue Service (IRS), Statistics of Income Division (SIS), PO Box 2608, Washington, DC, 20013-2608, (202) 874-0410, Fax: (202) 874-0964, www.irs.ustreas.gov; *Statistics of Income Bulletin; Statistics of Income Bulletin, Corporation Income Tax Returns;* and various fact sheets.

CORPORATIONS - SALES

Forbes, Inc., 60 Fifth Avenue, New York, NY 10011, (212) 366-8900, www.forbes.com; *America's Largest Private Companies.*

U.S. Census Bureau, Manufacturing and Construction Division, 4600 Silver Hill Road, Washington DC 20233, (301) 763-4673, www.census.gov/mcd; *Quarterly Financial Report for Manufacturing, Mining and Trade Corporations.*

CORPORATIONS - STOCKS AND BONDS

Board of Governors of the Federal Reserve System, Constitution Avenue, NW, Washington, DC 20551, (202) 452-3000, www.federalreserve.gov; *Federal Reserve Bulletin.*

Standard and Poor's Corporation, 55 Water Street, New York, NY 10041, (212) 438-1000, www.standardandpoors.com; *Market Insight.*

United Nations Conference on Trade and Development (UNCTAD), DC2-1120, United Nations, New York, NY 10017, (212) 963-0027, www.unctad.org; Foreign Direct Investment (FDI).

CORPORATIONS - TAXES - CORPORATE INCOME TAX

Bureau of Economic Analysis (BEA), U.S. Department of Commerce (DOC), 1441 L Street NW, Washington, DC 20230, (202) 606-9900, www.bea.gov; *2007 Annual Revision of the National Income and Product Accounts (NIPA)* and *Survey of Current Business (SCB).*

Economic and Policy Analysis Research Center (EPARC), University of Missouri-Columbia, 10 Professional Building, Columbia, MO 65211, (573) 882-4805, Fax: (573) 882-5563, http://econ.missouri.edu/eparc; *Missouri Historical Tax Summary 1965-2007* and *Tax Expenditure Report 2007.*

CORPORATIONS - TAXES - RETURNS

U.S. Department of the Treasury (DOT), Internal Revenue Service (IRS), Statistics of Income Division (SIS), PO Box 2608, Washington, DC, 20013-2608, (202) 874-0410, Fax: (202) 874-0964, www.irs.ustreas.gov; *Statistics of Income Bulletin; Statistics of Income Bulletin, Corporation Income Tax Returns;* unpublished data; and various fact sheets.

CORRECTIONAL INSTITUTIONS

See also PRISONS AND PRISONERS

Australian Institute of Criminology, 74 Leichhardt Street, Griffith ACT 2603 Australia, www.aic.gov.au/; *Deaths in Custody in Australia: National Deaths in Custody Program Annual Report 2004.*

Justice Research and Statistics Association (JRSA), 777 N. Capitol Street, NE, Suite 801, Washington, DC 20002, (202) 842-9330, Fax: (202) 842-9329, www.jrsa.org; *The Forum; JRP Digest; Justice Research and Policy;* and *SAC Publication Digest.*

Lesotho Bureau of Statistics, Ministry of Finance and Development Planning, PO Box 455, Maseru 100, Lesotho, www.bos.gov.ls; *Crime Statistics 2005* and *Prison Statistics.*

National Center for Juvenile Justice (NCJJ), 3700 South Water Street, Suite 200, Pittsburgh, PA 15203, (412) 227-6950, Fax: (412) 227-6955, http://ncjj.servehttp.com/NCJJWebsite/main.htm; *Juveniles in Corrections (2004).*

National Correctional Industries Association (NCIA), 1202 North Charles Street, Baltimore, MD 21201, (410) 230-3972, Fax: (410) 230-3981, www.nationalcia.org; unpublished data.

U.S. Department of Justice (DOJ), Bureau of Justice Statistics, 810 Seventh Street, NW, Washington, DC 20531, (202) 307-0765, www.ojp.usdoj.gov/bjs/; *Census of Jails; Census of State and Federal Correctional Facilities; Challenging the Conditions of Prisons and Jails: A Report on Section 1983 Litigation; Data Collections for the Prison Rape Elimination Act of 2003; Jails in Indian Country, 2003; National Corrections Reporting Program; Sexual Violence Reported by Correctional Authorities, 2005; The Sourcebook of Criminal Justice Statistics, 2003;* and *Veterans in Prison or Jail.*

U.S. Department of Justice (DOJ), National Institute of Justice (NIJ), 810 Seventh Street, NW, Washington, DC 20531, (202) 307-2942, Fax: (202) 616-0275, www.ojp.usdoj.gov/nij/; *Correctional Boot Camps: Lessons From a Decade of Research.*

CORRECTIONAL INSTITUTIONS - EMPLOYMENT

U.S. Bureau of Labor Statistics (BLS), Postal Square Building, 2 Massachusetts Avenue, NE, Washington, DC 20212-0001, (202) 691-5200, Fax: (202) 691-6325, www.bls.gov; *Employment and Earnings (EE); Monthly Labor Review (MLR);* and unpublished data.

CORRECTIONAL INSTITUTIONS - EXPENDITURES

U.S. Census Bureau, Governments Division, 4600 Silver Hill Road, Washington DC 20233, (800) 242-2184, www.census.gov/govs/www; *2002 Census of Governments, Government Finances.*

U.S. Department of Justice (DOJ), Bureau of Justice Statistics, 810 Seventh Street, NW, Washington, DC 20531, (202) 307-0765, www.ojp.usdoj.gov/bjs/; *State Prison Expenditures.*

CORRECTIONAL INSTITUTIONS - FACILITIES

U.S. Department of Justice (DOJ), Bureau of Justice Statistics, 810 Seventh Street, NW, Washington, DC 20531, (202) 307-0765, www.ojp.usdoj.gov/bjs/; *Census of State and Federal Correctional Facilities.*

CORRECTIONAL INSTITUTIONS - PRISONERS

Australian Institute of Criminology, 74 Leichhardt Street, Griffith ACT 2603 Australia, www.aic.gov.au/; *Deaths in Custody in Australia: National Deaths in Custody Program Annual Report 2004.*

National Center for Juvenile Justice (NCJJ), 3700 South Water Street, Suite 200, Pittsburgh, PA 15203, (412) 227-6950, Fax: (412) 227-6955, http://ncjj.servehttp.com/NCJJWebsite/main.htm; *Juveniles in Corrections (2004).*

Public/Private Ventures (P/PV), 2000 Market Street, Suite 600, Philadelphia, PA 19103, (215) 557-4400, Fax: (215) 557 4469, www.ppv.org; *When the Gates Open: Ready4Work - A National Response to the Prisoner Reentry Crisis.*

U.S. Department of Justice (DOJ), Bureau of Justice Statistics, 810 Seventh Street, NW, Washington, DC

20531, (202) 307-0765, www.ojp.usdoj.gov/bjs/; *Census of Jails; Correctional Populations in the United States; Education and Correctional Populations; Hepatitis Testing and Treatment in State Prisons; HIV in Prisons, 2004; Medical Problems of Jail Inmates; Mental Health Problems of Prison and Jail Inmates; Mental Health Treatment in State Prisons, 2000; National Corrections Reporting Program; Prevalence of Imprisonment in the U.S. Population, 1974-2001; Prison and Jail Inmates at Midyear 2005; Prisoner Petitions Filed in U.S. District Courts, 2000, with Trends, 1980-2000; Prisoners in 2004; Probation and Parole in the United States, 2004; Profile of Jail Inmates, 2002; Profile of Nonviolent Offenders Exiting State Prisons; Substance Dependence, Abuse, and Treatment of Jail Inmates, 2002;* and *Veterans in Prison or Jail.*

U.S. Department of Justice (DOJ), National Institute of Justice (NIJ), 810 Seventh Street, NW, Washington, DC 20531, (202) 307-2942, Fax: (202) 616-0275, www.ojp.usdoj.gov/nij/; *Correctional Boot Camps: Lessons From a Decade of Research* and *Does Parental Incarceration Increase a Child's Risk for Foster Care Placement?*

U.S. Library of Congress (LOC), Congressional Research Service (CRS), The Library of Congress, 101 Independence Avenue, SE, Washington, DC 20540-7500, (202) 707-5700, www.loc.gov/crsinfo; *Offender Reentry: Correctional Statistics, Reintegration into the Community, and Recidivism.*

The Urban Institute, 2100 M Street, N.W., Washington, DC 20037, (202) 833-7200, www.urban.org; *Beyond the Prison Gates: The State of Parole in America; Does Parole Work?: Analyzing the Impact of Postprison Supervision on Rearrest Outcomes; The Influences of Truth-in-Sentencing Reforms on Changes in States' Sentencing Practices and Prison Populations; Instituting Lasting Reforms for Prisoner Reentry in Philadelphia; National Portrait of SVORI: Serious and Violent Offender Reentry Initiative; Number of Prisoners Released in Ohio Triples in 2 Decades: 62 Percent Head for 7 Counties, Led by Cuyahoga; A Portrait of Prisoner Reentry in Illinois; A Portrait of Prisoner Reentry in Maryland; Prisoner Reentry in Idaho;* and *Study Finds Parole Has Little Effect on Rearrest Rates.*

CORRUPTION

Internet Center for Corruption Research (ICCR), Innstrasse 27, D-94032 Passau, Germany, www.icgg.org; *2007 Corruption Perceptions Index (CPI).*

U.S. Department of Justice (DOJ), Criminal Division, 950 Pennsylvania Ave., Washington, DC 20530-0001, (202) 514-2601, www.usdoj.gov/criminal/; *Report to Congress on the Activities and Operations of the Public Integrity Section.*

COSMETICS, PERFUME, ETC. - ADVERTISING EXPENDITURES

The NPD Group, Port Washington, 900 West Shore Road, Port Washington, NY 11050, (866) 444-1411, www.npd.com; *Market Research for the Beauty Industry.*

COSMETICS, PERFUME, ETC. - INTERNATIONAL TRADE

The NPD Group, Port Washington, 900 West Shore Road, Port Washington, NY 11050, (866) 444-1411, www.npd.com; *Market Research for the Beauty Industry.*

U.S. Census Bureau, Foreign Trade Division, 4700 Silver Hill Road, Washington DC 20233-0001, (301) 763-3030, www.census.gov/foreign-trade/www/; *U.S. International Trade in Goods and Services.*

COSMETICS, PERFUME, ETC. - SALES

The NPD Group, Port Washington, 900 West Shore Road, Port Washington, NY 11050, (866) 444-1411, www.npd.com; *Market Research for the Beauty Industry.*

Office of Trade and Industry Information (OTII), Manufacturing and Services, International Trade Administration, U.S. Department of Commerce, 1401 Constitution Ave, NW, Washington, DC 20230, (800) USA TRAD(E), http://trade.gov/index.asp; *TradeStats Express.*

U.S. Census Bureau, Center for Economic Studies, 4600 Silver Hill Road, Washington DC 20233, (301) 457-1235, www.ces.census.gov; *2002 Economic Census, Retail Trade* and *2002 Economic Census, Wholesale Trade.*

COST OF LIVING INDEXES

See CONSUMER PRICE INDEXES

COSTA RICA - NATIONAL STATISTICAL OFFICE

Instituto Nacional de Estadistica y Censos (INEC), de la Rotonda de La Bandera, 450 metros oeste, Calle Los Negritos, Edificio Ana Lorena, Mercedes de Montes de Oca, San Jose, Costa Rica, www.inec.go.cr; National Data Center.

COSTA RICA - PRIMARY STATISTICS SOURCES

Instituto Nacional de Estadistica y Censos (INEC), de la Rotonda de La Bandera, 450 metros oeste, Calle Los Negritos, Edificio Ana Lorena, Mercedes de Montes de Oca, San Jose, Costa Rica, www.inec.go.cr; *Anuario Estadistico 2005.*

COSTA RICA - AGRICULTURAL MACHINERY

Economist Intelligence Unit, 111 West 57th Street, New York, NY 10019, (212) 554-0600, Fax: (212) 586-1181, www.eiu.com; *Business Latin America.*

United Nations Statistics Division, New York, NY 10017, (800) 253-9646, Fax: (212) 963-4116, http://unstats.un.org; *Statistical Yearbook.*

COSTA RICA - AGRICULTURE

Economist Intelligence Unit, 111 West 57th Street, New York, NY 10019, (212) 554-0600, Fax: (212) 586-1181, www.eiu.com; *Business Latin America* and *Costa Rica Country Report.*

Euromonitor International, Inc., 224 S. Michigan Avenue, Suite 1500, Chicago, IL 60604, (312) 922-1115, Fax: (312) 922-1157, www.euromonitor.com; *International Marketing Data and Statistics 2008* and *World Marketing Data and Statistics.*

Inter-American Development Bank (IDB), 1300 New York Avenue, NW, Washington, DC 20577, (202) 623-1000, Fax: (202) 623-3096, www.iadb.org; *The Politics of Policies: Economic and Social Progress in Latin America - 2006 Report.*

M.E. Sharpe, 80 Business Park Drive, Armonk, NY 10504, (800) 541-6563, Fax: (914) 273-2106, www.mesharpe.com; *The Illustrated Book of World Rankings.*

Palgrave Macmillan Ltd., Houndmills, Basingstoke, Hampshire, RG21 6XS, England, (Telephone in U.S. (888) 330-8477), (Fax in U.S. (800) 672-2054), www.palgrave.com; *The Statesman's Yearbook 2008.*

Taylor and Francis Group, An Informa Business, 2 Park Square, Milton Park, Abingdon, Oxford OX14 4RN, United Kingdom, (Dial from U.S. (212) 216-7800), (Fax from U.S. (212) 564-7854), www.tandf.co.uk; *The Europa World Year Book.*

United Nations Conference on Trade and Development (UNCTAD), DC2-1120, United Nations, New York, NY 10017, (212) 963-0027, www.unctad.org; *UNCTAD Commodity Yearbook.*

United Nations Food and Agricultural Organization (FAO), Viale delle Terme di Caracalla, 00100 Rome, Italy, (Dial from U.S. (202) 653-2400), (Fax from U.S. (202) 653 5760), www.fao.org; AQUASTAT; *FAO Production Yearbook 2002; FAO Trade Yearbook;* and *The State of Food and Agriculture (SOFA) 2006.*

United Nations Statistics Division, New York, NY 10017, (800) 253-9646, Fax: (212) 963-4116, http://unstats.un.org; *Statistical Yearbook* and *Statistical Yearbook for Latin America and the Caribbean 2004.*

The World Bank, 1818 H Street, NW, Washington, DC 20433, (202) 473-1000, Fax: (202) 477-6391, www.worldbank.org; *Costa Rica* and *World Development Indicators (WDI) 2008.*

COSTA RICA - AIRLINES

Economist Intelligence Unit, 111 West 57th Street, New York, NY 10019, (212) 554-0600, Fax: (212) 586-1181, www.eiu.com; *Business Latin America.*

International Civil Aviation Organization (ICAO), External Relations and Public Information Office (EPO), 999 University Street, Montreal, Quebec H3C 5H7, Canada, (Dial from U.S. (514) 954-8219), (Fax from U.S. (514) 954-6077), www.icao.int; *Civil Aviation Statistics of the World.*

M.E. Sharpe, 80 Business Park Drive, Armonk, NY 10504, (800) 541-6563, Fax: (914) 273-2106, www.mesharpe.com; *The Illustrated Book of World Rankings.*

Palgrave Macmillan Ltd., Houndmills, Basingstoke, Hampshire, RG21 6XS, England, (Telephone in U.S. (888) 330-8477), (Fax in U.S. (800) 672-2054), www.palgrave.com; *The Statesman's Yearbook 2008.*

Taylor and Francis Group, An Informa Business, 2 Park Square, Milton Park, Abingdon, Oxford OX14 4RN, United Kingdom, (Dial from U.S. (212) 216-7800), (Fax from U.S. (212) 564-7854), www.tandf.co.uk; *The Europa World Year Book.*

COSTA RICA - AIRPORTS

Central Intelligence Agency, Office of Public Affairs, Washington, DC 20505, (703) 482-0623, Fax: (703) 482-1739, www.cia.gov; *The World Factbook.*

COSTA RICA - ALUMINUM PRODUCTION

See COSTA RICA - MINERAL INDUSTRIES

COSTA RICA - AREA

Economist Intelligence Unit, 111 West 57th Street, New York, NY 10019, (212) 554-0600, Fax: (212) 586-1181, www.eiu.com; *Business Latin America.*

COSTA RICA - ARMED FORCES

Central Intelligence Agency, Office of Public Affairs, Washington, DC 20505, (703) 482-0623, Fax: (703) 482-1739, www.cia.gov; *The World Factbook.*

Economist Intelligence Unit, 111 West 57th Street, New York, NY 10019, (212) 554-0600, Fax: (212) 586-1181, www.eiu.com; *Business Latin America.*

Euromonitor International, Inc., 224 S. Michigan Avenue, Suite 1500, Chicago, IL 60604, (312) 922-1115, Fax: (312) 922-1157, www.euromonitor.com; *World Marketing Data and Statistics.*

International Institute for Strategic Studies (IISS), Arundel House, 13-15 Arundel Street, Temple Place, London WC2R 3DX, England, www.iiss.org; *The Military Balance 2007.*

International Monetary Fund (IMF), 700 Nineteenth Street, NW, Washington, DC 20431, (202) 623-7000, Fax: (202) 623-4661, www.imf.org; *Government Finance Statistics Yearbook (2008 Edition).*

Palgrave Macmillan Ltd., Houndmills, Basingstoke, Hampshire, RG21 6XS, England, (Telephone in U.S. (888) 330-8477), (Fax in U.S. (800) 672-2054), www.palgrave.com; *The Statesman's Yearbook 2008.*

U.S. Department of State (DOS), 2201 C Street NW, Washington, DC 20520, (202) 647-4000, www.state.gov; *World Military Expenditures and Arms Transfers (WMEAT).*

UCLA Latin American Institute, 10343 Bunche Hall, Box 951447, Los Angeles, CA 90095-1447, (310) 825-4571, Fax: (310) 206-6859, www.international.ucla.edu/lac; *Statistical Abstract of Latin America.*

United Nations Statistics Division, New York, NY 10017, (800) 253-9646, Fax: (212) 963-4116, http://unstats.un.org; *Human Development Report 2006.*

COSTA RICA - BALANCE OF PAYMENTS

Economist Intelligence Unit, 111 West 57th Street, New York, NY 10019, (212) 554-0600, Fax: (212) 586-1181, www.eiu.com; *Business Latin America.*

Inter-American Development Bank (IDB), 1300 New York Avenue, NW, Washington, DC 20577, (202) 623-1000, Fax: (202) 623-3096, www.iadb.org; *The Politics of Policies: Economic and Social Progress in Latin America - 2006 Report.*

International Monetary Fund (IMF), 700 Nineteenth Street, NW, Washington, DC 20431, (202) 623-7000, Fax: (202) 623-4661, www.imf.org; *Balance of Payments Statistics Newsletter* and *Balance of Payments Statistics Yearbook 2007.*

Organization of American States (OAS), 17th Street Constitution Avenue NW, Washington, DC 20006, (202) 458-3000, www.oas.org; *The OAS in Transition: 1994-2004.*

Taylor and Francis Group, An Informa Business, 2 Park Square, Milton Park, Abingdon, Oxford OX14 4RN, United Kingdom, (Dial from U.S. (212) 216-7800), (Fax from U.S. (212) 564-7854), www.tandf.co.uk; *The Europa World Year Book.*

UCLA Latin American Institute, 10343 Bunche Hall, Box 951447, Los Angeles, CA 90095-1447, (310) 825-4571, Fax: (310) 206-6859, www.international.ucla.edu/lac; *Statistical Abstract of Latin America.*

United Nations Conference on Trade and Development (UNCTAD), DC2-1120, United Nations, New York, NY 10017, (212) 963-0027, www.unctad.org; *Handbook of Statistics 2005.*

United Nations Statistics Division, New York, NY 10017, (800) 253-9646, Fax: (212) 963-4116, http://unstats.un.org; *Economic Survey of Latin America and the Caribbean 2004-2005* and *Statistical Yearbook for Latin America and the Caribbean 2004.*

The World Bank, 1818 H Street, NW, Washington, DC 20433, (202) 473-1000, Fax: (202) 477-6391, www.worldbank.org; *Costa Rica; World Development Indicators (WDI) 2008;* and *World Development Report 2008.*

COSTA RICA - BANANAS

See COSTA RICA - CROPS

COSTA RICA - BANKS AND BANKING

Euromonitor International, Inc., 224 S. Michigan Avenue, Suite 1500, Chicago, IL 60604, (312) 922-1115, Fax: (312) 922-1157, www.euromonitor.com; *World Marketing Data and Statistics.*

Inter-American Development Bank (IDB), 1300 New York Avenue, NW, Washington, DC 20577, (202) 623-1000, Fax: (202) 623-3096, www.iadb.org; *The Politics of Policies: Economic and Social Progress in Latin America - 2006 Report.*

International Monetary Fund (IMF), 700 Nineteenth Street, NW, Washington, DC 20431, (202) 623-7000, Fax: (202) 623-4661, www.imf.org; *Government Finance Statistics Yearbook (2008 Edition)* and *International Financial Statistics Yearbook 2007.*

M.E. Sharpe, 80 Business Park Drive, Armonk, NY 10504, (800) 541-6563, Fax: (914) 273-2106, www.mesharpe.com; *The Illustrated Book of World Rankings.*

Palgrave Macmillan Ltd., Houndmills, Basingstoke, Hampshire, RG21 6XS, England, (Telephone in U.S. (888) 330-8477), (Fax in U.S. (800) 672-2054), www.palgrave.com; *The Statesman's Yearbook 2008.*

Taylor and Francis Group, An Informa Business, 2 Park Square, Milton Park, Abingdon, Oxford OX14 4RN, United Kingdom, (Dial from U.S. (212) 216-7800), (Fax from U.S. (212) 564-7854), www.tandf.co.uk; *The Europa World Year Book.*

United Nations Statistics Division, New York, NY 10017, (800) 253-9646, Fax: (212) 963-4116, http://unstats.un.org; *Statistical Yearbook* and *Statistical Yearbook for Latin America and the Caribbean 2004.*

COSTA RICA - BARLEY PRODUCTION

See COSTA RICA - CROPS

COSTA RICA - BEVERAGE INDUSTRY

M.E. Sharpe, 80 Business Park Drive, Armonk, NY 10504, (800) 541-6563, Fax: (914) 273-2106, www.mesharpe.com; *The Illustrated Book of World Rankings.*

United Nations Statistics Division, New York, NY 10017, (800) 253-9646, Fax: (212) 963-4116, http://unstats.un.org; *Statistical Yearbook.*

COSTA RICA - BIRTH CONTROL

UCLA Latin American Institute, 10343 Bunche Hall, Box 951447, Los Angeles, CA 90095-1447, (310) 825-4571, Fax: (310) 206-6859, www.international.ucla.edu/lac; *Statistical Abstract of Latin America.*

COSTA RICA - BONDS

Inter-American Development Bank (IDB), 1300 New York Avenue, NW, Washington, DC 20577, (202) 623-1000, Fax: (202) 623-3096, www.iadb.org; *The Politics of Policies: Economic and Social Progress in Latin America - 2006 Report.*

International Monetary Fund (IMF), 700 Nineteenth Street, NW, Washington, DC 20431, (202) 623-7000, Fax: (202) 623-4661, www.imf.org; *Government Finance Statistics Yearbook (2008 Edition).*

COSTA RICA - BROADCASTING

Central Intelligence Agency, Office of Public Affairs, Washington, DC 20505, (703) 482-0623, Fax: (703) 482-1739, www.cia.gov; *The World Factbook.*

Euromonitor International, Inc., 224 S. Michigan Avenue, Suite 1500, Chicago, IL 60604, (312) 922-1115, Fax: (312) 922-1157, www.euromonitor.com; *World Marketing Data and Statistics.*

M.E. Sharpe, 80 Business Park Drive, Armonk, NY 10504, (800) 541-6563, Fax: (914) 273-2106, www.mesharpe.com; *The Illustrated Book of World Rankings.*

Palgrave Macmillan Ltd., Houndmills, Basingstoke, Hampshire, RG21 6XS, England, (Telephone in U.S. (888) 330-8477), (Fax in U.S. (800) 672-2054), www.palgrave.com; *The Statesman's Yearbook 2008.*

WRTH Publications Limited, PO Box 290, Oxford OX2 7FT, UK, www.wrth.com; *World Radio TV Handbook 2007.*

COSTA RICA - BUDGET

Central Intelligence Agency, Office of Public Affairs, Washington, DC 20505, (703) 482-0623, Fax: (703) 482-1739, www.cia.gov; *The World Factbook.*

COSTA RICA - BUSINESS

Inter-American Development Bank (IDB), 1300 New York Avenue, NW, Washington, DC 20577, (202) 623-1000, Fax: (202) 623-3096, www.iadb.org; *The Politics of Policies: Economic and Social Progress in Latin America - 2006 Report.*

COSTA RICA - CAPITAL INVESTMENTS

Inter-American Development Bank (IDB), 1300 New York Avenue, NW, Washington, DC 20577, (202) 623-1000, Fax: (202) 623-3096, www.iadb.org; *The Politics of Policies: Economic and Social Progress in Latin America - 2006 Report.*

COSTA RICA - CAPITAL LEVY

Inter-American Development Bank (IDB), 1300 New York Avenue, NW, Washington, DC 20577, (202) 623-1000, Fax: (202) 623-3096, www.iadb.org; *The Politics of Policies: Economic and Social Progress in Latin America - 2006 Report.*

International Monetary Fund (IMF), 700 Nineteenth Street, NW, Washington, DC 20431, (202) 623-7000, Fax: (202) 623-4661, www.imf.org; *Government Finance Statistics Yearbook (2008 Edition).*

COSTA RICA - CATTLE

See COSTA RICA - LIVESTOCK

COSTA RICA - CHICKENS

See COSTA RICA - LIVESTOCK

COSTA RICA - CHILDBIRTH - STATISTICS

Central Intelligence Agency, Office of Public Affairs, Washington, DC 20505, (703) 482-0623, Fax: (703) 482-1739, www.cia.gov; *The World Factbook.*

Euromonitor International, Inc., 224 S. Michigan Avenue, Suite 1500, Chicago, IL 60604, (312) 922-1115, Fax: (312) 922-1157, www.euromonitor.com; *International Marketing Data and Statistics 2008* and *The World Economic Factbook 2008.*

M.E. Sharpe, 80 Business Park Drive, Armonk, NY 10504, (800) 541-6563, Fax: (914) 273-2106, www.mesharpe.com; *The Illustrated Book of World Rankings.*

Taylor and Francis Group, An Informa Business, 2 Park Square, Milton Park, Abingdon, Oxford OX14 4RN, United Kingdom, (Dial from U.S. (212) 216-7800), (Fax from U.S. (212) 564-7854), www.tandf.co.uk; *The Europa World Year Book.*

United Nations Statistics Division, New York, NY 10017, (800) 253-9646, Fax: (212) 963-4116, http://unstats.un.org; *Demographic Yearbook* and *Statistical Yearbook.*

The World Bank, 1818 H Street, NW, Washington, DC 20433, (202) 473-1000, Fax: (202) 477-6391, www.worldbank.org; *World Development Indicators (WDI) 2008.*

World Health Organization (WHO), Avenue Appia 20, 1211 Geneve 27, Switzerland, (Telephone in U.S. (212) 331-9081), www.who.int; *World Health Report 2006.*

COSTA RICA - CLIMATE

M.E. Sharpe, 80 Business Park Drive, Armonk, NY 10504, (800) 541-6563, Fax: (914) 273-2106, www.mesharpe.com; *The Illustrated Book of World Rankings.*

Palgrave Macmillan Ltd., Houndmills, Basingstoke, Hampshire, RG21 6XS, England, (Telephone in U.S. (888) 330-8477), (Fax in U.S. (800) 672-2054), www.palgrave.com; *The Statesman's Yearbook 2008.*

COSTA RICA - COAL PRODUCTION

See COSTA RICA - MINERAL INDUSTRIES

COSTA RICA - COCOA PRODUCTION

See COSTA RICA - CROPS

COSTA RICA - COFFEE

See COSTA RICA - CROPS

COSTA RICA - COMMERCE

Palgrave Macmillan Ltd., Houndmills, Basingstoke, Hampshire, RG21 6XS, England, (Telephone in U.S. (888) 330-8477), (Fax in U.S. (800) 672-2054), www.palgrave.com; *The Statesman's Yearbook 2008.*

COSTA RICA - COMMODITY EXCHANGES

Commodity Research Bureau, 330 South Wells Street, Suite 612, Chicago, IL 60606-7110, (800) 621-5271, Fax: (312) 939-4135, www.crbtrader.com; *2006 CRB Commodity Yearbook and CD.*

International Monetary Fund (IMF), 700 Nineteenth Street, NW, Washington, DC 20431, (202) 623-7000, Fax: (202) 623-4661, www.imf.org; *IMF Primary Commodity Prices.*

United Nations Food and Agricultural Organization (FAO), Viale delle Terme di Caracalla, 00100 Rome, Italy, (Dial from U.S. (202) 653-2400), (Fax from U.S. (202) 653 5760), www.fao.org; *The State of Food and Agriculture (SOFA) 2006.*

COSTA RICA - COMMUNICATION AND TRAFFIC

United Nations Statistics Division, New York, NY 10017, (800) 253-9646, Fax: (212) 963-4116, http://unstats.un.org; *Statistical Yearbook.*

COSTA RICA - CONSTRUCTION INDUSTRY

Economist Intelligence Unit, 111 West 57th Street, New York, NY 10019, (212) 554-0600, Fax: (212) 586-1181, www.eiu.com; *Business Latin America.*

Inter-American Development Bank (IDB), 1300 New York Avenue, NW, Washington, DC 20577, (202)

623-1000, Fax: (202) 623-3096, www.iadb.org; *The Politics of Policies: Economic and Social Progress in Latin America - 2006 Report.*

M.E. Sharpe, 80 Business Park Drive, Armonk, NY 10504, (800) 541-6563, Fax: (914) 273-2106, www.mesharpe.com; *The Illustrated Book of World Rankings.*

UCLA Latin American Institute, 10343 Bunche Hall, Box 951447, Los Angeles, CA 90095-1447, (310) 825-4571, Fax: (310) 206-6859, www.international.ucla.edu/lac; *Statistical Abstract of Latin America.*

COSTA RICA - CONSUMER COOPERATIVES

UCLA Latin American Institute, 10343 Bunche Hall, Box 951447, Los Angeles, CA 90095-1447, (310) 825-4571, Fax: (310) 206-6859, www.international.ucla.edu/lac; *Statistical Abstract of Latin America.*

COSTA RICA - CONSUMER PRICE INDEXES

Taylor and Francis Group, An Informa Business, 2 Park Square, Milton Park, Abingdon, Oxford OX14 4RN, United Kingdom, (Dial from U.S. (212) 216-7800), (Fax from U.S. (212) 564-7854), www.tandf.co.uk; *The Europa World Year Book.*

United Nations Statistics Division, New York, NY 10017, (800) 253-9646, Fax: (212) 963-4116, http://unstats.un.org; *Statistical Yearbook.*

The World Bank, 1818 H Street, NW, Washington, DC 20433, (202) 473-1000, Fax: (202) 477-6391, www.worldbank.org; *Costa Rica.*

COSTA RICA - CONSUMPTION (ECONOMICS)

Economist Intelligence Unit, 111 West 57th Street, New York, NY 10019, (212) 554-0600, Fax: (212) 586-1181, www.eiu.com; *Business Latin America.*

Inter-American Development Bank (IDB), 1300 New York Avenue, NW, Washington, DC 20577, (202) 623-1000, Fax: (202) 623-3096, www.iadb.org; *The Politics of Policies: Economic and Social Progress in Latin America - 2006 Report.*

United Nations Statistics Division, New York, NY 10017, (800) 253-9646, Fax: (212) 963-4116, http://unstats.un.org; *Statistical Yearbook for Latin America and the Caribbean 2004.*

The World Bank, 1818 H Street, NW, Washington, DC 20433, (202) 473-1000, Fax: (202) 477-6391, www.worldbank.org; *World Development Report 2008.*

COSTA RICA - COPPER INDUSTRY AND TRADE

See COSTA RICA - MINERAL INDUSTRIES

COSTA RICA - CORN INDUSTRY

See COSTA RICA - CROPS

COSTA RICA - COST AND STANDARD OF LIVING

International Monetary Fund (IMF), 700 Nineteenth Street, NW, Washington, DC 20431, (202) 623-7000, Fax: (202) 623-4661, www.imf.org; *Government Finance Statistics Yearbook (2008 Edition).*

COSTA RICA - COTTON

See COSTA RICA - CROPS

COSTA RICA - CRIME

International Criminal Police Organization (INTERPOL), General Secretariat, 200 quai Charles de Gaulle, 69006 Lyon, France, www.interpol.int; *International Crime Statistics.*

U.S. Department of Justice (DOJ), Bureau of Justice Statistics, 810 Seventh Street, NW, Washington, DC 20531, (202) 307-0765, www.ojp.usdoj.gov/bjs/; *The World Factbook of Criminal Justice Systems* and *The World Factbook of Criminal Justice Systems.*

COSTA RICA - CROPS

Economist Intelligence Unit, 111 West 57th Street, New York, NY 10019, (212) 554-0600, Fax: (212) 586-1181, www.eiu.com; *Business Latin America.*

International Monetary Fund (IMF), 700 Nineteenth Street, NW, Washington, DC 20431, (202) 623-7000, Fax: (202) 623-4661, www.imf.org; *International Financial Statistics Yearbook 2007.*

M.E. Sharpe, 80 Business Park Drive, Armonk, NY 10504, (800) 541-6563, Fax: (914) 273-2106, www.mesharpe.com; *The Illustrated Book of World Rankings.*

Organization of American States (OAS), 17th Street Constitution Avenue NW, Washington, DC 20006, (202) 458-3000, www.oas.org; *The OAS in Transition: 1994-2004.*

Palgrave Macmillan Ltd., Houndmills, Basingstoke, Hampshire, RG21 6XS, England, (Telephone in U.S. (888) 330-8477), (Fax in U.S. (800) 672-2054), www.palgrave.com; *The Statesman's Yearbook 2008.*

Taylor and Francis Group, An Informa Business, 2 Park Square, Milton Park, Abingdon, Oxford OX14 4RN, United Kingdom, (Dial from U.S. (212) 216-7800), (Fax from U.S. (212) 564-7854), www.tandf.co.uk; *The Europa World Year Book.*

United Nations Conference on Trade and Development (UNCTAD), DC2-1120, United Nations, New York, NY 10017, (212) 963-0027, www.unctad.org; *UNCTAD Commodity Yearbook.*

United Nations Food and Agricultural Organization (FAO), Viale delle Terme di Caracalla, 00100 Rome, Italy, (Dial from U.S. (202) 653-2400), (Fax from U.S. (202) 653 5760), www.fao.org; *FAO Production Yearbook 2002* and *The State of Food and Agriculture (SOFA) 2006.*

United Nations Statistics Division, New York, NY 10017, (800) 253-9646, Fax: (212) 963-4116, http://unstats.un.org; *Statistical Yearbook.*

COSTA RICA - CUSTOMS ADMINISTRATION

Inter-American Development Bank (IDB), 1300 New York Avenue, NW, Washington, DC 20577, (202) 623-1000, Fax: (202) 623-3096, www.iadb.org; *The Politics of Policies: Economic and Social Progress in Latin America - 2006 Report.*

International Monetary Fund (IMF), 700 Nineteenth Street, NW, Washington, DC 20431, (202) 623-7000, Fax: (202) 623-4661, www.imf.org; *Government Finance Statistics Yearbook (2008 Edition).*

COSTA RICA - DAIRY PROCESSING

M.E. Sharpe, 80 Business Park Drive, Armonk, NY 10504, (800) 541-6563, Fax: (914) 273-2106, www.mesharpe.com; *The Illustrated Book of World Rankings.*

Palgrave Macmillan Ltd., Houndmills, Basingstoke, Hampshire, RG21 6XS, England, (Telephone in U.S. (888) 330-8477), (Fax in U.S. (800) 672-2054), www.palgrave.com; *The Statesman's Yearbook 2008.*

Taylor and Francis Group, An Informa Business, 2 Park Square, Milton Park, Abingdon, Oxford OX14 4RN, United Kingdom, (Dial from U.S. (212) 216-7800), (Fax from U.S. (212) 564-7854), www.tandf.co.uk; *The Europa World Year Book.*

United Nations Food and Agricultural Organization (FAO), Viale delle Terme di Caracalla, 00100 Rome, Italy, (Dial from U.S. (202) 653-2400), (Fax from U.S. (202) 653 5760), www.fao.org; *The State of Food and Agriculture (SOFA) 2006.*

United Nations Statistics Division, New York, NY 10017, (800) 253-9646, Fax: (212) 963-4116, http://unstats.un.org; *Statistical Yearbook.*

COSTA RICA - DEATH RATES

See COSTA RICA - MORTALITY

COSTA RICA - DEBT

Economist Intelligence Unit, 111 West 57th Street, New York, NY 10019, (212) 554-0600, Fax: (212) 586-1181, www.eiu.com; *Business Latin America.*

The World Bank, 1818 H Street, NW, Washington, DC 20433, (202) 473-1000, Fax: (202) 477-6391, www.worldbank.org; *Global Development Finance 2007.*

COSTA RICA - DEBTS, EXTERNAL

Economist Intelligence Unit, 111 West 57th Street, New York, NY 10019, (212) 554-0600, Fax: (212) 586-1181, www.eiu.com; *Business Latin America.*

Inter-American Development Bank (IDB), 1300 New York Avenue, NW, Washington, DC 20577, (202) 623-1000, Fax: (202) 623-3096, www.iadb.org; *The Politics of Policies: Economic and Social Progress in Latin America - 2006 Report.*

International Monetary Fund (IMF), 700 Nineteenth Street, NW, Washington, DC 20431, (202) 623-7000, Fax: (202) 623-4661, www.imf.org; *Government Finance Statistics Yearbook (2008 Edition).*

United Nations Statistics Division, New York, NY 10017, (800) 253-9646, Fax: (212) 963-4116, http://unstats.un.org; *Economic Survey of Latin America and the Caribbean 2004-2005* and *Statistical Yearbook for Latin America and the Caribbean 2004.*

The World Bank, 1818 H Street, NW, Washington, DC 20433, (202) 473-1000, Fax: (202) 477-6391, www.worldbank.org; *Global Development Finance 2007; World Development Indicators (WDI) 2008;* and *World Development Report 2008.*

COSTA RICA - DEBTS, PUBLIC

United Nations Statistics Division, New York, NY 10017, (800) 253-9646, Fax: (212) 963-4116, http://unstats.un.org; *Statistical Yearbook.*

The World Bank, 1818 H Street, NW, Washington, DC 20433, (202) 473-1000, Fax: (202) 477-6391, www.worldbank.org; *Global Development Finance 2007.*

COSTA RICA - DEFENSE EXPENDITURES

See COSTA RICA - ARMED FORCES

COSTA RICA - DEMOGRAPHY

Euromonitor International, Inc., 224 S. Michigan Avenue, Suite 1500, Chicago, IL 60604, (312) 922-1115, Fax: (312) 922-1157, www.euromonitor.com; *International Marketing Data and Statistics 2008; The World Economic Factbook 2008;* and *World Marketing Data and Statistics.*

M.E. Sharpe, 80 Business Park Drive, Armonk, NY 10504, (800) 541-6563, Fax: (914) 273-2106, www.mesharpe.com; *The Illustrated Book of World Rankings.*

United Nations Statistics Division, New York, NY 10017, (800) 253-9646, Fax: (212) 963-4116, http://unstats.un.org; *Human Development Report 2006.*

The World Bank, 1818 H Street, NW, Washington, DC 20433, (202) 473-1000, Fax: (202) 477-6391, www.worldbank.org; *Costa Rica.*

COSTA RICA - DIAMONDS

See COSTA RICA - MINERAL INDUSTRIES

COSTA RICA - DISPOSABLE INCOME

Inter-American Development Bank (IDB), 1300 New York Avenue, NW, Washington, DC 20577, (202) 623-1000, Fax: (202) 623-3096, www.iadb.org; *The Politics of Policies: Economic and Social Progress in Latin America - 2006 Report.*

M.E. Sharpe, 80 Business Park Drive, Armonk, NY 10504, (800) 541-6563, Fax: (914) 273-2106, www.mesharpe.com; *The Illustrated Book of World Rankings.*

United Nations Statistics Division, New York, NY 10017, (800) 253-9646, Fax: (212) 963-4116, http://unstats.un.org; *Statistical Yearbook* and *Statistical Yearbook for Latin America and the Caribbean 2004.*

COSTA RICA - DIVORCE

M.E. Sharpe, 80 Business Park Drive, Armonk, NY 10504, (800) 541-6563, Fax: (914) 273-2106, www.mesharpe.com; *The Illustrated Book of World Rankings.*

United Nations Statistics Division, New York, NY 10017, (800) 253-9646, Fax: (212) 963-4116, http://unstats.un.org; *Demographic Yearbook* and *Statistical Yearbook.*

COSTA RICA - ECONOMIC ASSISTANCE

Inter-American Development Bank (IDB), 1300 New York Avenue, NW, Washington, DC 20577, (202) 623-1000, Fax: (202) 623-3096, www.iadb.org; *The Politics of Policies: Economic and Social Progress in Latin America - 2006 Report.*

United Nations Statistics Division, New York, NY 10017, (800) 253-9646, Fax: (212) 963-4116, http://unstats.un.org; *Statistical Yearbook.*

COSTA RICA - ECONOMIC CONDITIONS

Center for International Business Education Research (CIBER), Columbia Business School and School of International and Public Affairs, Uris Hall, Room 212, 3022 Broadway, New York, NY 10027-6902, Mr. Joshua Safier, (212) 854-4750, Fax: (212) 222-9821, www.columbia.edu/cu/ciber/; Datastream International.

Central Intelligence Agency, Office of Public Affairs, Washington, DC 20505, (703) 482-0623, Fax: (703) 482-1739, www.cia.gov; *The World Factbook.*

DSI Data Service Information, Xantener Strasse 51a, D-47495 Rheinberg, Germany, www.dsidata.com; *Campus Solution.*

Dun and Bradstreet (DB) Corporation, 103 JFK Parkway, Short Hills, NJ 07078, (973) 921-5500, www.dnb.com; *Country Report.*

Economist Intelligence Unit, 111 West 57th Street, New York, NY 10019, (212) 554-0600, Fax: (212) 586-1181, www.eiu.com; *Costa Rica Country Report.*

Euromonitor International, Inc., 224 S. Michigan Avenue, Suite 1500, Chicago, IL 60604, (312) 922-1115, Fax: (312) 922-1157, www.euromonitor.com; *International Marketing Data and Statistics 2008; The World Economic Factbook 2008;* and *World Marketing Data and Statistics.*

Inter-American Development Bank (IDB), 1300 New York Avenue, NW, Washington, DC 20577, (202) 623-1000, Fax: (202) 623-3096, www.iadb.org; *The Politics of Policies: Economic and Social Progress in Latin America - 2006 Report.*

International Monetary Fund (IMF), 700 Nineteenth Street, NW, Washington, DC 20431, (202) 623-7000, Fax: (202) 623-4661, www.imf.org; *World Economic Outlook Reports.*

M.E. Sharpe, 80 Business Park Drive, Armonk, NY 10504, (800) 541-6563, Fax: (914) 273-2106, www.mesharpe.com; *The Illustrated Book of World Rankings.*

Organization of American States (OAS), 17th Street Constitution Avenue NW, Washington, DC 20006, (202) 458-3000, www.oas.org; *The OAS in Transition: 1994-2004.*

Palgrave Macmillan Ltd., Houndmills, Basingstoke, Hampshire, RG21 6XS, England, (Telephone in U.S. (888) 330-8477), (Fax in U.S. (800) 672-2054), www.palgrave.com; *The Statesman's Yearbook 2008.*

Taylor and Francis Group, An Informa Business, 2 Park Square, Milton Park, Abingdon, Oxford OX14 4RN, United Kingdom, (Dial from U.S. (212) 216-7800), (Fax from U.S. (212) 564-7854), www.tandf.co.uk; *The Europa World Year Book.*

UCLA Latin American Institute, 10343 Bunche Hall, Box 951447, Los Angeles, CA 90095-1447, (310) 825-4571, Fax: (310) 206-6859, www.international.ucla.edu/lac; *Statistical Abstract of Latin America.*

United Nations Statistics Division, New York, NY 10017, (800) 253-9646, Fax: (212) 963-4116, http://unstats.un.org; *Economic Survey of Latin America and the Caribbean 2004-2005* and *World Statistics Pocketbook.*

The World Bank, 1818 H Street, NW, Washington, DC 20433, (202) 473-1000, Fax: (202) 477-6391, www.worldbank.org; *Costa Rica; Global Economic Monitor (GEM); Global Economic Prospects 2008; The World Bank Atlas 2003-2004;* and *World Development Report 2008.*

COSTA RICA - ECONOMICS - SOCIOLOGICAL ASPECTS

Inter-American Development Bank (IDB), 1300 New York Avenue, NW, Washington, DC 20577, (202) 623-1000, Fax: (202) 623-3096, www.iadb.org; *The Politics of Policies: Economic and Social Progress in Latin America - 2006 Report.*

UCLA Latin American Institute, 10343 Bunche Hall, Box 951447, Los Angeles, CA 90095-1447, (310) 825-4571, Fax: (310) 206-6859, www.international.ucla.edu/lac; *Statistical Abstract of Latin America.*

COSTA RICA - EDUCATION

Economist Intelligence Unit, 111 West 57th Street, New York, NY 10019, (212) 554-0600, Fax: (212) 586-1181, www.eiu.com; *Business Latin America.*

Euromonitor International, Inc., 224 S. Michigan Avenue, Suite 1500, Chicago, IL 60604, (312) 922-1115, Fax: (312) 922-1157, www.euromonitor.com; *International Marketing Data and Statistics 2008* and *World Marketing Data and Statistics.*

International Monetary Fund (IMF), 700 Nineteenth Street, NW, Washington, DC 20431, (202) 623-7000, Fax: (202) 623-4661, www.imf.org; *Government Finance Statistics Yearbook (2008 Edition).*

M.E. Sharpe, 80 Business Park Drive, Armonk, NY 10504, (800) 541-6563, Fax: (914) 273-2106, www.mesharpe.com; *The Illustrated Book of World Rankings.*

Palgrave Macmillan Ltd., Houndmills, Basingstoke, Hampshire, RG21 6XS, England, (Telephone in U.S. (888) 330-8477), (Fax in U.S. (800) 672-2054), www.palgrave.com; *The Statesman's Yearbook 2008.*

Taylor and Francis Group, An Informa Business, 2 Park Square, Milton Park, Abingdon, Oxford OX14 4RN, United Kingdom, (Dial from U.S. (212) 216-7800), (Fax from U.S. (212) 564-7854), www.tandf.co.uk; *The Europa World Year Book.*

UCLA Latin American Institute, 10343 Bunche Hall, Box 951447, Los Angeles, CA 90095-1447, (310) 825-4571, Fax: (310) 206-6859, www.international.ucla.edu/lac; *Statistical Abstract of Latin America.*

UNESCO Institute for Statistics, C.P. 6128 Succursale Centre-Ville, Montreal, Quebec, H3C 3J7 Canada, (Dial from U.S. (514) 343-6880), (Fax from U.S. (514) 343 6882), www.uis.unesco.org; *Statistical Tables.*

United Nations Statistics Division, New York, NY 10017, (800) 253-9646, Fax: (212) 963-4116, http://unstats.un.org; *Human Development Report 2006* and *Statistical Yearbook for Latin America and the Caribbean 2004.*

The World Bank, 1818 H Street, NW, Washington, DC 20433, (202) 473-1000, Fax: (202) 477-6391, www.worldbank.org; *Costa Rica; World Development Indicators (WDI) 2008;* and *World Development Report 2008.*

COSTA RICA - ELECTRICITY

Economist Intelligence Unit, 111 West 57th Street, New York, NY 10019, (212) 554-0600, Fax: (212) 586-1181, www.eiu.com; *Business Latin America.*

Inter-American Development Bank (IDB), 1300 New York Avenue, NW, Washington, DC 20577, (202) 623-1000, Fax: (202) 623-3096, www.iadb.org; *The Politics of Policies: Economic and Social Progress in Latin America - 2006 Report.*

M.E. Sharpe, 80 Business Park Drive, Armonk, NY 10504, (800) 541-6563, Fax: (914) 273-2106, www.mesharpe.com; *The Illustrated Book of World Rankings.*

Organization of American States (OAS), 17th Street Constitution Avenue NW, Washington, DC 20006, (202) 458-3000, www.oas.org; *The OAS in Transition: 1994-2004.*

Palgrave Macmillan Ltd., Houndmills, Basingstoke, Hampshire, RG21 6XS, England, (Telephone in U.S. (888) 330-8477), (Fax in U.S. (800) 672-2054), www.palgrave.com; *The Statesman's Yearbook 2008.*

U.S. Department of Energy (DOE), Energy Information Administration (EIA), 1000 Independence Avenue, SW, Washington, DC 20585, (202) 586-8800, www.eia.doe.gov; *International Energy Annual 2004* and *International Energy Outlook 2006.*

United Nations Statistics Division, New York, NY 10017, (800) 253-9646, Fax: (212) 963-4116, http://unstats.un.org; *Human Development Report 2006* and *Statistical Yearbook.*

COSTA RICA - EMIGRATION AND IMMIGRATION

UCLA Latin American Institute, 10343 Bunche Hall, Box 951447, Los Angeles, CA 90095-1447, (310) 825-4571, Fax: (310) 206-6859, www.international.ucla.edu/lac; *Statistical Abstract of Latin America.*

COSTA RICA - EMPLOYMENT

Euromonitor International, Inc., 224 S. Michigan Avenue, Suite 1500, Chicago, IL 60604, (312) 922-1115, Fax: (312) 922-1157, www.euromonitor.com; *International Marketing Data and Statistics 2008.*

International Labour Office, I.L.O. Publications, 4 route des Morillons, CH-1211 Geneva 22, Switzerland, (Telephone in U.S. (202) 653-7652), (Fax in U.S. (202) 653-7687), www.ilo.org; *Yearbook of Labour Statistics 2006.*

M.E. Sharpe, 80 Business Park Drive, Armonk, NY 10504, (800) 541-6563, Fax: (914) 273-2106, www.mesharpe.com; *The Illustrated Book of World Rankings.*

Organization of American States (OAS), 17th Street Constitution Avenue NW, Washington, DC 20006, (202) 458-3000, www.oas.org; *The OAS in Transition: 1994-2004.*

UCLA Latin American Institute, 10343 Bunche Hall, Box 951447, Los Angeles, CA 90095-1447, (310) 825-4571, Fax: (310) 206-6859, www.international.ucla.edu/lac; *Statistical Abstract of Latin America.*

United Nations Statistics Division, New York, NY 10017, (800) 253-9646, Fax: (212) 963-4116, http://unstats.un.org; *Statistical Yearbook for Latin America and the Caribbean 2004.*

The World Bank, 1818 H Street, NW, Washington, DC 20433, (202) 473-1000, Fax: (202) 477-6391, www.worldbank.org; *Costa Rica.*

COSTA RICA - ENVIRONMENTAL CONDITIONS

DSI Data Service Information, Xantener Strasse 51a, D-47495 Rheinberg, Germany, www.dsidata.com; *Campus Solution* and *DSI's Global Environmental Database.*

Economist Intelligence Unit, 111 West 57th Street, New York, NY 10019, (212) 554-0600, Fax: (212) 586-1181, www.eiu.com; *Costa Rica Country Report.*

United Nations Statistics Division, New York, NY 10017, (800) 253-9646, Fax: (212) 963-4116, http://unstats.un.org; *World Statistics Pocketbook.*

COSTA RICA - EXPENDITURES, PUBLIC

Inter-American Development Bank (IDB), 1300 New York Avenue, NW, Washington, DC 20577, (202) 623-1000, Fax: (202) 623-3096, www.iadb.org; *The Politics of Policies: Economic and Social Progress in Latin America - 2006 Report.*

Organization of American States (OAS), 17th Street Constitution Avenue NW, Washington, DC 20006, (202) 458-3000, www.oas.org; *The OAS in Transition: 1994-2004.*

United Nations Statistics Division, New York, NY 10017, (800) 253-9646, Fax: (212) 963-4116, http://unstats.un.org; *Statistical Yearbook for Latin America and the Caribbean 2004.*

COSTA RICA - EXPORTS

Central Intelligence Agency, Office of Public Affairs, Washington, DC 20505, (703) 482-0623, Fax: (703) 482-1739, www.cia.gov; *The World Factbook.*

Economist Intelligence Unit, 111 West 57th Street, New York, NY 10019, (212) 554-0600, Fax: (212) 586-1181, www.eiu.com; *Business Latin America* and *Costa Rica Country Report.*

Euromonitor International, Inc., 224 S. Michigan Avenue, Suite 1500, Chicago, IL 60604, (312) 922-1115, Fax: (312) 922-1157, www.euromonitor.com; *International Marketing Data and Statistics 2008* and *The World Economic Factbook 2008.*

Inter-American Development Bank (IDB), 1300 New York Avenue, NW, Washington, DC 20577, (202) 623-1000, Fax: (202) 623-3096, www.iadb.org; *The Politics of Policies: Economic and Social Progress in Latin America - 2006 Report.*

International Monetary Fund (IMF), 700 Nineteenth Street, NW, Washington, DC 20431, (202) 623-7000, Fax: (202) 623-4661, www.imf.org; *Direction of Trade Statistics Yearbook 2007; Government Finance Statistics Yearbook (2008 Edition);* and *International Financial Statistics Yearbook 2007.*

Organization of American States (OAS), 17th Street Constitution Avenue NW, Washington, DC 20006, (202) 458-3000, www.oas.org; *The OAS in Transition: 1994-2004.*

Palgrave Macmillan Ltd., Houndmills, Basingstoke, Hampshire, RG21 6XS, England, (Telephone in U.S. (888) 330-8477), (Fax in U.S. (800) 672-2054), www.palgrave.com; *The Statesman's Yearbook 2008.*

Taylor and Francis Group, An Informa Business, 2 Park Square, Milton Park, Abingdon, Oxford OX14 4RN, United Kingdom, (Dial from U.S. (212) 216-7800), (Fax from U.S. (212) 564-7854), www.tandf.co.uk; *The Europa World Year Book.*

United Nations Conference on Trade and Development (UNCTAD), DC2-1120, United Nations, New York, NY 10017, (212) 963-0027, www.unctad.org; *Handbook of Statistics 2005.*

United Nations Food and Agricultural Organization (FAO), Viale delle Terme di Caracalla, 00100 Rome, Italy, (Dial from U.S. (202) 653-2400), (Fax from U.S. (202) 653 5760), www.fao.org; *The State of Food and Agriculture (SOFA) 2006.*

United Nations Statistics Division, New York, NY 10017, (800) 253-9646, Fax: (212) 963-4116, http://unstats.un.org; *Statistical Yearbook for Latin America and the Caribbean 2004.*

The World Bank, 1818 H Street, NW, Washington, DC 20433, (202) 473-1000, Fax: (202) 477-6391, www.worldbank.org; *World Development Indicators (WDI) 2008* and *World Development Report 2008.*

COSTA RICA - FEMALE WORKING POPULATION

See COSTA RICA - EMPLOYMENT

COSTA RICA - FERTILITY, HUMAN

Central Intelligence Agency, Office of Public Affairs, Washington, DC 20505, (703) 482-0623, Fax: (703) 482-1739, www.cia.gov; *The World Factbook.*

M.E. Sharpe, 80 Business Park Drive, Armonk, NY 10504, (800) 541-6563, Fax: (914) 273-2106, www.mesharpe.com; *The Illustrated Book of World Rankings.*

United Nations Statistics Division, New York, NY 10017, (800) 253-9646, Fax: (212) 963-4116, http://unstats.un.org; *Human Development Report 2006.*

The World Bank, 1818 H Street, NW, Washington, DC 20433, (202) 473-1000, Fax: (202) 477-6391, www.worldbank.org; *The World Bank Atlas 2003-2004; World Development Indicators (WDI) 2008;* and *World Development Report 2008.*

COSTA RICA - FERTILIZER INDUSTRY

Economist Intelligence Unit, 111 West 57th Street, New York, NY 10019, (212) 554-0600, Fax: (212) 586-1181, www.eiu.com; *Business Latin America.*

United Nations Food and Agricultural Organization (FAO), Viale delle Terme di Caracalla, 00100 Rome, Italy, (Dial from U.S. (202) 653-2400), (Fax from U.S. (202) 653 5760), www.fao.org; *FAO Fertilizer Yearbook* and *The State of Food and Agriculture (SOFA) 2006.*

United Nations Statistics Division, New York, NY 10017, (800) 253-9646, Fax: (212) 963-4116, http://unstats.un.org; *Statistical Yearbook.*

COSTA RICA - FETAL MORTALITY

See COSTA RICA - MORTALITY

COSTA RICA - FINANCE

Inter-American Development Bank (IDB), 1300 New York Avenue, NW, Washington, DC 20577, (202) 623-1000, Fax: (202) 623-3096, www.iadb.org; *The Politics of Policies: Economic and Social Progress in Latin America - 2006 Report.*

Organization of American States (OAS), 17th Street Constitution Avenue NW, Washington, DC 20006, (202) 458-3000, www.oas.org; *The OAS in Transition: 1994-2004.*

Taylor and Francis Group, An Informa Business, 2 Park Square, Milton Park, Abingdon, Oxford OX14 4RN, United Kingdom, (Dial from U.S. (212) 216-7800), (Fax from U.S. (212) 564-7854), www.tandf.co.uk; *The Europa World Year Book.*

UCLA Latin American Institute, 10343 Bunche Hall, Box 951447, Los Angeles, CA 90095-1447, (310) 825-4571, Fax: (310) 206-6859, www.international.ucla.edu/lac; *Statistical Abstract of Latin America.*

United Nations Statistics Division, New York, NY 10017, (800) 253-9646, Fax: (212) 963-4116, http://unstats.un.org; *National Accounts Statistics: Compendium of Income Distribution Statistics* and *Statistical Yearbook.*

The World Bank, 1818 H Street, NW, Washington, DC 20433, (202) 473-1000, Fax: (202) 477-6391, www.worldbank.org; *Costa Rica.*

COSTA RICA - FINANCE, PUBLIC

Banque de France, 48 rue Croix des Petits champs, 75001 Paris, France, www.banque-france.fr/home.htm; *Public Finance.*

Bernan Essential Government Publications, 4611-F Assembly Drive, Lanham MD, 20706-4391, (301) 459-2255, Fax: (800) 865-3450, www.bernan.com; *National Accounts Statistics.*

Economist Intelligence Unit, 111 West 57th Street, New York, NY 10019, (212) 554-0600, Fax: (212) 586-1181, www.eiu.com; *Costa Rica Country Report.*

Inter-American Development Bank (IDB), 1300 New York Avenue, NW, Washington, DC 20577, (202) 623-1000, Fax: (202) 623-3096, www.iadb.org; *The Politics of Policies: Economic and Social Progress in Latin America - 2006 Report.*

International Monetary Fund (IMF), 700 Nineteenth Street, NW, Washington, DC 20431, (202) 623-7000, Fax: (202) 623-4661, www.imf.org; *Government Finance Statistics Yearbook (2008 Edition); International Financial Statistics; International Financial Statistics Online Service;* and *International Financial Statistics Yearbook 2007.*

M.E. Sharpe, 80 Business Park Drive, Armonk, NY 10504, (800) 541-6563, Fax: (914) 273-2106, www.mesharpe.com; *The Illustrated Book of World Rankings.*

Organization of American States (OAS), 17th Street Constitution Avenue NW, Washington, DC 20006, (202) 458-3000, www.oas.org; *The OAS in Transition: 1994-2004.*

Palgrave Macmillan Ltd., Houndmills, Basingstoke, Hampshire, RG21 6XS, England, (Telephone in U.S. (888) 330-8477), (Fax in U.S. (800) 672-2054), www.palgrave.com; *The Statesman's Yearbook 2008.*

Taylor and Francis Group, An Informa Business, 2 Park Square, Milton Park, Abingdon, Oxford OX14 4RN, United Kingdom, (Dial from U.S. (212) 216-7800), (Fax from U.S. (212) 564-7854), www.tandf.co.uk; *The Europa World Year Book.*

UCLA Latin American Institute, 10343 Bunche Hall, Box 951447, Los Angeles, CA 90095-1447, (310) 825-4571, Fax: (310) 206-6859, www.international.ucla.edu/lac; *Statistical Abstract of Latin America.*

The World Bank, 1818 H Street, NW, Washington, DC 20433, (202) 473-1000, Fax: (202) 477-6391, www.worldbank.org; *Costa Rica.*

COSTA RICA - FISHERIES

Inter-American Development Bank (IDB), 1300 New York Avenue, NW, Washington, DC 20577, (202) 623-1000, Fax: (202) 623-3096, www.iadb.org; *The Politics of Policies: Economic and Social Progress in Latin America - 2006 Report.*

M.E. Sharpe, 80 Business Park Drive, Armonk, NY 10504, (800) 541-6563, Fax: (914) 273-2106, www.mesharpe.com; *The Illustrated Book of World Rankings.*

Palgrave Macmillan Ltd., Houndmills, Basingstoke, Hampshire, RG21 6XS, England, (Telephone in U.S. (888) 330-8477), (Fax in U.S. (800) 672-2054), www.palgrave.com; *The Statesman's Yearbook 2008.*

Taylor and Francis Group, An Informa Business, 2 Park Square, Milton Park, Abingdon, Oxford OX14 4RN, United Kingdom, (Dial from U.S. (212) 216-7800), (Fax from U.S. (212) 564-7854), www.tandf.co.uk; *The Europa World Year Book.*

UCLA Latin American Institute, 10343 Bunche Hall, Box 951447, Los Angeles, CA 90095-1447, (310) 825-4571, Fax: (310) 206-6859, www.international.ucla.edu/lac; *Statistical Abstract of Latin America.*

United Nations Conference on Trade and Development (UNCTAD), DC2-1120, United Nations, New York, NY 10017, (212) 963-0027, www.unctad.org; *UNCTAD Commodity Yearbook.*

United Nations Food and Agricultural Organization (FAO), Viale delle Terme di Caracalla, 00100 Rome, Italy, (Dial from U.S. (202) 653-2400), (Fax from U.S. (202) 653 5760), www.fao.org; *FAO Yearbook of Fishery Statistics;* Fishery Databases; FISHSTAT Database. Subjects covered include: Aquaculture production, capture production, fishery commodities; and *The State of Food and Agriculture (SOFA) 2006.*

United Nations Statistics Division, New York, NY 10017, (800) 253-9646, Fax: (212) 963-4116, http://unstats.un.org; *Statistical Yearbook.*

The World Bank, 1818 H Street, NW, Washington, DC 20433, (202) 473-1000, Fax: (202) 477-6391, www.worldbank.org; *Costa Rica.*

COSTA RICA - FOOD

United Nations Conference on Trade and Development (UNCTAD), DC2-1120, United Nations, New York, NY 10017, (212) 963-0027, www.unctad.org; *UNCTAD Commodity Yearbook.*

United Nations Food and Agricultural Organization (FAO), Viale delle Terme di Caracalla, 00100 Rome, Italy, (Dial from U.S. (202) 653-2400), (Fax from U.S. (202) 653 5760), www.fao.org; *FAO Production Yearbook 2002* and *The State of Food and Agriculture (SOFA) 2006.*

United Nations Statistics Division, New York, NY 10017, (800) 253-9646, Fax: (212) 963-4116, http://unstats.un.org; *Human Development Report 2006.*

COSTA RICA - FOREIGN EXCHANGE RATES

Central Intelligence Agency, Office of Public Affairs, Washington, DC 20505, (703) 482-0623, Fax: (703) 482-1739, www.cia.gov; *The World Factbook.*

Euromonitor International, Inc., 224 S. Michigan Avenue, Suite 1500, Chicago, IL 60604, (312) 922-1115, Fax: (312) 922-1157, www.euromonitor.com; *International Marketing Data and Statistics 2008* and *The World Economic Factbook 2008.*

Inter-American Development Bank (IDB), 1300 New York Avenue, NW, Washington, DC 20577, (202) 623-1000, Fax: (202) 623-3096, www.iadb.org; *The Politics of Policies: Economic and Social Progress in Latin America - 2006 Report.*

International Civil Aviation Organization (ICAO), External Relations and Public Information Office (EPO), 999 University Street, Montreal, Quebec H3C 5H7, Canada, (Dial from U.S. (514) 954-8219),

(Fax from U.S. (514) 954-6077), www.icao.int; *Civil Aviation Statistics of the World.*

International Monetary Fund (IMF), 700 Nineteenth Street, NW, Washington, DC 20431, (202) 623-7000, Fax: (202) 623-4661, www.imf.org; *International Financial Statistics Yearbook 2007.*

Organization of American States (OAS), 17th Street Constitution Avenue NW, Washington, DC 20006, (202) 458-3000, www.oas.org; *The OAS in Transition: 1994-2004.*

Taylor and Francis Group, An Informa Business, 2 Park Square, Milton Park, Abingdon, Oxford OX14 4RN, United Kingdom, (Dial from U.S. (212) 216-7800), (Fax from U.S. (212) 564-7854), www.tandf.co.uk; *The Europa World Year Book.*

UCLA Latin American Institute, 10343 Bunche Hall, Box 951447, Los Angeles, CA 90095-1447, (310) 825-4571, Fax: (310) 206-6859, www.international.ucla.edu/lac; *Statistical Abstract of Latin America.*

United Nations Statistics Division, New York, NY 10017, (800) 253-9646, Fax: (212) 963-4116, http://unstats.un.org; *Statistical Yearbook* and *World Statistics Pocketbook.*

COSTA RICA - FORESTS AND FORESTRY

Economist Intelligence Unit, 111 West 57th Street, New York, NY 10019, (212) 554-0600, Fax: (212) 586-1181, www.eiu.com; *Business Latin America.*

Inter-American Development Bank (IDB), 1300 New York Avenue, NW, Washington, DC 20577, (202) 623-1000, Fax: (202) 623-3096, www.iadb.org; *The Politics of Policies: Economic and Social Progress in Latin America - 2006 Report.*

M.E. Sharpe, 80 Business Park Drive, Armonk, NY 10504, (800) 541-6563, Fax: (914) 273-2106, www.mesharpe.com; *The Illustrated Book of World Rankings.*

Palgrave Macmillan Ltd., Houndmills, Basingstoke, Hampshire, RG21 6XS, England, (Telephone in U.S. (888) 330-8477), (Fax in U.S. (800) 672-2054), www.palgrave.com; *The Statesman's Yearbook 2008.*

Taylor and Francis Group, An Informa Business, 2 Park Square, Milton Park, Abingdon, Oxford OX14 4RN, United Kingdom, (Dial from U.S. (212) 216-7800), (Fax from U.S. (212) 564-7854), www.tandf.co.uk; *The Europa World Year Book.*

UCLA Latin American Institute, 10343 Bunche Hall, Box 951447, Los Angeles, CA 90095-1447, (310) 825-4571, Fax: (310) 206-6859, www.international.ucla.edu/lac; *Statistical Abstract of Latin America.*

UNESCO Institute for Statistics, C.P. 6128 Succursale Centre-Ville, Montreal, Quebec, H3C 3J7 Canada, (Dial from U.S. (514) 343-6880), (Fax from U.S. (514) 343 6882), www.uis.unesco.org; *Statistical Tables.*

United Nations Conference on Trade and Development (UNCTAD), DC2-1120, United Nations, New York, NY 10017, (212) 963-0027, www.unctad.org; *UNCTAD Commodity Yearbook.*

United Nations Food and Agricultural Organization (FAO), Viale delle Terme di Caracalla, 00100 Rome, Italy, (Dial from U.S. (202) 653-2400), (Fax from U.S. (202) 653 5760), www.fao.org; *FAO Yearbook of Forest Products* and *The State of Food and Agriculture (SOFA) 2006.*

United Nations Statistics Division, New York, NY 10017, (800) 253-9646, Fax: (212) 963-4116, http://unstats.un.org; *Statistical Yearbook.*

The World Bank, 1818 H Street, NW, Washington, DC 20433, (202) 473-1000, Fax: (202) 477-6391, www.worldbank.org; *Costa Rica* and *World Development Report 2008.*

COSTA RICA - GAS PRODUCTION

See COSTA RICA - MINERAL INDUSTRIES

COSTA RICA - GEOGRAPHIC INFORMATION SYSTEMS

M.E. Sharpe, 80 Business Park Drive, Armonk, NY 10504, (800) 541-6563, Fax: (914) 273-2106, www.mesharpe.com; *The Illustrated Book of World Rankings.*

UCLA Latin American Institute, 10343 Bunche Hall, Box 951447, Los Angeles, CA 90095-1447, (310) 825-4571, Fax: (310) 206-6859, www.international.ucla.edu/lac; *Statistical Abstract of Latin America.*

The World Bank, 1818 H Street, NW, Washington, DC 20433, (202) 473-1000, Fax: (202) 477-6391, www.worldbank.org; *Costa Rica.*

COSTA RICA - GOLD INDUSTRY

Economist Intelligence Unit, 111 West 57th Street, New York, NY 10019, (212) 554-0600, Fax: (212) 586-1181, www.eiu.com; *Business Latin America.*

International Monetary Fund (IMF), 700 Nineteenth Street, NW, Washington, DC 20431, (202) 623-7000, Fax: (202) 623-4661, www.imf.org; *International Financial Statistics Yearbook 2007.*

United Nations Statistics Division, New York, NY 10017, (800) 253-9646, Fax: (212) 963-4116, http://unstats.un.org; *Statistical Yearbook.*

The World Bank, 1818 H Street, NW, Washington, DC 20433, (202) 473-1000, Fax: (202) 477-6391, www.worldbank.org; *World Development Indicators (WDI) 2008.*

COSTA RICA - GOLD PRODUCTION

See COSTA RICA - MINERAL INDUSTRIES

COSTA RICA - GRANTS-IN-AID

International Monetary Fund (IMF), 700 Nineteenth Street, NW, Washington, DC 20431, (202) 623-7000, Fax: (202) 623-4661, www.imf.org; *Government Finance Statistics Yearbook (2008 Edition).*

COSTA RICA - GROSS DOMESTIC PRODUCT

Economist Intelligence Unit, 111 West 57th Street, New York, NY 10019, (212) 554-0600, Fax: (212) 586-1181, www.eiu.com; *Business Latin America* and *Costa Rica Country Report.*

Euromonitor International, Inc., 224 S. Michigan Avenue, Suite 1500, Chicago, IL 60604, (312) 922-1115, Fax: (312) 922-1157, www.euromonitor.com; *International Marketing Data and Statistics 2008* and *The World Economic Factbook 2008.*

Inter-American Development Bank (IDB), 1300 New York Avenue, NW, Washington, DC 20577, (202) 623-1000, Fax: (202) 623-3096, www.iadb.org; *The Politics of Policies: Economic and Social Progress in Latin America - 2006 Report.*

M.E. Sharpe, 80 Business Park Drive, Armonk, NY 10504, (800) 541-6563, Fax: (914) 273-2106, www.mesharpe.com; *The Illustrated Book of World Rankings.*

Organization of American States (OAS), 17th Street Constitution Avenue NW, Washington, DC 20006, (202) 458-3000, www.oas.org; *The OAS in Transition: 1994-2004.*

Taylor and Francis Group, An Informa Business, 2 Park Square, Milton Park, Abingdon, Oxford OX14 4RN, United Kingdom, (Dial from U.S. (212) 216-7800), (Fax from U.S. (212) 564-7854), www.tandf.co.uk; *The Europa World Year Book.*

UCLA Latin American Institute, 10343 Bunche Hall, Box 951447, Los Angeles, CA 90095-1447, (310) 825-4571, Fax: (310) 206-6859, www.international.ucla.edu/lac; *Statistical Abstract of Latin America.*

United Nations Statistics Division, New York, NY 10017, (800) 253-9646, Fax: (212) 963-4116, http://unstats.un.org; *Human Development Report 2006; National Accounts Statistics: Compendium of Income Distribution Statistics; Statistical Yearbook;* and *Statistical Yearbook for Latin America and the Caribbean 2004.*

The World Bank, 1818 H Street, NW, Washington, DC 20433, (202) 473-1000, Fax: (202) 477-6391, www.worldbank.org; *World Development Indicators (WDI) 2008* and *World Development Report 2008.*

COSTA RICA - GROSS NATIONAL PRODUCT

Euromonitor International, Inc., 224 S. Michigan Avenue, Suite 1500, Chicago, IL 60604, (312) 922-1115, Fax: (312) 922-1157, www.euromonitor.com; *International Marketing Data and Statistics 2008.*

Inter-American Development Bank (IDB), 1300 New York Avenue, NW, Washington, DC 20577, (202) 623-1000, Fax: (202) 623-3096, www.iadb.org; *The Politics of Policies: Economic and Social Progress in Latin America - 2006 Report.*

M.E. Sharpe, 80 Business Park Drive, Armonk, NY 10504, (800) 541-6563, Fax: (914) 273-2106, www.mesharpe.com; *The Illustrated Book of World Rankings.*

Palgrave Macmillan Ltd., Houndmills, Basingstoke, Hampshire, RG21 6XS, England, (Telephone in U.S. (888) 330-8477), (Fax in U.S. (800) 672-2054), www.palgrave.com; *The Statesman's Yearbook 2008.*

U.S. Department of State (DOS), 2201 C Street NW, Washington, DC 20520, (202) 647-4000, www.state.gov; *World Military Expenditures and Arms Transfers (WMEAT).*

United Nations Statistics Division, New York, NY 10017, (800) 253-9646, Fax: (212) 963-4116, http://unstats.un.org; *Statistical Yearbook.*

The World Bank, 1818 H Street, NW, Washington, DC 20433, (202) 473-1000, Fax: (202) 477-6391, www.worldbank.org; *The World Bank Atlas 2003-2004; World Development Indicators (WDI) 2008;* and *World Development Report 2008.*

COSTA RICA - HIDES AND SKINS INDUSTRY

United Nations Food and Agricultural Organization (FAO), Viale delle Terme di Caracalla, 00100 Rome, Italy, (Dial from U.S. (202) 653-2400), (Fax from U.S. (202) 653 5760), www.fao.org; *FAO Production Yearbook 2002.*

COSTA RICA - HOUSING

Euromonitor International, Inc., 224 S. Michigan Avenue, Suite 1500, Chicago, IL 60604, (312) 922-1115, Fax: (312) 922-1157, www.euromonitor.com; *World Marketing Data and Statistics.*

M.E. Sharpe, 80 Business Park Drive, Armonk, NY 10504, (800) 541-6563, Fax: (914) 273-2106, www.mesharpe.com; *The Illustrated Book of World Rankings.*

UCLA Latin American Institute, 10343 Bunche Hall, Box 951447, Los Angeles, CA 90095-1447, (310) 825-4571, Fax: (310) 206-6859, www.international.ucla.edu/lac; *Statistical Abstract of Latin America.*

United Nations Statistics Division, New York, NY 10017, (800) 253-9646, Fax: (212) 963-4116, http://unstats.un.org; *Statistical Yearbook for Latin America and the Caribbean 2004.*

COSTA RICA - ILLITERATE PERSONS

Euromonitor International, Inc., 224 S. Michigan Avenue, Suite 1500, Chicago, IL 60604, (312) 922-1115, Fax: (312) 922-1157, www.euromonitor.com; *The World Economic Factbook 2008.*

Palgrave Macmillan Ltd., Houndmills, Basingstoke, Hampshire, RG21 6XS, England, (Telephone in U.S. (888) 330-8477), (Fax in U.S. (800) 672-2054), www.palgrave.com; *The Statesman's Yearbook 2008.*

UNESCO Institute for Statistics, C.P. 6128 Succursale Centre-Ville, Montreal, Quebec, H3C 3J7 Canada, (Dial from U.S. (514) 343-6880), (Fax from U.S. (514) 343 6882), www.uis.unesco.org; *Statistical Tables.*

United Nations Statistics Division, New York, NY 10017, (800) 253-9646, Fax: (212) 963-4116, http://unstats.un.org; *Human Development Report 2006* and *Statistical Yearbook for Latin America and the Caribbean 2004.*

COSTA RICA - IMPORTS

Central Intelligence Agency, Office of Public Affairs, Washington, DC 20505, (703) 482-0623, Fax: (703) 482-1739, www.cia.gov; *The World Factbook*.

Economist Intelligence Unit, 111 West 57th Street, New York, NY 10019, (212) 554-0600, Fax: (212) 586-1181, www.eiu.com; *Business Latin America* and *Costa Rica Country Report*.

Euromonitor International, Inc., 224 S. Michigan Avenue, Suite 1500, Chicago, IL 60604, (312) 922-1115, Fax: (312) 922-1157, www.euromonitor.com; *International Marketing Data and Statistics 2008* and *The World Economic Factbook 2008*.

Inter-American Development Bank (IDB), 1300 New York Avenue, NW, Washington, DC 20577, (202) 623-1000, Fax: (202) 623-3096, www.iadb.org; *The Politics of Policies: Economic and Social Progress in Latin America - 2006 Report*.

International Monetary Fund (IMF), 700 Nineteenth Street, NW, Washington, DC 20431, (202) 623-7000, Fax: (202) 623-4661, www.imf.org; *Direction of Trade Statistics Yearbook 2007; Government Finance Statistics Yearbook (2008 Edition);* and *International Financial Statistics Yearbook 2007*.

Organization of American States (OAS), 17th Street Constitution Avenue NW, Washington, DC 20006, (202) 458-3000, www.oas.org; *The OAS in Transition: 1994-2004*.

Palgrave Macmillan Ltd., Houndmills, Basingstoke, Hampshire, RG21 6XS, England, (Telephone in U.S. (888) 330-8477), (Fax in U.S. (800) 672-2054), www.palgrave.com; *The Statesman's Yearbook 2008*.

Taylor and Francis Group, An Informa Business, 2 Park Square, Milton Park, Abingdon, Oxford OX14 4RN, United Kingdom, (Dial from U.S. (212) 216-7800), (Fax from U.S. (212) 564-7854), www.tandf.co.uk; *The Europa World Year Book*.

United Nations Conference on Trade and Development (UNCTAD), DC2-1120, United Nations, New York, NY 10017, (212) 963-0027, www.unctad.org; *Handbook of Statistics 2005*.

United Nations Food and Agricultural Organization (FAO), Viale delle Terme di Caracalla, 00100 Rome, Italy, (Dial from U.S. (202) 653-2400), (Fax from U.S. (202) 653 5760), www.fao.org; *The State of Food and Agriculture (SOFA) 2006*.

United Nations Statistics Division, New York, NY 10017, (800) 253-9646, Fax: (212) 963-4116, http://unstats.un.org; *Statistical Yearbook for Latin America and the Caribbean 2004*.

The World Bank, 1818 H Street, NW, Washington, DC 20433, (202) 473-1000, Fax: (202) 477-6391, www.worldbank.org; *World Development Indicators (WDI) 2008* and *World Development Report 2008*.

COSTA RICA - INCOME DISTRIBUTION

UCLA Latin American Institute, 10343 Bunche Hall, Box 951447, Los Angeles, CA 90095-1447, (310) 825-4571, Fax: (310) 206-6859, www.international.ucla.edu/lac; *Statistical Abstract of Latin America*.

United Nations Statistics Division, New York, NY 10017, (800) 253-9646, Fax: (212) 963-4116, http://unstats.un.org; *Statistical Yearbook for Latin America and the Caribbean 2004*.

COSTA RICA - INCOME TAXES

See COSTA RICA - TAXATION

COSTA RICA - INDUSTRIAL PRODUCTIVITY

Euromonitor International, Inc., 224 S. Michigan Avenue, Suite 1500, Chicago, IL 60604, (312) 922-1115, Fax: (312) 922-1157, www.euromonitor.com; *International Marketing Data and Statistics 2008*.

M.E. Sharpe, 80 Business Park Drive, Armonk, NY 10504, (800) 541-6563, Fax: (914) 273-2106, www.mesharpe.com; *The Illustrated Book of World Rankings*.

COSTA RICA - INDUSTRIAL PROPERTY

United Nations Statistics Division, New York, NY 10017, (800) 253-9646, Fax: (212) 963-4116, http://unstats.un.org; *Statistical Yearbook*.

COSTA RICA - INDUSTRIES

Central Intelligence Agency, Office of Public Affairs, Washington, DC 20505, (703) 482-0623, Fax: (703) 482-1739, www.cia.gov; *The World Factbook*.

Economist Intelligence Unit, 111 West 57th Street, New York, NY 10019, (212) 554-0600, Fax: (212) 586-1181, www.eiu.com; *Costa Rica Country Report*.

Euromonitor International, Inc., 224 S. Michigan Avenue, Suite 1500, Chicago, IL 60604, (312) 922-1115, Fax: (312) 922-1157, www.euromonitor.com; *International Marketing Data and Statistics 2008; The World Economic Factbook 2008;* and *World Marketing Data and Statistics*.

International Labour Office, I.L.O. Publications, 4 route des Morillons, CH-1211 Geneva 22, Switzerland, (Telephone in U.S. (202) 653-7652), (Fax in U.S. (202) 653-7687), www.ilo.org; *Yearbook of Labour Statistics 2006*.

M.E. Sharpe, 80 Business Park Drive, Armonk, NY 10504, (800) 541-6563, Fax: (914) 273-2106, www.mesharpe.com; *The Illustrated Book of World Rankings*.

Palgrave Macmillan Ltd., Houndmills, Basingstoke, Hampshire, RG21 6XS, England, (Telephone in U.S. (888) 330-8477), (Fax in U.S. (800) 672-2054), www.palgrave.com; *The Statesman's Yearbook 2008*.

Taylor and Francis Group, An Informa Business, 2 Park Square, Milton Park, Abingdon, Oxford OX14 4RN, United Kingdom, (Dial from U.S. (212) 216-7800), (Fax from U.S. (212) 564-7854), www.tandf.co.uk; *The Europa World Year Book*.

UCLA Latin American Institute, 10343 Bunche Hall, Box 951447, Los Angeles, CA 90095-1447, (310) 825-4571, Fax: (310) 206-6859, www.international.ucla.edu/lac; *Statistical Abstract of Latin America*.

United Nations Industrial Development Organization (UNIDO), 1 United Nations Plaza, New York, NY 10017, (212) 963 6890, Fax: (212) 963-7904, http://unido.org; Industrial Statistics Database 2008 (INDSTAT) and *The International Yearbook of Industrial Statistics 2008*.

United Nations Statistics Division, New York, NY 10017, (800) 253-9646, Fax: (212) 963-4116, http://unstats.un.org; *Economic Survey of Latin America and the Caribbean 2004-2005* and *Statistical Yearbook*.

The World Bank, 1818 H Street, NW, Washington, DC 20433, (202) 473-1000, Fax: (202) 477-6391, www.worldbank.org; *Costa Rica* and *World Development Indicators (WDI) 2008*.

COSTA RICA - INFANT AND MATERNAL MORTALITY

See COSTA RICA - MORTALITY

COSTA RICA - INFLATION (FINANCE)

United Nations Statistics Division, New York, NY 10017, (800) 253-9646, Fax: (212) 963-4116, http://unstats.un.org; *Economic Survey of Latin America and the Caribbean 2004-2005*.

COSTA RICA - INTEREST RATES

Inter-American Development Bank (IDB), 1300 New York Avenue, NW, Washington, DC 20577, (202) 623-1000, Fax: (202) 623-3096, www.iadb.org; *The Politics of Policies: Economic and Social Progress in Latin America - 2006 Report*.

Organization of American States (OAS), 17th Street Constitution Avenue NW, Washington, DC 20006, (202) 458-3000, www.oas.org; *The OAS in Transition: 1994-2004*.

COSTA RICA - INTERNAL REVENUE

Inter-American Development Bank (IDB), 1300 New York Avenue, NW, Washington, DC 20577, (202) 623-1000, Fax: (202) 623-3096, www.iadb.org; *The Politics of Policies: Economic and Social Progress in Latin America - 2006 Report*.

Organization of American States (OAS), 17th Street Constitution Avenue NW, Washington, DC 20006, (202) 458-3000, www.oas.org; *The OAS in Transition: 1994-2004*.

COSTA RICA - INTERNATIONAL FINANCE

Inter-American Development Bank (IDB), 1300 New York Avenue, NW, Washington, DC 20577, (202) 623-1000, Fax: (202) 623-3096, www.iadb.org; *The Politics of Policies: Economic and Social Progress in Latin America - 2006 Report*.

UCLA Latin American Institute, 10343 Bunche Hall, Box 951447, Los Angeles, CA 90095-1447, (310) 825-4571, Fax: (310) 206-6859, www.international.ucla.edu/lac; *Statistical Abstract of Latin America*.

United Nations Statistics Division, New York, NY 10017, (800) 253-9646, Fax: (212) 963-4116, http://unstats.un.org; *Statistical Yearbook for Latin America and the Caribbean 2004*.

COSTA RICA - INTERNATIONAL LIQUIDITY

Inter-American Development Bank (IDB), 1300 New York Avenue, NW, Washington, DC 20577, (202) 623-1000, Fax: (202) 623-3096, www.iadb.org; *The Politics of Policies: Economic and Social Progress in Latin America - 2006 Report*.

International Monetary Fund (IMF), 700 Nineteenth Street, NW, Washington, DC 20431, (202) 623-7000, Fax: (202) 623-4661, www.imf.org; *International Financial Statistics Yearbook 2007*.

COSTA RICA - INTERNATIONAL STATISTICS

Inter-American Development Bank (IDB), 1300 New York Avenue, NW, Washington, DC 20577, (202) 623-1000, Fax: (202) 623-3096, www.iadb.org; *The Politics of Policies: Economic and Social Progress in Latin America - 2006 Report*.

UCLA Latin American Institute, 10343 Bunche Hall, Box 951447, Los Angeles, CA 90095-1447, (310) 825-4571, Fax: (310) 206-6859, www.international.ucla.edu/lac; *Statistical Abstract of Latin America*.

COSTA RICA - INTERNATIONAL TRADE

Banque de France, 48 rue Croix des Petits champs, 75001 Paris, France, www.banque-france.fr/home.htm; *Monthly Business Survey Overview*.

Economist Intelligence Unit, 111 West 57th Street, New York, NY 10019, (212) 554-0600, Fax: (212) 586-1181, www.eiu.com; *Business Latin America* and *Costa Rica Country Report*.

Euromonitor International, Inc., 224 S. Michigan Avenue, Suite 1500, Chicago, IL 60604, (312) 922-1115, Fax: (312) 922-1157, www.euromonitor.com; *International Marketing Data and Statistics 2008; The World Economic Factbook 2008;* and *World Marketing Data and Statistics*.

Inter-American Development Bank (IDB), 1300 New York Avenue, NW, Washington, DC 20577, (202) 623-1000, Fax: (202) 623-3096, www.iadb.org; *The Politics of Policies: Economic and Social Progress in Latin America - 2006 Report*.

International Monetary Fund (IMF), 700 Nineteenth Street, NW, Washington, DC 20431, (202) 623-7000, Fax: (202) 623-4661, www.imf.org; *International Financial Statistics Yearbook 2007*.

M.E. Sharpe, 80 Business Park Drive, Armonk, NY 10504, (800) 541-6563, Fax: (914) 273-2106, www.mesharpe.com; *The Illustrated Book of World Rankings*.

Organisation for Economic Cooperation and Development (OECD), 2 rue Andre Pascal, F-75775 Paris Cedex 16, France, (Telephone in U.S. (202) 785-6323), (Fax in U.S. (202) 785-0350), www.oecd.org; *International Trade by Commodity Statistics (ITCS)*.

Palgrave Macmillan Ltd., Houndmills, Basingstoke, Hampshire, RG21 6XS, England, (Telephone in U.S.

(888) 330-8477), (Fax in U.S. (800) 672-2054), www.palgrave.com; *The Statesman's Yearbook 2008.*

Taylor and Francis Group, An Informa Business, 2 Park Square, Milton Park, Abingdon, Oxford OX14 4RN, United Kingdom, (Dial from U.S. (212) 216-7800), (Fax from U.S. (212) 564-7854), www.tandf.co.uk; *The Europa World Year Book.*

UCLA Latin American Institute, 10343 Bunche Hall, Box 951447, Los Angeles, CA 90095-1447, (310) 825-4571, Fax: (310) 206-6859, www.international.ucla.edu/lac; *Statistical Abstract of Latin America.*

United Nations Conference on Trade and Development (UNCTAD), DC2-1120, United Nations, New York, NY 10017, (212) 963-0027, www.unctad.org; *UNCTAD Commodity Yearbook.*

United Nations Food and Agricultural Organization (FAO), Viale delle Terme di Caracalla, 00100 Rome, Italy, (Dial from U.S. (202) 653-2400), (Fax from U.S. (202) 653 5760), www.fao.org; *The State of Food and Agriculture (SOFA) 2006.*

United Nations Statistics Division, New York, NY 10017, (800) 253-9646, Fax: (212) 963-4116, http://unstats.un.org; *Economic Survey of Latin America and the Caribbean 2004-2005; International Trade Statistics Yearbook; Statistical Yearbook;* and *Statistical Yearbook for Latin America and the Caribbean 2004.*

The World Bank, 1818 H Street, NW, Washington, DC 20433, (202) 473-1000, Fax: (202) 477-6391, www.worldbank.org; *Costa Rica; World Development Indicators (WDI) 2008;* and *World Development Report 2008.*

World Trade Organization (WTO), Centre William Rappard, Rue de Lausanne 154, CH-1211 Geneva 21, Switzerland, www.wto.org; *International Trade Statistics 2006.*

COSTA RICA - INTERNET USERS

International Telecommunication Union (ITU), Place des Nations, 1211 Geneva 20, Switzerland, www.itu.int; *World Telecommunication/ICT Indicators Database on CD-ROM; World Telecommunication/ICT Indicators Database Online;* and *Yearbook of Statistics - Telecommunication Services (Chronological Time Series 1997-2006).*

The World Bank, 1818 H Street, NW, Washington, DC 20433, (202) 473-1000, Fax: (202) 477-6391, www.worldbank.org; *Costa Rica.*

COSTA RICA - INVESTMENTS

Inter-American Development Bank (IDB), 1300 New York Avenue, NW, Washington, DC 20577, (202) 623-1000, Fax: (202) 623-3096, www.iadb.org; *The Politics of Policies: Economic and Social Progress in Latin America - 2006 Report.*

United Nations Statistics Division, New York, NY 10017, (800) 253-9646, Fax: (212) 963-4116, http://unstats.un.org; *Statistical Yearbook for Latin America and the Caribbean 2004.*

COSTA RICA - INVESTMENTS, FOREIGN

Economist Intelligence Unit, 111 West 57th Street, New York, NY 10019, (212) 554-0600, Fax: (212) 586-1181, www.eiu.com; *Business Latin America.*

COSTA RICA - IRON AND IRON ORE PRODUCTION

See COSTA RICA - MINERAL INDUSTRIES

COSTA RICA - IRRIGATION

Euromonitor International, Inc., 224 S. Michigan Avenue, Suite 1500, Chicago, IL 60604, (312) 922-1115, Fax: (312) 922-1157, www.euromonitor.com; *International Marketing Data and Statistics 2008.*

Inter-American Development Bank (IDB), 1300 New York Avenue, NW, Washington, DC 20577, (202) 623-1000, Fax: (202) 623-3096, www.iadb.org; *The Politics of Policies: Economic and Social Progress in Latin America - 2006 Report.*

COSTA RICA - LABOR

Central Intelligence Agency, Office of Public Affairs, Washington, DC 20505, (703) 482-0623, Fax: (703) 482-1739, www.cia.gov; *The World Factbook.*

Economist Intelligence Unit, 111 West 57th Street, New York, NY 10019, (212) 554-0600, Fax: (212) 586-1181, www.eiu.com; *Business Latin America.*

Euromonitor International, Inc., 224 S. Michigan Avenue, Suite 1500, Chicago, IL 60604, (312) 922-1115, Fax: (312) 922-1157, www.euromonitor.com; *International Marketing Data and Statistics 2008* and *World Marketing Data and Statistics.*

International Labour Office, I.L.O. Publications, 4 route des Morillons, CH-1211 Geneva 22, Switzerland, (Telephone in U.S. (202) 653-7652), (Fax in U.S. (202) 653-7687), www.ilo.org; *Yearbook of Labour Statistics 2006.*

M.E. Sharpe, 80 Business Park Drive, Armonk, NY 10504, (800) 541-6563, Fax: (914) 273-2106, www.mesharpe.com; *The Illustrated Book of World Rankings.*

Palgrave Macmillan Ltd., Houndmills, Basingstoke, Hampshire, RG21 6XS, England, (Telephone in U.S. (888) 330-8477), (Fax in U.S. (800) 672-2054), www.palgrave.com; *The Statesman's Yearbook 2008.*

Taylor and Francis Group, An Informa Business, 2 Park Square, Milton Park, Abingdon, Oxford OX14 4RN, United Kingdom, (Dial from U.S. (212) 216-7800), (Fax from U.S. (212) 564-7854), www.tandf.co.uk; *The Europa World Year Book.*

United Nations Food and Agricultural Organization (FAO), Viale delle Terme di Caracalla, 00100 Rome, Italy, (Dial from U.S. (202) 653-2400), (Fax from U.S. (202) 653 5760), www.fao.org; *The State of Food and Agriculture (SOFA) 2006.*

United Nations Statistics Division, New York, NY 10017, (800) 253-9646, Fax: (212) 963-4116, http://unstats.un.org; *Human Development Report 2006.*

The World Bank, 1818 H Street, NW, Washington, DC 20433, (202) 473-1000, Fax: (202) 477-6391, www.worldbank.org; *The World Bank Atlas 2003-2004; World Development Indicators (WDI) 2008;* and *World Development Report 2008.*

COSTA RICA - LAND USE

Central Intelligence Agency, Office of Public Affairs, Washington, DC 20505, (703) 482-0623, Fax: (703) 482-1739, www.cia.gov; *The World Factbook.*

Euromonitor International, Inc., 224 S. Michigan Avenue, Suite 1500, Chicago, IL 60604, (312) 922-1115, Fax: (312) 922-1157, www.euromonitor.com; *International Marketing Data and Statistics 2008.*

Inter-American Development Bank (IDB), 1300 New York Avenue, NW, Washington, DC 20577, (202) 623-1000, Fax: (202) 623-3096, www.iadb.org; *The Politics of Policies: Economic and Social Progress in Latin America - 2006 Report.*

United Nations Food and Agricultural Organization (FAO), Viale delle Terme di Caracalla, 00100 Rome, Italy, (Dial from U.S. (202) 653-2400), (Fax from U.S. (202) 653 5760), www.fao.org; *FAO Production Yearbook 2002.*

The World Bank, 1818 H Street, NW, Washington, DC 20433, (202) 473-1000, Fax: (202) 477-6391, www.worldbank.org; *World Development Report 2008.*

COSTA RICA - LIBRARIES

M.E. Sharpe, 80 Business Park Drive, Armonk, NY 10504, (800) 541-6563, Fax: (914) 273-2106, www.mesharpe.com; *The Illustrated Book of World Rankings.*

UNESCO Institute for Statistics, C.P. 6128 Succursale Centre-Ville, Montreal, Quebec, H3C 3J7 Canada, (Dial from U.S. (514) 343-6880), (Fax from U.S. (514) 343 6882), www.uis.unesco.org; *Statistical Tables.*

COSTA RICA - LIFE EXPECTANCY

Central Intelligence Agency, Office of Public Affairs, Washington, DC 20505, (703) 482-0623, Fax: (703) 482-1739, www.cia.gov; *The World Factbook.*

Economist Intelligence Unit, 111 West 57th Street, New York, NY 10019, (212) 554-0600, Fax: (212) 586-1181, www.eiu.com; *Business Latin America.*

Euromonitor International, Inc., 224 S. Michigan Avenue, Suite 1500, Chicago, IL 60604, (312) 922-1115, Fax: (312) 922-1157, www.euromonitor.com; *The World Economic Factbook 2008.*

United Nations Statistics Division, New York, NY 10017, (800) 253-9646, Fax: (212) 963-4116, http://unstats.un.org; *Human Development Report 2006; Statistical Yearbook for Latin America and the Caribbean 2004;* and *World Statistics Pocketbook.*

The World Bank, 1818 H Street, NW, Washington, DC 20433, (202) 473-1000, Fax: (202) 477-6391, www.worldbank.org; *The World Bank Atlas 2003-2004* and *World Development Report 2008.*

COSTA RICA - LITERACY

Economist Intelligence Unit, 111 West 57th Street, New York, NY 10019, (212) 554-0600, Fax: (212) 586-1181, www.eiu.com; *Business Latin America.*

Euromonitor International, Inc., 224 S. Michigan Avenue, Suite 1500, Chicago, IL 60604, (312) 922-1115, Fax: (312) 922-1157, www.euromonitor.com; *World Marketing Data and Statistics.*

COSTA RICA - LIVESTOCK

Euromonitor International, Inc., 224 S. Michigan Avenue, Suite 1500, Chicago, IL 60604, (312) 922-1115, Fax: (312) 922-1157, www.euromonitor.com; *International Marketing Data and Statistics 2008.*

M.E. Sharpe, 80 Business Park Drive, Armonk, NY 10504, (800) 541-6563, Fax: (914) 273-2106, www.mesharpe.com; *The Illustrated Book of World Rankings.*

Palgrave Macmillan Ltd., Houndmills, Basingstoke, Hampshire, RG21 6XS, England, (Telephone in U.S. (888) 330-8477), (Fax in U.S. (800) 672-2054), www.palgrave.com; *The Statesman's Yearbook 2008.*

Taylor and Francis Group, An Informa Business, 2 Park Square, Milton Park, Abingdon, Oxford OX14 4RN, United Kingdom, (Dial from U.S. (212) 216-7800), (Fax from U.S. (212) 564-7854), www.tandf.co.uk; *The Europa World Year Book.*

United Nations Conference on Trade and Development (UNCTAD), DC2-1120, United Nations, New York, NY 10017, (212) 963-0027, www.unctad.org; *UNCTAD Commodity Yearbook.*

United Nations Food and Agricultural Organization (FAO), Viale delle Terme di Caracalla, 00100 Rome, Italy, (Dial from U.S. (202) 653-2400), (Fax from U.S. (202) 653 5760), www.fao.org; *FAO Production Yearbook 2002* and *The State of Food and Agriculture (SOFA) 2006.*

United Nations Statistics Division, New York, NY 10017, (800) 253-9646, Fax: (212) 963-4116, http://unstats.un.org; *Statistical Yearbook.*

COSTA RICA - MANUFACTURES

Economist Intelligence Unit, 111 West 57th Street, New York, NY 10019, (212) 554-0600, Fax: (212) 586-1181, www.eiu.com; *Business Latin America.*

Inter-American Development Bank (IDB), 1300 New York Avenue, NW, Washington, DC 20577, (202) 623-1000, Fax: (202) 623-3096, www.iadb.org; *The Politics of Policies: Economic and Social Progress in Latin America - 2006 Report.*

M.E. Sharpe, 80 Business Park Drive, Armonk, NY 10504, (800) 541-6563, Fax: (914) 273-2106, www.mesharpe.com; *The Illustrated Book of World Rankings.*

United Nations Statistics Division, New York, NY 10017, (800) 253-9646, Fax: (212) 963-4116, http://unstats.un.org; *Statistical Yearbook* and *Statistical Yearbook for Latin America and the Caribbean 2004.*

The World Bank, 1818 H Street, NW, Washington, DC 20433, (202) 473-1000, Fax: (202) 477-6391, www.worldbank.org; *World Development Indicators (WDI) 2008.*

COSTA RICA - MARRIAGE

M.E. Sharpe, 80 Business Park Drive, Armonk, NY 10504, (800) 541-6563, Fax: (914) 273-2106, www.mesharpe.com; *The Illustrated Book of World Rankings.*

Taylor and Francis Group, An Informa Business, 2 Park Square, Milton Park, Abingdon, Oxford OX14 4RN, United Kingdom, (Dial from U.S. (212) 216-7800), (Fax from U.S. (212) 564-7854), www.tandf.co.uk; *The Europa World Year Book.*

United Nations Statistics Division, New York, NY 10017, (800) 253-9646, Fax: (212) 963-4116, http://unstats.un.org; *Demographic Yearbook* and *Statistical Yearbook.*

COSTA RICA - MEAT INDUSTRY AND TRADE

International Monetary Fund (IMF), 700 Nineteenth Street, NW, Washington, DC 20431, (202) 623-7000, Fax: (202) 623-4661, www.imf.org; *International Financial Statistics Yearbook 2007.*

Organization of American States (OAS), 17th Street Constitution Avenue NW, Washington, DC 20006, (202) 458-3000, www.oas.org; *The OAS in Transition: 1994-2004.*

COSTA RICA - MEDICAL PERSONNEL

UCLA Latin American Institute, 10343 Bunche Hall, Box 951447, Los Angeles, CA 90095-1447, (310) 825-4571, Fax: (310) 206-6859, www.international.ucla.edu/lac; *Statistical Abstract of Latin America.*

COSTA RICA - MILK PRODUCTION

See COSTA RICA - DAIRY PROCESSING

COSTA RICA - MINERAL INDUSTRIES

Economist Intelligence Unit, 111 West 57th Street, New York, NY 10019, (212) 554-0600, Fax: (212) 586-1181, www.eiu.com; *Business Latin America.*

Inter-American Development Bank (IDB), 1300 New York Avenue, NW, Washington, DC 20577, (202) 623-1000, Fax: (202) 623-3096, www.iadb.org; *The Politics of Policies: Economic and Social Progress in Latin America - 2006 Report.*

Palgrave Macmillan Ltd., Houndmills, Basingstoke, Hampshire, RG21 6XS, England, (Telephone in U.S. (888) 330-8477), (Fax in U.S. (800) 672-2054), www.palgrave.com; *The Statesman's Yearbook 2008.*

Taylor and Francis Group, An Informa Business, 2 Park Square, Milton Park, Abingdon, Oxford OX14 4RN, United Kingdom, (Dial from U.S. (212) 216-7800), (Fax from U.S. (212) 564-7854), www.tandf.co.uk; *The Europa World Year Book.*

UCLA Latin American Institute, 10343 Bunche Hall, Box 951447, Los Angeles, CA 90095-1447, (310) 825-4571, Fax: (310) 206-6859, www.international.ucla.edu/lac; *Statistical Abstract of Latin America.*

United Nations Conference on Trade and Development (UNCTAD), DC2-1120, United Nations, New York, NY 10017, (212) 963-0027, www.unctad.org; *UNCTAD Commodity Yearbook.*

United Nations Statistics Division, New York, NY 10017, (800) 253-9646, Fax: (212) 963-4116, http://unstats.un.org; *Statistical Yearbook for Latin America and the Caribbean 2004.*

COSTA RICA - MONEY EXCHANGE RATES

See COSTA RICA - FOREIGN EXCHANGE RATES

COSTA RICA - MONEY SUPPLY

Economist Intelligence Unit, 111 West 57th Street, New York, NY 10019, (212) 554-0600, Fax: (212) 586-1181, www.eiu.com; *Costa Rica Country Report.*

Euromonitor International, Inc., 224 S. Michigan Avenue, Suite 1500, Chicago, IL 60604, (312) 922-1115, Fax: (312) 922-1157, www.euromonitor.com; *International Marketing Data and Statistics 2008.*

Inter-American Development Bank (IDB), 1300 New York Avenue, NW, Washington, DC 20577, (202) 623-1000, Fax: (202) 623-3096, www.iadb.org; *The Politics of Policies: Economic and Social Progress in Latin America - 2006 Report.*

International Monetary Fund (IMF), 700 Nineteenth Street, NW, Washington, DC 20431, (202) 623-7000, Fax: (202) 623-4661, www.imf.org; *International Financial Statistics Yearbook 2007.*

Taylor and Francis Group, An Informa Business, 2 Park Square, Milton Park, Abingdon, Oxford OX14 4RN, United Kingdom, (Dial from U.S. (212) 216-7800), (Fax from U.S. (212) 564-7854), www.tandf.co.uk; *The Europa World Year Book.*

UCLA Latin American Institute, 10343 Bunche Hall, Box 951447, Los Angeles, CA 90095-1447, (310) 825-4571, Fax: (310) 206-6859, www.international.ucla.edu/lac; *Statistical Abstract of Latin America.*

United Nations Statistics Division, New York, NY 10017, (800) 253-9646, Fax: (212) 963-4116, http://unstats.un.org; *Statistical Yearbook.*

The World Bank, 1818 H Street, NW, Washington, DC 20433, (202) 473-1000, Fax: (202) 477-6391, www.worldbank.org; *Costa Rica* and *World Development Indicators (WDI) 2008.*

COSTA RICA - MORTALITY

Central Intelligence Agency, Office of Public Affairs, Washington, DC 20505, (703) 482-0623, Fax: (703) 482-1739, www.cia.gov; *The World Factbook.*

Economist Intelligence Unit, 111 West 57th Street, New York, NY 10019, (212) 554-0600, Fax: (212) 586-1181, www.eiu.com; *Business Latin America.*

Euromonitor International, Inc., 224 S. Michigan Avenue, Suite 1500, Chicago, IL 60604, (312) 922-1115, Fax: (312) 922-1157, www.euromonitor.com; *International Marketing Data and Statistics 2008* and *The World Economic Factbook 2008.*

Taylor and Francis Group, An Informa Business, 2 Park Square, Milton Park, Abingdon, Oxford OX14 4RN, United Kingdom, (Dial from U.S. (212) 216-7800), (Fax from U.S. (212) 564-7854), www.tandf.co.uk; *The Europa World Year Book.*

UNICEF, 3 United Nations Plaza, New York, NY 10017, (800) 253-9646, Fax: (212) 887-7465, www.unicef.org; *The State of the World's Children 2008.*

United Nations Statistics Division, New York, NY 10017, (800) 253-9646, Fax: (212) 963-4116, http://unstats.un.org; *Demographic Yearbook; Human Development Report 2006; Statistical Yearbook; Statistical Yearbook for Latin America and the Caribbean 2004;* and *World Statistics Pocketbook.*

The World Bank, 1818 H Street, NW, Washington, DC 20433, (202) 473-1000, Fax: (202) 477-6391, www.worldbank.org; *The World Bank Atlas 2003-2004; World Development Indicators (WDI) 2008;* and *World Development Report 2008.*

World Health Organization (WHO), Avenue Appia 20, 1211 Geneve 27, Switzerland, (Telephone in U.S. (212) 331-9081), www.who.int; The WHO Global Atlas of Infectious Diseases and *World Health Report 2006.*

COSTA RICA - MOTION PICTURES

Palgrave Macmillan Ltd., Houndmills, Basingstoke, Hampshire, RG21 6XS, England, (Telephone in U.S. (888) 330-8477), (Fax in U.S. (800) 672-2054), www.palgrave.com; *The Statesman's Yearbook 2008.*

COSTA RICA - MOTOR VEHICLES

Economist Intelligence Unit, 111 West 57th Street, New York, NY 10019, (212) 554-0600, Fax: (212) 586-1181, www.eiu.com; *Business Latin America.*

Taylor and Francis Group, An Informa Business, 2 Park Square, Milton Park, Abingdon, Oxford OX14 4RN, United Kingdom, (Dial from U.S. (212) 216-7800), (Fax from U.S. (212) 564-7854), www.tandf.co.uk; *The Europa World Year Book.*

United Nations Statistics Division, New York, NY 10017, (800) 253-9646, Fax: (212) 963-4116, http://unstats.un.org; *Statistical Yearbook.*

COSTA RICA - MUSEUMS

M.E. Sharpe, 80 Business Park Drive, Armonk, NY 10504, (800) 541-6563, Fax: (914) 273-2106, www.mesharpe.com; *The Illustrated Book of World Rankings.*

UNESCO Institute for Statistics, C.P. 6128 Succursale Centre-Ville, Montreal, Quebec, H3C 3J7 Canada, (Dial from U.S. (514) 343-6880), (Fax from U.S. (514) 343 6882), www.uis.unesco.org; *Statistical Tables.*

COSTA RICA - NATURAL GAS PRODUCTION

See COSTA RICA - MINERAL INDUSTRIES

COSTA RICA - NUTRITION

United Nations Food and Agricultural Organization (FAO), Viale delle Terme di Caracalla, 00100 Rome, Italy, (Dial from U.S. (202) 653-2400), (Fax from U.S. (202) 653 5760), www.fao.org; *The State of Food and Agriculture (SOFA) 2006.*

United Nations Statistics Division, New York, NY 10017, (800) 253-9646, Fax: (212) 963-4116, http://unstats.un.org; *Statistical Yearbook for Latin America and the Caribbean 2004.*

COSTA RICA - OLDER PEOPLE

M.E. Sharpe, 80 Business Park Drive, Armonk, NY 10504, (800) 541-6563, Fax: (914) 273-2106, www.mesharpe.com; *The Illustrated Book of World Rankings.*

COSTA RICA - PALM OIL PRODUCTION

See COSTA RICA - CROPS

COSTA RICA - PAPER

See COSTA RICA - FORESTS AND FORESTRY

COSTA RICA - PEANUT PRODUCTION

See COSTA RICA - CROPS

COSTA RICA - PESTICIDES

United Nations Food and Agricultural Organization (FAO), Viale delle Terme di Caracalla, 00100 Rome, Italy, (Dial from U.S. (202) 653-2400), (Fax from U.S. (202) 653 5760), www.fao.org; *The State of Food and Agriculture (SOFA) 2006.*

COSTA RICA - PETROLEUM INDUSTRY AND TRADE

Economist Intelligence Unit, 111 West 57th Street, New York, NY 10019, (212) 554-0600, Fax: (212) 586-1181, www.eiu.com; *Business Latin America.*

Inter-American Development Bank (IDB), 1300 New York Avenue, NW, Washington, DC 20577, (202) 623-1000, Fax: (202) 623-3096, www.iadb.org; *The Politics of Policies: Economic and Social Progress in Latin America - 2006 Report.*

M.E. Sharpe, 80 Business Park Drive, Armonk, NY 10504, (800) 541-6563, Fax: (914) 273-2106, www.mesharpe.com; *The Illustrated Book of World Rankings.*

PennWell Corporation, 1421 South Sheridan Road, Tulsa, OK 74112, (918) 835-3161, www.pennwell.com; *International Petroleum Encyclopedia 2007.*

U.S. Department of Energy (DOE), Energy Information Administration (EIA), 1000 Independence Avenue, SW, Washington, DC 20585, (202) 586-8800, www.eia.doe.gov; *International Energy Annual 2004* and *International Energy Outlook 2006.*

United Nations Conference on Trade and Development (UNCTAD), DC2-1120, United Nations, New York, NY 10017, (212) 963-0027, www.unctad.org; *UNCTAD Commodity Yearbook.*

United Nations Food and Agricultural Organization (FAO), Viale delle Terme di Caracalla, 00100 Rome, Italy, (Dial from U.S. (202) 653-2400), (Fax from U.S. (202) 653 5760), www.fao.org; *The State of Food and Agriculture (SOFA) 2006.*

United Nations Statistics Division, New York, NY 10017, (800) 253-9646, Fax: (212) 963-4116, http://unstats.un.org; *Statistical Yearbook.*

COSTA RICA - POLITICAL SCIENCE

Central Intelligence Agency, Office of Public Affairs, Washington, DC 20505, (703) 482-0623, Fax: (703) 482-1739, www.cia.gov; *The World Factbook.*

Inter-American Development Bank (IDB), 1300 New York Avenue, NW, Washington, DC 20577, (202) 623-1000, Fax: (202) 623-3096, www.iadb.org; *The Politics of Policies: Economic and Social Progress in Latin America - 2006 Report.*

International Monetary Fund (IMF), 700 Nineteenth Street, NW, Washington, DC 20431, (202) 623-7000, Fax: (202) 623-4661, www.imf.org; *Government Finance Statistics Yearbook (2008 Edition).*

Palgrave Macmillan Ltd., Houndmills, Basingstoke, Hampshire, RG21 6XS, England, (Telephone in U.S. (888) 330-8477), (Fax in U.S. (800) 672-2054), www.palgrave.com; *The Statesman's Yearbook 2008.*

Taylor and Francis Group, An Informa Business, 2 Park Square, Milton Park, Abingdon, Oxford OX14 4RN, United Kingdom, (Dial from U.S. (212) 216-7800), (Fax from U.S. (212) 564-7854), www.tandf.co.uk; *The Europa World Year Book.*

UCLA Latin American Institute, 10343 Bunche Hall, Box 951447, Los Angeles, CA 90095-1447, (310) 825-4571, Fax: (310) 206-6859, www.international.ucla.edu/lac; *Statistical Abstract of Latin America.*

United Nations Statistics Division, New York, NY 10017, (800) 253-9646, Fax: (212) 963-4116, http://unstats.un.org; *National Accounts Statistics: Compendium of Income Distribution Statistics* and *Statistical Yearbook.*

The World Bank, 1818 H Street, NW, Washington, DC 20433, (202) 473-1000, Fax: (202) 477-6391, www.worldbank.org; *World Development Indicators (WDI) 2008* and *World Development Report 2008.*

COSTA RICA - POPULATION

Central Intelligence Agency, Office of Public Affairs, Washington, DC 20505, (703) 482-0623, Fax: (703) 482-1739, www.cia.gov; *The World Factbook.*

Economist Intelligence Unit, 111 West 57th Street, New York, NY 10019, (212) 554-0600, Fax: (212) 586-1181, www.eiu.com; *Business Latin America* and *Costa Rica Country Report.*

Euromonitor International, Inc., 224 S. Michigan Avenue, Suite 1500, Chicago, IL 60604, (312) 922-1115, Fax: (312) 922-1157, www.euromonitor.com; *International Marketing Data and Statistics 2008* and *The World Economic Factbook 2008.*

Inter-American Development Bank (IDB), 1300 New York Avenue, NW, Washington, DC 20577, (202) 623-1000, Fax: (202) 623-3096, www.iadb.org; *The Politics of Policies: Economic and Social Progress in Latin America - 2006 Report.*

International Labour Office, I.L.O. Publications, 4 route des Morillons, CH-1211 Geneva 22, Switzerland, (Telephone in U.S. (202) 653-7652), (Fax in U.S. (202) 653-7687), www.ilo.org; *Yearbook of Labour Statistics 2006.*

M.E. Sharpe, 80 Business Park Drive, Armonk, NY 10504, (800) 541-6563, Fax: (914) 273-2106, www.mesharpe.com; *The Illustrated Book of World Rankings.*

Organization of American States (OAS), 17th Street Constitution Avenue NW, Washington, DC 20006, (202) 458-3000, www.oas.org; *The OAS in Transition: 1994-2004.*

Palgrave Macmillan Ltd., Houndmills, Basingstoke, Hampshire, RG21 6XS, England, (Telephone in U.S. (888) 330-8477), (Fax in U.S. (800) 672-2054), www.palgrave.com; *The Statesman's Yearbook 2008.*

Taylor and Francis Group, An Informa Business, 2 Park Square, Milton Park, Abingdon, Oxford OX14 4RN, United Kingdom, (Dial from U.S. (212) 216-7800), (Fax from U.S. (212) 564-7854), www.tandf.co.uk; *The Europa World Year Book.*

U.S. Department of State (DOS), 2201 C Street NW, Washington, DC 20520, (202) 647-4000, www.state.gov; *World Military Expenditures and Arms Transfers (WMEAT).*

UCLA Latin American Institute, 10343 Bunche Hall, Box 951447, Los Angeles, CA 90095-1447, (310) 825-4571, Fax: (310) 206-6859, www.international.ucla.edu/lac; *Statistical Abstract of Latin America.*

United Nations Food and Agricultural Organization (FAO), Viale delle Terme di Caracalla, 00100 Rome, Italy, (Dial from U.S. (202) 653-2400), (Fax from U.S. (202) 653 5760), www.fao.org; *FAO Production Yearbook 2002.*

United Nations Statistics Division, New York, NY 10017, (800) 253-9646, Fax: (212) 963-4116, http://unstats.un.org; *Demographic Yearbook; Human Development Report 2006; Statistical Yearbook; Statistical Yearbook for Latin America and the Caribbean 2004;* and *World Statistics Pocketbook.*

The World Bank, 1818 H Street, NW, Washington, DC 20433, (202) 473-1000, Fax: (202) 477-6391, www.worldbank.org; *Costa Rica; The World Bank Atlas 2003-2004;* and *World Development Report 2008.*

World Health Organization (WHO), Avenue Appia 20, 1211 Geneve 27, Switzerland, (Telephone in U.S. (212) 331-9081), www.who.int; *World Health Report 2006.*

COSTA RICA - POPULATION DENSITY

Central Intelligence Agency, Office of Public Affairs, Washington, DC 20505, (703) 482-0623, Fax: (703) 482-1739, www.cia.gov; *The World Factbook.*

Euromonitor International, Inc., 224 S. Michigan Avenue, Suite 1500, Chicago, IL 60604, (312) 922-1115, Fax: (312) 922-1157, www.euromonitor.com; *International Marketing Data and Statistics 2008* and *The World Economic Factbook 2008.*

Inter-American Development Bank (IDB), 1300 New York Avenue, NW, Washington, DC 20577, (202) 623-1000, Fax: (202) 623-3096, www.iadb.org; *The Politics of Policies: Economic and Social Progress in Latin America - 2006 Report.*

M.E. Sharpe, 80 Business Park Drive, Armonk, NY 10504, (800) 541-6563, Fax: (914) 273-2106, www.mesharpe.com; *The Illustrated Book of World Rankings.*

Palgrave Macmillan Ltd., Houndmills, Basingstoke, Hampshire, RG21 6XS, England, (Telephone in U.S. (888) 330-8477), (Fax in U.S. (800) 672-2054), www.palgrave.com; *The Statesman's Yearbook 2008.*

Taylor and Francis Group, An Informa Business, 2 Park Square, Milton Park, Abingdon, Oxford OX14 4RN, United Kingdom, (Dial from U.S. (212) 216-7800), (Fax from U.S. (212) 564-7854), www.tandf.co.uk; *The Europa World Year Book.*

UNESCO Institute for Statistics, C.P. 6128 Succursale Centre-Ville, Montreal, Quebec, H3C 3J7 Canada, (Dial from U.S. (514) 343-6880), (Fax from U.S. (514) 343 6882), www.uis.unesco.org; *Statistical Tables.*

United Nations Food and Agricultural Organization (FAO), Viale delle Terme di Caracalla, 00100 Rome, Italy, (Dial from U.S. (202) 653-2400), (Fax from U.S. (202) 653 5760), www.fao.org; *The State of Food and Agriculture (SOFA) 2006.*

United Nations Statistics Division, New York, NY 10017, (800) 253-9646, Fax: (212) 963-4116, http://unstats.un.org; *Statistical Yearbook.*

The World Bank, 1818 H Street, NW, Washington, DC 20433, (202) 473-1000, Fax: (202) 477-6391, www.worldbank.org; *Costa Rica* and *World Development Report 2008.*

COSTA RICA - POSTAL SERVICE

M.E. Sharpe, 80 Business Park Drive, Armonk, NY 10504, (800) 541-6563, Fax: (914) 273-2106, www.mesharpe.com; *The Illustrated Book of World Rankings.*

COSTA RICA - POWER RESOURCES

Economist Intelligence Unit, 111 West 57th Street, New York, NY 10019, (212) 554-0600, Fax: (212) 586-1181, www.eiu.com; *Business Latin America.*

Euromonitor International, Inc., 224 S. Michigan Avenue, Suite 1500, Chicago, IL 60604, (312) 922-1115, Fax: (312) 922-1157, www.euromonitor.com; *International Marketing Data and Statistics 2008; The World Economic Factbook 2008;* and *World Marketing Data and Statistics.*

M.E. Sharpe, 80 Business Park Drive, Armonk, NY 10504, (800) 541-6563, Fax: (914) 273-2106, www.mesharpe.com; *The Illustrated Book of World Rankings.*

Palgrave Macmillan Ltd., Houndmills, Basingstoke, Hampshire, RG21 6XS, England, (Telephone in U.S. (888) 330-8477), (Fax in U.S. (800) 672-2054), www.palgrave.com; *The Statesman's Yearbook 2008.*

Platts, 2 Penn Plaza, 25th Floor, New York, NY 10121-2298, (212) 904-3070, www.platts.com; *Energy Economist.*

U.S. Department of Energy (DOE), Energy Information Administration (EIA), 1000 Independence Avenue, SW, Washington, DC 20585, (202) 586-8800, www.eia.doe.gov; *International Energy Annual 2004* and *International Energy Outlook 2006.*

UCLA Latin American Institute, 10343 Bunche Hall, Box 951447, Los Angeles, CA 90095-1447, (310) 825-4571, Fax: (310) 206-6859, www.international.ucla.edu/lac; *Statistical Abstract of Latin America.*

United Nations Food and Agricultural Organization (FAO), Viale delle Terme di Caracalla, 00100 Rome, Italy, (Dial from U.S. (202) 653-2400), (Fax from U.S. (202) 653 5760), www.fao.org; *The State of Food and Agriculture (SOFA) 2006.*

United Nations Statistics Division, New York, NY 10017, (800) 253-9646, Fax: (212) 963-4116, http://unstats.un.org; *Energy Statistics Yearbook 2003; Human Development Report 2006; Statistical Yearbook; Statistical Yearbook for Latin America and the Caribbean 2004;* and *World Statistics Pocketbook.*

The World Bank, 1818 H Street, NW, Washington, DC 20433, (202) 473-1000, Fax: (202) 477-6391, www.worldbank.org; *The World Bank Atlas 2003-2004* and *World Development Report 2008.*

COSTA RICA - PRICES

Economist Intelligence Unit, 111 West 57th Street, New York, NY 10019, (212) 554-0600, Fax: (212) 586-1181, www.eiu.com; *Business Latin America.*

Euromonitor International, Inc., 224 S. Michigan Avenue, Suite 1500, Chicago, IL 60604, (312) 922-1115, Fax: (312) 922-1157, www.euromonitor.com; *World Marketing Data and Statistics.*

International Labour Office, I.L.O. Publications, 4 route des Morillons, CH-1211 Geneva 22, Switzerland, (Telephone in U.S. (202) 653-7652), (Fax in U.S. (202) 653-7687), www.ilo.org; *Yearbook of Labour Statistics 2006.*

International Monetary Fund (IMF), 700 Nineteenth Street, NW, Washington, DC 20431, (202) 623-7000, Fax: (202) 623-4661, www.imf.org; *International Financial Statistics Yearbook 2007.*

M.E. Sharpe, 80 Business Park Drive, Armonk, NY 10504, (800) 541-6563, Fax: (914) 273-2106, www.mesharpe.com; *The Illustrated Book of World Rankings.*

Organization of American States (OAS), 17th Street Constitution Avenue NW, Washington, DC 20006, (202) 458-3000, www.oas.org; *The OAS in Transition: 1994-2004.*

UCLA Latin American Institute, 10343 Bunche Hall, Box 951447, Los Angeles, CA 90095-1447, (310) 825-4571, Fax: (310) 206-6859, www.international.ucla.edu/lac; *Statistical Abstract of Latin America.*

United Nations Food and Agricultural Organization (FAO), Viale delle Terme di Caracalla, 00100 Rome, Italy, (Dial from U.S. (202) 653-2400), (Fax from U.S. (202) 653 5760), www.fao.org; *FAO Production Yearbook 2002* and *The State of Food and Agriculture (SOFA) 2006.*

United Nations Statistics Division, New York, NY 10017, (800) 253-9646, Fax: (212) 963-4116, http://unstats.un.org; *Economic Survey of Latin America and the Caribbean 2004-2005* and *Statistical Yearbook for Latin America and the Caribbean 2004.*

The World Bank, 1818 H Street, NW, Washington, DC 20433, (202) 473-1000, Fax: (202) 477-6391, www.worldbank.org; *Costa Rica.*

COSTA RICA - PROFESSIONS

UCLA Latin American Institute, 10343 Bunche Hall, Box 951447, Los Angeles, CA 90095-1447, (310) 825-4571, Fax: (310) 206-6859, www.international.ucla.edu/lac; *Statistical Abstract of Latin America.*

COSTA RICA - PUBLIC HEALTH

Economist Intelligence Unit, 111 West 57th Street, New York, NY 10019, (212) 554-0600, Fax: (212) 586-1181, www.eiu.com; *Business Latin America.*

Euromonitor International, Inc., 224 S. Michigan Avenue, Suite 1500, Chicago, IL 60604, (312) 922-1115, Fax: (312) 922-1157, www.euromonitor.com; *World Marketing Data and Statistics.*

International Monetary Fund (IMF), 700 Nineteenth Street, NW, Washington, DC 20431, (202) 623-7000, Fax: (202) 623-4661, www.imf.org; *Government Finance Statistics Yearbook (2008 Edition).*

M.E. Sharpe, 80 Business Park Drive, Armonk, NY 10504, (800) 541-6563, Fax: (914) 273-2106, www.mesharpe.com; *The Illustrated Book of World Rankings.*

Palgrave Macmillan Ltd., Houndmills, Basingstoke, Hampshire, RG21 6XS, England, (Telephone in U.S. (888) 330-8477), (Fax in U.S. (800) 672-2054), www.palgrave.com; *The Statesman's Yearbook 2008.*

UCLA Latin American Institute, 10343 Bunche Hall, Box 951447, Los Angeles, CA 90095-1447, (310) 825-4571, Fax: (310) 206-6859, www.international.ucla.edu/lac; *Statistical Abstract of Latin America.*

UNICEF, 3 United Nations Plaza, New York, NY 10017, (800) 253-9646, Fax: (212) 887-7465, www.unicef.org; *The State of the World's Children 2008.*

United Nations Statistics Division, New York, NY 10017, (800) 253-9646, Fax: (212) 963-4116, http://unstats.un.org; *Human Development Report 2006* and *Statistical Yearbook.*

The World Bank, 1818 H Street, NW, Washington, DC 20433, (202) 473-1000, Fax: (202) 477-6391, www.worldbank.org; *Costa Rica* and *World Development Report 2008.*

World Health Organization (WHO), Avenue Appia 20, 1211 Geneve 27, Switzerland, (Telephone in U.S. (212) 331-9081), www.who.int; The WHO Global Atlas of Infectious Diseases and *World Health Report 2006.*

COSTA RICA - PUBLIC UTILITIES

UCLA Latin American Institute, 10343 Bunche Hall, Box 951447, Los Angeles, CA 90095-1447, (310) 825-4571, Fax: (310) 206-6859, www.international.ucla.edu/lac; *Statistical Abstract of Latin America.*

COSTA RICA - PUBLISHERS AND PUBLISHING

UNESCO Institute for Statistics, C.P. 6128 Succursale Centre-Ville, Montreal, Quebec, H3C 3J7 Canada, (Dial from U.S. (514) 343-6880), (Fax from U.S. (514) 343 6882), www.uis.unesco.org; *Statistical Tables.*

COSTA RICA - RADIO BROADCASTING

Palgrave Macmillan Ltd., Houndmills, Basingstoke, Hampshire, RG21 6XS, England, (Telephone in U.S. (888) 330-8477), (Fax in U.S. (800) 672-2054), www.palgrave.com; *The Statesman's Yearbook 2008.*

COSTA RICA - RAILROADS

Economist Intelligence Unit, 111 West 57th Street, New York, NY 10019, (212) 554-0600, Fax: (212) 586-1181, www.eiu.com; *Business Latin America.*

Jane's Information Group, 110 North Royal Street, Suite 200, Alexandria, VA 22314, (703) 683-3700, Fax: (800) 836-0297, www.janes.com; *Jane's World Railways.*

Palgrave Macmillan Ltd., Houndmills, Basingstoke, Hampshire, RG21 6XS, England, (Telephone in U.S. (888) 330-8477), (Fax in U.S. (800) 672-2054), www.palgrave.com; *The Statesman's Yearbook 2008.*

Taylor and Francis Group, An Informa Business, 2 Park Square, Milton Park, Abingdon, Oxford OX14 4RN, United Kingdom, (Dial from U.S. (212) 216-7800), (Fax from U.S. (212) 564-7854), www.tandf.co.uk; *The Europa World Year Book.*

United Nations Statistics Division, New York, NY 10017, (800) 253-9646, Fax: (212) 963-4116, http://unstats.un.org; *Statistical Yearbook.*

COSTA RICA - RANCHING

UCLA Latin American Institute, 10343 Bunche Hall, Box 951447, Los Angeles, CA 90095-1447, (310) 825-4571, Fax: (310) 206-6859, www.international.ucla.edu/lac; *Statistical Abstract of Latin America.*

COSTA RICA - RELIGION

Central Intelligence Agency, Office of Public Affairs, Washington, DC 20505, (703) 482-0623, Fax: (703) 482-1739, www.cia.gov; *The World Factbook.*

M.E. Sharpe, 80 Business Park Drive, Armonk, NY 10504, (800) 541-6563, Fax: (914) 273-2106, www.mesharpe.com; *The Illustrated Book of World Rankings.*

Palgrave Macmillan Ltd., Houndmills, Basingstoke, Hampshire, RG21 6XS, England, (Telephone in U.S. (888) 330-8477), (Fax in U.S. (800) 672-2054), www.palgrave.com; *The Statesman's Yearbook 2008.*

UCLA Latin American Institute, 10343 Bunche Hall, Box 951447, Los Angeles, CA 90095-1447, (310) 825-4571, Fax: (310) 206-6859, www.international.ucla.edu/lac; *Statistical Abstract of Latin America.*

COSTA RICA - RENT CHARGES

International Labour Office, I.L.O. Publications, 4 route des Morillons, CH-1211 Geneva 22, Switzerland, (Telephone in U.S. (202) 653-7652), (Fax in U.S. (202) 653-7687), www.ilo.org; *Yearbook of Labour Statistics 2006.*

COSTA RICA - RESERVES (ACCOUNTING)

Economist Intelligence Unit, 111 West 57th Street, New York, NY 10019, (212) 554-0600, Fax: (212) 586-1181, www.eiu.com; *Business Latin America.*

Euromonitor International, Inc., 224 S. Michigan Avenue, Suite 1500, Chicago, IL 60604, (312) 922-1115, Fax: (312) 922-1157, www.euromonitor.com; *International Marketing Data and Statistics 2008.*

Inter-American Development Bank (IDB), 1300 New York Avenue, NW, Washington, DC 20577, (202) 623-1000, Fax: (202) 623-3096, www.iadb.org; *The Politics of Policies: Economic and Social Progress in Latin America - 2006 Report.*

Organization of American States (OAS), 17th Street Constitution Avenue NW, Washington, DC 20006, (202) 458-3000, www.oas.org; *The OAS in Transition: 1994-2004.*

The World Bank, 1818 H Street, NW, Washington, DC 20433, (202) 473-1000, Fax: (202) 477-6391, www.worldbank.org; *World Development Indicators (WDI) 2008.*

COSTA RICA - RETAIL TRADE

Banque de France, 48 rue Croix des Petits champs, 75001 Paris, France, www.banque-france.fr/home.htm; *Monthly Business Survey Overview.*

Economist Intelligence Unit, 111 West 57th Street, New York, NY 10019, (212) 554-0600, Fax: (212) 586-1181, www.eiu.com; *Business Latin America.*

Euromonitor International, Inc., 224 S. Michigan Avenue, Suite 1500, Chicago, IL 60604, (312) 922-1115, Fax: (312) 922-1157, www.euromonitor.com; *World Marketing Data and Statistics.*

Inter-American Development Bank (IDB), 1300 New York Avenue, NW, Washington, DC 20577, (202) 623-1000, Fax: (202) 623-3096, www.iadb.org; *The Politics of Policies: Economic and Social Progress in Latin America - 2006 Report.*

M.E. Sharpe, 80 Business Park Drive, Armonk, NY 10504, (800) 541-6563, Fax: (914) 273-2106, www.mesharpe.com; *The Illustrated Book of World Rankings.*

COSTA RICA - RICE TRADE

United Nations Statistics Division, New York, NY 10017, (800) 253-9646, Fax: (212) 963-4116, http://unstats.un.org; *Statistical Yearbook.*

COSTA RICA - ROADS

Central Intelligence Agency, Office of Public Affairs, Washington, DC 20505, (703) 482-0623, Fax: (703) 482-1739, www.cia.gov; *The World Factbook.*

Economist Intelligence Unit, 111 West 57th Street, New York, NY 10019, (212) 554-0600, Fax: (212) 586-1181, www.eiu.com; *Business Latin America.*

International Road Federation (IFR), Madison Place, 500 Montgomery Street, 5th Floor, Alexandria, VA 22314, (703) 535-1001, Fax: (703) 535-1007, www.irfnet.org; *World Road Statistics 2006.*

Palgrave Macmillan Ltd., Houndmills, Basingstoke, Hampshire, RG21 6XS, England, (Telephone in U.S. (888) 330-8477), (Fax in U.S. (800) 672-2054), www.palgrave.com; *The Statesman's Yearbook 2008.*

COSTA RICA - RUBBER INDUSTRY AND TRADE

International Rubber Study Group (IRSG), 1st Floor, Heron House, 109/115 Wembley Hill Road, Wembley, Middlesex HA9 8DA, United Kingdom, www.rubberstudy.com; *Rubber Statistical Bulletin; Summary of World Rubber Statistics 2005; World Rubber Statistics Handbook (Volume 6, 1975-2001);* and *World Rubber Statistics Historic Handbook.*

M.E. Sharpe, 80 Business Park Drive, Armonk, NY 10504, (800) 541-6563, Fax: (914) 273-2106, www.mesharpe.com; *The Illustrated Book of World Rankings.*

COSTA RICA - SALT PRODUCTION

See COSTA RICA - MINERAL INDUSTRIES

COSTA RICA - SHEEP

See COSTA RICA - LIVESTOCK

COSTA RICA - SHIPPING

Palgrave Macmillan Ltd., Houndmills, Basingstoke, Hampshire, RG21 6XS, England, (Telephone in U.S. (888) 330-8477), (Fax in U.S. (800) 672-2054), www.palgrave.com; *The Statesman's Yearbook 2008.*

Taylor and Francis Group, An Informa Business, 2 Park Square, Milton Park, Abingdon, Oxford OX14 4RN, United Kingdom, (Dial from U.S. (212) 216-7800), (Fax from U.S. (212) 564-7854), www.tandf.co.uk; *The Europa World Year Book.*

United Nations Statistics Division, New York, NY 10017, (800) 253-9646, Fax: (212) 963-4116, http://unstats.un.org; *Statistical Yearbook.*

COSTA RICA - SILVER PRODUCTION

See COSTA RICA - MINERAL INDUSTRIES

COSTA RICA - SOCIAL ECOLOGY

M.E. Sharpe, 80 Business Park Drive, Armonk, NY 10504, (800) 541-6563, Fax: (914) 273-2106, www.mesharpe.com; *The Illustrated Book of World Rankings.*

UCLA Latin American Institute, 10343 Bunche Hall, Box 951447, Los Angeles, CA 90095-1447, (310) 825-4571, Fax: (310) 206-6859, www.international.ucla.edu/lac; *Statistical Abstract of Latin America.*

United Nations Statistics Division, New York, NY 10017, (800) 253-9646, Fax: (212) 963-4116, http://unstats.un.org; *World Statistics Pocketbook.*

COSTA RICA - SOCIAL SECURITY

Inter-American Development Bank (IDB), 1300 New York Avenue, NW, Washington, DC 20577, (202) 623-1000, Fax: (202) 623-3096, www.iadb.org; *The Politics of Policies: Economic and Social Progress in Latin America - 2006 Report.*

International Monetary Fund (IMF), 700 Nineteenth Street, NW, Washington, DC 20431, (202) 623-

7000, Fax: (202) 623-4661, www.imf.org; *Government Finance Statistics Yearbook (2008 Edition).*

United Nations Statistics Division, New York, NY 10017, (800) 253-9646, Fax: (212) 963-4116, http://unstats.un.org; *National Accounts Statistics: Compendium of Income Distribution Statistics.*

COSTA RICA - SOYBEAN PRODUCTION

See COSTA RICA - CROPS

COSTA RICA - STEEL PRODUCTION

See COSTA RICA - MINERAL INDUSTRIES

COSTA RICA - SUGAR PRODUCTION

See COSTA RICA - CROPS

COSTA RICA - TAXATION

Inter-American Development Bank (IDB), 1300 New York Avenue, NW, Washington, DC 20577, (202) 623-1000, Fax: (202) 623-3096, www.iadb.org; *The Politics of Policies: Economic and Social Progress in Latin America - 2006 Report.*

International Monetary Fund (IMF), 700 Nineteenth Street, NW, Washington, DC 20431, (202) 623-7000, Fax: (202) 623-4661, www.imf.org; *Government Finance Statistics Yearbook (2008 Edition).*

International Road Federation (IFR), Madison Place, 500 Montgomery Street, 5th Floor, Alexandria, VA 22314, (703) 535-1001, Fax: (703) 535-1007, www.irfnet.org; *World Road Statistics 2006.*

Palgrave Macmillan Ltd., Houndmills, Basingstoke, Hampshire, RG21 6XS, England, (Telephone in U.S. (888) 330-8477), (Fax in U.S. (800) 672-2054), www.palgrave.com; *The Statesman's Yearbook 2008.*

Taylor and Francis Group, An Informa Business, 2 Park Square, Milton Park, Abingdon, Oxford OX14 4RN, United Kingdom, (Dial from U.S. (212) 216-7800), (Fax from U.S. (212) 564-7854), www.tandf.co.uk; *The Europa World Year Book.*

United Nations Statistics Division, New York, NY 10017, (800) 253-9646, Fax: (212) 963-4116, http://unstats.un.org; *Statistical Yearbook for Latin America and the Caribbean 2004.*

The World Bank, 1818 H Street, NW, Washington, DC 20433, (202) 473-1000, Fax: (202) 477-6391, www.worldbank.org; *World Development Indicators (WDI) 2008.*

COSTA RICA - TELEPHONE

Economist Intelligence Unit, 111 West 57th Street, New York, NY 10019, (212) 554-0600, Fax: (212) 586-1181, www.eiu.com; *Business Latin America.*

International Telecommunication Union (ITU), Place des Nations, 1211 Geneva 20, Switzerland, www.itu.int; World Telecommunication Indicators Database.

Palgrave Macmillan Ltd., Houndmills, Basingstoke, Hampshire, RG21 6XS, England, (Telephone in U.S. (888) 330-8477), (Fax in U.S. (800) 672-2054), www.palgrave.com; *The Statesman's Yearbook 2008.*

Taylor and Francis Group, An Informa Business, 2 Park Square, Milton Park, Abingdon, Oxford OX14 4RN, United Kingdom, (Dial from U.S. (212) 216-7800), (Fax from U.S. (212) 564-7854), www.tandf.co.uk; *The Europa World Year Book.*

United Nations Statistics Division, New York, NY 10017, (800) 253-9646, Fax: (212) 963-4116, http://unstats.un.org; *Statistical Yearbook* and *World Statistics Pocketbook.*

COSTA RICA - TEXTILE INDUSTRY

M.E. Sharpe, 80 Business Park Drive, Armonk, NY 10504, (800) 541-6563, Fax: (914) 273-2106, www.mesharpe.com; *The Illustrated Book of World Rankings.*

Palgrave Macmillan Ltd., Houndmills, Basingstoke, Hampshire, RG21 6XS, England, (Telephone in U.S. (888) 330-8477), (Fax in U.S. (800) 672-2054), www.palgrave.com; *The Statesman's Yearbook 2008.*

United Nations Conference on Trade and Development (UNCTAD), DC2-1120, United Nations, New York, NY 10017, (212) 963-0027, www.unctad.org; *UNCTAD Commodity Yearbook.*

COSTA RICA - THEATER

UNESCO Institute for Statistics, C.P. 6128 Succursale Centre-Ville, Montreal, Quebec, H3C 3J7 Canada, (Dial from U.S. (514) 343-6880), (Fax from U.S. (514) 343 6882), www.uis.unesco.org; *Statistical Tables.*

COSTA RICA - TOBACCO INDUSTRY

Foreign Agricultural Service (FAS), U.S. Department of Agriculture (USDA), 1400 Independence Avenue, SW, Washington, DC 20250, (202) 720-3935, www.fas.usda.gov; *Tobacco: World Markets and Trade.*

M.E. Sharpe, 80 Business Park Drive, Armonk, NY 10504, (800) 541-6563, Fax: (914) 273-2106, www.mesharpe.com; *The Illustrated Book of World Rankings.*

United Nations Statistics Division, New York, NY 10017, (800) 253-9646, Fax: (212) 963-4116, http://unstats.un.org; *Statistical Yearbook.*

COSTA RICA - TOURISM

Economist Intelligence Unit, 111 West 57th Street, New York, NY 10019, (212) 554-0600, Fax: (212) 586-1181, www.eiu.com; *Business Latin America.*

Euromonitor International, Inc., 224 S. Michigan Avenue, Suite 1500, Chicago, IL 60604, (312) 922-1115, Fax: (312) 922-1157, www.euromonitor.com; *The World Economic Factbook 2008* and *World Marketing Data and Statistics.*

M.E. Sharpe, 80 Business Park Drive, Armonk, NY 10504, (800) 541-6563, Fax: (914) 273-2106, www.mesharpe.com; *The Illustrated Book of World Rankings.*

Organization of American States (OAS), 17th Street Constitution Avenue NW, Washington, DC 20006, (202) 458-3000, www.oas.org; *The OAS in Transition: 1994-2004.*

Palgrave Macmillan Ltd., Houndmills, Basingstoke, Hampshire, RG21 6XS, England, (Telephone in U.S. (888) 330-8477), (Fax in U.S. (800) 672-2054), www.palgrave.com; *The Statesman's Yearbook 2008.*

Taylor and Francis Group, An Informa Business, 2 Park Square, Milton Park, Abingdon, Oxford OX14 4RN, United Kingdom, (Dial from U.S. (212) 216-7800), (Fax from U.S. (212) 564-7854), www.tandf.co.uk; *The Europa World Year Book.*

UCLA Latin American Institute, 10343 Bunche Hall, Box 951447, Los Angeles, CA 90095-1447, (310) 825-4571, Fax: (310) 206-6859, www.international.ucla.edu/lac; *Statistical Abstract of Latin America.*

United Nations Statistics Division, New York, NY 10017, (800) 253-9646, Fax: (212) 963-4116, http://unstats.un.org; *Statistical Yearbook* and *Statistical Yearbook for Latin America and the Caribbean 2004.*

United Nations World Tourism Organization (UNWTO), Capitan Haya 42, 28020 Madrid, Spain, www.world-tourism.org; *Yearbook of Tourism Statistics.*

The World Bank, 1818 H Street, NW, Washington, DC 20433, (202) 473-1000, Fax: (202) 477-6391, www.worldbank.org; *Costa Rica.*

COSTA RICA - TRADE

See COSTA RICA - INTERNATIONAL TRADE

COSTA RICA - TRANSPORTATION

Central Intelligence Agency, Office of Public Affairs, Washington, DC 20505, (703) 482-0623, Fax: (703) 482-1739, www.cia.gov; *The World Factbook.*

Economist Intelligence Unit, 111 West 57th Street, New York, NY 10019, (212) 554-0600, Fax: (212) 586-1181, www.eiu.com; *Business Latin America.*

Euromonitor International, Inc., 224 S. Michigan Avenue, Suite 1500, Chicago, IL 60604, (312) 922-1115, Fax: (312) 922-1157, www.euromonitor.com; *International Marketing Data and Statistics 2008* and *World Marketing Data and Statistics.*

Inter-American Development Bank (IDB), 1300 New York Avenue, NW, Washington, DC 20577, (202) 623-1000, Fax: (202) 623-3096, www.iadb.org; *The Politics of Policies: Economic and Social Progress in Latin America - 2006 Report.*

M.E. Sharpe, 80 Business Park Drive, Armonk, NY 10504, (800) 541-6563, Fax: (914) 273-2106, www.mesharpe.com; *The Illustrated Book of World Rankings.*

Palgrave Macmillan Ltd., Houndmills, Basingstoke, Hampshire, RG21 6XS, England, (Telephone in U.S. (888) 330-8477), (Fax in U.S. (800) 672-2054), www.palgrave.com; *The Statesman's Yearbook 2008.*

Taylor and Francis Group, An Informa Business, 2 Park Square, Milton Park, Abingdon, Oxford OX14 4RN, United Kingdom, (Dial from U.S. (212) 216-7800), (Fax from U.S. (212) 564-7854), www.tandf.co.uk; *The Europa World Year Book.*

UCLA Latin American Institute, 10343 Bunche Hall, Box 951447, Los Angeles, CA 90095-1447, (310) 825-4571, Fax: (310) 206-6859, www.international.ucla.edu/lac; *Statistical Abstract of Latin America.*

United Nations Statistics Division, New York, NY 10017, (800) 253-9646, Fax: (212) 963-4116, http://unstats.un.org; *Human Development Report 2006* and *Statistical Yearbook for Latin America and the Caribbean 2004.*

The World Bank, 1818 H Street, NW, Washington, DC 20433, (202) 473-1000, Fax: (202) 477-6391, www.worldbank.org; *Costa Rica.*

COSTA RICA - UNEMPLOYMENT

Central Intelligence Agency, Office of Public Affairs, Washington, DC 20505, (703) 482-0623, Fax: (703) 482-1739, www.cia.gov; *The World Factbook.*

Economist Intelligence Unit, 111 West 57th Street, New York, NY 10019, (212) 554-0600, Fax: (212) 586-1181, www.eiu.com; *Business Latin America.*

Euromonitor International, Inc., 224 S. Michigan Avenue, Suite 1500, Chicago, IL 60604, (312) 922-1115, Fax: (312) 922-1157, www.euromonitor.com; *International Marketing Data and Statistics 2008.*

International Labour Office, I.L.O. Publications, 4 route des Morillons, CH-1211 Geneva 22, Switzerland, (Telephone in U.S. (202) 653-7652), (Fax in U.S. (202) 653-7687), www.ilo.org; *Yearbook of Labour Statistics 2006.*

UCLA Latin American Institute, 10343 Bunche Hall, Box 951447, Los Angeles, CA 90095-1447, (310) 825-4571, Fax: (310) 206-6859, www.international.ucla.edu/lac; *Statistical Abstract of Latin America.*

United Nations Statistics Division, New York, NY 10017, (800) 253-9646, Fax: (212) 963-4116, http://unstats.un.org; *Statistical Yearbook.*

COSTA RICA - VITAL STATISTICS

Euromonitor International, Inc., 224 S. Michigan Avenue, Suite 1500, Chicago, IL 60604, (312) 922-1115, Fax: (312) 922-1157, www.euromonitor.com; *International Marketing Data and Statistics 2008.*

United Nations Statistics Division, New York, NY 10017, (800) 253-9646, Fax: (212) 963-4116, http://unstats.un.org; *Statistical Yearbook.*

World Health Organization (WHO), Avenue Appia 20, 1211 Geneve 27, Switzerland, (Telephone in U.S. (212) 331-9081), www.who.int; *World Health Report 2006.*

COSTA RICA - WAGES

International Labour Office, I.L.O. Publications, 4 route des Morillons, CH-1211 Geneva 22, Switzerland, (Telephone in U.S. (202) 653-7652), (Fax in U.S. (202) 653-7687), www.ilo.org; *Yearbook of Labour Statistics 2006.*

Organization of American States (OAS), 17th Street Constitution Avenue NW, Washington, DC 20006, (202) 458-3000, www.oas.org; *The OAS in Transition: 1994-2004.*

UCLA Latin American Institute, 10343 Bunche Hall, Box 951447, Los Angeles, CA 90095-1447, (310) 825-4571, Fax: (310) 206-6859, www.international.ucla.edu/lac; *Statistical Abstract of Latin America.*

The World Bank, 1818 H Street, NW, Washington, DC 20433, (202) 473-1000, Fax: (202) 477-6391, www.worldbank.org; *Costa Rica.*

COSTA RICA - WEATHER

See COSTA RICA - CLIMATE

COSTA RICA - WELFARE STATE

Inter-American Development Bank (IDB), 1300 New York Avenue, NW, Washington, DC 20577, (202) 623-1000, Fax: (202) 623-3096, www.iadb.org; *The Politics of Policies: Economic and Social Progress in Latin America - 2006 Report.*

International Monetary Fund (IMF), 700 Nineteenth Street, NW, Washington, DC 20431, (202) 623-7000, Fax: (202) 623-4661, www.imf.org; *Government Finance Statistics Yearbook (2008 Edition).*

COSTA RICA - WHEAT PRODUCTION

See COSTA RICA - CROPS

COSTA RICA - WHOLESALE PRICE INDEXES

Inter-American Development Bank (IDB), 1300 New York Avenue, NW, Washington, DC 20577, (202) 623-1000, Fax: (202) 623-3096, www.iadb.org; *The Politics of Policies: Economic and Social Progress in Latin America - 2006 Report.*

International Monetary Fund (IMF), 700 Nineteenth Street, NW, Washington, DC 20431, (202) 623-7000, Fax: (202) 623-4661, www.imf.org; *International Financial Statistics Yearbook 2007.*

Organization of American States (OAS), 17th Street Constitution Avenue NW, Washington, DC 20006, (202) 458-3000, www.oas.org; *The OAS in Transition: 1994-2004.*

United Nations Statistics Division, New York, NY 10017, (800) 253-9646, Fax: (212) 963-4116, http://unstats.un.org; *Statistical Yearbook.*

COSTA RICA - WHOLESALE TRADE

Inter-American Development Bank (IDB), 1300 New York Avenue, NW, Washington, DC 20577, (202) 623-1000, Fax: (202) 623-3096, www.iadb.org; *The Politics of Policies: Economic and Social Progress in Latin America - 2006 Report.*

COSTA RICA - WINE PRODUCTION

See COSTA RICA - BEVERAGE INDUSTRY

COSTA RICA - WOOL PRODUCTION

See COSTA RICA - TEXTILE INDUSTRY

COSTUME JEWELRY AND NOTIONS - MANUFACTURING - EARNINGS

U.S. Census Bureau, Manufacturing and Construction Division, 4600 Silver Hill Road, Washington DC 20233, (301) 763-4673, www.census.gov/mcd; *Annual Survey of Manufactures (ASM)* and *Census of Manufactures.*

COSTUME JEWELRY AND NOTIONS - MANUFACTURING - EMPLOYEES

U.S. Census Bureau, Manufacturing and Construction Division, 4600 Silver Hill Road, Washington DC 20233, (301) 763-4673, www.census.gov/mcd; *Annual Survey of Manufactures (ASM)* and *Census of Manufactures.*

COTE D'IVOIRE - NATIONAL STATISTICAL OFFICE

Institut National de la Statistique, V 55, Abidjan 01, Cote d'Ivoire, www.ins.ci; National Data Center.

COTE D'IVOIRE - PRIMARY STATISTICS SOURCES

Institut National de la Statistique, V 55, Abidjan 01, Cote d'Ivoire, www.ins.ci; *Bulletin Mensuel de la Statistique* (Monthly Bulletin of Statistics).

COTE d'IVOIRE - AGRICULTURAL MACHINERY

United Nations Statistics Division, New York, NY 10017, (800) 253-9646, Fax: (212) 963-4116, http://unstats.un.org; *Statistical Yearbook.*

COTE d'IVOIRE - AGRICULTURE

Economist Intelligence Unit, 111 West 57th Street, New York, NY 10019, (212) 554-0600, Fax: (212) 586-1181, www.eiu.com; *Cote d'Ivoire Country Report.*

Euromonitor International, Inc., 224 S. Michigan Avenue, Suite 1500, Chicago, IL 60604, (312) 922-1115, Fax: (312) 922-1157, www.euromonitor.com; *International Marketing Data and Statistics 2008* and *World Marketing Data and Statistics.*

M.E. Sharpe, 80 Business Park Drive, Armonk, NY 10504, (800) 541-6563, Fax: (914) 273-2106, www.mesharpe.com; *The Illustrated Book of World Rankings.*

Palgrave Macmillan Ltd., Houndmills, Basingstoke, Hampshire, RG21 6XS, England, (Telephone in U.S. (888) 330-8477), (Fax in U.S. (800) 672-2054), www.palgrave.com; *The Statesman's Yearbook 2008.*

Taylor and Francis Group, An Informa Business, 2 Park Square, Milton Park, Abingdon, Oxford OX14 4RN, United Kingdom, (Dial from U.S. (212) 216-7800), (Fax from U.S. (212) 564-7854), www.tandf.co.uk; *The Europa World Year Book.*

United Nations Conference on Trade and Development (UNCTAD), DC2-1120, United Nations, New York, NY 10017, (212) 963-0027, www.unctad.org; *UNCTAD Commodity Yearbook.*

United Nations Economic Commission for Africa (ECA), PO Box 3001, Addis Ababa, Ethiopia, (Telephone in U.S. (212) 963-4957), www.uneca.org; *African Statistical Yearbook 2006.*

United Nations Food and Agricultural Organization (FAO), Viale delle Terme di Caracalla, 00100 Rome, Italy, (Dial from U.S. (202) 653-2400), (Fax from U.S. (202) 653 5760), www.fao.org; AQUASTAT; *FAO Production Yearbook 2002; FAO Trade Yearbook;* and *The State of Food and Agriculture (SOFA) 2006.*

United Nations Statistics Division, New York, NY 10017, (800) 253-9646, Fax: (212) 963-4116, http://unstats.un.org; *Statistical Yearbook* and *Survey of Economic and Social Conditions in Africa 2005.*

The World Bank, 1818 H Street, NW, Washington, DC 20433, (202) 473-1000, Fax: (202) 477-6391, www.worldbank.org; *Africa Live Database (LDB); African Development Indicators (ADI) 2007; Cote d'Ivoire;* and *World Development Indicators (WDI) 2008.*

COTE d'IVOIRE - AIRLINES

M.E. Sharpe, 80 Business Park Drive, Armonk, NY 10504, (800) 541-6563, Fax: (914) 273-2106, www.mesharpe.com; *The Illustrated Book of World Rankings.*

Palgrave Macmillan Ltd., Houndmills, Basingstoke, Hampshire, RG21 6XS, England, (Telephone in U.S. (888) 330-8477), (Fax in U.S. (800) 672-2054), www.palgrave.com; *The Statesman's Yearbook 2008.*

Taylor and Francis Group, An Informa Business, 2 Park Square, Milton Park, Abingdon, Oxford OX14 4RN, United Kingdom, (Dial from U.S. (212) 216-7800), (Fax from U.S. (212) 564-7854), www.tandf.co.uk; *The Europa World Year Book.*

United Nations Economic Commission for Africa (ECA), PO Box 3001, Addis Ababa, Ethiopia, (Telephone in U.S. (212) 963-4957), www.uneca.org; *African Statistical Yearbook 2006.*

United Nations Statistics Division, New York, NY 10017, (800) 253-9646, Fax: (212) 963-4116, http://unstats.un.org; *Statistical Yearbook.*

COTE d'IVOIRE - AIRPORTS

Central Intelligence Agency, Office of Public Affairs, Washington, DC 20505, (703) 482-0623, Fax: (703) 482-1739, www.cia.gov; *The World Factbook.*

COTE d'IVOIRE - ALUMINUM PRODUCTION

See COTE d'IVOIRE - MINERAL INDUSTRIES

COTE d'IVOIRE - ARMED FORCES

Central Intelligence Agency, Office of Public Affairs, Washington, DC 20505, (703) 482-0623, Fax: (703) 482-1739, www.cia.gov; *The World Factbook.*

Euromonitor International, Inc., 224 S. Michigan Avenue, Suite 1500, Chicago, IL 60604, (312) 922-1115, Fax: (312) 922-1157, www.euromonitor.com; *World Marketing Data and Statistics.*

International Institute for Strategic Studies (IISS), Arundel House, 13-15 Arundel Street, Temple Place, London WC2R 3DX, England, www.iiss.org; *The Military Balance 2007.*

Palgrave Macmillan Ltd., Houndmills, Basingstoke, Hampshire, RG21 6XS, England, (Telephone in U.S. (888) 330-8477), (Fax in U.S. (800) 672-2054), www.palgrave.com; *The Statesman's Yearbook 2008.*

U.S. Department of State (DOS), 2201 C Street NW, Washington, DC 20520, (202) 647-4000, www.state.gov; *World Military Expenditures and Arms Transfers (WMEAT).*

United Nations Statistics Division, New York, NY 10017, (800) 253-9646, Fax: (212) 963-4116, http://unstats.un.org; *Human Development Report 2006.*

COTE d'IVOIRE - AUTOMOBILE INDUSTRY AND TRADE

United Nations Statistics Division, New York, NY 10017, (800) 253-9646, Fax: (212) 963-4116, http://unstats.un.org; *Statistical Yearbook.*

COTE d'IVOIRE - BALANCE OF PAYMENTS

African Development Bank Group, Rue Joseph Anoma, 01 BP 1387 Abidjan 01, Cote d'Ivoire, www.afdb.org; *Statistics Pocketbook 2008.*

International Monetary Fund (IMF), 700 Nineteenth Street, NW, Washington, DC 20431, (202) 623-7000, Fax: (202) 623-4661, www.imf.org; *Balance of Payments Statistics Newsletter* and *Balance of Payments Statistics Yearbook 2007.*

Taylor and Francis Group, An Informa Business, 2 Park Square, Milton Park, Abingdon, Oxford OX14 4RN, United Kingdom, (Dial from U.S. (212) 216-7800), (Fax from U.S. (212) 564-7854), www.tandf.co.uk; *The Europa World Year Book.*

United Nations Conference on Trade and Development (UNCTAD), DC2-1120, United Nations, New York, NY 10017, (212) 963-0027, www.unctad.org; *Handbook of Statistics 2005.*

United Nations Economic Commission for Africa (ECA), PO Box 3001, Addis Ababa, Ethiopia, (Telephone in U.S. (212) 963-4957), www.uneca.org; *African Statistical Yearbook 2006.*

The World Bank, 1818 H Street, NW, Washington, DC 20433, (202) 473-1000, Fax: (202) 477-6391, www.worldbank.org; *Cote d'Ivoire; World Development Indicators (WDI) 2008;* and *World Development Report 2008.*

COTE d'IVOIRE - BANKS AND BANKING

Euromonitor International, Inc., 224 S. Michigan Avenue, Suite 1500, Chicago, IL 60604, (312) 922-1115, Fax: (312) 922-1157, www.euromonitor.com; *World Marketing Data and Statistics.*

M.E. Sharpe, 80 Business Park Drive, Armonk, NY 10504, (800) 541-6563, Fax: (914) 273-2106, www.mesharpe.com; *The Illustrated Book of World Rankings.*

Palgrave Macmillan Ltd., Houndmills, Basingstoke, Hampshire, RG21 6XS, England, (Telephone in U.S. (888) 330-8477), (Fax in U.S. (800) 672-2054), www.palgrave.com; *The Statesman's Yearbook 2008.*

Taylor and Francis Group, An Informa Business, 2 Park Square, Milton Park, Abingdon, Oxford OX14 4RN, United Kingdom, (Dial from U.S. (212) 216-

7800), (Fax from U.S. (212) 564-7854), www.tandf.co.uk; *The Europa World Year Book.*

United Nations Economic Commission for Africa (ECA), PO Box 3001, Addis Ababa, Ethiopia, (Telephone in U.S. (212) 963-4957), www.uneca.org; *African Statistical Yearbook 2006.*

United Nations Statistics Division, New York, NY 10017, (800) 253-9646, Fax: (212) 963-4116, http://unstats.un.org; *Statistical Yearbook.*

COTE d'IVOIRE - BARLEY PRODUCTION

See COTE d'IVOIRE - CROPS

COTE d'IVOIRE - BEVERAGE INDUSTRY

M.E. Sharpe, 80 Business Park Drive, Armonk, NY 10504, (800) 541-6563, Fax: (914) 273-2106, www.mesharpe.com; *The Illustrated Book of World Rankings.*

United Nations Statistics Division, New York, NY 10017, (800) 253-9646, Fax: (212) 963-4116, http://unstats.un.org; *Statistical Yearbook.*

COTE d'IVOIRE - BROADCASTING

Central Intelligence Agency, Office of Public Affairs, Washington, DC 20505, (703) 482-0623, Fax: (703) 482-1739, www.cia.gov; *The World Factbook.*

Euromonitor International, Inc., 224 S. Michigan Avenue, Suite 1500, Chicago, IL 60604, (312) 922-1115, Fax: (312) 922-1157, www.euromonitor.com; *World Marketing Data and Statistics.*

M.E. Sharpe, 80 Business Park Drive, Armonk, NY 10504, (800) 541-6563, Fax: (914) 273-2106, www.mesharpe.com; *The Illustrated Book of World Rankings.*

Palgrave Macmillan Ltd., Houndmills, Basingstoke, Hampshire, RG21 6XS, England, (Telephone in U.S. (888) 330-8477), (Fax in U.S. (800) 672-2054), www.palgrave.com; *The Statesman's Yearbook 2008.*

UNESCO Institute for Statistics, C.P. 6128 Succursale Centre-Ville, Montreal, Quebec, H3C 3J7 Canada, (Dial from U.S. (514) 343-6880), (Fax from U.S. (514) 343 6882), www.uis.unesco.org; *Statistical Tables.*

WRTH Publications Limited, PO Box 290, Oxford OX2 7FT, UK, www.wrth.com; *World Radio TV Handbook 2007.*

COTE d'IVOIRE - BUDGET

Central Intelligence Agency, Office of Public Affairs, Washington, DC 20505, (703) 482-0623, Fax: (703) 482-1739, www.cia.gov; *The World Factbook.*

COTE d'IVOIRE - CATTLE

See COTE d'IVOIRE - LIVESTOCK

COTE d'IVOIRE - CHICKENS

See COTE d'IVOIRE - LIVESTOCK

COTE d'IVOIRE - CHILDBIRTH - STATISTICS

Central Intelligence Agency, Office of Public Affairs, Washington, DC 20505, (703) 482-0623, Fax: (703) 482-1739, www.cia.gov; *The World Factbook.*

Euromonitor International, Inc., 224 S. Michigan Avenue, Suite 1500, Chicago, IL 60604, (312) 922-1115, Fax: (312) 922-1157, www.euromonitor.com; *International Marketing Data and Statistics 2008* and *The World Economic Factbook 2008.*

M.E. Sharpe, 80 Business Park Drive, Armonk, NY 10504, (800) 541-6563, Fax: (914) 273-2106, www.mesharpe.com; *The Illustrated Book of World Rankings.*

Taylor and Francis Group, An Informa Business, 2 Park Square, Milton Park, Abingdon, Oxford OX14 4RN, United Kingdom, (Dial from U.S. (212) 216-7800), (Fax from U.S. (212) 564-7854), www.tandf.co.uk; *The Europa World Year Book.*

United Nations Statistics Division, New York, NY 10017, (800) 253-9646, Fax: (212) 963-4116, http://unstats.un.org; *Demographic Yearbook; Statistical Yearbook;* and *Survey of Economic and Social Conditions in Africa 2005.*

The World Bank, 1818 H Street, NW, Washington, DC 20433, (202) 473-1000, Fax: (202) 477-6391, www.worldbank.org; *World Development Indicators (WDI) 2008.*

COTE d'IVOIRE - CLIMATE

International Institute for Environment and Development (IIED), 3 Endsleigh Street, London, England, WC1H 0DD, United Kingdom, www.iied.org; *Environment Urbanization* and *Haramata - Bulletin of the Drylands.*

M.E. Sharpe, 80 Business Park Drive, Armonk, NY 10504, (800) 541-6563, Fax: (914) 273-2106, www.mesharpe.com; *The Illustrated Book of World Rankings.*

Palgrave Macmillan Ltd., Houndmills, Basingstoke, Hampshire, RG21 6XS, England, (Telephone in U.S. (888) 330-8477), (Fax in U.S. (800) 672-2054), www.palgrave.com; *The Statesman's Yearbook 2008.*

COTE d'IVOIRE - COAL PRODUCTION

See COTE d'IVOIRE - MINERAL INDUSTRIES

COTE d'IVOIRE - COCOA PRODUCTION

See COTE d'IVOIRE - CROPS

COTE d'IVOIRE - COFFEE

See COTE d'IVOIRE - CROPS

COTE d'IVOIRE - COMMERCE

Palgrave Macmillan Ltd., Houndmills, Basingstoke, Hampshire, RG21 6XS, England, (Telephone in U.S. (888) 330-8477), (Fax in U.S. (800) 672-2054), www.palgrave.com; *The Statesman's Yearbook 2008.*

COTE d'IVOIRE - COMMODITY EXCHANGES

United Nations Food and Agricultural Organization (FAO), Viale delle Terme di Caracalla, 00100 Rome, Italy, (Dial from U.S. (202) 653-2400), (Fax from U.S. (202) 653 5760), www.fao.org; *The State of Food and Agriculture (SOFA) 2006.*

COTE d'IVOIRE - COMMUNICATION AND TRAFFIC

United Nations Statistics Division, New York, NY 10017, (800) 253-9646, Fax: (212) 963-4116, http://unstats.un.org; *Statistical Yearbook.*

COTE d'IVOIRE - CONSTRUCTION INDUSTRY

M.E. Sharpe, 80 Business Park Drive, Armonk, NY 10504, (800) 541-6563, Fax: (914) 273-2106, www.mesharpe.com; *The Illustrated Book of World Rankings.*

United Nations Economic Commission for Africa (ECA), PO Box 3001, Addis Ababa, Ethiopia, (Telephone in U.S. (212) 963-4957), www.uneca.org; *African Statistical Yearbook 2006.*

United Nations Statistics Division, New York, NY 10017, (800) 253-9646, Fax: (212) 963-4116, http://unstats.un.org; *Statistical Yearbook.*

COTE d'IVOIRE - CONSUMER PRICE INDEXES

Taylor and Francis Group, An Informa Business, 2 Park Square, Milton Park, Abingdon, Oxford OX14 4RN, United Kingdom, (Dial from U.S. (212) 216-7800), (Fax from U.S. (212) 564-7854), www.tandf.co.uk; *The Europa World Year Book.*

United Nations Economic Commission for Africa (ECA), PO Box 3001, Addis Ababa, Ethiopia, (Telephone in U.S. (212) 963-4957), www.uneca.org; *African Statistical Yearbook 2006.*

United Nations Statistics Division, New York, NY 10017, (800) 253-9646, Fax: (212) 963-4116, http://unstats.un.org; *Statistical Yearbook* and *Survey of Economic and Social Conditions in Africa 2005.*

COTE d'IVOIRE - CONSUMPTION (ECONOMICS)

African Development Bank Group, Rue Joseph Anoma, 01 BP 1387 Abidjan 01, Cote d'Ivoire, www.afdb.org; *Statistics Pocketbook 2008.*

United Nations Statistics Division, New York, NY 10017, (800) 253-9646, Fax: (212) 963-4116, http://unstats.un.org; *Survey of Economic and Social Conditions in Africa 2005.*

The World Bank, 1818 H Street, NW, Washington, DC 20433, (202) 473-1000, Fax: (202) 477-6391, www.worldbank.org; *World Development Report 2008.*

COTE d'IVOIRE - COPPER INDUSTRY AND TRADE

See COTE d'IVOIRE - MINERAL INDUSTRIES

COTE d'IVOIRE - CORN INDUSTRY

See COTE d'IVOIRE - CROPS

COTE d'IVOIRE - COTTON

See COTE d'IVOIRE - CROPS

COTE d'IVOIRE - CRIME

International Criminal Police Organization (INTERPOL), General Secretariat, 200 quai Charles de Gaulle, 69006 Lyon, France, www.interpol.int; *International Crime Statistics.*

Yale University Press, PO Box 209040, New Haven, CT 06520-9040, (203) 432-0960, Fax: (203) 432-0948, http://yalepress.yale.edu/yupbooks; *Violence and Crime in Cross-National Perspective.*

COTE d'IVOIRE - CROPS

M.E. Sharpe, 80 Business Park Drive, Armonk, NY 10504, (800) 541-6563, Fax: (914) 273-2106, www.mesharpe.com; *The Illustrated Book of World Rankings.*

Palgrave Macmillan Ltd., Houndmills, Basingstoke, Hampshire, RG21 6XS, England, (Telephone in U.S. (888) 330-8477), (Fax in U.S. (800) 672-2054), www.palgrave.com; *The Statesman's Yearbook 2008.*

Taylor and Francis Group, An Informa Business, 2 Park Square, Milton Park, Abingdon, Oxford OX14 4RN, United Kingdom, (Dial from U.S. (212) 216-7800), (Fax from U.S. (212) 564-7854), www.tandf.co.uk; *The Europa World Year Book.*

United Nations Conference on Trade and Development (UNCTAD), DC2-1120, United Nations, New York, NY 10017, (212) 963-0027, www.unctad.org; *UNCTAD Commodity Yearbook.*

United Nations Economic Commission for Africa (ECA), PO Box 3001, Addis Ababa, Ethiopia, (Telephone in U.S. (212) 963-4957), www.uneca.org; *African Statistical Yearbook 2006.*

United Nations Food and Agricultural Organization (FAO), Viale delle Terme di Caracalla, 00100 Rome, Italy, (Dial from U.S. (202) 653-2400), (Fax from U.S. (202) 653 5760), www.fao.org; *FAO Production Yearbook 2002* and *The State of Food and Agriculture (SOFA) 2006.*

United Nations Statistics Division, New York, NY 10017, (800) 253-9646, Fax: (212) 963-4116, http://unstats.un.org; *Statistical Yearbook.*

COTE d'IVOIRE - CUSTOMS ADMINISTRATION

Palgrave Macmillan Ltd., Houndmills, Basingstoke, Hampshire, RG21 6XS, England, (Telephone in U.S. (888) 330-8477), (Fax in U.S. (800) 672-2054), www.palgrave.com; *The Statesman's Yearbook 2008.*

COTE d'IVOIRE - DAIRY PROCESSING

M.E. Sharpe, 80 Business Park Drive, Armonk, NY 10504, (800) 541-6563, Fax: (914) 273-2106, www.mesharpe.com; *The Illustrated Book of World Rankings.*

Palgrave Macmillan Ltd., Houndmills, Basingstoke, Hampshire, RG21 6XS, England, (Telephone in U.S. (888) 330-8477), (Fax in U.S. (800) 672-2054), www.palgrave.com; *The Statesman's Yearbook 2008.*

Taylor and Francis Group, An Informa Business, 2 Park Square, Milton Park, Abingdon, Oxford OX14 4RN, United Kingdom, (Dial from U.S. (212) 216-7800), (Fax from U.S. (212) 564-7854), www.tandf.co.uk; *The Europa World Year Book.*

United Nations Food and Agricultural Organization (FAO), Viale delle Terme di Caracalla, 00100 Rome, Italy, (Dial from U.S. (202) 653-2400), (Fax from U.S. (202) 653 5760), www.fao.org; *The State of Food and Agriculture (SOFA) 2006.*

United Nations Statistics Division, New York, NY 10017, (800) 253-9646, Fax: (212) 963-4116, http://unstats.un.org; *Statistical Yearbook.*

COTE d'IVOIRE - DEATH RATES

See COTE d'IVOIRE - MORTALITY

COTE d'IVOIRE - DEBTS, EXTERNAL

African Development Bank Group, Rue Joseph Anoma, 01 BP 1387 Abidjan 01, Cote d'Ivoire, www.afdb.org; *Statistics Pocketbook 2008.*

Palgrave Macmillan Ltd., Houndmills, Basingstoke, Hampshire, RG21 6XS, England, (Telephone in U.S. (888) 330-8477), (Fax in U.S. (800) 672-2054), www.palgrave.com; *The Statesman's Yearbook 2008.*

United Nations Statistics Division, New York, NY 10017, (800) 253-9646, Fax: (212) 963-4116, http://unstats.un.org; *Survey of Economic and Social Conditions in Africa 2005.*

The World Bank, 1818 H Street, NW, Washington, DC 20433, (202) 473-1000, Fax: (202) 477-6391, www.worldbank.org; *Africa Live Database (LDB); African Development Indicators (ADI) 2007; World Development Indicators (WDI) 2008;* and *World Development Report 2008.*

COTE d'IVOIRE - DEFENSE EXPENDITURES

See COTE d'IVOIRE - ARMED FORCES

COTE d'IVOIRE - DEMOGRAPHY

Euromonitor International, Inc., 224 S. Michigan Avenue, Suite 1500, Chicago, IL 60604, (312) 922-1115, Fax: (312) 922-1157, www.euromonitor.com; *International Marketing Data and Statistics 2008; The World Economic Factbook 2008;* and *World Marketing Data and Statistics.*

M.E. Sharpe, 80 Business Park Drive, Armonk, NY 10504, (800) 541-6563, Fax: (914) 273-2106, www.mesharpe.com; *The Illustrated Book of World Rankings.*

United Nations Statistics Division, New York, NY 10017, (800) 253-9646, Fax: (212) 963-4116, http://unstats.un.org; *Human Development Report 2006* and *Survey of Economic and Social Conditions in Africa 2005.*

The World Bank, 1818 H Street, NW, Washington, DC 20433, (202) 473-1000, Fax: (202) 477-6391, www.worldbank.org; *Cote d'Ivoire.*

COTE d'IVOIRE - DIAMONDS

See COTE d'IVOIRE - MINERAL INDUSTRIES

COTE d'IVOIRE - DISPOSABLE INCOME

M.E. Sharpe, 80 Business Park Drive, Armonk, NY 10504, (800) 541-6563, Fax: (914) 273-2106, www.mesharpe.com; *The Illustrated Book of World Rankings.*

United Nations Statistics Division, New York, NY 10017, (800) 253-9646, Fax: (212) 963-4116, http://unstats.un.org; *National Accounts Statistics: Compendium of Income Distribution Statistics* and *Statistical Yearbook.*

COTE d'IVOIRE - DIVORCE

M.E. Sharpe, 80 Business Park Drive, Armonk, NY 10504, (800) 541-6563, Fax: (914) 273-2106, www.mesharpe.com; *The Illustrated Book of World Rankings.*

United Nations Statistics Division, New York, NY 10017, (800) 253-9646, Fax: (212) 963-4116, http://unstats.un.org; *Demographic Yearbook.*

COTE d'IVOIRE - ECONOMIC ASSISTANCE

United Nations Statistics Division, New York, NY 10017, (800) 253-9646, Fax: (212) 963-4116, http://unstats.un.org; *Statistical Yearbook.*

COTE d'IVOIRE - ECONOMIC CONDITIONS

African Development Bank Group, Rue Joseph Anoma, 01 BP 1387 Abidjan 01, Cote d'Ivoire, www.afdb.org; *The African Statistical Journal; Gender, Poverty and Environmental Indicators on African Countries 2007; Selected Statistics on African Countries 2007;* and *Statistics Pocketbook 2008.*

Central Intelligence Agency, Office of Public Affairs, Washington, DC 20505, (703) 482-0623, Fax: (703) 482-1739, www.cia.gov; *The World Factbook.*

Economist Intelligence Unit, 111 West 57th Street, New York, NY 10019, (212) 554-0600, Fax: (212) 586-1181, www.eiu.com; *Business Africa* and *Cote d'Ivoire Country Report.*

Euromonitor International, Inc., 224 S. Michigan Avenue, Suite 1500, Chicago, IL 60604, (312) 922-1115, Fax: (312) 922-1157, www.euromonitor.com; *International Marketing Data and Statistics 2008; The World Economic Factbook 2008;* and *World Marketing Data and Statistics.*

M.E. Sharpe, 80 Business Park Drive, Armonk, NY 10504, (800) 541-6563, Fax: (914) 273-2106, www.mesharpe.com; *The Illustrated Book of World Rankings.*

Palgrave Macmillan Ltd., Houndmills, Basingstoke, Hampshire, RG21 6XS, England, (Telephone in U.S. (888) 330-8477), (Fax in U.S. (800) 672-2054), www.palgrave.com; *The Statesman's Yearbook 2008.*

Taylor and Francis Group, An Informa Business, 2 Park Square, Milton Park, Abingdon, Oxford OX14 4RN, United Kingdom, (Dial from U.S. (212) 216-7800), (Fax from U.S. (212) 564-7854), www.tandf.co.uk; *The Europa World Year Book.*

United Nations Statistics Division, New York, NY 10017, (800) 253-9646, Fax: (212) 963-4116, http://unstats.un.org; *Compendium of Intra-African and Related Foreign Trade Statistics 2003* and *World Statistics Pocketbook.*

The World Bank, 1818 H Street, NW, Washington, DC 20433, (202) 473-1000, Fax: (202) 477-6391, www.worldbank.org; *Africa Household Survey Databank; Africa Live Database (LDB); Africa Standardized Files and Indicators; African Development Indicators (ADI) 2007; Cote d'Ivoire; The World Bank Atlas 2003-2004;* and *World Development Report 2008.*

COTE d'IVOIRE - EDUCATION

African Development Bank Group, Rue Joseph Anoma, 01 BP 1387 Abidjan 01, Cote d'Ivoire, www.afdb.org; *Statistics Pocketbook 2008.*

Euromonitor International, Inc., 224 S. Michigan Avenue, Suite 1500, Chicago, IL 60604, (312) 922-1115, Fax: (312) 922-1157, www.euromonitor.com; *International Marketing Data and Statistics 2008* and *World Marketing Data and Statistics.*

M.E. Sharpe, 80 Business Park Drive, Armonk, NY 10504, (800) 541-6563, Fax: (914) 273-2106, www.mesharpe.com; *The Illustrated Book of World Rankings.*

Palgrave Macmillan Ltd., Houndmills, Basingstoke, Hampshire, RG21 6XS, England, (Telephone in U.S. (888) 330-8477), (Fax in U.S. (800) 672-2054), www.palgrave.com; *The Statesman's Yearbook 2008.*

Taylor and Francis Group, An Informa Business, 2 Park Square, Milton Park, Abingdon, Oxford OX14 4RN, United Kingdom, (Dial from U.S. (212) 216-7800), (Fax from U.S. (212) 564-7854), www.tandf.co.uk; *The Europa World Year Book.*

UNESCO Institute for Statistics, C.P. 6128 Succursale Centre-Ville, Montreal, Quebec, H3C 3J7 Canada, (Dial from U.S. (514) 343-6880), (Fax from U.S. (514) 343 6882), www.uis.unesco.org; *Statistical Tables.*

United Nations Economic Commission for Africa (ECA), PO Box 3001, Addis Ababa, Ethiopia, (Telephone in U.S. (212) 963-4957), www.uneca.org; *African Statistical Yearbook 2006.*

United Nations Statistics Division, New York, NY 10017, (800) 253-9646, Fax: (212) 963-4116, http://unstats.un.org; *Human Development Report 2006* and *Survey of Economic and Social Conditions in Africa 2005.*

The World Bank, 1818 H Street, NW, Washington, DC 20433, (202) 473-1000, Fax: (202) 477-6391, www.worldbank.org; *Cote d'Ivoire; World Development Indicators (WDI) 2008;* and *World Development Report 2008.*

COTE d'IVOIRE - EGGPLANT PRODUCTION

See COTE d'IVOIRE - CROPS

COTE d'IVOIRE - ELECTRICITY

M.E. Sharpe, 80 Business Park Drive, Armonk, NY 10504, (800) 541-6563, Fax: (914) 273-2106, www.mesharpe.com; *The Illustrated Book of World Rankings.*

Organisation for Economic Cooperation and Development (OECD), 2 rue Andre Pascal, F-75775 Paris Cedex 16, France, (Telephone in U.S. (202) 785-6323), (Fax in U.S. (202) 785-0350), www.oecd.org; *World Energy Outlook 2007.*

Palgrave Macmillan Ltd., Houndmills, Basingstoke, Hampshire, RG21 6XS, England, (Telephone in U.S. (888) 330-8477), (Fax in U.S. (800) 672-2054), www.palgrave.com; *The Statesman's Yearbook 2008.*

U.S. Department of Energy (DOE), Energy Information Administration (EIA), 1000 Independence Avenue, SW, Washington, DC 20585, (202) 586-8800, www.eia.doe.gov; *International Energy Annual 2004* and *International Energy Outlook 2006.*

United Nations Economic Commission for Africa (ECA), PO Box 3001, Addis Ababa, Ethiopia, (Telephone in U.S. (212) 963-4957), www.uneca.org; *African Statistical Yearbook 2006.*

United Nations Statistics Division, New York, NY 10017, (800) 253-9646, Fax: (212) 963-4116, http://unstats.un.org; *Human Development Report 2006; Statistical Yearbook;* and *Survey of Economic and Social Conditions in Africa 2005.*

COTE d'IVOIRE - EMPLOYMENT

Euromonitor International, Inc., 224 S. Michigan Avenue, Suite 1500, Chicago, IL 60604, (312) 922-1115, Fax: (312) 922-1157, www.euromonitor.com; *International Marketing Data and Statistics 2008.*

M.E. Sharpe, 80 Business Park Drive, Armonk, NY 10504, (800) 541-6563, Fax: (914) 273-2106, www.mesharpe.com; *The Illustrated Book of World Rankings.*

United Nations Economic Commission for Africa (ECA), PO Box 3001, Addis Ababa, Ethiopia, (Telephone in U.S. (212) 963-4957), www.uneca.org; *African Statistical Yearbook 2006.*

United Nations Statistics Division, New York, NY 10017, (800) 253-9646, Fax: (212) 963-4116, http://unstats.un.org; *Statistical Yearbook* and *Survey of Economic and Social Conditions in Africa 2005.*

The World Bank, 1818 H Street, NW, Washington, DC 20433, (202) 473-1000, Fax: (202) 477-6391, www.worldbank.org; *Cote d'Ivoire.*

COTE d'IVOIRE - ENVIRONMENTAL CONDITIONS

DSI Data Service Information, Xantener Strasse 51a, D-47495 Rheinberg, Germany, www.dsidata.com; *Campus Solution.*

Economist Intelligence Unit, 111 West 57th Street, New York, NY 10019, (212) 554-0600, Fax: (212) 586-1181, www.eiu.com; *Cote d'Ivoire Country Report.*

International Institute for Environment and Development (IIED), 3 Endsleigh Street, London, England, WC1H 0DD, United Kingdom, www.iied.org; *Environment Urbanization* and *Haramata - Bulletin of the Drylands.*

United Nations Statistics Division, New York, NY 10017, (800) 253-9646, Fax: (212) 963-4116, http://unstats.un.org; *World Statistics Pocketbook.*

COTE d'IVOIRE - EXPORTS

African Development Bank Group, Rue Joseph Anoma, 01 BP 1387 Abidjan 01, Cote d'Ivoire, www.afdb.org; *Statistics Pocketbook 2008.*

Central Intelligence Agency, Office of Public Affairs, Washington, DC 20505, (703) 482-0623, Fax: (703) 482-1739, www.cia.gov; *The World Factbook.*

Economist Intelligence Unit, 111 West 57th Street, New York, NY 10019, (212) 554-0600, Fax: (212) 586-1181, www.eiu.com; *Cote d'Ivoire Country Report.*

Euromonitor International, Inc., 224 S. Michigan Avenue, Suite 1500, Chicago, IL 60604, (312) 922-1115, Fax: (312) 922-1157, www.euromonitor.com; *International Marketing Data and Statistics 2008* and *The World Economic Factbook 2008.*

International Monetary Fund (IMF), 700 Nineteenth Street, NW, Washington, DC 20431, (202) 623-7000, Fax: (202) 623-4661, www.imf.org; *Direction of Trade Statistics Yearbook 2007.*

Palgrave Macmillan Ltd., Houndmills, Basingstoke, Hampshire, RG21 6XS, England, (Telephone in U.S. (888) 330-8477), (Fax in U.S. (800) 672-2054), www.palgrave.com; *The Statesman's Yearbook 2008.*

Taylor and Francis Group, An Informa Business, 2 Park Square, Milton Park, Abingdon, Oxford OX14 4RN, United Kingdom, (Dial from U.S. (212) 216-7800), (Fax from U.S. (212) 564-7854), www.tandf.co.uk; *The Europa World Year Book.*

United Nations Conference on Trade and Development (UNCTAD), DC2-1120, United Nations, New York, NY 10017, (212) 963-0027, www.unctad.org; *Handbook of Statistics 2005.*

United Nations Economic Commission for Africa (ECA), PO Box 3001, Addis Ababa, Ethiopia, (Telephone in U.S. (212) 963-4957), www.uneca.org; *African Statistical Yearbook 2006.*

United Nations Food and Agricultural Organization (FAO), Viale delle Terme di Caracalla, 00100 Rome, Italy, (Dial from U.S. (202) 653-2400), (Fax from U.S. (202) 653 5760), www.fao.org; *The State of Food and Agriculture (SOFA) 2006.*

United Nations Statistics Division, New York, NY 10017, (800) 253-9646, Fax: (212) 963-4116, http://unstats.un.org; *Compendium of Intra-African and Related Foreign Trade Statistics 2003* and *Survey of Economic and Social Conditions in Africa 2005.*

The World Bank, 1818 H Street, NW, Washington, DC 20433, (202) 473-1000, Fax: (202) 477-6391, www.worldbank.org; *World Development Indicators (WDI) 2008* and *World Development Report 2008.*

COTE d'IVOIRE - FEMALE WORKING POPULATION

See COTE d'IVOIRE - EMPLOYMENT

COTE d'IVOIRE - FERTILITY, HUMAN

Central Intelligence Agency, Office of Public Affairs, Washington, DC 20505, (703) 482-0623, Fax: (703) 482-1739, www.cia.gov; *The World Factbook.*

M.E. Sharpe, 80 Business Park Drive, Armonk, NY 10504, (800) 541-6563, Fax: (914) 273-2106, www.mesharpe.com; *The Illustrated Book of World Rankings.*

United Nations Statistics Division, New York, NY 10017, (800) 253-9646, Fax: (212) 963-4116, http://unstats.un.org; *Human Development Report 2006* and *Survey of Economic and Social Conditions in Africa 2005.*

The World Bank, 1818 H Street, NW, Washington, DC 20433, (202) 473-1000, Fax: (202) 477-6391, www.worldbank.org; *The World Bank Atlas 2003-2004; World Development Indicators (WDI) 2008;* and *World Development Report 2008.*

COTE d'IVOIRE - FERTILIZER INDUSTRY

United Nations Food and Agricultural Organization (FAO), Viale delle Terme di Caracalla, 00100 Rome, Italy, (Dial from U.S. (202) 653-2400), (Fax from U.S. (202) 653 5760), www.fao.org; *FAO Fertilizer Yearbook* and *The State of Food and Agriculture (SOFA) 2006.*

United Nations Statistics Division, New York, NY 10017, (800) 253-9646, Fax: (212) 963-4116, http://unstats.un.org; *Statistical Yearbook.*

COTE d'IVOIRE - FETAL MORTALITY

See COTE d'IVOIRE - MORTALITY

COTE d'IVOIRE - FILM

See COTE d'IVOIRE - MOTION PICTURES

COTE d'IVOIRE - FINANCE

Taylor and Francis Group, An Informa Business, 2 Park Square, Milton Park, Abingdon, Oxford OX14 4RN, United Kingdom, (Dial from U.S. (212) 216-7800), (Fax from U.S. (212) 564-7854), www.tandf.co.uk; *The Europa World Year Book.*

United Nations Economic Commission for Africa (ECA), PO Box 3001, Addis Ababa, Ethiopia, (Telephone in U.S. (212) 963-4957), www.uneca.org; *African Statistical Yearbook 2006.*

United Nations Statistics Division, New York, NY 10017, (800) 253-9646, Fax: (212) 963-4116, http://unstats.un.org; *National Accounts Statistics: Compendium of Income Distribution Statistics* and *Statistical Yearbook.*

The World Bank, 1818 H Street, NW, Washington, DC 20433, (202) 473-1000, Fax: (202) 477-6391, www.worldbank.org; *Cote d'Ivoire.*

COTE d'IVOIRE - FINANCE, PUBLIC

African Development Bank Group, Rue Joseph Anoma, 01 BP 1387 Abidjan 01, Cote d'Ivoire, www.afdb.org; *Statistics Pocketbook 2008.*

Economist Intelligence Unit, 111 West 57th Street, New York, NY 10019, (212) 554-0600, Fax: (212) 586-1181, www.eiu.com; *Cote d'Ivoire Country Report.*

International Monetary Fund (IMF), 700 Nineteenth Street, NW, Washington, DC 20431, (202) 623-7000, Fax: (202) 623-4661, www.imf.org; *International Financial Statistics Yearbook 2007.*

M.E. Sharpe, 80 Business Park Drive, Armonk, NY 10504, (800) 541-6563, Fax: (914) 273-2106, www.mesharpe.com; *The Illustrated Book of World Rankings.*

Palgrave Macmillan Ltd., Houndmills, Basingstoke, Hampshire, RG21 6XS, England, (Telephone in U.S. (888) 330-8477), (Fax in U.S. (800) 672-2054), www.palgrave.com; *The Statesman's Yearbook 2008.*

Taylor and Francis Group, An Informa Business, 2 Park Square, Milton Park, Abingdon, Oxford OX14 4RN, United Kingdom, (Dial from U.S. (212) 216-7800), (Fax from U.S. (212) 564-7854), www.tandf.co.uk; *The Europa World Year Book.*

United Nations Economic Commission for Africa (ECA), PO Box 3001, Addis Ababa, Ethiopia, (Telephone in U.S. (212) 963-4957), www.uneca.org; *African Statistical Yearbook 2006.*

The World Bank, 1818 H Street, NW, Washington, DC 20433, (202) 473-1000, Fax: (202) 477-6391, www.worldbank.org; *Cote d'Ivoire.*

COTE d'IVOIRE - FISHERIES

M.E. Sharpe, 80 Business Park Drive, Armonk, NY 10504, (800) 541-6563, Fax: (914) 273-2106, www.mesharpe.com; *The Illustrated Book of World Rankings.*

Palgrave Macmillan Ltd., Houndmills, Basingstoke, Hampshire, RG21 6XS, England, (Telephone in U.S. (888) 330-8477), (Fax in U.S. (800) 672-2054), www.palgrave.com; *The Statesman's Yearbook 2008.*

Taylor and Francis Group, An Informa Business, 2 Park Square, Milton Park, Abingdon, Oxford OX14 4RN, United Kingdom, (Dial from U.S. (212) 216-7800), (Fax from U.S. (212) 564-7854), www.tandf.co.uk; *The Europa World Year Book.*

United Nations Conference on Trade and Development (UNCTAD), DC2-1120, United Nations, New York, NY 10017, (212) 963-0027, www.unctad.org; *UNCTAD Commodity Yearbook.*

United Nations Economic Commission for Africa (ECA), PO Box 3001, Addis Ababa, Ethiopia, (Telephone in U.S. (212) 963-4957), www.uneca.org; *African Statistical Yearbook 2006.*

United Nations Food and Agricultural Organization (FAO), Viale delle Terme di Caracalla, 00100 Rome, Italy, (Dial from U.S. (202) 653-2400), (Fax from U.S. (202) 653 5760), www.fao.org; *FAO Yearbook of Fishery Statistics;* Fishery Databases; FISHSTAT Database. Subjects covered include: Aquaculture production, capture production, fishery commodities; and *The State of Food and Agriculture (SOFA) 2006.*

United Nations Statistics Division, New York, NY 10017, (800) 253-9646, Fax: (212) 963-4116, http://unstats.un.org; *Statistical Yearbook* and *Survey of Economic and Social Conditions in Africa 2005.*

The World Bank, 1818 H Street, NW, Washington, DC 20433, (202) 473-1000, Fax: (202) 477-6391, www.worldbank.org; *Cote d'Ivoire.*

COTE d'IVOIRE - FLOUR INDUSTRY

United Nations Statistics Division, New York, NY 10017, (800) 253-9646, Fax: (212) 963-4116, http://unstats.un.org; *Statistical Yearbook.*

COTE d'IVOIRE - FOOD

African Development Bank Group, Rue Joseph Anoma, 01 BP 1387 Abidjan 01, Cote d'Ivoire, www.afdb.org; *Statistics Pocketbook 2008.*

United Nations Conference on Trade and Development (UNCTAD), DC2-1120, United Nations, New York, NY 10017, (212) 963-0027, www.unctad.org; *UNCTAD Commodity Yearbook.*

United Nations Food and Agricultural Organization (FAO), Viale delle Terme di Caracalla, 00100 Rome, Italy, (Dial from U.S. (202) 653-2400), (Fax from U.S. (202) 653 5760), www.fao.org; *FAO Production Yearbook 2002* and *The State of Food and Agriculture (SOFA) 2006.*

United Nations Statistics Division, New York, NY 10017, (800) 253-9646, Fax: (212) 963-4116, http://unstats.un.org; *Human Development Report 2006.*

COTE d'IVOIRE - FOREIGN EXCHANGE RATES

African Development Bank Group, Rue Joseph Anoma, 01 BP 1387 Abidjan 01, Cote d'Ivoire, www.afdb.org; *Statistics Pocketbook 2008.*

Central Intelligence Agency, Office of Public Affairs, Washington, DC 20505, (703) 482-0623, Fax: (703) 482-1739, www.cia.gov; *The World Factbook.*

Euromonitor International, Inc., 224 S. Michigan Avenue, Suite 1500, Chicago, IL 60604, (312) 922-1115, Fax: (312) 922-1157, www.euromonitor.com; *International Marketing Data and Statistics 2008* and *The World Economic Factbook 2008.*

Taylor and Francis Group, An Informa Business, 2 Park Square, Milton Park, Abingdon, Oxford OX14 4RN, United Kingdom, (Dial from U.S. (212) 216-7800), (Fax from U.S. (212) 564-7854), www.tandf.co.uk; *The Europa World Year Book.*

United Nations Statistics Division, New York, NY 10017, (800) 253-9646, Fax: (212) 963-4116, http://unstats.un.org; *Compendium of Intra-African and Related Foreign Trade Statistics 2003; Statistical Yearbook;* and *World Statistics Pocketbook.*

COTE d'IVOIRE - FORESTS AND FORESTRY

M.E. Sharpe, 80 Business Park Drive, Armonk, NY 10504, (800) 541-6563, Fax: (914) 273-2106, www.mesharpe.com; *The Illustrated Book of World Rankings.*

Palgrave Macmillan Ltd., Houndmills, Basingstoke, Hampshire, RG21 6XS, England, (Telephone in U.S. (888) 330-8477), (Fax in U.S. (800) 672-2054), www.palgrave.com; *The Statesman's Yearbook 2008.*

Taylor and Francis Group, An Informa Business, 2 Park Square, Milton Park, Abingdon, Oxford OX14 4RN, United Kingdom, (Dial from U.S. (212) 216-7800), (Fax from U.S. (212) 564-7854), www.tandf.co.uk; *The Europa World Year Book.*

UNESCO Institute for Statistics, C.P. 6128 Succursale Centre-Ville, Montreal, Quebec, H3C 3J7 Canada, (Dial from U.S. (514) 343-6880), (Fax from U.S. (514) 343 6882), www.uis.unesco.org; *Statistical Tables.*

United Nations Conference on Trade and Development (UNCTAD), DC2-1120, United Nations, New York, NY 10017, (212) 963-0027, www.unctad.org; *UNCTAD Commodity Yearbook.*

United Nations Economic Commission for Africa (ECA), PO Box 3001, Addis Ababa, Ethiopia, (Telephone in U.S. (212) 963-4957), www.uneca.org; *African Statistical Yearbook 2006.*

United Nations Food and Agricultural Organization (FAO), Viale delle Terme di Caracalla, 00100 Rome, Italy, (Dial from U.S. (202) 653-2400), (Fax from U.S. (202) 653 5760), www.fao.org; *FAO Yearbook of Forest Products* and *The State of Food and Agriculture (SOFA) 2006.*

United Nations Statistics Division, New York, NY 10017, (800) 253-9646, Fax: (212) 963-4116, http://unstats.un.org; *Statistical Yearbook.*

The World Bank, 1818 H Street, NW, Washington, DC 20433, (202) 473-1000, Fax: (202) 477-6391, www.worldbank.org; *Cote d'Ivoire* and *World Development Report 2008.*

COTE d'IVOIRE - GAS PRODUCTION

See COTE d'IVOIRE - MINERAL INDUSTRIES

COTE d'IVOIRE - GEOGRAPHIC INFORMATION SYSTEMS

M.E. Sharpe, 80 Business Park Drive, Armonk, NY 10504, (800) 541-6563, Fax: (914) 273-2106, www.mesharpe.com; *The Illustrated Book of World Rankings.*

COTE d'IVOIRE - GOLD INDUSTRY

United Nations Statistics Division, New York, NY 10017, (800) 253-9646, Fax: (212) 963-4116, http://unstats.un.org; *Statistical Yearbook.*

The World Bank, 1818 H Street, NW, Washington, DC 20433, (202) 473-1000, Fax: (202) 477-6391, www.worldbank.org; *World Development Indicators (WDI) 2008.*

COTE d'IVOIRE - GOLD PRODUCTION

See COTE d'IVOIRE - MINERAL INDUSTRIES

COTE d'IVOIRE - GREEN PEPPER AND CHILIE PRODUCTION

See COTE d'IVOIRE - CROPS

COTE d'IVOIRE - GROSS DOMESTIC PRODUCT

African Development Bank Group, Rue Joseph Anoma, 01 BP 1387 Abidjan 01, Cote d'Ivoire, www.afdb.org; *Statistics Pocketbook 2008.*

Economist Intelligence Unit, 111 West 57th Street, New York, NY 10019, (212) 554-0600, Fax: (212) 586-1181, www.eiu.com; *Cote d'Ivoire Country Report.*

Euromonitor International, Inc., 224 S. Michigan Avenue, Suite 1500, Chicago, IL 60604, (312) 922-1115, Fax: (312) 922-1157, www.euromonitor.com; *International Marketing Data and Statistics 2008* and *The World Economic Factbook 2008.*

M.E. Sharpe, 80 Business Park Drive, Armonk, NY 10504, (800) 541-6563, Fax: (914) 273-2106, www.mesharpe.com; *The Illustrated Book of World Rankings.*

Taylor and Francis Group, An Informa Business, 2 Park Square, Milton Park, Abingdon, Oxford OX14 4RN, United Kingdom, (Dial from U.S. (212) 216-7800), (Fax from U.S. (212) 564-7854), www.tandf.co.uk; *The Europa World Year Book.*

United Nations Economic Commission for Africa (ECA), PO Box 3001, Addis Ababa, Ethiopia, (Telephone in U.S. (212) 963-4957), www.uneca.org; *African Statistical Yearbook 2006.*

United Nations Statistics Division, New York, NY 10017, (800) 253-9646, Fax: (212) 963-4116, http://unstats.un.org; *Human Development Report 2006; National Accounts Statistics: Compendium of Income Distribution Statistics; Statistical Yearbook;* and *Survey of Economic and Social Conditions in Africa 2005.*

The World Bank, 1818 H Street, NW, Washington, DC 20433, (202) 473-1000, Fax: (202) 477-6391, www.worldbank.org; *World Development Indicators (WDI) 2008* and *World Development Report 2008.*

COTE d'IVOIRE - GROSS NATIONAL PRODUCT

Euromonitor International, Inc., 224 S. Michigan Avenue, Suite 1500, Chicago, IL 60604, (312) 922-1115, Fax: (312) 922-1157, www.euromonitor.com; *International Marketing Data and Statistics 2008.*

M.E. Sharpe, 80 Business Park Drive, Armonk, NY 10504, (800) 541-6563, Fax: (914) 273-2106, www.mesharpe.com; *The Illustrated Book of World Rankings.*

Taylor and Francis Group, An Informa Business, 2 Park Square, Milton Park, Abingdon, Oxford OX14 4RN, United Kingdom, (Dial from U.S. (212) 216-7800), (Fax from U.S. (212) 564-7854), www.tandf.co.uk; *The Europa World Year Book.*

U.S. Department of State (DOS), 2201 C Street NW, Washington, DC 20520, (202) 647-4000, www.state.gov; *World Military Expenditures and Arms Transfers (WMEAT).*

United Nations Statistics Division, New York, NY 10017, (800) 253-9646, Fax: (212) 963-4116, http://unstats.un.org; *Statistical Yearbook.*

The World Bank, 1818 H Street, NW, Washington, DC 20433, (202) 473-1000, Fax: (202) 477-6391, www.worldbank.org; *The World Bank Atlas 2003-2004; World Development Indicators (WDI) 2008;* and *World Development Report 2008.*

COTE d'IVOIRE - HIDES AND SKINS INDUSTRY

United Nations Food and Agricultural Organization (FAO), Viale delle Terme di Caracalla, 00100 Rome, Italy, (Dial from U.S. (202) 653-2400), (Fax from U.S. (202) 653 5760), www.fao.org; *FAO Production Yearbook 2002.*

COTE d'IVOIRE - HOUSING

Euromonitor International, Inc., 224 S. Michigan Avenue, Suite 1500, Chicago, IL 60604, (312) 922-1115, Fax: (312) 922-1157, www.euromonitor.com; *World Marketing Data and Statistics.*

M.E. Sharpe, 80 Business Park Drive, Armonk, NY 10504, (800) 541-6563, Fax: (914) 273-2106, www.mesharpe.com; *The Illustrated Book of World Rankings.*

COTE d'IVOIRE - ILLITERATE PERSONS

Euromonitor International, Inc., 224 S. Michigan Avenue, Suite 1500, Chicago, IL 60604, (312) 922-1115, Fax: (312) 922-1157, www.euromonitor.com; *The World Economic Factbook 2008.*

UNESCO Institute for Statistics, C.P. 6128 Succursale Centre-Ville, Montreal, Quebec, H3C 3J7 Canada, (Dial from U.S. (514) 343-6880), (Fax from U.S. (514) 343 6882), www.uis.unesco.org; *Statistical Tables.*

United Nations Statistics Division, New York, NY 10017, (800) 253-9646, Fax: (212) 963-4116, http://unstats.un.org; *Human Development Report 2006.*

COTE d'IVOIRE - IMPORTS

Central Intelligence Agency, Office of Public Affairs, Washington, DC 20505, (703) 482-0623, Fax: (703) 482-1739, www.cia.gov; *The World Factbook.*

Economist Intelligence Unit, 111 West 57th Street, New York, NY 10019, (212) 554-0600, Fax: (212) 586-1181, www.eiu.com; *Cote d'Ivoire Country Report.*

Euromonitor International, Inc., 224 S. Michigan Avenue, Suite 1500, Chicago, IL 60604, (312) 922-1115, Fax: (312) 922-1157, www.euromonitor.com; *International Marketing Data and Statistics 2008* and *The World Economic Factbook 2008.*

International Monetary Fund (IMF), 700 Nineteenth Street, NW, Washington, DC 20431, (202) 623-7000, Fax: (202) 623-4661, www.imf.org; *Direction of Trade Statistics Yearbook 2007.*

Palgrave Macmillan Ltd., Houndmills, Basingstoke, Hampshire, RG21 6XS, England, (Telephone in U.S. (888) 330-8477), (Fax in U.S. (800) 672-2054), www.palgrave.com; *The Statesman's Yearbook 2008.*

Taylor and Francis Group, An Informa Business, 2 Park Square, Milton Park, Abingdon, Oxford OX14 4RN, United Kingdom, (Dial from U.S. (212) 216-7800), (Fax from U.S. (212) 564-7854), www.tandf.co.uk; *The Europa World Year Book.*

United Nations Conference on Trade and Development (UNCTAD), DC2-1120, United Nations, New York, NY 10017, (212) 963-0027, www.unctad.org; *Handbook of Statistics 2005.*

United Nations Economic Commission for Africa (ECA), PO Box 3001, Addis Ababa, Ethiopia, (Telephone in U.S. (212) 963-4957), www.uneca.org; *African Statistical Yearbook 2006.*

United Nations Food and Agricultural Organization (FAO), Viale delle Terme di Caracalla, 00100 Rome, Italy, (Dial from U.S. (202) 653-2400), (Fax from U.S. (202) 653 5760), www.fao.org; *The State of Food and Agriculture (SOFA) 2006.*

United Nations Statistics Division, New York, NY 10017, (800) 253-9646, Fax: (212) 963-4116, http://unstats.un.org; *Compendium of Intra-African and Related Foreign Trade Statistics 2003* and *Survey of Economic and Social Conditions in Africa 2005.*

The World Bank, 1818 H Street, NW, Washington, DC 20433, (202) 473-1000, Fax: (202) 477-6391, www.worldbank.org; *World Development Indicators (WDI) 2008* and *World Development Report 2008.*

COTE d'IVOIRE - INDUSTRIAL PRODUCTIVITY

Euromonitor International, Inc., 224 S. Michigan Avenue, Suite 1500, Chicago, IL 60604, (312) 922-1115, Fax: (312) 922-1157, www.euromonitor.com; *International Marketing Data and Statistics 2008.*

M.E. Sharpe, 80 Business Park Drive, Armonk, NY 10504, (800) 541-6563, Fax: (914) 273-2106, www.mesharpe.com; *The Illustrated Book of World Rankings.*

COTE d'IVOIRE - INDUSTRIES

Central Intelligence Agency, Office of Public Affairs, Washington, DC 20505, (703) 482-0623, Fax: (703) 482-1739, www.cia.gov; *The World Factbook.*

Economist Intelligence Unit, 111 West 57th Street, New York, NY 10019, (212) 554-0600, Fax: (212) 586-1181, www.eiu.com; *Cote d'Ivoire Country Report.*

Euromonitor International, Inc., 224 S. Michigan Avenue, Suite 1500, Chicago, IL 60604, (312) 922-1115, Fax: (312) 922-1157, www.euromonitor.com; *International Marketing Data and Statistics 2008; The World Economic Factbook 2008;* and *World Marketing Data and Statistics.*

M.E. Sharpe, 80 Business Park Drive, Armonk, NY 10504, (800) 541-6563, Fax: (914) 273-2106, www.mesharpe.com; *The Illustrated Book of World Rankings.*

Palgrave Macmillan Ltd., Houndmills, Basingstoke, Hampshire, RG21 6XS, England, (Telephone in U.S. (888) 330-8477), (Fax in U.S. (800) 672-2054), www.palgrave.com; *The Statesman's Yearbook 2008.*

Taylor and Francis Group, An Informa Business, 2 Park Square, Milton Park, Abingdon, Oxford OX14 4RN, United Kingdom, (Dial from U.S. (212) 216-7800), (Fax from U.S. (212) 564-7854), www.tandf.co.uk; *The Europa World Year Book.*

United Nations Economic Commission for Africa (ECA), PO Box 3001, Addis Ababa, Ethiopia, (Telephone in U.S. (212) 963-4957), www.uneca.org; *African Statistical Yearbook 2006.*

United Nations Statistics Division, New York, NY 10017, (800) 253-9646, Fax: (212) 963-4116, http://unstats.un.org; *2004 Industrial Commodity Statistics Yearbook* and *Survey of Economic and Social Conditions in Africa 2005.*

The World Bank, 1818 H Street, NW, Washington, DC 20433, (202) 473-1000, Fax: (202) 477-6391, www.worldbank.org; *Cote d'Ivoire* and *World Development Indicators (WDI) 2008.*

COTE d'IVOIRE - INFANT AND MATERNAL MORTALITY

See COTE d'IVOIRE - MORTALITY

COTE d'IVOIRE - INTERNATIONAL TRADE

African Development Bank Group, Rue Joseph Anoma, 01 BP 1387 Abidjan 01, Cote d'Ivoire, www.afdb.org; *Statistics Pocketbook 2008.*

Economist Intelligence Unit, 111 West 57th Street, New York, NY 10019, (212) 554-0600, Fax: (212) 586-1181, www.eiu.com; *Cote d'Ivoire Country Report.*

Euromonitor International, Inc., 224 S. Michigan Avenue, Suite 1500, Chicago, IL 60604, (312) 922-1115, Fax: (312) 922-1157, www.euromonitor.com; *International Marketing Data and Statistics 2008; The World Economic Factbook 2008;* and *World Marketing Data and Statistics.*

M.E. Sharpe, 80 Business Park Drive, Armonk, NY 10504, (800) 541-6563, Fax: (914) 273-2106, www.mesharpe.com; *The Illustrated Book of World Rankings.*

Palgrave Macmillan Ltd., Houndmills, Basingstoke, Hampshire, RG21 6XS, England, (Telephone in U.S. (888) 330-8477), (Fax in U.S. (800) 672-2054), www.palgrave.com; *The Statesman's Yearbook 2008.*

Taylor and Francis Group, An Informa Business, 2 Park Square, Milton Park, Abingdon, Oxford OX14 4RN, United Kingdom, (Dial from U.S. (212) 216-7800), (Fax from U.S. (212) 564-7854), www.tandf.co.uk; *The Europa World Year Book.*

United Nations Conference on Trade and Development (UNCTAD), DC2-1120, United Nations, New York, NY 10017, (212) 963-0027, www.unctad.org; *UNCTAD Commodity Yearbook.*

United Nations Economic Commission for Africa (ECA), PO Box 3001, Addis Ababa, Ethiopia, (Telephone in U.S. (212) 963-4957), www.uneca.org; *African Statistical Yearbook 2006.*

United Nations Food and Agricultural Organization (FAO), Viale delle Terme di Caracalla, 00100 Rome, Italy, (Dial from U.S. (202) 653-2400), (Fax from U.S. (202) 653 5760), www.fao.org; *FAO Trade Yearbook* and *The State of Food and Agriculture (SOFA) 2006.*

United Nations Statistics Division, New York, NY 10017, (800) 253-9646, Fax: (212) 963-4116, http://unstats.un.org; *Compendium of Intra-African and Related Foreign Trade Statistics 2003; International Trade Statistics Yearbook;* and *Statistical Yearbook.*

The World Bank, 1818 H Street, NW, Washington, DC 20433, (202) 473-1000, Fax: (202) 477-6391, www.worldbank.org; *Cote d'Ivoire; World Development Indicators (WDI) 2008;* and *World Development Report 2008.*

World Trade Organization (WTO), Centre William Rappard, Rue de Lausanne 154, CH-1211 Geneva 21, Switzerland, www.wto.org; *International Trade Statistics 2006.*

COTE d'IVOIRE - IRON AND IRON ORE PRODUCTION

See COTE d'IVOIRE - MINERAL INDUSTRIES

COTE d'IVOIRE - IRRIGATION

Euromonitor International, Inc., 224 S. Michigan Avenue, Suite 1500, Chicago, IL 60604, (312) 922-1115, Fax: (312) 922-1157, www.euromonitor.com; *International Marketing Data and Statistics 2008.*

COTE d'IVOIRE - LABOR

African Development Bank Group, Rue Joseph Anoma, 01 BP 1387 Abidjan 01, Cote d'Ivoire, www.afdb.org; *Statistics Pocketbook 2008.*

Central Intelligence Agency, Office of Public Affairs, Washington, DC 20505, (703) 482-0623, Fax: (703) 482-1739, www.cia.gov; *The World Factbook.*

Euromonitor International, Inc., 224 S. Michigan Avenue, Suite 1500, Chicago, IL 60604, (312) 922-1115, Fax: (312) 922-1157, www.euromonitor.com; *International Marketing Data and Statistics 2008* and *World Marketing Data and Statistics.*

M.E. Sharpe, 80 Business Park Drive, Armonk, NY 10504, (800) 541-6563, Fax: (914) 273-2106, www.mesharpe.com; *The Illustrated Book of World Rankings.*

Palgrave Macmillan Ltd., Houndmills, Basingstoke, Hampshire, RG21 6XS, England, (Telephone in U.S. (888) 330-8477), (Fax in U.S. (800) 672-2054), www.palgrave.com; *The Statesman's Yearbook 2008.*

U.S. Department of Energy (DOE), Energy Information Administration (EIA), 1000 Independence Avenue, SW, Washington, DC 20585, (202) 586-8800, www.eia.doe.gov; *International Energy Annual 2004* and *International Energy Outlook 2006.*

United Nations Food and Agricultural Organization (FAO), Viale delle Terme di Caracalla, 00100 Rome, Italy, (Dial from U.S. (202) 653-2400), (Fax from U.S. (202) 653 5760), www.fao.org; *The State of Food and Agriculture (SOFA) 2006.*

United Nations Statistics Division, New York, NY 10017, (800) 253-9646, Fax: (212) 963-4116, http://unstats.un.org; *Human Development Report 2006.*

The World Bank, 1818 H Street, NW, Washington, DC 20433, (202) 473-1000, Fax: (202) 477-6391, www.worldbank.org; *The World Bank Atlas 2003-2004; World Development Indicators (WDI) 2008;* and *World Development Report 2008.*

COTE d'IVOIRE - LAND USE

Central Intelligence Agency, Office of Public Affairs, Washington, DC 20505, (703) 482-0623, Fax: (703) 482-1739, www.cia.gov; *The World Factbook.*

Euromonitor International, Inc., 224 S. Michigan Avenue, Suite 1500, Chicago, IL 60604, (312) 922-1115, Fax: (312) 922-1157, www.euromonitor.com; *International Marketing Data and Statistics 2008.*

United Nations Food and Agricultural Organization (FAO), Viale delle Terme di Caracalla, 00100 Rome, Italy, (Dial from U.S. (202) 653-2400), (Fax from U.S. (202) 653 5760), www.fao.org; *FAO Production Yearbook 2002.*

The World Bank, 1818 H Street, NW, Washington, DC 20433, (202) 473-1000, Fax: (202) 477-6391, www.worldbank.org; *World Development Report 2008.*

COTE d'IVOIRE - LIBRARIES

M.E. Sharpe, 80 Business Park Drive, Armonk, NY 10504, (800) 541-6563, Fax: (914) 273-2106, www.mesharpe.com; *The Illustrated Book of World Rankings.*

UNESCO Institute for Statistics, C.P. 6128 Succursale Centre-Ville, Montreal, Quebec, H3C 3J7 Canada, (Dial from U.S. (514) 343-6880), (Fax from U.S. (514) 343 6882), www.uis.unesco.org; *Statistical Tables.*

COTE d'IVOIRE - LIFE EXPECTANCY

African Development Bank Group, Rue Joseph Anoma, 01 BP 1387 Abidjan 01, Cote d'Ivoire, www.afdb.org; *Statistics Pocketbook 2008.*

Central Intelligence Agency, Office of Public Affairs, Washington, DC 20505, (703) 482-0623, Fax: (703) 482-1739, www.cia.gov; *The World Factbook.*

Euromonitor International, Inc., 224 S. Michigan Avenue, Suite 1500, Chicago, IL 60604, (312) 922-1115, Fax: (312) 922-1157, www.euromonitor.com; *The World Economic Factbook 2008.*

United Nations Statistics Division, New York, NY 10017, (800) 253-9646, Fax: (212) 963-4116, http://unstats.un.org; *Human Development Report 2006* and *World Statistics Pocketbook.*

The World Bank, 1818 H Street, NW, Washington, DC 20433, (202) 473-1000, Fax: (202) 477-6391, www.worldbank.org; *The World Bank Atlas 2003-2004* and *World Development Report 2008.*

COTE d'IVOIRE - LITERACY

Euromonitor International, Inc., 224 S. Michigan Avenue, Suite 1500, Chicago, IL 60604, (312) 922-1115, Fax: (312) 922-1157, www.euromonitor.com; *World Marketing Data and Statistics.*

United Nations Statistics Division, New York, NY 10017, (800) 253-9646, Fax: (212) 963-4116, http://unstats.un.org; *Survey of Economic and Social Conditions in Africa 2005.*

COTE d'IVOIRE - LIVESTOCK

Euromonitor International, Inc., 224 S. Michigan Avenue, Suite 1500, Chicago, IL 60604, (312) 922-1115, Fax: (312) 922-1157, www.euromonitor.com; *International Marketing Data and Statistics 2008.*

M.E. Sharpe, 80 Business Park Drive, Armonk, NY 10504, (800) 541-6563, Fax: (914) 273-2106, www.mesharpe.com; *The Illustrated Book of World Rankings.*

Palgrave Macmillan Ltd., Houndmills, Basingstoke, Hampshire, RG21 6XS, England, (Telephone in U.S. (888) 330-8477), (Fax in U.S. (800) 672-2054), www.palgrave.com; *The Statesman's Yearbook 2008.*

Taylor and Francis Group, An Informa Business, 2 Park Square, Milton Park, Abingdon, Oxford OX14 4RN, United Kingdom, (Dial from U.S. (212) 216-7800), (Fax from U.S. (212) 564-7854), www.tandf.co.uk; *The Europa World Year Book.*

United Nations Conference on Trade and Development (UNCTAD), DC2-1120, United Nations, New York, NY 10017, (212) 963-0027, www.unctad.org; *UNCTAD Commodity Yearbook.*

United Nations Economic Commission for Africa (ECA), PO Box 3001, Addis Ababa, Ethiopia, (Telephone in U.S. (212) 963-4957), www.uneca.org; *African Statistical Yearbook 2006.*

United Nations Food and Agricultural Organization (FAO), Viale delle Terme di Caracalla, 00100 Rome, Italy, (Dial from U.S. (202) 653-2400), (Fax from U.S. (202) 653 5760), www.fao.org; *FAO Production Yearbook 2002* and *The State of Food and Agriculture (SOFA) 2006.*

United Nations Statistics Division, New York, NY 10017, (800) 253-9646, Fax: (212) 963-4116, http://unstats.un.org; *Statistical Yearbook* and *Survey of Economic and Social Conditions in Africa 2005.*

COTE d'IVOIRE - LOCAL TAXATION

Euromonitor International, Inc., 224 S. Michigan Avenue, Suite 1500, Chicago, IL 60604, (312) 922-1115, Fax: (312) 922-1157, www.euromonitor.com; *International Marketing Data and Statistics 2008.*

COTE d'IVOIRE - MANUFACTURES

M.E. Sharpe, 80 Business Park Drive, Armonk, NY 10504, (800) 541-6563, Fax: (914) 273-2106, www.mesharpe.com; *The Illustrated Book of World Rankings.*

United Nations Economic Commission for Africa (ECA), PO Box 3001, Addis Ababa, Ethiopia, (Telephone in U.S. (212) 963-4957), www.uneca.org; *African Statistical Yearbook 2006.*

United Nations Statistics Division, New York, NY 10017, (800) 253-9646, Fax: (212) 963-4116, http://unstats.un.org; *Statistical Yearbook* and *Survey of Economic and Social Conditions in Africa 2005.*

The World Bank, 1818 H Street, NW, Washington, DC 20433, (202) 473-1000, Fax: (202) 477-6391, www.worldbank.org; *World Development Indicators (WDI) 2008.*

COTE d'IVOIRE - MARRIAGE

M.E. Sharpe, 80 Business Park Drive, Armonk, NY 10504, (800) 541-6563, Fax: (914) 273-2106, www.mesharpe.com; *The Illustrated Book of World Rankings.*

United Nations Statistics Division, New York, NY 10017, (800) 253-9646, Fax: (212) 963-4116, http://unstats.un.org; *Demographic Yearbook.*

COTE d'IVOIRE - MILK PRODUCTION

See COTE d'IVOIRE - DAIRY PROCESSING

COTE d'IVOIRE - MINERAL INDUSTRIES

M.E. Sharpe, 80 Business Park Drive, Armonk, NY 10504, (800) 541-6563, Fax: (914) 273-2106, www.mesharpe.com; *The Illustrated Book of World Rankings.*

Organisation for Economic Cooperation and Development (OECD), 2 rue Andre Pascal, F-75775 Paris Cedex 16, France, (Telephone in U.S. (202) 785-6323), (Fax in U.S. (202) 785-0350), www.oecd.org; *World Energy Outlook 2007.*

Palgrave Macmillan Ltd., Houndmills, Basingstoke, Hampshire, RG21 6XS, England, (Telephone in U.S. (888) 330-8477), (Fax in U.S. (800) 672-2054), www.palgrave.com; *The Statesman's Yearbook 2008.*

Taylor and Francis Group, An Informa Business, 2 Park Square, Milton Park, Abingdon, Oxford OX14 4RN, United Kingdom, (Dial from U.S. (212) 216-7800), (Fax from U.S. (212) 564-7854), www.tandf.co.uk; *The Europa World Year Book.*

United Nations Conference on Trade and Development (UNCTAD), DC2-1120, United Nations, New York, NY 10017, (212) 963-0027, www.unctad.org; *UNCTAD Commodity Yearbook.*

United Nations Economic Commission for Africa (ECA), PO Box 3001, Addis Ababa, Ethiopia, (Telephone in U.S. (212) 963-4957), www.uneca.org; *African Statistical Yearbook 2006.*

United Nations Statistics Division, New York, NY 10017, (800) 253-9646, Fax: (212) 963-4116, http://unstats.un.org; *Statistical Yearbook.*

COTE d'IVOIRE - MONEY EXCHANGE RATES

See COTE d'IVOIRE - FOREIGN EXCHANGE RATES

COTE d'IVOIRE - MONEY SUPPLY

African Development Bank Group, Rue Joseph Anoma, 01 BP 1387 Abidjan 01, Cote d'Ivoire, www.afdb.org; *Statistics Pocketbook 2008.*

Economist Intelligence Unit, 111 West 57th Street, New York, NY 10019, (212) 554-0600, Fax: (212) 586-1181, www.eiu.com; *Cote d'Ivoire Country Report.*

Euromonitor International, Inc., 224 S. Michigan Avenue, Suite 1500, Chicago, IL 60604, (312) 922-1115, Fax: (312) 922-1157, www.euromonitor.com; *International Marketing Data and Statistics 2008.*

Taylor and Francis Group, An Informa Business, 2 Park Square, Milton Park, Abingdon, Oxford OX14 4RN, United Kingdom, (Dial from U.S. (212) 216-7800), (Fax from U.S. (212) 564-7854), www.tandf.co.uk; *The Europa World Year Book.*

United Nations Statistics Division, New York, NY 10017, (800) 253-9646, Fax: (212) 963-4116, http://unstats.un.org; *Statistical Yearbook.*

The World Bank, 1818 H Street, NW, Washington, DC 20433, (202) 473-1000, Fax: (202) 477-6391, www.worldbank.org; *Cote d'Ivoire* and *World Development Indicators (WDI) 2008.*

COTE d'IVOIRE - MORTALITY

Central Intelligence Agency, Office of Public Affairs, Washington, DC 20505, (703) 482-0623, Fax: (703) 482-1739, www.cia.gov; *The World Factbook.*

Euromonitor International, Inc., 224 S. Michigan Avenue, Suite 1500, Chicago, IL 60604, (312) 922-1115, Fax: (312) 922-1157, www.euromonitor.com; *International Marketing Data and Statistics 2008* and *The World Economic Factbook 2008.*

Taylor and Francis Group, An Informa Business, 2 Park Square, Milton Park, Abingdon, Oxford OX14 4RN, United Kingdom, (Dial from U.S. (212) 216-7800), (Fax from U.S. (212) 564-7854), www.tandf.co.uk; *The Europa World Year Book.*

UNICEF, 3 United Nations Plaza, New York, NY 10017, (800) 253-9646, Fax: (212) 887-7465, www.unicef.org; *The State of the World's Children 2008.*

United Nations Statistics Division, New York, NY 10017, (800) 253-9646, Fax: (212) 963-4116, http://unstats.un.org; *Demographic Yearbook; Human Development Report 2006; Statistical Yearbook; Survey of Economic and Social Conditions in Africa 2005;* and *World Statistics Pocketbook.*

The World Bank, 1818 H Street, NW, Washington, DC 20433, (202) 473-1000, Fax: (202) 477-6391, www.worldbank.org; *The World Bank Atlas 2003-2004; World Development Indicators (WDI) 2008;* and *World Development Report 2008.*

COTE d'IVOIRE - MOTION PICTURES

UNESCO Institute for Statistics, C.P. 6128 Succursale Centre-Ville, Montreal, Quebec, H3C 3J7 Canada, (Dial from U.S. (514) 343-6880), (Fax from U.S. (514) 343 6882), www.uis.unesco.org; *Statistical Tables.*

United Nations Statistics Division, New York, NY 10017, (800) 253-9646, Fax: (212) 963-4116, http://unstats.un.org; *Statistical Yearbook.*

COTE d'IVOIRE - MOTOR VEHICLES

International Road Federation (IFR), Madison Place, 500 Montgomery Street, 5th Floor, Alexandria, VA 22314, (703) 535-1001, Fax: (703) 535-1007, www.irfnet.org; *World Road Statistics 2006.*

Taylor and Francis Group, An Informa Business, 2 Park Square, Milton Park, Abingdon, Oxford OX14 4RN, United Kingdom, (Dial from U.S. (212) 216-7800), (Fax from U.S. (212) 564-7854), www.tandf.co.uk; *The Europa World Year Book.*

United Nations Statistics Division, New York, NY 10017, (800) 253-9646, Fax: (212) 963-4116, http://unstats.un.org; *Statistical Yearbook* and *Survey of Economic and Social Conditions in Africa 2005.*

COTE d'IVOIRE - MUSEUMS

M.E. Sharpe, 80 Business Park Drive, Armonk, NY 10504, (800) 541-6563, Fax: (914) 273-2106, www.mesharpe.com; *The Illustrated Book of World Rankings.*

COTE d'IVOIRE - NATURAL GAS PRODUCTION

See COTE d'IVOIRE - MINERAL INDUSTRIES

COTE d'IVOIRE - NUTRITION

African Development Bank Group, Rue Joseph Anoma, 01 BP 1387 Abidjan 01, Cote d'Ivoire, www.afdb.org; *Statistics Pocketbook 2008.*

United Nations Food and Agricultural Organization (FAO), Viale delle Terme di Caracalla, 00100 Rome, Italy, (Dial from U.S. (202) 653-2400), (Fax from U.S. (202) 653 5760), www.fao.org; *The State of Food and Agriculture (SOFA) 2006.*

COTE d'IVOIRE - OLDER PEOPLE

M.E. Sharpe, 80 Business Park Drive, Armonk, NY 10504, (800) 541-6563, Fax: (914) 273-2106, www.mesharpe.com; *The Illustrated Book of World Rankings.*

COTE d'IVOIRE - PALM OIL PRODUCTION

See COTE d'IVOIRE - CROPS

COTE d'IVOIRE - PAPER

See COTE d'IVOIRE - FORESTS AND FORESTRY

COTE d'IVOIRE - PEANUT PRODUCTION

See COTE d'IVOIRE - CROPS

COTE d'IVOIRE - PERIODICALS

UNESCO Institute for Statistics, C.P. 6128 Succursale Centre-Ville, Montreal, Quebec, H3C 3J7 Canada, (Dial from U.S. (514) 343-6880), (Fax from U.S. (514) 343 6882), www.uis.unesco.org; *Statistical Tables.*

COTE d'IVOIRE - PESTICIDES

United Nations Food and Agricultural Organization (FAO), Viale delle Terme di Caracalla, 00100 Rome, Italy, (Dial from U.S. (202) 653-2400), (Fax from U.S. (202) 653 5760), www.fao.org; *The State of Food and Agriculture (SOFA) 2006.*

COTE d'IVOIRE - PETROLEUM INDUSTRY AND TRADE

M.E. Sharpe, 80 Business Park Drive, Armonk, NY 10504, (800) 541-6563, Fax: (914) 273-2106, www.mesharpe.com; *The Illustrated Book of World Rankings.*

Organisation for Economic Cooperation and Development (OECD), 2 rue Andre Pascal, F-75775 Paris Cedex 16, France, (Telephone in U.S. (202) 785-6323), (Fax in U.S. (202) 785-0350), www.oecd.org; *World Energy Outlook 2007.*

PennWell Corporation, 1421 South Sheridan Road, Tulsa, OK 74112, (918) 835-3161, www.pennwell.com; *International Petroleum Encyclopedia 2007.*

U.S. Department of Energy (DOE), Energy Information Administration (EIA), 1000 Independence Avenue, SW, Washington, DC 20585, (202) 586-8800, www.eia.doe.gov; *International Energy Annual 2004* and *International Energy Outlook 2006.*

United Nations Conference on Trade and Development (UNCTAD), DC2-1120, United Nations, New York, NY 10017, (212) 963-0027, www.unctad.org; *UNCTAD Commodity Yearbook.*

United Nations Food and Agricultural Organization (FAO), Viale delle Terme di Caracalla, 00100 Rome, Italy, (Dial from U.S. (202) 653-2400), (Fax from U.S. (202) 653 5760), www.fao.org; *The State of Food and Agriculture (SOFA) 2006.*

United Nations Statistics Division, New York, NY 10017, (800) 253-9646, Fax: (212) 963-4116, http://unstats.un.org; *Statistical Yearbook.*

COTE d'IVOIRE - POLITICAL SCIENCE

Central Intelligence Agency, Office of Public Affairs, Washington, DC 20505, (703) 482-0623, Fax: (703) 482-1739, www.cia.gov; *The World Factbook.*

Palgrave Macmillan Ltd., Houndmills, Basingstoke, Hampshire, RG21 6XS, England, (Telephone in U.S. (888) 330-8477), (Fax in U.S. (800) 672-2054), www.palgrave.com; *The Statesman's Yearbook 2008.*

Taylor and Francis Group, An Informa Business, 2 Park Square, Milton Park, Abingdon, Oxford OX14 4RN, United Kingdom, (Dial from U.S. (212) 216-7800), (Fax from U.S. (212) 564-7854), www.tandf.co.uk; *The Europa World Year Book.*

United Nations Statistics Division, New York, NY 10017, (800) 253-9646, Fax: (212) 963-4116, http://unstats.un.org; *National Accounts Statistics: Compendium of Income Distribution Statistics; Statistical Yearbook;* and *Survey of Economic and Social Conditions in Africa 2005.*

The World Bank, 1818 H Street, NW, Washington, DC 20433, (202) 473-1000, Fax: (202) 477-6391, www.worldbank.org; *World Development Indicators (WDI) 2008* and *World Development Report 2008.*

COTE d'IVOIRE - POPULATION

African Development Bank Group, Rue Joseph Anoma, 01 BP 1387 Abidjan 01, Cote d'Ivoire, www.afdb.org; *The African Statistical Journal; Gender, Poverty and Environmental Indicators on African Countries 2007; Selected Statistics on African Countries 2007;* and *Statistics Pocketbook 2008.*

Central Intelligence Agency, Office of Public Affairs, Washington, DC 20505, (703) 482-0623, Fax: (703) 482-1739, www.cia.gov; *The World Factbook.*

Economist Intelligence Unit, 111 West 57th Street, New York, NY 10019, (212) 554-0600, Fax: (212) 586-1181, www.eiu.com; *Cote d'Ivoire Country Report.*

Euromonitor International, Inc., 224 S. Michigan Avenue, Suite 1500, Chicago, IL 60604, (312) 922-1115, Fax: (312) 922-1157, www.euromonitor.com; *International Marketing Data and Statistics 2008* and *The World Economic Factbook 2008.*

Eurostat, Batiment Jean Monnet, Rue Alcide de Gasperi, L-2920 Luxembourg, http://epp.eurostat.ec.europa.eu; *Demographic Indicators - Population by Age-Classes.*

International Labour Office, I.L.O. Publications, 4 route des Morillons, CH-1211 Geneva 22, Switzerland, (Telephone in U.S. (202) 653-7652), (Fax in U.S. (202) 653-7687), www.ilo.org; *Yearbook of Labour Statistics 2006.*

M.E. Sharpe, 80 Business Park Drive, Armonk, NY 10504, (800) 541-6563, Fax: (914) 273-2106, www.mesharpe.com; *The Illustrated Book of World Rankings.*

Palgrave Macmillan Ltd., Houndmills, Basingstoke, Hampshire, RG21 6XS, England, (Telephone in U.S. (888) 330-8477), (Fax in U.S. (800) 672-2054), www.palgrave.com; *The Statesman's Yearbook 2008.*

Taylor and Francis Group, An Informa Business, 2 Park Square, Milton Park, Abingdon, Oxford OX14 4RN, United Kingdom, (Dial from U.S. (212) 216-7800), (Fax from U.S. (212) 564-7854), www.tandf.co.uk; *The Europa World Year Book.*

U.S. Department of State (DOS), 2201 C Street NW, Washington, DC 20520, (202) 647-4000, www.state.gov; *World Military Expenditures and Arms Transfers (WMEAT).*

UNESCO Institute for Statistics, C.P. 6128 Succursale Centre-Ville, Montreal, Quebec, H3C 3J7 Canada, (Dial from U.S. (514) 343-6880), (Fax from U.S. (514) 343 6882), www.uis.unesco.org; *Statistical Tables.*

United Nations Food and Agricultural Organization (FAO), Viale delle Terme di Caracalla, 00100 Rome, Italy, (Dial from U.S. (202) 653-2400), (Fax from U.S. (202) 653 5760), www.fao.org; *FAO Production Yearbook 2002.*

United Nations Statistics Division, New York, NY 10017, (800) 253-9646, Fax: (212) 963-4116, http://unstats.un.org; *Demographic Yearbook; Human Development Report 2006; Statistical Yearbook; Survey of Economic and Social Conditions in Africa 2005;* and *World Statistics Pocketbook.*

The World Bank, 1818 H Street, NW, Washington, DC 20433, (202) 473-1000, Fax: (202) 477-6391, www.worldbank.org; *Cote d'Ivoire; The World Bank Atlas 2003-2004;* and *World Development Report 2008.*

World Health Organization (WHO), Avenue Appia 20, 1211 Geneve 27, Switzerland, (Telephone in U.S. (212) 331-9081), www.who.int; *World Health Report 2006.*

COTE d'IVOIRE - POPULATION DENSITY

African Development Bank Group, Rue Joseph Anoma, 01 BP 1387 Abidjan 01, Cote d'Ivoire, www.afdb.org; *Statistics Pocketbook 2008.*

Central Intelligence Agency, Office of Public Affairs, Washington, DC 20505, (703) 482-0623, Fax: (703) 482-1739, www.cia.gov; *The World Factbook.*

Euromonitor International, Inc., 224 S. Michigan Avenue, Suite 1500, Chicago, IL 60604, (312) 922-1115, Fax: (312) 922-1157, www.euromonitor.com; *International Marketing Data and Statistics 2008* and *The World Economic Factbook 2008.*

M.E. Sharpe, 80 Business Park Drive, Armonk, NY 10504, (800) 541-6563, Fax: (914) 273-2106, www.mesharpe.com; *The Illustrated Book of World Rankings.*

Palgrave Macmillan Ltd., Houndmills, Basingstoke, Hampshire, RG21 6XS, England, (Telephone in U.S. (888) 330-8477), (Fax in U.S. (800) 672-2054), www.palgrave.com; *The Statesman's Yearbook 2008.*

Taylor and Francis Group, An Informa Business, 2 Park Square, Milton Park, Abingdon, Oxford OX14 4RN, United Kingdom, (Dial from U.S. (212) 216-7800), (Fax from U.S. (212) 564-7854), www.tandf.co.uk; *The Europa World Year Book.*

UNESCO Institute for Statistics, C.P. 6128 Succursale Centre-Ville, Montreal, Quebec, H3C 3J7 Canada, (Dial from U.S. (514) 343-6880), (Fax from U.S. (514) 343 6882), www.uis.unesco.org; *Statistical Tables.*

United Nations Food and Agricultural Organization (FAO), Viale delle Terme di Caracalla, 00100 Rome, Italy, (Dial from U.S. (202) 653-2400), (Fax from U.S. (202) 653 5760), www.fao.org; *The State of Food and Agriculture (SOFA) 2006.*

United Nations Statistics Division, New York, NY 10017, (800) 253-9646, Fax: (212) 963-4116, http://unstats.un.org; *Statistical Yearbook* and *Survey of Economic and Social Conditions in Africa 2005.*

The World Bank, 1818 H Street, NW, Washington, DC 20433, (202) 473-1000, Fax: (202) 477-6391, www.worldbank.org; *Cote d'Ivoire* and *World Development Report 2008.*

COTE d'IVOIRE - POSTAL SERVICE

M.E. Sharpe, 80 Business Park Drive, Armonk, NY 10504, (800) 541-6563, Fax: (914) 273-2106, www.mesharpe.com; *The Illustrated Book of World Rankings.*

United Nations Statistics Division, New York, NY 10017, (800) 253-9646, Fax: (212) 963-4116, http://unstats.un.org; *Statistical Yearbook.*

COTE d'IVOIRE - POWER RESOURCES

Euromonitor International, Inc., 224 S. Michigan Avenue, Suite 1500, Chicago, IL 60604, (312) 922-1115, Fax: (312) 922-1157, www.euromonitor.com; *International Marketing Data and Statistics 2008; The World Economic Factbook 2008;* and *World Marketing Data and Statistics.*

M.E. Sharpe, 80 Business Park Drive, Armonk, NY 10504, (800) 541-6563, Fax: (914) 273-2106, www.mesharpe.com; *The Illustrated Book of World Rankings.*

Organisation for Economic Cooperation and Development (OECD), 2 rue Andre Pascal, F-75775 Paris Cedex 16, France, (Telephone in U.S. (202) 785-6323), (Fax in U.S. (202) 785-0350), www.oecd.org; *World Energy Outlook 2007.*

Palgrave Macmillan Ltd., Houndmills, Basingstoke, Hampshire, RG21 6XS, England, (Telephone in U.S. (888) 330-8477), (Fax in U.S. (800) 672-2054), www.palgrave.com; *The Statesman's Yearbook 2008.*

Platts, 2 Penn Plaza, 25th Floor, New York, NY 10121-2298, (212) 904-3070, www.platts.com; *Energy Economist.*

U.S. Department of Energy (DOE), Energy Information Administration (EIA), 1000 Independence Avenue, SW, Washington, DC 20585, (202) 586-8800, www.eia.doe.gov; *International Energy Annual 2004* and *International Energy Outlook 2006.*

United Nations Economic Commission for Africa (ECA), PO Box 3001, Addis Ababa, Ethiopia, (Telephone in U.S. (212) 963-4957), www.uneca.org; *African Statistical Yearbook 2006.*

United Nations Food and Agricultural Organization (FAO), Viale delle Terme di Caracalla, 00100 Rome, Italy, (Dial from U.S. (202) 653-2400), (Fax from U.S. (202) 653 5760), www.fao.org; *The State of Food and Agriculture (SOFA) 2006.*

United Nations Statistics Division, New York, NY 10017, (800) 253-9646, Fax: (212) 963-4116, http://unstats.un.org; *Energy Statistics Yearbook 2003; Human Development Report 2006; Statistical Yearbook;* and *World Statistics Pocketbook.*

The World Bank, 1818 H Street, NW, Washington, DC 20433, (202) 473-1000, Fax: (202) 477-6391, www.worldbank.org; *The World Bank Atlas 2003-2004* and *World Development Report 2008.*

COTE d'IVOIRE - PRICES

Euromonitor International, Inc., 224 S. Michigan Avenue, Suite 1500, Chicago, IL 60604, (312) 922-1115, Fax: (312) 922-1157, www.euromonitor.com; *World Marketing Data and Statistics.*

International Labour Office, I.L.O. Publications, 4 route des Morillons, CH-1211 Geneva 22, Switzerland, (Telephone in U.S. (202) 653-7652), (Fax in U.S. (202) 653-7687), www.ilo.org; *Yearbook of Labour Statistics 2006.*

M.E. Sharpe, 80 Business Park Drive, Armonk, NY 10504, (800) 541-6563, Fax: (914) 273-2106, www.mesharpe.com; *The Illustrated Book of World Rankings.*

United Nations Economic Commission for Africa (ECA), PO Box 3001, Addis Ababa, Ethiopia, (Telephone in U.S. (212) 963-4957), www.uneca.org; *African Statistical Yearbook 2006.*

United Nations Food and Agricultural Organization (FAO), Viale delle Terme di Caracalla, 00100 Rome, Italy, (Dial from U.S. (202) 653-2400), (Fax from U.S. (202) 653 5760), www.fao.org; *FAO Production Yearbook 2002* and *The State of Food and Agriculture (SOFA) 2006.*

The World Bank, 1818 H Street, NW, Washington, DC 20433, (202) 473-1000, Fax: (202) 477-6391, www.worldbank.org; *Cote d'Ivoire.*

COTE d'IVOIRE - PROFESSIONS

UNESCO Institute for Statistics, C.P. 6128 Succursale Centre-Ville, Montreal, Quebec, H3C 3J7 Canada, (Dial from U.S. (514) 343-6880), (Fax from U.S. (514) 343 6882), www.uis.unesco.org; *Statistical Tables.*

United Nations Statistics Division, New York, NY 10017, (800) 253-9646, Fax: (212) 963-4116, http://unstats.un.org; *Statistical Yearbook.*

COTE d'IVOIRE - PUBLIC HEALTH

African Development Bank Group, Rue Joseph Anoma, 01 BP 1387 Abidjan 01, Cote d'Ivoire, www.afdb.org; *Statistics Pocketbook 2008.*

Euromonitor International, Inc., 224 S. Michigan Avenue, Suite 1500, Chicago, IL 60604, (312) 922-1115, Fax: (312) 922-1157, www.euromonitor.com; *World Marketing Data and Statistics.*

M.E. Sharpe, 80 Business Park Drive, Armonk, NY 10504, (800) 541-6563, Fax: (914) 273-2106, www.mesharpe.com; *The Illustrated Book of World Rankings.*

Palgrave Macmillan Ltd., Houndmills, Basingstoke, Hampshire, RG21 6XS, England, (Telephone in U.S. (888) 330-8477), (Fax in U.S. (800) 672-2054), www.palgrave.com; *The Statesman's Yearbook 2008.*

UNICEF, 3 United Nations Plaza, New York, NY 10017, (800) 253-9646, Fax: (212) 887-7465, www.unicef.org; *The State of the World's Children 2008.*

United Nations Economic Commission for Africa (ECA), PO Box 3001, Addis Ababa, Ethiopia, (Telephone in U.S. (212) 963-4957), www.uneca.org; *African Statistical Yearbook 2006.*

United Nations Statistics Division, New York, NY 10017, (800) 253-9646, Fax: (212) 963-4116, http://unstats.un.org; *Human Development Report 2006* and *Statistical Yearbook.*

The World Bank, 1818 H Street, NW, Washington, DC 20433, (202) 473-1000, Fax: (202) 477-6391, www.worldbank.org; *Cote d'Ivoire* and *World Development Report 2008.*

COTE d'IVOIRE - PUBLISHERS AND PUBLISHING

Taylor and Francis Group, An Informa Business, 2 Park Square, Milton Park, Abingdon, Oxford OX14 4RN, United Kingdom, (Dial from U.S. (212) 216-7800), (Fax from U.S. (212) 564-7854), www.tandf.co.uk; *The Europa World Year Book.*

UNESCO Institute for Statistics, C.P. 6128 Succursale Centre-Ville, Montreal, Quebec, H3C 3J7 Canada, (Dial from U.S. (514) 343-6880), (Fax from U.S. (514) 343 6882), www.uis.unesco.org; *Statistical Tables.*

COTE d'IVOIRE - RADIO - RECEIVERS AND RECEPTION

Palgrave Macmillan Ltd., Houndmills, Basingstoke, Hampshire, RG21 6XS, England, (Telephone in U.S. (888) 330-8477), (Fax in U.S. (800) 672-2054), www.palgrave.com; *The Statesman's Yearbook 2008.*

United Nations Statistics Division, New York, NY 10017, (800) 253-9646, Fax: (212) 963-4116, http://unstats.un.org; *Statistical Yearbook.*

COTE d'IVOIRE - RAILROADS

Jane's Information Group, 110 North Royal Street, Suite 200, Alexandria, VA 22314, (703) 683-3700, Fax: (800) 836-0297, www.janes.com; *Jane's World Railways.*

Palgrave Macmillan Ltd., Houndmills, Basingstoke, Hampshire, RG21 6XS, England, (Telephone in U.S. (888) 330-8477), (Fax in U.S. (800) 672-2054), www.palgrave.com; *The Statesman's Yearbook 2008.*

Taylor and Francis Group, An Informa Business, 2 Park Square, Milton Park, Abingdon, Oxford OX14 4RN, United Kingdom, (Dial from U.S. (212) 216-7800), (Fax from U.S. (212) 564-7854), www.tandf.co.uk; *The Europa World Year Book.*

United Nations Economic Commission for Africa (ECA), PO Box 3001, Addis Ababa, Ethiopia, (Telephone in U.S. (212) 963-4957), www.uneca.org; *African Statistical Yearbook 2006.*

United Nations Statistics Division, New York, NY 10017, (800) 253-9646, Fax: (212) 963-4116, http://unstats.un.org; *Statistical Yearbook* and *Survey of Economic and Social Conditions in Africa 2005.*

COTE d'IVOIRE - RELIGION

Central Intelligence Agency, Office of Public Affairs, Washington, DC 20505, (703) 482-0623, Fax: (703) 482-1739, www.cia.gov; *The World Factbook.*

M.E. Sharpe, 80 Business Park Drive, Armonk, NY 10504, (800) 541-6563, Fax: (914) 273-2106, www.mesharpe.com; *The Illustrated Book of World Rankings.*

Palgrave Macmillan Ltd., Houndmills, Basingstoke, Hampshire, RG21 6XS, England, (Telephone in U.S. (888) 330-8477), (Fax in U.S. (800) 672-2054), www.palgrave.com; *The Statesman's Yearbook 2008.*

COTE d'IVOIRE - RESERVES (ACCOUNTING)

African Development Bank Group, Rue Joseph Anoma, 01 BP 1387 Abidjan 01, Cote d'Ivoire, www.afdb.org; *Statistics Pocketbook 2008.*

Euromonitor International, Inc., 224 S. Michigan Avenue, Suite 1500, Chicago, IL 60604, (312) 922-1115, Fax: (312) 922-1157, www.euromonitor.com; *International Marketing Data and Statistics 2008.*

United Nations Statistics Division, New York, NY 10017, (800) 253-9646, Fax: (212) 963-4116, http://unstats.un.org; *Statistical Yearbook.*

The World Bank, 1818 H Street, NW, Washington, DC 20433, (202) 473-1000, Fax: (202) 477-6391, www.worldbank.org; *World Development Indicators (WDI) 2008.*

COTE d'IVOIRE - RETAIL TRADE

Euromonitor International, Inc., 224 S. Michigan Avenue, Suite 1500, Chicago, IL 60604, (312) 922-1115, Fax: (312) 922-1157, www.euromonitor.com; *World Marketing Data and Statistics.*

COTE d'IVOIRE - RICE PRODUCTION

See COTE d'IVOIRE - CROPS

COTE d'IVOIRE - ROADS

Central Intelligence Agency, Office of Public Affairs, Washington, DC 20505, (703) 482-0623, Fax: (703) 482-1739, www.cia.gov; *The World Factbook.*

International Road Federation (IFR), Madison Place, 500 Montgomery Street, 5th Floor, Alexandria, VA 22314, (703) 535-1001, Fax: (703) 535-1007, www.irfnet.org; *World Road Statistics 2006.*

Palgrave Macmillan Ltd., Houndmills, Basingstoke, Hampshire, RG21 6XS, England, (Telephone in U.S. (888) 330-8477), (Fax in U.S. (800) 672-2054), www.palgrave.com; *The Statesman's Yearbook 2008.*

United Nations Economic Commission for Africa (ECA), PO Box 3001, Addis Ababa, Ethiopia, (Telephone in U.S. (212) 963-4957), www.uneca.org; *African Statistical Yearbook 2006.*

United Nations Statistics Division, New York, NY 10017, (800) 253-9646, Fax: (212) 963-4116, http://unstats.un.org; *Survey of Economic and Social Conditions in Africa 2005.*

COTE d'IVOIRE - RUBBER INDUSTRY AND TRADE

International Rubber Study Group (IRSG), 1st Floor, Heron House, 109/115 Wembley Hill Road, Wembley, Middlesex HA9 8DA, United Kingdom, www.rubberstudy.com; *Rubber Statistical Bulletin; Summary of World Rubber Statistics 2005; World Rubber Statistics Handbook (Volume 6, 1975-2001);* and *World Rubber Statistics Historic Handbook.*

M.E. Sharpe, 80 Business Park Drive, Armonk, NY 10504, (800) 541-6563, Fax: (914) 273-2106, www.mesharpe.com; *The Illustrated Book of World Rankings.*

United Nations Statistics Division, New York, NY 10017, (800) 253-9646, Fax: (212) 963-4116, http://unstats.un.org; *Statistical Yearbook.*

COTE d'IVOIRE - SHEEP

See COTE d'IVOIRE - LIVESTOCK

COTE d'IVOIRE - SHIPPING

Palgrave Macmillan Ltd., Houndmills, Basingstoke, Hampshire, RG21 6XS, England, (Telephone in U.S. (888) 330-8477), (Fax in U.S. (800) 672-2054), www.palgrave.com; *The Statesman's Yearbook 2008.*

Taylor and Francis Group, An Informa Business, 2 Park Square, Milton Park, Abingdon, Oxford OX14 4RN, United Kingdom, (Dial from U.S. (212) 216-7800), (Fax from U.S. (212) 564-7854), www.tandf.co.uk; *The Europa World Year Book.*

U.S. Department of Transportation (DOT), Maritime Administration (MARAD), West Building, Southeast Federal Center, 1200 New Jersey Avenue, SE, Washington, DC 20590, (800) 99-MARAD, www.marad.dot.gov; *World Merchant Fleet 2005.*

United Nations Economic Commission for Africa (ECA), PO Box 3001, Addis Ababa, Ethiopia, (Telephone in U.S. (212) 963-4957), www.uneca.org; *African Statistical Yearbook 2006.*

United Nations Statistics Division, New York, NY 10017, (800) 253-9646, Fax: (212) 963-4116, http://unstats.un.org; *Statistical Yearbook.*

COTE d'IVOIRE - SILVER PRODUCTION

See COTE d'IVOIRE - MINERAL INDUSTRIES

COTE d'IVOIRE - SOCIAL ECOLOGY

M.E. Sharpe, 80 Business Park Drive, Armonk, NY 10504, (800) 541-6563, Fax: (914) 273-2106, www.mesharpe.com; *The Illustrated Book of World Rankings.*

United Nations Statistics Division, New York, NY 10017, (800) 253-9646, Fax: (212) 963-4116, http://unstats.un.org; *World Statistics Pocketbook.*

COTE d'IVOIRE - STEEL PRODUCTION

See COTE d'IVOIRE - MINERAL INDUSTRIES

COTE d'IVOIRE - SUGAR PRODUCTION

See COTE d'IVOIRE - CROPS

COTE d'IVOIRE - TAXATION

International Road Federation (IFR), Madison Place, 500 Montgomery Street, 5th Floor, Alexandria, VA 22314, (703) 535-1001, Fax: (703) 535-1007, www.irfnet.org; *World Road Statistics 2006.*

Taylor and Francis Group, An Informa Business, 2 Park Square, Milton Park, Abingdon, Oxford OX14 4RN, United Kingdom, (Dial from U.S. (212) 216-7800), (Fax from U.S. (212) 564-7854), www.tandf.co.uk; *The Europa World Year Book.*

The World Bank, 1818 H Street, NW, Washington, DC 20433, (202) 473-1000, Fax: (202) 477-6391, www.worldbank.org; *World Development Indicators (WDI) 2008.*

COTE d'IVOIRE - TELEPHONE

International Telecommunication Union (ITU), Place des Nations, 1211 Geneva 20, Switzerland, www.itu.int; World Telecommunication Indicators Database.

Palgrave Macmillan Ltd., Houndmills, Basingstoke, Hampshire, RG21 6XS, England, (Telephone in U.S. (888) 330-8477), (Fax in U.S. (800) 672-2054), www.palgrave.com; *The Statesman's Yearbook 2008.*

Taylor and Francis Group, An Informa Business, 2 Park Square, Milton Park, Abingdon, Oxford OX14 4RN, United Kingdom, (Dial from U.S. (212) 216-7800), (Fax from U.S. (212) 564-7854), www.tandf.co.uk; *The Europa World Year Book.*

United Nations Statistics Division, New York, NY 10017, (800) 253-9646, Fax: (212) 963-4116, http://unstats.un.org; *Statistical Yearbook* and *World Statistics Pocketbook.*

COTE d'IVOIRE - TEXTILE INDUSTRY

M.E. Sharpe, 80 Business Park Drive, Armonk, NY 10504, (800) 541-6563, Fax: (914) 273-2106, www.mesharpe.com; *The Illustrated Book of World Rankings.*

Palgrave Macmillan Ltd., Houndmills, Basingstoke, Hampshire, RG21 6XS, England, (Telephone in U.S. (888) 330-8477), (Fax in U.S. (800) 672-2054), www.palgrave.com; *The Statesman's Yearbook 2008.*

United Nations Conference on Trade and Development (UNCTAD), DC2-1120, United Nations, New York, NY 10017, (212) 963-0027, www.unctad.org; *UNCTAD Commodity Yearbook.*

United Nations Statistics Division, New York, NY 10017, (800) 253-9646, Fax: (212) 963-4116, http://unstats.un.org; *Statistical Yearbook.*

COTE d'IVOIRE - TOBACCO INDUSTRY

Foreign Agricultural Service (FAS), U.S. Department of Agriculture (USDA), 1400 Independence Avenue, SW, Washington, DC 20250, (202) 720-3935, www.fas.usda.gov; *Tobacco: World Markets and Trade.*

M.E. Sharpe, 80 Business Park Drive, Armonk, NY 10504, (800) 541-6563, Fax: (914) 273-2106, www.mesharpe.com; *The Illustrated Book of World Rankings.*

United Nations Statistics Division, New York, NY 10017, (800) 253-9646, Fax: (212) 963-4116, http://unstats.un.org; *Statistical Yearbook.*

COTE d'IVOIRE - TOURISM

Euromonitor International, Inc., 224 S. Michigan Avenue, Suite 1500, Chicago, IL 60604, (312) 922-

1115, Fax: (312) 922-1157, www.euromonitor.com; *The World Economic Factbook 2008* and *World Marketing Data and Statistics.*

M.E. Sharpe, 80 Business Park Drive, Armonk, NY 10504, (800) 541-6563, Fax: (914) 273-2106, www.mesharpe.com; *The Illustrated Book of World Rankings.*

Taylor and Francis Group, An Informa Business, 2 Park Square, Milton Park, Abingdon, Oxford OX14 4RN, United Kingdom, (Dial from U.S. (212) 216-7800), (Fax from U.S. (212) 564-7854), www.tandf.co.uk; *The Europa World Year Book.*

United Nations Economic Commission for Africa (ECA), PO Box 3001, Addis Ababa, Ethiopia, (Telephone in U.S. (212) 963-4957), www.uneca.org; *African Statistical Yearbook 2006.*

United Nations Statistics Division, New York, NY 10017, (800) 253-9646, Fax: (212) 963-4116, http://unstats.un.org; *Statistical Yearbook.*

United Nations World Tourism Organization (UN-WTO), Capitan Haya 42, 28020 Madrid, Spain, www.world-tourism.org; *Yearbook of Tourism Statistics.*

The World Bank, 1818 H Street, NW, Washington, DC 20433, (202) 473-1000, Fax: (202) 477-6391, www.worldbank.org; *Cote d'Ivoire.*

COTE d'IVOIRE - TRADE

See COTE d'IVOIRE - INTERNATIONAL TRADE

COTE d'IVOIRE - TRANSPORTATION

Central Intelligence Agency, Office of Public Affairs, Washington, DC 20505, (703) 482-0623, Fax: (703) 482-1739, www.cia.gov; *The World Factbook.*

Euromonitor International, Inc., 224 S. Michigan Avenue, Suite 1500, Chicago, IL 60604, (312) 922-1115, Fax: (312) 922-1157, www.euromonitor.com; *International Marketing Data and Statistics 2008* and *World Marketing Data and Statistics.*

M.E. Sharpe, 80 Business Park Drive, Armonk, NY 10504, (800) 541-6563, Fax: (914) 273-2106, www.mesharpe.com; *The Illustrated Book of World Rankings.*

Palgrave Macmillan Ltd., Houndmills, Basingstoke, Hampshire, RG21 6XS, England, (Telephone in U.S. (888) 330-8477), (Fax in U.S. (800) 672-2054), www.palgrave.com; *The Statesman's Yearbook 2008.*

Taylor and Francis Group, An Informa Business, 2 Park Square, Milton Park, Abingdon, Oxford OX14 4RN, United Kingdom, (Dial from U.S. (212) 216-7800), (Fax from U.S. (212) 564-7854), www.tandf.co.uk; *The Europa World Year Book.*

United Nations Economic Commission for Africa (ECA), PO Box 3001, Addis Ababa, Ethiopia, (Telephone in U.S. (212) 963-4957), www.uneca.org; *African Statistical Yearbook 2006.*

United Nations Statistics Division, New York, NY 10017, (800) 253-9646, Fax: (212) 963-4116, http://unstats.un.org; *Human Development Report 2006.*

The World Bank, 1818 H Street, NW, Washington, DC 20433, (202) 473-1000, Fax: (202) 477-6391, www.worldbank.org; *Africa Live Database (LDB)* and *Cote d'Ivoire.*

COTE d'IVOIRE - UNEMPLOYMENT

Central Intelligence Agency, Office of Public Affairs, Washington, DC 20505, (703) 482-0623, Fax: (703) 482-1739, www.cia.gov; *The World Factbook.*

Euromonitor International, Inc., 224 S. Michigan Avenue, Suite 1500, Chicago, IL 60604, (312) 922-1115, Fax: (312) 922-1157, www.euromonitor.com; *International Marketing Data and Statistics 2008.*

COTE d'IVOIRE - VITAL STATISTICS

Euromonitor International, Inc., 224 S. Michigan Avenue, Suite 1500, Chicago, IL 60604, (312) 922-1115, Fax: (312) 922-1157, www.euromonitor.com; *International Marketing Data and Statistics 2008.*

United Nations Statistics Division, New York, NY 10017, (800) 253-9646, Fax: (212) 963-4116, http://unstats.un.org; *Statistical Yearbook.*

World Health Organization (WHO), Avenue Appia 20, 1211 Geneve 27, Switzerland, (Telephone in U.S. (212) 331-9081), www.who.int; *World Health Report 2006.*

COTE d'IVOIRE - WAGES

The World Bank, 1818 H Street, NW, Washington, DC 20433, (202) 473-1000, Fax: (202) 477-6391, www.worldbank.org; *Cote d'Ivoire.*

COTE d'IVOIRE - WHEAT PRODUCTION

See COTE d'IVOIRE - CROPS

COTE d'IVOIRE - WHOLESALE PRICE INDEXES

United Nations Statistics Division, New York, NY 10017, (800) 253-9646, Fax: (212) 963-4116, http://unstats.un.org; *Statistical Yearbook.*

COTE d'IVOIRE - WINE PRODUCTION

See COTE d'IVOIRE - BEVERAGE INDUSTRY

COTE d'IVOIRE - WOOL PRODUCTION

See COTE d'IVOIRE - TEXTILE INDUSTRY

COTE d'IVOIRE - YARN PRODUCTION

See COTE d'IVOIRE - TEXTILE INDUSTRY

COTTON - ACREAGE

National Agricultural Statistics Service (NASS), U.S. Department of Agriculture (USDA), 1400 Independence Avenue, SW, Washington, DC 20250, (800) 727-9540, Fax: (202) 690-2090, www.nass.usda.gov; *Crop Production* and *Crop Values 2007 Summary.*

COTTON - ACREAGE - GENETICALLY MODIFIED SEED PLANTINGS

National Agricultural Statistics Service (NASS), U.S. Department of Agriculture (USDA), 1400 Independence Avenue, SW, Washington, DC 20250, (800) 727-9540, Fax: (202) 690-2090, www.nass.usda.gov; *Acreage.*

COTTON - CONSUMPTION

Fiber Economics Bureau (FEB), 1530 Wilson Boulevard, Suite 690, Arlington VA 22209, (703) 875-0676, Fax: (703) 875-0675, www.fibereconomics.com; *Manufactured Fiber Handbook* and *Manufactured Fiber Review.*

COTTON - INTERNATIONAL TRADE

Economic Research Service (ERS), U.S. Department of Agriculture (USDA), 1800 M Street, NW, Washington, DC 20036-5831, (202) 694-5050, Fax: (202) 694-5689, www.ers.usda.gov; *Agricultural Outlook; Agricultural Statistics; Cotton and Wool Outlook: 2008; Foreign Agricultural Trade of the United States (FATUS); U.S. Agricultural Trade Update: 2006;* and *World Agricultural Supply and Demand Estimates (WASDE): 2008.*

Fiber Economics Bureau (FEB), 1530 Wilson Boulevard, Suite 690, Arlington VA 22209, (703) 875-0676, Fax: (703) 875-0675, www.fibereconomics.com; *Manufactured Fiber Handbook* and *Manufactured Fiber Review.*

Foreign Agricultural Service (FAS), U.S. Department of Agriculture (USDA), 1400 Independence Avenue, SW, Washington, DC 20250, (202) 720-3935, www.fas.usda.gov; Foreign Agricultural Service's U.S. Trade Internet System.

National Agricultural Statistics Service (NASS), U.S. Department of Agriculture (USDA), 1400 Independence Avenue, SW, Washington, DC 20250, (800) 727-9540, Fax: (202) 690-2090, www.nass.usda.gov; *Crop Production* and *Crop Values 2007 Summary.*

U.S. Census Bureau, Foreign Trade Division, 4700 Silver Hill Road, Washington DC 20233-0001, (301) 763-3030, www.census.gov/foreign-trade/www/; *U.S. International Trade in Goods and Services.*

COTTON - PESTICIDES

Foreign Agricultural Service (FAS), U.S. Department of Agriculture (USDA), 1400 Independence Avenue, SW, Washington, DC 20250, (202) 720-3935, www.fas.usda.gov; Production, Supply and Distribution Online (PSD) Online.

COTTON - PRICES

Economic Research Service (ERS), U.S. Department of Agriculture (USDA), 1800 M Street, NW, Washington, DC 20036-5831, (202) 694-5050, Fax: (202) 694-5689, www.ers.usda.gov; *Agricultural Outlook; Agricultural Statistics; Cotton and Wool Outlook: 2008;* and *World Agricultural Supply and Demand Estimates (WASDE): 2008.*

National Agricultural Statistics Service (NASS), U.S. Department of Agriculture (USDA), 1400 Independence Avenue, SW, Washington, DC 20250, (800) 727-9540, Fax: (202) 690-2090, www.nass.usda.gov; *Agricultural Prices; Crop Production;* and *Crop Values 2007 Summary.*

COTTON - PRODUCTION

Economic Research Service (ERS), U.S. Department of Agriculture (USDA), 1800 M Street, NW, Washington, DC 20036-5831, (202) 694-5050, Fax: (202) 694-5689, www.ers.usda.gov; *Agricultural Outlook; Agricultural Statistics; Cotton and Wool Outlook: 2008;* and *World Agricultural Supply and Demand Estimates (WASDE): 2008.*

Foreign Agricultural Service (FAS), U.S. Department of Agriculture (USDA), 1400 Independence Avenue, SW, Washington, DC 20250, (202) 720-3935, www.fas.usda.gov; Foreign Agricultural Service's U.S. Trade Internet System.

National Agricultural Statistics Service (NASS), U.S. Department of Agriculture (USDA), 1400 Independence Avenue, SW, Washington, DC 20250, (800) 727-9540, Fax: (202) 690-2090, www.nass.usda.gov; *Crop Production* and *Crop Values 2007 Summary.*

COTTON - PRODUCTION - WORLD

Foreign Agricultural Service (FAS), U.S. Department of Agriculture (USDA), 1400 Independence Avenue, SW, Washington, DC 20250, (202) 720-3935, www.fas.usda.gov; Foreign Agricultural Service's U.S. Trade Internet System.

United Nations Statistics Division, New York, NY 10017, (800) 253-9646, Fax: (212) 963-4116, http://unstats.un.org; *Monthly Bulletin of Statistics.*

COTTON - SUPPLY AND DISAPPEARANCE

Economic Research Service (ERS), U.S. Department of Agriculture (USDA), 1800 M Street, NW, Washington, DC 20036-5831, (202) 694-5050, Fax: (202) 694-5689, www.ers.usda.gov; *Agricultural Outlook; Agricultural Statistics; Cotton and Wool Outlook: 2008;* and *World Agricultural Supply and Demand Estimates (WASDE): 2008.*

COUNTY GOVERNMENTS

U.S. Census Bureau, Governments Division, 4600 Silver Hill Road, Washington DC 20233, (800) 242-2184, www.census.gov/govs/www; *2002 Census of Governments, Government Organization.*

COUNTY GOVERNMENTS - DEBT

U.S. Census Bureau, Governments Division, 4600 Silver Hill Road, Washington DC 20233, (800) 242-2184, www.census.gov/govs/www; *2002 Census of Governments, Government Finances.*

COUNTY GOVERNMENTS - ELECTED OFFICIALS

Joint Center for Political and Economic Studies, 1090 Vermont Avenue, NW, Suite 1100, Washington, DC 20005-4928, (202) 789-3500, Fax: (202) 789-6390, www.jointcenter.org; *Black Elected Officials: A Statistical Summary.*

National Association of Latino Elected and Appointed Officials (NALEO) Educational Fund, 1122 West Washington Blvd., 3rd Floor, Los Angeles CA 90015, (213) 747-7606, Fax: (213) 747-7664, www.naleo.org; *2006 National Directory of Latino Elected Officials.*

COUNTY GOVERNMENTS - EMPLOYEES, EARNINGS, PAYROLL

U.S. Census Bureau, Governments Division, 4600 Silver Hill Road, Washington DC 20233, (800) 242-2184, www.census.gov/govs/www; *2002 Census of Governments, Public Employment and Payroll.*

COUNTY GOVERNMENTS - FINANCES OF COUNTY GOVERNMENTS

U.S. Census Bureau, Governments Division, 4600 Silver Hill Road, Washington DC 20233, (800) 242-2184, www.census.gov/govs/www; *2002 Census of Governments, Government Finances.*

COURIERS AND MESSENGERS - EARNINGS

U.S. Census Bureau, Center for Economic Studies, 4600 Silver Hill Road, Washington DC 20233, (301) 457-1235, www.ces.census.gov; *2002 Economic Census, Transportation and Warehousing.*

U.S. Census Bureau, Company Statistics Division, 4700 Silver Hill Road, Washington DC 20233-0001, (301) 763-3030, www.census.gov/csd/; *County Business Patterns 2004.*

COURIERS AND MESSENGERS - EMPLOYEES

U.S. Census Bureau, Center for Economic Studies, 4600 Silver Hill Road, Washington DC 20233, (301) 457-1235, www.ces.census.gov; *2002 Economic Census, Transportation and Warehousing.*

U.S. Census Bureau, Company Statistics Division, 4700 Silver Hill Road, Washington DC 20233-0001, (301) 763-3030, www.census.gov/csd/; *County Business Patterns 2004.*

COURIERS AND MESSENGERS - ESTABLISHMENTS

U.S. Census Bureau, Center for Economic Studies, 4600 Silver Hill Road, Washington DC 20233, (301) 457-1235, www.ces.census.gov; *2002 Economic Census, Transportation and Warehousing.*

U.S. Census Bureau, Company Statistics Division, 4700 Silver Hill Road, Washington DC 20233-0001, (301) 763-3030, www.census.gov/csd/; *County Business Patterns 2004.*

COURIERS AND MESSENGERS - REVENUE

U.S. Census Bureau, Center for Economic Studies, 4600 Silver Hill Road, Washington DC 20233, (301) 457-1235, www.ces.census.gov; *2002 Economic Census, Transportation and Warehousing.*

U.S. Census Bureau, Company Statistics Division, 4700 Silver Hill Road, Washington DC 20233-0001, (301) 763-3030, www.census.gov/csd/; *County Business Patterns 2004.*

U.S. Census Bureau, Service Sector Statistics Division, 4700 Silver Hill Road, Washington DC 20233-0001, (301) 763-3030, www.census.gov/svsd/www/economic.html; *2004 Service Annual Survey: Truck Transportation, Messenger Services and Warehousing.*

COURTS

Australian Institute of Criminology, 74 Leichhardt Street, Griffith ACT 2603 Australia, www.aic.gov.au/; *Final report on the North Queensland Drug Court.*

Congressional Quarterly, Inc., 1255 22nd Street, NW, Washington, DC 20037, (202) 419-8500, www.cq.com; *Supreme Court Compendium.*

Home Office Research Development and Statistics (RDS), Direct Communications Unit, 2 Marsham Street, London SW1P 4DF, United Kingdom, www.homeoffice.gov.uk/rds/; *Local Sentencing Patterns in Magistrates' Courts, 2000; Probation Statistics England and Wales 2002; Race and the Criminal Justice System: An Overview to the Complete Statistics 2004-2005;* and *Statistics on Women and the Criminal Justice System - 2004/05.*

Justice Research and Statistics Association (JRSA), 777 N. Capitol Street, NE, Suite 801, Washington, DC 20002, (202) 842-9330, Fax: (202) 842-9329, www.jrsa.org; *Directory of Justice Issues in the States; Documenting the Extent and Nature of Drug and Violent Crime: Developing Jurisdiction-Specific Profiles of the Criminal Justice System; The Forum;* InfoBase of State Activities and Research (ISAR); *JRP Digest; Justice Research and Policy;* and *SAC Publication Digest.*

National Center for Juvenile Justice (NCJJ), 3700 South Water Street, Suite 200, Pittsburgh, PA 15203, (412) 227-6950, Fax: (412) 227-6955, http://ncjj.servehttp.com/NCJJWebsite/main.htm; *Detention and Delinquency Cases 1990-1999 (2003); Good News: Measuring Juvenile Court Outcomes at Case Closing, 2003 (2003); How Does the Juvenile Justice System Measure Up? Applying Performance Measures in Five Jurisdictions (2006); Jury Trial in Abuse, Neglect, Dependency Cases; Jury Trial in Termination of Parental Rights (2005 Update);* and *Juvenile Court Statistics 2000 (2004).*

National Center for State Courts (NCSC), 300 Newport Avenue, Williamsburg, VA 23185-4147, (800) 616-6164, Fax: (757) 564-2022, www.ncsconline.org; *Examining the Work of State Courts, 2004; Maryland Attorney Staff Workload Assessment, 2005; Minnesota Court Staff Workload Assessment, 2004; State Court Organization, 2004; The State Courts in 2006: Surviving Anti-Court Initiatives and Demonstrating High Performance;* and *Trust and Confidence in the California Courts, 2005, A Survey of the Public and Attorneys.*

National Criminal Justice Reference Service (NCJRS), PO Box 6000, Rockville, MD 20849-6000, (800) 851-3420, Fax: (301) 519-5212, www.ncjrs.org; *New Jersey's "No Early Release Act": Its Impact on Prosecution, Sentencing, Corrections, and Victim Satisfaction, Final Report.*

Office of Public Affairs, Administrative Office of the United States Courts, Washington, DC 20544, (202) 502-2600, www.uscourts.gov; *Statistical Tables for the Federal Judiciary.*

Supreme Court of the United States, Office of the Clerk, United States Supreme Court Building, One First Street, NE, Washington, DC 20543, (202) 479-3000, www.supremecourtus.gov; unpublished data.

U.S. Department of Justice (DOJ), Bureau of Justice Statistics, 810 Seventh Street, NW, Washington, DC 20531, (202) 307-0765, www.ojp.usdoj.gov/bjs/; *Appeals from General Civil Trials in 46 Large Counties, 2001-2005; Contract Trials and Verdicts in Large Counties, 2001; Defense Counsel in Criminal Cases; Drugs Crime Facts; Federal Criminal Justice Trends, 2003; Federal Justice Statistics Resource Center; Federal Prosecution of Human Trafficking, 2001-2005; Felony Defendants in Large Urban Counties, 2002; Justice Expenditure and Employment in the United States 2003; Money Laundering Offenders, 1994-2001; Prosecutors in State Courts, 2005; Reporting by Prosecutors' Offices to Repositories of Criminal History Records; State Court Organization, 2004; State Court Prosecutors in Large Districts, 2001; State Court Prosecutors in Small Districts, 2001; State Court Sentencing of Convicted Felons;* and *Tort Trials and Verdicts in Large Counties, 2001.*

U.S. Department of Justice (DOJ), Drug Enforcement Administration (DEA), 2401 Jefferson Davis Highway, Alexandria, VA 22301, (202) 307-1000, www.usdoj.gov/dea; *State Factsheets* and *2005 US Money Laundering Threat Assessment.*

U.S. Department of Justice (DOJ), National Institute of Justice (NIJ), 810 Seventh Street, NW, Washington, DC 20531, (202) 307-2942, Fax: (202) 616-0275, www.ojp.usdoj.gov/nij/; *Drug Courts: The Second Decade.*

U.S. Department of Justice (DOJ), Office of the Attorney General, 950 Pennsylvania Avenue, NW, Washington, DC 20530-0001, (202) 353-1555, www.usdoj.gov/ag; *Assessment of U.S. Government Activities to Combat Trafficking in Persons.*

The Urban Institute, 2100 M Street, N.W., Washington, DC 20037, (202) 833-7200, www.urban.org; *Federal Criminal Case Processing, 2000: With Trends 1982-2000.*

COURTS - DISTRICT COURTS, UNITED STATES

Center for Substance Abuse Research (CESAR), 4321 Hartwick Road, Suite 501, College Park, MD 20740, (301) 405-9770, Fax: (301) 403-8342, www.cesar.umd.edu; *Assessment and Treatment of DWI Offenders in Maryland, 1995-2003: Current Findings.*

National Center for State Courts (NCSC), 300 Newport Avenue, Williamsburg, VA 23185-4147, (800) 616-6164, Fax: (757) 564-2022, www.ncsconline.org; *Examining the Work of State Courts, 2004; Maryland Attorney Staff Workload Assessment, 2005; Minnesota Court Staff Workload Assessment, 2004; State Court Organization, 2004; The State Courts in 2006: Surviving Anti-Court Initiatives and Demonstrating High Performance;* and *Trust and Confidence in the California Courts, 2005, A Survey of the Public and Attorneys.*

Office of Public Affairs, Administrative Office of the United States Courts, Washington, DC 20544, (202) 502-2600, www.uscourts.gov; *Statistical Tables for the Federal Judiciary.*

U.S. Department of Justice (DOJ), Bureau of Justice Statistics, 810 Seventh Street, NW, Washington, DC 20531, (202) 307-0765, www.ojp.usdoj.gov/bjs/; *Civil Rights Complaints in U.S. District Courts, 2000; Civil Trial Cases and Verdicts in Large Counties, 2001; Compendium of Federal Justice Statistics, 2003; Federal Justice Statistics Resource Center; Federal Tort Trials and Verdicts, 2002-03; Medical Malpractice Trials and Verdicts in Large Counties, 2001; Prisoner Petitions Filed in U.S. District Courts, 2000, with Trends, 1980-2000; Punitive Damage Awards in Large Counties, 2001; State Court Organization, 2004; State Court Prosecutors in Large Districts, 2001; State Court Prosecutors in Small Districts, 2001; State Court Sentencing of Convicted Felons;* and *Tort Trials and Verdicts in Large Counties, 2001.*

U.S. Department of Justice (DOJ), National Institute of Justice (NIJ), 810 Seventh Street, NW, Washington, DC 20531, (202) 307-2942, Fax: (202) 616-0275, www.ojp.usdoj.gov/nij/; *Drug Courts: The Second Decade.*

COURTS - JUVENILE COURT CASES HANDLED

National Center for Juvenile Justice (NCJJ), 3700 South Water Street, Suite 200, Pittsburgh, PA 15203, (412) 227-6950, Fax: (412) 227-6955, http://ncjj.servehttp.com/NCJJWebsite/main.htm; *Detention and Delinquency Cases 1990-1999 (2003); Good News: Measuring Juvenile Court Outcomes at Case Closing, 2003 (2003); How Does the Juvenile Justice System Measure Up? Applying Performance Measures in Five Jurisdictions (2006); Jury Trial in Abuse, Neglect, Dependency Cases; Jury Trial in Termination of Parental Rights (2005 Update); Juvenile Arrests 2003 (2005); Juvenile Court Statistics 2000 (2004); Juvenile Offenders and Victims: 2006 National Report; Juveniles in Corrections (2004);* and *Person Offenses in Juvenile Court, 1990-1999 (2003).*

National Criminal Justice Reference Service (NCJRS), PO Box 6000, Rockville, MD 20849-6000, (800) 851-3420, Fax: (301) 519-5212, www.ncjrs.org; *Delaware Juvenile Recidivism 1994-2005 Juvenile Level III, IV and V Recidivism Study* and *Presence of Learning Disabled Youth in Our Juvenile Institutions: Excusable or Gross Negligence?*

Office of Juvenile Justice and Delinquency Prevention (OJJDP), 810 Seventh Street, NW, Washington, DC 20531, (202) 307-5911, www.ojjdp.ncjrs.org; *Statistical Briefing Book (SBB).*

U.S. Department of Justice (DOJ), Bureau of Justice Statistics, 810 Seventh Street, NW, Washington, DC 20531, (202) 307-0765, www.ojp.usdoj.gov/bjs/; *Juvenile Victimization and Offending, 1993-2003; State Court Prosecutors in Large Districts, 2001;* and *State Court Prosecutors in Small Districts, 2001.*

U.S. Department of Justice (DOJ), National Institute of Justice (NIJ), 810 Seventh Street, NW, Washington, DC 20531, (202) 307-2942, Fax: (202) 616-0275, www.ojp.usdoj.gov/nij/; *Co-Offending and Patterns of Juvenile Crime.*

The Urban Institute, 2100 M Street, N.W., Washington, DC 20037, (202) 833-7200, www.urban.org; *Juvenile Crime in Washington, D.C.; The Rise and Fall of American Youth Violence: 1980 to 2000;* and *Youth Crime Drop.*

COURTS - PUBLIC OFFICIALS - PROSECUTIONS

U.S. Department of Justice (DOJ), Bureau of Justice Statistics, 810 Seventh Street, NW, Washington, DC 20531, (202) 307-0765, www.ojp.usdoj.gov/bjs/; *Reporting by Prosecutors' Offices to Repositories of Criminal History Records; State Court Prosecutors in Large Districts, 2001;* and *State Court Prosecutors in Small Districts, 2001.*

U.S. Department of Justice (DOJ), Criminal Division, 950 Pennsylvania Ave., Washington, DC 20530-0001, (202) 514-2601, www.usdoj.gov/criminal/; *Report to Congress on the Activities and Operations of the Public Integrity Section.*

COURTS - SENTENCING

Home Office Research Development and Statistics (RDS), Direct Communications Unit, 2 Marsham Street, London SW1P 4DF, United Kingdom, www.homeoffice.gov.uk/rds/; *Local Sentencing Patterns in Magistrates' Courts, 2000; Probation Statistics England and Wales 2002;* and *Race and the Criminal Justice System: An Overview to the Complete Statistics 2004-2005.*

National Center for Juvenile Justice (NCJJ), 3700 South Water Street, Suite 200, Pittsburgh, PA 15203, (412) 227-6950, Fax: (412) 227-6955, http://ncjj.servehttp.com/NCJJWebsite/main.htm; *Good News: Measuring Juvenile Court Outcomes at Case Closing, 2003 (2003)* and *How Does the Juvenile Justice System Measure Up? Applying Performance Measures in Five Jurisdictions (2006).*

National Criminal Justice Reference Service (NCJRS), PO Box 6000, Rockville, MD 20849-6000, (800) 851-3420, Fax: (301) 519-5212, www.ncjrs.org; *New Jersey's "No Early Release Act": Its Impact on Prosecution, Sentencing, Corrections, and Victim Satisfaction, Final Report.*

U.S. Department of Justice (DOJ), Bureau of Justice Statistics, 810 Seventh Street, NW, Washington, DC 20531, (202) 307-0765, www.ojp.usdoj.gov/bjs/; *Civil Trial Cases and Verdicts in Large Counties, 2001; Compendium of Federal Justice Statistics, 2003; Contract Trials and Verdicts in Large Counties, 2001; Felony Sentences in State Courts, 2002; Medical Malpractice Trials and Verdicts in Large Counties, 2001; Punitive Damage Awards in Large Counties, 2001;* and *State Court Sentencing of Convicted Felons.*

The Urban Institute, 2100 M Street, N.W., Washington, DC 20037, (202) 833-7200, www.urban.org; *The Influences of Truth-in-Sentencing Reforms on Changes in States' Sentencing Practices and Prison Populations.*

COURTS - SUPREME COURT, UNITED STATES

Office of Public Affairs, Administrative Office of the United States Courts, Washington, DC 20544, (202) 502-2600, www.uscourts.gov; unpublished data.

U.S. Library of Congress (LOC), Congressional Research Service (CRS), The Library of Congress, 101 Independence Avenue, SE, Washington, DC 20540-7500, (202) 707-5700, www.loc.gov/crsinfo; *Speed of Presidential and Senate Actions on Supreme Court Nominations, 1900-2005.*

COWS

National Agricultural Statistics Service (NASS), U.S. Department of Agriculture (USDA), 1400 Independence Avenue, SW, Washington, DC 20250, (800) 727-9540, Fax: (202) 690-2090, www.nass.usda.gov; *Dairy Products* and *Milk Cows and Milk Production.*

CRABS

National Marine Fisheries Service (NMFS), National Oceanic and Atmospheric Administration (NOAA), Office of Constituent Services, 1315 East West Highway, 9th Floor, Silver Spring, MD 20910, (301) 713-2379, Fax: (301) 713-2385, www.nmfs.noaa.gov; *Fisheries of the United States - 2006.*

CRACK COCAINE

Substance Abuse and Mental Health Services Administration (SAMHSA), 1 Choke Cherry Road, Rockville, MD 20857, (240) 777-1311, www.oas.samhsa.gov; *National Survey on Drug Use Health (NSDUH).*

U.S. Department of Justice (DOJ), National Institute of Justice (NIJ), 810 Seventh Street, NW, Washington, DC 20531, (202) 307-2942, Fax: (202) 616-0275, www.ojp.usdoj.gov/nij/; *ADAM Preliminary 2000 Findings on Drug Use Drug Markets: Adult Male Arrestees; Drug Courts: The Second Decade;* and *I-ADAM in Eight Countries: Approaches and Challenges.*

CRANBERRIES

National Agricultural Statistics Service (NASS), U.S. Department of Agriculture (USDA), 1400 Independence Avenue, SW, Washington, DC 20250, (800) 727-9540, Fax: (202) 690-2090, www.nass.usda.gov; *Noncitrus Fruits and Nuts: Final Estimates 1998-2003.*

CREDIT CARDS

Board of Governors of the Federal Reserve System, Constitution Avenue, NW, Washington, DC 20551, (202) 452-3000, www.federalreserve.gov; *Federal Reserve Bulletin* and unpublished data.

Federal Financial Institutions Examination Council (FFIEC), 3501 Fairfax Drive, Room D8073A, Arlington, VA 22226, (202) 872-7500, www.ffiec.gov; *Uniform Bank Performance Report (UBPR).*

National Center for Education Statistics (NCES), 1990 K Street, NW, Washington, DC 20006, (202) 502-7300, http://nces.ed.gov; *Profile of Undergraduates in U.S. Postsecondary Education Institutions: 2003-04, With a Special Analysis of Community College Students.*

The Nilson Report, 1110 Eugenia Place, Suite 100, Carpinteria, CA 93013-9921, (805) 684-8800, Fax: (805) 684-8825, www.nilsonreport.com; *The Nilson Report.*

CREDIT MARKETS

Board of Governors of the Federal Reserve System, Constitution Avenue, NW, Washington, DC 20551, (202) 452-3000, www.federalreserve.gov; *Federal Reserve Bulletin; Flow of Funds Accounts of the United States; Statistical Digest;* and unpublished data.

CREDIT MARKETS - FEDERAL PARTICIPATION

The Office of Management and Budget (OMB), 725 17th Street, NW, Washington, DC 20503, (202) 395-3080, Fax: (202) 395-3888, www.whitehouse.gov/omb; *Analytical Perspectives, Budget of the United States Government, Fiscal Year 2009* and *Budget of the United States Government, Federal Year 2009.*

CREDIT UNIONS - EARNINGS

U.S. Census Bureau, Company Statistics Division, 4700 Silver Hill Road, Washington DC 20233-0001, (301) 763-3030, www.census.gov/csd/; *County Business Patterns 2004.*

CREDIT UNIONS - EMPLOYEES

U.S. Census Bureau, Company Statistics Division, 4700 Silver Hill Road, Washington DC 20233-0001, (301) 763-3030, www.census.gov/csd/; *County Business Patterns 2004.*

CREDIT UNIONS - ESTABLISHMENTS

Federal Deposit Insurance Corporation (FDIC), 550 Seventeenth Street, NW, Washington, DC 20429-0002, (877) 275-3342, www.fdic.gov; *State Banking Performance Summary.*

National Credit Union Administration (NCUA), 1775 Duke Street, Alexandria, VA 22314-3428, (703) 518-6300, www.ncua.gov; *Annual Report of NCUA (2007); Midyear Statistics for Federally Insured Credit Unions;* and *2007 Year End Statistics for Federally Insured Credit Unions.*

CREDIT UNIONS - FINANCES

Board of Governors of the Federal Reserve System, Constitution Avenue, NW, Washington, DC 20551, (202) 452-3000, www.federalreserve.gov; *Federal Reserve Bulletin; Flow of Funds Accounts of the United States;* and *Statistical Digest.*

Federal Deposit Insurance Corporation (FDIC), 550 Seventeenth Street, NW, Washington, DC 20429-0002, (877) 275-3342, www.fdic.gov; *State Banking Performance Summary.*

National Credit Union Administration (NCUA), 1775 Duke Street, Alexandria, VA 22314-3428, (703) 518-6300, www.ncua.gov; *Annual Report of NCUA (2007); Midyear Statistics for Federally Insured Credit Unions; 2007 Year End Statistics for Federally Insured Credit Unions;* and unpublished data.

CREDIT UNIONS - INDIVIDUAL RETIREMENT ACCOUNTS

Investment Company Institute (ICI), 1401 H Street, NW, Suite 1200, Washington, DC 20005-2040, (202) 326-5800, www.ici.org; *2007 Investment Company Fact Book.*

CREW

National Collegiate Athletic Association (NCAA), 700 West Washington Street, PO Box 6222, Indianapolis, IN 46206-6222, (317) 917-6222, Fax: (317) 917-6888, www.ncaa.org; *1982-2003 Sports Sponsorship and Participation Rates Report.*

CRIME

See also CRIMINAL VICTIMIZATION

Eurostat, Batiment Jean Monnet, Rue Alcide de Gasperi, L-2920 Luxembourg, http://epp.eurostat.ec.europa.eu; *Crime and Criminal Justice; General Government Expenditure and Revenue in the EU, 2006;* and *Study on Crime Victimisation.*

Federal Trade Commission (FTC), 600 Pennsylvania Avenue, NW, Washington, DC 20580, (202) 326-2222, www.ftc.gov; *2003 Identity Theft Survey Report; Identity Theft Victim Complaint Data 2006;* and *National and State Trends in Fraud and Identity Theft, January-December 2004.*

Home Office Research Development and Statistics (RDS), Direct Communications Unit, 2 Marsham Street, London SW1P 4DF, United Kingdom, www.homeoffice.gov.uk/rds/; *Crime in England and Wales 2005/2006; Evaluation of the Impact of the National Reassurance Policing Programme; National Reassurance Policing Programme: A Ten-Site Evaluation; Race and the Criminal Justice System: An Overview to the Complete Statistics 2004-2005;* and *Statistics on Women and the Criminal Justice System - 2004/05.*

International Organization for Migration (IOM), 17, Route des Morillons, CH-1211 Geneva 19, Switzerland, www.iom.int; *Migration, Human Smuggling and Trafficking from Nigeria to Europe.*

Justice Research and Statistics Association (JRSA), 777 N. Capitol Street, NE, Suite 801, Washington, DC 20002, (202) 842-9330, Fax: (202) 842-9329, www.jrsa.org; *The Forum; JRP Digest; Justice Research and Policy;* and *SAC Publication Digest.*

Lesotho Bureau of Statistics, Ministry of Finance and Development Planning, PO Box 455, Maseru 100, Lesotho, www.bos.gov.ls; *Crime Statistics 2005.*

Memorial Institute for the Prevention of Terrorism (MIPT), PO Box 889, Oklahoma City, Oklahoma 73101, (405) 278-6307, Fax: (405) 232-5132, www.mipt.org; *Terrorism Statistics 1980-1998.*

Metropolitan Police Department, 300 Indiana Avenue, NW, Washington, DC 20001, (202) 727-1000, http://mpdc.dc.gov/mpdc; *Annual Index Crime Totals, 1993-2005; District Crime Data at a Glance; Live Data Feeds of Crime Incidents and Other DC Services;* and *Monthly Preliminary Crime Statistics (2005-2006).*

National Center for Juvenile Justice (NCJJ), 3700 South Water Street, Suite 200, Pittsburgh, PA 15203, (412) 227-6950, Fax: (412) 227-6955, http://ncjj.servehttp.com/NCJJWebsite/main.htm; *Detention and Delinquency Cases 1990-1999 (2003); Good News: Measuring Juvenile Court Outcomes at Case Closing, 2003 (2003); How Does the Juvenile Justice System Measure Up? Applying Performance Measures in Five Jurisdictions (2006); Jury Trial in Abuse, Neglect, Dependency Cases; Jury Trial in Termination of Parental Rights (2005 Update); Juvenile Arrests 2003 (2005); Juvenile Court Statistics 2000 (2004); Juvenile Offenders and Victims: 2006 National Report; Juveniles in Corrections (2004);* and *Person Offenses in Juvenile Court, 1990-1999 (2003).*

The National Consortium for the Study of Terrorism and Responses to Terror (START), University of Maryland, College Park, MD 20742, (301) 405-6600, www.start.umd.edu; *Surveying State Police Agencies about Domestic Terrorism and Far-Right Extremists.*

National Counterterrorism Center (NCTC), Office of the Director of National Intelligence (ODNI), Washington, DC 20511, (703) 733-8600, www.nctc.gov; *2007 NCTC Report on Incidents of Terrorism* and *Worldwide Incidents Tracking System (WITS).*

National Criminal Justice Reference Service (NCJRS), PO Box 6000, Rockville, MD 20849-6000, (800) 851-3420, Fax: (301) 519-5212, www.ncjrs.org; *Changing the Landscape: The Effectiveness of Grant Programs Under the Violence Against Women Act: 2002 Biennial Report to Congress; Delaware Juvenile Recidivism 1994-2005 Juvenile Level III, IV and V Recidivism Study;* and *Presence of Learning Disabled Youth in Our Juvenile Institutions: Excusable or Gross Negligence?*

Robert Wood Johnson Foundation, PO Box 2316, College Road East and Route 1, Princeton, NJ 08543, (877) 843-7953, www.rwjf.org; *Community-Based Prevention Programs in the War on Drugs: Findings from the "Fighting Back" Demonstration; Community-Based Prevention Programs in the War on Drugs: Findings from the "Fighting Back" Demonstration;* and *Neighborhood Crime Victimization, Drug Use and Drug Sales: Results from the "Fighting Back" Evaluation.*

Royal Canadian Mounted Police (RCMP), 1200 Vanier Parkway, Ottawa, ON K1A 0R2, Canada, (613) 993-7267, www.rcmp-grc.gc.ca; *The Direct and Indirect Impacts of Organized Crime on Youth, as Offenders and Victims.*

U.S. Department of Justice (DOJ), Bureau of Justice Statistics, 810 Seventh Street, NW, Washington, DC 20531, (202) 307-0765, www.ojp.usdoj.gov/bjs/; *American Indians and Crime: A BJS Statistical Profile, 1992-2002; Bureau of Justice Statistics, 2002: At a Glance; Census of Jails; Characteristics of Drivers Stopped by Police, 2002; Citizen Complaints about Police Use of Force; Cross-National Studies in Crime and Justice; Drugs Crime Facts; Effects of NIBRS on Crime Statistics; Federal Criminal Justice Trends, 2003; Federal Prosecution of Human Trafficking, 2001-2005; Felony Defendants in Large Urban Counties, 2002; Felony Sentences in State Courts, 2002; Firearm Use by Offenders; Immigration Offenders in the Federal Criminal Justice System, 2000; Intimate Partner Violence; Intimate Partner Violence and Age of Victim, 1993-99; Juvenile Victimization and Offending, 1993-2003; Money Laundering Offenders, 1994-2001; Police Departments in Large Cities, 1990-2000; Profile of Nonviolent Offenders Exiting State Prisons; Punitive Damage Awards in Large Counties, 2001; Rape and Sexual Assault: Reporting to Police and Medical Attention, 1992-2000; Sexual Assault of Young Children as Reported to Law Enforcement: Victim, Incident, and Offender Characteristics; Sexual Victimization of College Women; Sheriffs' Offices, 2003; The Sourcebook of Criminal Justice Statistics, 2003; Trends in State Parole, 1990-2000;* and *Violent Felons in Large Urban Counties.*

U.S. Department of Justice (DOJ), Drug Enforcement Administration (DEA), 2401 Jefferson Davis Highway, Alexandria, VA 22301, (202) 307-1000, www.usdoj.gov/dea; *State Factsheets* and *2005 US Money Laundering Threat Assessment.*

U.S. Department of Justice (DOJ), National Institute of Justice (NIJ), 810 Seventh Street, NW, Washington, DC 20531, (202) 307-2942, Fax: (202) 616-0275, www.ojp.usdoj.gov/nij/; *ADAM Preliminary 2000 Findings on Drug Use Drug Markets: Adult Male Arrestees; Assessing Risk Factors for Intimate Partner Homicide; Co-Offending and Patterns of Juvenile Crime; Do Batterer Intervention Programs Work? Two Studies; Do Domestic Violence Services Save Lives?; The Effectiveness and Safety of Pepper Spray ; Fighting Crime with COPS Citizens; Has Rape Reporting Increased Over Time?; I-ADAM in Eight Countries: Approaches and Challenges; Intimate Partner Homicide: An Overview; Responding to Gangs: Evaluation and Research; Reviewing Domestic Violence Deaths; Risky Mix: Drinking, Drug Use, and Homicide; Statistical Validation of the Individuality of Guns Using 3D Images of Bullets; When Violence Hits Home: How Economics and Neighborhood Play a Role;* and *Youth Victimization: Prevalence and Implications* .

U.S. Department of Justice (DOJ), Office of the Attorney General, 950 Pennsylvania Avenue, NW, Washington, DC 20530-0001, (202) 353-1555, www.usdoj.gov/ag; *Assessment of U.S. Government Activities to Combat Trafficking in Persons.*

U.S. Department of Justice (DOJ), Office on Violence Against Women (OVW), 950 Pennsylvania Avenue, NW, Washington, DC 20530-0001, (202) 514-2000, www.usdoj.gov/ovw; unpublished data.

U.S. Department of State (DOS), 2201 C Street NW, Washington, DC 20520, (202) 647-4000, www.state.gov; *Patterns of Global Terrorism.*

U.S. Department of State (DOS) Office of the Coordinator for Counterterrorism, Office of Public Affairs, Room 2509, 2201 C Street NW, Washington, DC 20520, (202) 647-4000, www.state.gov/s/ct; *Country Reports on Terrorism 2007.*

U.S. Library of Congress (LOC), Congressional Research Service (CRS), The Library of Congress, 101 Independence Avenue, SE, Washington, DC 20540-7500, (202) 707-5700, www.loc.gov/crsinfo; *The Economic Impact of Cyber-Attacks* and *Offender Reentry: Correctional Statistics, Reintegration into the Community, and Recidivism.*

The Urban Institute, 2100 M Street, N.W., Washington, DC 20037, (202) 833-7200, www.urban.org; *Beyond the Prison Gates: The State of Parole in America; Does Parole Work?: Analyzing the Impact of Postprison Supervision on Rearrest Outcomes; Federal Criminal Case Processing, 2000: With Trends 1982-2000; The Influences of Truth-in-Sentencing Reforms on Changes in States' Sentencing Practices and Prison Populations; Juvenile Crime in Washington, D.C.; A Portrait of Prisoner Reentry in Illinois; A Portrait of Prisoner Reentry in Maryland; Prisoner Reentry in Idaho; The Rise and Fall of American Youth Violence: 1980 to 2000; Study Finds Parole Has Little Effect on Rearrest Rates;* and *Youth Crime Drop.*

CRIME - ASSAULT

Australian Government Office for Women, Department of Families, Community Services and Indigenous Affairs, Box 7788, Canberra Mail Centre ACT 2610, Australia, http://ofw.facsia.gov.au; *Cost of Domestic Violence to the Australian Economy.*

Federal Bureau of Investigation (FBI), J. Edgar Hoover Building, 935 Pennsylvania Avenue, NW, Washington, DC 20535-0001, (202) 324-3000, www.fbi.gov; *Crime in the United States (CIUS) 2007 (Preliminary).*

Justice Research and Statistics Association (JRSA), 777 N. Capitol Street, NE, Suite 801, Washington, DC 20002, (202) 842-9330, Fax: (202) 842-9329, www.jrsa.org; *Crime and Justice Atlas 2001* and *Domestic Violence and Sexual Assault Data Collection Systems in the States.*

U.S. Department of Justice (DOJ), Bureau of Justice Statistics, 810 Seventh Street, NW, Washington, DC 20531, (202) 307-0765, www.ojp.usdoj.gov/bjs/; *American Indians and Crime: A BJS Statistical Profile, 1992-2002; Cross-National Studies in Crime and Justice; Intimate Partner Violence; Intimate Partner Violence and Age of Victim, 1993-99; Rape and Sexual Assault: Reporting to Police and Medical Attention, 1992-2000; Sexual Victimization of College Women; Violence by Gang Members, 1993-2003; Violent Felons in Large Urban Counties;* and *Weapon Use and Violent Crime, 1993-2001.*

U.S. Department of Justice (DOJ), National Institute of Justice (NIJ), 810 Seventh Street, NW, Washington, DC 20531, (202) 307-2942, Fax: (202) 616-0275, www.ojp.usdoj.gov/nij/; *Do Batterer Intervention Programs Work? Two Studies; Risky Mix: Drinking, Drug Use, and Homicide;* and *Youth Victimization: Prevalence and Implications* .

U.S. Department of Justice (DOJ), Office on Violence Against Women (OVW), 950 Pennsylvania Avenue, NW, Washington, DC 20530-0001, (202) 514-2000, www.usdoj.gov/ovw; unpublished data.

CRIME - AVERAGE VALUE LOST

Federal Bureau of Investigation (FBI), J. Edgar Hoover Building, 935 Pennsylvania Avenue, NW, Washington, DC 20535-0001, (202) 324-3000, www.fbi.gov; *Crime in the United States (CIUS) 2007 (Preliminary).*

Justice Research and Statistics Association (JRSA), 777 N. Capitol Street, NE, Suite 801, Washington, DC 20002, (202) 842-9330, Fax: (202) 842-9329, www.jrsa.org; *Crime and Justice Atlas 2001.*

CRIME - BURGLARY

Federal Bureau of Investigation (FBI), J. Edgar Hoover Building, 935 Pennsylvania Avenue, NW, Washington, DC 20535-0001, (202) 324-3000, www.fbi.gov; *Crime in the United States (CIUS) 2007 (Preliminary).*

Justice Research and Statistics Association (JRSA), 777 N. Capitol Street, NE, Suite 801, Washington, DC 20002, (202) 842-9330, Fax: (202) 842-9329, www.jrsa.org; *Crime and Justice Atlas 2001.*

U.S. Department of Justice (DOJ), Bureau of Justice Statistics, 810 Seventh Street, NW, Washington, DC 20531, (202) 307-0765, www.ojp.usdoj.gov/bjs/; *American Indians and Crime: A BJS Statistical Profile, 1992-2002; Carjacking, 1993-2002; Crime and the Nation's Households, 2004; Criminal Victimization, 2005;* and *Cross-National Studies in Crime and Justice.*

CRIME - CHILD ABUSE AND NEGLECT

Administration for Children and Families (ACF), U.S. Department of Health and Human Services (HHS), 370 L'Enfant Promenade, SW, Washington, DC 20447, (202) 401-2337, www.acf.hhs.gov; *Child Maltreatment 2006.*

Child Welfare Information Gateway, Children's Bureau/ACYF, 1250 Maryland Avenue, SW, Eighth Floor, Washington, DC 20024, (800) 394-3366, Fax: (703) 385-3206, www.childwelfare.gov; *Alternative Responses to Child Maltreatment: Findings from NCANDS* and *Child Abuse and Neglect Fatalities: Statistics and Interventions.*

National Center for Juvenile Justice (NCJJ), 3700 South Water Street, Suite 200, Pittsburgh, PA 15203, (412) 227-6950, Fax: (412) 227-6955, http://ncjj.servehttp.com/NCJJWebsite/main.htm; *Jury*

Trial in Abuse, Neglect, Dependency Cases and *Jury Trial in Termination of Parental Rights (2005 Update).*

U.S. Department of Justice (DOJ), Bureau of Justice Statistics, 810 Seventh Street, NW, Washington, DC 20531, (202) 307-0765, www.ojp.usdoj.gov/bjs/; *Family Violence Statistics: Including Statistics on Strangers and Acquaintances; Federal Criminal Case Processing, 2002: With trends 1982-2002, Reconciled Data;* and *Sexual Assault of Young Children as Reported to Law Enforcement: Victim, Incident, and Offender Characteristics.*

U.S. Department of Justice (DOJ), National Institute of Justice (NIJ), 810 Seventh Street, NW, Washington, DC 20531, (202) 307-2942, Fax: (202) 616-0275, www.ojp.usdoj.gov/nij/; *Youth Victimization: Prevalence and Implications* .

CRIME - CONTACT WITH POLICE

Home Office Research Development and Statistics (RDS), Direct Communications Unit, 2 Marsham Street, London SW1P 4DF, United Kingdom, www.homeoffice.gov.uk/rds/; *Evaluation of the Impact of the National Reassurance Policing Programme* and *National Reassurance Policing Programme: A Ten-Site Evaluation.*

Justice Research and Statistics Association (JRSA), 777 N. Capitol Street, NE, Suite 801, Washington, DC 20002, (202) 842-9330, Fax: (202) 842-9329, www.jrsa.org; *An Analysis of Variables Affecting the Clearance of Homicides: A Multistate Study* and *Domestic Violence and Sexual Assault Data Collection Systems in the States.*

RAND Corporation, 1776 Main Street, PO Box 2138, Santa Monica, CA 90407-2138, (310) 393-0411, www.rand.org; *Police-Community Relations in Cincinnati.*

U.S. Department of Justice (DOJ), Bureau of Justice Statistics, 810 Seventh Street, NW, Washington, DC 20531, (202) 307-0765, www.ojp.usdoj.gov/bjs/; *Bridging Gaps in Police Crime Data; Characteristics of Drivers Stopped by Police, 2002; Citizen Complaints about Police Use of Force; Contacts between Police and the Public: Findings from the 2002 National Survey; Federal Criminal Justice Trends, 2003; National Data Collection on Police Use of Force; Rape and Sexual Assault: Reporting to Police and Medical Attention, 1992-2000;* and *Reporting Crime to the Police, 1992-2000.*

U.S. Department of Justice (DOJ), National Institute of Justice (NIJ), 810 Seventh Street, NW, Washington, DC 20531, (202) 307-2942, Fax: (202) 616-0275, www.ojp.usdoj.gov/nij/; *Community Policing and "The New Immigrants": Latinos in Chicago; Factors That Influence Public Opinion of the Police; Fighting Crime with COPS Citizens; Has Rape Reporting Increased Over Time?; Reducing Gun Violence: Evaluation of the Indianapolis Police Department's Directed Patrol Project ; Responding to Gangs: Evaluation and Research; Satisfaction With Police--What Matters?;* and *Taking Stock: Community Policing in Chicago.*

CRIME - DRUG ABUSE VIOLATIONS

Australian Institute of Criminology, 74 Leichhardt Street, Griffith ACT 2603 Australia, www.aic.gov.au/; *Final report on the North Queensland Drug Court.*

Federal Bureau of Investigation (FBI), J. Edgar Hoover Building, 935 Pennsylvania Avenue, NW, Washington, DC 20535-0001, (202) 324-3000, www.fbi.gov; *Crime in the United States (CIUS) 2007 (Preliminary).*

Justice Research and Statistics Association (JRSA), 777 N. Capitol Street, NE, Suite 801, Washington, DC 20002, (202) 842-9330, Fax: (202) 842-9329, www.jrsa.org; *Crime and Justice Atlas 2001* and *Documenting the Extent and Nature of Drug and Violent Crime: Developing Jurisdiction-Specific Profiles of the Criminal Justice System.*

National Center for Juvenile Justice (NCJJ), 3700 South Water Street, Suite 200, Pittsburgh, PA 15203, (412) 227-6950, Fax: (412) 227-6955, http://ncjj.servehttp.com/NCJJWebsite/main.htm; *Jury Trial in Abuse, Neglect, Dependency Cases.*

Robert Wood Johnson Foundation, PO Box 2316, College Road East and Route 1, Princeton, NJ 08543, (877) 843-7953, www.rwjf.org; *Community-Based Prevention Programs in the War on Drugs: Findings from the "Fighting Back" Demonstration; Community-Based Substance Abuse Reduction and the Gap Between Treatment Need and Treatment Utilization: Analysis of Data From the "Fighting Back" General Population Survey; Neighborhood Crime Victimization, Drug Use and Drug Sales: Results from the "Fighting Back" Evaluation;* and *Varieties of Substance Use and Visible Drug Problems: Individual and Neighborhood Factors.*

U.S. Department of Justice (DOJ), Bureau of Justice Statistics, 810 Seventh Street, NW, Washington, DC 20531, (202) 307-0765, www.ojp.usdoj.gov/bjs/; *American Indians and Crime: A BJS Statistical Profile, 1992-2002; Compendium of Federal Justice Statistics, 2003;* and *Drugs Crime Facts.*

U.S. Department of Justice (DOJ), Drug Enforcement Administration (DEA), 2401 Jefferson Davis Highway, Alexandria, VA 22301, (202) 307-1000, www.usdoj.gov/dea; *State Factsheets.*

U.S. Department of Justice (DOJ), National Institute of Justice (NIJ), 810 Seventh Street, NW, Washington, DC 20531, (202) 307-2942, Fax: (202) 616-0275, www.ojp.usdoj.gov/nij/; *ADAM Preliminary 2000 Findings on Drug Use Drug Markets: Adult Male Arrestees; Drug Courts: The Second Decade;* and *I-ADAM in Eight Countries: Approaches and Challenges.*

United Nations Office on Drugs and Crime (UNODC), Vienna International Centre, PO Box 500, A-1400 Vienna, Austria, www.unodc.org; *World Drug Report 2006.*

CRIME - FRAUD

Federal Trade Commission (FTC), 600 Pennsylvania Avenue, NW, Washington, DC 20580, (202) 326-2222, www.ftc.gov; *National and State Trends in Fraud and Identity Theft, January-December 2004.*

U.S. Library of Congress (LOC), Congressional Research Service (CRS), The Library of Congress, 101 Independence Avenue, SE, Washington, DC 20540-7500, (202) 707-5700, www.loc.gov/crsinfo; *Immigration Fraud: Policies, Investigations, and Issues.*

CRIME - HATE CRIMES

Federal Bureau of Investigation (FBI), J. Edgar Hoover Building, 935 Pennsylvania Avenue, NW, Washington, DC 20535-0001, (202) 324-3000, www.fbi.gov; *Hate Crime Statistics, 2006.*

Justice Research and Statistics Association (JRSA), 777 N. Capitol Street, NE, Suite 801, Washington, DC 20002, (202) 842-9330, Fax: (202) 842-9329, www.jrsa.org; *Improving the Quality and Accuracy of Bias Crime Statistics Nationally: An Assessment of the First Ten Years of Bias Crime Data Collection.*

U.S. Department of Justice (DOJ), Bureau of Justice Statistics, 810 Seventh Street, NW, Washington, DC 20531, (202) 307-0765, www.ojp.usdoj.gov/bjs/; *American Indians and Crime: A BJS Statistical Profile, 1992-2002* and *Hate Crimes Reported by Victims and Police.*

CRIME - HOMICIDES

Justice Research and Statistics Association (JRSA), 777 N. Capitol Street, NE, Suite 801, Washington, DC 20002, (202) 842-9330, Fax: (202) 842-9329, www.jrsa.org; *An Analysis of Variables Affecting the Clearance of Homicides: A Multistate Study.*

U.S. Department of Justice (DOJ), Bureau of Justice Statistics, 810 Seventh Street, NW, Washington, DC 20531, (202) 307-0765, www.ojp.usdoj.gov/bjs/; *Age Patterns in Violent Victimization, 1976-2000; Homicide Trends in the United States: 2002 Update;* and *Weapon Use and Violent Crime, 1993-2001.*

U.S. Department of Justice (DOJ), National Institute of Justice (NIJ), 810 Seventh Street, NW, Washington, DC 20531, (202) 307-2942, Fax: (202) 616-0275, www.ojp.usdoj.gov/nij/; *Assessing Risk Factors for Intimate Partner Homicide; Intimate Partner Homicide: An Overview; Reviewing Domestic Violence Deaths;* and *Risky Mix: Drinking, Drug Use, and Homicide.*

CRIME - HOMICIDES - RACE AND SEX

National Center for Health Statistics (NCHS), Centers for Disease Control and Prevention (CDC), U.S. Department of Health and Human Services (HHS), 3311 Toledo Road, Hyattsville, MD 20782, (866) 232-4636, www.cdc.gov/nchs; *Vital Statistics of the United States (VSUS)* and unpublished data.

U.S. Department of Justice (DOJ), Bureau of Justice Statistics, 810 Seventh Street, NW, Washington, DC 20531, (202) 307-0765, www.ojp.usdoj.gov/bjs/; *American Indians and Crime: A BJS Statistical Profile, 1992-2002* and *Suicide and Homicide in State Prisons and Local Jails.*

CRIME - HUMAN TRAFFICKING

Inter-American Commission of Women (CIM), Organization of American States (OAS), 17th Street and Constitution Avenue, NW, Washington, D.C. 20006, (202) 458-3000, www.oas.org/CIM/english/About.htm; *Trafficking in Women and Children: Research Findings and Follow-Up.*

International Organization for Migration (IOM), 17, Route des Morillons, CH-1211 Geneva 19, Switzerland, www.iom.int; *Migration, Human Smuggling and Trafficking from Nigeria to Europe* and *Trafficking in Human Beings and the 2006 World Cup in Germany.*

U.S. Department of Justice (DOJ), Bureau of Justice Statistics, 810 Seventh Street, NW, Washington, DC 20531, (202) 307-0765, www.ojp.usdoj.gov/bjs/; *Federal Prosecution of Human Trafficking, 2001-2005.*

U.S. Department of Justice (DOJ), Office of the Attorney General, 950 Pennsylvania Avenue, NW, Washington, DC 20530-0001, (202) 353-1555, www.usdoj.gov/ag; *Assessment of U.S. Government Activities to Combat Trafficking in Persons.*

CRIME - IDENTITY THEFT

Federal Trade Commission (FTC), 600 Pennsylvania Avenue, NW, Washington, DC 20580, (202) 326-2222, www.ftc.gov; *National and State Trends in Fraud and Identity Theft, January-December 2004.*

U.S. Library of Congress (LOC), Congressional Research Service (CRS), The Library of Congress, 101 Independence Avenue, SE, Washington, DC 20540-7500, (202) 707-5700, www.loc.gov/crsinfo; *The Economic Impact of Cyber-Attacks.*

CRIME - IMMIGRATION VIOLATIONS

International Organization for Migration (IOM), 17, Route des Morillons, CH-1211 Geneva 19, Switzerland, www.iom.int; *Migration, Human Smuggling and Trafficking from Nigeria to Europe* and *Trafficking in Human Beings and the 2006 World Cup in Germany.*

U.S. Citizenship and Immigration Services (USCIS), Washington District Office, 2675 Prosperity Avenue, Fairfax, VA 22031, (800) 375-5283, http://uscis.gov; *2005 Yearbook of Immigration Statistics.*

U.S. Department of Justice (DOJ), Bureau of Justice Statistics, 810 Seventh Street, NW, Washington, DC 20531, (202) 307-0765, www.ojp.usdoj.gov/bjs/; *Immigration Offenders in the Federal Criminal Justice System, 2000.*

U.S. Library of Congress (LOC), Congressional Research Service (CRS), The Library of Congress, 101 Independence Avenue, SE, Washington, DC 20540-7500, (202) 707-5700, www.loc.gov/crsinfo; *Border Security: The Role of the U.S. Border Patrol* and *Immigration Fraud: Policies, Investigations, and Issues.*

CRIME - LARCENY - THEFT

Federal Bureau of Investigation (FBI), J. Edgar Hoover Building, 935 Pennsylvania Avenue, NW, Washington, DC 20535-0001, (202) 324-3000, www.fbi.gov; *Crime in the United States (CIUS) 2007 (Preliminary).*

Justice Research and Statistics Association (JRSA), 777 N. Capitol Street, NE, Suite 801, Washington, DC 20002, (202) 842-9330, Fax: (202) 842-9329, www.jrsa.org; *Crime and Justice Atlas 2001.*

U.S. Department of Justice (DOJ), Bureau of Justice Statistics, 810 Seventh Street, NW, Washington, DC 20531, (202) 307-0765, www.ojp.usdoj.gov/bjs/; *Identity Theft, 2004* and *Intellectual Property Theft, 2002.*

U.S. Government Accountablity Office (GAO), 441 G Street, NW, Washington, DC 20548, (202) 512-3000, www.gao.gov; *Identity Theft: Greater Awareness and Use of Existing Data Are Needed.*

CRIME - MOTOR VEHICLE THEFT

Federal Bureau of Investigation (FBI), J. Edgar Hoover Building, 935 Pennsylvania Avenue, NW, Washington, DC 20535-0001, (202) 324-3000, www.fbi.gov; *Crime in the United States (CIUS) 2007 (Preliminary).*

Justice Research and Statistics Association (JRSA), 777 N. Capitol Street, NE, Suite 801, Washington, DC 20002, (202) 842-9330, Fax: (202) 842-9329, www.jrsa.org; *Crime and Justice Atlas 2001.*

U.S. Department of Justice (DOJ), Bureau of Justice Statistics, 810 Seventh Street, NW, Washington, DC 20531, (202) 307-0765, www.ojp.usdoj.gov/bjs/; *Carjacking, 1993-2002; Criminal Victimization, 2005;* and *Cross-National Studies in Crime and Justice.*

CRIME - MURDER

U.S. Department of Justice (DOJ), Bureau of Justice Statistics, 810 Seventh Street, NW, Washington, DC 20531, (202) 307-0765, www.ojp.usdoj.gov/bjs/; *Cross-National Studies in Crime and Justice* and *Violent Felons in Large Urban Counties.*

U.S. Department of Justice (DOJ), National Institute of Justice (NIJ), 810 Seventh Street, NW, Washington, DC 20531, (202) 307-2942, Fax: (202) 616-0275, www.ojp.usdoj.gov/nij/; *Reviewing Domestic Violence Deaths.*

CRIME - MURDER - MURDER CIRCUMSTANCES

Federal Bureau of Investigation (FBI), J. Edgar Hoover Building, 935 Pennsylvania Avenue, NW, Washington, DC 20535-0001, (202) 324-3000, www.fbi.gov; *Crime in the United States (CIUS) 2007 (Preliminary).*

Justice Research and Statistics Association (JRSA), 777 N. Capitol Street, NE, Suite 801, Washington, DC 20002, (202) 842-9330, Fax: (202) 842-9329, www.jrsa.org; *Crime and Justice Atlas 2001.*

U.S. Department of Justice (DOJ), Bureau of Justice Statistics, 810 Seventh Street, NW, Washington, DC 20531, (202) 307-0765, www.ojp.usdoj.gov/bjs/; *Age Patterns in Violent Victimization, 1976-2000; American Indians and Crime: A BJS Statistical Profile, 1992-2002; Homicide Trends in the United States: 2002 Update;* and *Weapon Use and Violent Crime, 1993-2001.*

U.S. Department of Justice (DOJ), National Institute of Justice (NIJ), 810 Seventh Street, NW, Washington, DC 20531, (202) 307-2942, Fax: (202) 616-0275, www.ojp.usdoj.gov/nij/; *Assessing Risk Factors for Intimate Partner Homicide; Intimate Partner Homicide: An Overview; Reviewing Domestic Violence Deaths;* and *Risky Mix: Drinking, Drug Use, and Homicide.*

CRIME - PLACE AND TIME OF OCCURRENCE

U.S. Department of Justice (DOJ), Bureau of Justice Statistics, 810 Seventh Street, NW, Washington, DC 20531, (202) 307-0765, www.ojp.usdoj.gov/bjs/; *Criminal Victimization, 2005.*

CRIME - POLICE OFFICERS ASSAULTED, KILLED

Federal Bureau of Investigation (FBI), J. Edgar Hoover Building, 935 Pennsylvania Avenue, NW, Washington, DC 20535-0001, (202) 324-3000, www.fbi.gov; *Law Enforcement Officers Killed and Assaulted (LEOKA) 2007 (Preliminary).*

U.S. Department of Justice (DOJ), Bureau of Justice Statistics, 810 Seventh Street, NW, Washington, DC 20531, (202) 307-0765, www.ojp.usdoj.gov/bjs/; *Homicide Trends in the United States: 2002 Update.*

CRIME - PROPERTY CRIME

Federal Bureau of Investigation (FBI), J. Edgar Hoover Building, 935 Pennsylvania Avenue, NW, Washington, DC 20535-0001, (202) 324-3000, www.fbi.gov; *Crime in the United States (CIUS) 2007 (Preliminary).*

Justice Research and Statistics Association (JRSA), 777 N. Capitol Street, NE, Suite 801, Washington, DC 20002, (202) 842-9330, Fax: (202) 842-9329, www.jrsa.org; *Crime and Justice Atlas 2001.*

U.S. Department of Justice (DOJ), Bureau of Justice Statistics, 810 Seventh Street, NW, Washington, DC 20531, (202) 307-0765, www.ojp.usdoj.gov/bjs/; *Crime and the Nation's Households, 2004.*

CRIME - RAPE, FORCIBLE

Federal Bureau of Investigation (FBI), J. Edgar Hoover Building, 935 Pennsylvania Avenue, NW, Washington, DC 20535-0001, (202) 324-3000, www.fbi.gov; *Crime in the United States (CIUS) 2007 (Preliminary).*

Justice Research and Statistics Association (JRSA), 777 N. Capitol Street, NE, Suite 801, Washington, DC 20002, (202) 842-9330, Fax: (202) 842-9329, www.jrsa.org; *Crime and Justice Atlas 2001.*

U.S. Department of Justice (DOJ), Bureau of Justice Statistics, 810 Seventh Street, NW, Washington, DC 20531, (202) 307-0765, www.ojp.usdoj.gov/bjs/; *American Indians and Crime: A BJS Statistical Profile, 1992-2002; Cross-National Studies in Crime and Justice; Intimate Partner Violence; Intimate Partner Violence and Age of Victim, 1993-99; Rape and Sexual Assault: Reporting to Police and Medical Attention, 1992-2000; Sexual Assault of Young Children as Reported to Law Enforcement: Victim, Incident, and Offender Characteristics; Sexual Victimization of College Women; Sexual Violence Reported by Correctional Authorities, 2005;* and *Violent Felons in Large Urban Counties.*

U.S. Department of Justice (DOJ), National Institute of Justice (NIJ), 810 Seventh Street, NW, Washington, DC 20531, (202) 307-2942, Fax: (202) 616-0275, www.ojp.usdoj.gov/nij/; *Has Rape Reporting Increased Over Time?*

U.S. Department of Justice (DOJ), Office of Community Oriented Policing Services (COPS), 1100 Vermont Avenue, NW, Washington, DC 20530, (202) 307-1480, www.cops.usdoj.gov; *Acquaintance Rape of College Students.*

U.S. Department of Justice (DOJ), Office on Violence Against Women (OVW), 950 Pennsylvania Avenue, NW, Washington, DC 20530-0001, (202) 514-2000, www.usdoj.gov/ovw; unpublished data.

CRIME - ROBBERY

Federal Bureau of Investigation (FBI), J. Edgar Hoover Building, 935 Pennsylvania Avenue, NW, Washington, DC 20535-0001, (202) 324-3000, www.fbi.gov; *Crime in the United States (CIUS) 2007 (Preliminary).*

Justice Research and Statistics Association (JRSA), 777 N. Capitol Street, NE, Suite 801, Washington, DC 20002, (202) 842-9330, Fax: (202) 842-9329, www.jrsa.org; *Crime and Justice Atlas 2001.*

U.S. Department of Justice (DOJ), Bureau of Justice Statistics, 810 Seventh Street, NW, Washington, DC 20531, (202) 307-0765, www.ojp.usdoj.gov/bjs/; *American Indians and Crime: A BJS Statistical Profile, 1992-2002; Carjacking, 1993-2002; Crime and the Nation's Households, 2004;* and *Cross-National Studies in Crime and Justice.*

CRIME - SHOPLIFTING

Federal Bureau of Investigation (FBI), J. Edgar Hoover Building, 935 Pennsylvania Avenue, NW, Washington, DC 20535-0001, (202) 324-3000, www.fbi.gov; *Crime in the United States (CIUS) 2007 (Preliminary).*

Justice Research and Statistics Association (JRSA), 777 N. Capitol Street, NE, Suite 801, Washington, DC 20002, (202) 842-9330, Fax: (202) 842-9329, www.jrsa.org; *Crime and Justice Atlas 2001.*

CRIME - VIOLENT CRIME

Australian Government Office for Women, Department of Families, Community Services and Indigenous Affairs, Box 7788, Canberra Mail Centre ACT 2610, Australia, http://ofw.facsia.gov.au; *Cost of Domestic Violence to the Australian Economy.*

Federal Bureau of Investigation (FBI), J. Edgar Hoover Building, 935 Pennsylvania Avenue, NW, Washington, DC 20535-0001, (202) 324-3000, www.fbi.gov; *Crime in the United States (CIUS) 2007 (Preliminary).*

Justice Research and Statistics Association (JRSA), 777 N. Capitol Street, NE, Suite 801, Washington, DC 20002, (202) 842-9330, Fax: (202) 842-9329, www.jrsa.org; *Crime and Justice Atlas 2001; Documenting the Extent and Nature of Drug and Violent Crime: Developing Jurisdiction-Specific Profiles of the Criminal Justice System;* and *Domestic Violence and Sexual Assault Data Collection Systems in the States.*

The National Consortium for the Study of Terrorism and Responses to Terror (START), University of Maryland, College Park, MD 20742, (301) 405-6600, www.start.umd.edu; *Surveying State Police Agencies about Domestic Terrorism and Far-Right Extremists.*

National Counterterrorism Center (NCTC), Office of the Director of National Intelligence (ODNI), Washington, DC 20511, (703) 733-8600, www.nctc.gov; *2007 NCTC Report on Incidents of Terrorism.*

U.S. Department of Justice (DOJ), Bureau of Justice Statistics, 810 Seventh Street, NW, Washington, DC 20531, (202) 307-0765, www.ojp.usdoj.gov/bjs/; *Age Patterns in Violent Victimization, 1976-2000; Crime and the Nation's Households, 2004; Criminal Victimization, 2005; Family Violence Statistics: Including Statistics on Strangers and Acquaintances; Federal Criminal Case Processing, 2002: With trends 1982-2002, Reconciled Data; Hispanic Victims of Violent Crime, 1993-2000; Intimate Partner Violence; Intimate Partner Violence and Age of Victim, 1993-99; Intimate Partner Violence and Age of Victim, 1993-99; Sexual Violence Reported by Correctional Authorities, 2005; Violence by Gang Members, 1993-2003; Violent Felons in Large Urban Counties; Violent Victimization of College Students, 1995-2002;* and *Weapon Use and Violent Crime, 1993-2001.*

U.S. Department of Justice (DOJ), National Institute of Justice (NIJ), 810 Seventh Street, NW, Washington, DC 20531, (202) 307-2942, Fax: (202) 616-0275, www.ojp.usdoj.gov/nij/; *Assessing Risk Factors for Intimate Partner Homicide; Do Batterer Intervention Programs Work? Two Studies; Intimate Partner Homicide: An Overview; Reducing Gun Violence: Evaluation of the Indianapolis Police Department's Directed Patrol Project ; Responding to Gangs: Evaluation and Research; Reviewing Domestic Violence Deaths; Risky Mix: Drinking, Drug Use, and Homicide; When Violence Hits Home: How Economics and Neighborhood Play a Role;* and *Youth Victimization: Prevalence and Implications .*

U.S. Department of State (DOS), 2201 C Street NW, Washington, DC 20520, (202) 647-4000, www.state.gov; *Patterns of Global Terrorism.*

U.S. Department of State (DOS) Office of the Coordinator for Counterterrorism, Office of Public Affairs, Room 2509, 2201 C Street NW, Washington, DC 20520, (202) 647-4000, www.state.gov/s/ct; *Country Reports on Terrorism 2007.*

The Urban Institute, 2100 M Street, N.W., Washington, DC 20037, (202) 833-7200, www.urban.org; *National Portrait of SVORI: Serious and Violent Offender Reentry Initiative* and *The Rise and Fall of American Youth Violence: 1980 to 2000.*

CRIME - WORKPLACE

U.S. Bureau of Labor Statistics (BLS), Postal Square Building, 2 Massachusetts Avenue, NE, Washington, DC 20212-0001, (202) 691-5200, Fax: (202) 691-6325, www.bls.gov; *Monthly Labor Review (MLR)* and unpublished data.

U.S. Department of Justice (DOJ), Bureau of Justice Statistics, 810 Seventh Street, NW, Washington, DC 20531, (202) 307-0765, www.ojp.usdoj.gov/bjs/; *Cybercrime against Businesses: Pilot Test Results, 2001 Computer Security Survey.*

CRIMINAL INVESTIGATION

Child Welfare Information Gateway, Children's Bureau/ACYF, 1250 Maryland Avenue, SW, Eighth Floor, Washington, DC 20024, (800) 394-3366, Fax: (703) 385-3206, www.childwelfare.gov; *Alternative Responses to Child Maltreatment: Findings from NCANDS.*

Justice Research and Statistics Association (JRSA), 777 N. Capitol Street, NE, Suite 801, Washington, DC 20002, (202) 842-9330, Fax: (202) 842-9329, www.jrsa.org; *An Analysis of Variables Affecting the Clearance of Homicides: A Multistate Study; The Forum; JRP Digest; Justice Research and Policy;* and *SAC Publication Digest.*

Metropolitan Police Department, 300 Indiana Avenue, NW, Washington, DC 20001, (202) 727-1000, http://mpdc.dc.gov/mpdc; *Annual Index Crime Totals, 1993-2005; District Crime Data at a Glance; Live Data Feeds of Crime Incidents and Other DC Services;* and *Monthly Preliminary Crime Statistics (2005-2006).*

RAND Corporation, 1776 Main Street, PO Box 2138, Santa Monica, CA 90407-2138, (310) 393-0411, www.rand.org; *Police-Community Relations in Cincinnati.*

U.S. Department of Justice (DOJ), Bureau of Justice Statistics, 810 Seventh Street, NW, Washington, DC 20531, (202) 307-0765, www.ojp.usdoj.gov/bjs/; *Bridging Gaps in Police Crime Data; Census of Publicly Funded Forensic Crime Laboratories, 2002; Citizen Complaints about Police Use of Force; Compendium of State Security and Privacy Legislation: Overview 2002; Cross-National Studies in Crime and Justice; Defense Counsel in Criminal Cases; Drugs Crime Facts; Effects of NIBRS on Crime Statistics; Federal Criminal Justice Trends, 2003; Federal Justice Statistics Resource Center; Federal Prosecution of Human Trafficking, 2001-2005; Immigration Offenders in the Federal Criminal Justice System, 2000; Improving Access to and Integrity of Criminal History Records; Improving Criminal History Records for Background Checks, 2005; Justice Assistance Grant (JAG) Program, 2005; Justice Expenditure and Employment in the United States 2003; Police Departments in Large Cities, 1990-2000; Reporting by Prosecutors' Offices to Repositories of Criminal History Records; Survey of DNA Crime Laboratories, 2001; Survey of State Criminal History Information Systems, 2003; Survey of State Records Included in Presale Background Checks: Mental Health Records, Domestic Violence Misdemeanor Records, and Restraining Orders, 2003; Traffic Stop Data Collection Policies for State Police, 2004;* and *Tribal Law Enforcement, 2000.*

U.S. Department of Justice (DOJ), Drug Enforcement Administration (DEA), 2401 Jefferson Davis Highway, Alexandria, VA 22301, (202) 307-1000, www.usdoj.gov/dea; *State Factsheets.*

U.S. Department of Justice (DOJ), National Institute of Justice (NIJ), 810 Seventh Street, NW, Washington, DC 20531, (202) 307-2942, Fax: (202) 616-0275, www.ojp.usdoj.gov/nij/; *Police Innovations and the Structure of Informal Communication Between Police Agencies: Network and LEMAS Data; Reviewing Domestic Violence Deaths; Statistical Validation of the Individuality of Guns Using 3D Images of Bullets;* and *Victim Satisfaction With the Criminal Justice System.*

U.S. Department of Justice (DOJ), Office of the Attorney General, 950 Pennsylvania Avenue, NW, Washington, DC 20530-0001, (202) 353-1555, www.usdoj.gov/ag; *Assessment of U.S. Government Activities to Combat Trafficking in Persons.*

CRIMINAL JUSTICE, ADMINISTRATION OF

Death Penalty Information Center, 1101 Vermont Avenue, NW, Suite 701, Washington, DC 20005, (202) 289-2275, www.deathpenaltyinfo.org; *Blind Justice: Juries Deciding Life and Death with Only Half the Truth; A Crisis of Confidence: Americans' Doubts About the Death Penalty; The Death Penalty in 2005: Death Sentences Reach Record Lows as Country Turns to Life Without Parole; The Death Penalty in 2006: Use of the Death Penalty Declines in 2006; The Death Penalty in 2007: Execution Chambers Silent as Supreme Court Considers Next Step; The Death Penalty in Black and White: Who Lives, Who Dies, Who Decides; Innocence and the Crisis in the American Death Penalty;* and *International Perspectives on the Death Penalty: A Costly Isolation for the U.S.*

Home Office Research Development and Statistics (RDS), Direct Communications Unit, 2 Marsham Street, London SW1P 4DF, United Kingdom, www.homeoffice.gov.uk/rds/; *Digest 4 - Information on the Criminal Justice System (A Statistical Summary); Local Sentencing Patterns in Magistrates' Courts, 2000; Probation Statistics England and Wales 2002; Race and the Criminal Justice System: An Overview to the Complete Statistics 2004-2005;* and *Statistics on Women and the Criminal Justice System - 2004/05.*

Justice Research and Statistics Association (JRSA), 777 N. Capitol Street, NE, Suite 801, Washington, DC 20002, (202) 842-9330, Fax: (202) 842-9329, www.jrsa.org; *Crime and Justice Atlas 2001; Directory of Justice Issues in the States; Documenting the Extent and Nature of Drug and Violent Crime: Developing Jurisdiction-Specific Profiles of the Criminal Justice System; Domestic Violence and Sexual Assault Data Collection Systems in the States; The Forum;* InfoBase of State Activities and Research (ISAR); *JRP Digest; Justice Research and Policy;* and *SAC Publication Digest.*

Metropolitan Police Department, 300 Indiana Avenue, NW, Washington, DC 20001, (202) 727-1000, http://mpdc.dc.gov/mpdc; *Annual Index Crime Totals, 1993-2005; District Crime Data at a Glance; Live Data Feeds of Crime Incidents and Other DC Services;* and *Monthly Preliminary Crime Statistics (2005-2006).*

National Center for Juvenile Justice (NCJJ), 3700 South Water Street, Suite 200, Pittsburgh, PA 15203, (412) 227-6950, Fax: (412) 227-6955, http://ncjj.servehttp.com/NCJJWebsite/main.htm; *How Does the Juvenile Justice System Measure Up? Applying Performance Measures in Five Jurisdictions (2006).*

National Center for State Courts (NCSC), 300 Newport Avenue, Williamsburg, VA 23185-4147, (800) 616-6164, Fax: (757) 564-2022, www.ncsconline.org; *Examining the Work of State Courts, 2004; Maryland Attorney Staff Workload Assessment, 2005; Minnesota Court Staff Workload Assessment, 2004; State Court Organization, 2004; The State Courts in 2006: Surviving Anti-Court Initiatives and Demonstrating High Performance;* and *Trust and Confidence in the California Courts, 2005, A Survey of the Public and Attorneys.*

National Criminal Justice Reference Service (NCJRS), PO Box 6000, Rockville, MD 20849-6000, (800) 851-3420, Fax: (301) 519-5212, www.ncjrs.org; *American Terrorism Study: Patterns of Behavior, Investigation and Prosecution of American Terrorists; Changing the Landscape: The Effectiveness of Grant Programs Under the Violence Against Women Act: 2002 Biennial Report to Congress;* and *New Jersey's "No Early Release Act": Its Impact on Prosecution, Sentencing, Corrections, and Victim Satisfaction, Final Report.*

U.S. Department of Justice (DOJ), Bureau of Justice Statistics, 810 Seventh Street, NW, Washington, DC 20531, (202) 307-0765, www.ojp.usdoj.gov/bjs/; *Bridging Gaps in Police Crime Data; Bureau of Justice Statistics, 2002: At a Glance; Census of Tribal Justice Agencies in Indian Country, 2002; Citizen Complaints about Police Use of Force; Defense Counsel in Criminal Cases; Drugs Crime Facts; Federal Criminal Justice Trends, 2003; Federal Justice Statistics Resource Center; Federal Prosecution of Human Trafficking, 2001-2005; Immigration Offenders in the Federal Criminal Justice System, 2000; Improving Access to and Integrity of Criminal History Records; Improving Criminal History Records for Background Checks, 2005; Justice Assistance Grant (JAG) Program, 2005; Justice Expenditure and Employment Extracts Series; Justice Expenditure and Employment in the United States 2003; National Corrections Reporting Program; Prisoner Petitions Filed in U.S. District Courts, 2000, with Trends, 1980-2000; Reporting by Prosecutors' Offices to Repositories of Criminal History Records; The Sourcebook of Criminal Justice Statistics, 2003; State Court Organization, 2004; State Court Prosecutors in Large Districts, 2001; State Court Prosecutors in Small Districts, 2001; State Court Sentencing of Convicted Felons; Summary of Human Subjects Protections Issues Related to Large Sample Surveys; Summary of State Sex Offender Registries, 2001; Survey of DNA Crime Laboratories, 2001; Survey of State Criminal History Information Systems, 2003; Trends in State Parole, 1990-2000; Tribal Law Enforcement, 2000;* and *Violent Felons in Large Urban Counties.*

U.S. Department of Justice (DOJ), Criminal Division, 950 Pennsylvania Ave., Washington, DC 20530-0001, (202) 514-2601, www.usdoj.gov/criminal/; *Report to Congress on the Activities and Operations of the Public Integrity Section.*

U.S. Department of Justice (DOJ), Drug Enforcement Administration (DEA), 2401 Jefferson Davis Highway, Alexandria, VA 22301, (202) 307-1000, www.usdoj.gov/dea; *State Factsheets.*

U.S. Department of Justice (DOJ), National Institute of Justice (NIJ), 810 Seventh Street, NW, Washington, DC 20531, (202) 307-2942, Fax: (202) 616-0275, www.ojp.usdoj.gov/nij/; *Correctional Boot Camps: Lessons From a Decade of Research; Police Innovations and the Structure of Informal Communication Between Police Agencies: Network and LEMAS Data; Reviewing Domestic Violence Deaths;* and *Victim Satisfaction With the Criminal Justice System.*

U.S. Department of Justice (DOJ), Office of the Attorney General, 950 Pennsylvania Avenue, NW, Washington, DC 20530-0001, (202) 353-1555, www.usdoj.gov/ag; *Assessment of U.S. Government Activities to Combat Trafficking in Persons.*

The Urban Institute, 2100 M Street, N.W., Washington, DC 20037, (202) 833-7200, www.urban.org; *Beyond the Prison Gates: The State of Parole in America; Does Parole Work?: Analyzing the Impact of Postprison Supervision on Rearrest Outcomes; Federal Criminal Case Processing, 2000: With Trends 1982-2000; The Influences of Truth-in-Sentencing Reforms on Changes in States' Sentencing Practices and Prison Populations; Number of Prisoners Released in Ohio Triples in 2 Decades: 62 Percent Head for 7 Counties, Led by Cuyahoga; A Portrait of Prisoner Reentry in Illinois; A Portrait of Prisoner Reentry in Maryland; Prisoner Reentry in Idaho; The Rise and Fall of American Youth Violence: 1980 to 2000;* and *Study Finds Parole Has Little Effect on Rearrest Rates.*

CRIMINAL VICTIMIZATION

Eurostat, Batiment Jean Monnet, Rue Alcide de Gasperi, L-2920 Luxembourg, http://epp.eurostat.ec.europa.eu; *Crime and Criminal Justice; General Government Expenditure and Revenue in the EU, 2006;* and *Study on Crime Victimisation.*

Federal Bureau of Investigation (FBI), J. Edgar Hoover Building, 935 Pennsylvania Avenue, NW, Washington, DC 20535-0001, (202) 324-3000, www.fbi.gov; *NCIC Missing Person and Unidentified Person Statistics for 2007.*

Federal Trade Commission (FTC), 600 Pennsylvania Avenue, NW, Washington, DC 20580, (202) 326-2222, www.ftc.gov; *Identity Theft Victim Complaint Data 2006* and *National and State Trends in Fraud and Identity Theft, January-December 2004.*

Home Office Research Development and Statistics (RDS), Direct Communications Unit, 2 Marsham Street, London SW1P 4DF, United Kingdom, www.homeoffice.gov.uk/rds/; *Crime in England and Wales 2005/2006.*

Inter-American Commission of Women (CIM), Organization of American States (OAS), 17th Street and Constitution Avenue, NW, Washington, D.C. 20006, (202) 458-3000, www.oas.org/CIM/english/About.htm; *Trafficking in Women and Children: Research Findings and Follow-Up.*

Metropolitan Police Department, 300 Indiana Avenue, NW, Washington, DC 20001, (202) 727-1000, http://mpdc.dc.gov/mpdc; *Annual Index Crime Totals, 1993-2005; District Crime Data at a Glance; Live Data Feeds of Crime Incidents and Other DC Services;* and *Monthly Preliminary Crime Statistics (2005-2006).*

National Center for Juvenile Justice (NCJJ), 3700 South Water Street, Suite 200, Pittsburgh, PA 15203, (412) 227-6950, Fax: (412) 227-6955, http://ncjj.servehttp.com/NCJJWebsite/main.htm; *Juvenile Offenders and Victims: 2006 National Report.*

Robert Wood Johnson Foundation, PO Box 2316, College Road East and Route 1, Princeton, NJ 08543, (877) 843-7953, www.rwjf.org; *Community-Based Prevention Programs in the War on Drugs: Findings from the "Fighting Back" Demonstration; Community-Based Prevention Programs in the War on Drugs: Findings from the "Fighting Back" Demonstration;* and *Neighborhood Crime Victimization, Drug Use and Drug Sales: Results from the "Fighting Back" Evaluation.*

Royal Canadian Mounted Police (RCMP), 1200 Vanier Parkway, Ottawa, ON K1A 0R2, Canada, (613) 993-7267, www.rcmp-grc.gc.ca; *The Direct and Indirect Impacts of Organized Crime on Youth, as Offenders and Victims.*

U.S. Department of Justice (DOJ), Bureau of Justice Statistics, 810 Seventh Street, NW, Washington, DC 20531, (202) 307-0765, www.ojp.usdoj.gov/bjs/; *Age Patterns in Violent Victimization, 1976-2000; American Indians and Crime: A BJS Statistical Profile, 1992-2002; Crimes Against Persons Age 65 or Older, 1993-2002; Criminal Victimization, 2005; Family Violence Statistics: Including Statistics on Strangers and Acquaintances; Federal Criminal Case Processing, 2002: With trends 1982-2002, Reconciled Data; Hate Crimes Reported by Victims and Police; Hispanic Victims of Violent Crime, 1993-2000; Identity Theft, 2004; Indicators of School Crime and Safety, 2005; Intimate Partner Violence; Intimate Partner Violence and Age of Victim, 1993-99; Juvenile Victimization and Offending, 1993-2003; Reporting Crime to the Police, 1992-2000; Sexual Assault of Young Children as Reported to Law Enforcement: Victim, Incident, and Offender Characteristics; Sexual Victimization of College Women; The Sourcebook of Criminal Justice Statistics, 2003; Violent Felons in Large Urban Counties;* and *Violent Victimization of College Students, 1995-2002.*

U.S. Department of Justice (DOJ), National Institute of Justice (NIJ), 810 Seventh Street, NW, Washington, DC 20531, (202) 307-2942, Fax: (202) 616-0275, www.ojp.usdoj.gov/nij/; *Co-Offending and Patterns of Juvenile Crime; Do Domestic Violence Services Save Lives?; The Effectiveness and Safety of Pepper Spray ; Intimate Partner Homicide: An Overview; Risky Mix: Drinking, Drug Use, and Homicide; Victim Satisfaction With the Criminal Justice System; When Violence Hits Home: How Economics and Neighborhood Play a Role;* and *Youth Victimization: Prevalence and Implications .*

U.S. Department of Justice (DOJ), Office of the Attorney General, 950 Pennsylvania Avenue, NW, Washington, DC 20530-0001, (202) 353-1555, www.usdoj.gov/ag; *Assessment of U.S. Government Activities to Combat Trafficking in Persons.*

U.S. Department of Justice (DOJ), Office on Violence Against Women (OVW), 950 Pennsylvania Avenue, NW, Washington, DC 20530-0001, (202) 514-2000, www.usdoj.gov/ovw; unpublished data.

U.S. Government Accountablity Office (GAO), 441 G Street, NW, Washington, DC 20548, (202) 512-3000, www.gao.gov; *Identity Theft: Greater Awareness and Use of Existing Data Are Needed.*

CRIMINAL VICTIMIZATION - HOUSEHOLDS

U.S. Department of Justice (DOJ), Bureau of Justice Statistics, 810 Seventh Street, NW, Washington, DC 20531, (202) 307-0765, www.ojp.usdoj.gov/bjs/; *Crime and the Nation's Households, 2004.*

U.S. Department of Justice (DOJ), National Institute of Justice (NIJ), 810 Seventh Street, NW, Washington, DC 20531, (202) 307-2942, Fax: (202) 616-0275, www.ojp.usdoj.gov/nij/; *Assessing Risk Factors for Intimate Partner Homicide; Do Domestic Violence Services Save Lives?; Intimate Partner Homicide: An Overview; Reviewing Domestic Violence Deaths; Risky Mix: Drinking, Drug Use, and Homicide; When Violence Hits Home: How Economics and Neighborhood Play a Role;* and *Youth Victimization: Prevalence and Implications .*

CRIMINAL VICTIMIZATION - PLACE OF OCCURRENCE

U.S. Department of Justice (DOJ), Bureau of Justice Statistics, 810 Seventh Street, NW, Washington, DC 20531, (202) 307-0765, www.ojp.usdoj.gov/bjs/; *Criminal Victimization, 2005.*

CRIMINAL VICTIMIZATION - WEAPONS INVOLVED

U.S. Department of Justice (DOJ), Bureau of Justice Statistics, 810 Seventh Street, NW, Washington, DC 20531, (202) 307-0765, www.ojp.usdoj.gov/bjs/; *Criminal Victimization, 2005* and *Weapon Use and Violent Crime, 1993-2001.*

CRIMINAL VICTIMIZATION - WORKPLACE

U.S. Bureau of Labor Statistics (BLS), Postal Square Building, 2 Massachusetts Avenue, NE, Washington, DC 20212-0001, (202) 691-5200, Fax: (202) 691-6325, www.bls.gov; *Monthly Labor Review (MLR)* and unpublished data.

CROAKER

National Marine Fisheries Service (NMFS), National Oceanic and Atmospheric Administration (NOAA), Office of Constituent Services, 1315 East West Highway, 9th Floor, Silver Spring, MD 20910, (301) 713-2379, Fax: (301) 713-2385, www.nmfs.noaa.gov; *Fisheries of the United States - 2006.*

CROATIA - NATIONAL STATISTICAL OFFICE

Croatian Bureau of Statistics, Ilica 3, 10000 Zagreb, Croatia, www.dzs.hr; National Data Center.

CROATIA - PRIMARY STATISTICS SOURCES

Croatian Bureau of Statistics, Ilica 3, 10000 Zagreb, Croatia, www.dzs.hr; *Statistical Yearbook 2006.*

Eurostat, Batiment Jean Monnet, Rue Alcide de Gasperi, L-2920 Luxembourg, http://epp.eurostat.ec.europa.eu; *Pocketbook on Candidate and Potential Candidate Countries.*

CROATIA - ABORTION

United Nations Statistics Division, New York, NY 10017, (800) 253-9646, Fax: (212) 963-4116, http://unstats.un.org; *Trends in Europe and North America: The Statistical Yearbook of the ECE 2005.*

CROATIA - AGRICULTURE

Economist Intelligence Unit, 111 West 57th Street, New York, NY 10019, (212) 554-0600, Fax: (212) 586-1181, www.eiu.com; *Croatia Country Report.*

Euromonitor International, Inc., 224 S. Michigan Avenue, Suite 1500, Chicago, IL 60604, (312) 922-1115, Fax: (312) 922-1157, www.euromonitor.com; *World Marketing Data and Statistics.*

Palgrave Macmillan Ltd., Houndmills, Basingstoke, Hampshire, RG21 6XS, England, (Telephone in U.S. (888) 330-8477), (Fax in U.S. (800) 672-2054), www.palgrave.com; *The Statesman's Yearbook 2008.*

Taylor and Francis Group, An Informa Business, 2 Park Square, Milton Park, Abingdon, Oxford OX14 4RN, United Kingdom, (Dial from U.S. (212) 216-7800), (Fax from U.S. (212) 564-7854), www.tandf.co.uk; *The Europa World Year Book.*

United Nations Food and Agricultural Organization (FAO), Viale delle Terme di Caracalla, 00100 Rome, Italy, (Dial from U.S. (202) 653-2400), (Fax from U.S. (202) 653 5760), www.fao.org; AQUASTAT; *FAO Production Yearbook 2002; FAO Trade Yearbook;* and *The State of Food and Agriculture (SOFA) 2006.*

United Nations Statistics Division, New York, NY 10017, (800) 253-9646, Fax: (212) 963-4116, http://unstats.un.org; *2004 Industrial Commodity Statistics Yearbook* and *Statistical Yearbook.*

The World Bank, 1818 H Street, NW, Washington, DC 20433, (202) 473-1000, Fax: (202) 477-6391, www.worldbank.org; *Croatia.*

CROATIA - AIRLINES

International Civil Aviation Organization (ICAO), External Relations and Public Information Office (EPO), 999 University Street, Montreal, Quebec H3C 5H7, Canada, (Dial from U.S. (514) 954-8219), (Fax from U.S. (514) 954-6077), www.icao.int; *Civil Aviation Statistics of the World.*

Palgrave Macmillan Ltd., Houndmills, Basingstoke, Hampshire, RG21 6XS, England, (Telephone in U.S. (888) 330-8477), (Fax in U.S. (800) 672-2054), www.palgrave.com; *The Statesman's Yearbook 2008.*

United Nations Statistics Division, New York, NY 10017, (800) 253-9646, Fax: (212) 963-4116, http://unstats.un.org; *Statistical Yearbook.*

CROATIA - AIRPORTS

Central Intelligence Agency, Office of Public Affairs, Washington, DC 20505, (703) 482-0623, Fax: (703) 482-1739, www.cia.gov; *The World Factbook.*

CROATIA - ARMED FORCES

Central Intelligence Agency, Office of Public Affairs, Washington, DC 20505, (703) 482-0623, Fax: (703) 482-1739, www.cia.gov; *The World Factbook.*

Euromonitor International, Inc., 224 S. Michigan Avenue, Suite 1500, Chicago, IL 60604, (312) 922-1115, Fax: (312) 922-1157, www.euromonitor.com; *World Marketing Data and Statistics.*

International Institute for Strategic Studies (IISS), Arundel House, 13-15 Arundel Street, Temple Place, London WC2R 3DX, England, www.iiss.org; *The Military Balance 2007.*

Palgrave Macmillan Ltd., Houndmills, Basingstoke, Hampshire, RG21 6XS, England, (Telephone in U.S. (888) 330-8477), (Fax in U.S. (800) 672-2054), www.palgrave.com; *The Statesman's Yearbook 2008.*

United Nations Statistics Division, New York, NY 10017, (800) 253-9646, Fax: (212) 963-4116, http://unstats.un.org; *Human Development Report 2006.*

CROATIA - AUTOMOBILE INDUSTRY AND TRADE

United Nations Statistics Division, New York, NY 10017, (800) 253-9646, Fax: (212) 963-4116, http://unstats.un.org; *Statistical Yearbook.*

CROATIA - BALANCE OF PAYMENTS

Taylor and Francis Group, An Informa Business, 2 Park Square, Milton Park, Abingdon, Oxford OX14 4RN, United Kingdom, (Dial from U.S. (212) 216-7800), (Fax from U.S. (212) 564-7854), www.tandf.co.uk; *The Europa World Year Book.*

United Nations Conference on Trade and Development (UNCTAD), DC2-1120, United Nations, New York, NY 10017, (212) 963-0027, www.unctad.org; *Handbook of Statistics 2005*.

The World Bank, 1818 H Street, NW, Washington, DC 20433, (202) 473-1000, Fax: (202) 477-6391, www.worldbank.org; *Croatia* and *World Development Report 2008*.

CROATIA - BANKS AND BANKING

Euromonitor International, Inc., 224 S. Michigan Avenue, Suite 1500, Chicago, IL 60604, (312) 922-1115, Fax: (312) 922-1157, www.euromonitor.com; *World Marketing Data and Statistics*.

Palgrave Macmillan Ltd., Houndmills, Basingstoke, Hampshire, RG21 6XS, England, (Telephone in U.S. (888) 330-8477), (Fax in U.S. (800) 672-2054), www.palgrave.com; *The Statesman's Yearbook 2008*.

CROATIA - BEVERAGE INDUSTRY

United Nations Statistics Division, New York, NY 10017, (800) 253-9646, Fax: (212) 963-4116, http://unstats.un.org; *Statistical Yearbook*.

CROATIA - BROADCASTING

Central Intelligence Agency, Office of Public Affairs, Washington, DC 20505, (703) 482-0623, Fax: (703) 482-1739, www.cia.gov; *The World Factbook*.

Euromonitor International, Inc., 224 S. Michigan Avenue, Suite 1500, Chicago, IL 60604, (312) 922-1115, Fax: (312) 922-1157, www.euromonitor.com; *World Marketing Data and Statistics*.

Palgrave Macmillan Ltd., Houndmills, Basingstoke, Hampshire, RG21 6XS, England, (Telephone in U.S. (888) 330-8477), (Fax in U.S. (800) 672-2054), www.palgrave.com; *The Statesman's Yearbook 2008*.

UNESCO Institute for Statistics, C.P. 6128 Succursale Centre-Ville, Montreal, Quebec, H3C 3J7 Canada, (Dial from U.S. (514) 343-6880), (Fax from U.S. (514) 343 6882), www.uis.unesco.org; *Statistical Tables*.

United Nations Statistics Division, New York, NY 10017, (800) 253-9646, Fax: (212) 963-4116, http://unstats.un.org; *Trends in Europe and North America: The Statistical Yearbook of the ECE 2005*.

CROATIA - BUDGET

Central Intelligence Agency, Office of Public Affairs, Washington, DC 20505, (703) 482-0623, Fax: (703) 482-1739, www.cia.gov; *The World Factbook*.

CROATIA - BUSINESS

Economist Intelligence Unit, 111 West 57th Street, New York, NY 10019, (212) 554-0600, Fax: (212) 586-1181, www.eiu.com; *Business Eastern Europe*.

United Nations Statistics Division, New York, NY 10017, (800) 253-9646, Fax: (212) 963-4116, http://unstats.un.org; *Statistical Yearbook*.

CROATIA - CHILDBIRTH - STATISTICS

Central Intelligence Agency, Office of Public Affairs, Washington, DC 20505, (703) 482-0623, Fax: (703) 482-1739, www.cia.gov; *The World Factbook*.

Euromonitor International, Inc., 224 S. Michigan Avenue, Suite 1500, Chicago, IL 60604, (312) 922-1115, Fax: (312) 922-1157, www.euromonitor.com; *The World Economic Factbook 2008*.

Palgrave Macmillan Ltd., Houndmills, Basingstoke, Hampshire, RG21 6XS, England, (Telephone in U.S. (888) 330-8477), (Fax in U.S. (800) 672-2054), www.palgrave.com; *The Statesman's Yearbook 2008*.

Taylor and Francis Group, An Informa Business, 2 Park Square, Milton Park, Abingdon, Oxford OX14 4RN, United Kingdom, (Dial from U.S. (212) 216-7800), (Fax from U.S. (212) 564-7854), www.tandf.co.uk; *The Europa World Year Book*.

United Nations Statistics Division, New York, NY 10017, (800) 253-9646, Fax: (212) 963-4116, http://unstats.un.org; *Statistical Yearbook*.

CROATIA - CLIMATE

Palgrave Macmillan Ltd., Houndmills, Basingstoke, Hampshire, RG21 6XS, England, (Telephone in U.S. (888) 330-8477), (Fax in U.S. (800) 672-2054), www.palgrave.com; *The Statesman's Yearbook 2008*.

CROATIA - COMMERCE

Palgrave Macmillan Ltd., Houndmills, Basingstoke, Hampshire, RG21 6XS, England, (Telephone in U.S. (888) 330-8477), (Fax in U.S. (800) 672-2054), www.palgrave.com; *The Statesman's Yearbook 2008*.

CROATIA - CONSTRUCTION INDUSTRY

United Nations Statistics Division, New York, NY 10017, (800) 253-9646, Fax: (212) 963-4116, http://unstats.un.org; *Statistical Yearbook*.

CROATIA - CONSUMER PRICE INDEXES

Taylor and Francis Group, An Informa Business, 2 Park Square, Milton Park, Abingdon, Oxford OX14 4RN, United Kingdom, (Dial from U.S. (212) 216-7800), (Fax from U.S. (212) 564-7854), www.tandf.co.uk; *The Europa World Year Book*.

United Nations Statistics Division, New York, NY 10017, (800) 253-9646, Fax: (212) 963-4116, http://unstats.un.org; *Statistical Yearbook* and *Trends in Europe and North America: The Statistical Yearbook of the ECE 2005*.

The World Bank, 1818 H Street, NW, Washington, DC 20433, (202) 473-1000, Fax: (202) 477-6391, www.worldbank.org; *Croatia*.

CROATIA - CONSUMPTION (ECONOMICS)

The World Bank, 1818 H Street, NW, Washington, DC 20433, (202) 473-1000, Fax: (202) 477-6391, www.worldbank.org; *World Development Report 2008*.

CROATIA - CRIME

United Nations Statistics Division, New York, NY 10017, (800) 253-9646, Fax: (212) 963-4116, http://unstats.un.org; *Trends in Europe and North America: The Statistical Yearbook of the ECE 2005*.

CROATIA - CROPS

Palgrave Macmillan Ltd., Houndmills, Basingstoke, Hampshire, RG21 6XS, England, (Telephone in U.S. (888) 330-8477), (Fax in U.S. (800) 672-2054), www.palgrave.com; *The Statesman's Yearbook 2008*.

Taylor and Francis Group, An Informa Business, 2 Park Square, Milton Park, Abingdon, Oxford OX14 4RN, United Kingdom, (Dial from U.S. (212) 216-7800), (Fax from U.S. (212) 564-7854), www.tandf.co.uk; *The Europa World Year Book*.

United Nations Food and Agricultural Organization (FAO), Viale delle Terme di Caracalla, 00100 Rome, Italy, (Dial from U.S. (202) 653-2400), (Fax from U.S. (202) 653 5760), www.fao.org; *FAO Production Yearbook 2002* and *The State of Food and Agriculture (SOFA) 2006*.

United Nations Statistics Division, New York, NY 10017, (800) 253-9646, Fax: (212) 963-4116, http://unstats.un.org; *2004 Industrial Commodity Statistics Yearbook* and *Statistical Yearbook*.

CROATIA - CUSTOMS ADMINISTRATION

Palgrave Macmillan Ltd., Houndmills, Basingstoke, Hampshire, RG21 6XS, England, (Telephone in U.S. (888) 330-8477), (Fax in U.S. (800) 672-2054), www.palgrave.com; *The Statesman's Yearbook 2008*.

CROATIA - DAIRY PROCESSING

Palgrave Macmillan Ltd., Houndmills, Basingstoke, Hampshire, RG21 6XS, England, (Telephone in U.S. (888) 330-8477), (Fax in U.S. (800) 672-2054), www.palgrave.com; *The Statesman's Yearbook 2008*.

Taylor and Francis Group, An Informa Business, 2 Park Square, Milton Park, Abingdon, Oxford OX14 4RN, United Kingdom, (Dial from U.S. (212) 216-7800), (Fax from U.S. (212) 564-7854), www.tandf.co.uk; *The Europa World Year Book*.

United Nations Food and Agricultural Organization (FAO), Viale delle Terme di Caracalla, 00100 Rome, Italy, (Dial from U.S. (202) 653-2400), (Fax from U.S. (202) 653 5760), www.fao.org; *FAO Production Yearbook 2002* and *The State of Food and Agriculture (SOFA) 2006*.

United Nations Statistics Division, New York, NY 10017, (800) 253-9646, Fax: (212) 963-4116, http://unstats.un.org; *2004 Industrial Commodity Statistics Yearbook* and *Statistical Yearbook*.

CROATIA - DEATH RATES

See CROATIA - MORTALITY

CROATIA - DEBTS, EXTERNAL

The World Bank, 1818 H Street, NW, Washington, DC 20433, (202) 473-1000, Fax: (202) 477-6391, www.worldbank.org; *Global Development Finance 2007* and *World Development Report 2008*.

CROATIA - DEMOGRAPHY

Euromonitor International, Inc., 224 S. Michigan Avenue, Suite 1500, Chicago, IL 60604, (312) 922-1115, Fax: (312) 922-1157, www.euromonitor.com; *The World Economic Factbook 2008* and *World Marketing Data and Statistics*.

United Nations Statistics Division, New York, NY 10017, (800) 253-9646, Fax: (212) 963-4116, http://unstats.un.org; *Demographic Yearbook* and *Human Development Report 2006*.

The World Bank, 1818 H Street, NW, Washington, DC 20433, (202) 473-1000, Fax: (202) 477-6391, www.worldbank.org; *Croatia*.

CROATIA - DISPOSABLE INCOME

United Nations Statistics Division, New York, NY 10017, (800) 253-9646, Fax: (212) 963-4116, http://unstats.un.org; *Statistical Yearbook*.

CROATIA - DIVORCE

United Nations Statistics Division, New York, NY 10017, (800) 253-9646, Fax: (212) 963-4116, http://unstats.un.org; *Demographic Yearbook; Statistical Yearbook;* and *Trends in Europe and North America: The Statistical Yearbook of the ECE 2005*.

CROATIA - ECONOMIC CONDITIONS

Center for International Business Education Research (CIBER), Columbia Business School and School of International and Public Affairs, Uris Hall, Room 212, 3022 Broadway, New York, NY 10027-6902, Mr. Joshua Safier, (212) 854-4750, Fax: (212) 222-9821, www.columbia.edu/cu/ciber/; Datastream International.

Central Intelligence Agency, Office of Public Affairs, Washington, DC 20505, (703) 482-0623, Fax: (703) 482-1739, www.cia.gov; *The World Factbook*.

DSI Data Service Information, Xantener Strasse 51a, D-47495 Rheinberg, Germany, www.dsidata.com; *Campus Solution*.

Dun and Bradstreet (DB) Corporation, 103 JFK Parkway, Short Hills, NJ 07078, (973) 921-5500, www.dnb.com; *Country Report*.

Economist Intelligence Unit, 111 West 57th Street, New York, NY 10019, (212) 554-0600, Fax: (212) 586-1181, www.eiu.com; *Croatia Country Report*.

Euromonitor International, Inc., 224 S. Michigan Avenue, Suite 1500, Chicago, IL 60604, (312) 922-1115, Fax: (312) 922-1157, www.euromonitor.com; *The World Economic Factbook 2008* and *World Marketing Data and Statistics*.

Eurostat, Batiment Jean Monnet, Rue Alcide de Gasperi, L-2920 Luxembourg, http://epp.eurostat.ec.europa.eu; *Consumers in Europe - Facts and Figures on Services of General Interest*.

International Monetary Fund (IMF), 700 Nineteenth Street, NW, Washington, DC 20431, (202) 623-7000, Fax: (202) 623-4661, www.imf.org; *World Economic Outlook Reports*.

Palgrave Macmillan Ltd., Houndmills, Basingstoke, Hampshire, RG21 6XS, England, (Telephone in U.S.

(888) 330-8477), (Fax in U.S. (800) 672-2054), www.palgrave.com; *The Statesman's Yearbook 2008.*

Taylor and Francis Group, An Informa Business, 2 Park Square, Milton Park, Abingdon, Oxford OX14 4RN, United Kingdom, (Dial from U.S. (212) 216-7800), (Fax from U.S. (212) 564-7854), www.tandf.co.uk; *The Europa World Year Book.*

United Nations Statistics Division, New York, NY 10017, (800) 253-9646, Fax: (212) 963-4116, http://unstats.un.org; *World Statistics Pocketbook.*

The World Bank, 1818 H Street, NW, Washington, DC 20433, (202) 473-1000, Fax: (202) 477-6391, www.worldbank.org; *Croatia; Global Economic Monitor (GEM); Global Economic Prospects 2008; The World Bank Atlas 2003-2004;* and *World Development Report 2008.*

CROATIA - EDUCATION

Euromonitor International, Inc., 224 S. Michigan Avenue, Suite 1500, Chicago, IL 60604, (312) 922-1115, Fax: (312) 922-1157, www.euromonitor.com; *World Marketing Data and Statistics.*

European Union, Delegation of the European Commission to the United States, 2300 M Street, NW, Washington, DC 20037, (202) 862-9500, Fax: (202) 429-1766, www.eurunion.org; *Education across Europe 2003.*

Palgrave Macmillan Ltd., Houndmills, Basingstoke, Hampshire, RG21 6XS, England, (Telephone in U.S. (888) 330-8477), (Fax in U.S. (800) 672-2054), www.palgrave.com; *The Statesman's Yearbook 2008.*

Taylor and Francis Group, An Informa Business, 2 Park Square, Milton Park, Abingdon, Oxford OX14 4RN, United Kingdom, (Dial from U.S. (212) 216-7800), (Fax from U.S. (212) 564-7854), www.tandf.co.uk; *The Europa World Year Book.*

UNESCO Institute for Statistics, C.P. 6128 Succursale Centre-Ville, Montreal, Quebec, H3C 3J7 Canada, (Dial from U.S. (514) 343-6880), (Fax from U.S. (514) 343 6882), www.uis.unesco.org; *Statistical Tables.*

United Nations Statistics Division, New York, NY 10017, (800) 253-9646, Fax: (212) 963-4116, http://unstats.un.org; *Human Development Report 2006* and *Trends in Europe and North America: The Statistical Yearbook of the ECE 2005.*

The World Bank, 1818 H Street, NW, Washington, DC 20433, (202) 473-1000, Fax: (202) 477-6391, www.worldbank.org; *Croatia* and *World Development Report 2008.*

CROATIA - ELECTRICITY

Central Intelligence Agency, Office of Public Affairs, Washington, DC 20505, (703) 482-0623, Fax: (703) 482-1739, www.cia.gov; *The World Factbook.*

Palgrave Macmillan Ltd., Houndmills, Basingstoke, Hampshire, RG21 6XS, England, (Telephone in U.S. (888) 330-8477), (Fax in U.S. (800) 672-2054), www.palgrave.com; *The Statesman's Yearbook 2008.*

Platts, 2 Penn Plaza, 25th Floor, New York, NY 10121-2298, (212) 904-3070, www.platts.com; *Energy Economist* and *European Electricity Review 2004.*

U.S. Department of Energy (DOE), Energy Information Administration (EIA), 1000 Independence Avenue, SW, Washington, DC 20585, (202) 586-8800, www.eia.doe.gov; *International Energy Annual 2004* and *International Energy Outlook 2006.*

United Nations Statistics Division, New York, NY 10017, (800) 253-9646, Fax: (212) 963-4116, http://unstats.un.org; *Energy Statistics Yearbook 2003; Human Development Report 2006; Statistical Yearbook;* and *Trends in Europe and North America: The Statistical Yearbook of the ECE 2005.*

CROATIA - EMPLOYMENT

United Nations Statistics Division, New York, NY 10017, (800) 253-9646, Fax: (212) 963-4116, http://unstats.un.org; *Statistical Yearbook* and *Trends in Europe and North America: The Statistical Yearbook of the ECE 2005.*

The World Bank, 1818 H Street, NW, Washington, DC 20433, (202) 473-1000, Fax: (202) 477-6391, www.worldbank.org; *Croatia.*

CROATIA - ENERGY INDUSTRIES

Platts, 2 Penn Plaza, 25th Floor, New York, NY 10121-2298, (212) 904-3070, www.platts.com; *Energy in East Europe.*

Selig Center for Economic Growth, Terry College of Business, University of Georgia, Athens, GA 30602-6269, Mr. Jeffrey M. Humphreys, Director, (706) 425-2962, www.selig.uga.edu; *Georgia Economic Outlook.*

CROATIA - ENVIRONMENTAL CONDITIONS

DSI Data Service Information, Xantener Strasse 51a, D-47495 Rheinberg, Germany, www.dsidata.com; *Campus Solution* and *DSI's Global Environmental Database.*

Economist Intelligence Unit, 111 West 57th Street, New York, NY 10019, (212) 554-0600, Fax: (212) 586-1181, www.eiu.com; *Croatia Country Report.*

United Nations Statistics Division, New York, NY 10017, (800) 253-9646, Fax: (212) 963-4116, http://unstats.un.org; *Statistical Yearbook; Trends in Europe and North America: The Statistical Yearbook of the ECE 2005;* and *World Statistics Pocketbook.*

CROATIA - EXPORTS

Central Intelligence Agency, Office of Public Affairs, Washington, DC 20505, (703) 482-0623, Fax: (703) 482-1739, www.cia.gov; *The World Factbook.*

Economist Intelligence Unit, 111 West 57th Street, New York, NY 10019, (212) 554-0600, Fax: (212) 586-1181, www.eiu.com; *Croatia Country Report.*

Euromonitor International, Inc., 224 S. Michigan Avenue, Suite 1500, Chicago, IL 60604, (312) 922-1115, Fax: (312) 922-1157, www.euromonitor.com; *The World Economic Factbook 2008.*

Palgrave Macmillan Ltd., Houndmills, Basingstoke, Hampshire, RG21 6XS, England, (Telephone in U.S. (888) 330-8477), (Fax in U.S. (800) 672-2054), www.palgrave.com; *The Statesman's Yearbook 2008.*

Taylor and Francis Group, An Informa Business, 2 Park Square, Milton Park, Abingdon, Oxford OX14 4RN, United Kingdom, (Dial from U.S. (212) 216-7800), (Fax from U.S. (212) 564-7854), www.tandf.co.uk; *The Europa World Year Book.*

United Nations Conference on Trade and Development (UNCTAD), DC2-1120, United Nations, New York, NY 10017, (212) 963-0027, www.unctad.org; *Handbook of Statistics 2005.*

United Nations Statistics Division, New York, NY 10017, (800) 253-9646, Fax: (212) 963-4116, http://unstats.un.org; *International Trade Statistics Yearbook* and *Trends in Europe and North America: The Statistical Yearbook of the ECE 2005.*

The World Bank, 1818 H Street, NW, Washington, DC 20433, (202) 473-1000, Fax: (202) 477-6391, www.worldbank.org; *World Development Report 2008.*

CROATIA - FERTILITY, HUMAN

United Nations Statistics Division, New York, NY 10017, (800) 253-9646, Fax: (212) 963-4116, http://unstats.un.org; *Human Development Report 2006* and *Trends in Europe and North America: The Statistical Yearbook of the ECE 2005.*

The World Bank, 1818 H Street, NW, Washington, DC 20433, (202) 473-1000, Fax: (202) 477-6391, www.worldbank.org; *The World Bank Atlas 2003-2004* and *World Development Report 2008.*

CROATIA - FERTILIZER INDUSTRY

United Nations Food and Agricultural Organization (FAO), Viale delle Terme di Caracalla, 00100 Rome, Italy, (Dial from U.S. (202) 653-2400), (Fax from U.S. (202) 653 5760), www.fao.org; *FAO Fertilizer Yearbook.*

United Nations Statistics Division, New York, NY 10017, (800) 253-9646, Fax: (212) 963-4116, http://unstats.un.org; *2004 Industrial Commodity Statistics Yearbook* and *Statistical Yearbook.*

CROATIA - FINANCE

Taylor and Francis Group, An Informa Business, 2 Park Square, Milton Park, Abingdon, Oxford OX14 4RN, United Kingdom, (Dial from U.S. (212) 216-7800), (Fax from U.S. (212) 564-7854), www.tandf.co.uk; *The Europa World Year Book.*

United Nations Statistics Division, New York, NY 10017, (800) 253-9646, Fax: (212) 963-4116, http://unstats.un.org; *National Accounts Statistics: Compendium of Income Distribution Statistics* and *Statistical Yearbook.*

The World Bank, 1818 H Street, NW, Washington, DC 20433, (202) 473-1000, Fax: (202) 477-6391, www.worldbank.org; *Croatia.*

CROATIA - FINANCE, PUBLIC

Bernan Essential Government Publications, 4611-F Assembly Drive, Lanham MD, 20706-4391, (301) 459-2255, Fax: (800) 865-3450, www.bernan.com; *National Accounts Statistics.*

Economist Intelligence Unit, 111 West 57th Street, New York, NY 10019, (212) 554-0600, Fax: (212) 586-1181, www.eiu.com; *Croatia Country Report.*

International Monetary Fund (IMF), 700 Nineteenth Street, NW, Washington, DC 20431, (202) 623-7000, Fax: (202) 623-4661, www.imf.org; *International Financial Statistics* and *International Financial Statistics Online Service.*

Palgrave Macmillan Ltd., Houndmills, Basingstoke, Hampshire, RG21 6XS, England, (Telephone in U.S. (888) 330-8477), (Fax in U.S. (800) 672-2054), www.palgrave.com; *The Statesman's Yearbook 2008.*

Taylor and Francis Group, An Informa Business, 2 Park Square, Milton Park, Abingdon, Oxford OX14 4RN, United Kingdom, (Dial from U.S. (212) 216-7800), (Fax from U.S. (212) 564-7854), www.tandf.co.uk; *The Europa World Year Book.*

The World Bank, 1818 H Street, NW, Washington, DC 20433, (202) 473-1000, Fax: (202) 477-6391, www.worldbank.org; *Croatia.*

CROATIA - FISHERIES

Palgrave Macmillan Ltd., Houndmills, Basingstoke, Hampshire, RG21 6XS, England, (Telephone in U.S. (888) 330-8477), (Fax in U.S. (800) 672-2054), www.palgrave.com; *The Statesman's Yearbook 2008.*

Taylor and Francis Group, An Informa Business, 2 Park Square, Milton Park, Abingdon, Oxford OX14 4RN, United Kingdom, (Dial from U.S. (212) 216-7800), (Fax from U.S. (212) 564-7854), www.tandf.co.uk; *The Europa World Year Book.*

United Nations Food and Agricultural Organization (FAO), Viale delle Terme di Caracalla, 00100 Rome, Italy, (Dial from U.S. (202) 653-2400), (Fax from U.S. (202) 653 5760), www.fao.org; *FAO Yearbook of Fishery Statistics;* Fishery Databases; FISHSTAT Database. Subjects covered include: Aquaculture production, capture production, fishery commodities; and *The State of Food and Agriculture (SOFA) 2006.*

United Nations Statistics Division, New York, NY 10017, (800) 253-9646, Fax: (212) 963-4116, http://unstats.un.org; *2004 Industrial Commodity Statistics Yearbook* and *Statistical Yearbook.*

The World Bank, 1818 H Street, NW, Washington, DC 20433, (202) 473-1000, Fax: (202) 477-6391, www.worldbank.org; *Croatia.*

CROATIA - FOOD

United Nations Food and Agricultural Organization (FAO), Viale delle Terme di Caracalla, 00100 Rome, Italy, (Dial from U.S. (202) 653-2400), (Fax from U.S. (202) 653 5760), www.fao.org; *FAO Production Yearbook 2002* and *The State of Food and Agriculture (SOFA) 2006.*

United Nations Statistics Division, New York, NY 10017, (800) 253-9646, Fax: (212) 963-4116, http://

unstats.un.org; *Human Development Report 2006* and *2004 Industrial Commodity Statistics Yearbook.*

CROATIA - FOREIGN EXCHANGE RATES

Central Intelligence Agency, Office of Public Affairs, Washington, DC 20505, (703) 482-0623, Fax: (703) 482-1739, www.cia.gov; *The World Factbook.*

Euromonitor International, Inc., 224 S. Michigan Avenue, Suite 1500, Chicago, IL 60604, (312) 922-1115, Fax: (312) 922-1157, www.euromonitor.com; *The World Economic Factbook 2008.*

Taylor and Francis Group, An Informa Business, 2 Park Square, Milton Park, Abingdon, Oxford OX14 4RN, United Kingdom, (Dial from U.S. (212) 216-7800), (Fax from U.S. (212) 564-7854), www.tandf.co.uk; *The Europa World Year Book.*

United Nations Statistics Division, New York, NY 10017, (800) 253-9646, Fax: (212) 963-4116, http://unstats.un.org; *Statistical Yearbook; Trends in Europe and North America: The Statistical Yearbook of the ECE 2005;* and *World Statistics Pocketbook.*

CROATIA - FORESTS AND FORESTRY

Palgrave Macmillan Ltd., Houndmills, Basingstoke, Hampshire, RG21 6XS, England, (Telephone in U.S. (888) 330-8477), (Fax in U.S. (800) 672-2054), www.palgrave.com; *The Statesman's Yearbook 2008.*

Taylor and Francis Group, An Informa Business, 2 Park Square, Milton Park, Abingdon, Oxford OX14 4RN, United Kingdom, (Dial from U.S. (212) 216-7800), (Fax from U.S. (212) 564-7854), www.tandf.co.uk; *The Europa World Year Book.*

UNESCO Institute for Statistics, C.P. 6128 Succursale Centre-Ville, Montreal, Quebec, H3C 3J7 Canada, (Dial from U.S. (514) 343-6880), (Fax from U.S. (514) 343 6882), www.uis.unesco.org; *Statistical Tables.*

United Nations Food and Agricultural Organization (FAO), Viale delle Terme di Caracalla, 00100 Rome, Italy, (Dial from U.S. (202) 653-2400), (Fax from U.S. (202) 653 5760), www.fao.org; *FAO Yearbook of Forest Products* and *The State of Food and Agriculture (SOFA) 2006.*

United Nations Statistics Division, New York, NY 10017, (800) 253-9646, Fax: (212) 963-4116, http://unstats.un.org; *2004 Industrial Commodity Statistics Yearbook; Statistical Yearbook;* and *Trends in Europe and North America: The Statistical Yearbook of the ECE 2005.*

The World Bank, 1818 H Street, NW, Washington, DC 20433, (202) 473-1000, Fax: (202) 477-6391, www.worldbank.org; *Croatia* and *World Development Report 2008.*

CROATIA - GROSS DOMESTIC PRODUCT

Economist Intelligence Unit, 111 West 57th Street, New York, NY 10019, (212) 554-0600, Fax: (212) 586-1181, www.eiu.com; *Croatia Country Report.*

Euromonitor International, Inc., 224 S. Michigan Avenue, Suite 1500, Chicago, IL 60604, (312) 922-1115, Fax: (312) 922-1157, www.euromonitor.com; *The World Economic Factbook 2008.*

United Nations Statistics Division, New York, NY 10017, (800) 253-9646, Fax: (212) 963-4116, http://unstats.un.org; *Human Development Report 2006; National Accounts Statistics: Compendium of Income Distribution Statistics; Statistical Yearbook;* and *Trends in Europe and North America: The Statistical Yearbook of the ECE 2005.*

The World Bank, 1818 H Street, NW, Washington, DC 20433, (202) 473-1000, Fax: (202) 477-6391, www.worldbank.org; *World Development Report 2008.*

CROATIA - GROSS NATIONAL PRODUCT

Palgrave Macmillan Ltd., Houndmills, Basingstoke, Hampshire, RG21 6XS, England, (Telephone in U.S. (888) 330-8477), (Fax in U.S. (800) 672-2054), www.palgrave.com; *The Statesman's Yearbook 2008.*

United Nations Statistics Division, New York, NY 10017, (800) 253-9646, Fax: (212) 963-4116, http://unstats.un.org; *Statistical Yearbook.*

The World Bank, 1818 H Street, NW, Washington, DC 20433, (202) 473-1000, Fax: (202) 477-6391, www.worldbank.org; *The World Bank Atlas 2003-2004* and *World Development Report 2008.*

CROATIA - HOUSING

Euromonitor International, Inc., 224 S. Michigan Avenue, Suite 1500, Chicago, IL 60604, (312) 922-1115, Fax: (312) 922-1157, www.euromonitor.com; *World Marketing Data and Statistics.*

United Nations Statistics Division, New York, NY 10017, (800) 253-9646, Fax: (212) 963-4116, http://unstats.un.org; *Trends in Europe and North America: The Statistical Yearbook of the ECE 2005.*

CROATIA - ILLITERATE PERSONS

Euromonitor International, Inc., 224 S. Michigan Avenue, Suite 1500, Chicago, IL 60604, (312) 922-1115, Fax: (312) 922-1157, www.euromonitor.com; *The World Economic Factbook 2008.*

UNESCO Institute for Statistics, C.P. 6128 Succursale Centre-Ville, Montreal, Quebec, H3C 3J7 Canada, (Dial from U.S. (514) 343-6880), (Fax from U.S. (514) 343 6882), www.uis.unesco.org; *Statistical Tables.*

United Nations Statistics Division, New York, NY 10017, (800) 253-9646, Fax: (212) 963-4116, http://unstats.un.org; *Human Development Report 2006.*

CROATIA - IMPORTS

Central Intelligence Agency, Office of Public Affairs, Washington, DC 20505, (703) 482-0623, Fax: (703) 482-1739, www.cia.gov; *The World Factbook.*

Economist Intelligence Unit, 111 West 57th Street, New York, NY 10019, (212) 554-0600, Fax: (212) 586-1181, www.eiu.com; *Croatia Country Report.*

Euromonitor International, Inc., 224 S. Michigan Avenue, Suite 1500, Chicago, IL 60604, (312) 922-1115, Fax: (312) 922-1157, www.euromonitor.com; *The World Economic Factbook 2008.*

Palgrave Macmillan Ltd., Houndmills, Basingstoke, Hampshire, RG21 6XS, England, (Telephone in U.S. (888) 330-8477), (Fax in U.S. (800) 672-2054), www.palgrave.com; *The Statesman's Yearbook 2008.*

Taylor and Francis Group, An Informa Business, 2 Park Square, Milton Park, Abingdon, Oxford OX14 4RN, United Kingdom, (Dial from U.S. (212) 216-7800), (Fax from U.S. (212) 564-7854), www.tandf.co.uk; *The Europa World Year Book.*

United Nations Conference on Trade and Development (UNCTAD), DC2-1120, United Nations, New York, NY 10017, (212) 963-0027, www.unctad.org; *Handbook of Statistics 2005.*

United Nations Statistics Division, New York, NY 10017, (800) 253-9646, Fax: (212) 963-4116, http://unstats.un.org; *International Trade Statistics Yearbook* and *Trends in Europe and North America: The Statistical Yearbook of the ECE 2005.*

The World Bank, 1818 H Street, NW, Washington, DC 20433, (202) 473-1000, Fax: (202) 477-6391, www.worldbank.org; *World Development Report 2008.*

CROATIA - INDUSTRIAL PROPERTY

United Nations Statistics Division, New York, NY 10017, (800) 253-9646, Fax: (212) 963-4116, http://unstats.un.org; *Statistical Yearbook.*

CROATIA - INDUSTRIES

Central Intelligence Agency, Office of Public Affairs, Washington, DC 20505, (703) 482-0623, Fax: (703) 482-1739, www.cia.gov; *The World Factbook.*

Economist Intelligence Unit, 111 West 57th Street, New York, NY 10019, (212) 554-0600, Fax: (212) 586-1181, www.eiu.com; *Croatia Country Report.*

Euromonitor International, Inc., 224 S. Michigan Avenue, Suite 1500, Chicago, IL 60604, (312) 922-1115, Fax: (312) 922-1157, www.euromonitor.com; *The World Economic Factbook 2008* and *World Marketing Data and Statistics.*

Palgrave Macmillan Ltd., Houndmills, Basingstoke, Hampshire, RG21 6XS, England, (Telephone in U.S. (888) 330-8477), (Fax in U.S. (800) 672-2054), www.palgrave.com; *The Statesman's Yearbook 2008.*

Taylor and Francis Group, An Informa Business, 2 Park Square, Milton Park, Abingdon, Oxford OX14 4RN, United Kingdom, (Dial from U.S. (212) 216-7800), (Fax from U.S. (212) 564-7854), www.tandf.co.uk; *The Europa World Year Book.*

United Nations Industrial Development Organization (UNIDO), 1 United Nations Plaza, New York, NY 10017, (212) 963 6890, Fax: (212) 963-7904, http://unido.org; Industrial Statistics Database 2008 (INDSTAT) and *The International Yearbook of Industrial Statistics 2008.*

United Nations Statistics Division, New York, NY 10017, (800) 253-9646, Fax: (212) 963-4116, http://unstats.un.org; *2004 Industrial Commodity Statistics Yearbook; Statistical Yearbook;* and *Trends in Europe and North America: The Statistical Yearbook of the ECE 2005.*

The World Bank, 1818 H Street, NW, Washington, DC 20433, (202) 473-1000, Fax: (202) 477-6391, www.worldbank.org; *Croatia.*

CROATIA - INTERNATIONAL TRADE

Economist Intelligence Unit, 111 West 57th Street, New York, NY 10019, (212) 554-0600, Fax: (212) 586-1181, www.eiu.com; *Croatia Country Report.*

Euromonitor International, Inc., 224 S. Michigan Avenue, Suite 1500, Chicago, IL 60604, (312) 922-1115, Fax: (312) 922-1157, www.euromonitor.com; *The World Economic Factbook 2008* and *World Marketing Data and Statistics.*

Palgrave Macmillan Ltd., Houndmills, Basingstoke, Hampshire, RG21 6XS, England, (Telephone in U.S. (888) 330-8477), (Fax in U.S. (800) 672-2054), www.palgrave.com; *The Statesman's Yearbook 2008.*

Taylor and Francis Group, An Informa Business, 2 Park Square, Milton Park, Abingdon, Oxford OX14 4RN, United Kingdom, (Dial from U.S. (212) 216-7800), (Fax from U.S. (212) 564-7854), www.tandf.co.uk; *The Europa World Year Book.*

United Nations Food and Agricultural Organization (FAO), Viale delle Terme di Caracalla, 00100 Rome, Italy, (Dial from U.S. (202) 653-2400), (Fax from U.S. (202) 653 5760), www.fao.org; *FAO Trade Yearbook.*

United Nations Statistics Division, New York, NY 10017, (800) 253-9646, Fax: (212) 963-4116, http://unstats.un.org; *International Trade Statistics Yearbook* and *Statistical Yearbook.*

The World Bank, 1818 H Street, NW, Washington, DC 20433, (202) 473-1000, Fax: (202) 477-6391, www.worldbank.org; *Croatia* and *World Development Report 2008.*

World Trade Organization (WTO), Centre William Rappard, Rue de Lausanne 154, CH-1211 Geneva 21, Switzerland, www.wto.org; *International Trade Statistics 2006.*

CROATIA - INTERNET USERS

International Telecommunication Union (ITU), Place des Nations, 1211 Geneva 20, Switzerland, www.itu.int; *World Telecommunication/ICT Indicators Database on CD-ROM; World Telecommunication/ICT Indicators Database Online;* and *Yearbook of Statistics - Telecommunication Services (Chronological Time Series 1997-2006).*

The World Bank, 1818 H Street, NW, Washington, DC 20433, (202) 473-1000, Fax: (202) 477-6391, www.worldbank.org; *Croatia.*

CROATIA - LABOR

Central Intelligence Agency, Office of Public Affairs, Washington, DC 20505, (703) 482-0623, Fax: (703) 482-1739, www.cia.gov; *The World Factbook.*

Euromonitor International, Inc., 224 S. Michigan Avenue, Suite 1500, Chicago, IL 60604, (312) 922-1115, Fax: (312) 922-1157, www.euromonitor.com; *World Marketing Data and Statistics.*

Palgrave Macmillan Ltd., Houndmills, Basingstoke, Hampshire, RG21 6XS, England, (Telephone in U.S. (888) 330-8477), (Fax in U.S. (800) 672-2054), www.palgrave.com; *The Statesman's Yearbook 2008.*

United Nations Statistics Division, New York, NY 10017, (800) 253-9646, Fax: (212) 963-4116, http://unstats.un.org; *Human Development Report 2006* and *Statistical Yearbook.*

The World Bank, 1818 H Street, NW, Washington, DC 20433, (202) 473-1000, Fax: (202) 477-6391, www.worldbank.org; *The World Bank Atlas 2003-2004* and *World Development Report 2008.*

CROATIA - LAND USE

Central Intelligence Agency, Office of Public Affairs, Washington, DC 20505, (703) 482-0623, Fax: (703) 482-1739, www.cia.gov; *The World Factbook.*

United Nations Food and Agricultural Organization (FAO), Viale delle Terme di Caracalla, 00100 Rome, Italy, (Dial from U.S. (202) 653-2400), (Fax from U.S. (202) 653 5760), www.fao.org; *FAO Production Yearbook 2002.*

The World Bank, 1818 H Street, NW, Washington, DC 20433, (202) 473-1000, Fax: (202) 477-6391, www.worldbank.org; *World Development Report 2008.*

CROATIA - LIBRARIES

UNESCO Institute for Statistics, C.P. 6128 Succursale Centre-Ville, Montreal, Quebec, H3C 3J7 Canada, (Dial from U.S. (514) 343-6880), (Fax from U.S. (514) 343 6882), www.uis.unesco.org; *Statistical Tables.*

United Nations Statistics Division, New York, NY 10017, (800) 253-9646, Fax: (212) 963-4116, http://unstats.un.org; *Trends in Europe and North America: The Statistical Yearbook of the ECE 2005.*

CROATIA - LIFE EXPECTANCY

Central Intelligence Agency, Office of Public Affairs, Washington, DC 20505, (703) 482-0623, Fax: (703) 482-1739, www.cia.gov; *The World Factbook.*

Euromonitor International, Inc., 224 S. Michigan Avenue, Suite 1500, Chicago, IL 60604, (312) 922-1115, Fax: (312) 922-1157, www.euromonitor.com; *The World Economic Factbook 2008.*

United Nations Statistics Division, New York, NY 10017, (800) 253-9646, Fax: (212) 963-4116, http://unstats.un.org; *Demographic Yearbook; Human Development Report 2006; Trends in Europe and North America: The Statistical Yearbook of the ECE 2005;* and *World Statistics Pocketbook.*

The World Bank, 1818 H Street, NW, Washington, DC 20433, (202) 473-1000, Fax: (202) 477-6391, www.worldbank.org; *The World Bank Atlas 2003-2004* and *World Development Report 2008.*

CROATIA - LITERACY

Euromonitor International, Inc., 224 S. Michigan Avenue, Suite 1500, Chicago, IL 60604, (312) 922-1115, Fax: (312) 922-1157, www.euromonitor.com; *World Marketing Data and Statistics.*

CROATIA - LIVESTOCK

Palgrave Macmillan Ltd., Houndmills, Basingstoke, Hampshire, RG21 6XS, England, (Telephone in U.S. (888) 330-8477), (Fax in U.S. (800) 672-2054), www.palgrave.com; *The Statesman's Yearbook 2008.*

Taylor and Francis Group, An Informa Business, 2 Park Square, Milton Park, Abingdon, Oxford OX14 4RN, United Kingdom, (Dial from U.S. (212) 216-7800), (Fax from U.S. (212) 564-7854), www.tandf.co.uk; *The Europa World Year Book.*

United Nations Food and Agricultural Organization (FAO), Viale delle Terme di Caracalla, 00100 Rome, Italy, (Dial from U.S. (202) 653-2400), (Fax from U.S. (202) 653 5760), www.fao.org; *FAO Production Yearbook 2002* and *The State of Food and Agriculture (SOFA) 2006.*

United Nations Statistics Division, New York, NY 10017, (800) 253-9646, Fax: (212) 963-4116, http://unstats.un.org; *2004 Industrial Commodity Statistics Yearbook* and *Statistical Yearbook.*

CROATIA - MACHINERY

United Nations Statistics Division, New York, NY 10017, (800) 253-9646, Fax: (212) 963-4116, http://unstats.un.org; *2004 Industrial Commodity Statistics Yearbook.*

CROATIA - MANUFACTURES

United Nations Statistics Division, New York, NY 10017, (800) 253-9646, Fax: (212) 963-4116, http://unstats.un.org; *2004 Industrial Commodity Statistics Yearbook* and *Statistical Yearbook.*

CROATIA - MARRIAGE

Taylor and Francis Group, An Informa Business, 2 Park Square, Milton Park, Abingdon, Oxford OX14 4RN, United Kingdom, (Dial from U.S. (212) 216-7800), (Fax from U.S. (212) 564-7854), www.tandf.co.uk; *The Europa World Year Book.*

United Nations Statistics Division, New York, NY 10017, (800) 253-9646, Fax: (212) 963-4116, http://unstats.un.org; *Demographic Yearbook; Statistical Yearbook;* and *Trends in Europe and North America: The Statistical Yearbook of the ECE 2005.*

CROATIA - MINERAL INDUSTRIES

Platts, 2 Penn Plaza, 25th Floor, New York, NY 10121-2298, (212) 904-3070, www.platts.com; *Energy Economist* and *Energy in East Europe.*

Taylor and Francis Group, An Informa Business, 2 Park Square, Milton Park, Abingdon, Oxford OX14 4RN, United Kingdom, (Dial from U.S. (212) 216-7800), (Fax from U.S. (212) 564-7854), www.tandf.co.uk; *The Europa World Year Book.*

United Nations Statistics Division, New York, NY 10017, (800) 253-9646, Fax: (212) 963-4116, http://unstats.un.org; *Energy Statistics Yearbook 2003; 2004 Industrial Commodity Statistics Yearbook;* and *Statistical Yearbook.*

The World Bank, 1818 H Street, NW, Washington, DC 20433, (202) 473-1000, Fax: (202) 477-6391, www.worldbank.org; *Croatia.*

CROATIA - MONEY SUPPLY

Economist Intelligence Unit, 111 West 57th Street, New York, NY 10019, (212) 554-0600, Fax: (212) 586-1181, www.eiu.com; *Croatia Country Report.*

The World Bank, 1818 H Street, NW, Washington, DC 20433, (202) 473-1000, Fax: (202) 477-6391, www.worldbank.org; *Croatia.*

CROATIA - MONUMENTS AND HISTORIC SITES

Palgrave Macmillan Ltd., Houndmills, Basingstoke, Hampshire, RG21 6XS, England, (Telephone in U.S. (888) 330-8477), (Fax in U.S. (800) 672-2054), www.palgrave.com; *The Statesman's Yearbook 2008.*

UNESCO Institute for Statistics, C.P. 6128 Succursale Centre-Ville, Montreal, Quebec, H3C 3J7 Canada, (Dial from U.S. (514) 343-6880), (Fax from U.S. (514) 343 6882), www.uis.unesco.org; *Statistical Tables.*

CROATIA - MORTALITY

Central Intelligence Agency, Office of Public Affairs, Washington, DC 20505, (703) 482-0623, Fax: (703) 482-1739, www.cia.gov; *The World Factbook.*

Euromonitor International, Inc., 224 S. Michigan Avenue, Suite 1500, Chicago, IL 60604, (312) 922-1115, Fax: (312) 922-1157, www.euromonitor.com; *The World Economic Factbook 2008.*

Palgrave Macmillan Ltd., Houndmills, Basingstoke, Hampshire, RG21 6XS, England, (Telephone in U.S. (888) 330-8477), (Fax in U.S. (800) 672-2054), www.palgrave.com; *The Statesman's Yearbook 2008.*

Taylor and Francis Group, An Informa Business, 2 Park Square, Milton Park, Abingdon, Oxford OX14 4RN, United Kingdom, (Dial from U.S. (212) 216-7800), (Fax from U.S. (212) 564-7854), www.tandf.co.uk; *The Europa World Year Book.*

UNICEF, 3 United Nations Plaza, New York, NY 10017, (800) 253-9646, Fax: (212) 887-7465, www.unicef.org; *The State of the World's Children 2008.*

United Nations Statistics Division, New York, NY 10017, (800) 253-9646, Fax: (212) 963-4116, http://unstats.un.org; *Demographic Yearbook; Human Development Report 2006; Statistical Yearbook; Trends in Europe and North America: The Statistical Yearbook of the ECE 2005;* and *World Statistics Pocketbook.*

The World Bank, 1818 H Street, NW, Washington, DC 20433, (202) 473-1000, Fax: (202) 477-6391, www.worldbank.org; *The World Bank Atlas 2003-2004* and *World Development Report 2008.*

World Health Organization (WHO), Avenue Appia 20, 1211 Geneve 27, Switzerland, (Telephone in U.S. (212) 331-9081), www.who.int; The WHO Global Atlas of Infectious Diseases.

CROATIA - MOTION PICTURES

Palgrave Macmillan Ltd., Houndmills, Basingstoke, Hampshire, RG21 6XS, England, (Telephone in U.S. (888) 330-8477), (Fax in U.S. (800) 672-2054), www.palgrave.com; *The Statesman's Yearbook 2008.*

UNESCO Institute for Statistics, C.P. 6128 Succursale Centre-Ville, Montreal, Quebec, H3C 3J7 Canada, (Dial from U.S. (514) 343-6880), (Fax from U.S. (514) 343 6882), www.uis.unesco.org; *Statistical Tables.*

United Nations Statistics Division, New York, NY 10017, (800) 253-9646, Fax: (212) 963-4116, http://unstats.un.org; *Statistical Yearbook.*

CROATIA - MOTOR VEHICLES

Taylor and Francis Group, An Informa Business, 2 Park Square, Milton Park, Abingdon, Oxford OX14 4RN, United Kingdom, (Dial from U.S. (212) 216-7800), (Fax from U.S. (212) 564-7854), www.tandf.co.uk; *The Europa World Year Book.*

CROATIA - MUSEUMS

UNESCO Institute for Statistics, C.P. 6128 Succursale Centre-Ville, Montreal, Quebec, H3C 3J7 Canada, (Dial from U.S. (514) 343-6880), (Fax from U.S. (514) 343 6882), www.uis.unesco.org; *Statistical Tables.*

CROATIA - PERIODICALS

UNESCO Institute for Statistics, C.P. 6128 Succursale Centre-Ville, Montreal, Quebec, H3C 3J7 Canada, (Dial from U.S. (514) 343-6880), (Fax from U.S. (514) 343 6882), www.uis.unesco.org; *Statistical Tables.*

CROATIA - PETROLEUM INDUSTRY AND TRADE

Palgrave Macmillan Ltd., Houndmills, Basingstoke, Hampshire, RG21 6XS, England, (Telephone in U.S. (888) 330-8477), (Fax in U.S. (800) 672-2054), www.palgrave.com; *The Statesman's Yearbook 2008.*

PennWell Corporation, 1421 South Sheridan Road, Tulsa, OK 74112, (918) 835-3161, www.pennwell.com; *International Petroleum Encyclopedia 2007.*

Platts, 2 Penn Plaza, 25th Floor, New York, NY 10121-2298, (212) 904-3070, www.platts.com; *Energy Economist.*

U.S. Department of Energy (DOE), Energy Information Administration (EIA), 1000 Independence Avenue, SW, Washington, DC 20585, (202) 586-8800, www.eia.doe.gov; *International Energy Annual 2004* and *International Energy Outlook 2006.*

United Nations Food and Agricultural Organization (FAO), Viale delle Terme di Caracalla, 00100 Rome, Italy, (Dial from U.S. (202) 653-2400), (Fax from U.S. (202) 653 5760), www.fao.org; *The State of Food and Agriculture (SOFA) 2006.*

United Nations Statistics Division, New York, NY 10017, (800) 253-9646, Fax: (212) 963-4116, http://

unstats.un.org; *Energy Statistics Yearbook 2003; 2004 Industrial Commodity Statistics Yearbook; Statistical Yearbook;* and *Trends in Europe and North America: The Statistical Yearbook of the ECE 2005.*

CROATIA - POLITICAL SCIENCE

Central Intelligence Agency, Office of Public Affairs, Washington, DC 20505, (703) 482-0623, Fax: (703) 482-1739, www.cia.gov; *The World Factbook.*

Palgrave Macmillan Ltd., Houndmills, Basingstoke, Hampshire, RG21 6XS, England, (Telephone in U.S. (888) 330-8477), (Fax in U.S. (800) 672-2054), www.palgrave.com; *The Statesman's Yearbook 2008.*

Taylor and Francis Group, An Informa Business, 2 Park Square, Milton Park, Abingdon, Oxford OX14 4RN, United Kingdom, (Dial from U.S. (212) 216-7800), (Fax from U.S. (212) 564-7854), www.tandf.co.uk; *The Europa World Year Book.*

United Nations Statistics Division, New York, NY 10017, (800) 253-9646, Fax: (212) 963-4116, http://unstats.un.org; *Statistical Yearbook.*

The World Bank, 1818 H Street, NW, Washington, DC 20433, (202) 473-1000, Fax: (202) 477-6391, www.worldbank.org; *World Development Report 2008.*

CROATIA - POPULATION

Central Intelligence Agency, Office of Public Affairs, Washington, DC 20505, (703) 482-0623, Fax: (703) 482-1739, www.cia.gov; *The World Factbook.*

Economist Intelligence Unit, 111 West 57th Street, New York, NY 10019, (212) 554-0600, Fax: (212) 586-1181, www.eiu.com; *Croatia Country Report.*

Euromonitor International, Inc., 224 S. Michigan Avenue, Suite 1500, Chicago, IL 60604, (312) 922-1115, Fax: (312) 922-1157, www.euromonitor.com; *The World Economic Factbook 2008.*

Palgrave Macmillan Ltd., Houndmills, Basingstoke, Hampshire, RG21 6XS, England, (Telephone in U.S. (888) 330-8477), (Fax in U.S. (800) 672-2054), www.palgrave.com; *The Statesman's Yearbook 2008.*

Taylor and Francis Group, An Informa Business, 2 Park Square, Milton Park, Abingdon, Oxford OX14 4RN, United Kingdom, (Dial from U.S. (212) 216-7800), (Fax from U.S. (212) 564-7854), www.tandf.co.uk; *The Europa World Year Book.*

UNESCO Institute for Statistics, C.P. 6128 Succursale Centre-Ville, Montreal, Quebec, H3C 3J7 Canada, (Dial from U.S. (514) 343-6880), (Fax from U.S. (514) 343 6882), www.uis.unesco.org; *Statistical Tables.*

United Nations Food and Agricultural Organization (FAO), Viale delle Terme di Caracalla, 00100 Rome, Italy, (Dial from U.S. (202) 653-2400), (Fax from U.S. (202) 653 5760), www.fao.org; *FAO Production Yearbook 2002.*

United Nations Statistics Division, New York, NY 10017, (800) 253-9646, Fax: (212) 963-4116, http://unstats.un.org; *Demographic Yearbook; Human Development Report 2006; Statistical Yearbook; Trends in Europe and North America: The Statistical Yearbook of the ECE 2005;* and *World Statistics Pocketbook.*

The World Bank, 1818 H Street, NW, Washington, DC 20433, (202) 473-1000, Fax: (202) 477-6391, www.worldbank.org; *Croatia; The World Bank Atlas 2003-2004;* and *World Development Report 2008.*

CROATIA - POPULATION DENSITY

Central Intelligence Agency, Office of Public Affairs, Washington, DC 20505, (703) 482-0623, Fax: (703) 482-1739, www.cia.gov; *The World Factbook.*

Euromonitor International, Inc., 224 S. Michigan Avenue, Suite 1500, Chicago, IL 60604, (312) 922-1115, Fax: (312) 922-1157, www.euromonitor.com; *The World Economic Factbook 2008.*

Palgrave Macmillan Ltd., Houndmills, Basingstoke, Hampshire, RG21 6XS, England, (Telephone in U.S. (888) 330-8477), (Fax in U.S. (800) 672-2054), www.palgrave.com; *The Statesman's Yearbook 2008.*

Taylor and Francis Group, An Informa Business, 2 Park Square, Milton Park, Abingdon, Oxford OX14 4RN, United Kingdom, (Dial from U.S. (212) 216-7800), (Fax from U.S. (212) 564-7854), www.tandf.co.uk; *The Europa World Year Book.*

UNESCO Institute for Statistics, C.P. 6128 Succursale Centre-Ville, Montreal, Quebec, H3C 3J7 Canada, (Dial from U.S. (514) 343-6880), (Fax from U.S. (514) 343 6882), www.uis.unesco.org; *Statistical Tables.*

United Nations Statistics Division, New York, NY 10017, (800) 253-9646, Fax: (212) 963-4116, http://unstats.un.org; *Statistical Yearbook* and *Trends in Europe and North America: The Statistical Yearbook of the ECE 2005.*

The World Bank, 1818 H Street, NW, Washington, DC 20433, (202) 473-1000, Fax: (202) 477-6391, www.worldbank.org; *Croatia* and *World Development Report 2008.*

CROATIA - POSTAL SERVICE

United Nations Statistics Division, New York, NY 10017, (800) 253-9646, Fax: (212) 963-4116, http://unstats.un.org; *Statistical Yearbook* and *Trends in Europe and North America: The Statistical Yearbook of the ECE 2005.*

CROATIA - POWER RESOURCES

Euromonitor International, Inc., 224 S. Michigan Avenue, Suite 1500, Chicago, IL 60604, (312) 922-1115, Fax: (312) 922-1157, www.euromonitor.com; *The World Economic Factbook 2008* and *World Marketing Data and Statistics.*

Palgrave Macmillan Ltd., Houndmills, Basingstoke, Hampshire, RG21 6XS, England, (Telephone in U.S. (888) 330-8477), (Fax in U.S. (800) 672-2054), www.palgrave.com; *The Statesman's Yearbook 2008.*

Platts, 2 Penn Plaza, 25th Floor, New York, NY 10121-2298, (212) 904-3070, www.platts.com; *Energy Economist.*

U.S. Department of Energy (DOE), Energy Information Administration (EIA), 1000 Independence Avenue, SW, Washington, DC 20585, (202) 586-8800, www.eia.doe.gov; *International Energy Annual 2004* and *International Energy Outlook 2006.*

United Nations Statistics Division, New York, NY 10017, (800) 253-9646, Fax: (212) 963-4116, http://unstats.un.org; *Energy Statistics Yearbook 2003; Human Development Report 2006; Statistical Yearbook; Trends in Europe and North America: The Statistical Yearbook of the ECE 2005;* and *World Statistics Pocketbook.*

The World Bank, 1818 H Street, NW, Washington, DC 20433, (202) 473-1000, Fax: (202) 477-6391, www.worldbank.org; *The World Bank Atlas 2003-2004* and *World Development Report 2008.*

CROATIA - PRICES

Euromonitor International, Inc., 224 S. Michigan Avenue, Suite 1500, Chicago, IL 60604, (312) 922-1115, Fax: (312) 922-1157, www.euromonitor.com; *World Marketing Data and Statistics.*

United Nations Food and Agricultural Organization (FAO), Viale delle Terme di Caracalla, 00100 Rome, Italy, (Dial from U.S. (202) 653-2400), (Fax from U.S. (202) 653 5760), www.fao.org; *FAO Production Yearbook 2002.*

The World Bank, 1818 H Street, NW, Washington, DC 20433, (202) 473-1000, Fax: (202) 477-6391, www.worldbank.org; *Croatia.*

CROATIA - PROFESSIONS

United Nations Statistics Division, New York, NY 10017, (800) 253-9646, Fax: (212) 963-4116, http://unstats.un.org; *Statistical Yearbook.*

CROATIA - PUBLIC HEALTH

Euromonitor International, Inc., 224 S. Michigan Avenue, Suite 1500, Chicago, IL 60604, (312) 922-1115, Fax: (312) 922-1157, www.euromonitor.com; *World Health Databook 2007/2008* and *World Marketing Data and Statistics.*

Palgrave Macmillan Ltd., Houndmills, Basingstoke, Hampshire, RG21 6XS, England, (Telephone in U.S. (888) 330-8477), (Fax in U.S. (800) 672-2054), www.palgrave.com; *The Statesman's Yearbook 2008.*

UNICEF, 3 United Nations Plaza, New York, NY 10017, (800) 253-9646, Fax: (212) 887-7465, www.unicef.org; *The State of the World's Children 2008.*

United Nations Statistics Division, New York, NY 10017, (800) 253-9646, Fax: (212) 963-4116, http://unstats.un.org; *Human Development Report 2006; Statistical Yearbook;* and *Trends in Europe and North America: The Statistical Yearbook of the ECE 2005.*

The World Bank, 1818 H Street, NW, Washington, DC 20433, (202) 473-1000, Fax: (202) 477-6391, www.worldbank.org; *Croatia* and *World Development Report 2008.*

World Health Organization (WHO), Avenue Appia 20, 1211 Geneve 27, Switzerland, (Telephone in U.S. (212) 331-9081), www.who.int; The WHO Global Atlas of Infectious Diseases.

CROATIA - PUBLISHERS AND PUBLISHING

Taylor and Francis Group, An Informa Business, 2 Park Square, Milton Park, Abingdon, Oxford OX14 4RN, United Kingdom, (Dial from U.S. (212) 216-7800), (Fax from U.S. (212) 564-7854), www.tandf.co.uk; *The Europa World Year Book.*

UNESCO Institute for Statistics, C.P. 6128 Succursale Centre-Ville, Montreal, Quebec, H3C 3J7 Canada, (Dial from U.S. (514) 343-6880), (Fax from U.S. (514) 343 6882), www.uis.unesco.org; *Statistical Tables.*

United Nations Statistics Division, New York, NY 10017, (800) 253-9646, Fax: (212) 963-4116, http://unstats.un.org; *Trends in Europe and North America: The Statistical Yearbook of the ECE 2005.*

CROATIA - RADIO - RECEIVERS AND RECEPTION

Palgrave Macmillan Ltd., Houndmills, Basingstoke, Hampshire, RG21 6XS, England, (Telephone in U.S. (888) 330-8477), (Fax in U.S. (800) 672-2054), www.palgrave.com; *The Statesman's Yearbook 2008.*

United Nations Statistics Division, New York, NY 10017, (800) 253-9646, Fax: (212) 963-4116, http://unstats.un.org; *Statistical Yearbook.*

CROATIA - RAILROADS

Palgrave Macmillan Ltd., Houndmills, Basingstoke, Hampshire, RG21 6XS, England, (Telephone in U.S. (888) 330-8477), (Fax in U.S. (800) 672-2054), www.palgrave.com; *The Statesman's Yearbook 2008.*

Taylor and Francis Group, An Informa Business, 2 Park Square, Milton Park, Abingdon, Oxford OX14 4RN, United Kingdom, (Dial from U.S. (212) 216-7800), (Fax from U.S. (212) 564-7854), www.tandf.co.uk; *The Europa World Year Book.*

United Nations Statistics Division, New York, NY 10017, (800) 253-9646, Fax: (212) 963-4116, http://unstats.un.org; *Annual Bulletin of Transport Statistics for Europe and North America 2004; Statistical Yearbook;* and *Trends in Europe and North America: The Statistical Yearbook of the ECE 2005.*

CROATIA - RELIGION

Central Intelligence Agency, Office of Public Affairs, Washington, DC 20505, (703) 482-0623, Fax: (703) 482-1739, www.cia.gov; *The World Factbook.*

Palgrave Macmillan Ltd., Houndmills, Basingstoke, Hampshire, RG21 6XS, England, (Telephone in U.S. (888) 330-8477), (Fax in U.S. (800) 672-2054), www.palgrave.com; *The Statesman's Yearbook 2008.*

CROATIA - RETAIL TRADE

Euromonitor International, Inc., 224 S. Michigan Avenue, Suite 1500, Chicago, IL 60604, (312) 922-1115, Fax: (312) 922-1157, www.euromonitor.com; *World Marketing Data and Statistics.*

United Nations Statistics Division, New York, NY 10017, (800) 253-9646, Fax: (212) 963-4116, http://unstats.un.org; *Statistical Yearbook.*

CROATIA - ROADS

Central Intelligence Agency, Office of Public Affairs, Washington, DC 20505, (703) 482-0623, Fax: (703) 482-1739, www.cia.gov; *The World Factbook.*

Palgrave Macmillan Ltd., Houndmills, Basingstoke, Hampshire, RG21 6XS, England, (Telephone in U.S. (888) 330-8477), (Fax in U.S. (800) 672-2054), www.palgrave.com; *The Statesman's Yearbook 2008.*

United Nations Statistics Division, New York, NY 10017, (800) 253-9646, Fax: (212) 963-4116, http://unstats.un.org; *Annual Bulletin of Transport Statistics for Europe and North America 2004* and *Trends in Europe and North America: The Statistical Yearbook of the ECE 2005.*

CROATIA - RUBBER INDUSTRY AND TRADE

International Rubber Study Group (IRSG), 1st Floor, Heron House, 109/115 Wembley Hill Road, Wembley, Middlesex HA9 8DA, United Kingdom, www.rubberstudy.com; *Rubber Statistical Bulletin; Summary of World Rubber Statistics 2005; World Rubber Statistics Handbook (Volume 6, 1975-2001);* and *World Rubber Statistics Historic Handbook.*

United Nations Statistics Division, New York, NY 10017, (800) 253-9646, Fax: (212) 963-4116, http://unstats.un.org; *Statistical Yearbook.*

CROATIA - SHIPPING

Palgrave Macmillan Ltd., Houndmills, Basingstoke, Hampshire, RG21 6XS, England, (Telephone in U.S. (888) 330-8477), (Fax in U.S. (800) 672-2054), www.palgrave.com; *The Statesman's Yearbook 2008.*

Taylor and Francis Group, An Informa Business, 2 Park Square, Milton Park, Abingdon, Oxford OX14 4RN, United Kingdom, (Dial from U.S. (212) 216-7800), (Fax from U.S. (212) 564-7854), www.tandf.co.uk; *The Europa World Year Book.*

United Nations Statistics Division, New York, NY 10017, (800) 253-9646, Fax: (212) 963-4116, http://unstats.un.org; *Annual Bulletin of Transport Statistics for Europe and North America 2004* and *Statistical Yearbook.*

CROATIA - SOCIAL ECOLOGY

United Nations Statistics Division, New York, NY 10017, (800) 253-9646, Fax: (212) 963-4116, http://unstats.un.org; *World Statistics Pocketbook.*

CROATIA - SOCIAL SECURITY

Palgrave Macmillan Ltd., Houndmills, Basingstoke, Hampshire, RG21 6XS, England, (Telephone in U.S. (888) 330-8477), (Fax in U.S. (800) 672-2054), www.palgrave.com; *The Statesman's Yearbook 2008.*

United Nations Statistics Division, New York, NY 10017, (800) 253-9646, Fax: (212) 963-4116, http://unstats.un.org; *National Accounts Statistics: Compendium of Income Distribution Statistics.*

CROATIA - TAXATION

Taylor and Francis Group, An Informa Business, 2 Park Square, Milton Park, Abingdon, Oxford OX14 4RN, United Kingdom, (Dial from U.S. (212) 216-7800), (Fax from U.S. (212) 564-7854), www.tandf.co.uk; *The Europa World Year Book.*

CROATIA - TELEPHONE

Palgrave Macmillan Ltd., Houndmills, Basingstoke, Hampshire, RG21 6XS, England, (Telephone in U.S. (888) 330-8477), (Fax in U.S. (800) 672-2054), www.palgrave.com; *The Statesman's Yearbook 2008.*

Taylor and Francis Group, An Informa Business, 2 Park Square, Milton Park, Abingdon, Oxford OX14 4RN, United Kingdom, (Dial from U.S. (212) 216-7800), (Fax from U.S. (212) 564-7854), www.tandf.co.uk; *The Europa World Year Book.*

United Nations Statistics Division, New York, NY 10017, (800) 253-9646, Fax: (212) 963-4116, http://unstats.un.org; *Statistical Yearbook; Trends in Europe and North America: The Statistical Yearbook of the ECE 2005;* and *World Statistics Pocketbook.*

CROATIA - TEXTILE INDUSTRY

United Nations Statistics Division, New York, NY 10017, (800) 253-9646, Fax: (212) 963-4116, http://unstats.un.org; *2004 Industrial Commodity Statistics Yearbook* and *Statistical Yearbook.*

CROATIA - THEATER

UNESCO Institute for Statistics, C.P. 6128 Succursale Centre-Ville, Montreal, Quebec, H3C 3J7 Canada, (Dial from U.S. (514) 343-6880), (Fax from U.S. (514) 343 6882), www.uis.unesco.org; *Statistical Tables.*

CROATIA - TIRE INDUSTRY

United Nations Statistics Division, New York, NY 10017, (800) 253-9646, Fax: (212) 963-4116, http://unstats.un.org; *Statistical Yearbook.*

CROATIA - TOBACCO INDUSTRY

Foreign Agricultural Service (FAS), U.S. Department of Agriculture (USDA), 1400 Independence Avenue, SW, Washington, DC 20250, (202) 720-3935, www.fas.usda.gov; *Tobacco: World Markets and Trade.*

United Nations Statistics Division, New York, NY 10017, (800) 253-9646, Fax: (212) 963-4116, http://unstats.un.org; *Statistical Yearbook.*

CROATIA - TOURISM

Euromonitor International, Inc., 224 S. Michigan Avenue, Suite 1500, Chicago, IL 60604, (312) 922-1115, Fax: (312) 922-1157, www.euromonitor.com; *The World Economic Factbook 2008* and *World Marketing Data and Statistics.*

Palgrave Macmillan Ltd., Houndmills, Basingstoke, Hampshire, RG21 6XS, England, (Telephone in U.S. (888) 330-8477), (Fax in U.S. (800) 672-2054), www.palgrave.com; *The Statesman's Yearbook 2008.*

Taylor and Francis Group, An Informa Business, 2 Park Square, Milton Park, Abingdon, Oxford OX14 4RN, United Kingdom, (Dial from U.S. (212) 216-7800), (Fax from U.S. (212) 564-7854), www.tandf.co.uk; *The Europa World Year Book.*

United Nations Statistics Division, New York, NY 10017, (800) 253-9646, Fax: (212) 963-4116, http://unstats.un.org; *Statistical Yearbook* and *Trends in Europe and North America: The Statistical Yearbook of the ECE 2005.*

The World Bank, 1818 H Street, NW, Washington, DC 20433, (202) 473-1000, Fax: (202) 477-6391, www.worldbank.org; *Croatia.*

CROATIA - TRANSPORTATION

Central Intelligence Agency, Office of Public Affairs, Washington, DC 20505, (703) 482-0623, Fax: (703) 482-1739, www.cia.gov; *The World Factbook.*

Euromonitor International, Inc., 224 S. Michigan Avenue, Suite 1500, Chicago, IL 60604, (312) 922-1115, Fax: (312) 922-1157, www.euromonitor.com; *World Marketing Data and Statistics.*

Eurostat, Batiment Jean Monnet, Rue Alcide de Gasperi, L-2920 Luxembourg, http://epp.eurostat.ec.europa.eu; *Regional Passenger and Freight Air Transport in Europe in 2006* and *Regional Road and Rail Transport Networks.*

Palgrave Macmillan Ltd., Houndmills, Basingstoke, Hampshire, RG21 6XS, England, (Telephone in U.S. (888) 330-8477), (Fax in U.S. (800) 672-2054), www.palgrave.com; *The Statesman's Yearbook 2008.*

Taylor and Francis Group, An Informa Business, 2 Park Square, Milton Park, Abingdon, Oxford OX14 4RN, United Kingdom, (Dial from U.S. (212) 216-7800), (Fax from U.S. (212) 564-7854), www.tandf.co.uk; *The Europa World Year Book.*

United Nations Statistics Division, New York, NY 10017, (800) 253-9646, Fax: (212) 963-4116, http://unstats.un.org; *Annual Bulletin of Transport Statistics for Europe and North America 2004; Human Development Report 2006;* and *Trends in Europe and North America: The Statistical Yearbook of the ECE 2005.*

The World Bank, 1818 H Street, NW, Washington, DC 20433, (202) 473-1000, Fax: (202) 477-6391, www.worldbank.org; *Croatia.*

CROATIA - UNEMPLOYMENT

Central Intelligence Agency, Office of Public Affairs, Washington, DC 20505, (703) 482-0623, Fax: (703) 482-1739, www.cia.gov; *The World Factbook.*

Palgrave Macmillan Ltd., Houndmills, Basingstoke, Hampshire, RG21 6XS, England, (Telephone in U.S. (888) 330-8477), (Fax in U.S. (800) 672-2054), www.palgrave.com; *The Statesman's Yearbook 2008.*

United Nations Statistics Division, New York, NY 10017, (800) 253-9646, Fax: (212) 963-4116, http://unstats.un.org; *Statistical Yearbook* and *Trends in Europe and North America: The Statistical Yearbook of the ECE 2005.*

The World Bank, 1818 H Street, NW, Washington, DC 20433, (202) 473-1000, Fax: (202) 477-6391, www.worldbank.org; *Croatia.*

CROATIA - VITAL STATISTICS

Palgrave Macmillan Ltd., Houndmills, Basingstoke, Hampshire, RG21 6XS, England, (Telephone in U.S. (888) 330-8477), (Fax in U.S. (800) 672-2054), www.palgrave.com; *The Statesman's Yearbook 2008.*

United Nations Statistics Division, New York, NY 10017, (800) 253-9646, Fax: (212) 963-4116, http://unstats.un.org; *Statistical Yearbook.*

CROATIA - WAGES

United Nations Statistics Division, New York, NY 10017, (800) 253-9646, Fax: (212) 963-4116, http://unstats.un.org; *Statistical Yearbook.*

The World Bank, 1818 H Street, NW, Washington, DC 20433, (202) 473-1000, Fax: (202) 477-6391, www.worldbank.org; *Croatia.*

CROATIA - WHOLESALE PRICE INDEXES

United Nations Statistics Division, New York, NY 10017, (800) 253-9646, Fax: (212) 963-4116, http://unstats.un.org; *Statistical Yearbook.*

CROATIA - WHOLESALE TRADE

United Nations Statistics Division, New York, NY 10017, (800) 253-9646, Fax: (212) 963-4116, http://unstats.un.org; *Statistical Yearbook.*

CROPS

See also FARMS and Individual crops

Economic Research Service (ERS), U.S. Department of Agriculture (USDA), 1800 M Street, NW, Washington, DC 20036-5831, (202) 694-5050, Fax: (202) 694-5689, www.ers.usda.gov; *Floriculture and Nursery Crops: 2007.*

CROPS - ACREAGE

Economic Research Service (ERS), U.S. Department of Agriculture (USDA), 1800 M Street, NW, Washington, DC 20036-5831, (202) 694-5050, Fax: (202) 694-5689, www.ers.usda.gov; *Agricultural Resource Management Study (ARMS); Agricultural Resources and Environmental Indicators 2006;* and *Agricultural Statistics.*

National Agricultural Statistics Service (NASS), U.S. Department of Agriculture (USDA), 1400 Independence Avenue, SW, Washington, DC 20250, (800) 727-9540, Fax: (202) 690-2090, www.nass.usda.gov; *2006 Agricultural Statistics; Crop Production; Crop Values 2007 Summary;* and *Field Crops: Final Estimates 1997-2002.*

CROPS - FARM MARKETINGS, SALES

Economic Research Service (ERS), U.S. Department of Agriculture (USDA), 1800 M Street, NW, Washington, DC 20036-5831, (202) 694-5050, Fax: (202) 694-5689, www.ers.usda.gov; *2008 Farm Income Forecast.*

CROPS - INTERNATIONAL TRADE

Economic Research Service (ERS), U.S. Department of Agriculture (USDA), 1800 M Street, NW,

Washington, DC 20036-5831, (202) 694-5050, Fax: (202) 694-5689, www.ers.usda.gov; *Agricultural Outlook; Agricultural Statistics; Foreign Agricultural Trade of the United States (FATUS);* and *World Agricultural Supply and Demand Estimates (WASDE): 2008.*

National Agricultural Statistics Service (NASS), U.S. Department of Agriculture (USDA), 1400 Independence Avenue, SW, Washington, DC 20250, (800) 727-9540, Fax: (202) 690-2090, www.nass.usda.gov; *2006 Agricultural Statistics.*

CROPS - PRICES

Economic Research Service (ERS), U.S. Department of Agriculture (USDA), 1800 M Street, NW, Washington, DC 20036-5831, (202) 694-5050, Fax: (202) 694-5689, www.ers.usda.gov; *Agricultural Statistics.*

National Agricultural Statistics Service (NASS), U.S. Department of Agriculture (USDA), 1400 Independence Avenue, SW, Washington, DC 20250, (800) 727-9540, Fax: (202) 690-2090, www.nass.usda.gov; *Agricultural Prices; 2006 Agricultural Statistics; Crop Production;* and *Crop Values 2007 Summary.*

CROPS - PRODUCTION

Economic Research Service (ERS), U.S. Department of Agriculture (USDA), 1800 M Street, NW, Washington, DC 20036-5831, (202) 694-5050, Fax: (202) 694-5689, www.ers.usda.gov; *Agricultural Outlook* and *Agricultural Statistics.*

National Agricultural Statistics Service (NASS), U.S. Department of Agriculture (USDA), 1400 Independence Avenue, SW, Washington, DC 20250, (800) 727-9540, Fax: (202) 690-2090, www.nass.usda.gov; *2006 Agricultural Statistics; Crop Production;* and *Crop Values 2007 Summary.*

CROPS - PRODUCTIVITY

Economic Research Service (ERS), U.S. Department of Agriculture (USDA), 1800 M Street, NW, Washington, DC 20036-5831, (202) 694-5050, Fax: (202) 694-5689, www.ers.usda.gov; *Agricultural Resource Management Study (ARMS); Agricultural Resources and Environmental Indicators 2006;* and *Agricultural Statistics.*

CROPS - SUPPLY AND DISAPPEARANCE

Economic Research Service (ERS), U.S. Department of Agriculture (USDA), 1800 M Street, NW, Washington, DC 20036-5831, (202) 694-5050, Fax: (202) 694-5689, www.ers.usda.gov; *Agricultural Outlook; Agricultural Statistics; Cotton and Wool Outlook: 2008; Feed Yearbook: Report; Tobacco Outlook 2006; Wheat Yearbook;* and *World Agricultural Supply and Demand Estimates (WASDE): 2008.*

CROSS COUNTRY (RUNNING)

National Collegiate Athletic Association (NCAA), 700 West Washington Street, PO Box 6222, Indianapolis, IN 46206-6222, (317) 917-6222, Fax: (317) 917-6888, www.ncaa.org; *1982-2003 Sports Sponsorship and Participation Rates Report.*

National Federation of State High School Associations, PO Box 690, Indianapolis, IN 46206, (317) 972-6900, Fax: (317) 822-5700, www.nfhs.org; *2005-06 High School Athletics Participation Survey.*

CROSSWORD PUZZLES

Mediamark Research, Inc., 75 Ninth Avenue, 5th Floor, New York, NY 10011, (212) 884-9200, Fax: (212) 884-9339, www.mediamark.com; MRI+.

CRUDE MATERIALS

U.S. Department of Energy (DOE), Energy Information Administration (EIA), 1000 Independence Avenue, SW, Washington, DC 20585, (202) 586-8800, www.eia.doe.gov; *International Energy Annual 2004; International Energy Outlook 2006;* and *Monthly Energy Review (MER).*

CRUDE MATERIALS - PRODUCER PRICE INDEXES

U.S. Bureau of Labor Statistics (BLS), Postal Square Building, 2 Massachusetts Avenue, NE, Washington, DC 20212-0001, (202) 691-5200, Fax: (202) 691-6325, www.bls.gov; *Producer Price Indexes (PPI).*

CRUDE OIL

See also PETROLEUM INDUSTRY AND TRADE

American Petroleum Institute (API), 1220 L Street, NW, Washington, DC 20005-4070, (202) 682-8000, http://api-ec.api.org; *Monthly Statistical Report* and *Weekly Statistical Bulletin.*

Lundberg Survey, Incorporated (LSI), 911 Via Alondra, Camarillo, CA 93012, (805) 383-2400, Fax: (805) 383-2424, www.lundbergsurvey.com; *Energy Detente; Lundberg Letter; National Retail Gasoline and Diesel Price Survey;* and *National Share of Market Report.*

CRUDE OIL - INTERNATIONAL TRADE

American Petroleum Institute (API), 1220 L Street, NW, Washington, DC 20005-4070, (202) 682-8000, http://api-ec.api.org; *Crude Oil and Product Import Chart.*

U.S. Census Bureau, Foreign Trade Division, 4700 Silver Hill Road, Washington DC 20233-0001, (301) 763-3030, www.census.gov/foreign-trade/www/; *U.S. International Trade in Goods and Services.*

U.S. Department of Energy (DOE), Energy Information Administration (EIA), 1000 Independence Avenue, SW, Washington, DC 20585, (202) 586-8800, www.eia.doe.gov; *Annual Energy Outlook 2006; Annual Energy Review 2005; International Energy Annual 2004; International Energy Outlook 2006; Monthly Energy Review (MER); Petroleum Supply Annual 2004;* and *U.S. Crude Oil, Natural Gas, and Natural Gas Liquids Reserves, 2005 Annual Report.*

CRUDE OIL - PRICES

U.S. Department of Energy (DOE), Energy Information Administration (EIA), 1000 Independence Avenue, SW, Washington, DC 20585, (202) 586-8800, www.eia.doe.gov; *Annual Energy Review 2005.*

CRUDE OIL - PRODUCTION

U.S. Department of Energy (DOE), Energy Information Administration (EIA), 1000 Independence Avenue, SW, Washington, DC 20585, (202) 586-8800, www.eia.doe.gov; *Annual Energy Review 2005; Monthly Energy Review (MER); Petroleum Supply Annual 2004;* and *U.S. Crude Oil, Natural Gas, and Natural Gas Liquids Reserves, 2005 Annual Report.*

U.S. Department of the Interior (DOI), Minerals Management Service (MMS), 1849 C Street, NW, Washington, DC 20240, (202) 208-3985, www.mms.gov; *Federal Offshore Statistics.*

CRUDE OIL - WORLD PRODUCTION

PennWell Corporation, 1421 South Sheridan Road, Tulsa, OK 74112, (918) 835-3161, www.pennwell.com; *Oil and Gas Financial Journal; Oil and Gas Journal;* and *Oil Gas Journal Latinoamericana.*

U.S. Department of Energy (DOE), Energy Information Administration (EIA), 1000 Independence Avenue, SW, Washington, DC 20585, (202) 586-8800, www.eia.doe.gov; *International Energy Annual 2004* and *International Energy Outlook 2006.*

CRUISES

United Nations World Tourism Organization (UNWTO), Capitan Haya 42, 28020 Madrid, Spain, www.world-tourism.org; *Worldwide Cruise Ship Activity.*

CRYPTOSPORIDIOSIS

Centers for Disease Control and Prevention (CDC), U.S. Department of Health and Human Services (HHS), 1600 Clifton Road, Atlanta, GA 30333, (800) 311-3435, www.cdc.gov; *Morbidity and Mortality Weekly Report (MMWR)* and *Summary of Notifiable Diseases, United States, 2006.*

CUBA - NATIONAL STATISTICAL OFFICE

La Oficina Nacional de Estadisticas, Paseo No. 60 e/ 3ra y 5ta, Vedado, Plaza de la Revolucion, Ciudad de La Habana, Cuba, CP 10400, www.one.cu; National Data Center.

CUBA - PRIMARY STATISTICS SOURCES

La Oficina Nacional de Estadisticas, Paseo No. 60 e/ 3ra y 5ta, Vedado, Plaza de la Revolucion, Ciudad de La Habana, Cuba, CP 10400, www.one.cu; *Anuario Demografico 2006; Anuario estadistico de Cuba 2006* (Statistical Yearbook of Cuba 2006); and *Indicadores sociales y demograficos de Cuba por territorios.*

CUBA - AGRICULTURAL MACHINERY

United Nations Statistics Division, New York, NY 10017, (800) 253-9646, Fax: (212) 963-4116, http://unstats.un.org; *Statistical Yearbook.*

CUBA - AGRICULTURE

Economist Intelligence Unit, 111 West 57th Street, New York, NY 10019, (212) 554-0600, Fax: (212) 586-1181, www.eiu.com; *Cuba Country Report.*

Euromonitor International, Inc., 224 S. Michigan Avenue, Suite 1500, Chicago, IL 60604, (312) 922-1115, Fax: (312) 922-1157, www.euromonitor.com; *International Marketing Data and Statistics 2008* and *World Marketing Data and Statistics.*

M.E. Sharpe, 80 Business Park Drive, Armonk, NY 10504, (800) 541-6563, Fax: (914) 273-2106, www.mesharpe.com; *The Illustrated Book of World Rankings.*

Palgrave Macmillan Ltd., Houndmills, Basingstoke, Hampshire, RG21 6XS, England, (Telephone in U.S. (888) 330-8477), (Fax in U.S. (800) 672-2054), www.palgrave.com; *The Statesman's Yearbook 2008.*

Taylor and Francis Group, An Informa Business, 2 Park Square, Milton Park, Abingdon, Oxford OX14 4RN, United Kingdom, (Dial from U.S. (212) 216-7800), (Fax from U.S. (212) 564-7854), www.tandf.co.uk; *The Europa World Year Book.*

UCLA Latin American Institute, 10343 Bunche Hall, Box 951447, Los Angeles, CA 90095-1447, (310) 825-4571, Fax: (310) 206-6859, www.international.ucla.edu/lac; *Statistical Abstract of Latin America.*

United Nations Conference on Trade and Development (UNCTAD), DC2-1120, United Nations, New York, NY 10017, (212) 963-0027, www.unctad.org; *UNCTAD Commodity Yearbook.*

United Nations Food and Agricultural Organization (FAO), Viale delle Terme di Caracalla, 00100 Rome, Italy, (Dial from U.S. (202) 653-2400), (Fax from U.S. (202) 653 5760), www.fao.org; AQUASTAT; *FAO Production Yearbook 2002; FAO Trade Yearbook;* and *The State of Food and Agriculture (SOFA) 2006.*

United Nations Statistics Division, New York, NY 10017, (800) 253-9646, Fax: (212) 963-4116, http://unstats.un.org; *Statistical Yearbook.*

The World Bank, 1818 H Street, NW, Washington, DC 20433, (202) 473-1000, Fax: (202) 477-6391, www.worldbank.org; *Cuba.*

CUBA - AIRLINES

M.E. Sharpe, 80 Business Park Drive, Armonk, NY 10504, (800) 541-6563, Fax: (914) 273-2106, www.mesharpe.com; *The Illustrated Book of World Rankings.*

Palgrave Macmillan Ltd., Houndmills, Basingstoke, Hampshire, RG21 6XS, England, (Telephone in U.S. (888) 330-8477), (Fax in U.S. (800) 672-2054), www.palgrave.com; *The Statesman's Yearbook 2008.*

Taylor and Francis Group, An Informa Business, 2 Park Square, Milton Park, Abingdon, Oxford OX14

4RN, United Kingdom, (Dial from U.S. (212) 216-7800), (Fax from U.S. (212) 564-7854), www.tandf.co.uk; *The Europa World Year Book.*

United Nations Statistics Division, New York, NY 10017, (800) 253-9646, Fax: (212) 963-4116, http://unstats.un.org; *Statistical Yearbook.*

CUBA - AIRPORTS

Central Intelligence Agency, Office of Public Affairs, Washington, DC 20505, (703) 482-0623, Fax: (703) 482-1739, www.cia.gov; *The World Factbook.*

CUBA - ALUMINUM PRODUCTION

See CUBA - MINERAL INDUSTRIES

CUBA - ARMED FORCES

Central Intelligence Agency, Office of Public Affairs, Washington, DC 20505, (703) 482-0623, Fax: (703) 482-1739, www.cia.gov; *The World Factbook.*

Euromonitor International, Inc., 224 S. Michigan Avenue, Suite 1500, Chicago, IL 60604, (312) 922-1115, Fax: (312) 922-1157, www.euromonitor.com; *World Marketing Data and Statistics.*

International Institute for Strategic Studies (IISS), Arundel House, 13-15 Arundel Street, Temple Place, London WC2R 3DX, England, www.iiss.org; *The Military Balance 2007.*

Palgrave Macmillan Ltd., Houndmills, Basingstoke, Hampshire, RG21 6XS, England, (Telephone in U.S. (888) 330-8477), (Fax in U.S. (800) 672-2054), www.palgrave.com; *The Statesman's Yearbook 2008.*

U.S. Department of State (DOS), 2201 C Street NW, Washington, DC 20520, (202) 647-4000, www.state.gov; *World Military Expenditures and Arms Transfers (WMEAT).*

UCLA Latin American Institute, 10343 Bunche Hall, Box 951447, Los Angeles, CA 90095-1447, (310) 825-4571, Fax: (310) 206-6859, www.international.ucla.edu/lac; *Statistical Abstract of Latin America.*

United Nations Statistics Division, New York, NY 10017, (800) 253-9646, Fax: (212) 963-4116, http://unstats.un.org; *Human Development Report 2006.*

CUBA - BALANCE OF PAYMENTS

United Nations Statistics Division, New York, NY 10017, (800) 253-9646, Fax: (212) 963-4116, http://unstats.un.org; *Economic Survey of Latin America and the Caribbean 2004-2005.*

The World Bank, 1818 H Street, NW, Washington, DC 20433, (202) 473-1000, Fax: (202) 477-6391, www.worldbank.org; *Cuba.*

CUBA - BANKS AND BANKING

Euromonitor International, Inc., 224 S. Michigan Avenue, Suite 1500, Chicago, IL 60604, (312) 922-1115, Fax: (312) 922-1157, www.euromonitor.com; *World Marketing Data and Statistics.*

M.E. Sharpe, 80 Business Park Drive, Armonk, NY 10504, (800) 541-6563, Fax: (914) 273-2106, www.mesharpe.com; *The Illustrated Book of World Rankings.*

Palgrave Macmillan Ltd., Houndmills, Basingstoke, Hampshire, RG21 6XS, England, (Telephone in U.S. (888) 330-8477), (Fax in U.S. (800) 672-2054), www.palgrave.com; *The Statesman's Yearbook 2008.*

Taylor and Francis Group, An Informa Business, 2 Park Square, Milton Park, Abingdon, Oxford OX14 4RN, United Kingdom, (Dial from U.S. (212) 216-7800), (Fax from U.S. (212) 564-7854), www.tandf.co.uk; *The Europa World Year Book.*

CUBA - BARLEY PRODUCTION

See CUBA - CROPS

CUBA - BEVERAGE INDUSTRY

M.E. Sharpe, 80 Business Park Drive, Armonk, NY 10504, (800) 541-6563, Fax: (914) 273-2106, www.mesharpe.com; *The Illustrated Book of World Rankings.*

United Nations Statistics Division, New York, NY 10017, (800) 253-9646, Fax: (212) 963-4116, http://unstats.un.org; *Statistical Yearbook.*

CUBA - BIRTH CONTROL

UCLA Latin American Institute, 10343 Bunche Hall, Box 951447, Los Angeles, CA 90095-1447, (310) 825-4571, Fax: (310) 206-6859, www.international.ucla.edu/lac; *Statistical Abstract of Latin America.*

CUBA - BROADCASTING

Central Intelligence Agency, Office of Public Affairs, Washington, DC 20505, (703) 482-0623, Fax: (703) 482-1739, www.cia.gov; *The World Factbook.*

Euromonitor International, Inc., 224 S. Michigan Avenue, Suite 1500, Chicago, IL 60604, (312) 922-1115, Fax: (312) 922-1157, www.euromonitor.com; *World Marketing Data and Statistics.*

M.E. Sharpe, 80 Business Park Drive, Armonk, NY 10504, (800) 541-6563, Fax: (914) 273-2106, www.mesharpe.com; *The Illustrated Book of World Rankings.*

Palgrave Macmillan Ltd., Houndmills, Basingstoke, Hampshire, RG21 6XS, England, (Telephone in U.S. (888) 330-8477), (Fax in U.S. (800) 672-2054), www.palgrave.com; *The Statesman's Yearbook 2008.*

UNESCO Institute for Statistics, C.P. 6128 Succursale Centre-Ville, Montreal, Quebec, H3C 3J7 Canada, (Dial from U.S. (514) 343-6880), (Fax from U.S. (514) 343 6882), www.uis.unesco.org; *Statistical Tables.*

WRTH Publications Limited, PO Box 290, Oxford OX2 7FT, UK, www.wrth.com; *World Radio TV Handbook 2007.*

CUBA - BUDGET

Central Intelligence Agency, Office of Public Affairs, Washington, DC 20505, (703) 482-0623, Fax: (703) 482-1739, www.cia.gov; *The World Factbook.*

CUBA - CATTLE

See CUBA - LIVESTOCK

CUBA - CHICKENS

See CUBA - LIVESTOCK

CUBA - CHILDBIRTH - STATISTICS

Central Intelligence Agency, Office of Public Affairs, Washington, DC 20505, (703) 482-0623, Fax: (703) 482-1739, www.cia.gov; *The World Factbook.*

Euromonitor International, Inc., 224 S. Michigan Avenue, Suite 1500, Chicago, IL 60604, (312) 922-1115, Fax: (312) 922-1157, www.euromonitor.com; *International Marketing Data and Statistics 2008* and *The World Economic Factbook 2008.*

M.E. Sharpe, 80 Business Park Drive, Armonk, NY 10504, (800) 541-6563, Fax: (914) 273-2106, www.mesharpe.com; *The Illustrated Book of World Rankings.*

Taylor and Francis Group, An Informa Business, 2 Park Square, Milton Park, Abingdon, Oxford OX14 4RN, United Kingdom, (Dial from U.S. (212) 216-7800), (Fax from U.S. (212) 564-7854), www.tandf.co.uk; *The Europa World Year Book.*

United Nations Statistics Division, New York, NY 10017, (800) 253-9646, Fax: (212) 963-4116, http://unstats.un.org; *Demographic Yearbook* and *Statistical Yearbook.*

World Health Organization (WHO), Avenue Appia 20, 1211 Geneve 27, Switzerland, (Telephone in U.S. (212) 331-9081), www.who.int; *World Health Report 2006.*

CUBA - CLIMATE

M.E. Sharpe, 80 Business Park Drive, Armonk, NY 10504, (800) 541-6563, Fax: (914) 273-2106, www.mesharpe.com; *The Illustrated Book of World Rankings.*

Palgrave Macmillan Ltd., Houndmills, Basingstoke, Hampshire, RG21 6XS, England, (Telephone in U.S. (888) 330-8477), (Fax in U.S. (800) 672-2054), www.palgrave.com; *The Statesman's Yearbook 2008.*

CUBA - COAL PRODUCTION

See CUBA - MINERAL INDUSTRIES

CUBA - COBALT PRODUCTION

See CUBA - MINERAL INDUSTRIES

CUBA - COCOA PRODUCTION

See CUBA - CROPS

CUBA - COFFEE

See CUBA - CROPS

CUBA - COMMERCE

Palgrave Macmillan Ltd., Houndmills, Basingstoke, Hampshire, RG21 6XS, England, (Telephone in U.S. (888) 330-8477), (Fax in U.S. (800) 672-2054), www.palgrave.com; *The Statesman's Yearbook 2008.*

CUBA - COMMODITY EXCHANGES

Commodity Research Bureau, 330 South Wells Street, Suite 612, Chicago, IL 60606-7110, (800) 621-5271, Fax: (312) 939-4135, www.crbtrader.com; *2006 CRB Commodity Yearbook and CD.*

International Monetary Fund (IMF), 700 Nineteenth Street, NW, Washington, DC 20431, (202) 623-7000, Fax: (202) 623-4661, www.imf.org; *IMF Primary Commodity Prices.*

United Nations Food and Agricultural Organization (FAO), Viale delle Terme di Caracalla, 00100 Rome, Italy, (Dial from U.S. (202) 653-2400), (Fax from U.S. (202) 653 5760), www.fao.org; *The State of Food and Agriculture (SOFA) 2006.*

CUBA - COMMUNICATION AND TRAFFIC

United Nations Statistics Division, New York, NY 10017, (800) 253-9646, Fax: (212) 963-4116, http://unstats.un.org; *Statistical Yearbook.*

CUBA - CONSTRUCTION INDUSTRY

M.E. Sharpe, 80 Business Park Drive, Armonk, NY 10504, (800) 541-6563, Fax: (914) 273-2106, www.mesharpe.com; *The Illustrated Book of World Rankings.*

UCLA Latin American Institute, 10343 Bunche Hall, Box 951447, Los Angeles, CA 90095-1447, (310) 825-4571, Fax: (310) 206-6859, www.international.ucla.edu/lac; *Statistical Abstract of Latin America.*

United Nations Statistics Division, New York, NY 10017, (800) 253-9646, Fax: (212) 963-4116, http://unstats.un.org; *Statistical Yearbook.*

CUBA - CONSUMER COOPERATIVES

UCLA Latin American Institute, 10343 Bunche Hall, Box 951447, Los Angeles, CA 90095-1447, (310) 825-4571, Fax: (310) 206-6859, www.international.ucla.edu/lac; *Statistical Abstract of Latin America.*

CUBA - CONSUMER PRICE INDEXES

The World Bank, 1818 H Street, NW, Washington, DC 20433, (202) 473-1000, Fax: (202) 477-6391, www.worldbank.org; *Cuba.*

CUBA - COPPER INDUSTRY AND TRADE

See CUBA - MINERAL INDUSTRIES

CUBA - CORN INDUSTRY

See CUBA - CROPS

CUBA - COTTON

See CUBA - CROPS

CUBA - CRIME

U.S. Department of Justice (DOJ), Bureau of Justice Statistics, 810 Seventh Street, NW, Washington, DC 20531, (202) 307-0765, www.ojp.usdoj.gov/bjs/; *The World Factbook of Criminal Justice Systems.*

Yale University Press, PO Box 209040, New Haven, CT 06520-9040, (203) 432-0960, Fax: (203) 432-0948, http://yalepress.yale.edu/yupbooks; *Violence and Crime in Cross-National Perspective.*

CUBA - CROPS

M.E. Sharpe, 80 Business Park Drive, Armonk, NY 10504, (800) 541-6563, Fax: (914) 273-2106, www.mesharpe.com; *The Illustrated Book of World Rankings.*

Palgrave Macmillan Ltd., Houndmills, Basingstoke, Hampshire, RG21 6XS, England, (Telephone in U.S. (888) 330-8477), (Fax in U.S. (800) 672-2054), www.palgrave.com; *The Statesman's Yearbook 2008.*

Taylor and Francis Group, An Informa Business, 2 Park Square, Milton Park, Abingdon, Oxford OX14 4RN, United Kingdom, (Dial from U.S. (212) 216-7800), (Fax from U.S. (212) 564-7854), www.tandf.co.uk; *The Europa World Year Book.*

United Nations Conference on Trade and Development (UNCTAD), DC2-1120, United Nations, New York, NY 10017, (212) 963-0027, www.unctad.org; *UNCTAD Commodity Yearbook.*

United Nations Food and Agricultural Organization (FAO), Viale delle Terme di Caracalla, 00100 Rome, Italy, (Dial from U.S. (202) 653-2400), (Fax from U.S. (202) 653 5760), www.fao.org; *FAO Production Yearbook 2002* and *The State of Food and Agriculture (SOFA) 2006.*

United Nations Statistics Division, New York, NY 10017, (800) 253-9646, Fax: (212) 963-4116, http://unstats.un.org; *Statistical Yearbook.*

CUBA - CUSTOMS ADMINISTRATION

Palgrave Macmillan Ltd., Houndmills, Basingstoke, Hampshire, RG21 6XS, England, (Telephone in U.S. (888) 330-8477), (Fax in U.S. (800) 672-2054), www.palgrave.com; *The Statesman's Yearbook 2008.*

CUBA - DAIRY PROCESSING

M.E. Sharpe, 80 Business Park Drive, Armonk, NY 10504, (800) 541-6563, Fax: (914) 273-2106, www.mesharpe.com; *The Illustrated Book of World Rankings.*

Palgrave Macmillan Ltd., Houndmills, Basingstoke, Hampshire, RG21 6XS, England, (Telephone in U.S. (888) 330-8477), (Fax in U.S. (800) 672-2054), www.palgrave.com; *The Statesman's Yearbook 2008.*

Taylor and Francis Group, An Informa Business, 2 Park Square, Milton Park, Abingdon, Oxford OX14 4RN, United Kingdom, (Dial from U.S. (212) 216-7800), (Fax from U.S. (212) 564-7854), www.tandf.co.uk; *The Europa World Year Book.*

United Nations Food and Agricultural Organization (FAO), Viale delle Terme di Caracalla, 00100 Rome, Italy, (Dial from U.S. (202) 653-2400), (Fax from U.S. (202) 653 5760), www.fao.org; *FAO Production Yearbook 2002* and *The State of Food and Agriculture (SOFA) 2006.*

United Nations Statistics Division, New York, NY 10017, (800) 253-9646, Fax: (212) 963-4116, http://unstats.un.org; *Statistical Yearbook.*

CUBA - DEATH RATES

See CUBA - MORTALITY

CUBA - DEBTS, EXTERNAL

Palgrave Macmillan Ltd., Houndmills, Basingstoke, Hampshire, RG21 6XS, England, (Telephone in U.S. (888) 330-8477), (Fax in U.S. (800) 672-2054), www.palgrave.com; *The Statesman's Yearbook 2008.*

United Nations Statistics Division, New York, NY 10017, (800) 253-9646, Fax: (212) 963-4116, http://unstats.un.org; *Economic Survey of Latin America and the Caribbean 2004-2005.*

The World Bank, 1818 H Street, NW, Washington, DC 20433, (202) 473-1000, Fax: (202) 477-6391, www.worldbank.org; *Global Development Finance 2007.*

CUBA - DEFENSE EXPENDITURES

See CUBA - ARMED FORCES

CUBA - DEMOGRAPHY

Euromonitor International, Inc., 224 S. Michigan Avenue, Suite 1500, Chicago, IL 60604, (312) 922-1115, Fax: (312) 922-1157, www.euromonitor.com; *International Marketing Data and Statistics 2008; The World Economic Factbook 2008;* and *World Marketing Data and Statistics.*

M.E. Sharpe, 80 Business Park Drive, Armonk, NY 10504, (800) 541-6563, Fax: (914) 273-2106, www.mesharpe.com; *The Illustrated Book of World Rankings.*

La Oficina Nacional de Estadisticas, Paseo No. 60 e/ 3ra y 5ta, Vedado, Plaza de la Revolucion, Ciudad de La Habana, Cuba, CP 10400, www.one.cu; *Anuario Demografico 2006* and *Indicadores sociales y demograficos de Cuba por territorios.*

United Nations Statistics Division, New York, NY 10017, (800) 253-9646, Fax: (212) 963-4116, http://unstats.un.org; *Human Development Report 2006.*

The World Bank, 1818 H Street, NW, Washington, DC 20433, (202) 473-1000, Fax: (202) 477-6391, www.worldbank.org; *Cuba.*

CUBA - DIAMONDS

See CUBA - MINERAL INDUSTRIES

CUBA - DISPOSABLE INCOME

M.E. Sharpe, 80 Business Park Drive, Armonk, NY 10504, (800) 541-6563, Fax: (914) 273-2106, www.mesharpe.com; *The Illustrated Book of World Rankings.*

United Nations Statistics Division, New York, NY 10017, (800) 253-9646, Fax: (212) 963-4116, http://unstats.un.org; *National Accounts Statistics: Compendium of Income Distribution Statistics* and *Statistical Yearbook.*

CUBA - DIVORCE

M.E. Sharpe, 80 Business Park Drive, Armonk, NY 10504, (800) 541-6563, Fax: (914) 273-2106, www.mesharpe.com; *The Illustrated Book of World Rankings.*

United Nations Statistics Division, New York, NY 10017, (800) 253-9646, Fax: (212) 963-4116, http://unstats.un.org; *Demographic Yearbook* and *Statistical Yearbook.*

CUBA - ECONOMIC ASSISTANCE

United Nations Statistics Division, New York, NY 10017, (800) 253-9646, Fax: (212) 963-4116, http://unstats.un.org; *Statistical Yearbook.*

CUBA - ECONOMIC CONDITIONS

Center for International Business Education Research (CIBER), Columbia Business School and School of International and Public Affairs, Uris Hall, Room 212, 3022 Broadway, New York, NY 10027-6902, Mr. Joshua Safier, (212) 854-4750, Fax: (212) 222-9821, www.columbia.edu/cu/ciber/; Datastream International.

Central Intelligence Agency, Office of Public Affairs, Washington, DC 20505, (703) 482-0623, Fax: (703) 482-1739, www.cia.gov; *The World Factbook.*

DSI Data Service Information, Xantener Strasse 51a, D-47495 Rheinberg, Germany, www.dsidata.com; *Campus Solution.*

Dun and Bradstreet (DB) Corporation, 103 JFK Parkway, Short Hills, NJ 07078, (973) 921-5500, www.dnb.com; *Country Report.*

Economist Intelligence Unit, 111 West 57th Street, New York, NY 10019, (212) 554-0600, Fax: (212) 586-1181, www.eiu.com; *Cuba Country Report.*

Euromonitor International, Inc., 224 S. Michigan Avenue, Suite 1500, Chicago, IL 60604, (312) 922-1115, Fax: (312) 922-1157, www.euromonitor.com; *International Marketing Data and Statistics 2008; The World Economic Factbook 2008;* and *World Marketing Data and Statistics.*

International Monetary Fund (IMF), 700 Nineteenth Street, NW, Washington, DC 20431, (202) 623-7000, Fax: (202) 623-4661, www.imf.org; *World Economic Outlook Reports.*

M.E. Sharpe, 80 Business Park Drive, Armonk, NY 10504, (800) 541-6563, Fax: (914) 273-2106, www.mesharpe.com; *The Illustrated Book of World Rankings.*

Palgrave Macmillan Ltd., Houndmills, Basingstoke, Hampshire, RG21 6XS, England, (Telephone in U.S. (888) 330-8477), (Fax in U.S. (800) 672-2054), www.palgrave.com; *The Statesman's Yearbook 2008.*

Taylor and Francis Group, An Informa Business, 2 Park Square, Milton Park, Abingdon, Oxford OX14 4RN, United Kingdom, (Dial from U.S. (212) 216-7800), (Fax from U.S. (212) 564-7854), www.tandf.co.uk; *The Europa World Year Book.*

UCLA Latin American Institute, 10343 Bunche Hall, Box 951447, Los Angeles, CA 90095-1447, (310) 825-4571, Fax: (310) 206-6859, www.international.ucla.edu/lac; *Statistical Abstract of Latin America.*

United Nations Statistics Division, New York, NY 10017, (800) 253-9646, Fax: (212) 963-4116, http://unstats.un.org; *Economic Survey of Latin America and the Caribbean 2004-2005* and *World Statistics Pocketbook.*

The World Bank, 1818 H Street, NW, Washington, DC 20433, (202) 473-1000, Fax: (202) 477-6391, www.worldbank.org; *Cuba; Global Economic Monitor (GEM); Global Economic Prospects 2008;* and *The World Bank Atlas 2003-2004.*

CUBA - ECONOMICS - SOCIOLOGICAL ASPECTS

UCLA Latin American Institute, 10343 Bunche Hall, Box 951447, Los Angeles, CA 90095-1447, (310) 825-4571, Fax: (310) 206-6859, www.international.ucla.edu/lac; *Statistical Abstract of Latin America.*

CUBA - EDUCATION

Euromonitor International, Inc., 224 S. Michigan Avenue, Suite 1500, Chicago, IL 60604, (312) 922-1115, Fax: (312) 922-1157, www.euromonitor.com; *International Marketing Data and Statistics 2008* and *World Marketing Data and Statistics.*

M.E. Sharpe, 80 Business Park Drive, Armonk, NY 10504, (800) 541-6563, Fax: (914) 273-2106, www.mesharpe.com; *The Illustrated Book of World Rankings.*

La Oficina Nacional de Estadisticas, Paseo No. 60 e/ 3ra y 5ta, Vedado, Plaza de la Revolucion, Ciudad de La Habana, Cuba, CP 10400, www.one.cu; *Educacion en Cifras, 1958-2002.*

Palgrave Macmillan Ltd., Houndmills, Basingstoke, Hampshire, RG21 6XS, England, (Telephone in U.S. (888) 330-8477), (Fax in U.S. (800) 672-2054), www.palgrave.com; *The Statesman's Yearbook 2008.*

Taylor and Francis Group, An Informa Business, 2 Park Square, Milton Park, Abingdon, Oxford OX14 4RN, United Kingdom, (Dial from U.S. (212) 216-7800), (Fax from U.S. (212) 564-7854), www.tandf.co.uk; *The Europa World Year Book.*

UCLA Latin American Institute, 10343 Bunche Hall, Box 951447, Los Angeles, CA 90095-1447, (310) 825-4571, Fax: (310) 206-6859, www.international.ucla.edu/lac; *Statistical Abstract of Latin America.*

UNESCO Institute for Statistics, C.P. 6128 Succursale Centre-Ville, Montreal, Quebec, H3C 3J7 Canada, (Dial from U.S. (514) 343-6880), (Fax from U.S. (514) 343 6882), www.uis.unesco.org; *Statistical Tables.*

United Nations Statistics Division, New York, NY 10017, (800) 253-9646, Fax: (212) 963-4116, http://unstats.un.org; *Human Development Report 2006.*

The World Bank, 1818 H Street, NW, Washington, DC 20433, (202) 473-1000, Fax: (202) 477-6391, www.worldbank.org; *Cuba.*

CUBA - ELECTRICITY

M.E. Sharpe, 80 Business Park Drive, Armonk, NY 10504, (800) 541-6563, Fax: (914) 273-2106, www.mesharpe.com; *The Illustrated Book of World Rankings.*

Organisation for Economic Cooperation and Development (OECD), 2 rue Andre Pascal, F-75775 Paris Cedex 16, France, (Telephone in U.S. (202) 785-6323), (Fax in U.S. (202) 785-0350), www.oecd.org; *World Energy Outlook 2007.*

Palgrave Macmillan Ltd., Houndmills, Basingstoke, Hampshire, RG21 6XS, England, (Telephone in U.S. (888) 330-8477), (Fax in U.S. (800) 672-2054), www.palgrave.com; *The Statesman's Yearbook 2008.*

U.S. Department of Energy (DOE), Energy Information Administration (EIA), 1000 Independence Avenue, SW, Washington, DC 20585, (202) 586-8800, www.eia.doe.gov; *International Energy Annual 2004* and *International Energy Outlook 2006.*

United Nations Statistics Division, New York, NY 10017, (800) 253-9646, Fax: (212) 963-4116, http://unstats.un.org; *Human Development Report 2006* and *Statistical Yearbook.*

CUBA - EMIGRATION AND IMMIGRATION

UCLA Latin American Institute, 10343 Bunche Hall, Box 951447, Los Angeles, CA 90095-1447, (310) 825-4571, Fax: (310) 206-6859, www.international.ucla.edu/lac; *Statistical Abstract of Latin America.*

CUBA - EMPLOYMENT

Euromonitor International, Inc., 224 S. Michigan Avenue, Suite 1500, Chicago, IL 60604, (312) 922-1115, Fax: (312) 922-1157, www.euromonitor.com; *International Marketing Data and Statistics 2008.*

International Labour Office, I.L.O. Publications, 4 route des Morillons, CH-1211 Geneva 22, Switzerland, (Telephone in U.S. (202) 653-7652), (Fax in U.S. (202) 653-7687), www.ilo.org; *Yearbook of Labour Statistics 2006.*

M.E. Sharpe, 80 Business Park Drive, Armonk, NY 10504, (800) 541-6563, Fax: (914) 273-2106, www.mesharpe.com; *The Illustrated Book of World Rankings.*

UCLA Latin American Institute, 10343 Bunche Hall, Box 951447, Los Angeles, CA 90095-1447, (310) 825-4571, Fax: (310) 206-6859, www.international.ucla.edu/lac; *Statistical Abstract of Latin America.*

United Nations Statistics Division, New York, NY 10017, (800) 253-9646, Fax: (212) 963-4116, http://unstats.un.org; *Statistical Yearbook.*

The World Bank, 1818 H Street, NW, Washington, DC 20433, (202) 473-1000, Fax: (202) 477-6391, www.worldbank.org; *Cuba.*

CUBA - ENVIRONMENTAL CONDITIONS

DSI Data Service Information, Xantener Strasse 51a, D-47495 Rheinberg, Germany, www.dsidata.com; *Campus Solution* and *DSI's Global Environmental Database.*

Economist Intelligence Unit, 111 West 57th Street, New York, NY 10019, (212) 554-0600, Fax: (212) 586-1181, www.eiu.com; *Cuba Country Report.*

United Nations Statistics Division, New York, NY 10017, (800) 253-9646, Fax: (212) 963-4116, http://unstats.un.org; *World Statistics Pocketbook.*

CUBA - EXPORTS

Central Intelligence Agency, Office of Public Affairs, Washington, DC 20505, (703) 482-0623, Fax: (703) 482-1739, www.cia.gov; *The World Factbook.*

Economist Intelligence Unit, 111 West 57th Street, New York, NY 10019, (212) 554-0600, Fax: (212) 586-1181, www.eiu.com; *Cuba Country Report.*

Euromonitor International, Inc., 224 S. Michigan Avenue, Suite 1500, Chicago, IL 60604, (312) 922-1115, Fax: (312) 922-1157, www.euromonitor.com; *International Marketing Data and Statistics 2008* and *The World Economic Factbook 2008.*

International Monetary Fund (IMF), 700 Nineteenth Street, NW, Washington, DC 20431, (202) 623-7000, Fax: (202) 623-4661, www.imf.org; *Direction of Trade Statistics Yearbook 2007.*

Palgrave Macmillan Ltd., Houndmills, Basingstoke, Hampshire, RG21 6XS, England, (Telephone in U.S. (888) 330-8477), (Fax in U.S. (800) 672-2054), www.palgrave.com; *The Statesman's Yearbook 2008.*

Taylor and Francis Group, An Informa Business, 2 Park Square, Milton Park, Abingdon, Oxford OX14 4RN, United Kingdom, (Dial from U.S. (212) 216-7800), (Fax from U.S. (212) 564-7854), www.tandf.co.uk; *The Europa World Year Book.*

United Nations Food and Agricultural Organization (FAO), Viale delle Terme di Caracalla, 00100 Rome, Italy, (Dial from U.S. (202) 653-2400), (Fax from U.S. (202) 653 5760), www.fao.org; *The State of Food and Agriculture (SOFA) 2006.*

CUBA - FEMALE WORKING POPULATION

See CUBA - EMPLOYMENT

CUBA - FERTILITY, HUMAN

Central Intelligence Agency, Office of Public Affairs, Washington, DC 20505, (703) 482-0623, Fax: (703) 482-1739, www.cia.gov; *The World Factbook.*

M.E. Sharpe, 80 Business Park Drive, Armonk, NY 10504, (800) 541-6563, Fax: (914) 273-2106, www.mesharpe.com; *The Illustrated Book of World Rankings.*

United Nations Statistics Division, New York, NY 10017, (800) 253-9646, Fax: (212) 963-4116, http://unstats.un.org; *Human Development Report 2006.*

The World Bank, 1818 H Street, NW, Washington, DC 20433, (202) 473-1000, Fax: (202) 477-6391, www.worldbank.org; *The World Bank Atlas 2003-2004.*

CUBA - FERTILIZER INDUSTRY

United Nations Food and Agricultural Organization (FAO), Viale delle Terme di Caracalla, 00100 Rome, Italy, (Dial from U.S. (202) 653-2400), (Fax from U.S. (202) 653 5760), www.fao.org; *FAO Fertilizer Yearbook* and *The State of Food and Agriculture (SOFA) 2006.*

United Nations Statistics Division, New York, NY 10017, (800) 253-9646, Fax: (212) 963-4116, http://unstats.un.org; *Statistical Yearbook.*

CUBA - FETAL MORTALITY

See CUBA - MORTALITY

CUBA - FILM

See CUBA - MOTION PICTURES

CUBA - FINANCE

Taylor and Francis Group, An Informa Business, 2 Park Square, Milton Park, Abingdon, Oxford OX14 4RN, United Kingdom, (Dial from U.S. (212) 216-7800), (Fax from U.S. (212) 564-7854), www.tandf.co.uk; *The Europa World Year Book.*

UCLA Latin American Institute, 10343 Bunche Hall, Box 951447, Los Angeles, CA 90095-1447, (310) 825-4571, Fax: (310) 206-6859, www.international.ucla.edu/lac; *Statistical Abstract of Latin America.*

United Nations Statistics Division, New York, NY 10017, (800) 253-9646, Fax: (212) 963-4116, http://unstats.un.org; *National Accounts Statistics: Compendium of Income Distribution Statistics* and *Statistical Yearbook.*

The World Bank, 1818 H Street, NW, Washington, DC 20433, (202) 473-1000, Fax: (202) 477-6391, www.worldbank.org; *Cuba.*

CUBA - FINANCE, PUBLIC

Bernan Essential Government Publications, 4611-F Assembly Drive, Lanham MD, 20706-4391, (301) 459-2255, Fax: (800) 865-3450, www.bernan.com; *National Accounts Statistics.*

Economist Intelligence Unit, 111 West 57th Street, New York, NY 10019, (212) 554-0600, Fax: (212) 586-1181, www.eiu.com; *Cuba Country Report.*

International Monetary Fund (IMF), 700 Nineteenth Street, NW, Washington, DC 20431, (202) 623-7000, Fax: (202) 623-4661, www.imf.org; *International Financial Statistics* and *International Financial Statistics Online Service.*

M.E. Sharpe, 80 Business Park Drive, Armonk, NY 10504, (800) 541-6563, Fax: (914) 273-2106, www.mesharpe.com; *The Illustrated Book of World Rankings.*

Palgrave Macmillan Ltd., Houndmills, Basingstoke, Hampshire, RG21 6XS, England, (Telephone in U.S. (888) 330-8477), (Fax in U.S. (800) 672-2054), www.palgrave.com; *The Statesman's Yearbook 2008.*

Taylor and Francis Group, An Informa Business, 2 Park Square, Milton Park, Abingdon, Oxford OX14 4RN, United Kingdom, (Dial from U.S. (212) 216-7800), (Fax from U.S. (212) 564-7854), www.tandf.co.uk; *The Europa World Year Book.*

UCLA Latin American Institute, 10343 Bunche Hall, Box 951447, Los Angeles, CA 90095-1447, (310) 825-4571, Fax: (310) 206-6859, www.international.ucla.edu/lac; *Statistical Abstract of Latin America.*

The World Bank, 1818 H Street, NW, Washington, DC 20433, (202) 473-1000, Fax: (202) 477-6391, www.worldbank.org; *Cuba.*

CUBA - FISHERIES

M.E. Sharpe, 80 Business Park Drive, Armonk, NY 10504, (800) 541-6563, Fax: (914) 273-2106, www.mesharpe.com; *The Illustrated Book of World Rankings.*

Palgrave Macmillan Ltd., Houndmills, Basingstoke, Hampshire, RG21 6XS, England, (Telephone in U.S. (888) 330-8477), (Fax in U.S. (800) 672-2054), www.palgrave.com; *The Statesman's Yearbook 2008.*

Taylor and Francis Group, An Informa Business, 2 Park Square, Milton Park, Abingdon, Oxford OX14 4RN, United Kingdom, (Dial from U.S. (212) 216-7800), (Fax from U.S. (212) 564-7854), www.tandf.co.uk; *The Europa World Year Book.*

UCLA Latin American Institute, 10343 Bunche Hall, Box 951447, Los Angeles, CA 90095-1447, (310) 825-4571, Fax: (310) 206-6859, www.international.ucla.edu/lac; *Statistical Abstract of Latin America.*

United Nations Conference on Trade and Development (UNCTAD), DC2-1120, United Nations, New York, NY 10017, (212) 963-0027, www.unctad.org; *UNCTAD Commodity Yearbook.*

United Nations Food and Agricultural Organization (FAO), Viale delle Terme di Caracalla, 00100 Rome, Italy, (Dial from U.S. (202) 653-2400), (Fax from U.S. (202) 653 5760), www.fao.org; *FAO Yearbook of Fishery Statistics*; Fishery Databases; FISHSTAT Database. Subjects covered include: Aquaculture production, capture production, fishery commodities; and *The State of Food and Agriculture (SOFA) 2006.*

United Nations Statistics Division, New York, NY 10017, (800) 253-9646, Fax: (212) 963-4116, http://unstats.un.org; *Statistical Yearbook.*

The World Bank, 1818 H Street, NW, Washington, DC 20433, (202) 473-1000, Fax: (202) 477-6391, www.worldbank.org; *Cuba.*

CUBA - FLOUR INDUSTRY

United Nations Statistics Division, New York, NY 10017, (800) 253-9646, Fax: (212) 963-4116, http://unstats.un.org; *Statistical Yearbook.*

CUBA - FOOD

United Nations Conference on Trade and Development (UNCTAD), DC2-1120, United Nations, New York, NY 10017, (212) 963-0027, www.unctad.org; *UNCTAD Commodity Yearbook.*

United Nations Food and Agricultural Organization (FAO), Viale delle Terme di Caracalla, 00100 Rome, Italy, (Dial from U.S. (202) 653-2400), (Fax from U.S. (202) 653 5760), www.fao.org; *FAO Production Yearbook 2002* and *The State of Food and Agriculture (SOFA) 2006.*

United Nations Statistics Division, New York, NY 10017, (800) 253-9646, Fax: (212) 963-4116, http://unstats.un.org; *Human Development Report 2006.*

CUBA - FOREIGN EXCHANGE RATES

Central Intelligence Agency, Office of Public Affairs, Washington, DC 20505, (703) 482-0623, Fax: (703) 482-1739, www.cia.gov; *The World Factbook.*

Euromonitor International, Inc., 224 S. Michigan Avenue, Suite 1500, Chicago, IL 60604, (312) 922-1115, Fax: (312) 922-1157, www.euromonitor.com; *International Marketing Data and Statistics 2008* and *The World Economic Factbook 2008.*

Taylor and Francis Group, An Informa Business, 2 Park Square, Milton Park, Abingdon, Oxford OX14 4RN, United Kingdom, (Dial from U.S. (212) 216-7800), (Fax from U.S. (212) 564-7854), www.tandf.co.uk; *The Europa World Year Book.*

UCLA Latin American Institute, 10343 Bunche Hall, Box 951447, Los Angeles, CA 90095-1447, (310) 825-4571, Fax: (310) 206-6859, www.international.ucla.edu/lac; *Statistical Abstract of Latin America.*

United Nations Statistics Division, New York, NY 10017, (800) 253-9646, Fax: (212) 963-4116, http://unstats.un.org; *Statistical Yearbook* and *World Statistics Pocketbook.*

CUBA - FORESTS AND FORESTRY

M.E. Sharpe, 80 Business Park Drive, Armonk, NY 10504, (800) 541-6563, Fax: (914) 273-2106, www.mesharpe.com; *The Illustrated Book of World Rankings.*

Palgrave Macmillan Ltd., Houndmills, Basingstoke, Hampshire, RG21 6XS, England, (Telephone in U.S. (888) 330-8477), (Fax in U.S. (800) 672-2054), www.palgrave.com; *The Statesman's Yearbook 2008.*

Taylor and Francis Group, An Informa Business, 2 Park Square, Milton Park, Abingdon, Oxford OX14 4RN, United Kingdom, (Dial from U.S. (212) 216-7800), (Fax from U.S. (212) 564-7854), www.tandf.co.uk; *The Europa World Year Book.*

UCLA Latin American Institute, 10343 Bunche Hall, Box 951447, Los Angeles, CA 90095-1447, (310) 825-4571, Fax: (310) 206-6859, www.international.ucla.edu/lac; *Statistical Abstract of Latin America.*

UNESCO Institute for Statistics, C.P. 6128 Succursale Centre-Ville, Montreal, Quebec, H3C 3J7 Canada, (Dial from U.S. (514) 343-6880), (Fax from U.S. (514) 343 6882), www.uis.unesco.org; *Statistical Tables.*

United Nations Conference on Trade and Development (UNCTAD), DC2-1120, United Nations, New York, NY 10017, (212) 963-0027, www.unctad.org; *UNCTAD Commodity Yearbook.*

United Nations Food and Agricultural Organization (FAO), Viale delle Terme di Caracalla, 00100 Rome, Italy, (Dial from U.S. (202) 653-2400), (Fax from U.S. (202) 653 5760), www.fao.org; *FAO Yearbook of Forest Products* and *The State of Food and Agriculture (SOFA) 2006.*

United Nations Statistics Division, New York, NY 10017, (800) 253-9646, Fax: (212) 963-4116, http://unstats.un.org; *Statistical Yearbook.*

The World Bank, 1818 H Street, NW, Washington, DC 20433, (202) 473-1000, Fax: (202) 477-6391, www.worldbank.org; *Cuba.*

CUBA - GAS PRODUCTION

See CUBA - MINERAL INDUSTRIES

CUBA - GEOGRAPHIC INFORMATION SYSTEMS

M.E. Sharpe, 80 Business Park Drive, Armonk, NY 10504, (800) 541-6563, Fax: (914) 273-2106, www.mesharpe.com; *The Illustrated Book of World Rankings.*

UCLA Latin American Institute, 10343 Bunche Hall, Box 951447, Los Angeles, CA 90095-1447, (310) 825-4571, Fax: (310) 206-6859, www.international.ucla.edu/lac; *Statistical Abstract of Latin America.*

The World Bank, 1818 H Street, NW, Washington, DC 20433, (202) 473-1000, Fax: (202) 477-6391, www.worldbank.org; *Cuba.*

CUBA - GOATS

Euromonitor International, Inc., 224 S. Michigan Avenue, Suite 1500, Chicago, IL 60604, (312) 922-1115, Fax: (312) 922-1157, www.euromonitor.com; *International Marketing Data and Statistics 2008.*

CUBA - GOLD PRODUCTION

See CUBA - MINERAL INDUSTRIES

CUBA - GREEN PEPPER AND CHILIE PRODUCTION

See CUBA - CROPS

CUBA - GROSS DOMESTIC PRODUCT

Economist Intelligence Unit, 111 West 57th Street, New York, NY 10019, (212) 554-0600, Fax: (212) 586-1181, www.eiu.com; *Cuba Country Report.*

Euromonitor International, Inc., 224 S. Michigan Avenue, Suite 1500, Chicago, IL 60604, (312) 922-1115, Fax: (312) 922-1157, www.euromonitor.com; *International Marketing Data and Statistics 2008* and *The World Economic Factbook 2008.*

M.E. Sharpe, 80 Business Park Drive, Armonk, NY 10504, (800) 541-6563, Fax: (914) 273-2106, www.mesharpe.com; *The Illustrated Book of World Rankings.*

United Nations Statistics Division, New York, NY 10017, (800) 253-9646, Fax: (212) 963-4116, http://unstats.un.org; *Human Development Report 2006; National Accounts Statistics: Compendium of Income Distribution Statistics;* and *Statistical Yearbook.*

CUBA - GROSS NATIONAL PRODUCT

Euromonitor International, Inc., 224 S. Michigan Avenue, Suite 1500, Chicago, IL 60604, (312) 922-1115, Fax: (312) 922-1157, www.euromonitor.com; *International Marketing Data and Statistics 2008.*

M.E. Sharpe, 80 Business Park Drive, Armonk, NY 10504, (800) 541-6563, Fax: (914) 273-2106, www.mesharpe.com; *The Illustrated Book of World Rankings.*

U.S. Department of State (DOS), 2201 C Street NW, Washington, DC 20520, (202) 647-4000, www.state.gov; *World Military Expenditures and Arms Transfers (WMEAT).*

United Nations Statistics Division, New York, NY 10017, (800) 253-9646, Fax: (212) 963-4116, http://unstats.un.org; *Statistical Yearbook.*

The World Bank, 1818 H Street, NW, Washington, DC 20433, (202) 473-1000, Fax: (202) 477-6391, www.worldbank.org; *The World Bank Atlas 2003-2004.*

CUBA - HIDES AND SKINS INDUSTRY

United Nations Food and Agricultural Organization (FAO), Viale delle Terme di Caracalla, 00100 Rome, Italy, (Dial from U.S. (202) 653-2400), (Fax from U.S. (202) 653 5760), www.fao.org; *FAO Production Yearbook 2002.*

CUBA - HOUSING

Euromonitor International, Inc., 224 S. Michigan Avenue, Suite 1500, Chicago, IL 60604, (312) 922-1115, Fax: (312) 922-1157, www.euromonitor.com; *World Marketing Data and Statistics.*

M.E. Sharpe, 80 Business Park Drive, Armonk, NY 10504, (800) 541-6563, Fax: (914) 273-2106, www.mesharpe.com; *The Illustrated Book of World Rankings.*

UCLA Latin American Institute, 10343 Bunche Hall, Box 951447, Los Angeles, CA 90095-1447, (310) 825-4571, Fax: (310) 206-6859, www.international.ucla.edu/lac; *Statistical Abstract of Latin America.*

CUBA - ILLITERATE PERSONS

Euromonitor International, Inc., 224 S. Michigan Avenue, Suite 1500, Chicago, IL 60604, (312) 922-1115, Fax: (312) 922-1157, www.euromonitor.com; *The World Economic Factbook 2008.*

Palgrave Macmillan Ltd., Houndmills, Basingstoke, Hampshire, RG21 6XS, England, (Telephone in U.S. (888) 330-8477), (Fax in U.S. (800) 672-2054), www.palgrave.com; *The Statesman's Yearbook 2008.*

UNESCO Institute for Statistics, C.P. 6128 Succursale Centre-Ville, Montreal, Quebec, H3C 3J7 Canada, (Dial from U.S. (514) 343-6880), (Fax from U.S. (514) 343 6882), www.uis.unesco.org; *Statistical Tables.*

United Nations Statistics Division, New York, NY 10017, (800) 253-9646, Fax: (212) 963-4116, http://unstats.un.org; *Human Development Report 2006.*

CUBA - IMPORTS

Central Intelligence Agency, Office of Public Affairs, Washington, DC 20505, (703) 482-0623, Fax: (703) 482-1739, www.cia.gov; *The World Factbook.*

Economist Intelligence Unit, 111 West 57th Street, New York, NY 10019, (212) 554-0600, Fax: (212) 586-1181, www.eiu.com; *Cuba Country Report.*

Euromonitor International, Inc., 224 S. Michigan Avenue, Suite 1500, Chicago, IL 60604, (312) 922-1115, Fax: (312) 922-1157, www.euromonitor.com; *International Marketing Data and Statistics 2008* and *The World Economic Factbook 2008.*

International Monetary Fund (IMF), 700 Nineteenth Street, NW, Washington, DC 20431, (202) 623-7000, Fax: (202) 623-4661, www.imf.org; *Direction of Trade Statistics Yearbook 2007.*

Palgrave Macmillan Ltd., Houndmills, Basingstoke, Hampshire, RG21 6XS, England, (Telephone in U.S. (888) 330-8477), (Fax in U.S. (800) 672-2054), www.palgrave.com; *The Statesman's Yearbook 2008.*

Taylor and Francis Group, An Informa Business, 2 Park Square, Milton Park, Abingdon, Oxford OX14 4RN, United Kingdom, (Dial from U.S. (212) 216-7800), (Fax from U.S. (212) 564-7854), www.tandf.co.uk; *The Europa World Year Book.*

United Nations Food and Agricultural Organization (FAO), Viale delle Terme di Caracalla, 00100 Rome, Italy, (Dial from U.S. (202) 653-2400), (Fax from U.S. (202) 653 5760), www.fao.org; *The State of Food and Agriculture (SOFA) 2006.*

CUBA - INCOME DISTRIBUTION

UCLA Latin American Institute, 10343 Bunche Hall, Box 951447, Los Angeles, CA 90095-1447, (310) 825-4571, Fax: (310) 206-6859, www.international.ucla.edu/lac; *Statistical Abstract of Latin America.*

CUBA - INDUSTRIAL METALS PRODUCTION

See CUBA - MINERAL INDUSTRIES

CUBA - INDUSTRIAL PRODUCTIVITY

Euromonitor International, Inc., 224 S. Michigan Avenue, Suite 1500, Chicago, IL 60604, (312) 922-1115, Fax: (312) 922-1157, www.euromonitor.com; *International Marketing Data and Statistics 2008.*

M.E. Sharpe, 80 Business Park Drive, Armonk, NY 10504, (800) 541-6563, Fax: (914) 273-2106, www.mesharpe.com; *The Illustrated Book of World Rankings.*

CUBA - INDUSTRIAL PROPERTY

United Nations Statistics Division, New York, NY 10017, (800) 253-9646, Fax: (212) 963-4116, http://unstats.un.org; *Statistical Yearbook.*

World Intellectual Property Organization (WIPO), PO Box 18, CH-1211 Geneva 20, Switzerland, www.wipo.int; *Industrial Property Statistics* and *Industrial Property Statistics Online Directory.*

CUBA - INDUSTRIES

Central Intelligence Agency, Office of Public Affairs, Washington, DC 20505, (703) 482-0623, Fax: (703) 482-1739, www.cia.gov; *The World Factbook.*

Economist Intelligence Unit, 111 West 57th Street, New York, NY 10019, (212) 554-0600, Fax: (212) 586-1181, www.eiu.com; *Cuba Country Report.*

Euromonitor International, Inc., 224 S. Michigan Avenue, Suite 1500, Chicago, IL 60604, (312) 922-1115, Fax: (312) 922-1157, www.euromonitor.com; *International Marketing Data and Statistics 2008; The World Economic Factbook 2008;* and *World Marketing Data and Statistics.*

International Labour Office, I.L.O. Publications, 4 route des Morillons, CH-1211 Geneva 22, Switzerland, (Telephone in U.S. (202) 653-7652), (Fax in U.S. (202) 653-7687), www.ilo.org; *Yearbook of Labour Statistics 2006.*

M.E. Sharpe, 80 Business Park Drive, Armonk, NY 10504, (800) 541-6563, Fax: (914) 273-2106, www.mesharpe.com; *The Illustrated Book of World Rankings.*

Palgrave Macmillan Ltd., Houndmills, Basingstoke, Hampshire, RG21 6XS, England, (Telephone in U.S. (888) 330-8477), (Fax in U.S. (800) 672-2054), www.palgrave.com; *The Statesman's Yearbook 2008.*

Taylor and Francis Group, An Informa Business, 2 Park Square, Milton Park, Abingdon, Oxford OX14 4RN, United Kingdom, (Dial from U.S. (212) 216-7800), (Fax from U.S. (212) 564-7854), www.tandf.co.uk; *The Europa World Year Book.*

UCLA Latin American Institute, 10343 Bunche Hall, Box 951447, Los Angeles, CA 90095-1447, (310) 825-4571, Fax: (310) 206-6859, www.international.ucla.edu/lac; *Statistical Abstract of Latin America.*

United Nations Industrial Development Organization (UNIDO), 1 United Nations Plaza, New York, NY 10017, (212) 963 6890, Fax: (212) 963-7904, http://unido.org; Industrial Statistics Database 2008 (INDSTAT) and *The International Yearbook of Industrial Statistics 2008.*

United Nations Statistics Division, New York, NY 10017, (800) 253-9646, Fax: (212) 963-4116, http://unstats.un.org; *Economic Survey of Latin America and the Caribbean 2004-2005.*

The World Bank, 1818 H Street, NW, Washington, DC 20433, (202) 473-1000, Fax: (202) 477-6391, www.worldbank.org; *Cuba.*

CUBA - INFANT AND MATERNAL MORTALITY

See CUBA - MORTALITY

CUBA - INFLATION (FINANCE)

United Nations Statistics Division, New York, NY 10017, (800) 253-9646, Fax: (212) 963-4116, http://unstats.un.org; *Economic Survey of Latin America and the Caribbean 2004-2005.*

CUBA - INORGANIC ACIDS

United Nations Statistics Division, New York, NY 10017, (800) 253-9646, Fax: (212) 963-4116, http://unstats.un.org; *Statistical Yearbook.*

CUBA - INTERNATIONAL FINANCE

UCLA Latin American Institute, 10343 Bunche Hall, Box 951447, Los Angeles, CA 90095-1447, (310) 825-4571, Fax: (310) 206-6859, www.international.ucla.edu/lac; *Statistical Abstract of Latin America.*

CUBA - INTERNATIONAL STATISTICS

UCLA Latin American Institute, 10343 Bunche Hall, Box 951447, Los Angeles, CA 90095-1447, (310) 825-4571, Fax: (310) 206-6859, www.international.ucla.edu/lac; *Statistical Abstract of Latin America.*

CUBA - INTERNATIONAL TRADE

Economist Intelligence Unit, 111 West 57th Street, New York, NY 10019, (212) 554-0600, Fax: (212) 586-1181, www.eiu.com; *Cuba Country Report.*

Euromonitor International, Inc., 224 S. Michigan Avenue, Suite 1500, Chicago, IL 60604, (312) 922-1115, Fax: (312) 922-1157, www.euromonitor.com; *International Marketing Data and Statistics 2008; The World Economic Factbook 2008;* and *World Marketing Data and Statistics.*

M.E. Sharpe, 80 Business Park Drive, Armonk, NY 10504, (800) 541-6563, Fax: (914) 273-2106, www.mesharpe.com; *The Illustrated Book of World Rankings.*

Organisation for Economic Cooperation and Development (OECD), 2 rue Andre Pascal, F-75775 Paris Cedex 16, France, (Telephone in U.S. (202) 785-6323), (Fax in U.S. (202) 785-0350), www.oecd.org; *International Trade by Commodity Statistics (ITCS).*

Palgrave Macmillan Ltd., Houndmills, Basingstoke, Hampshire, RG21 6XS, England, (Telephone in U.S. (888) 330-8477), (Fax in U.S. (800) 672-2054), www.palgrave.com; *The Statesman's Yearbook 2008.*

Taylor and Francis Group, An Informa Business, 2 Park Square, Milton Park, Abingdon, Oxford OX14 4RN, United Kingdom, (Dial from U.S. (212) 216-7800), (Fax from U.S. (212) 564-7854), www.tandf.co.uk; *The Europa World Year Book.*

UCLA Latin American Institute, 10343 Bunche Hall, Box 951447, Los Angeles, CA 90095-1447, (310) 825-4571, Fax: (310) 206-6859, www.international.ucla.edu/lac; *Statistical Abstract of Latin America.*

United Nations Conference on Trade and Development (UNCTAD), DC2-1120, United Nations, New York, NY 10017, (212) 963-0027, www.unctad.org; *UNCTAD Commodity Yearbook.*

United Nations Food and Agricultural Organization (FAO), Viale delle Terme di Caracalla, 00100 Rome, Italy, (Dial from U.S. (202) 653-2400), (Fax from U.S. (202) 653 5760), www.fao.org; *FAO Trade Yearbook* and *The State of Food and Agriculture (SOFA) 2006.*

United Nations Statistics Division, New York, NY 10017, (800) 253-9646, Fax: (212) 963-4116, http://unstats.un.org; *Economic Survey of Latin America and the Caribbean 2004-2005; International Trade Statistics Yearbook;* and *Statistical Yearbook.*

The World Bank, 1818 H Street, NW, Washington, DC 20433, (202) 473-1000, Fax: (202) 477-6391, www.worldbank.org; *Cuba.*

World Trade Organization (WTO), Centre William Rappard, Rue de Lausanne 154, CH-1211 Geneva 21, Switzerland, www.wto.org; *International Trade Statistics 2006.*

CUBA - INTERNET USERS

International Telecommunication Union (ITU), Place des Nations, 1211 Geneva 20, Switzerland, www.itu.int; *World Telecommunication/ICT Indicators Database on CD-ROM; World Telecommunication/ICT Indicators Database Online;* and *Yearbook of Statistics - Telecommunication Services (Chronological Time Series 1997-2006).*

The World Bank, 1818 H Street, NW, Washington, DC 20433, (202) 473-1000, Fax: (202) 477-6391, www.worldbank.org; *Cuba.*

CUBA - IRON AND IRON ORE PRODUCTION

See CUBA - MINERAL INDUSTRIES

CUBA - IRRIGATION

Euromonitor International, Inc., 224 S. Michigan Avenue, Suite 1500, Chicago, IL 60604, (312) 922-1115, Fax: (312) 922-1157, www.euromonitor.com; *International Marketing Data and Statistics 2008.*

CUBA - JUTE PRODUCTION

See CUBA - CROPS

CUBA - LABOR

Central Intelligence Agency, Office of Public Affairs, Washington, DC 20505, (703) 482-0623, Fax: (703) 482-1739, www.cia.gov; *The World Factbook.*

Euromonitor International, Inc., 224 S. Michigan Avenue, Suite 1500, Chicago, IL 60604, (312) 922-1115, Fax: (312) 922-1157, www.euromonitor.com; *International Marketing Data and Statistics 2008* and *World Marketing Data and Statistics.*

International Labour Office, I.L.O. Publications, 4 route des Morillons, CH-1211 Geneva 22, Switzerland, (Telephone in U.S. (202) 653-7652), (Fax in U.S. (202) 653-7687), www.ilo.org; *Yearbook of Labour Statistics 2006.*

M.E. Sharpe, 80 Business Park Drive, Armonk, NY 10504, (800) 541-6563, Fax: (914) 273-2106, www.mesharpe.com; *The Illustrated Book of World Rankings.*

Palgrave Macmillan Ltd., Houndmills, Basingstoke, Hampshire, RG21 6XS, England, (Telephone in U.S. (888) 330-8477), (Fax in U.S. (800) 672-2054), www.palgrave.com; *The Statesman's Yearbook 2008.*

Taylor and Francis Group, An Informa Business, 2 Park Square, Milton Park, Abingdon, Oxford OX14 4RN, United Kingdom, (Dial from U.S. (212) 216-7800), (Fax from U.S. (212) 564-7854), www.tandf.co.uk; *The Europa World Year Book.*

United Nations Food and Agricultural Organization (FAO), Viale delle Terme di Caracalla, 00100 Rome, Italy, (Dial from U.S. (202) 653-2400), (Fax from U.S. (202) 653 5760), www.fao.org; *The State of Food and Agriculture (SOFA) 2006.*

United Nations Statistics Division, New York, NY 10017, (800) 253-9646, Fax: (212) 963-4116, http://unstats.un.org; *Human Development Report 2006.*

The World Bank, 1818 H Street, NW, Washington, DC 20433, (202) 473-1000, Fax: (202) 477-6391, www.worldbank.org; *The World Bank Atlas 2003-2004.*

CUBA - LAND USE

Central Intelligence Agency, Office of Public Affairs, Washington, DC 20505, (703) 482-0623, Fax: (703) 482-1739, www.cia.gov; *The World Factbook.*

Euromonitor International, Inc., 224 S. Michigan Avenue, Suite 1500, Chicago, IL 60604, (312) 922-1115, Fax: (312) 922-1157, www.euromonitor.com; *International Marketing Data and Statistics 2008.*

United Nations Food and Agricultural Organization (FAO), Viale delle Terme di Caracalla, 00100 Rome, Italy, (Dial from U.S. (202) 653-2400), (Fax from U.S. (202) 653 5760), www.fao.org; *FAO Production Yearbook 2002.*

CUBA - LIBRARIES

M.E. Sharpe, 80 Business Park Drive, Armonk, NY 10504, (800) 541-6563, Fax: (914) 273-2106, www.mesharpe.com; *The Illustrated Book of World Rankings.*

CUBA - LIFE EXPECTANCY

Central Intelligence Agency, Office of Public Affairs, Washington, DC 20505, (703) 482-0623, Fax: (703) 482-1739, www.cia.gov; *The World Factbook.*

Euromonitor International, Inc., 224 S. Michigan Avenue, Suite 1500, Chicago, IL 60604, (312) 922-1115, Fax: (312) 922-1157, www.euromonitor.com; *The World Economic Factbook 2008.*

United Nations Statistics Division, New York, NY 10017, (800) 253-9646, Fax: (212) 963-4116, http://unstats.un.org; *Human Development Report 2006* and *World Statistics Pocketbook.*

The World Bank, 1818 H Street, NW, Washington, DC 20433, (202) 473-1000, Fax: (202) 477-6391, www.worldbank.org; *The World Bank Atlas 2003-2004.*

CUBA - LITERACY

Euromonitor International, Inc., 224 S. Michigan Avenue, Suite 1500, Chicago, IL 60604, (312) 922-1115, Fax: (312) 922-1157, www.euromonitor.com; *World Marketing Data and Statistics.*

CUBA - LIVESTOCK

Euromonitor International, Inc., 224 S. Michigan Avenue, Suite 1500, Chicago, IL 60604, (312) 922-1115, Fax: (312) 922-1157, www.euromonitor.com; *International Marketing Data and Statistics 2008.*

M.E. Sharpe, 80 Business Park Drive, Armonk, NY 10504, (800) 541-6563, Fax: (914) 273-2106, www.mesharpe.com; *The Illustrated Book of World Rankings.*

Palgrave Macmillan Ltd., Houndmills, Basingstoke, Hampshire, RG21 6XS, England, (Telephone in U.S.

(888) 330-8477), (Fax in U.S. (800) 672-2054), www.palgrave.com; *The Statesman's Yearbook 2008.*

Taylor and Francis Group, An Informa Business, 2 Park Square, Milton Park, Abingdon, Oxford OX14 4RN, United Kingdom, (Dial from U.S. (212) 216-7800), (Fax from U.S. (212) 564-7854), www.tandf.co.uk; *The Europa World Year Book.*

United Nations Conference on Trade and Development (UNCTAD), DC2-1120, United Nations, New York, NY 10017, (212) 963-0027, www.unctad.org; *UNCTAD Commodity Yearbook.*

United Nations Food and Agricultural Organization (FAO), Viale delle Terme di Caracalla, 00100 Rome, Italy, (Dial from U.S. (202) 653-2400), (Fax from U.S. (202) 653 5760), www.fao.org; *FAO Production Yearbook 2002* and *The State of Food and Agriculture (SOFA) 2006.*

United Nations Statistics Division, New York, NY 10017, (800) 253-9646, Fax: (212) 963-4116, http://unstats.un.org; *Statistical Yearbook.*

CUBA - LOCAL TAXATION

Euromonitor International, Inc., 224 S. Michigan Avenue, Suite 1500, Chicago, IL 60604, (312) 922-1115, Fax: (312) 922-1157, www.euromonitor.com; *International Marketing Data and Statistics 2008.*

CUBA - MANUFACTURES

M.E. Sharpe, 80 Business Park Drive, Armonk, NY 10504, (800) 541-6563, Fax: (914) 273-2106, www.mesharpe.com; *The Illustrated Book of World Rankings.*

CUBA - MARRIAGE

M.E. Sharpe, 80 Business Park Drive, Armonk, NY 10504, (800) 541-6563, Fax: (914) 273-2106, www.mesharpe.com; *The Illustrated Book of World Rankings.*

Taylor and Francis Group, An Informa Business, 2 Park Square, Milton Park, Abingdon, Oxford OX14 4RN, United Kingdom, (Dial from U.S. (212) 216-7800), (Fax from U.S. (212) 564-7854), www.tandf.co.uk; *The Europa World Year Book.*

United Nations Statistics Division, New York, NY 10017, (800) 253-9646, Fax: (212) 963-4116, http://unstats.un.org; *Demographic Yearbook* and *Statistical Yearbook.*

CUBA - MEDICAL PERSONNEL

UCLA Latin American Institute, 10343 Bunche Hall, Box 951447, Los Angeles, CA 90095-1447, (310) 825-4571, Fax: (310) 206-6859, www.international.ucla.edu/lac; *Statistical Abstract of Latin America.*

CUBA - MILK PRODUCTION

See CUBA - DAIRY PROCESSING

CUBA - MINERAL INDUSTRIES

Commodity Research Bureau, 330 South Wells Street, Suite 612, Chicago, IL 60606-7110, (800) 621-5271, Fax: (312) 939-4135, www.crbtrader.com; *2006 CRB Commodity Yearbook and CD.*

M.E. Sharpe, 80 Business Park Drive, Armonk, NY 10504, (800) 541-6563, Fax: (914) 273-2106, www.mesharpe.com; *The Illustrated Book of World Rankings.*

Organisation for Economic Cooperation and Development (OECD), 2 rue Andre Pascal, F-75775 Paris Cedex 16, France, (Telephone in U.S. (202) 785-6323), (Fax in U.S. (202) 785-0350), www.oecd.org; *World Energy Outlook 2007.*

Palgrave Macmillan Ltd., Houndmills, Basingstoke, Hampshire, RG21 6XS, England, (Telephone in U.S. (888) 330-8477), (Fax in U.S. (800) 672-2054), www.palgrave.com; *The Statesman's Yearbook 2008.*

Taylor and Francis Group, An Informa Business, 2 Park Square, Milton Park, Abingdon, Oxford OX14 4RN, United Kingdom, (Dial from U.S. (212) 216-7800), (Fax from U.S. (212) 564-7854), www.tandf.co.uk; *The Europa World Year Book.*

UCLA Latin American Institute, 10343 Bunche Hall, Box 951447, Los Angeles, CA 90095-1447, (310) 825-4571, Fax: (310) 206-6859, www.international.ucla.edu/lac; *Statistical Abstract of Latin America.*

United Nations Conference on Trade and Development (UNCTAD), DC2-1120, United Nations, New York, NY 10017, (212) 963-0027, www.unctad.org; *UNCTAD Commodity Yearbook.*

United Nations Statistics Division, New York, NY 10017, (800) 253-9646, Fax: (212) 963-4116, http://unstats.un.org; *Statistical Yearbook.*

CUBA - MOLASSES PRODUCTION

See CUBA - CROPS

CUBA - MONEY EXCHANGE RATES

See CUBA - FOREIGN EXCHANGE RATES

CUBA - MONEY SUPPLY

Economist Intelligence Unit, 111 West 57th Street, New York, NY 10019, (212) 554-0600, Fax: (212) 586-1181, www.eiu.com; *Cuba Country Report.*

Euromonitor International, Inc., 224 S. Michigan Avenue, Suite 1500, Chicago, IL 60604, (312) 922-1115, Fax: (312) 922-1157, www.euromonitor.com; *International Marketing Data and Statistics 2008.*

UCLA Latin American Institute, 10343 Bunche Hall, Box 951447, Los Angeles, CA 90095-1447, (310) 825-4571, Fax: (310) 206-6859, www.international.ucla.edu/lac; *Statistical Abstract of Latin America.*

The World Bank, 1818 H Street, NW, Washington, DC 20433, (202) 473-1000, Fax: (202) 477-6391, www.worldbank.org; *Cuba.*

CUBA - MORTALITY

Central Intelligence Agency, Office of Public Affairs, Washington, DC 20505, (703) 482-0623, Fax: (703) 482-1739, www.cia.gov; *The World Factbook.*

Euromonitor International, Inc., 224 S. Michigan Avenue, Suite 1500, Chicago, IL 60604, (312) 922-1115, Fax: (312) 922-1157, www.euromonitor.com; *International Marketing Data and Statistics 2008* and *The World Economic Factbook 2008.*

Taylor and Francis Group, An Informa Business, 2 Park Square, Milton Park, Abingdon, Oxford OX14 4RN, United Kingdom, (Dial from U.S. (212) 216-7800), (Fax from U.S. (212) 564-7854), www.tandf.co.uk; *The Europa World Year Book.*

UNICEF, 3 United Nations Plaza, New York, NY 10017, (800) 253-9646, Fax: (212) 887-7465, www.unicef.org; *The State of the World's Children 2008.*

United Nations Statistics Division, New York, NY 10017, (800) 253-9646, Fax: (212) 963-4116, http://unstats.un.org; *Demographic Yearbook; Human Development Report 2006; Statistical Yearbook;* and *World Statistics Pocketbook.*

The World Bank, 1818 H Street, NW, Washington, DC 20433, (202) 473-1000, Fax: (202) 477-6391, www.worldbank.org; *The World Bank Atlas 2003-2004.*

World Health Organization (WHO), Avenue Appia 20, 1211 Geneve 27, Switzerland, (Telephone in U.S. (212) 331-9081), www.who.int; The WHO Global Atlas of Infectious Diseases and *World Health Report 2006.*

CUBA - MOTION PICTURES

Palgrave Macmillan Ltd., Houndmills, Basingstoke, Hampshire, RG21 6XS, England, (Telephone in U.S. (888) 330-8477), (Fax in U.S. (800) 672-2054), www.palgrave.com; *The Statesman's Yearbook 2008.*

UNESCO Institute for Statistics, C.P. 6128 Succursale Centre-Ville, Montreal, Quebec, H3C 3J7 Canada, (Dial from U.S. (514) 343-6880), (Fax from U.S. (514) 343 6882), www.uis.unesco.org; *Statistical Tables.*

United Nations Statistics Division, New York, NY 10017, (800) 253-9646, Fax: (212) 963-4116, http://unstats.un.org; *Statistical Yearbook.*

CUBA - MOTOR VEHICLES

Taylor and Francis Group, An Informa Business, 2 Park Square, Milton Park, Abingdon, Oxford OX14 4RN, United Kingdom, (Dial from U.S. (212) 216-7800), (Fax from U.S. (212) 564-7854), www.tandf.co.uk; *The Europa World Year Book.*

United Nations Statistics Division, New York, NY 10017, (800) 253-9646, Fax: (212) 963-4116, http://unstats.un.org; *Statistical Yearbook.*

CUBA - MUSEUMS

M.E. Sharpe, 80 Business Park Drive, Armonk, NY 10504, (800) 541-6563, Fax: (914) 273-2106, www.mesharpe.com; *The Illustrated Book of World Rankings.*

UNESCO Institute for Statistics, C.P. 6128 Succursale Centre-Ville, Montreal, Quebec, H3C 3J7 Canada, (Dial from U.S. (514) 343-6880), (Fax from U.S. (514) 343 6882), www.uis.unesco.org; *Statistical Tables.*

CUBA - NATIONAL INCOME

United Nations Statistics Division, New York, NY 10017, (800) 253-9646, Fax: (212) 963-4116, http://unstats.un.org; *Statistical Yearbook.*

CUBA - NATURAL GAS PRODUCTION

See CUBA - MINERAL INDUSTRIES

CUBA - NICKEL AND NICKEL ORE

See CUBA - MINERAL INDUSTRIES

CUBA - NUTRITION

United Nations Food and Agricultural Organization (FAO), Viale delle Terme di Caracalla, 00100 Rome, Italy, (Dial from U.S. (202) 653-2400), (Fax from U.S. (202) 653 5760), www.fao.org; *The State of Food and Agriculture (SOFA) 2006.*

CUBA - OLDER PEOPLE

M.E. Sharpe, 80 Business Park Drive, Armonk, NY 10504, (800) 541-6563, Fax: (914) 273-2106, www.mesharpe.com; *The Illustrated Book of World Rankings.*

CUBA - PAPER

See CUBA - FORESTS AND FORESTRY

CUBA - PEANUT PRODUCTION

See CUBA - CROPS

CUBA - PERIODICALS

UNESCO Institute for Statistics, C.P. 6128 Succursale Centre-Ville, Montreal, Quebec, H3C 3J7 Canada, (Dial from U.S. (514) 343-6880), (Fax from U.S. (514) 343 6882), www.uis.unesco.org; *Statistical Tables.*

CUBA - PESTICIDES

United Nations Food and Agricultural Organization (FAO), Viale delle Terme di Caracalla, 00100 Rome, Italy, (Dial from U.S. (202) 653-2400), (Fax from U.S. (202) 653 5760), www.fao.org; *The State of Food and Agriculture (SOFA) 2006.*

CUBA - PETROLEUM INDUSTRY AND TRADE

M.E. Sharpe, 80 Business Park Drive, Armonk, NY 10504, (800) 541-6563, Fax: (914) 273-2106, www.mesharpe.com; *The Illustrated Book of World Rankings.*

Organisation for Economic Cooperation and Development (OECD), 2 rue Andre Pascal, F-75775 Paris Cedex 16, France, (Telephone in U.S. (202) 785-6323), (Fax in U.S. (202) 785-0350), www.oecd.org; *World Energy Outlook 2007.*

Palgrave Macmillan Ltd., Houndmills, Basingstoke, Hampshire, RG21 6XS, England, (Telephone in U.S. (888) 330-8477), (Fax in U.S. (800) 672-2054), www.palgrave.com; *The Statesman's Yearbook 2008.*

PennWell Corporation, 1421 South Sheridan Road, Tulsa, OK 74112, (918) 835-3161, www.pennwell.com; *International Petroleum Encyclopedia 2007.*

U.S. Department of Energy (DOE), Energy Information Administration (EIA), 1000 Independence Avenue, SW, Washington, DC 20585, (202) 586-8800, www.eia.doe.gov; *International Energy Annual 2004* and *International Energy Outlook 2006.*

United Nations Conference on Trade and Development (UNCTAD), DC2-1120, United Nations, New York, NY 10017, (212) 963-0027, www.unctad.org; *UNCTAD Commodity Yearbook.*

United Nations Food and Agricultural Organization (FAO), Viale delle Terme di Caracalla, 00100 Rome, Italy, (Dial from U.S. (202) 653-2400), (Fax from U.S. (202) 653 5760), www.fao.org; *The State of Food and Agriculture (SOFA) 2006.*

United Nations Statistics Division, New York, NY 10017, (800) 253-9646, Fax: (212) 963-4116, http://unstats.un.org; *Statistical Yearbook.*

CUBA - POLITICAL SCIENCE

Central Intelligence Agency, Office of Public Affairs, Washington, DC 20505, (703) 482-0623, Fax: (703) 482-1739, www.cia.gov; *The World Factbook.*

Palgrave Macmillan Ltd., Houndmills, Basingstoke, Hampshire, RG21 6XS, England, (Telephone in U.S. (888) 330-8477), (Fax in U.S. (800) 672-2054), www.palgrave.com; *The Statesman's Yearbook 2008.*

Taylor and Francis Group, An Informa Business, 2 Park Square, Milton Park, Abingdon, Oxford OX14 4RN, United Kingdom, (Dial from U.S. (212) 216-7800), (Fax from U.S. (212) 564-7854), www.tandf.co.uk; *The Europa World Year Book.*

UCLA Latin American Institute, 10343 Bunche Hall, Box 951447, Los Angeles, CA 90095-1447, (310) 825-4571, Fax: (310) 206-6859, www.international.ucla.edu/lac; *Statistical Abstract of Latin America.*

United Nations Statistics Division, New York, NY 10017, (800) 253-9646, Fax: (212) 963-4116, http://unstats.un.org; *National Accounts Statistics: Compendium of Income Distribution Statistics.*

CUBA - POPULATION

Central Intelligence Agency, Office of Public Affairs, Washington, DC 20505, (703) 482-0623, Fax: (703) 482-1739, www.cia.gov; *The World Factbook.*

Economist Intelligence Unit, 111 West 57th Street, New York, NY 10019, (212) 554-0600, Fax: (212) 586-1181, www.eiu.com; *Cuba Country Report.*

Euromonitor International, Inc., 224 S. Michigan Avenue, Suite 1500, Chicago, IL 60604, (312) 922-1115, Fax: (312) 922-1157, www.euromonitor.com; *International Marketing Data and Statistics 2008* and *The World Economic Factbook 2008.*

Eurostat, Batiment Jean Monnet, Rue Alcide de Gasperi, L-2920 Luxembourg, http://epp.eurostat.ec.europa.eu; *Demographic Indicators - Population by Age-Classes.*

International Labour Office, I.L.O. Publications, 4 route des Morillons, CH-1211 Geneva 22, Switzerland, (Telephone in U.S. (202) 653-7652), (Fax in U.S. (202) 653-7687), www.ilo.org; *Yearbook of Labour Statistics 2006.*

M.E. Sharpe, 80 Business Park Drive, Armonk, NY 10504, (800) 541-6563, Fax: (914) 273-2106, www.mesharpe.com; *The Illustrated Book of World Rankings.*

Palgrave Macmillan Ltd., Houndmills, Basingstoke, Hampshire, RG21 6XS, England, (Telephone in U.S. (888) 330-8477), (Fax in U.S. (800) 672-2054), www.palgrave.com; *The Statesman's Yearbook 2008.*

Taylor and Francis Group, An Informa Business, 2 Park Square, Milton Park, Abingdon, Oxford OX14 4RN, United Kingdom, (Dial from U.S. (212) 216-7800), (Fax from U.S. (212) 564-7854), www.tandf.co.uk; *The Europa World Year Book.*

U.S. Department of State (DOS), 2201 C Street NW, Washington, DC 20520, (202) 647-4000, www.state.gov; *World Military Expenditures and Arms Transfers (WMEAT).*

UCLA Latin American Institute, 10343 Bunche Hall, Box 951447, Los Angeles, CA 90095-1447, (310) 825-4571, Fax: (310) 206-6859, www.international.ucla.edu/lac; *Statistical Abstract of Latin America.*

UNESCO Institute for Statistics, C.P. 6128 Succursale Centre-Ville, Montreal, Quebec, H3C 3J7 Canada, (Dial from U.S. (514) 343-6880), (Fax from U.S. (514) 343 6882), www.uis.unesco.org; *Statistical Tables.*

United Nations Food and Agricultural Organization (FAO), Viale delle Terme di Caracalla, 00100 Rome, Italy, (Dial from U.S. (202) 653-2400), (Fax from U.S. (202) 653 5760), www.fao.org; *FAO Production Yearbook 2002.*

United Nations Statistics Division, New York, NY 10017, (800) 253-9646, Fax: (212) 963-4116, http://unstats.un.org; *Demographic Yearbook; Human Development Report 2006; Statistical Yearbook;* and *World Statistics Pocketbook.*

The World Bank, 1818 H Street, NW, Washington, DC 20433, (202) 473-1000, Fax: (202) 477-6391, www.worldbank.org; *Cuba* and *The World Bank Atlas 2003-2004.*

World Health Organization (WHO), Avenue Appia 20, 1211 Geneve 27, Switzerland, (Telephone in U.S. (212) 331-9081), www.who.int; *World Health Report 2006.*

CUBA - POPULATION DENSITY

Central Intelligence Agency, Office of Public Affairs, Washington, DC 20505, (703) 482-0623, Fax: (703) 482-1739, www.cia.gov; *The World Factbook.*

Euromonitor International, Inc., 224 S. Michigan Avenue, Suite 1500, Chicago, IL 60604, (312) 922-1115, Fax: (312) 922-1157, www.euromonitor.com; *International Marketing Data and Statistics 2008* and *The World Economic Factbook 2008.*

M.E. Sharpe, 80 Business Park Drive, Armonk, NY 10504, (800) 541-6563, Fax: (914) 273-2106, www.mesharpe.com; *The Illustrated Book of World Rankings.*

Palgrave Macmillan Ltd., Houndmills, Basingstoke, Hampshire, RG21 6XS, England, (Telephone in U.S. (888) 330-8477), (Fax in U.S. (800) 672-2054), www.palgrave.com; *The Statesman's Yearbook 2008.*

Taylor and Francis Group, An Informa Business, 2 Park Square, Milton Park, Abingdon, Oxford OX14 4RN, United Kingdom, (Dial from U.S. (212) 216-7800), (Fax from U.S. (212) 564-7854), www.tandf.co.uk; *The Europa World Year Book.*

UNESCO Institute for Statistics, C.P. 6128 Succursale Centre-Ville, Montreal, Quebec, H3C 3J7 Canada, (Dial from U.S. (514) 343-6880), (Fax from U.S. (514) 343 6882), www.uis.unesco.org; *Statistical Tables.*

United Nations Food and Agricultural Organization (FAO), Viale delle Terme di Caracalla, 00100 Rome, Italy, (Dial from U.S. (202) 653-2400), (Fax from U.S. (202) 653 5760), www.fao.org; *The State of Food and Agriculture (SOFA) 2006.*

United Nations Statistics Division, New York, NY 10017, (800) 253-9646, Fax: (212) 963-4116, http://unstats.un.org; *Statistical Yearbook.*

The World Bank, 1818 H Street, NW, Washington, DC 20433, (202) 473-1000, Fax: (202) 477-6391, www.worldbank.org; *Cuba.*

CUBA - POSTAL SERVICE

M.E. Sharpe, 80 Business Park Drive, Armonk, NY 10504, (800) 541-6563, Fax: (914) 273-2106, www.mesharpe.com; *The Illustrated Book of World Rankings.*

United Nations Statistics Division, New York, NY 10017, (800) 253-9646, Fax: (212) 963-4116, http://unstats.un.org; *Statistical Yearbook.*

CUBA - POWER RESOURCES

Euromonitor International, Inc., 224 S. Michigan Avenue, Suite 1500, Chicago, IL 60604, (312) 922-1115, Fax: (312) 922-1157, www.euromonitor.com; *International Marketing Data and Statistics 2008; The World Economic Factbook 2008;* and *World Marketing Data and Statistics.*

M.E. Sharpe, 80 Business Park Drive, Armonk, NY 10504, (800) 541-6563, Fax: (914) 273-2106, www.mesharpe.com; *The Illustrated Book of World Rankings.*

Organisation for Economic Cooperation and Development (OECD), 2 rue Andre Pascal, F-75775 Paris Cedex 16, France, (Telephone in U.S. (202) 785-6323), (Fax in U.S. (202) 785-0350), www.oecd.org; *World Energy Outlook 2007.*

Palgrave Macmillan Ltd., Houndmills, Basingstoke, Hampshire, RG21 6XS, England, (Telephone in U.S. (888) 330-8477), (Fax in U.S. (800) 672-2054), www.palgrave.com; *The Statesman's Yearbook 2008.*

Platts, 2 Penn Plaza, 25th Floor, New York, NY 10121-2298, (212) 904-3070, www.platts.com; *Energy Economist.*

U.S. Department of Energy (DOE), Energy Information Administration (EIA), 1000 Independence Avenue, SW, Washington, DC 20585, (202) 586-8800, www.eia.doe.gov; *International Energy Annual 2004* and *International Energy Outlook 2006.*

UCLA Latin American Institute, 10343 Bunche Hall, Box 951447, Los Angeles, CA 90095-1447, (310) 825-4571, Fax: (310) 206-6859, www.international.ucla.edu/lac; *Statistical Abstract of Latin America.*

United Nations Food and Agricultural Organization (FAO), Viale delle Terme di Caracalla, 00100 Rome, Italy, (Dial from U.S. (202) 653-2400), (Fax from U.S. (202) 653 5760), www.fao.org; *The State of Food and Agriculture (SOFA) 2006.*

United Nations Statistics Division, New York, NY 10017, (800) 253-9646, Fax: (212) 963-4116, http://unstats.un.org; *Energy Statistics Yearbook 2003; Human Development Report 2006; Statistical Yearbook;* and *World Statistics Pocketbook.*

The World Bank, 1818 H Street, NW, Washington, DC 20433, (202) 473-1000, Fax: (202) 477-6391, www.worldbank.org; *The World Bank Atlas 2003-2004.*

CUBA - PRICES

Euromonitor International, Inc., 224 S. Michigan Avenue, Suite 1500, Chicago, IL 60604, (312) 922-1115, Fax: (312) 922-1157, www.euromonitor.com; *World Marketing Data and Statistics.*

International Labour Office, I.L.O. Publications, 4 route des Morillons, CH-1211 Geneva 22, Switzerland, (Telephone in U.S. (202) 653-7652), (Fax in U.S. (202) 653-7687), www.ilo.org; *Yearbook of Labour Statistics 2006.*

M.E. Sharpe, 80 Business Park Drive, Armonk, NY 10504, (800) 541-6563, Fax: (914) 273-2106, www.mesharpe.com; *The Illustrated Book of World Rankings.*

United Nations Food and Agricultural Organization (FAO), Viale delle Terme di Caracalla, 00100 Rome, Italy, (Dial from U.S. (202) 653-2400), (Fax from U.S. (202) 653 5760), www.fao.org; *FAO Production Yearbook 2002* and *The State of Food and Agriculture (SOFA) 2006.*

United Nations Statistics Division, New York, NY 10017, (800) 253-9646, Fax: (212) 963-4116, http://unstats.un.org; *Economic Survey of Latin America and the Caribbean 2004-2005.*

The World Bank, 1818 H Street, NW, Washington, DC 20433, (202) 473-1000, Fax: (202) 477-6391, www.worldbank.org; *Cuba.*

CUBA - PROFESSIONS

UCLA Latin American Institute, 10343 Bunche Hall, Box 951447, Los Angeles, CA 90095-1447, (310) 825-4571, Fax: (310) 206-6859, www.international.ucla.edu/lac; *Statistical Abstract of Latin America.*

CUBA - PUBLIC HEALTH

Euromonitor International, Inc., 224 S. Michigan Avenue, Suite 1500, Chicago, IL 60604, (312) 922-

1115, Fax: (312) 922-1157, www.euromonitor.com; *World Marketing Data and Statistics.*

M.E. Sharpe, 80 Business Park Drive, Armonk, NY 10504, (800) 541-6563, Fax: (914) 273-2106, www.mesharpe.com; *The Illustrated Book of World Rankings.*

Palgrave Macmillan Ltd., Houndmills, Basingstoke, Hampshire, RG21 6XS, England, (Telephone in U.S. (888) 330-8477), (Fax in U.S. (800) 672-2054), www.palgrave.com; *The Statesman's Yearbook 2008.*

UCLA Latin American Institute, 10343 Bunche Hall, Box 951447, Los Angeles, CA 90095-1447, (310) 825-4571, Fax: (310) 206-6859, www.international.ucla.edu/lac; *Statistical Abstract of Latin America.*

UNICEF, 3 United Nations Plaza, New York, NY 10017, (800) 253-9646, Fax: (212) 887-7465, www.unicef.org; *The State of the World's Children 2008.*

United Nations Statistics Division, New York, NY 10017, (800) 253-9646, Fax: (212) 963-4116, http://unstats.un.org; *Human Development Report 2006* and *Statistical Yearbook.*

The World Bank, 1818 H Street, NW, Washington, DC 20433, (202) 473-1000, Fax: (202) 477-6391, www.worldbank.org; *Cuba.*

World Health Organization (WHO), Avenue Appia 20, 1211 Geneve 27, Switzerland, (Telephone in U.S. (212) 331-9081), www.who.int; The WHO Global Atlas of Infectious Diseases and *World Health Report 2006.*

CUBA - PUBLIC UTILITIES

UCLA Latin American Institute, 10343 Bunche Hall, Box 951447, Los Angeles, CA 90095-1447, (310) 825-4571, Fax: (310) 206-6859, www.international.ucla.edu/lac; *Statistical Abstract of Latin America.*

CUBA - PUBLISHERS AND PUBLISHING

UNESCO Institute for Statistics, C.P. 6128 Succursale Centre-Ville, Montreal, Quebec, H3C 3J7 Canada, (Dial from U.S. (514) 343-6880), (Fax from U.S. (514) 343 6882), www.uis.unesco.org; *Statistical Tables.*

CUBA - RADIO - RECEIVERS AND RECEPTION

Palgrave Macmillan Ltd., Houndmills, Basingstoke, Hampshire, RG21 6XS, England, (Telephone in U.S. (888) 330-8477), (Fax in U.S. (800) 672-2054), www.palgrave.com; *The Statesman's Yearbook 2008.*

United Nations Statistics Division, New York, NY 10017, (800) 253-9646, Fax: (212) 963-4116, http://unstats.un.org; *Statistical Yearbook.*

CUBA - RAILROADS

Jane's Information Group, 110 North Royal Street, Suite 200, Alexandria, VA 22314, (703) 683-3700, Fax: (800) 836-0297, www.janes.com; *Jane's World Railways.*

Palgrave Macmillan Ltd., Houndmills, Basingstoke, Hampshire, RG21 6XS, England, (Telephone in U.S. (888) 330-8477), (Fax in U.S. (800) 672-2054), www.palgrave.com; *The Statesman's Yearbook 2008.*

Taylor and Francis Group, An Informa Business, 2 Park Square, Milton Park, Abingdon, Oxford OX14 4RN, United Kingdom, (Dial from U.S. (212) 216-7800), (Fax from U.S. (212) 564-7854), www.tandf.co.uk; *The Europa World Year Book.*

United Nations Statistics Division, New York, NY 10017, (800) 253-9646, Fax: (212) 963-4116, http://unstats.un.org; *Statistical Yearbook.*

CUBA - RANCHING

UCLA Latin American Institute, 10343 Bunche Hall, Box 951447, Los Angeles, CA 90095-1447, (310) 825-4571, Fax: (310) 206-6859, www.international.ucla.edu/lac; *Statistical Abstract of Latin America.*

CUBA - RELIGION

Central Intelligence Agency, Office of Public Affairs, Washington, DC 20505, (703) 482-0623, Fax: (703) 482-1739, www.cia.gov; *The World Factbook.*

M.E. Sharpe, 80 Business Park Drive, Armonk, NY 10504, (800) 541-6563, Fax: (914) 273-2106, www.mesharpe.com; *The Illustrated Book of World Rankings.*

Palgrave Macmillan Ltd., Houndmills, Basingstoke, Hampshire, RG21 6XS, England, (Telephone in U.S. (888) 330-8477), (Fax in U.S. (800) 672-2054), www.palgrave.com; *The Statesman's Yearbook 2008.*

UCLA Latin American Institute, 10343 Bunche Hall, Box 951447, Los Angeles, CA 90095-1447, (310) 825-4571, Fax: (310) 206-6859, www.international.ucla.edu/lac; *Statistical Abstract of Latin America.*

CUBA - RESERVES (ACCOUNTING)

Euromonitor International, Inc., 224 S. Michigan Avenue, Suite 1500, Chicago, IL 60604, (312) 922-1115, Fax: (312) 922-1157, www.euromonitor.com; *International Marketing Data and Statistics 2008.*

CUBA - RETAIL TRADE

Euromonitor International, Inc., 224 S. Michigan Avenue, Suite 1500, Chicago, IL 60604, (312) 922-1115, Fax: (312) 922-1157, www.euromonitor.com; *World Marketing Data and Statistics.*

United Nations Statistics Division, New York, NY 10017, (800) 253-9646, Fax: (212) 963-4116, http://unstats.un.org; *Statistical Yearbook.*

CUBA - RICE PRODUCTION

See CUBA - CROPS

CUBA - ROADS

Central Intelligence Agency, Office of Public Affairs, Washington, DC 20505, (703) 482-0623, Fax: (703) 482-1739, www.cia.gov; *The World Factbook.*

Palgrave Macmillan Ltd., Houndmills, Basingstoke, Hampshire, RG21 6XS, England, (Telephone in U.S. (888) 330-8477), (Fax in U.S. (800) 672-2054), www.palgrave.com; *The Statesman's Yearbook 2008.*

CUBA - RUBBER INDUSTRY AND TRADE

International Rubber Study Group (IRSG), 1st Floor, Heron House, 109/115 Wembley Hill Road, Wembley, Middlesex HA9 8DA, United Kingdom, www.rubberstudy.com; *Rubber Statistical Bulletin; Summary of World Rubber Statistics 2005; World Rubber Statistics Handbook (Volume 6, 1975-2001);* and *World Rubber Statistics Historic Handbook.*

M.E. Sharpe, 80 Business Park Drive, Armonk, NY 10504, (800) 541-6563, Fax: (914) 273-2106, www.mesharpe.com; *The Illustrated Book of World Rankings.*

CUBA - SALT PRODUCTION

See CUBA - MINERAL INDUSTRIES

CUBA - SHEEP

See CUBA - LIVESTOCK

CUBA - SHIPPING

Palgrave Macmillan Ltd., Houndmills, Basingstoke, Hampshire, RG21 6XS, England, (Telephone in U.S. (888) 330-8477), (Fax in U.S. (800) 672-2054), www.palgrave.com; *The Statesman's Yearbook 2008.*

Taylor and Francis Group, An Informa Business, 2 Park Square, Milton Park, Abingdon, Oxford OX14 4RN, United Kingdom, (Dial from U.S. (212) 216-7800), (Fax from U.S. (212) 564-7854), www.tandf.co.uk; *The Europa World Year Book.*

U.S. Department of Transportation (DOT), Maritime Administration (MARAD), West Building, Southeast Federal Center, 1200 New Jersey Avenue, SE, Washington, DC 20590, (800) 99-MARAD, www.marad.dot.gov; *World Merchant Fleet 2005.*

United Nations Statistics Division, New York, NY 10017, (800) 253-9646, Fax: (212) 963-4116, http://unstats.un.org; *Statistical Yearbook.*

CUBA - SILVER PRODUCTION

See CUBA - MINERAL INDUSTRIES

CUBA - SOCIAL ECOLOGY

M.E. Sharpe, 80 Business Park Drive, Armonk, NY 10504, (800) 541-6563, Fax: (914) 273-2106, www.mesharpe.com; *The Illustrated Book of World Rankings.*

UCLA Latin American Institute, 10343 Bunche Hall, Box 951447, Los Angeles, CA 90095-1447, (310) 825-4571, Fax: (310) 206-6859, www.international.ucla.edu/lac; *Statistical Abstract of Latin America.*

United Nations Statistics Division, New York, NY 10017, (800) 253-9646, Fax: (212) 963-4116, http://unstats.un.org; *World Statistics Pocketbook.*

CUBA - SOCIAL SECURITY

United Nations Statistics Division, New York, NY 10017, (800) 253-9646, Fax: (212) 963-4116, http://unstats.un.org; *National Accounts Statistics: Compendium of Income Distribution Statistics.*

CUBA - STEEL PRODUCTION

See CUBA - MINERAL INDUSTRIES

CUBA - SUGAR PRODUCTION

See CUBA - CROPS

CUBA - TELEPHONE

International Telecommunication Union (ITU), Place des Nations, 1211 Geneva 20, Switzerland, www.itu.int; World Telecommunication Indicators Database.

Palgrave Macmillan Ltd., Houndmills, Basingstoke, Hampshire, RG21 6XS, England, (Telephone in U.S. (888) 330-8477), (Fax in U.S. (800) 672-2054), www.palgrave.com; *The Statesman's Yearbook 2008.*

Taylor and Francis Group, An Informa Business, 2 Park Square, Milton Park, Abingdon, Oxford OX14 4RN, United Kingdom, (Dial from U.S. (212) 216-7800), (Fax from U.S. (212) 564-7854), www.tandf.co.uk; *The Europa World Year Book.*

United Nations Statistics Division, New York, NY 10017, (800) 253-9646, Fax: (212) 963-4116, http://unstats.un.org; *Statistical Yearbook* and *World Statistics Pocketbook.*

CUBA - TEXTILE INDUSTRY

M.E. Sharpe, 80 Business Park Drive, Armonk, NY 10504, (800) 541-6563, Fax: (914) 273-2106, www.mesharpe.com; *The Illustrated Book of World Rankings.*

Palgrave Macmillan Ltd., Houndmills, Basingstoke, Hampshire, RG21 6XS, England, (Telephone in U.S. (888) 330-8477), (Fax in U.S. (800) 672-2054), www.palgrave.com; *The Statesman's Yearbook 2008.*

United Nations Conference on Trade and Development (UNCTAD), DC2-1120, United Nations, New York, NY 10017, (212) 963-0027, www.unctad.org; *UNCTAD Commodity Yearbook.*

United Nations Statistics Division, New York, NY 10017, (800) 253-9646, Fax: (212) 963-4116, http://unstats.un.org; *Statistical Yearbook.*

CUBA - TIN PRODUCTION

See CUBA - MINERAL INDUSTRIES

CUBA - TIRE INDUSTRY

United Nations Statistics Division, New York, NY 10017, (800) 253-9646, Fax: (212) 963-4116, http://unstats.un.org; *Statistical Yearbook.*

CUBA - TOBACCO INDUSTRY

Foreign Agricultural Service (FAS), U.S. Department of Agriculture (USDA), 1400 Independence Avenue, SW, Washington, DC 20250, (202) 720-3935, www.fas.usda.gov; *Tobacco: World Markets and Trade.*

M.E. Sharpe, 80 Business Park Drive, Armonk, NY 10504, (800) 541-6563, Fax: (914) 273-2106, www.mesharpe.com; *The Illustrated Book of World Rankings.*

United Nations Statistics Division, New York, NY 10017, (800) 253-9646, Fax: (212) 963-4116, http://unstats.un.org; *Statistical Yearbook.*

CUBA - TOURISM

Euromonitor International, Inc., 224 S. Michigan Avenue, Suite 1500, Chicago, IL 60604, (312) 922-1115, Fax: (312) 922-1157, www.euromonitor.com; *The World Economic Factbook 2008* and *World Marketing Data and Statistics.*

M.E. Sharpe, 80 Business Park Drive, Armonk, NY 10504, (800) 541-6563, Fax: (914) 273-2106, www.mesharpe.com; *The Illustrated Book of World Rankings.*

Palgrave Macmillan Ltd., Houndmills, Basingstoke, Hampshire, RG21 6XS, England, (Telephone in U.S. (888) 330-8477), (Fax in U.S. (800) 672-2054), www.palgrave.com; *The Statesman's Yearbook 2008.*

Taylor and Francis Group, An Informa Business, 2 Park Square, Milton Park, Abingdon, Oxford OX14 4RN, United Kingdom, (Dial from U.S. (212) 216-7800), (Fax from U.S. (212) 564-7854), www.tandf.co.uk; *The Europa World Year Book.*

UCLA Latin American Institute, 10343 Bunche Hall, Box 951447, Los Angeles, CA 90095-1447, (310) 825-4571, Fax: (310) 206-6859, www.international.ucla.edu/lac; *Statistical Abstract of Latin America.*

United Nations World Tourism Organization (UNWTO), Capitan Haya 42, 28020 Madrid, Spain, www.world-tourism.org; *Yearbook of Tourism Statistics.*

The World Bank, 1818 H Street, NW, Washington, DC 20433, (202) 473-1000, Fax: (202) 477-6391, www.worldbank.org; *Cuba.*

CUBA - TRADE

See CUBA - INTERNATIONAL TRADE

CUBA - TRANSPORTATION

Central Intelligence Agency, Office of Public Affairs, Washington, DC 20505, (703) 482-0623, Fax: (703) 482-1739, www.cia.gov; *The World Factbook.*

Euromonitor International, Inc., 224 S. Michigan Avenue, Suite 1500, Chicago, IL 60604, (312) 922-1115, Fax: (312) 922-1157, www.euromonitor.com; *International Marketing Data and Statistics 2008.*

CUBA - UNEMPLOYMENT

Central Intelligence Agency, Office of Public Affairs, Washington, DC 20505, (703) 482-0623, Fax: (703) 482-1739, www.cia.gov; *The World Factbook.*

Euromonitor International, Inc., 224 S. Michigan Avenue, Suite 1500, Chicago, IL 60604, (312) 922-1115, Fax: (312) 922-1157, www.euromonitor.com; *International Marketing Data and Statistics 2008.*

International Labour Office, I.L.O. Publications, 4 route des Morillons, CH-1211 Geneva 22, Switzerland, (Telephone in U.S. (202) 653-7652), (Fax in U.S. (202) 653-7687), www.ilo.org; *Yearbook of Labour Statistics 2006.*

UCLA Latin American Institute, 10343 Bunche Hall, Box 951447, Los Angeles, CA 90095-1447, (310) 825-4571, Fax: (310) 206-6859, www.international.ucla.edu/lac; *Statistical Abstract of Latin America.*

United Nations Statistics Division, New York, NY 10017, (800) 253-9646, Fax: (212) 963-4116, http://unstats.un.org; *Statistical Yearbook.*

CUBA - VITAL STATISTICS

Euromonitor International, Inc., 224 S. Michigan Avenue, Suite 1500, Chicago, IL 60604, (312) 922-1115, Fax: (312) 922-1157, www.euromonitor.com; *International Marketing Data and Statistics 2008.*

La Oficina Nacional de Estadisticas, Paseo No. 60 e/ 3ra y 5ta, Vedado, Plaza de la Revolucion, Ciudad de La Habana, Cuba, CP 10400, www.one.cu; *Anuario Demografico 2006* and *Indicadores sociales y demograficos de Cuba por territorios.*

World Health Organization (WHO), Avenue Appia 20, 1211 Geneve 27, Switzerland, (Telephone in U.S. (212) 331-9081), www.who.int; *World Health Report 2006.*

CUBA - WAGES

International Labour Office, I.L.O. Publications, 4 route des Morillons, CH-1211 Geneva 22, Switzerland, (Telephone in U.S. (202) 653-7652), (Fax in U.S. (202) 653-7687), www.ilo.org; *Yearbook of Labour Statistics 2006.*

UCLA Latin American Institute, 10343 Bunche Hall, Box 951447, Los Angeles, CA 90095-1447, (310) 825-4571, Fax: (310) 206-6859, www.international.ucla.edu/lac; *Statistical Abstract of Latin America.*

United Nations Statistics Division, New York, NY 10017, (800) 253-9646, Fax: (212) 963-4116, http://unstats.un.org; *Statistical Yearbook.*

The World Bank, 1818 H Street, NW, Washington, DC 20433, (202) 473-1000, Fax: (202) 477-6391, www.worldbank.org; *Cuba.*

CUBA - WHEAT PRODUCTION

See CUBA - CROPS

CUBA - WHOLESALE TRADE

United Nations Statistics Division, New York, NY 10017, (800) 253-9646, Fax: (212) 963-4116, http://unstats.un.org; *Statistical Yearbook.*

CUBA - WINE PRODUCTION

See CUBA - BEVERAGE INDUSTRY

CUBA - WOOL PRODUCTION

See CUBA - TEXTILE INDUSTRY

CUBA - YARN PRODUCTION

See CUBA - TEXTILE INDUSTRY

CUBAN POPULATION

See also HISPANIC ORIGIN POPULATION

Population Reference Bureau, 1875 Connecticut Avenue, NW, Suite 520, Washington, DC, 20009-5728, (800) 877-9881, Fax: (202) 328-3937, www.prb.org; *The American People Series.*

RAND Corporation, 1776 Main Street, PO Box 2138, Santa Monica, CA 90407-2138, (310) 393-0411, www.rand.org; *Asthma Mortality in U.S. Hispanics of Mexican, Puerto Rican, and Cuban Heritage, 1990-1995.*

U.S. Census Bureau, 4700 Silver Hill Road, Washington DC 20233-0001, (301) 763-3030, www.census.gov; unpublished data.

U.S. Census Bureau, Population Division, 4700 Silver Hill Road, Washington DC 20233-0001, (301) 763-3030, www.census.gov/population/www/; *Census 2000 Profiles of General Demographic Characteristics.*

CUBAN POPULATION - EDUCATIONAL ATTAINMENT

U.S. Census Bureau, 4700 Silver Hill Road, Washington DC 20233-0001, (301) 763-3030, www.census.gov; unpublished data.

U.S. Census Bureau, Housing and Household Economics Statistics Division, 4700 Silver Hill Road, Washington DC 20233-0001, (301) 763-3030, www.census.gov/hhes/www; Decennial Census of Population and Housing (web app).

U.S. Census Bureau, Population Division, 4700 Silver Hill Road, Washington DC 20233-0001, (301) 763-3030, www.census.gov/population/www/; *Current Population Reports.*

CUBAN POPULATION - LABOR FORCE

U.S. Bureau of Labor Statistics (BLS), Postal Square Building, 2 Massachusetts Avenue, NE, Washington, DC 20212-0001, (202) 691-5200, Fax: (202) 691-6325, www.bls.gov; *Employment and Earnings (EE).*

CUCUMBERS

Economic Research Service (ERS), U.S. Department of Agriculture (USDA), 1800 M Street, NW, Washington, DC 20036-5831, (202) 694-5050, Fax: (202) 694-5689, www.ers.usda.gov; *Agricultural Outlook; Agricultural Statistics;* and *Food CPI, Prices, and Expenditures.*

National Agricultural Statistics Service (NASS), U.S. Department of Agriculture (USDA), 1400 Independence Avenue, SW, Washington, DC 20250, (800) 727-9540, Fax: (202) 690-2090, www.nass.usda.gov; *Vegetables: 2004 Annual Summary.*

CURRENCY - FOREIGN EXCHANGE RATE

International Monetary Fund (IMF), 700 Nineteenth Street, NW, Washington, DC 20431, (202) 623-7000, Fax: (202) 623-4661, www.imf.org; *International Financial Statistics Yearbook 2007.*

International Trade Administration (ITA), U.S. Department of Commerce (DOC), 1401 Constitution Avenue, NW, Washington, DC 20230, (800) USA-TRAD(E), Fax: (202) 482-4473, www.ita.doc.gov; unpublished data.

CURRENCY - PERSONAL SAVING COMPONENT

Bureau of Economic Analysis (BEA), U.S. Department of Commerce (DOC), 1441 L Street NW, Washington, DC 20230, (202) 606-9900, www.bea.gov; *2007 Annual Revision of the National Income and Product Accounts (NIPA)* and *Survey of Current Business (SCB).*

CURRENCY - SUPPLY

Board of Governors of the Federal Reserve System, Constitution Avenue, NW, Washington, DC 20551, (202) 452-3000, www.federalreserve.gov; *Federal Reserve Board Statistical Release; Federal Reserve Bulletin;* and *Money Stock Measures.*

CUSTOMS

The Office of Management and Budget (OMB), 725 17th Street, NW, Washington, DC 20503, (202) 395-3080, Fax: (202) 395-3888, www.whitehouse.gov/omb; *Historical Tables.*

U.S. Customs and Border Protection (CBP), U.S. Department of Homeland Security (DHS), 1300 Pennsylvania Avenue, NW Washington, DC 20004-3002, (202) 354-1000, www.cbp.gov; *National Workload Statistics.*

CYCLONES

National Climatic Data Center (NCDC), National Oceanic and Atmospheric Administration (NOAA), Federal Building, 151 Patton Avenue, Asheville, NC 28801-5001, (828) 271-4800, Fax: (828) 271-4876, www.ncdc.noaa.gov; *Storm Data 2006.*

CYPRUS - NATIONAL STATISTICAL OFFICE

Statistical Service of the Republic of Cyprus (CYSTAT), Michalakis Karaolis Street, 1444 Nicosia, Cyprus, www.mof.gov.cy/cystat; National Data Center.

CYPRUS - PRIMARY STATISTICS SOURCES

Eurostat, Batiment Jean Monnet, Rue Alcide de Gasperi, L-2920 Luxembourg, http://epp.eurostat.ec.europa.eu; *Pocketbook on Candidate and Potential Candidate Countries.*

CYPRUS - ABORTION

United Nations Statistics Division, New York, NY 10017, (800) 253-9646, Fax: (212) 963-4116, http://unstats.un.org; *Trends in Europe and North America: The Statistical Yearbook of the ECE 2005.*

CYPRUS - AGRICULTURAL MACHINERY

United Nations Statistics Division, New York, NY 10017, (800) 253-9646, Fax: (212) 963-4116, http://unstats.un.org; *Statistical Yearbook.*

CYPRUS - AGRICULTURE

Economist Intelligence Unit, 111 West 57th Street, New York, NY 10019, (212) 554-0600, Fax: (212) 586-1181, www.eiu.com; *Cyprus Country Report.*

Euromonitor International, Inc., 224 S. Michigan Avenue, Suite 1500, Chicago, IL 60604, (312) 922-1115, Fax: (312) 922-1157, www.euromonitor.com; *World Marketing Data and Statistics.*

Eurostat, Batiment Jean Monnet, Rue Alcide de Gasperi, L-2920 Luxembourg, http://epp.eurostat.ec.europa.eu; *EU Agricultural Prices in 2007.*

M.E. Sharpe, 80 Business Park Drive, Armonk, NY 10504, (800) 541-6563, Fax: (914) 273-2106, www.mesharpe.com; *The Illustrated Book of World Rankings.*

Palgrave Macmillan Ltd., Houndmills, Basingstoke, Hampshire, RG21 6XS, England, (Telephone in U.S. (888) 330-8477), (Fax in U.S. (800) 672-2054), www.palgrave.com; *The Statesman's Yearbook 2008.*

Taylor and Francis Group, An Informa Business, 2 Park Square, Milton Park, Abingdon, Oxford OX14 4RN, United Kingdom, (Dial from U.S. (212) 216-7800), (Fax from U.S. (212) 564-7854), www.tandf.co.uk; *The Europa World Year Book.*

United Nations Conference on Trade and Development (UNCTAD), DC2-1120, United Nations, New York, NY 10017, (212) 963-0027, www.unctad.org; *UNCTAD Commodity Yearbook.*

United Nations Food and Agricultural Organization (FAO), Viale delle Terme di Caracalla, 00100 Rome, Italy, (Dial from U.S. (202) 653-2400), (Fax from U.S. (202) 653 5760), www.fao.org; AQUASTAT; *FAO Production Yearbook 2002; FAO Trade Yearbook;* and *The State of Food and Agriculture (SOFA) 2006.*

United Nations Statistics Division, New York, NY 10017, (800) 253-9646, Fax: (212) 963-4116, http://unstats.un.org; *Statistical Yearbook.*

The World Bank, 1818 H Street, NW, Washington, DC 20433, (202) 473-1000, Fax: (202) 477-6391, www.worldbank.org; *Cyprus* and *World Development Indicators (WDI) 2008.*

CYPRUS - AIRLINES

Eurostat, Batiment Jean Monnet, Rue Alcide de Gasperi, L-2920 Luxembourg, http://epp.eurostat.ec.europa.eu; *Regional Passenger and Freight Air Transport in Europe in 2006.*

International Civil Aviation Organization (ICAO), External Relations and Public Information Office (EPO), 999 University Street, Montreal, Quebec H3C 5H7, Canada, (Dial from U.S. (514) 954-8219), (Fax from U.S. (514) 954-6077), www.icao.int; *Civil Aviation Statistics of the World.*

M.E. Sharpe, 80 Business Park Drive, Armonk, NY 10504, (800) 541-6563, Fax: (914) 273-2106, www.mesharpe.com; *The Illustrated Book of World Rankings.*

Palgrave Macmillan Ltd., Houndmills, Basingstoke, Hampshire, RG21 6XS, England, (Telephone in U.S. (888) 330-8477), (Fax in U.S. (800) 672-2054), www.palgrave.com; *The Statesman's Yearbook 2008.*

Taylor and Francis Group, An Informa Business, 2 Park Square, Milton Park, Abingdon, Oxford OX14 4RN, United Kingdom, (Dial from U.S. (212) 216-7800), (Fax from U.S. (212) 564-7854), www.tandf.co.uk; *The Europa World Year Book.*

United Nations Statistics Division, New York, NY 10017, (800) 253-9646, Fax: (212) 963-4116, http://unstats.un.org; *Statistical Yearbook.*

CYPRUS - AIRPORTS

Central Intelligence Agency, Office of Public Affairs, Washington, DC 20505, (703) 482-0623, Fax: (703) 482-1739, www.cia.gov; *The World Factbook.*

CYPRUS - ALMOND PRODUCTION

See CYPRUS - CROPS

CYPRUS - ALUMINUM PRODUCTION

See CYPRUS - MINERAL INDUSTRIES

CYPRUS - ARMED FORCES

Central Intelligence Agency, Office of Public Affairs, Washington, DC 20505, (703) 482-0623, Fax: (703) 482-1739, www.cia.gov; *The World Factbook.*

Euromonitor International, Inc., 224 S. Michigan Avenue, Suite 1500, Chicago, IL 60604, (312) 922-1115, Fax: (312) 922-1157, www.euromonitor.com; *World Marketing Data and Statistics.*

International Institute for Strategic Studies (IISS), Arundel House, 13-15 Arundel Street, Temple Place, London WC2R 3DX, England, www.iiss.org; *The Military Balance 2007.*

International Monetary Fund (IMF), 700 Nineteenth Street, NW, Washington, DC 20431, (202) 623-7000, Fax: (202) 623-4661, www.imf.org; *Government Finance Statistics Yearbook (2008 Edition).*

Palgrave Macmillan Ltd., Houndmills, Basingstoke, Hampshire, RG21 6XS, England, (Telephone in U.S. (888) 330-8477), (Fax in U.S. (800) 672-2054), www.palgrave.com; *The Statesman's Yearbook 2008.*

U.S. Department of State (DOS), 2201 C Street NW, Washington, DC 20520, (202) 647-4000, www.state.gov; *World Military Expenditures and Arms Transfers (WMEAT).*

United Nations Statistics Division, New York, NY 10017, (800) 253-9646, Fax: (212) 963-4116, http://unstats.un.org; *Human Development Report 2006.*

CYPRUS - ARTICHOKE PRODUCTION

See CYPRUS - CROPS

CYPRUS - BALANCE OF PAYMENTS

International Monetary Fund (IMF), 700 Nineteenth Street, NW, Washington, DC 20431, (202) 623-7000, Fax: (202) 623-4661, www.imf.org; *Balance of Payments Statistics Newsletter* and *Balance of Payments Statistics Yearbook 2007.*

Taylor and Francis Group, An Informa Business, 2 Park Square, Milton Park, Abingdon, Oxford OX14 4RN, United Kingdom, (Dial from U.S. (212) 216-7800), (Fax from U.S. (212) 564-7854), www.tandf.co.uk; *The Europa World Year Book.*

United Nations Conference on Trade and Development (UNCTAD), DC2-1120, United Nations, New York, NY 10017, (212) 963-0027, www.unctad.org; *Handbook of Statistics 2005.*

The World Bank, 1818 H Street, NW, Washington, DC 20433, (202) 473-1000, Fax: (202) 477-6391, www.worldbank.org; *Cyprus* and *World Development Indicators (WDI) 2008.*

CYPRUS - BANKS AND BANKING

Euromonitor International, Inc., 224 S. Michigan Avenue, Suite 1500, Chicago, IL 60604, (312) 922-1115, Fax: (312) 922-1157, www.euromonitor.com; *World Marketing Data and Statistics.*

European Union, Delegation of the European Commission to the United States, 2300 M Street, NW, Washington, DC 20037, (202) 862-9500, Fax: (202) 429-1766, www.eurunion.org; *The EU Economy, 2007 Review: Moving Europe's Productivity Frontier.*

International Monetary Fund (IMF), 700 Nineteenth Street, NW, Washington, DC 20431, (202) 623-7000, Fax: (202) 623-4661, www.imf.org; *Government Finance Statistics Yearbook (2008 Edition)* and *International Financial Statistics Yearbook 2007.*

M.E. Sharpe, 80 Business Park Drive, Armonk, NY 10504, (800) 541-6563, Fax: (914) 273-2106, www.mesharpe.com; *The Illustrated Book of World Rankings.*

Palgrave Macmillan Ltd., Houndmills, Basingstoke, Hampshire, RG21 6XS, England, (Telephone in U.S. (888) 330-8477), (Fax in U.S. (800) 672-2054), www.palgrave.com; *The Statesman's Yearbook 2008.*

Taylor and Francis Group, An Informa Business, 2 Park Square, Milton Park, Abingdon, Oxford OX14 4RN, United Kingdom, (Dial from U.S. (212) 216-7800), (Fax from U.S. (212) 564-7854), www.tandf.co.uk; *The Europa World Year Book.*

CYPRUS - BARLEY PRODUCTION

See CYPRUS - CROPS

CYPRUS - BEVERAGE INDUSTRY

International Monetary Fund (IMF), 700 Nineteenth Street, NW, Washington, DC 20431, (202) 623-7000, Fax: (202) 623-4661, www.imf.org; *International Financial Statistics Yearbook 2007.*

M.E. Sharpe, 80 Business Park Drive, Armonk, NY 10504, (800) 541-6563, Fax: (914) 273-2106, www.mesharpe.com; *The Illustrated Book of World Rankings.*

United Nations Statistics Division, New York, NY 10017, (800) 253-9646, Fax: (212) 963-4116, http://unstats.un.org; *Statistical Yearbook.*

CYPRUS - BONDS

International Monetary Fund (IMF), 700 Nineteenth Street, NW, Washington, DC 20431, (202) 623-7000, Fax: (202) 623-4661, www.imf.org; *Government Finance Statistics Yearbook (2008 Edition).*

CYPRUS - BROADCASTING

Central Intelligence Agency, Office of Public Affairs, Washington, DC 20505, (703) 482-0623, Fax: (703) 482-1739, www.cia.gov; *The World Factbook.*

Euromonitor International, Inc., 224 S. Michigan Avenue, Suite 1500, Chicago, IL 60604, (312) 922-1115, Fax: (312) 922-1157, www.euromonitor.com; *World Marketing Data and Statistics.*

Palgrave Macmillan Ltd., Houndmills, Basingstoke, Hampshire, RG21 6XS, England, (Telephone in U.S. (888) 330-8477), (Fax in U.S. (800) 672-2054), www.palgrave.com; *The Statesman's Yearbook 2008.*

UNESCO Institute for Statistics, C.P. 6128 Succursale Centre-Ville, Montreal, Quebec, H3C 3J7 Canada, (Dial from U.S. (514) 343-6880), (Fax from U.S. (514) 343 6882), www.uis.unesco.org; *Statistical Tables.*

United Nations Statistics Division, New York, NY 10017, (800) 253-9646, Fax: (212) 963-4116, http://unstats.un.org; *Trends in Europe and North America: The Statistical Yearbook of the ECE 2005.*

WRTH Publications Limited, PO Box 290, Oxford OX2 7FT, UK, www.wrth.com; *World Radio TV Handbook 2007.*

CYPRUS - BUDGET

Central Intelligence Agency, Office of Public Affairs, Washington, DC 20505, (703) 482-0623, Fax: (703) 482-1739, www.cia.gov; *The World Factbook.*

Eurostat, Batiment Jean Monnet, Rue Alcide de Gasperi, L-2920 Luxembourg, http://epp.eurostat.ec.europa.eu; *Government Budgets.*

CYPRUS - CAPITAL LEVY

International Monetary Fund (IMF), 700 Nineteenth Street, NW, Washington, DC 20431, (202) 623-7000, Fax: (202) 623-4661, www.imf.org; *Government Finance Statistics Yearbook (2008 Edition).*

CYPRUS - CATTLE

See CYPRUS - LIVESTOCK

CYPRUS - CHICK PEA PRODUCTION

See CYPRUS - CROPS

CYPRUS - CHILDBIRTH - STATISTICS

Central Intelligence Agency, Office of Public Affairs, Washington, DC 20505, (703) 482-0623, Fax: (703) 482-1739, www.cia.gov; *The World Factbook.*

Euromonitor International, Inc., 224 S. Michigan Avenue, Suite 1500, Chicago, IL 60604, (312) 922-1115, Fax: (312) 922-1157, www.euromonitor.com; *The World Economic Factbook 2008.*

M.E. Sharpe, 80 Business Park Drive, Armonk, NY 10504, (800) 541-6563, Fax: (914) 273-2106, www.mesharpe.com; *The Illustrated Book of World Rankings.*

Taylor and Francis Group, An Informa Business, 2 Park Square, Milton Park, Abingdon, Oxford OX14 4RN, United Kingdom, (Dial from U.S. (212) 216-7800), (Fax from U.S. (212) 564-7854), www.tandf.co.uk; *The Europa World Year Book.*

United Nations Statistics Division, New York, NY 10017, (800) 253-9646, Fax: (212) 963-4116, http://unstats.un.org; *Demographic Yearbook* and *Statistical Yearbook.*

The World Bank, 1818 H Street, NW, Washington, DC 20433, (202) 473-1000, Fax: (202) 477-6391, www.worldbank.org; *World Development Indicators (WDI) 2008.*

World Health Organization (WHO), Avenue Appia 20, 1211 Geneve 27, Switzerland, (Telephone in U.S. (212) 331-9081), www.who.int; *World Health Report 2006.*

CYPRUS - CLIMATE

M.E. Sharpe, 80 Business Park Drive, Armonk, NY 10504, (800) 541-6563, Fax: (914) 273-2106, www.mesharpe.com; *The Illustrated Book of World Rankings.*

Palgrave Macmillan Ltd., Houndmills, Basingstoke, Hampshire, RG21 6XS, England, (Telephone in U.S. (888) 330-8477), (Fax in U.S. (800) 672-2054), www.palgrave.com; *The Statesman's Yearbook 2008.*

CYPRUS - COAL PRODUCTION

See CYPRUS - MINERAL INDUSTRIES

CYPRUS - COFFEE

See CYPRUS - CROPS

CYPRUS - COMMERCE

Palgrave Macmillan Ltd., Houndmills, Basingstoke, Hampshire, RG21 6XS, England, (Telephone in U.S. (888) 330-8477), (Fax in U.S. (800) 672-2054), www.palgrave.com; *The Statesman's Yearbook 2008.*

CYPRUS - COMMODITY EXCHANGES

Commodity Research Bureau, 330 South Wells Street, Suite 612, Chicago, IL 60606-7110, (800) 621-5271, Fax: (312) 939-4135, www.crbtrader.com; *2006 CRB Commodity Yearbook and CD.*

International Monetary Fund (IMF), 700 Nineteenth Street, NW, Washington, DC 20431, (202) 623-7000, Fax: (202) 623-4661, www.imf.org; *IMF Primary Commodity Prices.*

United Nations Food and Agricultural Organization (FAO), Viale delle Terme di Caracalla, 00100 Rome, Italy, (Dial from U.S. (202) 653-2400), (Fax from U.S. (202) 653 5760), www.fao.org; *The State of Food and Agriculture (SOFA) 2006.*

CYPRUS - COMMUNICATION AND TRAFFIC

United Nations Statistics Division, New York, NY 10017, (800) 253-9646, Fax: (212) 963-4116, http://unstats.un.org; *Statistical Yearbook.*

CYPRUS - CONSTRUCTION INDUSTRY

M.E. Sharpe, 80 Business Park Drive, Armonk, NY 10504, (800) 541-6563, Fax: (914) 273-2106, www.mesharpe.com; *The Illustrated Book of World Rankings.*

United Nations Statistics Division, New York, NY 10017, (800) 253-9646, Fax: (212) 963-4116, http://unstats.un.org; *Statistical Yearbook.*

CYPRUS - CONSUMER PRICE INDEXES

Taylor and Francis Group, An Informa Business, 2 Park Square, Milton Park, Abingdon, Oxford OX14 4RN, United Kingdom, (Dial from U.S. (212) 216-7800), (Fax from U.S. (212) 564-7854), www.tandf.co.uk; *The Europa World Year Book.*

United Nations Statistics Division, New York, NY 10017, (800) 253-9646, Fax: (212) 963-4116, http://unstats.un.org; *Statistical Yearbook* and *Trends in Europe and North America: The Statistical Yearbook of the ECE 2005.*

The World Bank, 1818 H Street, NW, Washington, DC 20433, (202) 473-1000, Fax: (202) 477-6391, www.worldbank.org; *Cyprus.*

CYPRUS - COPPER INDUSTRY AND TRADE

See CYPRUS - MINERAL INDUSTRIES

CYPRUS - CORN INDUSTRY

See CYPRUS - CROPS

CYPRUS - COST AND STANDARD OF LIVING

International Monetary Fund (IMF), 700 Nineteenth Street, NW, Washington, DC 20431, (202) 623-7000, Fax: (202) 623-4661, www.imf.org; *Government Finance Statistics Yearbook (2008 Edition).*

CYPRUS - COTTON

See CYPRUS - CROPS

CYPRUS - CRIME

Eurostat, Batiment Jean Monnet, Rue Alcide de Gasperi, L-2920 Luxembourg, http://epp.eurostat.ec.europa.eu; *Crime and Criminal Justice; General Government Expenditure and Revenue in the EU, 2006;* and *Study on Crime Victimisation.*

International Criminal Police Organization (INTERPOL), General Secretariat, 200 quai Charles de Gaulle, 69006 Lyon, France, www.interpol.int; *International Crime Statistics.*

United Nations Statistics Division, New York, NY 10017, (800) 253-9646, Fax: (212) 963-4116, http://unstats.un.org; *Trends in Europe and North America: The Statistical Yearbook of the ECE 2005.*

Yale University Press, PO Box 209040, New Haven, CT 06520-9040, (203) 432-0960, Fax: (203) 432-0948, http://yalepress.yale.edu/yupbooks; *Violence and Crime in Cross-National Perspective.*

CYPRUS - CROPS

Euromonitor International, Inc., 224 S. Michigan Avenue, Suite 1500, Chicago, IL 60604, (312) 922-1115, Fax: (312) 922-1157, www.euromonitor.com; *European Marketing Data and Statistics 2008.*

International Monetary Fund (IMF), 700 Nineteenth Street, NW, Washington, DC 20431, (202) 623-7000, Fax: (202) 623-4661, www.imf.org; *International Financial Statistics Yearbook 2007.*

M.E. Sharpe, 80 Business Park Drive, Armonk, NY 10504, (800) 541-6563, Fax: (914) 273-2106, www.mesharpe.com; *The Illustrated Book of World Rankings.*

Palgrave Macmillan Ltd., Houndmills, Basingstoke, Hampshire, RG21 6XS, England, (Telephone in U.S. (888) 330-8477), (Fax in U.S. (800) 672-2054), www.palgrave.com; *The Statesman's Yearbook 2008.*

Taylor and Francis Group, An Informa Business, 2 Park Square, Milton Park, Abingdon, Oxford OX14 4RN, United Kingdom, (Dial from U.S. (212) 216-7800), (Fax from U.S. (212) 564-7854), www.tandf.co.uk; *The Europa World Year Book.*

United Nations Conference on Trade and Development (UNCTAD), DC2-1120, United Nations, New York, NY 10017, (212) 963-0027, www.unctad.org; *UNCTAD Commodity Yearbook.*

United Nations Food and Agricultural Organization (FAO), Viale delle Terme di Caracalla, 00100 Rome, Italy, (Dial from U.S. (202) 653-2400), (Fax from U.S. (202) 653 5760), www.fao.org; *FAO Production Yearbook 2002* and *The State of Food and Agriculture (SOFA) 2006.*

United Nations Statistics Division, New York, NY 10017, (800) 253-9646, Fax: (212) 963-4116, http://unstats.un.org; *Statistical Yearbook.*

CYPRUS - CUSTOMS ADMINISTRATION

International Monetary Fund (IMF), 700 Nineteenth Street, NW, Washington, DC 20431, (202) 623-7000, Fax: (202) 623-4661, www.imf.org; *Government Finance Statistics Yearbook (2008 Edition).*

Palgrave Macmillan Ltd., Houndmills, Basingstoke, Hampshire, RG21 6XS, England, (Telephone in U.S. (888) 330-8477), (Fax in U.S. (800) 672-2054), www.palgrave.com; *The Statesman's Yearbook 2008.*

CYPRUS - DAIRY PROCESSING

M.E. Sharpe, 80 Business Park Drive, Armonk, NY 10504, (800) 541-6563, Fax: (914) 273-2106, www.mesharpe.com; *The Illustrated Book of World Rankings.*

Palgrave Macmillan Ltd., Houndmills, Basingstoke, Hampshire, RG21 6XS, England, (Telephone in U.S. (888) 330-8477), (Fax in U.S. (800) 672-2054), www.palgrave.com; *The Statesman's Yearbook 2008.*

United Nations Food and Agricultural Organization (FAO), Viale delle Terme di Caracalla, 00100 Rome, Italy, (Dial from U.S. (202) 653-2400), (Fax from U.S. (202) 653 5760), www.fao.org; *FAO Production Yearbook 2002* and *The State of Food and Agriculture (SOFA) 2006.*

United Nations Statistics Division, New York, NY 10017, (800) 253-9646, Fax: (212) 963-4116, http://unstats.un.org; *Statistical Yearbook.*

CYPRUS - DEATH RATES

See CYPRUS - MORTALITY

CYPRUS - DEBTS, EXTERNAL

International Monetary Fund (IMF), 700 Nineteenth Street, NW, Washington, DC 20431, (202) 623-7000, Fax: (202) 623-4661, www.imf.org; *Government Finance Statistics Yearbook (2008 Edition).*

Palgrave Macmillan Ltd., Houndmills, Basingstoke, Hampshire, RG21 6XS, England, (Telephone in U.S. (888) 330-8477), (Fax in U.S. (800) 672-2054), www.palgrave.com; *The Statesman's Yearbook 2008.*

The World Bank, 1818 H Street, NW, Washington, DC 20433, (202) 473-1000, Fax: (202) 477-6391, www.worldbank.org; *Global Development Finance 2007* and *World Development Indicators (WDI) 2008.*

CYPRUS - DEFENSE EXPENDITURES

See CYPRUS - ARMED FORCES

CYPRUS - DEMOGRAPHY

Euromonitor International, Inc., 224 S. Michigan Avenue, Suite 1500, Chicago, IL 60604, (312) 922-1115, Fax: (312) 922-1157, www.euromonitor.com; *The World Economic Factbook 2008* and *World Marketing Data and Statistics.*

Eurostat, Batiment Jean Monnet, Rue Alcide de Gasperi, L-2920 Luxembourg, http://epp.eurostat.ec.europa.eu; *Demographic Outlook - National Reports on the Demographic Developments in 2006.*

M.E. Sharpe, 80 Business Park Drive, Armonk, NY 10504, (800) 541-6563, Fax: (914) 273-2106, www.mesharpe.com; *The Illustrated Book of World Rankings.*

United Nations Statistics Division, New York, NY 10017, (800) 253-9646, Fax: (212) 963-4116, http://unstats.un.org; *Human Development Report 2006.*

The World Bank, 1818 H Street, NW, Washington, DC 20433, (202) 473-1000, Fax: (202) 477-6391, www.worldbank.org; *Cyprus.*

CYPRUS - DIAMONDS

See CYPRUS - MINERAL INDUSTRIES

CYPRUS - DISPOSABLE INCOME

M.E. Sharpe, 80 Business Park Drive, Armonk, NY 10504, (800) 541-6563, Fax: (914) 273-2106, www.mesharpe.com; *The Illustrated Book of World Rankings.*

United Nations Statistics Division, New York, NY 10017, (800) 253-9646, Fax: (212) 963-4116, http://unstats.un.org; *Statistical Yearbook.*

CYPRUS - DIVORCE

M.E. Sharpe, 80 Business Park Drive, Armonk, NY 10504, (800) 541-6563, Fax: (914) 273-2106, www.mesharpe.com; *The Illustrated Book of World Rankings.*

United Nations Statistics Division, New York, NY 10017, (800) 253-9646, Fax: (212) 963-4116, http://unstats.un.org; *Demographic Yearbook; Statistical Yearbook;* and *Trends in Europe and North America: The Statistical Yearbook of the ECE 2005.*

CYPRUS - ECONOMIC ASSISTANCE

United Nations Statistics Division, New York, NY 10017, (800) 253-9646, Fax: (212) 963-4116, http://unstats.un.org; *Statistical Yearbook.*

CYPRUS - ECONOMIC CONDITIONS

Center for International Business Education Research (CIBER), Columbia Business School and School of International and Public Affairs, Uris Hall, Room 212, 3022 Broadway, New York, NY 10027-6902, Mr. Joshua Safier, (212) 854-4750, Fax: (212) 222-9821, www.columbia.edu/cu/ciber/; Datastream International.

Central Intelligence Agency, Office of Public Affairs, Washington, DC 20505, (703) 482-0623, Fax: (703) 482-1739, www.cia.gov; *The World Factbook.*

DSI Data Service Information, Xantener Strasse 51a, D-47495 Rheinberg, Germany, www.dsidata.com; *Campus Solution.*

Dun and Bradstreet (DB) Corporation, 103 JFK Parkway, Short Hills, NJ 07078, (973) 921-5500, www.dnb.com; *Country Report.*

Economist Intelligence Unit, 111 West 57th Street, New York, NY 10019, (212) 554-0600, Fax: (212) 586-1181, www.eiu.com; *Cyprus Country Report.*

Euromonitor International, Inc., 224 S. Michigan Avenue, Suite 1500, Chicago, IL 60604, (312) 922-1115, Fax: (312) 922-1157, www.euromonitor.com; *European Marketing Data and Statistics 2008; The World Economic Factbook 2008;* and *World Marketing Data and Statistics.*

European Union, Delegation of the European Commission to the United States, 2300 M Street, NW, Washington, DC 20037, (202) 862-9500, Fax: (202) 429-1766, www.eurunion.org; *The EU Economy, 2007 Review: Moving Europe's Productivity Frontier.*

Eurostat, Batiment Jean Monnet, Rue Alcide de Gasperi, L-2920 Luxembourg, http://epp.eurostat.ec.europa.eu; *Consumers in Europe - Facts and Figures on Services of General Interest* and *EU Economic Data Pocketbook.*

International Monetary Fund (IMF), 700 Nineteenth Street, NW, Washington, DC 20431, (202) 623-7000, Fax: (202) 623-4661, www.imf.org; *World Economic Outlook Reports.*

M.E. Sharpe, 80 Business Park Drive, Armonk, NY 10504, (800) 541-6563, Fax: (914) 273-2106, www.mesharpe.com; *The Illustrated Book of World Rankings.*

Nomura Research Institute (NRI), 2 World Financial Center, Building B, 19th Fl., New York, NY 10281-1198, (212) 667-1670, www.nri.co.jp/english; *Asian Economic Outlook 2003-2004.*

Palgrave Macmillan Ltd., Houndmills, Basingstoke, Hampshire, RG21 6XS, England, (Telephone in U.S. (888) 330-8477), (Fax in U.S. (800) 672-2054), www.palgrave.com; *The Statesman's Yearbook 2008.*

Statistical Service of the Republic of Cyprus (CYSTAT), Michalakis Karaolis Street, 1444 Nicosia, Cyprus, www.mof.gov.cy/cystat; *Consolidated Accounts of Central Government.*

Taylor and Francis Group, An Informa Business, 2 Park Square, Milton Park, Abingdon, Oxford OX14 4RN, United Kingdom, (Dial from U.S. (212) 216-7800), (Fax from U.S. (212) 564-7854), www.tandf.co.uk; *The Europa World Year Book.*

United Nations Economic and Social Commission for Western Asia (ESCWA), PO Box 11-8575, Riad el-Solh Square, Beirut, Lebanon, www.escwa.un.org; *Annual Report 2006; Bulletin on Population and Vital Statistics in the ESCWA Region;* and *Survey of Economic and Social Developments in the ESCWA Region 2006-2007.*

United Nations Statistics Division, New York, NY 10017, (800) 253-9646, Fax: (212) 963-4116, http://unstats.un.org; *World Statistics Pocketbook.*

The World Bank, 1818 H Street, NW, Washington, DC 20433, (202) 473-1000, Fax: (202) 477-6391, www.worldbank.org; *Cyprus; Global Economic Monitor (GEM); Global Economic Prospects 2008;* and *The World Bank Atlas 2003-2004.*

CYPRUS - EDUCATION

Euromonitor International, Inc., 224 S. Michigan Avenue, Suite 1500, Chicago, IL 60604, (312) 922-1115, Fax: (312) 922-1157, www.euromonitor.com; *European Marketing Data and Statistics 2008* and *World Marketing Data and Statistics.*

European Union, Delegation of the European Commission to the United States, 2300 M Street, NW, Washington, DC 20037, (202) 862-9500, Fax: (202) 429-1766, www.eurunion.org; *Education across Europe 2003.*

Eurostat, Batiment Jean Monnet, Rue Alcide de Gasperi, L-2920 Luxembourg, http://epp.eurostat.ec.europa.eu; *Education, Science and Culture Statistics.*

International Monetary Fund (IMF), 700 Nineteenth Street, NW, Washington, DC 20431, (202) 623-7000, Fax: (202) 623-4661, www.imf.org; *Government Finance Statistics Yearbook (2008 Edition).*

M.E. Sharpe, 80 Business Park Drive, Armonk, NY 10504, (800) 541-6563, Fax: (914) 273-2106, www.mesharpe.com; *The Illustrated Book of World Rankings.*

Palgrave Macmillan Ltd., Houndmills, Basingstoke, Hampshire, RG21 6XS, England, (Telephone in U.S. (888) 330-8477), (Fax in U.S. (800) 672-2054), www.palgrave.com; *The Statesman's Yearbook 2008.*

UNESCO Institute for Statistics, C.P. 6128 Succursale Centre-Ville, Montreal, Quebec, H3C 3J7 Canada, (Dial from U.S. (514) 343-6880), (Fax from U.S. (514) 343 6882), www.uis.unesco.org; *Statistical Tables.*

United Nations Statistics Division, New York, NY 10017, (800) 253-9646, Fax: (212) 963-4116, http://unstats.un.org; *Human Development Report 2006* and *Trends in Europe and North America: The Statistical Yearbook of the ECE 2005.*

The World Bank, 1818 H Street, NW, Washington, DC 20433, (202) 473-1000, Fax: (202) 477-6391, www.worldbank.org; *Cyprus* and *World Development Indicators (WDI) 2008.*

CYPRUS - ELECTRICITY

Eurostat, Batiment Jean Monnet, Rue Alcide de Gasperi, L-2920 Luxembourg, http://epp.eurostat.ec.europa.eu; *Energy - Monthly Statistics* and *Panorama of Energy - 2007 Edition.*

M.E. Sharpe, 80 Business Park Drive, Armonk, NY 10504, (800) 541-6563, Fax: (914) 273-2106, www.mesharpe.com; *The Illustrated Book of World Rankings.*

Palgrave Macmillan Ltd., Houndmills, Basingstoke, Hampshire, RG21 6XS, England, (Telephone in U.S. (888) 330-8477), (Fax in U.S. (800) 672-2054), www.palgrave.com; *The Statesman's Yearbook 2008.*

Platts, 2 Penn Plaza, 25th Floor, New York, NY 10121-2298, (212) 904-3070, www.platts.com; *EU Energy* and *European Electricity Review 2004.*

U.S. Department of Energy (DOE), Energy Information Administration (EIA), 1000 Independence Avenue, SW, Washington, DC 20585, (202) 586-8800, www.eia.doe.gov; *International Energy Annual 2004* and *International Energy Outlook 2006.*

United Nations Statistics Division, New York, NY 10017, (800) 253-9646, Fax: (212) 963-4116, http://unstats.un.org; *Human Development Report 2006; Statistical Yearbook;* and *Trends in Europe and North America: The Statistical Yearbook of the ECE 2005.*

CYPRUS - EMPLOYMENT

Euromonitor International, Inc., 224 S. Michigan Avenue, Suite 1500, Chicago, IL 60604, (312) 922-1115, Fax: (312) 922-1157, www.euromonitor.com; *European Marketing Data and Statistics 2008.*

International Labour Office, I.L.O. Publications, 4 route des Morillons, CH-1211 Geneva 22, Switzerland, (Telephone in U.S. (202) 653-7652), (Fax in U.S. (202) 653-7687), www.ilo.org; *Yearbook of Labour Statistics 2006.*

M.E. Sharpe, 80 Business Park Drive, Armonk, NY 10504, (800) 541-6563, Fax: (914) 273-2106, www.mesharpe.com; *The Illustrated Book of World Rankings.*

United Nations Statistics Division, New York, NY 10017, (800) 253-9646, Fax: (212) 963-4116, http://unstats.un.org; *Statistical Yearbook* and *Trends in Europe and North America: The Statistical Yearbook of the ECE 2005.*

The World Bank, 1818 H Street, NW, Washington, DC 20433, (202) 473-1000, Fax: (202) 477-6391, www.worldbank.org; *Cyprus.*

CYPRUS - ENERGY INDUSTRIES

Eurostat, Batiment Jean Monnet, Rue Alcide de Gasperi, L-2920 Luxembourg, http://epp.eurostat.ec.europa.eu; *Energy - Monthly Statistics* and *Panorama of Energy - 2007 Edition.*

Platts, 2 Penn Plaza, 25th Floor, New York, NY 10121-2298, (212) 904-3070, www.platts.com; *EU Energy.*

CYPRUS - ENVIRONMENTAL CONDITIONS

DSI Data Service Information, Xantener Strasse 51a, D-47495 Rheinberg, Germany, www.dsidata.com; *Campus Solution* and *DSI's Global Environmental Database.*

Economist Intelligence Unit, 111 West 57th Street, New York, NY 10019, (212) 554-0600, Fax: (212) 586-1181, www.eiu.com; *Cyprus Country Report.*

United Nations Statistics Division, New York, NY 10017, (800) 253-9646, Fax: (212) 963-4116, http://unstats.un.org; *Trends in Europe and North America: The Statistical Yearbook of the ECE 2005* and *World Statistics Pocketbook.*

CYPRUS - EXPENDITURES, PUBLIC

Eurostat, Batiment Jean Monnet, Rue Alcide de Gasperi, L-2920 Luxembourg, http://epp.eurostat.ec.europa.eu; *European Social Statistics - Social Protection Expenditure and Receipts - Data 1997-2005.*

CYPRUS - EXPORTS

Central Intelligence Agency, Office of Public Affairs, Washington, DC 20505, (703) 482-0623, Fax: (703) 482-1739, www.cia.gov; *The World Factbook.*

Economist Intelligence Unit, 111 West 57th Street, New York, NY 10019, (212) 554-0600, Fax: (212) 586-1181, www.eiu.com; *Cyprus Country Report.*

Euromonitor International, Inc., 224 S. Michigan Avenue, Suite 1500, Chicago, IL 60604, (312) 922-1115, Fax: (312) 922-1157, www.euromonitor.com; *The World Economic Factbook 2008.*

International Monetary Fund (IMF), 700 Nineteenth Street, NW, Washington, DC 20431, (202) 623-7000, Fax: (202) 623-4661, www.imf.org; *Direction of Trade Statistics Yearbook 2007* and *International Financial Statistics Yearbook 2007.*

Palgrave Macmillan Ltd., Houndmills, Basingstoke, Hampshire, RG21 6XS, England, (Telephone in U.S. (888) 330-8477), (Fax in U.S. (800) 672-2054), www.palgrave.com; *The Statesman's Yearbook 2008.*

Taylor and Francis Group, An Informa Business, 2 Park Square, Milton Park, Abingdon, Oxford OX14

4RN, United Kingdom, (Dial from U.S. (212) 216-7800), (Fax from U.S. (212) 564-7854), www.tandf.co.uk; *The Europa World Year Book.*

United Nations Conference on Trade and Development (UNCTAD), DC2-1120, United Nations, New York, NY 10017, (212) 963-0027, www.unctad.org; *Handbook of Statistics 2005.*

United Nations Food and Agricultural Organization (FAO), Viale delle Terme di Caracalla, 00100 Rome, Italy, (Dial from U.S. (202) 653-2400), (Fax from U.S. (202) 653 5760), www.fao.org; *The State of Food and Agriculture (SOFA) 2006.*

United Nations Statistics Division, New York, NY 10017, (800) 253-9646, Fax: (212) 963-4116, http://unstats.un.org; *Trends in Europe and North America: The Statistical Yearbook of the ECE 2005.*

The World Bank, 1818 H Street, NW, Washington, DC 20433, (202) 473-1000, Fax: (202) 477-6391, www.worldbank.org; *World Development Indicators (WDI) 2008.*

CYPRUS - FERTILITY, HUMAN

Central Intelligence Agency, Office of Public Affairs, Washington, DC 20505, (703) 482-0623, Fax: (703) 482-1739, www.cia.gov; *The World Factbook.*

M.E. Sharpe, 80 Business Park Drive, Armonk, NY 10504, (800) 541-6563, Fax: (914) 273-2106, www.mesharpe.com; *The Illustrated Book of World Rankings.*

United Nations Statistics Division, New York, NY 10017, (800) 253-9646, Fax: (212) 963-4116, http://unstats.un.org; *Human Development Report 2006* and *Trends in Europe and North America: The Statistical Yearbook of the ECE 2005.*

The World Bank, 1818 H Street, NW, Washington, DC 20433, (202) 473-1000, Fax: (202) 477-6391, www.worldbank.org; *The World Bank Atlas 2003-2004* and *World Development Indicators (WDI) 2008.*

CYPRUS - FERTILIZER INDUSTRY

United Nations Food and Agricultural Organization (FAO), Viale delle Terme di Caracalla, 00100 Rome, Italy, (Dial from U.S. (202) 653-2400), (Fax from U.S. (202) 653 5760), www.fao.org; *FAO Fertilizer Yearbook* and *The State of Food and Agriculture (SOFA) 2006.*

United Nations Statistics Division, New York, NY 10017, (800) 253-9646, Fax: (212) 963-4116, http://unstats.un.org; *Statistical Yearbook.*

CYPRUS - FETAL MORTALITY

See CYPRUS - MORTALITY

CYPRUS - FINANCE

United Nations Statistics Division, New York, NY 10017, (800) 253-9646, Fax: (212) 963-4116, http://unstats.un.org; *National Accounts Statistics: Compendium of Income Distribution Statistics* and *Statistical Yearbook.*

The World Bank, 1818 H Street, NW, Washington, DC 20433, (202) 473-1000, Fax: (202) 477-6391, www.worldbank.org; *Cyprus.*

CYPRUS - FINANCE, PUBLIC

Bernan Essential Government Publications, 4611-F Assembly Drive, Lanham MD, 20706-4391, (301) 459-2255, Fax: (800) 865-3450, www.bernan.com; *National Accounts Statistics.*

Economist Intelligence Unit, 111 West 57th Street, New York, NY 10019, (212) 554-0600, Fax: (212) 586-1181, www.eiu.com; *Cyprus Country Report.*

International Monetary Fund (IMF), 700 Nineteenth Street, NW, Washington, DC 20431, (202) 623-7000, Fax: (202) 623-4661, www.imf.org; *Government Finance Statistics Yearbook (2008 Edition); International Financial Statistics; International Financial Statistics Online Service;* and *International Financial Statistics Yearbook 2007.*

M.E. Sharpe, 80 Business Park Drive, Armonk, NY 10504, (800) 541-6563, Fax: (914) 273-2106, www.mesharpe.com; *The Illustrated Book of World Rankings.*

Palgrave Macmillan Ltd., Houndmills, Basingstoke, Hampshire, RG21 6XS, England, (Telephone in U.S. (888) 330-8477), (Fax in U.S. (800) 672-2054), www.palgrave.com; *The Statesman's Yearbook 2008.*

Taylor and Francis Group, An Informa Business, 2 Park Square, Milton Park, Abingdon, Oxford OX14 4RN, United Kingdom, (Dial from U.S. (212) 216-7800), (Fax from U.S. (212) 564-7854), www.tandf.co.uk; *The Europa World Year Book.*

The World Bank, 1818 H Street, NW, Washington, DC 20433, (202) 473-1000, Fax: (202) 477-6391, www.worldbank.org; *Cyprus.*

CYPRUS - FISHERIES

Euromonitor International, Inc., 224 S. Michigan Avenue, Suite 1500, Chicago, IL 60604, (312) 922-1115, Fax: (312) 922-1157, www.euromonitor.com; *European Marketing Data and Statistics 2008.*

M.E. Sharpe, 80 Business Park Drive, Armonk, NY 10504, (800) 541-6563, Fax: (914) 273-2106, www.mesharpe.com; *The Illustrated Book of World Rankings.*

Palgrave Macmillan Ltd., Houndmills, Basingstoke, Hampshire, RG21 6XS, England, (Telephone in U.S. (888) 330-8477), (Fax in U.S. (800) 672-2054), www.palgrave.com; *The Statesman's Yearbook 2008.*

Taylor and Francis Group, An Informa Business, 2 Park Square, Milton Park, Abingdon, Oxford OX14 4RN, United Kingdom, (Dial from U.S. (212) 216-7800), (Fax from U.S. (212) 564-7854), www.tandf.co.uk; *The Europa World Year Book.*

United Nations Conference on Trade and Development (UNCTAD), DC2-1120, United Nations, New York, NY 10017, (212) 963-0027, www.unctad.org; *UNCTAD Commodity Yearbook.*

United Nations Food and Agricultural Organization (FAO), Viale delle Terme di Caracalla, 00100 Rome, Italy, (Dial from U.S. (202) 653-2400), (Fax from U.S. (202) 653 5760), www.fao.org; *FAO Yearbook of Fishery Statistics;* Fishery Databases; FISHSTAT Database. Subjects covered include: Aquaculture production, capture production, fishery commodities; and *The State of Food and Agriculture (SOFA) 2006.*

United Nations Statistics Division, New York, NY 10017, (800) 253-9646, Fax: (212) 963-4116, http://unstats.un.org; *Statistical Yearbook.*

The World Bank, 1818 H Street, NW, Washington, DC 20433, (202) 473-1000, Fax: (202) 477-6391, www.worldbank.org; *Cyprus.*

CYPRUS - FOOD

United Nations Conference on Trade and Development (UNCTAD), DC2-1120, United Nations, New York, NY 10017, (212) 963-0027, www.unctad.org; *UNCTAD Commodity Yearbook.*

United Nations Food and Agricultural Organization (FAO), Viale delle Terme di Caracalla, 00100 Rome, Italy, (Dial from U.S. (202) 653-2400), (Fax from U.S. (202) 653 5760), www.fao.org; *FAO Production Yearbook 2002* and *The State of Food and Agriculture (SOFA) 2006.*

United Nations Statistics Division, New York, NY 10017, (800) 253-9646, Fax: (212) 963-4116, http://unstats.un.org; *Human Development Report 2006.*

CYPRUS - FOREIGN EXCHANGE RATES

Central Intelligence Agency, Office of Public Affairs, Washington, DC 20505, (703) 482-0623, Fax: (703) 482-1739, www.cia.gov; *The World Factbook.*

Euromonitor International, Inc., 224 S. Michigan Avenue, Suite 1500, Chicago, IL 60604, (312) 922-1115, Fax: (312) 922-1157, www.euromonitor.com; *The World Economic Factbook 2008.*

International Civil Aviation Organization (ICAO), External Relations and Public Information Office (EPO), 999 University Street, Montreal, Quebec H3C 5H7, Canada, (Dial from U.S. (514) 954-8219), (Fax from U.S. (514) 954-6077), www.icao.int; *Civil Aviation Statistics of the World.*

International Monetary Fund (IMF), 700 Nineteenth Street, NW, Washington, DC 20431, (202) 623-7000, Fax: (202) 623-4661, www.imf.org; *International Financial Statistics Yearbook 2007.*

Taylor and Francis Group, An Informa Business, 2 Park Square, Milton Park, Abingdon, Oxford OX14 4RN, United Kingdom, (Dial from U.S. (212) 216-7800), (Fax from U.S. (212) 564-7854), www.tandf.co.uk; *The Europa World Year Book.*

United Nations Statistics Division, New York, NY 10017, (800) 253-9646, Fax: (212) 963-4116, http://unstats.un.org; *Statistical Yearbook; Trends in Europe and North America: The Statistical Yearbook of the ECE 2005;* and *World Statistics Pocketbook.*

CYPRUS - FORESTS AND FORESTRY

Euromonitor International, Inc., 224 S. Michigan Avenue, Suite 1500, Chicago, IL 60604, (312) 922-1115, Fax: (312) 922-1157, www.euromonitor.com; *European Marketing Data and Statistics 2008.*

M.E. Sharpe, 80 Business Park Drive, Armonk, NY 10504, (800) 541-6563, Fax: (914) 273-2106, www.mesharpe.com; *The Illustrated Book of World Rankings.*

Palgrave Macmillan Ltd., Houndmills, Basingstoke, Hampshire, RG21 6XS, England, (Telephone in U.S. (888) 330-8477), (Fax in U.S. (800) 672-2054), www.palgrave.com; *The Statesman's Yearbook 2008.*

UNESCO Institute for Statistics, C.P. 6128 Succursale Centre-Ville, Montreal, Quebec, H3C 3J7 Canada, (Dial from U.S. (514) 343-6880), (Fax from U.S. (514) 343 6882), www.uis.unesco.org; *Statistical Tables.*

United Nations Conference on Trade and Development (UNCTAD), DC2-1120, United Nations, New York, NY 10017, (212) 963-0027, www.unctad.org; *UNCTAD Commodity Yearbook.*

United Nations Food and Agricultural Organization (FAO), Viale delle Terme di Caracalla, 00100 Rome, Italy, (Dial from U.S. (202) 653-2400), (Fax from U.S. (202) 653 5760), www.fao.org; *FAO Yearbook of Forest Products* and *The State of Food and Agriculture (SOFA) 2006.*

United Nations Statistics Division, New York, NY 10017, (800) 253-9646, Fax: (212) 963-4116, http://unstats.un.org; *Statistical Yearbook* and *Trends in Europe and North America: The Statistical Yearbook of the ECE 2005.*

The World Bank, 1818 H Street, NW, Washington, DC 20433, (202) 473-1000, Fax: (202) 477-6391, www.worldbank.org; *Cyprus.*

CYPRUS - FRUIT TRADE

International Monetary Fund (IMF), 700 Nineteenth Street, NW, Washington, DC 20431, (202) 623-7000, Fax: (202) 623-4661, www.imf.org; *International Financial Statistics Yearbook 2007.*

CYPRUS - GAS PRODUCTION

See CYPRUS - MINERAL INDUSTRIES

CYPRUS - GEOGRAPHIC INFORMATION SYSTEMS

M.E. Sharpe, 80 Business Park Drive, Armonk, NY 10504, (800) 541-6563, Fax: (914) 273-2106, www.mesharpe.com; *The Illustrated Book of World Rankings.*

The World Bank, 1818 H Street, NW, Washington, DC 20433, (202) 473-1000, Fax: (202) 477-6391, www.worldbank.org; *Cyprus.*

CYPRUS - GOLD INDUSTRY

International Monetary Fund (IMF), 700 Nineteenth Street, NW, Washington, DC 20431, (202) 623-7000, Fax: (202) 623-4661, www.imf.org; *International Financial Statistics Yearbook 2007.*

United Nations Statistics Division, New York, NY 10017, (800) 253-9646, Fax: (212) 963-4116, http://unstats.un.org; *Statistical Yearbook.*

The World Bank, 1818 H Street, NW, Washington, DC 20433, (202) 473-1000, Fax: (202) 477-6391, www.worldbank.org; *World Development Indicators (WDI) 2008.*

CYPRUS - GOLD PRODUCTION

See CYPRUS - MINERAL INDUSTRIES

CYPRUS - GRANTS-IN-AID

International Monetary Fund (IMF), 700 Nineteenth Street, NW, Washington, DC 20431, (202) 623-7000, Fax: (202) 623-4661, www.imf.org; *Government Finance Statistics Yearbook (2008 Edition).*

CYPRUS - GROSS DOMESTIC PRODUCT

Economist Intelligence Unit, 111 West 57th Street, New York, NY 10019, (212) 554-0600, Fax: (212) 586-1181, www.eiu.com; *Cyprus Country Report.*

Euromonitor International, Inc., 224 S. Michigan Avenue, Suite 1500, Chicago, IL 60604, (312) 922-1115, Fax: (312) 922-1157, www.euromonitor.com; *The World Economic Factbook 2008.*

M.E. Sharpe, 80 Business Park Drive, Armonk, NY 10504, (800) 541-6563, Fax: (914) 273-2106, www.mesharpe.com; *The Illustrated Book of World Rankings.*

Taylor and Francis Group, An Informa Business, 2 Park Square, Milton Park, Abingdon, Oxford OX14 4RN, United Kingdom, (Dial from U.S. (212) 216-7800), (Fax from U.S. (212) 564-7854), www.tandf.co.uk; *The Europa World Year Book.*

United Nations Statistics Division, New York, NY 10017, (800) 253-9646, Fax: (212) 963-4116, http://unstats.un.org; *Human Development Report 2006; National Accounts Statistics: Compendium of Income Distribution Statistics; Statistical Yearbook;* and *Trends in Europe and North America: The Statistical Yearbook of the ECE 2005.*

The World Bank, 1818 H Street, NW, Washington, DC 20433, (202) 473-1000, Fax: (202) 477-6391, www.worldbank.org; *World Development Indicators (WDI) 2008.*

CYPRUS - GROSS NATIONAL PRODUCT

European Union, Delegation of the European Commission to the United States, 2300 M Street, NW, Washington, DC 20037, (202) 862-9500, Fax: (202) 429-1766, www.eurunion.org; *The EU Economy, 2007 Review: Moving Europe's Productivity Frontier.*

M.E. Sharpe, 80 Business Park Drive, Armonk, NY 10504, (800) 541-6563, Fax: (914) 273-2106, www.mesharpe.com; *The Illustrated Book of World Rankings.*

Palgrave Macmillan Ltd., Houndmills, Basingstoke, Hampshire, RG21 6XS, England, (Telephone in U.S. (888) 330-8477), (Fax in U.S. (800) 672-2054), www.palgrave.com; *The Statesman's Yearbook 2008.*

U.S. Department of State (DOS), 2201 C Street NW, Washington, DC 20520, (202) 647-4000, www.state.gov; *World Military Expenditures and Arms Transfers (WMEAT).*

United Nations Statistics Division, New York, NY 10017, (800) 253-9646, Fax: (212) 963-4116, http://unstats.un.org; *Statistical Yearbook.*

The World Bank, 1818 H Street, NW, Washington, DC 20433, (202) 473-1000, Fax: (202) 477-6391, www.worldbank.org; *The World Bank Atlas 2003-2004* and *World Development Indicators (WDI) 2008.*

CYPRUS - HAZELNUT PRODUCTION

See CYPRUS - CROPS

CYPRUS - HIDES AND SKINS INDUSTRY

United Nations Food and Agricultural Organization (FAO), Viale delle Terme di Caracalla, 00100 Rome, Italy, (Dial from U.S. (202) 653-2400), (Fax from U.S. (202) 653 5760), www.fao.org; *FAO Production Yearbook 2002.*

CYPRUS - HOUSING

Euromonitor International, Inc., 224 S. Michigan Avenue, Suite 1500, Chicago, IL 60604, (312) 922-1115, Fax: (312) 922-1157, www.euromonitor.com; *World Marketing Data and Statistics.*

M.E. Sharpe, 80 Business Park Drive, Armonk, NY 10504, (800) 541-6563, Fax: (914) 273-2106, www.mesharpe.com; *The Illustrated Book of World Rankings.*

United Nations Statistics Division, New York, NY 10017, (800) 253-9646, Fax: (212) 963-4116, http://unstats.un.org; *Trends in Europe and North America: The Statistical Yearbook of the ECE 2005.*

CYPRUS - ILLITERATE PERSONS

Euromonitor International, Inc., 224 S. Michigan Avenue, Suite 1500, Chicago, IL 60604, (312) 922-1115, Fax: (312) 922-1157, www.euromonitor.com; *The World Economic Factbook 2008.*

UNESCO Institute for Statistics, C.P. 6128 Succursale Centre-Ville, Montreal, Quebec, H3C 3J7 Canada, (Dial from U.S. (514) 343-6880), (Fax from U.S. (514) 343 6882), www.uis.unesco.org; *Statistical Tables.*

United Nations Statistics Division, New York, NY 10017, (800) 253-9646, Fax: (212) 963-4116, http://unstats.un.org; *Human Development Report 2006.*

CYPRUS - IMPORTS

Central Intelligence Agency, Office of Public Affairs, Washington, DC 20505, (703) 482-0623, Fax: (703) 482-1739, www.cia.gov; *The World Factbook.*

Economist Intelligence Unit, 111 West 57th Street, New York, NY 10019, (212) 554-0600, Fax: (212) 586-1181, www.eiu.com; *Cyprus Country Report.*

Euromonitor International, Inc., 224 S. Michigan Avenue, Suite 1500, Chicago, IL 60604, (312) 922-1115, Fax: (312) 922-1157, www.euromonitor.com; *The World Economic Factbook 2008.*

International Monetary Fund (IMF), 700 Nineteenth Street, NW, Washington, DC 20431, (202) 623-7000, Fax: (202) 623-4661, www.imf.org; *Direction of Trade Statistics Yearbook 2007; Government Finance Statistics Yearbook (2008 Edition);* and *International Financial Statistics Yearbook 2007.*

Palgrave Macmillan Ltd., Houndmills, Basingstoke, Hampshire, RG21 6XS, England, (Telephone in U.S. (888) 330-8477), (Fax in U.S. (800) 672-2054), www.palgrave.com; *The Statesman's Yearbook 2008.*

Taylor and Francis Group, An Informa Business, 2 Park Square, Milton Park, Abingdon, Oxford OX14 4RN, United Kingdom, (Dial from U.S. (212) 216-7800), (Fax from U.S. (212) 564-7854), www.tandf.co.uk; *The Europa World Year Book.*

United Nations Conference on Trade and Development (UNCTAD), DC2-1120, United Nations, New York, NY 10017, (212) 963-0027, www.unctad.org; *Handbook of Statistics 2005.*

United Nations Food and Agricultural Organization (FAO), Viale delle Terme di Caracalla, 00100 Rome, Italy, (Dial from U.S. (202) 653-2400), (Fax from U.S. (202) 653 5760), www.fao.org; *The State of Food and Agriculture (SOFA) 2006.*

United Nations Statistics Division, New York, NY 10017, (800) 253-9646, Fax: (212) 963-4116, http://unstats.un.org; *Trends in Europe and North America: The Statistical Yearbook of the ECE 2005.*

The World Bank, 1818 H Street, NW, Washington, DC 20433, (202) 473-1000, Fax: (202) 477-6391, www.worldbank.org; *World Development Indicators (WDI) 2008.*

CYPRUS - INCOME TAXES

See CYPRUS - TAXATION

CYPRUS - INDUSTRIAL PRODUCTIVITY

M.E. Sharpe, 80 Business Park Drive, Armonk, NY 10504, (800) 541-6563, Fax: (914) 273-2106, www.mesharpe.com; *The Illustrated Book of World Rankings.*

CYPRUS - INDUSTRIAL PROPERTY

United Nations Statistics Division, New York, NY 10017, (800) 253-9646, Fax: (212) 963-4116, http://unstats.un.org; *Statistical Yearbook.*

World Intellectual Property Organization (WIPO), PO Box 18, CH-1211 Geneva 20, Switzerland, www.wipo.int; *Industrial Property Statistics* and *Industrial Property Statistics Online Directory.*

CYPRUS - INDUSTRIES

Central Intelligence Agency, Office of Public Affairs, Washington, DC 20505, (703) 482-0623, Fax: (703) 482-1739, www.cia.gov; *The World Factbook.*

Economist Intelligence Unit, 111 West 57th Street, New York, NY 10019, (212) 554-0600, Fax: (212) 586-1181, www.eiu.com; *Cyprus Country Report.*

Euromonitor International, Inc., 224 S. Michigan Avenue, Suite 1500, Chicago, IL 60604, (312) 922-1115, Fax: (312) 922-1157, www.euromonitor.com; *The World Economic Factbook 2008* and *World Marketing Data and Statistics.*

International Labour Office, I.L.O. Publications, 4 route des Morillons, CH-1211 Geneva 22, Switzerland, (Telephone in U.S. (202) 653-7652), (Fax in U.S. (202) 653-7687), www.ilo.org; *Yearbook of Labour Statistics 2006.*

International Monetary Fund (IMF), 700 Nineteenth Street, NW, Washington, DC 20431, (202) 623-7000, Fax: (202) 623-4661, www.imf.org; *International Financial Statistics Yearbook 2007.*

M.E. Sharpe, 80 Business Park Drive, Armonk, NY 10504, (800) 541-6563, Fax: (914) 273-2106, www.mesharpe.com; *The Illustrated Book of World Rankings.*

Palgrave Macmillan Ltd., Houndmills, Basingstoke, Hampshire, RG21 6XS, England, (Telephone in U.S. (888) 330-8477), (Fax in U.S. (800) 672-2054), www.palgrave.com; *The Statesman's Yearbook 2008.*

Taylor and Francis Group, An Informa Business, 2 Park Square, Milton Park, Abingdon, Oxford OX14 4RN, United Kingdom, (Dial from U.S. (212) 216-7800), (Fax from U.S. (212) 564-7854), www.tandf.co.uk; *The Europa World Year Book.*

United Nations Industrial Development Organization (UNIDO), 1 United Nations Plaza, New York, NY 10017, (212) 963 6890, Fax: (212) 963-7904, http://unido.org; Industrial Statistics Database 2008 (INDSTAT) and *The International Yearbook of Industrial Statistics 2008.*

United Nations Statistics Division, New York, NY 10017, (800) 253-9646, Fax: (212) 963-4116, http://unstats.un.org; *2004 Industrial Commodity Statistics Yearbook* and *Trends in Europe and North America: The Statistical Yearbook of the ECE 2005.*

The World Bank, 1818 H Street, NW, Washington, DC 20433, (202) 473-1000, Fax: (202) 477-6391, www.worldbank.org; *Cyprus* and *World Development Indicators (WDI) 2008.*

CYPRUS - INFANT AND MATERNAL MORTALITY

See CYPRUS - MORTALITY

CYPRUS - INTERNATIONAL LIQUIDITY

International Monetary Fund (IMF), 700 Nineteenth Street, NW, Washington, DC 20431, (202) 623-7000, Fax: (202) 623-4661, www.imf.org; *International Financial Statistics Yearbook 2007.*

CYPRUS - INTERNATIONAL TRADE

Economist Intelligence Unit, 111 West 57th Street, New York, NY 10019, (212) 554-0600, Fax: (212) 586-1181, www.eiu.com; *Cyprus Country Report.*

Euromonitor International, Inc., 224 S. Michigan Avenue, Suite 1500, Chicago, IL 60604, (312) 922-1115, Fax: (312) 922-1157, www.euromonitor.com; *European Marketing Data and Statistics 2008; The World Economic Factbook 2008;* and *World Marketing Data and Statistics.*

Eurostat, Batiment Jean Monnet, Rue Alcide de Gasperi, L-2920 Luxembourg, http://epp.eurostat.ec.europa.eu; Intra- and Extra-EU Trade.

International Monetary Fund (IMF), 700 Nineteenth Street, NW, Washington, DC 20431, (202) 623-

7000, Fax: (202) 623-4661, www.imf.org; *International Financial Statistics Yearbook 2007.*

M.E. Sharpe, 80 Business Park Drive, Armonk, NY 10504, (800) 541-6563, Fax: (914) 273-2106, www.mesharpe.com; *The Illustrated Book of World Rankings.*

Palgrave Macmillan Ltd., Houndmills, Basingstoke, Hampshire, RG21 6XS, England, (Telephone in U.S. (888) 330-8477), (Fax in U.S. (800) 672-2054), www.palgrave.com; *The Statesman's Yearbook 2008.*

Taylor and Francis Group, An Informa Business, 2 Park Square, Milton Park, Abingdon, Oxford OX14 4RN, United Kingdom, (Dial from U.S. (212) 216-7800), (Fax from U.S. (212) 564-7854), www.tandf.co.uk; *The Europa World Year Book.*

United Nations Conference on Trade and Development (UNCTAD), DC2-1120, United Nations, New York, NY 10017, (212) 963-0027, www.unctad.org; *UNCTAD Commodity Yearbook.*

United Nations Food and Agricultural Organization (FAO), Viale delle Terme di Caracalla, 00100 Rome, Italy, (Dial from U.S. (202) 653-2400), (Fax from U.S. (202) 653 5760), www.fao.org; *FAO Trade Yearbook* and *The State of Food and Agriculture (SOFA) 2006.*

United Nations Statistics Division, New York, NY 10017, (800) 253-9646, Fax: (212) 963-4116, http://unstats.un.org; *International Trade Statistics Yearbook* and *Statistical Yearbook.*

The World Bank, 1818 H Street, NW, Washington, DC 20433, (202) 473-1000, Fax: (202) 477-6391, www.worldbank.org; *Cyprus* and *World Development Indicators (WDI) 2008.*

World Trade Organization (WTO), Centre William Rappard, Rue de Lausanne 154, CH-1211 Geneva 21, Switzerland, www.wto.org; *International Trade Statistics 2006.*

CYPRUS - INTERNET USERS

Eurostat, Batiment Jean Monnet, Rue Alcide de Gasperi, L-2920 Luxembourg, http://epp.eurostat.ec.europa.eu; *Internet Usage by Enterprises 2007.*

International Telecommunication Union (ITU), Place des Nations, 1211 Geneva 20, Switzerland, www.itu.int; *World Telecommunication/ICT Indicators Database on CD-ROM; World Telecommunication/ICT Indicators Database Online;* and *Yearbook of Statistics - Telecommunication Services (Chronological Time Series 1997-2006).*

The World Bank, 1818 H Street, NW, Washington, DC 20433, (202) 473-1000, Fax: (202) 477-6391, www.worldbank.org; *Cyprus.*

CYPRUS - IRON AND IRON ORE PRODUCTION

See CYPRUS - MINERAL INDUSTRIES

CYPRUS - LABOR

Central Intelligence Agency, Office of Public Affairs, Washington, DC 20505, (703) 482-0623, Fax: (703) 482-1739, www.cia.gov; *The World Factbook.*

Euromonitor International, Inc., 224 S. Michigan Avenue, Suite 1500, Chicago, IL 60604, (312) 922-1115, Fax: (312) 922-1157, www.euromonitor.com; *World Marketing Data and Statistics.*

International Labour Office, I.L.O. Publications, 4 route des Morillons, CH-1211 Geneva 22, Switzerland, (Telephone in U.S. (202) 653-7652), (Fax in U.S. (202) 653-7687), www.ilo.org; *Yearbook of Labour Statistics 2006.*

M.E. Sharpe, 80 Business Park Drive, Armonk, NY 10504, (800) 541-6563, Fax: (914) 273-2106, www.mesharpe.com; *The Illustrated Book of World Rankings.*

Palgrave Macmillan Ltd., Houndmills, Basingstoke, Hampshire, RG21 6XS, England, (Telephone in U.S. (888) 330-8477), (Fax in U.S. (800) 672-2054), www.palgrave.com; *The Statesman's Yearbook 2008.*

United Nations Food and Agricultural Organization (FAO), Viale delle Terme di Caracalla, 00100 Rome, Italy, (Dial from U.S. (202) 653-2400), (Fax from U.S. (202) 653 5760), www.fao.org; *The State of Food and Agriculture (SOFA) 2006.*

United Nations Statistics Division, New York, NY 10017, (800) 253-9646, Fax: (212) 963-4116, http://unstats.un.org; *Human Development Report 2006.*

The World Bank, 1818 H Street, NW, Washington, DC 20433, (202) 473-1000, Fax: (202) 477-6391, www.worldbank.org; *The World Bank Atlas 2003-2004* and *World Development Indicators (WDI) 2008.*

CYPRUS - LAND USE

Central Intelligence Agency, Office of Public Affairs, Washington, DC 20505, (703) 482-0623, Fax: (703) 482-1739, www.cia.gov; *The World Factbook.*

Euromonitor International, Inc., 224 S. Michigan Avenue, Suite 1500, Chicago, IL 60604, (312) 922-1115, Fax: (312) 922-1157, www.euromonitor.com; *European Marketing Data and Statistics 2008.*

United Nations Food and Agricultural Organization (FAO), Viale delle Terme di Caracalla, 00100 Rome, Italy, (Dial from U.S. (202) 653-2400), (Fax from U.S. (202) 653 5760), www.fao.org; *FAO Production Yearbook 2002.*

CYPRUS - LIBRARIES

Euromonitor International, Inc., 224 S. Michigan Avenue, Suite 1500, Chicago, IL 60604, (312) 922-1115, Fax: (312) 922-1157, www.euromonitor.com; *European Marketing Data and Statistics 2008.*

M.E. Sharpe, 80 Business Park Drive, Armonk, NY 10504, (800) 541-6563, Fax: (914) 273-2106, www.mesharpe.com; *The Illustrated Book of World Rankings.*

UNESCO Institute for Statistics, C.P. 6128 Succursale Centre-Ville, Montreal, Quebec, H3C 3J7 Canada, (Dial from U.S. (514) 343-6880), (Fax from U.S. (514) 343 6882), www.uis.unesco.org; *Statistical Tables.*

United Nations Statistics Division, New York, NY 10017, (800) 253-9646, Fax: (212) 963-4116, http://unstats.un.org; *Trends in Europe and North America: The Statistical Yearbook of the ECE 2005.*

CYPRUS - LICENSES

International Monetary Fund (IMF), 700 Nineteenth Street, NW, Washington, DC 20431, (202) 623-7000, Fax: (202) 623-4661, www.imf.org; *Government Finance Statistics Yearbook (2008 Edition).*

CYPRUS - LIFE EXPECTANCY

Central Intelligence Agency, Office of Public Affairs, Washington, DC 20505, (703) 482-0623, Fax: (703) 482-1739, www.cia.gov; *The World Factbook.*

Euromonitor International, Inc., 224 S. Michigan Avenue, Suite 1500, Chicago, IL 60604, (312) 922-1115, Fax: (312) 922-1157, www.euromonitor.com; *The World Economic Factbook 2008.*

United Nations Statistics Division, New York, NY 10017, (800) 253-9646, Fax: (212) 963-4116, http://unstats.un.org; *Human Development Report 2006; Trends in Europe and North America: The Statistical Yearbook of the ECE 2005;* and *World Statistics Pocketbook.*

The World Bank, 1818 H Street, NW, Washington, DC 20433, (202) 473-1000, Fax: (202) 477-6391, www.worldbank.org; *The World Bank Atlas 2003-2004.*

CYPRUS - LIVESTOCK

Euromonitor International, Inc., 224 S. Michigan Avenue, Suite 1500, Chicago, IL 60604, (312) 922-1115, Fax: (312) 922-1157, www.euromonitor.com; *European Marketing Data and Statistics 2008.*

M.E. Sharpe, 80 Business Park Drive, Armonk, NY 10504, (800) 541-6563, Fax: (914) 273-2106, www.mesharpe.com; *The Illustrated Book of World Rankings.*

Palgrave Macmillan Ltd., Houndmills, Basingstoke, Hampshire, RG21 6XS, England, (Telephone in U.S. (888) 330-8477), (Fax in U.S. (800) 672-2054), www.palgrave.com; *The Statesman's Yearbook 2008.*

Taylor and Francis Group, An Informa Business, 2 Park Square, Milton Park, Abingdon, Oxford OX14 4RN, United Kingdom, (Dial from U.S. (212) 216-7800), (Fax from U.S. (212) 564-7854), www.tandf.co.uk; *The Europa World Year Book.*

United Nations Conference on Trade and Development (UNCTAD), DC2-1120, United Nations, New York, NY 10017, (212) 963-0027, www.unctad.org; *UNCTAD Commodity Yearbook.*

United Nations Food and Agricultural Organization (FAO), Viale delle Terme di Caracalla, 00100 Rome, Italy, (Dial from U.S. (202) 653-2400), (Fax from U.S. (202) 653 5760), www.fao.org; *FAO Production Yearbook 2002* and *The State of Food and Agriculture (SOFA) 2006.*

United Nations Statistics Division, New York, NY 10017, (800) 253-9646, Fax: (212) 963-4116, http://unstats.un.org; *Statistical Yearbook.*

CYPRUS - MANUFACTURES

M.E. Sharpe, 80 Business Park Drive, Armonk, NY 10504, (800) 541-6563, Fax: (914) 273-2106, www.mesharpe.com; *The Illustrated Book of World Rankings.*

United Nations Statistics Division, New York, NY 10017, (800) 253-9646, Fax: (212) 963-4116, http://unstats.un.org; *Statistical Yearbook.*

The World Bank, 1818 H Street, NW, Washington, DC 20433, (202) 473-1000, Fax: (202) 477-6391, www.worldbank.org; *World Development Indicators (WDI) 2008.*

CYPRUS - MARRIAGE

M.E. Sharpe, 80 Business Park Drive, Armonk, NY 10504, (800) 541-6563, Fax: (914) 273-2106, www.mesharpe.com; *The Illustrated Book of World Rankings.*

United Nations Statistics Division, New York, NY 10017, (800) 253-9646, Fax: (212) 963-4116, http://unstats.un.org; *Demographic Yearbook; Statistical Yearbook;* and *Trends in Europe and North America: The Statistical Yearbook of the ECE 2005.*

CYPRUS - MILK PRODUCTION

See CYPRUS - DAIRY PROCESSING

CYPRUS - MINERAL INDUSTRIES

Eurostat, Batiment Jean Monnet, Rue Alcide de Gasperi, L-2920 Luxembourg, http://epp.eurostat.ec.europa.eu; *Energy - Monthly Statistics* and *Panorama of Energy - 2007 Edition.*

International Monetary Fund (IMF), 700 Nineteenth Street, NW, Washington, DC 20431, (202) 623-7000, Fax: (202) 623-4661, www.imf.org; *International Financial Statistics Yearbook 2007.*

M.E. Sharpe, 80 Business Park Drive, Armonk, NY 10504, (800) 541-6563, Fax: (914) 273-2106, www.mesharpe.com; *The Illustrated Book of World Rankings.*

Palgrave Macmillan Ltd., Houndmills, Basingstoke, Hampshire, RG21 6XS, England, (Telephone in U.S. (888) 330-8477), (Fax in U.S. (800) 672-2054), www.palgrave.com; *The Statesman's Yearbook 2008.*

Platts, 2 Penn Plaza, 25th Floor, New York, NY 10121-2298, (212) 904-3070, www.platts.com; *EU Energy.*

Taylor and Francis Group, An Informa Business, 2 Park Square, Milton Park, Abingdon, Oxford OX14 4RN, United Kingdom, (Dial from U.S. (212) 216-7800), (Fax from U.S. (212) 564-7854), www.tandf.co.uk; *The Europa World Year Book.*

United Nations Conference on Trade and Development (UNCTAD), DC2-1120, United Nations, New York, NY 10017, (212) 963-0027, www.unctad.org; *UNCTAD Commodity Yearbook.*

United Nations Statistics Division, New York, NY 10017, (800) 253-9646, Fax: (212) 963-4116, http://unstats.un.org; *Statistical Yearbook.*

The World Bank, 1818 H Street, NW, Washington, DC 20433, (202) 473-1000, Fax: (202) 477-6391, www.worldbank.org; *Cyprus.*

CYPRUS - MONEY EXCHANGE RATES

See CYPRUS - FOREIGN EXCHANGE RATES

CYPRUS - MONEY SUPPLY

Economist Intelligence Unit, 111 West 57th Street, New York, NY 10019, (212) 554-0600, Fax: (212) 586-1181, www.eiu.com; *Cyprus Country Report.*

International Monetary Fund (IMF), 700 Nineteenth Street, NW, Washington, DC 20431, (202) 623-7000, Fax: (202) 623-4661, www.imf.org; *International Financial Statistics Yearbook 2007.*

Taylor and Francis Group, An Informa Business, 2 Park Square, Milton Park, Abingdon, Oxford OX14 4RN, United Kingdom, (Dial from U.S. (212) 216-7800), (Fax from U.S. (212) 564-7854), www.tandf.co.uk; *The Europa World Year Book.*

United Nations Statistics Division, New York, NY 10017, (800) 253-9646, Fax: (212) 963-4116, http://unstats.un.org; *Statistical Yearbook.*

The World Bank, 1818 H Street, NW, Washington, DC 20433, (202) 473-1000, Fax: (202) 477-6391, www.worldbank.org; *Cyprus* and *World Development Indicators (WDI) 2008.*

CYPRUS - MONUMENTS AND HISTORIC SITES

UNESCO Institute for Statistics, C.P. 6128 Succursale Centre-Ville, Montreal, Quebec, H3C 3J7 Canada, (Dial from U.S. (514) 343-6880), (Fax from U.S. (514) 343 6882), www.uis.unesco.org; *Statistical Tables.*

CYPRUS - MORTALITY

Central Intelligence Agency, Office of Public Affairs, Washington, DC 20505, (703) 482-0623, Fax: (703) 482-1739, www.cia.gov; *The World Factbook.*

Euromonitor International, Inc., 224 S. Michigan Avenue, Suite 1500, Chicago, IL 60604, (312) 922-1115, Fax: (312) 922-1157, www.euromonitor.com; *The World Economic Factbook 2008.*

Palgrave Macmillan Ltd., Houndmills, Basingstoke, Hampshire, RG21 6XS, England, (Telephone in U.S. (888) 330-8477), (Fax in U.S. (800) 672-2054), www.palgrave.com; *The Statesman's Yearbook 2008.*

Taylor and Francis Group, An Informa Business, 2 Park Square, Milton Park, Abingdon, Oxford OX14 4RN, United Kingdom, (Dial from U.S. (212) 216-7800), (Fax from U.S. (212) 564-7854), www.tandf.co.uk; *The Europa World Year Book.*

United Nations Statistics Division, New York, NY 10017, (800) 253-9646, Fax: (212) 963-4116, http://unstats.un.org; *Demographic Yearbook; Human Development Report 2006; Statistical Yearbook; Trends in Europe and North America: The Statistical Yearbook of the ECE 2005;* and *World Statistics Pocketbook.*

The World Bank, 1818 H Street, NW, Washington, DC 20433, (202) 473-1000, Fax: (202) 477-6391, www.worldbank.org; *The World Bank Atlas 2003-2004* and *World Development Indicators (WDI) 2008.*

World Health Organization (WHO), Avenue Appia 20, 1211 Geneve 27, Switzerland, (Telephone in U.S. (212) 331-9081), www.who.int; The WHO Global Atlas of Infectious Diseases and *World Health Report 2006.*

CYPRUS - MOTION PICTURES

Palgrave Macmillan Ltd., Houndmills, Basingstoke, Hampshire, RG21 6XS, England, (Telephone in U.S. (888) 330-8477), (Fax in U.S. (800) 672-2054), www.palgrave.com; *The Statesman's Yearbook 2008.*

United Nations Statistics Division, New York, NY 10017, (800) 253-9646, Fax: (212) 963-4116, http://unstats.un.org; *Statistical Yearbook.*

CYPRUS - MOTOR VEHICLES

International Road Federation (IFR), Madison Place, 500 Montgomery Street, 5th Floor, Alexandria, VA 22314, (703) 535-1001, Fax: (703) 535-1007, www.irfnet.org; *World Road Statistics 2006.*

Taylor and Francis Group, An Informa Business, 2 Park Square, Milton Park, Abingdon, Oxford OX14 4RN, United Kingdom, (Dial from U.S. (212) 216-7800), (Fax from U.S. (212) 564-7854), www.tandf.co.uk; *The Europa World Year Book.*

United Nations Statistics Division, New York, NY 10017, (800) 253-9646, Fax: (212) 963-4116, http://unstats.un.org; *Statistical Yearbook.*

CYPRUS - MUSEUMS

M.E. Sharpe, 80 Business Park Drive, Armonk, NY 10504, (800) 541-6563, Fax: (914) 273-2106, www.mesharpe.com; *The Illustrated Book of World Rankings.*

UNESCO Institute for Statistics, C.P. 6128 Succursale Centre-Ville, Montreal, Quebec, H3C 3J7 Canada, (Dial from U.S. (514) 343-6880), (Fax from U.S. (514) 343 6882), www.uis.unesco.org; *Statistical Tables.*

CYPRUS - NATURAL GAS PRODUCTION

See CYPRUS - MINERAL INDUSTRIES

CYPRUS - NUPTIALITY

See CYPRUS - MARRIAGE

CYPRUS - NUTRITION

United Nations Food and Agricultural Organization (FAO), Viale delle Terme di Caracalla, 00100 Rome, Italy, (Dial from U.S. (202) 653-2400), (Fax from U.S. (202) 653 5760), www.fao.org; *The State of Food and Agriculture (SOFA) 2006.*

CYPRUS - OLDER PEOPLE

M.E. Sharpe, 80 Business Park Drive, Armonk, NY 10504, (800) 541-6563, Fax: (914) 273-2106, www.mesharpe.com; *The Illustrated Book of World Rankings.*

CYPRUS - PAPER

See CYPRUS - FORESTS AND FORESTRY

CYPRUS - PEANUT PRODUCTION

See CYPRUS - CROPS

CYPRUS - PERIODICALS

UNESCO Institute for Statistics, C.P. 6128 Succursale Centre-Ville, Montreal, Quebec, H3C 3J7 Canada, (Dial from U.S. (514) 343-6880), (Fax from U.S. (514) 343 6882), www.uis.unesco.org; *Statistical Tables.*

CYPRUS - PESTICIDES

United Nations Food and Agricultural Organization (FAO), Viale delle Terme di Caracalla, 00100 Rome, Italy, (Dial from U.S. (202) 653-2400), (Fax from U.S. (202) 653 5760), www.fao.org; *The State of Food and Agriculture (SOFA) 2006.*

CYPRUS - PETROLEUM INDUSTRY AND TRADE

Euromonitor International, Inc., 224 S. Michigan Avenue, Suite 1500, Chicago, IL 60604, (312) 922-1115, Fax: (312) 922-1157, www.euromonitor.com; *European Marketing Data and Statistics 2008.*

M.E. Sharpe, 80 Business Park Drive, Armonk, NY 10504, (800) 541-6563, Fax: (914) 273-2106, www.mesharpe.com; *The Illustrated Book of World Rankings.*

PennWell Corporation, 1421 South Sheridan Road, Tulsa, OK 74112, (918) 835-3161, www.pennwell.com; *International Petroleum Encyclopedia 2007.*

U.S. Department of Energy (DOE), Energy Information Administration (EIA), 1000 Independence Avenue, SW, Washington, DC 20585, (202) 586-8800, www.eia.doe.gov; *International Energy Annual 2004* and *International Energy Outlook 2006.*

United Nations Conference on Trade and Development (UNCTAD), DC2-1120, United Nations, New York, NY 10017, (212) 963-0027, www.unctad.org; *UNCTAD Commodity Yearbook.*

United Nations Food and Agricultural Organization (FAO), Viale delle Terme di Caracalla, 00100 Rome, Italy, (Dial from U.S. (202) 653-2400), (Fax from U.S. (202) 653 5760), www.fao.org; *The State of Food and Agriculture (SOFA) 2006.*

United Nations Statistics Division, New York, NY 10017, (800) 253-9646, Fax: (212) 963-4116, http://unstats.un.org; *Statistical Yearbook* and *Trends in Europe and North America: The Statistical Yearbook of the ECE 2005.*

CYPRUS - POLITICAL SCIENCE

Central Intelligence Agency, Office of Public Affairs, Washington, DC 20505, (703) 482-0623, Fax: (703) 482-1739, www.cia.gov; *The World Factbook.*

International Monetary Fund (IMF), 700 Nineteenth Street, NW, Washington, DC 20431, (202) 623-7000, Fax: (202) 623-4661, www.imf.org; *Government Finance Statistics Yearbook (2008 Edition)* and *International Financial Statistics Yearbook 2007.*

Palgrave Macmillan Ltd., Houndmills, Basingstoke, Hampshire, RG21 6XS, England, (Telephone in U.S. (888) 330-8477), (Fax in U.S. (800) 672-2054), www.palgrave.com; *The Statesman's Yearbook 2008.*

Taylor and Francis Group, An Informa Business, 2 Park Square, Milton Park, Abingdon, Oxford OX14 4RN, United Kingdom, (Dial from U.S. (212) 216-7800), (Fax from U.S. (212) 564-7854), www.tandf.co.uk; *The Europa World Year Book.*

United Nations Statistics Division, New York, NY 10017, (800) 253-9646, Fax: (212) 963-4116, http://unstats.un.org; *National Accounts Statistics: Compendium of Income Distribution Statistics* and *Statistical Yearbook.*

The World Bank, 1818 H Street, NW, Washington, DC 20433, (202) 473-1000, Fax: (202) 477-6391, www.worldbank.org; *World Development Indicators (WDI) 2008.*

CYPRUS - POPULATION

Central Intelligence Agency, Office of Public Affairs, Washington, DC 20505, (703) 482-0623, Fax: (703) 482-1739, www.cia.gov; *The World Factbook.*

Economist Intelligence Unit, 111 West 57th Street, New York, NY 10019, (212) 554-0600, Fax: (212) 586-1181, www.eiu.com; *Cyprus Country Report.*

Euromonitor International, Inc., 224 S. Michigan Avenue, Suite 1500, Chicago, IL 60604, (312) 922-1115, Fax: (312) 922-1157, www.euromonitor.com; *European Marketing Data and Statistics 2008* and *The World Economic Factbook 2008.*

Eurostat, Batiment Jean Monnet, Rue Alcide de Gasperi, L-2920 Luxembourg, http://epp.eurostat.ec.europa.eu; *The Life of Women and Men in Europe - A Statistical Portrait.*

International Labour Office, I.L.O. Publications, 4 route des Morillons, CH-1211 Geneva 22, Switzerland, (Telephone in U.S. (202) 653-7652), (Fax in U.S. (202) 653-7687), www.ilo.org; *Yearbook of Labour Statistics 2006.*

M.E. Sharpe, 80 Business Park Drive, Armonk, NY 10504, (800) 541-6563, Fax: (914) 273-2106, www.mesharpe.com; *The Illustrated Book of World Rankings.*

Palgrave Macmillan Ltd., Houndmills, Basingstoke, Hampshire, RG21 6XS, England, (Telephone in U.S. (888) 330-8477), (Fax in U.S. (800) 672-2054), www.palgrave.com; *The Statesman's Yearbook 2008.*

Taylor and Francis Group, An Informa Business, 2 Park Square, Milton Park, Abingdon, Oxford OX14 4RN, United Kingdom, (Dial from U.S. (212) 216-7800), (Fax from U.S. (212) 564-7854), www.tandf.co.uk; *The Europa World Year Book.*

U.S. Department of State (DOS), 2201 C Street NW, Washington, DC 20520, (202) 647-4000, www.state.gov; *World Military Expenditures and Arms Transfers (WMEAT).*

UNESCO Institute for Statistics, C.P. 6128 Succursale Centre-Ville, Montreal, Quebec, H3C 3J7 Canada, (Dial from U.S. (514) 343-6880), (Fax from U.S. (514) 343 6882), www.uis.unesco.org; *Statistical Tables.*

United Nations Food and Agricultural Organization (FAO), Viale delle Terme di Caracalla, 00100 Rome, Italy, (Dial from U.S. (202) 653-2400), (Fax from U.S. (202) 653 5760), www.fao.org; *FAO Production Yearbook 2002.*

United Nations Statistics Division, New York, NY 10017, (800) 253-9646, Fax: (212) 963-4116, http://unstats.un.org; *Demographic Yearbook; Human Development Report 2006; Statistical Yearbook; Trends in Europe and North America: The Statistical Yearbook of the ECE 2005;* and *World Statistics Pocketbook.*

The World Bank, 1818 H Street, NW, Washington, DC 20433, (202) 473-1000, Fax: (202) 477-6391, www.worldbank.org; *Cyprus* and *The World Bank Atlas 2003-2004.*

World Health Organization (WHO), Avenue Appia 20, 1211 Geneve 27, Switzerland, (Telephone in U.S. (212) 331-9081), www.who.int; *World Health Report 2006.*

CYPRUS - POPULATION DENSITY

Central Intelligence Agency, Office of Public Affairs, Washington, DC 20505, (703) 482-0623, Fax: (703) 482-1739, www.cia.gov; *The World Factbook.*

Euromonitor International, Inc., 224 S. Michigan Avenue, Suite 1500, Chicago, IL 60604, (312) 922-1115, Fax: (312) 922-1157, www.euromonitor.com; *The World Economic Factbook 2008.*

M.E. Sharpe, 80 Business Park Drive, Armonk, NY 10504, (800) 541-6563, Fax: (914) 273-2106, www.mesharpe.com; *The Illustrated Book of World Rankings.*

Palgrave Macmillan Ltd., Houndmills, Basingstoke, Hampshire, RG21 6XS, England, (Telephone in U.S. (888) 330-8477), (Fax in U.S. (800) 672-2054), www.palgrave.com; *The Statesman's Yearbook 2008.*

Taylor and Francis Group, An Informa Business, 2 Park Square, Milton Park, Abingdon, Oxford OX14 4RN, United Kingdom, (Dial from U.S. (212) 216-7800), (Fax from U.S. (212) 564-7854), www.tandf.co.uk; *The Europa World Year Book.*

UNESCO Institute for Statistics, C.P. 6128 Succursale Centre-Ville, Montreal, Quebec, H3C 3J7 Canada, (Dial from U.S. (514) 343-6880), (Fax from U.S. (514) 343 6882), www.uis.unesco.org; *Statistical Tables.*

United Nations Food and Agricultural Organization (FAO), Viale delle Terme di Caracalla, 00100 Rome, Italy, (Dial from U.S. (202) 653-2400), (Fax from U.S. (202) 653 5760), www.fao.org; *The State of Food and Agriculture (SOFA) 2006.*

United Nations Statistics Division, New York, NY 10017, (800) 253-9646, Fax: (212) 963-4116, http://unstats.un.org; *Statistical Yearbook* and *Trends in Europe and North America: The Statistical Yearbook of the ECE 2005.*

The World Bank, 1818 H Street, NW, Washington, DC 20433, (202) 473-1000, Fax: (202) 477-6391, www.worldbank.org; *Cyprus.*

CYPRUS - POSTAL SERVICE

M.E. Sharpe, 80 Business Park Drive, Armonk, NY 10504, (800) 541-6563, Fax: (914) 273-2106, www.mesharpe.com; *The Illustrated Book of World Rankings.*

Palgrave Macmillan Ltd., Houndmills, Basingstoke, Hampshire, RG21 6XS, England, (Telephone in U.S. (888) 330-8477), (Fax in U.S. (800) 672-2054), www.palgrave.com; *The Statesman's Yearbook 2008.*

United Nations Statistics Division, New York, NY 10017, (800) 253-9646, Fax: (212) 963-4116, http://unstats.un.org; *Statistical Yearbook* and *Trends in Europe and North America: The Statistical Yearbook of the ECE 2005.*

CYPRUS - POWER RESOURCES

Euromonitor International, Inc., 224 S. Michigan Avenue, Suite 1500, Chicago, IL 60604, (312) 922-1115, Fax: (312) 922-1157, www.euromonitor.com; *European Marketing Data and Statistics 2008; The World Economic Factbook 2008;* and *World Marketing Data and Statistics.*

M.E. Sharpe, 80 Business Park Drive, Armonk, NY 10504, (800) 541-6563, Fax: (914) 273-2106, www.mesharpe.com; *The Illustrated Book of World Rankings.*

Palgrave Macmillan Ltd., Houndmills, Basingstoke, Hampshire, RG21 6XS, England, (Telephone in U.S. (888) 330-8477), (Fax in U.S. (800) 672-2054), www.palgrave.com; *The Statesman's Yearbook 2008.*

Platts, 2 Penn Plaza, 25th Floor, New York, NY 10121-2298, (212) 904-3070, www.platts.com; *Energy Economist* and *European Power Daily.*

U.S. Department of Energy (DOE), Energy Information Administration (EIA), 1000 Independence Avenue, SW, Washington, DC 20585, (202) 586-8800, www.eia.doe.gov; *International Energy Annual 2004* and *International Energy Outlook 2006.*

United Nations Food and Agricultural Organization (FAO), Viale delle Terme di Caracalla, 00100 Rome, Italy, (Dial from U.S. (202) 653-2400), (Fax from U.S. (202) 653 5760), www.fao.org; *The State of Food and Agriculture (SOFA) 2006.*

United Nations Statistics Division, New York, NY 10017, (800) 253-9646, Fax: (212) 963-4116, http://unstats.un.org; *Energy Statistics Yearbook 2003; Human Development Report 2006; Statistical Yearbook; Trends in Europe and North America: The Statistical Yearbook of the ECE 2005;* and *World Statistics Pocketbook.*

The World Bank, 1818 H Street, NW, Washington, DC 20433, (202) 473-1000, Fax: (202) 477-6391, www.worldbank.org; *The World Bank Atlas 2003-2004.*

CYPRUS - PRICES

Euromonitor International, Inc., 224 S. Michigan Avenue, Suite 1500, Chicago, IL 60604, (312) 922-1115, Fax: (312) 922-1157, www.euromonitor.com; *European Marketing Data and Statistics 2008* and *World Marketing Data and Statistics.*

International Labour Office, I.L.O. Publications, 4 route des Morillons, CH-1211 Geneva 22, Switzerland, (Telephone in U.S. (202) 653-7652), (Fax in U.S. (202) 653-7687), www.ilo.org; *Yearbook of Labour Statistics 2006.*

International Monetary Fund (IMF), 700 Nineteenth Street, NW, Washington, DC 20431, (202) 623-7000, Fax: (202) 623-4661, www.imf.org; *International Financial Statistics Yearbook 2007.*

M.E. Sharpe, 80 Business Park Drive, Armonk, NY 10504, (800) 541-6563, Fax: (914) 273-2106, www.mesharpe.com; *The Illustrated Book of World Rankings.*

United Nations Food and Agricultural Organization (FAO), Viale delle Terme di Caracalla, 00100 Rome, Italy, (Dial from U.S. (202) 653-2400), (Fax from U.S. (202) 653 5760), www.fao.org; *FAO Production Yearbook 2002* and *The State of Food and Agriculture (SOFA) 2006.*

The World Bank, 1818 H Street, NW, Washington, DC 20433, (202) 473-1000, Fax: (202) 477-6391, www.worldbank.org; *Cyprus.*

CYPRUS - PROFESSIONS

United Nations Statistics Division, New York, NY 10017, (800) 253-9646, Fax: (212) 963-4116, http://unstats.un.org; *Statistical Yearbook.*

CYPRUS - PUBLIC HEALTH

Euromonitor International, Inc., 224 S. Michigan Avenue, Suite 1500, Chicago, IL 60604, (312) 922-1115, Fax: (312) 922-1157, www.euromonitor.com; *World Marketing Data and Statistics.*

Health and Consumer Protection Directorate-General, European Commission, B-1049 Brussels, Belgium, http://ec.europa.eu/dgs/health_consumer/index_en.htm; *Injuries in the European Union: Statistics Summary 2002-2004.*

International Monetary Fund (IMF), 700 Nineteenth Street, NW, Washington, DC 20431, (202) 623-7000, Fax: (202) 623-4661, www.imf.org; *Government Finance Statistics Yearbook (2008 Edition).*

M.E. Sharpe, 80 Business Park Drive, Armonk, NY 10504, (800) 541-6563, Fax: (914) 273-2106, www.mesharpe.com; *The Illustrated Book of World Rankings.*

Robert Koch Institute, Nordufer 20, D 13353 Berlin, Germany, www.rki.de; *EUVAC-NET Report: Pertussis-Surveillance 1998-2002.*

United Nations Statistics Division, New York, NY 10017, (800) 253-9646, Fax: (212) 963-4116, http://unstats.un.org; *Human Development Report 2006; Statistical Yearbook;* and *Trends in Europe and North America: The Statistical Yearbook of the ECE 2005.*

The World Bank, 1818 H Street, NW, Washington, DC 20433, (202) 473-1000, Fax: (202) 477-6391, www.worldbank.org; *Cyprus.*

World Health Organization (WHO), Avenue Appia 20, 1211 Geneve 27, Switzerland, (Telephone in U.S. (212) 331-9081), www.who.int; The WHO Global Atlas of Infectious Diseases and *World Health Report 2006.*

CYPRUS - PUBLISHERS AND PUBLISHING

UNESCO Institute for Statistics, C.P. 6128 Succursale Centre-Ville, Montreal, Quebec, H3C 3J7 Canada, (Dial from U.S. (514) 343-6880), (Fax from U.S. (514) 343 6882), www.uis.unesco.org; *Statistical Tables.*

United Nations Statistics Division, New York, NY 10017, (800) 253-9646, Fax: (212) 963-4116, http://unstats.un.org; *Trends in Europe and North America: The Statistical Yearbook of the ECE 2005.*

CYPRUS - RADIO BROADCASTING

Palgrave Macmillan Ltd., Houndmills, Basingstoke, Hampshire, RG21 6XS, England, (Telephone in U.S. (888) 330-8477), (Fax in U.S. (800) 672-2054), www.palgrave.com; *The Statesman's Yearbook 2008.*

CYPRUS - RAILROADS

Euromonitor International, Inc., 224 S. Michigan Avenue, Suite 1500, Chicago, IL 60604, (312) 922-1115, Fax: (312) 922-1157, www.euromonitor.com; *European Marketing Data and Statistics 2008.*

United Nations Statistics Division, New York, NY 10017, (800) 253-9646, Fax: (212) 963-4116, http://unstats.un.org; *Trends in Europe and North America: The Statistical Yearbook of the ECE 2005.*

CYPRUS - RELIGION

Central Intelligence Agency, Office of Public Affairs, Washington, DC 20505, (703) 482-0623, Fax: (703) 482-1739, www.cia.gov; *The World Factbook.*

M.E. Sharpe, 80 Business Park Drive, Armonk, NY 10504, (800) 541-6563, Fax: (914) 273-2106, www.mesharpe.com; *The Illustrated Book of World Rankings.*

Palgrave Macmillan Ltd., Houndmills, Basingstoke, Hampshire, RG21 6XS, England, (Telephone in U.S. (888) 330-8477), (Fax in U.S. (800) 672-2054), www.palgrave.com; *The Statesman's Yearbook 2008.*

CYPRUS - RENT CHARGES

International Labour Office, I.L.O. Publications, 4 route des Morillons, CH-1211 Geneva 22, Switzerland, (Telephone in U.S. (202) 653-7652), (Fax in U.S. (202) 653-7687), www.ilo.org; *Yearbook of Labour Statistics 2006.*

CYPRUS - RESERVES (ACCOUNTING)

The World Bank, 1818 H Street, NW, Washington, DC 20433, (202) 473-1000, Fax: (202) 477-6391, www.worldbank.org; *World Development Indicators (WDI) 2008.*

CYPRUS - RETAIL TRADE

Euromonitor International, Inc., 224 S. Michigan Avenue, Suite 1500, Chicago, IL 60604, (312) 922-1115, Fax: (312) 922-1157, www.euromonitor.com; *World Marketing Data and Statistics.*

United Nations Statistics Division, New York, NY 10017, (800) 253-9646, Fax: (212) 963-4116, http://unstats.un.org; *Statistical Yearbook.*

CYPRUS - RICE PRODUCTION

See CYPRUS - CROPS

CYPRUS - ROADS

Central Intelligence Agency, Office of Public Affairs, Washington, DC 20505, (703) 482-0623, Fax: (703) 482-1739, www.cia.gov; *The World Factbook.*

International Road Federation (IFR), Madison Place, 500 Montgomery Street, 5th Floor, Alexandria, VA 22314, (703) 535-1001, Fax: (703) 535-1007, www.irfnet.org; *World Road Statistics 2006.*

Palgrave Macmillan Ltd., Houndmills, Basingstoke, Hampshire, RG21 6XS, England, (Telephone in U.S. (888) 330-8477), (Fax in U.S. (800) 672-2054), www.palgrave.com; *The Statesman's Yearbook 2008.*

United Nations Statistics Division, New York, NY 10017, (800) 253-9646, Fax: (212) 963-4116, http://unstats.un.org; *Annual Bulletin of Transport Statistics for Europe and North America 2004* and *Trends in Europe and North America: The Statistical Yearbook of the ECE 2005.*

CYPRUS - RUBBER INDUSTRY AND TRADE

International Rubber Study Group (IRSG), 1st Floor, Heron House, 109/115 Wembley Hill Road, Wembley, Middlesex HA9 8DA, United Kingdom, www.rubberstudy.com; *Rubber Statistical Bulletin; Summary of World Rubber Statistics 2005; World Rubber Statistics Handbook (Volume 6, 1975-2001);* and *World Rubber Statistics Historic Handbook.*

M.E. Sharpe, 80 Business Park Drive, Armonk, NY 10504, (800) 541-6563, Fax: (914) 273-2106, www.mesharpe.com; *The Illustrated Book of World Rankings.*

CYPRUS - SALT PRODUCTION

See CYPRUS - MINERAL INDUSTRIES

CYPRUS - SHEEP

See CYPRUS - LIVESTOCK

CYPRUS - SHIPPING

Lloyd's Register - Fairplay, 8410 N.W. 53rd Terrace, Suite 207, Miami FL 33166, (305) 718-9929, Fax: (305) 718-9663, www.lrfairplay.com; *Register of Ships 2007-2008; World Casualty Statistics 2007; World Fleet Statistics 2006; World Marine Propulsion Report 2006-2010; World Shipbuilding Statistics 2007;* and The World Shipping Encyclopaedia.

Palgrave Macmillan Ltd., Houndmills, Basingstoke, Hampshire, RG21 6XS, England, (Telephone in U.S. (888) 330-8477), (Fax in U.S. (800) 672-2054), www.palgrave.com; *The Statesman's Yearbook 2008.*

Taylor and Francis Group, An Informa Business, 2 Park Square, Milton Park, Abingdon, Oxford OX14 4RN, United Kingdom, (Dial from U.S. (212) 216-7800), (Fax from U.S. (212) 564-7854), www.tandf.co.uk; *The Europa World Year Book.*

U.S. Department of Transportation (DOT), Maritime Administration (MARAD), West Building, Southeast Federal Center, 1200 New Jersey Avenue, SE, Washington, DC 20590, (800) 99-MARAD, www.marad.dot.gov; *World Merchant Fleet 2005.*

United Nations Statistics Division, New York, NY 10017, (800) 253-9646, Fax: (212) 963-4116, http://unstats.un.org; *Statistical Yearbook.*

CYPRUS - SILVER PRODUCTION

See CYPRUS - MINERAL INDUSTRIES

CYPRUS - SOCIAL ECOLOGY

M.E. Sharpe, 80 Business Park Drive, Armonk, NY 10504, (800) 541-6563, Fax: (914) 273-2106, www.mesharpe.com; *The Illustrated Book of World Rankings.*

United Nations Statistics Division, New York, NY 10017, (800) 253-9646, Fax: (212) 963-4116, http://unstats.un.org; *World Statistics Pocketbook.*

CYPRUS - SOCIAL SECURITY

International Monetary Fund (IMF), 700 Nineteenth Street, NW, Washington, DC 20431, (202) 623-7000, Fax: (202) 623-4661, www.imf.org; *Government Finance Statistics Yearbook (2008 Edition).*

Palgrave Macmillan Ltd., Houndmills, Basingstoke, Hampshire, RG21 6XS, England, (Telephone in U.S. (888) 330-8477), (Fax in U.S. (800) 672-2054), www.palgrave.com; *The Statesman's Yearbook 2008.*

United Nations Statistics Division, New York, NY 10017, (800) 253-9646, Fax: (212) 963-4116, http://unstats.un.org; *National Accounts Statistics: Compendium of Income Distribution Statistics.*

CYPRUS - STEEL PRODUCTION

See CYPRUS - MINERAL INDUSTRIES

CYPRUS - SUGAR PRODUCTION

See CYPRUS - CROPS

CYPRUS - TAXATION

Eurostat, Batiment Jean Monnet, Rue Alcide de Gasperi, L-2920 Luxembourg, http://epp.eurostat.ec.europa.eu; *Taxation Trends in the European Union - Data for the EU Member States and Norway.*

International Monetary Fund (IMF), 700 Nineteenth Street, NW, Washington, DC 20431, (202) 623-7000, Fax: (202) 623-4661, www.imf.org; *Government Finance Statistics Yearbook (2008 Edition).*

Taylor and Francis Group, An Informa Business, 2 Park Square, Milton Park, Abingdon, Oxford OX14 4RN, United Kingdom, (Dial from U.S. (212) 216-7800), (Fax from U.S. (212) 564-7854), www.tandf.co.uk; *The Europa World Year Book.*

The World Bank, 1818 H Street, NW, Washington, DC 20433, (202) 473-1000, Fax: (202) 477-6391, www.worldbank.org; *World Development Indicators (WDI) 2008.*

CYPRUS - TELEPHONE

International Telecommunication Union (ITU), Place des Nations, 1211 Geneva 20, Switzerland, www.itu.int; World Telecommunication Indicators Database.

Palgrave Macmillan Ltd., Houndmills, Basingstoke, Hampshire, RG21 6XS, England, (Telephone in U.S. (888) 330-8477), (Fax in U.S. (800) 672-2054), www.palgrave.com; *The Statesman's Yearbook 2008.*

United Nations Statistics Division, New York, NY 10017, (800) 253-9646, Fax: (212) 963-4116, http://unstats.un.org; *Statistical Yearbook; Trends in Europe and North America: The Statistical Yearbook of the ECE 2005;* and *World Statistics Pocketbook.*

CYPRUS - TEXTILE INDUSTRY

M.E. Sharpe, 80 Business Park Drive, Armonk, NY 10504, (800) 541-6563, Fax: (914) 273-2106, www.mesharpe.com; *The Illustrated Book of World Rankings.*

Palgrave Macmillan Ltd., Houndmills, Basingstoke, Hampshire, RG21 6XS, England, (Telephone in U.S. (888) 330-8477), (Fax in U.S. (800) 672-2054), www.palgrave.com; *The Statesman's Yearbook 2008.*

United Nations Conference on Trade and Development (UNCTAD), DC2-1120, United Nations, New York, NY 10017, (212) 963-0027, www.unctad.org; *UNCTAD Commodity Yearbook.*

CYPRUS - THEATER

UNESCO Institute for Statistics, C.P. 6128 Succursale Centre-Ville, Montreal, Quebec, H3C 3J7 Canada, (Dial from U.S. (514) 343-6880), (Fax from U.S. (514) 343 6882), www.uis.unesco.org; *Statistical Tables.*

CYPRUS - TOBACCO INDUSTRY

Euromonitor International, Inc., 224 S. Michigan Avenue, Suite 1500, Chicago, IL 60604, (312) 922-1115, Fax: (312) 922-1157, www.euromonitor.com; *European Marketing Data and Statistics 2008.*

Foreign Agricultural Service (FAS), U.S. Department of Agriculture (USDA), 1400 Independence Avenue, SW, Washington, DC 20250, (202) 720-3935, www.fas.usda.gov; *Tobacco: World Markets and Trade.*

M.E. Sharpe, 80 Business Park Drive, Armonk, NY 10504, (800) 541-6563, Fax: (914) 273-2106, www.mesharpe.com; *The Illustrated Book of World Rankings.*

United Nations Statistics Division, New York, NY 10017, (800) 253-9646, Fax: (212) 963-4116, http://unstats.un.org; *Statistical Yearbook.*

CYPRUS - TOURISM

Euromonitor International, Inc., 224 S. Michigan Avenue, Suite 1500, Chicago, IL 60604, (312) 922-1115, Fax: (312) 922-1157, www.euromonitor.com; *European Marketing Data and Statistics 2008; The World Economic Factbook 2008;* and *World Marketing Data and Statistics.*

International Road Federation (IFR), Madison Place, 500 Montgomery Street, 5th Floor, Alexandria, VA 22314, (703) 535-1001, Fax: (703) 535-1007, www.irfnet.org; *World Road Statistics 2006.*

M.E. Sharpe, 80 Business Park Drive, Armonk, NY 10504, (800) 541-6563, Fax: (914) 273-2106, www.mesharpe.com; *The Illustrated Book of World Rankings.*

Palgrave Macmillan Ltd., Houndmills, Basingstoke, Hampshire, RG21 6XS, England, (Telephone in U.S. (888) 330-8477), (Fax in U.S. (800) 672-2054), www.palgrave.com; *The Statesman's Yearbook 2008.*

Statistical Service of the Republic of Cyprus (CYSTAT), Michalakis Karaolis Street, 1444 Nicosia, Cyprus, www.mof.gov.cy/cystat; *Tourism, January 2008.*

Taylor and Francis Group, An Informa Business, 2 Park Square, Milton Park, Abingdon, Oxford OX14 4RN, United Kingdom, (Dial from U.S. (212) 216-7800), (Fax from U.S. (212) 564-7854), www.tandf.co.uk; *The Europa World Year Book.*

United Nations Statistics Division, New York, NY 10017, (800) 253-9646, Fax: (212) 963-4116, http://unstats.un.org; *Statistical Yearbook* and *Trends in Europe and North America: The Statistical Yearbook of the ECE 2005.*

United Nations World Tourism Organization (UNWTO), Capitan Haya 42, 28020 Madrid, Spain, www.world-tourism.org; *Yearbook of Tourism Statistics.*

The World Bank, 1818 H Street, NW, Washington, DC 20433, (202) 473-1000, Fax: (202) 477-6391, www.worldbank.org; *Cyprus.*

CYPRUS - TRADE

See CYPRUS - INTERNATIONAL TRADE

CYPRUS - TRANSPORTATION

Central Intelligence Agency, Office of Public Affairs, Washington, DC 20505, (703) 482-0623, Fax: (703) 482-1739, www.cia.gov; *The World Factbook.*

Euromonitor International, Inc., 224 S. Michigan Avenue, Suite 1500, Chicago, IL 60604, (312) 922-1115, Fax: (312) 922-1157, www.euromonitor.com; *World Marketing Data and Statistics.*

Eurostat, Batiment Jean Monnet, Rue Alcide de Gasperi, L-2920 Luxembourg, http://epp.eurostat.ec.europa.eu; *Regional Passenger and Freight Air Transport in Europe in 2006* and *Regional Road and Rail Transport Networks.*

M.E. Sharpe, 80 Business Park Drive, Armonk, NY 10504, (800) 541-6563, Fax: (914) 273-2106, www.mesharpe.com; *The Illustrated Book of World Rankings.*

Palgrave Macmillan Ltd., Houndmills, Basingstoke, Hampshire, RG21 6XS, England, (Telephone in U.S. (888) 330-8477), (Fax in U.S. (800) 672-2054), www.palgrave.com; *The Statesman's Yearbook 2008.*

Taylor and Francis Group, An Informa Business, 2 Park Square, Milton Park, Abingdon, Oxford OX14 4RN, United Kingdom, (Dial from U.S. (212) 216-7800), (Fax from U.S. (212) 564-7854), www.tandf.co.uk; *The Europa World Year Book.*

United Nations Statistics Division, New York, NY 10017, (800) 253-9646, Fax: (212) 963-4116, http://unstats.un.org; *Human Development Report 2006* and *Trends in Europe and North America: The Statistical Yearbook of the ECE 2005.*

The World Bank, 1818 H Street, NW, Washington, DC 20433, (202) 473-1000, Fax: (202) 477-6391, www.worldbank.org; *Cyprus.*

CYPRUS - TURKEYS

See CYPRUS - LIVESTOCK

CYPRUS - UNEMPLOYMENT

Central Intelligence Agency, Office of Public Affairs, Washington, DC 20505, (703) 482-0623, Fax: (703) 482-1739, www.cia.gov; *The World Factbook.*

Euromonitor International, Inc., 224 S. Michigan Avenue, Suite 1500, Chicago, IL 60604, (312) 922-1115, Fax: (312) 922-1157, www.euromonitor.com; *European Marketing Data and Statistics 2008.*

International Labour Office, I.L.O. Publications, 4 route des Morillons, CH-1211 Geneva 22, Switzerland, (Telephone in U.S. (202) 653-7652), (Fax in U.S. (202) 653-7687), www.ilo.org; *Yearbook of Labour Statistics 2006.*

Palgrave Macmillan Ltd., Houndmills, Basingstoke, Hampshire, RG21 6XS, England, (Telephone in U.S. (888) 330-8477), (Fax in U.S. (800) 672-2054), www.palgrave.com; *The Statesman's Yearbook 2008.*

United Nations Statistics Division, New York, NY 10017, (800) 253-9646, Fax: (212) 963-4116, http://unstats.un.org; *Statistical Yearbook* and *Trends in Europe and North America: The Statistical Yearbook of the ECE 2005.*

The World Bank, 1818 H Street, NW, Washington, DC 20433, (202) 473-1000, Fax: (202) 477-6391, www.worldbank.org; *Cyprus.*

CYPRUS - VITAL STATISTICS

Palgrave Macmillan Ltd., Houndmills, Basingstoke, Hampshire, RG21 6XS, England, (Telephone in U.S. (888) 330-8477), (Fax in U.S. (800) 672-2054), www.palgrave.com; *The Statesman's Yearbook 2008.*

United Nations Economic and Social Commission for Western Asia (ESCWA), PO Box 11-8575, Riad el-Solh Square, Beirut, Lebanon, www.escwa.un.org; *Annual Report 2006; Bulletin on Population and Vital Statistics in the ESCWA Region;* and *Survey of Economic and Social Developments in the ESCWA Region 2006-2007.*

United Nations Statistics Division, New York, NY 10017, (800) 253-9646, Fax: (212) 963-4116, http://unstats.un.org; *Statistical Yearbook.*

World Health Organization (WHO), Avenue Appia 20, 1211 Geneve 27, Switzerland, (Telephone in U.S. (212) 331-9081), www.who.int; *World Health Report 2006.*

CYPRUS - WAGES

Euromonitor International, Inc., 224 S. Michigan Avenue, Suite 1500, Chicago, IL 60604, (312) 922-1115, Fax: (312) 922-1157, www.euromonitor.com; *European Marketing Data and Statistics 2008.*

International Labour Office, I.L.O. Publications, 4 route des Morillons, CH-1211 Geneva 22, Switzerland, (Telephone in U.S. (202) 653-7652), (Fax in U.S. (202) 653-7687), www.ilo.org; *Yearbook of Labour Statistics 2006.*

United Nations Statistics Division, New York, NY 10017, (800) 253-9646, Fax: (212) 963-4116, http://unstats.un.org; *Statistical Yearbook.*

The World Bank, 1818 H Street, NW, Washington, DC 20433, (202) 473-1000, Fax: (202) 477-6391, www.worldbank.org; *Cyprus.*

CYPRUS - WALNUT PRODUCTION

See CYPRUS - CROPS

CYPRUS - WELFARE STATE

International Monetary Fund (IMF), 700 Nineteenth Street, NW, Washington, DC 20431, (202) 623-7000, Fax: (202) 623-4661, www.imf.org; *Government Finance Statistics Yearbook (2008 Edition).*

CYPRUS - WHEAT PRODUCTION

See CYPRUS - CROPS

CYPRUS - WHOLESALE PRICE INDEXES

International Monetary Fund (IMF), 700 Nineteenth Street, NW, Washington, DC 20431, (202) 623-7000, Fax: (202) 623-4661, www.imf.org; *International Financial Statistics Yearbook 2007.*

United Nations Statistics Division, New York, NY 10017, (800) 253-9646, Fax: (212) 963-4116, http://unstats.un.org; *Statistical Yearbook.*

CYPRUS - WHOLESALE TRADE

United Nations Statistics Division, New York, NY 10017, (800) 253-9646, Fax: (212) 963-4116, http://unstats.un.org; *Statistical Yearbook.*

CYPRUS - WINE PRODUCTION

See CYPRUS - BEVERAGE INDUSTRY

CYPRUS - WOOL PRODUCTION

See CYPRUS - TEXTILE INDUSTRY

CZECH REPUBLIC - NATIONAL STATISTICAL OFFICE

Czech Statistical Office, Na padesatem 81, 100 82 Praha 10, Strasnice, Czech Republic, www.czso.cz; National Data Center.

CZECH REPUBLIC - PRIMARY STATISTICS SOURCES

Czech Statistical Office, Na padesatem 81, 100 82 Praha 10, Strasnice, Czech Republic, www.czso.cz; *Analysis of Macroeconomic Development 2008* and *Statistical Yearbook of the Czech Republic 2007.*

Eurostat, Batiment Jean Monnet, Rue Alcide de Gasperi, L-2920 Luxembourg, http://epp.eurostat.ec.europa.eu; *Pocketbook on Candidate and Potential Candidate Countries.*

CZECH REPUBLIC - ABORTION

United Nations Statistics Division, New York, NY 10017, (800) 253-9646, Fax: (212) 963-4116, http://unstats.un.org; *Demographic Yearbook* and *Trends in Europe and North America: The Statistical Yearbook of the ECE 2005.*

CZECH REPUBLIC - AGRICULTURAL MACHINERY

United Nations Statistics Division, New York, NY 10017, (800) 253-9646, Fax: (212) 963-4116, http://unstats.un.org; *Statistical Yearbook.*

CZECH REPUBLIC - AGRICULTURE

Economist Intelligence Unit, 111 West 57th Street, New York, NY 10019, (212) 554-0600, Fax: (212) 586-1181, www.eiu.com; *Czech Republic Country Report.*

Euromonitor International, Inc., 224 S. Michigan Avenue, Suite 1500, Chicago, IL 60604, (312) 922-1115, Fax: (312) 922-1157, www.euromonitor.com; *World Marketing Data and Statistics.*

Eurostat, Batiment Jean Monnet, Rue Alcide de Gasperi, L-2920 Luxembourg, http://epp.eurostat.ec.europa.eu; *EU Agricultural Prices in 2007.*

M.E. Sharpe, 80 Business Park Drive, Armonk, NY 10504, (800) 541-6563, Fax: (914) 273-2106, www.mesharpe.com; *The Illustrated Book of World Rankings.*

Organisation for Economic Cooperation and Development (OECD), 2 rue Andre Pascal, F-75775 Paris Cedex 16, France, (Telephone in U.S. (202) 785-6323), (Fax in U.S. (202) 785-0350), www.oecd.org; *OECD Agricultural Outlook: 2007-2016* and *OECD Economic Survey - Czech Republic 2008.*

Palgrave Macmillan Ltd., Houndmills, Basingstoke, Hampshire, RG21 6XS, England, (Telephone in U.S. (888) 330-8477), (Fax in U.S. (800) 672-2054), www.palgrave.com; *The Statesman's Yearbook 2008.*

Taylor and Francis Group, An Informa Business, 2 Park Square, Milton Park, Abingdon, Oxford OX14 4RN, United Kingdom, (Dial from U.S. (212) 216-7800), (Fax from U.S. (212) 564-7854), www.tandf.co.uk; *The Europa World Year Book.*

United Nations Conference on Trade and Development (UNCTAD), DC2-1120, United Nations, New York, NY 10017, (212) 963-0027, www.unctad.org; *UNCTAD Commodity Yearbook.*

United Nations Food and Agricultural Organization (FAO), Viale delle Terme di Caracalla, 00100 Rome, Italy, (Dial from U.S. (202) 653-2400), (Fax from U.S. (202) 653 5760), www.fao.org; AQUASTAT; *FAO Production Yearbook 2002; FAO Trade Yearbook;* and *The State of Food and Agriculture (SOFA) 2006.*

United Nations Statistics Division, New York, NY 10017, (800) 253-9646, Fax: (212) 963-4116, http://unstats.un.org; *2004 Industrial Commodity Statistics Yearbook* and *Statistical Yearbook.*

The World Bank, 1818 H Street, NW, Washington, DC 20433, (202) 473-1000, Fax: (202) 477-6391, www.worldbank.org; *Czech Republic.*

CZECH REPUBLIC - AIRLINES

Eurostat, Batiment Jean Monnet, Rue Alcide de Gasperi, L-2920 Luxembourg, http://epp.eurostat.ec.europa.eu; *Regional Passenger and Freight Air Transport in Europe in 2006.*

International Civil Aviation Organization (ICAO), External Relations and Public Information Office (EPO), 999 University Street, Montreal, Quebec H3C 5H7, Canada, (Dial from U.S. (514) 954-8219), (Fax from U.S. (514) 954-6077), www.icao.int; *Civil Aviation Statistics of the World.*

M.E. Sharpe, 80 Business Park Drive, Armonk, NY 10504, (800) 541-6563, Fax: (914) 273-2106, www.mesharpe.com; *The Illustrated Book of World Rankings.*

Palgrave Macmillan Ltd., Houndmills, Basingstoke, Hampshire, RG21 6XS, England, (Telephone in U.S. (888) 330-8477), (Fax in U.S. (800) 672-2054), www.palgrave.com; *The Statesman's Yearbook 2008.*

Taylor and Francis Group, An Informa Business, 2 Park Square, Milton Park, Abingdon, Oxford OX14 4RN, United Kingdom, (Dial from U.S. (212) 216-7800), (Fax from U.S. (212) 564-7854), www.tandf.co.uk; *The Europa World Year Book.*

United Nations Statistics Division, New York, NY 10017, (800) 253-9646, Fax: (212) 963-4116, http://unstats.un.org; *Statistical Yearbook.*

CZECH REPUBLIC - AIRPORTS

Central Intelligence Agency, Office of Public Affairs, Washington, DC 20505, (703) 482-0623, Fax: (703) 482-1739, www.cia.gov; *The World Factbook.*

CZECH REPUBLIC - ALUMINUM PRODUCTION

See CZECH REPUBLIC - MINERAL INDUSTRIES

CZECH REPUBLIC - ARMED FORCES

Central Intelligence Agency, Office of Public Affairs, Washington, DC 20505, (703) 482-0623, Fax: (703) 482-1739, www.cia.gov; *The World Factbook.*

Euromonitor International, Inc., 224 S. Michigan Avenue, Suite 1500, Chicago, IL 60604, (312) 922-1115, Fax: (312) 922-1157, www.euromonitor.com; *World Marketing Data and Statistics.*

International Institute for Strategic Studies (IISS), Arundel House, 13-15 Arundel Street, Temple Place, London WC2R 3DX, England, www.iiss.org; *The Military Balance 2007.*

Palgrave Macmillan Ltd., Houndmills, Basingstoke, Hampshire, RG21 6XS, England, (Telephone in U.S. (888) 330-8477), (Fax in U.S. (800) 672-2054), www.palgrave.com; *The Statesman's Yearbook 2008.*

U.S. Department of State (DOS), 2201 C Street NW, Washington, DC 20520, (202) 647-4000, www.state.gov; *World Military Expenditures and Arms Transfers (WMEAT).*

United Nations Statistics Division, New York, NY 10017, (800) 253-9646, Fax: (212) 963-4116, http://unstats.un.org; *Human Development Report 2006.*

CZECH REPUBLIC - AUTOMOBILE INDUSTRY AND TRADE

United Nations Statistics Division, New York, NY 10017, (800) 253-9646, Fax: (212) 963-4116, http://unstats.un.org; *Statistical Yearbook.*

CZECH REPUBLIC - BALANCE OF PAYMENTS

Organisation for Economic Cooperation and Development (OECD), 2 rue Andre Pascal, F-75775 Paris Cedex 16, France, (Telephone in U.S. (202) 785-6323), (Fax in U.S. (202) 785-0350), www.oecd.org; *OECD Economic Survey - Czech Republic 2008.*

Taylor and Francis Group, An Informa Business, 2 Park Square, Milton Park, Abingdon, Oxford OX14 4RN, United Kingdom, (Dial from U.S. (212) 216-7800), (Fax from U.S. (212) 564-7854), www.tandf.co.uk; *The Europa World Year Book.*

United Nations Conference on Trade and Development (UNCTAD), DC2-1120, United Nations, New York, NY 10017, (212) 963-0027, www.unctad.org; *Handbook of Statistics 2005.*

The World Bank, 1818 H Street, NW, Washington, DC 20433, (202) 473-1000, Fax: (202) 477-6391, www.worldbank.org; *Czech Republic* and *World Development Report 2008.*

CZECH REPUBLIC - BANKS AND BANKING

Euromonitor International, Inc., 224 S. Michigan Avenue, Suite 1500, Chicago, IL 60604, (312) 922-1115, Fax: (312) 922-1157, www.euromonitor.com; *World Marketing Data and Statistics.*

European Union, Delegation of the European Commission to the United States, 2300 M Street, NW, Washington, DC 20037, (202) 862-9500, Fax: (202) 429-1766, www.eurunion.org; *The EU Economy, 2007 Review: Moving Europe's Productivity Frontier.*

M.E. Sharpe, 80 Business Park Drive, Armonk, NY 10504, (800) 541-6563, Fax: (914) 273-2106, www.mesharpe.com; *The Illustrated Book of World Rankings.*

Organisation for Economic Cooperation and Development (OECD), 2 rue Andre Pascal, F-75775 Paris Cedex 16, France, (Telephone in U.S. (202) 785-6323), (Fax in U.S. (202) 785-0350), www.oecd.org; *OECD Economic Survey - Czech Republic 2008.*

Palgrave Macmillan Ltd., Houndmills, Basingstoke, Hampshire, RG21 6XS, England, (Telephone in U.S. (888) 330-8477), (Fax in U.S. (800) 672-2054), www.palgrave.com; *The Statesman's Yearbook 2008.*

Taylor and Francis Group, An Informa Business, 2 Park Square, Milton Park, Abingdon, Oxford OX14 4RN, United Kingdom, (Dial from U.S. (212) 216-7800), (Fax from U.S. (212) 564-7854), www.tandf.co.uk; *The Europa World Year Book.*

CZECH REPUBLIC - BARLEY PRODUCTION

See CZECH REPUBLIC - CROPS

CZECH REPUBLIC - BEVERAGE INDUSTRY

M.E. Sharpe, 80 Business Park Drive, Armonk, NY 10504, (800) 541-6563, Fax: (914) 273-2106, www.mesharpe.com; *The Illustrated Book of World Rankings.*

United Nations Statistics Division, New York, NY 10017, (800) 253-9646, Fax: (212) 963-4116, http://unstats.un.org; *Statistical Yearbook.*

CZECH REPUBLIC - BROADCASTING

Central Intelligence Agency, Office of Public Affairs, Washington, DC 20505, (703) 482-0623, Fax: (703) 482-1739, www.cia.gov; *The World Factbook.*

Euromonitor International, Inc., 224 S. Michigan Avenue, Suite 1500, Chicago, IL 60604, (312) 922-1115, Fax: (312) 922-1157, www.euromonitor.com; *World Marketing Data and Statistics.*

M.E. Sharpe, 80 Business Park Drive, Armonk, NY 10504, (800) 541-6563, Fax: (914) 273-2106, www.mesharpe.com; *The Illustrated Book of World Rankings.*

Palgrave Macmillan Ltd., Houndmills, Basingstoke, Hampshire, RG21 6XS, England, (Telephone in U.S. (888) 330-8477), (Fax in U.S. (800) 672-2054), www.palgrave.com; *The Statesman's Yearbook 2008.*

United Nations Statistics Division, New York, NY 10017, (800) 253-9646, Fax: (212) 963-4116, http://unstats.un.org; *Trends in Europe and North America: The Statistical Yearbook of the ECE 2005.*

WRTH Publications Limited, PO Box 290, Oxford OX2 7FT, UK, www.wrth.com; *World Radio TV Handbook 2007.*

CZECH REPUBLIC - BUDGET

Central Intelligence Agency, Office of Public Affairs, Washington, DC 20505, (703) 482-0623, Fax: (703) 482-1739, www.cia.gov; *The World Factbook.*

Eurostat, Batiment Jean Monnet, Rue Alcide de Gasperi, L-2920 Luxembourg, http://epp.eurostat.ec.europa.eu; *Government Budgets.*

CZECH REPUBLIC - BUSINESS

Economist Intelligence Unit, 111 West 57th Street, New York, NY 10019, (212) 554-0600, Fax: (212) 586-1181, www.eiu.com; *Business Eastern Europe.*

United Nations Statistics Division, New York, NY 10017, (800) 253-9646, Fax: (212) 963-4116, http://unstats.un.org; *Statistical Yearbook.*

CZECH REPUBLIC - CATTLE

See CZECH REPUBLIC - LIVESTOCK

CZECH REPUBLIC - CHILDBIRTH - STATISTICS

Central Intelligence Agency, Office of Public Affairs, Washington, DC 20505, (703) 482-0623, Fax: (703) 482-1739, www.cia.gov; *The World Factbook.*

Euromonitor International, Inc., 224 S. Michigan Avenue, Suite 1500, Chicago, IL 60604, (312) 922-1115, Fax: (312) 922-1157, www.euromonitor.com; *The World Economic Factbook 2008.*

M.E. Sharpe, 80 Business Park Drive, Armonk, NY 10504, (800) 541-6563, Fax: (914) 273-2106, www.mesharpe.com; *The Illustrated Book of World Rankings.*

Palgrave Macmillan Ltd., Houndmills, Basingstoke, Hampshire, RG21 6XS, England, (Telephone in U.S. (888) 330-8477), (Fax in U.S. (800) 672-2054), www.palgrave.com; *The Statesman's Yearbook 2008.*

Taylor and Francis Group, An Informa Business, 2 Park Square, Milton Park, Abingdon, Oxford OX14 4RN, United Kingdom, (Dial from U.S. (212) 216-7800), (Fax from U.S. (212) 564-7854), www.tandf.co.uk; *The Europa World Year Book.*

United Nations Statistics Division, New York, NY 10017, (800) 253-9646, Fax: (212) 963-4116, http://unstats.un.org; *Demographic Yearbook* and *Statistical Yearbook.*

World Health Organization (WHO), Avenue Appia 20, 1211 Geneve 27, Switzerland, (Telephone in U.S. (212) 331-9081), www.who.int; *World Health Report 2006.*

CZECH REPUBLIC - CLIMATE

M.E. Sharpe, 80 Business Park Drive, Armonk, NY 10504, (800) 541-6563, Fax: (914) 273-2106, www.mesharpe.com; *The Illustrated Book of World Rankings.*

Palgrave Macmillan Ltd., Houndmills, Basingstoke, Hampshire, RG21 6XS, England, (Telephone in U.S. (888) 330-8477), (Fax in U.S. (800) 672-2054), www.palgrave.com; *The Statesman's Yearbook 2008.*

CZECH REPUBLIC - COAL PRODUCTION

See CZECH REPUBLIC - MINERAL INDUSTRIES

CZECH REPUBLIC - COFFEE

See CZECH REPUBLIC - CROPS

CZECH REPUBLIC - COMMERCE

Palgrave Macmillan Ltd., Houndmills, Basingstoke, Hampshire, RG21 6XS, England, (Telephone in U.S. (888) 330-8477), (Fax in U.S. (800) 672-2054), www.palgrave.com; *The Statesman's Yearbook 2008.*

CZECH REPUBLIC - COMMODITY EXCHANGES

Commodity Research Bureau, 330 South Wells Street, Suite 612, Chicago, IL 60606-7110, (800) 621-5271, Fax: (312) 939-4135, www.crbtrader.com; *2006 CRB Commodity Yearbook and CD.*

International Lead and Zinc Study Group (ILZSG), Rua Almirante Barroso 38, 5th Floor, Lisbon 1000 - 013, Portugal, www.ilzsg.org; Interactive Statistical Database.

International Monetary Fund (IMF), 700 Nineteenth Street, NW, Washington, DC 20431, (202) 623-7000, Fax: (202) 623-4661, www.imf.org; *IMF Primary Commodity Prices.*

United Nations Food and Agricultural Organization (FAO), Viale delle Terme di Caracalla, 00100 Rome, Italy, (Dial from U.S. (202) 653-2400), (Fax from U.S. (202) 653 5760), www.fao.org; *The State of Food and Agriculture (SOFA) 2006.*

CZECH REPUBLIC - COMMUNICATION AND TRAFFIC

United Nations Statistics Division, New York, NY 10017, (800) 253-9646, Fax: (212) 963-4116, http://unstats.un.org; *Statistical Yearbook.*

CZECH REPUBLIC - CONSTRUCTION INDUSTRY

M.E. Sharpe, 80 Business Park Drive, Armonk, NY 10504, (800) 541-6563, Fax: (914) 273-2106, www.mesharpe.com; *The Illustrated Book of World Rankings.*

Organisation for Economic Cooperation and Development (OECD), 2 rue Andre Pascal, F-75775 Paris Cedex 16, France, (Telephone in U.S. (202) 785-6323), (Fax in U.S. (202) 785-0350), www.oecd.org; *OECD Economic Survey - Czech Republic 2008.*

United Nations Statistics Division, New York, NY 10017, (800) 253-9646, Fax: (212) 963-4116, http://unstats.un.org; *Statistical Yearbook.*

CZECH REPUBLIC - CONSUMER PRICE INDEXES

Taylor and Francis Group, An Informa Business, 2 Park Square, Milton Park, Abingdon, Oxford OX14 4RN, United Kingdom, (Dial from U.S. (212) 216-7800), (Fax from U.S. (212) 564-7854), www.tandf.co.uk; *The Europa World Year Book.*

United Nations Statistics Division, New York, NY 10017, (800) 253-9646, Fax: (212) 963-4116, http://unstats.un.org; *Statistical Yearbook* and *Trends in Europe and North America: The Statistical Yearbook of the ECE 2005.*

The World Bank, 1818 H Street, NW, Washington, DC 20433, (202) 473-1000, Fax: (202) 477-6391, www.worldbank.org; *Czech Republic.*

CZECH REPUBLIC - CONSUMPTION (ECONOMICS)

International Lead and Zinc Study Group (ILZSG), Rua Almirante Barroso 38, 5th Floor, Lisbon 1000 - 013, Portugal, www.ilzsg.org; Interactive Statistical Database.

Organisation for Economic Cooperation and Development (OECD), 2 rue Andre Pascal, F-75775 Paris Cedex 16, France, (Telephone in U.S. (202) 785-6323), (Fax in U.S. (202) 785-0350), www.oecd.org; *Towards Sustainable Household Consumption?: Trends and Policies in OECD Countries.*

The World Bank, 1818 H Street, NW, Washington, DC 20433, (202) 473-1000, Fax: (202) 477-6391, www.worldbank.org; *World Development Report 2008.*

CZECH REPUBLIC - COPPER INDUSTRY AND TRADE

See CZECH REPUBLIC - MINERAL INDUSTRIES

CZECH REPUBLIC - CORN INDUSTRY

See CZECH REPUBLIC - CROPS

CZECH REPUBLIC - COTTON

See CZECH REPUBLIC - CROPS

CZECH REPUBLIC - CRIME

Eurostat, Batiment Jean Monnet, Rue Alcide de Gasperi, L-2920 Luxembourg, http://epp.eurostat.ec.europa.eu; *Crime and Criminal Justice; General Government Expenditure and Revenue in the EU, 2006;* and *Study on Crime Victimisation.*

U.S. Department of Justice (DOJ), Bureau of Justice Statistics, 810 Seventh Street, NW, Washington, DC 20531, (202) 307-0765, www.ojp.usdoj.gov/bjs/; *The World Factbook of Criminal Justice Systems.*

United Nations Statistics Division, New York, NY 10017, (800) 253-9646, Fax: (212) 963-4116, http://unstats.un.org; *Trends in Europe and North America: The Statistical Yearbook of the ECE 2005.*

CZECH REPUBLIC - CROPS

Euromonitor International, Inc., 224 S. Michigan Avenue, Suite 1500, Chicago, IL 60604, (312) 922-1115, Fax: (312) 922-1157, www.euromonitor.com; *European Marketing Data and Statistics 2008.*

M.E. Sharpe, 80 Business Park Drive, Armonk, NY 10504, (800) 541-6563, Fax: (914) 273-2106, www.mesharpe.com; *The Illustrated Book of World Rankings.*

Palgrave Macmillan Ltd., Houndmills, Basingstoke, Hampshire, RG21 6XS, England, (Telephone in U.S. (888) 330-8477), (Fax in U.S. (800) 672-2054), www.palgrave.com; *The Statesman's Yearbook 2008.*

Taylor and Francis Group, An Informa Business, 2 Park Square, Milton Park, Abingdon, Oxford OX14 4RN, United Kingdom, (Dial from U.S. (212) 216-7800), (Fax from U.S. (212) 564-7854), www.tandf.co.uk; *The Europa World Year Book.*

United Nations Conference on Trade and Development (UNCTAD), DC2-1120, United Nations, New York, NY 10017, (212) 963-0027, www.unctad.org; *UNCTAD Commodity Yearbook.*

United Nations Food and Agricultural Organization (FAO), Viale delle Terme di Caracalla, 00100 Rome, Italy, (Dial from U.S. (202) 653-2400), (Fax from U.S. (202) 653 5760), www.fao.org; *FAO Production Yearbook 2002* and *The State of Food and Agriculture (SOFA) 2006.*

United Nations Statistics Division, New York, NY 10017, (800) 253-9646, Fax: (212) 963-4116, http://unstats.un.org; *2004 Industrial Commodity Statistics Yearbook* and *Statistical Yearbook.*

CZECH REPUBLIC - CUSTOMS ADMINISTRATION

Palgrave Macmillan Ltd., Houndmills, Basingstoke, Hampshire, RG21 6XS, England, (Telephone in U.S. (888) 330-8477), (Fax in U.S. (800) 672-2054), www.palgrave.com; *The Statesman's Yearbook 2008.*

CZECH REPUBLIC - DAIRY PROCESSING

Euromonitor International, Inc., 224 S. Michigan Avenue, Suite 1500, Chicago, IL 60604, (312) 922-1115, Fax: (312) 922-1157, www.euromonitor.com; *European Marketing Data and Statistics 2008.*

Palgrave Macmillan Ltd., Houndmills, Basingstoke, Hampshire, RG21 6XS, England, (Telephone in U.S. (888) 330-8477), (Fax in U.S. (800) 672-2054), www.palgrave.com; *The Statesman's Yearbook 2008.*

Taylor and Francis Group, An Informa Business, 2 Park Square, Milton Park, Abingdon, Oxford OX14 4RN, United Kingdom, (Dial from U.S. (212) 216-7800), (Fax from U.S. (212) 564-7854), www.tandf.co.uk; *The Europa World Year Book.*

United Nations Food and Agricultural Organization (FAO), Viale delle Terme di Caracalla, 00100 Rome, Italy, (Dial from U.S. (202) 653-2400), (Fax from U.S. (202) 653 5760), www.fao.org; *FAO Production Yearbook 2002* and *The State of Food and Agriculture (SOFA) 2006.*

United Nations Statistics Division, New York, NY 10017, (800) 253-9646, Fax: (212) 963-4116, http://unstats.un.org; *2004 Industrial Commodity Statistics Yearbook* and *Statistical Yearbook.*

CZECH REPUBLIC - DEATH RATES

See CZECH REPUBLIC - MORTALITY

CZECH REPUBLIC - DEBTS, EXTERNAL

The World Bank, 1818 H Street, NW, Washington, DC 20433, (202) 473-1000, Fax: (202) 477-6391, www.worldbank.org; *Global Development Finance 2007* and *World Development Report 2008.*

CZECH REPUBLIC - DEFENSE EXPENDITURES

See CZECH REPUBLIC - ARMED FORCES

CZECH REPUBLIC - DEMOGRAPHY

Euromonitor International, Inc., 224 S. Michigan Avenue, Suite 1500, Chicago, IL 60604, (312) 922-1115, Fax: (312) 922-1157, www.euromonitor.com; *The World Economic Factbook 2008* and *World Marketing Data and Statistics.*

Eurostat, Batiment Jean Monnet, Rue Alcide de Gasperi, L-2920 Luxembourg, http://epp.eurostat.ec.europa.eu; *Demographic Outlook - National Reports on the Demographic Developments in 2006.*

M.E. Sharpe, 80 Business Park Drive, Armonk, NY 10504, (800) 541-6563, Fax: (914) 273-2106, www.mesharpe.com; *The Illustrated Book of World Rankings.*

United Nations Statistics Division, New York, NY 10017, (800) 253-9646, Fax: (212) 963-4116, http://unstats.un.org; *Demographic Yearbook* and *Human Development Report 2006.*

The World Bank, 1818 H Street, NW, Washington, DC 20433, (202) 473-1000, Fax: (202) 477-6391, www.worldbank.org; *Czech Republic.*

CZECH REPUBLIC - DIAMONDS

See CZECH REPUBLIC - MINERAL INDUSTRIES

CZECH REPUBLIC - DISPOSABLE INCOME

M.E. Sharpe, 80 Business Park Drive, Armonk, NY 10504, (800) 541-6563, Fax: (914) 273-2106, www.mesharpe.com; *The Illustrated Book of World Rankings.*

United Nations Statistics Division, New York, NY 10017, (800) 253-9646, Fax: (212) 963-4116, http://unstats.un.org; *National Accounts Statistics: Compendium of Income Distribution Statistics* and *Statistical Yearbook.*

CZECH REPUBLIC - DIVORCE

M.E. Sharpe, 80 Business Park Drive, Armonk, NY 10504, (800) 541-6563, Fax: (914) 273-2106, www.mesharpe.com; *The Illustrated Book of World Rankings.*

United Nations Statistics Division, New York, NY 10017, (800) 253-9646, Fax: (212) 963-4116, http://unstats.un.org; *Demographic Yearbook; Statistical Yearbook;* and *Trends in Europe and North America: The Statistical Yearbook of the ECE 2005.*

CZECH REPUBLIC - ECONOMIC ASSISTANCE

United Nations Statistics Division, New York, NY 10017, (800) 253-9646, Fax: (212) 963-4116, http://unstats.un.org; *Statistical Yearbook.*

CZECH REPUBLIC - ECONOMIC CONDITIONS

Banque de France, 48 rue Croix des Petits champs, 75001 Paris, France, www.banque-france.fr/home.htm; *Key Data for the Euro Area.*

Center for International Business Education Research (CIBER), Columbia Business School and School of International and Public Affairs, Uris Hall, Room 212, 3022 Broadway, New York, NY 10027-6902, Mr. Joshua Safier, (212) 854-4750, Fax: (212) 222-9821, www.columbia.edu/cu/ciber/; Datastream International.

Central Intelligence Agency, Office of Public Affairs, Washington, DC 20505, (703) 482-0623, Fax: (703) 482-1739, www.cia.gov; *The World Factbook.*

DSI Data Service Information, Xantener Strasse 51a, D-47495 Rheinberg, Germany, www.dsidata.com; *Campus Solution.*

Dun and Bradstreet (DB) Corporation, 103 JFK Parkway, Short Hills, NJ 07078, (973) 921-5500, www.dnb.com; *Country Report.*

Economist Intelligence Unit, 111 West 57th Street, New York, NY 10019, (212) 554-0600, Fax: (212) 586-1181, www.eiu.com; *Czech Republic Country Report.*

Euromonitor International, Inc., 224 S. Michigan Avenue, Suite 1500, Chicago, IL 60604, (312) 922-1115, Fax: (312) 922-1157, www.euromonitor.com; *European Marketing Data and Statistics 2008; The World Economic Factbook 2008;* and *World Marketing Data and Statistics.*

European Union, Delegation of the European Commission to the United States, 2300 M Street, NW, Washington, DC 20037, (202) 862-9500, Fax: (202) 429-1766, www.eurunion.org; *The EU Economy, 2007 Review: Moving Europe's Productivity Frontier.*

Eurostat, Batiment Jean Monnet, Rue Alcide de Gasperi, L-2920 Luxembourg, http://epp.eurostat.ec.europa.eu; *Consumers in Europe - Facts and Figures on Services of General Interest* and *EU Economic Data Pocketbook.*

Federal Statistical Office Germany, D-65180 Wiesbaden, Germany, www.destatis.de; *Czech Republic 2005.*

International Monetary Fund (IMF), 700 Nineteenth Street, NW, Washington, DC 20431, (202) 623-7000, Fax: (202) 623-4661, www.imf.org; *World Economic Outlook Reports.*

M.E. Sharpe, 80 Business Park Drive, Armonk, NY 10504, (800) 541-6563, Fax: (914) 273-2106, www.mesharpe.com; *The Illustrated Book of World Rankings.*

Organisation for Economic Cooperation and Development (OECD), 2 rue Andre Pascal, F-75775 Paris Cedex 16, France, (Telephone in U.S. (202) 785-6323), (Fax in U.S. (202) 785-0350), www.oecd.org; *ICT Sector Data and Metadata by Country; Labour Force Statistics: 1986-2005, 2007 Edition; OECD Composite Leading Indicators (CLIs), Updated September 2007; OECD Economic Survey - Czech Republic 2008;* and *OECD in Figures 2007.*

Palgrave Macmillan Ltd., Houndmills, Basingstoke, Hampshire, RG21 6XS, England, (Telephone in U.S. (888) 330-8477), (Fax in U.S. (800) 672-2054), www.palgrave.com; *The Statesman's Yearbook 2008.*

Taylor and Francis Group, An Informa Business, 2 Park Square, Milton Park, Abingdon, Oxford OX14 4RN, United Kingdom, (Dial from U.S. (212) 216-7800), (Fax from U.S. (212) 564-7854), www.tandf.co.uk; *The Europa World Year Book.*

United Nations Statistics Division, New York, NY 10017, (800) 253-9646, Fax: (212) 963-4116, http://unstats.un.org; *World Statistics Pocketbook.*

The World Bank, 1818 H Street, NW, Washington, DC 20433, (202) 473-1000, Fax: (202) 477-6391, www.worldbank.org; *Czech Republic; Global Economic Monitor (GEM); Global Economic Prospects 2008; The World Bank Atlas 2003-2004;* and *World Development Report 2008.*

CZECH REPUBLIC - EDUCATION

Euromonitor International, Inc., 224 S. Michigan Avenue, Suite 1500, Chicago, IL 60604, (312) 922-1115, Fax: (312) 922-1157, www.euromonitor.com; *European Marketing Data and Statistics 2008* and *World Marketing Data and Statistics.*

European Union, Delegation of the European Commission to the United States, 2300 M Street, NW, Washington, DC 20037, (202) 862-9500, Fax: (202) 429-1766, www.eurunion.org; *Education across Europe 2003.*

Eurostat, Batiment Jean Monnet, Rue Alcide de Gasperi, L-2920 Luxembourg, http://epp.eurostat.ec.europa.eu; *Education, Science and Culture Statistics.*

M.E. Sharpe, 80 Business Park Drive, Armonk, NY 10504, (800) 541-6563, Fax: (914) 273-2106, www.mesharpe.com; *The Illustrated Book of World Rankings.*

Taylor and Francis Group, An Informa Business, 2 Park Square, Milton Park, Abingdon, Oxford OX14 4RN, United Kingdom, (Dial from U.S. (212) 216-7800), (Fax from U.S. (212) 564-7854), www.tandf.co.uk; *The Europa World Year Book.*

UNESCO Institute for Statistics, C.P. 6128 Succursale Centre-Ville, Montreal, Quebec, H3C 3J7 Canada, (Dial from U.S. (514) 343-6880), (Fax from U.S. (514) 343 6882), www.uis.unesco.org; *Statistical Tables.*

United Nations Statistics Division, New York, NY 10017, (800) 253-9646, Fax: (212) 963-4116, http://unstats.un.org; *Human Development Report 2006* and *Trends in Europe and North America: The Statistical Yearbook of the ECE 2005.*

The World Bank, 1818 H Street, NW, Washington, DC 20433, (202) 473-1000, Fax: (202) 477-6391, www.worldbank.org; *Czech Republic* and *World Development Report 2008.*

CZECH REPUBLIC - ELECTRICITY

Eurostat, Batiment Jean Monnet, Rue Alcide de Gasperi, L-2920 Luxembourg, http://epp.eurostat.ec.europa.eu; *Energy - Monthly Statistics* and *Panorama of Energy - 2007 Edition.*

M.E. Sharpe, 80 Business Park Drive, Armonk, NY 10504, (800) 541-6563, Fax: (914) 273-2106, www.mesharpe.com; *The Illustrated Book of World Rankings.*

Organisation for Economic Cooperation and Development (OECD), 2 rue Andre Pascal, F-75775 Paris Cedex 16, France, (Telephone in U.S. (202) 785-6323), (Fax in U.S. (202) 785-0350), www.oecd.org; *World Energy Outlook 2007.*

Palgrave Macmillan Ltd., Houndmills, Basingstoke, Hampshire, RG21 6XS, England, (Telephone in U.S. (888) 330-8477), (Fax in U.S. (800) 672-2054), www.palgrave.com; *The Statesman's Yearbook 2008.*

Platts, 2 Penn Plaza, 25th Floor, New York, NY 10121-2298, (212) 904-3070, www.platts.com; *Energy Economist; EU Energy; European Electricity Review 2004;* and *European Electricity Review 2004.*

U.S. Department of Energy (DOE), Energy Information Administration (EIA), 1000 Independence Avenue, SW, Washington, DC 20585, (202) 586-8800, www.eia.doe.gov; *International Energy Annual 2004* and *International Energy Outlook 2006.*

United Nations Statistics Division, New York, NY 10017, (800) 253-9646, Fax: (212) 963-4116, http://unstats.un.org; *Energy Statistics Yearbook 2003; Human Development Report 2006; Statistical Yearbook;* and *Trends in Europe and North America: The Statistical Yearbook of the ECE 2005.*

CZECH REPUBLIC - EMPLOYMENT

Bernan Essential Government Publications, 4611-F Assembly Drive, Lanham MD, 20706-4391, (301) 459-2255, Fax: (800) 865-3450, www.bernan.com; *OECD Factbook 2006.*

Euromonitor International, Inc., 224 S. Michigan Avenue, Suite 1500, Chicago, IL 60604, (312) 922-1115, Fax: (312) 922-1157, www.euromonitor.com; *European Marketing Data and Statistics 2008.*

International Labour Office, I.L.O. Publications, 4 route des Morillons, CH-1211 Geneva 22, Switzerland, (Telephone in U.S. (202) 653-7652), (Fax in U.S. (202) 653-7687), www.ilo.org; *Yearbook of Labour Statistics 2006.*

M.E. Sharpe, 80 Business Park Drive, Armonk, NY 10504, (800) 541-6563, Fax: (914) 273-2106, www.mesharpe.com; *The Illustrated Book of World Rankings.*

Organisation for Economic Cooperation and Development (OECD), 2 rue Andre Pascal, F-75775 Paris Cedex 16, France, (Telephone in U.S. (202) 785-6323), (Fax in U.S. (202) 785-0350), www.oecd.org; *ICT Sector Data and Metadata by Country; Labour Force Statistics: 1986-2005, 2007 Edition; OECD Composite Leading Indicators (CLIs), Updated September 2007; OECD Economic Survey - Czech Republic 2008;* and *OECD in Figures 2007.*

United Nations Statistics Division, New York, NY 10017, (800) 253-9646, Fax: (212) 963-4116, http://unstats.un.org; *Statistical Yearbook* and *Trends in Europe and North America: The Statistical Yearbook of the ECE 2005.*

The World Bank, 1818 H Street, NW, Washington, DC 20433, (202) 473-1000, Fax: (202) 477-6391, www.worldbank.org; *Czech Republic.*

CZECH REPUBLIC - ENERGY INDUSTRIES

Enerdata, 10 Rue Royale, 75008 Paris, France, www.enerdata.fr; *Global Energy Market Data.*

Eurostat, Batiment Jean Monnet, Rue Alcide de Gasperi, L-2920 Luxembourg, http://epp.eurostat.ec.europa.eu; *Energy - Monthly Statistics* and *Panorama of Energy - 2007 Edition.*

International Energy Agency (IEA), 9, rue de la Federation, 75739 Paris Cedex 15, France, www.iea.org; *Key World Energy Statistics 2007.*

Organisation for Economic Cooperation and Development (OECD), 2 rue Andre Pascal, F-75775 Paris Cedex 16, France, (Telephone in U.S. (202) 785-6323), (Fax in U.S. (202) 785-0350), www.oecd.org; *Towards Sustainable Household Consumption?: Trends and Policies in OECD Countries.*

Platts, 2 Penn Plaza, 25th Floor, New York, NY 10121-2298, (212) 904-3070, www.platts.com; *Energy in East Europe; EU Energy;* and *European Power Daily.*

United Nations Statistics Division, New York, NY 10017, (800) 253-9646, Fax: (212) 963-4116, http://unstats.un.org; *Statistical Yearbook.*

The World Bank, 1818 H Street, NW, Washington, DC 20433, (202) 473-1000, Fax: (202) 477-6391, www.worldbank.org; *Czech Republic.*

CZECH REPUBLIC - ENVIRONMENTAL CONDITIONS

Center for Research on the Epidemiology of Disasters (CRED), Universite Catholique de Louvain, Ecole de Sante Publique, 30.94 Clos Chapelle-aux-Champs, 1200 Brussels, Belgium, www.cred.be; *Three Decades of Floods in Europe: A Preliminary Analysis of EMDAT Data.*

DSI Data Service Information, Xantener Strasse 51a, D-47495 Rheinberg, Germany, www.dsidata.com; *Campus Solution* and *DSI's Global Environmental Database.*

Economist Intelligence Unit, 111 West 57th Street, New York, NY 10019, (212) 554-0600, Fax: (212) 586-1181, www.eiu.com; *Czech Republic Country Report.*

Eurostat, Batiment Jean Monnet, Rue Alcide de Gasperi, L-2920 Luxembourg, http://epp.eurostat.ec.europa.eu; *Environmental Protection Expenditure in Europe.*

Federal Statistical Office Germany, D-65180 Wiesbaden, Germany, www.destatis.de; *Czech Republic 2005.*

Platts, 2 Penn Plaza, 25th Floor, New York, NY 10121-2298, (212) 904-3070, www.platts.com; *Emissions Daily.*

United Nations Statistics Division, New York, NY 10017, (800) 253-9646, Fax: (212) 963-4116, http://unstats.un.org; *Statistical Yearbook; Trends in Europe and North America: The Statistical Yearbook of the ECE 2005;* and *World Statistics Pocketbook.*

CZECH REPUBLIC - EXPENDITURES, PUBLIC

Eurostat, Batiment Jean Monnet, Rue Alcide de Gasperi, L-2920 Luxembourg, http://epp.eurostat.ec.europa.eu; *European Social Statistics - Social Protection Expenditure and Receipts - Data 1997-2005.*

CZECH REPUBLIC - EXPORTS

Central Intelligence Agency, Office of Public Affairs, Washington, DC 20505, (703) 482-0623, Fax: (703) 482-1739, www.cia.gov; *The World Factbook.*

Economist Intelligence Unit, 111 West 57th Street, New York, NY 10019, (212) 554-0600, Fax: (212) 586-1181, www.eiu.com; *Czech Republic Country Report.*

Euromonitor International, Inc., 224 S. Michigan Avenue, Suite 1500, Chicago, IL 60604, (312) 922-1115, Fax: (312) 922-1157, www.euromonitor.com; *The World Economic Factbook 2008.*

International Lead and Zinc Study Group (ILZSG), Rua Almirante Barroso 38, 5th Floor, Lisbon 1000 - 013, Portugal, www.ilzsg.org; Interactive Statistical Database.

International Monetary Fund (IMF), 700 Nineteenth Street, NW, Washington, DC 20431, (202) 623-7000, Fax: (202) 623-4661, www.imf.org; *Direction of Trade Statistics Yearbook 2007.*

Organisation for Economic Cooperation and Development (OECD), 2 rue Andre Pascal, F-75775 Paris Cedex 16, France, (Telephone in U.S. (202) 785-6323), (Fax in U.S. (202) 785-0350), www.oecd.org; *OECD Economic Survey - Czech Republic 2008.*

Palgrave Macmillan Ltd., Houndmills, Basingstoke, Hampshire, RG21 6XS, England, (Telephone in U.S. (888) 330-8477), (Fax in U.S. (800) 672-2054), www.palgrave.com; *The Statesman's Yearbook 2008.*

Taylor and Francis Group, An Informa Business, 2 Park Square, Milton Park, Abingdon, Oxford OX14 4RN, United Kingdom, (Dial from U.S. (212) 216-7800), (Fax from U.S. (212) 564-7854), www.tandf.co.uk; *The Europa World Year Book.*

United Nations Conference on Trade and Development (UNCTAD), DC2-1120, United Nations, New York, NY 10017, (212) 963-0027, www.unctad.org; *Handbook of Statistics 2005.*

United Nations Food and Agricultural Organization (FAO), Viale delle Terme di Caracalla, 00100 Rome, Italy, (Dial from U.S. (202) 653-2400), (Fax from U.S. (202) 653 5760), www.fao.org; *The State of Food and Agriculture (SOFA) 2006.*

United Nations Statistics Division, New York, NY 10017, (800) 253-9646, Fax: (212) 963-4116, http://unstats.un.org; *International Trade Statistics Yearbook* and *Trends in Europe and North America: The Statistical Yearbook of the ECE 2005.*

The World Bank, 1818 H Street, NW, Washington, DC 20433, (202) 473-1000, Fax: (202) 477-6391, www.worldbank.org; *World Development Report 2008.*

CZECH REPUBLIC - FERTILITY, HUMAN

Central Intelligence Agency, Office of Public Affairs, Washington, DC 20505, (703) 482-0623, Fax: (703) 482-1739, www.cia.gov; *The World Factbook.*

M.E. Sharpe, 80 Business Park Drive, Armonk, NY 10504, (800) 541-6563, Fax: (914) 273-2106, www.mesharpe.com; *The Illustrated Book of World Rankings.*

United Nations Statistics Division, New York, NY 10017, (800) 253-9646, Fax: (212) 963-4116, http://unstats.un.org; *Human Development Report 2006* and *Trends in Europe and North America: The Statistical Yearbook of the ECE 2005.*

The World Bank, 1818 H Street, NW, Washington, DC 20433, (202) 473-1000, Fax: (202) 477-6391, www.worldbank.org; *The World Bank Atlas 2003-2004* and *World Development Report 2008.*

CZECH REPUBLIC - FERTILIZER INDUSTRY

United Nations Food and Agricultural Organization (FAO), Viale delle Terme di Caracalla, 00100 Rome, Italy, (Dial from U.S. (202) 653-2400), (Fax from U.S. (202) 653 5760), www.fao.org; *FAO Fertilizer Yearbook* and *The State of Food and Agriculture (SOFA) 2006.*

United Nations Statistics Division, New York, NY 10017, (800) 253-9646, Fax: (212) 963-4116, http://unstats.un.org; *2004 Industrial Commodity Statistics Yearbook* and *Statistical Yearbook.*

CZECH REPUBLIC - FETAL MORTALITY

See CZECH REPUBLIC - MORTALITY

CZECH REPUBLIC - FILM

See CZECH REPUBLIC - MOTION PICTURES

CZECH REPUBLIC - FINANCE

Taylor and Francis Group, An Informa Business, 2 Park Square, Milton Park, Abingdon, Oxford OX14 4RN, United Kingdom, (Dial from U.S. (212) 216-7800), (Fax from U.S. (212) 564-7854), www.tandf.co.uk; *The Europa World Year Book.*

United Nations Statistics Division, New York, NY 10017, (800) 253-9646, Fax: (212) 963-4116, http://unstats.un.org; *National Accounts Statistics: Compendium of Income Distribution Statistics* and *Statistical Yearbook.*

The World Bank, 1818 H Street, NW, Washington, DC 20433, (202) 473-1000, Fax: (202) 477-6391, www.worldbank.org; *Czech Republic.*

CZECH REPUBLIC - FINANCE, PUBLIC

Banque de France, 48 rue Croix des Petits champs, 75001 Paris, France, www.banque-france.fr/home.htm; *Key Data for the Euro Area* and *Public Finance.*

Bernan Essential Government Publications, 4611-F Assembly Drive, Lanham MD, 20706-4391, (301) 459-2255, Fax: (800) 865-3450, www.bernan.com; *National Accounts Statistics.*

Economist Intelligence Unit, 111 West 57th Street, New York, NY 10019, (212) 554-0600, Fax: (212) 586-1181, www.eiu.com; *Czech Republic Country Report.*

International Monetary Fund (IMF), 700 Nineteenth Street, NW, Washington, DC 20431, (202) 623-7000, Fax: (202) 623-4661, www.imf.org; *International Financial Statistics* and *International Financial Statistics Online Service.*

M.E. Sharpe, 80 Business Park Drive, Armonk, NY 10504, (800) 541-6563, Fax: (914) 273-2106, www.mesharpe.com; *The Illustrated Book of World Rankings.*

Palgrave Macmillan Ltd., Houndmills, Basingstoke, Hampshire, RG21 6XS, England, (Telephone in U.S. (888) 330-8477), (Fax in U.S. (800) 672-2054), www.palgrave.com; *The Statesman's Yearbook 2008.*

Taylor and Francis Group, An Informa Business, 2 Park Square, Milton Park, Abingdon, Oxford OX14 4RN, United Kingdom, (Dial from U.S. (212) 216-7800), (Fax from U.S. (212) 564-7854), www.tandf.co.uk; *The Europa World Year Book.*

The World Bank, 1818 H Street, NW, Washington, DC 20433, (202) 473-1000, Fax: (202) 477-6391, www.worldbank.org; *Czech Republic.*

CZECH REPUBLIC - FISHERIES

Euromonitor International, Inc., 224 S. Michigan Avenue, Suite 1500, Chicago, IL 60604, (312) 922-1115, Fax: (312) 922-1157, www.euromonitor.com; *European Marketing Data and Statistics 2008.*

M.E. Sharpe, 80 Business Park Drive, Armonk, NY 10504, (800) 541-6563, Fax: (914) 273-2106, www.mesharpe.com; *The Illustrated Book of World Rankings.*

Taylor and Francis Group, An Informa Business, 2 Park Square, Milton Park, Abingdon, Oxford OX14 4RN, United Kingdom, (Dial from U.S. (212) 216-7800), (Fax from U.S. (212) 564-7854), www.tandf.co.uk; *The Europa World Year Book.*

United Nations Conference on Trade and Development (UNCTAD), DC2-1120, United Nations, New York, NY 10017, (212) 963-0027, www.unctad.org; *UNCTAD Commodity Yearbook.*

United Nations Food and Agricultural Organization (FAO), Viale delle Terme di Caracalla, 00100 Rome, Italy, (Dial from U.S. (202) 653-2400), (Fax from U.S. (202) 653 5760), www.fao.org; *FAO Yearbook of Fishery Statistics;* Fishery Databases; FISHSTAT Database. Subjects covered include: Aquaculture production, capture production, fishery commodities; and *The State of Food and Agriculture (SOFA) 2006.*

United Nations Statistics Division, New York, NY 10017, (800) 253-9646, Fax: (212) 963-4116, http://unstats.un.org; *2004 Industrial Commodity Statistics Yearbook* and *Statistical Yearbook.*

The World Bank, 1818 H Street, NW, Washington, DC 20433, (202) 473-1000, Fax: (202) 477-6391, www.worldbank.org; *Czech Republic.*

CZECH REPUBLIC - FLOUR INDUSTRY

United Nations Statistics Division, New York, NY 10017, (800) 253-9646, Fax: (212) 963-4116, http://unstats.un.org; *Statistical Yearbook.*

CZECH REPUBLIC - FOOD

Euromonitor International, Inc., 224 S. Michigan Avenue, Suite 1500, Chicago, IL 60604, (312) 922-1115, Fax: (312) 922-1157, www.euromonitor.com; *Retail Trade International 2007.*

United Nations Conference on Trade and Development (UNCTAD), DC2-1120, United Nations, New York, NY 10017, (212) 963-0027, www.unctad.org; *UNCTAD Commodity Yearbook.*

United Nations Food and Agricultural Organization (FAO), Viale delle Terme di Caracalla, 00100 Rome, Italy, (Dial from U.S. (202) 653-2400), (Fax from U.S. (202) 653 5760), www.fao.org; *FAO Production Yearbook 2002* and *The State of Food and Agriculture (SOFA) 2006.*

United Nations Statistics Division, New York, NY 10017, (800) 253-9646, Fax: (212) 963-4116, http://unstats.un.org; *Human Development Report 2006* and *2004 Industrial Commodity Statistics Yearbook.*

CZECH REPUBLIC - FOREIGN EXCHANGE RATES

Central Intelligence Agency, Office of Public Affairs, Washington, DC 20505, (703) 482-0623, Fax: (703) 482-1739, www.cia.gov; *The World Factbook.*

Euromonitor International, Inc., 224 S. Michigan Avenue, Suite 1500, Chicago, IL 60604, (312) 922-1115, Fax: (312) 922-1157, www.euromonitor.com; *The World Economic Factbook 2008.*

Taylor and Francis Group, An Informa Business, 2 Park Square, Milton Park, Abingdon, Oxford OX14 4RN, United Kingdom, (Dial from U.S. (212) 216-7800), (Fax from U.S. (212) 564-7854), www.tandf.co.uk; *The Europa World Year Book.*

United Nations Statistics Division, New York, NY 10017, (800) 253-9646, Fax: (212) 963-4116, http://unstats.un.org; *Statistical Yearbook; Trends in Europe and North America: The Statistical Yearbook of the ECE 2005;* and *World Statistics Pocketbook.*

CZECH REPUBLIC - FORESTS AND FORESTRY

Euromonitor International, Inc., 224 S. Michigan Avenue, Suite 1500, Chicago, IL 60604, (312) 922-1115, Fax: (312) 922-1157, www.euromonitor.com; *European Marketing Data and Statistics 2008.*

M.E. Sharpe, 80 Business Park Drive, Armonk, NY 10504, (800) 541-6563, Fax: (914) 273-2106, www.mesharpe.com; *The Illustrated Book of World Rankings.*

Palgrave Macmillan Ltd., Houndmills, Basingstoke, Hampshire, RG21 6XS, England, (Telephone in U.S. (888) 330-8477), (Fax in U.S. (800) 672-2054), www.palgrave.com; *The Statesman's Yearbook 2008.*

Taylor and Francis Group, An Informa Business, 2 Park Square, Milton Park, Abingdon, Oxford OX14 4RN, United Kingdom, (Dial from U.S. (212) 216-7800), (Fax from U.S. (212) 564-7854), www.tandf.co.uk; *The Europa World Year Book.*

UNESCO Institute for Statistics, C.P. 6128 Succursale Centre-Ville, Montreal, Quebec, H3C 3J7 Canada, (Dial from U.S. (514) 343-6880), (Fax from U.S. (514) 343 6882), www.uis.unesco.org; *Statistical Tables.*

United Nations Conference on Trade and Development (UNCTAD), DC2-1120, United Nations, New York, NY 10017, (212) 963-0027, www.unctad.org; *UNCTAD Commodity Yearbook.*

United Nations Food and Agricultural Organization (FAO), Viale delle Terme di Caracalla, 00100 Rome, Italy, (Dial from U.S. (202) 653-2400), (Fax from U.S. (202) 653 5760), www.fao.org; *FAO Yearbook of Forest Products* and *The State of Food and Agriculture (SOFA) 2006.*

United Nations Statistics Division, New York, NY 10017, (800) 253-9646, Fax: (212) 963-4116, http://unstats.un.org; *2004 Industrial Commodity Statistics Yearbook; Statistical Yearbook;* and *Trends in Europe and North America: The Statistical Yearbook of the ECE 2005.*

The World Bank, 1818 H Street, NW, Washington, DC 20433, (202) 473-1000, Fax: (202) 477-6391, www.worldbank.org; *Czech Republic* and *World Development Report 2008.*

CZECH REPUBLIC - GAS PRODUCTION

See CZECH REPUBLIC - MINERAL INDUSTRIES

CZECH REPUBLIC - GEOGRAPHIC INFORMATION SYSTEMS

M.E. Sharpe, 80 Business Park Drive, Armonk, NY 10504, (800) 541-6563, Fax: (914) 273-2106, www.mesharpe.com; *The Illustrated Book of World Rankings.*

The World Bank, 1818 H Street, NW, Washington, DC 20433, (202) 473-1000, Fax: (202) 477-6391, www.worldbank.org; *Czech Republic.*

CZECH REPUBLIC - GOLD PRODUCTION

See CZECH REPUBLIC - MINERAL INDUSTRIES

CZECH REPUBLIC - GREEN PEPPER AND CHILIE PRODUCTION

See CZECH REPUBLIC - CROPS

CZECH REPUBLIC - GROSS DOMESTIC PRODUCT

Economist Intelligence Unit, 111 West 57th Street, New York, NY 10019, (212) 554-0600, Fax: (212) 586-1181, www.eiu.com; *Czech Republic Country Report.*

Euromonitor International, Inc., 224 S. Michigan Avenue, Suite 1500, Chicago, IL 60604, (312) 922-1115, Fax: (312) 922-1157, www.euromonitor.com; *The World Economic Factbook 2008.*

M.E. Sharpe, 80 Business Park Drive, Armonk, NY 10504, (800) 541-6563, Fax: (914) 273-2106, www.mesharpe.com; *The Illustrated Book of World Rankings.*

Organisation for Economic Cooperation and Development (OECD), 2 rue Andre Pascal, F-75775 Paris Cedex 16, France, (Telephone in U.S. (202) 785-6323), (Fax in U.S. (202) 785-0350), www.oecd.org; *Comparison of Gross Domestic Product (GDP) for OECD Countries.*

United Nations Statistics Division, New York, NY 10017, (800) 253-9646, Fax: (212) 963-4116, http://unstats.un.org; *Human Development Report 2006; National Accounts Statistics: Compendium of Income Distribution Statistics; Statistical Yearbook;* and *Trends in Europe and North America: The Statistical Yearbook of the ECE 2005.*

The World Bank, 1818 H Street, NW, Washington, DC 20433, (202) 473-1000, Fax: (202) 477-6391, www.worldbank.org; *World Development Report 2008.*

CZECH REPUBLIC - GROSS NATIONAL PRODUCT

European Union, Delegation of the European Commission to the United States, 2300 M Street, NW, Washington, DC 20037, (202) 862-9500, Fax: (202) 429-1766, www.eurunion.org; *The EU Economy, 2007 Review: Moving Europe's Productivity Frontier.*

M.E. Sharpe, 80 Business Park Drive, Armonk, NY 10504, (800) 541-6563, Fax: (914) 273-2106, www.mesharpe.com; *The Illustrated Book of World Rankings.*

Organisation for Economic Cooperation and Development (OECD), 2 rue Andre Pascal, F-75775 Paris Cedex 16, France, (Telephone in U.S. (202) 785-6323), (Fax in U.S. (202) 785-0350), www.oecd.org; *OECD Composite Leading Indicators (CLIs), Updated September 2007.*

U.S. Department of State (DOS), 2201 C Street NW, Washington, DC 20520, (202) 647-4000, www.state.gov; *World Military Expenditures and Arms Transfers (WMEAT).*

United Nations Statistics Division, New York, NY 10017, (800) 253-9646, Fax: (212) 963-4116, http://unstats.un.org; *Statistical Yearbook.*

The World Bank, 1818 H Street, NW, Washington, DC 20433, (202) 473-1000, Fax: (202) 477-6391, www.worldbank.org; *The World Bank Atlas 2003-2004* and *World Development Report 2008.*

CZECH REPUBLIC - HEMP FIBRE PRODUCTION

See CZECH REPUBLIC - TEXTILE INDUSTRY

CZECH REPUBLIC - HIDES AND SKINS INDUSTRY

United Nations Food and Agricultural Organization (FAO), Viale delle Terme di Caracalla, 00100 Rome, Italy, (Dial from U.S. (202) 653-2400), (Fax from U.S. (202) 653 5760), www.fao.org; *FAO Production Yearbook 2002.*

CZECH REPUBLIC - HOPS PRODUCTION

See CZECH REPUBLIC - CROPS

CZECH REPUBLIC - HOUSING

Euromonitor International, Inc., 224 S. Michigan Avenue, Suite 1500, Chicago, IL 60604, (312) 922-1115, Fax: (312) 922-1157, www.euromonitor.com; *World Marketing Data and Statistics.*

M.E. Sharpe, 80 Business Park Drive, Armonk, NY 10504, (800) 541-6563, Fax: (914) 273-2106, www.mesharpe.com; *The Illustrated Book of World Rankings.*

United Nations Statistics Division, New York, NY 10017, (800) 253-9646, Fax: (212) 963-4116, http://unstats.un.org; *Trends in Europe and North America: The Statistical Yearbook of the ECE 2005.*

CZECH REPUBLIC - ILLITERATE PERSONS

Euromonitor International, Inc., 224 S. Michigan Avenue, Suite 1500, Chicago, IL 60604, (312) 922-1115, Fax: (312) 922-1157, www.euromonitor.com; *The World Economic Factbook 2008.*

UNESCO Institute for Statistics, C.P. 6128 Succursale Centre-Ville, Montreal, Quebec, H3C 3J7 Canada, (Dial from U.S. (514) 343-6880), (Fax from U.S. (514) 343 6882), www.uis.unesco.org; *Statistical Tables.*

United Nations Statistics Division, New York, NY 10017, (800) 253-9646, Fax: (212) 963-4116, http://unstats.un.org; *Human Development Report 2006.*

CZECH REPUBLIC - IMPORTS

Central Intelligence Agency, Office of Public Affairs, Washington, DC 20505, (703) 482-0623, Fax: (703) 482-1739, www.cia.gov; *The World Factbook.*

Economist Intelligence Unit, 111 West 57th Street, New York, NY 10019, (212) 554-0600, Fax: (212) 586-1181, www.eiu.com; *Czech Republic Country Report.*

Euromonitor International, Inc., 224 S. Michigan Avenue, Suite 1500, Chicago, IL 60604, (312) 922-1115, Fax: (312) 922-1157, www.euromonitor.com; *The World Economic Factbook 2008.*

International Lead and Zinc Study Group (ILZSG), Rua Almirante Barroso 38, 5th Floor, Lisbon 1000 - 013, Portugal, www.ilzsg.org; Interactive Statistical Database.

International Monetary Fund (IMF), 700 Nineteenth Street, NW, Washington, DC 20431, (202) 623-7000, Fax: (202) 623-4661, www.imf.org; *Direction of Trade Statistics Yearbook 2007.*

Organisation for Economic Cooperation and Development (OECD), 2 rue Andre Pascal, F-75775 Paris Cedex 16, France, (Telephone in U.S. (202) 785-6323), (Fax in U.S. (202) 785-0350), www.oecd.org; *OECD Economic Survey - Czech Republic 2008.*

Palgrave Macmillan Ltd., Houndmills, Basingstoke, Hampshire, RG21 6XS, England, (Telephone in U.S. (888) 330-8477), (Fax in U.S. (800) 672-2054), www.palgrave.com; *The Statesman's Yearbook 2008.*

Taylor and Francis Group, An Informa Business, 2 Park Square, Milton Park, Abingdon, Oxford OX14 4RN, United Kingdom, (Dial from U.S. (212) 216-7800), (Fax from U.S. (212) 564-7854), www.tandf.co.uk; *The Europa World Year Book.*

United Nations Conference on Trade and Development (UNCTAD), DC2-1120, United Nations, New York, NY 10017, (212) 963-0027, www.unctad.org; *Handbook of Statistics 2005.*

United Nations Food and Agricultural Organization (FAO), Viale delle Terme di Caracalla, 00100 Rome, Italy, (Dial from U.S. (202) 653-2400), (Fax from U.S. (202) 653 5760), www.fao.org; *The State of Food and Agriculture (SOFA) 2006.*

United Nations Statistics Division, New York, NY 10017, (800) 253-9646, Fax: (212) 963-4116, http://unstats.un.org; *International Trade Statistics Yearbook* and *Trends in Europe and North America: The Statistical Yearbook of the ECE 2005.*

The World Bank, 1818 H Street, NW, Washington, DC 20433, (202) 473-1000, Fax: (202) 477-6391, www.worldbank.org; *World Development Report 2008.*

CZECH REPUBLIC - INDUSTRIAL METALS PRODUCTION

See CZECH REPUBLIC - MINERAL INDUSTRIES

CZECH REPUBLIC - INDUSTRIAL PRODUCTIVITY

International Lead and Zinc Study Group (ILZSG), Rua Almirante Barroso 38, 5th Floor, Lisbon 1000 - 013, Portugal, www.ilzsg.org; Interactive Statistical Database.

M.E. Sharpe, 80 Business Park Drive, Armonk, NY 10504, (800) 541-6563, Fax: (914) 273-2106, www.mesharpe.com; *The Illustrated Book of World Rankings.*

CZECH REPUBLIC - INDUSTRIAL PROPERTY

United Nations Statistics Division, New York, NY 10017, (800) 253-9646, Fax: (212) 963-4116, http://unstats.un.org; *Statistical Yearbook.*

World Intellectual Property Organization (WIPO), PO Box 18, CH-1211 Geneva 20, Switzerland, www.wipo.int; *Industrial Property Statistics* and *Industrial Property Statistics Online Directory.*

CZECH REPUBLIC - INDUSTRIES

Central Intelligence Agency, Office of Public Affairs, Washington, DC 20505, (703) 482-0623, Fax: (703) 482-1739, www.cia.gov; *The World Factbook.*

Economist Intelligence Unit, 111 West 57th Street, New York, NY 10019, (212) 554-0600, Fax: (212) 586-1181, www.eiu.com; *Czech Republic Country Report.*

Euromonitor International, Inc., 224 S. Michigan Avenue, Suite 1500, Chicago, IL 60604, (312) 922-1115, Fax: (312) 922-1157, www.euromonitor.com; *The World Economic Factbook 2008* and *World Marketing Data and Statistics.*

International Labour Office, I.L.O. Publications, 4 route des Morillons, CH-1211 Geneva 22, Switzerland, (Telephone in U.S. (202) 653-7652), (Fax in U.S. (202) 653-7687), www.ilo.org; *Yearbook of Labour Statistics 2006.*

M.E. Sharpe, 80 Business Park Drive, Armonk, NY 10504, (800) 541-6563, Fax: (914) 273-2106, www.mesharpe.com; *The Illustrated Book of World Rankings.*

Palgrave Macmillan Ltd., Houndmills, Basingstoke, Hampshire, RG21 6XS, England, (Telephone in U.S. (888) 330-8477), (Fax in U.S. (800) 672-2054), www.palgrave.com; *The Statesman's Yearbook 2008.*

Taylor and Francis Group, An Informa Business, 2 Park Square, Milton Park, Abingdon, Oxford OX14 4RN, United Kingdom, (Dial from U.S. (212) 216-7800), (Fax from U.S. (212) 564-7854), www.tandf.co.uk; *The Europa World Year Book.*

United Nations Industrial Development Organization (UNIDO), 1 United Nations Plaza, New York, NY 10017, (212) 963 6890, Fax: (212) 963-7904, http://unido.org; Industrial Statistics Database 2008 (INDSTAT) and *The International Yearbook of Industrial Statistics 2008.*

United Nations Statistics Division, New York, NY 10017, (800) 253-9646, Fax: (212) 963-4116, http://unstats.un.org; *2004 Industrial Commodity Statistics Yearbook; Statistical Yearbook;* and *Trends in Europe and North America: The Statistical Yearbook of the ECE 2005.*

The World Bank, 1818 H Street, NW, Washington, DC 20433, (202) 473-1000, Fax: (202) 477-6391, www.worldbank.org; *Czech Republic.*

CZECH REPUBLIC - INFANT AND MATERNAL MORTALITY

See CZECH REPUBLIC - MORTALITY

CZECH REPUBLIC - INORGANIC ACIDS

United Nations Statistics Division, New York, NY 10017, (800) 253-9646, Fax: (212) 963-4116, http://unstats.un.org; *Statistical Yearbook.*

CZECH REPUBLIC - INTERNATIONAL TRADE

Banque de France, 48 rue Croix des Petits champs, 75001 Paris, France, www.banque-france.fr/home.htm; *Monthly Business Survey Overview.*

Bernan Essential Government Publications, 4611-F Assembly Drive, Lanham MD, 20706-4391, (301) 459-2255, Fax: (800) 865-3450, www.bernan.com; *OECD Factbook 2006.*

Economist Intelligence Unit, 111 West 57th Street, New York, NY 10019, (212) 554-0600, Fax: (212) 586-1181, www.eiu.com; *Czech Republic Country Report.*

Euromonitor International, Inc., 224 S. Michigan Avenue, Suite 1500, Chicago, IL 60604, (312) 922-

1115, Fax: (312) 922-1157, www.euromonitor.com; *European Marketing Data and Statistics 2008; The World Economic Factbook 2008;* and *World Marketing Data and Statistics.*

Eurostat, Batiment Jean Monnet, Rue Alcide de Gasperi, L-2920 Luxembourg, http://epp.eurostat.ec.europa.eu; Intra- and Extra-EU Trade.

M.E. Sharpe, 80 Business Park Drive, Armonk, NY 10504, (800) 541-6563, Fax: (914) 273-2106, www.mesharpe.com; *The Illustrated Book of World Rankings.*

Organisation for Economic Cooperation and Development (OECD), 2 rue Andre Pascal, F-75775 Paris Cedex 16, France, (Telephone in U.S. (202) 785-6323), (Fax in U.S. (202) 785-0350), www.oecd.org; *OECD Economic Survey - Czech Republic 2008* and *OECD in Figures 2007.*

Palgrave Macmillan Ltd., Houndmills, Basingstoke, Hampshire, RG21 6XS, England, (Telephone in U.S. (888) 330-8477), (Fax in U.S. (800) 672-2054), www.palgrave.com; *The Statesman's Yearbook 2008.*

Taylor and Francis Group, An Informa Business, 2 Park Square, Milton Park, Abingdon, Oxford OX14 4RN, United Kingdom, (Dial from U.S. (212) 216-7800), (Fax from U.S. (212) 564-7854), www.tandf.co.uk; *The Europa World Year Book.*

United Nations Conference on Trade and Development (UNCTAD), DC2-1120, United Nations, New York, NY 10017, (212) 963-0027, www.unctad.org; *UNCTAD Commodity Yearbook.*

United Nations Food and Agricultural Organization (FAO), Viale delle Terme di Caracalla, 00100 Rome, Italy, (Dial from U.S. (202) 653-2400), (Fax from U.S. (202) 653 5760), www.fao.org; *FAO Trade Yearbook* and *The State of Food and Agriculture (SOFA) 2006.*

United Nations Statistics Division, New York, NY 10017, (800) 253-9646, Fax: (212) 963-4116, http://unstats.un.org; *International Trade Statistics Yearbook* and *Statistical Yearbook.*

The World Bank, 1818 H Street, NW, Washington, DC 20433, (202) 473-1000, Fax: (202) 477-6391, www.worldbank.org; *Czech Republic* and *World Development Report 2008.*

World Trade Organization (WTO), Centre William Rappard, Rue de Lausanne 154, CH-1211 Geneva 21, Switzerland, www.wto.org; *International Trade Statistics 2006.*

CZECH REPUBLIC - INTERNET USERS

Eurostat, Batiment Jean Monnet, Rue Alcide de Gasperi, L-2920 Luxembourg, http://epp.eurostat.ec.europa.eu; *Internet Usage by Enterprises 2007.*

International Telecommunication Union (ITU), Place des Nations, 1211 Geneva 20, Switzerland, www.itu.int; *World Telecommunication/ICT Indicators Database on CD-ROM; World Telecommunication/ICT Indicators Database Online;* and *Yearbook of Statistics - Telecommunication Services (Chronological Time Series 1997-2006).*

The World Bank, 1818 H Street, NW, Washington, DC 20433, (202) 473-1000, Fax: (202) 477-6391, www.worldbank.org; *Czech Republic.*

CZECH REPUBLIC - IRON AND IRON ORE PRODUCTION

See CZECH REPUBLIC - MINERAL INDUSTRIES

CZECH REPUBLIC - LABOR

Central Intelligence Agency, Office of Public Affairs, Washington, DC 20505, (703) 482-0623, Fax: (703) 482-1739, www.cia.gov; *The World Factbook.*

Euromonitor International, Inc., 224 S. Michigan Avenue, Suite 1500, Chicago, IL 60604, (312) 922-1115, Fax: (312) 922-1157, www.euromonitor.com; *World Marketing Data and Statistics.*

Federal Statistical Office Germany, D-65180 Wiesbaden, Germany, www.destatis.de; *Czech Republic 2005.*

International Labour Office, I.L.O. Publications, 4 route des Morillons, CH-1211 Geneva 22, Switzerland, (Telephone in U.S. (202) 653-7652), (Fax in U.S. (202) 653-7687), www.ilo.org; *Yearbook of Labour Statistics 2006.*

M.E. Sharpe, 80 Business Park Drive, Armonk, NY 10504, (800) 541-6563, Fax: (914) 273-2106, www.mesharpe.com; *The Illustrated Book of World Rankings.*

Organisation for Economic Cooperation and Development (OECD), 2 rue Andre Pascal, F-75775 Paris Cedex 16, France, (Telephone in U.S. (202) 785-6323), (Fax in U.S. (202) 785-0350), www.oecd.org; *OECD Economic Survey - Czech Republic 2008.*

Palgrave Macmillan Ltd., Houndmills, Basingstoke, Hampshire, RG21 6XS, England, (Telephone in U.S. (888) 330-8477), (Fax in U.S. (800) 672-2054), www.palgrave.com; *The Statesman's Yearbook 2008.*

United Nations Food and Agricultural Organization (FAO), Viale delle Terme di Caracalla, 00100 Rome, Italy, (Dial from U.S. (202) 653-2400), (Fax from U.S. (202) 653 5760), www.fao.org; *The State of Food and Agriculture (SOFA) 2006.*

United Nations Statistics Division, New York, NY 10017, (800) 253-9646, Fax: (212) 963-4116, http://unstats.un.org; *Human Development Report 2006* and *Statistical Yearbook.*

The World Bank, 1818 H Street, NW, Washington, DC 20433, (202) 473-1000, Fax: (202) 477-6391, www.worldbank.org; *The World Bank Atlas 2003-2004* and *World Development Report 2008.*

CZECH REPUBLIC - LAND USE

Central Intelligence Agency, Office of Public Affairs, Washington, DC 20505, (703) 482-0623, Fax: (703) 482-1739, www.cia.gov; *The World Factbook.*

Euromonitor International, Inc., 224 S. Michigan Avenue, Suite 1500, Chicago, IL 60604, (312) 922-1115, Fax: (312) 922-1157, www.euromonitor.com; *European Marketing Data and Statistics 2008.*

United Nations Food and Agricultural Organization (FAO), Viale delle Terme di Caracalla, 00100 Rome, Italy, (Dial from U.S. (202) 653-2400), (Fax from U.S. (202) 653 5760), www.fao.org; *FAO Production Yearbook 2002.*

CZECH REPUBLIC - LIBRARIES

M.E. Sharpe, 80 Business Park Drive, Armonk, NY 10504, (800) 541-6563, Fax: (914) 273-2106, www.mesharpe.com; *The Illustrated Book of World Rankings.*

UNESCO Institute for Statistics, C.P. 6128 Succursale Centre-Ville, Montreal, Quebec, H3C 3J7 Canada, (Dial from U.S. (514) 343-6880), (Fax from U.S. (514) 343 6882), www.uis.unesco.org; *Statistical Tables.*

United Nations Statistics Division, New York, NY 10017, (800) 253-9646, Fax: (212) 963-4116, http://unstats.un.org; *Trends in Europe and North America: The Statistical Yearbook of the ECE 2005.*

CZECH REPUBLIC - LIFE EXPECTANCY

Central Intelligence Agency, Office of Public Affairs, Washington, DC 20505, (703) 482-0623, Fax: (703) 482-1739, www.cia.gov; *The World Factbook.*

Euromonitor International, Inc., 224 S. Michigan Avenue, Suite 1500, Chicago, IL 60604, (312) 922-1115, Fax: (312) 922-1157, www.euromonitor.com; *The World Economic Factbook 2008.*

United Nations Statistics Division, New York, NY 10017, (800) 253-9646, Fax: (212) 963-4116, http://unstats.un.org; *Demographic Yearbook; Human Development Report 2006; Trends in Europe and North America: The Statistical Yearbook of the ECE 2005;* and *World Statistics Pocketbook.*

The World Bank, 1818 H Street, NW, Washington, DC 20433, (202) 473-1000, Fax: (202) 477-6391, www.worldbank.org; *The World Bank Atlas 2003-2004* and *World Development Report 2008.*

CZECH REPUBLIC - LITERACY

Euromonitor International, Inc., 224 S. Michigan Avenue, Suite 1500, Chicago, IL 60604, (312) 922-1115, Fax: (312) 922-1157, www.euromonitor.com; *World Marketing Data and Statistics.*

CZECH REPUBLIC - LIVESTOCK

Euromonitor International, Inc., 224 S. Michigan Avenue, Suite 1500, Chicago, IL 60604, (312) 922-1115, Fax: (312) 922-1157, www.euromonitor.com; *European Marketing Data and Statistics 2008.*

M.E. Sharpe, 80 Business Park Drive, Armonk, NY 10504, (800) 541-6563, Fax: (914) 273-2106, www.mesharpe.com; *The Illustrated Book of World Rankings.*

Palgrave Macmillan Ltd., Houndmills, Basingstoke, Hampshire, RG21 6XS, England, (Telephone in U.S. (888) 330-8477), (Fax in U.S. (800) 672-2054), www.palgrave.com; *The Statesman's Yearbook 2008.*

Taylor and Francis Group, An Informa Business, 2 Park Square, Milton Park, Abingdon, Oxford OX14 4RN, United Kingdom, (Dial from U.S. (212) 216-7800), (Fax from U.S. (212) 564-7854), www.tandf.co.uk; *The Europa World Year Book.*

United Nations Conference on Trade and Development (UNCTAD), DC2-1120, United Nations, New York, NY 10017, (212) 963-0027, www.unctad.org; *UNCTAD Commodity Yearbook.*

United Nations Food and Agricultural Organization (FAO), Viale delle Terme di Caracalla, 00100 Rome, Italy, (Dial from U.S. (202) 653-2400), (Fax from U.S. (202) 653 5760), www.fao.org; *FAO Production Yearbook 2002* and *The State of Food and Agriculture (SOFA) 2006.*

United Nations Statistics Division, New York, NY 10017, (800) 253-9646, Fax: (212) 963-4116, http://unstats.un.org; *2004 Industrial Commodity Statistics Yearbook* and *Statistical Yearbook.*

CZECH REPUBLIC - MACHINERY

United Nations Statistics Division, New York, NY 10017, (800) 253-9646, Fax: (212) 963-4116, http://unstats.un.org; *2004 Industrial Commodity Statistics Yearbook.*

CZECH REPUBLIC - MANUFACTURES

M.E. Sharpe, 80 Business Park Drive, Armonk, NY 10504, (800) 541-6563, Fax: (914) 273-2106, www.mesharpe.com; *The Illustrated Book of World Rankings.*

Organisation for Economic Cooperation and Development (OECD), 2 rue Andre Pascal, F-75775 Paris Cedex 16, France, (Telephone in U.S. (202) 785-6323), (Fax in U.S. (202) 785-0350), www.oecd.org; *OECD Economic Survey - Czech Republic 2008.*

United Nations Statistics Division, New York, NY 10017, (800) 253-9646, Fax: (212) 963-4116, http://unstats.un.org; *2004 Industrial Commodity Statistics Yearbook* and *Statistical Yearbook.*

CZECH REPUBLIC - MARRIAGE

M.E. Sharpe, 80 Business Park Drive, Armonk, NY 10504, (800) 541-6563, Fax: (914) 273-2106, www.mesharpe.com; *The Illustrated Book of World Rankings.*

Taylor and Francis Group, An Informa Business, 2 Park Square, Milton Park, Abingdon, Oxford OX14 4RN, United Kingdom, (Dial from U.S. (212) 216-7800), (Fax from U.S. (212) 564-7854), www.tandf.co.uk; *The Europa World Year Book.*

UNESCO Institute for Statistics, C.P. 6128 Succursale Centre-Ville, Montreal, Quebec, H3C 3J7 Canada, (Dial from U.S. (514) 343-6880), (Fax from U.S. (514) 343 6882), www.uis.unesco.org; *Statistical Tables.*

United Nations Statistics Division, New York, NY 10017, (800) 253-9646, Fax: (212) 963-4116, http://unstats.un.org; *Demographic Yearbook; Statistical Yearbook;* and *Trends in Europe and North America: The Statistical Yearbook of the ECE 2005.*

CZECH REPUBLIC - MERCURY PRODUCTION

See CZECH REPUBLIC - MINERAL INDUSTRIES

CZECH REPUBLIC - MILK PRODUCTION

See CZECH REPUBLIC - DAIRY PROCESSING

CZECH REPUBLIC - MINERAL INDUSTRIES

Commodity Research Bureau, 330 South Wells Street, Suite 612, Chicago, IL 60606-7110, (800) 621-5271, Fax: (312) 939-4135, www.crbtrader.com; *2006 CRB Commodity Yearbook and CD.*

Eurostat, Batiment Jean Monnet, Rue Alcide de Gasperi, L-2920 Luxembourg, http://epp.eurostat.ec.europa.eu; *Energy - Monthly Statistics* and *Panorama of Energy - 2007 Edition.*

International Energy Agency (IEA), 9, rue de la Federation, 75739 Paris Cedex 15, France, www.iea.org; *Key World Energy Statistics 2007.*

International Lead and Zinc Study Group (ILZSG), Rua Almirante Barroso 38, 5th Floor, Lisbon 1000 - 013, Portugal, www.ilzsg.org; Interactive Statistical Database.

M.E. Sharpe, 80 Business Park Drive, Armonk, NY 10504, (800) 541-6563, Fax: (914) 273-2106, www.mesharpe.com; *The Illustrated Book of World Rankings.*

Organisation for Economic Cooperation and Development (OECD), 2 rue Andre Pascal, F-75775 Paris Cedex 16, France, (Telephone in U.S. (202) 785-6323), (Fax in U.S. (202) 785-0350), www.oecd.org; *World Energy Outlook 2007.*

Palgrave Macmillan Ltd., Houndmills, Basingstoke, Hampshire, RG21 6XS, England, (Telephone in U.S. (888) 330-8477), (Fax in U.S. (800) 672-2054), www.palgrave.com; *The Statesman's Yearbook 2008.*

Platts, 2 Penn Plaza, 25th Floor, New York, NY 10121-2298, (212) 904-3070, www.platts.com; *Energy Economist; Energy in East Europe;* and *EU Energy.*

Taylor and Francis Group, An Informa Business, 2 Park Square, Milton Park, Abingdon, Oxford OX14 4RN, United Kingdom, (Dial from U.S. (212) 216-7800), (Fax from U.S. (212) 564-7854), www.tandf.co.uk; *The Europa World Year Book.*

United Nations Conference on Trade and Development (UNCTAD), DC2-1120, United Nations, New York, NY 10017, (212) 963-0027, www.unctad.org; *UNCTAD Commodity Yearbook.*

United Nations Statistics Division, New York, NY 10017, (800) 253-9646, Fax: (212) 963-4116, http://unstats.un.org; *Energy Statistics Yearbook 2003; 2004 Industrial Commodity Statistics Yearbook;* and *Statistical Yearbook.*

The World Bank, 1818 H Street, NW, Washington, DC 20433, (202) 473-1000, Fax: (202) 477-6391, www.worldbank.org; *Czech Republic.*

CZECH REPUBLIC - MONEY EXCHANGE RATES

See CZECH REPUBLIC - FOREIGN EXCHANGE RATES

CZECH REPUBLIC - MONEY SUPPLY

Economist Intelligence Unit, 111 West 57th Street, New York, NY 10019, (212) 554-0600, Fax: (212) 586-1181, www.eiu.com; *Czech Republic Country Report.*

Organisation for Economic Cooperation and Development (OECD), 2 rue Andre Pascal, F-75775 Paris Cedex 16, France, (Telephone in U.S. (202) 785-6323), (Fax in U.S. (202) 785-0350), www.oecd.org; *OECD Economic Survey - Czech Republic 2008.*

Taylor and Francis Group, An Informa Business, 2 Park Square, Milton Park, Abingdon, Oxford OX14 4RN, United Kingdom, (Dial from U.S. (212) 216-7800), (Fax from U.S. (212) 564-7854), www.tandf.co.uk; *The Europa World Year Book.*

The World Bank, 1818 H Street, NW, Washington, DC 20433, (202) 473-1000, Fax: (202) 477-6391, www.worldbank.org; *Czech Republic.*

CZECH REPUBLIC - MONUMENTS AND HISTORIC SITES

UNESCO Institute for Statistics, C.P. 6128 Succursale Centre-Ville, Montreal, Quebec, H3C 3J7 Canada, (Dial from U.S. (514) 343-6880), (Fax from U.S. (514) 343 6882), www.uis.unesco.org; *Statistical Tables.*

CZECH REPUBLIC - MORTALITY

Central Intelligence Agency, Office of Public Affairs, Washington, DC 20505, (703) 482-0623, Fax: (703) 482-1739, www.cia.gov; *The World Factbook.*

Euromonitor International, Inc., 224 S. Michigan Avenue, Suite 1500, Chicago, IL 60604, (312) 922-1115, Fax: (312) 922-1157, www.euromonitor.com; *The World Economic Factbook 2008.*

Palgrave Macmillan Ltd., Houndmills, Basingstoke, Hampshire, RG21 6XS, England, (Telephone in U.S. (888) 330-8477), (Fax in U.S. (800) 672-2054), www.palgrave.com; *The Statesman's Yearbook 2008.*

Taylor and Francis Group, An Informa Business, 2 Park Square, Milton Park, Abingdon, Oxford OX14 4RN, United Kingdom, (Dial from U.S. (212) 216-7800), (Fax from U.S. (212) 564-7854), www.tandf.co.uk; *The Europa World Year Book.*

UNICEF, 3 United Nations Plaza, New York, NY 10017, (800) 253-9646, Fax: (212) 887-7465, www.unicef.org; *The State of the World's Children 2008.*

United Nations Statistics Division, New York, NY 10017, (800) 253-9646, Fax: (212) 963-4116, http://unstats.un.org; *Demographic Yearbook; Human Development Report 2006; Statistical Yearbook; Trends in Europe and North America: The Statistical Yearbook of the ECE 2005;* and *World Statistics Pocketbook.*

The World Bank, 1818 H Street, NW, Washington, DC 20433, (202) 473-1000, Fax: (202) 477-6391, www.worldbank.org; *The World Bank Atlas 2003-2004* and *World Development Report 2008.*

World Health Organization (WHO), Avenue Appia 20, 1211 Geneve 27, Switzerland, (Telephone in U.S. (212) 331-9081), www.who.int; The WHO Global Atlas of Infectious Diseases and *World Health Report 2006.*

CZECH REPUBLIC - MOTION PICTURES

UNESCO Institute for Statistics, C.P. 6128 Succursale Centre-Ville, Montreal, Quebec, H3C 3J7 Canada, (Dial from U.S. (514) 343-6880), (Fax from U.S. (514) 343 6882), www.uis.unesco.org; *Statistical Tables.*

United Nations Statistics Division, New York, NY 10017, (800) 253-9646, Fax: (212) 963-4116, http://unstats.un.org; *Statistical Yearbook.*

CZECH REPUBLIC - MOTOR VEHICLES

International Road Federation (IRF), Madison Place, 500 Montgomery Street, 5th Floor, Alexandria, VA 22314, (703) 535-1001, Fax: (703) 535-1007, www.irfnet.org; *World Road Statistics 2006.*

Taylor and Francis Group, An Informa Business, 2 Park Square, Milton Park, Abingdon, Oxford OX14 4RN, United Kingdom, (Dial from U.S. (212) 216-7800), (Fax from U.S. (212) 564-7854), www.tandf.co.uk; *The Europa World Year Book.*

United Nations Statistics Division, New York, NY 10017, (800) 253-9646, Fax: (212) 963-4116, http://unstats.un.org; *Statistical Yearbook.*

CZECH REPUBLIC - MUSEUMS

M.E. Sharpe, 80 Business Park Drive, Armonk, NY 10504, (800) 541-6563, Fax: (914) 273-2106, www.mesharpe.com; *The Illustrated Book of World Rankings.*

UNESCO Institute for Statistics, C.P. 6128 Succursale Centre-Ville, Montreal, Quebec, H3C 3J7 Canada, (Dial from U.S. (514) 343-6880), (Fax from U.S. (514) 343 6882), www.uis.unesco.org; *Statistical Tables.*

CZECH REPUBLIC - NATIONAL INCOME

United Nations Statistics Division, New York, NY 10017, (800) 253-9646, Fax: (212) 963-4116, http://unstats.un.org; *Statistical Yearbook.*

CZECH REPUBLIC - NATURAL GAS PRODUCTION

See CZECH REPUBLIC - MINERAL INDUSTRIES

CZECH REPUBLIC - NICKEL AND NICKEL ORE

See CZECH REPUBLIC - MINERAL INDUSTRIES

CZECH REPUBLIC - NUTRITION

United Nations Food and Agricultural Organization (FAO), Viale delle Terme di Caracalla, 00100 Rome, Italy, (Dial from U.S. (202) 653-2400), (Fax from U.S. (202) 653 5760), www.fao.org; *The State of Food and Agriculture (SOFA) 2006.*

CZECH REPUBLIC - OATS PRODUCTION

See CZECH REPUBLIC - CROPS

CZECH REPUBLIC - OLDER PEOPLE

M.E. Sharpe, 80 Business Park Drive, Armonk, NY 10504, (800) 541-6563, Fax: (914) 273-2106, www.mesharpe.com; *The Illustrated Book of World Rankings.*

CZECH REPUBLIC - PAPER

See CZECH REPUBLIC - FORESTS AND FORESTRY

CZECH REPUBLIC - PEANUT PRODUCTION

See CZECH REPUBLIC - CROPS

CZECH REPUBLIC - PERIODICALS

UNESCO Institute for Statistics, C.P. 6128 Succursale Centre-Ville, Montreal, Quebec, H3C 3J7 Canada, (Dial from U.S. (514) 343-6880), (Fax from U.S. (514) 343 6882), www.uis.unesco.org; *Statistical Tables.*

CZECH REPUBLIC - PESTICIDES

United Nations Food and Agricultural Organization (FAO), Viale delle Terme di Caracalla, 00100 Rome, Italy, (Dial from U.S. (202) 653-2400), (Fax from U.S. (202) 653 5760), www.fao.org; *The State of Food and Agriculture (SOFA) 2006.*

CZECH REPUBLIC - PETROLEUM INDUSTRY AND TRADE

Euromonitor International, Inc., 224 S. Michigan Avenue, Suite 1500, Chicago, IL 60604, (312) 922-1115, Fax: (312) 922-1157, www.euromonitor.com; *European Marketing Data and Statistics 2008.*

International Energy Agency (IEA), 9, rue de la Federation, 75739 Paris Cedex 15, France, www.iea.org; *Key World Energy Statistics 2007.*

M.E. Sharpe, 80 Business Park Drive, Armonk, NY 10504, (800) 541-6563, Fax: (914) 273-2106, www.mesharpe.com; *The Illustrated Book of World Rankings.*

Organisation for Economic Cooperation and Development (OECD), 2 rue Andre Pascal, F-75775 Paris Cedex 16, France, (Telephone in U.S. (202) 785-6323), (Fax in U.S. (202) 785-0350), www.oecd.org; *World Energy Outlook 2007.*

PennWell Corporation, 1421 South Sheridan Road, Tulsa, OK 74112, (918) 835-3161, www.pennwell.com; *International Petroleum Encyclopedia 2007.*

Platts, 2 Penn Plaza, 25th Floor, New York, NY 10121-2298, (212) 904-3070, www.platts.com; *Energy Economist.*

U.S. Department of Energy (DOE), Energy Information Administration (EIA), 1000 Independence Avenue, SW, Washington, DC 20585, (202) 586-8800, www.eia.doe.gov; *International Energy Annual 2004* and *International Energy Outlook 2006.*

United Nations Conference on Trade and Development (UNCTAD), DC2-1120, United Nations, New York, NY 10017, (212) 963-0027, www.unctad.org; *UNCTAD Commodity Yearbook.*

United Nations Food and Agricultural Organization (FAO), Viale delle Terme di Caracalla, 00100 Rome, Italy, (Dial from U.S. (202) 653-2400), (Fax from U.S. (202) 653 5760), www.fao.org; *The State of Food and Agriculture (SOFA) 2006.*

United Nations Statistics Division, New York, NY 10017, (800) 253-9646, Fax: (212) 963-4116, http://unstats.un.org; *Energy Statistics Yearbook 2003; 2004 Industrial Commodity Statistics Yearbook; Statistical Yearbook;* and *Trends in Europe and North America: The Statistical Yearbook of the ECE 2005.*

CZECH REPUBLIC - PIPELINES

United Nations Statistics Division, New York, NY 10017, (800) 253-9646, Fax: (212) 963-4116, http://unstats.un.org; *Annual Bulletin of Transport Statistics for Europe and North America 2004.*

CZECH REPUBLIC - PLASTICS INDUSTRY AND TRADE

United Nations Statistics Division, New York, NY 10017, (800) 253-9646, Fax: (212) 963-4116, http://unstats.un.org; *Statistical Yearbook.*

CZECH REPUBLIC - POLITICAL SCIENCE

Central Intelligence Agency, Office of Public Affairs, Washington, DC 20505, (703) 482-0623, Fax: (703) 482-1739, www.cia.gov; *The World Factbook.*

Palgrave Macmillan Ltd., Houndmills, Basingstoke, Hampshire, RG21 6XS, England, (Telephone in U.S. (888) 330-8477), (Fax in U.S. (800) 672-2054), www.palgrave.com; *The Statesman's Yearbook 2008.*

Taylor and Francis Group, An Informa Business, 2 Park Square, Milton Park, Abingdon, Oxford OX14 4RN, United Kingdom, (Dial from U.S. (212) 216-7800), (Fax from U.S. (212) 564-7854), www.tandf.co.uk; *The Europa World Year Book.*

United Nations Statistics Division, New York, NY 10017, (800) 253-9646, Fax: (212) 963-4116, http://unstats.un.org; *National Accounts Statistics: Compendium of Income Distribution Statistics* and *Statistical Yearbook.*

The World Bank, 1818 H Street, NW, Washington, DC 20433, (202) 473-1000, Fax: (202) 477-6391, www.worldbank.org; *World Development Report 2008.*

CZECH REPUBLIC - POPULATION

Banque de France, 48 rue Croix des Petits champs, 75001 Paris, France, www.banque-france.fr/home.htm; *Key Data for the Euro Area.*

Central Intelligence Agency, Office of Public Affairs, Washington, DC 20505, (703) 482-0623, Fax: (703) 482-1739, www.cia.gov; *The World Factbook.*

Economist Intelligence Unit, 111 West 57th Street, New York, NY 10019, (212) 554-0600, Fax: (212) 586-1181, www.eiu.com; *Czech Republic Country Report.*

Euromonitor International, Inc., 224 S. Michigan Avenue, Suite 1500, Chicago, IL 60604, (312) 922-1115, Fax: (312) 922-1157, www.euromonitor.com; *European Marketing Data and Statistics 2008* and *The World Economic Factbook 2008.*

Eurostat, Batiment Jean Monnet, Rue Alcide de Gasperi, L-2920 Luxembourg, http://epp.eurostat.ec.europa.eu; *The Life of Women and Men in Europe - A Statistical Portrait.*

Federal Statistical Office Germany, D-65180 Wiesbaden, Germany, www.destatis.de; *Czech Republic 2005.*

International Labour Office, I.L.O. Publications, 4 route des Morillons, CH-1211 Geneva 22, Switzerland, (Telephone in U.S. (202) 653-7652), (Fax in U.S. (202) 653-7687), www.ilo.org; *Yearbook of Labour Statistics 2006.*

M.E. Sharpe, 80 Business Park Drive, Armonk, NY 10504, (800) 541-6563, Fax: (914) 273-2106, www.mesharpe.com; *The Illustrated Book of World Rankings.*

Organisation for Economic Cooperation and Development (OECD), 2 rue Andre Pascal, F-75775 Paris Cedex 16, France, (Telephone in U.S. (202) 785-6323), (Fax in U.S. (202) 785-0350), www.oecd.org; *Labour Force Statistics: 1986-2005, 2007 Edition.*

Palgrave Macmillan Ltd., Houndmills, Basingstoke, Hampshire, RG21 6XS, England, (Telephone in U.S. (888) 330-8477), (Fax in U.S. (800) 672-2054), www.palgrave.com; *The Statesman's Yearbook 2008.*

Taylor and Francis Group, An Informa Business, 2 Park Square, Milton Park, Abingdon, Oxford OX14 4RN, United Kingdom, (Dial from U.S. (212) 216-7800), (Fax from U.S. (212) 564-7854), www.tandf.co.uk; *The Europa World Year Book.*

U.S. Department of State (DOS), 2201 C Street NW, Washington, DC 20520, (202) 647-4000, www.state.gov; *World Military Expenditures and Arms Transfers (WMEAT).*

UNESCO Institute for Statistics, C.P. 6128 Succursale Centre-Ville, Montreal, Quebec, H3C 3J7 Canada, (Dial from U.S. (514) 343-6880), (Fax from U.S. (514) 343 6882), www.uis.unesco.org; *Statistical Tables.*

United Nations Food and Agricultural Organization (FAO), Viale delle Terme di Caracalla, 00100 Rome, Italy, (Dial from U.S. (202) 653-2400), (Fax from U.S. (202) 653 5760), www.fao.org; *FAO Production Yearbook 2002.*

United Nations Statistics Division, New York, NY 10017, (800) 253-9646, Fax: (212) 963-4116, http://unstats.un.org; *Demographic Yearbook; Human Development Report 2006; Statistical Yearbook; Trends in Europe and North America: The Statistical Yearbook of the ECE 2005;* and *World Statistics Pocketbook.*

The World Bank, 1818 H Street, NW, Washington, DC 20433, (202) 473-1000, Fax: (202) 477-6391, www.worldbank.org; *Czech Republic; The World Bank Atlas 2003-2004;* and *World Development Report 2008.*

World Health Organization (WHO), Avenue Appia 20, 1211 Geneve 27, Switzerland, (Telephone in U.S. (212) 331-9081), www.who.int; *World Health Report 2006.*

CZECH REPUBLIC - POPULATION DENSITY

Central Intelligence Agency, Office of Public Affairs, Washington, DC 20505, (703) 482-0623, Fax: (703) 482-1739, www.cia.gov; *The World Factbook.*

Euromonitor International, Inc., 224 S. Michigan Avenue, Suite 1500, Chicago, IL 60604, (312) 922-1115, Fax: (312) 922-1157, www.euromonitor.com; *The World Economic Factbook 2008.*

M.E. Sharpe, 80 Business Park Drive, Armonk, NY 10504, (800) 541-6563, Fax: (914) 273-2106, www.mesharpe.com; *The Illustrated Book of World Rankings.*

Palgrave Macmillan Ltd., Houndmills, Basingstoke, Hampshire, RG21 6XS, England, (Telephone in U.S. (888) 330-8477), (Fax in U.S. (800) 672-2054), www.palgrave.com; *The Statesman's Yearbook 2008.*

Taylor and Francis Group, An Informa Business, 2 Park Square, Milton Park, Abingdon, Oxford OX14 4RN, United Kingdom, (Dial from U.S. (212) 216-7800), (Fax from U.S. (212) 564-7854), www.tandf.co.uk; *The Europa World Year Book.*

UNESCO Institute for Statistics, C.P. 6128 Succursale Centre-Ville, Montreal, Quebec, H3C 3J7 Canada, (Dial from U.S. (514) 343-6880), (Fax from U.S. (514) 343 6882), www.uis.unesco.org; *Statistical Tables.*

United Nations Food and Agricultural Organization (FAO), Viale delle Terme di Caracalla, 00100 Rome, Italy, (Dial from U.S. (202) 653-2400), (Fax from U.S. (202) 653 5760), www.fao.org; *The State of Food and Agriculture (SOFA) 2006.*

United Nations Statistics Division, New York, NY 10017, (800) 253-9646, Fax: (212) 963-4116, http://unstats.un.org; *Statistical Yearbook* and *Trends in Europe and North America: The Statistical Yearbook of the ECE 2005.*

The World Bank, 1818 H Street, NW, Washington, DC 20433, (202) 473-1000, Fax: (202) 477-6391, www.worldbank.org; *Czech Republic* and *World Development Report 2008.*

CZECH REPUBLIC - POSTAL SERVICE

M.E. Sharpe, 80 Business Park Drive, Armonk, NY 10504, (800) 541-6563, Fax: (914) 273-2106, www.mesharpe.com; *The Illustrated Book of World Rankings.*

United Nations Statistics Division, New York, NY 10017, (800) 253-9646, Fax: (212) 963-4116, http://unstats.un.org; *Statistical Yearbook* and *Trends in Europe and North America: The Statistical Yearbook of the ECE 2005.*

CZECH REPUBLIC - POWER RESOURCES

Euromonitor International, Inc., 224 S. Michigan Avenue, Suite 1500, Chicago, IL 60604, (312) 922-1115, Fax: (312) 922-1157, www.euromonitor.com; *European Marketing Data and Statistics 2008; The World Economic Factbook 2008;* and *World Marketing Data and Statistics.*

M.E. Sharpe, 80 Business Park Drive, Armonk, NY 10504, (800) 541-6563, Fax: (914) 273-2106, www.mesharpe.com; *The Illustrated Book of World Rankings.*

Organisation for Economic Cooperation and Development (OECD), 2 rue Andre Pascal, F-75775 Paris Cedex 16, France, (Telephone in U.S. (202) 785-6323), (Fax in U.S. (202) 785-0350), www.oecd.org; *World Energy Outlook 2007.*

Palgrave Macmillan Ltd., Houndmills, Basingstoke, Hampshire, RG21 6XS, England, (Telephone in U.S. (888) 330-8477), (Fax in U.S. (800) 672-2054), www.palgrave.com; *The Statesman's Yearbook 2008.*

Platts, 2 Penn Plaza, 25th Floor, New York, NY 10121-2298, (212) 904-3070, www.platts.com; *Energy Economist* and *European Power Daily.*

U.S. Department of Energy (DOE), Energy Information Administration (EIA), 1000 Independence Avenue, SW, Washington, DC 20585, (202) 586-8800, www.eia.doe.gov; *International Energy Annual 2004* and *International Energy Outlook 2006.*

United Nations Food and Agricultural Organization (FAO), Viale delle Terme di Caracalla, 00100 Rome, Italy, (Dial from U.S. (202) 653-2400), (Fax from U.S. (202) 653 5760), www.fao.org; *The State of Food and Agriculture (SOFA) 2006.*

United Nations Statistics Division, New York, NY 10017, (800) 253-9646, Fax: (212) 963-4116, http://unstats.un.org; *Energy Statistics Yearbook 2003; Human Development Report 2006; Statistical Yearbook; Trends in Europe and North America: The Statistical Yearbook of the ECE 2005;* and *World Statistics Pocketbook.*

The World Bank, 1818 H Street, NW, Washington, DC 20433, (202) 473-1000, Fax: (202) 477-6391, www.worldbank.org; *The World Bank Atlas 2003-2004* and *World Development Report 2008.*

CZECH REPUBLIC - PRICES

Euromonitor International, Inc., 224 S. Michigan Avenue, Suite 1500, Chicago, IL 60604, (312) 922-1115, Fax: (312) 922-1157, www.euromonitor.com; *European Marketing Data and Statistics 2008* and *World Marketing Data and Statistics.*

International Labour Office, I.L.O. Publications, 4 route des Morillons, CH-1211 Geneva 22, Switzerland, (Telephone in U.S. (202) 653-7652), (Fax in U.S. (202) 653-7687), www.ilo.org; *Yearbook of Labour Statistics 2006.*

International Lead and Zinc Study Group (ILZSG), Rua Almirante Barroso 38, 5th Floor, Lisbon 1000 - 013, Portugal, www.ilzsg.org; Interactive Statistical Database.

M.E. Sharpe, 80 Business Park Drive, Armonk, NY 10504, (800) 541-6563, Fax: (914) 273-2106, www.mesharpe.com; *The Illustrated Book of World Rankings.*

United Nations Food and Agricultural Organization (FAO), Viale delle Terme di Caracalla, 00100 Rome, Italy, (Dial from U.S. (202) 653-2400), (Fax from U.S. (202) 653 5760), www.fao.org; *FAO Production Yearbook 2002* and *The State of Food and Agriculture (SOFA) 2006.*

The World Bank, 1818 H Street, NW, Washington, DC 20433, (202) 473-1000, Fax: (202) 477-6391, www.worldbank.org; *Czech Republic.*

CZECH REPUBLIC - PROFESSIONS

United Nations Statistics Division, New York, NY 10017, (800) 253-9646, Fax: (212) 963-4116, http://unstats.un.org; *Statistical Yearbook.*

CZECH REPUBLIC - PUBLIC HEALTH

Euromonitor International, Inc., 224 S. Michigan Avenue, Suite 1500, Chicago, IL 60604, (312) 922-1115, Fax: (312) 922-1157, www.euromonitor.com; *World Health Databook 2007/2008* and *World Marketing Data and Statistics.*

European Centre for Disease Prevention and Control (ECDC), 171 83 Stockholm, Sweden, www.ecdc.europa.eu; *Eurosurveillance.*

Health and Consumer Protection Directorate-General, European Commission, B-1049 Brussels, Belgium, http://ec.europa.eu/dgs/health_consumer/index_en.htm; *Injuries in the European Union: Statistics Summary 2002-2004.*

M.E. Sharpe, 80 Business Park Drive, Armonk, NY 10504, (800) 541-6563, Fax: (914) 273-2106, www.mesharpe.com; *The Illustrated Book of World Rankings.*

UNICEF, 3 United Nations Plaza, New York, NY 10017, (800) 253-9646, Fax: (212) 887-7465, www.unicef.org; *The State of the World's Children 2008.*

United Nations Statistics Division, New York, NY 10017, (800) 253-9646, Fax: (212) 963-4116, http://unstats.un.org; *Human Development Report 2006; Statistical Yearbook;* and *Trends in Europe and North America: The Statistical Yearbook of the ECE 2005.*

The World Bank, 1818 H Street, NW, Washington, DC 20433, (202) 473-1000, Fax: (202) 477-6391, www.worldbank.org; *Czech Republic* and *World Development Report 2008.*

World Health Organization (WHO), Avenue Appia 20, 1211 Geneve 27, Switzerland, (Telephone in U.S. (212) 331-9081), www.who.int; The WHO Global Atlas of Infectious Diseases.

CZECH REPUBLIC - PUBLISHERS AND PUBLISHING

Taylor and Francis Group, An Informa Business, 2 Park Square, Milton Park, Abingdon, Oxford OX14 4RN, United Kingdom, (Dial from U.S. (212) 216-7800), (Fax from U.S. (212) 564-7854), www.tandf.co.uk; *The Europa World Year Book.*

UNESCO Institute for Statistics, C.P. 6128 Succursale Centre-Ville, Montreal, Quebec, H3C 3J7 Canada, (Dial from U.S. (514) 343-6880), (Fax from U.S. (514) 343 6882), www.uis.unesco.org; *Statistical Tables.*

United Nations Statistics Division, New York, NY 10017, (800) 253-9646, Fax: (212) 963-4116, http://unstats.un.org; *Trends in Europe and North America: The Statistical Yearbook of the ECE 2005.*

CZECH REPUBLIC - RADIO - RECEIVERS AND RECEPTION

Palgrave Macmillan Ltd., Houndmills, Basingstoke, Hampshire, RG21 6XS, England, (Telephone in U.S. (888) 330-8477), (Fax in U.S. (800) 672-2054), www.palgrave.com; *The Statesman's Yearbook 2008.*

United Nations Statistics Division, New York, NY 10017, (800) 253-9646, Fax: (212) 963-4116, http://unstats.un.org; *Statistical Yearbook.*

CZECH REPUBLIC - RAILROADS

Euromonitor International, Inc., 224 S. Michigan Avenue, Suite 1500, Chicago, IL 60604, (312) 922-1115, Fax: (312) 922-1157, www.euromonitor.com; *European Marketing Data and Statistics 2008.*

Jane's Information Group, 110 North Royal Street, Suite 200, Alexandria, VA 22314, (703) 683-3700, Fax: (800) 836-0297, www.janes.com; *Jane's World Railways.*

Palgrave Macmillan Ltd., Houndmills, Basingstoke, Hampshire, RG21 6XS, England, (Telephone in U.S. (888) 330-8477), (Fax in U.S. (800) 672-2054), www.palgrave.com; *The Statesman's Yearbook 2008.*

Taylor and Francis Group, An Informa Business, 2 Park Square, Milton Park, Abingdon, Oxford OX14 4RN, United Kingdom, (Dial from U.S. (212) 216-7800), (Fax from U.S. (212) 564-7854), www.tandf.co.uk; *The Europa World Year Book.*

United Nations Statistics Division, New York, NY 10017, (800) 253-9646, Fax: (212) 963-4116, http://unstats.un.org; *Annual Bulletin of Transport Statistics for Europe and North America 2004; Statistical Yearbook;* and *Trends in Europe and North America: The Statistical Yearbook of the ECE 2005.*

CZECH REPUBLIC - RELIGION

Central Intelligence Agency, Office of Public Affairs, Washington, DC 20505, (703) 482-0623, Fax: (703) 482-1739, www.cia.gov; *The World Factbook.*

M.E. Sharpe, 80 Business Park Drive, Armonk, NY 10504, (800) 541-6563, Fax: (914) 273-2106, www.mesharpe.com; *The Illustrated Book of World Rankings.*

Palgrave Macmillan Ltd., Houndmills, Basingstoke, Hampshire, RG21 6XS, England, (Telephone in U.S. (888) 330-8477), (Fax in U.S. (800) 672-2054), www.palgrave.com; *The Statesman's Yearbook 2008.*

CZECH REPUBLIC - RETAIL TRADE

Banque de France, 48 rue Croix des Petits champs, 75001 Paris, France, www.banque-france.fr/home.htm; *Monthly Business Survey Overview.*

Euromonitor International, Inc., 224 S. Michigan Avenue, Suite 1500, Chicago, IL 60604, (312) 922-1115, Fax: (312) 922-1157, www.euromonitor.com; *Retail Trade International 2007* and *World Marketing Data and Statistics.*

United Nations Statistics Division, New York, NY 10017, (800) 253-9646, Fax: (212) 963-4116, http://unstats.un.org; *Statistical Yearbook.*

CZECH REPUBLIC - RICE PRODUCTION

See CZECH REPUBLIC - CROPS

CZECH REPUBLIC - ROADS

Central Intelligence Agency, Office of Public Affairs, Washington, DC 20505, (703) 482-0623, Fax: (703) 482-1739, www.cia.gov; *The World Factbook.*

International Road Federation (IFR), Madison Place, 500 Montgomery Street, 5th Floor, Alexandria, VA 22314, (703) 535-1001, Fax: (703) 535-1007, www.irfnet.org; *World Road Statistics 2006.*

Palgrave Macmillan Ltd., Houndmills, Basingstoke, Hampshire, RG21 6XS, England, (Telephone in U.S. (888) 330-8477), (Fax in U.S. (800) 672-2054), www.palgrave.com; *The Statesman's Yearbook 2008.*

United Nations Statistics Division, New York, NY 10017, (800) 253-9646, Fax: (212) 963-4116, http://unstats.un.org; *Annual Bulletin of Transport Statistics for Europe and North America 2004* and *Trends in Europe and North America: The Statistical Yearbook of the ECE 2005.*

CZECH REPUBLIC - RUBBER INDUSTRY AND TRADE

International Rubber Study Group (IRSG), 1st Floor, Heron House, 109/115 Wembley Hill Road, Wembley, Middlesex HA9 8DA, United Kingdom, www.rubberstudy.com; *Rubber Statistical Bulletin; Summary of World Rubber Statistics 2005; World Rubber Statistics Handbook (Volume 6, 1975-2001);* and *World Rubber Statistics Historic Handbook.*

M.E. Sharpe, 80 Business Park Drive, Armonk, NY 10504, (800) 541-6563, Fax: (914) 273-2106, www.mesharpe.com; *The Illustrated Book of World Rankings.*

United Nations Statistics Division, New York, NY 10017, (800) 253-9646, Fax: (212) 963-4116, http://unstats.un.org; *Statistical Yearbook.*

CZECH REPUBLIC - RYE PRODUCTION

See CZECH REPUBLIC - CROPS

CZECH REPUBLIC - SALT PRODUCTION

See CZECH REPUBLIC - MINERAL INDUSTRIES

CZECH REPUBLIC - SHEEP

See CZECH REPUBLIC - LIVESTOCK

CZECH REPUBLIC - SHIPPING

Palgrave Macmillan Ltd., Houndmills, Basingstoke, Hampshire, RG21 6XS, England, (Telephone in U.S. (888) 330-8477), (Fax in U.S. (800) 672-2054), www.palgrave.com; *The Statesman's Yearbook 2008.*

Taylor and Francis Group, An Informa Business, 2 Park Square, Milton Park, Abingdon, Oxford OX14 4RN, United Kingdom, (Dial from U.S. (212) 216-7800), (Fax from U.S. (212) 564-7854), www.tandf.co.uk; *The Europa World Year Book.*

U.S. Department of State (DOS), 2201 C Street NW, Washington, DC 20520, (202) 647-4000, www.state.gov; *World Military Expenditures and Arms Transfers (WMEAT).*

United Nations Statistics Division, New York, NY 10017, (800) 253-9646, Fax: (212) 963-4116, http://unstats.un.org; *Annual Bulletin of Transport Statistics for Europe and North America 2004* and *Statistical Yearbook.*

CZECH REPUBLIC - SILVER PRODUCTION

See CZECH REPUBLIC - MINERAL INDUSTRIES

CZECH REPUBLIC - SOCIAL ECOLOGY

M.E. Sharpe, 80 Business Park Drive, Armonk, NY 10504, (800) 541-6563, Fax: (914) 273-2106, www.mesharpe.com; *The Illustrated Book of World Rankings.*

United Nations Statistics Division, New York, NY 10017, (800) 253-9646, Fax: (212) 963-4116, http://unstats.un.org; *World Statistics Pocketbook.*

CZECH REPUBLIC - SOCIAL SECURITY

Palgrave Macmillan Ltd., Houndmills, Basingstoke, Hampshire, RG21 6XS, England, (Telephone in U.S. (888) 330-8477), (Fax in U.S. (800) 672-2054), www.palgrave.com; *The Statesman's Yearbook 2008.*

United Nations Statistics Division, New York, NY 10017, (800) 253-9646, Fax: (212) 963-4116, http://unstats.un.org; *National Accounts Statistics: Compendium of Income Distribution Statistics.*

CZECH REPUBLIC - STEEL PRODUCTION

See CZECH REPUBLIC - MINERAL INDUSTRIES

CZECH REPUBLIC - SUGAR PRODUCTION

See CZECH REPUBLIC - CROPS

CZECH REPUBLIC - TAXATION

Eurostat, Batiment Jean Monnet, Rue Alcide de Gasperi, L-2920 Luxembourg, http://epp.eurostat.ec.europa.eu; *Taxation Trends in the European Union - Data for the EU Member States and Norway.*

International Road Federation (IFR), Madison Place, 500 Montgomery Street, 5th Floor, Alexandria, VA 22314, (703) 535-1001, Fax: (703) 535-1007, www.irfnet.org; *World Road Statistics 2006.*

Taylor and Francis Group, An Informa Business, 2 Park Square, Milton Park, Abingdon, Oxford OX14 4RN, United Kingdom, (Dial from U.S. (212) 216-7800), (Fax from U.S. (212) 564-7854), www.tandf.co.uk; *The Europa World Year Book.*

CZECH REPUBLIC - TEA PRODUCTION

See CZECH REPUBLIC - CROPS

CZECH REPUBLIC - TELEPHONE

International Telecommunication Union (ITU), Place des Nations, 1211 Geneva 20, Switzerland, www.itu.int; World Telecommunication Indicators Database.

Palgrave Macmillan Ltd., Houndmills, Basingstoke, Hampshire, RG21 6XS, England, (Telephone in U.S. (888) 330-8477), (Fax in U.S. (800) 672-2054), www.palgrave.com; *The Statesman's Yearbook 2008.*

Taylor and Francis Group, An Informa Business, 2 Park Square, Milton Park, Abingdon, Oxford OX14 4RN, United Kingdom, (Dial from U.S. (212) 216-7800), (Fax from U.S. (212) 564-7854), www.tandf.co.uk; *The Europa World Year Book.*

United Nations Statistics Division, New York, NY 10017, (800) 253-9646, Fax: (212) 963-4116, http://unstats.un.org; *Statistical Yearbook; Trends in Europe and North America: The Statistical Yearbook of the ECE 2005;* and *World Statistics Pocketbook.*

CZECH REPUBLIC - TELEVISION - RECEIVERS AND RECEPTION

United Nations Statistics Division, New York, NY 10017, (800) 253-9646, Fax: (212) 963-4116, http://unstats.un.org; *Statistical Yearbook.*

CZECH REPUBLIC - TEXTILE INDUSTRY

Euromonitor International, Inc., 224 S. Michigan Avenue, Suite 1500, Chicago, IL 60604, (312) 922-1115, Fax: (312) 922-1157, www.euromonitor.com; *Retail Trade International 2007.*

Palgrave Macmillan Ltd., Houndmills, Basingstoke, Hampshire, RG21 6XS, England, (Telephone in U.S. (888) 330-8477), (Fax in U.S. (800) 672-2054), www.palgrave.com; *The Statesman's Yearbook 2008.*

United Nations Conference on Trade and Development (UNCTAD), DC2-1120, United Nations, New York, NY 10017, (212) 963-0027, www.unctad.org; *UNCTAD Commodity Yearbook.*

United Nations Food and Agricultural Organization (FAO), Viale delle Terme di Caracalla, 00100 Rome, Italy, (Dial from U.S. (202) 653-2400), (Fax from U.S. (202) 653 5760), www.fao.org; *FAO Production Yearbook 2002.*

United Nations Statistics Division, New York, NY 10017, (800) 253-9646, Fax: (212) 963-4116, http://unstats.un.org; *2004 Industrial Commodity Statistics Yearbook* and *Statistical Yearbook.*

CZECH REPUBLIC - THEATER

UNESCO Institute for Statistics, C.P. 6128 Succursale Centre-Ville, Montreal, Quebec, H3C 3J7 Canada, (Dial from U.S. (514) 343-6880), (Fax from U.S. (514) 343 6882), www.uis.unesco.org; *Statistical Tables.*

CZECH REPUBLIC - TIN PRODUCTION

See CZECH REPUBLIC - MINERAL INDUSTRIES

CZECH REPUBLIC - TIRE INDUSTRY

United Nations Statistics Division, New York, NY 10017, (800) 253-9646, Fax: (212) 963-4116, http://unstats.un.org; *Statistical Yearbook.*

CZECH REPUBLIC - TOBACCO INDUSTRY

Euromonitor International, Inc., 224 S. Michigan Avenue, Suite 1500, Chicago, IL 60604, (312) 922-1115, Fax: (312) 922-1157, www.euromonitor.com; *European Marketing Data and Statistics 2008.*

Foreign Agricultural Service (FAS), U.S. Department of Agriculture (USDA), 1400 Independence Avenue, SW, Washington, DC 20250, (202) 720-3935, www.fas.usda.gov; *Tobacco: World Markets and Trade.*

M.E. Sharpe, 80 Business Park Drive, Armonk, NY 10504, (800) 541-6563, Fax: (914) 273-2106, www.mesharpe.com; *The Illustrated Book of World Rankings.*

United Nations Statistics Division, New York, NY 10017, (800) 253-9646, Fax: (212) 963-4116, http://unstats.un.org; *Statistical Yearbook.*

CZECH REPUBLIC - TOURISM

Euromonitor International, Inc., 224 S. Michigan Avenue, Suite 1500, Chicago, IL 60604, (312) 922-1115, Fax: (312) 922-1157, www.euromonitor.com; *The World Economic Factbook 2008* and *World Marketing Data and Statistics.*

Eurostat, Batiment Jean Monnet, Rue Alcide de Gasperi, L-2920 Luxembourg, http://epp.eurostat.ec.europa.eu; *Tourism in Europe: First Results for 2007.*

International Road Federation (IFR), Madison Place, 500 Montgomery Street, 5th Floor, Alexandria, VA 22314, (703) 535-1001, Fax: (703) 535-1007, www.irfnet.org; *World Road Statistics 2006.*

M.E. Sharpe, 80 Business Park Drive, Armonk, NY 10504, (800) 541-6563, Fax: (914) 273-2106, www.mesharpe.com; *The Illustrated Book of World Rankings.*

Taylor and Francis Group, An Informa Business, 2 Park Square, Milton Park, Abingdon, Oxford OX14 4RN, United Kingdom, (Dial from U.S. (212) 216-7800), (Fax from U.S. (212) 564-7854), www.tandf.co.uk; *The Europa World Year Book.*

United Nations Statistics Division, New York, NY 10017, (800) 253-9646, Fax: (212) 963-4116, http://unstats.un.org; *Statistical Yearbook* and *Trends in Europe and North America: The Statistical Yearbook of the ECE 2005.*

United Nations World Tourism Organization (UNWTO), Capitan Haya 42, 28020 Madrid, Spain, www.world-tourism.org; *Tourism Market Trends 2004 - Europe* and *Yearbook of Tourism Statistics.*

The World Bank, 1818 H Street, NW, Washington, DC 20433, (202) 473-1000, Fax: (202) 477-6391, www.worldbank.org; *Czech Republic.*

CZECH REPUBLIC - TRADE

See CZECH REPUBLIC - INTERNATIONAL TRADE

CZECH REPUBLIC - TRANSPORTATION

Central Intelligence Agency, Office of Public Affairs, Washington, DC 20505, (703) 482-0623, Fax: (703) 482-1739, www.cia.gov; *The World Factbook.*

Euromonitor International, Inc., 224 S. Michigan Avenue, Suite 1500, Chicago, IL 60604, (312) 922-1115, Fax: (312) 922-1157, www.euromonitor.com; *World Marketing Data and Statistics.*

Eurostat, Batiment Jean Monnet, Rue Alcide de Gasperi, L-2920 Luxembourg, http://epp.eurostat.ec.europa.eu; *Regional Passenger and Freight Air Transport in Europe in 2006* and *Regional Road and Rail Transport Networks.*

M.E. Sharpe, 80 Business Park Drive, Armonk, NY 10504, (800) 541-6563, Fax: (914) 273-2106, www.mesharpe.com; *The Illustrated Book of World Rankings.*

Palgrave Macmillan Ltd., Houndmills, Basingstoke, Hampshire, RG21 6XS, England, (Telephone in U.S. (888) 330-8477), (Fax in U.S. (800) 672-2054), www.palgrave.com; *The Statesman's Yearbook 2008.*

Taylor and Francis Group, An Informa Business, 2 Park Square, Milton Park, Abingdon, Oxford OX14 4RN, United Kingdom, (Dial from U.S. (212) 216-7800), (Fax from U.S. (212) 564-7854), www.tandf.co.uk; *The Europa World Year Book.*

United Nations Statistics Division, New York, NY 10017, (800) 253-9646, Fax: (212) 963-4116, http://unstats.un.org; *Annual Bulletin of Transport Statistics for Europe and North America 2004; Human Development Report 2006;* and *Trends in Europe and North America: The Statistical Yearbook of the ECE 2005.*

The World Bank, 1818 H Street, NW, Washington, DC 20433, (202) 473-1000, Fax: (202) 477-6391, www.worldbank.org; *Czech Republic.*

CZECH REPUBLIC - TURKEYS

See CZECH REPUBLIC - LIVESTOCK

CZECH REPUBLIC - UNEMPLOYMENT

Central Intelligence Agency, Office of Public Affairs, Washington, DC 20505, (703) 482-0623, Fax: (703) 482-1739, www.cia.gov; *The World Factbook.*

Euromonitor International, Inc., 224 S. Michigan Avenue, Suite 1500, Chicago, IL 60604, (312) 922-1115, Fax: (312) 922-1157, www.euromonitor.com; *European Marketing Data and Statistics 2008.*

International Labour Office, I.L.O. Publications, 4 route des Morillons, CH-1211 Geneva 22, Switzerland, (Telephone in U.S. (202) 653-7652), (Fax in U.S. (202) 653-7687), www.ilo.org; *Yearbook of Labour Statistics 2006.*

Organisation for Economic Cooperation and Development (OECD), 2 rue Andre Pascal, F-75775 Paris Cedex 16, France, (Telephone in U.S. (202) 785-6323), (Fax in U.S. (202) 785-0350), www.oecd.org; *Labour Force Statistics: 1986-2005, 2007 Edition; OECD Composite Leading Indicators (CLIs), Updated September 2007;* and *OECD Economic Survey - Czech Republic 2008.*

Palgrave Macmillan Ltd., Houndmills, Basingstoke, Hampshire, RG21 6XS, England, (Telephone in U.S. (888) 330-8477), (Fax in U.S. (800) 672-2054), www.palgrave.com; *The Statesman's Yearbook 2008.*

United Nations Statistics Division, New York, NY 10017, (800) 253-9646, Fax: (212) 963-4116, http://unstats.un.org; *Statistical Yearbook* and *Trends in Europe and North America: The Statistical Yearbook of the ECE 2005.*

The World Bank, 1818 H Street, NW, Washington, DC 20433, (202) 473-1000, Fax: (202) 477-6391, www.worldbank.org; *Czech Republic.*

CZECH REPUBLIC - VITAL STATISTICS

Palgrave Macmillan Ltd., Houndmills, Basingstoke, Hampshire, RG21 6XS, England, (Telephone in U.S. (888) 330-8477), (Fax in U.S. (800) 672-2054), www.palgrave.com; *The Statesman's Yearbook 2008.*

United Nations Statistics Division, New York, NY 10017, (800) 253-9646, Fax: (212) 963-4116, http://unstats.un.org; *Statistical Yearbook.*

World Health Organization (WHO), Avenue Appia 20, 1211 Geneve 27, Switzerland, (Telephone in U.S. (212) 331-9081), www.who.int; *World Health Report 2006.*

CZECH REPUBLIC - WAGES

Euromonitor International, Inc., 224 S. Michigan Avenue, Suite 1500, Chicago, IL 60604, (312) 922-1115, Fax: (312) 922-1157, www.euromonitor.com; *European Marketing Data and Statistics 2008.*

International Labour Office, I.L.O. Publications, 4 route des Morillons, CH-1211 Geneva 22, Switzerland, (Telephone in U.S. (202) 653-7652), (Fax in U.S. (202) 653-7687), www.ilo.org; *Yearbook of Labour Statistics 2006.*

Organisation for Economic Cooperation and Development (OECD), 2 rue Andre Pascal, F-75775 Paris Cedex 16, France, (Telephone in U.S. (202) 785-6323), (Fax in U.S. (202) 785-0350), www.oecd.org; *ICT Sector Data and Metadata by Country.*

United Nations Statistics Division, New York, NY 10017, (800) 253-9646, Fax: (212) 963-4116, http://unstats.un.org; *Statistical Yearbook.*

The World Bank, 1818 H Street, NW, Washington, DC 20433, (202) 473-1000, Fax: (202) 477-6391, www.worldbank.org; *Czech Republic.*

CZECH REPUBLIC - WALNUT PRODUCTION

See CZECH REPUBLIC - CROPS

CZECH REPUBLIC - WATERWAYS

United Nations Statistics Division, New York, NY 10017, (800) 253-9646, Fax: (212) 963-4116, http://unstats.un.org; *Annual Bulletin of Transport Statistics for Europe and North America 2004.*

CZECH REPUBLIC - WHEAT PRODUCTION

See CZECH REPUBLIC - CROPS

CZECH REPUBLIC - WHOLESALE PRICE INDEXES

United Nations Statistics Division, New York, NY 10017, (800) 253-9646, Fax: (212) 963-4116, http://unstats.un.org; *Statistical Yearbook.*

CZECH REPUBLIC - WHOLESALE TRADE

United Nations Statistics Division, New York, NY 10017, (800) 253-9646, Fax: (212) 963-4116, http://unstats.un.org; *Statistical Yearbook.*STATISTICS SOURCES, Thirty-second Edition - 2009STATISTICS SOURCES, Thirty-second Edition - 2009

DAIRY PRODUCTS - CALCIUM SOURCE

Center for Nutrition Policy and Promotion (CNPP), U.S. Department of Agriculture (USDA), 3101 Park Center Drive, 10th Floor, Alexandria, VA 22302-1594, (703) 305-7600, Fax: (703) 305-3300, www.usda.gov/cnpp; *Nutrient Content of the U.S. Food Supply Summary Report 2005.*

DAIRY PRODUCTS - CHOLESTEROL SOURCE

Center for Nutrition Policy and Promotion (CNPP), U.S. Department of Agriculture (USDA), 3101 Park Center Drive, 10th Floor, Alexandria, VA 22302-1594, (703) 305-7600, Fax: (703) 305-3300, www.usda.gov/cnpp; *Nutrient Content of the U.S. Food Supply Summary Report 2005.*

DAIRY PRODUCTS - CONSUMER EXPENDITURES

U.S. Bureau of Labor Statistics (BLS), Postal Square Building, 2 Massachusetts Avenue, NE, Washington, DC 20212-0001, (202) 691-5200, Fax: (202) 691-6325, www.bls.gov; *Consumer Expenditures in 2006.*

DAIRY PRODUCTS - CONSUMPTION

Economic Research Service (ERS), U.S. Department of Agriculture (USDA), 1800 M Street, NW, Washington, DC 20036-5831, (202) 694-5050, Fax: (202) 694-5689, www.ers.usda.gov; *Agricultural Outlook* and *Food CPI, Prices, and Expenditures.*

DAIRY PRODUCTS - FARM MARKETINGS - SALES

Economic Research Service (ERS), U.S. Department of Agriculture (USDA), 1800 M Street, NW, Washington, DC 20036-5831, (202) 694-5050, Fax: (202) 694-5689, www.ers.usda.gov; *Agricultural Income and Finance Outlook* and *Farm Income: Data Files.*

National Agricultural Statistics Service (NASS), U.S. Department of Agriculture (USDA), 1400 Independence Avenue, SW, Washington, DC 20250, (800) 727-9540, Fax: (202) 690-2090, www.nass.usda.gov; *Dairy Products* and *Milk Cows and Milk Production.*

DAIRY PRODUCTS - INTERNATIONAL TRADE

Economic Research Service (ERS), U.S. Department of Agriculture (USDA), 1800 M Street, NW, Washington, DC 20036-5831, (202) 694-5050, Fax: (202) 694-5689, www.ers.usda.gov; *Food CPI, Prices, and Expenditures; Foreign Agricultural Trade of the United States (FATUS);* and *U.S. Agricultural Trade Update: 2006.*

U.S. Census Bureau, Foreign Trade Division, 4700 Silver Hill Road, Washington DC 20233-0001, (301) 763-3030, www.census.gov/foreign-trade/www/; *U.S. International Trade in Goods and Services.*

DAIRY PRODUCTS - IRON (DIETARY) SOURCE

Center for Nutrition Policy and Promotion (CNPP), U.S. Department of Agriculture (USDA), 3101 Park Center Drive, 10th Floor, Alexandria, VA 22302-1594, (703) 305-7600, Fax: (703) 305-3300, www.usda.gov/cnpp; *Nutrient Content of the U.S. Food Supply Summary Report 2005.*

DAIRY PRODUCTS - MANUFACTURING

National Agricultural Statistics Service (NASS), U.S. Department of Agriculture (USDA), 1400 Independence Avenue, SW, Washington, DC 20250, (800) 727-9540, Fax: (202) 690-2090, www.nass.usda.gov; *Dairy Products* and *Milk Cows and Milk Production.*

DAIRY PRODUCTS - PRICES

National Agricultural Statistics Service (NASS), U.S. Department of Agriculture (USDA), 1400 Independence Avenue, SW, Washington, DC 20250, (800) 727-9540, Fax: (202) 690-2090, www.nass.usda.gov; *Agricultural Prices.*

DAIRY PRODUCTS - PRODUCTION

Economic Research Service (ERS), U.S. Department of Agriculture (USDA), 1800 M Street, NW, Washington, DC 20036-5831, (202) 694-5050, Fax: (202) 694-5689, www.ers.usda.gov; *Agricultural Outlook.*

Executive Office of the President, Council of Economic Advisors, The White House, 1600 Pennsylvania Avenue NW, Washington, DC 20500, (202) 456-1414, www.whitehouse.gov/cea; *2007 Economic Report of the President.*

National Agricultural Statistics Service (NASS), U.S. Department of Agriculture (USDA), 1400 Independence Avenue, SW, Washington, DC 20250, (800) 727-9540, Fax: (202) 690-2090, www.nass.usda.gov; *Dairy Products* and *Milk Cows and Milk Production.*

DANCE

National Endowment for the Arts (NEA), 1100 Pennsylvania Avenue, NW, Washington, DC 20506-0001, (202) 682-5400, www.arts.gov; *Raising the Barre: The Geographic, Financial, and Economic Trends of Nonprofit Dance Companies* and *2002 Survey of Public Participation in the Arts.*

DART THROWING

National Sporting Goods Association (NSGA), 1601 Feehanville Drive, Suite 300, Mount Prospect, IL 60056, (847) 296-6742, Fax: (847) 391-9827, www.nsga.org; *2006 Sports Participation.*

DATES

National Agricultural Statistics Service (NASS), U.S. Department of Agriculture (USDA), 1400 Independence Avenue, SW, Washington, DC 20250, (800) 727-9540, Fax: (202) 690-2090, www.nass.usda.gov; *Noncitrus Fruits and Nuts: Final Estimates 1998-2003.*

DAY CARE

See CHILD DAY CARE SERVICES

DEATH AND DEATH RATES

See MORTALITY

DEATH PENALTY

Death Penalty Information Center, 1101 Vermont Avenue, NW, Suite 701, Washington, DC 20005, (202) 289-2275, www.deathpenaltyinfo.org; *Blind Justice: Juries Deciding Life and Death with Only Half the Truth; A Crisis of Confidence: Americans' Doubts About the Death Penalty; The Death Penalty in 2005: Death Sentences Reach Record Lows as Country Turns to Life Without Parole; The Death Penalty in 2006: Use of the Death Penalty Declines in 2006; The Death Penalty in 2007: Execution Chambers Silent as Supreme Court Considers Next Step; The Death Penalty in Black and White: Who Lives, Who Dies, Who Decides; Innocence and the Crisis in the American Death Penalty;* and *International Perspectives on the Death Penalty: A Costly Isolation for the U.S.*

U.S. Department of Justice (DOJ), Bureau of Justice Statistics, 810 Seventh Street, NW, Washington, DC 20531, (202) 307-0765, www.ojp.usdoj.gov/bjs/; *Capital Punishment, 2004* and *Correctional Populations in the United States.*

DEBIT CARDS

The Nilson Report, 1110 Eugenia Place, Suite 100, Carpinteria, CA 93013-9921, (805) 684-8800, Fax: (805) 684-8825, www.nilsonreport.com; *The Nilson Report.*

DEBT - CITY

U.S. Census Bureau, 4700 Silver Hill Road, Washington DC 20233-0001, (301) 763-3030, www.census.gov; unpublished data.

DEBT - CONSUMER

Board of Governors of the Federal Reserve System, Constitution Avenue, NW, Washington, DC 20551, (202) 452-3000, www.federalreserve.gov; *Federal Reserve Bulletin; Household Debt Service and Financial Obligations Ratios; Statistical Digest;* and unpublished data.

DEBT - COUNTY GOVERNMENTS

U.S. Census Bureau, 4700 Silver Hill Road, Washington DC 20233-0001, (301) 763-3030, www.census.gov; unpublished data.

DEBT - FARM

Economic Research Service (ERS), U.S. Department of Agriculture (USDA), 1800 M Street, NW, Washington, DC 20036-5831, (202) 694-5050, Fax:

(202) 694-5689, www.ers.usda.gov; *Agricultural Income and Finance Outlook; Amber Waves: The Economics of Food, Farming, Natural Resources, and Rural America; Farm Balance Sheet;* and *Farm Income: Data Files.*

DEBT - FEDERAL GOVERNMENT

The Office of Management and Budget (OMB), 725 17th Street, NW, Washington, DC 20503, (202) 395-3080, Fax: (202) 395-3888, www.whitehouse.gov/omb; *Historical Tables.*

U.S. Census Bureau, Governments Division, 4600 Silver Hill Road, Washington DC 20233, (800) 242-2184, www.census.gov/govs/www; *2002 Census of Governments* and *2002 Census of Governments, Government Finances.*

U.S. Department of the Treasury (DOT), 1500 Pennsylvania Avenue, NW, Washington, DC 20220, (202) 622-2000, Fax: (202) 622-6415, www.ustreas.gov; *Treasury Bulletin.*

U.S. Department of the Treasury (DOT), Internal Revenue Service (IRS), Statistics of Income Division (SIS), PO Box 2608, Washington, DC, 20013-2608, (202) 874-0410, Fax: (202) 874-0964, www.irs.ustreas.gov; *Statistics of Income Bulletin, Individual Income Tax Returns.*

DEBT - FOREIGN COUNTRIES

International Monetary Fund (IMF), 700 Nineteenth Street, NW, Washington, DC 20431, (202) 623-7000, Fax: (202) 623-4661, www.imf.org; *Joint BIS-IMF-OECD-World Bank Statistics on External Debt.*

The World Bank, 1818 H Street, NW, Washington, DC 20433, (202) 473-1000, Fax: (202) 477-6391, www.worldbank.org; *World Development Indicators (WDI) 2008.*

DEBT - HOUSEHOLDS

Board of Governors of the Federal Reserve System, Constitution Avenue, NW, Washington, DC 20551, (202) 452-3000, www.federalreserve.gov; *Federal Reserve Board Statistical Release; Federal Reserve Bulletin;* and *Flow of Funds Accounts of the United States.*

DEBT - LOCAL GOVERNMENTS

U.S. Census Bureau, 4700 Silver Hill Road, Washington DC 20233-0001, (301) 763-3030, www.census.gov; unpublished data.

U.S. Census Bureau, Governments Division, 4600 Silver Hill Road, Washington DC 20233, (800) 242-2184, www.census.gov/govs/www; *2002 Census of Governments; 2002 Census of Governments, Government Finances;* and *Federal Aid to States for Fiscal Year 2004.*

DEBT - PUBLIC - STATE AND LOCAL GOVERNMENT - HIGHWAYS

U.S. Department of Transportation (DOT), Federal Highway Administration (FHA), 1200 New Jersey Avenue, SE, Washington, DC 20590, (202) 366-0660, www.fhwa.dot.gov; *Highway Statistics 2006.*

DEBT - PUBLIC - STATE GOVERNMENT

U.S. Census Bureau, 4700 Silver Hill Road, Washington DC 20233-0001, (301) 763-3030, www.census.gov; unpublished data.

U.S. Census Bureau, Governments Division, 4600 Silver Hill Road, Washington DC 20233, (800) 242-2184, www.census.gov/govs/www; *2002 Census of Governments, Government Finances.*

DEBT - STATE AND LOCAL GOVERNMENTS

U.S. Census Bureau, Governments Division, 4600 Silver Hill Road, Washington DC 20233, (800) 242-2184, www.census.gov/govs/www; *2002 Census of Governments, Government Finances.*

DEDUCTIONS (TAXES)

U.S. Department of the Treasury (DOT), Internal Revenue Service (IRS), Statistics of Income Division (SIS), PO Box 2608, Washington, DC, 20013-2608, (202) 874-0410, Fax: (202) 874-0964, www.irs.ustreas.gov; *Statistics of Income Bulletin, Individual Income Tax Returns.*

DEFENSE, DEPARTMENT OF - BUDGET AUTHORITY, OUTLAYS

The Office of Management and Budget (OMB), 725 17th Street, NW, Washington, DC 20503, (202) 395-3080, Fax: (202) 395-3888, www.whitehouse.gov/omb; *Historical Tables.*

DEFENSE, DEPARTMENT OF - CONTRACT AWARDS - STATES

U.S. Department of Defense (DOD), Statistical Information Analysis Division (SIAD), The Pentagon, Washington, DC 20301, (703) 545-6700, http://siadapp.dior.whs.mil/; *Atlas/Data Abstract for the United States and Selected Areas, Fiscal Year 2005.*

DEFENSE, DEPARTMENT OF - EMPLOYEES - CIVILIAN

U.S. Department of Defense (DOD), Statistical Information Analysis Division (SIAD), The Pentagon, Washington, DC 20301, (703) 545-6700, http://siadapp.dior.whs.mil/; *Atlas/Data Abstract for the United States and Selected Areas, Fiscal Year 2005; Selected Manpower Statistics, Fiscal Year 2005;* and *Worldwide Manpower Distribution by Geographical Area.*

DEFENSE, DEPARTMENT OF - EXPENDITURES

The Office of Management and Budget (OMB), 725 17th Street, NW, Washington, DC 20503, (202) 395-3080, Fax: (202) 395-3888, www.whitehouse.gov/omb; *Historical Tables.*

U.S. Department of Defense (DOD), Statistical Information Analysis Division (SIAD), The Pentagon, Washington, DC 20301, (703) 545-6700, http://siadapp.dior.whs.mil/; *Atlas/Data Abstract for the United States and Selected Areas, Fiscal Year 2005.*

DEFENSE, DEPARTMENT OF - EXPENDITURES - HEALTH AND MEDICAL CARE

Centers for Medicare and Medicaid Services (CMS), U.S. Department of Health and Human Services (HHS), 7500 Security Boulevard, Baltimore, MD 21244-1850, (410) 786-3000, http://cms.hhs.gov; *Health Care Financing Review.*

DEFENSE, DEPARTMENT OF - FUNDS AVAILABLE AND OUTLAYS

The Office of Management and Budget (OMB), 725 17th Street, NW, Washington, DC 20503, (202) 395-3080, Fax: (202) 395-3888, www.whitehouse.gov/omb; *Historical Tables.*

DEFENSE, DEPARTMENT OF - MILITARY BASES

U.S. Department of Defense (DOD), Statistical Information Analysis Division (SIAD), The Pentagon, Washington, DC 20301, (703) 545-6700, http://siadapp.dior.whs.mil/; *Selected Manpower Statistics, Fiscal Year 2005.*

DEFENSE, DEPARTMENT OF - MILITARY PERSONNEL

U.S. Department of Defense (DOD), Statistical Information Analysis Division (SIAD), The Pentagon, Washington, DC 20301, (703) 545-6700, http://siadapp.dior.whs.mil/; *Distribution of Personnel by State and by Selected Locations; Selected Manpower Statistics, Fiscal Year 2005;* and *Worldwide Manpower Distribution by Geographical Area.*

DEFENSE, DEPARTMENT OF - MILITARY RETIREES

U.S. Department of Defense (DOD), Statistical Information Analysis Division (SIAD), The Pentagon, Washington, DC 20301, (703) 545-6700, http://siadapp.dior.whs.mil/; *Selected Manpower Statistics, Fiscal Year 2005.*

DEFENSE, DEPARTMENT OF - PROPERTY - REAL AND PERSONAL

General Services Administration (GSA), 1800 F Street, NW, Washington, DC 20405, (202) 708-5082, www.gsa.gov; *Federal Real Property Profile 2004 (FRPP).*

DEGREES CONFERRED

See also Individual Fields

National Center for Education Statistics (NCES), 1990 K Street, NW, Washington, DC 20006, (202) 502-7300, http://nces.ed.gov; *Digest of Education Statistics 2007.*

National Science Foundation, Division of Science Resources Statistics (SRS), 4201 Wilson Boulevard, Arlington, VA 22230, (703) 292-8780, Fax: (703) 292-9092, www.nsf.gov; *National Survey of Recent College Graduates: 2006; Selected Data on Science and Engineering Doctorate Awards;* and *Survey of Earned Doctorates 2006.*

DEGREES CONFERRED - SALARY OFFERS

National Association of Colleges and Employers (NACE), 62 Highland Avenue, Bethlehem, PA 18017, (800) 544-5272, Fax: (610) 868-0208, www.naceweb.org; *Salary Survey.*

DELAWARE

See also - STATE DATA (FOR INDIVIDUAL STATES)

DELAWARE - STATE DATA CENTERS

Delaware Economic Development Office (DEDO), 99 Kings Highway, Dover, DE 19901, (302) 739-4271, Fax: (302) 739-5749, www.state.de.us/dedo/default.shtml; State Data Center.

Research and Data Management Services (RDMS), University of Delaware, 002 Smith Hall, Newark, DE 19716, (302) 831-DATA, Fax: (302) 831-4205, http://maps.rdms.udel.edu/census; State Data Center.

School of Urban Affairs and Public Policy, University of Delaware, 182 Graham Hall, Newark, DE 19716, (302) 831-1687, Fax: (302) 831-3296, www.udel.edu/suapp; State Data Center.

DELAWARE - PRIMARY STATISTICS SOURCES

Delaware Economic Development Office (DEDO), 99 Kings Highway, Dover, DE 19901, (302) 739-4271, Fax: (302) 739-5749, www.state.de.us/dedo/default.shtml; *Delaware Statistical Overview.*

DELINQUENCY

See JUVENILES

National Center for Juvenile Justice (NCJJ), 3700 South Water Street, Suite 200, Pittsburgh, PA 15203, (412) 227-6950, Fax: (412) 227-6955, http://ncjj.servehttp.com/NCJJWebsite/main.htm; *Juvenile Offenders and Victims: 2006 National Report.*

DEMOCRATIC KAMPUCHEA

See CAMBODIA

DENMARK - NATIONAL STATISTICAL OFFICE

Statistics Denmark (Danmarks Statistik), Sejroegade 11, 2100 Copenhagen Oe, Denmark, www.dst.dk/HomeUK.aspx; National Data Center.

DENMARK - PRIMARY STATISTICS SOURCES

Eurostat, Batiment Jean Monnet, Rue Alcide de Gasperi, L-2920 Luxembourg, http://epp.eurostat.ec.europa.eu; *Pocketbook on Candidate and Potential Candidate Countries.*

Statistics Denmark (Danmarks Statistik), Sejroegade 11, 2100 Copenhagen Oe, Denmark, www.dst.dk/HomeUK.aspx; *Statistical News* (Statistiske Efterretninger) and *Statistical Yearbook 2008.*

DENMARK - DATABASES

Danmarks Turistrad (tourist board), Vesterbrogade 6 D, DK-1620 Copenhagen V, Denmark; STABAS database. Subject coverage: travel and tourism in Denmark.

EMD International A/S, Niels Jernesvej 10, 9220 Aalborg O, Denmark, www.emd.dk; VE-databasen. Subject coverage: historical and actual data regarding the Danish energy market.

Statistics Denmark (Danmarks Statistik), Sejroegade 11, 2100 Copenhagen Oe, Denmark, www.dst.dk/HomeUK.aspx; Statbank Denmark.

DENMARK - ABORTION

European Union, Delegation of the European Commission to the United States, 2300 M Street, NW, Washington, DC 20037, (202) 862-9500, Fax: (202) 429-1766, www.eurunion.org; *First Demographic Estimates for 2006.*

Nordic Council of Ministers, Store Strandstraede 18, DK-1255 Copenhagen K, Denmark, www.norden.org; *Nordic Statistical Yearbook 2004-2006.*

United Nations Statistics Division, New York, NY 10017, (800) 253-9646, Fax: (212) 963-4116, http://unstats.un.org; *Demographic Yearbook* and *Trends in Europe and North America: The Statistical Yearbook of the ECE 2005.*

DENMARK - AGRICULTURAL MACHINERY

European Union, Delegation of the European Commission to the United States, 2300 M Street, NW, Washington, DC 20037, (202) 862-9500, Fax: (202) 429-1766, www.eurunion.org; *Statistical Overview of Transport in the European Union (Data 1970-2001).*

United Nations Statistics Division, New York, NY 10017, (800) 253-9646, Fax: (212) 963-4116, http://unstats.un.org; *Statistical Yearbook.*

DENMARK - AGRICULTURE

Economist Intelligence Unit, 111 West 57th Street, New York, NY 10019, (212) 554-0600, Fax: (212) 586-1181, www.eiu.com; *Denmark Country Report.*

Euromonitor International, Inc., 224 S. Michigan Avenue, Suite 1500, Chicago, IL 60604, (312) 922-1115, Fax: (312) 922-1157, www.euromonitor.com; *World Marketing Data and Statistics.*

European Union, Delegation of the European Commission to the United States, 2300 M Street, NW, Washington, DC 20037, (202) 862-9500, Fax: (202) 429-1766, www.eurunion.org; *Agricultural Statistics: Data 1995-2005; European Union Labour Force Survey; Eurostatistics: Data for Short-Term Economic Analysis (2007 edition);* and *Regions - Statistical Yearbook 2006.*

Eurostat, Batiment Jean Monnet, Rue Alcide de Gasperi, L-2920 Luxembourg, http://epp.eurostat.ec.europa.eu; *EU Agricultural Prices in 2007* and *Eurostat Yearbook 2006-2007.*

International Monetary Fund (IMF), 700 Nineteenth Street, NW, Washington, DC 20431, (202) 623-7000, Fax: (202) 623-4661, www.imf.org; *International Financial Statistics Yearbook 2007.*

M.E. Sharpe, 80 Business Park Drive, Armonk, NY 10504, (800) 541-6563, Fax: (914) 273-2106, www.mesharpe.com; *The Illustrated Book of World Rankings.*

Nordic Council of Ministers, Store Strandstraede 18, DK-1255 Copenhagen K, Denmark, www.norden.org; *Nordic Statistical Yearbook 2004-2006.*

Organisation for Economic Cooperation and Development (OECD), 2 rue Andre Pascal, F-75775 Paris Cedex 16, France, (Telephone in U.S. (202) 785-6323), (Fax in U.S. (202) 785-0350), www.oecd.org; *Indicators of Industrial Activity; 2005 OECD Agricultural Outlook Tables, 1970-2014; OECD Agricultural Outlook: 2007-2016; OECD Economic Survey - Denmark 2008;* and STructural ANalysis (STAN) database.

Palgrave Macmillan Ltd., Houndmills, Basingstoke, Hampshire, RG21 6XS, England, (Telephone in U.S. (888) 330-8477), (Fax in U.S. (800) 672-2054), www.palgrave.com; *The Statesman's Yearbook 2008.*

Taylor and Francis Group, An Informa Business, 2 Park Square, Milton Park, Abingdon, Oxford OX14 4RN, United Kingdom, (Dial from U.S. (212) 216-7800), (Fax from U.S. (212) 564-7854), www.tandf.co.uk; *The Europa World Year Book.*

United Nations Conference on Trade and Development (UNCTAD), DC2-1120, United Nations, New York, NY 10017, (212) 963-0027, www.unctad.org; *UNCTAD Commodity Yearbook.*

United Nations Food and Agricultural Organization (FAO), Viale delle Terme di Caracalla, 00100 Rome, Italy, (Dial from U.S. (202) 653-2400), (Fax from U.S. (202) 653 5760), www.fao.org; AQUASTAT; *FAO Production Yearbook 2002; FAO Trade Yearbook;* and *The State of Food and Agriculture (SOFA) 2006.*

United Nations Statistics Division, New York, NY 10017, (800) 253-9646, Fax: (212) 963-4116, http://unstats.un.org; *Statistical Yearbook.*

The World Bank, 1818 H Street, NW, Washington, DC 20433, (202) 473-1000, Fax: (202) 477-6391, www.worldbank.org; *Denmark* and *World Development Indicators (WDI) 2008.*

DENMARK - AIRLINES

European Union, Delegation of the European Commission to the United States, 2300 M Street, NW, Washington, DC 20037, (202) 862-9500, Fax: (202) 429-1766, www.eurunion.org; *Regions - Statistical Yearbook 2006* and *Statistical Overview of Transport in the European Union (Data 1970-2001).*

Eurostat, Batiment Jean Monnet, Rue Alcide de Gasperi, L-2920 Luxembourg, http://epp.eurostat.ec.europa.eu; *Eurostat Yearbook 2006-2007* and *Regional Passenger and Freight Air Transport in Europe in 2006.*

International Civil Aviation Organization (ICAO), External Relations and Public Information Office (EPO), 999 University Street, Montreal, Quebec H3C 5H7, Canada, (Dial from U.S. (514) 954-8219), (Fax from U.S. (514) 954-6077), www.icao.int; *Civil Aviation Statistics of the World.*

M.E. Sharpe, 80 Business Park Drive, Armonk, NY 10504, (800) 541-6563, Fax: (914) 273-2106, www.mesharpe.com; *The Illustrated Book of World Rankings.*

Nordic Council of Ministers, Store Strandstraede 18, DK-1255 Copenhagen K, Denmark, www.norden.org; *Nordic Statistical Yearbook 2004-2006.*

Organisation for Economic Cooperation and Development (OECD), 2 rue Andre Pascal, F-75775 Paris Cedex 16, France, (Telephone in U.S. (202) 785-6323), (Fax in U.S. (202) 785-0350), www.oecd.org; *Household, Tourism, Travel: Trends, Environmental Impacts and Policy Responses.*

Palgrave Macmillan Ltd., Houndmills, Basingstoke, Hampshire, RG21 6XS, England, (Telephone in U.S. (888) 330-8477), (Fax in U.S. (800) 672-2054), www.palgrave.com; *The Statesman's Yearbook 2008.*

Taylor and Francis Group, An Informa Business, 2 Park Square, Milton Park, Abingdon, Oxford OX14 4RN, United Kingdom, (Dial from U.S. (212) 216-7800), (Fax from U.S. (212) 564-7854), www.tandf.co.uk; *The Europa World Year Book.*

United Nations Statistics Division, New York, NY 10017, (800) 253-9646, Fax: (212) 963-4116, http://unstats.un.org; *Statistical Yearbook.*

DENMARK - AIRPORTS

Central Intelligence Agency, Office of Public Affairs, Washington, DC 20505, (703) 482-0623, Fax: (703) 482-1739, www.cia.gov; *The World Factbook.*

DENMARK - ALMOND PRODUCTION

See DENMARK - CROPS

DENMARK - ALUMINUM PRODUCTION

See DENMARK - MINERAL INDUSTRIES

DENMARK - ANIMAL FEEDING

Organisation for Economic Cooperation and Development (OECD), 2 rue Andre Pascal, F-75775 Paris Cedex 16, France, (Telephone in U.S. (202) 785-6323), (Fax in U.S. (202) 785-0350), www.oecd.org; *International Trade by Commodity Statistics (ITCS).*

United Nations Statistics Division, New York, NY 10017, (800) 253-9646, Fax: (212) 963-4116, http://unstats.un.org; *Statistical Yearbook.*

DENMARK - APPLE PRODUCTION

See DENMARK - CROPS

DENMARK - ARMED FORCES

Central Intelligence Agency, Office of Public Affairs, Washington, DC 20505, (703) 482-0623, Fax: (703) 482-1739, www.cia.gov; *The World Factbook.*

Euromonitor International, Inc., 224 S. Michigan Avenue, Suite 1500, Chicago, IL 60604, (312) 922-1115, Fax: (312) 922-1157, www.euromonitor.com; *World Marketing Data and Statistics.*

European Union, Delegation of the European Commission to the United States, 2300 M Street, NW, Washington, DC 20037, (202) 862-9500, Fax: (202) 429-1766, www.eurunion.org; *RD Expenditure in Europe (2006 edition).*

International Institute for Strategic Studies (IISS), Arundel House, 13-15 Arundel Street, Temple Place, London WC2R 3DX, England, www.iiss.org; *The Military Balance 2007.*

International Monetary Fund (IMF), 700 Nineteenth Street, NW, Washington, DC 20431, (202) 623-7000, Fax: (202) 623-4661, www.imf.org; *Government Finance Statistics Yearbook (2008 Edition).*

Nordic Council of Ministers, Store Strandstraede 18, DK-1255 Copenhagen K, Denmark, www.norden.org; *Nordic Statistical Yearbook 2004-2006.*

Palgrave Macmillan Ltd., Houndmills, Basingstoke, Hampshire, RG21 6XS, England, (Telephone in U.S. (888) 330-8477), (Fax in U.S. (800) 672-2054), www.palgrave.com; *The Statesman's Yearbook 2008.*

U.S. Department of State (DOS), 2201 C Street NW, Washington, DC 20520, (202) 647-4000, www.state.gov; *World Military Expenditures and Arms Transfers (WMEAT).*

United Nations Statistics Division, New York, NY 10017, (800) 253-9646, Fax: (212) 963-4116, http://unstats.un.org; *Human Development Report 2006.*

DENMARK - AUTOMOBILE INDUSTRY AND TRADE

European Union, Delegation of the European Commission to the United States, 2300 M Street, NW, Washington, DC 20037, (202) 862-9500, Fax: (202) 429-1766, www.eurunion.org; *Eurostatistics: Data for Short-Term Economic Analysis (2007 edition).*

Eurostat, Batiment Jean Monnet, Rue Alcide de Gasperi, L-2920 Luxembourg, http://epp.eurostat.ec.europa.eu; *Eurostat Yearbook 2006-2007.*

Organisation for Economic Cooperation and Development (OECD), 2 rue Andre Pascal, F-75775 Paris Cedex 16, France, (Telephone in U.S. (202) 785-6323), (Fax in U.S. (202) 785-0350), www.oecd.org; *Indicators of Industrial Activity* and *International Trade by Commodity Statistics (ITCS).*

United Nations Statistics Division, New York, NY 10017, (800) 253-9646, Fax: (212) 963-4116, http://unstats.un.org; *Statistical Yearbook.*

DENMARK - BALANCE OF PAYMENTS

European Union, Delegation of the European Commission to the United States, 2300 M Street, NW, Washington, DC 20037, (202) 862-9500, Fax: (202)

429-1766, www.eurunion.org; *Eurostatistics: Data for Short-Term Economic Analysis (2007 edition).*

Eurostat, Batiment Jean Monnet, Rue Alcide de Gasperi, L-2920 Luxembourg, http://epp.eurostat.ec.europa.eu; *Eurostat Yearbook 2006-2007.*

International Monetary Fund (IMF), 700 Nineteenth Street, NW, Washington, DC 20431, (202) 623-7000, Fax: (202) 623-4661, www.imf.org; *Balance of Payments Statistics Newsletter; Balance of Payments Statistics Yearbook 2007;* and *International Financial Statistics Yearbook 2007.*

Nordic Council of Ministers, Store Strandstraede 18, DK-1255 Copenhagen K, Denmark, www.norden.org; *Nordic Statistical Yearbook 2004-2006.*

Organisation for Economic Cooperation and Development (OECD), 2 rue Andre Pascal, F-75775 Paris Cedex 16, France, (Telephone in U.S. (202) 785-6323), (Fax in U.S. (202) 785-0350), www.oecd.org; *Geographical Distribution of Financial Flows to Aid Recipients 2002-2006; OECD Economic Outlook 2008;* and *OECD Economic Survey - Denmark 2008.*

Platts, 2 Penn Plaza, 25th Floor, New York, NY 10121-2298, (212) 904-3070, www.platts.com; *Energy Economist.*

Taylor and Francis Group, An Informa Business, 2 Park Square, Milton Park, Abingdon, Oxford OX14 4RN, United Kingdom, (Dial from U.S. (212) 216-7800), (Fax from U.S. (212) 564-7854), www.tandf.co.uk; *The Europa World Year Book.*

United Nations Conference on Trade and Development (UNCTAD), DC2-1120, United Nations, New York, NY 10017, (212) 963-0027, www.unctad.org; *Handbook of Statistics 2005.*

United Nations Statistics Division, New York, NY 10017, (800) 253-9646, Fax: (212) 963-4116, http://unstats.un.org; *Energy Statistics Yearbook 2003.*

The World Bank, 1818 H Street, NW, Washington, DC 20433, (202) 473-1000, Fax: (202) 477-6391, www.worldbank.org; *Denmark; World Development Indicators (WDI) 2008;* and *World Development Report 2008.*

DENMARK - BANANAS

See DENMARK - CROPS

DENMARK - BANKS AND BANKING

Euromonitor International, Inc., 224 S. Michigan Avenue, Suite 1500, Chicago, IL 60604, (312) 922-1115, Fax: (312) 922-1157, www.euromonitor.com; *World Marketing Data and Statistics.*

European Union, Delegation of the European Commission to the United States, 2300 M Street, NW, Washington, DC 20037, (202) 862-9500, Fax: (202) 429-1766, www.eurunion.org; *The EU Economy, 2007 Review: Moving Europe's Productivity Frontier* and *Eurostatistics: Data for Short-Term Economic Analysis (2007 edition).*

Eurostat, Batiment Jean Monnet, Rue Alcide de Gasperi, L-2920 Luxembourg, http://epp.eurostat.ec.europa.eu; *Eurostat Yearbook 2006-2007.*

International Monetary Fund (IMF), 700 Nineteenth Street, NW, Washington, DC 20431, (202) 623-7000, Fax: (202) 623-4661, www.imf.org; *International Financial Statistics Yearbook 2007.*

M.E. Sharpe, 80 Business Park Drive, Armonk, NY 10504, (800) 541-6563, Fax: (914) 273-2106, www.mesharpe.com; *The Illustrated Book of World Rankings.*

Nordic Council of Ministers, Store Strandstraede 18, DK-1255 Copenhagen K, Denmark, www.norden.org; *Nordic Statistical Yearbook 2004-2006.*

Organisation for Economic Cooperation and Development (OECD), 2 rue Andre Pascal, F-75775 Paris Cedex 16, France, (Telephone in U.S. (202) 785-6323), (Fax in U.S. (202) 785-0350), www.oecd.org; *Financial Market Trends: OECD Periodical; OECD Economic Outlook 2008;* and *OECD Economic Survey - Denmark 2008.*

Palgrave Macmillan Ltd., Houndmills, Basingstoke, Hampshire, RG21 6XS, England, (Telephone in U.S. (888) 330-8477), (Fax in U.S. (800) 672-2054), www.palgrave.com; *The Statesman's Yearbook 2008.*

Taylor and Francis Group, An Informa Business, 2 Park Square, Milton Park, Abingdon, Oxford OX14 4RN, United Kingdom, (Dial from U.S. (212) 216-7800), (Fax from U.S. (212) 564-7854), www.tandf.co.uk; *The Europa World Year Book.*

United Nations Statistics Division, New York, NY 10017, (800) 253-9646, Fax: (212) 963-4116, http://unstats.un.org; *Statistical Yearbook.*

DENMARK - BARLEY PRODUCTION

See DENMARK - CROPS

DENMARK - BEVERAGE INDUSTRY

Eurostat, Batiment Jean Monnet, Rue Alcide de Gasperi, L-2920 Luxembourg, http://epp.eurostat.ec.europa.eu; *Eurostat Yearbook 2006-2007.*

M.E. Sharpe, 80 Business Park Drive, Armonk, NY 10504, (800) 541-6563, Fax: (914) 273-2106, www.mesharpe.com; *The Illustrated Book of World Rankings.*

Organisation for Economic Cooperation and Development (OECD), 2 rue Andre Pascal, F-75775 Paris Cedex 16, France, (Telephone in U.S. (202) 785-6323), (Fax in U.S. (202) 785-0350), www.oecd.org; *Indicators of Industrial Activity.*

United Nations Statistics Division, New York, NY 10017, (800) 253-9646, Fax: (212) 963-4116, http://unstats.un.org; *Statistical Yearbook.*

DENMARK - BONDS

Eurostat, Batiment Jean Monnet, Rue Alcide de Gasperi, L-2920 Luxembourg, http://epp.eurostat.ec.europa.eu; *Eurostat Yearbook 2006-2007.*

Organisation for Economic Cooperation and Development (OECD), 2 rue Andre Pascal, F-75775 Paris Cedex 16, France, (Telephone in U.S. (202) 785-6323), (Fax in U.S. (202) 785-0350), www.oecd.org; *Financial Market Trends: OECD Periodical.*

United Nations Statistics Division, New York, NY 10017, (800) 253-9646, Fax: (212) 963-4116, http://unstats.un.org; *Statistical Yearbook.*

DENMARK - BROADCASTING

Central Intelligence Agency, Office of Public Affairs, Washington, DC 20505, (703) 482-0623, Fax: (703) 482-1739, www.cia.gov; *The World Factbook.*

Euromonitor International, Inc., 224 S. Michigan Avenue, Suite 1500, Chicago, IL 60604, (312) 922-1115, Fax: (312) 922-1157, www.euromonitor.com; *World Marketing Data and Statistics.*

Eurostat, Batiment Jean Monnet, Rue Alcide de Gasperi, L-2920 Luxembourg, http://epp.eurostat.ec.europa.eu; *Eurostat Yearbook 2006-2007.*

M.E. Sharpe, 80 Business Park Drive, Armonk, NY 10504, (800) 541-6563, Fax: (914) 273-2106, www.mesharpe.com; *The Illustrated Book of World Rankings.*

Nordic Council of Ministers, Store Strandstraede 18, DK-1255 Copenhagen K, Denmark, www.norden.org; *Nordic Statistical Yearbook 2004-2006.*

Palgrave Macmillan Ltd., Houndmills, Basingstoke, Hampshire, RG21 6XS, England, (Telephone in U.S. (888) 330-8477), (Fax in U.S. (800) 672-2054), www.palgrave.com; *The Statesman's Yearbook 2008.*

UNESCO Institute for Statistics, C.P. 6128 Succursale Centre-Ville, Montreal, Quebec, H3C 3J7 Canada, (Dial from U.S. (514) 343-6880), (Fax from U.S. (514) 343 6882), www.uis.unesco.org; *Statistical Tables.*

United Nations Statistics Division, New York, NY 10017, (800) 253-9646, Fax: (212) 963-4116, http://unstats.un.org; *Trends in Europe and North America: The Statistical Yearbook of the ECE 2005.*

WRTH Publications Limited, PO Box 290, Oxford OX2 7FT, UK, www.wrth.com; *World Radio TV Handbook 2007.*

DENMARK - BUDGET

Central Intelligence Agency, Office of Public Affairs, Washington, DC 20505, (703) 482-0623, Fax: (703) 482-1739, www.cia.gov; *The World Factbook.*

Eurostat, Batiment Jean Monnet, Rue Alcide de Gasperi, L-2920 Luxembourg, http://epp.eurostat.ec.europa.eu; *Government Budgets.*

DENMARK - BUSINESS

Eurostat, Batiment Jean Monnet, Rue Alcide de Gasperi, L-2920 Luxembourg, http://epp.eurostat.ec.europa.eu; *Eurostat Yearbook 2006-2007.*

Nordic Council of Ministers, Store Strandstraede 18, DK-1255 Copenhagen K, Denmark, www.norden.org; *Nordic Statistical Yearbook 2004-2006.*

DENMARK - CADMIUM PRODUCTION

See DENMARK - MINERAL INDUSTRIES

DENMARK - CAPITAL INVESTMENTS

Organisation for Economic Cooperation and Development (OECD), 2 rue Andre Pascal, F-75775 Paris Cedex 16, France, (Telephone in U.S. (202) 785-6323), (Fax in U.S. (202) 785-0350), www.oecd.org; *Financial Market Trends: OECD Periodical* and *OECD Economic Outlook 2008.*

DENMARK - CAPITAL LEVY

International Monetary Fund (IMF), 700 Nineteenth Street, NW, Washington, DC 20431, (202) 623-7000, Fax: (202) 623-4661, www.imf.org; *Government Finance Statistics Yearbook (2008 Edition).*

Organisation for Economic Cooperation and Development (OECD), 2 rue Andre Pascal, F-75775 Paris Cedex 16, France, (Telephone in U.S. (202) 785-6323), (Fax in U.S. (202) 785-0350), www.oecd.org; *Financial Market Trends: OECD Periodical* and *OECD Economic Outlook 2008.*

DENMARK - CATTLE

See DENMARK - LIVESTOCK

DENMARK - CHESTNUT PRODUCTION

See DENMARK - CROPS

DENMARK - CHICKENS

See DENMARK - LIVESTOCK

DENMARK - CHILDBIRTH - STATISTICS

Central Intelligence Agency, Office of Public Affairs, Washington, DC 20505, (703) 482-0623, Fax: (703) 482-1739, www.cia.gov; *The World Factbook.*

Euromonitor International, Inc., 224 S. Michigan Avenue, Suite 1500, Chicago, IL 60604, (312) 922-1115, Fax: (312) 922-1157, www.euromonitor.com; *The World Economic Factbook 2008.*

European Union, Delegation of the European Commission to the United States, 2300 M Street, NW, Washington, DC 20037, (202) 862-9500, Fax: (202) 429-1766, www.eurunion.org; *First Demographic Estimates for 2006.*

Eurostat, Batiment Jean Monnet, Rue Alcide de Gasperi, L-2920 Luxembourg, http://epp.eurostat.ec.europa.eu; *Eurostat Yearbook 2006-2007.*

M.E. Sharpe, 80 Business Park Drive, Armonk, NY 10504, (800) 541-6563, Fax: (914) 273-2106, www.mesharpe.com; *The Illustrated Book of World Rankings.*

Nordic Council of Ministers, Store Strandstraede 18, DK-1255 Copenhagen K, Denmark, www.norden.org; *Nordic Statistical Yearbook 2004-2006.*

Palgrave Macmillan Ltd., Houndmills, Basingstoke, Hampshire, RG21 6XS, England, (Telephone in U.S. (888) 330-8477), (Fax in U.S. (800) 672-2054), www.palgrave.com; *The Statesman's Yearbook 2008.*

Taylor and Francis Group, An Informa Business, 2 Park Square, Milton Park, Abingdon, Oxford OX14 4RN, United Kingdom, (Dial from U.S. (212) 216-

7800), (Fax from U.S. (212) 564-7854), www.tandf.co.uk; *The Europa World Year Book.*

United Nations Statistics Division, New York, NY 10017, (800) 253-9646, Fax: (212) 963-4116, http://unstats.un.org; *Demographic Yearbook* and *Statistical Yearbook.*

The World Bank, 1818 H Street, NW, Washington, DC 20433, (202) 473-1000, Fax: (202) 477-6391, www.worldbank.org; *World Development Indicators (WDI) 2008.*

World Health Organization (WHO), Avenue Appia 20, 1211 Geneve 27, Switzerland, (Telephone in U.S. (212) 331-9081), www.who.int; *World Health Report 2006.*

DENMARK - CLIMATE

Danish Energy Authority, Amaliegade 44, DK 1256 Copenhagen K, Denmark, www.ens.dk; *Energy in Denmark 2006* and *Energy Statistics 2006.*

M.E. Sharpe, 80 Business Park Drive, Armonk, NY 10504, (800) 541-6563, Fax: (914) 273-2106, www.mesharpe.com; *The Illustrated Book of World Rankings.*

Nordic Council of Ministers, Store Strandstraede 18, DK-1255 Copenhagen K, Denmark, www.norden.org; *Nordic Statistical Yearbook 2004-2006.*

Palgrave Macmillan Ltd., Houndmills, Basingstoke, Hampshire, RG21 6XS, England, (Telephone in U.S. (888) 330-8477), (Fax in U.S. (800) 672-2054), www.palgrave.com; *The Statesman's Yearbook 2008.*

DENMARK - CLOTHING EXPORTS AND IMPORTS

See DENMARK - TEXTILE INDUSTRY

DENMARK - COAL PRODUCTION

See DENMARK - MINERAL INDUSTRIES

DENMARK - COBALT PRODUCTION

See DENMARK - MINERAL INDUSTRIES

DENMARK - COCOA PRODUCTION

See DENMARK - CROPS

DENMARK - COFFEE

See DENMARK - CROPS

DENMARK - COMMERCE

Palgrave Macmillan Ltd., Houndmills, Basingstoke, Hampshire, RG21 6XS, England, (Telephone in U.S. (888) 330-8477), (Fax in U.S. (800) 672-2054), www.palgrave.com; *The Statesman's Yearbook 2008.*

DENMARK - COMMODITY EXCHANGES

Commodity Research Bureau, 330 South Wells Street, Suite 612, Chicago, IL 60606-7110, (800) 621-5271, Fax: (312) 939-4135, www.crbtrader.com; *2006 CRB Commodity Yearbook and CD.*

International Lead and Zinc Study Group (ILZSG), Rua Almirante Barroso 38, 5th Floor, Lisbon 1000 - 013, Portugal, www.ilzsg.org; Interactive Statistical Database.

International Monetary Fund (IMF), 700 Nineteenth Street, NW, Washington, DC 20431, (202) 623-7000, Fax: (202) 623-4661, www.imf.org; *IMF Primary Commodity Prices.*

United Nations Food and Agricultural Organization (FAO), Viale delle Terme di Caracalla, 00100 Rome, Italy, (Dial from U.S. (202) 653-2400), (Fax from U.S. (202) 653 5760), www.fao.org; *The State of Food and Agriculture (SOFA) 2006.*

World Bureau of Metal Statistics (WBMS), 27a High Street, Ware, Hertfordshire, SG12 9BA, United Kingdom, www.world-bureau.com; *Annual Stainless Steel Statistics; World Flow Charts; World Metal Statistics; World Nickel Statistics;* and *World Tin Statistics.*

DENMARK - COMMUNICATION AND TRAFFIC

European Union, Delegation of the European Commission to the United States, 2300 M Street, NW, Washington, DC 20037, (202) 862-9500, Fax: (202) 429-1766, www.eurunion.org; *Statistical Overview of Transport in the European Union (Data 1970-2001).*

Nordic Council of Ministers, Store Strandstraede 18, DK-1255 Copenhagen K, Denmark, www.norden.org; *Nordic Statistical Yearbook 2004-2006.*

United Nations Statistics Division, New York, NY 10017, (800) 253-9646, Fax: (212) 963-4116, http://unstats.un.org; *Statistical Yearbook.*

DENMARK - CONSTRUCTION INDUSTRY

European Union, Delegation of the European Commission to the United States, 2300 M Street, NW, Washington, DC 20037, (202) 862-9500, Fax: (202) 429-1766, www.eurunion.org; *European Union Labour Force Survey.*

Eurostat, Batiment Jean Monnet, Rue Alcide de Gasperi, L-2920 Luxembourg, http://epp.eurostat.ec.europa.eu; *Eurostat Yearbook 2006-2007.*

M.E. Sharpe, 80 Business Park Drive, Armonk, NY 10504, (800) 541-6563, Fax: (914) 273-2106, www.mesharpe.com; *The Illustrated Book of World Rankings.*

Nordic Council of Ministers, Store Strandstraede 18, DK-1255 Copenhagen K, Denmark, www.norden.org; *Nordic Statistical Yearbook 2004-2006.*

Organisation for Economic Cooperation and Development (OECD), 2 rue Andre Pascal, F-75775 Paris Cedex 16, France, (Telephone in U.S. (202) 785-6323), (Fax in U.S. (202) 785-0350), www.oecd.org; *Iron and Steel Industry in 2004 (2006 Edition); OECD Economic Survey - Denmark 2008;* and STructural ANalysis (STAN) database.

Palgrave Macmillan Ltd., Houndmills, Basingstoke, Hampshire, RG21 6XS, England, (Telephone in U.S. (888) 330-8477), (Fax in U.S. (800) 672-2054), www.palgrave.com; *The Statesman's Yearbook 2008.*

United Nations Statistics Division, New York, NY 10017, (800) 253-9646, Fax: (212) 963-4116, http://unstats.un.org; *Statistical Yearbook.*

DENMARK - CONSUMER PRICE INDEXES

Eurostat, Batiment Jean Monnet, Rue Alcide de Gasperi, L-2920 Luxembourg, http://epp.eurostat.ec.europa.eu; *Eurostat Yearbook 2006-2007.*

Nordic Council of Ministers, Store Strandstraede 18, DK-1255 Copenhagen K, Denmark, www.norden.org; *Nordic Statistical Yearbook 2004-2006.*

Organisation for Economic Cooperation and Development (OECD), 2 rue Andre Pascal, F-75775 Paris Cedex 16, France, (Telephone in U.S. (202) 785-6323), (Fax in U.S. (202) 785-0350), www.oecd.org; *OECD Economic Outlook 2008.*

Taylor and Francis Group, An Informa Business, 2 Park Square, Milton Park, Abingdon, Oxford OX14 4RN, United Kingdom, (Dial from U.S. (212) 216-7800), (Fax from U.S. (212) 564-7854), www.tandf.co.uk; *The Europa World Year Book.*

United Nations Statistics Division, New York, NY 10017, (800) 253-9646, Fax: (212) 963-4116, http://unstats.un.org; *Statistical Yearbook* and *Trends in Europe and North America: The Statistical Yearbook of the ECE 2005.*

The World Bank, 1818 H Street, NW, Washington, DC 20433, (202) 473-1000, Fax: (202) 477-6391, www.worldbank.org; *Denmark.*

DENMARK - CONSUMPTION (ECONOMICS)

Eurostat, Batiment Jean Monnet, Rue Alcide de Gasperi, L-2920 Luxembourg, http://epp.eurostat.ec.europa.eu; *Eurostat Yearbook 2006-2007.*

International Lead and Zinc Study Group (ILZSG), Rua Almirante Barroso 38, 5th Floor, Lisbon 1000 - 013, Portugal, www.ilzsg.org; Interactive Statistical Database.

Nordic Council of Ministers, Store Strandstraede 18, DK-1255 Copenhagen K, Denmark, www.norden.org; *Nordic Statistical Yearbook 2004-2006.*

Organisation for Economic Cooperation and Development (OECD), 2 rue Andre Pascal, F-75775 Paris Cedex 16, France, (Telephone in U.S. (202) 785-6323), (Fax in U.S. (202) 785-0350), www.oecd.org; *Environmental Impacts of Foreign Direct Investment in the Mining Sector in the Newly Independent States (NIS); Iron and Steel Industry in 2004 (2006 Edition); A New World Map in Textiles and Clothing: Adjusting to Change; 2005 OECD Agricultural Outlook Tables, 1970-2014; Revenue Statistics 1965-2006 - 2007 Edition;* and *Towards Sustainable Household Consumption?: Trends and Policies in OECD Countries.*

Technical Association of the Pulp and Paper Industry (TAPPI), 15 Technology Parkway South, Norcross, GA 30092, (770) 446-1400, Fax: (770) 446-6947, www.tappi.org; *TAPPI Annual Report.*

The World Bank, 1818 H Street, NW, Washington, DC 20433, (202) 473-1000, Fax: (202) 477-6391, www.worldbank.org; *World Development Report 2008.*

DENMARK - COPPER INDUSTRY AND TRADE

See DENMARK - MINERAL INDUSTRIES

DENMARK - CORN INDUSTRY

See DENMARK - CROPS

DENMARK - COST AND STANDARD OF LIVING

Eurostat, Batiment Jean Monnet, Rue Alcide de Gasperi, L-2920 Luxembourg, http://epp.eurostat.ec.europa.eu; *Eurostat Yearbook 2006-2007.*

International Monetary Fund (IMF), 700 Nineteenth Street, NW, Washington, DC 20431, (202) 623-7000, Fax: (202) 623-4661, www.imf.org; *Government Finance Statistics Yearbook (2008 Edition).*

DENMARK - COTTON

See DENMARK - CROPS

DENMARK - CRIME

Eurostat, Batiment Jean Monnet, Rue Alcide de Gasperi, L-2920 Luxembourg, http://epp.eurostat.ec.europa.eu; *Crime and Criminal Justice; General Government Expenditure and Revenue in the EU, 2006;* and *Study on Crime Victimisation.*

International Criminal Police Organization (INTERPOL), General Secretariat, 200 quai Charles de Gaulle, 69006 Lyon, France, www.interpol.int; *International Crime Statistics.*

Nordic Council of Ministers, Store Strandstraede 18, DK-1255 Copenhagen K, Denmark, www.norden.org; *Nordic Statistical Yearbook 2004-2006.*

U.S. Department of Justice (DOJ), Bureau of Justice Statistics, 810 Seventh Street, NW, Washington, DC 20531, (202) 307-0765, www.ojp.usdoj.gov/bjs/; *The World Factbook of Criminal Justice Systems.*

United Nations Statistics Division, New York, NY 10017, (800) 253-9646, Fax: (212) 963-4116, http://unstats.un.org; *Trends in Europe and North America: The Statistical Yearbook of the ECE 2005.*

Yale University Press, PO Box 209040, New Haven, CT 06520-9040, (203) 432-0960, Fax: (203) 432-0948, http://yalepress.yale.edu/yupbooks; *Violence and Crime in Cross-National Perspective.*

DENMARK - CROPS

Euromonitor International, Inc., 224 S. Michigan Avenue, Suite 1500, Chicago, IL 60604, (312) 922-1115, Fax: (312) 922-1157, www.euromonitor.com; *European Marketing Data and Statistics 2008.*

European Union, Delegation of the European Commission to the United States, 2300 M Street, NW, Washington, DC 20037, (202) 862-9500, Fax: (202) 429-1766, www.eurunion.org; *Agricultural Statistics: Data 1995-2005; Agriculture in the European Union: Statistical and Economic Information 2006; Eurostatistics: Data for Short-Term Economic Analysis (2007 edition);* and *Regions - Statistical Yearbook 2006.*

Eurostat, Batiment Jean Monnet, Rue Alcide de Gasperi, L-2920 Luxembourg, http://epp.eurostat.ec.europa.eu; *Eurostat Yearbook 2006-2007.*

International Grains Council (IGC), 1 Canada Square, Canary Wharf, London E14 5AE, England, www.igc.org.uk; *Grain Market Report.*

M.E. Sharpe, 80 Business Park Drive, Armonk, NY 10504, (800) 541-6563, Fax: (914) 273-2106, www.mesharpe.com; *The Illustrated Book of World Rankings.*

Organisation for Economic Cooperation and Development (OECD), 2 rue Andre Pascal, F-75775 Paris Cedex 16, France, (Telephone in U.S. (202) 785-6323), (Fax in U.S. (202) 785-0350), www.oecd.org; *International Trade by Commodity Statistics (ITCS)* and *2005 OECD Agricultural Outlook Tables, 1970-2014.*

Palgrave Macmillan Ltd., Houndmills, Basingstoke, Hampshire, RG21 6XS, England, (Telephone in U.S. (888) 330-8477), (Fax in U.S. (800) 672-2054), www.palgrave.com; *The Statesman's Yearbook 2008.*

Taylor and Francis Group, An Informa Business, 2 Park Square, Milton Park, Abingdon, Oxford OX14 4RN, United Kingdom, (Dial from U.S. (212) 216-7800), (Fax from U.S. (212) 564-7854), www.tandf.co.uk; *The Europa World Year Book.*

United Nations Conference on Trade and Development (UNCTAD), DC2-1120, United Nations, New York, NY 10017, (212) 963-0027, www.unctad.org; *UNCTAD Commodity Yearbook.*

United Nations Food and Agricultural Organization (FAO), Viale delle Terme di Caracalla, 00100 Rome, Italy, (Dial from U.S. (202) 653-2400), (Fax from U.S. (202) 653 5760), www.fao.org; *FAO Production Yearbook 2002* and *The State of Food and Agriculture (SOFA) 2006.*

United Nations Statistics Division, New York, NY 10017, (800) 253-9646, Fax: (212) 963-4116, http://unstats.un.org; *Statistical Yearbook.*

DENMARK - CUSTOMS ADMINISTRATION

Eurostat, Batiment Jean Monnet, Rue Alcide de Gasperi, L-2920 Luxembourg, http://epp.eurostat.ec.europa.eu; *Eurostat Yearbook 2006-2007.*

International Monetary Fund (IMF), 700 Nineteenth Street, NW, Washington, DC 20431, (202) 623-7000, Fax: (202) 623-4661, www.imf.org; *Government Finance Statistics Yearbook (2008 Edition).*

Organisation for Economic Cooperation and Development (OECD), 2 rue Andre Pascal, F-75775 Paris Cedex 16, France, (Telephone in U.S. (202) 785-6323), (Fax in U.S. (202) 785-0350), www.oecd.org; *Environmental Impacts of Foreign Direct Investment in the Mining Sector in the Newly Independent States (NIS).*

Palgrave Macmillan Ltd., Houndmills, Basingstoke, Hampshire, RG21 6XS, England, (Telephone in U.S. (888) 330-8477), (Fax in U.S. (800) 672-2054), www.palgrave.com; *The Statesman's Yearbook 2008.*

DENMARK - DAIRY PROCESSING

European Union, Delegation of the European Commission to the United States, 2300 M Street, NW, Washington, DC 20037, (202) 862-9500, Fax: (202) 429-1766, www.eurunion.org; *Eurostatistics: Data for Short-Term Economic Analysis (2007 edition).*

Eurostat, Batiment Jean Monnet, Rue Alcide de Gasperi, L-2920 Luxembourg, http://epp.eurostat.ec.europa.eu; *Eurostat Yearbook 2006-2007.*

M.E. Sharpe, 80 Business Park Drive, Armonk, NY 10504, (800) 541-6563, Fax: (914) 273-2106, www.mesharpe.com; *The Illustrated Book of World Rankings.*

Organisation for Economic Cooperation and Development (OECD), 2 rue Andre Pascal, F-75775 Paris Cedex 16, France, (Telephone in U.S. (202) 785-6323), (Fax in U.S. (202) 785-0350), www.oecd.org; *2005 OECD Agricultural Outlook Tables, 1970-2014.*

Palgrave Macmillan Ltd., Houndmills, Basingstoke, Hampshire, RG21 6XS, England, (Telephone in U.S. (888) 330-8477), (Fax in U.S. (800) 672-2054), www.palgrave.com; *The Statesman's Yearbook 2008.*

Taylor and Francis Group, An Informa Business, 2 Park Square, Milton Park, Abingdon, Oxford OX14 4RN, United Kingdom, (Dial from U.S. (212) 216-7800), (Fax from U.S. (212) 564-7854), www.tandf.co.uk; *The Europa World Year Book.*

United Nations Food and Agricultural Organization (FAO), Viale delle Terme di Caracalla, 00100 Rome, Italy, (Dial from U.S. (202) 653-2400), (Fax from U.S. (202) 653 5760), www.fao.org; *FAO Production Yearbook 2002* and *The State of Food and Agriculture (SOFA) 2006.*

United Nations Statistics Division, New York, NY 10017, (800) 253-9646, Fax: (212) 963-4116, http://unstats.un.org; *Statistical Yearbook.*

DENMARK - DEATH RATES

See DENMARK - MORTALITY

DENMARK - DEBTS, EXTERNAL

Organisation for Economic Cooperation and Development (OECD), 2 rue Andre Pascal, F-75775 Paris Cedex 16, France, (Telephone in U.S. (202) 785-6323), (Fax in U.S. (202) 785-0350), www.oecd.org; *Financial Market Trends: OECD Periodical; Geographical Distribution of Financial Flows to Aid Recipients 2002-2006;* and *OECD Economic Outlook 2008.*

Palgrave Macmillan Ltd., Houndmills, Basingstoke, Hampshire, RG21 6XS, England, (Telephone in U.S. (888) 330-8477), (Fax in U.S. (800) 672-2054), www.palgrave.com; *The Statesman's Yearbook 2008.*

The World Bank, 1818 H Street, NW, Washington, DC 20433, (202) 473-1000, Fax: (202) 477-6391, www.worldbank.org; *Global Development Finance 2007; World Development Indicators (WDI) 2008;* and *World Development Report 2008.*

DENMARK - DEFENSE EXPENDITURES

See DENMARK - ARMED FORCES

DENMARK - DEMOGRAPHY

Euromonitor International, Inc., 224 S. Michigan Avenue, Suite 1500, Chicago, IL 60604, (312) 922-1115, Fax: (312) 922-1157, www.euromonitor.com; *The World Economic Factbook 2008* and *World Marketing Data and Statistics.*

European Union, Delegation of the European Commission to the United States, 2300 M Street, NW, Washington, DC 20037, (202) 862-9500, Fax: (202) 429-1766, www.eurunion.org; *First Demographic Estimates for 2006* and *Regions - Statistical Yearbook 2006.*

Eurostat, Batiment Jean Monnet, Rue Alcide de Gasperi, L-2920 Luxembourg, http://epp.eurostat.ec.europa.eu; *Demographic Outlook - National Reports on the Demographic Developments in 2006* and *Eurostat Yearbook 2006-2007.*

M.E. Sharpe, 80 Business Park Drive, Armonk, NY 10504, (800) 541-6563, Fax: (914) 273-2106, www.mesharpe.com; *The Illustrated Book of World Rankings.*

Nordic Council of Ministers, Store Strandstraede 18, DK-1255 Copenhagen K, Denmark, www.norden.org; *Nordic Statistical Yearbook 2004-2006.*

United Nations Statistics Division, New York, NY 10017, (800) 253-9646, Fax: (212) 963-4116, http://unstats.un.org; *Human Development Report 2006.*

The World Bank, 1818 H Street, NW, Washington, DC 20433, (202) 473-1000, Fax: (202) 477-6391, www.worldbank.org; *Denmark.*

DENMARK - DIAMONDS

See DENMARK - MINERAL INDUSTRIES

DENMARK - DISPOSABLE INCOME

M.E. Sharpe, 80 Business Park Drive, Armonk, NY 10504, (800) 541-6563, Fax: (914) 273-2106, www.mesharpe.com; *The Illustrated Book of World Rankings.*

Nordic Council of Ministers, Store Strandstraede 18, DK-1255 Copenhagen K, Denmark, www.norden.org; *Nordic Statistical Yearbook 2004-2006.*

Organisation for Economic Cooperation and Development (OECD), 2 rue Andre Pascal, F-75775 Paris Cedex 16, France, (Telephone in U.S. (202) 785-6323), (Fax in U.S. (202) 785-0350), www.oecd.org; *OECD Economic Outlook 2008.*

United Nations Statistics Division, New York, NY 10017, (800) 253-9646, Fax: (212) 963-4116, http://unstats.un.org; *National Accounts Statistics: Compendium of Income Distribution Statistics* and *Statistical Yearbook.*

DENMARK - DIVORCE

European Union, Delegation of the European Commission to the United States, 2300 M Street, NW, Washington, DC 20037, (202) 862-9500, Fax: (202) 429-1766, www.eurunion.org; *First Demographic Estimates for 2006.*

M.E. Sharpe, 80 Business Park Drive, Armonk, NY 10504, (800) 541-6563, Fax: (914) 273-2106, www.mesharpe.com; *The Illustrated Book of World Rankings.*

Nordic Council of Ministers, Store Strandstraede 18, DK-1255 Copenhagen K, Denmark, www.norden.org; *Nordic Statistical Yearbook 2004-2006.*

United Nations Statistics Division, New York, NY 10017, (800) 253-9646, Fax: (212) 963-4116, http://unstats.un.org; *Demographic Yearbook; Statistical Yearbook;* and *Trends in Europe and North America: The Statistical Yearbook of the ECE 2005.*

DENMARK - ECONOMIC ASSISTANCE

European Union, Delegation of the European Commission to the United States, 2300 M Street, NW, Washington, DC 20037, (202) 862-9500, Fax: (202) 429-1766, www.eurunion.org; *RD Expenditure in Europe (2006 edition).*

Eurostat, Batiment Jean Monnet, Rue Alcide de Gasperi, L-2920 Luxembourg, http://epp.eurostat.ec.europa.eu; *Eurostat Yearbook 2006-2007.*

Organisation for Economic Cooperation and Development (OECD), 2 rue Andre Pascal, F-75775 Paris Cedex 16, France, (Telephone in U.S. (202) 785-6323), (Fax in U.S. (202) 785-0350), www.oecd.org; *Geographical Distribution of Financial Flows to Aid Recipients 2002-2006.*

United Nations Statistics Division, New York, NY 10017, (800) 253-9646, Fax: (212) 963-4116, http://unstats.un.org; *Statistical Yearbook.*

DENMARK - ECONOMIC CONDITIONS

Banque de France, 48 rue Croix des Petits champs, 75001 Paris, France, www.banque-france.fr/home.htm; *Key Data for the Euro Area.*

Center for International Business Education Research (CIBER), Columbia Business School and School of International and Public Affairs, Uris Hall, Room 212, 3022 Broadway, New York, NY 10027-6902, Mr. Joshua Safier, (212) 854-4750, Fax: (212) 222-9821, www.columbia.edu/cu/ciber/; Datastream International.

Central Intelligence Agency, Office of Public Affairs, Washington, DC 20505, (703) 482-0623, Fax: (703) 482-1739, www.cia.gov; *The World Factbook.*

DSI Data Service Information, Xantener Strasse 51a, D-47495 Rheinberg, Germany, www.dsidata.com; *Campus Solution.*

Dun and Bradstreet (DB) Corporation, 103 JFK Parkway, Short Hills, NJ 07078, (973) 921-5500, www.dnb.com; *Country Report.*

Economist Intelligence Unit, 111 West 57th Street, New York, NY 10019, (212) 554-0600, Fax: (212) 586-1181, www.eiu.com; *Denmark Country Report.*

Euromonitor International, Inc., 224 S. Michigan Avenue, Suite 1500, Chicago, IL 60604, (312) 922-1115, Fax: (312) 922-1157, www.euromonitor.com; *European Marketing Data and Statistics 2008; The World Economic Factbook 2008;* and *World Marketing Data and Statistics.*

European Union, Delegation of the European Commission to the United States, 2300 M Street, NW, Washington, DC 20037, (202) 862-9500, Fax: (202) 429-1766, www.eurunion.org; *The EU Economy, 2007 Review: Moving Europe's Productivity Frontier* and *European Union Labour Force Survey.*

Eurostat, Batiment Jean Monnet, Rue Alcide de Gasperi, L-2920 Luxembourg, http://epp.eurostat.ec.europa.eu; *Consumers in Europe - Facts and Figures on Services of General Interest; EU Economic Data Pocketbook;* and *Eurostat Yearbook 2006-2007.*

Federal Statistical Office Germany, D-65180 Wiesbaden, Germany, www.destatis.de; *Denmark 2005.*

International Monetary Fund (IMF), 700 Nineteenth Street, NW, Washington, DC 20431, (202) 623-7000, Fax: (202) 623-4661, www.imf.org; *World Economic Outlook Reports.*

M.E. Sharpe, 80 Business Park Drive, Armonk, NY 10504, (800) 541-6563, Fax: (914) 273-2106, www.mesharpe.com; *The Illustrated Book of World Rankings.*

Organisation for Economic Cooperation and Development (OECD), 2 rue Andre Pascal, F-75775 Paris Cedex 16, France, (Telephone in U.S. (202) 785-6323), (Fax in U.S. (202) 785-0350), www.oecd.org; *Geographical Distribution of Financial Flows to Aid Recipients 2002-2006; ICT Sector Data and Metadata by Country; Labour Force Statistics: 1986-2005, 2007 Edition; OECD Composite Leading Indicators (CLIs), Updated September 2007; OECD Economic Outlook 2008; OECD Economic Survey - Denmark 2008; OECD Employment Outlook 2007; OECD in Figures 2007;* and *OECD Main Economic Indicators (MEI).*

Palgrave Macmillan Ltd., Houndmills, Basingstoke, Hampshire, RG21 6XS, England, (Telephone in U.S. (888) 330-8477), (Fax in U.S. (800) 672-2054), www.palgrave.com; *The Statesman's Yearbook 2008.*

Platts, 2 Penn Plaza, 25th Floor, New York, NY 10121-2298, (212) 904-3070, www.platts.com; *Energy Economist.*

Taylor and Francis Group, An Informa Business, 2 Park Square, Milton Park, Abingdon, Oxford OX14 4RN, United Kingdom, (Dial from U.S. (212) 216-7800), (Fax from U.S. (212) 564-7854), www.tandf.co.uk; *The Europa World Year Book.*

United Nations Statistics Division, New York, NY 10017, (800) 253-9646, Fax: (212) 963-4116, http://unstats.un.org; *Energy Statistics Yearbook 2003; Statistical Yearbook;* and *World Statistics Pocketbook.*

The World Bank, 1818 H Street, NW, Washington, DC 20433, (202) 473-1000, Fax: (202) 477-6391, www.worldbank.org; *Denmark; Global Economic Monitor (GEM); Global Economic Prospects 2008; The World Bank Atlas 2003-2004;* and *World Development Report 2008.*

DENMARK - ECONOMICS - SOCIOLOGICAL ASPECTS

Eurostat, Batiment Jean Monnet, Rue Alcide de Gasperi, L-2920 Luxembourg, http://epp.eurostat.ec.europa.eu; *Eurostat Yearbook 2006-2007.*

Organisation for Economic Cooperation and Development (OECD), 2 rue Andre Pascal, F-75775 Paris Cedex 16, France, (Telephone in U.S. (202) 785-6323), (Fax in U.S. (202) 785-0350), www.oecd.org; *OECD Economic Outlook 2008.*

DENMARK - EDUCATION

Euromonitor International, Inc., 224 S. Michigan Avenue, Suite 1500, Chicago, IL 60604, (312) 922-1115, Fax: (312) 922-1157, www.euromonitor.com; *European Marketing Data and Statistics 2008* and *World Marketing Data and Statistics.*

European Union, Delegation of the European Commission to the United States, 2300 M Street, NW, Washington, DC 20037, (202) 862-9500, Fax: (202) 429-1766, www.eurunion.org; *Education across Europe 2003* and *Regions - Statistical Yearbook 2006.*

Eurostat, Batiment Jean Monnet, Rue Alcide de Gasperi, L-2920 Luxembourg, http://epp.eurostat.ec.europa.eu; *Education, Science and Culture Statistics* and *Eurostat Yearbook 2006-2007.*

International Monetary Fund (IMF), 700 Nineteenth Street, NW, Washington, DC 20431, (202) 623-7000, Fax: (202) 623-4661, www.imf.org; *Government Finance Statistics Yearbook (2008 Edition).*

M.E. Sharpe, 80 Business Park Drive, Armonk, NY 10504, (800) 541-6563, Fax: (914) 273-2106, www.mesharpe.com; *The Illustrated Book of World Rankings.*

Nordic Council of Ministers, Store Strandstraede 18, DK-1255 Copenhagen K, Denmark, www.norden.org; *Nordic Statistical Yearbook 2004-2006.*

Organisation for Economic Cooperation and Development (OECD), 2 rue Andre Pascal, F-75775 Paris Cedex 16, France, (Telephone in U.S. (202) 785-6323), (Fax in U.S. (202) 785-0350), www.oecd.org; *Education at a Glance* (2007 Edition).

Palgrave Macmillan Ltd., Houndmills, Basingstoke, Hampshire, RG21 6XS, England, (Telephone in U.S. (888) 330-8477), (Fax in U.S. (800) 672-2054), www.palgrave.com; *The Statesman's Yearbook 2008.*

Taylor and Francis Group, An Informa Business, 2 Park Square, Milton Park, Abingdon, Oxford OX14 4RN, United Kingdom, (Dial from U.S. (212) 216-7800), (Fax from U.S. (212) 564-7854), www.tandf.co.uk; *The Europa World Year Book.*

UNESCO Institute for Statistics, C.P. 6128 Succursale Centre-Ville, Montreal, Quebec, H3C 3J7 Canada, (Dial from U.S. (514) 343-6880), (Fax from U.S. (514) 343 6882), www.uis.unesco.org; *Statistical Tables.*

United Nations Statistics Division, New York, NY 10017, (800) 253-9646, Fax: (212) 963-4116, http://unstats.un.org; *Human Development Report 2006* and *Trends in Europe and North America: The Statistical Yearbook of the ECE 2005.*

The World Bank, 1818 H Street, NW, Washington, DC 20433, (202) 473-1000, Fax: (202) 477-6391, www.worldbank.org; *Denmark; World Development Indicators (WDI) 2008;* and *World Development Report 2008.*

DENMARK - ELECTRICITY

Danish Energy Authority, Amaliegade 44, DK 1256 Copenhagen K, Denmark, www.ens.dk; *Energy in Denmark 2006* and *Energy Statistics 2006.*

European Union, Delegation of the European Commission to the United States, 2300 M Street, NW, Washington, DC 20037, (202) 862-9500, Fax: (202) 429-1766, www.eurunion.org; *European Union Energy Transport in Figures 2006; Eurostatistics: Data for Short-Term Economic Analysis (2007 edition);* and *Regions - Statistical Yearbook 2006.*

Eurostat, Batiment Jean Monnet, Rue Alcide de Gasperi, L-2920 Luxembourg, http://epp.eurostat.ec.europa.eu; *Energy - Monthly Statistics; Eurostat Yearbook 2006-2007;* and *Panorama of Energy - 2007 Edition.*

M.E. Sharpe, 80 Business Park Drive, Armonk, NY 10504, (800) 541-6563, Fax: (914) 273-2106, www.mesharpe.com; *The Illustrated Book of World Rankings.*

Nordic Council of Ministers, Store Strandstraede 18, DK-1255 Copenhagen K, Denmark, www.norden.org; *Nordic Statistical Yearbook 2004-2006.*

Organisation for Economic Cooperation and Development (OECD), 2 rue Andre Pascal, F-75775 Paris Cedex 16, France, (Telephone in U.S. (202) 785-6323), (Fax in U.S. (202) 785-0350), www.oecd.org; *Coal Information: 2007 Edition; Energy Statistics of OECD Countries* (2007 Edition); *Indicators of Industrial Activity;* STructural ANalysis (STAN) database; and *World Energy Outlook 2007.*

Palgrave Macmillan Ltd., Houndmills, Basingstoke, Hampshire, RG21 6XS, England, (Telephone in U.S. (888) 330-8477), (Fax in U.S. (800) 672-2054), www.palgrave.com; *The Statesman's Yearbook 2008.*

Platts, 2 Penn Plaza, 25th Floor, New York, NY 10121-2298, (212) 904-3070, www.platts.com; *Energy Economist; EU Energy;* and *European Electricity Review 2004.*

U.S. Department of Energy (DOE), Energy Information Administration (EIA), 1000 Independence Avenue, SW, Washington, DC 20585, (202) 586-8800, www.eia.doe.gov; *International Energy Annual 2004* and *International Energy Outlook 2006.*

United Nations Statistics Division, New York, NY 10017, (800) 253-9646, Fax: (212) 963-4116, http://unstats.un.org; *Energy Statistics Yearbook 2003; Human Development Report 2006; Statistical Yearbook;* and *Trends in Europe and North America: The Statistical Yearbook of the ECE 2005.*

DENMARK - EMPLOYMENT

Bernan Essential Government Publications, 4611-F Assembly Drive, Lanham MD, 20706-4391, (301) 459-2255, Fax: (800) 865-3450, www.bernan.com; *OECD Factbook 2006.*

Euromonitor International, Inc., 224 S. Michigan Avenue, Suite 1500, Chicago, IL 60604, (312) 922-1115, Fax: (312) 922-1157, www.euromonitor.com; *European Marketing Data and Statistics 2008.*

European Union, Delegation of the European Commission to the United States, 2300 M Street, NW, Washington, DC 20037, (202) 862-9500, Fax: (202) 429-1766, www.eurunion.org; *Agriculture in the European Union: Statistical and Economic Information 2006; European Union Labour Force Survey; Eurostatistics: Data for Short-Term Economic Analysis (2007 edition);* and *Iron and Steel.*

Eurostat, Batiment Jean Monnet, Rue Alcide de Gasperi, L-2920 Luxembourg, http://epp.eurostat.ec.europa.eu; *Eurostat Yearbook 2006-2007.*

International Labour Office, I.L.O. Publications, 4 route des Morillons, CH-1211 Geneva 22, Switzerland, (Telephone in U.S. (202) 653-7652), (Fax in U.S. (202) 653-7687), www.ilo.org; *Yearbook of Labour Statistics 2006.*

M.E. Sharpe, 80 Business Park Drive, Armonk, NY 10504, (800) 541-6563, Fax: (914) 273-2106, www.mesharpe.com; *The Illustrated Book of World Rankings.*

Nordic Council of Ministers, Store Strandstraede 18, DK-1255 Copenhagen K, Denmark, www.norden.org; *Nordic Statistical Yearbook 2004-2006.*

Organisation for Economic Cooperation and Development (OECD), 2 rue Andre Pascal, F-75775 Paris Cedex 16, France, (Telephone in U.S. (202) 785-6323), (Fax in U.S. (202) 785-0350), www.oecd.org; *ICT Sector Data and Metadata by Country; Iron and Steel Industry in 2004 (2006 Edition); Labour Force Statistics: 1986-2005, 2007 Edition; A New World Map in Textiles and Clothing: Adjusting to Change; OECD Composite Leading Indicators (CLIs), Updated September 2007; OECD Economic Outlook 2008; OECD Economic Survey - Denmark 2008; OECD Employment Outlook 2007;* and *OECD in Figures 2007.*

United Nations Statistics Division, New York, NY 10017, (800) 253-9646, Fax: (212) 963-4116, http://unstats.un.org; *Statistical Yearbook* and *Trends in Europe and North America: The Statistical Yearbook of the ECE 2005.*

The World Bank, 1818 H Street, NW, Washington, DC 20433, (202) 473-1000, Fax: (202) 477-6391, www.worldbank.org; *Denmark.*

DENMARK - ENERGY INDUSTRIES

Danish Energy Authority, Amaliegade 44, DK 1256 Copenhagen K, Denmark, www.ens.dk; *Energy in Denmark 2006* and *Energy Statistics 2006.*

Enerdata, 10 Rue Royale, 75008 Paris, France, www.enerdata.fr; *Global Energy Market Data.*

Eurostat, Batiment Jean Monnet, Rue Alcide de Gasperi, L-2920 Luxembourg, http://epp.eurostat.ec.europa.eu; *Energy - Monthly Statistics; Eurostat Yearbook 2006-2007;* and *Panorama of Energy - 2007 Edition.*

International Energy Agency (IEA), 9, rue de la Federation, 75739 Paris Cedex 15, France, www.iea.org; *Key World Energy Statistics 2007.*

Organisation for Economic Cooperation and Development (OECD), 2 rue Andre Pascal, F-75775 Paris Cedex 16, France, (Telephone in U.S. (202) 785-6323), (Fax in U.S. (202) 785-0350), www.oecd.org; *Towards Sustainable Household Consumption?: Trends and Policies in OECD Countries.*

Platts, 2 Penn Plaza, 25th Floor, New York, NY 10121-2298, (212) 904-3070, www.platts.com; *EU Energy* and *European Power Daily.*

DENMARK - ENVIRONMENTAL CONDITIONS

Center for Research on the Epidemiology of Disasters (CRED), Universite Catholique de Louvain, Ecole de Sante Publique, 30.94 Clos Chapelle-aux-Champs, 1200 Brussels, Belgium, www.cred.be; *Three Decades of Floods in Europe: A Preliminary Analysis of EMDAT Data.*

Danish Energy Authority, Amaliegade 44, DK 1256 Copenhagen K, Denmark, www.ens.dk; *Energy in Denmark 2006* and *Energy Statistics 2006.*

DSI Data Service Information, Xantener Strasse 51a, D-47495 Rheinberg, Germany, www.dsidata.com; *Campus Solution* and *DSI's Global Environmental Database.*

Economist Intelligence Unit, 111 West 57th Street, New York, NY 10019, (212) 554-0600, Fax: (212) 586-1181, www.eiu.com; *Denmark Country Report.*

Eurostat, Batiment Jean Monnet, Rue Alcide de Gasperi, L-2920 Luxembourg, http://epp.eurostat.ec.europa.eu; *Environmental Protection Expenditure in Europe.*

Federal Statistical Office Germany, D-65180 Wiesbaden, Germany, www.destatis.de; *Denmark 2005.*

Organisation for Economic Cooperation and Development (OECD), 2 rue Andre Pascal, F-75775 Paris Cedex 16, France, (Telephone in U.S. (202) 785-6323), (Fax in U.S. (202) 785-0350), www.oecd.org; *Key Environmental Indicators 2004.*

Platts, 2 Penn Plaza, 25th Floor, New York, NY 10121-2298, (212) 904-3070, www.platts.com; *Emissions Daily.*

United Nations Statistics Division, New York, NY 10017, (800) 253-9646, Fax: (212) 963-4116, http://unstats.un.org; *Trends in Europe and North America: The Statistical Yearbook of the ECE 2005* and *World Statistics Pocketbook.*

DENMARK - EXPENDITURES, PUBLIC

Eurostat, Batiment Jean Monnet, Rue Alcide de Gasperi, L-2920 Luxembourg, http://epp.eurostat.ec.europa.eu; *European Social Statistics - Social Protection Expenditure and Receipts - Data 1997-2005* and *Eurostat Yearbook 2006-2007.*

Organisation for Economic Cooperation and Development (OECD), 2 rue Andre Pascal, F-75775 Paris Cedex 16, France, (Telephone in U.S. (202) 785-6323), (Fax in U.S. (202) 785-0350), www.oecd.org; *Revenue Statistics 1965-2006 - 2007 Edition.*

DENMARK - EXPORTS

Central Intelligence Agency, Office of Public Affairs, Washington, DC 20505, (703) 482-0623, Fax: (703) 482-1739, www.cia.gov; *The World Factbook.*

Economist Intelligence Unit, 111 West 57th Street, New York, NY 10019, (212) 554-0600, Fax: (212) 586-1181, www.eiu.com; *Denmark Country Report.*

Euromonitor International, Inc., 224 S. Michigan Avenue, Suite 1500, Chicago, IL 60604, (312) 922-1115, Fax: (312) 922-1157, www.euromonitor.com; *The World Economic Factbook 2008.*

European Union, Delegation of the European Commission to the United States, 2300 M Street, NW, Washington, DC 20037, (202) 862-9500, Fax: (202) 429-1766, www.eurunion.org; *European Union Energy Transport in Figures 2006; Eurostatistics: Data for Short-Term Economic Analysis (2007 edition); External and Intra-European Union Trade: Data 1958-2002; External and Intra-European Union Trade: Data 1999-2004;* and *Fishery Statistics - 1990-2006.*

Eurostat, Batiment Jean Monnet, Rue Alcide de Gasperi, L-2920 Luxembourg, http://epp.eurostat.ec.europa.eu; *Eurostat Yearbook 2006-2007.*

International Lead and Zinc Study Group (ILZSG), Rua Almirante Barroso 38, 5th Floor, Lisbon 1000 - 013, Portugal, www.ilzsg.org; Interactive Statistical Database.

International Monetary Fund (IMF), 700 Nineteenth Street, NW, Washington, DC 20431, (202) 623-7000, Fax: (202) 623-4661, www.imf.org; *Direction of Trade Statistics Yearbook 2007; Government Finance Statistics Yearbook (2008 Edition);* and *International Financial Statistics Yearbook 2007.*

Nordic Council of Ministers, Store Strandstraede 18, DK-1255 Copenhagen K, Denmark, www.norden.org; *Nordic Statistical Yearbook 2004-2006.*

Organisation for Economic Cooperation and Development (OECD), 2 rue Andre Pascal, F-75775 Paris Cedex 16, France, (Telephone in U.S. (202) 785-6323), (Fax in U.S. (202) 785-0350), www.oecd.org; *Geographical Distribution of Financial Flows to Aid Recipients 2002-2006; International Trade by Commodity Statistics (ITCS); Iron and Steel Industry in 2004 (2006 Edition); 2005 OECD Agricultural Outlook Tables, 1970-2014; OECD Economic Outlook 2008; OECD Economic Survey - Denmark 2008; Review of Fisheries in OECD Countries: Country Statistics 2001 to 2003 - 2005 Edition;* and STructural ANalysis (STAN) database.

Palgrave Macmillan Ltd., Houndmills, Basingstoke, Hampshire, RG21 6XS, England, (Telephone in U.S. (888) 330-8477), (Fax in U.S. (800) 672-2054), www.palgrave.com; *The Statesman's Yearbook 2008.*

Platts, 2 Penn Plaza, 25th Floor, New York, NY 10121-2298, (212) 904-3070, www.platts.com; *Energy Economist.*

Taylor and Francis Group, An Informa Business, 2 Park Square, Milton Park, Abingdon, Oxford OX14 4RN, United Kingdom, (Dial from U.S. (212) 216-7800), (Fax from U.S. (212) 564-7854), www.tandf.co.uk; *The Europa World Year Book.*

Technical Association of the Pulp and Paper Industry (TAPPI), 15 Technology Parkway South, Norcross, GA 30092, (770) 446-1400, Fax: (770) 446-6947, www.tappi.org; *TAPPI Annual Report.*

United Nations Conference on Trade and Development (UNCTAD), DC2-1120, United Nations, New York, NY 10017, (212) 963-0027, www.unctad.org; *Handbook of Statistics 2005.*

United Nations Food and Agricultural Organization (FAO), Viale delle Terme di Caracalla, 00100 Rome, Italy, (Dial from U.S. (202) 653-2400), (Fax from U.S. (202) 653 5760), www.fao.org; *The State of Food and Agriculture (SOFA) 2006.*

United Nations Statistics Division, New York, NY 10017, (800) 253-9646, Fax: (212) 963-4116, http://unstats.un.org; *Energy Statistics Yearbook 2003* and *Trends in Europe and North America: The Statistical Yearbook of the ECE 2005.*

The World Bank, 1818 H Street, NW, Washington, DC 20433, (202) 473-1000, Fax: (202) 477-6391, www.worldbank.org; *World Development Indicators (WDI) 2008* and *World Development Report 2008.*

DENMARK - FEMALE WORKING POPULATION

See DENMARK - EMPLOYMENT

DENMARK - FERTILITY, HUMAN

Central Intelligence Agency, Office of Public Affairs, Washington, DC 20505, (703) 482-0623, Fax: (703) 482-1739, www.cia.gov; *The World Factbook.*

European Union, Delegation of the European Commission to the United States, 2300 M Street, NW, Washington, DC 20037, (202) 862-9500, Fax: (202) 429-1766, www.eurunion.org; *First Demographic Estimates for 2006.*

M.E. Sharpe, 80 Business Park Drive, Armonk, NY 10504, (800) 541-6563, Fax: (914) 273-2106, www.mesharpe.com; *The Illustrated Book of World Rankings.*

Nordic Council of Ministers, Store Strandstraede 18, DK-1255 Copenhagen K, Denmark, www.norden.org; *Nordic Statistical Yearbook 2004-2006.*

United Nations Statistics Division, New York, NY 10017, (800) 253-9646, Fax: (212) 963-4116, http://unstats.un.org; *Human Development Report 2006* and *Trends in Europe and North America: The Statistical Yearbook of the ECE 2005.*

The World Bank, 1818 H Street, NW, Washington, DC 20433, (202) 473-1000, Fax: (202) 477-6391, www.worldbank.org; *The World Bank Atlas 2003-2004; World Development Indicators (WDI) 2008;* and *World Development Report 2008.*

DENMARK - FERTILIZER INDUSTRY

Eurostat, Batiment Jean Monnet, Rue Alcide de Gasperi, L-2920 Luxembourg, http://epp.eurostat.ec.europa.eu; *Eurostat Yearbook 2006-2007.*

Organisation for Economic Cooperation and Development (OECD), 2 rue Andre Pascal, F-75775 Paris Cedex 16, France, (Telephone in U.S. (202) 785-6323), (Fax in U.S. (202) 785-0350), www.oecd.org; *International Trade by Commodity Statistics (ITCS)* and *2005 OECD Agricultural Outlook Tables, 1970-2014.*

United Nations Food and Agricultural Organization (FAO), Viale delle Terme di Caracalla, 00100 Rome, Italy, (Dial from U.S. (202) 653-2400), (Fax from U.S. (202) 653 5760), www.fao.org; *FAO Fertilizer Yearbook* and *The State of Food and Agriculture (SOFA) 2006.*

United Nations Statistics Division, New York, NY 10017, (800) 253-9646, Fax: (212) 963-4116, http://unstats.un.org; *Statistical Yearbook.*

DENMARK - FETAL MORTALITY

See DENMARK - MORTALITY

DENMARK - FILM

See DENMARK - MOTION PICTURES

DENMARK - FINANCE

European Union, Delegation of the European Commission to the United States, 2300 M Street, NW, Washington, DC 20037, (202) 862-9500, Fax: (202) 429-1766, www.eurunion.org; *Eurostatistics: Data for Short-Term Economic Analysis (2007 edition).*

Eurostat, Batiment Jean Monnet, Rue Alcide de Gasperi, L-2920 Luxembourg, http://epp.eurostat.ec.europa.eu; *Eurostat Yearbook 2006-2007.*

International Monetary Fund (IMF), 700 Nineteenth Street, NW, Washington, DC 20431, (202) 623-7000, Fax: (202) 623-4661, www.imf.org; *International Financial Statistics Yearbook 2007.*

Nordic Council of Ministers, Store Strandstraede 18, DK-1255 Copenhagen K, Denmark, www.norden.org; *Nordic Statistical Yearbook 2004-2006.*

Organisation for Economic Cooperation and Development (OECD), 2 rue Andre Pascal, F-75775 Paris Cedex 16, France, (Telephone in U.S. (202) 785-6323), (Fax in U.S. (202) 785-0350), www.oecd.org; *OECD Economic Outlook 2008.*

Taylor and Francis Group, An Informa Business, 2 Park Square, Milton Park, Abingdon, Oxford OX14 4RN, United Kingdom, (Dial from U.S. (212) 216-7800), (Fax from U.S. (212) 564-7854), www.tandf.co.uk; *The Europa World Year Book.*

United Nations Statistics Division, New York, NY 10017, (800) 253-9646, Fax: (212) 963-4116, http://unstats.un.org; *National Accounts Statistics: Compendium of Income Distribution Statistics* and *Statistical Yearbook.*

The World Bank, 1818 H Street, NW, Washington, DC 20433, (202) 473-1000, Fax: (202) 477-6391, www.worldbank.org; *Denmark.*

DENMARK - FINANCE, PUBLIC

Banque de France, 48 rue Croix des Petits champs, 75001 Paris, France, www.banque-france.fr/home.htm; *Key Data for the Euro Area* and *Public Finance.*

Bernan Essential Government Publications, 4611-F Assembly Drive, Lanham MD, 20706-4391, (301) 459-2255, Fax: (800) 865-3450, www.bernan.com; *National Accounts Statistics.*

Economist Intelligence Unit, 111 West 57th Street, New York, NY 10019, (212) 554-0600, Fax: (212) 586-1181, www.eiu.com; *Denmark Country Report.*

European Union, Delegation of the European Commission to the United States, 2300 M Street, NW, Washington, DC 20037, (202) 862-9500, Fax: (202) 429-1766, www.eurunion.org; *Eurostatistics: Data for Short-Term Economic Analysis (2007 edition).*

Eurostat, Batiment Jean Monnet, Rue Alcide de Gasperi, L-2920 Luxembourg, http://epp.eurostat.ec.europa.eu; *Eurostat Yearbook 2006-2007.*

International Monetary Fund (IMF), 700 Nineteenth Street, NW, Washington, DC 20431, (202) 623-7000, Fax: (202) 623-4661, www.imf.org; *International Financial Statistics; International Financial Statistics Online Service;* and *International Financial Statistics Yearbook 2007.*

M.E. Sharpe, 80 Business Park Drive, Armonk, NY 10504, (800) 541-6563, Fax: (914) 273-2106, www.mesharpe.com; *The Illustrated Book of World Rankings.*

Organisation for Economic Cooperation and Development (OECD), 2 rue Andre Pascal, F-75775 Paris Cedex 16, France, (Telephone in U.S. (202) 785-6323), (Fax in U.S. (202) 785-0350), www.oecd.org; *Financial Market Trends: OECD Periodical; Geographical Distribution of Financial Flows to Aid Recipients 2002-2006; OECD Economic Outlook 2008;* and *Revenue Statistics 1965-2006 - 2007 Edition.*

Palgrave Macmillan Ltd., Houndmills, Basingstoke, Hampshire, RG21 6XS, England, (Telephone in U.S. (888) 330-8477), (Fax in U.S. (800) 672-2054), www.palgrave.com; *The Statesman's Yearbook 2008.*

Taylor and Francis Group, An Informa Business, 2 Park Square, Milton Park, Abingdon, Oxford OX14 4RN, United Kingdom, (Dial from U.S. (212) 216-7800), (Fax from U.S. (212) 564-7854), www.tandf.co.uk; *The Europa World Year Book.*

The World Bank, 1818 H Street, NW, Washington, DC 20433, (202) 473-1000, Fax: (202) 477-6391, www.worldbank.org; *Denmark.*

DENMARK - FISHERIES

Euromonitor International, Inc., 224 S. Michigan Avenue, Suite 1500, Chicago, IL 60604, (312) 922-1115, Fax: (312) 922-1157, www.euromonitor.com; *European Marketing Data and Statistics 2008.*

European Union, Delegation of the European Commission to the United States, 2300 M Street, NW, Washington, DC 20037, (202) 862-9500, Fax: (202) 429-1766, www.eurunion.org; *Agricultural Statistics: Data 1995-2005* and *Fishery Statistics - 1990-2006.*

Eurostat, Batiment Jean Monnet, Rue Alcide de Gasperi, L-2920 Luxembourg, http://epp.eurostat.ec.europa.eu; *Eurostat Yearbook 2006-2007.*

M.E. Sharpe, 80 Business Park Drive, Armonk, NY 10504, (800) 541-6563, Fax: (914) 273-2106, www.mesharpe.com; *The Illustrated Book of World Rankings.*

Nordic Council of Ministers, Store Strandstraede 18, DK-1255 Copenhagen K, Denmark, www.norden.org; *Nordic Statistical Yearbook 2004-2006.*

Organisation for Economic Cooperation and Development (OECD), 2 rue Andre Pascal, F-75775 Paris Cedex 16, France, (Telephone in U.S. (202) 785-6323), (Fax in U.S. (202) 785-0350), www.oecd.org; *International Trade by Commodity Statistics (ITCS); Review of Fisheries in OECD Countries: Country Statistics 2001 to 2003 - 2005 Edition;* and STructural ANalysis (STAN) database.

Palgrave Macmillan Ltd., Houndmills, Basingstoke, Hampshire, RG21 6XS, England, (Telephone in U.S. (888) 330-8477), (Fax in U.S. (800) 672-2054), www.palgrave.com; *The Statesman's Yearbook 2008.*

Taylor and Francis Group, An Informa Business, 2 Park Square, Milton Park, Abingdon, Oxford OX14 4RN, United Kingdom, (Dial from U.S. (212) 216-7800), (Fax from U.S. (212) 564-7854), www.tandf.co.uk; *The Europa World Year Book.*

United Nations Conference on Trade and Development (UNCTAD), DC2-1120, United Nations, New York, NY 10017, (212) 963-0027, www.unctad.org; *UNCTAD Commodity Yearbook.*

United Nations Food and Agricultural Organization (FAO), Viale delle Terme di Caracalla, 00100 Rome, Italy, (Dial from U.S. (202) 653-2400), (Fax from U.S. (202) 653 5760), www.fao.org; *FAO Yearbook of Fishery Statistics;* Fishery Databases; FISHSTAT Database. Subjects covered include: Aquaculture production, capture production, fishery commodities; and *The State of Food and Agriculture (SOFA) 2006.*

United Nations Statistics Division, New York, NY 10017, (800) 253-9646, Fax: (212) 963-4116, http://unstats.un.org; *Statistical Yearbook.*

The World Bank, 1818 H Street, NW, Washington, DC 20433, (202) 473-1000, Fax: (202) 477-6391, www.worldbank.org; *Denmark.*

DENMARK - FLOUR INDUSTRY

Eurostat, Batiment Jean Monnet, Rue Alcide de Gasperi, L-2920 Luxembourg, http://epp.eurostat.ec.europa.eu; *Eurostat Yearbook 2006-2007.*

United Nations Statistics Division, New York, NY 10017, (800) 253-9646, Fax: (212) 963-4116, http://unstats.un.org; *Statistical Yearbook.*

DENMARK - FOOD

Euromonitor International, Inc., 224 S. Michigan Avenue, Suite 1500, Chicago, IL 60604, (312) 922-1115, Fax: (312) 922-1157, www.euromonitor.com; *Retail Trade International 2007.*

Eurostat, Batiment Jean Monnet, Rue Alcide de Gasperi, L-2920 Luxembourg, http://epp.eurostat.ec.europa.eu; *Eurostat Yearbook 2006-2007.*

Organisation for Economic Cooperation and Development (OECD), 2 rue Andre Pascal, F-75775 Paris Cedex 16, France, (Telephone in U.S. (202) 785-6323), (Fax in U.S. (202) 785-0350), www.oecd.org; *International Trade by Commodity Statistics (ITCS)* and *Towards Sustainable Household Consumption?: Trends and Policies in OECD Countries.*

United Nations Conference on Trade and Development (UNCTAD), DC2-1120, United Nations, New York, NY 10017, (212) 963-0027, www.unctad.org; *UNCTAD Commodity Yearbook.*

United Nations Food and Agricultural Organization (FAO), Viale delle Terme di Caracalla, 00100 Rome, Italy, (Dial from U.S. (202) 653-2400), (Fax from U.S. (202) 653 5760), www.fao.org; *The State of Food and Agriculture (SOFA) 2006.*

United Nations Statistics Division, New York, NY 10017, (800) 253-9646, Fax: (212) 963-4116, http://unstats.un.org; *Human Development Report 2006.*

DENMARK - FOOTWEAR

Organisation for Economic Cooperation and Development (OECD), 2 rue Andre Pascal, F-75775 Paris Cedex 16, France, (Telephone in U.S. (202) 785-6323), (Fax in U.S. (202) 785-0350), www.oecd.org; *Indicators of Industrial Activity.*

DENMARK - FOREIGN EXCHANGE RATES

Central Intelligence Agency, Office of Public Affairs, Washington, DC 20505, (703) 482-0623, Fax: (703) 482-1739, www.cia.gov; *The World Factbook.*

Euromonitor International, Inc., 224 S. Michigan Avenue, Suite 1500, Chicago, IL 60604, (312) 922-1115, Fax: (312) 922-1157, www.euromonitor.com; *The World Economic Factbook 2008.*

European Union, Delegation of the European Commission to the United States, 2300 M Street, NW, Washington, DC 20037, (202) 862-9500, Fax: (202) 429-1766, www.eurunion.org; *Eurostatistics: Data for Short-Term Economic Analysis (2007 edition).*

Eurostat, Batiment Jean Monnet, Rue Alcide de Gasperi, L-2920 Luxembourg, http://epp.eurostat.ec.europa.eu; *Eurostat Yearbook 2006-2007.*

International Civil Aviation Organization (ICAO), External Relations and Public Information Office (EPO), 999 University Street, Montreal, Quebec H3C 5H7, Canada, (Dial from U.S. (514) 954-8219), (Fax from U.S. (514) 954-6077), www.icao.int; *Civil Aviation Statistics of the World.*

International Monetary Fund (IMF), 700 Nineteenth Street, NW, Washington, DC 20431, (202) 623-7000, Fax: (202) 623-4661, www.imf.org; *International Financial Statistics Yearbook 2007.*

Nordic Council of Ministers, Store Strandstraede 18, DK-1255 Copenhagen K, Denmark, www.norden.org; *Nordic Statistical Yearbook 2004-2006.*

Organisation for Economic Cooperation and Development (OECD), 2 rue Andre Pascal, F-75775 Paris Cedex 16, France, (Telephone in U.S. (202) 785-6323), (Fax in U.S. (202) 785-0350), www.oecd.org; *Financial Market Trends: OECD Periodical; Household, Tourism, Travel: Trends, Environmental Impacts and Policy Responses; OECD Economic Outlook 2008;* and *Revenue Statistics 1965-2006 - 2007 Edition.*

Taylor and Francis Group, An Informa Business, 2 Park Square, Milton Park, Abingdon, Oxford OX14 4RN, United Kingdom, (Dial from U.S. (212) 216-7800), (Fax from U.S. (212) 564-7854), www.tandf.co.uk; *The Europa World Year Book.*

United Nations Statistics Division, New York, NY 10017, (800) 253-9646, Fax: (212) 963-4116, http://unstats.un.org; *Statistical Yearbook; Trends in Europe and North America: The Statistical Yearbook of the ECE 2005;* and *World Statistics Pocketbook.*

DENMARK - FORESTS AND FORESTRY

American Forest Paper Association (AFPA), 1111 Nineteenth Street, NW, Suite 800, Washington, DC 20036, (800) 878-8878, www.afandpa.org; *2007 Annual Statistics of Paper, Paperboard, and Wood Pulp.*

Euromonitor International, Inc., 224 S. Michigan Avenue, Suite 1500, Chicago, IL 60604, (312) 922-1115, Fax: (312) 922-1157, www.euromonitor.com; *European Marketing Data and Statistics 2008.*

European Union, Delegation of the European Commission to the United States, 2300 M Street, NW, Washington, DC 20037, (202) 862-9500, Fax: (202) 429-1766, www.eurunion.org; *Agricultural Statistics: Data 1995-2005.*

Eurostat, Batiment Jean Monnet, Rue Alcide de Gasperi, L-2920 Luxembourg, http://epp.eurostat.ec.europa.eu; *Eurostat Yearbook 2006-2007.*

M.E. Sharpe, 80 Business Park Drive, Armonk, NY 10504, (800) 541-6563, Fax: (914) 273-2106, www.mesharpe.com; *The Illustrated Book of World Rankings.*

Nordic Council of Ministers, Store Strandstraede 18, DK-1255 Copenhagen K, Denmark, www.norden.org; *Nordic Statistical Yearbook 2004-2006.*

Organisation for Economic Cooperation and Development (OECD), 2 rue Andre Pascal, F-75775 Paris Cedex 16, France, (Telephone in U.S. (202) 785-6323), (Fax in U.S. (202) 785-0350), www.oecd.org; *Indicators of Industrial Activity; International Trade by Commodity Statistics (ITCS);* and STructural ANalysis (STAN) database.

Palgrave Macmillan Ltd., Houndmills, Basingstoke, Hampshire, RG21 6XS, England, (Telephone in U.S. (888) 330-8477), (Fax in U.S. (800) 672-2054), www.palgrave.com; *The Statesman's Yearbook 2008.*

Taylor and Francis Group, An Informa Business, 2 Park Square, Milton Park, Abingdon, Oxford OX14 4RN, United Kingdom, (Dial from U.S. (212) 216-

7800), (Fax from U.S. (212) 564-7854), www.tandf.co.uk; *The Europa World Year Book.*

Technical Association of the Pulp and Paper Industry (TAPPI), 15 Technology Parkway South, Norcross, GA 30092, (770) 446-1400, Fax: (770) 446-6947, www.tappi.org; *TAPPI Annual Report.*

UNESCO Institute for Statistics, C.P. 6128 Succursale Centre-Ville, Montreal, Quebec, H3C 3J7 Canada, (Dial from U.S. (514) 343-6880), (Fax from U.S. (514) 343 6882), www.uis.unesco.org; *Statistical Tables.*

United Nations Conference on Trade and Development (UNCTAD), DC2-1120, United Nations, New York, NY 10017, (212) 963-0027, www.unctad.org; *UNCTAD Commodity Yearbook.*

United Nations Food and Agricultural Organization (FAO), Viale delle Terme di Caracalla, 00100 Rome, Italy, (Dial from U.S. (202) 653-2400), (Fax from U.S. (202) 653 5760), www.fao.org; *FAO Yearbook of Forest Products* and *The State of Food and Agriculture (SOFA) 2006.*

United Nations Statistics Division, New York, NY 10017, (800) 253-9646, Fax: (212) 963-4116, http://unstats.un.org; *Statistical Yearbook* and *Trends in Europe and North America: The Statistical Yearbook of the ECE 2005.*

The World Bank, 1818 H Street, NW, Washington, DC 20433, (202) 473-1000, Fax: (202) 477-6391, www.worldbank.org; *Denmark* and *World Development Report 2008.*

DENMARK - FRUIT PRODUCTION

See DENMARK - CROPS

DENMARK - GAS PRODUCTION

See DENMARK - MINERAL INDUSTRIES

DENMARK - GEOGRAPHIC INFORMATION SYSTEMS

Eurostat, Batiment Jean Monnet, Rue Alcide de Gasperi, L-2920 Luxembourg, http://epp.eurostat.ec.europa.eu; *Eurostat Yearbook 2006-2007.*

M.E. Sharpe, 80 Business Park Drive, Armonk, NY 10504, (800) 541-6563, Fax: (914) 273-2106, www.mesharpe.com; *The Illustrated Book of World Rankings.*

The World Bank, 1818 H Street, NW, Washington, DC 20433, (202) 473-1000, Fax: (202) 477-6391, www.worldbank.org; *Denmark.*

DENMARK - GLASS TRADE

Organisation for Economic Cooperation and Development (OECD), 2 rue Andre Pascal, F-75775 Paris Cedex 16, France, (Telephone in U.S. (202) 785-6323), (Fax in U.S. (202) 785-0350), www.oecd.org; *Indicators of Industrial Activity.*

DENMARK - GOLD INDUSTRY

International Monetary Fund (IMF), 700 Nineteenth Street, NW, Washington, DC 20431, (202) 623-7000, Fax: (202) 623-4661, www.imf.org; *International Financial Statistics Yearbook 2007.*

United Nations Statistics Division, New York, NY 10017, (800) 253-9646, Fax: (212) 963-4116, http://unstats.un.org; *Statistical Yearbook.*

The World Bank, 1818 H Street, NW, Washington, DC 20433, (202) 473-1000, Fax: (202) 477-6391, www.worldbank.org; *World Development Indicators (WDI) 2008.*

DENMARK - GOLD PRODUCTION

See DENMARK - MINERAL INDUSTRIES

DENMARK - GRANTS-IN-AID

International Monetary Fund (IMF), 700 Nineteenth Street, NW, Washington, DC 20431, (202) 623-7000, Fax: (202) 623-4661, www.imf.org; *Government Finance Statistics Yearbook (2008 Edition).*

Organisation for Economic Cooperation and Development (OECD), 2 rue Andre Pascal, F-75775 Paris Cedex 16, France, (Telephone in U.S. (202) 785-6323), (Fax in U.S. (202) 785-0350), www.oecd.org; *Geographical Distribution of Financial Flows to Aid Recipients 2002-2006.*

DENMARK - GREEN PEPPER AND CHILIE PRODUCTION

See DENMARK - CROPS

DENMARK - GROSS DOMESTIC PRODUCT

Economist Intelligence Unit, 111 West 57th Street, New York, NY 10019, (212) 554-0600, Fax: (212) 586-1181, www.eiu.com; *Denmark Country Report.*

Euromonitor International, Inc., 224 S. Michigan Avenue, Suite 1500, Chicago, IL 60604, (312) 922-1115, Fax: (312) 922-1157, www.euromonitor.com; *The World Economic Factbook 2008.*

European Union, Delegation of the European Commission to the United States, 2300 M Street, NW, Washington, DC 20037, (202) 862-9500, Fax: (202) 429-1766, www.eurunion.org; *Eurostatistics: Data for Short-Term Economic Analysis (2007 edition); Iron and Steel;* and *RD Expenditure in Europe (2006 edition).*

Eurostat, Batiment Jean Monnet, Rue Alcide de Gasperi, L-2920 Luxembourg, http://epp.eurostat.ec.europa.eu; *Eurostat Yearbook 2006-2007.*

M.E. Sharpe, 80 Business Park Drive, Armonk, NY 10504, (800) 541-6563, Fax: (914) 273-2106, www.mesharpe.com; *The Illustrated Book of World Rankings.*

Nordic Council of Ministers, Store Strandstraede 18, DK-1255 Copenhagen K, Denmark, www.norden.org; *Nordic Statistical Yearbook 2004-2006.*

Organisation for Economic Cooperation and Development (OECD), 2 rue Andre Pascal, F-75775 Paris Cedex 16, France, (Telephone in U.S. (202) 785-6323), (Fax in U.S. (202) 785-0350), www.oecd.org; *Comparison of Gross Domestic Product (GDP) for OECD Countries; Geographical Distribution of Financial Flows to Aid Recipients 2002-2006; OECD Economic Outlook 2008;* and *Revenue Statistics 1965-2006 - 2007 Edition.*

United Nations Statistics Division, New York, NY 10017, (800) 253-9646, Fax: (212) 963-4116, http://unstats.un.org; *Human Development Report 2006; National Accounts Statistics: Compendium of Income Distribution Statistics; Statistical Yearbook;* and *Trends in Europe and North America: The Statistical Yearbook of the ECE 2005.*

The World Bank, 1818 H Street, NW, Washington, DC 20433, (202) 473-1000, Fax: (202) 477-6391, www.worldbank.org; *World Development Indicators (WDI) 2008* and *World Development Report 2008.*

DENMARK - GROSS NATIONAL PRODUCT

European Union, Delegation of the European Commission to the United States, 2300 M Street, NW, Washington, DC 20037, (202) 862-9500, Fax: (202) 429-1766, www.eurunion.org; *The EU Economy, 2007 Review: Moving Europe's Productivity Frontier.*

Eurostat, Batiment Jean Monnet, Rue Alcide de Gasperi, L-2920 Luxembourg, http://epp.eurostat.ec.europa.eu; *Eurostat Yearbook 2006-2007.*

M.E. Sharpe, 80 Business Park Drive, Armonk, NY 10504, (800) 541-6563, Fax: (914) 273-2106, www.mesharpe.com; *The Illustrated Book of World Rankings.*

Organisation for Economic Cooperation and Development (OECD), 2 rue Andre Pascal, F-75775 Paris Cedex 16, France, (Telephone in U.S. (202) 785-6323), (Fax in U.S. (202) 785-0350), www.oecd.org; *Geographical Distribution of Financial Flows to Aid Recipients 2002-2006; OECD Composite Leading Indicators (CLIs), Updated September 2007;* and *OECD Economic Outlook 2008.*

Palgrave Macmillan Ltd., Houndmills, Basingstoke, Hampshire, RG21 6XS, England, (Telephone in U.S. (888) 330-8477), (Fax in U.S. (800) 672-2054), www.palgrave.com; *The Statesman's Yearbook 2008.*

U.S. Department of State (DOS), 2201 C Street NW, Washington, DC 20520, (202) 647-4000, www.state.gov; *World Military Expenditures and Arms Transfers (WMEAT).*

United Nations Statistics Division, New York, NY 10017, (800) 253-9646, Fax: (212) 963-4116, http://unstats.un.org; *Statistical Yearbook.*

The World Bank, 1818 H Street, NW, Washington, DC 20433, (202) 473-1000, Fax: (202) 477-6391, www.worldbank.org; *The World Bank Atlas 2003-2004; World Development Indicators (WDI) 2008;* and *World Development Report 2008.*

DENMARK - HAY PRODUCTION

See DENMARK - CROPS

DENMARK - HAZELNUT PRODUCTION

See DENMARK - CROPS

DENMARK - HEALTH

See DENMARK - PUBLIC HEALTH

DENMARK - HEMP FIBRE PRODUCTION

See DENMARK - TEXTILE INDUSTRY

DENMARK - HIDES AND SKINS INDUSTRY

Organisation for Economic Cooperation and Development (OECD), 2 rue Andre Pascal, F-75775 Paris Cedex 16, France, (Telephone in U.S. (202) 785-6323), (Fax in U.S. (202) 785-0350), www.oecd.org; *Indicators of Industrial Activity* and *International Trade by Commodity Statistics (ITCS).*

United Nations Food and Agricultural Organization (FAO), Viale delle Terme di Caracalla, 00100 Rome, Italy, (Dial from U.S. (202) 653-2400), (Fax from U.S. (202) 653 5760), www.fao.org; *FAO Production Yearbook 2002.*

DENMARK - HOPS PRODUCTION

See DENMARK - CROPS

DENMARK - HOUSING

Euromonitor International, Inc., 224 S. Michigan Avenue, Suite 1500, Chicago, IL 60604, (312) 922-1115, Fax: (312) 922-1157, www.euromonitor.com; *World Marketing Data and Statistics.*

European Union, Delegation of the European Commission to the United States, 2300 M Street, NW, Washington, DC 20037, (202) 862-9500, Fax: (202) 429-1766, www.eurunion.org; *European Union Labour Force Survey* and *Regions - Statistical Yearbook 2006.*

Eurostat, Batiment Jean Monnet, Rue Alcide de Gasperi, L-2920 Luxembourg, http://epp.eurostat.ec.europa.eu; *Eurostat Yearbook 2006-2007.*

M.E. Sharpe, 80 Business Park Drive, Armonk, NY 10504, (800) 541-6563, Fax: (914) 273-2106, www.mesharpe.com; *The Illustrated Book of World Rankings.*

Nordic Council of Ministers, Store Strandstraede 18, DK-1255 Copenhagen K, Denmark, www.norden.org; *Nordic Statistical Yearbook 2004-2006.*

United Nations Statistics Division, New York, NY 10017, (800) 253-9646, Fax: (212) 963-4116, http://unstats.un.org; *Trends in Europe and North America: The Statistical Yearbook of the ECE 2005.*

DENMARK - HOUSING CONSTRUCTION

See DENMARK - CONSTRUCTION INDUSTRY

DENMARK - ILLITERATE PERSONS

Euromonitor International, Inc., 224 S. Michigan Avenue, Suite 1500, Chicago, IL 60604, (312) 922-1115, Fax: (312) 922-1157, www.euromonitor.com; *The World Economic Factbook 2008.*

Palgrave Macmillan Ltd., Houndmills, Basingstoke, Hampshire, RG21 6XS, England, (Telephone in U.S.

(888) 330-8477), (Fax in U.S. (800) 672-2054), www.palgrave.com; *The Statesman's Yearbook 2008.*

United Nations Statistics Division, New York, NY 10017, (800) 253-9646, Fax: (212) 963-4116, http://unstats.un.org; *Human Development Report 2006.*

DENMARK - IMPORTS

Central Intelligence Agency, Office of Public Affairs, Washington, DC 20505, (703) 482-0623, Fax: (703) 482-1739, www.cia.gov; *The World Factbook.*

Economist Intelligence Unit, 111 West 57th Street, New York, NY 10019, (212) 554-0600, Fax: (212) 586-1181, www.eiu.com; *Denmark Country Report.*

Euromonitor International, Inc., 224 S. Michigan Avenue, Suite 1500, Chicago, IL 60604, (312) 922-1115, Fax: (312) 922-1157, www.euromonitor.com; *The World Economic Factbook 2008.*

European Union, Delegation of the European Commission to the United States, 2300 M Street, NW, Washington, DC 20037, (202) 862-9500, Fax: (202) 429-1766, www.eurunion.org; *European Union Energy Transport in Figures 2006; Eurostatistics: Data for Short-Term Economic Analysis (2007 edition); External and Intra-European Union Trade: Data 1958-2002; External and Intra-European Union Trade: Data 1999-2004;* and *Fishery Statistics - 1990-2006.*

Eurostat, Batiment Jean Monnet, Rue Alcide de Gasperi, L-2920 Luxembourg, http://epp.eurostat.ec.europa.eu; *Eurostat Yearbook 2006-2007.*

International Lead and Zinc Study Group (ILZSG), Rua Almirante Barroso 38, 5th Floor, Lisbon 1000 - 013, Portugal, www.ilzsg.org; Interactive Statistical Database.

International Monetary Fund (IMF), 700 Nineteenth Street, NW, Washington, DC 20431, (202) 623-7000, Fax: (202) 623-4661, www.imf.org; *Direction of Trade Statistics Yearbook 2007; Government Finance Statistics Yearbook (2008 Edition);* and *International Financial Statistics Yearbook 2007.*

Nordic Council of Ministers, Store Strandstraede 18, DK-1255 Copenhagen K, Denmark, www.norden.org; *Nordic Statistical Yearbook 2004-2006.*

Organisation for Economic Cooperation and Development (OECD), 2 rue Andre Pascal, F-75775 Paris Cedex 16, France, (Telephone in U.S. (202) 785-6323), (Fax in U.S. (202) 785-0350), www.oecd.org; *Iron and Steel Industry in 2004 (2006 Edition); 2005 OECD Agricultural Outlook Tables, 1970-2014; OECD Economic Outlook 2008; OECD Economic Survey - Denmark 2008; Review of Fisheries in OECD Countries: Country Statistics 2001 to 2003 - 2005 Edition;* and STructural ANalysis (STAN) database.

Palgrave Macmillan Ltd., Houndmills, Basingstoke, Hampshire, RG21 6XS, England, (Telephone in U.S. (888) 330-8477), (Fax in U.S. (800) 672-2054), www.palgrave.com; *The Statesman's Yearbook 2008.*

Platts, 2 Penn Plaza, 25th Floor, New York, NY 10121-2298, (212) 904-3070, www.platts.com; *Energy Economist.*

Taylor and Francis Group, An Informa Business, 2 Park Square, Milton Park, Abingdon, Oxford OX14 4RN, United Kingdom, (Dial from U.S. (212) 216-7800), (Fax from U.S. (212) 564-7854), www.tandf.co.uk; *The Europa World Year Book.*

Technical Association of the Pulp and Paper Industry (TAPPI), 15 Technology Parkway South, Norcross, GA 30092, (770) 446-1400, Fax: (770) 446-6947, www.tappi.org; *TAPPI Annual Report.*

United Nations Conference on Trade and Development (UNCTAD), DC2-1120, United Nations, New York, NY 10017, (212) 963-0027, www.unctad.org; *Handbook of Statistics 2005.*

United Nations Food and Agricultural Organization (FAO), Viale delle Terme di Caracalla, 00100 Rome, Italy, (Dial from U.S. (202) 653-2400), (Fax from U.S. (202) 653 5760), www.fao.org; *The State of Food and Agriculture (SOFA) 2006.*

United Nations Statistics Division, New York, NY 10017, (800) 253-9646, Fax: (212) 963-4116, http://unstats.un.org; *Energy Statistics Yearbook 2003* and *Trends in Europe and North America: The Statistical Yearbook of the ECE 2005.*

The World Bank, 1818 H Street, NW, Washington, DC 20433, (202) 473-1000, Fax: (202) 477-6391, www.worldbank.org; *World Development Indicators (WDI) 2008* and *World Development Report 2008.*

DENMARK - INCOME TAXES

See DENMARK - TAXATION

DENMARK - INDUSTRIAL METALS PRODUCTION

See DENMARK - MINERAL INDUSTRIES

DENMARK - INDUSTRIAL PRODUCTIVITY

European Union, Delegation of the European Commission to the United States, 2300 M Street, NW, Washington, DC 20037, (202) 862-9500, Fax: (202) 429-1766, www.eurunion.org; *Eurostatistics: Data for Short-Term Economic Analysis (2007 edition); Fishery Statistics - 1990-2006;* and *RD Expenditure in Europe (2006 edition).*

Eurostat, Batiment Jean Monnet, Rue Alcide de Gasperi, L-2920 Luxembourg, http://epp.eurostat.ec.europa.eu; *Eurostat Yearbook 2006-2007.*

International Lead and Zinc Study Group (ILZSG), Rua Almirante Barroso 38, 5th Floor, Lisbon 1000 - 013, Portugal, www.ilzsg.org; Interactive Statistical Database.

M.E. Sharpe, 80 Business Park Drive, Armonk, NY 10504, (800) 541-6563, Fax: (914) 273-2106, www.mesharpe.com; *The Illustrated Book of World Rankings.*

Organisation for Economic Cooperation and Development (OECD), 2 rue Andre Pascal, F-75775 Paris Cedex 16, France, (Telephone in U.S. (202) 785-6323), (Fax in U.S. (202) 785-0350), www.oecd.org; *Environmental Impacts of Foreign Direct Investment in the Mining Sector in the Newly Independent States (NIS); Indicators of Industrial Activity; Iron and Steel Industry in 2004 (2006 Edition); A New World Map in Textiles and Clothing: Adjusting to Change; 2005 OECD Agricultural Outlook Tables, 1970-2014; OECD Economic Outlook 2008;* and STructural ANalysis (STAN) database.

Technical Association of the Pulp and Paper Industry (TAPPI), 15 Technology Parkway South, Norcross, GA 30092, (770) 446-1400, Fax: (770) 446-6947, www.tappi.org; *TAPPI Annual Report.*

DENMARK - INDUSTRIAL PROPERTY

Nordic Council of Ministers, Store Strandstraede 18, DK-1255 Copenhagen K, Denmark, www.norden.org; *Nordic Statistical Yearbook 2004-2006.*

United Nations Statistics Division, New York, NY 10017, (800) 253-9646, Fax: (212) 963-4116, http://unstats.un.org; *Statistical Yearbook.*

World Intellectual Property Organization (WIPO), PO Box 18, CH-1211 Geneva 20, Switzerland, www.wipo.int; *Industrial Property Statistics* and *Industrial Property Statistics Online Directory.*

DENMARK - INDUSTRIES

Central Intelligence Agency, Office of Public Affairs, Washington, DC 20505, (703) 482-0623, Fax: (703) 482-1739, www.cia.gov; *The World Factbook.*

Danish Energy Authority, Amaliegade 44, DK 1256 Copenhagen K, Denmark, www.ens.dk; *Energy in Denmark 2006* and *Energy Statistics 2006.*

Economist Intelligence Unit, 111 West 57th Street, New York, NY 10019, (212) 554-0600, Fax: (212) 586-1181, www.eiu.com; *Denmark Country Report.*

Euromonitor International, Inc., 224 S. Michigan Avenue, Suite 1500, Chicago, IL 60604, (312) 922-1115, Fax: (312) 922-1157, www.euromonitor.com; *The World Economic Factbook 2008* and *World Marketing Data and Statistics.*

European Union, Delegation of the European Commission to the United States, 2300 M Street, NW, Washington, DC 20037, (202) 862-9500, Fax: (202) 429-1766, www.eurunion.org; *European Union Labour Force Survey* and *Eurostatistics: Data for Short-Term Economic Analysis (2007 edition).*

Eurostat, Batiment Jean Monnet, Rue Alcide de Gasperi, L-2920 Luxembourg, http://epp.eurostat.ec.europa.eu; *Eurostat Yearbook 2006-2007.*

International Labour Office, I.L.O. Publications, 4 route des Morillons, CH-1211 Geneva 22, Switzerland, (Telephone in U.S. (202) 653-7652), (Fax in U.S. (202) 653-7687), www.ilo.org; *Yearbook of Labour Statistics 2006.*

M.E. Sharpe, 80 Business Park Drive, Armonk, NY 10504, (800) 541-6563, Fax: (914) 273-2106, www.mesharpe.com; *The Illustrated Book of World Rankings.*

Nordic Council of Ministers, Store Strandstraede 18, DK-1255 Copenhagen K, Denmark, www.norden.org; *Nordic Statistical Yearbook 2004-2006.*

Organisation for Economic Cooperation and Development (OECD), 2 rue Andre Pascal, F-75775 Paris Cedex 16, France, (Telephone in U.S. (202) 785-6323), (Fax in U.S. (202) 785-0350), www.oecd.org; *Key Environmental Indicators 2004; OECD Economic Outlook 2008;* and STructural ANalysis (STAN) database.

Palgrave Macmillan Ltd., Houndmills, Basingstoke, Hampshire, RG21 6XS, England, (Telephone in U.S. (888) 330-8477), (Fax in U.S. (800) 672-2054), www.palgrave.com; *The Statesman's Yearbook 2008.*

Taylor and Francis Group, An Informa Business, 2 Park Square, Milton Park, Abingdon, Oxford OX14 4RN, United Kingdom, (Dial from U.S. (212) 216-7800), (Fax from U.S. (212) 564-7854), www.tandf.co.uk; *The Europa World Year Book.*

United Nations Industrial Development Organization (UNIDO), 1 United Nations Plaza, New York, NY 10017, (212) 963 6890, Fax: (212) 963-7904, http://unido.org; Industrial Statistics Database 2008 (INDSTAT) and *The International Yearbook of Industrial Statistics 2008.*

United Nations Statistics Division, New York, NY 10017, (800) 253-9646, Fax: (212) 963-4116, http://unstats.un.org; *2004 Industrial Commodity Statistics Yearbook; Statistical Yearbook;* and *Trends in Europe and North America: The Statistical Yearbook of the ECE 2005.*

The World Bank, 1818 H Street, NW, Washington, DC 20433, (202) 473-1000, Fax: (202) 477-6391, www.worldbank.org; *Denmark* and *World Development Indicators (WDI) 2008.*

DENMARK - INFANT AND MATERNAL MORTALITY

See DENMARK - MORTALITY

DENMARK - INORGANIC ACIDS

Eurostat, Batiment Jean Monnet, Rue Alcide de Gasperi, L-2920 Luxembourg, http://epp.eurostat.ec.europa.eu; *Eurostat Yearbook 2006-2007.*

United Nations Statistics Division, New York, NY 10017, (800) 253-9646, Fax: (212) 963-4116, http://unstats.un.org; *Statistical Yearbook.*

DENMARK - INTEREST RATES

Eurostat, Batiment Jean Monnet, Rue Alcide de Gasperi, L-2920 Luxembourg, http://epp.eurostat.ec.europa.eu; *Eurostat Yearbook 2006-2007.*

Organisation for Economic Cooperation and Development (OECD), 2 rue Andre Pascal, F-75775 Paris Cedex 16, France, (Telephone in U.S. (202) 785-6323), (Fax in U.S. (202) 785-0350), www.oecd.org; *Financial Market Trends: OECD Periodical* and *OECD Economic Outlook 2008.*

DENMARK - INTERNAL REVENUE

Organisation for Economic Cooperation and Development (OECD), 2 rue Andre Pascal, F-75775 Paris Cedex 16, France, (Telephone in U.S. (202) 785-6323), (Fax in U.S. (202) 785-0350), www.oecd.org; *Revenue Statistics 1965-2006 - 2007 Edition.*

DENMARK - INTERNATIONAL FINANCE

Eurostat, Batiment Jean Monnet, Rue Alcide de Gasperi, L-2920 Luxembourg, http://epp.eurostat.ec.europa.eu; *Eurostat Yearbook 2006-2007.*

Organisation for Economic Cooperation and Development (OECD), 2 rue Andre Pascal, F-75775 Paris Cedex 16, France, (Telephone in U.S. (202) 785-6323), (Fax in U.S. (202) 785-0350), www.oecd.org; *Financial Market Trends: OECD Periodical* and *OECD Economic Outlook 2008.*

DENMARK - INTERNATIONAL LIQUIDITY

International Monetary Fund (IMF), 700 Nineteenth Street, NW, Washington, DC 20431, (202) 623-7000, Fax: (202) 623-4661, www.imf.org; *International Financial Statistics Yearbook 2007.*

Organisation for Economic Cooperation and Development (OECD), 2 rue Andre Pascal, F-75775 Paris Cedex 16, France, (Telephone in U.S. (202) 785-6323), (Fax in U.S. (202) 785-0350), www.oecd.org; *Financial Market Trends: OECD Periodical* and *OECD Economic Outlook 2008.*

DENMARK - INTERNATIONAL STATISTICS

Organisation for Economic Cooperation and Development (OECD), 2 rue Andre Pascal, F-75775 Paris Cedex 16, France, (Telephone in U.S. (202) 785-6323), (Fax in U.S. (202) 785-0350), www.oecd.org; *Financial Market Trends: OECD Periodical* and *Household, Tourism, Travel: Trends, Environmental Impacts and Policy Responses.*

DENMARK - INTERNATIONAL TRADE

Banque de France, 48 rue Croix des Petits champs, 75001 Paris, France, www.banque-france.fr/home.htm; *Monthly Business Survey Overview.*

Bernan Essential Government Publications, 4611-F Assembly Drive, Lanham MD, 20706-4391, (301) 459-2255, Fax: (800) 865-3450, www.bernan.com; *OECD Factbook 2006.*

Economist Intelligence Unit, 111 West 57th Street, New York, NY 10019, (212) 554-0600, Fax: (212) 586-1181, www.eiu.com; *Denmark Country Report.*

Euromonitor International, Inc., 224 S. Michigan Avenue, Suite 1500, Chicago, IL 60604, (312) 922-1115, Fax: (312) 922-1157, www.euromonitor.com; *The World Economic Factbook 2008* and *World Marketing Data and Statistics.*

European Union, Delegation of the European Commission to the United States, 2300 M Street, NW, Washington, DC 20037, (202) 862-9500, Fax: (202) 429-1766, www.eurunion.org; *Eurostatistics: Data for Short-Term Economic Analysis (2007 edition); External and Intra-European Union Trade: Data 1958-2002; External and Intra-European Union Trade: Data 1999-2004;* and *Iron and Steel.*

Eurostat, Batiment Jean Monnet, Rue Alcide de Gasperi, L-2920 Luxembourg, http://epp.eurostat.ec.europa.eu; *Eurostat Yearbook 2006-2007* and Intra- and Extra-EU Trade.

International Monetary Fund (IMF), 700 Nineteenth Street, NW, Washington, DC 20431, (202) 623-7000, Fax: (202) 623-4661, www.imf.org; *International Financial Statistics Yearbook 2007.*

M.E. Sharpe, 80 Business Park Drive, Armonk, NY 10504, (800) 541-6563, Fax: (914) 273-2106, www.mesharpe.com; *The Illustrated Book of World Rankings.*

Nordic Council of Ministers, Store Strandstraede 18, DK-1255 Copenhagen K, Denmark, www.norden.org; *Nordic Statistical Yearbook 2004-2006.*

Organisation for Economic Cooperation and Development (OECD), 2 rue Andre Pascal, F-75775 Paris Cedex 16, France, (Telephone in U.S. (202) 785-6323), (Fax in U.S. (202) 785-0350), www.oecd.org; *International Trade by Commodity Statistics (ITCS); 2005 OECD Agricultural Outlook Tables, 1970-2014; OECD Economic Outlook 2008; OECD Economic Survey - Denmark 2008; OECD in Figures 2007;* and *Statistics on Ship Production, Exports and Orders in 2004.*

Palgrave Macmillan Ltd., Houndmills, Basingstoke, Hampshire, RG21 6XS, England, (Telephone in U.S. (888) 330-8477), (Fax in U.S. (800) 672-2054), www.palgrave.com; *The Statesman's Yearbook 2008.*

Taylor and Francis Group, An Informa Business, 2 Park Square, Milton Park, Abingdon, Oxford OX14 4RN, United Kingdom, (Dial from U.S. (212) 216-7800), (Fax from U.S. (212) 564-7854), www.tandf.co.uk; *The Europa World Year Book.*

United Nations Conference on Trade and Development (UNCTAD), DC2-1120, United Nations, New York, NY 10017, (212) 963-0027, www.unctad.org; *UNCTAD Commodity Yearbook.*

United Nations Food and Agricultural Organization (FAO), Viale delle Terme di Caracalla, 00100 Rome, Italy, (Dial from U.S. (202) 653-2400), (Fax from U.S. (202) 653 5760), www.fao.org; *FAO Trade Yearbook* and *The State of Food and Agriculture (SOFA) 2006.*

United Nations Statistics Division, New York, NY 10017, (800) 253-9646, Fax: (212) 963-4116, http://unstats.un.org; *International Trade Statistics Yearbook* and *Statistical Yearbook.*

The World Bank, 1818 H Street, NW, Washington, DC 20433, (202) 473-1000, Fax: (202) 477-6391, www.worldbank.org; *Denmark; World Development Indicators (WDI) 2008;* and *World Development Report 2008.*

World Bureau of Metal Statistics (WBMS), 27a High Street, Ware, Hertfordshire, SG12 9BA, United Kingdom, www.world-bureau.com; *World Flow Charts* and *World Metal Statistics.*

World Trade Organization (WTO), Centre William Rappard, Rue de Lausanne 154, CH-1211 Geneva 21, Switzerland, www.wto.org; *International Trade Statistics 2006.*

DENMARK - INTERNET USERS

Eurostat, Batiment Jean Monnet, Rue Alcide de Gasperi, L-2920 Luxembourg, http://epp.eurostat.ec.europa.eu; *Internet Usage by Enterprises 2007.*

International Telecommunication Union (ITU), Place des Nations, 1211 Geneva 20, Switzerland, www.itu.int; *World Telecommunication/ICT Indicators Database on CD-ROM; World Telecommunication/ICT Indicators Database Online;* and *Yearbook of Statistics - Telecommunication Services (Chronological Time Series 1997-2006).*

The World Bank, 1818 H Street, NW, Washington, DC 20433, (202) 473-1000, Fax: (202) 477-6391, www.worldbank.org; *Denmark.*

DENMARK - INVESTMENTS

International Monetary Fund (IMF), 700 Nineteenth Street, NW, Washington, DC 20431, (202) 623-7000, Fax: (202) 623-4661, www.imf.org; *International Financial Statistics Yearbook 2007.*

Organisation for Economic Cooperation and Development (OECD), 2 rue Andre Pascal, F-75775 Paris Cedex 16, France, (Telephone in U.S. (202) 785-6323), (Fax in U.S. (202) 785-0350), www.oecd.org; *Financial Market Trends: OECD Periodical; Iron and Steel Industry in 2004 (2006 Edition); A New World Map in Textiles and Clothing: Adjusting to Change; OECD Economic Outlook 2008;* and STructural ANalysis (STAN) database.

DENMARK - IRON AND IRON ORE PRODUCTION

See DENMARK - MINERAL INDUSTRIES

DENMARK - JUTE PRODUCTION

See DENMARK - CROPS

DENMARK - LABOR

Central Intelligence Agency, Office of Public Affairs, Washington, DC 20505, (703) 482-0623, Fax: (703) 482-1739, www.cia.gov; *The World Factbook.*

Euromonitor International, Inc., 224 S. Michigan Avenue, Suite 1500, Chicago, IL 60604, (312) 922-1115, Fax: (312) 922-1157, www.euromonitor.com; *World Marketing Data and Statistics.*

European Union, Delegation of the European Commission to the United States, 2300 M Street, NW, Washington, DC 20037, (202) 862-9500, Fax: (202) 429-1766, www.eurunion.org; *European Union Labour Force Survey* and *Regions - Statistical Yearbook 2006.*

Eurostat, Batiment Jean Monnet, Rue Alcide de Gasperi, L-2920 Luxembourg, http://epp.eurostat.ec.europa.eu; *Eurostat Yearbook 2006-2007.*

Federal Statistical Office Germany, D-65180 Wiesbaden, Germany, www.destatis.de; *Denmark 2005.*

International Labour Office, I.L.O. Publications, 4 route des Morillons, CH-1211 Geneva 22, Switzerland, (Telephone in U.S. (202) 653-7652), (Fax in U.S. (202) 653-7687), www.ilo.org; *Yearbook of Labour Statistics 2006.*

M.E. Sharpe, 80 Business Park Drive, Armonk, NY 10504, (800) 541-6563, Fax: (914) 273-2106, www.mesharpe.com; *The Illustrated Book of World Rankings.*

Nordic Council of Ministers, Store Strandstraede 18, DK-1255 Copenhagen K, Denmark, www.norden.org; *Nordic Statistical Yearbook 2004-2006.*

Organisation for Economic Cooperation and Development (OECD), 2 rue Andre Pascal, F-75775 Paris Cedex 16, France, (Telephone in U.S. (202) 785-6323), (Fax in U.S. (202) 785-0350), www.oecd.org; *Iron and Steel Industry in 2004 (2006 Edition); A New World Map in Textiles and Clothing: Adjusting to Change; OECD Economic Outlook 2008; OECD Economic Survey - Denmark 2008; OECD Employment Outlook 2007;* and *Statistics on Ship Production, Exports and Orders in 2004.*

Palgrave Macmillan Ltd., Houndmills, Basingstoke, Hampshire, RG21 6XS, England, (Telephone in U.S. (888) 330-8477), (Fax in U.S. (800) 672-2054), www.palgrave.com; *The Statesman's Yearbook 2008.*

United Nations Food and Agricultural Organization (FAO), Viale delle Terme di Caracalla, 00100 Rome, Italy, (Dial from U.S. (202) 653-2400), (Fax from U.S. (202) 653 5760), www.fao.org; *The State of Food and Agriculture (SOFA) 2006.*

United Nations Statistics Division, New York, NY 10017, (800) 253-9646, Fax: (212) 963-4116, http://unstats.un.org; *Human Development Report 2006.*

The World Bank, 1818 H Street, NW, Washington, DC 20433, (202) 473-1000, Fax: (202) 477-6391, www.worldbank.org; *The World Bank Atlas 2003-2004; World Development Indicators (WDI) 2008;* and *World Development Report 2008.*

DENMARK - LAND USE

Central Intelligence Agency, Office of Public Affairs, Washington, DC 20505, (703) 482-0623, Fax: (703) 482-1739, www.cia.gov; *The World Factbook.*

Euromonitor International, Inc., 224 S. Michigan Avenue, Suite 1500, Chicago, IL 60604, (312) 922-1115, Fax: (312) 922-1157, www.euromonitor.com; *European Marketing Data and Statistics 2008.*

European Union, Delegation of the European Commission to the United States, 2300 M Street, NW, Washington, DC 20037, (202) 862-9500, Fax: (202) 429-1766, www.eurunion.org; *Agricultural Statistics: Data 1995-2005; Agriculture in the European Union: Statistical and Economic Information 2006;* and *Regions - Statistical Yearbook 2006.*

Eurostat, Batiment Jean Monnet, Rue Alcide de Gasperi, L-2920 Luxembourg, http://epp.eurostat.ec.europa.eu; *Eurostat Yearbook 2006-2007.*

United Nations Food and Agricultural Organization (FAO), Viale delle Terme di Caracalla, 00100 Rome, Italy, (Dial from U.S. (202) 653-2400), (Fax from U.S. (202) 653 5760), www.fao.org; *FAO Production Yearbook 2002.*

The World Bank, 1818 H Street, NW, Washington, DC 20433, (202) 473-1000, Fax: (202) 477-6391, www.worldbank.org; *World Development Report 2008.*

DENMARK - LEATHER INDUSTRY AND TRADE

Eurostat, Batiment Jean Monnet, Rue Alcide de Gasperi, L-2920 Luxembourg, http://epp.eurostat.ec.europa.eu; *Eurostat Yearbook 2006-2007.*

Organisation for Economic Cooperation and Development (OECD), 2 rue Andre Pascal, F-75775 Paris Cedex 16, France, (Telephone in U.S. (202) 785-6323), (Fax in U.S. (202) 785-0350), www.oecd.org; *Indicators of Industrial Activity.*

DENMARK - LIBRARIES

M.E. Sharpe, 80 Business Park Drive, Armonk, NY 10504, (800) 541-6563, Fax: (914) 273-2106, www.mesharpe.com; *The Illustrated Book of World Rankings.*

Nordic Council of Ministers, Store Strandstraede 18, DK-1255 Copenhagen K, Denmark, www.norden.org; *Nordic Statistical Yearbook 2004-2006.*

UNESCO Institute for Statistics, C.P. 6128 Succursale Centre-Ville, Montreal, Quebec, H3C 3J7 Canada, (Dial from U.S. (514) 343-6880), (Fax from U.S. (514) 343 6882), www.uis.unesco.org; *Statistical Tables.*

United Nations Statistics Division, New York, NY 10017, (800) 253-9646, Fax: (212) 963-4116, http://unstats.un.org; *Trends in Europe and North America: The Statistical Yearbook of the ECE 2005.*

DENMARK - LICENSES

International Monetary Fund (IMF), 700 Nineteenth Street, NW, Washington, DC 20431, (202) 623-7000, Fax: (202) 623-4661, www.imf.org; *Government Finance Statistics Yearbook (2008 Edition).*

DENMARK - LIFE EXPECTANCY

Central Intelligence Agency, Office of Public Affairs, Washington, DC 20505, (703) 482-0623, Fax: (703) 482-1739, www.cia.gov; *The World Factbook.*

Euromonitor International, Inc., 224 S. Michigan Avenue, Suite 1500, Chicago, IL 60604, (312) 922-1115, Fax: (312) 922-1157, www.euromonitor.com; *The World Economic Factbook 2008.*

Organisation for Economic Cooperation and Development (OECD), 2 rue Andre Pascal, F-75775 Paris Cedex 16, France, (Telephone in U.S. (202) 785-6323), (Fax in U.S. (202) 785-0350), www.oecd.org; *OECD Economic Outlook 2008.*

United Nations Statistics Division, New York, NY 10017, (800) 253-9646, Fax: (212) 963-4116, http://unstats.un.org; *Human Development Report 2006; Trends in Europe and North America: The Statistical Yearbook of the ECE 2005;* and *World Statistics Pocketbook.*

The World Bank, 1818 H Street, NW, Washington, DC 20433, (202) 473-1000, Fax: (202) 477-6391, www.worldbank.org; *The World Bank Atlas 2003-2004* and *World Development Report 2008.*

DENMARK - LITERACY

Euromonitor International, Inc., 224 S. Michigan Avenue, Suite 1500, Chicago, IL 60604, (312) 922-1115, Fax: (312) 922-1157, www.euromonitor.com; *World Marketing Data and Statistics.*

DENMARK - LIVESTOCK

Euromonitor International, Inc., 224 S. Michigan Avenue, Suite 1500, Chicago, IL 60604, (312) 922-1115, Fax: (312) 922-1157, www.euromonitor.com; *European Marketing Data and Statistics 2008.*

European Union, Delegation of the European Commission to the United States, 2300 M Street, NW, Washington, DC 20037, (202) 862-9500, Fax: (202) 429-1766, www.eurunion.org; *Agricultural Statistics: Data 1995-2005; Eurostatistics: Data for Short-Term Economic Analysis (2007 edition);* and *Regions - Statistical Yearbook 2006.*

Eurostat, Batiment Jean Monnet, Rue Alcide de Gasperi, L-2920 Luxembourg, http://epp.eurostat.ec.europa.eu; *Eurostat Yearbook 2006-2007.*

M.E. Sharpe, 80 Business Park Drive, Armonk, NY 10504, (800) 541-6563, Fax: (914) 273-2106, www.mesharpe.com; *The Illustrated Book of World Rankings.*

Nordic Council of Ministers, Store Strandstraede 18, DK-1255 Copenhagen K, Denmark, www.norden.org; *Nordic Statistical Yearbook 2004-2006.*

Organisation for Economic Cooperation and Development (OECD), 2 rue Andre Pascal, F-75775 Paris Cedex 16, France, (Telephone in U.S. (202) 785-6323), (Fax in U.S. (202) 785-0350), www.oecd.org; *2005 OECD Agricultural Outlook Tables, 1970-2014.*

Palgrave Macmillan Ltd., Houndmills, Basingstoke, Hampshire, RG21 6XS, England, (Telephone in U.S. (888) 330-8477), (Fax in U.S. (800) 672-2054), www.palgrave.com; *The Statesman's Yearbook 2008.*

Taylor and Francis Group, An Informa Business, 2 Park Square, Milton Park, Abingdon, Oxford OX14 4RN, United Kingdom, (Dial from U.S. (212) 216-7800), (Fax from U.S. (212) 564-7854), www.tandf.co.uk; *The Europa World Year Book.*

United Nations Conference on Trade and Development (UNCTAD), DC2-1120, United Nations, New York, NY 10017, (212) 963-0027, www.unctad.org; *UNCTAD Commodity Yearbook.*

United Nations Food and Agricultural Organization (FAO), Viale delle Terme di Caracalla, 00100 Rome, Italy, (Dial from U.S. (202) 653-2400), (Fax from U.S. (202) 653 5760), www.fao.org; *FAO Production Yearbook 2002* and *The State of Food and Agriculture (SOFA) 2006.*

United Nations Statistics Division, New York, NY 10017, (800) 253-9646, Fax: (212) 963-4116, http://unstats.un.org; *Statistical Yearbook.*

DENMARK - MACHINERY

Organisation for Economic Cooperation and Development (OECD), 2 rue Andre Pascal, F-75775 Paris Cedex 16, France, (Telephone in U.S. (202) 785-6323), (Fax in U.S. (202) 785-0350), www.oecd.org; *Indicators of Industrial Activity.*

DENMARK - MAGNESIUM PRODUCTION AND CONSUMPTION

See DENMARK - MINERAL INDUSTRIES

DENMARK - MANUFACTURES

European Union, Delegation of the European Commission to the United States, 2300 M Street, NW, Washington, DC 20037, (202) 862-9500, Fax: (202) 429-1766, www.eurunion.org; *European Union Labour Force Survey; Eurostatistics: Data for Short-Term Economic Analysis (2007 edition);* and *The Textile Industry in the EU.*

Eurostat, Batiment Jean Monnet, Rue Alcide de Gasperi, L-2920 Luxembourg, http://epp.eurostat.ec.europa.eu; *Eurostat Yearbook 2006-2007.*

International Monetary Fund (IMF), 700 Nineteenth Street, NW, Washington, DC 20431, (202) 623-7000, Fax: (202) 623-4661, www.imf.org; *International Financial Statistics Yearbook 2007.*

M.E. Sharpe, 80 Business Park Drive, Armonk, NY 10504, (800) 541-6563, Fax: (914) 273-2106, www.mesharpe.com; *The Illustrated Book of World Rankings.*

Nordic Council of Ministers, Store Strandstraede 18, DK-1255 Copenhagen K, Denmark, www.norden.org; *Nordic Statistical Yearbook 2004-2006.*

Organisation for Economic Cooperation and Development (OECD), 2 rue Andre Pascal, F-75775 Paris Cedex 16, France, (Telephone in U.S. (202) 785-6323), (Fax in U.S. (202) 785-0350), www.oecd.org; *Indicators of Industrial Activity; International Trade by Commodity Statistics (ITCS); OECD Economic Survey - Denmark 2008;* and STructural ANalysis (STAN) database.

United Nations Statistics Division, New York, NY 10017, (800) 253-9646, Fax: (212) 963-4116, http://unstats.un.org; *Statistical Yearbook.*

The World Bank, 1818 H Street, NW, Washington, DC 20433, (202) 473-1000, Fax: (202) 477-6391, www.worldbank.org; *World Development Indicators (WDI) 2008.*

DENMARK - MARRIAGE

Eurostat, Batiment Jean Monnet, Rue Alcide de Gasperi, L-2920 Luxembourg, http://epp.eurostat.ec.europa.eu; *Eurostat Yearbook 2006-2007.*

M.E. Sharpe, 80 Business Park Drive, Armonk, NY 10504, (800) 541-6563, Fax: (914) 273-2106, www.mesharpe.com; *The Illustrated Book of World Rankings.*

Nordic Council of Ministers, Store Strandstraede 18, DK-1255 Copenhagen K, Denmark, www.norden.org; *Nordic Statistical Yearbook 2004-2006.*

Taylor and Francis Group, An Informa Business, 2 Park Square, Milton Park, Abingdon, Oxford OX14 4RN, United Kingdom, (Dial from U.S. (212) 216-7800), (Fax from U.S. (212) 564-7854), www.tandf.co.uk; *The Europa World Year Book.*

United Nations Statistics Division, New York, NY 10017, (800) 253-9646, Fax: (212) 963-4116, http://unstats.un.org; *Demographic Yearbook; Statistical Yearbook;* and *Trends in Europe and North America: The Statistical Yearbook of the ECE 2005.*

DENMARK - MERCURY PRODUCTION

See DENMARK - MINERAL INDUSTRIES

DENMARK - METAL PRODUCTS

Eurostat, Batiment Jean Monnet, Rue Alcide de Gasperi, L-2920 Luxembourg, http://epp.eurostat.ec.europa.eu; *Eurostat Yearbook 2006-2007.*

DENMARK - MILK PRODUCTION

See DENMARK - DAIRY PROCESSING

DENMARK - MINERAL INDUSTRIES

Danish Energy Authority, Amaliegade 44, DK 1256 Copenhagen K, Denmark, www.ens.dk; *Energy in Denmark 2006* and *Energy Statistics 2006.*

European Union, Delegation of the European Commission to the United States, 2300 M Street, NW, Washington, DC 20037, (202) 862-9500, Fax: (202) 429-1766, www.eurunion.org; *European Union Energy Transport in Figures 2006; Eurostatistics: Data for Short-Term Economic Analysis (2007 edition); Iron and Steel;* and *Regions - Statistical Yearbook 2006.*

Eurostat, Batiment Jean Monnet, Rue Alcide de Gasperi, L-2920 Luxembourg, http://epp.eurostat.ec.europa.eu; *Energy - Monthly Statistics; Eurostat Yearbook 2006-2007;* and *Panorama of Energy - 2007 Edition.*

International Energy Agency (IEA), 9, rue de la Federation, 75739 Paris Cedex 15, France, www.iea.org; *Key World Energy Statistics 2007.*

International Lead and Zinc Study Group (ILZSG), Rua Almirante Barroso 38, 5th Floor, Lisbon 1000 - 013, Portugal, www.ilzsg.org; Interactive Statistical Database.

M.E. Sharpe, 80 Business Park Drive, Armonk, NY 10504, (800) 541-6563, Fax: (914) 273-2106, www.mesharpe.com; *The Illustrated Book of World Rankings.*

Nordic Council of Ministers, Store Strandstraede 18, DK-1255 Copenhagen K, Denmark, www.norden.org; *Nordic Statistical Yearbook 2004-2006.*

Organisation for Economic Cooperation and Development (OECD), 2 rue Andre Pascal, F-75775 Paris Cedex 16, France, (Telephone in U.S. (202) 785-6323), (Fax in U.S. (202) 785-0350), www.oecd.org; *Coal Information: 2007 Edition; Energy Statistics of OECD Countries* (2007 Edition); *Environmental Impacts of Foreign Direct Investment in the Mining Sector in the Newly Independent States (NIS); Indicators of Industrial Activity; International Trade by Commodity Statistics (ITCS); Iron and Steel Industry in 2004 (2006 Edition); OECD Economic Survey -*

Denmark 2008; STructural ANalysis (STAN) database; and World Energy Outlook 2007.

Palgrave Macmillan Ltd., Houndmills, Basingstoke, Hampshire, RG21 6XS, England, (Telephone in U.S. (888) 330-8477), (Fax in U.S. (800) 672-2054), www.palgrave.com; *The Statesman's Yearbook 2008.*

Platts, 2 Penn Plaza, 25th Floor, New York, NY 10121-2298, (212) 904-3070, www.platts.com; *Energy Economist* and *EU Energy.*

Taylor and Francis Group, An Informa Business, 2 Park Square, Milton Park, Abingdon, Oxford OX14 4RN, United Kingdom, (Dial from U.S. (212) 216-7800), (Fax from U.S. (212) 564-7854), www.tandf.co.uk; *The Europa World Year Book.*

United Nations Conference on Trade and Development (UNCTAD), DC2-1120, United Nations, New York, NY 10017, (212) 963-0027, www.unctad.org; *UNCTAD Commodity Yearbook.*

United Nations Statistics Division, New York, NY 10017, (800) 253-9646, Fax: (212) 963-4116, http://unstats.un.org; *Energy Statistics Yearbook 2003* and *Statistical Yearbook.*

World Bureau of Metal Statistics (WBMS), 27a High Street, Ware, Hertfordshire, SG12 9BA, United Kingdom, www.world-bureau.com; *Annual Stainless Steel Statistics; World Flow Charts; World Metal Statistics; World Nickel Statistics;* and *World Tin Statistics.*

DENMARK - MONEY

European Central Bank (ECB), Postfach 160319, D-60066 Frankfurt am Main, Germany, www.ecb.int; *Monetary Developments in the Euro Area; Monthly Bulletin;* and *Statistics Pocket Book.*

Organisation for Economic Cooperation and Development (OECD), 2 rue Andre Pascal, F-75775 Paris Cedex 16, France, (Telephone in U.S. (202) 785-6323), (Fax in U.S. (202) 785-0350), www.oecd.org; *OECD Economic Survey - Denmark 2008.*

DENMARK - MONEY EXCHANGE RATES

See DENMARK - FOREIGN EXCHANGE RATES

DENMARK - MONEY SUPPLY

Economist Intelligence Unit, 111 West 57th Street, New York, NY 10019, (212) 554-0600, Fax: (212) 586-1181, www.eiu.com; *Denmark Country Report.*

European Union, Delegation of the European Commission to the United States, 2300 M Street, NW, Washington, DC 20037, (202) 862-9500, Fax: (202) 429-1766, www.eurunion.org; *Eurostatistics: Data for Short-Term Economic Analysis (2007 edition).*

Eurostat, Batiment Jean Monnet, Rue Alcide de Gasperi, L-2920 Luxembourg, http://epp.eurostat.ec.europa.eu; *Eurostat Yearbook 2006-2007.*

International Monetary Fund (IMF), 700 Nineteenth Street, NW, Washington, DC 20431, (202) 623-7000, Fax: (202) 623-4661, www.imf.org; *International Financial Statistics Yearbook 2007.*

Nordic Council of Ministers, Store Strandstraede 18, DK-1255 Copenhagen K, Denmark, www.norden.org; *Nordic Statistical Yearbook 2004-2006.*

Organisation for Economic Cooperation and Development (OECD), 2 rue Andre Pascal, F-75775 Paris Cedex 16, France, (Telephone in U.S. (202) 785-6323), (Fax in U.S. (202) 785-0350), www.oecd.org; *OECD Economic Outlook 2008.*

Taylor and Francis Group, An Informa Business, 2 Park Square, Milton Park, Abingdon, Oxford OX14 4RN, United Kingdom, (Dial from U.S. (212) 216-7800), (Fax from U.S. (212) 564-7854), www.tandf.co.uk; *The Europa World Year Book.*

United Nations Statistics Division, New York, NY 10017, (800) 253-9646, Fax: (212) 963-4116, http://unstats.un.org; *Statistical Yearbook.*

The World Bank, 1818 H Street, NW, Washington, DC 20433, (202) 473-1000, Fax: (202) 477-6391, www.worldbank.org; *Denmark* and *World Development Indicators (WDI) 2008.*

DENMARK - MONUMENTS AND HISTORIC SITES

UNESCO Institute for Statistics, C.P. 6128 Succursale Centre-Ville, Montreal, Quebec, H3C 3J7 Canada, (Dial from U.S. (514) 343-6880), (Fax from U.S. (514) 343 6882), www.uis.unesco.org; *Statistical Tables.*

DENMARK - MORTALITY

Central Intelligence Agency, Office of Public Affairs, Washington, DC 20505, (703) 482-0623, Fax: (703) 482-1739, www.cia.gov; *The World Factbook.*

Euromonitor International, Inc., 224 S. Michigan Avenue, Suite 1500, Chicago, IL 60604, (312) 922-1115, Fax: (312) 922-1157, www.euromonitor.com; *The World Economic Factbook 2008.*

European Union, Delegation of the European Commission to the United States, 2300 M Street, NW, Washington, DC 20037, (202) 862-9500, Fax: (202) 429-1766, www.eurunion.org; *First Demographic Estimates for 2006.*

Eurostat, Batiment Jean Monnet, Rue Alcide de Gasperi, L-2920 Luxembourg, http://epp.eurostat.ec.europa.eu; *Eurostat Yearbook 2006-2007.*

Nordic Council of Ministers, Store Strandstraede 18, DK-1255 Copenhagen K, Denmark, www.norden.org; *Nordic Statistical Yearbook 2004-2006.*

Palgrave Macmillan Ltd., Houndmills, Basingstoke, Hampshire, RG21 6XS, England, (Telephone in U.S. (888) 330-8477), (Fax in U.S. (800) 672-2054), www.palgrave.com; *The Statesman's Yearbook 2008.*

Taylor and Francis Group, An Informa Business, 2 Park Square, Milton Park, Abingdon, Oxford OX14 4RN, United Kingdom, (Dial from U.S. (212) 216-7800), (Fax from U.S. (212) 564-7854), www.tandf.co.uk; *The Europa World Year Book.*

United Nations Conference on Trade and Development (UNCTAD), DC2-1120, United Nations, New York, NY 10017, (212) 963-0027, www.unctad.org; *Handbook of Statistics 2005.*

United Nations Statistics Division, New York, NY 10017, (800) 253-9646, Fax: (212) 963-4116, http://unstats.un.org; *Demographic Yearbook; Human Development Report 2006; Statistical Yearbook; Trends in Europe and North America: The Statistical Yearbook of the ECE 2005;* and *World Statistics Pocketbook.*

The World Bank, 1818 H Street, NW, Washington, DC 20433, (202) 473-1000, Fax: (202) 477-6391, www.worldbank.org; *The World Bank Atlas 2003-2004; World Development Indicators (WDI) 2008;* and *World Development Report 2008.*

World Health Organization (WHO), Avenue Appia 20, 1211 Geneve 27, Switzerland, (Telephone in U.S. (212) 331-9081), www.who.int; *The WHO Global Atlas of Infectious Diseases* and *World Health Report 2006.*

DENMARK - MOTION PICTURES

Palgrave Macmillan Ltd., Houndmills, Basingstoke, Hampshire, RG21 6XS, England, (Telephone in U.S. (888) 330-8477), (Fax in U.S. (800) 672-2054), www.palgrave.com; *The Statesman's Yearbook 2008.*

UNESCO Institute for Statistics, C.P. 6128 Succursale Centre-Ville, Montreal, Quebec, H3C 3J7 Canada, (Dial from U.S. (514) 343-6880), (Fax from U.S. (514) 343 6882), www.uis.unesco.org; *Statistical Tables.*

United Nations Statistics Division, New York, NY 10017, (800) 253-9646, Fax: (212) 963-4116, http://unstats.un.org; *Statistical Yearbook.*

DENMARK - MOTOR VEHICLES

European Union, Delegation of the European Commission to the United States, 2300 M Street, NW, Washington, DC 20037, (202) 862-9500, Fax: (202) 429-1766, www.eurunion.org; *Statistical Overview of Transport in the European Union (Data 1970-2001).*

Eurostat, Batiment Jean Monnet, Rue Alcide de Gasperi, L-2920 Luxembourg, http://epp.eurostat.ec.europa.eu; *Eurostat Yearbook 2006-2007.*

International Road Federation (IFR), Madison Place, 500 Montgomery Street, 5th Floor, Alexandria, VA 22314, (703) 535-1001, Fax: (703) 535-1007, www.irfnet.org; *World Road Statistics 2006.*

Nordic Council of Ministers, Store Strandstraede 18, DK-1255 Copenhagen K, Denmark, www.norden.org; *Nordic Statistical Yearbook 2004-2006.*

Taylor and Francis Group, An Informa Business, 2 Park Square, Milton Park, Abingdon, Oxford OX14 4RN, United Kingdom, (Dial from U.S. (212) 216-7800), (Fax from U.S. (212) 564-7854), www.tandf.co.uk; *The Europa World Year Book.*

United Nations Statistics Division, New York, NY 10017, (800) 253-9646, Fax: (212) 963-4116, http://unstats.un.org; *Statistical Yearbook.*

DENMARK - MUSEUMS

M.E. Sharpe, 80 Business Park Drive, Armonk, NY 10504, (800) 541-6563, Fax: (914) 273-2106, www.mesharpe.com; *The Illustrated Book of World Rankings.*

Nordic Council of Ministers, Store Strandstraede 18, DK-1255 Copenhagen K, Denmark, www.norden.org; *Nordic Statistical Yearbook 2004-2006.*

UNESCO Institute for Statistics, C.P. 6128 Succursale Centre-Ville, Montreal, Quebec, H3C 3J7 Canada, (Dial from U.S. (514) 343-6880), (Fax from U.S. (514) 343 6882), www.uis.unesco.org; *Statistical Tables.*

DENMARK - NATURAL GAS PRODUCTION

See DENMARK - MINERAL INDUSTRIES

DENMARK - NICKEL AND NICKEL ORE

See DENMARK - MINERAL INDUSTRIES

DENMARK - NUTRITION

United Nations Food and Agricultural Organization (FAO), Viale delle Terme di Caracalla, 00100 Rome, Italy, (Dial from U.S. (202) 653-2400), (Fax from U.S. (202) 653 5760), www.fao.org; *The State of Food and Agriculture (SOFA) 2006.*

DENMARK - OATS PRODUCTION

See DENMARK - CROPS

DENMARK - OILSEED PLANTS

Eurostat, Batiment Jean Monnet, Rue Alcide de Gasperi, L-2920 Luxembourg, http://epp.eurostat.ec.europa.eu; *Eurostat Yearbook 2006-2007.*

Organisation for Economic Cooperation and Development (OECD), 2 rue Andre Pascal, F-75775 Paris Cedex 16, France, (Telephone in U.S. (202) 785-6323), (Fax in U.S. (202) 785-0350), www.oecd.org; *International Trade by Commodity Statistics (ITCS).*

DENMARK - OLDER PEOPLE

M.E. Sharpe, 80 Business Park Drive, Armonk, NY 10504, (800) 541-6563, Fax: (914) 273-2106, www.mesharpe.com; *The Illustrated Book of World Rankings.*

DENMARK - ONION PRODUCTION

See DENMARK - CROPS

DENMARK - PALM OIL PRODUCTION

See DENMARK - CROPS

DENMARK - PAPER

See DENMARK - FORESTS AND FORESTRY

DENMARK - PEANUT PRODUCTION

See DENMARK - CROPS

DENMARK - PEPPER PRODUCTION

See DENMARK - CROPS

DENMARK - PERIODICALS

UNESCO Institute for Statistics, C.P. 6128 Succursale Centre-Ville, Montreal, Quebec, H3C 3J7 Canada, (Dial from U.S. (514) 343-6880), (Fax from U.S. (514) 343 6882), www.uis.unesco.org; *Statistical Tables.*

DENMARK - PESTICIDES

United Nations Food and Agricultural Organization (FAO), Viale delle Terme di Caracalla, 00100 Rome, Italy, (Dial from U.S. (202) 653-2400), (Fax from U.S. (202) 653 5760), www.fao.org; *The State of Food and Agriculture (SOFA) 2006.*

DENMARK - PETROLEUM INDUSTRY AND TRADE

Danish Energy Authority, Amaliegade 44, DK 1256 Copenhagen K, Denmark, www.ens.dk; *Energy in Denmark 2006* and *Energy Statistics 2006.*

Euromonitor International, Inc., 224 S. Michigan Avenue, Suite 1500, Chicago, IL 60604, (312) 922-1115, Fax: (312) 922-1157, www.euromonitor.com; *European Marketing Data and Statistics 2008.*

Eurostat, Batiment Jean Monnet, Rue Alcide de Gasperi, L-2920 Luxembourg, http://epp.eurostat.ec.europa.eu; *Eurostat Yearbook 2006-2007.*

International Energy Agency (IEA), 9, rue de la Federation, 75739 Paris Cedex 15, France, www.iea.org; *Key World Energy Statistics 2007.*

M.E. Sharpe, 80 Business Park Drive, Armonk, NY 10504, (800) 541-6563, Fax: (914) 273-2106, www.mesharpe.com; *The Illustrated Book of World Rankings.*

Organisation for Economic Cooperation and Development (OECD), 2 rue Andre Pascal, F-75775 Paris Cedex 16, France, (Telephone in U.S. (202) 785-6323), (Fax in U.S. (202) 785-0350), www.oecd.org; *Energy Statistics of OECD Countries* (2007 Edition); *Indicators of Industrial Activity; International Trade by Commodity Statistics (ITCS); Oil Information 2006 Edition;* and *World Energy Outlook 2007.*

Palgrave Macmillan Ltd., Houndmills, Basingstoke, Hampshire, RG21 6XS, England, (Telephone in U.S. (888) 330-8477), (Fax in U.S. (800) 672-2054), www.palgrave.com; *The Statesman's Yearbook 2008.*

PennWell Corporation, 1421 South Sheridan Road, Tulsa, OK 74112, (918) 835-3161, www.pennwell.com; *International Petroleum Encyclopedia 2007.*

Platts, 2 Penn Plaza, 25th Floor, New York, NY 10121-2298, (212) 904-3070, www.platts.com; *Energy Economist.*

U.S. Department of Energy (DOE), Energy Information Administration (EIA), 1000 Independence Avenue, SW, Washington, DC 20585, (202) 586-8800, www.eia.doe.gov; *International Energy Annual 2004* and *International Energy Outlook 2006.*

United Nations Conference on Trade and Development (UNCTAD), DC2-1120, United Nations, New York, NY 10017, (212) 963-0027, www.unctad.org; *UNCTAD Commodity Yearbook.*

United Nations Food and Agricultural Organization (FAO), Viale delle Terme di Caracalla, 00100 Rome, Italy, (Dial from U.S. (202) 653-2400), (Fax from U.S. (202) 653 5760), www.fao.org; *The State of Food and Agriculture (SOFA) 2006.*

United Nations Statistics Division, New York, NY 10017, (800) 253-9646, Fax: (212) 963-4116, http://unstats.un.org; *Energy Statistics Yearbook 2003; Statistical Yearbook;* and *Trends in Europe and North America: The Statistical Yearbook of the ECE 2005.*

DENMARK - PHOSPHATES PRODUCTION

See DENMARK - MINERAL INDUSTRIES

DENMARK - PIPELINES

European Union, Delegation of the European Commission to the United States, 2300 M Street, NW, Washington, DC 20037, (202) 862-9500, Fax: (202) 429-1766, www.eurunion.org; *Statistical Overview of Transport in the European Union (Data 1970-2001).*

United Nations Statistics Division, New York, NY 10017, (800) 253-9646, Fax: (212) 963-4116, http://unstats.un.org; *Annual Bulletin of Transport Statistics for Europe and North America 2004.*

DENMARK - PLASTICS INDUSTRY AND TRADE

Eurostat, Batiment Jean Monnet, Rue Alcide de Gasperi, L-2920 Luxembourg, http://epp.eurostat.ec.europa.eu; *Eurostat Yearbook 2006-2007.*

Organisation for Economic Cooperation and Development (OECD), 2 rue Andre Pascal, F-75775 Paris Cedex 16, France, (Telephone in U.S. (202) 785-6323), (Fax in U.S. (202) 785-0350), www.oecd.org; *International Trade by Commodity Statistics (ITCS).*

United Nations Statistics Division, New York, NY 10017, (800) 253-9646, Fax: (212) 963-4116, http://unstats.un.org; *Statistical Yearbook.*

DENMARK - PLATINUM PRODUCTION

See DENMARK - MINERAL INDUSTRIES

DENMARK - POLITICAL SCIENCE

Central Intelligence Agency, Office of Public Affairs, Washington, DC 20505, (703) 482-0623, Fax: (703) 482-1739, www.cia.gov; *The World Factbook.*

European Union, Delegation of the European Commission to the United States, 2300 M Street, NW, Washington, DC 20037, (202) 862-9500, Fax: (202) 429-1766, www.eurunion.org; *RD Expenditure in Europe (2006 edition).*

Eurostat, Batiment Jean Monnet, Rue Alcide de Gasperi, L-2920 Luxembourg, http://epp.eurostat.ec.europa.eu; *Eurostat Yearbook 2006-2007.*

International Monetary Fund (IMF), 700 Nineteenth Street, NW, Washington, DC 20431, (202) 623-7000, Fax: (202) 623-4661, www.imf.org; *Government Finance Statistics Yearbook (2008 Edition)* and *International Financial Statistics Yearbook 2007.*

Nordic Council of Ministers, Store Strandstraede 18, DK-1255 Copenhagen K, Denmark, www.norden.org; *Nordic Statistical Yearbook 2004-2006.*

Organisation for Economic Cooperation and Development (OECD), 2 rue Andre Pascal, F-75775 Paris Cedex 16, France, (Telephone in U.S. (202) 785-6323), (Fax in U.S. (202) 785-0350), www.oecd.org; *OECD Economic Outlook 2008* and *Revenue Statistics 1965-2006 - 2007 Edition.*

Palgrave Macmillan Ltd., Houndmills, Basingstoke, Hampshire, RG21 6XS, England, (Telephone in U.S. (888) 330-8477), (Fax in U.S. (800) 672-2054), www.palgrave.com; *The Statesman's Yearbook 2008.*

Taylor and Francis Group, An Informa Business, 2 Park Square, Milton Park, Abingdon, Oxford OX14 4RN, United Kingdom, (Dial from U.S. (212) 216-7800), (Fax from U.S. (212) 564-7854), www.tandf.co.uk; *The Europa World Year Book.*

United Nations Statistics Division, New York, NY 10017, (800) 253-9646, Fax: (212) 963-4116, http://unstats.un.org; *National Accounts Statistics: Compendium of Income Distribution Statistics* and *Statistical Yearbook.*

The World Bank, 1818 H Street, NW, Washington, DC 20433, (202) 473-1000, Fax: (202) 477-6391, www.worldbank.org; *World Development Indicators (WDI) 2008* and *World Development Report 2008.*

DENMARK - POPULATION

Banque de France, 48 rue Croix des Petits champs, 75001 Paris, France, www.banque-france.fr/home.htm; *Key Data for the Euro Area.*

Central Intelligence Agency, Office of Public Affairs, Washington, DC 20505, (703) 482-0623, Fax: (703) 482-1739, www.cia.gov; *The World Factbook.*

Economist Intelligence Unit, 111 West 57th Street, New York, NY 10019, (212) 554-0600, Fax: (212) 586-1181, www.eiu.com; *Denmark Country Report.*

Euromonitor International, Inc., 224 S. Michigan Avenue, Suite 1500, Chicago, IL 60604, (312) 922-1115, Fax: (312) 922-1157, www.euromonitor.com; *European Marketing Data and Statistics 2008* and *The World Economic Factbook 2008.*

European Union, Delegation of the European Commission to the United States, 2300 M Street, NW, Washington, DC 20037, (202) 862-9500, Fax: (202) 429-1766, www.eurunion.org; *European Union Labour Force Survey; First Demographic Estimates for 2006;* and *Regions - Statistical Yearbook 2006.*

Eurostat, Batiment Jean Monnet, Rue Alcide de Gasperi, L-2920 Luxembourg, http://epp.eurostat.ec.europa.eu; *Eurostat Yearbook 2006-2007* and *The Life of Women and Men in Europe - A Statistical Portrait.*

Federal Statistical Office Germany, D-65180 Wiesbaden, Germany, www.destatis.de; *Denmark 2005.*

International Labour Office, I.L.O. Publications, 4 route des Morillons, CH-1211 Geneva 22, Switzerland, (Telephone in U.S. (202) 653-7652), (Fax in U.S. (202) 653-7687), www.ilo.org; *Yearbook of Labour Statistics 2006.*

M.E. Sharpe, 80 Business Park Drive, Armonk, NY 10504, (800) 541-6563, Fax: (914) 273-2106, www.mesharpe.com; *The Illustrated Book of World Rankings.*

Nordic Council of Ministers, Store Strandstraede 18, DK-1255 Copenhagen K, Denmark, www.norden.org; *Nordic Statistical Yearbook 2004-2006.*

Organisation for Economic Cooperation and Development (OECD), 2 rue Andre Pascal, F-75775 Paris Cedex 16, France, (Telephone in U.S. (202) 785-6323), (Fax in U.S. (202) 785-0350), www.oecd.org; *Labour Force Statistics: 1986-2005, 2007 Edition.*

Palgrave Macmillan Ltd., Houndmills, Basingstoke, Hampshire, RG21 6XS, England, (Telephone in U.S. (888) 330-8477), (Fax in U.S. (800) 672-2054), www.palgrave.com; *The Statesman's Yearbook 2008.*

Taylor and Francis Group, An Informa Business, 2 Park Square, Milton Park, Abingdon, Oxford OX14 4RN, United Kingdom, (Dial from U.S. (212) 216-7800), (Fax from U.S. (212) 564-7854), www.tandf.co.uk; *The Europa World Year Book.*

U.S. Department of State (DOS), 2201 C Street NW, Washington, DC 20520, (202) 647-4000, www.state.gov; *World Military Expenditures and Arms Transfers (WMEAT).*

UNESCO Institute for Statistics, C.P. 6128 Succursale Centre-Ville, Montreal, Quebec, H3C 3J7 Canada, (Dial from U.S. (514) 343-6880), (Fax from U.S. (514) 343 6882), www.uis.unesco.org; *Statistical Tables.*

United Nations Food and Agricultural Organization (FAO), Viale delle Terme di Caracalla, 00100 Rome, Italy, (Dial from U.S. (202) 653-2400), (Fax from U.S. (202) 653 5760), www.fao.org; *FAO Production Yearbook 2002.*

United Nations Statistics Division, New York, NY 10017, (800) 253-9646, Fax: (212) 963-4116, http://unstats.un.org; *Demographic Yearbook; Human Development Report 2006; Statistical Yearbook; Trends in Europe and North America: The Statistical Yearbook of the ECE 2005;* and *World Statistics Pocketbook.*

The World Bank, 1818 H Street, NW, Washington, DC 20433, (202) 473-1000, Fax: (202) 477-6391, www.worldbank.org; *Denmark; The World Bank Atlas 2003-2004;* and *World Development Report 2008.*

World Health Organization (WHO), Avenue Appia 20, 1211 Geneve 27, Switzerland, (Telephone in U.S. (212) 331-9081), www.who.int; *World Health Report 2006.*

DENMARK - POPULATION DENSITY

Central Intelligence Agency, Office of Public Affairs, Washington, DC 20505, (703) 482-0623, Fax: (703) 482-1739, www.cia.gov; *The World Factbook.*

Euromonitor International, Inc., 224 S. Michigan Avenue, Suite 1500, Chicago, IL 60604, (312) 922-1115, Fax: (312) 922-1157, www.euromonitor.com; *The World Economic Factbook 2008.*

European Union, Delegation of the European Commission to the United States, 2300 M Street, NW, Washington, DC 20037, (202) 862-9500, Fax: (202) 429-1766, www.eurunion.org; *First Demographic Estimates for 2006.*

Eurostat, Batiment Jean Monnet, Rue Alcide de Gasperi, L-2920 Luxembourg, http://epp.eurostat.ec.europa.eu; *Eurostat Yearbook 2006-2007.*

M.E. Sharpe, 80 Business Park Drive, Armonk, NY 10504, (800) 541-6563, Fax: (914) 273-2106, www.mesharpe.com; *The Illustrated Book of World Rankings.*

Nordic Council of Ministers, Store Strandstraede 18, DK-1255 Copenhagen K, Denmark, www.norden.org; *Nordic Statistical Yearbook 2004-2006.*

Palgrave Macmillan Ltd., Houndmills, Basingstoke, Hampshire, RG21 6XS, England, (Telephone in U.S. (888) 330-8477), (Fax in U.S. (800) 672-2054), www.palgrave.com; *The Statesman's Yearbook 2008.*

Taylor and Francis Group, An Informa Business, 2 Park Square, Milton Park, Abingdon, Oxford OX14 4RN, United Kingdom, (Dial from U.S. (212) 216-7800), (Fax from U.S. (212) 564-7854), www.tandf.co.uk; *The Europa World Year Book.*

UNESCO Institute for Statistics, C.P. 6128 Succursale Centre-Ville, Montreal, Quebec, H3C 3J7 Canada, (Dial from U.S. (514) 343-6880), (Fax from U.S. (514) 343 6882), www.uis.unesco.org; *Statistical Tables.*

United Nations Food and Agricultural Organization (FAO), Viale delle Terme di Caracalla, 00100 Rome, Italy, (Dial from U.S. (202) 653-2400), (Fax from U.S. (202) 653 5760), www.fao.org; *The State of Food and Agriculture (SOFA) 2006.*

United Nations Statistics Division, New York, NY 10017, (800) 253-9646, Fax: (212) 963-4116, http://unstats.un.org; *Statistical Yearbook* and *Trends in Europe and North America: The Statistical Yearbook of the ECE 2005.*

The World Bank, 1818 H Street, NW, Washington, DC 20433, (202) 473-1000, Fax: (202) 477-6391, www.worldbank.org; *Denmark* and *World Development Report 2008.*

DENMARK - POSTAL SERVICE

European Union, Delegation of the European Commission to the United States, 2300 M Street, NW, Washington, DC 20037, (202) 862-9500, Fax: (202) 429-1766, www.eurunion.org; *Statistical Overview of Transport in the European Union (Data 1970-2001).*

M.E. Sharpe, 80 Business Park Drive, Armonk, NY 10504, (800) 541-6563, Fax: (914) 273-2106, www.mesharpe.com; *The Illustrated Book of World Rankings.*

Nordic Council of Ministers, Store Strandstraede 18, DK-1255 Copenhagen K, Denmark, www.norden.org; *Nordic Statistical Yearbook 2004-2006.*

Palgrave Macmillan Ltd., Houndmills, Basingstoke, Hampshire, RG21 6XS, England, (Telephone in U.S. (888) 330-8477), (Fax in U.S. (800) 672-2054), www.palgrave.com; *The Statesman's Yearbook 2008.*

United Nations Statistics Division, New York, NY 10017, (800) 253-9646, Fax: (212) 963-4116, http://unstats.un.org; *Statistical Yearbook* and *Trends in Europe and North America: The Statistical Yearbook of the ECE 2005.*

DENMARK - POULTRY

See DENMARK - LIVESTOCK

DENMARK - POWER RESOURCES

Danish Energy Authority, Amaliegade 44, DK 1256 Copenhagen K, Denmark, www.ens.dk; *Energy in Denmark 2006* and *Energy Statistics 2006.*

Euromonitor International, Inc., 224 S. Michigan Avenue, Suite 1500, Chicago, IL 60604, (312) 922-1115, Fax: (312) 922-1157, www.euromonitor.com; *European Marketing Data and Statistics 2008; The World Economic Factbook 2008;* and *World Marketing Data and Statistics.*

European Union, Delegation of the European Commission to the United States, 2300 M Street, NW, Washington, DC 20037, (202) 862-9500, Fax: (202) 429-1766, www.eurunion.org; *European Union Energy Transport in Figures 2006; Regions - Statistical Yearbook 2006;* and *Statistical Overview of Transport in the European Union (Data 1970-2001).*

Eurostat, Batiment Jean Monnet, Rue Alcide de Gasperi, L-2920 Luxembourg, http://epp.eurostat.ec.europa.eu; *Eurostat Yearbook 2006-2007.*

M.E. Sharpe, 80 Business Park Drive, Armonk, NY 10504, (800) 541-6563, Fax: (914) 273-2106, www.mesharpe.com; *The Illustrated Book of World Rankings.*

Nordic Council of Ministers, Store Strandstraede 18, DK-1255 Copenhagen K, Denmark, www.norden.org; *Nordic Statistical Yearbook 2004-2006.*

Organisation for Economic Cooperation and Development (OECD), 2 rue Andre Pascal, F-75775 Paris Cedex 16, France, (Telephone in U.S. (202) 785-6323), (Fax in U.S. (202) 785-0350), www.oecd.org; *Coal Information: 2007 Edition; Energy Statistics of OECD Countries* (2007 Edition); *Key Environmental Indicators 2004; Oil Information 2006 Edition;* and *World Energy Outlook 2007.*

Palgrave Macmillan Ltd., Houndmills, Basingstoke, Hampshire, RG21 6XS, England, (Telephone in U.S. (888) 330-8477), (Fax in U.S. (800) 672-2054), www.palgrave.com; *The Statesman's Yearbook 2008.*

Platts, 2 Penn Plaza, 25th Floor, New York, NY 10121-2298, (212) 904-3070, www.platts.com; *Energy Economist* and *European Power Daily.*

U.S. Department of Energy (DOE), Energy Information Administration (EIA), 1000 Independence Avenue, SW, Washington, DC 20585, (202) 586-8800, www.eia.doe.gov; *International Energy Annual 2004* and *International Energy Outlook 2006.*

United Nations Food and Agricultural Organization (FAO), Viale delle Terme di Caracalla, 00100 Rome, Italy, (Dial from U.S. (202) 653-2400), (Fax from U.S. (202) 653 5760), www.fao.org; *The State of Food and Agriculture (SOFA) 2006.*

United Nations Statistics Division, New York, NY 10017, (800) 253-9646, Fax: (212) 963-4116, http://unstats.un.org; *Energy Statistics Yearbook 2003; Human Development Report 2006; Statistical Yearbook; Trends in Europe and North America: The Statistical Yearbook of the ECE 2005;* and *World Statistics Pocketbook.*

The World Bank, 1818 H Street, NW, Washington, DC 20433, (202) 473-1000, Fax: (202) 477-6391, www.worldbank.org; *The World Bank Atlas 2003-2004* and *World Development Report 2008.*

DENMARK - PRICES

Euromonitor International, Inc., 224 S. Michigan Avenue, Suite 1500, Chicago, IL 60604, (312) 922-1115, Fax: (312) 922-1157, www.euromonitor.com; *European Marketing Data and Statistics 2008* and *World Marketing Data and Statistics.*

European Union, Delegation of the European Commission to the United States, 2300 M Street, NW, Washington, DC 20037, (202) 862-9500, Fax: (202) 429-1766, www.eurunion.org; *Eurostatistics: Data for Short-Term Economic Analysis (2007 edition).*

Eurostat, Batiment Jean Monnet, Rue Alcide de Gasperi, L-2920 Luxembourg, http://epp.eurostat.ec.europa.eu; *Eurostat Yearbook 2006-2007.*

International Labour Office, I.L.O. Publications, 4 route des Morillons, CH-1211 Geneva 22, Switzerland, (Telephone in U.S. (202) 653-7652), (Fax in U.S. (202) 653-7687), www.ilo.org; *Yearbook of Labour Statistics 2006.*

International Lead and Zinc Study Group (ILZSG), Rua Almirante Barroso 38, 5th Floor, Lisbon 1000 - 013, Portugal, www.ilzsg.org; Interactive Statistical Database.

International Monetary Fund (IMF), 700 Nineteenth Street, NW, Washington, DC 20431, (202) 623-7000, Fax: (202) 623-4661, www.imf.org; *International Financial Statistics Yearbook 2007.*

M.E. Sharpe, 80 Business Park Drive, Armonk, NY 10504, (800) 541-6563, Fax: (914) 273-2106, www.mesharpe.com; *The Illustrated Book of World Rankings.*

Nordic Council of Ministers, Store Strandstraede 18, DK-1255 Copenhagen K, Denmark, www.norden.org; *Nordic Statistical Yearbook 2004-2006.*

Organisation for Economic Cooperation and Development (OECD), 2 rue Andre Pascal, F-75775 Paris Cedex 16, France, (Telephone in U.S. (202) 785-6323), (Fax in U.S. (202) 785-0350), www.oecd.org; *Indicators of Industrial Activity; Iron and Steel Industry in 2004 (2006 Edition);* and *OECD Economic Outlook 2008.*

Technical Association of the Pulp and Paper Industry (TAPPI), 15 Technology Parkway South, Norcross, GA 30092, (770) 446-1400, Fax: (770) 446-6947, www.tappi.org; *TAPPI Annual Report.*

United Nations Food and Agricultural Organization (FAO), Viale delle Terme di Caracalla, 00100 Rome, Italy, (Dial from U.S. (202) 653-2400), (Fax from U.S. (202) 653 5760), www.fao.org; *FAO Production Yearbook 2002* and *The State of Food and Agriculture (SOFA) 2006.*

The World Bank, 1818 H Street, NW, Washington, DC 20433, (202) 473-1000, Fax: (202) 477-6391, www.worldbank.org; *Denmark.*

World Bureau of Metal Statistics (WBMS), 27a High Street, Ware, Hertfordshire, SG12 9BA, United Kingdom, www.world-bureau.com; *World Flow Charts* and *World Metal Statistics.*

DENMARK - PROFESSIONS

Eurostat, Batiment Jean Monnet, Rue Alcide de Gasperi, L-2920 Luxembourg, http://epp.eurostat.ec.europa.eu; *Eurostat Yearbook 2006-2007.*

United Nations Statistics Division, New York, NY 10017, (800) 253-9646, Fax: (212) 963-4116, http://unstats.un.org; *Statistical Yearbook.*

DENMARK - PUBLIC HEALTH

Euromonitor International, Inc., 224 S. Michigan Avenue, Suite 1500, Chicago, IL 60604, (312) 922-1115, Fax: (312) 922-1157, www.euromonitor.com; *World Health Databook 2007/2008* and *World Marketing Data and Statistics.*

European Union, Delegation of the European Commission to the United States, 2300 M Street, NW, Washington, DC 20037, (202) 862-9500, Fax: (202) 429-1766, www.eurunion.org; *Regions - Statistical Yearbook 2006.*

Eurostat, Batiment Jean Monnet, Rue Alcide de Gasperi, L-2920 Luxembourg, http://epp.eurostat.ec.europa.eu; *Eurostat Yearbook 2006-2007.*

Health and Consumer Protection Directorate-General, European Commission, B-1049 Brussels, Belgium, http://ec.europa.eu/dgs/health_consumer/index_en.htm; *Injuries in the European Union: Statistics Summary 2002-2004.*

M.E. Sharpe, 80 Business Park Drive, Armonk, NY 10504, (800) 541-6563, Fax: (914) 273-2106, www.mesharpe.com; *The Illustrated Book of World Rankings.*

Nordic Council of Ministers, Store Strandstraede 18, DK-1255 Copenhagen K, Denmark, www.norden.org; *Nordic Statistical Yearbook 2004-2006.*

Organisation for Economic Cooperation and Development (OECD), 2 rue Andre Pascal, F-75775 Paris Cedex 16, France, (Telephone in U.S. (202) 785-6323), (Fax in U.S. (202) 785-0350), www.oecd.org; *Health at a Glance 2007 - OECD Indicators.*

Robert Koch Institute, Nordufer 20, D 13353 Berlin, Germany, www.rki.de; *EUVAC-NET Report: Pertussis-Surveillance 1998-2002.*

United Nations Conference on Trade and Development (UNCTAD), DC2-1120, United Nations, New York, NY 10017, (212) 963-0027, www.unctad.org; *Handbook of Statistics 2005.*

United Nations Statistics Division, New York, NY 10017, (800) 253-9646, Fax: (212) 963-4116, http://

unstats.un.org; *Human Development Report 2006; Statistical Yearbook;* and *Trends in Europe and North America: The Statistical Yearbook of the ECE 2005.*

The World Bank, 1818 H Street, NW, Washington, DC 20433, (202) 473-1000, Fax: (202) 477-6391, www.worldbank.org; *Denmark* and *World Development Report 2008.*

World Health Organization (WHO), Avenue Appia 20, 1211 Geneve 27, Switzerland, (Telephone in U.S. (212) 331-9081), www.who.int; The WHO Global Atlas of Infectious Diseases and *World Health Report 2006.*

DENMARK - PUBLIC UTILITIES

Danish Energy Authority, Amaliegade 44, DK 1256 Copenhagen K, Denmark, www.ens.dk; *Energy in Denmark 2006* and *Energy Statistics 2006.*

Eurostat, Batiment Jean Monnet, Rue Alcide de Gasperi, L-2920 Luxembourg, http://epp.eurostat.ec.europa.eu; *Eurostat Yearbook 2006-2007.*

DENMARK - PUBLISHERS AND PUBLISHING

Nordic Council of Ministers, Store Strandstraede 18, DK-1255 Copenhagen K, Denmark, www.norden.org; *Nordic Statistical Yearbook 2004-2006.*

Organisation for Economic Cooperation and Development (OECD), 2 rue Andre Pascal, F-75775 Paris Cedex 16, France, (Telephone in U.S. (202) 785-6323), (Fax in U.S. (202) 785-0350), www.oecd.org; *Indicators of Industrial Activity.*

Palgrave Macmillan Ltd., Houndmills, Basingstoke, Hampshire, RG21 6XS, England, (Telephone in U.S. (888) 330-8477), (Fax in U.S. (800) 672-2054), www.palgrave.com; *The Statesman's Yearbook 2008.*

Taylor and Francis Group, An Informa Business, 2 Park Square, Milton Park, Abingdon, Oxford OX14 4RN, United Kingdom, (Dial from U.S. (212) 216-7800), (Fax from U.S. (212) 564-7854), www.tandf.co.uk; *The Europa World Year Book.*

UNESCO Institute for Statistics, C.P. 6128 Succursale Centre-Ville, Montreal, Quebec, H3C 3J7 Canada, (Dial from U.S. (514) 343-6880), (Fax from U.S. (514) 343 6882), www.uis.unesco.org; *Statistical Tables.*

United Nations Statistics Division, New York, NY 10017, (800) 253-9646, Fax: (212) 963-4116, http://unstats.un.org; *Trends in Europe and North America: The Statistical Yearbook of the ECE 2005.*

DENMARK - RADIO - RECEIVERS AND RECEPTION

Palgrave Macmillan Ltd., Houndmills, Basingstoke, Hampshire, RG21 6XS, England, (Telephone in U.S. (888) 330-8477), (Fax in U.S. (800) 672-2054), www.palgrave.com; *The Statesman's Yearbook 2008.*

United Nations Statistics Division, New York, NY 10017, (800) 253-9646, Fax: (212) 963-4116, http://unstats.un.org; *Statistical Yearbook.*

DENMARK - RAILROADS

Euromonitor International, Inc., 224 S. Michigan Avenue, Suite 1500, Chicago, IL 60604, (312) 922-1115, Fax: (312) 922-1157, www.euromonitor.com; *European Marketing Data and Statistics 2008.*

European Union, Delegation of the European Commission to the United States, 2300 M Street, NW, Washington, DC 20037, (202) 862-9500, Fax: (202) 429-1766, www.eurunion.org; *Regions - Statistical Yearbook 2006* and *Statistical Overview of Transport in the European Union (Data 1970-2001).*

Eurostat, Batiment Jean Monnet, Rue Alcide de Gasperi, L-2920 Luxembourg, http://epp.eurostat.ec.europa.eu; *Eurostat Yearbook 2006-2007.*

Jane's Information Group, 110 North Royal Street, Suite 200, Alexandria, VA 22314, (703) 683-3700, Fax: (800) 836-0297, www.janes.com; *Jane's World Railways.*

Nordic Council of Ministers, Store Strandstraede 18, DK-1255 Copenhagen K, Denmark, www.norden.org; *Nordic Statistical Yearbook 2004-2006.*

Palgrave Macmillan Ltd., Houndmills, Basingstoke, Hampshire, RG21 6XS, England, (Telephone in U.S. (888) 330-8477), (Fax in U.S. (800) 672-2054), www.palgrave.com; *The Statesman's Yearbook 2008.*

Taylor and Francis Group, An Informa Business, 2 Park Square, Milton Park, Abingdon, Oxford OX14 4RN, United Kingdom, (Dial from U.S. (212) 216-7800), (Fax from U.S. (212) 564-7854), www.tandf.co.uk; *The Europa World Year Book.*

United Nations Statistics Division, New York, NY 10017, (800) 253-9646, Fax: (212) 963-4116, http://unstats.un.org; *Annual Bulletin of Transport Statistics for Europe and North America 2004; Statistical Yearbook;* and *Trends in Europe and North America: The Statistical Yearbook of the ECE 2005.*

DENMARK - RANCHING

Eurostat, Batiment Jean Monnet, Rue Alcide de Gasperi, L-2920 Luxembourg, http://epp.eurostat.ec.europa.eu; *Eurostat Yearbook 2006-2007.*

DENMARK - RELIGION

Central Intelligence Agency, Office of Public Affairs, Washington, DC 20505, (703) 482-0623, Fax: (703) 482-1739, www.cia.gov; *The World Factbook.*

M.E. Sharpe, 80 Business Park Drive, Armonk, NY 10504, (800) 541-6563, Fax: (914) 273-2106, www.mesharpe.com; *The Illustrated Book of World Rankings.*

Palgrave Macmillan Ltd., Houndmills, Basingstoke, Hampshire, RG21 6XS, England, (Telephone in U.S. (888) 330-8477), (Fax in U.S. (800) 672-2054), www.palgrave.com; *The Statesman's Yearbook 2008.*

DENMARK - RENT CHARGES

International Labour Office, I.L.O. Publications, 4 route des Morillons, CH-1211 Geneva 22, Switzerland, (Telephone in U.S. (202) 653-7652), (Fax in U.S. (202) 653-7687), www.ilo.org; *Yearbook of Labour Statistics 2006.*

DENMARK - RESERVES (ACCOUNTING)

Eurostat, Batiment Jean Monnet, Rue Alcide de Gasperi, L-2920 Luxembourg, http://epp.eurostat.ec.europa.eu; *Eurostat Yearbook 2006-2007.*

Organisation for Economic Cooperation and Development (OECD), 2 rue Andre Pascal, F-75775 Paris Cedex 16, France, (Telephone in U.S. (202) 785-6323), (Fax in U.S. (202) 785-0350), www.oecd.org; *Financial Market Trends: OECD Periodical* and *OECD Economic Outlook 2008.*

The World Bank, 1818 H Street, NW, Washington, DC 20433, (202) 473-1000, Fax: (202) 477-6391, www.worldbank.org; *World Development Indicators (WDI) 2008.*

DENMARK - RETAIL TRADE

Banque de France, 48 rue Croix des Petits champs, 75001 Paris, France, www.banque-france.fr/home.htm; *Monthly Business Survey Overview.*

Euromonitor International, Inc., 224 S. Michigan Avenue, Suite 1500, Chicago, IL 60604, (312) 922-1115, Fax: (312) 922-1157, www.euromonitor.com; *Retail Trade International 2007* and *World Marketing Data and Statistics.*

European Union, Delegation of the European Commission to the United States, 2300 M Street, NW, Washington, DC 20037, (202) 862-9500, Fax: (202) 429-1766, www.eurunion.org; *Eurostatistics: Data for Short-Term Economic Analysis (2007 edition).*

Eurostat, Batiment Jean Monnet, Rue Alcide de Gasperi, L-2920 Luxembourg, http://epp.eurostat.ec.europa.eu; *Eurostat Yearbook 2006-2007.*

United Nations Statistics Division, New York, NY 10017, (800) 253-9646, Fax: (212) 963-4116, http://unstats.un.org; *Statistical Yearbook.*

DENMARK - RICE PRODUCTION

See DENMARK - CROPS

DENMARK - ROADS

Central Intelligence Agency, Office of Public Affairs, Washington, DC 20505, (703) 482-0623, Fax: (703) 482-1739, www.cia.gov; *The World Factbook.*

European Union, Delegation of the European Commission to the United States, 2300 M Street, NW, Washington, DC 20037, (202) 862-9500, Fax: (202) 429-1766, www.eurunion.org; *Statistical Overview of Transport in the European Union (Data 1970-2001).*

Eurostat, Batiment Jean Monnet, Rue Alcide de Gasperi, L-2920 Luxembourg, http://epp.eurostat.ec.europa.eu; *Eurostat Yearbook 2006-2007.*

International Road Federation (IFR), Madison Place, 500 Montgomery Street, 5th Floor, Alexandria, VA 22314, (703) 535-1001, Fax: (703) 535-1007, www.irfnet.org; *World Road Statistics 2006.*

Nordic Council of Ministers, Store Strandstraede 18, DK-1255 Copenhagen K, Denmark, www.norden.org; *Nordic Statistical Yearbook 2004-2006.*

Palgrave Macmillan Ltd., Houndmills, Basingstoke, Hampshire, RG21 6XS, England, (Telephone in U.S. (888) 330-8477), (Fax in U.S. (800) 672-2054), www.palgrave.com; *The Statesman's Yearbook 2008.*

United Nations Statistics Division, New York, NY 10017, (800) 253-9646, Fax: (212) 963-4116, http://unstats.un.org; *Annual Bulletin of Transport Statistics for Europe and North America 2004* and *Trends in Europe and North America: The Statistical Yearbook of the ECE 2005.*

DENMARK - RUBBER INDUSTRY AND TRADE

Eurostat, Batiment Jean Monnet, Rue Alcide de Gasperi, L-2920 Luxembourg, http://epp.eurostat.ec.europa.eu; *Eurostat Yearbook 2006-2007.*

International Rubber Study Group (IRSG), 1st Floor, Heron House, 109/115 Wembley Hill Road, Wembley, Middlesex HA9 8DA, United Kingdom, www.rubberstudy.com; *Rubber Statistical Bulletin; Summary of World Rubber Statistics 2005; World Rubber Statistics Handbook (Volume 6, 1975-2001);* and *World Rubber Statistics Historic Handbook.*

M.E. Sharpe, 80 Business Park Drive, Armonk, NY 10504, (800) 541-6563, Fax: (914) 273-2106, www.mesharpe.com; *The Illustrated Book of World Rankings.*

Organisation for Economic Cooperation and Development (OECD), 2 rue Andre Pascal, F-75775 Paris Cedex 16, France, (Telephone in U.S. (202) 785-6323), (Fax in U.S. (202) 785-0350), www.oecd.org; *International Trade by Commodity Statistics (ITCS).*

DENMARK - RYE PRODUCTION

See DENMARK - CROPS

DENMARK - SAFFLOWER SEED PRODUCTION

See DENMARK - CROPS

DENMARK - SALT PRODUCTION

See DENMARK - MINERAL INDUSTRIES

DENMARK - SAVINGS ACCOUNT DEPOSITS

See DENMARK - BANKS AND BANKING

DENMARK - SHEEP

See DENMARK - LIVESTOCK

DENMARK - SHIPBUILDING

Organisation for Economic Cooperation and Development (OECD), 2 rue Andre Pascal, F-75775 Paris Cedex 16, France, (Telephone in U.S. (202) 785-6323), (Fax in U.S. (202) 785-0350), www.oecd.org; *Indicators of Industrial Activity.*

DENMARK - SHIPPING

European Union, Delegation of the European Commission to the United States, 2300 M Street, NW, Washington, DC 20037, (202) 862-9500, Fax: (202) 429-1766, www.eurunion.org; *Fishery Statistics - 1990-2006; Regions - Statistical Yearbook 2006;*

and *Statistical Overview of Transport in the European Union (Data 1970-2001).*

Eurostat, Batiment Jean Monnet, Rue Alcide de Gasperi, L-2920 Luxembourg, http://epp.eurostat.ec.europa.eu; *Eurostat Yearbook 2006-2007.*

Lloyd's Register - Fairplay, 8410 N.W. 53rd Terrace, Suite 207, Miami FL 33166, (305) 718-9929, Fax: (305) 718-9663, www.lrfairplay.com; *Register of Ships 2007-2008; World Casualty Statistics 2007; World Fleet Statistics 2006; World Marine Propulsion Report 2006-2010; World Shipbuilding Statistics 2007;* and The World Shipping Encyclopaedia.

Nordic Council of Ministers, Store Strandstraede 18, DK-1255 Copenhagen K, Denmark, www.norden.org; *Nordic Statistical Yearbook 2004-2006.*

Organisation for Economic Cooperation and Development (OECD), 2 rue Andre Pascal, F-75775 Paris Cedex 16, France, (Telephone in U.S. (202) 785-6323), (Fax in U.S. (202) 785-0350), www.oecd.org; *Statistics on Ship Production, Exports and Orders in 2004.*

Palgrave Macmillan Ltd., Houndmills, Basingstoke, Hampshire, RG21 6XS, England, (Telephone in U.S. (888) 330-8477), (Fax in U.S. (800) 672-2054), www.palgrave.com; *The Statesman's Yearbook 2008.*

Taylor and Francis Group, An Informa Business, 2 Park Square, Milton Park, Abingdon, Oxford OX14 4RN, United Kingdom, (Dial from U.S. (212) 216-7800), (Fax from U.S. (212) 564-7854), www.tandf.co.uk; *The Europa World Year Book.*

U.S. Department of Transportation (DOT), Maritime Administration (MARAD), West Building, Southeast Federal Center, 1200 New Jersey Avenue, SE, Washington, DC 20590, (800) 99-MARAD, www.marad.dot.gov; *World Merchant Fleet 2005.*

United Nations Statistics Division, New York, NY 10017, (800) 253-9646, Fax: (212) 963-4116, http://unstats.un.org; *Statistical Yearbook.*

DENMARK - SILVER PRODUCTION

See DENMARK - MINERAL INDUSTRIES

DENMARK - SOCIAL CLASSES

European Union, Delegation of the European Commission to the United States, 2300 M Street, NW, Washington, DC 20037, (202) 862-9500, Fax: (202) 429-1766, www.eurunion.org; *European Union Labour Force Survey.*

Eurostat, Batiment Jean Monnet, Rue Alcide de Gasperi, L-2920 Luxembourg, http://epp.eurostat.ec.europa.eu; *Eurostat Yearbook 2006-2007.*

DENMARK - SOCIAL ECOLOGY

Eurostat, Batiment Jean Monnet, Rue Alcide de Gasperi, L-2920 Luxembourg, http://epp.eurostat.ec.europa.eu; *Eurostat Yearbook 2006-2007.*

M.E. Sharpe, 80 Business Park Drive, Armonk, NY 10504, (800) 541-6563, Fax: (914) 273-2106, www.mesharpe.com; *The Illustrated Book of World Rankings.*

United Nations Statistics Division, New York, NY 10017, (800) 253-9646, Fax: (212) 963-4116, http://unstats.un.org; *World Statistics Pocketbook.*

DENMARK - SOCIAL SECURITY

Eurostat, Batiment Jean Monnet, Rue Alcide de Gasperi, L-2920 Luxembourg, http://epp.eurostat.ec.europa.eu; *Eurostat Yearbook 2006-2007.*

International Monetary Fund (IMF), 700 Nineteenth Street, NW, Washington, DC 20431, (202) 623-7000, Fax: (202) 623-4661, www.imf.org; *Government Finance Statistics Yearbook (2008 Edition).*

Nordic Council of Ministers, Store Strandstraede 18, DK-1255 Copenhagen K, Denmark, www.norden.org; *Nordic Statistical Yearbook 2004-2006.*

Organisation for Economic Cooperation and Development (OECD), 2 rue Andre Pascal, F-75775 Paris Cedex 16, France, (Telephone in U.S. (202) 785-6323), (Fax in U.S. (202) 785-0350), www.oecd.org; *Revenue Statistics 1965-2006 - 2007 Edition.*

Palgrave Macmillan Ltd., Houndmills, Basingstoke, Hampshire, RG21 6XS, England, (Telephone in U.S. (888) 330-8477), (Fax in U.S. (800) 672-2054), www.palgrave.com; *The Statesman's Yearbook 2008.*

United Nations Statistics Division, New York, NY 10017, (800) 253-9646, Fax: (212) 963-4116, http://unstats.un.org; *National Accounts Statistics: Compendium of Income Distribution Statistics.*

DENMARK - SOYBEAN PRODUCTION

See DENMARK - CROPS

DENMARK - STEEL PRODUCTION

See DENMARK - MINERAL INDUSTRIES

DENMARK - STRAW PRODUCTION

See DENMARK - CROPS

DENMARK - SUGAR PRODUCTION

See DENMARK - CROPS

DENMARK - SULPHUR PRODUCTION

See DENMARK - MINERAL INDUSTRIES

DENMARK - SUNFLOWER PRODUCTION

See DENMARK - CROPS

DENMARK - TAXATION

Eurostat, Batiment Jean Monnet, Rue Alcide de Gasperi, L-2920 Luxembourg, http://epp.eurostat.ec.europa.eu; *Eurostat Yearbook 2006-2007* and *Taxation Trends in the European Union - Data for the EU Member States and Norway.*

International Monetary Fund (IMF), 700 Nineteenth Street, NW, Washington, DC 20431, (202) 623-7000, Fax: (202) 623-4661, www.imf.org; *Government Finance Statistics Yearbook (2008 Edition).*

International Road Federation (IFR), Madison Place, 500 Montgomery Street, 5th Floor, Alexandria, VA 22314, (703) 535-1001, Fax: (703) 535-1007, www.irfnet.org; *World Road Statistics 2006.*

Nordic Council of Ministers, Store Strandstraede 18, DK-1255 Copenhagen K, Denmark, www.norden.org; *Nordic Statistical Yearbook 2004-2006.*

Organisation for Economic Cooperation and Development (OECD), 2 rue Andre Pascal, F-75775 Paris Cedex 16, France, (Telephone in U.S. (202) 785-6323), (Fax in U.S. (202) 785-0350), www.oecd.org; *Revenue Statistics 1965-2006 - 2007 Edition.*

Palgrave Macmillan Ltd., Houndmills, Basingstoke, Hampshire, RG21 6XS, England, (Telephone in U.S. (888) 330-8477), (Fax in U.S. (800) 672-2054), www.palgrave.com; *The Statesman's Yearbook 2008.*

Taylor and Francis Group, An Informa Business, 2 Park Square, Milton Park, Abingdon, Oxford OX14 4RN, United Kingdom, (Dial from U.S. (212) 216-7800), (Fax from U.S. (212) 564-7854), www.tandf.co.uk; *The Europa World Year Book.*

The World Bank, 1818 H Street, NW, Washington, DC 20433, (202) 473-1000, Fax: (202) 477-6391, www.worldbank.org; *World Development Indicators (WDI) 2008.*

DENMARK - TEA PRODUCTION

See DENMARK - CROPS

DENMARK - TELEPHONE

European Union, Delegation of the European Commission to the United States, 2300 M Street, NW, Washington, DC 20037, (202) 862-9500, Fax: (202) 429-1766, www.eurunion.org; *Statistical Overview of Transport in the European Union (Data 1970-2001).*

Eurostat, Batiment Jean Monnet, Rue Alcide de Gasperi, L-2920 Luxembourg, http://epp.eurostat.ec.europa.eu; *Eurostat Yearbook 2006-2007.*

International Telecommunication Union (ITU), Place des Nations, 1211 Geneva 20, Switzerland, www.itu.int; World Telecommunication Indicators Database.

Nordic Council of Ministers, Store Strandstraede 18, DK-1255 Copenhagen K, Denmark, www.norden.org; *Nordic Statistical Yearbook 2004-2006.*

Palgrave Macmillan Ltd., Houndmills, Basingstoke, Hampshire, RG21 6XS, England, (Telephone in U.S. (888) 330-8477), (Fax in U.S. (800) 672-2054), www.palgrave.com; *The Statesman's Yearbook 2008.*

Taylor and Francis Group, An Informa Business, 2 Park Square, Milton Park, Abingdon, Oxford OX14 4RN, United Kingdom, (Dial from U.S. (212) 216-7800), (Fax from U.S. (212) 564-7854), www.tandf.co.uk; *The Europa World Year Book.*

United Nations Statistics Division, New York, NY 10017, (800) 253-9646, Fax: (212) 963-4116, http://unstats.un.org; *Statistical Yearbook; Trends in Europe and North America: The Statistical Yearbook of the ECE 2005;* and *World Statistics Pocketbook.*

DENMARK - TELEVISION - RECEIVERS AND RECEPTION

Eurostat, Batiment Jean Monnet, Rue Alcide de Gasperi, L-2920 Luxembourg, http://epp.eurostat.ec.europa.eu; *Eurostat Yearbook 2006-2007.*

United Nations Statistics Division, New York, NY 10017, (800) 253-9646, Fax: (212) 963-4116, http://unstats.un.org; *Statistical Yearbook.*

DENMARK - TEXTILE INDUSTRY

Euromonitor International, Inc., 224 S. Michigan Avenue, Suite 1500, Chicago, IL 60604, (312) 922-1115, Fax: (312) 922-1157, www.euromonitor.com; *Retail Trade International 2007.*

European Union, Delegation of the European Commission to the United States, 2300 M Street, NW, Washington, DC 20037, (202) 862-9500, Fax: (202) 429-1766, www.eurunion.org; *Eurostatistics: Data for Short-Term Economic Analysis (2007 edition)* and *The Textile Industry in the EU.*

Eurostat, Batiment Jean Monnet, Rue Alcide de Gasperi, L-2920 Luxembourg, http://epp.eurostat.ec.europa.eu; *Eurostat Yearbook 2006-2007.*

M.E. Sharpe, 80 Business Park Drive, Armonk, NY 10504, (800) 541-6563, Fax: (914) 273-2106, www.mesharpe.com; *The Illustrated Book of World Rankings.*

Organisation for Economic Cooperation and Development (OECD), 2 rue Andre Pascal, F-75775 Paris Cedex 16, France, (Telephone in U.S. (202) 785-6323), (Fax in U.S. (202) 785-0350), www.oecd.org; *Indicators of Industrial Activity; International Trade by Commodity Statistics (ITCS); A New World Map in Textiles and Clothing: Adjusting to Change; 2005 OECD Agricultural Outlook Tables, 1970-2014;* and STructural ANalysis (STAN) database.

Palgrave Macmillan Ltd., Houndmills, Basingstoke, Hampshire, RG21 6XS, England, (Telephone in U.S. (888) 330-8477), (Fax in U.S. (800) 672-2054), www.palgrave.com; *The Statesman's Yearbook 2008.*

United Nations Conference on Trade and Development (UNCTAD), DC2-1120, United Nations, New York, NY 10017, (212) 963-0027, www.unctad.org; *UNCTAD Commodity Yearbook.*

United Nations Statistics Division, New York, NY 10017, (800) 253-9646, Fax: (212) 963-4116, http://unstats.un.org; Commodity Trade Statistics Database (COMTRADE) and *Statistical Yearbook.*

DENMARK - TIN PRODUCTION

See DENMARK - MINERAL INDUSTRIES

DENMARK - TOBACCO INDUSTRY

Euromonitor International, Inc., 224 S. Michigan Avenue, Suite 1500, Chicago, IL 60604, (312) 922-1115, Fax: (312) 922-1157, www.euromonitor.com; *European Marketing Data and Statistics 2008.*

Eurostat, Batiment Jean Monnet, Rue Alcide de Gasperi, L-2920 Luxembourg, http://epp.eurostat.ec.europa.eu; *Eurostat Yearbook 2006-2007.*

Foreign Agricultural Service (FAS), U.S. Department of Agriculture (USDA), 1400 Independence Avenue,

SW, Washington, DC 20250, (202) 720-3935, www.fas.usda.gov; *Tobacco: World Markets and Trade.*

M.E. Sharpe, 80 Business Park Drive, Armonk, NY 10504, (800) 541-6563, Fax: (914) 273-2106, www.mesharpe.com; *The Illustrated Book of World Rankings.*

Organisation for Economic Cooperation and Development (OECD), 2 rue Andre Pascal, F-75775 Paris Cedex 16, France, (Telephone in U.S. (202) 785-6323), (Fax in U.S. (202) 785-0350), www.oecd.org; *Indicators of Industrial Activity; International Trade by Commodity Statistics (ITCS);* and STructural ANalysis (STAN) database.

United Nations Statistics Division, New York, NY 10017, (800) 253-9646, Fax: (212) 963-4116, http://unstats.un.org; *Statistical Yearbook.*

DENMARK - TOURISM

Euromonitor International, Inc., 224 S. Michigan Avenue, Suite 1500, Chicago, IL 60604, (312) 922-1115, Fax: (312) 922-1157, www.euromonitor.com; *European Marketing Data and Statistics 2008; The World Economic Factbook 2008;* and *World Marketing Data and Statistics.*

European Union, Delegation of the European Commission to the United States, 2300 M Street, NW, Washington, DC 20037, (202) 862-9500, Fax: (202) 429-1766, www.eurunion.org; *Statistical Overview of Transport in the European Union (Data 1970-2001).*

Eurostat, Batiment Jean Monnet, Rue Alcide de Gasperi, L-2920 Luxembourg, http://epp.eurostat.ec.europa.eu; *Tourism in Europe: First Results for 2007.*

M.E. Sharpe, 80 Business Park Drive, Armonk, NY 10504, (800) 541-6563, Fax: (914) 273-2106, www.mesharpe.com; *The Illustrated Book of World Rankings.*

Organisation for Economic Cooperation and Development (OECD), 2 rue Andre Pascal, F-75775 Paris Cedex 16, France, (Telephone in U.S. (202) 785-6323), (Fax in U.S. (202) 785-0350), www.oecd.org; *Household, Tourism, Travel: Trends, Environmental Impacts and Policy Responses.*

Palgrave Macmillan Ltd., Houndmills, Basingstoke, Hampshire, RG21 6XS, England, (Telephone in U.S. (888) 330-8477), (Fax in U.S. (800) 672-2054), www.palgrave.com; *The Statesman's Yearbook 2008.*

Taylor and Francis Group, An Informa Business, 2 Park Square, Milton Park, Abingdon, Oxford OX14 4RN, United Kingdom, (Dial from U.S. (212) 216-7800), (Fax from U.S. (212) 564-7854), www.tandf.co.uk; *The Europa World Year Book.*

United Nations Statistics Division, New York, NY 10017, (800) 253-9646, Fax: (212) 963-4116, http://unstats.un.org; *Statistical Yearbook* and *Trends in Europe and North America: The Statistical Yearbook of the ECE 2005.*

United Nations World Tourism Organization (UNWTO), Capitan Haya 42, 28020 Madrid, Spain, www.world-tourism.org; *Tourism Market Trends 2004 - Europe* and *Yearbook of Tourism Statistics.*

The World Bank, 1818 H Street, NW, Washington, DC 20433, (202) 473-1000, Fax: (202) 477-6391, www.worldbank.org; *Denmark.*

DENMARK - TRADE

See DENMARK - INTERNATIONAL TRADE

DENMARK - TRANSPORTATION

Central Intelligence Agency, Office of Public Affairs, Washington, DC 20505, (703) 482-0623, Fax: (703) 482-1739, www.cia.gov; *The World Factbook.*

Euromonitor International, Inc., 224 S. Michigan Avenue, Suite 1500, Chicago, IL 60604, (312) 922-1115, Fax: (312) 922-1157, www.euromonitor.com; *World Marketing Data and Statistics.*

European Union, Delegation of the European Commission to the United States, 2300 M Street, NW, Washington, DC 20037, (202) 862-9500, Fax: (202) 429-1766, www.eurunion.org; *Regions - Statistical Yearbook 2006* and *Statistical Overview of Transport in the European Union (Data 1970-2001).*

Eurostat, Batiment Jean Monnet, Rue Alcide de Gasperi, L-2920 Luxembourg, http://epp.eurostat.ec.europa.eu; *Eurostat Yearbook 2006-2007; Regional Passenger and Freight Air Transport in Europe in 2006;* and *Regional Road and Rail Transport Networks.*

M.E. Sharpe, 80 Business Park Drive, Armonk, NY 10504, (800) 541-6563, Fax: (914) 273-2106, www.mesharpe.com; *The Illustrated Book of World Rankings.*

Nordic Council of Ministers, Store Strandstraede 18, DK-1255 Copenhagen K, Denmark, www.norden.org; *Nordic Statistical Yearbook 2004-2006.*

Palgrave Macmillan Ltd., Houndmills, Basingstoke, Hampshire, RG21 6XS, England, (Telephone in U.S. (888) 330-8477), (Fax in U.S. (800) 672-2054), www.palgrave.com; *The Statesman's Yearbook 2008.*

Platts, 2 Penn Plaza, 25th Floor, New York, NY 10121-2298, (212) 904-3070, www.platts.com; *Energy Economist.*

Taylor and Francis Group, An Informa Business, 2 Park Square, Milton Park, Abingdon, Oxford OX14 4RN, United Kingdom, (Dial from U.S. (212) 216-7800), (Fax from U.S. (212) 564-7854), www.tandf.co.uk; *The Europa World Year Book.*

United Nations Statistics Division, New York, NY 10017, (800) 253-9646, Fax: (212) 963-4116, http://unstats.un.org; *Energy Statistics Yearbook 2003; Human Development Report 2006;* and *Trends in Europe and North America: The Statistical Yearbook of the ECE 2005.*

The World Bank, 1818 H Street, NW, Washington, DC 20433, (202) 473-1000, Fax: (202) 477-6391, www.worldbank.org; *Denmark.*

DENMARK - TURKEYS

See DENMARK - LIVESTOCK

DENMARK - UNEMPLOYMENT

Central Intelligence Agency, Office of Public Affairs, Washington, DC 20505, (703) 482-0623, Fax: (703) 482-1739, www.cia.gov; *The World Factbook.*

Euromonitor International, Inc., 224 S. Michigan Avenue, Suite 1500, Chicago, IL 60604, (312) 922-1115, Fax: (312) 922-1157, www.euromonitor.com; *European Marketing Data and Statistics 2008.*

European Union, Delegation of the European Commission to the United States, 2300 M Street, NW, Washington, DC 20037, (202) 862-9500, Fax: (202) 429-1766, www.eurunion.org; *European Union Labour Force Survey; Eurostatistics: Data for Short-Term Economic Analysis (2007 edition);* and *Regions - Statistical Yearbook 2006.*

Eurostat, Batiment Jean Monnet, Rue Alcide de Gasperi, L-2920 Luxembourg, http://epp.eurostat.ec.europa.eu; *Eurostat Yearbook 2006-2007.*

International Labour Office, I.L.O. Publications, 4 route des Morillons, CH-1211 Geneva 22, Switzerland, (Telephone in U.S. (202) 653-7652), (Fax in U.S. (202) 653-7687), www.ilo.org; *Yearbook of Labour Statistics 2006.*

Nordic Council of Ministers, Store Strandstraede 18, DK-1255 Copenhagen K, Denmark, www.norden.org; *Nordic Statistical Yearbook 2004-2006.*

Organisation for Economic Cooperation and Development (OECD), 2 rue Andre Pascal, F-75775 Paris Cedex 16, France, (Telephone in U.S. (202) 785-6323), (Fax in U.S. (202) 785-0350), www.oecd.org; *Labour Force Statistics: 1986-2005, 2007 Edition; OECD Composite Leading Indicators (CLIs), Updated September 2007; OECD Economic Outlook 2008; OECD Economic Survey - Denmark 2008;* and *OECD Employment Outlook 2007.*

Palgrave Macmillan Ltd., Houndmills, Basingstoke, Hampshire, RG21 6XS, England, (Telephone in U.S. (888) 330-8477), (Fax in U.S. (800) 672-2054), www.palgrave.com; *The Statesman's Yearbook 2008.*

United Nations Statistics Division, New York, NY 10017, (800) 253-9646, Fax: (212) 963-4116, http://unstats.un.org; *Statistical Yearbook* and *Trends in Europe and North America: The Statistical Yearbook of the ECE 2005.*

DENMARK - URANIUM PRODUCTION AND CONSUMPTION

See DENMARK - MINERAL INDUSTRIES

DENMARK - VITAL STATISTICS

Danish Energy Authority, Amaliegade 44, DK 1256 Copenhagen K, Denmark, www.ens.dk; *Energy in Denmark 2006* and *Energy Statistics 2006.*

Eurostat, Batiment Jean Monnet, Rue Alcide de Gasperi, L-2920 Luxembourg, http://epp.eurostat.ec.europa.eu; *Eurostat Yearbook 2006-2007.*

Nordic Council of Ministers, Store Strandstraede 18, DK-1255 Copenhagen K, Denmark, www.norden.org; *Nordic Statistical Yearbook 2004-2006.*

Palgrave Macmillan Ltd., Houndmills, Basingstoke, Hampshire, RG21 6XS, England, (Telephone in U.S. (888) 330-8477), (Fax in U.S. (800) 672-2054), www.palgrave.com; *The Statesman's Yearbook 2008.*

United Nations Statistics Division, New York, NY 10017, (800) 253-9646, Fax: (212) 963-4116, http://unstats.un.org; *Statistical Yearbook.*

World Health Organization (WHO), Avenue Appia 20, 1211 Geneve 27, Switzerland, (Telephone in U.S. (212) 331-9081), www.who.int; *World Health Report 2006.*

DENMARK - WAGES

Euromonitor International, Inc., 224 S. Michigan Avenue, Suite 1500, Chicago, IL 60604, (312) 922-1115, Fax: (312) 922-1157, www.euromonitor.com; *European Marketing Data and Statistics 2008.*

European Union, Delegation of the European Commission to the United States, 2300 M Street, NW, Washington, DC 20037, (202) 862-9500, Fax: (202) 429-1766, www.eurunion.org; *Agriculture in the European Union: Statistical and Economic Information 2006* and *Eurostatistics: Data for Short-Term Economic Analysis (2007 edition).*

Eurostat, Batiment Jean Monnet, Rue Alcide de Gasperi, L-2920 Luxembourg, http://epp.eurostat.ec.europa.eu; *Eurostat Yearbook 2006-2007.*

International Labour Office, I.L.O. Publications, 4 route des Morillons, CH-1211 Geneva 22, Switzerland, (Telephone in U.S. (202) 653-7652), (Fax in U.S. (202) 653-7687), www.ilo.org; *Yearbook of Labour Statistics 2006.*

Nordic Council of Ministers, Store Strandstraede 18, DK-1255 Copenhagen K, Denmark, www.norden.org; *Nordic Statistical Yearbook 2004-2006.*

Organisation for Economic Cooperation and Development (OECD), 2 rue Andre Pascal, F-75775 Paris Cedex 16, France, (Telephone in U.S. (202) 785-6323), (Fax in U.S. (202) 785-0350), www.oecd.org; *ICT Sector Data and Metadata by Country; OECD Economic Outlook 2008;* and STructural ANalysis (STAN) database.

United Nations Statistics Division, New York, NY 10017, (800) 253-9646, Fax: (212) 963-4116, http://unstats.un.org; *Statistical Yearbook.*

The World Bank, 1818 H Street, NW, Washington, DC 20433, (202) 473-1000, Fax: (202) 477-6391, www.worldbank.org; *Denmark.*

DENMARK - WALNUT PRODUCTION

See DENMARK - CROPS

DENMARK - WEATHER

See DENMARK - CLIMATE

DENMARK - WELFARE STATE

Eurostat, Batiment Jean Monnet, Rue Alcide de Gasperi, L-2920 Luxembourg, http://epp.eurostat.ec.europa.eu; *Eurostat Yearbook 2006-2007.*

International Monetary Fund (IMF), 700 Nineteenth Street, NW, Washington, DC 20431, (202) 623-7000, Fax: (202) 623-4661, www.imf.org; *Government Finance Statistics Yearbook (2008 Edition).*

Nordic Council of Ministers, Store Strandstraede 18, DK-1255 Copenhagen K, Denmark, www.norden.org; *Nordic Statistical Yearbook 2004-2006.*

DENMARK - WHALES

See DENMARK - FISHERIES

DENMARK - WHEAT PRODUCTION

See DENMARK - CROPS

DENMARK - WHOLESALE PRICE INDEXES

Eurostat, Batiment Jean Monnet, Rue Alcide de Gasperi, L-2920 Luxembourg, http://epp.eurostat.ec.europa.eu; *Eurostat Yearbook 2006-2007.*

Nordic Council of Ministers, Store Strandstraede 18, DK-1255 Copenhagen K, Denmark, www.norden.org; *Nordic Statistical Yearbook 2004-2006.*

United Nations Statistics Division, New York, NY 10017, (800) 253-9646, Fax: (212) 963-4116, http://unstats.un.org; *Statistical Yearbook.*

DENMARK - WHOLESALE TRADE

Eurostat, Batiment Jean Monnet, Rue Alcide de Gasperi, L-2920 Luxembourg, http://epp.eurostat.ec.europa.eu; *Eurostat Yearbook 2006-2007.*

United Nations Statistics Division, New York, NY 10017, (800) 253-9646, Fax: (212) 963-4116, http://unstats.un.org; *Statistical Yearbook.*

DENMARK - WINE PRODUCTION

See DENMARK - BEVERAGE INDUSTRY

DENMARK - WOOD AND WOOD PULP

See DENMARK - FORESTS AND FORESTRY

DENMARK - WOOD PRODUCTS

Eurostat, Batiment Jean Monnet, Rue Alcide de Gasperi, L-2920 Luxembourg, http://epp.eurostat.ec.europa.eu; *Eurostat Yearbook 2006-2007.*

Organisation for Economic Cooperation and Development (OECD), 2 rue Andre Pascal, F-75775 Paris Cedex 16, France, (Telephone in U.S. (202) 785-6323), (Fax in U.S. (202) 785-0350), www.oecd.org; *International Trade by Commodity Statistics (ITCS)* and STructural ANalysis (STAN) database.

DENMARK - WOOL PRODUCTION

See DENMARK - TEXTILE INDUSTRY

DENMARK - YARN PRODUCTION

See DENMARK - TEXTILE INDUSTRY

DENMARK - ZINC AND ZINC ORE

See DENMARK - MINERAL INDUSTRIES

DENMARK - ZOOS

UNESCO Institute for Statistics, C.P. 6128 Succursale Centre-Ville, Montreal, Quebec, H3C 3J7 Canada, (Dial from U.S. (514) 343-6880), (Fax from U.S. (514) 343 6882), www.uis.unesco.org; *Statistical Tables.*

DENTISTS

U.S. Bureau of Labor Statistics (BLS), Postal Square Building, 2 Massachusetts Avenue, NE, Washington, DC 20212-0001, (202) 691-5200, Fax: (202) 691-6325, www.bls.gov; *Employment and Earnings (EE).*

DENTISTS - CHARGES AND EXPENDITURES FOR

Centers for Medicare and Medicaid Services (CMS), U.S. Department of Health and Human Services (HHS), 7500 Security Boulevard, Baltimore, MD 21244-1850, (410) 786-3000, http://cms.hhs.gov; *Health Care Financing Review.*

U.S. Bureau of Labor Statistics (BLS), Postal Square Building, 2 Massachusetts Avenue, NE, Washington, DC 20212-0001, (202) 691-5200, Fax: (202) 691-6325, www.bls.gov; *Consumer Price Index Detailed Report.*

DENTISTS - DENTAL SCHOOLS - STUDENTS, AND GRADUATES

National Center for Education Statistics (NCES), 1990 K Street, NW, Washington, DC 20006, (202) 502-7300, http://nces.ed.gov; *Digest of Education Statistics 2007.*

National Center for Health Statistics (NCHS), Centers for Disease Control and Prevention (CDC), U.S. Department of Health and Human Services (HHS), 3311 Toledo Road, Hyattsville, MD 20782, (866) 232-4636, www.cdc.gov/nchs; *Health, United States, 2006, with Chartbook on Trends in the Health of Americans with Special Feature on Pain.*

DENTISTS - MEDICAID PAYMENTS AND RECIPIENTS

Centers for Medicare and Medicaid Services (CMS), U.S. Department of Health and Human Services (HHS), 7500 Security Boulevard, Baltimore, MD 21244-1850, (410) 786-3000, http://cms.hhs.gov; The Medicare Current Beneficiary Survey (MCBS) (web app).

DENTISTS - OFFICES

U.S. Census Bureau, 4700 Silver Hill Road, Washington DC 20233-0001, (301) 763-3030, www.census.gov; unpublished data.

U.S. Census Bureau, Center for Economic Studies, 4600 Silver Hill Road, Washington DC 20233, (301) 457-1235, www.ces.census.gov; *2002 Economic Census, Professional, Scientific and Technical Services.*

U.S. Census Bureau, Company Statistics Division, 4700 Silver Hill Road, Washington DC 20233-0001, (301) 763-3030, www.census.gov/csd/; *County Business Patterns 2004* and *Current Business Reports.*

DEPARTMENT STORES - EARNINGS

Office of Trade and Industry Information (OTII), Manufacturing and Services, International Trade Administration, U.S. Department of Commerce, 1401 Constitution Ave, NW, Washington, DC 20230, (800) USA TRAD(E), http://trade.gov/index.asp; *TradeStats Express.*

U.S. Census Bureau, Center for Economic Studies, 4600 Silver Hill Road, Washington DC 20233, (301) 457-1235, www.ces.census.gov; *2002 Economic Census, Retail Trade* and *2002 Economic Census, Wholesale Trade.*

U.S. Census Bureau, Company Statistics Division, 4700 Silver Hill Road, Washington DC 20233-0001, (301) 763-3030, www.census.gov/csd/; *County Business Patterns 2004.*

DEPARTMENT STORES - EMPLOYEES

U.S. Census Bureau, Center for Economic Studies, 4600 Silver Hill Road, Washington DC 20233, (301) 457-1235, www.ces.census.gov; *2002 Economic Census, Retail Trade.*

U.S. Census Bureau, Company Statistics Division, 4700 Silver Hill Road, Washington DC 20233-0001, (301) 763-3030, www.census.gov/csd/; *County Business Patterns 2004.*

DEPARTMENT STORES - ESTABLISHMENTS

Office of Trade and Industry Information (OTII), Manufacturing and Services, International Trade Administration, U.S. Department of Commerce, 1401 Constitution Ave, NW, Washington, DC 20230, (800) USA TRAD(E), http://trade.gov/index.asp; *TradeStats Express.*

U.S. Census Bureau, Center for Economic Studies, 4600 Silver Hill Road, Washington DC 20233, (301) 457-1235, www.ces.census.gov; *2002 Economic Census, Retail Trade.*

U.S. Census Bureau, Company Statistics Division, 4700 Silver Hill Road, Washington DC 20233-0001, (301) 763-3030, www.census.gov/csd/; *County Business Patterns 2004.*

DEPARTMENT STORES - INVENTORIES

Office of Trade and Industry Information (OTII), Manufacturing and Services, International Trade Administration, U.S. Department of Commerce, 1401 Constitution Ave, NW, Washington, DC 20230, (800) USA TRAD(E), http://trade.gov/index.asp; *TradeStats Express.*

U.S. Census Bureau, 4700 Silver Hill Road, Washington DC 20233-0001, (301) 763-3030, www.census.gov; unpublished data.

U.S. Census Bureau, Center for Economic Studies, 4600 Silver Hill Road, Washington DC 20233, (301) 457-1235, www.ces.census.gov; *2002 Economic Census, Retail Trade.*

DEPARTMENT STORES - PRODUCTIVITY

U.S. Bureau of Labor Statistics (BLS), Postal Square Building, 2 Massachusetts Avenue, NE, Washington, DC 20212-0001, (202) 691-5200, Fax: (202) 691-6325, www.bls.gov; *Current Employment Statistics Survey (CES).*

DEPARTMENT STORES - SALES

Claritas, 5375 Mira Sorrento Place, Suite 400, San Diego, CA 92121, (800) 866-6520, Fax: (858) 550-5800, www.claritas.com; *Consumer Buying Power.*

Office of Trade and Industry Information (OTII), Manufacturing and Services, International Trade Administration, U.S. Department of Commerce, 1401 Constitution Ave, NW, Washington, DC 20230, (800) USA TRAD(E), http://trade.gov/index.asp; *TradeStats Express.*

U.S. Census Bureau, 4700 Silver Hill Road, Washington DC 20233-0001, (301) 763-3030, www.census.gov; unpublished data.

U.S. Census Bureau, Center for Economic Studies, 4600 Silver Hill Road, Washington DC 20233, (301) 457-1235, www.ces.census.gov; *2002 Economic Census, Retail Trade.*

U.S. Census Bureau, Company Statistics Division, 4700 Silver Hill Road, Washington DC 20233-0001, (301) 763-3030, www.census.gov/csd/; *Current Business Reports.*

DEPOSITS

See BANKS, COMMERCIAL - DEPOSITS

DERMATOLOGISTS

American Medical Association, 515 North State Street, Chicago, IL 60610, (800) 621-8335, www.ama-assn.org; *Physician Characteristics and Distribution in the United States, 2008* and *Physician Compensation and Production Survey: 2007 Report Based on 2006 Data.*

DESERT

International Institute for Environment and Development (IIED), 3 Endsleigh Street, London, England, WC1H 0DD, United Kingdom, www.iied.org; *Environment Urbanization* and *Haramata - Bulletin of the Drylands.*

United Nations Environment Programme (UNEP), PO Box 30552, Nairobi, Kenya, www.unep.org; *World Atlas of Desertification.*

DIABETES

Australian Institute of Health and Welfare (AIHW), GPO Box 570, Canberra ACT 2601, Australia, www.aihw.gov.au; *Diabetes: Australian Facts 2008.*

Bernan Essential Government Publications, 4611-F Assembly Drive, Lanham MD, 20706-4391, (301) 459-2255, Fax: (800) 865-3450, www.bernan.com; *Vital Statistics of the United States: Births, Life Expectancy, Deaths, and Selected Health Data.*

National Center for Chronic Disease Prevention and Health Promotion (NCCDPHP), Centers for Disease

Control and Prevention (CDC), 4770 Buford Hwy, NE, MS K-40, Atlanta, GA 30341-3717, (404) 639-3311, www.cdc.gov/nccdphp; *Diabetes: Disabling, Deadly, and on the Rise* and *Racial and Ethnic Approaches to Community Health (REACH 2010): Addressing Disparities in Health.*

National Center for Health Statistics (NCHS), Centers for Disease Control and Prevention (CDC), U.S. Department of Health and Human Services (HHS), 3311 Toledo Road, Hyattsville, MD 20782, (866) 232-4636, www.cdc.gov/nchs; *Faststats A to Z; National Vital Statistics Reports (NVSR); Vital Statistics of the United States (VSUS);* and unpublished data.

Netherlands Institute for Health Services Research (NIVEL), PO Box 1568, 3500 BN Utrecht, The Netherlands, www.nivel.eu; *Health Care Use by Diabetic Patients in the Netherlands: Patterns and Predicting Factors.*

DIAGNOSTIC HEALTH PROCEDURES

National Center for Health Statistics (NCHS), Centers for Disease Control and Prevention (CDC), U.S. Department of Health and Human Services (HHS), 3311 Toledo Road, Hyattsville, MD 20782, (866) 232-4636, www.cdc.gov/nchs; unpublished data.

DIAMONDS

U.S. Department of the Interior (DOI), U.S. Geological Survey (USGS), Office of Minerals Information, 12201 Sunrise Valley Drive, Reston, VA 20192, Mr. Kenneth A. Beckman, (703) 648-4916, Fax: (703) 648-4995, http://minerals.usgs.gov/minerals; *Mineral Commodity Summaries* and *Minerals Yearbook.*

DIAMONDS - INTERNATIONAL TRADE

U.S. Census Bureau, Foreign Trade Division, 4700 Silver Hill Road, Washington DC 20233-0001, (301) 763-3030, www.census.gov/foreign-trade/www/; *U.S. International Trade in Goods and Services.*

DIAMONDS - WORLD PRODUCTION

U.S. Department of the Interior (DOI), U.S. Geological Survey (USGS), Office of Minerals Information, 12201 Sunrise Valley Drive, Reston, VA 20192, Mr. Kenneth A. Beckman, (703) 648-4916, Fax: (703) 648-4995, http://minerals.usgs.gov/minerals; *Mineral Commodity Summaries* and *Minerals Yearbook.*

DIATOMITE

U.S. Department of the Interior (DOI), U.S. Geological Survey (USGS), Office of Minerals Information, 12201 Sunrise Valley Drive, Reston, VA 20192, Mr. Kenneth A. Beckman, (703) 648-4916, Fax: (703) 648-4995, http://minerals.usgs.gov/minerals; *Mineral Commodity Summaries* and *Minerals Yearbook.*

DIETICIANS AND THERAPISTS

U.S. Bureau of Labor Statistics (BLS), Postal Square Building, 2 Massachusetts Avenue, NE, Washington, DC 20212-0001, (202) 691-5200, Fax: (202) 691-6325, www.bls.gov; *Employment and Earnings (EE)* and unpublished data.

DIPHTHERIA

Centers for Disease Control and Prevention (CDC), U.S. Department of Health and Human Services (HHS), 1600 Clifton Road, Atlanta, GA 30333, (800) 311-3435, www.cdc.gov; *Immunization Coverage in the U.S.* and *Morbidity and Mortality Weekly Report (MMWR).*

National Center for Health Statistics (NCHS), Centers for Disease Control and Prevention (CDC), U.S. Department of Health and Human Services (HHS), 3311 Toledo Road, Hyattsville, MD 20782, (866) 232-4636, www.cdc.gov/nchs; *2005 National Immunization Survey (NIS).*

DIRECT MAIL ADVERTISING EXPENDITURES

McCann Erickson Worldwide, 622 Third Avenue, New York, NY 10017, (646) 865-2000, www.mccann.com; unpublished data.

DISABILITY

British Columbia Vital Statistics Agency, PO Box 9657 STN PROV GOVT, Victoria BC V8W 9P3, Canada, (Dial from U.S. (250) 952-2681), (Fax from U.S. (250) 952-2527), www.vs.gov.bc.ca; *Health Status Registry Report, 2005.*

LISU, Holywell Park, Loughborough University, Leicestershire, LE11 3TU, United Kingdom, www.lboro.ac.uk/departments/dis/lisu; *Availability of Accessible Publications.*

National Center for Health Statistics (NCHS), Centers for Disease Control and Prevention (CDC), U.S. Department of Health and Human Services (HHS), 3311 Toledo Road, Hyattsville, MD 20782, (866) 232-4636, www.cdc.gov/nchs; *Faststats A to Z.*

National Criminal Justice Reference Service (NCJRS), PO Box 6000, Rockville, MD 20849-6000, (800) 851-3420, Fax: (301) 519-5212, www.ncjrs.org; *Presence of Learning Disabled Youth in Our Juvenile Institutions: Excusable or Gross Negligence?*

National Safety Council (NSC), 1121 Spring Lake Drive, Itasca, IL 60143-3201, (630) 285-1121, www.nsc.org; *Injury Facts.*

U.S. Census Bureau, 4700 Silver Hill Road, Washington DC 20233-0001, (301) 763-3030, www.census.gov; unpublished data.

U.S. Census Bureau, Population Division, 4700 Silver Hill Road, Washington DC 20233-0001, (301) 763-3030, www.census.gov/population/www/; *Current Population Reports.*

U.S. Department of Education (ED), Office of Special Education and Rehabilitative Services (OSERS), 400 Maryland Ave., SW, Washington, DC 20202-7100, (202) 245-7468, www.ed.gov/osers; *Twenty-Seventh Annual Report to Congress on the Implementation of the Individuals with Disabilities Education Act.*

DISABILITY - BENEFICIARIES

National Center for Children in Poverty (NCCP), 215 W. 125th Street, 3rd Floor, New York, NY 10027, (646) 284-9600, Fax: (646) 284-9623, www.nccp.org; *Social Security Resources.*

Social Security Administration (SSA), Office of Public Inquiries, Windsor Park Building, 6401 Security Boulevard, Baltimore, MD 21235, (800) 772-1213, www.ssa.gov; *Annual Statistical Supplement, 2007* and unpublished data.

DISABILITY - BENEFITS PAID

Social Security Administration (SSA), Office of Public Inquiries, Windsor Park Building, 6401 Security Boulevard, Baltimore, MD 21235, (800) 772-1213, www.ssa.gov; *2006 Annual Report of the Board of Trustees of the Federal Old-Age and Survivors Insurance and Disability Insurance Trust Funds; Annual Statistical Supplement, 2007; Social Security Bulletin;* and unpublished data.

DISABILITY - CHILDREN

Centers for Disease Control and Prevention (CDC), U.S. Department of Health and Human Services (HHS), 1600 Clifton Road, Atlanta, GA 30333, (800) 311-3435, www.cdc.gov; *Morbidity and Mortality Weekly Report (MMWR).*

DISABILITY - GOVERNMENT TRANSFER PAYMENTS

Bureau of Economic Analysis (BEA), U.S. Department of Commerce (DOC), 1441 L Street NW, Washington, DC 20230, (202) 606-9900, www.bea.gov; State Annual Personal Income (SPI) (web app).

DISABILITY - MEDICAID PAYMENTS AND RECIPIENTS

Centers for Medicare and Medicaid Services (CMS), U.S. Department of Health and Human Services (HHS), 7500 Security Boulevard, Baltimore, MD 21244-1850, (410) 786-3000, http://cms.hhs.gov; The Medicare Current Beneficiary Survey (MCBS) (web app).

U.S. Census Bureau, 4700 Silver Hill Road, Washington DC 20233-0001, (301) 763-3030, www.census.gov; unpublished data.

DISABILITY - PAYMENTS

Social Security Administration (SSA), Office of Public Inquiries, Windsor Park Building, 6401 Security Boulevard, Baltimore, MD 21235, (800) 772-1213, www.ssa.gov; *Social Security Bulletin* and unpublished data.

DISABILITY - PERSONS WITH DISABILITY

Population Reference Bureau, 1875 Connecticut Avenue, NW, Suite 520, Washington, DC, 20009-5728, (800) 877-9881, Fax: (202) 328-3937, www.prb.org; *The American People Series.*

U.S. Census Bureau, 4700 Silver Hill Road, Washington DC 20233-0001, (301) 763-3030, www.census.gov; American FactFinder (web app); *County and City Data Book 2007; State and County QuickFacts;* and unpublished data.

U.S. Census Bureau, Demographic Surveys Division, 4700 Silver Hill Road, Washington DC 20233-0001, (301) 763-3030, www.census.gov; *Demographic Profiles: 100-percent and Sample Data.*

U.S. Census Bureau, Population Division, 4700 Silver Hill Road, Washington DC 20233-0001, (301) 763-3030, www.census.gov/population/www/; *Census 2000 Profiles of General Demographic Characteristics.*

U.S. Department of Education (ED), Office of Special Education and Rehabilitative Services (OSERS), 400 Maryland Ave., SW, Washington, DC 20202-7100, (202) 245-7468, www.ed.gov/osers; *Twenty-Seventh Annual Report to Congress on the Implementation of the Individuals with Disabilities Education Act.*

DISABILITY - POVERTY

U.S. Census Bureau, Population Division, 4700 Silver Hill Road, Washington DC 20233-0001, (301) 763-3030, www.census.gov/population/www/; *Current Population Reports.*

DISABILITY - PUBLIC ASSISTANCE RECIPIENTS AND/OR PAYMENTS

Social Security Administration (SSA), Office of Public Inquiries, Windsor Park Building, 6401 Security Boulevard, Baltimore, MD 21235, (800) 772-1213, www.ssa.gov; *Annual Statistical Supplement, 2007* and *Social Security Bulletin.*

U.S. Census Bureau, 4700 Silver Hill Road, Washington DC 20233-0001, (301) 763-3030, www.census.gov; unpublished data.

DISABILITY - SOCIAL SECURITY RECIPIENTS

National Center for Children in Poverty (NCCP), 215 W. 125th Street, 3rd Floor, New York, NY 10027, (646) 284-9600, Fax: (646) 284-9623, www.nccp.org; *Social Security Resources.*

Social Security Administration (SSA), Office of Public Inquiries, Windsor Park Building, 6401 Security Boulevard, Baltimore, MD 21235, (800) 772-1213, www.ssa.gov; *Annual Statistical Supplement, 2007; Social Security Bulletin;* and unpublished data.

DISABILITY - STUDENTS WITH DISABILITIES

National Center for Education Statistics (NCES), 1990 K Street, NW, Washington, DC 20006, (202) 502-7300, http://nces.ed.gov; *Profile of Undergraduates in U.S. Postsecondary Education Institutions: 2003-04, With a Special Analysis of Community College Students.*

U.S. Department of Education (ED), Office of Special Education and Rehabilitative Services (OSERS), 400 Maryland Ave., SW, Washington, DC 20202-7100, (202) 245-7468, www.ed.gov/osers;

Twenty-Seventh Annual Report to Congress on the Implementation of the Individuals with Disabilities Education Act.

DISABILITY - SUPPLEMENTAL SECURITY INCOME RECIPIENTS AND PAYMENTS

Social Security Administration (SSA), Office of Public Inquiries, Windsor Park Building, 6401 Security Boulevard, Baltimore, MD 21235, (800) 772-1213, www.ssa.gov; *Annual Statistical Supplement, 2007* and *Social Security Bulletin.*

DISABILITY - VETERANS RECEIVING COMPENSATION

U.S. Department of Veterans Affairs (VA), 810 Vermont Avenue, NW, Washington, DC 20420-0001, (202) 273-5400, www.va.gov; *Annual Accountability Report Statistical Appendix; Fact Sheets;* and unpublished data.

DISABILITY INSURANCE TRUST FUND (SOCIAL SECURITY)

The Office of Management and Budget (OMB), 725 17th Street, NW, Washington, DC 20503, (202) 395-3080, Fax: (202) 395-3888, www.whitehouse.gov/omb; *Analytical Perspectives, Budget of the United States Government, Fiscal Year 2009.*

Social Security Administration (SSA), Office of Public Inquiries, Windsor Park Building, 6401 Security Boulevard, Baltimore, MD 21235, (800) 772-1213, www.ssa.gov; *2006 Annual Report of the Board of Trustees of the Federal Old-Age and Survivors Insurance and Disability Insurance Trust Funds* and *Social Security Bulletin.*

U.S. Census Bureau, Population Division, 4700 Silver Hill Road, Washington DC 20233-0001, (301) 763-3030, www.census.gov/population/www/; *Current Population Reports.*

DISAPPEARED PERSONS

Federal Bureau of Investigation (FBI), J. Edgar Hoover Building, 935 Pennsylvania Avenue, NW, Washington, DC 20535-0001, (202) 324-3000, www.fbi.gov; *NCIC Missing Person and Unidentified Person Statistics for 2007.*

DISASTERS (TORNADOES, FLOODS, ETC.)

The Brookings Institution, 1775 Massachusetts Avenue, NW, Washington, DC 20036, (202) 797-6000, Fax: (202) 797-6004, www.brook.edu; *Katrina Index: Tracking Variables of Post-Katrina Recovery* and *Special Edition of the Katrina Index: A One-Year Review of Key Indicators of Recovery in Post-Storm New Orleans.*

Center for Research on the Epidemiology of Disasters (CRED), Universite Catholique de Louvain, Ecole de Sante Publique, 30.94 Clos Chapelle-aux-Champs, 1200 Brussels, Belgium, www.cred.be; *An Analytical Review of Selected Data Sets on Natural Disasters and Impacts;* Complex Emergency Database (CE-DAT): A Database on the Human Impact of Complex Emergencies; *EM-DAT: The International Disaster Database; Quality and Accuracy of Disaster Data: A Comparative Analysis of Three Global Data Sets; Thirty Years of Natural Disasters 1974-2003: The Numbers;* and *Three Decades of Floods in Europe: A Preliminary Analysis of EMDAT Data.*

Eurostat, Batiment Jean Monnet, Rue Alcide de Gasperi, L-2920 Luxembourg, http://epp.eurostat.ec.europa.eu; *Environmental Protection Expenditure in Europe.*

International Organization for Migration (IOM), 17, Route des Morillons, CH-1211 Geneva 19, Switzerland, www.iom.int; *Migration, Development and Natural Disasters: Insights from the Indian Ocean Tsunami.*

National Center for Children in Poverty (NCCP), 215 W. 125th Street, 3rd Floor, New York, NY 10027, (646) 284-9600, Fax: (646) 284-9623, www.nccp.org; *Child Poverty in 21st Century America* and *Child Poverty in States Hit by Hurricane Katrina.*

National Climatic Data Center (NCDC), National Oceanic and Atmospheric Administration (NOAA), Federal Building, 151 Patton Avenue, Asheville, NC 28801-5001, (828) 271-4800, Fax: (828) 271-4876, www.ncdc.noaa.gov; *Billion Dollar U.S. Weather Disasters, 1980-2007* and *Storm Data 2006.*

National Oceanic and Atmospheric Administration (NOAA), 1401 Constitution Avenue, NW, Room 6217, Washington, DC 20230, (202) 482-6090, Fax: (202) 482-3154, www.noaa.gov; *The Deadliest, Costliest, and Most Intense United States Tropical Cyclones from 1851 to 2006* and *Economic Statistics for NOAA.*

Netherlands Institute for Health Services Research (NIVEL), PO Box 1568, 3500 BN Utrecht, The Netherlands, www.nivel.eu; *Health Problems of Victims Before and After Disaster: A Longitudinal Study in General Practice.*

U.S. Census Bureau, Center for Economic Studies, 4600 Silver Hill Road, Washington DC 20233, (301) 457-1235, www.ces.census.gov; *The Impact of Hurricanes Katrina, Rita and Wilma on Business Establishments: A GIS Approach.*

U.S. Department of Labor (DOL), Bureau of Labor Statistics (BLS), Postal Square Building, 2 Massachusetts Avenue, NE, Washington, DC 20212-0001, (202) 691-5200, Fax: (202) 691-6325, www.bls.gov; *Hurricane Information: Katrina and Rita.*

United Nations Inter-Agency Secretariat of the International Strategy for Disaster Reduction (UN/ISDR), Palais des Nations, CH 1211 Geneva 10, Switzerland, www.unisdr.org; *Disaster Statistics 1991-2005.*

DISCOUNT RATES - FEDERAL RESERVE BANK OF NEW YORK

Board of Governors of the Federal Reserve System, Constitution Avenue, NW, Washington, DC 20551, (202) 452-3000, www.federalreserve.gov; *Federal Reserve Bulletin* and *Statistical Digest.*

DISCRIMINATION

Federal Bureau of Investigation (FBI), J. Edgar Hoover Building, 935 Pennsylvania Avenue, NW, Washington, DC 20535-0001, (202) 324-3000, www.fbi.gov; *FBI Equal Employment Opportunity Report 1999-2004.*

State of Connecticut, Department of Economic and Community Development (DECD), 505 Hudson Street, Hartford, CT 06106-7107, (860) 270-8000, www.ct.gov/ecd/; *State of Connecticut Analysis of Impediments to Fair Housing Choice Update.*

U.S. Equal Employment Opportunity Commission (EEOC), 1801 L Street, N.W., Washington, D.C. 20507, (800) 669-4000, www.eeoc.gov; *Annual Report on the Federal Work Force, Fiscal Year 2005; EEOC Litigation Statistics, Federal Year 1992 through Federal Year 2005; Equal Employment Opportunity Data Posted Pursuant to the No Fear Act;* and *Information on the Census 2000 Special EEO File.*

DISEASES

Australian Institute of Health and Welfare (AIHW), GPO Box 570, Canberra ACT 2601, Australia, www.aihw.gov.au; *Diabetes: Australian Facts 2008* and *Indicators for Chronic Diseases and Their Determinants 2008.*

Caribbean Epidemiology Centre (CAREC), 16-18 Jamaica Boulevard, Federation Park, PO Box 164, Port of Spain, Republic of Trinidad and Tobago, (Dial from U.S. (868) 622-4261), (Fax from U.S. (868) 622-2792), www.carec.org; *20 Years of the HIV/AIDS Epidemic in the Caribbean* and AIDS Statistics.

Centers for Disease Control and Prevention (CDC), U.S. Department of Health and Human Services (HHS), 1600 Clifton Road, Atlanta, GA 30333, (800) 311-3435, www.cdc.gov; *Morbidity and Mortality Weekly Report (MMWR)* and *Summary of Notifiable Diseases, United States, 2006.*

Environmental Defense Fund, 257 Park Avenue South, New York, NY 10010, (800) 684-3322, www.edf.org; *Smokestacks on Rails: Locomotive Pollution Impacts Public Health.*

EpiNorth, c/o Norwegian Institute of Public Health, PO Box 4404 Nydalen, N-0430 Oslo, Norway, www.epinorth.org; www.epinorth.org.

European Centre for Disease Prevention and Control (ECDC), 171 83 Stockholm, Sweden, www.ecdc.europa.eu; *Avian Influenza A/H5N1 in Bathing and Potable (Drinking) Water and Risks to Human Health; The Community Summary Report on Trends and Sources of Zoonoses, Zoonotic Agents, Antimicrobial resistance and Foodborne outbreaks in the European Union in 2006; The ECDC Avian Influenza Portofolio; Emergence of Clostridium Difficile-Associated Disease in Canada, the United States of America and Europe; Eurosurveillance; The First European Communicable Disease Epidemiological Report; HIV Infection in Europe: 25 Years into the Pandemic; Infant and Children Seasonal Immunisation Against Influenza on a Routine Basis During Inter-pandemic Period; Pandemic Preparedness in the European Union and European Economic Area - 2007; Sudden Deaths and Influenza Vaccinations in Israel - ECDC Interim Risk Assessment; Technical Report of the Scientific Panel on Influenza in Reply to Eight Questions Concerning Avian Flu;* and *Vaccines and Immunisation - VI news.*

Health Protection Agency, 7th Floor, Holborn Gate, 330 High Holborn, London WC1V 7PP, United Kingdom, www.hpa.org.uk; *Antimicrobial Resistance in England, Wales, and Northern Ireland; Communicable Disease in London 2002-05; Foreign Travel Associated Illness, England, Wales, and Northern Ireland: 2007 Report; Fungal Diseases in the UK; Hepatitis C in England; Indications of Public Health in the English Regions: Sexual Health (November 2006); Migrant Health: Infectious Diseases in Non-UK Born Populations in England, Wales and Northern Ireland (A Baseline Report - 2006); Surveillance of Healthcare Associated Infections Report 2007; Testing Times - HIV and other Sexually Transmitted Infections in the United Kingdom: 2007;* and *Tuberculosis in the UK: Annual Report on Tuberculosis Surveillance and Control in the UK 2007.*

Health Protection Surveillance Centre (HPSC), 25-27 Middle Gardiner Street, Dublin 1, Ireland, www.ndsc.ie/hpsc; *Acute Gastroenteritis in Ireland, North and South: A Telephone Survey* and *Report on the Epidemiology of Tuberculosis in Ireland 2005.*

HealthLeaders-InterStudy, One Vantage Way, B-300, Nashville, TN 37203, (615) 385-4131, Fax: (615) 385-4979, www.hmodata.com; *Strategic Assessment of Managed Markets (SAMM).*

National Cancer Institute (NCI), National Institutes of Health (NIH), Public Inquiries Office, 6116 Executive Boulevard, Room 3036A, Bethesda, MD 20892-8322, (800) 422-6237, www.cancer.gov; *2006-2007 Annual Report to the Nation; Assessing Progress, Advancing Change: 2005-2006 Annual President's Cancer Panel; Atlas of Cancer Mortality in the United States, 1950-94; Cancer Epidemiology in Older Adolescents and Young Adults 15 to 29 Years of Age, Including SEER Incidence and Survival: 1975-2000; Cancer Research Across Borders: Second Report 2001-2002; Decades of Progress 1983 to 2003 Community Clinical Oncology Program; Pancreatic Cancer: An Agenda for Action: Report of the Pancreatic Cancer Progress Review Group, February 2001; Report of the Brain Tumor Progress Review Group, November 2000; Report of the Gynecologic Cancers Progress Review Group, November 2001; Report of the Leukemia, Lymphoma, and Myeloma Progress Review Group, May 2001; Report of the Lung Cancer Progress Review Group, August 2001; Report of the Sarcoma Progress Review Group, A Roadmap for Sarcoma Research, January 2004;* and *SEER Cancer Statistics Review, 1975-2005.*

National Center for Chronic Disease Prevention and Health Promotion (NCCDPHP), Centers for Disease Control and Prevention (CDC), 4770 Buford Hwy, NE, MS K-40, Atlanta, GA 30341-3717, (404) 639-3311, www.cdc.gov/nccdphp; *The Atlas of Heart Disease and Stroke; The Burden of Chronic Disease and the Future of Public Health; The Burden of*

Chronic Diseases and Their Risk Factors: National and State Perspectives 2004; Chronic Disease Prevention Databases; Chronic Diseases: The Leading Causes of Death; Diabetes: Disabling, Deadly, and on the Rise; and *Racial and Ethnic Approaches to Community Health (REACH 2010): Addressing Disparities in Health.*

National Center for Health Statistics (NCHS), Centers for Disease Control and Prevention (CDC), U.S. Department of Health and Human Services (HHS), 3311 Toledo Road, Hyattsville, MD 20782, (866) 232-4636, www.cdc.gov/nchs; *Faststats A to Z; Health, United States, 2006, with Chartbook on Trends in the Health of Americans with Special Feature on Pain;* and unpublished data.

National Institute for Public Health and the Environment (RIVM), PO Box 1, 3720 BA Bilthoven, The Netherlands, www.rivm.nl/en; *Disease Burden and Related Costs of Cryptosporidiosis and Giardiasis in the Netherlands* and unpublished data.

Netherlands Institute for Health Services Research (NIVEL), PO Box 1568, 3500 BN Utrecht, The Netherlands, www.nivel.eu; *Health Care Needs of Patients with Rare Diseases* and *Health Care Use by Diabetic Patients in the Netherlands: Patterns and Predicting Factors.*

Robert Koch Institute, Nordufer 20, D 13353 Berlin, Germany, www.rki.de; *EUVAC-NET Report: Pertussis-Surveillance 1998-2002* and *Health in Germany 2006.*

U.S. Department of Justice (DOJ), Bureau of Justice Statistics, 810 Seventh Street, NW, Washington, DC 20531, (202) 307-0765, www.ojp.usdoj.gov/bjs/; *Hepatitis Testing and Treatment in State Prisons.*

UNAIDS, 20, Avenue Appia, CH-1211 Geneva 27, Switzerland, www.unaids.org; *2007 AIDS Epidemic Update.*

World Health Organization (WHO), Avenue Appia 20, 1211 Geneve 27, Switzerland, (Telephone in U.S. (212) 331-9081), www.who.int; The WHO Global Atlas of Infectious Diseases.

DISEASES - DEATHS FROM

Bernan Essential Government Publications, 4611-F Assembly Drive, Lanham MD, 20706-4391, (301) 459-2255, Fax: (800) 865-3450, www.bernan.com; *Vital Statistics of the United States: Births, Life Expectancy, Deaths, and Selected Health Data.*

Centers for Disease Control and Prevention (CDC), U.S. Department of Health and Human Services (HHS), 1600 Clifton Road, Atlanta, GA 30333, (800) 311-3435, www.cdc.gov; *HIV/AIDS Surveillance Report.*

Health Protection Agency, 7th Floor, Holborn Gate, 330 High Holborn, London WC1V 7PP, United Kingdom, www.hpa.org.uk; *National Confidential Study of Deaths Following Meticillin Resistant Staphylococcus aureus (MRSA) Infection.*

National Center for Chronic Disease Prevention and Health Promotion (NCCDPHP), Centers for Disease Control and Prevention (CDC), 4770 Buford Hwy, NE, MS K-40, Atlanta, GA 30341-3717, (404) 639-3311, www.cdc.gov/nccdphp; *Actual Causes of Death in the United States; The Burden of Chronic Disease and the Future of Public Health; The Burden of Chronic Diseases and Their Risk Factors: National and State Perspectives 2004; Chronic Diseases: The Leading Causes of Death;* and *Diabetes: Disabling, Deadly, and on the Rise.*

National Center for Health Statistics (NCHS), Centers for Disease Control and Prevention (CDC), U.S. Department of Health and Human Services (HHS), 3311 Toledo Road, Hyattsville, MD 20782, (866) 232-4636, www.cdc.gov/nchs; *Faststats A to Z; National Vital Statistics Reports (NVSR); Vital Statistics of the United States (VSUS);* and unpublished data.

DISKETTES

U.S. Census Bureau, Manufacturing and Construction Division, 4600 Silver Hill Road, Washington DC 20233, (301) 763-4673, www.census.gov/mcd; *Current Industrial Reports* and *Current Industrial Reports, Manufacturing Profiles.*

DISPOSABLE PERSONAL INCOME

See also INCOME

Board of Governors of the Federal Reserve System, Constitution Avenue, NW, Washington, DC 20551, (202) 452-3000, www.federalreserve.gov; *Household Debt Service and Financial Obligations Ratios.*

Bureau of Economic Analysis (BEA), U.S. Department of Commerce (DOC), 1441 L Street NW, Washington, DC 20230, (202) 606-9900, www.bea.gov; *2007 Annual Revision of the National Income and Product Accounts (NIPA); Survey of Current Business (SCB);* and unpublished data.

DISTANCE EDUCATION

National Center for Education Statistics (NCES), 1990 K Street, NW, Washington, DC 20006, (202) 502-7300, http://nces.ed.gov; *Distance Education at Degree-Granting Postsecondary Institutions: 2000-2001; Distance Education at Degree-Granting Postsecondary Institutions: 2000-2001;* and *Distance Education at Higher Education Institutions: 2000-01.*

North Carolina Office of State Budget and Management, 116 West Jones Street, Raleigh, NC 27603-8005, (919) 804-4700, Fax: (919) 733-0640, www.osbm.state.nc.us; *North Carolina University System Study of Distance Education.*

DISTRICT COURTS, UNITED STATES

Justice Research and Statistics Association (JRSA), 777 N. Capitol Street, NE, Suite 801, Washington, DC 20002, (202) 842-9330, Fax: (202) 842-9329, www.jrsa.org; *Directory of Justice Issues in the States; Documenting the Extent and Nature of Drug and Violent Crime: Developing Jurisdiction-Specific Profiles of the Criminal Justice System; The Forum;* InfoBase of State Activities and Research (ISAR); *JRP Digest; Justice Research and Policy;* and *SAC Publication Digest.*

Office of Public Affairs, Administrative Office of the United States Courts, Washington, DC 20544, (202) 502-2600, www.uscourts.gov; *Statistical Tables for the Federal Judiciary.*

U.S. Department of Justice (DOJ), Bureau of Justice Statistics, 810 Seventh Street, NW, Washington, DC 20531, (202) 307-0765, www.ojp.usdoj.gov/bjs/; *Appeals from General Civil Trials in 46 Large Counties, 2001-2005; Civil Trial Cases and Verdicts in Large Counties, 2001; Compendium of Federal Justice Statistics, 2003; Contract Trials and Verdicts in Large Counties, 2001; Prosecutors in State Courts, 2005;* and *Punitive Damage Awards in Large Counties, 2001.*

DISTRICT OF COLUMBIA - STATE DATA CENTERS

District of Columbia, Office of Planning, 801 N. Capitol Street, NE, Suite 4000, Washington, DC 20002, (202) 442-7600, www.planning.dc.gov; State Data Center.

Metropolitan Washington Council of Governments (COG), Suite 300, 777 North Capitol Street, NE, Washington, DC 20002, (202) 962-3200, Fax: (202) 962-3201, www.mwcog.org; State Data Center.

NeighborhoodInfo DC, c/o The Urban Institute, 2100 M Street, NW, Washington, DC 20037, (202) 261-5760, Fax: (202) 872-9322, www.neighborhoodinfodc.org; State Data Center.

Office of Planning, District of Columbia, 801 North Capitol Street, NE, Suite 4000, Washington, DC 20002, (202) 442-7600, Fax: (202) 442-7637, www.planning.dc.gov; State Data Center.

DISTRICT OF COLUMBIA - PRIMARY STATISTICS SOURCES

Office of Planning, District of Columbia, 801 North Capitol Street, NE, Suite 4000, Washington, DC 20002, (202) 442-7600, Fax: (202) 442-7637, www.planning.dc.gov; *Census 2000 - Demographic Profiles; Census 2000 - Wards and Tracts;* and *Key Indicators 1990-2000.*

Office of Policy and Legislative Affairs, Executive Office of the Mayor, John A. Wilson Building, 1350 Pennsylvania Avenue, NW, Suite 511, Washington, DC 20004, (202) 727-6979, Fax: (202) 727-3765; *Indices - A Statistical Index to District of Columbia Services.*

DISTRICT OF COLUMBIA

See also - STATE DATA (FOR INDIVIDUAL STATES)

The Brookings Institution, 1775 Massachusetts Avenue, NW, Washington, DC 20036, (202) 797-6000, Fax: (202) 797-6004, www.brook.edu; *Health Status and Access to Care Among Low-Income Washington, D.C. Residents.*

Casey Trees Endowment Fund, 1425 K St NW, Suite 1050, Washington, DC, 20005, (202) 833-4010, Fax: (202) 833-4092, www.caseytrees.org; *Casey Trees Tree Map.*

District of Columbia Department of Employment Services, 609 H Street, NE, Washington, DC 20002, (202) 724-7000, http://does.dc.gov/does; *Labor Market Snap Shot; Labor Market Trends Newsletter;* and unpublished data.

District of Columbia Government, Office of Revenue Analysis, John A. Wilson Building, 1350 Pennsylvania Avenue, NW, Washington, DC 20004, (202) 727-1000, www.dc.gov; *Tax Rates and Tax Burdens in the District of Columbia - A Nationwide Comparison 2005.*

Greater Washington Initiative (GWI), 1725 I Street, NW, Washington, DC 20006, (202) 857-5999, www.greaterwashington.org; *Greater Washington Regional Report.*

Metropolitan Police Department, 300 Indiana Avenue, NW, Washington, DC 20001, (202) 727-1000, http://mpdc.dc.gov/mpdc; *Annual Index Crime Totals, 1993-2005; District Crime Data at a Glance; Live Data Feeds of Crime Incidents and Other DC Services;* and *Monthly Preliminary Crime Statistics (2005-2006).*

Office of Planning, District of Columbia, 801 North Capitol Street, NE, Suite 4000, Washington, DC 20002, (202) 442-7600, Fax: (202) 442-7637, www.planning.dc.gov; *District of Columbia Census 2000 Key Demographic Indicators; District of Columbia Population and Housing Trends;* and *Income and Poverty in the District of Columbia: 1990-2004.*

The Urban Institute, 2100 M Street, N.W., Washington, DC 20037, (202) 833-7200, www.urban.org; *Juvenile Crime in Washington, D.C.*

DIVIDENDS - CORPORATION

Bureau of Economic Analysis (BEA), U.S. Department of Commerce (DOC), 1441 L Street NW, Washington, DC 20230, (202) 606-9900, www.bea.gov; *2007 Annual Revision of the National Income and Product Accounts (NIPA)* and *Survey of Current Business (SCB).*

DIVIDENDS - INDIVIDUAL INCOME TAX RETURNS

U.S. Department of the Treasury (DOT), Internal Revenue Service (IRS), Statistics of Income Division (SIS), PO Box 2608, Washington, DC, 20013-2608, (202) 874-0410, Fax: (202) 874-0964, www.irs.ustreas.gov; *Statistics of Income Bulletin.*

DIVIDENDS - NATIONAL AND/OR PERSONAL INCOME COMPONENTS

Bureau of Economic Analysis (BEA), U.S. Department of Commerce (DOC), 1441 L Street NW, Washington, DC 20230, (202) 606-9900, www.bea.gov; *2007 Annual Revision of the National Income and Product Accounts (NIPA)* and *Survey of Current Business (SCB).*

DIVIDENDS - RAILROAD STOCK

Association of American Railroads (AAR), 50 F Street, NW, Washington, DC 20001-1564, (202)

639-2100, www.aar.org; *Analysis of Class I Railroads* and *Railroad Facts.*

DIVORCE

See MARITAL STATUS

DJIBOUTI - NATIONAL STATISTICAL OFFICE

Ministere de l'Economie, des Finances et de la Planification Charge de la Privatisation, BP 13, Djibouti, Djibouti, www.ministere-finances.dj; National Data Center.

DJIBOUTI - PRIMARY STATISTICS SOURCES

Ministere de l'Economie, des Finances et de la Planification Charge de la Privatisation, BP 13, Djibouti, Djibouti, www.ministere-finances.dj; *Annuaire Statistique* (Annual Statistics).

DJIBOUTI - AGRICULTURAL MACHINERY

United Nations Statistics Division, New York, NY 10017, (800) 253-9646, Fax: (212) 963-4116, http://unstats.un.org; *Statistical Yearbook.*

DJIBOUTI - AGRICULTURE

Economist Intelligence Unit, 111 West 57th Street, New York, NY 10019, (212) 554-0600, Fax: (212) 586-1181, www.eiu.com; *Djibouti Country Report.*

Euromonitor International, Inc., 224 S. Michigan Avenue, Suite 1500, Chicago, IL 60604, (312) 922-1115, Fax: (312) 922-1157, www.euromonitor.com; *World Marketing Data and Statistics.*

Palgrave Macmillan Ltd., Houndmills, Basingstoke, Hampshire, RG21 6XS, England, (Telephone in U.S. (888) 330-8477), (Fax in U.S. (800) 672-2054), www.palgrave.com; *The Statesman's Yearbook 2008.*

Taylor and Francis Group, An Informa Business, 2 Park Square, Milton Park, Abingdon, Oxford OX14 4RN, United Kingdom, (Dial from U.S. (212) 216-7800), (Fax from U.S. (212) 564-7854), www.tandf.co.uk; *The Europa World Year Book.*

United Nations Conference on Trade and Development (UNCTAD), DC2-1120, United Nations, New York, NY 10017, (212) 963-0027, www.unctad.org; *UNCTAD Commodity Yearbook.*

United Nations Economic Commission for Africa (ECA), PO Box 3001, Addis Ababa, Ethiopia, (Telephone in U.S. (212) 963-4957), www.uneca.org; *African Statistical Yearbook 2006.*

United Nations Food and Agricultural Organization (FAO), Viale delle Terme di Caracalla, 00100 Rome, Italy, (Dial from U.S. (202) 653-2400), (Fax from U.S. (202) 653 5760), www.fao.org; AQUASTAT; *FAO Production Yearbook 2002; FAO Trade Yearbook;* and *The State of Food and Agriculture (SOFA) 2006.*

United Nations Statistics Division, New York, NY 10017, (800) 253-9646, Fax: (212) 963-4116, http://unstats.un.org; *Statistical Yearbook* and *Survey of Economic and Social Conditions in Africa 2005.*

The World Bank, 1818 H Street, NW, Washington, DC 20433, (202) 473-1000, Fax: (202) 477-6391, www.worldbank.org; *Africa Live Database (LDB); African Development Indicators (ADI) 2007;* and *Djibouti.*

DJIBOUTI - AIRLINES

Palgrave Macmillan Ltd., Houndmills, Basingstoke, Hampshire, RG21 6XS, England, (Telephone in U.S. (888) 330-8477), (Fax in U.S. (800) 672-2054), www.palgrave.com; *The Statesman's Yearbook 2008.*

Taylor and Francis Group, An Informa Business, 2 Park Square, Milton Park, Abingdon, Oxford OX14 4RN, United Kingdom, (Dial from U.S. (212) 216-7800), (Fax from U.S. (212) 564-7854), www.tandf.co.uk; *The Europa World Year Book.*

United Nations Economic Commission for Africa (ECA), PO Box 3001, Addis Ababa, Ethiopia, (Telephone in U.S. (212) 963-4957), www.uneca.org; *African Statistical Yearbook 2006.*

DJIBOUTI - AIRPORTS

Central Intelligence Agency, Office of Public Affairs, Washington, DC 20505, (703) 482-0623, Fax: (703) 482-1739, www.cia.gov; *The World Factbook.*

DJIBOUTI - ARMED FORCES

Central Intelligence Agency, Office of Public Affairs, Washington, DC 20505, (703) 482-0623, Fax: (703) 482-1739, www.cia.gov; *The World Factbook.*

Euromonitor International, Inc., 224 S. Michigan Avenue, Suite 1500, Chicago, IL 60604, (312) 922-1115, Fax: (312) 922-1157, www.euromonitor.com; *World Marketing Data and Statistics.*

International Institute for Strategic Studies (IISS), Arundel House, 13-15 Arundel Street, Temple Place, London WC2R 3DX, England, www.iiss.org; *The Military Balance 2007.*

International Monetary Fund (IMF), 700 Nineteenth Street, NW, Washington, DC 20431, (202) 623-7000, Fax: (202) 623-4661, www.imf.org; *Government Finance Statistics Yearbook (2008 Edition).*

Palgrave Macmillan Ltd., Houndmills, Basingstoke, Hampshire, RG21 6XS, England, (Telephone in U.S. (888) 330-8477), (Fax in U.S. (800) 672-2054), www.palgrave.com; *The Statesman's Yearbook 2008.*

United Nations Statistics Division, New York, NY 10017, (800) 253-9646, Fax: (212) 963-4116, http://unstats.un.org; *Human Development Report 2006.*

DJIBOUTI - BALANCE OF PAYMENTS

African Development Bank Group, Rue Joseph Anoma, 01 BP 1387 Abidjan 01, Cote d'Ivoire, www.afdb.org; *Statistics Pocketbook 2008.*

Taylor and Francis Group, An Informa Business, 2 Park Square, Milton Park, Abingdon, Oxford OX14 4RN, United Kingdom, (Dial from U.S. (212) 216-7800), (Fax from U.S. (212) 564-7854), www.tandf.co.uk; *The Europa World Year Book.*

United Nations Conference on Trade and Development (UNCTAD), DC2-1120, United Nations, New York, NY 10017, (212) 963-0027, www.unctad.org; *Handbook of Statistics 2005.*

United Nations Economic Commission for Africa (ECA), PO Box 3001, Addis Ababa, Ethiopia, (Telephone in U.S. (212) 963-4957), www.uneca.org; *African Statistical Yearbook 2006.*

The World Bank, 1818 H Street, NW, Washington, DC 20433, (202) 473-1000, Fax: (202) 477-6391, www.worldbank.org; *Djibouti.*

DJIBOUTI - BANKS AND BANKING

Euromonitor International, Inc., 224 S. Michigan Avenue, Suite 1500, Chicago, IL 60604, (312) 922-1115, Fax: (312) 922-1157, www.euromonitor.com; *World Marketing Data and Statistics.*

Palgrave Macmillan Ltd., Houndmills, Basingstoke, Hampshire, RG21 6XS, England, (Telephone in U.S. (888) 330-8477), (Fax in U.S. (800) 672-2054), www.palgrave.com; *The Statesman's Yearbook 2008.*

Taylor and Francis Group, An Informa Business, 2 Park Square, Milton Park, Abingdon, Oxford OX14 4RN, United Kingdom, (Dial from U.S. (212) 216-7800), (Fax from U.S. (212) 564-7854), www.tandf.co.uk; *The Europa World Year Book.*

United Nations Economic Commission for Africa (ECA), PO Box 3001, Addis Ababa, Ethiopia, (Telephone in U.S. (212) 963-4957), www.uneca.org; *African Statistical Yearbook 2006.*

DJIBOUTI - BROADCASTING

Central Intelligence Agency, Office of Public Affairs, Washington, DC 20505, (703) 482-0623, Fax: (703) 482-1739, www.cia.gov; *The World Factbook.*

Euromonitor International, Inc., 224 S. Michigan Avenue, Suite 1500, Chicago, IL 60604, (312) 922-1115, Fax: (312) 922-1157, www.euromonitor.com; *World Marketing Data and Statistics.*

Palgrave Macmillan Ltd., Houndmills, Basingstoke, Hampshire, RG21 6XS, England, (Telephone in U.S. (888) 330-8477), (Fax in U.S. (800) 672-2054), www.palgrave.com; *The Statesman's Yearbook 2008.*

WRTH Publications Limited, PO Box 290, Oxford OX2 7FT, UK, www.wrth.com; *World Radio TV Handbook 2007.*

DJIBOUTI - BUDGET

Central Intelligence Agency, Office of Public Affairs, Washington, DC 20505, (703) 482-0623, Fax: (703) 482-1739, www.cia.gov; *The World Factbook.*

DJIBOUTI - CAPITAL LEVY

International Monetary Fund (IMF), 700 Nineteenth Street, NW, Washington, DC 20431, (202) 623-7000, Fax: (202) 623-4661, www.imf.org; *Government Finance Statistics Yearbook (2008 Edition).*

DJIBOUTI - CATTLE

See DJIBOUTI - LIVESTOCK

DJIBOUTI - CHILDBIRTH - STATISTICS

Central Intelligence Agency, Office of Public Affairs, Washington, DC 20505, (703) 482-0623, Fax: (703) 482-1739, www.cia.gov; *The World Factbook.*

Euromonitor International, Inc., 224 S. Michigan Avenue, Suite 1500, Chicago, IL 60604, (312) 922-1115, Fax: (312) 922-1157, www.euromonitor.com; *International Marketing Data and Statistics 2008* and *The World Economic Factbook 2008.*

Palgrave Macmillan Ltd., Houndmills, Basingstoke, Hampshire, RG21 6XS, England, (Telephone in U.S. (888) 330-8477), (Fax in U.S. (800) 672-2054), www.palgrave.com; *The Statesman's Yearbook 2008.*

Taylor and Francis Group, An Informa Business, 2 Park Square, Milton Park, Abingdon, Oxford OX14 4RN, United Kingdom, (Dial from U.S. (212) 216-7800), (Fax from U.S. (212) 564-7854), www.tandf.co.uk; *The Europa World Year Book.*

United Nations Statistics Division, New York, NY 10017, (800) 253-9646, Fax: (212) 963-4116, http://unstats.un.org; *Demographic Yearbook; Statistical Yearbook;* and *Survey of Economic and Social Conditions in Africa 2005.*

DJIBOUTI - CLIMATE

International Institute for Environment and Development (IIED), 3 Endsleigh Street, London, England, WC1H 0DD, United Kingdom, www.iied.org; *Environment Urbanization* and *Haramata - Bulletin of the Drylands.*

Palgrave Macmillan Ltd., Houndmills, Basingstoke, Hampshire, RG21 6XS, England, (Telephone in U.S. (888) 330-8477), (Fax in U.S. (800) 672-2054), www.palgrave.com; *The Statesman's Yearbook 2008.*

DJIBOUTI - COAL PRODUCTION

See DJIBOUTI - MINERAL INDUSTRIES

DJIBOUTI - COMMERCE

Palgrave Macmillan Ltd., Houndmills, Basingstoke, Hampshire, RG21 6XS, England, (Telephone in U.S. (888) 330-8477), (Fax in U.S. (800) 672-2054), www.palgrave.com; *The Statesman's Yearbook 2008.*

DJIBOUTI - COMMODITY EXCHANGES

Commodity Research Bureau, 330 South Wells Street, Suite 612, Chicago, IL 60606-7110, (800) 621-5271, Fax: (312) 939-4135, www.crbtrader.com; *2006 CRB Commodity Yearbook and CD.*

International Monetary Fund (IMF), 700 Nineteenth Street, NW, Washington, DC 20431, (202) 623-7000, Fax: (202) 623-4661, www.imf.org; *IMF Primary Commodity Prices.*

United Nations Food and Agricultural Organization (FAO), Viale delle Terme di Caracalla, 00100 Rome, Italy, (Dial from U.S. (202) 653-2400), (Fax from

U.S. (202) 653 5760), www.fao.org; *The State of Food and Agriculture (SOFA) 2006.*

DJIBOUTI - COMMUNICATION AND TRAFFIC

United Nations Statistics Division, New York, NY 10017, (800) 253-9646, Fax: (212) 963-4116, http://unstats.un.org; *Statistical Yearbook.*

DJIBOUTI - CONSTRUCTION INDUSTRY

Palgrave Macmillan Ltd., Houndmills, Basingstoke, Hampshire, RG21 6XS, England, (Telephone in U.S. (888) 330-8477), (Fax in U.S. (800) 672-2054), www.palgrave.com; *The Statesman's Yearbook 2008.*

United Nations Economic Commission for Africa (ECA), PO Box 3001, Addis Ababa, Ethiopia, (Telephone in U.S. (212) 963-4957), www.uneca.org; *African Statistical Yearbook 2006.*

United Nations Statistics Division, New York, NY 10017, (800) 253-9646, Fax: (212) 963-4116, http://unstats.un.org; *Statistical Yearbook.*

DJIBOUTI - CONSUMER PRICE INDEXES

United Nations Economic Commission for Africa (ECA), PO Box 3001, Addis Ababa, Ethiopia, (Telephone in U.S. (212) 963-4957), www.uneca.org; *African Statistical Yearbook 2006.*

United Nations Statistics Division, New York, NY 10017, (800) 253-9646, Fax: (212) 963-4116, http://unstats.un.org; *Survey of Economic and Social Conditions in Africa 2005.*

The World Bank, 1818 H Street, NW, Washington, DC 20433, (202) 473-1000, Fax: (202) 477-6391, www.worldbank.org; *Djibouti.*

DJIBOUTI - CONSUMPTION (ECONOMICS)

African Development Bank Group, Rue Joseph Anoma, 01 BP 1387 Abidjan 01, Cote d'Ivoire, www.afdb.org; *Statistics Pocketbook 2008.*

United Nations Statistics Division, New York, NY 10017, (800) 253-9646, Fax: (212) 963-4116, http://unstats.un.org; *Survey of Economic and Social Conditions in Africa 2005.*

DJIBOUTI - CORN INDUSTRY

See DJIBOUTI - CROPS

DJIBOUTI - CROPS

Palgrave Macmillan Ltd., Houndmills, Basingstoke, Hampshire, RG21 6XS, England, (Telephone in U.S. (888) 330-8477), (Fax in U.S. (800) 672-2054), www.palgrave.com; *The Statesman's Yearbook 2008.*

Taylor and Francis Group, An Informa Business, 2 Park Square, Milton Park, Abingdon, Oxford OX14 4RN, United Kingdom, (Dial from U.S. (212) 216-7800), (Fax from U.S. (212) 564-7854), www.tandf.co.uk; *The Europa World Year Book.*

United Nations Conference on Trade and Development (UNCTAD), DC2-1120, United Nations, New York, NY 10017, (212) 963-0027, www.unctad.org; *UNCTAD Commodity Yearbook.*

United Nations Economic Commission for Africa (ECA), PO Box 3001, Addis Ababa, Ethiopia, (Telephone in U.S. (212) 963-4957), www.uneca.org; *African Statistical Yearbook 2006.*

United Nations Food and Agricultural Organization (FAO), Viale delle Terme di Caracalla, 00100 Rome, Italy, (Dial from U.S. (202) 653-2400), (Fax from U.S. (202) 653 5760), www.fao.org; *The State of Food and Agriculture (SOFA) 2006.*

DJIBOUTI - DAIRY PROCESSING

Taylor and Francis Group, An Informa Business, 2 Park Square, Milton Park, Abingdon, Oxford OX14 4RN, United Kingdom, (Dial from U.S. (212) 216-7800), (Fax from U.S. (212) 564-7854), www.tandf.co.uk; *The Europa World Year Book.*

United Nations Food and Agricultural Organization (FAO), Viale delle Terme di Caracalla, 00100 Rome, Italy, (Dial from U.S. (202) 653-2400), (Fax from U.S. (202) 653 5760), www.fao.org; *The State of Food and Agriculture (SOFA) 2006.*

DJIBOUTI - DEATH RATES

See DJIBOUTI - MORTALITY

DJIBOUTI - DEBTS, EXTERNAL

African Development Bank Group, Rue Joseph Anoma, 01 BP 1387 Abidjan 01, Cote d'Ivoire, www.afdb.org; *Statistics Pocketbook 2008.*

Palgrave Macmillan Ltd., Houndmills, Basingstoke, Hampshire, RG21 6XS, England, (Telephone in U.S. (888) 330-8477), (Fax in U.S. (800) 672-2054), www.palgrave.com; *The Statesman's Yearbook 2008.*

United Nations Statistics Division, New York, NY 10017, (800) 253-9646, Fax: (212) 963-4116, http://unstats.un.org; *Survey of Economic and Social Conditions in Africa 2005.*

The World Bank, 1818 H Street, NW, Washington, DC 20433, (202) 473-1000, Fax: (202) 477-6391, www.worldbank.org; *Africa Live Database (LDB); African Development Indicators (ADI) 2007;* and *Global Development Finance 2007.*

DJIBOUTI - DEFENSE EXPENDITURES

See DJIBOUTI - ARMED FORCES

DJIBOUTI - DEMOGRAPHY

Euromonitor International, Inc., 224 S. Michigan Avenue, Suite 1500, Chicago, IL 60604, (312) 922-1115, Fax: (312) 922-1157, www.euromonitor.com; *International Marketing Data and Statistics 2008; The World Economic Factbook 2008;* and *World Marketing Data and Statistics.*

United Nations Statistics Division, New York, NY 10017, (800) 253-9646, Fax: (212) 963-4116, http://unstats.un.org; *Human Development Report 2006* and *Survey of Economic and Social Conditions in Africa 2005.*

The World Bank, 1818 H Street, NW, Washington, DC 20433, (202) 473-1000, Fax: (202) 477-6391, www.worldbank.org; *Djibouti.*

DJIBOUTI - DISPOSABLE INCOME

United Nations Statistics Division, New York, NY 10017, (800) 253-9646, Fax: (212) 963-4116, http://unstats.un.org; *National Accounts Statistics: Compendium of Income Distribution Statistics* and *Statistical Yearbook.*

DJIBOUTI - DIVORCE

United Nations Statistics Division, New York, NY 10017, (800) 253-9646, Fax: (212) 963-4116, http://unstats.un.org; *Demographic Yearbook* and *Statistical Yearbook.*

DJIBOUTI - ECONOMIC ASSISTANCE

United Nations Statistics Division, New York, NY 10017, (800) 253-9646, Fax: (212) 963-4116, http://unstats.un.org; *Statistical Yearbook.*

DJIBOUTI - ECONOMIC CONDITIONS

African Development Bank Group, Rue Joseph Anoma, 01 BP 1387 Abidjan 01, Cote d'Ivoire, www.afdb.org; *The African Statistical Journal; Gender, Poverty and Environmental Indicators on African Countries 2007; Selected Statistics on African Countries 2007;* and *Statistics Pocketbook 2008.*

Center for International Business Education Research (CIBER), Columbia Business School and School of International and Public Affairs, Uris Hall, Room 212, 3022 Broadway, New York, NY 10027-6902, Mr. Joshua Safier, (212) 854-4750, Fax: (212) 222-9821, www.columbia.edu/cu/ciber/; Datastream International.

Central Intelligence Agency, Office of Public Affairs, Washington, DC 20505, (703) 482-0623, Fax: (703) 482-1739, www.cia.gov; *The World Factbook.*

DSI Data Service Information, Xantener Strasse 51a, D-47495 Rheinberg, Germany, www.dsidata.com; *Campus Solution.*

Dun and Bradstreet (DB) Corporation, 103 JFK Parkway, Short Hills, NJ 07078, (973) 921-5500, www.dnb.com; *Country Report.*

Economist Intelligence Unit, 111 West 57th Street, New York, NY 10019, (212) 554-0600, Fax: (212) 586-1181, www.eiu.com; *Business Africa* and *Djibouti Country Report.*

Euromonitor International, Inc., 224 S. Michigan Avenue, Suite 1500, Chicago, IL 60604, (312) 922-1115, Fax: (312) 922-1157, www.euromonitor.com; *The World Economic Factbook 2008* and *World Marketing Data and Statistics.*

International Monetary Fund (IMF), 700 Nineteenth Street, NW, Washington, DC 20431, (202) 623-7000, Fax: (202) 623-4661, www.imf.org; *World Economic Outlook Reports.*

Palgrave Macmillan Ltd., Houndmills, Basingstoke, Hampshire, RG21 6XS, England, (Telephone in U.S. (888) 330-8477), (Fax in U.S. (800) 672-2054), www.palgrave.com; *The Statesman's Yearbook 2008.*

United Nations Statistics Division, New York, NY 10017, (800) 253-9646, Fax: (212) 963-4116, http://unstats.un.org; *Compendium of Intra-African and Related Foreign Trade Statistics 2003* and *World Statistics Pocketbook.*

The World Bank, 1818 H Street, NW, Washington, DC 20433, (202) 473-1000, Fax: (202) 477-6391, www.worldbank.org; *Africa Household Survey Databank; Africa Live Database (LDB); Africa Standardized Files and Indicators; African Development Indicators (ADI) 2007; Djibouti; Global Economic Monitor (GEM); Global Economic Prospects 2008;* and *The World Bank Atlas 2003-2004.*

DJIBOUTI - EDUCATION

African Development Bank Group, Rue Joseph Anoma, 01 BP 1387 Abidjan 01, Cote d'Ivoire, www.afdb.org; *Statistics Pocketbook 2008.*

Euromonitor International, Inc., 224 S. Michigan Avenue, Suite 1500, Chicago, IL 60604, (312) 922-1115, Fax: (312) 922-1157, www.euromonitor.com; *International Marketing Data and Statistics 2008* and *World Marketing Data and Statistics.*

International Monetary Fund (IMF), 700 Nineteenth Street, NW, Washington, DC 20431, (202) 623-7000, Fax: (202) 623-4661, www.imf.org; *Government Finance Statistics Yearbook (2008 Edition).*

Palgrave Macmillan Ltd., Houndmills, Basingstoke, Hampshire, RG21 6XS, England, (Telephone in U.S. (888) 330-8477), (Fax in U.S. (800) 672-2054), www.palgrave.com; *The Statesman's Yearbook 2008.*

Taylor and Francis Group, An Informa Business, 2 Park Square, Milton Park, Abingdon, Oxford OX14 4RN, United Kingdom, (Dial from U.S. (212) 216-7800), (Fax from U.S. (212) 564-7854), www.tandf.co.uk; *The Europa World Year Book.*

UNESCO Institute for Statistics, C.P. 6128 Succursale Centre-Ville, Montreal, Quebec, H3C 3J7 Canada, (Dial from U.S. (514) 343-6880), (Fax from U.S. (514) 343 6882), www.uis.unesco.org; *Statistical Tables.*

United Nations Economic Commission for Africa (ECA), PO Box 3001, Addis Ababa, Ethiopia, (Telephone in U.S. (212) 963-4957), www.uneca.org; *African Statistical Yearbook 2006.*

United Nations Statistics Division, New York, NY 10017, (800) 253-9646, Fax: (212) 963-4116, http://unstats.un.org; *Human Development Report 2006* and *Survey of Economic and Social Conditions in Africa 2005.*

The World Bank, 1818 H Street, NW, Washington, DC 20433, (202) 473-1000, Fax: (202) 477-6391, www.worldbank.org; *Djibouti.*

DJIBOUTI - ELECTRICITY

Palgrave Macmillan Ltd., Houndmills, Basingstoke, Hampshire, RG21 6XS, England, (Telephone in U.S. (888) 330-8477), (Fax in U.S. (800) 672-2054), www.palgrave.com; *The Statesman's Yearbook 2008.*

United Nations Economic Commission for Africa (ECA), PO Box 3001, Addis Ababa, Ethiopia,

(Telephone in U.S. (212) 963-4957), www.uneca.org; *African Statistical Yearbook 2006.*

United Nations Statistics Division, New York, NY 10017, (800) 253-9646, Fax: (212) 963-4116, http://unstats.un.org; *Human Development Report 2006; Statistical Yearbook;* and *Survey of Economic and Social Conditions in Africa 2005.*

DJIBOUTI - EMPLOYMENT

Euromonitor International, Inc., 224 S. Michigan Avenue, Suite 1500, Chicago, IL 60604, (312) 922-1115, Fax: (312) 922-1157, www.euromonitor.com; *International Marketing Data and Statistics 2008.*

International Labour Office, I.L.O. Publications, 4 route des Morillons, CH-1211 Geneva 22, Switzerland, (Telephone in U.S. (202) 653-7652), (Fax in U.S. (202) 653-7687), www.ilo.org; *Yearbook of Labour Statistics 2006.*

United Nations Economic Commission for Africa (ECA), PO Box 3001, Addis Ababa, Ethiopia, (Telephone in U.S. (212) 963-4957), www.uneca.org; *African Statistical Yearbook 2006.*

United Nations Statistics Division, New York, NY 10017, (800) 253-9646, Fax: (212) 963-4116, http://unstats.un.org; *Bulletin of Industrial Statistics for the Arab Countries* and *Survey of Economic and Social Conditions in Africa 2005.*

The World Bank, 1818 H Street, NW, Washington, DC 20433, (202) 473-1000, Fax: (202) 477-6391, www.worldbank.org; *Djibouti.*

DJIBOUTI - ENVIRONMENTAL CONDITIONS

DSI Data Service Information, Xantener Strasse 51a, D-47495 Rheinberg, Germany, www.dsidata.com; *Campus Solution* and *DSI's Global Environmental Database.*

Economist Intelligence Unit, 111 West 57th Street, New York, NY 10019, (212) 554-0600, Fax: (212) 586-1181, www.eiu.com; *Djibouti Country Report.*

International Institute for Environment and Development (IIED), 3 Endsleigh Street, London, England, WC1H 0DD, United Kingdom, www.iied.org; *Environment Urbanization* and *Haramata - Bulletin of the Drylands.*

United Nations Statistics Division, New York, NY 10017, (800) 253-9646, Fax: (212) 963-4116, http://unstats.un.org; *World Statistics Pocketbook.*

DJIBOUTI - EXPORTS

African Development Bank Group, Rue Joseph Anoma, 01 BP 1387 Abidjan 01, Cote d'Ivoire, www.afdb.org; *Statistics Pocketbook 2008.*

Central Intelligence Agency, Office of Public Affairs, Washington, DC 20505, (703) 482-0623, Fax: (703) 482-1739, www.cia.gov; *The World Factbook.*

Economist Intelligence Unit, 111 West 57th Street, New York, NY 10019, (212) 554-0600, Fax: (212) 586-1181, www.eiu.com; *Djibouti Country Report.*

Euromonitor International, Inc., 224 S. Michigan Avenue, Suite 1500, Chicago, IL 60604, (312) 922-1115, Fax: (312) 922-1157, www.euromonitor.com; *International Marketing Data and Statistics 2008* and *The World Economic Factbook 2008.*

Inter-American Development Bank (IDB), 1300 New York Avenue, NW, Washington, DC 20577, (202) 623-1000, Fax: (202) 623-3096, www.iadb.org; *The Politics of Policies: Economic and Social Progress in Latin America - 2006 Report.*

International Monetary Fund (IMF), 700 Nineteenth Street, NW, Washington, DC 20431, (202) 623-7000, Fax: (202) 623-4661, www.imf.org; *Government Finance Statistics Yearbook (2008 Edition)* and *International Financial Statistics Yearbook 2007.*

Taylor and Francis Group, An Informa Business, 2 Park Square, Milton Park, Abingdon, Oxford OX14 4RN, United Kingdom, (Dial from U.S. (212) 216-7800), (Fax from U.S. (212) 564-7854), www.tandf.co.uk; *The Europa World Year Book.*

United Nations Conference on Trade and Development (UNCTAD), DC2-1120, United Nations, New York, NY 10017, (212) 963-0027, www.unctad.org; *Handbook of Statistics 2005.*

United Nations Economic Commission for Africa (ECA), PO Box 3001, Addis Ababa, Ethiopia, (Telephone in U.S. (212) 963-4957), www.uneca.org; *African Statistical Yearbook 2006.*

United Nations Food and Agricultural Organization (FAO), Viale delle Terme di Caracalla, 00100 Rome, Italy, (Dial from U.S. (202) 653-2400), (Fax from U.S. (202) 653 5760), www.fao.org; *The State of Food and Agriculture (SOFA) 2006.*

United Nations Statistics Division, New York, NY 10017, (800) 253-9646, Fax: (212) 963-4116, http://unstats.un.org; *Bulletin of Industrial Statistics for the Arab Countries; Compendium of Intra-African and Related Foreign Trade Statistics 2003;* and *Survey of Economic and Social Conditions in Africa 2005.*

DJIBOUTI - FERTILITY, HUMAN

Central Intelligence Agency, Office of Public Affairs, Washington, DC 20505, (703) 482-0623, Fax: (703) 482-1739, www.cia.gov; *The World Factbook.*

United Nations Statistics Division, New York, NY 10017, (800) 253-9646, Fax: (212) 963-4116, http://unstats.un.org; *Human Development Report 2006* and *Survey of Economic and Social Conditions in Africa 2005.*

The World Bank, 1818 H Street, NW, Washington, DC 20433, (202) 473-1000, Fax: (202) 477-6391, www.worldbank.org; *The World Bank Atlas 2003-2004.*

DJIBOUTI - FERTILIZER INDUSTRY

United Nations Food and Agricultural Organization (FAO), Viale delle Terme di Caracalla, 00100 Rome, Italy, (Dial from U.S. (202) 653-2400), (Fax from U.S. (202) 653 5760), www.fao.org; *The State of Food and Agriculture (SOFA) 2006.*

DJIBOUTI - FETAL MORTALITY

See DJIBOUTI - MORTALITY

DJIBOUTI - FINANCE

United Nations Economic Commission for Africa (ECA), PO Box 3001, Addis Ababa, Ethiopia, (Telephone in U.S. (212) 963-4957), www.uneca.org; *African Statistical Yearbook 2006.*

United Nations Statistics Division, New York, NY 10017, (800) 253-9646, Fax: (212) 963-4116, http://unstats.un.org; *National Accounts Statistics: Compendium of Income Distribution Statistics.*

The World Bank, 1818 H Street, NW, Washington, DC 20433, (202) 473-1000, Fax: (202) 477-6391, www.worldbank.org; *Djibouti.*

DJIBOUTI - FINANCE, PUBLIC

African Development Bank Group, Rue Joseph Anoma, 01 BP 1387 Abidjan 01, Cote d'Ivoire, www.afdb.org; *Statistics Pocketbook 2008.*

Bernan Essential Government Publications, 4611-F Assembly Drive, Lanham MD, 20706-4391, (301) 459-2255, Fax: (800) 865-3450, www.bernan.com; *National Accounts Statistics.*

Economist Intelligence Unit, 111 West 57th Street, New York, NY 10019, (212) 554-0600, Fax: (212) 586-1181, www.eiu.com; *Djibouti Country Report.*

International Monetary Fund (IMF), 700 Nineteenth Street, NW, Washington, DC 20431, (202) 623-7000, Fax: (202) 623-4661, www.imf.org; *Government Finance Statistics Yearbook (2008 Edition); International Financial Statistics;* and *International Financial Statistics Online Service.*

Palgrave Macmillan Ltd., Houndmills, Basingstoke, Hampshire, RG21 6XS, England, (Telephone in U.S. (888) 330-8477), (Fax in U.S. (800) 672-2054), www.palgrave.com; *The Statesman's Yearbook 2008.*

Taylor and Francis Group, An Informa Business, 2 Park Square, Milton Park, Abingdon, Oxford OX14 4RN, United Kingdom, (Dial from U.S. (212) 216-7800), (Fax from U.S. (212) 564-7854), www.tandf.co.uk; *The Europa World Year Book.*

United Nations Economic Commission for Africa (ECA), PO Box 3001, Addis Ababa, Ethiopia, (Telephone in U.S. (212) 963-4957), www.uneca.org; *African Statistical Yearbook 2006.*

The World Bank, 1818 H Street, NW, Washington, DC 20433, (202) 473-1000, Fax: (202) 477-6391, www.worldbank.org; *Djibouti.*

DJIBOUTI - FISHERIES

Palgrave Macmillan Ltd., Houndmills, Basingstoke, Hampshire, RG21 6XS, England, (Telephone in U.S. (888) 330-8477), (Fax in U.S. (800) 672-2054), www.palgrave.com; *The Statesman's Yearbook 2008.*

Taylor and Francis Group, An Informa Business, 2 Park Square, Milton Park, Abingdon, Oxford OX14 4RN, United Kingdom, (Dial from U.S. (212) 216-7800), (Fax from U.S. (212) 564-7854), www.tandf.co.uk; *The Europa World Year Book.*

United Nations Conference on Trade and Development (UNCTAD), DC2-1120, United Nations, New York, NY 10017, (212) 963-0027, www.unctad.org; *UNCTAD Commodity Yearbook.*

United Nations Economic Commission for Africa (ECA), PO Box 3001, Addis Ababa, Ethiopia, (Telephone in U.S. (212) 963-4957), www.uneca.org; *African Statistical Yearbook 2006.*

United Nations Food and Agricultural Organization (FAO), Viale delle Terme di Caracalla, 00100 Rome, Italy, (Dial from U.S. (202) 653-2400), (Fax from U.S. (202) 653 5760), www.fao.org; *FAO Yearbook of Fishery Statistics;* Fishery Databases; FISHSTAT Database. Subjects covered include: Aquaculture production, capture production, fishery commodities; and *The State of Food and Agriculture (SOFA) 2006.*

The World Bank, 1818 H Street, NW, Washington, DC 20433, (202) 473-1000, Fax: (202) 477-6391, www.worldbank.org; *Djibouti.*

DJIBOUTI - FOOD

African Development Bank Group, Rue Joseph Anoma, 01 BP 1387 Abidjan 01, Cote d'Ivoire, www.afdb.org; *Statistics Pocketbook 2008.*

United Nations Conference on Trade and Development (UNCTAD), DC2-1120, United Nations, New York, NY 10017, (212) 963-0027, www.unctad.org; *UNCTAD Commodity Yearbook.*

United Nations Food and Agricultural Organization (FAO), Viale delle Terme di Caracalla, 00100 Rome, Italy, (Dial from U.S. (202) 653-2400), (Fax from U.S. (202) 653 5760), www.fao.org; *FAO Production Yearbook 2002* and *The State of Food and Agriculture (SOFA) 2006.*

United Nations Statistics Division, New York, NY 10017, (800) 253-9646, Fax: (212) 963-4116, http://unstats.un.org; *Human Development Report 2006.*

DJIBOUTI - FOREIGN EXCHANGE RATES

African Development Bank Group, Rue Joseph Anoma, 01 BP 1387 Abidjan 01, Cote d'Ivoire, www.afdb.org; *Statistics Pocketbook 2008.*

Central Intelligence Agency, Office of Public Affairs, Washington, DC 20505, (703) 482-0623, Fax: (703) 482-1739, www.cia.gov; *The World Factbook.*

Euromonitor International, Inc., 224 S. Michigan Avenue, Suite 1500, Chicago, IL 60604, (312) 922-1115, Fax: (312) 922-1157, www.euromonitor.com; *International Marketing Data and Statistics 2008* and *The World Economic Factbook 2008.*

Inter-American Development Bank (IDB), 1300 New York Avenue, NW, Washington, DC 20577, (202) 623-1000, Fax: (202) 623-3096, www.iadb.org; *The Politics of Policies: Economic and Social Progress in Latin America - 2006 Report.*

Taylor and Francis Group, An Informa Business, 2 Park Square, Milton Park, Abingdon, Oxford OX14 4RN, United Kingdom, (Dial from U.S. (212) 216-7800), (Fax from U.S. (212) 564-7854), www.tandf.co.uk; *The Europa World Year Book.*

United Nations Statistics Division, New York, NY 10017, (800) 253-9646, Fax: (212) 963-4116, http://unstats.un.org; *Bulletin of Industrial Statistics for the Arab Countries; Compendium of Intra-African and Related Foreign Trade Statistics 2003;* and *World Statistics Pocketbook.*

DJIBOUTI - FORESTS AND FORESTRY

UNESCO Institute for Statistics, C.P. 6128 Succursale Centre-Ville, Montreal, Quebec, H3C 3J7 Canada, (Dial from U.S. (514) 343-6880), (Fax from U.S. (514) 343 6882), www.uis.unesco.org; *Statistical Tables.*

United Nations Conference on Trade and Development (UNCTAD), DC2-1120, United Nations, New York, NY 10017, (212) 963-0027, www.unctad.org; *UNCTAD Commodity Yearbook.*

United Nations Economic Commission for Africa (ECA), PO Box 3001, Addis Ababa, Ethiopia, (Telephone in U.S. (212) 963-4957), www.uneca.org; *African Statistical Yearbook 2006.*

United Nations Food and Agricultural Organization (FAO), Viale delle Terme di Caracalla, 00100 Rome, Italy, (Dial from U.S. (202) 653-2400), (Fax from U.S. (202) 653 5760), www.fao.org; *FAO Yearbook of Forest Products* and *The State of Food and Agriculture (SOFA) 2006.*

United Nations Statistics Division, New York, NY 10017, (800) 253-9646, Fax: (212) 963-4116, http://unstats.un.org; *Statistical Yearbook.*

The World Bank, 1818 H Street, NW, Washington, DC 20433, (202) 473-1000, Fax: (202) 477-6391, www.worldbank.org; *Djibouti.*

DJIBOUTI - GEOGRAPHIC INFORMATION SYSTEMS

The World Bank, 1818 H Street, NW, Washington, DC 20433, (202) 473-1000, Fax: (202) 477-6391, www.worldbank.org; *Djibouti.*

DJIBOUTI - GRANTS-IN-AID

International Monetary Fund (IMF), 700 Nineteenth Street, NW, Washington, DC 20431, (202) 623-7000, Fax: (202) 623-4661, www.imf.org; *Government Finance Statistics Yearbook (2008 Edition).*

DJIBOUTI - GROSS DOMESTIC PRODUCT

African Development Bank Group, Rue Joseph Anoma, 01 BP 1387 Abidjan 01, Cote d'Ivoire, www.afdb.org; *Statistics Pocketbook 2008.*

Economist Intelligence Unit, 111 West 57th Street, New York, NY 10019, (212) 554-0600, Fax: (212) 586-1181, www.eiu.com; *Djibouti Country Report.*

Euromonitor International, Inc., 224 S. Michigan Avenue, Suite 1500, Chicago, IL 60604, (312) 922-1115, Fax: (312) 922-1157, www.euromonitor.com; *International Marketing Data and Statistics 2008* and *The World Economic Factbook 2008.*

Taylor and Francis Group, An Informa Business, 2 Park Square, Milton Park, Abingdon, Oxford OX14 4RN, United Kingdom, (Dial from U.S. (212) 216-7800), (Fax from U.S. (212) 564-7854), www.tandf.co.uk; *The Europa World Year Book.*

United Nations Economic Commission for Africa (ECA), PO Box 3001, Addis Ababa, Ethiopia, (Telephone in U.S. (212) 963-4957), www.uneca.org; *African Statistical Yearbook 2006.*

United Nations Statistics Division, New York, NY 10017, (800) 253-9646, Fax: (212) 963-4116, http://unstats.un.org; *Bulletin of Industrial Statistics for the Arab Countries; Human Development Report 2006; National Accounts Statistics: Compendium of Income Distribution Statistics; Statistical Yearbook;* and *Survey of Economic and Social Conditions in Africa 2005.*

DJIBOUTI - GROSS NATIONAL PRODUCT

Palgrave Macmillan Ltd., Houndmills, Basingstoke, Hampshire, RG21 6XS, England, (Telephone in U.S. (888) 330-8477), (Fax in U.S. (800) 672-2054), www.palgrave.com; *The Statesman's Yearbook 2008.*

United Nations Statistics Division, New York, NY 10017, (800) 253-9646, Fax: (212) 963-4116, http://unstats.un.org; *Statistical Yearbook.*

The World Bank, 1818 H Street, NW, Washington, DC 20433, (202) 473-1000, Fax: (202) 477-6391, www.worldbank.org; *The World Bank Atlas 2003-2004.*

DJIBOUTI - HIDES AND SKINS INDUSTRY

United Nations Food and Agricultural Organization (FAO), Viale delle Terme di Caracalla, 00100 Rome, Italy, (Dial from U.S. (202) 653-2400), (Fax from U.S. (202) 653 5760), www.fao.org; *FAO Production Yearbook 2002.*

DJIBOUTI - HOUSING

Euromonitor International, Inc., 224 S. Michigan Avenue, Suite 1500, Chicago, IL 60604, (312) 922-1115, Fax: (312) 922-1157, www.euromonitor.com; *World Marketing Data and Statistics.*

International Monetary Fund (IMF), 700 Nineteenth Street, NW, Washington, DC 20431, (202) 623-7000, Fax: (202) 623-4661, www.imf.org; *Government Finance Statistics Yearbook (2008 Edition).*

DJIBOUTI - ILLITERATE PERSONS

Euromonitor International, Inc., 224 S. Michigan Avenue, Suite 1500, Chicago, IL 60604, (312) 922-1115, Fax: (312) 922-1157, www.euromonitor.com; *The World Economic Factbook 2008.*

United Nations Statistics Division, New York, NY 10017, (800) 253-9646, Fax: (212) 963-4116, http://unstats.un.org; *Human Development Report 2006.*

DJIBOUTI - IMPORTS

Central Intelligence Agency, Office of Public Affairs, Washington, DC 20505, (703) 482-0623, Fax: (703) 482-1739, www.cia.gov; *The World Factbook.*

Economist Intelligence Unit, 111 West 57th Street, New York, NY 10019, (212) 554-0600, Fax: (212) 586-1181, www.eiu.com; *Djibouti Country Report.*

Euromonitor International, Inc., 224 S. Michigan Avenue, Suite 1500, Chicago, IL 60604, (312) 922-1115, Fax: (312) 922-1157, www.euromonitor.com; *International Marketing Data and Statistics 2008* and *The World Economic Factbook 2008.*

Inter-American Development Bank (IDB), 1300 New York Avenue, NW, Washington, DC 20577, (202) 623-1000, Fax: (202) 623-3096, www.iadb.org; *The Politics of Policies: Economic and Social Progress in Latin America - 2006 Report.*

International Monetary Fund (IMF), 700 Nineteenth Street, NW, Washington, DC 20431, (202) 623-7000, Fax: (202) 623-4661, www.imf.org; *Direction of Trade Statistics Yearbook 2007.*

Palgrave Macmillan Ltd., Houndmills, Basingstoke, Hampshire, RG21 6XS, England, (Telephone in U.S. (888) 330-8477), (Fax in U.S. (800) 672-2054), www.palgrave.com; *The Statesman's Yearbook 2008.*

Taylor and Francis Group, An Informa Business, 2 Park Square, Milton Park, Abingdon, Oxford OX14 4RN, United Kingdom, (Dial from U.S. (212) 216-7800), (Fax from U.S. (212) 564-7854), www.tandf.co.uk; *The Europa World Year Book.*

United Nations Conference on Trade and Development (UNCTAD), DC2-1120, United Nations, New York, NY 10017, (212) 963-0027, www.unctad.org; *Handbook of Statistics 2005.*

United Nations Economic Commission for Africa (ECA), PO Box 3001, Addis Ababa, Ethiopia, (Telephone in U.S. (212) 963-4957), www.uneca.org; *African Statistical Yearbook 2006.*

United Nations Food and Agricultural Organization (FAO), Viale delle Terme di Caracalla, 00100 Rome, Italy, (Dial from U.S. (202) 653-2400), (Fax from U.S. (202) 653 5760), www.fao.org; *The State of Food and Agriculture (SOFA) 2006.*

United Nations Statistics Division, New York, NY 10017, (800) 253-9646, Fax: (212) 963-4116, http://unstats.un.org; *Bulletin of Industrial Statistics for the Arab Countries; Compendium of Intra-African and Related Foreign Trade Statistics 2003;* and *Survey of Economic and Social Conditions in Africa 2005.*

DJIBOUTI - INDUSTRIES

Central Intelligence Agency, Office of Public Affairs, Washington, DC 20505, (703) 482-0623, Fax: (703) 482-1739, www.cia.gov; *The World Factbook.*

Economist Intelligence Unit, 111 West 57th Street, New York, NY 10019, (212) 554-0600, Fax: (212) 586-1181, www.eiu.com; *Djibouti Country Report.*

Euromonitor International, Inc., 224 S. Michigan Avenue, Suite 1500, Chicago, IL 60604, (312) 922-1115, Fax: (312) 922-1157, www.euromonitor.com; *The World Economic Factbook 2008* and *World Marketing Data and Statistics.*

International Labour Office, I.L.O. Publications, 4 route des Morillons, CH-1211 Geneva 22, Switzerland, (Telephone in U.S. (202) 653-7652), (Fax in U.S. (202) 653-7687), www.ilo.org; *Yearbook of Labour Statistics 2006.*

Palgrave Macmillan Ltd., Houndmills, Basingstoke, Hampshire, RG21 6XS, England, (Telephone in U.S. (888) 330-8477), (Fax in U.S. (800) 672-2054), www.palgrave.com; *The Statesman's Yearbook 2008.*

Taylor and Francis Group, An Informa Business, 2 Park Square, Milton Park, Abingdon, Oxford OX14 4RN, United Kingdom, (Dial from U.S. (212) 216-7800), (Fax from U.S. (212) 564-7854), www.tandf.co.uk; *The Europa World Year Book.*

United Nations Economic Commission for Africa (ECA), PO Box 3001, Addis Ababa, Ethiopia, (Telephone in U.S. (212) 963-4957), www.uneca.org; *African Statistical Yearbook 2006.*

United Nations Industrial Development Organization (UNIDO), 1 United Nations Plaza, New York, NY 10017, (212) 963 6890, Fax: (212) 963-7904, http://unido.org; Industrial Statistics Database 2008 (INDSTAT) and *The International Yearbook of Industrial Statistics 2008.*

United Nations Statistics Division, New York, NY 10017, (800) 253-9646, Fax: (212) 963-4116, http://unstats.un.org; *Bulletin of Industrial Statistics for the Arab Countries* and *Survey of Economic and Social Conditions in Africa 2005.*

The World Bank, 1818 H Street, NW, Washington, DC 20433, (202) 473-1000, Fax: (202) 477-6391, www.worldbank.org; *Djibouti.*

DJIBOUTI - INFANT AND MATERNAL MORTALITY

See DJIBOUTI - MORTALITY

DJIBOUTI - INTERNATIONAL TRADE

African Development Bank Group, Rue Joseph Anoma, 01 BP 1387 Abidjan 01, Cote d'Ivoire, www.afdb.org; *Statistics Pocketbook 2008.*

Economist Intelligence Unit, 111 West 57th Street, New York, NY 10019, (212) 554-0600, Fax: (212) 586-1181, www.eiu.com; *Djibouti Country Report.*

Euromonitor International, Inc., 224 S. Michigan Avenue, Suite 1500, Chicago, IL 60604, (312) 922-1115, Fax: (312) 922-1157, www.euromonitor.com; *The World Economic Factbook 2008* and *World Marketing Data and Statistics.*

Inter-American Development Bank (IDB), 1300 New York Avenue, NW, Washington, DC 20577, (202) 623-1000, Fax: (202) 623-3096, www.iadb.org; *The Politics of Policies: Economic and Social Progress in Latin America - 2006 Report.*

Palgrave Macmillan Ltd., Houndmills, Basingstoke, Hampshire, RG21 6XS, England, (Telephone in U.S. (888) 330-8477), (Fax in U.S. (800) 672-2054), www.palgrave.com; *The Statesman's Yearbook 2008.*

Taylor and Francis Group, An Informa Business, 2 Park Square, Milton Park, Abingdon, Oxford OX14 4RN, United Kingdom, (Dial from U.S. (212) 216-7800), (Fax from U.S. (212) 564-7854), www.tandf.co.uk; *The Europa World Year Book.*

United Nations Conference on Trade and Development (UNCTAD), DC2-1120, United Nations, New

York, NY 10017, (212) 963-0027, www.unctad.org; *UNCTAD Commodity Yearbook.*

United Nations Economic Commission for Africa (ECA), PO Box 3001, Addis Ababa, Ethiopia, (Telephone in U.S. (212) 963-4957), www.uneca.org; *African Statistical Yearbook 2006.*

United Nations Food and Agricultural Organization (FAO), Viale delle Terme di Caracalla, 00100 Rome, Italy, (Dial from U.S. (202) 653-2400), (Fax from U.S. (202) 653 5760), www.fao.org; *FAO Trade Yearbook* and *The State of Food and Agriculture (SOFA) 2006.*

United Nations Statistics Division, New York, NY 10017, (800) 253-9646, Fax: (212) 963-4116, http://unstats.un.org; *Bulletin of Industrial Statistics for the Arab Countries; Compendium of Intra-African and Related Foreign Trade Statistics 2003;* and *Statistical Yearbook.*

The World Bank, 1818 H Street, NW, Washington, DC 20433, (202) 473-1000, Fax: (202) 477-6391, www.worldbank.org; *Djibouti.*

World Trade Organization (WTO), Centre William Rappard, Rue de Lausanne 154, CH-1211 Geneva 21, Switzerland, www.wto.org; *International Trade Statistics 2006.*

DJIBOUTI - INTERNET USERS

International Telecommunication Union (ITU), Place des Nations, 1211 Geneva 20, Switzerland, www.itu.int; *World Telecommunication/ICT Indicators Database on CD-ROM; World Telecommunication/ICT Indicators Database Online;* and *Yearbook of Statistics - Telecommunication Services (Chronological Time Series 1997-2006).*

The World Bank, 1818 H Street, NW, Washington, DC 20433, (202) 473-1000, Fax: (202) 477-6391, www.worldbank.org; *Djibouti.*

DJIBOUTI - LABOR

African Development Bank Group, Rue Joseph Anoma, 01 BP 1387 Abidjan 01, Cote d'Ivoire, www.afdb.org; *Statistics Pocketbook 2008.*

Central Intelligence Agency, Office of Public Affairs, Washington, DC 20505, (703) 482-0623, Fax: (703) 482-1739, www.cia.gov; *The World Factbook.*

Euromonitor International, Inc., 224 S. Michigan Avenue, Suite 1500, Chicago, IL 60604, (312) 922-1115, Fax: (312) 922-1157, www.euromonitor.com; *International Marketing Data and Statistics 2008* and *World Marketing Data and Statistics.*

International Labour Office, I.L.O. Publications, 4 route des Morillons, CH-1211 Geneva 22, Switzerland, (Telephone in U.S. (202) 653-7652), (Fax in U.S. (202) 653-7687), www.ilo.org; *Yearbook of Labour Statistics 2006.*

Palgrave Macmillan Ltd., Houndmills, Basingstoke, Hampshire, RG21 6XS, England, (Telephone in U.S. (888) 330-8477), (Fax in U.S. (800) 672-2054), www.palgrave.com; *The Statesman's Yearbook 2008.*

United Nations Food and Agricultural Organization (FAO), Viale delle Terme di Caracalla, 00100 Rome, Italy, (Dial from U.S. (202) 653-2400), (Fax from U.S. (202) 653 5760), www.fao.org; *The State of Food and Agriculture (SOFA) 2006.*

United Nations Statistics Division, New York, NY 10017, (800) 253-9646, Fax: (212) 963-4116, http://unstats.un.org; *Human Development Report 2006.*

The World Bank, 1818 H Street, NW, Washington, DC 20433, (202) 473-1000, Fax: (202) 477-6391, www.worldbank.org; *The World Bank Atlas 2003-2004.*

DJIBOUTI - LAND USE

Central Intelligence Agency, Office of Public Affairs, Washington, DC 20505, (703) 482-0623, Fax: (703) 482-1739, www.cia.gov; *The World Factbook.*

Euromonitor International, Inc., 224 S. Michigan Avenue, Suite 1500, Chicago, IL 60604, (312) 922-1115, Fax: (312) 922-1157, www.euromonitor.com; *International Marketing Data and Statistics 2008.*

United Nations Food and Agricultural Organization (FAO), Viale delle Terme di Caracalla, 00100 Rome, Italy, (Dial from U.S. (202) 653-2400), (Fax from U.S. (202) 653 5760), www.fao.org; *FAO Production Yearbook 2002.*

DJIBOUTI - LIBRARIES

UNESCO Institute for Statistics, C.P. 6128 Succursale Centre-Ville, Montreal, Quebec, H3C 3J7 Canada, (Dial from U.S. (514) 343-6880), (Fax from U.S. (514) 343 6882), www.uis.unesco.org; *Statistical Tables.*

DJIBOUTI - LICENSES

International Monetary Fund (IMF), 700 Nineteenth Street, NW, Washington, DC 20431, (202) 623-7000, Fax: (202) 623-4661, www.imf.org; *Government Finance Statistics Yearbook (2008 Edition).*

DJIBOUTI - LIFE EXPECTANCY

African Development Bank Group, Rue Joseph Anoma, 01 BP 1387 Abidjan 01, Cote d'Ivoire, www.afdb.org; *Statistics Pocketbook 2008.*

Central Intelligence Agency, Office of Public Affairs, Washington, DC 20505, (703) 482-0623, Fax: (703) 482-1739, www.cia.gov; *The World Factbook.*

Euromonitor International, Inc., 224 S. Michigan Avenue, Suite 1500, Chicago, IL 60604, (312) 922-1115, Fax: (312) 922-1157, www.euromonitor.com; *The World Economic Factbook 2008.*

Palgrave Macmillan Ltd., Houndmills, Basingstoke, Hampshire, RG21 6XS, England, (Telephone in U.S. (888) 330-8477), (Fax in U.S. (800) 672-2054), www.palgrave.com; *The Statesman's Yearbook 2008.*

United Nations Statistics Division, New York, NY 10017, (800) 253-9646, Fax: (212) 963-4116, http://unstats.un.org; *Human Development Report 2006* and *World Statistics Pocketbook.*

The World Bank, 1818 H Street, NW, Washington, DC 20433, (202) 473-1000, Fax: (202) 477-6391, www.worldbank.org; *The World Bank Atlas 2003-2004.*

DJIBOUTI - LITERACY

Euromonitor International, Inc., 224 S. Michigan Avenue, Suite 1500, Chicago, IL 60604, (312) 922-1115, Fax: (312) 922-1157, www.euromonitor.com; *World Marketing Data and Statistics.*

United Nations Statistics Division, New York, NY 10017, (800) 253-9646, Fax: (212) 963-4116, http://unstats.un.org; *Survey of Economic and Social Conditions in Africa 2005.*

DJIBOUTI - LIVESTOCK

Palgrave Macmillan Ltd., Houndmills, Basingstoke, Hampshire, RG21 6XS, England, (Telephone in U.S. (888) 330-8477), (Fax in U.S. (800) 672-2054), www.palgrave.com; *The Statesman's Yearbook 2008.*

Taylor and Francis Group, An Informa Business, 2 Park Square, Milton Park, Abingdon, Oxford OX14 4RN, United Kingdom, (Dial from U.S. (212) 216-7800), (Fax from U.S. (212) 564-7854), www.tandf.co.uk; *The Europa World Year Book.*

United Nations Conference on Trade and Development (UNCTAD), DC2-1120, United Nations, New York, NY 10017, (212) 963-0027, www.unctad.org; *UNCTAD Commodity Yearbook.*

United Nations Economic Commission for Africa (ECA), PO Box 3001, Addis Ababa, Ethiopia, (Telephone in U.S. (212) 963-4957), www.uneca.org; *African Statistical Yearbook 2006.*

United Nations Food and Agricultural Organization (FAO), Viale delle Terme di Caracalla, 00100 Rome, Italy, (Dial from U.S. (202) 653-2400), (Fax from U.S. (202) 653 5760), www.fao.org; *FAO Production Yearbook 2002* and *The State of Food and Agriculture (SOFA) 2006.*

United Nations Statistics Division, New York, NY 10017, (800) 253-9646, Fax: (212) 963-4116, http://unstats.un.org; *Statistical Yearbook* and *Survey of Economic and Social Conditions in Africa 2005.*

DJIBOUTI - MANUFACTURES

United Nations Statistics Division, New York, NY 10017, (800) 253-9646, Fax: (212) 963-4116, http://unstats.un.org; *Bulletin of Industrial Statistics for the Arab Countries* and *Survey of Economic and Social Conditions in Africa 2005.*

DJIBOUTI - MARRIAGE

United Nations Statistics Division, New York, NY 10017, (800) 253-9646, Fax: (212) 963-4116, http://unstats.un.org; *Demographic Yearbook.*

DJIBOUTI - MEDICAL CARE, COST OF

International Monetary Fund (IMF), 700 Nineteenth Street, NW, Washington, DC 20431, (202) 623-7000, Fax: (202) 623-4661, www.imf.org; *Government Finance Statistics Yearbook (2008 Edition).*

DJIBOUTI - MINERAL INDUSTRIES

Palgrave Macmillan Ltd., Houndmills, Basingstoke, Hampshire, RG21 6XS, England, (Telephone in U.S. (888) 330-8477), (Fax in U.S. (800) 672-2054), www.palgrave.com; *The Statesman's Yearbook 2008.*

United Nations Conference on Trade and Development (UNCTAD), DC2-1120, United Nations, New York, NY 10017, (212) 963-0027, www.unctad.org; *UNCTAD Commodity Yearbook.*

United Nations Economic Commission for Africa (ECA), PO Box 3001, Addis Ababa, Ethiopia, (Telephone in U.S. (212) 963-4957), www.uneca.org; *African Statistical Yearbook 2006.*

United Nations Statistics Division, New York, NY 10017, (800) 253-9646, Fax: (212) 963-4116, http://unstats.un.org; *Bulletin of Industrial Statistics for the Arab Countries.*

DJIBOUTI - MONEY SUPPLY

African Development Bank Group, Rue Joseph Anoma, 01 BP 1387 Abidjan 01, Cote d'Ivoire, www.afdb.org; *Statistics Pocketbook 2008.*

Economist Intelligence Unit, 111 West 57th Street, New York, NY 10019, (212) 554-0600, Fax: (212) 586-1181, www.eiu.com; *Djibouti Country Report.*

Taylor and Francis Group, An Informa Business, 2 Park Square, Milton Park, Abingdon, Oxford OX14 4RN, United Kingdom, (Dial from U.S. (212) 216-7800), (Fax from U.S. (212) 564-7854), www.tandf.co.uk; *The Europa World Year Book.*

The World Bank, 1818 H Street, NW, Washington, DC 20433, (202) 473-1000, Fax: (202) 477-6391, www.worldbank.org; *Djibouti.*

DJIBOUTI - MORTALITY

Central Intelligence Agency, Office of Public Affairs, Washington, DC 20505, (703) 482-0623, Fax: (703) 482-1739, www.cia.gov; *The World Factbook.*

Euromonitor International, Inc., 224 S. Michigan Avenue, Suite 1500, Chicago, IL 60604, (312) 922-1115, Fax: (312) 922-1157, www.euromonitor.com; *International Marketing Data and Statistics 2008* and *The World Economic Factbook 2008.*

Palgrave Macmillan Ltd., Houndmills, Basingstoke, Hampshire, RG21 6XS, England, (Telephone in U.S. (888) 330-8477), (Fax in U.S. (800) 672-2054), www.palgrave.com; *The Statesman's Yearbook 2008.*

Taylor and Francis Group, An Informa Business, 2 Park Square, Milton Park, Abingdon, Oxford OX14 4RN, United Kingdom, (Dial from U.S. (212) 216-7800), (Fax from U.S. (212) 564-7854), www.tandf.co.uk; *The Europa World Year Book.*

United Nations Statistics Division, New York, NY 10017, (800) 253-9646, Fax: (212) 963-4116, http://unstats.un.org; *Demographic Yearbook; Statistical Yearbook; Survey of Economic and Social Conditions in Africa 2005;* and *World Statistics Pocketbook.*

The World Bank, 1818 H Street, NW, Washington, DC 20433, (202) 473-1000, Fax: (202) 477-6391, www.worldbank.org; *The World Bank Atlas 2003-2004.*

World Health Organization (WHO), Avenue Appia 20, 1211 Geneve 27, Switzerland, (Telephone in U.S. (212) 331-9081), www.who.int; The WHO Global Atlas of Infectious Diseases.

DJIBOUTI - MOTION PICTURES

United Nations Statistics Division, New York, NY 10017, (800) 253-9646, Fax: (212) 963-4116, http://unstats.un.org; *Statistical Yearbook.*

DJIBOUTI - MOTOR VEHICLES

Taylor and Francis Group, An Informa Business, 2 Park Square, Milton Park, Abingdon, Oxford OX14 4RN, United Kingdom, (Dial from U.S. (212) 216-7800), (Fax from U.S. (212) 564-7854), www.tandf.co.uk; *The Europa World Year Book.*

United Nations Statistics Division, New York, NY 10017, (800) 253-9646, Fax: (212) 963-4116, http://unstats.un.org; *Statistical Yearbook* and *Survey of Economic and Social Conditions in Africa 2005.*

DJIBOUTI - NUTRITION

African Development Bank Group, Rue Joseph Anoma, 01 BP 1387 Abidjan 01, Cote d'Ivoire, www.afdb.org; *Statistics Pocketbook 2008.*

United Nations Food and Agricultural Organization (FAO), Viale delle Terme di Caracalla, 00100 Rome, Italy, (Dial from U.S. (202) 653-2400), (Fax from U.S. (202) 653 5760), www.fao.org; *The State of Food and Agriculture (SOFA) 2006.*

DJIBOUTI - PAPER

See DJIBOUTI - FORESTS AND FORESTRY

DJIBOUTI - PERIODICALS

UNESCO Institute for Statistics, C.P. 6128 Succursale Centre-Ville, Montreal, Quebec, H3C 3J7 Canada, (Dial from U.S. (514) 343-6880), (Fax from U.S. (514) 343 6882), www.uis.unesco.org; *Statistical Tables.*

DJIBOUTI - PESTICIDES

United Nations Food and Agricultural Organization (FAO), Viale delle Terme di Caracalla, 00100 Rome, Italy, (Dial from U.S. (202) 653-2400), (Fax from U.S. (202) 653 5760), www.fao.org; *The State of Food and Agriculture (SOFA) 2006.*

DJIBOUTI - PETROLEUM INDUSTRY AND TRADE

PennWell Corporation, 1421 South Sheridan Road, Tulsa, OK 74112, (918) 835-3161, www.pennwell.com; *International Petroleum Encyclopedia 2007.*

United Nations Conference on Trade and Development (UNCTAD), DC2-1120, United Nations, New York, NY 10017, (212) 963-0027, www.unctad.org; *UNCTAD Commodity Yearbook.*

United Nations Food and Agricultural Organization (FAO), Viale delle Terme di Caracalla, 00100 Rome, Italy, (Dial from U.S. (202) 653-2400), (Fax from U.S. (202) 653 5760), www.fao.org; *The State of Food and Agriculture (SOFA) 2006.*

DJIBOUTI - POLITICAL SCIENCE

Central Intelligence Agency, Office of Public Affairs, Washington, DC 20505, (703) 482-0623, Fax: (703) 482-1739, www.cia.gov; *The World Factbook.*

International Monetary Fund (IMF), 700 Nineteenth Street, NW, Washington, DC 20431, (202) 623-7000, Fax: (202) 623-4661, www.imf.org; *Government Finance Statistics Yearbook (2008 Edition).*

Palgrave Macmillan Ltd., Houndmills, Basingstoke, Hampshire, RG21 6XS, England, (Telephone in U.S. (888) 330-8477), (Fax in U.S. (800) 672-2054), www.palgrave.com; *The Statesman's Yearbook 2008.*

Taylor and Francis Group, An Informa Business, 2 Park Square, Milton Park, Abingdon, Oxford OX14 4RN, United Kingdom, (Dial from U.S. (212) 216-7800), (Fax from U.S. (212) 564-7854), www.tandf.co.uk; *The Europa World Year Book.*

United Nations Statistics Division, New York, NY 10017, (800) 253-9646, Fax: (212) 963-4116, http://unstats.un.org; *National Accounts Statistics: Compendium of Income Distribution Statistics* and *Survey of Economic and Social Conditions in Africa 2005.*

DJIBOUTI - POPULATION

African Development Bank Group, Rue Joseph Anoma, 01 BP 1387 Abidjan 01, Cote d'Ivoire, www.afdb.org; *The African Statistical Journal; Gender, Poverty and Environmental Indicators on African Countries 2007; Selected Statistics on African Countries 2007;* and *Statistics Pocketbook 2008.*

Central Intelligence Agency, Office of Public Affairs, Washington, DC 20505, (703) 482-0623, Fax: (703) 482-1739, www.cia.gov; *The World Factbook.*

Economist Intelligence Unit, 111 West 57th Street, New York, NY 10019, (212) 554-0600, Fax: (212) 586-1181, www.eiu.com; *Djibouti Country Report.*

Euromonitor International, Inc., 224 S. Michigan Avenue, Suite 1500, Chicago, IL 60604, (312) 922-1115, Fax: (312) 922-1157, www.euromonitor.com; *International Marketing Data and Statistics 2008* and *The World Economic Factbook 2008.*

Eurostat, Batiment Jean Monnet, Rue Alcide de Gasperi, L-2920 Luxembourg, http://epp.eurostat.ec.europa.eu; *Demographic Indicators - Population by Age-Classes.*

International Labour Office, I.L.O. Publications, 4 route des Morillons, CH-1211 Geneva 22, Switzerland, (Telephone in U.S. (202) 653-7652), (Fax in U.S. (202) 653-7687), www.ilo.org; *Yearbook of Labour Statistics 2006.*

Palgrave Macmillan Ltd., Houndmills, Basingstoke, Hampshire, RG21 6XS, England, (Telephone in U.S. (888) 330-8477), (Fax in U.S. (800) 672-2054), www.palgrave.com; *The Statesman's Yearbook 2008.*

Taylor and Francis Group, An Informa Business, 2 Park Square, Milton Park, Abingdon, Oxford OX14 4RN, United Kingdom, (Dial from U.S. (212) 216-7800), (Fax from U.S. (212) 564-7854), www.tandf.co.uk; *The Europa World Year Book.*

United Nations Food and Agricultural Organization (FAO), Viale delle Terme di Caracalla, 00100 Rome, Italy, (Dial from U.S. (202) 653-2400), (Fax from U.S. (202) 653 5760), www.fao.org; *FAO Production Yearbook 2002.*

United Nations Statistics Division, New York, NY 10017, (800) 253-9646, Fax: (212) 963-4116, http://unstats.un.org; *Demographic Yearbook; Human Development Report 2006; Statistical Yearbook; Survey of Economic and Social Conditions in Africa 2005;* and *World Statistics Pocketbook.*

The World Bank, 1818 H Street, NW, Washington, DC 20433, (202) 473-1000, Fax: (202) 477-6391, www.worldbank.org; *Djibouti* and *The World Bank Atlas 2003-2004.*

World Health Organization (WHO), Avenue Appia 20, 1211 Geneve 27, Switzerland, (Telephone in U.S. (212) 331-9081), www.who.int; *World Health Report 2006.*

DJIBOUTI - POPULATION DENSITY

African Development Bank Group, Rue Joseph Anoma, 01 BP 1387 Abidjan 01, Cote d'Ivoire, www.afdb.org; *Statistics Pocketbook 2008.*

Central Intelligence Agency, Office of Public Affairs, Washington, DC 20505, (703) 482-0623, Fax: (703) 482-1739, www.cia.gov; *The World Factbook.*

Euromonitor International, Inc., 224 S. Michigan Avenue, Suite 1500, Chicago, IL 60604, (312) 922-1115, Fax: (312) 922-1157, www.euromonitor.com; *The World Economic Factbook 2008.*

Palgrave Macmillan Ltd., Houndmills, Basingstoke, Hampshire, RG21 6XS, England, (Telephone in U.S. (888) 330-8477), (Fax in U.S. (800) 672-2054), www.palgrave.com; *The Statesman's Yearbook 2008.*

Taylor and Francis Group, An Informa Business, 2 Park Square, Milton Park, Abingdon, Oxford OX14 4RN, United Kingdom, (Dial from U.S. (212) 216-7800), (Fax from U.S. (212) 564-7854), www.tandf.co.uk; *The Europa World Year Book.*

United Nations Food and Agricultural Organization (FAO), Viale delle Terme di Caracalla, 00100 Rome, Italy, (Dial from U.S. (202) 653-2400), (Fax from U.S. (202) 653 5760), www.fao.org; *The State of Food and Agriculture (SOFA) 2006.*

United Nations Statistics Division, New York, NY 10017, (800) 253-9646, Fax: (212) 963-4116, http://unstats.un.org; *Statistical Yearbook* and *Survey of Economic and Social Conditions in Africa 2005.*

The World Bank, 1818 H Street, NW, Washington, DC 20433, (202) 473-1000, Fax: (202) 477-6391, www.worldbank.org; *Djibouti.*

DJIBOUTI - POSTAL SERVICE

United Nations Statistics Division, New York, NY 10017, (800) 253-9646, Fax: (212) 963-4116, http://unstats.un.org; *Statistical Yearbook.*

DJIBOUTI - POWER RESOURCES

Euromonitor International, Inc., 224 S. Michigan Avenue, Suite 1500, Chicago, IL 60604, (312) 922-1115, Fax: (312) 922-1157, www.euromonitor.com; *International Marketing Data and Statistics 2008; The World Economic Factbook 2008;* and *World Marketing Data and Statistics.*

Palgrave Macmillan Ltd., Houndmills, Basingstoke, Hampshire, RG21 6XS, England, (Telephone in U.S. (888) 330-8477), (Fax in U.S. (800) 672-2054), www.palgrave.com; *The Statesman's Yearbook 2008.*

United Nations Economic Commission for Africa (ECA), PO Box 3001, Addis Ababa, Ethiopia, (Telephone in U.S. (212) 963-4957), www.uneca.org; *African Statistical Yearbook 2006.*

United Nations Food and Agricultural Organization (FAO), Viale delle Terme di Caracalla, 00100 Rome, Italy, (Dial from U.S. (202) 653-2400), (Fax from U.S. (202) 653 5760), www.fao.org; *The State of Food and Agriculture (SOFA) 2006.*

United Nations Statistics Division, New York, NY 10017, (800) 253-9646, Fax: (212) 963-4116, http://unstats.un.org; *Human Development Report 2006; Statistical Yearbook;* and *World Statistics Pocketbook.*

The World Bank, 1818 H Street, NW, Washington, DC 20433, (202) 473-1000, Fax: (202) 477-6391, www.worldbank.org; *The World Bank Atlas 2003-2004.*

DJIBOUTI - PRICES

Euromonitor International, Inc., 224 S. Michigan Avenue, Suite 1500, Chicago, IL 60604, (312) 922-1115, Fax: (312) 922-1157, www.euromonitor.com; *World Marketing Data and Statistics.*

International Labour Office, I.L.O. Publications, 4 route des Morillons, CH-1211 Geneva 22, Switzerland, (Telephone in U.S. (202) 653-7652), (Fax in U.S. (202) 653-7687), www.ilo.org; *Yearbook of Labour Statistics 2006.*

United Nations Economic Commission for Africa (ECA), PO Box 3001, Addis Ababa, Ethiopia, (Telephone in U.S. (212) 963-4957), www.uneca.org; *African Statistical Yearbook 2006.*

United Nations Food and Agricultural Organization (FAO), Viale delle Terme di Caracalla, 00100 Rome, Italy, (Dial from U.S. (202) 653-2400), (Fax from U.S. (202) 653 5760), www.fao.org; *FAO Production Yearbook 2002* and *The State of Food and Agriculture (SOFA) 2006.*

The World Bank, 1818 H Street, NW, Washington, DC 20433, (202) 473-1000, Fax: (202) 477-6391, www.worldbank.org; *Djibouti.*

DJIBOUTI - PROFESSIONS

United Nations Statistics Division, New York, NY 10017, (800) 253-9646, Fax: (212) 963-4116, http://unstats.un.org; *Statistical Yearbook.*

DJIBOUTI - PUBLIC HEALTH

African Development Bank Group, Rue Joseph Anoma, 01 BP 1387 Abidjan 01, Cote d'Ivoire, www.afdb.org; *Statistics Pocketbook 2008.*

Euromonitor International, Inc., 224 S. Michigan Avenue, Suite 1500, Chicago, IL 60604, (312) 922-1115, Fax: (312) 922-1157, www.euromonitor.com; *World Marketing Data and Statistics.*

Palgrave Macmillan Ltd., Houndmills, Basingstoke, Hampshire, RG21 6XS, England, (Telephone in U.S. (888) 330-8477), (Fax in U.S. (800) 672-2054), www.palgrave.com; *The Statesman's Yearbook 2008.*

United Nations Economic Commission for Africa (ECA), PO Box 3001, Addis Ababa, Ethiopia, (Telephone in U.S. (212) 963-4957), www.uneca.org; *African Statistical Yearbook 2006.*

United Nations Statistics Division, New York, NY 10017, (800) 253-9646, Fax: (212) 963-4116, http://unstats.un.org; *Human Development Report 2006* and *Statistical Yearbook.*

The World Bank, 1818 H Street, NW, Washington, DC 20433, (202) 473-1000, Fax: (202) 477-6391, www.worldbank.org; *Djibouti.*

World Health Organization (WHO), Avenue Appia 20, 1211 Geneve 27, Switzerland, (Telephone in U.S. (212) 331-9081), www.who.int; The WHO Global Atlas of Infectious Diseases.

DJIBOUTI - RADIO BROADCASTING

Palgrave Macmillan Ltd., Houndmills, Basingstoke, Hampshire, RG21 6XS, England, (Telephone in U.S. (888) 330-8477), (Fax in U.S. (800) 672-2054), www.palgrave.com; *The Statesman's Yearbook 2008.*

DJIBOUTI - RAILROADS

Palgrave Macmillan Ltd., Houndmills, Basingstoke, Hampshire, RG21 6XS, England, (Telephone in U.S. (888) 330-8477), (Fax in U.S. (800) 672-2054), www.palgrave.com; *The Statesman's Yearbook 2008.*

Taylor and Francis Group, An Informa Business, 2 Park Square, Milton Park, Abingdon, Oxford OX14 4RN, United Kingdom, (Dial from U.S. (212) 216-7800), (Fax from U.S. (212) 564-7854), www.tandf.co.uk; *The Europa World Year Book.*

United Nations Economic Commission for Africa (ECA), PO Box 3001, Addis Ababa, Ethiopia, (Telephone in U.S. (212) 963-4957), www.uneca.org; *African Statistical Yearbook 2006.*

United Nations Statistics Division, New York, NY 10017, (800) 253-9646, Fax: (212) 963-4116, http://unstats.un.org; *Survey of Economic and Social Conditions in Africa 2005.*

DJIBOUTI - RELIGION

Central Intelligence Agency, Office of Public Affairs, Washington, DC 20505, (703) 482-0623, Fax: (703) 482-1739, www.cia.gov; *The World Factbook.*

Palgrave Macmillan Ltd., Houndmills, Basingstoke, Hampshire, RG21 6XS, England, (Telephone in U.S. (888) 330-8477), (Fax in U.S. (800) 672-2054), www.palgrave.com; *The Statesman's Yearbook 2008.*

DJIBOUTI - RESERVES (ACCOUNTING)

African Development Bank Group, Rue Joseph Anoma, 01 BP 1387 Abidjan 01, Cote d'Ivoire, www.afdb.org; *Statistics Pocketbook 2008.*

DJIBOUTI - RETAIL TRADE

Euromonitor International, Inc., 224 S. Michigan Avenue, Suite 1500, Chicago, IL 60604, (312) 922-1115, Fax: (312) 922-1157, www.euromonitor.com; *World Marketing Data and Statistics.*

DJIBOUTI - ROADS

Central Intelligence Agency, Office of Public Affairs, Washington, DC 20505, (703) 482-0623, Fax: (703) 482-1739, www.cia.gov; *The World Factbook.*

Palgrave Macmillan Ltd., Houndmills, Basingstoke, Hampshire, RG21 6XS, England, (Telephone in U.S. (888) 330-8477), (Fax in U.S. (800) 672-2054), www.palgrave.com; *The Statesman's Yearbook 2008.*

United Nations Economic Commission for Africa (ECA), PO Box 3001, Addis Ababa, Ethiopia, (Telephone in U.S. (212) 963-4957), www.uneca.org; *African Statistical Yearbook 2006.*

United Nations Statistics Division, New York, NY 10017, (800) 253-9646, Fax: (212) 963-4116, http://unstats.un.org; *Survey of Economic and Social Conditions in Africa 2005.*

DJIBOUTI - SHEEP

See DJIBOUTI - LIVESTOCK

DJIBOUTI - SHELLFISH FISHERIES

International Monetary Fund (IMF), 700 Nineteenth Street, NW, Washington, DC 20431, (202) 623-7000, Fax: (202) 623-4661, www.imf.org; *Government Finance Statistics Yearbook (2008 Edition).*

DJIBOUTI - SHIPPING

Palgrave Macmillan Ltd., Houndmills, Basingstoke, Hampshire, RG21 6XS, England, (Telephone in U.S. (888) 330-8477), (Fax in U.S. (800) 672-2054), www.palgrave.com; *The Statesman's Yearbook 2008.*

Taylor and Francis Group, An Informa Business, 2 Park Square, Milton Park, Abingdon, Oxford OX14 4RN, United Kingdom, (Dial from U.S. (212) 216-7800), (Fax from U.S. (212) 564-7854), www.tandf.co.uk; *The Europa World Year Book.*

United Nations Economic Commission for Africa (ECA), PO Box 3001, Addis Ababa, Ethiopia, (Telephone in U.S. (212) 963-4957), www.uneca.org; *African Statistical Yearbook 2006.*

United Nations Statistics Division, New York, NY 10017, (800) 253-9646, Fax: (212) 963-4116, http://unstats.un.org; *Statistical Yearbook.*

DJIBOUTI - SOCIAL ECOLOGY

United Nations Statistics Division, New York, NY 10017, (800) 253-9646, Fax: (212) 963-4116, http://unstats.un.org; *World Statistics Pocketbook.*

DJIBOUTI - SOCIAL SECURITY

International Monetary Fund (IMF), 700 Nineteenth Street, NW, Washington, DC 20431, (202) 623-7000, Fax: (202) 623-4661, www.imf.org; *Government Finance Statistics Yearbook (2008 Edition).*

United Nations Statistics Division, New York, NY 10017, (800) 253-9646, Fax: (212) 963-4116, http://unstats.un.org; *National Accounts Statistics: Compendium of Income Distribution Statistics.*

DJIBOUTI - TAXATION

International Monetary Fund (IMF), 700 Nineteenth Street, NW, Washington, DC 20431, (202) 623-7000, Fax: (202) 623-4661, www.imf.org; *Government Finance Statistics Yearbook (2008 Edition).*

Taylor and Francis Group, An Informa Business, 2 Park Square, Milton Park, Abingdon, Oxford OX14 4RN, United Kingdom, (Dial from U.S. (212) 216-7800), (Fax from U.S. (212) 564-7854), www.tandf.co.uk; *The Europa World Year Book.*

DJIBOUTI - TELEPHONE

International Telecommunication Union (ITU), Place des Nations, 1211 Geneva 20, Switzerland, www.itu.int; World Telecommunication Indicators Database.

Palgrave Macmillan Ltd., Houndmills, Basingstoke, Hampshire, RG21 6XS, England, (Telephone in U.S. (888) 330-8477), (Fax in U.S. (800) 672-2054), www.palgrave.com; *The Statesman's Yearbook 2008.*

Taylor and Francis Group, An Informa Business, 2 Park Square, Milton Park, Abingdon, Oxford OX14 4RN, United Kingdom, (Dial from U.S. (212) 216-7800), (Fax from U.S. (212) 564-7854), www.tandf.co.uk; *The Europa World Year Book.*

United Nations Statistics Division, New York, NY 10017, (800) 253-9646, Fax: (212) 963-4116, http://unstats.un.org; *Statistical Yearbook* and *World Statistics Pocketbook.*

DJIBOUTI - TEXTILE INDUSTRY

United Nations Conference on Trade and Development (UNCTAD), DC2-1120, United Nations, New York, NY 10017, (212) 963-0027, www.unctad.org; *UNCTAD Commodity Yearbook.*

DJIBOUTI - TOURISM

Euromonitor International, Inc., 224 S. Michigan Avenue, Suite 1500, Chicago, IL 60604, (312) 922-1115, Fax: (312) 922-1157, www.euromonitor.com; *The World Economic Factbook 2008* and *World Marketing Data and Statistics.*

Palgrave Macmillan Ltd., Houndmills, Basingstoke, Hampshire, RG21 6XS, England, (Telephone in U.S. (888) 330-8477), (Fax in U.S. (800) 672-2054), www.palgrave.com; *The Statesman's Yearbook 2008.*

Taylor and Francis Group, An Informa Business, 2 Park Square, Milton Park, Abingdon, Oxford OX14 4RN, United Kingdom, (Dial from U.S. (212) 216-7800), (Fax from U.S. (212) 564-7854), www.tandf.co.uk; *The Europa World Year Book.*

United Nations Economic Commission for Africa (ECA), PO Box 3001, Addis Ababa, Ethiopia, (Telephone in U.S. (212) 963-4957), www.uneca.org; *African Statistical Yearbook 2006.*

The World Bank, 1818 H Street, NW, Washington, DC 20433, (202) 473-1000, Fax: (202) 477-6391, www.worldbank.org; *Djibouti.*

DJIBOUTI - TRADE

See DJIBOUTI - INTERNATIONAL TRADE

DJIBOUTI - TRANSPORTATION

Central Intelligence Agency, Office of Public Affairs, Washington, DC 20505, (703) 482-0623, Fax: (703) 482-1739, www.cia.gov; *The World Factbook.*

Euromonitor International, Inc., 224 S. Michigan Avenue, Suite 1500, Chicago, IL 60604, (312) 922-1115, Fax: (312) 922-1157, www.euromonitor.com; *International Marketing Data and Statistics 2008* and *World Marketing Data and Statistics.*

Palgrave Macmillan Ltd., Houndmills, Basingstoke, Hampshire, RG21 6XS, England, (Telephone in U.S. (888) 330-8477), (Fax in U.S. (800) 672-2054), www.palgrave.com; *The Statesman's Yearbook 2008.*

Taylor and Francis Group, An Informa Business, 2 Park Square, Milton Park, Abingdon, Oxford OX14 4RN, United Kingdom, (Dial from U.S. (212) 216-7800), (Fax from U.S. (212) 564-7854), www.tandf.co.uk; *The Europa World Year Book.*

United Nations Economic Commission for Africa (ECA), PO Box 3001, Addis Ababa, Ethiopia, (Telephone in U.S. (212) 963-4957), www.uneca.org; *African Statistical Yearbook 2006.*

United Nations Statistics Division, New York, NY 10017, (800) 253-9646, Fax: (212) 963-4116, http://unstats.un.org; *Human Development Report 2006.*

The World Bank, 1818 H Street, NW, Washington, DC 20433, (202) 473-1000, Fax: (202) 477-6391, www.worldbank.org; *Africa Live Database (LDB)* and *Djibouti.*

DJIBOUTI - UNEMPLOYMENT

Central Intelligence Agency, Office of Public Affairs, Washington, DC 20505, (703) 482-0623, Fax: (703) 482-1739, www.cia.gov; *The World Factbook.*

International Labour Office, I.L.O. Publications, 4 route des Morillons, CH-1211 Geneva 22, Switzerland, (Telephone in U.S. (202) 653-7652), (Fax in U.S. (202) 653-7687), www.ilo.org; *Yearbook of Labour Statistics 2006.*

DJIBOUTI - VITAL STATISTICS

Palgrave Macmillan Ltd., Houndmills, Basingstoke, Hampshire, RG21 6XS, England, (Telephone in U.S. (888) 330-8477), (Fax in U.S. (800) 672-2054), www.palgrave.com; *The Statesman's Yearbook 2008.*

United Nations Statistics Division, New York, NY 10017, (800) 253-9646, Fax: (212) 963-4116, http://unstats.un.org; *Statistical Yearbook.*

World Health Organization (WHO), Avenue Appia 20, 1211 Geneve 27, Switzerland, (Telephone in U.S. (212) 331-9081), www.who.int; *World Health Report 2006.*

DJIBOUTI - WAGES

International Labour Office, I.L.O. Publications, 4 route des Morillons, CH-1211 Geneva 22, Switzerland, (Telephone in U.S. (202) 653-7652), (Fax in U.S. (202) 653-7687), www.ilo.org; *Yearbook of Labour Statistics 2006*.

The World Bank, 1818 H Street, NW, Washington, DC 20433, (202) 473-1000, Fax: (202) 477-6391, www.worldbank.org; *Djibouti*.

DJIBOUTI - WELFARE STATE

International Monetary Fund (IMF), 700 Nineteenth Street, NW, Washington, DC 20431, (202) 623-7000, Fax: (202) 623-4661, www.imf.org; *Government Finance Statistics Yearbook (2008 Edition)*.

DOCTORS, M.D.'s

See PHYSICIANS

DOGS - OWNERSHIP

American Humane, 63 Inverness Drive East, Englewood, CO 80112, (303) 792-9900, Fax: (303) 792-5333, www.americanhumane.org; unpublished data.

American Veterinary Medical Association (AVMA), 1931 North Meacham Road, Suite 100, Schaumburg, IL 60173, (847) 925-8070, Fax: (847) 925-1329, www.avma.org; *U.S. Pet Ownership and Demographics Sourcebook*.

DOGS - RACING

Association of Racing Commissioners International (RCI), 2343 Alexandria Drive, Suite 200, Lexington, KY 40504, (859) 224-7070, Fax: (859) 224-7071, www.arci.com; unpublished data.

DOMESTIC SERVICE

National Institute of Statistics (NIS), Ministry of Planning, Preah Monivong Boulevard, Sankat Boeung Keng Kang 1, Phnom Penh, Cambodia, www.nis.gov.kh; *Child Domestic Worker Survey Phnom Penh 2003*.

U.S. Bureau of Labor Statistics (BLS), Postal Square Building, 2 Massachusetts Avenue, NE, Washington, DC 20212-0001, (202) 691-5200, Fax: (202) 691-6325, www.bls.gov; *Employment and Earnings (EE)* and unpublished data.

DOMINICA - NATIONAL STATISTICAL OFFICE

Central Statistical Office, Ministry of Finance, Kennedy Avenue, Roseau, Dominica, (Dial from U.S. (767) 266-3401), (Fax from U.S. (767) 449-9128); National Data Center.

DOMINICA - PRIMARY STATISTICS SOURCES

Central Statistical Office, Ministry of Finance, Kennedy Avenue, Roseau, Dominica, (Dial from U.S. (767) 266-3401), (Fax from U.S. (767) 449-9128); *Statistical Digest*.

DOMINICA - AGRICULTURAL MACHINERY

United Nations Statistics Division, New York, NY 10017, (800) 253-9646, Fax: (212) 963-4116, http://unstats.un.org; *Statistical Yearbook*.

DOMINICA - AGRICULTURE

Economist Intelligence Unit, 111 West 57th Street, New York, NY 10019, (212) 554-0600, Fax: (212) 586-1181, www.eiu.com; *Organisation of Eastern Caribbean States*.

Euromonitor International, Inc., 224 S. Michigan Avenue, Suite 1500, Chicago, IL 60604, (312) 922-1115, Fax: (312) 922-1157, www.euromonitor.com; *World Marketing Data and Statistics*.

Palgrave Macmillan Ltd., Houndmills, Basingstoke, Hampshire, RG21 6XS, England, (Telephone in U.S. (888) 330-8477), (Fax in U.S. (800) 672-2054), www.palgrave.com; *The Statesman's Yearbook 2008*.

Taylor and Francis Group, An Informa Business, 2 Park Square, Milton Park, Abingdon, Oxford OX14 4RN, United Kingdom, (Dial from U.S. (212) 216-7800), (Fax from U.S. (212) 564-7854), www.tandf.co.uk; *The Europa World Year Book*.

United Nations Conference on Trade and Development (UNCTAD), DC2-1120, United Nations, New York, NY 10017, (212) 963-0027, www.unctad.org; *UNCTAD Commodity Yearbook*.

United Nations Food and Agricultural Organization (FAO), Viale delle Terme di Caracalla, 00100 Rome, Italy, (Dial from U.S. (202) 653-2400), (Fax from U.S. (202) 653 5760), www.fao.org; AQUASTAT; *FAO Production Yearbook 2002; FAO Trade Yearbook;* and *The State of Food and Agriculture (SOFA) 2006*.

United Nations Statistics Division, New York, NY 10017, (800) 253-9646, Fax: (212) 963-4116, http://unstats.un.org; *Statistical Yearbook*.

The World Bank, 1818 H Street, NW, Washington, DC 20433, (202) 473-1000, Fax: (202) 477-6391, www.worldbank.org; *Dominica* and *World Development Indicators (WDI) 2008*.

DOMINICA - AIRLINES

Taylor and Francis Group, An Informa Business, 2 Park Square, Milton Park, Abingdon, Oxford OX14 4RN, United Kingdom, (Dial from U.S. (212) 216-7800), (Fax from U.S. (212) 564-7854), www.tandf.co.uk; *The Europa World Year Book*.

DOMINICA - AIRPORTS

Central Intelligence Agency, Office of Public Affairs, Washington, DC 20505, (703) 482-0623, Fax: (703) 482-1739, www.cia.gov; *The World Factbook*.

DOMINICA - ARMED FORCES

Central Intelligence Agency, Office of Public Affairs, Washington, DC 20505, (703) 482-0623, Fax: (703) 482-1739, www.cia.gov; *The World Factbook*.

Euromonitor International, Inc., 224 S. Michigan Avenue, Suite 1500, Chicago, IL 60604, (312) 922-1115, Fax: (312) 922-1157, www.euromonitor.com; *World Marketing Data and Statistics*.

International Monetary Fund (IMF), 700 Nineteenth Street, NW, Washington, DC 20431, (202) 623-7000, Fax: (202) 623-4661, www.imf.org; *Government Finance Statistics Yearbook (2008 Edition)*.

United Nations Statistics Division, New York, NY 10017, (800) 253-9646, Fax: (212) 963-4116, http://unstats.un.org; *Human Development Report 2006*.

DOMINICA - BALANCE OF PAYMENTS

Taylor and Francis Group, An Informa Business, 2 Park Square, Milton Park, Abingdon, Oxford OX14 4RN, United Kingdom, (Dial from U.S. (212) 216-7800), (Fax from U.S. (212) 564-7854), www.tandf.co.uk; *The Europa World Year Book*.

United Nations Conference on Trade and Development (UNCTAD), DC2-1120, United Nations, New York, NY 10017, (212) 963-0027, www.unctad.org; *Handbook of Statistics 2005*.

United Nations Statistics Division, New York, NY 10017, (800) 253-9646, Fax: (212) 963-4116, http://unstats.un.org; *Economic Survey of Latin America and the Caribbean 2004-2005*.

The World Bank, 1818 H Street, NW, Washington, DC 20433, (202) 473-1000, Fax: (202) 477-6391, www.worldbank.org; *Dominica* and *World Development Indicators (WDI) 2008*.

DOMINICA - BANKS AND BANKING

Euromonitor International, Inc., 224 S. Michigan Avenue, Suite 1500, Chicago, IL 60604, (312) 922-1115, Fax: (312) 922-1157, www.euromonitor.com; *World Marketing Data and Statistics*.

Palgrave Macmillan Ltd., Houndmills, Basingstoke, Hampshire, RG21 6XS, England, (Telephone in U.S. (888) 330-8477), (Fax in U.S. (800) 672-2054), www.palgrave.com; *The Statesman's Yearbook 2008*.

Taylor and Francis Group, An Informa Business, 2 Park Square, Milton Park, Abingdon, Oxford OX14 4RN, United Kingdom, (Dial from U.S. (212) 216-7800), (Fax from U.S. (212) 564-7854), www.tandf.co.uk; *The Europa World Year Book*.

DOMINICA - BROADCASTING

Central Intelligence Agency, Office of Public Affairs, Washington, DC 20505, (703) 482-0623, Fax: (703) 482-1739, www.cia.gov; *The World Factbook*.

Euromonitor International, Inc., 224 S. Michigan Avenue, Suite 1500, Chicago, IL 60604, (312) 922-1115, Fax: (312) 922-1157, www.euromonitor.com; *World Marketing Data and Statistics*.

Palgrave Macmillan Ltd., Houndmills, Basingstoke, Hampshire, RG21 6XS, England, (Telephone in U.S. (888) 330-8477), (Fax in U.S. (800) 672-2054), www.palgrave.com; *The Statesman's Yearbook 2008*.

WRTH Publications Limited, PO Box 290, Oxford OX2 7FT, UK, www.wrth.com; *World Radio TV Handbook 2007*.

DOMINICA - BUDGET

Central Intelligence Agency, Office of Public Affairs, Washington, DC 20505, (703) 482-0623, Fax: (703) 482-1739, www.cia.gov; *The World Factbook*.

DOMINICA - CAPITAL LEVY

International Monetary Fund (IMF), 700 Nineteenth Street, NW, Washington, DC 20431, (202) 623-7000, Fax: (202) 623-4661, www.imf.org; *Government Finance Statistics Yearbook (2008 Edition)*.

DOMINICA - CATTLE

See DOMINICA - LIVESTOCK

DOMINICA - CHILDBIRTH - STATISTICS

Central Intelligence Agency, Office of Public Affairs, Washington, DC 20505, (703) 482-0623, Fax: (703) 482-1739, www.cia.gov; *The World Factbook*.

Euromonitor International, Inc., 224 S. Michigan Avenue, Suite 1500, Chicago, IL 60604, (312) 922-1115, Fax: (312) 922-1157, www.euromonitor.com; *International Marketing Data and Statistics 2008* and *The World Economic Factbook 2008*.

Taylor and Francis Group, An Informa Business, 2 Park Square, Milton Park, Abingdon, Oxford OX14 4RN, United Kingdom, (Dial from U.S. (212) 216-7800), (Fax from U.S. (212) 564-7854), www.tandf.co.uk; *The Europa World Year Book*.

United Nations Statistics Division, New York, NY 10017, (800) 253-9646, Fax: (212) 963-4116, http://unstats.un.org; *Demographic Yearbook* and *Statistical Yearbook*.

The World Bank, 1818 H Street, NW, Washington, DC 20433, (202) 473-1000, Fax: (202) 477-6391, www.worldbank.org; *World Development Indicators (WDI) 2008*.

World Health Organization (WHO), Avenue Appia 20, 1211 Geneve 27, Switzerland, (Telephone in U.S. (212) 331-9081), www.who.int; *World Health Report 2006*.

DOMINICA - CLIMATE

Palgrave Macmillan Ltd., Houndmills, Basingstoke, Hampshire, RG21 6XS, England, (Telephone in U.S. (888) 330-8477), (Fax in U.S. (800) 672-2054), www.palgrave.com; *The Statesman's Yearbook 2008*.

DOMINICA - COCOA PRODUCTION

See DOMINICA - CROPS

DOMINICA - COMMERCE

Palgrave Macmillan Ltd., Houndmills, Basingstoke, Hampshire, RG21 6XS, England, (Telephone in U.S.

(888) 330-8477), (Fax in U.S. (800) 672-2054), www.palgrave.com; *The Statesman's Yearbook 2008.*

DOMINICA - COMMODITY EXCHANGES

Commodity Research Bureau, 330 South Wells Street, Suite 612, Chicago, IL 60606-7110, (800) 621-5271, Fax: (312) 939-4135, www.crbtrader.com; *2006 CRB Commodity Yearbook and CD.*

International Monetary Fund (IMF), 700 Nineteenth Street, NW, Washington, DC 20431, (202) 623-7000, Fax: (202) 623-4661, www.imf.org; *IMF Primary Commodity Prices.*

United Nations Food and Agricultural Organization (FAO), Viale delle Terme di Caracalla, 00100 Rome, Italy, (Dial from U.S. (202) 653-2400), (Fax from U.S. (202) 653 5760), www.fao.org; *The State of Food and Agriculture (SOFA) 2006.*

DOMINICA - CONSUMER PRICE INDEXES

Taylor and Francis Group, An Informa Business, 2 Park Square, Milton Park, Abingdon, Oxford OX14 4RN, United Kingdom, (Dial from U.S. (212) 216-7800), (Fax from U.S. (212) 564-7854), www.tandf.co.uk; *The Europa World Year Book.*

United Nations Statistics Division, New York, NY 10017, (800) 253-9646, Fax: (212) 963-4116, http://unstats.un.org; *Statistical Yearbook.*

The World Bank, 1818 H Street, NW, Washington, DC 20433, (202) 473-1000, Fax: (202) 477-6391, www.worldbank.org; *Dominica.*

DOMINICA - CORN INDUSTRY

See DOMINICA - CROPS

DOMINICA - COST AND STANDARD OF LIVING

International Monetary Fund (IMF), 700 Nineteenth Street, NW, Washington, DC 20431, (202) 623-7000, Fax: (202) 623-4661, www.imf.org; *Government Finance Statistics Yearbook (2008 Edition).*

DOMINICA - CROPS

Palgrave Macmillan Ltd., Houndmills, Basingstoke, Hampshire, RG21 6XS, England, (Telephone in U.S. (888) 330-8477), (Fax in U.S. (800) 672-2054), www.palgrave.com; *The Statesman's Yearbook 2008.*

Taylor and Francis Group, An Informa Business, 2 Park Square, Milton Park, Abingdon, Oxford OX14 4RN, United Kingdom, (Dial from U.S. (212) 216-7800), (Fax from U.S. (212) 564-7854), www.tandf.co.uk; *The Europa World Year Book.*

United Nations Conference on Trade and Development (UNCTAD), DC2-1120, United Nations, New York, NY 10017, (212) 963-0027, www.unctad.org; *UNCTAD Commodity Yearbook.*

United Nations Food and Agricultural Organization (FAO), Viale delle Terme di Caracalla, 00100 Rome, Italy, (Dial from U.S. (202) 653-2400), (Fax from U.S. (202) 653 5760), www.fao.org; *FAO Production Yearbook 2002* and *The State of Food and Agriculture (SOFA) 2006.*

United Nations Statistics Division, New York, NY 10017, (800) 253-9646, Fax: (212) 963-4116, http://unstats.un.org; *Statistical Yearbook.*

DOMINICA - CUSTOMS ADMINISTRATION

International Monetary Fund (IMF), 700 Nineteenth Street, NW, Washington, DC 20431, (202) 623-7000, Fax: (202) 623-4661, www.imf.org; *Government Finance Statistics Yearbook (2008 Edition).*

Palgrave Macmillan Ltd., Houndmills, Basingstoke, Hampshire, RG21 6XS, England, (Telephone in U.S. (888) 330-8477), (Fax in U.S. (800) 672-2054), www.palgrave.com; *The Statesman's Yearbook 2008.*

DOMINICA - DAIRY PROCESSING

Taylor and Francis Group, An Informa Business, 2 Park Square, Milton Park, Abingdon, Oxford OX14 4RN, United Kingdom, (Dial from U.S. (212) 216-7800), (Fax from U.S. (212) 564-7854), www.tandf.co.uk; *The Europa World Year Book.*

United Nations Food and Agricultural Organization (FAO), Viale delle Terme di Caracalla, 00100 Rome, Italy, (Dial from U.S. (202) 653-2400), (Fax from U.S. (202) 653 5760), www.fao.org; *The State of Food and Agriculture (SOFA) 2006.*

DOMINICA - DEATH RATES

See DOMINICA - MORTALITY

DOMINICA - DEBTS, EXTERNAL

United Nations Statistics Division, New York, NY 10017, (800) 253-9646, Fax: (212) 963-4116, http://unstats.un.org; *Economic Survey of Latin America and the Caribbean 2004-2005.*

The World Bank, 1818 H Street, NW, Washington, DC 20433, (202) 473-1000, Fax: (202) 477-6391, www.worldbank.org; *Global Development Finance 2007* and *World Development Indicators (WDI) 2008.*

DOMINICA - DEFENSE EXPENDITURES

See DOMINICA - ARMED FORCES

DOMINICA - DEMOGRAPHY

Euromonitor International, Inc., 224 S. Michigan Avenue, Suite 1500, Chicago, IL 60604, (312) 922-1115, Fax: (312) 922-1157, www.euromonitor.com; *International Marketing Data and Statistics 2008; The World Economic Factbook 2008;* and *World Marketing Data and Statistics.*

United Nations Statistics Division, New York, NY 10017, (800) 253-9646, Fax: (212) 963-4116, http://unstats.un.org; *Human Development Report 2006.*

The World Bank, 1818 H Street, NW, Washington, DC 20433, (202) 473-1000, Fax: (202) 477-6391, www.worldbank.org; *Dominica.*

DOMINICA - DISPOSABLE INCOME

United Nations Statistics Division, New York, NY 10017, (800) 253-9646, Fax: (212) 963-4116, http://unstats.un.org; *National Accounts Statistics: Compendium of Income Distribution Statistics* and *Statistical Yearbook.*

DOMINICA - DIVORCE

United Nations Statistics Division, New York, NY 10017, (800) 253-9646, Fax: (212) 963-4116, http://unstats.un.org; *Demographic Yearbook* and *Statistical Yearbook.*

DOMINICA - ECONOMIC CONDITIONS

Center for International Business Education Research (CIBER), Columbia Business School and School of International and Public Affairs, Uris Hall, Room 212, 3022 Broadway, New York, NY 10027-6902, Mr. Joshua Safier, (212) 854-4750, Fax: (212) 222-9821, www.columbia.edu/cu/ciber/; Datastream International.

Central Intelligence Agency, Office of Public Affairs, Washington, DC 20505, (703) 482-0623, Fax: (703) 482-1739, www.cia.gov; *The World Factbook.*

DSI Data Service Information, Xantener Strasse 51a, D-47495 Rheinberg, Germany, www.dsidata.com; *Campus Solution.*

Dun and Bradstreet (DB) Corporation, 103 JFK Parkway, Short Hills, NJ 07078, (973) 921-5500, www.dnb.com; *Country Report.*

Economist Intelligence Unit, 111 West 57th Street, New York, NY 10019, (212) 554-0600, Fax: (212) 586-1181, www.eiu.com; *Organisation of Eastern Caribbean States.*

Euromonitor International, Inc., 224 S. Michigan Avenue, Suite 1500, Chicago, IL 60604, (312) 922-1115, Fax: (312) 922-1157, www.euromonitor.com; *The World Economic Factbook 2008* and *World Marketing Data and Statistics.*

International Monetary Fund (IMF), 700 Nineteenth Street, NW, Washington, DC 20431, (202) 623-7000, Fax: (202) 623-4661, www.imf.org; *World Economic Outlook Reports.*

Palgrave Macmillan Ltd., Houndmills, Basingstoke, Hampshire, RG21 6XS, England, (Telephone in U.S. (888) 330-8477), (Fax in U.S. (800) 672-2054), www.palgrave.com; *The Statesman's Yearbook 2008.*

Taylor and Francis Group, An Informa Business, 2 Park Square, Milton Park, Abingdon, Oxford OX14 4RN, United Kingdom, (Dial from U.S. (212) 216-7800), (Fax from U.S. (212) 564-7854), www.tandf.co.uk; *The Europa World Year Book.*

United Nations Statistics Division, New York, NY 10017, (800) 253-9646, Fax: (212) 963-4116, http://unstats.un.org; *Economic Survey of Latin America and the Caribbean 2004-2005* and *World Statistics Pocketbook.*

The World Bank, 1818 H Street, NW, Washington, DC 20433, (202) 473-1000, Fax: (202) 477-6391, www.worldbank.org; *Dominica; Global Economic Monitor (GEM); Global Economic Prospects 2008;* and *The World Bank Atlas 2003-2004.*

DOMINICA - EDUCATION

Euromonitor International, Inc., 224 S. Michigan Avenue, Suite 1500, Chicago, IL 60604, (312) 922-1115, Fax: (312) 922-1157, www.euromonitor.com; *International Marketing Data and Statistics 2008.*

International Monetary Fund (IMF), 700 Nineteenth Street, NW, Washington, DC 20431, (202) 623-7000, Fax: (202) 623-4661, www.imf.org; *Government Finance Statistics Yearbook (2008 Edition).*

Palgrave Macmillan Ltd., Houndmills, Basingstoke, Hampshire, RG21 6XS, England, (Telephone in U.S. (888) 330-8477), (Fax in U.S. (800) 672-2054), www.palgrave.com; *The Statesman's Yearbook 2008.*

Taylor and Francis Group, An Informa Business, 2 Park Square, Milton Park, Abingdon, Oxford OX14 4RN, United Kingdom, (Dial from U.S. (212) 216-7800), (Fax from U.S. (212) 564-7854), www.tandf.co.uk; *The Europa World Year Book.*

UNESCO Institute for Statistics, C.P. 6128 Succursale Centre-Ville, Montreal, Quebec, H3C 3J7 Canada, (Dial from U.S. (514) 343-6880), (Fax from U.S. (514) 343 6882), www.uis.unesco.org; *Statistical Tables.*

United Nations Statistics Division, New York, NY 10017, (800) 253-9646, Fax: (212) 963-4116, http://unstats.un.org; *Human Development Report 2006.*

The World Bank, 1818 H Street, NW, Washington, DC 20433, (202) 473-1000, Fax: (202) 477-6391, www.worldbank.org; *Dominica* and *World Development Indicators (WDI) 2008.*

DOMINICA - ELECTRICITY

Palgrave Macmillan Ltd., Houndmills, Basingstoke, Hampshire, RG21 6XS, England, (Telephone in U.S. (888) 330-8477), (Fax in U.S. (800) 672-2054), www.palgrave.com; *The Statesman's Yearbook 2008.*

United Nations Statistics Division, New York, NY 10017, (800) 253-9646, Fax: (212) 963-4116, http://unstats.un.org; *Human Development Report 2006.*

DOMINICA - EMPLOYMENT

Euromonitor International, Inc., 224 S. Michigan Avenue, Suite 1500, Chicago, IL 60604, (312) 922-1115, Fax: (312) 922-1157, www.euromonitor.com; *International Marketing Data and Statistics 2008.*

International Labour Office, I.L.O. Publications, 4 route des Morillons, CH-1211 Geneva 22, Switzerland, (Telephone in U.S. (202) 653-7652), (Fax in U.S. (202) 653-7687), www.ilo.org; *Yearbook of Labour Statistics 2006.*

The World Bank, 1818 H Street, NW, Washington, DC 20433, (202) 473-1000, Fax: (202) 477-6391, www.worldbank.org; *Dominica.*

DOMINICA - ENVIRONMENTAL CONDITIONS

DSI Data Service Information, Xantener Strasse 51a, D-47495 Rheinberg, Germany, www.dsidata.com; *Campus Solution* and *DSI's Global Environmental Database.*

Economist Intelligence Unit, 111 West 57th Street, New York, NY 10019, (212) 554-0600, Fax: (212) 586-1181, www.eiu.com; *Organisation of Eastern Caribbean States.*

United Nations Statistics Division, New York, NY 10017, (800) 253-9646, Fax: (212) 963-4116, http://unstats.un.org; *World Statistics Pocketbook.*

DOMINICA - EXCISE TAX

Euromonitor International, Inc., 224 S. Michigan Avenue, Suite 1500, Chicago, IL 60604, (312) 922-1115, Fax: (312) 922-1157, www.euromonitor.com; *International Marketing Data and Statistics 2008* and *The World Economic Factbook 2008.*

International Monetary Fund (IMF), 700 Nineteenth Street, NW, Washington, DC 20431, (202) 623-7000, Fax: (202) 623-4661, www.imf.org; *Government Finance Statistics Yearbook (2008 Edition).*

Taylor and Francis Group, An Informa Business, 2 Park Square, Milton Park, Abingdon, Oxford OX14 4RN, United Kingdom, (Dial from U.S. (212) 216-7800), (Fax from U.S. (212) 564-7854), www.tandf.co.uk; *The Europa World Year Book.*

United Nations Statistics Division, New York, NY 10017, (800) 253-9646, Fax: (212) 963-4116, http://unstats.un.org; *World Statistics Pocketbook.*

DOMINICA - EXPORTS

Central Intelligence Agency, Office of Public Affairs, Washington, DC 20505, (703) 482-0623, Fax: (703) 482-1739, www.cia.gov; *The World Factbook.*

Economist Intelligence Unit, 111 West 57th Street, New York, NY 10019, (212) 554-0600, Fax: (212) 586-1181, www.eiu.com; *Organisation of Eastern Caribbean States.*

Euromonitor International, Inc., 224 S. Michigan Avenue, Suite 1500, Chicago, IL 60604, (312) 922-1115, Fax: (312) 922-1157, www.euromonitor.com; *International Marketing Data and Statistics 2008* and *The World Economic Factbook 2008.*

International Monetary Fund (IMF), 700 Nineteenth Street, NW, Washington, DC 20431, (202) 623-7000, Fax: (202) 623-4661, www.imf.org; *Government Finance Statistics Yearbook (2008 Edition).*

Palgrave Macmillan Ltd., Houndmills, Basingstoke, Hampshire, RG21 6XS, England, (Telephone in U.S. (888) 330-8477), (Fax in U.S. (800) 672-2054), www.palgrave.com; *The Statesman's Yearbook 2008.*

Taylor and Francis Group, An Informa Business, 2 Park Square, Milton Park, Abingdon, Oxford OX14 4RN, United Kingdom, (Dial from U.S. (212) 216-7800), (Fax from U.S. (212) 564-7854), www.tandf.co.uk; *The Europa World Year Book.*

United Nations Conference on Trade and Development (UNCTAD), DC2-1120, United Nations, New York, NY 10017, (212) 963-0027, www.unctad.org; *Handbook of Statistics 2005.*

United Nations Food and Agricultural Organization (FAO), Viale delle Terme di Caracalla, 00100 Rome, Italy, (Dial from U.S. (202) 653-2400), (Fax from U.S. (202) 653 5760), www.fao.org; *The State of Food and Agriculture (SOFA) 2006.*

The World Bank, 1818 H Street, NW, Washington, DC 20433, (202) 473-1000, Fax: (202) 477-6391, www.worldbank.org; *World Development Indicators (WDI) 2008.*

DOMINICA - FERTILITY, HUMAN

Central Intelligence Agency, Office of Public Affairs, Washington, DC 20505, (703) 482-0623, Fax: (703) 482-1739, www.cia.gov; *The World Factbook.*

United Nations Statistics Division, New York, NY 10017, (800) 253-9646, Fax: (212) 963-4116, http://unstats.un.org; *Human Development Report 2006.*

The World Bank, 1818 H Street, NW, Washington, DC 20433, (202) 473-1000, Fax: (202) 477-6391, www.worldbank.org; *The World Bank Atlas 2003-2004* and *World Development Indicators (WDI) 2008.*

DOMINICA - FERTILIZER INDUSTRY

United Nations Food and Agricultural Organization (FAO), Viale delle Terme di Caracalla, 00100 Rome, Italy, (Dial from U.S. (202) 653-2400), (Fax from U.S. (202) 653 5760), www.fao.org; *The State of Food and Agriculture (SOFA) 2006.*

DOMINICA - FETAL MORTALITY

See DOMINICA - MORTALITY

DOMINICA - FINANCE

Taylor and Francis Group, An Informa Business, 2 Park Square, Milton Park, Abingdon, Oxford OX14 4RN, United Kingdom, (Dial from U.S. (212) 216-7800), (Fax from U.S. (212) 564-7854), www.tandf.co.uk; *The Europa World Year Book.*

United Nations Statistics Division, New York, NY 10017, (800) 253-9646, Fax: (212) 963-4116, http://unstats.un.org; *National Accounts Statistics: Compendium of Income Distribution Statistics* and *Statistical Yearbook.*

The World Bank, 1818 H Street, NW, Washington, DC 20433, (202) 473-1000, Fax: (202) 477-6391, www.worldbank.org; *Dominica.*

DOMINICA - FINANCE, PUBLIC

Bernan Essential Government Publications, 4611-F Assembly Drive, Lanham MD, 20706-4391, (301) 459-2255, Fax: (800) 865-3450, www.bernan.com; *National Accounts Statistics.*

Economist Intelligence Unit, 111 West 57th Street, New York, NY 10019, (212) 554-0600, Fax: (212) 586-1181, www.eiu.com; *Organisation of Eastern Caribbean States.*

International Monetary Fund (IMF), 700 Nineteenth Street, NW, Washington, DC 20431, (202) 623-7000, Fax: (202) 623-4661, www.imf.org; *International Financial Statistics* and *International Financial Statistics Online Service.*

Palgrave Macmillan Ltd., Houndmills, Basingstoke, Hampshire, RG21 6XS, England, (Telephone in U.S. (888) 330-8477), (Fax in U.S. (800) 672-2054), www.palgrave.com; *The Statesman's Yearbook 2008.*

Taylor and Francis Group, An Informa Business, 2 Park Square, Milton Park, Abingdon, Oxford OX14 4RN, United Kingdom, (Dial from U.S. (212) 216-7800), (Fax from U.S. (212) 564-7854), www.tandf.co.uk; *The Europa World Year Book.*

The World Bank, 1818 H Street, NW, Washington, DC 20433, (202) 473-1000, Fax: (202) 477-6391, www.worldbank.org; *Dominica.*

DOMINICA - FISHERIES

Taylor and Francis Group, An Informa Business, 2 Park Square, Milton Park, Abingdon, Oxford OX14 4RN, United Kingdom, (Dial from U.S. (212) 216-7800), (Fax from U.S. (212) 564-7854), www.tandf.co.uk; *The Europa World Year Book.*

United Nations Conference on Trade and Development (UNCTAD), DC2-1120, United Nations, New York, NY 10017, (212) 963-0027, www.unctad.org; *UNCTAD Commodity Yearbook.*

United Nations Food and Agricultural Organization (FAO), Viale delle Terme di Caracalla, 00100 Rome, Italy, (Dial from U.S. (202) 653-2400), (Fax from U.S. (202) 653 5760), www.fao.org; *FAO Yearbook of Fishery Statistics;* Fishery Databases; FISHSTAT Database. Subjects covered include: Aquaculture production, capture production, fishery commodities; and *The State of Food and Agriculture (SOFA) 2006.*

The World Bank, 1818 H Street, NW, Washington, DC 20433, (202) 473-1000, Fax: (202) 477-6391, www.worldbank.org; *Dominica.*

DOMINICA - FOOD

United Nations Conference on Trade and Development (UNCTAD), DC2-1120, United Nations, New York, NY 10017, (212) 963-0027, www.unctad.org; *UNCTAD Commodity Yearbook.*

United Nations Food and Agricultural Organization (FAO), Viale delle Terme di Caracalla, 00100 Rome, Italy, (Dial from U.S. (202) 653-2400), (Fax from U.S. (202) 653 5760), www.fao.org; *The State of Food and Agriculture (SOFA) 2006.*

United Nations Statistics Division, New York, NY 10017, (800) 253-9646, Fax: (212) 963-4116, http://unstats.un.org; *Human Development Report 2006.*

DOMINICA - FORESTS AND FORESTRY

Taylor and Francis Group, An Informa Business, 2 Park Square, Milton Park, Abingdon, Oxford OX14 4RN, United Kingdom, (Dial from U.S. (212) 216-7800), (Fax from U.S. (212) 564-7854), www.tandf.co.uk; *The Europa World Year Book.*

United Nations Conference on Trade and Development (UNCTAD), DC2-1120, United Nations, New York, NY 10017, (212) 963-0027, www.unctad.org; *UNCTAD Commodity Yearbook.*

United Nations Food and Agricultural Organization (FAO), Viale delle Terme di Caracalla, 00100 Rome, Italy, (Dial from U.S. (202) 653-2400), (Fax from U.S. (202) 653 5760), www.fao.org; *FAO Yearbook of Forest Products* and *The State of Food and Agriculture (SOFA) 2006.*

The World Bank, 1818 H Street, NW, Washington, DC 20433, (202) 473-1000, Fax: (202) 477-6391, www.worldbank.org; *Dominica.*

DOMINICA - GOLD INDUSTRY

The World Bank, 1818 H Street, NW, Washington, DC 20433, (202) 473-1000, Fax: (202) 477-6391, www.worldbank.org; *World Development Indicators (WDI) 2008.*

DOMINICA - GRANTS-IN-AID

International Monetary Fund (IMF), 700 Nineteenth Street, NW, Washington, DC 20431, (202) 623-7000, Fax: (202) 623-4661, www.imf.org; *Government Finance Statistics Yearbook (2008 Edition).*

DOMINICA - GROSS DOMESTIC PRODUCT

Economist Intelligence Unit, 111 West 57th Street, New York, NY 10019, (212) 554-0600, Fax: (212) 586-1181, www.eiu.com; *Organisation of Eastern Caribbean States.*

Euromonitor International, Inc., 224 S. Michigan Avenue, Suite 1500, Chicago, IL 60604, (312) 922-1115, Fax: (312) 922-1157, www.euromonitor.com; *International Marketing Data and Statistics 2008* and *The World Economic Factbook 2008.*

Taylor and Francis Group, An Informa Business, 2 Park Square, Milton Park, Abingdon, Oxford OX14 4RN, United Kingdom, (Dial from U.S. (212) 216-7800), (Fax from U.S. (212) 564-7854), www.tandf.co.uk; *The Europa World Year Book.*

United Nations Statistics Division, New York, NY 10017, (800) 253-9646, Fax: (212) 963-4116, http://unstats.un.org; *Human Development Report 2006; National Accounts Statistics: Compendium of Income Distribution Statistics;* and *Statistical Yearbook.*

The World Bank, 1818 H Street, NW, Washington, DC 20433, (202) 473-1000, Fax: (202) 477-6391, www.worldbank.org; *World Development Indicators (WDI) 2008.*

DOMINICA - GROSS NATIONAL PRODUCT

Palgrave Macmillan Ltd., Houndmills, Basingstoke, Hampshire, RG21 6XS, England, (Telephone in U.S. (888) 330-8477), (Fax in U.S. (800) 672-2054), www.palgrave.com; *The Statesman's Yearbook 2008.*

The World Bank, 1818 H Street, NW, Washington, DC 20433, (202) 473-1000, Fax: (202) 477-6391, www.worldbank.org; *The World Bank Atlas 2003-2004* and *World Development Indicators (WDI) 2008.*

DOMINICA - HIDES AND SKINS INDUSTRY

United Nations Food and Agricultural Organization (FAO), Viale delle Terme di Caracalla, 00100 Rome,

Italy, (Dial from U.S. (202) 653-2400), (Fax from U.S. (202) 653 5760), www.fao.org; *FAO Production Yearbook 2002.*

DOMINICA - HOUSING

Euromonitor International, Inc., 224 S. Michigan Avenue, Suite 1500, Chicago, IL 60604, (312) 922-1115, Fax: (312) 922-1157, www.euromonitor.com; *World Marketing Data and Statistics.*

United Nations Statistics Division, New York, NY 10017, (800) 253-9646, Fax: (212) 963-4116, http://unstats.un.org; *Statistical Yearbook.*

DOMINICA - ILLITERATE PERSONS

Euromonitor International, Inc., 224 S. Michigan Avenue, Suite 1500, Chicago, IL 60604, (312) 922-1115, Fax: (312) 922-1157, www.euromonitor.com; *The World Economic Factbook 2008.*

UNESCO Institute for Statistics, C.P. 6128 Succursale Centre-Ville, Montreal, Quebec, H3C 3J7 Canada, (Dial from U.S. (514) 343-6880), (Fax from U.S. (514) 343 6882), www.uis.unesco.org; *Statistical Tables.*

United Nations Statistics Division, New York, NY 10017, (800) 253-9646, Fax: (212) 963-4116, http://unstats.un.org; *Human Development Report 2006.*

DOMINICA - IMPORTS

Central Intelligence Agency, Office of Public Affairs, Washington, DC 20505, (703) 482-0623, Fax: (703) 482-1739, www.cia.gov; *The World Factbook.*

Economist Intelligence Unit, 111 West 57th Street, New York, NY 10019, (212) 554-0600, Fax: (212) 586-1181, www.eiu.com; *Organisation of Eastern Caribbean States.*

Euromonitor International, Inc., 224 S. Michigan Avenue, Suite 1500, Chicago, IL 60604, (312) 922-1115, Fax: (312) 922-1157, www.euromonitor.com; *International Marketing Data and Statistics 2008* and *The World Economic Factbook 2008.*

International Monetary Fund (IMF), 700 Nineteenth Street, NW, Washington, DC 20431, (202) 623-7000, Fax: (202) 623-4661, www.imf.org; *Government Finance Statistics Yearbook (2008 Edition).*

Palgrave Macmillan Ltd., Houndmills, Basingstoke, Hampshire, RG21 6XS, England, (Telephone in U.S. (888) 330-8477), (Fax in U.S. (800) 672-2054), www.palgrave.com; *The Statesman's Yearbook 2008.*

Taylor and Francis Group, An Informa Business, 2 Park Square, Milton Park, Abingdon, Oxford OX14 4RN, United Kingdom, (Dial from U.S. (212) 216-7800), (Fax from U.S. (212) 564-7854), www.tandf.co.uk; *The Europa World Year Book.*

United Nations Conference on Trade and Development (UNCTAD), DC2-1120, United Nations, New York, NY 10017, (212) 963-0027, www.unctad.org; *Handbook of Statistics 2005.*

United Nations Food and Agricultural Organization (FAO), Viale delle Terme di Caracalla, 00100 Rome, Italy, (Dial from U.S. (202) 653-2400), (Fax from U.S. (202) 653 5760), www.fao.org; *The State of Food and Agriculture (SOFA) 2006.*

The World Bank, 1818 H Street, NW, Washington, DC 20433, (202) 473-1000, Fax: (202) 477-6391, www.worldbank.org; *World Development Indicators (WDI) 2008.*

DOMINICA - INCOME TAXES

See DOMINICA - TAXATION

DOMINICA - INDUSTRIES

Central Intelligence Agency, Office of Public Affairs, Washington, DC 20505, (703) 482-0623, Fax: (703) 482-1739, www.cia.gov; *The World Factbook.*

Economist Intelligence Unit, 111 West 57th Street, New York, NY 10019, (212) 554-0600, Fax: (212) 586-1181, www.eiu.com; *Organisation of Eastern Caribbean States.*

Euromonitor International, Inc., 224 S. Michigan Avenue, Suite 1500, Chicago, IL 60604, (312) 922-1115, Fax: (312) 922-1157, www.euromonitor.com; *World Marketing Data and Statistics.*

International Labour Office, I.L.O. Publications, 4 route des Morillons, CH-1211 Geneva 22, Switzerland, (Telephone in U.S. (202) 653-7652), (Fax in U.S. (202) 653-7687), www.ilo.org; *Yearbook of Labour Statistics 2006.*

Taylor and Francis Group, An Informa Business, 2 Park Square, Milton Park, Abingdon, Oxford OX14 4RN, United Kingdom, (Dial from U.S. (212) 216-7800), (Fax from U.S. (212) 564-7854), www.tandf.co.uk; *The Europa World Year Book.*

United Nations Industrial Development Organization (UNIDO), 1 United Nations Plaza, New York, NY 10017, (212) 963 6890, Fax: (212) 963-7904, http://unido.org; Industrial Statistics Database 2008 (INDSTAT) and *The International Yearbook of Industrial Statistics 2008.*

United Nations Statistics Division, New York, NY 10017, (800) 253-9646, Fax: (212) 963-4116, http://unstats.un.org; *Economic Survey of Latin America and the Caribbean 2004-2005.*

The World Bank, 1818 H Street, NW, Washington, DC 20433, (202) 473-1000, Fax: (202) 477-6391, www.worldbank.org; *World Development Indicators (WDI) 2008.*

DOMINICA - INFANT AND MATERNAL MORTALITY

See DOMINICA - MORTALITY

DOMINICA - INFLATION (FINANCE)

United Nations Statistics Division, New York, NY 10017, (800) 253-9646, Fax: (212) 963-4116, http://unstats.un.org; *Economic Survey of Latin America and the Caribbean 2004-2005.*

DOMINICA - INTERNATIONAL TRADE

Economist Intelligence Unit, 111 West 57th Street, New York, NY 10019, (212) 554-0600, Fax: (212) 586-1181, www.eiu.com; *Organisation of Eastern Caribbean States.*

Euromonitor International, Inc., 224 S. Michigan Avenue, Suite 1500, Chicago, IL 60604, (312) 922-1115, Fax: (312) 922-1157, www.euromonitor.com; *The World Economic Factbook 2008* and *World Marketing Data and Statistics.*

Organisation for Economic Cooperation and Development (OECD), 2 rue Andre Pascal, F-75775 Paris Cedex 16, France, (Telephone in U.S. (202) 785-6323), (Fax in U.S. (202) 785-0350), www.oecd.org; *International Trade by Commodity Statistics (ITCS).*

Palgrave Macmillan Ltd., Houndmills, Basingstoke, Hampshire, RG21 6XS, England, (Telephone in U.S. (888) 330-8477), (Fax in U.S. (800) 672-2054), www.palgrave.com; *The Statesman's Yearbook 2008.*

Taylor and Francis Group, An Informa Business, 2 Park Square, Milton Park, Abingdon, Oxford OX14 4RN, United Kingdom, (Dial from U.S. (212) 216-7800), (Fax from U.S. (212) 564-7854), www.tandf.co.uk; *The Europa World Year Book.*

United Nations Conference on Trade and Development (UNCTAD), DC2-1120, United Nations, New York, NY 10017, (212) 963-0027, www.unctad.org; *UNCTAD Commodity Yearbook.*

United Nations Food and Agricultural Organization (FAO), Viale delle Terme di Caracalla, 00100 Rome, Italy, (Dial from U.S. (202) 653-2400), (Fax from U.S. (202) 653 5760), www.fao.org; *FAO Trade Yearbook* and *The State of Food and Agriculture (SOFA) 2006.*

United Nations Statistics Division, New York, NY 10017, (800) 253-9646, Fax: (212) 963-4116, http://unstats.un.org; *Economic Survey of Latin America and the Caribbean 2004-2005* and *International Trade Statistics Yearbook.*

The World Bank, 1818 H Street, NW, Washington, DC 20433, (202) 473-1000, Fax: (202) 477-6391, www.worldbank.org; *Dominica* and *World Development Indicators (WDI) 2008.*

World Trade Organization (WTO), Centre William Rappard, Rue de Lausanne 154, CH-1211 Geneva 21, Switzerland, www.wto.org; *International Trade Statistics 2006.*

DOMINICA - INTERNET USERS

International Telecommunication Union (ITU), Place des Nations, 1211 Geneva 20, Switzerland, www.itu.int; *World Telecommunication/ICT Indicators Database on CD-ROM; World Telecommunication/ICT Indicators Database Online;* and *Yearbook of Statistics - Telecommunication Services (Chronological Time Series 1997-2006).*

The World Bank, 1818 H Street, NW, Washington, DC 20433, (202) 473-1000, Fax: (202) 477-6391, www.worldbank.org; *Dominica.*

DOMINICA - LABOR

Central Intelligence Agency, Office of Public Affairs, Washington, DC 20505, (703) 482-0623, Fax: (703) 482-1739, www.cia.gov; *The World Factbook.*

Euromonitor International, Inc., 224 S. Michigan Avenue, Suite 1500, Chicago, IL 60604, (312) 922-1115, Fax: (312) 922-1157, www.euromonitor.com; *International Marketing Data and Statistics 2008* and *World Marketing Data and Statistics.*

International Labour Office, I.L.O. Publications, 4 route des Morillons, CH-1211 Geneva 22, Switzerland, (Telephone in U.S. (202) 653-7652), (Fax in U.S. (202) 653-7687), www.ilo.org; *Yearbook of Labour Statistics 2006.*

United Nations Food and Agricultural Organization (FAO), Viale delle Terme di Caracalla, 00100 Rome, Italy, (Dial from U.S. (202) 653-2400), (Fax from U.S. (202) 653 5760), www.fao.org; *The State of Food and Agriculture (SOFA) 2006.*

United Nations Statistics Division, New York, NY 10017, (800) 253-9646, Fax: (212) 963-4116, http://unstats.un.org; *Human Development Report 2006.*

The World Bank, 1818 H Street, NW, Washington, DC 20433, (202) 473-1000, Fax: (202) 477-6391, www.worldbank.org; *The World Bank Atlas 2003-2004* and *World Development Indicators (WDI) 2008.*

DOMINICA - LAND USE

Central Intelligence Agency, Office of Public Affairs, Washington, DC 20505, (703) 482-0623, Fax: (703) 482-1739, www.cia.gov; *The World Factbook.*

Euromonitor International, Inc., 224 S. Michigan Avenue, Suite 1500, Chicago, IL 60604, (312) 922-1115, Fax: (312) 922-1157, www.euromonitor.com; *International Marketing Data and Statistics 2008.*

United Nations Food and Agricultural Organization (FAO), Viale delle Terme di Caracalla, 00100 Rome, Italy, (Dial from U.S. (202) 653-2400), (Fax from U.S. (202) 653 5760), www.fao.org; *FAO Production Yearbook 2002.*

DOMINICA - LICENSES

International Monetary Fund (IMF), 700 Nineteenth Street, NW, Washington, DC 20431, (202) 623-7000, Fax: (202) 623-4661, www.imf.org; *Government Finance Statistics Yearbook (2008 Edition).*

DOMINICA - LIFE EXPECTANCY

Central Intelligence Agency, Office of Public Affairs, Washington, DC 20505, (703) 482-0623, Fax: (703) 482-1739, www.cia.gov; *The World Factbook.*

Euromonitor International, Inc., 224 S. Michigan Avenue, Suite 1500, Chicago, IL 60604, (312) 922-1115, Fax: (312) 922-1157, www.euromonitor.com; *The World Economic Factbook 2008.*

United Nations Statistics Division, New York, NY 10017, (800) 253-9646, Fax: (212) 963-4116, http://unstats.un.org; *Human Development Report 2006* and *World Statistics Pocketbook.*

The World Bank, 1818 H Street, NW, Washington, DC 20433, (202) 473-1000, Fax: (202) 477-6391, www.worldbank.org; *The World Bank Atlas 2003-2004.*

DOMINICA - LITERACY

Euromonitor International, Inc., 224 S. Michigan Avenue, Suite 1500, Chicago, IL 60604, (312) 922-1115, Fax: (312) 922-1157, www.euromonitor.com; *World Marketing Data and Statistics.*

DOMINICA - LIVESTOCK

Palgrave Macmillan Ltd., Houndmills, Basingstoke, Hampshire, RG21 6XS, England, (Telephone in U.S. (888) 330-8477), (Fax in U.S. (800) 672-2054), www.palgrave.com; *The Statesman's Yearbook 2008.*

Taylor and Francis Group, An Informa Business, 2 Park Square, Milton Park, Abingdon, Oxford OX14 4RN, United Kingdom, (Dial from U.S. (212) 216-7800), (Fax from U.S. (212) 564-7854), www.tandf.co.uk; *The Europa World Year Book.*

United Nations Conference on Trade and Development (UNCTAD), DC2-1120, United Nations, New York, NY 10017, (212) 963-0027, www.unctad.org; *UNCTAD Commodity Yearbook.*

United Nations Food and Agricultural Organization (FAO), Viale delle Terme di Caracalla, 00100 Rome, Italy, (Dial from U.S. (202) 653-2400), (Fax from U.S. (202) 653 5760), www.fao.org; *FAO Production Yearbook 2002* and *The State of Food and Agriculture (SOFA) 2006.*

United Nations Statistics Division, New York, NY 10017, (800) 253-9646, Fax: (212) 963-4116, http://unstats.un.org; *Statistical Yearbook.*

DOMINICA - MANUFACTURES

The World Bank, 1818 H Street, NW, Washington, DC 20433, (202) 473-1000, Fax: (202) 477-6391, www.worldbank.org; *World Development Indicators (WDI) 2008.*

DOMINICA - MARRIAGE

Taylor and Francis Group, An Informa Business, 2 Park Square, Milton Park, Abingdon, Oxford OX14 4RN, United Kingdom, (Dial from U.S. (212) 216-7800), (Fax from U.S. (212) 564-7854), www.tandf.co.uk; *The Europa World Year Book.*

United Nations Statistics Division, New York, NY 10017, (800) 253-9646, Fax: (212) 963-4116, http://unstats.un.org; *Demographic Yearbook* and *Statistical Yearbook.*

DOMINICA - MEDICAL CARE, COST OF

International Monetary Fund (IMF), 700 Nineteenth Street, NW, Washington, DC 20431, (202) 623-7000, Fax: (202) 623-4661, www.imf.org; *Government Finance Statistics Yearbook (2008 Edition).*

DOMINICA - MINERAL INDUSTRIES

Taylor and Francis Group, An Informa Business, 2 Park Square, Milton Park, Abingdon, Oxford OX14 4RN, United Kingdom, (Dial from U.S. (212) 216-7800), (Fax from U.S. (212) 564-7854), www.tandf.co.uk; *The Europa World Year Book.*

United Nations Conference on Trade and Development (UNCTAD), DC2-1120, United Nations, New York, NY 10017, (212) 963-0027, www.unctad.org; *UNCTAD Commodity Yearbook.*

DOMINICA - MONEY SUPPLY

Economist Intelligence Unit, 111 West 57th Street, New York, NY 10019, (212) 554-0600, Fax: (212) 586-1181, www.eiu.com; *Organisation of Eastern Caribbean States.*

Taylor and Francis Group, An Informa Business, 2 Park Square, Milton Park, Abingdon, Oxford OX14 4RN, United Kingdom, (Dial from U.S. (212) 216-7800), (Fax from U.S. (212) 564-7854), www.tandf.co.uk; *The Europa World Year Book.*

The World Bank, 1818 H Street, NW, Washington, DC 20433, (202) 473-1000, Fax: (202) 477-6391, www.worldbank.org; *Dominica* and *World Development Indicators (WDI) 2008.*

DOMINICA - MORTALITY

Central Intelligence Agency, Office of Public Affairs, Washington, DC 20505, (703) 482-0623, Fax: (703) 482-1739, www.cia.gov; *The World Factbook.*

Euromonitor International, Inc., 224 S. Michigan Avenue, Suite 1500, Chicago, IL 60604, (312) 922-1115, Fax: (312) 922-1157, www.euromonitor.com; *International Marketing Data and Statistics 2008* and *The World Economic Factbook 2008.*

Taylor and Francis Group, An Informa Business, 2 Park Square, Milton Park, Abingdon, Oxford OX14 4RN, United Kingdom, (Dial from U.S. (212) 216-7800), (Fax from U.S. (212) 564-7854), www.tandf.co.uk; *The Europa World Year Book.*

UNICEF, 3 United Nations Plaza, New York, NY 10017, (800) 253-9646, Fax: (212) 887-7465, www.unicef.org; *The State of the World's Children 2008.*

United Nations Statistics Division, New York, NY 10017, (800) 253-9646, Fax: (212) 963-4116, http://unstats.un.org; *Demographic Yearbook; Human Development Report 2006; Statistical Yearbook;* and *World Statistics Pocketbook.*

The World Bank, 1818 H Street, NW, Washington, DC 20433, (202) 473-1000, Fax: (202) 477-6391, www.worldbank.org; *The World Bank Atlas 2003-2004* and *World Development Indicators (WDI) 2008.*

World Health Organization (WHO), Avenue Appia 20, 1211 Geneve 27, Switzerland, (Telephone in U.S. (212) 331-9081), www.who.int; The WHO Global Atlas of Infectious Diseases and *World Health Report 2006.*

DOMINICA - MOTION PICTURES

Palgrave Macmillan Ltd., Houndmills, Basingstoke, Hampshire, RG21 6XS, England, (Telephone in U.S. (888) 330-8477), (Fax in U.S. (800) 672-2054), www.palgrave.com; *The Statesman's Yearbook 2008.*

DOMINICA - MOTOR VEHICLES

Taylor and Francis Group, An Informa Business, 2 Park Square, Milton Park, Abingdon, Oxford OX14 4RN, United Kingdom, (Dial from U.S. (212) 216-7800), (Fax from U.S. (212) 564-7854), www.tandf.co.uk; *The Europa World Year Book.*

DOMINICA - NUTRITION

United Nations Food and Agricultural Organization (FAO), Viale delle Terme di Caracalla, 00100 Rome, Italy, (Dial from U.S. (202) 653-2400), (Fax from U.S. (202) 653 5760), www.fao.org; *The State of Food and Agriculture (SOFA) 2006.*

DOMINICA - PESTICIDES

United Nations Food and Agricultural Organization (FAO), Viale delle Terme di Caracalla, 00100 Rome, Italy, (Dial from U.S. (202) 653-2400), (Fax from U.S. (202) 653 5760), www.fao.org; *The State of Food and Agriculture (SOFA) 2006.*

DOMINICA - PETROLEUM INDUSTRY AND TRADE

PennWell Corporation, 1421 South Sheridan Road, Tulsa, OK 74112, (918) 835-3161, www.pennwell.com; *International Petroleum Encyclopedia 2007.*

United Nations Conference on Trade and Development (UNCTAD), DC2-1120, United Nations, New York, NY 10017, (212) 963-0027, www.unctad.org; *UNCTAD Commodity Yearbook.*

United Nations Food and Agricultural Organization (FAO), Viale delle Terme di Caracalla, 00100 Rome, Italy, (Dial from U.S. (202) 653-2400), (Fax from U.S. (202) 653 5760), www.fao.org; *The State of Food and Agriculture (SOFA) 2006.*

DOMINICA - POLITICAL SCIENCE

Central Intelligence Agency, Office of Public Affairs, Washington, DC 20505, (703) 482-0623, Fax: (703) 482-1739, www.cia.gov; *The World Factbook.*

International Monetary Fund (IMF), 700 Nineteenth Street, NW, Washington, DC 20431, (202) 623-7000, Fax: (202) 623-4661, www.imf.org; *Government Finance Statistics Yearbook (2008 Edition).*

Palgrave Macmillan Ltd., Houndmills, Basingstoke, Hampshire, RG21 6XS, England, (Telephone in U.S. (888) 330-8477), (Fax in U.S. (800) 672-2054), www.palgrave.com; *The Statesman's Yearbook 2008.*

Taylor and Francis Group, An Informa Business, 2 Park Square, Milton Park, Abingdon, Oxford OX14 4RN, United Kingdom, (Dial from U.S. (212) 216-7800), (Fax from U.S. (212) 564-7854), www.tandf.co.uk; *The Europa World Year Book.*

United Nations Statistics Division, New York, NY 10017, (800) 253-9646, Fax: (212) 963-4116, http://unstats.un.org; *National Accounts Statistics: Compendium of Income Distribution Statistics.*

The World Bank, 1818 H Street, NW, Washington, DC 20433, (202) 473-1000, Fax: (202) 477-6391, www.worldbank.org; *World Development Indicators (WDI) 2008.*

DOMINICA - POPULATION

Caribbean Epidemiology Centre (CAREC), 16-18 Jamaica Boulevard, Federation Park, PO Box 164, Port of Spain, Republic of Trinidad and Tobago, (Dial from U.S. (868) 622-4261), (Fax from U.S. (868) 622-2792), www.carec.org; *Population Data.*

Central Intelligence Agency, Office of Public Affairs, Washington, DC 20505, (703) 482-0623, Fax: (703) 482-1739, www.cia.gov; *The World Factbook.*

Economist Intelligence Unit, 111 West 57th Street, New York, NY 10019, (212) 554-0600, Fax: (212) 586-1181, www.eiu.com; *Organisation of Eastern Caribbean States.*

Euromonitor International, Inc., 224 S. Michigan Avenue, Suite 1500, Chicago, IL 60604, (312) 922-1115, Fax: (312) 922-1157, www.euromonitor.com; *International Marketing Data and Statistics 2008* and *The World Economic Factbook 2008.*

Eurostat, Batiment Jean Monnet, Rue Alcide de Gasperi, L-2920 Luxembourg, http://epp.eurostat.ec.europa.eu; *Demographic Indicators - Population by Age-Classes.*

International Labour Office, I.L.O. Publications, 4 route des Morillons, CH-1211 Geneva 22, Switzerland, (Telephone in U.S. (202) 653-7652), (Fax in U.S. (202) 653-7687), www.ilo.org; *Yearbook of Labour Statistics 2006.*

Organization of American States (OAS), 17th Street Constitution Avenue NW, Washington, DC 20006, (202) 458-3000, www.oas.org; *The OAS in Transition: 1994-2004.*

Palgrave Macmillan Ltd., Houndmills, Basingstoke, Hampshire, RG21 6XS, England, (Telephone in U.S. (888) 330-8477), (Fax in U.S. (800) 672-2054), www.palgrave.com; *The Statesman's Yearbook 2008.*

Taylor and Francis Group, An Informa Business, 2 Park Square, Milton Park, Abingdon, Oxford OX14 4RN, United Kingdom, (Dial from U.S. (212) 216-7800), (Fax from U.S. (212) 564-7854), www.tandf.co.uk; *The Europa World Year Book.*

UNESCO Institute for Statistics, C.P. 6128 Succursale Centre-Ville, Montreal, Quebec, H3C 3J7 Canada, (Dial from U.S. (514) 343-6880), (Fax from U.S. (514) 343 6882), www.uis.unesco.org; *Statistical Tables.*

United Nations Food and Agricultural Organization (FAO), Viale delle Terme di Caracalla, 00100 Rome, Italy, (Dial from U.S. (202) 653-2400), (Fax from U.S. (202) 653 5760), www.fao.org; *FAO Production Yearbook 2002.*

United Nations Statistics Division, New York, NY 10017, (800) 253-9646, Fax: (212) 963-4116, http://unstats.un.org; *Demographic Yearbook; Human Development Report 2006; Statistical Yearbook;* and *World Statistics Pocketbook.*

The World Bank, 1818 H Street, NW, Washington, DC 20433, (202) 473-1000, Fax: (202) 477-6391, www.worldbank.org; *Dominica* and *The World Bank Atlas 2003-2004.*

World Health Organization (WHO), Avenue Appia 20, 1211 Geneve 27, Switzerland, (Telephone in U.S. (212) 331-9081), www.who.int; *World Health Report 2006.*

DOMINICA - POPULATION DENSITY

Central Intelligence Agency, Office of Public Affairs, Washington, DC 20505, (703) 482-0623, Fax: (703) 482-1739, www.cia.gov; *The World Factbook.*

Euromonitor International, Inc., 224 S. Michigan Avenue, Suite 1500, Chicago, IL 60604, (312) 922-1115, Fax: (312) 922-1157, www.euromonitor.com; *The World Economic Factbook 2008.*

Palgrave Macmillan Ltd., Houndmills, Basingstoke, Hampshire, RG21 6XS, England, (Telephone in U.S. (888) 330-8477), (Fax in U.S. (800) 672-2054), www.palgrave.com; *The Statesman's Yearbook 2008.*

Taylor and Francis Group, An Informa Business, 2 Park Square, Milton Park, Abingdon, Oxford OX14 4RN, United Kingdom, (Dial from U.S. (212) 216-7800), (Fax from U.S. (212) 564-7854), www.tandf.co.uk; *The Europa World Year Book.*

UNESCO Institute for Statistics, C.P. 6128 Succursale Centre-Ville, Montreal, Quebec, H3C 3J7 Canada, (Dial from U.S. (514) 343-6880), (Fax from U.S. (514) 343 6882), www.uis.unesco.org; *Statistical Tables.*

United Nations Food and Agricultural Organization (FAO), Viale delle Terme di Caracalla, 00100 Rome, Italy, (Dial from U.S. (202) 653-2400), (Fax from U.S. (202) 653 5760), www.fao.org; *The State of Food and Agriculture (SOFA) 2006.*

United Nations Statistics Division, New York, NY 10017, (800) 253-9646, Fax: (212) 963-4116, http://unstats.un.org; *Statistical Yearbook.*

The World Bank, 1818 H Street, NW, Washington, DC 20433, (202) 473-1000, Fax: (202) 477-6391, www.worldbank.org; *Dominica.*

DOMINICA - POWER RESOURCES

Euromonitor International, Inc., 224 S. Michigan Avenue, Suite 1500, Chicago, IL 60604, (312) 922-1115, Fax: (312) 922-1157, www.euromonitor.com; *International Marketing Data and Statistics 2008* and *The World Economic Factbook 2008.*

Palgrave Macmillan Ltd., Houndmills, Basingstoke, Hampshire, RG21 6XS, England, (Telephone in U.S. (888) 330-8477), (Fax in U.S. (800) 672-2054), www.palgrave.com; *The Statesman's Yearbook 2008.*

Platts, 2 Penn Plaza, 25th Floor, New York, NY 10121-2298, (212) 904-3070, www.platts.com; *Energy Economist.*

United Nations Food and Agricultural Organization (FAO), Viale delle Terme di Caracalla, 00100 Rome, Italy, (Dial from U.S. (202) 653-2400), (Fax from U.S. (202) 653 5760), www.fao.org; *The State of Food and Agriculture (SOFA) 2006.*

United Nations Statistics Division, New York, NY 10017, (800) 253-9646, Fax: (212) 963-4116, http://unstats.un.org; *Energy Statistics Yearbook 2003; Human Development Report 2006;* and *World Statistics Pocketbook.*

The World Bank, 1818 H Street, NW, Washington, DC 20433, (202) 473-1000, Fax: (202) 477-6391, www.worldbank.org; *The World Bank Atlas 2003-2004.*

DOMINICA - PRICES

Euromonitor International, Inc., 224 S. Michigan Avenue, Suite 1500, Chicago, IL 60604, (312) 922-1115, Fax: (312) 922-1157, www.euromonitor.com; *World Marketing Data and Statistics.*

International Labour Office, I.L.O. Publications, 4 route des Morillons, CH-1211 Geneva 22, Switzerland, (Telephone in U.S. (202) 653-7652), (Fax in U.S. (202) 653-7687), www.ilo.org; *Yearbook of Labour Statistics 2006.*

United Nations Food and Agricultural Organization (FAO), Viale delle Terme di Caracalla, 00100 Rome, Italy, (Dial from U.S. (202) 653-2400), (Fax from U.S. (202) 653 5760), www.fao.org; *FAO Production Yearbook 2002* and *The State of Food and Agriculture (SOFA) 2006.*

United Nations Statistics Division, New York, NY 10017, (800) 253-9646, Fax: (212) 963-4116, http://unstats.un.org; *Economic Survey of Latin America and the Caribbean 2004-2005.*

DOMINICA - PUBLIC HEALTH

Euromonitor International, Inc., 224 S. Michigan Avenue, Suite 1500, Chicago, IL 60604, (312) 922-1115, Fax: (312) 922-1157, www.euromonitor.com; *World Marketing Data and Statistics.*

Palgrave Macmillan Ltd., Houndmills, Basingstoke, Hampshire, RG21 6XS, England, (Telephone in U.S. (888) 330-8477), (Fax in U.S. (800) 672-2054), www.palgrave.com; *The Statesman's Yearbook 2008.*

UNICEF, 3 United Nations Plaza, New York, NY 10017, (800) 253-9646, Fax: (212) 887-7465, www.unicef.org; *The State of the World's Children 2008.*

United Nations Statistics Division, New York, NY 10017, (800) 253-9646, Fax: (212) 963-4116, http://unstats.un.org; *Human Development Report 2006* and *Statistical Yearbook.*

The World Bank, 1818 H Street, NW, Washington, DC 20433, (202) 473-1000, Fax: (202) 477-6391, www.worldbank.org; *Dominica.*

World Health Organization (WHO), Avenue Appia 20, 1211 Geneve 27, Switzerland, (Telephone in U.S. (212) 331-9081), www.who.int; The WHO Global Atlas of Infectious Diseases and *World Health Report 2006.*

DOMINICA - RADIO BROADCASTING

Palgrave Macmillan Ltd., Houndmills, Basingstoke, Hampshire, RG21 6XS, England, (Telephone in U.S. (888) 330-8477), (Fax in U.S. (800) 672-2054), www.palgrave.com; *The Statesman's Yearbook 2008.*

DOMINICA - RELIGION

Central Intelligence Agency, Office of Public Affairs, Washington, DC 20505, (703) 482-0623, Fax: (703) 482-1739, www.cia.gov; *The World Factbook.*

Palgrave Macmillan Ltd., Houndmills, Basingstoke, Hampshire, RG21 6XS, England, (Telephone in U.S. (888) 330-8477), (Fax in U.S. (800) 672-2054), www.palgrave.com; *The Statesman's Yearbook 2008.*

DOMINICA - RENT CHARGES

International Labour Office, I.L.O. Publications, 4 route des Morillons, CH-1211 Geneva 22, Switzerland, (Telephone in U.S. (202) 653-7652), (Fax in U.S. (202) 653-7687), www.ilo.org; *Yearbook of Labour Statistics 2006.*

DOMINICA - RESERVES (ACCOUNTING)

The World Bank, 1818 H Street, NW, Washington, DC 20433, (202) 473-1000, Fax: (202) 477-6391, www.worldbank.org; *World Development Indicators (WDI) 2008.*

DOMINICA - RETAIL TRADE

Euromonitor International, Inc., 224 S. Michigan Avenue, Suite 1500, Chicago, IL 60604, (312) 922-1115, Fax: (312) 922-1157, www.euromonitor.com; *World Marketing Data and Statistics.*

DOMINICA - ROADS

Central Intelligence Agency, Office of Public Affairs, Washington, DC 20505, (703) 482-0623, Fax: (703) 482-1739, www.cia.gov; *The World Factbook.*

Palgrave Macmillan Ltd., Houndmills, Basingstoke, Hampshire, RG21 6XS, England, (Telephone in U.S. (888) 330-8477), (Fax in U.S. (800) 672-2054), www.palgrave.com; *The Statesman's Yearbook 2008.*

DOMINICA - SHEEP

See DOMINICA - LIVESTOCK

DOMINICA - SHIPPING

Taylor and Francis Group, An Informa Business, 2 Park Square, Milton Park, Abingdon, Oxford OX14 4RN, United Kingdom, (Dial from U.S. (212) 216-7800), (Fax from U.S. (212) 564-7854), www.tandf.co.uk; *The Europa World Year Book.*

United Nations Statistics Division, New York, NY 10017, (800) 253-9646, Fax: (212) 963-4116, http://unstats.un.org; *Statistical Yearbook.*

DOMINICA - SOCIAL ECOLOGY

United Nations Statistics Division, New York, NY 10017, (800) 253-9646, Fax: (212) 963-4116, http://unstats.un.org; *World Statistics Pocketbook.*

DOMINICA - SOCIAL SECURITY

International Monetary Fund (IMF), 700 Nineteenth Street, NW, Washington, DC 20431, (202) 623-7000, Fax: (202) 623-4661, www.imf.org; *Government Finance Statistics Yearbook (2008 Edition).*

United Nations Statistics Division, New York, NY 10017, (800) 253-9646, Fax: (212) 963-4116, http://unstats.un.org; *National Accounts Statistics: Compendium of Income Distribution Statistics.*

DOMINICA - TAXATION

International Monetary Fund (IMF), 700 Nineteenth Street, NW, Washington, DC 20431, (202) 623-7000, Fax: (202) 623-4661, www.imf.org; *Government Finance Statistics Yearbook (2008 Edition).*

The World Bank, 1818 H Street, NW, Washington, DC 20433, (202) 473-1000, Fax: (202) 477-6391, www.worldbank.org; *World Development Indicators (WDI) 2008.*

DOMINICA - TELEPHONE

International Telecommunication Union (ITU), Place des Nations, 1211 Geneva 20, Switzerland, www.itu.int; World Telecommunication Indicators Database.

Palgrave Macmillan Ltd., Houndmills, Basingstoke, Hampshire, RG21 6XS, England, (Telephone in U.S. (888) 330-8477), (Fax in U.S. (800) 672-2054), www.palgrave.com; *The Statesman's Yearbook 2008.*

Taylor and Francis Group, An Informa Business, 2 Park Square, Milton Park, Abingdon, Oxford OX14 4RN, United Kingdom, (Dial from U.S. (212) 216-7800), (Fax from U.S. (212) 564-7854), www.tandf.co.uk; *The Europa World Year Book.*

United Nations Statistics Division, New York, NY 10017, (800) 253-9646, Fax: (212) 963-4116, http://unstats.un.org; *Statistical Yearbook* and *World Statistics Pocketbook.*

DOMINICA - TEXTILE INDUSTRY

United Nations Conference on Trade and Development (UNCTAD), DC2-1120, United Nations, New York, NY 10017, (212) 963-0027, www.unctad.org; *UNCTAD Commodity Yearbook.*

DOMINICA - TOURISM

Euromonitor International, Inc., 224 S. Michigan Avenue, Suite 1500, Chicago, IL 60604, (312) 922-1115, Fax: (312) 922-1157, www.euromonitor.com; *The World Economic Factbook 2008* and *World Marketing Data and Statistics.*

Palgrave Macmillan Ltd., Houndmills, Basingstoke, Hampshire, RG21 6XS, England, (Telephone in U.S. (888) 330-8477), (Fax in U.S. (800) 672-2054), www.palgrave.com; *The Statesman's Yearbook 2008.*

Taylor and Francis Group, An Informa Business, 2 Park Square, Milton Park, Abingdon, Oxford OX14 4RN, United Kingdom, (Dial from U.S. (212) 216-7800), (Fax from U.S. (212) 564-7854), www.tandf.co.uk; *The Europa World Year Book.*

United Nations World Tourism Organization (UNWTO), Capitan Haya 42, 28020 Madrid, Spain, www.world-tourism.org; *Yearbook of Tourism Statistics.*

The World Bank, 1818 H Street, NW, Washington, DC 20433, (202) 473-1000, Fax: (202) 477-6391, www.worldbank.org; *Dominica.*

DOMINICA - TRADE

See DOMINICA - INTERNATIONAL TRADE

DOMINICA - TRANSPORTATION

Central Intelligence Agency, Office of Public Affairs, Washington, DC 20505, (703) 482-0623, Fax: (703) 482-1739, www.cia.gov; *The World Factbook.*

Euromonitor International, Inc., 224 S. Michigan Avenue, Suite 1500, Chicago, IL 60604, (312) 922-1115, Fax: (312) 922-1157, www.euromonitor.com; *International Marketing Data and Statistics 2008* and *World Marketing Data and Statistics.*

Palgrave Macmillan Ltd., Houndmills, Basingstoke, Hampshire, RG21 6XS, England, (Telephone in U.S. (888) 330-8477), (Fax in U.S. (800) 672-2054), www.palgrave.com; *The Statesman's Yearbook 2008.*

Taylor and Francis Group, An Informa Business, 2 Park Square, Milton Park, Abingdon, Oxford OX14 4RN, United Kingdom, (Dial from U.S. (212) 216-7800), (Fax from U.S. (212) 564-7854), www.tandf.co.uk; *The Europa World Year Book.*

United Nations Statistics Division, New York, NY 10017, (800) 253-9646, Fax: (212) 963-4116, http://unstats.un.org; *Human Development Report 2006.*

The World Bank, 1818 H Street, NW, Washington, DC 20433, (202) 473-1000, Fax: (202) 477-6391, www.worldbank.org; *Dominica.*

DOMINICA - UNEMPLOYMENT

Central Intelligence Agency, Office of Public Affairs, Washington, DC 20505, (703) 482-0623, Fax: (703) 482-1739, www.cia.gov; *The World Factbook.*

International Labour Office, I.L.O. Publications, 4 route des Morillons, CH-1211 Geneva 22, Switzerland, (Telephone in U.S. (202) 653-7652), (Fax in U.S. (202) 653-7687), www.ilo.org; *Yearbook of Labour Statistics 2006.*

DOMINICA - VITAL STATISTICS

World Health Organization (WHO), Avenue Appia 20, 1211 Geneve 27, Switzerland, (Telephone in U.S. (212) 331-9081), www.who.int; *World Health Report 2006.*

DOMINICA - WAGES

International Labour Office, I.L.O. Publications, 4 route des Morillons, CH-1211 Geneva 22, Switzerland, (Telephone in U.S. (202) 653-7652), (Fax in U.S. (202) 653-7687), www.ilo.org; *Yearbook of Labour Statistics 2006.*

The World Bank, 1818 H Street, NW, Washington, DC 20433, (202) 473-1000, Fax: (202) 477-6391, www.worldbank.org; *Dominica.*

DOMINICA - WELFARE STATE

International Monetary Fund (IMF), 700 Nineteenth Street, NW, Washington, DC 20431, (202) 623-7000, Fax: (202) 623-4661, www.imf.org; *Government Finance Statistics Yearbook (2008 Edition).*

DOMINICAN REPUBLIC - NATIONAL STATISTICAL OFFICE

Oficina Nacional de Estadistica, Av. Mexico Esq. Leopoldo Navarro, Edif. Oficinas Gubernamntales Juan Pablo Duarte, Piso 9, Santo Domingo, Dominican Republic, (Dial from U.S. (809) 682-7777 ext. 277), (Fax from U.S. (809) 685-4424), www.one.gov.do; National Data Center.

DOMINICAN REPUBLIC - PRIMARY STATISTICS SOURCES

Oficina Nacional de Estadistica, Av. Mexico Esq. Leopoldo Navarro, Edif. Oficinas Gubernamntales Juan Pablo Duarte, Piso 9, Santo Domingo, Dominican Republic, (Dial from U.S. (809) 682-7777 ext. 277), (Fax from U.S. (809) 685-4424), www.one.gov.do; *Republica Dominicana en Cifras 2006* (The Dominican Republic in Figures 2006).

DOMINICAN REPUBLIC - AGRICULTURAL MACHINERY

Economist Intelligence Unit, 111 West 57th Street, New York, NY 10019, (212) 554-0600, Fax: (212) 586-1181, www.eiu.com; *Business Latin America.*

United Nations Statistics Division, New York, NY 10017, (800) 253-9646, Fax: (212) 963-4116, http://unstats.un.org; *Statistical Yearbook.*

DOMINICAN REPUBLIC - AGRICULTURE

Economist Intelligence Unit, 111 West 57th Street, New York, NY 10019, (212) 554-0600, Fax: (212) 586-1181, www.eiu.com; *Business Latin America* and *Dominican Republic Country Report.*

Euromonitor International, Inc., 224 S. Michigan Avenue, Suite 1500, Chicago, IL 60604, (312) 922-1115, Fax: (312) 922-1157, www.euromonitor.com; *International Marketing Data and Statistics 2008* and *World Marketing Data and Statistics.*

Inter-American Development Bank (IDB), 1300 New York Avenue, NW, Washington, DC 20577, (202) 623-1000, Fax: (202) 623-3096, www.iadb.org; *The Politics of Policies: Economic and Social Progress in Latin America - 2006 Report.*

M.E. Sharpe, 80 Business Park Drive, Armonk, NY 10504, (800) 541-6563, Fax: (914) 273-2106, www.mesharpe.com; *The Illustrated Book of World Rankings.*

Palgrave Macmillan Ltd., Houndmills, Basingstoke, Hampshire, RG21 6XS, England, (Telephone in U.S. (888) 330-8477), (Fax in U.S. (800) 672-2054), www.palgrave.com; *The Statesman's Yearbook 2008.*

Taylor and Francis Group, An Informa Business, 2 Park Square, Milton Park, Abingdon, Oxford OX14 4RN, United Kingdom, (Dial from U.S. (212) 216-7800), (Fax from U.S. (212) 564-7854), www.tandf.co.uk; *The Europa World Year Book.*

UCLA Latin American Institute, 10343 Bunche Hall, Box 951447, Los Angeles, CA 90095-1447, (310) 825-4571, Fax: (310) 206-6859, www.international.ucla.edu/lac; *Statistical Abstract of Latin America.*

United Nations Conference on Trade and Development (UNCTAD), DC2-1120, United Nations, New York, NY 10017, (212) 963-0027, www.unctad.org; *UNCTAD Commodity Yearbook.*

United Nations Food and Agricultural Organization (FAO), Viale delle Terme di Caracalla, 00100 Rome, Italy, (Dial from U.S. (202) 653-2400), (Fax from U.S. (202) 653 5760), www.fao.org; AQUASTAT; *FAO Production Yearbook 2002; FAO Trade Yearbook;* and *The State of Food and Agriculture (SOFA) 2006.*

United Nations Statistics Division, New York, NY 10017, (800) 253-9646, Fax: (212) 963-4116, http://unstats.un.org; *Statistical Yearbook* and *Statistical Yearbook for Latin America and the Caribbean 2004.*

The World Bank, 1818 H Street, NW, Washington, DC 20433, (202) 473-1000, Fax: (202) 477-6391, www.worldbank.org; *Dominican Republic* and *World Development Indicators (WDI) 2008.*

DOMINICAN REPUBLIC - AIRLINES

Economist Intelligence Unit, 111 West 57th Street, New York, NY 10019, (212) 554-0600, Fax: (212) 586-1181, www.eiu.com; *Business Latin America.*

International Civil Aviation Organization (ICAO), External Relations and Public Information Office (EPO), 999 University Street, Montreal, Quebec H3C 5H7, Canada, (Dial from U.S. (514) 954-8219), (Fax from U.S. (514) 954-6077), www.icao.int; *Civil Aviation Statistics of the World.*

M.E. Sharpe, 80 Business Park Drive, Armonk, NY 10504, (800) 541-6563, Fax: (914) 273-2106, www.mesharpe.com; *The Illustrated Book of World Rankings.*

Palgrave Macmillan Ltd., Houndmills, Basingstoke, Hampshire, RG21 6XS, England, (Telephone in U.S. (888) 330-8477), (Fax in U.S. (800) 672-2054), www.palgrave.com; *The Statesman's Yearbook 2008.*

Taylor and Francis Group, An Informa Business, 2 Park Square, Milton Park, Abingdon, Oxford OX14 4RN, United Kingdom, (Dial from U.S. (212) 216-7800), (Fax from U.S. (212) 564-7854), www.tandf.co.uk; *The Europa World Year Book.*

DOMINICAN REPUBLIC - AIRPORTS

Central Intelligence Agency, Office of Public Affairs, Washington, DC 20505, (703) 482-0623, Fax: (703) 482-1739, www.cia.gov; *The World Factbook.*

DOMINICAN REPUBLIC - ALUMINUM PRODUCTION

See DOMINICAN REPUBLIC - MINERAL INDUSTRIES

DOMINICAN REPUBLIC - AREA

Economist Intelligence Unit, 111 West 57th Street, New York, NY 10019, (212) 554-0600, Fax: (212) 586-1181, www.eiu.com; *Business Latin America.*

DOMINICAN REPUBLIC - ARMED FORCES

Central Intelligence Agency, Office of Public Affairs, Washington, DC 20505, (703) 482-0623, Fax: (703) 482-1739, www.cia.gov; *The World Factbook.*

Economist Intelligence Unit, 111 West 57th Street, New York, NY 10019, (212) 554-0600, Fax: (212) 586-1181, www.eiu.com; *Business Latin America.*

Euromonitor International, Inc., 224 S. Michigan Avenue, Suite 1500, Chicago, IL 60604, (312) 922-1115, Fax: (312) 922-1157, www.euromonitor.com; *World Marketing Data and Statistics.*

International Institute for Strategic Studies (IISS), Arundel House, 13-15 Arundel Street, Temple Place, London WC2R 3DX, England, www.iiss.org; *The Military Balance 2007.*

International Monetary Fund (IMF), 700 Nineteenth Street, NW, Washington, DC 20431, (202) 623-7000, Fax: (202) 623-4661, www.imf.org; *Government Finance Statistics Yearbook (2008 Edition).*

Palgrave Macmillan Ltd., Houndmills, Basingstoke, Hampshire, RG21 6XS, England, (Telephone in U.S. (888) 330-8477), (Fax in U.S. (800) 672-2054), www.palgrave.com; *The Statesman's Yearbook 2008.*

U.S. Department of State (DOS), 2201 C Street NW, Washington, DC 20520, (202) 647-4000, www.state.gov; *World Military Expenditures and Arms Transfers (WMEAT).*

UCLA Latin American Institute, 10343 Bunche Hall, Box 951447, Los Angeles, CA 90095-1447, (310) 825-4571, Fax: (310) 206-6859, www.international.ucla.edu/lac; *Statistical Abstract of Latin America.*

United Nations Statistics Division, New York, NY 10017, (800) 253-9646, Fax: (212) 963-4116, http://unstats.un.org; *Human Development Report 2006.*

DOMINICAN REPUBLIC - BALANCE OF PAYMENTS

Economist Intelligence Unit, 111 West 57th Street, New York, NY 10019, (212) 554-0600, Fax: (212) 586-1181, www.eiu.com; *Business Latin America.*

Inter-American Development Bank (IDB), 1300 New York Avenue, NW, Washington, DC 20577, (202) 623-1000, Fax: (202) 623-3096, www.iadb.org; *The Politics of Policies: Economic and Social Progress in Latin America - 2006 Report.*

International Monetary Fund (IMF), 700 Nineteenth Street, NW, Washington, DC 20431, (202) 623-7000, Fax: (202) 623-4661, www.imf.org; *Balance of Payments Statistics Newsletter* and *Balance of Payments Statistics Yearbook 2007.*

Organization of American States (OAS), 17th Street Constitution Avenue NW, Washington, DC 20006, (202) 458-3000, www.oas.org; *The OAS in Transition: 1994-2004.*

Taylor and Francis Group, An Informa Business, 2 Park Square, Milton Park, Abingdon, Oxford OX14 4RN, United Kingdom, (Dial from U.S. (212) 216-7800), (Fax from U.S. (212) 564-7854), www.tandf.co.uk; *The Europa World Year Book.*

UCLA Latin American Institute, 10343 Bunche Hall, Box 951447, Los Angeles, CA 90095-1447, (310) 825-4571, Fax: (310) 206-6859, www.international.ucla.edu/lac; *Statistical Abstract of Latin America.*

United Nations Conference on Trade and Development (UNCTAD), DC2-1120, United Nations, New York, NY 10017, (212) 963-0027, www.unctad.org; *Handbook of Statistics 2005.*

United Nations Statistics Division, New York, NY 10017, (800) 253-9646, Fax: (212) 963-4116, http://unstats.un.org; *Statistical Yearbook for Latin America and the Caribbean 2004.*

The World Bank, 1818 H Street, NW, Washington, DC 20433, (202) 473-1000, Fax: (202) 477-6391, www.worldbank.org; *Dominican Republic; World Development Indicators (WDI) 2008;* and *World Development Report 2008.*

DOMINICAN REPUBLIC - BANKS AND BANKING

Euromonitor International, Inc., 224 S. Michigan Avenue, Suite 1500, Chicago, IL 60604, (312) 922-1115, Fax: (312) 922-1157, www.euromonitor.com; *World Marketing Data and Statistics.*

Inter-American Development Bank (IDB), 1300 New York Avenue, NW, Washington, DC 20577, (202) 623-1000, Fax: (202) 623-3096, www.iadb.org; *The Politics of Policies: Economic and Social Progress in Latin America - 2006 Report.*

International Monetary Fund (IMF), 700 Nineteenth Street, NW, Washington, DC 20431, (202) 623-7000, Fax: (202) 623-4661, www.imf.org; *International Financial Statistics Yearbook 2007.*

M.E. Sharpe, 80 Business Park Drive, Armonk, NY 10504, (800) 541-6563, Fax: (914) 273-2106, www.mesharpe.com; *The Illustrated Book of World Rankings.*

Palgrave Macmillan Ltd., Houndmills, Basingstoke, Hampshire, RG21 6XS, England, (Telephone in U.S. (888) 330-8477), (Fax in U.S. (800) 672-2054), www.palgrave.com; *The Statesman's Yearbook 2008.*

Taylor and Francis Group, An Informa Business, 2 Park Square, Milton Park, Abingdon, Oxford OX14 4RN, United Kingdom, (Dial from U.S. (212) 216-7800), (Fax from U.S. (212) 564-7854), www.tandf.co.uk; *The Europa World Year Book.*

United Nations Statistics Division, New York, NY 10017, (800) 253-9646, Fax: (212) 963-4116, http://unstats.un.org; *Statistical Yearbook for Latin America and the Caribbean 2004.*

DOMINICAN REPUBLIC - BARLEY PRODUCTION

See DOMINICAN REPUBLIC - CROPS

DOMINICAN REPUBLIC - BEVERAGE INDUSTRY

M.E. Sharpe, 80 Business Park Drive, Armonk, NY 10504, (800) 541-6563, Fax: (914) 273-2106, www.mesharpe.com; *The Illustrated Book of World Rankings.*

United Nations Statistics Division, New York, NY 10017, (800) 253-9646, Fax: (212) 963-4116, http://unstats.un.org; *Statistical Yearbook.*

DOMINICAN REPUBLIC - BIRTH CONTROL

UCLA Latin American Institute, 10343 Bunche Hall, Box 951447, Los Angeles, CA 90095-1447, (310) 825-4571, Fax: (310) 206-6859, www.international.ucla.edu/lac; *Statistical Abstract of Latin America.*

DOMINICAN REPUBLIC - BONDS

Inter-American Development Bank (IDB), 1300 New York Avenue, NW, Washington, DC 20577, (202) 623-1000, Fax: (202) 623-3096, www.iadb.org; *The Politics of Policies: Economic and Social Progress in Latin America - 2006 Report.*

DOMINICAN REPUBLIC - BROADCASTING

Central Intelligence Agency, Office of Public Affairs, Washington, DC 20505, (703) 482-0623, Fax: (703) 482-1739, www.cia.gov; *The World Factbook.*

Euromonitor International, Inc., 224 S. Michigan Avenue, Suite 1500, Chicago, IL 60604, (312) 922-1115, Fax: (312) 922-1157, www.euromonitor.com; *World Marketing Data and Statistics.*

M.E. Sharpe, 80 Business Park Drive, Armonk, NY 10504, (800) 541-6563, Fax: (914) 273-2106, www.mesharpe.com; *The Illustrated Book of World Rankings.*

Palgrave Macmillan Ltd., Houndmills, Basingstoke, Hampshire, RG21 6XS, England, (Telephone in U.S. (888) 330-8477), (Fax in U.S. (800) 672-2054), www.palgrave.com; *The Statesman's Yearbook 2008.*

WRTH Publications Limited, PO Box 290, Oxford OX2 7FT, UK, www.wrth.com; *World Radio TV Handbook 2007.*

DOMINICAN REPUBLIC - BUDGET

Central Intelligence Agency, Office of Public Affairs, Washington, DC 20505, (703) 482-0623, Fax: (703) 482-1739, www.cia.gov; *The World Factbook.*

DOMINICAN REPUBLIC - BUSINESS

Inter-American Development Bank (IDB), 1300 New York Avenue, NW, Washington, DC 20577, (202) 623-1000, Fax: (202) 623-3096, www.iadb.org; *The Politics of Policies: Economic and Social Progress in Latin America - 2006 Report.*

United Nations Statistics Division, New York, NY 10017, (800) 253-9646, Fax: (212) 963-4116, http://unstats.un.org; *Statistical Yearbook.*

DOMINICAN REPUBLIC - CACAO

See DOMINICAN REPUBLIC - CROPS

DOMINICAN REPUBLIC - CAPITAL INVESTMENTS

Inter-American Development Bank (IDB), 1300 New York Avenue, NW, Washington, DC 20577, (202) 623-1000, Fax: (202) 623-3096, www.iadb.org; *The Politics of Policies: Economic and Social Progress in Latin America - 2006 Report.*

DOMINICAN REPUBLIC - CAPITAL LEVY

Inter-American Development Bank (IDB), 1300 New York Avenue, NW, Washington, DC 20577, (202) 623-1000, Fax: (202) 623-3096, www.iadb.org; *The Politics of Policies: Economic and Social Progress in Latin America - 2006 Report.*

International Monetary Fund (IMF), 700 Nineteenth Street, NW, Washington, DC 20431, (202) 623-7000, Fax: (202) 623-4661, www.imf.org; *Government Finance Statistics Yearbook (2008 Edition).*

DOMINICAN REPUBLIC - CATTLE

See DOMINICAN REPUBLIC - LIVESTOCK

DOMINICAN REPUBLIC - CHICKENS

See DOMINICAN REPUBLIC - LIVESTOCK

DOMINICAN REPUBLIC - CHILDBIRTH - STATISTICS

Central Intelligence Agency, Office of Public Affairs, Washington, DC 20505, (703) 482-0623, Fax: (703) 482-1739, www.cia.gov; *The World Factbook.*

Euromonitor International, Inc., 224 S. Michigan Avenue, Suite 1500, Chicago, IL 60604, (312) 922-1115, Fax: (312) 922-1157, www.euromonitor.com; *International Marketing Data and Statistics 2008* and *The World Economic Factbook 2008.*

M.E. Sharpe, 80 Business Park Drive, Armonk, NY 10504, (800) 541-6563, Fax: (914) 273-2106, www.mesharpe.com; *The Illustrated Book of World Rankings.*

Taylor and Francis Group, An Informa Business, 2 Park Square, Milton Park, Abingdon, Oxford OX14 4RN, United Kingdom, (Dial from U.S. (212) 216-7800), (Fax from U.S. (212) 564-7854), www.tandf.co.uk; *The Europa World Year Book.*

United Nations Statistics Division, New York, NY 10017, (800) 253-9646, Fax: (212) 963-4116, http://unstats.un.org; *Demographic Yearbook; Statistical Yearbook;* and *Statistical Yearbook for Latin America and the Caribbean 2004.*

The World Bank, 1818 H Street, NW, Washington, DC 20433, (202) 473-1000, Fax: (202) 477-6391, www.worldbank.org; *World Development Indicators (WDI) 2008.*

World Health Organization (WHO), Avenue Appia 20, 1211 Geneve 27, Switzerland, (Telephone in U.S. (212) 331-9081), www.who.int; *World Health Report 2006.*

DOMINICAN REPUBLIC - CLIMATE

M.E. Sharpe, 80 Business Park Drive, Armonk, NY 10504, (800) 541-6563, Fax: (914) 273-2106, www.mesharpe.com; *The Illustrated Book of World Rankings.*

Palgrave Macmillan Ltd., Houndmills, Basingstoke, Hampshire, RG21 6XS, England, (Telephone in U.S. (888) 330-8477), (Fax in U.S. (800) 672-2054), www.palgrave.com; *The Statesman's Yearbook 2008.*

DOMINICAN REPUBLIC - COAL PRODUCTION

See DOMINICAN REPUBLIC - MINERAL INDUSTRIES

DOMINICAN REPUBLIC - COCOA PRODUCTION

See DOMINICAN REPUBLIC - CROPS

DOMINICAN REPUBLIC - COFFEE

See DOMINICAN REPUBLIC - CROPS

DOMINICAN REPUBLIC - COMMERCE

Palgrave Macmillan Ltd., Houndmills, Basingstoke, Hampshire, RG21 6XS, England, (Telephone in U.S. (888) 330-8477), (Fax in U.S. (800) 672-2054), www.palgrave.com; *The Statesman's Yearbook 2008.*

DOMINICAN REPUBLIC - COMMODITY EXCHANGES

Commodity Research Bureau, 330 South Wells Street, Suite 612, Chicago, IL 60606-7110, (800) 621-5271, Fax: (312) 939-4135, www.crbtrader.com; *2006 CRB Commodity Yearbook and CD.*

International Monetary Fund (IMF), 700 Nineteenth Street, NW, Washington, DC 20431, (202) 623-7000, Fax: (202) 623-4661, www.imf.org; *IMF Primary Commodity Prices.*

United Nations Food and Agricultural Organization (FAO), Viale delle Terme di Caracalla, 00100 Rome, Italy, (Dial from U.S. (202) 653-2400), (Fax from U.S. (202) 653 5760), www.fao.org; *The State of Food and Agriculture (SOFA) 2006.*

DOMINICAN REPUBLIC - CONSTRUCTION INDUSTRY

Economist Intelligence Unit, 111 West 57th Street, New York, NY 10019, (212) 554-0600, Fax: (212) 586-1181, www.eiu.com; *Business Latin America.*

Inter-American Development Bank (IDB), 1300 New York Avenue, NW, Washington, DC 20577, (202) 623-1000, Fax: (202) 623-3096, www.iadb.org; *The Politics of Policies: Economic and Social Progress in Latin America - 2006 Report.*

M.E. Sharpe, 80 Business Park Drive, Armonk, NY 10504, (800) 541-6563, Fax: (914) 273-2106, www.mesharpe.com; *The Illustrated Book of World Rankings.*

UCLA Latin American Institute, 10343 Bunche Hall, Box 951447, Los Angeles, CA 90095-1447, (310) 825-4571, Fax: (310) 206-6859, www.international.ucla.edu/lac; *Statistical Abstract of Latin America.*

United Nations Statistics Division, New York, NY 10017, (800) 253-9646, Fax: (212) 963-4116, http://unstats.un.org; *Statistical Yearbook.*

DOMINICAN REPUBLIC - CONSUMER COOPERATIVES

UCLA Latin American Institute, 10343 Bunche Hall, Box 951447, Los Angeles, CA 90095-1447, (310)

825-4571, Fax: (310) 206-6859, www.international.ucla.edu/lac; *Statistical Abstract of Latin America.*

DOMINICAN REPUBLIC - CONSUMER PRICE INDEXES

International Labour Office, I.L.O. Publications, 4 route des Morillons, CH-1211 Geneva 22, Switzerland, (Telephone in U.S. (202) 653-7652), (Fax in U.S. (202) 653-7687), www.ilo.org; *Yearbook of Labour Statistics 2006.*

Taylor and Francis Group, An Informa Business, 2 Park Square, Milton Park, Abingdon, Oxford OX14 4RN, United Kingdom, (Dial from U.S. (212) 216-7800), (Fax from U.S. (212) 564-7854), www.tandf.co.uk; *The Europa World Year Book.*

United Nations Statistics Division, New York, NY 10017, (800) 253-9646, Fax: (212) 963-4116, http://unstats.un.org; *Statistical Yearbook.*

The World Bank, 1818 H Street, NW, Washington, DC 20433, (202) 473-1000, Fax: (202) 477-6391, www.worldbank.org; *Dominican Republic.*

DOMINICAN REPUBLIC - CONSUMPTION (ECONOMICS)

Economist Intelligence Unit, 111 West 57th Street, New York, NY 10019, (212) 554-0600, Fax: (212) 586-1181, www.eiu.com; *Business Latin America.*

Inter-American Development Bank (IDB), 1300 New York Avenue, NW, Washington, DC 20577, (202) 623-1000, Fax: (202) 623-3096, www.iadb.org; *The Politics of Policies: Economic and Social Progress in Latin America - 2006 Report.*

United Nations Statistics Division, New York, NY 10017, (800) 253-9646, Fax: (212) 963-4116, http://unstats.un.org; *Statistical Yearbook for Latin America and the Caribbean 2004.*

The World Bank, 1818 H Street, NW, Washington, DC 20433, (202) 473-1000, Fax: (202) 477-6391, www.worldbank.org; *World Development Report 2008.*

DOMINICAN REPUBLIC - COPPER INDUSTRY AND TRADE

See DOMINICAN REPUBLIC - MINERAL INDUSTRIES

DOMINICAN REPUBLIC - CORN INDUSTRY

See DOMINICAN REPUBLIC - CROPS

DOMINICAN REPUBLIC - COST AND STANDARD OF LIVING

International Monetary Fund (IMF), 700 Nineteenth Street, NW, Washington, DC 20431, (202) 623-7000, Fax: (202) 623-4661, www.imf.org; *Government Finance Statistics Yearbook (2008 Edition).*

DOMINICAN REPUBLIC - COTTON

See DOMINICAN REPUBLIC - CROPS

DOMINICAN REPUBLIC - CRIME

Yale University Press, PO Box 209040, New Haven, CT 06520-9040, (203) 432-0960, Fax: (203) 432-0948, http://yalepress.yale.edu/yupbooks; *Violence and Crime in Cross-National Perspective.*

DOMINICAN REPUBLIC - CROPS

Economist Intelligence Unit, 111 West 57th Street, New York, NY 10019, (212) 554-0600, Fax: (212) 586-1181, www.eiu.com; *Business Latin America.*

International Monetary Fund (IMF), 700 Nineteenth Street, NW, Washington, DC 20431, (202) 623-7000, Fax: (202) 623-4661, www.imf.org; *International Financial Statistics Yearbook 2007.*

M.E. Sharpe, 80 Business Park Drive, Armonk, NY 10504, (800) 541-6563, Fax: (914) 273-2106, www.mesharpe.com; *The Illustrated Book of World Rankings.*

Organization of American States (OAS), 17th Street Constitution Avenue NW, Washington, DC 20006, (202) 458-3000, www.oas.org; *The OAS in Transition: 1994-2004.*

Palgrave Macmillan Ltd., Houndmills, Basingstoke, Hampshire, RG21 6XS, England, (Telephone in U.S. (888) 330-8477), (Fax in U.S. (800) 672-2054), www.palgrave.com; *The Statesman's Yearbook 2008.*

Taylor and Francis Group, An Informa Business, 2 Park Square, Milton Park, Abingdon, Oxford OX14 4RN, United Kingdom, (Dial from U.S. (212) 216-7800), (Fax from U.S. (212) 564-7854), www.tandf.co.uk; *The Europa World Year Book.*

United Nations Conference on Trade and Development (UNCTAD), DC2-1120, United Nations, New York, NY 10017, (212) 963-0027, www.unctad.org; *UNCTAD Commodity Yearbook.*

United Nations Food and Agricultural Organization (FAO), Viale delle Terme di Caracalla, 00100 Rome, Italy, (Dial from U.S. (202) 653-2400), (Fax from U.S. (202) 653 5760), www.fao.org; *FAO Production Yearbook 2002* and *The State of Food and Agriculture (SOFA) 2006.*

United Nations Statistics Division, New York, NY 10017, (800) 253-9646, Fax: (212) 963-4116, http://unstats.un.org; *Statistical Yearbook.*

DOMINICAN REPUBLIC - CUSTOMS ADMINISTRATION

Inter-American Development Bank (IDB), 1300 New York Avenue, NW, Washington, DC 20577, (202) 623-1000, Fax: (202) 623-3096, www.iadb.org; *The Politics of Policies: Economic and Social Progress in Latin America - 2006 Report.*

International Monetary Fund (IMF), 700 Nineteenth Street, NW, Washington, DC 20431, (202) 623-7000, Fax: (202) 623-4661, www.imf.org; *Government Finance Statistics Yearbook (2008 Edition).*

Palgrave Macmillan Ltd., Houndmills, Basingstoke, Hampshire, RG21 6XS, England, (Telephone in U.S. (888) 330-8477), (Fax in U.S. (800) 672-2054), www.palgrave.com; *The Statesman's Yearbook 2008.*

DOMINICAN REPUBLIC - DAIRY PROCESSING

M.E. Sharpe, 80 Business Park Drive, Armonk, NY 10504, (800) 541-6563, Fax: (914) 273-2106, www.mesharpe.com; *The Illustrated Book of World Rankings.*

Palgrave Macmillan Ltd., Houndmills, Basingstoke, Hampshire, RG21 6XS, England, (Telephone in U.S. (888) 330-8477), (Fax in U.S. (800) 672-2054), www.palgrave.com; *The Statesman's Yearbook 2008.*

Taylor and Francis Group, An Informa Business, 2 Park Square, Milton Park, Abingdon, Oxford OX14 4RN, United Kingdom, (Dial from U.S. (212) 216-7800), (Fax from U.S. (212) 564-7854), www.tandf.co.uk; *The Europa World Year Book.*

United Nations Food and Agricultural Organization (FAO), Viale delle Terme di Caracalla, 00100 Rome, Italy, (Dial from U.S. (202) 653-2400), (Fax from U.S. (202) 653 5760), www.fao.org; *The State of Food and Agriculture (SOFA) 2006.*

United Nations Statistics Division, New York, NY 10017, (800) 253-9646, Fax: (212) 963-4116, http://unstats.un.org; *Statistical Yearbook.*

DOMINICAN REPUBLIC - DEATH RATES

See DOMINICAN REPUBLIC - MORTALITY

DOMINICAN REPUBLIC - DEBT

Economist Intelligence Unit, 111 West 57th Street, New York, NY 10019, (212) 554-0600, Fax: (212) 586-1181, www.eiu.com; *Business Latin America.*

The World Bank, 1818 H Street, NW, Washington, DC 20433, (202) 473-1000, Fax: (202) 477-6391, www.worldbank.org; *Global Development Finance 2007.*

DOMINICAN REPUBLIC - DEBTS, EXTERNAL

Economist Intelligence Unit, 111 West 57th Street, New York, NY 10019, (212) 554-0600, Fax: (212) 586-1181, www.eiu.com; *Business Latin America.*

Inter-American Development Bank (IDB), 1300 New York Avenue, NW, Washington, DC 20577, (202) 623-1000, Fax: (202) 623-3096, www.iadb.org; *The Politics of Policies: Economic and Social Progress in Latin America - 2006 Report.*

Palgrave Macmillan Ltd., Houndmills, Basingstoke, Hampshire, RG21 6XS, England, (Telephone in U.S. (888) 330-8477), (Fax in U.S. (800) 672-2054), www.palgrave.com; *The Statesman's Yearbook 2008.*

United Nations Statistics Division, New York, NY 10017, (800) 253-9646, Fax: (212) 963-4116, http://unstats.un.org; *Statistical Yearbook for Latin America and the Caribbean 2004.*

The World Bank, 1818 H Street, NW, Washington, DC 20433, (202) 473-1000, Fax: (202) 477-6391, www.worldbank.org; *Global Development Finance 2007; World Development Indicators (WDI) 2008;* and *World Development Report 2008.*

DOMINICAN REPUBLIC - DEFENSE EXPENDITURES

See DOMINICAN REPUBLIC - ARMED FORCES

DOMINICAN REPUBLIC - DEMOGRAPHY

Euromonitor International, Inc., 224 S. Michigan Avenue, Suite 1500, Chicago, IL 60604, (312) 922-1115, Fax: (312) 922-1157, www.euromonitor.com; *International Marketing Data and Statistics 2008; The World Economic Factbook 2008;* and *World Marketing Data and Statistics.*

M.E. Sharpe, 80 Business Park Drive, Armonk, NY 10504, (800) 541-6563, Fax: (914) 273-2106, www.mesharpe.com; *The Illustrated Book of World Rankings.*

United Nations Statistics Division, New York, NY 10017, (800) 253-9646, Fax: (212) 963-4116, http://unstats.un.org; *Human Development Report 2006.*

The World Bank, 1818 H Street, NW, Washington, DC 20433, (202) 473-1000, Fax: (202) 477-6391, www.worldbank.org; *Dominican Republic.*

DOMINICAN REPUBLIC - DIAMONDS

See DOMINICAN REPUBLIC - MINERAL INDUSTRIES

DOMINICAN REPUBLIC - DISPOSABLE INCOME

Inter-American Development Bank (IDB), 1300 New York Avenue, NW, Washington, DC 20577, (202) 623-1000, Fax: (202) 623-3096, www.iadb.org; *The Politics of Policies: Economic and Social Progress in Latin America - 2006 Report.*

M.E. Sharpe, 80 Business Park Drive, Armonk, NY 10504, (800) 541-6563, Fax: (914) 273-2106, www.mesharpe.com; *The Illustrated Book of World Rankings.*

United Nations Statistics Division, New York, NY 10017, (800) 253-9646, Fax: (212) 963-4116, http://unstats.un.org; *National Accounts Statistics: Compendium of Income Distribution Statistics* and *Statistical Yearbook.*

DOMINICAN REPUBLIC - DIVORCE

M.E. Sharpe, 80 Business Park Drive, Armonk, NY 10504, (800) 541-6563, Fax: (914) 273-2106, www.mesharpe.com; *The Illustrated Book of World Rankings.*

United Nations Statistics Division, New York, NY 10017, (800) 253-9646, Fax: (212) 963-4116, http://unstats.un.org; *Demographic Yearbook* and *Statistical Yearbook.*

DOMINICAN REPUBLIC - ECONOMIC ASSISTANCE

Inter-American Development Bank (IDB), 1300 New York Avenue, NW, Washington, DC 20577, (202) 623-1000, Fax: (202) 623-3096, www.iadb.org; *The Politics of Policies: Economic and Social Progress in Latin America - 2006 Report.*

United Nations Statistics Division, New York, NY 10017, (800) 253-9646, Fax: (212) 963-4116, http://unstats.un.org; *Statistical Yearbook.*

DOMINICAN REPUBLIC - ECONOMIC CONDITIONS

Center for International Business Education Research (CIBER), Columbia Business School and School of International and Public Affairs, Uris Hall, Room 212, 3022 Broadway, New York, NY 10027-6902, Mr. Joshua Safier, (212) 854-4750, Fax: (212) 222-9821, www.columbia.edu/cu/ciber/; Datastream International.

Central Intelligence Agency, Office of Public Affairs, Washington, DC 20505, (703) 482-0623, Fax: (703) 482-1739, www.cia.gov; *The World Factbook.*

DSI Data Service Information, Xantener Strasse 51a, D-47495 Rheinberg, Germany, www.dsidata.com; *Campus Solution.*

Dun and Bradstreet (DB) Corporation, 103 JFK Parkway, Short Hills, NJ 07078, (973) 921-5500, www.dnb.com; *Country Report.*

Economist Intelligence Unit, 111 West 57th Street, New York, NY 10019, (212) 554-0600, Fax: (212) 586-1181, www.eiu.com; *Dominican Republic Country Report.*

Euromonitor International, Inc., 224 S. Michigan Avenue, Suite 1500, Chicago, IL 60604, (312) 922-1115, Fax: (312) 922-1157, www.euromonitor.com; *International Marketing Data and Statistics 2008; The World Economic Factbook 2008;* and *World Marketing Data and Statistics.*

Inter-American Development Bank (IDB), 1300 New York Avenue, NW, Washington, DC 20577, (202) 623-1000, Fax: (202) 623-3096, www.iadb.org; *The Politics of Policies: Economic and Social Progress in Latin America - 2006 Report.*

International Monetary Fund (IMF), 700 Nineteenth Street, NW, Washington, DC 20431, (202) 623-7000, Fax: (202) 623-4661, www.imf.org; *World Economic Outlook Reports.*

M.E. Sharpe, 80 Business Park Drive, Armonk, NY 10504, (800) 541-6563, Fax: (914) 273-2106, www.mesharpe.com; *The Illustrated Book of World Rankings.*

Organization of American States (OAS), 17th Street Constitution Avenue NW, Washington, DC 20006, (202) 458-3000, www.oas.org; *The OAS in Transition: 1994-2004.*

Palgrave Macmillan Ltd., Houndmills, Basingstoke, Hampshire, RG21 6XS, England, (Telephone in U.S. (888) 330-8477), (Fax in U.S. (800) 672-2054), www.palgrave.com; *The Statesman's Yearbook 2008.*

Taylor and Francis Group, An Informa Business, 2 Park Square, Milton Park, Abingdon, Oxford OX14 4RN, United Kingdom, (Dial from U.S. (212) 216-7800), (Fax from U.S. (212) 564-7854), www.tandf.co.uk; *The Europa World Year Book.*

UCLA Latin American Institute, 10343 Bunche Hall, Box 951447, Los Angeles, CA 90095-1447, (310) 825-4571, Fax: (310) 206-6859, www.international.ucla.edu/lac; *Statistical Abstract of Latin America.*

United Nations Statistics Division, New York, NY 10017, (800) 253-9646, Fax: (212) 963-4116, http://unstats.un.org; *World Statistics Pocketbook.*

The World Bank, 1818 H Street, NW, Washington, DC 20433, (202) 473-1000, Fax: (202) 477-6391, www.worldbank.org; *Dominican Republic; Global Economic Monitor (GEM); Global Economic Prospects 2008; The World Bank Atlas 2003-2004;* and *World Development Report 2008.*

DOMINICAN REPUBLIC - ECONOMICS - SOCIOLOGICAL ASPECTS

Inter-American Development Bank (IDB), 1300 New York Avenue, NW, Washington, DC 20577, (202) 623-1000, Fax: (202) 623-3096, www.iadb.org; *The Politics of Policies: Economic and Social Progress in Latin America - 2006 Report.*

UCLA Latin American Institute, 10343 Bunche Hall, Box 951447, Los Angeles, CA 90095-1447, (310) 825-4571, Fax: (310) 206-6859, www.international.ucla.edu/lac; *Statistical Abstract of Latin America.*

DOMINICAN REPUBLIC - EDUCATION

Economist Intelligence Unit, 111 West 57th Street, New York, NY 10019, (212) 554-0600, Fax: (212) 586-1181, www.eiu.com; *Business Latin America.*

Euromonitor International, Inc., 224 S. Michigan Avenue, Suite 1500, Chicago, IL 60604, (312) 922-1115, Fax: (312) 922-1157, www.euromonitor.com; *International Marketing Data and Statistics 2008* and *World Marketing Data and Statistics.*

International Monetary Fund (IMF), 700 Nineteenth Street, NW, Washington, DC 20431, (202) 623-7000, Fax: (202) 623-4661, www.imf.org; *Government Finance Statistics Yearbook (2008 Edition).*

M.E. Sharpe, 80 Business Park Drive, Armonk, NY 10504, (800) 541-6563, Fax: (914) 273-2106, www.mesharpe.com; *The Illustrated Book of World Rankings.*

Palgrave Macmillan Ltd., Houndmills, Basingstoke, Hampshire, RG21 6XS, England, (Telephone in U.S. (888) 330-8477), (Fax in U.S. (800) 672-2054), www.palgrave.com; *The Statesman's Yearbook 2008.*

Taylor and Francis Group, An Informa Business, 2 Park Square, Milton Park, Abingdon, Oxford OX14 4RN, United Kingdom, (Dial from U.S. (212) 216-7800), (Fax from U.S. (212) 564-7854), www.tandf.co.uk; *The Europa World Year Book.*

UCLA Latin American Institute, 10343 Bunche Hall, Box 951447, Los Angeles, CA 90095-1447, (310) 825-4571, Fax: (310) 206-6859, www.international.ucla.edu/lac; *Statistical Abstract of Latin America.*

UNESCO Institute for Statistics, C.P. 6128 Succursale Centre-Ville, Montreal, Quebec, H3C 3J7 Canada, (Dial from U.S. (514) 343-6880), (Fax from U.S. (514) 343 6882), www.uis.unesco.org; *Statistical Tables.*

United Nations Statistics Division, New York, NY 10017, (800) 253-9646, Fax: (212) 963-4116, http://unstats.un.org; *Human Development Report 2006* and *Statistical Yearbook for Latin America and the Caribbean 2004.*

The World Bank, 1818 H Street, NW, Washington, DC 20433, (202) 473-1000, Fax: (202) 477-6391, www.worldbank.org; *Dominican Republic; World Development Indicators (WDI) 2008;* and *World Development Report 2008.*

DOMINICAN REPUBLIC - ELECTRICITY

Economist Intelligence Unit, 111 West 57th Street, New York, NY 10019, (212) 554-0600, Fax: (212) 586-1181, www.eiu.com; *Business Latin America.*

Inter-American Development Bank (IDB), 1300 New York Avenue, NW, Washington, DC 20577, (202) 623-1000, Fax: (202) 623-3096, www.iadb.org; *The Politics of Policies: Economic and Social Progress in Latin America - 2006 Report.*

M.E. Sharpe, 80 Business Park Drive, Armonk, NY 10504, (800) 541-6563, Fax: (914) 273-2106, www.mesharpe.com; *The Illustrated Book of World Rankings.*

Palgrave Macmillan Ltd., Houndmills, Basingstoke, Hampshire, RG21 6XS, England, (Telephone in U.S. (888) 330-8477), (Fax in U.S. (800) 672-2054), www.palgrave.com; *The Statesman's Yearbook 2008.*

U.S. Department of Energy (DOE), Energy Information Administration (EIA), 1000 Independence Avenue, SW, Washington, DC 20585, (202) 586-8800, www.eia.doe.gov; *International Energy Annual 2004* and *International Energy Outlook 2006.*

United Nations Statistics Division, New York, NY 10017, (800) 253-9646, Fax: (212) 963-4116, http://unstats.un.org; *Human Development Report 2006* and *Statistical Yearbook.*

DOMINICAN REPUBLIC - EMIGRATION AND IMMIGRATION

UCLA Latin American Institute, 10343 Bunche Hall, Box 951447, Los Angeles, CA 90095-1447, (310) 825-4571, Fax: (310) 206-6859, www.international.ucla.edu/lac; *Statistical Abstract of Latin America.*

DOMINICAN REPUBLIC - EMPLOYMENT

Euromonitor International, Inc., 224 S. Michigan Avenue, Suite 1500, Chicago, IL 60604, (312) 922-1115, Fax: (312) 922-1157, www.euromonitor.com; *International Marketing Data and Statistics 2008.*

International Labour Office, I.L.O. Publications, 4 route des Morillons, CH-1211 Geneva 22, Switzerland, (Telephone in U.S. (202) 653-7652), (Fax in U.S. (202) 653-7687), www.ilo.org; *Yearbook of Labour Statistics 2006.*

M.E. Sharpe, 80 Business Park Drive, Armonk, NY 10504, (800) 541-6563, Fax: (914) 273-2106, www.mesharpe.com; *The Illustrated Book of World Rankings.*

UCLA Latin American Institute, 10343 Bunche Hall, Box 951447, Los Angeles, CA 90095-1447, (310) 825-4571, Fax: (310) 206-6859, www.international.ucla.edu/lac; *Statistical Abstract of Latin America.*

United Nations Statistics Division, New York, NY 10017, (800) 253-9646, Fax: (212) 963-4116, http://unstats.un.org; *Statistical Yearbook* and *Statistical Yearbook for Latin America and the Caribbean 2004.*

The World Bank, 1818 H Street, NW, Washington, DC 20433, (202) 473-1000, Fax: (202) 477-6391, www.worldbank.org; *Dominican Republic.*

DOMINICAN REPUBLIC - ENERGY INDUSTRIES

Enerdata, 10 Rue Royale, 75008 Paris, France, www.enerdata.fr; *Global Energy Market Data.*

United Nations Statistics Division, New York, NY 10017, (800) 253-9646, Fax: (212) 963-4116, http://unstats.un.org; *Statistical Yearbook.*

DOMINICAN REPUBLIC - ENVIRONMENTAL CONDITIONS

DSI Data Service Information, Xantener Strasse 51a, D-47495 Rheinberg, Germany, www.dsidata.com; *Campus Solution* and *DSI's Global Environmental Database.*

Economist Intelligence Unit, 111 West 57th Street, New York, NY 10019, (212) 554-0600, Fax: (212) 586-1181, www.eiu.com; *Dominican Republic Country Report.*

United Nations Statistics Division, New York, NY 10017, (800) 253-9646, Fax: (212) 963-4116, http://unstats.un.org; *World Statistics Pocketbook.*

DOMINICAN REPUBLIC - EXPENDITURES, PUBLIC

Inter-American Development Bank (IDB), 1300 New York Avenue, NW, Washington, DC 20577, (202) 623-1000, Fax: (202) 623-3096, www.iadb.org; *The Politics of Policies: Economic and Social Progress in Latin America - 2006 Report.*

Organization of American States (OAS), 17th Street Constitution Avenue NW, Washington, DC 20006, (202) 458-3000, www.oas.org; *The OAS in Transition: 1994-2004.*

United Nations Statistics Division, New York, NY 10017, (800) 253-9646, Fax: (212) 963-4116, http://unstats.un.org; *Statistical Yearbook for Latin America and the Caribbean 2004.*

DOMINICAN REPUBLIC - EXPORTS

Central Intelligence Agency, Office of Public Affairs, Washington, DC 20505, (703) 482-0623, Fax: (703) 482-1739, www.cia.gov; *The World Factbook.*

Economist Intelligence Unit, 111 West 57th Street, New York, NY 10019, (212) 554-0600, Fax: (212) 586-1181, www.eiu.com; *Business Latin America* and *Dominican Republic Country Report.*

Euromonitor International, Inc., 224 S. Michigan Avenue, Suite 1500, Chicago, IL 60604, (312) 922-1115, Fax: (312) 922-1157, www.euromonitor.com; *International Marketing Data and Statistics 2008* and *The World Economic Factbook 2008.*

Inter-American Development Bank (IDB), 1300 New York Avenue, NW, Washington, DC 20577, (202)

623-1000, Fax: (202) 623-3096, www.iadb.org; *The Politics of Policies: Economic and Social Progress in Latin America - 2006 Report.*

International Monetary Fund (IMF), 700 Nineteenth Street, NW, Washington, DC 20431, (202) 623-7000, Fax: (202) 623-4661, www.imf.org; *Direction of Trade Statistics Yearbook 2007* and *International Financial Statistics Yearbook 2007.*

Organization of American States (OAS), 17th Street Constitution Avenue NW, Washington, DC 20006, (202) 458-3000, www.oas.org; *The OAS in Transition: 1994-2004.*

Palgrave Macmillan Ltd., Houndmills, Basingstoke, Hampshire, RG21 6XS, England, (Telephone in U.S. (888) 330-8477), (Fax in U.S. (800) 672-2054), www.palgrave.com; *The Statesman's Yearbook 2008.*

Taylor and Francis Group, An Informa Business, 2 Park Square, Milton Park, Abingdon, Oxford OX14 4RN, United Kingdom, (Dial from U.S. (212) 216-7800), (Fax from U.S. (212) 564-7854), www.tandf.co.uk; *The Europa World Year Book.*

United Nations Conference on Trade and Development (UNCTAD), DC2-1120, United Nations, New York, NY 10017, (212) 963-0027, www.unctad.org; *Handbook of Statistics 2005.*

United Nations Food and Agricultural Organization (FAO), Viale delle Terme di Caracalla, 00100 Rome, Italy, (Dial from U.S. (202) 653-2400), (Fax from U.S. (202) 653 5760), www.fao.org; *The State of Food and Agriculture (SOFA) 2006.*

United Nations Statistics Division, New York, NY 10017, (800) 253-9646, Fax: (212) 963-4116, http://unstats.un.org; *Statistical Yearbook for Latin America and the Caribbean 2004.*

The World Bank, 1818 H Street, NW, Washington, DC 20433, (202) 473-1000, Fax: (202) 477-6391, www.worldbank.org; *World Development Indicators (WDI) 2008* and *World Development Report 2008.*

DOMINICAN REPUBLIC - FEMALE WORKING POPULATION

See DOMINICAN REPUBLIC - EMPLOYMENT

DOMINICAN REPUBLIC - FERTILITY, HUMAN

Central Intelligence Agency, Office of Public Affairs, Washington, DC 20505, (703) 482-0623, Fax: (703) 482-1739, www.cia.gov; *The World Factbook.*

M.E. Sharpe, 80 Business Park Drive, Armonk, NY 10504, (800) 541-6563, Fax: (914) 273-2106, www.mesharpe.com; *The Illustrated Book of World Rankings.*

United Nations Statistics Division, New York, NY 10017, (800) 253-9646, Fax: (212) 963-4116, http://unstats.un.org; *Human Development Report 2006.*

The World Bank, 1818 H Street, NW, Washington, DC 20433, (202) 473-1000, Fax: (202) 477-6391, www.worldbank.org; *The World Bank Atlas 2003-2004; World Development Indicators (WDI) 2008;* and *World Development Report 2008.*

DOMINICAN REPUBLIC - FERTILIZER INDUSTRY

Economist Intelligence Unit, 111 West 57th Street, New York, NY 10019, (212) 554-0600, Fax: (212) 586-1181, www.eiu.com; *Business Latin America.*

United Nations Food and Agricultural Organization (FAO), Viale delle Terme di Caracalla, 00100 Rome, Italy, (Dial from U.S. (202) 653-2400), (Fax from U.S. (202) 653 5760), www.fao.org; *FAO Fertilizer Yearbook* and *The State of Food and Agriculture (SOFA) 2006.*

United Nations Statistics Division, New York, NY 10017, (800) 253-9646, Fax: (212) 963-4116, http://unstats.un.org; *Statistical Yearbook.*

DOMINICAN REPUBLIC - FETAL MORTALITY

See DOMINICAN REPUBLIC - MORTALITY

DOMINICAN REPUBLIC - FINANCE

Inter-American Development Bank (IDB), 1300 New York Avenue, NW, Washington, DC 20577, (202) 623-1000, Fax: (202) 623-3096, www.iadb.org; *The Politics of Policies: Economic and Social Progress in Latin America - 2006 Report.*

International Monetary Fund (IMF), 700 Nineteenth Street, NW, Washington, DC 20431, (202) 623-7000, Fax: (202) 623-4661, www.imf.org; *International Financial Statistics Yearbook 2007.*

Organization of American States (OAS), 17th Street Constitution Avenue NW, Washington, DC 20006, (202) 458-3000, www.oas.org; *The OAS in Transition: 1994-2004.*

Taylor and Francis Group, An Informa Business, 2 Park Square, Milton Park, Abingdon, Oxford OX14 4RN, United Kingdom, (Dial from U.S. (212) 216-7800), (Fax from U.S. (212) 564-7854), www.tandf.co.uk; *The Europa World Year Book.*

UCLA Latin American Institute, 10343 Bunche Hall, Box 951447, Los Angeles, CA 90095-1447, (310) 825-4571, Fax: (310) 206-6859, www.international.ucla.edu/lac; *Statistical Abstract of Latin America.*

United Nations Statistics Division, New York, NY 10017, (800) 253-9646, Fax: (212) 963-4116, http://unstats.un.org; *National Accounts Statistics: Compendium of Income Distribution Statistics* and *Statistical Yearbook.*

The World Bank, 1818 H Street, NW, Washington, DC 20433, (202) 473-1000, Fax: (202) 477-6391, www.worldbank.org; *Dominican Republic.*

DOMINICAN REPUBLIC - FINANCE, PUBLIC

Bernan Essential Government Publications, 4611-F Assembly Drive, Lanham MD, 20706-4391, (301) 459-2255, Fax: (800) 865-3450, www.bernan.com; *National Accounts Statistics.*

Economist Intelligence Unit, 111 West 57th Street, New York, NY 10019, (212) 554-0600, Fax: (212) 586-1181, www.eiu.com; *Dominican Republic Country Report.*

Inter-American Development Bank (IDB), 1300 New York Avenue, NW, Washington, DC 20577, (202) 623-1000, Fax: (202) 623-3096, www.iadb.org; *The Politics of Policies: Economic and Social Progress in Latin America - 2006 Report.*

International Monetary Fund (IMF), 700 Nineteenth Street, NW, Washington, DC 20431, (202) 623-7000, Fax: (202) 623-4661, www.imf.org; *International Financial Statistics; International Financial Statistics Online Service;* and *International Financial Statistics Yearbook 2007.*

M.E. Sharpe, 80 Business Park Drive, Armonk, NY 10504, (800) 541-6563, Fax: (914) 273-2106, www.mesharpe.com; *The Illustrated Book of World Rankings.*

Organization of American States (OAS), 17th Street Constitution Avenue NW, Washington, DC 20006, (202) 458-3000, www.oas.org; *The OAS in Transition: 1994-2004.*

Palgrave Macmillan Ltd., Houndmills, Basingstoke, Hampshire, RG21 6XS, England, (Telephone in U.S. (888) 330-8477), (Fax in U.S. (800) 672-2054), www.palgrave.com; *The Statesman's Yearbook 2008.*

Taylor and Francis Group, An Informa Business, 2 Park Square, Milton Park, Abingdon, Oxford OX14 4RN, United Kingdom, (Dial from U.S. (212) 216-7800), (Fax from U.S. (212) 564-7854), www.tandf.co.uk; *The Europa World Year Book.*

UCLA Latin American Institute, 10343 Bunche Hall, Box 951447, Los Angeles, CA 90095-1447, (310) 825-4571, Fax: (310) 206-6859, www.international.ucla.edu/lac; *Statistical Abstract of Latin America.*

The World Bank, 1818 H Street, NW, Washington, DC 20433, (202) 473-1000, Fax: (202) 477-6391, www.worldbank.org; *Dominican Republic.*

DOMINICAN REPUBLIC - FISHERIES

Inter-American Development Bank (IDB), 1300 New York Avenue, NW, Washington, DC 20577, (202) 623-1000, Fax: (202) 623-3096, www.iadb.org; *The Politics of Policies: Economic and Social Progress in Latin America - 2006 Report.*

M.E. Sharpe, 80 Business Park Drive, Armonk, NY 10504, (800) 541-6563, Fax: (914) 273-2106, www.mesharpe.com; *The Illustrated Book of World Rankings.*

Palgrave Macmillan Ltd., Houndmills, Basingstoke, Hampshire, RG21 6XS, England, (Telephone in U.S. (888) 330-8477), (Fax in U.S. (800) 672-2054), www.palgrave.com; *The Statesman's Yearbook 2008.*

Taylor and Francis Group, An Informa Business, 2 Park Square, Milton Park, Abingdon, Oxford OX14 4RN, United Kingdom, (Dial from U.S. (212) 216-7800), (Fax from U.S. (212) 564-7854), www.tandf.co.uk; *The Europa World Year Book.*

UCLA Latin American Institute, 10343 Bunche Hall, Box 951447, Los Angeles, CA 90095-1447, (310) 825-4571, Fax: (310) 206-6859, www.international.ucla.edu/lac; *Statistical Abstract of Latin America.*

United Nations Conference on Trade and Development (UNCTAD), DC2-1120, United Nations, New York, NY 10017, (212) 963-0027, www.unctad.org; *UNCTAD Commodity Yearbook.*

United Nations Food and Agricultural Organization (FAO), Viale delle Terme di Caracalla, 00100 Rome, Italy, (Dial from U.S. (202) 653-2400), (Fax from U.S. (202) 653 5760), www.fao.org; *FAO Yearbook of Fishery Statistics;* Fishery Databases; FISHSTAT Database. Subjects covered include: Aquaculture production, capture production, fishery commodities; and *The State of Food and Agriculture (SOFA) 2006.*

United Nations Statistics Division, New York, NY 10017, (800) 253-9646, Fax: (212) 963-4116, http://unstats.un.org; *Statistical Yearbook.*

The World Bank, 1818 H Street, NW, Washington, DC 20433, (202) 473-1000, Fax: (202) 477-6391, www.worldbank.org; *Dominican Republic.*

DOMINICAN REPUBLIC - FLOUR INDUSTRY

United Nations Statistics Division, New York, NY 10017, (800) 253-9646, Fax: (212) 963-4116, http://unstats.un.org; *Statistical Yearbook.*

DOMINICAN REPUBLIC - FOOD

United Nations Conference on Trade and Development (UNCTAD), DC2-1120, United Nations, New York, NY 10017, (212) 963-0027, www.unctad.org; *UNCTAD Commodity Yearbook.*

United Nations Food and Agricultural Organization (FAO), Viale delle Terme di Caracalla, 00100 Rome, Italy, (Dial from U.S. (202) 653-2400), (Fax from U.S. (202) 653 5760), www.fao.org; *FAO Production Yearbook 2002* and *The State of Food and Agriculture (SOFA) 2006.*

United Nations Statistics Division, New York, NY 10017, (800) 253-9646, Fax: (212) 963-4116, http://unstats.un.org; *Human Development Report 2006.*

DOMINICAN REPUBLIC - FOREIGN EXCHANGE RATES

Central Intelligence Agency, Office of Public Affairs, Washington, DC 20505, (703) 482-0623, Fax: (703) 482-1739, www.cia.gov; *The World Factbook.*

Euromonitor International, Inc., 224 S. Michigan Avenue, Suite 1500, Chicago, IL 60604, (312) 922-1115, Fax: (312) 922-1157, www.euromonitor.com; *International Marketing Data and Statistics 2008* and *The World Economic Factbook 2008.*

Inter-American Development Bank (IDB), 1300 New York Avenue, NW, Washington, DC 20577, (202) 623-1000, Fax: (202) 623-3096, www.iadb.org; *The Politics of Policies: Economic and Social Progress in Latin America - 2006 Report.*

International Civil Aviation Organization (ICAO), External Relations and Public Information Office (EPO), 999 University Street, Montreal, Quebec H3C 5H7, Canada, (Dial from U.S. (514) 954-8219), (Fax from U.S. (514) 954-6077), www.icao.int; *Civil Aviation Statistics of the World.*

International Monetary Fund (IMF), 700 Nineteenth Street, NW, Washington, DC 20431, (202) 623-7000, Fax: (202) 623-4661, www.imf.org; *International Financial Statistics Yearbook 2007.*

Organization of American States (OAS), 17th Street Constitution Avenue NW, Washington, DC 20006, (202) 458-3000, www.oas.org; *The OAS in Transition: 1994-2004.*

Taylor and Francis Group, An Informa Business, 2 Park Square, Milton Park, Abingdon, Oxford OX14 4RN, United Kingdom, (Dial from U.S. (212) 216-7800), (Fax from U.S. (212) 564-7854), www.tandf.co.uk; *The Europa World Year Book.*

UCLA Latin American Institute, 10343 Bunche Hall, Box 951447, Los Angeles, CA 90095-1447, (310) 825-4571, Fax: (310) 206-6859, www.international.ucla.edu/lac; *Statistical Abstract of Latin America.*

United Nations Statistics Division, New York, NY 10017, (800) 253-9646, Fax: (212) 963-4116, http://unstats.un.org; *Statistical Yearbook* and *World Statistics Pocketbook.*

DOMINICAN REPUBLIC - FORESTS AND FORESTRY

Economist Intelligence Unit, 111 West 57th Street, New York, NY 10019, (212) 554-0600, Fax: (212) 586-1181, www.eiu.com; *Business Latin America.*

Inter-American Development Bank (IDB), 1300 New York Avenue, NW, Washington, DC 20577, (202) 623-1000, Fax: (202) 623-3096, www.iadb.org; *The Politics of Policies: Economic and Social Progress in Latin America - 2006 Report.*

M.E. Sharpe, 80 Business Park Drive, Armonk, NY 10504, (800) 541-6563, Fax: (914) 273-2106, www.mesharpe.com; *The Illustrated Book of World Rankings.*

Palgrave Macmillan Ltd., Houndmills, Basingstoke, Hampshire, RG21 6XS, England, (Telephone in U.S. (888) 330-8477), (Fax in U.S. (800) 672-2054), www.palgrave.com; *The Statesman's Yearbook 2008.*

Taylor and Francis Group, An Informa Business, 2 Park Square, Milton Park, Abingdon, Oxford OX14 4RN, United Kingdom, (Dial from U.S. (212) 216-7800), (Fax from U.S. (212) 564-7854), www.tandf.co.uk; *The Europa World Year Book.*

UCLA Latin American Institute, 10343 Bunche Hall, Box 951447, Los Angeles, CA 90095-1447, (310) 825-4571, Fax: (310) 206-6859, www.international.ucla.edu/lac; *Statistical Abstract of Latin America.*

UNESCO Institute for Statistics, C.P. 6128 Succursale Centre-Ville, Montreal, Quebec, H3C 3J7 Canada, (Dial from U.S. (514) 343-6880), (Fax from U.S. (514) 343 6882), www.uis.unesco.org; *Statistical Tables.*

United Nations Conference on Trade and Development (UNCTAD), DC2-1120, United Nations, New York, NY 10017, (212) 963-0027, www.unctad.org; *UNCTAD Commodity Yearbook.*

United Nations Food and Agricultural Organization (FAO), Viale delle Terme di Caracalla, 00100 Rome, Italy, (Dial from U.S. (202) 653-2400), (Fax from U.S. (202) 653 5760), www.fao.org; *FAO Yearbook of Forest Products* and *The State of Food and Agriculture (SOFA) 2006.*

United Nations Statistics Division, New York, NY 10017, (800) 253-9646, Fax: (212) 963-4116, http://unstats.un.org; *Statistical Yearbook.*

The World Bank, 1818 H Street, NW, Washington, DC 20433, (202) 473-1000, Fax: (202) 477-6391, www.worldbank.org; *Dominican Republic* and *World Development Report 2008.*

DOMINICAN REPUBLIC - GAS PRODUCTION

See DOMINICAN REPUBLIC - MINERAL INDUSTRIES

DOMINICAN REPUBLIC - GEOGRAPHIC INFORMATION SYSTEMS

M.E. Sharpe, 80 Business Park Drive, Armonk, NY 10504, (800) 541-6563, Fax: (914) 273-2106, www.mesharpe.com; *The Illustrated Book of World Rankings.*

UCLA Latin American Institute, 10343 Bunche Hall, Box 951447, Los Angeles, CA 90095-1447, (310) 825-4571, Fax: (310) 206-6859, www.international.ucla.edu/lac; *Statistical Abstract of Latin America.*

The World Bank, 1818 H Street, NW, Washington, DC 20433, (202) 473-1000, Fax: (202) 477-6391, www.worldbank.org; *Dominican Republic.*

DOMINICAN REPUBLIC - GOLD INDUSTRY

Economist Intelligence Unit, 111 West 57th Street, New York, NY 10019, (212) 554-0600, Fax: (212) 586-1181, www.eiu.com; *Business Latin America.*

International Monetary Fund (IMF), 700 Nineteenth Street, NW, Washington, DC 20431, (202) 623-7000, Fax: (202) 623-4661, www.imf.org; *International Financial Statistics Yearbook 2007.*

United Nations Statistics Division, New York, NY 10017, (800) 253-9646, Fax: (212) 963-4116, http://unstats.un.org; *Statistical Yearbook.*

The World Bank, 1818 H Street, NW, Washington, DC 20433, (202) 473-1000, Fax: (202) 477-6391, www.worldbank.org; *World Development Indicators (WDI) 2008.*

DOMINICAN REPUBLIC - GOLD PRODUCTION

See DOMINICAN REPUBLIC - MINERAL INDUSTRIES

DOMINICAN REPUBLIC - GRANTS-IN-AID

International Monetary Fund (IMF), 700 Nineteenth Street, NW, Washington, DC 20431, (202) 623-7000, Fax: (202) 623-4661, www.imf.org; *Government Finance Statistics Yearbook (2008 Edition).*

DOMINICAN REPUBLIC - GREEN PEPPER AND CHILIE PRODUCTION

See DOMINICAN REPUBLIC - CROPS

DOMINICAN REPUBLIC - GROSS DOMESTIC PRODUCT

Economist Intelligence Unit, 111 West 57th Street, New York, NY 10019, (212) 554-0600, Fax: (212) 586-1181, www.eiu.com; *Business Latin America* and *Dominican Republic Country Report.*

Euromonitor International, Inc., 224 S. Michigan Avenue, Suite 1500, Chicago, IL 60604, (312) 922-1115, Fax: (312) 922-1157, www.euromonitor.com; *International Marketing Data and Statistics 2008* and *The World Economic Factbook 2008.*

Inter-American Development Bank (IDB), 1300 New York Avenue, NW, Washington, DC 20577, (202) 623-1000, Fax: (202) 623-3096, www.iadb.org; *The Politics of Policies: Economic and Social Progress in Latin America - 2006 Report.*

M.E. Sharpe, 80 Business Park Drive, Armonk, NY 10504, (800) 541-6563, Fax: (914) 273-2106, www.mesharpe.com; *The Illustrated Book of World Rankings.*

Organization of American States (OAS), 17th Street Constitution Avenue NW, Washington, DC 20006, (202) 458-3000, www.oas.org; *The OAS in Transition: 1994-2004.*

Taylor and Francis Group, An Informa Business, 2 Park Square, Milton Park, Abingdon, Oxford OX14 4RN, United Kingdom, (Dial from U.S. (212) 216-7800), (Fax from U.S. (212) 564-7854), www.tandf.co.uk; *The Europa World Year Book.*

UCLA Latin American Institute, 10343 Bunche Hall, Box 951447, Los Angeles, CA 90095-1447, (310) 825-4571, Fax: (310) 206-6859, www.international.ucla.edu/lac; *Statistical Abstract of Latin America.*

United Nations Statistics Division, New York, NY 10017, (800) 253-9646, Fax: (212) 963-4116, http://unstats.un.org; *Human Development Report 2006; National Accounts Statistics: Compendium of Income Distribution Statistics; Statistical Yearbook;* and *Statistical Yearbook for Latin America and the Caribbean 2004.*

The World Bank, 1818 H Street, NW, Washington, DC 20433, (202) 473-1000, Fax: (202) 477-6391, www.worldbank.org; *World Development Indicators (WDI) 2008* and *World Development Report 2008.*

DOMINICAN REPUBLIC - GROSS NATIONAL PRODUCT

Euromonitor International, Inc., 224 S. Michigan Avenue, Suite 1500, Chicago, IL 60604, (312) 922-1115, Fax: (312) 922-1157, www.euromonitor.com; *International Marketing Data and Statistics 2008.*

Inter-American Development Bank (IDB), 1300 New York Avenue, NW, Washington, DC 20577, (202) 623-1000, Fax: (202) 623-3096, www.iadb.org; *The Politics of Policies: Economic and Social Progress in Latin America - 2006 Report.*

M.E. Sharpe, 80 Business Park Drive, Armonk, NY 10504, (800) 541-6563, Fax: (914) 273-2106, www.mesharpe.com; *The Illustrated Book of World Rankings.*

Palgrave Macmillan Ltd., Houndmills, Basingstoke, Hampshire, RG21 6XS, England, (Telephone in U.S. (888) 330-8477), (Fax in U.S. (800) 672-2054), www.palgrave.com; *The Statesman's Yearbook 2008.*

Taylor and Francis Group, An Informa Business, 2 Park Square, Milton Park, Abingdon, Oxford OX14 4RN, United Kingdom, (Dial from U.S. (212) 216-7800), (Fax from U.S. (212) 564-7854), www.tandf.co.uk; *The Europa World Year Book.*

U.S. Department of State (DOS), 2201 C Street NW, Washington, DC 20520, (202) 647-4000, www.state.gov; *World Military Expenditures and Arms Transfers (WMEAT).*

United Nations Statistics Division, New York, NY 10017, (800) 253-9646, Fax: (212) 963-4116, http://unstats.un.org; *Statistical Yearbook.*

The World Bank, 1818 H Street, NW, Washington, DC 20433, (202) 473-1000, Fax: (202) 477-6391, www.worldbank.org; *The World Bank Atlas 2003-2004; World Development Indicators (WDI) 2008;* and *World Development Report 2008.*

DOMINICAN REPUBLIC - HARDWOOD INDUSTRY

Inter-American Development Bank (IDB), 1300 New York Avenue, NW, Washington, DC 20577, (202) 623-1000, Fax: (202) 623-3096, www.iadb.org; *The Politics of Policies: Economic and Social Progress in Latin America - 2006 Report.*

United Nations Food and Agricultural Organization (FAO), Viale delle Terme di Caracalla, 00100 Rome, Italy, (Dial from U.S. (202) 653-2400), (Fax from U.S. (202) 653 5760), www.fao.org; *FAO Yearbook of Forest Products.*

United Nations Statistics Division, New York, NY 10017, (800) 253-9646, Fax: (212) 963-4116, http://unstats.un.org; *Statistical Yearbook.*

DOMINICAN REPUBLIC - HIDES AND SKINS INDUSTRY

United Nations Food and Agricultural Organization (FAO), Viale delle Terme di Caracalla, 00100 Rome, Italy, (Dial from U.S. (202) 653-2400), (Fax from U.S. (202) 653 5760), www.fao.org; *FAO Production Yearbook 2002.*

DOMINICAN REPUBLIC - HOUSING

Euromonitor International, Inc., 224 S. Michigan Avenue, Suite 1500, Chicago, IL 60604, (312) 922-1115, Fax: (312) 922-1157, www.euromonitor.com; *World Marketing Data and Statistics.*

M.E. Sharpe, 80 Business Park Drive, Armonk, NY 10504, (800) 541-6563, Fax: (914) 273-2106, www.mesharpe.com; *The Illustrated Book of World Rankings.*

UCLA Latin American Institute, 10343 Bunche Hall, Box 951447, Los Angeles, CA 90095-1447, (310) 825-4571, Fax: (310) 206-6859, www.international.ucla.edu/lac; *Statistical Abstract of Latin America.*

United Nations Statistics Division, New York, NY 10017, (800) 253-9646, Fax: (212) 963-4116, http://unstats.un.org; *Statistical Yearbook for Latin America and the Caribbean 2004.*

DOMINICAN REPUBLIC - ILLITERATE PERSONS

Economist Intelligence Unit, 111 West 57th Street, New York, NY 10019, (212) 554-0600, Fax: (212) 586-1181, www.eiu.com; *Business Latin America.*

Euromonitor International, Inc., 224 S. Michigan Avenue, Suite 1500, Chicago, IL 60604, (312) 922-1115, Fax: (312) 922-1157, www.euromonitor.com; *The World Economic Factbook 2008.*

UNESCO Institute for Statistics, C.P. 6128 Succursale Centre-Ville, Montreal, Quebec, H3C 3J7 Canada, (Dial from U.S. (514) 343-6880), (Fax from U.S. (514) 343 6882), www.uis.unesco.org; *Statistical Tables.*

United Nations Statistics Division, New York, NY 10017, (800) 253-9646, Fax: (212) 963-4116, http://unstats.un.org; *Human Development Report 2006* and *Statistical Yearbook for Latin America and the Caribbean 2004.*

DOMINICAN REPUBLIC - IMPORTS

Central Intelligence Agency, Office of Public Affairs, Washington, DC 20505, (703) 482-0623, Fax: (703) 482-1739, www.cia.gov; *The World Factbook.*

Economist Intelligence Unit, 111 West 57th Street, New York, NY 10019, (212) 554-0600, Fax: (212) 586-1181, www.eiu.com; *Business Latin America* and *Dominican Republic Country Report.*

Euromonitor International, Inc., 224 S. Michigan Avenue, Suite 1500, Chicago, IL 60604, (312) 922-1115, Fax: (312) 922-1157, www.euromonitor.com; *International Marketing Data and Statistics 2008* and *The World Economic Factbook 2008.*

Inter-American Development Bank (IDB), 1300 New York Avenue, NW, Washington, DC 20577, (202) 623-1000, Fax: (202) 623-3096, www.iadb.org; *The Politics of Policies: Economic and Social Progress in Latin America - 2006 Report.*

International Monetary Fund (IMF), 700 Nineteenth Street, NW, Washington, DC 20431, (202) 623-7000, Fax: (202) 623-4661, www.imf.org; *Direction of Trade Statistics Yearbook 2007; Government Finance Statistics Yearbook (2008 Edition);* and *International Financial Statistics Yearbook 2007.*

Organization of American States (OAS), 17th Street Constitution Avenue NW, Washington, DC 20006, (202) 458-3000, www.oas.org; *The OAS in Transition: 1994-2004.*

Palgrave Macmillan Ltd., Houndmills, Basingstoke, Hampshire, RG21 6XS, England, (Telephone in U.S. (888) 330-8477), (Fax in U.S. (800) 672-2054), www.palgrave.com; *The Statesman's Yearbook 2008.*

Taylor and Francis Group, An Informa Business, 2 Park Square, Milton Park, Abingdon, Oxford OX14 4RN, United Kingdom, (Dial from U.S. (212) 216-7800), (Fax from U.S. (212) 564-7854), www.tandf.co.uk; *The Europa World Year Book.*

United Nations Conference on Trade and Development (UNCTAD), DC2-1120, United Nations, New York, NY 10017, (212) 963-0027, www.unctad.org; *Handbook of Statistics 2005.*

United Nations Food and Agricultural Organization (FAO), Viale delle Terme di Caracalla, 00100 Rome, Italy, (Dial from U.S. (202) 653-2400), (Fax from U.S. (202) 653 5760), www.fao.org; *The State of Food and Agriculture (SOFA) 2006.*

United Nations Statistics Division, New York, NY 10017, (800) 253-9646, Fax: (212) 963-4116, http://unstats.un.org; *Statistical Yearbook for Latin America and the Caribbean 2004.*

The World Bank, 1818 H Street, NW, Washington, DC 20433, (202) 473-1000, Fax: (202) 477-6391, www.worldbank.org; *World Development Indicators (WDI) 2008* and *World Development Report 2008.*

DOMINICAN REPUBLIC - INCOME DISTRIBUTION

UCLA Latin American Institute, 10343 Bunche Hall, Box 951447, Los Angeles, CA 90095-1447, (310) 825-4571, Fax: (310) 206-6859, www.international.ucla.edu/lac; *Statistical Abstract of Latin America.*

United Nations Statistics Division, New York, NY 10017, (800) 253-9646, Fax: (212) 963-4116, http://unstats.un.org; *Statistical Yearbook for Latin America and the Caribbean 2004.*

DOMINICAN REPUBLIC - INCOME TAXES

See DOMINICAN REPUBLIC - TAXATION

DOMINICAN REPUBLIC - INDUSTRIAL PRODUCTIVITY

Euromonitor International, Inc., 224 S. Michigan Avenue, Suite 1500, Chicago, IL 60604, (312) 922-1115, Fax: (312) 922-1157, www.euromonitor.com; *International Marketing Data and Statistics 2008.*

M.E. Sharpe, 80 Business Park Drive, Armonk, NY 10504, (800) 541-6563, Fax: (914) 273-2106, www.mesharpe.com; *The Illustrated Book of World Rankings.*

DOMINICAN REPUBLIC - INDUSTRIAL PROPERTY

United Nations Statistics Division, New York, NY 10017, (800) 253-9646, Fax: (212) 963-4116, http://unstats.un.org; *Statistical Yearbook.*

DOMINICAN REPUBLIC - INDUSTRIES

Central Intelligence Agency, Office of Public Affairs, Washington, DC 20505, (703) 482-0623, Fax: (703) 482-1739, www.cia.gov; *The World Factbook.*

Economist Intelligence Unit, 111 West 57th Street, New York, NY 10019, (212) 554-0600, Fax: (212) 586-1181, www.eiu.com; *Dominican Republic Country Report.*

Euromonitor International, Inc., 224 S. Michigan Avenue, Suite 1500, Chicago, IL 60604, (312) 922-1115, Fax: (312) 922-1157, www.euromonitor.com; *International Marketing Data and Statistics 2008; The World Economic Factbook 2008;* and *World Marketing Data and Statistics.*

International Labour Office, I.L.O. Publications, 4 route des Morillons, CH-1211 Geneva 22, Switzerland, (Telephone in U.S. (202) 653-7652), (Fax in U.S. (202) 653-7687), www.ilo.org; *Yearbook of Labour Statistics 2006.*

M.E. Sharpe, 80 Business Park Drive, Armonk, NY 10504, (800) 541-6563, Fax: (914) 273-2106, www.mesharpe.com; *The Illustrated Book of World Rankings.*

Palgrave Macmillan Ltd., Houndmills, Basingstoke, Hampshire, RG21 6XS, England, (Telephone in U.S. (888) 330-8477), (Fax in U.S. (800) 672-2054), www.palgrave.com; *The Statesman's Yearbook 2008.*

Taylor and Francis Group, An Informa Business, 2 Park Square, Milton Park, Abingdon, Oxford OX14 4RN, United Kingdom, (Dial from U.S. (212) 216-7800), (Fax from U.S. (212) 564-7854), www.tandf.co.uk; *The Europa World Year Book.*

UCLA Latin American Institute, 10343 Bunche Hall, Box 951447, Los Angeles, CA 90095-1447, (310) 825-4571, Fax: (310) 206-6859, www.international.ucla.edu/lac; *Statistical Abstract of Latin America.*

United Nations Industrial Development Organization (UNIDO), 1 United Nations Plaza, New York, NY 10017, (212) 963 6890, Fax: (212) 963-7904, http://unido.org; Industrial Statistics Database 2008 (INDSTAT) and *The International Yearbook of Industrial Statistics 2008.*

United Nations Statistics Division, New York, NY 10017, (800) 253-9646, Fax: (212) 963-4116, http://unstats.un.org; *2004 Industrial Commodity Statistics Yearbook* and *Statistical Yearbook.*

The World Bank, 1818 H Street, NW, Washington, DC 20433, (202) 473-1000, Fax: (202) 477-6391, www.worldbank.org; *Dominican Republic* and *World Development Indicators (WDI) 2008.*

DOMINICAN REPUBLIC - INFANT AND MATERNAL MORTALITY

See DOMINICAN REPUBLIC - MORTALITY

DOMINICAN REPUBLIC - INTEREST RATES

Inter-American Development Bank (IDB), 1300 New York Avenue, NW, Washington, DC 20577, (202) 623-1000, Fax: (202) 623-3096, www.iadb.org; *The Politics of Policies: Economic and Social Progress in Latin America - 2006 Report.*

DOMINICAN REPUBLIC - INTERNAL REVENUE

Inter-American Development Bank (IDB), 1300 New York Avenue, NW, Washington, DC 20577, (202) 623-1000, Fax: (202) 623-3096, www.iadb.org; *The Politics of Policies: Economic and Social Progress in Latin America - 2006 Report.*

Organization of American States (OAS), 17th Street Constitution Avenue NW, Washington, DC 20006, (202) 458-3000, www.oas.org; *The OAS in Transition: 1994-2004.*

DOMINICAN REPUBLIC - INTERNATIONAL FINANCE

Inter-American Development Bank (IDB), 1300 New York Avenue, NW, Washington, DC 20577, (202) 623-1000, Fax: (202) 623-3096, www.iadb.org; *The Politics of Policies: Economic and Social Progress in Latin America - 2006 Report.*

UCLA Latin American Institute, 10343 Bunche Hall, Box 951447, Los Angeles, CA 90095-1447, (310) 825-4571, Fax: (310) 206-6859, www.international.ucla.edu/lac; *Statistical Abstract of Latin America.*

United Nations Statistics Division, New York, NY 10017, (800) 253-9646, Fax: (212) 963-4116, http://unstats.un.org; *Statistical Yearbook for Latin America and the Caribbean 2004.*

DOMINICAN REPUBLIC - INTERNATIONAL LIQUIDITY

Inter-American Development Bank (IDB), 1300 New York Avenue, NW, Washington, DC 20577, (202) 623-1000, Fax: (202) 623-3096, www.iadb.org; *The Politics of Policies: Economic and Social Progress in Latin America - 2006 Report.*

International Monetary Fund (IMF), 700 Nineteenth Street, NW, Washington, DC 20431, (202) 623-7000, Fax: (202) 623-4661, www.imf.org; *International Financial Statistics Yearbook 2007.*

DOMINICAN REPUBLIC - INTERNATIONAL STATISTICS

Inter-American Development Bank (IDB), 1300 New York Avenue, NW, Washington, DC 20577, (202) 623-1000, Fax: (202) 623-3096, www.iadb.org; *The Politics of Policies: Economic and Social Progress in Latin America - 2006 Report.*

UCLA Latin American Institute, 10343 Bunche Hall, Box 951447, Los Angeles, CA 90095-1447, (310) 825-4571, Fax: (310) 206-6859, www.international.ucla.edu/lac; *Statistical Abstract of Latin America.*

DOMINICAN REPUBLIC - INTERNATIONAL TRADE

Economist Intelligence Unit, 111 West 57th Street, New York, NY 10019, (212) 554-0600, Fax: (212) 586-1181, www.eiu.com; *Business Latin America* and *Dominican Republic Country Report.*

Euromonitor International, Inc., 224 S. Michigan Avenue, Suite 1500, Chicago, IL 60604, (312) 922-1115, Fax: (312) 922-1157, www.euromonitor.com; *International Marketing Data and Statistics 2008; The World Economic Factbook 2008;* and *World Marketing Data and Statistics.*

Inter-American Development Bank (IDB), 1300 New York Avenue, NW, Washington, DC 20577, (202) 623-1000, Fax: (202) 623-3096, www.iadb.org; *The Politics of Policies: Economic and Social Progress in Latin America - 2006 Report.*

International Monetary Fund (IMF), 700 Nineteenth Street, NW, Washington, DC 20431, (202) 623-7000, Fax: (202) 623-4661, www.imf.org; *International Financial Statistics Yearbook 2007.*

M.E. Sharpe, 80 Business Park Drive, Armonk, NY 10504, (800) 541-6563, Fax: (914) 273-2106, www.mesharpe.com; *The Illustrated Book of World Rankings.*

Organisation for Economic Cooperation and Development (OECD), 2 rue Andre Pascal, F-75775 Paris Cedex 16, France, (Telephone in U.S. (202) 785-6323), (Fax in U.S. (202) 785-0350), www.oecd.org; *International Trade by Commodity Statistics (ITCS).*

Palgrave Macmillan Ltd., Houndmills, Basingstoke, Hampshire, RG21 6XS, England, (Telephone in U.S. (888) 330-8477), (Fax in U.S. (800) 672-2054), www.palgrave.com; *The Statesman's Yearbook 2008.*

Taylor and Francis Group, An Informa Business, 2 Park Square, Milton Park, Abingdon, Oxford OX14 4RN, United Kingdom, (Dial from U.S. (212) 216-7800), (Fax from U.S. (212) 564-7854), www.tandf.co.uk; *The Europa World Year Book.*

UCLA Latin American Institute, 10343 Bunche Hall, Box 951447, Los Angeles, CA 90095-1447, (310) 825-4571, Fax: (310) 206-6859, www.international.ucla.edu/lac; *Statistical Abstract of Latin America.*

United Nations Conference on Trade and Development (UNCTAD), DC2-1120, United Nations, New York, NY 10017, (212) 963-0027, www.unctad.org; *UNCTAD Commodity Yearbook.*

United Nations Food and Agricultural Organization (FAO), Viale delle Terme di Caracalla, 00100 Rome, Italy, (Dial from U.S. (202) 653-2400), (Fax from U.S. (202) 653 5760), www.fao.org; *FAO Trade Yearbook* and *The State of Food and Agriculture (SOFA) 2006.*

United Nations Statistics Division, New York, NY 10017, (800) 253-9646, Fax: (212) 963-4116, http://unstats.un.org; *International Trade Statistics Yearbook; Statistical Yearbook;* and *Statistical Yearbook for Latin America and the Caribbean 2004.*

The World Bank, 1818 H Street, NW, Washington, DC 20433, (202) 473-1000, Fax: (202) 477-6391, www.worldbank.org; *Dominican Republic; World Development Indicators (WDI) 2008;* and *World Development Report 2008.*

World Trade Organization (WTO), Centre William Rappard, Rue de Lausanne 154, CH-1211 Geneva 21, Switzerland, www.wto.org; *International Trade Statistics 2006.*

DOMINICAN REPUBLIC - INTERNET USERS

International Telecommunication Union (ITU), Place des Nations, 1211 Geneva 20, Switzerland, www.itu.int; *World Telecommunication/ICT Indicators Database on CD-ROM; World Telecommunication/ICT Indicators Database Online;* and *Yearbook of Statistics - Telecommunication Services (Chronological Time Series 1997-2006).*

The World Bank, 1818 H Street, NW, Washington, DC 20433, (202) 473-1000, Fax: (202) 477-6391, www.worldbank.org; *Dominican Republic.*

DOMINICAN REPUBLIC - INVESTMENTS

Inter-American Development Bank (IDB), 1300 New York Avenue, NW, Washington, DC 20577, (202) 623-1000, Fax: (202) 623-3096, www.iadb.org; *The Politics of Policies: Economic and Social Progress in Latin America - 2006 Report.*

United Nations Statistics Division, New York, NY 10017, (800) 253-9646, Fax: (212) 963-4116, http://unstats.un.org; *Statistical Yearbook for Latin America and the Caribbean 2004.*

DOMINICAN REPUBLIC - INVESTMENTS, FOREIGN

Economist Intelligence Unit, 111 West 57th Street, New York, NY 10019, (212) 554-0600, Fax: (212) 586-1181, www.eiu.com; *Business Latin America.*

DOMINICAN REPUBLIC - IRON AND IRON ORE PRODUCTION

See DOMINICAN REPUBLIC - MINERAL INDUSTRIES

DOMINICAN REPUBLIC - IRRIGATION

Euromonitor International, Inc., 224 S. Michigan Avenue, Suite 1500, Chicago, IL 60604, (312) 922-1115, Fax: (312) 922-1157, www.euromonitor.com; *International Marketing Data and Statistics 2008.*

Inter-American Development Bank (IDB), 1300 New York Avenue, NW, Washington, DC 20577, (202) 623-1000, Fax: (202) 623-3096, www.iadb.org; *The Politics of Policies: Economic and Social Progress in Latin America - 2006 Report.*

DOMINICAN REPUBLIC - LABOR

Central Intelligence Agency, Office of Public Affairs, Washington, DC 20505, (703) 482-0623, Fax: (703) 482-1739, www.cia.gov; *The World Factbook.*

Economist Intelligence Unit, 111 West 57th Street, New York, NY 10019, (212) 554-0600, Fax: (212) 586-1181, www.eiu.com; *Business Latin America.*

Euromonitor International, Inc., 224 S. Michigan Avenue, Suite 1500, Chicago, IL 60604, (312) 922-1115, Fax: (312) 922-1157, www.euromonitor.com; *International Marketing Data and Statistics 2008* and *World Marketing Data and Statistics.*

International Labour Office, I.L.O. Publications, 4 route des Morillons, CH-1211 Geneva 22, Switzerland, (Telephone in U.S. (202) 653-7652), (Fax in U.S. (202) 653-7687), www.ilo.org; *Yearbook of Labour Statistics 2006.*

M.E. Sharpe, 80 Business Park Drive, Armonk, NY 10504, (800) 541-6563, Fax: (914) 273-2106, www.mesharpe.com; *The Illustrated Book of World Rankings.*

Palgrave Macmillan Ltd., Houndmills, Basingstoke, Hampshire, RG21 6XS, England, (Telephone in U.S. (888) 330-8477), (Fax in U.S. (800) 672-2054), www.palgrave.com; *The Statesman's Yearbook 2008.*

Taylor and Francis Group, An Informa Business, 2 Park Square, Milton Park, Abingdon, Oxford OX14 4RN, United Kingdom, (Dial from U.S. (212) 216-7800), (Fax from U.S. (212) 564-7854), www.tandf.co.uk; *The Europa World Year Book.*

U.S. Department of Energy (DOE), Energy Information Administration (EIA), 1000 Independence Avenue, SW, Washington, DC 20585, (202) 586-8800, www.eia.doe.gov; *International Energy Annual 2004* and *International Energy Outlook 2006.*

U.S. Department of Labor (DOL), Bureau of International Labor Affairs (ILAB), Frances Perkins Building, Room C-4325, 200 Constitution Avenue, NW, Washington, DC 20210, (202) 693-4770, Fax: (202) 693-4780, www.dol.gov/ilab; *Labor Rights Report.*

United Nations Food and Agricultural Organization (FAO), Viale delle Terme di Caracalla, 00100 Rome, Italy, (Dial from U.S. (202) 653-2400), (Fax from U.S. (202) 653 5760), www.fao.org; *The State of Food and Agriculture (SOFA) 2006.*

United Nations Statistics Division, New York, NY 10017, (800) 253-9646, Fax: (212) 963-4116, http://unstats.un.org; *Human Development Report 2006.*

The World Bank, 1818 H Street, NW, Washington, DC 20433, (202) 473-1000, Fax: (202) 477-6391, www.worldbank.org; *The World Bank Atlas 2003-2004; World Development Indicators (WDI) 2008;* and *World Development Report 2008.*

DOMINICAN REPUBLIC - LAND USE

Central Intelligence Agency, Office of Public Affairs, Washington, DC 20505, (703) 482-0623, Fax: (703) 482-1739, www.cia.gov; *The World Factbook.*

Euromonitor International, Inc., 224 S. Michigan Avenue, Suite 1500, Chicago, IL 60604, (312) 922-1115, Fax: (312) 922-1157, www.euromonitor.com; *International Marketing Data and Statistics 2008.*

Inter-American Development Bank (IDB), 1300 New York Avenue, NW, Washington, DC 20577, (202) 623-1000, Fax: (202) 623-3096, www.iadb.org; *The Politics of Policies: Economic and Social Progress in Latin America - 2006 Report.*

United Nations Food and Agricultural Organization (FAO), Viale delle Terme di Caracalla, 00100 Rome, Italy, (Dial from U.S. (202) 653-2400), (Fax from U.S. (202) 653 5760), www.fao.org; *FAO Production Yearbook 2002.*

The World Bank, 1818 H Street, NW, Washington, DC 20433, (202) 473-1000, Fax: (202) 477-6391, www.worldbank.org; *World Development Report 2008.*

DOMINICAN REPUBLIC - LIBRARIES

M.E. Sharpe, 80 Business Park Drive, Armonk, NY 10504, (800) 541-6563, Fax: (914) 273-2106, www.mesharpe.com; *The Illustrated Book of World Rankings.*

DOMINICAN REPUBLIC - LICENSES

International Monetary Fund (IMF), 700 Nineteenth Street, NW, Washington, DC 20431, (202) 623-7000, Fax: (202) 623-4661, www.imf.org; *Government Finance Statistics Yearbook (2008 Edition).*

DOMINICAN REPUBLIC - LIFE EXPECTANCY

Central Intelligence Agency, Office of Public Affairs, Washington, DC 20505, (703) 482-0623, Fax: (703) 482-1739, www.cia.gov; *The World Factbook.*

Economist Intelligence Unit, 111 West 57th Street, New York, NY 10019, (212) 554-0600, Fax: (212) 586-1181, www.eiu.com; *Business Latin America.*

Euromonitor International, Inc., 224 S. Michigan Avenue, Suite 1500, Chicago, IL 60604, (312) 922-1115, Fax: (312) 922-1157, www.euromonitor.com; *The World Economic Factbook 2008.*

United Nations Statistics Division, New York, NY 10017, (800) 253-9646, Fax: (212) 963-4116, http://unstats.un.org; *Human Development Report 2006; Statistical Yearbook for Latin America and the Caribbean 2004;* and *World Statistics Pocketbook.*

The World Bank, 1818 H Street, NW, Washington, DC 20433, (202) 473-1000, Fax: (202) 477-6391, www.worldbank.org; *The World Bank Atlas 2003-2004* and *World Development Report 2008.*

DOMINICAN REPUBLIC - LITERACY

Euromonitor International, Inc., 224 S. Michigan Avenue, Suite 1500, Chicago, IL 60604, (312) 922-1115, Fax: (312) 922-1157, www.euromonitor.com; *World Marketing Data and Statistics.*

DOMINICAN REPUBLIC - LIVESTOCK

Euromonitor International, Inc., 224 S. Michigan Avenue, Suite 1500, Chicago, IL 60604, (312) 922-1115, Fax: (312) 922-1157, www.euromonitor.com; *International Marketing Data and Statistics 2008.*

M.E. Sharpe, 80 Business Park Drive, Armonk, NY 10504, (800) 541-6563, Fax: (914) 273-2106, www.mesharpe.com; *The Illustrated Book of World Rankings.*

Palgrave Macmillan Ltd., Houndmills, Basingstoke, Hampshire, RG21 6XS, England, (Telephone in U.S. (888) 330-8477), (Fax in U.S. (800) 672-2054), www.palgrave.com; *The Statesman's Yearbook 2008.*

Taylor and Francis Group, An Informa Business, 2 Park Square, Milton Park, Abingdon, Oxford OX14 4RN, United Kingdom, (Dial from U.S. (212) 216-7800), (Fax from U.S. (212) 564-7854), www.tandf.co.uk; *The Europa World Year Book.*

United Nations Conference on Trade and Development (UNCTAD), DC2-1120, United Nations, New York, NY 10017, (212) 963-0027, www.unctad.org; *UNCTAD Commodity Yearbook.*

United Nations Food and Agricultural Organization (FAO), Viale delle Terme di Caracalla, 00100 Rome, Italy, (Dial from U.S. (202) 653-2400), (Fax from U.S. (202) 653 5760), www.fao.org; *FAO Production Yearbook 2002* and *The State of Food and Agriculture (SOFA) 2006.*

United Nations Statistics Division, New York, NY 10017, (800) 253-9646, Fax: (212) 963-4116, http://unstats.un.org; *Statistical Yearbook.*

DOMINICAN REPUBLIC - LOCAL TAXATION

Euromonitor International, Inc., 224 S. Michigan Avenue, Suite 1500, Chicago, IL 60604, (312) 922-1115, Fax: (312) 922-1157, www.euromonitor.com; *International Marketing Data and Statistics 2008.*

Inter-American Development Bank (IDB), 1300 New York Avenue, NW, Washington, DC 20577, (202) 623-1000, Fax: (202) 623-3096, www.iadb.org; *The Politics of Policies: Economic and Social Progress in Latin America - 2006 Report.*

DOMINICAN REPUBLIC - MANUFACTURES

Economist Intelligence Unit, 111 West 57th Street, New York, NY 10019, (212) 554-0600, Fax: (212) 586-1181, www.eiu.com; *Business Latin America.*

Inter-American Development Bank (IDB), 1300 New York Avenue, NW, Washington, DC 20577, (202) 623-1000, Fax: (202) 623-3096, www.iadb.org; *The Politics of Policies: Economic and Social Progress in Latin America - 2006 Report.*

M.E. Sharpe, 80 Business Park Drive, Armonk, NY 10504, (800) 541-6563, Fax: (914) 273-2106, www.mesharpe.com; *The Illustrated Book of World Rankings.*

United Nations Statistics Division, New York, NY 10017, (800) 253-9646, Fax: (212) 963-4116, http://unstats.un.org; *Statistical Yearbook* and *Statistical Yearbook for Latin America and the Caribbean 2004.*

The World Bank, 1818 H Street, NW, Washington, DC 20433, (202) 473-1000, Fax: (202) 477-6391, www.worldbank.org; *World Development Indicators (WDI) 2008.*

DOMINICAN REPUBLIC - MARRIAGE

M.E. Sharpe, 80 Business Park Drive, Armonk, NY 10504, (800) 541-6563, Fax: (914) 273-2106, www.mesharpe.com; *The Illustrated Book of World Rankings.*

United Nations Statistics Division, New York, NY 10017, (800) 253-9646, Fax: (212) 963-4116, http://unstats.un.org; *Demographic Yearbook* and *Statistical Yearbook.*

DOMINICAN REPUBLIC - MEDICAL CARE, COST OF

International Monetary Fund (IMF), 700 Nineteenth Street, NW, Washington, DC 20431, (202) 623-7000, Fax: (202) 623-4661, www.imf.org; *Government Finance Statistics Yearbook (2008 Edition).*

United Nations Statistics Division, New York, NY 10017, (800) 253-9646, Fax: (212) 963-4116, http://unstats.un.org; *Statistical Yearbook for Latin America and the Caribbean 2004.*

DOMINICAN REPUBLIC - MEDICAL PERSONNEL

UCLA Latin American Institute, 10343 Bunche Hall, Box 951447, Los Angeles, CA 90095-1447, (310) 825-4571, Fax: (310) 206-6859, www.international.ucla.edu/lac; *Statistical Abstract of Latin America.*

DOMINICAN REPUBLIC - MILK PRODUCTION

See DOMINICAN REPUBLIC - DAIRY PROCESSING

DOMINICAN REPUBLIC - MINERAL INDUSTRIES

Economist Intelligence Unit, 111 West 57th Street, New York, NY 10019, (212) 554-0600, Fax: (212) 586-1181, www.eiu.com; *Business Latin America.*

Inter-American Development Bank (IDB), 1300 New York Avenue, NW, Washington, DC 20577, (202) 623-1000, Fax: (202) 623-3096, www.iadb.org; *The Politics of Policies: Economic and Social Progress in Latin America - 2006 Report.*

International Monetary Fund (IMF), 700 Nineteenth Street, NW, Washington, DC 20431, (202) 623-7000, Fax: (202) 623-4661, www.imf.org; *International Financial Statistics Yearbook 2007.*

M.E. Sharpe, 80 Business Park Drive, Armonk, NY 10504, (800) 541-6563, Fax: (914) 273-2106, www.mesharpe.com; *The Illustrated Book of World Rankings.*

Organization of American States (OAS), 17th Street Constitution Avenue NW, Washington, DC 20006, (202) 458-3000, www.oas.org; *The OAS in Transition: 1994-2004.*

Palgrave Macmillan Ltd., Houndmills, Basingstoke, Hampshire, RG21 6XS, England, (Telephone in U.S. (888) 330-8477), (Fax in U.S. (800) 672-2054), www.palgrave.com; *The Statesman's Yearbook 2008.*

Taylor and Francis Group, An Informa Business, 2 Park Square, Milton Park, Abingdon, Oxford OX14 4RN, United Kingdom, (Dial from U.S. (212) 216-7800), (Fax from U.S. (212) 564-7854), www.tandf.co.uk; *The Europa World Year Book.*

UCLA Latin American Institute, 10343 Bunche Hall, Box 951447, Los Angeles, CA 90095-1447, (310) 825-4571, Fax: (310) 206-6859, www.international.ucla.edu/lac; *Statistical Abstract of Latin America.*

United Nations Conference on Trade and Development (UNCTAD), DC2-1120, United Nations, New York, NY 10017, (212) 963-0027, www.unctad.org; *UNCTAD Commodity Yearbook.*

United Nations Statistics Division, New York, NY 10017, (800) 253-9646, Fax: (212) 963-4116, http://unstats.un.org; *Statistical Yearbook* and *Statistical Yearbook for Latin America and the Caribbean 2004.*

DOMINICAN REPUBLIC - MONEY EXCHANGE RATES

See DOMINICAN REPUBLIC - FOREIGN EXCHANGE RATES

DOMINICAN REPUBLIC - MONEY SUPPLY

Economist Intelligence Unit, 111 West 57th Street, New York, NY 10019, (212) 554-0600, Fax: (212) 586-1181, www.eiu.com; *Dominican Republic Country Report.*

Euromonitor International, Inc., 224 S. Michigan Avenue, Suite 1500, Chicago, IL 60604, (312) 922-1115, Fax: (312) 922-1157, www.euromonitor.com; *International Marketing Data and Statistics 2008.*

Inter-American Development Bank (IDB), 1300 New York Avenue, NW, Washington, DC 20577, (202) 623-1000, Fax: (202) 623-3096, www.iadb.org; *The Politics of Policies: Economic and Social Progress in Latin America - 2006 Report.*

International Monetary Fund (IMF), 700 Nineteenth Street, NW, Washington, DC 20431, (202) 623-7000, Fax: (202) 623-4661, www.imf.org; *International Financial Statistics Yearbook 2007.*

Taylor and Francis Group, An Informa Business, 2 Park Square, Milton Park, Abingdon, Oxford OX14 4RN, United Kingdom, (Dial from U.S. (212) 216-7800), (Fax from U.S. (212) 564-7854), www.tandf.co.uk; *The Europa World Year Book.*

UCLA Latin American Institute, 10343 Bunche Hall, Box 951447, Los Angeles, CA 90095-1447, (310) 825-4571, Fax: (310) 206-6859, www.international.ucla.edu/lac; *Statistical Abstract of Latin America.*

United Nations Statistics Division, New York, NY 10017, (800) 253-9646, Fax: (212) 963-4116, http://unstats.un.org; *Statistical Yearbook.*

The World Bank, 1818 H Street, NW, Washington, DC 20433, (202) 473-1000, Fax: (202) 477-6391, www.worldbank.org; *Dominican Republic* and *World Development Indicators (WDI) 2008.*

DOMINICAN REPUBLIC - MORTALITY

Central Intelligence Agency, Office of Public Affairs, Washington, DC 20505, (703) 482-0623, Fax: (703) 482-1739, www.cia.gov; *The World Factbook.*

Economist Intelligence Unit, 111 West 57th Street, New York, NY 10019, (212) 554-0600, Fax: (212) 586-1181, www.eiu.com; *Business Latin America.*

Euromonitor International, Inc., 224 S. Michigan Avenue, Suite 1500, Chicago, IL 60604, (312) 922-1115, Fax: (312) 922-1157, www.euromonitor.com; *International Marketing Data and Statistics 2008* and *The World Economic Factbook 2008.*

Taylor and Francis Group, An Informa Business, 2 Park Square, Milton Park, Abingdon, Oxford OX14 4RN, United Kingdom, (Dial from U.S. (212) 216-7800), (Fax from U.S. (212) 564-7854), www.tandf.co.uk; *The Europa World Year Book.*

United Nations Statistics Division, New York, NY 10017, (800) 253-9646, Fax: (212) 963-4116, http://unstats.un.org; *Demographic Yearbook; Human Development Report 2006; Statistical Yearbook; Statistical Yearbook for Latin America and the Caribbean 2004;* and *World Statistics Pocketbook.*

The World Bank, 1818 H Street, NW, Washington, DC 20433, (202) 473-1000, Fax: (202) 477-6391, www.worldbank.org; *The World Bank Atlas 2003-2004; World Development Indicators (WDI) 2008;* and *World Development Report 2008.*

World Health Organization (WHO), Avenue Appia 20, 1211 Geneve 27, Switzerland, (Telephone in U.S. (212) 331-9081), www.who.int; The WHO Global Atlas of Infectious Diseases and *World Health Report 2006.*

DOMINICAN REPUBLIC - MOTOR VEHICLES

Economist Intelligence Unit, 111 West 57th Street, New York, NY 10019, (212) 554-0600, Fax: (212) 586-1181, www.eiu.com; *Business Latin America.*

International Road Federation (IFR), Madison Place, 500 Montgomery Street, 5th Floor, Alexandria, VA 22314, (703) 535-1001, Fax: (703) 535-1007, www.irfnet.org; *World Road Statistics 2006.*

Taylor and Francis Group, An Informa Business, 2 Park Square, Milton Park, Abingdon, Oxford OX14 4RN, United Kingdom, (Dial from U.S. (212) 216-7800), (Fax from U.S. (212) 564-7854), www.tandf.co.uk; *The Europa World Year Book.*

United Nations Statistics Division, New York, NY 10017, (800) 253-9646, Fax: (212) 963-4116, http://unstats.un.org; *Statistical Yearbook.*

DOMINICAN REPUBLIC - MUSEUMS

M.E. Sharpe, 80 Business Park Drive, Armonk, NY 10504, (800) 541-6563, Fax: (914) 273-2106, www.mesharpe.com; *The Illustrated Book of World Rankings.*

UNESCO Institute for Statistics, C.P. 6128 Succursale Centre-Ville, Montreal, Quebec, H3C 3J7 Canada, (Dial from U.S. (514) 343-6880), (Fax from U.S. (514) 343 6882), www.uis.unesco.org; *Statistical Tables.*

DOMINICAN REPUBLIC - NATURAL GAS PRODUCTION

See DOMINICAN REPUBLIC - MINERAL INDUSTRIES

DOMINICAN REPUBLIC - NICKEL AND NICKEL ORE

See DOMINICAN REPUBLIC - MINERAL INDUSTRIES

DOMINICAN REPUBLIC - NUTRITION

United Nations Food and Agricultural Organization (FAO), Viale delle Terme di Caracalla, 00100 Rome, Italy, (Dial from U.S. (202) 653-2400), (Fax from U.S. (202) 653 5760), www.fao.org; *The State of Food and Agriculture (SOFA) 2006.*

United Nations Statistics Division, New York, NY 10017, (800) 253-9646, Fax: (212) 963-4116, http://

unstats.un.org; *Statistical Yearbook for Latin America and the Caribbean 2004.*

DOMINICAN REPUBLIC - OLDER PEOPLE

M.E. Sharpe, 80 Business Park Drive, Armonk, NY 10504, (800) 541-6563, Fax: (914) 273-2106, www.mesharpe.com; *The Illustrated Book of World Rankings.*

DOMINICAN REPUBLIC - PAPER

See DOMINICAN REPUBLIC - FORESTS AND FORESTRY

DOMINICAN REPUBLIC - PEANUT PRODUCTION

See DOMINICAN REPUBLIC - CROPS

DOMINICAN REPUBLIC - PESTICIDES

United Nations Food and Agricultural Organization (FAO), Viale delle Terme di Caracalla, 00100 Rome, Italy, (Dial from U.S. (202) 653-2400), (Fax from U.S. (202) 653 5760), www.fao.org; *The State of Food and Agriculture (SOFA) 2006.*

DOMINICAN REPUBLIC - PETROLEUM INDUSTRY AND TRADE

Economist Intelligence Unit, 111 West 57th Street, New York, NY 10019, (212) 554-0600, Fax: (212) 586-1181, www.eiu.com; *Business Latin America.*

Inter-American Development Bank (IDB), 1300 New York Avenue, NW, Washington, DC 20577, (202) 623-1000, Fax: (202) 623-3096, www.iadb.org; *The Politics of Policies: Economic and Social Progress in Latin America - 2006 Report.*

M.E. Sharpe, 80 Business Park Drive, Armonk, NY 10504, (800) 541-6563, Fax: (914) 273-2106, www.mesharpe.com; *The Illustrated Book of World Rankings.*

PennWell Corporation, 1421 South Sheridan Road, Tulsa, OK 74112, (918) 835-3161, www.pennwell.com; *International Petroleum Encyclopedia 2007.*

U.S. Department of Energy (DOE), Energy Information Administration (EIA), 1000 Independence Avenue, SW, Washington, DC 20585, (202) 586-8800, www.eia.doe.gov; *International Energy Annual 2004* and *International Energy Outlook 2006.*

United Nations Conference on Trade and Development (UNCTAD), DC2-1120, United Nations, New York, NY 10017, (212) 963-0027, www.unctad.org; *UNCTAD Commodity Yearbook.*

United Nations Food and Agricultural Organization (FAO), Viale delle Terme di Caracalla, 00100 Rome, Italy, (Dial from U.S. (202) 653-2400), (Fax from U.S. (202) 653 5760), www.fao.org; *The State of Food and Agriculture (SOFA) 2006.*

United Nations Statistics Division, New York, NY 10017, (800) 253-9646, Fax: (212) 963-4116, http://unstats.un.org; *Statistical Yearbook.*

DOMINICAN REPUBLIC - POLITICAL SCIENCE

Central Intelligence Agency, Office of Public Affairs, Washington, DC 20505, (703) 482-0623, Fax: (703) 482-1739, www.cia.gov; *The World Factbook.*

Inter-American Development Bank (IDB), 1300 New York Avenue, NW, Washington, DC 20577, (202) 623-1000, Fax: (202) 623-3096, www.iadb.org; *The Politics of Policies: Economic and Social Progress in Latin America - 2006 Report.*

International Monetary Fund (IMF), 700 Nineteenth Street, NW, Washington, DC 20431, (202) 623-7000, Fax: (202) 623-4661, www.imf.org; *Government Finance Statistics Yearbook (2008 Edition).*

Palgrave Macmillan Ltd., Houndmills, Basingstoke, Hampshire, RG21 6XS, England, (Telephone in U.S. (888) 330-8477), (Fax in U.S. (800) 672-2054), www.palgrave.com; *The Statesman's Yearbook 2008.*

Taylor and Francis Group, An Informa Business, 2 Park Square, Milton Park, Abingdon, Oxford OX14 4RN, United Kingdom, (Dial from U.S. (212) 216-7800), (Fax from U.S. (212) 564-7854), www.tandf.co.uk; *The Europa World Year Book.*

UCLA Latin American Institute, 10343 Bunche Hall, Box 951447, Los Angeles, CA 90095-1447, (310) 825-4571, Fax: (310) 206-6859, www.international.ucla.edu/lac; *Statistical Abstract of Latin America.*

United Nations Statistics Division, New York, NY 10017, (800) 253-9646, Fax: (212) 963-4116, http://unstats.un.org; *National Accounts Statistics: Compendium of Income Distribution Statistics* and *Statistical Yearbook.*

The World Bank, 1818 H Street, NW, Washington, DC 20433, (202) 473-1000, Fax: (202) 477-6391, www.worldbank.org; *World Development Indicators (WDI) 2008* and *World Development Report 2008.*

DOMINICAN REPUBLIC - POPULATION

Central Intelligence Agency, Office of Public Affairs, Washington, DC 20505, (703) 482-0623, Fax: (703) 482-1739, www.cia.gov; *The World Factbook.*

Economist Intelligence Unit, 111 West 57th Street, New York, NY 10019, (212) 554-0600, Fax: (212) 586-1181, www.eiu.com; *Business Latin America* and *Dominican Republic Country Report.*

Euromonitor International, Inc., 224 S. Michigan Avenue, Suite 1500, Chicago, IL 60604, (312) 922-1115, Fax: (312) 922-1157, www.euromonitor.com; *International Marketing Data and Statistics 2008* and *The World Economic Factbook 2008.*

Eurostat, Batiment Jean Monnet, Rue Alcide de Gasperi, L-2920 Luxembourg, http://epp.eurostat.ec.europa.eu; *Demographic Indicators - Population by Age-Classes.*

Inter-American Development Bank (IDB), 1300 New York Avenue, NW, Washington, DC 20577, (202) 623-1000, Fax: (202) 623-3096, www.iadb.org; *The Politics of Policies: Economic and Social Progress in Latin America - 2006 Report.*

International Labour Office, I.L.O. Publications, 4 route des Morillons, CH-1211 Geneva 22, Switzerland, (Telephone in U.S. (202) 653-7652), (Fax in U.S. (202) 653-7687), www.ilo.org; *Yearbook of Labour Statistics 2006.*

M.E. Sharpe, 80 Business Park Drive, Armonk, NY 10504, (800) 541-6563, Fax: (914) 273-2106, www.mesharpe.com; *The Illustrated Book of World Rankings.*

Organization of American States (OAS), 17th Street Constitution Avenue NW, Washington, DC 20006, (202) 458-3000, www.oas.org; *The OAS in Transition: 1994-2004.*

Palgrave Macmillan Ltd., Houndmills, Basingstoke, Hampshire, RG21 6XS, England, (Telephone in U.S. (888) 330-8477), (Fax in U.S. (800) 672-2054), www.palgrave.com; *The Statesman's Yearbook 2008.*

Taylor and Francis Group, An Informa Business, 2 Park Square, Milton Park, Abingdon, Oxford OX14 4RN, United Kingdom, (Dial from U.S. (212) 216-7800), (Fax from U.S. (212) 564-7854), www.tandf.co.uk; *The Europa World Year Book.*

U.S. Department of State (DOS), 2201 C Street NW, Washington, DC 20520, (202) 647-4000, www.state.gov; *World Military Expenditures and Arms Transfers (WMEAT).*

UCLA Latin American Institute, 10343 Bunche Hall, Box 951447, Los Angeles, CA 90095-1447, (310) 825-4571, Fax: (310) 206-6859, www.international.ucla.edu/lac; *Statistical Abstract of Latin America.*

UNESCO Institute for Statistics, C.P. 6128 Succursale Centre-Ville, Montreal, Quebec, H3C 3J7 Canada, (Dial from U.S. (514) 343-6880), (Fax from U.S. (514) 343 6882), www.uis.unesco.org; *Statistical Tables.*

United Nations Food and Agricultural Organization (FAO), Viale delle Terme di Caracalla, 00100 Rome, Italy, (Dial from U.S. (202) 653-2400), (Fax from U.S. (202) 653 5760), www.fao.org; *FAO Production Yearbook 2002.*

United Nations Statistics Division, New York, NY 10017, (800) 253-9646, Fax: (212) 963-4116, http://unstats.un.org; *Demographic Yearbook; Human Development Report 2006; Statistical Yearbook; Statistical Yearbook for Latin America and the Caribbean 2004;* and *World Statistics Pocketbook.*

The World Bank, 1818 H Street, NW, Washington, DC 20433, (202) 473-1000, Fax: (202) 477-6391, www.worldbank.org; *Dominican Republic; The World Bank Atlas 2003-2004;* and *World Development Report 2008.*

World Health Organization (WHO), Avenue Appia 20, 1211 Geneve 27, Switzerland, (Telephone in U.S. (212) 331-9081), www.who.int; *World Health Report 2006.*

DOMINICAN REPUBLIC - POPULATION DENSITY

Central Intelligence Agency, Office of Public Affairs, Washington, DC 20505, (703) 482-0623, Fax: (703) 482-1739, www.cia.gov; *The World Factbook.*

Euromonitor International, Inc., 224 S. Michigan Avenue, Suite 1500, Chicago, IL 60604, (312) 922-1115, Fax: (312) 922-1157, www.euromonitor.com; *International Marketing Data and Statistics 2008* and *The World Economic Factbook 2008.*

Inter-American Development Bank (IDB), 1300 New York Avenue, NW, Washington, DC 20577, (202) 623-1000, Fax: (202) 623-3096, www.iadb.org; *The Politics of Policies: Economic and Social Progress in Latin America - 2006 Report.*

M.E. Sharpe, 80 Business Park Drive, Armonk, NY 10504, (800) 541-6563, Fax: (914) 273-2106, www.mesharpe.com; *The Illustrated Book of World Rankings.*

Palgrave Macmillan Ltd., Houndmills, Basingstoke, Hampshire, RG21 6XS, England, (Telephone in U.S. (888) 330-8477), (Fax in U.S. (800) 672-2054), www.palgrave.com; *The Statesman's Yearbook 2008.*

Taylor and Francis Group, An Informa Business, 2 Park Square, Milton Park, Abingdon, Oxford OX14 4RN, United Kingdom, (Dial from U.S. (212) 216-7800), (Fax from U.S. (212) 564-7854), www.tandf.co.uk; *The Europa World Year Book.*

United Nations Food and Agricultural Organization (FAO), Viale delle Terme di Caracalla, 00100 Rome, Italy, (Dial from U.S. (202) 653-2400), (Fax from U.S. (202) 653 5760), www.fao.org; *The State of Food and Agriculture (SOFA) 2006.*

The World Bank, 1818 H Street, NW, Washington, DC 20433, (202) 473-1000, Fax: (202) 477-6391, www.worldbank.org; *Dominican Republic* and *World Development Report 2008.*

DOMINICAN REPUBLIC - POSTAL SERVICE

M.E. Sharpe, 80 Business Park Drive, Armonk, NY 10504, (800) 541-6563, Fax: (914) 273-2106, www.mesharpe.com; *The Illustrated Book of World Rankings.*

United Nations Statistics Division, New York, NY 10017, (800) 253-9646, Fax: (212) 963-4116, http://unstats.un.org; *Statistical Yearbook.*

DOMINICAN REPUBLIC - POWER RESOURCES

Economist Intelligence Unit, 111 West 57th Street, New York, NY 10019, (212) 554-0600, Fax: (212) 586-1181, www.eiu.com; *Business Latin America.*

Euromonitor International, Inc., 224 S. Michigan Avenue, Suite 1500, Chicago, IL 60604, (312) 922-1115, Fax: (312) 922-1157, www.euromonitor.com; *International Marketing Data and Statistics 2008; The World Economic Factbook 2008;* and *World Marketing Data and Statistics.*

M.E. Sharpe, 80 Business Park Drive, Armonk, NY 10504, (800) 541-6563, Fax: (914) 273-2106, www.mesharpe.com; *The Illustrated Book of World Rankings.*

Palgrave Macmillan Ltd., Houndmills, Basingstoke, Hampshire, RG21 6XS, England, (Telephone in U.S. (888) 330-8477), (Fax in U.S. (800) 672-2054), www.palgrave.com; *The Statesman's Yearbook 2008.*

Platts, 2 Penn Plaza, 25th Floor, New York, NY 10121-2298, (212) 904-3070, www.platts.com; *Energy Economist.*

U.S. Department of Energy (DOE), Energy Information Administration (EIA), 1000 Independence Avenue, SW, Washington, DC 20585, (202) 586-8800, www.eia.doe.gov; *International Energy Annual 2004* and *International Energy Outlook 2006.*

UCLA Latin American Institute, 10343 Bunche Hall, Box 951447, Los Angeles, CA 90095-1447, (310) 825-4571, Fax: (310) 206-6859, www.international.ucla.edu/lac; *Statistical Abstract of Latin America.*

United Nations Food and Agricultural Organization (FAO), Viale delle Terme di Caracalla, 00100 Rome, Italy, (Dial from U.S. (202) 653-2400), (Fax from U.S. (202) 653 5760), www.fao.org; *The State of Food and Agriculture (SOFA) 2006.*

United Nations Statistics Division, New York, NY 10017, (800) 253-9646, Fax: (212) 963-4116, http://unstats.un.org; *Energy Statistics Yearbook 2003; Human Development Report 2006; Statistical Yearbook; Statistical Yearbook for Latin America and the Caribbean 2004;* and *World Statistics Pocketbook.*

The World Bank, 1818 H Street, NW, Washington, DC 20433, (202) 473-1000, Fax: (202) 477-6391, www.worldbank.org; *The World Bank Atlas 2003-2004* and *World Development Report 2008.*

DOMINICAN REPUBLIC - PRICES

Economist Intelligence Unit, 111 West 57th Street, New York, NY 10019, (212) 554-0600, Fax: (212) 586-1181, www.eiu.com; *Business Latin America.*

Euromonitor International, Inc., 224 S. Michigan Avenue, Suite 1500, Chicago, IL 60604, (312) 922-1115, Fax: (312) 922-1157, www.euromonitor.com; *World Marketing Data and Statistics.*

International Labour Office, I.L.O. Publications, 4 route des Morillons, CH-1211 Geneva 22, Switzerland, (Telephone in U.S. (202) 653-7652), (Fax in U.S. (202) 653-7687), www.ilo.org; *Yearbook of Labour Statistics 2006.*

International Monetary Fund (IMF), 700 Nineteenth Street, NW, Washington, DC 20431, (202) 623-7000, Fax: (202) 623-4661, www.imf.org; *International Financial Statistics Yearbook 2007.*

M.E. Sharpe, 80 Business Park Drive, Armonk, NY 10504, (800) 541-6563, Fax: (914) 273-2106, www.mesharpe.com; *The Illustrated Book of World Rankings.*

Organization of American States (OAS), 17th Street Constitution Avenue NW, Washington, DC 20006, (202) 458-3000, www.oas.org; *The OAS in Transition: 1994-2004.*

UCLA Latin American Institute, 10343 Bunche Hall, Box 951447, Los Angeles, CA 90095-1447, (310) 825-4571, Fax: (310) 206-6859, www.international.ucla.edu/lac; *Statistical Abstract of Latin America.*

United Nations Food and Agricultural Organization (FAO), Viale delle Terme di Caracalla, 00100 Rome, Italy, (Dial from U.S. (202) 653-2400), (Fax from U.S. (202) 653 5760), www.fao.org; *FAO Production Yearbook 2002* and *The State of Food and Agriculture (SOFA) 2006.*

United Nations Statistics Division, New York, NY 10017, (800) 253-9646, Fax: (212) 963-4116, http://unstats.un.org; *Statistical Yearbook for Latin America and the Caribbean 2004.*

The World Bank, 1818 H Street, NW, Washington, DC 20433, (202) 473-1000, Fax: (202) 477-6391, www.worldbank.org; *Dominican Republic.*

DOMINICAN REPUBLIC - PROFESSIONS

UCLA Latin American Institute, 10343 Bunche Hall, Box 951447, Los Angeles, CA 90095-1447, (310) 825-4571, Fax: (310) 206-6859, www.international.ucla.edu/lac; *Statistical Abstract of Latin America.*

DOMINICAN REPUBLIC - PUBLIC HEALTH

Economist Intelligence Unit, 111 West 57th Street, New York, NY 10019, (212) 554-0600, Fax: (212) 586-1181, www.eiu.com; *Business Latin America.*

Euromonitor International, Inc., 224 S. Michigan Avenue, Suite 1500, Chicago, IL 60604, (312) 922-1115, Fax: (312) 922-1157, www.euromonitor.com; *World Marketing Data and Statistics.*

M.E. Sharpe, 80 Business Park Drive, Armonk, NY 10504, (800) 541-6563, Fax: (914) 273-2106, www.mesharpe.com; *The Illustrated Book of World Rankings.*

Palgrave Macmillan Ltd., Houndmills, Basingstoke, Hampshire, RG21 6XS, England, (Telephone in U.S. (888) 330-8477), (Fax in U.S. (800) 672-2054), www.palgrave.com; *The Statesman's Yearbook 2008.*

UCLA Latin American Institute, 10343 Bunche Hall, Box 951447, Los Angeles, CA 90095-1447, (310) 825-4571, Fax: (310) 206-6859, www.international.ucla.edu/lac; *Statistical Abstract of Latin America.*

United Nations Statistics Division, New York, NY 10017, (800) 253-9646, Fax: (212) 963-4116, http://unstats.un.org; *Human Development Report 2006* and *Statistical Yearbook.*

The World Bank, 1818 H Street, NW, Washington, DC 20433, (202) 473-1000, Fax: (202) 477-6391, www.worldbank.org; *Dominican Republic* and *World Development Report 2008.*

World Health Organization (WHO), Avenue Appia 20, 1211 Geneve 27, Switzerland, (Telephone in U.S. (212) 331-9081), www.who.int; The WHO Global Atlas of Infectious Diseases and *World Health Report 2006.*

DOMINICAN REPUBLIC - PUBLIC UTILITIES

UCLA Latin American Institute, 10343 Bunche Hall, Box 951447, Los Angeles, CA 90095-1447, (310) 825-4571, Fax: (310) 206-6859, www.international.ucla.edu/lac; *Statistical Abstract of Latin America.*

DOMINICAN REPUBLIC - RADIO BROADCASTING

Palgrave Macmillan Ltd., Houndmills, Basingstoke, Hampshire, RG21 6XS, England, (Telephone in U.S. (888) 330-8477), (Fax in U.S. (800) 672-2054), www.palgrave.com; *The Statesman's Yearbook 2008.*

DOMINICAN REPUBLIC - RAILROADS

Economist Intelligence Unit, 111 West 57th Street, New York, NY 10019, (212) 554-0600, Fax: (212) 586-1181, www.eiu.com; *Business Latin America.*

Jane's Information Group, 110 North Royal Street, Suite 200, Alexandria, VA 22314, (703) 683-3700, Fax: (800) 836-0297, www.janes.com; *Jane's World Railways.*

Palgrave Macmillan Ltd., Houndmills, Basingstoke, Hampshire, RG21 6XS, England, (Telephone in U.S. (888) 330-8477), (Fax in U.S. (800) 672-2054), www.palgrave.com; *The Statesman's Yearbook 2008.*

DOMINICAN REPUBLIC - RANCHING

UCLA Latin American Institute, 10343 Bunche Hall, Box 951447, Los Angeles, CA 90095-1447, (310) 825-4571, Fax: (310) 206-6859, www.international.ucla.edu/lac; *Statistical Abstract of Latin America.*

DOMINICAN REPUBLIC - RELIGION

Central Intelligence Agency, Office of Public Affairs, Washington, DC 20505, (703) 482-0623, Fax: (703) 482-1739, www.cia.gov; *The World Factbook.*

M.E. Sharpe, 80 Business Park Drive, Armonk, NY 10504, (800) 541-6563, Fax: (914) 273-2106, www.mesharpe.com; *The Illustrated Book of World Rankings.*

Palgrave Macmillan Ltd., Houndmills, Basingstoke, Hampshire, RG21 6XS, England, (Telephone in U.S. (888) 330-8477), (Fax in U.S. (800) 672-2054), www.palgrave.com; *The Statesman's Yearbook 2008.*

UCLA Latin American Institute, 10343 Bunche Hall, Box 951447, Los Angeles, CA 90095-1447, (310) 825-4571, Fax: (310) 206-6859, www.international.ucla.edu/lac; *Statistical Abstract of Latin America.*

DOMINICAN REPUBLIC - RENT CHARGES

International Labour Office, I.L.O. Publications, 4 route des Morillons, CH-1211 Geneva 22, Switzerland, (Telephone in U.S. (202) 653-7652), (Fax in U.S. (202) 653-7687), www.ilo.org; *Yearbook of Labour Statistics 2006.*

DOMINICAN REPUBLIC - RESERVES (ACCOUNTING)

Economist Intelligence Unit, 111 West 57th Street, New York, NY 10019, (212) 554-0600, Fax: (212) 586-1181, www.eiu.com; *Business Latin America.*

Euromonitor International, Inc., 224 S. Michigan Avenue, Suite 1500, Chicago, IL 60604, (312) 922-1115, Fax: (312) 922-1157, www.euromonitor.com; *International Marketing Data and Statistics 2008.*

Inter-American Development Bank (IDB), 1300 New York Avenue, NW, Washington, DC 20577, (202) 623-1000, Fax: (202) 623-3096, www.iadb.org; *The Politics of Policies: Economic and Social Progress in Latin America - 2006 Report.*

Organization of American States (OAS), 17th Street Constitution Avenue NW, Washington, DC 20006, (202) 458-3000, www.oas.org; *The OAS in Transition: 1994-2004.*

The World Bank, 1818 H Street, NW, Washington, DC 20433, (202) 473-1000, Fax: (202) 477-6391, www.worldbank.org; *World Development Indicators (WDI) 2008.*

DOMINICAN REPUBLIC - RETAIL TRADE

Euromonitor International, Inc., 224 S. Michigan Avenue, Suite 1500, Chicago, IL 60604, (312) 922-1115, Fax: (312) 922-1157, www.euromonitor.com; *World Marketing Data and Statistics.*

Inter-American Development Bank (IDB), 1300 New York Avenue, NW, Washington, DC 20577, (202) 623-1000, Fax: (202) 623-3096, www.iadb.org; *The Politics of Policies: Economic and Social Progress in Latin America - 2006 Report.*

DOMINICAN REPUBLIC - RICE PRODUCTION

See DOMINICAN REPUBLIC - CROPS

DOMINICAN REPUBLIC - ROADS

Central Intelligence Agency, Office of Public Affairs, Washington, DC 20505, (703) 482-0623, Fax: (703) 482-1739, www.cia.gov; *The World Factbook.*

Economist Intelligence Unit, 111 West 57th Street, New York, NY 10019, (212) 554-0600, Fax: (212) 586-1181, www.eiu.com; *Business Latin America.*

International Road Federation (IFR), Madison Place, 500 Montgomery Street, 5th Floor, Alexandria, VA 22314, (703) 535-1001, Fax: (703) 535-1007, www.irfnet.org; *World Road Statistics 2006.*

Palgrave Macmillan Ltd., Houndmills, Basingstoke, Hampshire, RG21 6XS, England, (Telephone in U.S. (888) 330-8477), (Fax in U.S. (800) 672-2054), www.palgrave.com; *The Statesman's Yearbook 2008.*

DOMINICAN REPUBLIC - RUBBER INDUSTRY AND TRADE

International Rubber Study Group (IRSG), 1st Floor, Heron House, 109/115 Wembley Hill Road, Wembley, Middlesex HA9 8DA, United Kingdom, www.rubberstudy.com; *Rubber Statistical Bulletin; Summary of World Rubber Statistics 2005; World Rubber Statistics Handbook (Volume 6, 1975-2001);* and *World Rubber Statistics Historic Handbook.*

M.E. Sharpe, 80 Business Park Drive, Armonk, NY 10504, (800) 541-6563, Fax: (914) 273-2106, www.mesharpe.com; *The Illustrated Book of World Rankings.*

DOMINICAN REPUBLIC - SALT PRODUCTION

See DOMINICAN REPUBLIC - MINERAL INDUSTRIES

DOMINICAN REPUBLIC - SHEEP

See DOMINICAN REPUBLIC - LIVESTOCK

DOMINICAN REPUBLIC - SHIPPING

Palgrave Macmillan Ltd., Houndmills, Basingstoke, Hampshire, RG21 6XS, England, (Telephone in U.S. (888) 330-8477), (Fax in U.S. (800) 672-2054), www.palgrave.com; *The Statesman's Yearbook 2008.*

Taylor and Francis Group, An Informa Business, 2 Park Square, Milton Park, Abingdon, Oxford OX14 4RN, United Kingdom, (Dial from U.S. (212) 216-7800), (Fax from U.S. (212) 564-7854), www.tandf.co.uk; *The Europa World Year Book.*

U.S. Department of Transportation (DOT), Maritime Administration (MARAD), West Building, Southeast Federal Center, 1200 New Jersey Avenue, SE, Washington, DC 20590, (800) 99-MARAD, www.marad.dot.gov; *World Merchant Fleet 2005.*

United Nations Statistics Division, New York, NY 10017, (800) 253-9646, Fax: (212) 963-4116, http://unstats.un.org; *Statistical Yearbook.*

DOMINICAN REPUBLIC - SILVER PRODUCTION

See DOMINICAN REPUBLIC - MINERAL INDUSTRIES

DOMINICAN REPUBLIC - SOCIAL ECOLOGY

M.E. Sharpe, 80 Business Park Drive, Armonk, NY 10504, (800) 541-6563, Fax: (914) 273-2106, www.mesharpe.com; *The Illustrated Book of World Rankings.*

UCLA Latin American Institute, 10343 Bunche Hall, Box 951447, Los Angeles, CA 90095-1447, (310) 825-4571, Fax: (310) 206-6859, www.international.ucla.edu/lac; *Statistical Abstract of Latin America.*

United Nations Statistics Division, New York, NY 10017, (800) 253-9646, Fax: (212) 963-4116, http://unstats.un.org; *World Statistics Pocketbook.*

DOMINICAN REPUBLIC - SOCIAL SECURITY

Inter-American Development Bank (IDB), 1300 New York Avenue, NW, Washington, DC 20577, (202) 623-1000, Fax: (202) 623-3096, www.iadb.org; *The Politics of Policies: Economic and Social Progress in Latin America - 2006 Report.*

International Monetary Fund (IMF), 700 Nineteenth Street, NW, Washington, DC 20431, (202) 623-7000, Fax: (202) 623-4661, www.imf.org; *Government Finance Statistics Yearbook (2008 Edition).*

United Nations Statistics Division, New York, NY 10017, (800) 253-9646, Fax: (212) 963-4116, http://unstats.un.org; *National Accounts Statistics: Compendium of Income Distribution Statistics.*

DOMINICAN REPUBLIC - SOYBEAN PRODUCTION

See DOMINICAN REPUBLIC - CROPS

DOMINICAN REPUBLIC - STEEL PRODUCTION

See DOMINICAN REPUBLIC - MINERAL INDUSTRIES

DOMINICAN REPUBLIC - SUGAR PRODUCTION

See DOMINICAN REPUBLIC - CROPS

DOMINICAN REPUBLIC - TAXATION

Inter-American Development Bank (IDB), 1300 New York Avenue, NW, Washington, DC 20577, (202) 623-1000, Fax: (202) 623-3096, www.iadb.org; *The Politics of Policies: Economic and Social Progress in Latin America - 2006 Report.*

International Monetary Fund (IMF), 700 Nineteenth Street, NW, Washington, DC 20431, (202) 623-7000, Fax: (202) 623-4661, www.imf.org; *Government Finance Statistics Yearbook (2008 Edition).*

International Road Federation (IFR), Madison Place, 500 Montgomery Street, 5th Floor, Alexandria, VA 22314, (703) 535-1001, Fax: (703) 535-1007, www.irfnet.org; *World Road Statistics 2006.*

Taylor and Francis Group, An Informa Business, 2 Park Square, Milton Park, Abingdon, Oxford OX14 4RN, United Kingdom, (Dial from U.S. (212) 216-7800), (Fax from U.S. (212) 564-7854), www.tandf.co.uk; *The Europa World Year Book.*

United Nations Statistics Division, New York, NY 10017, (800) 253-9646, Fax: (212) 963-4116, http://unstats.un.org; *Statistical Yearbook for Latin America and the Caribbean 2004.*

The World Bank, 1818 H Street, NW, Washington, DC 20433, (202) 473-1000, Fax: (202) 477-6391, www.worldbank.org; *World Development Indicators (WDI) 2008.*

DOMINICAN REPUBLIC - TELEPHONE

Economist Intelligence Unit, 111 West 57th Street, New York, NY 10019, (212) 554-0600, Fax: (212) 586-1181, www.eiu.com; *Business Latin America.*

International Telecommunication Union (ITU), Place des Nations, 1211 Geneva 20, Switzerland, www.itu.int; World Telecommunication Indicators Database.

Palgrave Macmillan Ltd., Houndmills, Basingstoke, Hampshire, RG21 6XS, England, (Telephone in U.S. (888) 330-8477), (Fax in U.S. (800) 672-2054), www.palgrave.com; *The Statesman's Yearbook 2008.*

United Nations Statistics Division, New York, NY 10017, (800) 253-9646, Fax: (212) 963-4116, http://unstats.un.org; *World Statistics Pocketbook.*

DOMINICAN REPUBLIC - TEXTILE INDUSTRY

M.E. Sharpe, 80 Business Park Drive, Armonk, NY 10504, (800) 541-6563, Fax: (914) 273-2106, www.mesharpe.com; *The Illustrated Book of World Rankings.*

United Nations Conference on Trade and Development (UNCTAD), DC2-1120, United Nations, New York, NY 10017, (212) 963-0027, www.unctad.org; *UNCTAD Commodity Yearbook.*

United Nations Statistics Division, New York, NY 10017, (800) 253-9646, Fax: (212) 963-4116, http://unstats.un.org; *Statistical Yearbook.*

DOMINICAN REPUBLIC - TOBACCO INDUSTRY

Foreign Agricultural Service (FAS), U.S. Department of Agriculture (USDA), 1400 Independence Avenue, SW, Washington, DC 20250, (202) 720-3935, www.fas.usda.gov; *Tobacco: World Markets and Trade.*

International Monetary Fund (IMF), 700 Nineteenth Street, NW, Washington, DC 20431, (202) 623-7000, Fax: (202) 623-4661, www.imf.org; *International Financial Statistics Yearbook 2007.*

M.E. Sharpe, 80 Business Park Drive, Armonk, NY 10504, (800) 541-6563, Fax: (914) 273-2106, www.mesharpe.com; *The Illustrated Book of World Rankings.*

United Nations Statistics Division, New York, NY 10017, (800) 253-9646, Fax: (212) 963-4116, http://unstats.un.org; *Statistical Yearbook.*

DOMINICAN REPUBLIC - TOURISM

Economist Intelligence Unit, 111 West 57th Street, New York, NY 10019, (212) 554-0600, Fax: (212) 586-1181, www.eiu.com; *Business Latin America.*

Euromonitor International, Inc., 224 S. Michigan Avenue, Suite 1500, Chicago, IL 60604, (312) 922-1115, Fax: (312) 922-1157, www.euromonitor.com; *The World Economic Factbook 2008* and *World Marketing Data and Statistics.*

M.E. Sharpe, 80 Business Park Drive, Armonk, NY 10504, (800) 541-6563, Fax: (914) 273-2106, www.mesharpe.com; *The Illustrated Book of World Rankings.*

Palgrave Macmillan Ltd., Houndmills, Basingstoke, Hampshire, RG21 6XS, England, (Telephone in U.S. (888) 330-8477), (Fax in U.S. (800) 672-2054), www.palgrave.com; *The Statesman's Yearbook 2008.*

Taylor and Francis Group, An Informa Business, 2 Park Square, Milton Park, Abingdon, Oxford OX14 4RN, United Kingdom, (Dial from U.S. (212) 216-7800), (Fax from U.S. (212) 564-7854), www.tandf.co.uk; *The Europa World Year Book.*

UCLA Latin American Institute, 10343 Bunche Hall, Box 951447, Los Angeles, CA 90095-1447, (310) 825-4571, Fax: (310) 206-6859, www.international.ucla.edu/lac; *Statistical Abstract of Latin America.*

United Nations Statistics Division, New York, NY 10017, (800) 253-9646, Fax: (212) 963-4116, http://unstats.un.org; *Statistical Yearbook* and *Statistical Yearbook for Latin America and the Caribbean 2004.*

United Nations World Tourism Organization (UNWTO), Capitan Haya 42, 28020 Madrid, Spain, www.world-tourism.org; *Yearbook of Tourism Statistics.*

The World Bank, 1818 H Street, NW, Washington, DC 20433, (202) 473-1000, Fax: (202) 477-6391, www.worldbank.org; *Dominican Republic.*

DOMINICAN REPUBLIC - TRADE

See DOMINICAN REPUBLIC - INTERNATIONAL TRADE

DOMINICAN REPUBLIC - TRANSPORTATION

Central Intelligence Agency, Office of Public Affairs, Washington, DC 20505, (703) 482-0623, Fax: (703) 482-1739, www.cia.gov; *The World Factbook.*

Economist Intelligence Unit, 111 West 57th Street, New York, NY 10019, (212) 554-0600, Fax: (212) 586-1181, www.eiu.com; *Business Latin America.*

Euromonitor International, Inc., 224 S. Michigan Avenue, Suite 1500, Chicago, IL 60604, (312) 922-1115, Fax: (312) 922-1157, www.euromonitor.com; *International Marketing Data and Statistics 2008* and *World Marketing Data and Statistics.*

Inter-American Development Bank (IDB), 1300 New York Avenue, NW, Washington, DC 20577, (202) 623-1000, Fax: (202) 623-3096, www.iadb.org; *The Politics of Policies: Economic and Social Progress in Latin America - 2006 Report.*

M.E. Sharpe, 80 Business Park Drive, Armonk, NY 10504, (800) 541-6563, Fax: (914) 273-2106, www.mesharpe.com; *The Illustrated Book of World Rankings.*

Palgrave Macmillan Ltd., Houndmills, Basingstoke, Hampshire, RG21 6XS, England, (Telephone in U.S. (888) 330-8477), (Fax in U.S. (800) 672-2054), www.palgrave.com; *The Statesman's Yearbook 2008.*

Taylor and Francis Group, An Informa Business, 2 Park Square, Milton Park, Abingdon, Oxford OX14 4RN, United Kingdom, (Dial from U.S. (212) 216-7800), (Fax from U.S. (212) 564-7854), www.tandf.co.uk; *The Europa World Year Book.*

UCLA Latin American Institute, 10343 Bunche Hall, Box 951447, Los Angeles, CA 90095-1447, (310) 825-4571, Fax: (310) 206-6859, www.international.ucla.edu/lac; *Statistical Abstract of Latin America.*

United Nations Statistics Division, New York, NY 10017, (800) 253-9646, Fax: (212) 963-4116, http://unstats.un.org; *Human Development Report 2006* and *Statistical Yearbook for Latin America and the Caribbean 2004.*

The World Bank, 1818 H Street, NW, Washington, DC 20433, (202) 473-1000, Fax: (202) 477-6391, www.worldbank.org; *Dominican Republic.*

DOMINICAN REPUBLIC - TRAVEL COSTS

International Monetary Fund (IMF), 700 Nineteenth Street, NW, Washington, DC 20431, (202) 623-7000, Fax: (202) 623-4661, www.imf.org; *Government Finance Statistics Yearbook (2008 Edition).*

DOMINICAN REPUBLIC - TURKEYS

See DOMINICAN REPUBLIC - LIVESTOCK

DOMINICAN REPUBLIC - UNEMPLOYMENT

Central Intelligence Agency, Office of Public Affairs, Washington, DC 20505, (703) 482-0623, Fax: (703) 482-1739, www.cia.gov; *The World Factbook.*

Economist Intelligence Unit, 111 West 57th Street, New York, NY 10019, (212) 554-0600, Fax: (212) 586-1181, www.eiu.com; *Business Latin America.*

Euromonitor International, Inc., 224 S. Michigan Avenue, Suite 1500, Chicago, IL 60604, (312) 922-1115, Fax: (312) 922-1157, www.euromonitor.com; *International Marketing Data and Statistics 2008.*

International Labour Office, I.L.O. Publications, 4 route des Morillons, CH-1211 Geneva 22, Switzerland, (Telephone in U.S. (202) 653-7652), (Fax in U.S. (202) 653-7687), www.ilo.org; *Yearbook of Labour Statistics 2006.*

UCLA Latin American Institute, 10343 Bunche Hall, Box 951447, Los Angeles, CA 90095-1447, (310) 825-4571, Fax: (310) 206-6859, www.international.ucla.edu/lac; *Statistical Abstract of Latin America.*

DOMINICAN REPUBLIC - VITAL STATISTICS

Euromonitor International, Inc., 224 S. Michigan Avenue, Suite 1500, Chicago, IL 60604, (312) 922-1115, Fax: (312) 922-1157, www.euromonitor.com; *International Marketing Data and Statistics 2008.*

United Nations Statistics Division, New York, NY 10017, (800) 253-9646, Fax: (212) 963-4116, http://unstats.un.org; *Statistical Yearbook.*

World Health Organization (WHO), Avenue Appia 20, 1211 Geneve 27, Switzerland, (Telephone in U.S. (212) 331-9081), www.who.int; *World Health Report 2006.*

DOMINICAN REPUBLIC - WAGES

International Labour Office, I.L.O. Publications, 4 route des Morillons, CH-1211 Geneva 22, Switzerland, (Telephone in U.S. (202) 653-7652), (Fax in U.S. (202) 653-7687), www.ilo.org; *Yearbook of Labour Statistics 2006.*

UCLA Latin American Institute, 10343 Bunche Hall, Box 951447, Los Angeles, CA 90095-1447, (310) 825-4571, Fax: (310) 206-6859, www.international.ucla.edu/lac; *Statistical Abstract of Latin America.*

United Nations Statistics Division, New York, NY 10017, (800) 253-9646, Fax: (212) 963-4116, http://unstats.un.org; *Statistical Yearbook.*

The World Bank, 1818 H Street, NW, Washington, DC 20433, (202) 473-1000, Fax: (202) 477-6391, www.worldbank.org; *Dominican Republic.*

DOMINICAN REPUBLIC - WELFARE STATE

Inter-American Development Bank (IDB), 1300 New York Avenue, NW, Washington, DC 20577, (202) 623-1000, Fax: (202) 623-3096, www.iadb.org; *The Politics of Policies: Economic and Social Progress in Latin America - 2006 Report.*

International Monetary Fund (IMF), 700 Nineteenth Street, NW, Washington, DC 20431, (202) 623-7000, Fax: (202) 623-4661, www.imf.org; *Government Finance Statistics Yearbook (2008 Edition).*

DOMINICAN REPUBLIC - WHEAT PRODUCTION

See DOMINICAN REPUBLIC - CROPS

DOMINICAN REPUBLIC - WHOLESALE PRICE INDEXES

Inter-American Development Bank (IDB), 1300 New York Avenue, NW, Washington, DC 20577, (202) 623-1000, Fax: (202) 623-3096, www.iadb.org; *The Politics of Policies: Economic and Social Progress in Latin America - 2006 Report.*

Organization of American States (OAS), 17th Street Constitution Avenue NW, Washington, DC 20006, (202) 458-3000, www.oas.org; *The OAS in Transition: 1994-2004.*

United Nations Statistics Division, New York, NY 10017, (800) 253-9646, Fax: (212) 963-4116, http://unstats.un.org; *Statistical Yearbook.*

DOMINICAN REPUBLIC - WHOLESALE TRADE

Inter-American Development Bank (IDB), 1300 New York Avenue, NW, Washington, DC 20577, (202) 623-1000, Fax: (202) 623-3096, www.iadb.org; *The Politics of Policies: Economic and Social Progress in Latin America - 2006 Report.*

DOMINICAN REPUBLIC - WINE PRODUCTION

See DOMINICAN REPUBLIC - BEVERAGE INDUSTRY

DOMINICAN REPUBLIC - WOOL PRODUCTION

See DOMINICAN REPUBLIC - TEXTILE INDUSTRY

DOMINICAN REPUBLIC - YARN PRODUCTION

See DOMINICAN REPUBLIC - TEXTILE INDUSTRY

DORMITORIES - COLLEGE

Population Reference Bureau, 1875 Connecticut Avenue, NW, Suite 520, Washington, DC, 20009-5728, (800) 877-9881, Fax: (202) 328-3937, www.prb.org; *The American People Series.*

U.S. Census Bureau, Housing and Household Economics Statistics Division, 4700 Silver Hill Road, Washington DC 20233-0001, (301) 763-3030, www.census.gov/hhes/www; *Census 2000 Summary File 1.*

U.S. Census Bureau, Population Division, 4700 Silver Hill Road, Washington DC 20233-0001, (301) 763-3030, www.census.gov/population/www/; *Census 2000 Profiles of General Demographic Characteristics.*

DOW JONES STOCK INDICES

Board of Governors of the Federal Reserve System, Constitution Avenue, NW, Washington, DC 20551, (202) 452-3000, www.federalreserve.gov; *Annual Report to the Congress on Retail Fees and Services of Depository Institutions.*

Global Financial Data, Inc., 784 Fremont Villas, Los Angeles, CA 90042, (323) 924-1016, www.globalfindata.com; *Dow Jones Industrial Average.*

DRINKING PLACES

See FOOD SERVICE AND DRINKING PLACES

DRIVING

See also MOTOR VEHICLES

National Center for Statistics and Analysis (NCSA) of the National Highway Traffic Safety Administration, West Building, 1200 New Jersey Avenue, S.E., Washington, DC 20590, (202) 366-1503, Fax: (202) 366-7078, www.nhtsa.gov; *Drivers' Perceptions of Headlight Glare from Oncoming and Following Vehicles; Most Fatalities in Young (15- to 20-Year-Old) Driver Crashes Are Young Drivers and Their Young Passengers; Pedestrian Roadway Fatalities; The Rollover Propensity of Fifteen-Passenger Vans; Seat Belt Use in 2006 - Overall Results; States With Primary Enforcement Laws Have Lower Fatality Rates; Traffic Safety Fact Sheets, 2006 Data - Children; Traffic Safety Fact Sheets, 2006 Data - Pedestrians; Traffic Safety Fact Sheets, 2006 Data - Speeding; Traffic Safety Fact Sheets, 2006 Data - Young Drivers;* and *Traffic Safety Facts Annual Report: 2005.*

National Transportation Safety Board (NTSB), 490 L'Enfant Plaza, SW, Washington, DC 20594, (202) 314-6000, www.ntsb.gov; *Transportation Safety Databases* and *Vehicle- and Infrastructure-based Technology for the Prevention of Rear-end Collisions.*

DRIVING - FATAL ACCIDENTS

National Transportation Safety Board (NTSB), 490 L'Enfant Plaza, SW, Washington, DC 20594, (202) 314-6000, www.ntsb.gov; *Transportation Safety Databases.*

U.S. Department of Transportation (DOT), Research and Innovative Technology Administration (RITA), Bureau of Transportation Statistics (BTS), 1200 New Jersey Avenue, SE, Washington, DC 20590, (800) 853-1351, www.bts.gov; *TranStats.*

DRIVING - INTOXICATED

Center for Substance Abuse Research (CESAR), 4321 Hartwick Road, Suite 501, College Park, MD 20740, (301) 405-9770, Fax: (301) 403-8342, www.cesar.umd.edu; *Assessment and Treatment of DWI Offenders in Maryland, 1995-2003: Current Findings.*

National Center for Statistics and Analysis (NCSA) of the National Highway Traffic Safety Administration, West Building, 1200 New Jersey Avenue, S.E., Washington, DC 20590, (202) 366-1503, Fax: (202) 366-7078, www.nhtsa.gov; *Alcohol Involvement in Fatal Motor Vehicle Traffic Crashes, 2003; Impaired Motorcycle Operators Involved in Fatal Crashes;*

Individual State Data from the State Alcohol Related Fatality Report; Large-Truck Crash Causation Study: An Initial Overview; State Alcohol-Related Fatality Rates 2003; Total and Alcohol-Related Fatality Rates by State, 2003-2004; Traffic Safety Fact Sheets, 2005 Data - State Alcohol Estimates; Traffic Safety Fact Sheets, 2006 Data - Alcohol-Impaired Driving; Traffic Safety Facts Annual Report: 2005; and unpublished data.

National Criminal Justice Reference Service (NCJRS), PO Box 6000, Rockville, MD 20849-6000, (800) 851-3420, Fax: (301) 519-5212, www.ncjrs.org; *Driving Under the Influence in the City and County of Honolulu.*

DRIVING - LICENSED DRIVERS

U.S. Department of Transportation (DOT), Federal Highway Administration (FHA), 1200 New Jersey Avenue, SE, Washington, DC 20590, (202) 366-0660, www.fhwa.dot.gov; *Highway Statistics 2006* and unpublished data.

DRIVING - TRAFFIC OFFENSE

Federal Bureau of Investigation (FBI), J. Edgar Hoover Building, 935 Pennsylvania Avenue, NW, Washington, DC 20535-0001, (202) 324-3000, www.fbi.gov; *Crime in the United States (CIUS) 2007 (Preliminary).*

Justice Research and Statistics Association (JRSA), 777 N. Capitol Street, NE, Suite 801, Washington, DC 20002, (202) 842-9330, Fax: (202) 842-9329, www.jrsa.org; *Crime and Justice Atlas 2001.*

National Center for Statistics and Analysis (NCSA) of the National Highway Traffic Safety Administration, West Building, 1200 New Jersey Avenue, S.E., Washington, DC 20590, (202) 366-1503, Fax: (202) 366-7078, www.nhtsa.gov; *Large-Truck Crash Causation Study: An Initial Overview; Traffic Safety Fact Sheets, 2006 Data - Speeding;* and *Traffic Safety Facts Annual Report: 2005.*

U.S. Department of Justice (DOJ), Bureau of Justice Statistics, 810 Seventh Street, NW, Washington, DC 20531, (202) 307-0765, www.ojp.usdoj.gov/bjs/; *Characteristics of Drivers Stopped by Police, 2002; Contacts between Police and the Public: Findings from the 2002 National Survey;* and *Traffic Stop Data Collection Policies for State Police, 2004.*

DRUG STORES AND PROPRIETARY STORES

See PHARMACIES AND DRUG STORES

DRUGS (ILLEGAL)

The Annie E. Casey Foundation, 701 Saint Paul Street, Baltimore, MD 21202, (410) 547-6600, Fax: (410) 547-3610, www.aecf.org; *Faith Matters: Race/Ethnicity, Religion, and Substance Abuse* and *Lessons from the Field.*

Australian Institute of Criminology, 74 Leichhardt Street, Griffith ACT 2603 Australia, www.aic.gov.au/; *Final report on the North Queensland Drug Court.*

Center for Substance Abuse Research (CESAR), 4321 Hartwick Road, Suite 501, College Park, MD 20740, (301) 405-9770, Fax: (301) 403-8342, www.cesar.umd.edu; *College Students' Perceptions of Non-Medical Use of Prescription Stimulants by Their Peers: Findings From the April 2005 Administration of the Student Drug Research (SDR) Survey; DEWS Investigates: A Pilot Study to Enhance the Understanding of Methadone Intoxication Deaths in Maryland; DEWS Investigates: Identifying Maryland Public School Students Who Have Tried Multiple Drugs;* and *DEWS Investigates: Perceptions of Prescription Stimulant Misuse Among College Students at High and Low Risk of Drug Use.*

Health Protection Agency, 7th Floor, Holborn Gate, 330 High Holborn, London WC1V 7PP, United Kingdom, www.hpa.org.uk; *Shooting Up: Infections Among Injecting Drug Users in the United Kingdom 2006 (An Update: 2007).*

Robert Wood Johnson Foundation, PO Box 2316, College Road East and Route 1, Princeton, NJ 08543, (877) 843-7953, www.rwjf.org; *Community-Based Prevention Programs in the War on Drugs: Findings from the "Fighting Back" Demonstration; Neighborhood Crime Victimization, Drug Use and Drug Sales: Results from the "Fighting Back" Evaluation;* and *Varieties of Substance Use and Visible Drug Problems: Individual and Neighborhood Factors.*

Royal Canadian Mounted Police (RCMP), 1200 Vanier Parkway, Ottawa, ON K1A 0R2, Canada, (613) 993-7267, www.rcmp-grc.gc.ca; *Drug Situation in Canada - 2004.*

U.S. Department of Justice (DOJ), Bureau of Justice Statistics, 810 Seventh Street, NW, Washington, DC 20531, (202) 307-0765, www.ojp.usdoj.gov/bjs/; *Drug Use and Dependence, State and Federal Prisoners, 2004; Drug Use, Testing, and Treatment in Jails; Drugs Crime Facts;* and *Substance Dependence, Abuse, and Treatment of Jail Inmates, 2002.*

U.S. Department of Justice (DOJ), Drug Enforcement Administration (DEA), 2401 Jefferson Davis Highway, Alexandria, VA 22301, (202) 307-1000, www.usdoj.gov/dea; *State Factsheets.*

U.S. Department of Justice (DOJ), National Drug Intelligence Center, 319 Washington Street, 5th Floor, Johnstown, PA 15901-1622, (814) 532-4601, Fax: (814) 532-4690, www.usdoj.gov/ndic; *Drug Assessments* and *National Drug Threat Assessment 2007.*

U.S. Department of Justice (DOJ), National Institute of Justice (NIJ), 810 Seventh Street, NW, Washington, DC 20531, (202) 307-2942, Fax: (202) 616-0275, www.ojp.usdoj.gov/nij/; *ADAM Preliminary 2000 Findings on Drug Use Drug Markets: Adult Male Arrestees; Drug Courts: The Second Decade; I-ADAM in Eight Countries: Approaches and Challenges; Methamphetamine Abuse: Challenges for Law Enforcement and Communities;* and *Risky Mix: Drinking, Drug Use, and Homicide.*

United Nations Office on Drugs and Crime (UNODC), Vienna International Centre, PO Box 500, A-1400 Vienna, Austria, www.unodc.org; *World Drug Report 2006* and *World Drug Report 2006.*

DRUGS (ILLEGAL) - ARRESTS

Federal Bureau of Investigation (FBI), J. Edgar Hoover Building, 935 Pennsylvania Avenue, NW, Washington, DC 20535-0001, (202) 324-3000, www.fbi.gov; *Crime in the United States (CIUS) 2007 (Preliminary).*

Justice Research and Statistics Association (JRSA), 777 N. Capitol Street, NE, Suite 801, Washington, DC 20002, (202) 842-9330, Fax: (202) 842-9329, www.jrsa.org; *Crime and Justice Atlas 2001.*

U.S. Citizenship and Immigration Services (USCIS), Washington District Office, 2675 Prosperity Avenue, Fairfax, VA 22031, (800) 375-5283, http://uscis.gov; *2005 Yearbook of Immigration Statistics.*

U.S. Department of Justice (DOJ), Bureau of Justice Statistics, 810 Seventh Street, NW, Washington, DC 20531, (202) 307-0765, www.ojp.usdoj.gov/bjs/; *Drugs Crime Facts* and *Federal Criminal Justice Trends, 2003.*

U.S. Department of Justice (DOJ), Drug Enforcement Administration (DEA), 2401 Jefferson Davis Highway, Alexandria, VA 22301, (202) 307-1000, www.usdoj.gov/dea; *State Factsheets.*

U.S. Department of Justice (DOJ), National Institute of Justice (NIJ), 810 Seventh Street, NW, Washington, DC 20531, (202) 307-2942, Fax: (202) 616-0275, www.ojp.usdoj.gov/nij/; *ADAM Preliminary 2000 Findings on Drug Use Drug Markets: Adult Male Arrestees; Drug Courts: The Second Decade; I-ADAM in Eight Countries: Approaches and Challenges;* and *Methamphetamine Abuse: Challenges for Law Enforcement and Communities.*

DRUGS (ILLEGAL) - COURT CASES

Australian Institute of Criminology, 74 Leichhardt Street, Griffith ACT 2603 Australia, www.aic.gov.au/; *Final report on the North Queensland Drug Court.*

Australian Institute of Health and Welfare (AIHW), GPO Box 570, Canberra ACT 2601, Australia, www.aihw.gov.au; *The Effectiveness of the Illicit Drug Diversion Initiative in Rural and Remote Australia.*

Justice Research and Statistics Association (JRSA), 777 N. Capitol Street, NE, Suite 801, Washington, DC 20002, (202) 842-9330, Fax: (202) 842-9329, www.jrsa.org; *Documenting the Extent and Nature of Drug and Violent Crime: Developing Jurisdiction-Specific Profiles of the Criminal Justice System; JRP Digest; Justice Research and Policy;* and *SAC Publication Digest.*

National Center for Juvenile Justice (NCJJ), 3700 South Water Street, Suite 200, Pittsburgh, PA 15203, (412) 227-6950, Fax: (412) 227-6955, http://ncjj.servehttp.com/NCJJWebsite/main.htm; *Jury Trial in Abuse, Neglect, Dependency Cases.*

U.S. Department of Justice (DOJ), Bureau of Justice Statistics, 810 Seventh Street, NW, Washington, DC 20531, (202) 307-0765, www.ojp.usdoj.gov/bjs/; *Compendium of Federal Justice Statistics, 2003* and *Drugs Crime Facts.*

U.S. Department of Justice (DOJ), Drug Enforcement Administration (DEA), 2401 Jefferson Davis Highway, Alexandria, VA 22301, (202) 307-1000, www.usdoj.gov/dea; *State Factsheets.*

U.S. Department of Justice (DOJ), National Institute of Justice (NIJ), 810 Seventh Street, NW, Washington, DC 20531, (202) 307-2942, Fax: (202) 616-0275, www.ojp.usdoj.gov/nij/; *ADAM Preliminary 2000 Findings on Drug Use Drug Markets: Adult Male Arrestees; Drug Courts: The Second Decade;* and *I-ADAM in Eight Countries: Approaches and Challenges.*

United Nations Office on Drugs and Crime (UNODC), Vienna International Centre, PO Box 500, A-1400 Vienna, Austria, www.unodc.org; *World Drug Report 2006.*

DRUGS (ILLEGAL) - DRUG ABUSE TREATMENT

Australian Institute of Health and Welfare (AIHW), GPO Box 570, Canberra ACT 2601, Australia, www.aihw.gov.au; *The Effectiveness of the Illicit Drug Diversion Initiative in Rural and Remote Australia.*

Robert Wood Johnson Foundation, PO Box 2316, College Road East and Route 1, Princeton, NJ 08543, (877) 843-7953, www.rwjf.org; *Changes in the Number of Methadone Maintenance Slots as Measures of "Fighting Back" Program Effectiveness* and *Community-Based Substance Abuse Reduction and the Gap Between Treatment Need and Treatment Utilization: Analysis of Data From the "Fighting Back" General Population Survey.*

Substance Abuse and Mental Health Services Administration (SAMHSA), 1 Choke Cherry Road, Rockville, MD 20857, (240) 777-1311, www.oas.samhsa.gov; *Health Services Utilization by Individuals with Substance Abuse and Mental Disorders* and *National Survey of Substance Abuse Treatment Services (N-SSATS).*

U.S. Department of Justice (DOJ), Bureau of Justice Statistics, 810 Seventh Street, NW, Washington, DC 20531, (202) 307-0765, www.ojp.usdoj.gov/bjs/; *Drug Use, Testing, and Treatment in Jails* and *Substance Dependence, Abuse, and Treatment of Jail Inmates, 2002.*

DRUGS (ILLEGAL) - ENFORCEMENT ACTIVITIES

The Annie E. Casey Foundation, 701 Saint Paul Street, Baltimore, MD 21202, (410) 547-6600, Fax: (410) 547-3610, www.aecf.org; *Lessons from the Field.*

Australian Institute of Criminology, 74 Leichhardt Street, Griffith ACT 2603 Australia, www.aic.gov.au/; *Final report on the North Queensland Drug Court.*

Australian Institute of Health and Welfare (AIHW), GPO Box 570, Canberra ACT 2601, Australia, www.aihw.gov.au; *The Effectiveness of the Illicit Drug Diversion Initiative in Rural and Remote Australia.*

Robert Wood Johnson Foundation, PO Box 2316, College Road East and Route 1, Princeton, NJ 08543, (877) 843-7953, www.rwjf.org; *Community-Based Prevention Programs in the War on Drugs: Findings from the "Fighting Back" Demonstration* and *Neighborhood Crime Victimization, Drug Use and Drug Sales: Results from the "Fighting Back" Evaluation.*

Royal Canadian Mounted Police (RCMP), 1200 Vanier Parkway, Ottawa, ON K1A 0R2, Canada, (613) 993-7267, www.rcmp-grc.gc.ca; *Drug Situation in Canada - 2004.*

U.S. Citizenship and Immigration Services (USCIS), Washington District Office, 2675 Prosperity Avenue, Fairfax, VA 22031, (800) 375-5283, http://uscis.gov; *2005 Yearbook of Immigration Statistics.*

U.S. Department of Justice (DOJ), Bureau of Justice Statistics, 810 Seventh Street, NW, Washington, DC 20531, (202) 307-0765, www.ojp.usdoj.gov/bjs/; *Drugs Crime Facts.*

U.S. Department of Justice (DOJ), Drug Enforcement Administration (DEA), 2401 Jefferson Davis Highway, Alexandria, VA 22301, (202) 307-1000, www.usdoj.gov/dea; *State Factsheets* and *State Factsheets.*

U.S. Department of Justice (DOJ), National Drug Intelligence Center, 319 Washington Street, 5th Floor, Johnstown, PA 15901-1622, (814) 532-4601, Fax: (814) 532-4690, www.usdoj.gov/ndic; *Drug Assessments* and *National Drug Threat Assessment 2007.*

U.S. Department of Justice (DOJ), National Institute of Justice (NIJ), 810 Seventh Street, NW, Washington, DC 20531, (202) 307-2942, Fax: (202) 616-0275, www.ojp.usdoj.gov/nij/; *ADAM Preliminary 2000 Findings on Drug Use Drug Markets: Adult Male Arrestees; Drug Courts: The Second Decade; I-ADAM in Eight Countries: Approaches and Challenges;* and *Methamphetamine Abuse: Challenges for Law Enforcement and Communities.*

United Nations Office on Drugs and Crime (UNODC), Vienna International Centre, PO Box 500, A-1400 Vienna, Austria, www.unodc.org; *World Drug Report 2006* and *World Drug Report 2006.*

DRUGS (ILLEGAL) - JUVENILES

Center for Substance Abuse Research (CESAR), 4321 Hartwick Road, Suite 501, College Park, MD 20740, (301) 405-9770, Fax: (301) 403-8342, www.cesar.umd.edu; *Juvenile Offender Population Urinalysis Screening Program (OPUS) Detention Study, February-June 2005.*

National Center for Juvenile Justice (NCJJ), 3700 South Water Street, Suite 200, Pittsburgh, PA 15203, (412) 227-6950, Fax: (412) 227-6955, http://ncjj.servehttp.com/NCJJWebsite/main.htm; *Detention and Delinquency Cases 1990-1999 (2003); Jury Trial in Abuse, Neglect, Dependency Cases; Juvenile Arrests 2003 (2005);* and *Juvenile Court Statistics 2000 (2004).*

Office of Juvenile Justice and Delinquency Prevention (OJJDP), 810 Seventh Street, NW, Washington, DC 20531, (202) 307-5911, www.ojjdp.ncjrs.org; *Statistical Briefing Book (SBB).*

U.S. Department of Justice (DOJ), Bureau of Justice Statistics, 810 Seventh Street, NW, Washington, DC 20531, (202) 307-0765, www.ojp.usdoj.gov/bjs/; *Drugs Crime Facts* and *Juvenile Victimization and Offending, 1993-2003.*

U.S. Department of Justice (DOJ), Drug Enforcement Administration (DEA), 2401 Jefferson Davis Highway, Alexandria, VA 22301, (202) 307-1000, www.usdoj.gov/dea; *State Factsheets.*

United Nations Office on Drugs and Crime (UNODC), Vienna International Centre, PO Box 500, A-1400 Vienna, Austria, www.unodc.org; *World Drug Report 2006.*

DRUGS (ILLEGAL) - USAGE

Center for Substance Abuse Research (CESAR), 4321 Hartwick Road, Suite 501, College Park, MD 20740, (301) 405-9770, Fax: (301) 403-8342, www.cesar.umd.edu; *College Students' Perceptions of Non-Medical Use of Prescription Stimulants by Their Peers: Findings From the April 2005 Administration of the Student Drug Research (SDR) Survey; DEWS Investigates: Perceptions of Prescription Stimulant Misuse Among College Students at High and Low Risk of Drug Use;* and *Juvenile Offender Population Urinalysis Screening Program (OPUS) Detention Study, February-June 2005.*

Federal Bureau of Investigation (FBI), J. Edgar Hoover Building, 935 Pennsylvania Avenue, NW, Washington, DC 20535-0001, (202) 324-3000, www.fbi.gov; *Crime in the United States (CIUS) 2007 (Preliminary).*

Justice Research and Statistics Association (JRSA), 777 N. Capitol Street, NE, Suite 801, Washington, DC 20002, (202) 842-9330, Fax: (202) 842-9329, www.jrsa.org; *Crime and Justice Atlas 2001.*

Robert Wood Johnson Foundation, PO Box 2316, College Road East and Route 1, Princeton, NJ 08543, (877) 843-7953, www.rwjf.org; *Varieties of Substance Use and Visible Drug Problems: Individual and Neighborhood Factors.*

Royal Canadian Mounted Police (RCMP), 1200 Vanier Parkway, Ottawa, ON K1A 0R2, Canada, (613) 993-7267, www.rcmp-grc.gc.ca; *Drug Situation in Canada - 2004.*

Substance Abuse and Mental Health Services Administration (SAMHSA), 1 Choke Cherry Road, Rockville, MD 20857, (240) 777-1311, www.oas.samhsa.gov; *Alcohol and Drug Services Study (ADSS)* and *National Survey on Drug Use Health (NSDUH).*

U.S. Department of Justice (DOJ), Bureau of Justice Statistics, 810 Seventh Street, NW, Washington, DC 20531, (202) 307-0765, www.ojp.usdoj.gov/bjs/; *Drug Use and Dependence, State and Federal Prisoners, 2004; Drug Use, Testing, and Treatment in Jails;* and *Drugs Crime Facts.*

U.S. Department of Justice (DOJ), National Drug Intelligence Center, 319 Washington Street, 5th Floor, Johnstown, PA 15901-1622, (814) 532-4601, Fax: (814) 532-4690, www.usdoj.gov/ndic; *Drug Assessments* and *National Drug Threat Assessment 2007.*

U.S. Department of Justice (DOJ), National Institute of Justice (NIJ), 810 Seventh Street, NW, Washington, DC 20531, (202) 307-2942, Fax: (202) 616-0275, www.ojp.usdoj.gov/nij/; *Annual Report; Methamphetamine Abuse: Challenges for Law Enforcement and Communities;* and *Risky Mix: Drinking, Drug Use, and Homicide.*

United Nations Office on Drugs and Crime (UNODC), Vienna International Centre, PO Box 500, A-1400 Vienna, Austria, www.unodc.org; *World Drug Report 2006.*

DRUGS AND MEDICINES

Center for Substance Abuse Research (CESAR), 4321 Hartwick Road, Suite 501, College Park, MD 20740, (301) 405-9770, Fax: (301) 403-8342, www.cesar.umd.edu; *DEWS Investigates: A Pilot Study to Enhance the Understanding of Methadone Intoxication Deaths in Maryland.*

HealthLeaders-InterStudy, One Vantage Way, B-300, Nashville, TN 37203, (615) 385-4131, Fax: (615) 385-4979, www.hmodata.com; *Strategic Assessment of Managed Markets (SAMM).*

Office of Trade and Industry Information (OTII), Manufacturing and Services, International Trade Administration, U.S. Department of Commerce, 1401 Constitution Ave, NW, Washington, DC 20230, (800) USA TRAD(E), http://trade.gov/index.asp; *TradeStats Express.*

Thomson Healthcare, 200 First Stamford Place, 4th Floor, Stamford, CT 06902, (203) 539-8000, www.thomson.com; *Medstat Advantage Suite* and *Medstat Modeler.*

U.S. Census Bureau, 4700 Silver Hill Road, Washington DC 20233-0001, (301) 763-3030, www.census.gov; *2006 E-Commerce Multi-Sector Report* and *E-Stats - Measuring the Electronic Economy.*

U.S. Census Bureau, Center for Economic Studies, 4600 Silver Hill Road, Washington DC 20233, (301) 457-1235, www.ces.census.gov; *2002 Economic Census, Retail Trade* and *2002 Economic Census, Wholesale Trade.*

DRUGS AND MEDICINES - ADVERTISING EXPENDITURES

Magazine Publishers of America (MPA), 810 Seventh Avenue, 24th Floor, New York, NY 10019, (212) 872-3700, www.magazine.org; *The Media Research Index.*

DRUGS AND MEDICINES - CONSUMER PRICE INDEXES

U.S. Bureau of Labor Statistics (BLS), Postal Square Building, 2 Massachusetts Avenue, NE, Washington, DC 20212-0001, (202) 691-5200, Fax: (202) 691-6325, www.bls.gov; *Consumer Price Index Detailed Report* and *Monthly Labor Review (MLR).*

DRUGS AND MEDICINES - DRUG ABUSE TREATMENT

Robert Wood Johnson Foundation, PO Box 2316, College Road East and Route 1, Princeton, NJ 08543, (877) 843-7953, www.rwjf.org; *Changes in the Number of Methadone Maintenance Slots as Measures of "Fighting Back" Program Effectiveness.*

Substance Abuse and Mental Health Services Administration (SAMHSA), 1 Choke Cherry Road, Rockville, MD 20857, (240) 777-1311, www.oas.samhsa.gov; *National Survey of Substance Abuse Treatment Services (N-SSATS).*

U.S. Department of Justice (DOJ), Bureau of Justice Statistics, 810 Seventh Street, NW, Washington, DC 20531, (202) 307-0765, www.ojp.usdoj.gov/bjs/; *Substance Dependence, Abuse, and Treatment of Jail Inmates, 2002.*

DRUGS AND MEDICINES - EXPENDITURES FOR

Centers for Medicare and Medicaid Services (CMS), U.S. Department of Health and Human Services (HHS), 7500 Security Boulevard, Baltimore, MD 21244-1850, (410) 786-3000, http://cms.hhs.gov; *Health Care Financing Review.*

HealthLeaders-InterStudy, One Vantage Way, B-300, Nashville, TN 37203, (615) 385-4131, Fax: (615) 385-4979, www.hmodata.com; *Strategic Assessment of Managed Markets (SAMM).*

U.S. Bureau of Labor Statistics (BLS), Postal Square Building, 2 Massachusetts Avenue, NE, Washington, DC 20212-0001, (202) 691-5200, Fax: (202) 691-6325, www.bls.gov; *Consumer Expenditures in 2006.*

DRUGS AND MEDICINES - INTERNATIONAL TRADE

U.S. Census Bureau, Foreign Trade Division, 4700 Silver Hill Road, Washington DC 20233-0001, (301)

763-3030, www.census.gov/foreign-trade/www/; *U.S. International Trade in Goods and Services.*

DRUGS AND MEDICINES - MEDICAID PAYMENTS AND RECIPIENTS

Centers for Medicare and Medicaid Services (CMS), U.S. Department of Health and Human Services (HHS), 7500 Security Boulevard, Baltimore, MD 21244-1850, (410) 786-3000, http://cms.hhs.gov; The Medicare Current Beneficiary Survey (MCBS) (web app).

DRUGS AND MEDICINES - NONMEDICAL USE

Center for Substance Abuse Research (CESAR), 4321 Hartwick Road, Suite 501, College Park, MD 20740, (301) 405-9770, Fax: (301) 403-8342, www.cesar.umd.edu; *College Students' Perceptions of Non-Medical Use of Prescription Stimulants by Their Peers: Findings From the April 2005 Administration of the Student Drug Research (SDR) Survey; DEWS Investigates: Perceptions of Prescription Stimulant Misuse Among College Students at High and Low Risk of Drug Use;* and *DEWS Investigates: Who Is Entering Treatment for Narcotic Pain Relievers in Maryland?*

DRUGS AND MEDICINES - PRICE INDEXES

U.S. Bureau of Labor Statistics (BLS), Postal Square Building, 2 Massachusetts Avenue, NE, Washington, DC 20212-0001, (202) 691-5200, Fax: (202) 691-6325, www.bls.gov; *Consumer Price Index Detailed Report* and *Monthly Labor Review (MLR).*

DRUNK DRIVING - ARRESTS

Federal Bureau of Investigation (FBI), J. Edgar Hoover Building, 935 Pennsylvania Avenue, NW, Washington, DC 20535-0001, (202) 324-3000, www.fbi.gov; *Crime in the United States (CIUS) 2007 (Preliminary).*

Justice Research and Statistics Association (JRSA), 777 N. Capitol Street, NE, Suite 801, Washington, DC 20002, (202) 842-9330, Fax: (202) 842-9329, www.jrsa.org; *Crime and Justice Atlas 2001.*

DRYCLEANING AND LAUNDRY SERVICES - EARNINGS

U.S. Bureau of Labor Statistics (BLS), Postal Square Building, 2 Massachusetts Avenue, NE, Washington, DC 20212-0001, (202) 691-5200, Fax: (202) 691-6325, www.bls.gov; *Current Employment Statistics Survey (CES)* and *Employment and Earnings (EE).*

U.S. Census Bureau, Company Statistics Division, 4700 Silver Hill Road, Washington DC 20233-0001, (301) 763-3030, www.census.gov/csd/; *County Business Patterns 2004.*

DRYCLEANING AND LAUNDRY SERVICES - EMPLOYEES

U.S. Bureau of Labor Statistics (BLS), Postal Square Building, 2 Massachusetts Avenue, NE, Washington, DC 20212-0001, (202) 691-5200, Fax: (202) 691-6325, www.bls.gov; *Current Employment Statistics Survey (CES)* and *Employment and Earnings (EE).*

U.S. Census Bureau, Center for Economic Studies, 4600 Silver Hill Road, Washington DC 20233, (301) 457-1235, www.ces.census.gov; *2002 Economic Census, Other Services (except Public Administration).*

U.S. Census Bureau, Company Statistics Division, 4700 Silver Hill Road, Washington DC 20233-0001, (301) 763-3030, www.census.gov/csd/; *County Business Patterns 2004.*

DRYCLEANING AND LAUNDRY SERVICES - ESTABLISHMENTS

U.S. Census Bureau, Center for Economic Studies, 4600 Silver Hill Road, Washington DC 20233, (301) 457-1235, www.ces.census.gov; *2002 Economic Census, Other Services (except Public Administration).*

U.S. Census Bureau, Company Statistics Division, 4700 Silver Hill Road, Washington DC 20233-0001, (301) 763-3030, www.census.gov/csd/; *County Business Patterns 2004.*

DRYCLEANING AND LAUNDRY SERVICES - PRODUCTIVITY

U.S. Bureau of Labor Statistics (BLS), Postal Square Building, 2 Massachusetts Avenue, NE, Washington, DC 20212-0001, (202) 691-5200, Fax: (202) 691-6325, www.bls.gov; *Industry Productivity and Costs.*

DRYCLEANING AND LAUNDRY SERVICES - RECEIPTS

U.S. Census Bureau, Center for Economic Studies, 4600 Silver Hill Road, Washington DC 20233, (301) 457-1235, www.ces.census.gov; *2002 Economic Census, Other Services (except Public Administration).*STATISTICS SOURCES, Thirty-second Edition - 2009STATISTICS SOURCES, Thirty-second Edition - 2009

E COLI

Centers for Disease Control and Prevention (CDC), U.S. Department of Health and Human Services (HHS), 1600 Clifton Road, Atlanta, GA 30333, (800) 311-3435, www.cdc.gov; *Morbidity and Mortality Weekly Report (MMWR)* and *Summary of Notifiable Diseases, United States, 2006.*

E-COMMERCE

See ELECTRONIC COMMERCE (E-COMMERCE)

EARNINGS - AGRICULTURE FORESTRY, FISHERIES

U.S. Census Bureau, Company Statistics Division, 4700 Silver Hill Road, Washington DC 20233-0001, (301) 763-3030, www.census.gov/csd/; *County Business Patterns 2004.*

EARNINGS - AIRLINES

Air Transport Association of America, 1301 Pennsylvania Avenue, NW, Suite 1100, Washington, DC 20004-7017, (202) 626-4000, Fax: (202) 626-6584, www.air-transport.org; *Air Transportation and the Economy: A State-by-State Review* and *2007 Economic Report.*

EARNINGS - COLLEGE FACULTY

American Association of University Professors, 1012 14th Street, NW, Suite 500, Washington, DC 20005-3465, (202) 737-5900, Fax: (202) 737-5526, www.aaup.org; *AAUP Annual Report on the Economic Status of the Profession.*

EARNINGS - COLLEGE GRADUATES, STARTING SALARIES

National Association of Colleges and Employers (NACE), 62 Highland Avenue, Bethlehem, PA 18017, (800) 544-5272, Fax: (610) 868-0208, www.naceweb.org; *Salary Survey.*

EARNINGS - CONSTRUCTION INDUSTRY

U.S. Census Bureau, Center for Economic Studies, 4600 Silver Hill Road, Washington DC 20233, (301) 457-1235, www.ces.census.gov; *2002 Economic Census, Transportation and Warehousing.*

U.S. Census Bureau, Company Statistics Division, 4700 Silver Hill Road, Washington DC 20233-0001, (301) 763-3030, www.census.gov/csd/; *County Business Patterns 2004.*

EARNINGS - EDUCATIONAL ATTAINMENT

U.S. Census Bureau, 4700 Silver Hill Road, Washington DC 20233-0001, (301) 763-3030, www.census.gov; *Survey of Income and Program Participation (SIPP).*

U.S. Census Bureau, Population Division, 4700 Silver Hill Road, Washington DC 20233-0001, (301) 763-3030, www.census.gov/population/www/; *Current Population Reports.*

EARNINGS - EMPLOYMENT COVERED BY SOCIAL INSURANCE

National Academy of Social Insurance (NASI), 1776 Massachusetts Avenue, NW, Suite 615, Washington, DC 20036, (202) 452-8097, Fax: (202) 452-8111, www.nasi.org; *Workers' Compensation: Benefits, Coverage, and Costs, 2004.*

Social Security Administration (SSA), Office of Public Inquiries, Windsor Park Building, 6401 Security Boulevard, Baltimore, MD 21235, (800) 772-1213, www.ssa.gov; *Annual Statistical Supplement, 2007* and unpublished data.

U.S. Department of Labor (DOL), Employment and Training Administration (ETA), Frances Perkins Building, 200 Constitution Avenue, NW, Washington, DC 20210, (877) US-2JOBS, www.doleta.gov; unpublished data.

EARNINGS - FAMILY TYPE

U.S. Bureau of Labor Statistics (BLS), Postal Square Building, 2 Massachusetts Avenue, NE, Washington, DC 20212-0001, (202) 691-5200, Fax: (202) 691-6325, www.bls.gov; *Current Population Survey (CPS).*

U.S. Census Bureau, Housing and Household Economics Statistics Division, 4700 Silver Hill Road, Washington DC 20233-0001, (301) 763-3030, www.census.gov/hhes/www; *2006 American Community Survey (ACS).*

EARNINGS - GOVERNMENT EMPLOYEES - FEDERAL

U.S. Census Bureau, Governments Division, 4600 Silver Hill Road, Washington DC 20233, (800) 242-2184, www.census.gov/govs/www; *2002 Census of Governments, Public Employment and Payroll.*

U.S. Library of Congress (LOC), Congressional Research Service (CRS), The Library of Congress, 101 Independence Avenue, SE, Washington, DC 20540-7500, (202) 707-5700, www.loc.gov/crsinfo; *Federal Employees: Pay and Pension Increases Since 1969.*

U.S. Office of Personnel Management (OPM), 1900 E Street, NW, Washington, DC 20415-1000, (202) 606-1800, www.opm.gov; *Biennial Report of Employment by Geographic Area; 2004 Demographic Profile of the Federal Workforce;* and *Employment and Trends.*

United States Office of Personnel Management (OMB), 1900 E Street, NW, Washington, DC 20415-1000, (202) 606-1800, www.opm.gov; *Employment and Trends of Federal Civilian Workforce Statistics* and *Pay Structure of the Federal Civil Service.*

EARNINGS - GOVERNMENT EMPLOYEES - STATE AND LOCAL

U.S. Census Bureau, Governments Division, 4600 Silver Hill Road, Washington DC 20233, (800) 242-2184, www.census.gov/govs/www; *2002 Census of Governments, Government Finances* and *2002 Census of Governments, Public Employment and Payroll.*

EARNINGS - INCOME TAX RETURNS (REPORTED TOTALS)

U.S. Department of the Treasury (DOT), Internal Revenue Service (IRS), Statistics of Income Division (SIS), PO Box 2608, Washington, DC, 20013-2608, (202) 874-0410, Fax: (202) 874-0964, www.irs.ustreas.gov; *Statistics of Income Bulletin* and *Statistics of Income Bulletin, Individual Income Tax Returns.*

EARNINGS - INDUSTRY

Bureau of Economic Analysis (BEA), U.S. Department of Commerce (DOC), 1441 L Street NW, Washington, DC 20230, (202) 606-9900, www.bea.gov; *2007 Annual Revision of the National Income and Product Accounts (NIPA)* and *Survey of Current Business (SCB).*

U.S. Bureau of Labor Statistics (BLS), Postal Square Building, 2 Massachusetts Avenue, NE, Washington, DC 20212-0001, (202) 691-5200, Fax: (202) 691-6325, www.bls.gov; *Current Employment Statistics Survey (CES); Employment and Earnings (EE);* and *Monthly Labor Review (MLR).*

U.S. Census Bureau, Company Statistics Division, 4700 Silver Hill Road, Washington DC 20233-0001, (301) 763-3030, www.census.gov/csd/; *County Business Patterns 2004.*

EARNINGS - MANUFACTURING

U.S. Census Bureau, Company Statistics Division, 4700 Silver Hill Road, Washington DC 20233-0001, (301) 763-3030, www.census.gov/csd/; *County Business Patterns 2004.*

EARNINGS - METROPOLITAN AREAS

U.S. Bureau of Labor Statistics (BLS), Postal Square Building, 2 Massachusetts Avenue, NE, Washington, DC 20212-0001, (202) 691-5200, Fax: (202) 691-6325, www.bls.gov; *Average Annual Pay Levels in Metropolitan Areas* and unpublished data.

EARNINGS - MINERAL INDUSTRIES

U.S. Bureau of Labor Statistics (BLS), Postal Square Building, 2 Massachusetts Avenue, NE, Washington, DC 20212-0001, (202) 691-5200, Fax: (202) 691-6325, www.bls.gov; *Current Employment Statistics Survey (CES)* and *Employment and Earnings (EE).*

U.S. Department of the Interior (DOI), U.S. Geological Survey (USGS), Office of Minerals Information, 12201 Sunrise Valley Drive, Reston, VA 20192, Mr. Kenneth A. Beckman, (703) 648-4916, Fax: (703) 648-4995, http://minerals.usgs.gov/minerals; *Minerals Yearbook* and *Nonmetallic Mineral Products Industry Indexes.*

EARNINGS - MINIMUM WAGE WORKERS

National Center for Children in Poverty (NCCP), 215 W. 125th Street, 3rd Floor, New York, NY 10027, (646) 284-9600, Fax: (646) 284-9623, www.nccp.org; *Living at the Edge* and *When Work Doesn't Pay: What Every Policymaker Should Know.*

U.S. Bureau of Labor Statistics (BLS), Postal Square Building, 2 Massachusetts Avenue, NE, Washington, DC 20212-0001, (202) 691-5200, Fax: (202) 691-6325, www.bls.gov; unpublished data.

U.S. Department of Labor (DOL), Employment Standards Administration (ESA), Frances Perkins Building, 200 Constitution Avenue, NW, Washington, DC 20210, (866) 4-USA-DOL, www.dol.gov/esa; *2007 Statistics Fact Sheet.*

EARNINGS - MINING INDUSTRY

U.S. Census Bureau, Center for Economic Studies, 4600 Silver Hill Road, Washington DC 20233, (301) 457-1235, www.ces.census.gov; *2002 Economic Census, Transportation and Warehousing.*

U.S. Census Bureau, Company Statistics Division, 4700 Silver Hill Road, Washington DC 20233-0001, (301) 763-3030, www.census.gov/csd/; *County Business Patterns 2004.*

U.S. Census Bureau, Manufacturing and Construction Division, 4600 Silver Hill Road, Washington DC 20233, (301) 763-4673, www.census.gov/mcd; *Census of Mineral Industries.*

EARNINGS - MUNICIPAL EMPLOYEES

U.S. Census Bureau, 4700 Silver Hill Road, Washington DC 20233-0001, (301) 763-3030, www.census.gov; unpublished data.

U.S. Census Bureau, Governments Division, 4600 Silver Hill Road, Washington DC 20233, (800) 242-2184, www.census.gov/govs/www; *2002 Census of Governments, Public Employment and Payroll.*

EARNINGS - OCCUPATIONS

U.S. Bureau of Labor Statistics (BLS), Postal Square Building, 2 Massachusetts Avenue, NE, Washington, DC 20212-0001, (202) 691-5200, Fax: (202) 691-6325, www.bls.gov; *Current Population Survey (CPS); Employment and Earnings (EE);* and unpublished data.

U.S. Census Bureau, Population Division, 4700 Silver Hill Road, Washington DC 20233-0001, (301) 763-3030, www.census.gov/population/www/; *Current Population Reports.*

U.S. Department of Labor (DOL), Bureau of Labor Statistics (BLS), Postal Square Building, 2 Massachusetts Avenue, NE, Washington, DC 20212-0001, (202) 691-5200, Fax: (202) 691-6325, www.bls.gov; *Current Employment Statistics (CES)* and *Employment and Wages, Annual Averages 2005.*

U.S. Government Printing Office (GPO), Office of Congressional Publishing Services (OCPS), 732 North Capitol Street NW, Washington, DC 20401, (202) 512-0224, www.gpo.gov/customerservices/cps.htm; *Occupational Outlook Handbook, 2008-09.*

EARNINGS - PERSONAL INCOME

Bureau of Economic Analysis (BEA), U.S. Department of Commerce (DOC), 1441 L Street NW, Washington, DC 20230, (202) 606-9900, www.bea.gov; *2007 Annual Revision of the National Income and Product Accounts (NIPA); Survey of Current Business (SCB);* and unpublished data.

National Center for Children in Poverty (NCCP), 215 W. 125th Street, 3rd Floor, New York, NY 10027, (646) 284-9600, Fax: (646) 284-9623, www.nccp.org; *When Work Doesn't Pay: What Every Policymaker Should Know.*

State of Hawaii Department of Business, Economic Development Tourism (DBEDT), Research and Economic Analysis Division (READ), PO Box 2359 Honolulu, HI 96804, (808) 586-2423, Fax: (808) 587-2790, www.hawaii.gov/dbedt/info/economic/census; *Wage and Employment Structure: Comparing Recent Trends for Hawaii vs. the U.S.*

EARNINGS - PHYSICIANS

American Medical Association, 515 North State Street, Chicago, IL 60610, (800) 621-8335, www.ama-assn.org; *Physician Socioeconomic Statistics.*

EARNINGS - PRIVATE EMPLOYER FIRMS

Small Business Administration (SBA), 409 3rd Street, SW, Washington, DC 20024-3212, (202) 205-6533, Fax: (202) 206-6928, www.sba.gov; unpublished data.

EARNINGS - RAILROADS

Association of American Railroads (AAR), 50 F Street, NW, Washington, DC 20001-1564, (202) 639-2100, www.aar.org; *Analysis of Class I Railroads* and *Railroad Facts.*

EARNINGS - RETAIL TRADE

Progressive Grocer, 770 Broadway, New York, NY 10003, (866) 890-8541, www.progressivegrocer.com; *2006 Consumer Expenditures Study.*

U.S. Census Bureau, Company Statistics Division, 4700 Silver Hill Road, Washington DC 20233-0001, (301) 763-3030, www.census.gov/csd/; *County Business Patterns 2004.*

EARNINGS - SCHOOL TEACHERS

National Center for Education Statistics (NCES), 1990 K Street, NW, Washington, DC 20006, (202) 502-7300, http://nces.ed.gov; *Digest of Education Statistics 2007* and unpublished data.

National Education Association (NEA), 1201 Sixteenth Street, NW, Washington, DC 20036-3290, (202) 833-4000, Fax: (202) 822-7974, www.nea.org; *Education Statistics: Rankings and Estimates 2006-2007.*

EARNINGS - SEAMEN

U.S. Department of Transportation (DOT), Maritime Administration (MARAD), West Building, Southeast Federal Center, 1200 New Jersey Avenue, SE, Washington, DC 20590, (800) 99-MARAD, www.marad.dot.gov; *U.S.-Flag Oceangoing Fleet 2005* and unpublished data.

EARNINGS - STATES

U.S. Bureau of Labor Statistics (BLS), Postal Square Building, 2 Massachusetts Avenue, NE, Washington, DC 20212-0001, (202) 691-5200, Fax: (202) 691-6325, www.bls.gov; *Average Annual Pay by State and Industry* and unpublished data.

EARNINGS - TELEPHONE SYSTEMS, EMPLOYEES

Federal Communications Commission (FCC), Wireline Competition Bureau (WCB), 445 12th Street, SW, Washington, DC 20554, (202) 418-1500, Fax: (202) 418-2825, www.fcc.gov/wcb; *Statistical Trends in Telephony 2007* and *Statistics of Communications Common Carriers 2005/2006.*

United States Telecom Association (USTelecom), 607 14th Street, NW, Suite 400, Washington, DC 20005, (202) 326-7300, Fax: (202) 326-7333, www.usta.org; *Telecom Statistics.*

EARNINGS - TRANSPORTATION

U.S. Census Bureau, Company Statistics Division, 4700 Silver Hill Road, Washington DC 20233-0001, (301) 763-3030, www.census.gov/csd/; *County Business Patterns 2004.*

EARNINGS - UNION MEMBERS

U.S. Bureau of Labor Statistics (BLS), Postal Square Building, 2 Massachusetts Avenue, NE, Washington, DC 20212-0001, (202) 691-5200, Fax: (202) 691-6325, www.bls.gov; *Employment and Earnings (EE).*

EARNINGS - WHOLESALE TRADE

Office of Trade and Industry Information (OTII), Manufacturing and Services, International Trade Administration, U.S. Department of Commerce, 1401 Constitution Ave, NW, Washington, DC 20230, (800) USA TRAD(E), http://trade.gov/index.asp; *TradeStats Express.*

U.S. Census Bureau, Company Statistics Division, 4700 Silver Hill Road, Washington DC 20233-0001, (301) 763-3030, www.census.gov/csd/; *County Business Patterns 2004.*

EARNINGS - WOMEN-OWNED BUSINESSES

U.S. Census Bureau, Company Statistics Division, 4700 Silver Hill Road, Washington DC 20233-0001, (301) 763-3030, www.census.gov/csd/; *Survey of Women-Owned Businesses.*

EARTH SCIENCES - DEGREES CONFERRED

National Science Foundation, Division of Science Resources Statistics (SRS), 4201 Wilson Boulevard, Arlington, VA 22230, (703) 292-8780, Fax: (703) 292-9092, www.nsf.gov; *Selected Data on Science and Engineering Doctorate Awards* and *Survey of Earned Doctorates 2006.*

EAST TIMOR - NATIONAL STATISTICAL OFFICE

Ministry of Planning and Finance, PO Box 10, Dili, Timor-Leste; National Data Center.

EAST TIMOR - AGRICULTURAL MACHINERY

United Nations Statistics Division, New York, NY 10017, (800) 253-9646, Fax: (212) 963-4116, http://unstats.un.org; *Statistical Yearbook.*

EAST TIMOR - AGRICULTURE

Economist Intelligence Unit, 111 West 57th Street, New York, NY 10019, (212) 554-0600, Fax: (212) 586-1181, www.eiu.com; *East Timor Country Report.*

United Nations Food and Agricultural Organization (FAO), Viale delle Terme di Caracalla, 00100 Rome, Italy, (Dial from U.S. (202) 653-2400), (Fax from U.S. (202) 653 5760), www.fao.org; AQUASTAT; *FAO Production Yearbook 2002; FAO Trade Yearbook;* and *The State of Food and Agriculture (SOFA) 2006.*

United Nations Statistics Division, New York, NY 10017, (800) 253-9646, Fax: (212) 963-4116, http://unstats.un.org; *Statistical Yearbook.*

The World Bank, 1818 H Street, NW, Washington, DC 20433, (202) 473-1000, Fax: (202) 477-6391, www.worldbank.org; *Timor-Leste.*

EAST TIMOR - CATTLE

See EAST TIMOR - LIVESTOCK

EAST TIMOR - CHILDBIRTH - STATISTICS

United Nations Statistics Division, New York, NY 10017, (800) 253-9646, Fax: (212) 963-4116, http://unstats.un.org; *Demographic Yearbook* and *Statistical Yearbook.*

EAST TIMOR - COAL PRODUCTION

See EAST TIMOR - MINERAL INDUSTRIES

EAST TIMOR - COMMODITY EXCHANGES

Commodity Research Bureau, 330 South Wells Street, Suite 612, Chicago, IL 60606-7110, (800) 621-5271, Fax: (312) 939-4135, www.crbtrader.com; *2006 CRB Commodity Yearbook and CD.*

International Monetary Fund (IMF), 700 Nineteenth Street, NW, Washington, DC 20431, (202) 623-7000, Fax: (202) 623-4661, www.imf.org; *IMF Primary Commodity Prices.*

United Nations Food and Agricultural Organization (FAO), Viale delle Terme di Caracalla, 00100 Rome, Italy, (Dial from U.S. (202) 653-2400), (Fax from U.S. (202) 653 5760), www.fao.org; *The State of Food and Agriculture (SOFA) 2006.*

EAST TIMOR - CORN INDUSTRY

See EAST TIMOR - CROPS

EAST TIMOR - CROPS

United Nations Food and Agricultural Organization (FAO), Viale delle Terme di Caracalla, 00100 Rome, Italy, (Dial from U.S. (202) 653-2400), (Fax from U.S. (202) 653 5760), www.fao.org; *FAO Production Yearbook 2002* and *The State of Food and Agriculture (SOFA) 2006.*

United Nations Statistics Division, New York, NY 10017, (800) 253-9646, Fax: (212) 963-4116, http://unstats.un.org; *Statistical Yearbook.*

EAST TIMOR - DAIRY PROCESSING

United Nations Food and Agricultural Organization (FAO), Viale delle Terme di Caracalla, 00100 Rome, Italy, (Dial from U.S. (202) 653-2400), (Fax from U.S. (202) 653 5760), www.fao.org; *FAO Production Yearbook 2002* and *The State of Food and Agriculture (SOFA) 2006.*

EAST TIMOR - DEATH RATES

See EAST TIMOR - MORTALITY

EAST TIMOR - DISPOSABLE INCOME

United Nations Statistics Division, New York, NY 10017, (800) 253-9646, Fax: (212) 963-4116, http://unstats.un.org; *Statistical Yearbook.*

EAST TIMOR - DIVORCE

United Nations Statistics Division, New York, NY 10017, (800) 253-9646, Fax: (212) 963-4116, http://unstats.un.org; *Demographic Yearbook.*

EAST TIMOR - ECONOMIC ASSISTANCE

United Nations Statistics Division, New York, NY 10017, (800) 253-9646, Fax: (212) 963-4116, http://unstats.un.org; *Statistical Yearbook.*

EAST TIMOR - ECONOMIC CONDITIONS

Center for International Business Education Research (CIBER), Columbia Business School and School of International and Public Affairs, Uris Hall, Room 212, 3022 Broadway, New York, NY 10027-6902, Mr. Joshua Safier, (212) 854-4750, Fax: (212) 222-9821, www.columbia.edu/cu/ciber/; Datastream International.

DSI Data Service Information, Xantener Strasse 51a, D-47495 Rheinberg, Germany, www.dsidata.com; *Campus Solution.*

Dun and Bradstreet (DB) Corporation, 103 JFK Parkway, Short Hills, NJ 07078, (973) 921-5500, www.dnb.com; *Country Report.*

Economist Intelligence Unit, 111 West 57th Street, New York, NY 10019, (212) 554-0600, Fax: (212) 586-1181, www.eiu.com; *East Timor Country Report.*

International Monetary Fund (IMF), 700 Nineteenth Street, NW, Washington, DC 20431, (202) 623-7000, Fax: (202) 623-4661, www.imf.org; *World Economic Outlook Reports.*

United Nations Statistics Division, New York, NY 10017, (800) 253-9646, Fax: (212) 963-4116, http://unstats.un.org; *World Statistics Pocketbook.*

The World Bank, 1818 H Street, NW, Washington, DC 20433, (202) 473-1000, Fax: (202) 477-6391, www.worldbank.org; *Global Economic Monitor (GEM); Global Economic Prospects 2008;* and *Timor-Leste.*

EAST TIMOR - ENVIRONMENTAL CONDITIONS

DSI Data Service Information, Xantener Strasse 51a, D-47495 Rheinberg, Germany, www.dsidata.com; *Campus Solution* and *DSI's Global Environmental Database.*

Economist Intelligence Unit, 111 West 57th Street, New York, NY 10019, (212) 554-0600, Fax: (212) 586-1181, www.eiu.com; *East Timor Country Report.*

United Nations Statistics Division, New York, NY 10017, (800) 253-9646, Fax: (212) 963-4116, http://unstats.un.org; *World Statistics Pocketbook.*

EAST TIMOR - EXPORTS

Economist Intelligence Unit, 111 West 57th Street, New York, NY 10019, (212) 554-0600, Fax: (212) 586-1181, www.eiu.com; *East Timor Country Report.*

United Nations Food and Agricultural Organization (FAO), Viale delle Terme di Caracalla, 00100 Rome, Italy, (Dial from U.S. (202) 653-2400), (Fax from U.S. (202) 653 5760), www.fao.org; *The State of Food and Agriculture (SOFA) 2006.*

EAST TIMOR - FERTILIZER INDUSTRY

United Nations Food and Agricultural Organization (FAO), Viale delle Terme di Caracalla, 00100 Rome, Italy, (Dial from U.S. (202) 653-2400), (Fax from U.S. (202) 653 5760), www.fao.org; *The State of Food and Agriculture (SOFA) 2006.*

EAST TIMOR - FETAL MORTALITY

See EAST TIMOR - MORTALITY

EAST TIMOR - FINANCE, PUBLIC

Bernan Essential Government Publications, 4611-F Assembly Drive, Lanham MD, 20706-4391, (301) 459-2255, Fax: (800) 865-3450, www.bernan.com; *National Accounts Statistics.*

Economist Intelligence Unit, 111 West 57th Street, New York, NY 10019, (212) 554-0600, Fax: (212) 586-1181, www.eiu.com; *East Timor Country Report.*

International Monetary Fund (IMF), 700 Nineteenth Street, NW, Washington, DC 20431, (202) 623-7000, Fax: (202) 623-4661, www.imf.org; *International Financial Statistics* and *International Financial Statistics Online Service.*

The World Bank, 1818 H Street, NW, Washington, DC 20433, (202) 473-1000, Fax: (202) 477-6391, www.worldbank.org; *Timor-Leste.*

EAST TIMOR - FISHERIES

United Nations Food and Agricultural Organization (FAO), Viale delle Terme di Caracalla, 00100 Rome, Italy, (Dial from U.S. (202) 653-2400), (Fax from U.S. (202) 653 5760), www.fao.org; *FAO Yearbook of Fishery Statistics;* Fishery Databases; FISHSTAT Database. Subjects covered include: Aquaculture production, capture production, fishery commodities; and *The State of Food and Agriculture (SOFA) 2006.*

The World Bank, 1818 H Street, NW, Washington, DC 20433, (202) 473-1000, Fax: (202) 477-6391, www.worldbank.org; *Timor-Leste.*

EAST TIMOR - FOOD

United Nations Food and Agricultural Organization (FAO), Viale delle Terme di Caracalla, 00100 Rome, Italy, (Dial from U.S. (202) 653-2400), (Fax from U.S. (202) 653 5760), www.fao.org; *FAO Production Yearbook 2002* and *The State of Food and Agriculture (SOFA) 2006.*

EAST TIMOR - FOREIGN EXCHANGE RATES

United Nations Statistics Division, New York, NY 10017, (800) 253-9646, Fax: (212) 963-4116, http://unstats.un.org; *World Statistics Pocketbook.*

EAST TIMOR - FORESTS AND FORESTRY

UNESCO Institute for Statistics, C.P. 6128 Succursale Centre-Ville, Montreal, Quebec, H3C 3J7 Canada, (Dial from U.S. (514) 343-6880), (Fax from U.S. (514) 343 6882), www.uis.unesco.org; *Statistical Tables.*

United Nations Food and Agricultural Organization (FAO), Viale delle Terme di Caracalla, 00100 Rome, Italy, (Dial from U.S. (202) 653-2400), (Fax from U.S. (202) 653 5760), www.fao.org; *FAO Yearbook of Forest Products* and *The State of Food and Agriculture (SOFA) 2006.*

United Nations Statistics Division, New York, NY 10017, (800) 253-9646, Fax: (212) 963-4116, http://unstats.un.org; *Demographic Yearbook.*

The World Bank, 1818 H Street, NW, Washington, DC 20433, (202) 473-1000, Fax: (202) 477-6391, www.worldbank.org; *Timor-Leste.*

EAST TIMOR - GROSS DOMESTIC PRODUCT

Economist Intelligence Unit, 111 West 57th Street, New York, NY 10019, (212) 554-0600, Fax: (212) 586-1181, www.eiu.com; *East Timor Country Report.*

United Nations Statistics Division, New York, NY 10017, (800) 253-9646, Fax: (212) 963-4116, http://unstats.un.org; *Statistical Yearbook.*

EAST TIMOR - HIDES AND SKINS INDUSTRY

United Nations Food and Agricultural Organization (FAO), Viale delle Terme di Caracalla, 00100 Rome, Italy, (Dial from U.S. (202) 653-2400), (Fax from U.S. (202) 653 5760), www.fao.org; *FAO Production Yearbook 2002.*

EAST TIMOR - IMPORTS

Economist Intelligence Unit, 111 West 57th Street, New York, NY 10019, (212) 554-0600, Fax: (212) 586-1181, www.eiu.com; *East Timor Country Report.*

United Nations Food and Agricultural Organization (FAO), Viale delle Terme di Caracalla, 00100 Rome, Italy, (Dial from U.S. (202) 653-2400), (Fax from U.S. (202) 653 5760), www.fao.org; *The State of Food and Agriculture (SOFA) 2006.*

EAST TIMOR - INDUSTRIES

Economist Intelligence Unit, 111 West 57th Street, New York, NY 10019, (212) 554-0600, Fax: (212) 586-1181, www.eiu.com; *East Timor Country Report.*

United Nations Industrial Development Organization (UNIDO), 1 United Nations Plaza, New York, NY 10017, (212) 963 6890, Fax: (212) 963-7904, http://unido.org; Industrial Statistics Database 2008 (INDSTAT) and *The International Yearbook of Industrial Statistics 2008.*

The World Bank, 1818 H Street, NW, Washington, DC 20433, (202) 473-1000, Fax: (202) 477-6391, www.worldbank.org; *Timor-Leste.*

EAST TIMOR - INFANT AND MATERNAL MORTALITY

See EAST TIMOR - MORTALITY

EAST TIMOR - INTERNATIONAL TRADE

Economist Intelligence Unit, 111 West 57th Street, New York, NY 10019, (212) 554-0600, Fax: (212) 586-1181, www.eiu.com; *East Timor Country Report.*

United Nations Food and Agricultural Organization (FAO), Viale delle Terme di Caracalla, 00100 Rome, Italy, (Dial from U.S. (202) 653-2400), (Fax from U.S. (202) 653 5760), www.fao.org; *FAO Trade Yearbook* and *The State of Food and Agriculture (SOFA) 2006.*

The World Bank, 1818 H Street, NW, Washington, DC 20433, (202) 473-1000, Fax: (202) 477-6391, www.worldbank.org; *Timor-Leste.*

World Trade Organization (WTO), Centre William Rappard, Rue de Lausanne 154, CH-1211 Geneva 21, Switzerland, www.wto.org; *International Trade Statistics 2006.*

EAST TIMOR - INTERNET USERS

International Telecommunication Union (ITU), Place des Nations, 1211 Geneva 20, Switzerland, www.itu.int; *World Telecommunication/ICT Indicators Database on CD-ROM; World Telecommunication/ICT Indicators Database Online;* and *Yearbook of Statistics - Telecommunication Services (Chronological Time Series 1997-2006).*

The World Bank, 1818 H Street, NW, Washington, DC 20433, (202) 473-1000, Fax: (202) 477-6391, www.worldbank.org; *Timor-Leste.*

EAST TIMOR - LABOR

United Nations Food and Agricultural Organization (FAO), Viale delle Terme di Caracalla, 00100 Rome,

Italy, (Dial from U.S. (202) 653-2400), (Fax from U.S. (202) 653 5760), www.fao.org; *The State of Food and Agriculture (SOFA) 2006.*

EAST TIMOR - LAND USE

United Nations Food and Agricultural Organization (FAO), Viale delle Terme di Caracalla, 00100 Rome, Italy, (Dial from U.S. (202) 653-2400), (Fax from U.S. (202) 653 5760), www.fao.org; *FAO Production Yearbook 2002.*

EAST TIMOR - LIBRARIES

UNESCO Institute for Statistics, C.P. 6128 Succursale Centre-Ville, Montreal, Quebec, H3C 3J7 Canada, (Dial from U.S. (514) 343-6880), (Fax from U.S. (514) 343 6882), www.uis.unesco.org; *Statistical Tables.*

EAST TIMOR - LIFE EXPECTANCY

United Nations Statistics Division, New York, NY 10017, (800) 253-9646, Fax: (212) 963-4116, http://unstats.un.org; *World Statistics Pocketbook.*

EAST TIMOR - LIVESTOCK

United Nations Food and Agricultural Organization (FAO), Viale delle Terme di Caracalla, 00100 Rome, Italy, (Dial from U.S. (202) 653-2400), (Fax from U.S. (202) 653 5760), www.fao.org; *FAO Production Yearbook 2002* and *The State of Food and Agriculture (SOFA) 2006.*

United Nations Statistics Division, New York, NY 10017, (800) 253-9646, Fax: (212) 963-4116, http://unstats.un.org; *Statistical Yearbook.*

EAST TIMOR - MARRIAGE

United Nations Statistics Division, New York, NY 10017, (800) 253-9646, Fax: (212) 963-4116, http://unstats.un.org; *Demographic Yearbook* and *Statistical Yearbook.*

EAST TIMOR - MILK PRODUCTION

See EAST TIMOR - DAIRY PROCESSING

EAST TIMOR - MONEY SUPPLY

Economist Intelligence Unit, 111 West 57th Street, New York, NY 10019, (212) 554-0600, Fax: (212) 586-1181, www.eiu.com; *East Timor Country Report.*

The World Bank, 1818 H Street, NW, Washington, DC 20433, (202) 473-1000, Fax: (202) 477-6391, www.worldbank.org; *Timor-Leste.*

EAST TIMOR - MORTALITY

United Nations Statistics Division, New York, NY 10017, (800) 253-9646, Fax: (212) 963-4116, http://unstats.un.org; *Demographic Yearbook; Statistical Yearbook;* and *World Statistics Pocketbook.*

World Health Organization (WHO), Avenue Appia 20, 1211 Geneve 27, Switzerland, (Telephone in U.S. (212) 331-9081), www.who.int; The WHO Global Atlas of Infectious Diseases.

EAST TIMOR - NUTRITION

United Nations Food and Agricultural Organization (FAO), Viale delle Terme di Caracalla, 00100 Rome, Italy, (Dial from U.S. (202) 653-2400), (Fax from U.S. (202) 653 5760), www.fao.org; *The State of Food and Agriculture (SOFA) 2006.*

EAST TIMOR - PALM OIL PRODUCTION

See EAST TIMOR - CROPS

EAST TIMOR - PAPER

See EAST TIMOR - FORESTS AND FORESTRY

EAST TIMOR - PESTICIDES

United Nations Food and Agricultural Organization (FAO), Viale delle Terme di Caracalla, 00100 Rome, Italy, (Dial from U.S. (202) 653-2400), (Fax from U.S. (202) 653 5760), www.fao.org; *The State of Food and Agriculture (SOFA) 2006.*

EAST TIMOR - PETROLEUM INDUSTRY AND TRADE

PennWell Corporation, 1421 South Sheridan Road, Tulsa, OK 74112, (918) 835-3161, www.pennwell.com; *International Petroleum Encyclopedia 2007.*

United Nations Food and Agricultural Organization (FAO), Viale delle Terme di Caracalla, 00100 Rome, Italy, (Dial from U.S. (202) 653-2400), (Fax from U.S. (202) 653 5760), www.fao.org; *The State of Food and Agriculture (SOFA) 2006.*

EAST TIMOR - POPULATION

Economist Intelligence Unit, 111 West 57th Street, New York, NY 10019, (212) 554-0600, Fax: (212) 586-1181, www.eiu.com; *East Timor Country Report.*

United Nations Food and Agricultural Organization (FAO), Viale delle Terme di Caracalla, 00100 Rome, Italy, (Dial from U.S. (202) 653-2400), (Fax from U.S. (202) 653 5760), www.fao.org; *FAO Production Yearbook 2002.*

United Nations Statistics Division, New York, NY 10017, (800) 253-9646, Fax: (212) 963-4116, http://unstats.un.org; *Demographic Yearbook; Statistical Yearbook;* and *World Statistics Pocketbook.*

The World Bank, 1818 H Street, NW, Washington, DC 20433, (202) 473-1000, Fax: (202) 477-6391, www.worldbank.org; *Timor-Leste.*

World Health Organization (WHO), Avenue Appia 20, 1211 Geneve 27, Switzerland, (Telephone in U.S. (212) 331-9081), www.who.int; *World Health Report 2006.*

EAST TIMOR - POPULATION DENSITY

United Nations Food and Agricultural Organization (FAO), Viale delle Terme di Caracalla, 00100 Rome, Italy, (Dial from U.S. (202) 653-2400), (Fax from U.S. (202) 653 5760), www.fao.org; *The State of Food and Agriculture (SOFA) 2006.*

United Nations Statistics Division, New York, NY 10017, (800) 253-9646, Fax: (212) 963-4116, http://unstats.un.org; *Statistical Yearbook.*

The World Bank, 1818 H Street, NW, Washington, DC 20433, (202) 473-1000, Fax: (202) 477-6391, www.worldbank.org; *Timor-Leste.*

EAST TIMOR - POSTAL SERVICE

United Nations Statistics Division, New York, NY 10017, (800) 253-9646, Fax: (212) 963-4116, http://unstats.un.org; *Statistical Yearbook.*

EAST TIMOR - POWER RESOURCES

United Nations Food and Agricultural Organization (FAO), Viale delle Terme di Caracalla, 00100 Rome, Italy, (Dial from U.S. (202) 653-2400), (Fax from U.S. (202) 653 5760), www.fao.org; *The State of Food and Agriculture (SOFA) 2006.*

United Nations Statistics Division, New York, NY 10017, (800) 253-9646, Fax: (212) 963-4116, http://unstats.un.org; *Statistical Yearbook* and *World Statistics Pocketbook.*

EAST TIMOR - PRICES

United Nations Food and Agricultural Organization (FAO), Viale delle Terme di Caracalla, 00100 Rome, Italy, (Dial from U.S. (202) 653-2400), (Fax from U.S. (202) 653 5760), www.fao.org; *FAO Production Yearbook 2002* and *The State of Food and Agriculture (SOFA) 2006.*

The World Bank, 1818 H Street, NW, Washington, DC 20433, (202) 473-1000, Fax: (202) 477-6391, www.worldbank.org; *Timor-Leste.*

EAST TIMOR - PUBLIC HEALTH

United Nations Statistics Division, New York, NY 10017, (800) 253-9646, Fax: (212) 963-4116, http://unstats.un.org; *Statistical Yearbook.*

The World Bank, 1818 H Street, NW, Washington, DC 20433, (202) 473-1000, Fax: (202) 477-6391, www.worldbank.org; *Timor-Leste.*

World Health Organization (WHO), Avenue Appia 20, 1211 Geneve 27, Switzerland, (Telephone in U.S. (212) 331-9081), www.who.int; The WHO Global Atlas of Infectious Diseases.

EAST TIMOR - RICE PRODUCTION

See EAST TIMOR - CROPS

EAST TIMOR - SHIPPING

United Nations Statistics Division, New York, NY 10017, (800) 253-9646, Fax: (212) 963-4116, http://unstats.un.org; *Statistical Yearbook.*

EAST TIMOR - SOCIAL ECOLOGY

United Nations Statistics Division, New York, NY 10017, (800) 253-9646, Fax: (212) 963-4116, http://unstats.un.org; *World Statistics Pocketbook.*

EAST TIMOR - TELEPHONE

United Nations Statistics Division, New York, NY 10017, (800) 253-9646, Fax: (212) 963-4116, http://unstats.un.org; *World Statistics Pocketbook.*

EAST TIMOR - TOBACCO INDUSTRY

Foreign Agricultural Service (FAS), U.S. Department of Agriculture (USDA), 1400 Independence Avenue, SW, Washington, DC 20250, (202) 720-3935, www.fas.usda.gov; *Tobacco: World Markets and Trade.*

United Nations Statistics Division, New York, NY 10017, (800) 253-9646, Fax: (212) 963-4116, http://unstats.un.org; *Statistical Yearbook.*

EAST TIMOR - TRADE

See EAST TIMOR - INTERNATIONAL TRADE

EAST TIMOR - VITAL STATISTICS

United Nations Statistics Division, New York, NY 10017, (800) 253-9646, Fax: (212) 963-4116, http://unstats.un.org; *Statistical Yearbook.*

World Health Organization (WHO), Avenue Appia 20, 1211 Geneve 27, Switzerland, (Telephone in U.S. (212) 331-9081), www.who.int; *World Health Report 2006.*

EATING AND DRINKING PLACES

See FOOD SERVICES AND DRINKING PLACES

ECONOMIC ASSISTANCE - FOREIGN

U.S. Agency for International Development (USAID), Information Center, Ronald Reagan Building, Washington, D.C. 20523, (202) 712-0000, Fax: (202) 216-3524, www.usaid.gov; *U.S. Overseas Loans and Grants and Assistance from International Organizations.*

ECONOMIC GROWTH RATES

Bureau of Economic Analysis (BEA), U.S. Department of Commerce (DOC), 1441 L Street NW, Washington, DC 20230, (202) 606-9900, www.bea.gov; *2007 Annual Revision of the National Income and Product Accounts (NIPA)* and *Survey of Current Business (SCB).*

ECONOMIC INDICATORS

AFL-CIO, 815 Sixteenth Street, NW, Washington, DC 20006-4104, (202) 637-5000, www.aflcio.org; *A Summary of Economic Markers.*

Bernan Essential Government Publications, 4611-F Assembly Drive, Lanham MD, 20706-4391, (301) 459-2255, Fax: (800) 865-3450, www.bernan.com; *Business Statistics of the United States: Patterns of Economic Change .*

The Brookings Institution, 1775 Massachusetts Avenue, NW, Washington, DC 20036, (202) 797-6000, Fax: (202) 797-6004, www.brook.edu; *Downtown Detroit In Focus: A Profile of Market Opportunity; The Economic Potential of American Cities;* and *Finding Exurbia: America's Fast-Growing Communities at the Metropolitan Fringe.*

Central Administration for Statistics (CAS), PO Box 50-346, Furn el Chebbak, Baabda 1011 2030, Lebanon, www.cas.gov.lb/Index_en.asp; *The National Survey of Household Living Conditions 2004.*

The Conference Board, 845 Third Avenue, New York, NY 10022-6679, (212) 759-0900, Fax: (212) 980-7014, www.conference-board.org; *Business Cycle Indicators.*

Economic and Business Research, Eller College of Management, The University of Arizona, PO Box 210108, Tucson, AZ 85721-0108, (520) 621-2155, Fax: (520) 621-2150, http://ebr.eller.arizona.edu/; *Outlook 2007/2008.*

Economic and Policy Analysis Research Center (EPARC), University of Missouri-Columbia, 10 Professional Building, Columbia, MO 65211, (573) 882-4805, Fax: (573) 882-5563, http://econ.missouri.edu/eparc; *Effect of Wal-Mart Stores on Economic Environment of Rural Communities.*

Economist Intelligence Unit, 111 West 57th Street, New York, NY 10019, (212) 554-0600, Fax: (212) 586-1181, www.eiu.com; *United States of America Country Report.*

Editor and Publisher, 770 Broadway, New York, NY 10003-9595, (800) 336-4380, Fax: (646) 654-5370, www.editorandpublisher.com; *Market Guide 2006.*

National Bureau of Economic Research, Inc. (NBER), 1050 Massachusetts Avenue, Cambridge, MA 02138-5398, (617) 868-3900, Fax: (617) 868-2742, www.nber.org; unpublished data.

Progressive Grocer, 770 Broadway, New York, NY 10003, (866) 890-8541, www.progressivegrocer.com; *The VNU Retail Index.*

STAT-USA, HCHB Room 4885, U.S. Department of Commerce, Washington, DC 20230, (202) 482-1986, Fax: (202) 482-2164, www.stat-usa.gov; STAT-USA/Internet.

Thomson Financial, 195 Broadway, New York, NY 10007, (646) 822-2000, www.thomson.com; *Thomson Financial News.*

U.S. Census Bureau, Center for Economic Studies, 4600 Silver Hill Road, Washington DC 20233, (301) 457-1235, www.ces.census.gov; Economic Census (web app).

U.S. Department of Commerce (DOC), Economics and Statistics Administration (ESA), 1401 Constitution Avenue, NW, Washington, DC 20230, (800) 782-8872, www.esa.doc.gov; *Impact of Increased Natural Gas Prices on U.S. Economy and Industries: Report to Congress* and *Overview of the Nation's Economy.*

U.S. Library of Congress (LOC), Congressional Research Service (CRS), The Library of Congress, 101 Independence Avenue, SE, Washington, DC 20540-7500, (202) 707-5700, www.loc.gov/crsinfo; *The Economic Impact of Cyber-Attacks.*

ECONOMIC INDICATORS - FOREIGN COUNTRIES

Banque de France, 48 rue Croix des Petits champs, 75001 Paris, France, www.banque-france.fr/home.htm; *Key Data for the Euro Area* and *Public Finance.*

Central Statistical Organization (CSO), Ministry of National Planning and Economic Development, Building 32, Nay Pyi Taw, Myanmar, www.csostat.gov.mm; *Selected Monthly Economic Indicators (December 2007).*

Department of Statistics (DOS), PO Box 2015, Amman 11181, Jordan, www.dos.gov.jo; Economic Surveys.

Economics, Statistics Fiscal Analysis Division, Department of Provincial Treasury, PO Box 2000, Charlottetown, Prince Edward Island C1A 7N8, Canada, (Dial from U.S. (902) 368-4050), (Fax from U.S. (902) 368-6575), www.gov.pe.ca/pt/index.php3; *A First Look at the 2001 Census of Population* and *2006 Progress Report on the PEI Economy.*

Eurostat, Batiment Jean Monnet, Rue Alcide de Gasperi, L-2920 Luxembourg, http://epp.eurostat.ec.europa.eu; *Consumers in Europe - Facts and Figures on Services of General Interest.*

International Food Policy Research Institute (IFPRI), 2033 K Street, NW, Washington, D.C., 2006, (202) 862-5600, www.ifpri.org; *The World Food Situation: New Driving Forces and Required Actions.*

International Monetary Fund (IMF), 700 Nineteenth Street, NW, Washington, DC 20431, (202) 623-7000, Fax: (202) 623-4661, www.imf.org; *GFSR Market Update; Global Financial Stability Report (April 2008 Edition);* and *World Economic Outlook Database (April 2008 Edition).*

International Organization for Migration (IOM), 17, Route des Morillons, CH-1211 Geneva 19, Switzerland, www.iom.int; *Migration and Development: New Strategic Outlooks and Practical Ways Forward - The Cases of Angola and Zambia; Migration and Poverty Alleviation in China;* and *World Migration 2005: Costs and Benefits of International Migration.*

International Trade Administration (ITA), U.S. Department of Commerce (DOC), 1401 Constitution Avenue, NW, Washington, DC 20230, (800) USA-TRAD(E), Fax: (202) 482-4473, www.ita.doc.gov; unpublished data.

Organisation for Economic Cooperation and Development (OECD), 2 rue Andre Pascal, F-75775 Paris Cedex 16, France, (Telephone in U.S. (202) 785-6323), (Fax in U.S. (202) 785-0350), www.oecd.org; *OECD Science, Technology and Industry Outlook 2006.*

Thomson Financial, 195 Broadway, New York, NY 10007, (646) 822-2000, www.thomson.com; *International Financing Review (IFR).*

United Nations Conference on Trade and Development (UNCTAD), DC2-1120, United Nations, New York, NY 10017, (212) 963-0027, www.unctad.org; *Development and Globalization: Facts and Figures.*

United Nations Economic Commission for Europe (UNECE), Information Service, Palais des Nations, CH - 1211 Geneva 10, Switzerland, www.unece.org; *statunece Database.*

ECONOMISTS - LABOR FORCE

U.S. Bureau of Labor Statistics (BLS), Postal Square Building, 2 Massachusetts Avenue, NE, Washington, DC 20212-0001, (202) 691-5200, Fax: (202) 691-6325, www.bls.gov; *Employment and Earnings (EE)* and unpublished data.

ECOTOURISM

United Nations World Tourism Organization (UNWTO), Capitan Haya 42, 28020 Madrid, Spain, www.world-tourism.org; *The British Ecotourism Market; The Canadian Ecotourism Market; The French Ecotourism Market; The German Ecotourism Market;* and *The Italian Ecotourism Market.*

ECSTASY (DRUG)

Royal Canadian Mounted Police (RCMP), 1200 Vanier Parkway, Ottawa, ON K1A 0R2, Canada, (613) 993-7267, www.rcmp-grc.gc.ca; *Drug Situation in Canada - 2004.*

United Nations Office on Drugs and Crime (UNODC), Vienna International Centre, PO Box 500, A-1400 Vienna, Austria, www.unodc.org; *World Drug Report 2006.*

ECUADOR - NATIONAL STATISTICAL OFFICE

Instituto Nacional de Estadistica y Censos (INEC), 10 de Agosto 229, Quito, Ecuador, www.inec.gov.ec; National Data Center.

ECUADOR - PRIMARY STATISTICS SOURCES

Banco Central del Ecuador, Av. Amazonas N34-451 y Av. Atahualpa, Quito, Ecuador, www.bce.fin.ec; *Boletin anuario (Annual Bulletin)* and unpublished data.

Instituto Nacional de Estadistica y Censos (INEC), 10 de Agosto 229, Quito, Ecuador, www.inec.gov.ec; *Censo de Poblacion y Vivienda 2001* (Census of Population and Housing 2001).

ECUADOR - AGRICULTURAL MACHINERY

Economist Intelligence Unit, 111 West 57th Street, New York, NY 10019, (212) 554-0600, Fax: (212) 586-1181, www.eiu.com; *Business Latin America.*

United Nations Statistics Division, New York, NY 10017, (800) 253-9646, Fax: (212) 963-4116, http://unstats.un.org; *Statistical Yearbook.*

ECUADOR - AGRICULTURE

Economist Intelligence Unit, 111 West 57th Street, New York, NY 10019, (212) 554-0600, Fax: (212) 586-1181, www.eiu.com; *Business Latin America* and *Ecuador Country Report.*

Euromonitor International, Inc., 224 S. Michigan Avenue, Suite 1500, Chicago, IL 60604, (312) 922-1115, Fax: (312) 922-1157, www.euromonitor.com; *International Marketing Data and Statistics 2008* and *World Marketing Data and Statistics.*

Inter-American Development Bank (IDB), 1300 New York Avenue, NW, Washington, DC 20577, (202) 623-1000, Fax: (202) 623-3096, www.iadb.org; *The Politics of Policies: Economic and Social Progress in Latin America - 2006 Report.*

M.E. Sharpe, 80 Business Park Drive, Armonk, NY 10504, (800) 541-6563, Fax: (914) 273-2106, www.mesharpe.com; *The Illustrated Book of World Rankings.*

Palgrave Macmillan Ltd., Houndmills, Basingstoke, Hampshire, RG21 6XS, England, (Telephone in U.S. (888) 330-8477), (Fax in U.S. (800) 672-2054), www.palgrave.com; *The Statesman's Yearbook 2008.*

Taylor and Francis Group, An Informa Business, 2 Park Square, Milton Park, Abingdon, Oxford OX14 4RN, United Kingdom, (Dial from U.S. (212) 216-7800), (Fax from U.S. (212) 564-7854), www.tandf.co.uk; *The Europa World Year Book.*

UCLA Latin American Institute, 10343 Bunche Hall, Box 951447, Los Angeles, CA 90095-1447, (310) 825-4571, Fax: (310) 206-6859, www.international.ucla.edu/lac; *Statistical Abstract of Latin America.*

United Nations Conference on Trade and Development (UNCTAD), DC2-1120, United Nations, New York, NY 10017, (212) 963-0027, www.unctad.org; *UNCTAD Commodity Yearbook.*

United Nations Food and Agricultural Organization (FAO), Viale delle Terme di Caracalla, 00100 Rome, Italy, (Dial from U.S. (202) 653-2400), (Fax from U.S. (202) 653 5760), www.fao.org; AQUASTAT; *FAO Production Yearbook 2002; FAO Trade Yearbook;* and *The State of Food and Agriculture (SOFA) 2006.*

United Nations Statistics Division, New York, NY 10017, (800) 253-9646, Fax: (212) 963-4116, http://unstats.un.org; *Statistical Yearbook* and *Statistical Yearbook for Latin America and the Caribbean 2004.*

The World Bank, 1818 H Street, NW, Washington, DC 20433, (202) 473-1000, Fax: (202) 477-6391, www.worldbank.org; *Ecuador* and *World Development Indicators (WDI) 2008.*

ECUADOR - AIRLINES

Central Intelligence Agency, Office of Public Affairs, Washington, DC 20505, (703) 482-0623, Fax: (703) 482-1739, www.cia.gov; *The World Factbook.*

Economist Intelligence Unit, 111 West 57th Street, New York, NY 10019, (212) 554-0600, Fax: (212) 586-1181, www.eiu.com; *Business Latin America.*

International Civil Aviation Organization (ICAO), External Relations and Public Information Office (EPO), 999 University Street, Montreal, Quebec H3C 5H7, Canada, (Dial from U.S. (514) 954-8219), (Fax from U.S. (514) 954-6077), www.icao.int; *Civil Aviation Statistics of the World.*

M.E. Sharpe, 80 Business Park Drive, Armonk, NY 10504, (800) 541-6563, Fax: (914) 273-2106, www.mesharpe.com; *The Illustrated Book of World Rankings.*

Palgrave Macmillan Ltd., Houndmills, Basingstoke, Hampshire, RG21 6XS, England, (Telephone in U.S. (888) 330-8477), (Fax in U.S. (800) 672-2054), www.palgrave.com; *The Statesman's Yearbook 2008.*

Taylor and Francis Group, An Informa Business, 2 Park Square, Milton Park, Abingdon, Oxford OX14 4RN, United Kingdom, (Dial from U.S. (212) 216-7800), (Fax from U.S. (212) 564-7854), www.tandf.co.uk; *The Europa World Year Book.*

United Nations Statistics Division, New York, NY 10017, (800) 253-9646, Fax: (212) 963-4116, http://unstats.un.org; *Statistical Yearbook.*

ECUADOR - ALUMINUM PRODUCTION

See ECUADOR - MINERAL INDUSTRIES

ECUADOR - AREA

Economist Intelligence Unit, 111 West 57th Street, New York, NY 10019, (212) 554-0600, Fax: (212) 586-1181, www.eiu.com; *Business Latin America.*

ECUADOR - ARMED FORCES

Central Intelligence Agency, Office of Public Affairs, Washington, DC 20505, (703) 482-0623, Fax: (703) 482-1739, www.cia.gov; *The World Factbook.*

Economist Intelligence Unit, 111 West 57th Street, New York, NY 10019, (212) 554-0600, Fax: (212) 586-1181, www.eiu.com; *Business Latin America.*

Euromonitor International, Inc., 224 S. Michigan Avenue, Suite 1500, Chicago, IL 60604, (312) 922-1115, Fax: (312) 922-1157, www.euromonitor.com; *World Marketing Data and Statistics.*

International Institute for Strategic Studies (IISS), Arundel House, 13-15 Arundel Street, Temple Place, London WC2R 3DX, England, www.iiss.org; *The Military Balance 2007.*

International Monetary Fund (IMF), 700 Nineteenth Street, NW, Washington, DC 20431, (202) 623-7000, Fax: (202) 623-4661, www.imf.org; *Government Finance Statistics Yearbook (2008 Edition).*

Palgrave Macmillan Ltd., Houndmills, Basingstoke, Hampshire, RG21 6XS, England, (Telephone in U.S. (888) 330-8477), (Fax in U.S. (800) 672-2054), www.palgrave.com; *The Statesman's Yearbook 2008.*

U.S. Department of State (DOS), 2201 C Street NW, Washington, DC 20520, (202) 647-4000, www.state.gov; *World Military Expenditures and Arms Transfers (WMEAT).*

UCLA Latin American Institute, 10343 Bunche Hall, Box 951447, Los Angeles, CA 90095-1447, (310) 825-4571, Fax: (310) 206-6859, www.international.ucla.edu/lac; *Statistical Abstract of Latin America.*

United Nations Statistics Division, New York, NY 10017, (800) 253-9646, Fax: (212) 963-4116, http://unstats.un.org; *Human Development Report 2006.*

ECUADOR - BALANCE OF PAYMENTS

Economist Intelligence Unit, 111 West 57th Street, New York, NY 10019, (212) 554-0600, Fax: (212) 586-1181, www.eiu.com; *Business Latin America.*

Inter-American Development Bank (IDB), 1300 New York Avenue, NW, Washington, DC 20577, (202) 623-1000, Fax: (202) 623-3096, www.iadb.org; *The Politics of Policies: Economic and Social Progress in Latin America - 2006 Report.*

International Monetary Fund (IMF), 700 Nineteenth Street, NW, Washington, DC 20431, (202) 623-7000, Fax: (202) 623-4661, www.imf.org; *Balance of Payments Statistics Newsletter; Balance of Payments Statistics Yearbook 2007;* and *International Financial Statistics Yearbook 2007.*

Organization of American States (OAS), 17th Street Constitution Avenue NW, Washington, DC 20006, (202) 458-3000, www.oas.org; *The OAS in Transition: 1994-2004.*

Taylor and Francis Group, An Informa Business, 2 Park Square, Milton Park, Abingdon, Oxford OX14 4RN, United Kingdom, (Dial from U.S. (212) 216-7800), (Fax from U.S. (212) 564-7854), www.tandf.co.uk; *The Europa World Year Book.*

UCLA Latin American Institute, 10343 Bunche Hall, Box 951447, Los Angeles, CA 90095-1447, (310) 825-4571, Fax: (310) 206-6859, www.international.ucla.edu/lac; *Statistical Abstract of Latin America.*

United Nations Conference on Trade and Development (UNCTAD), DC2-1120, United Nations, New York, NY 10017, (212) 963-0027, www.unctad.org; *Handbook of Statistics 2005.*

United Nations Statistics Division, New York, NY 10017, (800) 253-9646, Fax: (212) 963-4116, http://unstats.un.org; *Economic Survey of Latin America and the Caribbean 2004-2005* and *Statistical Yearbook for Latin America and the Caribbean 2004.*

The World Bank, 1818 H Street, NW, Washington, DC 20433, (202) 473-1000, Fax: (202) 477-6391, www.worldbank.org; *Ecuador; World Development Indicators (WDI) 2008;* and *World Development Report 2008.*

ECUADOR - BANANAS

See ECUADOR - CROPS

ECUADOR - BANKS AND BANKING

Euromonitor International, Inc., 224 S. Michigan Avenue, Suite 1500, Chicago, IL 60604, (312) 922-1115, Fax: (312) 922-1157, www.euromonitor.com; *World Marketing Data and Statistics.*

Inter-American Development Bank (IDB), 1300 New York Avenue, NW, Washington, DC 20577, (202) 623-1000, Fax: (202) 623-3096, www.iadb.org; *The Politics of Policies: Economic and Social Progress in Latin America - 2006 Report.*

International Monetary Fund (IMF), 700 Nineteenth Street, NW, Washington, DC 20431, (202) 623-7000, Fax: (202) 623-4661, www.imf.org; *International Financial Statistics Yearbook 2007.*

M.E. Sharpe, 80 Business Park Drive, Armonk, NY 10504, (800) 541-6563, Fax: (914) 273-2106, www.mesharpe.com; *The Illustrated Book of World Rankings.*

Palgrave Macmillan Ltd., Houndmills, Basingstoke, Hampshire, RG21 6XS, England, (Telephone in U.S. (888) 330-8477), (Fax in U.S. (800) 672-2054), www.palgrave.com; *The Statesman's Yearbook 2008.*

Taylor and Francis Group, An Informa Business, 2 Park Square, Milton Park, Abingdon, Oxford OX14 4RN, United Kingdom, (Dial from U.S. (212) 216-7800), (Fax from U.S. (212) 564-7854), www.tandf.co.uk; *The Europa World Year Book.*

United Nations Statistics Division, New York, NY 10017, (800) 253-9646, Fax: (212) 963-4116, http://unstats.un.org; *Statistical Yearbook* and *Statistical Yearbook for Latin America and the Caribbean 2004.*

ECUADOR - BARLEY PRODUCTION

See ECUADOR - CROPS

ECUADOR - BEVERAGE INDUSTRY

M.E. Sharpe, 80 Business Park Drive, Armonk, NY 10504, (800) 541-6563, Fax: (914) 273-2106, www.mesharpe.com; *The Illustrated Book of World Rankings.*

United Nations Statistics Division, New York, NY 10017, (800) 253-9646, Fax: (212) 963-4116, http://unstats.un.org; *Statistical Yearbook.*

ECUADOR - BIRTH CONTROL

UCLA Latin American Institute, 10343 Bunche Hall, Box 951447, Los Angeles, CA 90095-1447, (310) 825-4571, Fax: (310) 206-6859, www.international.ucla.edu/lac; *Statistical Abstract of Latin America.*

ECUADOR - BONDS

Inter-American Development Bank (IDB), 1300 New York Avenue, NW, Washington, DC 20577, (202) 623-1000, Fax: (202) 623-3096, www.iadb.org; *The Politics of Policies: Economic and Social Progress in Latin America - 2006 Report.*

ECUADOR - BROADCASTING

Central Intelligence Agency, Office of Public Affairs, Washington, DC 20505, (703) 482-0623, Fax: (703) 482-1739, www.cia.gov; *The World Factbook.*

Euromonitor International, Inc., 224 S. Michigan Avenue, Suite 1500, Chicago, IL 60604, (312) 922-1115, Fax: (312) 922-1157, www.euromonitor.com; *World Marketing Data and Statistics.*

M.E. Sharpe, 80 Business Park Drive, Armonk, NY 10504, (800) 541-6563, Fax: (914) 273-2106, www.mesharpe.com; *The Illustrated Book of World Rankings.*

Palgrave Macmillan Ltd., Houndmills, Basingstoke, Hampshire, RG21 6XS, England, (Telephone in U.S. (888) 330-8477), (Fax in U.S. (800) 672-2054), www.palgrave.com; *The Statesman's Yearbook 2008.*

WRTH Publications Limited, PO Box 290, Oxford OX2 7FT, UK, www.wrth.com; *World Radio TV Handbook 2007.*

ECUADOR - BUDGET

Central Intelligence Agency, Office of Public Affairs, Washington, DC 20505, (703) 482-0623, Fax: (703) 482-1739, www.cia.gov; *The World Factbook.*

ECUADOR - BUSINESS

Inter-American Development Bank (IDB), 1300 New York Avenue, NW, Washington, DC 20577, (202) 623-1000, Fax: (202) 623-3096, www.iadb.org; *The Politics of Policies: Economic and Social Progress in Latin America - 2006 Report.*

United Nations Statistics Division, New York, NY 10017, (800) 253-9646, Fax: (212) 963-4116, http://unstats.un.org; *Statistical Yearbook.*

ECUADOR - CACAO

See ECUADOR - CROPS

ECUADOR - CAPITAL INVESTMENTS

Inter-American Development Bank (IDB), 1300 New York Avenue, NW, Washington, DC 20577, (202) 623-1000, Fax: (202) 623-3096, www.iadb.org; *The Politics of Policies: Economic and Social Progress in Latin America - 2006 Report.*

ECUADOR - CAPITAL LEVY

Inter-American Development Bank (IDB), 1300 New York Avenue, NW, Washington, DC 20577, (202) 623-1000, Fax: (202) 623-3096, www.iadb.org; *The Politics of Policies: Economic and Social Progress in Latin America - 2006 Report.*

International Monetary Fund (IMF), 700 Nineteenth Street, NW, Washington, DC 20431, (202) 623-7000, Fax: (202) 623-4661, www.imf.org; *Government Finance Statistics Yearbook (2008 Edition).*

ECUADOR - CATTLE

See ECUADOR - LIVESTOCK

ECUADOR - CHICKENS

See ECUADOR - LIVESTOCK

ECUADOR - CHILDBIRTH - STATISTICS

Central Intelligence Agency, Office of Public Affairs, Washington, DC 20505, (703) 482-0623, Fax: (703) 482-1739, www.cia.gov; *The World Factbook.*

Euromonitor International, Inc., 224 S. Michigan Avenue, Suite 1500, Chicago, IL 60604, (312) 922-1115, Fax: (312) 922-1157, www.euromonitor.com; *International Marketing Data and Statistics 2008* and *The World Economic Factbook 2008.*

M.E. Sharpe, 80 Business Park Drive, Armonk, NY 10504, (800) 541-6563, Fax: (914) 273-2106, www.mesharpe.com; *The Illustrated Book of World Rankings.*

Palgrave Macmillan Ltd., Houndmills, Basingstoke, Hampshire, RG21 6XS, England, (Telephone in U.S. (888) 330-8477), (Fax in U.S. (800) 672-2054), www.palgrave.com; *The Statesman's Yearbook 2008.*

Taylor and Francis Group, An Informa Business, 2 Park Square, Milton Park, Abingdon, Oxford OX14 4RN, United Kingdom, (Dial from U.S. (212) 216-7800), (Fax from U.S. (212) 564-7854), www.tandf.co.uk; *The Europa World Year Book.*

United Nations Statistics Division, New York, NY 10017, (800) 253-9646, Fax: (212) 963-4116, http://unstats.un.org; *Demographic Yearbook.*

The World Bank, 1818 H Street, NW, Washington, DC 20433, (202) 473-1000, Fax: (202) 477-6391, www.worldbank.org; *World Development Indicators (WDI) 2008.*

World Health Organization (WHO), Avenue Appia 20, 1211 Geneve 27, Switzerland, (Telephone in U.S. (212) 331-9081), www.who.int; *World Health Report 2006.*

ECUADOR - CLIMATE

M.E. Sharpe, 80 Business Park Drive, Armonk, NY 10504, (800) 541-6563, Fax: (914) 273-2106, www.mesharpe.com; *The Illustrated Book of World Rankings.*

Palgrave Macmillan Ltd., Houndmills, Basingstoke, Hampshire, RG21 6XS, England, (Telephone in U.S. (888) 330-8477), (Fax in U.S. (800) 672-2054), www.palgrave.com; *The Statesman's Yearbook 2008.*

ECUADOR - COAL PRODUCTION

See ECUADOR - MINERAL INDUSTRIES

ECUADOR - COCOA PRODUCTION

See ECUADOR - CROPS

ECUADOR - COFFEE

See ECUADOR - CROPS

ECUADOR - COMMERCE

Palgrave Macmillan Ltd., Houndmills, Basingstoke, Hampshire, RG21 6XS, England, (Telephone in U.S. (888) 330-8477), (Fax in U.S. (800) 672-2054), www.palgrave.com; *The Statesman's Yearbook 2008.*

ECUADOR - COMMODITY EXCHANGES

Commodity Research Bureau, 330 South Wells Street, Suite 612, Chicago, IL 60606-7110, (800) 621-5271, Fax: (312) 939-4135, www.crbtrader.com; *2006 CRB Commodity Yearbook and CD.*

International Monetary Fund (IMF), 700 Nineteenth Street, NW, Washington, DC 20431, (202) 623-7000, Fax: (202) 623-4661, www.imf.org; *IMF Primary Commodity Prices.*

United Nations Food and Agricultural Organization (FAO), Viale delle Terme di Caracalla, 00100 Rome, Italy, (Dial from U.S. (202) 653-2400), (Fax from U.S. (202) 653 5760), www.fao.org; *The State of Food and Agriculture (SOFA) 2006.*

ECUADOR - COMMUNICATION AND TRAFFIC

United Nations Statistics Division, New York, NY 10017, (800) 253-9646, Fax: (212) 963-4116, http://unstats.un.org; *Statistical Yearbook.*

ECUADOR - CONSTRUCTION INDUSTRY

Economist Intelligence Unit, 111 West 57th Street, New York, NY 10019, (212) 554-0600, Fax: (212) 586-1181, www.eiu.com; *Business Latin America.*

Inter-American Development Bank (IDB), 1300 New York Avenue, NW, Washington, DC 20577, (202) 623-1000, Fax: (202) 623-3096, www.iadb.org; *The Politics of Policies: Economic and Social Progress in Latin America - 2006 Report.*

M.E. Sharpe, 80 Business Park Drive, Armonk, NY 10504, (800) 541-6563, Fax: (914) 273-2106, www.mesharpe.com; *The Illustrated Book of World Rankings.*

UCLA Latin American Institute, 10343 Bunche Hall, Box 951447, Los Angeles, CA 90095-1447, (310) 825-4571, Fax: (310) 206-6859, www.international.ucla.edu/lac; *Statistical Abstract of Latin America.*

United Nations Statistics Division, New York, NY 10017, (800) 253-9646, Fax: (212) 963-4116, http://unstats.un.org; *Statistical Yearbook.*

ECUADOR - CONSUMER COOPERATIVES

UCLA Latin American Institute, 10343 Bunche Hall, Box 951447, Los Angeles, CA 90095-1447, (310) 825-4571, Fax: (310) 206-6859, www.international.ucla.edu/lac; *Statistical Abstract of Latin America.*

ECUADOR - CONSUMER PRICE INDEXES

International Labour Office, I.L.O. Publications, 4 route des Morillons, CH-1211 Geneva 22, Switzerland, (Telephone in U.S. (202) 653-7652), (Fax in U.S. (202) 653-7687), www.ilo.org; *Yearbook of Labour Statistics 2006.*

Taylor and Francis Group, An Informa Business, 2 Park Square, Milton Park, Abingdon, Oxford OX14 4RN, United Kingdom, (Dial from U.S. (212) 216-7800), (Fax from U.S. (212) 564-7854), www.tandf.co.uk; *The Europa World Year Book.*

United Nations Statistics Division, New York, NY 10017, (800) 253-9646, Fax: (212) 963-4116, http://unstats.un.org; *Statistical Yearbook.*

The World Bank, 1818 H Street, NW, Washington, DC 20433, (202) 473-1000, Fax: (202) 477-6391, www.worldbank.org; *Ecuador.*

ECUADOR - CONSUMPTION (ECONOMICS)

Economist Intelligence Unit, 111 West 57th Street, New York, NY 10019, (212) 554-0600, Fax: (212) 586-1181, www.eiu.com; *Business Latin America.*

Inter-American Development Bank (IDB), 1300 New York Avenue, NW, Washington, DC 20577, (202) 623-1000, Fax: (202) 623-3096, www.iadb.org; *The Politics of Policies: Economic and Social Progress in Latin America - 2006 Report.*

United Nations Statistics Division, New York, NY 10017, (800) 253-9646, Fax: (212) 963-4116, http://unstats.un.org; *Statistical Yearbook for Latin America and the Caribbean 2004.*

The World Bank, 1818 H Street, NW, Washington, DC 20433, (202) 473-1000, Fax: (202) 477-6391, www.worldbank.org; *World Development Report 2008.*

ECUADOR - COPPER INDUSTRY AND TRADE

See ECUADOR - MINERAL INDUSTRIES

ECUADOR - CORN INDUSTRY

See ECUADOR - CROPS

ECUADOR - COTTON

See ECUADOR - CROPS

ECUADOR - CRIME

International Criminal Police Organization (INTERPOL), General Secretariat, 200 quai Charles de Gaulle, 69006 Lyon, France, www.interpol.int; *International Crime Statistics.*

ECUADOR - CROPS

Economist Intelligence Unit, 111 West 57th Street, New York, NY 10019, (212) 554-0600, Fax: (212) 586-1181, www.eiu.com; *Business Latin America.*

International Monetary Fund (IMF), 700 Nineteenth Street, NW, Washington, DC 20431, (202) 623-7000, Fax: (202) 623-4661, www.imf.org; *International Financial Statistics Yearbook 2007.*

M.E. Sharpe, 80 Business Park Drive, Armonk, NY 10504, (800) 541-6563, Fax: (914) 273-2106, www.mesharpe.com; *The Illustrated Book of World Rankings.*

Organization of American States (OAS), 17th Street Constitution Avenue NW, Washington, DC 20006, (202) 458-3000, www.oas.org; *The OAS in Transition: 1994-2004.*

Palgrave Macmillan Ltd., Houndmills, Basingstoke, Hampshire, RG21 6XS, England, (Telephone in U.S. (888) 330-8477), (Fax in U.S. (800) 672-2054), www.palgrave.com; *The Statesman's Yearbook 2008.*

Taylor and Francis Group, An Informa Business, 2 Park Square, Milton Park, Abingdon, Oxford OX14 4RN, United Kingdom, (Dial from U.S. (212) 216-7800), (Fax from U.S. (212) 564-7854), www.tandf.co.uk; *The Europa World Year Book.*

United Nations Conference on Trade and Development (UNCTAD), DC2-1120, United Nations, New York, NY 10017, (212) 963-0027, www.unctad.org; *UNCTAD Commodity Yearbook.*

United Nations Food and Agricultural Organization (FAO), Viale delle Terme di Caracalla, 00100 Rome, Italy, (Dial from U.S. (202) 653-2400), (Fax from U.S. (202) 653 5760), www.fao.org; *FAO Production Yearbook 2002* and *The State of Food and Agriculture (SOFA) 2006.*

United Nations Statistics Division, New York, NY 10017, (800) 253-9646, Fax: (212) 963-4116, http://unstats.un.org; *Statistical Yearbook.*

ECUADOR - CUSTOMS ADMINISTRATION

Inter-American Development Bank (IDB), 1300 New York Avenue, NW, Washington, DC 20577, (202) 623-1000, Fax: (202) 623-3096, www.iadb.org; *The Politics of Policies: Economic and Social Progress in Latin America - 2006 Report.*

International Monetary Fund (IMF), 700 Nineteenth Street, NW, Washington, DC 20431, (202) 623-7000, Fax: (202) 623-4661, www.imf.org; *Government Finance Statistics Yearbook (2008 Edition).*

Palgrave Macmillan Ltd., Houndmills, Basingstoke, Hampshire, RG21 6XS, England, (Telephone in U.S. (888) 330-8477), (Fax in U.S. (800) 672-2054), www.palgrave.com; *The Statesman's Yearbook 2008.*

ECUADOR - DAIRY PROCESSING

M.E. Sharpe, 80 Business Park Drive, Armonk, NY 10504, (800) 541-6563, Fax: (914) 273-2106, www.mesharpe.com; *The Illustrated Book of World Rankings.*

Palgrave Macmillan Ltd., Houndmills, Basingstoke, Hampshire, RG21 6XS, England, (Telephone in U.S. (888) 330-8477), (Fax in U.S. (800) 672-2054), www.palgrave.com; *The Statesman's Yearbook 2008.*

Taylor and Francis Group, An Informa Business, 2 Park Square, Milton Park, Abingdon, Oxford OX14 4RN, United Kingdom, (Dial from U.S. (212) 216-7800), (Fax from U.S. (212) 564-7854), www.tandf.co.uk; *The Europa World Year Book.*

United Nations Food and Agricultural Organization (FAO), Viale delle Terme di Caracalla, 00100 Rome, Italy, (Dial from U.S. (202) 653-2400), (Fax from U.S. (202) 653 5760), www.fao.org; *The State of Food and Agriculture (SOFA) 2006.*

United Nations Statistics Division, New York, NY 10017, (800) 253-9646, Fax: (212) 963-4116, http://unstats.un.org; *Statistical Yearbook.*

ECUADOR - DEATH RATES

See ECUADOR - MORTALITY

ECUADOR - DEBT

Economist Intelligence Unit, 111 West 57th Street, New York, NY 10019, (212) 554-0600, Fax: (212) 586-1181, www.eiu.com; *Business Latin America.*

The World Bank, 1818 H Street, NW, Washington, DC 20433, (202) 473-1000, Fax: (202) 477-6391, www.worldbank.org; *Global Development Finance 2007.*

ECUADOR - DEBTS, EXTERNAL

Economist Intelligence Unit, 111 West 57th Street, New York, NY 10019, (212) 554-0600, Fax: (212) 586-1181, www.eiu.com; *Business Latin America.*

Inter-American Development Bank (IDB), 1300 New York Avenue, NW, Washington, DC 20577, (202) 623-1000, Fax: (202) 623-3096, www.iadb.org; *The Politics of Policies: Economic and Social Progress in Latin America - 2006 Report.*

Palgrave Macmillan Ltd., Houndmills, Basingstoke, Hampshire, RG21 6XS, England, (Telephone in U.S. (888) 330-8477), (Fax in U.S. (800) 672-2054), www.palgrave.com; *The Statesman's Yearbook 2008.*

United Nations Statistics Division, New York, NY 10017, (800) 253-9646, Fax: (212) 963-4116, http://unstats.un.org; *Economic Survey of Latin America and the Caribbean 2004-2005.*

The World Bank, 1818 H Street, NW, Washington, DC 20433, (202) 473-1000, Fax: (202) 477-6391, www.worldbank.org; *Global Development Finance 2007; World Development Indicators (WDI) 2008;* and *World Development Report 2008.*

ECUADOR - DEFENSE EXPENDITURES

See ECUADOR - ARMED FORCES

ECUADOR - DEMOGRAPHY

Euromonitor International, Inc., 224 S. Michigan Avenue, Suite 1500, Chicago, IL 60604, (312) 922-1115, Fax: (312) 922-1157, www.euromonitor.com; *International Marketing Data and Statistics 2008; The World Economic Factbook 2008;* and *World Marketing Data and Statistics.*

M.E. Sharpe, 80 Business Park Drive, Armonk, NY 10504, (800) 541-6563, Fax: (914) 273-2106, www.mesharpe.com; *The Illustrated Book of World Rankings.*

UCLA Latin American Institute, 10343 Bunche Hall, Box 951447, Los Angeles, CA 90095-1447, (310) 825-4571, Fax: (310) 206-6859, www.international.ucla.edu/lac; *Statistical Abstract of Latin America.*

United Nations Statistics Division, New York, NY 10017, (800) 253-9646, Fax: (212) 963-4116, http://unstats.un.org; *Human Development Report 2006.*

The World Bank, 1818 H Street, NW, Washington, DC 20433, (202) 473-1000, Fax: (202) 477-6391, www.worldbank.org; *Ecuador.*

ECUADOR - DIAMONDS

See ECUADOR - MINERAL INDUSTRIES

ECUADOR - DISPOSABLE INCOME

Inter-American Development Bank (IDB), 1300 New York Avenue, NW, Washington, DC 20577, (202) 623-1000, Fax: (202) 623-3096, www.iadb.org; *The Politics of Policies: Economic and Social Progress in Latin America - 2006 Report.*

International Monetary Fund (IMF), 700 Nineteenth Street, NW, Washington, DC 20431, (202) 623-7000, Fax: (202) 623-4661, www.imf.org; *International Financial Statistics Yearbook 2007.*

M.E. Sharpe, 80 Business Park Drive, Armonk, NY 10504, (800) 541-6563, Fax: (914) 273-2106, www.mesharpe.com; *The Illustrated Book of World Rankings.*

United Nations Statistics Division, New York, NY 10017, (800) 253-9646, Fax: (212) 963-4116, http://unstats.un.org; *National Accounts Statistics: Compendium of Income Distribution Statistics; Statistical Yearbook;* and *Statistical Yearbook for Latin America and the Caribbean 2004.*

ECUADOR - DIVORCE

M.E. Sharpe, 80 Business Park Drive, Armonk, NY 10504, (800) 541-6563, Fax: (914) 273-2106, www.mesharpe.com; *The Illustrated Book of World Rankings.*

United Nations Statistics Division, New York, NY 10017, (800) 253-9646, Fax: (212) 963-4116, http://unstats.un.org; *Demographic Yearbook* and *Statistical Yearbook.*

ECUADOR - ECONOMIC ASSISTANCE

Inter-American Development Bank (IDB), 1300 New York Avenue, NW, Washington, DC 20577, (202) 623-1000, Fax: (202) 623-3096, www.iadb.org; *The Politics of Policies: Economic and Social Progress in Latin America - 2006 Report.*

United Nations Statistics Division, New York, NY 10017, (800) 253-9646, Fax: (212) 963-4116, http://unstats.un.org; *Statistical Yearbook.*

ECUADOR - ECONOMIC CONDITIONS

Center for International Business Education Research (CIBER), Columbia Business School and School of International and Public Affairs, Uris Hall, Room 212, 3022 Broadway, New York, NY 10027-6902, Mr. Joshua Safier, (212) 854-4750, Fax: (212) 222-9821, www.columbia.edu/cu/ciber/; Datastream International.

Central Intelligence Agency, Office of Public Affairs, Washington, DC 20505, (703) 482-0623, Fax: (703) 482-1739, www.cia.gov; *The World Factbook.*

DSI Data Service Information, Xantener Strasse 51a, D-47495 Rheinberg, Germany, www.dsidata.com; *Campus Solution.*

Dun and Bradstreet (DB) Corporation, 103 JFK Parkway, Short Hills, NJ 07078, (973) 921-5500, www.dnb.com; *Country Report.*

Economist Intelligence Unit, 111 West 57th Street, New York, NY 10019, (212) 554-0600, Fax: (212) 586-1181, www.eiu.com; *Ecuador Country Report.*

Euromonitor International, Inc., 224 S. Michigan Avenue, Suite 1500, Chicago, IL 60604, (312) 922-1115, Fax: (312) 922-1157, www.euromonitor.com; *International Marketing Data and Statistics 2008; The World Economic Factbook 2008;* and *World Marketing Data and Statistics.*

Inter-American Development Bank (IDB), 1300 New York Avenue, NW, Washington, DC 20577, (202) 623-1000, Fax: (202) 623-3096, www.iadb.org; *The Politics of Policies: Economic and Social Progress in Latin America - 2006 Report.*

International Monetary Fund (IMF), 700 Nineteenth Street, NW, Washington, DC 20431, (202) 623-7000, Fax: (202) 623-4661, www.imf.org; *World Economic Outlook Reports.*

M.E. Sharpe, 80 Business Park Drive, Armonk, NY 10504, (800) 541-6563, Fax: (914) 273-2106, www.mesharpe.com; *The Illustrated Book of World Rankings.*

Organization of American States (OAS), 17th Street Constitution Avenue NW, Washington, DC 20006, (202) 458-3000, www.oas.org; *The OAS in Transition: 1994-2004.*

Palgrave Macmillan Ltd., Houndmills, Basingstoke, Hampshire, RG21 6XS, England, (Telephone in U.S. (888) 330-8477), (Fax in U.S. (800) 672-2054), www.palgrave.com; *The Statesman's Yearbook 2008.*

Taylor and Francis Group, An Informa Business, 2 Park Square, Milton Park, Abingdon, Oxford OX14 4RN, United Kingdom, (Dial from U.S. (212) 216-7800), (Fax from U.S. (212) 564-7854), www.tandf.co.uk; *The Europa World Year Book.*

UCLA Latin American Institute, 10343 Bunche Hall, Box 951447, Los Angeles, CA 90095-1447, (310) 825-4571, Fax: (310) 206-6859, www.international.ucla.edu/lac; *Statistical Abstract of Latin America.*

United Nations Statistics Division, New York, NY 10017, (800) 253-9646, Fax: (212) 963-4116, http://unstats.un.org; *Economic Survey of Latin America and the Caribbean 2004-2005* and *World Statistics Pocketbook.*

The World Bank, 1818 H Street, NW, Washington, DC 20433, (202) 473-1000, Fax: (202) 477-6391, www.worldbank.org; *Ecuador; Global Economic Monitor (GEM); Global Economic Prospects 2008; The World Bank Atlas 2003-2004;* and *World Development Report 2008.*

ECUADOR - ECONOMICS - SOCIOLOGICAL ASPECTS

Inter-American Development Bank (IDB), 1300 New York Avenue, NW, Washington, DC 20577, (202) 623-1000, Fax: (202) 623-3096, www.iadb.org; *The Politics of Policies: Economic and Social Progress in Latin America - 2006 Report.*

UCLA Latin American Institute, 10343 Bunche Hall, Box 951447, Los Angeles, CA 90095-1447, (310) 825-4571, Fax: (310) 206-6859, www.international.ucla.edu/lac; *Statistical Abstract of Latin America.*

ECUADOR - EDUCATION

Economist Intelligence Unit, 111 West 57th Street, New York, NY 10019, (212) 554-0600, Fax: (212) 586-1181, www.eiu.com; *Business Latin America.*

Euromonitor International, Inc., 224 S. Michigan Avenue, Suite 1500, Chicago, IL 60604, (312) 922-1115, Fax: (312) 922-1157, www.euromonitor.com; *International Marketing Data and Statistics 2008* and *World Marketing Data and Statistics.*

International Monetary Fund (IMF), 700 Nineteenth Street, NW, Washington, DC 20431, (202) 623-7000, Fax: (202) 623-4661, www.imf.org; *Government Finance Statistics Yearbook (2008 Edition).*

M.E. Sharpe, 80 Business Park Drive, Armonk, NY 10504, (800) 541-6563, Fax: (914) 273-2106, www.mesharpe.com; *The Illustrated Book of World Rankings.*

Palgrave Macmillan Ltd., Houndmills, Basingstoke, Hampshire, RG21 6XS, England, (Telephone in U.S. (888) 330-8477), (Fax in U.S. (800) 672-2054), www.palgrave.com; *The Statesman's Yearbook 2008.*

Taylor and Francis Group, An Informa Business, 2 Park Square, Milton Park, Abingdon, Oxford OX14 4RN, United Kingdom, (Dial from U.S. (212) 216-7800), (Fax from U.S. (212) 564-7854), www.tandf.co.uk; *The Europa World Year Book.*

UCLA Latin American Institute, 10343 Bunche Hall, Box 951447, Los Angeles, CA 90095-1447, (310) 825-4571, Fax: (310) 206-6859, www.international.ucla.edu/lac; *Statistical Abstract of Latin America.*

UNESCO Institute for Statistics, C.P. 6128 Succursale Centre-Ville, Montreal, Quebec, H3C 3J7 Canada, (Dial from U.S. (514) 343-6880), (Fax from U.S. (514) 343 6882), www.uis.unesco.org; *Statistical Tables.*

United Nations Statistics Division, New York, NY 10017, (800) 253-9646, Fax: (212) 963-4116, http://unstats.un.org; *Human Development Report 2006* and *Statistical Yearbook for Latin America and the Caribbean 2004.*

The World Bank, 1818 H Street, NW, Washington, DC 20433, (202) 473-1000, Fax: (202) 477-6391, www.worldbank.org; *Ecuador; World Development Indicators (WDI) 2008;* and *World Development Report 2008.*

ECUADOR - ELECTRICITY

Economist Intelligence Unit, 111 West 57th Street, New York, NY 10019, (212) 554-0600, Fax: (212) 586-1181, www.eiu.com; *Business Latin America.*

Inter-American Development Bank (IDB), 1300 New York Avenue, NW, Washington, DC 20577, (202) 623-1000, Fax: (202) 623-3096, www.iadb.org; *The Politics of Policies: Economic and Social Progress in Latin America - 2006 Report.*

M.E. Sharpe, 80 Business Park Drive, Armonk, NY 10504, (800) 541-6563, Fax: (914) 273-2106, www.mesharpe.com; *The Illustrated Book of World Rankings.*

Organisation for Economic Cooperation and Development (OECD), 2 rue Andre Pascal, F-75775 Paris Cedex 16, France, (Telephone in U.S. (202) 785-6323), (Fax in U.S. (202) 785-0350), www.oecd.org; *World Energy Outlook 2007.*

Palgrave Macmillan Ltd., Houndmills, Basingstoke, Hampshire, RG21 6XS, England, (Telephone in U.S. (888) 330-8477), (Fax in U.S. (800) 672-2054), www.palgrave.com; *The Statesman's Yearbook 2008.*

U.S. Department of Energy (DOE), Energy Information Administration (EIA), 1000 Independence Avenue, SW, Washington, DC 20585, (202) 586-8800, www.eia.doe.gov; *International Energy Annual 2004* and *International Energy Outlook 2006.*

United Nations Statistics Division, New York, NY 10017, (800) 253-9646, Fax: (212) 963-4116, http://unstats.un.org; *Human Development Report 2006* and *Statistical Yearbook.*

ECUADOR - EMIGRATION AND IMMIGRATION

UCLA Latin American Institute, 10343 Bunche Hall, Box 951447, Los Angeles, CA 90095-1447, (310) 825-4571, Fax: (310) 206-6859, www.international.ucla.edu/lac; *Statistical Abstract of Latin America.*

ECUADOR - EMPLOYMENT

Euromonitor International, Inc., 224 S. Michigan Avenue, Suite 1500, Chicago, IL 60604, (312) 922-1115, Fax: (312) 922-1157, www.euromonitor.com; *International Marketing Data and Statistics 2008.*

International Labour Office, I.L.O. Publications, 4 route des Morillons, CH-1211 Geneva 22, Switzerland, (Telephone in U.S. (202) 653-7652), (Fax in U.S. (202) 653-7687), www.ilo.org; *Yearbook of Labour Statistics 2006.*

M.E. Sharpe, 80 Business Park Drive, Armonk, NY 10504, (800) 541-6563, Fax: (914) 273-2106, www.mesharpe.com; *The Illustrated Book of World Rankings.*

Organization of American States (OAS), 17th Street Constitution Avenue NW, Washington, DC 20006, (202) 458-3000, www.oas.org; *The OAS in Transition: 1994-2004.*

UCLA Latin American Institute, 10343 Bunche Hall, Box 951447, Los Angeles, CA 90095-1447, (310) 825-4571, Fax: (310) 206-6859, www.international.ucla.edu/lac; *Statistical Abstract of Latin America.*

United Nations Statistics Division, New York, NY 10017, (800) 253-9646, Fax: (212) 963-4116, http://unstats.un.org; *Statistical Yearbook* and *Statistical Yearbook for Latin America and the Caribbean 2004.*

The World Bank, 1818 H Street, NW, Washington, DC 20433, (202) 473-1000, Fax: (202) 477-6391, www.worldbank.org; *Ecuador.*

ECUADOR - ENVIRONMENTAL CONDITIONS

DSI Data Service Information, Xantener Strasse 51a, D-47495 Rheinberg, Germany, www.dsidata.com; *Campus Solution* and *DSI's Global Environmental Database.*

Economist Intelligence Unit, 111 West 57th Street, New York, NY 10019, (212) 554-0600, Fax: (212) 586-1181, www.eiu.com; *Ecuador Country Report.*

United Nations Statistics Division, New York, NY 10017, (800) 253-9646, Fax: (212) 963-4116, http://unstats.un.org; *World Statistics Pocketbook.*

ECUADOR - EXCISE TAX

Inter-American Development Bank (IDB), 1300 New York Avenue, NW, Washington, DC 20577, (202) 623-1000, Fax: (202) 623-3096, www.iadb.org; *The Politics of Policies: Economic and Social Progress in Latin America - 2006 Report.*

International Monetary Fund (IMF), 700 Nineteenth Street, NW, Washington, DC 20431, (202) 623-7000, Fax: (202) 623-4661, www.imf.org; *Government Finance Statistics Yearbook (2008 Edition).*

ECUADOR - EXPENDITURES, PUBLIC

Inter-American Development Bank (IDB), 1300 New York Avenue, NW, Washington, DC 20577, (202) 623-1000, Fax: (202) 623-3096, www.iadb.org; *The Politics of Policies: Economic and Social Progress in Latin America - 2006 Report.*

Organization of American States (OAS), 17th Street Constitution Avenue NW, Washington, DC 20006, (202) 458-3000, www.oas.org; *The OAS in Transition: 1994-2004.*

United Nations Statistics Division, New York, NY 10017, (800) 253-9646, Fax: (212) 963-4116, http://unstats.un.org; *Statistical Yearbook for Latin America and the Caribbean 2004.*

ECUADOR - EXPORTS

Central Intelligence Agency, Office of Public Affairs, Washington, DC 20505, (703) 482-0623, Fax: (703) 482-1739, www.cia.gov; *The World Factbook.*

Economist Intelligence Unit, 111 West 57th Street, New York, NY 10019, (212) 554-0600, Fax: (212) 586-1181, www.eiu.com; *Business Latin America* and *Ecuador Country Report.*

Euromonitor International, Inc., 224 S. Michigan Avenue, Suite 1500, Chicago, IL 60604, (312) 922-1115, Fax: (312) 922-1157, www.euromonitor.com; *International Marketing Data and Statistics 2008* and *The World Economic Factbook 2008.*

Inter-American Development Bank (IDB), 1300 New York Avenue, NW, Washington, DC 20577, (202) 623-1000, Fax: (202) 623-3096, www.iadb.org; *The Politics of Policies: Economic and Social Progress in Latin America - 2006 Report.*

International Monetary Fund (IMF), 700 Nineteenth Street, NW, Washington, DC 20431, (202) 623-7000, Fax: (202) 623-4661, www.imf.org; *Direction of Trade Statistics Yearbook 2007* and *International Financial Statistics Yearbook 2007.*

Organization of American States (OAS), 17th Street Constitution Avenue NW, Washington, DC 20006, (202) 458-3000, www.oas.org; *The OAS in Transition: 1994-2004.*

Organization of Petroleum Exporting Countries (OPEC), Obere Donaustrasse 93, A-1020, Vienna, Austria, www.opec.org; *Annual Statistical Bulletin 2006.*

Palgrave Macmillan Ltd., Houndmills, Basingstoke, Hampshire, RG21 6XS, England, (Telephone in U.S. (888) 330-8477), (Fax in U.S. (800) 672-2054), www.palgrave.com; *The Statesman's Yearbook 2008.*

Taylor and Francis Group, An Informa Business, 2 Park Square, Milton Park, Abingdon, Oxford OX14 4RN, United Kingdom, (Dial from U.S. (212) 216-7800), (Fax from U.S. (212) 564-7854), www.tandf.co.uk; *The Europa World Year Book.*

United Nations Conference on Trade and Development (UNCTAD), DC2-1120, United Nations, New York, NY 10017, (212) 963-0027, www.unctad.org; *Handbook of Statistics 2005.*

United Nations Food and Agricultural Organization (FAO), Viale delle Terme di Caracalla, 00100 Rome, Italy, (Dial from U.S. (202) 653-2400), (Fax from U.S. (202) 653 5760), www.fao.org; *The State of Food and Agriculture (SOFA) 2006.*

United Nations Statistics Division, New York, NY 10017, (800) 253-9646, Fax: (212) 963-4116, http://unstats.un.org; *Statistical Yearbook for Latin America and the Caribbean 2004.*

The World Bank, 1818 H Street, NW, Washington, DC 20433, (202) 473-1000, Fax: (202) 477-6391, www.worldbank.org; *World Development Indicators (WDI) 2008* and *World Development Report 2008.*

ECUADOR - FEMALE WORKING POPULATION

See ECUADOR - EMPLOYMENT

ECUADOR - FERTILITY, HUMAN

Central Intelligence Agency, Office of Public Affairs, Washington, DC 20505, (703) 482-0623, Fax: (703) 482-1739, www.cia.gov; *The World Factbook.*

M.E. Sharpe, 80 Business Park Drive, Armonk, NY 10504, (800) 541-6563, Fax: (914) 273-2106, www.mesharpe.com; *The Illustrated Book of World Rankings.*

United Nations Statistics Division, New York, NY 10017, (800) 253-9646, Fax: (212) 963-4116, http://unstats.un.org; *Human Development Report 2006.*

The World Bank, 1818 H Street, NW, Washington, DC 20433, (202) 473-1000, Fax: (202) 477-6391, www.worldbank.org; *The World Bank Atlas 2003-2004; World Development Indicators (WDI) 2008;* and *World Development Report 2008.*

ECUADOR - FERTILIZER INDUSTRY

Economist Intelligence Unit, 111 West 57th Street, New York, NY 10019, (212) 554-0600, Fax: (212) 586-1181, www.eiu.com; *Business Latin America.*

United Nations Food and Agricultural Organization (FAO), Viale delle Terme di Caracalla, 00100 Rome, Italy, (Dial from U.S. (202) 653-2400), (Fax from U.S. (202) 653 5760), www.fao.org; *FAO Fertilizer Yearbook* and *The State of Food and Agriculture (SOFA) 2006.*

United Nations Statistics Division, New York, NY 10017, (800) 253-9646, Fax: (212) 963-4116, http://unstats.un.org; *Statistical Yearbook.*

ECUADOR - FETAL MORTALITY

See ECUADOR - MORTALITY

ECUADOR - FINANCE

Inter-American Development Bank (IDB), 1300 New York Avenue, NW, Washington, DC 20577, (202) 623-1000, Fax: (202) 623-3096, www.iadb.org; *The Politics of Policies: Economic and Social Progress in Latin America - 2006 Report.*

International Monetary Fund (IMF), 700 Nineteenth Street, NW, Washington, DC 20431, (202) 623-7000, Fax: (202) 623-4661, www.imf.org; *International Financial Statistics Yearbook 2007.*

Organization of American States (OAS), 17th Street Constitution Avenue NW, Washington, DC 20006, (202) 458-3000, www.oas.org; *The OAS in Transition: 1994-2004.*

Taylor and Francis Group, An Informa Business, 2 Park Square, Milton Park, Abingdon, Oxford OX14 4RN, United Kingdom, (Dial from U.S. (212) 216-7800), (Fax from U.S. (212) 564-7854), www.tandf.co.uk; *The Europa World Year Book.*

UCLA Latin American Institute, 10343 Bunche Hall, Box 951447, Los Angeles, CA 90095-1447, (310) 825-4571, Fax: (310) 206-6859, www.international.ucla.edu/lac; *Statistical Abstract of Latin America.*

United Nations Statistics Division, New York, NY 10017, (800) 253-9646, Fax: (212) 963-4116, http://unstats.un.org; *National Accounts Statistics: Compendium of Income Distribution Statistics* and *Statistical Yearbook.*

The World Bank, 1818 H Street, NW, Washington, DC 20433, (202) 473-1000, Fax: (202) 477-6391, www.worldbank.org; *Ecuador.*

ECUADOR - FINANCE, PUBLIC

Bernan Essential Government Publications, 4611-F Assembly Drive, Lanham MD, 20706-4391, (301) 459-2255, Fax: (800) 865-3450, www.bernan.com; *National Accounts Statistics.*

Economist Intelligence Unit, 111 West 57th Street, New York, NY 10019, (212) 554-0600, Fax: (212) 586-1181, www.eiu.com; *Ecuador Country Report.*

Inter-American Development Bank (IDB), 1300 New York Avenue, NW, Washington, DC 20577, (202) 623-1000, Fax: (202) 623-3096, www.iadb.org; *The Politics of Policies: Economic and Social Progress in Latin America - 2006 Report.*

International Monetary Fund (IMF), 700 Nineteenth Street, NW, Washington, DC 20431, (202) 623-7000, Fax: (202) 623-4661, www.imf.org; *International Financial Statistics; International Financial Statistics Online Service;* and *International Financial Statistics Yearbook 2007.*

M.E. Sharpe, 80 Business Park Drive, Armonk, NY 10504, (800) 541-6563, Fax: (914) 273-2106, www.mesharpe.com; *The Illustrated Book of World Rankings.*

Organization of American States (OAS), 17th Street Constitution Avenue NW, Washington, DC 20006, (202) 458-3000, www.oas.org; *The OAS in Transition: 1994-2004.*

Palgrave Macmillan Ltd., Houndmills, Basingstoke, Hampshire, RG21 6XS, England, (Telephone in U.S. (888) 330-8477), (Fax in U.S. (800) 672-2054), www.palgrave.com; *The Statesman's Yearbook 2008.*

Taylor and Francis Group, An Informa Business, 2 Park Square, Milton Park, Abingdon, Oxford OX14 4RN, United Kingdom, (Dial from U.S. (212) 216-7800), (Fax from U.S. (212) 564-7854), www.tandf.co.uk; *The Europa World Year Book.*

UCLA Latin American Institute, 10343 Bunche Hall, Box 951447, Los Angeles, CA 90095-1447, (310) 825-4571, Fax: (310) 206-6859, www.international.ucla.edu/lac; *Statistical Abstract of Latin America.*

The World Bank, 1818 H Street, NW, Washington, DC 20433, (202) 473-1000, Fax: (202) 477-6391, www.worldbank.org; *Ecuador.*

ECUADOR - FISHERIES

Inter-American Development Bank (IDB), 1300 New York Avenue, NW, Washington, DC 20577, (202) 623-1000, Fax: (202) 623-3096, www.iadb.org; *The Politics of Policies: Economic and Social Progress in Latin America - 2006 Report.*

M.E. Sharpe, 80 Business Park Drive, Armonk, NY 10504, (800) 541-6563, Fax: (914) 273-2106, www.mesharpe.com; *The Illustrated Book of World Rankings.*

Palgrave Macmillan Ltd., Houndmills, Basingstoke, Hampshire, RG21 6XS, England, (Telephone in U.S. (888) 330-8477), (Fax in U.S. (800) 672-2054), www.palgrave.com; *The Statesman's Yearbook 2008.*

Taylor and Francis Group, An Informa Business, 2 Park Square, Milton Park, Abingdon, Oxford OX14 4RN, United Kingdom, (Dial from U.S. (212) 216-7800), (Fax from U.S. (212) 564-7854), www.tandf.co.uk; *The Europa World Year Book.*

UCLA Latin American Institute, 10343 Bunche Hall, Box 951447, Los Angeles, CA 90095-1447, (310) 825-4571, Fax: (310) 206-6859, www.international.ucla.edu/lac; *Statistical Abstract of Latin America.*

United Nations Conference on Trade and Development (UNCTAD), DC2-1120, United Nations, New York, NY 10017, (212) 963-0027, www.unctad.org; *UNCTAD Commodity Yearbook.*

United Nations Food and Agricultural Organization (FAO), Viale delle Terme di Caracalla, 00100 Rome, Italy, (Dial from U.S. (202) 653-2400), (Fax from U.S. (202) 653 5760), www.fao.org; *FAO Yearbook of Fishery Statistics;* Fishery Databases; FISHSTAT Database. Subjects covered include: Aquaculture production, capture production, fishery commodities; and *The State of Food and Agriculture (SOFA) 2006.*

United Nations Statistics Division, New York, NY 10017, (800) 253-9646, Fax: (212) 963-4116, http://unstats.un.org; *Statistical Yearbook.*

The World Bank, 1818 H Street, NW, Washington, DC 20433, (202) 473-1000, Fax: (202) 477-6391, www.worldbank.org; *Ecuador.*

ECUADOR - FLOUR INDUSTRY

United Nations Statistics Division, New York, NY 10017, (800) 253-9646, Fax: (212) 963-4116, http://unstats.un.org; *Statistical Yearbook.*

ECUADOR - FOOD

United Nations Conference on Trade and Development (UNCTAD), DC2-1120, United Nations, New York, NY 10017, (212) 963-0027, www.unctad.org; *UNCTAD Commodity Yearbook.*

United Nations Food and Agricultural Organization (FAO), Viale delle Terme di Caracalla, 00100 Rome, Italy, (Dial from U.S. (202) 653-2400), (Fax from U.S. (202) 653 5760), www.fao.org; *FAO Production Yearbook 2002* and *The State of Food and Agriculture (SOFA) 2006.*

United Nations Statistics Division, New York, NY 10017, (800) 253-9646, Fax: (212) 963-4116, http://unstats.un.org; *Human Development Report 2006.*

ECUADOR - FOREIGN EXCHANGE RATES

Central Intelligence Agency, Office of Public Affairs, Washington, DC 20505, (703) 482-0623, Fax: (703) 482-1739, www.cia.gov; *The World Factbook.*

Euromonitor International, Inc., 224 S. Michigan Avenue, Suite 1500, Chicago, IL 60604, (312) 922-1115, Fax: (312) 922-1157, www.euromonitor.com; *International Marketing Data and Statistics 2008* and *The World Economic Factbook 2008.*

Inter-American Development Bank (IDB), 1300 New York Avenue, NW, Washington, DC 20577, (202) 623-1000, Fax: (202) 623-3096, www.iadb.org; *The Politics of Policies: Economic and Social Progress in Latin America - 2006 Report.*

International Civil Aviation Organization (ICAO), External Relations and Public Information Office (EPO), 999 University Street, Montreal, Quebec H3C 5H7, Canada, (Dial from U.S. (514) 954-8219), (Fax from U.S. (514) 954-6077), www.icao.int; *Civil Aviation Statistics of the World.*

International Monetary Fund (IMF), 700 Nineteenth Street, NW, Washington, DC 20431, (202) 623-7000, Fax: (202) 623-4661, www.imf.org; *International Financial Statistics Yearbook 2007.*

Organization of American States (OAS), 17th Street Constitution Avenue NW, Washington, DC 20006, (202) 458-3000, www.oas.org; *The OAS in Transition: 1994-2004.*

Organization of Petroleum Exporting Countries (OPEC), Obere Donaustrasse 93, A-1020, Vienna, Austria, www.opec.org; *Annual Statistical Bulletin 2006.*

Taylor and Francis Group, An Informa Business, 2 Park Square, Milton Park, Abingdon, Oxford OX14 4RN, United Kingdom, (Dial from U.S. (212) 216-7800), (Fax from U.S. (212) 564-7854), www.tandf.co.uk; *The Europa World Year Book.*

UCLA Latin American Institute, 10343 Bunche Hall, Box 951447, Los Angeles, CA 90095-1447, (310) 825-4571, Fax: (310) 206-6859, www.international.ucla.edu/lac; *Statistical Abstract of Latin America.*

United Nations Statistics Division, New York, NY 10017, (800) 253-9646, Fax: (212) 963-4116, http://unstats.un.org; *Statistical Yearbook* and *World Statistics Pocketbook.*

ECUADOR - FORESTS AND FORESTRY

American Forest Paper Association (AFPA), 1111 Nineteenth Street, NW, Suite 800, Washington, DC 20036, (800) 878-8878, www.afandpa.org; *2007 Annual Statistics of Paper, Paperboard, and Wood Pulp.*

Inter-American Development Bank (IDB), 1300 New York Avenue, NW, Washington, DC 20577, (202) 623-1000, Fax: (202) 623-3096, www.iadb.org; *The Politics of Policies: Economic and Social Progress in Latin America - 2006 Report.*

M.E. Sharpe, 80 Business Park Drive, Armonk, NY 10504, (800) 541-6563, Fax: (914) 273-2106, www.mesharpe.com; *The Illustrated Book of World Rankings.*

Palgrave Macmillan Ltd., Houndmills, Basingstoke, Hampshire, RG21 6XS, England, (Telephone in U.S. (888) 330-8477), (Fax in U.S. (800) 672-2054), www.palgrave.com; *The Statesman's Yearbook 2008.*

Taylor and Francis Group, An Informa Business, 2 Park Square, Milton Park, Abingdon, Oxford OX14 4RN, United Kingdom, (Dial from U.S. (212) 216-7800), (Fax from U.S. (212) 564-7854), www.tandf.co.uk; *The Europa World Year Book.*

UCLA Latin American Institute, 10343 Bunche Hall, Box 951447, Los Angeles, CA 90095-1447, (310) 825-4571, Fax: (310) 206-6859, www.international.ucla.edu/lac; *Statistical Abstract of Latin America.*

UNESCO Institute for Statistics, C.P. 6128 Succursale Centre-Ville, Montreal, Quebec, H3C 3J7 Canada, (Dial from U.S. (514) 343-6880), (Fax from U.S. (514) 343 6882), www.uis.unesco.org; *Statistical Tables.*

United Nations Conference on Trade and Development (UNCTAD), DC2-1120, United Nations, New York, NY 10017, (212) 963-0027, www.unctad.org; *UNCTAD Commodity Yearbook.*

United Nations Food and Agricultural Organization (FAO), Viale delle Terme di Caracalla, 00100 Rome, Italy, (Dial from U.S. (202) 653-2400), (Fax from U.S. (202) 653 5760), www.fao.org; *FAO Yearbook of Forest Products* and *The State of Food and Agriculture (SOFA) 2006.*

The World Bank, 1818 H Street, NW, Washington, DC 20433, (202) 473-1000, Fax: (202) 477-6391, www.worldbank.org; *Ecuador* and *World Development Report 2008.*

ECUADOR - GAS PRODUCTION

See ECUADOR - MINERAL INDUSTRIES

ECUADOR - GEOGRAPHIC INFORMATION SYSTEMS

M.E. Sharpe, 80 Business Park Drive, Armonk, NY 10504, (800) 541-6563, Fax: (914) 273-2106, www.mesharpe.com; *The Illustrated Book of World Rankings.*

UCLA Latin American Institute, 10343 Bunche Hall, Box 951447, Los Angeles, CA 90095-1447, (310) 825-4571, Fax: (310) 206-6859, www.international.ucla.edu/lac; *Statistical Abstract of Latin America.*

The World Bank, 1818 H Street, NW, Washington, DC 20433, (202) 473-1000, Fax: (202) 477-6391, www.worldbank.org; *Ecuador.*

ECUADOR - GOLD INDUSTRY

Economist Intelligence Unit, 111 West 57th Street, New York, NY 10019, (212) 554-0600, Fax: (212) 586-1181, www.eiu.com; *Business Latin America.*

International Monetary Fund (IMF), 700 Nineteenth Street, NW, Washington, DC 20431, (202) 623-7000, Fax: (202) 623-4661, www.imf.org; *International Financial Statistics Yearbook 2007.*

United Nations Statistics Division, New York, NY 10017, (800) 253-9646, Fax: (212) 963-4116, http://unstats.un.org; *Statistical Yearbook.*

The World Bank, 1818 H Street, NW, Washington, DC 20433, (202) 473-1000, Fax: (202) 477-6391, www.worldbank.org; *World Development Indicators (WDI) 2008.*

ECUADOR - GOLD PRODUCTION

See ECUADOR - MINERAL INDUSTRIES

ECUADOR - GRANTS-IN-AID

International Monetary Fund (IMF), 700 Nineteenth Street, NW, Washington, DC 20431, (202) 623-7000, Fax: (202) 623-4661, www.imf.org; *Government Finance Statistics Yearbook (2008 Edition).*

ECUADOR - GREEN PEPPER AND CHILIE PRODUCTION

See ECUADOR - CROPS

ECUADOR - GROSS DOMESTIC PRODUCT

Economist Intelligence Unit, 111 West 57th Street, New York, NY 10019, (212) 554-0600, Fax: (212) 586-1181, www.eiu.com; *Business Latin America* and *Ecuador Country Report.*

Euromonitor International, Inc., 224 S. Michigan Avenue, Suite 1500, Chicago, IL 60604, (312) 922-1115, Fax: (312) 922-1157, www.euromonitor.com; *International Marketing Data and Statistics 2008* and *The World Economic Factbook 2008.*

Inter-American Development Bank (IDB), 1300 New York Avenue, NW, Washington, DC 20577, (202) 623-1000, Fax: (202) 623-3096, www.iadb.org; *The Politics of Policies: Economic and Social Progress in Latin America - 2006 Report.*

M.E. Sharpe, 80 Business Park Drive, Armonk, NY 10504, (800) 541-6563, Fax: (914) 273-2106, www.mesharpe.com; *The Illustrated Book of World Rankings.*

Organization of American States (OAS), 17th Street Constitution Avenue NW, Washington, DC 20006, (202) 458-3000, www.oas.org; *The OAS in Transition: 1994-2004.*

UCLA Latin American Institute, 10343 Bunche Hall, Box 951447, Los Angeles, CA 90095-1447, (310) 825-4571, Fax: (310) 206-6859, www.international.ucla.edu/lac; *Statistical Abstract of Latin America.*

United Nations Statistics Division, New York, NY 10017, (800) 253-9646, Fax: (212) 963-4116, http://unstats.un.org; *Human Development Report 2006; National Accounts Statistics: Compendium of Income Distribution Statistics; Statistical Yearbook;* and *Statistical Yearbook for Latin America and the Caribbean 2004.*

The World Bank, 1818 H Street, NW, Washington, DC 20433, (202) 473-1000, Fax: (202) 477-6391, www.worldbank.org; *World Development Indicators (WDI) 2008* and *World Development Report 2008.*

ECUADOR - GROSS NATIONAL PRODUCT

Euromonitor International, Inc., 224 S. Michigan Avenue, Suite 1500, Chicago, IL 60604, (312) 922-1115, Fax: (312) 922-1157, www.euromonitor.com; *International Marketing Data and Statistics 2008.*

Inter-American Development Bank (IDB), 1300 New York Avenue, NW, Washington, DC 20577, (202) 623-1000, Fax: (202) 623-3096, www.iadb.org; *The Politics of Policies: Economic and Social Progress in Latin America - 2006 Report.*

M.E. Sharpe, 80 Business Park Drive, Armonk, NY 10504, (800) 541-6563, Fax: (914) 273-2106, www.mesharpe.com; *The Illustrated Book of World Rankings.*

Organization of Petroleum Exporting Countries (OPEC), Obere Donaustrasse 93, A-1020, Vienna, Austria, www.opec.org; *Annual Statistical Bulletin 2006.*

Palgrave Macmillan Ltd., Houndmills, Basingstoke, Hampshire, RG21 6XS, England, (Telephone in U.S. (888) 330-8477), (Fax in U.S. (800) 672-2054), www.palgrave.com; *The Statesman's Yearbook 2008.*

U.S. Department of State (DOS), 2201 C Street NW, Washington, DC 20520, (202) 647-4000, www.state.gov; *World Military Expenditures and Arms Transfers (WMEAT).*

United Nations Statistics Division, New York, NY 10017, (800) 253-9646, Fax: (212) 963-4116, http://unstats.un.org; *Statistical Yearbook.*

The World Bank, 1818 H Street, NW, Washington, DC 20433, (202) 473-1000, Fax: (202) 477-6391, www.worldbank.org; *The World Bank Atlas 2003-2004; World Development Indicators (WDI) 2008;* and *World Development Report 2008.*

ECUADOR - HARDWOOD INDUSTRY

Economist Intelligence Unit, 111 West 57th Street, New York, NY 10019, (212) 554-0600, Fax: (212) 586-1181, www.eiu.com; *Business Latin America.*

Inter-American Development Bank (IDB), 1300 New York Avenue, NW, Washington, DC 20577, (202) 623-1000, Fax: (202) 623-3096, www.iadb.org; *The Politics of Policies: Economic and Social Progress in Latin America - 2006 Report.*

United Nations Food and Agricultural Organization (FAO), Viale delle Terme di Caracalla, 00100 Rome, Italy, (Dial from U.S. (202) 653-2400), (Fax from U.S. (202) 653 5760), www.fao.org; *FAO Yearbook of Forest Products.*

United Nations Statistics Division, New York, NY 10017, (800) 253-9646, Fax: (212) 963-4116, http://unstats.un.org; *Statistical Yearbook.*

ECUADOR - HIDES AND SKINS INDUSTRY

United Nations Food and Agricultural Organization (FAO), Viale delle Terme di Caracalla, 00100 Rome, Italy, (Dial from U.S. (202) 653-2400), (Fax from U.S. (202) 653 5760), www.fao.org; *FAO Production Yearbook 2002.*

ECUADOR - HOUSING

Euromonitor International, Inc., 224 S. Michigan Avenue, Suite 1500, Chicago, IL 60604, (312) 922-1115, Fax: (312) 922-1157, www.euromonitor.com; *World Marketing Data and Statistics.*

M.E. Sharpe, 80 Business Park Drive, Armonk, NY 10504, (800) 541-6563, Fax: (914) 273-2106, www.mesharpe.com; *The Illustrated Book of World Rankings.*

UCLA Latin American Institute, 10343 Bunche Hall, Box 951447, Los Angeles, CA 90095-1447, (310) 825-4571, Fax: (310) 206-6859, www.international.ucla.edu/lac; *Statistical Abstract of Latin America.*

United Nations Statistics Division, New York, NY 10017, (800) 253-9646, Fax: (212) 963-4116, http://unstats.un.org; *Statistical Yearbook for Latin America and the Caribbean 2004.*

ECUADOR - ILLITERATE PERSONS

UNESCO Institute for Statistics, C.P. 6128 Succursale Centre-Ville, Montreal, Quebec, H3C 3J7 Canada, (Dial from U.S. (514) 343-6880), (Fax from U.S. (514) 343 6882), www.uis.unesco.org; *Statistical Tables.*

United Nations Statistics Division, New York, NY 10017, (800) 253-9646, Fax: (212) 963-4116, http://unstats.un.org; *Human Development Report 2006* and *Statistical Yearbook for Latin America and the Caribbean 2004.*

ECUADOR - IMPORTS

Central Intelligence Agency, Office of Public Affairs, Washington, DC 20505, (703) 482-0623, Fax: (703) 482-1739, www.cia.gov; *The World Factbook.*

Economist Intelligence Unit, 111 West 57th Street, New York, NY 10019, (212) 554-0600, Fax: (212) 586-1181, www.eiu.com; *Business Latin America* and *Ecuador Country Report.*

Euromonitor International, Inc., 224 S. Michigan Avenue, Suite 1500, Chicago, IL 60604, (312) 922-1115, Fax: (312) 922-1157, www.euromonitor.com; *International Marketing Data and Statistics 2008* and *The World Economic Factbook 2008.*

Inter-American Development Bank (IDB), 1300 New York Avenue, NW, Washington, DC 20577, (202) 623-1000, Fax: (202) 623-3096, www.iadb.org; *The Politics of Policies: Economic and Social Progress in Latin America - 2006 Report.*

International Monetary Fund (IMF), 700 Nineteenth Street, NW, Washington, DC 20431, (202) 623-7000, Fax: (202) 623-4661, www.imf.org; *Direction of Trade Statistics Yearbook 2007; Government Finance Statistics Yearbook (2008 Edition);* and *International Financial Statistics Yearbook 2007.*

Organization of American States (OAS), 17th Street Constitution Avenue NW, Washington, DC 20006, (202) 458-3000, www.oas.org; *The OAS in Transition: 1994-2004.*

Palgrave Macmillan Ltd., Houndmills, Basingstoke, Hampshire, RG21 6XS, England, (Telephone in U.S. (888) 330-8477), (Fax in U.S. (800) 672-2054), www.palgrave.com; *The Statesman's Yearbook 2008.*

Taylor and Francis Group, An Informa Business, 2 Park Square, Milton Park, Abingdon, Oxford OX14 4RN, United Kingdom, (Dial from U.S. (212) 216-7800), (Fax from U.S. (212) 564-7854), www.tandf.co.uk; *The Europa World Year Book.*

United Nations Conference on Trade and Development (UNCTAD), DC2-1120, United Nations, New York, NY 10017, (212) 963-0027, www.unctad.org; *Handbook of Statistics 2005.*

United Nations Food and Agricultural Organization (FAO), Viale delle Terme di Caracalla, 00100 Rome, Italy, (Dial from U.S. (202) 653-2400), (Fax from U.S. (202) 653 5760), www.fao.org; *The State of Food and Agriculture (SOFA) 2006.*

United Nations Statistics Division, New York, NY 10017, (800) 253-9646, Fax: (212) 963-4116, http://unstats.un.org; *Statistical Yearbook for Latin America and the Caribbean 2004.*

The World Bank, 1818 H Street, NW, Washington, DC 20433, (202) 473-1000, Fax: (202) 477-6391, www.worldbank.org; *World Development Indicators (WDI) 2008* and *World Development Report 2008.*

ECUADOR - INCOME DISTRIBUTION

UCLA Latin American Institute, 10343 Bunche Hall, Box 951447, Los Angeles, CA 90095-1447, (310) 825-4571, Fax: (310) 206-6859, www.international.ucla.edu/lac; *Statistical Abstract of Latin America.*

United Nations Statistics Division, New York, NY 10017, (800) 253-9646, Fax: (212) 963-4116, http://unstats.un.org; *Statistical Yearbook for Latin America and the Caribbean 2004.*

ECUADOR - INCOME TAXES

See ECUADOR - TAXATION

ECUADOR - INDUSTRIAL PRODUCTIVITY

Euromonitor International, Inc., 224 S. Michigan Avenue, Suite 1500, Chicago, IL 60604, (312) 922-1115, Fax: (312) 922-1157, www.euromonitor.com; *International Marketing Data and Statistics 2008.*

M.E. Sharpe, 80 Business Park Drive, Armonk, NY 10504, (800) 541-6563, Fax: (914) 273-2106, www.mesharpe.com; *The Illustrated Book of World Rankings.*

ECUADOR - INDUSTRIAL PROPERTY

United Nations Statistics Division, New York, NY 10017, (800) 253-9646, Fax: (212) 963-4116, http://unstats.un.org; *Statistical Yearbook.*

ECUADOR - INDUSTRIES

Central Intelligence Agency, Office of Public Affairs, Washington, DC 20505, (703) 482-0623, Fax: (703) 482-1739, www.cia.gov; *The World Factbook.*

Economist Intelligence Unit, 111 West 57th Street, New York, NY 10019, (212) 554-0600, Fax: (212) 586-1181, www.eiu.com; *Ecuador Country Report.*

Euromonitor International, Inc., 224 S. Michigan Avenue, Suite 1500, Chicago, IL 60604, (312) 922-1115, Fax: (312) 922-1157, www.euromonitor.com; *International Marketing Data and Statistics 2008; The World Economic Factbook 2008;* and *World Marketing Data and Statistics.*

International Labour Office, I.L.O. Publications, 4 route des Morillons, CH-1211 Geneva 22, Switzerland, (Telephone in U.S. (202) 653-7652), (Fax in U.S. (202) 653-7687), www.ilo.org; *Yearbook of Labour Statistics 2006.*

M.E. Sharpe, 80 Business Park Drive, Armonk, NY 10504, (800) 541-6563, Fax: (914) 273-2106, www.mesharpe.com; *The Illustrated Book of World Rankings.*

Palgrave Macmillan Ltd., Houndmills, Basingstoke, Hampshire, RG21 6XS, England, (Telephone in U.S. (888) 330-8477), (Fax in U.S. (800) 672-2054), www.palgrave.com; *The Statesman's Yearbook 2008.*

Taylor and Francis Group, An Informa Business, 2 Park Square, Milton Park, Abingdon, Oxford OX14 4RN, United Kingdom, (Dial from U.S. (212) 216-7800), (Fax from U.S. (212) 564-7854), www.tandf.co.uk; *The Europa World Year Book.*

UCLA Latin American Institute, 10343 Bunche Hall, Box 951447, Los Angeles, CA 90095-1447, (310) 825-4571, Fax: (310) 206-6859, www.international.ucla.edu/lac; *Statistical Abstract of Latin America.*

United Nations Industrial Development Organization (UNIDO), 1 United Nations Plaza, New York, NY 10017, (212) 963 6890, Fax: (212) 963-7904, http://unido.org; Industrial Statistics Database 2008 (INDSTAT) and *The International Yearbook of Industrial Statistics 2008.*

United Nations Statistics Division, New York, NY 10017, (800) 253-9646, Fax: (212) 963-4116, http://unstats.un.org; *Economic Survey of Latin America and the Caribbean 2004-2005; 2004 Industrial Commodity Statistics Yearbook;* and *Statistical Yearbook.*

The World Bank, 1818 H Street, NW, Washington, DC 20433, (202) 473-1000, Fax: (202) 477-6391, www.worldbank.org; *Ecuador* and *World Development Indicators (WDI) 2008.*

ECUADOR - INFANT AND MATERNAL MORTALITY

See ECUADOR - MORTALITY

ECUADOR - INFLATION (FINANCE)

United Nations Statistics Division, New York, NY 10017, (800) 253-9646, Fax: (212) 963-4116, http://unstats.un.org; *Economic Survey of Latin America and the Caribbean 2004-2005.*

ECUADOR - INTEREST RATES

Inter-American Development Bank (IDB), 1300 New York Avenue, NW, Washington, DC 20577, (202) 623-1000, Fax: (202) 623-3096, www.iadb.org; *The Politics of Policies: Economic and Social Progress in Latin America - 2006 Report.*

Organization of American States (OAS), 17th Street Constitution Avenue NW, Washington, DC 20006, (202) 458-3000, www.oas.org; *The OAS in Transition: 1994-2004.*

ECUADOR - INTERNAL REVENUE

Inter-American Development Bank (IDB), 1300 New York Avenue, NW, Washington, DC 20577, (202) 623-1000, Fax: (202) 623-3096, www.iadb.org; *The Politics of Policies: Economic and Social Progress in Latin America - 2006 Report.*

Organization of American States (OAS), 17th Street Constitution Avenue NW, Washington, DC 20006, (202) 458-3000, www.oas.org; *The OAS in Transition: 1994-2004.*

ECUADOR - INTERNATIONAL FINANCE

Inter-American Development Bank (IDB), 1300 New York Avenue, NW, Washington, DC 20577, (202) 623-1000, Fax: (202) 623-3096, www.iadb.org; *The Politics of Policies: Economic and Social Progress in Latin America - 2006 Report.*

UCLA Latin American Institute, 10343 Bunche Hall, Box 951447, Los Angeles, CA 90095-1447, (310) 825-4571, Fax: (310) 206-6859, www.international.ucla.edu/lac; *Statistical Abstract of Latin America.*

United Nations Statistics Division, New York, NY 10017, (800) 253-9646, Fax: (212) 963-4116, http://unstats.un.org; *Statistical Yearbook for Latin America and the Caribbean 2004.*

ECUADOR - INTERNATIONAL LIQUIDITY

Inter-American Development Bank (IDB), 1300 New York Avenue, NW, Washington, DC 20577, (202) 623-1000, Fax: (202) 623-3096, www.iadb.org; *The Politics of Policies: Economic and Social Progress in Latin America - 2006 Report.*

International Monetary Fund (IMF), 700 Nineteenth Street, NW, Washington, DC 20431, (202) 623-7000, Fax: (202) 623-4661, www.imf.org; *International Financial Statistics Yearbook 2007.*

ECUADOR - INTERNATIONAL STATISTICS

Inter-American Development Bank (IDB), 1300 New York Avenue, NW, Washington, DC 20577, (202) 623-1000, Fax: (202) 623-3096, www.iadb.org; *The Politics of Policies: Economic and Social Progress in Latin America - 2006 Report.*

UCLA Latin American Institute, 10343 Bunche Hall, Box 951447, Los Angeles, CA 90095-1447, (310) 825-4571, Fax: (310) 206-6859, www.international.ucla.edu/lac; *Statistical Abstract of Latin America.*

ECUADOR - INTERNATIONAL TRADE

Economist Intelligence Unit, 111 West 57th Street, New York, NY 10019, (212) 554-0600, Fax: (212) 586-1181, www.eiu.com; *Business Latin America* and *Ecuador Country Report.*

Euromonitor International, Inc., 224 S. Michigan Avenue, Suite 1500, Chicago, IL 60604, (312) 922-1115, Fax: (312) 922-1157, www.euromonitor.com; *International Marketing Data and Statistics 2008; The World Economic Factbook 2008;* and *World Marketing Data and Statistics.*

Inter-American Development Bank (IDB), 1300 New York Avenue, NW, Washington, DC 20577, (202) 623-1000, Fax: (202) 623-3096, www.iadb.org; *The Politics of Policies: Economic and Social Progress in Latin America - 2006 Report.*

International Monetary Fund (IMF), 700 Nineteenth Street, NW, Washington, DC 20431, (202) 623-7000, Fax: (202) 623-4661, www.imf.org; *International Financial Statistics Yearbook 2007.*

M.E. Sharpe, 80 Business Park Drive, Armonk, NY 10504, (800) 541-6563, Fax: (914) 273-2106, www.mesharpe.com; *The Illustrated Book of World Rankings.*

Organisation for Economic Cooperation and Development (OECD), 2 rue Andre Pascal, F-75775 Paris Cedex 16, France, (Telephone in U.S. (202) 785-6323), (Fax in U.S. (202) 785-0350), www.oecd.org; *International Trade by Commodity Statistics (ITCS).*

Palgrave Macmillan Ltd., Houndmills, Basingstoke, Hampshire, RG21 6XS, England, (Telephone in U.S. (888) 330-8477), (Fax in U.S. (800) 672-2054), www.palgrave.com; *The Statesman's Yearbook 2008.*

Taylor and Francis Group, An Informa Business, 2 Park Square, Milton Park, Abingdon, Oxford OX14 4RN, United Kingdom, (Dial from U.S. (212) 216-7800), (Fax from U.S. (212) 564-7854), www.tandf.co.uk; *The Europa World Year Book.*

UCLA Latin American Institute, 10343 Bunche Hall, Box 951447, Los Angeles, CA 90095-1447, (310) 825-4571, Fax: (310) 206-6859, www.international.ucla.edu/lac; *Statistical Abstract of Latin America.*

United Nations Conference on Trade and Development (UNCTAD), DC2-1120, United Nations, New York, NY 10017, (212) 963-0027, www.unctad.org; *UNCTAD Commodity Yearbook.*

United Nations Food and Agricultural Organization (FAO), Viale delle Terme di Caracalla, 00100 Rome, Italy, (Dial from U.S. (202) 653-2400), (Fax from U.S. (202) 653 5760), www.fao.org; *FAO Trade Yearbook* and *The State of Food and Agriculture (SOFA) 2006.*

United Nations Statistics Division, New York, NY 10017, (800) 253-9646, Fax: (212) 963-4116, http://unstats.un.org; *Economic Survey of Latin America and the Caribbean 2004-2005; International Trade Statistics Yearbook; Statistical Yearbook;* and *Statistical Yearbook for Latin America and the Caribbean 2004.*

The World Bank, 1818 H Street, NW, Washington, DC 20433, (202) 473-1000, Fax: (202) 477-6391, www.worldbank.org; *Ecuador; World Development Indicators (WDI) 2008;* and *World Development Report 2008.*

World Trade Organization (WTO), Centre William Rappard, Rue de Lausanne 154, CH-1211 Geneva 21, Switzerland, www.wto.org; *International Trade Statistics 2006.*

ECUADOR - INTERNET USERS

International Telecommunication Union (ITU), Place des Nations, 1211 Geneva 20, Switzerland, www.itu.int; *World Telecommunication/ICT Indicators Database on CD-ROM; World Telecommunication/ICT Indicators Database Online;* and *Yearbook of Statistics - Telecommunication Services (Chronological Time Series 1997-2006).*

The World Bank, 1818 H Street, NW, Washington, DC 20433, (202) 473-1000, Fax: (202) 477-6391, www.worldbank.org; *Ecuador.*

ECUADOR - INVESTMENTS

Inter-American Development Bank (IDB), 1300 New York Avenue, NW, Washington, DC 20577, (202) 623-1000, Fax: (202) 623-3096, www.iadb.org; *The Politics of Policies: Economic and Social Progress in Latin America - 2006 Report.*

United Nations Statistics Division, New York, NY 10017, (800) 253-9646, Fax: (212) 963-4116, http://unstats.un.org; *Statistical Yearbook for Latin America and the Caribbean 2004.*

ECUADOR - INVESTMENTS, FOREIGN

Economist Intelligence Unit, 111 West 57th Street, New York, NY 10019, (212) 554-0600, Fax: (212) 586-1181, www.eiu.com; *Business Latin America.*

ECUADOR - IRON AND IRON ORE PRODUCTION

See ECUADOR - MINERAL INDUSTRIES

ECUADOR - IRRIGATION

Euromonitor International, Inc., 224 S. Michigan Avenue, Suite 1500, Chicago, IL 60604, (312) 922-1115, Fax: (312) 922-1157, www.euromonitor.com; *International Marketing Data and Statistics 2008.*

Inter-American Development Bank (IDB), 1300 New York Avenue, NW, Washington, DC 20577, (202) 623-1000, Fax: (202) 623-3096, www.iadb.org; *The Politics of Policies: Economic and Social Progress in Latin America - 2006 Report.*

ECUADOR - LABOR

Central Intelligence Agency, Office of Public Affairs, Washington, DC 20505, (703) 482-0623, Fax: (703) 482-1739, www.cia.gov; *The World Factbook.*

Economist Intelligence Unit, 111 West 57th Street, New York, NY 10019, (212) 554-0600, Fax: (212) 586-1181, www.eiu.com; *Business Latin America.*

Euromonitor International, Inc., 224 S. Michigan Avenue, Suite 1500, Chicago, IL 60604, (312) 922-1115, Fax: (312) 922-1157, www.euromonitor.com; *International Marketing Data and Statistics 2008* and *World Marketing Data and Statistics.*

International Labour Office, I.L.O. Publications, 4 route des Morillons, CH-1211 Geneva 22, Switzerland, (Telephone in U.S. (202) 653-7652), (Fax in U.S. (202) 653-7687), www.ilo.org; *Yearbook of Labour Statistics 2006.*

M.E. Sharpe, 80 Business Park Drive, Armonk, NY 10504, (800) 541-6563, Fax: (914) 273-2106, www.mesharpe.com; *The Illustrated Book of World Rankings.*

Palgrave Macmillan Ltd., Houndmills, Basingstoke, Hampshire, RG21 6XS, England, (Telephone in U.S. (888) 330-8477), (Fax in U.S. (800) 672-2054), www.palgrave.com; *The Statesman's Yearbook 2008.*

Taylor and Francis Group, An Informa Business, 2 Park Square, Milton Park, Abingdon, Oxford OX14 4RN, United Kingdom, (Dial from U.S. (212) 216-7800), (Fax from U.S. (212) 564-7854), www.tandf.co.uk; *The Europa World Year Book.*

United Nations Food and Agricultural Organization (FAO), Viale delle Terme di Caracalla, 00100 Rome, Italy, (Dial from U.S. (202) 653-2400), (Fax from U.S. (202) 653 5760), www.fao.org; *The State of Food and Agriculture (SOFA) 2006.*

United Nations Statistics Division, New York, NY 10017, (800) 253-9646, Fax: (212) 963-4116, http://unstats.un.org; *Human Development Report 2006.*

The World Bank, 1818 H Street, NW, Washington, DC 20433, (202) 473-1000, Fax: (202) 477-6391, www.worldbank.org; *The World Bank Atlas 2003-2004; World Development Indicators (WDI) 2008;* and *World Development Report 2008.*

ECUADOR - LAND USE

Central Intelligence Agency, Office of Public Affairs, Washington, DC 20505, (703) 482-0623, Fax: (703) 482-1739, www.cia.gov; *The World Factbook.*

Euromonitor International, Inc., 224 S. Michigan Avenue, Suite 1500, Chicago, IL 60604, (312) 922-1115, Fax: (312) 922-1157, www.euromonitor.com; *International Marketing Data and Statistics 2008.*

Inter-American Development Bank (IDB), 1300 New York Avenue, NW, Washington, DC 20577, (202) 623-1000, Fax: (202) 623-3096, www.iadb.org; *The Politics of Policies: Economic and Social Progress in Latin America - 2006 Report.*

United Nations Food and Agricultural Organization (FAO), Viale delle Terme di Caracalla, 00100 Rome, Italy, (Dial from U.S. (202) 653-2400), (Fax from U.S. (202) 653 5760), www.fao.org; *FAO Production Yearbook 2002.*

The World Bank, 1818 H Street, NW, Washington, DC 20433, (202) 473-1000, Fax: (202) 477-6391, www.worldbank.org; *World Development Report 2008.*

ECUADOR - LIBRARIES

M.E. Sharpe, 80 Business Park Drive, Armonk, NY 10504, (800) 541-6563, Fax: (914) 273-2106, www.mesharpe.com; *The Illustrated Book of World Rankings.*

ECUADOR - LIFE EXPECTANCY

Central Intelligence Agency, Office of Public Affairs, Washington, DC 20505, (703) 482-0623, Fax: (703) 482-1739, www.cia.gov; *The World Factbook.*

Economist Intelligence Unit, 111 West 57th Street, New York, NY 10019, (212) 554-0600, Fax: (212) 586-1181, www.eiu.com; *Business Latin America.*

Euromonitor International, Inc., 224 S. Michigan Avenue, Suite 1500, Chicago, IL 60604, (312) 922-1115, Fax: (312) 922-1157, www.euromonitor.com; *The World Economic Factbook 2008.*

Palgrave Macmillan Ltd., Houndmills, Basingstoke, Hampshire, RG21 6XS, England, (Telephone in U.S. (888) 330-8477), (Fax in U.S. (800) 672-2054), www.palgrave.com; *The Statesman's Yearbook 2008.*

United Nations Statistics Division, New York, NY 10017, (800) 253-9646, Fax: (212) 963-4116, http://unstats.un.org; *Human Development Report 2006; Statistical Yearbook for Latin America and the Caribbean 2004;* and *World Statistics Pocketbook.*

The World Bank, 1818 H Street, NW, Washington, DC 20433, (202) 473-1000, Fax: (202) 477-6391, www.worldbank.org; *The World Bank Atlas 2003-2004* and *World Development Report 2008.*

ECUADOR - LITERACY

Central Intelligence Agency, Office of Public Affairs, Washington, DC 20505, (703) 482-0623, Fax: (703) 482-1739, www.cia.gov; *The World Factbook.*

Economist Intelligence Unit, 111 West 57th Street, New York, NY 10019, (212) 554-0600, Fax: (212) 586-1181, www.eiu.com; *Business Latin America.*

Euromonitor International, Inc., 224 S. Michigan Avenue, Suite 1500, Chicago, IL 60604, (312) 922-1115, Fax: (312) 922-1157, www.euromonitor.com; *The World Economic Factbook 2008.*

ECUADOR - LIVESTOCK

Euromonitor International, Inc., 224 S. Michigan Avenue, Suite 1500, Chicago, IL 60604, (312) 922-1115, Fax: (312) 922-1157, www.euromonitor.com; *International Marketing Data and Statistics 2008.*

M.E. Sharpe, 80 Business Park Drive, Armonk, NY 10504, (800) 541-6563, Fax: (914) 273-2106, www.mesharpe.com; *The Illustrated Book of World Rankings.*

Palgrave Macmillan Ltd., Houndmills, Basingstoke, Hampshire, RG21 6XS, England, (Telephone in U.S. (888) 330-8477), (Fax in U.S. (800) 672-2054), www.palgrave.com; *The Statesman's Yearbook 2008.*

Taylor and Francis Group, An Informa Business, 2 Park Square, Milton Park, Abingdon, Oxford OX14 4RN, United Kingdom, (Dial from U.S. (212) 216-7800), (Fax from U.S. (212) 564-7854), www.tandf.co.uk; *The Europa World Year Book.*

United Nations Conference on Trade and Development (UNCTAD), DC2-1120, United Nations, New York, NY 10017, (212) 963-0027, www.unctad.org; *UNCTAD Commodity Yearbook.*

United Nations Food and Agricultural Organization (FAO), Viale delle Terme di Caracalla, 00100 Rome, Italy, (Dial from U.S. (202) 653-2400), (Fax from U.S. (202) 653 5760), www.fao.org; *FAO Production Yearbook 2002* and *The State of Food and Agriculture (SOFA) 2006.*

United Nations Statistics Division, New York, NY 10017, (800) 253-9646, Fax: (212) 963-4116, http://unstats.un.org; *Statistical Yearbook.*

ECUADOR - LOCAL TAXATION

Euromonitor International, Inc., 224 S. Michigan Avenue, Suite 1500, Chicago, IL 60604, (312) 922-1115, Fax: (312) 922-1157, www.euromonitor.com; *International Marketing Data and Statistics 2008.*

Inter-American Development Bank (IDB), 1300 New York Avenue, NW, Washington, DC 20577, (202) 623-1000, Fax: (202) 623-3096, www.iadb.org; *The Politics of Policies: Economic and Social Progress in Latin America - 2006 Report.*

ECUADOR - MANUFACTURES

Economist Intelligence Unit, 111 West 57th Street, New York, NY 10019, (212) 554-0600, Fax: (212) 586-1181, www.eiu.com; *Business Latin America.*

Inter-American Development Bank (IDB), 1300 New York Avenue, NW, Washington, DC 20577, (202) 623-1000, Fax: (202) 623-3096, www.iadb.org; *The Politics of Policies: Economic and Social Progress in Latin America - 2006 Report.*

M.E. Sharpe, 80 Business Park Drive, Armonk, NY 10504, (800) 541-6563, Fax: (914) 273-2106, www.mesharpe.com; *The Illustrated Book of World Rankings.*

United Nations Statistics Division, New York, NY 10017, (800) 253-9646, Fax: (212) 963-4116, http://unstats.un.org; *Statistical Yearbook* and *Statistical Yearbook for Latin America and the Caribbean 2004.*

The World Bank, 1818 H Street, NW, Washington, DC 20433, (202) 473-1000, Fax: (202) 477-6391, www.worldbank.org; *World Development Indicators (WDI) 2008.*

ECUADOR - MARRIAGE

M.E. Sharpe, 80 Business Park Drive, Armonk, NY 10504, (800) 541-6563, Fax: (914) 273-2106, www.mesharpe.com; *The Illustrated Book of World Rankings.*

Taylor and Francis Group, An Informa Business, 2 Park Square, Milton Park, Abingdon, Oxford OX14 4RN, United Kingdom, (Dial from U.S. (212) 216-7800), (Fax from U.S. (212) 564-7854), www.tandf.co.uk; *The Europa World Year Book.*

United Nations Statistics Division, New York, NY 10017, (800) 253-9646, Fax: (212) 963-4116, http://unstats.un.org; *Demographic Yearbook* and *Statistical Yearbook.*

ECUADOR - MEDICAL CARE, COST OF

International Monetary Fund (IMF), 700 Nineteenth Street, NW, Washington, DC 20431, (202) 623-7000, Fax: (202) 623-4661, www.imf.org; *Government Finance Statistics Yearbook (2008 Edition).*

United Nations Statistics Division, New York, NY 10017, (800) 253-9646, Fax: (212) 963-4116, http://unstats.un.org; *Statistical Yearbook for Latin America and the Caribbean 2004.*

ECUADOR - MEDICAL PERSONNEL

UCLA Latin American Institute, 10343 Bunche Hall, Box 951447, Los Angeles, CA 90095-1447, (310) 825-4571, Fax: (310) 206-6859, www.international.ucla.edu/lac; *Statistical Abstract of Latin America.*

ECUADOR - MILK PRODUCTION

See ECUADOR - DAIRY PROCESSING

ECUADOR - MINERAL INDUSTRIES

Economist Intelligence Unit, 111 West 57th Street, New York, NY 10019, (212) 554-0600, Fax: (212) 586-1181, www.eiu.com; *Business Latin America.*

Inter-American Development Bank (IDB), 1300 New York Avenue, NW, Washington, DC 20577, (202) 623-1000, Fax: (202) 623-3096, www.iadb.org; *The Politics of Policies: Economic and Social Progress in Latin America - 2006 Report.*

M.E. Sharpe, 80 Business Park Drive, Armonk, NY 10504, (800) 541-6563, Fax: (914) 273-2106, www.mesharpe.com; *The Illustrated Book of World Rankings.*

Organisation for Economic Cooperation and Development (OECD), 2 rue Andre Pascal, F-75775 Paris Cedex 16, France, (Telephone in U.S. (202) 785-6323), (Fax in U.S. (202) 785-0350), www.oecd.org; *World Energy Outlook 2007.*

Organization of Petroleum Exporting Countries (OPEC), Obere Donaustrasse 93, A-1020, Vienna, Austria, www.opec.org; *Annual Statistical Bulletin 2006.*

Palgrave Macmillan Ltd., Houndmills, Basingstoke, Hampshire, RG21 6XS, England, (Telephone in U.S. (888) 330-8477), (Fax in U.S. (800) 672-2054), www.palgrave.com; *The Statesman's Yearbook 2008.*

PennWell Corporation, 1421 South Sheridan Road, Tulsa, OK 74112, (918) 835-3161, www.pennwell.com; *Oil Gas Journal Latinoamericana.*

Taylor and Francis Group, An Informa Business, 2 Park Square, Milton Park, Abingdon, Oxford OX14 4RN, United Kingdom, (Dial from U.S. (212) 216-7800), (Fax from U.S. (212) 564-7854), www.tandf.co.uk; *The Europa World Year Book.*

UCLA Latin American Institute, 10343 Bunche Hall, Box 951447, Los Angeles, CA 90095-1447, (310) 825-4571, Fax: (310) 206-6859, www.international.ucla.edu/lac; *Statistical Abstract of Latin America.*

United Nations Conference on Trade and Development (UNCTAD), DC2-1120, United Nations, New York, NY 10017, (212) 963-0027, www.unctad.org; *UNCTAD Commodity Yearbook.*

United Nations Statistics Division, New York, NY 10017, (800) 253-9646, Fax: (212) 963-4116, http://unstats.un.org; *Statistical Yearbook* and *Statistical Yearbook for Latin America and the Caribbean 2004.*

ECUADOR - MONEY EXCHANGE RATES

See ECUADOR - FOREIGN EXCHANGE RATES

ECUADOR - MONEY SUPPLY

Economist Intelligence Unit, 111 West 57th Street, New York, NY 10019, (212) 554-0600, Fax: (212) 586-1181, www.eiu.com; *Ecuador Country Report.*

Euromonitor International, Inc., 224 S. Michigan Avenue, Suite 1500, Chicago, IL 60604, (312) 922-1115, Fax: (312) 922-1157, www.euromonitor.com; *International Marketing Data and Statistics 2008.*

Inter-American Development Bank (IDB), 1300 New York Avenue, NW, Washington, DC 20577, (202) 623-1000, Fax: (202) 623-3096, www.iadb.org; *The Politics of Policies: Economic and Social Progress in Latin America - 2006 Report.*

International Monetary Fund (IMF), 700 Nineteenth Street, NW, Washington, DC 20431, (202) 623-7000, Fax: (202) 623-4661, www.imf.org; *International Financial Statistics Yearbook 2007.*

Taylor and Francis Group, An Informa Business, 2 Park Square, Milton Park, Abingdon, Oxford OX14 4RN, United Kingdom, (Dial from U.S. (212) 216-7800), (Fax from U.S. (212) 564-7854), www.tandf.co.uk; *The Europa World Year Book.*

UCLA Latin American Institute, 10343 Bunche Hall, Box 951447, Los Angeles, CA 90095-1447, (310) 825-4571, Fax: (310) 206-6859, www.international.ucla.edu/lac; *Statistical Abstract of Latin America.*

United Nations Statistics Division, New York, NY 10017, (800) 253-9646, Fax: (212) 963-4116, http://unstats.un.org; *Statistical Yearbook.*

The World Bank, 1818 H Street, NW, Washington, DC 20433, (202) 473-1000, Fax: (202) 477-6391, www.worldbank.org; *Ecuador* and *World Development Indicators (WDI) 2008.*

ECUADOR - MORTALITY

Central Intelligence Agency, Office of Public Affairs, Washington, DC 20505, (703) 482-0623, Fax: (703) 482-1739, www.cia.gov; *The World Factbook.*

Economist Intelligence Unit, 111 West 57th Street, New York, NY 10019, (212) 554-0600, Fax: (212) 586-1181, www.eiu.com; *Business Latin America.*

Euromonitor International, Inc., 224 S. Michigan Avenue, Suite 1500, Chicago, IL 60604, (312) 922-1115, Fax: (312) 922-1157, www.euromonitor.com; *International Marketing Data and Statistics 2008* and *The World Economic Factbook 2008.*

Palgrave Macmillan Ltd., Houndmills, Basingstoke, Hampshire, RG21 6XS, England, (Telephone in U.S.

(888) 330-8477), (Fax in U.S. (800) 672-2054), www.palgrave.com; *The Statesman's Yearbook 2008.*

Taylor and Francis Group, An Informa Business, 2 Park Square, Milton Park, Abingdon, Oxford OX14 4RN, United Kingdom, (Dial from U.S. (212) 216-7800), (Fax from U.S. (212) 564-7854), www.tandf.co.uk; *The Europa World Year Book.*

UNICEF, 3 United Nations Plaza, New York, NY 10017, (800) 253-9646, Fax: (212) 887-7465, www.unicef.org; *The State of the World's Children 2008.*

United Nations Statistics Division, New York, NY 10017, (800) 253-9646, Fax: (212) 963-4116, http://unstats.un.org; *Demographic Yearbook; Human Development Report 2006; Statistical Yearbook; Statistical Yearbook for Latin America and the Caribbean 2004;* and *World Statistics Pocketbook.*

The World Bank, 1818 H Street, NW, Washington, DC 20433, (202) 473-1000, Fax: (202) 477-6391, www.worldbank.org; *The World Bank Atlas 2003-2004; World Development Indicators (WDI) 2008;* and *World Development Report 2008.*

World Health Organization (WHO), Avenue Appia 20, 1211 Geneve 27, Switzerland, (Telephone in U.S. (212) 331-9081), www.who.int; The WHO Global Atlas of Infectious Diseases and *World Health Report 2006.*

ECUADOR - MOTION PICTURES

United Nations Statistics Division, New York, NY 10017, (800) 253-9646, Fax: (212) 963-4116, http://unstats.un.org; *Statistical Yearbook.*

ECUADOR - MOTOR VEHICLES

Economist Intelligence Unit, 111 West 57th Street, New York, NY 10019, (212) 554-0600, Fax: (212) 586-1181, www.eiu.com; *Business Latin America.*

International Road Federation (IFR), Madison Place, 500 Montgomery Street, 5th Floor, Alexandria, VA 22314, (703) 535-1001, Fax: (703) 535-1007, www.irfnet.org; *World Road Statistics 2006.*

Taylor and Francis Group, An Informa Business, 2 Park Square, Milton Park, Abingdon, Oxford OX14 4RN, United Kingdom, (Dial from U.S. (212) 216-7800), (Fax from U.S. (212) 564-7854), www.tandf.co.uk; *The Europa World Year Book.*

United Nations Statistics Division, New York, NY 10017, (800) 253-9646, Fax: (212) 963-4116, http://unstats.un.org; *Statistical Yearbook.*

ECUADOR - MUSEUMS

M.E. Sharpe, 80 Business Park Drive, Armonk, NY 10504, (800) 541-6563, Fax: (914) 273-2106, www.mesharpe.com; *The Illustrated Book of World Rankings.*

ECUADOR - NATURAL GAS PRODUCTION

See ECUADOR - MINERAL INDUSTRIES

ECUADOR - NUTRITION

United Nations Food and Agricultural Organization (FAO), Viale delle Terme di Caracalla, 00100 Rome, Italy, (Dial from U.S. (202) 653-2400), (Fax from U.S. (202) 653 5760), www.fao.org; *The State of Food and Agriculture (SOFA) 2006.*

United Nations Statistics Division, New York, NY 10017, (800) 253-9646, Fax: (212) 963-4116, http://unstats.un.org; *Statistical Yearbook for Latin America and the Caribbean 2004.*

ECUADOR - OLDER PEOPLE

M.E. Sharpe, 80 Business Park Drive, Armonk, NY 10504, (800) 541-6563, Fax: (914) 273-2106, www.mesharpe.com; *The Illustrated Book of World Rankings.*

ECUADOR - PALM OIL PRODUCTION

See ECUADOR - CROPS

ECUADOR - PAPER MANUFACTURING

UNESCO Institute for Statistics, C.P. 6128 Succursale Centre-Ville, Montreal, Quebec, H3C 3J7 Canada, (Dial from U.S. (514) 343-6880), (Fax from U.S. (514) 343 6882), www.uis.unesco.org; *Statistical Tables.*

United Nations Statistics Division, New York, NY 10017, (800) 253-9646, Fax: (212) 963-4116, http://unstats.un.org; *Statistical Yearbook.*

ECUADOR - PEANUT PRODUCTION

See ECUADOR - CROPS

ECUADOR - PERIODICALS

UNESCO Institute for Statistics, C.P. 6128 Succursale Centre-Ville, Montreal, Quebec, H3C 3J7 Canada, (Dial from U.S. (514) 343-6880), (Fax from U.S. (514) 343 6882), www.uis.unesco.org; *Statistical Tables.*

ECUADOR - PESTICIDES

United Nations Food and Agricultural Organization (FAO), Viale delle Terme di Caracalla, 00100 Rome, Italy, (Dial from U.S. (202) 653-2400), (Fax from U.S. (202) 653 5760), www.fao.org; *The State of Food and Agriculture (SOFA) 2006.*

ECUADOR - PETROLEUM INDUSTRY AND TRADE

Economist Intelligence Unit, 111 West 57th Street, New York, NY 10019, (212) 554-0600, Fax: (212) 586-1181, www.eiu.com; *Business Latin America.*

Inter-American Development Bank (IDB), 1300 New York Avenue, NW, Washington, DC 20577, (202) 623-1000, Fax: (202) 623-3096, www.iadb.org; *The Politics of Policies: Economic and Social Progress in Latin America - 2006 Report.*

M.E. Sharpe, 80 Business Park Drive, Armonk, NY 10504, (800) 541-6563, Fax: (914) 273-2106, www.mesharpe.com; *The Illustrated Book of World Rankings.*

Organisation for Economic Cooperation and Development (OECD), 2 rue Andre Pascal, F-75775 Paris Cedex 16, France, (Telephone in U.S. (202) 785-6323), (Fax in U.S. (202) 785-0350), www.oecd.org; *World Energy Outlook 2007.*

Organization of American States (OAS), 17th Street Constitution Avenue NW, Washington, DC 20006, (202) 458-3000, www.oas.org; *The OAS in Transition: 1994-2004.*

Organization of Petroleum Exporting Countries (OPEC), Obere Donaustrasse 93, A-1020, Vienna, Austria, www.opec.org; *Annual Statistical Bulletin 2006.*

Palgrave Macmillan Ltd., Houndmills, Basingstoke, Hampshire, RG21 6XS, England, (Telephone in U.S. (888) 330-8477), (Fax in U.S. (800) 672-2054), www.palgrave.com; *The Statesman's Yearbook 2008.*

PennWell Corporation, 1421 South Sheridan Road, Tulsa, OK 74112, (918) 835-3161, www.pennwell.com; *International Petroleum Encyclopedia 2007.*

U.S. Department of Energy (DOE), Energy Information Administration (EIA), 1000 Independence Avenue, SW, Washington, DC 20585, (202) 586-8800, www.eia.doe.gov; *International Energy Annual 2004* and *International Energy Outlook 2006.*

United Nations Conference on Trade and Development (UNCTAD), DC2-1120, United Nations, New York, NY 10017, (212) 963-0027, www.unctad.org; *UNCTAD Commodity Yearbook.*

United Nations Food and Agricultural Organization (FAO), Viale delle Terme di Caracalla, 00100 Rome, Italy, (Dial from U.S. (202) 653-2400), (Fax from U.S. (202) 653 5760), www.fao.org; *The State of Food and Agriculture (SOFA) 2006.*

United Nations Statistics Division, New York, NY 10017, (800) 253-9646, Fax: (212) 963-4116, http://unstats.un.org; *Statistical Yearbook.*

ECUADOR - PIPELINES

Organization of Petroleum Exporting Countries (OPEC), Obere Donaustrasse 93, A-1020, Vienna, Austria, www.opec.org; *Annual Statistical Bulletin 2006.*

ECUADOR - POLITICAL SCIENCE

Central Intelligence Agency, Office of Public Affairs, Washington, DC 20505, (703) 482-0623, Fax: (703) 482-1739, www.cia.gov; *The World Factbook.*

Inter-American Development Bank (IDB), 1300 New York Avenue, NW, Washington, DC 20577, (202) 623-1000, Fax: (202) 623-3096, www.iadb.org; *The Politics of Policies: Economic and Social Progress in Latin America - 2006 Report.*

International Monetary Fund (IMF), 700 Nineteenth Street, NW, Washington, DC 20431, (202) 623-7000, Fax: (202) 623-4661, www.imf.org; *Government Finance Statistics Yearbook (2008 Edition).*

Palgrave Macmillan Ltd., Houndmills, Basingstoke, Hampshire, RG21 6XS, England, (Telephone in U.S. (888) 330-8477), (Fax in U.S. (800) 672-2054), www.palgrave.com; *The Statesman's Yearbook 2008.*

Taylor and Francis Group, An Informa Business, 2 Park Square, Milton Park, Abingdon, Oxford OX14 4RN, United Kingdom, (Dial from U.S. (212) 216-7800), (Fax from U.S. (212) 564-7854), www.tandf.co.uk; *The Europa World Year Book.*

UCLA Latin American Institute, 10343 Bunche Hall, Box 951447, Los Angeles, CA 90095-1447, (310) 825-4571, Fax: (310) 206-6859, www.international.ucla.edu/lac; *Statistical Abstract of Latin America.*

United Nations Statistics Division, New York, NY 10017, (800) 253-9646, Fax: (212) 963-4116, http://unstats.un.org; *National Accounts Statistics: Compendium of Income Distribution Statistics* and *Statistical Yearbook.*

The World Bank, 1818 H Street, NW, Washington, DC 20433, (202) 473-1000, Fax: (202) 477-6391, www.worldbank.org; *World Development Indicators (WDI) 2008* and *World Development Report 2008.*

ECUADOR - POPULATION

Central Intelligence Agency, Office of Public Affairs, Washington, DC 20505, (703) 482-0623, Fax: (703) 482-1739, www.cia.gov; *The World Factbook.*

Economist Intelligence Unit, 111 West 57th Street, New York, NY 10019, (212) 554-0600, Fax: (212) 586-1181, www.eiu.com; *Business Latin America* and *Ecuador Country Report.*

Euromonitor International, Inc., 224 S. Michigan Avenue, Suite 1500, Chicago, IL 60604, (312) 922-1115, Fax: (312) 922-1157, www.euromonitor.com; *International Marketing Data and Statistics 2008* and *The World Economic Factbook 2008.*

Inter-American Development Bank (IDB), 1300 New York Avenue, NW, Washington, DC 20577, (202) 623-1000, Fax: (202) 623-3096, www.iadb.org; *The Politics of Policies: Economic and Social Progress in Latin America - 2006 Report.*

International Labour Office, I.L.O. Publications, 4 route des Morillons, CH-1211 Geneva 22, Switzerland, (Telephone in U.S. (202) 653-7652), (Fax in U.S. (202) 653-7687), www.ilo.org; *Yearbook of Labour Statistics 2006.*

M.E. Sharpe, 80 Business Park Drive, Armonk, NY 10504, (800) 541-6563, Fax: (914) 273-2106, www.mesharpe.com; *The Illustrated Book of World Rankings.*

Organization of American States (OAS), 17th Street Constitution Avenue NW, Washington, DC 20006, (202) 458-3000, www.oas.org; *The OAS in Transition: 1994-2004.*

Palgrave Macmillan Ltd., Houndmills, Basingstoke, Hampshire, RG21 6XS, England, (Telephone in U.S. (888) 330-8477), (Fax in U.S. (800) 672-2054), www.palgrave.com; *The Statesman's Yearbook 2008.*

Taylor and Francis Group, An Informa Business, 2 Park Square, Milton Park, Abingdon, Oxford OX14 4RN, United Kingdom, (Dial from U.S. (212) 216-7800), (Fax from U.S. (212) 564-7854), www.tandf.co.uk; *The Europa World Year Book.*

U.S. Department of State (DOS), 2201 C Street NW, Washington, DC 20520, (202) 647-4000, www.state.gov; *World Military Expenditures and Arms Transfers (WMEAT).*

UCLA Latin American Institute, 10343 Bunche Hall, Box 951447, Los Angeles, CA 90095-1447, (310) 825-4571, Fax: (310) 206-6859, www.international.ucla.edu/lac; *Statistical Abstract of Latin America.*

UNESCO Institute for Statistics, C.P. 6128 Succursale Centre-Ville, Montreal, Quebec, H3C 3J7 Canada, (Dial from U.S. (514) 343-6880), (Fax from U.S. (514) 343 6882), www.uis.unesco.org; *Statistical Tables.*

United Nations Food and Agricultural Organization (FAO), Viale delle Terme di Caracalla, 00100 Rome, Italy, (Dial from U.S. (202) 653-2400), (Fax from U.S. (202) 653 5760), www.fao.org; *FAO Production Yearbook 2002.*

United Nations Statistics Division, New York, NY 10017, (800) 253-9646, Fax: (212) 963-4116, http://unstats.un.org; *Demographic Yearbook; Human Development Report 2006; Statistical Yearbook; Statistical Yearbook for Latin America and the Caribbean 2004;* and *World Statistics Pocketbook.*

The World Bank, 1818 H Street, NW, Washington, DC 20433, (202) 473-1000, Fax: (202) 477-6391, www.worldbank.org; *Ecuador; The World Bank Atlas 2003-2004;* and *World Development Report 2008.*

World Health Organization (WHO), Avenue Appia 20, 1211 Geneve 27, Switzerland, (Telephone in U.S. (212) 331-9081), www.who.int; *World Health Report 2006.*

ECUADOR - POPULATION DENSITY

Central Intelligence Agency, Office of Public Affairs, Washington, DC 20505, (703) 482-0623, Fax: (703) 482-1739, www.cia.gov; *The World Factbook.*

Euromonitor International, Inc., 224 S. Michigan Avenue, Suite 1500, Chicago, IL 60604, (312) 922-1115, Fax: (312) 922-1157, www.euromonitor.com; *International Marketing Data and Statistics 2008* and *The World Economic Factbook 2008.*

Inter-American Development Bank (IDB), 1300 New York Avenue, NW, Washington, DC 20577, (202) 623-1000, Fax: (202) 623-3096, www.iadb.org; *The Politics of Policies: Economic and Social Progress in Latin America - 2006 Report.*

M.E. Sharpe, 80 Business Park Drive, Armonk, NY 10504, (800) 541-6563, Fax: (914) 273-2106, www.mesharpe.com; *The Illustrated Book of World Rankings.*

Palgrave Macmillan Ltd., Houndmills, Basingstoke, Hampshire, RG21 6XS, England, (Telephone in U.S. (888) 330-8477), (Fax in U.S. (800) 672-2054), www.palgrave.com; *The Statesman's Yearbook 2008.*

Taylor and Francis Group, An Informa Business, 2 Park Square, Milton Park, Abingdon, Oxford OX14 4RN, United Kingdom, (Dial from U.S. (212) 216-7800), (Fax from U.S. (212) 564-7854), www.tandf.co.uk; *The Europa World Year Book.*

UNESCO Institute for Statistics, C.P. 6128 Succursale Centre-Ville, Montreal, Quebec, H3C 3J7 Canada, (Dial from U.S. (514) 343-6880), (Fax from U.S. (514) 343 6882), www.uis.unesco.org; *Statistical Tables.*

United Nations Food and Agricultural Organization (FAO), Viale delle Terme di Caracalla, 00100 Rome, Italy, (Dial from U.S. (202) 653-2400), (Fax from U.S. (202) 653 5760), www.fao.org; *The State of Food and Agriculture (SOFA) 2006.*

United Nations Statistics Division, New York, NY 10017, (800) 253-9646, Fax: (212) 963-4116, http://unstats.un.org; *Statistical Yearbook.*

The World Bank, 1818 H Street, NW, Washington, DC 20433, (202) 473-1000, Fax: (202) 477-6391, www.worldbank.org; *Ecuador* and *World Development Report 2008.*

ECUADOR - POSTAL SERVICE

M.E. Sharpe, 80 Business Park Drive, Armonk, NY 10504, (800) 541-6563, Fax: (914) 273-2106, www.mesharpe.com; *The Illustrated Book of World Rankings.*

United Nations Statistics Division, New York, NY 10017, (800) 253-9646, Fax: (212) 963-4116, http://unstats.un.org; *Statistical Yearbook.*

ECUADOR - POWER RESOURCES

Economist Intelligence Unit, 111 West 57th Street, New York, NY 10019, (212) 554-0600, Fax: (212) 586-1181, www.eiu.com; *Business Latin America.*

Euromonitor International, Inc., 224 S. Michigan Avenue, Suite 1500, Chicago, IL 60604, (312) 922-1115, Fax: (312) 922-1157, www.euromonitor.com; *International Marketing Data and Statistics 2008; The World Economic Factbook 2008;* and *World Marketing Data and Statistics.*

M.E. Sharpe, 80 Business Park Drive, Armonk, NY 10504, (800) 541-6563, Fax: (914) 273-2106, www.mesharpe.com; *The Illustrated Book of World Rankings.*

Organisation for Economic Cooperation and Development (OECD), 2 rue Andre Pascal, F-75775 Paris Cedex 16, France, (Telephone in U.S. (202) 785-6323), (Fax in U.S. (202) 785-0350), www.oecd.org; *World Energy Outlook 2007.*

Palgrave Macmillan Ltd., Houndmills, Basingstoke, Hampshire, RG21 6XS, England, (Telephone in U.S. (888) 330-8477), (Fax in U.S. (800) 672-2054), www.palgrave.com; *The Statesman's Yearbook 2008.*

Platts, 2 Penn Plaza, 25th Floor, New York, NY 10121-2298, (212) 904-3070, www.platts.com; *Energy Economist.*

U.S. Department of Energy (DOE), Energy Information Administration (EIA), 1000 Independence Avenue, SW, Washington, DC 20585, (202) 586-8800, www.eia.doe.gov; *International Energy Annual 2004* and *International Energy Outlook 2006.*

UCLA Latin American Institute, 10343 Bunche Hall, Box 951447, Los Angeles, CA 90095-1447, (310) 825-4571, Fax: (310) 206-6859, www.international.ucla.edu/lac; *Statistical Abstract of Latin America.*

United Nations Food and Agricultural Organization (FAO), Viale delle Terme di Caracalla, 00100 Rome, Italy, (Dial from U.S. (202) 653-2400), (Fax from U.S. (202) 653 5760), www.fao.org; *The State of Food and Agriculture (SOFA) 2006.*

United Nations Statistics Division, New York, NY 10017, (800) 253-9646, Fax: (212) 963-4116, http://unstats.un.org; *Energy Statistics Yearbook 2003; Human Development Report 2006; Statistical Yearbook; Statistical Yearbook for Latin America and the Caribbean 2004;* and *World Statistics Pocketbook.*

The World Bank, 1818 H Street, NW, Washington, DC 20433, (202) 473-1000, Fax: (202) 477-6391, www.worldbank.org; *The World Bank Atlas 2003-2004* and *World Development Report 2008.*

ECUADOR - PRICES

Economist Intelligence Unit, 111 West 57th Street, New York, NY 10019, (212) 554-0600, Fax: (212) 586-1181, www.eiu.com; *Business Latin America.*

Euromonitor International, Inc., 224 S. Michigan Avenue, Suite 1500, Chicago, IL 60604, (312) 922-1115, Fax: (312) 922-1157, www.euromonitor.com; *World Marketing Data and Statistics.*

International Labour Office, I.L.O. Publications, 4 route des Morillons, CH-1211 Geneva 22, Switzerland, (Telephone in U.S. (202) 653-7652), (Fax in U.S. (202) 653-7687), www.ilo.org; *Yearbook of Labour Statistics 2006.*

International Monetary Fund (IMF), 700 Nineteenth Street, NW, Washington, DC 20431, (202) 623-7000, Fax: (202) 623-4661, www.imf.org; *International Financial Statistics Yearbook 2007.*

M.E. Sharpe, 80 Business Park Drive, Armonk, NY 10504, (800) 541-6563, Fax: (914) 273-2106, www.mesharpe.com; *The Illustrated Book of World Rankings.*

Organization of American States (OAS), 17th Street Constitution Avenue NW, Washington, DC 20006, (202) 458-3000, www.oas.org; *The OAS in Transition: 1994-2004.*

UCLA Latin American Institute, 10343 Bunche Hall, Box 951447, Los Angeles, CA 90095-1447, (310) 825-4571, Fax: (310) 206-6859, www.international.ucla.edu/lac; *Statistical Abstract of Latin America.*

United Nations Food and Agricultural Organization (FAO), Viale delle Terme di Caracalla, 00100 Rome, Italy, (Dial from U.S. (202) 653-2400), (Fax from U.S. (202) 653 5760), www.fao.org; *FAO Production Yearbook 2002* and *The State of Food and Agriculture (SOFA) 2006.*

United Nations Statistics Division, New York, NY 10017, (800) 253-9646, Fax: (212) 963-4116, http://unstats.un.org; *Economic Survey of Latin America and the Caribbean 2004-2005* and *Statistical Yearbook for Latin America and the Caribbean 2004.*

The World Bank, 1818 H Street, NW, Washington, DC 20433, (202) 473-1000, Fax: (202) 477-6391, www.worldbank.org; *Ecuador.*

ECUADOR - PROFESSIONS

UCLA Latin American Institute, 10343 Bunche Hall, Box 951447, Los Angeles, CA 90095-1447, (310) 825-4571, Fax: (310) 206-6859, www.international.ucla.edu/lac; *Statistical Abstract of Latin America.*

United Nations Statistics Division, New York, NY 10017, (800) 253-9646, Fax: (212) 963-4116, http://unstats.un.org; *Statistical Yearbook.*

ECUADOR - PUBLIC HEALTH

Economist Intelligence Unit, 111 West 57th Street, New York, NY 10019, (212) 554-0600, Fax: (212) 586-1181, www.eiu.com; *Business Latin America.*

Euromonitor International, Inc., 224 S. Michigan Avenue, Suite 1500, Chicago, IL 60604, (312) 922-1115, Fax: (312) 922-1157, www.euromonitor.com; *World Marketing Data and Statistics.*

M.E. Sharpe, 80 Business Park Drive, Armonk, NY 10504, (800) 541-6563, Fax: (914) 273-2106, www.mesharpe.com; *The Illustrated Book of World Rankings.*

Palgrave Macmillan Ltd., Houndmills, Basingstoke, Hampshire, RG21 6XS, England, (Telephone in U.S. (888) 330-8477), (Fax in U.S. (800) 672-2054), www.palgrave.com; *The Statesman's Yearbook 2008.*

UCLA Latin American Institute, 10343 Bunche Hall, Box 951447, Los Angeles, CA 90095-1447, (310) 825-4571, Fax: (310) 206-6859, www.international.ucla.edu/lac; *Statistical Abstract of Latin America.*

UNICEF, 3 United Nations Plaza, New York, NY 10017, (800) 253-9646, Fax: (212) 887-7465, www.unicef.org; *The State of the World's Children 2008.*

United Nations Statistics Division, New York, NY 10017, (800) 253-9646, Fax: (212) 963-4116, http://unstats.un.org; *Human Development Report 2006* and *Statistical Yearbook.*

The World Bank, 1818 H Street, NW, Washington, DC 20433, (202) 473-1000, Fax: (202) 477-6391, www.worldbank.org; *Ecuador* and *World Development Report 2008.*

World Health Organization (WHO), Avenue Appia 20, 1211 Geneve 27, Switzerland, (Telephone in U.S. (212) 331-9081), www.who.int; The WHO Global Atlas of Infectious Diseases and *World Health Report 2006.*

ECUADOR - PUBLIC UTILITIES

UCLA Latin American Institute, 10343 Bunche Hall, Box 951447, Los Angeles, CA 90095-1447, (310) 825-4571, Fax: (310) 206-6859, www.international.ucla.edu/lac; *Statistical Abstract of Latin America.*

ECUADOR - RADIO - RECEIVERS AND RECEPTION

Palgrave Macmillan Ltd., Houndmills, Basingstoke, Hampshire, RG21 6XS, England, (Telephone in U.S. (888) 330-8477), (Fax in U.S. (800) 672-2054), www.palgrave.com; *The Statesman's Yearbook 2008.*

United Nations Statistics Division, New York, NY 10017, (800) 253-9646, Fax: (212) 963-4116, http://unstats.un.org; *Statistical Yearbook.*

ECUADOR - RAILROADS

Economist Intelligence Unit, 111 West 57th Street, New York, NY 10019, (212) 554-0600, Fax: (212) 586-1181, www.eiu.com; *Business Latin America.*

Jane's Information Group, 110 North Royal Street, Suite 200, Alexandria, VA 22314, (703) 683-3700, Fax: (800) 836-0297, www.janes.com; *Jane's World Railways.*

Palgrave Macmillan Ltd., Houndmills, Basingstoke, Hampshire, RG21 6XS, England, (Telephone in U.S. (888) 330-8477), (Fax in U.S. (800) 672-2054), www.palgrave.com; *The Statesman's Yearbook 2008.*

Taylor and Francis Group, An Informa Business, 2 Park Square, Milton Park, Abingdon, Oxford OX14 4RN, United Kingdom, (Dial from U.S. (212) 216-7800), (Fax from U.S. (212) 564-7854), www.tandf.co.uk; *The Europa World Year Book.*

United Nations Statistics Division, New York, NY 10017, (800) 253-9646, Fax: (212) 963-4116, http://unstats.un.org; *Statistical Yearbook.*

ECUADOR - RANCHING

UCLA Latin American Institute, 10343 Bunche Hall, Box 951447, Los Angeles, CA 90095-1447, (310) 825-4571, Fax: (310) 206-6859, www.international.ucla.edu/lac; *Statistical Abstract of Latin America.*

ECUADOR - RELIGION

Central Intelligence Agency, Office of Public Affairs, Washington, DC 20505, (703) 482-0623, Fax: (703) 482-1739, www.cia.gov; *The World Factbook.*

M.E. Sharpe, 80 Business Park Drive, Armonk, NY 10504, (800) 541-6563, Fax: (914) 273-2106, www.mesharpe.com; *The Illustrated Book of World Rankings.*

Palgrave Macmillan Ltd., Houndmills, Basingstoke, Hampshire, RG21 6XS, England, (Telephone in U.S. (888) 330-8477), (Fax in U.S. (800) 672-2054), www.palgrave.com; *The Statesman's Yearbook 2008.*

UCLA Latin American Institute, 10343 Bunche Hall, Box 951447, Los Angeles, CA 90095-1447, (310) 825-4571, Fax: (310) 206-6859, www.international.ucla.edu/lac; *Statistical Abstract of Latin America.*

ECUADOR - RENT CHARGES

International Labour Office, I.L.O. Publications, 4 route des Morillons, CH-1211 Geneva 22, Switzerland, (Telephone in U.S. (202) 653-7652), (Fax in U.S. (202) 653-7687), www.ilo.org; *Yearbook of Labour Statistics 2006.*

ECUADOR - RESERVES (ACCOUNTING)

Economist Intelligence Unit, 111 West 57th Street, New York, NY 10019, (212) 554-0600, Fax: (212) 586-1181, www.eiu.com; *Business Latin America.*

Euromonitor International, Inc., 224 S. Michigan Avenue, Suite 1500, Chicago, IL 60604, (312) 922-1115, Fax: (312) 922-1157, www.euromonitor.com; *International Marketing Data and Statistics 2008.*

Inter-American Development Bank (IDB), 1300 New York Avenue, NW, Washington, DC 20577, (202) 623-1000, Fax: (202) 623-3096, www.iadb.org; *The Politics of Policies: Economic and Social Progress in Latin America - 2006 Report.*

Organization of American States (OAS), 17th Street Constitution Avenue NW, Washington, DC 20006, (202) 458-3000, www.oas.org; *The OAS in Transition: 1994-2004.*

United Nations Statistics Division, New York, NY 10017, (800) 253-9646, Fax: (212) 963-4116, http://unstats.un.org; *Statistical Yearbook.*

The World Bank, 1818 H Street, NW, Washington, DC 20433, (202) 473-1000, Fax: (202) 477-6391, www.worldbank.org; *World Development Indicators (WDI) 2008.*

ECUADOR - RETAIL TRADE

Euromonitor International, Inc., 224 S. Michigan Avenue, Suite 1500, Chicago, IL 60604, (312) 922-1115, Fax: (312) 922-1157, www.euromonitor.com; *World Marketing Data and Statistics.*

Inter-American Development Bank (IDB), 1300 New York Avenue, NW, Washington, DC 20577, (202) 623-1000, Fax: (202) 623-3096, www.iadb.org; *The Politics of Policies: Economic and Social Progress in Latin America - 2006 Report.*

United Nations Statistics Division, New York, NY 10017, (800) 253-9646, Fax: (212) 963-4116, http://unstats.un.org; *Statistical Yearbook.*

ECUADOR - RICE PRODUCTION

See ECUADOR - CROPS

ECUADOR - ROADS

Central Intelligence Agency, Office of Public Affairs, Washington, DC 20505, (703) 482-0623, Fax: (703) 482-1739, www.cia.gov; *The World Factbook.*

Economist Intelligence Unit, 111 West 57th Street, New York, NY 10019, (212) 554-0600, Fax: (212) 586-1181, www.eiu.com; *Business Latin America.*

International Road Federation (IFR), Madison Place, 500 Montgomery Street, 5th Floor, Alexandria, VA 22314, (703) 535-1001, Fax: (703) 535-1007, www.irfnet.org; *World Road Statistics 2006.*

Palgrave Macmillan Ltd., Houndmills, Basingstoke, Hampshire, RG21 6XS, England, (Telephone in U.S. (888) 330-8477), (Fax in U.S. (800) 672-2054), www.palgrave.com; *The Statesman's Yearbook 2008.*

ECUADOR - RUBBER INDUSTRY AND TRADE

International Rubber Study Group (IRSG), 1st Floor, Heron House, 109/115 Wembley Hill Road, Wembley, Middlesex HA9 8DA, United Kingdom, www.rubberstudy.com; *Rubber Statistical Bulletin; Summary of World Rubber Statistics 2005; World Rubber Statistics Handbook (Volume 6, 1975-2001);* and *World Rubber Statistics Historic Handbook.*

M.E. Sharpe, 80 Business Park Drive, Armonk, NY 10504, (800) 541-6563, Fax: (914) 273-2106, www.mesharpe.com; *The Illustrated Book of World Rankings.*

ECUADOR - SALT PRODUCTION

See ECUADOR - MINERAL INDUSTRIES

ECUADOR - SHEEP

See ECUADOR - LIVESTOCK

ECUADOR - SHIPPING

Organization of Petroleum Exporting Countries (OPEC), Obere Donaustrasse 93, A-1020, Vienna, Austria, www.opec.org; *Annual Statistical Bulletin 2006.*

Palgrave Macmillan Ltd., Houndmills, Basingstoke, Hampshire, RG21 6XS, England, (Telephone in U.S. (888) 330-8477), (Fax in U.S. (800) 672-2054), www.palgrave.com; *The Statesman's Yearbook 2008.*

Taylor and Francis Group, An Informa Business, 2 Park Square, Milton Park, Abingdon, Oxford OX14 4RN, United Kingdom, (Dial from U.S. (212) 216-7800), (Fax from U.S. (212) 564-7854), www.tandf.co.uk; *The Europa World Year Book.*

U.S. Department of Transportation (DOT), Maritime Administration (MARAD), West Building, Southeast Federal Center, 1200 New Jersey Avenue, SE, Washington, DC 20590, (800) 99-MARAD, www.marad.dot.gov; *World Merchant Fleet 2005.*

United Nations Statistics Division, New York, NY 10017, (800) 253-9646, Fax: (212) 963-4116, http://unstats.un.org; *Statistical Yearbook.*

ECUADOR - SILVER PRODUCTION

See ECUADOR - MINERAL INDUSTRIES

ECUADOR - SOCIAL ECOLOGY

M.E. Sharpe, 80 Business Park Drive, Armonk, NY 10504, (800) 541-6563, Fax: (914) 273-2106, www.mesharpe.com; *The Illustrated Book of World Rankings.*

UCLA Latin American Institute, 10343 Bunche Hall, Box 951447, Los Angeles, CA 90095-1447, (310) 825-4571, Fax: (310) 206-6859, www.international.ucla.edu/lac; *Statistical Abstract of Latin America.*

United Nations Statistics Division, New York, NY 10017, (800) 253-9646, Fax: (212) 963-4116, http://unstats.un.org; *World Statistics Pocketbook.*

ECUADOR - SOCIAL SECURITY

Inter-American Development Bank (IDB), 1300 New York Avenue, NW, Washington, DC 20577, (202) 623-1000, Fax: (202) 623-3096, www.iadb.org; *The Politics of Policies: Economic and Social Progress in Latin America - 2006 Report.*

International Monetary Fund (IMF), 700 Nineteenth Street, NW, Washington, DC 20431, (202) 623-7000, Fax: (202) 623-4661, www.imf.org; *Government Finance Statistics Yearbook (2008 Edition).*

United Nations Statistics Division, New York, NY 10017, (800) 253-9646, Fax: (212) 963-4116, http://unstats.un.org; *National Accounts Statistics: Compendium of Income Distribution Statistics.*

ECUADOR - SOYBEAN PRODUCTION

See ECUADOR - CROPS

ECUADOR - STEEL PRODUCTION

See ECUADOR - MINERAL INDUSTRIES

ECUADOR - SUGAR PRODUCTION

See ECUADOR - CROPS

ECUADOR - TAXATION

Inter-American Development Bank (IDB), 1300 New York Avenue, NW, Washington, DC 20577, (202) 623-1000, Fax: (202) 623-3096, www.iadb.org; *The Politics of Policies: Economic and Social Progress in Latin America - 2006 Report.*

International Monetary Fund (IMF), 700 Nineteenth Street, NW, Washington, DC 20431, (202) 623-7000, Fax: (202) 623-4661, www.imf.org; *Government Finance Statistics Yearbook (2008 Edition).*

Taylor and Francis Group, An Informa Business, 2 Park Square, Milton Park, Abingdon, Oxford OX14 4RN, United Kingdom, (Dial from U.S. (212) 216-7800), (Fax from U.S. (212) 564-7854), www.tandf.co.uk; *The Europa World Year Book.*

United Nations Statistics Division, New York, NY 10017, (800) 253-9646, Fax: (212) 963-4116, http://unstats.un.org; *Statistical Yearbook for Latin America and the Caribbean 2004.*

The World Bank, 1818 H Street, NW, Washington, DC 20433, (202) 473-1000, Fax: (202) 477-6391, www.worldbank.org; *World Development Indicators (WDI) 2008.*

ECUADOR - TELEPHONE

Economist Intelligence Unit, 111 West 57th Street, New York, NY 10019, (212) 554-0600, Fax: (212) 586-1181, www.eiu.com; *Business Latin America.*

International Telecommunication Union (ITU), Place des Nations, 1211 Geneva 20, Switzerland, www.itu.int; World Telecommunication Indicators Database.

Palgrave Macmillan Ltd., Houndmills, Basingstoke, Hampshire, RG21 6XS, England, (Telephone in U.S. (888) 330-8477), (Fax in U.S. (800) 672-2054), www.palgrave.com; *The Statesman's Yearbook 2008.*

Taylor and Francis Group, An Informa Business, 2 Park Square, Milton Park, Abingdon, Oxford OX14 4RN, United Kingdom, (Dial from U.S. (212) 216-7800), (Fax from U.S. (212) 564-7854), www.tandf.co.uk; *The Europa World Year Book.*

United Nations Statistics Division, New York, NY 10017, (800) 253-9646, Fax: (212) 963-4116, http://unstats.un.org; *Statistical Yearbook* and *World Statistics Pocketbook.*

ECUADOR - TELEVISION - RECEIVERS AND RECEPTION

United Nations Statistics Division, New York, NY 10017, (800) 253-9646, Fax: (212) 963-4116, http://unstats.un.org; *Statistical Yearbook.*

ECUADOR - TEXTILE INDUSTRY

M.E. Sharpe, 80 Business Park Drive, Armonk, NY 10504, (800) 541-6563, Fax: (914) 273-2106, www.mesharpe.com; *The Illustrated Book of World Rankings.*

United Nations Conference on Trade and Development (UNCTAD), DC2-1120, United Nations, New York, NY 10017, (212) 963-0027, www.unctad.org; *UNCTAD Commodity Yearbook.*

United Nations Statistics Division, New York, NY 10017, (800) 253-9646, Fax: (212) 963-4116, http://unstats.un.org; *Statistical Yearbook.*

ECUADOR - TIRE INDUSTRY

United Nations Statistics Division, New York, NY 10017, (800) 253-9646, Fax: (212) 963-4116, http://unstats.un.org; *Statistical Yearbook.*

ECUADOR - TOBACCO INDUSTRY

Foreign Agricultural Service (FAS), U.S. Department of Agriculture (USDA), 1400 Independence Avenue, SW, Washington, DC 20250, (202) 720-3935, www.fas.usda.gov; *Tobacco: World Markets and Trade.*

M.E. Sharpe, 80 Business Park Drive, Armonk, NY 10504, (800) 541-6563, Fax: (914) 273-2106, www.mesharpe.com; *The Illustrated Book of World Rankings.*

United Nations Statistics Division, New York, NY 10017, (800) 253-9646, Fax: (212) 963-4116, http://unstats.un.org; *Statistical Yearbook.*

ECUADOR - TOURISM

Economist Intelligence Unit, 111 West 57th Street, New York, NY 10019, (212) 554-0600, Fax: (212) 586-1181, www.eiu.com; *Business Latin America.*

Euromonitor International, Inc., 224 S. Michigan Avenue, Suite 1500, Chicago, IL 60604, (312) 922-1115, Fax: (312) 922-1157, www.euromonitor.com; *The World Economic Factbook 2008* and *World Marketing Data and Statistics.*

M.E. Sharpe, 80 Business Park Drive, Armonk, NY 10504, (800) 541-6563, Fax: (914) 273-2106, www.mesharpe.com; *The Illustrated Book of World Rankings.*

Palgrave Macmillan Ltd., Houndmills, Basingstoke, Hampshire, RG21 6XS, England, (Telephone in U.S. (888) 330-8477), (Fax in U.S. (800) 672-2054), www.palgrave.com; *The Statesman's Yearbook 2008.*

Taylor and Francis Group, An Informa Business, 2 Park Square, Milton Park, Abingdon, Oxford OX14 4RN, United Kingdom, (Dial from U.S. (212) 216-7800), (Fax from U.S. (212) 564-7854), www.tandf.co.uk; *The Europa World Year Book.*

UCLA Latin American Institute, 10343 Bunche Hall, Box 951447, Los Angeles, CA 90095-1447, (310) 825-4571, Fax: (310) 206-6859, www.international.ucla.edu/lac; *Statistical Abstract of Latin America.*

United Nations Statistics Division, New York, NY 10017, (800) 253-9646, Fax: (212) 963-4116, http://unstats.un.org; *Statistical Yearbook* and *Statistical Yearbook for Latin America and the Caribbean 2004.*

United Nations World Tourism Organization (UNWTO), Capitan Haya 42, 28020 Madrid, Spain, www.world-tourism.org; *Yearbook of Tourism Statistics.*

The World Bank, 1818 H Street, NW, Washington, DC 20433, (202) 473-1000, Fax: (202) 477-6391, www.worldbank.org; *Ecuador.*

ECUADOR - TRADE

See ECUADOR - INTERNATIONAL TRADE

ECUADOR - TRANSPORTATION

Central Intelligence Agency, Office of Public Affairs, Washington, DC 20505, (703) 482-0623, Fax: (703) 482-1739, www.cia.gov; *The World Factbook.*

Economist Intelligence Unit, 111 West 57th Street, New York, NY 10019, (212) 554-0600, Fax: (212) 586-1181, www.eiu.com; *Business Latin America.*

Euromonitor International, Inc., 224 S. Michigan Avenue, Suite 1500, Chicago, IL 60604, (312) 922-1115, Fax: (312) 922-1157, www.euromonitor.com; *International Marketing Data and Statistics 2008* and *World Marketing Data and Statistics.*

Inter-American Development Bank (IDB), 1300 New York Avenue, NW, Washington, DC 20577, (202) 623-1000, Fax: (202) 623-3096, www.iadb.org; *The Politics of Policies: Economic and Social Progress in Latin America - 2006 Report.*

M.E. Sharpe, 80 Business Park Drive, Armonk, NY 10504, (800) 541-6563, Fax: (914) 273-2106, www.mesharpe.com; *The Illustrated Book of World Rankings.*

Palgrave Macmillan Ltd., Houndmills, Basingstoke, Hampshire, RG21 6XS, England, (Telephone in U.S. (888) 330-8477), (Fax in U.S. (800) 672-2054), www.palgrave.com; *The Statesman's Yearbook 2008.*

Taylor and Francis Group, An Informa Business, 2 Park Square, Milton Park, Abingdon, Oxford OX14 4RN, United Kingdom, (Dial from U.S. (212) 216-7800), (Fax from U.S. (212) 564-7854), www.tandf.co.uk; *The Europa World Year Book.*

UCLA Latin American Institute, 10343 Bunche Hall, Box 951447, Los Angeles, CA 90095-1447, (310) 825-4571, Fax: (310) 206-6859, www.international.ucla.edu/lac; *Statistical Abstract of Latin America.*

United Nations Statistics Division, New York, NY 10017, (800) 253-9646, Fax: (212) 963-4116, http://unstats.un.org; *Human Development Report 2006* and *Statistical Yearbook for Latin America and the Caribbean 2004.*

The World Bank, 1818 H Street, NW, Washington, DC 20433, (202) 473-1000, Fax: (202) 477-6391, www.worldbank.org; *Ecuador.*

ECUADOR - TURKEYS

See ECUADOR - LIVESTOCK

ECUADOR - UNEMPLOYMENT

Central Intelligence Agency, Office of Public Affairs, Washington, DC 20505, (703) 482-0623, Fax: (703) 482-1739, www.cia.gov; *The World Factbook.*

Economist Intelligence Unit, 111 West 57th Street, New York, NY 10019, (212) 554-0600, Fax: (212) 586-1181, www.eiu.com; *Business Latin America.*

Euromonitor International, Inc., 224 S. Michigan Avenue, Suite 1500, Chicago, IL 60604, (312) 922-1115, Fax: (312) 922-1157, www.euromonitor.com; *International Marketing Data and Statistics 2008.*

International Labour Office, I.L.O. Publications, 4 route des Morillons, CH-1211 Geneva 22, Switzerland, (Telephone in U.S. (202) 653-7652), (Fax in U.S. (202) 653-7687), www.ilo.org; *Yearbook of Labour Statistics 2006.*

UCLA Latin American Institute, 10343 Bunche Hall, Box 951447, Los Angeles, CA 90095-1447, (310) 825-4571, Fax: (310) 206-6859, www.international.ucla.edu/lac; *Statistical Abstract of Latin America.*

ECUADOR - VITAL STATISTICS

Euromonitor International, Inc., 224 S. Michigan Avenue, Suite 1500, Chicago, IL 60604, (312) 922-1115, Fax: (312) 922-1157, www.euromonitor.com; *International Marketing Data and Statistics 2008.*

Palgrave Macmillan Ltd., Houndmills, Basingstoke, Hampshire, RG21 6XS, England, (Telephone in U.S. (888) 330-8477), (Fax in U.S. (800) 672-2054), www.palgrave.com; *The Statesman's Yearbook 2008.*

United Nations Statistics Division, New York, NY 10017, (800) 253-9646, Fax: (212) 963-4116, http://unstats.un.org; *Statistical Yearbook.*

World Health Organization (WHO), Avenue Appia 20, 1211 Geneve 27, Switzerland, (Telephone in U.S. (212) 331-9081), www.who.int; *World Health Report 2006.*

ECUADOR - WAGES

International Labour Office, I.L.O. Publications, 4 route des Morillons, CH-1211 Geneva 22, Switzerland, (Telephone in U.S. (202) 653-7652), (Fax in U.S. (202) 653-7687), www.ilo.org; *Yearbook of Labour Statistics 2006.*

Organization of American States (OAS), 17th Street Constitution Avenue NW, Washington, DC 20006, (202) 458-3000, www.oas.org; *The OAS in Transition: 1994-2004.*

UCLA Latin American Institute, 10343 Bunche Hall, Box 951447, Los Angeles, CA 90095-1447, (310) 825-4571, Fax: (310) 206-6859, www.international.ucla.edu/lac; *Statistical Abstract of Latin America.*

United Nations Statistics Division, New York, NY 10017, (800) 253-9646, Fax: (212) 963-4116, http://unstats.un.org; *Statistical Yearbook.*

The World Bank, 1818 H Street, NW, Washington, DC 20433, (202) 473-1000, Fax: (202) 477-6391, www.worldbank.org; *Ecuador.*

ECUADOR - WELFARE STATE

Inter-American Development Bank (IDB), 1300 New York Avenue, NW, Washington, DC 20577, (202) 623-1000, Fax: (202) 623-3096, www.iadb.org; *The Politics of Policies: Economic and Social Progress in Latin America - 2006 Report.*

International Monetary Fund (IMF), 700 Nineteenth Street, NW, Washington, DC 20431, (202) 623-7000, Fax: (202) 623-4661, www.imf.org; *Government Finance Statistics Yearbook (2008 Edition).*

ECUADOR - WHEAT PRODUCTION

See ECUADOR - CROPS

ECUADOR - WHOLESALE PRICE INDEXES

Inter-American Development Bank (IDB), 1300 New York Avenue, NW, Washington, DC 20577, (202) 623-1000, Fax: (202) 623-3096, www.iadb.org; *The Politics of Policies: Economic and Social Progress in Latin America - 2006 Report.*

International Monetary Fund (IMF), 700 Nineteenth Street, NW, Washington, DC 20431, (202) 623-7000, Fax: (202) 623-4661, www.imf.org; *International Financial Statistics Yearbook 2007.*

Organization of American States (OAS), 17th Street Constitution Avenue NW, Washington, DC 20006, (202) 458-3000, www.oas.org; *The OAS in Transition: 1994-2004.*

ECUADOR - WHOLESALE TRADE

Inter-American Development Bank (IDB), 1300 New York Avenue, NW, Washington, DC 20577, (202) 623-1000, Fax: (202) 623-3096, www.iadb.org; *The Politics of Policies: Economic and Social Progress in Latin America - 2006 Report.*

United Nations Statistics Division, New York, NY 10017, (800) 253-9646, Fax: (212) 963-4116, http://unstats.un.org; *Statistical Yearbook.*

ECUADOR - WINE PRODUCTION

See ECUADOR - BEVERAGE INDUSTRY

ECUADOR - WOOD AND WOOD PULP

See ECUADOR - FORESTS AND FORESTRY

ECUADOR - WOOL PRODUCTION

See ECUADOR - TEXTILE INDUSTRY

ECUADOR - YARN PRODUCTION

See ECUADOR - TEXTILE INDUSTRY

EDUCATION

The Annie E. Casey Foundation, 701 Saint Paul Street, Baltimore, MD 21202, (410) 547-6600, Fax: (410) 547-3610, www.aecf.org; *Improving School Readiness Outcomes; Making Connections to Improve Education: A Snapshot of School-Based Education Investments in Seven Making Connections Sites; Maryland's Early Care and Education Committee Progress Report; Of, By, And For the Community: The Story of PUENTE Learning Center;*

School Choice: Doing It the Right Way Makes a Difference; and *Schools Uniting Neighborhoods: Successful Collaboration in an Environment of Constant Change.*

The Brookings Institution, 1775 Massachusetts Avenue, NW, Washington, DC 20036, (202) 797-6000, Fax: (202) 797-6004, www.brook.edu; *How Well Are American Students Learning?*

Center for Social Organization of Schools (CSOS), Johns Hopkins University, 3003 North Charles Street, Suite 200, Baltimore, MD 21218, (410) 516-8800, Fax: (410) 516-8890, www.csos.jhu.edu; unpublished data.

Coalition for Community Schools, 4455 Connecticut Avenue, NW, Suite 310, Washington, DC, 20008, (202) 822-8405, Fax: (202) 872-4050, www.communityschools.org; *Evaluation of Community Schools: An Early Look* and *Making the Difference: Research and Practice in Community Schools.*

Editorial Projects in Education, Inc., 6935 Arlington Road, Suite 100, Bethesda, MD 20814-5233, (301) 280-3100, www2.edweek.org/info/about; *Education Week* and *Teacher Magazine.*

Lesotho Bureau of Statistics, Ministry of Finance and Development Planning, PO Box 455, Maseru 100, Lesotho, www.bos.gov.ls; *Education Statistical Report 2003.*

Market Data Retrieval (MDR), 6 Armstrong Road, Shelton, CT 06484, (800) 333-8802, www.schooldata.com; *Email Trends in the Education Market 2007.*

Standard and Poor's Corporation, 55 Water Street, New York, NY 10041, (212) 438-1000, www.standardandpoors.com; *SchoolMatters.*

U.S. Bureau of Labor Statistics (BLS), Postal Square Building, 2 Massachusetts Avenue, NE, Washington, DC 20212-0001, (202) 691-5200, Fax: (202) 691-6325, www.bls.gov; *Industries at a Glance.*

U.S. Department of Education (ED), Institute of Education Sciences (IES), 400 Maryland Avenue, SW, Washington, DC 20202-7100, (800) USA-LEARN, Fax: (202) 401-0689, www.ed.gov/ies; ERIC Database (Education Resources Information Center).

U.S. Department of Justice (DOJ), Bureau of Justice Statistics, 810 Seventh Street, NW, Washington, DC 20531, (202) 307-0765, www.ojp.usdoj.gov/bjs/; *Education and Correctional Populations.*

The Wallace Foundation, 5 Penn Plaza, 7th Floor, New York, NY 10001, (212) 251-9700, www.wallacefoundation.org; *Knowledge Center.*

World Food Programme, Via C.G.Viola 68, Parco dei Medici, 00148 Rome, Italy, www.wfp.org; *World Hunger Series 2006: Hunger and Learning.*

EDUCATION - ACCESS

The Annie E. Casey Foundation, 701 Saint Paul Street, Baltimore, MD 21202, (410) 547-6600, Fax: (410) 547-3610, www.aecf.org; *City and Rural KIDS COUNT Data Book* and *Of, By, And For the Community: The Story of PUENTE Learning Center.*

EDUCATION - ADULT EDUCATION

The Annie E. Casey Foundation, 701 Saint Paul Street, Baltimore, MD 21202, (410) 547-6600, Fax: (410) 547-3610, www.aecf.org; *Of, By, And For the Community: The Story of PUENTE Learning Center.*

National Center for Education Statistics (NCES), 1990 K Street, NW, Washington, DC 20006, (202) 502-7300, http://nces.ed.gov; *The National Household Education Surveys Program (NHES).*

U.S. Census Bureau, Center for Economic Studies, 4600 Silver Hill Road, Washington DC 20233, (301) 457-1235, www.ces.census.gov; *2002 Economic Census, Educational Services.*

EDUCATION - ADVANCED PLACEMENT EXAMS

College Board, 45 Columbus Avenue, New York, NY 10023, (212) 713-8000, www.collegeboard.com; *College-Bound Seniors 2006.*

EDUCATION - AMERICAN COLLEGE TESTING (ACT) PROGRAM

ACT, 500 ACT Drive, Box 168, Iowa City, IA 52243-0168, (319) 337-1000, Fax: (319) 339-3020, www.act.org; *ACT National and State Scores.*

EDUCATION - ARTS EDUCATION

National Assembly of State Arts Agencies (NASAA), 1029 Vermont Avenue, NW, 2nd Floor, Washington, DC 20005, (202) 347-6352, Fax: (202) 737-0526, www.nasaa-arts.org; *Critical Evidence: How the Arts Benefit Student Achievement.*

National Center for Education Statistics (NCES), 1990 K Street, NW, Washington, DC 20006, (202) 502-7300, http://nces.ed.gov; *Arts Education in Public Elementary and Secondary Schools.*

EDUCATION - ATTAINMENT

The Brookings Institution, 1775 Massachusetts Avenue, NW, Washington, DC 20036, (202) 797-6000, Fax: (202) 797-6004, www.brook.edu; *How Well Are American Students Learning?*

Editorial Projects in Education, Inc., 6935 Arlington Road, Suite 100, Bethesda, MD 20814-5233, (301) 280-3100, www2.edweek.org/info/about; *Education Week.*

Higher Education Research Institute (HERI), University of California, Los Angeles, 3005 Moore Hall/Box 951521, Los Angeles, CA 90095-1521, (310) 825-1925, Fax: (310) 206-2228, www.gseis.ucla.edu/heri/index.php; *Degree Attainment Rates at Colleges and Universities.*

Robert Wood Johnson Foundation, PO Box 2316, College Road East and Route 1, Princeton, NJ 08543, (877) 843-7953, www.rwjf.org; *Race Ethnicity, and the Education Gradient in Health.*

Standard and Poor's Corporation, 55 Water Street, New York, NY 10041, (212) 438-1000, www.standardandpoors.com; *SchoolMatters.*

U.S. Census Bureau, 4700 Silver Hill Road, Washington DC 20233-0001, (301) 763-3030, www.census.gov; *State and County QuickFacts* and unpublished data.

U.S. Census Bureau, Housing and Household Economics Statistics Division, 4700 Silver Hill Road, Washington DC 20233-0001, (301) 763-3030, www.census.gov/hhes/www; Decennial Census of Population and Housing (web app).

U.S. Census Bureau, Population Division, 4700 Silver Hill Road, Washington DC 20233-0001, (301) 763-3030, www.census.gov/population/www/; *Current Population Reports.*

US Charter Schools, www.uscharterschools.org; *Charter Achievement Among Low-Income Students; State of the Charter School Movement 2005: Trends, Issues, and Indicators;* and *A Straightforward Comparison of Charter Schools and Regular Public Schools in the United States.*

EDUCATION - ATTAINMENT - ASIAN AND PACIFIC ISLANDER POPULATION

U.S. Census Bureau, 4700 Silver Hill Road, Washington DC 20233-0001, (301) 763-3030, www.census.gov; unpublished data.

U.S. Census Bureau, Population Division, 4700 Silver Hill Road, Washington DC 20233-0001, (301) 763-3030, www.census.gov/population/www/; *The Asian and Pacific Islander Population in the United States* and *Current Population Reports.*

EDUCATION - ATTAINMENT - BLACK POPULATION

U.S. Census Bureau, 4700 Silver Hill Road, Washington DC 20233-0001, (301) 763-3030, www.census.gov; unpublished data.

U.S. Census Bureau, Population Division, 4700 Silver Hill Road, Washington DC 20233-0001, (301) 763-3030, www.census.gov/population/www/; *The Black Population in the United States* and *Current Population Reports.*

EDUCATION - ATTAINMENT - CIGARETTE SMOKING

Centers for Disease Control and Prevention (CDC), U.S. Department of Health and Human Services (HHS), 1600 Clifton Road, Atlanta, GA 30333, (800) 311-3435, www.cdc.gov; *Morbidity and Mortality Weekly Report (MMWR).*

National Center for Health Statistics (NCHS), Centers for Disease Control and Prevention (CDC), U.S. Department of Health and Human Services (HHS), 3311 Toledo Road, Hyattsville, MD 20782, (866) 232-4636, www.cdc.gov/nchs; *Health, United States, 2006, with Chartbook on Trends in the Health of Americans with Special Feature on Pain.*

EDUCATION - ATTAINMENT - COMPUTER USE

National Telecommunications and Information Administration (NTIA), U.S. Department of Commerce (DOC), 1401 Constitution Avenue, NW, Washington, DC 20230, (202) 482-7002, www.ntia.doc.gov; *A Nation Online: Entering the Broadband Age.*

EDUCATION - ATTAINMENT - GENERAL EDUCATION DEVELOPMENT CERTIFICATES (GEDs)

National Center for Education Statistics (NCES), 1990 K Street, NW, Washington, DC 20006, (202) 502-7300, http://nces.ed.gov; *Digest of Education Statistics 2007.*

EDUCATION - ATTAINMENT - HISPANIC ORIGIN POPULATION

National Center for Education Statistics (NCES), 1990 K Street, NW, Washington, DC 20006, (202) 502-7300, http://nces.ed.gov; *Digest of Education Statistics 2007.*

U.S. Census Bureau, 4700 Silver Hill Road, Washington DC 20233-0001, (301) 763-3030, www.census.gov; unpublished data.

U.S. Census Bureau, Population Division, 4700 Silver Hill Road, Washington DC 20233-0001, (301) 763-3030, www.census.gov/population/www/; *The Hispanic Population in the United States.*

EDUCATION - ATTAINMENT - INCOME

U.S. Census Bureau, 4700 Silver Hill Road, Washington DC 20233-0001, (301) 763-3030, www.census.gov; unpublished data.

U.S. Census Bureau, Population Division, 4700 Silver Hill Road, Washington DC 20233-0001, (301) 763-3030, www.census.gov/population/www/; *Current Population Reports.*

US Charter Schools, www.uscharterschools.org; *Charter Achievement Among Low-Income Students.*

EDUCATION - ATTAINMENT - LABOR FORCE STATUS

U.S. Bureau of Labor Statistics (BLS), Postal Square Building, 2 Massachusetts Avenue, NE, Washington, DC 20212-0001, (202) 691-5200, Fax: (202) 691-6325, www.bls.gov; *Current Population Survey (CPS)* and unpublished data.

EDUCATION - ATTAINMENT - MEDIA USERS

Mediamark Research, Inc., 75 Ninth Avenue, 5th Floor, New York, NY 10011, (212) 884-9200, Fax: (212) 884-9339, www.mediamark.com; MRI+.

EDUCATION - ATTAINMENT - OCCUPATION

U.S. Bureau of Labor Statistics (BLS), Postal Square Building, 2 Massachusetts Avenue, NE, Washington, DC 20212-0001, (202) 691-5200, Fax: (202) 691-6325, www.bls.gov; unpublished data.

EDUCATION - ATTAINMENT - OLDER PEOPLE

U.S. Census Bureau, 4700 Silver Hill Road, Washington DC 20233-0001, (301) 763-3030, www.census.gov; unpublished data.

U.S. Census Bureau, Population Division, 4700 Silver Hill Road, Washington DC 20233-0001, (301) 763-3030, www.census.gov/population/www/; *Current Population Reports.*

EDUCATION - ATTAINMENT - POVERTY

U.S. Census Bureau, Population Division, 4700 Silver Hill Road, Washington DC 20233-0001, (301) 763-3030, www.census.gov/population/www/; *Current Population Reports.*

US Charter Schools, www.uscharterschools.org; *Charter Achievement Among Low-Income Students.*

World Food Programme, Via C.G.Viola 68, Parco dei Medici, 00148 Rome, Italy, www.wfp.org; *World Hunger Series 2006: Hunger and Learning.*

EDUCATION - ATTAINMENT - RACE

U.S. Census Bureau, 4700 Silver Hill Road, Washington DC 20233-0001, (301) 763-3030, www.census.gov; unpublished data.

U.S. Census Bureau, Population Division, 4700 Silver Hill Road, Washington DC 20233-0001, (301) 763-3030, www.census.gov/population/www/; *Current Population Reports.*

EDUCATION - ATTAINMENT - STATES

The Brookings Institution, 1775 Massachusetts Avenue, NW, Washington, DC 20036, (202) 797-6000, Fax: (202) 797-6004, www.brook.edu; *How Well Are American Students Learning?*

U.S. Census Bureau, Population Division, 4700 Silver Hill Road, Washington DC 20233-0001, (301) 763-3030, www.census.gov/population/www/; *Current Population Reports.*

EDUCATION - ATTAINMENT - WOMEN

U.S. Census Bureau, 4700 Silver Hill Road, Washington DC 20233-0001, (301) 763-3030, www.census.gov; unpublished data.

U.S. Census Bureau, Housing and Household Economics Statistics Division, 4700 Silver Hill Road, Washington DC 20233-0001, (301) 763-3030, www.census.gov/hhes/www; Decennial Census of Population and Housing (web app).

U.S. Census Bureau, Population Division, 4700 Silver Hill Road, Washington DC 20233-0001, (301) 763-3030, www.census.gov/population/www/; *Current Population Reports.*

EDUCATION - CATHOLIC SCHOOLS

National Center for Education Statistics (NCES), 1990 K Street, NW, Washington, DC 20006, (202) 502-7300, http://nces.ed.gov; *Private School Universe Survey 2005-2006.*

EDUCATION - CHARITABLE CONTRIBUTIONS

Independent Sector, 1200 Eighteenth Street, NW, Suite 200, Washington, DC 20036, (202) 467-6100, Fax: (202) 467-6101, www.independentsector.org; *Giving and Volunteering in the United States 2001.*

EDUCATION - CHARTER SCHOOLS

US Charter Schools, www.uscharterschools.org; *Charter Achievement Among Low-Income Students; State of the Charter School Movement 2005: Trends, Issues, and Indicators;* and *A Straightforward Comparison of Charter Schools and Regular Public Schools in the United States.*

U.S. Department of Education (ED), Office of Innovation and Improvement (OII), 400 Maryland Avenue, SW, Washington, DC 20202, (202) 205-4500, www.ed.gov/oii; *Evaluation of the Public Charter Schools Program (PCSP)* and *Public Charter Schools Program.*

EDUCATION - COMMUNITY SCHOOLS

Coalition for Community Schools, 4455 Connecticut Avenue, NW, Suite 310, Washington, DC, 20008, (202) 822-8405, Fax: (202) 872-4050, www.communityschools.org; *Evaluation of Community Schools: An Early Look* and *Making the Difference: Research and Practice in Community Schools.*

EDUCATION - COMMUNITY SERVICE (STUDENTS)

National Center for Education Statistics (NCES), 1990 K Street, NW, Washington, DC 20006, (202) 502-7300, http://nces.ed.gov; various fact sheets.

Public/Private Ventures (P/PV), 2000 Market Street, Suite 600, Philadelphia, PA 19103, (215) 557-4400, Fax: (215) 557 4469, www.ppv.org; *College Students as Mentors for At-Risk Youth: A Study of Six Campus Partners in Learning Programs.*

EDUCATION - COMPUTER USE

Market Data Retrieval (MDR), 6 Armstrong Road, Shelton, CT 06484, (800) 333-8802, www.schooldata.com; *The K-12 Technology Review 2005.*

National Center for Education Statistics (NCES), 1990 K Street, NW, Washington, DC 20006, (202) 502-7300, http://nces.ed.gov; *Internet Access in U.S. Public Schools and Classrooms: 1994-2005* and *Teacher Use of Computers and the Internet in Public Schools.*

EDUCATION - CONTINUING EDUCATION

Organisation for Economic Cooperation and Development (OECD), 2 rue Andre Pascal, F-75775 Paris Cedex 16, France, (Telephone in U.S. (202) 785-6323), (Fax in U.S. (202) 785-0350), www.oecd.org; *Education at a Glance* (2007 Edition).

U.S. Census Bureau, Center for Economic Studies, 4600 Silver Hill Road, Washington DC 20233, (301) 457-1235, www.ces.census.gov; *2002 Economic Census, Educational Services.*

EDUCATION - CREDIT CARD USE

Higher Education Research Institute (HERI), University of California, Los Angeles, 3005 Moore Hall/Box 951521, Los Angeles, CA 90095-1521, (310) 825-1925, Fax: (310) 206-2228, www.gseis.ucla.edu/heri/index.php; *The American Freshman: National Norms for 2006.*

EDUCATION - CRIMINAL STATISTICS

U.S. Department of Justice (DOJ), Bureau of Justice Statistics, 810 Seventh Street, NW, Washington, DC 20531, (202) 307-0765, www.ojp.usdoj.gov/bjs/; *Criminal Victimization, 2005* and *Indicators of School Crime and Safety, 2005.*

EDUCATION - DEGREES CONFERRED

National Center for Education Statistics (NCES), 1990 K Street, NW, Washington, DC 20006, (202) 502-7300, http://nces.ed.gov; *Digest of Education Statistics 2007.*

National Science Foundation, Division of Science Resources Statistics (SRS), 4201 Wilson Boulevard, Arlington, VA 22230, (703) 292-8780, Fax: (703) 292-9092, www.nsf.gov; *National Survey of Recent College Graduates: 2006; Selected Data on Science and Engineering Doctorate Awards;* and *Survey of Earned Doctorates 2006.*

U.S. Census Bureau, 4700 Silver Hill Road, Washington DC 20233-0001, (301) 763-3030, www.census.gov; unpublished data.

EDUCATION - DEGREES CONFERRED - NON-RESIDENT ALIENS

National Center for Education Statistics (NCES), 1990 K Street, NW, Washington, DC 20006, (202) 502-7300, http://nces.ed.gov; *Digest of Education Statistics 2007.*

EDUCATION - DEGREES CONFERRED - SALARY OFFERS

National Association of Colleges and Employers (NACE), 62 Highland Avenue, Bethlehem, PA 18017, (800) 544-5272, Fax: (610) 868-0208, www.naceweb.org; *Salary Survey.*

EDUCATION - DENTAL SCHOOLS - STUDENTS - GRADUATES

National Center for Health Statistics (NCHS), Centers for Disease Control and Prevention (CDC), U.S. Department of Health and Human Services (HHS), 3311 Toledo Road, Hyattsville, MD 20782, (866) 232-4636, www.cdc.gov/nchs; *Health, United States, 2006, with Chartbook on Trends in the Health of Americans with Special Feature on Pain.*

EDUCATION - DISABLED STUDENTS

National Center for Education Statistics (NCES), 1990 K Street, NW, Washington, DC 20006, (202) 502-7300, http://nces.ed.gov; Data Analysis System (DAS) and *Profile of Undergraduates in U.S. Postsecondary Education Institutions: 2003-04, With a Special Analysis of Community College Students.*

U.S. Department of Education (ED), Office of Special Education and Rehabilitative Services (OSERS), 400 Maryland Ave., SW, Washington, DC 20202-7100, (202) 245-7468, www.ed.gov/osers; *Twenty-Seventh Annual Report to Congress on the Implementation of the Individuals with Disabilities Education Act.*

EDUCATION - DISTANCE EDUCATION

National Center for Education Statistics (NCES), 1990 K Street, NW, Washington, DC 20006, (202) 502-7300, http://nces.ed.gov; *Distance Education at Degree-Granting Postsecondary Institutions: 2000-2001; Distance Education at Degree-Granting Postsecondary Institutions: 2000-2001;* and *Distance Education at Higher Education Institutions: 2000-01.*

North Carolina Office of State Budget and Management, 116 West Jones Street, Raleigh, NC 27603-8005, (919) 804-4700, Fax: (919) 733-0640, www.osbm.state.nc.us; *North Carolina University System Study of Distance Education.*

EDUCATION - EMPLOYED STUDENTS

U.S. Bureau of Labor Statistics (BLS), Postal Square Building, 2 Massachusetts Avenue, NE, Washington, DC 20212-0001, (202) 691-5200, Fax: (202) 691-6325, www.bls.gov; *Employment Experience of Youths: Results From a Longitudinal Survey.*

EDUCATION - EMPLOYMENT - STATE AND LOCAL GOVERNMENT

U.S. Census Bureau, Governments Division, 4600 Silver Hill Road, Washington DC 20233, (800) 242-2184, www.census.gov/govs/www; *2002 Census of Governments, Public Employment and Payroll.*

EDUCATION - EMPLOYMENT STATUS OF HIGH SCHOOL GRADUATES AND DROPOUTS

U.S. Bureau of Labor Statistics (BLS), Postal Square Building, 2 Massachusetts Avenue, NE, Washington, DC 20212-0001, (202) 691-5200, Fax: (202) 691-6325, www.bls.gov; *Current Population Survey (CPS); Monthly Labor Review (MLR);* and unpublished data.

EDUCATION - ENROLLMENT

The Brookings Institution, 1775 Massachusetts Avenue, NW, Washington, DC 20036, (202) 797-6000, Fax: (202) 797-6004, www.brook.edu; *How Well Are American Students Learning?*

Editorial Projects in Education, Inc., 6935 Arlington Road, Suite 100, Bethesda, MD 20814-5233, (301) 280-3100, www2.edweek.org/info/about; *Education Week.*

Market Data Retrieval (MDR), 6 Armstrong Road, Shelton, CT 06484, (800) 333-8802, www.schooldata.com; *MDR's Enrollment Comparison Report, 2007-2008.*

National Center for Education Statistics (NCES), 1990 K Street, NW, Washington, DC 20006, (202) 502-7300, http://nces.ed.gov; *Digest of Education Statistics 2007; Dual Enrollment of High School Students at Postsecondary Institutions: 2002-03; Projections of Education Statistics to 2016;* and unpublished data.

National Education Association (NEA), 1201 Sixteenth Street, NW, Washington, DC 20036-3290, (202) 833-4000, Fax: (202) 822-7974, www.nea.org; *Education Statistics: Rankings and Estimates 2006-2007.*

Standard and Poor's Corporation, 55 Water Street, New York, NY 10041, (212) 438-1000, www.standardandpoors.com; *SchoolMatters.*

U.S. Census Bureau, Housing and Household Economics Statistics Division, 4700 Silver Hill Road, Washington DC 20233-0001, (301) 763-3030, www.census.gov/hhes/www; Decennial Census of Population and Housing (web app).

U.S. Census Bureau, Population Division, 4700 Silver Hill Road, Washington DC 20233-0001, (301) 763-3030, www.census.gov/population/www/; *Current Population Reports.*

EDUCATION - ENROLLMENT - CATHOLIC SCHOOLS

National Center for Education Statistics (NCES), 1990 K Street, NW, Washington, DC 20006, (202) 502-7300, http://nces.ed.gov; *Private School Universe Survey 2005-2006.*

EDUCATION - ENROLLMENT - FOREIGN BORN STUDENTS

U.S. Census Bureau, Population Division, 4700 Silver Hill Road, Washington DC 20233-0001, (301) 763-3030, www.census.gov/population/www/; *Foreign-Born Population in the U.S. 2003.*

EDUCATION - ENROLLMENT - HOME-SCHOOLED

National Center for Education Statistics (NCES), 1990 K Street, NW, Washington, DC 20006, (202) 502-7300, http://nces.ed.gov; *1.1 Million Homeschooled Students in the United States in 2003* and *Homeschooling in the United States: 2003.*

EDUCATION - ENROLLMENT - OUTLYING AREAS OF THE UNITED STATES

National Center for Education Statistics (NCES), 1990 K Street, NW, Washington, DC 20006, (202) 502-7300, http://nces.ed.gov; *Digest of Education Statistics 2007* and unpublished data.

Oficina del Censo, Programa de Planificacion Economica y Social, Junta de Planificacion, PO Box 41119, Santurce, Puerto Rico 00940, (Dial from U.S. (787) 723-6200), (Fax from U.S. (787) 268-0506), www.censo.gobierno.pr; unpublished data.

EDUCATION - ENROLLMENT - PREPRIMARY SCHOOLS

U.S. Census Bureau, Population Division, 4700 Silver Hill Road, Washington DC 20233-0001, (301) 763-3030, www.census.gov/population/www/; *Current Population Reports.*

EDUCATION - ENROLLMENT - STATES

National Center for Education Statistics (NCES), 1990 K Street, NW, Washington, DC 20006, (202) 502-7300, http://nces.ed.gov; *Digest of Education Statistics 2007.*

EDUCATION - EXPENDITURES - ASSISTANCE FOR PERSONS WITH LIMITED INCOME

U.S. Library of Congress (LOC), Congressional Research Service (CRS), The Library of Congress, 101 Independence Avenue, SE, Washington, DC 20540-7500, (202) 707-5700, www.loc.gov/crsinfo; *Cash and Non-cash Benefits for Persons With Limited Income: Eligibility Rules, Recipient and Expenditure Data.*

EDUCATION - EXPENDITURES - CITY GOVERNMENT

National Education Association (NEA), 1201 Sixteenth Street, NW, Washington, DC 20036-3290, (202) 833-4000, Fax: (202) 822-7974, www.nea.org; *Rankings and Estimates: Rankings of the States 2006 and Estimates of School Statistics 2007.*

U.S. Census Bureau, 4700 Silver Hill Road, Washington DC 20233-0001, (301) 763-3030, www.census.gov; unpublished data.

EDUCATION - EXPENDITURES - COUNTY GOVERNMENT

National Education Association (NEA), 1201 Sixteenth Street, NW, Washington, DC 20036-3290, (202) 833-4000, Fax: (202) 822-7974, www.nea.org; *Rankings and Estimates: Rankings of the States 2006 and Estimates of School Statistics 2007.*

U.S. Census Bureau, 4700 Silver Hill Road, Washington DC 20233-0001, (301) 763-3030, www.census.gov; unpublished data.

EDUCATION - EXPENDITURES - LOCAL GOVERNMENT

Educational Research Service (ERS), 1001 North Fairfax Street, Suite 500, Alexandria, VA 22314-1587, (703) 243-2100, Fax: (703) 243-1985, www.ers.org; *Budgeted Revenues and Expenditures in Public School Systems: Current Status and Trends, Update 2006.*

National Education Association (NEA), 1201 Sixteenth Street, NW, Washington, DC 20036-3290, (202) 833-4000, Fax: (202) 822-7974, www.nea.org; *Rankings and Estimates: Rankings of the States 2006 and Estimates of School Statistics 2007.*

U.S. Census Bureau, 4700 Silver Hill Road, Washington DC 20233-0001, (301) 763-3030, www.census.gov; unpublished data.

EDUCATION - EXPENDITURES - PRIVATE

National Center for Education Statistics (NCES), 1990 K Street, NW, Washington, DC 20006, (202) 502-7300, http://nces.ed.gov; *Digest of Education Statistics 2007* and unpublished data.

Social Security Administration (SSA), Office of Public Inquiries, Windsor Park Building, 6401 Security Boulevard, Baltimore, MD 21235, (800) 772-1213, www.ssa.gov; *Annual Statistical Supplement, 2007.*

U.S. Department of Labor (DOL), Bureau of Labor Statistics (BLS), Postal Square Building, 2 Massachusetts Avenue, NE, Washington, DC 20212-0001, (202) 691-5200, Fax: (202) 691-6325, www.bls.gov; *Consumer Price Indexes (CPI).*

EDUCATION - EXPENDITURES - STATE AND LOCAL GOVERNMENTS

National Center for Education Statistics (NCES), 1990 K Street, NW, Washington, DC 20006, (202) 502-7300, http://nces.ed.gov; *Digest of Education Statistics 2007* and unpublished data.

National Education Association (NEA), 1201 Sixteenth Street, NW, Washington, DC 20036-3290, (202) 833-4000, Fax: (202) 822-7974, www.nea.org; *Rankings and Estimates: Rankings of the States 2006 and Estimates of School Statistics 2007.*

Standard and Poor's Corporation, 55 Water Street, New York, NY 10041, (212) 438-1000, www.standardandpoors.com; *SchoolMatters.*

U.S. Census Bureau, Governments Division, 4600 Silver Hill Road, Washington DC 20233, (800) 242-2184, www.census.gov/govs/www; *2002 Census of Governments, Government Finances.*

EDUCATION - FEDERAL AID

National Center for Education Statistics (NCES), 1990 K Street, NW, Washington, DC 20006, (202) 502-7300, http://nces.ed.gov; *Digest of Education Statistics 2007* and unpublished data.

EDUCATION - FOREIGN COUNTRIES

Lesotho Bureau of Statistics, Ministry of Finance and Development Planning, PO Box 455, Maseru 100, Lesotho, www.bos.gov.ls; *Education Statistical Report 2003.*

LISU, Holywell Park, Loughborough University, Leicestershire, LE11 3TU, United Kingdom, www.lboro.ac.uk/departments/dis/lisu; *A Survey of Library Services to Schools and Children in the UK 2005-06.*

Ministry of Statistics and Analysis of the Republic of Belarus, 12 Partizansky Avenue, Minsk 220070, Belarus, www.belstat.gov.by; *Education in the Republic of Belarus.*

Organisation for Economic Cooperation and Development (OECD), 2 rue Andre Pascal, F-75775 Paris Cedex 16, France, (Telephone in U.S. (202) 785-6323), (Fax in U.S. (202) 785-0350), www.oecd.org; *Education at a Glance* (2007 Edition).

World Food Programme, Via C.G.Viola 68, Parco dei Medici, 00148 Rome, Italy, www.wfp.org; *World Hunger Series 2006: Hunger and Learning.*

EDUCATION - FOREIGN LANGUAGE ENROLLMENT

American Council on the Teaching of Foreign Languages (ACTFL), 700 S. Washington Street, Suite 210, Alexandria, VA 22314, (703) 894-2900, Fax: (703) 894-2905, www.actfl.org; *Foreign Language Enrollments.*

Association of Departments of Foreign Languages (ADFL), 26 Broadway, 3rd Floor, New York, NY 10004-1789, (646) 576-5140, www.adfl.org; *ADFL Bulletin.*

EDUCATION - GENERAL EDUCATION DEVELOPMENT (GEDs)

National Center for Education Statistics (NCES), 1990 K Street, NW, Washington, DC 20006, (202) 502-7300, http://nces.ed.gov; *Digest of Education Statistics 2007.*

EDUCATION - GRANTS TO INSTITUTIONS FROM FOUNDATIONS

The Foundation Center, 79 Fifth Avenue, New York, NY 10003-3076, (212) 620-4230, Fax: (212) 807-3677, www.fdncenter.org; *FC Stats - Grantmaker; FC Stats - Grants; Foundation Growth and Giving Estimates: Current Outlook (2008 Edition);* and *Top Funders: Top 100 U.S. Foundations by Asset Size.*

EDUCATION - HANDICAPPED STUDENTS

National Center for Education Statistics (NCES), 1990 K Street, NW, Washington, DC 20006, (202) 502-7300, http://nces.ed.gov; Data Analysis System (DAS) and *An Institutional Perspective on Students With Disabilities in Postsecondary Education.*

EDUCATION - HIGH SCHOOL DROPOUTS

U.S. Bureau of Labor Statistics (BLS), Postal Square Building, 2 Massachusetts Avenue, NE, Washington, DC 20212-0001, (202) 691-5200, Fax: (202) 691-6325, www.bls.gov; *Current Population Survey (CPS)* and unpublished data.

U.S. Census Bureau, Housing and Household Economics Statistics Division, 4700 Silver Hill Road, Washington DC 20233-0001, (301) 763-3030, www.census.gov/hhes/www; Decennial Census of Population and Housing (web app).

U.S. Census Bureau, Population Division, 4700 Silver Hill Road, Washington DC 20233-0001, (301) 763-3030, www.census.gov/population/www/; *Current Population Reports.*

EDUCATION - HIGH SCHOOL STUDENTS

The Brookings Institution, 1775 Massachusetts Avenue, NW, Washington, DC 20036, (202) 797-6000, Fax: (202) 797-6004, www.brook.edu; *How Well Are American Students Learning?*

Editorial Projects in Education, Inc., 6935 Arlington Road, Suite 100, Bethesda, MD 20814-5233, (301) 280-3100, www2.edweek.org/info/about; *Education Week.*

EDUCATION - HIGHER EDUCATION INSTITUTIONS

Market Data Retrieval (MDR), 6 Armstrong Road, Shelton, CT 06484, (800) 333-8802, www.schooldata.com; *The College Technology Review 2006.*

North Carolina Office of State Budget and Management, 116 West Jones Street, Raleigh, NC 27603-8005, (919) 804-4700, Fax: (919) 733-0640, www.osbm.state.nc.us; *North Carolina University System Study of Distance Education.*

TheCenter, PO Box 112012, Gainesville FL, 32611-2012, (352) 846-3501, Fax: (352) 392-8774, http://thecenter.ufl.edu; *Top American Research Universities: An Overview.*

EDUCATION - HIGHER EDUCATION INSTITUTIONS - BEGINNING SALARY OFFERS, COLLEGE GRADUATES

National Association of Colleges and Employers (NACE), 62 Highland Avenue, Bethlehem, PA 18017, (800) 544-5272, Fax: (610) 868-0208, www.naceweb.org; *Salary Survey.*

EDUCATION - HIGHER EDUCATION INSTITUTIONS - CHARGES FOR ROOM AND BOARD

National Center for Education Statistics (NCES), 1990 K Street, NW, Washington, DC 20006, (202) 502-7300, http://nces.ed.gov; *Digest of Education Statistics 2007.*

EDUCATION - HIGHER EDUCATION INSTITUTIONS - CRIMINAL STATISTICS

U.S. Department of Justice (DOJ), Bureau of Justice Statistics, 810 Seventh Street, NW, Washington, DC 20531, (202) 307-0765, www.ojp.usdoj.gov/bjs/; *Violent Victimization of College Students, 1995-2002.*

EDUCATION - HIGHER EDUCATION INSTITUTIONS - DEGREES CONFERRED

Higher Education Research Institute (HERI), University of California, Los Angeles, 3005 Moore Hall/Box 951521, Los Angeles, CA 90095-1521, (310) 825-1925, Fax: (310) 206-2228, www.gseis.ucla.edu/heri/index.php; *Degree Attainment Rates at Colleges and Universities.*

National Center for Education Statistics (NCES), 1990 K Street, NW, Washington, DC 20006, (202) 502-7300, http://nces.ed.gov; *Digest of Education Statistics 2007* and *Projections of Education Statistics to 2016.*

National Science Foundation, Division of Science Resources Statistics (SRS), 4201 Wilson Boulevard, Arlington, VA 22230, (703) 292-8780, Fax: (703) 292-9092, www.nsf.gov; *Microdata Files; Selected Data on Science and Engineering Doctorate Awards;* and *Survey of Earned Doctorates 2006.*

EDUCATION - HIGHER EDUCATION INSTITUTIONS - DEGREES CONFERRED - NON-RESIDENT ALIENS

National Center for Education Statistics (NCES), 1990 K Street, NW, Washington, DC 20006, (202) 502-7300, http://nces.ed.gov; *Digest of Education Statistics 2007.*

EDUCATION - HIGHER EDUCATION INSTITUTIONS - DORMITORIES

Population Reference Bureau, 1875 Connecticut Avenue, NW, Suite 520, Washington, DC, 20009-5728, (800) 877-9881, Fax: (202) 328-3937, www.prb.org; *The American People Series.*

U.S. Census Bureau, Housing and Household Economics Statistics Division, 4700 Silver Hill Road, Washington DC 20233-0001, (301) 763-3030, www.census.gov/hhes/www; *Census 2000 Summary File 1.*

U.S. Census Bureau, Population Division, 4700 Silver Hill Road, Washington DC 20233-0001, (301) 763-3030, www.census.gov/population/www/; *Census 2000 Profiles of General Demographic Characteristics.*

EDUCATION - HIGHER EDUCATION INSTITUTIONS - ENROLLMENT

Council of Graduate Schools, One Dupont Circle NW, Suite 230, Washington, DC 20036, (202) 223-3791, www.cgsnet.org; *Findings from the 2007 CGS International Graduate Admissions Survey: Phase I - Applications; Findings from the 2007 CGS International Graduate Admissions Survey: Phase II - Final Applications and Initial Offers of Acceptance; Findings from the 2007 CGS International Graduate Amissions Survey: Phase III - Admissions and Enrollment; Graduate Enrollment and Degrees Report;* and *Graduate Enrollment and Degrees: 1996 to 2006.*

Higher Education Research Institute (HERI), University of California, Los Angeles, 3005 Moore Hall/Box 951521, Los Angeles, CA 90095-1521, (310) 825-1925, Fax: (310) 206-2228, www.gseis.ucla.edu/heri/index.php; *How Service Learning Affects Students.*

Institute of International Education (IIE), 809 United Nations Plaza, New York, NY 10017-3580, (212) 883-8200, Fax: (212) 984-5452, www.iie.org; *International Student Enrollment Survey: Survey Report Fall 2007; Open Doors 1948-2004: CD-ROM;* and *Open Doors 2007.*

National Center for Education Statistics (NCES), 1990 K Street, NW, Washington, DC 20006, (202) 502-7300, http://nces.ed.gov; *Digest of Education Statistics 2007; Dual Enrollment of High School Students at Postsecondary Institutions: 2002-03; Projections of Education Statistics to 2016; Remedial Education at Degree-Granting Postsecondary Institutions in Fall 2000;* and unpublished data.

U.S. Census Bureau, 4700 Silver Hill Road, Washington DC 20233-0001, (301) 763-3030, www.census.gov; unpublished data.

U.S. Census Bureau, Housing and Household Economics Statistics Division, 4700 Silver Hill Road, Washington DC 20233-0001, (301) 763-3030, www.census.gov/hhes/www; Decennial Census of Population and Housing (web app).

U.S. Census Bureau, Population Division, 4700 Silver Hill Road, Washington DC 20233-0001, (301) 763-3030, www.census.gov/population/www/; *Current Population Reports.*

U.S. Department of Education (ED), Institute of Education Sciences (IES), 400 Maryland Avenue, SW, Washington, DC 20202-7100, (800) USA-LEARN, Fax: (202) 401-0689, www.ed.gov/ies; *Principal Indicators of Student Academic Histories in Postsecondary Education, 1972-2000.*

EDUCATION - HIGHER EDUCATION INSTITUTIONS - ENROLLMENT - COLLEGE FRESHMEN

Higher Education Research Institute (HERI), University of California, Los Angeles, 3005 Moore Hall/Box 951521, Los Angeles, CA 90095-1521, (310) 825-1925, Fax: (310) 206-2228, www.gseis.ucla.edu/heri/index.php; *The American Freshman: National Norms for 2006; American Freshman: National Norms for 2006;* and *The 2007 Your First College Year (YFCY) Survey.*

EDUCATION - HIGHER EDUCATION INSTITUTIONS - ENROLLMENT - CREDIT CARD USE

Higher Education Research Institute (HERI), University of California, Los Angeles, 3005 Moore Hall/Box 951521, Los Angeles, CA 90095-1521, (310) 825-1925, Fax: (310) 206-2228, www.gseis.ucla.edu/heri/index.php; *The American Freshman: National Norms for 2006.*

EDUCATION - HIGHER EDUCATION INSTITUTIONS - ENROLLMENT - DISABLED

National Center for Education Statistics (NCES), 1990 K Street, NW, Washington, DC 20006, (202) 502-7300, http://nces.ed.gov; Data Analysis System (DAS) and *Profile of Undergraduates in U.S. Postsecondary Education Institutions: 2003-04, With a Special Analysis of Community College Students.*

EDUCATION - HIGHER EDUCATION INSTITUTIONS - ENROLLMENT - DISTANCE EDUCATION

National Center for Education Statistics (NCES), 1990 K Street, NW, Washington, DC 20006, (202) 502-7300, http://nces.ed.gov; *Distance Education at Degree-Granting Postsecondary Institutions: 2000-2001; Distance Education at Higher Education Institutions: 2000-01;* and *Profile of Undergraduates in U.S. Postsecondary Education Institutions: 2003-04, With a Special Analysis of Community College Students.*

North Carolina Office of State Budget and Management, 116 West Jones Street, Raleigh, NC 27603-8005, (919) 804-4700, Fax: (919) 733-0640, www.osbm.state.nc.us; *North Carolina University System Study of Distance Education.*

EDUCATION - HIGHER EDUCATION INSTITUTIONS - ENROLLMENT - FOREIGN BORN

U.S. Census Bureau, Population Division, 4700 Silver Hill Road, Washington DC 20233-0001, (301) 763-3030, www.census.gov/population/www/; *Foreign-Born Population in the U.S. 2003.*

EDUCATION - HIGHER EDUCATION INSTITUTIONS - ENROLLMENT - FOREIGN LANGUAGES

Association of Departments of Foreign Languages (ADFL), 26 Broadway, 3rd Floor, New York, NY 10004-1789, (646) 576-5140, www.adfl.org; *ADFL Bulletin.*

EDUCATION - HIGHER EDUCATION INSTITUTIONS - ENROLLMENT - FOREIGN STUDENTS

Institute of International Education (IIE), 809 United Nations Plaza, New York, NY 10017-3580, (212) 883-8200, Fax: (212) 984-5452, www.iie.org; *Open Doors 2007.*

National Center for Education Statistics (NCES), 1990 K Street, NW, Washington, DC 20006, (202) 502-7300, http://nces.ed.gov; *Digest of Education Statistics 2007.*

EDUCATION - HIGHER EDUCATION INSTITUTIONS - ENROLLMENT - PROJECTIONS

National Center for Education Statistics (NCES), 1990 K Street, NW, Washington, DC 20006, (202) 502-7300, http://nces.ed.gov; *Digest of Education Statistics 2007; Projections of Education Statistics to 2016;* and unpublished data.

EDUCATION - HIGHER EDUCATION INSTITUTIONS - ENROLLMENT - SPORTS PARTICIPATION

Centers for Disease Control and Prevention (CDC), U.S. Department of Health and Human Services (HHS), 1600 Clifton Road, Atlanta, GA 30333, (800) 311-3435, www.cdc.gov; *Morbidity and Mortality Weekly Report (MMWR)* and *Youth Risk Behavior Surveillance - United States, 2007.*

National Collegiate Athletic Association (NCAA), 700 West Washington Street, PO Box 6222, Indianapolis, IN 46206-6222, (317) 917-6222, Fax: (317) 917-6888, www.ncaa.org; *1982-2003 Sports Sponsorship and Participation Rates Report.*

National Federation of State High School Associations, PO Box 690, Indianapolis, IN 46206, (317) 972-6900, Fax: (317) 822-5700, www.nfhs.org; *2005-06 High School Athletics Participation Survey.*

EDUCATION - HIGHER EDUCATION INSTITUTIONS - ENROLLMENT - STATES

National Center for Education Statistics (NCES), 1990 K Street, NW, Washington, DC 20006, (202) 502-7300, http://nces.ed.gov; *Digest of Education Statistics 2007.*

TheCenter, PO Box 112012, Gainesville FL, 32611-2012, (352) 846-3501, Fax: (352) 392-8774, http://thecenter.ufl.edu; *The Top American Research Universities.*

EDUCATION - HIGHER EDUCATION INSTITUTIONS - ENROLLMENT - UNITED STATES SERVICE SCHOOLS

National Center for Education Statistics (NCES), 1990 K Street, NW, Washington, DC 20006, (202) 502-7300, http://nces.ed.gov; *Digest of Education Statistics 2007.*

EDUCATION - HIGHER EDUCATION INSTITUTIONS - EXPENDITURES

Bureau of Business and Economic Research, University of North Dakota, PO Box 8369, Grand

Forks, ND 58202, (701) 777-3351, Fax: (701) 777-3365, http://business.und.edu/bber/; *The Economic Impact of Research at the University of North Dakota: Fiscal Year 2003.*

Council for Aid to Education (CAE), 215 Lexington Avenue, 21st Floor, New York, NY 10016-6023, (212) 661-5800, Fax: (212) 661-9766, www.cae.org; *Voluntary Support of Education (VSE) 2005.*

LISU, Holywell Park, Loughborough University, Leicestershire, LE11 3TU, United Kingdom, www.lboro.ac.uk/departments/dis/lisu; *The Cost of Copyright Compliance in Further and Higher Education Institutions.*

National Center for Education Statistics (NCES), 1990 K Street, NW, Washington, DC 20006, (202) 502-7300, http://nces.ed.gov; *Digest of Education Statistics 2007.*

EDUCATION - HIGHER EDUCATION INSTITUTIONS - EXPENDITURES - PRICE INDEXES

TheCenter, PO Box 112012, Gainesville FL, 32611-2012, (352) 846-3501, Fax: (352) 392-8774, http://thecenter.ufl.edu; *The Top American Research Universities.*

U.S. Department of Labor (DOL), Bureau of Labor Statistics (BLS), Postal Square Building, 2 Massachusetts Avenue, NE, Washington, DC 20212-0001, (202) 691-5200, Fax: (202) 691-6325, www.bls.gov; *Consumer Price Indexes (CPI).*

EDUCATION - HIGHER EDUCATION INSTITUTIONS - EXPENDITURES - SCIENTIFIC PURPOSES BY TYPE

National Science Foundation, Division of Science Resources Statistics (SRS), 4201 Wilson Boulevard, Arlington, VA 22230, (703) 292-8780, Fax: (703) 292-9092, www.nsf.gov; *Survey of Research and Development Expenditures at Universities and Colleges.*

EDUCATION - HIGHER EDUCATION INSTITUTIONS - FACULTY

American Association of University Professors, 1012 14th Street, NW, Suite 500, Washington, DC 20005-3465, (202) 737-5900, Fax: (202) 737-5526, www.aaup.org; *AAUP Annual Report on the Economic Status of the Profession.*

Higher Education Research Institute (HERI), University of California, Los Angeles, 3005 Moore Hall/Box 951521, Los Angeles, CA 90095-1521, (310) 825-1925, Fax: (310) 206-2228, www.gseis.ucla.edu/heri/index.php; *The American College Teacher: National Norms for the 2004-2005 HERI Faculty Study* and *Race and Ethnicity in the American Professoriate.*

National Center for Education Statistics (NCES), 1990 K Street, NW, Washington, DC 20006, (202) 502-7300, http://nces.ed.gov; *Digest of Education Statistics 2007; Projections of Education Statistics to 2016; Staff in Postsecondary Institutions, Fall 2003, and Salaries of Full-Time Instructional Faculty, 2003-04;* and unpublished data.

EDUCATION - HIGHER EDUCATION INSTITUTIONS - FINANCES

National Center for Education Statistics (NCES), 1990 K Street, NW, Washington, DC 20006, (202) 502-7300, http://nces.ed.gov; *Digest of Education Statistics 2007; Projections of Education Statistics to 2016;* and unpublished data.

National Education Association (NEA), 1201 Sixteenth Street, NW, Washington, DC 20036-3290, (202) 833-4000, Fax: (202) 822-7974, www.nea.org; *Rankings and Estimates: Rankings of the States 2006 and Estimates of School Statistics 2007.*

TheCenter, PO Box 112012, Gainesville FL, 32611-2012, (352) 846-3501, Fax: (352) 392-8774, http://thecenter.ufl.edu; *The Top American Research Universities.*

EDUCATION - HIGHER EDUCATION INSTITUTIONS - FINANCIAL AID

National Center for Education Statistics (NCES), 1990 K Street, NW, Washington, DC 20006, (202) 502-7300, http://nces.ed.gov; *Digest of Education Statistics 2007* and unpublished data.

U.S. Department of Education (ED), Office of Special Education and Rehabilitative Services (OSERS), 400 Maryland Ave., SW, Washington, DC 20202-7100, (202) 245-7468, www.ed.gov/osers; *Federal Campus-Based Programs Data Book 2007.*

EDUCATION - HIGHER EDUCATION INSTITUTIONS - LIBRARIES

American Library Association, Association of College and Research Libraries (ACRL), 50 East Huron Street, Chicago, IL 60611, (800) 545-2433, Fax: (312) 280-2520, www.ala.org; *2005 Academic Library Trends and Statistics* and *Statistical Summaries for Academic Libraries.*

Information Today, Inc., 143 Old Marlton Pike, Medford, NJ 08055-8750, (609) 654-6266, Fax: (609) 654-4309, www.infotoday.com; *American Library Directory 2007-2008* and *The Bowker Annual Library and Book Trade Almanac 2006.*

LISU, Holywell Park, Loughborough University, Leicestershire, LE11 3TU, United Kingdom, www.lboro.ac.uk/departments/dis/lisu; *Clearing the Way: Copyright Clearance in UK Libraries; Digest of Statistics; 2004 Library and Information Statistics Tables; Statistics in Practice - Measuring and Managing; A Survey of NHS Libraries: Statistics From the NHS Regional Librarians Group;* and *Trend Analysis of Monograph Acquisitions in Public and University Libraries in the UK.*

National Center for Education Statistics (NCES), 1990 K Street, NW, Washington, DC 20006, (202) 502-7300, http://nces.ed.gov; *Public Libraries in the United States, Fiscal Year 2005.*

EDUCATION - HIGHER EDUCATION INSTITUTIONS - NUMBER

National Center for Education Statistics (NCES), 1990 K Street, NW, Washington, DC 20006, (202) 502-7300, http://nces.ed.gov; *Digest of Education Statistics 2007; Projections of Education Statistics to 2016;* and unpublished data.

EDUCATION - HIGHER EDUCATION INSTITUTIONS - PRICE INDEXES

TheCenter, PO Box 112012, Gainesville FL, 32611-2012, (352) 846-3501, Fax: (352) 392-8774, http://thecenter.ufl.edu; *The Top American Research Universities.*

U.S. Department of Labor (DOL), Bureau of Labor Statistics (BLS), Postal Square Building, 2 Massachusetts Avenue, NE, Washington, DC 20212-0001, (202) 691-5200, Fax: (202) 691-6325, www.bls.gov; *Consumer Price Indexes (CPI).*

EDUCATION - HIGHER EDUCATION INSTITUTIONS - REMEDIAL TEACHING

National Center for Education Statistics (NCES), 1990 K Street, NW, Washington, DC 20006, (202) 502-7300, http://nces.ed.gov; *Remedial Education at Degree-Granting Postsecondary Institutions in Fall 2000.*

EDUCATION - HIGHER EDUCATION INSTITUTIONS - TUITION AND FEES

Investment Company Institute (ICI), 1401 H Street, NW, Suite 1200, Washington, DC 20005-2040, (202) 326-5800, www.ici.org; *Profile of Households Saving for College.*

National Center for Education Statistics (NCES), 1990 K Street, NW, Washington, DC 20006, (202) 502-7300, http://nces.ed.gov; *Digest of Education Statistics 2007.*

EDUCATION - HIGHER EDUCATION INSTITUTIONS - VOLUNTARY FINANCIAL SUPPORT

Council for Aid to Education (CAE), 215 Lexington Avenue, 21st Floor, New York, NY 10016-6023, (212) 661-5800, Fax: (212) 661-9766, www.cae.org; *Voluntary Support of Education (VSE) 2005.*

EDUCATION - HOMESCHOOLED

National Center for Education Statistics (NCES), 1990 K Street, NW, Washington, DC 20006, (202) 502-7300, http://nces.ed.gov; *Homeschooling in the United States: 2003.*

EDUCATION - INTERNET ACCESS

Market Data Retrieval (MDR), 6 Armstrong Road, Shelton, CT 06484, (800) 333-8802, www.school-data.com; *The K-12 Technology Review 2005.*

Mediamark Research, Inc., 75 Ninth Avenue, 5th Floor, New York, NY 10011, (212) 884-9200, Fax: (212) 884-9339, www.mediamark.com; MRI+.

National Center for Education Statistics (NCES), 1990 K Street, NW, Washington, DC 20006, (202) 502-7300, http://nces.ed.gov; *Advanced Telecommunications in U.S. Private Schools; Fast Response Survey System (FRSS); Internet Access in U.S. Public Schools and Classrooms: 1994-2005;* and *Teacher Use of Computers and the Internet in Public Schools.*

National Telecommunications and Information Administration (NTIA), U.S. Department of Commerce (DOC), 1401 Constitution Avenue, NW, Washington, DC 20230, (202) 482-7002, www.ntia.doc.gov; *A Nation Online: Entering the Broadband Age.*

EDUCATION - LOANS AND GRANTS - FEDERAL GOVERNMENT

U.S. Department of Education (ED), Office of Postsecondary Education (OPE), 1990 K Street, NW, Washington, DC 20006, (202) 502-7750, www.ed.gov/ope; *Meeting the Highly Qualified Teachers Challenge: The Secretary's Third Annual Report on Teacher Quality.*

U.S. Department of Education (ED), Office of Special Education and Rehabilitative Services (OSERS), 400 Maryland Ave., SW, Washington, DC 20202-7100, (202) 245-7468, www.ed.gov/osers; *Federal Campus-Based Programs Data Book 2007.*

EDUCATION - MEDICAL SCHOOLS - STUDENTS AND GRADUATES

National Center for Health Statistics (NCHS), Centers for Disease Control and Prevention (CDC), U.S. Department of Health and Human Services (HHS), 3311 Toledo Road, Hyattsville, MD 20782, (866) 232-4636, www.cdc.gov/nchs; *Health, United States, 2006, with Chartbook on Trends in the Health of Americans with Special Feature on Pain.*

EDUCATION - MONTESSORI SCHOOLS

National Center for Education Statistics (NCES), 1990 K Street, NW, Washington, DC 20006, (202) 502-7300, http://nces.ed.gov; *Private School Universe Survey 2005-2006.*

EDUCATION - NATIONAL ASSESSMENT OF EDUCATIONAL PROGRESS TESTS (NAEP)

National Center for Education Statistics (NCES), 1990 K Street, NW, Washington, DC 20006, (202) 502-7300, http://nces.ed.gov; *Digest of Education Statistics 2007.*

EDUCATION - NURSING PROGRAMS - STUDENTS - GRADUATES

National Center for Health Statistics (NCHS), Centers for Disease Control and Prevention (CDC), U.S. Department of Health and Human Services (HHS), 3311 Toledo Road, Hyattsville, MD 20782, (866) 232-4636, www.cdc.gov/nchs; *Health, United States, 2006, with Chartbook on Trends in the Health of Americans with Special Feature on Pain.*

EDUCATION - OPTOMETRY SCHOOLS - STUDENTS - GRADUATES

National Center for Health Statistics (NCHS), Centers for Disease Control and Prevention (CDC), U.S. Department of Health and Human Services (HHS), 3311 Toledo Road, Hyattsville, MD 20782,

(866) 232-4636, www.cdc.gov/nchs; *Health, United States, 2006, with Chartbook on Trends in the Health of Americans with Special Feature on Pain.*

EDUCATION - OUTLYING AREAS OF THE UNITED STATES

National Center for Education Statistics (NCES), 1990 K Street, NW, Washington, DC 20006, (202) 502-7300, http://nces.ed.gov; *Digest of Education Statistics 2007* and unpublished data.

Oficina del Censo, Programa de Planificacion Economica y Social, Junta de Planificacion, PO Box 41119, Santurce, Puerto Rico 00940, (Dial from U.S. (787) 723-6200), (Fax from U.S. (787) 268-0506), www.censo.gobierno.pr; unpublished data.

EDUCATION - PARENTAL INVOLVEMENT

The Annie E. Casey Foundation, 701 Saint Paul Street, Baltimore, MD 21202, (410) 547-6600, Fax: (410) 547-3610, www.aecf.org; *Schools Uniting Neighborhoods: Successful Collaboration in an Environment of Constant Change.*

National Center for Education Statistics (NCES), 1990 K Street, NW, Washington, DC 20006, (202) 502-7300, http://nces.ed.gov; *The National Household Education Surveys Program (NHES)* and *Parent Involvement in Children's Education: Efforts by Public Elementary Schools.*

EDUCATION - PHARMACY SCHOOLS - STUDENTS - GRADUATES

National Center for Health Statistics (NCHS), Centers for Disease Control and Prevention (CDC), U.S. Department of Health and Human Services (HHS), 3311 Toledo Road, Hyattsville, MD 20782, (866) 232-4636, www.cdc.gov/nchs; *Health, United States, 2006, with Chartbook on Trends in the Health of Americans with Special Feature on Pain.*

EDUCATION - PHILANTHROPY

The Foundation Center, 79 Fifth Avenue, New York, NY 10003-3076, (212) 620-4230, Fax: (212) 807-3677, www.fdncenter.org; *Foundation Growth and Giving Estimates: Current Outlook (2008 Edition).*

The Giving Institute, 4700 W. Lake Ave, Glenview, IL 60025, (800) 462-2372, Fax: (866) 607-0913, www.aafrc.org; *Giving USA 2006.*

Independent Sector, 1200 Eighteenth Street, NW, Suite 200, Washington, DC 20036, (202) 467-6100, Fax: (202) 467-6101, www.independentsector.org; *Giving and Volunteering in the United States 2001.*

EDUCATION - PRICE INDEXES

U.S. Bureau of Labor Statistics (BLS), Postal Square Building, 2 Massachusetts Avenue, NE, Washington, DC 20212-0001, (202) 691-5200, Fax: (202) 691-6325, www.bls.gov; *Consumer Price Index Detailed Report* and *Monthly Labor Review (MLR).*

U.S. Department of Labor (DOL), Bureau of Labor Statistics (BLS), Postal Square Building, 2 Massachusetts Avenue, NE, Washington, DC 20212-0001, (202) 691-5200, Fax: (202) 691-6325, www.bls.gov; *Consumer Price Indexes (CPI).*

EDUCATION - PRIVATE ELEMENTARY AND SECONDARY SCHOOLS

The Brookings Institution, 1775 Massachusetts Avenue, NW, Washington, DC 20036, (202) 797-6000, Fax: (202) 797-6004, www.brook.edu; *How Well Are American Students Learning?*

Editorial Projects in Education, Inc., 6935 Arlington Road, Suite 100, Bethesda, MD 20814-5233, (301) 280-3100, www2.edweek.org/info/about; *Education Week.*

National Catholic Educational Association (NCEA), 1077 30th Street, NW, Suite 100, Washington, DC 20007-3852, (202) 337-6232, Fax: (202) 333-6706, www.ncea.org; *United States Catholic Elementary and Secondary Schools 2004-2005.*

National Center for Education Statistics (NCES), 1990 K Street, NW, Washington, DC 20006, (202) 502-7300, http://nces.ed.gov; *Digest of Education Statistics 2007; Private School Universe Survey 2005-2006; Projections of Education Statistics to 2016;* and unpublished data.

U.S. Census Bureau, 4700 Silver Hill Road, Washington DC 20233-0001, (301) 763-3030, www.census.gov; unpublished data.

U.S. Census Bureau, Population Division, 4700 Silver Hill Road, Washington DC 20233-0001, (301) 763-3030, www.census.gov/population/www/; *Current Population Reports.*

U.S. Department of Education (ED), Office of Innovation and Improvement (OII), 400 Maryland Avenue, SW, Washington, DC 20202, (202) 205-4500, www.ed.gov/oii; *Characteristics of Private Schools in the United States: Results From the 2001-2002 Private School Universe Survey.*

EDUCATION - PRIVATE ELEMENTARY AND SECONDARY SCHOOLS - COMPUTER USE

Market Data Retrieval (MDR), 6 Armstrong Road, Shelton, CT 06484, (800) 333-8802, www.schooldata.com; *The K-12 Technology Review 2005.*

National Center for Education Statistics (NCES), 1990 K Street, NW, Washington, DC 20006, (202) 502-7300, http://nces.ed.gov; *Advanced Telecommunications in U.S. Private Schools.*

EDUCATION - PRIVATE ELEMENTARY AND SECONDARY SCHOOLS - EXPENDITURES

National Center for Education Statistics (NCES), 1990 K Street, NW, Washington, DC 20006, (202) 502-7300, http://nces.ed.gov; *Digest of Education Statistics 2007.*

EDUCATION - PRIVATE ELEMENTARY AND SECONDARY SCHOOLS - INTERNET ACCESS

Market Data Retrieval (MDR), 6 Armstrong Road, Shelton, CT 06484, (800) 333-8802, www.schooldata.com; *The K-12 Technology Review 2005.*

National Center for Education Statistics (NCES), 1990 K Street, NW, Washington, DC 20006, (202) 502-7300, http://nces.ed.gov; *Advanced Telecommunications in U.S. Private Schools.*

EDUCATION - PRIVATE ELEMENTARY AND SECONDARY SCHOOLS - TEACHERS

National Center for Education Statistics (NCES), 1990 K Street, NW, Washington, DC 20006, (202) 502-7300, http://nces.ed.gov; *Digest of Education Statistics 2007.*

EDUCATION - PUBLIC ELEMENTARY AND SECONDARY SCHOOLS

The Annie E. Casey Foundation, 701 Saint Paul Street, Baltimore, MD 21202, (410) 547-6600, Fax: (410) 547-3610, www.aecf.org; *Schools Uniting Neighborhoods: Successful Collaboration in an Environment of Constant Change.*

The Brookings Institution, 1775 Massachusetts Avenue, NW, Washington, DC 20036, (202) 797-6000, Fax: (202) 797-6004, www.brook.edu; *How Well Are American Students Learning?*

Center for Substance Abuse Research (CESAR), 4321 Hartwick Road, Suite 501, College Park, MD 20740, (301) 405-9770, Fax: (301) 403-8342, www.cesar.umd.edu; *DEWS Investigates: Identifying Maryland Public School Students Who Have Tried Multiple Drugs.*

Council of the Great City Schools (CGCS), 1301 Pennsylvania Avenue, NW, Suite 702, Washington DC, 20004, (202) 393-2427, www.cgcs.org; *Critical Trends in Urban Education: Fifth Biennial Survey of America's Great City Schools; Foundations for Success: Case Studies of How Urban School Systems Improve Student Achievement;* and *Urban Indicator: Urban School Superintendents - Characteristics, Tenure, and Salary.*

Editorial Projects in Education, Inc., 6935 Arlington Road, Suite 100, Bethesda, MD 20814-5233, (301) 280-3100, www2.edweek.org/info/about; *Education Week.*

National Center for Education Statistics (NCES), 1990 K Street, NW, Washington, DC 20006, (202) 502-7300, http://nces.ed.gov; Common Core of Data (CCD).

North Carolina Office of State Budget and Management, 116 West Jones Street, Raleigh, NC 27603-8005, (919) 804-4700, Fax: (919) 733-0640, www.osbm.state.nc.us; *Cost of Collecting Civil Penalties for Public Schools.*

Public/Private Ventures (P/PV), 2000 Market Street, Suite 600, Philadelphia, PA 19103, (215) 557-4400, Fax: (215) 557 4469, www.ppv.org; *Beacons In Brief* and *Promoting Emotional and Behavioral Health in Preteens: Benchmarks of Success and Challenges Among Programs in Santa Clara and San Mateo Counties.*

Standard and Poor's Corporation, 55 Water Street, New York, NY 10041, (212) 438-1000, www.standardandpoors.com; *SchoolMatters.*

US Charter Schools, www.uscharterschools.org; *A Straightforward Comparison of Charter Schools and Regular Public Schools in the United States.*

EDUCATION - PUBLIC ELEMENTARY AND SECONDARY SCHOOLS - CHARTER SCHOOLS

US Charter Schools, www.uscharterschools.org; *Charter Achievement Among Low-Income Students; State of the Charter School Movement 2005: Trends, Issues, and Indicators;* and *A Straightforward Comparison of Charter Schools and Regular Public Schools in the United States.*

U.S. Department of Education (ED), Office of Innovation and Improvement (OII), 400 Maryland Avenue, SW, Washington, DC 20202, (202) 205-4500, www.ed.gov/oii; *Evaluation of the Public Charter Schools Program (PCSP).*

EDUCATION - PUBLIC ELEMENTARY AND SECONDARY SCHOOLS - COMPUTER USE

Market Data Retrieval (MDR), 6 Armstrong Road, Shelton, CT 06484, (800) 333-8802, www.schooldata.com; *The K-12 Technology Review 2005.*

National Center for Education Statistics (NCES), 1990 K Street, NW, Washington, DC 20006, (202) 502-7300, http://nces.ed.gov; *Internet Access in U.S. Public Schools and Classrooms: 1994-2005* and *Teacher Use of Computers and the Internet in Public Schools.*

EDUCATION - PUBLIC ELEMENTARY AND SECONDARY SCHOOLS - CRIMES REPORTED

U.S. Department of Justice (DOJ), Bureau of Justice Statistics, 810 Seventh Street, NW, Washington, DC 20531, (202) 307-0765, www.ojp.usdoj.gov/bjs/; *Indicators of School Crime and Safety, 2005.*

EDUCATION - PUBLIC ELEMENTARY AND SECONDARY SCHOOLS - ENROLLMENT

National Center for Education Statistics (NCES), 1990 K Street, NW, Washington, DC 20006, (202) 502-7300, http://nces.ed.gov; *Digest of Education Statistics 2007; Projections of Education Statistics to 2016;* and unpublished data.

National Education Association (NEA), 1201 Sixteenth Street, NW, Washington, DC 20036-3290, (202) 833-4000, Fax: (202) 822-7974, www.nea.org; *Education Statistics: Rankings and Estimates 2006-2007.*

Standard and Poor's Corporation, 55 Water Street, New York, NY 10041, (212) 438-1000, www.standardandpoors.com; *SchoolMatters.*

U.S. Census Bureau, Population Division, 4700 Silver Hill Road, Washington DC 20233-0001, (301) 763-3030, www.census.gov/population/www/; *Current Population Reports.*

EDUCATION - PUBLIC ELEMENTARY AND SECONDARY SCHOOLS - ENROLLMENT - PROJECTIONS

National Center for Education Statistics (NCES), 1990 K Street, NW, Washington, DC 20006, (202) 502-7300, http://nces.ed.gov; *Digest of Education Statistics 2007; Projections of Education Statistics to 2016;* and unpublished data.

EDUCATION - PUBLIC ELEMENTARY AND SECONDARY SCHOOLS - ENROLLMENT - SIZE

National Center for Education Statistics (NCES), 1990 K Street, NW, Washington, DC 20006, (202) 502-7300, http://nces.ed.gov; *Digest of Education Statistics 2007.*

EDUCATION - PUBLIC ELEMENTARY AND SECONDARY SCHOOLS - ENROLLMENT - STATES

National Center for Education Statistics (NCES), 1990 K Street, NW, Washington, DC 20006, (202) 502-7300, http://nces.ed.gov; *Digest of Education Statistics 2007.*

Standard and Poor's Corporation, 55 Water Street, New York, NY 10041, (212) 438-1000, www.standardandpoors.com; *SchoolMatters.*

EDUCATION - PUBLIC ELEMENTARY AND SECONDARY SCHOOLS - FINANCES

Educational Research Service (ERS), 1001 North Fairfax Street, Suite 500, Alexandria, VA 22314-1587, (703) 243-2100, Fax: (703) 243-1985, www.ers.org; *Budgeted Revenues and Expenditures in Public School Systems: Current Status and Trends, Update 2006.*

National Center for Education Statistics (NCES), 1990 K Street, NW, Washington, DC 20006, (202) 502-7300, http://nces.ed.gov; *Digest of Education Statistics 2007; Projections of Education Statistics to 2016;* and unpublished data.

National Education Association (NEA), 1201 Sixteenth Street, NW, Washington, DC 20036-3290, (202) 833-4000, Fax: (202) 822-7974, www.nea.org; *Education Statistics: Rankings and Estimates 2006-2007.*

Standard and Poor's Corporation, 55 Water Street, New York, NY 10041, (212) 438-1000, www.standardandpoors.com; *SchoolMatters.*

EDUCATION - PUBLIC ELEMENTARY AND SECONDARY SCHOOLS - HIGH SCHOOL GRADUATES

National Center for Education Statistics (NCES), 1990 K Street, NW, Washington, DC 20006, (202) 502-7300, http://nces.ed.gov; *Digest of Education Statistics 2007.*

EDUCATION - PUBLIC ELEMENTARY AND SECONDARY SCHOOLS - INTERNET ACCESS

National Center for Education Statistics (NCES), 1990 K Street, NW, Washington, DC 20006, (202) 502-7300, http://nces.ed.gov; *Internet Access in U.S. Public Schools and Classrooms: 1994-2005.*

EDUCATION - PUBLIC ELEMENTARY AND SECONDARY SCHOOLS - NUMBER

National Center for Education Statistics (NCES), 1990 K Street, NW, Washington, DC 20006, (202) 502-7300, http://nces.ed.gov; *Digest of Education Statistics 2007.*

EDUCATION - PUBLIC ELEMENTARY AND SECONDARY SCHOOLS - PERSONNEL SALARIES

Educational Research Service (ERS), 1001 North Fairfax Street, Suite 500, Alexandria, VA 22314-1587, (703) 243-2100, Fax: (703) 243-1985, www.ers.org; *Salaries and Wages for Professional and Support Personnel in Public Schools, 2005-2006.*

EDUCATION - PUBLIC ELEMENTARY AND SECONDARY SCHOOLS - PRICE INDEXES

TheCenter, PO Box 112012, Gainesville FL, 32611-2012, (352) 846-3501, Fax: (352) 392-8774, http://thecenter.ufl.edu; *The Top American Research Universities.*

EDUCATION - PUBLIC ELEMENTARY AND SECONDARY SCHOOLS - SPECIAL EDUCATION PROGRAMS

National Center for Education Statistics (NCES), 1990 K Street, NW, Washington, DC 20006, (202) 502-7300, http://nces.ed.gov; Data Analysis System (DAS).

EDUCATION - PUBLIC ELEMENTARY AND SECONDARY SCHOOLS - TEACHERS

National Center for Education Statistics (NCES), 1990 K Street, NW, Washington, DC 20006, (202) 502-7300, http://nces.ed.gov; *Digest of Education Statistics 2007; Projections of Education Statistics to 2016;* and unpublished data.

National Education Association (NEA), 1201 Sixteenth Street, NW, Washington, DC 20036-3290, (202) 833-4000, Fax: (202) 822-7974, www.nea.org; *Education Statistics: Rankings and Estimates 2006-2007* and *Status of the American Public School Teacher, 2000-2001.*

EDUCATION - PUBLIC ELEMENTARY AND SECONDARY SCHOOLS - TEACHERS - PROJECTIONS

National Center for Education Statistics (NCES), 1990 K Street, NW, Washington, DC 20006, (202) 502-7300, http://nces.ed.gov; *Digest of Education Statistics 2007* and *Projections of Education Statistics to 2016.*

EDUCATION - SCHOLASTIC ASSESSMENT TEST

College Board, 45 Columbus Avenue, New York, NY 10023, (212) 713-8000, www.collegeboard.com; *College-Bound Seniors 2006.*

EDUCATION - SCHOOL ACTIVITIES

National Center for Education Statistics (NCES), 1990 K Street, NW, Washington, DC 20006, (202) 502-7300, http://nces.ed.gov; *The National Household Education Surveys Program (NHES).*

EDUCATION - SCHOOL DISTRICTS

Educational Research Service (ERS), 1001 North Fairfax Street, Suite 500, Alexandria, VA 22314-1587, (703) 243-2100, Fax: (703) 243-1985, www.ers.org; *Budgeted Revenues and Expenditures in Public School Systems: Current Status and Trends, Update 2006.*

U.S. Census Bureau, Governments Division, 4600 Silver Hill Road, Washington DC 20233, (800) 242-2184, www.census.gov/govs/www; *2002 Census of Governments, Government Organization.*

EDUCATION - SPECIAL EDUCATION PROGRAMS

National Center for Education Statistics (NCES), 1990 K Street, NW, Washington, DC 20006, (202) 502-7300, http://nces.ed.gov; Data Analysis System (DAS).

EDUCATION - STATE DATA - ELEMENTARY AND SECONDARY SCHOOLS

Congressional Quarterly, Inc., 1255 22nd Street, NW, Washington, DC 20037, (202) 419-8500, www.cq.com; *CQ's State Fact Finder 2007: Rankings Across America.*

Council of the Great City Schools (CGCS), 1301 Pennsylvania Avenue, NW, Suite 702, Washington DC, 20004, (202) 393-2427, www.cgcs.org; *Beating the Odds VII: An Analysis of Student Performance and Achievement Gaps on State Assessments - Results from the 2005-2006 School Year; Critical Trends in Urban Education: Fifth Biennial Survey of America's Great City Schools;* and *Foundations for Success: Case Studies of How Urban School Systems Improve Student Achievement.*

National Center for Education Statistics (NCES), 1990 K Street, NW, Washington, DC 20006, (202) 502-7300, http://nces.ed.gov; *Digest of Education Statistics 2007.*

National Education Association (NEA), 1201 Sixteenth Street, NW, Washington, DC 20036-3290, (202) 833-4000, Fax: (202) 822-7974, www.nea.org; *Education Statistics: Rankings and Estimates 2006-2007.*

Public/Private Ventures (P/PV), 2000 Market Street, Suite 600, Philadelphia, PA 19103, (215) 557-4400, Fax: (215) 557 4469, www.ppv.org; *After-School Pursuits: An Examination of Outcomes in the San Francisco Beacon Initiative; Beacons In Brief; The Costs of Out-of-School-Time Programs: A Review of the Available Evidence; Launching Literacy in After-School Programs: Early Lessons from the CORAL Initiative;* and *Promoting Emotional and Behavioral Health in Preteens: Benchmarks of Success and Challenges Among Programs in Santa Clara and San Mateo Counties.*

Standard and Poor's Corporation, 55 Water Street, New York, NY 10041, (212) 438-1000, www.standardandpoors.com; *SchoolMatters.*

EDUCATION - STATE DATA - HIGHER EDUCATION

Congressional Quarterly, Inc., 1255 22nd Street, NW, Washington, DC 20037, (202) 419-8500, www.cq.com; *CQ's State Fact Finder 2007: Rankings Across America.*

National Center for Education Statistics (NCES), 1990 K Street, NW, Washington, DC 20006, (202) 502-7300, http://nces.ed.gov; *Digest of Education Statistics 2007.*

TheCenter, PO Box 112012, Gainesville FL, 32611-2012, (352) 846-3501, Fax: (352) 392-8774, http://thecenter.ufl.edu; *The Top American Research Universities.*

EDUCATION - TEACHERS

National Education Association (NEA), 1201 Sixteenth Street, NW, Washington, DC 20036-3290, (202) 833-4000, Fax: (202) 822-7974, www.nea.org; *Status of the American Public School Teacher, 2000-2001.*

EDUCATION - TEACHERS - CATHOLIC SCHOOLS

National Center for Education Statistics (NCES), 1990 K Street, NW, Washington, DC 20006, (202) 502-7300, http://nces.ed.gov; *Private School Universe Survey 2005-2006.*

EDUCATION - TEACHERS - ELEMENTARY AND SECONDARY

National Center for Education Statistics (NCES), 1990 K Street, NW, Washington, DC 20006, (202) 502-7300, http://nces.ed.gov; *Digest of Education Statistics 2007.*

National Education Association (NEA), 1201 Sixteenth Street, NW, Washington, DC 20036-3290, (202) 833-4000, Fax: (202) 822-7974, www.nea.org; *Education Statistics: Rankings and Estimates 2006-2007.*

EDUCATION - TEACHERS - EMPLOYMENT PROJECTIONS

National Center for Education Statistics (NCES), 1990 K Street, NW, Washington, DC 20006, (202) 502-7300, http://nces.ed.gov; *Digest of Education Statistics 2007* and *Projections of Education Statistics to 2016.*

U.S. Bureau of Labor Statistics (BLS), Postal Square Building, 2 Massachusetts Avenue, NE, Washington, DC 20212-0001, (202) 691-5200, Fax: (202) 691-6325, www.bls.gov; *Monthly Labor Review (MLR).*

EDUCATION - TEACHERS - HIGHER EDUCATION

American Association of University Professors, 1012 14th Street, NW, Suite 500, Washington, DC 20005-3465, (202) 737-5900, Fax: (202) 737-5526, www.aaup.org; *AAUP Annual Report on the Economic Status of the Profession.*

National Center for Education Statistics (NCES), 1990 K Street, NW, Washington, DC 20006, (202) 502-7300, http://nces.ed.gov; *Digest of Education Statistics 2007; Projections of Education Statistics to 2016;* and unpublished data.

U.S. Department of Education (ED), Office of Postsecondary Education (OPE), 1990 K Street, NW, Washington, DC 20006, (202) 502-7750, www.ed.gov/ope; *Meeting the Highly Qualified Teachers Challenge: The Secretary's Third Annual Report on Teacher Quality.*

EDUCATION - TEACHERS - INTERNET USE

National Center for Education Statistics (NCES), 1990 K Street, NW, Washington, DC 20006, (202) 502-7300, http://nces.ed.gov; *Fast Response Survey System (FRSS)* and *Teacher Use of Computers and the Internet in Public Schools.*

EDUCATION - TESTS - ADVANCED PLACEMENT EXAMS

College Board, 45 Columbus Avenue, New York, NY 10023, (212) 713-8000, www.collegeboard.com; *College-Bound Seniors 2006.*

EDUCATION - TESTS - AMERICAN COLLEGE TESTING PROGRAM

ACT, 500 ACT Drive, Box 168, Iowa City, IA 52243-0168, (319) 337-1000, Fax: (319) 339-3020, www.act.org; *ACT National and State Scores.*

EDUCATION - TESTS - NATIONAL ASSESSMENT OF EDUCATIONAL PROGRESS (NAEP) TESTS

Council of the Great City Schools (CGCS), 1301 Pennsylvania Avenue, NW, Suite 702, Washington DC, 20004, (202) 393-2427, www.cgcs.org; *Beating the Odds VII: An Analysis of Student Performance and Achievement Gaps on State Assessments - Results from the 2005-2006 School Year.*

National Center for Education Statistics (NCES), 1990 K Street, NW, Washington, DC 20006, (202) 502-7300, http://nces.ed.gov; *Digest of Education Statistics 2007.*

EDUCATION - TESTS - SCHOLASTIC ASSESSMENT TEST (SAT)

College Board, 45 Columbus Avenue, New York, NY 10023, (212) 713-8000, www.collegeboard.com; *College-Bound Seniors 2006.*

EDUCATION - VOLUNTEERS

Independent Sector, 1200 Eighteenth Street, NW, Suite 200, Washington, DC 20036, (202) 467-6100, Fax: (202) 467-6101, www.independentsector.org; *Giving and Volunteering in the United States 2001.*

EDUCATIONAL EXPENSE INDEXES

U.S. Bureau of Labor Statistics (BLS), Postal Square Building, 2 Massachusetts Avenue, NE, Washington, DC 20212-0001, (202) 691-5200, Fax: (202) 691-6325, www.bls.gov; *Consumer Price Index Detailed Report* and *Monthly Labor Review (MLR).*

EDUCATIONAL SERVICES

U.S. Census Bureau, Center for Economic Studies, 4600 Silver Hill Road, Washington DC 20233, (301) 457-1235, www.ces.census.gov; Economic Census (web app).

EDUCATIONAL SERVICES - EARNINGS

U.S. Bureau of Labor Statistics (BLS), Postal Square Building, 2 Massachusetts Avenue, NE, Washington, DC 20212-0001, (202) 691-5200, Fax: (202) 691-6325, www.bls.gov; *Current Employment Statistics Survey (CES)* and *Employment and Earnings (EE).*

U.S. Census Bureau, Center for Economic Studies, 4600 Silver Hill Road, Washington DC 20233, (301) 457-1235, www.ces.census.gov; *2002 Economic Census, Educational Services.*

U.S. Census Bureau, Company Statistics Division, 4700 Silver Hill Road, Washington DC 20233-0001, (301) 763-3030, www.census.gov/csd/; *County Business Patterns 2004* and *Statistics of U.S. Businesses (SUSB).*

U.S. Census Bureau, Service Sector Statistics Division, 4700 Silver Hill Road, Washington DC 20233-0001, (301) 763-3030, www.census.gov/svsd/www/economic.html; *2004 Service Annual Survey.*

EDUCATIONAL SERVICES - EMPLOYEES

U.S. Bureau of Labor Statistics (BLS), Postal Square Building, 2 Massachusetts Avenue, NE, Washington, DC 20212-0001, (202) 691-5200, Fax: (202) 691-6325, www.bls.gov; *Current Employment Statistics Survey (CES)* and *Employment and Earnings (EE).*

U.S. Census Bureau, Center for Economic Studies, 4600 Silver Hill Road, Washington DC 20233, (301) 457-1235, www.ces.census.gov; *2002 Economic Census, Educational Services.*

U.S. Census Bureau, Company Statistics Division, 4700 Silver Hill Road, Washington DC 20233-0001, (301) 763-3030, www.census.gov/csd/; *County Business Patterns 2004* and *Statistics of U.S. Businesses (SUSB).*

U.S. Census Bureau, Service Sector Statistics Division, 4700 Silver Hill Road, Washington DC 20233-0001, (301) 763-3030, www.census.gov/svsd/www/economic.html; *2004 Service Annual Survey.*

EDUCATIONAL SERVICES - ESTABLISHMENTS

U.S. Census Bureau, Center for Economic Studies, 4600 Silver Hill Road, Washington DC 20233, (301) 457-1235, www.ces.census.gov; *2002 Economic Census, Educational Services.*

U.S. Census Bureau, Company Statistics Division, 4700 Silver Hill Road, Washington DC 20233-0001, (301) 763-3030, www.census.gov/csd/; *County Business Patterns 2004* and *Statistics of U.S. Businesses (SUSB).*

U.S. Census Bureau, Service Sector Statistics Division, 4700 Silver Hill Road, Washington DC 20233-0001, (301) 763-3030, www.census.gov/svsd/www/economic.html; *2004 Service Annual Survey.*

EDUCATIONAL SERVICES - FINANCES

U.S. Census Bureau, Company Statistics Division, 4700 Silver Hill Road, Washington DC 20233-0001, (301) 763-3030, www.census.gov/csd/; *Statistics of U.S. Businesses (SUSB).*

U.S. Census Bureau, Service Sector Statistics Division, 4700 Silver Hill Road, Washington DC 20233-0001, (301) 763-3030, www.census.gov/svsd/www/economic.html; *2004 Service Annual Survey.*

EDUCATIONAL SERVICES - GROSS DOMESTIC PRODUCT

Bureau of Economic Analysis (BEA), U.S. Department of Commerce (DOC), 1441 L Street NW, Washington, DC 20230, (202) 606-9900, www.bea.gov; *Survey of Current Business (SCB).*

EDUCATIONAL SERVICES - INDUSTRIAL SAFETY

U.S. Bureau of Labor Statistics (BLS), Postal Square Building, 2 Massachusetts Avenue, NE, Washington, DC 20212-0001, (202) 691-5200, Fax: (202) 691-6325, www.bls.gov; *Injuries, Illnesses, and Fatalities (IIF).*

EDUCATIONAL SERVICES - INDUSTRY

U.S. Census Bureau, 4700 Silver Hill Road, Washington DC 20233-0001, (301) 763-3030, www.census.gov; *2002 Economic Census, Nonemployer Statistics.*

U.S. Census Bureau, Center for Economic Studies, 4600 Silver Hill Road, Washington DC 20233, (301) 457-1235, www.ces.census.gov; *2002 Economic Census, Geographic Area Series.*

EDUCATIONAL SERVICES - NONEMPLOYERS

U.S. Census Bureau, 4700 Silver Hill Road, Washington DC 20233-0001, (301) 763-3030, www.census.gov; *2002 Economic Census, Nonemployer Statistics.*

EDUCATIONAL SERVICES - RECEIPTS

U.S. Census Bureau, Center for Economic Studies, 4600 Silver Hill Road, Washington DC 20233, (301) 457-1235, www.ces.census.gov; *2002 Economic Census, Educational Services.*

U.S. Census Bureau, Service Sector Statistics Division, 4700 Silver Hill Road, Washington DC 20233-0001, (301) 763-3030, www.census.gov/svsd/www/economic.html; *2004 Service Annual Survey.*

EGGS - CHOLESTEROL SOURCE

Center for Nutrition Policy and Promotion (CNPP), U.S. Department of Agriculture (USDA), 3101 Park Center Drive, 10th Floor, Alexandria, VA 22302-1594, (703) 305-7600, Fax: (703) 305-3300, www.usda.gov/cnpp; *Nutrient Content of the U.S. Food Supply Summary Report 2005.*

EGGS - CONSUMPTION

Economic Research Service (ERS), U.S. Department of Agriculture (USDA), 1800 M Street, NW, Washington, DC 20036-5831, (202) 694-5050, Fax: (202) 694-5689, www.ers.usda.gov; *Agricultural Outlook* and *Food CPI, Prices, and Expenditures.*

State of Connecticut, Department of Economic and Community Development (DECD), 505 Hudson Street, Hartford, CT 06106-7107, (860) 270-8000, www.ct.gov/ecd/; *The Economic Impact of Avian Influenza on Connecticut's Egg Industry.*

EGGS - FARM MARKETINGS, SALES

Economic Research Service (ERS), U.S. Department of Agriculture (USDA), 1800 M Street, NW, Washington, DC 20036-5831, (202) 694-5050, Fax: (202) 694-5689, www.ers.usda.gov; *Agricultural Income and Finance Outlook* and *Farm Income: Data Files.*

EGGS - IRON (DIETARY) SOURCE

Center for Nutrition Policy and Promotion (CNPP), U.S. Department of Agriculture (USDA), 3101 Park Center Drive, 10th Floor, Alexandria, VA 22302-1594, (703) 305-7600, Fax: (703) 305-3300, www.usda.gov/cnpp; *Nutrient Content of the U.S. Food Supply Summary Report 2005.*

EGGS - PRICES

Economic Research Service (ERS), U.S. Department of Agriculture (USDA), 1800 M Street, NW, Washington, DC 20036-5831, (202) 694-5050, Fax: (202) 694-5689, www.ers.usda.gov; *Agricultural Outlook.*

National Agricultural Statistics Service (NASS), U.S. Department of Agriculture (USDA), 1400 Independence Avenue, SW, Washington, DC 20250, (800) 727-9540, Fax: (202) 690-2090, www.nass.usda.gov; *Chickens Eggs: Final Estimates, 1998-2003.*

U.S. Bureau of Labor Statistics (BLS), Postal Square Building, 2 Massachusetts Avenue, NE, Washington, DC 20212-0001, (202) 691-5200, Fax: (202) 691-6325, www.bls.gov; *Consumer Price Index Detailed Report* and *Monthly Labor Review (MLR).*

EGGS - PRODUCTION

Economic Research Service (ERS), U.S. Department of Agriculture (USDA), 1800 M Street, NW,

Washington, DC 20036-5831, (202) 694-5050, Fax: (202) 694-5689, www.ers.usda.gov; *Agricultural Outlook.*

National Agricultural Statistics Service (NASS), U.S. Department of Agriculture (USDA), 1400 Independence Avenue, SW, Washington, DC 20250, (800) 727-9540, Fax: (202) 690-2090, www.nass.usda.gov; *Chickens Eggs: Final Estimates, 1998-2003.*

State of Connecticut, Department of Economic and Community Development (DECD), 505 Hudson Street, Hartford, CT 06106-7107, (860) 270-8000, www.ct.gov/ecd/; *The Economic Impact of Avian Influenza on Connecticut's Egg Industry.*

EGYPT - NATIONAL STATISTICAL OFFICE

Central Agency for Public Mobilization and Statistics (CAPMAS), PO 2080, Selah Salem Nasr City, Egypt, www.capmas.gov.eg/eng_ver/homeE.htm; National Data Center.

EGYPT - PRIMARY STATISTICS SOURCES

Egypt State Information Service (SIS), 3 Al Estad Al Bahary Street, Nasr City, Cairo, Egypt, www.sis.gov.eg; *Statistical Yearbook 2006.*

EGYPT - AGRICULTURE

Economist Intelligence Unit, 111 West 57th Street, New York, NY 10019, (212) 554-0600, Fax: (212) 586-1181, www.eiu.com; *Egypt Country Report.*

Euromonitor International, Inc., 224 S. Michigan Avenue, Suite 1500, Chicago, IL 60604, (312) 922-1115, Fax: (312) 922-1157, www.euromonitor.com; *International Marketing Data and Statistics 2008* and *World Marketing Data and Statistics.*

M.E. Sharpe, 80 Business Park Drive, Armonk, NY 10504, (800) 541-6563, Fax: (914) 273-2106, www.mesharpe.com; *The Illustrated Book of World Rankings.*

Palgrave Macmillan Ltd., Houndmills, Basingstoke, Hampshire, RG21 6XS, England, (Telephone in U.S. (888) 330-8477), (Fax in U.S. (800) 672-2054), www.palgrave.com; *The Statesman's Yearbook 2008.*

Taylor and Francis Group, An Informa Business, 2 Park Square, Milton Park, Abingdon, Oxford OX14 4RN, United Kingdom, (Dial from U.S. (212) 216-7800), (Fax from U.S. (212) 564-7854), www.tandf.co.uk; *The Europa World Year Book.*

United Nations Conference on Trade and Development (UNCTAD), DC2-1120, United Nations, New York, NY 10017, (212) 963-0027, www.unctad.org; *UNCTAD Commodity Yearbook.*

United Nations Economic and Social Commission for Western Asia (ESCWA), PO Box 11-8575, Riad el-Solh Square, Beirut, Lebanon, www.escwa.un.org; *Annual Report 2006* and *Statistical Abstract of the ESCWA Region 2007.*

United Nations Economic Commission for Africa (ECA), PO Box 3001, Addis Ababa, Ethiopia, (Telephone in U.S. (212) 963-4957), www.uneca.org; *African Statistical Yearbook 2006.*

United Nations Food and Agricultural Organization (FAO), Viale delle Terme di Caracalla, 00100 Rome, Italy, (Dial from U.S. (202) 653-2400), (Fax from U.S. (202) 653 5760), www.fao.org; AQUASTAT; *FAO Trade Yearbook;* and *The State of Food and Agriculture (SOFA) 2006.*

United Nations Statistics Division, New York, NY 10017, (800) 253-9646, Fax: (212) 963-4116, http://unstats.un.org; *Statistical Yearbook* and *Survey of Economic and Social Conditions in Africa 2005.*

The World Bank, 1818 H Street, NW, Washington, DC 20433, (202) 473-1000, Fax: (202) 477-6391, www.worldbank.org; *Africa Live Database (LDB); African Development Indicators (ADI) 2007;* and *Egypt, Arab Republic.*

EGYPT - AIRLINES

International Civil Aviation Organization (ICAO), External Relations and Public Information Office (EPO), 999 University Street, Montreal, Quebec H3C 5H7, Canada, (Dial from U.S. (514) 954-8219), (Fax from U.S. (514) 954-6077), www.icao.int; *Civil Aviation Statistics of the World.*

M.E. Sharpe, 80 Business Park Drive, Armonk, NY 10504, (800) 541-6563, Fax: (914) 273-2106, www.mesharpe.com; *The Illustrated Book of World Rankings.*

Palgrave Macmillan Ltd., Houndmills, Basingstoke, Hampshire, RG21 6XS, England, (Telephone in U.S. (888) 330-8477), (Fax in U.S. (800) 672-2054), www.palgrave.com; *The Statesman's Yearbook 2008.*

Taylor and Francis Group, An Informa Business, 2 Park Square, Milton Park, Abingdon, Oxford OX14 4RN, United Kingdom, (Dial from U.S. (212) 216-7800), (Fax from U.S. (212) 564-7854), www.tandf.co.uk; *The Europa World Year Book.*

United Nations Economic Commission for Africa (ECA), PO Box 3001, Addis Ababa, Ethiopia, (Telephone in U.S. (212) 963-4957), www.uneca.org; *African Statistical Yearbook 2006.*

United Nations Statistics Division, New York, NY 10017, (800) 253-9646, Fax: (212) 963-4116, http://unstats.un.org; *Statistical Yearbook.*

EGYPT - AIRPORTS

Central Intelligence Agency, Office of Public Affairs, Washington, DC 20505, (703) 482-0623, Fax: (703) 482-1739, www.cia.gov; *The World Factbook.*

EGYPT - ALUMINUM PRODUCTION

See EGYPT - MINERAL INDUSTRIES

EGYPT - ARMED FORCES

Central Intelligence Agency, Office of Public Affairs, Washington, DC 20505, (703) 482-0623, Fax: (703) 482-1739, www.cia.gov; *The World Factbook.*

Euromonitor International, Inc., 224 S. Michigan Avenue, Suite 1500, Chicago, IL 60604, (312) 922-1115, Fax: (312) 922-1157, www.euromonitor.com; *World Marketing Data and Statistics.*

International Institute for Strategic Studies (IISS), Arundel House, 13-15 Arundel Street, Temple Place, London WC2R 3DX, England, www.iiss.org; *The Military Balance 2007.*

International Monetary Fund (IMF), 700 Nineteenth Street, NW, Washington, DC 20431, (202) 623-7000, Fax: (202) 623-4661, www.imf.org; *Government Finance Statistics Yearbook (2008 Edition).*

Palgrave Macmillan Ltd., Houndmills, Basingstoke, Hampshire, RG21 6XS, England, (Telephone in U.S. (888) 330-8477), (Fax in U.S. (800) 672-2054), www.palgrave.com; *The Statesman's Yearbook 2008.*

U.S. Department of State (DOS), 2201 C Street NW, Washington, DC 20520, (202) 647-4000, www.state.gov; *World Military Expenditures and Arms Transfers (WMEAT).*

United Nations Statistics Division, New York, NY 10017, (800) 253-9646, Fax: (212) 963-4116, http://unstats.un.org; *Human Development Report 2006.*

EGYPT - ARTICHOKE PRODUCTION

See EGYPT - CROPS

EGYPT - AUTOMOBILE INDUSTRY AND TRADE

Taylor and Francis Group, An Informa Business, 2 Park Square, Milton Park, Abingdon, Oxford OX14 4RN, United Kingdom, (Dial from U.S. (212) 216-7800), (Fax from U.S. (212) 564-7854), www.tandf.co.uk; *The Europa World Year Book.*

United Nations Statistics Division, New York, NY 10017, (800) 253-9646, Fax: (212) 963-4116, http://unstats.un.org; *Statistical Yearbook.*

EGYPT - BALANCE OF PAYMENTS

African Development Bank Group, Rue Joseph Anoma, 01 BP 1387 Abidjan 01, Cote d'Ivoire, www.afdb.org; *Statistics Pocketbook 2008.*

International Monetary Fund (IMF), 700 Nineteenth Street, NW, Washington, DC 20431, (202) 623-7000, Fax: (202) 623-4661, www.imf.org; *Balance of Payments Statistics Newsletter* and *Balance of Payments Statistics Yearbook 2007.*

Taylor and Francis Group, An Informa Business, 2 Park Square, Milton Park, Abingdon, Oxford OX14 4RN, United Kingdom, (Dial from U.S. (212) 216-7800), (Fax from U.S. (212) 564-7854), www.tandf.co.uk; *The Europa World Year Book.*

United Nations Conference on Trade and Development (UNCTAD), DC2-1120, United Nations, New York, NY 10017, (212) 963-0027, www.unctad.org; *Handbook of Statistics 2005.*

United Nations Economic and Social Commission for Western Asia (ESCWA), PO Box 11-8575, Riad el-Solh Square, Beirut, Lebanon, www.escwa.un.org; *Annual Report 2006* and *Statistical Abstract of the ESCWA Region 2007.*

United Nations Economic Commission for Africa (ECA), PO Box 3001, Addis Ababa, Ethiopia, (Telephone in U.S. (212) 963-4957), www.uneca.org; *African Statistical Yearbook 2006.*

The World Bank, 1818 H Street, NW, Washington, DC 20433, (202) 473-1000, Fax: (202) 477-6391, www.worldbank.org; *Egypt, Arab Republic* and *World Development Report 2008.*

EGYPT - BANKS AND BANKING

Euromonitor International, Inc., 224 S. Michigan Avenue, Suite 1500, Chicago, IL 60604, (312) 922-1115, Fax: (312) 922-1157, www.euromonitor.com; *World Marketing Data and Statistics.*

International Monetary Fund (IMF), 700 Nineteenth Street, NW, Washington, DC 20431, (202) 623-7000, Fax: (202) 623-4661, www.imf.org; *International Financial Statistics Yearbook 2007.*

M.E. Sharpe, 80 Business Park Drive, Armonk, NY 10504, (800) 541-6563, Fax: (914) 273-2106, www.mesharpe.com; *The Illustrated Book of World Rankings.*

Palgrave Macmillan Ltd., Houndmills, Basingstoke, Hampshire, RG21 6XS, England, (Telephone in U.S. (888) 330-8477), (Fax in U.S. (800) 672-2054), www.palgrave.com; *The Statesman's Yearbook 2008.*

Taylor and Francis Group, An Informa Business, 2 Park Square, Milton Park, Abingdon, Oxford OX14 4RN, United Kingdom, (Dial from U.S. (212) 216-7800), (Fax from U.S. (212) 564-7854), www.tandf.co.uk; *The Europa World Year Book.*

United Nations Economic and Social Commission for Western Asia (ESCWA), PO Box 11-8575, Riad el-Solh Square, Beirut, Lebanon, www.escwa.un.org; *Annual Report 2006* and *Statistical Abstract of the ESCWA Region 2007.*

United Nations Economic Commission for Africa (ECA), PO Box 3001, Addis Ababa, Ethiopia, (Telephone in U.S. (212) 963-4957), www.uneca.org; *African Statistical Yearbook 2006.*

United Nations Statistics Division, New York, NY 10017, (800) 253-9646, Fax: (212) 963-4116, http://unstats.un.org; *Statistical Yearbook.*

EGYPT - BARLEY PRODUCTION

See EGYPT - CROPS

EGYPT - BEVERAGE INDUSTRY

M.E. Sharpe, 80 Business Park Drive, Armonk, NY 10504, (800) 541-6563, Fax: (914) 273-2106, www.mesharpe.com; *The Illustrated Book of World Rankings.*

United Nations Statistics Division, New York, NY 10017, (800) 253-9646, Fax: (212) 963-4116, http://unstats.un.org; *Statistical Yearbook.*

EGYPT - BONDS

International Monetary Fund (IMF), 700 Nineteenth Street, NW, Washington, DC 20431, (202) 623-7000, Fax: (202) 623-4661, www.imf.org; *Government Finance Statistics Yearbook (2008 Edition).*

United Nations Statistics Division, New York, NY 10017, (800) 253-9646, Fax: (212) 963-4116, http://unstats.un.org; *Statistical Yearbook.*

EGYPT - BROADCASTING

Central Intelligence Agency, Office of Public Affairs, Washington, DC 20505, (703) 482-0623, Fax: (703) 482-1739, www.cia.gov; *The World Factbook.*

Euromonitor International, Inc., 224 S. Michigan Avenue, Suite 1500, Chicago, IL 60604, (312) 922-1115, Fax: (312) 922-1157, www.euromonitor.com; *World Marketing Data and Statistics.*

M.E. Sharpe, 80 Business Park Drive, Armonk, NY 10504, (800) 541-6563, Fax: (914) 273-2106, www.mesharpe.com; *The Illustrated Book of World Rankings.*

Palgrave Macmillan Ltd., Houndmills, Basingstoke, Hampshire, RG21 6XS, England, (Telephone in U.S. (888) 330-8477), (Fax in U.S. (800) 672-2054), www.palgrave.com; *The Statesman's Yearbook 2008.*

WRTH Publications Limited, PO Box 290, Oxford OX2 7FT, UK, www.wrth.com; *World Radio TV Handbook 2007.*

EGYPT - BUDGET

Central Intelligence Agency, Office of Public Affairs, Washington, DC 20505, (703) 482-0623, Fax: (703) 482-1739, www.cia.gov; *The World Factbook.*

EGYPT - CAPITAL LEVY

International Monetary Fund (IMF), 700 Nineteenth Street, NW, Washington, DC 20431, (202) 623-7000, Fax: (202) 623-4661, www.imf.org; *Government Finance Statistics Yearbook (2008 Edition).*

EGYPT - CATTLE

See EGYPT - LIVESTOCK

EGYPT - CHICK PEA PRODUCTION

See EGYPT - CROPS

EGYPT - CHICKENS

See EGYPT - LIVESTOCK

EGYPT - CHILDBIRTH - STATISTICS

Central Intelligence Agency, Office of Public Affairs, Washington, DC 20505, (703) 482-0623, Fax: (703) 482-1739, www.cia.gov; *The World Factbook.*

Euromonitor International, Inc., 224 S. Michigan Avenue, Suite 1500, Chicago, IL 60604, (312) 922-1115, Fax: (312) 922-1157, www.euromonitor.com; *International Marketing Data and Statistics 2008* and *The World Economic Factbook 2008.*

M.E. Sharpe, 80 Business Park Drive, Armonk, NY 10504, (800) 541-6563, Fax: (914) 273-2106, www.mesharpe.com; *The Illustrated Book of World Rankings.*

Palgrave Macmillan Ltd., Houndmills, Basingstoke, Hampshire, RG21 6XS, England, (Telephone in U.S. (888) 330-8477), (Fax in U.S. (800) 672-2054), www.palgrave.com; *The Statesman's Yearbook 2008.*

Taylor and Francis Group, An Informa Business, 2 Park Square, Milton Park, Abingdon, Oxford OX14 4RN, United Kingdom, (Dial from U.S. (212) 216-7800), (Fax from U.S. (212) 564-7854), www.tandf.co.uk; *The Europa World Year Book.*

United Nations Statistics Division, New York, NY 10017, (800) 253-9646, Fax: (212) 963-4116, http://unstats.un.org; *Demographic Yearbook; Statistical Yearbook;* and *Survey of Economic and Social Conditions in Africa 2005.*

World Health Organization (WHO), Avenue Appia 20, 1211 Geneve 27, Switzerland, (Telephone in U.S. (212) 331-9081), www.who.int; *World Health Report 2006.*

EGYPT - CLIMATE

International Institute for Environment and Development (IIED), 3 Endsleigh Street, London, England, WC1H 0DD, United Kingdom, www.iied.org; *Environment Urbanization* and *Haramata - Bulletin of the Drylands.*

M.E. Sharpe, 80 Business Park Drive, Armonk, NY 10504, (800) 541-6563, Fax: (914) 273-2106, www.mesharpe.com; *The Illustrated Book of World Rankings.*

Palgrave Macmillan Ltd., Houndmills, Basingstoke, Hampshire, RG21 6XS, England, (Telephone in U.S. (888) 330-8477), (Fax in U.S. (800) 672-2054), www.palgrave.com; *The Statesman's Yearbook 2008.*

EGYPT - COAL PRODUCTION

See EGYPT - MINERAL INDUSTRIES

EGYPT - COFFEE

See EGYPT - CROPS

EGYPT - COMMERCE

Palgrave Macmillan Ltd., Houndmills, Basingstoke, Hampshire, RG21 6XS, England, (Telephone in U.S. (888) 330-8477), (Fax in U.S. (800) 672-2054), www.palgrave.com; *The Statesman's Yearbook 2008.*

EGYPT - COMMODITY EXCHANGES

Commodity Research Bureau, 330 South Wells Street, Suite 612, Chicago, IL 60606-7110, (800) 621-5271, Fax: (312) 939-4135, www.crbtrader.com; *2006 CRB Commodity Yearbook and CD.*

International Monetary Fund (IMF), 700 Nineteenth Street, NW, Washington, DC 20431, (202) 623-7000, Fax: (202) 623-4661, www.imf.org; *IMF Primary Commodity Prices.*

United Nations Food and Agricultural Organization (FAO), Viale delle Terme di Caracalla, 00100 Rome, Italy, (Dial from U.S. (202) 653-2400), (Fax from U.S. (202) 653 5760), www.fao.org; *The State of Food and Agriculture (SOFA) 2006.*

EGYPT - CONSTRUCTION INDUSTRY

M.E. Sharpe, 80 Business Park Drive, Armonk, NY 10504, (800) 541-6563, Fax: (914) 273-2106, www.mesharpe.com; *The Illustrated Book of World Rankings.*

Palgrave Macmillan Ltd., Houndmills, Basingstoke, Hampshire, RG21 6XS, England, (Telephone in U.S. (888) 330-8477), (Fax in U.S. (800) 672-2054), www.palgrave.com; *The Statesman's Yearbook 2008.*

United Nations Economic Commission for Africa (ECA), PO Box 3001, Addis Ababa, Ethiopia, (Telephone in U.S. (212) 963-4957), www.uneca.org; *African Statistical Yearbook 2006.*

United Nations Statistics Division, New York, NY 10017, (800) 253-9646, Fax: (212) 963-4116, http://unstats.un.org; *Statistical Yearbook.*

EGYPT - CONSUMER PRICE INDEXES

Taylor and Francis Group, An Informa Business, 2 Park Square, Milton Park, Abingdon, Oxford OX14 4RN, United Kingdom, (Dial from U.S. (212) 216-7800), (Fax from U.S. (212) 564-7854), www.tandf.co.uk; *The Europa World Year Book.*

United Nations Economic Commission for Africa (ECA), PO Box 3001, Addis Ababa, Ethiopia, (Telephone in U.S. (212) 963-4957), www.uneca.org; *African Statistical Yearbook 2006.*

United Nations Statistics Division, New York, NY 10017, (800) 253-9646, Fax: (212) 963-4116, http://unstats.un.org; *Statistical Yearbook* and *Survey of Economic and Social Conditions in Africa 2005.*

The World Bank, 1818 H Street, NW, Washington, DC 20433, (202) 473-1000, Fax: (202) 477-6391, www.worldbank.org; *Egypt, Arab Republic.*

EGYPT - CONSUMPTION (ECONOMICS)

African Development Bank Group, Rue Joseph Anoma, 01 BP 1387 Abidjan 01, Cote d'Ivoire, www.afdb.org; *Statistics Pocketbook 2008.*

United Nations Statistics Division, New York, NY 10017, (800) 253-9646, Fax: (212) 963-4116, http://unstats.un.org; *Survey of Economic and Social Conditions in Africa 2005.*

The World Bank, 1818 H Street, NW, Washington, DC 20433, (202) 473-1000, Fax: (202) 477-6391, www.worldbank.org; *World Development Report 2008.*

EGYPT - COPPER INDUSTRY AND TRADE

See EGYPT - MINERAL INDUSTRIES

EGYPT - CORN INDUSTRY

See EGYPT - CROPS

EGYPT - COST AND STANDARD OF LIVING

International Monetary Fund (IMF), 700 Nineteenth Street, NW, Washington, DC 20431, (202) 623-7000, Fax: (202) 623-4661, www.imf.org; *Government Finance Statistics Yearbook (2008 Edition).*

EGYPT - COTTON

See EGYPT - CROPS

EGYPT - CRIME

International Criminal Police Organization (INTERPOL), General Secretariat, 200 quai Charles de Gaulle, 69006 Lyon, France, www.interpol.int; *International Crime Statistics.*

Yale University Press, PO Box 209040, New Haven, CT 06520-9040, (203) 432-0960, Fax: (203) 432-0948, http://yalepress.yale.edu/yupbooks; *Violence and Crime in Cross-National Perspective.*

EGYPT - CROPS

International Monetary Fund (IMF), 700 Nineteenth Street, NW, Washington, DC 20431, (202) 623-7000, Fax: (202) 623-4661, www.imf.org; *International Financial Statistics Yearbook 2007.*

M.E. Sharpe, 80 Business Park Drive, Armonk, NY 10504, (800) 541-6563, Fax: (914) 273-2106, www.mesharpe.com; *The Illustrated Book of World Rankings.*

Palgrave Macmillan Ltd., Houndmills, Basingstoke, Hampshire, RG21 6XS, England, (Telephone in U.S. (888) 330-8477), (Fax in U.S. (800) 672-2054), www.palgrave.com; *The Statesman's Yearbook 2008.*

Taylor and Francis Group, An Informa Business, 2 Park Square, Milton Park, Abingdon, Oxford OX14 4RN, United Kingdom, (Dial from U.S. (212) 216-7800), (Fax from U.S. (212) 564-7854), www.tandf.co.uk; *The Europa World Year Book.*

United Nations Conference on Trade and Development (UNCTAD), DC2-1120, United Nations, New York, NY 10017, (212) 963-0027, www.unctad.org; *UNCTAD Commodity Yearbook.*

United Nations Economic Commission for Africa (ECA), PO Box 3001, Addis Ababa, Ethiopia, (Telephone in U.S. (212) 963-4957), www.uneca.org; *African Statistical Yearbook 2006.*

United Nations Food and Agricultural Organization (FAO), Viale delle Terme di Caracalla, 00100 Rome, Italy, (Dial from U.S. (202) 653-2400), (Fax from U.S. (202) 653 5760), www.fao.org; *FAO Production Yearbook 2002* and *The State of Food and Agriculture (SOFA) 2006.*

United Nations Statistics Division, New York, NY 10017, (800) 253-9646, Fax: (212) 963-4116, http://unstats.un.org; *Statistical Yearbook.*

EGYPT - CUSTOMS ADMINISTRATION

International Monetary Fund (IMF), 700 Nineteenth Street, NW, Washington, DC 20431, (202) 623-7000, Fax: (202) 623-4661, www.imf.org; *Government Finance Statistics Yearbook (2008 Edition).*

Palgrave Macmillan Ltd., Houndmills, Basingstoke, Hampshire, RG21 6XS, England, (Telephone in U.S. (888) 330-8477), (Fax in U.S. (800) 672-2054), www.palgrave.com; *The Statesman's Yearbook 2008.*

EGYPT - DAIRY PROCESSING

M.E. Sharpe, 80 Business Park Drive, Armonk, NY 10504, (800) 541-6563, Fax: (914) 273-2106, www.mesharpe.com; *The Illustrated Book of World Rankings.*

Palgrave Macmillan Ltd., Houndmills, Basingstoke, Hampshire, RG21 6XS, England, (Telephone in U.S. (888) 330-8477), (Fax in U.S. (800) 672-2054), www.palgrave.com; *The Statesman's Yearbook 2008.*

Taylor and Francis Group, An Informa Business, 2 Park Square, Milton Park, Abingdon, Oxford OX14 4RN, United Kingdom, (Dial from U.S. (212) 216-7800), (Fax from U.S. (212) 564-7854), www.tandf.co.uk; *The Europa World Year Book.*

United Nations Food and Agricultural Organization (FAO), Viale delle Terme di Caracalla, 00100 Rome, Italy, (Dial from U.S. (202) 653-2400), (Fax from U.S. (202) 653 5760), www.fao.org; *FAO Production Yearbook 2002* and *The State of Food and Agriculture (SOFA) 2006.*

United Nations Statistics Division, New York, NY 10017, (800) 253-9646, Fax: (212) 963-4116, http://unstats.un.org; *Statistical Yearbook.*

EGYPT - DEATH RATES

See EGYPT - MORTALITY

EGYPT - DEBTS, EXTERNAL

African Development Bank Group, Rue Joseph Anoma, 01 BP 1387 Abidjan 01, Cote d'Ivoire, www.afdb.org; *Statistics Pocketbook 2008.*

United Nations Statistics Division, New York, NY 10017, (800) 253-9646, Fax: (212) 963-4116, http://unstats.un.org; *Survey of Economic and Social Conditions in Africa 2005.*

The World Bank, 1818 H Street, NW, Washington, DC 20433, (202) 473-1000, Fax: (202) 477-6391, www.worldbank.org; *Africa Live Database (LDB); African Development Indicators (ADI) 2007; Global Development Finance 2007;* and *World Development Report 2008.*

EGYPT - DEFENSE EXPENDITURES

See EGYPT - ARMED FORCES

EGYPT - DEMOGRAPHY

Euromonitor International, Inc., 224 S. Michigan Avenue, Suite 1500, Chicago, IL 60604, (312) 922-1115, Fax: (312) 922-1157, www.euromonitor.com; *International Marketing Data and Statistics 2008; The World Economic Factbook 2008;* and *World Marketing Data and Statistics.*

M.E. Sharpe, 80 Business Park Drive, Armonk, NY 10504, (800) 541-6563, Fax: (914) 273-2106, www.mesharpe.com; *The Illustrated Book of World Rankings.*

United Nations Statistics Division, New York, NY 10017, (800) 253-9646, Fax: (212) 963-4116, http://unstats.un.org; *Human Development Report 2006* and *Survey of Economic and Social Conditions in Africa 2005.*

The World Bank, 1818 H Street, NW, Washington, DC 20433, (202) 473-1000, Fax: (202) 477-6391, www.worldbank.org; *Egypt, Arab Republic.*

EGYPT - DIAMONDS

See EGYPT - MINERAL INDUSTRIES

EGYPT - DISPOSABLE INCOME

International Monetary Fund (IMF), 700 Nineteenth Street, NW, Washington, DC 20431, (202) 623-7000, Fax: (202) 623-4661, www.imf.org; *International Financial Statistics Yearbook 2007.*

M.E. Sharpe, 80 Business Park Drive, Armonk, NY 10504, (800) 541-6563, Fax: (914) 273-2106, www.mesharpe.com; *The Illustrated Book of World Rankings.*

United Nations Statistics Division, New York, NY 10017, (800) 253-9646, Fax: (212) 963-4116, http://unstats.un.org; *National Accounts Statistics: Compendium of Income Distribution Statistics* and *Statistical Yearbook.*

EGYPT - DIVORCE

M.E. Sharpe, 80 Business Park Drive, Armonk, NY 10504, (800) 541-6563, Fax: (914) 273-2106, www.mesharpe.com; *The Illustrated Book of World Rankings.*

United Nations Statistics Division, New York, NY 10017, (800) 253-9646, Fax: (212) 963-4116, http://unstats.un.org; *Demographic Yearbook* and *Statistical Yearbook.*

EGYPT - ECONOMIC ASSISTANCE

United Nations Statistics Division, New York, NY 10017, (800) 253-9646, Fax: (212) 963-4116, http://unstats.un.org; *Statistical Yearbook.*

EGYPT - ECONOMIC CONDITIONS

African Development Bank Group, Rue Joseph Anoma, 01 BP 1387 Abidjan 01, Cote d'Ivoire, www.afdb.org; *The African Statistical Journal; Gender, Poverty and Environmental Indicators on African Countries 2007; Selected Statistics on African Countries 2007;* and *Statistics Pocketbook 2008.*

Center for International Business Education Research (CIBER), Columbia Business School and School of International and Public Affairs, Uris Hall, Room 212, 3022 Broadway, New York, NY 10027-6902, Mr. Joshua Safier, (212) 854-4750, Fax: (212) 222-9821, www.columbia.edu/cu/ciber/; Datastream International.

Central Intelligence Agency, Office of Public Affairs, Washington, DC 20505, (703) 482-0623, Fax: (703) 482-1739, www.cia.gov; *The World Factbook.*

DSI Data Service Information, Xantener Strasse 51a, D-47495 Rheinberg, Germany, www.dsidata.com; *Campus Solution.*

Dun and Bradstreet (DB) Corporation, 103 JFK Parkway, Short Hills, NJ 07078, (973) 921-5500, www.dnb.com; *Country Report.*

Economist Intelligence Unit, 111 West 57th Street, New York, NY 10019, (212) 554-0600, Fax: (212) 586-1181, www.eiu.com; *Business Africa* and *Egypt Country Report.*

Euromonitor International, Inc., 224 S. Michigan Avenue, Suite 1500, Chicago, IL 60604, (312) 922-1115, Fax: (312) 922-1157, www.euromonitor.com; *International Marketing Data and Statistics 2008; The World Economic Factbook 2008;* and *World Marketing Data and Statistics.*

International Monetary Fund (IMF), 700 Nineteenth Street, NW, Washington, DC 20431, (202) 623-7000, Fax: (202) 623-4661, www.imf.org; *World Economic Outlook Reports.*

M.E. Sharpe, 80 Business Park Drive, Armonk, NY 10504, (800) 541-6563, Fax: (914) 273-2106, www.mesharpe.com; *The Illustrated Book of World Rankings.*

Palgrave Macmillan Ltd., Houndmills, Basingstoke, Hampshire, RG21 6XS, England, (Telephone in U.S. (888) 330-8477), (Fax in U.S. (800) 672-2054), www.palgrave.com; *The Statesman's Yearbook 2008.*

Taylor and Francis Group, An Informa Business, 2 Park Square, Milton Park, Abingdon, Oxford OX14 4RN, United Kingdom, (Dial from U.S. (212) 216-7800), (Fax from U.S. (212) 564-7854), www.tandf.co.uk; *The Europa World Year Book.*

United Nations Statistics Division, New York, NY 10017, (800) 253-9646, Fax: (212) 963-4116, http://unstats.un.org; *Compendium of Intra-African and Related Foreign Trade Statistics 2003* and *World Statistics Pocketbook.*

The World Bank, 1818 H Street, NW, Washington, DC 20433, (202) 473-1000, Fax: (202) 477-6391, www.worldbank.org; *Africa Household Survey Databank; Africa Live Database (LDB); Africa Standardized Files and Indicators; African Development Indicators (ADI) 2007; Egypt, Arab Republic; Global Economic Monitor (GEM); Global Economic Prospects 2008; The World Bank Atlas 2003-2004;* and *World Development Report 2008.*

EGYPT - EDUCATION

African Development Bank Group, Rue Joseph Anoma, 01 BP 1387 Abidjan 01, Cote d'Ivoire, www.afdb.org; *Statistics Pocketbook 2008.*

Euromonitor International, Inc., 224 S. Michigan Avenue, Suite 1500, Chicago, IL 60604, (312) 922-1115, Fax: (312) 922-1157, www.euromonitor.com; *International Marketing Data and Statistics 2008* and *World Marketing Data and Statistics.*

International Monetary Fund (IMF), 700 Nineteenth Street, NW, Washington, DC 20431, (202) 623-7000, Fax: (202) 623-4661, www.imf.org; *Government Finance Statistics Yearbook (2008 Edition).*

M.E. Sharpe, 80 Business Park Drive, Armonk, NY 10504, (800) 541-6563, Fax: (914) 273-2106, www.mesharpe.com; *The Illustrated Book of World Rankings.*

Palgrave Macmillan Ltd., Houndmills, Basingstoke, Hampshire, RG21 6XS, England, (Telephone in U.S. (888) 330-8477), (Fax in U.S. (800) 672-2054), www.palgrave.com; *The Statesman's Yearbook 2008.*

Taylor and Francis Group, An Informa Business, 2 Park Square, Milton Park, Abingdon, Oxford OX14 4RN, United Kingdom, (Dial from U.S. (212) 216-7800), (Fax from U.S. (212) 564-7854), www.tandf.co.uk; *The Europa World Year Book.*

UNESCO Institute for Statistics, C.P. 6128 Succursale Centre-Ville, Montreal, Quebec, H3C 3J7 Canada, (Dial from U.S. (514) 343-6880), (Fax from U.S. (514) 343 6882), www.uis.unesco.org; *Statistical Tables.*

United Nations Economic and Social Commission for Western Asia (ESCWA), PO Box 11-8575, Riad el-Solh Square, Beirut, Lebanon, www.escwa.un.org; *Annual Report 2006* and *Statistical Abstract of the ESCWA Region 2007.*

United Nations Economic Commission for Africa (ECA), PO Box 3001, Addis Ababa, Ethiopia, (Telephone in U.S. (212) 963-4957), www.uneca.org; *African Statistical Yearbook 2006.*

United Nations Statistics Division, New York, NY 10017, (800) 253-9646, Fax: (212) 963-4116, http://unstats.un.org; *Human Development Report 2006* and *Survey of Economic and Social Conditions in Africa 2005.*

The World Bank, 1818 H Street, NW, Washington, DC 20433, (202) 473-1000, Fax: (202) 477-6391, www.worldbank.org; *Egypt, Arab Republic* and *World Development Report 2008.*

EGYPT - EGGPLANT PRODUCTION

See EGYPT - CROPS

EGYPT - ELECTRICITY

M.E. Sharpe, 80 Business Park Drive, Armonk, NY 10504, (800) 541-6563, Fax: (914) 273-2106, www.mesharpe.com; *The Illustrated Book of World Rankings.*

Organisation for Economic Cooperation and Development (OECD), 2 rue Andre Pascal, F-75775 Paris Cedex 16, France, (Telephone in U.S. (202) 785-6323), (Fax in U.S. (202) 785-0350), www.oecd.org; *World Energy Outlook 2007.*

Palgrave Macmillan Ltd., Houndmills, Basingstoke, Hampshire, RG21 6XS, England, (Telephone in U.S. (888) 330-8477), (Fax in U.S. (800) 672-2054), www.palgrave.com; *The Statesman's Yearbook 2008.*

U.S. Department of Energy (DOE), Energy Information Administration (EIA), 1000 Independence Avenue, SW, Washington, DC 20585, (202) 586-8800, www.eia.doe.gov; *International Energy Annual 2004* and *International Energy Outlook 2006.*

United Nations Economic Commission for Africa (ECA), PO Box 3001, Addis Ababa, Ethiopia, (Telephone in U.S. (212) 963-4957), www.uneca.org; *African Statistical Yearbook 2006.*

United Nations Statistics Division, New York, NY 10017, (800) 253-9646, Fax: (212) 963-4116, http://unstats.un.org; *Human Development Report 2006; Statistical Yearbook;* and *Survey of Economic and Social Conditions in Africa 2005.*

EGYPT - EMPLOYMENT

Euromonitor International, Inc., 224 S. Michigan Avenue, Suite 1500, Chicago, IL 60604, (312) 922-1115, Fax: (312) 922-1157, www.euromonitor.com; *International Marketing Data and Statistics 2008.*

International Labour Office, I.L.O. Publications, 4 route des Morillons, CH-1211 Geneva 22, Switzerland, (Telephone in U.S. (202) 653-7652), (Fax in U.S. (202) 653-7687), www.ilo.org; *Yearbook of Labour Statistics 2006.*

M.E. Sharpe, 80 Business Park Drive, Armonk, NY 10504, (800) 541-6563, Fax: (914) 273-2106, www.mesharpe.com; *The Illustrated Book of World Rankings.*

United Nations Economic and Social Commission for Western Asia (ESCWA), PO Box 11-8575, Riad el-Solh Square, Beirut, Lebanon, www.escwa.un.org; *Annual Report 2006* and *Statistical Abstract of the ESCWA Region 2007.*

United Nations Economic Commission for Africa (ECA), PO Box 3001, Addis Ababa, Ethiopia, (Telephone in U.S. (212) 963-4957), www.uneca.org; *African Statistical Yearbook 2006.*

United Nations Statistics Division, New York, NY 10017, (800) 253-9646, Fax: (212) 963-4116, http://unstats.un.org; *Bulletin of Industrial Statistics for the Arab Countries; Statistical Yearbook;* and *Survey of Economic and Social Conditions in Africa 2005.*

The World Bank, 1818 H Street, NW, Washington, DC 20433, (202) 473-1000, Fax: (202) 477-6391, www.worldbank.org; *Egypt, Arab Republic.*

EGYPT - ENERGY INDUSTRIES

Enerdata, 10 Rue Royale, 75008 Paris, France, www.enerdata.fr; *Global Energy Market Data.*

United Nations Statistics Division, New York, NY 10017, (800) 253-9646, Fax: (212) 963-4116, http://unstats.un.org; *Statistical Yearbook.*

The World Bank, 1818 H Street, NW, Washington, DC 20433, (202) 473-1000, Fax: (202) 477-6391, www.worldbank.org; *Egypt, Arab Republic.*

EGYPT - ENVIRONMENTAL CONDITIONS

DSI Data Service Information, Xantener Strasse 51a, D-47495 Rheinberg, Germany, www.dsidata.com; *Campus Solution* and *DSI's Global Environmental Database.*

Economist Intelligence Unit, 111 West 57th Street, New York, NY 10019, (212) 554-0600, Fax: (212) 586-1181, www.eiu.com; *Egypt Country Report.*

International Institute for Environment and Development (IIED), 3 Endsleigh Street, London, England, WC1H 0DD, United Kingdom, www.iied.org; *Environment Urbanization* and *Haramata - Bulletin of the Drylands.*

United Nations Statistics Division, New York, NY 10017, (800) 253-9646, Fax: (212) 963-4116, http://unstats.un.org; *World Statistics Pocketbook.*

EGYPT - EXPORTS

African Development Bank Group, Rue Joseph Anoma, 01 BP 1387 Abidjan 01, Cote d'Ivoire, www.afdb.org; *Statistics Pocketbook 2008.*

Central Intelligence Agency, Office of Public Affairs, Washington, DC 20505, (703) 482-0623, Fax: (703) 482-1739, www.cia.gov; *The World Factbook.*

Economist Intelligence Unit, 111 West 57th Street, New York, NY 10019, (212) 554-0600, Fax: (212) 586-1181, www.eiu.com; *Egypt Country Report.*

Euromonitor International, Inc., 224 S. Michigan Avenue, Suite 1500, Chicago, IL 60604, (312) 922-1115, Fax: (312) 922-1157, www.euromonitor.com; *International Marketing Data and Statistics 2008* and *The World Economic Factbook 2008.*

International Monetary Fund (IMF), 700 Nineteenth Street, NW, Washington, DC 20431, (202) 623-7000, Fax: (202) 623-4661, www.imf.org; *Direction of Trade Statistics Yearbook 2007* and *International Financial Statistics Yearbook 2007.*

Palgrave Macmillan Ltd., Houndmills, Basingstoke, Hampshire, RG21 6XS, England, (Telephone in U.S. (888) 330-8477), (Fax in U.S. (800) 672-2054), www.palgrave.com; *The Statesman's Yearbook 2008.*

Taylor and Francis Group, An Informa Business, 2 Park Square, Milton Park, Abingdon, Oxford OX14 4RN, United Kingdom, (Dial from U.S. (212) 216-7800), (Fax from U.S. (212) 564-7854), www.tandf.co.uk; *The Europa World Year Book.*

United Nations Conference on Trade and Development (UNCTAD), DC2-1120, United Nations, New York, NY 10017, (212) 963-0027, www.unctad.org; *Handbook of Statistics 2005.*

United Nations Economic and Social Commission for Western Asia (ESCWA), PO Box 11-8575, Riad el-Solh Square, Beirut, Lebanon, www.escwa.un.org; *Annual Report 2006* and *Statistical Abstract of the ESCWA Region 2007.*

United Nations Economic Commission for Africa (ECA), PO Box 3001, Addis Ababa, Ethiopia, (Telephone in U.S. (212) 963-4957), www.uneca.org; *African Statistical Yearbook 2006.*

United Nations Food and Agricultural Organization (FAO), Viale delle Terme di Caracalla, 00100 Rome, Italy, (Dial from U.S. (202) 653-2400), (Fax from U.S. (202) 653 5760), www.fao.org; *The State of Food and Agriculture (SOFA) 2006.*

United Nations Statistics Division, New York, NY 10017, (800) 253-9646, Fax: (212) 963-4116, http://unstats.un.org; *Bulletin of Industrial Statistics for the Arab Countries; Compendium of Intra-African and Related Foreign Trade Statistics 2003;* and *Survey of Economic and Social Conditions in Africa 2005.*

The World Bank, 1818 H Street, NW, Washington, DC 20433, (202) 473-1000, Fax: (202) 477-6391, www.worldbank.org; *World Development Report 2008.*

EGYPT - FEMALE WORKING POPULATION

See EGYPT - EMPLOYMENT

EGYPT - FERTILITY, HUMAN

Central Intelligence Agency, Office of Public Affairs, Washington, DC 20505, (703) 482-0623, Fax: (703) 482-1739, www.cia.gov; *The World Factbook.*

M.E. Sharpe, 80 Business Park Drive, Armonk, NY 10504, (800) 541-6563, Fax: (914) 273-2106, www.mesharpe.com; *The Illustrated Book of World Rankings.*

United Nations Statistics Division, New York, NY 10017, (800) 253-9646, Fax: (212) 963-4116, http://unstats.un.org; *Human Development Report 2006* and *Survey of Economic and Social Conditions in Africa 2005.*

The World Bank, 1818 H Street, NW, Washington, DC 20433, (202) 473-1000, Fax: (202) 477-6391, www.worldbank.org; *The World Bank Atlas 2003-2004* and *World Development Report 2008.*

EGYPT - FERTILIZER INDUSTRY

United Nations Food and Agricultural Organization (FAO), Viale delle Terme di Caracalla, 00100 Rome, Italy, (Dial from U.S. (202) 653-2400), (Fax from U.S. (202) 653 5760), www.fao.org; *FAO Fertilizer Yearbook* and *The State of Food and Agriculture (SOFA) 2006.*

United Nations Statistics Division, New York, NY 10017, (800) 253-9646, Fax: (212) 963-4116, http://unstats.un.org; *Statistical Yearbook.*

EGYPT - FETAL MORTALITY

See EGYPT - MORTALITY

EGYPT - FILM

See EGYPT - MOTION PICTURES

EGYPT - FINANCE

International Monetary Fund (IMF), 700 Nineteenth Street, NW, Washington, DC 20431, (202) 623-7000, Fax: (202) 623-4661, www.imf.org; *International Financial Statistics Yearbook 2007.*

Taylor and Francis Group, An Informa Business, 2 Park Square, Milton Park, Abingdon, Oxford OX14 4RN, United Kingdom, (Dial from U.S. (212) 216-7800), (Fax from U.S. (212) 564-7854), www.tandf.co.uk; *The Europa World Year Book.*

United Nations Economic and Social Commission for Western Asia (ESCWA), PO Box 11-8575, Riad el-Solh Square, Beirut, Lebanon, www.escwa.un.org; *Annual Report 2006* and *Statistical Abstract of the ESCWA Region 2007.*

United Nations Economic Commission for Africa (ECA), PO Box 3001, Addis Ababa, Ethiopia, (Telephone in U.S. (212) 963-4957), www.uneca.org; *African Statistical Yearbook 2006.*

United Nations Statistics Division, New York, NY 10017, (800) 253-9646, Fax: (212) 963-4116, http://unstats.un.org; *National Accounts Statistics: Compendium of Income Distribution Statistics* and *Statistical Yearbook.*

The World Bank, 1818 H Street, NW, Washington, DC 20433, (202) 473-1000, Fax: (202) 477-6391, www.worldbank.org; *Egypt, Arab Republic.*

EGYPT - FINANCE, PUBLIC

African Development Bank Group, Rue Joseph Anoma, 01 BP 1387 Abidjan 01, Cote d'Ivoire, www.afdb.org; *Statistics Pocketbook 2008.*

Bernan Essential Government Publications, 4611-F Assembly Drive, Lanham MD, 20706-4391, (301) 459-2255, Fax: (800) 865-3450, www.bernan.com; *National Accounts Statistics.*

Economist Intelligence Unit, 111 West 57th Street, New York, NY 10019, (212) 554-0600, Fax: (212) 586-1181, www.eiu.com; *Egypt Country Report.*

International Monetary Fund (IMF), 700 Nineteenth Street, NW, Washington, DC 20431, (202) 623-7000, Fax: (202) 623-4661, www.imf.org; *Government Finance Statistics Yearbook (2008 Edition); International Financial Statistics; International Financial Statistics Online Service;* and *International Financial Statistics Yearbook 2007.*

M.E. Sharpe, 80 Business Park Drive, Armonk, NY 10504, (800) 541-6563, Fax: (914) 273-2106, www.mesharpe.com; *The Illustrated Book of World Rankings.*

Palgrave Macmillan Ltd., Houndmills, Basingstoke, Hampshire, RG21 6XS, England, (Telephone in U.S. (888) 330-8477), (Fax in U.S. (800) 672-2054), www.palgrave.com; *The Statesman's Yearbook 2008.*

Taylor and Francis Group, An Informa Business, 2 Park Square, Milton Park, Abingdon, Oxford OX14 4RN, United Kingdom, (Dial from U.S. (212) 216-7800), (Fax from U.S. (212) 564-7854), www.tandf.co.uk; *The Europa World Year Book.*

United Nations Economic and Social Commission for Western Asia (ESCWA), PO Box 11-8575, Riad el-Solh Square, Beirut, Lebanon, www.escwa.un.org; *Annual Report 2006* and *Statistical Abstract of the ESCWA Region 2007.*

United Nations Economic Commission for Africa (ECA), PO Box 3001, Addis Ababa, Ethiopia, (Telephone in U.S. (212) 963-4957), www.uneca.org; *African Statistical Yearbook 2006.*

The World Bank, 1818 H Street, NW, Washington, DC 20433, (202) 473-1000, Fax: (202) 477-6391, www.worldbank.org; *Egypt, Arab Republic.*

EGYPT - FISHERIES

M.E. Sharpe, 80 Business Park Drive, Armonk, NY 10504, (800) 541-6563, Fax: (914) 273-2106, www.mesharpe.com; *The Illustrated Book of World Rankings.*

Palgrave Macmillan Ltd., Houndmills, Basingstoke, Hampshire, RG21 6XS, England, (Telephone in U.S. (888) 330-8477), (Fax in U.S. (800) 672-2054), www.palgrave.com; *The Statesman's Yearbook 2008.*

Taylor and Francis Group, An Informa Business, 2 Park Square, Milton Park, Abingdon, Oxford OX14 4RN, United Kingdom, (Dial from U.S. (212) 216-7800), (Fax from U.S. (212) 564-7854), www.tandf.co.uk; *The Europa World Year Book.*

United Nations Conference on Trade and Development (UNCTAD), DC2-1120, United Nations, New

York, NY 10017, (212) 963-0027, www.unctad.org; *UNCTAD Commodity Yearbook.*

United Nations Economic and Social Commission for Western Asia (ESCWA), PO Box 11-8575, Riad el-Solh Square, Beirut, Lebanon, www.escwa.un.org; *Annual Report 2006* and *Statistical Abstract of the ESCWA Region 2007.*

United Nations Economic Commission for Africa (ECA), PO Box 3001, Addis Ababa, Ethiopia, (Telephone in U.S. (212) 963-4957), www.uneca.org; *African Statistical Yearbook 2006.*

United Nations Food and Agricultural Organization (FAO), Viale delle Terme di Caracalla, 00100 Rome, Italy, (Dial from U.S. (202) 653-2400), (Fax from U.S. (202) 653 5760), www.fao.org; *FAO Yearbook of Fishery Statistics;* Fishery Databases; FISHSTAT Database. Subjects covered include: Aquaculture production, capture production, fishery commodities; and *The State of Food and Agriculture (SOFA) 2006.*

United Nations Statistics Division, New York, NY 10017, (800) 253-9646, Fax: (212) 963-4116, http://unstats.un.org; *Statistical Yearbook* and *Survey of Economic and Social Conditions in Africa 2005.*

The World Bank, 1818 H Street, NW, Washington, DC 20433, (202) 473-1000, Fax: (202) 477-6391, www.worldbank.org; *Egypt, Arab Republic.*

EGYPT - FLOUR INDUSTRY

United Nations Statistics Division, New York, NY 10017, (800) 253-9646, Fax: (212) 963-4116, http://unstats.un.org; *Statistical Yearbook.*

EGYPT - FOOD

African Development Bank Group, Rue Joseph Anoma, 01 BP 1387 Abidjan 01, Cote d'Ivoire, www.afdb.org; *Statistics Pocketbook 2008.*

United Nations Conference on Trade and Development (UNCTAD), DC2-1120, United Nations, New York, NY 10017, (212) 963-0027, www.unctad.org; *UNCTAD Commodity Yearbook.*

United Nations Food and Agricultural Organization (FAO), Viale delle Terme di Caracalla, 00100 Rome, Italy, (Dial from U.S. (202) 653-2400), (Fax from U.S. (202) 653 5760), www.fao.org; *FAO Production Yearbook 2002* and *The State of Food and Agriculture (SOFA) 2006.*

United Nations Statistics Division, New York, NY 10017, (800) 253-9646, Fax: (212) 963-4116, http://unstats.un.org; *Human Development Report 2006.*

EGYPT - FOREIGN EXCHANGE RATES

African Development Bank Group, Rue Joseph Anoma, 01 BP 1387 Abidjan 01, Cote d'Ivoire, www.afdb.org; *Statistics Pocketbook 2008.*

Central Intelligence Agency, Office of Public Affairs, Washington, DC 20505, (703) 482-0623, Fax: (703) 482-1739, www.cia.gov; *The World Factbook.*

Euromonitor International, Inc., 224 S. Michigan Avenue, Suite 1500, Chicago, IL 60604, (312) 922-1115, Fax: (312) 922-1157, www.euromonitor.com; *International Marketing Data and Statistics 2008* and *The World Economic Factbook 2008.*

International Civil Aviation Organization (ICAO), External Relations and Public Information Office (EPO), 999 University Street, Montreal, Quebec H3C 5H7, Canada, (Dial from U.S. (514) 954-8219), (Fax from U.S. (514) 954-6077), www.icao.int; *Civil Aviation Statistics of the World.*

International Monetary Fund (IMF), 700 Nineteenth Street, NW, Washington, DC 20431, (202) 623-7000, Fax: (202) 623-4661, www.imf.org; *International Financial Statistics Yearbook 2007.*

Taylor and Francis Group, An Informa Business, 2 Park Square, Milton Park, Abingdon, Oxford OX14 4RN, United Kingdom, (Dial from U.S. (212) 216-7800), (Fax from U.S. (212) 564-7854), www.tandf.co.uk; *The Europa World Year Book.*

United Nations Statistics Division, New York, NY 10017, (800) 253-9646, Fax: (212) 963-4116, http://unstats.un.org; *Bulletin of Industrial Statistics for the Arab Countries; Compendium of Intra-African and Related Foreign Trade Statistics 2003; Statistical Yearbook;* and *World Statistics Pocketbook.*

EGYPT - FORESTS AND FORESTRY

American Forest Paper Association (AFPA), 1111 Nineteenth Street, NW, Suite 800, Washington, DC 20036, (800) 878-8878, www.afandpa.org; *2007 Annual Statistics of Paper, Paperboard, and Wood Pulp.*

M.E. Sharpe, 80 Business Park Drive, Armonk, NY 10504, (800) 541-6563, Fax: (914) 273-2106, www.mesharpe.com; *The Illustrated Book of World Rankings.*

Palgrave Macmillan Ltd., Houndmills, Basingstoke, Hampshire, RG21 6XS, England, (Telephone in U.S. (888) 330-8477), (Fax in U.S. (800) 672-2054), www.palgrave.com; *The Statesman's Yearbook 2008.*

Taylor and Francis Group, An Informa Business, 2 Park Square, Milton Park, Abingdon, Oxford OX14 4RN, United Kingdom, (Dial from U.S. (212) 216-7800), (Fax from U.S. (212) 564-7854), www.tandf.co.uk; *The Europa World Year Book.*

UNESCO Institute for Statistics, C.P. 6128 Succursale Centre-Ville, Montreal, Quebec, H3C 3J7 Canada, (Dial from U.S. (514) 343-6880), (Fax from U.S. (514) 343 6882), www.uis.unesco.org; *Statistical Tables.*

United Nations Conference on Trade and Development (UNCTAD), DC2-1120, United Nations, New York, NY 10017, (212) 963-0027, www.unctad.org; *UNCTAD Commodity Yearbook.*

United Nations Economic Commission for Africa (ECA), PO Box 3001, Addis Ababa, Ethiopia, (Telephone in U.S. (212) 963-4957), www.uneca.org; *African Statistical Yearbook 2006.*

United Nations Food and Agricultural Organization (FAO), Viale delle Terme di Caracalla, 00100 Rome, Italy, (Dial from U.S. (202) 653-2400), (Fax from U.S. (202) 653 5760), www.fao.org; *FAO Yearbook of Forest Products* and *The State of Food and Agriculture (SOFA) 2006.*

United Nations Statistics Division, New York, NY 10017, (800) 253-9646, Fax: (212) 963-4116, http://unstats.un.org; *Statistical Yearbook.*

The World Bank, 1818 H Street, NW, Washington, DC 20433, (202) 473-1000, Fax: (202) 477-6391, www.worldbank.org; *Egypt, Arab Republic* and *World Development Report 2008.*

EGYPT - GAS PRODUCTION

See EGYPT - MINERAL INDUSTRIES

EGYPT - GEOGRAPHIC INFORMATION SYSTEMS

M.E. Sharpe, 80 Business Park Drive, Armonk, NY 10504, (800) 541-6563, Fax: (914) 273-2106, www.mesharpe.com; *The Illustrated Book of World Rankings.*

The World Bank, 1818 H Street, NW, Washington, DC 20433, (202) 473-1000, Fax: (202) 477-6391, www.worldbank.org; *Egypt, Arab Republic.*

EGYPT - GOLD INDUSTRY

International Monetary Fund (IMF), 700 Nineteenth Street, NW, Washington, DC 20431, (202) 623-7000, Fax: (202) 623-4661, www.imf.org; *International Financial Statistics Yearbook 2007.*

United Nations Statistics Division, New York, NY 10017, (800) 253-9646, Fax: (212) 963-4116, http://unstats.un.org; *Statistical Yearbook.*

EGYPT - GOLD PRODUCTION

See EGYPT - MINERAL INDUSTRIES

EGYPT - GRANTS-IN-AID

International Monetary Fund (IMF), 700 Nineteenth Street, NW, Washington, DC 20431, (202) 623-7000, Fax: (202) 623-4661, www.imf.org; *Government Finance Statistics Yearbook (2008 Edition).*

EGYPT - GREEN PEPPER AND CHILIE PRODUCTION

See EGYPT - CROPS

EGYPT - GROSS DOMESTIC PRODUCT

African Development Bank Group, Rue Joseph Anoma, 01 BP 1387 Abidjan 01, Cote d'Ivoire, www.afdb.org; *Statistics Pocketbook 2008.*

Economist Intelligence Unit, 111 West 57th Street, New York, NY 10019, (212) 554-0600, Fax: (212) 586-1181, www.eiu.com; *Egypt Country Report.*

Euromonitor International, Inc., 224 S. Michigan Avenue, Suite 1500, Chicago, IL 60604, (312) 922-1115, Fax: (312) 922-1157, www.euromonitor.com; *International Marketing Data and Statistics 2008* and *The World Economic Factbook 2008.*

M.E. Sharpe, 80 Business Park Drive, Armonk, NY 10504, (800) 541-6563, Fax: (914) 273-2106, www.mesharpe.com; *The Illustrated Book of World Rankings.*

Taylor and Francis Group, An Informa Business, 2 Park Square, Milton Park, Abingdon, Oxford OX14 4RN, United Kingdom, (Dial from U.S. (212) 216-7800), (Fax from U.S. (212) 564-7854), www.tandf.co.uk; *The Europa World Year Book.*

United Nations Economic and Social Commission for Western Asia (ESCWA), PO Box 11-8575, Riad el-Solh Square, Beirut, Lebanon, www.escwa.un.org; *Annual Report 2006* and *Statistical Abstract of the ESCWA Region 2007.*

United Nations Economic Commission for Africa (ECA), PO Box 3001, Addis Ababa, Ethiopia, (Telephone in U.S. (212) 963-4957), www.uneca.org; *African Statistical Yearbook 2006.*

United Nations Statistics Division, New York, NY 10017, (800) 253-9646, Fax: (212) 963-4116, http://unstats.un.org; *Bulletin of Industrial Statistics for the Arab Countries; Human Development Report 2006; National Accounts Statistics: Compendium of Income Distribution Statistics; Statistical Yearbook;* and *Survey of Economic and Social Conditions in Africa 2005.*

The World Bank, 1818 H Street, NW, Washington, DC 20433, (202) 473-1000, Fax: (202) 477-6391, www.worldbank.org; *World Development Report 2008.*

EGYPT - GROSS NATIONAL PRODUCT

Euromonitor International, Inc., 224 S. Michigan Avenue, Suite 1500, Chicago, IL 60604, (312) 922-1115, Fax: (312) 922-1157, www.euromonitor.com; *International Marketing Data and Statistics 2008.*

M.E. Sharpe, 80 Business Park Drive, Armonk, NY 10504, (800) 541-6563, Fax: (914) 273-2106, www.mesharpe.com; *The Illustrated Book of World Rankings.*

Palgrave Macmillan Ltd., Houndmills, Basingstoke, Hampshire, RG21 6XS, England, (Telephone in U.S. (888) 330-8477), (Fax in U.S. (800) 672-2054), www.palgrave.com; *The Statesman's Yearbook 2008.*

U.S. Department of State (DOS), 2201 C Street NW, Washington, DC 20520, (202) 647-4000, www.state.gov; *World Military Expenditures and Arms Transfers (WMEAT).*

United Nations Statistics Division, New York, NY 10017, (800) 253-9646, Fax: (212) 963-4116, http://unstats.un.org; *Statistical Yearbook.*

The World Bank, 1818 H Street, NW, Washington, DC 20433, (202) 473-1000, Fax: (202) 477-6391, www.worldbank.org; *The World Bank Atlas 2003-2004* and *World Development Report 2008.*

EGYPT - HIDES AND SKINS INDUSTRY

United Nations Food and Agricultural Organization (FAO), Viale delle Terme di Caracalla, 00100 Rome, Italy, (Dial from U.S. (202) 653-2400), (Fax from U.S. (202) 653 5760), www.fao.org; *FAO Production Yearbook 2002.*

EGYPT - HOUSING

Euromonitor International, Inc., 224 S. Michigan Avenue, Suite 1500, Chicago, IL 60604, (312) 922-1115, Fax: (312) 922-1157, www.euromonitor.com; *World Marketing Data and Statistics.*

M.E. Sharpe, 80 Business Park Drive, Armonk, NY 10504, (800) 541-6563, Fax: (914) 273-2106, www.mesharpe.com; *The Illustrated Book of World Rankings.*

United Nations Statistics Division, New York, NY 10017, (800) 253-9646, Fax: (212) 963-4116, http://unstats.un.org; *Statistical Yearbook.*

EGYPT - ILLITERATE PERSONS

Euromonitor International, Inc., 224 S. Michigan Avenue, Suite 1500, Chicago, IL 60604, (312) 922-1115, Fax: (312) 922-1157, www.euromonitor.com; *The World Economic Factbook 2008.*

Palgrave Macmillan Ltd., Houndmills, Basingstoke, Hampshire, RG21 6XS, England, (Telephone in U.S. (888) 330-8477), (Fax in U.S. (800) 672-2054), www.palgrave.com; *The Statesman's Yearbook 2008.*

UNESCO Institute for Statistics, C.P. 6128 Succursale Centre-Ville, Montreal, Quebec, H3C 3J7 Canada, (Dial from U.S. (514) 343-6880), (Fax from U.S. (514) 343 6882), www.uis.unesco.org; *Statistical Tables.*

United Nations Statistics Division, New York, NY 10017, (800) 253-9646, Fax: (212) 963-4116, http://unstats.un.org; *Human Development Report 2006.*

EGYPT - IMPORTS

Central Intelligence Agency, Office of Public Affairs, Washington, DC 20505, (703) 482-0623, Fax: (703) 482-1739, www.cia.gov; *The World Factbook.*

Economist Intelligence Unit, 111 West 57th Street, New York, NY 10019, (212) 554-0600, Fax: (212) 586-1181, www.eiu.com; *Egypt Country Report.*

Euromonitor International, Inc., 224 S. Michigan Avenue, Suite 1500, Chicago, IL 60604, (312) 922-1115, Fax: (312) 922-1157, www.euromonitor.com; *International Marketing Data and Statistics 2008* and *The World Economic Factbook 2008.*

International Monetary Fund (IMF), 700 Nineteenth Street, NW, Washington, DC 20431, (202) 623-7000, Fax: (202) 623-4661, www.imf.org; *Direction of Trade Statistics Yearbook 2007; Government Finance Statistics Yearbook (2008 Edition);* and *International Financial Statistics Yearbook 2007.*

Palgrave Macmillan Ltd., Houndmills, Basingstoke, Hampshire, RG21 6XS, England, (Telephone in U.S. (888) 330-8477), (Fax in U.S. (800) 672-2054), www.palgrave.com; *The Statesman's Yearbook 2008.*

Taylor and Francis Group, An Informa Business, 2 Park Square, Milton Park, Abingdon, Oxford OX14 4RN, United Kingdom, (Dial from U.S. (212) 216-7800), (Fax from U.S. (212) 564-7854), www.tandf.co.uk; *The Europa World Year Book.*

United Nations Conference on Trade and Development (UNCTAD), DC2-1120, United Nations, New York, NY 10017, (212) 963-0027, www.unctad.org; *Handbook of Statistics 2005.*

United Nations Economic and Social Commission for Western Asia (ESCWA), PO Box 11-8575, Riad el-Solh Square, Beirut, Lebanon, www.escwa.un.org; *Annual Report 2006* and *Statistical Abstract of the ESCWA Region 2007.*

United Nations Economic Commission for Africa (ECA), PO Box 3001, Addis Ababa, Ethiopia, (Telephone in U.S. (212) 963-4957), www.uneca.org; *African Statistical Yearbook 2006.*

United Nations Food and Agricultural Organization (FAO), Viale delle Terme di Caracalla, 00100 Rome, Italy, (Dial from U.S. (202) 653-2400), (Fax from U.S. (202) 653 5760), www.fao.org; *The State of Food and Agriculture (SOFA) 2006.*

United Nations Statistics Division, New York, NY 10017, (800) 253-9646, Fax: (212) 963-4116, http://unstats.un.org; *Bulletin of Industrial Statistics for the Arab Countries; Compendium of Intra-African and Related Foreign Trade Statistics 2003;* and *Survey of Economic and Social Conditions in Africa 2005.*

The World Bank, 1818 H Street, NW, Washington, DC 20433, (202) 473-1000, Fax: (202) 477-6391, www.worldbank.org; *World Development Report 2008.*

EGYPT - INCOME TAXES

See EGYPT - TAXATION

EGYPT - INDUSTRIAL PRODUCTIVITY

Euromonitor International, Inc., 224 S. Michigan Avenue, Suite 1500, Chicago, IL 60604, (312) 922-1115, Fax: (312) 922-1157, www.euromonitor.com; *International Marketing Data and Statistics 2008.*

M.E. Sharpe, 80 Business Park Drive, Armonk, NY 10504, (800) 541-6563, Fax: (914) 273-2106, www.mesharpe.com; *The Illustrated Book of World Rankings.*

EGYPT - INDUSTRIAL PROPERTY

United Nations Statistics Division, New York, NY 10017, (800) 253-9646, Fax: (212) 963-4116, http://unstats.un.org; *Statistical Yearbook.*

EGYPT - INDUSTRIES

Central Intelligence Agency, Office of Public Affairs, Washington, DC 20505, (703) 482-0623, Fax: (703) 482-1739, www.cia.gov; *The World Factbook.*

Economist Intelligence Unit, 111 West 57th Street, New York, NY 10019, (212) 554-0600, Fax: (212) 586-1181, www.eiu.com; *Egypt Country Report.*

Euromonitor International, Inc., 224 S. Michigan Avenue, Suite 1500, Chicago, IL 60604, (312) 922-1115, Fax: (312) 922-1157, www.euromonitor.com; *International Marketing Data and Statistics 2008; The World Economic Factbook 2008;* and *World Marketing Data and Statistics.*

International Labour Office, I.L.O. Publications, 4 route des Morillons, CH-1211 Geneva 22, Switzerland, (Telephone in U.S. (202) 653-7652), (Fax in U.S. (202) 653-7687), www.ilo.org; *Yearbook of Labour Statistics 2006.*

M.E. Sharpe, 80 Business Park Drive, Armonk, NY 10504, (800) 541-6563, Fax: (914) 273-2106, www.mesharpe.com; *The Illustrated Book of World Rankings.*

Taylor and Francis Group, An Informa Business, 2 Park Square, Milton Park, Abingdon, Oxford OX14 4RN, United Kingdom, (Dial from U.S. (212) 216-7800), (Fax from U.S. (212) 564-7854), www.tandf.co.uk; *The Europa World Year Book.*

United Nations Economic Commission for Africa (ECA), PO Box 3001, Addis Ababa, Ethiopia, (Telephone in U.S. (212) 963-4957), www.uneca.org; *African Statistical Yearbook 2006.*

United Nations Industrial Development Organization (UNIDO), 1 United Nations Plaza, New York, NY 10017, (212) 963 6890, Fax: (212) 963-7904, http://unido.org; Industrial Statistics Database 2008 (INDSTAT) and *The International Yearbook of Industrial Statistics 2008.*

United Nations Statistics Division, New York, NY 10017, (800) 253-9646, Fax: (212) 963-4116, http://unstats.un.org; *Bulletin of Industrial Statistics for the Arab Countries; 2004 Industrial Commodity Statistics Yearbook;* and *Survey of Economic and Social Conditions in Africa 2005.*

The World Bank, 1818 H Street, NW, Washington, DC 20433, (202) 473-1000, Fax: (202) 477-6391, www.worldbank.org; *Egypt, Arab Republic.*

EGYPT - INFANT AND MATERNAL MORTALITY

See EGYPT - MORTALITY

EGYPT - INORGANIC ACIDS

United Nations Statistics Division, New York, NY 10017, (800) 253-9646, Fax: (212) 963-4116, http://unstats.un.org; *Statistical Yearbook.*

EGYPT - INTERNATIONAL LIQUIDITY

International Monetary Fund (IMF), 700 Nineteenth Street, NW, Washington, DC 20431, (202) 623-7000, Fax: (202) 623-4661, www.imf.org; *International Financial Statistics Yearbook 2007.*

EGYPT - INTERNATIONAL TRADE

African Development Bank Group, Rue Joseph Anoma, 01 BP 1387 Abidjan 01, Cote d'Ivoire, www.afdb.org; *Statistics Pocketbook 2008.*

Economist Intelligence Unit, 111 West 57th Street, New York, NY 10019, (212) 554-0600, Fax: (212) 586-1181, www.eiu.com; *Egypt Country Report.*

Euromonitor International, Inc., 224 S. Michigan Avenue, Suite 1500, Chicago, IL 60604, (312) 922-1115, Fax: (312) 922-1157, www.euromonitor.com; *International Marketing Data and Statistics 2008; The World Economic Factbook 2008;* and *World Marketing Data and Statistics.*

International Monetary Fund (IMF), 700 Nineteenth Street, NW, Washington, DC 20431, (202) 623-7000, Fax: (202) 623-4661, www.imf.org; *International Financial Statistics Yearbook 2007.*

M.E. Sharpe, 80 Business Park Drive, Armonk, NY 10504, (800) 541-6563, Fax: (914) 273-2106, www.mesharpe.com; *The Illustrated Book of World Rankings.*

Palgrave Macmillan Ltd., Houndmills, Basingstoke, Hampshire, RG21 6XS, England, (Telephone in U.S. (888) 330-8477), (Fax in U.S. (800) 672-2054), www.palgrave.com; *The Statesman's Yearbook 2008.*

Taylor and Francis Group, An Informa Business, 2 Park Square, Milton Park, Abingdon, Oxford OX14 4RN, United Kingdom, (Dial from U.S. (212) 216-7800), (Fax from U.S. (212) 564-7854), www.tandf.co.uk; *The Europa World Year Book.*

United Nations Conference on Trade and Development (UNCTAD), DC2-1120, United Nations, New York, NY 10017, (212) 963-0027, www.unctad.org; *UNCTAD Commodity Yearbook.*

United Nations Economic and Social Commission for Western Asia (ESCWA), PO Box 11-8575, Riad el-Solh Square, Beirut, Lebanon, www.escwa.un.org; *Annual Report 2006* and *Statistical Abstract of the ESCWA Region 2007.*

United Nations Economic Commission for Africa (ECA), PO Box 3001, Addis Ababa, Ethiopia, (Telephone in U.S. (212) 963-4957), www.uneca.org; *African Statistical Yearbook 2006.*

United Nations Food and Agricultural Organization (FAO), Viale delle Terme di Caracalla, 00100 Rome, Italy, (Dial from U.S. (202) 653-2400), (Fax from U.S. (202) 653 5760), www.fao.org; *FAO Trade Yearbook* and *The State of Food and Agriculture (SOFA) 2006.*

United Nations Statistics Division, New York, NY 10017, (800) 253-9646, Fax: (212) 963-4116, http://unstats.un.org; *Bulletin of Industrial Statistics for the Arab Countries; Compendium of Intra-African and Related Foreign Trade Statistics 2003; International Trade Statistics Yearbook;* and *Statistical Yearbook.*

The World Bank, 1818 H Street, NW, Washington, DC 20433, (202) 473-1000, Fax: (202) 477-6391, www.worldbank.org; *Egypt, Arab Republic* and *World Development Report 2008.*

World Trade Organization (WTO), Centre William Rappard, Rue de Lausanne 154, CH-1211 Geneva 21, Switzerland, www.wto.org; *International Trade Statistics 2006.*

EGYPT - INTERNET USERS

International Telecommunication Union (ITU), Place des Nations, 1211 Geneva 20, Switzerland, www.itu.int; *World Telecommunication/ICT Indicators Database on CD-ROM; World Telecommunication/ICT Indicators Database Online;* and *Yearbook of Statistics - Telecommunication Services (Chronological Time Series 1997-2006).*

The World Bank, 1818 H Street, NW, Washington, DC 20433, (202) 473-1000, Fax: (202) 477-6391, www.worldbank.org; *Egypt, Arab Republic.*

EGYPT - IRON AND IRON ORE PRODUCTION

See EGYPT - MINERAL INDUSTRIES

EGYPT - IRRIGATION

Euromonitor International, Inc., 224 S. Michigan Avenue, Suite 1500, Chicago, IL 60604, (312) 922-1115, Fax: (312) 922-1157, www.euromonitor.com; *International Marketing Data and Statistics 2008.*

EGYPT - LABOR

African Development Bank Group, Rue Joseph Anoma, 01 BP 1387 Abidjan 01, Cote d'Ivoire, www.afdb.org; *Statistics Pocketbook 2008.*

Central Intelligence Agency, Office of Public Affairs, Washington, DC 20505, (703) 482-0623, Fax: (703) 482-1739, www.cia.gov; *The World Factbook.*

Euromonitor International, Inc., 224 S. Michigan Avenue, Suite 1500, Chicago, IL 60604, (312) 922-1115, Fax: (312) 922-1157, www.euromonitor.com; *International Marketing Data and Statistics 2008* and *World Marketing Data and Statistics.*

International Labour Office, I.L.O. Publications, 4 route des Morillons, CH-1211 Geneva 22, Switzerland, (Telephone in U.S. (202) 653-7652), (Fax in U.S. (202) 653-7687), www.ilo.org; *Yearbook of Labour Statistics 2006.*

M.E. Sharpe, 80 Business Park Drive, Armonk, NY 10504, (800) 541-6563, Fax: (914) 273-2106, www.mesharpe.com; *The Illustrated Book of World Rankings.*

Palgrave Macmillan Ltd., Houndmills, Basingstoke, Hampshire, RG21 6XS, England, (Telephone in U.S. (888) 330-8477), (Fax in U.S. (800) 672-2054), www.palgrave.com; *The Statesman's Yearbook 2008.*

Taylor and Francis Group, An Informa Business, 2 Park Square, Milton Park, Abingdon, Oxford OX14 4RN, United Kingdom, (Dial from U.S. (212) 216-7800), (Fax from U.S. (212) 564-7854), www.tandf.co.uk; *The Europa World Year Book.*

United Nations Economic and Social Commission for Western Asia (ESCWA), PO Box 11-8575, Riad el-Solh Square, Beirut, Lebanon, www.escwa.un.org; *Annual Report 2006* and *Statistical Abstract of the ESCWA Region 2007.*

United Nations Food and Agricultural Organization (FAO), Viale delle Terme di Caracalla, 00100 Rome, Italy, (Dial from U.S. (202) 653-2400), (Fax from U.S. (202) 653 5760), www.fao.org; *The State of Food and Agriculture (SOFA) 2006.*

United Nations Statistics Division, New York, NY 10017, (800) 253-9646, Fax: (212) 963-4116, http://unstats.un.org; *Human Development Report 2006.*

The World Bank, 1818 H Street, NW, Washington, DC 20433, (202) 473-1000, Fax: (202) 477-6391, www.worldbank.org; *The World Bank Atlas 2003-2004* and *World Development Report 2008.*

EGYPT - LAND USE

Central Intelligence Agency, Office of Public Affairs, Washington, DC 20505, (703) 482-0623, Fax: (703) 482-1739, www.cia.gov; *The World Factbook.*

Euromonitor International, Inc., 224 S. Michigan Avenue, Suite 1500, Chicago, IL 60604, (312) 922-1115, Fax: (312) 922-1157, www.euromonitor.com; *International Marketing Data and Statistics 2008.*

United Nations Economic and Social Commission for Western Asia (ESCWA), PO Box 11-8575, Riad el-Solh Square, Beirut, Lebanon, www.escwa.un.org; *Annual Report 2006* and *Statistical Abstract of the ESCWA Region 2007.*

United Nations Food and Agricultural Organization (FAO), Viale delle Terme di Caracalla, 00100 Rome, Italy, (Dial from U.S. (202) 653-2400), (Fax from U.S. (202) 653 5760), www.fao.org; *FAO Production Yearbook 2002.*

The World Bank, 1818 H Street, NW, Washington, DC 20433, (202) 473-1000, Fax: (202) 477-6391, www.worldbank.org; *World Development Report 2008.*

EGYPT - LIBRARIES

M.E. Sharpe, 80 Business Park Drive, Armonk, NY 10504, (800) 541-6563, Fax: (914) 273-2106, www.mesharpe.com; *The Illustrated Book of World Rankings.*

UNESCO Institute for Statistics, C.P. 6128 Succursale Centre-Ville, Montreal, Quebec, H3C 3J7 Canada, (Dial from U.S. (514) 343-6880), (Fax from U.S. (514) 343 6882), www.uis.unesco.org; *Statistical Tables.*

EGYPT - LICENSES

International Monetary Fund (IMF), 700 Nineteenth Street, NW, Washington, DC 20431, (202) 623-7000, Fax: (202) 623-4661, www.imf.org; *Government Finance Statistics Yearbook (2008 Edition).*

EGYPT - LIFE EXPECTANCY

African Development Bank Group, Rue Joseph Anoma, 01 BP 1387 Abidjan 01, Cote d'Ivoire, www.afdb.org; *Statistics Pocketbook 2008.*

Central Intelligence Agency, Office of Public Affairs, Washington, DC 20505, (703) 482-0623, Fax: (703) 482-1739, www.cia.gov; *The World Factbook.*

Euromonitor International, Inc., 224 S. Michigan Avenue, Suite 1500, Chicago, IL 60604, (312) 922-1115, Fax: (312) 922-1157, www.euromonitor.com; *The World Economic Factbook 2008.*

Palgrave Macmillan Ltd., Houndmills, Basingstoke, Hampshire, RG21 6XS, England, (Telephone in U.S. (888) 330-8477), (Fax in U.S. (800) 672-2054), www.palgrave.com; *The Statesman's Yearbook 2008.*

United Nations Statistics Division, New York, NY 10017, (800) 253-9646, Fax: (212) 963-4116, http://unstats.un.org; *Human Development Report 2006* and *World Statistics Pocketbook.*

The World Bank, 1818 H Street, NW, Washington, DC 20433, (202) 473-1000, Fax: (202) 477-6391, www.worldbank.org; *The World Bank Atlas 2003-2004* and *World Development Report 2008.*

EGYPT - LITERACY

Euromonitor International, Inc., 224 S. Michigan Avenue, Suite 1500, Chicago, IL 60604, (312) 922-1115, Fax: (312) 922-1157, www.euromonitor.com; *World Marketing Data and Statistics.*

United Nations Statistics Division, New York, NY 10017, (800) 253-9646, Fax: (212) 963-4116, http://unstats.un.org; *Survey of Economic and Social Conditions in Africa 2005.*

EGYPT - LIVESTOCK

Euromonitor International, Inc., 224 S. Michigan Avenue, Suite 1500, Chicago, IL 60604, (312) 922-1115, Fax: (312) 922-1157, www.euromonitor.com; *International Marketing Data and Statistics 2008.*

M.E. Sharpe, 80 Business Park Drive, Armonk, NY 10504, (800) 541-6563, Fax: (914) 273-2106, www.mesharpe.com; *The Illustrated Book of World Rankings.*

Palgrave Macmillan Ltd., Houndmills, Basingstoke, Hampshire, RG21 6XS, England, (Telephone in U.S. (888) 330-8477), (Fax in U.S. (800) 672-2054), www.palgrave.com; *The Statesman's Yearbook 2008.*

Taylor and Francis Group, An Informa Business, 2 Park Square, Milton Park, Abingdon, Oxford OX14 4RN, United Kingdom, (Dial from U.S. (212) 216-7800), (Fax from U.S. (212) 564-7854), www.tandf.co.uk; *The Europa World Year Book.*

United Nations Conference on Trade and Development (UNCTAD), DC2-1120, United Nations, New York, NY 10017, (212) 963-0027, www.unctad.org; *UNCTAD Commodity Yearbook.*

United Nations Economic and Social Commission for Western Asia (ESCWA), PO Box 11-8575, Riad el-Solh Square, Beirut, Lebanon, www.escwa.un.org; *Annual Report 2006* and *Statistical Abstract of the ESCWA Region 2007.*

United Nations Economic Commission for Africa (ECA), PO Box 3001, Addis Ababa, Ethiopia, (Telephone in U.S. (212) 963-4957), www.uneca.org; *African Statistical Yearbook 2006.*

United Nations Food and Agricultural Organization (FAO), Viale delle Terme di Caracalla, 00100 Rome, Italy, (Dial from U.S. (202) 653-2400), (Fax from U.S. (202) 653 5760), www.fao.org; *FAO Production Yearbook 2002* and *The State of Food and Agriculture (SOFA) 2006.*

United Nations Statistics Division, New York, NY 10017, (800) 253-9646, Fax: (212) 963-4116, http://unstats.un.org; *Statistical Yearbook* and *Survey of Economic and Social Conditions in Africa 2005.*

EGYPT - LOCAL TAXATION

Euromonitor International, Inc., 224 S. Michigan Avenue, Suite 1500, Chicago, IL 60604, (312) 922-1115, Fax: (312) 922-1157, www.euromonitor.com; *International Marketing Data and Statistics 2008.*

EGYPT - MANUFACTURES

M.E. Sharpe, 80 Business Park Drive, Armonk, NY 10504, (800) 541-6563, Fax: (914) 273-2106, www.mesharpe.com; *The Illustrated Book of World Rankings.*

United Nations Economic Commission for Africa (ECA), PO Box 3001, Addis Ababa, Ethiopia, (Telephone in U.S. (212) 963-4957), www.uneca.org; *African Statistical Yearbook 2006.*

United Nations Statistics Division, New York, NY 10017, (800) 253-9646, Fax: (212) 963-4116, http://unstats.un.org; *Bulletin of Industrial Statistics for the Arab Countries; Statistical Yearbook;* and *Survey of Economic and Social Conditions in Africa 2005.*

EGYPT - MARRIAGE

M.E. Sharpe, 80 Business Park Drive, Armonk, NY 10504, (800) 541-6563, Fax: (914) 273-2106, www.mesharpe.com; *The Illustrated Book of World Rankings.*

Taylor and Francis Group, An Informa Business, 2 Park Square, Milton Park, Abingdon, Oxford OX14 4RN, United Kingdom, (Dial from U.S. (212) 216-7800), (Fax from U.S. (212) 564-7854), www.tandf.co.uk; *The Europa World Year Book.*

United Nations Statistics Division, New York, NY 10017, (800) 253-9646, Fax: (212) 963-4116, http://unstats.un.org; *Demographic Yearbook* and *Statistical Yearbook.*

EGYPT - MILK PRODUCTION

See EGYPT - DAIRY PROCESSING

EGYPT - MINERAL INDUSTRIES

M.E. Sharpe, 80 Business Park Drive, Armonk, NY 10504, (800) 541-6563, Fax: (914) 273-2106, www.mesharpe.com; *The Illustrated Book of World Rankings.*

Organisation for Economic Cooperation and Development (OECD), 2 rue Andre Pascal, F-75775 Paris Cedex 16, France, (Telephone in U.S. (202) 785-6323), (Fax in U.S. (202) 785-0350), www.oecd.org; *World Energy Outlook 2007.*

Palgrave Macmillan Ltd., Houndmills, Basingstoke, Hampshire, RG21 6XS, England, (Telephone in U.S. (888) 330-8477), (Fax in U.S. (800) 672-2054), www.palgrave.com; *The Statesman's Yearbook 2008.*

Taylor and Francis Group, An Informa Business, 2 Park Square, Milton Park, Abingdon, Oxford OX14 4RN, United Kingdom, (Dial from U.S. (212) 216-7800), (Fax from U.S. (212) 564-7854), www.tandf.co.uk; *The Europa World Year Book.*

United Nations Conference on Trade and Development (UNCTAD), DC2-1120, United Nations, New York, NY 10017, (212) 963-0027, www.unctad.org; *UNCTAD Commodity Yearbook.*

United Nations Economic and Social Commission for Western Asia (ESCWA), PO Box 11-8575, Riad el-Solh Square, Beirut, Lebanon, www.escwa.un.org; *Annual Report 2006* and *Statistical Abstract of the ESCWA Region 2007.*

United Nations Economic Commission for Africa (ECA), PO Box 3001, Addis Ababa, Ethiopia, (Telephone in U.S. (212) 963-4957), www.uneca.org; *African Statistical Yearbook 2006.*

United Nations Statistics Division, New York, NY 10017, (800) 253-9646, Fax: (212) 963-4116, http://unstats.un.org; *Bulletin of Industrial Statistics for the Arab Countries* and *Statistical Yearbook.*

The World Bank, 1818 H Street, NW, Washington, DC 20433, (202) 473-1000, Fax: (202) 477-6391, www.worldbank.org; *Egypt, Arab Republic.*

EGYPT - MONEY EXCHANGE RATES

See EGYPT - FOREIGN EXCHANGE RATES

EGYPT - MONEY SUPPLY

African Development Bank Group, Rue Joseph Anoma, 01 BP 1387 Abidjan 01, Cote d'Ivoire, www.afdb.org; *Statistics Pocketbook 2008.*

Economist Intelligence Unit, 111 West 57th Street, New York, NY 10019, (212) 554-0600, Fax: (212) 586-1181, www.eiu.com; *Egypt Country Report.*

Euromonitor International, Inc., 224 S. Michigan Avenue, Suite 1500, Chicago, IL 60604, (312) 922-1115, Fax: (312) 922-1157, www.euromonitor.com; *International Marketing Data and Statistics 2008.*

International Monetary Fund (IMF), 700 Nineteenth Street, NW, Washington, DC 20431, (202) 623-7000, Fax: (202) 623-4661, www.imf.org; *International Financial Statistics Yearbook 2007.*

Taylor and Francis Group, An Informa Business, 2 Park Square, Milton Park, Abingdon, Oxford OX14 4RN, United Kingdom, (Dial from U.S. (212) 216-7800), (Fax from U.S. (212) 564-7854), www.tandf.co.uk; *The Europa World Year Book.*

United Nations Economic and Social Commission for Western Asia (ESCWA), PO Box 11-8575, Riad el-Solh Square, Beirut, Lebanon, www.escwa.un.org; *Annual Report 2006* and *Statistical Abstract of the ESCWA Region 2007.*

United Nations Statistics Division, New York, NY 10017, (800) 253-9646, Fax: (212) 963-4116, http://unstats.un.org; *Statistical Yearbook.*

The World Bank, 1818 H Street, NW, Washington, DC 20433, (202) 473-1000, Fax: (202) 477-6391, www.worldbank.org; *Egypt, Arab Republic.*

EGYPT - MORTALITY

Central Intelligence Agency, Office of Public Affairs, Washington, DC 20505, (703) 482-0623, Fax: (703) 482-1739, www.cia.gov; *The World Factbook.*

Euromonitor International, Inc., 224 S. Michigan Avenue, Suite 1500, Chicago, IL 60604, (312) 922-1115, Fax: (312) 922-1157, www.euromonitor.com; *International Marketing Data and Statistics 2008* and *The World Economic Factbook 2008.*

Palgrave Macmillan Ltd., Houndmills, Basingstoke, Hampshire, RG21 6XS, England, (Telephone in U.S. (888) 330-8477), (Fax in U.S. (800) 672-2054), www.palgrave.com; *The Statesman's Yearbook 2008.*

Taylor and Francis Group, An Informa Business, 2 Park Square, Milton Park, Abingdon, Oxford OX14 4RN, United Kingdom, (Dial from U.S. (212) 216-7800), (Fax from U.S. (212) 564-7854), www.tandf.co.uk; *The Europa World Year Book.*

UNICEF, 3 United Nations Plaza, New York, NY 10017, (800) 253-9646, Fax: (212) 887-7465, www.unicef.org; *The State of the World's Children 2008.*

United Nations Statistics Division, New York, NY 10017, (800) 253-9646, Fax: (212) 963-4116, http://unstats.un.org; *Demographic Yearbook; Human Development Report 2006; Statistical Yearbook; Survey of Economic and Social Conditions in Africa 2005;* and *World Statistics Pocketbook.*

The World Bank, 1818 H Street, NW, Washington, DC 20433, (202) 473-1000, Fax: (202) 477-6391, www.worldbank.org; *The World Bank Atlas 2003-2004* and *World Development Report 2008.*

World Health Organization (WHO), Avenue Appia 20, 1211 Geneve 27, Switzerland, (Telephone in U.S. (212) 331-9081), www.who.int; *The WHO Global Atlas of Infectious Diseases* and *World Health Report 2006.*

EGYPT - MOTION PICTURES

Palgrave Macmillan Ltd., Houndmills, Basingstoke, Hampshire, RG21 6XS, England, (Telephone in U.S. (888) 330-8477), (Fax in U.S. (800) 672-2054), www.palgrave.com; *The Statesman's Yearbook 2008.*

UNESCO Institute for Statistics, C.P. 6128 Succursale Centre-Ville, Montreal, Quebec, H3C 3J7 Canada, (Dial from U.S. (514) 343-6880), (Fax from U.S. (514) 343 6882), www.uis.unesco.org; *Statistical Tables.*

EGYPT - MOTOR VEHICLES

International Road Federation (IFR), Madison Place, 500 Montgomery Street, 5th Floor, Alexandria, VA 22314, (703) 535-1001, Fax: (703) 535-1007, www.irfnet.org; *World Road Statistics 2006.*

United Nations Statistics Division, New York, NY 10017, (800) 253-9646, Fax: (212) 963-4116, http://unstats.un.org; *Statistical Yearbook* and *Survey of Economic and Social Conditions in Africa 2005.*

EGYPT - MUSEUMS

M.E. Sharpe, 80 Business Park Drive, Armonk, NY 10504, (800) 541-6563, Fax: (914) 273-2106, www.mesharpe.com; *The Illustrated Book of World Rankings.*

UNESCO Institute for Statistics, C.P. 6128 Succursale Centre-Ville, Montreal, Quebec, H3C 3J7 Canada, (Dial from U.S. (514) 343-6880), (Fax from U.S. (514) 343 6882), www.uis.unesco.org; *Statistical Tables.*

EGYPT - NATURAL GAS PRODUCTION

See EGYPT - MINERAL INDUSTRIES

EGYPT - NUTRITION

African Development Bank Group, Rue Joseph Anoma, 01 BP 1387 Abidjan 01, Cote d'Ivoire, www.afdb.org; *Statistics Pocketbook 2008.*

United Nations Food and Agricultural Organization (FAO), Viale delle Terme di Caracalla, 00100 Rome, Italy, (Dial from U.S. (202) 653-2400), (Fax from U.S. (202) 653 5760), www.fao.org; *The State of Food and Agriculture (SOFA) 2006.*

EGYPT - OLDER PEOPLE

M.E. Sharpe, 80 Business Park Drive, Armonk, NY 10504, (800) 541-6563, Fax: (914) 273-2106, www.mesharpe.com; *The Illustrated Book of World Rankings.*

EGYPT - ONION PRODUCTION

See EGYPT - CROPS

EGYPT - PAPER

See EGYPT - FORESTS AND FORESTRY

EGYPT - PEANUT PRODUCTION

See EGYPT - CROPS

EGYPT - PERIODICALS

UNESCO Institute for Statistics, C.P. 6128 Succursale Centre-Ville, Montreal, Quebec, H3C 3J7 Canada, (Dial from U.S. (514) 343-6880), (Fax from U.S. (514) 343 6882), www.uis.unesco.org; *Statistical Tables.*

EGYPT - PESTICIDES

United Nations Food and Agricultural Organization (FAO), Viale delle Terme di Caracalla, 00100 Rome, Italy, (Dial from U.S. (202) 653-2400), (Fax from U.S. (202) 653 5760), www.fao.org; *The State of Food and Agriculture (SOFA) 2006.*

EGYPT - PETROLEUM INDUSTRY AND TRADE

M.E. Sharpe, 80 Business Park Drive, Armonk, NY 10504, (800) 541-6563, Fax: (914) 273-2106, www.mesharpe.com; *The Illustrated Book of World Rankings.*

Organisation for Economic Cooperation and Development (OECD), 2 rue Andre Pascal, F-75775 Paris Cedex 16, France, (Telephone in U.S. (202) 785-6323), (Fax in U.S. (202) 785-0350), www.oecd.org; *World Energy Outlook 2007.*

Palgrave Macmillan Ltd., Houndmills, Basingstoke, Hampshire, RG21 6XS, England, (Telephone in U.S. (888) 330-8477), (Fax in U.S. (800) 672-2054), www.palgrave.com; *The Statesman's Yearbook 2008.*

PennWell Corporation, 1421 South Sheridan Road, Tulsa, OK 74112, (918) 835-3161, www.pennwell.com; *International Petroleum Encyclopedia 2007.*

U.S. Department of Energy (DOE), Energy Information Administration (EIA), 1000 Independence Avenue, SW, Washington, DC 20585, (202) 586-8800, www.eia.doe.gov; *International Energy Annual 2004* and *International Energy Outlook 2006.*

United Nations Conference on Trade and Development (UNCTAD), DC2-1120, United Nations, New York, NY 10017, (212) 963-0027, www.unctad.org; *UNCTAD Commodity Yearbook.*

United Nations Food and Agricultural Organization (FAO), Viale delle Terme di Caracalla, 00100 Rome, Italy, (Dial from U.S. (202) 653-2400), (Fax from U.S. (202) 653 5760), www.fao.org; *The State of Food and Agriculture (SOFA) 2006.*

United Nations Statistics Division, New York, NY 10017, (800) 253-9646, Fax: (212) 963-4116, http://unstats.un.org; *Statistical Yearbook.*

EGYPT - PHOSPHATES PRODUCTION

See EGYPT - MINERAL INDUSTRIES

EGYPT - POLITICAL SCIENCE

Central Intelligence Agency, Office of Public Affairs, Washington, DC 20505, (703) 482-0623, Fax: (703) 482-1739, www.cia.gov; *The World Factbook.*

International Monetary Fund (IMF), 700 Nineteenth Street, NW, Washington, DC 20431, (202) 623-7000, Fax: (202) 623-4661, www.imf.org; *Government Finance Statistics Yearbook (2008 Edition).*

Palgrave Macmillan Ltd., Houndmills, Basingstoke, Hampshire, RG21 6XS, England, (Telephone in U.S. (888) 330-8477), (Fax in U.S. (800) 672-2054), www.palgrave.com; *The Statesman's Yearbook 2008.*

Taylor and Francis Group, An Informa Business, 2 Park Square, Milton Park, Abingdon, Oxford OX14 4RN, United Kingdom, (Dial from U.S. (212) 216-7800), (Fax from U.S. (212) 564-7854), www.tandf.co.uk; *The Europa World Year Book.*

United Nations Statistics Division, New York, NY 10017, (800) 253-9646, Fax: (212) 963-4116, http://unstats.un.org; *National Accounts Statistics: Compendium of Income Distribution Statistics; Statistical Yearbook;* and *Survey of Economic and Social Conditions in Africa 2005.*

The World Bank, 1818 H Street, NW, Washington, DC 20433, (202) 473-1000, Fax: (202) 477-6391, www.worldbank.org; *World Development Report 2008.*

EGYPT - POPULATION

African Development Bank Group, Rue Joseph Anoma, 01 BP 1387 Abidjan 01, Cote d'Ivoire, www.afdb.org; *The African Statistical Journal; Gender, Poverty and Environmental Indicators on African Countries 2007; Selected Statistics on African Countries 2007;* and *Statistics Pocketbook 2008.*

Central Intelligence Agency, Office of Public Affairs, Washington, DC 20505, (703) 482-0623, Fax: (703) 482-1739, www.cia.gov; *The World Factbook.*

Economist Intelligence Unit, 111 West 57th Street, New York, NY 10019, (212) 554-0600, Fax: (212) 586-1181, www.eiu.com; *Egypt Country Report.*

Euromonitor International, Inc., 224 S. Michigan Avenue, Suite 1500, Chicago, IL 60604, (312) 922-1115, Fax: (312) 922-1157, www.euromonitor.com; *International Marketing Data and Statistics 2008* and *The World Economic Factbook 2008.*

Eurostat, Batiment Jean Monnet, Rue Alcide de Gasperi, L-2920 Luxembourg, http://epp.eurostat.ec.europa.eu; *Demographic Indicators - Population by Age-Classes.*

International Labour Office, I.L.O. Publications, 4 route des Morillons, CH-1211 Geneva 22, Switzerland, (Telephone in U.S. (202) 653-7652), (Fax in U.S. (202) 653-7687), www.ilo.org; *Yearbook of Labour Statistics 2006.*

M.E. Sharpe, 80 Business Park Drive, Armonk, NY 10504, (800) 541-6563, Fax: (914) 273-2106, www.mesharpe.com; *The Illustrated Book of World Rankings.*

Palgrave Macmillan Ltd., Houndmills, Basingstoke, Hampshire, RG21 6XS, England, (Telephone in U.S. (888) 330-8477), (Fax in U.S. (800) 672-2054), www.palgrave.com; *The Statesman's Yearbook 2008.*

Taylor and Francis Group, An Informa Business, 2 Park Square, Milton Park, Abingdon, Oxford OX14 4RN, United Kingdom, (Dial from U.S. (212) 216-7800), (Fax from U.S. (212) 564-7854), www.tandf.co.uk; *The Europa World Year Book.*

U.S. Department of State (DOS), 2201 C Street NW, Washington, DC 20520, (202) 647-4000, www.state.gov; *World Military Expenditures and Arms Transfers (WMEAT).*

UNESCO Institute for Statistics, C.P. 6128 Succursale Centre-Ville, Montreal, Quebec, H3C 3J7 Canada, (Dial from U.S. (514) 343-6880), (Fax from U.S. (514) 343 6882), www.uis.unesco.org; *Statistical Tables.*

United Nations Economic and Social Commission for Western Asia (ESCWA), PO Box 11-8575, Riad el-Solh Square, Beirut, Lebanon, www.escwa.un.org; *Annual Report 2006* and *Statistical Abstract of the ESCWA Region 2007.*

United Nations Food and Agricultural Organization (FAO), Viale delle Terme di Caracalla, 00100 Rome, Italy, (Dial from U.S. (202) 653-2400), (Fax from U.S. (202) 653 5760), www.fao.org; *FAO Production Yearbook 2002.*

United Nations Statistics Division, New York, NY 10017, (800) 253-9646, Fax: (212) 963-4116, http://unstats.un.org; *Demographic Yearbook; Human Development Report 2006; Statistical Yearbook; Survey of Economic and Social Conditions in Africa 2005;* and *World Statistics Pocketbook.*

The World Bank, 1818 H Street, NW, Washington, DC 20433, (202) 473-1000, Fax: (202) 477-6391, www.worldbank.org; *Egypt, Arab Republic; The World Bank Atlas 2003-2004;* and *World Development Report 2008.*

World Health Organization (WHO), Avenue Appia 20, 1211 Geneve 27, Switzerland, (Telephone in U.S. (212) 331-9081), www.who.int; *World Health Report 2006.*

EGYPT - POPULATION DENSITY

African Development Bank Group, Rue Joseph Anoma, 01 BP 1387 Abidjan 01, Cote d'Ivoire, www.afdb.org; *Statistics Pocketbook 2008.*

Central Intelligence Agency, Office of Public Affairs, Washington, DC 20505, (703) 482-0623, Fax: (703) 482-1739, www.cia.gov; *The World Factbook.*

Euromonitor International, Inc., 224 S. Michigan Avenue, Suite 1500, Chicago, IL 60604, (312) 922-1115, Fax: (312) 922-1157, www.euromonitor.com; *International Marketing Data and Statistics 2008* and *The World Economic Factbook 2008.*

M.E. Sharpe, 80 Business Park Drive, Armonk, NY 10504, (800) 541-6563, Fax: (914) 273-2106, www.mesharpe.com; *The Illustrated Book of World Rankings.*

Palgrave Macmillan Ltd., Houndmills, Basingstoke, Hampshire, RG21 6XS, England, (Telephone in U.S. (888) 330-8477), (Fax in U.S. (800) 672-2054), www.palgrave.com; *The Statesman's Yearbook 2008.*

Taylor and Francis Group, An Informa Business, 2 Park Square, Milton Park, Abingdon, Oxford OX14 4RN, United Kingdom, (Dial from U.S. (212) 216-7800), (Fax from U.S. (212) 564-7854), www.tandf.co.uk; *The Europa World Year Book.*

UNESCO Institute for Statistics, C.P. 6128 Succursale Centre-Ville, Montreal, Quebec, H3C 3J7 Canada, (Dial from U.S. (514) 343-6880), (Fax from U.S. (514) 343 6882), www.uis.unesco.org; *Statistical Tables.*

United Nations Food and Agricultural Organization (FAO), Viale delle Terme di Caracalla, 00100 Rome, Italy, (Dial from U.S. (202) 653-2400), (Fax from U.S. (202) 653 5760), www.fao.org; *The State of Food and Agriculture (SOFA) 2006.*

United Nations Statistics Division, New York, NY 10017, (800) 253-9646, Fax: (212) 963-4116, http://unstats.un.org; *Statistical Yearbook* and *Survey of Economic and Social Conditions in Africa 2005.*

The World Bank, 1818 H Street, NW, Washington, DC 20433, (202) 473-1000, Fax: (202) 477-6391, www.worldbank.org; *Egypt, Arab Republic* and *World Development Report 2008.*

EGYPT - POSTAL SERVICE

M.E. Sharpe, 80 Business Park Drive, Armonk, NY 10504, (800) 541-6563, Fax: (914) 273-2106, www.mesharpe.com; *The Illustrated Book of World Rankings.*

United Nations Statistics Division, New York, NY 10017, (800) 253-9646, Fax: (212) 963-4116, http://unstats.un.org; *Statistical Yearbook.*

EGYPT - POWER RESOURCES

Euromonitor International, Inc., 224 S. Michigan Avenue, Suite 1500, Chicago, IL 60604, (312) 922-1115, Fax: (312) 922-1157, www.euromonitor.com; *International Marketing Data and Statistics 2008; The World Economic Factbook 2008;* and *World Marketing Data and Statistics.*

M.E. Sharpe, 80 Business Park Drive, Armonk, NY 10504, (800) 541-6563, Fax: (914) 273-2106, www.mesharpe.com; *The Illustrated Book of World Rankings.*

Organisation for Economic Cooperation and Development (OECD), 2 rue Andre Pascal, F-75775 Paris Cedex 16, France, (Telephone in U.S. (202) 785-6323), (Fax in U.S. (202) 785-0350), www.oecd.org; *World Energy Outlook 2007.*

Palgrave Macmillan Ltd., Houndmills, Basingstoke, Hampshire, RG21 6XS, England, (Telephone in U.S. (888) 330-8477), (Fax in U.S. (800) 672-2054), www.palgrave.com; *The Statesman's Yearbook 2008.*

Platts, 2 Penn Plaza, 25th Floor, New York, NY 10121-2298, (212) 904-3070, www.platts.com; *Energy Economist.*

U.S. Department of Energy (DOE), Energy Information Administration (EIA), 1000 Independence Avenue, SW, Washington, DC 20585, (202) 586-8800, www.eia.doe.gov; *International Energy Annual 2004* and *International Energy Outlook 2006.*

United Nations Economic and Social Commission for Western Asia (ESCWA), PO Box 11-8575, Riad el-Solh Square, Beirut, Lebanon, www.escwa.un.org; *Annual Report 2006* and *Statistical Abstract of the ESCWA Region 2007.*

United Nations Economic Commission for Africa (ECA), PO Box 3001, Addis Ababa, Ethiopia, (Telephone in U.S. (212) 963-4957), www.uneca.org; *African Statistical Yearbook 2006.*

United Nations Food and Agricultural Organization (FAO), Viale delle Terme di Caracalla, 00100 Rome, Italy, (Dial from U.S. (202) 653-2400), (Fax from U.S. (202) 653 5760), www.fao.org; *The State of Food and Agriculture (SOFA) 2006.*

United Nations Statistics Division, New York, NY 10017, (800) 253-9646, Fax: (212) 963-4116, http://unstats.un.org; *Energy Statistics Yearbook 2003; Human Development Report 2006; Statistical Yearbook;* and *World Statistics Pocketbook.*

The World Bank, 1818 H Street, NW, Washington, DC 20433, (202) 473-1000, Fax: (202) 477-6391, www.worldbank.org; *The World Bank Atlas 2003-2004* and *World Development Report 2008.*

EGYPT - PRICES

Euromonitor International, Inc., 224 S. Michigan Avenue, Suite 1500, Chicago, IL 60604, (312) 922-1115, Fax: (312) 922-1157, www.euromonitor.com; *World Marketing Data and Statistics.*

International Labour Office, I.L.O. Publications, 4 route des Morillons, CH-1211 Geneva 22, Switzerland, (Telephone in U.S. (202) 653-7652), (Fax in U.S. (202) 653-7687), www.ilo.org; *Yearbook of Labour Statistics 2006.*

International Monetary Fund (IMF), 700 Nineteenth Street, NW, Washington, DC 20431, (202) 623-7000, Fax: (202) 623-4661, www.imf.org; *International Financial Statistics Yearbook 2007.*

M.E. Sharpe, 80 Business Park Drive, Armonk, NY 10504, (800) 541-6563, Fax: (914) 273-2106, www.mesharpe.com; *The Illustrated Book of World Rankings.*

United Nations Economic Commission for Africa (ECA), PO Box 3001, Addis Ababa, Ethiopia, (Telephone in U.S. (212) 963-4957), www.uneca.org; *African Statistical Yearbook 2006.*

United Nations Food and Agricultural Organization (FAO), Viale delle Terme di Caracalla, 00100 Rome, Italy, (Dial from U.S. (202) 653-2400), (Fax from U.S. (202) 653 5760), www.fao.org; *FAO Production Yearbook 2002* and *The State of Food and Agriculture (SOFA) 2006.*

The World Bank, 1818 H Street, NW, Washington, DC 20433, (202) 473-1000, Fax: (202) 477-6391, www.worldbank.org; *Egypt, Arab Republic.*

EGYPT - PROFESSIONS

UNESCO Institute for Statistics, C.P. 6128 Succursale Centre-Ville, Montreal, Quebec, H3C 3J7 Canada, (Dial from U.S. (514) 343-6880), (Fax from U.S. (514) 343 6882), www.uis.unesco.org; *Statistical Tables.*

United Nations Statistics Division, New York, NY 10017, (800) 253-9646, Fax: (212) 963-4116, http://unstats.un.org; *Statistical Yearbook.*

EGYPT - PUBLIC HEALTH

African Development Bank Group, Rue Joseph Anoma, 01 BP 1387 Abidjan 01, Cote d'Ivoire, www.afdb.org; *Statistics Pocketbook 2008.*

Euromonitor International, Inc., 224 S. Michigan Avenue, Suite 1500, Chicago, IL 60604, (312) 922-1115, Fax: (312) 922-1157, www.euromonitor.com; *World Health Databook 2007/2008* and *World Marketing Data and Statistics.*

International Monetary Fund (IMF), 700 Nineteenth Street, NW, Washington, DC 20431, (202) 623-7000, Fax: (202) 623-4661, www.imf.org; *Government Finance Statistics Yearbook (2008 Edition).*

M.E. Sharpe, 80 Business Park Drive, Armonk, NY 10504, (800) 541-6563, Fax: (914) 273-2106, www.mesharpe.com; *The Illustrated Book of World Rankings.*

Palgrave Macmillan Ltd., Houndmills, Basingstoke, Hampshire, RG21 6XS, England, (Telephone in U.S. (888) 330-8477), (Fax in U.S. (800) 672-2054), www.palgrave.com; *The Statesman's Yearbook 2008.*

UNICEF, 3 United Nations Plaza, New York, NY 10017, (800) 253-9646, Fax: (212) 887-7465, www.unicef.org; *The State of the World's Children 2008.*

United Nations Economic and Social Commission for Western Asia (ESCWA), PO Box 11-8575, Riad el-Solh Square, Beirut, Lebanon, www.escwa.un.org; *Annual Report 2006* and *Statistical Abstract of the ESCWA Region 2007.*

United Nations Economic Commission for Africa (ECA), PO Box 3001, Addis Ababa, Ethiopia, (Telephone in U.S. (212) 963-4957), www.uneca.org; *African Statistical Yearbook 2006.*

United Nations Statistics Division, New York, NY 10017, (800) 253-9646, Fax: (212) 963-4116, http://unstats.un.org; *Human Development Report 2006* and *Statistical Yearbook.*

The World Bank, 1818 H Street, NW, Washington, DC 20433, (202) 473-1000, Fax: (202) 477-6391, www.worldbank.org; *Egypt, Arab Republic* and *World Development Report 2008.*

World Health Organization (WHO), Avenue Appia 20, 1211 Geneve 27, Switzerland, (Telephone in U.S. (212) 331-9081), www.who.int; The WHO Global Atlas of Infectious Diseases and *World Health Report 2006.*

EGYPT - PUBLISHERS AND PUBLISHING

UNESCO Institute for Statistics, C.P. 6128 Succursale Centre-Ville, Montreal, Quebec, H3C 3J7 Canada, (Dial from U.S. (514) 343-6880), (Fax from U.S. (514) 343 6882), www.uis.unesco.org; *Statistical Tables.*

EGYPT - RADIO - RECEIVERS AND RECEPTION

Palgrave Macmillan Ltd., Houndmills, Basingstoke, Hampshire, RG21 6XS, England, (Telephone in U.S. (888) 330-8477), (Fax in U.S. (800) 672-2054), www.palgrave.com; *The Statesman's Yearbook 2008.*

United Nations Statistics Division, New York, NY 10017, (800) 253-9646, Fax: (212) 963-4116, http://unstats.un.org; *Statistical Yearbook.*

EGYPT - RAILROADS

Jane's Information Group, 110 North Royal Street, Suite 200, Alexandria, VA 22314, (703) 683-3700, Fax: (800) 836-0297, www.janes.com; *Jane's World Railways.*

Palgrave Macmillan Ltd., Houndmills, Basingstoke, Hampshire, RG21 6XS, England, (Telephone in U.S. (888) 330-8477), (Fax in U.S. (800) 672-2054), www.palgrave.com; *The Statesman's Yearbook 2008.*

Taylor and Francis Group, An Informa Business, 2 Park Square, Milton Park, Abingdon, Oxford OX14 4RN, United Kingdom, (Dial from U.S. (212) 216-7800), (Fax from U.S. (212) 564-7854), www.tandf.co.uk; *The Europa World Year Book.*

United Nations Economic Commission for Africa (ECA), PO Box 3001, Addis Ababa, Ethiopia, (Telephone in U.S. (212) 963-4957), www.uneca.org; *African Statistical Yearbook 2006.*

United Nations Statistics Division, New York, NY 10017, (800) 253-9646, Fax: (212) 963-4116, http://unstats.un.org; *Statistical Yearbook* and *Survey of Economic and Social Conditions in Africa 2005.*

EGYPT - RELIGION

Central Intelligence Agency, Office of Public Affairs, Washington, DC 20505, (703) 482-0623, Fax: (703) 482-1739, www.cia.gov; *The World Factbook.*

M.E. Sharpe, 80 Business Park Drive, Armonk, NY 10504, (800) 541-6563, Fax: (914) 273-2106, www.mesharpe.com; *The Illustrated Book of World Rankings.*

Palgrave Macmillan Ltd., Houndmills, Basingstoke, Hampshire, RG21 6XS, England, (Telephone in U.S. (888) 330-8477), (Fax in U.S. (800) 672-2054), www.palgrave.com; *The Statesman's Yearbook 2008.*

EGYPT - RENT CHARGES

International Labour Office, I.L.O. Publications, 4 route des Morillons, CH-1211 Geneva 22, Switzerland, (Telephone in U.S. (202) 653-7652), (Fax in U.S. (202) 653-7687), www.ilo.org; *Yearbook of Labour Statistics 2006.*

EGYPT - RESERVES (ACCOUNTING)

African Development Bank Group, Rue Joseph Anoma, 01 BP 1387 Abidjan 01, Cote d'Ivoire, www.afdb.org; *Statistics Pocketbook 2008.*

Euromonitor International, Inc., 224 S. Michigan Avenue, Suite 1500, Chicago, IL 60604, (312) 922-1115, Fax: (312) 922-1157, www.euromonitor.com; *International Marketing Data and Statistics 2008.*

EGYPT - RETAIL TRADE

Euromonitor International, Inc., 224 S. Michigan Avenue, Suite 1500, Chicago, IL 60604, (312) 922-1115, Fax: (312) 922-1157, www.euromonitor.com; *World Marketing Data and Statistics.*

United Nations Statistics Division, New York, NY 10017, (800) 253-9646, Fax: (212) 963-4116, http://unstats.un.org; *Statistical Yearbook.*

EGYPT - RICE PRODUCTION

See EGYPT - CROPS

EGYPT - ROADS

Central Intelligence Agency, Office of Public Affairs, Washington, DC 20505, (703) 482-0623, Fax: (703) 482-1739, www.cia.gov; *The World Factbook.*

International Road Federation (IFR), Madison Place, 500 Montgomery Street, 5th Floor, Alexandria, VA 22314, (703) 535-1001, Fax: (703) 535-1007, www.irfnet.org; *World Road Statistics 2006.*

Palgrave Macmillan Ltd., Houndmills, Basingstoke, Hampshire, RG21 6XS, England, (Telephone in U.S. (888) 330-8477), (Fax in U.S. (800) 672-2054), www.palgrave.com; *The Statesman's Yearbook 2008.*

United Nations Economic Commission for Africa (ECA), PO Box 3001, Addis Ababa, Ethiopia, (Telephone in U.S. (212) 963-4957), www.uneca.org; *African Statistical Yearbook 2006.*

United Nations Statistics Division, New York, NY 10017, (800) 253-9646, Fax: (212) 963-4116, http://unstats.un.org; *Survey of Economic and Social Conditions in Africa 2005.*

EGYPT - RUBBER INDUSTRY AND TRADE

International Rubber Study Group (IRSG), 1st Floor, Heron House, 109/115 Wembley Hill Road, Wembley, Middlesex HA9 8DA, United Kingdom, www.rubberstudy.com; *Rubber Statistical Bulletin; Summary of World Rubber Statistics 2005; World Rubber Statistics Handbook (Volume 6, 1975-2001);* and *World Rubber Statistics Historic Handbook.*

M.E. Sharpe, 80 Business Park Drive, Armonk, NY 10504, (800) 541-6563, Fax: (914) 273-2106, www.mesharpe.com; *The Illustrated Book of World Rankings.*

EGYPT - SALT PRODUCTION

See EGYPT - MINERAL INDUSTRIES

EGYPT - SHEEP

See EGYPT - LIVESTOCK

EGYPT - SHIPPING

Lloyd's Register - Fairplay, 8410 N.W. 53rd Terrace, Suite 207, Miami FL 33166, (305) 718-9929, Fax: (305) 718-9663, www.lrfairplay.com; *Register of Ships 2007-2008; World Casualty Statistics 2007; World Fleet Statistics 2006; World Marine Propulsion Report 2006-2010; World Shipbuilding Statistics 2007;* and The World Shipping Encyclopaedia.

Palgrave Macmillan Ltd., Houndmills, Basingstoke, Hampshire, RG21 6XS, England, (Telephone in U.S. (888) 330-8477), (Fax in U.S. (800) 672-2054), www.palgrave.com; *The Statesman's Yearbook 2008.*

Taylor and Francis Group, An Informa Business, 2 Park Square, Milton Park, Abingdon, Oxford OX14 4RN, United Kingdom, (Dial from U.S. (212) 216-7800), (Fax from U.S. (212) 564-7854), www.tandf.co.uk; *The Europa World Year Book.*

United Nations Economic Commission for Africa (ECA), PO Box 3001, Addis Ababa, Ethiopia, (Telephone in U.S. (212) 963-4957), www.uneca.org; *African Statistical Yearbook 2006.*

United Nations Statistics Division, New York, NY 10017, (800) 253-9646, Fax: (212) 963-4116, http://unstats.un.org; *Statistical Yearbook.*

EGYPT - SILVER PRODUCTION

See EGYPT - MINERAL INDUSTRIES

EGYPT - SOCIAL ECOLOGY

M.E. Sharpe, 80 Business Park Drive, Armonk, NY 10504, (800) 541-6563, Fax: (914) 273-2106, www.mesharpe.com; *The Illustrated Book of World Rankings.*

United Nations Statistics Division, New York, NY 10017, (800) 253-9646, Fax: (212) 963-4116, http://unstats.un.org; *World Statistics Pocketbook.*

EGYPT - SOCIAL SECURITY

International Monetary Fund (IMF), 700 Nineteenth Street, NW, Washington, DC 20431, (202) 623-7000, Fax: (202) 623-4661, www.imf.org; *Government Finance Statistics Yearbook (2008 Edition).*

United Nations Statistics Division, New York, NY 10017, (800) 253-9646, Fax: (212) 963-4116, http://unstats.un.org; *National Accounts Statistics: Compendium of Income Distribution Statistics.*

EGYPT - SOYBEAN PRODUCTION

See EGYPT - CROPS

EGYPT - STEEL PRODUCTION

See EGYPT - MINERAL INDUSTRIES

EGYPT - SUGAR PRODUCTION

See EGYPT - CROPS

EGYPT - TAXATION

International Monetary Fund (IMF), 700 Nineteenth Street, NW, Washington, DC 20431, (202) 623-7000, Fax: (202) 623-4661, www.imf.org; *Government Finance Statistics Yearbook (2008 Edition).*

International Road Federation (IFR), Madison Place, 500 Montgomery Street, 5th Floor, Alexandria, VA 22314, (703) 535-1001, Fax: (703) 535-1007, www.irfnet.org; *World Road Statistics 2006.*

Palgrave Macmillan Ltd., Houndmills, Basingstoke, Hampshire, RG21 6XS, England, (Telephone in U.S. (888) 330-8477), (Fax in U.S. (800) 672-2054), www.palgrave.com; *The Statesman's Yearbook 2008.*

Taylor and Francis Group, An Informa Business, 2 Park Square, Milton Park, Abingdon, Oxford OX14 4RN, United Kingdom, (Dial from U.S. (212) 216-7800), (Fax from U.S. (212) 564-7854), www.tandf.co.uk; *The Europa World Year Book.*

EGYPT - TEA PRODUCTION

See EGYPT - CROPS

EGYPT - TELEPHONE

International Telecommunication Union (ITU), Place des Nations, 1211 Geneva 20, Switzerland, www.itu.int; World Telecommunication Indicators Database.

Palgrave Macmillan Ltd., Houndmills, Basingstoke, Hampshire, RG21 6XS, England, (Telephone in U.S. (888) 330-8477), (Fax in U.S. (800) 672-2054), www.palgrave.com; *The Statesman's Yearbook 2008.*

United Nations Statistics Division, New York, NY 10017, (800) 253-9646, Fax: (212) 963-4116, http://unstats.un.org; *Statistical Yearbook* and *World Statistics Pocketbook.*

EGYPT - TELEVISION - RECEIVERS AND RECEPTION

United Nations Statistics Division, New York, NY 10017, (800) 253-9646, Fax: (212) 963-4116, http://unstats.un.org; *Statistical Yearbook.*

EGYPT - TEXTILE INDUSTRY

M.E. Sharpe, 80 Business Park Drive, Armonk, NY 10504, (800) 541-6563, Fax: (914) 273-2106, www.mesharpe.com; *The Illustrated Book of World Rankings.*

Palgrave Macmillan Ltd., Houndmills, Basingstoke, Hampshire, RG21 6XS, England, (Telephone in U.S. (888) 330-8477), (Fax in U.S. (800) 672-2054), www.palgrave.com; *The Statesman's Yearbook 2008.*

United Nations Conference on Trade and Development (UNCTAD), DC2-1120, United Nations, New York, NY 10017, (212) 963-0027, www.unctad.org; *UNCTAD Commodity Yearbook.*

United Nations Statistics Division, New York, NY 10017, (800) 253-9646, Fax: (212) 963-4116, http://unstats.un.org; *Statistical Yearbook.*

EGYPT - THEATER

UNESCO Institute for Statistics, C.P. 6128 Succursale Centre-Ville, Montreal, Quebec, H3C 3J7 Canada, (Dial from U.S. (514) 343-6880), (Fax from U.S. (514) 343 6882), www.uis.unesco.org; *Statistical Tables.*

EGYPT - TIN PRODUCTION

See EGYPT - MINERAL INDUSTRIES

EGYPT - TIRE INDUSTRY

United Nations Statistics Division, New York, NY 10017, (800) 253-9646, Fax: (212) 963-4116, http://unstats.un.org; *Statistical Yearbook.*

EGYPT - TOBACCO INDUSTRY

Foreign Agricultural Service (FAS), U.S. Department of Agriculture (USDA), 1400 Independence Avenue, SW, Washington, DC 20250, (202) 720-3935, www.fas.usda.gov; *Tobacco: World Markets and Trade.*

M.E. Sharpe, 80 Business Park Drive, Armonk, NY 10504, (800) 541-6563, Fax: (914) 273-2106, www.mesharpe.com; *The Illustrated Book of World Rankings.*

United Nations Statistics Division, New York, NY 10017, (800) 253-9646, Fax: (212) 963-4116, http://unstats.un.org; *Statistical Yearbook.*

EGYPT - TOURISM

Euromonitor International, Inc., 224 S. Michigan Avenue, Suite 1500, Chicago, IL 60604, (312) 922-1115, Fax: (312) 922-1157, www.euromonitor.com; *The World Economic Factbook 2008* and *World Marketing Data and Statistics.*

M.E. Sharpe, 80 Business Park Drive, Armonk, NY 10504, (800) 541-6563, Fax: (914) 273-2106, www.mesharpe.com; *The Illustrated Book of World Rankings.*

Palgrave Macmillan Ltd., Houndmills, Basingstoke, Hampshire, RG21 6XS, England, (Telephone in U.S. (888) 330-8477), (Fax in U.S. (800) 672-2054), www.palgrave.com; *The Statesman's Yearbook 2008.*

Taylor and Francis Group, An Informa Business, 2 Park Square, Milton Park, Abingdon, Oxford OX14 4RN, United Kingdom, (Dial from U.S. (212) 216-7800), (Fax from U.S. (212) 564-7854), www.tandf.co.uk; *The Europa World Year Book.*

United Nations Economic and Social Commission for Western Asia (ESCWA), PO Box 11-8575, Riad el-Solh Square, Beirut, Lebanon, www.escwa.un.org; *Annual Report 2006* and *Statistical Abstract of the ESCWA Region 2007.*

United Nations Economic Commission for Africa (ECA), PO Box 3001, Addis Ababa, Ethiopia, (Telephone in U.S. (212) 963-4957), www.uneca.org; *African Statistical Yearbook 2006.*

United Nations Statistics Division, New York, NY 10017, (800) 253-9646, Fax: (212) 963-4116, http://unstats.un.org; *Statistical Yearbook.*

The World Bank, 1818 H Street, NW, Washington, DC 20433, (202) 473-1000, Fax: (202) 477-6391, www.worldbank.org; *Egypt, Arab Republic.*

EGYPT - TRADE

See EGYPT - INTERNATIONAL TRADE

EGYPT - TRANSPORTATION

Central Intelligence Agency, Office of Public Affairs, Washington, DC 20505, (703) 482-0623, Fax: (703) 482-1739, www.cia.gov; *The World Factbook.*

Euromonitor International, Inc., 224 S. Michigan Avenue, Suite 1500, Chicago, IL 60604, (312) 922-1115, Fax: (312) 922-1157, www.euromonitor.com; *International Marketing Data and Statistics 2008* and *World Marketing Data and Statistics.*

M.E. Sharpe, 80 Business Park Drive, Armonk, NY 10504, (800) 541-6563, Fax: (914) 273-2106, www.mesharpe.com; *The Illustrated Book of World Rankings.*

Palgrave Macmillan Ltd., Houndmills, Basingstoke, Hampshire, RG21 6XS, England, (Telephone in U.S. (888) 330-8477), (Fax in U.S. (800) 672-2054), www.palgrave.com; *The Statesman's Yearbook 2008.*

Taylor and Francis Group, An Informa Business, 2 Park Square, Milton Park, Abingdon, Oxford OX14 4RN, United Kingdom, (Dial from U.S. (212) 216-7800), (Fax from U.S. (212) 564-7854), www.tandf.co.uk; *The Europa World Year Book.*

United Nations Economic and Social Commission for Western Asia (ESCWA), PO Box 11-8575, Riad el-Solh Square, Beirut, Lebanon, www.escwa.un.org; *Annual Report 2006* and *Statistical Abstract of the ESCWA Region 2007.*

United Nations Economic Commission for Africa (ECA), PO Box 3001, Addis Ababa, Ethiopia, (Telephone in U.S. (212) 963-4957), www.uneca.org; *African Statistical Yearbook 2006.*

United Nations Statistics Division, New York, NY 10017, (800) 253-9646, Fax: (212) 963-4116, http://unstats.un.org; *Human Development Report 2006.*

The World Bank, 1818 H Street, NW, Washington, DC 20433, (202) 473-1000, Fax: (202) 477-6391, www.worldbank.org; *Africa Live Database (LDB)* and *Egypt, Arab Republic.*

EGYPT - TRAVEL COSTS

International Monetary Fund (IMF), 700 Nineteenth Street, NW, Washington, DC 20431, (202) 623-7000, Fax: (202) 623-4661, www.imf.org; *Government Finance Statistics Yearbook (2008 Edition).*

EGYPT - TURKEYS

See EGYPT - LIVESTOCK

EGYPT - UNEMPLOYMENT

Central Intelligence Agency, Office of Public Affairs, Washington, DC 20505, (703) 482-0623, Fax: (703) 482-1739, www.cia.gov; *The World Factbook.*

Euromonitor International, Inc., 224 S. Michigan Avenue, Suite 1500, Chicago, IL 60604, (312) 922-1115, Fax: (312) 922-1157, www.euromonitor.com; *International Marketing Data and Statistics 2008.*

International Labour Office, I.L.O. Publications, 4 route des Morillons, CH-1211 Geneva 22, Switzerland, (Telephone in U.S. (202) 653-7652), (Fax in U.S. (202) 653-7687), www.ilo.org; *Yearbook of Labour Statistics 2006.*

Palgrave Macmillan Ltd., Houndmills, Basingstoke, Hampshire, RG21 6XS, England, (Telephone in U.S. (888) 330-8477), (Fax in U.S. (800) 672-2054), www.palgrave.com; *The Statesman's Yearbook 2008.*

United Nations Statistics Division, New York, NY 10017, (800) 253-9646, Fax: (212) 963-4116, http://unstats.un.org; *Statistical Yearbook.*

The World Bank, 1818 H Street, NW, Washington, DC 20433, (202) 473-1000, Fax: (202) 477-6391, www.worldbank.org; *Egypt, Arab Republic.*

EGYPT - VITAL STATISTICS

Euromonitor International, Inc., 224 S. Michigan Avenue, Suite 1500, Chicago, IL 60604, (312) 922-1115, Fax: (312) 922-1157, www.euromonitor.com; *International Marketing Data and Statistics 2008.*

Palgrave Macmillan Ltd., Houndmills, Basingstoke, Hampshire, RG21 6XS, England, (Telephone in U.S. (888) 330-8477), (Fax in U.S. (800) 672-2054), www.palgrave.com; *The Statesman's Yearbook 2008.*

World Health Organization (WHO), Avenue Appia 20, 1211 Geneve 27, Switzerland, (Telephone in U.S. (212) 331-9081), www.who.int; *World Health Report 2006.*

EGYPT - WAGES

International Labour Office, I.L.O. Publications, 4 route des Morillons, CH-1211 Geneva 22, Switzerland, (Telephone in U.S. (202) 653-7652), (Fax in U.S. (202) 653-7687), www.ilo.org; *Yearbook of Labour Statistics 2006.*

United Nations Statistics Division, New York, NY 10017, (800) 253-9646, Fax: (212) 963-4116, http://unstats.un.org; *Statistical Yearbook.*

The World Bank, 1818 H Street, NW, Washington, DC 20433, (202) 473-1000, Fax: (202) 477-6391, www.worldbank.org; *Egypt, Arab Republic.*

EGYPT - WEATHER

See EGYPT - CLIMATE

EGYPT - WELFARE STATE

International Monetary Fund (IMF), 700 Nineteenth Street, NW, Washington, DC 20431, (202) 623-7000, Fax: (202) 623-4661, www.imf.org; *Government Finance Statistics Yearbook (2008 Edition).*

EGYPT - WHEAT PRODUCTION

See EGYPT - CROPS

EGYPT - WHOLESALE PRICE INDEXES

International Monetary Fund (IMF), 700 Nineteenth Street, NW, Washington, DC 20431, (202) 623-7000, Fax: (202) 623-4661, www.imf.org; *International Financial Statistics Yearbook 2007.*

United Nations Statistics Division, New York, NY 10017, (800) 253-9646, Fax: (212) 963-4116, http://unstats.un.org; *Statistical Yearbook.*

EGYPT - WHOLESALE TRADE

United Nations Statistics Division, New York, NY 10017, (800) 253-9646, Fax: (212) 963-4116, http://unstats.un.org; *Statistical Yearbook.*

EGYPT - WINE PRODUCTION

See EGYPT - BEVERAGE INDUSTRY

EGYPT - WOOD AND WOOD PULP

See EGYPT - FORESTS AND FORESTRY

EGYPT - WOOL PRODUCTION

See EGYPT - TEXTILE INDUSTRY

EGYPT - YARN PRODUCTION

See EGYPT - TEXTILE INDUSTRY

EGYPT - ZOOS

UNESCO Institute for Statistics, C.P. 6128 Succursale Centre-Ville, Montreal, Quebec, H3C 3J7 Canada, (Dial from U.S. (514) 343-6880), (Fax from U.S. (514) 343 6882), www.uis.unesco.org; *Statistical Tables.*

EIRE

See IRELAND

EL SALVADOR - NATIONAL STATISTICAL OFFICE

Direccion General de Estadistica y Censos (DIGESTYC), Avenida Juan Bertis No. 79 Ciudad Delgado, Aptdo. Postal No. 2670, San Salvador, El Salvador, www.digestyc.gob.sv; National Data Center.

EL SALVADOR - PRIMARY STATISTICS SOURCES

Direccion General de Estadistica y Censos (DIGESTYC), Avenida Juan Bertis No. 79 Ciudad Delgado, Aptdo. Postal No. 2670, San Salvador, El Salvador, www.digestyc.gob.sv; *Anuario Estadistico* (Statistical Yearbook) and *Estadisticas Demograficas* (Demographic Statistics).

EL SALVADOR - AGRICULTURAL MACHINERY

Economist Intelligence Unit, 111 West 57th Street, New York, NY 10019, (212) 554-0600, Fax: (212) 586-1181, www.eiu.com; *Business Latin America.*

United Nations Statistics Division, New York, NY 10017, (800) 253-9646, Fax: (212) 963-4116, http://unstats.un.org; *Statistical Yearbook.*

EL SALVADOR - AGRICULTURE

Economist Intelligence Unit, 111 West 57th Street, New York, NY 10019, (212) 554-0600, Fax: (212) 586-1181, www.eiu.com; *Business Latin America* and *El Salvador Country Report.*

Euromonitor International, Inc., 224 S. Michigan Avenue, Suite 1500, Chicago, IL 60604, (312) 922-1115, Fax: (312) 922-1157, www.euromonitor.com; *International Marketing Data and Statistics 2008* and *World Marketing Data and Statistics.*

Inter-American Development Bank (IDB), 1300 New York Avenue, NW, Washington, DC 20577, (202) 623-1000, Fax: (202) 623-3096, www.iadb.org; *The Politics of Policies: Economic and Social Progress in Latin America - 2006 Report.*

M.E. Sharpe, 80 Business Park Drive, Armonk, NY 10504, (800) 541-6563, Fax: (914) 273-2106, www.mesharpe.com; *The Illustrated Book of World Rankings.*

Palgrave Macmillan Ltd., Houndmills, Basingstoke, Hampshire, RG21 6XS, England, (Telephone in U.S. (888) 330-8477), (Fax in U.S. (800) 672-2054), www.palgrave.com; *The Statesman's Yearbook 2008.*

Taylor and Francis Group, An Informa Business, 2 Park Square, Milton Park, Abingdon, Oxford OX14 4RN, United Kingdom, (Dial from U.S. (212) 216-7800), (Fax from U.S. (212) 564-7854), www.tandf.co.uk; *The Europa World Year Book.*

UCLA Latin American Institute, 10343 Bunche Hall, Box 951447, Los Angeles, CA 90095-1447, (310) 825-4571, Fax: (310) 206-6859, www.international.ucla.edu/lac; *Statistical Abstract of Latin America.*

United Nations Conference on Trade and Development (UNCTAD), DC2-1120, United Nations, New York, NY 10017, (212) 963-0027, www.unctad.org; *UNCTAD Commodity Yearbook.*

United Nations Food and Agricultural Organization (FAO), Viale delle Terme di Caracalla, 00100 Rome, Italy, (Dial from U.S. (202) 653-2400), (Fax from U.S. (202) 653 5760), www.fao.org; AQUASTAT; *FAO Production Yearbook 2002; FAO Trade Yearbook;* and *The State of Food and Agriculture (SOFA) 2006.*

United Nations Statistics Division, New York, NY 10017, (800) 253-9646, Fax: (212) 963-4116, http://unstats.un.org; *Statistical Yearbook* and *Statistical Yearbook for Latin America and the Caribbean 2004.*

The World Bank, 1818 H Street, NW, Washington, DC 20433, (202) 473-1000, Fax: (202) 477-6391, www.worldbank.org; *El Salvador.*

EL SALVADOR - AIRLINES

Economist Intelligence Unit, 111 West 57th Street, New York, NY 10019, (212) 554-0600, Fax: (212) 586-1181, www.eiu.com; *Business Latin America.*

International Civil Aviation Organization (ICAO), External Relations and Public Information Office (EPO), 999 University Street, Montreal, Quebec H3C 5H7, Canada, (Dial from U.S. (514) 954-8219), (Fax from U.S. (514) 954-6077), www.icao.int; *Civil Aviation Statistics of the World.*

M.E. Sharpe, 80 Business Park Drive, Armonk, NY 10504, (800) 541-6563, Fax: (914) 273-2106, www.mesharpe.com; *The Illustrated Book of World Rankings.*

Palgrave Macmillan Ltd., Houndmills, Basingstoke, Hampshire, RG21 6XS, England, (Telephone in U.S. (888) 330-8477), (Fax in U.S. (800) 672-2054), www.palgrave.com; *The Statesman's Yearbook 2008.*

Taylor and Francis Group, An Informa Business, 2 Park Square, Milton Park, Abingdon, Oxford OX14 4RN, United Kingdom, (Dial from U.S. (212) 216-7800), (Fax from U.S. (212) 564-7854), www.tandf.co.uk; *The Europa World Year Book.*

EL SALVADOR - AIRPORTS

Central Intelligence Agency, Office of Public Affairs, Washington, DC 20505, (703) 482-0623, Fax: (703) 482-1739, www.cia.gov; *The World Factbook.*

EL SALVADOR - ALUMINUM PRODUCTION

See EL SALVADOR - MINERAL INDUSTRIES

EL SALVADOR - AREA

Economist Intelligence Unit, 111 West 57th Street, New York, NY 10019, (212) 554-0600, Fax: (212) 586-1181, www.eiu.com; *Business Latin America.*

EL SALVADOR - ARMED FORCES

Central Intelligence Agency, Office of Public Affairs, Washington, DC 20505, (703) 482-0623, Fax: (703) 482-1739, www.cia.gov; *The World Factbook.*

Economist Intelligence Unit, 111 West 57th Street, New York, NY 10019, (212) 554-0600, Fax: (212) 586-1181, www.eiu.com; *Business Latin America.*

Euromonitor International, Inc., 224 S. Michigan Avenue, Suite 1500, Chicago, IL 60604, (312) 922-1115, Fax: (312) 922-1157, www.euromonitor.com; *World Marketing Data and Statistics.*

International Institute for Strategic Studies (IISS), Arundel House, 13-15 Arundel Street, Temple Place, London WC2R 3DX, England, www.iiss.org; *The Military Balance 2007.*

International Monetary Fund (IMF), 700 Nineteenth Street, NW, Washington, DC 20431, (202) 623-7000, Fax: (202) 623-4661, www.imf.org; *Government Finance Statistics Yearbook (2008 Edition).*

Palgrave Macmillan Ltd., Houndmills, Basingstoke, Hampshire, RG21 6XS, England, (Telephone in U.S. (888) 330-8477), (Fax in U.S. (800) 672-2054), www.palgrave.com; *The Statesman's Yearbook 2008.*

U.S. Department of State (DOS), 2201 C Street NW, Washington, DC 20520, (202) 647-4000, www.state.gov; *World Military Expenditures and Arms Transfers (WMEAT).*

UCLA Latin American Institute, 10343 Bunche Hall, Box 951447, Los Angeles, CA 90095-1447, (310) 825-4571, Fax: (310) 206-6859, www.international.ucla.edu/lac; *Statistical Abstract of Latin America.*

United Nations Statistics Division, New York, NY 10017, (800) 253-9646, Fax: (212) 963-4116, http://unstats.un.org; *Human Development Report 2006.*

EL SALVADOR - AUTOMOBILE INDUSTRY AND TRADE

Taylor and Francis Group, An Informa Business, 2 Park Square, Milton Park, Abingdon, Oxford OX14 4RN, United Kingdom, (Dial from U.S. (212) 216-7800), (Fax from U.S. (212) 564-7854), www.tandf.co.uk; *The Europa World Year Book.*

United Nations Statistics Division, New York, NY 10017, (800) 253-9646, Fax: (212) 963-4116, http://unstats.un.org; *Statistical Yearbook.*

EL SALVADOR - BALANCE OF PAYMENTS

Economist Intelligence Unit, 111 West 57th Street, New York, NY 10019, (212) 554-0600, Fax: (212) 586-1181, www.eiu.com; *Business Latin America.*

Inter-American Development Bank (IDB), 1300 New York Avenue, NW, Washington, DC 20577, (202) 623-1000, Fax: (202) 623-3096, www.iadb.org; *The Politics of Policies: Economic and Social Progress in Latin America - 2006 Report.*

International Monetary Fund (IMF), 700 Nineteenth Street, NW, Washington, DC 20431, (202) 623-7000, Fax: (202) 623-4661, www.imf.org; *Balance of Payments Statistics Newsletter; Balance of Payments Statistics Yearbook 2007;* and *International Financial Statistics Yearbook 2007.*

Organization of American States (OAS), 17th Street Constitution Avenue NW, Washington, DC 20006, (202) 458-3000, www.oas.org; *The OAS in Transition: 1994-2004.*

Taylor and Francis Group, An Informa Business, 2 Park Square, Milton Park, Abingdon, Oxford OX14 4RN, United Kingdom, (Dial from U.S. (212) 216-7800), (Fax from U.S. (212) 564-7854), www.tandf.co.uk; *The Europa World Year Book.*

UCLA Latin American Institute, 10343 Bunche Hall, Box 951447, Los Angeles, CA 90095-1447, (310) 825-4571, Fax: (310) 206-6859, www.international.ucla.edu/lac; *Statistical Abstract of Latin America.*

United Nations Conference on Trade and Development (UNCTAD), DC2-1120, United Nations, New York, NY 10017, (212) 963-0027, www.unctad.org; *Handbook of Statistics 2005.*

United Nations Statistics Division, New York, NY 10017, (800) 253-9646, Fax: (212) 963-4116, http://unstats.un.org; *Economic Survey of Latin America and the Caribbean 2004-2005* and *Statistical Yearbook for Latin America and the Caribbean 2004.*

The World Bank, 1818 H Street, NW, Washington, DC 20433, (202) 473-1000, Fax: (202) 477-6391, www.worldbank.org; *El Salvador* and *World Development Report 2008.*

EL SALVADOR - BANKS AND BANKING

Euromonitor International, Inc., 224 S. Michigan Avenue, Suite 1500, Chicago, IL 60604, (312) 922-1115, Fax: (312) 922-1157, www.euromonitor.com; *World Marketing Data and Statistics.*

Inter-American Development Bank (IDB), 1300 New York Avenue, NW, Washington, DC 20577, (202) 623-1000, Fax: (202) 623-3096, www.iadb.org; *The Politics of Policies: Economic and Social Progress in Latin America - 2006 Report.*

International Monetary Fund (IMF), 700 Nineteenth Street, NW, Washington, DC 20431, (202) 623-7000, Fax: (202) 623-4661, www.imf.org; *Government Finance Statistics Yearbook (2008 Edition)* and *International Financial Statistics Yearbook 2007.*

M.E. Sharpe, 80 Business Park Drive, Armonk, NY 10504, (800) 541-6563, Fax: (914) 273-2106, www.mesharpe.com; *The Illustrated Book of World Rankings.*

Palgrave Macmillan Ltd., Houndmills, Basingstoke, Hampshire, RG21 6XS, England, (Telephone in U.S. (888) 330-8477), (Fax in U.S. (800) 672-2054), www.palgrave.com; *The Statesman's Yearbook 2008.*

Taylor and Francis Group, An Informa Business, 2 Park Square, Milton Park, Abingdon, Oxford OX14 4RN, United Kingdom, (Dial from U.S. (212) 216-7800), (Fax from U.S. (212) 564-7854), www.tandf.co.uk; *The Europa World Year Book.*

EL SALVADOR - BARLEY PRODUCTION

See EL SALVADOR - CROPS

EL SALVADOR - BEVERAGE INDUSTRY

M.E. Sharpe, 80 Business Park Drive, Armonk, NY 10504, (800) 541-6563, Fax: (914) 273-2106, www.mesharpe.com; *The Illustrated Book of World Rankings.*

United Nations Statistics Division, New York, NY 10017, (800) 253-9646, Fax: (212) 963-4116, http://unstats.un.org; *Statistical Yearbook.*

EL SALVADOR - BIRTH CONTROL

UCLA Latin American Institute, 10343 Bunche Hall, Box 951447, Los Angeles, CA 90095-1447, (310) 825-4571, Fax: (310) 206-6859, www.international.ucla.edu/lac; *Statistical Abstract of Latin America.*

EL SALVADOR - BONDS

Inter-American Development Bank (IDB), 1300 New York Avenue, NW, Washington, DC 20577, (202) 623-1000, Fax: (202) 623-3096, www.iadb.org; *The Politics of Policies: Economic and Social Progress in Latin America - 2006 Report.*

International Monetary Fund (IMF), 700 Nineteenth Street, NW, Washington, DC 20431, (202) 623-7000, Fax: (202) 623-4661, www.imf.org; *Government Finance Statistics Yearbook (2008 Edition).*

EL SALVADOR - BROADCASTING

Central Intelligence Agency, Office of Public Affairs, Washington, DC 20505, (703) 482-0623, Fax: (703) 482-1739, www.cia.gov; *The World Factbook.*

Euromonitor International, Inc., 224 S. Michigan Avenue, Suite 1500, Chicago, IL 60604, (312) 922-1115, Fax: (312) 922-1157, www.euromonitor.com; *World Marketing Data and Statistics.*

M.E. Sharpe, 80 Business Park Drive, Armonk, NY 10504, (800) 541-6563, Fax: (914) 273-2106, www.mesharpe.com; *The Illustrated Book of World Rankings.*

Palgrave Macmillan Ltd., Houndmills, Basingstoke, Hampshire, RG21 6XS, England, (Telephone in U.S. (888) 330-8477), (Fax in U.S. (800) 672-2054), www.palgrave.com; *The Statesman's Yearbook 2008.*

WRTH Publications Limited, PO Box 290, Oxford OX2 7FT, UK, www.wrth.com; *World Radio TV Handbook 2007.*

EL SALVADOR - BUDGET

Central Intelligence Agency, Office of Public Affairs, Washington, DC 20505, (703) 482-0623, Fax: (703) 482-1739, www.cia.gov; *The World Factbook.*

EL SALVADOR - BUSINESS

Inter-American Development Bank (IDB), 1300 New York Avenue, NW, Washington, DC 20577, (202) 623-1000, Fax: (202) 623-3096, www.iadb.org; *The Politics of Policies: Economic and Social Progress in Latin America - 2006 Report.*

EL SALVADOR - CAPITAL INVESTMENTS

Inter-American Development Bank (IDB), 1300 New York Avenue, NW, Washington, DC 20577, (202) 623-1000, Fax: (202) 623-3096, www.iadb.org; *The Politics of Policies: Economic and Social Progress in Latin America - 2006 Report.*

EL SALVADOR - CAPITAL LEVY

Inter-American Development Bank (IDB), 1300 New York Avenue, NW, Washington, DC 20577, (202) 623-1000, Fax: (202) 623-3096, www.iadb.org; *The Politics of Policies: Economic and Social Progress in Latin America - 2006 Report.*

International Monetary Fund (IMF), 700 Nineteenth Street, NW, Washington, DC 20431, (202) 623-7000, Fax: (202) 623-4661, www.imf.org; *Government Finance Statistics Yearbook (2008 Edition).*

EL SALVADOR - CATTLE

See EL SALVADOR - LIVESTOCK

EL SALVADOR - CHICKENS

See EL SALVADOR - LIVESTOCK

EL SALVADOR - CHILDBIRTH - STATISTICS

Central Intelligence Agency, Office of Public Affairs, Washington, DC 20505, (703) 482-0623, Fax: (703) 482-1739, www.cia.gov; *The World Factbook.*

Euromonitor International, Inc., 224 S. Michigan Avenue, Suite 1500, Chicago, IL 60604, (312) 922-1115, Fax: (312) 922-1157, www.euromonitor.com; *International Marketing Data and Statistics 2008* and *The World Economic Factbook 2008.*

M.E. Sharpe, 80 Business Park Drive, Armonk, NY 10504, (800) 541-6563, Fax: (914) 273-2106, www.mesharpe.com; *The Illustrated Book of World Rankings.*

Palgrave Macmillan Ltd., Houndmills, Basingstoke, Hampshire, RG21 6XS, England, (Telephone in U.S. (888) 330-8477), (Fax in U.S. (800) 672-2054), www.palgrave.com; *The Statesman's Yearbook 2008.*

Taylor and Francis Group, An Informa Business, 2 Park Square, Milton Park, Abingdon, Oxford OX14 4RN, United Kingdom, (Dial from U.S. (212) 216-7800), (Fax from U.S. (212) 564-7854), www.tandf.co.uk; *The Europa World Year Book.*

United Nations Statistics Division, New York, NY 10017, (800) 253-9646, Fax: (212) 963-4116, http://unstats.un.org; *Demographic Yearbook; Statistical Yearbook;* and *Statistical Yearbook for Latin America and the Caribbean 2004.*

World Health Organization (WHO), Avenue Appia 20, 1211 Geneve 27, Switzerland, (Telephone in U.S. (212) 331-9081), www.who.int; *World Health Report 2006.*

EL SALVADOR - CLIMATE

M.E. Sharpe, 80 Business Park Drive, Armonk, NY 10504, (800) 541-6563, Fax: (914) 273-2106, www.mesharpe.com; *The Illustrated Book of World Rankings.*

Palgrave Macmillan Ltd., Houndmills, Basingstoke, Hampshire, RG21 6XS, England, (Telephone in U.S. (888) 330-8477), (Fax in U.S. (800) 672-2054), www.palgrave.com; *The Statesman's Yearbook 2008.*

EL SALVADOR - COAL PRODUCTION

See EL SALVADOR - MINERAL INDUSTRIES

EL SALVADOR - COCOA PRODUCTION

See EL SALVADOR - CROPS

EL SALVADOR - COFFEE

See EL SALVADOR - CROPS

EL SALVADOR - COMMERCE

Palgrave Macmillan Ltd., Houndmills, Basingstoke, Hampshire, RG21 6XS, England, (Telephone in U.S. (888) 330-8477), (Fax in U.S. (800) 672-2054), www.palgrave.com; *The Statesman's Yearbook 2008.*

EL SALVADOR - COMMODITY EXCHANGES

Commodity Research Bureau, 330 South Wells Street, Suite 612, Chicago, IL 60606-7110, (800) 621-5271, Fax: (312) 939-4135, www.crbtrader.com; *2006 CRB Commodity Yearbook and CD.*

International Monetary Fund (IMF), 700 Nineteenth Street, NW, Washington, DC 20431, (202) 623-7000, Fax: (202) 623-4661, www.imf.org; *IMF Primary Commodity Prices.*

United Nations Food and Agricultural Organization (FAO), Viale delle Terme di Caracalla, 00100 Rome, Italy, (Dial from U.S. (202) 653-2400), (Fax from U.S. (202) 653 5760), www.fao.org; *The State of Food and Agriculture (SOFA) 2006.*

EL SALVADOR - COMMUNICATION AND TRAFFIC

United Nations Statistics Division, New York, NY 10017, (800) 253-9646, Fax: (212) 963-4116, http://unstats.un.org; *Statistical Yearbook.*

EL SALVADOR - CONSTRUCTION INDUSTRY

Economist Intelligence Unit, 111 West 57th Street, New York, NY 10019, (212) 554-0600, Fax: (212) 586-1181, www.eiu.com; *Business Latin America.*

Inter-American Development Bank (IDB), 1300 New York Avenue, NW, Washington, DC 20577, (202) 623-1000, Fax: (202) 623-3096, www.iadb.org; *The Politics of Policies: Economic and Social Progress in Latin America - 2006 Report.*

M.E. Sharpe, 80 Business Park Drive, Armonk, NY 10504, (800) 541-6563, Fax: (914) 273-2106, www.mesharpe.com; *The Illustrated Book of World Rankings.*

Organization of American States (OAS), 17th Street Constitution Avenue NW, Washington, DC 20006, (202) 458-3000, www.oas.org; *The OAS in Transition: 1994-2004.*

United Nations Statistics Division, New York, NY 10017, (800) 253-9646, Fax: (212) 963-4116, http://unstats.un.org; *Statistical Yearbook.*

EL SALVADOR - CONSUMER COOPERATIVES

UCLA Latin American Institute, 10343 Bunche Hall, Box 951447, Los Angeles, CA 90095-1447, (310) 825-4571, Fax: (310) 206-6859, www.international.ucla.edu/lac; *Statistical Abstract of Latin America.*

EL SALVADOR - CONSUMER PRICE INDEXES

Taylor and Francis Group, An Informa Business, 2 Park Square, Milton Park, Abingdon, Oxford OX14 4RN, United Kingdom, (Dial from U.S. (212) 216-7800), (Fax from U.S. (212) 564-7854), www.tandf.co.uk; *The Europa World Year Book.*

United Nations Statistics Division, New York, NY 10017, (800) 253-9646, Fax: (212) 963-4116, http://unstats.un.org; *Statistical Yearbook.*

The World Bank, 1818 H Street, NW, Washington, DC 20433, (202) 473-1000, Fax: (202) 477-6391, www.worldbank.org; *El Salvador.*

EL SALVADOR - CONSUMPTION (ECONOMICS)

Economist Intelligence Unit, 111 West 57th Street, New York, NY 10019, (212) 554-0600, Fax: (212) 586-1181, www.eiu.com; *Business Latin America.*

Inter-American Development Bank (IDB), 1300 New York Avenue, NW, Washington, DC 20577, (202) 623-1000, Fax: (202) 623-3096, www.iadb.org; *The Politics of Policies: Economic and Social Progress in Latin America - 2006 Report.*

United Nations Statistics Division, New York, NY 10017, (800) 253-9646, Fax: (212) 963-4116, http://unstats.un.org; *Statistical Yearbook for Latin America and the Caribbean 2004.*

The World Bank, 1818 H Street, NW, Washington, DC 20433, (202) 473-1000, Fax: (202) 477-6391, www.worldbank.org; *World Development Report 2008.*

EL SALVADOR - COPPER INDUSTRY AND TRADE

See EL SALVADOR - MINERAL INDUSTRIES

EL SALVADOR - CORN INDUSTRY

See EL SALVADOR - CROPS

EL SALVADOR - COST AND STANDARD OF LIVING

International Monetary Fund (IMF), 700 Nineteenth Street, NW, Washington, DC 20431, (202) 623-7000, Fax: (202) 623-4661, www.imf.org; *Government Finance Statistics Yearbook (2008 Edition).*

EL SALVADOR - COTTON

See EL SALVADOR - CROPS

EL SALVADOR - CRIME

Yale University Press, PO Box 209040, New Haven, CT 06520-9040, (203) 432-0960, Fax: (203) 432-0948, http://yalepress.yale.edu/yupbooks; *Violence and Crime in Cross-National Perspective.*

EL SALVADOR - CROPS

Economist Intelligence Unit, 111 West 57th Street, New York, NY 10019, (212) 554-0600, Fax: (212) 586-1181, www.eiu.com; *Business Latin America.*

International Monetary Fund (IMF), 700 Nineteenth Street, NW, Washington, DC 20431, (202) 623-7000, Fax: (202) 623-4661, www.imf.org; *International Financial Statistics Yearbook 2007.*

M.E. Sharpe, 80 Business Park Drive, Armonk, NY 10504, (800) 541-6563, Fax: (914) 273-2106, www.mesharpe.com; *The Illustrated Book of World Rankings.*

Organization of American States (OAS), 17th Street Constitution Avenue NW, Washington, DC 20006, (202) 458-3000, www.oas.org; *The OAS in Transition: 1994-2004*.

Palgrave Macmillan Ltd., Houndmills, Basingstoke, Hampshire, RG21 6XS, England, (Telephone in U.S. (888) 330-8477), (Fax in U.S. (800) 672-2054), www.palgrave.com; *The Statesman's Yearbook 2008*.

Taylor and Francis Group, An Informa Business, 2 Park Square, Milton Park, Abingdon, Oxford OX14 4RN, United Kingdom, (Dial from U.S. (212) 216-7800), (Fax from U.S. (212) 564-7854), www.tandf.co.uk; *The Europa World Year Book*.

United Nations Conference on Trade and Development (UNCTAD), DC2-1120, United Nations, New York, NY 10017, (212) 963-0027, www.unctad.org; *UNCTAD Commodity Yearbook*.

United Nations Food and Agricultural Organization (FAO), Viale delle Terme di Caracalla, 00100 Rome, Italy, (Dial from U.S. (202) 653-2400), (Fax from U.S. (202) 653 5760), www.fao.org; *FAO Production Yearbook 2002* and *The State of Food and Agriculture (SOFA) 2006*.

United Nations Statistics Division, New York, NY 10017, (800) 253-9646, Fax: (212) 963-4116, http://unstats.un.org; *Statistical Yearbook*.

EL SALVADOR - CUSTOMS ADMINISTRATION

Inter-American Development Bank (IDB), 1300 New York Avenue, NW, Washington, DC 20577, (202) 623-1000, Fax: (202) 623-3096, www.iadb.org; *The Politics of Policies: Economic and Social Progress in Latin America - 2006 Report*.

International Monetary Fund (IMF), 700 Nineteenth Street, NW, Washington, DC 20431, (202) 623-7000, Fax: (202) 623-4661, www.imf.org; *Government Finance Statistics Yearbook (2008 Edition)*.

EL SALVADOR - DAIRY PROCESSING

M.E. Sharpe, 80 Business Park Drive, Armonk, NY 10504, (800) 541-6563, Fax: (914) 273-2106, www.mesharpe.com; *The Illustrated Book of World Rankings*.

Palgrave Macmillan Ltd., Houndmills, Basingstoke, Hampshire, RG21 6XS, England, (Telephone in U.S. (888) 330-8477), (Fax in U.S. (800) 672-2054), www.palgrave.com; *The Statesman's Yearbook 2008*.

Taylor and Francis Group, An Informa Business, 2 Park Square, Milton Park, Abingdon, Oxford OX14 4RN, United Kingdom, (Dial from U.S. (212) 216-7800), (Fax from U.S. (212) 564-7854), www.tandf.co.uk; *The Europa World Year Book*.

United Nations Food and Agricultural Organization (FAO), Viale delle Terme di Caracalla, 00100 Rome, Italy, (Dial from U.S. (202) 653-2400), (Fax from U.S. (202) 653 5760), www.fao.org; *FAO Production Yearbook 2002* and *The State of Food and Agriculture (SOFA) 2006*.

United Nations Statistics Division, New York, NY 10017, (800) 253-9646, Fax: (212) 963-4116, http://unstats.un.org; *Statistical Yearbook*.

EL SALVADOR - DEATH RATES

See EL SALVADOR - MORTALITY

EL SALVADOR - DEBT

Economist Intelligence Unit, 111 West 57th Street, New York, NY 10019, (212) 554-0600, Fax: (212) 586-1181, www.eiu.com; *Business Latin America*.

The World Bank, 1818 H Street, NW, Washington, DC 20433, (202) 473-1000, Fax: (202) 477-6391, www.worldbank.org; *Global Development Finance 2007*.

EL SALVADOR - DEBTS, EXTERNAL

Economist Intelligence Unit, 111 West 57th Street, New York, NY 10019, (212) 554-0600, Fax: (212) 586-1181, www.eiu.com; *Business Latin America*.

Inter-American Development Bank (IDB), 1300 New York Avenue, NW, Washington, DC 20577, (202) 623-1000, Fax: (202) 623-3096, www.iadb.org; *The Politics of Policies: Economic and Social Progress in Latin America - 2006 Report*.

International Monetary Fund (IMF), 700 Nineteenth Street, NW, Washington, DC 20431, (202) 623-7000, Fax: (202) 623-4661, www.imf.org; *Government Finance Statistics Yearbook (2008 Edition)*.

Palgrave Macmillan Ltd., Houndmills, Basingstoke, Hampshire, RG21 6XS, England, (Telephone in U.S. (888) 330-8477), (Fax in U.S. (800) 672-2054), www.palgrave.com; *The Statesman's Yearbook 2008*.

United Nations Statistics Division, New York, NY 10017, (800) 253-9646, Fax: (212) 963-4116, http://unstats.un.org; *Economic Survey of Latin America and the Caribbean 2004-2005* and *Statistical Yearbook for Latin America and the Caribbean 2004*.

The World Bank, 1818 H Street, NW, Washington, DC 20433, (202) 473-1000, Fax: (202) 477-6391, www.worldbank.org; *Global Development Finance 2007* and *World Development Report 2008*.

EL SALVADOR - DEFENSE EXPENDITURES

See EL SALVADOR - ARMED FORCES

EL SALVADOR - DEMOGRAPHY

Euromonitor International, Inc., 224 S. Michigan Avenue, Suite 1500, Chicago, IL 60604, (312) 922-1115, Fax: (312) 922-1157, www.euromonitor.com; *International Marketing Data and Statistics 2008; The World Economic Factbook 2008;* and *World Marketing Data and Statistics*.

M.E. Sharpe, 80 Business Park Drive, Armonk, NY 10504, (800) 541-6563, Fax: (914) 273-2106, www.mesharpe.com; *The Illustrated Book of World Rankings*.

United Nations Statistics Division, New York, NY 10017, (800) 253-9646, Fax: (212) 963-4116, http://unstats.un.org; *Human Development Report 2006*.

The World Bank, 1818 H Street, NW, Washington, DC 20433, (202) 473-1000, Fax: (202) 477-6391, www.worldbank.org; *El Salvador*.

EL SALVADOR - DIAMONDS

See EL SALVADOR - MINERAL INDUSTRIES

EL SALVADOR - DISPOSABLE INCOME

Inter-American Development Bank (IDB), 1300 New York Avenue, NW, Washington, DC 20577, (202) 623-1000, Fax: (202) 623-3096, www.iadb.org; *The Politics of Policies: Economic and Social Progress in Latin America - 2006 Report*.

International Monetary Fund (IMF), 700 Nineteenth Street, NW, Washington, DC 20431, (202) 623-7000, Fax: (202) 623-4661, www.imf.org; *International Financial Statistics Yearbook 2007*.

M.E. Sharpe, 80 Business Park Drive, Armonk, NY 10504, (800) 541-6563, Fax: (914) 273-2106, www.mesharpe.com; *The Illustrated Book of World Rankings*.

United Nations Statistics Division, New York, NY 10017, (800) 253-9646, Fax: (212) 963-4116, http://unstats.un.org; *National Accounts Statistics: Compendium of Income Distribution Statistics* and *Statistical Yearbook*.

EL SALVADOR - DIVORCE

M.E. Sharpe, 80 Business Park Drive, Armonk, NY 10504, (800) 541-6563, Fax: (914) 273-2106, www.mesharpe.com; *The Illustrated Book of World Rankings*.

United Nations Statistics Division, New York, NY 10017, (800) 253-9646, Fax: (212) 963-4116, http://unstats.un.org; *Demographic Yearbook* and *Statistical Yearbook*.

EL SALVADOR - ECONOMIC ASSISTANCE

Inter-American Development Bank (IDB), 1300 New York Avenue, NW, Washington, DC 20577, (202) 623-1000, Fax: (202) 623-3096, www.iadb.org; *The Politics of Policies: Economic and Social Progress in Latin America - 2006 Report*.

United Nations Statistics Division, New York, NY 10017, (800) 253-9646, Fax: (212) 963-4116, http://unstats.un.org; *Statistical Yearbook*.

EL SALVADOR - ECONOMIC CONDITIONS

Center for International Business Education Research (CIBER), Columbia Business School and School of International and Public Affairs, Uris Hall, Room 212, 3022 Broadway, New York, NY 10027-6902, Mr. Joshua Safier, (212) 854-4750, Fax: (212) 222-9821, www.columbia.edu/cu/ciber/; Datastream International.

Central Intelligence Agency, Office of Public Affairs, Washington, DC 20505, (703) 482-0623, Fax: (703) 482-1739, www.cia.gov; *The World Factbook*.

DSI Data Service Information, Xantener Strasse 51a, D-47495 Rheinberg, Germany, www.dsidata.com; *Campus Solution*.

Dun and Bradstreet (DB) Corporation, 103 JFK Parkway, Short Hills, NJ 07078, (973) 921-5500, www.dnb.com; *Country Report*.

Economist Intelligence Unit, 111 West 57th Street, New York, NY 10019, (212) 554-0600, Fax: (212) 586-1181, www.eiu.com; *El Salvador Country Report*.

Euromonitor International, Inc., 224 S. Michigan Avenue, Suite 1500, Chicago, IL 60604, (312) 922-1115, Fax: (312) 922-1157, www.euromonitor.com; *International Marketing Data and Statistics 2008; The World Economic Factbook 2008;* and *World Marketing Data and Statistics*.

Inter-American Development Bank (IDB), 1300 New York Avenue, NW, Washington, DC 20577, (202) 623-1000, Fax: (202) 623-3096, www.iadb.org; *The Politics of Policies: Economic and Social Progress in Latin America - 2006 Report*.

International Monetary Fund (IMF), 700 Nineteenth Street, NW, Washington, DC 20431, (202) 623-7000, Fax: (202) 623-4661, www.imf.org; *World Economic Outlook Reports*.

M.E. Sharpe, 80 Business Park Drive, Armonk, NY 10504, (800) 541-6563, Fax: (914) 273-2106, www.mesharpe.com; *The Illustrated Book of World Rankings*.

Organization of American States (OAS), 17th Street Constitution Avenue NW, Washington, DC 20006, (202) 458-3000, www.oas.org; *The OAS in Transition: 1994-2004*.

Palgrave Macmillan Ltd., Houndmills, Basingstoke, Hampshire, RG21 6XS, England, (Telephone in U.S. (888) 330-8477), (Fax in U.S. (800) 672-2054), www.palgrave.com; *The Statesman's Yearbook 2008*.

Taylor and Francis Group, An Informa Business, 2 Park Square, Milton Park, Abingdon, Oxford OX14 4RN, United Kingdom, (Dial from U.S. (212) 216-7800), (Fax from U.S. (212) 564-7854), www.tandf.co.uk; *The Europa World Year Book*.

UCLA Latin American Institute, 10343 Bunche Hall, Box 951447, Los Angeles, CA 90095-1447, (310) 825-4571, Fax: (310) 206-6859, www.international.ucla.edu/lac; *Statistical Abstract of Latin America*.

United Nations Statistics Division, New York, NY 10017, (800) 253-9646, Fax: (212) 963-4116, http://unstats.un.org; *Economic Survey of Latin America and the Caribbean 2004-2005* and *World Statistics Pocketbook*.

The World Bank, 1818 H Street, NW, Washington, DC 20433, (202) 473-1000, Fax: (202) 477-6391, www.worldbank.org; *El Salvador; Global Economic Monitor (GEM); Global Economic Prospects 2008; The World Bank Atlas 2003-2004;* and *World Development Report 2008*.

EL SALVADOR - ECONOMICS - SOCIOLOGICAL ASPECTS

Inter-American Development Bank (IDB), 1300 New York Avenue, NW, Washington, DC 20577, (202)

623-1000, Fax: (202) 623-3096, www.iadb.org; *The Politics of Policies: Economic and Social Progress in Latin America - 2006 Report.*

UCLA Latin American Institute, 10343 Bunche Hall, Box 951447, Los Angeles, CA 90095-1447, (310) 825-4571, Fax: (310) 206-6859, www.international.ucla.edu/lac; *Statistical Abstract of Latin America.*

EL SALVADOR - EDUCATION

Economist Intelligence Unit, 111 West 57th Street, New York, NY 10019, (212) 554-0600, Fax: (212) 586-1181, www.eiu.com; *Business Latin America.*

Euromonitor International, Inc., 224 S. Michigan Avenue, Suite 1500, Chicago, IL 60604, (312) 922-1115, Fax: (312) 922-1157, www.euromonitor.com; *International Marketing Data and Statistics 2008* and *World Marketing Data and Statistics.*

International Monetary Fund (IMF), 700 Nineteenth Street, NW, Washington, DC 20431, (202) 623-7000, Fax: (202) 623-4661, www.imf.org; *Government Finance Statistics Yearbook (2008 Edition).*

M.E. Sharpe, 80 Business Park Drive, Armonk, NY 10504, (800) 541-6563, Fax: (914) 273-2106, www.mesharpe.com; *The Illustrated Book of World Rankings.*

Palgrave Macmillan Ltd., Houndmills, Basingstoke, Hampshire, RG21 6XS, England, (Telephone in U.S. (888) 330-8477), (Fax in U.S. (800) 672-2054), www.palgrave.com; *The Statesman's Yearbook 2008.*

Taylor and Francis Group, An Informa Business, 2 Park Square, Milton Park, Abingdon, Oxford OX14 4RN, United Kingdom, (Dial from U.S. (212) 216-7800), (Fax from U.S. (212) 564-7854), www.tandf.co.uk; *The Europa World Year Book.*

UCLA Latin American Institute, 10343 Bunche Hall, Box 951447, Los Angeles, CA 90095-1447, (310) 825-4571, Fax: (310) 206-6859, www.international.ucla.edu/lac; *Statistical Abstract of Latin America.*

UNESCO Institute for Statistics, C.P. 6128 Succursale Centre-Ville, Montreal, Quebec, H3C 3J7 Canada, (Dial from U.S. (514) 343-6880), (Fax from U.S. (514) 343 6882), www.uis.unesco.org; *Statistical Tables.*

United Nations Statistics Division, New York, NY 10017, (800) 253-9646, Fax: (212) 963-4116, http://unstats.un.org; *Human Development Report 2006* and *Statistical Yearbook for Latin America and the Caribbean 2004.*

The World Bank, 1818 H Street, NW, Washington, DC 20433, (202) 473-1000, Fax: (202) 477-6391, www.worldbank.org; *El Salvador* and *World Development Report 2008.*

EL SALVADOR - ELECTRICITY

Central Intelligence Agency, Office of Public Affairs, Washington, DC 20505, (703) 482-0623, Fax: (703) 482-1739, www.cia.gov; *The World Factbook.*

Economist Intelligence Unit, 111 West 57th Street, New York, NY 10019, (212) 554-0600, Fax: (212) 586-1181, www.eiu.com; *Business Latin America.*

Inter-American Development Bank (IDB), 1300 New York Avenue, NW, Washington, DC 20577, (202) 623-1000, Fax: (202) 623-3096, www.iadb.org; *The Politics of Policies: Economic and Social Progress in Latin America - 2006 Report.*

M.E. Sharpe, 80 Business Park Drive, Armonk, NY 10504, (800) 541-6563, Fax: (914) 273-2106, www.mesharpe.com; *The Illustrated Book of World Rankings.*

Organization of American States (OAS), 17th Street Constitution Avenue NW, Washington, DC 20006, (202) 458-3000, www.oas.org; *The OAS in Transition: 1994-2004.*

Palgrave Macmillan Ltd., Houndmills, Basingstoke, Hampshire, RG21 6XS, England, (Telephone in U.S. (888) 330-8477), (Fax in U.S. (800) 672-2054), www.palgrave.com; *The Statesman's Yearbook 2008.*

U.S. Department of Energy (DOE), Energy Information Administration (EIA), 1000 Independence Avenue, SW, Washington, DC 20585, (202) 586-8800, www.eia.doe.gov; *International Energy Annual 2004* and *International Energy Outlook 2006.*

United Nations Statistics Division, New York, NY 10017, (800) 253-9646, Fax: (212) 963-4116, http://unstats.un.org; *Human Development Report 2006.*

EL SALVADOR - EMIGRATION AND IMMIGRATION

UCLA Latin American Institute, 10343 Bunche Hall, Box 951447, Los Angeles, CA 90095-1447, (310) 825-4571, Fax: (310) 206-6859, www.international.ucla.edu/lac; *Statistical Abstract of Latin America.*

EL SALVADOR - EMPLOYMENT

Euromonitor International, Inc., 224 S. Michigan Avenue, Suite 1500, Chicago, IL 60604, (312) 922-1115, Fax: (312) 922-1157, www.euromonitor.com; *International Marketing Data and Statistics 2008.*

International Labour Office, I.L.O. Publications, 4 route des Morillons, CH-1211 Geneva 22, Switzerland, (Telephone in U.S. (202) 653-7652), (Fax in U.S. (202) 653-7687), www.ilo.org; *Yearbook of Labour Statistics 2006.*

M.E. Sharpe, 80 Business Park Drive, Armonk, NY 10504, (800) 541-6563, Fax: (914) 273-2106, www.mesharpe.com; *The Illustrated Book of World Rankings.*

Organization of American States (OAS), 17th Street Constitution Avenue NW, Washington, DC 20006, (202) 458-3000, www.oas.org; *The OAS in Transition: 1994-2004.*

UCLA Latin American Institute, 10343 Bunche Hall, Box 951447, Los Angeles, CA 90095-1447, (310) 825-4571, Fax: (310) 206-6859, www.international.ucla.edu/lac; *Statistical Abstract of Latin America.*

United Nations Statistics Division, New York, NY 10017, (800) 253-9646, Fax: (212) 963-4116, http://unstats.un.org; *Statistical Yearbook for Latin America and the Caribbean 2004.*

The World Bank, 1818 H Street, NW, Washington, DC 20433, (202) 473-1000, Fax: (202) 477-6391, www.worldbank.org; *El Salvador.*

EL SALVADOR - ENVIRONMENTAL CONDITIONS

DSI Data Service Information, Xantener Strasse 51a, D-47495 Rheinberg, Germany, www.dsidata.com; *Campus Solution* and *DSI's Global Environmental Database.*

Economist Intelligence Unit, 111 West 57th Street, New York, NY 10019, (212) 554-0600, Fax: (212) 586-1181, www.eiu.com; *El Salvador Country Report.*

United Nations Statistics Division, New York, NY 10017, (800) 253-9646, Fax: (212) 963-4116, http://unstats.un.org; *World Statistics Pocketbook.*

EL SALVADOR - EXPENDITURES, PUBLIC

Inter-American Development Bank (IDB), 1300 New York Avenue, NW, Washington, DC 20577, (202) 623-1000, Fax: (202) 623-3096, www.iadb.org; *The Politics of Policies: Economic and Social Progress in Latin America - 2006 Report.*

Organization of American States (OAS), 17th Street Constitution Avenue NW, Washington, DC 20006, (202) 458-3000, www.oas.org; *The OAS in Transition: 1994-2004.*

United Nations Statistics Division, New York, NY 10017, (800) 253-9646, Fax: (212) 963-4116, http://unstats.un.org; *Statistical Yearbook for Latin America and the Caribbean 2004.*

EL SALVADOR - EXPORTS

Central Intelligence Agency, Office of Public Affairs, Washington, DC 20505, (703) 482-0623, Fax: (703) 482-1739, www.cia.gov; *The World Factbook.*

Economist Intelligence Unit, 111 West 57th Street, New York, NY 10019, (212) 554-0600, Fax: (212) 586-1181, www.eiu.com; *Business Latin America* and *El Salvador Country Report.*

Euromonitor International, Inc., 224 S. Michigan Avenue, Suite 1500, Chicago, IL 60604, (312) 922-1115, Fax: (312) 922-1157, www.euromonitor.com; *International Marketing Data and Statistics 2008* and *The World Economic Factbook 2008.*

Inter-American Development Bank (IDB), 1300 New York Avenue, NW, Washington, DC 20577, (202) 623-1000, Fax: (202) 623-3096, www.iadb.org; *The Politics of Policies: Economic and Social Progress in Latin America - 2006 Report.*

International Monetary Fund (IMF), 700 Nineteenth Street, NW, Washington, DC 20431, (202) 623-7000, Fax: (202) 623-4661, www.imf.org; *Direction of Trade Statistics Yearbook 2007; Government Finance Statistics Yearbook (2008 Edition);* and *International Financial Statistics Yearbook 2007.*

Organization of American States (OAS), 17th Street Constitution Avenue NW, Washington, DC 20006, (202) 458-3000, www.oas.org; *The OAS in Transition: 1994-2004.*

Palgrave Macmillan Ltd., Houndmills, Basingstoke, Hampshire, RG21 6XS, England, (Telephone in U.S. (888) 330-8477), (Fax in U.S. (800) 672-2054), www.palgrave.com; *The Statesman's Yearbook 2008.*

Taylor and Francis Group, An Informa Business, 2 Park Square, Milton Park, Abingdon, Oxford OX14 4RN, United Kingdom, (Dial from U.S. (212) 216-7800), (Fax from U.S. (212) 564-7854), www.tandf.co.uk; *The Europa World Year Book.*

United Nations Conference on Trade and Development (UNCTAD), DC2-1120, United Nations, New York, NY 10017, (212) 963-0027, www.unctad.org; *Handbook of Statistics 2005.*

United Nations Food and Agricultural Organization (FAO), Viale delle Terme di Caracalla, 00100 Rome, Italy, (Dial from U.S. (202) 653-2400), (Fax from U.S. (202) 653 5760), www.fao.org; *The State of Food and Agriculture (SOFA) 2006.*

United Nations Statistics Division, New York, NY 10017, (800) 253-9646, Fax: (212) 963-4116, http://unstats.un.org; *Statistical Yearbook for Latin America and the Caribbean 2004.*

The World Bank, 1818 H Street, NW, Washington, DC 20433, (202) 473-1000, Fax: (202) 477-6391, www.worldbank.org; *World Development Report 2008.*

EL SALVADOR - FEMALE WORKING POPULATION

See EL SALVADOR - EMPLOYMENT

EL SALVADOR - FERTILITY, HUMAN

Central Intelligence Agency, Office of Public Affairs, Washington, DC 20505, (703) 482-0623, Fax: (703) 482-1739, www.cia.gov; *The World Factbook.*

M.E. Sharpe, 80 Business Park Drive, Armonk, NY 10504, (800) 541-6563, Fax: (914) 273-2106, www.mesharpe.com; *The Illustrated Book of World Rankings.*

United Nations Statistics Division, New York, NY 10017, (800) 253-9646, Fax: (212) 963-4116, http://unstats.un.org; *Human Development Report 2006.*

The World Bank, 1818 H Street, NW, Washington, DC 20433, (202) 473-1000, Fax: (202) 477-6391, www.worldbank.org; *The World Bank Atlas 2003-2004* and *World Development Report 2008.*

EL SALVADOR - FERTILIZER INDUSTRY

Economist Intelligence Unit, 111 West 57th Street, New York, NY 10019, (212) 554-0600, Fax: (212) 586-1181, www.eiu.com; *Business Latin America.*

United Nations Food and Agricultural Organization (FAO), Viale delle Terme di Caracalla, 00100 Rome, Italy, (Dial from U.S. (202) 653-2400), (Fax from U.S. (202) 653 5760), www.fao.org; *FAO Fertilizer Yearbook* and *The State of Food and Agriculture (SOFA) 2006.*

United Nations Statistics Division, New York, NY 10017, (800) 253-9646, Fax: (212) 963-4116, http://unstats.un.org; *Statistical Yearbook.*

EL SALVADOR - FETAL MORTALITY

See EL SALVADOR - MORTALITY

EL SALVADOR - FINANCE

Inter-American Development Bank (IDB), 1300 New York Avenue, NW, Washington, DC 20577, (202) 623-1000, Fax: (202) 623-3096, www.iadb.org; *The Politics of Policies: Economic and Social Progress in Latin America - 2006 Report.*

International Monetary Fund (IMF), 700 Nineteenth Street, NW, Washington, DC 20431, (202) 623-7000, Fax: (202) 623-4661, www.imf.org; *International Financial Statistics Yearbook 2007.*

Organization of American States (OAS), 17th Street Constitution Avenue NW, Washington, DC 20006, (202) 458-3000, www.oas.org; *The OAS in Transition: 1994-2004.*

Taylor and Francis Group, An Informa Business, 2 Park Square, Milton Park, Abingdon, Oxford OX14 4RN, United Kingdom, (Dial from U.S. (212) 216-7800), (Fax from U.S. (212) 564-7854), www.tandf.co.uk; *The Europa World Year Book.*

UCLA Latin American Institute, 10343 Bunche Hall, Box 951447, Los Angeles, CA 90095-1447, (310) 825-4571, Fax: (310) 206-6859, www.international.ucla.edu/lac; *Statistical Abstract of Latin America.*

United Nations Statistics Division, New York, NY 10017, (800) 253-9646, Fax: (212) 963-4116, http://unstats.un.org; *National Accounts Statistics: Compendium of Income Distribution Statistics* and *Statistical Yearbook.*

The World Bank, 1818 H Street, NW, Washington, DC 20433, (202) 473-1000, Fax: (202) 477-6391, www.worldbank.org; *El Salvador.*

EL SALVADOR - FINANCE, PUBLIC

Bernan Essential Government Publications, 4611-F Assembly Drive, Lanham MD, 20706-4391, (301) 459-2255, Fax: (800) 865-3450, www.bernan.com; *National Accounts Statistics.*

Economist Intelligence Unit, 111 West 57th Street, New York, NY 10019, (212) 554-0600, Fax: (212) 586-1181, www.eiu.com; *El Salvador Country Report.*

Inter-American Development Bank (IDB), 1300 New York Avenue, NW, Washington, DC 20577, (202) 623-1000, Fax: (202) 623-3096, www.iadb.org; *The Politics of Policies: Economic and Social Progress in Latin America - 2006 Report.*

International Monetary Fund (IMF), 700 Nineteenth Street, NW, Washington, DC 20431, (202) 623-7000, Fax: (202) 623-4661, www.imf.org; *Government Finance Statistics Yearbook (2008 Edition); International Financial Statistics; International Financial Statistics Online Service;* and *International Financial Statistics Yearbook 2007.*

M.E. Sharpe, 80 Business Park Drive, Armonk, NY 10504, (800) 541-6563, Fax: (914) 273-2106, www.mesharpe.com; *The Illustrated Book of World Rankings.*

Organization of American States (OAS), 17th Street Constitution Avenue NW, Washington, DC 20006, (202) 458-3000, www.oas.org; *The OAS in Transition: 1994-2004.*

Palgrave Macmillan Ltd., Houndmills, Basingstoke, Hampshire, RG21 6XS, England, (Telephone in U.S. (888) 330-8477), (Fax in U.S. (800) 672-2054), www.palgrave.com; *The Statesman's Yearbook 2008.*

Taylor and Francis Group, An Informa Business, 2 Park Square, Milton Park, Abingdon, Oxford OX14 4RN, United Kingdom, (Dial from U.S. (212) 216-7800), (Fax from U.S. (212) 564-7854), www.tandf.co.uk; *The Europa World Year Book.*

UCLA Latin American Institute, 10343 Bunche Hall, Box 951447, Los Angeles, CA 90095-1447, (310) 825-4571, Fax: (310) 206-6859, www.international.ucla.edu/lac; *Statistical Abstract of Latin America.*

The World Bank, 1818 H Street, NW, Washington, DC 20433, (202) 473-1000, Fax: (202) 477-6391, www.worldbank.org; *El Salvador.*

EL SALVADOR - FISHERIES

Inter-American Development Bank (IDB), 1300 New York Avenue, NW, Washington, DC 20577, (202) 623-1000, Fax: (202) 623-3096, www.iadb.org; *The Politics of Policies: Economic and Social Progress in Latin America - 2006 Report.*

M.E. Sharpe, 80 Business Park Drive, Armonk, NY 10504, (800) 541-6563, Fax: (914) 273-2106, www.mesharpe.com; *The Illustrated Book of World Rankings.*

Palgrave Macmillan Ltd., Houndmills, Basingstoke, Hampshire, RG21 6XS, England, (Telephone in U.S. (888) 330-8477), (Fax in U.S. (800) 672-2054), www.palgrave.com; *The Statesman's Yearbook 2008.*

Taylor and Francis Group, An Informa Business, 2 Park Square, Milton Park, Abingdon, Oxford OX14 4RN, United Kingdom, (Dial from U.S. (212) 216-7800), (Fax from U.S. (212) 564-7854), www.tandf.co.uk; *The Europa World Year Book.*

UCLA Latin American Institute, 10343 Bunche Hall, Box 951447, Los Angeles, CA 90095-1447, (310) 825-4571, Fax: (310) 206-6859, www.international.ucla.edu/lac; *Statistical Abstract of Latin America.*

United Nations Conference on Trade and Development (UNCTAD), DC2-1120, United Nations, New York, NY 10017, (212) 963-0027, www.unctad.org; *UNCTAD Commodity Yearbook.*

United Nations Food and Agricultural Organization (FAO), Viale delle Terme di Caracalla, 00100 Rome, Italy, (Dial from U.S. (202) 653-2400), (Fax from U.S. (202) 653 5760), www.fao.org; *FAO Yearbook of Fishery Statistics;* Fishery Databases; FISHSTAT Database. Subjects covered include: Aquaculture production, capture production, fishery commodities; and *The State of Food and Agriculture (SOFA) 2006.*

United Nations Statistics Division, New York, NY 10017, (800) 253-9646, Fax: (212) 963-4116, http://unstats.un.org; *Statistical Yearbook.*

The World Bank, 1818 H Street, NW, Washington, DC 20433, (202) 473-1000, Fax: (202) 477-6391, www.worldbank.org; *El Salvador.*

EL SALVADOR - FLOUR INDUSTRY

United Nations Statistics Division, New York, NY 10017, (800) 253-9646, Fax: (212) 963-4116, http://unstats.un.org; *Statistical Yearbook.*

EL SALVADOR - FOOD

United Nations Conference on Trade and Development (UNCTAD), DC2-1120, United Nations, New York, NY 10017, (212) 963-0027, www.unctad.org; *UNCTAD Commodity Yearbook.*

United Nations Food and Agricultural Organization (FAO), Viale delle Terme di Caracalla, 00100 Rome, Italy, (Dial from U.S. (202) 653-2400), (Fax from U.S. (202) 653 5760), www.fao.org; *FAO Production Yearbook 2002* and *The State of Food and Agriculture (SOFA) 2006.*

United Nations Statistics Division, New York, NY 10017, (800) 253-9646, Fax: (212) 963-4116, http://unstats.un.org; *Human Development Report 2006.*

EL SALVADOR - FOREIGN EXCHANGE RATES

Central Intelligence Agency, Office of Public Affairs, Washington, DC 20505, (703) 482-0623, Fax: (703) 482-1739, www.cia.gov; *The World Factbook.*

Euromonitor International, Inc., 224 S. Michigan Avenue, Suite 1500, Chicago, IL 60604, (312) 922-1115, Fax: (312) 922-1157, www.euromonitor.com; *International Marketing Data and Statistics 2008* and *The World Economic Factbook 2008.*

Inter-American Development Bank (IDB), 1300 New York Avenue, NW, Washington, DC 20577, (202) 623-1000, Fax: (202) 623-3096, www.iadb.org; *The Politics of Policies: Economic and Social Progress in Latin America - 2006 Report.*

International Civil Aviation Organization (ICAO), External Relations and Public Information Office (EPO), 999 University Street, Montreal, Quebec H3C 5H7, Canada, (Dial from U.S. (514) 954-8219), (Fax from U.S. (514) 954-6077), www.icao.int; *Civil Aviation Statistics of the World.*

International Monetary Fund (IMF), 700 Nineteenth Street, NW, Washington, DC 20431, (202) 623-7000, Fax: (202) 623-4661, www.imf.org; *International Financial Statistics Yearbook 2007.*

Organization of American States (OAS), 17th Street Constitution Avenue NW, Washington, DC 20006, (202) 458-3000, www.oas.org; *The OAS in Transition: 1994-2004.*

Taylor and Francis Group, An Informa Business, 2 Park Square, Milton Park, Abingdon, Oxford OX14 4RN, United Kingdom, (Dial from U.S. (212) 216-7800), (Fax from U.S. (212) 564-7854), www.tandf.co.uk; *The Europa World Year Book.*

UCLA Latin American Institute, 10343 Bunche Hall, Box 951447, Los Angeles, CA 90095-1447, (310) 825-4571, Fax: (310) 206-6859, www.international.ucla.edu/lac; *Statistical Abstract of Latin America.*

United Nations Statistics Division, New York, NY 10017, (800) 253-9646, Fax: (212) 963-4116, http://unstats.un.org; *Statistical Yearbook* and *World Statistics Pocketbook.*

EL SALVADOR - FORESTS AND FORESTRY

Economist Intelligence Unit, 111 West 57th Street, New York, NY 10019, (212) 554-0600, Fax: (212) 586-1181, www.eiu.com; *Business Latin America.*

Inter-American Development Bank (IDB), 1300 New York Avenue, NW, Washington, DC 20577, (202) 623-1000, Fax: (202) 623-3096, www.iadb.org; *The Politics of Policies: Economic and Social Progress in Latin America - 2006 Report.*

M.E. Sharpe, 80 Business Park Drive, Armonk, NY 10504, (800) 541-6563, Fax: (914) 273-2106, www.mesharpe.com; *The Illustrated Book of World Rankings.*

Palgrave Macmillan Ltd., Houndmills, Basingstoke, Hampshire, RG21 6XS, England, (Telephone in U.S. (888) 330-8477), (Fax in U.S. (800) 672-2054), www.palgrave.com; *The Statesman's Yearbook 2008.*

Taylor and Francis Group, An Informa Business, 2 Park Square, Milton Park, Abingdon, Oxford OX14 4RN, United Kingdom, (Dial from U.S. (212) 216-7800), (Fax from U.S. (212) 564-7854), www.tandf.co.uk; *The Europa World Year Book.*

UCLA Latin American Institute, 10343 Bunche Hall, Box 951447, Los Angeles, CA 90095-1447, (310) 825-4571, Fax: (310) 206-6859, www.international.ucla.edu/lac; *Statistical Abstract of Latin America.*

UNESCO Institute for Statistics, C.P. 6128 Succursale Centre-Ville, Montreal, Quebec, H3C 3J7 Canada, (Dial from U.S. (514) 343-6880), (Fax from U.S. (514) 343 6882), www.uis.unesco.org; *Statistical Tables.*

United Nations Conference on Trade and Development (UNCTAD), DC2-1120, United Nations, New York, NY 10017, (212) 963-0027, www.unctad.org; *UNCTAD Commodity Yearbook.*

United Nations Food and Agricultural Organization (FAO), Viale delle Terme di Caracalla, 00100 Rome, Italy, (Dial from U.S. (202) 653-2400), (Fax from U.S. (202) 653 5760), www.fao.org; *FAO Yearbook of Forest Products* and *The State of Food and Agriculture (SOFA) 2006.*

United Nations Statistics Division, New York, NY 10017, (800) 253-9646, Fax: (212) 963-4116, http://unstats.un.org; *Statistical Yearbook.*

The World Bank, 1818 H Street, NW, Washington, DC 20433, (202) 473-1000, Fax: (202) 477-6391, www.worldbank.org; *El Salvador* and *World Development Report 2008.*

EL SALVADOR - GAS PRODUCTION

See EL SALVADOR - MINERAL INDUSTRIES

EL SALVADOR - GEOGRAPHIC INFORMATION SYSTEMS

M.E. Sharpe, 80 Business Park Drive, Armonk, NY 10504, (800) 541-6563, Fax: (914) 273-2106, www.mesharpe.com; *The Illustrated Book of World Rankings.*

UCLA Latin American Institute, 10343 Bunche Hall, Box 951447, Los Angeles, CA 90095-1447, (310) 825-4571, Fax: (310) 206-6859, www.international.ucla.edu/lac; *Statistical Abstract of Latin America.*

The World Bank, 1818 H Street, NW, Washington, DC 20433, (202) 473-1000, Fax: (202) 477-6391, www.worldbank.org; *El Salvador.*

EL SALVADOR - GOLD INDUSTRY

Economist Intelligence Unit, 111 West 57th Street, New York, NY 10019, (212) 554-0600, Fax: (212) 586-1181, www.eiu.com; *Business Latin America.*

International Monetary Fund (IMF), 700 Nineteenth Street, NW, Washington, DC 20431, (202) 623-7000, Fax: (202) 623-4661, www.imf.org; *International Financial Statistics Yearbook 2007.*

United Nations Statistics Division, New York, NY 10017, (800) 253-9646, Fax: (212) 963-4116, http://unstats.un.org; *Statistical Yearbook.*

EL SALVADOR - GOLD PRODUCTION

See EL SALVADOR - MINERAL INDUSTRIES

EL SALVADOR - GRANTS-IN-AID

International Monetary Fund (IMF), 700 Nineteenth Street, NW, Washington, DC 20431, (202) 623-7000, Fax: (202) 623-4661, www.imf.org; *Government Finance Statistics Yearbook (2008 Edition).*

EL SALVADOR - GROSS DOMESTIC PRODUCT

Economist Intelligence Unit, 111 West 57th Street, New York, NY 10019, (212) 554-0600, Fax: (212) 586-1181, www.eiu.com; *Business Latin America* and *El Salvador Country Report.*

Euromonitor International, Inc., 224 S. Michigan Avenue, Suite 1500, Chicago, IL 60604, (312) 922-1115, Fax: (312) 922-1157, www.euromonitor.com; *International Marketing Data and Statistics 2008* and *The World Economic Factbook 2008.*

Inter-American Development Bank (IDB), 1300 New York Avenue, NW, Washington, DC 20577, (202) 623-1000, Fax: (202) 623-3096, www.iadb.org; *The Politics of Policies: Economic and Social Progress in Latin America - 2006 Report.*

M.E. Sharpe, 80 Business Park Drive, Armonk, NY 10504, (800) 541-6563, Fax: (914) 273-2106, www.mesharpe.com; *The Illustrated Book of World Rankings.*

Organization of American States (OAS), 17th Street Constitution Avenue NW, Washington, DC 20006, (202) 458-3000, www.oas.org; *The OAS in Transition: 1994-2004.*

Taylor and Francis Group, An Informa Business, 2 Park Square, Milton Park, Abingdon, Oxford OX14 4RN, United Kingdom, (Dial from U.S. (212) 216-7800), (Fax from U.S. (212) 564-7854), www.tandf.co.uk; *The Europa World Year Book.*

UCLA Latin American Institute, 10343 Bunche Hall, Box 951447, Los Angeles, CA 90095-1447, (310) 825-4571, Fax: (310) 206-6859, www.international.ucla.edu/lac; *Statistical Abstract of Latin America.*

United Nations Statistics Division, New York, NY 10017, (800) 253-9646, Fax: (212) 963-4116, http://unstats.un.org; *Human Development Report 2006; National Accounts Statistics: Compendium of Income Distribution Statistics; Statistical Yearbook;* and *Statistical Yearbook for Latin America and the Caribbean 2004.*

The World Bank, 1818 H Street, NW, Washington, DC 20433, (202) 473-1000, Fax: (202) 477-6391, www.worldbank.org; *World Development Report 2008.*

EL SALVADOR - GROSS NATIONAL PRODUCT

Euromonitor International, Inc., 224 S. Michigan Avenue, Suite 1500, Chicago, IL 60604, (312) 922-1115, Fax: (312) 922-1157, www.euromonitor.com; *International Marketing Data and Statistics 2008.*

Inter-American Development Bank (IDB), 1300 New York Avenue, NW, Washington, DC 20577, (202) 623-1000, Fax: (202) 623-3096, www.iadb.org; *The Politics of Policies: Economic and Social Progress in Latin America - 2006 Report.*

M.E. Sharpe, 80 Business Park Drive, Armonk, NY 10504, (800) 541-6563, Fax: (914) 273-2106, www.mesharpe.com; *The Illustrated Book of World Rankings.*

Palgrave Macmillan Ltd., Houndmills, Basingstoke, Hampshire, RG21 6XS, England, (Telephone in U.S. (888) 330-8477), (Fax in U.S. (800) 672-2054), www.palgrave.com; *The Statesman's Yearbook 2008.*

Taylor and Francis Group, An Informa Business, 2 Park Square, Milton Park, Abingdon, Oxford OX14 4RN, United Kingdom, (Dial from U.S. (212) 216-7800), (Fax from U.S. (212) 564-7854), www.tandf.co.uk; *The Europa World Year Book.*

U.S. Department of State (DOS), 2201 C Street NW, Washington, DC 20520, (202) 647-4000, www.state.gov; *World Military Expenditures and Arms Transfers (WMEAT).*

United Nations Statistics Division, New York, NY 10017, (800) 253-9646, Fax: (212) 963-4116, http://unstats.un.org; *Statistical Yearbook.*

The World Bank, 1818 H Street, NW, Washington, DC 20433, (202) 473-1000, Fax: (202) 477-6391, www.worldbank.org; *The World Bank Atlas 2003-2004* and *World Development Report 2008.*

EL SALVADOR - HIDES AND SKINS INDUSTRY

United Nations Food and Agricultural Organization (FAO), Viale delle Terme di Caracalla, 00100 Rome, Italy, (Dial from U.S. (202) 653-2400), (Fax from U.S. (202) 653 5760), www.fao.org; *FAO Production Yearbook 2002.*

EL SALVADOR - HOUSING

M.E. Sharpe, 80 Business Park Drive, Armonk, NY 10504, (800) 541-6563, Fax: (914) 273-2106, www.mesharpe.com; *The Illustrated Book of World Rankings.*

UCLA Latin American Institute, 10343 Bunche Hall, Box 951447, Los Angeles, CA 90095-1447, (310) 825-4571, Fax: (310) 206-6859, www.international.ucla.edu/lac; *Statistical Abstract of Latin America.*

United Nations Statistics Division, New York, NY 10017, (800) 253-9646, Fax: (212) 963-4116, http://unstats.un.org; *Statistical Yearbook for Latin America and the Caribbean 2004.*

EL SALVADOR - ILLITERATE PERSONS

Economist Intelligence Unit, 111 West 57th Street, New York, NY 10019, (212) 554-0600, Fax: (212) 586-1181, www.eiu.com; *Business Latin America.*

Euromonitor International, Inc., 224 S. Michigan Avenue, Suite 1500, Chicago, IL 60604, (312) 922-1115, Fax: (312) 922-1157, www.euromonitor.com; *The World Economic Factbook 2008.*

UNESCO Institute for Statistics, C.P. 6128 Succursale Centre-Ville, Montreal, Quebec, H3C 3J7 Canada, (Dial from U.S. (514) 343-6880), (Fax from U.S. (514) 343 6882), www.uis.unesco.org; *Statistical Tables.*

United Nations Statistics Division, New York, NY 10017, (800) 253-9646, Fax: (212) 963-4116, http://unstats.un.org; *Human Development Report 2006* and *Statistical Yearbook for Latin America and the Caribbean 2004.*

EL SALVADOR - IMPORTS

Central Intelligence Agency, Office of Public Affairs, Washington, DC 20505, (703) 482-0623, Fax: (703) 482-1739, www.cia.gov; *The World Factbook.*

Economist Intelligence Unit, 111 West 57th Street, New York, NY 10019, (212) 554-0600, Fax: (212) 586-1181, www.eiu.com; *Business Latin America* and *El Salvador Country Report.*

Euromonitor International, Inc., 224 S. Michigan Avenue, Suite 1500, Chicago, IL 60604, (312) 922-1115, Fax: (312) 922-1157, www.euromonitor.com; *International Marketing Data and Statistics 2008* and *The World Economic Factbook 2008.*

Inter-American Development Bank (IDB), 1300 New York Avenue, NW, Washington, DC 20577, (202) 623-1000, Fax: (202) 623-3096, www.iadb.org; *The Politics of Policies: Economic and Social Progress in Latin America - 2006 Report.*

International Monetary Fund (IMF), 700 Nineteenth Street, NW, Washington, DC 20431, (202) 623-7000, Fax: (202) 623-4661, www.imf.org; *Direction of Trade Statistics Yearbook 2007; Government Finance Statistics Yearbook (2008 Edition);* and *International Financial Statistics Yearbook 2007.*

Organization of American States (OAS), 17th Street Constitution Avenue NW, Washington, DC 20006, (202) 458-3000, www.oas.org; *The OAS in Transition: 1994-2004.*

Palgrave Macmillan Ltd., Houndmills, Basingstoke, Hampshire, RG21 6XS, England, (Telephone in U.S. (888) 330-8477), (Fax in U.S. (800) 672-2054), www.palgrave.com; *The Statesman's Yearbook 2008.*

Taylor and Francis Group, An Informa Business, 2 Park Square, Milton Park, Abingdon, Oxford OX14 4RN, United Kingdom, (Dial from U.S. (212) 216-7800), (Fax from U.S. (212) 564-7854), www.tandf.co.uk; *The Europa World Year Book.*

United Nations Conference on Trade and Development (UNCTAD), DC2-1120, United Nations, New York, NY 10017, (212) 963-0027, www.unctad.org; *Handbook of Statistics 2005.*

United Nations Food and Agricultural Organization (FAO), Viale delle Terme di Caracalla, 00100 Rome, Italy, (Dial from U.S. (202) 653-2400), (Fax from U.S. (202) 653 5760), www.fao.org; *The State of Food and Agriculture (SOFA) 2006.*

United Nations Statistics Division, New York, NY 10017, (800) 253-9646, Fax: (212) 963-4116, http://unstats.un.org; *Statistical Yearbook for Latin America and the Caribbean 2004.*

The World Bank, 1818 H Street, NW, Washington, DC 20433, (202) 473-1000, Fax: (202) 477-6391, www.worldbank.org; *World Development Report 2008.*

EL SALVADOR - INCOME DISTRIBUTION

UCLA Latin American Institute, 10343 Bunche Hall, Box 951447, Los Angeles, CA 90095-1447, (310) 825-4571, Fax: (310) 206-6859, www.international.ucla.edu/lac; *Statistical Abstract of Latin America.*

United Nations Statistics Division, New York, NY 10017, (800) 253-9646, Fax: (212) 963-4116, http://unstats.un.org; *Statistical Yearbook for Latin America and the Caribbean 2004.*

EL SALVADOR - INCOME TAXES

See EL SALVADOR - TAXATION

EL SALVADOR - INDUSTRIAL PRODUCTIVITY

Euromonitor International, Inc., 224 S. Michigan Avenue, Suite 1500, Chicago, IL 60604, (312) 922-1115, Fax: (312) 922-1157, www.euromonitor.com; *International Marketing Data and Statistics 2008.*

M.E. Sharpe, 80 Business Park Drive, Armonk, NY 10504, (800) 541-6563, Fax: (914) 273-2106, www.mesharpe.com; *The Illustrated Book of World Rankings.*

EL SALVADOR - INDUSTRIAL PROPERTY

United Nations Statistics Division, New York, NY 10017, (800) 253-9646, Fax: (212) 963-4116, http://unstats.un.org; *Statistical Yearbook.*

World Intellectual Property Organization (WIPO), PO Box 18, CH-1211 Geneva 20, Switzerland, www.wipo.int; *Industrial Property Statistics* and *Industrial Property Statistics Online Directory.*

EL SALVADOR - INDUSTRIES

Central Intelligence Agency, Office of Public Affairs, Washington, DC 20505, (703) 482-0623, Fax: (703) 482-1739, www.cia.gov; *The World Factbook.*

Economist Intelligence Unit, 111 West 57th Street, New York, NY 10019, (212) 554-0600, Fax: (212) 586-1181, www.eiu.com; *El Salvador Country Report.*

Euromonitor International, Inc., 224 S. Michigan Avenue, Suite 1500, Chicago, IL 60604, (312) 922-1115, Fax: (312) 922-1157, www.euromonitor.com; *International Marketing Data and Statistics 2008; The World Economic Factbook 2008;* and *World Marketing Data and Statistics.*

International Labour Office, I.L.O. Publications, 4 route des Morillons, CH-1211 Geneva 22, Switzerland, (Telephone in U.S. (202) 653-7652), (Fax in U.S. (202) 653-7687), www.ilo.org; *Yearbook of Labour Statistics 2006.*

M.E. Sharpe, 80 Business Park Drive, Armonk, NY 10504, (800) 541-6563, Fax: (914) 273-2106, www.mesharpe.com; *The Illustrated Book of World Rankings.*

Palgrave Macmillan Ltd., Houndmills, Basingstoke, Hampshire, RG21 6XS, England, (Telephone in U.S. (888) 330-8477), (Fax in U.S. (800) 672-2054), www.palgrave.com; *The Statesman's Yearbook 2008.*

Taylor and Francis Group, An Informa Business, 2 Park Square, Milton Park, Abingdon, Oxford OX14 4RN, United Kingdom, (Dial from U.S. (212) 216-7800), (Fax from U.S. (212) 564-7854), www.tandf.co.uk; *The Europa World Year Book.*

UCLA Latin American Institute, 10343 Bunche Hall, Box 951447, Los Angeles, CA 90095-1447, (310) 825-4571, Fax: (310) 206-6859, www.international.ucla.edu/lac; *Statistical Abstract of Latin America.*

United Nations Industrial Development Organization (UNIDO), 1 United Nations Plaza, New York, NY 10017, (212) 963 6890, Fax: (212) 963-7904, http://unido.org; Industrial Statistics Database 2008 (INDSTAT) and *The International Yearbook of Industrial Statistics 2008.*

United Nations Statistics Division, New York, NY 10017, (800) 253-9646, Fax: (212) 963-4116, http://unstats.un.org; *Economic Survey of Latin America and the Caribbean 2004-2005; 2004 Industrial Commodity Statistics Yearbook;* and *Statistical Yearbook.*

The World Bank, 1818 H Street, NW, Washington, DC 20433, (202) 473-1000, Fax: (202) 477-6391, www.worldbank.org; *El Salvador.*

EL SALVADOR - INFANT AND MATERNAL MORTALITY

See EL SALVADOR - MORTALITY

EL SALVADOR - INFLATION (FINANCE)

United Nations Statistics Division, New York, NY 10017, (800) 253-9646, Fax: (212) 963-4116, http://unstats.un.org; *Economic Survey of Latin America and the Caribbean 2004-2005.*

EL SALVADOR - INORGANIC ACIDS

United Nations Statistics Division, New York, NY 10017, (800) 253-9646, Fax: (212) 963-4116, http://unstats.un.org; *Statistical Yearbook.*

EL SALVADOR - INTEREST RATES

Inter-American Development Bank (IDB), 1300 New York Avenue, NW, Washington, DC 20577, (202) 623-1000, Fax: (202) 623-3096, www.iadb.org; *The Politics of Policies: Economic and Social Progress in Latin America - 2006 Report.*

EL SALVADOR - INTERNAL REVENUE

Inter-American Development Bank (IDB), 1300 New York Avenue, NW, Washington, DC 20577, (202) 623-1000, Fax: (202) 623-3096, www.iadb.org; *The Politics of Policies: Economic and Social Progress in Latin America - 2006 Report.*

Organization of American States (OAS), 17th Street Constitution Avenue NW, Washington, DC 20006, (202) 458-3000, www.oas.org; *The OAS in Transition: 1994-2004.*

EL SALVADOR - INTERNATIONAL FINANCE

Inter-American Development Bank (IDB), 1300 New York Avenue, NW, Washington, DC 20577, (202) 623-1000, Fax: (202) 623-3096, www.iadb.org; *The Politics of Policies: Economic and Social Progress in Latin America - 2006 Report.*

UCLA Latin American Institute, 10343 Bunche Hall, Box 951447, Los Angeles, CA 90095-1447, (310) 825-4571, Fax: (310) 206-6859, www.international.ucla.edu/lac; *Statistical Abstract of Latin America.*

United Nations Statistics Division, New York, NY 10017, (800) 253-9646, Fax: (212) 963-4116, http://unstats.un.org; *Statistical Yearbook for Latin America and the Caribbean 2004.*

EL SALVADOR - INTERNATIONAL LIQUIDITY

Inter-American Development Bank (IDB), 1300 New York Avenue, NW, Washington, DC 20577, (202) 623-1000, Fax: (202) 623-3096, www.iadb.org; *The Politics of Policies: Economic and Social Progress in Latin America - 2006 Report.*

International Monetary Fund (IMF), 700 Nineteenth Street, NW, Washington, DC 20431, (202) 623-7000, Fax: (202) 623-4661, www.imf.org; *International Financial Statistics Yearbook 2007.*

EL SALVADOR - INTERNATIONAL STATISTICS

Inter-American Development Bank (IDB), 1300 New York Avenue, NW, Washington, DC 20577, (202) 623-1000, Fax: (202) 623-3096, www.iadb.org; *The Politics of Policies: Economic and Social Progress in Latin America - 2006 Report.*

UCLA Latin American Institute, 10343 Bunche Hall, Box 951447, Los Angeles, CA 90095-1447, (310) 825-4571, Fax: (310) 206-6859, www.international.ucla.edu/lac; *Statistical Abstract of Latin America.*

EL SALVADOR - INTERNATIONAL TRADE

Economist Intelligence Unit, 111 West 57th Street, New York, NY 10019, (212) 554-0600, Fax: (212) 586-1181, www.eiu.com; *Business Latin America* and *El Salvador Country Report.*

Euromonitor International, Inc., 224 S. Michigan Avenue, Suite 1500, Chicago, IL 60604, (312) 922-1115, Fax: (312) 922-1157, www.euromonitor.com; *International Marketing Data and Statistics 2008; The World Economic Factbook 2008;* and *World Marketing Data and Statistics.*

Inter-American Development Bank (IDB), 1300 New York Avenue, NW, Washington, DC 20577, (202) 623-1000, Fax: (202) 623-3096, www.iadb.org; *The Politics of Policies: Economic and Social Progress in Latin America - 2006 Report.*

International Monetary Fund (IMF), 700 Nineteenth Street, NW, Washington, DC 20431, (202) 623-7000, Fax: (202) 623-4661, www.imf.org; *International Financial Statistics Yearbook 2007.*

M.E. Sharpe, 80 Business Park Drive, Armonk, NY 10504, (800) 541-6563, Fax: (914) 273-2106, www.mesharpe.com; *The Illustrated Book of World Rankings.*

Palgrave Macmillan Ltd., Houndmills, Basingstoke, Hampshire, RG21 6XS, England, (Telephone in U.S. (888) 330-8477), (Fax in U.S. (800) 672-2054), www.palgrave.com; *The Statesman's Yearbook 2008.*

Taylor and Francis Group, An Informa Business, 2 Park Square, Milton Park, Abingdon, Oxford OX14 4RN, United Kingdom, (Dial from U.S. (212) 216-7800), (Fax from U.S. (212) 564-7854), www.tandf.co.uk; *The Europa World Year Book.*

UCLA Latin American Institute, 10343 Bunche Hall, Box 951447, Los Angeles, CA 90095-1447, (310) 825-4571, Fax: (310) 206-6859, www.international.ucla.edu/lac; *Statistical Abstract of Latin America.*

United Nations Conference on Trade and Development (UNCTAD), DC2-1120, United Nations, New York, NY 10017, (212) 963-0027, www.unctad.org; *UNCTAD Commodity Yearbook.*

United Nations Food and Agricultural Organization (FAO), Viale delle Terme di Caracalla, 00100 Rome, Italy, (Dial from U.S. (202) 653-2400), (Fax from U.S. (202) 653 5760), www.fao.org; *FAO Trade Yearbook* and *The State of Food and Agriculture (SOFA) 2006.*

United Nations Statistics Division, New York, NY 10017, (800) 253-9646, Fax: (212) 963-4116, http://unstats.un.org; *Economic Survey of Latin America and the Caribbean 2004-2005; International Trade Statistics Yearbook; Statistical Yearbook;* and *Statistical Yearbook for Latin America and the Caribbean 2004.*

The World Bank, 1818 H Street, NW, Washington, DC 20433, (202) 473-1000, Fax: (202) 477-6391, www.worldbank.org; *El Salvador* and *World Development Report 2008.*

World Trade Organization (WTO), Centre William Rappard, Rue de Lausanne 154, CH-1211 Geneva 21, Switzerland, www.wto.org; *International Trade Statistics 2006.*

EL SALVADOR - INTERNET USERS

International Telecommunication Union (ITU), Place des Nations, 1211 Geneva 20, Switzerland, www.itu.int; *World Telecommunication/ICT Indicators Database on CD-ROM; World Telecommunication/ICT Indicators Database Online;* and *Yearbook of Statistics - Telecommunication Services (Chronological Time Series 1997-2006).*

The World Bank, 1818 H Street, NW, Washington, DC 20433, (202) 473-1000, Fax: (202) 477-6391, www.worldbank.org; *El Salvador.*

EL SALVADOR - INVESTMENTS

Inter-American Development Bank (IDB), 1300 New York Avenue, NW, Washington, DC 20577, (202) 623-1000, Fax: (202) 623-3096, www.iadb.org; *The Politics of Policies: Economic and Social Progress in Latin America - 2006 Report.*

United Nations Statistics Division, New York, NY 10017, (800) 253-9646, Fax: (212) 963-4116, http://unstats.un.org; *Statistical Yearbook for Latin America and the Caribbean 2004.*

EL SALVADOR - INVESTMENTS, FOREIGN

Economist Intelligence Unit, 111 West 57th Street, New York, NY 10019, (212) 554-0600, Fax: (212) 586-1181, www.eiu.com; *Business Latin America.*

EL SALVADOR - IRON AND IRON ORE PRODUCTION

See EL SALVADOR - MINERAL INDUSTRIES

EL SALVADOR - IRRIGATION

Euromonitor International, Inc., 224 S. Michigan Avenue, Suite 1500, Chicago, IL 60604, (312) 922-1115, Fax: (312) 922-1157, www.euromonitor.com; *International Marketing Data and Statistics 2008.*

Inter-American Development Bank (IDB), 1300 New York Avenue, NW, Washington, DC 20577, (202) 623-1000, Fax: (202) 623-3096, www.iadb.org; *The Politics of Policies: Economic and Social Progress in Latin America - 2006 Report.*

EL SALVADOR - JUTE PRODUCTION

See EL SALVADOR - CROPS

EL SALVADOR - LABOR

Central Intelligence Agency, Office of Public Affairs, Washington, DC 20505, (703) 482-0623, Fax: (703) 482-1739, www.cia.gov; *The World Factbook.*

Economist Intelligence Unit, 111 West 57th Street, New York, NY 10019, (212) 554-0600, Fax: (212) 586-1181, www.eiu.com; *Business Latin America.*

Euromonitor International, Inc., 224 S. Michigan Avenue, Suite 1500, Chicago, IL 60604, (312) 922-1115, Fax: (312) 922-1157, www.euromonitor.com; *International Marketing Data and Statistics 2008* and *World Marketing Data and Statistics.*

International Labour Office, I.L.O. Publications, 4 route des Morillons, CH-1211 Geneva 22, Switzerland, (Telephone in U.S. (202) 653-7652), (Fax in U.S. (202) 653-7687), www.ilo.org; *Yearbook of Labour Statistics 2006.*

M.E. Sharpe, 80 Business Park Drive, Armonk, NY 10504, (800) 541-6563, Fax: (914) 273-2106, www.mesharpe.com; *The Illustrated Book of World Rankings.*

Palgrave Macmillan Ltd., Houndmills, Basingstoke, Hampshire, RG21 6XS, England, (Telephone in U.S. (888) 330-8477), (Fax in U.S. (800) 672-2054), www.palgrave.com; *The Statesman's Yearbook 2008.*

Taylor and Francis Group, An Informa Business, 2 Park Square, Milton Park, Abingdon, Oxford OX14 4RN, United Kingdom, (Dial from U.S. (212) 216-7800), (Fax from U.S. (212) 564-7854), www.tandf.co.uk; *The Europa World Year Book.*

United Nations Food and Agricultural Organization (FAO), Viale delle Terme di Caracalla, 00100 Rome, Italy, (Dial from U.S. (202) 653-2400), (Fax from U.S. (202) 653 5760), www.fao.org; *The State of Food and Agriculture (SOFA) 2006.*

United Nations Statistics Division, New York, NY 10017, (800) 253-9646, Fax: (212) 963-4116, http://unstats.un.org; *Human Development Report 2006.*

The World Bank, 1818 H Street, NW, Washington, DC 20433, (202) 473-1000, Fax: (202) 477-6391, www.worldbank.org; *The World Bank Atlas 2003-2004* and *World Development Report 2008.*

EL SALVADOR - LAND USE

Central Intelligence Agency, Office of Public Affairs, Washington, DC 20505, (703) 482-0623, Fax: (703) 482-1739, www.cia.gov; *The World Factbook.*

Euromonitor International, Inc., 224 S. Michigan Avenue, Suite 1500, Chicago, IL 60604, (312) 922-1115, Fax: (312) 922-1157, www.euromonitor.com; *International Marketing Data and Statistics 2008.*

Inter-American Development Bank (IDB), 1300 New York Avenue, NW, Washington, DC 20577, (202) 623-1000, Fax: (202) 623-3096, www.iadb.org; *The Politics of Policies: Economic and Social Progress in Latin America - 2006 Report.*

United Nations Food and Agricultural Organization (FAO), Viale delle Terme di Caracalla, 00100 Rome, Italy, (Dial from U.S. (202) 653-2400), (Fax from U.S. (202) 653 5760), www.fao.org; *FAO Production Yearbook 2002.*

The World Bank, 1818 H Street, NW, Washington, DC 20433, (202) 473-1000, Fax: (202) 477-6391, www.worldbank.org; *World Development Report 2008.*

EL SALVADOR - LIBRARIES

M.E. Sharpe, 80 Business Park Drive, Armonk, NY 10504, (800) 541-6563, Fax: (914) 273-2106, www.mesharpe.com; *The Illustrated Book of World Rankings.*

UNESCO Institute for Statistics, C.P. 6128 Succursale Centre-Ville, Montreal, Quebec, H3C 3J7 Canada, (Dial from U.S. (514) 343-6880), (Fax from U.S. (514) 343 6882), www.uis.unesco.org; *Statistical Tables.*

EL SALVADOR - LICENSES

International Monetary Fund (IMF), 700 Nineteenth Street, NW, Washington, DC 20431, (202) 623-7000, Fax: (202) 623-4661, www.imf.org; *Government Finance Statistics Yearbook (2008 Edition).*

EL SALVADOR - LIFE EXPECTANCY

Central Intelligence Agency, Office of Public Affairs, Washington, DC 20505, (703) 482-0623, Fax: (703) 482-1739, www.cia.gov; *The World Factbook.*

Economist Intelligence Unit, 111 West 57th Street, New York, NY 10019, (212) 554-0600, Fax: (212) 586-1181, www.eiu.com; *Business Latin America.*

Euromonitor International, Inc., 224 S. Michigan Avenue, Suite 1500, Chicago, IL 60604, (312) 922-1115, Fax: (312) 922-1157, www.euromonitor.com; *The World Economic Factbook 2008.*

Palgrave Macmillan Ltd., Houndmills, Basingstoke, Hampshire, RG21 6XS, England, (Telephone in U.S. (888) 330-8477), (Fax in U.S. (800) 672-2054), www.palgrave.com; *The Statesman's Yearbook 2008.*

United Nations Statistics Division, New York, NY 10017, (800) 253-9646, Fax: (212) 963-4116, http://unstats.un.org; *Human Development Report 2006; Statistical Yearbook for Latin America and the Caribbean 2004;* and *World Statistics Pocketbook.*

The World Bank, 1818 H Street, NW, Washington, DC 20433, (202) 473-1000, Fax: (202) 477-6391, www.worldbank.org; *The World Bank Atlas 2003-2004* and *World Development Report 2008.*

EL SALVADOR - LITERACY

Euromonitor International, Inc., 224 S. Michigan Avenue, Suite 1500, Chicago, IL 60604, (312) 922-1115, Fax: (312) 922-1157, www.euromonitor.com; *World Marketing Data and Statistics.*

EL SALVADOR - LIVESTOCK

Euromonitor International, Inc., 224 S. Michigan Avenue, Suite 1500, Chicago, IL 60604, (312) 922-1115, Fax: (312) 922-1157, www.euromonitor.com; *International Marketing Data and Statistics 2008.*

M.E. Sharpe, 80 Business Park Drive, Armonk, NY 10504, (800) 541-6563, Fax: (914) 273-2106, www.mesharpe.com; *The Illustrated Book of World Rankings.*

Palgrave Macmillan Ltd., Houndmills, Basingstoke, Hampshire, RG21 6XS, England, (Telephone in U.S. (888) 330-8477), (Fax in U.S. (800) 672-2054), www.palgrave.com; *The Statesman's Yearbook 2008.*

Taylor and Francis Group, An Informa Business, 2 Park Square, Milton Park, Abingdon, Oxford OX14 4RN, United Kingdom, (Dial from U.S. (212) 216-7800), (Fax from U.S. (212) 564-7854), www.tandf.co.uk; *The Europa World Year Book.*

United Nations Conference on Trade and Development (UNCTAD), DC2-1120, United Nations, New York, NY 10017, (212) 963-0027, www.unctad.org; *UNCTAD Commodity Yearbook.*

United Nations Food and Agricultural Organization (FAO), Viale delle Terme di Caracalla, 00100 Rome, Italy, (Dial from U.S. (202) 653-2400), (Fax from U.S. (202) 653 5760), www.fao.org; *FAO Production Yearbook 2002* and *The State of Food and Agriculture (SOFA) 2006.*

United Nations Statistics Division, New York, NY 10017, (800) 253-9646, Fax: (212) 963-4116, http://unstats.un.org; *Statistical Yearbook.*

EL SALVADOR - LOCAL TAXATION

Euromonitor International, Inc., 224 S. Michigan Avenue, Suite 1500, Chicago, IL 60604, (312) 922-1115, Fax: (312) 922-1157, www.euromonitor.com; *International Marketing Data and Statistics 2008.*

Inter-American Development Bank (IDB), 1300 New York Avenue, NW, Washington, DC 20577, (202) 623-1000, Fax: (202) 623-3096, www.iadb.org; *The Politics of Policies: Economic and Social Progress in Latin America - 2006 Report.*

EL SALVADOR - MANUFACTURES

Economist Intelligence Unit, 111 West 57th Street, New York, NY 10019, (212) 554-0600, Fax: (212) 586-1181, www.eiu.com; *Business Latin America.*

Inter-American Development Bank (IDB), 1300 New York Avenue, NW, Washington, DC 20577, (202) 623-1000, Fax: (202) 623-3096, www.iadb.org; *The Politics of Policies: Economic and Social Progress in Latin America - 2006 Report.*

M.E. Sharpe, 80 Business Park Drive, Armonk, NY 10504, (800) 541-6563, Fax: (914) 273-2106, www.mesharpe.com; *The Illustrated Book of World Rankings.*

United Nations Statistics Division, New York, NY 10017, (800) 253-9646, Fax: (212) 963-4116, http://unstats.un.org; *Statistical Yearbook* and *Statistical Yearbook for Latin America and the Caribbean 2004.*

EL SALVADOR - MARRIAGE

M.E. Sharpe, 80 Business Park Drive, Armonk, NY 10504, (800) 541-6563, Fax: (914) 273-2106, www.mesharpe.com; *The Illustrated Book of World Rankings.*

Taylor and Francis Group, An Informa Business, 2 Park Square, Milton Park, Abingdon, Oxford OX14 4RN, United Kingdom, (Dial from U.S. (212) 216-7800), (Fax from U.S. (212) 564-7854), www.tandf.co.uk; *The Europa World Year Book.*

United Nations Statistics Division, New York, NY 10017, (800) 253-9646, Fax: (212) 963-4116, http://unstats.un.org; *Demographic Yearbook* and *Statistical Yearbook.*

EL SALVADOR - MEDICAL PERSONNEL

UCLA Latin American Institute, 10343 Bunche Hall, Box 951447, Los Angeles, CA 90095-1447, (310) 825-4571, Fax: (310) 206-6859, www.international.ucla.edu/lac; *Statistical Abstract of Latin America.*

EL SALVADOR - MILK PRODUCTION

See EL SALVADOR - DAIRY PROCESSING

EL SALVADOR - MINERAL INDUSTRIES

Economist Intelligence Unit, 111 West 57th Street, New York, NY 10019, (212) 554-0600, Fax: (212) 586-1181, www.eiu.com; *Business Latin America.*

Inter-American Development Bank (IDB), 1300 New York Avenue, NW, Washington, DC 20577, (202) 623-1000, Fax: (202) 623-3096, www.iadb.org; *The Politics of Policies: Economic and Social Progress in Latin America - 2006 Report.*

Palgrave Macmillan Ltd., Houndmills, Basingstoke, Hampshire, RG21 6XS, England, (Telephone in U.S. (888) 330-8477), (Fax in U.S. (800) 672-2054), www.palgrave.com; *The Statesman's Yearbook 2008.*

PennWell Corporation, 1421 South Sheridan Road, Tulsa, OK 74112, (918) 835-3161, www.pennwell.com; *Oil Gas Journal Latinoamericana.*

UCLA Latin American Institute, 10343 Bunche Hall, Box 951447, Los Angeles, CA 90095-1447, (310) 825-4571, Fax: (310) 206-6859, www.international.ucla.edu/lac; *Statistical Abstract of Latin America.*

United Nations Conference on Trade and Development (UNCTAD), DC2-1120, United Nations, New York, NY 10017, (212) 963-0027, www.unctad.org; *UNCTAD Commodity Yearbook.*

United Nations Statistics Division, New York, NY 10017, (800) 253-9646, Fax: (212) 963-4116, http://unstats.un.org; *Statistical Yearbook for Latin America and the Caribbean 2004.*

EL SALVADOR - MONEY EXCHANGE RATES

See EL SALVADOR - FOREIGN EXCHANGE RATES

EL SALVADOR - MONEY SUPPLY

Economist Intelligence Unit, 111 West 57th Street, New York, NY 10019, (212) 554-0600, Fax: (212) 586-1181, www.eiu.com; *El Salvador Country Report.*

Euromonitor International, Inc., 224 S. Michigan Avenue, Suite 1500, Chicago, IL 60604, (312) 922-1115, Fax: (312) 922-1157, www.euromonitor.com; *International Marketing Data and Statistics 2008.*

Inter-American Development Bank (IDB), 1300 New York Avenue, NW, Washington, DC 20577, (202) 623-1000, Fax: (202) 623-3096, www.iadb.org; *The*

Politics of Policies: Economic and Social Progress in Latin America - 2006 Report.

International Monetary Fund (IMF), 700 Nineteenth Street, NW, Washington, DC 20431, (202) 623-7000, Fax: (202) 623-4661, www.imf.org; *International Financial Statistics Yearbook 2007.*

Taylor and Francis Group, An Informa Business, 2 Park Square, Milton Park, Abingdon, Oxford OX14 4RN, United Kingdom, (Dial from U.S. (212) 216-7800), (Fax from U.S. (212) 564-7854), www.tandf.co.uk; *The Europa World Year Book.*

UCLA Latin American Institute, 10343 Bunche Hall, Box 951447, Los Angeles, CA 90095-1447, (310) 825-4571, Fax: (310) 206-6859, www.international.ucla.edu/lac; *Statistical Abstract of Latin America.*

United Nations Statistics Division, New York, NY 10017, (800) 253-9646, Fax: (212) 963-4116, http://unstats.un.org; *Statistical Yearbook.*

The World Bank, 1818 H Street, NW, Washington, DC 20433, (202) 473-1000, Fax: (202) 477-6391, www.worldbank.org; *El Salvador.*

EL SALVADOR - MORTALITY

Central Intelligence Agency, Office of Public Affairs, Washington, DC 20505, (703) 482-0623, Fax: (703) 482-1739, www.cia.gov; *The World Factbook.*

Economist Intelligence Unit, 111 West 57th Street, New York, NY 10019, (212) 554-0600, Fax: (212) 586-1181, www.eiu.com; *Business Latin America.*

Euromonitor International, Inc., 224 S. Michigan Avenue, Suite 1500, Chicago, IL 60604, (312) 922-1115, Fax: (312) 922-1157, www.euromonitor.com; *International Marketing Data and Statistics 2008* and *The World Economic Factbook 2008.*

Palgrave Macmillan Ltd., Houndmills, Basingstoke, Hampshire, RG21 6XS, England, (Telephone in U.S. (888) 330-8477), (Fax in U.S. (800) 672-2054), www.palgrave.com; *The Statesman's Yearbook 2008.*

Taylor and Francis Group, An Informa Business, 2 Park Square, Milton Park, Abingdon, Oxford OX14 4RN, United Kingdom, (Dial from U.S. (212) 216-7800), (Fax from U.S. (212) 564-7854), www.tandf.co.uk; *The Europa World Year Book.*

UNICEF, 3 United Nations Plaza, New York, NY 10017, (800) 253-9646, Fax: (212) 887-7465, www.unicef.org; *The State of the World's Children 2008.*

United Nations Statistics Division, New York, NY 10017, (800) 253-9646, Fax: (212) 963-4116, http://unstats.un.org; *Demographic Yearbook; Human Development Report 2006; Statistical Yearbook; Statistical Yearbook for Latin America and the Caribbean 2004;* and *World Statistics Pocketbook.*

The World Bank, 1818 H Street, NW, Washington, DC 20433, (202) 473-1000, Fax: (202) 477-6391, www.worldbank.org; *The World Bank Atlas 2003-2004* and *World Development Report 2008.*

World Health Organization (WHO), Avenue Appia 20, 1211 Geneve 27, Switzerland, (Telephone in U.S. (212) 331-9081), www.who.int; The WHO Global Atlas of Infectious Diseases and *World Health Report 2006.*

EL SALVADOR - MOTION PICTURES

Palgrave Macmillan Ltd., Houndmills, Basingstoke, Hampshire, RG21 6XS, England, (Telephone in U.S. (888) 330-8477), (Fax in U.S. (800) 672-2054), www.palgrave.com; *The Statesman's Yearbook 2008.*

United Nations Statistics Division, New York, NY 10017, (800) 253-9646, Fax: (212) 963-4116, http://unstats.un.org; *Statistical Yearbook.*

EL SALVADOR - MOTOR VEHICLES

Economist Intelligence Unit, 111 West 57th Street, New York, NY 10019, (212) 554-0600, Fax: (212) 586-1181, www.eiu.com; *Business Latin America.*

International Road Federation (IFR), Madison Place, 500 Montgomery Street, 5th Floor, Alexandria, VA 22314, (703) 535-1001, Fax: (703) 535-1007, www.irfnet.org; *World Road Statistics 2006.*

United Nations Statistics Division, New York, NY 10017, (800) 253-9646, Fax: (212) 963-4116, http://unstats.un.org; *Statistical Yearbook.*

EL SALVADOR - MUSEUMS

M.E. Sharpe, 80 Business Park Drive, Armonk, NY 10504, (800) 541-6563, Fax: (914) 273-2106, www.mesharpe.com; *The Illustrated Book of World Rankings.*

UNESCO Institute for Statistics, C.P. 6128 Succursale Centre-Ville, Montreal, Quebec, H3C 3J7 Canada, (Dial from U.S. (514) 343-6880), (Fax from U.S. (514) 343 6882), www.uis.unesco.org; *Statistical Tables.*

EL SALVADOR - NATURAL GAS PRODUCTION

See EL SALVADOR - MINERAL INDUSTRIES

EL SALVADOR - NUTRITION

United Nations Food and Agricultural Organization (FAO), Viale delle Terme di Caracalla, 00100 Rome, Italy, (Dial from U.S. (202) 653-2400), (Fax from U.S. (202) 653 5760), www.fao.org; *The State of Food and Agriculture (SOFA) 2006.*

United Nations Statistics Division, New York, NY 10017, (800) 253-9646, Fax: (212) 963-4116, http://unstats.un.org; *Statistical Yearbook for Latin America and the Caribbean 2004.*

EL SALVADOR - OLDER PEOPLE

M.E. Sharpe, 80 Business Park Drive, Armonk, NY 10504, (800) 541-6563, Fax: (914) 273-2106, www.mesharpe.com; *The Illustrated Book of World Rankings.*

EL SALVADOR - PAPER

See EL SALVADOR - FORESTS AND FORESTRY

EL SALVADOR - PEANUT PRODUCTION

See EL SALVADOR - CROPS

EL SALVADOR - PESTICIDES

United Nations Food and Agricultural Organization (FAO), Viale delle Terme di Caracalla, 00100 Rome, Italy, (Dial from U.S. (202) 653-2400), (Fax from U.S. (202) 653 5760), www.fao.org; *The State of Food and Agriculture (SOFA) 2006.*

EL SALVADOR - PETROLEUM INDUSTRY AND TRADE

Economist Intelligence Unit, 111 West 57th Street, New York, NY 10019, (212) 554-0600, Fax: (212) 586-1181, www.eiu.com; *Business Latin America.*

Inter-American Development Bank (IDB), 1300 New York Avenue, NW, Washington, DC 20577, (202) 623-1000, Fax: (202) 623-3096, www.iadb.org; *The Politics of Policies: Economic and Social Progress in Latin America - 2006 Report.*

M.E. Sharpe, 80 Business Park Drive, Armonk, NY 10504, (800) 541-6563, Fax: (914) 273-2106, www.mesharpe.com; *The Illustrated Book of World Rankings.*

Palgrave Macmillan Ltd., Houndmills, Basingstoke, Hampshire, RG21 6XS, England, (Telephone in U.S. (888) 330-8477), (Fax in U.S. (800) 672-2054), www.palgrave.com; *The Statesman's Yearbook 2008.*

PennWell Corporation, 1421 South Sheridan Road, Tulsa, OK 74112, (918) 835-3161, www.pennwell.com; *International Petroleum Encyclopedia 2007.*

U.S. Department of Energy (DOE), Energy Information Administration (EIA), 1000 Independence Avenue, SW, Washington, DC 20585, (202) 586-8800, www.eia.doe.gov; *International Energy Annual 2004* and *International Energy Outlook 2006.*

United Nations Conference on Trade and Development (UNCTAD), DC2-1120, United Nations, New York, NY 10017, (212) 963-0027, www.unctad.org; *UNCTAD Commodity Yearbook.*

United Nations Food and Agricultural Organization (FAO), Viale delle Terme di Caracalla, 00100 Rome, Italy, (Dial from U.S. (202) 653-2400), (Fax from U.S. (202) 653 5760), www.fao.org; *The State of Food and Agriculture (SOFA) 2006.*

United Nations Statistics Division, New York, NY 10017, (800) 253-9646, Fax: (212) 963-4116, http://unstats.un.org; *Statistical Yearbook.*

EL SALVADOR - POLITICAL SCIENCE

Central Intelligence Agency, Office of Public Affairs, Washington, DC 20505, (703) 482-0623, Fax: (703) 482-1739, www.cia.gov; *The World Factbook.*

Inter-American Development Bank (IDB), 1300 New York Avenue, NW, Washington, DC 20577, (202) 623-1000, Fax: (202) 623-3096, www.iadb.org; *The Politics of Policies: Economic and Social Progress in Latin America - 2006 Report.*

International Monetary Fund (IMF), 700 Nineteenth Street, NW, Washington, DC 20431, (202) 623-7000, Fax: (202) 623-4661, www.imf.org; *Government Finance Statistics Yearbook (2008 Edition).*

Palgrave Macmillan Ltd., Houndmills, Basingstoke, Hampshire, RG21 6XS, England, (Telephone in U.S. (888) 330-8477), (Fax in U.S. (800) 672-2054), www.palgrave.com; *The Statesman's Yearbook 2008.*

Taylor and Francis Group, An Informa Business, 2 Park Square, Milton Park, Abingdon, Oxford OX14 4RN, United Kingdom, (Dial from U.S. (212) 216-7800), (Fax from U.S. (212) 564-7854), www.tandf.co.uk; *The Europa World Year Book.*

UCLA Latin American Institute, 10343 Bunche Hall, Box 951447, Los Angeles, CA 90095-1447, (310) 825-4571, Fax: (310) 206-6859, www.international.ucla.edu/lac; *Statistical Abstract of Latin America.*

United Nations Statistics Division, New York, NY 10017, (800) 253-9646, Fax: (212) 963-4116, http://unstats.un.org; *National Accounts Statistics: Compendium of Income Distribution Statistics* and *Statistical Yearbook.*

The World Bank, 1818 H Street, NW, Washington, DC 20433, (202) 473-1000, Fax: (202) 477-6391, www.worldbank.org; *World Development Report 2008.*

EL SALVADOR - POPULATION

Central Intelligence Agency, Office of Public Affairs, Washington, DC 20505, (703) 482-0623, Fax: (703) 482-1739, www.cia.gov; *The World Factbook.*

Economist Intelligence Unit, 111 West 57th Street, New York, NY 10019, (212) 554-0600, Fax: (212) 586-1181, www.eiu.com; *Business Latin America* and *El Salvador Country Report.*

Euromonitor International, Inc., 224 S. Michigan Avenue, Suite 1500, Chicago, IL 60604, (312) 922-1115, Fax: (312) 922-1157, www.euromonitor.com; *International Marketing Data and Statistics 2008* and *The World Economic Factbook 2008.*

Inter-American Development Bank (IDB), 1300 New York Avenue, NW, Washington, DC 20577, (202) 623-1000, Fax: (202) 623-3096, www.iadb.org; *The Politics of Policies: Economic and Social Progress in Latin America - 2006 Report.*

International Labour Office, I.L.O. Publications, 4 route des Morillons, CH-1211 Geneva 22, Switzerland, (Telephone in U.S. (202) 653-7652), (Fax in U.S. (202) 653-7687), www.ilo.org; *Yearbook of Labour Statistics 2006.*

M.E. Sharpe, 80 Business Park Drive, Armonk, NY 10504, (800) 541-6563, Fax: (914) 273-2106, www.mesharpe.com; *The Illustrated Book of World Rankings.*

Organization of American States (OAS), 17th Street Constitution Avenue NW, Washington, DC 20006, (202) 458-3000, www.oas.org; *The OAS in Transition: 1994-2004.*

Palgrave Macmillan Ltd., Houndmills, Basingstoke, Hampshire, RG21 6XS, England, (Telephone in U.S. (888) 330-8477), (Fax in U.S. (800) 672-2054), www.palgrave.com; *The Statesman's Yearbook 2008.*

Taylor and Francis Group, An Informa Business, 2 Park Square, Milton Park, Abingdon, Oxford OX14 4RN, United Kingdom, (Dial from U.S. (212) 216-7800), (Fax from U.S. (212) 564-7854), www.tandf.co.uk; *The Europa World Year Book.*

U.S. Department of State (DOS), 2201 C Street NW, Washington, DC 20520, (202) 647-4000, www.state.gov; *World Military Expenditures and Arms Transfers (WMEAT).*

UCLA Latin American Institute, 10343 Bunche Hall, Box 951447, Los Angeles, CA 90095-1447, (310) 825-4571, Fax: (310) 206-6859, www.international.ucla.edu/lac; *Statistical Abstract of Latin America.*

UNESCO Institute for Statistics, C.P. 6128 Succursale Centre-Ville, Montreal, Quebec, H3C 3J7 Canada, (Dial from U.S. (514) 343-6880), (Fax from U.S. (514) 343 6882), www.uis.unesco.org; *Statistical Tables.*

United Nations Food and Agricultural Organization (FAO), Viale delle Terme di Caracalla, 00100 Rome, Italy, (Dial from U.S. (202) 653-2400), (Fax from U.S. (202) 653 5760), www.fao.org; *FAO Production Yearbook 2002.*

United Nations Statistics Division, New York, NY 10017, (800) 253-9646, Fax: (212) 963-4116, http://unstats.un.org; *Demographic Yearbook; Human Development Report 2006; Statistical Yearbook; Statistical Yearbook for Latin America and the Caribbean 2004;* and *World Statistics Pocketbook.*

The World Bank, 1818 H Street, NW, Washington, DC 20433, (202) 473-1000, Fax: (202) 477-6391, www.worldbank.org; *El Salvador; The World Bank Atlas 2003-2004;* and *World Development Report 2008.*

World Health Organization (WHO), Avenue Appia 20, 1211 Geneve 27, Switzerland, (Telephone in U.S. (212) 331-9081), www.who.int; *World Health Report 2006.*

EL SALVADOR - POPULATION DENSITY

Central Intelligence Agency, Office of Public Affairs, Washington, DC 20505, (703) 482-0623, Fax: (703) 482-1739, www.cia.gov; *The World Factbook.*

Euromonitor International, Inc., 224 S. Michigan Avenue, Suite 1500, Chicago, IL 60604, (312) 922-1115, Fax: (312) 922-1157, www.euromonitor.com; *International Marketing Data and Statistics 2008* and *The World Economic Factbook 2008.*

Inter-American Development Bank (IDB), 1300 New York Avenue, NW, Washington, DC 20577, (202) 623-1000, Fax: (202) 623-3096, www.iadb.org; *The Politics of Policies: Economic and Social Progress in Latin America - 2006 Report.*

M.E. Sharpe, 80 Business Park Drive, Armonk, NY 10504, (800) 541-6563, Fax: (914) 273-2106, www.mesharpe.com; *The Illustrated Book of World Rankings.*

Palgrave Macmillan Ltd., Houndmills, Basingstoke, Hampshire, RG21 6XS, England, (Telephone in U.S. (888) 330-8477), (Fax in U.S. (800) 672-2054), www.palgrave.com; *The Statesman's Yearbook 2008.*

Taylor and Francis Group, An Informa Business, 2 Park Square, Milton Park, Abingdon, Oxford OX14 4RN, United Kingdom, (Dial from U.S. (212) 216-7800), (Fax from U.S. (212) 564-7854), www.tandf.co.uk; *The Europa World Year Book.*

UNESCO Institute for Statistics, C.P. 6128 Succursale Centre-Ville, Montreal, Quebec, H3C 3J7 Canada, (Dial from U.S. (514) 343-6880), (Fax from U.S. (514) 343 6882), www.uis.unesco.org; *Statistical Tables.*

United Nations Food and Agricultural Organization (FAO), Viale delle Terme di Caracalla, 00100 Rome, Italy, (Dial from U.S. (202) 653-2400), (Fax from U.S. (202) 653 5760), www.fao.org; *The State of Food and Agriculture (SOFA) 2006.*

United Nations Statistics Division, New York, NY 10017, (800) 253-9646, Fax: (212) 963-4116, http://unstats.un.org; *Statistical Yearbook.*

The World Bank, 1818 H Street, NW, Washington, DC 20433, (202) 473-1000, Fax: (202) 477-6391, www.worldbank.org; *El Salvador* and *World Development Report 2008.*

EL SALVADOR - POSTAL SERVICE

M.E. Sharpe, 80 Business Park Drive, Armonk, NY 10504, (800) 541-6563, Fax: (914) 273-2106, www.mesharpe.com; *The Illustrated Book of World Rankings.*

United Nations Statistics Division, New York, NY 10017, (800) 253-9646, Fax: (212) 963-4116, http://unstats.un.org; *Statistical Yearbook.*

EL SALVADOR - POWER RESOURCES

Economist Intelligence Unit, 111 West 57th Street, New York, NY 10019, (212) 554-0600, Fax: (212) 586-1181, www.eiu.com; *Business Latin America.*

Euromonitor International, Inc., 224 S. Michigan Avenue, Suite 1500, Chicago, IL 60604, (312) 922-1115, Fax: (312) 922-1157, www.euromonitor.com; *International Marketing Data and Statistics 2008; The World Economic Factbook 2008;* and *World Marketing Data and Statistics.*

M.E. Sharpe, 80 Business Park Drive, Armonk, NY 10504, (800) 541-6563, Fax: (914) 273-2106, www.mesharpe.com; *The Illustrated Book of World Rankings.*

Palgrave Macmillan Ltd., Houndmills, Basingstoke, Hampshire, RG21 6XS, England, (Telephone in U.S. (888) 330-8477), (Fax in U.S. (800) 672-2054), www.palgrave.com; *The Statesman's Yearbook 2008.*

Platts, 2 Penn Plaza, 25th Floor, New York, NY 10121-2298, (212) 904-3070, www.platts.com; *Energy Economist.*

U.S. Department of Energy (DOE), Energy Information Administration (EIA), 1000 Independence Avenue, SW, Washington, DC 20585, (202) 586-8800, www.eia.doe.gov; *International Energy Annual 2004* and *International Energy Outlook 2006.*

UCLA Latin American Institute, 10343 Bunche Hall, Box 951447, Los Angeles, CA 90095-1447, (310) 825-4571, Fax: (310) 206-6859, www.international.ucla.edu/lac; *Statistical Abstract of Latin America.*

United Nations Food and Agricultural Organization (FAO), Viale delle Terme di Caracalla, 00100 Rome, Italy, (Dial from U.S. (202) 653-2400), (Fax from U.S. (202) 653 5760), www.fao.org; *The State of Food and Agriculture (SOFA) 2006.*

United Nations Statistics Division, New York, NY 10017, (800) 253-9646, Fax: (212) 963-4116, http://unstats.un.org; *Energy Statistics Yearbook 2003; Human Development Report 2006; Statistical Yearbook; Statistical Yearbook for Latin America and the Caribbean 2004;* and *World Statistics Pocketbook.*

The World Bank, 1818 H Street, NW, Washington, DC 20433, (202) 473-1000, Fax: (202) 477-6391, www.worldbank.org; *The World Bank Atlas 2003-2004* and *World Development Report 2008.*

EL SALVADOR - PRICES

Economist Intelligence Unit, 111 West 57th Street, New York, NY 10019, (212) 554-0600, Fax: (212) 586-1181, www.eiu.com; *Business Latin America.*

Euromonitor International, Inc., 224 S. Michigan Avenue, Suite 1500, Chicago, IL 60604, (312) 922-1115, Fax: (312) 922-1157, www.euromonitor.com; *World Marketing Data and Statistics.*

International Labour Office, I.L.O. Publications, 4 route des Morillons, CH-1211 Geneva 22, Switzerland, (Telephone in U.S. (202) 653-7652), (Fax in U.S. (202) 653-7687), www.ilo.org; *Yearbook of Labour Statistics 2006.*

International Monetary Fund (IMF), 700 Nineteenth Street, NW, Washington, DC 20431, (202) 623-7000, Fax: (202) 623-4661, www.imf.org; *International Financial Statistics Yearbook 2007.*

M.E. Sharpe, 80 Business Park Drive, Armonk, NY 10504, (800) 541-6563, Fax: (914) 273-2106, www.mesharpe.com; *The Illustrated Book of World Rankings.*

Organization of American States (OAS), 17th Street Constitution Avenue NW, Washington, DC 20006, (202) 458-3000, www.oas.org; *The OAS in Transition: 1994-2004.*

UCLA Latin American Institute, 10343 Bunche Hall, Box 951447, Los Angeles, CA 90095-1447, (310) 825-4571, Fax: (310) 206-6859, www.international.ucla.edu/lac; *Statistical Abstract of Latin America.*

United Nations Food and Agricultural Organization (FAO), Viale delle Terme di Caracalla, 00100 Rome, Italy, (Dial from U.S. (202) 653-2400), (Fax from U.S. (202) 653 5760), www.fao.org; *FAO Production Yearbook 2002* and *The State of Food and Agriculture (SOFA) 2006.*

United Nations Statistics Division, New York, NY 10017, (800) 253-9646, Fax: (212) 963-4116, http://unstats.un.org; *Statistical Yearbook for Latin America and the Caribbean 2004.*

The World Bank, 1818 H Street, NW, Washington, DC 20433, (202) 473-1000, Fax: (202) 477-6391, www.worldbank.org; *El Salvador.*

EL SALVADOR - PROFESSIONS

UCLA Latin American Institute, 10343 Bunche Hall, Box 951447, Los Angeles, CA 90095-1447, (310) 825-4571, Fax: (310) 206-6859, www.international.ucla.edu/lac; *Statistical Abstract of Latin America.*

United Nations Statistics Division, New York, NY 10017, (800) 253-9646, Fax: (212) 963-4116, http://unstats.un.org; *Statistical Yearbook.*

EL SALVADOR - PUBLIC HEALTH

Economist Intelligence Unit, 111 West 57th Street, New York, NY 10019, (212) 554-0600, Fax: (212) 586-1181, www.eiu.com; *Business Latin America.*

Euromonitor International, Inc., 224 S. Michigan Avenue, Suite 1500, Chicago, IL 60604, (312) 922-1115, Fax: (312) 922-1157, www.euromonitor.com; *World Marketing Data and Statistics.*

International Monetary Fund (IMF), 700 Nineteenth Street, NW, Washington, DC 20431, (202) 623-7000, Fax: (202) 623-4661, www.imf.org; *Government Finance Statistics Yearbook (2008 Edition).*

M.E. Sharpe, 80 Business Park Drive, Armonk, NY 10504, (800) 541-6563, Fax: (914) 273-2106, www.mesharpe.com; *The Illustrated Book of World Rankings.*

Palgrave Macmillan Ltd., Houndmills, Basingstoke, Hampshire, RG21 6XS, England, (Telephone in U.S. (888) 330-8477), (Fax in U.S. (800) 672-2054), www.palgrave.com; *The Statesman's Yearbook 2008.*

UCLA Latin American Institute, 10343 Bunche Hall, Box 951447, Los Angeles, CA 90095-1447, (310) 825-4571, Fax: (310) 206-6859, www.international.ucla.edu/lac; *Statistical Abstract of Latin America.*

UNICEF, 3 United Nations Plaza, New York, NY 10017, (800) 253-9646, Fax: (212) 887-7465, www.unicef.org; *The State of the World's Children 2008.*

United Nations Statistics Division, New York, NY 10017, (800) 253-9646, Fax: (212) 963-4116, http://unstats.un.org; *Human Development Report 2006; Statistical Yearbook;* and *Statistical Yearbook for Latin America and the Caribbean 2004.*

The World Bank, 1818 H Street, NW, Washington, DC 20433, (202) 473-1000, Fax: (202) 477-6391, www.worldbank.org; *El Salvador* and *World Development Report 2008.*

World Health Organization (WHO), Avenue Appia 20, 1211 Geneve 27, Switzerland, (Telephone in U.S. (212) 331-9081), www.who.int; The WHO Global Atlas of Infectious Diseases and *World Health Report 2006.*

EL SALVADOR - PUBLIC UTILITIES

UCLA Latin American Institute, 10343 Bunche Hall, Box 951447, Los Angeles, CA 90095-1447, (310) 825-4571, Fax: (310) 206-6859, www.international.ucla.edu/lac; *Statistical Abstract of Latin America.*

EL SALVADOR - PUBLISHERS AND PUBLISHING

UNESCO Institute for Statistics, C.P. 6128 Succursale Centre-Ville, Montreal, Quebec, H3C 3J7 Canada, (Dial from U.S. (514) 343-6880), (Fax from U.S. (514) 343 6882), www.uis.unesco.org; *Statistical Tables.*

EL SALVADOR - RADIO BROADCASTING

Palgrave Macmillan Ltd., Houndmills, Basingstoke, Hampshire, RG21 6XS, England, (Telephone in U.S. (888) 330-8477), (Fax in U.S. (800) 672-2054), www.palgrave.com; *The Statesman's Yearbook 2008.*

EL SALVADOR - RAILROADS

Economist Intelligence Unit, 111 West 57th Street, New York, NY 10019, (212) 554-0600, Fax: (212) 586-1181, www.eiu.com; *Business Latin America.*

Jane's Information Group, 110 North Royal Street, Suite 200, Alexandria, VA 22314, (703) 683-3700, Fax: (800) 836-0297, www.janes.com; *Jane's World Railways.*

Palgrave Macmillan Ltd., Houndmills, Basingstoke, Hampshire, RG21 6XS, England, (Telephone in U.S. (888) 330-8477), (Fax in U.S. (800) 672-2054), www.palgrave.com; *The Statesman's Yearbook 2008.*

Taylor and Francis Group, An Informa Business, 2 Park Square, Milton Park, Abingdon, Oxford OX14 4RN, United Kingdom, (Dial from U.S. (212) 216-7800), (Fax from U.S. (212) 564-7854), www.tandf.co.uk; *The Europa World Year Book.*

EL SALVADOR - RANCHING

UCLA Latin American Institute, 10343 Bunche Hall, Box 951447, Los Angeles, CA 90095-1447, (310) 825-4571, Fax: (310) 206-6859, www.international.ucla.edu/lac; *Statistical Abstract of Latin America.*

EL SALVADOR - RELIGION

Central Intelligence Agency, Office of Public Affairs, Washington, DC 20505, (703) 482-0623, Fax: (703) 482-1739, www.cia.gov; *The World Factbook.*

M.E. Sharpe, 80 Business Park Drive, Armonk, NY 10504, (800) 541-6563, Fax: (914) 273-2106, www.mesharpe.com; *The Illustrated Book of World Rankings.*

Palgrave Macmillan Ltd., Houndmills, Basingstoke, Hampshire, RG21 6XS, England, (Telephone in U.S. (888) 330-8477), (Fax in U.S. (800) 672-2054), www.palgrave.com; *The Statesman's Yearbook 2008.*

UCLA Latin American Institute, 10343 Bunche Hall, Box 951447, Los Angeles, CA 90095-1447, (310) 825-4571, Fax: (310) 206-6859, www.international.ucla.edu/lac; *Statistical Abstract of Latin America.*

EL SALVADOR - RENT CHARGES

International Labour Office, I.L.O. Publications, 4 route des Morillons, CH-1211 Geneva 22, Switzerland, (Telephone in U.S. (202) 653-7652), (Fax in U.S. (202) 653-7687), www.ilo.org; *Yearbook of Labour Statistics 2006.*

EL SALVADOR - RESERVES (ACCOUNTING)

Economist Intelligence Unit, 111 West 57th Street, New York, NY 10019, (212) 554-0600, Fax: (212) 586-1181, www.eiu.com; *Business Latin America.*

Euromonitor International, Inc., 224 S. Michigan Avenue, Suite 1500, Chicago, IL 60604, (312) 922-1115, Fax: (312) 922-1157, www.euromonitor.com; *International Marketing Data and Statistics 2008.*

Inter-American Development Bank (IDB), 1300 New York Avenue, NW, Washington, DC 20577, (202) 623-1000, Fax: (202) 623-3096, www.iadb.org; *The Politics of Policies: Economic and Social Progress in Latin America - 2006 Report.*

United Nations Statistics Division, New York, NY 10017, (800) 253-9646, Fax: (212) 963-4116, http://unstats.un.org; *Statistical Yearbook.*

EL SALVADOR - RETAIL TRADE

Euromonitor International, Inc., 224 S. Michigan Avenue, Suite 1500, Chicago, IL 60604, (312) 922-1115, Fax: (312) 922-1157, www.euromonitor.com; *World Marketing Data and Statistics.*

Inter-American Development Bank (IDB), 1300 New York Avenue, NW, Washington, DC 20577, (202) 623-1000, Fax: (202) 623-3096, www.iadb.org; *The Politics of Policies: Economic and Social Progress in Latin America - 2006 Report.*

United Nations Statistics Division, New York, NY 10017, (800) 253-9646, Fax: (212) 963-4116, http://unstats.un.org; *Statistical Yearbook.*

EL SALVADOR - RICE PRODUCTION

See EL SALVADOR - CROPS

EL SALVADOR - ROADS

Central Intelligence Agency, Office of Public Affairs, Washington, DC 20505, (703) 482-0623, Fax: (703) 482-1739, www.cia.gov; *The World Factbook.*

Economist Intelligence Unit, 111 West 57th Street, New York, NY 10019, (212) 554-0600, Fax: (212) 586-1181, www.eiu.com; *Business Latin America.*

International Road Federation (IFR), Madison Place, 500 Montgomery Street, 5th Floor, Alexandria, VA 22314, (703) 535-1001, Fax: (703) 535-1007, www.irfnet.org; *World Road Statistics 2006.*

Palgrave Macmillan Ltd., Houndmills, Basingstoke, Hampshire, RG21 6XS, England, (Telephone in U.S. (888) 330-8477), (Fax in U.S. (800) 672-2054), www.palgrave.com; *The Statesman's Yearbook 2008.*

EL SALVADOR - RUBBER INDUSTRY AND TRADE

International Rubber Study Group (IRSG), 1st Floor, Heron House, 109/115 Wembley Hill Road, Wembley, Middlesex HA9 8DA, United Kingdom, www.rubberstudy.com; *Rubber Statistical Bulletin; Summary of World Rubber Statistics 2005; World Rubber Statistics Handbook (Volume 6, 1975-2001);* and *World Rubber Statistics Historic Handbook.*

M.E. Sharpe, 80 Business Park Drive, Armonk, NY 10504, (800) 541-6563, Fax: (914) 273-2106, www.mesharpe.com; *The Illustrated Book of World Rankings.*

EL SALVADOR - SHEEP

See EL SALVADOR - LIVESTOCK

EL SALVADOR - SHIPPING

Palgrave Macmillan Ltd., Houndmills, Basingstoke, Hampshire, RG21 6XS, England, (Telephone in U.S. (888) 330-8477), (Fax in U.S. (800) 672-2054), www.palgrave.com; *The Statesman's Yearbook 2008.*

Taylor and Francis Group, An Informa Business, 2 Park Square, Milton Park, Abingdon, Oxford OX14 4RN, United Kingdom, (Dial from U.S. (212) 216-7800), (Fax from U.S. (212) 564-7854), www.tandf.co.uk; *The Europa World Year Book.*

U.S. Department of Transportation (DOT), Maritime Administration (MARAD), West Building, Southeast Federal Center, 1200 New Jersey Avenue, SE, Washington, DC 20590, (800) 99-MARAD, www.marad.dot.gov; *World Merchant Fleet 2005.*

United Nations Statistics Division, New York, NY 10017, (800) 253-9646, Fax: (212) 963-4116, http://unstats.un.org; *Statistical Yearbook.*

EL SALVADOR - SILVER PRODUCTION

See EL SALVADOR - MINERAL INDUSTRIES

EL SALVADOR - SOCIAL ECOLOGY

M.E. Sharpe, 80 Business Park Drive, Armonk, NY 10504, (800) 541-6563, Fax: (914) 273-2106, www.mesharpe.com; *The Illustrated Book of World Rankings.*

UCLA Latin American Institute, 10343 Bunche Hall, Box 951447, Los Angeles, CA 90095-1447, (310) 825-4571, Fax: (310) 206-6859, www.international.ucla.edu/lac; *Statistical Abstract of Latin America.*

United Nations Statistics Division, New York, NY 10017, (800) 253-9646, Fax: (212) 963-4116, http://unstats.un.org; *World Statistics Pocketbook.*

EL SALVADOR - SOCIAL SECURITY

Inter-American Development Bank (IDB), 1300 New York Avenue, NW, Washington, DC 20577, (202) 623-1000, Fax: (202) 623-3096, www.iadb.org; *The Politics of Policies: Economic and Social Progress in Latin America - 2006 Report.*

International Monetary Fund (IMF), 700 Nineteenth Street, NW, Washington, DC 20431, (202) 623-7000, Fax: (202) 623-4661, www.imf.org; *Government Finance Statistics Yearbook (2008 Edition).*

Palgrave Macmillan Ltd., Houndmills, Basingstoke, Hampshire, RG21 6XS, England, (Telephone in U.S. (888) 330-8477), (Fax in U.S. (800) 672-2054), www.palgrave.com; *The Statesman's Yearbook 2008.*

United Nations Statistics Division, New York, NY 10017, (800) 253-9646, Fax: (212) 963-4116, http://unstats.un.org; *National Accounts Statistics: Compendium of Income Distribution Statistics.*

EL SALVADOR - SOYBEAN PRODUCTION

See EL SALVADOR - CROPS

EL SALVADOR - STEEL PRODUCTION

See EL SALVADOR - MINERAL INDUSTRIES

EL SALVADOR - SUGAR PRODUCTION

See EL SALVADOR - CROPS

EL SALVADOR - TAXATION

Inter-American Development Bank (IDB), 1300 New York Avenue, NW, Washington, DC 20577, (202) 623-1000, Fax: (202) 623-3096, www.iadb.org; *The Politics of Policies: Economic and Social Progress in Latin America - 2006 Report.*

International Monetary Fund (IMF), 700 Nineteenth Street, NW, Washington, DC 20431, (202) 623-7000, Fax: (202) 623-4661, www.imf.org; *Government Finance Statistics Yearbook (2008 Edition).*

International Road Federation (IFR), Madison Place, 500 Montgomery Street, 5th Floor, Alexandria, VA 22314, (703) 535-1001, Fax: (703) 535-1007, www.irfnet.org; *World Road Statistics 2006.*

Taylor and Francis Group, An Informa Business, 2 Park Square, Milton Park, Abingdon, Oxford OX14 4RN, United Kingdom, (Dial from U.S. (212) 216-7800), (Fax from U.S. (212) 564-7854), www.tandf.co.uk; *The Europa World Year Book.*

United Nations Statistics Division, New York, NY 10017, (800) 253-9646, Fax: (212) 963-4116, http://unstats.un.org; *Statistical Yearbook for Latin America and the Caribbean 2004.*

EL SALVADOR - TELEPHONE

Economist Intelligence Unit, 111 West 57th Street, New York, NY 10019, (212) 554-0600, Fax: (212) 586-1181, www.eiu.com; *Business Latin America.*

International Telecommunication Union (ITU), Place des Nations, 1211 Geneva 20, Switzerland, www.itu.int; World Telecommunication Indicators Database.

Palgrave Macmillan Ltd., Houndmills, Basingstoke, Hampshire, RG21 6XS, England, (Telephone in U.S. (888) 330-8477), (Fax in U.S. (800) 672-2054), www.palgrave.com; *The Statesman's Yearbook 2008.*

Taylor and Francis Group, An Informa Business, 2 Park Square, Milton Park, Abingdon, Oxford OX14 4RN, United Kingdom, (Dial from U.S. (212) 216-7800), (Fax from U.S. (212) 564-7854), www.tandf.co.uk; *The Europa World Year Book.*

United Nations Statistics Division, New York, NY 10017, (800) 253-9646, Fax: (212) 963-4116, http://unstats.un.org; *Statistical Yearbook* and *World Statistics Pocketbook.*

EL SALVADOR - TELEVISION - RECEIVERS AND RECEPTION

United Nations Statistics Division, New York, NY 10017, (800) 253-9646, Fax: (212) 963-4116, http://unstats.un.org; *Statistical Yearbook.*

EL SALVADOR - TEXTILE INDUSTRY

M.E. Sharpe, 80 Business Park Drive, Armonk, NY 10504, (800) 541-6563, Fax: (914) 273-2106, www.mesharpe.com; *The Illustrated Book of World Rankings.*

United Nations Conference on Trade and Development (UNCTAD), DC2-1120, United Nations, New York, NY 10017, (212) 963-0027, www.unctad.org; *UNCTAD Commodity Yearbook.*

United Nations Statistics Division, New York, NY 10017, (800) 253-9646, Fax: (212) 963-4116, http://unstats.un.org; *Statistical Yearbook.*

EL SALVADOR - TOBACCO INDUSTRY

Foreign Agricultural Service (FAS), U.S. Department of Agriculture (USDA), 1400 Independence Avenue, SW, Washington, DC 20250, (202) 720-3935, www.fas.usda.gov; *Tobacco: World Markets and Trade.*

M.E. Sharpe, 80 Business Park Drive, Armonk, NY 10504, (800) 541-6563, Fax: (914) 273-2106, www.mesharpe.com; *The Illustrated Book of World Rankings.*

United Nations Statistics Division, New York, NY 10017, (800) 253-9646, Fax: (212) 963-4116, http://unstats.un.org; *Statistical Yearbook.*

EL SALVADOR - TOURISM

Economist Intelligence Unit, 111 West 57th Street, New York, NY 10019, (212) 554-0600, Fax: (212) 586-1181, www.eiu.com; *Business Latin America.*

Euromonitor International, Inc., 224 S. Michigan Avenue, Suite 1500, Chicago, IL 60604, (312) 922-1115, Fax: (312) 922-1157, www.euromonitor.com; *World Marketing Data and Statistics.*

M.E. Sharpe, 80 Business Park Drive, Armonk, NY 10504, (800) 541-6563, Fax: (914) 273-2106, www.mesharpe.com; *The Illustrated Book of World Rankings.*

Palgrave Macmillan Ltd., Houndmills, Basingstoke, Hampshire, RG21 6XS, England, (Telephone in U.S. (888) 330-8477), (Fax in U.S. (800) 672-2054), www.palgrave.com; *The Statesman's Yearbook 2008.*

Taylor and Francis Group, An Informa Business, 2 Park Square, Milton Park, Abingdon, Oxford OX14 4RN, United Kingdom, (Dial from U.S. (212) 216-7800), (Fax from U.S. (212) 564-7854), www.tandf.co.uk; *The Europa World Year Book.*

UCLA Latin American Institute, 10343 Bunche Hall, Box 951447, Los Angeles, CA 90095-1447, (310) 825-4571, Fax: (310) 206-6859, www.international.ucla.edu/lac; *Statistical Abstract of Latin America.*

United Nations Statistics Division, New York, NY 10017, (800) 253-9646, Fax: (212) 963-4116, http://unstats.un.org; *Statistical Yearbook* and *Statistical Yearbook for Latin America and the Caribbean 2004.*

United Nations World Tourism Organization (UNWTO), Capitan Haya 42, 28020 Madrid, Spain, www.world-tourism.org; *Yearbook of Tourism Statistics.*

The World Bank, 1818 H Street, NW, Washington, DC 20433, (202) 473-1000, Fax: (202) 477-6391, www.worldbank.org; *El Salvador.*

EL SALVADOR - TRADE

See EL SALVADOR - INTERNATIONAL TRADE

EL SALVADOR - TRANSPORTATION

Central Intelligence Agency, Office of Public Affairs, Washington, DC 20505, (703) 482-0623, Fax: (703) 482-1739, www.cia.gov; *The World Factbook.*

Economist Intelligence Unit, 111 West 57th Street, New York, NY 10019, (212) 554-0600, Fax: (212) 586-1181, www.eiu.com; *Business Latin America.*

Euromonitor International, Inc., 224 S. Michigan Avenue, Suite 1500, Chicago, IL 60604, (312) 922-1115, Fax: (312) 922-1157, www.euromonitor.com; *International Marketing Data and Statistics 2008* and *World Marketing Data and Statistics.*

Inter-American Development Bank (IDB), 1300 New York Avenue, NW, Washington, DC 20577, (202) 623-1000, Fax: (202) 623-3096, www.iadb.org; *The Politics of Policies: Economic and Social Progress in Latin America - 2006 Report.*

M.E. Sharpe, 80 Business Park Drive, Armonk, NY 10504, (800) 541-6563, Fax: (914) 273-2106, www.mesharpe.com; *The Illustrated Book of World Rankings.*

Palgrave Macmillan Ltd., Houndmills, Basingstoke, Hampshire, RG21 6XS, England, (Telephone in U.S. (888) 330-8477), (Fax in U.S. (800) 672-2054), www.palgrave.com; *The Statesman's Yearbook 2008.*

Taylor and Francis Group, An Informa Business, 2 Park Square, Milton Park, Abingdon, Oxford OX14 4RN, United Kingdom, (Dial from U.S. (212) 216-7800), (Fax from U.S. (212) 564-7854), www.tandf.co.uk; *The Europa World Year Book.*

UCLA Latin American Institute, 10343 Bunche Hall, Box 951447, Los Angeles, CA 90095-1447, (310) 825-4571, Fax: (310) 206-6859, www.international.ucla.edu/lac; *Statistical Abstract of Latin America.*

United Nations Statistics Division, New York, NY 10017, (800) 253-9646, Fax: (212) 963-4116, http://unstats.un.org; *Human Development Report 2006* and *Statistical Yearbook for Latin America and the Caribbean 2004.*

The World Bank, 1818 H Street, NW, Washington, DC 20433, (202) 473-1000, Fax: (202) 477-6391, www.worldbank.org; *El Salvador.*

EL SALVADOR - UNEMPLOYMENT

Central Intelligence Agency, Office of Public Affairs, Washington, DC 20505, (703) 482-0623, Fax: (703) 482-1739, www.cia.gov; *The World Factbook.*

Economist Intelligence Unit, 111 West 57th Street, New York, NY 10019, (212) 554-0600, Fax: (212) 586-1181, www.eiu.com; *Business Latin America.*

Euromonitor International, Inc., 224 S. Michigan Avenue, Suite 1500, Chicago, IL 60604, (312) 922-1115, Fax: (312) 922-1157, www.euromonitor.com; *International Marketing Data and Statistics 2008.*

International Labour Office, I.L.O. Publications, 4 route des Morillons, CH-1211 Geneva 22, Switzerland, (Telephone in U.S. (202) 653-7652), (Fax in U.S. (202) 653-7687), www.ilo.org; *Yearbook of Labour Statistics 2006.*

Palgrave Macmillan Ltd., Houndmills, Basingstoke, Hampshire, RG21 6XS, England, (Telephone in U.S. (888) 330-8477), (Fax in U.S. (800) 672-2054), www.palgrave.com; *The Statesman's Yearbook 2008.*

UCLA Latin American Institute, 10343 Bunche Hall, Box 951447, Los Angeles, CA 90095-1447, (310) 825-4571, Fax: (310) 206-6859, www.international.ucla.edu/lac; *Statistical Abstract of Latin America.*

EL SALVADOR - VITAL STATISTICS

Euromonitor International, Inc., 224 S. Michigan Avenue, Suite 1500, Chicago, IL 60604, (312) 922-1115, Fax: (312) 922-1157, www.euromonitor.com; *International Marketing Data and Statistics 2008.*

Palgrave Macmillan Ltd., Houndmills, Basingstoke, Hampshire, RG21 6XS, England, (Telephone in U.S. (888) 330-8477), (Fax in U.S. (800) 672-2054), www.palgrave.com; *The Statesman's Yearbook 2008.*

United Nations Statistics Division, New York, NY 10017, (800) 253-9646, Fax: (212) 963-4116, http://unstats.un.org; *Statistical Yearbook.*

World Health Organization (WHO), Avenue Appia 20, 1211 Geneve 27, Switzerland, (Telephone in U.S. (212) 331-9081), www.who.int; *World Health Report 2006.*

EL SALVADOR - WAGES

International Labour Office, I.L.O. Publications, 4 route des Morillons, CH-1211 Geneva 22, Switzerland, (Telephone in U.S. (202) 653-7652), (Fax in U.S. (202) 653-7687), www.ilo.org; *Yearbook of Labour Statistics 2006.*

UCLA Latin American Institute, 10343 Bunche Hall, Box 951447, Los Angeles, CA 90095-1447, (310) 825-4571, Fax: (310) 206-6859, www.international.ucla.edu/lac; *Statistical Abstract of Latin America.*

United Nations Statistics Division, New York, NY 10017, (800) 253-9646, Fax: (212) 963-4116, http://unstats.un.org; *Statistical Yearbook.*

The World Bank, 1818 H Street, NW, Washington, DC 20433, (202) 473-1000, Fax: (202) 477-6391, www.worldbank.org; *El Salvador.*

EL SALVADOR - WEATHER

See EL SALVADOR - CLIMATE

EL SALVADOR - WELFARE STATE

Inter-American Development Bank (IDB), 1300 New York Avenue, NW, Washington, DC 20577, (202) 623-1000, Fax: (202) 623-3096, www.iadb.org; *The Politics of Policies: Economic and Social Progress in Latin America - 2006 Report.*

International Monetary Fund (IMF), 700 Nineteenth Street, NW, Washington, DC 20431, (202) 623-7000, Fax: (202) 623-4661, www.imf.org; *Government Finance Statistics Yearbook (2008 Edition).*

Palgrave Macmillan Ltd., Houndmills, Basingstoke, Hampshire, RG21 6XS, England, (Telephone in U.S. (888) 330-8477), (Fax in U.S. (800) 672-2054), www.palgrave.com; *The Statesman's Yearbook 2008.*

EL SALVADOR - WHEAT PRODUCTION

See EL SALVADOR - CROPS

EL SALVADOR - WHOLESALE PRICE INDEXES

Inter-American Development Bank (IDB), 1300 New York Avenue, NW, Washington, DC 20577, (202) 623-1000, Fax: (202) 623-3096, www.iadb.org; *The Politics of Policies: Economic and Social Progress in Latin America - 2006 Report.*

International Monetary Fund (IMF), 700 Nineteenth Street, NW, Washington, DC 20431, (202) 623-7000, Fax: (202) 623-4661, www.imf.org; *International Financial Statistics Yearbook 2007.*

Organization of American States (OAS), 17th Street Constitution Avenue NW, Washington, DC 20006, (202) 458-3000, www.oas.org; *The OAS in Transition: 1994-2004.*

United Nations Statistics Division, New York, NY 10017, (800) 253-9646, Fax: (212) 963-4116, http://unstats.un.org; *Statistical Yearbook.*

EL SALVADOR - WHOLESALE TRADE

Inter-American Development Bank (IDB), 1300 New York Avenue, NW, Washington, DC 20577, (202) 623-1000, Fax: (202) 623-3096, www.iadb.org; *The Politics of Policies: Economic and Social Progress in Latin America - 2006 Report.*

United Nations Statistics Division, New York, NY 10017, (800) 253-9646, Fax: (212) 963-4116, http://unstats.un.org; *Statistical Yearbook.*

EL SALVADOR - WINE PRODUCTION

See EL SALVADOR - BEVERAGE INDUSTRY

EL SALVADOR - WOOL PRODUCTION

See EL SALVADOR - TEXTILE INDUSTRY

EL SALVADOR - YARN PRODUCTION

See EL SALVADOR - TEXTILE INDUSTRY

ELDERLY

See OLDER PEOPLE

ELECTIONS

Congressional Quarterly, Inc., 1255 22nd Street, NW, Washington, DC 20037, (202) 419-8500, www.cq.com; *Political Handbook of the World 2008.*

Electoral Vote Predictor, www.electoral-vote.com; www.electoral-vote.com.

PollingReport.com, www.pollingreport.com; *Election 2008.*

United Nations Development Programme, One United Nations Plaza, New York, NY 10017, (212) 906-5000, Fax: (212) 906-5364, www.undp.org; *Getting to the CORE: A Global Survey on the Cost of Registration and Elections.*

ELECTIONS - BLACK ELECTED OFFICIALS

Joint Center for Political and Economic Studies, 1090 Vermont Avenue, NW, Suite 1100, Washington, DC 20005-4928, (202) 789-3500, Fax: (202) 789-6390, www.jointcenter.org; *Black Elected Officials: A Statistical Summary.*

ELECTIONS - CAMPAIGN FINANCES

Federal Election Commission (FEC), 999 E Street, NW, Washington, DC 20463, (800) 424-9530, www.fec.gov; *Annual Report 2006; Combined Federal/State Disclosure and Election Directory 2008;* and unpublished data.

ELECTIONS - CONGRESSIONAL

Congressional Quarterly, Inc., 1255 22nd Street, NW, Washington, DC 20037, (202) 419-8500, www.cq.com; *America Votes 27: Election Returns by State, 2005-2006; Congressional Quarterly Weekly Report; CQ Congress Collection; CQ's Politics in America 2006: The 109th Congress;* and *Statistical History of the American Electorate.*

Electoral Vote Predictor, www.electoral-vote.com; www.electoral-vote.com.

Federal Election Commission (FEC), 999 E Street, NW, Washington, DC 20463, (800) 424-9530, www.fec.gov; *Federal Elections 2006: Election Results for the U.S. Senate and the U.S. House of Representatives.*

The Green Papers, www.thegreenpapers.com; www.thegreenpapers.com.

PollingReport.com, www.pollingreport.com; *Election 2008.*

ELECTIONS - GUBERNATORIAL

The Green Papers, www.thegreenpapers.com; www.thegreenpapers.com.

National Governors Association (NGA), Hall of the States, Suite 267, 444 North Capitol Street, NW, Washington, DC 20001-1512, (202) 624-5300, Fax: (202) 624-5313, www.nga.org; *Governors Database.*

ELECTIONS - HISPANIC ORIGIN OFFICIALS

National Association of Latino Elected and Appointed Officials (NALEO) Educational Fund, 1122 West Washington Blvd., 3rd Floor, Los Angeles CA 90015, (213) 747-7606, Fax: (213) 747-7664, www.naleo.org; *2006 National Directory of Latino Elected Officials.*

ELECTIONS - POLITICAL ACTION COMMITTEES (PACS)

Federal Election Commission (FEC), 999 E Street, NW, Washington, DC 20463, (800) 424-9530, www.fec.gov; *Annual Report 2006; Combined Federal/State Disclosure and Election Directory 2008;* and unpublished data.

ELECTIONS - PRESIDENTIAL

Congressional Quarterly, Inc., 1255 22nd Street, NW, Washington, DC 20037, (202) 419-8500, www.cq.com; *America at the Polls, 1960-2004; America Votes 27: Election Returns by State, 2005-2006; Historical Atlas of U.S. Presidential Elections 1789-2004; Statistical History of the American Electorate;* and *Vital Statistics on American Politics 2007-2008.*

Electoral Vote Predictor, www.electoral-vote.com; www.electoral-vote.com.

Federal Election Commission (FEC), 999 E Street, NW, Washington, DC 20463, (800) 424-9530, www.fec.gov; unpublished data.

The Green Papers, www.thegreenpapers.com; www.thegreenpapers.com.

PollingReport.com, www.pollingreport.com; *Election 2008.*

U.S. Congress, Office of the Clerk, U.S. Capitol, Room H154, Washington, DC 20515-6601, (202) 225-7000, http://clerk.house.gov; *Statistics of the Presidential and Congressional Election.*

ELECTIONS - STATE LEGISLATURES

Congressional Quarterly, Inc., 1255 22nd Street, NW, Washington, DC 20037, (202) 419-8500, www.cq.com; *Almanac of State Legislatures.*

Council of State Governments (CSG), 2760 Research Park Drive, PO Box 11910, Lexington, KY 40511-1910, (859) 244-8000, Fax: (859) 244-8001, www.csg.org; *CSG Directory One: Elective Officials, 2006.*

The Green Papers, www.thegreenpapers.com; www.thegreenpapers.com.

National Conference of State Legislatures (NCSL), 7700 East First Place, Denver, CO 80230, (303) 364-7700, Fax: (303) 364-7800, www.ncsl.org; *State Legislatures* and unpublished data.

ELECTIONS - VOTER REGISTRATION

Congressional Quarterly, Inc., 1255 22nd Street, NW, Washington, DC 20037, (202) 419-8500, www.cq.com; *America Votes 27: Election Returns by State, 2005-2006; Congressional Quarterly Weekly Report; CQ Congress Collection;* and *Statistical History of the American Electorate.*

U.S. Census Bureau, 4700 Silver Hill Road, Washington DC 20233-0001, (301) 763-3030, www.census.gov; unpublished data.

U.S. Census Bureau, Population Division, 4700 Silver Hill Road, Washington DC 20233-0001, (301) 763-3030, www.census.gov/population/www/; *Current Population Reports.*

United Nations Development Programme, One United Nations Plaza, New York, NY 10017, (212) 906-5000, Fax: (212) 906-5364, www.undp.org; *Getting to the CORE: A Global Survey on the Cost of Registration and Elections.*

ELECTIONS - VOTER TURNOUT

Congressional Quarterly, Inc., 1255 22nd Street, NW, Washington, DC 20037, (202) 419-8500, www.cq.com; *Congressional Quarterly Weekly Report* and *CQ Congress Collection.*

U.S. Census Bureau, 4700 Silver Hill Road, Washington DC 20233-0001, (301) 763-3030, www.census.gov; unpublished data.

U.S. Census Bureau, Population Division, 4700 Silver Hill Road, Washington DC 20233-0001, (301) 763-3030, www.census.gov/population/www/; *Current Population Reports.*

ELECTIONS - VOTES CAST

Congressional Quarterly, Inc., 1255 22nd Street, NW, Washington, DC 20037, (202) 419-8500, www.cq.com; *America Votes 27: Election Returns by State, 2005-2006; Congressional Quarterly Weekly Report; CQ Congress Collection; Presidential Primaries and Caucuses; Statistical History of the American Electorate;* and *Vital Statistics on American Politics 2007-2008.*

The Eagleton Institute of Politics, Rutgers, The State University of New Jersey, 191 Ryders Lane, New Brunswick, NJ 08901-8557, (732) 932-9384, Fax: (732) 932-6778, www.eagleton.rutgers.edu; *America's Newest Voters: Understanding Immigrant and Minority Voting Behavior.*

U.S. Census Bureau, 4700 Silver Hill Road, Washington DC 20233-0001, (301) 763-3030, www.census.gov; unpublished data.

U.S. Congress, Office of the Clerk, U.S. Capitol, Room H154, Washington, DC 20515-6601, (202) 225-7000, http://clerk.house.gov; *Statistics of the Presidential and Congressional Election.*

ELECTIONS - VOTING AGE POPULATION

Congressional Quarterly, Inc., 1255 22nd Street, NW, Washington, DC 20037, (202) 419-8500, www.cq.com; *Congressional Quarterly Weekly Report* and *CQ Congress Collection.*

U.S. Census Bureau, 4700 Silver Hill Road, Washington DC 20233-0001, (301) 763-3030, www.census.gov; unpublished data.

U.S. Census Bureau, Population Division, 4700 Silver Hill Road, Washington DC 20233-0001, (301) 763-3030, www.census.gov/population/www/; *Current Population Reports.*

ELECTIONS - WOMEN IN PUBLIC OFFICE

The Eagleton Institute of Politics, Rutgers, The State University of New Jersey, 191 Ryders Lane, New Brunswick, NJ 08901-8557, (732) 932-9384, Fax: (732) 932-6778, www.eagleton.rutgers.edu; unpublished data.

ELECTRIC LIGHT AND POWER INDUSTRY

Federal Bureau of Statistics (FBS), 5-SLIC Building, F-6/4, Blue Area, Islamabad, Pakistan, www.statpak.gov.pk/depts; *Census of Electricity Establishments 2003-04.*

U.S. Library of Congress (LOC), Congressional Research Service (CRS), The Library of Congress, 101 Independence Avenue, SE, Washington, DC 20540-7500, (202) 707-5700, www.loc.gov/crsinfo; *Energy: Selected Facts and Numbers.*

ELECTRIC LIGHT AND POWER INDUSTRY - CAPITAL EXPENDITURES

U.S. Census Bureau, Company Statistics Division, 4700 Silver Hill Road, Washington DC 20233-0001, (301) 763-3030, www.census.gov/csd/; *Annual Capital Expenditures Survey (ACES).*

ELECTRIC LIGHT AND POWER INDUSTRY - CONSTRUCTION COSTS

U.S. Census Bureau, Manufacturing and Construction Division, 4600 Silver Hill Road, Washington DC 20233, (301) 763-4673, www.census.gov/mcd; *Census of Construction Industries* and *Current Construction Reports.*

ELECTRIC LIGHT AND POWER INDUSTRY - CUSTOMERS

American Gas Association, 400 North Capitol Street, NW, Washington, DC 20001-1535, (202) 824-7000, www.aga.org; *Gas Facts.*

Edison Electric Institute (EEI), 701 Pennsylvania Avenue, NW, Washington, DC 20004-2696, (202) 508-5000, www.eei.org; *Weekly Electric Output* and *Statistical Yearbook of the Electric Power Industry - 2005 Data.*

ELECTRIC LIGHT AND POWER INDUSTRY - EMISSIONS

Platts, 2 Penn Plaza, 25th Floor, New York, NY 10121-2298, (212) 904-3070, www.platts.com; *Emissions Daily.*

U.S. Department of Energy (DOE), Energy Information Administration (EIA), 1000 Independence Avenue, SW, Washington, DC 20585, (202) 586-8800, www.eia.doe.gov; *Emissions of Greenhouse Gases in the United States 2005.*

U.S. Environmental Protection Agency (EPA), Ariel Rios Building, 1200 Pennsylvania Avenue, NW, Washington, DC 20460, (202) 272-0167, www.epa.gov; *National Emission Inventory (NEI) Database.*

ELECTRIC LIGHT AND POWER INDUSTRY - FINANCES

Edison Electric Institute (EEI), 701 Pennsylvania Avenue, NW, Washington, DC 20004-2696, (202) 508-5000, www.eei.org; *Historical Statistics of the Electric Utility Industry through 1992; Profiles and Rankings Data Tables - May 2007;* and *Profiles and Rankings of Shareholder-Owned Electric Companies - May 2007.*

U.S. Census Bureau, Center for Economic Studies, 4600 Silver Hill Road, Washington DC 20233, (301) 457-1235, www.ces.census.gov; *2002 Economic Census, Utilities.*

U.S. Department of Energy (DOE), Energy Information Administration (EIA), 1000 Independence Avenue, SW, Washington, DC 20585, (202) 586-8800, www.eia.doe.gov; *Electric Power Annual.*

ELECTRIC LIGHT AND POWER INDUSTRY - GENERAL CAPABILITY

Edison Electric Institute (EEI), 701 Pennsylvania Avenue, NW, Washington, DC 20004-2696, (202) 508-5000, www.eei.org; *Historical Statistics of the Electric Utility Industry through 1992* and *Statistical Yearbook of the Electric Power Industry - 2005 Data.*

U.S. Department of Energy (DOE), Energy Information Administration (EIA), 1000 Independence Avenue, SW, Washington, DC 20585, (202) 586-8800, www.eia.doe.gov; *Annual Energy Review 2005; Electric Power Annual;* and unpublished data.

ELECTRIC LIGHT AND POWER INDUSTRY - GENERAL CAPACITY, INSTALLED

Edison Electric Institute (EEI), 701 Pennsylvania Avenue, NW, Washington, DC 20004-2696, (202) 508-5000, www.eei.org; *Historical Statistics of the Electric Utility Industry through 1992.*

U.S. Department of Energy (DOE), Energy Information Administration (EIA), 1000 Independence Avenue, SW, Washington, DC 20585, (202) 586-8800, www.eia.doe.gov; *Electric Power Annual; Electric Power Monthly (EPM);* and *Inventory of Electric Utility Power Plants in the United States 2000.*

ELECTRIC LIGHT AND POWER INDUSTRY - MULTINATIONAL COMPANIES

Bureau of Economic Analysis (BEA), U.S. Department of Commerce (DOC), 1441 L Street NW, Washington, DC 20230, (202) 606-9900, www.bea.gov; *Survey of Current Business (SCB).*

ELECTRIC LIGHT AND POWER INDUSTRY - OWNERSHIP - CLASS OF

Edison Electric Institute (EEI), 701 Pennsylvania Avenue, NW, Washington, DC 20004-2696, (202) 508-5000, www.eei.org; *Historical Statistics of the Electric Utility Industry through 1992* and *Profiles and Rankings Data Tables - May 2007.*

U.S. Department of Energy (DOE), Energy Information Administration (EIA), 1000 Independence Avenue, SW, Washington, DC 20585, (202) 586-8800, www.eia.doe.gov; *Annual Energy Review 2005; Electric Power Annual;* and unpublished data.

ELECTRIC LIGHT AND POWER INDUSTRY - PEAK LOAD

Edison Electric Institute (EEI), 701 Pennsylvania Avenue, NW, Washington, DC 20004-2696, (202) 508-5000, www.eei.org; *Statistical Yearbook of the Electric Power Industry - 2005 Data.*

ELECTRIC LIGHT AND POWER INDUSTRY - WATER USE

U.S. Department of the Interior (DOI), U.S. Geological Survey (USGS), Water Resources Discipline (WRD), 12201 Sunrise Valley Drive, Reston, VA 20192, (888) 275-8747, http://water.usgs.gov; *Estimated Use of Water in the United States.*

ELECTRICAL EQUIPMENT MANUFACTURING - CAPITAL

Bureau of Economic Analysis (BEA), U.S. Department of Commerce (DOC), 1441 L Street NW, Washington, DC 20230, (202) 606-9900, www.bea.gov; *Survey of Current Business (SCB).*

ELECTRICAL EQUIPMENT MANUFACTURING - EARNINGS

U.S. Census Bureau, Manufacturing and Construction Division, 4600 Silver Hill Road, Washington DC 20233, (301) 763-4673, www.census.gov/mcd; *Annual Survey of Manufactures (ASM)* and *Census of Manufactures.*

U.S. Department of Commerce (DOC), Economics and Statistics Administration (ESA), 1401 Constitution Avenue, NW, Washington, DC 20230, (800) 782-8872, www.esa.doc.gov; *The Digital Economy 2003.*

ELECTRICAL EQUIPMENT MANUFACTURING - EMPLOYEES

U.S. Bureau of Labor Statistics (BLS), Postal Square Building, 2 Massachusetts Avenue, NE, Washington, DC 20212-0001, (202) 691-5200, Fax: (202) 691-6325, www.bls.gov; *Current Employment Statistics Survey (CES); Employment and Earnings (EE);* and *Monthly Labor Review (MLR).*

U.S. Census Bureau, Manufacturing and Construction Division, 4600 Silver Hill Road, Washington DC 20233, (301) 763-4673, www.census.gov/mcd; *Annual Survey of Manufactures (ASM)* and *Census of Manufactures.*

ELECTRICAL EQUIPMENT MANUFACTURING - ENERGY CONSUMPTION

U.S. Department of Energy (DOE), Energy Information Administration (EIA), 1000 Independence Avenue, SW, Washington, DC 20585, (202) 586-8800, www.eia.doe.gov; *Manufacturing Energy Consumption Survey (MECS) 2002.*

ELECTRICAL EQUIPMENT MANUFACTURING - FINANCES

Bureau of Economic Analysis (BEA), U.S. Department of Commerce (DOC), 1441 L Street NW, Washington, DC 20230, (202) 606-9900, www.bea.gov; *2007 Annual Revision of the National Income and Product Accounts (NIPA)* and *Survey of Current Business (SCB).*

Forbes, Inc., 60 Fifth Avenue, New York, NY 10011, (212) 366-8900, www.forbes.com; *America's Largest Private Companies.*

ELECTRICAL EQUIPMENT MANUFACTURING - GROSS DOMESTIC PRODUCT

Bureau of Economic Analysis (BEA), U.S. Department of Commerce (DOC), 1441 L Street NW, Washington, DC 20230, (202) 606-9900, www.bea.gov; *Survey of Current Business (SCB).*

U.S. Department of Commerce (DOC), Economics and Statistics Administration (ESA), 1401 Constitution Avenue, NW, Washington, DC 20230, (800) 782-8872, www.esa.doc.gov; *The Digital Economy 2003.*

ELECTRICAL EQUIPMENT MANUFACTURING - INDUSTRIAL SAFETY

U.S. Bureau of Labor Statistics (BLS), Postal Square Building, 2 Massachusetts Avenue, NE, Washington, DC 20212-0001, (202) 691-5200, Fax: (202) 691-6325, www.bls.gov; *Injuries, Illnesses, and Fatalities (IIF).*

ELECTRICAL EQUIPMENT MANUFACTURING - INTERNATIONAL TRADE

U.S. Census Bureau, Foreign Trade Division, 4700 Silver Hill Road, Washington DC 20233-0001, (301) 763-3030, www.census.gov/foreign-trade/www/; *U.S. International Trade in Goods and Services.*

ELECTRICAL EQUIPMENT MANUFACTURING - MERGERS AND ACQUISITIONS

Thomson Financial, 195 Broadway, New York, NY 10007, (646) 822-2000, www.thomson.com; Thomson Research.

ELECTRICAL EQUIPMENT MANUFACTURING - PRODUCTIVITY

Board of Governors of the Federal Reserve System, Constitution Avenue, NW, Washington, DC 20551, (202) 452-3000, www.federalreserve.gov; *Federal Reserve Bulletin* and *Industrial Production and Capacity Utilization.*

U.S. Bureau of Labor Statistics (BLS), Postal Square Building, 2 Massachusetts Avenue, NE, Washington, DC 20212-0001, (202) 691-5200, Fax: (202) 691-6325, www.bls.gov; *Industry Productivity and Costs.*

ELECTRICAL EQUIPMENT MANUFACTURING - PROFITS

Bureau of Economic Analysis (BEA), U.S. Department of Commerce (DOC), 1441 L Street NW, Washington, DC 20230, (202) 606-9900, www.bea.gov; *2007 Annual Revision of the National Income and Product Accounts (NIPA)* and *Survey of Current Business (SCB).*

Forbes, Inc., 60 Fifth Avenue, New York, NY 10011, (212) 366-8900, www.forbes.com; *America's Largest Private Companies.*

U.S. Census Bureau, Manufacturing and Construction Division, 4600 Silver Hill Road, Washington DC 20233, (301) 763-4673, www.census.gov/mcd; *Quarterly Financial Report for Manufacturing, Mining and Trade Corporations.*

ELECTRICAL EQUIPMENT MANUFACTURING - RESEARCH AND DEVELOPMENT

National Science Foundation, Division of Science Resources Statistics (SRS), 4201 Wilson Boulevard, Arlington, VA 22230, (703) 292-8780, Fax: (703) 292-9092, www.nsf.gov; *Research and Development in Industry: 2003.*

ELECTRICAL EQUIPMENT MANUFACTURING - SHIPMENTS

U.S. Census Bureau, Manufacturing and Construction Division, 4600 Silver Hill Road, Washington DC 20233, (301) 763-4673, www.census.gov/mcd; *Annual Survey of Manufactures (ASM).*

ELECTRICAL EQUIPMENT MANUFACTURING - TOXIC CHEMICAL RELEASES

U.S. Environmental Protection Agency (EPA), Ariel Rios Building, 1200 Pennsylvania Avenue, NW, Washington, DC 20460, (202) 272-0167, www.epa.gov; Toxics Release Inventory (TRI) Database.

ELECTRICAL EQUIPMENT MANUFACTURING - VALUE ADDED

U.S. Census Bureau, Manufacturing and Construction Division, 4600 Silver Hill Road, Washington DC 20233, (301) 763-4673, www.census.gov/mcd; *Annual Survey of Manufactures (ASM); Census of Manufactures; Current Industrial Reports;* and *Manufacturers Shipments, Inventories and Orders.*

ELECTRICITY - CAPABILITY

Edison Electric Institute (EEI), 701 Pennsylvania Avenue, NW, Washington, DC 20004-2696, (202) 508-5000, www.eei.org; *Historical Statistics of the Electric Utility Industry through 1992* and *Statistical Yearbook of the Electric Power Industry - 2005 Data.*

Platts, 2 Penn Plaza, 25th Floor, New York, NY 10121-2298, (212) 904-3070, www.platts.com; *Asian Electricity Outlook 2006.*

U.S. Department of Energy (DOE), Energy Information Administration (EIA), 1000 Independence Avenue, SW, Washington, DC 20585, (202) 586-8800, www.eia.doe.gov; *Annual Energy Review 2005; Electric Power Annual;* and unpublished data.

ELECTRICITY - COMMERCIAL BUILDINGS

U.S. Census Bureau, Center for Economic Studies, 4600 Silver Hill Road, Washington DC 20233, (301) 457-1235, www.ces.census.gov; *2002 Economic Census, Construction.*

U.S. Department of Energy (DOE), Energy Information Administration (EIA), 1000 Independence

Avenue, SW, Washington, DC 20585, (202) 586-8800, www.eia.doe.gov; *Commercial Buildings Energy Consumption Survey (CBECS).*

ELECTRICITY - CONSUMPTION

Edison Electric Institute (EEI), 701 Pennsylvania Avenue, NW, Washington, DC 20004-2696, (202) 508-5000, www.eei.org; *Historical Statistics of the Electric Utility Industry through 1992* and *Statistical Yearbook of the Electric Power Industry - 2005 Data.*

Platts, 2 Penn Plaza, 25th Floor, New York, NY 10121-2298, (212) 904-3070, www.platts.com; *Asian Electricity Outlook 2006; Electric Power Daily;* and *Electric Utility Week.*

U.S. Department of Energy (DOE), Energy Information Administration (EIA), 1000 Independence Avenue, SW, Washington, DC 20585, (202) 586-8800, www.eia.doe.gov; *Annual Energy Review 2005; Commercial Buildings Energy Consumption Survey (CBECS); Electric Power Annual; Residential Energy Consumption Survey (RECS);* and unpublished data.

ELECTRICITY - EXPENDITURES

Platts, 2 Penn Plaza, 25th Floor, New York, NY 10121-2298, (212) 904-3070, www.platts.com; *Asian Electricity Outlook 2006; Electric Power Daily; Electric Utility Week;* and *Historical Price Data.*

U.S. Bureau of Labor Statistics (BLS), Postal Square Building, 2 Massachusetts Avenue, NE, Washington, DC 20212-0001, (202) 691-5200, Fax: (202) 691-6325, www.bls.gov; *Consumer Expenditures in 2006* and unpublished data.

U.S. Department of Energy (DOE), Energy Information Administration (EIA), 1000 Independence Avenue, SW, Washington, DC 20585, (202) 586-8800, www.eia.doe.gov; *Residential Energy Consumption Survey (RECS)* and *State Energy Data 2003 Price and Expenditure Data.*

U.S. Library of Congress (LOC), Congressional Research Service (CRS), The Library of Congress, 101 Independence Avenue, SE, Washington, DC 20540-7500, (202) 707-5700, www.loc.gov/crsinfo; *Energy: Selected Facts and Numbers* and *The Low-Income Home Energy Assistance Program (LIHEAP): Program and Funding Issues.*

ELECTRICITY - FOREIGN COUNTRIES

Platts, 2 Penn Plaza, 25th Floor, New York, NY 10121-2298, (212) 904-3070, www.platts.com; *Asian Electricity Outlook 2006; Electric Power Daily; Electric Utility Week; Emissions Daily; European Electricity Review 2004; Historical Price Data;* and *Nucleonics Week.*

U.S. Department of Energy (DOE), Energy Information Administration (EIA), 1000 Independence Avenue, SW, Washington, DC 20585, (202) 586-8800, www.eia.doe.gov; *International Energy Annual 2004* and *International Energy Outlook 2006.*

ELECTRICITY - HYDROELECTRIC POWER

Edison Electric Institute (EEI), 701 Pennsylvania Avenue, NW, Washington, DC 20004-2696, (202) 508-5000, www.eei.org; *Historical Statistics of the Electric Utility Industry through 1992.*

International Energy Agency (IEA), 9, rue de la Federation, 75739 Paris Cedex 15, France, www.iea.org; *Key World Energy Statistics 2007.*

U.S. Department of Energy (DOE), Energy Information Administration (EIA), 1000 Independence Avenue, SW, Washington, DC 20585, (202) 586-8800, www.eia.doe.gov; *Annual Energy Review 2005; Electric Power Annual; Electric Power Monthly (EPM); Monthly Energy Review (MER); State Energy Data Report;* and unpublished data.

U.S. Department of Energy (DOE), Federal Energy Regulatory Commission (FERC), 888 First Street, NE, Washington, DC 20426, (866) 208-3372, www.ferc.gov; *Historical Hydroelectric Generation Compared to 16 Year Average for 1991-2006* and unpublished data.

ELECTRICITY - NUCLEAR

Edison Electric Institute (EEI), 701 Pennsylvania Avenue, NW, Washington, DC 20004-2696, (202) 508-5000, www.eei.org; *Historical Statistics of the Electric Utility Industry through 1992.*

International Energy Agency (IEA), 9, rue de la Federation, 75739 Paris Cedex 15, France, www.iea.org; *Key World Energy Statistics 2007.*

Platts, 2 Penn Plaza, 25th Floor, New York, NY 10121-2298, (212) 904-3070, www.platts.com; *Nucleonics Week.*

U.S. Department of Energy (DOE), Energy Information Administration (EIA), 1000 Independence Avenue, SW, Washington, DC 20585, (202) 586-8800, www.eia.doe.gov; *Annual Energy Review 2005; Electric Power Annual; Monthly Energy Review (MER); State Energy Data Report;* and unpublished data.

ELECTRICITY - PRICE INDEXES

Bureau of Economic Analysis (BEA), U.S. Department of Commerce (DOC), 1441 L Street NW, Washington, DC 20230, (202) 606-9900, www.bea.gov; *2007 Annual Revision of the National Income and Product Accounts (NIPA)* and *Survey of Current Business (SCB).*

Platts, 2 Penn Plaza, 25th Floor, New York, NY 10121-2298, (212) 904-3070, www.platts.com; *Asian Electricity Outlook 2006; Electric Power Daily; Electric Utility Week;* and *Historical Price Data.*

U.S. Bureau of Labor Statistics (BLS), Postal Square Building, 2 Massachusetts Avenue, NE, Washington, DC 20212-0001, (202) 691-5200, Fax: (202) 691-6325, www.bls.gov; *Consumer Price Index Detailed Report* and *Monthly Labor Review (MLR).*

ELECTRICITY - PRICES

Platts, 2 Penn Plaza, 25th Floor, New York, NY 10121-2298, (212) 904-3070, www.platts.com; *Asian Electricity Outlook 2006; Electric Power Daily; Electric Utility Week; European Electricity Review 2004;* and *Historical Price Data.*

U.S. Department of Energy (DOE), Energy Information Administration (EIA), 1000 Independence Avenue, SW, Washington, DC 20585, (202) 586-8800, www.eia.doe.gov; *Annual Energy Review 2005.*

ELECTRICITY - PRODUCTION

Edison Electric Institute (EEI), 701 Pennsylvania Avenue, NW, Washington, DC 20004-2696, (202) 508-5000, www.eei.org; *Historical Statistics of the Electric Utility Industry through 1992.*

U.S. Department of Energy (DOE), Energy Information Administration (EIA), 1000 Independence Avenue, SW, Washington, DC 20585, (202) 586-8800, www.eia.doe.gov; *Annual Energy Review 2005; Electric Power Annual; Electric Power Monthly (EPM); Inventory of Electric Utility Power Plants in the United States 2000;* and unpublished data.

U.S. Library of Congress (LOC), Congressional Research Service (CRS), The Library of Congress, 101 Independence Avenue, SE, Washington, DC 20540-7500, (202) 707-5700, www.loc.gov/crsinfo; *Energy: Selected Facts and Numbers.*

ELECTRICITY - PRODUCTION - WORLD

Platts, 2 Penn Plaza, 25th Floor, New York, NY 10121-2298, (212) 904-3070, www.platts.com; *Asian Electricity Outlook 2006* and *European Electricity Review 2004.*

U.S. Department of Energy (DOE), Energy Information Administration (EIA), 1000 Independence Avenue, SW, Washington, DC 20585, (202) 586-8800, www.eia.doe.gov; *International Energy Annual 2004* and *International Energy Outlook 2006.*

ELECTRICITY - RESIDENTIAL

Edison Electric Institute (EEI), 701 Pennsylvania Avenue, NW, Washington, DC 20004-2696, (202) 508-5000, www.eei.org; *Statistical Yearbook of the Electric Power Industry - 2005 Data.*

U.S. Census Bureau, Center for Economic Studies, 4600 Silver Hill Road, Washington DC 20233, (301) 457-1235, www.ces.census.gov; *2002 Economic Census, Construction.*

U.S. Department of Energy (DOE), Energy Information Administration (EIA), 1000 Independence Avenue, SW, Washington, DC 20585, (202) 586-8800, www.eia.doe.gov; *Annual Energy Outlook 2006; Natural Gas Annual 2004; Petroleum Supply Annual 2004;* and *Residential Energy Consumption Survey (RECS).*

U.S. Library of Congress (LOC), Congressional Research Service (CRS), The Library of Congress, 101 Independence Avenue, SE, Washington, DC 20540-7500, (202) 707-5700, www.loc.gov/crsinfo; *The Low-Income Home Energy Assistance Program (LIHEAP): Program and Funding Issues.*

ELECTRICITY - SALES

Edison Electric Institute (EEI), 701 Pennsylvania Avenue, NW, Washington, DC 20004-2696, (202) 508-5000, www.eei.org; *Historical Statistics of the Electric Utility Industry through 1992* and *Statistical Yearbook of the Electric Power Industry - 2005 Data.*

Platts, 2 Penn Plaza, 25th Floor, New York, NY 10121-2298, (212) 904-3070, www.platts.com; *Asian Electricity Outlook 2006; Electric Power Daily; Electric Utility Week;* and *European Electricity Review 2004.*

U.S. Department of Energy (DOE), Energy Information Administration (EIA), 1000 Independence Avenue, SW, Washington, DC 20585, (202) 586-8800, www.eia.doe.gov; *Annual Energy Review 2005; Electric Power Annual;* and *Electric Power Monthly (EPM).*

ELECTRONIC COMMERCE (E-COMMERCE) - BUSINESS SALES

Forrester Research, Inc., 400 Technology Square, Cambridge, MA 02139, (617) 613-6000, www.forrester.com; *US Online Retail.*

ELECTRONIC COMMERCE (E-COMMERCE) - CONSUMER SALES

Forrester Research, Inc., 400 Technology Square, Cambridge, MA 02139, (617) 613-6000, www.forrester.com; *US Online Retail.*

JupiterResearch, 233 Broadway, Suite 1005, New York, NY 10279, USA, (212) 857-0700, Fax: (212) 857-0701, www.jupiterresearch.com; unpublished data.

ELECTRONIC COMMERCE (E-COMMERCE) - MANUFACTURING

U.S. Census Bureau, 4700 Silver Hill Road, Washington DC 20233-0001, (301) 763-3030, www.census.gov; *E-Stats - Measuring the Electronic Economy.*

ELECTRONIC COMMERCE (E-COMMERCE) - RETAIL TRADE

U.S. Census Bureau, 4700 Silver Hill Road, Washington DC 20233-0001, (301) 763-3030, www.census.gov; *2006 E-Commerce Multi-Sector Report* and *E-Stats - Measuring the Electronic Economy.*

ELECTRONIC COMMERCE (E-COMMERCE) - SERVICES

U.S. Census Bureau, 4700 Silver Hill Road, Washington DC 20233-0001, (301) 763-3030, www.census.gov; *2006 E-Commerce Multi-Sector Report* and *E-Stats - Measuring the Electronic Economy.*

ELECTRONIC COMMERCE (E-COMMERCE) - WHOLESALE

U.S. Census Bureau, 4700 Silver Hill Road, Washington DC 20233-0001, (301) 763-3030, www.census.gov; *2006 E-Commerce Multi-Sector Report* and *E-Stats - Measuring the Electronic Economy.*

ELECTRONIC FUNDS TRANSFER PAYMENTS

The Nilson Report, 1110 Eugenia Place, Suite 100, Carpinteria, CA 93013-9921, (805) 684-8800, Fax: (805) 684-8825, www.nilsonreport.com; *The Nilson Report.*

ELECTRONIC GOODS

Mediamark Research, Inc., 75 Ninth Avenue, 5th Floor, New York, NY 10011, (212) 884-9200, Fax: (212) 884-9339, www.mediamark.com; *The American Kids Study.*

ELECTRONIC GOODS - CONSUMER PRICE INDEXES

U.S. Department of Labor (DOL), Bureau of Labor Statistics (BLS), Postal Square Building, 2 Massachusetts Avenue, NE, Washington, DC 20212-0001, (202) 691-5200, Fax: (202) 691-6325, www.bls.gov; *Consumer Price Indexes (CPI).*

ELECTRONIC GOODS - INTERNATIONAL TRADE

U.S. Census Bureau, Foreign Trade Division, 4700 Silver Hill Road, Washington DC 20233-0001, (301) 763-3030, www.census.gov/foreign-trade/www/; *U.S. International Trade in Goods and Services.*

ELECTRONIC GOODS - SALES, SHIPMENTS AND RECEIPTS

Consumer Electronics Association (CEA), 2500 Wilson Boulevard, Arlington, VA 22201-3834, (703) 907-7600, Fax: (703) 907 7675, www.ce.org; *Digital America 2006.*

Electronic Industries Alliance (EIA), 2500 Wilson Boulevard, Arlington, VA 22201, (703) 907-7500, www.eia.org; unpublished data.

U.S. Census Bureau, Manufacturing and Construction Division, 4600 Silver Hill Road, Washington DC 20233, (301) 763-4673, www.census.gov/mcd; *Annual Survey of Manufactures, Statistics for Industry Groups and Industries* and *Current Industrial Reports, Manufacturing Profiles.*

ELECTRONICS AND APPLIANCE STORES - EARNINGS

The NPD Group, Port Washington, 900 West Shore Road, Port Washington, NY 11050, (866) 444-1411, www.npd.com; *Market Research for the Appliances, Home Improvement, Home Textiles, and Housewares Industries.*

Office of Trade and Industry Information (OTII), Manufacturing and Services, International Trade Administration, U.S. Department of Commerce, 1401 Constitution Ave, NW, Washington, DC 20230, (800) USA TRAD(E), http://trade.gov/index.asp; *TradeStats Express.*

U.S. Census Bureau, Center for Economic Studies, 4600 Silver Hill Road, Washington DC 20233, (301) 457-1235, www.ces.census.gov; *2002 Economic Census, Retail Trade.*

U.S. Census Bureau, Company Statistics Division, 4700 Silver Hill Road, Washington DC 20233-0001, (301) 763-3030, www.census.gov/csd/; *County Business Patterns 2004.*

ELECTRONICS AND APPLIANCE STORES - ELECTRONIC COMMERCE

U.S. Census Bureau, 4700 Silver Hill Road, Washington DC 20233-0001, (301) 763-3030, www.census.gov; *2006 E-Commerce Multi-Sector Report* and *E-Stats - Measuring the Electronic Economy.*

ELECTRONICS AND APPLIANCE STORES - EMPLOYEES

U.S. Census Bureau, Center for Economic Studies, 4600 Silver Hill Road, Washington DC 20233, (301) 457-1235, www.ces.census.gov; *2002 Economic Census, Retail Trade.*

U.S. Census Bureau, Company Statistics Division, 4700 Silver Hill Road, Washington DC 20233-0001, (301) 763-3030, www.census.gov/csd/; *County Business Patterns 2004.*

ELECTRONICS AND APPLIANCE STORES - ESTABLISHMENTS

The NPD Group, Port Washington, 900 West Shore Road, Port Washington, NY 11050, (866) 444-1411, www.npd.com; *Market Research for the Appliances, Home Improvement, Home Textiles, and Housewares Industries.*

Office of Trade and Industry Information (OTII), Manufacturing and Services, International Trade Administration, U.S. Department of Commerce, 1401 Constitution Ave, NW, Washington, DC 20230, (800) USA TRAD(E), http://trade.gov/index.asp; *TradeStats Express.*

U.S. Census Bureau, 4700 Silver Hill Road, Washington DC 20233-0001, (301) 763-3030, www.census.gov; *2002 Economic Census, Nonemployer Statistics.*

U.S. Census Bureau, Center for Economic Studies, 4600 Silver Hill Road, Washington DC 20233, (301) 457-1235, www.ces.census.gov; *2002 Economic Census, Retail Trade* and *2002 Economic Census, Wholesale Trade.*

U.S. Census Bureau, Company Statistics Division, 4700 Silver Hill Road, Washington DC 20233-0001, (301) 763-3030, www.census.gov/csd/; *County Business Patterns 2004.*

ELECTRONICS AND APPLIANCE STORES - NONEMPLOYERS

U.S. Census Bureau, 4700 Silver Hill Road, Washington DC 20233-0001, (301) 763-3030, www.census.gov; *2002 Economic Census, Nonemployer Statistics.*

ELECTRONICS AND APPLIANCE STORES - PURCHASES

Office of Trade and Industry Information (OTII), Manufacturing and Services, International Trade Administration, U.S. Department of Commerce, 1401 Constitution Ave, NW, Washington, DC 20230, (800) USA TRAD(E), http://trade.gov/index.asp; *TradeStats Express.*

U.S. Census Bureau, 4700 Silver Hill Road, Washington DC 20233-0001, (301) 763-3030, www.census.gov; unpublished data.

U.S. Census Bureau, Center for Economic Studies, 4600 Silver Hill Road, Washington DC 20233, (301) 457-1235, www.ces.census.gov; *2002 Economic Census, Retail Trade.*

U.S. Census Bureau, Company Statistics Division, 4700 Silver Hill Road, Washington DC 20233-0001, (301) 763-3030, www.census.gov/csd/; *Current Business Reports.*

ELECTRONICS AND APPLIANCE STORES - SALES

Consumer Electronics Association (CEA), 2500 Wilson Boulevard, Arlington, VA 22201-3834, (703) 907-7600, Fax: (703) 907 7675, www.ce.org; *Digital America 2006.*

The NPD Group, Port Washington, 900 West Shore Road, Port Washington, NY 11050, (866) 444-1411, www.npd.com; *Market Research for the Appliances, Home Improvement, Home Textiles, and Housewares Industries.*

Office of Trade and Industry Information (OTII), Manufacturing and Services, International Trade Administration, U.S. Department of Commerce, 1401 Constitution Ave, NW, Washington, DC 20230, (800) USA TRAD(E), http://trade.gov/index.asp; *TradeStats Express.*

U.S. Census Bureau, 4700 Silver Hill Road, Washington DC 20233-0001, (301) 763-3030, www.census.gov; *2006 E-Commerce Multi-Sector Report; E-Stats - Measuring the Electronic Economy;* and *2002 Economic Census, Nonemployer Statistics.*

U.S. Census Bureau, Center for Economic Studies, 4600 Silver Hill Road, Washington DC 20233, (301) 457-1235, www.ces.census.gov; *2002 Economic Census, Retail Trade* and *2002 Economic Census, Wholesale Trade.*

U.S. Census Bureau, Company Statistics Division, 4700 Silver Hill Road, Washington DC 20233-0001, (301) 763-3030, www.census.gov/csd/; *Current Business Reports.*

EMERGENCY MEDICINE

American Medical Association, 515 North State Street, Chicago, IL 60610, (800) 621-8335, www.ama-assn.org; *Physician Characteristics and Distribution in the United States, 2008* and *Physician Compensation and Production Survey: 2007 Report Based on 2006 Data.*

National Center for Health Statistics (NCHS), Centers for Disease Control and Prevention (CDC), U.S. Department of Health and Human Services (HHS), 3311 Toledo Road, Hyattsville, MD 20782, (866) 232-4636, www.cdc.gov/nchs; unpublished data.

National Council on Compensation Insurance, Inc. (NCCI), 901 Peninsula Corporate Circle, Boca Raton, FL 33487, (800) NCCI-123, www.ncci.com; *NCCI Examines Emergency Room Treatment of Younger Workers vs. Older Workers - Fall 2007.*

EMPHYSEMA

Bernan Essential Government Publications, 4611-F Assembly Drive, Lanham MD, 20706-4391, (301) 459-2255, Fax: (800) 865-3450, www.bernan.com; *Vital Statistics of the United States: Births, Life Expectancy, Deaths, and Selected Health Data.*

National Center for Health Statistics (NCHS), Centers for Disease Control and Prevention (CDC), U.S. Department of Health and Human Services (HHS), 3311 Toledo Road, Hyattsville, MD 20782, (866) 232-4636, www.cdc.gov/nchs; *Health, United States, 2006, with Chartbook on Trends in the Health of Americans with Special Feature on Pain; National Vital Statistics Reports (NVSR); Vital Statistics of the United States (VSUS);* and unpublished data.

World Health Organization (WHO), Avenue Appia 20, 1211 Geneve 27, Switzerland, (Telephone in U.S. (212) 331-9081), www.who.int; *World Health Report 2006.*

EMPLOYEE BENEFITS

Agency for Healthcare Research and Quality (AHRQ), Office of Communications and Knowledge Transfer, 540 Gaither Road, Suite 2000, Rockville, MD 20850, (301) 427-1364, www.ahrq.gov; The Healthcare Cost and Utilization Project (HCUP) and *Medical Expenditure Panel Survey (MEPS).*

Economic Policy Institute (EPI), 1333 H Street, NW, Suite 300, East Tower, Washington, DC 20005-4707, (202) 775-8810, www.epi.org; *Hardships in America: The Real Story of Working Families; The State of Working America 2006/2007;* and *The Teaching Penalty.*

HealthLeaders-InterStudy, One Vantage Way, B-300, Nashville, TN 37203, (615) 385-4131, Fax: (615) 385-4979, www.hmodata.com; *Employer Vantage.*

National Center for Employee Ownership (NCEO), 1736 Franklin Street, 8th Floor, Oakland, CA 94612, (510) 208-1300, Fax: (510) 272-9510, www.nceo.org; unpublished data.

National Center for Health Statistics (NCHS), Centers for Disease Control and Prevention (CDC), U.S. Department of Health and Human Services (HHS), 3311 Toledo Road, Hyattsville, MD 20782, (866) 232-4636, www.cdc.gov/nchs; *Data on Health Insurance and Access to Care.*

Robert Wood Johnson Foundation, PO Box 2316, College Road East and Route 1, Princeton, NJ 08543, (877) 843-7953, www.rwjf.org; *Report from Massachusetts: Employers Largely Support Health Care Reform, and Few Signs of Crowd-Out Appear.*

Thomson Tax and Accounting, 395 Hudson Street, New York, NY 10014, (888) 833-6578, Fax: (800) 487-8488, www.thomson.com; *RIA/WGL Pension Benefits Research Products.*

U.S. Bureau of Labor Statistics (BLS), Postal Square Building, 2 Massachusetts Avenue, NE,

Washington, DC 20212-0001, (202) 691-5200, Fax: (202) 691-6325, www.bls.gov; *Employee Benefits in Medium and Large Private Establishments; Employer Costs for Employee Compensation;* and unpublished data.

U.S. Census Bureau, 4700 Silver Hill Road, Washington DC 20233-0001, (301) 763-3030, www.census.gov; unpublished data.

U.S. Library of Congress (LOC), Congressional Research Service (CRS), The Library of Congress, 101 Independence Avenue, SE, Washington, DC 20540-7500, (202) 707-5700, www.loc.gov/crsinfo; *Pension Sponsorship and Participation: Summary of Recent Trends.*

Vermont Department of Labor, Labor Market Information Section, PO Box 488, Montpelier, VT 05601-0488, (802) 828-4202, Fax: (802) 828-4050, www.vtlmi.com; *Fringe Benefits in Vermont 2005.*

EMPLOYEE BENEFITS - GOVERNMENT EMPLOYEES

U.S. Library of Congress (LOC), Congressional Research Service (CRS), The Library of Congress, 101 Independence Avenue, SE, Washington, DC 20540-7500, (202) 707-5700, www.loc.gov/crsinfo; *Federal Employees: Pay and Pension Increases Since 1969.*

EMPLOYEE OWNERSHIP

National Center for Employee Ownership (NCEO), 1736 Franklin Street, 8th Floor, Oakland, CA 94612, (510) 208-1300, Fax: (510) 272-9510, www.nceo.org; unpublished data.

EMPLOYEE TURNOVER

The Annie E. Casey Foundation, 701 Saint Paul Street, Baltimore, MD 21202, (410) 547-6600, Fax: (410) 547-3610, www.aecf.org; *The Road to Good Employment Retention: Three Successful Programs from the Jobs Initiative.*

United States Office of Personnel Management (OMB), 1900 E Street, NW, Washington, DC 20415-1000, (202) 606-1800, www.opm.gov; *The Fact Book (Federal Civilian Workforce) (2005 edition).*

EMPLOYMENT

See LABOR FORCE EMPLOYMENT AND EARNINGS

ENDANGERED SPECIES

U.S. Department of the Interior (DOI), Fish Wildlife Service (FWS), 1849 C Street, NW, Washington, DC 20240, (800) 344-WILD, www.fws.gov; *Endangered Species Bulletin* and Environmental Conservation Online System (ECOS).

ENERGY

See also ELECTRIC LIGHT AND POWER INDUSTRY

American Petroleum Institute (API), 1220 L Street, NW, Washington, DC 20005-4070, (202) 682-8000, http://api-ec.api.org; *Petroleum Facts at a Glance.*

Congressional Quarterly, Inc., 1255 22nd Street, NW, Washington, DC 20037, (202) 419-8500, www.cq.com; *World at Risk: A Global Issues Sourcebook.*

Danish Energy Authority, Amaliegade 44, DK 1256 Copenhagen K, Denmark, www.ens.dk; *Energy in Denmark 2006* and *Energy Statistics 2006.*

Enerdata, 10 Rue Royale, 75008 Paris, France, www.enerdata.fr; *EmissionStat; Enerdata Yearbook 2007 Edition; EnerFuture Forecasts; Energy Prices Forecasts; European Energy Utilities Watch; Global Energy Market Data; Odyssee: Energy Efficiency Indicators in Europe;* and *Profiles: International Energy Market Research Online.*

Environmental Business International, Inc., 4452 Park Boulevard, Suite 306, San Diego, CA 92116, (619) 295-7685, Fax: (619) 295-5743, www.ebiusa.com; *Environmental Business Journal (EBJ) 2006; Environmental Market Reports;* and *U.S. and Global Environmental Market Data.*

International Energy Agency (IEA), 9, rue de la Federation, 75739 Paris Cedex 15, France, www.iea.org; Research and Development Statistics and *World Energy Statistics and Balances (2007 edition).*

Organisation for Economic Cooperation and Development (OECD), 2 rue Andre Pascal, F-75775 Paris Cedex 16, France, (Telephone in U.S. (202) 785-6323), (Fax in U.S. (202) 785-0350), www.oecd.org; *World Energy Outlook 2007.*

Platts, 2 Penn Plaza, 25th Floor, New York, NY 10121-2298, (212) 904-3070, www.platts.com; *Energy in East Europe* and *European Electricity Review 2004.*

United Nations Statistics Division, New York, NY 10017, (800) 253-9646, Fax: (212) 963-4116, http://unstats.un.org; *World Energy Assessment 2004 Update: Overview.*

ENERGY - AIR POLLUTANT EMISSIONS

Platts, 2 Penn Plaza, 25th Floor, New York, NY 10121-2298, (212) 904-3070, www.platts.com; *Emissions Daily; European Power Daily;* and *2007 Global Energy Outlook.*

U.S. Department of Energy (DOE), Energy Information Administration (EIA), 1000 Independence Avenue, SW, Washington, DC 20585, (202) 586-8800, www.eia.doe.gov; *Emissions of Greenhouse Gases in the United States 2005.*

United Nations Environment Programme (UNEP), PO Box 30552, Nairobi, Kenya, www.unep.org; *Climate Action; One Planet, Many People: Atlas of Our Changing Environment; Our Planet Magazine; Planet in Peril: Atlas of Current Threats to People and the Environment;* The UNEP Year Book 2008; and *World Atlas of Biodiversity: Earth's Living Resources in the 21st Century.*

ENERGY - AIR POLLUTANT EMISSIONS - FOREIGN COUNTRIES

Organisation for Economic Cooperation and Development (OECD), 2 rue Andre Pascal, F-75775 Paris Cedex 16, France, (Telephone in U.S. (202) 785-6323), (Fax in U.S. (202) 785-0350), www.oecd.org; *Key Environmental Indicators 2004.*

Platts, 2 Penn Plaza, 25th Floor, New York, NY 10121-2298, (212) 904-3070, www.platts.com; *Emissions Daily; European Power Daily;* and *2007 Global Energy Outlook.*

U.S. Department of Energy (DOE), Energy Information Administration (EIA), 1000 Independence Avenue, SW, Washington, DC 20585, (202) 586-8800, www.eia.doe.gov; *International Energy Annual 2004; International Energy Outlook 2006;* and *International Energy Outlook 2006.*

ENERGY - ASSISTANCE FOR PERSONS WITH LIMITED INCOME

U.S. Library of Congress (LOC), Congressional Research Service (CRS), The Library of Congress, 101 Independence Avenue, SE, Washington, DC 20540-7500, (202) 707-5700, www.loc.gov/crsinfo; *Cash and Non-cash Benefits for Persons With Limited Income: Eligibility Rules, Recipient and Expenditure Data.*

ENERGY - COMMERCIAL BUILDINGS

U.S. Department of Energy (DOE), Energy Information Administration (EIA), 1000 Independence Avenue, SW, Washington, DC 20585, (202) 586-8800, www.eia.doe.gov; *Commercial Buildings Energy Consumption Survey (CBECS)* and *Residential Energy Consumption Survey (RECS).*

ENERGY - CONSUMPTION

Edison Electric Institute (EEI), 701 Pennsylvania Avenue, NW, Washington, DC 20004-2696, (202) 508-5000, www.eei.org; *Weekly Electric Output.*

International Energy Agency (IEA), 9, rue de la Federation, 75739 Paris Cedex 15, France, www.iea.org; *Key World Energy Statistics 2007.*

McGraw-Hill Construction, Dodge Analytics, 1221 Avenue of The Americas, Manhattan, NY 10020, (800) 393-6343, http://dodge.construction.com/analytics; *Green Building SmartMarket Report 2006.*

Platts, 2 Penn Plaza, 25th Floor, New York, NY 10121-2298, (212) 904-3070, www.platts.com; *Energy Economist* and *Global Power Report.*

U.S. Department of Energy (DOE), Energy Information Administration (EIA), 1000 Independence Avenue, SW, Washington, DC 20585, (202) 586-8800, www.eia.doe.gov; *Annual Energy Review 2005; Monthly Energy Review (MER); Residential Energy Consumption Survey (RECS);* and *State Energy Data Report.*

United Nations Environment Programme (UNEP), PO Box 30552, Nairobi, Kenya, www.unep.org; *Climate Action.*

United Nations Statistics Division, New York, NY 10017, (800) 253-9646, Fax: (212) 963-4116, http://unstats.un.org; *Energy Statistics Yearbook 2003.*

ENERGY - CONSUMPTION - END USE SECTOR

U.S. Department of Energy (DOE), Energy Information Administration (EIA), 1000 Independence Avenue, SW, Washington, DC 20585, (202) 586-8800, www.eia.doe.gov; *Annual Energy Review 2005; Monthly Energy Review (MER); State Energy Data 2003 Price and Expenditure Data;* and *State Energy Data Report.*

ENERGY - CONSUMPTION - FOREIGN COUNTRIES

Enerdata, 10 Rue Royale, 75008 Paris, France, www.enerdata.fr; *EmissionStat; Enerdata Yearbook 2007 Edition; EnerFuture Forecasts; Energy Prices Forecasts; European Energy Utilities Watch; Global Energy Market Data; Odyssee: Energy Efficiency Indicators in Europe;* and *Profiles: International Energy Market Research Online.*

Platts, 2 Penn Plaza, 25th Floor, New York, NY 10121-2298, (212) 904-3070, www.platts.com; *Energy Economist.*

U.S. Department of Energy (DOE), Energy Information Administration (EIA), 1000 Independence Avenue, SW, Washington, DC 20585, (202) 586-8800, www.eia.doe.gov; *International Energy Annual 2004* and *International Energy Outlook 2006.*

United Nations Statistics Division, New York, NY 10017, (800) 253-9646, Fax: (212) 963-4116, http://unstats.un.org; *Energy Statistics Yearbook 2003* and United Nations Common Database (UNCDB).

ENERGY - CONSUMPTION - RENEWABLE SOURCES

Enerdata, 10 Rue Royale, 75008 Paris, France, www.enerdata.fr; *EmissionStat; Enerdata Yearbook 2007 Edition; EnerFuture Forecasts; Energy Prices Forecasts; European Energy Utilities Watch; Global Energy Market Data; Odyssee: Energy Efficiency Indicators in Europe;* and *Profiles: International Energy Market Research Online.*

U.S. Department of Energy (DOE), Energy Information Administration (EIA), 1000 Independence Avenue, SW, Washington, DC 20585, (202) 586-8800, www.eia.doe.gov; *Annual Energy Review 2005.*

ENERGY - CONSUMPTION - SOURCE

International Energy Agency (IEA), 9, rue de la Federation, 75739 Paris Cedex 15, France, www.iea.org; *Key World Energy Statistics 2007.*

U.S. Department of Energy (DOE), Energy Information Administration (EIA), 1000 Independence Avenue, SW, Washington, DC 20585, (202) 586-8800, www.eia.doe.gov; *Annual Energy Review 2005* and *Monthly Energy Review (MER).*

ENERGY - END USE SECTOR

U.S. Department of Energy (DOE), Energy Information Administration (EIA), 1000 Independence Avenue, SW, Washington, DC 20585, (202) 586-8800, www.eia.doe.gov; *Annual Energy Review*

2005; Monthly Energy Review (MER); State Energy Data 2003 Price and Expenditure Data; and *State Energy Data Report.*

ENERGY - EXPENDITURES

Enerdata, 10 Rue Royale, 75008 Paris, France, www.enerdata.fr; *EmissionStat; Enerdata Yearbook 2007 Edition; EnerFuture Forecasts; Energy Prices Forecasts; European Energy Utilities Watch; Global Energy Market Data; Odyssee: Energy Efficiency Indicators in Europe;* and *Profiles: International Energy Market Research Online.*

U.S. Department of Energy (DOE), Energy Information Administration (EIA), 1000 Independence Avenue, SW, Washington, DC 20585, (202) 586-8800, www.eia.doe.gov; *Commercial Buildings Energy Consumption Survey (CBECS); Residential Energy Consumption Survey (RECS);* and *State Energy Data 2003 Price and Expenditure Data.*

U.S. Library of Congress (LOC), Congressional Research Service (CRS), The Library of Congress, 101 Independence Avenue, SE, Washington, DC 20540-7500, (202) 707-5700, www.loc.gov/crsinfo; *Energy: Selected Facts and Numbers* and *The Low-Income Home Energy Assistance Program (LIHEAP): Program and Funding Issues.*

ENERGY - EXPENDITURES - COMMERCIAL

U.S. Department of Energy (DOE), Energy Information Administration (EIA), 1000 Independence Avenue, SW, Washington, DC 20585, (202) 586-8800, www.eia.doe.gov; *Commercial Buildings Energy Consumption Survey (CBECS).*

ENERGY - EXPENDITURES - RESIDENTIAL

U.S. Department of Energy (DOE), Energy Information Administration (EIA), 1000 Independence Avenue, SW, Washington, DC 20585, (202) 586-8800, www.eia.doe.gov; *Residential Energy Consumption Survey (RECS).*

ENERGY - FEDERAL OUTLAYS

The Office of Management and Budget (OMB), 725 17th Street, NW, Washington, DC 20503, (202) 395-3080, Fax: (202) 395-3888, www.whitehouse.gov/omb; *Historical Tables.*

ENERGY - PRICE INDEXES - CONSUMER

U.S. Bureau of Labor Statistics (BLS), Postal Square Building, 2 Massachusetts Avenue, NE, Washington, DC 20212-0001, (202) 691-5200, Fax: (202) 691-6325, www.bls.gov; *Consumer Price Index Detailed Report* and *Monthly Labor Review (MLR).*

U.S. Department of Energy (DOE), Energy Information Administration (EIA), 1000 Independence Avenue, SW, Washington, DC 20585, (202) 586-8800, www.eia.doe.gov; *International Energy Annual 2004* and *International Energy Outlook 2006.*

ENERGY - PRICE INDEXES - EXPORT AND IMPORT

U.S. Bureau of Labor Statistics (BLS), Postal Square Building, 2 Massachusetts Avenue, NE, Washington, DC 20212-0001, (202) 691-5200, Fax: (202) 691-6325, www.bls.gov; *U.S. Import and Export Price Indexes.*

ENERGY - PRICE INDEXES - PRODUCER

U.S. Bureau of Labor Statistics (BLS), Postal Square Building, 2 Massachusetts Avenue, NE, Washington, DC 20212-0001, (202) 691-5200, Fax: (202) 691-6325, www.bls.gov; *Producer Price Indexes (PPI).*

ENERGY - PRICES

Enerdata, 10 Rue Royale, 75008 Paris, France, www.enerdata.fr; *EmissionStat; Enerdata Yearbook 2007 Edition; EnerFuture Forecasts; Energy Prices Forecasts; European Energy Utilities Watch; Global Energy Market Data; Odyssee: Energy Efficiency Indicators in Europe;* and *Profiles: International Energy Market Research Online.*

International Energy Agency (IEA), 9, rue de la Federation, 75739 Paris Cedex 15, France, www.iea.org; *Key World Energy Statistics 2007.*

U.S. Bureau of Labor Statistics (BLS), Postal Square Building, 2 Massachusetts Avenue, NE, Washington, DC 20212-0001, (202) 691-5200, Fax: (202) 691-6325, www.bls.gov; *Consumer Price Index Detailed Report.*

U.S. Library of Congress (LOC), Congressional Research Service (CRS), The Library of Congress, 101 Independence Avenue, SE, Washington, DC 20540-7500, (202) 707-5700, www.loc.gov/crsinfo; *Energy: Selected Facts and Numbers.*

ENERGY - SOLAR COLLECTORS - MANUFACTURER'S SHIPMENTS

U.S. Department of Energy (DOE), Energy Information Administration (EIA), 1000 Independence Avenue, SW, Washington, DC 20585, (202) 586-8800, www.eia.doe.gov; *Solar Thermal and Photovoltaic Collector Manufacturing Activities 2005.*

ENGINEERING

National Science Foundation, Division of Science Resources Statistics (SRS), 4201 Wilson Boulevard, Arlington, VA 22230, (703) 292-8780, Fax: (703) 292-9092, www.nsf.gov; *Integrated Science and Engineering Resources Data System (WebCASPAR).*

National Technical Information Service (NTIS), U.S. Department of Commerce (DOC), 5285 Port Royal Road, Springfield, VA 22161, (703) 605-6000, www.ntis.gov; unpublished data.

ENGINEERING AND ARCHITECTURAL SERVICES - EARNINGS

U.S. Census Bureau, Center for Economic Studies, 4600 Silver Hill Road, Washington DC 20233, (301) 457-1235, www.ces.census.gov; *2002 Economic Census, Construction* and *2002 Economic Census, Professional, Scientific and Technical Services.*

ENGINEERING AND ARCHITECTURAL SERVICES - EMPLOYEES

U.S. Census Bureau, Center for Economic Studies, 4600 Silver Hill Road, Washington DC 20233, (301) 457-1235, www.ces.census.gov; *2002 Economic Census, Professional, Scientific and Technical Services.*

ENGINEERING AND ARCHITECTURAL SERVICES - ESTABLISHMENTS

U.S. Census Bureau, Center for Economic Studies, 4600 Silver Hill Road, Washington DC 20233, (301) 457-1235, www.ces.census.gov; *2002 Economic Census, Professional, Scientific and Technical Services.*

ENGINEERING AND ARCHITECTURAL SERVICES - RECEIPTS

U.S. Census Bureau, 4700 Silver Hill Road, Washington DC 20233-0001, (301) 763-3030, www.census.gov; unpublished data.

U.S. Census Bureau, Center for Economic Studies, 4600 Silver Hill Road, Washington DC 20233, (301) 457-1235, www.ces.census.gov; *2002 Economic Census, Construction.*

U.S. Census Bureau, Company Statistics Division, 4700 Silver Hill Road, Washington DC 20233-0001, (301) 763-3030, www.census.gov/csd/; *Current Business Reports.*

ENGINEERS AND SCIENTISTS

National Science Foundation, Division of Science Resources Statistics (SRS), 4201 Wilson Boulevard, Arlington, VA 22230, (703) 292-8780, Fax: (703) 292-9092, www.nsf.gov; *Scientists and Engineers Statistical Data System (SESTAT).*

ENGINEERS AND SCIENTISTS - DEGREES CONFERRED

National Center for Education Statistics (NCES), 1990 K Street, NW, Washington, DC 20006, (202) 502-7300, http://nces.ed.gov; *Digest of Education Statistics 2007.*

National Science Foundation, Division of Science Resources Statistics (SRS), 4201 Wilson Boulevard, Arlington, VA 22230, (703) 292-8780, Fax: (703) 292-9092, www.nsf.gov; *National Survey of Recent College Graduates: 2006; Selected Data on Science and Engineering Doctorate Awards;* and *Survey of Earned Doctorates 2006.*

U.S. Census Bureau, 4700 Silver Hill Road, Washington DC 20233-0001, (301) 763-3030, www.census.gov; unpublished data.

ENGINEERS AND SCIENTISTS - EMPLOYMENT

National Science Foundation, Division of Science Resources Statistics (SRS), 4201 Wilson Boulevard, Arlington, VA 22230, (703) 292-8780, Fax: (703) 292-9092, www.nsf.gov; *Research and Development in Industry: 2003.*

U.S. Bureau of Labor Statistics (BLS), Postal Square Building, 2 Massachusetts Avenue, NE, Washington, DC 20212-0001, (202) 691-5200, Fax: (202) 691-6325, www.bls.gov; *Employment and Earnings (EE); Monthly Labor Review (MLR);* and unpublished data.

ENGINEERS AND SCIENTISTS - RESEARCH AND DEVELOPMENT

National Science Foundation, Division of Science Resources Statistics (SRS), 4201 Wilson Boulevard, Arlington, VA 22230, (703) 292-8780, Fax: (703) 292-9092, www.nsf.gov; *Research and Development in Industry: 2003* and *Survey of Research and Development Expenditures at Universities and Colleges.*

ENGINEERS AND SCIENTISTS - SALARY OFFERS

National Association of Colleges and Employers (NACE), 62 Highland Avenue, Bethlehem, PA 18017, (800) 544-5272, Fax: (610) 868-0208, www.naceweb.org; *Salary Survey.*

ENGINES

U.S. Census Bureau, Manufacturing and Construction Division, 4600 Silver Hill Road, Washington DC 20233, (301) 763-4673, www.census.gov/mcd; *Current Industrial Reports.*

ENGLAND

See UNITED KINGDOM

ENTERTAINMENT

See also RECREATION

ENTERTAINMENT - CONSUMER PRICE INDEXES

U.S. Bureau of Labor Statistics (BLS), Postal Square Building, 2 Massachusetts Avenue, NE, Washington, DC 20212-0001, (202) 691-5200, Fax: (202) 691-6325, www.bls.gov; *Consumer Price Index Detailed Report* and *Monthly Labor Review (MLR).*

ENTERTAINMENT - PERSONAL EXPENDITURES

U.S. Bureau of Labor Statistics (BLS), Postal Square Building, 2 Massachusetts Avenue, NE, Washington, DC 20212-0001, (202) 691-5200, Fax: (202) 691-6325, www.bls.gov; *Consumer Expenditures in 2006; Consumer Price Index Detailed Report; Monthly Labor Review (MLR);* and unpublished data.

ENVIRONMENT

See also POLLUTION

Casey Trees Endowment Fund, 1425 K St NW, Suite 1050, Washington, DC, 20005, (202) 833-4010, Fax: (202) 833-4092, www.caseytrees.org; *Casey Trees Tree Map.*

Congressional Quarterly, Inc., 1255 22nd Street, NW, Washington, DC 20037, (202) 419-8500, www.cq.com; *World at Risk: A Global Issues Sourcebook.*

Department of Statistics (DOS), PO Box 2015, Amman 11181, Jordan, www.dos.gov.jo; *Annual Environmental Statistic 2006.*

Economist Intelligence Unit, 111 West 57th Street, New York, NY 10019, (212) 554-0600, Fax: (212) 586-1181, www.eiu.com; *United States of America Country Report.*

Environmental Defense Fund, 257 Park Avenue South, New York, NY 10010, (800) 684-3322, www.edf.org; *All Choked Up: Heavy Traffic, Dirty Air and the Risk to New Yorkers; Cars and Climate Change: How Automakers Stack Up;* and *Smokestacks on Rails: Locomotive Pollution Impacts Public Health.*

Intergovernmental Panel on Climate Change (IPCC), www.ipcc.ch; *Carbon Dioxide Capture and Storage; Climate Change 2007: Working Group II Report - Impacts, Adaptation and Vulnerability; The Regional Impacts of Climate Change: An Assessment of Vulnerability;* and *Safeguarding the Ozone Layer and the Global Climate System: Issues Related to Hydrofluorocarbons and Perfluorocarbons.*

International Institute for Environment and Development (IIED), 3 Endsleigh Street, London, England, WC1H 0DD, United Kingdom, www.iied.org; *Environment Urbanization; Tiempo: A Bulletin on Climate Change and Development; Up in Smoke? Asia and the Pacific;* and *Urban Environments, Wealth and Health: Shifting Burdens and Possible Responses in Low and Middle-Income Nations.*

Lithuanian Department of Statistics (Statistics Lithuania), Gedimino av. 29, LT-01500 Vilnius, Lithuania, www.stat.gov.lt/en; *Natural Resources and Environment Protection 2008.*

Ministry of Statistics and Analysis of the Republic of Belarus, 12 Partizansky Avenue, Minsk 220070, Belarus, www.belstat.gov.by; *Environment and Natural Resources in the Republic of Belarus.*

National Oceanic and Atmospheric Administration (NOAA), 1401 Constitution Avenue, NW, Room 6217, Washington, DC 20230, (202) 482-6090, Fax: (202) 482-3154, www.noaa.gov; *U.S. Climate at a Glance.*

National Oceanographic Data Center (NOCD), National Oceanic and Atmospheric Administration (NOAA), SSMC3, 4th Floor, 1315 East-West Highway, Silver Spring, MD 20910-3282, (301) 713-3277, Fax: (301) 713-3302, www.nodc.noaa.gov; *Climatic Atlas of the Arctic Seas 2004; Heat Content 2004; Linear Trends in Salinity for the World Ocean, 1955-1998; On the Variability of Dissolved Oxygen and Apparent Oxygen Utilization Content for the Upper World Ocean: 1955 to 1998; Warming of the World Ocean, 1955-2003; World Ocean Atlas 2005;* and *World Ocean Database Select and Search (WODselect).*

Organisation for Economic Cooperation and Development (OECD), 2 rue Andre Pascal, F-75775 Paris Cedex 16, France, (Telephone in U.S. (202) 785-6323), (Fax in U.S. (202) 785-0350), www.oecd.org; *OECD Environmental Data Compendium 2004.*

Platts, 2 Penn Plaza, 25th Floor, New York, NY 10121-2298, (212) 904-3070, www.platts.com; *Emissions Daily.*

Population Reference Bureau, 1875 Connecticut Avenue, NW, Suite 520, Washington, DC, 20009-5728, (800) 877-9881, Fax: (202) 328-3937, www.prb.org; *Making the Link: Population, Health, Environment.*

Saint Lucia Government Statistics Department, Chreiki Building, Micoud Street, Castries, Saint Lucia, (Dial from U.S. (758) 453-7670), (Fax from U.S. (758) 451-8254), www.stats.gov.lc; *Education Statistical Digest 2005.*

Statistical Institute of Jamaica (STATIN), 7 Cecelio Avenue, Kingston 10, Jamaica, (Dial from U.S. (876) 926-5311), (Fax from U.S. (876) 926-1138), www.statinja.com; *Environmental Statistics 2001.*

Statistics Iceland, Borgartuni 21a, 150 Reykjavik, Iceland, www.statice.is; *Environment and Pollutant Emissions.*

Statistics Indonesia (Badan Pusat Statistik (BPS)), Jl. Dr. Sutomo 6-8, Jakarta 10710, Indonesia, www.bps.go.id; *Environmental Statistical of Indonesia 2005.*

U.S. Census Bureau, 4700 Silver Hill Road, Washington DC 20233-0001, (301) 763-3030, www.census.gov; *LandView 6.*

U.S. Department of the Interior (DOI), Fish Wildlife Service (FWS), 1849 C Street, NW, Washington, DC 20240, (800) 344-WILD, www.fws.gov; Environmental Conservation Online System (ECOS).

U.S. Environmental Protection Agency (EPA) National Center for Environmental Research (NCER), Ariel Rios Building, 1200 Pennsylvania Avenue, NW, Washington, D.C. 20460, http://es.epa.gov/ncer; *Combustion Emissions from Hazardous Waste Incinerators, Boilers and Industrial Furnaces, and Municipal Solid Waste Incinerators - Results from Five STAR Grants and Research Needs* and *A Decade of Children's Environmental Health Research: Highlights from EPA's Science to Achieve Results Program.*

United Nations Environment Programme (UNEP), PO Box 30552, Nairobi, Kenya, www.unep.org; *Africa's Lakes: Atlas of Our Changing Environment; Atlas of International Freshwater Agreements; Climate Action; Eastern African Atlas of Coastal Resources; One Planet, Many People: Atlas of Our Changing Environment; Our Planet Magazine; Planet in Peril: Atlas of Current Threats to People and the Environment;* The UNEP Year Book 2008; *World Atlas of Biodiversity: Earth's Living Resources in the 21st Century; World Atlas of Coral Reefs; World Atlas of Desertification; World Atlas of Great Apes and Their Conservation;* and *World Atlas of Seagrasses.*

World Resources Institute (WRI), 10 G Street, NE, Suite 800 Washington, DC 20002, (202) 729-7600, www.wri.org; *Charting the Midwest: An Inventory and Analysis of Greenhouse Gas Emissions in America's Heartland; Eutrophication and Hypoxia in Coastal Areas: A Global Assessment of the State of Knowledge; Nature's Benefits in Kenya: An Atlas of Ecosystems and Human Well-Being; Painting the Global Picture of Tree Cover Change: Tree Cover Loss in the Humid Tropics; Thirst for Corn: What 2007 Plantings Could Mean for the Environment;* and *Undermining Grassland Management through Centralized Environmental Politics in Inner Mongolia.*

ENVIRONMENT - ENFORCEMENT ACTIONS

Platts, 2 Penn Plaza, 25th Floor, New York, NY 10121-2298, (212) 904-3070, www.platts.com; *Emissions Daily.*

U.S. Department of Justice (DOJ), Bureau of Justice Statistics, 810 Seventh Street, NW, Washington, DC 20531, (202) 307-0765, www.ojp.usdoj.gov/bjs/; *Federal Enforcement of Environmental Laws.*

United Nations Environment Programme (UNEP), PO Box 30552, Nairobi, Kenya, www.unep.org; *Atlas of International Freshwater Agreements.*

ENVIRONMENT - WETLANDS

U.S. Department of the Interior (DOI), Fish Wildlife Service (FWS), 1849 C Street, NW, Washington, DC 20240, (800) 344-WILD, www.fws.gov; *Status and Trends of Wetlands in the Conterminous United States, 1986 to 1997.*

ENVIRONMENTAL INDUSTRY

McGraw-Hill Construction, Dodge Analytics, 1221 Avenue of The Americas, Manhattan, NY 10020, (800) 393-6343, http://dodge.construction.com/analytics; *Green Building SmartMarket Report 2006.*

Platts, 2 Penn Plaza, 25th Floor, New York, NY 10121-2298, (212) 904-3070, www.platts.com; *Emissions Daily.*

Statistics Canada, 100 Tunney's Pasture Driveway, Ottawa, Ontario K1A 0T6, (Dial from U.S. (800) 263-1136), (Fax from U.S. (877) 287-4369), www.statcan.ca; *Greenhouse Gas Reduction Technologies: Industry Expenditures and Business Opportunities* and *Measuring Employment in the Environment Industry.*

ENVIRONMENTAL INDUSTRY - AGENCIES

Environmental Business International, Inc., 4452 Park Boulevard, Suite 306, San Diego, CA 92116, (619) 295-7685, Fax: (619) 295-5743, www.ebiusa.com; *Environmental Business Journal (EBJ) 2006; Environmental Market Reports;* and *U.S. and Global Environmental Market Data.*

ENVIRONMENTAL PROTECTION AGENCY - EMPLOYMENT

United States Office of Personnel Management (OMB), 1900 E Street, NW, Washington, DC 20415-1000, (202) 606-1800, www.opm.gov; *Employment and Trends of Federal Civilian Workforce Statistics.*

ENVIRONMENTAL PROTECTION AGENCY - WASTE TREATMENT FACILITIES - FEDERAL AID TO STATE AND LOCAL GOVERNMENTS

U.S. Census Bureau, Governments Division, 4600 Silver Hill Road, Washington DC 20233, (800) 242-2184, www.census.gov/govs/www; *Federal Aid to States for Fiscal Year 2004.*

EPIDEMICS

Caribbean Epidemiology Centre (CAREC), 16-18 Jamaica Boulevard, Federation Park, PO Box 164, Port of Spain, Republic of Trinidad and Tobago, (Dial from U.S. (868) 622-4261), (Fax from U.S. (868) 622-2792), www.carec.org; *20 Years of the HIV/AIDS Epidemic in the Caribbean* and AIDS Statistics.

European Centre for Disease Prevention and Control (ECDC), 171 83 Stockholm, Sweden, www.ecdc.europa.eu; *The First European Communicable Disease Epidemiological Report* and *Pandemic Preparedness in the European Union and European Economic Area - 2007.*

Health Protection Surveillance Centre (HPSC), 25-27 Middle Gardiner Street, Dublin 1, Ireland, www.ndsc.ie/hpsc; *Acute Gastroenteritis in Ireland, North and South: A Telephone Survey* and *Report on the Epidemiology of Tuberculosis in Ireland 2005.*

EQUATORIAL GUINEA - NATIONAL STATISTICAL OFFICE

Direccion General de Estadistica y Cuentas Nacionales (DGECN), Ministerio de Planificacion, Desarrollo Economico e Inversiones Publicas, Malabo, Equatorial Guinea, www.dgecnstat-ge.org; National Data Center.

EQUATORIAL GUINEA - PRIMARY STATISTICS SOURCES

Direccion General de Estadistica y Cuentas Nacionales (DGECN), Ministerio de Planificacion, Desarrollo Economico e Inversiones Publicas, Malabo, Equatorial Guinea, www.dgecnstat-ge.org; *Boletin estadistico 1990-2003* (Statistical Bulletin 1990-2003).

EQUATORIAL GUINEA - AGRICULTURAL MACHINERY

United Nations Statistics Division, New York, NY 10017, (800) 253-9646, Fax: (212) 963-4116, http://unstats.un.org; *Statistical Yearbook.*

EQUATORIAL GUINEA - AGRICULTURE

Economist Intelligence Unit, 111 West 57th Street, New York, NY 10019, (212) 554-0600, Fax: (212) 586-1181, www.eiu.com; *Equatorial Guinea Country Report.*

Euromonitor International, Inc., 224 S. Michigan Avenue, Suite 1500, Chicago, IL 60604, (312) 922-1115, Fax: (312) 922-1157, www.euromonitor.com; *World Marketing Data and Statistics.*

Palgrave Macmillan Ltd., Houndmills, Basingstoke, Hampshire, RG21 6XS, England, (Telephone in U.S. (888) 330-8477), (Fax in U.S. (800) 672-2054), www.palgrave.com; *The Statesman's Yearbook 2008.*

Taylor and Francis Group, An Informa Business, 2 Park Square, Milton Park, Abingdon, Oxford OX14 4RN, United Kingdom, (Dial from U.S. (212) 216-7800), (Fax from U.S. (212) 564-7854), www.tandf.co.uk; *The Europa World Year Book.*

United Nations Conference on Trade and Development (UNCTAD), DC2-1120, United Nations, New York, NY 10017, (212) 963-0027, www.unctad.org; *UNCTAD Commodity Yearbook.*

United Nations Economic Commission for Africa (ECA), PO Box 3001, Addis Ababa, Ethiopia, (Telephone in U.S. (212) 963-4957), www.uneca.org; *African Statistical Yearbook 2006.*

United Nations Food and Agricultural Organization (FAO), Viale delle Terme di Caracalla, 00100 Rome, Italy, (Dial from U.S. (202) 653-2400), (Fax from U.S. (202) 653 5760), www.fao.org; AQUASTAT; *FAO Production Yearbook 2002; FAO Trade Yearbook;* and *The State of Food and Agriculture (SOFA) 2006.*

United Nations Statistics Division, New York, NY 10017, (800) 253-9646, Fax: (212) 963-4116, http://unstats.un.org; *Statistical Yearbook* and *Survey of Economic and Social Conditions in Africa 2005.*

The World Bank, 1818 H Street, NW, Washington, DC 20433, (202) 473-1000, Fax: (202) 477-6391, www.worldbank.org; *Africa Live Database (LDB); African Development Indicators (ADI) 2007;* and *Equatorial Guinea.*

EQUATORIAL GUINEA - AIRLINES

Palgrave Macmillan Ltd., Houndmills, Basingstoke, Hampshire, RG21 6XS, England, (Telephone in U.S. (888) 330-8477), (Fax in U.S. (800) 672-2054), www.palgrave.com; *The Statesman's Yearbook 2008.*

Taylor and Francis Group, An Informa Business, 2 Park Square, Milton Park, Abingdon, Oxford OX14 4RN, United Kingdom, (Dial from U.S. (212) 216-7800), (Fax from U.S. (212) 564-7854), www.tandf.co.uk; *The Europa World Year Book.*

United Nations Economic Commission for Africa (ECA), PO Box 3001, Addis Ababa, Ethiopia, (Telephone in U.S. (212) 963-4957), www.uneca.org; *African Statistical Yearbook 2006.*

EQUATORIAL GUINEA - AIRPORTS

Central Intelligence Agency, Office of Public Affairs, Washington, DC 20505, (703) 482-0623, Fax: (703) 482-1739, www.cia.gov; *The World Factbook.*

EQUATORIAL GUINEA - ARMED FORCES

Central Intelligence Agency, Office of Public Affairs, Washington, DC 20505, (703) 482-0623, Fax: (703) 482-1739, www.cia.gov; *The World Factbook.*

Euromonitor International, Inc., 224 S. Michigan Avenue, Suite 1500, Chicago, IL 60604, (312) 922-1115, Fax: (312) 922-1157, www.euromonitor.com; *World Marketing Data and Statistics.*

International Institute for Strategic Studies (IISS), Arundel House, 13-15 Arundel Street, Temple Place, London WC2R 3DX, England, www.iiss.org; *The Military Balance 2007.*

Palgrave Macmillan Ltd., Houndmills, Basingstoke, Hampshire, RG21 6XS, England, (Telephone in U.S. (888) 330-8477), (Fax in U.S. (800) 672-2054), www.palgrave.com; *The Statesman's Yearbook 2008.*

U.S. Department of State (DOS), 2201 C Street NW, Washington, DC 20520, (202) 647-4000, www.state.gov; *World Military Expenditures and Arms Transfers (WMEAT).*

United Nations Statistics Division, New York, NY 10017, (800) 253-9646, Fax: (212) 963-4116, http://unstats.un.org; *Human Development Report 2006.*

EQUATORIAL GUINEA - BALANCE OF PAYMENTS

African Development Bank Group, Rue Joseph Anoma, 01 BP 1387 Abidjan 01, Cote d'Ivoire, www.afdb.org; *Statistics Pocketbook 2008.*

International Monetary Fund (IMF), 700 Nineteenth Street, NW, Washington, DC 20431, (202) 623-7000, Fax: (202) 623-4661, www.imf.org; *Balance of Payments Statistics Newsletter* and *Balance of Payments Statistics Yearbook 2007.*

Taylor and Francis Group, An Informa Business, 2 Park Square, Milton Park, Abingdon, Oxford OX14 4RN, United Kingdom, (Dial from U.S. (212) 216-7800), (Fax from U.S. (212) 564-7854), www.tandf.co.uk; *The Europa World Year Book.*

United Nations Conference on Trade and Development (UNCTAD), DC2-1120, United Nations, New York, NY 10017, (212) 963-0027, www.unctad.org; *Handbook of Statistics 2005.*

United Nations Economic Commission for Africa (ECA), PO Box 3001, Addis Ababa, Ethiopia, (Telephone in U.S. (212) 963-4957), www.uneca.org; *African Statistical Yearbook 2006.*

The World Bank, 1818 H Street, NW, Washington, DC 20433, (202) 473-1000, Fax: (202) 477-6391, www.worldbank.org; *Equatorial Guinea.*

EQUATORIAL GUINEA - BANKS AND BANKING

Euromonitor International, Inc., 224 S. Michigan Avenue, Suite 1500, Chicago, IL 60604, (312) 922-1115, Fax: (312) 922-1157, www.euromonitor.com; *World Marketing Data and Statistics.*

Palgrave Macmillan Ltd., Houndmills, Basingstoke, Hampshire, RG21 6XS, England, (Telephone in U.S. (888) 330-8477), (Fax in U.S. (800) 672-2054), www.palgrave.com; *The Statesman's Yearbook 2008.*

Taylor and Francis Group, An Informa Business, 2 Park Square, Milton Park, Abingdon, Oxford OX14 4RN, United Kingdom, (Dial from U.S. (212) 216-7800), (Fax from U.S. (212) 564-7854), www.tandf.co.uk; *The Europa World Year Book.*

United Nations Economic Commission for Africa (ECA), PO Box 3001, Addis Ababa, Ethiopia, (Telephone in U.S. (212) 963-4957), www.uneca.org; *African Statistical Yearbook 2006.*

EQUATORIAL GUINEA - BROADCASTING

Central Intelligence Agency, Office of Public Affairs, Washington, DC 20505, (703) 482-0623, Fax: (703) 482-1739, www.cia.gov; *The World Factbook.*

Euromonitor International, Inc:, 224 S. Michigan Avenue, Suite 1500, Chicago, IL 60604, (312) 922-1115, Fax: (312) 922-1157, www.euromonitor.com; *World Marketing Data and Statistics.*

Palgrave Macmillan Ltd., Houndmills, Basingstoke, Hampshire, RG21 6XS, England, (Telephone in U.S. (888) 330-8477), (Fax in U.S. (800) 672-2054), www.palgrave.com; *The Statesman's Yearbook 2008.*

WRTH Publications Limited, PO Box 290, Oxford OX2 7FT, UK, www.wrth.com; *World Radio TV Handbook 2007.*

EQUATORIAL GUINEA - BUDGET

Central Intelligence Agency, Office of Public Affairs, Washington, DC 20505, (703) 482-0623, Fax: (703) 482-1739, www.cia.gov; *The World Factbook.*

EQUATORIAL GUINEA - CATTLE

See EQUATORIAL GUINEA - LIVESTOCK

EQUATORIAL GUINEA - CHILDBIRTH - STATISTICS

Central Intelligence Agency, Office of Public Affairs, Washington, DC 20505, (703) 482-0623, Fax: (703) 482-1739, www.cia.gov; *The World Factbook.*

Euromonitor International, Inc., 224 S. Michigan Avenue, Suite 1500, Chicago, IL 60604, (312) 922-1115, Fax: (312) 922-1157, www.euromonitor.com; *International Marketing Data and Statistics 2008.*

Palgrave Macmillan Ltd., Houndmills, Basingstoke, Hampshire, RG21 6XS, England, (Telephone in U.S. (888) 330-8477), (Fax in U.S. (800) 672-2054), www.palgrave.com; *The Statesman's Yearbook 2008.*

Taylor and Francis Group, An Informa Business, 2 Park Square, Milton Park, Abingdon, Oxford OX14 4RN, United Kingdom, (Dial from U.S. (212) 216-7800), (Fax from U.S. (212) 564-7854), www.tandf.co.uk; *The Europa World Year Book.*

United Nations Statistics Division, New York, NY 10017, (800) 253-9646, Fax: (212) 963-4116, http://unstats.un.org; *Demographic Yearbook; Statistical Yearbook;* and *Survey of Economic and Social Conditions in Africa 2005.*

EQUATORIAL GUINEA - CLIMATE

International Institute for Environment and Development (IIED), 3 Endsleigh Street, London, England, WC1H 0DD, United Kingdom, www.iied.org; *Environment Urbanization* and *Haramata - Bulletin of the Drylands.*

Palgrave Macmillan Ltd., Houndmills, Basingstoke, Hampshire, RG21 6XS, England, (Telephone in U.S. (888) 330-8477), (Fax in U.S. (800) 672-2054), www.palgrave.com; *The Statesman's Yearbook 2008.*

EQUATORIAL GUINEA - COAL PRODUCTION

See EQUATORIAL GUINEA - MINERAL INDUSTRIES

EQUATORIAL GUINEA - COCOA PRODUCTION

See EQUATORIAL GUINEA - CROPS

EQUATORIAL GUINEA - COFFEE

See EQUATORIAL GUINEA - CROPS

EQUATORIAL GUINEA - COMMERCE

Palgrave Macmillan Ltd., Houndmills, Basingstoke, Hampshire, RG21 6XS, England, (Telephone in U.S. (888) 330-8477), (Fax in U.S. (800) 672-2054), www.palgrave.com; *The Statesman's Yearbook 2008.*

EQUATORIAL GUINEA - COMMODITY EXCHANGES

Commodity Research Bureau, 330 South Wells Street, Suite 612, Chicago, IL 60606-7110, (800) 621-5271, Fax: (312) 939-4135, www.crbtrader.com; *2006 CRB Commodity Yearbook and CD.*

International Monetary Fund (IMF), 700 Nineteenth Street, NW, Washington, DC 20431, (202) 623-7000, Fax: (202) 623-4661, www.imf.org; *IMF Primary Commodity Prices.*

United Nations Food and Agricultural Organization (FAO), Viale delle Terme di Caracalla, 00100 Rome, Italy, (Dial from U.S. (202) 653-2400), (Fax from U.S. (202) 653 5760), www.fao.org; *The State of Food and Agriculture (SOFA) 2006.*

EQUATORIAL GUINEA - CONSUMER PRICE INDEXES

Taylor and Francis Group, An Informa Business, 2 Park Square, Milton Park, Abingdon, Oxford OX14 4RN, United Kingdom, (Dial from U.S. (212) 216-7800), (Fax from U.S. (212) 564-7854), www.tandf.co.uk; *The Europa World Year Book.*

United Nations Statistics Division, New York, NY 10017, (800) 253-9646, Fax: (212) 963-4116, http://unstats.un.org; *Survey of Economic and Social Conditions in Africa 2005.*

The World Bank, 1818 H Street, NW, Washington, DC 20433, (202) 473-1000, Fax: (202) 477-6391, www.worldbank.org; *Equatorial Guinea.*

EQUATORIAL GUINEA - CONSUMPTION (ECONOMICS)

African Development Bank Group, Rue Joseph Anoma, 01 BP 1387 Abidjan 01, Cote d'Ivoire, www.afdb.org; *Statistics Pocketbook 2008.*

United Nations Statistics Division, New York, NY 10017, (800) 253-9646, Fax: (212) 963-4116, http://unstats.un.org; *Survey of Economic and Social Conditions in Africa 2005.*

EQUATORIAL GUINEA - CORN INDUSTRY

See EQUATORIAL GUINEA - CROPS

EQUATORIAL GUINEA - CROPS

Palgrave Macmillan Ltd., Houndmills, Basingstoke, Hampshire, RG21 6XS, England, (Telephone in U.S. (888) 330-8477), (Fax in U.S. (800) 672-2054), www.palgrave.com; *The Statesman's Yearbook 2008.*

Taylor and Francis Group, An Informa Business, 2 Park Square, Milton Park, Abingdon, Oxford OX14 4RN, United Kingdom, (Dial from U.S. (212) 216-7800), (Fax from U.S. (212) 564-7854), www.tandf.co.uk; *The Europa World Year Book.*

United Nations Conference on Trade and Development (UNCTAD), DC2-1120, United Nations, New York, NY 10017, (212) 963-0027, www.unctad.org; *UNCTAD Commodity Yearbook.*

United Nations Economic Commission for Africa (ECA), PO Box 3001, Addis Ababa, Ethiopia, (Telephone in U.S. (212) 963-4957), www.uneca.org; *African Statistical Yearbook 2006.*

United Nations Food and Agricultural Organization (FAO), Viale delle Terme di Caracalla, 00100 Rome, Italy, (Dial from U.S. (202) 653-2400), (Fax from U.S. (202) 653 5760), www.fao.org; *FAO Production Yearbook 2002* and *The State of Food and Agriculture (SOFA) 2006.*

United Nations Statistics Division, New York, NY 10017, (800) 253-9646, Fax: (212) 963-4116, http://unstats.un.org; *Statistical Yearbook.*

EQUATORIAL GUINEA - DAIRY PROCESSING

Organisation for Economic Cooperation and Development (OECD), 2 rue Andre Pascal, F-75775 Paris Cedex 16, France, (Telephone in U.S. (202) 785-6323), (Fax in U.S. (202) 785-0350), www.oecd.org; *Indicators of Industrial Activity.*

Palgrave Macmillan Ltd., Houndmills, Basingstoke, Hampshire, RG21 6XS, England, (Telephone in U.S. (888) 330-8477), (Fax in U.S. (800) 672-2054), www.palgrave.com; *The Statesman's Yearbook 2008.*

EQUATORIAL GUINEA - DEATH RATES

See EQUATORIAL GUINEA - MORTALITY

EQUATORIAL GUINEA - DEBTS, EXTERNAL

African Development Bank Group, Rue Joseph Anoma, 01 BP 1387 Abidjan 01, Cote d'Ivoire, www.afdb.org; *Statistics Pocketbook 2008.*

United Nations Statistics Division, New York, NY 10017, (800) 253-9646, Fax: (212) 963-4116, http://unstats.un.org; *Survey of Economic and Social Conditions in Africa 2005.*

The World Bank, 1818 H Street, NW, Washington, DC 20433, (202) 473-1000, Fax: (202) 477-6391, www.worldbank.org; *Africa Live Database (LDB); African Development Indicators (ADI) 2007;* and *Global Development Finance 2007.*

EQUATORIAL GUINEA - DEFENSE EXPENDITURES

See EQUATORIAL GUINEA - ARMED FORCES

EQUATORIAL GUINEA - DEMOGRAPHY

Euromonitor International, Inc., 224 S. Michigan Avenue, Suite 1500, Chicago, IL 60604, (312) 922-1115, Fax: (312) 922-1157, www.euromonitor.com; *International Marketing Data and Statistics 2008* and *World Marketing Data and Statistics.*

Palgrave Macmillan Ltd., Houndmills, Basingstoke, Hampshire, RG21 6XS, England, (Telephone in U.S. (888) 330-8477), (Fax in U.S. (800) 672-2054), www.palgrave.com; *The Statesman's Yearbook 2008.*

United Nations Statistics Division, New York, NY 10017, (800) 253-9646, Fax: (212) 963-4116, http://unstats.un.org; *Human Development Report 2006* and *Survey of Economic and Social Conditions in Africa 2005.*

The World Bank, 1818 H Street, NW, Washington, DC 20433, (202) 473-1000, Fax: (202) 477-6391, www.worldbank.org; *Equatorial Guinea.*

EQUATORIAL GUINEA - DISPOSABLE INCOME

United Nations Statistics Division, New York, NY 10017, (800) 253-9646, Fax: (212) 963-4116, http://unstats.un.org; *National Accounts Statistics: Compendium of Income Distribution Statistics* and *Statistical Yearbook.*

EQUATORIAL GUINEA - DIVORCE

United Nations Statistics Division, New York, NY 10017, (800) 253-9646, Fax: (212) 963-4116, http://unstats.un.org; *Demographic Yearbook.*

EQUATORIAL GUINEA - ECONOMIC ASSISTANCE

United Nations Statistics Division, New York, NY 10017, (800) 253-9646, Fax: (212) 963-4116, http://unstats.un.org; *Statistical Yearbook.*

EQUATORIAL GUINEA - ECONOMIC CONDITIONS

African Development Bank Group, Rue Joseph Anoma, 01 BP 1387 Abidjan 01, Cote d'Ivoire, www.afdb.org; *The African Statistical Journal; Gender, Poverty and Environmental Indicators on African Countries 2007; Selected Statistics on African Countries 2007;* and *Statistics Pocketbook 2008.*

Center for International Business Education Research (CIBER), Columbia Business School and School of International and Public Affairs, Uris Hall, Room 212, 3022 Broadway, New York, NY 10027-6902, Mr. Joshua Safier, (212) 854-4750, Fax: (212) 222-9821, www.columbia.edu/cu/ciber/; Datastream International.

Central Intelligence Agency, Office of Public Affairs, Washington, DC 20505, (703) 482-0623, Fax: (703) 482-1739, www.cia.gov; *The World Factbook.*

DSI Data Service Information, Xantener Strasse 51a, D-47495 Rheinberg, Germany, www.dsidata.com; *Campus Solution.*

Dun and Bradstreet (DB) Corporation, 103 JFK Parkway, Short Hills, NJ 07078, (973) 921-5500, www.dnb.com; *Country Report.*

Economist Intelligence Unit, 111 West 57th Street, New York, NY 10019, (212) 554-0600, Fax: (212) 586-1181, www.eiu.com; *Business Africa* and *Equatorial Guinea Country Report.*

Euromonitor International, Inc., 224 S. Michigan Avenue, Suite 1500, Chicago, IL 60604, (312) 922-1115, Fax: (312) 922-1157, www.euromonitor.com; *World Marketing Data and Statistics.*

International Monetary Fund (IMF), 700 Nineteenth Street, NW, Washington, DC 20431, (202) 623-7000, Fax: (202) 623-4661, www.imf.org; *World Economic Outlook Reports.*

Palgrave Macmillan Ltd., Houndmills, Basingstoke, Hampshire, RG21 6XS, England, (Telephone in U.S. (888) 330-8477), (Fax in U.S. (800) 672-2054), www.palgrave.com; *The Statesman's Yearbook 2008.*

Taylor and Francis Group, An Informa Business, 2 Park Square, Milton Park, Abingdon, Oxford OX14 4RN, United Kingdom, (Dial from U.S. (212) 216-7800), (Fax from U.S. (212) 564-7854), www.tandf.co.uk; *The Europa World Year Book.*

United Nations Statistics Division, New York, NY 10017, (800) 253-9646, Fax: (212) 963-4116, http://unstats.un.org; *World Statistics Pocketbook.*

The World Bank, 1818 H Street, NW, Washington, DC 20433, (202) 473-1000, Fax: (202) 477-6391, www.worldbank.org; *Africa Household Survey Databank; Africa Live Database (LDB); Africa Standardized Files and Indicators; African Development Indicators (ADI) 2007; Equatorial Guinea; Global Economic Monitor (GEM); Global Economic Prospects 2008;* and *The World Bank Atlas 2003-2004.*

EQUATORIAL GUINEA - EDUCATION

African Development Bank Group, Rue Joseph Anoma, 01 BP 1387 Abidjan 01, Cote d'Ivoire, www.afdb.org; *Statistics Pocketbook 2008.*

Euromonitor International, Inc., 224 S. Michigan Avenue, Suite 1500, Chicago, IL 60604, (312) 922-1115, Fax: (312) 922-1157, www.euromonitor.com; *International Marketing Data and Statistics 2008* and *World Marketing Data and Statistics.*

Palgrave Macmillan Ltd., Houndmills, Basingstoke, Hampshire, RG21 6XS, England, (Telephone in U.S. (888) 330-8477), (Fax in U.S. (800) 672-2054), www.palgrave.com; *The Statesman's Yearbook 2008.*

Taylor and Francis Group, An Informa Business, 2 Park Square, Milton Park, Abingdon, Oxford OX14 4RN, United Kingdom, (Dial from U.S. (212) 216-7800), (Fax from U.S. (212) 564-7854), www.tandf.co.uk; *The Europa World Year Book.*

United Nations Economic Commission for Africa (ECA), PO Box 3001, Addis Ababa, Ethiopia, (Telephone in U.S. (212) 963-4957), www.uneca.org; *African Statistical Yearbook 2006.*

United Nations Statistics Division, New York, NY 10017, (800) 253-9646, Fax: (212) 963-4116, http://unstats.un.org; *Human Development Report 2006* and *Survey of Economic and Social Conditions in Africa 2005.*

The World Bank, 1818 H Street, NW, Washington, DC 20433, (202) 473-1000, Fax: (202) 477-6391, www.worldbank.org; *Equatorial Guinea.*

EQUATORIAL GUINEA - ELECTRICITY

Palgrave Macmillan Ltd., Houndmills, Basingstoke, Hampshire, RG21 6XS, England, (Telephone in U.S. (888) 330-8477), (Fax in U.S. (800) 672-2054), www.palgrave.com; *The Statesman's Yearbook 2008.*

United Nations Economic Commission for Africa (ECA), PO Box 3001, Addis Ababa, Ethiopia, (Telephone in U.S. (212) 963-4957), www.uneca.org; *African Statistical Yearbook 2006.*

United Nations Statistics Division, New York, NY 10017, (800) 253-9646, Fax: (212) 963-4116, http://unstats.un.org; *Human Development Report 2006* and *Survey of Economic and Social Conditions in Africa 2005.*

EQUATORIAL GUINEA - EMPLOYMENT

Euromonitor International, Inc., 224 S. Michigan Avenue, Suite 1500, Chicago, IL 60604, (312) 922-1115, Fax: (312) 922-1157, www.euromonitor.com; *International Marketing Data and Statistics 2008.*

United Nations Economic Commission for Africa (ECA), PO Box 3001, Addis Ababa, Ethiopia, (Telephone in U.S. (212) 963-4957), www.uneca.org; *African Statistical Yearbook 2006.*

United Nations Statistics Division, New York, NY 10017, (800) 253-9646, Fax: (212) 963-4116, http://unstats.un.org; *Survey of Economic and Social Conditions in Africa 2005.*

The World Bank, 1818 H Street, NW, Washington, DC 20433, (202) 473-1000, Fax: (202) 477-6391, www.worldbank.org; *Equatorial Guinea.*

EQUATORIAL GUINEA - ENVIRONMENTAL CONDITIONS

DSI Data Service Information, Xantener Strasse 51a, D-47495 Rheinberg, Germany, www.dsidata.com; *Campus Solution* and *DSI's Global Environmental Database.*

Economist Intelligence Unit, 111 West 57th Street, New York, NY 10019, (212) 554-0600, Fax: (212) 586-1181, www.eiu.com; *Equatorial Guinea Country Report.*

International Institute for Environment and Development (IIED), 3 Endsleigh Street, London, England, WC1H 0DD, United Kingdom, www.iied.org; *Environment Urbanization* and *Haramata - Bulletin of the Drylands.*

United Nations Statistics Division, New York, NY 10017, (800) 253-9646, Fax: (212) 963-4116, http://unstats.un.org; *World Statistics Pocketbook.*

EQUATORIAL GUINEA - EXPORTS

African Development Bank Group, Rue Joseph Anoma, 01 BP 1387 Abidjan 01, Cote d'Ivoire, www.afdb.org; *Statistics Pocketbook 2008.*

Central Intelligence Agency, Office of Public Affairs, Washington, DC 20505, (703) 482-0623, Fax: (703) 482-1739, www.cia.gov; *The World Factbook.*

Economist Intelligence Unit, 111 West 57th Street, New York, NY 10019, (212) 554-0600, Fax: (212) 586-1181, www.eiu.com; *Equatorial Guinea Country Report.*

Euromonitor International, Inc., 224 S. Michigan Avenue, Suite 1500, Chicago, IL 60604, (312) 922-1115, Fax: (312) 922-1157, www.euromonitor.com; *International Marketing Data and Statistics 2008.*

International Monetary Fund (IMF), 700 Nineteenth Street, NW, Washington, DC 20431, (202) 623-7000, Fax: (202) 623-4661, www.imf.org; *Direction of Trade Statistics Yearbook 2007.*

Palgrave Macmillan Ltd., Houndmills, Basingstoke, Hampshire, RG21 6XS, England, (Telephone in U.S. (888) 330-8477), (Fax in U.S. (800) 672-2054), www.palgrave.com; *The Statesman's Yearbook 2008.*

Taylor and Francis Group, An Informa Business, 2 Park Square, Milton Park, Abingdon, Oxford OX14 4RN, United Kingdom, (Dial from U.S. (212) 216-7800), (Fax from U.S. (212) 564-7854), www.tandf.co.uk; *The Europa World Year Book.*

United Nations Conference on Trade and Development (UNCTAD), DC2-1120, United Nations, New York, NY 10017, (212) 963-0027, www.unctad.org; *Handbook of Statistics 2005.*

United Nations Economic Commission for Africa (ECA), PO Box 3001, Addis Ababa, Ethiopia, (Telephone in U.S. (212) 963-4957), www.uneca.org; *African Statistical Yearbook 2006.*

United Nations Food and Agricultural Organization (FAO), Viale delle Terme di Caracalla, 00100 Rome, Italy, (Dial from U.S. (202) 653-2400), (Fax from U.S. (202) 653 5760), www.fao.org; *The State of Food and Agriculture (SOFA) 2006.*

United Nations Statistics Division, New York, NY 10017, (800) 253-9646, Fax: (212) 963-4116, http://unstats.un.org; *Survey of Economic and Social Conditions in Africa 2005.*

EQUATORIAL GUINEA - FERTILITY, HUMAN

Central Intelligence Agency, Office of Public Affairs, Washington, DC 20505, (703) 482-0623, Fax: (703) 482-1739, www.cia.gov; *The World Factbook.*

United Nations Statistics Division, New York, NY 10017, (800) 253-9646, Fax: (212) 963-4116, http://unstats.un.org; *Human Development Report 2006* and *Survey of Economic and Social Conditions in Africa 2005.*

The World Bank, 1818 H Street, NW, Washington, DC 20433, (202) 473-1000, Fax: (202) 477-6391, www.worldbank.org; *The World Bank Atlas 2003-2004.*

EQUATORIAL GUINEA - FERTILIZER INDUSTRY

United Nations Food and Agricultural Organization (FAO), Viale delle Terme di Caracalla, 00100 Rome, Italy, (Dial from U.S. (202) 653-2400), (Fax from U.S. (202) 653 5760), www.fao.org; *FAO Fertilizer Yearbook* and *The State of Food and Agriculture (SOFA) 2006.*

United Nations Statistics Division, New York, NY 10017, (800) 253-9646, Fax: (212) 963-4116, http://unstats.un.org; *Statistical Yearbook.*

EQUATORIAL GUINEA - FETAL MORTALITY

See EQUATORIAL GUINEA - MORTALITY

EQUATORIAL GUINEA - FINANCE

International Monetary Fund (IMF), 700 Nineteenth Street, NW, Washington, DC 20431, (202) 623-7000, Fax: (202) 623-4661, www.imf.org; *International Financial Statistics Yearbook 2007.*

United Nations Economic Commission for Africa (ECA), PO Box 3001, Addis Ababa, Ethiopia, (Telephone in U.S. (212) 963-4957), www.uneca.org; *African Statistical Yearbook 2006.*

United Nations Statistics Division, New York, NY 10017, (800) 253-9646, Fax: (212) 963-4116, http://unstats.un.org; *Statistical Yearbook.*

The World Bank, 1818 H Street, NW, Washington, DC 20433, (202) 473-1000, Fax: (202) 477-6391, www.worldbank.org; *Equatorial Guinea.*

EQUATORIAL GUINEA - FINANCE, PUBLIC

African Development Bank Group, Rue Joseph Anoma, 01 BP 1387 Abidjan 01, Cote d'Ivoire, www.afdb.org; *Statistics Pocketbook 2008.*

Bernan Essential Government Publications, 4611-F Assembly Drive, Lanham MD, 20706-4391, (301) 459-2255, Fax: (800) 865-3450, www.bernan.com; *National Accounts Statistics.*

Economist Intelligence Unit, 111 West 57th Street, New York, NY 10019, (212) 554-0600, Fax: (212) 586-1181, www.eiu.com; *Equatorial Guinea Country Report.*

International Monetary Fund (IMF), 700 Nineteenth Street, NW, Washington, DC 20431, (202) 623-7000, Fax: (202) 623-4661, www.imf.org; *International Financial Statistics; International Financial Statistics Online Service;* and *International Financial Statistics Yearbook 2007.*

Taylor and Francis Group, An Informa Business, 2 Park Square, Milton Park, Abingdon, Oxford OX14 4RN, United Kingdom, (Dial from U.S. (212) 216-7800), (Fax from U.S. (212) 564-7854), www.tandf.co.uk; *The Europa World Year Book.*

United Nations Economic Commission for Africa (ECA), PO Box 3001, Addis Ababa, Ethiopia, (Telephone in U.S. (212) 963-4957), www.uneca.org; *African Statistical Yearbook 2006.*

The World Bank, 1818 H Street, NW, Washington, DC 20433, (202) 473-1000, Fax: (202) 477-6391, www.worldbank.org; *Equatorial Guinea.*

EQUATORIAL GUINEA - FISHERIES

Palgrave Macmillan Ltd., Houndmills, Basingstoke, Hampshire, RG21 6XS, England, (Telephone in U.S. (888) 330-8477), (Fax in U.S. (800) 672-2054), www.palgrave.com; *The Statesman's Yearbook 2008.*

Taylor and Francis Group, An Informa Business, 2 Park Square, Milton Park, Abingdon, Oxford OX14 4RN, United Kingdom, (Dial from U.S. (212) 216-7800), (Fax from U.S. (212) 564-7854), www.tandf.co.uk; *The Europa World Year Book.*

United Nations Conference on Trade and Development (UNCTAD), DC2-1120, United Nations, New York, NY 10017, (212) 963-0027, www.unctad.org; *UNCTAD Commodity Yearbook.*

United Nations Economic Commission for Africa (ECA), PO Box 3001, Addis Ababa, Ethiopia, (Telephone in U.S. (212) 963-4957), www.uneca.org; *African Statistical Yearbook 2006.*

United Nations Food and Agricultural Organization (FAO), Viale delle Terme di Caracalla, 00100 Rome, Italy, (Dial from U.S. (202) 653-2400), (Fax from U.S. (202) 653 5760), www.fao.org; *FAO Yearbook of Fishery Statistics;* Fishery Databases; FISHSTAT Database. Subjects covered include: Aquaculture production, capture production, fishery commodities; and *The State of Food and Agriculture (SOFA) 2006.*

United Nations Statistics Division, New York, NY 10017, (800) 253-9646, Fax: (212) 963-4116, http://unstats.un.org; *Survey of Economic and Social Conditions in Africa 2005.*

The World Bank, 1818 H Street, NW, Washington, DC 20433, (202) 473-1000, Fax: (202) 477-6391, www.worldbank.org; *Equatorial Guinea.*

EQUATORIAL GUINEA - FOOD

African Development Bank Group, Rue Joseph Anoma, 01 BP 1387 Abidjan 01, Cote d'Ivoire, www.afdb.org; *Statistics Pocketbook 2008.*

United Nations Conference on Trade and Development (UNCTAD), DC2-1120, United Nations, New York, NY 10017, (212) 963-0027, www.unctad.org; *UNCTAD Commodity Yearbook.*

United Nations Food and Agricultural Organization (FAO), Viale delle Terme di Caracalla, 00100 Rome, Italy, (Dial from U.S. (202) 653-2400), (Fax from U.S. (202) 653 5760), www.fao.org; *FAO Production Yearbook 2002* and *The State of Food and Agriculture (SOFA) 2006.*

United Nations Statistics Division, New York, NY 10017, (800) 253-9646, Fax: (212) 963-4116, http://unstats.un.org; *Human Development Report 2006.*

EQUATORIAL GUINEA - FOREIGN EXCHANGE RATES

African Development Bank Group, Rue Joseph Anoma, 01 BP 1387 Abidjan 01, Cote d'Ivoire, www.afdb.org; *Statistics Pocketbook 2008.*

Central Intelligence Agency, Office of Public Affairs, Washington, DC 20505, (703) 482-0623, Fax: (703) 482-1739, www.cia.gov; *The World Factbook.*

Euromonitor International, Inc., 224 S. Michigan Avenue, Suite 1500, Chicago, IL 60604, (312) 922-1115, Fax: (312) 922-1157, www.euromonitor.com; *International Marketing Data and Statistics 2008.*

Palgrave Macmillan Ltd., Houndmills, Basingstoke, Hampshire, RG21 6XS, England, (Telephone in U.S. (888) 330-8477), (Fax in U.S. (800) 672-2054), www.palgrave.com; *The Statesman's Yearbook 2008.*

Taylor and Francis Group, An Informa Business, 2 Park Square, Milton Park, Abingdon, Oxford OX14 4RN, United Kingdom, (Dial from U.S. (212) 216-7800), (Fax from U.S. (212) 564-7854), www.tandf.co.uk; *The Europa World Year Book.*

United Nations Statistics Division, New York, NY 10017, (800) 253-9646, Fax: (212) 963-4116, http://unstats.un.org; *Statistical Yearbook* and *World Statistics Pocketbook.*

EQUATORIAL GUINEA - FORESTS AND FORESTRY

Palgrave Macmillan Ltd., Houndmills, Basingstoke, Hampshire, RG21 6XS, England, (Telephone in U.S. (888) 330-8477), (Fax in U.S. (800) 672-2054), www.palgrave.com; *The Statesman's Yearbook 2008.*

Taylor and Francis Group, An Informa Business, 2 Park Square, Milton Park, Abingdon, Oxford OX14 4RN, United Kingdom, (Dial from U.S. (212) 216-7800), (Fax from U.S. (212) 564-7854), www.tandf.co.uk; *The Europa World Year Book.*

UNESCO Institute for Statistics, C.P. 6128 Succursale Centre-Ville, Montreal, Quebec, H3C 3J7 Canada, (Dial from U.S. (514) 343-6880), (Fax from U.S. (514) 343 6882), www.uis.unesco.org; *Statistical Tables.*

United Nations Conference on Trade and Development (UNCTAD), DC2-1120, United Nations, New York, NY 10017, (212) 963-0027, www.unctad.org; *UNCTAD Commodity Yearbook.*

United Nations Economic Commission for Africa (ECA), PO Box 3001, Addis Ababa, Ethiopia, (Telephone in U.S. (212) 963-4957), www.uneca.org; *African Statistical Yearbook 2006.*

United Nations Food and Agricultural Organization (FAO), Viale delle Terme di Caracalla, 00100 Rome,

Italy, (Dial from U.S. (202) 653-2400), (Fax from U.S. (202) 653 5760), www.fao.org; *FAO Yearbook of Forest Products* and *The State of Food and Agriculture (SOFA) 2006.*

The World Bank, 1818 H Street, NW, Washington, DC 20433, (202) 473-1000, Fax: (202) 477-6391, www.worldbank.org; *Equatorial Guinea.*

EQUATORIAL GUINEA - GROSS DOMESTIC PRODUCT

African Development Bank Group, Rue Joseph Anoma, 01 BP 1387 Abidjan 01, Cote d'Ivoire, www.afdb.org; *Statistics Pocketbook 2008.*

Economist Intelligence Unit, 111 West 57th Street, New York, NY 10019, (212) 554-0600, Fax: (212) 586-1181, www.eiu.com; *Equatorial Guinea Country Report.*

Euromonitor International, Inc., 224 S. Michigan Avenue, Suite 1500, Chicago, IL 60604, (312) 922-1115, Fax: (312) 922-1157, www.euromonitor.com; *International Marketing Data and Statistics 2008.*

Palgrave Macmillan Ltd., Houndmills, Basingstoke, Hampshire, RG21 6XS, England, (Telephone in U.S. (888) 330-8477), (Fax in U.S. (800) 672-2054), www.palgrave.com; *The Statesman's Yearbook 2008.*

Taylor and Francis Group, An Informa Business, 2 Park Square, Milton Park, Abingdon, Oxford OX14 4RN, United Kingdom, (Dial from U.S. (212) 216-7800), (Fax from U.S. (212) 564-7854), www.tandf.co.uk; *The Europa World Year Book.*

United Nations Economic Commission for Africa (ECA), PO Box 3001, Addis Ababa, Ethiopia, (Telephone in U.S. (212) 963-4957), www.uneca.org; *African Statistical Yearbook 2006.*

United Nations Statistics Division, New York, NY 10017, (800) 253-9646, Fax: (212) 963-4116, http://unstats.un.org; *Human Development Report 2006; National Accounts Statistics: Compendium of Income Distribution Statistics; Statistical Yearbook;* and *Survey of Economic and Social Conditions in Africa 2005.*

EQUATORIAL GUINEA - GROSS NATIONAL PRODUCT

Palgrave Macmillan Ltd., Houndmills, Basingstoke, Hampshire, RG21 6XS, England, (Telephone in U.S. (888) 330-8477), (Fax in U.S. (800) 672-2054), www.palgrave.com; *The Statesman's Yearbook 2008.*

U.S. Department of State (DOS), 2201 C Street NW, Washington, DC 20520, (202) 647-4000, www.state.gov; *World Military Expenditures and Arms Transfers (WMEAT).*

The World Bank, 1818 H Street, NW, Washington, DC 20433, (202) 473-1000, Fax: (202) 477-6391, www.worldbank.org; *The World Bank Atlas 2003-2004.*

EQUATORIAL GUINEA - HIDES AND SKINS INDUSTRY

United Nations Food and Agricultural Organization (FAO), Viale delle Terme di Caracalla, 00100 Rome, Italy, (Dial from U.S. (202) 653-2400), (Fax from U.S. (202) 653 5760), www.fao.org; *FAO Production Yearbook 2002.*

EQUATORIAL GUINEA - HOUSING

Euromonitor International, Inc., 224 S. Michigan Avenue, Suite 1500, Chicago, IL 60604, (312) 922-1115, Fax: (312) 922-1157, www.euromonitor.com; *World Marketing Data and Statistics.*

EQUATORIAL GUINEA - ILLITERATE PERSONS

Palgrave Macmillan Ltd., Houndmills, Basingstoke, Hampshire, RG21 6XS, England, (Telephone in U.S. (888) 330-8477), (Fax in U.S. (800) 672-2054), www.palgrave.com; *The Statesman's Yearbook 2008.*

United Nations Statistics Division, New York, NY 10017, (800) 253-9646, Fax: (212) 963-4116, http://unstats.un.org; *Human Development Report 2006.*

EQUATORIAL GUINEA - IMPORTS

Central Intelligence Agency, Office of Public Affairs, Washington, DC 20505, (703) 482-0623, Fax: (703) 482-1739, www.cia.gov; *The World Factbook.*

Economist Intelligence Unit, 111 West 57th Street, New York, NY 10019, (212) 554-0600, Fax: (212) 586-1181, www.eiu.com; *Equatorial Guinea Country Report.*

Euromonitor International, Inc., 224 S. Michigan Avenue, Suite 1500, Chicago, IL 60604, (312) 922-1115, Fax: (312) 922-1157, www.euromonitor.com; *International Marketing Data and Statistics 2008.*

International Monetary Fund (IMF), 700 Nineteenth Street, NW, Washington, DC 20431, (202) 623-7000, Fax: (202) 623-4661, www.imf.org; *Direction of Trade Statistics Yearbook 2007.*

Palgrave Macmillan Ltd., Houndmills, Basingstoke, Hampshire, RG21 6XS, England, (Telephone in U.S. (888) 330-8477), (Fax in U.S. (800) 672-2054), www.palgrave.com; *The Statesman's Yearbook 2008.*

Taylor and Francis Group, An Informa Business, 2 Park Square, Milton Park, Abingdon, Oxford OX14 4RN, United Kingdom, (Dial from U.S. (212) 216-7800), (Fax from U.S. (212) 564-7854), www.tandf.co.uk; *The Europa World Year Book.*

United Nations Conference on Trade and Development (UNCTAD), DC2-1120, United Nations, New York, NY 10017, (212) 963-0027, www.unctad.org; *Handbook of Statistics 2005.*

United Nations Food and Agricultural Organization (FAO), Viale delle Terme di Caracalla, 00100 Rome, Italy, (Dial from U.S. (202) 653-2400), (Fax from U.S. (202) 653 5760), www.fao.org; *The State of Food and Agriculture (SOFA) 2006.*

United Nations Statistics Division, New York, NY 10017, (800) 253-9646, Fax: (212) 963-4116, http://unstats.un.org; *Survey of Economic and Social Conditions in Africa 2005.*

EQUATORIAL GUINEA - INDUSTRIES

Central Intelligence Agency, Office of Public Affairs, Washington, DC 20505, (703) 482-0623, Fax: (703) 482-1739, www.cia.gov; *The World Factbook.*

Economist Intelligence Unit, 111 West 57th Street, New York, NY 10019, (212) 554-0600, Fax: (212) 586-1181, www.eiu.com; *Equatorial Guinea Country Report.*

Euromonitor International, Inc., 224 S. Michigan Avenue, Suite 1500, Chicago, IL 60604, (312) 922-1115, Fax: (312) 922-1157, www.euromonitor.com; *World Marketing Data and Statistics.*

Palgrave Macmillan Ltd., Houndmills, Basingstoke, Hampshire, RG21 6XS, England, (Telephone in U.S. (888) 330-8477), (Fax in U.S. (800) 672-2054), www.palgrave.com; *The Statesman's Yearbook 2008.*

Taylor and Francis Group, An Informa Business, 2 Park Square, Milton Park, Abingdon, Oxford OX14 4RN, United Kingdom, (Dial from U.S. (212) 216-7800), (Fax from U.S. (212) 564-7854), www.tandf.co.uk; *The Europa World Year Book.*

United Nations Economic Commission for Africa (ECA), PO Box 3001, Addis Ababa, Ethiopia, (Telephone in U.S. (212) 963-4957), www.uneca.org; *African Statistical Yearbook 2006.*

United Nations Industrial Development Organization (UNIDO), 1 United Nations Plaza, New York, NY 10017, (212) 963 6890, Fax: (212) 963-7904, http://unido.org; Industrial Statistics Database 2008 (INDSTAT) and *The International Yearbook of Industrial Statistics 2008.*

United Nations Statistics Division, New York, NY 10017, (800) 253-9646, Fax: (212) 963-4116, http://unstats.un.org; *Survey of Economic and Social Conditions in Africa 2005.*

The World Bank, 1818 H Street, NW, Washington, DC 20433, (202) 473-1000, Fax: (202) 477-6391, www.worldbank.org; *Equatorial Guinea.*

EQUATORIAL GUINEA - INFANT AND MATERNAL MORTALITY

See EQUATORIAL GUINEA - MORTALITY

EQUATORIAL GUINEA - INTERNATIONAL TRADE

African Development Bank Group, Rue Joseph Anoma, 01 BP 1387 Abidjan 01, Cote d'Ivoire, www.afdb.org; *Statistics Pocketbook 2008.*

Economist Intelligence Unit, 111 West 57th Street, New York, NY 10019, (212) 554-0600, Fax: (212) 586-1181, www.eiu.com; *Equatorial Guinea Country Report.*

Euromonitor International, Inc., 224 S. Michigan Avenue, Suite 1500, Chicago, IL 60604, (312) 922-1115, Fax: (312) 922-1157, www.euromonitor.com; *World Marketing Data and Statistics.*

Palgrave Macmillan Ltd., Houndmills, Basingstoke, Hampshire, RG21 6XS, England, (Telephone in U.S. (888) 330-8477), (Fax in U.S. (800) 672-2054), www.palgrave.com; *The Statesman's Yearbook 2008.*

Taylor and Francis Group, An Informa Business, 2 Park Square, Milton Park, Abingdon, Oxford OX14 4RN, United Kingdom, (Dial from U.S. (212) 216-7800), (Fax from U.S. (212) 564-7854), www.tandf.co.uk; *The Europa World Year Book.*

United Nations Conference on Trade and Development (UNCTAD), DC2-1120, United Nations, New York, NY 10017, (212) 963-0027, www.unctad.org; *UNCTAD Commodity Yearbook.*

United Nations Economic Commission for Africa (ECA), PO Box 3001, Addis Ababa, Ethiopia, (Telephone in U.S. (212) 963-4957), www.uneca.org; *African Statistical Yearbook 2006.*

United Nations Food and Agricultural Organization (FAO), Viale delle Terme di Caracalla, 00100 Rome, Italy, (Dial from U.S. (202) 653-2400), (Fax from U.S. (202) 653 5760), www.fao.org; *FAO Trade Yearbook* and *The State of Food and Agriculture (SOFA) 2006.*

The World Bank, 1818 H Street, NW, Washington, DC 20433, (202) 473-1000, Fax: (202) 477-6391, www.worldbank.org; *Equatorial Guinea.*

World Trade Organization (WTO), Centre William Rappard, Rue de Lausanne 154, CH-1211 Geneva 21, Switzerland, www.wto.org; *International Trade Statistics 2006.*

EQUATORIAL GUINEA - INTERNET USERS

International Telecommunication Union (ITU), Place des Nations, 1211 Geneva 20, Switzerland, www.itu.int; *World Telecommunication/ICT Indicators Database on CD-ROM; World Telecommunication/ICT Indicators Database Online;* and *Yearbook of Statistics - Telecommunication Services (Chronological Time Series 1997-2006).*

The World Bank, 1818 H Street, NW, Washington, DC 20433, (202) 473-1000, Fax: (202) 477-6391, www.worldbank.org; *Equatorial Guinea.*

EQUATORIAL GUINEA - LABOR

African Development Bank Group, Rue Joseph Anoma, 01 BP 1387 Abidjan 01, Cote d'Ivoire, www.afdb.org; *Statistics Pocketbook 2008.*

Central Intelligence Agency, Office of Public Affairs, Washington, DC 20505, (703) 482-0623, Fax: (703) 482-1739, www.cia.gov; *The World Factbook.*

Euromonitor International, Inc., 224 S. Michigan Avenue, Suite 1500, Chicago, IL 60604, (312) 922-1115, Fax: (312) 922-1157, www.euromonitor.com; *International Marketing Data and Statistics 2008* and *World Marketing Data and Statistics.*

Palgrave Macmillan Ltd., Houndmills, Basingstoke, Hampshire, RG21 6XS, England, (Telephone in U.S. (888) 330-8477), (Fax in U.S. (800) 672-2054), www.palgrave.com; *The Statesman's Yearbook 2008.*

Taylor and Francis Group, An Informa Business, 2 Park Square, Milton Park, Abingdon, Oxford OX14 4RN, United Kingdom, (Dial from U.S. (212) 216-

7800), (Fax from U.S. (212) 564-7854), www.tandf.co.uk; *The Europa World Year Book.*

United Nations Food and Agricultural Organization (FAO), Viale delle Terme di Caracalla, 00100 Rome, Italy, (Dial from U.S. (202) 653-2400), (Fax from U.S. (202) 653 5760), www.fao.org; *The State of Food and Agriculture (SOFA) 2006.*

United Nations Statistics Division, New York, NY 10017, (800) 253-9646, Fax: (212) 963-4116, http://unstats.un.org; *Human Development Report 2006.*

The World Bank, 1818 H Street, NW, Washington, DC 20433, (202) 473-1000, Fax: (202) 477-6391, www.worldbank.org; *The World Bank Atlas 2003-2004.*

EQUATORIAL GUINEA - LAND USE

Central Intelligence Agency, Office of Public Affairs, Washington, DC 20505, (703) 482-0623, Fax: (703) 482-1739, www.cia.gov; *The World Factbook.*

Euromonitor International, Inc., 224 S. Michigan Avenue, Suite 1500, Chicago, IL 60604, (312) 922-1115, Fax: (312) 922-1157, www.euromonitor.com; *International Marketing Data and Statistics 2008.*

United Nations Food and Agricultural Organization (FAO), Viale delle Terme di Caracalla, 00100 Rome, Italy, (Dial from U.S. (202) 653-2400), (Fax from U.S. (202) 653 5760), www.fao.org; *FAO Production Yearbook 2002.*

EQUATORIAL GUINEA - LIFE EXPECTANCY

African Development Bank Group, Rue Joseph Anoma, 01 BP 1387 Abidjan 01, Cote d'Ivoire, www.afdb.org; *Statistics Pocketbook 2008.*

Central Intelligence Agency, Office of Public Affairs, Washington, DC 20505, (703) 482-0623, Fax: (703) 482-1739, www.cia.gov; *The World Factbook.*

Palgrave Macmillan Ltd., Houndmills, Basingstoke, Hampshire, RG21 6XS, England, (Telephone in U.S. (888) 330-8477), (Fax in U.S. (800) 672-2054), www.palgrave.com; *The Statesman's Yearbook 2008.*

United Nations Statistics Division, New York, NY 10017, (800) 253-9646, Fax: (212) 963-4116, http://unstats.un.org; *Human Development Report 2006* and *World Statistics Pocketbook.*

The World Bank, 1818 H Street, NW, Washington, DC 20433, (202) 473-1000, Fax: (202) 477-6391, www.worldbank.org; *The World Bank Atlas 2003-2004.*

EQUATORIAL GUINEA - LITERACY

Euromonitor International, Inc., 224 S. Michigan Avenue, Suite 1500, Chicago, IL 60604, (312) 922-1115, Fax: (312) 922-1157, www.euromonitor.com; *World Marketing Data and Statistics.*

United Nations Statistics Division, New York, NY 10017, (800) 253-9646, Fax: (212) 963-4116, http://unstats.un.org; *Survey of Economic and Social Conditions in Africa 2005.*

EQUATORIAL GUINEA - LIVESTOCK

Palgrave Macmillan Ltd., Houndmills, Basingstoke, Hampshire, RG21 6XS, England, (Telephone in U.S. (888) 330-8477), (Fax in U.S. (800) 672-2054), www.palgrave.com; *The Statesman's Yearbook 2008.*

Taylor and Francis Group, An Informa Business, 2 Park Square, Milton Park, Abingdon, Oxford OX14 4RN, United Kingdom, (Dial from U.S. (212) 216-7800), (Fax from U.S. (212) 564-7854), www.tandf.co.uk; *The Europa World Year Book.*

United Nations Conference on Trade and Development (UNCTAD), DC2-1120, United Nations, New York, NY 10017, (212) 963-0027, www.unctad.org; *UNCTAD Commodity Yearbook.*

United Nations Economic Commission for Africa (ECA), PO Box 3001, Addis Ababa, Ethiopia, (Telephone in U.S. (212) 963-4957), www.uneca.org; *African Statistical Yearbook 2006.*

United Nations Food and Agricultural Organization (FAO), Viale delle Terme di Caracalla, 00100 Rome, Italy, (Dial from U.S. (202) 653-2400), (Fax from U.S. (202) 653 5760), www.fao.org; *FAO Production Yearbook 2002* and *The State of Food and Agriculture (SOFA) 2006.*

United Nations Statistics Division, New York, NY 10017, (800) 253-9646, Fax: (212) 963-4116, http://unstats.un.org; *Statistical Yearbook* and *Survey of Economic and Social Conditions in Africa 2005.*

EQUATORIAL GUINEA - MANUFACTURES

United Nations Statistics Division, New York, NY 10017, (800) 253-9646, Fax: (212) 963-4116, http://unstats.un.org; *Survey of Economic and Social Conditions in Africa 2005.*

EQUATORIAL GUINEA - MARRIAGE

United Nations Statistics Division, New York, NY 10017, (800) 253-9646, Fax: (212) 963-4116, http://unstats.un.org; *Demographic Yearbook* and *Statistical Yearbook.*

EQUATORIAL GUINEA - MINERAL INDUSTRIES

United Nations Conference on Trade and Development (UNCTAD), DC2-1120, United Nations, New York, NY 10017, (212) 963-0027, www.unctad.org; *UNCTAD Commodity Yearbook.*

United Nations Economic Commission for Africa (ECA), PO Box 3001, Addis Ababa, Ethiopia, (Telephone in U.S. (212) 963-4957), www.uneca.org; *African Statistical Yearbook 2006.*

EQUATORIAL GUINEA - MONEY EXCHANGE RATES

See EQUATORIAL GUINEA - FOREIGN EXCHANGE RATES

EQUATORIAL GUINEA - MONEY SUPPLY

African Development Bank Group, Rue Joseph Anoma, 01 BP 1387 Abidjan 01, Cote d'Ivoire, www.afdb.org; *Statistics Pocketbook 2008.*

Economist Intelligence Unit, 111 West 57th Street, New York, NY 10019, (212) 554-0600, Fax: (212) 586-1181, www.eiu.com; *Equatorial Guinea Country Report.*

Taylor and Francis Group, An Informa Business, 2 Park Square, Milton Park, Abingdon, Oxford OX14 4RN, United Kingdom, (Dial from U.S. (212) 216-7800), (Fax from U.S. (212) 564-7854), www.tandf.co.uk; *The Europa World Year Book.*

The World Bank, 1818 H Street, NW, Washington, DC 20433, (202) 473-1000, Fax: (202) 477-6391, www.worldbank.org; *Equatorial Guinea.*

EQUATORIAL GUINEA - MORTALITY

Central Intelligence Agency, Office of Public Affairs, Washington, DC 20505, (703) 482-0623, Fax: (703) 482-1739, www.cia.gov; *The World Factbook.*

Euromonitor International, Inc., 224 S. Michigan Avenue, Suite 1500, Chicago, IL 60604, (312) 922-1115, Fax: (312) 922-1157, www.euromonitor.com; *International Marketing Data and Statistics 2008.*

Palgrave Macmillan Ltd., Houndmills, Basingstoke, Hampshire, RG21 6XS, England, (Telephone in U.S. (888) 330-8477), (Fax in U.S. (800) 672-2054), www.palgrave.com; *The Statesman's Yearbook 2008.*

Taylor and Francis Group, An Informa Business, 2 Park Square, Milton Park, Abingdon, Oxford OX14 4RN, United Kingdom, (Dial from U.S. (212) 216-7800), (Fax from U.S. (212) 564-7854), www.tandf.co.uk; *The Europa World Year Book.*

United Nations Statistics Division, New York, NY 10017, (800) 253-9646, Fax: (212) 963-4116, http://unstats.un.org; *Demographic Yearbook; Human Development Report 2006; Statistical Yearbook; Survey of Economic and Social Conditions in Africa 2005;* and *World Statistics Pocketbook.*

The World Bank, 1818 H Street, NW, Washington, DC 20433, (202) 473-1000, Fax: (202) 477-6391, www.worldbank.org; *The World Bank Atlas 2003-2004.*

World Health Organization (WHO), Avenue Appia 20, 1211 Geneve 27, Switzerland, (Telephone in U.S. (212) 331-9081), www.who.int; The WHO Global Atlas of Infectious Diseases.

EQUATORIAL GUINEA - MOTION PICTURES

United Nations Statistics Division, New York, NY 10017, (800) 253-9646, Fax: (212) 963-4116, http://unstats.un.org; *Statistical Yearbook.*

EQUATORIAL GUINEA - MOTOR VEHICLES

United Nations Statistics Division, New York, NY 10017, (800) 253-9646, Fax: (212) 963-4116, http://unstats.un.org; *Survey of Economic and Social Conditions in Africa 2005.*

EQUATORIAL GUINEA - MUSEUMS

UNESCO Institute for Statistics, C.P. 6128 Succursale Centre-Ville, Montreal, Quebec, H3C 3J7 Canada, (Dial from U.S. (514) 343-6880), (Fax from U.S. (514) 343 6882), www.uis.unesco.org; *Statistical Tables.*

EQUATORIAL GUINEA - NUTRITION

African Development Bank Group, Rue Joseph Anoma, 01 BP 1387 Abidjan 01, Cote d'Ivoire, www.afdb.org; *Statistics Pocketbook 2008.*

United Nations Food and Agricultural Organization (FAO), Viale delle Terme di Caracalla, 00100 Rome, Italy, (Dial from U.S. (202) 653-2400), (Fax from U.S. (202) 653 5760), www.fao.org; *The State of Food and Agriculture (SOFA) 2006.*

EQUATORIAL GUINEA - PALM OIL PRODUCTION

See EQUATORIAL GUINEA - CROPS

EQUATORIAL GUINEA - PESTICIDES

United Nations Food and Agricultural Organization (FAO), Viale delle Terme di Caracalla, 00100 Rome, Italy, (Dial from U.S. (202) 653-2400), (Fax from U.S. (202) 653 5760), www.fao.org; *The State of Food and Agriculture (SOFA) 2006.*

EQUATORIAL GUINEA - PETROLEUM INDUSTRY AND TRADE

PennWell Corporation, 1421 South Sheridan Road, Tulsa, OK 74112, (918) 835-3161, www.pennwell.com; *International Petroleum Encyclopedia 2007.*

United Nations Conference on Trade and Development (UNCTAD), DC2-1120, United Nations, New York, NY 10017, (212) 963-0027, www.unctad.org; *UNCTAD Commodity Yearbook.*

United Nations Food and Agricultural Organization (FAO), Viale delle Terme di Caracalla, 00100 Rome, Italy, (Dial from U.S. (202) 653-2400), (Fax from U.S. (202) 653 5760), www.fao.org; *The State of Food and Agriculture (SOFA) 2006.*

EQUATORIAL GUINEA - POLITICAL SCIENCE

Central Intelligence Agency, Office of Public Affairs, Washington, DC 20505, (703) 482-0623, Fax: (703) 482-1739, www.cia.gov; *The World Factbook.*

Palgrave Macmillan Ltd., Houndmills, Basingstoke, Hampshire, RG21 6XS, England, (Telephone in U.S. (888) 330-8477), (Fax in U.S. (800) 672-2054), www.palgrave.com; *The Statesman's Yearbook 2008.*

Taylor and Francis Group, An Informa Business, 2 Park Square, Milton Park, Abingdon, Oxford OX14 4RN, United Kingdom, (Dial from U.S. (212) 216-7800), (Fax from U.S. (212) 564-7854), www.tandf.co.uk; *The Europa World Year Book.*

United Nations Statistics Division, New York, NY 10017, (800) 253-9646, Fax: (212) 963-4116, http://unstats.un.org; *National Accounts Statistics: Compendium of Income Distribution Statistics* and *Survey of Economic and Social Conditions in Africa 2005.*

EQUATORIAL GUINEA - POPULATION

African Development Bank Group, Rue Joseph Anoma, 01 BP 1387 Abidjan 01, Cote d'Ivoire, www.afdb.org; *The African Statistical Journal; Gender, Poverty and Environmental Indicators on African Countries 2007; Selected Statistics on African Countries 2007;* and *Statistics Pocketbook 2008.*

Central Intelligence Agency, Office of Public Affairs, Washington, DC 20505, (703) 482-0623, Fax: (703) 482-1739, www.cia.gov; *The World Factbook.*

Economist Intelligence Unit, 111 West 57th Street, New York, NY 10019, (212) 554-0600, Fax: (212) 586-1181, www.eiu.com; *Equatorial Guinea Country Report.*

Euromonitor International, Inc., 224 S. Michigan Avenue, Suite 1500, Chicago, IL 60604, (312) 922-1115, Fax: (312) 922-1157, www.euromonitor.com; *International Marketing Data and Statistics 2008.*

Eurostat, Batiment Jean Monnet, Rue Alcide de Gasperi, L-2920 Luxembourg, http://epp.eurostat.ec.europa.eu; *Demographic Indicators - Population by Age-Classes.*

Palgrave Macmillan Ltd., Houndmills, Basingstoke, Hampshire, RG21 6XS, England, (Telephone in U.S. (888) 330-8477), (Fax in U.S. (800) 672-2054), www.palgrave.com; *The Statesman's Yearbook 2008.*

Taylor and Francis Group, An Informa Business, 2 Park Square, Milton Park, Abingdon, Oxford OX14 4RN, United Kingdom, (Dial from U.S. (212) 216-7800), (Fax from U.S. (212) 564-7854), www.tandf.co.uk; *The Europa World Year Book.*

U.S. Department of State (DOS), 2201 C Street NW, Washington, DC 20520, (202) 647-4000, www.state.gov; *World Military Expenditures and Arms Transfers (WMEAT).*

United Nations Food and Agricultural Organization (FAO), Viale delle Terme di Caracalla, 00100 Rome, Italy, (Dial from U.S. (202) 653-2400), (Fax from U.S. (202) 653 5760), www.fao.org; *FAO Production Yearbook 2002.*

United Nations Statistics Division, New York, NY 10017, (800) 253-9646, Fax: (212) 963-4116, http://unstats.un.org; *Demographic Yearbook; Human Development Report 2006; Statistical Yearbook; Survey of Economic and Social Conditions in Africa 2005;* and *World Statistics Pocketbook.*

The World Bank, 1818 H Street, NW, Washington, DC 20433, (202) 473-1000, Fax: (202) 477-6391, www.worldbank.org; *Equatorial Guinea* and *The World Bank Atlas 2003-2004.*

World Health Organization (WHO), Avenue Appia 20, 1211 Geneve 27, Switzerland, (Telephone in U.S. (212) 331-9081), www.who.int; *World Health Report 2006.*

EQUATORIAL GUINEA - POPULATION DENSITY

African Development Bank Group, Rue Joseph Anoma, 01 BP 1387 Abidjan 01, Cote d'Ivoire, www.afdb.org; *Statistics Pocketbook 2008.*

Central Intelligence Agency, Office of Public Affairs, Washington, DC 20505, (703) 482-0623, Fax: (703) 482-1739, www.cia.gov; *The World Factbook.*

Palgrave Macmillan Ltd., Houndmills, Basingstoke, Hampshire, RG21 6XS, England, (Telephone in U.S. (888) 330-8477), (Fax in U.S. (800) 672-2054), www.palgrave.com; *The Statesman's Yearbook 2008.*

Taylor and Francis Group, An Informa Business, 2 Park Square, Milton Park, Abingdon, Oxford OX14 4RN, United Kingdom, (Dial from U.S. (212) 216-7800), (Fax from U.S. (212) 564-7854), www.tandf.co.uk; *The Europa World Year Book.*

United Nations Food and Agricultural Organization (FAO), Viale delle Terme di Caracalla, 00100 Rome, Italy, (Dial from U.S. (202) 653-2400), (Fax from U.S. (202) 653 5760), www.fao.org; *The State of Food and Agriculture (SOFA) 2006.*

United Nations Statistics Division, New York, NY 10017, (800) 253-9646, Fax: (212) 963-4116, http://unstats.un.org; *Statistical Yearbook* and *Survey of Economic and Social Conditions in Africa 2005.*

The World Bank, 1818 H Street, NW, Washington, DC 20433, (202) 473-1000, Fax: (202) 477-6391, www.worldbank.org; *Equatorial Guinea.*

EQUATORIAL GUINEA - POWER RESOURCES

Euromonitor International, Inc., 224 S. Michigan Avenue, Suite 1500, Chicago, IL 60604, (312) 922-1115, Fax: (312) 922-1157, www.euromonitor.com; *International Marketing Data and Statistics 2008* and *World Marketing Data and Statistics.*

Palgrave Macmillan Ltd., Houndmills, Basingstoke, Hampshire, RG21 6XS, England, (Telephone in U.S. (888) 330-8477), (Fax in U.S. (800) 672-2054), www.palgrave.com; *The Statesman's Yearbook 2008.*

United Nations Economic Commission for Africa (ECA), PO Box 3001, Addis Ababa, Ethiopia, (Telephone in U.S. (212) 963-4957), www.uneca.org; *African Statistical Yearbook 2006.*

United Nations Food and Agricultural Organization (FAO), Viale delle Terme di Caracalla, 00100 Rome, Italy, (Dial from U.S. (202) 653-2400), (Fax from U.S. (202) 653 5760), www.fao.org; *The State of Food and Agriculture (SOFA) 2006.*

United Nations Statistics Division, New York, NY 10017, (800) 253-9646, Fax: (212) 963-4116, http://unstats.un.org; *Human Development Report 2006; Statistical Yearbook;* and *World Statistics Pocketbook.*

The World Bank, 1818 H Street, NW, Washington, DC 20433, (202) 473-1000, Fax: (202) 477-6391, www.worldbank.org; *The World Bank Atlas 2003-2004.*

EQUATORIAL GUINEA - PRICES

Euromonitor International, Inc., 224 S. Michigan Avenue, Suite 1500, Chicago, IL 60604, (312) 922-1115, Fax: (312) 922-1157, www.euromonitor.com; *World Marketing Data and Statistics.*

United Nations Food and Agricultural Organization (FAO), Viale delle Terme di Caracalla, 00100 Rome, Italy, (Dial from U.S. (202) 653-2400), (Fax from U.S. (202) 653 5760), www.fao.org; *FAO Production Yearbook 2002* and *The State of Food and Agriculture (SOFA) 2006.*

The World Bank, 1818 H Street, NW, Washington, DC 20433, (202) 473-1000, Fax: (202) 477-6391, www.worldbank.org; *Equatorial Guinea.*

EQUATORIAL GUINEA - PUBLIC HEALTH

African Development Bank Group, Rue Joseph Anoma, 01 BP 1387 Abidjan 01, Cote d'Ivoire, www.afdb.org; *Statistics Pocketbook 2008.*

Euromonitor International, Inc., 224 S. Michigan Avenue, Suite 1500, Chicago, IL 60604, (312) 922-1115, Fax: (312) 922-1157, www.euromonitor.com; *World Marketing Data and Statistics.*

United Nations Economic Commission for Africa (ECA), PO Box 3001, Addis Ababa, Ethiopia, (Telephone in U.S. (212) 963-4957), www.uneca.org; *African Statistical Yearbook 2006.*

United Nations Statistics Division, New York, NY 10017, (800) 253-9646, Fax: (212) 963-4116, http://unstats.un.org; *Human Development Report 2006* and *Statistical Yearbook.*

The World Bank, 1818 H Street, NW, Washington, DC 20433, (202) 473-1000, Fax: (202) 477-6391, www.worldbank.org; *Equatorial Guinea.*

World Health Organization (WHO), Avenue Appia 20, 1211 Geneve 27, Switzerland, (Telephone in U.S. (212) 331-9081), www.who.int; The WHO Global Atlas of Infectious Diseases.

EQUATORIAL GUINEA - PUBLISHERS AND PUBLISHING

Taylor and Francis Group, An Informa Business, 2 Park Square, Milton Park, Abingdon, Oxford OX14 4RN, United Kingdom, (Dial from U.S. (212) 216-7800), (Fax from U.S. (212) 564-7854), www.tandf.co.uk; *The Europa World Year Book.*

EQUATORIAL GUINEA - RADIO BROADCASTING

Palgrave Macmillan Ltd., Houndmills, Basingstoke, Hampshire, RG21 6XS, England, (Telephone in U.S. (888) 330-8477), (Fax in U.S. (800) 672-2054), www.palgrave.com; *The Statesman's Yearbook 2008.*

EQUATORIAL GUINEA - RAILROADS

United Nations Economic Commission for Africa (ECA), PO Box 3001, Addis Ababa, Ethiopia, (Telephone in U.S. (212) 963-4957), www.uneca.org; *African Statistical Yearbook 2006.*

EQUATORIAL GUINEA - RELIGION

Central Intelligence Agency, Office of Public Affairs, Washington, DC 20505, (703) 482-0623, Fax: (703) 482-1739, www.cia.gov; *The World Factbook.*

Palgrave Macmillan Ltd., Houndmills, Basingstoke, Hampshire, RG21 6XS, England, (Telephone in U.S. (888) 330-8477), (Fax in U.S. (800) 672-2054), www.palgrave.com; *The Statesman's Yearbook 2008.*

EQUATORIAL GUINEA - RESERVES (ACCOUNTING)

African Development Bank Group, Rue Joseph Anoma, 01 BP 1387 Abidjan 01, Cote d'Ivoire, www.afdb.org; *Statistics Pocketbook 2008.*

EQUATORIAL GUINEA - RETAIL TRADE

Euromonitor International, Inc., 224 S. Michigan Avenue, Suite 1500, Chicago, IL 60604, (312) 922-1115, Fax: (312) 922-1157, www.euromonitor.com; *World Marketing Data and Statistics.*

EQUATORIAL GUINEA - ROADS

Central Intelligence Agency, Office of Public Affairs, Washington, DC 20505, (703) 482-0623, Fax: (703) 482-1739, www.cia.gov; *The World Factbook.*

Palgrave Macmillan Ltd., Houndmills, Basingstoke, Hampshire, RG21 6XS, England, (Telephone in U.S. (888) 330-8477), (Fax in U.S. (800) 672-2054), www.palgrave.com; *The Statesman's Yearbook 2008.*

United Nations Economic Commission for Africa (ECA), PO Box 3001, Addis Ababa, Ethiopia, (Telephone in U.S. (212) 963-4957), www.uneca.org; *African Statistical Yearbook 2006.*

United Nations Statistics Division, New York, NY 10017, (800) 253-9646, Fax: (212) 963-4116, http://unstats.un.org; *Survey of Economic and Social Conditions in Africa 2005.*

EQUATORIAL GUINEA - SHEEP

See EQUATORIAL GUINEA - LIVESTOCK

EQUATORIAL GUINEA - SHIPPING

Palgrave Macmillan Ltd., Houndmills, Basingstoke, Hampshire, RG21 6XS, England, (Telephone in U.S. (888) 330-8477), (Fax in U.S. (800) 672-2054), www.palgrave.com; *The Statesman's Yearbook 2008.*

Taylor and Francis Group, An Informa Business, 2 Park Square, Milton Park, Abingdon, Oxford OX14 4RN, United Kingdom, (Dial from U.S. (212) 216-7800), (Fax from U.S. (212) 564-7854), www.tandf.co.uk; *The Europa World Year Book.*

United Nations Economic Commission for Africa (ECA), PO Box 3001, Addis Ababa, Ethiopia, (Telephone in U.S. (212) 963-4957), www.uneca.org; *African Statistical Yearbook 2006.*

United Nations Statistics Division, New York, NY 10017, (800) 253-9646, Fax: (212) 963-4116, http://unstats.un.org; *Statistical Yearbook.*

EQUATORIAL GUINEA - SOCIAL ECOLOGY

United Nations Statistics Division, New York, NY 10017, (800) 253-9646, Fax: (212) 963-4116, http://unstats.un.org; *World Statistics Pocketbook.*

EQUATORIAL GUINEA - SOCIAL SECURITY

United Nations Statistics Division, New York, NY 10017, (800) 253-9646, Fax: (212) 963-4116, http://unstats.un.org; *National Accounts Statistics: Compendium of Income Distribution Statistics.*

EQUATORIAL GUINEA - TAXATION

Taylor and Francis Group, An Informa Business, 2 Park Square, Milton Park, Abingdon, Oxford OX14 4RN, United Kingdom, (Dial from U.S. (212) 216-7800), (Fax from U.S. (212) 564-7854), www.tandf.co.uk; *The Europa World Year Book.*

EQUATORIAL GUINEA - TELEPHONE

International Telecommunication Union (ITU), Place des Nations, 1211 Geneva 20, Switzerland, www.itu.int; World Telecommunication Indicators Database.

United Nations Statistics Division, New York, NY 10017, (800) 253-9646, Fax: (212) 963-4116, http://unstats.un.org; *World Statistics Pocketbook.*

EQUATORIAL GUINEA - TEXTILE INDUSTRY

United Nations Conference on Trade and Development (UNCTAD), DC2-1120, United Nations, New York, NY 10017, (212) 963-0027, www.unctad.org; *UNCTAD Commodity Yearbook.*

EQUATORIAL GUINEA - THEATER

UNESCO Institute for Statistics, C.P. 6128 Succursale Centre-Ville, Montreal, Quebec, H3C 3J7 Canada, (Dial from U.S. (514) 343-6880), (Fax from U.S. (514) 343 6882), www.uis.unesco.org; *Statistical Tables.*

EQUATORIAL GUINEA - TOURISM

Euromonitor International, Inc., 224 S. Michigan Avenue, Suite 1500, Chicago, IL 60604, (312) 922-1115, Fax: (312) 922-1157, www.euromonitor.com; *World Marketing Data and Statistics.*

Palgrave Macmillan Ltd., Houndmills, Basingstoke, Hampshire, RG21 6XS, England, (Telephone in U.S. (888) 330-8477), (Fax in U.S. (800) 672-2054), www.palgrave.com; *The Statesman's Yearbook 2008.*

United Nations Economic Commission for Africa (ECA), PO Box 3001, Addis Ababa, Ethiopia, (Telephone in U.S. (212) 963-4957), www.uneca.org; *African Statistical Yearbook 2006.*

The World Bank, 1818 H Street, NW, Washington, DC 20433, (202) 473-1000, Fax: (202) 477-6391, www.worldbank.org; *Equatorial Guinea.*

EQUATORIAL GUINEA - TRADE

See EQUATORIAL GUINEA - INTERNATIONAL TRADE

EQUATORIAL GUINEA - TRANSPORTATION

Central Intelligence Agency, Office of Public Affairs, Washington, DC 20505, (703) 482-0623, Fax: (703) 482-1739, www.cia.gov; *The World Factbook.*

Euromonitor International, Inc., 224 S. Michigan Avenue, Suite 1500, Chicago, IL 60604, (312) 922-1115, Fax: (312) 922-1157, www.euromonitor.com; *International Marketing Data and Statistics 2008* and *World Marketing Data and Statistics.*

Palgrave Macmillan Ltd., Houndmills, Basingstoke, Hampshire, RG21 6XS, England, (Telephone in U.S. (888) 330-8477), (Fax in U.S. (800) 672-2054), www.palgrave.com; *The Statesman's Yearbook 2008.*

Taylor and Francis Group, An Informa Business, 2 Park Square, Milton Park, Abingdon, Oxford OX14 4RN, United Kingdom, (Dial from U.S. (212) 216-7800), (Fax from U.S. (212) 564-7854), www.tandf.co.uk; *The Europa World Year Book.*

United Nations Economic Commission for Africa (ECA), PO Box 3001, Addis Ababa, Ethiopia, (Telephone in U.S. (212) 963-4957), www.uneca.org; *African Statistical Yearbook 2006.*

United Nations Statistics Division, New York, NY 10017, (800) 253-9646, Fax: (212) 963-4116, http://unstats.un.org; *Human Development Report 2006.*

The World Bank, 1818 H Street, NW, Washington, DC 20433, (202) 473-1000, Fax: (202) 477-6391, www.worldbank.org; *Africa Live Database (LDB)* and *Equatorial Guinea.*

EQUATORIAL GUINEA - UNEMPLOYMENT

Central Intelligence Agency, Office of Public Affairs, Washington, DC 20505, (703) 482-0623, Fax: (703) 482-1739, www.cia.gov; *The World Factbook.*

EQUATORIAL GUINEA - VITAL STATISTICS

United Nations Statistics Division, New York, NY 10017, (800) 253-9646, Fax: (212) 963-4116, http://unstats.un.org; *Statistical Yearbook.*

World Health Organization (WHO), Avenue Appia 20, 1211 Geneve 27, Switzerland, (Telephone in U.S. (212) 331-9081), www.who.int; *World Health Report 2006.*

EQUATORIAL GUINEA - WAGES

The World Bank, 1818 H Street, NW, Washington, DC 20433, (202) 473-1000, Fax: (202) 477-6391, www.worldbank.org; *Equatorial Guinea.*

ERITREA - NATIONAL STATISTICAL OFFICE

National Statistics Office, PO Box 5838, Asmara, Eritrea; National Data Center.

ERITREA - AGRICULTURE

Economist Intelligence Unit, 111 West 57th Street, New York, NY 10019, (212) 554-0600, Fax: (212) 586-1181, www.eiu.com; *Eritrea Country Report.*

Euromonitor International, Inc., 224 S. Michigan Avenue, Suite 1500, Chicago, IL 60604, (312) 922-1115, Fax: (312) 922-1157, www.euromonitor.com; *World Marketing Data and Statistics.*

Palgrave Macmillan Ltd., Houndmills, Basingstoke, Hampshire, RG21 6XS, England, (Telephone in U.S. (888) 330-8477), (Fax in U.S. (800) 672-2054), www.palgrave.com; *The Statesman's Yearbook 2008.*

United Nations Food and Agricultural Organization (FAO), Viale delle Terme di Caracalla, 00100 Rome, Italy, (Dial from U.S. (202) 653-2400), (Fax from U.S. (202) 653 5760), www.fao.org; AQUASTAT; *FAO Production Yearbook 2002; FAO Trade Yearbook;* and *The State of Food and Agriculture (SOFA) 2006.*

United Nations Statistics Division, New York, NY 10017, (800) 253-9646, Fax: (212) 963-4116, http://unstats.un.org; *2004 Industrial Commodity Statistics Yearbook* and *Statistical Yearbook.*

The World Bank, 1818 H Street, NW, Washington, DC 20433, (202) 473-1000, Fax: (202) 477-6391, www.worldbank.org; *Africa Live Database (LDB); African Development Indicators (ADI) 2007;* and *Eritrea.*

ERITREA - AIRLINES

United Nations Statistics Division, New York, NY 10017, (800) 253-9646, Fax: (212) 963-4116, http://unstats.un.org; *Statistical Yearbook.*

ERITREA - AIRPORTS

Central Intelligence Agency, Office of Public Affairs, Washington, DC 20505, (703) 482-0623, Fax: (703) 482-1739, www.cia.gov; *The World Factbook.*

ERITREA - ARMED FORCES

Central Intelligence Agency, Office of Public Affairs, Washington, DC 20505, (703) 482-0623, Fax: (703) 482-1739, www.cia.gov; *The World Factbook.*

Euromonitor International, Inc., 224 S. Michigan Avenue, Suite 1500, Chicago, IL 60604, (312) 922-1115, Fax: (312) 922-1157, www.euromonitor.com; *World Marketing Data and Statistics.*

Palgrave Macmillan Ltd., Houndmills, Basingstoke, Hampshire, RG21 6XS, England, (Telephone in U.S. (888) 330-8477), (Fax in U.S. (800) 672-2054), www.palgrave.com; *The Statesman's Yearbook 2008.*

United Nations Statistics Division, New York, NY 10017, (800) 253-9646, Fax: (212) 963-4116, http://unstats.un.org; *Human Development Report 2006.*

ERITREA - AUTOMOBILE INDUSTRY AND TRADE

United Nations Statistics Division, New York, NY 10017, (800) 253-9646, Fax: (212) 963-4116, http://unstats.un.org; *Statistical Yearbook.*

ERITREA - BANKS AND BANKING

Euromonitor International, Inc., 224 S. Michigan Avenue, Suite 1500, Chicago, IL 60604, (312) 922-1115, Fax: (312) 922-1157, www.euromonitor.com; *World Marketing Data and Statistics.*

Palgrave Macmillan Ltd., Houndmills, Basingstoke, Hampshire, RG21 6XS, England, (Telephone in U.S. (888) 330-8477), (Fax in U.S. (800) 672-2054), www.palgrave.com; *The Statesman's Yearbook 2008.*

ERITREA - BEVERAGE INDUSTRY

United Nations Statistics Division, New York, NY 10017, (800) 253-9646, Fax: (212) 963-4116, http://unstats.un.org; *Statistical Yearbook.*

ERITREA - BROADCASTING

Central Intelligence Agency, Office of Public Affairs, Washington, DC 20505, (703) 482-0623, Fax: (703) 482-1739, www.cia.gov; *The World Factbook.*

Euromonitor International, Inc., 224 S. Michigan Avenue, Suite 1500, Chicago, IL 60604, (312) 922-1115, Fax: (312) 922-1157, www.euromonitor.com; *World Marketing Data and Statistics.*

UNESCO Institute for Statistics, C.P. 6128 Succursale Centre-Ville, Montreal, Quebec, H3C 3J7 Canada, (Dial from U.S. (514) 343-6880), (Fax from U.S. (514) 343 6882), www.uis.unesco.org; *Statistical Tables.*

ERITREA - BUDGET

Central Intelligence Agency, Office of Public Affairs, Washington, DC 20505, (703) 482-0623, Fax: (703) 482-1739, www.cia.gov; *The World Factbook.*

ERITREA - BUSINESS

Economist Intelligence Unit, 111 West 57th Street, New York, NY 10019, (212) 554-0600, Fax: (212) 586-1181, www.eiu.com; *Business Africa.*

United Nations Statistics Division, New York, NY 10017, (800) 253-9646, Fax: (212) 963-4116, http://unstats.un.org; *Statistical Yearbook.*

ERITREA - CHILDBIRTH - STATISTICS

Central Intelligence Agency, Office of Public Affairs, Washington, DC 20505, (703) 482-0623, Fax: (703) 482-1739, www.cia.gov; *The World Factbook.*

Euromonitor International, Inc., 224 S. Michigan Avenue, Suite 1500, Chicago, IL 60604, (312) 922-1115, Fax: (312) 922-1157, www.euromonitor.com; *International Marketing Data and Statistics 2008* and *The World Economic Factbook 2008.*

United Nations Statistics Division, New York, NY 10017, (800) 253-9646, Fax: (212) 963-4116, http://unstats.un.org; *Statistical Yearbook.*

ERITREA - CLIMATE

International Institute for Environment and Development (IIED), 3 Endsleigh Street, London, England, WC1H 0DD, United Kingdom, www.iied.org; *Environment Urbanization* and *Haramata - Bulletin of the Drylands.*

Palgrave Macmillan Ltd., Houndmills, Basingstoke, Hampshire, RG21 6XS, England, (Telephone in U.S. (888) 330-8477), (Fax in U.S. (800) 672-2054), www.palgrave.com; *The Statesman's Yearbook 2008.*

ERITREA - COMMERCE

Palgrave Macmillan Ltd., Houndmills, Basingstoke, Hampshire, RG21 6XS, England, (Telephone in U.S. (888) 330-8477), (Fax in U.S. (800) 672-2054), www.palgrave.com; *The Statesman's Yearbook 2008.*

ERITREA - CONSTRUCTION INDUSTRY

United Nations Statistics Division, New York, NY 10017, (800) 253-9646, Fax: (212) 963-4116, http://unstats.un.org; *Statistical Yearbook.*

ERITREA - CONSUMER PRICE INDEXES

United Nations Statistics Division, New York, NY 10017, (800) 253-9646, Fax: (212) 963-4116, http://unstats.un.org; *Statistical Yearbook.*

The World Bank, 1818 H Street, NW, Washington, DC 20433, (202) 473-1000, Fax: (202) 477-6391, www.worldbank.org; *Eritrea.*

ERITREA - CROPS

Palgrave Macmillan Ltd., Houndmills, Basingstoke, Hampshire, RG21 6XS, England, (Telephone in U.S. (888) 330-8477), (Fax in U.S. (800) 672-2054), www.palgrave.com; *The Statesman's Yearbook 2008.*

United Nations Food and Agricultural Organization (FAO), Viale delle Terme di Caracalla, 00100 Rome, Italy, (Dial from U.S. (202) 653-2400), (Fax from U.S. (202) 653 5760), www.fao.org; *FAO Production Yearbook 2002* and *The State of Food and Agriculture (SOFA) 2006.*

United Nations Statistics Division, New York, NY 10017, (800) 253-9646, Fax: (212) 963-4116, http://unstats.un.org; *2004 Industrial Commodity Statistics Yearbook* and *Statistical Yearbook.*

ERITREA - DAIRY PROCESSING

United Nations Food and Agricultural Organization (FAO), Viale delle Terme di Caracalla, 00100 Rome, Italy, (Dial from U.S. (202) 653-2400), (Fax from U.S. (202) 653 5760), www.fao.org; *FAO Production Yearbook 2002* and *The State of Food and Agriculture (SOFA) 2006.*

United Nations Statistics Division, New York, NY 10017, (800) 253-9646, Fax: (212) 963-4116, http://unstats.un.org; *2004 Industrial Commodity Statistics Yearbook* and *Statistical Yearbook.*

ERITREA - DEMOGRAPHY

Euromonitor International, Inc., 224 S. Michigan Avenue, Suite 1500, Chicago, IL 60604, (312) 922-1115, Fax: (312) 922-1157, www.euromonitor.com; *International Marketing Data and Statistics 2008; The World Economic Factbook 2008;* and *World Marketing Data and Statistics.*

United Nations Statistics Division, New York, NY 10017, (800) 253-9646, Fax: (212) 963-4116, http://unstats.un.org; *Demographic Yearbook* and *Human Development Report 2006.*

The World Bank, 1818 H Street, NW, Washington, DC 20433, (202) 473-1000, Fax: (202) 477-6391, www.worldbank.org; *Eritrea.*

ERITREA - DISPOSABLE INCOME

United Nations Statistics Division, New York, NY 10017, (800) 253-9646, Fax: (212) 963-4116, http://unstats.un.org; *Statistical Yearbook.*

ERITREA - DIVORCE

United Nations Statistics Division, New York, NY 10017, (800) 253-9646, Fax: (212) 963-4116, http://unstats.un.org; *Demographic Yearbook* and *Statistical Yearbook.*

ERITREA - ECONOMIC CONDITIONS

African Development Bank Group, Rue Joseph Anoma, 01 BP 1387 Abidjan 01, Cote d'Ivoire, www.afdb.org; *The African Statistical Journal; Gender, Poverty and Environmental Indicators on African Countries 2007;* and *Selected Statistics on African Countries 2007.*

Central Intelligence Agency, Office of Public Affairs, Washington, DC 20505, (703) 482-0623, Fax: (703) 482-1739, www.cia.gov; *The World Factbook.*

Economist Intelligence Unit, 111 West 57th Street, New York, NY 10019, (212) 554-0600, Fax: (212) 586-1181, www.eiu.com; *Business Africa* and *Eritrea Country Report.*

Euromonitor International, Inc., 224 S. Michigan Avenue, Suite 1500, Chicago, IL 60604, (312) 922-1115, Fax: (312) 922-1157, www.euromonitor.com; *The World Economic Factbook 2008* and *World Marketing Data and Statistics.*

United Nations Statistics Division, New York, NY 10017, (800) 253-9646, Fax: (212) 963-4116, http://unstats.un.org; *World Statistics Pocketbook.*

The World Bank, 1818 H Street, NW, Washington, DC 20433, (202) 473-1000, Fax: (202) 477-6391, www.worldbank.org; *Africa Household Survey Databank; Africa Live Database (LDB); Africa Standardized Files and Indicators; African Development Indicators (ADI) 2007; Eritrea;* and *The World Bank Atlas 2003-2004.*

ERITREA - EDUCATION

Euromonitor International, Inc., 224 S. Michigan Avenue, Suite 1500, Chicago, IL 60604, (312) 922-1115, Fax: (312) 922-1157, www.euromonitor.com; *International Marketing Data and Statistics 2008* and *World Marketing Data and Statistics.*

UNESCO Institute for Statistics, C.P. 6128 Succursale Centre-Ville, Montreal, Quebec, H3C 3J7 Canada, (Dial from U.S. (514) 343-6880), (Fax from U.S. (514) 343 6882), www.uis.unesco.org; *Statistical Tables.*

United Nations Statistics Division, New York, NY 10017, (800) 253-9646, Fax: (212) 963-4116, http://unstats.un.org; *Human Development Report 2006.*

The World Bank, 1818 H Street, NW, Washington, DC 20433, (202) 473-1000, Fax: (202) 477-6391, www.worldbank.org; *Eritrea.*

ERITREA - ELECTRICITY

Platts, 2 Penn Plaza, 25th Floor, New York, NY 10121-2298, (212) 904-3070, www.platts.com; *Energy Economist.*

United Nations Statistics Division, New York, NY 10017, (800) 253-9646, Fax: (212) 963-4116, http://unstats.un.org; *Energy Statistics Yearbook 2003; Human Development Report 2006;* and *Statistical Yearbook.*

ERITREA - EMPLOYMENT

Euromonitor International, Inc., 224 S. Michigan Avenue, Suite 1500, Chicago, IL 60604, (312) 922-1115, Fax: (312) 922-1157, www.euromonitor.com; *International Marketing Data and Statistics 2008.*

United Nations Statistics Division, New York, NY 10017, (800) 253-9646, Fax: (212) 963-4116, http://unstats.un.org; *Statistical Yearbook.*

The World Bank, 1818 H Street, NW, Washington, DC 20433, (202) 473-1000, Fax: (202) 477-6391, www.worldbank.org; *Eritrea.*

ERITREA - ENVIRONMENTAL CONDITIONS

DSI Data Service Information, Xantener Strasse 51a, D-47495 Rheinberg, Germany, www.dsidata.com; *Campus Solution.*

Economist Intelligence Unit, 111 West 57th Street, New York, NY 10019, (212) 554-0600, Fax: (212) 586-1181, www.eiu.com; *Eritrea Country Report.*

International Institute for Environment and Development (IIED), 3 Endsleigh Street, London, England, WC1H 0DD, United Kingdom, www.iied.org; *Environment Urbanization* and *Haramata - Bulletin of the Drylands.*

United Nations Statistics Division, New York, NY 10017, (800) 253-9646, Fax: (212) 963-4116, http://unstats.un.org; *Statistical Yearbook* and *World Statistics Pocketbook.*

ERITREA - EXPORTS

Central Intelligence Agency, Office of Public Affairs, Washington, DC 20505, (703) 482-0623, Fax: (703) 482-1739, www.cia.gov; *The World Factbook.*

Economist Intelligence Unit, 111 West 57th Street, New York, NY 10019, (212) 554-0600, Fax: (212) 586-1181, www.eiu.com; *Eritrea Country Report.*

Euromonitor International, Inc., 224 S. Michigan Avenue, Suite 1500, Chicago, IL 60604, (312) 922-1115, Fax: (312) 922-1157, www.euromonitor.com; *International Marketing Data and Statistics 2008* and *The World Economic Factbook 2008.*

United Nations Statistics Division, New York, NY 10017, (800) 253-9646, Fax: (212) 963-4116, http://unstats.un.org; *International Trade Statistics Yearbook.*

ERITREA - FERTILITY, HUMAN

Central Intelligence Agency, Office of Public Affairs, Washington, DC 20505, (703) 482-0623, Fax: (703) 482-1739, www.cia.gov; *The World Factbook.*

United Nations Statistics Division, New York, NY 10017, (800) 253-9646, Fax: (212) 963-4116, http://unstats.un.org; *Human Development Report 2006.*

The World Bank, 1818 H Street, NW, Washington, DC 20433, (202) 473-1000, Fax: (202) 477-6391, www.worldbank.org; *The World Bank Atlas 2003-2004.*

ERITREA - FERTILIZER INDUSTRY

United Nations Food and Agricultural Organization (FAO), Viale delle Terme di Caracalla, 00100 Rome, Italy, (Dial from U.S. (202) 653-2400), (Fax from U.S. (202) 653 5760), www.fao.org; *FAO Fertilizer Yearbook.*

United Nations Statistics Division, New York, NY 10017, (800) 253-9646, Fax: (212) 963-4116, http://unstats.un.org; *2004 Industrial Commodity Statistics Yearbook* and *Statistical Yearbook.*

ERITREA - FINANCE

United Nations Statistics Division, New York, NY 10017, (800) 253-9646, Fax: (212) 963-4116, http://unstats.un.org; *National Accounts Statistics: Compendium of Income Distribution Statistics* and *Statistical Yearbook.*

The World Bank, 1818 H Street, NW, Washington, DC 20433, (202) 473-1000, Fax: (202) 477-6391, www.worldbank.org; *Eritrea.*

ERITREA - FINANCE, PUBLIC

Economist Intelligence Unit, 111 West 57th Street, New York, NY 10019, (212) 554-0600, Fax: (212) 586-1181, www.eiu.com; *Eritrea Country Report.*

Taylor and Francis Group, An Informa Business, 2 Park Square, Milton Park, Abingdon, Oxford OX14 4RN, United Kingdom, (Dial from U.S. (212) 216-7800), (Fax from U.S. (212) 564-7854), www.tandf.co.uk; *The Europa World Year Book.*

The World Bank, 1818 H Street, NW, Washington, DC 20433, (202) 473-1000, Fax: (202) 477-6391, www.worldbank.org; *Eritrea.*

ERITREA - FISHERIES

United Nations Food and Agricultural Organization (FAO), Viale delle Terme di Caracalla, 00100 Rome, Italy, (Dial from U.S. (202) 653-2400), (Fax from U.S. (202) 653 5760), www.fao.org; *FAO Yearbook of Fishery Statistics;* Fishery Databases; FISHSTAT Database. Subjects covered include: Aquaculture production, capture production, fishery commodities; and *The State of Food and Agriculture (SOFA) 2006.*

United Nations Statistics Division, New York, NY 10017, (800) 253-9646, Fax: (212) 963-4116, http://

unstats.un.org; *2004 Industrial Commodity Statistics Yearbook* and *Statistical Yearbook*.

The World Bank, 1818 H Street, NW, Washington, DC 20433, (202) 473-1000, Fax: (202) 477-6391, www.worldbank.org; *Eritrea*.

ERITREA - FOOD

United Nations Food and Agricultural Organization (FAO), Viale delle Terme di Caracalla, 00100 Rome, Italy, (Dial from U.S. (202) 653-2400), (Fax from U.S. (202) 653 5760), www.fao.org; *FAO Production Yearbook 2002* and *The State of Food and Agriculture (SOFA) 2006*.

United Nations Statistics Division, New York, NY 10017, (800) 253-9646, Fax: (212) 963-4116, http://unstats.un.org; *Human Development Report 2006* and *2004 Industrial Commodity Statistics Yearbook*.

ERITREA - FOREIGN EXCHANGE RATES

Central Intelligence Agency, Office of Public Affairs, Washington, DC 20505, (703) 482-0623, Fax: (703) 482-1739, www.cia.gov; *The World Factbook*.

Euromonitor International, Inc., 224 S. Michigan Avenue, Suite 1500, Chicago, IL 60604, (312) 922-1115, Fax: (312) 922-1157, www.euromonitor.com; *International Marketing Data and Statistics 2008* and *The World Economic Factbook 2008*.

Taylor and Francis Group, An Informa Business, 2 Park Square, Milton Park, Abingdon, Oxford OX14 4RN, United Kingdom, (Dial from U.S. (212) 216-7800), (Fax from U.S. (212) 564-7854), www.tandf.co.uk; *The Europa World Year Book*.

United Nations Statistics Division, New York, NY 10017, (800) 253-9646, Fax: (212) 963-4116, http://unstats.un.org; *Statistical Yearbook* and *World Statistics Pocketbook*.

ERITREA - FORESTS AND FORESTRY

UNESCO Institute for Statistics, C.P. 6128 Succursale Centre-Ville, Montreal, Quebec, H3C 3J7 Canada, (Dial from U.S. (514) 343-6880), (Fax from U.S. (514) 343 6882), www.uis.unesco.org; *Statistical Tables*.

United Nations Food and Agricultural Organization (FAO), Viale delle Terme di Caracalla, 00100 Rome, Italy, (Dial from U.S. (202) 653-2400), (Fax from U.S. (202) 653 5760), www.fao.org; *FAO Yearbook of Forest Products* and *The State of Food and Agriculture (SOFA) 2006*.

United Nations Statistics Division, New York, NY 10017, (800) 253-9646, Fax: (212) 963-4116, http://unstats.un.org; *2004 Industrial Commodity Statistics Yearbook* and *Statistical Yearbook*.

The World Bank, 1818 H Street, NW, Washington, DC 20433, (202) 473-1000, Fax: (202) 477-6391, www.worldbank.org; *Eritrea*.

ERITREA - GROSS DOMESTIC PRODUCT

Economist Intelligence Unit, 111 West 57th Street, New York, NY 10019, (212) 554-0600, Fax: (212) 586-1181, www.eiu.com; *Eritrea Country Report*.

Euromonitor International, Inc., 224 S. Michigan Avenue, Suite 1500, Chicago, IL 60604, (312) 922-1115, Fax: (312) 922-1157, www.euromonitor.com; *International Marketing Data and Statistics 2008* and *The World Economic Factbook 2008*.

United Nations Statistics Division, New York, NY 10017, (800) 253-9646, Fax: (212) 963-4116, http://unstats.un.org; *Human Development Report 2006* and *National Accounts Statistics: Compendium of Income Distribution Statistics*.

ERITREA - GROSS NATIONAL PRODUCT

Palgrave Macmillan Ltd., Houndmills, Basingstoke, Hampshire, RG21 6XS, England, (Telephone in U.S. (888) 330-8477), (Fax in U.S. (800) 672-2054), www.palgrave.com; *The Statesman's Yearbook 2008*.

United Nations Statistics Division, New York, NY 10017, (800) 253-9646, Fax: (212) 963-4116, http://unstats.un.org; *Statistical Yearbook*.

The World Bank, 1818 H Street, NW, Washington, DC 20433, (202) 473-1000, Fax: (202) 477-6391, www.worldbank.org; *The World Bank Atlas 2003-2004*.

ERITREA - HOUSING

Euromonitor International, Inc., 224 S. Michigan Avenue, Suite 1500, Chicago, IL 60604, (312) 922-1115, Fax: (312) 922-1157, www.euromonitor.com; *World Marketing Data and Statistics*.

ERITREA - ILLITERATE PERSONS

Euromonitor International, Inc., 224 S. Michigan Avenue, Suite 1500, Chicago, IL 60604, (312) 922-1115, Fax: (312) 922-1157, www.euromonitor.com; *The World Economic Factbook 2008*.

UNESCO Institute for Statistics, C.P. 6128 Succursale Centre-Ville, Montreal, Quebec, H3C 3J7 Canada, (Dial from U.S. (514) 343-6880), (Fax from U.S. (514) 343 6882), www.uis.unesco.org; *Statistical Tables*.

United Nations Statistics Division, New York, NY 10017, (800) 253-9646, Fax: (212) 963-4116, http://unstats.un.org; *Human Development Report 2006*.

ERITREA - IMPORTS

Central Intelligence Agency, Office of Public Affairs, Washington, DC 20505, (703) 482-0623, Fax: (703) 482-1739, www.cia.gov; *The World Factbook*.

Economist Intelligence Unit, 111 West 57th Street, New York, NY 10019, (212) 554-0600, Fax: (212) 586-1181, www.eiu.com; *Eritrea Country Report*.

Euromonitor International, Inc., 224 S. Michigan Avenue, Suite 1500, Chicago, IL 60604, (312) 922-1115, Fax: (312) 922-1157, www.euromonitor.com; *International Marketing Data and Statistics 2008* and *The World Economic Factbook 2008*.

United Nations Statistics Division, New York, NY 10017, (800) 253-9646, Fax: (212) 963-4116, http://unstats.un.org; *International Trade Statistics Yearbook*.

ERITREA - INDUSTRIAL PROPERTY

United Nations Statistics Division, New York, NY 10017, (800) 253-9646, Fax: (212) 963-4116, http://unstats.un.org; *Statistical Yearbook*.

ERITREA - INDUSTRIES

Central Intelligence Agency, Office of Public Affairs, Washington, DC 20505, (703) 482-0623, Fax: (703) 482-1739, www.cia.gov; *The World Factbook*.

Economist Intelligence Unit, 111 West 57th Street, New York, NY 10019, (212) 554-0600, Fax: (212) 586-1181, www.eiu.com; *Eritrea Country Report*.

Euromonitor International, Inc., 224 S. Michigan Avenue, Suite 1500, Chicago, IL 60604, (312) 922-1115, Fax: (312) 922-1157, www.euromonitor.com; *The World Economic Factbook 2008* and *World Marketing Data and Statistics*.

United Nations Statistics Division, New York, NY 10017, (800) 253-9646, Fax: (212) 963-4116, http://unstats.un.org; *2004 Industrial Commodity Statistics Yearbook* and *Statistical Yearbook*.

The World Bank, 1818 H Street, NW, Washington, DC 20433, (202) 473-1000, Fax: (202) 477-6391, www.worldbank.org; *Eritrea*.

ERITREA - INTERNATIONAL TRADE

Economist Intelligence Unit, 111 West 57th Street, New York, NY 10019, (212) 554-0600, Fax: (212) 586-1181, www.eiu.com; *Eritrea Country Report*.

Euromonitor International, Inc., 224 S. Michigan Avenue, Suite 1500, Chicago, IL 60604, (312) 922-1115, Fax: (312) 922-1157, www.euromonitor.com; *The World Economic Factbook 2008* and *World Marketing Data and Statistics*.

United Nations Food and Agricultural Organization (FAO), Viale delle Terme di Caracalla, 00100 Rome, Italy, (Dial from U.S. (202) 653-2400), (Fax from U.S. (202) 653 5760), www.fao.org; *FAO Trade Yearbook*.

United Nations Statistics Division, New York, NY 10017, (800) 253-9646, Fax: (212) 963-4116, http://unstats.un.org; *International Trade Statistics Yearbook* and *Statistical Yearbook*.

The World Bank, 1818 H Street, NW, Washington, DC 20433, (202) 473-1000, Fax: (202) 477-6391, www.worldbank.org; *Eritrea*.

World Trade Organization (WTO), Centre William Rappard, Rue de Lausanne 154, CH-1211 Geneva 21, Switzerland, www.wto.org; *International Trade Statistics 2006*.

ERITREA - LABOR

Central Intelligence Agency, Office of Public Affairs, Washington, DC 20505, (703) 482-0623, Fax: (703) 482-1739, www.cia.gov; *The World Factbook*.

Euromonitor International, Inc., 224 S. Michigan Avenue, Suite 1500, Chicago, IL 60604, (312) 922-1115, Fax: (312) 922-1157, www.euromonitor.com; *International Marketing Data and Statistics 2008* and *World Marketing Data and Statistics*.

United Nations Statistics Division, New York, NY 10017, (800) 253-9646, Fax: (212) 963-4116, http://unstats.un.org; *Human Development Report 2006* and *Statistical Yearbook*.

The World Bank, 1818 H Street, NW, Washington, DC 20433, (202) 473-1000, Fax: (202) 477-6391, www.worldbank.org; *The World Bank Atlas 2003-2004*.

ERITREA - LAND USE

Central Intelligence Agency, Office of Public Affairs, Washington, DC 20505, (703) 482-0623, Fax: (703) 482-1739, www.cia.gov; *The World Factbook*.

Euromonitor International, Inc., 224 S. Michigan Avenue, Suite 1500, Chicago, IL 60604, (312) 922-1115, Fax: (312) 922-1157, www.euromonitor.com; *International Marketing Data and Statistics 2008*.

United Nations Food and Agricultural Organization (FAO), Viale delle Terme di Caracalla, 00100 Rome, Italy, (Dial from U.S. (202) 653-2400), (Fax from U.S. (202) 653 5760), www.fao.org; *FAO Production Yearbook 2002*.

ERITREA - LIBRARIES

UNESCO Institute for Statistics, C.P. 6128 Succursale Centre-Ville, Montreal, Quebec, H3C 3J7 Canada, (Dial from U.S. (514) 343-6880), (Fax from U.S. (514) 343 6882), www.uis.unesco.org; *Statistical Tables*.

ERITREA - LIFE EXPECTANCY

Central Intelligence Agency, Office of Public Affairs, Washington, DC 20505, (703) 482-0623, Fax: (703) 482-1739, www.cia.gov; *The World Factbook*.

Euromonitor International, Inc., 224 S. Michigan Avenue, Suite 1500, Chicago, IL 60604, (312) 922-1115, Fax: (312) 922-1157, www.euromonitor.com; *The World Economic Factbook 2008*.

United Nations Statistics Division, New York, NY 10017, (800) 253-9646, Fax: (212) 963-4116, http://unstats.un.org; *Demographic Yearbook; Human Development Report 2006;* and *World Statistics Pocketbook*.

The World Bank, 1818 H Street, NW, Washington, DC 20433, (202) 473-1000, Fax: (202) 477-6391, www.worldbank.org; *The World Bank Atlas 2003-2004*.

ERITREA - LITERACY

Euromonitor International, Inc., 224 S. Michigan Avenue, Suite 1500, Chicago, IL 60604, (312) 922-1115, Fax: (312) 922-1157, www.euromonitor.com; *World Marketing Data and Statistics*.

ERITREA - LIVESTOCK

Palgrave Macmillan Ltd., Houndmills, Basingstoke, Hampshire, RG21 6XS, England, (Telephone in U.S. (888) 330-8477), (Fax in U.S. (800) 672-2054), www.palgrave.com; *The Statesman's Yearbook 2008*.

United Nations Food and Agricultural Organization (FAO), Viale delle Terme di Caracalla, 00100 Rome, Italy, (Dial from U.S. (202) 653-2400), (Fax from U.S. (202) 653 5760), www.fao.org; *FAO Production Yearbook 2002* and *The State of Food and Agriculture (SOFA) 2006.*

United Nations Statistics Division, New York, NY 10017, (800) 253-9646, Fax: (212) 963-4116, http://unstats.un.org; *2004 Industrial Commodity Statistics Yearbook* and *Statistical Yearbook.*

ERITREA - MACHINERY

United Nations Statistics Division, New York, NY 10017, (800) 253-9646, Fax: (212) 963-4116, http://unstats.un.org; *2004 Industrial Commodity Statistics Yearbook.*

ERITREA - MANUFACTURES

United Nations Statistics Division, New York, NY 10017, (800) 253-9646, Fax: (212) 963-4116, http://unstats.un.org; *2004 Industrial Commodity Statistics Yearbook* and *Statistical Yearbook.*

ERITREA - MARRIAGE

United Nations Statistics Division, New York, NY 10017, (800) 253-9646, Fax: (212) 963-4116, http://unstats.un.org; *Demographic Yearbook* and *Statistical Yearbook.*

ERITREA - MINERAL INDUSTRIES

Palgrave Macmillan Ltd., Houndmills, Basingstoke, Hampshire, RG21 6XS, England, (Telephone in U.S. (888) 330-8477), (Fax in U.S. (800) 672-2054), www.palgrave.com; *The Statesman's Yearbook 2008.*

Platts, 2 Penn Plaza, 25th Floor, New York, NY 10121-2298, (212) 904-3070, www.platts.com; *Energy Economist.*

United Nations Statistics Division, New York, NY 10017, (800) 253-9646, Fax: (212) 963-4116, http://unstats.un.org; *Energy Statistics Yearbook 2003; 2004 Industrial Commodity Statistics Yearbook;* and *Statistical Yearbook.*

The World Bank, 1818 H Street, NW, Washington, DC 20433, (202) 473-1000, Fax: (202) 477-6391, www.worldbank.org; *Eritrea.*

ERITREA - MONEY SUPPLY

Economist Intelligence Unit, 111 West 57th Street, New York, NY 10019, (212) 554-0600, Fax: (212) 586-1181, www.eiu.com; *Eritrea Country Report.*

The World Bank, 1818 H Street, NW, Washington, DC 20433, (202) 473-1000, Fax: (202) 477-6391, www.worldbank.org; *Eritrea.*

ERITREA - MONUMENTS AND HISTORIC SITES

UNESCO Institute for Statistics, C.P. 6128 Succursale Centre-Ville, Montreal, Quebec, H3C 3J7 Canada, (Dial from U.S. (514) 343-6880), (Fax from U.S. (514) 343 6882), www.uis.unesco.org; *Statistical Tables.*

ERITREA - MORTALITY

Central Intelligence Agency, Office of Public Affairs, Washington, DC 20505, (703) 482-0623, Fax: (703) 482-1739, www.cia.gov; *The World Factbook.*

Euromonitor International, Inc., 224 S. Michigan Avenue, Suite 1500, Chicago, IL 60604, (312) 922-1115, Fax: (312) 922-1157, www.euromonitor.com; *International Marketing Data and Statistics 2008* and *The World Economic Factbook 2008.*

UNICEF, 3 United Nations Plaza, New York, NY 10017, (800) 253-9646, Fax: (212) 887-7465, www.unicef.org; *The State of the World's Children 2008.*

United Nations Statistics Division, New York, NY 10017, (800) 253-9646, Fax: (212) 963-4116, http://unstats.un.org; *Demographic Yearbook; Human Development Report 2006; Statistical Yearbook;* and *World Statistics Pocketbook.*

The World Bank, 1818 H Street, NW, Washington, DC 20433, (202) 473-1000, Fax: (202) 477-6391, www.worldbank.org; *The World Bank Atlas 2003-2004.*

ERITREA - MOTION PICTURES

UNESCO Institute for Statistics, C.P. 6128 Succursale Centre-Ville, Montreal, Quebec, H3C 3J7 Canada, (Dial from U.S. (514) 343-6880), (Fax from U.S. (514) 343 6882), www.uis.unesco.org; *Statistical Tables.*

United Nations Statistics Division, New York, NY 10017, (800) 253-9646, Fax: (212) 963-4116, http://unstats.un.org; *Statistical Yearbook.*

ERITREA - MUSEUMS

UNESCO Institute for Statistics, C.P. 6128 Succursale Centre-Ville, Montreal, Quebec, H3C 3J7 Canada, (Dial from U.S. (514) 343-6880), (Fax from U.S. (514) 343 6882), www.uis.unesco.org; *Statistical Tables.*

ERITREA - PERIODICALS

UNESCO Institute for Statistics, C.P. 6128 Succursale Centre-Ville, Montreal, Quebec, H3C 3J7 Canada, (Dial from U.S. (514) 343-6880), (Fax from U.S. (514) 343 6882), www.uis.unesco.org; *Statistical Tables.*

ERITREA - PETROLEUM INDUSTRY AND TRADE

PennWell Corporation, 1421 South Sheridan Road, Tulsa, OK 74112, (918) 835-3161, www.pennwell.com; *International Petroleum Encyclopedia 2007.*

Platts, 2 Penn Plaza, 25th Floor, New York, NY 10121-2298, (212) 904-3070, www.platts.com; *Energy Economist.*

United Nations Food and Agricultural Organization (FAO), Viale delle Terme di Caracalla, 00100 Rome, Italy, (Dial from U.S. (202) 653-2400), (Fax from U.S. (202) 653 5760), www.fao.org; *The State of Food and Agriculture (SOFA) 2006.*

United Nations Statistics Division, New York, NY 10017, (800) 253-9646, Fax: (212) 963-4116, http://unstats.un.org; *Energy Statistics Yearbook 2003; 2004 Industrial Commodity Statistics Yearbook;* and *Statistical Yearbook.*

ERITREA - POLITICAL SCIENCE

Central Intelligence Agency, Office of Public Affairs, Washington, DC 20505, (703) 482-0623, Fax: (703) 482-1739, www.cia.gov; *The World Factbook.*

Palgrave Macmillan Ltd., Houndmills, Basingstoke, Hampshire, RG21 6XS, England, (Telephone in U.S. (888) 330-8477), (Fax in U.S. (800) 672-2054), www.palgrave.com; *The Statesman's Yearbook 2008.*

United Nations Statistics Division, New York, NY 10017, (800) 253-9646, Fax: (212) 963-4116, http://unstats.un.org; *Statistical Yearbook.*

ERITREA - POPULATION

African Development Bank Group, Rue Joseph Anoma, 01 BP 1387 Abidjan 01, Cote d'Ivoire, www.afdb.org; *The African Statistical Journal; Gender, Poverty and Environmental Indicators on African Countries 2007;* and *Selected Statistics on African Countries 2007.*

Central Intelligence Agency, Office of Public Affairs, Washington, DC 20505, (703) 482-0623, Fax: (703) 482-1739, www.cia.gov; *The World Factbook.*

Economist Intelligence Unit, 111 West 57th Street, New York, NY 10019, (212) 554-0600, Fax: (212) 586-1181, www.eiu.com; *Eritrea Country Report.*

Euromonitor International, Inc., 224 S. Michigan Avenue, Suite 1500, Chicago, IL 60604, (312) 922-1115, Fax: (312) 922-1157, www.euromonitor.com; *International Marketing Data and Statistics 2008* and *The World Economic Factbook 2008.*

Eurostat, Batiment Jean Monnet, Rue Alcide de Gasperi, L-2920 Luxembourg, http://epp.eurostat.ec.europa.eu; *Demographic Indicators - Population by Age-Classes.*

Palgrave Macmillan Ltd., Houndmills, Basingstoke, Hampshire, RG21 6XS, England, (Telephone in U.S. (888) 330-8477), (Fax in U.S. (800) 672-2054), www.palgrave.com; *The Statesman's Yearbook 2008.*

Taylor and Francis Group, An Informa Business, 2 Park Square, Milton Park, Abingdon, Oxford OX14 4RN, United Kingdom, (Dial from U.S. (212) 216-7800), (Fax from U.S. (212) 564-7854), www.tandf.co.uk; *The Europa World Year Book.*

UNESCO Institute for Statistics, C.P. 6128 Succursale Centre-Ville, Montreal, Quebec, H3C 3J7 Canada, (Dial from U.S. (514) 343-6880), (Fax from U.S. (514) 343 6882), www.uis.unesco.org; *Statistical Tables.*

United Nations Food and Agricultural Organization (FAO), Viale delle Terme di Caracalla, 00100 Rome, Italy, (Dial from U.S. (202) 653-2400), (Fax from U.S. (202) 653 5760), www.fao.org; *FAO Production Yearbook 2002.*

United Nations Statistics Division, New York, NY 10017, (800) 253-9646, Fax: (212) 963-4116, http://unstats.un.org; *Demographic Yearbook; Human Development Report 2006; Statistical Yearbook;* and *World Statistics Pocketbook.*

The World Bank, 1818 H Street, NW, Washington, DC 20433, (202) 473-1000, Fax: (202) 477-6391, www.worldbank.org; *Eritrea* and *The World Bank Atlas 2003-2004.*

ERITREA - POPULATION DENSITY

Central Intelligence Agency, Office of Public Affairs, Washington, DC 20505, (703) 482-0623, Fax: (703) 482-1739, www.cia.gov; *The World Factbook.*

Euromonitor International, Inc., 224 S. Michigan Avenue, Suite 1500, Chicago, IL 60604, (312) 922-1115, Fax: (312) 922-1157, www.euromonitor.com; *The World Economic Factbook 2008.*

Palgrave Macmillan Ltd., Houndmills, Basingstoke, Hampshire, RG21 6XS, England, (Telephone in U.S. (888) 330-8477), (Fax in U.S. (800) 672-2054), www.palgrave.com; *The Statesman's Yearbook 2008.*

Taylor and Francis Group, An Informa Business, 2 Park Square, Milton Park, Abingdon, Oxford OX14 4RN, United Kingdom, (Dial from U.S. (212) 216-7800), (Fax from U.S. (212) 564-7854), www.tandf.co.uk; *The Europa World Year Book.*

UNESCO Institute for Statistics, C.P. 6128 Succursale Centre-Ville, Montreal, Quebec, H3C 3J7 Canada, (Dial from U.S. (514) 343-6880), (Fax from U.S. (514) 343 6882), www.uis.unesco.org; *Statistical Tables.*

United Nations Statistics Division, New York, NY 10017, (800) 253-9646, Fax: (212) 963-4116, http://unstats.un.org; *Statistical Yearbook.*

The World Bank, 1818 H Street, NW, Washington, DC 20433, (202) 473-1000, Fax: (202) 477-6391, www.worldbank.org; *Eritrea.*

ERITREA - POSTAL SERVICE

United Nations Statistics Division, New York, NY 10017, (800) 253-9646, Fax: (212) 963-4116, http://unstats.un.org; *Statistical Yearbook.*

ERITREA - POWER RESOURCES

Euromonitor International, Inc., 224 S. Michigan Avenue, Suite 1500, Chicago, IL 60604, (312) 922-1115, Fax: (312) 922-1157, www.euromonitor.com; *International Marketing Data and Statistics 2008; The World Economic Factbook 2008;* and *World Marketing Data and Statistics.*

Platts, 2 Penn Plaza, 25th Floor, New York, NY 10121-2298, (212) 904-3070, www.platts.com; *Energy Economist* and *European Power Daily.*

United Nations Statistics Division, New York, NY 10017, (800) 253-9646, Fax: (212) 963-4116, http://unstats.un.org; *Energy Statistics Yearbook 2003; Human Development Report 2006; Statistical Yearbook;* and *World Statistics Pocketbook.*

The World Bank, 1818 H Street, NW, Washington, DC 20433, (202) 473-1000, Fax: (202) 477-6391, www.worldbank.org; *The World Bank Atlas 2003-2004.*

ERITREA - PRICES

Euromonitor International, Inc., 224 S. Michigan Avenue, Suite 1500, Chicago, IL 60604, (312) 922-1115, Fax: (312) 922-1157, www.euromonitor.com; *World Marketing Data and Statistics.*

United Nations Food and Agricultural Organization (FAO), Viale delle Terme di Caracalla, 00100 Rome, Italy, (Dial from U.S. (202) 653-2400), (Fax from U.S. (202) 653 5760), www.fao.org; *FAO Production Yearbook 2002.*

The World Bank, 1818 H Street, NW, Washington, DC 20433, (202) 473-1000, Fax: (202) 477-6391, www.worldbank.org; *Eritrea.*

ERITREA - PROFESSIONS

United Nations Statistics Division, New York, NY 10017, (800) 253-9646, Fax: (212) 963-4116, http://unstats.un.org; *Statistical Yearbook.*

ERITREA - PUBLIC HEALTH

Euromonitor International, Inc., 224 S. Michigan Avenue, Suite 1500, Chicago, IL 60604, (312) 922-1115, Fax: (312) 922-1157, www.euromonitor.com; *World Marketing Data and Statistics.*

UNICEF, 3 United Nations Plaza, New York, NY 10017, (800) 253-9646, Fax: (212) 887-7465, www.unicef.org; *The State of the World's Children 2008.*

United Nations Statistics Division, New York, NY 10017, (800) 253-9646, Fax: (212) 963-4116, http://unstats.un.org; *Human Development Report 2006* and *Statistical Yearbook.*

The World Bank, 1818 H Street, NW, Washington, DC 20433, (202) 473-1000, Fax: (202) 477-6391, www.worldbank.org; *Eritrea.*

ERITREA - PUBLISHERS AND PUBLISHING

UNESCO Institute for Statistics, C.P. 6128 Succursale Centre-Ville, Montreal, Quebec, H3C 3J7 Canada, (Dial from U.S. (514) 343-6880), (Fax from U.S. (514) 343 6882), www.uis.unesco.org; *Statistical Tables.*

ERITREA - RADIO - RECEIVERS AND RECEPTION

United Nations Statistics Division, New York, NY 10017, (800) 253-9646, Fax: (212) 963-4116, http://unstats.un.org; *Statistical Yearbook.*

ERITREA - RAILROADS

United Nations Statistics Division, New York, NY 10017, (800) 253-9646, Fax: (212) 963-4116, http://unstats.un.org; *Statistical Yearbook.*

ERITREA - RELIGION

Central Intelligence Agency, Office of Public Affairs, Washington, DC 20505, (703) 482-0623, Fax: (703) 482-1739, www.cia.gov; *The World Factbook.*

Palgrave Macmillan Ltd., Houndmills, Basingstoke, Hampshire, RG21 6XS, England, (Telephone in U.S. (888) 330-8477), (Fax in U.S. (800) 672-2054), www.palgrave.com; *The Statesman's Yearbook 2008.*

ERITREA - RETAIL TRADE

Euromonitor International, Inc., 224 S. Michigan Avenue, Suite 1500, Chicago, IL 60604, (312) 922-1115, Fax: (312) 922-1157, www.euromonitor.com; *World Marketing Data and Statistics.*

United Nations Statistics Division, New York, NY 10017, (800) 253-9646, Fax: (212) 963-4116, http://unstats.un.org; *Statistical Yearbook.*

ERITREA - ROADS

Central Intelligence Agency, Office of Public Affairs, Washington, DC 20505, (703) 482-0623, Fax: (703) 482-1739, www.cia.gov; *The World Factbook.*

ERITREA - RUBBER INDUSTRY AND TRADE

International Rubber Study Group (IRSG), 1st Floor, Heron House, 109/115 Wembley Hill Road, Wembley, Middlesex HA9 8DA, United Kingdom, www.rubberstudy.com; *Rubber Statistical Bulletin; Summary of World Rubber Statistics 2005; World Rubber Statistics Handbook (Volume 6, 1975-2001);* and *World Rubber Statistics Historic Handbook.*

United Nations Statistics Division, New York, NY 10017, (800) 253-9646, Fax: (212) 963-4116, http://unstats.un.org; *Statistical Yearbook.*

ERITREA - SHIPPING

United Nations Statistics Division, New York, NY 10017, (800) 253-9646, Fax: (212) 963-4116, http://unstats.un.org; *Statistical Yearbook.*

ERITREA - SOCIAL ECOLOGY

United Nations Statistics Division, New York, NY 10017, (800) 253-9646, Fax: (212) 963-4116, http://unstats.un.org; *World Statistics Pocketbook.*

ERITREA - TELEPHONE

United Nations Statistics Division, New York, NY 10017, (800) 253-9646, Fax: (212) 963-4116, http://unstats.un.org; *Statistical Yearbook* and *World Statistics Pocketbook.*

ERITREA - TEXTILE INDUSTRY

United Nations Statistics Division, New York, NY 10017, (800) 253-9646, Fax: (212) 963-4116, http://unstats.un.org; *2004 Industrial Commodity Statistics Yearbook* and *Statistical Yearbook.*

ERITREA - TIRE INDUSTRY

United Nations Statistics Division, New York, NY 10017, (800) 253-9646, Fax: (212) 963-4116, http://unstats.un.org; *Statistical Yearbook.*

ERITREA - TOBACCO INDUSTRY

Foreign Agricultural Service (FAS), U.S. Department of Agriculture (USDA), 1400 Independence Avenue, SW, Washington, DC 20250, (202) 720-3935, www.fas.usda.gov; *Tobacco: World Markets and Trade.*

United Nations Statistics Division, New York, NY 10017, (800) 253-9646, Fax: (212) 963-4116, http://unstats.un.org; *Statistical Yearbook.*

ERITREA - TOURISM

Euromonitor International, Inc., 224 S. Michigan Avenue, Suite 1500, Chicago, IL 60604, (312) 922-1115, Fax: (312) 922-1157, www.euromonitor.com; *The World Economic Factbook 2008* and *World Marketing Data and Statistics.*

United Nations Statistics Division, New York, NY 10017, (800) 253-9646, Fax: (212) 963-4116, http://unstats.un.org; *Statistical Yearbook.*

The World Bank, 1818 H Street, NW, Washington, DC 20433, (202) 473-1000, Fax: (202) 477-6391, www.worldbank.org; *Eritrea.*

ERITREA - TRANSPORTATION

Central Intelligence Agency, Office of Public Affairs, Washington, DC 20505, (703) 482-0623, Fax: (703) 482-1739, www.cia.gov; *The World Factbook.*

Euromonitor International, Inc., 224 S. Michigan Avenue, Suite 1500, Chicago, IL 60604, (312) 922-1115, Fax: (312) 922-1157, www.euromonitor.com; *International Marketing Data and Statistics 2008* and *World Marketing Data and Statistics.*

United Nations Statistics Division, New York, NY 10017, (800) 253-9646, Fax: (212) 963-4116, http://unstats.un.org; *Human Development Report 2006.*

The World Bank, 1818 H Street, NW, Washington, DC 20433, (202) 473-1000, Fax: (202) 477-6391, www.worldbank.org; *Africa Live Database (LDB)* and *Eritrea.*

ERITREA - UNEMPLOYMENT

Central Intelligence Agency, Office of Public Affairs, Washington, DC 20505, (703) 482-0623, Fax: (703) 482-1739, www.cia.gov; *The World Factbook.*

United Nations Statistics Division, New York, NY 10017, (800) 253-9646, Fax: (212) 963-4116, http://unstats.un.org; *Statistical Yearbook.*

The World Bank, 1818 H Street, NW, Washington, DC 20433, (202) 473-1000, Fax: (202) 477-6391, www.worldbank.org; *Eritrea.*

ERITREA - VITAL STATISTICS

United Nations Statistics Division, New York, NY 10017, (800) 253-9646, Fax: (212) 963-4116, http://unstats.un.org; *Statistical Yearbook.*

ERITREA - WAGES

United Nations Statistics Division, New York, NY 10017, (800) 253-9646, Fax: (212) 963-4116, http://unstats.un.org; *Statistical Yearbook.*

The World Bank, 1818 H Street, NW, Washington, DC 20433, (202) 473-1000, Fax: (202) 477-6391, www.worldbank.org; *Eritrea.*

ERITREA - WHOLESALE PRICE INDEXES

United Nations Statistics Division, New York, NY 10017, (800) 253-9646, Fax: (212) 963-4116, http://unstats.un.org; *Statistical Yearbook.*

ERITREA - WHOLESALE TRADE

United Nations Statistics Division, New York, NY 10017, (800) 253-9646, Fax: (212) 963-4116, http://unstats.un.org; *Statistical Yearbook.*

ESKIMO POPULATION

U.S. Census Bureau, Population Division, 4700 Silver Hill Road, Washington DC 20233-0001, (301) 763-3030, www.census.gov/population/www/; *The Asian and Pacific Islander Population in the United States* and *Current Population Reports.*

ESTATE AND GIFT TAXES

The Office of Management and Budget (OMB), 725 17th Street, NW, Washington, DC 20503, (202) 395-3080, Fax: (202) 395-3888, www.whitehouse.gov/omb; *Budget of the United States Government, Federal Year 2009* and *Historical Tables.*

U.S. Census Bureau, Governments Division, 4600 Silver Hill Road, Washington DC 20233, (800) 242-2184, www.census.gov/govs/www; *2002 Census of Governments, Government Finances.*

U.S. Department of the Treasury (DOT), Internal Revenue Service (IRS), Statistics of Income Division (SIS), PO Box 2608, Washington, DC, 20013-2608, (202) 874-0410, Fax: (202) 874-0964, www.irs.ustreas.gov; *IRS Data Book 2004-2005.*

ESTONIA - NATIONAL STATISTICAL OFFICE

Statistical Office of Estonia (Statistikaamet), Endla 15, 15174 Tallinn, Estonia, www.stat.ee; National Data Center.

ESTONIA - PRIMARY STATISTICS SOURCES

Central Statistical Bureau of Latvia (CSB) (Latvijas Republikas Centrala Statistikas Parvalde), 1 Lacplesa Street, Riga LV-1301, Latvia, www.csb.gov.lv; *Estonia, Latvia, Lithuania in Figures 2006.*

Eurostat, Batiment Jean Monnet, Rue Alcide de Gasperi, L-2920 Luxembourg, http://epp.eurostat.ec.europa.eu; *Pocketbook on Candidate and Potential Candidate Countries.*

Statistical Office of Estonia (Statistikaamet), Endla 15, 15174 Tallinn, Estonia, www.stat.ee; *Statistical Yearbook of Estonia 2006* (Eesti statistika aastaraamat 2005).

ESTONIA - ABORTION

United Nations Statistics Division, New York, NY 10017, (800) 253-9646, Fax: (212) 963-4116, http://

unstats.un.org; *Trends in Europe and North America: The Statistical Yearbook of the ECE 2005.*

ESTONIA - AGRICULTURE

Academic International Press, PO Box 1111, Gulf Breeze, FL 32562-1111, Fax: (850) 934-0953, www.ai-press.com; *Russia and Eurasia Facts and Figures Annual.*

Economist Intelligence Unit, 111 West 57th Street, New York, NY 10019, (212) 554-0600, Fax: (212) 586-1181, www.eiu.com; *Estonia Country Report.*

Euromonitor International, Inc., 224 S. Michigan Avenue, Suite 1500, Chicago, IL 60604, (312) 922-1115, Fax: (312) 922-1157, www.euromonitor.com; *World Marketing Data and Statistics.*

Eurostat, Batiment Jean Monnet, Rue Alcide de Gasperi, L-2920 Luxembourg, http://epp.eurostat.ec.europa.eu; *EU Agricultural Prices in 2007.*

Palgrave Macmillan Ltd., Houndmills, Basingstoke, Hampshire, RG21 6XS, England, (Telephone in U.S. (888) 330-8477), (Fax in U.S. (800) 672-2054), www.palgrave.com; *The Statesman's Yearbook 2008.*

Taylor and Francis Group, An Informa Business, 2 Park Square, Milton Park, Abingdon, Oxford OX14 4RN, United Kingdom, (Dial from U.S. (212) 216-7800), (Fax from U.S. (212) 564-7854), www.tandf.co.uk; *The Europa World Year Book.*

United Nations Food and Agricultural Organization (FAO), Viale delle Terme di Caracalla, 00100 Rome, Italy, (Dial from U.S. (202) 653-2400), (Fax from U.S. (202) 653 5760), www.fao.org; AQUASTAT; *FAO Production Yearbook 2002; FAO Trade Yearbook;* and *The State of Food and Agriculture (SOFA) 2006.*

United Nations Statistics Division, New York, NY 10017, (800) 253-9646, Fax: (212) 963-4116, http://unstats.un.org; *2004 Industrial Commodity Statistics Yearbook* and *Statistical Yearbook.*

The World Bank, 1818 H Street, NW, Washington, DC 20433, (202) 473-1000, Fax: (202) 477-6391, www.worldbank.org; *Estonia; Statistical Handbook: States of the Former USSR;* and *World Development Indicators (WDI) 2008.*

ESTONIA - AIRLINES

Eurostat, Batiment Jean Monnet, Rue Alcide de Gasperi, L-2920 Luxembourg, http://epp.eurostat.ec.europa.eu; *Regional Passenger and Freight Air Transport in Europe in 2006.*

International Civil Aviation Organization (ICAO), External Relations and Public Information Office (EPO), 999 University Street, Montreal, Quebec H3C 5H7, Canada, (Dial from U.S. (514) 954-8219), (Fax from U.S. (514) 954-6077), www.icao.int; *Civil Aviation Statistics of the World.*

Palgrave Macmillan Ltd., Houndmills, Basingstoke, Hampshire, RG21 6XS, England, (Telephone in U.S. (888) 330-8477), (Fax in U.S. (800) 672-2054), www.palgrave.com; *The Statesman's Yearbook 2008.*

Taylor and Francis Group, An Informa Business, 2 Park Square, Milton Park, Abingdon, Oxford OX14 4RN, United Kingdom, (Dial from U.S. (212) 216-7800), (Fax from U.S. (212) 564-7854), www.tandf.co.uk; *The Europa World Year Book.*

United Nations Statistics Division, New York, NY 10017, (800) 253-9646, Fax: (212) 963-4116, http://unstats.un.org; *Statistical Yearbook.*

ESTONIA - AIRPORTS

Central Intelligence Agency, Office of Public Affairs, Washington, DC 20505, (703) 482-0623, Fax: (703) 482-1739, www.cia.gov; *The World Factbook.*

ESTONIA - ARMED FORCES

Academic International Press, PO Box 1111, Gulf Breeze, FL 32562-1111, Fax: (850) 934-0953, www.ai-press.com; *Russia and Eurasia Facts and Figures Annual.*

Central Intelligence Agency, Office of Public Affairs, Washington, DC 20505, (703) 482-0623, Fax: (703) 482-1739, www.cia.gov; *The World Factbook.*

Euromonitor International, Inc., 224 S. Michigan Avenue, Suite 1500, Chicago, IL 60604, (312) 922-1115, Fax: (312) 922-1157, www.euromonitor.com; *World Marketing Data and Statistics.*

International Institute for Strategic Studies (IISS), Arundel House, 13-15 Arundel Street, Temple Place, London WC2R 3DX, England, www.iiss.org; *The Military Balance 2007.*

Palgrave Macmillan Ltd., Houndmills, Basingstoke, Hampshire, RG21 6XS, England, (Telephone in U.S. (888) 330-8477), (Fax in U.S. (800) 672-2054), www.palgrave.com; *The Statesman's Yearbook 2008.*

United Nations Statistics Division, New York, NY 10017, (800) 253-9646, Fax: (212) 963-4116, http://unstats.un.org; *Human Development Report 2006.*

ESTONIA - BALANCE OF PAYMENTS

Taylor and Francis Group, An Informa Business, 2 Park Square, Milton Park, Abingdon, Oxford OX14 4RN, United Kingdom, (Dial from U.S. (212) 216-7800), (Fax from U.S. (212) 564-7854), www.tandf.co.uk; *The Europa World Year Book.*

United Nations Conference on Trade and Development (UNCTAD), DC2-1120, United Nations, New York, NY 10017, (212) 963-0027, www.unctad.org; *Handbook of Statistics 2005.*

The World Bank, 1818 H Street, NW, Washington, DC 20433, (202) 473-1000, Fax: (202) 477-6391, www.worldbank.org; *Estonia; World Development Indicators (WDI) 2008;* and *World Development Report 2008.*

ESTONIA - BANKS AND BANKING

Euromonitor International, Inc., 224 S. Michigan Avenue, Suite 1500, Chicago, IL 60604, (312) 922-1115, Fax: (312) 922-1157, www.euromonitor.com; *World Marketing Data and Statistics.*

European Union, Delegation of the European Commission to the United States, 2300 M Street, NW, Washington, DC 20037, (202) 862-9500, Fax: (202) 429-1766, www.eurunion.org; *The EU Economy, 2007 Review: Moving Europe's Productivity Frontier.*

Palgrave Macmillan Ltd., Houndmills, Basingstoke, Hampshire, RG21 6XS, England, (Telephone in U.S. (888) 330-8477), (Fax in U.S. (800) 672-2054), www.palgrave.com; *The Statesman's Yearbook 2008.*

Taylor and Francis Group, An Informa Business, 2 Park Square, Milton Park, Abingdon, Oxford OX14 4RN, United Kingdom, (Dial from U.S. (212) 216-7800), (Fax from U.S. (212) 564-7854), www.tandf.co.uk; *The Europa World Year Book.*

ESTONIA - BEVERAGE INDUSTRY

United Nations Statistics Division, New York, NY 10017, (800) 253-9646, Fax: (212) 963-4116, http://unstats.un.org; *Statistical Yearbook.*

ESTONIA - BROADCASTING

Central Intelligence Agency, Office of Public Affairs, Washington, DC 20505, (703) 482-0623, Fax: (703) 482-1739, www.cia.gov; *The World Factbook.*

Euromonitor International, Inc., 224 S. Michigan Avenue, Suite 1500, Chicago, IL 60604, (312) 922-1115, Fax: (312) 922-1157, www.euromonitor.com; *World Marketing Data and Statistics.*

Palgrave Macmillan Ltd., Houndmills, Basingstoke, Hampshire, RG21 6XS, England, (Telephone in U.S. (888) 330-8477), (Fax in U.S. (800) 672-2054), www.palgrave.com; *The Statesman's Yearbook 2008.*

UNESCO Institute for Statistics, C.P. 6128 Succursale Centre-Ville, Montreal, Quebec, H3C 3J7 Canada, (Dial from U.S. (514) 343-6880), (Fax from U.S. (514) 343 6882), www.uis.unesco.org; *Statistical Tables.*

United Nations Statistics Division, New York, NY 10017, (800) 253-9646, Fax: (212) 963-4116, http://unstats.un.org; *Trends in Europe and North America: The Statistical Yearbook of the ECE 2005.*

ESTONIA - BUDGET

Central Intelligence Agency, Office of Public Affairs, Washington, DC 20505, (703) 482-0623, Fax: (703) 482-1739, www.cia.gov; *The World Factbook.*

Eurostat, Batiment Jean Monnet, Rue Alcide de Gasperi, L-2920 Luxembourg, http://epp.eurostat.ec.europa.eu; *Government Budgets.*

ESTONIA - BUSINESS

Economist Intelligence Unit, 111 West 57th Street, New York, NY 10019, (212) 554-0600, Fax: (212) 586-1181, www.eiu.com; *Business Eastern Europe.*

United Nations Statistics Division, New York, NY 10017, (800) 253-9646, Fax: (212) 963-4116, http://unstats.un.org; *Statistical Yearbook.*

ESTONIA - CAPITAL INVESTMENTS

The World Bank, 1818 H Street, NW, Washington, DC 20433, (202) 473-1000, Fax: (202) 477-6391, www.worldbank.org; *Statistical Handbook: States of the Former USSR.*

ESTONIA - CATTLE

See ESTONIA - LIVESTOCK

ESTONIA - CHILDBIRTH - STATISTICS

Central Intelligence Agency, Office of Public Affairs, Washington, DC 20505, (703) 482-0623, Fax: (703) 482-1739, www.cia.gov; *The World Factbook.*

Euromonitor International, Inc., 224 S. Michigan Avenue, Suite 1500, Chicago, IL 60604, (312) 922-1115, Fax: (312) 922-1157, www.euromonitor.com; *The World Economic Factbook 2008.*

Palgrave Macmillan Ltd., Houndmills, Basingstoke, Hampshire, RG21 6XS, England, (Telephone in U.S. (888) 330-8477), (Fax in U.S. (800) 672-2054), www.palgrave.com; *The Statesman's Yearbook 2008.*

Taylor and Francis Group, An Informa Business, 2 Park Square, Milton Park, Abingdon, Oxford OX14 4RN, United Kingdom, (Dial from U.S. (212) 216-7800), (Fax from U.S. (212) 564-7854), www.tandf.co.uk; *The Europa World Year Book.*

United Nations Statistics Division, New York, NY 10017, (800) 253-9646, Fax: (212) 963-4116, http://unstats.un.org; *Statistical Yearbook.*

World Health Organization (WHO), Avenue Appia 20, 1211 Geneve 27, Switzerland, (Telephone in U.S. (212) 331-9081), www.who.int; *World Health Report 2006.*

ESTONIA - CLIMATE

Palgrave Macmillan Ltd., Houndmills, Basingstoke, Hampshire, RG21 6XS, England, (Telephone in U.S. (888) 330-8477), (Fax in U.S. (800) 672-2054), www.palgrave.com; *The Statesman's Yearbook 2008.*

ESTONIA - COAL PRODUCTION

See ESTONIA - MINERAL INDUSTRIES

ESTONIA - COMMERCE

Palgrave Macmillan Ltd., Houndmills, Basingstoke, Hampshire, RG21 6XS, England, (Telephone in U.S. (888) 330-8477), (Fax in U.S. (800) 672-2054), www.palgrave.com; *The Statesman's Yearbook 2008.*

ESTONIA - CONSTRUCTION INDUSTRY

Academic International Press, PO Box 1111, Gulf Breeze, FL 32562-1111, Fax: (850) 934-0953, www.ai-press.com; *Russia and Eurasia Facts and Figures Annual.*

United Nations Statistics Division, New York, NY 10017, (800) 253-9646, Fax: (212) 963-4116, http://unstats.un.org; *Statistical Yearbook.*

ESTONIA - CONSUMER GOODS

International Labour Office, I.L.O. Publications, 4 route des Morillons, CH-1211 Geneva 22, Switzerland, (Telephone in U.S. (202) 653-7652), (Fax in U.S. (202) 653-7687), www.ilo.org; *Yearbook of Labour Statistics 2006.*

ESTONIA - CONSUMER PRICE INDEXES

Taylor and Francis Group, An Informa Business, 2 Park Square, Milton Park, Abingdon, Oxford OX14

4RN, United Kingdom, (Dial from U.S. (212) 216-7800), (Fax from U.S. (212) 564-7854), www.tandf.co.uk; *The Europa World Year Book.*

United Nations Statistics Division, New York, NY 10017, (800) 253-9646, Fax: (212) 963-4116, http://unstats.un.org; *Statistical Yearbook* and *Trends in Europe and North America: The Statistical Yearbook of the ECE 2005.*

The World Bank, 1818 H Street, NW, Washington, DC 20433, (202) 473-1000, Fax: (202) 477-6391, www.worldbank.org; *Estonia.*

ESTONIA - CONSUMPTION (ECONOMICS)

The World Bank, 1818 H Street, NW, Washington, DC 20433, (202) 473-1000, Fax: (202) 477-6391, www.worldbank.org; *Statistical Handbook: States of the Former USSR* and *World Development Report 2008.*

ESTONIA - COTTON

See ESTONIA - CROPS

ESTONIA - CRIME

Academic International Press, PO Box 1111, Gulf Breeze, FL 32562-1111, Fax: (850) 934-0953, www.ai-press.com; *Russia and Eurasia Facts and Figures Annual.*

Eurostat, Batiment Jean Monnet, Rue Alcide de Gasperi, L-2920 Luxembourg, http://epp.eurostat.ec.europa.eu; *Crime and Criminal Justice; General Government Expenditure and Revenue in the EU, 2006;* and *Study on Crime Victimisation.*

United Nations Statistics Division, New York, NY 10017, (800) 253-9646, Fax: (212) 963-4116, http://unstats.un.org; *Trends in Europe and North America: The Statistical Yearbook of the ECE 2005.*

ESTONIA - CROPS

Palgrave Macmillan Ltd., Houndmills, Basingstoke, Hampshire, RG21 6XS, England, (Telephone in U.S. (888) 330-8477), (Fax in U.S. (800) 672-2054), www.palgrave.com; *The Statesman's Yearbook 2008.*

Taylor and Francis Group, An Informa Business, 2 Park Square, Milton Park, Abingdon, Oxford OX14 4RN, United Kingdom, (Dial from U.S. (212) 216-7800), (Fax from U.S. (212) 564-7854), www.tandf.co.uk; *The Europa World Year Book.*

United Nations Food and Agricultural Organization (FAO), Viale delle Terme di Caracalla, 00100 Rome, Italy, (Dial from U.S. (202) 653-2400), (Fax from U.S. (202) 653 5760), www.fao.org; *FAO Production Yearbook 2002* and *The State of Food and Agriculture (SOFA) 2006.*

United Nations Statistics Division, New York, NY 10017, (800) 253-9646, Fax: (212) 963-4116, http://unstats.un.org; *2004 Industrial Commodity Statistics Yearbook* and *Statistical Yearbook.*

The World Bank, 1818 H Street, NW, Washington, DC 20433, (202) 473-1000, Fax: (202) 477-6391, www.worldbank.org; *Statistical Handbook: States of the Former USSR.*

ESTONIA - DAIRY PROCESSING

Palgrave Macmillan Ltd., Houndmills, Basingstoke, Hampshire, RG21 6XS, England, (Telephone in U.S. (888) 330-8477), (Fax in U.S. (800) 672-2054), www.palgrave.com; *The Statesman's Yearbook 2008.*

Taylor and Francis Group, An Informa Business, 2 Park Square, Milton Park, Abingdon, Oxford OX14 4RN, United Kingdom, (Dial from U.S. (212) 216-7800), (Fax from U.S. (212) 564-7854), www.tandf.co.uk; *The Europa World Year Book.*

United Nations Food and Agricultural Organization (FAO), Viale delle Terme di Caracalla, 00100 Rome, Italy, (Dial from U.S. (202) 653-2400), (Fax from U.S. (202) 653 5760), www.fao.org; *FAO Production Yearbook 2002* and *The State of Food and Agriculture (SOFA) 2006.*

United Nations Statistics Division, New York, NY 10017, (800) 253-9646, Fax: (212) 963-4116, http://unstats.un.org; *Statistical Yearbook.*

ESTONIA - DEATH RATES

See ESTONIA - MORTALITY

ESTONIA - DEBTS, EXTERNAL

The World Bank, 1818 H Street, NW, Washington, DC 20433, (202) 473-1000, Fax: (202) 477-6391, www.worldbank.org; *Global Development Finance 2007; World Development Indicators (WDI) 2008;* and *World Development Report 2008.*

ESTONIA - DEMOGRAPHY

Euromonitor International, Inc., 224 S. Michigan Avenue, Suite 1500, Chicago, IL 60604, (312) 922-1115, Fax: (312) 922-1157, www.euromonitor.com; *The World Economic Factbook 2008* and *World Marketing Data and Statistics.*

Eurostat, Batiment Jean Monnet, Rue Alcide de Gasperi, L-2920 Luxembourg, http://epp.eurostat.ec.europa.eu; *Demographic Outlook - National Reports on the Demographic Developments in 2006.*

United Nations Statistics Division, New York, NY 10017, (800) 253-9646, Fax: (212) 963-4116, http://unstats.un.org; *Demographic Yearbook* and *Human Development Report 2006.*

The World Bank, 1818 H Street, NW, Washington, DC 20433, (202) 473-1000, Fax: (202) 477-6391, www.worldbank.org; *Estonia* and *Statistical Handbook: States of the Former USSR.*

ESTONIA - DISPOSABLE INCOME

United Nations Statistics Division, New York, NY 10017, (800) 253-9646, Fax: (212) 963-4116, http://unstats.un.org; *National Accounts Statistics: Compendium of Income Distribution Statistics* and *Statistical Yearbook.*

ESTONIA - DIVORCE

United Nations Statistics Division, New York, NY 10017, (800) 253-9646, Fax: (212) 963-4116, http://unstats.un.org; *Demographic Yearbook; Statistical Yearbook;* and *Trends in Europe and North America: The Statistical Yearbook of the ECE 2005.*

ESTONIA - ECONOMIC CONDITIONS

Academic International Press, PO Box 1111, Gulf Breeze, FL 32562-1111, Fax: (850) 934-0953, www.ai-press.com; *Russia and Eurasia Facts and Figures Annual.*

Banque de France, 48 rue Croix des Petits champs, 75001 Paris, France, www.banque-france.fr/home.htm; *Key Data for the Euro Area.*

Center for International Business Education Research (CIBER), Columbia Business School and School of International and Public Affairs, Uris Hall, Room 212, 3022 Broadway, New York, NY 10027-6902, Mr. Joshua Safier, (212) 854-4750, Fax: (212) 222-9821, www.columbia.edu/cu/ciber/; Datastream International.

Central Intelligence Agency, Office of Public Affairs, Washington, DC 20505, (703) 482-0623, Fax: (703) 482-1739, www.cia.gov; *The World Factbook.*

DSI Data Service Information, Xantener Strasse 51a, D-47495 Rheinberg, Germany, www.dsidata.com; *Campus Solution.*

Dun and Bradstreet (DB) Corporation, 103 JFK Parkway, Short Hills, NJ 07078, (973) 921-5500, www.dnb.com; *Country Report.*

Economist Intelligence Unit, 111 West 57th Street, New York, NY 10019, (212) 554-0600, Fax: (212) 586-1181, www.eiu.com; *Estonia Country Report.*

Euromonitor International, Inc., 224 S. Michigan Avenue, Suite 1500, Chicago, IL 60604, (312) 922-1115, Fax: (312) 922-1157, www.euromonitor.com; *The World Economic Factbook 2008* and *World Marketing Data and Statistics.*

European Union, Delegation of the European Commission to the United States, 2300 M Street, NW, Washington, DC 20037, (202) 862-9500, Fax: (202) 429-1766, www.eurunion.org; *The EU Economy, 2007 Review: Moving Europe's Productivity Frontier.*

Eurostat, Batiment Jean Monnet, Rue Alcide de Gasperi, L-2920 Luxembourg, http://epp.eurostat.ec.europa.eu; *EU Economic Data Pocketbook.*

International Monetary Fund (IMF), 700 Nineteenth Street, NW, Washington, DC 20431, (202) 623-7000, Fax: (202) 623-4661, www.imf.org; *World Economic Outlook Reports.*

Palgrave Macmillan Ltd., Houndmills, Basingstoke, Hampshire, RG21 6XS, England, (Telephone in U.S. (888) 330-8477), (Fax in U.S. (800) 672-2054), www.palgrave.com; *The Statesman's Yearbook 2008.*

Taylor and Francis Group, An Informa Business, 2 Park Square, Milton Park, Abingdon, Oxford OX14 4RN, United Kingdom, (Dial from U.S. (212) 216-7800), (Fax from U.S. (212) 564-7854), www.tandf.co.uk; *The Europa World Year Book.*

United Nations Statistics Division, New York, NY 10017, (800) 253-9646, Fax: (212) 963-4116, http://unstats.un.org; *World Statistics Pocketbook.*

The World Bank, 1818 H Street, NW, Washington, DC 20433, (202) 473-1000, Fax: (202) 477-6391, www.worldbank.org; *Estonia; Global Economic Monitor (GEM); Global Economic Prospects 2008; The World Bank Atlas 2003-2004;* and *World Development Report 2008.*

ESTONIA - EDUCATION

Academic International Press, PO Box 1111, Gulf Breeze, FL 32562-1111, Fax: (850) 934-0953, www.ai-press.com; *Russia and Eurasia Facts and Figures Annual.*

Euromonitor International, Inc., 224 S. Michigan Avenue, Suite 1500, Chicago, IL 60604, (312) 922-1115, Fax: (312) 922-1157, www.euromonitor.com; *World Marketing Data and Statistics.*

European Union, Delegation of the European Commission to the United States, 2300 M Street, NW, Washington, DC 20037, (202) 862-9500, Fax: (202) 429-1766, www.eurunion.org; *Education across Europe 2003.*

Eurostat, Batiment Jean Monnet, Rue Alcide de Gasperi, L-2920 Luxembourg, http://epp.eurostat.ec.europa.eu; *Education, Science and Culture Statistics.*

Palgrave Macmillan Ltd., Houndmills, Basingstoke, Hampshire, RG21 6XS, England, (Telephone in U.S. (888) 330-8477), (Fax in U.S. (800) 672-2054), www.palgrave.com; *The Statesman's Yearbook 2008.*

Taylor and Francis Group, An Informa Business, 2 Park Square, Milton Park, Abingdon, Oxford OX14 4RN, United Kingdom, (Dial from U.S. (212) 216-7800), (Fax from U.S. (212) 564-7854), www.tandf.co.uk; *The Europa World Year Book.*

UNESCO Institute for Statistics, C.P. 6128 Succursale Centre-Ville, Montreal, Quebec, H3C 3J7 Canada, (Dial from U.S. (514) 343-6880), (Fax from U.S. (514) 343 6882), www.uis.unesco.org; *Statistical Tables.*

United Nations Statistics Division, New York, NY 10017, (800) 253-9646, Fax: (212) 963-4116, http://unstats.un.org; *Human Development Report 2006* and *Trends in Europe and North America: The Statistical Yearbook of the ECE 2005.*

The World Bank, 1818 H Street, NW, Washington, DC 20433, (202) 473-1000, Fax: (202) 477-6391, www.worldbank.org; *Estonia* and *World Development Report 2008.*

ESTONIA - ELECTRICITY

Eurostat, Batiment Jean Monnet, Rue Alcide de Gasperi, L-2920 Luxembourg, http://epp.eurostat.ec.europa.eu; *Energy - Monthly Statistics* and *Panorama of Energy - 2007 Edition.*

Palgrave Macmillan Ltd., Houndmills, Basingstoke, Hampshire, RG21 6XS, England, (Telephone in U.S. (888) 330-8477), (Fax in U.S. (800) 672-2054), www.palgrave.com; *The Statesman's Yearbook 2008.*

Platts, 2 Penn Plaza, 25th Floor, New York, NY 10121-2298, (212) 904-3070, www.platts.com; *En-*

ergy Economist; EU Energy; European Electricity Review 2004; and *European Electricity Review 2004.*

U.S. Department of Energy (DOE), Energy Information Administration (EIA), 1000 Independence Avenue, SW, Washington, DC 20585, (202) 586-8800, www.eia.doe.gov; *International Energy Annual 2004* and *International Energy Outlook 2006.*

United Nations Statistics Division, New York, NY 10017, (800) 253-9646, Fax: (212) 963-4116, http://unstats.un.org; *Energy Statistics Yearbook 2003; Human Development Report 2006; Statistical Yearbook;* and *Trends in Europe and North America: The Statistical Yearbook of the ECE 2005.*

The World Bank, 1818 H Street, NW, Washington, DC 20433, (202) 473-1000, Fax: (202) 477-6391, www.worldbank.org; *Statistical Handbook: States of the Former USSR.*

ESTONIA - EMPLOYMENT

International Labour Office, I.L.O. Publications, 4 route des Morillons, CH-1211 Geneva 22, Switzerland, (Telephone in U.S. (202) 653-7652), (Fax in U.S. (202) 653-7687), www.ilo.org; *Yearbook of Labour Statistics 2006.*

United Nations Statistics Division, New York, NY 10017, (800) 253-9646, Fax: (212) 963-4116, http://unstats.un.org; *Statistical Yearbook* and *Trends in Europe and North America: The Statistical Yearbook of the ECE 2005.*

The World Bank, 1818 H Street, NW, Washington, DC 20433, (202) 473-1000, Fax: (202) 477-6391, www.worldbank.org; *Estonia* and *Statistical Handbook: States of the Former USSR.*

ESTONIA - ENERGY INDUSTRIES

Eurostat, Batiment Jean Monnet, Rue Alcide de Gasperi, L-2920 Luxembourg, http://epp.eurostat.ec.europa.eu; *Energy - Monthly Statistics* and *Panorama of Energy - 2007 Edition.*

Platts, 2 Penn Plaza, 25th Floor, New York, NY 10121-2298, (212) 904-3070, www.platts.com; *Energy in East Europe* and *EU Energy.*

ESTONIA - ENVIRONMENTAL CONDITIONS

Center for Research on the Epidemiology of Disasters (CRED), Universite Catholique de Louvain, Ecole de Sante Publique, 30.94 Clos Chapelle-aux-Champs, 1200 Brussels, Belgium, www.cred.be; *Three Decades of Floods in Europe: A Preliminary Analysis of EMDAT Data.*

DSI Data Service Information, Xantener Strasse 51a, D-47495 Rheinberg, Germany, www.dsidata.com; *Campus Solution* and *DSI's Global Environmental Database.*

Economist Intelligence Unit, 111 West 57th Street, New York, NY 10019, (212) 554-0600, Fax: (212) 586-1181, www.eiu.com; *Estonia Country Report.*

Eurostat, Batiment Jean Monnet, Rue Alcide de Gasperi, L-2920 Luxembourg, http://epp.eurostat.ec.europa.eu; *Environmental Protection Expenditure in Europe.*

United Nations Statistics Division, New York, NY 10017, (800) 253-9646, Fax: (212) 963-4116, http://unstats.un.org; *Statistical Yearbook; Trends in Europe and North America: The Statistical Yearbook of the ECE 2005;* and *World Statistics Pocketbook.*

ESTONIA - EXPENDITURES, PUBLIC

Eurostat, Batiment Jean Monnet, Rue Alcide de Gasperi, L-2920 Luxembourg, http://epp.eurostat.ec.europa.eu; *European Social Statistics - Social Protection Expenditure and Receipts - Data 1997-2005.*

ESTONIA - EXPORTS

Academic International Press, PO Box 1111, Gulf Breeze, FL 32562-1111, Fax: (850) 934-0953, www.ai-press.com; *Russia and Eurasia Facts and Figures Annual.*

Central Intelligence Agency, Office of Public Affairs, Washington, DC 20505, (703) 482-0623, Fax: (703) 482-1739, www.cia.gov; *The World Factbook.*

Economist Intelligence Unit, 111 West 57th Street, New York, NY 10019, (212) 554-0600, Fax: (212) 586-1181, www.eiu.com; *Estonia Country Report.*

Euromonitor International, Inc., 224 S. Michigan Avenue, Suite 1500, Chicago, IL 60604, (312) 922-1115, Fax: (312) 922-1157, www.euromonitor.com; *The World Economic Factbook 2008.*

International Monetary Fund (IMF), 700 Nineteenth Street, NW, Washington, DC 20431, (202) 623-7000, Fax: (202) 623-4661, www.imf.org; *Direction of Trade Statistics Yearbook 2007.*

Taylor and Francis Group, An Informa Business, 2 Park Square, Milton Park, Abingdon, Oxford OX14 4RN, United Kingdom, (Dial from U.S. (212) 216-7800), (Fax from U.S. (212) 564-7854), www.tandf.co.uk; *The Europa World Year Book.*

United Nations Conference on Trade and Development (UNCTAD), DC2-1120, United Nations, New York, NY 10017, (212) 963-0027, www.unctad.org; *Handbook of Statistics 2005.*

United Nations Statistics Division, New York, NY 10017, (800) 253-9646, Fax: (212) 963-4116, http://unstats.un.org; *International Trade Statistics Yearbook* and *Trends in Europe and North America: The Statistical Yearbook of the ECE 2005.*

The World Bank, 1818 H Street, NW, Washington, DC 20433, (202) 473-1000, Fax: (202) 477-6391, www.worldbank.org; *Statistical Handbook: States of the Former USSR; World Development Indicators (WDI) 2008;* and *World Development Report 2008.*

ESTONIA - FERTILITY, HUMAN

Central Intelligence Agency, Office of Public Affairs, Washington, DC 20505, (703) 482-0623, Fax: (703) 482-1739, www.cia.gov; *The World Factbook.*

United Nations Statistics Division, New York, NY 10017, (800) 253-9646, Fax: (212) 963-4116, http://unstats.un.org; *Human Development Report 2006* and *Trends in Europe and North America: The Statistical Yearbook of the ECE 2005.*

The World Bank, 1818 H Street, NW, Washington, DC 20433, (202) 473-1000, Fax: (202) 477-6391, www.worldbank.org; *Statistical Handbook: States of the Former USSR; The World Bank Atlas 2003-2004; World Development Indicators (WDI) 2008;* and *World Development Report 2008.*

World Health Organization (WHO), Avenue Appia 20, 1211 Geneve 27, Switzerland, (Telephone in U.S. (212) 331-9081), www.who.int; *World Health Report 2006.*

ESTONIA - FERTILIZER INDUSTRY

United Nations Food and Agricultural Organization (FAO), Viale delle Terme di Caracalla, 00100 Rome, Italy, (Dial from U.S. (202) 653-2400), (Fax from U.S. (202) 653 5760), www.fao.org; *FAO Fertilizer Yearbook.*

United Nations Statistics Division, New York, NY 10017, (800) 253-9646, Fax: (212) 963-4116, http://unstats.un.org; *2004 Industrial Commodity Statistics Yearbook* and *Statistical Yearbook.*

ESTONIA - FINANCE

Taylor and Francis Group, An Informa Business, 2 Park Square, Milton Park, Abingdon, Oxford OX14 4RN, United Kingdom, (Dial from U.S. (212) 216-7800), (Fax from U.S. (212) 564-7854), www.tandf.co.uk; *The Europa World Year Book.*

United Nations Statistics Division, New York, NY 10017, (800) 253-9646, Fax: (212) 963-4116, http://unstats.un.org; *National Accounts Statistics: Compendium of Income Distribution Statistics* and *Statistical Yearbook.*

The World Bank, 1818 H Street, NW, Washington, DC 20433, (202) 473-1000, Fax: (202) 477-6391, www.worldbank.org; *Estonia* and *Statistical Handbook: States of the Former USSR.*

ESTONIA - FINANCE, PUBLIC

Banque de France, 48 rue Croix des Petits champs, 75001 Paris, France, www.banque-france.fr/home.htm; *Key Data for the Euro Area* and *Public Finance.*

Bernan Essential Government Publications, 4611-F Assembly Drive, Lanham MD, 20706-4391, (301) 459-2255, Fax: (800) 865-3450, www.bernan.com; *National Accounts Statistics.*

Economist Intelligence Unit, 111 West 57th Street, New York, NY 10019, (212) 554-0600, Fax: (212) 586-1181, www.eiu.com; *Estonia Country Report.*

International Monetary Fund (IMF), 700 Nineteenth Street, NW, Washington, DC 20431, (202) 623-7000, Fax: (202) 623-4661, www.imf.org; *International Financial Statistics* and *International Financial Statistics Online Service.*

Palgrave Macmillan Ltd., Houndmills, Basingstoke, Hampshire, RG21 6XS, England, (Telephone in U.S. (888) 330-8477), (Fax in U.S. (800) 672-2054), www.palgrave.com; *The Statesman's Yearbook 2008.*

Taylor and Francis Group, An Informa Business, 2 Park Square, Milton Park, Abingdon, Oxford OX14 4RN, United Kingdom, (Dial from U.S. (212) 216-7800), (Fax from U.S. (212) 564-7854), www.tandf.co.uk; *The Europa World Year Book.*

The World Bank, 1818 H Street, NW, Washington, DC 20433, (202) 473-1000, Fax: (202) 477-6391, www.worldbank.org; *Estonia* and *Statistical Handbook: States of the Former USSR.*

ESTONIA - FISHERIES

Taylor and Francis Group, An Informa Business, 2 Park Square, Milton Park, Abingdon, Oxford OX14 4RN, United Kingdom, (Dial from U.S. (212) 216-7800), (Fax from U.S. (212) 564-7854), www.tandf.co.uk; *The Europa World Year Book.*

United Nations Food and Agricultural Organization (FAO), Viale delle Terme di Caracalla, 00100 Rome, Italy, (Dial from U.S. (202) 653-2400), (Fax from U.S. (202) 653 5760), www.fao.org; *FAO Yearbook of Fishery Statistics;* Fishery Databases; FISHSTAT Database. Subjects covered include: Aquaculture production, capture production, fishery commodities; and *The State of Food and Agriculture (SOFA) 2006.*

United Nations Statistics Division, New York, NY 10017, (800) 253-9646, Fax: (212) 963-4116, http://unstats.un.org; *2004 Industrial Commodity Statistics Yearbook* and *Statistical Yearbook.*

The World Bank, 1818 H Street, NW, Washington, DC 20433, (202) 473-1000, Fax: (202) 477-6391, www.worldbank.org; *Estonia.*

ESTONIA - FOOD

United Nations Food and Agricultural Organization (FAO), Viale delle Terme di Caracalla, 00100 Rome, Italy, (Dial from U.S. (202) 653-2400), (Fax from U.S. (202) 653 5760), www.fao.org; *FAO Production Yearbook 2002.*

United Nations Statistics Division, New York, NY 10017, (800) 253-9646, Fax: (212) 963-4116, http://unstats.un.org; *Human Development Report 2006* and *2004 Industrial Commodity Statistics Yearbook.*

ESTONIA - FOREIGN EXCHANGE RATES

Central Intelligence Agency, Office of Public Affairs, Washington, DC 20505, (703) 482-0623, Fax: (703) 482-1739, www.cia.gov; *The World Factbook.*

Euromonitor International, Inc., 224 S. Michigan Avenue, Suite 1500, Chicago, IL 60604, (312) 922-1115, Fax: (312) 922-1157, www.euromonitor.com; *The World Economic Factbook 2008.*

Taylor and Francis Group, An Informa Business, 2 Park Square, Milton Park, Abingdon, Oxford OX14 4RN, United Kingdom, (Dial from U.S. (212) 216-7800), (Fax from U.S. (212) 564-7854), www.tandf.co.uk; *The Europa World Year Book.*

United Nations Statistics Division, New York, NY 10017, (800) 253-9646, Fax: (212) 963-4116, http://unstats.un.org; *Statistical Yearbook; Trends in*

Europe and North America: The Statistical Yearbook of the ECE 2005; and *World Statistics Pocketbook.*

ESTONIA - FORESTS AND FORESTRY

Academic International Press, PO Box 1111, Gulf Breeze, FL 32562-1111, Fax: (850) 934-0953, www.ai-press.com; *Russia and Eurasia Facts and Figures Annual.*

Palgrave Macmillan Ltd., Houndmills, Basingstoke, Hampshire, RG21 6XS, England, (Telephone in U.S. (888) 330-8477), (Fax in U.S. (800) 672-2054), www.palgrave.com; *The Statesman's Yearbook 2008.*

Taylor and Francis Group, An Informa Business, 2 Park Square, Milton Park, Abingdon, Oxford OX14 4RN, United Kingdom, (Dial from U.S. (212) 216-7800), (Fax from U.S. (212) 564-7854), www.tandf.co.uk; *The Europa World Year Book.*

UNESCO Institute for Statistics, C.P. 6128 Succursale Centre-Ville, Montreal, Quebec, H3C 3J7 Canada, (Dial from U.S. (514) 343-6880), (Fax from U.S. (514) 343 6882), www.uis.unesco.org; *Statistical Tables.*

United Nations Food and Agricultural Organization (FAO), Viale delle Terme di Caracalla, 00100 Rome, Italy, (Dial from U.S. (202) 653-2400), (Fax from U.S. (202) 653 5760), www.fao.org; *FAO Yearbook of Forest Products* and *The State of Food and Agriculture (SOFA) 2006.*

United Nations Statistics Division, New York, NY 10017, (800) 253-9646, Fax: (212) 963-4116, http://unstats.un.org; *2004 Industrial Commodity Statistics Yearbook; Statistical Yearbook;* and *Trends in Europe and North America: The Statistical Yearbook of the ECE 2005.*

The World Bank, 1818 H Street, NW, Washington, DC 20433, (202) 473-1000, Fax: (202) 477-6391, www.worldbank.org; *Estonia* and *World Development Report 2008.*

ESTONIA - GROSS DOMESTIC PRODUCT

Academic International Press, PO Box 1111, Gulf Breeze, FL 32562-1111, Fax: (850) 934-0953, www.ai-press.com; *Russia and Eurasia Facts and Figures Annual.*

Economist Intelligence Unit, 111 West 57th Street, New York, NY 10019, (212) 554-0600, Fax: (212) 586-1181, www.eiu.com; *Estonia Country Report.*

Euromonitor International, Inc., 224 S. Michigan Avenue, Suite 1500, Chicago, IL 60604, (312) 922-1115, Fax: (312) 922-1157, www.euromonitor.com; *The World Economic Factbook 2008.*

Taylor and Francis Group, An Informa Business, 2 Park Square, Milton Park, Abingdon, Oxford OX14 4RN, United Kingdom, (Dial from U.S. (212) 216-7800), (Fax from U.S. (212) 564-7854), www.tandf.co.uk; *The Europa World Year Book.*

United Nations Statistics Division, New York, NY 10017, (800) 253-9646, Fax: (212) 963-4116, http://unstats.un.org; *Human Development Report 2006; National Accounts Statistics: Compendium of Income Distribution Statistics; Statistical Yearbook;* and *Trends in Europe and North America: The Statistical Yearbook of the ECE 2005.*

The World Bank, 1818 H Street, NW, Washington, DC 20433, (202) 473-1000, Fax: (202) 477-6391, www.worldbank.org; *Statistical Handbook: States of the Former USSR; World Development Indicators (WDI) 2008;* and *World Development Report 2008.*

ESTONIA - GROSS NATIONAL PRODUCT

European Union, Delegation of the European Commission to the United States, 2300 M Street, NW, Washington, DC 20037, (202) 862-9500, Fax: (202) 429-1766, www.eurunion.org; *The EU Economy, 2007 Review: Moving Europe's Productivity Frontier.*

Palgrave Macmillan Ltd., Houndmills, Basingstoke, Hampshire, RG21 6XS, England, (Telephone in U.S. (888) 330-8477), (Fax in U.S. (800) 672-2054), www.palgrave.com; *The Statesman's Yearbook 2008.*

United Nations Statistics Division, New York, NY 10017, (800) 253-9646, Fax: (212) 963-4116, http://unstats.un.org; *Statistical Yearbook.*

The World Bank, 1818 H Street, NW, Washington, DC 20433, (202) 473-1000, Fax: (202) 477-6391, www.worldbank.org; *The World Bank Atlas 2003-2004; World Development Indicators (WDI) 2008;* and *World Development Report 2008.*

ESTONIA - HOUSING

Euromonitor International, Inc., 224 S. Michigan Avenue, Suite 1500, Chicago, IL 60604, (312) 922-1115, Fax: (312) 922-1157, www.euromonitor.com; *World Marketing Data and Statistics.*

United Nations Statistics Division, New York, NY 10017, (800) 253-9646, Fax: (212) 963-4116, http://unstats.un.org; *Trends in Europe and North America: The Statistical Yearbook of the ECE 2005.*

ESTONIA - ILLITERATE PERSONS

Euromonitor International, Inc., 224 S. Michigan Avenue, Suite 1500, Chicago, IL 60604, (312) 922-1115, Fax: (312) 922-1157, www.euromonitor.com; *The World Economic Factbook 2008.*

UNESCO Institute for Statistics, C.P. 6128 Succursale Centre-Ville, Montreal, Quebec, H3C 3J7 Canada, (Dial from U.S. (514) 343-6880), (Fax from U.S. (514) 343 6882), www.uis.unesco.org; *Statistical Tables.*

United Nations Statistics Division, New York, NY 10017, (800) 253-9646, Fax: (212) 963-4116, http://unstats.un.org; *Human Development Report 2006.*

ESTONIA - IMPORTS

Academic International Press, PO Box 1111, Gulf Breeze, FL 32562-1111, Fax: (850) 934-0953, www.ai-press.com; *Russia and Eurasia Facts and Figures Annual.*

Central Intelligence Agency, Office of Public Affairs, Washington, DC 20505, (703) 482-0623, Fax: (703) 482-1739, www.cia.gov; *The World Factbook.*

Economist Intelligence Unit, 111 West 57th Street, New York, NY 10019, (212) 554-0600, Fax: (212) 586-1181, www.eiu.com; *Estonia Country Report.*

Euromonitor International, Inc., 224 S. Michigan Avenue, Suite 1500, Chicago, IL 60604, (312) 922-1115, Fax: (312) 922-1157, www.euromonitor.com; *The World Economic Factbook 2008.*

International Monetary Fund (IMF), 700 Nineteenth Street, NW, Washington, DC 20431, (202) 623-7000, Fax: (202) 623-4661, www.imf.org; *Direction of Trade Statistics Yearbook 2007.*

Taylor and Francis Group, An Informa Business, 2 Park Square, Milton Park, Abingdon, Oxford OX14 4RN, United Kingdom, (Dial from U.S. (212) 216-7800), (Fax from U.S. (212) 564-7854), www.tandf.co.uk; *The Europa World Year Book.*

United Nations Conference on Trade and Development (UNCTAD), DC2-1120, United Nations, New York, NY 10017, (212) 963-0027, www.unctad.org; *Handbook of Statistics 2005.*

United Nations Statistics Division, New York, NY 10017, (800) 253-9646, Fax: (212) 963-4116, http://unstats.un.org; *International Trade Statistics Yearbook* and *Trends in Europe and North America: The Statistical Yearbook of the ECE 2005.*

The World Bank, 1818 H Street, NW, Washington, DC 20433, (202) 473-1000, Fax: (202) 477-6391, www.worldbank.org; *Statistical Handbook: States of the Former USSR; World Development Indicators (WDI) 2008;* and *World Development Report 2008.*

ESTONIA - INDUSTRIAL PRODUCTIVITY

The World Bank, 1818 H Street, NW, Washington, DC 20433, (202) 473-1000, Fax: (202) 477-6391, www.worldbank.org; *Statistical Handbook: States of the Former USSR.*

ESTONIA - INDUSTRIAL PROPERTY

United Nations Statistics Division, New York, NY 10017, (800) 253-9646, Fax: (212) 963-4116, http://unstats.un.org; *Statistical Yearbook.*

ESTONIA - INDUSTRIES

Academic International Press, PO Box 1111, Gulf Breeze, FL 32562-1111, Fax: (850) 934-0953, www.ai-press.com; *Russia and Eurasia Facts and Figures Annual.*

Central Intelligence Agency, Office of Public Affairs, Washington, DC 20505, (703) 482-0623, Fax: (703) 482-1739, www.cia.gov; *The World Factbook.*

Economist Intelligence Unit, 111 West 57th Street, New York, NY 10019, (212) 554-0600, Fax: (212) 586-1181, www.eiu.com; *Estonia Country Report.*

Euromonitor International, Inc., 224 S. Michigan Avenue, Suite 1500, Chicago, IL 60604, (312) 922-1115, Fax: (312) 922-1157, www.euromonitor.com; *The World Economic Factbook 2008* and *World Marketing Data and Statistics.*

International Labour Office, I.L.O. Publications, 4 route des Morillons, CH-1211 Geneva 22, Switzerland, (Telephone in U.S. (202) 653-7652), (Fax in U.S. (202) 653-7687), www.ilo.org; *Yearbook of Labour Statistics 2006.*

Palgrave Macmillan Ltd., Houndmills, Basingstoke, Hampshire, RG21 6XS, England, (Telephone in U.S. (888) 330-8477), (Fax in U.S. (800) 672-2054), www.palgrave.com; *The Statesman's Yearbook 2008.*

Taylor and Francis Group, An Informa Business, 2 Park Square, Milton Park, Abingdon, Oxford OX14 4RN, United Kingdom, (Dial from U.S. (212) 216-7800), (Fax from U.S. (212) 564-7854), www.tandf.co.uk; *The Europa World Year Book.*

United Nations Industrial Development Organization (UNIDO), 1 United Nations Plaza, New York, NY 10017, (212) 963 6890, Fax: (212) 963-7904, http://unido.org; Industrial Statistics Database 2008 (INDSTAT) and *The International Yearbook of Industrial Statistics 2008.*

United Nations Statistics Division, New York, NY 10017, (800) 253-9646, Fax: (212) 963-4116, http://unstats.un.org; *2004 Industrial Commodity Statistics Yearbook; Statistical Yearbook;* and *Trends in Europe and North America: The Statistical Yearbook of the ECE 2005.*

The World Bank, 1818 H Street, NW, Washington, DC 20433, (202) 473-1000, Fax: (202) 477-6391, www.worldbank.org; *Estonia; Statistical Handbook: States of the Former USSR;* and *World Development Indicators (WDI) 2008.*

ESTONIA - INFANT AND MATERNAL MORTALITY

See ESTONIA - MORTALITY

ESTONIA - INTERNATIONAL TRADE

Academic International Press, PO Box 1111, Gulf Breeze, FL 32562-1111, Fax: (850) 934-0953, www.ai-press.com; *Russia and Eurasia Facts and Figures Annual.*

Banque de France, 48 rue Croix des Petits champs, 75001 Paris, France, www.banque-france.fr/home.htm; *Monthly Business Survey Overview.*

Economist Intelligence Unit, 111 West 57th Street, New York, NY 10019, (212) 554-0600, Fax: (212) 586-1181, www.eiu.com; *Estonia Country Report.*

Euromonitor International, Inc., 224 S. Michigan Avenue, Suite 1500, Chicago, IL 60604, (312) 922-1115, Fax: (312) 922-1157, www.euromonitor.com; *The World Economic Factbook 2008* and *World Marketing Data and Statistics.*

Eurostat, Batiment Jean Monnet, Rue Alcide de Gasperi, L-2920 Luxembourg, http://epp.eurostat.ec.europa.eu; Intra- and Extra-EU Trade.

International Monetary Fund (IMF), 700 Nineteenth Street, NW, Washington, DC 20431, (202) 623-7000, Fax: (202) 623-4661, www.imf.org; *Direction of Trade Statistics Yearbook 2007.*

Palgrave Macmillan Ltd., Houndmills, Basingstoke, Hampshire, RG21 6XS, England, (Telephone in U.S. (888) 330-8477), (Fax in U.S. (800) 672-2054), www.palgrave.com; *The Statesman's Yearbook 2008.*

Taylor and Francis Group, An Informa Business, 2 Park Square, Milton Park, Abingdon, Oxford OX14 4RN, United Kingdom, (Dial from U.S. (212) 216-7800), (Fax from U.S. (212) 564-7854), www.tandf.co.uk; *The Europa World Year Book.*

United Nations Food and Agricultural Organization (FAO), Viale delle Terme di Caracalla, 00100 Rome, Italy, (Dial from U.S. (202) 653-2400), (Fax from U.S. (202) 653 5760), www.fao.org; *FAO Trade Yearbook.*

United Nations Statistics Division, New York, NY 10017, (800) 253-9646, Fax: (212) 963-4116, http://unstats.un.org; *International Trade Statistics Yearbook* and *Statistical Yearbook.*

The World Bank, 1818 H Street, NW, Washington, DC 20433, (202) 473-1000, Fax: (202) 477-6391, www.worldbank.org; *Estonia; Statistical Handbook: States of the Former USSR; World Development Indicators (WDI) 2008;* and *World Development Report 2008.*

World Trade Organization (WTO), Centre William Rappard, Rue de Lausanne 154, CH-1211 Geneva 21, Switzerland, www.wto.org; *International Trade Statistics 2006.*

ESTONIA - INTERNET USERS

Eurostat, Batiment Jean Monnet, Rue Alcide de Gasperi, L-2920 Luxembourg, http://epp.eurostat.ec.europa.eu; *Internet Usage by Enterprises 2007.*

International Telecommunication Union (ITU), Place des Nations, 1211 Geneva 20, Switzerland, www.itu.int; *World Telecommunication/ICT Indicators Database on CD-ROM; World Telecommunication/ICT Indicators Database Online;* and *Yearbook of Statistics - Telecommunication Services (Chronological Time Series 1997-2006).*

The World Bank, 1818 H Street, NW, Washington, DC 20433, (202) 473-1000, Fax: (202) 477-6391, www.worldbank.org; *Estonia.*

ESTONIA - LABOR

Academic International Press, PO Box 1111, Gulf Breeze, FL 32562-1111, Fax: (850) 934-0953, www.ai-press.com; *Russia and Eurasia Facts and Figures Annual.*

Central Intelligence Agency, Office of Public Affairs, Washington, DC 20505, (703) 482-0623, Fax: (703) 482-1739, www.cia.gov; *The World Factbook.*

Euromonitor International, Inc., 224 S. Michigan Avenue, Suite 1500, Chicago, IL 60604, (312) 922-1115, Fax: (312) 922-1157, www.euromonitor.com; *World Marketing Data and Statistics.*

International Labour Office, I.L.O. Publications, 4 route des Morillons, CH-1211 Geneva 22, Switzerland, (Telephone in U.S. (202) 653-7652), (Fax in U.S. (202) 653-7687), www.ilo.org; *Yearbook of Labour Statistics 2006.*

Palgrave Macmillan Ltd., Houndmills, Basingstoke, Hampshire, RG21 6XS, England, (Telephone in U.S. (888) 330-8477), (Fax in U.S. (800) 672-2054), www.palgrave.com; *The Statesman's Yearbook 2008.*

Taylor and Francis Group, An Informa Business, 2 Park Square, Milton Park, Abingdon, Oxford OX14 4RN, United Kingdom, (Dial from U.S. (212) 216-7800), (Fax from U.S. (212) 564-7854), www.tandf.co.uk; *The Europa World Year Book.*

United Nations Statistics Division, New York, NY 10017, (800) 253-9646, Fax: (212) 963-4116, http://unstats.un.org; *Human Development Report 2006* and *Statistical Yearbook.*

The World Bank, 1818 H Street, NW, Washington, DC 20433, (202) 473-1000, Fax: (202) 477-6391, www.worldbank.org; *Statistical Handbook: States of the Former USSR; The World Bank Atlas 2003-2004; World Development Indicators (WDI) 2008;* and *World Development Report 2008.*

ESTONIA - LAND USE

Central Intelligence Agency, Office of Public Affairs, Washington, DC 20505, (703) 482-0623, Fax: (703) 482-1739, www.cia.gov; *The World Factbook.*

United Nations Food and Agricultural Organization (FAO), Viale delle Terme di Caracalla, 00100 Rome, Italy, (Dial from U.S. (202) 653-2400), (Fax from U.S. (202) 653 5760), www.fao.org; *FAO Production Yearbook 2002.*

The World Bank, 1818 H Street, NW, Washington, DC 20433, (202) 473-1000, Fax: (202) 477-6391, www.worldbank.org; *World Development Report 2008.*

ESTONIA - LIBRARIES

UNESCO Institute for Statistics, C.P. 6128 Succursale Centre-Ville, Montreal, Quebec, H3C 3J7 Canada, (Dial from U.S. (514) 343-6880), (Fax from U.S. (514) 343 6882), www.uis.unesco.org; *Statistical Tables.*

United Nations Statistics Division, New York, NY 10017, (800) 253-9646, Fax: (212) 963-4116, http://unstats.un.org; *Trends in Europe and North America: The Statistical Yearbook of the ECE 2005.*

ESTONIA - LIFE EXPECTANCY

Central Intelligence Agency, Office of Public Affairs, Washington, DC 20505, (703) 482-0623, Fax: (703) 482-1739, www.cia.gov; *The World Factbook.*

Euromonitor International, Inc., 224 S. Michigan Avenue, Suite 1500, Chicago, IL 60604, (312) 922-1115, Fax: (312) 922-1157, www.euromonitor.com; *The World Economic Factbook 2008.*

Palgrave Macmillan Ltd., Houndmills, Basingstoke, Hampshire, RG21 6XS, England, (Telephone in U.S. (888) 330-8477), (Fax in U.S. (800) 672-2054), www.palgrave.com; *The Statesman's Yearbook 2008.*

United Nations Statistics Division, New York, NY 10017, (800) 253-9646, Fax: (212) 963-4116, http://unstats.un.org; *Demographic Yearbook; Human Development Report 2006; Trends in Europe and North America: The Statistical Yearbook of the ECE 2005;* and *World Statistics Pocketbook.*

The World Bank, 1818 H Street, NW, Washington, DC 20433, (202) 473-1000, Fax: (202) 477-6391, www.worldbank.org; *The World Bank Atlas 2003-2004; World Development Indicators (WDI) 2008;* and *World Development Report 2008.*

World Health Organization (WHO), Avenue Appia 20, 1211 Geneve 27, Switzerland, (Telephone in U.S. (212) 331-9081), www.who.int; *World Health Report 2006.*

ESTONIA - LITERACY

Euromonitor International, Inc., 224 S. Michigan Avenue, Suite 1500, Chicago, IL 60604, (312) 922-1115, Fax: (312) 922-1157, www.euromonitor.com; *World Marketing Data and Statistics.*

ESTONIA - LIVESTOCK

Academic International Press, PO Box 1111, Gulf Breeze, FL 32562-1111, Fax: (850) 934-0953, www.ai-press.com; *Russia and Eurasia Facts and Figures Annual.*

Palgrave Macmillan Ltd., Houndmills, Basingstoke, Hampshire, RG21 6XS, England, (Telephone in U.S. (888) 330-8477), (Fax in U.S. (800) 672-2054), www.palgrave.com; *The Statesman's Yearbook 2008.*

Taylor and Francis Group, An Informa Business, 2 Park Square, Milton Park, Abingdon, Oxford OX14 4RN, United Kingdom, (Dial from U.S. (212) 216-7800), (Fax from U.S. (212) 564-7854), www.tandf.co.uk; *The Europa World Year Book.*

United Nations Food and Agricultural Organization (FAO), Viale delle Terme di Caracalla, 00100 Rome, Italy, (Dial from U.S. (202) 653-2400), (Fax from U.S. (202) 653 5760), www.fao.org; *FAO Production Yearbook 2002* and *The State of Food and Agriculture (SOFA) 2006.*

United Nations Statistics Division, New York, NY 10017, (800) 253-9646, Fax: (212) 963-4116, http://unstats.un.org; *2004 Industrial Commodity Statistics Yearbook* and *Statistical Yearbook.*

ESTONIA - MACHINERY

United Nations Statistics Division, New York, NY 10017, (800) 253-9646, Fax: (212) 963-4116, http://unstats.un.org; *2004 Industrial Commodity Statistics Yearbook.*

ESTONIA - MANUFACTURES

United Nations Statistics Division, New York, NY 10017, (800) 253-9646, Fax: (212) 963-4116, http://unstats.un.org; *2004 Industrial Commodity Statistics Yearbook* and *Statistical Yearbook.*

The World Bank, 1818 H Street, NW, Washington, DC 20433, (202) 473-1000, Fax: (202) 477-6391, www.worldbank.org; *World Development Indicators (WDI) 2008.*

ESTONIA - MARRIAGE

Taylor and Francis Group, An Informa Business, 2 Park Square, Milton Park, Abingdon, Oxford OX14 4RN, United Kingdom, (Dial from U.S. (212) 216-7800), (Fax from U.S. (212) 564-7854), www.tandf.co.uk; *The Europa World Year Book.*

United Nations Statistics Division, New York, NY 10017, (800) 253-9646, Fax: (212) 963-4116, http://unstats.un.org; *Demographic Yearbook; Statistical Yearbook;* and *Trends in Europe and North America: The Statistical Yearbook of the ECE 2005.*

ESTONIA - MINERAL INDUSTRIES

Academic International Press, PO Box 1111, Gulf Breeze, FL 32562-1111, Fax: (850) 934-0953, www.ai-press.com; *Russia and Eurasia Facts and Figures Annual.*

Eurostat, Batiment Jean Monnet, Rue Alcide de Gasperi, L-2920 Luxembourg, http://epp.eurostat.ec.europa.eu; *Energy - Monthly Statistics* and *Panorama of Energy - 2007 Edition.*

Palgrave Macmillan Ltd., Houndmills, Basingstoke, Hampshire, RG21 6XS, England, (Telephone in U.S. (888) 330-8477), (Fax in U.S. (800) 672-2054), www.palgrave.com; *The Statesman's Yearbook 2008.*

Platts, 2 Penn Plaza, 25th Floor, New York, NY 10121-2298, (212) 904-3070, www.platts.com; *Energy Economist; Energy in East Europe;* and *EU Energy.*

Taylor and Francis Group, An Informa Business, 2 Park Square, Milton Park, Abingdon, Oxford OX14 4RN, United Kingdom, (Dial from U.S. (212) 216-7800), (Fax from U.S. (212) 564-7854), www.tandf.co.uk; *The Europa World Year Book.*

United Nations Statistics Division, New York, NY 10017, (800) 253-9646, Fax: (212) 963-4116, http://unstats.un.org; *Energy Statistics Yearbook 2003; 2004 Industrial Commodity Statistics Yearbook;* and *Statistical Yearbook.*

The World Bank, 1818 H Street, NW, Washington, DC 20433, (202) 473-1000, Fax: (202) 477-6391, www.worldbank.org; *Estonia.*

ESTONIA - MONEY SUPPLY

Economist Intelligence Unit, 111 West 57th Street, New York, NY 10019, (212) 554-0600, Fax: (212) 586-1181, www.eiu.com; *Estonia Country Report.*

Taylor and Francis Group, An Informa Business, 2 Park Square, Milton Park, Abingdon, Oxford OX14 4RN, United Kingdom, (Dial from U.S. (212) 216-7800), (Fax from U.S. (212) 564-7854), www.tandf.co.uk; *The Europa World Year Book.*

The World Bank, 1818 H Street, NW, Washington, DC 20433, (202) 473-1000, Fax: (202) 477-6391, www.worldbank.org; *Estonia.*

ESTONIA - MONUMENTS AND HISTORIC SITES

UNESCO Institute for Statistics, C.P. 6128 Succursale Centre-Ville, Montreal, Quebec, H3C 3J7 Canada, (Dial from U.S. (514) 343-6880), (Fax from U.S. (514) 343 6882), www.uis.unesco.org; *Statistical Tables.*

ESTONIA - MORTALITY

Central Intelligence Agency, Office of Public Affairs, Washington, DC 20505, (703) 482-0623, Fax: (703) 482-1739, www.cia.gov; *The World Factbook.*

Euromonitor International, Inc., 224 S. Michigan Avenue, Suite 1500, Chicago, IL 60604, (312) 922-1115, Fax: (312) 922-1157, www.euromonitor.com; *The World Economic Factbook 2008.*

Palgrave Macmillan Ltd., Houndmills, Basingstoke, Hampshire, RG21 6XS, England, (Telephone in U.S. (888) 330-8477), (Fax in U.S. (800) 672-2054), www.palgrave.com; *The Statesman's Yearbook 2008.*

Taylor and Francis Group, An Informa Business, 2 Park Square, Milton Park, Abingdon, Oxford OX14 4RN, United Kingdom, (Dial from U.S. (212) 216-7800), (Fax from U.S. (212) 564-7854), www.tandf.co.uk; *The Europa World Year Book.*

UNICEF, 3 United Nations Plaza, New York, NY 10017, (800) 253-9646, Fax: (212) 887-7465, www.unicef.org; *The State of the World's Children 2008.*

United Nations Statistics Division, New York, NY 10017, (800) 253-9646, Fax: (212) 963-4116, http://unstats.un.org; *Demographic Yearbook; Human Development Report 2006; Statistical Yearbook; Trends in Europe and North America: The Statistical Yearbook of the ECE 2005;* and *World Statistics Pocketbook.*

The World Bank, 1818 H Street, NW, Washington, DC 20433, (202) 473-1000, Fax: (202) 477-6391, www.worldbank.org; *The World Bank Atlas 2003-2004; World Development Indicators (WDI) 2008;* and *World Development Report 2008.*

World Health Organization (WHO), Avenue Appia 20, 1211 Geneve 27, Switzerland, (Telephone in U.S. (212) 331-9081), www.who.int; The WHO Global Atlas of Infectious Diseases and *World Health Report 2006.*

ESTONIA - MOTION PICTURES

UNESCO Institute for Statistics, C.P. 6128 Succursale Centre-Ville, Montreal, Quebec, H3C 3J7 Canada, (Dial from U.S. (514) 343-6880), (Fax from U.S. (514) 343 6882), www.uis.unesco.org; *Statistical Tables.*

United Nations Statistics Division, New York, NY 10017, (800) 253-9646, Fax: (212) 963-4116, http://unstats.un.org; *Statistical Yearbook.*

ESTONIA - MOTOR VEHICLES

Taylor and Francis Group, An Informa Business, 2 Park Square, Milton Park, Abingdon, Oxford OX14 4RN, United Kingdom, (Dial from U.S. (212) 216-7800), (Fax from U.S. (212) 564-7854), www.tandf.co.uk; *The Europa World Year Book.*

United Nations Statistics Division, New York, NY 10017, (800) 253-9646, Fax: (212) 963-4116, http://unstats.un.org; *Statistical Yearbook.*

ESTONIA - MUSEUMS

UNESCO Institute for Statistics, C.P. 6128 Succursale Centre-Ville, Montreal, Quebec, H3C 3J7 Canada, (Dial from U.S. (514) 343-6880), (Fax from U.S. (514) 343 6882), www.uis.unesco.org; *Statistical Tables.*

ESTONIA - PERIODICALS

UNESCO Institute for Statistics, C.P. 6128 Succursale Centre-Ville, Montreal, Quebec, H3C 3J7 Canada, (Dial from U.S. (514) 343-6880), (Fax from U.S. (514) 343 6882), www.uis.unesco.org; *Statistical Tables.*

ESTONIA - PETROLEUM INDUSTRY AND TRADE

Palgrave Macmillan Ltd., Houndmills, Basingstoke, Hampshire, RG21 6XS, England, (Telephone in U.S. (888) 330-8477), (Fax in U.S. (800) 672-2054), www.palgrave.com; *The Statesman's Yearbook 2008.*

PennWell Corporation, 1421 South Sheridan Road, Tulsa, OK 74112, (918) 835-3161, www.pennwell.com; *International Petroleum Encyclopedia 2007.*

Platts, 2 Penn Plaza, 25th Floor, New York, NY 10121-2298, (212) 904-3070, www.platts.com; *Energy Economist.*

U.S. Department of Energy (DOE), Energy Information Administration (EIA), 1000 Independence Avenue, SW, Washington, DC 20585, (202) 586-8800, www.eia.doe.gov; *International Energy Annual 2004* and *International Energy Outlook 2006.*

United Nations Food and Agricultural Organization (FAO), Viale delle Terme di Caracalla, 00100 Rome, Italy, (Dial from U.S. (202) 653-2400), (Fax from U.S. (202) 653 5760), www.fao.org; *The State of Food and Agriculture (SOFA) 2006.*

United Nations Statistics Division, New York, NY 10017, (800) 253-9646, Fax: (212) 963-4116, http://unstats.un.org; *Energy Statistics Yearbook 2003; 2004 Industrial Commodity Statistics Yearbook; Statistical Yearbook;* and *Trends in Europe and North America: The Statistical Yearbook of the ECE 2005.*

ESTONIA - POLITICAL SCIENCE

Academic International Press, PO Box 1111, Gulf Breeze, FL 32562-1111, Fax: (850) 934-0953, www.ai-press.com; *Russia and Eurasia Facts and Figures Annual.*

Central Intelligence Agency, Office of Public Affairs, Washington, DC 20505, (703) 482-0623, Fax: (703) 482-1739, www.cia.gov; *The World Factbook.*

Palgrave Macmillan Ltd., Houndmills, Basingstoke, Hampshire, RG21 6XS, England, (Telephone in U.S. (888) 330-8477), (Fax in U.S. (800) 672-2054), www.palgrave.com; *The Statesman's Yearbook 2008.*

Taylor and Francis Group, An Informa Business, 2 Park Square, Milton Park, Abingdon, Oxford OX14 4RN, United Kingdom, (Dial from U.S. (212) 216-7800), (Fax from U.S. (212) 564-7854), www.tandf.co.uk; *The Europa World Year Book.*

United Nations Statistics Division, New York, NY 10017, (800) 253-9646, Fax: (212) 963-4116, http://unstats.un.org; *National Accounts Statistics: Compendium of Income Distribution Statistics* and *Statistical Yearbook.*

The World Bank, 1818 H Street, NW, Washington, DC 20433, (202) 473-1000, Fax: (202) 477-6391, www.worldbank.org; *Statistical Handbook: States of the Former USSR* and *World Development Report 2008.*

ESTONIA - POPULATION

Academic International Press, PO Box 1111, Gulf Breeze, FL 32562-1111, Fax: (850) 934-0953, www.ai-press.com; *Russia and Eurasia Facts and Figures Annual.*

Banque de France, 48 rue Croix des Petits champs, 75001 Paris, France, www.banque-france.fr/home.htm; *Key Data for the Euro Area.*

Central Intelligence Agency, Office of Public Affairs, Washington, DC 20505, (703) 482-0623, Fax: (703) 482-1739, www.cia.gov; *The World Factbook.*

Economist Intelligence Unit, 111 West 57th Street, New York, NY 10019, (212) 554-0600, Fax: (212) 586-1181, www.eiu.com; *Estonia Country Report.*

Euromonitor International, Inc., 224 S. Michigan Avenue, Suite 1500, Chicago, IL 60604, (312) 922-1115, Fax: (312) 922-1157, www.euromonitor.com; *The World Economic Factbook 2008.*

Eurostat, Batiment Jean Monnet, Rue Alcide de Gasperi, L-2920 Luxembourg, http://epp.eurostat.ec.europa.eu; *The Life of Women and Men in Europe - A Statistical Portrait.*

International Labour Office, I.L.O. Publications, 4 route des Morillons, CH-1211 Geneva 22, Switzerland, (Telephone in U.S. (202) 653-7652), (Fax in U.S. (202) 653-7687), www.ilo.org; *Yearbook of Labour Statistics 2006.*

Palgrave Macmillan Ltd., Houndmills, Basingstoke, Hampshire, RG21 6XS, England, (Telephone in U.S. (888) 330-8477), (Fax in U.S. (800) 672-2054), www.palgrave.com; *The Statesman's Yearbook 2008.*

Taylor and Francis Group, An Informa Business, 2 Park Square, Milton Park, Abingdon, Oxford OX14 4RN, United Kingdom, (Dial from U.S. (212) 216-7800), (Fax from U.S. (212) 564-7854), www.tandf.co.uk; *The Europa World Year Book.*

UNESCO Institute for Statistics, C.P. 6128 Succursale Centre-Ville, Montreal, Quebec, H3C 3J7 Canada, (Dial from U.S. (514) 343-6880), (Fax from U.S. (514) 343 6882), www.uis.unesco.org; *Statistical Tables.*

United Nations Food and Agricultural Organization (FAO), Viale delle Terme di Caracalla, 00100 Rome, Italy, (Dial from U.S. (202) 653-2400), (Fax from U.S. (202) 653 5760), www.fao.org; *FAO Production Yearbook 2002.*

United Nations Statistics Division, New York, NY 10017, (800) 253-9646, Fax: (212) 963-4116, http://unstats.un.org; *Demographic Yearbook; Human Development Report 2006; Statistical Yearbook; Trends in Europe and North America: The Statistical Yearbook of the ECE 2005;* and *World Statistics Pocketbook.*

The World Bank, 1818 H Street, NW, Washington, DC 20433, (202) 473-1000, Fax: (202) 477-6391, www.worldbank.org; *Estonia; Statistical Handbook: States of the Former USSR; The World Bank Atlas 2003-2004; World Development Indicators (WDI) 2008;* and *World Development Report 2008.*

World Health Organization (WHO), Avenue Appia 20, 1211 Geneve 27, Switzerland, (Telephone in U.S. (212) 331-9081), www.who.int; *World Health Report 2006.*

ESTONIA - POPULATION DENSITY

Central Intelligence Agency, Office of Public Affairs, Washington, DC 20505, (703) 482-0623, Fax: (703) 482-1739, www.cia.gov; *The World Factbook.*

Euromonitor International, Inc., 224 S. Michigan Avenue, Suite 1500, Chicago, IL 60604, (312) 922-1115, Fax: (312) 922-1157, www.euromonitor.com; *The World Economic Factbook 2008.*

Palgrave Macmillan Ltd., Houndmills, Basingstoke, Hampshire, RG21 6XS, England, (Telephone in U.S. (888) 330-8477), (Fax in U.S. (800) 672-2054), www.palgrave.com; *The Statesman's Yearbook 2008.*

Taylor and Francis Group, An Informa Business, 2 Park Square, Milton Park, Abingdon, Oxford OX14 4RN, United Kingdom, (Dial from U.S. (212) 216-7800), (Fax from U.S. (212) 564-7854), www.tandf.co.uk; *The Europa World Year Book.*

UNESCO Institute for Statistics, C.P. 6128 Succursale Centre-Ville, Montreal, Quebec, H3C 3J7 Canada, (Dial from U.S. (514) 343-6880), (Fax from U.S. (514) 343 6882), www.uis.unesco.org; *Statistical Tables.*

United Nations Statistics Division, New York, NY 10017, (800) 253-9646, Fax: (212) 963-4116, http://unstats.un.org; *Statistical Yearbook* and *Trends in Europe and North America: The Statistical Yearbook of the ECE 2005.*

The World Bank, 1818 H Street, NW, Washington, DC 20433, (202) 473-1000, Fax: (202) 477-6391, www.worldbank.org; *Estonia* and *World Development Report 2008.*

ESTONIA - POSTAL SERVICE

Palgrave Macmillan Ltd., Houndmills, Basingstoke, Hampshire, RG21 6XS, England, (Telephone in U.S. (888) 330-8477), (Fax in U.S. (800) 672-2054), www.palgrave.com; *The Statesman's Yearbook 2008.*

United Nations Statistics Division, New York, NY 10017, (800) 253-9646, Fax: (212) 963-4116, http://unstats.un.org; *Statistical Yearbook* and *Trends in Europe and North America: The Statistical Yearbook of the ECE 2005.*

ESTONIA - POULTRY

See ESTONIA - LIVESTOCK

ESTONIA - POWER RESOURCES

Academic International Press, PO Box 1111, Gulf Breeze, FL 32562-1111, Fax: (850) 934-0953, www.ai-press.com; *Russia and Eurasia Facts and Figures Annual.*

Euromonitor International, Inc., 224 S. Michigan Avenue, Suite 1500, Chicago, IL 60604, (312) 922-1115, Fax: (312) 922-1157, www.euromonitor.com; *The World Economic Factbook 2008* and *World Marketing Data and Statistics.*

Palgrave Macmillan Ltd., Houndmills, Basingstoke, Hampshire, RG21 6XS, England, (Telephone in U.S. (888) 330-8477), (Fax in U.S. (800) 672-2054), www.palgrave.com; *The Statesman's Yearbook 2008.*

Platts, 2 Penn Plaza, 25th Floor, New York, NY 10121-2298, (212) 904-3070, www.platts.com; *Energy Economist* and *European Power Daily.*

U.S. Department of Energy (DOE), Energy Information Administration (EIA), 1000 Independence Avenue, SW, Washington, DC 20585, (202) 586-8800, www.eia.doe.gov; *International Energy Annual 2004* and *International Energy Outlook 2006.*

United Nations Statistics Division, New York, NY 10017, (800) 253-9646, Fax: (212) 963-4116, http://unstats.un.org; *Energy Statistics Yearbook 2003; Human Development Report 2006; Statistical Yearbook; Trends in Europe and North America: The Statistical Yearbook of the ECE 2005;* and *World Statistics Pocketbook.*

The World Bank, 1818 H Street, NW, Washington, DC 20433, (202) 473-1000, Fax: (202) 477-6391, www.worldbank.org; *Statistical Handbook: States of the Former USSR; The World Bank Atlas 2003-2004;* and *World Development Report 2008.*

ESTONIA - PRICES

Euromonitor International, Inc., 224 S. Michigan Avenue, Suite 1500, Chicago, IL 60604, (312) 922-1115, Fax: (312) 922-1157, www.euromonitor.com; *World Marketing Data and Statistics.*

International Labour Office, I.L.O. Publications, 4 route des Morillons, CH-1211 Geneva 22, Switzerland, (Telephone in U.S. (202) 653-7652), (Fax in U.S. (202) 653-7687), www.ilo.org; *Yearbook of Labour Statistics 2006.*

United Nations Food and Agricultural Organization (FAO), Viale delle Terme di Caracalla, 00100 Rome, Italy, (Dial from U.S. (202) 653-2400), (Fax from U.S. (202) 653 5760), www.fao.org; *FAO Production Yearbook 2002.*

The World Bank, 1818 H Street, NW, Washington, DC 20433, (202) 473-1000, Fax: (202) 477-6391, www.worldbank.org; *Estonia* and *Statistical Handbook: States of the Former USSR.*

ESTONIA - PROFESSIONS

United Nations Statistics Division, New York, NY 10017, (800) 253-9646, Fax: (212) 963-4116, http://unstats.un.org; *Statistical Yearbook.*

ESTONIA - PUBLIC HEALTH

Academic International Press, PO Box 1111, Gulf Breeze, FL 32562-1111, Fax: (850) 934-0953, www.ai-press.com; *Russia and Eurasia Facts and Figures Annual.*

Euromonitor International, Inc., 224 S. Michigan Avenue, Suite 1500, Chicago, IL 60604, (312) 922-1115, Fax: (312) 922-1157, www.euromonitor.com; *World Health Databook 2007/2008* and *World Marketing Data and Statistics.*

Health and Consumer Protection Directorate-General, European Commission, B-1049 Brussels, Belgium, http://ec.europa.eu/dgs/health_consumer/index_en.htm; *Injuries in the European Union: Statistics Summary 2002-2004.*

Palgrave Macmillan Ltd., Houndmills, Basingstoke, Hampshire, RG21 6XS, England, (Telephone in U.S. (888) 330-8477), (Fax in U.S. (800) 672-2054), www.palgrave.com; *The Statesman's Yearbook 2008.*

Robert Koch Institute, Nordufer 20, D 13353 Berlin, Germany, www.rki.de; *EUVAC-NET Report: Pertussis-Surveillance 1998-2002.*

UNICEF, 3 United Nations Plaza, New York, NY 10017, (800) 253-9646, Fax: (212) 887-7465, www.unicef.org; *The State of the World's Children 2008.*

United Nations Statistics Division, New York, NY 10017, (800) 253-9646, Fax: (212) 963-4116, http://unstats.un.org; *Human Development Report 2006; Statistical Yearbook;* and *Trends in Europe and North America: The Statistical Yearbook of the ECE 2005.*

The World Bank, 1818 H Street, NW, Washington, DC 20433, (202) 473-1000, Fax: (202) 477-6391, www.worldbank.org; *Estonia* and *World Development Report 2008.*

World Health Organization (WHO), Avenue Appia 20, 1211 Geneve 27, Switzerland, (Telephone in U.S. (212) 331-9081), www.who.int; The WHO Global Atlas of Infectious Diseases and *World Health Report 2006.*

ESTONIA - PUBLISHERS AND PUBLISHING

Palgrave Macmillan Ltd., Houndmills, Basingstoke, Hampshire, RG21 6XS, England, (Telephone in U.S. (888) 330-8477), (Fax in U.S. (800) 672-2054), www.palgrave.com; *The Statesman's Yearbook 2008.*

Taylor and Francis Group, An Informa Business, 2 Park Square, Milton Park, Abingdon, Oxford OX14 4RN, United Kingdom, (Dial from U.S. (212) 216-7800), (Fax from U.S. (212) 564-7854), www.tandf.co.uk; *The Europa World Year Book.*

UNESCO Institute for Statistics, C.P. 6128 Succursale Centre-Ville, Montreal, Quebec, H3C 3J7 Canada, (Dial from U.S. (514) 343-6880), (Fax from U.S. (514) 343 6882), www.uis.unesco.org; *Statistical Tables.*

United Nations Statistics Division, New York, NY 10017, (800) 253-9646, Fax: (212) 963-4116, http://unstats.un.org; *Trends in Europe and North America: The Statistical Yearbook of the ECE 2005.*

ESTONIA - RADIO - RECEIVERS AND RECEPTION

Palgrave Macmillan Ltd., Houndmills, Basingstoke, Hampshire, RG21 6XS, England, (Telephone in U.S. (888) 330-8477), (Fax in U.S. (800) 672-2054), www.palgrave.com; *The Statesman's Yearbook 2008.*

United Nations Statistics Division, New York, NY 10017, (800) 253-9646, Fax: (212) 963-4116, http://unstats.un.org; *Statistical Yearbook.*

ESTONIA - RAILROADS

Taylor and Francis Group, An Informa Business, 2 Park Square, Milton Park, Abingdon, Oxford OX14 4RN, United Kingdom, (Dial from U.S. (212) 216-7800), (Fax from U.S. (212) 564-7854), www.tandf.co.uk; *The Europa World Year Book.*

United Nations Statistics Division, New York, NY 10017, (800) 253-9646, Fax: (212) 963-4116, http://unstats.un.org; *Annual Bulletin of Transport Statistics for Europe and North America 2004; Statistical Yearbook;* and *Trends in Europe and North America: The Statistical Yearbook of the ECE 2005.*

ESTONIA - RELIGION

Academic International Press, PO Box 1111, Gulf Breeze, FL 32562-1111, Fax: (850) 934-0953, www.ai-press.com; *Russia and Eurasia Facts and Figures Annual.*

Central Intelligence Agency, Office of Public Affairs, Washington, DC 20505, (703) 482-0623, Fax: (703) 482-1739, www.cia.gov; *The World Factbook.*

Palgrave Macmillan Ltd., Houndmills, Basingstoke, Hampshire, RG21 6XS, England, (Telephone in U.S. (888) 330-8477), (Fax in U.S. (800) 672-2054), www.palgrave.com; *The Statesman's Yearbook 2008.*

ESTONIA - RENT CHARGES

International Labour Office, I.L.O. Publications, 4 route des Morillons, CH-1211 Geneva 22, Switzerland, (Telephone in U.S. (202) 653-7652), (Fax in U.S. (202) 653-7687), www.ilo.org; *Yearbook of Labour Statistics 2006.*

ESTONIA - RETAIL TRADE

Banque de France, 48 rue Croix des Petits champs, 75001 Paris, France, www.banque-france.fr/home.htm; *Monthly Business Survey Overview.*

Euromonitor International, Inc., 224 S. Michigan Avenue, Suite 1500, Chicago, IL 60604, (312) 922-1115, Fax: (312) 922-1157, www.euromonitor.com; *World Marketing Data and Statistics.*

United Nations Statistics Division, New York, NY 10017, (800) 253-9646, Fax: (212) 963-4116, http://unstats.un.org; *Statistical Yearbook.*

ESTONIA - ROADS

Central Intelligence Agency, Office of Public Affairs, Washington, DC 20505, (703) 482-0623, Fax: (703) 482-1739, www.cia.gov; *The World Factbook.*

Palgrave Macmillan Ltd., Houndmills, Basingstoke, Hampshire, RG21 6XS, England, (Telephone in U.S. (888) 330-8477), (Fax in U.S. (800) 672-2054), www.palgrave.com; *The Statesman's Yearbook 2008.*

United Nations Statistics Division, New York, NY 10017, (800) 253-9646, Fax: (212) 963-4116, http://unstats.un.org; *Annual Bulletin of Transport Statistics for Europe and North America 2004* and *Trends in Europe and North America: The Statistical Yearbook of the ECE 2005.*

ESTONIA - RUBBER INDUSTRY AND TRADE

International Rubber Study Group (IRSG), 1st Floor, Heron House, 109/115 Wembley Hill Road, Wembley, Middlesex HA9 8DA, United Kingdom, www.rubberstudy.com; *Rubber Statistical Bulletin; Summary of World Rubber Statistics 2005; World Rubber Statistics Handbook (Volume 6, 1975-2001);* and *World Rubber Statistics Historic Handbook.*

United Nations Statistics Division, New York, NY 10017, (800) 253-9646, Fax: (212) 963-4116, http://unstats.un.org; *Statistical Yearbook.*

ESTONIA - SHEEP

See ESTONIA - LIVESTOCK

ESTONIA - SHIPPING

Palgrave Macmillan Ltd., Houndmills, Basingstoke, Hampshire, RG21 6XS, England, (Telephone in U.S. (888) 330-8477), (Fax in U.S. (800) 672-2054), www.palgrave.com; *The Statesman's Yearbook 2008.*

Taylor and Francis Group, An Informa Business, 2 Park Square, Milton Park, Abingdon, Oxford OX14 4RN, United Kingdom, (Dial from U.S. (212) 216-7800), (Fax from U.S. (212) 564-7854), www.tandf.co.uk; *The Europa World Year Book.*

United Nations Statistics Division, New York, NY 10017, (800) 253-9646, Fax: (212) 963-4116, http://unstats.un.org; *Annual Bulletin of Transport Statistics for Europe and North America 2004* and *Statistical Yearbook.*

ESTONIA - SOCIAL ECOLOGY

United Nations Statistics Division, New York, NY 10017, (800) 253-9646, Fax: (212) 963-4116, http://unstats.un.org; *World Statistics Pocketbook.*

ESTONIA - SOCIAL SECURITY

United Nations Statistics Division, New York, NY 10017, (800) 253-9646, Fax: (212) 963-4116, http://unstats.un.org; *National Accounts Statistics: Compendium of Income Distribution Statistics.*

ESTONIA - STEEL PRODUCTION

See ESTONIA - MINERAL INDUSTRIES

ESTONIA - TAXATION

Eurostat, Batiment Jean Monnet, Rue Alcide de Gasperi, L-2920 Luxembourg, http://epp.eurostat.ec.europa.eu; *Taxation Trends in the European Union - Data for the EU Member States and Norway.*

Taylor and Francis Group, An Informa Business, 2 Park Square, Milton Park, Abingdon, Oxford OX14 4RN, United Kingdom, (Dial from U.S. (212) 216-7800), (Fax from U.S. (212) 564-7854), www.tandf.co.uk; *The Europa World Year Book.*

ESTONIA - TELEPHONE

Palgrave Macmillan Ltd., Houndmills, Basingstoke, Hampshire, RG21 6XS, England, (Telephone in U.S.

(888) 330-8477), (Fax in U.S. (800) 672-2054), www.palgrave.com; *The Statesman's Yearbook 2008.*

United Nations Statistics Division, New York, NY 10017, (800) 253-9646, Fax: (212) 963-4116, http://unstats.un.org; *Statistical Yearbook; Trends in Europe and North America: The Statistical Yearbook of the ECE 2005;* and *World Statistics Pocketbook.*

ESTONIA - TEXTILE INDUSTRY

United Nations Statistics Division, New York, NY 10017, (800) 253-9646, Fax: (212) 963-4116, http://unstats.un.org; *2004 Industrial Commodity Statistics Yearbook* and *Statistical Yearbook.*

ESTONIA - THEATER

UNESCO Institute for Statistics, C.P. 6128 Succursale Centre-Ville, Montreal, Quebec, H3C 3J7 Canada, (Dial from U.S. (514) 343-6880), (Fax from U.S. (514) 343 6882), www.uis.unesco.org; *Statistical Tables.*

ESTONIA - TIRE INDUSTRY

United Nations Statistics Division, New York, NY 10017, (800) 253-9646, Fax: (212) 963-4116, http://unstats.un.org; *Statistical Yearbook.*

ESTONIA - TOBACCO INDUSTRY

Foreign Agricultural Service (FAS), U.S. Department of Agriculture (USDA), 1400 Independence Avenue, SW, Washington, DC 20250, (202) 720-3935, www.fas.usda.gov; *Tobacco: World Markets and Trade.*

United Nations Statistics Division, New York, NY 10017, (800) 253-9646, Fax: (212) 963-4116, http://unstats.un.org; *Statistical Yearbook.*

ESTONIA - TOURISM

Euromonitor International, Inc., 224 S. Michigan Avenue, Suite 1500, Chicago, IL 60604, (312) 922-1115, Fax: (312) 922-1157, www.euromonitor.com; *The World Economic Factbook 2008* and *World Marketing Data and Statistics.*

Taylor and Francis Group, An Informa Business, 2 Park Square, Milton Park, Abingdon, Oxford OX14 4RN, United Kingdom, (Dial from U.S. (212) 216-7800), (Fax from U.S. (212) 564-7854), www.tandf.co.uk; *The Europa World Year Book.*

United Nations Statistics Division, New York, NY 10017, (800) 253-9646, Fax: (212) 963-4116, http://unstats.un.org; *Statistical Yearbook* and *Trends in Europe and North America: The Statistical Yearbook of the ECE 2005.*

The World Bank, 1818 H Street, NW, Washington, DC 20433, (202) 473-1000, Fax: (202) 477-6391, www.worldbank.org; *Estonia.*

ESTONIA - TRANSPORTATION

Academic International Press, PO Box 1111, Gulf Breeze, FL 32562-1111, Fax: (850) 934-0953, www.ai-press.com; *Russia and Eurasia Facts and Figures Annual.*

Central Intelligence Agency, Office of Public Affairs, Washington, DC 20505, (703) 482-0623, Fax: (703) 482-1739, www.cia.gov; *The World Factbook.*

Euromonitor International, Inc., 224 S. Michigan Avenue, Suite 1500, Chicago, IL 60604, (312) 922-1115, Fax: (312) 922-1157, www.euromonitor.com; *World Marketing Data and Statistics.*

Eurostat, Batiment Jean Monnet, Rue Alcide de Gasperi, L-2920 Luxembourg, http://epp.eurostat.ec.europa.eu; *Regional Passenger and Freight Air Transport in Europe in 2006* and *Regional Road and Rail Transport Networks.*

Palgrave Macmillan Ltd., Houndmills, Basingstoke, Hampshire, RG21 6XS, England, (Telephone in U.S. (888) 330-8477), (Fax in U.S. (800) 672-2054), www.palgrave.com; *The Statesman's Yearbook 2008.*

Taylor and Francis Group, An Informa Business, 2 Park Square, Milton Park, Abingdon, Oxford OX14 4RN, United Kingdom, (Dial from U.S. (212) 216-7800), (Fax from U.S. (212) 564-7854), www.tandf.co.uk; *The Europa World Year Book.*

United Nations Statistics Division, New York, NY 10017, (800) 253-9646, Fax: (212) 963-4116, http://unstats.un.org; *Annual Bulletin of Transport Statistics for Europe and North America 2004; Human Development Report 2006;* and *Trends in Europe and North America: The Statistical Yearbook of the ECE 2005.*

The World Bank, 1818 H Street, NW, Washington, DC 20433, (202) 473-1000, Fax: (202) 477-6391, www.worldbank.org; *Estonia.*

ESTONIA - UNEMPLOYMENT

Central Intelligence Agency, Office of Public Affairs, Washington, DC 20505, (703) 482-0623, Fax: (703) 482-1739, www.cia.gov; *The World Factbook.*

International Labour Office, I.L.O. Publications, 4 route des Morillons, CH-1211 Geneva 22, Switzerland, (Telephone in U.S. (202) 653-7652), (Fax in U.S. (202) 653-7687), www.ilo.org; *Yearbook of Labour Statistics 2006.*

United Nations Statistics Division, New York, NY 10017, (800) 253-9646, Fax: (212) 963-4116, http://unstats.un.org; *Statistical Yearbook* and *Trends in Europe and North America: The Statistical Yearbook of the ECE 2005.*

The World Bank, 1818 H Street, NW, Washington, DC 20433, (202) 473-1000, Fax: (202) 477-6391, www.worldbank.org; *Estonia.*

ESTONIA - VITAL STATISTICS

Palgrave Macmillan Ltd., Houndmills, Basingstoke, Hampshire, RG21 6XS, England, (Telephone in U.S. (888) 330-8477), (Fax in U.S. (800) 672-2054), www.palgrave.com; *The Statesman's Yearbook 2008.*

World Health Organization (WHO), Avenue Appia 20, 1211 Geneve 27, Switzerland, (Telephone in U.S. (212) 331-9081), www.who.int; *World Health Report 2006.*

ESTONIA - WAGES

International Labour Office, I.L.O. Publications, 4 route des Morillons, CH-1211 Geneva 22, Switzerland, (Telephone in U.S. (202) 653-7652), (Fax in U.S. (202) 653-7687), www.ilo.org; *Yearbook of Labour Statistics 2006.*

United Nations Statistics Division, New York, NY 10017, (800) 253-9646, Fax: (212) 963-4116, http://unstats.un.org; *Statistical Yearbook.*

The World Bank, 1818 H Street, NW, Washington, DC 20433, (202) 473-1000, Fax: (202) 477-6391, www.worldbank.org; *Estonia* and *Statistical Handbook: States of the Former USSR.*

ESTONIA - WELFARE STATE

Palgrave Macmillan Ltd., Houndmills, Basingstoke, Hampshire, RG21 6XS, England, (Telephone in U.S. (888) 330-8477), (Fax in U.S. (800) 672-2054), www.palgrave.com; *The Statesman's Yearbook 2008.*

ESTONIA - WHOLESALE PRICE INDEXES

United Nations Statistics Division, New York, NY 10017, (800) 253-9646, Fax: (212) 963-4116, http://unstats.un.org; *Statistical Yearbook.*

ESTONIA - WHOLESALE TRADE

United Nations Statistics Division, New York, NY 10017, (800) 253-9646, Fax: (212) 963-4116, http://unstats.un.org; *Statistical Yearbook.*

ESTONIA - WOOL PRODUCTION

See ESTONIA - TEXTILE INDUSTRY

ETHANE

U.S. Department of Energy (DOE), Energy Information Administration (EIA), 1000 Independence Avenue, SW, Washington, DC 20585, (202) 586-8800, www.eia.doe.gov; *Petroleum Supply Annual 2004.*

ETHANOL

World Resources Institute (WRI), 10 G Street, NE, Suite 800 Washington, DC 20002, (202) 729-7600, www.wri.org; *Thirst for Corn: What 2007 Plantings Could Mean for the Environment.*

ETHIOPIA - NATIONAL STATISTICAL OFFICE

Central Statistical Agency (CSA) of Ethiopia, PO Box 1143, Addis Ababa, Ethiopia, www.csa.gov.et; National Data Center.

ETHIOPIA - PRIMARY STATISTICS SOURCES

Central Statistical Agency (CSA) of Ethiopia, PO Box 1143, Addis Ababa, Ethiopia, www.csa.gov.et; *Statistical Abstract of Ethiopia.*

ETHIOPIA - AGRICULTURE

Central Statistical Agency (CSA) of Ethiopia, PO Box 1143, Addis Ababa, Ethiopia, www.csa.gov.et; *Statistical Abstract of Ethiopia.*

Economist Intelligence Unit, 111 West 57th Street, New York, NY 10019, (212) 554-0600, Fax: (212) 586-1181, www.eiu.com; *Ethiopia Country Report.*

Euromonitor International, Inc., 224 S. Michigan Avenue, Suite 1500, Chicago, IL 60604, (312) 922-1115, Fax: (312) 922-1157, www.euromonitor.com; *International Marketing Data and Statistics 2008* and *World Marketing Data and Statistics.*

Palgrave Macmillan Ltd., Houndmills, Basingstoke, Hampshire, RG21 6XS, England, (Telephone in U.S. (888) 330-8477), (Fax in U.S. (800) 672-2054), www.palgrave.com; *The Statesman's Yearbook 2008.*

Taylor and Francis Group, An Informa Business, 2 Park Square, Milton Park, Abingdon, Oxford OX14 4RN, United Kingdom, (Dial from U.S. (212) 216-7800), (Fax from U.S. (212) 564-7854), www.tandf.co.uk; *The Europa World Year Book.*

United Nations Conference on Trade and Development (UNCTAD), DC2-1120, United Nations, New York, NY 10017, (212) 963-0027, www.unctad.org; *UNCTAD Commodity Yearbook.*

United Nations Economic Commission for Africa (ECA), PO Box 3001, Addis Ababa, Ethiopia, (Telephone in U.S. (212) 963-4957), www.uneca.org; *African Statistical Yearbook 2006.*

United Nations Food and Agricultural Organization (FAO), Viale delle Terme di Caracalla, 00100 Rome, Italy, (Dial from U.S. (202) 653-2400), (Fax from U.S. (202) 653 5760), www.fao.org; AQUASTAT; *FAO Production Yearbook 2002; FAO Trade Yearbook;* and *The State of Food and Agriculture (SOFA) 2006.*

United Nations Statistics Division, New York, NY 10017, (800) 253-9646, Fax: (212) 963-4116, http://unstats.un.org; *Statistical Yearbook* and *Survey of Economic and Social Conditions in Africa 2005.*

The World Bank, 1818 H Street, NW, Washington, DC 20433, (202) 473-1000, Fax: (202) 477-6391, www.worldbank.org; *Africa Live Database (LDB); African Development Indicators (ADI) 2007;* and *Ethiopia.*

ETHIOPIA - AIRLINES

International Civil Aviation Organization (ICAO), External Relations and Public Information Office (EPO), 999 University Street, Montreal, Quebec H3C 5H7, Canada, (Dial from U.S. (514) 954-8219), (Fax from U.S. (514) 954-6077), www.icao.int; *Civil Aviation Statistics of the World.*

Palgrave Macmillan Ltd., Houndmills, Basingstoke, Hampshire, RG21 6XS, England, (Telephone in U.S. (888) 330-8477), (Fax in U.S. (800) 672-2054), www.palgrave.com; *The Statesman's Yearbook 2008.*

Taylor and Francis Group, An Informa Business, 2 Park Square, Milton Park, Abingdon, Oxford OX14 4RN, United Kingdom, (Dial from U.S. (212) 216-7800), (Fax from U.S. (212) 564-7854), www.tandf.co.uk; *The Europa World Year Book.*

United Nations Economic Commission for Africa (ECA), PO Box 3001, Addis Ababa, Ethiopia, (Telephone in U.S. (212) 963-4957), www.uneca.org; *African Statistical Yearbook 2006.*

United Nations Statistics Division, New York, NY 10017, (800) 253-9646, Fax: (212) 963-4116, http://unstats.un.org; *Statistical Yearbook.*

ETHIOPIA - AIRPORTS

Central Intelligence Agency, Office of Public Affairs, Washington, DC 20505, (703) 482-0623, Fax: (703) 482-1739, www.cia.gov; *The World Factbook.*

ETHIOPIA - ARMED FORCES

Central Intelligence Agency, Office of Public Affairs, Washington, DC 20505, (703) 482-0623, Fax: (703) 482-1739, www.cia.gov; *The World Factbook.*

Euromonitor International, Inc., 224 S. Michigan Avenue, Suite 1500, Chicago, IL 60604, (312) 922-1115, Fax: (312) 922-1157, www.euromonitor.com; *World Marketing Data and Statistics.*

International Institute for Strategic Studies (IISS), Arundel House, 13-15 Arundel Street, Temple Place, London WC2R 3DX, England, www.iiss.org; *The Military Balance 2007.*

International Monetary Fund (IMF), 700 Nineteenth Street, NW, Washington, DC 20431, (202) 623-7000, Fax: (202) 623-4661, www.imf.org; *Government Finance Statistics Yearbook (2008 Edition).*

Palgrave Macmillan Ltd., Houndmills, Basingstoke, Hampshire, RG21 6XS, England, (Telephone in U.S. (888) 330-8477), (Fax in U.S. (800) 672-2054), www.palgrave.com; *The Statesman's Yearbook 2008.*

U.S. Department of State (DOS), 2201 C Street NW, Washington, DC 20520, (202) 647-4000, www.state.gov; *World Military Expenditures and Arms Transfers (WMEAT).*

United Nations Statistics Division, New York, NY 10017, (800) 253-9646, Fax: (212) 963-4116, http://unstats.un.org; *Human Development Report 2006.*

ETHIOPIA - BALANCE OF PAYMENTS

African Development Bank Group, Rue Joseph Anoma, 01 BP 1387 Abidjan 01, Cote d'Ivoire, www.afdb.org; *Statistics Pocketbook 2008.*

Central Statistical Agency (CSA) of Ethiopia, PO Box 1143, Addis Ababa, Ethiopia, www.csa.gov.et; *Statistical Abstract of Ethiopia.*

International Monetary Fund (IMF), 700 Nineteenth Street, NW, Washington, DC 20431, (202) 623-7000, Fax: (202) 623-4661, www.imf.org; *Balance of Payments Statistics Newsletter; Balance of Payments Statistics Yearbook 2007;* and *International Financial Statistics Yearbook 2007.*

Taylor and Francis Group, An Informa Business, 2 Park Square, Milton Park, Abingdon, Oxford OX14 4RN, United Kingdom, (Dial from U.S. (212) 216-7800), (Fax from U.S. (212) 564-7854), www.tandf.co.uk; *The Europa World Year Book.*

United Nations Economic Commission for Africa (ECA), PO Box 3001, Addis Ababa, Ethiopia, (Telephone in U.S. (212) 963-4957), www.uneca.org; *African Statistical Yearbook 2006.*

The World Bank, 1818 H Street, NW, Washington, DC 20433, (202) 473-1000, Fax: (202) 477-6391, www.worldbank.org; *Ethiopia* and *World Development Report 2008.*

ETHIOPIA - BANKS AND BANKING

Central Statistical Agency (CSA) of Ethiopia, PO Box 1143, Addis Ababa, Ethiopia, www.csa.gov.et; *Statistical Abstract of Ethiopia.*

Euromonitor International, Inc., 224 S. Michigan Avenue, Suite 1500, Chicago, IL 60604, (312) 922-1115, Fax: (312) 922-1157, www.euromonitor.com; *World Marketing Data and Statistics.*

International Monetary Fund (IMF), 700 Nineteenth Street, NW, Washington, DC 20431, (202) 623-7000, Fax: (202) 623-4661, www.imf.org; *Government Finance Statistics Yearbook (2008 Edition)* and *International Financial Statistics Yearbook 2007.*

Palgrave Macmillan Ltd., Houndmills, Basingstoke, Hampshire, RG21 6XS, England, (Telephone in U.S. (888) 330-8477), (Fax in U.S. (800) 672-2054), www.palgrave.com; *The Statesman's Yearbook 2008.*

Taylor and Francis Group, An Informa Business, 2 Park Square, Milton Park, Abingdon, Oxford OX14 4RN, United Kingdom, (Dial from U.S. (212) 216-7800), (Fax from U.S. (212) 564-7854), www.tandf.co.uk; *The Europa World Year Book.*

United Nations Economic Commission for Africa (ECA), PO Box 3001, Addis Ababa, Ethiopia, (Telephone in U.S. (212) 963-4957), www.uneca.org; *African Statistical Yearbook 2006.*

ETHIOPIA - BARLEY PRODUCTION

See ETHIOPIA - CROPS

ETHIOPIA - BEVERAGE INDUSTRY

United Nations Statistics Division, New York, NY 10017, (800) 253-9646, Fax: (212) 963-4116, http://unstats.un.org; *Statistical Yearbook.*

ETHIOPIA - BONDS

International Monetary Fund (IMF), 700 Nineteenth Street, NW, Washington, DC 20431, (202) 623-7000, Fax: (202) 623-4661, www.imf.org; *Government Finance Statistics Yearbook (2008 Edition).*

ETHIOPIA - BROADCASTING

Central Intelligence Agency, Office of Public Affairs, Washington, DC 20505, (703) 482-0623, Fax: (703) 482-1739, www.cia.gov; *The World Factbook.*

Euromonitor International, Inc., 224 S. Michigan Avenue, Suite 1500, Chicago, IL 60604, (312) 922-1115, Fax: (312) 922-1157, www.euromonitor.com; *World Marketing Data and Statistics.*

Palgrave Macmillan Ltd., Houndmills, Basingstoke, Hampshire, RG21 6XS, England, (Telephone in U.S. (888) 330-8477), (Fax in U.S. (800) 672-2054), www.palgrave.com; *The Statesman's Yearbook 2008.*

WRTH Publications Limited, PO Box 290, Oxford OX2 7FT, UK, www.wrth.com; *World Radio TV Handbook 2007.*

ETHIOPIA - BUDGET

Central Intelligence Agency, Office of Public Affairs, Washington, DC 20505, (703) 482-0623, Fax: (703) 482-1739, www.cia.gov; *The World Factbook.*

ETHIOPIA - CAPITAL LEVY

International Monetary Fund (IMF), 700 Nineteenth Street, NW, Washington, DC 20431, (202) 623-7000, Fax: (202) 623-4661, www.imf.org; *Government Finance Statistics Yearbook (2008 Edition).*

ETHIOPIA - CATTLE

See ETHIOPIA - LIVESTOCK

ETHIOPIA - CHICK PEA PRODUCTION

See ETHIOPIA - CROPS

ETHIOPIA - CHICKENS

See ETHIOPIA - LIVESTOCK

ETHIOPIA - CHILDBIRTH - STATISTICS

Central Intelligence Agency, Office of Public Affairs, Washington, DC 20505, (703) 482-0623, Fax: (703) 482-1739, www.cia.gov; *The World Factbook.*

Euromonitor International, Inc., 224 S. Michigan Avenue, Suite 1500, Chicago, IL 60604, (312) 922-1115, Fax: (312) 922-1157, www.euromonitor.com; *International Marketing Data and Statistics 2008* and *The World Economic Factbook 2008.*

Taylor and Francis Group, An Informa Business, 2 Park Square, Milton Park, Abingdon, Oxford OX14 4RN, United Kingdom, (Dial from U.S. (212) 216-7800), (Fax from U.S. (212) 564-7854), www.tandf.co.uk; *The Europa World Year Book.*

United Nations Statistics Division, New York, NY 10017, (800) 253-9646, Fax: (212) 963-4116, http://unstats.un.org; *Demographic Yearbook; Statistical Yearbook;* and *Survey of Economic and Social Conditions in Africa 2005.*

ETHIOPIA - CLIMATE

Central Statistical Agency (CSA) of Ethiopia, PO Box 1143, Addis Ababa, Ethiopia, www.csa.gov.et; *Statistical Abstract of Ethiopia.*

International Institute for Environment and Development (IIED), 3 Endsleigh Street, London, England, WC1H 0DD, United Kingdom, www.iied.org; *Environment Urbanization* and *Haramata - Bulletin of the Drylands.*

Palgrave Macmillan Ltd., Houndmills, Basingstoke, Hampshire, RG21 6XS, England, (Telephone in U.S. (888) 330-8477), (Fax in U.S. (800) 672-2054), www.palgrave.com; *The Statesman's Yearbook 2008.*

ETHIOPIA - COAL PRODUCTION

See ETHIOPIA - MINERAL INDUSTRIES

ETHIOPIA - COFFEE

See ETHIOPIA - CROPS

ETHIOPIA - COMMERCE

Palgrave Macmillan Ltd., Houndmills, Basingstoke, Hampshire, RG21 6XS, England, (Telephone in U.S. (888) 330-8477), (Fax in U.S. (800) 672-2054), www.palgrave.com; *The Statesman's Yearbook 2008.*

ETHIOPIA - COMMODITY EXCHANGES

Commodity Research Bureau, 330 South Wells Street, Suite 612, Chicago, IL 60606-7110, (800) 621-5271, Fax: (312) 939-4135, www.crbtrader.com; *2006 CRB Commodity Yearbook and CD.*

International Monetary Fund (IMF), 700 Nineteenth Street, NW, Washington, DC 20431, (202) 623-7000, Fax: (202) 623-4661, www.imf.org; *IMF Primary Commodity Prices.*

United Nations Food and Agricultural Organization (FAO), Viale delle Terme di Caracalla, 00100 Rome, Italy, (Dial from U.S. (202) 653-2400), (Fax from U.S. (202) 653 5760), www.fao.org; *The State of Food and Agriculture (SOFA) 2006.*

ETHIOPIA - COMMUNICATION AND TRAFFIC

United Nations Statistics Division, New York, NY 10017, (800) 253-9646, Fax: (212) 963-4116, http://unstats.un.org; *Statistical Yearbook.*

ETHIOPIA - CONSTRUCTION INDUSTRY

Central Statistical Agency (CSA) of Ethiopia, PO Box 1143, Addis Ababa, Ethiopia, www.csa.gov.et; *Statistical Abstract of Ethiopia.*

United Nations Economic Commission for Africa (ECA), PO Box 3001, Addis Ababa, Ethiopia, (Telephone in U.S. (212) 963-4957), www.uneca.org; *African Statistical Yearbook 2006.*

United Nations Statistics Division, New York, NY 10017, (800) 253-9646, Fax: (212) 963-4116, http://unstats.un.org; *Statistical Yearbook.*

ETHIOPIA - CONSUMER PRICE INDEXES

Taylor and Francis Group, An Informa Business, 2 Park Square, Milton Park, Abingdon, Oxford OX14 4RN, United Kingdom, (Dial from U.S. (212) 216-7800), (Fax from U.S. (212) 564-7854), www.tandf.co.uk; *The Europa World Year Book.*

United Nations Economic Commission for Africa (ECA), PO Box 3001, Addis Ababa, Ethiopia, (Telephone in U.S. (212) 963-4957), www.uneca.org; *African Statistical Yearbook 2006.*

United Nations Statistics Division, New York, NY 10017, (800) 253-9646, Fax: (212) 963-4116, http://

unstats.un.org; *Statistical Yearbook* and *Survey of Economic and Social Conditions in Africa 2005.*

The World Bank, 1818 H Street, NW, Washington, DC 20433, (202) 473-1000, Fax: (202) 477-6391, www.worldbank.org; *Ethiopia.*

ETHIOPIA - CONSUMPTION (ECONOMICS)

African Development Bank Group, Rue Joseph Anoma, 01 BP 1387 Abidjan 01, Cote d'Ivoire, www.afdb.org; *Statistics Pocketbook 2008.*

United Nations Statistics Division, New York, NY 10017, (800) 253-9646, Fax: (212) 963-4116, http://unstats.un.org; *Survey of Economic and Social Conditions in Africa 2005.*

The World Bank, 1818 H Street, NW, Washington, DC 20433, (202) 473-1000, Fax: (202) 477-6391, www.worldbank.org; *World Development Report 2008.*

ETHIOPIA - CORN INDUSTRY

See ETHIOPIA - CROPS

ETHIOPIA - COST AND STANDARD OF LIVING

International Monetary Fund (IMF), 700 Nineteenth Street, NW, Washington, DC 20431, (202) 623-7000, Fax: (202) 623-4661, www.imf.org; *Government Finance Statistics Yearbook (2008 Edition).*

ETHIOPIA - COTTON

See ETHIOPIA - CROPS

ETHIOPIA - CRIME

Yale University Press, PO Box 209040, New Haven, CT 06520-9040, (203) 432-0960, Fax: (203) 432-0948, http://yalepress.yale.edu/yupbooks; *Violence and Crime in Cross-National Perspective.*

ETHIOPIA - CROPS

International Grains Council (IGC), 1 Canada Square, Canary Wharf, London E14 5AE, England, www.igc.org.uk; *Grain Market Report.*

International Monetary Fund (IMF), 700 Nineteenth Street, NW, Washington, DC 20431, (202) 623-7000, Fax: (202) 623-4661, www.imf.org; *International Financial Statistics Yearbook 2007.*

Palgrave Macmillan Ltd., Houndmills, Basingstoke, Hampshire, RG21 6XS, England, (Telephone in U.S. (888) 330-8477), (Fax in U.S. (800) 672-2054), www.palgrave.com; *The Statesman's Yearbook 2008.*

Taylor and Francis Group, An Informa Business, 2 Park Square, Milton Park, Abingdon, Oxford OX14 4RN, United Kingdom, (Dial from U.S. (212) 216-7800), (Fax from U.S. (212) 564-7854), www.tandf.co.uk; *The Europa World Year Book.*

United Nations Conference on Trade and Development (UNCTAD), DC2-1120, United Nations, New York, NY 10017, (212) 963-0027, www.unctad.org; *UNCTAD Commodity Yearbook.*

United Nations Economic Commission for Africa (ECA), PO Box 3001, Addis Ababa, Ethiopia, (Telephone in U.S. (212) 963-4957), www.uneca.org; *African Statistical Yearbook 2006.*

United Nations Food and Agricultural Organization (FAO), Viale delle Terme di Caracalla, 00100 Rome, Italy, (Dial from U.S. (202) 653-2400), (Fax from U.S. (202) 653 5760), www.fao.org; *FAO Production Yearbook 2002* and *The State of Food and Agriculture (SOFA) 2006.*

United Nations Statistics Division, New York, NY 10017, (800) 253-9646, Fax: (212) 963-4116, http://unstats.un.org; *Statistical Yearbook.*

ETHIOPIA - CUSTOMS ADMINISTRATION

International Monetary Fund (IMF), 700 Nineteenth Street, NW, Washington, DC 20431, (202) 623-7000, Fax: (202) 623-4661, www.imf.org; *Government Finance Statistics Yearbook (2008 Edition).*

ETHIOPIA - DAIRY PROCESSING

Palgrave Macmillan Ltd., Houndmills, Basingstoke, Hampshire, RG21 6XS, England, (Telephone in U.S. (888) 330-8477), (Fax in U.S. (800) 672-2054), www.palgrave.com; *The Statesman's Yearbook 2008.*

Taylor and Francis Group, An Informa Business, 2 Park Square, Milton Park, Abingdon, Oxford OX14 4RN, United Kingdom, (Dial from U.S. (212) 216-7800), (Fax from U.S. (212) 564-7854), www.tandf.co.uk; *The Europa World Year Book.*

United Nations Food and Agricultural Organization (FAO), Viale delle Terme di Caracalla, 00100 Rome, Italy, (Dial from U.S. (202) 653-2400), (Fax from U.S. (202) 653 5760), www.fao.org; *The State of Food and Agriculture (SOFA) 2006.*

United Nations Statistics Division, New York, NY 10017, (800) 253-9646, Fax: (212) 963-4116, http://unstats.un.org; *Statistical Yearbook.*

ETHIOPIA - DEATH RATES

See ETHIOPIA - MORTALITY

ETHIOPIA - DEBTS, EXTERNAL

African Development Bank Group, Rue Joseph Anoma, 01 BP 1387 Abidjan 01, Cote d'Ivoire, www.afdb.org; *Statistics Pocketbook 2008.*

International Monetary Fund (IMF), 700 Nineteenth Street, NW, Washington, DC 20431, (202) 623-7000, Fax: (202) 623-4661, www.imf.org; *Government Finance Statistics Yearbook (2008 Edition).*

United Nations Statistics Division, New York, NY 10017, (800) 253-9646, Fax: (212) 963-4116, http://unstats.un.org; *Survey of Economic and Social Conditions in Africa 2005.*

The World Bank, 1818 H Street, NW, Washington, DC 20433, (202) 473-1000, Fax: (202) 477-6391, www.worldbank.org; *Africa Live Database (LDB); African Development Indicators (ADI) 2007; Global Development Finance 2007;* and *World Development Report 2008.*

ETHIOPIA - DEFENSE EXPENDITURES

See ETHIOPIA - ARMED FORCES

ETHIOPIA - DEMOGRAPHY

Euromonitor International, Inc., 224 S. Michigan Avenue, Suite 1500, Chicago, IL 60604, (312) 922-1115, Fax: (312) 922-1157, www.euromonitor.com; *International Marketing Data and Statistics 2008; The World Economic Factbook 2008;* and *World Marketing Data and Statistics.*

Population Reference Bureau, 1875 Connecticut Avenue, NW, Suite 520, Washington, DC, 20009-5728, (800) 877-9881, Fax: (202) 328-3937, www.prb.org; *Ethiopia Demographic and Health Survey, 2005.*

United Nations Statistics Division, New York, NY 10017, (800) 253-9646, Fax: (212) 963-4116, http://unstats.un.org; *Human Development Report 2006* and *Survey of Economic and Social Conditions in Africa 2005.*

The World Bank, 1818 H Street, NW, Washington, DC 20433, (202) 473-1000, Fax: (202) 477-6391, www.worldbank.org; *Ethiopia.*

ETHIOPIA - DISPOSABLE INCOME

United Nations Statistics Division, New York, NY 10017, (800) 253-9646, Fax: (212) 963-4116, http://unstats.un.org; *National Accounts Statistics: Compendium of Income Distribution Statistics* and *Statistical Yearbook.*

ETHIOPIA - DIVORCE

United Nations Statistics Division, New York, NY 10017, (800) 253-9646, Fax: (212) 963-4116, http://unstats.un.org; *Demographic Yearbook.*

ETHIOPIA - ECONOMIC ASSISTANCE

United Nations Statistics Division, New York, NY 10017, (800) 253-9646, Fax: (212) 963-4116, http://unstats.un.org; *Statistical Yearbook.*

ETHIOPIA - ECONOMIC CONDITIONS

African Development Bank Group, Rue Joseph Anoma, 01 BP 1387 Abidjan 01, Cote d'Ivoire, www.afdb.org; *The African Statistical Journal; Gender, Poverty and Environmental Indicators on African Countries 2007; Selected Statistics on African Countries 2007;* and *Statistics Pocketbook 2008.*

Center for International Business Education Research (CIBER), Columbia Business School and School of International and Public Affairs, Uris Hall, Room 212, 3022 Broadway, New York, NY 10027-6902, Mr. Joshua Safier, (212) 854-4750, Fax: (212) 222-9821, www.columbia.edu/cu/ciber/; Datastream International.

Central Intelligence Agency, Office of Public Affairs, Washington, DC 20505, (703) 482-0623, Fax: (703) 482-1739, www.cia.gov; *The World Factbook.*

DSI Data Service Information, Xantener Strasse 51a, D-47495 Rheinberg, Germany, www.dsidata.com; *Campus Solution.*

Dun and Bradstreet (DB) Corporation, 103 JFK Parkway, Short Hills, NJ 07078, (973) 921-5500, www.dnb.com; *Country Report.*

Economist Intelligence Unit, 111 West 57th Street, New York, NY 10019, (212) 554-0600, Fax: (212) 586-1181, www.eiu.com; *Business Africa* and *Ethiopia Country Report.*

Euromonitor International, Inc., 224 S. Michigan Avenue, Suite 1500, Chicago, IL 60604, (312) 922-1115, Fax: (312) 922-1157, www.euromonitor.com; *International Marketing Data and Statistics 2008; The World Economic Factbook 2008;* and *World Marketing Data and Statistics.*

International Monetary Fund (IMF), 700 Nineteenth Street, NW, Washington, DC 20431, (202) 623-7000, Fax: (202) 623-4661, www.imf.org; *World Economic Outlook Reports.*

Palgrave Macmillan Ltd., Houndmills, Basingstoke, Hampshire, RG21 6XS, England, (Telephone in U.S. (888) 330-8477), (Fax in U.S. (800) 672-2054), www.palgrave.com; *The Statesman's Yearbook 2008.*

Taylor and Francis Group, An Informa Business, 2 Park Square, Milton Park, Abingdon, Oxford OX14 4RN, United Kingdom, (Dial from U.S. (212) 216-7800), (Fax from U.S. (212) 564-7854), www.tandf.co.uk; *The Europa World Year Book.*

United Nations Statistics Division, New York, NY 10017, (800) 253-9646, Fax: (212) 963-4116, http://unstats.un.org; *Compendium of Intra-African and Related Foreign Trade Statistics 2003* and *World Statistics Pocketbook.*

The World Bank, 1818 H Street, NW, Washington, DC 20433, (202) 473-1000, Fax: (202) 477-6391, www.worldbank.org; *Africa Household Survey Databank; Africa Live Database (LDB); Africa Standardized Files and Indicators; African Development Indicators (ADI) 2007; Ethiopia; Global Economic Monitor (GEM); Global Economic Prospects 2008; The World Bank Atlas 2003-2004;* and *World Development Report 2008.*

ETHIOPIA - EDUCATION

African Development Bank Group, Rue Joseph Anoma, 01 BP 1387 Abidjan 01, Cote d'Ivoire, www.afdb.org; *Statistics Pocketbook 2008.*

Central Statistical Agency (CSA) of Ethiopia, PO Box 1143, Addis Ababa, Ethiopia, www:csa.gov.et; *Statistical Abstract of Ethiopia.*

Euromonitor International, Inc., 224 S. Michigan Avenue, Suite 1500, Chicago, IL 60604, (312) 922-1115, Fax: (312) 922-1157, www.euromonitor.com; *International Marketing Data and Statistics 2008* and *World Marketing Data and Statistics.*

International Monetary Fund (IMF), 700 Nineteenth Street, NW, Washington, DC 20431, (202) 623-7000, Fax: (202) 623-4661, www.imf.org; *Government Finance Statistics Yearbook (2008 Edition).*

Taylor and Francis Group, An Informa Business, 2 Park Square, Milton Park, Abingdon, Oxford OX14 4RN, United Kingdom, (Dial from U.S. (212) 216-

7800), (Fax from U.S. (212) 564-7854), www.tandf.co.uk; *The Europa World Year Book.*

UNESCO Institute for Statistics, C.P. 6128 Succursale Centre-Ville, Montreal, Quebec, H3C 3J7 Canada, (Dial from U.S. (514) 343-6880), (Fax from U.S. (514) 343 6882), www.uis.unesco.org; *Statistical Tables.*

United Nations Economic Commission for Africa (ECA), PO Box 3001, Addis Ababa, Ethiopia, (Telephone in U.S. (212) 963-4957), www.uneca.org; *African Statistical Yearbook 2006.*

United Nations Statistics Division, New York, NY 10017, (800) 253-9646, Fax: (212) 963-4116, http://unstats.un.org; *Human Development Report 2006* and *Survey of Economic and Social Conditions in Africa 2005.*

The World Bank, 1818 H Street, NW, Washington, DC 20433, (202) 473-1000, Fax: (202) 477-6391, www.worldbank.org; *Ethiopia* and *World Development Report 2008.*

ETHIOPIA - ELECTRICITY

Palgrave Macmillan Ltd., Houndmills, Basingstoke, Hampshire, RG21 6XS, England, (Telephone in U.S. (888) 330-8477), (Fax in U.S. (800) 672-2054), www.palgrave.com; *The Statesman's Yearbook 2008.*

United Nations Economic Commission for Africa (ECA), PO Box 3001, Addis Ababa, Ethiopia, (Telephone in U.S. (212) 963-4957), www.uneca.org; *African Statistical Yearbook 2006.*

United Nations Statistics Division, New York, NY 10017, (800) 253-9646, Fax: (212) 963-4116, http://unstats.un.org; *Human Development Report 2006; Statistical Yearbook;* and *Survey of Economic and Social Conditions in Africa 2005.*

ETHIOPIA - EMPLOYMENT

Euromonitor International, Inc., 224 S. Michigan Avenue, Suite 1500, Chicago, IL 60604, (312) 922-1115, Fax: (312) 922-1157, www.euromonitor.com; *International Marketing Data and Statistics 2008.*

International Labour Office, I.L.O. Publications, 4 route des Morillons, CH-1211 Geneva 22, Switzerland, (Telephone in U.S. (202) 653-7652), (Fax in U.S. (202) 653-7687), www.ilo.org; *Yearbook of Labour Statistics 2006.*

U.S. Department of Energy (DOE), Energy Information Administration (EIA), 1000 Independence Avenue, SW, Washington, DC 20585, (202) 586-8800, www.eia.doe.gov; *International Energy Annual 2004* and *International Energy Outlook 2006.*

United Nations Economic Commission for Africa (ECA), PO Box 3001, Addis Ababa, Ethiopia, (Telephone in U.S. (212) 963-4957), www.uneca.org; *African Statistical Yearbook 2006.*

United Nations Statistics Division, New York, NY 10017, (800) 253-9646, Fax: (212) 963-4116, http://unstats.un.org; *Statistical Yearbook* and *Survey of Economic and Social Conditions in Africa 2005.*

The World Bank, 1818 H Street, NW, Washington, DC 20433, (202) 473-1000, Fax: (202) 477-6391, www.worldbank.org; *Ethiopia.*

ETHIOPIA - ENERGY INDUSTRIES

Enerdata, 10 Rue Royale, 75008 Paris, France, www.enerdata.fr; *Global Energy Market Data.*

United Nations Statistics Division, New York, NY 10017, (800) 253-9646, Fax: (212) 963-4116, http://unstats.un.org; *Statistical Yearbook.*

ETHIOPIA - ENVIRONMENTAL CONDITIONS

DSI Data Service Information, Xantener Strasse 51a, D-47495 Rheinberg, Germany, www.dsidata.com; *Campus Solution* and *DSI's Global Environmental Database.*

Economist Intelligence Unit, 111 West 57th Street, New York, NY 10019, (212) 554-0600, Fax: (212) 586-1181, www.eiu.com; *Ethiopia Country Report.*

International Institute for Environment and Development (IIED), 3 Endsleigh Street, London, England, WC1H 0DD, United Kingdom, www.iied.org; *Environment Urbanization* and *Haramata - Bulletin of the Drylands.*

United Nations Statistics Division, New York, NY 10017, (800) 253-9646, Fax: (212) 963-4116, http://unstats.un.org; *World Statistics Pocketbook.*

ETHIOPIA - EXPORTS

African Development Bank Group, Rue Joseph Anoma, 01 BP 1387 Abidjan 01, Cote d'Ivoire, www.afdb.org; *Statistics Pocketbook 2008.*

Central Intelligence Agency, Office of Public Affairs, Washington, DC 20505, (703) 482-0623, Fax: (703) 482-1739, www.cia.gov; *The World Factbook.*

Economist Intelligence Unit, 111 West 57th Street, New York, NY 10019, (212) 554-0600, Fax: (212) 586-1181, www.eiu.com; *Ethiopia Country Report.*

Euromonitor International, Inc., 224 S. Michigan Avenue, Suite 1500, Chicago, IL 60604, (312) 922-1115, Fax: (312) 922-1157, www.euromonitor.com; *International Marketing Data and Statistics 2008* and *The World Economic Factbook 2008.*

International Monetary Fund (IMF), 700 Nineteenth Street, NW, Washington, DC 20431, (202) 623-7000, Fax: (202) 623-4661, www.imf.org; *Direction of Trade Statistics Yearbook 2007; Government Finance Statistics Yearbook (2008 Edition);* and *International Financial Statistics Yearbook 2007.*

Palgrave Macmillan Ltd., Houndmills, Basingstoke, Hampshire, RG21 6XS, England, (Telephone in U.S. (888) 330-8477), (Fax in U.S. (800) 672-2054), www.palgrave.com; *The Statesman's Yearbook 2008.*

Taylor and Francis Group, An Informa Business, 2 Park Square, Milton Park, Abingdon, Oxford OX14 4RN, United Kingdom, (Dial from U.S. (212) 216-7800), (Fax from U.S. (212) 564-7854), www.tandf.co.uk; *The Europa World Year Book.*

United Nations Economic Commission for Africa (ECA), PO Box 3001, Addis Ababa, Ethiopia, (Telephone in U.S. (212) 963-4957), www.uneca.org; *African Statistical Yearbook 2006.*

United Nations Food and Agricultural Organization (FAO), Viale delle Terme di Caracalla, 00100 Rome, Italy, (Dial from U.S. (202) 653-2400), (Fax from U.S. (202) 653 5760), www.fao.org; *The State of Food and Agriculture (SOFA) 2006.*

United Nations Statistics Division, New York, NY 10017, (800) 253-9646, Fax: (212) 963-4116, http://unstats.un.org; *Compendium of Intra-African and Related Foreign Trade Statistics 2003* and *Survey of Economic and Social Conditions in Africa 2005.*

The World Bank, 1818 H Street, NW, Washington, DC 20433, (202) 473-1000, Fax: (202) 477-6391, www.worldbank.org; *World Development Report 2008.*

ETHIOPIA - FEMALE WORKING POPULATION

See ETHIOPIA - EMPLOYMENT

ETHIOPIA - FERTILITY, HUMAN

Central Intelligence Agency, Office of Public Affairs, Washington, DC 20505, (703) 482-0623, Fax: (703) 482-1739, www.cia.gov; *The World Factbook.*

United Nations Statistics Division, New York, NY 10017, (800) 253-9646, Fax: (212) 963-4116, http://unstats.un.org; *Human Development Report 2006* and *Survey of Economic and Social Conditions in Africa 2005.*

The World Bank, 1818 H Street, NW, Washington, DC 20433, (202) 473-1000, Fax: (202) 477-6391, www.worldbank.org; *The World Bank Atlas 2003-2004* and *World Development Report 2008.*

ETHIOPIA - FERTILIZER INDUSTRY

United Nations Food and Agricultural Organization (FAO), Viale delle Terme di Caracalla, 00100 Rome, Italy, (Dial from U.S. (202) 653-2400), (Fax from U.S. (202) 653 5760), www.fao.org; *FAO Fertilizer Yearbook* and *The State of Food and Agriculture (SOFA) 2006.*

United Nations Statistics Division, New York, NY 10017, (800) 253-9646, Fax: (212) 963-4116, http://unstats.un.org; *Statistical Yearbook.*

ETHIOPIA - FETAL MORTALITY

See ETHIOPIA - MORTALITY

ETHIOPIA - FINANCE

Central Statistical Agency (CSA) of Ethiopia, PO Box 1143, Addis Ababa, Ethiopia, www.csa.gov.et; *Statistical Abstract of Ethiopia.*

International Monetary Fund (IMF), 700 Nineteenth Street, NW, Washington, DC 20431, (202) 623-7000, Fax: (202) 623-4661, www.imf.org; *International Financial Statistics Yearbook 2007.*

Taylor and Francis Group, An Informa Business, 2 Park Square, Milton Park, Abingdon, Oxford OX14 4RN, United Kingdom, (Dial from U.S. (212) 216-7800), (Fax from U.S. (212) 564-7854), www.tandf.co.uk; *The Europa World Year Book.*

United Nations Economic Commission for Africa (ECA), PO Box 3001, Addis Ababa, Ethiopia, (Telephone in U.S. (212) 963-4957), www.uneca.org; *African Statistical Yearbook 2006.*

United Nations Statistics Division, New York, NY 10017, (800) 253-9646, Fax: (212) 963-4116, http://unstats.un.org; *National Accounts Statistics: Compendium of Income Distribution Statistics* and *Statistical Yearbook.*

The World Bank, 1818 H Street, NW, Washington, DC 20433, (202) 473-1000, Fax: (202) 477-6391, www.worldbank.org; *Ethiopia.*

ETHIOPIA - FINANCE, PUBLIC

African Development Bank Group, Rue Joseph Anoma, 01 BP 1387 Abidjan 01, Cote d'Ivoire, www.afdb.org; *Statistics Pocketbook 2008.*

Bernan Essential Government Publications, 4611-F Assembly Drive, Lanham MD, 20706-4391, (301) 459-2255, Fax: (800) 865-3450, www.bernan.com; *National Accounts Statistics.*

Central Statistical Agency (CSA) of Ethiopia, PO Box 1143, Addis Ababa, Ethiopia, www.csa.gov.et; *Statistical Abstract of Ethiopia.*

Economist Intelligence Unit, 111 West 57th Street, New York, NY 10019, (212) 554-0600, Fax: (212) 586-1181, www.eiu.com; *Ethiopia Country Report.*

International Monetary Fund (IMF), 700 Nineteenth Street, NW, Washington, DC 20431, (202) 623-7000, Fax: (202) 623-4661, www.imf.org; *Government Finance Statistics Yearbook (2008 Edition); International Financial Statistics; International Financial Statistics Online Service;* and *International Financial Statistics Yearbook 2007.*

Palgrave Macmillan Ltd., Houndmills, Basingstoke, Hampshire, RG21 6XS, England, (Telephone in U.S. (888) 330-8477), (Fax in U.S. (800) 672-2054), www.palgrave.com; *The Statesman's Yearbook 2008.*

Taylor and Francis Group, An Informa Business, 2 Park Square, Milton Park, Abingdon, Oxford OX14 4RN, United Kingdom, (Dial from U.S. (212) 216-7800), (Fax from U.S. (212) 564-7854), www.tandf.co.uk; *The Europa World Year Book.*

United Nations Economic Commission for Africa (ECA), PO Box 3001, Addis Ababa, Ethiopia, (Telephone in U.S. (212) 963-4957), www.uneca.org; *African Statistical Yearbook 2006.*

The World Bank, 1818 H Street, NW, Washington, DC 20433, (202) 473-1000, Fax: (202) 477-6391, www.worldbank.org; *Ethiopia.*

ETHIOPIA - FISHERIES

Taylor and Francis Group, An Informa Business, 2 Park Square, Milton Park, Abingdon, Oxford OX14 4RN, United Kingdom, (Dial from U.S. (212) 216-7800), (Fax from U.S. (212) 564-7854), www.tandf.co.uk; *The Europa World Year Book.*

United Nations Conference on Trade and Development (UNCTAD), DC2-1120, United Nations, New

York, NY 10017, (212) 963-0027, www.unctad.org; *UNCTAD Commodity Yearbook.*

United Nations Economic Commission for Africa (ECA), PO Box 3001, Addis Ababa, Ethiopia, (Telephone in U.S. (212) 963-4957), www.uneca.org; *African Statistical Yearbook 2006.*

United Nations Food and Agricultural Organization (FAO), Viale delle Terme di Caracalla, 00100 Rome, Italy, (Dial from U.S. (202) 653-2400), (Fax from U.S. (202) 653 5760), www.fao.org; *FAO Yearbook of Fishery Statistics;* Fishery Databases; FISHSTAT Database. Subjects covered include: Aquaculture production, capture production, fishery commodities; and *The State of Food and Agriculture (SOFA) 2006.*

United Nations Statistics Division, New York, NY 10017, (800) 253-9646, Fax: (212) 963-4116, http://unstats.un.org; *Statistical Yearbook* and *Survey of Economic and Social Conditions in Africa 2005.*

The World Bank, 1818 H Street, NW, Washington, DC 20433, (202) 473-1000, Fax: (202) 477-6391, www.worldbank.org; *Ethiopia.*

ETHIOPIA - FLOUR INDUSTRY

United Nations Statistics Division, New York, NY 10017, (800) 253-9646, Fax: (212) 963-4116, http://unstats.un.org; *Statistical Yearbook.*

ETHIOPIA - FOOD

African Development Bank Group, Rue Joseph Anoma, 01 BP 1387 Abidjan 01, Cote d'Ivoire, www.afdb.org; *Statistics Pocketbook 2008.*

United Nations Conference on Trade and Development (UNCTAD), DC2-1120, United Nations, New York, NY 10017, (212) 963-0027, www.unctad.org; *UNCTAD Commodity Yearbook.*

United Nations Food and Agricultural Organization (FAO), Viale delle Terme di Caracalla, 00100 Rome, Italy, (Dial from U.S. (202) 653-2400), (Fax from U.S. (202) 653 5760), www.fao.org; *FAO Production Yearbook 2002* and *The State of Food and Agriculture (SOFA) 2006.*

United Nations Statistics Division, New York, NY 10017, (800) 253-9646, Fax: (212) 963-4116, http://unstats.un.org; *Human Development Report 2006.*

ETHIOPIA - FOREIGN EXCHANGE RATES

African Development Bank Group, Rue Joseph Anoma, 01 BP 1387 Abidjan 01, Cote d'Ivoire, www.afdb.org; *Statistics Pocketbook 2008.*

Central Intelligence Agency, Office of Public Affairs, Washington, DC 20505, (703) 482-0623, Fax: (703) 482-1739, www.cia.gov; *The World Factbook.*

Euromonitor International, Inc., 224 S. Michigan Avenue, Suite 1500, Chicago, IL 60604, (312) 922-1115, Fax: (312) 922-1157, www.euromonitor.com; *International Marketing Data and Statistics 2008* and *The World Economic Factbook 2008.*

International Civil Aviation Organization (ICAO), External Relations and Public Information Office (EPO), 999 University Street, Montreal, Quebec H3C 5H7, Canada, (Dial from U.S. (514) 954-8219), (Fax from U.S. (514) 954-6077), www.icao.int; *Civil Aviation Statistics of the World.*

International Monetary Fund (IMF), 700 Nineteenth Street, NW, Washington, DC 20431, (202) 623-7000, Fax: (202) 623-4661, www.imf.org; *International Financial Statistics Yearbook 2007.*

Taylor and Francis Group, An Informa Business, 2 Park Square, Milton Park, Abingdon, Oxford OX14 4RN, United Kingdom, (Dial from U.S. (212) 216-7800), (Fax from U.S. (212) 564-7854), www.tandf.co.uk; *The Europa World Year Book.*

United Nations Statistics Division, New York, NY 10017, (800) 253-9646, Fax: (212) 963-4116, http://unstats.un.org; *Compendium of Intra-African and Related Foreign Trade Statistics 2003; Statistical Yearbook;* and *World Statistics Pocketbook.*

ETHIOPIA - FORESTS AND FORESTRY

Palgrave Macmillan Ltd., Houndmills, Basingstoke, Hampshire, RG21 6XS, England, (Telephone in U.S. (888) 330-8477), (Fax in U.S. (800) 672-2054), www.palgrave.com; *The Statesman's Yearbook 2008.*

Taylor and Francis Group, An Informa Business, 2 Park Square, Milton Park, Abingdon, Oxford OX14 4RN, United Kingdom, (Dial from U.S. (212) 216-7800), (Fax from U.S. (212) 564-7854), www.tandf.co.uk; *The Europa World Year Book.*

UNESCO Institute for Statistics, C.P. 6128 Succursale Centre-Ville, Montreal, Quebec, H3C 3J7 Canada, (Dial from U.S. (514) 343-6880), (Fax from U.S. (514) 343 6882), www.uis.unesco.org; *Statistical Tables.*

United Nations Conference on Trade and Development (UNCTAD), DC2-1120, United Nations, New York, NY 10017, (212) 963-0027, www.unctad.org; *UNCTAD Commodity Yearbook.*

United Nations Economic Commission for Africa (ECA), PO Box 3001, Addis Ababa, Ethiopia, (Telephone in U.S. (212) 963-4957), www.uneca.org; *African Statistical Yearbook 2006.*

United Nations Food and Agricultural Organization (FAO), Viale delle Terme di Caracalla, 00100 Rome, Italy, (Dial from U.S. (202) 653-2400), (Fax from U.S. (202) 653 5760), www.fao.org; *FAO Yearbook of Forest Products* and *The State of Food and Agriculture (SOFA) 2006.*

United Nations Statistics Division, New York, NY 10017, (800) 253-9646, Fax: (212) 963-4116, http://unstats.un.org; *Statistical Yearbook.*

The World Bank, 1818 H Street, NW, Washington, DC 20433, (202) 473-1000, Fax: (202) 477-6391, www.worldbank.org; *Ethiopia* and *World Development Report 2008.*

ETHIOPIA - GEOGRAPHIC INFORMATION SYSTEMS

The World Bank, 1818 H Street, NW, Washington, DC 20433, (202) 473-1000, Fax: (202) 477-6391, www.worldbank.org; *Ethiopia.*

ETHIOPIA - GOLD INDUSTRY

International Monetary Fund (IMF), 700 Nineteenth Street, NW, Washington, DC 20431, (202) 623-7000, Fax: (202) 623-4661, www.imf.org; *International Financial Statistics Yearbook 2007.*

United Nations Statistics Division, New York, NY 10017, (800) 253-9646, Fax: (212) 963-4116, http://unstats.un.org; *Statistical Yearbook.*

ETHIOPIA - GOLD PRODUCTION

See ETHIOPIA - MINERAL INDUSTRIES

ETHIOPIA - GRANTS-IN-AID

International Monetary Fund (IMF), 700 Nineteenth Street, NW, Washington, DC 20431, (202) 623-7000, Fax: (202) 623-4661, www.imf.org; *Government Finance Statistics Yearbook (2008 Edition).*

ETHIOPIA - GROSS DOMESTIC PRODUCT

African Development Bank Group, Rue Joseph Anoma, 01 BP 1387 Abidjan 01, Cote d'Ivoire, www.afdb.org; *Statistics Pocketbook 2008.*

Economist Intelligence Unit, 111 West 57th Street, New York, NY 10019, (212) 554-0600, Fax: (212) 586-1181, www.eiu.com; *Ethiopia Country Report.*

Euromonitor International, Inc., 224 S. Michigan Avenue, Suite 1500, Chicago, IL 60604, (312) 922-1115, Fax: (312) 922-1157, www.euromonitor.com; *International Marketing Data and Statistics 2008* and *The World Economic Factbook 2008.*

Taylor and Francis Group, An Informa Business, 2 Park Square, Milton Park, Abingdon, Oxford OX14 4RN, United Kingdom, (Dial from U.S. (212) 216-7800), (Fax from U.S. (212) 564-7854), www.tandf.co.uk; *The Europa World Year Book.*

United Nations Economic Commission for Africa (ECA), PO Box 3001, Addis Ababa, Ethiopia, (Telephone in U.S. (212) 963-4957), www.uneca.org; *African Statistical Yearbook 2006.*

United Nations Statistics Division, New York, NY 10017, (800) 253-9646, Fax: (212) 963-4116, http://unstats.un.org; *Human Development Report 2006; National Accounts Statistics: Compendium of Income Distribution Statistics; Statistical Yearbook;* and *Survey of Economic and Social Conditions in Africa 2005.*

The World Bank, 1818 H Street, NW, Washington, DC 20433, (202) 473-1000, Fax: (202) 477-6391, www.worldbank.org; *World Development Report 2008.*

ETHIOPIA - GROSS NATIONAL PRODUCT

Euromonitor International, Inc., 224 S. Michigan Avenue, Suite 1500, Chicago, IL 60604, (312) 922-1115, Fax: (312) 922-1157, www.euromonitor.com; *International Marketing Data and Statistics 2008.*

Palgrave Macmillan Ltd., Houndmills, Basingstoke, Hampshire, RG21 6XS, England, (Telephone in U.S. (888) 330-8477), (Fax in U.S. (800) 672-2054), www.palgrave.com; *The Statesman's Yearbook 2008.*

U.S. Department of State (DOS), 2201 C Street NW, Washington, DC 20520, (202) 647-4000, www.state.gov; *World Military Expenditures and Arms Transfers (WMEAT).*

United Nations Statistics Division, New York, NY 10017, (800) 253-9646, Fax: (212) 963-4116, http://unstats.un.org; *Statistical Yearbook.*

The World Bank, 1818 H Street, NW, Washington, DC 20433, (202) 473-1000, Fax: (202) 477-6391, www.worldbank.org; *The World Bank Atlas 2003-2004* and *World Development Report 2008.*

ETHIOPIA - HIDES AND SKINS INDUSTRY

International Monetary Fund (IMF), 700 Nineteenth Street, NW, Washington, DC 20431, (202) 623-7000, Fax: (202) 623-4661, www.imf.org; *International Financial Statistics Yearbook 2007.*

United Nations Food and Agricultural Organization (FAO), Viale delle Terme di Caracalla, 00100 Rome, Italy, (Dial from U.S. (202) 653-2400), (Fax from U.S. (202) 653 5760), www.fao.org; *FAO Production Yearbook 2002.*

ETHIOPIA - HONEY PRODUCTION

See ETHIOPIA - CROPS

ETHIOPIA - HOUSING

Euromonitor International, Inc., 224 S. Michigan Avenue, Suite 1500, Chicago, IL 60604, (312) 922-1115, Fax: (312) 922-1157, www.euromonitor.com; *World Marketing Data and Statistics.*

ETHIOPIA - ILLITERATE PERSONS

Euromonitor International, Inc., 224 S. Michigan Avenue, Suite 1500, Chicago, IL 60604, (312) 922-1115, Fax: (312) 922-1157, www.euromonitor.com; *The World Economic Factbook 2008.*

Palgrave Macmillan Ltd., Houndmills, Basingstoke, Hampshire, RG21 6XS, England, (Telephone in U.S. (888) 330-8477), (Fax in U.S. (800) 672-2054), www.palgrave.com; *The Statesman's Yearbook 2008.*

UNESCO Institute for Statistics, C.P. 6128 Succursale Centre-Ville, Montreal, Quebec, H3C 3J7 Canada, (Dial from U.S. (514) 343-6880), (Fax from U.S. (514) 343 6882), www.uis.unesco.org; *Statistical Tables.*

United Nations Statistics Division, New York, NY 10017, (800) 253-9646, Fax: (212) 963-4116, http://unstats.un.org; *Human Development Report 2006.*

ETHIOPIA - IMPORTS

Central Intelligence Agency, Office of Public Affairs, Washington, DC 20505, (703) 482-0623, Fax: (703) 482-1739, www.cia.gov; *The World Factbook.*

Economist Intelligence Unit, 111 West 57th Street, New York, NY 10019, (212) 554-0600, Fax: (212) 586-1181, www.eiu.com; *Ethiopia Country Report.*

Euromonitor International, Inc., 224 S. Michigan Avenue, Suite 1500, Chicago, IL 60604, (312) 922-

1115, Fax: (312) 922-1157, www.euromonitor.com; *International Marketing Data and Statistics 2008* and *The World Economic Factbook 2008.*

International Monetary Fund (IMF), 700 Nineteenth Street, NW, Washington, DC 20431, (202) 623-7000, Fax: (202) 623-4661, www.imf.org; *Direction of Trade Statistics Yearbook 2007; Government Finance Statistics Yearbook (2008 Edition);* and *International Financial Statistics Yearbook 2007.*

Palgrave Macmillan Ltd., Houndmills, Basingstoke, Hampshire, RG21 6XS, England, (Telephone in U.S. (888) 330-8477), (Fax in U.S. (800) 672-2054), www.palgrave.com; *The Statesman's Yearbook 2008.*

Taylor and Francis Group, An Informa Business, 2 Park Square, Milton Park, Abingdon, Oxford OX14 4RN, United Kingdom, (Dial from U.S. (212) 216-7800), (Fax from U.S. (212) 564-7854), www.tandf.co.uk; *The Europa World Year Book.*

United Nations Economic Commission for Africa (ECA), PO Box 3001, Addis Ababa, Ethiopia, (Telephone in U.S. (212) 963-4957), www.uneca.org; *African Statistical Yearbook 2006.*

United Nations Food and Agricultural Organization (FAO), Viale delle Terme di Caracalla, 00100 Rome, Italy, (Dial from U.S. (202) 653-2400), (Fax from U.S. (202) 653 5760), www.fao.org; *The State of Food and Agriculture (SOFA) 2006.*

United Nations Statistics Division, New York, NY 10017, (800) 253-9646, Fax: (212) 963-4116, http://unstats.un.org; *Compendium of Intra-African and Related Foreign Trade Statistics 2003* and *Survey of Economic and Social Conditions in Africa 2005.*

The World Bank, 1818 H Street, NW, Washington, DC 20433, (202) 473-1000, Fax: (202) 477-6391, www.worldbank.org; *World Development Report 2008.*

ETHIOPIA - INCOME TAXES

See ETHIOPIA - TAXATION

ETHIOPIA - INDUSTRIAL PRODUCTIVITY

Euromonitor International, Inc., 224 S. Michigan Avenue, Suite 1500, Chicago, IL 60604, (312) 922-1115, Fax: (312) 922-1157, www.euromonitor.com; *International Marketing Data and Statistics 2008.*

ETHIOPIA - INDUSTRIAL PROPERTY

United Nations Statistics Division, New York, NY 10017, (800) 253-9646, Fax: (212) 963-4116, http://unstats.un.org; *Statistical Yearbook.*

ETHIOPIA - INDUSTRIES

Central Intelligence Agency, Office of Public Affairs, Washington, DC 20505, (703) 482-0623, Fax: (703) 482-1739, www.cia.gov; *The World Factbook.*

Economist Intelligence Unit, 111 West 57th Street, New York, NY 10019, (212) 554-0600, Fax: (212) 586-1181, www.eiu.com; *Ethiopia Country Report.*

Euromonitor International, Inc., 224 S. Michigan Avenue, Suite 1500, Chicago, IL 60604, (312) 922-1115, Fax: (312) 922-1157, www.euromonitor.com; *International Marketing Data and Statistics 2008; The World Economic Factbook 2008;* and *World Marketing Data and Statistics.*

International Labour Office, I.L.O. Publications, 4 route des Morillons, CH-1211 Geneva 22, Switzerland, (Telephone in U.S. (202) 653-7652), (Fax in U.S. (202) 653-7687), www.ilo.org; *Yearbook of Labour Statistics 2006.*

Palgrave Macmillan Ltd., Houndmills, Basingstoke, Hampshire, RG21 6XS, England, (Telephone in U.S. (888) 330-8477), (Fax in U.S. (800) 672-2054), www.palgrave.com; *The Statesman's Yearbook 2008.*

Taylor and Francis Group, An Informa Business, 2 Park Square, Milton Park, Abingdon, Oxford OX14 4RN, United Kingdom, (Dial from U.S. (212) 216-7800), (Fax from U.S. (212) 564-7854), www.tandf.co.uk; *The Europa World Year Book.*

United Nations Economic Commission for Africa (ECA), PO Box 3001, Addis Ababa, Ethiopia, (Telephone in U.S. (212) 963-4957), www.uneca.org; *African Statistical Yearbook 2006.*

United Nations Industrial Development Organization (UNIDO), 1 United Nations Plaza, New York, NY 10017, (212) 963 6890, Fax: (212) 963-7904, http://unido.org; Industrial Statistics Database 2008 (INDSTAT) and *The International Yearbook of Industrial Statistics 2008.*

United Nations Statistics Division, New York, NY 10017, (800) 253-9646, Fax: (212) 963-4116, http://unstats.un.org; *2004 Industrial Commodity Statistics Yearbook* and *Survey of Economic and Social Conditions in Africa 2005.*

The World Bank, 1818 H Street, NW, Washington, DC 20433, (202) 473-1000, Fax: (202) 477-6391, www.worldbank.org; *Ethiopia.*

ETHIOPIA - INFANT AND MATERNAL MORTALITY

See ETHIOPIA - MORTALITY

ETHIOPIA - INSURANCE

Central Statistical Agency (CSA) of Ethiopia, PO Box 1143, Addis Ababa, Ethiopia, www.csa.gov.et; *Statistical Abstract of Ethiopia.*

ETHIOPIA - INTERNATIONAL LIQUIDITY

International Monetary Fund (IMF), 700 Nineteenth Street, NW, Washington, DC 20431, (202) 623-7000, Fax: (202) 623-4661, www.imf.org; *International Financial Statistics Yearbook 2007.*

ETHIOPIA - INTERNATIONAL TRADE

African Development Bank Group, Rue Joseph Anoma, 01 BP 1387 Abidjan 01, Cote d'Ivoire, www.afdb.org; *Statistics Pocketbook 2008.*

Central Statistical Agency (CSA) of Ethiopia, PO Box 1143, Addis Ababa, Ethiopia, www.csa.gov.et; *Statistical Abstract of Ethiopia.*

Economist Intelligence Unit, 111 West 57th Street, New York, NY 10019, (212) 554-0600, Fax: (212) 586-1181, www.eiu.com; *Ethiopia Country Report.*

Euromonitor International, Inc., 224 S. Michigan Avenue, Suite 1500, Chicago, IL 60604, (312) 922-1115, Fax: (312) 922-1157, www.euromonitor.com; *International Marketing Data and Statistics 2008; The World Economic Factbook 2008;* and *World Marketing Data and Statistics.*

International Monetary Fund (IMF), 700 Nineteenth Street, NW, Washington, DC 20431, (202) 623-7000, Fax: (202) 623-4661, www.imf.org; *International Financial Statistics Yearbook 2007.*

Organisation for Economic Cooperation and Development (OECD), 2 rue Andre Pascal, F-75775 Paris Cedex 16, France, (Telephone in U.S. (202) 785-6323), (Fax in U.S. (202) 785-0350), www.oecd.org; *International Trade by Commodity Statistics (ITCS).*

Palgrave Macmillan Ltd., Houndmills, Basingstoke, Hampshire, RG21 6XS, England, (Telephone in U.S. (888) 330-8477), (Fax in U.S. (800) 672-2054), www.palgrave.com; *The Statesman's Yearbook 2008.*

Taylor and Francis Group, An Informa Business, 2 Park Square, Milton Park, Abingdon, Oxford OX14 4RN, United Kingdom, (Dial from U.S. (212) 216-7800), (Fax from U.S. (212) 564-7854), www.tandf.co.uk; *The Europa World Year Book.*

United Nations Conference on Trade and Development (UNCTAD), DC2-1120, United Nations, New York, NY 10017, (212) 963-0027, www.unctad.org; *UNCTAD Commodity Yearbook.*

United Nations Economic Commission for Africa (ECA), PO Box 3001, Addis Ababa, Ethiopia, (Telephone in U.S. (212) 963-4957), www.uneca.org; *African Statistical Yearbook 2006.*

United Nations Food and Agricultural Organization (FAO), Viale delle Terme di Caracalla, 00100 Rome, Italy, (Dial from U.S. (202) 653-2400), (Fax from U.S. (202) 653 5760), www.fao.org; *FAO Trade Yearbook* and *The State of Food and Agriculture (SOFA) 2006.*

United Nations Statistics Division, New York, NY 10017, (800) 253-9646, Fax: (212) 963-4116, http://unstats.un.org; *Compendium of Intra-African and Related Foreign Trade Statistics 2003; International Trade Statistics Yearbook;* and *Statistical Yearbook.*

The World Bank, 1818 H Street, NW, Washington, DC 20433, (202) 473-1000, Fax: (202) 477-6391, www.worldbank.org; *Ethiopia* and *World Development Report 2008.*

World Trade Organization (WTO), Centre William Rappard, Rue de Lausanne 154, CH-1211 Geneva 21, Switzerland, www.wto.org; *International Trade Statistics 2006.*

ETHIOPIA - INTERNET USERS

International Telecommunication Union (ITU), Place des Nations, 1211 Geneva 20, Switzerland, www.itu.int; *World Telecommunication/ICT Indicators Database on CD-ROM; World Telecommunication/ICT Indicators Database Online;* and *Yearbook of Statistics - Telecommunication Services (Chronological Time Series 1997-2006).*

The World Bank, 1818 H Street, NW, Washington, DC 20433, (202) 473-1000, Fax: (202) 477-6391, www.worldbank.org; *Ethiopia.*

ETHIOPIA - INVESTMENTS

International Monetary Fund (IMF), 700 Nineteenth Street, NW, Washington, DC 20431, (202) 623-7000, Fax: (202) 623-4661, www.imf.org; *International Financial Statistics Yearbook 2007.*

ETHIOPIA - IRRIGATION

Euromonitor International, Inc., 224 S. Michigan Avenue, Suite 1500, Chicago, IL 60604, (312) 922-1115, Fax: (312) 922-1157, www.euromonitor.com; *International Marketing Data and Statistics 2008.*

ETHIOPIA - LABOR

African Development Bank Group, Rue Joseph Anoma, 01 BP 1387 Abidjan 01, Cote d'Ivoire, www.afdb.org; *Statistics Pocketbook 2008.*

Central Intelligence Agency, Office of Public Affairs, Washington, DC 20505, (703) 482-0623, Fax: (703) 482-1739, www.cia.gov; *The World Factbook.*

Euromonitor International, Inc., 224 S. Michigan Avenue, Suite 1500, Chicago, IL 60604, (312) 922-1115, Fax: (312) 922-1157, www.euromonitor.com; *International Marketing Data and Statistics 2008* and *World Marketing Data and Statistics.*

International Labour Office, I.L.O. Publications, 4 route des Morillons, CH-1211 Geneva 22, Switzerland, (Telephone in U.S. (202) 653-7652), (Fax in U.S. (202) 653-7687), www.ilo.org; *Yearbook of Labour Statistics 2006.*

Taylor and Francis Group, An Informa Business, 2 Park Square, Milton Park, Abingdon, Oxford OX14 4RN, United Kingdom, (Dial from U.S. (212) 216-7800), (Fax from U.S. (212) 564-7854), www.tandf.co.uk; *The Europa World Year Book.*

United Nations Food and Agricultural Organization (FAO), Viale delle Terme di Caracalla, 00100 Rome, Italy, (Dial from U.S. (202) 653-2400), (Fax from U.S. (202) 653 5760), www.fao.org; *The State of Food and Agriculture (SOFA) 2006.*

United Nations Statistics Division, New York, NY 10017, (800) 253-9646, Fax: (212) 963-4116, http://unstats.un.org; *Human Development Report 2006.*

The World Bank, 1818 H Street, NW, Washington, DC 20433, (202) 473-1000, Fax: (202) 477-6391, www.worldbank.org; *The World Bank Atlas 2003-2004* and *World Development Report 2008.*

ETHIOPIA - LAND USE

Central Intelligence Agency, Office of Public Affairs, Washington, DC 20505, (703) 482-0623, Fax: (703) 482-1739, www.cia.gov; *The World Factbook.*

Euromonitor International, Inc., 224 S. Michigan Avenue, Suite 1500, Chicago, IL 60604, (312) 922-1115, Fax: (312) 922-1157, www.euromonitor.com; *International Marketing Data and Statistics 2008.*

United Nations Food and Agricultural Organization (FAO), Viale delle Terme di Caracalla, 00100 Rome, Italy, (Dial from U.S. (202) 653-2400), (Fax from U.S. (202) 653 5760), www.fao.org; *FAO Production Yearbook 2002.*

The World Bank, 1818 H Street, NW, Washington, DC 20433, (202) 473-1000, Fax: (202) 477-6391, www.worldbank.org; *World Development Report 2008.*

ETHIOPIA - LIBRARIES

UNESCO Institute for Statistics, C.P. 6128 Succursale Centre-Ville, Montreal, Quebec, H3C 3J7 Canada, (Dial from U.S. (514) 343-6880), (Fax from U.S. (514) 343 6882), www.uis.unesco.org; *Statistical Tables.*

ETHIOPIA - LICENSES

International Monetary Fund (IMF), 700 Nineteenth Street, NW, Washington, DC 20431, (202) 623-7000, Fax: (202) 623-4661, www.imf.org; *Government Finance Statistics Yearbook (2008 Edition).*

ETHIOPIA - LIFE EXPECTANCY

African Development Bank Group, Rue Joseph Anoma, 01 BP 1387 Abidjan 01, Cote d'Ivoire, www.afdb.org; *Statistics Pocketbook 2008.*

Central Intelligence Agency, Office of Public Affairs, Washington, DC 20505, (703) 482-0623, Fax: (703) 482-1739, www.cia.gov; *The World Factbook.*

Euromonitor International, Inc., 224 S. Michigan Avenue, Suite 1500, Chicago, IL 60604, (312) 922-1115, Fax: (312) 922-1157, www.euromonitor.com; *The World Economic Factbook 2008.*

Palgrave Macmillan Ltd., Houndmills, Basingstoke, Hampshire, RG21 6XS, England, (Telephone in U.S. (888) 330-8477), (Fax in U.S. (800) 672-2054), www.palgrave.com; *The Statesman's Yearbook 2008.*

United Nations Statistics Division, New York, NY 10017, (800) 253-9646, Fax: (212) 963-4116, http://unstats.un.org; *Human Development Report 2006* and *World Statistics Pocketbook.*

The World Bank, 1818 H Street, NW, Washington, DC 20433, (202) 473-1000, Fax: (202) 477-6391, www.worldbank.org; *The World Bank Atlas 2003-2004* and *World Development Report 2008.*

ETHIOPIA - LITERACY

Euromonitor International, Inc., 224 S. Michigan Avenue, Suite 1500, Chicago, IL 60604, (312) 922-1115, Fax: (312) 922-1157, www.euromonitor.com; *World Marketing Data and Statistics.*

United Nations Statistics Division, New York, NY 10017, (800) 253-9646, Fax: (212) 963-4116, http://unstats.un.org; *Survey of Economic and Social Conditions in Africa 2005.*

ETHIOPIA - LIVESTOCK

Euromonitor International, Inc., 224 S. Michigan Avenue, Suite 1500, Chicago, IL 60604, (312) 922-1115, Fax: (312) 922-1157, www.euromonitor.com; *International Marketing Data and Statistics 2008.*

Palgrave Macmillan Ltd., Houndmills, Basingstoke, Hampshire, RG21 6XS, England, (Telephone in U.S. (888) 330-8477), (Fax in U.S. (800) 672-2054), www.palgrave.com; *The Statesman's Yearbook 2008.*

Taylor and Francis Group, An Informa Business, 2 Park Square, Milton Park, Abingdon, Oxford OX14 4RN, United Kingdom, (Dial from U.S. (212) 216-7800), (Fax from U.S. (212) 564-7854), www.tandf.co.uk; *The Europa World Year Book.*

United Nations Conference on Trade and Development (UNCTAD), DC2-1120, United Nations, New York, NY 10017, (212) 963-0027, www.unctad.org; *UNCTAD Commodity Yearbook.*

United Nations Economic Commission for Africa (ECA), PO Box 3001, Addis Ababa, Ethiopia, (Telephone in U.S. (212) 963-4957), www.uneca.org; *African Statistical Yearbook 2006.*

United Nations Food and Agricultural Organization (FAO), Viale delle Terme di Caracalla, 00100 Rome, Italy, (Dial from U.S. (202) 653-2400), (Fax from U.S. (202) 653 5760), www.fao.org; *FAO Production Yearbook 2002* and *The State of Food and Agriculture (SOFA) 2006.*

United Nations Statistics Division, New York, NY 10017, (800) 253-9646, Fax: (212) 963-4116, http://unstats.un.org; *Statistical Yearbook* and *Survey of Economic and Social Conditions in Africa 2005.*

ETHIOPIA - LOCAL TAXATION

Euromonitor International, Inc., 224 S. Michigan Avenue, Suite 1500, Chicago, IL 60604, (312) 922-1115, Fax: (312) 922-1157, www.euromonitor.com; *International Marketing Data and Statistics 2008.*

ETHIOPIA - MANUFACTURES

Central Statistical Agency (CSA) of Ethiopia, PO Box 1143, Addis Ababa, Ethiopia, www.csa.gov.et; *Statistical Abstract of Ethiopia.*

United Nations Economic Commission for Africa (ECA), PO Box 3001, Addis Ababa, Ethiopia, (Telephone in U.S. (212) 963-4957), www.uneca.org; *African Statistical Yearbook 2006.*

United Nations Statistics Division, New York, NY 10017, (800) 253-9646, Fax: (212) 963-4116, http://unstats.un.org; *Statistical Yearbook* and *Survey of Economic and Social Conditions in Africa 2005.*

ETHIOPIA - MARRIAGE

United Nations Statistics Division, New York, NY 10017, (800) 253-9646, Fax: (212) 963-4116, http://unstats.un.org; *Demographic Yearbook.*

ETHIOPIA - MEDICAL CARE, COST OF

International Monetary Fund (IMF), 700 Nineteenth Street, NW, Washington, DC 20431, (202) 623-7000, Fax: (202) 623-4661, www.imf.org; *Government Finance Statistics Yearbook (2008 Edition).*

ETHIOPIA - MILK PRODUCTION

See ETHIOPIA - DAIRY PROCESSING

ETHIOPIA - MINERAL INDUSTRIES

Central Statistical Agency (CSA) of Ethiopia, PO Box 1143, Addis Ababa, Ethiopia, www.csa.gov.et; *Statistical Abstract of Ethiopia.*

Commodity Research Bureau, 330 South Wells Street, Suite 612, Chicago, IL 60606-7110, (800) 621-5271, Fax: (312) 939-4135, www.crbtrader.com; *2006 CRB Commodity Yearbook and CD.*

Palgrave Macmillan Ltd., Houndmills, Basingstoke, Hampshire, RG21 6XS, England, (Telephone in U.S. (888) 330-8477), (Fax in U.S. (800) 672-2054), www.palgrave.com; *The Statesman's Yearbook 2008.*

Taylor and Francis Group, An Informa Business, 2 Park Square, Milton Park, Abingdon, Oxford OX14 4RN, United Kingdom, (Dial from U.S. (212) 216-7800), (Fax from U.S. (212) 564-7854), www.tandf.co.uk; *The Europa World Year Book.*

United Nations Conference on Trade and Development (UNCTAD), DC2-1120, United Nations, New York, NY 10017, (212) 963-0027, www.unctad.org; *UNCTAD Commodity Yearbook.*

United Nations Economic Commission for Africa (ECA), PO Box 3001, Addis Ababa, Ethiopia, (Telephone in U.S. (212) 963-4957), www.uneca.org; *African Statistical Yearbook 2006.*

United Nations Statistics Division, New York, NY 10017, (800) 253-9646, Fax: (212) 963-4116, http://unstats.un.org; *Statistical Yearbook.*

ETHIOPIA - MONEY EXCHANGE RATES

See ETHIOPIA - FOREIGN EXCHANGE RATES

ETHIOPIA - MONEY SUPPLY

African Development Bank Group, Rue Joseph Anoma, 01 BP 1387 Abidjan 01, Cote d'Ivoire, www.afdb.org; *Statistics Pocketbook 2008.*

Economist Intelligence Unit, 111 West 57th Street, New York, NY 10019, (212) 554-0600, Fax: (212) 586-1181, www.eiu.com; *Ethiopia Country Report.*

Euromonitor International, Inc., 224 S. Michigan Avenue, Suite 1500, Chicago, IL 60604, (312) 922-1115, Fax: (312) 922-1157, www.euromonitor.com; *International Marketing Data and Statistics 2008.*

International Monetary Fund (IMF), 700 Nineteenth Street, NW, Washington, DC 20431, (202) 623-7000, Fax: (202) 623-4661, www.imf.org; *International Financial Statistics Yearbook 2007.*

Taylor and Francis Group, An Informa Business, 2 Park Square, Milton Park, Abingdon, Oxford OX14 4RN, United Kingdom, (Dial from U.S. (212) 216-7800), (Fax from U.S. (212) 564-7854), www.tandf.co.uk; *The Europa World Year Book.*

United Nations Statistics Division, New York, NY 10017, (800) 253-9646, Fax: (212) 963-4116, http://unstats.un.org; *Statistical Yearbook.*

The World Bank, 1818 H Street, NW, Washington, DC 20433, (202) 473-1000, Fax: (202) 477-6391, www.worldbank.org; *Ethiopia.*

ETHIOPIA - MORTALITY

Central Intelligence Agency, Office of Public Affairs, Washington, DC 20505, (703) 482-0623, Fax: (703) 482-1739, www.cia.gov; *The World Factbook.*

Euromonitor International, Inc., 224 S. Michigan Avenue, Suite 1500, Chicago, IL 60604, (312) 922-1115, Fax: (312) 922-1157, www.euromonitor.com; *International Marketing Data and Statistics 2008* and *The World Economic Factbook 2008.*

Taylor and Francis Group, An Informa Business, 2 Park Square, Milton Park, Abingdon, Oxford OX14 4RN, United Kingdom, (Dial from U.S. (212) 216-7800), (Fax from U.S. (212) 564-7854), www.tandf.co.uk; *The Europa World Year Book.*

UNICEF, 3 United Nations Plaza, New York, NY 10017, (800) 253-9646, Fax: (212) 887-7465, www.unicef.org; *The State of the World's Children 2008.*

United Nations Statistics Division, New York, NY 10017, (800) 253-9646, Fax: (212) 963-4116, http://unstats.un.org; *Demographic Yearbook; Human Development Report 2006; Statistical Yearbook; Survey of Economic and Social Conditions in Africa 2005;* and *World Statistics Pocketbook.*

The World Bank, 1818 H Street, NW, Washington, DC 20433, (202) 473-1000, Fax: (202) 477-6391, www.worldbank.org; *The World Bank Atlas 2003-2004* and *World Development Report 2008.*

World Health Organization (WHO), Avenue Appia 20, 1211 Geneve 27, Switzerland, (Telephone in U.S. (212) 331-9081), www.who.int; The WHO Global Atlas of Infectious Diseases.

ETHIOPIA - MOTION PICTURES

United Nations Statistics Division, New York, NY 10017, (800) 253-9646, Fax: (212) 963-4116, http://unstats.un.org; *Statistical Yearbook.*

ETHIOPIA - MOTOR VEHICLES

International Road Federation (IFR), Madison Place, 500 Montgomery Street, 5th Floor, Alexandria, VA 22314, (703) 535-1001, Fax: (703) 535-1007, www.irfnet.org; *World Road Statistics 2006.*

Taylor and Francis Group, An Informa Business, 2 Park Square, Milton Park, Abingdon, Oxford OX14 4RN, United Kingdom, (Dial from U.S. (212) 216-7800), (Fax from U.S. (212) 564-7854), www.tandf.co.uk; *The Europa World Year Book.*

United Nations Statistics Division, New York, NY 10017, (800) 253-9646, Fax: (212) 963-4116, http://unstats.un.org; *Statistical Yearbook* and *Survey of Economic and Social Conditions in Africa 2005.*

ETHIOPIA - NUTRITION

African Development Bank Group, Rue Joseph Anoma, 01 BP 1387 Abidjan 01, Cote d'Ivoire, www.afdb.org; *Statistics Pocketbook 2008.*

United Nations Food and Agricultural Organization (FAO), Viale delle Terme di Caracalla, 00100 Rome,

Italy, (Dial from U.S. (202) 653-2400), (Fax from U.S. (202) 653 5760), www.fao.org; *The State of Food and Agriculture (SOFA) 2006.*

ETHIOPIA - OATS PRODUCTION

See ETHIOPIA - CROPS

ETHIOPIA - OILSEED PLANTS

International Monetary Fund (IMF), 700 Nineteenth Street, NW, Washington, DC 20431, (202) 623-7000, Fax: (202) 623-4661, www.imf.org; *International Financial Statistics Yearbook 2007.*

ETHIOPIA - PAPER

See ETHIOPIA - FORESTS AND FORESTRY

ETHIOPIA - PERIODICALS

UNESCO Institute for Statistics, C.P. 6128 Succursale Centre-Ville, Montreal, Quebec, H3C 3J7 Canada, (Dial from U.S. (514) 343-6880), (Fax from U.S. (514) 343 6882), www.uis.unesco.org; *Statistical Tables.*

ETHIOPIA - PESTICIDES

United Nations Food and Agricultural Organization (FAO), Viale delle Terme di Caracalla, 00100 Rome, Italy, (Dial from U.S. (202) 653-2400), (Fax from U.S. (202) 653 5760), www.fao.org; *The State of Food and Agriculture (SOFA) 2006.*

ETHIOPIA - PETROLEUM INDUSTRY AND TRADE

PennWell Corporation, 1421 South Sheridan Road, Tulsa, OK 74112, (918) 835-3161, www.pennwell.com; *International Petroleum Encyclopedia 2007.*

U.S. Department of Energy (DOE), Energy Information Administration (EIA), 1000 Independence Avenue, SW, Washington, DC 20585, (202) 586-8800, www.eia.doe.gov; *International Energy Annual 2004* and *International Energy Outlook 2006.*

United Nations Conference on Trade and Development (UNCTAD), DC2-1120, United Nations, New York, NY 10017, (212) 963-0027, www.unctad.org; *UNCTAD Commodity Yearbook.*

United Nations Food and Agricultural Organization (FAO), Viale delle Terme di Caracalla, 00100 Rome, Italy, (Dial from U.S. (202) 653-2400), (Fax from U.S. (202) 653 5760), www.fao.org; *The State of Food and Agriculture (SOFA) 2006.*

United Nations Statistics Division, New York, NY 10017, (800) 253-9646, Fax: (212) 963-4116, http://unstats.un.org; *Statistical Yearbook.*

ETHIOPIA - PLATINUM PRODUCTION

See ETHIOPIA - MINERAL INDUSTRIES

ETHIOPIA - POLITICAL SCIENCE

Central Intelligence Agency, Office of Public Affairs, Washington, DC 20505, (703) 482-0623, Fax: (703) 482-1739, www.cia.gov; *The World Factbook.*

International Monetary Fund (IMF), 700 Nineteenth Street, NW, Washington, DC 20431, (202) 623-7000, Fax: (202) 623-4661, www.imf.org; *Government Finance Statistics Yearbook (2008 Edition)* and *International Financial Statistics Yearbook 2007.*

Palgrave Macmillan Ltd., Houndmills, Basingstoke, Hampshire, RG21 6XS, England, (Telephone in U.S. (888) 330-8477), (Fax in U.S. (800) 672-2054), www.palgrave.com; *The Statesman's Yearbook 2008.*

Taylor and Francis Group, An Informa Business, 2 Park Square, Milton Park, Abingdon, Oxford OX14 4RN, United Kingdom, (Dial from U.S. (212) 216-7800), (Fax from U.S. (212) 564-7854), www.tandf.co.uk; *The Europa World Year Book.*

United Nations Statistics Division, New York, NY 10017, (800) 253-9646, Fax: (212) 963-4116, http://unstats.un.org; *National Accounts Statistics: Compendium of Income Distribution Statistics; Statistical Yearbook;* and *Survey of Economic and Social Conditions in Africa 2005.*

The World Bank, 1818 H Street, NW, Washington, DC 20433, (202) 473-1000, Fax: (202) 477-6391, www.worldbank.org; *World Development Report 2008.*

ETHIOPIA - POPULATION

African Development Bank Group, Rue Joseph Anoma, 01 BP 1387 Abidjan 01, Cote d'Ivoire, www.afdb.org; *The African Statistical Journal; Gender, Poverty and Environmental Indicators on African Countries 2007; Selected Statistics on African Countries 2007;* and *Statistics Pocketbook 2008.*

Central Intelligence Agency, Office of Public Affairs, Washington, DC 20505, (703) 482-0623, Fax: (703) 482-1739, www.cia.gov; *The World Factbook.*

Central Statistical Agency (CSA) of Ethiopia, PO Box 1143, Addis Ababa, Ethiopia, www.csa.gov.et; *Statistical Abstract of Ethiopia.*

Economist Intelligence Unit, 111 West 57th Street, New York, NY 10019, (212) 554-0600, Fax: (212) 586-1181, www.eiu.com; *Ethiopia Country Report.*

Euromonitor International, Inc., 224 S. Michigan Avenue, Suite 1500, Chicago, IL 60604, (312) 922-1115, Fax: (312) 922-1157, www.euromonitor.com; *International Marketing Data and Statistics 2008* and *The World Economic Factbook 2008.*

Eurostat, Batiment Jean Monnet, Rue Alcide de Gasperi, L-2920 Luxembourg, http://epp.eurostat.ec.europa.eu; *Demographic Indicators - Population by Age-Classes.*

International Labour Office, I.L.O. Publications, 4 route des Morillons, CH-1211 Geneva 22, Switzerland, (Telephone in U.S. (202) 653-7652), (Fax in U.S. (202) 653-7687), www.ilo.org; *Yearbook of Labour Statistics 2006.*

Palgrave Macmillan Ltd., Houndmills, Basingstoke, Hampshire, RG21 6XS, England, (Telephone in U.S. (888) 330-8477), (Fax in U.S. (800) 672-2054), www.palgrave.com; *The Statesman's Yearbook 2008.*

Population Reference Bureau, 1875 Connecticut Avenue, NW, Suite 520, Washington, DC, 20009-5728, (800) 877-9881, Fax: (202) 328-3937, www.prb.org; *Ethiopia Demographic and Health Survey, 2005.*

Taylor and Francis Group, An Informa Business, 2 Park Square, Milton Park, Abingdon, Oxford OX14 4RN, United Kingdom, (Dial from U.S. (212) 216-7800), (Fax from U.S. (212) 564-7854), www.tandf.co.uk; *The Europa World Year Book.*

U.S. Department of State (DOS), 2201 C Street NW, Washington, DC 20520, (202) 647-4000, www.state.gov; *World Military Expenditures and Arms Transfers (WMEAT).*

UNESCO Institute for Statistics, C.P. 6128 Succursale Centre-Ville, Montreal, Quebec, H3C 3J7 Canada, (Dial from U.S. (514) 343-6880), (Fax from U.S. (514) 343 6882), www.uis.unesco.org; *Statistical Tables.*

United Nations Food and Agricultural Organization (FAO), Viale delle Terme di Caracalla, 00100 Rome, Italy, (Dial from U.S. (202) 653-2400), (Fax from U.S. (202) 653 5760), www.fao.org; *FAO Production Yearbook 2002.*

United Nations Statistics Division, New York, NY 10017, (800) 253-9646, Fax: (212) 963-4116, http://unstats.un.org; *Demographic Yearbook; Human Development Report 2006; Statistical Yearbook; Survey of Economic and Social Conditions in Africa 2005;* and *World Statistics Pocketbook.*

The World Bank, 1818 H Street, NW, Washington, DC 20433, (202) 473-1000, Fax: (202) 477-6391, www.worldbank.org; *Ethiopia; The World Bank Atlas 2003-2004;* and *World Development Report 2008.*

World Health Organization (WHO), Avenue Appia 20, 1211 Geneve 27, Switzerland, (Telephone in U.S. (212) 331-9081), www.who.int; *World Health Report 2006.*

ETHIOPIA - POPULATION DENSITY

African Development Bank Group, Rue Joseph Anoma, 01 BP 1387 Abidjan 01, Cote d'Ivoire, www.afdb.org; *Statistics Pocketbook 2008.*

Central Intelligence Agency, Office of Public Affairs, Washington, DC 20505, (703) 482-0623, Fax: (703) 482-1739, www.cia.gov; *The World Factbook.*

Euromonitor International, Inc., 224 S. Michigan Avenue, Suite 1500, Chicago, IL 60604, (312) 922-1115, Fax: (312) 922-1157, www.euromonitor.com; *International Marketing Data and Statistics 2008* and *The World Economic Factbook 2008.*

Palgrave Macmillan Ltd., Houndmills, Basingstoke, Hampshire, RG21 6XS, England, (Telephone in U.S. (888) 330-8477), (Fax in U.S. (800) 672-2054), www.palgrave.com; *The Statesman's Yearbook 2008.*

Taylor and Francis Group, An Informa Business, 2 Park Square, Milton Park, Abingdon, Oxford OX14 4RN, United Kingdom, (Dial from U.S. (212) 216-7800), (Fax from U.S. (212) 564-7854), www.tandf.co.uk; *The Europa World Year Book.*

UNESCO Institute for Statistics, C.P. 6128 Succursale Centre-Ville, Montreal, Quebec, H3C 3J7 Canada, (Dial from U.S. (514) 343-6880), (Fax from U.S. (514) 343 6882), www.uis.unesco.org; *Statistical Tables.*

United Nations Food and Agricultural Organization (FAO), Viale delle Terme di Caracalla, 00100 Rome, Italy, (Dial from U.S. (202) 653-2400), (Fax from U.S. (202) 653 5760), www.fao.org; *The State of Food and Agriculture (SOFA) 2006.*

United Nations Statistics Division, New York, NY 10017, (800) 253-9646, Fax: (212) 963-4116, http://unstats.un.org; *Statistical Yearbook* and *Survey of Economic and Social Conditions in Africa 2005.*

The World Bank, 1818 H Street, NW, Washington, DC 20433, (202) 473-1000, Fax: (202) 477-6391, www.worldbank.org; *Ethiopia* and *World Development Report 2008.*

ETHIOPIA - POSTAL SERVICE

Palgrave Macmillan Ltd., Houndmills, Basingstoke, Hampshire, RG21 6XS, England, (Telephone in U.S. (888) 330-8477), (Fax in U.S. (800) 672-2054), www.palgrave.com; *The Statesman's Yearbook 2008.*

United Nations Statistics Division, New York, NY 10017, (800) 253-9646, Fax: (212) 963-4116, http://unstats.un.org; *Statistical Yearbook.*

ETHIOPIA - POWER RESOURCES

Euromonitor International, Inc., 224 S. Michigan Avenue, Suite 1500, Chicago, IL 60604, (312) 922-1115, Fax: (312) 922-1157, www.euromonitor.com; *International Marketing Data and Statistics 2008; The World Economic Factbook 2008;* and *World Marketing Data and Statistics.*

Palgrave Macmillan Ltd., Houndmills, Basingstoke, Hampshire, RG21 6XS, England, (Telephone in U.S. (888) 330-8477), (Fax in U.S. (800) 672-2054), www.palgrave.com; *The Statesman's Yearbook 2008.*

Platts, 2 Penn Plaza, 25th Floor, New York, NY 10121-2298, (212) 904-3070, www.platts.com; *Energy Economist.*

U.S. Department of Energy (DOE), Energy Information Administration (EIA), 1000 Independence Avenue, SW, Washington, DC 20585, (202) 586-8800, www.eia.doe.gov; *International Energy Annual 2004* and *International Energy Outlook 2006.*

United Nations Economic Commission for Africa (ECA), PO Box 3001, Addis Ababa, Ethiopia, (Telephone in U.S. (212) 963-4957), www.uneca.org; *African Statistical Yearbook 2006.*

United Nations Statistics Division, New York, NY 10017, (800) 253-9646, Fax: (212) 963-4116, http://unstats.un.org; *Energy Statistics Yearbook 2003; Human Development Report 2006; Statistical Yearbook;* and *World Statistics Pocketbook.*

The World Bank, 1818 H Street, NW, Washington, DC 20433, (202) 473-1000, Fax: (202) 477-6391, www.worldbank.org; *The World Bank Atlas 2003-2004* and *World Development Report 2008.*

ETHIOPIA - PRICES

Central Statistical Agency (CSA) of Ethiopia, PO Box 1143, Addis Ababa, Ethiopia, www.csa.gov.et; *Statistical Abstract of Ethiopia.*

Euromonitor International, Inc., 224 S. Michigan Avenue, Suite 1500, Chicago, IL 60604, (312) 922-1115, Fax: (312) 922-1157, www.euromonitor.com; *World Marketing Data and Statistics.*

International Labour Office, I.L.O. Publications, 4 route des Morillons, CH-1211 Geneva 22, Switzerland, (Telephone in U.S. (202) 653-7652), (Fax in U.S. (202) 653-7687), www.ilo.org; *Yearbook of Labour Statistics 2006.*

International Monetary Fund (IMF), 700 Nineteenth Street, NW, Washington, DC 20431, (202) 623-7000, Fax: (202) 623-4661, www.imf.org; *International Financial Statistics Yearbook 2007.*

United Nations Economic Commission for Africa (ECA), PO Box 3001, Addis Ababa, Ethiopia, (Telephone in U.S. (212) 963-4957), www.uneca.org; *African Statistical Yearbook 2006.*

United Nations Food and Agricultural Organization (FAO), Viale delle Terme di Caracalla, 00100 Rome, Italy, (Dial from U.S. (202) 653-2400), (Fax from U.S. (202) 653 5760), www.fao.org; *FAO Production Yearbook 2002* and *The State of Food and Agriculture (SOFA) 2006.*

The World Bank, 1818 H Street, NW, Washington, DC 20433, (202) 473-1000, Fax: (202) 477-6391, www.worldbank.org; *Ethiopia.*

ETHIOPIA - PUBLIC HEALTH

African Development Bank Group, Rue Joseph Anoma, 01 BP 1387 Abidjan 01, Cote d'Ivoire, www.afdb.org; *Statistics Pocketbook 2008.*

Central Statistical Agency (CSA) of Ethiopia, PO Box 1143, Addis Ababa, Ethiopia, www.csa.gov.et; *Statistical Abstract of Ethiopia.*

Euromonitor International, Inc., 224 S. Michigan Avenue, Suite 1500, Chicago, IL 60604, (312) 922-1115, Fax: (312) 922-1157, www.euromonitor.com; *World Marketing Data and Statistics.*

Palgrave Macmillan Ltd., Houndmills, Basingstoke, Hampshire, RG21 6XS, England, (Telephone in U.S. (888) 330-8477), (Fax in U.S. (800) 672-2054), www.palgrave.com; *The Statesman's Yearbook 2008.*

Population Reference Bureau, 1875 Connecticut Avenue, NW, Suite 520, Washington, DC, 20009-5728, (800) 877-9881, Fax: (202) 328-3937, www.prb.org; *Ethiopia Demographic and Health Survey, 2005.*

UNICEF, 3 United Nations Plaza, New York, NY 10017, (800) 253-9646, Fax: (212) 887-7465, www.unicef.org; *The State of the World's Children 2008.*

United Nations Economic Commission for Africa (ECA), PO Box 3001, Addis Ababa, Ethiopia, (Telephone in U.S. (212) 963-4957), www.uneca.org; *African Statistical Yearbook 2006.*

United Nations Statistics Division, New York, NY 10017, (800) 253-9646, Fax: (212) 963-4116, http://unstats.un.org; *Human Development Report 2006* and *Statistical Yearbook.*

The World Bank, 1818 H Street, NW, Washington, DC 20433, (202) 473-1000, Fax: (202) 477-6391, www.worldbank.org; *Ethiopia* and *World Development Report 2008.*

World Health Organization (WHO), Avenue Appia 20, 1211 Geneve 27, Switzerland, (Telephone in U.S. (212) 331-9081), www.who.int; The WHO Global Atlas of Infectious Diseases.

ETHIOPIA - PUBLISHERS AND PUBLISHING

Taylor and Francis Group, An Informa Business, 2 Park Square, Milton Park, Abingdon, Oxford OX14 4RN, United Kingdom, (Dial from U.S. (212) 216-7800), (Fax from U.S. (212) 564-7854), www.tandf.co.uk; *The Europa World Year Book.*

UNESCO Institute for Statistics, C.P. 6128 Succursale Centre-Ville, Montreal, Quebec, H3C 3J7 Canada, (Dial from U.S. (514) 343-6880), (Fax from U.S. (514) 343 6882), www.uis.unesco.org; *Statistical Tables.*

ETHIOPIA - RADIO BROADCASTING

Palgrave Macmillan Ltd., Houndmills, Basingstoke, Hampshire, RG21 6XS, England, (Telephone in U.S. (888) 330-8477), (Fax in U.S. (800) 672-2054), www.palgrave.com; *The Statesman's Yearbook 2008.*

ETHIOPIA - RAILROADS

Jane's Information Group, 110 North Royal Street, Suite 200, Alexandria, VA 22314, (703) 683-3700, Fax: (800) 836-0297, www.janes.com; *Jane's World Railways.*

Palgrave Macmillan Ltd., Houndmills, Basingstoke, Hampshire, RG21 6XS, England, (Telephone in U.S. (888) 330-8477), (Fax in U.S. (800) 672-2054), www.palgrave.com; *The Statesman's Yearbook 2008.*

Taylor and Francis Group, An Informa Business, 2 Park Square, Milton Park, Abingdon, Oxford OX14 4RN, United Kingdom, (Dial from U.S. (212) 216-7800), (Fax from U.S. (212) 564-7854), www.tandf.co.uk; *The Europa World Year Book.*

United Nations Economic Commission for Africa (ECA), PO Box 3001, Addis Ababa, Ethiopia, (Telephone in U.S. (212) 963-4957), www.uneca.org; *African Statistical Yearbook 2006.*

United Nations Statistics Division, New York, NY 10017, (800) 253-9646, Fax: (212) 963-4116, http://unstats.un.org; *Statistical Yearbook* and *Survey of Economic and Social Conditions in Africa 2005.*

ETHIOPIA - RELIGION

Central Intelligence Agency, Office of Public Affairs, Washington, DC 20505, (703) 482-0623, Fax: (703) 482-1739, www.cia.gov; *The World Factbook.*

Palgrave Macmillan Ltd., Houndmills, Basingstoke, Hampshire, RG21 6XS, England, (Telephone in U.S. (888) 330-8477), (Fax in U.S. (800) 672-2054), www.palgrave.com; *The Statesman's Yearbook 2008.*

ETHIOPIA - RESERVES (ACCOUNTING)

African Development Bank Group, Rue Joseph Anoma, 01 BP 1387 Abidjan 01, Cote d'Ivoire, www.afdb.org; *Statistics Pocketbook 2008.*

Euromonitor International, Inc., 224 S. Michigan Avenue, Suite 1500, Chicago, IL 60604, (312) 922-1115, Fax: (312) 922-1157, www.euromonitor.com; *International Marketing Data and Statistics 2008.*

ETHIOPIA - RETAIL TRADE

Euromonitor International, Inc., 224 S. Michigan Avenue, Suite 1500, Chicago, IL 60604, (312) 922-1115, Fax: (312) 922-1157, www.euromonitor.com; *World Marketing Data and Statistics.*

United Nations Statistics Division, New York, NY 10017, (800) 253-9646, Fax: (212) 963-4116, http://unstats.un.org; *Statistical Yearbook.*

ETHIOPIA - ROADS

Central Intelligence Agency, Office of Public Affairs, Washington, DC 20505, (703) 482-0623, Fax: (703) 482-1739, www.cia.gov; *The World Factbook.*

International Road Federation (IFR), Madison Place, 500 Montgomery Street, 5th Floor, Alexandria, VA 22314, (703) 535-1001, Fax: (703) 535-1007, www.irfnet.org; *World Road Statistics 2006.*

Palgrave Macmillan Ltd., Houndmills, Basingstoke, Hampshire, RG21 6XS, England, (Telephone in U.S. (888) 330-8477), (Fax in U.S. (800) 672-2054), www.palgrave.com; *The Statesman's Yearbook 2008.*

United Nations Economic Commission for Africa (ECA), PO Box 3001, Addis Ababa, Ethiopia, (Telephone in U.S. (212) 963-4957), www.uneca.org; *African Statistical Yearbook 2006.*

United Nations Statistics Division, New York, NY 10017, (800) 253-9646, Fax: (212) 963-4116, http://unstats.un.org; *Survey of Economic and Social Conditions in Africa 2005.*

ETHIOPIA - SAFFLOWER SEED PRODUCTION

See ETHIOPIA - CROPS

ETHIOPIA - SALT PRODUCTION

See ETHIOPIA - MINERAL INDUSTRIES

ETHIOPIA - SHEEP

See ETHIOPIA - LIVESTOCK

ETHIOPIA - SHIPPING

Taylor and Francis Group, An Informa Business, 2 Park Square, Milton Park, Abingdon, Oxford OX14 4RN, United Kingdom, (Dial from U.S. (212) 216-7800), (Fax from U.S. (212) 564-7854), www.tandf.co.uk; *The Europa World Year Book.*

U.S. Department of Transportation (DOT), Maritime Administration (MARAD), West Building, Southeast Federal Center, 1200 New Jersey Avenue, SE, Washington, DC 20590, (800) 99-MARAD, www.marad.dot.gov; *World Merchant Fleet 2005.*

United Nations Economic Commission for Africa (ECA), PO Box 3001, Addis Ababa, Ethiopia, (Telephone in U.S. (212) 963-4957), www.uneca.org; *African Statistical Yearbook 2006.*

United Nations Statistics Division, New York, NY 10017, (800) 253-9646, Fax: (212) 963-4116, http://unstats.un.org; *Statistical Yearbook.*

ETHIOPIA - SOCIAL ECOLOGY

United Nations Statistics Division, New York, NY 10017, (800) 253-9646, Fax: (212) 963-4116, http://unstats.un.org; *World Statistics Pocketbook.*

ETHIOPIA - SOCIAL SECURITY

International Monetary Fund (IMF), 700 Nineteenth Street, NW, Washington, DC 20431, (202) 623-7000, Fax: (202) 623-4661, www.imf.org; *Government Finance Statistics Yearbook (2008 Edition).*

United Nations Statistics Division, New York, NY 10017, (800) 253-9646, Fax: (212) 963-4116, http://unstats.un.org; *National Accounts Statistics: Compendium of Income Distribution Statistics.*

ETHIOPIA - STEEL PRODUCTION

See ETHIOPIA - MINERAL INDUSTRIES

ETHIOPIA - SUGAR PRODUCTION

See ETHIOPIA - CROPS

ETHIOPIA - TAXATION

International Monetary Fund (IMF), 700 Nineteenth Street, NW, Washington, DC 20431, (202) 623-7000, Fax: (202) 623-4661, www.imf.org; *Government Finance Statistics Yearbook (2008 Edition).*

Taylor and Francis Group, An Informa Business, 2 Park Square, Milton Park, Abingdon, Oxford OX14 4RN, United Kingdom, (Dial from U.S. (212) 216-7800), (Fax from U.S. (212) 564-7854), www.tandf.co.uk; *The Europa World Year Book.*

ETHIOPIA - TELEPHONE

International Telecommunication Union (ITU), Place des Nations, 1211 Geneva 20, Switzerland, www.itu.int; World Telecommunication Indicators Database.

Palgrave Macmillan Ltd., Houndmills, Basingstoke, Hampshire, RG21 6XS, England, (Telephone in U.S. (888) 330-8477), (Fax in U.S. (800) 672-2054), www.palgrave.com; *The Statesman's Yearbook 2008.*

Taylor and Francis Group, An Informa Business, 2 Park Square, Milton Park, Abingdon, Oxford OX14 4RN, United Kingdom, (Dial from U.S. (212) 216-7800), (Fax from U.S. (212) 564-7854), www.tandf.co.uk; *The Europa World Year Book.*

United Nations Statistics Division, New York, NY 10017, (800) 253-9646, Fax: (212) 963-4116, http://unstats.un.org; *Statistical Yearbook* and *World Statistics Pocketbook.*

ETHIOPIA - TEXTILE INDUSTRY

United Nations Conference on Trade and Development (UNCTAD), DC2-1120, United Nations, New York, NY 10017, (212) 963-0027, www.unctad.org; *UNCTAD Commodity Yearbook.*

United Nations Statistics Division, New York, NY 10017, (800) 253-9646, Fax: (212) 963-4116, http://unstats.un.org; *Statistical Yearbook.*

ETHIOPIA - THEATER

UNESCO Institute for Statistics, C.P. 6128 Succursale Centre-Ville, Montreal, Quebec, H3C 3J7 Canada, (Dial from U.S. (514) 343-6880), (Fax from U.S. (514) 343 6882), www.uis.unesco.org; *Statistical Tables.*

ETHIOPIA - TOBACCO INDUSTRY

Foreign Agricultural Service (FAS), U.S. Department of Agriculture (USDA), 1400 Independence Avenue, SW, Washington, DC 20250, (202) 720-3935, www.fas.usda.gov; *Tobacco: World Markets and Trade.*

United Nations Statistics Division, New York, NY 10017, (800) 253-9646, Fax: (212) 963-4116, http://unstats.un.org; *Statistical Yearbook.*

ETHIOPIA - TOURISM

Euromonitor International, Inc., 224 S. Michigan Avenue, Suite 1500, Chicago, IL 60604, (312) 922-1115, Fax: (312) 922-1157, www.euromonitor.com; *The World Economic Factbook 2008* and *World Marketing Data and Statistics.*

Taylor and Francis Group, An Informa Business, 2 Park Square, Milton Park, Abingdon, Oxford OX14 4RN, United Kingdom, (Dial from U.S. (212) 216-7800), (Fax from U.S. (212) 564-7854), www.tandf.co.uk; *The Europa World Year Book.*

United Nations Economic Commission for Africa (ECA), PO Box 3001, Addis Ababa, Ethiopia, (Telephone in U.S. (212) 963-4957), www.uneca.org; *African Statistical Yearbook 2006.*

United Nations Statistics Division, New York, NY 10017, (800) 253-9646, Fax: (212) 963-4116, http://unstats.un.org; *Statistical Yearbook.*

United Nations World Tourism Organization (UNWTO), Capitan Haya 42, 28020 Madrid, Spain, www.world-tourism.org; *Yearbook of Tourism Statistics.*

The World Bank, 1818 H Street, NW, Washington, DC 20433, (202) 473-1000, Fax: (202) 477-6391, www.worldbank.org; *Ethiopia.*

ETHIOPIA - TRADE

See ETHIOPIA - INTERNATIONAL TRADE

ETHIOPIA - TRANSPORTATION

Central Intelligence Agency, Office of Public Affairs, Washington, DC 20505, (703) 482-0623, Fax: (703) 482-1739, www.cia.gov; *The World Factbook.*

Central Statistical Agency (CSA) of Ethiopia, PO Box 1143, Addis Ababa, Ethiopia, www.csa.gov.et; *Statistical Abstract of Ethiopia.*

Euromonitor International, Inc., 224 S. Michigan Avenue, Suite 1500, Chicago, IL 60604, (312) 922-1115, Fax: (312) 922-1157, www.euromonitor.com; *International Marketing Data and Statistics 2008* and *World Marketing Data and Statistics.*

Palgrave Macmillan Ltd., Houndmills, Basingstoke, Hampshire, RG21 6XS, England, (Telephone in U.S. (888) 330-8477), (Fax in U.S. (800) 672-2054), www.palgrave.com; *The Statesman's Yearbook 2008.*

Taylor and Francis Group, An Informa Business, 2 Park Square, Milton Park, Abingdon, Oxford OX14 4RN, United Kingdom, (Dial from U.S. (212) 216-7800), (Fax from U.S. (212) 564-7854), www.tandf.co.uk; *The Europa World Year Book.*

United Nations Economic Commission for Africa (ECA), PO Box 3001, Addis Ababa, Ethiopia, (Telephone in U.S. (212) 963-4957), www.uneca.org; *African Statistical Yearbook 2006.*

United Nations Statistics Division, New York, NY 10017, (800) 253-9646, Fax: (212) 963-4116, http://unstats.un.org; *Human Development Report 2006.*

The World Bank, 1818 H Street, NW, Washington, DC 20433, (202) 473-1000, Fax: (202) 477-6391, www.worldbank.org; *Africa Live Database (LDB)* and *Ethiopia.*

ETHIOPIA - UNEMPLOYMENT

Central Intelligence Agency, Office of Public Affairs, Washington, DC 20505, (703) 482-0623, Fax: (703) 482-1739, www.cia.gov; *The World Factbook.*

Euromonitor International, Inc., 224 S. Michigan Avenue, Suite 1500, Chicago, IL 60604, (312) 922-1115, Fax: (312) 922-1157, www.euromonitor.com; *International Marketing Data and Statistics 2008.*

International Labour Office, I.L.O. Publications, 4 route des Morillons, CH-1211 Geneva 22, Switzerland, (Telephone in U.S. (202) 653-7652), (Fax in U.S. (202) 653-7687), www.ilo.org; *Yearbook of Labour Statistics 2006.*

ETHIOPIA - VITAL STATISTICS

Euromonitor International, Inc., 224 S. Michigan Avenue, Suite 1500, Chicago, IL 60604, (312) 922-1115, Fax: (312) 922-1157, www.euromonitor.com; *International Marketing Data and Statistics 2008.*

World Health Organization (WHO), Avenue Appia 20, 1211 Geneve 27, Switzerland, (Telephone in U.S. (212) 331-9081), www.who.int; *World Health Report 2006.*

ETHIOPIA - WAGES

International Labour Office, I.L.O. Publications, 4 route des Morillons, CH-1211 Geneva 22, Switzerland, (Telephone in U.S. (202) 653-7652), (Fax in U.S. (202) 653-7687), www.ilo.org; *Yearbook of Labour Statistics 2006.*

The World Bank, 1818 H Street, NW, Washington, DC 20433, (202) 473-1000, Fax: (202) 477-6391, www.worldbank.org; *Ethiopia.*

ETHIOPIA - WELFARE STATE

International Monetary Fund (IMF), 700 Nineteenth Street, NW, Washington, DC 20431, (202) 623-7000, Fax: (202) 623-4661, www.imf.org; *Government Finance Statistics Yearbook (2008 Edition).*

ETHIOPIA - WHEAT PRODUCTION

See ETHIOPIA - CROPS

ETHIOPIA - WHOLESALE PRICE INDEXES

United Nations Statistics Division, New York, NY 10017, (800) 253-9646, Fax: (212) 963-4116, http://unstats.un.org; *Statistical Yearbook.*

ETHIOPIA - WHOLESALE TRADE

United Nations Statistics Division, New York, NY 10017, (800) 253-9646, Fax: (212) 963-4116, http://unstats.un.org; *Statistical Yearbook.*

ETHIOPIA - YARN PRODUCTION

See ETHIOPIA - TEXTILE INDUSTRY

ETHNICITY

Higher Education Research Institute (HERI), University of California, Los Angeles, 3005 Moore Hall/Box 951521, Los Angeles, CA 90095-1521, (310) 825-1925, Fax: (310) 206-2228, www.gseis.ucla.edu/heri/index.php; *Race and Ethnicity in the American Professoriate.*

EUROPE

See Individual foreign countries

Eurostat, Batiment Jean Monnet, Rue Alcide de Gasperi, L-2920 Luxembourg, http://epp.eurostat.ec.europa.eu; *Tourism in Europe: First Results for 2007.*

United Nations World Tourism Organization (UNWTO), Capitan Haya 42, 28020 Madrid, Spain, www.world-tourism.org; *Tourism Market Trends 2004 - Europe.*

EUROPEAN UNION

Banque de France, 48 rue Croix des Petits champs, 75001 Paris, France, www.banque-france.fr/home.htm; *Monthly Business Survey Overview.*

Economist Intelligence Unit, 111 West 57th Street, New York, NY 10019, (212) 554-0600, Fax: (212) 586-1181, www.eiu.com; *Business Eastern Europe* and *European Union Country Report.*

European Union, Delegation of the European Commission to the United States, 2300 M Street, NW, Washington, DC 20037, (202) 862-9500, Fax: (202) 429-1766, www.eurunion.org; *Education across Europe 2003; The EU Economy, 2007 Review: Moving Europe's Productivity Frontier;* and *Regional Unemployment in the European Union and Candidate Countries in 2004.*

Eurostat, Batiment Jean Monnet, Rue Alcide de Gasperi, L-2920 Luxembourg, http://epp.eurostat.ec.europa.eu; *Education, Science and Culture Statistics; Euro-Indicators Newsletter; Euro-Mediterranean Statistics 2007;* and *Pocketbook on Candidate and Potential Candidate Countries.*

Federal Statistical Office Germany, D-65180 Wiesbaden, Germany, www.destatis.de; *The International Statistical Yearbook 2005.*

Organisation for Economic Cooperation and Development (OECD), 2 rue Andre Pascal, F-75775 Paris Cedex 16, France, (Telephone in U.S. (202) 785-6323), (Fax in U.S. (202) 785-0350), www.oecd.org; *Comparison of Gross Domestic Product (GDP) for OECD Countries.*

Statistics Netherlands, PO Box 4000, 2270 JM Voorburg, Netherlands, www.cbs.nl; *The EU-15's New Economy - A Statistical Portrait: How Are the Fifteen "Old" EU Countries Faring in the New Economy?*

United Nations Statistics Division, New York, NY 10017, (800) 253-9646, Fax: (212) 963-4116, http://unstats.un.org; *National Accounts Statistics: Compendium of Income Distribution Statistics.*

EUROPEAN UNION - AGRICULTURE

Economist Intelligence Unit, 111 West 57th Street, New York, NY 10019, (212) 554-0600, Fax: (212) 586-1181, www.eiu.com; *European Union Country Report.*

Eurostat, Batiment Jean Monnet, Rue Alcide de Gasperi, L-2920 Luxembourg, http://epp.eurostat.ec.europa.eu; *EU Agricultural Prices in 2007.*

EUROPEAN UNION - BUSINESS

Economist Intelligence Unit, 111 West 57th Street, New York, NY 10019, (212) 554-0600, Fax: (212) 586-1181, www.eiu.com; *Business Eastern Europe.*

Eurostat, Batiment Jean Monnet, Rue Alcide de Gasperi, L-2920 Luxembourg, http://epp.eurostat.ec.europa.eu; *Patent Applications to the EPO in the ICT Sector 1993 to 2003.*

EUROPEAN UNION - ECONOMIC CONDITIONS

Economist Intelligence Unit, 111 West 57th Street, New York, NY 10019, (212) 554-0600, Fax: (212) 586-1181, www.eiu.com; *European Union Country Report.*

Eurostat, Batiment Jean Monnet, Rue Alcide de Gasperi, L-2920 Luxembourg, http://epp.eurostat.ec.europa.eu; *Consumers in Europe - Facts and Figures on Services of General Interest; EU Agricultural Prices in 2007;* and *EU Economic Data Pocketbook.*

EUROPEAN UNION - ENVIRONMENTAL CONDITIONS

DSI Data Service Information, Xantener Strasse 51a, D-47495 Rheinberg, Germany, www.dsidata.com; *Campus Solution.*

Economist Intelligence Unit, 111 West 57th Street, New York, NY 10019, (212) 554-0600, Fax: (212) 586-1181, www.eiu.com; *European Union Country Report.*

Platts, 2 Penn Plaza, 25th Floor, New York, NY 10121-2298, (212) 904-3070, www.platts.com; *Emissions Daily.*

EUROPEAN UNION - EXPORTS

Economist Intelligence Unit, 111 West 57th Street, New York, NY 10019, (212) 554-0600, Fax: (212) 586-1181, www.eiu.com; *European Union Country Report.*

Eurostat, Batiment Jean Monnet, Rue Alcide de Gasperi, L-2920 Luxembourg, http://epp.eurostat.ec.europa.eu; Intra- and Extra-EU Trade.

EUROPEAN UNION - FINANCE, PUBLIC

Economist Intelligence Unit, 111 West 57th Street, New York, NY 10019, (212) 554-0600, Fax: (212) 586-1181, www.eiu.com; *European Union Country Report.*

Eurostat, Batiment Jean Monnet, Rue Alcide de Gasperi, L-2920 Luxembourg, http://epp.eurostat.ec.europa.eu; *European Social Statistics - Social Protection Expenditure and Receipts - Data 1997-2005.*

EUROPEAN UNION - GROSS DOMESTIC PRODUCT

Economist Intelligence Unit, 111 West 57th Street, New York, NY 10019, (212) 554-0600, Fax: (212) 586-1181, www.eiu.com; *European Union Country Report.*

EUROPEAN UNION - IMPORTS

Economist Intelligence Unit, 111 West 57th Street, New York, NY 10019, (212) 554-0600, Fax: (212) 586-1181, www.eiu.com; *European Union Country Report.*

Eurostat, Batiment Jean Monnet, Rue Alcide de Gasperi, L-2920 Luxembourg, http://epp.eurostat.ec.europa.eu; Intra- and Extra-EU Trade.

EUROPEAN UNION - INDUSTRIES

Economist Intelligence Unit, 111 West 57th Street, New York, NY 10019, (212) 554-0600, Fax: (212) 586-1181, www.eiu.com; *European Union Country Report.*

Eurostat, Batiment Jean Monnet, Rue Alcide de Gasperi, L-2920 Luxembourg, http://epp.eurostat.ec.europa.eu; *Patent Applications to the EPO in the ICT Sector 1993 to 2003.*

Platts, 2 Penn Plaza, 25th Floor, New York, NY 10121-2298, (212) 904-3070, www.platts.com; *Emissions Daily.*

EUROPEAN UNION - INTERNATIONAL TRADE

Economist Intelligence Unit, 111 West 57th Street, New York, NY 10019, (212) 554-0600, Fax: (212) 586-1181, www.eiu.com; *European Union Country Report.*

Eurostat, Batiment Jean Monnet, Rue Alcide de Gasperi, L-2920 Luxembourg, http://epp.eurostat.ec.europa.eu; Intra- and Extra-EU Trade.

World Trade Organization (WTO), Centre William Rappard, Rue de Lausanne 154, CH-1211 Geneva 21, Switzerland, www.wto.org; *International Trade Statistics 2006.*

EUROPEAN UNION - MONEY SUPPLY

Economist Intelligence Unit, 111 West 57th Street, New York, NY 10019, (212) 554-0600, Fax: (212) 586-1181, www.eiu.com; *European Union Country Report.*

EUROPEAN UNION - POPULATION

Economist Intelligence Unit, 111 West 57th Street, New York, NY 10019, (212) 554-0600, Fax: (212) 586-1181, www.eiu.com; *European Union Country Report.*

Eurostat, Batiment Jean Monnet, Rue Alcide de Gasperi, L-2920 Luxembourg, http://epp.eurostat.ec.europa.eu; *Consumers in Europe - Facts and Figures on Services of General Interest; Demographic Indicators - Population by Age-Classes; Demographic Outlook - National Reports on the Demographic Developments in 2006;* and *The Life of Women and Men in Europe - A Statistical Portrait.*

International Organization for Migration (IOM), 17, Route des Morillons, CH-1211 Geneva 19, Switzerland, www.iom.int; *Migration from Latin America to Europe: Trends and Policy Challenges; Migration, Human Smuggling and Trafficking from Nigeria to Europe;* and *Trafficking in Human Beings and the 2006 World Cup in Germany.*

Taylor and Francis Group, An Informa Business, 2 Park Square, Milton Park, Abingdon, Oxford OX14 4RN, United Kingdom, (Dial from U.S. (212) 216-7800), (Fax from U.S. (212) 564-7854), www.tandf.co.uk; *Europa World Plus.*

EUROPEAN UNION - PUBLIC HEALTH

EpiNorth, c/o Norwegian Institute of Public Health, PO Box 4404 Nydalen, N-0430 Oslo, Norway, www.epinorth.org; www.epinorth.org.

European Centre for Disease Prevention and Control (ECDC), 171 83 Stockholm, Sweden, www.ecdc.europa.eu; *The Community Summary Report on Trends and Sources of Zoonoses, Zoonotic Agents, Antimicrobial resistance and Foodborne outbreaks in the European Union in 2006; The First European Communicable Disease Epidemiological Report; HIV Infection in Europe: 25 Years into the Pandemic; HIV Infection in Europe: 25 Years into the Pandemic; Influenza News; Pandemic Preparedness in the European Union and European Economic Area - 2007; Technical Report of the Scientific Panel on Influenza in Reply to Eight Questions Concerning Avian Flu;* and *Vaccines and Immunisation - VI news.*

Health and Consumer Protection Directorate-General, European Commission, B-1049 Brussels, Belgium, http://ec.europa.eu/dgs/health_consumer/index_en.htm; *Injuries in the European Union: Statistics Summary 2002-2004.*

National Institute for Public Health and the Environment (RIVM), PO Box 1, 3720 BA Bilthoven, The Netherlands, www.rivm.nl/en; *Disease Burden and Related Costs of Cryptosporidiosis and Giardiasis in the Netherlands* and unpublished data.

Robert Koch Institute, Nordufer 20, D 13353 Berlin, Germany, www.rki.de; *EUVAC-NET Report: Pertussis-Surveillance 1998-2002.*

EVAPORATED AND CONDENSED MILK

Economic Research Service (ERS), U.S. Department of Agriculture (USDA), 1800 M Street, NW, Washington, DC 20036-5831, (202) 694-5050, Fax: (202) 694-5689, www.ers.usda.gov; *Agricultural Outlook* and *Food CPI, Prices, and Expenditures.*

National Agricultural Statistics Service (NASS), U.S. Department of Agriculture (USDA), 1400 Independence Avenue, SW, Washington, DC 20250, (800) 727-9540, Fax: (202) 690-2090, www.nass.usda.gov; *Dairy Products* and *Milk Cows and Milk Production.*

EXCISE TAXES

Alcohol and Tobacco Tax and Trade Bureau (TTB), U.S. Department of the Treasury (DOT), Public Information Officer, 1310 G Street, NW, Suite 300, Washington, D.C. 20220, (202) 927-5000, Fax: (202) 927-5611, www.ttb.gov; *Monthly Statistical Release - Tobacco Products.*

The Office of Management and Budget (OMB), 725 17th Street, NW, Washington, DC 20503, (202) 395-3080, Fax: (202) 395-3888, www.whitehouse.gov/omb; *Historical Tables.*

U.S. Department of the Treasury (DOT), Internal Revenue Service (IRS), Statistics of Income Division (SIS), PO Box 2608, Washington, DC, 20013-2608, (202) 874-0410, Fax: (202) 874-0964, www.irs.ustreas.gov; *IRS Data Book 2004-2005.*

EXECUTIONS

U.S. Department of Justice (DOJ), Bureau of Justice Statistics, 810 Seventh Street, NW, Washington, DC 20531, (202) 307-0765, www.ojp.usdoj.gov/bjs/; *Capital Punishment, 2004* and *Correctional Populations in the United States.*

EXECUTIVE OFFICE OF THE PRESIDENT (FEDERAL)

United States Office of Personnel Management (OMB), 1900 E Street, NW, Washington, DC 20415-1000, (202) 606-1800, www.opm.gov; *Employment and Trends of Federal Civilian Workforce Statistics* and unpublished data.

EXERCISE EQUIPMENT

National Sporting Goods Association (NSGA), 1601 Feehanville Drive, Suite 300, Mount Prospect, IL 60056, (847) 296-6742, Fax: (847) 391-9827, www.nsga.org; *Ten-Year History of Selected Sports Participation, 1996-2006.*

EXPECTATION OF LIFE (AVERAGE LIFETIME)

Bernan Essential Government Publications, 4611-F Assembly Drive, Lanham MD, 20706-4391, (301) 459-2255, Fax: (800) 865-3450, www.bernan.com; *Vital Statistics of the United States: Births, Life Expectancy, Deaths, and Selected Health Data.*

National Center for Health Statistics (NCHS), Centers for Disease Control and Prevention (CDC), U.S. Department of Health and Human Services (HHS), 3311 Toledo Road, Hyattsville, MD 20782, (866) 232-4636, www.cdc.gov/nchs; *National Vital Statistics Reports (NVSR); United States Life Tables, 2004; Vital Statistics of the United States (VSUS);* and unpublished data.

EXPECTATION OF LIFE (AVERAGE LIFETIME) - FOREIGN COUNTRIES

U.S. Census Bureau, Population Division, 4700 Silver Hill Road, Washington DC 20233-0001, (301) 763-3030, www.census.gov/population/www/; International Data Base (IDB).

EXPECTATION OF LIFE (AVERAGE LIFETIME) - PROJECTIONS

Bernan Essential Government Publications, 4611-F Assembly Drive, Lanham MD, 20706-4391, (301) 459-2255, Fax: (800) 865-3450, www.bernan.com; *Vital Statistics of the United States: Births, Life Expectancy, Deaths, and Selected Health Data.*

National Center for Health Statistics (NCHS), Centers for Disease Control and Prevention (CDC), U.S. Department of Health and Human Services (HHS), 3311 Toledo Road, Hyattsville, MD 20782, (866) 232-4636, www.cdc.gov/nchs; *National Vital Statistics Reports (NVSR); Vital Statistics of the United States (VSUS);* and unpublished data.

EXPENDITURES OF STATE AND LOCAL GOVERNMENT

See Individual governmental units

EXPENDITURES OF UNITED STATES GOVERNMENT

The Office of Management and Budget (OMB), 725 17th Street, NW, Washington, DC 20503, (202) 395-3080, Fax: (202) 395-3888, www.whitehouse.gov/omb; *Analytical Perspectives, Budget of the United States Government, Fiscal Year 2009* and *Historical Tables.*

Population Reference Bureau, 1875 Connecticut Avenue, NW, Suite 520, Washington, DC, 20009-5728, (800) 877-9881, Fax: (202) 328-3937, www.prb.org; *Government Spending in an Older America.*

U.S. Agency for International Development (USAID), Information Center, Ronald Reagan Building, Washington, D.C. 20523, (202) 712-0000, Fax: (202) 216-3524, www.usaid.gov; *U.S. Overseas Loans and Grants and Assistance from International Organizations* and unpublished data.

U.S. Census Bureau, 4700 Silver Hill Road, Washington DC 20233-0001, (301) 763-3030, www.census.gov; unpublished data.

U.S. Census Bureau, Governments Division, 4600 Silver Hill Road, Washington DC 20233, (800) 242-2184, www.census.gov/govs/www; *2002 Census of Governments* and *2002 Census of Governments, Government Finances.*

EXPENDITURES OF UNITED STATES GOVERNMENT - AID TO ARTS AND HUMANITIES

National Endowment for the Arts (NEA), 1100 Pennsylvania Avenue, NW, Washington, DC 20506-0001, (202) 682-5400, www.arts.gov; *2007 Annual Report.*

National Endowment for the Humanities (NEH), 1100 Pennsylvania Avenue, NW, Washington, DC 20506, (800) NEH-1121, www.neh.gov; *Annual Report.*

EXPENDITURES OF UNITED STATES GOVERNMENT - AID TO STATE AND LOCAL GOVERNMENT

The Office of Management and Budget (OMB), 725 17th Street, NW, Washington, DC 20503, (202) 395-3080, Fax: (202) 395-3888, www.whitehouse.gov/omb; *Budget of the United States Government, Federal Year 2009* and *Historical Tables.*

EXPENDITURES OF UNITED STATES GOVERNMENT - AID TO STATE AND LOCAL GOVERNMENT - BY FUNCTION

The Office of Management and Budget (OMB), 725 17th Street, NW, Washington, DC 20503, (202) 395-3080, Fax: (202) 395-3888, www.whitehouse.gov/omb; *Budget of the United States Government, Federal Year 2009* and *Historical Tables.*

EXPENDITURES OF UNITED STATES GOVERNMENT - ATOMIC ENERGY DEFENSE ACTIVITIES

The Office of Management and Budget (OMB), 725 17th Street, NW, Washington, DC 20503, (202) 395-3080, Fax: (202) 395-3888, www.whitehouse.gov/omb; *Budget of the United States Government, Federal Year 2009* and *Historical Tables.*

EXPENDITURES OF UNITED STATES GOVERNMENT - BUDGET OUTLAYS

The Office of Management and Budget (OMB), 725 17th Street, NW, Washington, DC 20503, (202) 395-3080, Fax: (202) 395-3888, www.whitehouse.gov/omb; *Analytical Perspectives, Budget of the United States Government, Fiscal Year 2009; Budget of the United States Government, Federal Year 2009;* and *Historical Tables.*

EXPENDITURES OF UNITED STATES GOVERNMENT - BY FUNCTION

The Office of Management and Budget (OMB), 725 17th Street, NW, Washington, DC 20503, (202) 395-3080, Fax: (202) 395-3888, www.whitehouse.gov/omb; *Historical Tables.*

EXPENDITURES OF UNITED STATES GOVERNMENT - BY SOURCE OF FUNDS

The Office of Management and Budget (OMB), 725 17th Street, NW, Washington, DC 20503, (202) 395-3080, Fax: (202) 395-3888, www.whitehouse.gov/omb; *Historical Tables.*

U.S. Census Bureau, Governments Division, 4600 Silver Hill Road, Washington DC 20233, (800) 242-2184, www.census.gov/govs/www; *2002 Census of Governments.*

EXPENDITURES OF UNITED STATES GOVERNMENT - CAPITAL OUTLAY

U.S. Census Bureau, 4700 Silver Hill Road, Washington DC 20233-0001, (301) 763-3030, www.census.gov; unpublished data.

U.S. Census Bureau, Governments Division, 4600 Silver Hill Road, Washington DC 20233, (800) 242-2184, www.census.gov/govs/www; *2002 Census of Governments* and *2002 Census of Governments, Government Finances.*

EXPENDITURES OF UNITED STATES GOVERNMENT - CAPITAL OUTLAY - CONTRACT AWARDS

U.S. Department of Defense (DOD), Statistical Information Analysis Division (SIAD), The Pentagon, Washington, DC 20301, (703) 545-6700, http://siadapp.dior.whs.mil/; *Atlas/Data Abstract for the United States and Selected Areas, Fiscal Year 2005.*

EXPENDITURES OF UNITED STATES GOVERNMENT - FOOD PROGRAMS - FEDERAL

Economic Research Service (ERS), U.S. Department of Agriculture (USDA), 1800 M Street, NW, Washington, DC 20036-5831, (202) 694-5050, Fax: (202) 694-5689, www.ers.usda.gov; *The Food Assistance Landscape: Federal Year 2007 Annual Report* and *Household Food Security in the United States, 2006.*

Social Security Administration (SSA), Office of Public Inquiries, Windsor Park Building, 6401 Security Boulevard, Baltimore, MD 21235, (800) 772-1213, www.ssa.gov; *Social Security Bulletin* and unpublished data.

U.S. Library of Congress (LOC), Congressional Research Service (CRS), The Library of Congress, 101 Independence Avenue, SE, Washington, DC 20540-7500, (202) 707-5700, www.loc.gov/crsinfo; *Cash and Non-cash Benefits for Persons With Limited Income: Eligibility Rules, Recipient and Expenditure Data.*

EXPENDITURES OF UNITED STATES GOVERNMENT - HEALTH

Centers for Medicare and Medicaid Services (CMS), U.S. Department of Health and Human Services (HHS), 7500 Security Boulevard, Baltimore, MD 21244-1850, (410) 786-3000, http://cms.hhs.gov; *Health Care Financing Review.*

EXPENDITURES OF UNITED STATES GOVERNMENT - HOSPITALS

American Hospital Association (AHA), One North Franklin, Chicago, IL 60606-3421, (312) 422-3000, www.aha.org; *Hospital Statistics 2008.*

EXPENDITURES OF UNITED STATES GOVERNMENT - JUSTICE

Justice Research and Statistics Association (JRSA), 777 N. Capitol Street, NE, Suite 801, Washington, DC 20002, (202) 842-9330, Fax: (202) 842-9329, www.jrsa.org; *Documenting the Extent and Nature of Drug and Violent Crime: Developing Jurisdiction-Specific Profiles of the Criminal Justice System; The Forum; JRP Digest; Justice Research and Policy;* and *SAC Publication Digest.*

U.S. Department of Justice (DOJ), Bureau of Justice Statistics, 810 Seventh Street, NW, Washington, DC 20531, (202) 307-0765, www.ojp.usdoj.gov/bjs/; *Justice Expenditure and Employment in the United States 2003.*

EXPENDITURES OF UNITED STATES GOVERNMENT - LAND AND BUILDINGS

General Services Administration (GSA), 1800 F Street, NW, Washington, DC 20405, (202) 708-5082, www.gsa.gov; *Federal Real Property Profile 2004 (FRPP).*

EXPENDITURES OF UNITED STATES GOVERNMENT - MILITARY PERSONNEL

U.S. Department of Defense (DOD), Statistical Information Analysis Division (SIAD), The Pentagon, Washington, DC 20301, (703) 545-6700, http://siadapp.dior.whs.mil/; *Atlas/Data Abstract for the United States and Selected Areas, Fiscal Year 2005; Selected Manpower Statistics, Fiscal Year 2005;* and unpublished data.

EXPENDITURES OF UNITED STATES GOVERNMENT - NATIONAL DEFENSE

The Office of Management and Budget (OMB), 725 17th Street, NW, Washington, DC 20503, (202) 395-3080, Fax: (202) 395-3888, www.whitehouse.gov/omb; *Historical Tables.*

U.S. Library of Congress (LOC), Congressional Research Service (CRS), The Library of Congress, 101 Independence Avenue, SE, Washington, DC 20540-7500, (202) 707-5700, www.loc.gov/crsinfo; *FY2006 Appropriations for State and Local Homeland Security; Homeland Security Department: FY2006 Appropriations;* and *Homeland Security Research and Development Funding, Organization, and Oversight.*

EXPENDITURES OF UNITED STATES GOVERNMENT - OUTLAYS BY AGENCY

The Office of Management and Budget (OMB), 725 17th Street, NW, Washington, DC 20503, (202) 395-3080, Fax: (202) 395-3888, www.whitehouse.gov/omb; *Budget of the United States Government, Federal Year 2009* and *Historical Tables.*

EXPENDITURES OF UNITED STATES GOVERNMENT - OUTLAYS BY FUNCTION

The Office of Management and Budget (OMB), 725 17th Street, NW, Washington, DC 20503, (202) 395-3080, Fax: (202) 395-3888, www.whitehouse.gov/omb; *Budget of the United States Government, Federal Year 2009* and *Historical Tables.*

EXPENDITURES OF UNITED STATES GOVERNMENT - PAYMENTS FOR PUBLIC ASSISTANCE

Social Security Administration (SSA), Office of Public Inquiries, Windsor Park Building, 6401 Security Boulevard, Baltimore, MD 21235, (800) 772-1213, www.ssa.gov; *Social Security Bulletin* and unpublished data.

U.S. Department of Labor (DOL), Employment and Training Administration (ETA), Frances Perkins Building, 200 Constitution Avenue, NW, Washington, DC 20210, (877) US-2JOBS, www.doleta.gov; *Unemployment Insurance Data Summary.*

U.S. Library of Congress (LOC), Congressional Research Service (CRS), The Library of Congress, 101 Independence Avenue, SE, Washington, DC 20540-7500, (202) 707-5700, www.loc.gov/crsinfo; *Cash and Non-cash Benefits for Persons With Limited Income: Eligibility Rules, Recipient and Expenditure Data* and *Social Security: The Cost-of-Living Adjustment in January 2003.*

EXPENDITURES OF UNITED STATES GOVERNMENT - PAYROLLS

U.S. Census Bureau, Governments Division, 4600 Silver Hill Road, Washington DC 20233, (800) 242-2184, www.census.gov/govs/www; *2002 Census of Governments, Government Finances* and *2002 Census of Governments, Public Employment and Payroll.*

United States Office of Personnel Management (OMB), 1900 E Street, NW, Washington, DC 20415-1000, (202) 606-1800, www.opm.gov; *Employment and Trends of Federal Civilian Workforce Statistics* and *Pay Structure of the Federal Civil Service.*

EXPENDITURES OF UNITED STATES GOVERNMENT - PUBLIC DEBT

The Office of Management and Budget (OMB), 725 17th Street, NW, Washington, DC 20503, (202) 395-3080, Fax: (202) 395-3888, www.whitehouse.gov/omb; *Historical Tables.*

U.S. Census Bureau, Governments Division, 4600 Silver Hill Road, Washington DC 20233, (800) 242-2184, www.census.gov/govs/www; *2002 Census of Governments* and *2002 Census of Governments, Government Finances.*

EXPENDITURES OF UNITED STATES GOVERNMENT - PUBLIC ROADS

U.S. Census Bureau, Governments Division, 4600 Silver Hill Road, Washington DC 20233, (800) 242-2184, www.census.gov/govs/www; *Federal Aid to States for Fiscal Year 2004.*

EXPENDITURES OF UNITED STATES GOVERNMENT - RESEARCH AND DEVELOPMENT

National Science Foundation, Division of Science Resources Statistics (SRS), 4201 Wilson Boulevard, Arlington, VA 22230, (703) 292-8780, Fax: (703) 292-9092, www.nsf.gov; *Federal Funds for Research and Development: Fiscal Years 2004-2006; Federal R D Funding by Budget Function: Fiscal Years 2004-06; National Patterns of Research and Development Resources: 2006 Data Update;* and *Science and Engineering Indicators 2008.*

U.S. Library of Congress (LOC), Congressional Research Service (CRS), The Library of Congress, 101 Independence Avenue, SE, Washington, DC 20540-7500, (202) 707-5700, www.loc.gov/crsinfo; *Homeland Security Research and Development Funding, Organization, and Oversight.*

EXPENDITURES OF UNITED STATES GOVERNMENT - RIVERS, HARBORS, AND FLOOD CONTROL

Center for Research on the Epidemiology of Disasters (CRED), Universite Catholique de Louvain, Ecole de Sante Publique, 30.94 Clos Chapelle-aux-Champs, 1200 Brussels, Belgium, www.cred.be; *An Analytical Review of Selected Data Sets on Natural Disasters and Impacts;* Complex Emergency Database (CE-DAT): A Database on the Human Impact of Complex Emergencies; *EM-DAT: The International Disaster Database;* and *Thirty Years of Natural Disasters 1974-2003: The Numbers.*

U.S. Army Corps of Engineers (USACE), 441 G Street, NW, Washington, DC 20314-1000, (202) 761-0011, www.usace.army.mil; *Annual Report of the Secretary of the Army on Civil Works Activities.*

U.S. Library of Congress (LOC), Congressional Research Service (CRS), The Library of Congress, 101 Independence Avenue, SE, Washington, DC 20540-7500, (202) 707-5700, www.loc.gov/crsinfo; *Port and Maritime Security: Background and Issues for Congress.*

EXPENDITURES OF UNITED STATES GOVERNMENT - SCHOOLS

National Center for Education Statistics (NCES), 1990 K Street, NW, Washington, DC 20006, (202) 502-7300, http://nces.ed.gov; *Digest of Education Statistics 2007.*

National Education Association (NEA), 1201 Sixteenth Street, NW, Washington, DC 20036-3290, (202) 833-4000, Fax: (202) 822-7974, www.nea.org; *Rankings and Estimates: Rankings of the States 2006 and Estimates of School Statistics 2007.*

EXPENDITURES OF UNITED STATES GOVERNMENT - SCIENCE AND SPACE PROGRAMS

The Office of Management and Budget (OMB), 725 17th Street, NW, Washington, DC 20503, (202) 395-3080, Fax: (202) 395-3888, www.whitehouse.gov/omb; *Budget of the United States Government, Federal Year 2009* and *Historical Tables.*

Satellite Industry Association (SIA), 1730 M. Street, NW, Suite 600, Washington, DC 20036, (202) 349-3650, Fax: (202) 349-3622, www.sia.org; *The Director's Report.*

United Nations Conference on Trade and Development (UNCTAD), DC2-1120, United Nations, New York, NY 10017, (212) 963-0027, www.unctad.org; *UNCTAD Commodity Yearbook.*

EXPENDITURES OF UNITED STATES GOVERNMENT - SOCIAL WELFARE PROGRAMS

Economic Policy Institute (EPI), 1333 H Street, NW, Suite 300, East Tower, Washington, DC 20005-4707, (202) 775-8810, www.epi.org; *The End of Welfare? Consequences of Federal Devolution for the Nation.*

Social Security Administration (SSA), Office of Public Inquiries, Windsor Park Building, 6401 Security Boulevard, Baltimore, MD 21235, (800) 772-1213, www.ssa.gov; *Annual Statistical Supplement, 2007; Social Security Bulletin;* and unpublished data.

U.S. Library of Congress (LOC), Congressional Research Service (CRS), The Library of Congress, 101 Independence Avenue, SE, Washington, DC 20540-7500, (202) 707-5700, www.loc.gov/crsinfo; *The Low-Income Home Energy Assistance Program (LIHEAP): Program and Funding Issues.*

EXPENDITURES OF UNITED STATES GOVERNMENT - TRUST FUNDS

The Office of Management and Budget (OMB), 725 17th Street, NW, Washington, DC 20503, (202) 395-3080, Fax: (202) 395-3888, www.whitehouse.gov/omb; *Analytical Perspectives, Budget of the United States Government, Fiscal Year 2009.*

EXPLOSIVE MATERIAL SHIPMENTS

U.S. Department of Transportation (DOT), Federal Highway Administration (FHA), 1200 New Jersey Avenue, SE, Washington, DC 20590, (202) 366-0660, www.fhwa.dot.gov; *Highway Statistics 2006.*

EXPLOSIVES

Bureau of Alcohol, Tobacco, Firearms and Explosives (ATF), Office of Public and Governmental Affairs, 99 New York Avenue, NE, Mail Stop 5S144, Washington, DC 20226, (202) 927-7890, www.atf.gov; *Explosive Incident Reports For Bombing.*

EXPORTS

See INTERNATIONAL TRADE

EXPRESS MAIL

U.S. Postal Service (USPS), 475 L'Enfant Plaza West, SW, Washington, DC 20260, (202) 268-2500, Fax: (202) 268-4860, www.usps.gov; *2005 Annual Report; 2005 Comprehensive Statement on Postal Operations; Postal Bulletin 2005 Annual Index; Quarterly Statistics Report (QSR);* and unpublished data.

EYE CARE PRICE INDEXES

U.S. Bureau of Labor Statistics (BLS), Postal Square Building, 2 Massachusetts Avenue, NE, Washington, DC 20212-0001, (202) 691-5200, Fax: (202) 691-6325, www.bls.gov; *Consumer Price Index Detailed Report* and *Monthly Labor Review (MLR).*

EYEGLASSES AND CONTACT LENSES

Centers for Medicare and Medicaid Services (CMS), U.S. Department of Health and Human Services (HHS), 7500 Security Boulevard, Baltimore, MD 21244-1850, (410) 786-3000, http://cms.hhs.gov; *Health Care Financing Review.*STATISTICS SOURCES, Thirty-second Edition - 2009STATISTICS SOURCES, Thirty-second Edition - 2009

FABRICATED METAL PRODUCTS INDUSTRY, MANUFACTURING - CAPITAL

Bureau of Economic Analysis (BEA), U.S. Department of Commerce (DOC), 1441 L Street NW, Washington, DC 20230, (202) 606-9900, www.bea.gov; *Survey of Current Business (SCB).*

International Trade Administration (ITA), U.S. Department of Commerce (DOC), 1401 Constitution Avenue, NW, Washington, DC 20230, (800) USA-TRAD(E), Fax: (202) 482-4473, www.ita.doc.gov; unpublished data.

FABRICATED METAL PRODUCTS INDUSTRY, MANUFACTURING - EARNINGS

U.S. Census Bureau, Center for Economic Studies, 4600 Silver Hill Road, Washington DC 20233, (301) 457-1235, www.ces.census.gov; *2002 Economic Census, Transportation and Warehousing.*

U.S. Census Bureau, Manufacturing and Construction Division, 4600 Silver Hill Road, Washington DC 20233, (301) 763-4673, www.census.gov/mcd; *Annual Survey of Manufactures (ASM)* and *Census of Manufactures.*

FABRICATED METAL PRODUCTS INDUSTRY, MANUFACTURING - EMPLOYEES

U.S. Census Bureau, Center for Economic Studies, 4600 Silver Hill Road, Washington DC 20233, (301) 457-1235, www.ces.census.gov; *2002 Economic Census, Manufacturing.*

U.S. Census Bureau, Manufacturing and Construction Division, 4600 Silver Hill Road, Washington DC 20233, (301) 763-4673, www.census.gov/mcd; *Annual Survey of Manufactures (ASM)* and *Census of Manufactures.*

FABRICATED METAL PRODUCTS INDUSTRY, MANUFACTURING - ENERGY CONSUMPTION

U.S. Department of Energy (DOE), Energy Information Administration (EIA), 1000 Independence Avenue, SW, Washington, DC 20585, (202) 586-8800, www.eia.doe.gov; *Manufacturing Energy Consumption Survey (MECS) 2002.*

FABRICATED METAL PRODUCTS INDUSTRY, MANUFACTURING - ESTABLISHMENTS

U.S. Census Bureau, Company Statistics Division, 4700 Silver Hill Road, Washington DC 20233-0001, (301) 763-3030, www.census.gov/csd/; *County Business Patterns 2004.*

FABRICATED METAL PRODUCTS INDUSTRY, MANUFACTURING - FINANCE

American Iron and Steel Institute, 1140 Connecticut Avenue, NW, Suite 705, Washington, DC 20036, (202) 452-7100, www.steel.org; *2005 Annual Statistical Report.*

FABRICATED METAL PRODUCTS INDUSTRY, MANUFACTURING - GROSS DOMESTIC PRODUCT

Bureau of Economic Analysis (BEA), U.S. Department of Commerce (DOC), 1441 L Street NW, Washington, DC 20230, (202) 606-9900, www.bea.gov; *Survey of Current Business (SCB).*

FABRICATED METAL PRODUCTS INDUSTRY, MANUFACTURING - INDUSTRIAL SAFETY

U.S. Bureau of Labor Statistics (BLS), Postal Square Building, 2 Massachusetts Avenue, NE, Washington, DC 20212-0001, (202) 691-5200, Fax: (202) 691-6325, www.bls.gov; *Injuries, Illnesses, and Fatalities (IIF).*

FABRICATED METAL PRODUCTS INDUSTRY, MANUFACTURING - PRODUCTIVITY

Board of Governors of the Federal Reserve System, Constitution Avenue, NW, Washington, DC 20551, (202) 452-3000, www.federalreserve.gov; *Federal Reserve Bulletin* and *Industrial Production and Capacity Utilization.*

U.S. Bureau of Labor Statistics (BLS), Postal Square Building, 2 Massachusetts Avenue, NE, Washington, DC 20212-0001, (202) 691-5200, Fax: (202) 691-6325, www.bls.gov; *Industry Productivity and Costs.*

FABRICATED METAL PRODUCTS INDUSTRY, MANUFACTURING - PROFITS

Bureau of Economic Analysis (BEA), U.S. Department of Commerce (DOC), 1441 L Street NW, Washington, DC 20230, (202) 606-9900, www.bea.gov; *2007 Annual Revision of the National Income and Product Accounts (NIPA)* and *Survey of Current Business (SCB).*

FABRICATED METAL PRODUCTS INDUSTRY, MANUFACTURING - SHIPMENTS

U.S. Census Bureau, Manufacturing and Construction Division, 4600 Silver Hill Road, Washington DC 20233, (301) 763-4673, www.census.gov/mcd; *Current Industrial Reports* and *Manufacturers Shipments, Inventories and Orders.*

FABRICATED METAL PRODUCTS INDUSTRY, MANUFACTURING - TOXIC CHEMICAL RELEASES

U.S. Environmental Protection Agency (EPA), Ariel Rios Building, 1200 Pennsylvania Avenue, NW, Washington, DC 20460, (202) 272-0167, www.epa.gov; Toxics Release Inventory (TRI) Database.

FABRICATED METAL PRODUCTS INDUSTRY, MANUFACTURING - VALUE ADDED

U.S. Census Bureau, Manufacturing and Construction Division, 4600 Silver Hill Road, Washington DC 20233, (301) 763-4673, www.census.gov/mcd; *Annual Survey of Manufactures (ASM)* and *Census of Manufactures.*

FABRICS

See TEXTILE MILL PRODUCTS

FALKLAND ISLANDS - NATIONAL STATISTICAL OFFICE

The Secretariat, Secretariat Building, Thatcher Drive, Stanley, Falkland Islands; National Data Center.

FALKLAND ISLANDS - AGRICULTURAL MACHINERY

United Nations Statistics Division, New York, NY 10017, (800) 253-9646, Fax: (212) 963-4116, http://unstats.un.org; *Statistical Yearbook.*

FALKLAND ISLANDS - AGRICULTURE

Palgrave Macmillan Ltd., Houndmills, Basingstoke, Hampshire, RG21 6XS, England, (Telephone in U.S. (888) 330-8477), (Fax in U.S. (800) 672-2054), www.palgrave.com; *The Statesman's Yearbook 2008.*

Taylor and Francis Group, An Informa Business, 2 Park Square, Milton Park, Abingdon, Oxford OX14 4RN, United Kingdom, (Dial from U.S. (212) 216-7800), (Fax from U.S. (212) 564-7854), www.tandf.co.uk; *The Europa World Year Book.*

United Nations Conference on Trade and Development (UNCTAD), DC2-1120, United Nations, New York, NY 10017, (212) 963-0027, www.unctad.org; *UNCTAD Commodity Yearbook.*

United Nations Food and Agricultural Organization (FAO), Viale delle Terme di Caracalla, 00100 Rome, Italy, (Dial from U.S. (202) 653-2400), (Fax from U.S. (202) 653 5760), www.fao.org; AQUASTAT; *FAO Production Yearbook 2002; FAO Trade Yearbook;* and *The State of Food and Agriculture (SOFA) 2006.*

United Nations Statistics Division, New York, NY 10017, (800) 253-9646, Fax: (212) 963-4116, http://unstats.un.org; *Statistical Yearbook.*

FALKLAND ISLANDS - AIRLINES

Palgrave Macmillan Ltd., Houndmills, Basingstoke, Hampshire, RG21 6XS, England, (Telephone in U.S. (888) 330-8477), (Fax in U.S. (800) 672-2054), www.palgrave.com; *The Statesman's Yearbook 2008.*

FALKLAND ISLANDS - AIRPORTS

Central Intelligence Agency, Office of Public Affairs, Washington, DC 20505, (703) 482-0623, Fax: (703) 482-1739, www.cia.gov; *The World Factbook.*

FALKLAND ISLANDS - ARMED FORCES

Central Intelligence Agency, Office of Public Affairs, Washington, DC 20505, (703) 482-0623, Fax: (703) 482-1739, www.cia.gov; *The World Factbook.*

Palgrave Macmillan Ltd., Houndmills, Basingstoke, Hampshire, RG21 6XS, England, (Telephone in U.S. (888) 330-8477), (Fax in U.S. (800) 672-2054), www.palgrave.com; *The Statesman's Yearbook 2008.*

FALKLAND ISLANDS - BANKS AND BANKING

Palgrave Macmillan Ltd., Houndmills, Basingstoke, Hampshire, RG21 6XS, England, (Telephone in U.S. (888) 330-8477), (Fax in U.S. (800) 672-2054), www.palgrave.com; *The Statesman's Yearbook 2008.*

FALKLAND ISLANDS - BROADCASTING

Central Intelligence Agency, Office of Public Affairs, Washington, DC 20505, (703) 482-0623, Fax: (703) 482-1739, www.cia.gov; *The World Factbook.*

Palgrave Macmillan Ltd., Houndmills, Basingstoke, Hampshire, RG21 6XS, England, (Telephone in U.S. (888) 330-8477), (Fax in U.S. (800) 672-2054), www.palgrave.com; *The Statesman's Yearbook 2008.*

UNESCO Institute for Statistics, C.P. 6128 Succursale Centre-Ville, Montreal, Quebec, H3C 3J7 Canada, (Dial from U.S. (514) 343-6880), (Fax from U.S. (514) 343 6882), www.uis.unesco.org; *Statistical Tables.*

WRTH Publications Limited, PO Box 290, Oxford OX2 7FT, UK, www.wrth.com; *World Radio TV Handbook 2007.*

FALKLAND ISLANDS - BUDGET

Central Intelligence Agency, Office of Public Affairs, Washington, DC 20505, (703) 482-0623, Fax: (703) 482-1739, www.cia.gov; *The World Factbook.*

FALKLAND ISLANDS - CATTLE

See FALKLAND ISLANDS - LIVESTOCK

FALKLAND ISLANDS - CHILDBIRTH - STATISTICS

Central Intelligence Agency, Office of Public Affairs, Washington, DC 20505, (703) 482-0623, Fax: (703) 482-1739, www.cia.gov; *The World Factbook.*

Taylor and Francis Group, An Informa Business, 2 Park Square, Milton Park, Abingdon, Oxford OX14 4RN, United Kingdom, (Dial from U.S. (212) 216-7800), (Fax from U.S. (212) 564-7854), www.tandf.co.uk; *The Europa World Year Book.*

United Nations Statistics Division, New York, NY 10017, (800) 253-9646, Fax: (212) 963-4116, http://unstats.un.org; *Demographic Yearbook* and *Statistical Yearbook.*

World Health Organization (WHO), Avenue Appia 20, 1211 Geneve 27, Switzerland, (Telephone in U.S. (212) 331-9081), www.who.int; *World Health Report 2006.*

FALKLAND ISLANDS - CLIMATE

Palgrave Macmillan Ltd., Houndmills, Basingstoke, Hampshire, RG21 6XS, England, (Telephone in U.S. (888) 330-8477), (Fax in U.S. (800) 672-2054), www.palgrave.com; *The Statesman's Yearbook 2008.*

FALKLAND ISLANDS - COMMODITY EXCHANGES

United Nations Food and Agricultural Organization (FAO), Viale delle Terme di Caracalla, 00100 Rome, Italy, (Dial from U.S. (202) 653-2400), (Fax from U.S. (202) 653 5760), www.fao.org; *The State of Food and Agriculture (SOFA) 2006.*

FALKLAND ISLANDS - CONSUMER PRICE INDEXES

Taylor and Francis Group, An Informa Business, 2 Park Square, Milton Park, Abingdon, Oxford OX14 4RN, United Kingdom, (Dial from U.S. (212) 216-7800), (Fax from U.S. (212) 564-7854), www.tandf.co.uk; *The Europa World Year Book.*

United Nations Statistics Division, New York, NY 10017, (800) 253-9646, Fax: (212) 963-4116, http://unstats.un.org; *Statistical Yearbook.*

FALKLAND ISLANDS - CORN INDUSTRY

See FALKLAND ISLANDS - CROPS

FALKLAND ISLANDS - CROPS

Palgrave Macmillan Ltd., Houndmills, Basingstoke, Hampshire, RG21 6XS, England, (Telephone in U.S. (888) 330-8477), (Fax in U.S. (800) 672-2054), www.palgrave.com; *The Statesman's Yearbook 2008.*

United Nations Conference on Trade and Development (UNCTAD), DC2-1120, United Nations, New York, NY 10017, (212) 963-0027, www.unctad.org; *UNCTAD Commodity Yearbook.*

United Nations Food and Agricultural Organization (FAO), Viale delle Terme di Caracalla, 00100 Rome, Italy, (Dial from U.S. (202) 653-2400), (Fax from U.S. (202) 653 5760), www.fao.org; *The State of Food and Agriculture (SOFA) 2006.*

FALKLAND ISLANDS - DAIRY PROCESSING

Palgrave Macmillan Ltd., Houndmills, Basingstoke, Hampshire, RG21 6XS, England, (Telephone in U.S. (888) 330-8477), (Fax in U.S. (800) 672-2054), www.palgrave.com; *The Statesman's Yearbook 2008.*

United Nations Food and Agricultural Organization (FAO), Viale delle Terme di Caracalla, 00100 Rome, Italy, (Dial from U.S. (202) 653-2400), (Fax from U.S. (202) 653 5760), www.fao.org; *The State of Food and Agriculture (SOFA) 2006.*

FALKLAND ISLANDS - DEATH RATES

See FALKLAND ISLANDS - MORTALITY

FALKLAND ISLANDS - DIVORCE

United Nations Statistics Division, New York, NY 10017, (800) 253-9646, Fax: (212) 963-4116, http://unstats.un.org; *Demographic Yearbook* and *Statistical Yearbook.*

FALKLAND ISLANDS - ECONOMIC CONDITIONS

Central Intelligence Agency, Office of Public Affairs, Washington, DC 20505, (703) 482-0623, Fax: (703) 482-1739, www.cia.gov; *The World Factbook.*

Palgrave Macmillan Ltd., Houndmills, Basingstoke, Hampshire, RG21 6XS, England, (Telephone in U.S. (888) 330-8477), (Fax in U.S. (800) 672-2054), www.palgrave.com; *The Statesman's Yearbook 2008.*

FALKLAND ISLANDS - EDUCATION

Palgrave Macmillan Ltd., Houndmills, Basingstoke, Hampshire, RG21 6XS, England, (Telephone in U.S. (888) 330-8477), (Fax in U.S. (800) 672-2054), www.palgrave.com; *The Statesman's Yearbook 2008.*

Taylor and Francis Group, An Informa Business, 2 Park Square, Milton Park, Abingdon, Oxford OX14 4RN, United Kingdom, (Dial from U.S. (212) 216-7800), (Fax from U.S. (212) 564-7854), www.tandf.co.uk; *The Europa World Year Book.*

UNESCO Institute for Statistics, C.P. 6128 Succursale Centre-Ville, Montreal, Quebec, H3C 3J7 Canada, (Dial from U.S. (514) 343-6880), (Fax from U.S. (514) 343 6882), www.uis.unesco.org; *Statistical Tables.*

FALKLAND ISLANDS - EMPLOYMENT

International Labour Office, I.L.O. Publications, 4 route des Morillons, CH-1211 Geneva 22, Switzerland, (Telephone in U.S. (202) 653-7652), (Fax in U.S. (202) 653-7687), www.ilo.org; *Yearbook of Labour Statistics 2006.*

FALKLAND ISLANDS - EXPORTS

Central Intelligence Agency, Office of Public Affairs, Washington, DC 20505, (703) 482-0623, Fax: (703) 482-1739, www.cia.gov; *The World Factbook.*

International Monetary Fund (IMF), 700 Nineteenth Street, NW, Washington, DC 20431, (202) 623-7000, Fax: (202) 623-4661, www.imf.org; *Direction of Trade Statistics Yearbook 2007.*

Palgrave Macmillan Ltd., Houndmills, Basingstoke, Hampshire, RG21 6XS, England, (Telephone in U.S. (888) 330-8477), (Fax in U.S. (800) 672-2054), www.palgrave.com; *The Statesman's Yearbook 2008.*

Taylor and Francis Group, An Informa Business, 2 Park Square, Milton Park, Abingdon, Oxford OX14 4RN, United Kingdom, (Dial from U.S. (212) 216-7800), (Fax from U.S. (212) 564-7854), www.tandf.co.uk; *The Europa World Year Book.*

United Nations Food and Agricultural Organization (FAO), Viale delle Terme di Caracalla, 00100 Rome, Italy, (Dial from U.S. (202) 653-2400), (Fax from U.S. (202) 653 5760), www.fao.org; *The State of Food and Agriculture (SOFA) 2006.*

FALKLAND ISLANDS - FERTILITY, HUMAN

Central Intelligence Agency, Office of Public Affairs, Washington, DC 20505, (703) 482-0623, Fax: (703) 482-1739, www.cia.gov; *The World Factbook.*

FALKLAND ISLANDS - FERTILIZER INDUSTRY

United Nations Food and Agricultural Organization (FAO), Viale delle Terme di Caracalla, 00100 Rome, Italy, (Dial from U.S. (202) 653-2400), (Fax from U.S. (202) 653 5760), www.fao.org; *The State of Food and Agriculture (SOFA) 2006.*

FALKLAND ISLANDS - FETAL MORTALITY

See FALKLAND ISLANDS - MORTALITY

FALKLAND ISLANDS - FINANCE, PUBLIC

Taylor and Francis Group, An Informa Business, 2 Park Square, Milton Park, Abingdon, Oxford OX14 4RN, United Kingdom, (Dial from U.S. (212) 216-7800), (Fax from U.S. (212) 564-7854), www.tandf.co.uk; *The Europa World Year Book.*

FALKLAND ISLANDS - FISHERIES

Palgrave Macmillan Ltd., Houndmills, Basingstoke, Hampshire, RG21 6XS, England, (Telephone in U.S. (888) 330-8477), (Fax in U.S. (800) 672-2054), www.palgrave.com; *The Statesman's Yearbook 2008.*

United Nations Conference on Trade and Development (UNCTAD), DC2-1120, United Nations, New York, NY 10017, (212) 963-0027, www.unctad.org; *UNCTAD Commodity Yearbook.*

United Nations Food and Agricultural Organization (FAO), Viale delle Terme di Caracalla, 00100 Rome, Italy, (Dial from U.S. (202) 653-2400), (Fax from U.S. (202) 653 5760), www.fao.org; *FAO Yearbook of Fishery Statistics;* Fishery Databases; FISHSTAT Database. Subjects covered include: Aquaculture production, capture production, fishery commodities; and *The State of Food and Agriculture (SOFA) 2006.*

FALKLAND ISLANDS - FOOD

United Nations Conference on Trade and Development (UNCTAD), DC2-1120, United Nations, New York, NY 10017, (212) 963-0027, www.unctad.org; *UNCTAD Commodity Yearbook.*

United Nations Food and Agricultural Organization (FAO), Viale delle Terme di Caracalla, 00100 Rome, Italy, (Dial from U.S. (202) 653-2400), (Fax from U.S. (202) 653 5760), www.fao.org; *FAO Production Yearbook 2002* and *The State of Food and Agriculture (SOFA) 2006.*

FALKLAND ISLANDS - FOREIGN EXCHANGE RATES

Central Intelligence Agency, Office of Public Affairs, Washington, DC 20505, (703) 482-0623, Fax: (703) 482-1739, www.cia.gov; *The World Factbook.*

Taylor and Francis Group, An Informa Business, 2 Park Square, Milton Park, Abingdon, Oxford OX14 4RN, United Kingdom, (Dial from U.S. (212) 216-7800), (Fax from U.S. (212) 564-7854), www.tandf.co.uk; *The Europa World Year Book.*

FALKLAND ISLANDS - FORESTS AND FORESTRY

United Nations Conference on Trade and Development (UNCTAD), DC2-1120, United Nations, New York, NY 10017, (212) 963-0027, www.unctad.org; *UNCTAD Commodity Yearbook.*

United Nations Food and Agricultural Organization (FAO), Viale delle Terme di Caracalla, 00100 Rome, Italy, (Dial from U.S. (202) 653-2400), (Fax from U.S. (202) 653 5760), www.fao.org; *The State of Food and Agriculture (SOFA) 2006.*

FALKLAND ISLANDS - HIDES AND SKINS INDUSTRY

United Nations Food and Agricultural Organization (FAO), Viale delle Terme di Caracalla, 00100 Rome, Italy, (Dial from U.S. (202) 653-2400), (Fax from U.S. (202) 653 5760), www.fao.org; *FAO Production Yearbook 2002.*

FALKLAND ISLANDS - IMPORTS

Central Intelligence Agency, Office of Public Affairs, Washington, DC 20505, (703) 482-0623, Fax: (703) 482-1739, www.cia.gov; *The World Factbook.*

International Monetary Fund (IMF), 700 Nineteenth Street, NW, Washington, DC 20431, (202) 623-7000, Fax: (202) 623-4661, www.imf.org; *Direction of Trade Statistics Yearbook 2007.*

Palgrave Macmillan Ltd., Houndmills, Basingstoke, Hampshire, RG21 6XS, England, (Telephone in U.S. (888) 330-8477), (Fax in U.S. (800) 672-2054), www.palgrave.com; *The Statesman's Yearbook 2008.*

Taylor and Francis Group, An Informa Business, 2 Park Square, Milton Park, Abingdon, Oxford OX14 4RN, United Kingdom, (Dial from U.S. (212) 216-7800), (Fax from U.S. (212) 564-7854), www.tandf.co.uk; *The Europa World Year Book.*

United Nations Food and Agricultural Organization (FAO), Viale delle Terme di Caracalla, 00100 Rome, Italy, (Dial from U.S. (202) 653-2400), (Fax from U.S. (202) 653 5760), www.fao.org; *The State of Food and Agriculture (SOFA) 2006.*

FALKLAND ISLANDS - INDUSTRIES

Central Intelligence Agency, Office of Public Affairs, Washington, DC 20505, (703) 482-0623, Fax: (703) 482-1739, www.cia.gov; *The World Factbook.*

International Labour Office, I.L.O. Publications, 4 route des Morillons, CH-1211 Geneva 22, Switzerland, (Telephone in U.S. (202) 653-7652), (Fax in U.S. (202) 653-7687), www.ilo.org; *Yearbook of Labour Statistics 2006.*

FALKLAND ISLANDS - INFANT AND MATERNAL MORTALITY

See FALKLAND ISLANDS - MORTALITY

FALKLAND ISLANDS - INTERNATIONAL TRADE

Organisation for Economic Cooperation and Development (OECD), 2 rue Andre Pascal, F-75775 Paris Cedex 16, France, (Telephone in U.S. (202) 785-6323), (Fax in U.S. (202) 785-0350), www.oecd.org; *International Trade by Commodity Statistics (ITCS).*

Palgrave Macmillan Ltd., Houndmills, Basingstoke, Hampshire, RG21 6XS, England, (Telephone in U.S. (888) 330-8477), (Fax in U.S. (800) 672-2054), www.palgrave.com; *The Statesman's Yearbook 2008.*

Taylor and Francis Group, An Informa Business, 2 Park Square, Milton Park, Abingdon, Oxford OX14 4RN, United Kingdom, (Dial from U.S. (212) 216-7800), (Fax from U.S. (212) 564-7854), www.tandf.co.uk; *The Europa World Year Book.*

United Nations Conference on Trade and Development (UNCTAD), DC2-1120, United Nations, New York, NY 10017, (212) 963-0027, www.unctad.org; *UNCTAD Commodity Yearbook.*

United Nations Food and Agricultural Organization (FAO), Viale delle Terme di Caracalla, 00100 Rome, Italy, (Dial from U.S. (202) 653-2400), (Fax from U.S. (202) 653 5760), www.fao.org; *FAO Trade Yearbook* and *The State of Food and Agriculture (SOFA) 2006.*

United Nations Statistics Division, New York, NY 10017, (800) 253-9646, Fax: (212) 963-4116, http://unstats.un.org; *International Trade Statistics Yearbook* and *Statistical Yearbook.*

World Trade Organization (WTO), Centre William Rappard, Rue de Lausanne 154, CH-1211 Geneva 21, Switzerland, www.wto.org; *International Trade Statistics 2006.*

FALKLAND ISLANDS - LABOR

Central Intelligence Agency, Office of Public Affairs, Washington, DC 20505, (703) 482-0623, Fax: (703) 482-1739, www.cia.gov; *The World Factbook.*

International Labour Office, I.L.O. Publications, 4 route des Morillons, CH-1211 Geneva 22, Switzerland, (Telephone in U.S. (202) 653-7652), (Fax in U.S. (202) 653-7687), www.ilo.org; *Yearbook of Labour Statistics 2006.*

Taylor and Francis Group, An Informa Business, 2 Park Square, Milton Park, Abingdon, Oxford OX14 4RN, United Kingdom, (Dial from U.S. (212) 216-7800), (Fax from U.S. (212) 564-7854), www.tandf.co.uk; *The Europa World Year Book.*

United Nations Food and Agricultural Organization (FAO), Viale delle Terme di Caracalla, 00100 Rome, Italy, (Dial from U.S. (202) 653-2400), (Fax from U.S. (202) 653 5760), www.fao.org; *The State of Food and Agriculture (SOFA) 2006.*

FALKLAND ISLANDS - LAND USE

Central Intelligence Agency, Office of Public Affairs, Washington, DC 20505, (703) 482-0623, Fax: (703) 482-1739, www.cia.gov; *The World Factbook.*

United Nations Food and Agricultural Organization (FAO), Viale delle Terme di Caracalla, 00100 Rome, Italy, (Dial from U.S. (202) 653-2400), (Fax from U.S. (202) 653 5760), www.fao.org; *FAO Production Yearbook 2002.*

FALKLAND ISLANDS - LIFE EXPECTANCY

Central Intelligence Agency, Office of Public Affairs, Washington, DC 20505, (703) 482-0623, Fax: (703) 482-1739, www.cia.gov; *The World Factbook.*

FALKLAND ISLANDS - LIVESTOCK

Palgrave Macmillan Ltd., Houndmills, Basingstoke, Hampshire, RG21 6XS, England, (Telephone in U.S. (888) 330-8477), (Fax in U.S. (800) 672-2054), www.palgrave.com; *The Statesman's Yearbook 2008.*

Taylor and Francis Group, An Informa Business, 2 Park Square, Milton Park, Abingdon, Oxford OX14 4RN, United Kingdom, (Dial from U.S. (212) 216-7800), (Fax from U.S. (212) 564-7854), www.tandf.co.uk; *The Europa World Year Book.*

United Nations Conference on Trade and Development (UNCTAD), DC2-1120, United Nations, New York, NY 10017, (212) 963-0027, www.unctad.org; *UNCTAD Commodity Yearbook.*

United Nations Food and Agricultural Organization (FAO), Viale delle Terme di Caracalla, 00100 Rome, Italy, (Dial from U.S. (202) 653-2400), (Fax from U.S. (202) 653 5760), www.fao.org; *FAO Production Yearbook 2002* and *The State of Food and Agriculture (SOFA) 2006.*

United Nations Statistics Division, New York, NY 10017, (800) 253-9646, Fax: (212) 963-4116, http://unstats.un.org; *Statistical Yearbook.*

FALKLAND ISLANDS - MARRIAGE

United Nations Statistics Division, New York, NY 10017, (800) 253-9646, Fax: (212) 963-4116, http://unstats.un.org; *Demographic Yearbook* and *Statistical Yearbook.*

FALKLAND ISLANDS - MINERAL INDUSTRIES

United Nations Conference on Trade and Development (UNCTAD), DC2-1120, United Nations, New York, NY 10017, (212) 963-0027, www.unctad.org; *UNCTAD Commodity Yearbook.*

FALKLAND ISLANDS - MORTALITY

Central Intelligence Agency, Office of Public Affairs, Washington, DC 20505, (703) 482-0623, Fax: (703) 482-1739, www.cia.gov; *The World Factbook.*

Taylor and Francis Group, An Informa Business, 2 Park Square, Milton Park, Abingdon, Oxford OX14 4RN, United Kingdom, (Dial from U.S. (212) 216-7800), (Fax from U.S. (212) 564-7854), www.tandf.co.uk; *The Europa World Year Book.*

United Nations Statistics Division, New York, NY 10017, (800) 253-9646, Fax: (212) 963-4116, http://unstats.un.org; *Demographic Yearbook* and *Statistical Yearbook.*

FALKLAND ISLANDS - MOTION PICTURES

United Nations Statistics Division, New York, NY 10017, (800) 253-9646, Fax: (212) 963-4116, http://unstats.un.org; *Statistical Yearbook.*

FALKLAND ISLANDS - MOTOR VEHICLES

Taylor and Francis Group, An Informa Business, 2 Park Square, Milton Park, Abingdon, Oxford OX14 4RN, United Kingdom, (Dial from U.S. (212) 216-7800), (Fax from U.S. (212) 564-7854), www.tandf.co.uk; *The Europa World Year Book.*

United Nations Statistics Division, New York, NY 10017, (800) 253-9646, Fax: (212) 963-4116, http://unstats.un.org; *Statistical Yearbook.*

FALKLAND ISLANDS - MUSEUMS

UNESCO Institute for Statistics, C.P. 6128 Succursale Centre-Ville, Montreal, Quebec, H3C 3J7 Canada, (Dial from U.S. (514) 343-6880), (Fax from U.S. (514) 343 6882), www.uis.unesco.org; *Statistical Tables.*

FALKLAND ISLANDS - NUTRITION

United Nations Food and Agricultural Organization (FAO), Viale delle Terme di Caracalla, 00100 Rome, Italy, (Dial from U.S. (202) 653-2400), (Fax from U.S. (202) 653 5760), www.fao.org; *The State of Food and Agriculture (SOFA) 2006.*

FALKLAND ISLANDS - PERIODICALS

UNESCO Institute for Statistics, C.P. 6128 Succursale Centre-Ville, Montreal, Quebec, H3C 3J7 Canada, (Dial from U.S. (514) 343-6880), (Fax from U.S. (514) 343 6882), www.uis.unesco.org; *Statistical Tables.*

FALKLAND ISLANDS - PESTICIDES

United Nations Food and Agricultural Organization (FAO), Viale delle Terme di Caracalla, 00100 Rome, Italy, (Dial from U.S. (202) 653-2400), (Fax from U.S. (202) 653 5760), www.fao.org; *The State of Food and Agriculture (SOFA) 2006.*

FALKLAND ISLANDS - PETROLEUM INDUSTRY AND TRADE

Palgrave Macmillan Ltd., Houndmills, Basingstoke, Hampshire, RG21 6XS, England, (Telephone in U.S. (888) 330-8477), (Fax in U.S. (800) 672-2054), www.palgrave.com; *The Statesman's Yearbook 2008.*

PennWell Corporation, 1421 South Sheridan Road, Tulsa, OK 74112, (918) 835-3161, www.pennwell.com; *International Petroleum Encyclopedia 2007.*

United Nations Conference on Trade and Development (UNCTAD), DC2-1120, United Nations, New York, NY 10017, (212) 963-0027, www.unctad.org; *UNCTAD Commodity Yearbook.*

United Nations Food and Agricultural Organization (FAO), Viale delle Terme di Caracalla, 00100 Rome, Italy, (Dial from U.S. (202) 653-2400), (Fax from U.S. (202) 653 5760), www.fao.org; *The State of Food and Agriculture (SOFA) 2006.*

FALKLAND ISLANDS - POLITICAL SCIENCE

Central Intelligence Agency, Office of Public Affairs, Washington, DC 20505, (703) 482-0623, Fax: (703) 482-1739, www.cia.gov; *The World Factbook.*

Palgrave Macmillan Ltd., Houndmills, Basingstoke, Hampshire, RG21 6XS, England, (Telephone in U.S. (888) 330-8477), (Fax in U.S. (800) 672-2054), www.palgrave.com; *The Statesman's Yearbook 2008.*

Taylor and Francis Group, An Informa Business, 2 Park Square, Milton Park, Abingdon, Oxford OX14 4RN, United Kingdom, (Dial from U.S. (212) 216-7800), (Fax from U.S. (212) 564-7854), www.tandf.co.uk; *The Europa World Year Book.*

FALKLAND ISLANDS - POPULATION

Central Intelligence Agency, Office of Public Affairs, Washington, DC 20505, (703) 482-0623, Fax: (703) 482-1739, www.cia.gov; *The World Factbook.*

International Labour Office, I.L.O. Publications, 4 route des Morillons, CH-1211 Geneva 22, Switzerland, (Telephone in U.S. (202) 653-7652), (Fax in U.S. (202) 653-7687), www.ilo.org; *Yearbook of Labour Statistics 2006.*

Palgrave Macmillan Ltd., Houndmills, Basingstoke, Hampshire, RG21 6XS, England, (Telephone in U.S. (888) 330-8477), (Fax in U.S. (800) 672-2054), www.palgrave.com; *The Statesman's Yearbook 2008.*

Taylor and Francis Group, An Informa Business, 2 Park Square, Milton Park, Abingdon, Oxford OX14 4RN, United Kingdom, (Dial from U.S. (212) 216-7800), (Fax from U.S. (212) 564-7854), www.tandf.co.uk; *The Europa World Year Book.*

UNESCO Institute for Statistics, C.P. 6128 Succursale Centre-Ville, Montreal, Quebec, H3C 3J7 Canada, (Dial from U.S. (514) 343-6880), (Fax from U.S. (514) 343 6882), www.uis.unesco.org; *Statistical Tables.*

United Nations Food and Agricultural Organization (FAO), Viale delle Terme di Caracalla, 00100 Rome, Italy, (Dial from U.S. (202) 653-2400), (Fax from U.S. (202) 653 5760), www.fao.org; *FAO Production Yearbook 2002.*

United Nations Statistics Division, New York, NY 10017, (800) 253-9646, Fax: (212) 963-4116, http://unstats.un.org; *Demographic Yearbook* and *Statistical Yearbook.*

World Health Organization (WHO), Avenue Appia 20, 1211 Geneve 27, Switzerland, (Telephone in U.S. (212) 331-9081), www.who.int; *World Health Report 2006.*

FALKLAND ISLANDS - POPULATION DENSITY

Central Intelligence Agency, Office of Public Affairs, Washington, DC 20505, (703) 482-0623, Fax: (703) 482-1739, www.cia.gov; *The World Factbook.*

Palgrave Macmillan Ltd., Houndmills, Basingstoke, Hampshire, RG21 6XS, England, (Telephone in U.S. (888) 330-8477), (Fax in U.S. (800) 672-2054), www.palgrave.com; *The Statesman's Yearbook 2008.*

Taylor and Francis Group, An Informa Business, 2 Park Square, Milton Park, Abingdon, Oxford OX14 4RN, United Kingdom, (Dial from U.S. (212) 216-7800), (Fax from U.S. (212) 564-7854), www.tandf.co.uk; *The Europa World Year Book.*

UNESCO Institute for Statistics, C.P. 6128 Succursale Centre-Ville, Montreal, Quebec, H3C 3J7 Canada, (Dial from U.S. (514) 343-6880), (Fax from U.S. (514) 343 6882), www.uis.unesco.org; *Statistical Tables.*

United Nations Food and Agricultural Organization (FAO), Viale delle Terme di Caracalla, 00100 Rome, Italy, (Dial from U.S. (202) 653-2400), (Fax from U.S. (202) 653 5760), www.fao.org; *The State of Food and Agriculture (SOFA) 2006.*

United Nations Statistics Division, New York, NY 10017, (800) 253-9646, Fax: (212) 963-4116, http://unstats.un.org; *Statistical Yearbook.*

FALKLAND ISLANDS - POSTAL SERVICE

United Nations Statistics Division, New York, NY 10017, (800) 253-9646, Fax: (212) 963-4116, http://unstats.un.org; *Statistical Yearbook.*

FALKLAND ISLANDS - POWER RESOURCES

Platts, 2 Penn Plaza, 25th Floor, New York, NY 10121-2298, (212) 904-3070, www.platts.com; *Energy Economist.*

United Nations Food and Agricultural Organization (FAO), Viale delle Terme di Caracalla, 00100 Rome, Italy, (Dial from U.S. (202) 653-2400), (Fax from U.S. (202) 653 5760), www.fao.org; *The State of Food and Agriculture (SOFA) 2006.*

United Nations Statistics Division, New York, NY 10017, (800) 253-9646, Fax: (212) 963-4116, http://unstats.un.org; *Energy Statistics Yearbook 2003* and *Statistical Yearbook.*

FALKLAND ISLANDS - PRICES

International Labour Office, I.L.O. Publications, 4 route des Morillons, CH-1211 Geneva 22, Switzerland, (Telephone in U.S. (202) 653-7652), (Fax in U.S. (202) 653-7687), www.ilo.org; *Yearbook of Labour Statistics 2006.*

United Nations Food and Agricultural Organization (FAO), Viale delle Terme di Caracalla, 00100 Rome, Italy, (Dial from U.S. (202) 653-2400), (Fax from U.S. (202) 653 5760), www.fao.org; *FAO Production Yearbook 2002* and *The State of Food and Agriculture (SOFA) 2006.*

FALKLAND ISLANDS - PROFESSIONS

UNESCO Institute for Statistics, C.P. 6128 Succursale Centre-Ville, Montreal, Quebec, H3C 3J7 Canada, (Dial from U.S. (514) 343-6880), (Fax from U.S. (514) 343 6882), www.uis.unesco.org; *Statistical Tables.*

FALKLAND ISLANDS - PUBLIC HEALTH

Palgrave Macmillan Ltd., Houndmills, Basingstoke, Hampshire, RG21 6XS, England, (Telephone in U.S. (888) 330-8477), (Fax in U.S. (800) 672-2054), www.palgrave.com; *The Statesman's Yearbook 2008.*

United Nations Statistics Division, New York, NY 10017, (800) 253-9646, Fax: (212) 963-4116, http://unstats.un.org; *Statistical Yearbook.*

FALKLAND ISLANDS - RADIO BROADCASTING

Palgrave Macmillan Ltd., Houndmills, Basingstoke, Hampshire, RG21 6XS, England, (Telephone in U.S. (888) 330-8477), (Fax in U.S. (800) 672-2054), www.palgrave.com; *The Statesman's Yearbook 2008.*

UNESCO Institute for Statistics, C.P. 6128 Succursale Centre-Ville, Montreal, Quebec, H3C 3J7 Canada, (Dial from U.S. (514) 343-6880), (Fax from U.S. (514) 343 6882), www.uis.unesco.org; *Statistical Tables.*

FALKLAND ISLANDS - RELIGION

Central Intelligence Agency, Office of Public Affairs, Washington, DC 20505, (703) 482-0623, Fax: (703) 482-1739, www.cia.gov; *The World Factbook.*

FALKLAND ISLANDS - ROADS

Central Intelligence Agency, Office of Public Affairs, Washington, DC 20505, (703) 482-0623, Fax: (703) 482-1739, www.cia.gov; *The World Factbook.*

Palgrave Macmillan Ltd., Houndmills, Basingstoke, Hampshire, RG21 6XS, England, (Telephone in U.S. (888) 330-8477), (Fax in U.S. (800) 672-2054), www.palgrave.com; *The Statesman's Yearbook 2008.*

FALKLAND ISLANDS - SHEEP

See FALKLAND ISLANDS - LIVESTOCK

FALKLAND ISLANDS - SHIPPING

Palgrave Macmillan Ltd., Houndmills, Basingstoke, Hampshire, RG21 6XS, England, (Telephone in U.S. (888) 330-8477), (Fax in U.S. (800) 672-2054), www.palgrave.com; *The Statesman's Yearbook 2008.*

Taylor and Francis Group, An Informa Business, 2 Park Square, Milton Park, Abingdon, Oxford OX14 4RN, United Kingdom, (Dial from U.S. (212) 216-7800), (Fax from U.S. (212) 564-7854), www.tandf.co.uk; *The Europa World Year Book.*

United Nations Statistics Division, New York, NY 10017, (800) 253-9646, Fax: (212) 963-4116, http://unstats.un.org; *Statistical Yearbook.*

FALKLAND ISLANDS - TELEPHONE

International Telecommunication Union (ITU), Place des Nations, 1211 Geneva 20, Switzerland, www.itu.int; *World Telecommunication Indicators Database.*

Palgrave Macmillan Ltd., Houndmills, Basingstoke, Hampshire, RG21 6XS, England, (Telephone in U.S. (888) 330-8477), (Fax in U.S. (800) 672-2054), www.palgrave.com; *The Statesman's Yearbook 2008.*

FALKLAND ISLANDS - TEXTILE INDUSTRY

United Nations Conference on Trade and Development (UNCTAD), DC2-1120, United Nations, New York, NY 10017, (212) 963-0027, www.unctad.org; *UNCTAD Commodity Yearbook.*

FALKLAND ISLANDS - TRADE

See FALKLAND ISLANDS - INTERNATIONAL TRADE

FALKLAND ISLANDS - TRANSPORTATION

Central Intelligence Agency, Office of Public Affairs, Washington, DC 20505, (703) 482-0623, Fax: (703) 482-1739, www.cia.gov; *The World Factbook.*

Palgrave Macmillan Ltd., Houndmills, Basingstoke, Hampshire, RG21 6XS, England, (Telephone in U.S. (888) 330-8477), (Fax in U.S. (800) 672-2054), www.palgrave.com; *The Statesman's Yearbook 2008.*

Taylor and Francis Group, An Informa Business, 2 Park Square, Milton Park, Abingdon, Oxford OX14 4RN, United Kingdom, (Dial from U.S. (212) 216-7800), (Fax from U.S. (212) 564-7854), www.tandf.co.uk; *The Europa World Year Book.*

FALKLAND ISLANDS - UNEMPLOYMENT

Central Intelligence Agency, Office of Public Affairs, Washington, DC 20505, (703) 482-0623, Fax: (703) 482-1739, www.cia.gov; *The World Factbook.*

International Labour Office, I.L.O. Publications, 4 route des Morillons, CH-1211 Geneva 22, Switzerland, (Telephone in U.S. (202) 653-7652), (Fax in U.S. (202) 653-7687), www.ilo.org; *Yearbook of Labour Statistics 2006.*

FALKLAND ISLANDS - VITAL STATISTICS

United Nations Statistics Division, New York, NY 10017, (800) 253-9646, Fax: (212) 963-4116, http://unstats.un.org; *Statistical Yearbook.*

World Health Organization (WHO), Avenue Appia 20, 1211 Geneve 27, Switzerland, (Telephone in U.S. (212) 331-9081), www.who.int; *World Health Report 2006.*

FALKLAND ISLANDS - WAGES

International Labour Office, I.L.O. Publications, 4 route des Morillons, CH-1211 Geneva 22, Switzerland, (Telephone in U.S. (202) 653-7652), (Fax in U.S. (202) 653-7687), www.ilo.org; *Yearbook of Labour Statistics 2006.*

FAMILIES

See HOUSEHOLDS OR FAMILIES

The Annie E. Casey Foundation, 701 Saint Paul Street, Baltimore, MD 21202, (410) 547-6600, Fax: (410) 547-3610, www.aecf.org; *Of, By, And For the Community: The Story of PUENTE Learning Center.*

FAMILY VIOLENCE

Australian Government Office for Women, Department of Families, Community Services and Indigenous Affairs, Box 7788, Canberra Mail Centre ACT 2610, Australia, http://ofw.facsia.gov.au; *Cost of Domestic Violence to the Australian Economy.*

Justice Research and Statistics Association (JRSA), 777 N. Capitol Street, NE, Suite 801, Washington, DC 20002, (202) 842-9330, Fax: (202) 842-9329, www.jrsa.org; *Documenting the Extent and Nature of Drug and Violent Crime: Developing Jurisdiction-Specific Profiles of the Criminal Justice System; Domestic Violence and Sexual Assault Data Collection Systems in the States; The Forum; JRP Digest; Justice Research and Policy;* and *SAC Publication Digest.*

U.S. Department of Justice (DOJ), Bureau of Justice Statistics, 810 Seventh Street, NW, Washington, DC 20531, (202) 307-0765, www.ojp.usdoj.gov/bjs/; *Crime and the Nation's Households, 2004; Family Violence Statistics: Including Statistics on Strangers and Acquaintances;* and *Federal Criminal Case Processing, 2002: With trends 1982-2002, Reconciled Data.*

U.S. Department of Justice (DOJ), National Institute of Justice (NIJ), 810 Seventh Street, NW, Washington, DC 20531, (202) 307-2942, Fax: (202) 616-0275, www.ojp.usdoj.gov/nij/; *Assessing Risk Factors for Intimate Partner Homicide; Do Batterer Intervention Programs Work? Two Studies; Do Domestic Violence Services Save Lives?; Intimate Partner Homicide: An Overview; Reviewing Domestic Violence Deaths; Risky Mix: Drinking, Drug Use, and Homicide; When Violence Hits Home: How Economics and Neighborhood Play a Role;* and *Youth Victimization: Prevalence and Implications* .

FAMILY-OWNED BUSINESS ENTERPRISES

U.S. Census Bureau, Company Statistics Division, 4700 Silver Hill Road, Washington DC 20233-0001, (301) 763-3030, www.census.gov/csd/; *2002 Survey of Business Owners (SBO).*

FARM AND GARDEN MACHINERY - MANUFACTURING - EARNINGS

U.S. Bureau of Labor Statistics (BLS), Postal Square Building, 2 Massachusetts Avenue, NE, Washington, DC 20212-0001, (202) 691-5200, Fax: (202) 691-6325, www.bls.gov; *Current Employment Statistics Survey (CES)* and *Employment and Earnings (EE).*

FARM AND GARDEN MACHINERY - MANUFACTURING - EMPLOYEES

U.S. Bureau of Labor Statistics (BLS), Postal Square Building, 2 Massachusetts Avenue, NE, Washington, DC 20212-0001, (202) 691-5200, Fax: (202) 691-6325, www.bls.gov; *Current Employment Statistics Survey (CES)* and *Employment and Earnings (EE).*

FARM AND GARDEN MACHINERY - MANUFACTURING - PRODUCTIVITY

U.S. Bureau of Labor Statistics (BLS), Postal Square Building, 2 Massachusetts Avenue, NE, Washington, DC 20212-0001, (202) 691-5200, Fax: (202) 691-6325, www.bls.gov; *Industry Productivity and Costs.*

FARM MORTGAGE LOANS

Board of Governors of the Federal Reserve System, Constitution Avenue, NW, Washington, DC 20551, (202) 452-3000, www.federalreserve.gov; *Federal Reserve Bulletin.*

HUD USER, PO Box 23268, Washington, DC 20026-3268, (800) 245-2691, Fax: (202) 708-9981, www.huduser.org; *Comprehensive Market Analysis Reports.*

FARMERS AND FARM WORKERS - EMPLOYMENT

Economic Research Service (ERS), U.S. Department of Agriculture (USDA), 1800 M Street, NW, Washington, DC 20036-5831, (202) 694-5050, Fax: (202) 694-5689, www.ers.usda.gov; *Amber Waves: The Economics of Food, Farming, Natural Resources, and Rural America.*

U.S. Bureau of Labor Statistics (BLS), Postal Square Building, 2 Massachusetts Avenue, NE, Washington, DC 20212-0001, (202) 691-5200, Fax: (202) 691-6325, www.bls.gov; *Employment and Earnings (EE)* and unpublished data.

FARMERS AND FARM WORKERS - INDEXES OF FARM INPUTS

Economic Research Service (ERS), U.S. Department of Agriculture (USDA), 1800 M Street, NW, Washington, DC 20036-5831, (202) 694-5050, Fax: (202) 694-5689, www.ers.usda.gov; *Agricultural Outlook.*

FARMERS AND FARM WORKERS - UNEMPLOYMENT

U.S. Bureau of Labor Statistics (BLS), Postal Square Building, 2 Massachusetts Avenue, NE, Washington, DC 20212-0001, (202) 691-5200, Fax: (202) 691-6325, www.bls.gov; *Employment and Earnings (EE).*

FARMS

Department of Agriculture and Rural Development (DARD), Dundonald House, Upper Newtownards Road, Belfast BT4 3SB, Northern Ireland, United Kingdom, www.dardni.gov.uk; *Agricultural Census in Northern Ireland 2007; European Union Farm Structure Survey 2007; Farm Business Data 2008; Farm Incomes in Northern Ireland 2006/07;* and *Statistical Review of Northern Ireland Agriculture 2007.*

Economic Research Service (ERS), U.S. Department of Agriculture (USDA), 1800 M Street, NW, Washington, DC 20036-5831, (202) 694-5050, Fax: (202) 694-5689, www.ers.usda.gov; *U.S. Organic Farming in 2000-2001: Adoption of Certified Systems.*

Lithuanian Department of Statistics (Statistics Lithuania), Gedimino av. 29, LT-01500 Vilnius, Lithuania, www.stat.gov.lt/en; *Agriculture in Lithuania 2008.*

National Agricultural Statistics Service (NASS), U.S. Department of Agriculture (USDA), 1400 Independence Avenue, SW, Washington, DC 20250, (800) 727-9540, Fax: (202) 690-2090, www.nass.usda.gov; *Hogs and Pigs.*

FARMS - ACREAGE

Economic Research Service (ERS), U.S. Department of Agriculture (USDA), 1800 M Street, NW, Washington, DC 20036-5831, (202) 694-5050, Fax: (202) 694-5689, www.ers.usda.gov; *Agricultural Outlook.*

National Agricultural Statistics Service (NASS), U.S. Department of Agriculture (USDA), 1400 Independence Avenue, SW, Washington, DC 20250, (800) 727-9540, Fax: (202) 690-2090, www.nass.usda.gov; *2007 Census of Agriculture* and *Farms, Land in Farms, Livestock Operations 2007 Summary.*

FARMS - ACREAGE - CROPLAND

Economic Research Service (ERS), U.S. Department of Agriculture (USDA), 1800 M Street, NW, Washington, DC 20036-5831, (202) 694-5050, Fax: (202) 694-5689, www.ers.usda.gov; *Agricultural Resources and Environmental Indicators 2006* and *Agricultural Statistics.*

National Agricultural Statistics Service (NASS), U.S. Department of Agriculture (USDA), 1400 Independence Avenue, SW, Washington, DC 20250, (800) 727-9540, Fax: (202) 690-2090, www.nass.usda.gov; *2007 Census of Agriculture.*

FARMS - ACREAGE - CROPS HARVESTED

See also Individual crops

Economic Research Service (ERS), U.S. Department of Agriculture (USDA), 1800 M Street, NW, Washington, DC 20036-5831, (202) 694-5050, Fax: (202) 694-5689, www.ers.usda.gov; *Agricultural Outlook; Agricultural Resources and Environmental Indicators 2006;* and *Agricultural Statistics.*

National Agricultural Statistics Service (NASS), U.S. Department of Agriculture (USDA), 1400 Independence Avenue, SW, Washington, DC 20250, (800) 727-9540, Fax: (202) 690-2090, www.nass.usda.gov; *Crop Production; Crop Values 2007 Summary; Field Crops: Final Estimates 1997-2002;* and *Vegetables: 2004 Annual Summary.*

FARMS - AGRICHEMICALS

Economic Research Service (ERS), U.S. Department of Agriculture (USDA), 1800 M Street, NW, Washington, DC 20036-5831, (202) 694-5050, Fax: (202) 694-5689, www.ers.usda.gov; *Agricultural Outlook.*

National Agricultural Statistics Service (NASS), U.S. Department of Agriculture (USDA), 1400 Independence Avenue, SW, Washington, DC 20250, (800) 727-9540, Fax: (202) 690-2090, www.nass.usda.gov; *Agricultural Prices.*

FARMS - AGRICULTURAL PRODUCTS - EXPORTS

International Trade Administration (ITA), U.S. Department of Commerce (DOC), 1401 Constitution Avenue, NW, Washington, DC 20230, (800) USA-TRAD(E), Fax: (202) 482-4473, www.ita.doc.gov; *U.S. Foreign Trade Highlights* and unpublished data.

Organisation for Economic Cooperation and Development (OECD), 2 rue Andre Pascal, F-75775 Paris Cedex 16, France, (Telephone in U.S. (202) 785-6323), (Fax in U.S. (202) 785-0350), www.oecd.org; *OECD Agricultural Outlook: 2007-2016.*

FARMS - AGRICULTURAL PRODUCTS - FOREIGN COUNTRIES

Foreign Agricultural Service (FAS), U.S. Department of Agriculture (USDA), 1400 Independence Avenue, SW, Washington, DC 20250, (202) 720-3935, www.fas.usda.gov; Production, Supply and Distribution Online (PSD) Online.

Teagasc, Oak Park, Carlow, Ireland, www.teagasc.ie; *Beef and Sheep Production Research* and *National Farm Survey 2005.*

United Nations Food and Agricultural Organization (FAO), Viale delle Terme di Caracalla, 00100 Rome, Italy, (Dial from U.S. (202) 653-2400), (Fax from U.S. (202) 653 5760), www.fao.org; *FAO Statistical Yearbook 2004* and FAOSTAT Database. Subjects covered include: Agriculture, nutrition, fisheries, forestry, food aid, land use and population.

United Nations Statistics Division, New York, NY 10017, (800) 253-9646, Fax: (212) 963-4116, http://unstats.un.org; *Statistical Yearbook* and United Nations Common Database (UNCDB).

FARMS - AGRICULTURAL PRODUCTS - RAILROAD CAR LOADINGS OF

Association of American Railroads (AAR), 50 F Street, NW, Washington, DC 20001-1564, (202) 639-2100, www.aar.org; *Freight Commodity Statistics; Freight Loss and Damage;* and *Weekly Railroad Traffic.*

FARMS - AGRICULTURAL PRODUCTS - WATERBORNE COMMERCE

Waterborne Commerce Statistics Center (WCSC), Navigation Data Center (NDC), U.S. Army Corps of Engineers, PO Box 61280, New Orleans, LA 70161-1280, (504) 862-1426, www.iwr.usace.army.mil/ndc/wcsc/wcsc.htm; *2006 Waterborne Commerce of the United States (WCUS).*

FARMS - AGRICULTURAL PRODUCTS - WORLD PRODUCTION

Economic Research Service (ERS), U.S. Department of Agriculture (USDA), 1800 M Street, NW, Washington, DC 20036-5831, (202) 694-5050, Fax: (202) 694-5689, www.ers.usda.gov; *Agricultural Outlook.*

Organisation for Economic Cooperation and Development (OECD), 2 rue Andre Pascal, F-75775 Paris Cedex 16, France, (Telephone in U.S. (202) 785-6323), (Fax in U.S. (202) 785-0350), www.oecd.org; *OECD Agricultural Outlook: 2007-2016.*

United Nations Food and Agricultural Organization (FAO), Viale delle Terme di Caracalla, 00100 Rome, Italy, (Dial from U.S. (202) 653-2400), (Fax from U.S. (202) 653 5760), www.fao.org; FAOSTAT Database. Subjects covered include: Agriculture, nutrition, fisheries, forestry, food aid, land use and population.

United Nations Statistics Division, New York, NY 10017, (800) 253-9646, Fax: (212) 963-4116, http://unstats.un.org; *Monthly Bulletin of Statistics.*

FARMS - ASSETS AND LIABILITIES

Board of Governors of the Federal Reserve System, Constitution Avenue, NW, Washington, DC 20551, (202) 452-3000, www.federalreserve.gov; *Flow of Funds Accounts of the United States.*

Economic Research Service (ERS), U.S. Department of Agriculture (USDA), 1800 M Street, NW, Washington, DC 20036-5831, (202) 694-5050, Fax: (202) 694-5689, www.ers.usda.gov; *Agricultural Income and Finance Outlook; Amber Waves: The Economics of Food, Farming, Natural Resources, and Rural America; Farm Balance Sheet;* and *Farm Income: Data Files.*

FARMS - CAPITAL STOCKS - FARM HOUSING

Bureau of Economic Analysis (BEA), U.S. Department of Commerce (DOC), 1441 L Street NW, Washington, DC 20230, (202) 606-9900, www.bea.gov; Fixed Assets Accounts Tables (web app) and *Survey of Current Business (SCB).*

FARMS - CONSTRUCTION VALUE - FARM NON-RESIDENTIAL

U.S. Census Bureau, Manufacturing and Construction Division, 4600 Silver Hill Road, Washington DC 20233, (301) 763-4673, www.census.gov/mcd; *Current Construction Reports.*

FARMS - CONTRACTS

Economic Research Service (ERS), U.S. Department of Agriculture (USDA), 1800 M Street, NW, Washington, DC 20036-5831, (202) 694-5050, Fax: (202) 694-5689, www.ers.usda.gov; *Agricultural Resource Management Study (ARMS).*

FARMS - CORPORATE

National Agricultural Statistics Service (NASS), U.S. Department of Agriculture (USDA), 1400 Independence Avenue, SW, Washington, DC 20250, (800) 727-9540, Fax: (202) 690-2090, www.nass.usda.gov; *2007 Census of Agriculture.*

FARMS - CROPS

See also Individual crops

National Agricultural Statistics Service (NASS), U.S. Department of Agriculture (USDA), 1400 Independence Avenue, SW, Washington, DC 20250, (800) 727-9540, Fax: (202) 690-2090, www.nass.usda.gov; *Rice Stocks.*

FARMS - CROPS - ACREAGE

Economic Research Service (ERS), U.S. Department of Agriculture (USDA), 1800 M Street, NW, Washington, DC 20036-5831, (202) 694-5050, Fax: (202) 694-5689, www.ers.usda.gov; *Agricultural Outlook; Agricultural Resources and Environmental Indicators 2006;* and *Agricultural Statistics.*

National Agricultural Statistics Service (NASS), U.S. Department of Agriculture (USDA), 1400 Independence Avenue, SW, Washington, DC 20250, (800) 727-9540, Fax: (202) 690-2090, www.nass.usda.gov; *Crop Production* and *Crop Values 2007 Summary.*

FARMS - CROPS - FRUITS AND NUTS

National Agricultural Statistics Service (NASS), U.S. Department of Agriculture (USDA), 1400 Independence Avenue, SW, Washington, DC 20250, (800) 727-9540, Fax: (202) 690-2090, www.nass.usda.gov; *Citrus Fruits* and *Noncitrus Fruits and Nuts: Final Estimates 1998-2003.*

FARMS - CROPS - INCOME

Economic Research Service (ERS), U.S. Department of Agriculture (USDA), 1800 M Street, NW, Washington, DC 20036-5831, (202) 694-5050, Fax: (202) 694-5689, www.ers.usda.gov; *Agricultural Income and Finance Outlook* and *2008 Farm Income Forecast.*

FARMS - CROPS - PRODUCTION

Economic Research Service (ERS), U.S. Department of Agriculture (USDA), 1800 M Street, NW, Washington, DC 20036-5831, (202) 694-5050, Fax: (202) 694-5689, www.ers.usda.gov; *Agricultural Outlook; Agricultural Resources and Environmental Indicators 2006;* and *Agricultural Statistics.*

Foreign Agricultural Service (FAS), U.S. Department of Agriculture (USDA), 1400 Independence Avenue, SW, Washington, DC 20250, (202) 720-3935, www.fas.usda.gov; Foreign Agricultural Service's U.S. Trade Internet System.

National Agricultural Statistics Service (NASS), U.S. Department of Agriculture (USDA), 1400 Independence Avenue, SW, Washington, DC 20250, (800) 727-9540, Fax: (202) 690-2090, www.nass.usda.gov; *2006 Agricultural Statistics.*

U.S. Department of Agriculture (USDA), 1400 Independence Ave, SW, Washington, DC 20250, (202) 264-8600, www.usda.gov; *The Agricultural Fact Book 2001-2002.*

FARMS - CROPS - PRODUCTION - WORLD

United Nations Food and Agricultural Organization (FAO), Viale delle Terme di Caracalla, 00100 Rome, Italy, (Dial from U.S. (202) 653-2400), (Fax from U.S. (202) 653 5760), www.fao.org; *FAO Statistical Yearbook 2004* and FAOSTAT Database. Subjects covered include: Agriculture, nutrition, fisheries, forestry, food aid, land use and population.

United Nations Statistics Division, New York, NY 10017, (800) 253-9646, Fax: (212) 963-4116, http://unstats.un.org; *Monthly Bulletin of Statistics.*

FARMS - CROPS - VEGETABLES

Economic Research Service (ERS), U.S. Department of Agriculture (USDA), 1800 M Street, NW, Washington, DC 20036-5831, (202) 694-5050, Fax: (202) 694-5689, www.ers.usda.gov; *Agricultural Statistics.*

National Agricultural Statistics Service (NASS), U.S. Department of Agriculture (USDA), 1400 Independence Avenue, SW, Washington, DC 20250, (800) 727-9540, Fax: (202) 690-2090, www.nass.usda.gov; *Vegetables: 2004 Annual Summary.*

FARMS - DEBT

Economic Research Service (ERS), U.S. Department of Agriculture (USDA), 1800 M Street, NW, Washington, DC 20036-5831, (202) 694-5050, Fax: (202) 694-5689, www.ers.usda.gov; *Agricultural Income and Finance Outlook; Farm Balance Sheet;* and *Farm Income: Data Files.*

FARMS - DEBT - MORTGAGE OUTSTANDING

Board of Governors of the Federal Reserve System, Constitution Avenue, NW, Washington, DC 20551, (202) 452-3000, www.federalreserve.gov; *Federal Reserve Bulletin.*

FARMS - EXPENSES

Economic Research Service (ERS), U.S. Department of Agriculture (USDA), 1800 M Street, NW, Washington, DC 20036-5831, (202) 694-5050, Fax: (202) 694-5689, www.ers.usda.gov; *Agricultural Income and Finance Outlook; Amber Waves: The Economics of Food, Farming, Natural Resources, and Rural America;* and *Farm Income: Data Files.*

FARMS - FARM PRODUCTS SOLD - MARKETING RECEIPTS

Bureau of Economic Analysis (BEA), U.S. Department of Commerce (DOC), 1441 L Street NW, Washington, DC 20230, (202) 606-9900, www.bea.gov; *2007 Annual Revision of the National Income and Product Accounts (NIPA)* and *Survey of Current Business (SCB).*

Economic Research Service (ERS), U.S. Department of Agriculture (USDA), 1800 M Street, NW, Washington, DC 20036-5831, (202) 694-5050, Fax: (202) 694-5689, www.ers.usda.gov; *Agricultural Income and Finance Outlook* and *Farm Income: Data Files.*

National Agricultural Statistics Service (NASS), U.S. Department of Agriculture (USDA), 1400 Independence Avenue, SW, Washington, DC 20250, (800) 727-9540, Fax: (202) 690-2090, www.nass.usda.gov; *2007 Census of Agriculture.*

FARMS - GOVERNMENT PAYMENTS TO FARMERS

Economic Research Service (ERS), U.S. Department of Agriculture (USDA), 1800 M Street, NW, Washington, DC 20036-5831, (202) 694-5050, Fax: (202) 694-5689, www.ers.usda.gov; *Agricultural Income and Finance Outlook* and *Farm Income: Data Files.*

FARMS - GROSS FARM PRODUCT

Bureau of Economic Analysis (BEA), U.S. Department of Commerce (DOC), 1441 L Street NW, Washington, DC 20230, (202) 606-9900, www.bea.gov; *2007 Annual Revision of the National Income and Product Accounts (NIPA)* and *Survey of Current Business (SCB).*

Economic Research Service (ERS), U.S. Department of Agriculture (USDA), 1800 M Street, NW, Washington, DC 20036-5831, (202) 694-5050, Fax: (202) 694-5689, www.ers.usda.gov; *2008 Farm Income Forecast.*

FARMS - HOUSING - RENTAL VALUE

Bureau of Economic Analysis (BEA), U.S. Department of Commerce (DOC), 1441 L Street NW, Washington, DC 20230, (202) 606-9900, www.bea.gov; *2007 Annual Revision of the National Income and Product Accounts (NIPA)* and *Survey of Current Business (SCB).*

FARMS - INCOME

Bureau of Economic Analysis (BEA), U.S. Department of Commerce (DOC), 1441 L Street NW, Washington, DC 20230, (202) 606-9900, www.bea.gov; *2007 Annual Revision of the National Income and Product Accounts (NIPA)* and *Survey of Current Business (SCB).*

Economic Research Service (ERS), U.S. Department of Agriculture (USDA), 1800 M Street, NW, Washington, DC 20036-5831, (202) 694-5050, Fax: (202) 694-5689, www.ers.usda.gov; *Agricultural Income and Finance Outlook; Amber Waves: The Economics of Food, Farming, Natural Resources, and Rural America;* and *2008 Farm Income Forecast.*

FARMS - INDIVIDUAL OR FAMILY

National Agricultural Statistics Service (NASS), U.S. Department of Agriculture (USDA), 1400 Independence Avenue, SW, Washington, DC 20250, (800) 727-9540, Fax: (202) 690-2090, www.nass.usda.gov; *2007 Census of Agriculture.*

FARMS - INPUT INDEXES

Economic Research Service (ERS), U.S. Department of Agriculture (USDA), 1800 M Street, NW, Washington, DC 20036-5831, (202) 694-5050, Fax: (202) 694-5689, www.ers.usda.gov; *Agricultural Outlook.*

FARMS - INVENTORIES - CHANGE IN

Bureau of Economic Analysis (BEA), U.S. Department of Commerce (DOC), 1441 L Street NW, Washington, DC 20230, (202) 606-9900, www.bea.gov; *2007 Annual Revision of the National Income and Product Accounts (NIPA)* and *Survey of Current Business (SCB)*.

FARMS - LABOR COSTS

Economic Research Service (ERS), U.S. Department of Agriculture (USDA), 1800 M Street, NW, Washington, DC 20036-5831, (202) 694-5050, Fax: (202) 694-5689, www.ers.usda.gov; *Agricultural Income and Finance Outlook* and *Farm Income: Data Files*.

National Agricultural Statistics Service (NASS), U.S. Department of Agriculture (USDA), 1400 Independence Avenue, SW, Washington, DC 20250, (800) 727-9540, Fax: (202) 690-2090, www.nass.usda.gov; *Agricultural Prices*.

FARMS - LABOR INPUTS

Economic Research Service (ERS), U.S. Department of Agriculture (USDA), 1800 M Street, NW, Washington, DC 20036-5831, (202) 694-5050, Fax: (202) 694-5689, www.ers.usda.gov; *Agricultural Outlook*.

National Agricultural Statistics Service (NASS), U.S. Department of Agriculture (USDA), 1400 Independence Avenue, SW, Washington, DC 20250, (800) 727-9540, Fax: (202) 690-2090, www.nass.usda.gov; *Farm Labor*.

FARMS - MACHINERY AND MOTOR VEHICLES

Economic Research Service (ERS), U.S. Department of Agriculture (USDA), 1800 M Street, NW, Washington, DC 20036-5831, (202) 694-5050, Fax: (202) 694-5689, www.ers.usda.gov; *Agricultural Outlook*.

U.S. Census Bureau, Foreign Trade Division, 4700 Silver Hill Road, Washington DC 20233-0001, (301) 763-3030, www.census.gov/foreign-trade/www/; *U.S. International Trade in Goods and Services*.

U.S. Census Bureau, Manufacturing and Construction Division, 4600 Silver Hill Road, Washington DC 20233, (301) 763-4673, www.census.gov/mcd; *Annual Survey of Manufactures (ASM)* and *Census of Manufactures*.

FARMS - MORTGAGE LOANS

Board of Governors of the Federal Reserve System, Constitution Avenue, NW, Washington, DC 20551, (202) 452-3000, www.federalreserve.gov; *Federal Reserve Bulletin*.

FARMS - NATIONAL INCOME - ORIGIN IN

Bureau of Economic Analysis (BEA), U.S. Department of Commerce (DOC), 1441 L Street NW, Washington, DC 20230, (202) 606-9900, www.bea.gov; *2007 Annual Revision of the National Income and Product Accounts (NIPA)* and *Survey of Current Business (SCB)*.

Economic Research Service (ERS), U.S. Department of Agriculture (USDA), 1800 M Street, NW, Washington, DC 20036-5831, (202) 694-5050, Fax: (202) 694-5689, www.ers.usda.gov; *2008 Farm Income Forecast*.

FARMS - NUMBER OF FARMS

National Agricultural Statistics Service (NASS), U.S. Department of Agriculture (USDA), 1400 Independence Avenue, SW, Washington, DC 20250, (800) 727-9540, Fax: (202) 690-2090, www.nass.usda.gov; *2007 Census of Agriculture* and *Farms, Land in Farms, Livestock Operations 2007 Summary*.

FARMS - OPERATOR CHARACTERISTICS

National Agricultural Statistics Service (NASS), U.S. Department of Agriculture (USDA), 1400 Independence Avenue, SW, Washington, DC 20250, (800) 727-9540, Fax: (202) 690-2090, www.nass.usda.gov; *2007 Census of Agriculture*.

FARMS - PARITY RATIO

National Agricultural Statistics Service (NASS), U.S. Department of Agriculture (USDA), 1400 Independence Avenue, SW, Washington, DC 20250, (800) 727-9540, Fax: (202) 690-2090, www.nass.usda.gov; *Agricultural Prices*.

FARMS - PARTNERSHIPS

National Agricultural Statistics Service (NASS), U.S. Department of Agriculture (USDA), 1400 Independence Avenue, SW, Washington, DC 20250, (800) 727-9540, Fax: (202) 690-2090, www.nass.usda.gov; *2007 Census of Agriculture*.

FARMS - PRICES - CROPS

Economic Research Service (ERS), U.S. Department of Agriculture (USDA), 1800 M Street, NW, Washington, DC 20036-5831, (202) 694-5050, Fax: (202) 694-5689, www.ers.usda.gov; *Agricultural Outlook* and *Agricultural Statistics*.

National Agricultural Statistics Service (NASS), U.S. Department of Agriculture (USDA), 1400 Independence Avenue, SW, Washington, DC 20250, (800) 727-9540, Fax: (202) 690-2090, www.nass.usda.gov; *Agricultural Prices; Crop Production; Crop Values 2007 Summary; Field Crops: Final Estimates 1997-2002;* and *Vegetables: 2004 Annual Summary*.

Organisation for Economic Cooperation and Development (OECD), 2 rue Andre Pascal, F-75775 Paris Cedex 16, France, (Telephone in U.S. (202) 785-6323), (Fax in U.S. (202) 785-0350), www.oecd.org; *OECD Agricultural Outlook: 2007-2016*.

FARMS - PRICES - LIVESTOCK AND PRODUCTS

Economic Research Service (ERS), U.S. Department of Agriculture (USDA), 1800 M Street, NW, Washington, DC 20036-5831, (202) 694-5050, Fax: (202) 694-5689, www.ers.usda.gov; *Agricultural Statistics*.

National Agricultural Statistics Service (NASS), U.S. Department of Agriculture (USDA), 1400 Independence Avenue, SW, Washington, DC 20250, (800) 727-9540, Fax: (202) 690-2090, www.nass.usda.gov; *Agricultural Prices* and *Meat Animals Production, Disposition, and Income*.

FARMS - REAL ESTATE - INPUT INDEXES

Economic Research Service (ERS), U.S. Department of Agriculture (USDA), 1800 M Street, NW, Washington, DC 20036-5831, (202) 694-5050, Fax: (202) 694-5689, www.ers.usda.gov; *Agricultural Outlook*.

FARMS - TAXES

Bureau of Economic Analysis (BEA), U.S. Department of Commerce (DOC), 1441 L Street NW, Washington, DC 20230, (202) 606-9900, www.bea.gov; *2007 Annual Revision of the National Income and Product Accounts (NIPA)* and *Survey of Current Business (SCB)*.

National Agricultural Statistics Service (NASS), U.S. Department of Agriculture (USDA), 1400 Independence Avenue, SW, Washington, DC 20250, (800) 727-9540, Fax: (202) 690-2090, www.nass.usda.gov; *Agricultural Prices*.

FARMS - TENURE OF OPERATOR

National Agricultural Statistics Service (NASS), U.S. Department of Agriculture (USDA), 1400 Independence Avenue, SW, Washington, DC 20250, (800) 727-9540, Fax: (202) 690-2090, www.nass.usda.gov; *2007 Census of Agriculture*.

FARMS - VALUE - FARM LAND AND BUILDINGS

Economic Research Service (ERS), U.S. Department of Agriculture (USDA), 1800 M Street, NW, Washington, DC 20036-5831, (202) 694-5050, Fax: (202) 694-5689, www.ers.usda.gov; *Agricultural Resources and Environmental Indicators 2006*.

National Agricultural Statistics Service (NASS), U.S. Department of Agriculture (USDA), 1400 Independence Avenue, SW, Washington, DC 20250, (800) 727-9540, Fax: (202) 690-2090, www.nass.usda.gov; *Agricultural Land Values and Cash Rents Annual Summary* and *2007 Census of Agriculture*.

FARMS - VALUE - FARM PRODUCTS SOLD - MARKETING RECEIPTS

Bureau of Economic Analysis (BEA), U.S. Department of Commerce (DOC), 1441 L Street NW, Washington, DC 20230, (202) 606-9900, www.bea.gov; *2007 Annual Revision of the National Income and Product Accounts (NIPA)* and *Survey of Current Business (SCB)*.

Economic Research Service (ERS), U.S. Department of Agriculture (USDA), 1800 M Street, NW, Washington, DC 20036-5831, (202) 694-5050, Fax: (202) 694-5689, www.ers.usda.gov; *Agricultural Income and Finance Outlook* and *Farm Income: Data Files*.

National Agricultural Statistics Service (NASS), U.S. Department of Agriculture (USDA), 1400 Independence Avenue, SW, Washington, DC 20250, (800) 727-9540, Fax: (202) 690-2090, www.nass.usda.gov; *2007 Census of Agriculture*.

FAROE ISLANDS - ABORTION

United Nations Statistics Division, New York, NY 10017, (800) 253-9646, Fax: (212) 963-4116, http://unstats.un.org; *Demographic Yearbook*.

FAROE ISLANDS - AGRICULTURE

Palgrave Macmillan Ltd., Houndmills, Basingstoke, Hampshire, RG21 6XS, England, (Telephone in U.S. (888) 330-8477), (Fax in U.S. (800) 672-2054), www.palgrave.com; *The Statesman's Yearbook 2008*.

Taylor and Francis Group, An Informa Business, 2 Park Square, Milton Park, Abingdon, Oxford OX14 4RN, United Kingdom, (Dial from U.S. (212) 216-7800), (Fax from U.S. (212) 564-7854), www.tandf.co.uk; *The Europa World Year Book*.

United Nations Conference on Trade and Development (UNCTAD), DC2-1120, United Nations, New York, NY 10017, (212) 963-0027, www.unctad.org; *UNCTAD Commodity Yearbook*.

United Nations Food and Agricultural Organization (FAO), Viale delle Terme di Caracalla, 00100 Rome, Italy, (Dial from U.S. (202) 653-2400), (Fax from U.S. (202) 653 5760), www.fao.org; AQUASTAT; *FAO Production Yearbook 2002; FAO Trade Yearbook;* and *The State of Food and Agriculture (SOFA) 2006*.

The World Bank, 1818 H Street, NW, Washington, DC 20433, (202) 473-1000, Fax: (202) 477-6391, www.worldbank.org; *Faeroe Islands*.

FAROE ISLANDS - AIRLINES

Palgrave Macmillan Ltd., Houndmills, Basingstoke, Hampshire, RG21 6XS, England, (Telephone in U.S. (888) 330-8477), (Fax in U.S. (800) 672-2054), www.palgrave.com; *The Statesman's Yearbook 2008*.

FAROE ISLANDS - BROADCASTING

Palgrave Macmillan Ltd., Houndmills, Basingstoke, Hampshire, RG21 6XS, England, (Telephone in U.S. (888) 330-8477), (Fax in U.S. (800) 672-2054), www.palgrave.com; *The Statesman's Yearbook 2008*.

WRTH Publications Limited, PO Box 290, Oxford OX2 7FT, UK, www.wrth.com; *World Radio TV Handbook 2007*.

FAROE ISLANDS - CATTLE

See FAROE ISLANDS - LIVESTOCK

FAROE ISLANDS - CHILDBIRTH - STATISTICS

Taylor and Francis Group, An Informa Business, 2 Park Square, Milton Park, Abingdon, Oxford OX14

4RN, United Kingdom, (Dial from U.S. (212) 216-7800), (Fax from U.S. (212) 564-7854), www.tandf.co.uk; *The Europa World Year Book.*

United Nations Statistics Division, New York, NY 10017, (800) 253-9646, Fax: (212) 963-4116, http://unstats.un.org; *Demographic Yearbook* and *Statistical Yearbook.*

World Health Organization (WHO), Avenue Appia 20, 1211 Geneve 27, Switzerland, (Telephone in U.S. (212) 331-9081), www.who.int; *World Health Report 2006.*

FAROE ISLANDS - COMMERCE

Palgrave Macmillan Ltd., Houndmills, Basingstoke, Hampshire, RG21 6XS, England, (Telephone in U.S. (888) 330-8477), (Fax in U.S. (800) 672-2054), www.palgrave.com; *The Statesman's Yearbook 2008.*

FAROE ISLANDS - COMMODITY EXCHANGES

United Nations Food and Agricultural Organization (FAO), Viale delle Terme di Caracalla, 00100 Rome, Italy, (Dial from U.S. (202) 653-2400), (Fax from U.S. (202) 653 5760), www.fao.org; *The State of Food and Agriculture (SOFA) 2006.*

FAROE ISLANDS - CONSUMER PRICE INDEXES

Taylor and Francis Group, An Informa Business, 2 Park Square, Milton Park, Abingdon, Oxford OX14 4RN, United Kingdom, (Dial from U.S. (212) 216-7800), (Fax from U.S. (212) 564-7854), www.tandf.co.uk; *The Europa World Year Book.*

United Nations Statistics Division, New York, NY 10017, (800) 253-9646, Fax: (212) 963-4116, http://unstats.un.org; *Statistical Yearbook.*

The World Bank, 1818 H Street, NW, Washington, DC 20433, (202) 473-1000, Fax: (202) 477-6391, www.worldbank.org; *Faeroe Islands.*

FAROE ISLANDS - CORN INDUSTRY

See FAROE ISLANDS - CROPS

FAROE ISLANDS - CROPS

Palgrave Macmillan Ltd., Houndmills, Basingstoke, Hampshire, RG21 6XS, England, (Telephone in U.S. (888) 330-8477), (Fax in U.S. (800) 672-2054), www.palgrave.com; *The Statesman's Yearbook 2008.*

Taylor and Francis Group, An Informa Business, 2 Park Square, Milton Park, Abingdon, Oxford OX14 4RN, United Kingdom, (Dial from U.S. (212) 216-7800), (Fax from U.S. (212) 564-7854), www.tandf.co.uk; *The Europa World Year Book.*

United Nations Conference on Trade and Development (UNCTAD), DC2-1120, United Nations, New York, NY 10017, (212) 963-0027, www.unctad.org; *UNCTAD Commodity Yearbook.*

United Nations Food and Agricultural Organization (FAO), Viale delle Terme di Caracalla, 00100 Rome, Italy, (Dial from U.S. (202) 653-2400), (Fax from U.S. (202) 653 5760), www.fao.org; *The State of Food and Agriculture (SOFA) 2006.*

United Nations Statistics Division, New York, NY 10017, (800) 253-9646, Fax: (212) 963-4116, http://unstats.un.org; *Statistical Yearbook.*

FAROE ISLANDS - DAIRY PROCESSING

United Nations Food and Agricultural Organization (FAO), Viale delle Terme di Caracalla, 00100 Rome, Italy, (Dial from U.S. (202) 653-2400), (Fax from U.S. (202) 653 5760), www.fao.org; *The State of Food and Agriculture (SOFA) 2006.*

FAROE ISLANDS - DEATH RATES

See FAROE ISLANDS - MORTALITY

FAROE ISLANDS - DIVORCE

United Nations Statistics Division, New York, NY 10017, (800) 253-9646, Fax: (212) 963-4116, http://unstats.un.org; *Demographic Yearbook* and *Statistical Yearbook.*

FAROE ISLANDS - ECONOMIC CONDITIONS

Palgrave Macmillan Ltd., Houndmills, Basingstoke, Hampshire, RG21 6XS, England, (Telephone in U.S. (888) 330-8477), (Fax in U.S. (800) 672-2054), www.palgrave.com; *The Statesman's Yearbook 2008.*

The World Bank, 1818 H Street, NW, Washington, DC 20433, (202) 473-1000, Fax: (202) 477-6391, www.worldbank.org; *Faeroe Islands; Faeroe Islands;* and *The World Bank Atlas 2003-2004.*

FAROE ISLANDS - EDUCATION

Palgrave Macmillan Ltd., Houndmills, Basingstoke, Hampshire, RG21 6XS, England, (Telephone in U.S. (888) 330-8477), (Fax in U.S. (800) 672-2054), www.palgrave.com; *The Statesman's Yearbook 2008.*

The World Bank, 1818 H Street, NW, Washington, DC 20433, (202) 473-1000, Fax: (202) 477-6391, www.worldbank.org; *Faeroe Islands.*

FAROE ISLANDS - ELECTRICITY

Palgrave Macmillan Ltd., Houndmills, Basingstoke, Hampshire, RG21 6XS, England, (Telephone in U.S. (888) 330-8477), (Fax in U.S. (800) 672-2054), www.palgrave.com; *The Statesman's Yearbook 2008.*

United Nations Statistics Division, New York, NY 10017, (800) 253-9646, Fax: (212) 963-4116, http://unstats.un.org; *Statistical Yearbook.*

FAROE ISLANDS - EMPLOYMENT

International Labour Office, I.L.O. Publications, 4 route des Morillons, CH-1211 Geneva 22, Switzerland, (Telephone in U.S. (202) 653-7652), (Fax in U.S. (202) 653-7687), www.ilo.org; *Yearbook of Labour Statistics 2006.*

The World Bank, 1818 H Street, NW, Washington, DC 20433, (202) 473-1000, Fax: (202) 477-6391, www.worldbank.org; *Faeroe Islands.*

FAROE ISLANDS - EXPORTS

International Monetary Fund (IMF), 700 Nineteenth Street, NW, Washington, DC 20431, (202) 623-7000, Fax: (202) 623-4661, www.imf.org; *Direction of Trade Statistics Yearbook 2007.*

Palgrave Macmillan Ltd., Houndmills, Basingstoke, Hampshire, RG21 6XS, England, (Telephone in U.S. (888) 330-8477), (Fax in U.S. (800) 672-2054), www.palgrave.com; *The Statesman's Yearbook 2008.*

Taylor and Francis Group, An Informa Business, 2 Park Square, Milton Park, Abingdon, Oxford OX14 4RN, United Kingdom, (Dial from U.S. (212) 216-7800), (Fax from U.S. (212) 564-7854), www.tandf.co.uk; *The Europa World Year Book.*

United Nations Food and Agricultural Organization (FAO), Viale delle Terme di Caracalla, 00100 Rome, Italy, (Dial from U.S. (202) 653-2400), (Fax from U.S. (202) 653 5760), www.fao.org; *The State of Food and Agriculture (SOFA) 2006.*

FAROE ISLANDS - FERTILITY, HUMAN

The World Bank, 1818 H Street, NW, Washington, DC 20433, (202) 473-1000, Fax: (202) 477-6391, www.worldbank.org; *The World Bank Atlas 2003-2004.*

FAROE ISLANDS - FERTILIZER INDUSTRY

United Nations Food and Agricultural Organization (FAO), Viale delle Terme di Caracalla, 00100 Rome, Italy, (Dial from U.S. (202) 653-2400), (Fax from U.S. (202) 653 5760), www.fao.org; *The State of Food and Agriculture (SOFA) 2006.*

FAROE ISLANDS - FETAL MORTALITY

See FAROE ISLANDS - MORTALITY

FAROE ISLANDS - FINANCE, PUBLIC

Banque de France, 48 rue Croix des Petits champs, 75001 Paris, France, www.banque-france.fr/home.htm; *Public Finance.*

Taylor and Francis Group, An Informa Business, 2 Park Square, Milton Park, Abingdon, Oxford OX14 4RN, United Kingdom, (Dial from U.S. (212) 216-7800), (Fax from U.S. (212) 564-7854), www.tandf.co.uk; *The Europa World Year Book.*

The World Bank, 1818 H Street, NW, Washington, DC 20433, (202) 473-1000, Fax: (202) 477-6391, www.worldbank.org; *Faeroe Islands.*

FAROE ISLANDS - FISHERIES

Palgrave Macmillan Ltd., Houndmills, Basingstoke, Hampshire, RG21 6XS, England, (Telephone in U.S. (888) 330-8477), (Fax in U.S. (800) 672-2054), www.palgrave.com; *The Statesman's Yearbook 2008.*

Taylor and Francis Group, An Informa Business, 2 Park Square, Milton Park, Abingdon, Oxford OX14 4RN, United Kingdom, (Dial from U.S. (212) 216-7800), (Fax from U.S. (212) 564-7854), www.tandf.co.uk; *The Europa World Year Book.*

United Nations Conference on Trade and Development (UNCTAD), DC2-1120, United Nations, New York, NY 10017, (212) 963-0027, www.unctad.org; *UNCTAD Commodity Yearbook.*

United Nations Food and Agricultural Organization (FAO), Viale delle Terme di Caracalla, 00100 Rome, Italy, (Dial from U.S. (202) 653-2400), (Fax from U.S. (202) 653 5760), www.fao.org; *FAO Yearbook of Fishery Statistics;* Fishery Databases; FISHSTAT Database. Subjects covered include: Aquaculture production, capture production, fishery commodities; and *The State of Food and Agriculture (SOFA) 2006.*

United Nations Statistics Division, New York, NY 10017, (800) 253-9646, Fax: (212) 963-4116, http://unstats.un.org; *Statistical Yearbook.*

The World Bank, 1818 H Street, NW, Washington, DC 20433, (202) 473-1000, Fax: (202) 477-6391, www.worldbank.org; *Faeroe Islands.*

FAROE ISLANDS - FOOD

United Nations Conference on Trade and Development (UNCTAD), DC2-1120, United Nations, New York, NY 10017, (212) 963-0027, www.unctad.org; *UNCTAD Commodity Yearbook.*

United Nations Food and Agricultural Organization (FAO), Viale delle Terme di Caracalla, 00100 Rome, Italy, (Dial from U.S. (202) 653-2400), (Fax from U.S. (202) 653 5760), www.fao.org; *FAO Production Yearbook 2002* and *The State of Food and Agriculture (SOFA) 2006.*

FAROE ISLANDS - FORESTS AND FORESTRY

United Nations Conference on Trade and Development (UNCTAD), DC2-1120, United Nations, New York, NY 10017, (212) 963-0027, www.unctad.org; *UNCTAD Commodity Yearbook.*

United Nations Food and Agricultural Organization (FAO), Viale delle Terme di Caracalla, 00100 Rome, Italy, (Dial from U.S. (202) 653-2400), (Fax from U.S. (202) 653 5760), www.fao.org; *The State of Food and Agriculture (SOFA) 2006.*

United Nations Statistics Division, New York, NY 10017, (800) 253-9646, Fax: (212) 963-4116, http://unstats.un.org; *Statistical Yearbook.*

The World Bank, 1818 H Street, NW, Washington, DC 20433, (202) 473-1000, Fax: (202) 477-6391, www.worldbank.org; *Faeroe Islands.*

FAROE ISLANDS - GROSS DOMESTIC PRODUCT

Taylor and Francis Group, An Informa Business, 2 Park Square, Milton Park, Abingdon, Oxford OX14 4RN, United Kingdom, (Dial from U.S. (212) 216-7800), (Fax from U.S. (212) 564-7854), www.tandf.co.uk; *The Europa World Year Book.*

FAROE ISLANDS - GROSS NATIONAL PRODUCT

The World Bank, 1818 H Street, NW, Washington, DC 20433, (202) 473-1000, Fax: (202) 477-6391, www.worldbank.org; *The World Bank Atlas 2003-2004.*

FAROE ISLANDS - HIDES AND SKINS INDUSTRY

United Nations Food and Agricultural Organization (FAO), Viale delle Terme di Caracalla, 00100 Rome, Italy, (Dial from U.S. (202) 653-2400), (Fax from U.S. (202) 653 5760), www.fao.org; *FAO Production Yearbook 2002.*

FAROE ISLANDS - IMPORTS

International Monetary Fund (IMF), 700 Nineteenth Street, NW, Washington, DC 20431, (202) 623-7000, Fax: (202) 623-4661, www.imf.org; *Direction of Trade Statistics Yearbook 2007.*

Palgrave Macmillan Ltd., Houndmills, Basingstoke, Hampshire, RG21 6XS, England, (Telephone in U.S. (888) 330-8477), (Fax in U.S. (800) 672-2054), www.palgrave.com; *The Statesman's Yearbook 2008.*

Taylor and Francis Group, An Informa Business, 2 Park Square, Milton Park, Abingdon, Oxford OX14 4RN, United Kingdom, (Dial from U.S. (212) 216-7800), (Fax from U.S. (212) 564-7854), www.tandf.co.uk; *The Europa World Year Book.*

United Nations Food and Agricultural Organization (FAO), Viale delle Terme di Caracalla, 00100 Rome, Italy, (Dial from U.S. (202) 653-2400), (Fax from U.S. (202) 653 5760), www.fao.org; *The State of Food and Agriculture (SOFA) 2006.*

FAROE ISLANDS - INDUSTRIES

Palgrave Macmillan Ltd., Houndmills, Basingstoke, Hampshire, RG21 6XS, England, (Telephone in U.S. (888) 330-8477), (Fax in U.S. (800) 672-2054), www.palgrave.com; *The Statesman's Yearbook 2008.*

Taylor and Francis Group, An Informa Business, 2 Park Square, Milton Park, Abingdon, Oxford OX14 4RN, United Kingdom, (Dial from U.S. (212) 216-7800), (Fax from U.S. (212) 564-7854), www.tandf.co.uk; *The Europa World Year Book.*

The World Bank, 1818 H Street, NW, Washington, DC 20433, (202) 473-1000, Fax: (202) 477-6391, www.worldbank.org; *Faeroe Islands.*

FAROE ISLANDS - INFANT AND MATERNAL MORTALITY

See FAROE ISLANDS - MORTALITY

FAROE ISLANDS - INTERNATIONAL TRADE

Banque de France, 48 rue Croix des Petits champs, 75001 Paris, France, www.banque-france.fr/home.htm; *Monthly Business Survey Overview.*

International Labour Office, I.L.O. Publications, 4 route des Morillons, CH-1211 Geneva 22, Switzerland, (Telephone in U.S. (202) 653-7652), (Fax in U.S. (202) 653-7687), www.ilo.org; *Yearbook of Labour Statistics 2006.*

Organisation for Economic Cooperation and Development (OECD), 2 rue Andre Pascal, F-75775 Paris Cedex 16, France, (Telephone in U.S. (202) 785-6323), (Fax in U.S. (202) 785-0350), www.oecd.org; *International Trade by Commodity Statistics (ITCS).*

Palgrave Macmillan Ltd., Houndmills, Basingstoke, Hampshire, RG21 6XS, England, (Telephone in U.S. (888) 330-8477), (Fax in U.S. (800) 672-2054), www.palgrave.com; *The Statesman's Yearbook 2008.*

Taylor and Francis Group, An Informa Business, 2 Park Square, Milton Park, Abingdon, Oxford OX14 4RN, United Kingdom, (Dial from U.S. (212) 216-7800), (Fax from U.S. (212) 564-7854), www.tandf.co.uk; *The Europa World Year Book.*

United Nations Conference on Trade and Development (UNCTAD), DC2-1120, United Nations, New York, NY 10017, (212) 963-0027, www.unctad.org; *UNCTAD Commodity Yearbook.*

United Nations Food and Agricultural Organization (FAO), Viale delle Terme di Caracalla, 00100 Rome, Italy, (Dial from U.S. (202) 653-2400), (Fax from U.S. (202) 653 5760), www.fao.org; *FAO Trade Yearbook* and *The State of Food and Agriculture (SOFA) 2006.*

United Nations Statistics Division, New York, NY 10017, (800) 253-9646, Fax: (212) 963-4116, http://unstats.un.org; *International Trade Statistics Yearbook* and *Statistical Yearbook.*

The World Bank, 1818 H Street, NW, Washington, DC 20433, (202) 473-1000, Fax: (202) 477-6391, www.worldbank.org; *Faeroe Islands.*

World Trade Organization (WTO), Centre William Rappard, Rue de Lausanne 154, CH-1211 Geneva 21, Switzerland, www.wto.org; *International Trade Statistics 2006.*

FAROE ISLANDS - LABOR

International Labour Office, I.L.O. Publications, 4 route des Morillons, CH-1211 Geneva 22, Switzerland, (Telephone in U.S. (202) 653-7652), (Fax in U.S. (202) 653-7687), www.ilo.org; *Yearbook of Labour Statistics 2006.*

Taylor and Francis Group, An Informa Business, 2 Park Square, Milton Park, Abingdon, Oxford OX14 4RN, United Kingdom, (Dial from U.S. (212) 216-7800), (Fax from U.S. (212) 564-7854), www.tandf.co.uk; *The Europa World Year Book.*

United Nations Food and Agricultural Organization (FAO), Viale delle Terme di Caracalla, 00100 Rome, Italy, (Dial from U.S. (202) 653-2400), (Fax from U.S. (202) 653 5760), www.fao.org; *The State of Food and Agriculture (SOFA) 2006.*

The World Bank, 1818 H Street, NW, Washington, DC 20433, (202) 473-1000, Fax: (202) 477-6391, www.worldbank.org; *The World Bank Atlas 2003-2004.*

FAROE ISLANDS - LAND USE

United Nations Food and Agricultural Organization (FAO), Viale delle Terme di Caracalla, 00100 Rome, Italy, (Dial from U.S. (202) 653-2400), (Fax from U.S. (202) 653 5760), www.fao.org; *FAO Production Yearbook 2002.*

FAROE ISLANDS - LIBRARIES

UNESCO Institute for Statistics, C.P. 6128 Succursale Centre-Ville, Montreal, Quebec, H3C 3J7 Canada, (Dial from U.S. (514) 343-6880), (Fax from U.S. (514) 343 6882), www.uis.unesco.org; *Statistical Tables.*

FAROE ISLANDS - LIFE EXPECTANCY

Palgrave Macmillan Ltd., Houndmills, Basingstoke, Hampshire, RG21 6XS, England, (Telephone in U.S. (888) 330-8477), (Fax in U.S. (800) 672-2054), www.palgrave.com; *The Statesman's Yearbook 2008.*

The World Bank, 1818 H Street, NW, Washington, DC 20433, (202) 473-1000, Fax: (202) 477-6391, www.worldbank.org; *The World Bank Atlas 2003-2004.*

FAROE ISLANDS - LIVESTOCK

Palgrave Macmillan Ltd., Houndmills, Basingstoke, Hampshire, RG21 6XS, England, (Telephone in U.S. (888) 330-8477), (Fax in U.S. (800) 672-2054), www.palgrave.com; *The Statesman's Yearbook 2008.*

Taylor and Francis Group, An Informa Business, 2 Park Square, Milton Park, Abingdon, Oxford OX14 4RN, United Kingdom, (Dial from U.S. (212) 216-7800), (Fax from U.S. (212) 564-7854), www.tandf.co.uk; *The Europa World Year Book.*

United Nations Conference on Trade and Development (UNCTAD), DC2-1120, United Nations, New York, NY 10017, (212) 963-0027, www.unctad.org; *UNCTAD Commodity Yearbook.*

United Nations Food and Agricultural Organization (FAO), Viale delle Terme di Caracalla, 00100 Rome, Italy, (Dial from U.S. (202) 653-2400), (Fax from U.S. (202) 653 5760), www.fao.org; *FAO Production Yearbook 2002* and *The State of Food and Agriculture (SOFA) 2006.*

United Nations Statistics Division, New York, NY 10017, (800) 253-9646, Fax: (212) 963-4116, http://unstats.un.org; *Statistical Yearbook.*

FAROE ISLANDS - MARRIAGE

United Nations Statistics Division, New York, NY 10017, (800) 253-9646, Fax: (212) 963-4116, http://unstats.un.org; *Demographic Yearbook* and *Statistical Yearbook.*

FAROE ISLANDS - MINERAL INDUSTRIES

United Nations Conference on Trade and Development (UNCTAD), DC2-1120, United Nations, New York, NY 10017, (212) 963-0027, www.unctad.org; *UNCTAD Commodity Yearbook.*

FAROE ISLANDS - MORTALITY

International Labour Office, I.L.O. Publications, 4 route des Morillons, CH-1211 Geneva 22, Switzerland, (Telephone in U.S. (202) 653-7652), (Fax in U.S. (202) 653-7687), www.ilo.org; *Yearbook of Labour Statistics 2006.*

Taylor and Francis Group, An Informa Business, 2 Park Square, Milton Park, Abingdon, Oxford OX14 4RN, United Kingdom, (Dial from U.S. (212) 216-7800), (Fax from U.S. (212) 564-7854), www.tandf.co.uk; *The Europa World Year Book.*

United Nations Statistics Division, New York, NY 10017, (800) 253-9646, Fax: (212) 963-4116, http://unstats.un.org; *Demographic Yearbook* and *Statistical Yearbook.*

The World Bank, 1818 H Street, NW, Washington, DC 20433, (202) 473-1000, Fax: (202) 477-6391, www.worldbank.org; *The World Bank Atlas 2003-2004.*

World Health Organization (WHO), Avenue Appia 20, 1211 Geneve 27, Switzerland, (Telephone in U.S. (212) 331-9081), www.who.int; *World Health Report 2006.*

FAROE ISLANDS - MOTOR VEHICLES

Taylor and Francis Group, An Informa Business, 2 Park Square, Milton Park, Abingdon, Oxford OX14 4RN, United Kingdom, (Dial from U.S. (212) 216-7800), (Fax from U.S. (212) 564-7854), www.tandf.co.uk; *The Europa World Year Book.*

FAROE ISLANDS - NUTRITION

United Nations Food and Agricultural Organization (FAO), Viale delle Terme di Caracalla, 00100 Rome, Italy, (Dial from U.S. (202) 653-2400), (Fax from U.S. (202) 653 5760), www.fao.org; *The State of Food and Agriculture (SOFA) 2006.*

FAROE ISLANDS - PESTICIDES

United Nations Food and Agricultural Organization (FAO), Viale delle Terme di Caracalla, 00100 Rome, Italy, (Dial from U.S. (202) 653-2400), (Fax from U.S. (202) 653 5760), www.fao.org; *The State of Food and Agriculture (SOFA) 2006.*

FAROE ISLANDS - PETROLEUM INDUSTRY AND TRADE

PennWell Corporation, 1421 South Sheridan Road, Tulsa, OK 74112, (918) 835-3161, www.pennwell.com; *International Petroleum Encyclopedia 2007.*

United Nations Conference on Trade and Development (UNCTAD), DC2-1120, United Nations, New York, NY 10017, (212) 963-0027, www.unctad.org; *UNCTAD Commodity Yearbook.*

United Nations Food and Agricultural Organization (FAO), Viale delle Terme di Caracalla, 00100 Rome, Italy, (Dial from U.S. (202) 653-2400), (Fax from U.S. (202) 653 5760), www.fao.org; *The State of Food and Agriculture (SOFA) 2006.*

FAROE ISLANDS - POLITICAL SCIENCE

Palgrave Macmillan Ltd., Houndmills, Basingstoke, Hampshire, RG21 6XS, England, (Telephone in U.S. (888) 330-8477), (Fax in U.S. (800) 672-2054), www.palgrave.com; *The Statesman's Yearbook 2008.*

Taylor and Francis Group, An Informa Business, 2 Park Square, Milton Park, Abingdon, Oxford OX14 4RN, United Kingdom, (Dial from U.S. (212) 216-

7800), (Fax from U.S. (212) 564-7854), www.tandf.co.uk; *The Europa World Year Book.*

FAROE ISLANDS - POPULATION

International Labour Office, I.L.O. Publications, 4 route des Morillons, CH-1211 Geneva 22, Switzerland, (Telephone in U.S. (202) 653-7652), (Fax in U.S. (202) 653-7687), www.ilo.org; *Yearbook of Labour Statistics 2006.*

Palgrave Macmillan Ltd., Houndmills, Basingstoke, Hampshire, RG21 6XS, England, (Telephone in U.S. (888) 330-8477), (Fax in U.S. (800) 672-2054), www.palgrave.com; *The Statesman's Yearbook 2008.*

Taylor and Francis Group, An Informa Business, 2 Park Square, Milton Park, Abingdon, Oxford OX14 4RN, United Kingdom, (Dial from U.S. (212) 216-7800), (Fax from U.S. (212) 564-7854), www.tandf.co.uk; *The Europa World Year Book.*

UNESCO Institute for Statistics, C.P. 6128 Succursale Centre-Ville, Montreal, Quebec, H3C 3J7 Canada, (Dial from U.S. (514) 343-6880), (Fax from U.S. (514) 343 6882), www.uis.unesco.org; *Statistical Tables.*

United Nations Food and Agricultural Organization (FAO), Viale delle Terme di Caracalla, 00100 Rome, Italy, (Dial from U.S. (202) 653-2400), (Fax from U.S. (202) 653 5760), www.fao.org; *FAO Production Yearbook 2002.*

United Nations Statistics Division, New York, NY 10017, (800) 253-9646, Fax: (212) 963-4116, http://unstats.un.org; *Demographic Yearbook* and *Statistical Yearbook.*

The World Bank, 1818 H Street, NW, Washington, DC 20433, (202) 473-1000, Fax: (202) 477-6391, www.worldbank.org; *Faeroe Islands* and *The World Bank Atlas 2003-2004.*

World Health Organization (WHO), Avenue Appia 20, 1211 Geneve 27, Switzerland, (Telephone in U.S. (212) 331-9081), www.who.int; *World Health Report 2006.*

FAROE ISLANDS - POPULATION DENSITY

Palgrave Macmillan Ltd., Houndmills, Basingstoke, Hampshire, RG21 6XS, England, (Telephone in U.S. (888) 330-8477), (Fax in U.S. (800) 672-2054), www.palgrave.com; *The Statesman's Yearbook 2008.*

Taylor and Francis Group, An Informa Business, 2 Park Square, Milton Park, Abingdon, Oxford OX14 4RN, United Kingdom, (Dial from U.S. (212) 216-7800), (Fax from U.S. (212) 564-7854), www.tandf.co.uk; *The Europa World Year Book.*

UNESCO Institute for Statistics, C.P. 6128 Succursale Centre-Ville, Montreal, Quebec, H3C 3J7 Canada, (Dial from U.S. (514) 343-6880), (Fax from U.S. (514) 343 6882), www.uis.unesco.org; *Statistical Tables.*

United Nations Food and Agricultural Organization (FAO), Viale delle Terme di Caracalla, 00100 Rome, Italy, (Dial from U.S. (202) 653-2400), (Fax from U.S. (202) 653 5760), www.fao.org; *The State of Food and Agriculture (SOFA) 2006.*

United Nations Statistics Division, New York, NY 10017, (800) 253-9646, Fax: (212) 963-4116, http://unstats.un.org; *Statistical Yearbook.*

The World Bank, 1818 H Street, NW, Washington, DC 20433, (202) 473-1000, Fax: (202) 477-6391, www.worldbank.org; *Faeroe Islands.*

FAROE ISLANDS - POWER RESOURCES

Palgrave Macmillan Ltd., Houndmills, Basingstoke, Hampshire, RG21 6XS, England, (Telephone in U.S. (888) 330-8477), (Fax in U.S. (800) 672-2054), www.palgrave.com; *The Statesman's Yearbook 2008.*

Platts, 2 Penn Plaza, 25th Floor, New York, NY 10121-2298, (212) 904-3070, www.platts.com; *Energy Economist.*

United Nations Food and Agricultural Organization (FAO), Viale delle Terme di Caracalla, 00100 Rome, Italy, (Dial from U.S. (202) 653-2400), (Fax from U.S. (202) 653 5760), www.fao.org; *The State of Food and Agriculture (SOFA) 2006.*

United Nations Statistics Division, New York, NY 10017, (800) 253-9646, Fax: (212) 963-4116, http://unstats.un.org; *Energy Statistics Yearbook 2003* and *Statistical Yearbook.*

The World Bank, 1818 H Street, NW, Washington, DC 20433, (202) 473-1000, Fax: (202) 477-6391, www.worldbank.org; *The World Bank Atlas 2003-2004.*

FAROE ISLANDS - PRICES

International Labour Office, I.L.O. Publications, 4 route des Morillons, CH-1211 Geneva 22, Switzerland, (Telephone in U.S. (202) 653-7652), (Fax in U.S. (202) 653-7687), www.ilo.org; *Yearbook of Labour Statistics 2006.*

United Nations Food and Agricultural Organization (FAO), Viale delle Terme di Caracalla, 00100 Rome, Italy, (Dial from U.S. (202) 653-2400), (Fax from U.S. (202) 653 5760), www.fao.org; *FAO Production Yearbook 2002* and *The State of Food and Agriculture (SOFA) 2006.*

The World Bank, 1818 H Street, NW, Washington, DC 20433, (202) 473-1000, Fax: (202) 477-6391, www.worldbank.org; *Faeroe Islands.*

FAROE ISLANDS - PUBLIC HEALTH

Palgrave Macmillan Ltd., Houndmills, Basingstoke, Hampshire, RG21 6XS, England, (Telephone in U.S. (888) 330-8477), (Fax in U.S. (800) 672-2054), www.palgrave.com; *The Statesman's Yearbook 2008.*

United Nations Statistics Division, New York, NY 10017, (800) 253-9646, Fax: (212) 963-4116, http://unstats.un.org; *Statistical Yearbook.*

The World Bank, 1818 H Street, NW, Washington, DC 20433, (202) 473-1000, Fax: (202) 477-6391, www.worldbank.org; *Faeroe Islands.*

World Health Organization (WHO), Avenue Appia 20, 1211 Geneve 27, Switzerland, (Telephone in U.S. (212) 331-9081), www.who.int; *World Health Report 2006.*

FAROE ISLANDS - PUBLISHERS AND PUBLISHING

Taylor and Francis Group, An Informa Business, 2 Park Square, Milton Park, Abingdon, Oxford OX14 4RN, United Kingdom, (Dial from U.S. (212) 216-7800), (Fax from U.S. (212) 564-7854), www.tandf.co.uk; *The Europa World Year Book.*

FAROE ISLANDS - RADIO BROADCASTING

Palgrave Macmillan Ltd., Houndmills, Basingstoke, Hampshire, RG21 6XS, England, (Telephone in U.S. (888) 330-8477), (Fax in U.S. (800) 672-2054), www.palgrave.com; *The Statesman's Yearbook 2008.*

FAROE ISLANDS - RELIGION

Palgrave Macmillan Ltd., Houndmills, Basingstoke, Hampshire, RG21 6XS, England, (Telephone in U.S. (888) 330-8477), (Fax in U.S. (800) 672-2054), www.palgrave.com; *The Statesman's Yearbook 2008.*

FAROE ISLANDS - RENT CHARGES

International Labour Office, I.L.O. Publications, 4 route des Morillons, CH-1211 Geneva 22, Switzerland, (Telephone in U.S. (202) 653-7652), (Fax in U.S. (202) 653-7687), www.ilo.org; *Yearbook of Labour Statistics 2006.*

FAROE ISLANDS - ROADS

Palgrave Macmillan Ltd., Houndmills, Basingstoke, Hampshire, RG21 6XS, England, (Telephone in U.S. (888) 330-8477), (Fax in U.S. (800) 672-2054), www.palgrave.com; *The Statesman's Yearbook 2008.*

FAROE ISLANDS - SHEEP

See FAROE ISLANDS - LIVESTOCK

FAROE ISLANDS - SHIPPING

Lloyd's Register - Fairplay, 8410 N.W. 53rd Terrace, Suite 207, Miami FL 33166, (305) 718-9929, Fax: (305) 718-9663, www.lrfairplay.com; *Register of Ships 2007-2008; World Casualty Statistics 2007; World Fleet Statistics 2006; World Marine Propulsion Report 2006-2010; World Shipbuilding Statistics 2007;* and The World Shipping Encyclopaedia.

Palgrave Macmillan Ltd., Houndmills, Basingstoke, Hampshire, RG21 6XS, England, (Telephone in U.S. (888) 330-8477), (Fax in U.S. (800) 672-2054), www.palgrave.com; *The Statesman's Yearbook 2008.*

Taylor and Francis Group, An Informa Business, 2 Park Square, Milton Park, Abingdon, Oxford OX14 4RN, United Kingdom, (Dial from U.S. (212) 216-7800), (Fax from U.S. (212) 564-7854), www.tandf.co.uk; *The Europa World Year Book.*

United Nations Statistics Division, New York, NY 10017, (800) 253-9646, Fax: (212) 963-4116, http://unstats.un.org; *Statistical Yearbook.*

FAROE ISLANDS - SOCIAL SECURITY

Palgrave Macmillan Ltd., Houndmills, Basingstoke, Hampshire, RG21 6XS, England, (Telephone in U.S. (888) 330-8477), (Fax in U.S. (800) 672-2054), www.palgrave.com; *The Statesman's Yearbook 2008.*

FAROE ISLANDS - TEXTILE INDUSTRY

United Nations Conference on Trade and Development (UNCTAD), DC2-1120, United Nations, New York, NY 10017, (212) 963-0027, www.unctad.org; *UNCTAD Commodity Yearbook.*

FAROE ISLANDS - TRADE

See FAROE ISLANDS - INTERNATIONAL TRADE

FAROE ISLANDS - TRANSPORTATION

Palgrave Macmillan Ltd., Houndmills, Basingstoke, Hampshire, RG21 6XS, England, (Telephone in U.S. (888) 330-8477), (Fax in U.S. (800) 672-2054), www.palgrave.com; *The Statesman's Yearbook 2008.*

Taylor and Francis Group, An Informa Business, 2 Park Square, Milton Park, Abingdon, Oxford OX14 4RN, United Kingdom, (Dial from U.S. (212) 216-7800), (Fax from U.S. (212) 564-7854), www.tandf.co.uk; *The Europa World Year Book.*

The World Bank, 1818 H Street, NW, Washington, DC 20433, (202) 473-1000, Fax: (202) 477-6391, www.worldbank.org; *Faeroe Islands.*

FAROE ISLANDS - UNEMPLOYMENT

International Labour Office, I.L.O. Publications, 4 route des Morillons, CH-1211 Geneva 22, Switzerland, (Telephone in U.S. (202) 653-7652), (Fax in U.S. (202) 653-7687), www.ilo.org; *Yearbook of Labour Statistics 2006.*

FAROE ISLANDS - VITAL STATISTICS

United Nations Statistics Division, New York, NY 10017, (800) 253-9646, Fax: (212) 963-4116, http://unstats.un.org; *Statistical Yearbook.*

FAROE ISLANDS - WAGES

International Labour Office, I.L.O. Publications, 4 route des Morillons, CH-1211 Geneva 22, Switzerland, (Telephone in U.S. (202) 653-7652), (Fax in U.S. (202) 653-7687), www.ilo.org; *Yearbook of Labour Statistics 2006.*

The World Bank, 1818 H Street, NW, Washington, DC 20433, (202) 473-1000, Fax: (202) 477-6391, www.worldbank.org; *Faeroe Islands.*

FAT - NUTRIENT AVAILABLE FOR CONSUMPTION

Center for Nutrition Policy and Promotion (CNPP), U.S. Department of Agriculture (USDA), 3101 Park Center Drive, 10th Floor, Alexandria, VA 22302-1594, (703) 305-7600, Fax: (703) 305-3300, www.usda.gov/cnpp; *Nutrient Content of the U.S. Food Supply Summary Report 2005.*

Food and Nutrition Service (FNS), U.S. Department of Agriculture (USDA), 3101 Park Center Drive, Alexandria, VA 22302, (703) 305-2062, www.fns.usda.gov/fns; unpublished data.

FATALITIES

See ACCIDENTS

FEDERAL AID TO EDUCATION

National Center for Education Statistics (NCES), 1990 K Street, NW, Washington, DC 20006, (202) 502-7300, http://nces.ed.gov; *Digest of Education Statistics 2007.*

The Office of Management and Budget (OMB), 725 17th Street, NW, Washington, DC 20503, (202) 395-3080, Fax: (202) 395-3888, www.whitehouse.gov/omb; *Historical Tables.*

U.S. Census Bureau, Governments Division, 4600 Silver Hill Road, Washington DC 20233, (800) 242-2184, www.census.gov/govs/www; *2002 Census of Governments, Government Finances* and *Federal Aid to States for Fiscal Year 2004.*

FEDERAL AID TO EDUCATION - ELEMENTARY AND SECONDARY EDUCATION

National Center for Education Statistics (NCES), 1990 K Street, NW, Washington, DC 20006, (202) 502-7300, http://nces.ed.gov; *Digest of Education Statistics 2007.*

FEDERAL AID TO EDUCATION - HIGHER EDUCATION INSTITUTIONS

National Center for Education Statistics (NCES), 1990 K Street, NW, Washington, DC 20006, (202) 502-7300, http://nces.ed.gov; *Digest of Education Statistics 2007* and unpublished data.

U.S. Department of Education (ED), Office of Postsecondary Education (OPE), 1990 K Street, NW, Washington, DC 20006, (202) 502-7750, www.ed.gov/ope; *Meeting the Highly Qualified Teachers Challenge: The Secretary's Third Annual Report on Teacher Quality.*

U.S. Department of Education (ED), Office of Special Education and Rehabilitative Services (OSERS), 400 Maryland Ave., SW, Washington, DC 20202-7100, (202) 245-7468, www.ed.gov/osers; *Federal Campus-Based Programs Data Book 2007.*

FEDERAL AID TO EDUCATION - RESEARCH AND DEVELOPMENT

National Science Foundation, Division of Science Resources Statistics (SRS), 4201 Wilson Boulevard, Arlington, VA 22230, (703) 292-8780, Fax: (703) 292-9092, www.nsf.gov; *Federal Science and Engineering Support to Universities, Colleges, and Nonprofit Institutions: Federal Year 2005* and *National Patterns of Research and Development Resources: 2006 Data Update.*

FEDERAL AID TO EDUCATION - SCIENCE AND ENGINEERING

National Science Foundation, Division of Science Resources Statistics (SRS), 4201 Wilson Boulevard, Arlington, VA 22230, (703) 292-8780, Fax: (703) 292-9092, www.nsf.gov; *Federal Science and Engineering Support to Universities, Colleges, and Nonprofit Institutions: Federal Year 2005* and *Survey of Research and Development Expenditures at Universities and Colleges.*

FEDERAL AID TO STATE AND LOCAL GOVERNMENT

The Office of Management and Budget (OMB), 725 17th Street, NW, Washington, DC 20503, (202) 395-3080, Fax: (202) 395-3888, www.whitehouse.gov/omb; *Historical Tables.*

U.S. Census Bureau, Governments Division, 4600 Silver Hill Road, Washington DC 20233, (800) 242-2184, www.census.gov/govs/www; *2002 Census of Governments, Government Finances.*

U.S. Department of Homeland Security (DHS), Washington, DC 20528, (202) 282-8000, www.dhs.gov; *2004 Counterterrorism Grants - State Allocations.*

FEDERAL BUDGET

See EXPENDITURES OF U.S. GOVERNMENT

FEDERAL DEBT

U.S. Department of the Treasury (DOT), 1500 Pennsylvania Avenue, NW, Washington, DC 20220, (202) 622-2000, Fax: (202) 622-6415, www.ustreas.gov; *Treasury Bulletin.*

FEDERAL EMPLOYEES RETIREMENT TRUST FUND

See GOVERNMENT

FEDERAL FUNDS - SUMMARY DISTRIBUTION BY STATE

U.S. Department of Homeland Security (DHS), Washington, DC 20528, (202) 282-8000, www.dhs.gov; *2004 Counterterrorism Grants - State Allocations.*

FEDERAL GOVERNMENT

See GOVERNMENT

FEDERAL GOVERNMENT FINANCES

See RECEIPTS

FEDERAL HOUSING ADMINISTRATION MORTGAGE LOANS

Board of Governors of the Federal Reserve System, Constitution Avenue, NW, Washington, DC 20551, (202) 452-3000, www.federalreserve.gov; *Federal Reserve Bulletin.*

Mortgage Bankers Association of America (MBA), 1919 Pennsylvania Avenue, NW, Washington, DC 20006-3404, (202) 557-2700, www.mbaa.org; *National Delinquency Survey.*

FEDERAL NATIONAL MORTGAGE ASSOCIATION LOANS

Board of Governors of the Federal Reserve System, Constitution Avenue, NW, Washington, DC 20551, (202) 452-3000, www.federalreserve.gov; *Federal Reserve Bulletin.*

FEDERAL REAL PROPERTY

General Services Administration (GSA), 1800 F Street, NW, Washington, DC 20405, (202) 708-5082, www.gsa.gov; *Federal Real Property Profile 2004 (FRPP).*

FEDERATED STATES OF MICRONESIA

See MICRONESIA, FEDERATED STATES OF

FEED

See GRAIN

FELDSPAR

U.S. Department of the Interior (DOI), U.S. Geological Survey (USGS), Office of Minerals Information, 12201 Sunrise Valley Drive, Reston, VA 20192, Mr. Kenneth A. Beckman, (703) 648-4916, Fax: (703) 648-4995, http://minerals.usgs.gov/minerals; *Mineral Commodity Summaries* and *Minerals Yearbook.*

FEMALE HOUSEHOLDER

See HOUSEHOLDS OR FAMILIES

FEMALE POPULATION

See WOMEN

FENCING

National Collegiate Athletic Association (NCAA), 700 West Washington Street, PO Box 6222, Indianapolis, IN 46206-6222, (317) 917-6222, Fax: (317) 917-6888, www.ncaa.org; *1982-2003 Sports Sponsorship and Participation Rates Report.*

FERTILITY RATE

National Center for Health Statistics (NCHS), Centers for Disease Control and Prevention (CDC), U.S. Department of Health and Human Services (HHS), 3311 Toledo Road, Hyattsville, MD 20782, (866) 232-4636, www.cdc.gov/nchs; *Vital Statistics of the United States (VSUS)* and unpublished data.

Statistical Centre of Iran (SCI), Dr. Fatemi Avenue, PO Box 14155-6133, Tehran 1414663111, Iran, www.sci.org.ir/portal/faces/public/sci_en/; *A Study on the Effects of Women's Activity on Fertility in Iran.*

U.S. Census Bureau, Population Division, 4700 Silver Hill Road, Washington DC 20233-0001, (301) 763-3030, www.census.gov/population/www/; *Current Population Reports.*

United Nations Statistics Division, New York, NY 10017, (800) 253-9646, Fax: (212) 963-4116, http://unstats.un.org; United Nations Common Database (UNCDB).

FERTILIZERS

United Nations Food and Agricultural Organization (FAO), Viale delle Terme di Caracalla, 00100 Rome, Italy, (Dial from U.S. (202) 653-2400), (Fax from U.S. (202) 653 5760), www.fao.org; *FAO Statistical Yearbook 2004* and FAOSTAT Database. Subjects covered include: Agriculture, nutrition, fisheries, forestry, food aid, land use and population.

FERTILIZERS - FARM EXPENDITURES FOR

Economic Research Service (ERS), U.S. Department of Agriculture (USDA), 1800 M Street, NW, Washington, DC 20036-5831, (202) 694-5050, Fax: (202) 694-5689, www.ers.usda.gov; *Agricultural Income and Finance Outlook* and *Farm Income: Data Files.*

FERTILIZERS - INTERNATIONAL TRADE

U.S. Census Bureau, Foreign Trade Division, 4700 Silver Hill Road, Washington DC 20233-0001, (301) 763-3030, www.census.gov/foreign-trade/www/; *U.S. International Trade in Goods and Services.*

FERTILIZERS - PRICES

National Agricultural Statistics Service (NASS), U.S. Department of Agriculture (USDA), 1400 Independence Avenue, SW, Washington, DC 20250, (800) 727-9540, Fax: (202) 690-2090, www.nass.usda.gov; *Agricultural Prices.*

FERTILIZERS - SHIPMENTS

U.S. Census Bureau, Manufacturing and Construction Division, 4600 Silver Hill Road, Washington DC 20233, (301) 763-4673, www.census.gov/mcd; *Annual Survey of Manufactures (ASM)* and *Census of Manufactures.*

FETAL DEATHS

Bernan Essential Government Publications, 4611-F Assembly Drive, Lanham MD, 20706-4391, (301) 459-2255, Fax: (800) 865-3450, www.bernan.com; *Vital Statistics of the United States: Births, Life Expectancy, Deaths, and Selected Health Data.*

National Center for Health Statistics (NCHS), Centers for Disease Control and Prevention (CDC), U.S. Department of Health and Human Services (HHS), 3311 Toledo Road, Hyattsville, MD 20782, (866) 232-4636, www.cdc.gov/nchs; *National Vital Statistics Reports (NVSR); Vital Statistics of the United States (VSUS);* and unpublished data.

FIBER - DIETARY

Center for Nutrition Policy and Promotion (CNPP), U.S. Department of Agriculture (USDA), 3101 Park Center Drive, 10th Floor, Alexandria, VA 22302-1594, (703) 305-7600, Fax: (703) 305-3300, www.usda.gov/cnpp; *Nutrient Content of the U.S. Food Supply Summary Report 2005.*

FIBERS

American Forest Paper Association (AFPA), 1111 Nineteenth Street, NW, Suite 800, Washington, DC 20036, (800) 878-8878, www.afandpa.org; *Annual Fiber Consumption Report.*

U.S. Census Bureau, Manufacturing and Construction Division, 4600 Silver Hill Road, Washington DC 20233, (301) 763-4673, www.census.gov/mcd; *Current Industrial Reports* and *Current Industrial Reports, Manufacturing Profiles.*

FIELD HOCKEY

National Collegiate Athletic Association (NCAA), 700 West Washington Street, PO Box 6222, Indianapolis, IN 46206-6222, (317) 917-6222, Fax: (317) 917-6888, www.ncaa.org; *1982-2003 Sports Sponsorship and Participation Rates Report.*

National Federation of State High School Associations, PO Box 690, Indianapolis, IN 46206, (317) 972-6900, Fax: (317) 822-5700, www.nfhs.org; *2005-06 High School Athletics Participation Survey.*

FIGURE SKATING

Mediamark Research, Inc., 75 Ninth Avenue, 5th Floor, New York, NY 10011, (212) 884-9200, Fax: (212) 884-9339, www.mediamark.com; MRI+.

National Sporting Goods Association (NSGA), 1601 Feehanville Drive, Suite 300, Mount Prospect, IL 60056, (847) 296-6742, Fax: (847) 391-9827, www.nsga.org; *2006 Sports Participation.*

FIJI - NATIONAL STATISTICAL OFFICE

Fiji Islands Bureau of Statistics (FIBOS), PO Box 2221, Government Buildings, Suva, Fiji, www.statsfiji.gov.fj; National Data Center.

FIJI - PRIMARY STATISTICS SOURCES

Fiji Islands Bureau of Statistics (FIBOS), PO Box 2221, Government Buildings, Suva, Fiji, www.statsfiji.gov.fj; *2007 Facts and Figures; Fiji Standard Industrial Classification (FSIC) 2004;* and *Key Statistics, September 2007.*

FIJI - AGRICULTURAL MACHINERY

United Nations Statistics Division, New York, NY 10017, (800) 253-9646, Fax: (212) 963-4116, http://unstats.un.org; *Statistical Yearbook.*

FIJI - AGRICULTURE

Asian Development Bank (ADB), PO Box 789, 0980 Manila, Philippines, www.adb.org; *Key Indicators of Developing Asian and Pacific Countries 2006.*

Economist Intelligence Unit, 111 West 57th Street, New York, NY 10019, (212) 554-0600, Fax: (212) 586-1181, www.eiu.com; *Fiji Country Report.*

Euromonitor International, Inc., 224 S. Michigan Avenue, Suite 1500, Chicago, IL 60604, (312) 922-1115, Fax: (312) 922-1157, www.euromonitor.com; *World Marketing Data and Statistics.*

M.E. Sharpe, 80 Business Park Drive, Armonk, NY 10504, (800) 541-6563, Fax: (914) 273-2106, www.mesharpe.com; *The Illustrated Book of World Rankings.*

Taylor and Francis Group, An Informa Business, 2 Park Square, Milton Park, Abingdon, Oxford OX14 4RN, United Kingdom, (Dial from U.S. (212) 216-7800), (Fax from U.S. (212) 564-7854), www.tandf.co.uk; *The Europa World Year Book.*

United Nations Conference on Trade and Development (UNCTAD), DC2-1120, United Nations, New York, NY 10017, (212) 963-0027, www.unctad.org; *UNCTAD Commodity Yearbook.*

United Nations Food and Agricultural Organization (FAO), Viale delle Terme di Caracalla, 00100 Rome, Italy, (Dial from U.S. (202) 653-2400), (Fax from U.S. (202) 653 5760), www.fao.org; AQUASTAT; *FAO Production Yearbook 2002; FAO Trade Yearbook;* and *The State of Food and Agriculture (SOFA) 2006.*

United Nations Statistics Division, New York, NY 10017, (800) 253-9646, Fax: (212) 963-4116, http://unstats.un.org; *Asia-Pacific in Figures 2004; Statistical Yearbook;* and *Statistical Yearbook for Asia and the Pacific 2004.*

The World Bank, 1818 H Street, NW, Washington, DC 20433, (202) 473-1000, Fax: (202) 477-6391, www.worldbank.org; *Fiji* and *World Development Indicators (WDI) 2008.*

FIJI - AIRLINES

M.E. Sharpe, 80 Business Park Drive, Armonk, NY 10504, (800) 541-6563, Fax: (914) 273-2106, www.mesharpe.com; *The Illustrated Book of World Rankings.*

Palgrave Macmillan Ltd., Houndmills, Basingstoke, Hampshire, RG21 6XS, England, (Telephone in U.S. (888) 330-8477), (Fax in U.S. (800) 672-2054), www.palgrave.com; *The Statesman's Yearbook 2008.*

Taylor and Francis Group, An Informa Business, 2 Park Square, Milton Park, Abingdon, Oxford OX14 4RN, United Kingdom, (Dial from U.S. (212) 216-7800), (Fax from U.S. (212) 564-7854), www.tandf.co.uk; *The Europa World Year Book.*

FIJI - AIRPORTS

Central Intelligence Agency, Office of Public Affairs, Washington, DC 20505, (703) 482-0623, Fax: (703) 482-1739, www.cia.gov; *The World Factbook.*

FIJI - ALUMINUM PRODUCTION

See FIJI - MINERAL INDUSTRIES

FIJI - ARMED FORCES

Central Intelligence Agency, Office of Public Affairs, Washington, DC 20505, (703) 482-0623, Fax: (703) 482-1739, www.cia.gov; *The World Factbook.*

Euromonitor International, Inc., 224 S. Michigan Avenue, Suite 1500, Chicago, IL 60604, (312) 922-1115, Fax: (312) 922-1157, www.euromonitor.com; *World Marketing Data and Statistics.*

International Institute for Strategic Studies (IISS), Arundel House, 13-15 Arundel Street, Temple Place, London WC2R 3DX, England, www.iiss.org; *The Military Balance 2007.*

International Monetary Fund (IMF), 700 Nineteenth Street, NW, Washington, DC 20431, (202) 623-7000, Fax: (202) 623-4661, www.imf.org; *Government Finance Statistics Yearbook (2008 Edition).*

Palgrave Macmillan Ltd., Houndmills, Basingstoke, Hampshire, RG21 6XS, England, (Telephone in U.S. (888) 330-8477), (Fax in U.S. (800) 672-2054), www.palgrave.com; *The Statesman's Yearbook 2008.*

U.S. Department of State (DOS), 2201 C Street NW, Washington, DC 20520, (202) 647-4000, www.state.gov; *World Military Expenditures and Arms Transfers (WMEAT).*

United Nations Statistics Division, New York, NY 10017, (800) 253-9646, Fax: (212) 963-4116, http://unstats.un.org; *Human Development Report 2006.*

FIJI - BALANCE OF PAYMENTS

International Monetary Fund (IMF), 700 Nineteenth Street, NW, Washington, DC 20431, (202) 623-7000, Fax: (202) 623-4661, www.imf.org; *Balance of Payments Statistics Newsletter* and *Balance of Payments Statistics Yearbook 2007.*

Taylor and Francis Group, An Informa Business, 2 Park Square, Milton Park, Abingdon, Oxford OX14 4RN, United Kingdom, (Dial from U.S. (212) 216-7800), (Fax from U.S. (212) 564-7854), www.tandf.co.uk; *The Europa World Year Book.*

United Nations Conference on Trade and Development (UNCTAD), DC2-1120, United Nations, New York, NY 10017, (212) 963-0027, www.unctad.org; *Handbook of Statistics 2005.*

The World Bank, 1818 H Street, NW, Washington, DC 20433, (202) 473-1000, Fax: (202) 477-6391, www.worldbank.org; *Fiji* and *World Development Indicators (WDI) 2008.*

FIJI - BANKS AND BANKING

Asian Development Bank (ADB), PO Box 789, 0980 Manila, Philippines, www.adb.org; *Key Indicators of Developing Asian and Pacific Countries 2006.*

Euromonitor International, Inc., 224 S. Michigan Avenue, Suite 1500, Chicago, IL 60604, (312) 922-1115, Fax: (312) 922-1157, www.euromonitor.com; *World Marketing Data and Statistics.*

International Monetary Fund (IMF), 700 Nineteenth Street, NW, Washington, DC 20431, (202) 623-7000, Fax: (202) 623-4661, www.imf.org; *Government Finance Statistics Yearbook (2008 Edition)* and *International Financial Statistics Yearbook 2007.*

M.E. Sharpe, 80 Business Park Drive, Armonk, NY 10504, (800) 541-6563, Fax: (914) 273-2106, www.mesharpe.com; *The Illustrated Book of World Rankings.*

Palgrave Macmillan Ltd., Houndmills, Basingstoke, Hampshire, RG21 6XS, England, (Telephone in U.S. (888) 330-8477), (Fax in U.S. (800) 672-2054), www.palgrave.com; *The Statesman's Yearbook 2008.*

Taylor and Francis Group, An Informa Business, 2 Park Square, Milton Park, Abingdon, Oxford OX14 4RN, United Kingdom, (Dial from U.S. (212) 216-7800), (Fax from U.S. (212) 564-7854), www.tandf.co.uk; *The Europa World Year Book.*

FIJI - BARLEY PRODUCTION

See FIJI - CROPS

FIJI - BEVERAGE INDUSTRY

M.E. Sharpe, 80 Business Park Drive, Armonk, NY 10504, (800) 541-6563, Fax: (914) 273-2106, www.mesharpe.com; *The Illustrated Book of World Rankings.*

United Nations Statistics Division, New York, NY 10017, (800) 253-9646, Fax: (212) 963-4116, http://unstats.un.org; *Statistical Yearbook.*

FIJI - BONDS

Asian Development Bank (ADB), PO Box 789, 0980 Manila, Philippines, www.adb.org; *Key Indicators of Developing Asian and Pacific Countries 2006.*

International Monetary Fund (IMF), 700 Nineteenth Street, NW, Washington, DC 20431, (202) 623-7000, Fax: (202) 623-4661, www.imf.org; *Government Finance Statistics Yearbook (2008 Edition).*

FIJI - BROADCASTING

Central Intelligence Agency, Office of Public Affairs, Washington, DC 20505, (703) 482-0623, Fax: (703) 482-1739, www.cia.gov; *The World Factbook.*

Euromonitor International, Inc., 224 S. Michigan Avenue, Suite 1500, Chicago, IL 60604, (312) 922-1115, Fax: (312) 922-1157, www.euromonitor.com; *World Marketing Data and Statistics.*

M.E. Sharpe, 80 Business Park Drive, Armonk, NY 10504, (800) 541-6563, Fax: (914) 273-2106, www.mesharpe.com; *The Illustrated Book of World Rankings.*

Palgrave Macmillan Ltd., Houndmills, Basingstoke, Hampshire, RG21 6XS, England, (Telephone in U.S. (888) 330-8477), (Fax in U.S. (800) 672-2054), www.palgrave.com; *The Statesman's Yearbook 2008.*

UNESCO Institute for Statistics, C.P. 6128 Succursale Centre-Ville, Montreal, Quebec, H3C 3J7 Canada, (Dial from U.S. (514) 343-6880), (Fax from U.S. (514) 343 6882), www.uis.unesco.org; *Statistical Tables.*

WRTH Publications Limited, PO Box 290, Oxford OX2 7FT, UK, www.wrth.com; *World Radio TV Handbook 2007.*

FIJI - BUDGET

Central Intelligence Agency, Office of Public Affairs, Washington, DC 20505, (703) 482-0623, Fax: (703) 482-1739, www.cia.gov; *The World Factbook.*

FIJI - BUSINESS

United Nations Statistics Division, New York, NY 10017, (800) 253-9646, Fax: (212) 963-4116, http://unstats.un.org; *Statistical Yearbook* and *Statistical Yearbook for Asia and the Pacific 2004.*

FIJI - CAPITAL INVESTMENTS

Asian Development Bank (ADB), PO Box 789, 0980 Manila, Philippines, www.adb.org; *Key Indicators of Developing Asian and Pacific Countries 2006.*

FIJI - CAPITAL LEVY

Asian Development Bank (ADB), PO Box 789, 0980 Manila, Philippines, www.adb.org; *Key Indicators of Developing Asian and Pacific Countries 2006.*

International Monetary Fund (IMF), 700 Nineteenth Street, NW, Washington, DC 20431, (202) 623-7000, Fax: (202) 623-4661, www.imf.org; *Government Finance Statistics Yearbook (2008 Edition).*

FIJI - CATTLE

See FIJI - LIVESTOCK

FIJI - CHILDBIRTH - STATISTICS

Central Intelligence Agency, Office of Public Affairs, Washington, DC 20505, (703) 482-0623, Fax: (703) 482-1739, www.cia.gov; *The World Factbook.*

Euromonitor International, Inc., 224 S. Michigan Avenue, Suite 1500, Chicago, IL 60604, (312) 922-1115, Fax: (312) 922-1157, www.euromonitor.com; *International Marketing Data and Statistics 2008* and *The World Economic Factbook 2008.*

M.E. Sharpe, 80 Business Park Drive, Armonk, NY 10504, (800) 541-6563, Fax: (914) 273-2106, www.mesharpe.com; *The Illustrated Book of World Rankings.*

Palgrave Macmillan Ltd., Houndmills, Basingstoke, Hampshire, RG21 6XS, England, (Telephone in U.S. (888) 330-8477), (Fax in U.S. (800) 672-2054), www.palgrave.com; *The Statesman's Yearbook 2008.*

Taylor and Francis Group, An Informa Business, 2 Park Square, Milton Park, Abingdon, Oxford OX14 4RN, United Kingdom, (Dial from U.S. (212) 216-7800), (Fax from U.S. (212) 564-7854), www.tandf.co.uk; *The Europa World Year Book.*

United Nations Statistics Division, New York, NY 10017, (800) 253-9646, Fax: (212) 963-4116, http://unstats.un.org; *Asia-Pacific in Figures 2004; Demographic Yearbook;* and *Statistical Yearbook.*

The World Bank, 1818 H Street, NW, Washington, DC 20433, (202) 473-1000, Fax: (202) 477-6391, www.worldbank.org; *World Development Indicators (WDI) 2008.*

World Health Organization (WHO), Avenue Appia 20, 1211 Geneve 27, Switzerland, (Telephone in U.S. (212) 331-9081), www.who.int; *World Health Report 2006.*

FIJI - CLIMATE

M.E. Sharpe, 80 Business Park Drive, Armonk, NY 10504, (800) 541-6563, Fax: (914) 273-2106, www.mesharpe.com; *The Illustrated Book of World Rankings.*

Palgrave Macmillan Ltd., Houndmills, Basingstoke, Hampshire, RG21 6XS, England, (Telephone in U.S. (888) 330-8477), (Fax in U.S. (800) 672-2054), www.palgrave.com; *The Statesman's Yearbook 2008.*

FIJI - CLOTHING EXPORTS AND IMPORTS

See FIJI - TEXTILE INDUSTRY

FIJI - COAL PRODUCTION

See FIJI - MINERAL INDUSTRIES

FIJI - COCOA PRODUCTION

See FIJI - CROPS

FIJI - COCONUT PRODUCTS

See FIJI - CROPS

FIJI - COFFEE

See FIJI - CROPS

FIJI - COMMERCE

Palgrave Macmillan Ltd., Houndmills, Basingstoke, Hampshire, RG21 6XS, England, (Telephone in U.S. (888) 330-8477), (Fax in U.S. (800) 672-2054), www.palgrave.com; *The Statesman's Yearbook 2008.*

FIJI - COMMODITY EXCHANGES

Commodity Research Bureau, 330 South Wells Street, Suite 612, Chicago, IL 60606-7110, (800) 621-5271, Fax: (312) 939-4135, www.crbtrader.com; *2006 CRB Commodity Yearbook and CD.*

International Monetary Fund (IMF), 700 Nineteenth Street, NW, Washington, DC 20431, (202) 623-7000, Fax: (202) 623-4661, www.imf.org; *IMF Primary Commodity Prices.*

United Nations Food and Agricultural Organization (FAO), Viale delle Terme di Caracalla, 00100 Rome, Italy, (Dial from U.S. (202) 653-2400), (Fax from U.S. (202) 653 5760), www.fao.org; *The State of Food and Agriculture (SOFA) 2006.*

FIJI - CONSTRUCTION INDUSTRY

M.E. Sharpe, 80 Business Park Drive, Armonk, NY 10504, (800) 541-6563, Fax: (914) 273-2106, www.mesharpe.com; *The Illustrated Book of World Rankings.*

United Nations Statistics Division, New York, NY 10017, (800) 253-9646, Fax: (212) 963-4116, http://unstats.un.org; *Statistical Yearbook.*

FIJI - CONSUMER PRICE INDEXES

Asian Development Bank (ADB), PO Box 789, 0980 Manila, Philippines, www.adb.org; *Key Indicators of Developing Asian and Pacific Countries 2006.*

Taylor and Francis Group, An Informa Business, 2 Park Square, Milton Park, Abingdon, Oxford OX14 4RN, United Kingdom, (Dial from U.S. (212) 216-7800), (Fax from U.S. (212) 564-7854), www.tandf.co.uk; *The Europa World Year Book.*

United Nations Statistics Division, New York, NY 10017, (800) 253-9646, Fax: (212) 963-4116, http://unstats.un.org; *Statistical Yearbook.*

The World Bank, 1818 H Street, NW, Washington, DC 20433, (202) 473-1000, Fax: (202) 477-6391, www.worldbank.org; *Fiji.*

FIJI - CONSUMPTION (ECONOMICS)

Secretariat of the Pacific Community (SPC), BP D5, 98848 Noumea Cedex, New Caledonia, www.spc.int/corp; *Selected Pacific Economies - a Statistical Summary (SPESS).*

FIJI - COPPER INDUSTRY AND TRADE

See FIJI - MINERAL INDUSTRIES

FIJI - CORN INDUSTRY

See FIJI - CROPS

FIJI - COST AND STANDARD OF LIVING

International Monetary Fund (IMF), 700 Nineteenth Street, NW, Washington, DC 20431, (202) 623-7000, Fax: (202) 623-4661, www.imf.org; *Government Finance Statistics Yearbook (2008 Edition).*

Secretariat of the Pacific Community (SPC), BP D5, 98848 Noumea Cedex, New Caledonia, www.spc.int/corp; *Selected Pacific Economies - a Statistical Summary (SPESS).*

FIJI - COTTON

See FIJI - CROPS

FIJI - CRIME

International Criminal Police Organization (INTERPOL), General Secretariat, 200 quai Charles de Gaulle, 69006 Lyon, France, www.interpol.int; *International Crime Statistics.*

Yale University Press, PO Box 209040, New Haven, CT 06520-9040, (203) 432-0960, Fax: (203) 432-0948, http://yalepress.yale.edu/yupbooks; *Violence and Crime in Cross-National Perspective.*

FIJI - CROPS

Asian Development Bank (ADB), PO Box 789, 0980 Manila, Philippines, www.adb.org; *Key Indicators of Developing Asian and Pacific Countries 2006.*

International Monetary Fund (IMF), 700 Nineteenth Street, NW, Washington, DC 20431, (202) 623-7000, Fax: (202) 623-4661, www.imf.org; *International Financial Statistics Yearbook 2007.*

M.E. Sharpe, 80 Business Park Drive, Armonk, NY 10504, (800) 541-6563, Fax: (914) 273-2106, www.mesharpe.com; *The Illustrated Book of World Rankings.*

Palgrave Macmillan Ltd., Houndmills, Basingstoke, Hampshire, RG21 6XS, England, (Telephone in U.S. (888) 330-8477), (Fax in U.S. (800) 672-2054), www.palgrave.com; *The Statesman's Yearbook 2008.*

Taylor and Francis Group, An Informa Business, 2 Park Square, Milton Park, Abingdon, Oxford OX14 4RN, United Kingdom, (Dial from U.S. (212) 216-7800), (Fax from U.S. (212) 564-7854), www.tandf.co.uk; *The Europa World Year Book.*

United Nations Conference on Trade and Development (UNCTAD), DC2-1120, United Nations, New York, NY 10017, (212) 963-0027, www.unctad.org; *UNCTAD Commodity Yearbook.*

United Nations Food and Agricultural Organization (FAO), Viale delle Terme di Caracalla, 00100 Rome, Italy, (Dial from U.S. (202) 653-2400), (Fax from U.S. (202) 653 5760), www.fao.org; *FAO Production Yearbook 2002* and *The State of Food and Agriculture (SOFA) 2006.*

United Nations Statistics Division, New York, NY 10017, (800) 253-9646, Fax: (212) 963-4116, http://unstats.un.org; *Statistical Yearbook.*

FIJI - CUSTOMS ADMINISTRATION

International Monetary Fund (IMF), 700 Nineteenth Street, NW, Washington, DC 20431, (202) 623-7000, Fax: (202) 623-4661, www.imf.org; *Government Finance Statistics Yearbook (2008 Edition).*

Palgrave Macmillan Ltd., Houndmills, Basingstoke, Hampshire, RG21 6XS, England, (Telephone in U.S. (888) 330-8477), (Fax in U.S. (800) 672-2054), www.palgrave.com; *The Statesman's Yearbook 2008.*

FIJI - DAIRY PROCESSING

M.E. Sharpe, 80 Business Park Drive, Armonk, NY 10504, (800) 541-6563, Fax: (914) 273-2106, www.mesharpe.com; *The Illustrated Book of World Rankings.*

Palgrave Macmillan Ltd., Houndmills, Basingstoke, Hampshire, RG21 6XS, England, (Telephone in U.S. (888) 330-8477), (Fax in U.S. (800) 672-2054), www.palgrave.com; *The Statesman's Yearbook 2008.*

United Nations Food and Agricultural Organization (FAO), Viale delle Terme di Caracalla, 00100 Rome, Italy, (Dial from U.S. (202) 653-2400), (Fax from U.S. (202) 653 5760), www.fao.org; *The State of Food and Agriculture (SOFA) 2006.*

FIJI - DEATH RATES

See FIJI - MORTALITY

FIJI - DEBTS, EXTERNAL

Asian Development Bank (ADB), PO Box 789, 0980 Manila, Philippines, www.adb.org; *Key Indicators of Developing Asian and Pacific Countries 2006.*

International Monetary Fund (IMF), 700 Nineteenth Street, NW, Washington, DC 20431, (202) 623-7000, Fax: (202) 623-4661, www.imf.org; *Government Finance Statistics Yearbook (2008 Edition).*

Palgrave Macmillan Ltd., Houndmills, Basingstoke, Hampshire, RG21 6XS, England, (Telephone in U.S. (888) 330-8477), (Fax in U.S. (800) 672-2054), www.palgrave.com; *The Statesman's Yearbook 2008.*

The World Bank, 1818 H Street, NW, Washington, DC 20433, (202) 473-1000, Fax: (202) 477-6391,

www.worldbank.org; *Global Development Finance 2007* and *World Development Indicators (WDI) 2008.*

Worldinformation.com, 2 Market Street, Saffron Walden, Essex CB10 1HZ, United Kingdom, www.worldinformation.com; The World of Information (www.worldinformation.com).

FIJI - DEFENSE EXPENDITURES

See FIJI - ARMED FORCES

FIJI - DEMOGRAPHY

Euromonitor International, Inc., 224 S. Michigan Avenue, Suite 1500, Chicago, IL 60604, (312) 922-1115, Fax: (312) 922-1157, www.euromonitor.com; *International Marketing Data and Statistics 2008; The World Economic Factbook 2008;* and *World Marketing Data and Statistics.*

M.E. Sharpe, 80 Business Park Drive, Armonk, NY 10504, (800) 541-6563, Fax: (914) 273-2106, www.mesharpe.com; *The Illustrated Book of World Rankings.*

United Nations Statistics Division, New York, NY 10017, (800) 253-9646, Fax: (212) 963-4116, http://unstats.un.org; *Asia-Pacific in Figures 2004* and *Human Development Report 2006.*

The World Bank, 1818 H Street, NW, Washington, DC 20433, (202) 473-1000, Fax: (202) 477-6391, www.worldbank.org; *Fiji.*

FIJI - DIAMONDS

See FIJI - MINERAL INDUSTRIES

FIJI - DISPOSABLE INCOME

M.E. Sharpe, 80 Business Park Drive, Armonk, NY 10504, (800) 541-6563, Fax: (914) 273-2106, www.mesharpe.com; *The Illustrated Book of World Rankings.*

United Nations Statistics Division, New York, NY 10017, (800) 253-9646, Fax: (212) 963-4116, http://unstats.un.org; *National Accounts Statistics: Compendium of Income Distribution Statistics* and *Statistical Yearbook.*

FIJI - DIVORCE

M.E. Sharpe, 80 Business Park Drive, Armonk, NY 10504, (800) 541-6563, Fax: (914) 273-2106, www.mesharpe.com; *The Illustrated Book of World Rankings.*

United Nations Statistics Division, New York, NY 10017, (800) 253-9646, Fax: (212) 963-4116, http://unstats.un.org; *Demographic Yearbook* and *Statistical Yearbook.*

FIJI - ECONOMIC ASSISTANCE

Asian Development Bank (ADB), PO Box 789, 0980 Manila, Philippines, www.adb.org; *Key Indicators of Developing Asian and Pacific Countries 2006.*

United Nations Statistics Division, New York, NY 10017, (800) 253-9646, Fax: (212) 963-4116, http://unstats.un.org; *Statistical Yearbook.*

FIJI - ECONOMIC CONDITIONS

Asian Development Bank (ADB), PO Box 789, 0980 Manila, Philippines, www.adb.org; *Key Indicators of Developing Asian and Pacific Countries 2006.*

Center for International Business Education Research (CIBER), Columbia Business School and School of International and Public Affairs, Uris Hall, Room 212, 3022 Broadway, New York, NY 10027-6902, Mr. Joshua Safier, (212) 854-4750, Fax: (212) 222-9821, www.columbia.edu/cu/ciber/; Datastream International.

Central Intelligence Agency, Office of Public Affairs, Washington, DC 20505, (703) 482-0623, Fax: (703) 482-1739, www.cia.gov; *The World Factbook.*

DSI Data Service Information, Xantener Strasse 51a, D-47495 Rheinberg, Germany, www.dsidata.com; *Campus Solution.*

Dun and Bradstreet (DB) Corporation, 103 JFK Parkway, Short Hills, NJ 07078, (973) 921-5500, www.dnb.com; *Country Report.*

Economist Intelligence Unit, 111 West 57th Street, New York, NY 10019, (212) 554-0600, Fax: (212) 586-1181, www.eiu.com; *Fiji Country Report.*

Euromonitor International, Inc., 224 S. Michigan Avenue, Suite 1500, Chicago, IL 60604, (312) 922-1115, Fax: (312) 922-1157, www.euromonitor.com; *The World Economic Factbook 2008* and *World Marketing Data and Statistics.*

International Monetary Fund (IMF), 700 Nineteenth Street, NW, Washington, DC 20431, (202) 623-7000, Fax: (202) 623-4661, www.imf.org; *World Economic Outlook Reports.*

M.E. Sharpe, 80 Business Park Drive, Armonk, NY 10504, (800) 541-6563, Fax: (914) 273-2106, www.mesharpe.com; *The Illustrated Book of World Rankings.*

Palgrave Macmillan Ltd., Houndmills, Basingstoke, Hampshire, RG21 6XS, England, (Telephone in U.S. (888) 330-8477), (Fax in U.S. (800) 672-2054), www.palgrave.com; *The Statesman's Yearbook 2008.*

Secretariat of the Pacific Community (SPC), BP D5, 98848 Noumea Cedex, New Caledonia, www.spc.int/corp; PRISM (Pacific Regional Information System).

Taylor and Francis Group, An Informa Business, 2 Park Square, Milton Park, Abingdon, Oxford OX14 4RN, United Kingdom, (Dial from U.S. (212) 216-7800), (Fax from U.S. (212) 564-7854), www.tandf.co.uk; *The Europa World Year Book.*

United Nations Statistics Division, New York, NY 10017, (800) 253-9646, Fax: (212) 963-4116, http://unstats.un.org; *World Statistics Pocketbook.*

The World Bank, 1818 H Street, NW, Washington, DC 20433, (202) 473-1000, Fax: (202) 477-6391, www.worldbank.org; *Fiji; Global Economic Monitor (GEM); Global Economic Prospects 2008;* and *The World Bank Atlas 2003-2004.*

FIJI - EDUCATION

Euromonitor International, Inc., 224 S. Michigan Avenue, Suite 1500, Chicago, IL 60604, (312) 922-1115, Fax: (312) 922-1157, www.euromonitor.com; *International Marketing Data and Statistics 2008* and *World Marketing Data and Statistics.*

International Monetary Fund (IMF), 700 Nineteenth Street, NW, Washington, DC 20431, (202) 623-7000, Fax: (202) 623-4661, www.imf.org; *Government Finance Statistics Yearbook (2008 Edition).*

M.E. Sharpe, 80 Business Park Drive, Armonk, NY 10504, (800) 541-6563, Fax: (914) 273-2106, www.mesharpe.com; *The Illustrated Book of World Rankings.*

Palgrave Macmillan Ltd., Houndmills, Basingstoke, Hampshire, RG21 6XS, England, (Telephone in U.S. (888) 330-8477), (Fax in U.S. (800) 672-2054), www.palgrave.com; *The Statesman's Yearbook 2008.*

Taylor and Francis Group, An Informa Business, 2 Park Square, Milton Park, Abingdon, Oxford OX14 4RN, United Kingdom, (Dial from U.S. (212) 216-7800), (Fax from U.S. (212) 564-7854), www.tandf.co.uk; *The Europa World Year Book.*

UNESCO Institute for Statistics, C.P. 6128 Succursale Centre-Ville, Montreal, Quebec, H3C 3J7 Canada, (Dial from U.S. (514) 343-6880), (Fax from U.S. (514) 343 6882), www.uis.unesco.org; *Statistical Tables.*

United Nations Statistics Division, New York, NY 10017, (800) 253-9646, Fax: (212) 963-4116, http://unstats.un.org; *Asia-Pacific in Figures 2004; Human Development Report 2006;* and *Statistical Yearbook for Asia and the Pacific 2004.*

The World Bank, 1818 H Street, NW, Washington, DC 20433, (202) 473-1000, Fax: (202) 477-6391, www.worldbank.org; *Fiji* and *World Development Indicators (WDI) 2008.*

FIJI - ELECTRICITY

Asian Development Bank (ADB), PO Box 789, 0980 Manila, Philippines, www.adb.org; *Key Indicators of Developing Asian and Pacific Countries 2006.*

M.E. Sharpe, 80 Business Park Drive, Armonk, NY 10504, (800) 541-6563, Fax: (914) 273-2106, www.mesharpe.com; *The Illustrated Book of World Rankings.*

Palgrave Macmillan Ltd., Houndmills, Basingstoke, Hampshire, RG21 6XS, England, (Telephone in U.S. (888) 330-8477), (Fax in U.S. (800) 672-2054), www.palgrave.com; *The Statesman's Yearbook 2008.*

U.S. Department of Energy (DOE), Energy Information Administration (EIA), 1000 Independence Avenue, SW, Washington, DC 20585, (202) 586-8800, www.eia.doe.gov; *International Energy Annual 2004* and *International Energy Outlook 2006.*

United Nations Statistics Division, New York, NY 10017, (800) 253-9646, Fax: (212) 963-4116, http://unstats.un.org; *Electric Power in Asia and the Pacific 2001 and 2002; Human Development Report 2006;* and *Statistical Yearbook.*

FIJI - EMPLOYMENT

Euromonitor International, Inc., 224 S. Michigan Avenue, Suite 1500, Chicago, IL 60604, (312) 922-1115, Fax: (312) 922-1157, www.euromonitor.com; *International Marketing Data and Statistics 2008.*

International Labour Office, I.L.O. Publications, 4 route des Morillons, CH-1211 Geneva 22, Switzerland, (Telephone in U.S. (202) 653-7652), (Fax in U.S. (202) 653-7687), www.ilo.org; *Yearbook of Labour Statistics 2006.*

M.E. Sharpe, 80 Business Park Drive, Armonk, NY 10504, (800) 541-6563, Fax: (914) 273-2106, www.mesharpe.com; *The Illustrated Book of World Rankings.*

United Nations Statistics Division, New York, NY 10017, (800) 253-9646, Fax: (212) 963-4116, http://unstats.un.org; *Asia-Pacific in Figures 2004* and *Statistical Yearbook.*

The World Bank, 1818 H Street, NW, Washington, DC 20433, (202) 473-1000, Fax: (202) 477-6391, www.worldbank.org; *Fiji.*

FIJI - ENERGY INDUSTRIES

Enerdata, 10 Rue Royale, 75008 Paris, France, www.enerdata.fr; *Global Energy Market Data.*

United Nations Statistics Division, New York, NY 10017, (800) 253-9646, Fax: (212) 963-4116, http://unstats.un.org; *Electric Power in Asia and the Pacific 2001 and 2002* and *Statistical Yearbook.*

FIJI - ENVIRONMENTAL CONDITIONS

DSI Data Service Information, Xantener Strasse 51a, D-47495 Rheinberg, Germany, www.dsidata.com; *Campus Solution* and *DSI's Global Environmental Database.*

Economist Intelligence Unit, 111 West 57th Street, New York, NY 10019, (212) 554-0600, Fax: (212) 586-1181, www.eiu.com; *Fiji Country Report.*

United Nations Statistics Division, New York, NY 10017, (800) 253-9646, Fax: (212) 963-4116, http://unstats.un.org; *World Statistics Pocketbook.*

FIJI - EXPORTS

Asian Development Bank (ADB), PO Box 789, 0980 Manila, Philippines, www.adb.org; *Key Indicators of Developing Asian and Pacific Countries 2006.*

Central Intelligence Agency, Office of Public Affairs, Washington, DC 20505, (703) 482-0623, Fax: (703) 482-1739, www.cia.gov; *The World Factbook.*

Economist Intelligence Unit, 111 West 57th Street, New York, NY 10019, (212) 554-0600, Fax: (212) 586-1181, www.eiu.com; *Fiji Country Report.*

Euromonitor International, Inc., 224 S. Michigan Avenue, Suite 1500, Chicago, IL 60604, (312) 922-1115, Fax: (312) 922-1157, www.euromonitor.com; *International Marketing Data and Statistics 2008* and *The World Economic Factbook 2008.*

International Monetary Fund (IMF), 700 Nineteenth Street, NW, Washington, DC 20431, (202) 623-7000, Fax: (202) 623-4661, www.imf.org; *Direction of Trade Statistics Yearbook 2007; Government Finance Statistics Yearbook (2008 Edition);* and *International Financial Statistics Yearbook 2007.*

Palgrave Macmillan Ltd., Houndmills, Basingstoke, Hampshire, RG21 6XS, England, (Telephone in U.S. (888) 330-8477), (Fax in U.S. (800) 672-2054), www.palgrave.com; *The Statesman's Yearbook 2008.*

Secretariat of the Pacific Community (SPC), BP D5, 98848 Noumea Cedex, New Caledonia, www.spc.int/corp; *Selected Pacific Economies - a Statistical Summary (SPESS).*

United Nations Conference on Trade and Development (UNCTAD), DC2-1120, United Nations, New York, NY 10017, (212) 963-0027, www.unctad.org; *Handbook of Statistics 2005.*

United Nations Food and Agricultural Organization (FAO), Viale delle Terme di Caracalla, 00100 Rome, Italy, (Dial from U.S. (202) 653-2400), (Fax from U.S. (202) 653 5760), www.fao.org; *The State of Food and Agriculture (SOFA) 2006.*

United Nations Statistics Division, New York, NY 10017, (800) 253-9646, Fax: (212) 963-4116, http://unstats.un.org; *Foreign Trade Statistics of Asia and the Pacific 1996-2000.*

The World Bank, 1818 H Street, NW, Washington, DC 20433, (202) 473-1000, Fax: (202) 477-6391, www.worldbank.org; *World Development Indicators (WDI) 2008.*

Worldinformation.com, 2 Market Street, Saffron Walden, Essex CB10 1HZ, United Kingdom, www.worldinformation.com; The World of Information (www.worldinformation.com).

FIJI - FERTILITY, HUMAN

Central Intelligence Agency, Office of Public Affairs, Washington, DC 20505, (703) 482-0623, Fax: (703) 482-1739, www.cia.gov; *The World Factbook.*

M.E. Sharpe, 80 Business Park Drive, Armonk, NY 10504, (800) 541-6563, Fax: (914) 273-2106, www.mesharpe.com; *The Illustrated Book of World Rankings.*

United Nations Statistics Division, New York, NY 10017, (800) 253-9646, Fax: (212) 963-4116, http://unstats.un.org; *Human Development Report 2006.*

The World Bank, 1818 H Street, NW, Washington, DC 20433, (202) 473-1000, Fax: (202) 477-6391, www.worldbank.org; *The World Bank Atlas 2003-2004* and *World Development Indicators (WDI) 2008.*

FIJI - FERTILIZER INDUSTRY

United Nations Food and Agricultural Organization (FAO), Viale delle Terme di Caracalla, 00100 Rome, Italy, (Dial from U.S. (202) 653-2400), (Fax from U.S. (202) 653 5760), www.fao.org; *FAO Fertilizer Yearbook* and *The State of Food and Agriculture (SOFA) 2006.*

United Nations Statistics Division, New York, NY 10017, (800) 253-9646, Fax: (212) 963-4116, http://unstats.un.org; *Statistical Yearbook.*

FIJI - FETAL MORTALITY

See FIJI - MORTALITY

FIJI - FINANCE

International Monetary Fund (IMF), 700 Nineteenth Street, NW, Washington, DC 20431, (202) 623-7000, Fax: (202) 623-4661, www.imf.org; *International Financial Statistics Yearbook 2007.*

United Nations Statistics Division, New York, NY 10017, (800) 253-9646, Fax: (212) 963-4116, http://unstats.un.org; *Asia-Pacific in Figures 2004; National Accounts Statistics: Compendium of Income Distribution Statistics; Statistical Yearbook;* and *Statistical Yearbook for Asia and the Pacific 2004.*

The World Bank, 1818 H Street, NW, Washington, DC 20433, (202) 473-1000, Fax: (202) 477-6391, www.worldbank.org; *Fiji.*

FIJI - FINANCE, PUBLIC

Asian Development Bank (ADB), PO Box 789, 0980 Manila, Philippines, www.adb.org; *Key Indicators of Developing Asian and Pacific Countries 2006.*

Bernan Essential Government Publications, 4611-F Assembly Drive, Lanham MD, 20706-4391, (301) 459-2255, Fax: (800) 865-3450, www.bernan.com; *National Accounts Statistics.*

Economist Intelligence Unit, 111 West 57th Street, New York, NY 10019, (212) 554-0600, Fax: (212) 586-1181, www.eiu.com; *Fiji Country Report.*

International Monetary Fund (IMF), 700 Nineteenth Street, NW, Washington, DC 20431, (202) 623-7000, Fax: (202) 623-4661, www.imf.org; *Government Finance Statistics Yearbook (2008 Edition); International Financial Statistics; International Financial Statistics Online Service;* and *International Financial Statistics Yearbook 2007.*

M.E. Sharpe, 80 Business Park Drive, Armonk, NY 10504, (800) 541-6563, Fax: (914) 273-2106, www.mesharpe.com; *The Illustrated Book of World Rankings.*

Palgrave Macmillan Ltd., Houndmills, Basingstoke, Hampshire, RG21 6XS, England, (Telephone in U.S. (888) 330-8477), (Fax in U.S. (800) 672-2054), www.palgrave.com; *The Statesman's Yearbook 2008.*

Taylor and Francis Group, An Informa Business, 2 Park Square, Milton Park, Abingdon, Oxford OX14 4RN, United Kingdom, (Dial from U.S. (212) 216-7800), (Fax from U.S. (212) 564-7854), www.tandf.co.uk; *The Europa World Year Book.*

United Nations Statistics Division, New York, NY 10017, (800) 253-9646, Fax: (212) 963-4116, http://unstats.un.org; *Statistical Yearbook for Asia and the Pacific 2004.*

The World Bank, 1818 H Street, NW, Washington, DC 20433, (202) 473-1000, Fax: (202) 477-6391, www.worldbank.org; *Fiji.*

FIJI - FISHERIES

M.E. Sharpe, 80 Business Park Drive, Armonk, NY 10504, (800) 541-6563, Fax: (914) 273-2106, www.mesharpe.com; *The Illustrated Book of World Rankings.*

Palgrave Macmillan Ltd., Houndmills, Basingstoke, Hampshire, RG21 6XS, England, (Telephone in U.S. (888) 330-8477), (Fax in U.S. (800) 672-2054), www.palgrave.com; *The Statesman's Yearbook 2008.*

Taylor and Francis Group, An Informa Business, 2 Park Square, Milton Park, Abingdon, Oxford OX14 4RN, United Kingdom, (Dial from U.S. (212) 216-7800), (Fax from U.S. (212) 564-7854), www.tandf.co.uk; *The Europa World Year Book.*

United Nations Conference on Trade and Development (UNCTAD), DC2-1120, United Nations, New York, NY 10017, (212) 963-0027, www.unctad.org; *UNCTAD Commodity Yearbook.*

United Nations Food and Agricultural Organization (FAO), Viale delle Terme di Caracalla, 00100 Rome, Italy, (Dial from U.S. (202) 653-2400), (Fax from U.S. (202) 653 5760), www.fao.org; *FAO Yearbook of Fishery Statistics;* Fishery Databases; FISHSTAT Database. Subjects covered include: Aquaculture production, capture production, fishery commodities; and *The State of Food and Agriculture (SOFA) 2006.*

United Nations Statistics Division, New York, NY 10017, (800) 253-9646, Fax: (212) 963-4116, http://unstats.un.org; *Statistical Yearbook.*

The World Bank, 1818 H Street, NW, Washington, DC 20433, (202) 473-1000, Fax: (202) 477-6391, www.worldbank.org; *Fiji.*

FIJI - FLOUR INDUSTRY

United Nations Statistics Division, New York, NY 10017, (800) 253-9646, Fax: (212) 963-4116, http://unstats.un.org; *Statistical Yearbook.*

FIJI - FOOD

Secretariat of the Pacific Community (SPC), BP D5, 98848 Noumea Cedex, New Caledonia, www.spc.int/corp; *Selected Pacific Economies - a Statistical Summary (SPESS).*

United Nations Conference on Trade and Development (UNCTAD), DC2-1120, United Nations, New York, NY 10017, (212) 963-0027, www.unctad.org; *UNCTAD Commodity Yearbook.*

United Nations Food and Agricultural Organization (FAO), Viale delle Terme di Caracalla, 00100 Rome, Italy, (Dial from U.S. (202) 653-2400), (Fax from U.S. (202) 653 5760), www.fao.org; *FAO Production Yearbook 2002* and *The State of Food and Agriculture (SOFA) 2006.*

United Nations Statistics Division, New York, NY 10017, (800) 253-9646, Fax: (212) 963-4116, http://unstats.un.org; *Human Development Report 2006* and *Statistical Yearbook for Asia and the Pacific 2004.*

FIJI - FOREIGN EXCHANGE RATES

Asian Development Bank (ADB), PO Box 789, 0980 Manila, Philippines, www.adb.org; *Key Indicators of Developing Asian and Pacific Countries 2006.*

Central Intelligence Agency, Office of Public Affairs, Washington, DC 20505, (703) 482-0623, Fax: (703) 482-1739, www.cia.gov; *The World Factbook.*

Euromonitor International, Inc., 224 S. Michigan Avenue, Suite 1500, Chicago, IL 60604, (312) 922-1115, Fax: (312) 922-1157, www.euromonitor.com; *The World Economic Factbook 2008.*

International Monetary Fund (IMF), 700 Nineteenth Street, NW, Washington, DC 20431, (202) 623-7000, Fax: (202) 623-4661, www.imf.org; *International Financial Statistics Yearbook 2007.*

Taylor and Francis Group, An Informa Business, 2 Park Square, Milton Park, Abingdon, Oxford OX14 4RN, United Kingdom, (Dial from U.S. (212) 216-7800), (Fax from U.S. (212) 564-7854), www.tandf.co.uk; *The Europa World Year Book.*

United Nations Statistics Division, New York, NY 10017, (800) 253-9646, Fax: (212) 963-4116, http://unstats.un.org; *Statistical Yearbook* and *World Statistics Pocketbook.*

Worldinformation.com, 2 Market Street, Saffron Walden, Essex CB10 1HZ, United Kingdom, www.worldinformation.com; The World of Information (www.worldinformation.com).

FIJI - FORESTS AND FORESTRY

M.E. Sharpe, 80 Business Park Drive, Armonk, NY 10504, (800) 541-6563, Fax: (914) 273-2106, www.mesharpe.com; *The Illustrated Book of World Rankings.*

Palgrave Macmillan Ltd., Houndmills, Basingstoke, Hampshire, RG21 6XS, England, (Telephone in U.S. (888) 330-8477), (Fax in U.S. (800) 672-2054), www.palgrave.com; *The Statesman's Yearbook 2008.*

Taylor and Francis Group, An Informa Business, 2 Park Square, Milton Park, Abingdon, Oxford OX14 4RN, United Kingdom, (Dial from U.S. (212) 216-7800), (Fax from U.S. (212) 564-7854), www.tandf.co.uk; *The Europa World Year Book.*

UNESCO Institute for Statistics, C.P. 6128 Succursale Centre-Ville, Montreal, Quebec, H3C 3J7 Canada, (Dial from U.S. (514) 343-6880), (Fax from U.S. (514) 343 6882), www.uis.unesco.org; *Statistical Tables.*

United Nations Conference on Trade and Development (UNCTAD), DC2-1120, United Nations, New York, NY 10017, (212) 963-0027, www.unctad.org; *UNCTAD Commodity Yearbook.*

United Nations Food and Agricultural Organization (FAO), Viale delle Terme di Caracalla, 00100 Rome, Italy, (Dial from U.S. (202) 653-2400), (Fax from U.S. (202) 653 5760), www.fao.org; *FAO Yearbook of Forest Products* and *The State of Food and Agriculture (SOFA) 2006.*

United Nations Statistics Division, New York, NY 10017, (800) 253-9646, Fax: (212) 963-4116, http://unstats.un.org; *Statistical Yearbook.*

The World Bank, 1818 H Street, NW, Washington, DC 20433, (202) 473-1000, Fax: (202) 477-6391, www.worldbank.org; *Fiji.*

FIJI - GAS PRODUCTION

See FIJI - MINERAL INDUSTRIES

FIJI - GEOGRAPHIC INFORMATION SYSTEMS

M.E. Sharpe, 80 Business Park Drive, Armonk, NY 10504, (800) 541-6563, Fax: (914) 273-2106, www.mesharpe.com; *The Illustrated Book of World Rankings.*

FIJI - GOLD INDUSTRY

International Monetary Fund (IMF), 700 Nineteenth Street, NW, Washington, DC 20431, (202) 623-7000, Fax: (202) 623-4661, www.imf.org; *International Financial Statistics Yearbook 2007.*

United Nations Statistics Division, New York, NY 10017, (800) 253-9646, Fax: (212) 963-4116, http://unstats.un.org; *Statistical Yearbook.*

The World Bank, 1818 H Street, NW, Washington, DC 20433, (202) 473-1000, Fax: (202) 477-6391, www.worldbank.org; *World Development Indicators (WDI) 2008.*

FIJI - GOLD PRODUCTION

See FIJI - MINERAL INDUSTRIES

FIJI - GRANTS-IN-AID

International Monetary Fund (IMF), 700 Nineteenth Street, NW, Washington, DC 20431, (202) 623-7000, Fax: (202) 623-4661, www.imf.org; *Government Finance Statistics Yearbook (2008 Edition).*

FIJI - GROSS DOMESTIC PRODUCT

Asian Development Bank (ADB), PO Box 789, 0980 Manila, Philippines, www.adb.org; *Key Indicators of Developing Asian and Pacific Countries 2006.*

Economist Intelligence Unit, 111 West 57th Street, New York, NY 10019, (212) 554-0600, Fax: (212) 586-1181, www.eiu.com; *Fiji Country Report.*

Euromonitor International, Inc., 224 S. Michigan Avenue, Suite 1500, Chicago, IL 60604, (312) 922-1115, Fax: (312) 922-1157, www.euromonitor.com; *International Marketing Data and Statistics 2008* and *The World Economic Factbook 2008.*

M.E. Sharpe, 80 Business Park Drive, Armonk, NY 10504, (800) 541-6563, Fax: (914) 273-2106, www.mesharpe.com; *The Illustrated Book of World Rankings.*

Taylor and Francis Group, An Informa Business, 2 Park Square, Milton Park, Abingdon, Oxford OX14 4RN, United Kingdom, (Dial from U.S. (212) 216-7800), (Fax from U.S. (212) 564-7854), www.tandf.co.uk; *The Europa World Year Book.*

United Nations Statistics Division, New York, NY 10017, (800) 253-9646, Fax: (212) 963-4116, http://unstats.un.org; *Human Development Report 2006; National Accounts Statistics: Compendium of Income Distribution Statistics;* and *Statistical Yearbook.*

The World Bank, 1818 H Street, NW, Washington, DC 20433, (202) 473-1000, Fax: (202) 477-6391, www.worldbank.org; *World Development Indicators (WDI) 2008.*

FIJI - GROSS NATIONAL PRODUCT

Asian Development Bank (ADB), PO Box 789, 0980 Manila, Philippines, www.adb.org; *Key Indicators of Developing Asian and Pacific Countries 2006.*

M.E. Sharpe, 80 Business Park Drive, Armonk, NY 10504, (800) 541-6563, Fax: (914) 273-2106, www.mesharpe.com; *The Illustrated Book of World Rankings.*

Palgrave Macmillan Ltd., Houndmills, Basingstoke, Hampshire, RG21 6XS, England, (Telephone in U.S. (888) 330-8477), (Fax in U.S. (800) 672-2054), www.palgrave.com; *The Statesman's Yearbook 2008.*

U.S. Department of State (DOS), 2201 C Street NW, Washington, DC 20520, (202) 647-4000, www.state.gov; *World Military Expenditures and Arms Transfers (WMEAT).*

United Nations Statistics Division, New York, NY 10017, (800) 253-9646, Fax: (212) 963-4116, http://unstats.un.org; *Statistical Yearbook.*

The World Bank, 1818 H Street, NW, Washington, DC 20433, (202) 473-1000, Fax: (202) 477-6391, www.worldbank.org; *The World Bank Atlas 2003-2004* and *World Development Indicators (WDI) 2008.*

Worldinformation.com, 2 Market Street, Saffron Walden, Essex CB10 1HZ, United Kingdom, www.worldinformation.com; The World of Information (www.worldinformation.com).

FIJI - HIDES AND SKINS INDUSTRY

United Nations Food and Agricultural Organization (FAO), Viale delle Terme di Caracalla, 00100 Rome, Italy, (Dial from U.S. (202) 653-2400), (Fax from U.S. (202) 653 5760), www.fao.org; *FAO Production Yearbook 2002.*

FIJI - HOUSING

Euromonitor International, Inc., 224 S. Michigan Avenue, Suite 1500, Chicago, IL 60604, (312) 922-1115, Fax: (312) 922-1157, www.euromonitor.com; *World Marketing Data and Statistics.*

M.E. Sharpe, 80 Business Park Drive, Armonk, NY 10504, (800) 541-6563, Fax: (914) 273-2106, www.mesharpe.com; *The Illustrated Book of World Rankings.*

Secretariat of the Pacific Community (SPC), BP D5, 98848 Noumea Cedex, New Caledonia, www.spc.int/corp; *Selected Pacific Economies - a Statistical Summary (SPESS).*

FIJI - ILLITERATE PERSONS

Euromonitor International, Inc., 224 S. Michigan Avenue, Suite 1500, Chicago, IL 60604, (312) 922-1115, Fax: (312) 922-1157, www.euromonitor.com; *The World Economic Factbook 2008.*

UNESCO Institute for Statistics, C.P. 6128 Succursale Centre-Ville, Montreal, Quebec, H3C 3J7 Canada, (Dial from U.S. (514) 343-6880), (Fax from U.S. (514) 343 6882), www.uis.unesco.org; *Statistical Tables.*

United Nations Statistics Division, New York, NY 10017, (800) 253-9646, Fax: (212) 963-4116, http://unstats.un.org; *Asia-Pacific in Figures 2004* and *Human Development Report 2006.*

FIJI - IMPORTS

Asian Development Bank (ADB), PO Box 789, 0980 Manila, Philippines, www.adb.org; *Key Indicators of Developing Asian and Pacific Countries 2006.*

Central Intelligence Agency, Office of Public Affairs, Washington, DC 20505, (703) 482-0623, Fax: (703) 482-1739, www.cia.gov; *The World Factbook.*

Economist Intelligence Unit, 111 West 57th Street, New York, NY 10019, (212) 554-0600, Fax: (212) 586-1181, www.eiu.com; *Fiji Country Report.*

Euromonitor International, Inc., 224 S. Michigan Avenue, Suite 1500, Chicago, IL 60604, (312) 922-1115, Fax: (312) 922-1157, www.euromonitor.com; *International Marketing Data and Statistics 2008* and *The World Economic Factbook 2008.*

International Monetary Fund (IMF), 700 Nineteenth Street, NW, Washington, DC 20431, (202) 623-7000, Fax: (202) 623-4661, www.imf.org; *Direction of Trade Statistics Yearbook 2007; Government Finance Statistics Yearbook (2008 Edition);* and *International Financial Statistics Yearbook 2007.*

Palgrave Macmillan Ltd., Houndmills, Basingstoke, Hampshire, RG21 6XS, England, (Telephone in U.S. (888) 330-8477), (Fax in U.S. (800) 672-2054), www.palgrave.com; *The Statesman's Yearbook 2008.*

Secretariat of the Pacific Community (SPC), BP D5, 98848 Noumea Cedex, New Caledonia, www.spc.int/corp; *Selected Pacific Economies - a Statistical Summary (SPESS).*

Taylor and Francis Group, An Informa Business, 2 Park Square, Milton Park, Abingdon, Oxford OX14 4RN, United Kingdom, (Dial from U.S. (212) 216-7800), (Fax from U.S. (212) 564-7854), www.tandf.co.uk; *The Europa World Year Book.*

United Nations Conference on Trade and Development (UNCTAD), DC2-1120, United Nations, New York, NY 10017, (212) 963-0027, www.unctad.org; *Handbook of Statistics 2005.*

United Nations Food and Agricultural Organization (FAO), Viale delle Terme di Caracalla, 00100 Rome, Italy, (Dial from U.S. (202) 653-2400), (Fax from U.S. (202) 653 5760), www.fao.org; *The State of Food and Agriculture (SOFA) 2006.*

United Nations Statistics Division, New York, NY 10017, (800) 253-9646, Fax: (212) 963-4116, http://unstats.un.org; *Foreign Trade Statistics of Asia and the Pacific 1996-2000.*

The World Bank, 1818 H Street, NW, Washington, DC 20433, (202) 473-1000, Fax: (202) 477-6391, www.worldbank.org; *World Development Indicators (WDI) 2008.*

Worldinformation.com, 2 Market Street, Saffron Walden, Essex CB10 1HZ, United Kingdom, www.worldinformation.com; The World of Information (www.worldinformation.com).

FIJI - INCOME TAXES

See FIJI - TAXATION

FIJI - INDUSTRIAL PRODUCTIVITY

M.E. Sharpe, 80 Business Park Drive, Armonk, NY 10504, (800) 541-6563, Fax: (914) 273-2106, www.mesharpe.com; *The Illustrated Book of World Rankings.*

FIJI - INDUSTRIAL PROPERTY

United Nations Statistics Division, New York, NY 10017, (800) 253-9646, Fax: (212) 963-4116, http://unstats.un.org; *Statistical Yearbook.*

FIJI - INDUSTRIES

Central Intelligence Agency, Office of Public Affairs, Washington, DC 20505, (703) 482-0623, Fax: (703) 482-1739, www.cia.gov; *The World Factbook.*

Economist Intelligence Unit, 111 West 57th Street, New York, NY 10019, (212) 554-0600, Fax: (212) 586-1181, www.eiu.com; *Fiji Country Report.*

Euromonitor International, Inc., 224 S. Michigan Avenue, Suite 1500, Chicago, IL 60604, (312) 922-1115, Fax: (312) 922-1157, www.euromonitor.com; *The World Economic Factbook 2008* and *World Marketing Data and Statistics.*

International Labour Office, I.L.O. Publications, 4 route des Morillons, CH-1211 Geneva 22, Switzerland, (Telephone in U.S. (202) 653-7652), (Fax in U.S. (202) 653-7687), www.ilo.org; *Yearbook of Labour Statistics 2006.*

M.E. Sharpe, 80 Business Park Drive, Armonk, NY 10504, (800) 541-6563, Fax: (914) 273-2106, www.mesharpe.com; *The Illustrated Book of World Rankings.*

Palgrave Macmillan Ltd., Houndmills, Basingstoke, Hampshire, RG21 6XS, England, (Telephone in U.S. (888) 330-8477), (Fax in U.S. (800) 672-2054), www.palgrave.com; *The Statesman's Yearbook 2008.*

Taylor and Francis Group, An Informa Business, 2 Park Square, Milton Park, Abingdon, Oxford OX14 4RN, United Kingdom, (Dial from U.S. (212) 216-7800), (Fax from U.S. (212) 564-7854), www.tandf.co.uk; *The Europa World Year Book.*

United Nations Industrial Development Organization (UNIDO), 1 United Nations Plaza, New York, NY

10017, (212) 963 6890, Fax: (212) 963-7904, http://unido.org; Industrial Statistics Database 2008 (INDSTAT) and *The International Yearbook of Industrial Statistics 2008.*

United Nations Statistics Division, New York, NY 10017, (800) 253-9646, Fax: (212) 963-4116, http://unstats.un.org; *Asia-Pacific in Figures 2004; 2004 Industrial Commodity Statistics Yearbook;* and *Statistical Yearbook for Asia and the Pacific 2004.*

The World Bank, 1818 H Street, NW, Washington, DC 20433, (202) 473-1000, Fax: (202) 477-6391, www.worldbank.org; *Fiji* and *World Development Indicators (WDI) 2008.*

FIJI - INFANT AND MATERNAL MORTALITY

See FIJI - MORTALITY

FIJI - INTERNATIONAL FINANCE

Asian Development Bank (ADB), PO Box 789, 0980 Manila, Philippines, www.adb.org; *Key Indicators of Developing Asian and Pacific Countries 2006.*

FIJI - INTERNATIONAL LIQUIDITY

International Monetary Fund (IMF), 700 Nineteenth Street, NW, Washington, DC 20431, (202) 623-7000, Fax: (202) 623-4661, www.imf.org; *International Financial Statistics Yearbook 2007.*

FIJI - INTERNATIONAL STATISTICS

Asian Development Bank (ADB), PO Box 789, 0980 Manila, Philippines, www.adb.org; *Key Indicators of Developing Asian and Pacific Countries 2006.*

FIJI - INTERNATIONAL TRADE

Asian Development Bank (ADB), PO Box 789, 0980 Manila, Philippines, www.adb.org; *Key Indicators of Developing Asian and Pacific Countries 2006.*

Economist Intelligence Unit, 111 West 57th Street, New York, NY 10019, (212) 554-0600, Fax: (212) 586-1181, www.eiu.com; *Fiji Country Report.*

Euromonitor International, Inc., 224 S. Michigan Avenue, Suite 1500, Chicago, IL 60604, (312) 922-1115, Fax: (312) 922-1157, www.euromonitor.com; *The World Economic Factbook 2008* and *World Marketing Data and Statistics.*

M.E. Sharpe, 80 Business Park Drive, Armonk, NY 10504, (800) 541-6563, Fax: (914) 273-2106, www.mesharpe.com; *The Illustrated Book of World Rankings.*

Organisation for Economic Cooperation and Development (OECD), 2 rue Andre Pascal, F-75775 Paris Cedex 16, France, (Telephone in U.S. (202) 785-6323), (Fax in U.S. (202) 785-0350), www.oecd.org; *International Trade by Commodity Statistics (ITCS).*

Palgrave Macmillan Ltd., Houndmills, Basingstoke, Hampshire, RG21 6XS, England, (Telephone in U.S. (888) 330-8477), (Fax in U.S. (800) 672-2054), www.palgrave.com; *The Statesman's Yearbook 2008.*

Secretariat of the Pacific Community (SPC), BP D5, 98848 Noumea Cedex, New Caledonia, www.spc.int/corp; *Selected Pacific Economies - a Statistical Summary (SPESS).*

Taylor and Francis Group, An Informa Business, 2 Park Square, Milton Park, Abingdon, Oxford OX14 4RN, United Kingdom, (Dial from U.S. (212) 216-7800), (Fax from U.S. (212) 564-7854), www.tandf.co.uk; *The Europa World Year Book.*

United Nations Conference on Trade and Development (UNCTAD), DC2-1120, United Nations, New York, NY 10017, (212) 963-0027, www.unctad.org; *UNCTAD Commodity Yearbook.*

United Nations Food and Agricultural Organization (FAO), Viale delle Terme di Caracalla, 00100 Rome, Italy, (Dial from U.S. (202) 653-2400), (Fax from U.S. (202) 653 5760), www.fao.org; *FAO Trade Yearbook* and *The State of Food and Agriculture (SOFA) 2006.*

United Nations Statistics Division, New York, NY 10017, (800) 253-9646, Fax: (212) 963-4116, http://unstats.un.org; *Asia-Pacific in Figures 2004; International Trade Statistics Yearbook;* and *Statistical Yearbook.*

The World Bank, 1818 H Street, NW, Washington, DC 20433, (202) 473-1000, Fax: (202) 477-6391, www.worldbank.org; *Fiji* and *World Development Indicators (WDI) 2008.*

World Trade Organization (WTO), Centre William Rappard, Rue de Lausanne 154, CH-1211 Geneva 21, Switzerland, www.wto.org; *International Trade Statistics 2006.*

FIJI - INTERNET USERS

International Telecommunication Union (ITU), Place des Nations, 1211 Geneva 20, Switzerland, www.itu.int; *World Telecommunication/ICT Indicators Database on CD-ROM; World Telecommunication/ICT Indicators Database Online;* and *Yearbook of Statistics - Telecommunication Services (Chronological Time Series 1997-2006).*

The World Bank, 1818 H Street, NW, Washington, DC 20433, (202) 473-1000, Fax: (202) 477-6391, www.worldbank.org; *Fiji.*

FIJI - IRON AND IRON ORE PRODUCTION

See FIJI - MINERAL INDUSTRIES

FIJI - LABOR

Central Intelligence Agency, Office of Public Affairs, Washington, DC 20505, (703) 482-0623, Fax: (703) 482-1739, www.cia.gov; *The World Factbook.*

Euromonitor International, Inc., 224 S. Michigan Avenue, Suite 1500, Chicago, IL 60604, (312) 922-1115, Fax: (312) 922-1157, www.euromonitor.com; *International Marketing Data and Statistics 2008* and *World Marketing Data and Statistics.*

International Labour Office, I.L.O. Publications, 4 route des Morillons, CH-1211 Geneva 22, Switzerland, (Telephone in U.S. (202) 653-7652), (Fax in U.S. (202) 653-7687), www.ilo.org; *Yearbook of Labour Statistics 2006.*

M.E. Sharpe, 80 Business Park Drive, Armonk, NY 10504, (800) 541-6563, Fax: (914) 273-2106, www.mesharpe.com; *The Illustrated Book of World Rankings.*

Palgrave Macmillan Ltd., Houndmills, Basingstoke, Hampshire, RG21 6XS, England, (Telephone in U.S. (888) 330-8477), (Fax in U.S. (800) 672-2054), www.palgrave.com; *The Statesman's Yearbook 2008.*

Taylor and Francis Group, An Informa Business, 2 Park Square, Milton Park, Abingdon, Oxford OX14 4RN, United Kingdom, (Dial from U.S. (212) 216-7800), (Fax from U.S. (212) 564-7854), www.tandf.co.uk; *The Europa World Year Book.*

United Nations Food and Agricultural Organization (FAO), Viale delle Terme di Caracalla, 00100 Rome, Italy, (Dial from U.S. (202) 653-2400), (Fax from U.S. (202) 653 5760), www.fao.org; *The State of Food and Agriculture (SOFA) 2006.*

United Nations Statistics Division, New York, NY 10017, (800) 253-9646, Fax: (212) 963-4116, http://unstats.un.org; *Human Development Report 2006.*

The World Bank, 1818 H Street, NW, Washington, DC 20433, (202) 473-1000, Fax: (202) 477-6391, www.worldbank.org; *The World Bank Atlas 2003-2004* and *World Development Indicators (WDI) 2008.*

FIJI - LAND USE

Central Intelligence Agency, Office of Public Affairs, Washington, DC 20505, (703) 482-0623, Fax: (703) 482-1739, www.cia.gov; *The World Factbook.*

Euromonitor International, Inc., 224 S. Michigan Avenue, Suite 1500, Chicago, IL 60604, (312) 922-1115, Fax: (312) 922-1157, www.euromonitor.com; *International Marketing Data and Statistics 2008.*

United Nations Food and Agricultural Organization (FAO), Viale delle Terme di Caracalla, 00100 Rome, Italy, (Dial from U.S. (202) 653-2400), (Fax from U.S. (202) 653 5760), www.fao.org; *FAO Production Yearbook 2002.*

FIJI - LIBRARIES

M.E. Sharpe, 80 Business Park Drive, Armonk, NY 10504, (800) 541-6563, Fax: (914) 273-2106, www.mesharpe.com; *The Illustrated Book of World Rankings.*

UNESCO Institute for Statistics, C.P. 6128 Succursale Centre-Ville, Montreal, Quebec, H3C 3J7 Canada, (Dial from U.S. (514) 343-6880), (Fax from U.S. (514) 343 6882), www.uis.unesco.org; *Statistical Tables.*

FIJI - LICENSES

International Monetary Fund (IMF), 700 Nineteenth Street, NW, Washington, DC 20431, (202) 623-7000, Fax: (202) 623-4661, www.imf.org; *Government Finance Statistics Yearbook (2008 Edition).*

FIJI - LIFE EXPECTANCY

Central Intelligence Agency, Office of Public Affairs, Washington, DC 20505, (703) 482-0623, Fax: (703) 482-1739, www.cia.gov; *The World Factbook.*

Euromonitor International, Inc., 224 S. Michigan Avenue, Suite 1500, Chicago, IL 60604, (312) 922-1115, Fax: (312) 922-1157, www.euromonitor.com; *The World Economic Factbook 2008.*

Palgrave Macmillan Ltd., Houndmills, Basingstoke, Hampshire, RG21 6XS, England, (Telephone in U.S. (888) 330-8477), (Fax in U.S. (800) 672-2054), www.palgrave.com; *The Statesman's Yearbook 2008.*

United Nations Statistics Division, New York, NY 10017, (800) 253-9646, Fax: (212) 963-4116, http://unstats.un.org; *Asia-Pacific in Figures 2004; Human Development Report 2006;* and *World Statistics Pocketbook.*

The World Bank, 1818 H Street, NW, Washington, DC 20433, (202) 473-1000, Fax: (202) 477-6391, www.worldbank.org; *The World Bank Atlas 2003-2004.*

FIJI - LITERACY

Euromonitor International, Inc., 224 S. Michigan Avenue, Suite 1500, Chicago, IL 60604, (312) 922-1115, Fax: (312) 922-1157, www.euromonitor.com; *World Marketing Data and Statistics.*

FIJI - LIVESTOCK

M.E. Sharpe, 80 Business Park Drive, Armonk, NY 10504, (800) 541-6563, Fax: (914) 273-2106, www.mesharpe.com; *The Illustrated Book of World Rankings.*

Palgrave Macmillan Ltd., Houndmills, Basingstoke, Hampshire, RG21 6XS, England, (Telephone in U.S. (888) 330-8477), (Fax in U.S. (800) 672-2054), www.palgrave.com; *The Statesman's Yearbook 2008.*

Taylor and Francis Group, An Informa Business, 2 Park Square, Milton Park, Abingdon, Oxford OX14 4RN, United Kingdom, (Dial from U.S. (212) 216-7800), (Fax from U.S. (212) 564-7854), www.tandf.co.uk; *The Europa World Year Book.*

United Nations Conference on Trade and Development (UNCTAD), DC2-1120, United Nations, New York, NY 10017, (212) 963-0027, www.unctad.org; *UNCTAD Commodity Yearbook.*

United Nations Food and Agricultural Organization (FAO), Viale delle Terme di Caracalla, 00100 Rome, Italy, (Dial from U.S. (202) 653-2400), (Fax from U.S. (202) 653 5760), www.fao.org; *FAO Production Yearbook 2002* and *The State of Food and Agriculture (SOFA) 2006.*

United Nations Statistics Division, New York, NY 10017, (800) 253-9646, Fax: (212) 963-4116, http://unstats.un.org; *Statistical Yearbook.*

FIJI - MANPOWER

United Nations Statistics Division, New York, NY 10017, (800) 253-9646, Fax: (212) 963-4116, http://unstats.un.org; *Statistical Yearbook for Asia and the Pacific 2004.*

FIJI - MANUFACTURES

Asian Development Bank (ADB), PO Box 789, 0980 Manila, Philippines, www.adb.org; *Key Indicators of Developing Asian and Pacific Countries 2006.*

M.E. Sharpe, 80 Business Park Drive, Armonk, NY 10504, (800) 541-6563, Fax: (914) 273-2106, www.mesharpe.com; *The Illustrated Book of World Rankings*.

United Nations Statistics Division, New York, NY 10017, (800) 253-9646, Fax: (212) 963-4116, http://unstats.un.org; *Statistical Yearbook*.

The World Bank, 1818 H Street, NW, Washington, DC 20433, (202) 473-1000, Fax: (202) 477-6391, www.worldbank.org; *World Development Indicators (WDI) 2008*.

FIJI - MARRIAGE

M.E. Sharpe, 80 Business Park Drive, Armonk, NY 10504, (800) 541-6563, Fax: (914) 273-2106, www.mesharpe.com; *The Illustrated Book of World Rankings*.

Taylor and Francis Group, An Informa Business, 2 Park Square, Milton Park, Abingdon, Oxford OX14 4RN, United Kingdom, (Dial from U.S. (212) 216-7800), (Fax from U.S. (212) 564-7854), www.tandf.co.uk; *The Europa World Year Book*.

United Nations Statistics Division, New York, NY 10017, (800) 253-9646, Fax: (212) 963-4116, http://unstats.un.org; *Demographic Yearbook* and *Statistical Yearbook*.

FIJI - MILK PRODUCTION

See FIJI - DAIRY PROCESSING

FIJI - MINERAL INDUSTRIES

Asian Development Bank (ADB), PO Box 789, 0980 Manila, Philippines, www.adb.org; *Key Indicators of Developing Asian and Pacific Countries 2006*.

M.E. Sharpe, 80 Business Park Drive, Armonk, NY 10504, (800) 541-6563, Fax: (914) 273-2106, www.mesharpe.com; *The Illustrated Book of World Rankings*.

Taylor and Francis Group, An Informa Business, 2 Park Square, Milton Park, Abingdon, Oxford OX14 4RN, United Kingdom, (Dial from U.S. (212) 216-7800), (Fax from U.S. (212) 564-7854), www.tandf.co.uk; *The Europa World Year Book*.

United Nations Conference on Trade and Development (UNCTAD), DC2-1120, United Nations, New York, NY 10017, (212) 963-0027, www.unctad.org; *UNCTAD Commodity Yearbook*.

United Nations Statistics Division, New York, NY 10017, (800) 253-9646, Fax: (212) 963-4116, http://unstats.un.org; *Statistical Yearbook*.

FIJI - MONEY EXCHANGE RATES

See FIJI - FOREIGN EXCHANGE RATES

FIJI - MONEY SUPPLY

Asian Development Bank (ADB), PO Box 789, 0980 Manila, Philippines, www.adb.org; *Key Indicators of Developing Asian and Pacific Countries 2006*.

Economist Intelligence Unit, 111 West 57th Street, New York, NY 10019, (212) 554-0600, Fax: (212) 586-1181, www.eiu.com; *Fiji Country Report*.

International Monetary Fund (IMF), 700 Nineteenth Street, NW, Washington, DC 20431, (202) 623-7000, Fax: (202) 623-4661, www.imf.org; *International Financial Statistics Yearbook 2007*.

Taylor and Francis Group, An Informa Business, 2 Park Square, Milton Park, Abingdon, Oxford OX14 4RN, United Kingdom, (Dial from U.S. (212) 216-7800), (Fax from U.S. (212) 564-7854), www.tandf.co.uk; *The Europa World Year Book*.

United Nations Statistics Division, New York, NY 10017, (800) 253-9646, Fax: (212) 963-4116, http://unstats.un.org; *Statistical Yearbook*.

The World Bank, 1818 H Street, NW, Washington, DC 20433, (202) 473-1000, Fax: (202) 477-6391, www.worldbank.org; *Fiji* and *World Development Indicators (WDI) 2008*.

FIJI - MORTALITY

Central Intelligence Agency, Office of Public Affairs, Washington, DC 20505, (703) 482-0623, Fax: (703) 482-1739, www.cia.gov; *The World Factbook*.

Euromonitor International, Inc., 224 S. Michigan Avenue, Suite 1500, Chicago, IL 60604, (312) 922-1115, Fax: (312) 922-1157, www.euromonitor.com; *International Marketing Data and Statistics 2008* and *The World Economic Factbook 2008*.

Palgrave Macmillan Ltd., Houndmills, Basingstoke, Hampshire, RG21 6XS, England, (Telephone in U.S. (888) 330-8477), (Fax in U.S. (800) 672-2054), www.palgrave.com; *The Statesman's Yearbook 2008*.

Taylor and Francis Group, An Informa Business, 2 Park Square, Milton Park, Abingdon, Oxford OX14 4RN, United Kingdom, (Dial from U.S. (212) 216-7800), (Fax from U.S. (212) 564-7854), www.tandf.co.uk; *The Europa World Year Book*.

United Nations Statistics Division, New York, NY 10017, (800) 253-9646, Fax: (212) 963-4116, http://unstats.un.org; *Asia-Pacific in Figures 2004; Demographic Yearbook; Human Development Report 2006; Statistical Yearbook;* and *World Statistics Pocketbook*.

The World Bank, 1818 H Street, NW, Washington, DC 20433, (202) 473-1000, Fax: (202) 477-6391, www.worldbank.org; *The World Bank Atlas 2003-2004* and *World Development Indicators (WDI) 2008*.

World Health Organization (WHO), Avenue Appia 20, 1211 Geneve 27, Switzerland, (Telephone in U.S. (212) 331-9081), www.who.int; The WHO Global Atlas of Infectious Diseases and *World Health Report 2006*.

FIJI - MOTION PICTURES

United Nations Statistics Division, New York, NY 10017, (800) 253-9646, Fax: (212) 963-4116, http://unstats.un.org; *Statistical Yearbook*.

FIJI - MOTOR VEHICLES

Taylor and Francis Group, An Informa Business, 2 Park Square, Milton Park, Abingdon, Oxford OX14 4RN, United Kingdom, (Dial from U.S. (212) 216-7800), (Fax from U.S. (212) 564-7854), www.tandf.co.uk; *The Europa World Year Book*.

United Nations Statistics Division, New York, NY 10017, (800) 253-9646, Fax: (212) 963-4116, http://unstats.un.org; *Statistical Yearbook*.

FIJI - MUSEUMS

M.E. Sharpe, 80 Business Park Drive, Armonk, NY 10504, (800) 541-6563, Fax: (914) 273-2106, www.mesharpe.com; *The Illustrated Book of World Rankings*.

UNESCO Institute for Statistics, C.P. 6128 Succursale Centre-Ville, Montreal, Quebec, H3C 3J7 Canada, (Dial from U.S. (514) 343-6880), (Fax from U.S. (514) 343 6882), www.uis.unesco.org; *Statistical Tables*.

FIJI - NATURAL GAS PRODUCTION

See FIJI - MINERAL INDUSTRIES

FIJI - NUTRITION

Asian Development Bank (ADB), PO Box 789, 0980 Manila, Philippines, www.adb.org; *Key Indicators of Developing Asian and Pacific Countries 2006*.

United Nations Food and Agricultural Organization (FAO), Viale delle Terme di Caracalla, 00100 Rome, Italy, (Dial from U.S. (202) 653-2400), (Fax from U.S. (202) 653 5760), www.fao.org; *The State of Food and Agriculture (SOFA) 2006*.

FIJI - OLDER PEOPLE

M.E. Sharpe, 80 Business Park Drive, Armonk, NY 10504, (800) 541-6563, Fax: (914) 273-2106, www.mesharpe.com; *The Illustrated Book of World Rankings*.

FIJI - PEANUT PRODUCTION

See FIJI - CROPS

FIJI - PERIODICALS

UNESCO Institute for Statistics, C.P. 6128 Succursale Centre-Ville, Montreal, Quebec, H3C 3J7 Canada, (Dial from U.S. (514) 343-6880), (Fax from U.S. (514) 343 6882), www.uis.unesco.org; *Statistical Tables*.

FIJI - PESTICIDES

United Nations Food and Agricultural Organization (FAO), Viale delle Terme di Caracalla, 00100 Rome, Italy, (Dial from U.S. (202) 653-2400), (Fax from U.S. (202) 653 5760), www.fao.org; *The State of Food and Agriculture (SOFA) 2006*.

FIJI - PETROLEUM INDUSTRY AND TRADE

Asian Development Bank (ADB), PO Box 789, 0980 Manila, Philippines, www.adb.org; *Key Indicators of Developing Asian and Pacific Countries 2006*.

M.E. Sharpe, 80 Business Park Drive, Armonk, NY 10504, (800) 541-6563, Fax: (914) 273-2106, www.mesharpe.com; *The Illustrated Book of World Rankings*.

PennWell Corporation, 1421 South Sheridan Road, Tulsa, OK 74112, (918) 835-3161, www.pennwell.com; *International Petroleum Encyclopedia 2007*.

U.S. Department of Energy (DOE), Energy Information Administration (EIA), 1000 Independence Avenue, SW, Washington, DC 20585, (202) 586-8800, www.eia.doe.gov; *International Energy Annual 2004* and *International Energy Outlook 2006*.

United Nations Conference on Trade and Development (UNCTAD), DC2-1120, United Nations, New York, NY 10017, (212) 963-0027, www.unctad.org; *UNCTAD Commodity Yearbook*.

United Nations Food and Agricultural Organization (FAO), Viale delle Terme di Caracalla, 00100 Rome, Italy, (Dial from U.S. (202) 653-2400), (Fax from U.S. (202) 653 5760), www.fao.org; *The State of Food and Agriculture (SOFA) 2006*.

FIJI - POLITICAL SCIENCE

Asian Development Bank (ADB), PO Box 789, 0980 Manila, Philippines, www.adb.org; *Key Indicators of Developing Asian and Pacific Countries 2006*.

Central Intelligence Agency, Office of Public Affairs, Washington, DC 20505, (703) 482-0623, Fax: (703) 482-1739, www.cia.gov; *The World Factbook*.

International Monetary Fund (IMF), 700 Nineteenth Street, NW, Washington, DC 20431, (202) 623-7000, Fax: (202) 623-4661, www.imf.org; *Government Finance Statistics Yearbook (2008 Edition)* and *International Financial Statistics Yearbook 2007*.

Palgrave Macmillan Ltd., Houndmills, Basingstoke, Hampshire, RG21 6XS, England, (Telephone in U.S. (888) 330-8477), (Fax in U.S. (800) 672-2054), www.palgrave.com; *The Statesman's Yearbook 2008*.

Taylor and Francis Group, An Informa Business, 2 Park Square, Milton Park, Abingdon, Oxford OX14 4RN, United Kingdom, (Dial from U.S. (212) 216-7800), (Fax from U.S. (212) 564-7854), www.tandf.co.uk; *The Europa World Year Book*.

United Nations Statistics Division, New York, NY 10017, (800) 253-9646, Fax: (212) 963-4116, http://unstats.un.org; *Asia-Pacific in Figures 2004; National Accounts Statistics: Compendium of Income Distribution Statistics;* and *Statistical Yearbook*.

The World Bank, 1818 H Street, NW, Washington, DC 20433, (202) 473-1000, Fax: (202) 477-6391, www.worldbank.org; *World Development Indicators (WDI) 2008*.

FIJI - POPULATION

Asian Development Bank (ADB), PO Box 789, 0980 Manila, Philippines, www.adb.org; *Key Indicators of Developing Asian and Pacific Countries 2006*.

Economist Intelligence Unit, 111 West 57th Street, New York, NY 10019, (212) 554-0600, Fax: (212) 586-1181, www.eiu.com; *Fiji Country Report*.

Euromonitor International, Inc., 224 S. Michigan Avenue, Suite 1500, Chicago, IL 60604, (312) 922-1115, Fax: (312) 922-1157, www.euromonitor.com; *International Marketing Data and Statistics 2008* and *The World Economic Factbook 2008*.

International Labour Office, I.L.O. Publications, 4 route des Morillons, CH-1211 Geneva 22, Switzerland, (Telephone in U.S. (202) 653-7652), (Fax in U.S. (202) 653-7687), www.ilo.org; *Yearbook of Labour Statistics 2006.*

M.E. Sharpe, 80 Business Park Drive, Armonk, NY 10504, (800) 541-6563, Fax: (914) 273-2106, www.mesharpe.com; *The Illustrated Book of World Rankings.*

Palgrave Macmillan Ltd., Houndmills, Basingstoke, Hampshire, RG21 6XS, England, (Telephone in U.S. (888) 330-8477), (Fax in U.S. (800) 672-2054), www.palgrave.com; *The Statesman's Yearbook 2008.*

Taylor and Francis Group, An Informa Business, 2 Park Square, Milton Park, Abingdon, Oxford OX14 4RN, United Kingdom, (Dial from U.S. (212) 216-7800), (Fax from U.S. (212) 564-7854), www.tandf.co.uk; *The Europa World Year Book.*

U.S. Department of State (DOS), 2201 C Street NW, Washington, DC 20520, (202) 647-4000, www.state.gov; *World Military Expenditures and Arms Transfers (WMEAT).*

UNESCO Institute for Statistics, C.P. 6128 Succursale Centre-Ville, Montreal, Quebec, H3C 3J7 Canada, (Dial from U.S. (514) 343-6880), (Fax from U.S. (514) 343 6882), www.uis.unesco.org; *Statistical Tables.*

United Nations Food and Agricultural Organization (FAO), Viale delle Terme di Caracalla, 00100 Rome, Italy, (Dial from U.S. (202) 653-2400), (Fax from U.S. (202) 653 5760), www.fao.org; *FAO Production Yearbook 2002.*

United Nations Statistics Division, New York, NY 10017, (800) 253-9646, Fax: (212) 963-4116, http://unstats.un.org; *Asia-Pacific in Figures 2004; Demographic Yearbook; Statistical Yearbook; Statistical Yearbook for Asia and the Pacific 2004;* and *World Statistics Pocketbook.*

The World Bank, 1818 H Street, NW, Washington, DC 20433, (202) 473-1000, Fax: (202) 477-6391, www.worldbank.org; *Fiji* and *The World Bank Atlas 2003-2004.*

World Health Organization (WHO), Avenue Appia 20, 1211 Geneve 27, Switzerland, (Telephone in U.S. (212) 331-9081), www.who.int; *World Health Report 2006.*

Worldinformation.com, 2 Market Street, Saffron Walden, Essex CB10 1HZ, United Kingdom, www.worldinformation.com; The World of Information (www.worldinformation.com).

FIJI - POPULATION DENSITY

Central Intelligence Agency, Office of Public Affairs, Washington, DC 20505, (703) 482-0623, Fax: (703) 482-1739, www.cia.gov; *The World Factbook.*

Euromonitor International, Inc., 224 S. Michigan Avenue, Suite 1500, Chicago, IL 60604, (312) 922-1115, Fax: (312) 922-1157, www.euromonitor.com; *The World Economic Factbook 2008.*

M.E. Sharpe, 80 Business Park Drive, Armonk, NY 10504, (800) 541-6563, Fax: (914) 273-2106, www.mesharpe.com; *The Illustrated Book of World Rankings.*

Palgrave Macmillan Ltd., Houndmills, Basingstoke, Hampshire, RG21 6XS, England, (Telephone in U.S. (888) 330-8477), (Fax in U.S. (800) 672-2054), www.palgrave.com; *The Statesman's Yearbook 2008.*

Taylor and Francis Group, An Informa Business, 2 Park Square, Milton Park, Abingdon, Oxford OX14 4RN, United Kingdom, (Dial from U.S. (212) 216-7800), (Fax from U.S. (212) 564-7854), www.tandf.co.uk; *The Europa World Year Book.*

UNESCO Institute for Statistics, C.P. 6128 Succursale Centre-Ville, Montreal, Quebec, H3C 3J7 Canada, (Dial from U.S. (514) 343-6880), (Fax from U.S. (514) 343 6882), www.uis.unesco.org; *Statistical Tables.*

United Nations Food and Agricultural Organization (FAO), Viale delle Terme di Caracalla, 00100 Rome, Italy, (Dial from U.S. (202) 653-2400), (Fax from U.S. (202) 653 5760), www.fao.org; *The State of Food and Agriculture (SOFA) 2006.*

United Nations Statistics Division, New York, NY 10017, (800) 253-9646, Fax: (212) 963-4116, http://unstats.un.org; *Statistical Yearbook.*

The World Bank, 1818 H Street, NW, Washington, DC 20433, (202) 473-1000, Fax: (202) 477-6391, www.worldbank.org; *Fiji.*

FIJI - POSTAL SERVICE

M.E. Sharpe, 80 Business Park Drive, Armonk, NY 10504, (800) 541-6563, Fax: (914) 273-2106, www.mesharpe.com; *The Illustrated Book of World Rankings.*

Palgrave Macmillan Ltd., Houndmills, Basingstoke, Hampshire, RG21 6XS, England, (Telephone in U.S. (888) 330-8477), (Fax in U.S. (800) 672-2054), www.palgrave.com; *The Statesman's Yearbook 2008.*

United Nations Statistics Division, New York, NY 10017, (800) 253-9646, Fax: (212) 963-4116, http://unstats.un.org; *Statistical Yearbook.*

FIJI - POWER RESOURCES

Euromonitor International, Inc., 224 S. Michigan Avenue, Suite 1500, Chicago, IL 60604, (312) 922-1115, Fax: (312) 922-1157, www.euromonitor.com; *The World Economic Factbook 2008* and *World Marketing Data and Statistics.*

M.E. Sharpe, 80 Business Park Drive, Armonk, NY 10504, (800) 541-6563, Fax: (914) 273-2106, www.mesharpe.com; *The Illustrated Book of World Rankings.*

Palgrave Macmillan Ltd., Houndmills, Basingstoke, Hampshire, RG21 6XS, England, (Telephone in U.S. (888) 330-8477), (Fax in U.S. (800) 672-2054), www.palgrave.com; *The Statesman's Yearbook 2008.*

Platts, 2 Penn Plaza, 25th Floor, New York, NY 10121-2298, (212) 904-3070, www.platts.com; *Energy Economist.*

U.S. Department of Energy (DOE), Energy Information Administration (EIA), 1000 Independence Avenue, SW, Washington, DC 20585, (202) 586-8800, www.eia.doe.gov; *International Energy Annual 2004* and *International Energy Outlook 2006.*

United Nations Food and Agricultural Organization (FAO), Viale delle Terme di Caracalla, 00100 Rome, Italy, (Dial from U.S. (202) 653-2400), (Fax from U.S. (202) 653 5760), www.fao.org; *The State of Food and Agriculture (SOFA) 2006.*

United Nations Statistics Division, New York, NY 10017, (800) 253-9646, Fax: (212) 963-4116, http://unstats.un.org; *Asia-Pacific in Figures 2004; Energy Statistics Yearbook 2003; Human Development Report 2006; Statistical Yearbook; Statistical Yearbook for Asia and the Pacific 2004;* and *World Statistics Pocketbook.*

The World Bank, 1818 H Street, NW, Washington, DC 20433, (202) 473-1000, Fax: (202) 477-6391, www.worldbank.org; *The World Bank Atlas 2003-2004.*

FIJI - PRICES

Asian Development Bank (ADB), PO Box 789, 0980 Manila, Philippines, www.adb.org; *Key Indicators of Developing Asian and Pacific Countries 2006.*

Euromonitor International, Inc., 224 S. Michigan Avenue, Suite 1500, Chicago, IL 60604, (312) 922-1115, Fax: (312) 922-1157, www.euromonitor.com; *World Marketing Data and Statistics.*

International Labour Office, I.L.O. Publications, 4 route des Morillons, CH-1211 Geneva 22, Switzerland, (Telephone in U.S. (202) 653-7652), (Fax in U.S. (202) 653-7687), www.ilo.org; *Yearbook of Labour Statistics 2006.*

International Monetary Fund (IMF), 700 Nineteenth Street, NW, Washington, DC 20431, (202) 623-7000, Fax: (202) 623-4661, www.imf.org; *International Financial Statistics Yearbook 2007.*

M.E. Sharpe, 80 Business Park Drive, Armonk, NY 10504, (800) 541-6563, Fax: (914) 273-2106, www.mesharpe.com; *The Illustrated Book of World Rankings.*

Secretariat of the Pacific Community (SPC), BP D5, 98848 Noumea Cedex, New Caledonia, www.spc.int/corp; *Selected Pacific Economies - a Statistical Summary (SPESS).*

United Nations Food and Agricultural Organization (FAO), Viale delle Terme di Caracalla, 00100 Rome, Italy, (Dial from U.S. (202) 653-2400), (Fax from U.S. (202) 653 5760), www.fao.org; *FAO Production Yearbook 2002* and *The State of Food and Agriculture (SOFA) 2006.*

FIJI - PUBLIC HEALTH

Euromonitor International, Inc., 224 S. Michigan Avenue, Suite 1500, Chicago, IL 60604, (312) 922-1115, Fax: (312) 922-1157, www.euromonitor.com; *World Marketing Data and Statistics.*

International Monetary Fund (IMF), 700 Nineteenth Street, NW, Washington, DC 20431, (202) 623-7000, Fax: (202) 623-4661, www.imf.org; *Government Finance Statistics Yearbook (2008 Edition).*

M.E. Sharpe, 80 Business Park Drive, Armonk, NY 10504, (800) 541-6563, Fax: (914) 273-2106, www.mesharpe.com; *The Illustrated Book of World Rankings.*

Palgrave Macmillan Ltd., Houndmills, Basingstoke, Hampshire, RG21 6XS, England, (Telephone in U.S. (888) 330-8477), (Fax in U.S. (800) 672-2054), www.palgrave.com; *The Statesman's Yearbook 2008.*

Secretariat of the Pacific Community (SPC), BP D5, 98848 Noumea Cedex, New Caledonia, www.spc.int/corp; *Selected Pacific Economies - a Statistical Summary (SPESS).*

United Nations Statistics Division, New York, NY 10017, (800) 253-9646, Fax: (212) 963-4116, http://unstats.un.org; *Asia-Pacific in Figures 2004; Human Development Report 2006;* and *Statistical Yearbook.*

The World Bank, 1818 H Street, NW, Washington, DC 20433, (202) 473-1000, Fax: (202) 477-6391, www.worldbank.org; *Fiji.*

World Health Organization (WHO), Avenue Appia 20, 1211 Geneve 27, Switzerland, (Telephone in U.S. (212) 331-9081), www.who.int; The WHO Global Atlas of Infectious Diseases and *World Health Report 2006.*

FIJI - PUBLIC UTILITIES

United Nations Statistics Division, New York, NY 10017, (800) 253-9646, Fax: (212) 963-4116, http://unstats.un.org; *Electric Power in Asia and the Pacific 2001 and 2002.*

FIJI - PUBLISHERS AND PUBLISHING

Taylor and Francis Group, An Informa Business, 2 Park Square, Milton Park, Abingdon, Oxford OX14 4RN, United Kingdom, (Dial from U.S. (212) 216-7800), (Fax from U.S. (212) 564-7854), www.tandf.co.uk; *The Europa World Year Book.*

FIJI - RADIO BROADCASTING

Palgrave Macmillan Ltd., Houndmills, Basingstoke, Hampshire, RG21 6XS, England, (Telephone in U.S. (888) 330-8477), (Fax in U.S. (800) 672-2054), www.palgrave.com; *The Statesman's Yearbook 2008.*

FIJI - RAILROADS

Palgrave Macmillan Ltd., Houndmills, Basingstoke, Hampshire, RG21 6XS, England, (Telephone in U.S. (888) 330-8477), (Fax in U.S. (800) 672-2054), www.palgrave.com; *The Statesman's Yearbook 2008.*

FIJI - RELIGION

M.E. Sharpe, 80 Business Park Drive, Armonk, NY 10504, (800) 541-6563, Fax: (914) 273-2106, www.mesharpe.com; *The Illustrated Book of World Rankings.*

Palgrave Macmillan Ltd., Houndmills, Basingstoke, Hampshire, RG21 6XS, England, (Telephone in U.S.

(888) 330-8477), (Fax in U.S. (800) 672-2054), www.palgrave.com; *The Statesman's Yearbook 2008.*

FIJI - RENT CHARGES

International Labour Office, I.L.O. Publications, 4 route des Morillons, CH-1211 Geneva 22, Switzerland, (Telephone in U.S. (202) 653-7652), (Fax in U.S. (202) 653-7687), www.ilo.org; *Yearbook of Labour Statistics 2006.*

FIJI - RESERVES (ACCOUNTING)

Asian Development Bank (ADB), PO Box 789, 0980 Manila, Philippines, www.adb.org; *Key Indicators of Developing Asian and Pacific Countries 2006.*

United Nations Statistics Division, New York, NY 10017, (800) 253-9646, Fax: (212) 963-4116, http://unstats.un.org; *Statistical Yearbook.*

The World Bank, 1818 H Street, NW, Washington, DC 20433, (202) 473-1000, Fax: (202) 477-6391, www.worldbank.org; *World Development Indicators (WDI) 2008.*

FIJI - RETAIL TRADE

Euromonitor International, Inc., 224 S. Michigan Avenue, Suite 1500, Chicago, IL 60604, (312) 922-1115, Fax: (312) 922-1157, www.euromonitor.com; *World Marketing Data and Statistics.*

United Nations Statistics Division, New York, NY 10017, (800) 253-9646, Fax: (212) 963-4116, http://unstats.un.org; *Statistical Yearbook.*

FIJI - RICE PRODUCTION

See FIJI - CROPS

FIJI - ROADS

Central Intelligence Agency, Office of Public Affairs, Washington, DC 20505, (703) 482-0623, Fax: (703) 482-1739, www.cia.gov; *The World Factbook.*

Palgrave Macmillan Ltd., Houndmills, Basingstoke, Hampshire, RG21 6XS, England, (Telephone in U.S. (888) 330-8477), (Fax in U.S. (800) 672-2054), www.palgrave.com; *The Statesman's Yearbook 2008.*

FIJI - RUBBER INDUSTRY AND TRADE

International Rubber Study Group (IRSG), 1st Floor, Heron House, 109/115 Wembley Hill Road, Wembley, Middlesex HA9 8DA, United Kingdom, www.rubberstudy.com; *Rubber Statistical Bulletin; Summary of World Rubber Statistics 2005; World Rubber Statistics Handbook (Volume 6, 1975-2001);* and *World Rubber Statistics Historic Handbook.*

M.E. Sharpe, 80 Business Park Drive, Armonk, NY 10504, (800) 541-6563, Fax: (914) 273-2106, www.mesharpe.com; *The Illustrated Book of World Rankings.*

FIJI - SHEEP

See FIJI - LIVESTOCK

FIJI - SHIPPING

Palgrave Macmillan Ltd., Houndmills, Basingstoke, Hampshire, RG21 6XS, England, (Telephone in U.S. (888) 330-8477), (Fax in U.S. (800) 672-2054), www.palgrave.com; *The Statesman's Yearbook 2008.*

Taylor and Francis Group, An Informa Business, 2 Park Square, Milton Park, Abingdon, Oxford OX14 4RN, United Kingdom, (Dial from U.S. (212) 216-7800), (Fax from U.S. (212) 564-7854), www.tandf.co.uk; *The Europa World Year Book.*

U.S. Department of Transportation (DOT), Maritime Administration (MARAD), West Building, Southeast Federal Center, 1200 New Jersey Avenue, SE, Washington, DC 20590, (800) 99-MARAD, www.marad.dot.gov; *World Merchant Fleet 2005.*

United Nations Statistics Division, New York, NY 10017, (800) 253-9646, Fax: (212) 963-4116, http://unstats.un.org; *Statistical Yearbook.*

FIJI - SILVER PRODUCTION

See FIJI - MINERAL INDUSTRIES

FIJI - SOCIAL ECOLOGY

Asian Development Bank (ADB), PO Box 789, 0980 Manila, Philippines, www.adb.org; *Key Indicators of Developing Asian and Pacific Countries 2006.*

M.E. Sharpe, 80 Business Park Drive, Armonk, NY 10504, (800) 541-6563, Fax: (914) 273-2106, www.mesharpe.com; *The Illustrated Book of World Rankings.*

United Nations Statistics Division, New York, NY 10017, (800) 253-9646, Fax: (212) 963-4116, http://unstats.un.org; *World Statistics Pocketbook.*

FIJI - SOCIAL SECURITY

International Monetary Fund (IMF), 700 Nineteenth Street, NW, Washington, DC 20431, (202) 623-7000, Fax: (202) 623-4661, www.imf.org; *Government Finance Statistics Yearbook (2008 Edition).*

United Nations Statistics Division, New York, NY 10017, (800) 253-9646, Fax: (212) 963-4116, http://unstats.un.org; *National Accounts Statistics: Compendium of Income Distribution Statistics.*

FIJI - STEEL PRODUCTION

See FIJI - MINERAL INDUSTRIES

FIJI - SUGAR PRODUCTION

See FIJI - CROPS

FIJI - TAXATION

International Monetary Fund (IMF), 700 Nineteenth Street, NW, Washington, DC 20431, (202) 623-7000, Fax: (202) 623-4661, www.imf.org; *Government Finance Statistics Yearbook (2008 Edition).*

Taylor and Francis Group, An Informa Business, 2 Park Square, Milton Park, Abingdon, Oxford OX14 4RN, United Kingdom, (Dial from U.S. (212) 216-7800), (Fax from U.S. (212) 564-7854), www.tandf.co.uk; *The Europa World Year Book.*

The World Bank, 1818 H Street, NW, Washington, DC 20433, (202) 473-1000, Fax: (202) 477-6391, www.worldbank.org; *World Development Indicators (WDI) 2008.*

FIJI - TELEPHONE

International Telecommunication Union (ITU), Place des Nations, 1211 Geneva 20, Switzerland, www.itu.int; World Telecommunication Indicators Database.

Palgrave Macmillan Ltd., Houndmills, Basingstoke, Hampshire, RG21 6XS, England, (Telephone in U.S. (888) 330-8477), (Fax in U.S. (800) 672-2054), www.palgrave.com; *The Statesman's Yearbook 2008.*

Taylor and Francis Group, An Informa Business, 2 Park Square, Milton Park, Abingdon, Oxford OX14 4RN, United Kingdom, (Dial from U.S. (212) 216-7800), (Fax from U.S. (212) 564-7854), www.tandf.co.uk; *The Europa World Year Book.*

United Nations Statistics Division, New York, NY 10017, (800) 253-9646, Fax: (212) 963-4116, http://unstats.un.org; *Statistical Yearbook* and *World Statistics Pocketbook.*

FIJI - TEXTILE INDUSTRY

M.E. Sharpe, 80 Business Park Drive, Armonk, NY 10504, (800) 541-6563, Fax: (914) 273-2106, www.mesharpe.com; *The Illustrated Book of World Rankings.*

Secretariat of the Pacific Community (SPC), BP D5, 98848 Noumea Cedex, New Caledonia, www.spc.int/corp; *Selected Pacific Economies - a Statistical Summary (SPESS).*

United Nations Conference on Trade and Development (UNCTAD), DC2-1120, United Nations, New York, NY 10017, (212) 963-0027, www.unctad.org; *UNCTAD Commodity Yearbook.*

FIJI - THEATER

UNESCO Institute for Statistics, C.P. 6128 Succursale Centre-Ville, Montreal, Quebec, H3C 3J7 Canada, (Dial from U.S. (514) 343-6880), (Fax from U.S. (514) 343 6882), www.uis.unesco.org; *Statistical Tables.*

FIJI - TOBACCO INDUSTRY

Foreign Agricultural Service (FAS), U.S. Department of Agriculture (USDA), 1400 Independence Avenue, SW, Washington, DC 20250, (202) 720-3935, www.fas.usda.gov; *Tobacco: World Markets and Trade.*

M.E. Sharpe, 80 Business Park Drive, Armonk, NY 10504, (800) 541-6563, Fax: (914) 273-2106, www.mesharpe.com; *The Illustrated Book of World Rankings.*

Secretariat of the Pacific Community (SPC), BP D5, 98848 Noumea Cedex, New Caledonia, www.spc.int/corp; *Selected Pacific Economies - a Statistical Summary (SPESS).*

United Nations Statistics Division, New York, NY 10017, (800) 253-9646, Fax: (212) 963-4116, http://unstats.un.org; *Statistical Yearbook.*

FIJI - TOURISM

Euromonitor International, Inc., 224 S. Michigan Avenue, Suite 1500, Chicago, IL 60604, (312) 922-1115, Fax: (312) 922-1157, www.euromonitor.com; *The World Economic Factbook 2008* and *World Marketing Data and Statistics.*

M.E. Sharpe, 80 Business Park Drive, Armonk, NY 10504, (800) 541-6563, Fax: (914) 273-2106, www.mesharpe.com; *The Illustrated Book of World Rankings.*

Palgrave Macmillan Ltd., Houndmills, Basingstoke, Hampshire, RG21 6XS, England, (Telephone in U.S. (888) 330-8477), (Fax in U.S. (800) 672-2054), www.palgrave.com; *The Statesman's Yearbook 2008.*

Taylor and Francis Group, An Informa Business, 2 Park Square, Milton Park, Abingdon, Oxford OX14 4RN, United Kingdom, (Dial from U.S. (212) 216-7800), (Fax from U.S. (212) 564-7854), www.tandf.co.uk; *The Europa World Year Book.*

United Nations Statistics Division, New York, NY 10017, (800) 253-9646, Fax: (212) 963-4116, http://unstats.un.org; *Statistical Yearbook.*

United Nations World Tourism Organization (UNWTO), Capitan Haya 42, 28020 Madrid, Spain, www.world-tourism.org; *Yearbook of Tourism Statistics.*

The World Bank, 1818 H Street, NW, Washington, DC 20433, (202) 473-1000, Fax: (202) 477-6391, www.worldbank.org; *Fiji.*

FIJI - TRADE

See FIJI - INTERNATIONAL TRADE

FIJI - TRANSPORTATION

Euromonitor International, Inc., 224 S. Michigan Avenue, Suite 1500, Chicago, IL 60604, (312) 922-1115, Fax: (312) 922-1157, www.euromonitor.com; *World Marketing Data and Statistics.*

M.E. Sharpe, 80 Business Park Drive, Armonk, NY 10504, (800) 541-6563, Fax: (914) 273-2106, www.mesharpe.com; *The Illustrated Book of World Rankings.*

Palgrave Macmillan Ltd., Houndmills, Basingstoke, Hampshire, RG21 6XS, England, (Telephone in U.S. (888) 330-8477), (Fax in U.S. (800) 672-2054), www.palgrave.com; *The Statesman's Yearbook 2008.*

Secretariat of the Pacific Community (SPC), BP D5, 98848 Noumea Cedex, New Caledonia, www.spc.int/corp; *Selected Pacific Economies - a Statistical Summary (SPESS).*

Taylor and Francis Group, An Informa Business, 2 Park Square, Milton Park, Abingdon, Oxford OX14 4RN, United Kingdom, (Dial from U.S. (212) 216-7800), (Fax from U.S. (212) 564-7854), www.tandf.co.uk; *The Europa World Year Book.*

United Nations Statistics Division, New York, NY 10017, (800) 253-9646, Fax: (212) 963-4116, http://unstats.un.org; *Human Development Report 2006* and *Statistical Yearbook for Asia and the Pacific 2004.*

The World Bank, 1818 H Street, NW, Washington, DC 20433, (202) 473-1000, Fax: (202) 477-6391, www.worldbank.org; *Fiji.*

FIJI - TURKEYS

See FIJI - LIVESTOCK

FIJI - UNEMPLOYMENT

International Labour Office, I.L.O. Publications, 4 route des Morillons, CH-1211 Geneva 22, Switzerland, (Telephone in U.S. (202) 653-7652), (Fax in U.S. (202) 653-7687), www.ilo.org; *Yearbook of Labour Statistics 2006.*

Palgrave Macmillan Ltd., Houndmills, Basingstoke, Hampshire, RG21 6XS, England, (Telephone in U.S. (888) 330-8477), (Fax in U.S. (800) 672-2054), www.palgrave.com; *The Statesman's Yearbook 2008.*

United Nations Statistics Division, New York, NY 10017, (800) 253-9646, Fax: (212) 963-4116, http://unstats.un.org; *Statistical Yearbook.*

FIJI - VITAL STATISTICS

Palgrave Macmillan Ltd., Houndmills, Basingstoke, Hampshire, RG21 6XS, England, (Telephone in U.S. (888) 330-8477), (Fax in U.S. (800) 672-2054), www.palgrave.com; *The Statesman's Yearbook 2008.*

United Nations Statistics Division, New York, NY 10017, (800) 253-9646, Fax: (212) 963-4116, http://unstats.un.org; *Statistical Yearbook.*

World Health Organization (WHO), Avenue Appia 20, 1211 Geneve 27, Switzerland, (Telephone in U.S. (212) 331-9081), www.who.int; *World Health Report 2006.*

FIJI - WAGES

International Labour Office, I.L.O. Publications, 4 route des Morillons, CH-1211 Geneva 22, Switzerland, (Telephone in U.S. (202) 653-7652), (Fax in U.S. (202) 653-7687), www.ilo.org; *Yearbook of Labour Statistics 2006.*

United Nations Statistics Division, New York, NY 10017, (800) 253-9646, Fax: (212) 963-4116, http://unstats.un.org; *Statistical Yearbook* and *Statistical Yearbook for Asia and the Pacific 2004.*

The World Bank, 1818 H Street, NW, Washington, DC 20433, (202) 473-1000, Fax: (202) 477-6391, www.worldbank.org; *Fiji.*

FIJI - WEATHER

See FIJI - CLIMATE

FIJI - WELFARE STATE

International Monetary Fund (IMF), 700 Nineteenth Street, NW, Washington, DC 20431, (202) 623-7000, Fax: (202) 623-4661, www.imf.org; *Government Finance Statistics Yearbook (2008 Edition).*

FIJI - WHEAT PRODUCTION

See FIJI - CROPS

FIJI - WHOLESALE PRICE INDEXES

Asian Development Bank (ADB), PO Box 789, 0980 Manila, Philippines, www.adb.org; *Key Indicators of Developing Asian and Pacific Countries 2006.*

FIJI - WHOLESALE TRADE

United Nations Statistics Division, New York, NY 10017, (800) 253-9646, Fax: (212) 963-4116, http://unstats.un.org; *Statistical Yearbook.*

FIJI - WINE PRODUCTION

See FIJI - BEVERAGE INDUSTRY

FIJI - WOOL PRODUCTION

See FIJI - TEXTILE INDUSTRY

FILBERTS

National Agricultural Statistics Service (NASS), U.S. Department of Agriculture (USDA), 1400 Independence Avenue, SW, Washington, DC 20250, (800) 727-9540, Fax: (202) 690-2090, www.nass.usda.gov; *Noncitrus Fruits and Nuts: Final Estimates 1998-2003.*

FILIPINO POPULATION

Population Reference Bureau, 1875 Connecticut Avenue, NW, Suite 520, Washington, DC, 20009-5728, (800) 877-9881, Fax: (202) 328-3937, www.prb.org; *The American People Series.*

U.S. Census Bureau, Population Division, 4700 Silver Hill Road, Washington DC 20233-0001, (301) 763-3030, www.census.gov/population/www/; *Census 2000 Profiles of General Demographic Characteristics.*

FINANCE

Board of Governors of the Federal Reserve System, Constitution Avenue, NW, Washington, DC 20551, (202) 452-3000, www.federalreserve.gov; *Flow of Funds Accounts of the United States.*

Economist Intelligence Unit, 111 West 57th Street, New York, NY 10019, (212) 554-0600, Fax: (212) 586-1181, www.eiu.com; *United States of America Country Report.*

International Monetary Fund (IMF), 700 Nineteenth Street, NW, Washington, DC 20431, (202) 623-7000, Fax: (202) 623-4661, www.imf.org; *GFSR Market Update* and *Global Financial Stability Report (April 2008 Edition).*

Thomson Financial, 195 Broadway, New York, NY 10007, (646) 822-2000, www.thomson.com; *Acquisitions Monthly; International Financing Review (IFR);* and *Thomson Financial News.*

The World Bank, 1818 H Street, NW, Washington, DC 20433, (202) 473-1000, Fax: (202) 477-6391, www.worldbank.org; *Global Development Finance 2007.*

FINANCE - CONSUMER INSTALLMENT CREDIT

Board of Governors of the Federal Reserve System, Constitution Avenue, NW, Washington, DC 20551, (202) 452-3000, www.federalreserve.gov; *Federal Reserve Bulletin* and *Statistical Digest.*

FINANCE - CORPORATE FUNDS

Board of Governors of the Federal Reserve System, Constitution Avenue, NW, Washington, DC 20551, (202) 452-3000, www.federalreserve.gov; *Flow of Funds Accounts of the United States.*

U.S. Census Bureau, Company Statistics Division, 4700 Silver Hill Road, Washington DC 20233-0001, (301) 763-3030, www.census.gov/csd/; *2002 Business Expenses Survey (BES).*

FINANCE, INSURANCE, AND REAL ESTATE INDUSTRY

DataQuick, 9620 Towne Centre Drive, San Diego, CA 92121, (858) 597-3100, www.dataquick.com; DQNews.com.

Federal Financial Institutions Examination Council (FFIEC), 3501 Fairfax Drive, Room D8073A, Arlington, VA 22226, (202) 872-7500, www.ffiec.gov; Trust Institutions Search.

Inman News, 1100 Marina Village Parkway, Suite 102, Alameda, CA 94501, (800) 775-4662, Fax: (510) 658-9317, www.inman.com; *Real Estate News.*

National Association of Realtors (NAR), 430 North Michigan Avenue, Chicago, IL 60611-4087, (800) 874-6500, www.realtor.org; *Existing-Home Sales (EHS); Field Guide to Quick Real Estate Statistics; 2006 NAR Baby Boomers and Real Estate: Today and Tomorrow; 2007 NAR Member Profile; 2007 NAR Profile of Buyer's Home Feature Preferences; 2006 NAR Profile of Home Buyers and Sellers; 2006 NAR Profile of Real Estate Firms: An Industry Overview; Pending Home Sales Index;* Real Estate Intelligence Online (REIO); and *Real Estate Outlook.*

U.S. Bureau of Labor Statistics (BLS), Postal Square Building, 2 Massachusetts Avenue, NE, Washington, DC 20212-0001, (202) 691-5200, Fax: (202) 691-6325, www.bls.gov; *Industries at a Glance.*

U.S. Census Bureau, Center for Economic Studies, 4600 Silver Hill Road, Washington DC 20233, (301) 457-1235, www.ces.census.gov; Economic Census (web app).

U.S. Library of Congress (LOC), Congressional Research Service (CRS), The Library of Congress, 101 Independence Avenue, SE, Washington, DC 20540-7500, (202) 707-5700, www.loc.gov/crsinfo; *Homeland Security Research and Development Funding, Organization, and Oversight.*

FINANCE, INSURANCE, AND REAL ESTATE INDUSTRY - CAPITAL

Board of Governors of the Federal Reserve System, Constitution Avenue, NW, Washington, DC 20551, (202) 452-3000, www.federalreserve.gov; *Federal Reserve Bulletin* and *Statistical Digest.*

U.S. Census Bureau, Center for Economic Studies, 4600 Silver Hill Road, Washington DC 20233, (301) 457-1235, www.ces.census.gov; *2002 Economic Census, Finance and Insurance* and *2002 Economic Census, Finance and Insurance.*

U.S. Census Bureau, Company Statistics Division, 4700 Silver Hill Road, Washington DC 20233-0001, (301) 763-3030, www.census.gov/csd/; *Annual Capital Expenditures Survey (ACES).*

FINANCE, INSURANCE, AND REAL ESTATE INDUSTRY - EARNINGS

Bureau of Economic Analysis (BEA), U.S. Department of Commerce (DOC), 1441 L Street NW, Washington, DC 20230, (202) 606-9900, www.bea.gov; *2007 Annual Revision of the National Income and Product Accounts (NIPA)* and *Survey of Current Business (SCB).*

Insurance Information Institute (III), 110 William Street, New York, NY 10038, (212) 346-5500, www.iii.org; *The Financial Services Fact Book 2008.*

U.S. Bureau of Labor Statistics (BLS), Postal Square Building, 2 Massachusetts Avenue, NE, Washington, DC 20212-0001, (202) 691-5200, Fax: (202) 691-6325, www.bls.gov; *Current Employment Statistics Survey (CES)* and *Employment and Earnings (EE).*

U.S. Census Bureau, Center for Economic Studies, 4600 Silver Hill Road, Washington DC 20233, (301) 457-1235, www.ces.census.gov; *2002 Economic Census, Finance and Insurance* and *2002 Economic Census, Professional, Scientific and Technical Services.*

U.S. Census Bureau, Company Statistics Division, 4700 Silver Hill Road, Washington DC 20233-0001, (301) 763-3030, www.census.gov/csd/; *County Business Patterns 2004; Statistics of U.S. Businesses (SUSB);* and *Statistics of U.S. Businesses (SUSB).*

FINANCE, INSURANCE, AND REAL ESTATE INDUSTRY - EMPLOYEES

U.S. Bureau of Labor Statistics (BLS), Postal Square Building, 2 Massachusetts Avenue, NE, Washington, DC 20212-0001, (202) 691-5200, Fax: (202) 691-6325, www.bls.gov; *Current Employment Statistics Survey (CES); Employment and Earnings (EE); Monthly Labor Review (MLR);* and unpublished data.

U.S. Census Bureau, Center for Economic Studies, 4600 Silver Hill Road, Washington DC 20233, (301) 457-1235, www.ces.census.gov; *2002 Economic Census, Professional, Scientific and Technical Services.*

U.S. Census Bureau, Company Statistics Division, 4700 Silver Hill Road, Washington DC 20233-0001, (301) 763-3030, www.census.gov/csd/; *County Business Patterns 2004; Statistics of U.S. Businesses (SUSB);* and *Statistics of U.S. Businesses (SUSB).*

FINANCE, INSURANCE, AND REAL ESTATE INDUSTRY - ESTABLISHMENTS

U.S. Census Bureau, Center for Economic Studies, 4600 Silver Hill Road, Washington DC 20233, (301)

457-1235, www.ces.census.gov; *2002 Economic Census, Finance and Insurance* and *2002 Economic Census, Professional, Scientific and Technical Services.*

U.S. Census Bureau, Company Statistics Division, 4700 Silver Hill Road, Washington DC 20233-0001, (301) 763-3030, www.census.gov/csd/; *County Business Patterns 2004; Statistics of U.S. Businesses (SUSB);* and *Statistics of U.S. Businesses (SUSB).*

FINANCE, INSURANCE, AND REAL ESTATE INDUSTRY - FINANCES

Board of Governors of the Federal Reserve System, Constitution Avenue, NW, Washington, DC 20551, (202) 452-3000, www.federalreserve.gov; *Federal Reserve Bulletin; Flow of Funds Accounts of the United States; Statistical Digest;* and unpublished data.

European Central Bank (ECB), Postfach 160319, D-60066 Frankfurt am Main, Germany, www.ecb.int; *Monetary Financial Institutions (MFI) Interest Rate Statistics (MIR).*

Federal Deposit Insurance Corporation (FDIC), 550 Seventeenth Street, NW, Washington, DC 20429-0002, (877) 275-3342, www.fdic.gov; *State Banking Performance Summary* and unpublished data.

Federal Financial Institutions Examination Council (FFIEC), 3501 Fairfax Drive, Room D8073A, Arlington, VA 22226, (202) 872-7500, www.ffiec.gov; *Annual Report 2006* and Call Report and Thrift Financial Report (TFR) Data.

U.S. Census Bureau, Center for Economic Studies, 4600 Silver Hill Road, Washington DC 20233, (301) 457-1235, www.ces.census.gov; *2002 Economic Census, Professional, Scientific and Technical Services.*

U.S. Census Bureau, Company Statistics Division, 4700 Silver Hill Road, Washington DC 20233-0001, (301) 763-3030, www.census.gov/csd/; *County Business Patterns 2004.*

U.S. Department of the Treasury (DOT), Internal Revenue Service (IRS), Statistics of Income Division (SIS), PO Box 2608, Washington, DC, 20013-2608, (202) 874-0410, Fax: (202) 874-0964, www.irs.ustreas.gov; *Statistics of Income Bulletin; Statistics of Income Bulletin, Corporation Income Tax Returns;* and unpublished data.

FINANCE, INSURANCE, AND REAL ESTATE INDUSTRY - FOREIGN INVESTMENT IN THE UNITED STATES

Bureau of Economic Analysis (BEA), U.S. Department of Commerce (DOC), 1441 L Street NW, Washington, DC 20230, (202) 606-9900, www.bea.gov; *Foreign Direct Investment in the United States (FDIUS); Survey of Current Business (SCB);* and *U.S. Direct Investment Abroad (USDIA).*

FINANCE, INSURANCE, AND REAL ESTATE INDUSTRY - GROSS DOMESTIC PRODUCT

Bureau of Economic Analysis (BEA), U.S. Department of Commerce (DOC), 1441 L Street NW, Washington, DC 20230, (202) 606-9900, www.bea.gov; *Survey of Current Business (SCB).*

FINANCE, INSURANCE, AND REAL ESTATE INDUSTRY - INDUSTRY

U.S. Census Bureau, 4700 Silver Hill Road, Washington DC 20233-0001, (301) 763-3030, www.census.gov; *2002 Economic Census, Nonemployer Statistics.*

U.S. Census Bureau, Center for Economic Studies, 4600 Silver Hill Road, Washington DC 20233, (301) 457-1235, www.ces.census.gov; *2002 Economic Census, Geographic Area Series.*

FINANCE, INSURANCE, AND REAL ESTATE INDUSTRY - MERGERS AND ACQUISITIONS

Thomson Financial, 195 Broadway, New York, NY 10007, (646) 822-2000, www.thomson.com; Thomson Research.

FINANCE, INSURANCE, AND REAL ESTATE INDUSTRY - MINORITY-OWNED BUSINESSES

U.S. Census Bureau, Company Statistics Division, 4700 Silver Hill Road, Washington DC 20233-0001, (301) 763-3030, www.census.gov/csd/; *Survey of Minority-Owned Business Enterprises.*

FINANCE, INSURANCE, AND REAL ESTATE INDUSTRY - MULTINATIONAL COMPANIES

Bureau of Economic Analysis (BEA), U.S. Department of Commerce (DOC), 1441 L Street NW, Washington, DC 20230, (202) 606-9900, www.bea.gov; *Survey of Current Business (SCB).*

FINANCE, INSURANCE, AND REAL ESTATE INDUSTRY - NONEMPLOYERS

U.S. Census Bureau, 4700 Silver Hill Road, Washington DC 20233-0001, (301) 763-3030, www.census.gov; *2002 Economic Census, Nonemployer Statistics.*

FINANCE, INSURANCE, AND REAL ESTATE INDUSTRY - PROFITS

Bureau of Economic Analysis (BEA), U.S. Department of Commerce (DOC), 1441 L Street NW, Washington, DC 20230, (202) 606-9900, www.bea.gov; *Survey of Current Business (SCB).*

Forbes, Inc., 60 Fifth Avenue, New York, NY 10011, (212) 366-8900, www.forbes.com; *America's Largest Private Companies.*

Insurance Information Institute (III), 110 William Street, New York, NY 10038, (212) 346-5500, www.iii.org; *The Financial Services Fact Book 2008.*

U.S. Census Bureau, Center for Economic Studies, 4600 Silver Hill Road, Washington DC 20233, (301) 457-1235, www.ces.census.gov; *2002 Economic Census, Finance and Insurance.*

U.S. Department of the Treasury (DOT), Internal Revenue Service (IRS), Statistics of Income Division (SIS), PO Box 2608, Washington, DC, 20013-2608, (202) 874-0410, Fax: (202) 874-0964, www.irs.ustreas.gov; *Statistics of Income Bulletin; Statistics of Income Bulletin, Corporation Income Tax Returns;* and various fact sheets.

FINANCE, INSURANCE, AND REAL ESTATE INDUSTRY - SALES, SHIPMENTS AND RECEIPTS

Forbes, Inc., 60 Fifth Avenue, New York, NY 10011, (212) 366-8900, www.forbes.com; *America's Largest Private Companies.*

U.S. Census Bureau, Center for Economic Studies, 4600 Silver Hill Road, Washington DC 20233, (301) 457-1235, www.ces.census.gov; *2002 Economic Census, Finance and Insurance.*

U.S. Census Bureau, Company Statistics Division, 4700 Silver Hill Road, Washington DC 20233-0001, (301) 763-3030, www.census.gov/csd/; *Statistics of U.S. Businesses (SUSB).*

U.S. Department of the Treasury (DOT), Internal Revenue Service (IRS), Statistics of Income Division (SIS), PO Box 2608, Washington, DC, 20013-2608, (202) 874-0410, Fax: (202) 874-0964, www.irs.ustreas.gov; *Statistics of Income Bulletin;* unpublished data; and various fact sheets.

FINANCE, INSURANCE, AND REAL ESTATE INDUSTRY - UNION MEMBERSHIP

U.S. Bureau of Labor Statistics (BLS), Postal Square Building, 2 Massachusetts Avenue, NE, Washington, DC 20212-0001, (202) 691-5200, Fax: (202) 691-6325, www.bls.gov; *Employment and Earnings (EE).*

FINANCE, INSURANCE, AND REAL ESTATE INDUSTRY - WOMEN-OWNED BUSINESSES

U.S. Census Bureau, Company Statistics Division, 4700 Silver Hill Road, Washington DC 20233-0001, (301) 763-3030, www.census.gov/csd/; *Survey of Women-Owned Businesses.*

FINLAND - NATIONAL STATISTICAL OFFICE

Statistics Finland, FI-00022, Helsinki, Finland, www.stat.fi/index_en.html; National Data Center.

FINLAND - PRIMARY STATISTICS SOURCES

Eurostat, Batiment Jean Monnet, Rue Alcide de Gasperi, L-2920 Luxembourg, http://epp.eurostat.ec.europa.eu; *Pocketbook on Candidate and Potential Candidate Countries.*

Statistics Finland, FI-00022, Helsinki, Finland, www.stat.fi/index_en.html; *Finland in Figures 2007* and *Statistical Yearbook of Finland 2007.*

Statistics Greenland, PO Box 1025, 3900 Nuuk, Greenland, www.statgreen.gl/english; *Statistical Yearbook 2001-2002.*

FINLAND - DATABASES

Statistics Finland, FI-00022, Helsinki, Finland, www.stat.fi/index_en.html; StatFin Online Service (web app).

FINLAND - ABORTION

Nordic Council of Ministers, Store Strandstraede 18, DK-1255 Copenhagen K, Denmark, www.norden.org; *Nordic Statistical Yearbook 2004-2006.*

United Nations Statistics Division, New York, NY 10017, (800) 253-9646, Fax: (212) 963-4116, http://unstats.un.org; *Demographic Yearbook* and *Trends in Europe and North America: The Statistical Yearbook of the ECE 2005.*

FINLAND - AGRICULTURAL MACHINERY

United Nations Statistics Division, New York, NY 10017, (800) 253-9646, Fax: (212) 963-4116, http://unstats.un.org; *Statistical Yearbook.*

FINLAND - AGRICULTURE

Economist Intelligence Unit, 111 West 57th Street, New York, NY 10019, (212) 554-0600, Fax: (212) 586-1181, www.eiu.com; *Finland Country Report.*

Euromonitor International, Inc., 224 S. Michigan Avenue, Suite 1500, Chicago, IL 60604, (312) 922-1115, Fax: (312) 922-1157, www.euromonitor.com; *World Marketing Data and Statistics.*

Eurostat, Batiment Jean Monnet, Rue Alcide de Gasperi, L-2920 Luxembourg, http://epp.eurostat.ec.europa.eu; *EU Agricultural Prices in 2007.*

M.E. Sharpe, 80 Business Park Drive, Armonk, NY 10504, (800) 541-6563, Fax: (914) 273-2106, www.mesharpe.com; *The Illustrated Book of World Rankings.*

Nordic Council of Ministers, Store Strandstraede 18, DK-1255 Copenhagen K, Denmark, www.norden.org; *Nordic Statistical Yearbook 2004-2006.*

Organisation for Economic Cooperation and Development (OECD), 2 rue Andre Pascal, F-75775 Paris Cedex 16, France, (Telephone in U.S. (202) 785-6323), (Fax in U.S. (202) 785-0350), www.oecd.org; *Indicators of Industrial Activity; 2005 OECD Agricultural Outlook Tables, 1970-2014; OECD Agricultural Outlook: 2007-2016; OECD Economic Survey - Finland 2008;* and STructural ANalysis (STAN) database.

Palgrave Macmillan Ltd., Houndmills, Basingstoke, Hampshire, RG21 6XS, England, (Telephone in U.S. (888) 330-8477), (Fax in U.S. (800) 672-2054), www.palgrave.com; *The Statesman's Yearbook 2008.*

Taylor and Francis Group, An Informa Business, 2 Park Square, Milton Park, Abingdon, Oxford OX14 4RN, United Kingdom, (Dial from U.S. (212) 216-

7800), (Fax from U.S. (212) 564-7854), www.tandf.co.uk; *The Europa World Year Book.*

United Nations Conference on Trade and Development (UNCTAD), DC2-1120, United Nations, New York, NY 10017, (212) 963-0027, www.unctad.org; *UNCTAD Commodity Yearbook.*

United Nations Food and Agricultural Organization (FAO), Viale delle Terme di Caracalla, 00100 Rome, Italy, (Dial from U.S. (202) 653-2400), (Fax from U.S. (202) 653 5760), www.fao.org; AQUASTAT; *FAO Production Yearbook 2002; FAO Trade Yearbook;* and *The State of Food and Agriculture (SOFA) 2006.*

United Nations Statistics Division, New York, NY 10017, (800) 253-9646, Fax: (212) 963-4116, http://unstats.un.org; *Statistical Yearbook.*

The World Bank, 1818 H Street, NW, Washington, DC 20433, (202) 473-1000, Fax: (202) 477-6391, www.worldbank.org; *Finland* and *World Development Indicators (WDI) 2008.*

FINLAND - AIRLINES

Eurostat, Batiment Jean Monnet, Rue Alcide de Gasperi, L-2920 Luxembourg, http://epp.eurostat.ec.europa.eu; *Regional Passenger and Freight Air Transport in Europe in 2006.*

International Civil Aviation Organization (ICAO), External Relations and Public Information Office (EPO), 999 University Street, Montreal, Quebec H3C 5H7, Canada, (Dial from U.S. (514) 954-8219), (Fax from U.S. (514) 954-6077), www.icao.int; *Civil Aviation Statistics of the World.*

M.E. Sharpe, 80 Business Park Drive, Armonk, NY 10504, (800) 541-6563, Fax: (914) 273-2106, www.mesharpe.com; *The Illustrated Book of World Rankings.*

Nordic Council of Ministers, Store Strandstraede 18, DK-1255 Copenhagen K, Denmark, www.norden.org; *Nordic Statistical Yearbook 2004-2006.*

Organisation for Economic Cooperation and Development (OECD), 2 rue Andre Pascal, F-75775 Paris Cedex 16, France, (Telephone in U.S. (202) 785-6323), (Fax in U.S. (202) 785-0350), www.oecd.org; *Household, Tourism, Travel: Trends, Environmental Impacts and Policy Responses.*

Palgrave Macmillan Ltd., Houndmills, Basingstoke, Hampshire, RG21 6XS, England, (Telephone in U.S. (888) 330-8477), (Fax in U.S. (800) 672-2054), www.palgrave.com; *The Statesman's Yearbook 2008.*

Taylor and Francis Group, An Informa Business, 2 Park Square, Milton Park, Abingdon, Oxford OX14 4RN, United Kingdom, (Dial from U.S. (212) 216-7800), (Fax from U.S. (212) 564-7854), www.tandf.co.uk; *The Europa World Year Book.*

United Nations Statistics Division, New York, NY 10017, (800) 253-9646, Fax: (212) 963-4116, http://unstats.un.org; *Statistical Yearbook.*

FINLAND - AIRPORTS

Central Intelligence Agency, Office of Public Affairs, Washington, DC 20505, (703) 482-0623, Fax: (703) 482-1739, www.cia.gov; *The World Factbook.*

FINLAND - ALUMINUM PRODUCTION

See FINLAND - MINERAL INDUSTRIES

FINLAND - ANIMAL FEEDING

Organisation for Economic Cooperation and Development (OECD), 2 rue Andre Pascal, F-75775 Paris Cedex 16, France, (Telephone in U.S. (202) 785-6323), (Fax in U.S. (202) 785-0350), www.oecd.org; *International Trade by Commodity Statistics (ITCS).*

FINLAND - ARMED FORCES

Central Intelligence Agency, Office of Public Affairs, Washington, DC 20505, (703) 482-0623, Fax: (703) 482-1739, www.cia.gov; *The World Factbook.*

Euromonitor International, Inc., 224 S. Michigan Avenue, Suite 1500, Chicago, IL 60604, (312) 922-1115, Fax: (312) 922-1157, www.euromonitor.com; *World Marketing Data and Statistics.*

International Institute for Strategic Studies (IISS), Arundel House, 13-15 Arundel Street, Temple Place, London WC2R 3DX, England, www.iiss.org; *The Military Balance 2007.*

International Monetary Fund (IMF), 700 Nineteenth Street, NW, Washington, DC 20431, (202) 623-7000, Fax: (202) 623-4661, www.imf.org; *Government Finance Statistics Yearbook (2008 Edition).*

Nordic Council of Ministers, Store Strandstraede 18, DK-1255 Copenhagen K, Denmark, www.norden.org; *Nordic Statistical Yearbook 2004-2006.*

Palgrave Macmillan Ltd., Houndmills, Basingstoke, Hampshire, RG21 6XS, England, (Telephone in U.S. (888) 330-8477), (Fax in U.S. (800) 672-2054), www.palgrave.com; *The Statesman's Yearbook 2008.*

U.S. Department of State (DOS), 2201 C Street NW, Washington, DC 20520, (202) 647-4000, www.state.gov; *World Military Expenditures and Arms Transfers (WMEAT).*

United Nations Statistics Division, New York, NY 10017, (800) 253-9646, Fax: (212) 963-4116, http://unstats.un.org; *Human Development Report 2006.*

FINLAND - AUTOMOBILE INDUSTRY AND TRADE

Organisation for Economic Cooperation and Development (OECD), 2 rue Andre Pascal, F-75775 Paris Cedex 16, France, (Telephone in U.S. (202) 785-6323), (Fax in U.S. (202) 785-0350), www.oecd.org; *Indicators of Industrial Activity* and *International Trade by Commodity Statistics (ITCS).*

United Nations Statistics Division, New York, NY 10017, (800) 253-9646, Fax: (212) 963-4116, http://unstats.un.org; *Statistical Yearbook.*

FINLAND - BALANCE OF PAYMENTS

International Monetary Fund (IMF), 700 Nineteenth Street, NW, Washington, DC 20431, (202) 623-7000, Fax: (202) 623-4661, www.imf.org; *Balance of Payments Statistics Newsletter; Balance of Payments Statistics Yearbook 2007;* and *International Financial Statistics Yearbook 2007.*

Nordic Council of Ministers, Store Strandstraede 18, DK-1255 Copenhagen K, Denmark, www.norden.org; *Nordic Statistical Yearbook 2004-2006.*

Organisation for Economic Cooperation and Development (OECD), 2 rue Andre Pascal, F-75775 Paris Cedex 16, France, (Telephone in U.S. (202) 785-6323), (Fax in U.S. (202) 785-0350), www.oecd.org; *Geographical Distribution of Financial Flows to Aid Recipients 2002-2006; OECD Economic Outlook 2008; OECD Economic Survey - Finland 2008;* and *OECD Main Economic Indicators (MEI).*

Taylor and Francis Group, An Informa Business, 2 Park Square, Milton Park, Abingdon, Oxford OX14 4RN, United Kingdom, (Dial from U.S. (212) 216-7800), (Fax from U.S. (212) 564-7854), www.tandf.co.uk; *The Europa World Year Book.*

United Nations Conference on Trade and Development (UNCTAD), DC2-1120, United Nations, New York, NY 10017, (212) 963-0027, www.unctad.org; *Handbook of Statistics 2005.*

The World Bank, 1818 H Street, NW, Washington, DC 20433, (202) 473-1000, Fax: (202) 477-6391, www.worldbank.org; *Finland; World Development Indicators (WDI) 2008;* and *World Development Report 2008.*

FINLAND - BANKS AND BANKING

Euromonitor International, Inc., 224 S. Michigan Avenue, Suite 1500, Chicago, IL 60604, (312) 922-1115, Fax: (312) 922-1157, www.euromonitor.com; *World Marketing Data and Statistics.*

European Union, Delegation of the European Commission to the United States, 2300 M Street, NW, Washington, DC 20037, (202) 862-9500, Fax: (202) 429-1766, www.eurunion.org; *The EU Economy, 2007 Review: Moving Europe's Productivity Frontier.*

International Monetary Fund (IMF), 700 Nineteenth Street, NW, Washington, DC 20431, (202) 623-7000, Fax: (202) 623-4661, www.imf.org; *International Financial Statistics Yearbook 2007.*

M.E. Sharpe, 80 Business Park Drive, Armonk, NY 10504, (800) 541-6563, Fax: (914) 273-2106, www.mesharpe.com; *The Illustrated Book of World Rankings.*

Nordic Council of Ministers, Store Strandstraede 18, DK-1255 Copenhagen K, Denmark, www.norden.org; *Nordic Statistical Yearbook 2004-2006.*

Organisation for Economic Cooperation and Development (OECD), 2 rue Andre Pascal, F-75775 Paris Cedex 16, France, (Telephone in U.S. (202) 785-6323), (Fax in U.S. (202) 785-0350), www.oecd.org; *Financial Market Trends: OECD Periodical; OECD Economic Outlook 2008;* and *OECD Economic Survey - Finland 2008.*

Palgrave Macmillan Ltd., Houndmills, Basingstoke, Hampshire, RG21 6XS, England, (Telephone in U.S. (888) 330-8477), (Fax in U.S. (800) 672-2054), www.palgrave.com; *The Statesman's Yearbook 2008.*

Taylor and Francis Group, An Informa Business, 2 Park Square, Milton Park, Abingdon, Oxford OX14 4RN, United Kingdom, (Dial from U.S. (212) 216-7800), (Fax from U.S. (212) 564-7854), www.tandf.co.uk; *The Europa World Year Book.*

United Nations Statistics Division, New York, NY 10017, (800) 253-9646, Fax: (212) 963-4116, http://unstats.un.org; *Statistical Yearbook.*

FINLAND - BARLEY PRODUCTION

See FINLAND - CROPS

FINLAND - BEVERAGE INDUSTRY

M.E. Sharpe, 80 Business Park Drive, Armonk, NY 10504, (800) 541-6563, Fax: (914) 273-2106, www.mesharpe.com; *The Illustrated Book of World Rankings.*

Organisation for Economic Cooperation and Development (OECD), 2 rue Andre Pascal, F-75775 Paris Cedex 16, France, (Telephone in U.S. (202) 785-6323), (Fax in U.S. (202) 785-0350), www.oecd.org; *Indicators of Industrial Activity.*

United Nations Statistics Division, New York, NY 10017, (800) 253-9646, Fax: (212) 963-4116, http://unstats.un.org; *Statistical Yearbook.*

FINLAND - BONDS

International Monetary Fund (IMF), 700 Nineteenth Street, NW, Washington, DC 20431, (202) 623-7000, Fax: (202) 623-4661, www.imf.org; *Government Finance Statistics Yearbook (2008 Edition).*

Organisation for Economic Cooperation and Development (OECD), 2 rue Andre Pascal, F-75775 Paris Cedex 16, France, (Telephone in U.S. (202) 785-6323), (Fax in U.S. (202) 785-0350), www.oecd.org; *Financial Market Trends: OECD Periodical.*

FINLAND - BROADCASTING

Central Intelligence Agency, Office of Public Affairs, Washington, DC 20505, (703) 482-0623, Fax: (703) 482-1739, www.cia.gov; *The World Factbook.*

Euromonitor International, Inc., 224 S. Michigan Avenue, Suite 1500, Chicago, IL 60604, (312) 922-1115, Fax: (312) 922-1157, www.euromonitor.com; *World Marketing Data and Statistics.*

M.E. Sharpe, 80 Business Park Drive, Armonk, NY 10504, (800) 541-6563, Fax: (914) 273-2106, www.mesharpe.com; *The Illustrated Book of World Rankings.*

Nordic Council of Ministers, Store Strandstraede 18, DK-1255 Copenhagen K, Denmark, www.norden.org; *Nordic Statistical Yearbook 2004-2006.*

Palgrave Macmillan Ltd., Houndmills, Basingstoke, Hampshire, RG21 6XS, England, (Telephone in U.S. (888) 330-8477), (Fax in U.S. (800) 672-2054), www.palgrave.com; *The Statesman's Yearbook 2008.*

UNESCO Institute for Statistics, C.P. 6128 Succursale Centre-Ville, Montreal, Quebec, H3C 3J7 Canada, (Dial from U.S. (514) 343-6880), (Fax from U.S. (514) 343 6882), www.uis.unesco.org; *Statistical Tables.*

United Nations Statistics Division, New York, NY 10017, (800) 253-9646, Fax: (212) 963-4116, http://unstats.un.org; *Trends in Europe and North America: The Statistical Yearbook of the ECE 2005.*

WRTH Publications Limited, PO Box 290, Oxford OX2 7FT, UK, www.wrth.com; *World Radio TV Handbook 2007.*

FINLAND - BUDGET

Central Intelligence Agency, Office of Public Affairs, Washington, DC 20505, (703) 482-0623, Fax: (703) 482-1739, www.cia.gov; *The World Factbook.*

Eurostat, Batiment Jean Monnet, Rue Alcide de Gasperi, L-2920 Luxembourg, http://epp.eurostat.ec.europa.eu; *Government Budgets.*

FINLAND - BUSINESS

Nordic Council of Ministers, Store Strandstraede 18, DK-1255 Copenhagen K, Denmark, www.norden.org; *Nordic Statistical Yearbook 2004-2006.*

Organisation for Economic Cooperation and Development (OECD), 2 rue Andre Pascal, F-75775 Paris Cedex 16, France, (Telephone in U.S. (202) 785-6323), (Fax in U.S. (202) 785-0350), www.oecd.org; *OECD Main Economic Indicators (MEI).*

FINLAND - CADMIUM PRODUCTION

See FINLAND - MINERAL INDUSTRIES

FINLAND - CAPITAL INVESTMENTS

Organisation for Economic Cooperation and Development (OECD), 2 rue Andre Pascal, F-75775 Paris Cedex 16, France, (Telephone in U.S. (202) 785-6323), (Fax in U.S. (202) 785-0350), www.oecd.org; *Financial Market Trends: OECD Periodical* and *OECD Economic Outlook 2008.*

FINLAND - CAPITAL LEVY

International Monetary Fund (IMF), 700 Nineteenth Street, NW, Washington, DC 20431, (202) 623-7000, Fax: (202) 623-4661, www.imf.org; *Government Finance Statistics Yearbook (2008 Edition).*

Organisation for Economic Cooperation and Development (OECD), 2 rue Andre Pascal, F-75775 Paris Cedex 16, France, (Telephone in U.S. (202) 785-6323), (Fax in U.S. (202) 785-0350), www.oecd.org; *Financial Market Trends: OECD Periodical* and *OECD Economic Outlook 2008.*

FINLAND - CATTLE

See FINLAND - LIVESTOCK

FINLAND - CHILDBIRTH - STATISTICS

Central Intelligence Agency, Office of Public Affairs, Washington, DC 20505, (703) 482-0623, Fax: (703) 482-1739, www.cia.gov; *The World Factbook.*

Euromonitor International, Inc., 224 S. Michigan Avenue, Suite 1500, Chicago, IL 60604, (312) 922-1115, Fax: (312) 922-1157, www.euromonitor.com; *The World Economic Factbook 2008.*

M.E. Sharpe, 80 Business Park Drive, Armonk, NY 10504, (800) 541-6563, Fax: (914) 273-2106, www.mesharpe.com; *The Illustrated Book of World Rankings.*

Nordic Council of Ministers, Store Strandstraede 18, DK-1255 Copenhagen K, Denmark, www.norden.org; *Nordic Statistical Yearbook 2004-2006.*

Palgrave Macmillan Ltd., Houndmills, Basingstoke, Hampshire, RG21 6XS, England, (Telephone in U.S. (888) 330-8477), (Fax in U.S. (800) 672-2054), www.palgrave.com; *The Statesman's Yearbook 2008.*

Taylor and Francis Group, An Informa Business, 2 Park Square, Milton Park, Abingdon, Oxford OX14 4RN, United Kingdom, (Dial from U.S. (212) 216-7800), (Fax from U.S. (212) 564-7854), www.tandf.co.uk; *The Europa World Year Book.*

United Nations Statistics Division, New York, NY 10017, (800) 253-9646, Fax: (212) 963-4116, http://unstats.un.org; *Demographic Yearbook* and *Statistical Yearbook.*

The World Bank, 1818 H Street, NW, Washington, DC 20433, (202) 473-1000, Fax: (202) 477-6391, www.worldbank.org; *World Development Indicators (WDI) 2008.*

World Health Organization (WHO), Avenue Appia 20, 1211 Geneve 27, Switzerland, (Telephone in U.S. (212) 331-9081), www.who.int; *World Health Report 2006.*

FINLAND - CLIMATE

M.E. Sharpe, 80 Business Park Drive, Armonk, NY 10504, (800) 541-6563, Fax: (914) 273-2106, www.mesharpe.com; *The Illustrated Book of World Rankings.*

Nordic Council of Ministers, Store Strandstraede 18, DK-1255 Copenhagen K, Denmark, www.norden.org; *Nordic Statistical Yearbook 2004-2006.*

Palgrave Macmillan Ltd., Houndmills, Basingstoke, Hampshire, RG21 6XS, England, (Telephone in U.S. (888) 330-8477), (Fax in U.S. (800) 672-2054), www.palgrave.com; *The Statesman's Yearbook 2008.*

FINLAND - CLOTHING EXPORTS AND IMPORTS

See FINLAND - TEXTILE INDUSTRY

FINLAND - COAL PRODUCTION

See FINLAND - MINERAL INDUSTRIES

FINLAND - COBALT PRODUCTION

See FINLAND - MINERAL INDUSTRIES

FINLAND - COFFEE

See FINLAND - CROPS

FINLAND - COMMERCE

Palgrave Macmillan Ltd., Houndmills, Basingstoke, Hampshire, RG21 6XS, England, (Telephone in U.S. (888) 330-8477), (Fax in U.S. (800) 672-2054), www.palgrave.com; *The Statesman's Yearbook 2008.*

FINLAND - COMMODITY EXCHANGES

Commodity Research Bureau, 330 South Wells Street, Suite 612, Chicago, IL 60606-7110, (800) 621-5271, Fax: (312) 939-4135, www.crbtrader.com; *2006 CRB Commodity Yearbook and CD.*

International Lead and Zinc Study Group (ILZSG), Rua Almirante Barroso 38, 5th Floor, Lisbon 1000 - 013, Portugal, www.ilzsg.org; Interactive Statistical Database.

International Monetary Fund (IMF), 700 Nineteenth Street, NW, Washington, DC 20431, (202) 623-7000, Fax: (202) 623-4661, www.imf.org; *IMF Primary Commodity Prices.*

United Nations Food and Agricultural Organization (FAO), Viale delle Terme di Caracalla, 00100 Rome, Italy, (Dial from U.S. (202) 653-2400), (Fax from U.S. (202) 653 5760), www.fao.org; *The State of Food and Agriculture (SOFA) 2006.*

United Nations Statistics Division, New York, NY 10017, (800) 253-9646, Fax: (212) 963-4116, http://unstats.un.org; *Statistical Yearbook.*

World Bureau of Metal Statistics (WBMS), 27a High Street, Ware, Hertfordshire, SG12 9BA, United Kingdom, www.world-bureau.com; *Annual Stainless Steel Statistics; World Flow Charts; World Metal Statistics; World Nickel Statistics;* and *World Tin Statistics.*

FINLAND - COMMUNICATION AND TRAFFIC

Nordic Council of Ministers, Store Strandstraede 18, DK-1255 Copenhagen K, Denmark, www.norden.org; *Nordic Statistical Yearbook 2004-2006.*

United Nations Statistics Division, New York, NY 10017, (800) 253-9646, Fax: (212) 963-4116, http://unstats.un.org; *Statistical Yearbook.*

FINLAND - CONSTRUCTION INDUSTRY

M.E. Sharpe, 80 Business Park Drive, Armonk, NY 10504, (800) 541-6563, Fax: (914) 273-2106, www.mesharpe.com; *The Illustrated Book of World Rankings.*

Organisation for Economic Cooperation and Development (OECD), 2 rue Andre Pascal, F-75775 Paris Cedex 16, France, (Telephone in U.S. (202) 785-6323), (Fax in U.S. (202) 785-0350). www.oecd.org; *OECD Economic Survey - Finland 2008; OECD Main Economic Indicators (MEI);* and STructural ANalysis (STAN) database.

United Nations Statistics Division, New York, NY 10017, (800) 253-9646, Fax: (212) 963-4116, http://unstats.un.org; *Statistical Yearbook.*

FINLAND - CONSUMER PRICE INDEXES

Nordic Council of Ministers, Store Strandstraede 18, DK-1255 Copenhagen K, Denmark, www.norden.org; *Nordic Statistical Yearbook 2004-2006.*

Organisation for Economic Cooperation and Development (OECD), 2 rue Andre Pascal, F-75775 Paris Cedex 16, France, (Telephone in U.S. (202) 785-6323), (Fax in U.S. (202) 785-0350), www.oecd.org; *OECD Economic Outlook 2008.*

Taylor and Francis Group, An Informa Business, 2 Park Square, Milton Park, Abingdon, Oxford OX14 4RN, United Kingdom, (Dial from U.S. (212) 216-7800), (Fax from U.S. (212) 564-7854), www.tandf.co.uk; *The Europa World Year Book.*

United Nations Statistics Division, New York, NY 10017, (800) 253-9646, Fax: (212) 963-4116, http://unstats.un.org; *Statistical Yearbook* and *Trends in Europe and North America: The Statistical Yearbook of the ECE 2005.*

The World Bank, 1818 H Street, NW, Washington, DC 20433, (202) 473-1000, Fax: (202) 477-6391, www.worldbank.org; *Finland.*

FINLAND - CONSUMPTION (ECONOMICS)

International Lead and Zinc Study Group (ILZSG), Rua Almirante Barroso 38, 5th Floor, Lisbon 1000 - 013, Portugal, www.ilzsg.org; Interactive Statistical Database.

International Monetary Fund (IMF), 700 Nineteenth Street, NW, Washington, DC 20431, (202) 623-7000, Fax: (202) 623-4661, www.imf.org; *International Financial Statistics Yearbook 2007.*

Nordic Council of Ministers, Store Strandstraede 18, DK-1255 Copenhagen K, Denmark, www.norden.org; *Nordic Statistical Yearbook 2004-2006.*

Organisation for Economic Cooperation and Development (OECD), 2 rue Andre Pascal, F-75775 Paris Cedex 16, France, (Telephone in U.S. (202) 785-6323), (Fax in U.S. (202) 785-0350), www.oecd.org; *Environmental Impacts of Foreign Direct Investment in the Mining Sector in the Newly Independent States (NIS); Iron and Steel Industry in 2004 (2006 Edition); A New World Map in Textiles and Clothing: Adjusting to Change; 2005 OECD Agricultural Outlook Tables, 1970-2014; Revenue Statistics 1965-2006 - 2007 Edition;* and *Towards Sustainable Household Consumption?: Trends and Policies in OECD Countries.*

Technical Association of the Pulp and Paper Industry (TAPPI), 15 Technology Parkway South, Norcross, GA 30092, (770) 446-1400, Fax: (770) 446-6947, www.tappi.org; *TAPPI Annual Report.*

The World Bank, 1818 H Street, NW, Washington, DC 20433, (202) 473-1000, Fax: (202) 477-6391, www.worldbank.org; *World Development Report 2008.*

FINLAND - COPPER INDUSTRY AND TRADE

See FINLAND - MINERAL INDUSTRIES

FINLAND - CORN INDUSTRY

See FINLAND - CROPS

FINLAND - COST AND STANDARD OF LIVING

International Monetary Fund (IMF), 700 Nineteenth Street, NW, Washington, DC 20431, (202) 623-7000, Fax: (202) 623-4661, www.imf.org; *Government Finance Statistics Yearbook (2008 Edition).*

Nordic Council of Ministers, Store Strandstraede 18, DK-1255 Copenhagen K, Denmark, www.norden.org; *Nordic Statistical Yearbook 2004-2006.*

Organisation for Economic Cooperation and Development (OECD), 2 rue Andre Pascal, F-75775 Paris Cedex 16, France, (Telephone in U.S. (202) 785-6323), (Fax in U.S. (202) 785-0350), www.oecd.org; *Iron and Steel Industry in 2004 (2006 Edition).*

FINLAND - COTTON

See FINLAND - CROPS

FINLAND - CRIME

Eurostat, Batiment Jean Monnet, Rue Alcide de Gasperi, L-2920 Luxembourg, http://epp.eurostat.ec.europa.eu; *Crime and Criminal Justice; General Government Expenditure and Revenue in the EU, 2006;* and *Study on Crime Victimisation.*

International Criminal Police Organization (INTERPOL), General Secretariat, 200 quai Charles de Gaulle, 69006 Lyon, France, www.interpol.int; *International Crime Statistics.*

Nordic Council of Ministers, Store Strandstraede 18, DK-1255 Copenhagen K, Denmark, www.norden.org; *Nordic Statistical Yearbook 2004-2006.*

U.S. Department of Justice (DOJ), Bureau of Justice Statistics, 810 Seventh Street, NW, Washington, DC 20531, (202) 307-0765, www.ojp.usdoj.gov/bjs/; *The World Factbook of Criminal Justice Systems.*

United Nations Statistics Division, New York, NY 10017, (800) 253-9646, Fax: (212) 963-4116, http://unstats.un.org; *Trends in Europe and North America: The Statistical Yearbook of the ECE 2005.*

FINLAND - CROPS

Euromonitor International, Inc., 224 S. Michigan Avenue, Suite 1500, Chicago, IL 60604, (312) 922-1115, Fax: (312) 922-1157, www.euromonitor.com; *European Marketing Data and Statistics 2008.*

M.E. Sharpe, 80 Business Park Drive, Armonk, NY 10504, (800) 541-6563, Fax: (914) 273-2106, www.mesharpe.com; *The Illustrated Book of World Rankings.*

Organisation for Economic Cooperation and Development (OECD), 2 rue Andre Pascal, F-75775 Paris Cedex 16, France, (Telephone in U.S. (202) 785-6323), (Fax in U.S. (202) 785-0350), www.oecd.org; *International Trade by Commodity Statistics (ITCS)* and *2005 OECD Agricultural Outlook Tables, 1970-2014.*

Palgrave Macmillan Ltd., Houndmills, Basingstoke, Hampshire, RG21 6XS, England, (Telephone in U.S. (888) 330-8477), (Fax in U.S. (800) 672-2054), www.palgrave.com; *The Statesman's Yearbook 2008.*

Taylor and Francis Group, An Informa Business, 2 Park Square, Milton Park, Abingdon, Oxford OX14 4RN, United Kingdom, (Dial from U.S. (212) 216-7800), (Fax from U.S. (212) 564-7854), www.tandf.co.uk; *The Europa World Year Book.*

United Nations Conference on Trade and Development (UNCTAD), DC2-1120, United Nations, New York, NY 10017, (212) 963-0027, www.unctad.org; *UNCTAD Commodity Yearbook.*

United Nations Food and Agricultural Organization (FAO), Viale delle Terme di Caracalla, 00100 Rome, Italy, (Dial from U.S. (202) 653-2400), (Fax from U.S. (202) 653 5760), www.fao.org; *FAO Production Yearbook 2002* and *The State of Food and Agriculture (SOFA) 2006.*

FINLAND - CUSTOMS ADMINISTRATION

International Monetary Fund (IMF), 700 Nineteenth Street, NW, Washington, DC 20431, (202) 623-7000, Fax: (202) 623-4661, www.imf.org; *Government Finance Statistics Yearbook (2008 Edition).*

Organisation for Economic Cooperation and Development (OECD), 2 rue Andre Pascal, F-75775 Paris Cedex 16, France, (Telephone in U.S. (202) 785-6323), (Fax in U.S. (202) 785-0350), www.oecd.org; *Environmental Impacts of Foreign Direct Investment in the Mining Sector in the Newly Independent States (NIS).*

Palgrave Macmillan Ltd., Houndmills, Basingstoke, Hampshire, RG21 6XS, England, (Telephone in U.S. (888) 330-8477), (Fax in U.S. (800) 672-2054), www.palgrave.com; *The Statesman's Yearbook 2008.*

FINLAND - DAIRY PROCESSING

M.E. Sharpe, 80 Business Park Drive, Armonk, NY 10504, (800) 541-6563, Fax: (914) 273-2106, www.mesharpe.com; *The Illustrated Book of World Rankings.*

Nordic Council of Ministers, Store Strandstraede 18, DK-1255 Copenhagen K, Denmark, www.norden.org; *Nordic Statistical Yearbook 2004-2006.*

Organisation for Economic Cooperation and Development (OECD), 2 rue Andre Pascal, F-75775 Paris Cedex 16, France, (Telephone in U.S. (202) 785-6323), (Fax in U.S. (202) 785-0350), www.oecd.org; *2005 OECD Agricultural Outlook Tables, 1970-2014.*

Palgrave Macmillan Ltd., Houndmills, Basingstoke, Hampshire, RG21 6XS, England, (Telephone in U.S. (888) 330-8477), (Fax in U.S. (800) 672-2054), www.palgrave.com; *The Statesman's Yearbook 2008.*

Taylor and Francis Group, An Informa Business, 2 Park Square, Milton Park, Abingdon, Oxford OX14 4RN, United Kingdom, (Dial from U.S. (212) 216-7800), (Fax from U.S. (212) 564-7854), www.tandf.co.uk; *The Europa World Year Book.*

United Nations Food and Agricultural Organization (FAO), Viale delle Terme di Caracalla, 00100 Rome, Italy, (Dial from U.S. (202) 653-2400), (Fax from U.S. (202) 653 5760), www.fao.org; *FAO Production Yearbook 2002* and *The State of Food and Agriculture (SOFA) 2006.*

United Nations Statistics Division, New York, NY 10017, (800) 253-9646, Fax: (212) 963-4116, http://unstats.un.org; *Statistical Yearbook.*

FINLAND - DEATH RATES

See FINLAND - MORTALITY

FINLAND - DEBTS, EXTERNAL

International Monetary Fund (IMF), 700 Nineteenth Street, NW, Washington, DC 20431, (202) 623-7000, Fax: (202) 623-4661, www.imf.org; *Government Finance Statistics Yearbook (2008 Edition).*

Organisation for Economic Cooperation and Development (OECD), 2 rue Andre Pascal, F-75775 Paris Cedex 16, France, (Telephone in U.S. (202) 785-6323), (Fax in U.S. (202) 785-0350), www.oecd.org; *Financial Market Trends: OECD Periodical; Geographical Distribution of Financial Flows to Aid Recipients 2002-2006;* and *OECD Economic Outlook 2008.*

Palgrave Macmillan Ltd., Houndmills, Basingstoke, Hampshire, RG21 6XS, England, (Telephone in U.S. (888) 330-8477), (Fax in U.S. (800) 672-2054), www.palgrave.com; *The Statesman's Yearbook 2008.*

The World Bank, 1818 H Street, NW, Washington, DC 20433, (202) 473-1000, Fax: (202) 477-6391, www.worldbank.org; *Global Development Finance 2007; World Development Indicators (WDI) 2008;* and *World Development Report 2008.*

FINLAND - DEFENSE EXPENDITURES

See FINLAND - ARMED FORCES

FINLAND - DEMOGRAPHY

Euromonitor International, Inc., 224 S. Michigan Avenue, Suite 1500, Chicago, IL 60604, (312) 922-1115, Fax: (312) 922-1157, www.euromonitor.com; *The World Economic Factbook 2008* and *World Marketing Data and Statistics.*

Eurostat, Batiment Jean Monnet, Rue Alcide de Gasperi, L-2920 Luxembourg, http://epp.eurostat.ec.europa.eu; *Demographic Outlook - National Reports on the Demographic Developments in 2006* and *Demographic Outlook - National Reports on the Demographic Developments in 2006.*

M.E. Sharpe, 80 Business Park Drive, Armonk, NY 10504, (800) 541-6563, Fax: (914) 273-2106, www.mesharpe.com; *The Illustrated Book of World Rankings.*

Nordic Council of Ministers, Store Strandstraede 18, DK-1255 Copenhagen K, Denmark, www.norden.org; *Nordic Statistical Yearbook 2004-2006.*

United Nations Statistics Division, New York, NY 10017, (800) 253-9646, Fax: (212) 963-4116, http://unstats.un.org; *Human Development Report 2006.*

The World Bank, 1818 H Street, NW, Washington, DC 20433, (202) 473-1000, Fax: (202) 477-6391, www.worldbank.org; *Finland.*

FINLAND - DIAMONDS

See FINLAND - MINERAL INDUSTRIES

FINLAND - DISPOSABLE INCOME

M.E. Sharpe, 80 Business Park Drive, Armonk, NY 10504, (800) 541-6563, Fax: (914) 273-2106, www.mesharpe.com; *The Illustrated Book of World Rankings.*

Nordic Council of Ministers, Store Strandstraede 18, DK-1255 Copenhagen K, Denmark, www.norden.org; *Nordic Statistical Yearbook 2004-2006.*

Organisation for Economic Cooperation and Development (OECD), 2 rue Andre Pascal, F-75775 Paris Cedex 16, France, (Telephone in U.S. (202) 785-6323), (Fax in U.S. (202) 785-0350), www.oecd.org; *OECD Economic Outlook 2008.*

United Nations Statistics Division, New York, NY 10017, (800) 253-9646, Fax: (212) 963-4116, http://unstats.un.org; *National Accounts Statistics: Compendium of Income Distribution Statistics* and *Statistical Yearbook.*

FINLAND - DIVORCE

M.E. Sharpe, 80 Business Park Drive, Armonk, NY 10504, (800) 541-6563, Fax: (914) 273-2106, www.mesharpe.com; *The Illustrated Book of World Rankings.*

Nordic Council of Ministers, Store Strandstraede 18, DK-1255 Copenhagen K, Denmark, www.norden.org; *Nordic Statistical Yearbook 2004-2006.*

United Nations Statistics Division, New York, NY 10017, (800) 253-9646, Fax: (212) 963-4116, http://unstats.un.org; *Demographic Yearbook; Statistical Yearbook;* and *Trends in Europe and North America: The Statistical Yearbook of the ECE 2005.*

FINLAND - ECONOMIC ASSISTANCE

Organisation for Economic Cooperation and Development (OECD), 2 rue Andre Pascal, F-75775 Paris Cedex 16, France, (Telephone in U.S. (202) 785-6323), (Fax in U.S. (202) 785-0350), www.oecd.org; *Geographical Distribution of Financial Flows to Aid Recipients 2002-2006.*

United Nations Statistics Division, New York, NY 10017, (800) 253-9646, Fax: (212) 963-4116, http://unstats.un.org; *Statistical Yearbook.*

FINLAND - ECONOMIC CONDITIONS

Banque de France, 48 rue Croix des Petits champs, 75001 Paris, France, www.banque-france.fr/home.htm; *Key Data for the Euro Area.*

Center for International Business Education Research (CIBER), Columbia Business School and School of International and Public Affairs, Uris Hall, Room 212, 3022 Broadway, New York, NY 10027-6902, Mr. Joshua Safier, (212) 854-4750, Fax: (212) 222-9821, www.columbia.edu/cu/ciber/; Datastream International.

Central Intelligence Agency, Office of Public Affairs, Washington, DC 20505, (703) 482-0623, Fax: (703) 482-1739, www.cia.gov; *The World Factbook.*

DSI Data Service Information, Xantener Strasse 51a, D-47495 Rheinberg, Germany, www.dsidata.com; *Campus Solution.*

Dun and Bradstreet (DB) Corporation, 103 JFK Parkway, Short Hills, NJ 07078, (973) 921-5500, www.dnb.com; *Country Report.*

Economist Intelligence Unit, 111 West 57th Street, New York, NY 10019, (212) 554-0600, Fax: (212) 586-1181, www.eiu.com; *Finland Country Report.*

Euromonitor International, Inc., 224 S. Michigan Avenue, Suite 1500, Chicago, IL 60604, (312) 922-1115, Fax: (312) 922-1157, www.euromonitor.com; *European Marketing Data and Statistics 2008; The World Economic Factbook 2008;* and *World Marketing Data and Statistics.*

European Union, Delegation of the European Commission to the United States, 2300 M Street, NW, Washington, DC 20037, (202) 862-9500, Fax: (202) 429-1766, www.eurunion.org; *The EU Economy, 2007 Review: Moving Europe's Productivity Frontier.*

Eurostat, Batiment Jean Monnet, Rue Alcide de Gasperi, L-2920 Luxembourg, http://epp.eurostat.ec.europa.eu; *Consumers in Europe - Facts and Figures on Services of General Interest* and *EU Economic Data Pocketbook.*

International Monetary Fund (IMF), 700 Nineteenth Street, NW, Washington, DC 20431, (202) 623-7000, Fax: (202) 623-4661, www.imf.org; *World Economic Outlook Reports.*

M.E. Sharpe, 80 Business Park Drive, Armonk, NY 10504, (800) 541-6563, Fax: (914) 273-2106, www.mesharpe.com; *The Illustrated Book of World Rankings.*

Organisation for Economic Cooperation and Development (OECD), 2 rue Andre Pascal, F-75775 Paris Cedex 16, France, (Telephone in U.S. (202) 785-6323), (Fax in U.S. (202) 785-0350), www.oecd.org; *Geographical Distribution of Financial Flows to Aid Recipients 2002-2006; ICT Sector Data and Metadata by Country; Labour Force Statistics: 1986-2005, 2007 Edition; OECD Composite Leading Indicators (CLIs), Updated September 2007; OECD Economic Outlook 2008; OECD Economic Survey - Finland 2008; OECD Employment Outlook 2007; OECD in Figures 2007;* and *OECD Main Economic Indicators (MEI).*

Palgrave Macmillan Ltd., Houndmills, Basingstoke, Hampshire, RG21 6XS, England, (Telephone in U.S. (888) 330-8477), (Fax in U.S. (800) 672-2054), www.palgrave.com; *The Statesman's Yearbook 2008.*

Taylor and Francis Group, An Informa Business, 2 Park Square, Milton Park, Abingdon, Oxford OX14 4RN, United Kingdom, (Dial from U.S. (212) 216-7800), (Fax from U.S. (212) 564-7854), www.tandf.co.uk; *The Europa World Year Book.*

United Nations Statistics Division, New York, NY 10017, (800) 253-9646, Fax: (212) 963-4116, http://unstats.un.org; *World Statistics Pocketbook.*

The World Bank, 1818 H Street, NW, Washington, DC 20433, (202) 473-1000, Fax: (202) 477-6391, www.worldbank.org; *Finland; Global Economic Monitor (GEM); Global Economic Prospects 2008; The World Bank Atlas 2003-2004;* and *World Development Report 2008.*

FINLAND - ECONOMICS - SOCIOLOGICAL ASPECTS

Organisation for Economic Cooperation and Development (OECD), 2 rue Andre Pascal, F-75775 Paris Cedex 16, France, (Telephone in U.S. (202) 785-6323), (Fax in U.S. (202) 785-0350), www.oecd.org; *OECD Economic Outlook 2008.*

FINLAND - EDUCATION

Euromonitor International, Inc., 224 S. Michigan Avenue, Suite 1500, Chicago, IL 60604, (312) 922-1115, Fax: (312) 922-1157, www.euromonitor.com; *European Marketing Data and Statistics 2008* and *World Marketing Data and Statistics.*

European Union, Delegation of the European Commission to the United States, 2300 M Street, NW, Washington, DC 20037, (202) 862-9500, Fax: (202) 429-1766, www.eurunion.org; *Education across Europe 2003.*

Eurostat, Batiment Jean Monnet, Rue Alcide de Gasperi, L-2920 Luxembourg, http://epp.eurostat.ec.europa.eu; *Education, Science and Culture Statistics.*

International Monetary Fund (IMF), 700 Nineteenth Street, NW, Washington, DC 20431, (202) 623-7000, Fax: (202) 623-4661, www.imf.org; *Government Finance Statistics Yearbook (2008 Edition).*

M.E. Sharpe, 80 Business Park Drive, Armonk, NY 10504, (800) 541-6563, Fax: (914) 273-2106, www.mesharpe.com; *The Illustrated Book of World Rankings.*

Nordic Council of Ministers, Store Strandstraede 18, DK-1255 Copenhagen K, Denmark, www.norden.org; *Nordic Statistical Yearbook 2004-2006.*

Organisation for Economic Cooperation and Development (OECD), 2 rue Andre Pascal, F-75775 Paris Cedex 16, France, (Telephone in U.S. (202) 785-6323), (Fax in U.S. (202) 785-0350), www.oecd.org; *Education at a Glance* (2007 Edition).

Palgrave Macmillan Ltd., Houndmills, Basingstoke, Hampshire, RG21 6XS, England, (Telephone in U.S. (888) 330-8477), (Fax in U.S. (800) 672-2054), www.palgrave.com; *The Statesman's Yearbook 2008.*

Taylor and Francis Group, An Informa Business, 2 Park Square, Milton Park, Abingdon, Oxford OX14 4RN, United Kingdom, (Dial from U.S. (212) 216-7800), (Fax from U.S. (212) 564-7854), www.tandf.co.uk; *The Europa World Year Book.*

UNESCO Institute for Statistics, C.P. 6128 Succursale Centre-Ville, Montreal, Quebec, H3C 3J7 Canada, (Dial from U.S. (514) 343-6880), (Fax from U.S. (514) 343 6882), www.uis.unesco.org; *Statistical Tables.*

United Nations Statistics Division, New York, NY 10017, (800) 253-9646, Fax: (212) 963-4116, http://unstats.un.org; *Human Development Report 2006* and *Trends in Europe and North America: The Statistical Yearbook of the ECE 2005.*

The World Bank, 1818 H Street, NW, Washington, DC 20433, (202) 473-1000, Fax: (202) 477-6391, www.worldbank.org; *Finland; World Development Indicators (WDI) 2008;* and *World Development Report 2008.*

FINLAND - ELECTRICITY

Eurostat, Batiment Jean Monnet, Rue Alcide de Gasperi, L-2920 Luxembourg, http://epp.eurostat.ec.europa.eu; *Energy - Monthly Statistics* and *Panorama of Energy - 2007 Edition.*

M.E. Sharpe, 80 Business Park Drive, Armonk, NY 10504, (800) 541-6563, Fax: (914) 273-2106, www.mesharpe.com; *The Illustrated Book of World Rankings.*

Nordic Council of Ministers, Store Strandstraede 18, DK-1255 Copenhagen K, Denmark, www.norden.org; *Nordic Statistical Yearbook 2004-2006.*

Organisation for Economic Cooperation and Development (OECD), 2 rue Andre Pascal, F-75775 Paris Cedex 16, France, (Telephone in U.S. (202) 785-6323), (Fax in U.S. (202) 785-0350), www.oecd.org; *Coal Information: 2007 Edition; Energy Statistics of OECD Countries* (2007 Edition); *Indicators of Industrial Activity;* and STructural ANalysis (STAN) database.

Palgrave Macmillan Ltd., Houndmills, Basingstoke, Hampshire, RG21 6XS, England, (Telephone in U.S. (888) 330-8477), (Fax in U.S. (800) 672-2054), www.palgrave.com; *The Statesman's Yearbook 2008.*

Platts, 2 Penn Plaza, 25th Floor, New York, NY 10121-2298, (212) 904-3070, www.platts.com; *EU Energy* and *European Electricity Review 2004.*

U.S. Department of Energy (DOE), Energy Information Administration (EIA), 1000 Independence Avenue, SW, Washington, DC 20585, (202) 586-8800, www.eia.doe.gov; *International Energy Annual 2004* and *International Energy Outlook 2006.*

United Nations Statistics Division, New York, NY 10017, (800) 253-9646, Fax: (212) 963-4116, http://unstats.un.org; *Human Development Report 2006; Statistical Yearbook;* and *Trends in Europe and North America: The Statistical Yearbook of the ECE 2005.*

FINLAND - EMPLOYMENT

Bernan Essential Government Publications, 4611-F Assembly Drive, Lanham MD, 20706-4391, (301) 459-2255, Fax: (800) 865-3450, www.bernan.com; *OECD Factbook 2006.*

Euromonitor International, Inc., 224 S. Michigan Avenue, Suite 1500, Chicago, IL 60604, (312) 922-1115, Fax: (312) 922-1157, www.euromonitor.com; *European Marketing Data and Statistics 2008.*

International Labour Office, I.L.O. Publications, 4 route des Morillons, CH-1211 Geneva 22, Switzerland, (Telephone in U.S. (202) 653-7652), (Fax in U.S. (202) 653-7687), www.ilo.org; *Yearbook of Labour Statistics 2006.*

M.E. Sharpe, 80 Business Park Drive, Armonk, NY 10504, (800) 541-6563, Fax: (914) 273-2106, www.mesharpe.com; *The Illustrated Book of World Rankings.*

Nordic Council of Ministers, Store Strandstraede 18, DK-1255 Copenhagen K, Denmark, www.norden.org; *Nordic Statistical Yearbook 2004-2006.*

Organisation for Economic Cooperation and Development (OECD), 2 rue Andre Pascal, F-75775 Paris Cedex 16, France, (Telephone in U.S. (202) 785-6323), (Fax in U.S. (202) 785-0350), www.oecd.org; *ICT Sector Data and Metadata by Country; Iron and Steel Industry in 2004 (2006 Edition); Labour Force Statistics: 1986-2005, 2007 Edition; A New World Map in Textiles and Clothing: Adjusting to Change; OECD Composite Leading Indicators (CLIs), Updated September 2007; OECD Economic Outlook 2008; OECD Economic Survey - Finland 2008; OECD Employment Outlook 2007;* and *OECD in Figures 2007.*

United Nations Statistics Division, New York, NY 10017, (800) 253-9646, Fax: (212) 963-4116, http://unstats.un.org; *Statistical Yearbook* and *Trends in Europe and North America: The Statistical Yearbook of the ECE 2005.*

The World Bank, 1818 H Street, NW, Washington, DC 20433, (202) 473-1000, Fax: (202) 477-6391, www.worldbank.org; *Finland.*

FINLAND - ENERGY INDUSTRIES

Enerdata, 10 Rue Royale, 75008 Paris, France, www.enerdata.fr; *Global Energy Market Data.*

Eurostat, Batiment Jean Monnet, Rue Alcide de Gasperi, L-2920 Luxembourg, http://epp.eurostat.ec.europa.eu; *Energy - Monthly Statistics* and *Panorama of Energy - 2007 Edition.*

International Energy Agency (IEA), 9, rue de la Federation, 75739 Paris Cedex 15, France, www.iea.org; *Key World Energy Statistics 2007.*

Organisation for Economic Cooperation and Development (OECD), 2 rue Andre Pascal, F-75775 Paris Cedex 16, France, (Telephone in U.S. (202) 785-6323), (Fax in U.S. (202) 785-0350), www.oecd.org; *Towards Sustainable Household Consumption?: Trends and Policies in OECD Countries.*

Platts, 2 Penn Plaza, 25th Floor, New York, NY 10121-2298, (212) 904-3070, www.platts.com; *EU Energy* and *European Power Daily.*

United Nations Statistics Division, New York, NY 10017, (800) 253-9646, Fax: (212) 963-4116, http://unstats.un.org; *Statistical Yearbook.*

FINLAND - ENVIRONMENTAL CONDITIONS

Center for Research on the Epidemiology of Disasters (CRED), Universite Catholique de Louvain, Ecole de Sante Publique, 30.94 Clos Chapelle-aux-Champs, 1200 Brussels, Belgium, www.cred.be; *Three Decades of Floods in Europe: A Preliminary Analysis of EMDAT Data.*

DSI Data Service Information, Xantener Strasse 51a, D-47495 Rheinberg, Germany, www.dsidata.com; *Campus Solution* and *DSI's Global Environmental Database.*

Economist Intelligence Unit, 111 West 57th Street, New York, NY 10019, (212) 554-0600, Fax: (212) 586-1181, www.eiu.com; *Finland Country Report.*

Eurostat, Batiment Jean Monnet, Rue Alcide de Gasperi, L-2920 Luxembourg, http://epp.eurostat.ec.europa.eu; *Environmental Protection Expenditure in Europe.*

Organisation for Economic Cooperation and Development (OECD), 2 rue Andre Pascal, F-75775 Paris Cedex 16, France, (Telephone in U.S. (202) 785-6323), (Fax in U.S. (202) 785-0350), www.oecd.org; *Key Environmental Indicators 2004.*

Platts, 2 Penn Plaza, 25th Floor, New York, NY 10121-2298, (212) 904-3070, www.platts.com; *Emissions Daily.*

United Nations Statistics Division, New York, NY 10017, (800) 253-9646, Fax: (212) 963-4116, http://unstats.un.org; *Trends in Europe and North America: The Statistical Yearbook of the ECE 2005* and *World Statistics Pocketbook.*

FINLAND - EXPENDITURES, PUBLIC

Eurostat, Batiment Jean Monnet, Rue Alcide de Gasperi, L-2920 Luxembourg, http://epp.eurostat.ec.europa.eu; *European Social Statistics - Social Protection Expenditure and Receipts - Data 1997-2005.*

Organisation for Economic Cooperation and Development (OECD), 2 rue Andre Pascal, F-75775 Paris Cedex 16, France, (Telephone in U.S. (202) 785-6323), (Fax in U.S. (202) 785-0350), www.oecd.org; *Revenue Statistics 1965-2006 - 2007 Edition.*

FINLAND - EXPORTS

Central Intelligence Agency, Office of Public Affairs, Washington, DC 20505, (703) 482-0623, Fax: (703) 482-1739, www.cia.gov; *The World Factbook.*

Economist Intelligence Unit, 111 West 57th Street, New York, NY 10019, (212) 554-0600, Fax: (212) 586-1181, www.eiu.com; *Finland Country Report.*

Euromonitor International, Inc., 224 S. Michigan Avenue, Suite 1500, Chicago, IL 60604, (312) 922-1115, Fax: (312) 922-1157, www.euromonitor.com; *The World Economic Factbook 2008.*

International Lead and Zinc Study Group (ILZSG), Rua Almirante Barroso 38, 5th Floor, Lisbon 1000 - 013, Portugal, www.ilzsg.org; Interactive Statistical Database.

International Monetary Fund (IMF), 700 Nineteenth Street, NW, Washington, DC 20431, (202) 623-7000, Fax: (202) 623-4661, www.imf.org; *Direction of Trade Statistics Yearbook 2007; Government Finance Statistics Yearbook (2008 Edition);* and *International Financial Statistics Yearbook 2007.*

Nordic Council of Ministers, Store Strandstraede 18, DK-1255 Copenhagen K, Denmark, www.norden.org; *Nordic Statistical Yearbook 2004-2006.*

Organisation for Economic Cooperation and Development (OECD), 2 rue Andre Pascal, F-75775 Paris Cedex 16, France, (Telephone in U.S. (202) 785-6323), (Fax in U.S. (202) 785-0350), www.oecd.org; *Geographical Distribution of Financial Flows to Aid Recipients 2002-2006; International Trade by Commodity Statistics (ITCS); Iron and Steel Industry in 2004 (2006 Edition); 2005 OECD Agricultural Outlook Tables, 1970-2014; OECD Economic Outlook 2008; OECD Economic Survey - Finland 2008; Review of Fisheries in OECD Countries: Country Statistics 2001 to 2003 - 2005 Edition;* and STructural ANalysis (STAN) database.

Palgrave Macmillan Ltd., Houndmills, Basingstoke, Hampshire, RG21 6XS, England, (Telephone in U.S. (888) 330-8477), (Fax in U.S. (800) 672-2054), www.palgrave.com; *The Statesman's Yearbook 2008.*

Taylor and Francis Group, An Informa Business, 2 Park Square, Milton Park, Abingdon, Oxford OX14 4RN, United Kingdom, (Dial from U.S. (212) 216-7800), (Fax from U.S. (212) 564-7854), www.tandf.co.uk; *The Europa World Year Book.*

Technical Association of the Pulp and Paper Industry (TAPPI), 15 Technology Parkway South, Norcross, GA 30092, (770) 446-1400, Fax: (770) 446-6947, www.tappi.org; *TAPPI Annual Report.*

United Nations Conference on Trade and Development (UNCTAD), DC2-1120, United Nations, New York, NY 10017, (212) 963-0027, www.unctad.org; *Handbook of Statistics 2005.*

United Nations Food and Agricultural Organization (FAO), Viale delle Terme di Caracalla, 00100 Rome, Italy, (Dial from U.S. (202) 653-2400), (Fax from U.S. (202) 653 5760), www.fao.org; *The State of Food and Agriculture (SOFA) 2006.*

United Nations Statistics Division, New York, NY 10017, (800) 253-9646, Fax: (212) 963-4116, http://unstats.un.org; *Trends in Europe and North America: The Statistical Yearbook of the ECE 2005.*

The World Bank, 1818 H Street, NW, Washington, DC 20433, (202) 473-1000, Fax: (202) 477-6391, www.worldbank.org; *World Development Indicators (WDI) 2008* and *World Development Report 2008.*

FINLAND - FERTILITY, HUMAN

Central Intelligence Agency, Office of Public Affairs, Washington, DC 20505, (703) 482-0623, Fax: (703) 482-1739, www.cia.gov; *The World Factbook.*

M.E. Sharpe, 80 Business Park Drive, Armonk, NY 10504, (800) 541-6563, Fax: (914) 273-2106, www.mesharpe.com; *The Illustrated Book of World Rankings.*

Nordic Council of Ministers, Store Strandstraede 18, DK-1255 Copenhagen K, Denmark, www.norden.org; *Nordic Statistical Yearbook 2004-2006.*

United Nations Statistics Division, New York, NY 10017, (800) 253-9646, Fax: (212) 963-4116, http://unstats.un.org; *Human Development Report 2006* and *Trends in Europe and North America: The Statistical Yearbook of the ECE 2005.*

The World Bank, 1818 H Street, NW, Washington, DC 20433, (202) 473-1000, Fax: (202) 477-6391, www.worldbank.org; *The World Bank Atlas 2003-2004; World Development Indicators (WDI) 2008;* and *World Development Report 2008.*

FINLAND - FERTILIZER INDUSTRY

Organisation for Economic Cooperation and Development (OECD), 2 rue Andre Pascal, F-75775 Paris Cedex 16, France, (Telephone in U.S. (202) 785-6323), (Fax in U.S. (202) 785-0350), www.oecd.org; *International Trade by Commodity Statistics (ITCS)* and *2005 OECD Agricultural Outlook Tables, 1970-2014.*

United Nations Food and Agricultural Organization (FAO), Viale delle Terme di Caracalla, 00100 Rome, Italy, (Dial from U.S. (202) 653-2400), (Fax from U.S. (202) 653 5760), www.fao.org; *FAO Fertilizer Yearbook* and *The State of Food and Agriculture (SOFA) 2006.*

United Nations Statistics Division, New York, NY 10017, (800) 253-9646, Fax: (212) 963-4116, http://unstats.un.org; *Statistical Yearbook.*

FINLAND - FETAL MORTALITY

See FINLAND - MORTALITY

FINLAND - FILM

See FINLAND - MOTION PICTURES

FINLAND - FINANCE

International Monetary Fund (IMF), 700 Nineteenth Street, NW, Washington, DC 20431, (202) 623-7000, Fax: (202) 623-4661, www.imf.org; *International Financial Statistics Yearbook 2007.*

Nordic Council of Ministers, Store Strandstraede 18, DK-1255 Copenhagen K, Denmark, www.norden.org; *Nordic Statistical Yearbook 2004-2006.*

Organisation for Economic Cooperation and Development (OECD), 2 rue Andre Pascal, F-75775 Paris Cedex 16, France, (Telephone in U.S. (202) 785-6323), (Fax in U.S. (202) 785-0350), www.oecd.org; *OECD Economic Outlook 2008.*

Taylor and Francis Group, An Informa Business, 2 Park Square, Milton Park, Abingdon, Oxford OX14 4RN, United Kingdom, (Dial from U.S. (212) 216-7800), (Fax from U.S. (212) 564-7854), www.tandf.co.uk; *The Europa World Year Book.*

United Nations Statistics Division, New York, NY 10017, (800) 253-9646, Fax: (212) 963-4116, http://unstats.un.org; *National Accounts Statistics: Compendium of Income Distribution Statistics* and *Statistical Yearbook.*

The World Bank, 1818 H Street, NW, Washington, DC 20433, (202) 473-1000, Fax: (202) 477-6391, www.worldbank.org; *Finland.*

FINLAND - FINANCE, PUBLIC

Banque de France, 48 rue Croix des Petits champs, 75001 Paris, France, www.banque-france.fr/home.htm; *Key Data for the Euro Area* and *Public Finance.*

Bernan Essential Government Publications, 4611-F Assembly Drive, Lanham MD, 20706-4391, (301) 459-2255, Fax: (800) 865-3450, www.bernan.com; *National Accounts Statistics.*

Economist Intelligence Unit, 111 West 57th Street, New York, NY 10019, (212) 554-0600, Fax: (212) 586-1181, www.eiu.com; *Finland Country Report.*

International Monetary Fund (IMF), 700 Nineteenth Street, NW, Washington, DC 20431, (202) 623-7000, Fax: (202) 623-4661, www.imf.org; *Government Finance Statistics Yearbook (2008 Edition); International Financial Statistics; International Financial Statistics Online Service;* and *International Financial Statistics Yearbook 2007.*

M.E. Sharpe, 80 Business Park Drive, Armonk, NY 10504, (800) 541-6563, Fax: (914) 273-2106, www.mesharpe.com; *The Illustrated Book of World Rankings.*

Nordic Council of Ministers, Store Strandstraede 18, DK-1255 Copenhagen K, Denmark, www.norden.org; *Nordic Statistical Yearbook 2004-2006.*

Organisation for Economic Cooperation and Development (OECD), 2 rue Andre Pascal, F-75775 Paris Cedex 16, France, (Telephone in U.S. (202) 785-6323), (Fax in U.S. (202) 785-0350), www.oecd.org; *Financial Market Trends: OECD Periodical; Geographical Distribution of Financial Flows to Aid Recipients 2002-2006; OECD Economic Outlook 2008;* and *Revenue Statistics 1965-2006 - 2007 Edition.*

Palgrave Macmillan Ltd., Houndmills, Basingstoke, Hampshire, RG21 6XS, England, (Telephone in U.S. (888) 330-8477), (Fax in U.S. (800) 672-2054), www.palgrave.com; *The Statesman's Yearbook 2008.*

Taylor and Francis Group, An Informa Business, 2 Park Square, Milton Park, Abingdon, Oxford OX14 4RN, United Kingdom, (Dial from U.S. (212) 216-7800), (Fax from U.S. (212) 564-7854), www.tandf.co.uk; *The Europa World Year Book.*

The World Bank, 1818 H Street, NW, Washington, DC 20433, (202) 473-1000, Fax: (202) 477-6391, www.worldbank.org; *Finland.*

FINLAND - FISHERIES

Euromonitor International, Inc., 224 S. Michigan Avenue, Suite 1500, Chicago, IL 60604, (312) 922-1115, Fax: (312) 922-1157, www.euromonitor.com; *European Marketing Data and Statistics 2008.*

M.E. Sharpe, 80 Business Park Drive, Armonk, NY 10504, (800) 541-6563, Fax: (914) 273-2106, www.mesharpe.com; *The Illustrated Book of World Rankings.*

Nordic Council of Ministers, Store Strandstraede 18, DK-1255 Copenhagen K, Denmark, www.norden.org; *Nordic Statistical Yearbook 2004-2006.*

Organisation for Economic Cooperation and Development (OECD), 2 rue Andre Pascal, F-75775 Paris Cedex 16, France, (Telephone in U.S. (202) 785-6323), (Fax in U.S. (202) 785-0350), www.oecd.org; *International Trade by Commodity Statistics (ITCS); Review of Fisheries in OECD Countries: Country Statistics 2001 to 2003 - 2005 Edition;* and STructural ANalysis (STAN) database.

Taylor and Francis Group, An Informa Business, 2 Park Square, Milton Park, Abingdon, Oxford OX14 4RN, United Kingdom, (Dial from U.S. (212) 216-7800), (Fax from U.S. (212) 564-7854), www.tandf.co.uk; *The Europa World Year Book.*

United Nations Conference on Trade and Development (UNCTAD), DC2-1120, United Nations, New York, NY 10017, (212) 963-0027, www.unctad.org; *UNCTAD Commodity Yearbook.*

United Nations Food and Agricultural Organization (FAO), Viale delle Terme di Caracalla, 00100 Rome, Italy, (Dial from U.S. (202) 653-2400), (Fax from U.S. (202) 653 5760), www.fao.org; *FAO Yearbook of Fishery Statistics;* Fishery Databases; FISHSTAT Database. Subjects covered include: Aquaculture production, capture production, fishery commodities; and *The State of Food and Agriculture (SOFA) 2006.*

United Nations Statistics Division, New York, NY 10017, (800) 253-9646, Fax: (212) 963-4116, http://unstats.un.org; *Statistical Yearbook.*

The World Bank, 1818 H Street, NW, Washington, DC 20433, (202) 473-1000, Fax: (202) 477-6391, www.worldbank.org; *Finland.*

FINLAND - FLOUR INDUSTRY

United Nations Statistics Division, New York, NY 10017, (800) 253-9646, Fax: (212) 963-4116, http://unstats.un.org; *Statistical Yearbook.*

FINLAND - FOOD

Euromonitor International, Inc., 224 S. Michigan Avenue, Suite 1500, Chicago, IL 60604, (312) 922-1115, Fax: (312) 922-1157, www.euromonitor.com; *Retail Trade International 2007.*

Organisation for Economic Cooperation and Development (OECD), 2 rue Andre Pascal, F-75775 Paris Cedex 16, France, (Telephone in U.S. (202) 785-6323), (Fax in U.S. (202) 785-0350), www.oecd.org; *International Trade by Commodity Statistics (ITCS)* and *Towards Sustainable Household Consumption?: Trends and Policies in OECD Countries.*

United Nations Conference on Trade and Development (UNCTAD), DC2-1120, United Nations, New York, NY 10017, (212) 963-0027, www.unctad.org; *UNCTAD Commodity Yearbook.*

United Nations Food and Agricultural Organization (FAO), Viale delle Terme di Caracalla, 00100 Rome, Italy, (Dial from U.S. (202) 653-2400), (Fax from U.S. (202) 653 5760), www.fao.org; *FAO Production Yearbook 2002* and *The State of Food and Agriculture (SOFA) 2006.*

United Nations Statistics Division, New York, NY 10017, (800) 253-9646, Fax: (212) 963-4116, http://unstats.un.org; *Human Development Report 2006* and *Statistical Yearbook.*

FINLAND - FOOTWEAR

Organisation for Economic Cooperation and Development (OECD), 2 rue Andre Pascal, F-75775 Paris Cedex 16, France, (Telephone in U.S. (202) 785-6323), (Fax in U.S. (202) 785-0350), www.oecd.org; *Indicators of Industrial Activity.*

FINLAND - FOREIGN EXCHANGE RATES

Central Intelligence Agency, Office of Public Affairs, Washington, DC 20505, (703) 482-0623, Fax: (703) 482-1739, www.cia.gov; *The World Factbook.*

Euromonitor International, Inc., 224 S. Michigan Avenue, Suite 1500, Chicago, IL 60604, (312) 922-1115, Fax: (312) 922-1157, www.euromonitor.com; *The World Economic Factbook 2008.*

International Civil Aviation Organization (ICAO), External Relations and Public Information Office (EPO), 999 University Street, Montreal, Quebec H3C 5H7, Canada, (Dial from U.S. (514) 954-8219), (Fax from U.S. (514) 954-6077), www.icao.int; *Civil Aviation Statistics of the World.*

International Monetary Fund (IMF), 700 Nineteenth Street, NW, Washington, DC 20431, (202) 623-7000, Fax: (202) 623-4661, www.imf.org; *International Financial Statistics Yearbook 2007.*

Nordic Council of Ministers, Store Strandstraede 18, DK-1255 Copenhagen K, Denmark, www.norden.org; *Nordic Statistical Yearbook 2004-2006.*

Organisation for Economic Cooperation and Development (OECD), 2 rue Andre Pascal, F-75775 Paris Cedex 16, France, (Telephone in U.S. (202) 785-6323), (Fax in U.S. (202) 785-0350), www.oecd.org; *Financial Market Trends: OECD Periodical; Household, Tourism, Travel: Trends, Environmental Impacts and Policy Responses; OECD Economic Outlook 2008;* and *Revenue Statistics 1965-2006 - 2007 Edition.*

Taylor and Francis Group, An Informa Business, 2 Park Square, Milton Park, Abingdon, Oxford OX14 4RN, United Kingdom, (Dial from U.S. (212) 216-7800), (Fax from U.S. (212) 564-7854), www.tandf.co.uk; *The Europa World Year Book.*

United Nations Statistics Division, New York, NY 10017, (800) 253-9646, Fax: (212) 963-4116, http://unstats.un.org; *Statistical Yearbook; Trends in Europe and North America: The Statistical Yearbook of the ECE 2005;* and *World Statistics Pocketbook.*

FINLAND - FORESTS AND FORESTRY

Euromonitor International, Inc., 224 S. Michigan Avenue, Suite 1500, Chicago, IL 60604, (312) 922-1115, Fax: (312) 922-1157, www.euromonitor.com; *European Marketing Data and Statistics 2008.*

International Monetary Fund (IMF), 700 Nineteenth Street, NW, Washington, DC 20431, (202) 623-7000, Fax: (202) 623-4661, www.imf.org; *International Financial Statistics Yearbook 2007.*

M.E. Sharpe, 80 Business Park Drive, Armonk, NY 10504, (800) 541-6563, Fax: (914) 273-2106, www.mesharpe.com; *The Illustrated Book of World Rankings.*

Nordic Council of Ministers, Store Strandstraede 18, DK-1255 Copenhagen K, Denmark, www.norden.org; *Nordic Statistical Yearbook 2004-2006.*

Organisation for Economic Cooperation and Development (OECD), 2 rue Andre Pascal, F-75775 Paris Cedex 16, France, (Telephone in U.S. (202) 785-6323), (Fax in U.S. (202) 785-0350), www.oecd.org; *Indicators of Industrial Activity; International Trade by Commodity Statistics (ITCS);* and STructural ANalysis (STAN) database.

Palgrave Macmillan Ltd., Houndmills, Basingstoke, Hampshire, RG21 6XS, England, (Telephone in U.S. (888) 330-8477), (Fax in U.S. (800) 672-2054), www.palgrave.com; *The Statesman's Yearbook 2008.*

Taylor and Francis Group, An Informa Business, 2 Park Square, Milton Park, Abingdon, Oxford OX14 4RN, United Kingdom, (Dial from U.S. (212) 216-7800), (Fax from U.S. (212) 564-7854), www.tandf.co.uk; *The Europa World Year Book.*

Technical Association of the Pulp and Paper Industry (TAPPI), 15 Technology Parkway South, Norcross, GA 30092, (770) 446-1400, Fax: (770) 446-6947, www.tappi.org; *TAPPI Annual Report.*

UNESCO Institute for Statistics, C.P. 6128 Succursale Centre-Ville, Montreal, Quebec, H3C 3J7 Canada, (Dial from U.S. (514) 343-6880), (Fax from U.S. (514) 343 6882), www.uis.unesco.org; *Statistical Tables.*

United Nations Conference on Trade and Development (UNCTAD), DC2-1120, United Nations, New York, NY 10017, (212) 963-0027, www.unctad.org; *UNCTAD Commodity Yearbook.*

United Nations Food and Agricultural Organization (FAO), Viale delle Terme di Caracalla, 00100 Rome, Italy, (Dial from U.S. (202) 653-2400), (Fax from U.S. (202) 653 5760), www.fao.org; *FAO Yearbook of Forest Products* and *The State of Food and Agriculture (SOFA) 2006.*

United Nations Statistics Division, New York, NY 10017, (800) 253-9646, Fax: (212) 963-4116, http://unstats.un.org; *Statistical Yearbook* and *Trends in Europe and North America: The Statistical Yearbook of the ECE 2005.*

The World Bank, 1818 H Street, NW, Washington, DC 20433, (202) 473-1000, Fax: (202) 477-6391, www.worldbank.org; *Finland* and *World Development Report 2008.*

FINLAND - FRUIT PRODUCTION

See FINLAND - CROPS

FINLAND - GAS PRODUCTION

See FINLAND - MINERAL INDUSTRIES

FINLAND - GEOGRAPHIC INFORMATION SYSTEMS

M.E. Sharpe, 80 Business Park Drive, Armonk, NY 10504, (800) 541-6563, Fax: (914) 273-2106, www.mesharpe.com; *The Illustrated Book of World Rankings.*

The World Bank, 1818 H Street, NW, Washington, DC 20433, (202) 473-1000, Fax: (202) 477-6391, www.worldbank.org; *Finland.*

FINLAND - GLASS TRADE

Organisation for Economic Cooperation and Development (OECD), 2 rue Andre Pascal, F-75775 Paris Cedex 16, France, (Telephone in U.S. (202) 785-6323), (Fax in U.S. (202) 785-0350), www.oecd.org; *Indicators of Industrial Activity.*

FINLAND - GOLD INDUSTRY

International Monetary Fund (IMF), 700 Nineteenth Street, NW, Washington, DC 20431, (202) 623-7000, Fax: (202) 623-4661, www.imf.org; *International Financial Statistics Yearbook 2007.*

United Nations Statistics Division, New York, NY 10017, (800) 253-9646, Fax: (212) 963-4116, http://unstats.un.org; *Statistical Yearbook.*

The World Bank, 1818 H Street, NW, Washington, DC 20433, (202) 473-1000, Fax: (202) 477-6391, www.worldbank.org; *World Development Indicators (WDI) 2008.*

FINLAND - GOLD PRODUCTION

See FINLAND - MINERAL INDUSTRIES

FINLAND - GRANTS-IN-AID

International Monetary Fund (IMF), 700 Nineteenth Street, NW, Washington, DC 20431, (202) 623-7000, Fax: (202) 623-4661, www.imf.org; *Government Finance Statistics Yearbook (2008 Edition).*

Organisation for Economic Cooperation and Development (OECD), 2 rue Andre Pascal, F-75775 Paris Cedex 16, France, (Telephone in U.S. (202) 785-6323), (Fax in U.S. (202) 785-0350), www.oecd.org; *Geographical Distribution of Financial Flows to Aid Recipients 2002-2006.*

FINLAND - GROSS DOMESTIC PRODUCT

Economist Intelligence Unit, 111 West 57th Street, New York, NY 10019, (212) 554-0600, Fax: (212) 586-1181, www.eiu.com; *Finland Country Report.*

Euromonitor International, Inc., 224 S. Michigan Avenue, Suite 1500, Chicago, IL 60604, (312) 922-1115, Fax: (312) 922-1157, www.euromonitor.com; *The World Economic Factbook 2008.*

International Monetary Fund (IMF), 700 Nineteenth Street, NW, Washington, DC 20431, (202) 623-7000, Fax: (202) 623-4661, www.imf.org; *International Financial Statistics Yearbook 2007.*

M.E. Sharpe, 80 Business Park Drive, Armonk, NY 10504, (800) 541-6563, Fax: (914) 273-2106, www.mesharpe.com; *The Illustrated Book of World Rankings.*

Nordic Council of Ministers, Store Strandstraede 18, DK-1255 Copenhagen K, Denmark, www.norden.org; *Nordic Statistical Yearbook 2004-2006.*

Organisation for Economic Cooperation and Development (OECD), 2 rue Andre Pascal, F-75775 Paris Cedex 16, France, (Telephone in U.S. (202) 785-6323), (Fax in U.S. (202) 785-0350), www.oecd.org; *Comparison of Gross Domestic Product (GDP) for OECD Countries; Geographical Distribution of Financial Flows to Aid Recipients 2002-2006; OECD Economic Outlook 2008;* and *Revenue Statistics 1965-2006 - 2007 Edition.*

Taylor and Francis Group, An Informa Business, 2 Park Square, Milton Park, Abingdon, Oxford OX14 4RN, United Kingdom, (Dial from U.S. (212) 216-7800), (Fax from U.S. (212) 564-7854), www.tandf.co.uk; *The Europa World Year Book.*

United Nations Statistics Division, New York, NY 10017, (800) 253-9646, Fax: (212) 963-4116, http://

unstats.un.org; *Human Development Report 2006; National Accounts Statistics: Compendium of Income Distribution Statistics; Statistical Yearbook;* and *Trends in Europe and North America: The Statistical Yearbook of the ECE 2005.*

The World Bank, 1818 H Street, NW, Washington, DC 20433, (202) 473-1000, Fax: (202) 477-6391, www.worldbank.org; *World Development Indicators (WDI) 2008* and *World Development Report 2008.*

FINLAND - GROSS NATIONAL PRODUCT

European Union, Delegation of the European Commission to the United States, 2300 M Street, NW, Washington, DC 20037, (202) 862-9500, Fax: (202) 429-1766, www.eurunion.org; *The EU Economy, 2007 Review: Moving Europe's Productivity Frontier.*

M.E. Sharpe, 80 Business Park Drive, Armonk, NY 10504, (800) 541-6563, Fax: (914) 273-2106, www.mesharpe.com; *The Illustrated Book of World Rankings.*

Organisation for Economic Cooperation and Development (OECD), 2 rue Andre Pascal, F-75775 Paris Cedex 16, France, (Telephone in U.S. (202) 785-6323), (Fax in U.S. (202) 785-0350), www.oecd.org; *Geographical Distribution of Financial Flows to Aid Recipients 2002-2006; OECD Composite Leading Indicators (CLIs), Updated September 2007;* and *OECD Economic Outlook 2008.*

Palgrave Macmillan Ltd., Houndmills, Basingstoke, Hampshire, RG21 6XS, England, (Telephone in U.S. (888) 330-8477), (Fax in U.S. (800) 672-2054), www.palgrave.com; *The Statesman's Yearbook 2008.*

Taylor and Francis Group, An Informa Business, 2 Park Square, Milton Park, Abingdon, Oxford OX14 4RN, United Kingdom, (Dial from U.S. (212) 216-7800), (Fax from U.S. (212) 564-7854), www.tandf.co.uk; *The Europa World Year Book.*

U.S. Department of State (DOS), 2201 C Street NW, Washington, DC 20520, (202) 647-4000, www.state.gov; *World Military Expenditures and Arms Transfers (WMEAT).*

United Nations Statistics Division, New York, NY 10017, (800) 253-9646, Fax: (212) 963-4116, http://unstats.un.org; *Statistical Yearbook.*

The World Bank, 1818 H Street, NW, Washington, DC 20433, (202) 473-1000, Fax: (202) 477-6391, www.worldbank.org; *The World Bank Atlas 2003-2004; World Development Indicators (WDI) 2008;* and *World Development Report 2008.*

FINLAND - HIDES AND SKINS INDUSTRY

Organisation for Economic Cooperation and Development (OECD), 2 rue Andre Pascal, F-75775 Paris Cedex 16, France, (Telephone in U.S. (202) 785-6323), (Fax in U.S. (202) 785-0350), www.oecd.org; *Indicators of Industrial Activity* and *International Trade by Commodity Statistics (ITCS).*

United Nations Food and Agricultural Organization (FAO), Viale delle Terme di Caracalla, 00100 Rome, Italy, (Dial from U.S. (202) 653-2400), (Fax from U.S. (202) 653 5760), www.fao.org; *FAO Production Yearbook 2002.*

FINLAND - HOUSING

Euromonitor International, Inc., 224 S. Michigan Avenue, Suite 1500, Chicago, IL 60604, (312) 922-1115, Fax: (312) 922-1157, www.euromonitor.com; *World Marketing Data and Statistics.*

M.E. Sharpe, 80 Business Park Drive, Armonk, NY 10504, (800) 541-6563, Fax: (914) 273-2106, www.mesharpe.com; *The Illustrated Book of World Rankings.*

Nordic Council of Ministers, Store Strandstraede 18, DK-1255 Copenhagen K, Denmark, www.norden.org; *Nordic Statistical Yearbook 2004-2006.*

United Nations Statistics Division, New York, NY 10017, (800) 253-9646, Fax: (212) 963-4116, http://unstats.un.org; *Trends in Europe and North America: The Statistical Yearbook of the ECE 2005.*

FINLAND - ILLITERATE PERSONS

Euromonitor International, Inc., 224 S. Michigan Avenue, Suite 1500, Chicago, IL 60604, (312) 922-1115, Fax: (312) 922-1157, www.euromonitor.com; *The World Economic Factbook 2008.*

United Nations Statistics Division, New York, NY 10017, (800) 253-9646, Fax: (212) 963-4116, http://unstats.un.org; *Human Development Report 2006.*

FINLAND - IMPORTS

Central Intelligence Agency, Office of Public Affairs, Washington, DC 20505, (703) 482-0623, Fax: (703) 482-1739, www.cia.gov; *The World Factbook.*

Economist Intelligence Unit, 111 West 57th Street, New York, NY 10019, (212) 554-0600, Fax: (212) 586-1181, www.eiu.com; *Finland Country Report.*

Euromonitor International, Inc., 224 S. Michigan Avenue, Suite 1500, Chicago, IL 60604, (312) 922-1115, Fax: (312) 922-1157, www.euromonitor.com; *The World Economic Factbook 2008.*

International Lead and Zinc Study Group (ILZSG), Rua Almirante Barroso 38, 5th Floor, Lisbon 1000 - 013, Portugal, www.ilzsg.org; Interactive Statistical Database.

International Monetary Fund (IMF), 700 Nineteenth Street, NW, Washington, DC 20431, (202) 623-7000, Fax: (202) 623-4661, www.imf.org; *Direction of Trade Statistics Yearbook 2007; Government Finance Statistics Yearbook (2008 Edition);* and *International Financial Statistics Yearbook 2007.*

Nordic Council of Ministers, Store Strandstraede 18, DK-1255 Copenhagen K, Denmark, www.norden.org; *Nordic Statistical Yearbook 2004-2006.*

Organisation for Economic Cooperation and Development (OECD), 2 rue Andre Pascal, F-75775 Paris Cedex 16, France, (Telephone in U.S. (202) 785-6323), (Fax in U.S. (202) 785-0350), www.oecd.org; *Iron and Steel Industry in 2004 (2006 Edition); 2005 OECD Agricultural Outlook Tables, 1970-2014; OECD Economic Outlook 2008; OECD Economic Survey - Finland 2008; Review of Fisheries in OECD Countries; Country Statistics 2001 to 2003 - 2005 Edition;* and STructural ANalysis (STAN) database.

Palgrave Macmillan Ltd., Houndmills, Basingstoke, Hampshire, RG21 6XS, England, (Telephone in U.S. (888) 330-8477), (Fax in U.S. (800) 672-2054), www.palgrave.com; *The Statesman's Yearbook 2008.*

Taylor and Francis Group, An Informa Business, 2 Park Square, Milton Park, Abingdon, Oxford OX14 4RN, United Kingdom, (Dial from U.S. (212) 216-7800), (Fax from U.S. (212) 564-7854), www.tandf.co.uk; *The Europa World Year Book.*

Technical Association of the Pulp and Paper Industry (TAPPI), 15 Technology Parkway South, Norcross, GA 30092, (770) 446-1400, Fax: (770) 446-6947, www.tappi.org; *TAPPI Annual Report.*

United Nations Conference on Trade and Development (UNCTAD), DC2-1120, United Nations, New York, NY 10017, (212) 963-0027, www.unctad.org; *Handbook of Statistics 2005.*

United Nations Food and Agricultural Organization (FAO), Viale delle Terme di Caracalla, 00100 Rome, Italy, (Dial from U.S. (202) 653-2400), (Fax from U.S. (202) 653 5760), www.fao.org; *The State of Food and Agriculture (SOFA) 2006.*

United Nations Statistics Division, New York, NY 10017, (800) 253-9646, Fax: (212) 963-4116, http://unstats.un.org; *Trends in Europe and North America: The Statistical Yearbook of the ECE 2005.*

The World Bank, 1818 H Street, NW, Washington, DC 20433, (202) 473-1000, Fax: (202) 477-6391, www.worldbank.org; *World Development Indicators (WDI) 2008* and *World Development Report 2008.*

FINLAND - INCOME TAXES

See FINLAND - TAXATION

FINLAND - INDUSTRIAL METALS PRODUCTION

See FINLAND - MINERAL INDUSTRIES

FINLAND - INDUSTRIAL PRODUCTIVITY

International Lead and Zinc Study Group (ILZSG), Rua Almirante Barroso 38, 5th Floor, Lisbon 1000 - 013, Portugal, www.ilzsg.org; Interactive Statistical Database.

M.E. Sharpe, 80 Business Park Drive, Armonk, NY 10504, (800) 541-6563, Fax: (914) 273-2106, www.mesharpe.com; *The Illustrated Book of World Rankings.*

Organisation for Economic Cooperation and Development (OECD), 2 rue Andre Pascal, F-75775 Paris Cedex 16, France, (Telephone in U.S. (202) 785-6323), (Fax in U.S. (202) 785-0350), www.oecd.org; *Environmental Impacts of Foreign Direct Investment in the Mining Sector in the Newly Independent States (NIS); Indicators of Industrial Activity; Iron and Steel Industry in 2004 (2006 Edition); A New World Map in Textiles and Clothing: Adjusting to Change; 2005 OECD Agricultural Outlook Tables, 1970-2014; OECD Economic Outlook 2008;* and STructural ANalysis (STAN) database.

Technical Association of the Pulp and Paper Industry (TAPPI), 15 Technology Parkway South, Norcross, GA 30092, (770) 446-1400, Fax: (770) 446-6947, www.tappi.org; *TAPPI Annual Report.*

FINLAND - INDUSTRIAL PROPERTY

Nordic Council of Ministers, Store Strandstraede 18, DK-1255 Copenhagen K, Denmark, www.norden.org; *Nordic Statistical Yearbook 2004-2006.*

United Nations Statistics Division, New York, NY 10017, (800) 253-9646, Fax: (212) 963-4116, http://unstats.un.org; *Statistical Yearbook.*

World Intellectual Property Organization (WIPO), PO Box 18, CH-1211 Geneva 20, Switzerland, www.wipo.int; *Industrial Property Statistics* and *Industrial Property Statistics Online Directory.*

FINLAND - INDUSTRIES

Central Intelligence Agency, Office of Public Affairs, Washington, DC 20505, (703) 482-0623, Fax: (703) 482-1739, www.cia.gov; *The World Factbook.*

Economist Intelligence Unit, 111 West 57th Street, New York, NY 10019, (212) 554-0600, Fax: (212) 586-1181, www.eiu.com; *Finland Country Report.*

Euromonitor International, Inc., 224 S. Michigan Avenue, Suite 1500, Chicago, IL 60604, (312) 922-1115, Fax: (312) 922-1157, www.euromonitor.com; *The World Economic Factbook 2008* and *World Marketing Data and Statistics.*

International Labour Office, I.L.O. Publications, 4 route des Morillons, CH-1211 Geneva 22, Switzerland, (Telephone in U.S. (202) 653-7652), (Fax in U.S. (202) 653-7687), www.ilo.org; *Yearbook of Labour Statistics 2006.*

M.E. Sharpe, 80 Business Park Drive, Armonk, NY 10504, (800) 541-6563, Fax: (914) 273-2106, www.mesharpe.com; *The Illustrated Book of World Rankings.*

Nordic Council of Ministers, Store Strandstraede 18, DK-1255 Copenhagen K, Denmark, www.norden.org; *Nordic Statistical Yearbook 2004-2006.*

Organisation for Economic Cooperation and Development (OECD), 2 rue Andre Pascal, F-75775 Paris Cedex 16, France, (Telephone in U.S. (202) 785-6323), (Fax in U.S. (202) 785-0350), www.oecd.org; *Indicators of Industrial Activity; Key Environmental Indicators 2004; OECD Economic Outlook 2008; OECD Main Economic Indicators (MEI);* and STructural ANalysis (STAN) database.

Palgrave Macmillan Ltd., Houndmills, Basingstoke, Hampshire, RG21 6XS, England, (Telephone in U.S. (888) 330-8477), (Fax in U.S. (800) 672-2054), www.palgrave.com; *The Statesman's Yearbook 2008.*

Taylor and Francis Group, An Informa Business, 2 Park Square, Milton Park, Abingdon, Oxford OX14 4RN, United Kingdom, (Dial from U.S. (212) 216-7800), (Fax from U.S. (212) 564-7854), www.tandf.co.uk; *The Europa World Year Book.*

United Nations Industrial Development Organization (UNIDO), 1 United Nations Plaza, New York, NY

10017, (212) 963 6890, Fax: (212) 963-7904, http://unido.org; Industrial Statistics Database 2008 (INDSTAT) and *The International Yearbook of Industrial Statistics 2008*.

United Nations Statistics Division, New York, NY 10017, (800) 253-9646, Fax: (212) 963-4116, http://unstats.un.org; *2004 Industrial Commodity Statistics Yearbook; Statistical Yearbook;* and *Trends in Europe and North America: The Statistical Yearbook of the ECE 2005*.

The World Bank, 1818 H Street, NW, Washington, DC 20433, (202) 473-1000, Fax: (202) 477-6391, www.worldbank.org; *Finland* and *World Development Indicators (WDI) 2008*.

FINLAND - INFANT AND MATERNAL MORTALITY

See FINLAND - MORTALITY

FINLAND - INORGANIC ACIDS

Organisation for Economic Cooperation and Development (OECD), 2 rue Andre Pascal, F-75775 Paris Cedex 16, France, (Telephone in U.S. (202) 785-6323), (Fax in U.S. (202) 785-0350), www.oecd.org; *Indicators of Industrial Activity*.

United Nations Statistics Division, New York, NY 10017, (800) 253-9646, Fax: (212) 963-4116, http://unstats.un.org; *Statistical Yearbook*.

FINLAND - INTEREST RATES

Organisation for Economic Cooperation and Development (OECD), 2 rue Andre Pascal, F-75775 Paris Cedex 16, France, (Telephone in U.S. (202) 785-6323), (Fax in U.S. (202) 785-0350), www.oecd.org; *Financial Market Trends: OECD Periodical* and *OECD Economic Outlook 2008*.

FINLAND - INTERNAL REVENUE

Organisation for Economic Cooperation and Development (OECD), 2 rue Andre Pascal, F-75775 Paris Cedex 16, France, (Telephone in U.S. (202) 785-6323), (Fax in U.S. (202) 785-0350), www.oecd.org; *Revenue Statistics 1965-2006 - 2007 Edition*.

FINLAND - INTERNATIONAL FINANCE

Organisation for Economic Cooperation and Development (OECD), 2 rue Andre Pascal, F-75775 Paris Cedex 16, France, (Telephone in U.S. (202) 785-6323), (Fax in U.S. (202) 785-0350), www.oecd.org; *Financial Market Trends: OECD Periodical; Household, Tourism, Travel: Trends, Environmental Impacts and Policy Responses;* and *OECD Economic Outlook 2008*.

FINLAND - INTERNATIONAL LIQUIDITY

International Monetary Fund (IMF), 700 Nineteenth Street, NW, Washington, DC 20431, (202) 623-7000, Fax: (202) 623-4661, www.imf.org; *International Financial Statistics Yearbook 2007*.

Organisation for Economic Cooperation and Development (OECD), 2 rue Andre Pascal, F-75775 Paris Cedex 16, France, (Telephone in U.S. (202) 785-6323), (Fax in U.S. (202) 785-0350), www.oecd.org; *Financial Market Trends: OECD Periodical* and *OECD Economic Outlook 2008*.

FINLAND - INTERNATIONAL STATISTICS

Organisation for Economic Cooperation and Development (OECD), 2 rue Andre Pascal, F-75775 Paris Cedex 16, France, (Telephone in U.S. (202) 785-6323), (Fax in U.S. (202) 785-0350), www.oecd.org; *Financial Market Trends: OECD Periodical*.

FINLAND - INTERNATIONAL TRADE

Banque de France, 48 rue Croix des Petits champs, 75001 Paris, France, www.banque-france.fr/home.htm; *Monthly Business Survey Overview*.

Bernan Essential Government Publications, 4611-F Assembly Drive, Lanham MD, 20706-4391, (301) 459-2255, Fax: (800) 865-3450, www.bernan.com; *OECD Factbook 2006*.

Economist Intelligence Unit, 111 West 57th Street, New York, NY 10019, (212) 554-0600, Fax: (212) 586-1181, www.eiu.com; *Finland Country Report*.

Euromonitor International, Inc., 224 S. Michigan Avenue, Suite 1500, Chicago, IL 60604, (312) 922-1115, Fax: (312) 922-1157, www.euromonitor.com; *European Marketing Data and Statistics 2008; The World Economic Factbook 2008;* and *World Marketing Data and Statistics*.

Eurostat, Batiment Jean Monnet, Rue Alcide de Gasperi, L-2920 Luxembourg, http://epp.eurostat.ec.europa.eu; Intra- and Extra-EU Trade.

M.E. Sharpe, 80 Business Park Drive, Armonk, NY 10504, (800) 541-6563, Fax: (914) 273-2106, www.mesharpe.com; *The Illustrated Book of World Rankings*.

Nordic Council of Ministers, Store Strandstraede 18, DK-1255 Copenhagen K, Denmark, www.norden.org; *Nordic Statistical Yearbook 2004-2006*.

Organisation for Economic Cooperation and Development (OECD), 2 rue Andre Pascal, F-75775 Paris Cedex 16, France, (Telephone in U.S. (202) 785-6323), (Fax in U.S. (202) 785-0350), www.oecd.org; *International Trade by Commodity Statistics (ITCS); 2005 OECD Agricultural Outlook Tables, 1970-2014; OECD Economic Outlook 2008; OECD Economic Survey - Finland 2008; OECD in Figures 2007; OECD Main Economic Indicators (MEI);* and *Statistics on Ship Production, Exports and Orders in 2004*.

Palgrave Macmillan Ltd., Houndmills, Basingstoke, Hampshire, RG21 6XS, England, (Telephone in U.S. (888) 330-8477), (Fax in U.S. (800) 672-2054), www.palgrave.com; *The Statesman's Yearbook 2008*.

Taylor and Francis Group, An Informa Business, 2 Park Square, Milton Park, Abingdon, Oxford OX14 4RN, United Kingdom, (Dial from U.S. (212) 216-7800), (Fax from U.S. (212) 564-7854), www.tandf.co.uk; *The Europa World Year Book*.

United Nations Conference on Trade and Development (UNCTAD), DC2-1120, United Nations, New York, NY 10017, (212) 963-0027, www.unctad.org; *UNCTAD Commodity Yearbook*.

United Nations Food and Agricultural Organization (FAO), Viale delle Terme di Caracalla, 00100 Rome, Italy, (Dial from U.S. (202) 653-2400), (Fax from U.S. (202) 653 5760), www.fao.org; *FAO Trade Yearbook* and *The State of Food and Agriculture (SOFA) 2006*.

United Nations Statistics Division, New York, NY 10017, (800) 253-9646, Fax: (212) 963-4116, http://unstats.un.org; *International Trade Statistics Yearbook* and *Statistical Yearbook*.

The World Bank, 1818 H Street, NW, Washington, DC 20433, (202) 473-1000, Fax: (202) 477-6391, www.worldbank.org; *Finland; World Development Indicators (WDI) 2008;* and *World Development Report 2008*.

World Bureau of Metal Statistics (WBMS), 27a High Street, Ware, Hertfordshire, SG12 9BA, United Kingdom, www.world-bureau.com; *World Flow Charts* and *World Metal Statistics*.

World Trade Organization (WTO), Centre William Rappard, Rue de Lausanne 154, CH-1211 Geneva 21, Switzerland, www.wto.org; *International Trade Statistics 2006*.

FINLAND - INTERNET USERS

Eurostat, Batiment Jean Monnet, Rue Alcide de Gasperi, L-2920 Luxembourg, http://epp.eurostat.ec.europa.eu; *Internet Usage by Enterprises 2007*.

International Telecommunication Union (ITU), Place des Nations, 1211 Geneva 20, Switzerland, www.itu.int; *World Telecommunication/ICT Indicators Database on CD-ROM; World Telecommunication/ICT Indicators Database Online;* and *Yearbook of Statistics - Telecommunication Services (Chronological Time Series 1997-2006)*.

The World Bank, 1818 H Street, NW, Washington, DC 20433, (202) 473-1000, Fax: (202) 477-6391, www.worldbank.org; *Finland*.

FINLAND - INVESTMENTS

International Monetary Fund (IMF), 700 Nineteenth Street, NW, Washington, DC 20431, (202) 623-7000, Fax: (202) 623-4661, www.imf.org; *International Financial Statistics Yearbook 2007*.

Organisation for Economic Cooperation and Development (OECD), 2 rue Andre Pascal, F-75775 Paris Cedex 16, France, (Telephone in U.S. (202) 785-6323), (Fax in U.S. (202) 785-0350), www.oecd.org; *Financial Market Trends: OECD Periodical; Iron and Steel Industry in 2004 (2006 Edition); A New World Map in Textiles and Clothing: Adjusting to Change; OECD Economic Outlook 2008;* and STructural ANalysis (STAN) database.

FINLAND - IRON AND IRON ORE PRODUCTION

See FINLAND - MINERAL INDUSTRIES

FINLAND - LABOR

Central Intelligence Agency, Office of Public Affairs, Washington, DC 20505, (703) 482-0623, Fax: (703) 482-1739, www.cia.gov; *The World Factbook*.

Euromonitor International, Inc., 224 S. Michigan Avenue, Suite 1500, Chicago, IL 60604, (312) 922-1115, Fax: (312) 922-1157, www.euromonitor.com; *World Marketing Data and Statistics*.

International Labour Office, I.L.O. Publications, 4 route des Morillons, CH-1211 Geneva 22, Switzerland, (Telephone in U.S. (202) 653-7652), (Fax in U.S. (202) 653-7687), www.ilo.org; *Yearbook of Labour Statistics 2006*.

M.E. Sharpe, 80 Business Park Drive, Armonk, NY 10504, (800) 541-6563, Fax: (914) 273-2106, www.mesharpe.com; *The Illustrated Book of World Rankings*.

Nordic Council of Ministers, Store Strandstraede 18, DK-1255 Copenhagen K, Denmark, www.norden.org; *Nordic Statistical Yearbook 2004-2006*.

Organisation for Economic Cooperation and Development (OECD), 2 rue Andre Pascal, F-75775 Paris Cedex 16, France, (Telephone in U.S. (202) 785-6323), (Fax in U.S. (202) 785-0350), www.oecd.org; *Iron and Steel Industry in 2004 (2006 Edition); A New World Map in Textiles and Clothing: Adjusting to Change; OECD Economic Outlook 2008; OECD Economic Survey - Finland 2008; OECD Employment Outlook 2007; OECD Main Economic Indicators (MEI);* and *Statistics on Ship Production, Exports and Orders in 2004*.

Palgrave Macmillan Ltd., Houndmills, Basingstoke, Hampshire, RG21 6XS, England, (Telephone in U.S. (888) 330-8477), (Fax in U.S. (800) 672-2054), www.palgrave.com; *The Statesman's Yearbook 2008*.

Taylor and Francis Group, An Informa Business, 2 Park Square, Milton Park, Abingdon, Oxford OX14 4RN, United Kingdom, (Dial from U.S. (212) 216-7800), (Fax from U.S. (212) 564-7854), www.tandf.co.uk; *The Europa World Year Book*.

United Nations Food and Agricultural Organization (FAO), Viale delle Terme di Caracalla, 00100 Rome, Italy, (Dial from U.S. (202) 653-2400), (Fax from U.S. (202) 653 5760), www.fao.org; *The State of Food and Agriculture (SOFA) 2006*.

United Nations Statistics Division, New York, NY 10017, (800) 253-9646, Fax: (212) 963-4116, http://unstats.un.org; *Human Development Report 2006*.

The World Bank, 1818 H Street, NW, Washington, DC 20433, (202) 473-1000, Fax: (202) 477-6391, www.worldbank.org; *The World Bank Atlas 2003-2004; World Development Indicators (WDI) 2008;* and *World Development Report 2008*.

FINLAND - LAND USE

Central Intelligence Agency, Office of Public Affairs, Washington, DC 20505, (703) 482-0623, Fax: (703) 482-1739, www.cia.gov; *The World Factbook*.

Euromonitor International, Inc., 224 S. Michigan Avenue, Suite 1500, Chicago, IL 60604, (312) 922-1115, Fax: (312) 922-1157, www.euromonitor.com; *European Marketing Data and Statistics 2008*.

United Nations Food and Agricultural Organization (FAO), Viale delle Terme di Caracalla, 00100 Rome, Italy, (Dial from U.S. (202) 653-2400), (Fax from U.S. (202) 653 5760), www.fao.org; *FAO Production Yearbook 2002.*

The World Bank, 1818 H Street, NW, Washington, DC 20433, (202) 473-1000, Fax: (202) 477-6391, www.worldbank.org; *World Development Report 2008.*

FINLAND - LEATHER INDUSTRY AND TRADE

Organisation for Economic Cooperation and Development (OECD), 2 rue Andre Pascal, F-75775 Paris Cedex 16, France, (Telephone in U.S. (202) 785-6323), (Fax in U.S. (202) 785-0350), www.oecd.org; *Indicators of Industrial Activity.*

FINLAND - LIBRARIES

Euromonitor International, Inc., 224 S. Michigan Avenue, Suite 1500, Chicago, IL 60604, (312) 922-1115, Fax: (312) 922-1157, www.euromonitor.com; *European Marketing Data and Statistics 2008.*

M.E. Sharpe, 80 Business Park Drive, Armonk, NY 10504, (800) 541-6563, Fax: (914) 273-2106, www.mesharpe.com; *The Illustrated Book of World Rankings.*

Nordic Council of Ministers, Store Strandstraede 18, DK-1255 Copenhagen K, Denmark, www.norden.org; *Nordic Statistical Yearbook 2004-2006.*

UNESCO Institute for Statistics, C.P. 6128 Succursale Centre-Ville, Montreal, Quebec, H3C 3J7 Canada, (Dial from U.S. (514) 343-6880), (Fax from U.S. (514) 343 6882), www.uis.unesco.org; *Statistical Tables.*

United Nations Statistics Division, New York, NY 10017, (800) 253-9646, Fax: (212) 963-4116, http://unstats.un.org; *Trends in Europe and North America: The Statistical Yearbook of the ECE 2005.*

FINLAND - LIFE EXPECTANCY

Central Intelligence Agency, Office of Public Affairs, Washington, DC 20505, (703) 482-0623, Fax: (703) 482-1739, www.cia.gov; *The World Factbook.*

Euromonitor International, Inc., 224 S. Michigan Avenue, Suite 1500, Chicago, IL 60604, (312) 922-1115, Fax: (312) 922-1157, www.euromonitor.com; *The World Economic Factbook 2008.*

Organisation for Economic Cooperation and Development (OECD), 2 rue Andre Pascal, F-75775 Paris Cedex 16, France, (Telephone in U.S. (202) 785-6323), (Fax in U.S. (202) 785-0350), www.oecd.org; *OECD Economic Outlook 2008.*

United Nations Statistics Division, New York, NY 10017, (800) 253-9646, Fax: (212) 963-4116, http://unstats.un.org; *Human Development Report 2006; Trends in Europe and North America: The Statistical Yearbook of the ECE 2005;* and *World Statistics Pocketbook.*

The World Bank, 1818 H Street, NW, Washington, DC 20433, (202) 473-1000, Fax: (202) 477-6391, www.worldbank.org; *The World Bank Atlas 2003-2004* and *World Development Report 2008.*

FINLAND - LITERACY

Euromonitor International, Inc., 224 S. Michigan Avenue, Suite 1500, Chicago, IL 60604, (312) 922-1115, Fax: (312) 922-1157, www.euromonitor.com; *World Marketing Data and Statistics.*

FINLAND - LIVESTOCK

Euromonitor International, Inc., 224 S. Michigan Avenue, Suite 1500, Chicago, IL 60604, (312) 922-1115, Fax: (312) 922-1157, www.euromonitor.com; *European Marketing Data and Statistics 2008.*

M.E. Sharpe, 80 Business Park Drive, Armonk, NY 10504, (800) 541-6563, Fax: (914) 273-2106, www.mesharpe.com; *The Illustrated Book of World Rankings.*

Nordic Council of Ministers, Store Strandstraede 18, DK-1255 Copenhagen K, Denmark, www.norden.org; *Nordic Statistical Yearbook 2004-2006.*

Organisation for Economic Cooperation and Development (OECD), 2 rue Andre Pascal, F-75775 Paris Cedex 16, France, (Telephone in U.S. (202) 785-6323), (Fax in U.S. (202) 785-0350), www.oecd.org; *2005 OECD Agricultural Outlook Tables, 1970-2014.*

Palgrave Macmillan Ltd., Houndmills, Basingstoke, Hampshire, RG21 6XS, England, (Telephone in U.S. (888) 330-8477), (Fax in U.S. (800) 672-2054), www.palgrave.com; *The Statesman's Yearbook 2008.*

Taylor and Francis Group, An Informa Business, 2 Park Square, Milton Park, Abingdon, Oxford OX14 4RN, United Kingdom, (Dial from U.S. (212) 216-7800), (Fax from U.S. (212) 564-7854), www.tandf.co.uk; *The Europa World Year Book.*

United Nations Conference on Trade and Development (UNCTAD), DC2-1120, United Nations, New York, NY 10017, (212) 963-0027, www.unctad.org; *UNCTAD Commodity Yearbook.*

United Nations Food and Agricultural Organization (FAO), Viale delle Terme di Caracalla, 00100 Rome, Italy, (Dial from U.S. (202) 653-2400), (Fax from U.S. (202) 653 5760), www.fao.org; *FAO Production Yearbook 2002* and *The State of Food and Agriculture (SOFA) 2006.*

United Nations Statistics Division, New York, NY 10017, (800) 253-9646, Fax: (212) 963-4116, http://unstats.un.org; *Statistical Yearbook.*

FINLAND - MACHINERY

Organisation for Economic Cooperation and Development (OECD), 2 rue Andre Pascal, F-75775 Paris Cedex 16, France, (Telephone in U.S. (202) 785-6323), (Fax in U.S. (202) 785-0350), www.oecd.org; *Indicators of Industrial Activity.*

FINLAND - MAGNESIUM PRODUCTION AND CONSUMPTION

See FINLAND - MINERAL INDUSTRIES

FINLAND - MANUFACTURES

M.E. Sharpe, 80 Business Park Drive, Armonk, NY 10504, (800) 541-6563, Fax: (914) 273-2106, www.mesharpe.com; *The Illustrated Book of World Rankings.*

Nordic Council of Ministers, Store Strandstraede 18, DK-1255 Copenhagen K, Denmark, www.norden.org; *Nordic Statistical Yearbook 2004-2006.*

Organisation for Economic Cooperation and Development (OECD), 2 rue Andre Pascal, F-75775 Paris Cedex 16, France, (Telephone in U.S. (202) 785-6323), (Fax in U.S. (202) 785-0350), www.oecd.org; *Indicators of Industrial Activity; International Trade by Commodity Statistics (ITCS); OECD Economic Survey - Finland 2008;* and STructural ANalysis (STAN) database.

United Nations Statistics Division, New York, NY 10017, (800) 253-9646, Fax: (212) 963-4116, http://unstats.un.org; *Statistical Yearbook.*

The World Bank, 1818 H Street, NW, Washington, DC 20433, (202) 473-1000, Fax: (202) 477-6391, www.worldbank.org; *World Development Indicators (WDI) 2008.*

FINLAND - MARRIAGE

M.E. Sharpe, 80 Business Park Drive, Armonk, NY 10504, (800) 541-6563, Fax: (914) 273-2106, www.mesharpe.com; *The Illustrated Book of World Rankings.*

Nordic Council of Ministers, Store Strandstraede 18, DK-1255 Copenhagen K, Denmark, www.norden.org; *Nordic Statistical Yearbook 2004-2006.*

Taylor and Francis Group, An Informa Business, 2 Park Square, Milton Park, Abingdon, Oxford OX14 4RN, United Kingdom, (Dial from U.S. (212) 216-7800), (Fax from U.S. (212) 564-7854), www.tandf.co.uk; *The Europa World Year Book.*

United Nations Statistics Division, New York, NY 10017, (800) 253-9646, Fax: (212) 963-4116, http://unstats.un.org; *Demographic Yearbook; Statistical Yearbook;* and *Trends in Europe and North America: The Statistical Yearbook of the ECE 2005.*

FINLAND - MERCURY PRODUCTION

See FINLAND - MINERAL INDUSTRIES

FINLAND - MILK PRODUCTION

See FINLAND - DAIRY PROCESSING

FINLAND - MINERAL INDUSTRIES

Commodity Research Bureau, 330 South Wells Street, Suite 612, Chicago, IL 60606-7110, (800) 621-5271, Fax: (312) 939-4135, www.crbtrader.com; *2006 CRB Commodity Yearbook and CD.*

Eurostat, Batiment Jean Monnet, Rue Alcide de Gasperi, L-2920 Luxembourg, http://epp.eurostat.ec.europa.eu; *Energy - Monthly Statistics* and *Panorama of Energy - 2007 Edition.*

International Energy Agency (IEA), 9, rue de la Federation, 75739 Paris Cedex 15, France, www.iea.org; *Key World Energy Statistics 2007.*

International Lead and Zinc Study Group (ILZSG), Rua Almirante Barroso 38, 5th Floor, Lisbon 1000 - 013, Portugal, www.ilzsg.org; Interactive Statistical Database.

M.E. Sharpe, 80 Business Park Drive, Armonk, NY 10504, (800) 541-6563, Fax: (914) 273-2106, www.mesharpe.com; *The Illustrated Book of World Rankings.*

Nordic Council of Ministers, Store Strandstraede 18, DK-1255 Copenhagen K, Denmark, www.norden.org; *Nordic Statistical Yearbook 2004-2006.*

Organisation for Economic Cooperation and Development (OECD), 2 rue Andre Pascal, F-75775 Paris Cedex 16, France, (Telephone in U.S. (202) 785-6323), (Fax in U.S. (202) 785-0350), www.oecd.org; *Coal Information: 2007 Edition; Energy Statistics of OECD Countries* (2007 Edition); *Environmental Impacts of Foreign Direct Investment in the Mining Sector in the Newly Independent States (NIS); Indicators of Industrial Activity; International Trade by Commodity Statistics (ITCS); Iron and Steel Industry in 2004 (2006 Edition); OECD Economic Survey - Finland 2008;* and STructural ANalysis (STAN) database.

Palgrave Macmillan Ltd., Houndmills, Basingstoke, Hampshire, RG21 6XS, England, (Telephone in U.S. (888) 330-8477), (Fax in U.S. (800) 672-2054), www.palgrave.com; *The Statesman's Yearbook 2008.*

Platts, 2 Penn Plaza, 25th Floor, New York, NY 10121-2298, (212) 904-3070, www.platts.com; *EU Energy.*

Taylor and Francis Group, An Informa Business, 2 Park Square, Milton Park, Abingdon, Oxford OX14 4RN, United Kingdom, (Dial from U.S. (212) 216-7800), (Fax from U.S. (212) 564-7854), www.tandf.co.uk; *The Europa World Year Book.*

United Nations Conference on Trade and Development (UNCTAD), DC2-1120, United Nations, New York, NY 10017, (212) 963-0027, www.unctad.org; *UNCTAD Commodity Yearbook.*

United Nations Statistics Division, New York, NY 10017, (800) 253-9646, Fax: (212) 963-4116, http://unstats.un.org; *Statistical Yearbook.*

World Bureau of Metal Statistics (WBMS), 27a High Street, Ware, Hertfordshire, SG12 9BA, United Kingdom, www.world-bureau.com; *Annual Stainless Steel Statistics; World Flow Charts; World Metal Statistics; World Nickel Statistics;* and *World Tin Statistics.*

FINLAND - MONEY

European Central Bank (ECB), Postfach 160319, D-60066 Frankfurt am Main, Germany, www.ecb.int; *Monetary Developments in the Euro Area; Monthly Bulletin;* and *Statistics Pocket Book.*

Organisation for Economic Cooperation and Development (OECD), 2 rue Andre Pascal, F-75775 Paris Cedex 16, France, (Telephone in U.S. (202) 785-6323), (Fax in U.S. (202) 785-0350), www.oecd.org; *OECD Economic Survey - Finland 2008.*

FINLAND - MONEY EXCHANGE RATES

See FINLAND - FOREIGN EXCHANGE RATES

FINLAND - MONEY SUPPLY

Economist Intelligence Unit, 111 West 57th Street, New York, NY 10019, (212) 554-0600, Fax: (212) 586-1181, www.eiu.com; *Finland Country Report.*

International Monetary Fund (IMF), 700 Nineteenth Street, NW, Washington, DC 20431, (202) 623-7000, Fax: (202) 623-4661, www.imf.org; *International Financial Statistics Yearbook 2007.*

Nordic Council of Ministers, Store Strandstraede 18, DK-1255 Copenhagen K, Denmark, www.norden.org; *Nordic Statistical Yearbook 2004-2006.*

Organisation for Economic Cooperation and Development (OECD), 2 rue Andre Pascal, F-75775 Paris Cedex 16, France, (Telephone in U.S. (202) 785-6323), (Fax in U.S. (202) 785-0350), www.oecd.org; *OECD Economic Outlook 2008.*

Taylor and Francis Group, An Informa Business, 2 Park Square, Milton Park, Abingdon, Oxford OX14 4RN, United Kingdom, (Dial from U.S. (212) 216-7800), (Fax from U.S. (212) 564-7854), www.tandf.co.uk; *The Europa World Year Book.*

United Nations Statistics Division, New York, NY 10017, (800) 253-9646, Fax: (212) 963-4116, http://unstats.un.org; *Statistical Yearbook.*

The World Bank, 1818 H Street, NW, Washington, DC 20433, (202) 473-1000, Fax: (202) 477-6391, www.worldbank.org; *Finland* and *World Development Indicators (WDI) 2008.*

FINLAND - MONUMENTS AND HISTORIC SITES

UNESCO Institute for Statistics, C.P. 6128 Succursale Centre-Ville, Montreal, Quebec, H3C 3J7 Canada, (Dial from U.S. (514) 343-6880), (Fax from U.S. (514) 343 6882), www.uis.unesco.org; *Statistical Tables.*

FINLAND - MORTALITY

Central Intelligence Agency, Office of Public Affairs, Washington, DC 20505, (703) 482-0623, Fax: (703) 482-1739, www.cia.gov; *The World Factbook.*

Euromonitor International, Inc., 224 S. Michigan Avenue, Suite 1500, Chicago, IL 60604, (312) 922-1115, Fax: (312) 922-1157, www.euromonitor.com; *The World Economic Factbook 2008.*

Nordic Council of Ministers, Store Strandstraede 18, DK-1255 Copenhagen K, Denmark, www.norden.org; *Nordic Statistical Yearbook 2004-2006.*

Palgrave Macmillan Ltd., Houndmills, Basingstoke, Hampshire, RG21 6XS, England, (Telephone in U.S. (888) 330-8477), (Fax in U.S. (800) 672-2054), www.palgrave.com; *The Statesman's Yearbook 2008.*

Taylor and Francis Group, An Informa Business, 2 Park Square, Milton Park, Abingdon, Oxford OX14 4RN, United Kingdom, (Dial from U.S. (212) 216-7800), (Fax from U.S. (212) 564-7854), www.tandf.co.uk; *The Europa World Year Book.*

UNICEF, 3 United Nations Plaza, New York, NY 10017, (800) 253-9646, Fax: (212) 887-7465, www.unicef.org; *The State of the World's Children 2008.*

United Nations Statistics Division, New York, NY 10017, (800) 253-9646, Fax: (212) 963-4116, http://unstats.un.org; *Demographic Yearbook; Human Development Report 2006; Statistical Yearbook; Trends in Europe and North America: The Statistical Yearbook of the ECE 2005;* and *World Statistics Pocketbook.*

The World Bank, 1818 H Street, NW, Washington, DC 20433, (202) 473-1000, Fax: (202) 477-6391, www.worldbank.org; *The World Bank Atlas 2003-2004; World Development Indicators (WDI) 2008;* and *World Development Report 2008.*

World Health Organization (WHO), Avenue Appia 20, 1211 Geneve 27, Switzerland, (Telephone in U.S. (212) 331-9081), www.who.int; The WHO Global Atlas of Infectious Diseases and *World Health Report 2006.*

FINLAND - MOTION PICTURES

Palgrave Macmillan Ltd., Houndmills, Basingstoke, Hampshire, RG21 6XS, England, (Telephone in U.S. (888) 330-8477), (Fax in U.S. (800) 672-2054), www.palgrave.com; *The Statesman's Yearbook 2008.*

UNESCO Institute for Statistics, C.P. 6128 Succursale Centre-Ville, Montreal, Quebec, H3C 3J7 Canada, (Dial from U.S. (514) 343-6880), (Fax from U.S. (514) 343 6882), www.uis.unesco.org; *Statistical Tables.*

United Nations Statistics Division, New York, NY 10017, (800) 253-9646, Fax: (212) 963-4116, http://unstats.un.org; *Statistical Yearbook.*

FINLAND - MOTOR VEHICLES

International Road Federation (IFR), Madison Place, 500 Montgomery Street, 5th Floor, Alexandria, VA 22314, (703) 535-1001, Fax: (703) 535-1007, www.irfnet.org; *World Road Statistics 2006.*

Nordic Council of Ministers, Store Strandstraede 18, DK-1255 Copenhagen K, Denmark, www.norden.org; *Nordic Statistical Yearbook 2004-2006.*

Taylor and Francis Group, An Informa Business, 2 Park Square, Milton Park, Abingdon, Oxford OX14 4RN, United Kingdom, (Dial from U.S. (212) 216-7800), (Fax from U.S. (212) 564-7854), www.tandf.co.uk; *The Europa World Year Book.*

United Nations Statistics Division, New York, NY 10017, (800) 253-9646, Fax: (212) 963-4116, http://unstats.un.org; *Statistical Yearbook.*

FINLAND - MUSEUMS

M.E. Sharpe, 80 Business Park Drive, Armonk, NY 10504, (800) 541-6563, Fax: (914) 273-2106, www.mesharpe.com; *The Illustrated Book of World Rankings.*

Nordic Council of Ministers, Store Strandstraede 18, DK-1255 Copenhagen K, Denmark, www.norden.org; *Nordic Statistical Yearbook 2004-2006.*

UNESCO Institute for Statistics, C.P. 6128 Succursale Centre-Ville, Montreal, Quebec, H3C 3J7 Canada, (Dial from U.S. (514) 343-6880), (Fax from U.S. (514) 343 6882), www.uis.unesco.org; *Statistical Tables.*

FINLAND - NATURAL GAS PRODUCTION

See FINLAND - MINERAL INDUSTRIES

FINLAND - NICKEL AND NICKEL ORE

See FINLAND - MINERAL INDUSTRIES

FINLAND - NUTRITION

United Nations Food and Agricultural Organization (FAO), Viale delle Terme di Caracalla, 00100 Rome, Italy, (Dial from U.S. (202) 653-2400), (Fax from U.S. (202) 653 5760), www.fao.org; *The State of Food and Agriculture (SOFA) 2006.*

FINLAND - OATS PRODUCTION

See FINLAND - CROPS

FINLAND - OILSEED PLANTS

Organisation for Economic Cooperation and Development (OECD), 2 rue Andre Pascal, F-75775 Paris Cedex 16, France, (Telephone in U.S. (202) 785-6323), (Fax in U.S. (202) 785-0350), www.oecd.org; *International Trade by Commodity Statistics (ITCS).*

FINLAND - OLDER PEOPLE

M.E. Sharpe, 80 Business Park Drive, Armonk, NY 10504, (800) 541-6563, Fax: (914) 273-2106, www.mesharpe.com; *The Illustrated Book of World Rankings.*

FINLAND - PAPER

See FINLAND - FORESTS AND FORESTRY

FINLAND - PEANUT PRODUCTION

See FINLAND - CROPS

FINLAND - PERIODICALS

UNESCO Institute for Statistics, C.P. 6128 Succursale Centre-Ville, Montreal, Quebec, H3C 3J7 Canada, (Dial from U.S. (514) 343-6880), (Fax from U.S. (514) 343 6882), www.uis.unesco.org; *Statistical Tables.*

FINLAND - PESTICIDES

United Nations Food and Agricultural Organization (FAO), Viale delle Terme di Caracalla, 00100 Rome, Italy, (Dial from U.S. (202) 653-2400), (Fax from U.S. (202) 653 5760), www.fao.org; *The State of Food and Agriculture (SOFA) 2006.*

FINLAND - PETROLEUM INDUSTRY AND TRADE

Euromonitor International, Inc., 224 S. Michigan Avenue, Suite 1500, Chicago, IL 60604, (312) 922-1115, Fax: (312) 922-1157, www.euromonitor.com; *European Marketing Data and Statistics 2008.*

International Energy Agency (IEA), 9, rue de la Federation, 75739 Paris Cedex 15, France, www.iea.org; *Key World Energy Statistics 2007.*

M.E. Sharpe, 80 Business Park Drive, Armonk, NY 10504, (800) 541-6563, Fax: (914) 273-2106, www.mesharpe.com; *The Illustrated Book of World Rankings.*

Organisation for Economic Cooperation and Development (OECD), 2 rue Andre Pascal, F-75775 Paris Cedex 16, France, (Telephone in U.S. (202) 785-6323), (Fax in U.S. (202) 785-0350), www.oecd.org; *Energy Statistics of OECD Countries* (2007 Edition); *Indicators of Industrial Activity; International Trade by Commodity Statistics (ITCS);* and *Oil Information 2006 Edition.*

PennWell Corporation, 1421 South Sheridan Road, Tulsa, OK 74112, (918) 835-3161, www.pennwell.com; *International Petroleum Encyclopedia 2007.*

U.S. Department of Energy (DOE), Energy Information Administration (EIA), 1000 Independence Avenue, SW, Washington, DC 20585, (202) 586-8800, www.eia.doe.gov; *International Energy Annual 2004* and *International Energy Outlook 2006.*

United Nations Conference on Trade and Development (UNCTAD), DC2-1120, United Nations, New York, NY 10017, (212) 963-0027, www.unctad.org; *UNCTAD Commodity Yearbook.*

United Nations Food and Agricultural Organization (FAO), Viale delle Terme di Caracalla, 00100 Rome, Italy, (Dial from U.S. (202) 653-2400), (Fax from U.S. (202) 653 5760), www.fao.org; *The State of Food and Agriculture (SOFA) 2006.*

United Nations Statistics Division, New York, NY 10017, (800) 253-9646, Fax: (212) 963-4116, http://unstats.un.org; *Statistical Yearbook* and *Trends in Europe and North America: The Statistical Yearbook of the ECE 2005.*

FINLAND - PHOSPHATES PRODUCTION

See FINLAND - MINERAL INDUSTRIES

FINLAND - PLASTICS INDUSTRY AND TRADE

Organisation for Economic Cooperation and Development (OECD), 2 rue Andre Pascal, F-75775 Paris Cedex 16, France, (Telephone in U.S. (202) 785-6323), (Fax in U.S. (202) 785-0350), www.oecd.org; *International Trade by Commodity Statistics (ITCS).*

United Nations Statistics Division, New York, NY 10017, (800) 253-9646, Fax: (212) 963-4116, http://unstats.un.org; *Statistical Yearbook.*

FINLAND - PLATINUM PRODUCTION

See FINLAND - MINERAL INDUSTRIES

FINLAND - POLITICAL SCIENCE

Central Intelligence Agency, Office of Public Affairs, Washington, DC 20505, (703) 482-0623, Fax: (703) 482-1739, www.cia.gov; *The World Factbook.*

International Monetary Fund (IMF), 700 Nineteenth Street, NW, Washington, DC 20431, (202) 623-7000, Fax: (202) 623-4661, www.imf.org; *Government Finance Statistics Yearbook (2008 Edition)* and *International Financial Statistics Yearbook 2007.*

Nordic Council of Ministers, Store Strandstraede 18, DK-1255 Copenhagen K, Denmark, www.norden.org; *Nordic Statistical Yearbook 2004-2006.*

Organisation for Economic Cooperation and Development (OECD), 2 rue Andre Pascal, F-75775 Paris Cedex 16, France, (Telephone in U.S. (202) 785-6323), (Fax in U.S. (202) 785-0350), www.oecd.org; *OECD Economic Outlook 2008* and *Revenue Statistics 1965-2006 - 2007 Edition.*

Palgrave Macmillan Ltd., Houndmills, Basingstoke, Hampshire, RG21 6XS, England, (Telephone in U.S. (888) 330-8477), (Fax in U.S. (800) 672-2054), www.palgrave.com; *The Statesman's Yearbook 2008.*

Taylor and Francis Group, An Informa Business, 2 Park Square, Milton Park, Abingdon, Oxford OX14 4RN, United Kingdom, (Dial from U.S. (212) 216-7800), (Fax from U.S. (212) 564-7854), www.tandf.co.uk; *The Europa World Year Book.*

United Nations Statistics Division, New York, NY 10017, (800) 253-9646, Fax: (212) 963-4116, http://unstats.un.org; *National Accounts Statistics: Compendium of Income Distribution Statistics* and *Statistical Yearbook.*

The World Bank, 1818 H Street, NW, Washington, DC 20433, (202) 473-1000, Fax: (202) 477-6391, www.worldbank.org; *World Development Indicators (WDI) 2008* and *World Development Report 2008.*

FINLAND - POPULATION

Banque de France, 48 rue Croix des Petits champs, 75001 Paris, France, www.banque-france.fr/home.htm; *Key Data for the Euro Area.*

Central Intelligence Agency, Office of Public Affairs, Washington, DC 20505, (703) 482-0623, Fax: (703) 482-1739, www.cia.gov; *The World Factbook.*

Economist Intelligence Unit, 111 West 57th Street, New York, NY 10019, (212) 554-0600, Fax: (212) 586-1181, www.eiu.com; *Finland Country Report.*

Euromonitor International, Inc., 224 S. Michigan Avenue, Suite 1500, Chicago, IL 60604, (312) 922-1115, Fax: (312) 922-1157, www.euromonitor.com; *European Marketing Data and Statistics 2008* and *The World Economic Factbook 2008.*

Eurostat, Batiment Jean Monnet, Rue Alcide de Gasperi, L-2920 Luxembourg, http://epp.eurostat.ec.europa.eu; *The Life of Women and Men in Europe - A Statistical Portrait.*

International Labour Office, I.L.O. Publications, 4 route des Morillons, CH-1211 Geneva 22, Switzerland, (Telephone in U.S. (202) 653-7652), (Fax in U.S. (202) 653-7687), www.ilo.org; *Yearbook of Labour Statistics 2006.*

M.E. Sharpe, 80 Business Park Drive, Armonk, NY 10504, (800) 541-6563, Fax: (914) 273-2106, www.mesharpe.com; *The Illustrated Book of World Rankings.*

Nordic Council of Ministers, Store Strandstraede 18, DK-1255 Copenhagen K, Denmark, www.norden.org; *Nordic Statistical Yearbook 2004-2006.*

Organisation for Economic Cooperation and Development (OECD), 2 rue Andre Pascal, F-75775 Paris Cedex 16, France, (Telephone in U.S. (202) 785-6323), (Fax in U.S. (202) 785-0350), www.oecd.org; *Labour Force Statistics: 1986-2005, 2007 Edition.*

Palgrave Macmillan Ltd., Houndmills, Basingstoke, Hampshire, RG21 6XS, England, (Telephone in U.S. (888) 330-8477), (Fax in U.S. (800) 672-2054), www.palgrave.com; *The Statesman's Yearbook 2008.*

Taylor and Francis Group, An Informa Business, 2 Park Square, Milton Park, Abingdon, Oxford OX14 4RN, United Kingdom, (Dial from U.S. (212) 216-7800), (Fax from U.S. (212) 564-7854), www.tandf.co.uk; *The Europa World Year Book.*

U.S. Department of State (DOS), 2201 C Street NW, Washington, DC 20520, (202) 647-4000, www.state.gov; *World Military Expenditures and Arms Transfers (WMEAT).*

UNESCO Institute for Statistics, C.P. 6128 Succursale Centre-Ville, Montreal, Quebec, H3C 3J7 Canada, (Dial from U.S. (514) 343-6880), (Fax from U.S. (514) 343 6882), www.uis.unesco.org; *Statistical Tables.*

United Nations Food and Agricultural Organization (FAO), Viale delle Terme di Caracalla, 00100 Rome, Italy, (Dial from U.S. (202) 653-2400), (Fax from U.S. (202) 653 5760), www.fao.org; *FAO Production Yearbook 2002.*

United Nations Statistics Division, New York, NY 10017, (800) 253-9646, Fax: (212) 963-4116, http://unstats.un.org; *Demographic Yearbook; Human Development Report 2006; Statistical Yearbook; Trends in Europe and North America: The Statistical Yearbook of the ECE 2005;* and *World Statistics Pocketbook.*

The World Bank, 1818 H Street, NW, Washington, DC 20433, (202) 473-1000, Fax: (202) 477-6391, www.worldbank.org; *Finland; The World Bank Atlas 2003-2004;* and *World Development Report 2008.*

World Health Organization (WHO), Avenue Appia 20, 1211 Geneve 27, Switzerland, (Telephone in U.S. (212) 331-9081), www.who.int; *World Health Report 2006.*

FINLAND - POPULATION DENSITY

Central Intelligence Agency, Office of Public Affairs, Washington, DC 20505, (703) 482-0623, Fax: (703) 482-1739, www.cia.gov; *The World Factbook.*

Euromonitor International, Inc., 224 S. Michigan Avenue, Suite 1500, Chicago, IL 60604, (312) 922-1115, Fax: (312) 922-1157, www.euromonitor.com; *The World Economic Factbook 2008.*

M.E. Sharpe, 80 Business Park Drive, Armonk, NY 10504, (800) 541-6563, Fax: (914) 273-2106, www.mesharpe.com; *The Illustrated Book of World Rankings.*

Nordic Council of Ministers, Store Strandstraede 18, DK-1255 Copenhagen K, Denmark, www.norden.org; *Nordic Statistical Yearbook 2004-2006.*

Palgrave Macmillan Ltd., Houndmills, Basingstoke, Hampshire, RG21 6XS, England, (Telephone in U.S. (888) 330-8477), (Fax in U.S. (800) 672-2054), www.palgrave.com; *The Statesman's Yearbook 2008.*

Taylor and Francis Group, An Informa Business, 2 Park Square, Milton Park, Abingdon, Oxford OX14 4RN, United Kingdom, (Dial from U.S. (212) 216-7800), (Fax from U.S. (212) 564-7854), www.tandf.co.uk; *The Europa World Year Book.*

United Nations Food and Agricultural Organization (FAO), Viale delle Terme di Caracalla, 00100 Rome, Italy, (Dial from U.S. (202) 653-2400), (Fax from U.S. (202) 653 5760), www.fao.org; *The State of Food and Agriculture (SOFA) 2006.*

United Nations Statistics Division, New York, NY 10017, (800) 253-9646, Fax: (212) 963-4116, http://unstats.un.org; *Statistical Yearbook* and *Trends in Europe and North America: The Statistical Yearbook of the ECE 2005.*

The World Bank, 1818 H Street, NW, Washington, DC 20433, (202) 473-1000, Fax: (202) 477-6391, www.worldbank.org; *Finland* and *World Development Report 2008.*

FINLAND - POSTAL SERVICE

M.E. Sharpe, 80 Business Park Drive, Armonk, NY 10504, (800) 541-6563, Fax: (914) 273-2106, www.mesharpe.com; *The Illustrated Book of World Rankings.*

Nordic Council of Ministers, Store Strandstraede 18, DK-1255 Copenhagen K, Denmark, www.norden.org; *Nordic Statistical Yearbook 2004-2006.*

Palgrave Macmillan Ltd., Houndmills, Basingstoke, Hampshire, RG21 6XS, England, (Telephone in U.S. (888) 330-8477), (Fax in U.S. (800) 672-2054), www.palgrave.com; *The Statesman's Yearbook 2008.*

United Nations Statistics Division, New York, NY 10017, (800) 253-9646, Fax: (212) 963-4116, http://unstats.un.org; *Statistical Yearbook* and *Trends in Europe and North America: The Statistical Yearbook of the ECE 2005.*

FINLAND - POULTRY

See FINLAND - LIVESTOCK

FINLAND - POWER RESOURCES

Euromonitor International, Inc., 224 S. Michigan Avenue, Suite 1500, Chicago, IL 60604, (312) 922-1115, Fax: (312) 922-1157, www.euromonitor.com; *European Marketing Data and Statistics 2008; The World Economic Factbook 2008;* and *World Marketing Data and Statistics.*

M.E. Sharpe, 80 Business Park Drive, Armonk, NY 10504, (800) 541-6563, Fax: (914) 273-2106, www.mesharpe.com; *The Illustrated Book of World Rankings.*

Nordic Council of Ministers, Store Strandstraede 18, DK-1255 Copenhagen K, Denmark, www.norden.org; *Nordic Statistical Yearbook 2004-2006.*

Organisation for Economic Cooperation and Development (OECD), 2 rue Andre Pascal, F-75775 Paris Cedex 16, France, (Telephone in U.S. (202) 785-6323), (Fax in U.S. (202) 785-0350), www.oecd.org; *Coal Information: 2007 Edition; Energy Statistics of OECD Countries* (2007 Edition); *Key Environmental Indicators 2004;* and *Oil Information 2006 Edition.*

Palgrave Macmillan Ltd., Houndmills, Basingstoke, Hampshire, RG21 6XS, England, (Telephone in U.S. (888) 330-8477), (Fax in U.S. (800) 672-2054), www.palgrave.com; *The Statesman's Yearbook 2008.*

Platts, 2 Penn Plaza, 25th Floor, New York, NY 10121-2298, (212) 904-3070, www.platts.com; *Energy Economist* and *European Power Daily.*

U.S. Department of Energy (DOE), Energy Information Administration (EIA), 1000 Independence Avenue, SW, Washington, DC 20585, (202) 586-8800, www.eia.doe.gov; *International Energy Annual 2004* and *International Energy Outlook 2006.*

United Nations Food and Agricultural Organization (FAO), Viale delle Terme di Caracalla, 00100 Rome, Italy, (Dial from U.S. (202) 653-2400), (Fax from U.S. (202) 653 5760), www.fao.org; *The State of Food and Agriculture (SOFA) 2006.*

United Nations Statistics Division, New York, NY 10017, (800) 253-9646, Fax: (212) 963-4116, http://unstats.un.org; *Energy Statistics Yearbook 2003; Human Development Report 2006; Statistical Yearbook; Trends in Europe and North America: The Statistical Yearbook of the ECE 2005;* and *World Statistics Pocketbook.*

The World Bank, 1818 H Street, NW, Washington, DC 20433, (202) 473-1000, Fax: (202) 477-6391, www.worldbank.org; *The World Bank Atlas 2003-2004* and *World Development Report 2008.*

FINLAND - PRICES

Euromonitor International, Inc., 224 S. Michigan Avenue, Suite 1500, Chicago, IL 60604, (312) 922-1115, Fax: (312) 922-1157, www.euromonitor.com; *European Marketing Data and Statistics 2008* and *World Marketing Data and Statistics.*

International Labour Office, I.L.O. Publications, 4 route des Morillons, CH-1211 Geneva 22, Switzerland, (Telephone in U.S. (202) 653-7652), (Fax in U.S. (202) 653-7687), www.ilo.org; *Yearbook of Labour Statistics 2006.*

International Lead and Zinc Study Group (ILZSG), Rua Almirante Barroso 38, 5th Floor, Lisbon 1000 - 013, Portugal, www.ilzsg.org; Interactive Statistical Database.

International Monetary Fund (IMF), 700 Nineteenth Street, NW, Washington, DC 20431, (202) 623-7000, Fax: (202) 623-4661, www.imf.org; *International Financial Statistics Yearbook 2007.*

M.E. Sharpe, 80 Business Park Drive, Armonk, NY 10504, (800) 541-6563, Fax: (914) 273-2106, www.mesharpe.com; *The Illustrated Book of World Rankings.*

Nordic Council of Ministers, Store Strandstraede 18, DK-1255 Copenhagen K, Denmark, www.norden.org; *Nordic Statistical Yearbook 2004-2006.*

Organisation for Economic Cooperation and Development (OECD), 2 rue Andre Pascal, F-75775 Paris

Cedex 16, France, (Telephone in U.S. (202) 785-6323), (Fax in U.S. (202) 785-0350), www.oecd.org; *Indicators of Industrial Activity; Iron and Steel Industry in 2004 (2006 Edition); OECD Economic Outlook 2008;* and *OECD Main Economic Indicators (MEI).*

Technical Association of the Pulp and Paper Industry (TAPPI), 15 Technology Parkway South, Norcross, GA 30092, (770) 446-1400, Fax: (770) 446-6947, www.tappi.org; *TAPPI Annual Report.*

United Nations Food and Agricultural Organization (FAO), Viale delle Terme di Caracalla, 00100 Rome, Italy, (Dial from U.S. (202) 653-2400), (Fax from U.S. (202) 653 5760), www.fao.org; *FAO Production Yearbook 2002* and *The State of Food and Agriculture (SOFA) 2006.*

The World Bank, 1818 H Street, NW, Washington, DC 20433, (202) 473-1000, Fax: (202) 477-6391, www.worldbank.org; *Finland.*

World Bureau of Metal Statistics (WBMS), 27a High Street, Ware, Hertfordshire, SG12 9BA, United Kingdom, www.world-bureau.com; *World Flow Charts* and *World Metal Statistics.*

FINLAND - PROFESSIONS

Organisation for Economic Cooperation and Development (OECD), 2 rue Andre Pascal, F-75775 Paris Cedex 16, France, (Telephone in U.S. (202) 785-6323), (Fax in U.S. (202) 785-0350), www.oecd.org; *OECD Employment Outlook 2007.*

United Nations Statistics Division, New York, NY 10017, (800) 253-9646, Fax: (212) 963-4116, http://unstats.un.org; *Statistical Yearbook.*

FINLAND - PUBLIC HEALTH

EpiNorth, c/o Norwegian Institute of Public Health, PO Box 4404 Nydalen, N-0430 Oslo, Norway, www.epinorth.org; www.epinorth.org.

Euromonitor International, Inc., 224 S. Michigan Avenue, Suite 1500, Chicago, IL 60604, (312) 922-1115, Fax: (312) 922-1157, www.euromonitor.com; *World Health Databook 2007/2008* and *World Marketing Data and Statistics.*

European Centre for Disease Prevention and Control (ECDC), 171 83 Stockholm, Sweden, www.ecdc.europa.eu; *Eurosurveillance.*

Health and Consumer Protection Directorate-General, European Commission, B-1049 Brussels, Belgium, http://ec.europa.eu/dgs/health_consumer/index_en.htm; *Injuries in the European Union: Statistics Summary 2002-2004.*

International Monetary Fund (IMF), 700 Nineteenth Street, NW, Washington, DC 20431, (202) 623-7000, Fax: (202) 623-4661, www.imf.org; *Government Finance Statistics Yearbook (2008 Edition).*

M.E. Sharpe, 80 Business Park Drive, Armonk, NY 10504, (800) 541-6563, Fax: (914) 273-2106, www.mesharpe.com; *The Illustrated Book of World Rankings.*

Nordic Council of Ministers, Store Strandstraede 18, DK-1255 Copenhagen K, Denmark, www.norden.org; *Nordic Statistical Yearbook 2004-2006.*

Organisation for Economic Cooperation and Development (OECD), 2 rue Andre Pascal, F-75775 Paris Cedex 16, France, (Telephone in U.S. (202) 785-6323), (Fax in U.S. (202) 785-0350), www.oecd.org; *Health at a Glance 2007 - OECD Indicators.*

Palgrave Macmillan Ltd., Houndmills, Basingstoke, Hampshire, RG21 6XS, England, (Telephone in U.S. (888) 330-8477), (Fax in U.S. (800) 672-2054), www.palgrave.com; *The Statesman's Yearbook 2008.*

Robert Koch Institute, Nordufer 20, D 13353 Berlin, Germany, www.rki.de; *EUVAC-NET Report: Pertussis-Surveillance 1998-2002.*

UNICEF, 3 United Nations Plaza, New York, NY 10017, (800) 253-9646, Fax: (212) 887-7465, www.unicef.org; *The State of the World's Children 2008.*

United Nations Statistics Division, New York, NY 10017, (800) 253-9646, Fax: (212) 963-4116, http://unstats.un.org; *Human Development Report 2006; Statistical Yearbook;* and *Trends in Europe and North America: The Statistical Yearbook of the ECE 2005.*

The World Bank, 1818 H Street, NW, Washington, DC 20433, (202) 473-1000, Fax: (202) 477-6391, www.worldbank.org; *Finland* and *World Development Report 2008.*

World Health Organization (WHO), Avenue Appia 20, 1211 Geneve 27, Switzerland, (Telephone in U.S. (212) 331-9081), www.who.int; The WHO Global Atlas of Infectious Diseases and *World Health Report 2006.*

FINLAND - PUBLISHERS AND PUBLISHING

Nordic Council of Ministers, Store Strandstraede 18, DK-1255 Copenhagen K, Denmark, www.norden.org; *Nordic Statistical Yearbook 2004-2006.*

Organisation for Economic Cooperation and Development (OECD), 2 rue Andre Pascal, F-75775 Paris Cedex 16, France, (Telephone in U.S. (202) 785-6323), (Fax in U.S. (202) 785-0350), www.oecd.org; *Indicators of Industrial Activity.*

Palgrave Macmillan Ltd., Houndmills, Basingstoke, Hampshire, RG21 6XS, England, (Telephone in U.S. (888) 330-8477), (Fax in U.S. (800) 672-2054), www.palgrave.com; *The Statesman's Yearbook 2008.*

Taylor and Francis Group, An Informa Business, 2 Park Square, Milton Park, Abingdon, Oxford OX14 4RN, United Kingdom, (Dial from U.S. (212) 216-7800), (Fax from U.S. (212) 564-7854), www.tandf.co.uk; *The Europa World Year Book.*

UNESCO Institute for Statistics, C.P. 6128 Succursale Centre-Ville, Montreal, Quebec, H3C 3J7 Canada, (Dial from U.S. (514) 343-6880), (Fax from U.S. (514) 343 6882), www.uis.unesco.org; *Statistical Tables.*

United Nations Statistics Division, New York, NY 10017, (800) 253-9646, Fax: (212) 963-4116, http://unstats.un.org; *Trends in Europe and North America: The Statistical Yearbook of the ECE 2005.*

FINLAND - RADIO - RECEIVERS AND RECEPTION

Palgrave Macmillan Ltd., Houndmills, Basingstoke, Hampshire, RG21 6XS, England, (Telephone in U.S. (888) 330-8477), (Fax in U.S. (800) 672-2054), www.palgrave.com; *The Statesman's Yearbook 2008.*

United Nations Statistics Division, New York, NY 10017, (800) 253-9646, Fax: (212) 963-4116, http://unstats.un.org; *Statistical Yearbook.*

FINLAND - RAILROADS

Euromonitor International, Inc., 224 S. Michigan Avenue, Suite 1500, Chicago, IL 60604, (312) 922-1115, Fax: (312) 922-1157, www.euromonitor.com; *European Marketing Data and Statistics 2008.*

Jane's Information Group, 110 North Royal Street, Suite 200, Alexandria, VA 22314, (703) 683-3700, Fax: (800) 836-0297, www.janes.com; *Jane's World Railways.*

Nordic Council of Ministers, Store Strandstraede 18, DK-1255 Copenhagen K, Denmark, www.norden.org; *Nordic Statistical Yearbook 2004-2006.*

Palgrave Macmillan Ltd., Houndmills, Basingstoke, Hampshire, RG21 6XS, England, (Telephone in U.S. (888) 330-8477), (Fax in U.S. (800) 672-2054), www.palgrave.com; *The Statesman's Yearbook 2008.*

Taylor and Francis Group, An Informa Business, 2 Park Square, Milton Park, Abingdon, Oxford OX14 4RN, United Kingdom, (Dial from U.S. (212) 216-7800), (Fax from U.S. (212) 564-7854), www.tandf.co.uk; *The Europa World Year Book.*

United Nations Statistics Division, New York, NY 10017, (800) 253-9646, Fax: (212) 963-4116, http://unstats.un.org; *Annual Bulletin of Transport Statistics for Europe and North America 2004; Statistical Yearbook;* and *Trends in Europe and North America: The Statistical Yearbook of the ECE 2005.*

FINLAND - RELIGION

Central Intelligence Agency, Office of Public Affairs, Washington, DC 20505, (703) 482-0623, Fax: (703) 482-1739, www.cia.gov; *The World Factbook.*

M.E. Sharpe, 80 Business Park Drive, Armonk, NY 10504, (800) 541-6563, Fax: (914) 273-2106, www.mesharpe.com; *The Illustrated Book of World Rankings.*

Palgrave Macmillan Ltd., Houndmills, Basingstoke, Hampshire, RG21 6XS, England, (Telephone in U.S. (888) 330-8477), (Fax in U.S. (800) 672-2054), www.palgrave.com; *The Statesman's Yearbook 2008.*

FINLAND - RENT CHARGES

International Labour Office, I.L.O. Publications, 4 route des Morillons, CH-1211 Geneva 22, Switzerland, (Telephone in U.S. (202) 653-7652), (Fax in U.S. (202) 653-7687), www.ilo.org; *Yearbook of Labour Statistics 2006.*

FINLAND - RESERVES (ACCOUNTING)

Organisation for Economic Cooperation and Development (OECD), 2 rue Andre Pascal, F-75775 Paris Cedex 16, France, (Telephone in U.S. (202) 785-6323), (Fax in U.S. (202) 785-0350), www.oecd.org; *Financial Market Trends: OECD Periodical* and *OECD Economic Outlook 2008.*

United Nations Statistics Division, New York, NY 10017, (800) 253-9646, Fax: (212) 963-4116, http://unstats.un.org; *Statistical Yearbook.*

The World Bank, 1818 H Street, NW, Washington, DC 20433, (202) 473-1000, Fax: (202) 477-6391, www.worldbank.org; *World Development Indicators (WDI) 2008.*

FINLAND - RETAIL TRADE

Banque de France, 48 rue Croix des Petits champs, 75001 Paris, France, www.banque-france.fr/home.htm; *Monthly Business Survey Overview.*

Euromonitor International, Inc., 224 S. Michigan Avenue, Suite 1500, Chicago, IL 60604, (312) 922-1115, Fax: (312) 922-1157, www.euromonitor.com; *Retail Trade International 2007* and *World Marketing Data and Statistics.*

United Nations Statistics Division, New York, NY 10017, (800) 253-9646, Fax: (212) 963-4116, http://unstats.un.org; *Statistical Yearbook.*

FINLAND - RICE PRODUCTION

See FINLAND - CROPS

FINLAND - ROADS

Central Intelligence Agency, Office of Public Affairs, Washington, DC 20505, (703) 482-0623, Fax: (703) 482-1739, www.cia.gov; *The World Factbook.*

International Road Federation (IFR), Madison Place, 500 Montgomery Street, 5th Floor, Alexandria, VA 22314, (703) 535-1001, Fax: (703) 535-1007, www.irfnet.org; *World Road Statistics 2006.*

Nordic Council of Ministers, Store Strandstraede 18, DK-1255 Copenhagen K, Denmark, www.norden.org; *Nordic Statistical Yearbook 2004-2006.*

Palgrave Macmillan Ltd., Houndmills, Basingstoke, Hampshire, RG21 6XS, England, (Telephone in U.S. (888) 330-8477), (Fax in U.S. (800) 672-2054), www.palgrave.com; *The Statesman's Yearbook 2008.*

United Nations Statistics Division, New York, NY 10017, (800) 253-9646, Fax: (212) 963-4116, http://unstats.un.org; *Annual Bulletin of Transport Statistics for Europe and North America 2004* and *Trends in Europe and North America: The Statistical Yearbook of the ECE 2005.*

FINLAND - RUBBER INDUSTRY AND TRADE

International Rubber Study Group (IRSG), 1st Floor, Heron House, 109/115 Wembley Hill Road, Wembley, Middlesex HA9 8DA, United Kingdom, www.rubberstudy.com; *Rubber Statistical Bulletin; Summary of World Rubber Statistics 2005; World Rubber*

Statistics Handbook (Volume 6, 1975-2001); and *World Rubber Statistics Historic Handbook.*

M.E. Sharpe, 80 Business Park Drive, Armonk, NY 10504, (800) 541-6563, Fax: (914) 273-2106, www.mesharpe.com; *The Illustrated Book of World Rankings.*

Organisation for Economic Cooperation and Development (OECD), 2 rue Andre Pascal, F-75775 Paris Cedex 16, France, (Telephone in U.S. (202) 785-6323), (Fax in U.S. (202) 785-0350), www.oecd.org; *International Trade by Commodity Statistics (ITCS).*

FINLAND - SALT PRODUCTION

See FINLAND - MINERAL INDUSTRIES

FINLAND - SHEEP

See FINLAND - LIVESTOCK

FINLAND - SHIPBUILDING

Organisation for Economic Cooperation and Development (OECD), 2 rue Andre Pascal, F-75775 Paris Cedex 16, France, (Telephone in U.S. (202) 785-6323), (Fax in U.S. (202) 785-0350), www.oecd.org; *Indicators of Industrial Activity.*

FINLAND - SHIPPING

Lloyd's Register - Fairplay, 8410 N.W. 53rd Terrace, Suite 207, Miami FL 33166, (305) 718-9929, Fax: (305) 718-9663, www.lrfairplay.com; *Register of Ships 2007-2008; World Casualty Statistics 2007; World Fleet Statistics 2006; World Marine Propulsion Report 2006-2010; World Shipbuilding Statistics 2007;* and The World Shipping Encyclopaedia.

Nordic Council of Ministers, Store Strandstraede 18, DK-1255 Copenhagen K, Denmark, www.norden.org; *Nordic Statistical Yearbook 2004-2006.*

Organisation for Economic Cooperation and Development (OECD), 2 rue Andre Pascal, F-75775 Paris Cedex 16, France, (Telephone in U.S. (202) 785-6323), (Fax in U.S. (202) 785-0350), www.oecd.org; *Statistics on Ship Production, Exports and Orders in 2004.*

Palgrave Macmillan Ltd., Houndmills, Basingstoke, Hampshire, RG21 6XS, England, (Telephone in U.S. (888) 330-8477), (Fax in U.S. (800) 672-2054), www.palgrave.com; *The Statesman's Yearbook 2008.*

Taylor and Francis Group, An Informa Business, 2 Park Square, Milton Park, Abingdon, Oxford OX14 4RN, United Kingdom, (Dial from U.S. (212) 216-7800), (Fax from U.S. (212) 564-7854), www.tandf.co.uk; *The Europa World Year Book.*

U.S. Department of Transportation (DOT), Maritime Administration (MARAD), West Building, Southeast Federal Center, 1200 New Jersey Avenue, SE, Washington, DC 20590, (800) 99-MARAD, www.marad.dot.gov; *World Merchant Fleet 2005.*

United Nations Statistics Division, New York, NY 10017, (800) 253-9646, Fax: (212) 963-4116, http://unstats.un.org; *Annual Bulletin of Transport Statistics for Europe and North America 2004* and *Statistical Yearbook.*

FINLAND - SILVER PRODUCTION

See FINLAND - MINERAL INDUSTRIES

FINLAND - SOCIAL ECOLOGY

M.E. Sharpe, 80 Business Park Drive, Armonk, NY 10504, (800) 541-6563, Fax: (914) 273-2106, www.mesharpe.com; *The Illustrated Book of World Rankings.*

United Nations Statistics Division, New York, NY 10017, (800) 253-9646, Fax: (212) 963-4116, http://unstats.un.org; *World Statistics Pocketbook.*

FINLAND - SOCIAL SECURITY

International Monetary Fund (IMF), 700 Nineteenth Street, NW, Washington, DC 20431, (202) 623-7000, Fax: (202) 623-4661, www.imf.org; *Government Finance Statistics Yearbook (2008 Edition).*

Nordic Council of Ministers, Store Strandstraede 18, DK-1255 Copenhagen K, Denmark, www.norden.org; *Nordic Statistical Yearbook 2004-2006.*

Organisation for Economic Cooperation and Development (OECD), 2 rue Andre Pascal, F-75775 Paris Cedex 16, France, (Telephone in U.S. (202) 785-6323), (Fax in U.S. (202) 785-0350), www.oecd.org; *Revenue Statistics 1965-2006 - 2007 Edition.*

Palgrave Macmillan Ltd., Houndmills, Basingstoke, Hampshire, RG21 6XS, England, (Telephone in U.S. (888) 330-8477), (Fax in U.S. (800) 672-2054), www.palgrave.com; *The Statesman's Yearbook 2008.*

FINLAND - STEEL PRODUCTION

See FINLAND - MINERAL INDUSTRIES

FINLAND - SUGAR PRODUCTION

See FINLAND - CROPS

FINLAND - SULPHUR PRODUCTION

See FINLAND - MINERAL INDUSTRIES

FINLAND - TAXATION

Eurostat, Batiment Jean Monnet, Rue Alcide de Gasperi, L-2920 Luxembourg, http://epp.eurostat.ec.europa.eu; *Taxation Trends in the European Union - Data for the EU Member States and Norway.*

International Monetary Fund (IMF), 700 Nineteenth Street, NW, Washington, DC 20431, (202) 623-7000, Fax: (202) 623-4661, www.imf.org; *Government Finance Statistics Yearbook (2008 Edition).*

International Road Federation (IFR), Madison Place, 500 Montgomery Street, 5th Floor, Alexandria, VA 22314, (703) 535-1001, Fax: (703) 535-1007, www.irfnet.org; *World Road Statistics 2006.*

Nordic Council of Ministers, Store Strandstraede 18, DK-1255 Copenhagen K, Denmark, www.norden.org; *Nordic Statistical Yearbook 2004-2006.*

Organisation for Economic Cooperation and Development (OECD), 2 rue Andre Pascal, F-75775 Paris Cedex 16, France, (Telephone in U.S. (202) 785-6323), (Fax in U.S. (202) 785-0350), www.oecd.org; *Revenue Statistics 1965-2006 - 2007 Edition.*

Taylor and Francis Group, An Informa Business, 2 Park Square, Milton Park, Abingdon, Oxford OX14 4RN, United Kingdom, (Dial from U.S. (212) 216-7800), (Fax from U.S. (212) 564-7854), www.tandf.co.uk; *The Europa World Year Book.*

The World Bank, 1818 H Street, NW, Washington, DC 20433, (202) 473-1000, Fax: (202) 477-6391, www.worldbank.org; *World Development Indicators (WDI) 2008.*

FINLAND - TELEPHONE

International Telecommunication Union (ITU), Place des Nations, 1211 Geneva 20, Switzerland, www.itu.int; World Telecommunication Indicators Database.

Nordic Council of Ministers, Store Strandstraede 18, DK-1255 Copenhagen K, Denmark, www.norden.org; *Nordic Statistical Yearbook 2004-2006.*

Palgrave Macmillan Ltd., Houndmills, Basingstoke, Hampshire, RG21 6XS, England, (Telephone in U.S. (888) 330-8477), (Fax in U.S. (800) 672-2054), www.palgrave.com; *The Statesman's Yearbook 2008.*

Taylor and Francis Group, An Informa Business, 2 Park Square, Milton Park, Abingdon, Oxford OX14 4RN, United Kingdom, (Dial from U.S. (212) 216-7800), (Fax from U.S. (212) 564-7854), www.tandf.co.uk; *The Europa World Year Book.*

United Nations Statistics Division, New York, NY 10017, (800) 253-9646, Fax: (212) 963-4116, http://unstats.un.org; *Statistical Yearbook; Trends in Europe and North America: The Statistical Yearbook of the ECE 2005;* and *World Statistics Pocketbook.*

FINLAND - TELEVISION BROADCASTING

United Nations Statistics Division, New York, NY 10017, (800) 253-9646, Fax: (212) 963-4116, http://unstats.un.org; *Statistical Yearbook.*

FINLAND - TEXTILE INDUSTRY

Euromonitor International, Inc., 224 S. Michigan Avenue, Suite 1500, Chicago, IL 60604, (312) 922-1115, Fax: (312) 922-1157, www.euromonitor.com; *Retail Trade International 2007.*

M.E. Sharpe, 80 Business Park Drive, Armonk, NY 10504, (800) 541-6563, Fax: (914) 273-2106, www.mesharpe.com; *The Illustrated Book of World Rankings.*

Organisation for Economic Cooperation and Development (OECD), 2 rue Andre Pascal, F-75775 Paris Cedex 16, France, (Telephone in U.S. (202) 785-6323), (Fax in U.S. (202) 785-0350), www.oecd.org; *Indicators of Industrial Activity; International Trade by Commodity Statistics (ITCS); A New World Map in Textiles and Clothing: Adjusting to Change; 2005 OECD Agricultural Outlook Tables, 1970-2014;* and STructural ANalysis (STAN) database.

Palgrave Macmillan Ltd., Houndmills, Basingstoke, Hampshire, RG21 6XS, England, (Telephone in U.S. (888) 330-8477), (Fax in U.S. (800) 672-2054), www.palgrave.com; *The Statesman's Yearbook 2008.*

United Nations Conference on Trade and Development (UNCTAD), DC2-1120, United Nations, New York, NY 10017, (212) 963-0027, www.unctad.org; *UNCTAD Commodity Yearbook.*

United Nations Statistics Division, New York, NY 10017, (800) 253-9646, Fax: (212) 963-4116, http://unstats.un.org; *Statistical Yearbook.*

FINLAND - THEATER

UNESCO Institute for Statistics, C.P. 6128 Succursale Centre-Ville, Montreal, Quebec, H3C 3J7 Canada, (Dial from U.S. (514) 343-6880), (Fax from U.S. (514) 343 6882), www.uis.unesco.org; *Statistical Tables.*

FINLAND - TIN PRODUCTION

See FINLAND - MINERAL INDUSTRIES

FINLAND - TIRE INDUSTRY

United Nations Statistics Division, New York, NY 10017, (800) 253-9646, Fax: (212) 963-4116, http://unstats.un.org; *Statistical Yearbook.*

FINLAND - TOBACCO INDUSTRY

Euromonitor International, Inc., 224 S. Michigan Avenue, Suite 1500, Chicago, IL 60604, (312) 922-1115, Fax: (312) 922-1157, www.euromonitor.com; *European Marketing Data and Statistics 2008.*

Foreign Agricultural Service (FAS), U.S. Department of Agriculture (USDA), 1400 Independence Avenue, SW, Washington, DC 20250, (202) 720-3935, www.fas.usda.gov; *Tobacco: World Markets and Trade.*

M.E. Sharpe, 80 Business Park Drive, Armonk, NY 10504, (800) 541-6563, Fax: (914) 273-2106, www.mesharpe.com; *The Illustrated Book of World Rankings.*

Organisation for Economic Cooperation and Development (OECD), 2 rue Andre Pascal, F-75775 Paris Cedex 16, France, (Telephone in U.S. (202) 785-6323), (Fax in U.S. (202) 785-0350), www.oecd.org; *Indicators of Industrial Activity; International Trade by Commodity Statistics (ITCS);* and STructural ANalysis (STAN) database.

United Nations Statistics Division, New York, NY 10017, (800) 253-9646, Fax: (212) 963-4116, http://unstats.un.org; *Statistical Yearbook.*

The World Bank, 1818 H Street, NW, Washington, DC 20433, (202) 473-1000, Fax: (202) 477-6391, www.worldbank.org; *World Development Indicators (WDI) 2008.*

FINLAND - TOURISM

Euromonitor International, Inc., 224 S. Michigan Avenue, Suite 1500, Chicago, IL 60604, (312) 922-1115, Fax: (312) 922-1157, www.euromonitor.com; *European Marketing Data and Statistics 2008; The World Economic Factbook 2008;* and *World Marketing Data and Statistics.*

Eurostat, Batiment Jean Monnet, Rue Alcide de Gasperi, L-2920 Luxembourg, http://epp.eurostat.ec.europa.eu; *Tourism in Europe: First Results for 2007.*

M.E. Sharpe, 80 Business Park Drive, Armonk, NY 10504, (800) 541-6563, Fax: (914) 273-2106, www.mesharpe.com; *The Illustrated Book of World Rankings.*

Organisation for Economic Cooperation and Development (OECD), 2 rue Andre Pascal, F-75775 Paris Cedex 16, France, (Telephone in U.S. (202) 785-6323), (Fax in U.S. (202) 785-0350), www.oecd.org; *Household, Tourism, Travel: Trends, Environmental Impacts and Policy Responses.*

Palgrave Macmillan Ltd., Houndmills, Basingstoke, Hampshire, RG21 6XS, England, (Telephone in U.S. (888) 330-8477), (Fax in U.S. (800) 672-2054), www.palgrave.com; *The Statesman's Yearbook 2008.*

Taylor and Francis Group, An Informa Business, 2 Park Square, Milton Park, Abingdon, Oxford OX14 4RN, United Kingdom, (Dial from U.S. (212) 216-7800), (Fax from U.S. (212) 564-7854), www.tandf.co.uk; *The Europa World Year Book.*

United Nations Statistics Division, New York, NY 10017, (800) 253-9646, Fax: (212) 963-4116, http://unstats.un.org; *Statistical Yearbook* and *Trends in Europe and North America: The Statistical Yearbook of the ECE 2005.*

United Nations World Tourism Organization (UNWTO), Capitan Haya 42, 28020 Madrid, Spain, www.world-tourism.org; *Tourism Market Trends 2004 - Europe* and *Yearbook of Tourism Statistics.*

The World Bank, 1818 H Street, NW, Washington, DC 20433, (202) 473-1000, Fax: (202) 477-6391, www.worldbank.org; *Finland.*

FINLAND - TRADE

See FINLAND - INTERNATIONAL TRADE

FINLAND - TRANSPORTATION

Central Intelligence Agency, Office of Public Affairs, Washington, DC 20505, (703) 482-0623, Fax: (703) 482-1739, www.cia.gov; *The World Factbook.*

Euromonitor International, Inc., 224 S. Michigan Avenue, Suite 1500, Chicago, IL 60604, (312) 922-1115, Fax: (312) 922-1157, www.euromonitor.com; *World Marketing Data and Statistics.*

Eurostat, Batiment Jean Monnet, Rue Alcide de Gasperi, L-2920 Luxembourg, http://epp.eurostat.ec.europa.eu; *Regional Passenger and Freight Air Transport in Europe in 2006* and *Regional Road and Rail Transport Networks.*

M.E. Sharpe, 80 Business Park Drive, Armonk, NY 10504, (800) 541-6563, Fax: (914) 273-2106, www.mesharpe.com; *The Illustrated Book of World Rankings.*

Nordic Council of Ministers, Store Strandstraede 18, DK-1255 Copenhagen K, Denmark, www.norden.org; *Nordic Statistical Yearbook 2004-2006.*

Palgrave Macmillan Ltd., Houndmills, Basingstoke, Hampshire, RG21 6XS, England, (Telephone in U.S. (888) 330-8477), (Fax in U.S. (800) 672-2054), www.palgrave.com; *The Statesman's Yearbook 2008.*

Taylor and Francis Group, An Informa Business, 2 Park Square, Milton Park, Abingdon, Oxford OX14 4RN, United Kingdom, (Dial from U.S. (212) 216-7800), (Fax from U.S. (212) 564-7854), www.tandf.co.uk; *The Europa World Year Book.*

United Nations Statistics Division, New York, NY 10017, (800) 253-9646, Fax: (212) 963-4116, http://unstats.un.org; *Human Development Report 2006* and *Trends in Europe and North America: The Statistical Yearbook of the ECE 2005.*

The World Bank, 1818 H Street, NW, Washington, DC 20433, (202) 473-1000, Fax: (202) 477-6391, www.worldbank.org; *Finland.*

FINLAND - UNEMPLOYMENT

Central Intelligence Agency, Office of Public Affairs, Washington, DC 20505, (703) 482-0623, Fax: (703) 482-1739, www.cia.gov; *The World Factbook.*

Euromonitor International, Inc., 224 S. Michigan Avenue, Suite 1500, Chicago, IL 60604, (312) 922-1115, Fax: (312) 922-1157, www.euromonitor.com; *European Marketing Data and Statistics 2008.*

International Labour Office, I.L.O. Publications, 4 route des Morillons, CH-1211 Geneva 22, Switzerland, (Telephone in U.S. (202) 653-7652), (Fax in U.S. (202) 653-7687), www.ilo.org; *Yearbook of Labour Statistics 2006.*

Nordic Council of Ministers, Store Strandstraede 18, DK-1255 Copenhagen K, Denmark, www.norden.org; *Nordic Statistical Yearbook 2004-2006.*

Organisation for Economic Cooperation and Development (OECD), 2 rue Andre Pascal, F-75775 Paris Cedex 16, France, (Telephone in U.S. (202) 785-6323), (Fax in U.S. (202) 785-0350), www.oecd.org; *Labour Force Statistics: 1986-2005, 2007 Edition; OECD Composite Leading Indicators (CLIs), Updated September 2007; OECD Economic Outlook 2008; OECD Economic Survey - Finland 2008;* and *OECD Employment Outlook 2007.*

Palgrave Macmillan Ltd., Houndmills, Basingstoke, Hampshire, RG21 6XS, England, (Telephone in U.S. (888) 330-8477), (Fax in U.S. (800) 672-2054), www.palgrave.com; *The Statesman's Yearbook 2008.*

United Nations Statistics Division, New York, NY 10017, (800) 253-9646, Fax: (212) 963-4116, http://unstats.un.org; *Statistical Yearbook* and *Trends in Europe and North America: The Statistical Yearbook of the ECE 2005.*

FINLAND - URANIUM PRODUCTION AND CONSUMPTION

See FINLAND - MINERAL INDUSTRIES

FINLAND - VITAL STATISTICS

Nordic Council of Ministers, Store Strandstraede 18, DK-1255 Copenhagen K, Denmark, www.norden.org; *Nordic Statistical Yearbook 2004-2006.*

Palgrave Macmillan Ltd., Houndmills, Basingstoke, Hampshire, RG21 6XS, England, (Telephone in U.S. (888) 330-8477), (Fax in U.S. (800) 672-2054), www.palgrave.com; *The Statesman's Yearbook 2008.*

United Nations Statistics Division, New York, NY 10017, (800) 253-9646, Fax: (212) 963-4116, http://unstats.un.org; *Statistical Yearbook.*

World Health Organization (WHO), Avenue Appia 20, 1211 Geneve 27, Switzerland, (Telephone in U.S. (212) 331-9081), www.who.int; *World Health Report 2006.*

FINLAND - WAGES

Euromonitor International, Inc., 224 S. Michigan Avenue, Suite 1500, Chicago, IL 60604, (312) 922-1115, Fax: (312) 922-1157, www.euromonitor.com; *European Marketing Data and Statistics 2008.*

International Labour Office, I.L.O. Publications, 4 route des Morillons, CH-1211 Geneva 22, Switzerland, (Telephone in U.S. (202) 653-7652), (Fax in U.S. (202) 653-7687), www.ilo.org; *Yearbook of Labour Statistics 2006.*

Nordic Council of Ministers, Store Strandstraede 18, DK-1255 Copenhagen K, Denmark, www.norden.org; *Nordic Statistical Yearbook 2004-2006.*

Organisation for Economic Cooperation and Development (OECD), 2 rue Andre Pascal, F-75775 Paris Cedex 16, France, (Telephone in U.S. (202) 785-6323), (Fax in U.S. (202) 785-0350), www.oecd.org; *ICT Sector Data and Metadata by Country; OECD Economic Outlook 2008; OECD Main Economic Indicators (MEI);* and STructural ANalysis (STAN) database.

United Nations Statistics Division, New York, NY 10017, (800) 253-9646, Fax: (212) 963-4116, http://unstats.un.org; *Statistical Yearbook.*

The World Bank, 1818 H Street, NW, Washington, DC 20433, (202) 473-1000, Fax: (202) 477-6391, www.worldbank.org; *Finland.*

FINLAND - WELFARE STATE

International Monetary Fund (IMF), 700 Nineteenth Street, NW, Washington, DC 20431, (202) 623-7000, Fax: (202) 623-4661, www.imf.org; *Government Finance Statistics Yearbook (2008 Edition).*

Nordic Council of Ministers, Store Strandstraede 18, DK-1255 Copenhagen K, Denmark, www.norden.org; *Nordic Statistical Yearbook 2004-2006.*

FINLAND - WHEAT PRODUCTION

See FINLAND - CROPS

FINLAND - WHOLESALE PRICE INDEXES

Nordic Council of Ministers, Store Strandstraede 18, DK-1255 Copenhagen K, Denmark, www.norden.org; *Nordic Statistical Yearbook 2004-2006.*

United Nations Statistics Division, New York, NY 10017, (800) 253-9646, Fax: (212) 963-4116, http://unstats.un.org; *Statistical Yearbook.*

FINLAND - WHOLESALE PRICES

Organisation for Economic Cooperation and Development (OECD), 2 rue Andre Pascal, F-75775 Paris Cedex 16, France, (Telephone in U.S. (202) 785-6323), (Fax in U.S. (202) 785-0350), www.oecd.org; *OECD Main Economic Indicators (MEI).*

FINLAND - WHOLESALE TRADE

United Nations Statistics Division, New York, NY 10017, (800) 253-9646, Fax: (212) 963-4116, http://unstats.un.org; *Statistical Yearbook.*

FINLAND - WINE PRODUCTION

See FINLAND - BEVERAGE INDUSTRY

FINLAND - WOOD AND WOOD PULP

See FINLAND - FORESTS AND FORESTRY

FINLAND - WOOD PRODUCTS

Organisation for Economic Cooperation and Development (OECD), 2 rue Andre Pascal, F-75775 Paris Cedex 16, France, (Telephone in U.S. (202) 785-6323), (Fax in U.S. (202) 785-0350), www.oecd.org; *International Trade by Commodity Statistics (ITCS)* and STructural ANalysis (STAN) database.

FINLAND - WOOL PRODUCTION

See FINLAND - TEXTILE INDUSTRY

FINLAND - YARN PRODUCTION

See FINLAND - TEXTILE INDUSTRY

FINLAND - ZINC AND ZINC ORE

See FINLAND - MINERAL INDUSTRIES

FINLAND - ZOOS

UNESCO Institute for Statistics, C.P. 6128 Succursale Centre-Ville, Montreal, Quebec, H3C 3J7 Canada, (Dial from U.S. (514) 343-6880), (Fax from U.S. (514) 343 6882), www.uis.unesco.org; *Statistical Tables.*

FIRE DEPARTMENTS

See PUBLIC SAFETY

FIRE INSURANCE

Insurance Information Institute (III), 110 William Street, New York, NY 10038, (212) 346-5500, www.iii.org; *Insurance Fact Book 2007.*

FIREARMS

Bernan Essential Government Publications, 4611-F Assembly Drive, Lanham MD, 20706-4391, (301) 459-2255, Fax: (800) 865-3450, www.bernan.com; *Vital Statistics of the United States: Births, Life Expectancy, Deaths, and Selected Health Data.*

Bureau of Alcohol, Tobacco, Firearms and Explosives (ATF), Office of Public and Governmental Affairs, 99 New York Avenue, NE, Mail Stop 5S144, Washington, DC 20226, (202) 927-7890, www.atf.gov; *2006 Annual Firearms Manufacturers And Export Report.*

Federal Bureau of Investigation (FBI), J. Edgar Hoover Building, 935 Pennsylvania Avenue, NW, Washington, DC 20535-0001, (202) 324-3000, www.fbi.gov; *Crime in the United States (CIUS) 2007 (Preliminary).*

Justice Research and Statistics Association (JRSA), 777 N. Capitol Street, NE, Suite 801, Washington, DC 20002, (202) 842-9330, Fax: (202) 842-9329, www.jrsa.org; *Crime and Justice Atlas 2001.*

National Center for Health Statistics (NCHS), Centers for Disease Control and Prevention (CDC), U.S. Department of Health and Human Services (HHS), 3311 Toledo Road, Hyattsville, MD 20782, (866) 232-4636, www.cdc.gov/nchs; *National Vital Statistics Reports (NVSR); Vital Statistics of the United States (VSUS);* and unpublished data.

National Sporting Goods Association (NSGA), 1601 Feehanville Drive, Suite 300, Mount Prospect, IL 60056, (847) 296-6742, Fax: (847) 391-9827, www.nsga.org; *Ten-Year History of Selected Sports Participation, 1996-2006.*

U.S. Department of Justice (DOJ), Bureau of Justice Statistics, 810 Seventh Street, NW, Washington, DC 20531, (202) 307-0765, www.ojp.usdoj.gov/bjs/; *Background Checks for Firearm Transfers, 2003: Trends for the Permanent Brady Period, 1999-2003; Background Checks for Firearm Transfers, 2004; Firearm Use by Offenders; Survey of State Procedures Related to Firearm Sales; Survey of State Records Included in Presale Background Checks: Mental Health Records, Domestic Violence Misdemeanor Records, and Restraining Orders, 2003;* and *Weapon Use and Violent Crime, 1993-2001.*

U.S. Department of Justice (DOJ), National Institute of Justice (NIJ), 810 Seventh Street, NW, Washington, DC 20531, (202) 307-2942, Fax: (202) 616-0275, www.ojp.usdoj.gov/nij/; *Reducing Gun Violence: Evaluation of the Indianapolis Police Department's Directed Patrol Project* and *Statistical Validation of the Individuality of Guns Using 3D Images of Bullets.*

U.S. Department of Transportation (DOT), Research and Innovative Technology Administration (RITA), Bureau of Transportation Statistics (BTS), 1200 New Jersey Avenue, SE, Washington, DC 20590, (800) 853-1351, www.bts.gov; *TranStats.*

FIREARMS - DEATHS

Bernan Essential Government Publications, 4611-F Assembly Drive, Lanham MD, 20706-4391, (301) 459-2255, Fax: (800) 865-3450, www.bernan.com; *Vital Statistics of the United States: Births, Life Expectancy, Deaths, and Selected Health Data.*

National Center for Health Statistics (NCHS), Centers for Disease Control and Prevention (CDC), U.S. Department of Health and Human Services (HHS), 3311 Toledo Road, Hyattsville, MD 20782, (866) 232-4636, www.cdc.gov/nchs; *National Vital Statistics Reports (NVSR); Vital Statistics of the United States (VSUS);* and unpublished data.

FIRES AND PROPERTY LOSS

Insurance Information Institute (III), 110 William Street, New York, NY 10038, (212) 346-5500, www.iii.org; *International Insurance Fact Book 2008-2009.*

National Fire Protection Association (NFPA), One Batterymarch Park, Quincy, MA 02169-7471, (617) 770-3000, Fax: (617) 770-0700, www.nfpa.org; *Fire statistics.*

FIRES AND PROPERTY LOSSES - ACCIDENTAL DEATHS

National Center for Health Statistics (NCHS), Centers for Disease Control and Prevention (CDC), U.S. Department of Health and Human Services (HHS), 3311 Toledo Road, Hyattsville, MD 20782, (866) 232-4636, www.cdc.gov/nchs; *Vital Statistics of the United States (VSUS)* and unpublished data.

National Fire Protection Association (NFPA), One Batterymarch Park, Quincy, MA 02169-7471, (617) 770-3000, Fax: (617) 770-0700, www.nfpa.org; *Fire statistics.*

FIRMS

See BUSINESS ENTERPRISE

FISH

United Nations Food and Agricultural Organization (FAO), Viale delle Terme di Caracalla, 00100 Rome, Italy, (Dial from U.S. (202) 653-2400), (Fax from U.S. (202) 653 5760), www.fao.org; *FAO Statistical Yearbook 2004* and FAOSTAT Database. Subjects covered include: Agriculture, nutrition, fisheries, forestry, food aid, land use and population.

World Resources Institute (WRI), 10 G Street, NE, Suite 800 Washington, DC 20002, (202) 729-7600, www.wri.org; *Dilemmas of Democratic Decentralization in Mangochi District, Malawi: Interest and Mistrust in Fisheries Management.*

FISH - AQUACULTURE

Economic Research Service (ERS), U.S. Department of Agriculture (USDA), 1800 M Street, NW, Washington, DC 20036-5831, (202) 694-5050, Fax: (202) 694-5689, www.ers.usda.gov; *Agricultural Income and Finance Outlook; Farm Balance Sheet;* and *Farm Income: Data Files.*

National Agricultural Statistics Service (NASS), U.S. Department of Agriculture (USDA), 1400 Independence Avenue, SW, Washington, DC 20250, (800) 727-9540, Fax: (202) 690-2090, www.nass.usda.gov; *Catfish Processing; Catfish Production;* and *Trout Production.*

FISH - CANNING AND PRESERVING

National Marine Fisheries Service (NMFS), National Oceanic and Atmospheric Administration (NOAA), Office of Constituent Services, 1315 East West Highway, 9th Floor, Silver Spring, MD 20910, (301) 713-2379, Fax: (301) 713-2385, www.nmfs.noaa.gov; *Fisheries of the United States - 2006.*

FISH - CATCH - QUANTITY AND VALUE

National Marine Fisheries Service (NMFS), National Oceanic and Atmospheric Administration (NOAA), Office of Constituent Services, 1315 East West Highway, 9th Floor, Silver Spring, MD 20910, (301) 713-2379, Fax: (301) 713-2385, www.nmfs.noaa.gov; *Fisheries of the United States - 2006.*

FISH - CONSUMER EXPENDITURES

U.S. Bureau of Labor Statistics (BLS), Postal Square Building, 2 Massachusetts Avenue, NE, Washington, DC 20212-0001, (202) 691-5200, Fax: (202) 691-6325, www.bls.gov; *Consumer Expenditures in 2006* and unpublished data.

FISH - CONSUMPTION

Economic Research Service (ERS), U.S. Department of Agriculture (USDA), 1800 M Street, NW, Washington, DC 20036-5831, (202) 694-5050, Fax: (202) 694-5689, www.ers.usda.gov; *Agricultural Outlook* and *Food CPI, Prices, and Expenditures.*

Netherlands Institute for Health Services Research (NIVEL), PO Box 1568, 3500 BN Utrecht, The Netherlands, www.nivel.eu; *Fatty Fish and Supplements Are the Greatest Modifiable Contributors to the Serum 25-Hydroxyvitamin D Concentration in a Multiethnic Population.*

FISH - INTERNATIONAL TRADE

National Marine Fisheries Service (NMFS), National Oceanic and Atmospheric Administration (NOAA), Office of Constituent Services, 1315 East West Highway, 9th Floor, Silver Spring, MD 20910, (301) 713-2379, Fax: (301) 713-2385, www.nmfs.noaa.gov; *Fisheries of the United States - 2006.*

U.S. Census Bureau, Foreign Trade Division, 4700 Silver Hill Road, Washington DC 20233-0001, (301) 763-3030, www.census.gov/foreign-trade/www/; *U.S. International Trade in Goods and Services.*

FISH - IRON (DIETARY) SOURCE

Center for Nutrition Policy and Promotion (CNPP), U.S. Department of Agriculture (USDA), 3101 Park Center Drive, 10th Floor, Alexandria, VA 22302-1594, (703) 305-7600, Fax: (703) 305-3300, www.usda.gov/cnpp; *Nutrient Content of the U.S. Food Supply Summary Report 2005.*

FISH - PRICES

National Marine Fisheries Service (NMFS), National Oceanic and Atmospheric Administration (NOAA), Office of Constituent Services, 1315 East West Highway, 9th Floor, Silver Spring, MD 20910, (301) 713-2379, Fax: (301) 713-2385, www.nmfs.noaa.gov; *Fisheries of the United States - 2006* and *Our Living Oceans: The Economic Status of U.S. Fisheries.*

U.S. Bureau of Labor Statistics (BLS), Postal Square Building, 2 Massachusetts Avenue, NE, Washington, DC 20212-0001, (202) 691-5200, Fax: (202) 691-6325, www.bls.gov; *Consumer Price Index Detailed Report* and *Monthly Labor Review (MLR).*

FISH - PRODUCTION AND VALUE - PROCESSED PRODUCTS

National Marine Fisheries Service (NMFS), National Oceanic and Atmospheric Administration (NOAA), Office of Constituent Services, 1315 East West Highway, 9th Floor, Silver Spring, MD 20910, (301) 713-2379, Fax: (301) 713-2385, www.nmfs.noaa.gov; *Fisheries of the United States - 2006.*

FISH - SUPPLY

National Marine Fisheries Service (NMFS), National Oceanic and Atmospheric Administration (NOAA), Office of Constituent Services, 1315 East West Highway, 9th Floor, Silver Spring, MD 20910, (301) 713-2379, Fax: (301) 713-2385, www.nmfs.noaa.gov; *Fisheries of the United States - 2006; Our Living Oceans: Report on the Status of U.S. Living Marine Resources;* and *Our Living Oceans: The Economic Status of U.S. Fisheries.*

FISHING AND HUNTING

National Sporting Goods Association (NSGA), 1601 Feehanville Drive, Suite 300, Mount Prospect, IL 60056, (847) 296-6742, Fax: (847) 391-9827, www.nsga.org; *2006 Sports Participation* and *Ten-Year History of Selected Sports Participation, 1996-2006.*

U.S. Census Bureau, Company Statistics Division, 4700 Silver Hill Road, Washington DC 20233-0001, (301) 763-3030, www.census.gov/csd/; *Statistics of U.S. Businesses (SUSB).*

U.S. Department of the Interior (DOI), Fish Wildlife Service (FWS), 1849 C Street, NW, Washington, DC 20240, (800) 344-WILD, www.fws.gov; *2006 National Survey of Fishing, Hunting, and Wildlife-Associated Recreation (FHWAR).*

FISHING, COMMERCIAL - CATCH - QUANTITY AND VALUE

National Marine Fisheries Service (NMFS), National Oceanic and Atmospheric Administration (NOAA), Office of Constituent Services, 1315 East West Highway, 9th Floor, Silver Spring, MD 20910, (301) 713-2379, Fax: (301) 713-2385, www.nmfs.noaa.gov; *Fisheries of the United States - 2006.*

FISHING, COMMERCIAL - INTERNATIONAL TRADE

National Marine Fisheries Service (NMFS), National Oceanic and Atmospheric Administration (NOAA), Office of Constituent Services, 1315 East West Highway, 9th Floor, Silver Spring, MD 20910, (301) 713-2379, Fax: (301) 713-2385, www.nmfs.noaa.gov; *Fisheries of the United States - 2006.*

U.S. Census Bureau, Foreign Trade Division, 4700 Silver Hill Road, Washington DC 20233-0001, (301) 763-3030, www.census.gov/foreign-trade/www/; *U.S. International Trade in Goods and Services.*

FISHING, COMMERCIAL - PRODUCTS

National Marine Fisheries Service (NMFS), National Oceanic and Atmospheric Administration (NOAA), Office of Constituent Services, 1315 East West

Highway, 9th Floor, Silver Spring, MD 20910, (301) 713-2379, Fax: (301) 713-2385, www.nmfs.noaa.gov; *Fisheries of the United States - 2006.*

FLAX PRODUCTION

National Agricultural Statistics Service (NASS), U.S. Department of Agriculture (USDA), 1400 Independence Avenue, SW, Washington, DC 20250, (800) 727-9540, Fax: (202) 690-2090, www.nass.usda.gov; *Grain Stocks.*

United Nations Statistics Division, New York, NY 10017, (800) 253-9646, Fax: (212) 963-4116, http://unstats.un.org; *Monthly Bulletin of Statistics.*

FLOODS

Center for Research on the Epidemiology of Disasters (CRED), Universite Catholique de Louvain, Ecole de Sante Publique, 30.94 Clos Chapelle-aux-Champs, 1200 Brussels, Belgium, www.cred.be; *An Analytical Review of Selected Data Sets on Natural Disasters and Impacts;* Complex Emergency Database (CE-DAT): A Database on the Human Impact of Complex Emergencies; *EM-DAT: The International Disaster Database; Quality and Accuracy of Disaster Data: A Comparative Analysis of Three Global Data Sets; Thirty Years of Natural Disasters 1974-2003: The Numbers;* and *Three Decades of Floods in Europe: A Preliminary Analysis of EMDAT Data.*

Eurostat, Batiment Jean Monnet, Rue Alcide de Gasperi, L-2920 Luxembourg, http://epp.eurostat.ec.europa.eu; *Environmental Protection Expenditure in Europe.*

International Organization for Migration (IOM), 17, Route des Morillons, CH-1211 Geneva 19, Switzerland, www.iom.int; *Migration, Development and Natural Disasters: Insights from the Indian Ocean Tsunami.*

National Climatic Data Center (NCDC), National Oceanic and Atmospheric Administration (NOAA), Federal Building, 151 Patton Avenue, Asheville, NC 28801-5001, (828) 271-4800, Fax: (828) 271-4876, www.ncdc.noaa.gov; *Billion Dollar U.S. Weather Disasters, 1980-2007* and *Storm Data 2006.*

National Oceanic and Atmospheric Administration (NOAA), 1401 Constitution Avenue, NW, Room 6217, Washington, DC 20230, (202) 482-6090, Fax: (202) 482-3154, www.noaa.gov; *Economic Statistics for NOAA.*

United Nations Inter-Agency Secretariat of the International Strategy for Disaster Reduction (UN/ISDR), Palais des Nations, CH 1211 Geneva 10, Switzerland, www.unisdr.org; *Disaster Statistics 1991-2005.*

FLORIDA

See also - STATE DATA (FOR INDIVIDUAL STATES)

Selig Center for Economic Growth, Terry College of Business, University of Georgia, Athens, GA 30602-6269, Mr. Jeffrey M. Humphreys, Director, (706) 425-2962, www.selig.uga.edu; *The Multicultural Economy: Minority Buying Power in 2006.*

FLORIDA - STATE DATA CENTERS

Center For Demography and Population Health, Florida State University, 601 Bellamy Building, 113 Collegiate Loop, Tallahassee, FL 32306-2240, (850) 644-1762, Fax: (850) 644-8818, www.fsu.edu/[]popctr/index.html; State Data Center.

Labor Market Statistics, Florida Agency for Workforce Innovation, MSC G-020, 107 E. Madison Street, Tallahassee, FL 32399-4111, (850) 245-7205, www.labormarketinfo.com; State Data Center.

State Library of Florida, 500 S. Bronough Street, Tallahassee, FL 32399-0250, (850) 245-6600, Fax: (850) 245-6651, http://dlis.dos.state.fl.us/stlib; State Data Center.

FLORIDA - PRIMARY STATISTICS SOURCES

Bureau of Economic Analysis Planning and Research, Florida Department of Commerce, 107 West Gaines Street, Collins Building, Suite 315, Tallahassee, FL 32399, (904) 487-3134, Fax: (904) 921-5395, http://www.gnet.org/government/stategov/1842.cfm; unpublished data.

Bureau of Economic and Business Research, University of Florida, Post Office Box 117145, Gainesville, FL 32611-7145, (352) 392-0171, Fax: (352) 392-4739, www.bebr.ufl.edu; *Florida Statistical Abstract.*

FLORISTS

Economic Research Service (ERS), U.S. Department of Agriculture (USDA), 1800 M Street, NW, Washington, DC 20036-5831, (202) 694-5050, Fax: (202) 694-5689, www.ers.usda.gov; *Floriculture and Nursery Crops: 2007.*

Office of Trade and Industry Information (OTII), Manufacturing and Services, International Trade Administration, U.S. Department of Commerce, 1401 Constitution Ave, NW, Washington, DC 20230, (800) USA TRAD(E), http://trade.gov/index.asp; *TradeStats Express.*

U.S. Census Bureau, Center for Economic Studies, 4600 Silver Hill Road, Washington DC 20233, (301) 457-1235, www.ces.census.gov; *2002 Economic Census, Retail Trade* and *2002 Economic Census, Wholesale Trade.*

U.S. Census Bureau, Company Statistics Division, 4700 Silver Hill Road, Washington DC 20233-0001, (301) 763-3030, www.census.gov/csd/; *County Business Patterns 2004.*

FLOUNDER

National Marine Fisheries Service (NMFS), National Oceanic and Atmospheric Administration (NOAA), Office of Constituent Services, 1315 East West Highway, 9th Floor, Silver Spring, MD 20910, (301) 713-2379, Fax: (301) 713-2385, www.nmfs.noaa.gov; *Fisheries of the United States - 2006.*

FLOUR - CONSUMPTION

See also GRAIN

Economic Research Service (ERS), U.S. Department of Agriculture (USDA), 1800 M Street, NW, Washington, DC 20036-5831, (202) 694-5050, Fax: (202) 694-5689, www.ers.usda.gov; *Agricultural Outlook* and *Food CPI, Prices, and Expenditures.*

FLOWERS

Foreign Agricultural Service (FAS), U.S. Department of Agriculture (USDA), 1400 Independence Avenue, SW, Washington, DC 20250, (202) 720-3935, www.fas.usda.gov; Production, Supply and Distribution Online (PSD) Online.

National Gardening Association, 1100 Dorset Street, South Burlington, VT 05403, (802) 863-5251, http://garden.org; *2007 National Gardening Survey.*

FLU

Bernan Essential Government Publications, 4611-F Assembly Drive, Lanham MD, 20706-4391, (301) 459-2255, Fax: (800) 865-3450, www.bernan.com; *Vital Statistics of the United States: Births, Life Expectancy, Deaths, and Selected Health Data.*

National Center for Health Statistics (NCHS), Centers for Disease Control and Prevention (CDC), U.S. Department of Health and Human Services (HHS), 3311 Toledo Road, Hyattsville, MD 20782, (866) 232-4636, www.cdc.gov/nchs; *National Vital Statistics Reports (NVSR); Vital Statistics of the United States (VSUS);* and unpublished data.

FLUORSPAR

U.S. Department of the Interior (DOI), U.S. Geological Survey (USGS), Office of Minerals Information, 12201 Sunrise Valley Drive, Reston, VA 20192, Mr. Kenneth A. Beckman, (703) 648-4916, Fax: (703) 648-4995, http://minerals.usgs.gov/minerals; *Mineral Commodity Summaries* and *Minerals Yearbook.*

FOLK ART

National Endowment for the Arts (NEA), 1100 Pennsylvania Avenue, NW, Washington, DC 20506-0001, (202) 682-5400, www.arts.gov; *The Changing Faces of Tradition: A Report on the Folk and Traditional Arts in the United States.*

FOOD - CAR LOADINGS

Association of American Railroads (AAR), 50 F Street, NW, Washington, DC 20001-1564, (202) 639-2100, www.aar.org; *Freight Commodity Statistics* and *Freight Loss and Damage.*

FOOD - COMMERCIAL VEGETABLES

Economic Research Service (ERS), U.S. Department of Agriculture (USDA), 1800 M Street, NW, Washington, DC 20036-5831, (202) 694-5050, Fax: (202) 694-5689, www.ers.usda.gov; *Agricultural Statistics.*

National Agricultural Statistics Service (NASS), U.S. Department of Agriculture (USDA), 1400 Independence Avenue, SW, Washington, DC 20250, (800) 727-9540, Fax: (202) 690-2090, www.nass.usda.gov; *2006 Agricultural Statistics* and *Vegetables: 2004 Annual Summary.*

FOOD - CONSUMPTION

Economic Research Service (ERS), U.S. Department of Agriculture (USDA), 1800 M Street, NW, Washington, DC 20036-5831, (202) 694-5050, Fax: (202) 694-5689, www.ers.usda.gov; *Agricultural Outlook;* The ERS Food Availability (Per Capita) Data System; and *Food CPI, Prices, and Expenditures.*

Foreign Agricultural Service (FAS), U.S. Department of Agriculture (USDA), 1400 Independence Avenue, SW, Washington, DC 20250, (202) 720-3935, www.fas.usda.gov; *Livestock and Poultry: World Markets and Trade* and Production, Supply and Distribution Online (PSD) Online.

The Norwegian Institute of Public Health (NIPH), PO Box 4404 Nydalen, N-0403 Oslo, Norway, www.fhi.no; *Rapport 2005: Interlaboratory Comparison on Dioxins in Food 2005.*

FOOD - EXPENDITURES

Economic Research Service (ERS), U.S. Department of Agriculture (USDA), 1800 M Street, NW, Washington, DC 20036-5831, (202) 694-5050, Fax: (202) 694-5689, www.ers.usda.gov; *Agricultural Statistics; Amber Waves: The Economics of Food, Farming, Natural Resources, and Rural America; Food CPI, Prices, and Expenditures;* and *Food Marketing and Price Spreads.*

Food and Nutrition Service (FNS), U.S. Department of Agriculture (USDA), 3101 Park Center Drive, Alexandria, VA 22302, (703) 305-2062, www.fns.usda.gov/fns; *Household Food Security in the United States, 2006.*

Foreign Agricultural Service (FAS), U.S. Department of Agriculture (USDA), 1400 Independence Avenue, SW, Washington, DC 20250, (202) 720-3935, www.fas.usda.gov; Production, Supply and Distribution Online (PSD) Online.

The NPD Group, Port Washington, 900 West Shore Road, Port Washington, NY 11050, (866) 444-1411, www.npd.com; Market Research for the Food and Beverage Industries and *Market Research for the Foodservice Industry.*

Progressive Grocer, 770 Broadway, New York, NY 10003, (866) 890-8541, www.progressivegrocer.com; *2006 Consumer Expenditures Study; Meat Operations Review 2008: Leaner Times; Progressive Grocer 2006 Bakery Study;* and *Progressive Grocer's 75th Annual Report of the Grocery Industry.*

U.S. Bureau of Labor Statistics (BLS), Postal Square Building, 2 Massachusetts Avenue, NE, Washington, DC 20212-0001, (202) 691-5200, Fax: (202) 691-6325, www.bls.gov; *Consumer Expenditures in 2006* and unpublished data.

World Food Programme, Via C.G.Viola 68, Parco dei Medici, 00148 Rome, Italy, www.wfp.org; *Enhanced Commitments to Women to Ensure Food Security.*

FOOD - FISH PRODUCTS

U.S. Bureau of Labor Statistics (BLS), Postal Square Building, 2 Massachusetts Avenue, NE, Washington, DC 20212-0001, (202) 691-5200, Fax: (202) 691-6325, www.bls.gov; *Consumer Expenditures in 2006.*

FOOD - FOOD COSTS

Council for Community and Economic Research (C2ER), PO Box 100127, Arlington, VA 22210, (703) 522-4980, Fax: (703) 522-4985, www.accra.org; *ACCRA Cost of Living Index.*

Foreign Agricultural Service (FAS), U.S. Department of Agriculture (USDA), 1400 Independence Avenue, SW, Washington, DC 20250, (202) 720-3935, www.fas.usda.gov; Production, Supply and Distribution Online (PSD) Online.

International Food Policy Research Institute (IFPRI), 2033 K Street, NW, Washington, D.C., 2006, (202) 862-5600, www.ifpri.org; *The World Food Situation: New Driving Forces and Required Actions.*

International Fund for Agricultural Development (IFAD), Via del Serafico, 107, 00142 Rome, Italy, www.ifad.org; *The World Food Price Situation and Its Implications for Action.*

The NPD Group, Port Washington, 900 West Shore Road, Port Washington, NY 11050, (866) 444-1411, www.npd.com; Market Research for the Food and Beverage Industries and *Market Research for the Foodservice Industry.*

U.S. Bureau of Labor Statistics (BLS), Postal Square Building, 2 Massachusetts Avenue, NE, Washington, DC 20212-0001, (202) 691-5200, Fax: (202) 691-6325, www.bls.gov; *Consumer Price Index Detailed Report.*

U.S. Department of Labor (DOL), Bureau of Labor Statistics (BLS), Postal Square Building, 2 Massachusetts Avenue, NE, Washington, DC 20212-0001, (202) 691-5200, Fax: (202) 691-6325, www.bls.gov; *Consumer Price Indexes (CPI).*

FOOD - HUNGER - INSECURITY

Economic Research Service (ERS), U.S. Department of Agriculture (USDA), 1800 M Street, NW, Washington, DC 20036-5831, (202) 694-5050, Fax: (202) 694-5689, www.ers.usda.gov; *2007 Food Assistance and Nutrition Research Innovation and Development Grants in Economics (RIDGE) Conference; Food Assistance and Nutrition Research Program, Final Report: Fiscal 2007 Activities; The Food Assistance Landscape: Federal Year 2007 Annual Report;* and *Household Food Security in the United States, 2006.*

Food and Nutrition Service (FNS), U.S. Department of Agriculture (USDA), 3101 Park Center Drive, Alexandria, VA 22302, (703) 305-2062, www.fns.usda.gov/fns; *Household Food Security in the United States, 2006.*

FOOD - PRICES

See also Individual Commodities

Bureau of Economic Analysis (BEA), U.S. Department of Commerce (DOC), 1441 L Street NW, Washington, DC 20230, (202) 606-9900, www.bea.gov; *2007 Annual Revision of the National Income and Product Accounts (NIPA)* and *Survey of Current Business (SCB).*

Foreign Agricultural Service (FAS), U.S. Department of Agriculture (USDA), 1400 Independence Avenue, SW, Washington, DC 20250, (202) 720-3935, www.fas.usda.gov; Production, Supply and Distribution Online (PSD) Online.

International Food Policy Research Institute (IFPRI), 2033 K Street, NW, Washington, D.C., 2006, (202) 862-5600, www.ifpri.org; *Food Prices, Biofuels, and Climate Change.*

The NPD Group, Port Washington, 900 West Shore Road, Port Washington, NY 11050, (866) 444-1411, www.npd.com; Market Research for the Food and Beverage Industries and *Market Research for the Foodservice Industry.*

U.S. Bureau of Labor Statistics (BLS), Postal Square Building, 2 Massachusetts Avenue, NE, Washington, DC 20212-0001, (202) 691-5200, Fax: (202) 691-6325, www.bls.gov; *Consumer Price Index Detailed Report* and *Monthly Labor Review (MLR).*

FOOD - SALES

The NPD Group, Port Washington, 900 West Shore Road, Port Washington, NY 11050, (866) 444-1411, www.npd.com; Market Research for the Food and Beverage Industries and *Market Research for the Foodservice Industry.*

Office of Trade and Industry Information (OTII), Manufacturing and Services, International Trade Administration, U.S. Department of Commerce, 1401 Constitution Ave, NW, Washington, DC 20230, (800) USA TRAD(E), http://trade.gov/index.asp; *TradeStats Express.*

Progressive Grocer, 770 Broadway, New York, NY 10003, (866) 890-8541, www.progressivegrocer.com; *2006 Consumer Expenditures Study; Marketing to American Latinos, Part I; Marketing to American Latinos, Part II; Meat Operations Review 2008: Leaner Times; Progressive Grocer 2006 Bakery Study;* and *Progressive Grocer's 75th Annual Report of the Grocery Industry.*

U.S. Census Bureau, 4700 Silver Hill Road, Washington DC 20233-0001, (301) 763-3030, www.census.gov; *2006 E-Commerce Multi-Sector Report* and *E-Stats - Measuring the Electronic Economy.*

U.S. Census Bureau, Center for Economic Studies, 4600 Silver Hill Road, Washington DC 20233, (301) 457-1235, www.ces.census.gov; *2002 Economic Census, Retail Trade* and *2002 Economic Census, Wholesale Trade.*

FOOD - SECURITY

Economic Research Service (ERS), U.S. Department of Agriculture (USDA), 1800 M Street, NW, Washington, DC 20036-5831, (202) 694-5050, Fax: (202) 694-5689, www.ers.usda.gov; *2007 Food Assistance and Nutrition Research Innovation and Development Grants in Economics (RIDGE) Conference; Food Assistance and Nutrition Research Program, Final Report: Fiscal 2007 Activities;* and *What Factors Account for State-to-State Differences in Food Security?*

Food and Nutrition Service (FNS), U.S. Department of Agriculture (USDA), 3101 Park Center Drive, Alexandria, VA 22302, (703) 305-2062, www.fns.usda.gov/fns; *Household Food Security in the United States, 2006.*

International Food Policy Research Institute (IFPRI), 2033 K Street, NW, Washington, D.C., 2006, (202) 862-5600, www.ifpri.org; *The World Food Situation: New Driving Forces and Required Actions.*

International Fund for Agricultural Development (IFAD), Via del Serafico, 107, 00142 Rome, Italy, www.ifad.org; *The World Food Price Situation and Its Implications for Action.*

World Food Programme, Via C.G.Viola 68, Parco dei Medici, 00148 Rome, Italy, www.wfp.org; *Enhanced Commitments to Women to Ensure Food Security.*

FOOD - WORLD PRODUCTION

Economic Research Service (ERS), U.S. Department of Agriculture (USDA), 1800 M Street, NW, Washington, DC 20036-5831, (202) 694-5050, Fax: (202) 694-5689, www.ers.usda.gov; *Agricultural Outlook.*

United Nations Food and Agricultural Organization (FAO), Viale delle Terme di Caracalla, 00100 Rome, Italy, (Dial from U.S. (202) 653-2400), (Fax from U.S. (202) 653 5760), www.fao.org; *FAO Statistical Yearbook 2004* and FAOSTAT Database. Subjects covered include: Agriculture, nutrition, fisheries, forestry, food aid, land use and population.

FOOD MANUFACTURING - CAPITAL

U.S. Census Bureau, Foreign Trade Division, 4700 Silver Hill Road, Washington DC 20233-0001, (301) 763-3030, www.census.gov/foreign-trade/www/; *U.S. International Trade in Goods and Services.*

FOOD MANUFACTURING - EARNINGS

The NPD Group, Port Washington, 900 West Shore Road, Port Washington, NY 11050, (866) 444-1411, www.npd.com; Market Research for the Food and Beverage Industries.

Progressive Grocer, 770 Broadway, New York, NY 10003, (866) 890-8541, www.progressivegrocer.com; *Meat Operations Review 2008: Leaner Times.*

U.S. Bureau of Labor Statistics (BLS), Postal Square Building, 2 Massachusetts Avenue, NE, Washington, DC 20212-0001, (202) 691-5200, Fax: (202) 691-6325, www.bls.gov; *Current Employment Statistics Survey (CES)* and *Employment and Earnings (EE).*

U.S. Census Bureau, Company Statistics Division, 4700 Silver Hill Road, Washington DC 20233-0001, (301) 763-3030, www.census.gov/csd/; *County Business Patterns 2004.*

U.S. Census Bureau, Foreign Trade Division, 4700 Silver Hill Road, Washington DC 20233-0001, (301) 763-3030, www.census.gov/foreign-trade/www/; *U.S. International Trade in Goods and Services.*

U.S. Census Bureau, Manufacturing and Construction Division, 4600 Silver Hill Road, Washington DC 20233, (301) 763-4673, www.census.gov/mcd; *Annual Survey of Manufactures (ASM)* and *Census of Manufactures.*

FOOD MANUFACTURING - EMPLOYEES

U.S. Bureau of Labor Statistics (BLS), Postal Square Building, 2 Massachusetts Avenue, NE, Washington, DC 20212-0001, (202) 691-5200, Fax: (202) 691-6325, www.bls.gov; *Monthly Labor Review (MLR).*

U.S. Census Bureau, Company Statistics Division, 4700 Silver Hill Road, Washington DC 20233-0001, (301) 763-3030, www.census.gov/csd/; *County Business Patterns 2004.*

U.S. Census Bureau, Foreign Trade Division, 4700 Silver Hill Road, Washington DC 20233-0001, (301) 763-3030, www.census.gov/foreign-trade/www/; *U.S. International Trade in Goods and Services.*

U.S. Census Bureau, Manufacturing and Construction Division, 4600 Silver Hill Road, Washington DC 20233, (301) 763-4673, www.census.gov/mcd; *Annual Survey of Manufactures (ASM)* and *Census of Manufactures.*

FOOD MANUFACTURING - ENERGY CONSUMPTION

U.S. Department of Energy (DOE), Energy Information Administration (EIA), 1000 Independence Avenue, SW, Washington, DC 20585, (202) 586-8800, www.eia.doe.gov; *Manufacturing Energy Consumption Survey (MECS) 2002.*

FOOD MANUFACTURING - ESTABLISHMENTS

U.S. Census Bureau, Center for Economic Studies, 4600 Silver Hill Road, Washington DC 20233, (301) 457-1235, www.ces.census.gov; *2002 Economic Census, Manufacturing.*

U.S. Census Bureau, Company Statistics Division, 4700 Silver Hill Road, Washington DC 20233-0001, (301) 763-3030, www.census.gov/csd/; *County Business Patterns 2004.*

FOOD MANUFACTURING - GROSS DOMESTIC PRODUCT

Bureau of Economic Analysis (BEA), U.S. Department of Commerce (DOC), 1441 L Street NW,

Washington, DC 20230, (202) 606-9900, www.bea.gov; *Survey of Current Business (SCB).*

FOOD MANUFACTURING - INDUSTRIAL SAFETY

U.S. Bureau of Labor Statistics (BLS), Postal Square Building, 2 Massachusetts Avenue, NE, Washington, DC 20212-0001, (202) 691-5200, Fax: (202) 691-6325, www.bls.gov; *Injuries, Illnesses, and Fatalities (IIF).*

FOOD MANUFACTURING - INTERNATIONAL TRADE

The NPD Group, Port Washington, 900 West Shore Road, Port Washington, NY 11050, (866) 444-1411, www.npd.com; Market Research for the Food and Beverage Industries.

U.S. Census Bureau, Foreign Trade Division, 4700 Silver Hill Road, Washington DC 20233-0001, (301) 763-3030, www.census.gov/foreign-trade/www/; *U.S. International Trade in Goods and Services.*

FOOD MANUFACTURING - MERGERS AND ACQUISITIONS

Thomson Financial, 195 Broadway, New York, NY 10007, (646) 822-2000, www.thomson.com; Thomson Research.

FOOD MANUFACTURING - PATENTS

U.S. Patent and Trademark Office (USPTO), PO Box 1450, Alexandria, VA 22313-1450, (571) 272-1000, www.uspto.gov; *Patenting Trends Calendar Year 2003.*

FOOD MANUFACTURING - PRODUCTIVITY

Board of Governors of the Federal Reserve System, Constitution Avenue, NW, Washington, DC 20551, (202) 452-3000, www.federalreserve.gov; *Federal Reserve Bulletin* and *Industrial Production and Capacity Utilization.*

The NPD Group, Port Washington, 900 West Shore Road, Port Washington, NY 11050, (866) 444-1411, www.npd.com; Market Research for the Food and Beverage Industries.

Progressive Grocer, 770 Broadway, New York, NY 10003, (866) 890-8541, www.progressivegrocer.com; *Progressive Grocer 2006 Bakery Study.*

U.S. Bureau of Labor Statistics (BLS), Postal Square Building, 2 Massachusetts Avenue, NE, Washington, DC 20212-0001, (202) 691-5200, Fax: (202) 691-6325, www.bls.gov; *Industry Productivity and Costs.*

FOOD MANUFACTURING - PROFITS

Bureau of Economic Analysis (BEA), U.S. Department of Commerce (DOC), 1441 L Street NW, Washington, DC 20230, (202) 606-9900, www.bea.gov; *2007 Annual Revision of the National Income and Product Accounts (NIPA)* and *Survey of Current Business (SCB).*

Executive Office of the President, Council of Economic Advisors, The White House, 1600 Pennsylvania Avenue NW, Washington, DC 20500, (202) 456-1414, www.whitehouse.gov/cea; *2007 Economic Report of the President.*

Federal Trade Commission (FTC), 600 Pennsylvania Avenue, NW, Washington, DC 20580, (202) 326-2222, www.ftc.gov; *Consumer Fraud in the United States: An FTC Survey.*

Forbes, Inc., 60 Fifth Avenue, New York, NY 10011, (212) 366-8900, www.forbes.com; *America's Largest Private Companies.*

The NPD Group, Port Washington, 900 West Shore Road, Port Washington, NY 11050, (866) 444-1411, www.npd.com; Market Research for the Food and Beverage Industries.

Progressive Grocer, 770 Broadway, New York, NY 10003, (866) 890-8541, www.progressivegrocer.com; *Progressive Grocer 2006 Bakery Study.*

FOOD MANUFACTURING - RESEARCH AND DEVELOPMENT

National Science Foundation, Division of Science Resources Statistics (SRS), 4201 Wilson Boulevard, Arlington, VA 22230, (703) 292-8780, Fax: (703) 292-9092, www.nsf.gov; *Research and Development in Industry: 2003.*

FOOD MANUFACTURING - SALES, SHIPMENTS AND RECEIPTS

Forbes, Inc., 60 Fifth Avenue, New York, NY 10011, (212) 366-8900, www.forbes.com; *America's Largest Private Companies.*

The NPD Group, Port Washington, 900 West Shore Road, Port Washington, NY 11050, (866) 444-1411, www.npd.com; Market Research for the Food and Beverage Industries.

Progressive Grocer, 770 Broadway, New York, NY 10003, (866) 890-8541, www.progressivegrocer.com; *2006 Consumer Expenditures Study; Meat Operations Review 2008: Leaner Times;* and *Progressive Grocer 2006 Bakery Study.*

U.S. Census Bureau, Center for Economic Studies, 4600 Silver Hill Road, Washington DC 20233, (301) 457-1235, www.ces.census.gov; *2002 Economic Census, Manufacturing.*

U.S. Census Bureau, Manufacturing and Construction Division, 4600 Silver Hill Road, Washington DC 20233, (301) 763-4673, www.census.gov/mcd; *Annual Survey of Manufactures (ASM)* and *Census of Manufactures.*

FOOD MANUFACTURING - TOXIC CHEMICAL RELEASES

U.S. Environmental Protection Agency (EPA), Ariel Rios Building, 1200 Pennsylvania Avenue, NW, Washington, DC 20460, (202) 272-0167, www.epa.gov; Toxics Release Inventory (TRI) Database.

FOOD SERVICE AND DRINKING PLACES

Economic Research Service (ERS), U.S. Department of Agriculture (USDA), 1800 M Street, NW, Washington, DC 20036-5831, (202) 694-5050, Fax: (202) 694-5689, www.ers.usda.gov; *Food Marketing and Price Spreads* and *Summer Food Service Program Map Machine.*

The NPD Group, Port Washington, 900 West Shore Road, Port Washington, NY 11050, (866) 444-1411, www.npd.com; *Market Research for the Foodservice Industry.*

U.S. Census Bureau, Center for Economic Studies, 4600 Silver Hill Road, Washington DC 20233, (301) 457-1235, www.ces.census.gov; *2002 Economic Census, Accommodation and Food Services.*

U.S. Census Bureau, Company Statistics Division, 4700 Silver Hill Road, Washington DC 20233-0001, (301) 763-3030, www.census.gov/csd/; *County Business Patterns 2004.*

FOOD SERVICE AND DRINKING PLACES - EARNINGS

The NPD Group, Port Washington, 900 West Shore Road, Port Washington, NY 11050, (866) 444-1411, www.npd.com; *Market Research for the Foodservice Industry.*

U.S. Bureau of Labor Statistics (BLS), Postal Square Building, 2 Massachusetts Avenue, NE, Washington, DC 20212-0001, (202) 691-5200, Fax: (202) 691-6325, www.bls.gov; *Current Employment Statistics Survey (CES)* and *Employment and Earnings (EE).*

U.S. Census Bureau, Center for Economic Studies, 4600 Silver Hill Road, Washington DC 20233, (301) 457-1235, www.ces.census.gov; *2002 Economic Census, Accommodation and Food Services.*

U.S. Census Bureau, Company Statistics Division, 4700 Silver Hill Road, Washington DC 20233-0001, (301) 763-3030, www.census.gov/csd/; *County Business Patterns 2004* and *Statistics of U.S. Businesses (SUSB).*

FOOD SERVICE AND DRINKING PLACES - EMPLOYEES

U.S. Bureau of Labor Statistics (BLS), Postal Square Building, 2 Massachusetts Avenue, NE, Washington, DC 20212-0001, (202) 691-5200, Fax: (202) 691-6325, www.bls.gov; *Current Employment Statistics Survey (CES)* and *Employment and Earnings (EE).*

U.S. Census Bureau, Center for Economic Studies, 4600 Silver Hill Road, Washington DC 20233, (301) 457-1235, www.ces.census.gov; *2002 Economic Census, Accommodation and Food Services.*

U.S. Census Bureau, Company Statistics Division, 4700 Silver Hill Road, Washington DC 20233-0001, (301) 763-3030, www.census.gov/csd/; *County Business Patterns 2004* and *Statistics of U.S. Businesses (SUSB).*

FOOD SERVICE AND DRINKING PLACES - FINANCES

The NPD Group, Port Washington, 900 West Shore Road, Port Washington, NY 11050, (866) 444-1411, www.npd.com; *Market Research for the Foodservice Industry.*

U.S. Census Bureau, Company Statistics Division, 4700 Silver Hill Road, Washington DC 20233-0001, (301) 763-3030, www.census.gov/csd/; *Statistics of U.S. Businesses (SUSB).*

U.S. Department of the Treasury (DOT), Internal Revenue Service (IRS), Statistics of Income Division (SIS), PO Box 2608, Washington, DC, 20013-2608, (202) 874-0410, Fax: (202) 874-0964, www.irs.ustreas.gov; *Statistics of Income Bulletin* and various fact sheets.

FOOD SERVICE AND DRINKING PLACES - MERGERS AND ACQUISITIONS

Thomson Financial, 195 Broadway, New York, NY 10007, (646) 822-2000, www.thomson.com; Thomson Research.

FOOD SERVICE AND DRINKING PLACES - PRODUCTIVITY

The NPD Group, Port Washington, 900 West Shore Road, Port Washington, NY 11050, (866) 444-1411, www.npd.com; *Market Research for the Foodservice Industry.*

U.S. Bureau of Labor Statistics (BLS), Postal Square Building, 2 Massachusetts Avenue, NE, Washington, DC 20212-0001, (202) 691-5200, Fax: (202) 691-6325, www.bls.gov; *Industry Productivity and Costs.*

FOOD SERVICE AND DRINKING PLACES - SALES

Claritas, 5375 Mira Sorrento Place, Suite 400, San Diego, CA 92121, (800) 866-6520, Fax: (858) 550-5800, www.claritas.com; *Consumer Buying Power.*

Economic Research Service (ERS), U.S. Department of Agriculture (USDA), 1800 M Street, NW, Washington, DC 20036-5831, (202) 694-5050, Fax: (202) 694-5689, www.ers.usda.gov; *Food CPI, Prices, and Expenditures* and *Food Marketing and Price Spreads.*

Foreign Agricultural Service (FAS), U.S. Department of Agriculture (USDA), 1400 Independence Avenue, SW, Washington, DC 20250, (202) 720-3935, www.fas.usda.gov; Production, Supply and Distribution Online (PSD) Online.

The NPD Group, Port Washington, 900 West Shore Road, Port Washington, NY 11050, (866) 444-1411, www.npd.com; *Market Research for the Foodservice Industry.*

Office of Trade and Industry Information (OTII), Manufacturing and Services, International Trade Administration, U.S. Department of Commerce, 1401 Constitution Ave, NW, Washington, DC 20230, (800) USA TRAD(E), http://trade.gov/index.asp; *TradeStats Express.*

U.S. Census Bureau, Center for Economic Studies, 4600 Silver Hill Road, Washington DC 20233, (301)

457-1235, www.ces.census.gov; *2002 Economic Census, Accommodation and Food Services; 2002 Economic Census, Retail Trade;* and *2002 Economic Census, Wholesale Trade.*

U.S. Census Bureau, Company Statistics Division, 4700 Silver Hill Road, Washington DC 20233-0001, (301) 763-3030, www.census.gov/csd/; *County Business Patterns 2004* and *Current Business Reports.*

U.S. Census Bureau, Service Sector Statistics Division, 4700 Silver Hill Road, Washington DC 20233-0001, (301) 763-3030, www.census.gov/svsd/www/economic.html; *Annual Benchmark Report for Wholesale Trade.*

FOOD SERVICE AND DRINKING PLACES - SALES - PRESCRIPTION DRUGS

National Association of Chain Drug Stores (NACDS) Foundation, 413 N. Lee Street, Alexandria, VA 22314, (703) 549-3001, Fax: (703) 836-4869, www.nacds.org; *Chain Pharmacy Industry Profile.*

FOOD STAMPS - PROGRAMS

Economic Research Service (ERS), U.S. Department of Agriculture (USDA), 1800 M Street, NW, Washington, DC 20036-5831, (202) 694-5050, Fax: (202) 694-5689, www.ers.usda.gov; *The Food Assistance Landscape: Federal Year 2007 Annual Report* and *Household Food Security in the United States, 2006.*

Food and Nutrition Service (FNS), U.S. Department of Agriculture (USDA), 3101 Park Center Drive, Alexandria, VA 22302, (703) 305-2062, www.fns.usda.gov/fns; *Characteristics of Food Stamp Households: Fiscal Year 2005; Reaching Those In Need: State Food Stamp Participation Rates in 2005;* and unpublished data.

Social Security Administration (SSA), Office of Public Inquiries, Windsor Park Building, 6401 Security Boulevard, Baltimore, MD 21235, (800) 772-1213, www.ssa.gov; *Social Security Bulletin* and unpublished data.

U.S. Census Bureau, 4700 Silver Hill Road, Washington DC 20233-0001, (301) 763-3030, www.census.gov; unpublished data.

U.S. Census Bureau, Population Division, 4700 Silver Hill Road, Washington DC 20233-0001, (301) 763-3030, www.census.gov/population/www/; *Current Population Reports.*

U.S. Library of Congress (LOC), Congressional Research Service (CRS), The Library of Congress, 101 Independence Avenue, SE, Washington, DC 20540-7500, (202) 707-5700, www.loc.gov/crsinfo; *Cash and Non-cash Benefits for Persons With Limited Income: Eligibility Rules, Recipient and Expenditure Data.*

FOOTBALL

Mediamark Research, Inc., 75 Ninth Avenue, 5th Floor, New York, NY 10011, (212) 884-9200, Fax: (212) 884-9339, www.mediamark.com; MRI+.

National Collegiate Athletic Association (NCAA), 700 West Washington Street, PO Box 6222, Indianapolis, IN 46206-6222, (317) 917-6222, Fax: (317) 917-6888, www.ncaa.org; *1982-2003 Sports Sponsorship and Participation Rates Report.*

National Federation of State High School Associations, PO Box 690, Indianapolis, IN 46206, (317) 972-6900, Fax: (317) 822-5700, www.nfhs.org; *2005-06 High School Athletics Participation Survey.*

National Football League (NFL), 280 Park Avenue, New York, NY 10017-1216, (212) 450-2000, www.nfl.com; unpublished data.

National Football League Players Association (NFLPA), 2021 L Street, NW, Suite 600, Washington, DC 20036-4909, (800) 372-2000, www.nflpa.org; unpublished data.

Sports Reference LLC, 6757 Greene Street, Suite 315, Philadelphia PA 19119, (215) 301-9181, www.sports-reference.com; *Pro-Football-Reference.com.*

FOOTWEAR

National Sporting Goods Association (NSGA), 1601 Feehanville Drive, Suite 300, Mount Prospect, IL 60056, (847) 296-6742, Fax: (847) 391-9827, www.nsga.org; *Ten-Year History of Selected Sports Participation, 1996-2006.*

The NPD Group, Port Washington, 900 West Shore Road, Port Washington, NY 11050, (866) 444-1411, www.npd.com; *Market Research for the Apparel and Footwear Industries.*

U.S. Bureau of Labor Statistics (BLS), Postal Square Building, 2 Massachusetts Avenue, NE, Washington, DC 20212-0001, (202) 691-5200, Fax: (202) 691-6325, www.bls.gov; *Consumer Expenditures in 2006; Consumer Price Index Detailed Report; Monthly Labor Review (MLR);* and unpublished data.

U.S. Census Bureau, Foreign Trade Division, 4700 Silver Hill Road, Washington DC 20233-0001, (301) 763-3030, www.census.gov/foreign-trade/www/; *U.S. International Trade in Goods and Services.*

U.S. Census Bureau, Manufacturing and Construction Division, 4600 Silver Hill Road, Washington DC 20233, (301) 763-4673, www.census.gov/mcd; *Current Industrial Reports, Manufacturing Profiles.*

FOOTWEAR - CONSUMER EXPENDITURES

The NPD Group, Port Washington, 900 West Shore Road, Port Washington, NY 11050, (866) 444-1411, www.npd.com; *Market Research for the Apparel and Footwear Industries.*

U.S. Bureau of Labor Statistics (BLS), Postal Square Building, 2 Massachusetts Avenue, NE, Washington, DC 20212-0001, (202) 691-5200, Fax: (202) 691-6325, www.bls.gov; *Consumer Expenditures in 2006.*

FOOTWEAR - INTERNATIONAL TRADE

The NPD Group, Port Washington, 900 West Shore Road, Port Washington, NY 11050, (866) 444-1411, www.npd.com; *Market Research for the Apparel and Footwear Industries.*

U.S. Census Bureau, Foreign Trade Division, 4700 Silver Hill Road, Washington DC 20233-0001, (301) 763-3030, www.census.gov/foreign-trade/www/; *U.S. International Trade in Goods and Services.*

U.S. Census Bureau, Manufacturing and Construction Division, 4600 Silver Hill Road, Washington DC 20233, (301) 763-4673, www.census.gov/mcd; *Current Industrial Reports.*

FOOTWEAR - SALES, SHIPMENTS AND RECEIPTS

The NPD Group, Port Washington, 900 West Shore Road, Port Washington, NY 11050, (866) 444-1411, www.npd.com; *Market Research for the Apparel and Footwear Industries.*

Office of Trade and Industry Information (OTII), Manufacturing and Services, International Trade Administration, U.S. Department of Commerce, 1401 Constitution Ave, NW, Washington, DC 20230, (800) USA TRAD(E), http://trade.gov/index.asp; *TradeStats Express.*

U.S. Census Bureau, Center for Economic Studies, 4600 Silver Hill Road, Washington DC 20233, (301) 457-1235, www.ces.census.gov; *2002 Economic Census, Retail Trade* and *2002 Economic Census, Wholesale Trade.*

U.S. Census Bureau, Manufacturing and Construction Division, 4600 Silver Hill Road, Washington DC 20233, (301) 763-4673, www.census.gov/mcd; *Current Industrial Reports.*

FOOTWEAR MANUFACTURING - EARNINGS

U.S. Bureau of Labor Statistics (BLS), Postal Square Building, 2 Massachusetts Avenue, NE, Washington, DC 20212-0001, (202) 691-5200, Fax: (202) 691-6325, www.bls.gov; *Current Employment Statistics Survey (CES)* and *Employment and Earnings (EE).*

U.S. Census Bureau, Foreign Trade Division, 4700 Silver Hill Road, Washington DC 20233-0001, (301) 763-3030, www.census.gov/foreign-trade/www/; *U.S. International Trade in Goods and Services.*

U.S. Census Bureau, Manufacturing and Construction Division, 4600 Silver Hill Road, Washington DC 20233, (301) 763-4673, www.census.gov/mcd; *Annual Survey of Manufactures (ASM)* and *Census of Manufactures.*

FOOTWEAR MANUFACTURING - EMPLOYEES

U.S. Bureau of Labor Statistics (BLS), Postal Square Building, 2 Massachusetts Avenue, NE, Washington, DC 20212-0001, (202) 691-5200, Fax: (202) 691-6325, www.bls.gov; *Current Employment Statistics Survey (CES)* and *Employment and Earnings (EE).*

U.S. Census Bureau, Foreign Trade Division, 4700 Silver Hill Road, Washington DC 20233-0001, (301) 763-3030, www.census.gov/foreign-trade/www/; *U.S. International Trade in Goods and Services.*

U.S. Census Bureau, Manufacturing and Construction Division, 4600 Silver Hill Road, Washington DC 20233, (301) 763-4673, www.census.gov/mcd; *Annual Survey of Manufactures (ASM)* and *Census of Manufactures.*

FOOTWEAR MANUFACTURING - PRODUCTIVITY

The NPD Group, Port Washington, 900 West Shore Road, Port Washington, NY 11050, (866) 444-1411, www.npd.com; *Market Research for the Apparel and Footwear Industries.*

U.S. Bureau of Labor Statistics (BLS), Postal Square Building, 2 Massachusetts Avenue, NE, Washington, DC 20212-0001, (202) 691-5200, Fax: (202) 691-6325, www.bls.gov; *Industry Productivity and Costs.*

FOREIGN AID OR ASSISTANCE

Bureau of Economic Analysis (BEA), U.S. Department of Commerce (DOC), 1441 L Street NW, Washington, DC 20230, (202) 606-9900, www.bea.gov; unpublished data.

Center for Research on the Epidemiology of Disasters (CRED), Universite Catholique de Louvain, Ecole de Sante Publique, 30.94 Clos Chapelle-aux-Champs, 1200 Brussels, Belgium, www.cred.be; *An Analytical Review of Selected Data Sets on Natural Disasters and Impacts;* Complex Emergency Database (CE-DAT): A Database on the Human Impact of Complex Emergencies; *EM-DAT: The International Disaster Database;* and *Thirty Years of Natural Disasters 1974-2003: The Numbers.*

International Food Policy Research Institute (IFPRI), 2033 K Street, NW, Washington, D.C., 2006, (202) 862-5600, www.ifpri.org; *Burkina Faso PNDSA II Impact Analysis Baseline Survey, 2002-2003.*

International Fund for Agricultural Development (IFAD), Via del Serafico, 107, 00142 Rome, Italy, www.ifad.org; *Rural Poverty Report 2001 - The Challenge of Ending Rural Poverty.*

Organisation for Economic Cooperation and Development (OECD), 2 rue Andre Pascal, F-75775 Paris Cedex 16, France, (Telephone in U.S. (202) 785-6323), (Fax in U.S. (202) 785-0350), www.oecd.org; International Development Statistics CD-ROM.

U.S. Agency for International Development (USAID), Information Center, Ronald Reagan Building, Washington, D.C. 20523, (202) 712-0000, Fax: (202) 216-3524, www.usaid.gov; *U.S. Overseas Loans and Grants and Assistance from International Organizations.*

United Nations Inter-Agency Secretariat of the International Strategy for Disaster Reduction (UN/ISDR), Palais des Nations, CH 1211 Geneva 10, Switzerland, www.unisdr.org; *Disaster Statistics 1991-2005.*

World Food Programme, Via C.G.Viola 68, Parco dei Medici, 00148 Rome, Italy, www.wfp.org; *Are We Reaching the Hungry?; Hunger Facts 2006; WFP in 2006;* and *WFP in Africa: 2006 Facts, Figures and Partners.*

FOREIGN BORN POPULATION

Migration Information Source, Migration Policy Institute (MPI), 1400 16th Street NW, Suite 300, Washington, DC 20036-2257, (202) 266-1940, Fax: (202) 266-1900, www.migrationinformation.org; *Maps of the Foreign Born in the United States; US Census Data on the Foreign Born; US Historical Trends;* and *Who's Where in the United States?*

National Center for Children in Poverty (NCCP), 215 W. 125th Street, 3rd Floor, New York, NY 10027, (646) 284-9600, Fax: (646) 284-9623, www.nccp.org; *Children in Low-Income Immigrant Families* and *Children of Immigrants: A Statistical Profile.*

U.S. Census Bureau, 4700 Silver Hill Road, Washington DC 20233-0001, (301) 763-3030, www.census.gov; American FactFinder (web app); *State and County QuickFacts;* and unpublished data.

U.S. Census Bureau, Housing and Household Economics Statistics Division, 4700 Silver Hill Road, Washington DC 20233-0001, (301) 763-3030, www.census.gov/hhes/www; Decennial Census of Population and Housing (web app).

U.S. Census Bureau, Population Division, 4700 Silver Hill Road, Washington DC 20233-0001, (301) 763-3030, www.census.gov/population/www/; *The Asian and Pacific Islander Population in the United States; Current Population Reports; Foreign-Born Population in the U.S. 2003;* and *National Population Estimates by Nativity.*

U.S. Department of Homeland Security (DHS), Office of Immigration Statistics, Washington, DC 20528, (202) 282-8000, www.dhs.gov; *Characteristics of Diversity Legal Permanent Residents: 2004; Characteristics of Employment-Based Legal Permanent Residents: 2004; Estimates of the Legal Permanent Resident Population and Population Eligible to Naturalize in 2004; Estimates of the Unauthorized Immigrant Population Residing in the United States: 1990 to 2000; Estimates of the Unauthorized Immigrant Population Residing in the United States: January 2005; Fiscal Year End Statistical Reports; Immigration Enforcement Actions: 2005; IRCA Legalization Effects: Lawful Permanent Residence and Naturalization through 2001; Legal Permanent Residents: 2005; Length of Visit of Nonimmigrants Departing the United States in 2003; Mapping Immigration: Legal Permanent Residents (LPRs); Mapping Trends in Naturalizations: 1980 to 2003; Mapping Trends in U.S. Legal Immigration: 1980 to 2003; Monthly Statistical Report; Naturalizations in the United States: 2005; Nonimmigrant Population Estimates: 2004; Profiles on Legal Permanent Residents; Profiles on Naturalized Citizens; Refugee Applicants and Admissions to the United States: 2004; Refugees and Asylees: 2005; Refugees and Asylees: 2005; Temporary Admissions of Nonimmigrants to the United States: 2005;* and *Temporary Admissions of Nonimmigrants to the United States: 2005.*

U.S. Department of Justice (DOJ), Bureau of Justice Statistics, 810 Seventh Street, NW, Washington, DC 20531, (202) 307-0765, www.ojp.usdoj.gov/bjs/; *Immigration Offenders in the Federal Criminal Justice System, 2000.*

FOREIGN BORN POPULATION - CITIES

Population Reference Bureau, 1875 Connecticut Avenue, NW, Suite 520, Washington, DC, 20009-5728, (800) 877-9881, Fax: (202) 328-3937, www.prb.org; *The American People Series.*

U.S. Census Bureau, 4700 Silver Hill Road, Washington DC 20233-0001, (301) 763-3030, www.census.gov; American FactFinder (web app) and *State and County QuickFacts.*

U.S. Census Bureau, Demographic Surveys Division, 4700 Silver Hill Road, Washington DC 20233-0001, (301) 763-3030, www.census.gov; *Demographic Profiles: 100-percent and Sample Data.*

U.S. Census Bureau, Population Division, 4700 Silver Hill Road, Washington DC 20233-0001, (301) 763-3030, www.census.gov/population/www/; *Census 2000 Profiles of General Demographic Characteristics.*

FOREIGN BORN POPULATION - FOREIGN COUNTRIES

Organisation for Economic Cooperation and Development (OECD), 2 rue Andre Pascal, F-75775 Paris Cedex 16, France, (Telephone in U.S. (202) 785-6323), (Fax in U.S. (202) 785-0350), www.oecd.org; *International Migration Outlook 2007.*

FOREIGN BORN POPULATION - METROPOLITAN AREAS

Population Reference Bureau, 1875 Connecticut Avenue, NW, Suite 520, Washington, DC, 20009-5728, (800) 877-9881, Fax: (202) 328-3937, www.prb.org; *The American People Series.*

U.S. Census Bureau, 4700 Silver Hill Road, Washington DC 20233-0001, (301) 763-3030, www.census.gov; American FactFinder (web app).

U.S. Census Bureau, Demographic Surveys Division, 4700 Silver Hill Road, Washington DC 20233-0001, (301) 763-3030, www.census.gov; *Demographic Profiles: 100-percent and Sample Data.*

U.S. Census Bureau, Population Division, 4700 Silver Hill Road, Washington DC 20233-0001, (301) 763-3030, www.census.gov/population/www/; *Census 2000 Profiles of General Demographic Characteristics.*

FOREIGN BORN POPULATION - STATES

Migration Information Source, Migration Policy Institute (MPI), 1400 16th Street NW, Suite 300, Washington, DC 20036-2257, (202) 266-1940, Fax: (202) 266-1900, www.migrationinformation.org; *Maps of the Foreign Born in the United States; US Census Data on the Foreign Born; US Historical Trends;* and *Who's Where in the United States?*

Population Reference Bureau, 1875 Connecticut Avenue, NW, Suite 520, Washington, DC, 20009-5728, (800) 877-9881, Fax: (202) 328-3937, www.prb.org; *The American People Series.*

U.S. Census Bureau, 4700 Silver Hill Road, Washington DC 20233-0001, (301) 763-3030, www.census.gov; American FactFinder (web app) and *State and County QuickFacts.*

U.S. Census Bureau, Demographic Surveys Division, 4700 Silver Hill Road, Washington DC 20233-0001, (301) 763-3030, www.census.gov; *Demographic Profiles: 100-percent and Sample Data.*

U.S. Census Bureau, Population Division, 4700 Silver Hill Road, Washington DC 20233-0001, (301) 763-3030, www.census.gov/population/www/; *Census 2000 Profiles of General Demographic Characteristics.*

FOREIGN COUNTRIES - AGRICULTURAL TRADE

Economic Research Service (ERS), U.S. Department of Agriculture (USDA), 1800 M Street, NW, Washington, DC 20036-5831, (202) 694-5050, Fax: (202) 694-5689, www.ers.usda.gov; *Agricultural Statistics* and *Foreign Agricultural Trade of the United States (FATUS).*

Statistical, Economic and Social Research and Training Centre for Islamic Countries (SESRIC), Attar Sokak, No. 4, Gaziosmanpasa, Ankara, 06700 Turkey, www.sesrtcic.org; *Agricultural Indicators in OIC Member Countries.*

Teagasc, Oak Park, Carlow, Ireland, www.teagasc.ie; *Beef and Sheep Production Research* and *National Farm Survey 2005.*

United Nations Food and Agricultural Organization (FAO), Viale delle Terme di Caracalla, 00100 Rome, Italy, (Dial from U.S. (202) 653-2400), (Fax from U.S. (202) 653 5760), www.fao.org; *FAO Statistical Yearbook 2004* and FAOSTAT Database. Subjects covered include: Agriculture, nutrition, fisheries, forestry, food aid, land use and population.

FOREIGN COUNTRIES - AID TO DEVELOPING COUNTRIES

Bureau of Economic Analysis (BEA), U.S. Department of Commerce (DOC), 1441 L Street NW, Washington, DC 20230, (202) 606-9900, www.bea.gov; unpublished data.

International Fund for Agricultural Development (IFAD), Via del Serafico, 107, 00142 Rome, Italy, www.ifad.org; *Rural Poverty Report 2001 - The Challenge of Ending Rural Poverty.*

International Organization for Migration (IOM), 17, Route des Morillons, CH-1211 Geneva 19, Switzerland, www.iom.int; *Migration and Development: New Strategic Outlooks and Practical Ways Forward - The Cases of Angola and Zambia.*

Organisation for Economic Cooperation and Development (OECD), 2 rue Andre Pascal, F-75775 Paris Cedex 16, France, (Telephone in U.S. (202) 785-6323), (Fax in U.S. (202) 785-0350), www.oecd.org; International Development Statistics CD-ROM.

U.S. Agency for International Development (USAID), Information Center, Ronald Reagan Building, Washington, D.C. 20523, (202) 712-0000, Fax: (202) 216-3524, www.usaid.gov; *U.S. Overseas Loans and Grants and Assistance from International Organizations.*

United Nations Conference on Trade and Development (UNCTAD), DC2-1120, United Nations, New York, NY 10017, (212) 963-0027, www.unctad.org; *Development and Globalization: Facts and Figures.*

World Food Programme, Via C.G.Viola 68, Parco dei Medici, 00148 Rome, Italy, www.wfp.org; *Are We Reaching the Hungry?; Hunger Facts 2006; WFP in 2006;* and *WFP in Africa: 2006 Facts, Figures and Partners.*

FOREIGN COUNTRIES - AIR POLLUTION EMISSIONS

International Institute for Environment and Development (IIED), 3 Endsleigh Street, London, England, WC1H 0DD, United Kingdom, www.iied.org; *Environment Urbanization.*

Organisation for Economic Cooperation and Development (OECD), 2 rue Andre Pascal, F-75775 Paris Cedex 16, France, (Telephone in U.S. (202) 785-6323), (Fax in U.S. (202) 785-0350), www.oecd.org; *Key Environmental Indicators 2004* and *OECD Environmental Data Compendium 2004.*

Platts, 2 Penn Plaza, 25th Floor, New York, NY 10121-2298, (212) 904-3070, www.platts.com; *Emissions Daily; European Power Daily;* and *2007 Global Energy Outlook.*

FOREIGN COUNTRIES - AREA

U.S. Census Bureau, Population Division, 4700 Silver Hill Road, Washington DC 20233-0001, (301) 763-3030, www.census.gov/population/www/; International Data Base (IDB).

FOREIGN COUNTRIES - ARMED FORCES PERSONNEL

U.S. Department of State (DOS), 2201 C Street NW, Washington, DC 20520, (202) 647-4000, www.state.gov; *World Military Expenditures and Arms Transfers (WMEAT).*

FOREIGN COUNTRIES - ARMS EXPORTS AND IMPORTS

U.S. Department of State (DOS), 2201 C Street NW, Washington, DC 20520, (202) 647-4000, www.state.gov; *World Military Expenditures and Arms Transfers (WMEAT).*

FOREIGN COUNTRIES - BALANCE OF PAYMENTS

DSI Data Service Information, Xantener Strasse 51a, D-47495 Rheinberg, Germany, www.dsidata.com; *International Statistical Yearbook 2007.*

Economist Intelligence Unit, 111 West 57th Street, New York, NY 10019, (212) 554-0600, Fax: (212) 586-1181, www.eiu.com; *Market Indicators and Forecasts.*

Eurostat, Batiment Jean Monnet, Rue Alcide de Gasperi, L-2920 Luxembourg, http://epp.eurostat.ec.europa.eu; *Government Budgets.*

International Monetary Fund (IMF), 700 Nineteenth Street, NW, Washington, DC 20431, (202) 623-

7000, Fax: (202) 623-4661, www.imf.org; *International Financial Statistics Yearbook 2007.*

National Bureau of Statistics of China (NBS), No. 57, Yuetan Nanjie, Sanlihe, Xicheng District, Beijing 100826, China, www.stats.gov.cn/english; *International Statistical Yearbook 2008.*

The World Bank, 1818 H Street, NW, Washington, DC 20433, (202) 473-1000, Fax: (202) 477-6391, www.worldbank.org; *Global Economic Monitor (GEM)* and *Global Economic Prospects 2008.*

FOREIGN COUNTRIES - CARBON DIOXIDE EMISSIONS

DSI Data Service Information, Xantener Strasse 51a, D-47495 Rheinberg, Germany, www.dsidata.com; *Campus Solution* and *DSI's Global Environmental Database.*

Enerdata, 10 Rue Royale, 75008 Paris, France, www.enerdata.fr; *EmissionStat; Enerdata Yearbook 2007 Edition; EnerFuture Forecasts; Energy Prices Forecasts; European Energy Utilities Watch; Global Energy Market Data; Odyssee: Energy Efficiency Indicators in Europe;* and *Profiles: International Energy Market Research Online.*

International Institute for Environment and Development (IIED), 3 Endsleigh Street, London, England, WC1H 0DD, United Kingdom, www.iied.org; *Environment Urbanization.*

Platts, 2 Penn Plaza, 25th Floor, New York, NY 10121-2298, (212) 904-3070, www.platts.com; *Emissions Daily; European Power Daily;* and *2007 Global Energy Outlook.*

Population Reference Bureau, 1875 Connecticut Avenue, NW, Suite 520, Washington, DC, 20009-5728, (800) 877-9881, Fax: (202) 328-3937, www.prb.org; *Making the Link: Population, Health, Environment.*

U.S. Department of Energy (DOE), Energy Information Administration (EIA), 1000 Independence Avenue, SW, Washington, DC 20585, (202) 586-8800, www.eia.doe.gov; *International Energy Annual 2004; International Energy Outlook 2006;* and *International Energy Outlook 2006.*

FOREIGN COUNTRIES - CHILDBIRTH - STATISTICS

Population Reference Bureau, 1875 Connecticut Avenue, NW, Suite 520, Washington, DC, 20009-5728, (800) 877-9881, Fax: (202) 328-3937, www.prb.org; *The Wealth Gap in Health.*

RAND Corporation, 1776 Main Street, PO Box 2138, Santa Monica, CA 90407-2138, (310) 393-0411, www.rand.org; *The Provision of Neonatal Services: Data for International Comparisons.*

FOREIGN COUNTRIES - COAL PRODUCTION

International Institute for Environment and Development (IIED), 3 Endsleigh Street, London, England, WC1H 0DD, United Kingdom, www.iied.org; *Charcoal - the Reality: A Study of Charcoal Consumption, Trade and Production in Malawi.*

U.S. Department of Energy (DOE), Energy Information Administration (EIA), 1000 Independence Avenue, SW, Washington, DC 20585, (202) 586-8800, www.eia.doe.gov; *Annual Coal Report 2005; Annual Energy Review 2005; International Energy Annual 2004; International Energy Outlook 2006;* and *International Energy Outlook 2006.*

FOREIGN COUNTRIES - COLLEGE STUDENTS ENROLLED IN THE UNITED STATES

Council of Graduate Schools, One Dupont Circle NW, Suite 230, Washington, DC 20036, (202) 223-3791, www.cgsnet.org; *Findings from the 2007 CGS International Graduate Admissions Survey: Phase I - Applications; Findings from the 2007 CGS International Graduate Admissions Survey: Phase II - Final Applications and Initial Offers of Acceptance; Findings from the 2007 CGS International Graduate Amissions Survey: Phase III - Admissions and Enrollment;* and *Graduate Enrollment and Degrees Report.*

Institute of International Education (IIE), 809 United Nations Plaza, New York, NY 10017-3580, (212) 883-8200, Fax: (212) 984-5452, www.iie.org; *International Student Enrollment Survey: Survey Report Fall 2007; Open Doors 1948-2004: CD-ROM;* and *Open Doors 2007.*

Organisation for Economic Cooperation and Development (OECD), 2 rue Andre Pascal, F-75775 Paris Cedex 16, France, (Telephone in U.S. (202) 785-6323), (Fax in U.S. (202) 785-0350), www.oecd.org; *Education at a Glance* (2007 Edition).

FOREIGN COUNTRIES - COMMUNICATIONS

Eurostat, Batiment Jean Monnet, Rue Alcide de Gasperi, L-2920 Luxembourg, http://epp.eurostat.ec.europa.eu; *Internet Usage by Enterprises 2007* and *Patent Applications to the EPO in the ICT Sector 1993 to 2003.*

International Telecommunication Union (ITU), Place des Nations, 1211 Geneva 20, Switzerland, www.itu.int; World Telecommunication Indicators Database.

UNESCO Institute for Statistics, C.P. 6128 Succursale Centre-Ville, Montreal, Quebec, H3C 3J7 Canada, (Dial from U.S. (514) 343-6880), (Fax from U.S. (514) 343 6882), www.uis.unesco.org; *Statistical Tables.*

FOREIGN COUNTRIES - CONSUMER PRICE INDEXES

DSI Data Service Information, Xantener Strasse 51a, D-47495 Rheinberg, Germany, www.dsidata.com; *International Statistical Yearbook 2007.*

International Monetary Fund (IMF), 700 Nineteenth Street, NW, Washington, DC 20431, (202) 623-7000, Fax: (202) 623-4661, www.imf.org; *International Financial Statistics Yearbook 2007.*

National Bureau of Statistics of China (NBS), No. 57, Yuetan Nanjie, Sanlihe, Xicheng District, Beijing 100826, China, www.stats.gov.cn/english; *International Statistical Yearbook 2008.*

Organisation for Economic Cooperation and Development (OECD), 2 rue Andre Pascal, F-75775 Paris Cedex 16, France, (Telephone in U.S. (202) 785-6323), (Fax in U.S. (202) 785-0350), www.oecd.org; *OECD Main Economic Indicators (MEI).*

The World Bank, 1818 H Street, NW, Washington, DC 20433, (202) 473-1000, Fax: (202) 477-6391, www.worldbank.org; *Global Economic Monitor (GEM)* and *Global Economic Prospects 2008.*

FOREIGN COUNTRIES - CRIMINAL JUSTICE, ADMINISTRATION OF

Death Penalty Information Center, 1101 Vermont Avenue, NW, Suite 701, Washington, DC 20005, (202) 289-2275, www.deathpenaltyinfo.org; *International Perspectives on the Death Penalty: A Costly Isolation for the U.S.*

FOREIGN COUNTRIES - CRUDE OIL

American Petroleum Institute (API), 1220 L Street, NW, Washington, DC 20005-4070, (202) 682-8000, http://api-ec.api.org; *Crude Oil and Product Import Chart; Monthly Statistical Report;* and *Weekly Statistical Bulletin.*

U.S. Department of Energy (DOE), Energy Information Administration (EIA), 1000 Independence Avenue, SW, Washington, DC 20585, (202) 586-8800, www.eia.doe.gov; *Annual Energy Review 2005; International Energy Annual 2004; International Energy Outlook 2006;* and *Petroleum Supply Annual 2004.*

FOREIGN COUNTRIES - DEATH AND DEATH RATES

Population Reference Bureau, 1875 Connecticut Avenue, NW, Suite 520, Washington, DC, 20009-5728, (800) 877-9881, Fax: (202) 328-3937, www.prb.org; *PRB Graphics Bank* and *The Wealth Gap in Health.*

U.S. Census Bureau, Population Division, 4700 Silver Hill Road, Washington DC 20233-0001, (301) 763-3030, www.census.gov/population/www/; International Data Base (IDB).

World Health Organization (WHO), Avenue Appia 20, 1211 Geneve 27, Switzerland, (Telephone in U.S. (212) 331-9081), www.who.int; *World Health Report 2006.*

FOREIGN COUNTRIES - DEBT

DSI Data Service Information, Xantener Strasse 51a, D-47495 Rheinberg, Germany, www.dsidata.com; *International Statistical Yearbook 2007.*

Statistical, Economic and Social Research and Training Centre for Islamic Countries (SESRIC), Attar Sokak, No. 4, Gaziosmanpasa, Ankara, 06700 Turkey, www.sesrtcic.org; *The External Debt Situation of African and Other OIC Member Countries.*

The World Bank, 1818 H Street, NW, Washington, DC 20433, (202) 473-1000, Fax: (202) 477-6391, www.worldbank.org; *Global Economic Monitor (GEM); Global Economic Prospects 2008;* and *World Development Indicators (WDI) 2008.*

FOREIGN COUNTRIES - ECONOMIC INDICATORS

Bank for International Settlements (BIS), CH-4002, Basel, Switzerland, www.bis.org; *Annual Report 2006/07.*

Center for International Business Education Research (CIBER), Columbia Business School and School of International and Public Affairs, Uris Hall, Room 212, 3022 Broadway, New York, NY 10027-6902, Mr. Joshua Safier, (212) 854-4750, Fax: (212) 222-9821, www.columbia.edu/cu/ciber/; Datastream International.

DSI Data Service Information, Xantener Strasse 51a, D-47495 Rheinberg, Germany, www.dsidata.com; *International Statistical Yearbook 2007.*

Economist Intelligence Unit, 111 West 57th Street, New York, NY 10019, (212) 554-0600, Fax: (212) 586-1181, www.eiu.com; *Market Indicators and Forecasts.*

Enerdata, 10 Rue Royale, 75008 Paris, France, www.enerdata.fr; *EmissionStat; Enerdata Yearbook 2007 Edition; EnerFuture Forecasts; Energy Prices Forecasts; European Energy Utilities Watch; Global Energy Market Data; Odyssee: Energy Efficiency Indicators in Europe;* and *Profiles: International Energy Market Research Online.*

ESDS (Economic and Social Data Service) International, Kilburn Building, University of Manchester, Oxford Road, Manchester M13 9PL, United Kingdom, www.esds.ac.uk/international; Database: Subjects covered a range of social science topics on various countries including household and demographic information, income, employment, education and housing and Database: Topics covered include various countries' national accounts, industrial production, employment, trade, demography, human development and other indicators of national performance and development.

International Food Policy Research Institute (IFPRI), 2033 K Street, NW, Washington, D.C., 2006, (202) 862-5600, www.ifpri.org; *Burkina Faso PNDSA II Impact Analysis Baseline Survey, 2002-2003; Public Spending and Poverty Reduction in an Oil-Based Economy: The Case of Yemen;* and *The World Food Situation: New Driving Forces and Required Actions.*

International Fund for Agricultural Development (IFAD), Via del Serafico, 107, 00142 Rome, Italy, www.ifad.org; *The World Food Price Situation and Its Implications for Action.*

International Institute for Environment and Development (IIED), 3 Endsleigh Street, London, England, WC1H 0DD, United Kingdom, www.iied.org; *Environment Urbanization; The Underestimation of Urban Poverty in Low and Middle-Income Nations;* and *Urban Environments, Wealth and Health: Shifting Burdens and Possible Responses in Low and Middle-Income Nations.*

International Organization for Migration (IOM), 17, Route des Morillons, CH-1211 Geneva 19, Switzerland, www.iom.int; *Migration and Development: New Strategic Outlooks and Practical Ways Forward - The Cases of Angola and Zambia; Migration and Poverty Alleviation in China; Migration, Development and Natural Disasters: Insights from the Indian Ocean Tsunami;* and *World Migration 2005: Costs and Benefits of International Migration.*

International Trade Administration (ITA), U.S. Department of Commerce (DOC), 1401 Constitution Avenue, NW, Washington, DC 20230, (800) USA-TRAD(E), Fax: (202) 482-4473, www.ita.doc.gov; unpublished data.

National Bureau of Statistics of China (NBS), No. 57, Yuetan Nanjie, Sanlihe, Xicheng District, Beijing 100826, China, www.stats.gov.cn/english; *International Statistical Yearbook 2008.*

Population Reference Bureau, 1875 Connecticut Avenue, NW, Suite 520, Washington, DC, 20009-5728, (800) 877-9881, Fax: (202) 328-3937, www.prb.org; *The Wealth Gap in Health.*

Statistical, Economic and Social Research and Training Centre for Islamic Countries (SESRIC), Attar Sokak, No. 4, Gaziosmanpasa, Ankara, 06700 Turkey, www.sesrtcic.org; *Annual Economic Report on the OIC Countries, 2005; Human Development Report (HDR) 2006;* and *Poverty in Sub-Saharan Africa: The Situation in the OIC Member Countries.*

Statistics South Africa, PO Box 44, Pretoria 0001, South Africa, www.statssa.gov.za; *Measuring Poverty in South Africa* and *Measuring Rural Development.*

Thomson Financial, 195 Broadway, New York, NY 10007, (646) 822-2000, www.thomson.com; *International Financing Review (IFR).*

Thomson Scientific, 3501 Market Street, Philadelphia, PA 19104-3302, (800) 336-4474, www.thomson.com; *Dialog TradStat.*

United Nations Conference on Trade and Development (UNCTAD), DC2-1120, United Nations, New York, NY 10017, (212) 963-0027, www.unctad.org; *Development and Globalization: Facts and Figures.*

United Nations Economic Commission for Europe (UNECE), Information Service, Palais des Nations, CH - 1211 Geneva 10, Switzerland, www.unece.org; *statunece Database.*

The World Bank, 1818 H Street, NW, Washington, DC 20433, (202) 473-1000, Fax: (202) 477-6391, www.worldbank.org; *Global Economic Monitor (GEM)* and *Global Economic Prospects 2008.*

FOREIGN COUNTRIES - EDUCATION

Organisation for Economic Cooperation and Development (OECD), 2 rue Andre Pascal, F-75775 Paris Cedex 16, France, (Telephone in U.S. (202) 785-6323), (Fax in U.S. (202) 785-0350), www.oecd.org; *Education at a Glance* (2007 Edition).

Statistical, Economic and Social Research and Training Centre for Islamic Countries (SESRIC), Attar Sokak, No. 4, Gaziosmanpasa, Ankara, 06700 Turkey, www.sesrtcic.org; *Academic Rankings of Universities in the OIC Member Countries; Basic Facts and Figures on OIC Member Countries 2006;* and Database: Basic Social and Economic Indicators (BASEIND) of the 57 OIC member countries.

FOREIGN COUNTRIES - ELECTRICITY GENERATION

Danish Energy Authority, Amaliegade 44, DK 1256 Copenhagen K, Denmark, www.ens.dk; *Energy in Denmark 2006* and *Energy Statistics 2006.*

DSI Data Service Information, Xantener Strasse 51a, D-47495 Rheinberg, Germany, www.dsidata.com; *Campus Solution.*

U.S. Department of Energy (DOE), Energy Information Administration (EIA), 1000 Independence Avenue, SW, Washington, DC 20585, (202) 586-8800, www.eia.doe.gov; *International Energy Annual 2004* and *International Energy Outlook 2006.*

FOREIGN COUNTRIES - EMPLOYMENT AND LABOR FORCE

National Bureau of Statistics of China (NBS), No. 57, Yuetan Nanjie, Sanlihe, Xicheng District, Beijing 100826, China, www.stats.gov.cn/english; *International Statistical Yearbook 2008.*

The Norwegian Institute of Public Health (NIPH), PO Box 4404 Nydalen, N-0403 Oslo, Norway, www.fhi.no; *Unemployment Rate 2007.*

U.S. Bureau of Labor Statistics (BLS), Postal Square Building, 2 Massachusetts Avenue, NE, Washington, DC 20212-0001, (202) 691-5200, Fax: (202) 691-6325, www.bls.gov; *Comparative Civilian Labor Force Statistics, Ten Countries, 1960-2007; Monthly Labor Review (MLR);* and unpublished data.

U.S. Department of Labor (DOL), Bureau of International Labor Affairs (ILAB), Frances Perkins Building, Room C-4325, 200 Constitution Avenue, NW, Washington, DC 20210, (202) 693-4770, Fax: (202) 693-4780, www.dol.gov/ilab; *The Department of Labor's 2005 Findings on the Worst Forms of Child Labor.*

FOREIGN COUNTRIES - ENERGY PRODUCTION

Danish Energy Authority, Amaliegade 44, DK 1256 Copenhagen K, Denmark, www.ens.dk; *Energy in Denmark 2006* and *Energy Statistics 2006.*

DSI Data Service Information, Xantener Strasse 51a, D-47495 Rheinberg, Germany, www.dsidata.com; *Campus Solution* and *DSI's Global Environmental Database.*

Enerdata, 10 Rue Royale, 75008 Paris, France, www.enerdata.fr; *EmissionStat; Enerdata Yearbook 2007 Edition; EnerFuture Forecasts; Energy Prices Forecasts; European Energy Utilities Watch; Global Energy Market Data; Odyssee: Energy Efficiency Indicators in Europe;* and *Profiles: International Energy Market Research Online.*

Statistical, Economic and Social Research and Training Centre for Islamic Countries (SESRIC), Attar Sokak, No. 4, Gaziosmanpasa, Ankara, 06700 Turkey, www.sesrtcic.org; *Environmental Sustainability Index Report (ESI) 2005.*

FOREIGN COUNTRIES - ENERGY PRODUCTION - CONSUMPTION AND PRICES

DSI Data Service Information, Xantener Strasse 51a, D-47495 Rheinberg, Germany, www.dsidata.com; *Campus Solution* and *DSI's Global Environmental Database.*

Enerdata, 10 Rue Royale, 75008 Paris, France, www.enerdata.fr; *EmissionStat; Enerdata Yearbook 2007 Edition; EnerFuture Forecasts; Energy Prices Forecasts; European Energy Utilities Watch; Global Energy Market Data; Odyssee: Energy Efficiency Indicators in Europe;* and *Profiles: International Energy Market Research Online.*

Platts, 2 Penn Plaza, 25th Floor, New York, NY 10121-2298, (212) 904-3070, www.platts.com; *European Power Daily.*

U.S. Department of Energy (DOE), Energy Information Administration (EIA), 1000 Independence Avenue, SW, Washington, DC 20585, (202) 586-8800, www.eia.doe.gov; *International Energy Annual 2004* and *International Energy Outlook 2006.*

FOREIGN COUNTRIES - ENVIRONMENT

Statistical, Economic and Social Research and Training Centre for Islamic Countries (SESRIC), Attar Sokak, No. 4, Gaziosmanpasa, Ankara, 06700 Turkey, www.sesrtcic.org; *Environmental Sustainability Index Report (ESI) 2005.*

FOREIGN COUNTRIES - EXCHANGE RATES

Federal Financial Institutions Examination Council (FFIEC), 3501 Fairfax Drive, Room D8073A, Arlington, VA 22226, (202) 872-7500, www.ffiec.gov; *Country Exposure Lending Survey.*

International Trade Administration (ITA), U.S. Department of Commerce (DOC), 1401 Constitution Avenue, NW, Washington, DC 20230, (800) USA-TRAD(E), Fax: (202) 482-4473, www.ita.doc.gov; unpublished data.

FOREIGN COUNTRIES - EXPORTS AND IMPORTS

DSI Data Service Information, Xantener Strasse 51a, D-47495 Rheinberg, Germany, www.dsidata.com; *International Statistical Yearbook 2007.*

Eurostat, Batiment Jean Monnet, Rue Alcide de Gasperi, L-2920 Luxembourg, http://epp.eurostat.ec.europa.eu; Intra- and Extra-EU Trade.

Foreign Agricultural Service (FAS), U.S. Department of Agriculture (USDA), 1400 Independence Avenue, SW, Washington, DC 20250, (202) 720-3935, www.fas.usda.gov; Production, Supply and Distribution Online (PSD) Online.

National Bureau of Statistics of China (NBS), No. 57, Yuetan Nanjie, Sanlihe, Xicheng District, Beijing 100826, China, www.stats.gov.cn/english; *International Statistical Yearbook 2008.*

Organisation for Economic Cooperation and Development (OECD), 2 rue Andre Pascal, F-75775 Paris Cedex 16, France, (Telephone in U.S. (202) 785-6323), (Fax in U.S. (202) 785-0350), www.oecd.org; *International Trade by Commodity Statistics (ITCS).*

Thomson Financial, 195 Broadway, New York, NY 10007, (646) 822-2000, www.thomson.com; *International Financing Review (IFR).*

U.S. Census Bureau, Foreign Trade Division, 4700 Silver Hill Road, Washington DC 20233-0001, (301) 763-3030, www.census.gov/foreign-trade/www/; *U.S. International Trade in Goods and Services.*

The World Bank, 1818 H Street, NW, Washington, DC 20433, (202) 473-1000, Fax: (202) 477-6391, www.worldbank.org; *Global Economic Monitor (GEM)* and *Global Economic Prospects 2008.*

World Trade Organization (WTO), Centre William Rappard, Rue de Lausanne 154, CH-1211 Geneva 21, Switzerland, www.wto.org; *Statistics Database.*

FOREIGN COUNTRIES - FINANCIAL ASSETS AND LIABILITIES (FLOW OF FUNDS)

Board of Governors of the Federal Reserve System, Constitution Avenue, NW, Washington, DC 20551, (202) 452-3000, www.federalreserve.gov; *Federal Reserve Board Statistical Release* and *Flow of Funds Accounts of the United States.*

International Institute for Environment and Development (IIED), 3 Endsleigh Street, London, England, WC1H 0DD, United Kingdom, www.iied.org; *The Underestimation of Urban Poverty in Low and Middle-Income Nations* and *Urban Environments, Wealth and Health: Shifting Burdens and Possible Responses in Low and Middle-Income Nations.*

FOREIGN COUNTRIES - FISH CATCHES

National Marine Fisheries Service (NMFS), National Oceanic and Atmospheric Administration (NOAA), Office of Constituent Services, 1315 East West Highway, 9th Floor, Silver Spring, MD 20910, (301) 713-2379, Fax: (301) 713-2385, www.nmfs.noaa.gov; *Fisheries of the United States - 2006.*

FOREIGN COUNTRIES - FOOD - CONSUMPTION

Foreign Agricultural Service (FAS), U.S. Department of Agriculture (USDA), 1400 Independence Avenue, SW, Washington, DC 20250, (202) 720-3935, www.fas.usda.gov; *Livestock and Poultry: World Markets and Trade.*

FOREIGN COUNTRIES - FORESTS AND FORESTRY

Foreign Agricultural Service (FAS), U.S. Department of Agriculture (USDA), 1400 Independence Avenue, SW, Washington, DC 20250, (202) 720-3935, www.fas.usda.gov; *Wood Products: International Trade and Foreign Markets.*

Organisation for Economic Cooperation and Development (OECD), 2 rue Andre Pascal, F-75775 Paris Cedex 16, France, (Telephone in U.S. (202) 785-6323), (Fax in U.S. (202) 785-0350), www.oecd.org; *OECD Environmental Data Compendium 2004.*

FOREIGN COUNTRIES - GEOTHERMAL ENERGY

U.S. Department of Energy (DOE), Energy Information Administration (EIA), 1000 Independence Avenue, SW, Washington, DC 20585, (202) 586-8800, www.eia.doe.gov; *International Energy Annual 2004* and *International Energy Outlook 2006.*

FOREIGN COUNTRIES - GOVERNMENT FINANCES

Eurostat, Batiment Jean Monnet, Rue Alcide de Gasperi, L-2920 Luxembourg, http://epp.eurostat.ec.europa.eu; *European Social Statistics - Social Protection Expenditure and Receipts - Data 1997-2005* and *Government Budgets.*

National Bureau of Statistics of China (NBS), No. 57, Yuetan Nanjie, Sanlihe, Xicheng District, Beijing 100826, China, www.stats.gov.cn/english; *International Statistical Yearbook 2008.*

Organisation for Economic Cooperation and Development (OECD), 2 rue Andre Pascal, F-75775 Paris Cedex 16, France, (Telephone in U.S. (202) 785-6323), (Fax in U.S. (202) 785-0350), www.oecd.org; *OECD Economic Outlook 2008* and *Revenue Statistics 1965-2006 - 2007 Edition.*

Tonga Statistics Department, PO Box 149, Nuku'alofa, Tonga, www.spc.int/prism/country/to/stats/; *National Accounts Statistics 2005.*

FOREIGN COUNTRIES - GROSS DOMESTIC PRODUCT

Organisation for Economic Cooperation and Development (OECD), 2 rue Andre Pascal, F-75775 Paris Cedex 16, France, (Telephone in U.S. (202) 785-6323), (Fax in U.S. (202) 785-0350), www.oecd.org; *Comparison of Gross Domestic Product (GDP) for OECD Countries.*

FOREIGN COUNTRIES - GROSS NATIONAL PRODUCT

DSI Data Service Information, Xantener Strasse 51a, D-47495 Rheinberg, Germany, www.dsidata.com; *International Statistical Yearbook 2007.*

U.S. Department of State (DOS), 2201 C Street NW, Washington, DC 20520, (202) 647-4000, www.state.gov; *World Military Expenditures and Arms Transfers (WMEAT).*

United Nations Conference on Trade and Development (UNCTAD), DC2-1120, United Nations, New York, NY 10017, (212) 963-0027, www.unctad.org; *Development and Globalization: Facts and Figures.*

The World Bank, 1818 H Street, NW, Washington, DC 20433, (202) 473-1000, Fax: (202) 477-6391, www.worldbank.org; *Global Economic Monitor (GEM)* and *Global Economic Prospects 2008.*

FOREIGN COUNTRIES - HEALTH CARE

Australian Government Department of Health and Ageing, GPO Box 9848, Canberra ACT 2601, Australia, www.health.gov.au; General Practice Statistics and *Medicare Statistics - December Quarter 2007.*

Australian Institute of Health and Welfare (AIHW), GPO Box 570, Canberra ACT 2601, Australia, www.aihw.gov.au; *Australia's Health 2006; Deaths and Hospitalisations Due to Drowning, Australia 1999-00 to 2003-04; Diabetes: Australian Facts 2008;* and *Key National Indicators of Children's Health, Development and Wellbeing: Indicator Framework of 'A Picture of Australia's Children 2009'.*

Eurostat, Batiment Jean Monnet, Rue Alcide de Gasperi, L-2920 Luxembourg, http://epp.eurostat.ec.europa.eu; *In-Patient Average Length of Stay (ISHMT, in Days).*

International Institute for Environment and Development (IIED), 3 Endsleigh Street, London, England, WC1H 0DD, United Kingdom, www.iied.org; *Urban Environments, Wealth and Health: Shifting Burdens and Possible Responses in Low and Middle-Income Nations.*

The Norwegian Institute of Public Health (NIPH), PO Box 4404 Nydalen, N-0403 Oslo, Norway, www.fhi.no; unpublished data.

FOREIGN COUNTRIES - HEALTH CARE EXPENDITURES

Australian Institute of Health and Welfare (AIHW), GPO Box 570, Canberra ACT 2601, Australia, www.aihw.gov.au; *Expenditures on Health for Aboriginal and Torres Strait Islander Peoples 2004-05; Key National Indicators of Children's Health, Development and Wellbeing: Indicator Framework of 'A Picture of Australia's Children 2009';* and *National Public Health Expenditure Report 2005-06.*

Organisation for Economic Cooperation and Development (OECD), 2 rue Andre Pascal, F-75775 Paris Cedex 16, France, (Telephone in U.S. (202) 785-6323), (Fax in U.S. (202) 785-0350), www.oecd.org; *OECD Health Data 2007* and *OECD in Figures 2007.*

Population Reference Bureau, 1875 Connecticut Avenue, NW, Suite 520, Washington, DC, 20009-5728, (800) 877-9881, Fax: (202) 328-3937, www.prb.org; *Making the Link: Population, Health, Environment* and *The Wealth Gap in Health.*

RAND Corporation, 1776 Main Street, PO Box 2138, Santa Monica, CA 90407-2138, (310) 393-0411, www.rand.org; *The Provision of Neonatal Services: Data for International Comparisons.*

FOREIGN COUNTRIES - HYDROELECTRIC POWER

Enerdata, 10 Rue Royale, 75008 Paris, France, www.enerdata.fr; *EmissionStat; Enerdata Yearbook 2007 Edition; EnerFuture Forecasts; Energy Prices Forecasts; European Energy Utilities Watch; Global Energy Market Data; Odyssee: Energy Efficiency Indicators in Europe;* and *Profiles: International Energy Market Research Online.*

International Energy Agency (IEA), 9, rue de la Federation, 75739 Paris Cedex 15, France, www.iea.org; *Key World Energy Statistics 2007.*

Platts, 2 Penn Plaza, 25th Floor, New York, NY 10121-2298, (212) 904-3070, www.platts.com; *European Power Daily.*

U.S. Department of Energy (DOE), Energy Information Administration (EIA), 1000 Independence Avenue, SW, Washington, DC 20585, (202) 586-8800, www.eia.doe.gov; *International Energy Annual 2004* and *International Energy Outlook 2006.*

FOREIGN COUNTRIES - IMMIGRANTS

International Organization for Migration (IOM), 17, Route des Morillons, CH-1211 Geneva 19, Switzerland, www.iom.int; *International Migration; IOM Worldwide; Migration from Latin America to Europe: Trends and Policy Challenges; Migration Health Annual Report 2006; Migration, Development and Natural Disasters: Insights from the Indian Ocean Tsunami; World Migration 2003: Managing Migration - Challenges and Responses for People on the Move; World Migration 2005: Costs and Benefits of International Migration;* and *World Migration Report 2000.*

Organisation for Economic Cooperation and Development (OECD), 2 rue Andre Pascal, F-75775 Paris Cedex 16, France, (Telephone in U.S. (202) 785-6323), (Fax in U.S. (202) 785-0350), www.oecd.org; *International Migration Outlook 2007.*

FOREIGN COUNTRIES - IMMIGRATION TO THE UNITED STATES

U.S. Citizenship and Immigration Services (USCIS), Washington District Office, 2675 Prosperity Avenue, Fairfax, VA 22031, (800) 375-5283, http://uscis.gov; *2005 Yearbook of Immigration Statistics.*

U.S. Library of Congress (LOC), Congressional Research Service (CRS), The Library of Congress, 101 Independence Avenue, SE, Washington, DC 20540-7500, (202) 707-5700, www.loc.gov/crsinfo; *Border Security: The Role of the U.S. Border Patrol.*

FOREIGN COUNTRIES - INCOME TAX

Organisation for Economic Cooperation and Development (OECD), 2 rue Andre Pascal, F-75775 Paris Cedex 16, France, (Telephone in U.S. (202) 785-6323), (Fax in U.S. (202) 785-0350), www.oecd.org; *Taxing Wages 2006/2007: 2007 Edition.*

FOREIGN COUNTRIES - INFORMATION AND COMMUNICATIONS SECTOR

Eurostat, Batiment Jean Monnet, Rue Alcide de Gasperi, L-2920 Luxembourg, http://epp.eurostat.ec.europa.eu; *Patent Applications to the EPO in the ICT Sector 1993 to 2003.*

Organisation for Economic Cooperation and Development (OECD), 2 rue Andre Pascal, F-75775 Paris Cedex 16, France, (Telephone in U.S. (202) 785-6323), (Fax in U.S. (202) 785-0350), www.oecd.org; *ICT Sector Data and Metadata by Country.*

FOREIGN COUNTRIES - INPATIENT CARE

Eurostat, Batiment Jean Monnet, Rue Alcide de Gasperi, L-2920 Luxembourg, http://epp.eurostat.ec.europa.eu; *In-Patient Average Length of Stay (ISHMT, in Days).*

Organisation for Economic Cooperation and Development (OECD), 2 rue Andre Pascal, F-75775 Paris Cedex 16, France, (Telephone in U.S. (202) 785-6323), (Fax in U.S. (202) 785-0350), www.oecd.org; *OECD Health Data 2007.*

FOREIGN COUNTRIES - INTERNATIONAL TRANSACTIONS - BALANCES

Bank for International Settlements (BIS), CH-4002, Basel, Switzerland, www.bis.org; *Annual Report 2006/07.*

Bureau of Economic Analysis (BEA), U.S. Department of Commerce (DOC), 1441 L Street NW, Washington, DC 20230, (202) 606-9900, www.bea.gov; *Survey of Current Business (SCB).*

Economist Intelligence Unit, 111 West 57th Street, New York, NY 10019, (212) 554-0600, Fax: (212) 586-1181, www.eiu.com; *Market Indicators and Forecasts.*

Eurostat, Batiment Jean Monnet, Rue Alcide de Gasperi, L-2920 Luxembourg, http://epp.eurostat.ec.europa.eu; Intra- and Extra-EU Trade.

National Bureau of Statistics of China (NBS), No. 57, Yuetan Nanjie, Sanlihe, Xicheng District, Beijing 100826, China, www.stats.gov.cn/english; *International Statistical Yearbook 2008.*

Thomson Financial, 195 Broadway, New York, NY 10007, (646) 822-2000, www.thomson.com; *International Financing Review (IFR).*

FOREIGN COUNTRIES - INVESTMENT IN THE UNITED STATES

Bureau of Economic Analysis (BEA), U.S. Department of Commerce (DOC), 1441 L Street NW, Washington, DC 20230, (202) 606-9900, www.bea.gov; *Foreign Direct Investment in the United States (FDIUS); Survey of Current Business (SCB);* and *U.S. Direct Investment Abroad (USDIA).*

Department of Employment and Economic Development, Minnesota Trade Office, 1st National Bank Building, Suite E200, 332 Minnesota Street, St. Paul, MN 55101-1351, (651) 297-4222, Fax: (651) 296-3555, http://www.exportminnesota.com/mtomap.htm; *Foreign Direct Investment in Minnesota.*

Thomson Financial, 195 Broadway, New York, NY 10007, (646) 822-2000, www.thomson.com; *International Financing Review (IFR).*

FOREIGN COUNTRIES - LABOR COSTS

Organisation for Economic Cooperation and Development (OECD), 2 rue Andre Pascal, F-75775 Paris Cedex 16, France, (Telephone in U.S. (202) 785-

6323), (Fax in U.S. (202) 785-0350), www.oecd.org; *Taxing Wages 2006/2007: 2007 Edition.*

U.S. Bureau of Labor Statistics (BLS), Postal Square Building, 2 Massachusetts Avenue, NE, Washington, DC 20212-0001, (202) 691-5200, Fax: (202) 691-6325, www.bls.gov; *Foreign Labor Statistics* and *Monthly Labor Review (MLR).*

U.S. Department of Labor (DOL), Bureau of International Labor Affairs (ILAB), Frances Perkins Building, Room C-4325, 200 Constitution Avenue, NW, Washington, DC 20210, (202) 693-4770, Fax: (202) 693-4780, www.dol.gov/ilab; *Foreign Labor Trends.*

FOREIGN COUNTRIES - LABOR FORCE

National Bureau of Statistics of China (NBS), No. 57, Yuetan Nanjie, Sanlihe, Xicheng District, Beijing 100826, China, www.stats.gov.cn/english; *International Statistical Yearbook 2008.*

Organisation for Economic Cooperation and Development (OECD), 2 rue Andre Pascal, F-75775 Paris Cedex 16, France, (Telephone in U.S. (202) 785-6323), (Fax in U.S. (202) 785-0350), www.oecd.org; *International Migration Outlook 2007.*

Statistical, Economic and Social Research and Training Centre for Islamic Countries (SESRIC), Attar Sokak, No. 4, Gaziosmanpasa, Ankara, 06700 Turkey, www.sesrtcic.org; *Basic Facts and Figures on OIC Member Countries 2006* and Database: Basic Social and Economic Indicators (BASEIND) of the 57 OIC member countries.

Tonga Statistics Department, PO Box 149, Nuku'alofa, Tonga, www.spc.int/prism/country/to/stats/; *Labour Force Survey Report 2003.*

U.S. Bureau of Labor Statistics (BLS), Postal Square Building, 2 Massachusetts Avenue, NE, Washington, DC 20212-0001, (202) 691-5200, Fax: (202) 691-6325, www.bls.gov; *Comparative Civilian Labor Force Statistics, Ten Countries, 1960-2007* and *Monthly Labor Review (MLR).*

U.S. Department of Labor (DOL), Bureau of International Labor Affairs (ILAB), Frances Perkins Building, Room C-4325, 200 Constitution Avenue, NW, Washington, DC 20210, (202) 693-4770, Fax: (202) 693-4780, www.dol.gov/ilab; *The Department of Labor's 2005 Findings on the Worst Forms of Child Labor; Foreign Labor Trends; Labor Rights Report;* and *United States Employment Impact Review.*

FOREIGN COUNTRIES - LABOR PRODUCTIVITY

The Conference Board, 845 Third Avenue, New York, NY 10022-6679, (212) 759-0900, Fax: (212) 980-7014, www.conference-board.org; *Business Cycle Indicators.*

U.S. Department of Labor (DOL), Bureau of International Labor Affairs (ILAB), Frances Perkins Building, Room C-4325, 200 Constitution Avenue, NW, Washington, DC 20210, (202) 693-4770, Fax: (202) 693-4780, www.dol.gov/ilab; *Foreign Labor Trends.*

FOREIGN COUNTRIES - LOANS - BY UNITED STATES COMMERCIAL BANKS

Board of Governors of the Federal Reserve System, Constitution Avenue, NW, Washington, DC 20551, (202) 452-3000, www.federalreserve.gov; *Federal Reserve Board Statistical Release.*

FOREIGN COUNTRIES - LUMBER

Foreign Agricultural Service (FAS), U.S. Department of Agriculture (USDA), 1400 Independence Avenue, SW, Washington, DC 20250, (202) 720-3935, www.fas.usda.gov; *Wood Products: International Trade and Foreign Markets.*

FOREIGN COUNTRIES - MANUFACTURES

Eurostat, Batiment Jean Monnet, Rue Alcide de Gasperi, L-2920 Luxembourg, http://epp.eurostat.ec.europa.eu; *Patent Applications to the EPO in the ICT Sector 1993 to 2003.*

National Bureau of Statistics of China (NBS), No. 57, Yuetan Nanjie, Sanlihe, Xicheng District, Beijing 100826, China, www.stats.gov.cn/english; *International Statistical Yearbook 2008.*

U.S. Bureau of Labor Statistics (BLS), Postal Square Building, 2 Massachusetts Avenue, NE, Washington, DC 20212-0001, (202) 691-5200, Fax: (202) 691-6325, www.bls.gov; *Monthly Labor Review (MLR).*

U.S. Department of Labor (DOL), Bureau of International Labor Affairs (ILAB), Frances Perkins Building, Room C-4325, 200 Constitution Avenue, NW, Washington, DC 20210, (202) 693-4770, Fax: (202) 693-4780, www.dol.gov/ilab; *United States Employment Impact Review.*

United Nations Conference on Trade and Development (UNCTAD), DC2-1120, United Nations, New York, NY 10017, (212) 963-0027, www.unctad.org; *Development and Globalization: Facts and Figures.*

FOREIGN COUNTRIES - MANUFACTURES - PRODUCTIVITY

U.S. Bureau of Labor Statistics (BLS), Postal Square Building, 2 Massachusetts Avenue, NE, Washington, DC 20212-0001, (202) 691-5200, Fax: (202) 691-6325, www.bls.gov; *Foreign Labor Statistics.*

FOREIGN COUNTRIES - MEAT INDUSTRY AND TRADE

Economic Research Service (ERS), U.S. Department of Agriculture (USDA), 1800 M Street, NW, Washington, DC 20036-5831, (202) 694-5050, Fax: (202) 694-5689, www.ers.usda.gov; *Agricultural Statistics.*

Foreign Agricultural Service (FAS), U.S. Department of Agriculture (USDA), 1400 Independence Avenue, SW, Washington, DC 20250, (202) 720-3935, www.fas.usda.gov; *Livestock and Poultry: World Markets and Trade.*

FOREIGN COUNTRIES - MERCHANT VESSELS

U.S. Department of Transportation (DOT), Maritime Administration (MARAD), West Building, Southeast Federal Center, 1200 New Jersey Avenue, SE, Washington, DC 20590, (800) 99-MARAD, www.marad.dot.gov; *World Merchant Fleet 2005* and unpublished data.

FOREIGN COUNTRIES - MILITARY EXPENDITURES

Center for Defense Information (CDI), 1779 Massachusetts Ave, NW, Washington, DC 20036-2109, (202) 332-0600, Fax: (202) 462-4559, www.cdi.org; *The Defense Monitor.*

FOREIGN COUNTRIES - MILITARY MANPOWER

Central Intelligence Agency, Office of Public Affairs, Washington, DC 20505, (703) 482-0623, Fax: (703) 482-1739, www.cia.gov; *The World Factbook.*

FOREIGN COUNTRIES - MILITARY PERSONNEL - UNITED STATES ON ACTIVE DUTY

U.S. Department of Defense (DOD), Statistical Information Analysis Division (SIAD), The Pentagon, Washington, DC 20301, (703) 545-6700, http://siadapp.dior.whs.mil/; *Selected Manpower Statistics, Fiscal Year 2005.*

FOREIGN COUNTRIES - MILITARY SALES

Defense Security Cooperation Agency (DSCA), U.S. Department of Defense (DOD), 2800 Defense Pentagon, Washington, DC 20301-2800, (703) 601-3710, www.dsca.mil; *DSCA Facts Book 2005.*

FOREIGN COUNTRIES - MOTOR VEHICLES

U.S. Department of Transportation (DOT), Federal Highway Administration (FHA), 1200 New Jersey Avenue, SE, Washington, DC 20590, (202) 366-0660, www.fhwa.dot.gov; *Highway Statistics 2006.*

FOREIGN COUNTRIES - MUNICIPAL WASTE

Organisation for Economic Cooperation and Development (OECD), 2 rue Andre Pascal, F-75775 Paris Cedex 16, France, (Telephone in U.S. (202) 785-6323), (Fax in U.S. (202) 785-0350), www.oecd.org; *OECD Environmental Data Compendium 2004.*

FOREIGN COUNTRIES - NATURAL GAS PRODUCTION

U.S. Department of Energy (DOE), Energy Information Administration (EIA), 1000 Independence Avenue, SW, Washington, DC 20585, (202) 586-8800, www.eia.doe.gov; *International Energy Annual 2004* and *International Energy Outlook 2006.*

FOREIGN COUNTRIES - NOBEL PRIZE LAUREATES

National Science Foundation, Division of Science Resources Statistics (SRS), 4201 Wilson Boulevard, Arlington, VA 22230, (703) 292-8780, Fax: (703) 292-9092, www.nsf.gov; unpublished data.

FOREIGN COUNTRIES - NUCLEAR POWER GENERATION

Enerdata, 10 Rue Royale, 75008 Paris, France, www.enerdata.fr; *EmissionStat; Enerdata Yearbook 2007 Edition; EnerFuture Forecasts; Energy Prices Forecasts; European Energy Utilities Watch; Global Energy Market Data; Odyssee: Energy Efficiency Indicators in Europe;* and *Profiles: International Energy Market Research Online.*

International Energy Agency (IEA), 9, rue de la Federation, 75739 Paris Cedex 15, France, www.iea.org; *Key World Energy Statistics 2007.*

Platts, 2 Penn Plaza, 25th Floor, New York, NY 10121-2298, (212) 904-3070, www.platts.com; *European Power Daily* and *Nucleonics Week.*

FOREIGN COUNTRIES - NUCLEAR WASTE

Enerdata, 10 Rue Royale, 75008 Paris, France, www.enerdata.fr; *EmissionStat; Enerdata Yearbook 2007 Edition; EnerFuture Forecasts; Energy Prices Forecasts; European Energy Utilities Watch; Global Energy Market Data; Odyssee: Energy Efficiency Indicators in Europe;* and *Profiles: International Energy Market Research Online.*

Organisation for Economic Cooperation and Development (OECD), 2 rue Andre Pascal, F-75775 Paris Cedex 16, France, (Telephone in U.S. (202) 785-6323), (Fax in U.S. (202) 785-0350), www.oecd.org; *OECD Environmental Data Compendium 2004.*

FOREIGN COUNTRIES - PATENTS

Eurostat, Batiment Jean Monnet, Rue Alcide de Gasperi, L-2920 Luxembourg, http://epp.eurostat.ec.europa.eu; *Patent Applications to the EPO in the ICT Sector 1993 to 2003.*

U.S. Patent and Trademark Office (USPTO), PO Box 1450, Alexandria, VA 22313-1450, (571) 272-1000, www.uspto.gov; *Trilateral Statistics Report.*

FOREIGN COUNTRIES - PERSONAL CONSUMPTION EXPENDITURES - FOOD AND BEVERAGE

Economic Research Service (ERS), U.S. Department of Agriculture (USDA), 1800 M Street, NW, Washington, DC 20036-5831, (202) 694-5050, Fax: (202) 694-5689, www.ers.usda.gov; *Food CPI, Prices, and Expenditures.*

FOREIGN COUNTRIES - PETROLEUM PRODUCTION

DSI Data Service Information, Xantener Strasse 51a, D-47495 Rheinberg, Germany, www.dsidata.com; *DSI's Global Environmental Database.*

Enerdata, 10 Rue Royale, 75008 Paris, France, www.enerdata.fr; *EmissionStat; Enerdata Yearbook 2007 Edition; EnerFuture Forecasts; Energy Prices Forecasts; European Energy Utilities Watch; Global Energy Market Data; Odyssee: Energy Efficiency*

Indicators in Europe; and *Profiles: International Energy Market Research Online.*

PennWell Corporation, 1421 South Sheridan Road, Tulsa, OK 74112, (918) 835-3161, www.pennwell.com; *International Petroleum Encyclopedia 2007.*

U.S. Department of Energy (DOE), Energy Information Administration (EIA), 1000 Independence Avenue, SW, Washington, DC 20585, (202) 586-8800, www.eia.doe.gov; *International Energy Annual 2004* and *International Energy Outlook 2006.*

FOREIGN COUNTRIES - PHYSICIANS

Organisation for Economic Cooperation and Development (OECD), 2 rue Andre Pascal, F-75775 Paris Cedex 16, France, (Telephone in U.S. (202) 785-6323), (Fax in U.S. (202) 785-0350), www.oecd.org; *OECD Health Data 2007.*

FOREIGN COUNTRIES - POPULATION

Australian Institute of Health and Welfare (AIHW), GPO Box 570, Canberra ACT 2601, Australia, www.aihw.gov.au; *Adoptions Australia 2006-07; Australia's Welfare 2007; Child Protection Australia 2006-07; Deaths and Hospitalisations Due to Drowning, Australia 1999-00 to 2003-04;* and *Diabetes: Australian Facts 2008.*

ESDS (Economic and Social Data Service) International, Kilburn Building, University of Manchester, Oxford Road, Manchester M13 9PL, United Kingdom, www.esds.ac.uk/international; Database: Subjects covered a range of social science topics on various countries including household and demographic information, income, employment, education and housing and Database: Topics covered include various countries' national accounts, industrial production, employment, trade, demography, human development and other indicators of national performance and development.

Eurostat, Batiment Jean Monnet, Rue Alcide de Gasperi, L-2920 Luxembourg, http://epp.eurostat.ec.europa.eu; *Demographic Indicators - Population by Age-Classes.*

International Food Policy Research Institute (IFPRI), 2033 K Street, NW, Washington, D.C., 2006, (202) 862-5600, www.ifpri.org; *Public Spending and Poverty Reduction in an Oil-Based Economy: The Case of Yemen.*

International Fund for Agricultural Development (IFAD), Via del Serafico, 107, 00142 Rome, Italy, www.ifad.org; *Rural Poverty Report 2001 - The Challenge of Ending Rural Poverty.*

International Organization for Migration (IOM), 17, Route des Morillons, CH-1211 Geneva 19, Switzerland, www.iom.int; *Domestic Migrant Remittances in China: Distribution, Channels and Livelihoods; Internal Migration and Development: A Global Perspective; International Migration; IOM Emergency Needs Assesments: Post-February 2006 Displacement in Iraq; IOM Monitoring and Needs Assessments: Assessment of Iraqi Return; IOM Worldwide; Irregular Migration in Turkey; Migration - December 2007; Migration and Development: New Strategic Outlooks and Practical Ways Forward - The Cases of Angola and Zambia; Migration and Poverty Alleviation in China; Migration from Latin America to Europe: Trends and Policy Challenges; Migration Health Annual Report 2006; Migration, Development and Natural Disasters: Insights from the Indian Ocean Tsunami; World Migration 2003: Managing Migration - Challenges and Responses for People on the Move; World Migration 2005: Costs and Benefits of International Migration;* and *World Migration Report 2000.*

National Bureau of Statistics of China (NBS), No. 57, Yuetan Nanjie, Sanlihe, Xicheng District, Beijing 100826, China, www.stats.gov.cn/english; *International Statistical Yearbook 2008.*

Organisation for Economic Cooperation and Development (OECD), 2 rue Andre Pascal, F-75775 Paris Cedex 16, France, (Telephone in U.S. (202) 785-6323), (Fax in U.S. (202) 785-0350), www.oecd.org; *International Migration Outlook 2007.*

Population Reference Bureau, 1875 Connecticut Avenue, NW, Suite 520, Washington, DC, 20009-5728, (800) 877-9881, Fax: (202) 328-3937, www.prb.org; *DataFinder; Making the Link: Population, Health, Environment; Population Bulletin; PRB Graphics Bank; The Wealth Gap in Health; 2005 Women of Our World; World Population Data Sheet;* and *World Population: More Than Just Numbers.*

Statistical, Economic and Social Research and Training Centre for Islamic Countries (SESRIC), Attar Sokak, No. 4, Gaziosmanpasa, Ankara, 06700 Turkey, www.sesrtcic.org; *Basic Facts and Figures on OIC Member Countries 2006;* Database: Basic Social and Economic Indicators (BASEIND) of the 57 OIC member countries; *Human Development Report (HDR) 2006; Poverty in Sub-Saharan Africa: The Situation in the OIC Member Countries;* and *Statistical Yearbook of the OIC Countries 2006.*

Taylor and Francis Group, An Informa Business, 2 Park Square, Milton Park, Abingdon, Oxford OX14 4RN, United Kingdom, (Dial from U.S. (212) 216-7800), (Fax from U.S. (212) 564-7854), www.tandf.co.uk; *Europa World Plus.*

U.S. Census Bureau, Population Division, 4700 Silver Hill Road, Washington DC 20233-0001, (301) 763-3030, www.census.gov/population/www/; International Data Base (IDB).

U.S. Department of Labor (DOL), Bureau of International Labor Affairs (ILAB), Frances Perkins Building, Room C-4325, 200 Constitution Avenue, NW, Washington, DC 20210, (202) 693-4770, Fax: (202) 693-4780, www.dol.gov/ilab; *The Department of Labor's 2005 Findings on the Worst Forms of Child Labor.*

United Nations Conference on Trade and Development (UNCTAD), DC2-1120, United Nations, New York, NY 10017, (212) 963-0027, www.unctad.org; *Development and Globalization: Facts and Figures.*

FOREIGN COUNTRIES - PRECIPITATION (CITIES)

National Climatic Data Center (NCDC), National Oceanic and Atmospheric Administration (NOAA), Federal Building, 151 Patton Avenue, Asheville, NC 28801-5001, (828) 271-4800, Fax: (828) 271-4876, www.ncdc.noaa.gov; *Climates of the World.*

FOREIGN COUNTRIES - PRICES

International Monetary Fund (IMF), 700 Nineteenth Street, NW, Washington, DC 20431, (202) 623-7000, Fax: (202) 623-4661, www.imf.org; *International Financial Statistics Yearbook 2007.*

Organisation for Economic Cooperation and Development (OECD), 2 rue Andre Pascal, F-75775 Paris Cedex 16, France, (Telephone in U.S. (202) 785-6323), (Fax in U.S. (202) 785-0350), www.oecd.org; *OECD Main Economic Indicators (MEI).*

FOREIGN COUNTRIES - PRODUCTION - CROPS

Foreign Agricultural Service (FAS), U.S. Department of Agriculture (USDA), 1400 Independence Avenue, SW, Washington, DC 20250, (202) 720-3935, www.fas.usda.gov; Production, Supply and Distribution Online (PSD) Online.

FOREIGN COUNTRIES - PRODUCTION - INDEXES

Organisation for Economic Cooperation and Development (OECD), 2 rue Andre Pascal, F-75775 Paris Cedex 16, France, (Telephone in U.S. (202) 785-6323), (Fax in U.S. (202) 785-0350), www.oecd.org; *OECD Composite Leading Indicators (CLIs), Updated September 2007* and *OECD Main Economic Indicators (MEI).*

FOREIGN COUNTRIES - PRODUCTION - MEAT

United Nations Food and Agricultural Organization (FAO), Viale delle Terme di Caracalla, 00100 Rome, Italy, (Dial from U.S. (202) 653-2400), (Fax from U.S. (202) 653 5760), www.fao.org; *FAO Statistical Yearbook 2004* and FAOSTAT Database. Subjects covered include: Agriculture, nutrition, fisheries, forestry, food aid, land use and population.

FOREIGN COUNTRIES - PRODUCTION - MINERALS

Enerdata, 10 Rue Royale, 75008 Paris, France, www.enerdata.fr; *EmissionStat; Enerdata Yearbook 2007 Edition; EnerFuture Forecasts; Energy Prices Forecasts; European Energy Utilities Watch; Global Energy Market Data; Odyssee: Energy Efficiency Indicators in Europe;* and *Profiles: International Energy Market Research Online.*

U.S. Department of the Interior (DOI), U.S. Geological Survey (USGS), Office of Minerals Information, 12201 Sunrise Valley Drive, Reston, VA 20192, Mr. Kenneth A. Beckman, (703) 648-4916, Fax: (703) 648-4995, http://minerals.usgs.gov/minerals; *Mineral Commodity Summaries* and *Minerals Yearbook.*

FOREIGN COUNTRIES - RAINFALL (CITIES)

National Climatic Data Center (NCDC), National Oceanic and Atmospheric Administration (NOAA), Federal Building, 151 Patton Avenue, Asheville, NC 28801-5001, (828) 271-4800, Fax: (828) 271-4876, www.ncdc.noaa.gov; *Climates of the World.*

FOREIGN COUNTRIES - REFUGEES ADMITTED TO THE UNITED STATES

The Brookings Institution, 1775 Massachusetts Avenue, NW, Washington, DC 20036, (202) 797-6000, Fax: (202) 797-6004, www.brook.edu; *From 'There' to 'Here': Refugee Resettlement in Metropolitan America.*

U.S. Citizenship and Immigration Services (USCIS), Washington District Office, 2675 Prosperity Avenue, Fairfax, VA 22031, (800) 375-5283, http://uscis.gov; *2005 Yearbook of Immigration Statistics.*

FOREIGN COUNTRIES - RESEARCH AND DEVELOPMENT EXPENDITURES

Lithuanian Department of Statistics (Statistics Lithuania), Gedimino av. 29, LT-01500 Vilnius, Lithuania, www.stat.gov.lt/en; *Research Activities 2006.*

National Science Foundation, Division of Science Resources Statistics (SRS), 4201 Wilson Boulevard, Arlington, VA 22230, (703) 292-8780, Fax: (703) 292-9092, www.nsf.gov; *National Patterns of Research and Development Resources: 2006 Data Update.*

FOREIGN COUNTRIES - RESERVES (ACCOUNTING)

International Monetary Fund (IMF), 700 Nineteenth Street, NW, Washington, DC 20431, (202) 623-7000, Fax: (202) 623-4661, www.imf.org; *International Financial Statistics Yearbook 2007.*

FOREIGN COUNTRIES - ROADS

U.S. Department of Transportation (DOT), Federal Highway Administration (FHA), 1200 New Jersey Avenue, SE, Washington, DC 20590, (202) 366-0660, www.fhwa.dot.gov; *Highway Statistics 2006.*

FOREIGN COUNTRIES - SALES AND ASSISTANCE BY UNITED STATES GOVERNMENT

Defense Security Cooperation Agency (DSCA), U.S. Department of Defense (DOD), 2800 Defense Pentagon, Washington, DC 20301-2800, (703) 601-3710, www.dsca.mil; *DSCA Facts Book 2005.*

FOREIGN COUNTRIES - SECURITIES

Bureau of Economic Analysis (BEA), U.S. Department of Commerce (DOC), 1441 L Street NW, Washington, DC 20230, (202) 606-9900, www.bea.gov; *Survey of Current Business (SCB).*

Dow Jones Company, 1 World Financial Center, 200 Liberty Street, New York, NY 10281, (212) 416-2000, www.dowjones.com; *Dow Jones Indexes.*

Standard and Poor's Corporation, 55 Water Street, New York, NY 10041, (212) 438-1000, www.standardandpoors.com; *SP Global Index Data.*

U.S. Department of the Treasury (DOT), 1500 Pennsylvania Avenue, NW, Washington, DC 20220, (202) 622-2000, Fax: (202) 622-6415, www.ustreas.gov; *Treasury Bulletin.*

FOREIGN COUNTRIES - SOCIAL SECURITY CONTRIBUTIONS

Organisation for Economic Cooperation and Development (OECD), 2 rue Andre Pascal, F-75775 Paris Cedex 16, France, (Telephone in U.S. (202) 785-6323), (Fax in U.S. (202) 785-0350), www.oecd.org; *Taxing Wages 2006/2007: 2007 Edition.*

FOREIGN COUNTRIES - TAXES (REVENUE)

Organisation for Economic Cooperation and Development (OECD), 2 rue Andre Pascal, F-75775 Paris Cedex 16, France, (Telephone in U.S. (202) 785-6323), (Fax in U.S. (202) 785-0350), www.oecd.org; *OECD Economic Outlook 2008* and *Revenue Statistics 1965-2006 - 2007 Edition.*

FOREIGN COUNTRIES - TELECOMMUNICATION SERVICES

Eurostat, Batiment Jean Monnet, Rue Alcide de Gasperi, L-2920 Luxembourg, http://epp.eurostat.ec.europa.eu; *Internet Usage by Enterprises 2007.*

International Telecommunication Union (ITU), Place des Nations, 1211 Geneva 20, Switzerland, www.itu.int; *Asia-Pacific Telecommunication Indicators.*

Lithuanian Department of Statistics (Statistics Lithuania), Gedimino av. 29, LT-01500 Vilnius, Lithuania, www.stat.gov.lt/en; *Transport and Communications 2006.*

Statistical, Economic and Social Research and Training Centre for Islamic Countries (SESRIC), Attar Sokak, No. 4, Gaziosmanpasa, Ankara, 06700 Turkey, www.sesrtcic.org; *Science and Technology in OIC Member Countries.*

FOREIGN COUNTRIES - TEMPERATURE (CITIES)

National Climatic Data Center (NCDC), National Oceanic and Atmospheric Administration (NOAA), Federal Building, 151 Patton Avenue, Asheville, NC 28801-5001, (828) 271-4800, Fax: (828) 271-4876, www.ncdc.noaa.gov; *Climates of the World.*

FOREIGN COUNTRIES - TOBACCO INDUSTRY

Foreign Agricultural Service (FAS), U.S. Department of Agriculture (USDA), 1400 Independence Avenue, SW, Washington, DC 20250, (202) 720-3935, www.fas.usda.gov; *Tobacco: World Markets and Trade* and *Tobacco: World Markets and Trade.*

FOREIGN COUNTRIES - TRADE WITH THE UNITED STATES

American Petroleum Institute (API), 1220 L Street, NW, Washington, DC 20005-4070, (202) 682-8000, http://api-ec.api.org; *Crude Oil and Product Import Chart; Monthly Statistical Report;* and *Weekly Statistical Bulletin.*

Bernan Essential Government Publications, 4611-F Assembly Drive, Lanham MD, 20706-4391, (301) 459-2255, Fax: (800) 865-3450, www.bernan.com; *United States Foreign Trade Highlights: Trends in the Global Market, 2007.*

Bureau of Economic Analysis (BEA), U.S. Department of Commerce (DOC), 1441 L Street NW, Washington, DC 20230, (202) 606-9900, www.bea.gov; *Survey of Current Business (SCB).*

Dun and Bradstreet (DB) Corporation, 103 JFK Parkway, Short Hills, NJ 07078, (973) 921-5500, www.dnb.com; *Country Report.*

Economic Research Service (ERS), U.S. Department of Agriculture (USDA), 1800 M Street, NW, Washington, DC 20036-5831, (202) 694-5050, Fax: (202) 694-5689, www.ers.usda.gov; *Foreign Agricultural Trade of the United States (FATUS).*

STAT-USA, HCHB Room 4885, U.S. Department of Commerce, Washington, DC 20230, (202) 482-1986, Fax: (202) 482-2164, www.stat-usa.gov; USA Trade Online.

U.S. Census Bureau, Foreign Trade Division, 4700 Silver Hill Road, Washington DC 20233-0001, (301) 763-3030, www.census.gov/foreign-trade/www/; *U.S. International Trade in Goods and Services.*

U.S. Customs and Border Protection (CBP), U.S. Department of Homeland Security (DHS), 1300 Pennsylvania Avenue, NW Washington, DC 20004-3002, (202) 354-1000, www.cbp.gov; *FY04 Year-End Import Trade Trends Report.*

U.S. Department of Labor (DOL), Bureau of International Labor Affairs (ILAB), Frances Perkins Building, Room C-4325, 200 Constitution Avenue, NW, Washington, DC 20210, (202) 693-4770, Fax: (202) 693-4780, www.dol.gov/ilab; *United States Employment Impact Review.*

United Nations Conference on Trade and Development (UNCTAD), DC2-1120, United Nations, New York, NY 10017, (212) 963-0027, www.unctad.org; *Development and Globalization: Facts and Figures.*

FOREIGN COUNTRIES - TRAVELERS AND EXPENDITURES

International Trade Administration (ITA), U.S. Department of Commerce (DOC), 1401 Constitution Avenue, NW, Washington, DC 20230, (800) USA-TRAD(E), Fax: (202) 482-4473, www.ita.doc.gov; unpublished data.

U.S. Citizenship and Immigration Services (USCIS), Washington District Office, 2675 Prosperity Avenue, Fairfax, VA 22031, (800) 375-5283, http://uscis.gov; *2005 Yearbook of Immigration Statistics.*

FOREIGN COUNTRIES - UNITED STATES INVESTMENT ABROAD

Bureau of Economic Analysis (BEA), U.S. Department of Commerce (DOC), 1441 L Street NW, Washington, DC 20230, (202) 606-9900, www.bea.gov; *Survey of Current Business (SCB).*

United Nations Conference on Trade and Development (UNCTAD), DC2-1120, United Nations, New York, NY 10017, (212) 963-0027, www.unctad.org; Foreign Direct Investment (FDI) and *World Investment Report, 2006.*

FOREIGN COUNTRIES - VISITORS FROM

U.S. Citizenship and Immigration Services (USCIS), Washington District Office, 2675 Prosperity Avenue, Fairfax, VA 22031, (800) 375-5283, http://uscis.gov; *2005 Yearbook of Immigration Statistics.*

FOREIGN COUNTRIES - VITAL STATISTICS

Australian Institute of Health and Welfare (AIHW), GPO Box 570, Canberra ACT 2601, Australia, www.aihw.gov.au; *Australia's Welfare 2007.*

ESDS (Economic and Social Data Service) International, Kilburn Building, University of Manchester, Oxford Road, Manchester M13 9PL, United Kingdom, www.esds.ac.uk/international; Database: Subjects covered a range of social science topics on various countries including household and demographic information, income, employment, education and housing and Database: Topics covered include various countries' national accounts, industrial production, employment, trade, demography, human development and other indicators of national performance and development.

International Organization for Migration (IOM), 17, Route des Morillons, CH-1211 Geneva 19, Switzerland, www.iom.int; *Domestic Migrant Remittances in China: Distribution, Channels and Livelihoods; Internal Migration and Development: A Global Perspective; International Migration; IOM Emergency Needs Assesments: Post-February 2006 Displacement in Iraq; IOM Monitoring and Needs Assessments: Assessment of Iraqi Return; IOM Worldwide; Irregular Migration in Turkey; Migration - December 2007; Migration and Poverty Alleviation in China; Migration from Latin America to Europe: Trends and Policy Challenges; Migration Health Annual Report 2006; Migration, Development and Natural Disasters: Insights from the Indian Ocean Tsunami; World Migration 2003: Managing Migration - Challenges and Responses for People on the Move; World Migration 2005: Costs and Benefits of International Migration;* and *World Migration Report 2000.*

National Bureau of Statistics of China (NBS), No. 57, Yuetan Nanjie, Sanlihe, Xicheng District, Beijing 100826, China, www.stats.gov.cn/english; *International Statistical Yearbook 2008.*

Population Reference Bureau, 1875 Connecticut Avenue, NW, Suite 520, Washington, DC, 20009-5728, (800) 877-9881, Fax: (202) 328-3937, www.prb.org; *PRB Graphics Bank* and *The Wealth Gap in Health.*

U.S. Census Bureau, Population Division, 4700 Silver Hill Road, Washington DC 20233-0001, (301) 763-3030, www.census.gov/population/www/; International Data Base (IDB).

U.S. Department of Labor (DOL), Bureau of International Labor Affairs (ILAB), Frances Perkins Building, Room C-4325, 200 Constitution Avenue, NW, Washington, DC 20210, (202) 693-4770, Fax: (202) 693-4780, www.dol.gov/ilab; *The Department of Labor's 2005 Findings on the Worst Forms of Child Labor.*

FOREIGN COUNTRIES - WEATHER

National Climatic Data Center (NCDC), National Oceanic and Atmospheric Administration (NOAA), Federal Building, 151 Patton Avenue, Asheville, NC 28801-5001, (828) 271-4800, Fax: (828) 271-4876, www.ncdc.noaa.gov; *Climates of the World.*

FOREIGN CURRENCY HOLDINGS

Board of Governors of the Federal Reserve System, Constitution Avenue, NW, Washington, DC 20551, (202) 452-3000, www.federalreserve.gov; *Flow of Funds Accounts of the United States* and *Statistical Digest.*

FOREIGN EXCHANGE RATES

DSI Data Service Information, Xantener Strasse 51a, D-47495 Rheinberg, Germany, www.dsidata.com; *International Statistical Yearbook 2007.*

Federal Financial Institutions Examination Council (FFIEC), 3501 Fairfax Drive, Room D8073A, Arlington, VA 22226, (202) 872-7500, www.ffiec.gov; *Country Exposure Lending Survey.*

International Monetary Fund (IMF), 700 Nineteenth Street, NW, Washington, DC 20431, (202) 623-7000, Fax: (202) 623-4661, www.imf.org; *International Financial Statistics Yearbook 2007.*

International Trade Administration (ITA), U.S. Department of Commerce (DOC), 1401 Constitution Avenue, NW, Washington, DC 20230, (800) USA-TRAD(E), Fax: (202) 482-4473, www.ita.doc.gov; unpublished data.

The World Bank, 1818 H Street, NW, Washington, DC 20433, (202) 473-1000, Fax: (202) 477-6391, www.worldbank.org; *Global Economic Monitor (GEM)* and *Global Economic Prospects 2008.*

FOREIGN GRANTS AND CREDITS - UNITED STATES GOVERNMENT

Bureau of Economic Analysis (BEA), U.S. Department of Commerce (DOC), 1441 L Street NW, Washington, DC 20230, (202) 606-9900, www.bea.gov; unpublished data.

FOREIGN INVESTMENTS IN UNITED STATES

Bureau of Economic Analysis (BEA), U.S. Department of Commerce (DOC), 1441 L Street NW, Washington, DC 20230, (202) 606-9900, www.bea.gov; *Foreign Direct Investment in the United States (FDIUS); Survey of Current Business (SCB);* and *U.S. Direct Investment Abroad (USDIA).*

FOREIGN LANGUAGES - DEGREES CONFERRED

National Center for Education Statistics (NCES), 1990 K Street, NW, Washington, DC 20006, (202) 502-7300, http://nces.ed.gov; *Digest of Education Statistics 2007.*

FOREIGN LANGUAGES - PERSONS SPEAKING

National Center for Education Statistics (NCES), 1990 K Street, NW, Washington, DC 20006, (202) 502-7300, http://nces.ed.gov; *Home Literacy Activities and Signs of Children's Emerging Literacy.*

FOREIGN LANGUAGES - STUDENTS ENROLLED

American Council on the Teaching of Foreign Languages (ACTFL), 700 S. Washington Street, Suite 210, Alexandria, VA 22314, (703) 894-2900, Fax: (703) 894-2905, www.actfl.org; *Foreign Language Enrollments.*

Association of Departments of Foreign Languages (ADFL), 26 Broadway, 3rd Floor, New York, NY 10004-1789, (646) 576-5140, www.adfl.org; *ADFL Bulletin.*

FOREIGN SALES AND ASSISTANCE BY U.S. GOVERNMENT

Bureau of Economic Analysis (BEA), U.S. Department of Commerce (DOC), 1441 L Street NW, Washington, DC 20230, (202) 606-9900, www.bea.gov; unpublished data.

U.S. Agency for International Development (USAID), Information Center, Ronald Reagan Building, Washington, D.C. 20523, (202) 712-0000, Fax: (202) 216-3524, www.usaid.gov; *U.S. Overseas Loans and Grants and Assistance from International Organizations.*

FOREIGN SALES AND ASSISTANCE BY U.S. GOVERNMENT - ECONOMIC ASSISTANCE

U.S. Agency for International Development (USAID), Information Center, Ronald Reagan Building, Washington, D.C. 20523, (202) 712-0000, Fax: (202) 216-3524, www.usaid.gov; *U.S. Overseas Loans and Grants and Assistance from International Organizations.*

FOREIGN SALES AND ASSISTANCE BY U.S. GOVERNMENT - MILITARY SALES AND ASSISTANCE

Defense Security Cooperation Agency (DSCA), U.S. Department of Defense (DOD), 2800 Defense Pentagon, Washington, DC 20301-2800, (703) 601-3710, www.dsca.mil; *DSCA Facts Book 2005.*

U.S. Agency for International Development (USAID), Information Center, Ronald Reagan Building, Washington, D.C. 20523, (202) 712-0000, Fax: (202) 216-3524, www.usaid.gov; *U.S. Overseas Loans and Grants and Assistance from International Organizations.*

FOREIGN STUDENTS - COLLEGE

Council of Graduate Schools, One Dupont Circle NW, Suite 230, Washington, DC 20036, (202) 223-3791, www.cgsnet.org; *Findings from the 2007 CGS International Graduate Admissions Survey: Phase I - Applications; Findings from the 2007 CGS International Graduate Admissions Survey: Phase II - Final Applications and Initial Offers of Acceptance; Findings from the 2007 CGS International Graduate Amissions Survey: Phase III - Admissions and Enrollment;* and *Graduate Enrollment and Degrees Report.*

Institute of International Education (IIE), 809 United Nations Plaza, New York, NY 10017-3580, (212) 883-8200, Fax: (212) 984-5452, www.iie.org; *International Student Enrollment Survey: Survey Report Fall 2007; Open Doors 1948-2004: CD-ROM;* and *Open Doors 2007.*

FOREIGN-STOCK POPULATION

U.S. Census Bureau, Population Division, 4700 Silver Hill Road, Washington DC 20233-0001, (301) 763-3030, www.census.gov/population/www/; *Current Population Reports.*

FOREST PRODUCTS - CAR LOADINGS

Association of American Railroads (AAR), 50 F Street, NW, Washington, DC 20001-1564, (202) 639-2100, www.aar.org; *Freight Commodity Statistics; Freight Loss and Damage;* and *Weekly Railroad Traffic.*

FOREST PRODUCTS - CONSUMPTION

American Forest Paper Association (AFPA), 1111 Nineteenth Street, NW, Suite 800, Washington, DC 20036, (800) 878-8878, www.afandpa.org; *Annual Fiber Consumption Report; Annual Statistical Summary of Recovered Paper Utilization; 2007 Annual Statistics of Paper, Paperboard, and Wood Pulp; The 48th Annual Survey of Paper, Paperboard and Pulp Capacity; Monthly Statistics of Paper, Paperboard and Wood Pulp (PPB1);* and unpublished data.

USDA Forest Service, 1400 Independence Ave, SW, Washington, DC 20250-0003, (202) 205-8333, www.fs.fed.us; *Timber Products Supply and Demand.*

FOREST PRODUCTS - FOREIGN COUNTRIES

Foreign Agricultural Service (FAS), U.S. Department of Agriculture (USDA), 1400 Independence Avenue, SW, Washington, DC 20250, (202) 720-3935, www.fas.usda.gov; *Wood Products: International Trade and Foreign Markets.*

Statistics Indonesia (Badan Pusat Statistik (BPS)), Jl. Dr. Sutomo 6-8, Jakarta 10710, Indonesia, www.bps.go.id; *Natural Forest Concession Enterprises.*

World Resources Institute (WRI), 10 G Street, NE, Suite 800 Washington, DC 20002, (202) 729-7600, www.wri.org; *Indigenous Peoples, Representation and Citizenship in Guatemalan Forestry.*

FOREST PRODUCTS - INTERNATIONAL TRADE

USDA Forest Service, 1400 Independence Ave, SW, Washington, DC 20250-0003, (202) 205-8333, www.fs.fed.us; *Timber Products Supply and Demand.*

FOREST PRODUCTS - PRODUCER - PRICES

U.S. Bureau of Labor Statistics (BLS), Postal Square Building, 2 Massachusetts Avenue, NE, Washington, DC 20212-0001, (202) 691-5200, Fax: (202) 691-6325, www.bls.gov; *Producer Price Indexes (PPI).*

FOREST PRODUCTS - SALES

Economic Research Service (ERS), U.S. Department of Agriculture (USDA), 1800 M Street, NW, Washington, DC 20036-5831, (202) 694-5050, Fax: (202) 694-5689, www.ers.usda.gov; *Agricultural Income and Finance Outlook* and *Farm Income: Data Files.*

FOREST PRODUCTS - SHIPMENTS

U.S. Department of Transportation (DOT), Research and Innovative Technology Administration (RITA), Bureau of Transportation Statistics (BTS), 1200 New Jersey Avenue, SE, Washington, DC 20590, (800) 853-1351, www.bts.gov; *2007 Commodity Flow Survey (CFS).*

FOREST PRODUCTS INDUSTRY - EARNINGS

Bureau of Economic Analysis (BEA), U.S. Department of Commerce (DOC), 1441 L Street NW, Washington, DC 20230, (202) 606-9900, www.bea.gov; *Survey of Current Business (SCB).*

U.S. Bureau of Labor Statistics (BLS), Postal Square Building, 2 Massachusetts Avenue, NE, Washington, DC 20212-0001, (202) 691-5200, Fax: (202) 691-6325, www.bls.gov; *Current Employment Statistics Survey (CES)* and *Employment and Earnings (EE).*

U.S. Census Bureau, Company Statistics Division, 4700 Silver Hill Road, Washington DC 20233-0001, (301) 763-3030, www.census.gov/csd/; *County Business Patterns 2004* and *Statistics of U.S. Businesses (SUSB).*

U.S. Census Bureau, Manufacturing and Construction Division, 4600 Silver Hill Road, Washington DC 20233, (301) 763-4673, www.census.gov/mcd; *Annual Survey of Manufactures, Statistics for Industry Groups and Industries.*

FOREST PRODUCTS INDUSTRY - ELECTRONIC COMMERCE

U.S. Census Bureau, 4700 Silver Hill Road, Washington DC 20233-0001, (301) 763-3030, www.census.gov; *E-Stats - Measuring the Electronic Economy.*

FOREST PRODUCTS INDUSTRY - EMPLOYEES

Bureau of Economic Analysis (BEA), U.S. Department of Commerce (DOC), 1441 L Street NW, Washington, DC 20230, (202) 606-9900, www.bea.gov; *Survey of Current Business (SCB).*

U.S. Bureau of Labor Statistics (BLS), Postal Square Building, 2 Massachusetts Avenue, NE, Washington, DC 20212-0001, (202) 691-5200, Fax: (202) 691-6325, www.bls.gov; *Current Employment Statistics Survey (CES)* and *Employment and Earnings (EE).*

U.S. Census Bureau, Company Statistics Division, 4700 Silver Hill Road, Washington DC 20233-0001, (301) 763-3030, www.census.gov/csd/; *County Business Patterns 2004* and *Statistics of U.S. Businesses (SUSB).*

U.S. Census Bureau, Manufacturing and Construction Division, 4600 Silver Hill Road, Washington DC 20233, (301) 763-4673, www.census.gov/mcd; *Annual Survey of Manufactures, Statistics for Industry Groups and Industries.*

FOREST PRODUCTS INDUSTRY - ENERGY CONSUMPTION

U.S. Department of Energy (DOE), Energy Information Administration (EIA), 1000 Independence Avenue, SW, Washington, DC 20585, (202) 586-8800, www.eia.doe.gov; *Manufacturing Energy Consumption Survey (MECS) 2002.*

FOREST PRODUCTS INDUSTRY - ESTABLISHMENTS

U.S. Census Bureau, Company Statistics Division, 4700 Silver Hill Road, Washington DC 20233-0001, (301) 763-3030, www.census.gov/csd/; *County Business Patterns 2004; Statistics of U.S. Businesses (SUSB);* and *Statistics of U.S. Businesses (SUSB).*

FOREST PRODUCTS INDUSTRY - GROSS DOMESTIC PRODUCT

Bureau of Economic Analysis (BEA), U.S. Department of Commerce (DOC), 1441 L Street NW, Washington, DC 20230, (202) 606-9900, www.bea.gov; National Income and Product Accounts (NIPA) Tables (web app) and *Survey of Current Business (SCB).*

FOREST PRODUCTS INDUSTRY - INDUSTRIAL SAFETY

U.S. Bureau of Labor Statistics (BLS), Postal Square Building, 2 Massachusetts Avenue, NE, Washington, DC 20212-0001, (202) 691-5200, Fax: (202) 691-6325, www.bls.gov; *Injuries, Illnesses, and Fatalities (IIF).*

FOREST PRODUCTS INDUSTRY - INTERNATIONAL TRADE

U.S. Census Bureau, 4700 Silver Hill Road, Washington DC 20233-0001, (301) 763-3030, www.census.gov; unpublished data.

U.S. Census Bureau, Foreign Trade Division, 4700 Silver Hill Road, Washington DC 20233-0001, (301) 763-3030, www.census.gov/foreign-trade/www/; *U.S. International Trade in Goods and Services.*

FOREST PRODUCTS INDUSTRY - MERGERS AND ACQUISITIONS

Thomson Financial, 195 Broadway, New York, NY 10007, (646) 822-2000, www.thomson.com; Thomson Research.

FOREST PRODUCTS INDUSTRY - PRICES

U.S. Bureau of Labor Statistics (BLS), Postal Square Building, 2 Massachusetts Avenue, NE, Washington, DC 20212-0001, (202) 691-5200, Fax: (202) 691-6325, www.bls.gov; *Producer Price Indexes (PPI).*

FOREST PRODUCTS INDUSTRY - PRODUCTIVITY

U.S. Bureau of Labor Statistics (BLS), Postal Square Building, 2 Massachusetts Avenue, NE, Washington, DC 20212-0001, (202) 691-5200, Fax: (202) 691-6325, www.bls.gov; *Industry Productivity and Costs.*

FOREST PRODUCTS INDUSTRY - RAILROAD CAR LOADINGS

Association of American Railroads (AAR), 50 F Street, NW, Washington, DC 20001-1564, (202) 639-2100, www.aar.org; *Freight Commodity Statistics; Freight Loss and Damage;* and *Weekly Railroad Traffic.*

FOREST PRODUCTS INDUSTRY - SHIPMENTS

U.S. Census Bureau, 4700 Silver Hill Road, Washington DC 20233-0001, (301) 763-3030, www.census.gov; *E-Stats - Measuring the Electronic Economy.*

U.S. Census Bureau, Manufacturing and Construction Division, 4600 Silver Hill Road, Washington DC 20233, (301) 763-4673, www.census.gov/mcd; *Annual Survey of Manufactures, Statistics for Industry Groups and Industries.*

FOREST PRODUCTS INDUSTRY - TOXIC CHEMICAL RELEASES

U.S. Environmental Protection Agency (EPA), Ariel Rios Building, 1200 Pennsylvania Avenue, NW, Washington, DC 20460, (202) 272-0167, www.epa.gov; Toxics Release Inventory (TRI) Database.

FORESTS - LAND - ACREAGE AND OWNERSHIP

USDA Forest Service, 1400 Independence Ave, SW, Washington, DC 20250-0003, (202) 205-8333, www.fs.fed.us; *Forest Resources of the United States, 2002.*

World Resources Institute (WRI), 10 G Street, NE, Suite 800 Washington, DC 20002, (202) 729-7600, www.wri.org; *Painting the Global Picture of Tree Cover Change: Tree Cover Loss in the Humid Tropics.*

FORESTS - NATIONAL

Economic Research Service (ERS), U.S. Department of Agriculture (USDA), 1800 M Street, NW, Washington, DC 20036-5831, (202) 694-5050, Fax: (202) 694-5689, www.ers.usda.gov; *Agricultural Statistics.*

Statistics Indonesia (Badan Pusat Statistik (BPS)), Jl. Dr. Sutomo 6-8, Jakarta 10710, Indonesia, www.bps.go.id; *Natural Forest Concession Enterprises.*

USDA Forest Service, 1400 Independence Ave, SW, Washington, DC 20250-0003, (202) 205-8333, www.fs.fed.us; *Land Areas of the National Forest System 2006* and *Timber Products Supply and Demand.*

World Resources Institute (WRI), 10 G Street, NE, Suite 800 Washington, DC 20002, (202) 729-7600, www.wri.org; *Indigenous Peoples, Representation and Citizenship in Guatemalan Forestry* and *Painting the Global Picture of Tree Cover Change: Tree Cover Loss in the Humid Tropics.*

FORESTS - NATIONAL - FINANCES

USDA Forest Service, 1400 Independence Ave, SW, Washington, DC 20250-0003, (202) 205-8333, www.fs.fed.us; *Timber Products Supply and Demand.*

FORGERY AND COUNTERFEITING (ARRESTS)

Federal Bureau of Investigation (FBI), J. Edgar Hoover Building, 935 Pennsylvania Avenue, NW, Washington, DC 20535-0001, (202) 324-3000, www.fbi.gov; *Crime in the United States (CIUS) 2007 (Preliminary).*

Justice Research and Statistics Association (JRSA), 777 N. Capitol Street, NE, Suite 801, Washington, DC 20002, (202) 842-9330, Fax: (202) 842-9329, www.jrsa.org; *Crime and Justice Atlas 2001.*

FOSTER CARE

Casey Family Programs, 1300 Dexter Avenue North, Floor 3, Seattle, WA 98109-3542, (206) 282-7300, Fax: (206) 282-3555, www.casey.org; *The Casey National Alumni Study; Focus on Foster Care: Committing to Diversity and Anti-Racism; The Indian Child Welfare Act: An Examination of State Compliance in Arizona; Northwest Foster Care Alumni Study;* and *Recruitment and Retention of Resource Families: A Report on the Use of the Breakthrough Series Collaborative Methodology for Foster Family Recruitment.*

National Council For Adoption (NCFA), 225 N. Washington Street, Alexandria, VA 22314-2561, (703) 299-6633, Fax: (703) 299-6004, www.ncfa-usa.org; *Adoption Factbook III.*

U.S. Department of Justice (DOJ), National Institute of Justice (NIJ), 810 Seventh Street, NW, Washington, DC 20531, (202) 307-2942, Fax: (202) 616-0275, www.ojp.usdoj.gov/nij/; *Does Parental Incarceration Increase a Child's Risk for Foster Care Placement?*

FOUNDATIONS - PHILANTHROPIC

The Foundation Center, 79 Fifth Avenue, New York, NY 10003-3076, (212) 620-4230, Fax: (212) 807-3677, www.fdncenter.org; *Foundation Growth and Giving Estimates: Current Outlook (2008 Edition)* and *Giving in the Aftermath of 9/11: Final Update on the Foundation and Corporate Response (2004).*

The Giving Institute, 4700 W. Lake Ave, Glenview, IL 60025, (800) 462-2372, Fax: (866) 607-0913, www.aafrc.org; *Giving USA 2006.*

Independent Sector, 1200 Eighteenth Street, NW, Suite 200, Washington, DC 20036, (202) 467-6100, Fax: (202) 467-6101, www.independentsector.org; *Giving and Volunteering in the United States 2001.*

FRANCE - NATIONAL STATISTICAL OFFICE

Centre de Renseignements Statistiques, Direction generale des douanes et droits indirects, 8 rue de la tour des Dames - piece 1110 - 75436 Paris Cedex 09, France, www.douane.gouv.fr; National Data Center.

National Institute for Statistics and Economic Studies (Institut National de la Statistique et des Etudes Economiques (INSEE)), Tour "Gamma A", 195 Rue de Bercy, 75582, Paris Cedex 12, France, www.insee.fr; National Data Center.

FRANCE - PRIMARY STATISTICS SOURCES

Eurostat, Batiment Jean Monnet, Rue Alcide de Gasperi, L-2920 Luxembourg, http://epp.eurostat.ec.europa.eu; *Euro-Mediterranean Statistics 2007* and *Pocketbook on Candidate and Potential Candidate Countries.*

National Institute for Statistics and Economic Studies (Institut National de la Statistique et des Etudes Economiques (INSEE)), Tour "Gamma A", 195 Rue de Bercy, 75582, Paris Cedex 12, France, www.insee.fr; *Annuaire Statistique de la France 2007* and *Bulletin mensuel de statistique.*

FRANCE - DATABASES

Institut Agronomique Mediterraneen de Montpellier (IAMM), 3191 rte de Mende, 34093 Montpellier Cedex 5, France, www.iamm.fr; Database. Subject coverage: Agriculture, agronomy, socio economics and demographics.

FRANCE - ABORTION

European Union, Delegation of the European Commission to the United States, 2300 M Street, NW, Washington, DC 20037, (202) 862-9500, Fax: (202) 429-1766, www.eurunion.org; *First Demographic Estimates for 2006.*

United Nations Statistics Division, New York, NY 10017, (800) 253-9646, Fax: (212) 963-4116, http://unstats.un.org; *Demographic Yearbook* and *Trends in Europe and North America: The Statistical Yearbook of the ECE 2005.*

FRANCE - AGRICULTURAL MACHINERY

European Union, Delegation of the European Commission to the United States, 2300 M Street, NW, Washington, DC 20037, (202) 862-9500, Fax: (202) 429-1766, www.eurunion.org; *Statistical Overview of Transport in the European Union (Data 1970-2001).*

United Nations Statistics Division, New York, NY 10017, (800) 253-9646, Fax: (212) 963-4116, http://unstats.un.org; *Statistical Yearbook.*

FRANCE - AGRICULTURE

Economist Intelligence Unit, 111 West 57th Street, New York, NY 10019, (212) 554-0600, Fax: (212) 586-1181, www.eiu.com; *France Country Report.*

Euromonitor International, Inc., 224 S. Michigan Avenue, Suite 1500, Chicago, IL 60604, (312) 922-1115, Fax: (312) 922-1157, www.euromonitor.com; *World Marketing Data and Statistics.*

European Union, Delegation of the European Commission to the United States, 2300 M Street, NW, Washington, DC 20037, (202) 862-9500, Fax: (202) 429-1766, www.eurunion.org; *Agricultural Statistics: Data 1995-2005; European Union Labour Force Survey; Eurostatistics: Data for Short-Term Economic Analysis (2007 edition);* and *Regions - Statistical Yearbook 2006.*

Eurostat, Batiment Jean Monnet, Rue Alcide de Gasperi, L-2920 Luxembourg, http://epp.eurostat.ec.europa.eu; *EU Agricultural Prices in 2007* and *Eurostat Yearbook 2006-2007.*

Federal Statistical Office Germany, D-65180 Wiesbaden, Germany, www.destatis.de; *France 2005.*

Organisation for Economic Cooperation and Development (OECD), 2 rue Andre Pascal, F-75775 Paris Cedex 16, France, (Telephone in U.S. (202) 785-6323), (Fax in U.S. (202) 785-0350), www.oecd.org; *Indicators of Industrial Activity; 2005 OECD Agricultural Outlook Tables, 1970-2014; OECD Agricultural Outlook: 2007-2016; OECD Economic Survey - France 2007;* and STructural ANalysis (STAN) database.

Palgrave Macmillan Ltd., Houndmills, Basingstoke, Hampshire, RG21 6XS, England, (Telephone in U.S. (888) 330-8477), (Fax in U.S. (800) 672-2054), www.palgrave.com; *The Statesman's Yearbook 2008.*

Taylor and Francis Group, An Informa Business, 2 Park Square, Milton Park, Abingdon, Oxford OX14 4RN, United Kingdom, (Dial from U.S. (212) 216-7800), (Fax from U.S. (212) 564-7854), www.tandf.co.uk; *The Europa World Year Book.*

United Nations Conference on Trade and Development (UNCTAD), DC2-1120, United Nations, New York, NY 10017, (212) 963-0027, www.unctad.org; *UNCTAD Commodity Yearbook.*

United Nations Food and Agricultural Organization (FAO), Viale delle Terme di Caracalla, 00100 Rome, Italy, (Dial from U.S. (202) 653-2400), (Fax from U.S. (202) 653 5760), www.fao.org; AQUASTAT; *FAO Production Yearbook 2002; FAO Trade Yearbook;* and *The State of Food and Agriculture (SOFA) 2006.*

United Nations Statistics Division, New York, NY 10017, (800) 253-9646, Fax: (212) 963-4116, http://unstats.un.org; *Statistical Yearbook.*

The World Bank, 1818 H Street, NW, Washington, DC 20433, (202) 473-1000, Fax: (202) 477-6391, www.worldbank.org; *France* and *World Development Indicators (WDI) 2008*.

FRANCE - AIRLINES

European Union, Delegation of the European Commission to the United States, 2300 M Street, NW, Washington, DC 20037, (202) 862-9500, Fax: (202) 429-1766, www.eurunion.org; *Regions - Statistical Yearbook 2006* and *Statistical Overview of Transport in the European Union (Data 1970-2001)*.

Eurostat, Batiment Jean Monnet, Rue Alcide de Gasperi, L-2920 Luxembourg, http://epp.eurostat.ec.europa.eu; *Eurostat Yearbook 2006-2007* and *Regional Passenger and Freight Air Transport in Europe in 2006*.

International Civil Aviation Organization (ICAO), External Relations and Public Information Office (EPO), 999 University Street, Montreal, Quebec H3C 5H7, Canada, (Dial from U.S. (514) 954-8219), (Fax from U.S. (514) 954-6077), www.icao.int; *Civil Aviation Statistics of the World*.

M.E. Sharpe, 80 Business Park Drive, Armonk, NY 10504, (800) 541-6563, Fax: (914) 273-2106, www.mesharpe.com; *The Illustrated Book of World Rankings*.

Organisation for Economic Cooperation and Development (OECD), 2 rue Andre Pascal, F-75775 Paris Cedex 16, France, (Telephone in U.S. (202) 785-6323), (Fax in U.S. (202) 785-0350), www.oecd.org; *Household, Tourism, Travel: Trends, Environmental Impacts and Policy Responses*.

Palgrave Macmillan Ltd., Houndmills, Basingstoke, Hampshire, RG21 6XS, England, (Telephone in U.S. (888) 330-8477), (Fax in U.S. (800) 672-2054), www.palgrave.com; *The Statesman's Yearbook 2008*.

Taylor and Francis Group, An Informa Business, 2 Park Square, Milton Park, Abingdon, Oxford OX14 4RN, United Kingdom, (Dial from U.S. (212) 216-7800), (Fax from U.S. (212) 564-7854), www.tandf.co.uk; *The Europa World Year Book*.

United Nations Statistics Division, New York, NY 10017, (800) 253-9646, Fax: (212) 963-4116, http://unstats.un.org; *Statistical Yearbook*.

FRANCE - AIRPORTS

Central Intelligence Agency, Office of Public Affairs, Washington, DC 20505, (703) 482-0623, Fax: (703) 482-1739, www.cia.gov; *The World Factbook*.

FRANCE - ALMOND PRODUCTION

See FRANCE - CROPS

FRANCE - ALUMINUM PRODUCTION

See FRANCE - MINERAL INDUSTRIES

FRANCE - ANIMAL FEEDING

Organisation for Economic Cooperation and Development (OECD), 2 rue Andre Pascal, F-75775 Paris Cedex 16, France, (Telephone in U.S. (202) 785-6323), (Fax in U.S. (202) 785-0350), www.oecd.org; *International Trade by Commodity Statistics (ITCS)*.

United Nations Statistics Division, New York, NY 10017, (800) 253-9646, Fax: (212) 963-4116, http://unstats.un.org; *Statistical Yearbook*.

FRANCE - APPLE PRODUCTION

See FRANCE - CROPS

FRANCE - ARMED FORCES

Central Intelligence Agency, Office of Public Affairs, Washington, DC 20505, (703) 482-0623, Fax: (703) 482-1739, www.cia.gov; *The World Factbook*.

Euromonitor International, Inc., 224 S. Michigan Avenue, Suite 1500, Chicago, IL 60604, (312) 922-1115, Fax: (312) 922-1157, www.euromonitor.com; *World Marketing Data and Statistics*.

European Union, Delegation of the European Commission to the United States, 2300 M Street, NW, Washington, DC 20037, (202) 862-9500, Fax: (202) 429-1766, www.eurunion.org; *RD Expenditure in Europe (2006 edition)*.

International Institute for Strategic Studies (IISS), Arundel House, 13-15 Arundel Street, Temple Place, London WC2R 3DX, England, www.iiss.org; *The Military Balance 2007*.

International Monetary Fund (IMF), 700 Nineteenth Street, NW, Washington, DC 20431, (202) 623-7000, Fax: (202) 623-4661, www.imf.org; *Government Finance Statistics Yearbook (2008 Edition)*.

Palgrave Macmillan Ltd., Houndmills, Basingstoke, Hampshire, RG21 6XS, England, (Telephone in U.S. (888) 330-8477), (Fax in U.S. (800) 672-2054), www.palgrave.com; *The Statesman's Yearbook 2008*.

U.S. Department of State (DOS), 2201 C Street NW, Washington, DC 20520, (202) 647-4000, www.state.gov; *World Military Expenditures and Arms Transfers (WMEAT)*.

United Nations Statistics Division, New York, NY 10017, (800) 253-9646, Fax: (212) 963-4116, http://unstats.un.org; *Human Development Report 2006*.

FRANCE - ARTICHOKE PRODUCTION

See FRANCE - CROPS

FRANCE - AUTOMOBILE INDUSTRY AND TRADE

European Union, Delegation of the European Commission to the United States, 2300 M Street, NW, Washington, DC 20037, (202) 862-9500, Fax: (202) 429-1766, www.eurunion.org; *Eurostatistics: Data for Short-Term Economic Analysis (2007 edition)*.

Eurostat, Batiment Jean Monnet, Rue Alcide de Gasperi, L-2920 Luxembourg, http://epp.eurostat.ec.europa.eu; *Eurostat Yearbook 2006-2007*.

Organisation for Economic Cooperation and Development (OECD), 2 rue Andre Pascal, F-75775 Paris Cedex 16, France, (Telephone in U.S. (202) 785-6323), (Fax in U.S. (202) 785-0350), www.oecd.org; *Indicators of Industrial Activity* and *International Trade by Commodity Statistics (ITCS)*.

United Nations Statistics Division, New York, NY 10017, (800) 253-9646, Fax: (212) 963-4116, http://unstats.un.org; *Statistical Yearbook*.

FRANCE - BALANCE OF PAYMENTS

European Union, Delegation of the European Commission to the United States, 2300 M Street, NW, Washington, DC 20037, (202) 862-9500, Fax: (202) 429-1766, www.eurunion.org; *Eurostatistics: Data for Short-Term Economic Analysis (2007 edition)*.

Eurostat, Batiment Jean Monnet, Rue Alcide de Gasperi, L-2920 Luxembourg, http://epp.eurostat.ec.europa.eu; *Eurostat Yearbook 2006-2007*.

International Monetary Fund (IMF), 700 Nineteenth Street, NW, Washington, DC 20431, (202) 623-7000, Fax: (202) 623-4661, www.imf.org; *Balance of Payments Statistics Newsletter; Balance of Payments Statistics Yearbook 2007;* and *International Financial Statistics Yearbook 2007*.

Organisation for Economic Cooperation and Development (OECD), 2 rue Andre Pascal, F-75775 Paris Cedex 16, France, (Telephone in U.S. (202) 785-6323), (Fax in U.S. (202) 785-0350), www.oecd.org; *Geographical Distribution of Financial Flows to Aid Recipients 2002-2006; OECD Economic Outlook 2008; OECD Economic Survey - France 2007;* and *OECD Main Economic Indicators (MEI)*.

Platts, 2 Penn Plaza, 25th Floor, New York, NY 10121-2298, (212) 904-3070, www.platts.com; *Energy Economist*.

Taylor and Francis Group, An Informa Business, 2 Park Square, Milton Park, Abingdon, Oxford OX14 4RN, United Kingdom, (Dial from U.S. (212) 216-7800), (Fax from U.S. (212) 564-7854), www.tandf.co.uk; *The Europa World Year Book*.

United Nations Conference on Trade and Development (UNCTAD), DC2-1120, United Nations, New York, NY 10017, (212) 963-0027, www.unctad.org; *Handbook of Statistics 2005*.

United Nations Statistics Division, New York, NY 10017, (800) 253-9646, Fax: (212) 963-4116, http://unstats.un.org; *Energy Statistics Yearbook 2003*.

The World Bank, 1818 H Street, NW, Washington, DC 20433, (202) 473-1000, Fax: (202) 477-6391, www.worldbank.org; *France; World Development Indicators (WDI) 2008;* and *World Development Report 2008*.

FRANCE - BANANAS

See FRANCE - CROPS

FRANCE - BANKS AND BANKING

Euromonitor International, Inc., 224 S. Michigan Avenue, Suite 1500, Chicago, IL 60604, (312) 922-1115, Fax: (312) 922-1157, www.euromonitor.com; *World Marketing Data and Statistics*.

European Union, Delegation of the European Commission to the United States, 2300 M Street, NW, Washington, DC 20037, (202) 862-9500, Fax: (202) 429-1766, www.eurunion.org; *The EU Economy, 2007 Review: Moving Europe's Productivity Frontier* and *Eurostatistics: Data for Short-Term Economic Analysis (2007 edition)*.

Eurostat, Batiment Jean Monnet, Rue Alcide de Gasperi, L-2920 Luxembourg, http://epp.eurostat.ec.europa.eu; *Eurostat Yearbook 2006-2007*.

International Monetary Fund (IMF), 700 Nineteenth Street, NW, Washington, DC 20431, (202) 623-7000, Fax: (202) 623-4661, www.imf.org; *Government Finance Statistics Yearbook (2008 Edition)* and *International Financial Statistics Yearbook 2007*.

M.E. Sharpe, 80 Business Park Drive, Armonk, NY 10504, (800) 541-6563, Fax: (914) 273-2106, www.mesharpe.com; *The Illustrated Book of World Rankings*.

Organisation for Economic Cooperation and Development (OECD), 2 rue Andre Pascal, F-75775 Paris Cedex 16, France, (Telephone in U.S. (202) 785-6323), (Fax in U.S. (202) 785-0350), www.oecd.org; *Financial Market Trends: OECD Periodical; OECD Economic Outlook 2008;* and *OECD Economic Survey - France 2007*.

Palgrave Macmillan Ltd., Houndmills, Basingstoke, Hampshire, RG21 6XS, England, (Telephone in U.S. (888) 330-8477), (Fax in U.S. (800) 672-2054), www.palgrave.com; *The Statesman's Yearbook 2008*.

Taylor and Francis Group, An Informa Business, 2 Park Square, Milton Park, Abingdon, Oxford OX14 4RN, United Kingdom, (Dial from U.S. (212) 216-7800), (Fax from U.S. (212) 564-7854), www.tandf.co.uk; *The Europa World Year Book*.

United Nations Statistics Division, New York, NY 10017, (800) 253-9646, Fax: (212) 963-4116, http://unstats.un.org; *Statistical Yearbook*.

FRANCE - BARLEY PRODUCTION

See FRANCE - CROPS

FRANCE - BEVERAGE INDUSTRY

Eurostat, Batiment Jean Monnet, Rue Alcide de Gasperi, L-2920 Luxembourg, http://epp.eurostat.ec.europa.eu; *Eurostat Yearbook 2006-2007*.

M.E. Sharpe, 80 Business Park Drive, Armonk, NY 10504, (800) 541-6563, Fax: (914) 273-2106, www.mesharpe.com; *The Illustrated Book of World Rankings*.

Organisation for Economic Cooperation and Development (OECD), 2 rue Andre Pascal, F-75775 Paris Cedex 16, France, (Telephone in U.S. (202) 785-6323), (Fax in U.S. (202) 785-0350), www.oecd.org; *Indicators of Industrial Activity*.

United Nations Statistics Division, New York, NY 10017, (800) 253-9646, Fax: (212) 963-4116, http://unstats.un.org; *Statistical Yearbook*.

FRANCE - BONDS

Eurostat, Batiment Jean Monnet, Rue Alcide de Gasperi, L-2920 Luxembourg, http://epp.eurostat.ec.europa.eu; *Eurostat Yearbook 2006-2007*.

International Monetary Fund (IMF), 700 Nineteenth Street, NW, Washington, DC 20431, (202) 623-7000, Fax: (202) 623-4661, www.imf.org; *Government Finance Statistics Yearbook (2008 Edition).*

Organisation for Economic Cooperation and Development (OECD), 2 rue Andre Pascal, F-75775 Paris Cedex 16, France, (Telephone in U.S. (202) 785-6323), (Fax in U.S. (202) 785-0350), www.oecd.org; *Financial Market Trends: OECD Periodical.*

United Nations Statistics Division, New York, NY 10017, (800) 253-9646, Fax: (212) 963-4116, http://unstats.un.org; *Statistical Yearbook.*

FRANCE - BROADCASTING

Central Intelligence Agency, Office of Public Affairs, Washington, DC 20505, (703) 482-0623, Fax: (703) 482-1739, www.cia.gov; *The World Factbook.*

Euromonitor International, Inc., 224 S. Michigan Avenue, Suite 1500, Chicago, IL 60604, (312) 922-1115, Fax: (312) 922-1157, www.euromonitor.com; *World Marketing Data and Statistics.*

Eurostat, Batiment Jean Monnet, Rue Alcide de Gasperi, L-2920 Luxembourg, http://epp.eurostat.ec.europa.eu; *Eurostat Yearbook 2006-2007.*

M.E. Sharpe, 80 Business Park Drive, Armonk, NY 10504, (800) 541-6563, Fax: (914) 273-2106, www.mesharpe.com; *The Illustrated Book of World Rankings.*

Palgrave Macmillan Ltd., Houndmills, Basingstoke, Hampshire, RG21 6XS, England, (Telephone in U.S. (888) 330-8477), (Fax in U.S. (800) 672-2054), www.palgrave.com; *The Statesman's Yearbook 2008.*

UNESCO Institute for Statistics, C.P. 6128 Succursale Centre-Ville, Montreal, Quebec, H3C 3J7 Canada, (Dial from U.S. (514) 343-6880), (Fax from U.S. (514) 343 6882), www.uis.unesco.org; *Statistical Tables.*

United Nations Statistics Division, New York, NY 10017, (800) 253-9646, Fax: (212) 963-4116, http://unstats.un.org; *Trends in Europe and North America: The Statistical Yearbook of the ECE 2005.*

WRTH Publications Limited, PO Box 290, Oxford OX2 7FT, UK, www.wrth.com; *World Radio TV Handbook 2007.*

FRANCE - BUDGET

Central Intelligence Agency, Office of Public Affairs, Washington, DC 20505, (703) 482-0623, Fax: (703) 482-1739, www.cia.gov; *The World Factbook.*

Eurostat, Batiment Jean Monnet, Rue Alcide de Gasperi, L-2920 Luxembourg, http://epp.eurostat.ec.europa.eu; *Government Budgets.*

FRANCE - BUSINESS

Eurostat, Batiment Jean Monnet, Rue Alcide de Gasperi, L-2920 Luxembourg, http://epp.eurostat.ec.europa.eu; *Eurostat Yearbook 2006-2007.*

Organisation for Economic Cooperation and Development (OECD), 2 rue Andre Pascal, F-75775 Paris Cedex 16, France, (Telephone in U.S. (202) 785-6323), (Fax in U.S. (202) 785-0350), www.oecd.org; *OECD Main Economic Indicators (MEI).*

United Nations Statistics Division, New York, NY 10017, (800) 253-9646, Fax: (212) 963-4116, http://unstats.un.org; *Statistical Yearbook.*

FRANCE - CADMIUM PRODUCTION

See FRANCE - MINERAL INDUSTRIES

FRANCE - CAPITAL INVESTMENTS

Organisation for Economic Cooperation and Development (OECD), 2 rue Andre Pascal, F-75775 Paris Cedex 16, France, (Telephone in U.S. (202) 785-6323), (Fax in U.S. (202) 785-0350), www.oecd.org; *Financial Market Trends: OECD Periodical* and *OECD Economic Outlook 2008.*

FRANCE - CAPITAL LEVY

International Monetary Fund (IMF), 700 Nineteenth Street, NW, Washington, DC 20431, (202) 623-7000, Fax: (202) 623-4661, www.imf.org; *Government Finance Statistics Yearbook (2008 Edition).*

Organisation for Economic Cooperation and Development (OECD), 2 rue Andre Pascal, F-75775 Paris Cedex 16, France, (Telephone in U.S. (202) 785-6323), (Fax in U.S. (202) 785-0350), www.oecd.org; *Financial Market Trends: OECD Periodical* and *OECD Economic Outlook 2008.*

FRANCE - CATTLE

See FRANCE - LIVESTOCK

FRANCE - CHESTNUT PRODUCTION

See FRANCE - CROPS

FRANCE - CHICKENS

See FRANCE - LIVESTOCK

FRANCE - CHILDBIRTH - STATISTICS

Central Intelligence Agency, Office of Public Affairs, Washington, DC 20505, (703) 482-0623, Fax: (703) 482-1739, www.cia.gov; *The World Factbook.*

Euromonitor International, Inc., 224 S. Michigan Avenue, Suite 1500, Chicago, IL 60604, (312) 922-1115, Fax: (312) 922-1157, www.euromonitor.com; *The World Economic Factbook 2008.*

European Union, Delegation of the European Commission to the United States, 2300 M Street, NW, Washington, DC 20037, (202) 862-9500, Fax: (202) 429-1766, www.eurunion.org; *First Demographic Estimates for 2006.*

Eurostat, Batiment Jean Monnet, Rue Alcide de Gasperi, L-2920 Luxembourg, http://epp.eurostat.ec.europa.eu; *Eurostat Yearbook 2006-2007.*

M.E. Sharpe, 80 Business Park Drive, Armonk, NY 10504, (800) 541-6563, Fax: (914) 273-2106, www.mesharpe.com; *The Illustrated Book of World Rankings.*

Palgrave Macmillan Ltd., Houndmills, Basingstoke, Hampshire, RG21 6XS, England, (Telephone in U.S. (888) 330-8477), (Fax in U.S. (800) 672-2054), www.palgrave.com; *The Statesman's Yearbook 2008.*

Taylor and Francis Group, An Informa Business, 2 Park Square, Milton Park, Abingdon, Oxford OX14 4RN, United Kingdom, (Dial from U.S. (212) 216-7800), (Fax from U.S. (212) 564-7854), www.tandf.co.uk; *The Europa World Year Book.*

United Nations Statistics Division, New York, NY 10017, (800) 253-9646, Fax: (212) 963-4116, http://unstats.un.org; *Demographic Yearbook* and *Statistical Yearbook.*

The World Bank, 1818 H Street, NW, Washington, DC 20433, (202) 473-1000, Fax: (202) 477-6391, www.worldbank.org; *World Development Indicators (WDI) 2008.*

World Health Organization (WHO), Avenue Appia 20, 1211 Geneve 27, Switzerland, (Telephone in U.S. (212) 331-9081), www.who.int; *World Health Report 2006.*

FRANCE - CLIMATE

M.E. Sharpe, 80 Business Park Drive, Armonk, NY 10504, (800) 541-6563, Fax: (914) 273-2106, www.mesharpe.com; *The Illustrated Book of World Rankings.*

Palgrave Macmillan Ltd., Houndmills, Basingstoke, Hampshire, RG21 6XS, England, (Telephone in U.S. (888) 330-8477), (Fax in U.S. (800) 672-2054), www.palgrave.com; *The Statesman's Yearbook 2008.*

FRANCE - CLOTHING EXPORTS AND IMPORTS

See FRANCE - TEXTILE INDUSTRY

FRANCE - COAL PRODUCTION

See FRANCE - MINERAL INDUSTRIES

FRANCE - COBALT PRODUCTION

See FRANCE - MINERAL INDUSTRIES

FRANCE - COCOA PRODUCTION

See FRANCE - CROPS

FRANCE - COFFEE

See FRANCE - CROPS

FRANCE - COMMERCE

Palgrave Macmillan Ltd., Houndmills, Basingstoke, Hampshire, RG21 6XS, England, (Telephone in U.S. (888) 330-8477), (Fax in U.S. (800) 672-2054), www.palgrave.com; *The Statesman's Yearbook 2008.*

FRANCE - COMMODITY EXCHANGES

Commodity Research Bureau, 330 South Wells Street, Suite 612, Chicago, IL 60606-7110, (800) 621-5271, Fax: (312) 939-4135, www.crbtrader.com; *2006 CRB Commodity Yearbook and CD.*

International Lead and Zinc Study Group (ILZSG), Rua Almirante Barroso 38, 5th Floor, Lisbon 1000-013, Portugal, www.ilzsg.org; Interactive Statistical Database.

International Monetary Fund (IMF), 700 Nineteenth Street, NW, Washington, DC 20431, (202) 623-7000, Fax: (202) 623-4661, www.imf.org; *IMF Primary Commodity Prices.*

United Nations Food and Agricultural Organization (FAO), Viale delle Terme di Caracalla, 00100 Rome, Italy, (Dial from U.S. (202) 653-2400), (Fax from U.S. (202) 653 5760), www.fao.org; *The State of Food and Agriculture (SOFA) 2006.*

United Nations Statistics Division, New York, NY 10017, (800) 253-9646, Fax: (212) 963-4116, http://unstats.un.org; *Statistical Yearbook.*

World Bureau of Metal Statistics (WBMS), 27a High Street, Ware, Hertfordshire, SG12 9BA, United Kingdom, www.world-bureau.com; *Annual Stainless Steel Statistics; World Flow Charts; World Metal Statistics; World Nickel Statistics;* and *World Tin Statistics.*

FRANCE - COMMUNICATION AND TRAFFIC

European Union, Delegation of the European Commission to the United States, 2300 M Street, NW, Washington, DC 20037, (202) 862-9500, Fax: (202) 429-1766, www.eurunion.org; *Statistical Overview of Transport in the European Union (Data 1970-2001).*

United Nations Statistics Division, New York, NY 10017, (800) 253-9646, Fax: (212) 963-4116, http://unstats.un.org; *Statistical Yearbook.*

FRANCE - CONSTRUCTION INDUSTRY

European Union, Delegation of the European Commission to the United States, 2300 M Street, NW, Washington, DC 20037, (202) 862-9500, Fax: (202) 429-1766, www.eurunion.org; *European Union Labour Force Survey.*

Eurostat, Batiment Jean Monnet, Rue Alcide de Gasperi, L-2920 Luxembourg, http://epp.eurostat.ec.europa.eu; *Eurostat Yearbook 2006-2007.*

M.E. Sharpe, 80 Business Park Drive, Armonk, NY 10504, (800) 541-6563, Fax: (914) 273-2106, www.mesharpe.com; *The Illustrated Book of World Rankings.*

Organisation for Economic Cooperation and Development (OECD), 2 rue Andre Pascal, F-75775 Paris Cedex 16, France, (Telephone in U.S. (202) 785-6323), (Fax in U.S. (202) 785-0350), www.oecd.org; *Iron and Steel Industry in 2004 (2006 Edition); OECD Economic Survey - France 2007; OECD Main Economic Indicators (MEI);* and STructural ANalysis (STAN) database.

Palgrave Macmillan Ltd., Houndmills, Basingstoke, Hampshire, RG21 6XS, England, (Telephone in U.S. (888) 330-8477), (Fax in U.S. (800) 672-2054), www.palgrave.com; *The Statesman's Yearbook 2008.*

United Nations Statistics Division, New York, NY 10017, (800) 253-9646, Fax: (212) 963-4116, http://unstats.un.org; *Statistical Yearbook.*

FRANCE - CONSUMER PRICE INDEXES

European Union, Delegation of the European Commission to the United States, 2300 M Street, NW, Washington, DC 20037, (202) 862-9500, Fax: (202) 429-1766, www.eurunion.org; *Eurostatistics: Data for Short-Term Economic Analysis (2007 edition).*

Eurostat, Batiment Jean Monnet, Rue Alcide de Gasperi, L-2920 Luxembourg, http://epp.eurostat.ec.europa.eu; *Eurostat Yearbook 2006-2007.*

Organisation for Economic Cooperation and Development (OECD), 2 rue Andre Pascal, F-75775 Paris Cedex 16, France, (Telephone in U.S. (202) 785-6323), (Fax in U.S. (202) 785-0350), www.oecd.org; *OECD Economic Outlook 2008.*

Taylor and Francis Group, An Informa Business, 2 Park Square, Milton Park, Abingdon, Oxford OX14 4RN, United Kingdom, (Dial from U.S. (212) 216-7800), (Fax from U.S. (212) 564-7854), www.tandf.co.uk; *The Europa World Year Book.*

United Nations Statistics Division, New York, NY 10017, (800) 253-9646, Fax: (212) 963-4116, http://unstats.un.org; *Statistical Yearbook* and *Trends in Europe and North America: The Statistical Yearbook of the ECE 2005.*

The World Bank, 1818 H Street, NW, Washington, DC 20433, (202) 473-1000, Fax: (202) 477-6391, www.worldbank.org; *France.*

FRANCE - CONSUMPTION (ECONOMICS)

Eurostat, Batiment Jean Monnet, Rue Alcide de Gasperi, L-2920 Luxembourg, http://epp.eurostat.ec.europa.eu; *Eurostat Yearbook 2006-2007.*

International Iron and Steel Institute (IISI), Rue Colonel Bourg 120, B-1140 Brussels, Belgium, www.worldsteel.org; *Steel Statistical Yearbook 2006.*

International Lead and Zinc Study Group (ILZSG), Rua Almirante Barroso 38, 5th Floor, Lisbon 1000 - 013, Portugal, www.ilzsg.org; Interactive Statistical Database.

International Monetary Fund (IMF), 700 Nineteenth Street, NW, Washington, DC 20431, (202) 623-7000, Fax: (202) 623-4661, www.imf.org; *International Financial Statistics Yearbook 2007.*

Organisation for Economic Cooperation and Development (OECD), 2 rue Andre Pascal, F-75775 Paris Cedex 16, France, (Telephone in U.S. (202) 785-6323), (Fax in U.S. (202) 785-0350), www.oecd.org; *Environmental Impacts of Foreign Direct Investment in the Mining Sector in the Newly Independent States (NIS); Iron and Steel Industry in 2004 (2006 Edition); A New World Map in Textiles and Clothing: Adjusting to Change; 2005 OECD Agricultural Outlook Tables, 1970-2014; Revenue Statistics 1965-2006 - 2007 Edition;* and *Towards Sustainable Household Consumption?: Trends and Policies in OECD Countries.*

Technical Association of the Pulp and Paper Industry (TAPPI), 15 Technology Parkway South, Norcross, GA 30092, (770) 446-1400, Fax: (770) 446-6947, www.tappi.org; *TAPPI Annual Report.*

The World Bank, 1818 H Street, NW, Washington, DC 20433, (202) 473-1000, Fax: (202) 477-6391, www.worldbank.org; *World Development Report 2008.*

FRANCE - COPPER INDUSTRY AND TRADE

See FRANCE - MINERAL INDUSTRIES

FRANCE - CORN INDUSTRY

See FRANCE - CROPS

FRANCE - COST AND STANDARD OF LIVING

Eurostat, Batiment Jean Monnet, Rue Alcide de Gasperi, L-2920 Luxembourg, http://epp.eurostat.ec.europa.eu; *Eurostat Yearbook 2006-2007.*

International Monetary Fund (IMF), 700 Nineteenth Street, NW, Washington, DC 20431, (202) 623-7000, Fax: (202) 623-4661, www.imf.org; *Government Finance Statistics Yearbook (2008 Edition).*

FRANCE - COTTON

See FRANCE - CROPS

FRANCE - CRIME

Eurostat, Batiment Jean Monnet, Rue Alcide de Gasperi, L-2920 Luxembourg, http://epp.eurostat.ec.europa.eu; *Crime and Criminal Justice; General Government Expenditure and Revenue in the EU, 2006;* and *Study on Crime Victimisation.*

International Criminal Police Organization (INTERPOL), General Secretariat, 200 quai Charles de Gaulle, 69006 Lyon, France, www.interpol.int; *International Crime Statistics.*

United Nations Statistics Division, New York, NY 10017, (800) 253-9646, Fax: (212) 963-4116, http://unstats.un.org; *Trends in Europe and North America: The Statistical Yearbook of the ECE 2005.*

Yale University Press, PO Box 209040, New Haven, CT 06520-9040, (203) 432-0960, Fax: (203) 432-0948, http://yalepress.yale.edu/yupbooks; *Violence and Crime in Cross-National Perspective.*

FRANCE - CROPS

Euromonitor International, Inc., 224 S. Michigan Avenue, Suite 1500, Chicago, IL 60604, (312) 922-1115, Fax: (312) 922-1157, www.euromonitor.com; *European Marketing Data and Statistics 2008.*

European Union, Delegation of the European Commission to the United States, 2300 M Street, NW, Washington, DC 20037, (202) 862-9500, Fax: (202) 429-1766, www.eurunion.org; *Agricultural Statistics: Data 1995-2005; Agriculture in the European Union: Statistical and Economic Information 2006; Eurostatistics: Data for Short-Term Economic Analysis (2007 edition);* and *Regions - Statistical Yearbook 2006.*

Eurostat, Batiment Jean Monnet, Rue Alcide de Gasperi, L-2920 Luxembourg, http://epp.eurostat.ec.europa.eu; *Eurostat Yearbook 2006-2007.*

International Grains Council (IGC), 1 Canada Square, Canary Wharf, London E14 5AE, England, www.igc.org.uk; *Grain Market Report.*

M.E. Sharpe, 80 Business Park Drive, Armonk, NY 10504, (800) 541-6563, Fax: (914) 273-2106, www.mesharpe.com; *The Illustrated Book of World Rankings.*

Organisation for Economic Cooperation and Development (OECD), 2 rue Andre Pascal, F-75775 Paris Cedex 16, France, (Telephone in U.S. (202) 785-6323), (Fax in U.S. (202) 785-0350), www.oecd.org; *International Trade by Commodity Statistics (ITCS)* and *2005 OECD Agricultural Outlook Tables, 1970-2014.*

Palgrave Macmillan Ltd., Houndmills, Basingstoke, Hampshire, RG21 6XS, England, (Telephone in U.S. (888) 330-8477), (Fax in U.S. (800) 672-2054), www.palgrave.com; *The Statesman's Yearbook 2008.*

Taylor and Francis Group, An Informa Business, 2 Park Square, Milton Park, Abingdon, Oxford OX14 4RN, United Kingdom, (Dial from U.S. (212) 216-7800), (Fax from U.S. (212) 564-7854), www.tandf.co.uk; *The Europa World Year Book.*

United Nations Conference on Trade and Development (UNCTAD), DC2-1120, United Nations, New York, NY 10017, (212) 963-0027, www.unctad.org; *UNCTAD Commodity Yearbook.*

United Nations Food and Agricultural Organization (FAO), Viale delle Terme di Caracalla, 00100 Rome, Italy, (Dial from U.S. (202) 653-2400), (Fax from U.S. (202) 653 5760), www.fao.org; *FAO Production Yearbook 2002* and *The State of Food and Agriculture (SOFA) 2006.*

United Nations Statistics Division, New York, NY 10017, (800) 253-9646, Fax: (212) 963-4116, http://unstats.un.org; *Statistical Yearbook.*

FRANCE - CUSTOMS ADMINISTRATION

Eurostat, Batiment Jean Monnet, Rue Alcide de Gasperi, L-2920 Luxembourg, http://epp.eurostat.ec.europa.eu; *Eurostat Yearbook 2006-2007.*

International Monetary Fund (IMF), 700 Nineteenth Street, NW, Washington, DC 20431, (202) 623-7000, Fax: (202) 623-4661, www.imf.org; *Government Finance Statistics Yearbook (2008 Edition).*

Organisation for Economic Cooperation and Development (OECD), 2 rue Andre Pascal, F-75775 Paris Cedex 16, France, (Telephone in U.S. (202) 785-6323), (Fax in U.S. (202) 785-0350), www.oecd.org; *Environmental Impacts of Foreign Direct Investment in the Mining Sector in the Newly Independent States (NIS).*

Palgrave Macmillan Ltd., Houndmills, Basingstoke, Hampshire, RG21 6XS, England, (Telephone in U.S. (888) 330-8477), (Fax in U.S. (800) 672-2054), www.palgrave.com; *The Statesman's Yearbook 2008.*

FRANCE - DAIRY PROCESSING

European Union, Delegation of the European Commission to the United States, 2300 M Street, NW, Washington, DC 20037, (202) 862-9500, Fax: (202) 429-1766, www.eurunion.org; *Eurostatistics: Data for Short-Term Economic Analysis (2007 edition).*

M.E. Sharpe, 80 Business Park Drive, Armonk, NY 10504, (800) 541-6563, Fax: (914) 273-2106, www.mesharpe.com; *The Illustrated Book of World Rankings.*

Organisation for Economic Cooperation and Development (OECD), 2 rue Andre Pascal, F-75775 Paris Cedex 16, France, (Telephone in U.S. (202) 785-6323), (Fax in U.S. (202) 785-0350), www.oecd.org; *2005 OECD Agricultural Outlook Tables, 1970-2014.*

Palgrave Macmillan Ltd., Houndmills, Basingstoke, Hampshire, RG21 6XS, England, (Telephone in U.S. (888) 330-8477), (Fax in U.S. (800) 672-2054), www.palgrave.com; *The Statesman's Yearbook 2008.*

Taylor and Francis Group, An Informa Business, 2 Park Square, Milton Park, Abingdon, Oxford OX14 4RN, United Kingdom, (Dial from U.S. (212) 216-7800), (Fax from U.S. (212) 564-7854), www.tandf.co.uk; *The Europa World Year Book.*

United Nations Food and Agricultural Organization (FAO), Viale delle Terme di Caracalla, 00100 Rome, Italy, (Dial from U.S. (202) 653-2400), (Fax from U.S. (202) 653 5760), www.fao.org; *The State of Food and Agriculture (SOFA) 2006.*

United Nations Statistics Division, New York, NY 10017, (800) 253-9646, Fax: (212) 963-4116, http://unstats.un.org; *Statistical Yearbook.*

FRANCE - DEATH RATES

See FRANCE - MORTALITY

FRANCE - DEBTS, EXTERNAL

Organisation for Economic Cooperation and Development (OECD), 2 rue Andre Pascal, F-75775 Paris Cedex 16, France, (Telephone in U.S. (202) 785-6323), (Fax in U.S. (202) 785-0350), www.oecd.org; *Financial Market Trends: OECD Periodical; Geographical Distribution of Financial Flows to Aid Recipients 2002-2006;* and *OECD Economic Outlook 2008.*

Palgrave Macmillan Ltd., Houndmills, Basingstoke, Hampshire, RG21 6XS, England, (Telephone in U.S. (888) 330-8477), (Fax in U.S. (800) 672-2054), www.palgrave.com; *The Statesman's Yearbook 2008.*

The World Bank, 1818 H Street, NW, Washington, DC 20433, (202) 473-1000, Fax: (202) 477-6391, www.worldbank.org; *Global Development Finance 2007; World Development Indicators (WDI) 2008;* and *World Development Report 2008.*

FRANCE - DEFENSE EXPENDITURES

See FRANCE - ARMED FORCES

FRANCE - DEMOGRAPHY

Euromonitor International, Inc., 224 S. Michigan Avenue, Suite 1500, Chicago, IL 60604, (312) 922-1115, Fax: (312) 922-1157, www.euromonitor.com; *The World Economic Factbook 2008* and *World Marketing Data and Statistics.*

European Union, Delegation of the European Commission to the United States, 2300 M Street, NW,

Washington, DC 20037, (202) 862-9500, Fax: (202) 429-1766, www.eurunion.org; *First Demographic Estimates for 2006* and *Regions - Statistical Yearbook 2006.*

Eurostat, Batiment Jean Monnet, Rue Alcide de Gasperi, L-2920 Luxembourg, http://epp.eurostat.ec.europa.eu; *Demographic Outlook - National Reports on the Demographic Developments in 2006; Demographic Outlook - National Reports on the Demographic Developments in 2006;* and *Eurostat Yearbook 2006-2007.*

Federal Statistical Office Germany, D-65180 Wiesbaden, Germany, www.destatis.de; *France 2005.*

M.E. Sharpe, 80 Business Park Drive, Armonk, NY 10504, (800) 541-6563, Fax: (914) 273-2106, www.mesharpe.com; *The Illustrated Book of World Rankings.*

United Nations Statistics Division, New York, NY 10017, (800) 253-9646, Fax: (212) 963-4116, http://unstats.un.org; *Human Development Report 2006.*

The World Bank, 1818 H Street, NW, Washington, DC 20433, (202) 473-1000, Fax: (202) 477-6391, www.worldbank.org; *France.*

FRANCE - DIAMONDS

See FRANCE - MINERAL INDUSTRIES

FRANCE - DISPOSABLE INCOME

M.E. Sharpe, 80 Business Park Drive, Armonk, NY 10504, (800) 541-6563, Fax: (914) 273-2106, www.mesharpe.com; *The Illustrated Book of World Rankings.*

Organisation for Economic Cooperation and Development (OECD), 2 rue Andre Pascal, F-75775 Paris Cedex 16, France, (Telephone in U.S. (202) 785-6323), (Fax in U.S. (202) 785-0350), www.oecd.org; *OECD Economic Outlook 2008.*

United Nations Statistics Division, New York, NY 10017, (800) 253-9646, Fax: (212) 963-4116, http://unstats.un.org; *National Accounts Statistics: Compendium of Income Distribution Statistics* and *Statistical Yearbook.*

FRANCE - DIVORCE

European Union, Delegation of the European Commission to the United States, 2300 M Street, NW, Washington, DC 20037, (202) 862-9500, Fax: (202) 429-1766, www.eurunion.org; *First Demographic Estimates for 2006.*

M.E. Sharpe, 80 Business Park Drive, Armonk, NY 10504, (800) 541-6563, Fax: (914) 273-2106, www.mesharpe.com; *The Illustrated Book of World Rankings.*

United Nations Statistics Division, New York, NY 10017, (800) 253-9646, Fax: (212) 963-4116, http://unstats.un.org; *Demographic Yearbook; Statistical Yearbook;* and *Trends in Europe and North America: The Statistical Yearbook of the ECE 2005.*

FRANCE - ECONOMIC ASSISTANCE

European Union, Delegation of the European Commission to the United States, 2300 M Street, NW, Washington, DC 20037, (202) 862-9500, Fax: (202) 429-1766, www.eurunion.org; *RD Expenditure in Europe (2006 edition).*

Eurostat, Batiment Jean Monnet, Rue Alcide de Gasperi, L-2920 Luxembourg, http://epp.eurostat.ec.europa.eu; *Eurostat Yearbook 2006-2007.*

Organisation for Economic Cooperation and Development (OECD), 2 rue Andre Pascal, F-75775 Paris Cedex 16, France, (Telephone in U.S. (202) 785-6323), (Fax in U.S. (202) 785-0350), www.oecd.org; *Geographical Distribution of Financial Flows to Aid Recipients 2002-2006.*

United Nations Statistics Division, New York, NY 10017, (800) 253-9646, Fax: (212) 963-4116, http://unstats.un.org; *Statistical Yearbook.*

FRANCE - ECONOMIC CONDITIONS

Banque de France, 48 rue Croix des Petits champs, 75001 Paris, France, www.banque-france.fr/home.htm; *Key Data for the Euro Area.*

Center for International Business Education Research (CIBER), Columbia Business School and School of International and Public Affairs, Uris Hall, Room 212, 3022 Broadway, New York, NY 10027-6902, Mr. Joshua Safier, (212) 854-4750, Fax: (212) 222-9821, www.columbia.edu/cu/ciber/; Datastream International.

Central Intelligence Agency, Office of Public Affairs, Washington, DC 20505, (703) 482-0623, Fax: (703) 482-1739, www.cia.gov; *The World Factbook.*

DSI Data Service Information, Xantener Strasse 51a, D-47495 Rheinberg, Germany, www.dsidata.com; *Campus Solution.*

Dun and Bradstreet (DB) Corporation, 103 JFK Parkway, Short Hills, NJ 07078, (973) 921-5500, www.dnb.com; *Country Report.*

Economist Intelligence Unit, 111 West 57th Street, New York, NY 10019, (212) 554-0600, Fax: (212) 586-1181, www.eiu.com; *France Country Report.*

Euromonitor International, Inc., 224 S. Michigan Avenue, Suite 1500, Chicago, IL 60604, (312) 922-1115, Fax: (312) 922-1157, www.euromonitor.com; *European Marketing Data and Statistics 2008; The World Economic Factbook 2008;* and *World Marketing Data and Statistics.*

European Union, Delegation of the European Commission to the United States, 2300 M Street, NW, Washington, DC 20037, (202) 862-9500, Fax: (202) 429-1766, www.eurunion.org; *The EU Economy, 2007 Review: Moving Europe's Productivity Frontier* and *European Union Labour Force Survey.*

Eurostat, Batiment Jean Monnet, Rue Alcide de Gasperi, L-2920 Luxembourg, http://epp.eurostat.ec.europa.eu; *Consumers in Europe - Facts and Figures on Services of General Interest; EU Economic Data Pocketbook;* and *Eurostat Yearbook 2006-2007.*

Federal Statistical Office Germany, D-65180 Wiesbaden, Germany, www.destatis.de; *France 2005.*

International Monetary Fund (IMF), 700 Nineteenth Street, NW, Washington, DC 20431, (202) 623-7000, Fax: (202) 623-4661, www.imf.org; *World Economic Outlook Reports.*

M.E. Sharpe, 80 Business Park Drive, Armonk, NY 10504, (800) 541-6563, Fax: (914) 273-2106, www.mesharpe.com; *The Illustrated Book of World Rankings.*

Organisation for Economic Cooperation and Development (OECD), 2 rue Andre Pascal, F-75775 Paris Cedex 16, France, (Telephone in U.S. (202) 785-6323), (Fax in U.S. (202) 785-0350), www.oecd.org; *Geographical Distribution of Financial Flows to Aid Recipients 2002-2006; ICT Sector Data and Metadata by Country; Labour Force Statistics: 1986-2005, 2007 Edition; OECD Composite Leading Indicators (CLIs), Updated September 2007; OECD Economic Outlook 2008; OECD Economic Survey - France 2007; OECD Employment Outlook 2007; OECD in Figures 2007;* and *OECD Main Economic Indicators (MEI).*

Palgrave Macmillan Ltd., Houndmills, Basingstoke, Hampshire, RG21 6XS, England, (Telephone in U.S. (888) 330-8477), (Fax in U.S. (800) 672-2054), www.palgrave.com; *The Statesman's Yearbook 2008.*

Platts, 2 Penn Plaza, 25th Floor, New York, NY 10121-2298, (212) 904-3070, www.platts.com; *Energy Economist.*

Taylor and Francis Group, An Informa Business, 2 Park Square, Milton Park, Abingdon, Oxford OX14 4RN, United Kingdom, (Dial from U.S. (212) 216-7800), (Fax from U.S. (212) 564-7854), www.tandf.co.uk; *The Europa World Year Book.*

United Nations Statistics Division, New York, NY 10017, (800) 253-9646, Fax: (212) 963-4116, http://unstats.un.org; *Energy Statistics Yearbook 2003* and *World Statistics Pocketbook.*

The World Bank, 1818 H Street, NW, Washington, DC 20433, (202) 473-1000, Fax: (202) 477-6391, www.worldbank.org; *France; Global Economic Monitor (GEM); Global Economic Prospects 2008; The World Bank Atlas 2003-2004;* and *World Development Report 2008.*

FRANCE - ECONOMICS - SOCIOLOGICAL ASPECTS

Eurostat, Batiment Jean Monnet, Rue Alcide de Gasperi, L-2920 Luxembourg, http://epp.eurostat.ec.europa.eu; *Eurostat Yearbook 2006-2007.*

Organisation for Economic Cooperation and Development (OECD), 2 rue Andre Pascal, F-75775 Paris Cedex 16, France, (Telephone in U.S. (202) 785-6323), (Fax in U.S. (202) 785-0350), www.oecd.org; *OECD Economic Outlook 2008.*

FRANCE - EDUCATION

Euromonitor International, Inc., 224 S. Michigan Avenue, Suite 1500, Chicago, IL 60604, (312) 922-1115, Fax: (312) 922-1157, www.euromonitor.com; *European Marketing Data and Statistics 2008* and *World Marketing Data and Statistics.*

European Union, Delegation of the European Commission to the United States, 2300 M Street, NW, Washington, DC 20037, (202) 862-9500, Fax: (202) 429-1766, www.eurunion.org; *Education across Europe 2003* and *Regions - Statistical Yearbook 2006.*

Eurostat, Batiment Jean Monnet, Rue Alcide de Gasperi, L-2920 Luxembourg, http://epp.eurostat.ec.europa.eu; *Education, Science and Culture Statistics* and *Eurostat Yearbook 2006-2007.*

Federal Statistical Office Germany, D-65180 Wiesbaden, Germany, www.destatis.de; *France 2005.*

International Monetary Fund (IMF), 700 Nineteenth Street, NW, Washington, DC 20431, (202) 623-7000, Fax: (202) 623-4661, www.imf.org; *Government Finance Statistics Yearbook (2008 Edition).*

M.E. Sharpe, 80 Business Park Drive, Armonk, NY 10504, (800) 541-6563, Fax: (914) 273-2106, www.mesharpe.com; *The Illustrated Book of World Rankings.*

Organisation for Economic Cooperation and Development (OECD), 2 rue Andre Pascal, F-75775 Paris Cedex 16, France, (Telephone in U.S. (202) 785-6323), (Fax in U.S. (202) 785-0350), www.oecd.org; *Education at a Glance* (2007 Edition).

Palgrave Macmillan Ltd., Houndmills, Basingstoke, Hampshire, RG21 6XS, England, (Telephone in U.S. (888) 330-8477), (Fax in U.S. (800) 672-2054), www.palgrave.com; *The Statesman's Yearbook 2008.*

Taylor and Francis Group, An Informa Business, 2 Park Square, Milton Park, Abingdon, Oxford OX14 4RN, United Kingdom, (Dial from U.S. (212) 216-7800), (Fax from U.S. (212) 564-7854), www.tandf.co.uk; *The Europa World Year Book.*

United Nations Statistics Division, New York, NY 10017, (800) 253-9646, Fax: (212) 963-4116, http://unstats.un.org; *Human Development Report 2006* and *Trends in Europe and North America: The Statistical Yearbook of the ECE 2005.*

The World Bank, 1818 H Street, NW, Washington, DC 20433, (202) 473-1000, Fax: (202) 477-6391, www.worldbank.org; *France; World Development Indicators (WDI) 2008;* and *World Development Report 2008.*

FRANCE - EGGPLANT PRODUCTION

See FRANCE - CROPS

FRANCE - ELECTRICITY

European Union, Delegation of the European Commission to the United States, 2300 M Street, NW, Washington, DC 20037, (202) 862-9500, Fax: (202) 429-1766, www.eurunion.org; *European Union Energy Transport in Figures 2006; Eurostatistics: Data for Short-Term Economic Analysis (2007 edition);* and *Regions - Statistical Yearbook 2006.*

Eurostat, Batiment Jean Monnet, Rue Alcide de Gasperi, L-2920 Luxembourg, http://epp.eurostat.ec.europa.eu; *Energy - Monthly Statistics; Eurostat Yearbook 2006-2007;* and *Panorama of Energy - 2007 Edition.*

M.E. Sharpe, 80 Business Park Drive, Armonk, NY 10504, (800) 541-6563, Fax: (914) 273-2106, www.mesharpe.com; *The Illustrated Book of World Rankings.*

Organisation for Economic Cooperation and Development (OECD), 2 rue Andre Pascal, F-75775 Paris Cedex 16, France, (Telephone in U.S. (202) 785-6323), (Fax in U.S. (202) 785-0350), www.oecd.org; *Coal Information: 2007 Edition; Energy Statistics of OECD Countries* (2007 Edition); *Indicators of Industrial Activity;* STructural ANalysis (STAN) database; and *World Energy Outlook 2007.*

Palgrave Macmillan Ltd., Houndmills, Basingstoke, Hampshire, RG21 6XS, England, (Telephone in U.S. (888) 330-8477), (Fax in U.S. (800) 672-2054), www.palgrave.com; *The Statesman's Yearbook 2008.*

Platts, 2 Penn Plaza, 25th Floor, New York, NY 10121-2298, (212) 904-3070, www.platts.com; *Energy Economist; EU Energy;* and *European Electricity Review 2004.*

U.S. Department of Energy (DOE), Energy Information Administration (EIA), 1000 Independence Avenue, SW, Washington, DC 20585, (202) 586-8800, www.eia.doe.gov; *International Energy Annual 2004* and *International Energy Outlook 2006.*

United Nations Statistics Division, New York, NY 10017, (800) 253-9646, Fax: (212) 963-4116, http://unstats.un.org; *Energy Statistics Yearbook 2003; Human Development Report 2006; Statistical Yearbook;* and *Trends in Europe and North America: The Statistical Yearbook of the ECE 2005.*

FRANCE - EMPLOYMENT

Bernan Essential Government Publications, 4611-F Assembly Drive, Lanham MD, 20706-4391, (301) 459-2255, Fax: (800) 865-3450, www.bernan.com; *OECD Factbook 2006.*

Euromonitor International, Inc., 224 S. Michigan Avenue, Suite 1500, Chicago, IL 60604, (312) 922-1115, Fax: (312) 922-1157, www.euromonitor.com; *European Marketing Data and Statistics 2008.*

European Union, Delegation of the European Commission to the United States, 2300 M Street, NW, Washington, DC 20037, (202) 862-9500, Fax: (202) 429-1766, www.eurunion.org; *Agriculture in the European Union: Statistical and Economic Information 2006; European Union Labour Force Survey; Eurostatistics: Data for Short-Term Economic Analysis (2007 edition); Iron and Steel;* and *Statistical Overview of Transport in the European Union (Data 1970-2001).*

Eurostat, Batiment Jean Monnet, Rue Alcide de Gasperi, L-2920 Luxembourg, http://epp.eurostat.ec.europa.eu; *Eurostat Yearbook 2006-2007.*

Federal Statistical Office Germany, D-65180 Wiesbaden, Germany, www.destatis.de; *France 2005.*

International Labour Office, I.L.O. Publications, 4 route des Morillons, CH-1211 Geneva 22, Switzerland, (Telephone in U.S. (202) 653-7652), (Fax in U.S. (202) 653-7687), www.ilo.org; *Yearbook of Labour Statistics 2006.*

M.E. Sharpe, 80 Business Park Drive, Armonk, NY 10504, (800) 541-6563, Fax: (914) 273-2106, www.mesharpe.com; *The Illustrated Book of World Rankings.*

Organisation for Economic Cooperation and Development (OECD), 2 rue Andre Pascal, F-75775 Paris Cedex 16, France, (Telephone in U.S. (202) 785-6323), (Fax in U.S. (202) 785-0350), www.oecd.org; *ICT Sector Data and Metadata by Country; Iron and Steel Industry in 2004 (2006 Edition); Labour Force Statistics: 1986-2005, 2007 Edition; A New World Map in Textiles and Clothing: Adjusting to Change; OECD Composite Leading Indicators (CLIs), Updated September 2007; OECD Economic Outlook 2008; OECD Economic Survey - France 2007; OECD Employment Outlook 2007;* and *OECD in Figures 2007.*

United Nations Statistics Division, New York, NY 10017, (800) 253-9646, Fax: (212) 963-4116, http://unstats.un.org; *Statistical Yearbook.*

The World Bank, 1818 H Street, NW, Washington, DC 20433, (202) 473-1000, Fax: (202) 477-6391, www.worldbank.org; *France.*

FRANCE - ENERGY INDUSTRIES

Enerdata, 10 Rue Royale, 75008 Paris, France, www.enerdata.fr; *Global Energy Market Data.*

Eurostat, Batiment Jean Monnet, Rue Alcide de Gasperi, L-2920 Luxembourg, http://epp.eurostat.ec.europa.eu; *Energy - Monthly Statistics; Eurostat Yearbook 2006-2007;* and *Panorama of Energy - 2007 Edition.*

International Energy Agency (IEA), 9, rue de la Federation, 75739 Paris Cedex 15, France, www.iea.org; *Key World Energy Statistics 2007.*

Organisation for Economic Cooperation and Development (OECD), 2 rue Andre Pascal, F-75775 Paris Cedex 16, France, (Telephone in U.S. (202) 785-6323), (Fax in U.S. (202) 785-0350), www.oecd.org; *Towards Sustainable Household Consumption?: Trends and Policies in OECD Countries.*

Platts, 2 Penn Plaza, 25th Floor, New York, NY 10121-2298, (212) 904-3070, www.platts.com; *EU Energy* and *European Power Daily.*

United Nations Statistics Division, New York, NY 10017, (800) 253-9646, Fax: (212) 963-4116, http://unstats.un.org; *Statistical Yearbook.*

FRANCE - ENVIRONMENTAL CONDITIONS

Center for Research on the Epidemiology of Disasters (CRED), Universite Catholique de Louvain, Ecole de Sante Publique, 30.94 Clos Chapelle-aux-Champs, 1200 Brussels, Belgium, www.cred.be; *Three Decades of Floods in Europe: A Preliminary Analysis of EMDAT Data.*

DSI Data Service Information, Xantener Strasse 51a, D-47495 Rheinberg, Germany, www.dsidata.com; *Campus Solution* and *DSI's Global Environmental Database.*

Economist Intelligence Unit, 111 West 57th Street, New York, NY 10019, (212) 554-0600, Fax: (212) 586-1181, www.eiu.com; *France Country Report.*

Eurostat, Batiment Jean Monnet, Rue Alcide de Gasperi, L-2920 Luxembourg, http://epp.eurostat.ec.europa.eu; *Environmental Protection Expenditure in Europe.*

Organisation for Economic Cooperation and Development (OECD), 2 rue Andre Pascal, F-75775 Paris Cedex 16, France, (Telephone in U.S. (202) 785-6323), (Fax in U.S. (202) 785-0350), www.oecd.org; *Key Environmental Indicators 2004.*

Platts, 2 Penn Plaza, 25th Floor, New York, NY 10121-2298, (212) 904-3070, www.platts.com; *Emissions Daily.*

United Nations Statistics Division, New York, NY 10017, (800) 253-9646, Fax: (212) 963-4116, http://unstats.un.org; *Trends in Europe and North America: The Statistical Yearbook of the ECE 2005* and *World Statistics Pocketbook.*

FRANCE - EXPENDITURES, PUBLIC

Eurostat, Batiment Jean Monnet, Rue Alcide de Gasperi, L-2920 Luxembourg, http://epp.eurostat.ec.europa.eu; *European Social Statistics - Social Protection Expenditure and Receipts - Data 1997-2005* and *Eurostat Yearbook 2006-2007.*

Organisation for Economic Cooperation and Development (OECD), 2 rue Andre Pascal, F-75775 Paris Cedex 16, France, (Telephone in U.S. (202) 785-6323), (Fax in U.S. (202) 785-0350), www.oecd.org; *Revenue Statistics 1965-2006 - 2007 Edition.*

FRANCE - EXPORTS

Central Intelligence Agency, Office of Public Affairs, Washington, DC 20505, (703) 482-0623, Fax: (703) 482-1739, www.cia.gov; *The World Factbook.*

Economist Intelligence Unit, 111 West 57th Street, New York, NY 10019, (212) 554-0600, Fax: (212) 586-1181, www.eiu.com; *France Country Report.*

Euromonitor International, Inc., 224 S. Michigan Avenue, Suite 1500, Chicago, IL 60604, (312) 922-1115, Fax: (312) 922-1157, www.euromonitor.com; *The World Economic Factbook 2008.*

European Union, Delegation of the European Commission to the United States, 2300 M Street, NW, Washington, DC 20037, (202) 862-9500, Fax: (202) 429-1766, www.eurunion.org; *European Union Energy Transport in Figures 2006; Eurostatistics: Data for Short-Term Economic Analysis (2007 edition); External and Intra-European Union Trade: Data 1958-2002; External and Intra-European Union Trade: Data 1999-2004;* and *Fishery Statistics - 1990-2006.*

Eurostat, Batiment Jean Monnet, Rue Alcide de Gasperi, L-2920 Luxembourg, http://epp.eurostat.ec.europa.eu; *Eurostat Yearbook 2006-2007.*

International Iron and Steel Institute (IISI), Rue Colonel Bourg 120, B-1140 Brussels, Belgium, www.worldsteel.org; *Steel Statistical Yearbook 2006.*

International Lead and Zinc Study Group (ILZSG), Rua Almirante Barroso 38, 5th Floor, Lisbon 1000 - 013, Portugal, www.ilzsg.org; Interactive Statistical Database.

International Monetary Fund (IMF), 700 Nineteenth Street, NW, Washington, DC 20431, (202) 623-7000, Fax: (202) 623-4661, www.imf.org; *Direction of Trade Statistics Yearbook 2007; Government Finance Statistics Yearbook (2008 Edition);* and *International Financial Statistics Yearbook 2007.*

Organisation for Economic Cooperation and Development (OECD), 2 rue Andre Pascal, F-75775 Paris Cedex 16, France, (Telephone in U.S. (202) 785-6323), (Fax in U.S. (202) 785-0350), www.oecd.org; *Geographical Distribution of Financial Flows to Aid Recipients 2002-2006; International Trade by Commodity Statistics (ITCS); Iron and Steel Industry in 2004 (2006 Edition); 2005 OECD Agricultural Outlook Tables, 1970-2014; OECD Economic Outlook 2008; OECD Economic Survey - France 2007; Review of Fisheries in OECD Countries: Country Statistics 2001 to 2003 - 2005 Edition;* and STructural ANalysis (STAN) database.

Platts, 2 Penn Plaza, 25th Floor, New York, NY 10121-2298, (212) 904-3070, www.platts.com; *Energy Economist.*

Taylor and Francis Group, An Informa Business, 2 Park Square, Milton Park, Abingdon, Oxford OX14 4RN, United Kingdom, (Dial from U.S. (212) 216-7800), (Fax from U.S. (212) 564-7854), www.tandf.co.uk; *The Europa World Year Book.*

Technical Association of the Pulp and Paper Industry (TAPPI), 15 Technology Parkway South, Norcross, GA 30092, (770) 446-1400, Fax: (770) 446-6947, www.tappi.org; *TAPPI Annual Report.*

United Nations Conference on Trade and Development (UNCTAD), DC2-1120, United Nations, New York, NY 10017, (212) 963-0027, www.unctad.org; *Handbook of Statistics 2005.*

United Nations Food and Agricultural Organization (FAO), Viale delle Terme di Caracalla, 00100 Rome, Italy, (Dial from U.S. (202) 653-2400), (Fax from U.S. (202) 653 5760), www.fao.org; *The State of Food and Agriculture (SOFA) 2006.*

United Nations Statistics Division, New York, NY 10017, (800) 253-9646, Fax: (212) 963-4116, http://unstats.un.org; *Energy Statistics Yearbook 2003* and *Trends in Europe and North America: The Statistical Yearbook of the ECE 2005.*

The World Bank, 1818 H Street, NW, Washington, DC 20433, (202) 473-1000, Fax: (202) 477-6391, www.worldbank.org; *World Development Indicators (WDI) 2008* and *World Development Report 2008.*

FRANCE - FEMALE WORKING POPULATION

See FRANCE - EMPLOYMENT

FRANCE - FERTILITY, HUMAN

Central Intelligence Agency, Office of Public Affairs, Washington, DC 20505, (703) 482-0623, Fax: (703) 482-1739, www.cia.gov; *The World Factbook.*

European Union, Delegation of the European Commission to the United States, 2300 M Street, NW, Washington, DC 20037, (202) 862-9500, Fax: (202) 429-1766, www.eurunion.org; *First Demographic Estimates for 2006.*

M.E. Sharpe, 80 Business Park Drive, Armonk, NY 10504, (800) 541-6563, Fax: (914) 273-2106, www.mesharpe.com; *The Illustrated Book of World Rankings.*

United Nations Statistics Division, New York, NY 10017, (800) 253-9646, Fax: (212) 963-4116, http://unstats.un.org; *Human Development Report 2006* and *Trends in Europe and North America: The Statistical Yearbook of the ECE 2005.*

The World Bank, 1818 H Street, NW, Washington, DC 20433, (202) 473-1000, Fax: (202) 477-6391, www.worldbank.org; *The World Bank Atlas 2003-2004; World Development Indicators (WDI) 2008;* and *World Development Report 2008.*

FRANCE - FERTILIZER INDUSTRY

Eurostat, Batiment Jean Monnet, Rue Alcide de Gasperi, L-2920 Luxembourg, http://epp.eurostat.ec.europa.eu; *Eurostat Yearbook 2006-2007.*

Organisation for Economic Cooperation and Development (OECD), 2 rue Andre Pascal, F-75775 Paris Cedex 16, France, (Telephone in U.S. (202) 785-6323), (Fax in U.S. (202) 785-0350), www.oecd.org; *International Trade by Commodity Statistics (ITCS); 2005 OECD Agricultural Outlook Tables, 1970-2014;* and *OECD Economic Survey - France 2007.*

United Nations Food and Agricultural Organization (FAO), Viale delle Terme di Caracalla, 00100 Rome, Italy, (Dial from U.S. (202) 653-2400), (Fax from U.S. (202) 653 5760), www.fao.org; *FAO Fertilizer Yearbook* and *The State of Food and Agriculture (SOFA) 2006.*

United Nations Statistics Division, New York, NY 10017, (800) 253-9646, Fax: (212) 963-4116, http://unstats.un.org; *Statistical Yearbook.*

FRANCE - FETAL MORTALITY

See FRANCE - MORTALITY

FRANCE - FILM

See FRANCE - MOTION PICTURES

FRANCE - FINANCE

European Union, Delegation of the European Commission to the United States, 2300 M Street, NW, Washington, DC 20037, (202) 862-9500, Fax: (202) 429-1766, www.eurunion.org; *Eurostatistics: Data for Short-Term Economic Analysis (2007 edition).*

Eurostat, Batiment Jean Monnet, Rue Alcide de Gasperi, L-2920 Luxembourg, http://epp.eurostat.ec.europa.eu; *Eurostat Yearbook 2006-2007.*

International Monetary Fund (IMF), 700 Nineteenth Street, NW, Washington, DC 20431, (202) 623-7000, Fax: (202) 623-4661, www.imf.org; *International Financial Statistics Yearbook 2007.*

Organisation for Economic Cooperation and Development (OECD), 2 rue Andre Pascal, F-75775 Paris Cedex 16, France, (Telephone in U.S. (202) 785-6323), (Fax in U.S. (202) 785-0350), www.oecd.org; *OECD Economic Outlook 2008.*

Taylor and Francis Group, An Informa Business, 2 Park Square, Milton Park, Abingdon, Oxford OX14 4RN, United Kingdom, (Dial from U.S. (212) 216-7800), (Fax from U.S. (212) 564-7854), www.tandf.co.uk; *The Europa World Year Book.*

United Nations Statistics Division, New York, NY 10017, (800) 253-9646, Fax: (212) 963-4116, http://unstats.un.org; *National Accounts Statistics: Compendium of Income Distribution Statistics* and *Statistical Yearbook.*

The World Bank, 1818 H Street, NW, Washington, DC 20433, (202) 473-1000, Fax: (202) 477-6391, www.worldbank.org; *France.*

FRANCE - FINANCE, PUBLIC

Banque de France, 48 rue Croix des Petits champs, 75001 Paris, France, www.banque-france.fr/home.htm; *Key Data for the Euro Area* and *Public Finance.*

Bernan Essential Government Publications, 4611-F Assembly Drive, Lanham MD, 20706-4391, (301) 459-2255, Fax: (800) 865-3450, www.bernan.com; *National Accounts Statistics.*

Economist Intelligence Unit, 111 West 57th Street, New York, NY 10019, (212) 554-0600, Fax: (212) 586-1181, www.eiu.com; *France Country Report.*

European Union, Delegation of the European Commission to the United States, 2300 M Street, NW, Washington, DC 20037, (202) 862-9500, Fax: (202) 429-1766, www.eurunion.org; *Eurostatistics: Data for Short-Term Economic Analysis (2007 edition).*

Eurostat, Batiment Jean Monnet, Rue Alcide de Gasperi, L-2920 Luxembourg, http://epp.eurostat.ec.europa.eu; *Eurostat Yearbook 2006-2007.*

International Monetary Fund (IMF), 700 Nineteenth Street, NW, Washington, DC 20431, (202) 623-7000, Fax: (202) 623-4661, www.imf.org; *Government Finance Statistics Yearbook (2008 Edition); International Financial Statistics; International Financial Statistics Online Service;* and *International Financial Statistics Yearbook 2007.*

M.E. Sharpe, 80 Business Park Drive, Armonk, NY 10504, (800) 541-6563, Fax: (914) 273-2106, www.mesharpe.com; *The Illustrated Book of World Rankings.*

Organisation for Economic Cooperation and Development (OECD), 2 rue Andre Pascal, F-75775 Paris Cedex 16, France, (Telephone in U.S. (202) 785-6323), (Fax in U.S. (202) 785-0350), www.oecd.org; *Financial Market Trends: OECD Periodical; Geographical Distribution of Financial Flows to Aid Recipients 2002-2006; OECD Economic Outlook 2008; OECD Main Economic Indicators (MEI);* and *Revenue Statistics 1965-2006 - 2007 Edition.*

Palgrave Macmillan Ltd., Houndmills, Basingstoke, Hampshire, RG21 6XS, England, (Telephone in U.S. (888) 330-8477), (Fax in U.S. (800) 672-2054), www.palgrave.com; *The Statesman's Yearbook 2008.*

Taylor and Francis Group, An Informa Business, 2 Park Square, Milton Park, Abingdon, Oxford OX14 4RN, United Kingdom, (Dial from U.S. (212) 216-7800), (Fax from U.S. (212) 564-7854), www.tandf.co.uk; *The Europa World Year Book.*

The World Bank, 1818 H Street, NW, Washington, DC 20433, (202) 473-1000, Fax: (202) 477-6391, www.worldbank.org; *France.*

FRANCE - FISHERIES

Euromonitor International, Inc., 224 S. Michigan Avenue, Suite 1500, Chicago, IL 60604, (312) 922-1115, Fax: (312) 922-1157, www.euromonitor.com; *European Marketing Data and Statistics 2008.*

European Union, Delegation of the European Commission to the United States, 2300 M Street, NW, Washington, DC 20037, (202) 862-9500, Fax: (202) 429-1766, www.eurunion.org; *Agricultural Statistics: Data 1995-2005* and *Fishery Statistics - 1990-2006.*

Eurostat, Batiment Jean Monnet, Rue Alcide de Gasperi, L-2920 Luxembourg, http://epp.eurostat.ec.europa.eu; *Eurostat Yearbook 2006-2007.*

M.E. Sharpe, 80 Business Park Drive, Armonk, NY 10504, (800) 541-6563, Fax: (914) 273-2106, www.mesharpe.com; *The Illustrated Book of World Rankings.*

Organisation for Economic Cooperation and Development (OECD), 2 rue Andre Pascal, F-75775 Paris Cedex 16, France, (Telephone in U.S. (202) 785-6323), (Fax in U.S. (202) 785-0350), www.oecd.org; *International Trade by Commodity Statistics (ITCS); Review of Fisheries in OECD Countries: Country Statistics 2001 to 2003 - 2005 Edition;* and STructural ANalysis (STAN) database.

Palgrave Macmillan Ltd., Houndmills, Basingstoke, Hampshire, RG21 6XS, England, (Telephone in U.S. (888) 330-8477), (Fax in U.S. (800) 672-2054), www.palgrave.com; *The Statesman's Yearbook 2008.*

Taylor and Francis Group, An Informa Business, 2 Park Square, Milton Park, Abingdon, Oxford OX14 4RN, United Kingdom, (Dial from U.S. (212) 216-7800), (Fax from U.S. (212) 564-7854), www.tandf.co.uk; *The Europa World Year Book.*

United Nations Conference on Trade and Development (UNCTAD), DC2-1120, United Nations, New York, NY 10017, (212) 963-0027, www.unctad.org; *UNCTAD Commodity Yearbook.*

United Nations Food and Agricultural Organization (FAO), Viale delle Terme di Caracalla, 00100 Rome, Italy, (Dial from U.S. (202) 653-2400), (Fax from U.S. (202) 653 5760), www.fao.org; *FAO Yearbook of Fishery Statistics;* Fishery Databases; FISHSTAT Database. Subjects covered include: Aquaculture production, capture production, fishery commodities; and *The State of Food and Agriculture (SOFA) 2006.*

United Nations Statistics Division, New York, NY 10017, (800) 253-9646, Fax: (212) 963-4116, http://unstats.un.org; *Statistical Yearbook.*

The World Bank, 1818 H Street, NW, Washington, DC 20433, (202) 473-1000, Fax: (202) 477-6391, www.worldbank.org; *France.*

FRANCE - FLOUR INDUSTRY

Eurostat, Batiment Jean Monnet, Rue Alcide de Gasperi, L-2920 Luxembourg, http://epp.eurostat.ec.europa.eu; *Eurostat Yearbook 2006-2007.*

United Nations Statistics Division, New York, NY 10017, (800) 253-9646, Fax: (212) 963-4116, http://unstats.un.org; *Statistical Yearbook.*

FRANCE - FOOD

Euromonitor International, Inc., 224 S. Michigan Avenue, Suite 1500, Chicago, IL 60604, (312) 922-1115, Fax: (312) 922-1157, www.euromonitor.com; *Retail Trade International 2007.*

Eurostat, Batiment Jean Monnet, Rue Alcide de Gasperi, L-2920 Luxembourg, http://epp.eurostat.ec.europa.eu; *Eurostat Yearbook 2006-2007.*

Organisation for Economic Cooperation and Development (OECD), 2 rue Andre Pascal, F-75775 Paris Cedex 16, France, (Telephone in U.S. (202) 785-6323), (Fax in U.S. (202) 785-0350), www.oecd.org; *International Trade by Commodity Statistics (ITCS)* and *Towards Sustainable Household Consumption?: Trends and Policies in OECD Countries.*

United Nations Conference on Trade and Development (UNCTAD), DC2-1120, United Nations, New York, NY 10017, (212) 963-0027, www.unctad.org; *UNCTAD Commodity Yearbook.*

United Nations Food and Agricultural Organization (FAO), Viale delle Terme di Caracalla, 00100 Rome, Italy, (Dial from U.S. (202) 653-2400), (Fax from U.S. (202) 653 5760), www.fao.org; *FAO Production Yearbook 2002* and *The State of Food and Agriculture (SOFA) 2006.*

United Nations Statistics Division, New York, NY 10017, (800) 253-9646, Fax: (212) 963-4116, http://unstats.un.org; *Human Development Report 2006* and *Statistical Yearbook.*

FRANCE - FOOTWEAR

Organisation for Economic Cooperation and Development (OECD), 2 rue Andre Pascal, F-75775 Paris Cedex 16, France, (Telephone in U.S. (202) 785-6323), (Fax in U.S. (202) 785-0350), www.oecd.org; *Indicators of Industrial Activity.*

FRANCE - FOREIGN EXCHANGE RATES

Central Intelligence Agency, Office of Public Affairs, Washington, DC 20505, (703) 482-0623, Fax: (703) 482-1739, www.cia.gov; *The World Factbook.*

Euromonitor International, Inc., 224 S. Michigan Avenue, Suite 1500, Chicago, IL 60604, (312) 922-1115, Fax: (312) 922-1157, www.euromonitor.com; *The World Economic Factbook 2008.*

European Union, Delegation of the European Commission to the United States, 2300 M Street, NW, Washington, DC 20037, (202) 862-9500, Fax: (202) 429-1766, www.eurunion.org; *Eurostatistics: Data for Short-Term Economic Analysis (2007 edition).*

Eurostat, Batiment Jean Monnet, Rue Alcide de Gasperi, L-2920 Luxembourg, http://epp.eurostat.ec.europa.eu; *Eurostat Yearbook 2006-2007.*

International Civil Aviation Organization (ICAO), External Relations and Public Information Office (EPO), 999 University Street, Montreal, Quebec H3C 5H7, Canada, (Dial from U.S. (514) 954-8219), (Fax from U.S. (514) 954-6077), www.icao.int; *Civil Aviation Statistics of the World.*

International Monetary Fund (IMF), 700 Nineteenth Street, NW, Washington, DC 20431, (202) 623-7000, Fax: (202) 623-4661, www.imf.org; *International Financial Statistics Yearbook 2007.*

Organisation for Economic Cooperation and Development (OECD), 2 rue Andre Pascal, F-75775 Paris Cedex 16, France, (Telephone in U.S. (202) 785-6323), (Fax in U.S. (202) 785-0350), www.oecd.org; *Financial Market Trends: OECD Periodical; Household, Tourism, Travel: Trends, Environmental Impacts and Policy Responses; OECD Economic Outlook 2008;* and *Revenue Statistics 1965-2006 - 2007 Edition.*

Taylor and Francis Group, An Informa Business, 2 Park Square, Milton Park, Abingdon, Oxford OX14 4RN, United Kingdom, (Dial from U.S. (212) 216-7800), (Fax from U.S. (212) 564-7854), www.tandf.co.uk; *The Europa World Year Book.*

United Nations Statistics Division, New York, NY 10017, (800) 253-9646, Fax: (212) 963-4116, http://unstats.un.org; *Statistical Yearbook; Trends in Europe and North America: The Statistical Yearbook of the ECE 2005;* and *World Statistics Pocketbook.*

FRANCE - FORESTS AND FORESTRY

American Forest Paper Association (AFPA), 1111 Nineteenth Street, NW, Suite 800, Washington, DC 20036, (800) 878-8878, www.afandpa.org; *2007 Annual Statistics of Paper, Paperboard, and Wood Pulp.*

Euromonitor International, Inc., 224 S. Michigan Avenue, Suite 1500, Chicago, IL 60604, (312) 922-1115, Fax: (312) 922-1157, www.euromonitor.com; *European Marketing Data and Statistics 2008.*

European Union, Delegation of the European Commission to the United States, 2300 M Street, NW, Washington, DC 20037, (202) 862-9500, Fax: (202) 429-1766, www.eurunion.org; *Agricultural Statistics: Data 1995-2005.*

Eurostat, Batiment Jean Monnet, Rue Alcide de Gasperi, L-2920 Luxembourg, http://epp.eurostat.ec.europa.eu; *Eurostat Yearbook 2006-2007.*

M.E. Sharpe, 80 Business Park Drive, Armonk, NY 10504, (800) 541-6563, Fax: (914) 273-2106, www.mesharpe.com; *The Illustrated Book of World Rankings.*

Organisation for Economic Cooperation and Development (OECD), 2 rue Andre Pascal, F-75775 Paris Cedex 16, France, (Telephone in U.S. (202) 785-6323), (Fax in U.S. (202) 785-0350), www.oecd.org; *Indicators of Industrial Activity; International Trade by Commodity Statistics (ITCS);* and STructural ANalysis (STAN) database.

Palgrave Macmillan Ltd., Houndmills, Basingstoke, Hampshire, RG21 6XS, England, (Telephone in U.S. (888) 330-8477), (Fax in U.S. (800) 672-2054), www.palgrave.com; *The Statesman's Yearbook 2008.*

Taylor and Francis Group, An Informa Business, 2 Park Square, Milton Park, Abingdon, Oxford OX14 4RN, United Kingdom, (Dial from U.S. (212) 216-7800), (Fax from U.S. (212) 564-7854), www.tandf.co.uk; *The Europa World Year Book.*

Technical Association of the Pulp and Paper Industry (TAPPI), 15 Technology Parkway South, Norcross, GA 30092, (770) 446-1400, Fax: (770) 446-6947, www.tappi.org; *TAPPI Annual Report.*

UNESCO Institute for Statistics, C.P. 6128 Succursale Centre-Ville, Montreal, Quebec, H3C 3J7 Canada, (Dial from U.S. (514) 343-6880), (Fax from U.S. (514) 343 6882), www.uis.unesco.org; *Statistical Tables.*

United Nations Conference on Trade and Development (UNCTAD), DC2-1120, United Nations, New York, NY 10017, (212) 963-0027, www.unctad.org; *UNCTAD Commodity Yearbook.*

United Nations Food and Agricultural Organization (FAO), Viale delle Terme di Caracalla, 00100 Rome, Italy, (Dial from U.S. (202) 653-2400), (Fax from U.S. (202) 653 5760), www.fao.org; *FAO Yearbook of Forest Products* and *The State of Food and Agriculture (SOFA) 2006.*

United Nations Statistics Division, New York, NY 10017, (800) 253-9646, Fax: (212) 963-4116, http://unstats.un.org; *Statistical Yearbook* and *Trends in Europe and North America: The Statistical Yearbook of the ECE 2005.*

The World Bank, 1818 H Street, NW, Washington, DC 20433, (202) 473-1000, Fax: (202) 477-6391, www.worldbank.org; *France* and *World Development Report 2008.*

FRANCE - FRUIT PRODUCTION

See FRANCE - CROPS

FRANCE - GAS PRODUCTION

See FRANCE - MINERAL INDUSTRIES

FRANCE - GEOGRAPHIC INFORMATION SYSTEMS

Eurostat, Batiment Jean Monnet, Rue Alcide de Gasperi, L-2920 Luxembourg, http://epp.eurostat.ec.europa.eu; *Eurostat Yearbook 2006-2007.*

M.E. Sharpe, 80 Business Park Drive, Armonk, NY 10504, (800) 541-6563, Fax: (914) 273-2106, www.mesharpe.com; *The Illustrated Book of World Rankings.*

The World Bank, 1818 H Street, NW, Washington, DC 20433, (202) 473-1000, Fax: (202) 477-6391, www.worldbank.org; *France.*

FRANCE - GLASS TRADE

Organisation for Economic Cooperation and Development (OECD), 2 rue Andre Pascal, F-75775 Paris Cedex 16, France, (Telephone in U.S. (202) 785-6323), (Fax in U.S. (202) 785-0350), www.oecd.org; *Indicators of Industrial Activity.*

FRANCE - GOLD INDUSTRY

International Monetary Fund (IMF), 700 Nineteenth Street, NW, Washington, DC 20431, (202) 623-7000, Fax: (202) 623-4661, www.imf.org; *International Financial Statistics Yearbook 2007.*

United Nations Statistics Division, New York, NY 10017, (800) 253-9646, Fax: (212) 963-4116, http://unstats.un.org; *Statistical Yearbook.*

The World Bank, 1818 H Street, NW, Washington, DC 20433, (202) 473-1000, Fax: (202) 477-6391, www.worldbank.org; *World Development Indicators (WDI) 2008.*

FRANCE - GOLD PRODUCTION

See FRANCE - MINERAL INDUSTRIES

FRANCE - GRANTS-IN-AID

International Monetary Fund (IMF), 700 Nineteenth Street, NW, Washington, DC 20431, (202) 623-7000, Fax: (202) 623-4661, www.imf.org; *Government Finance Statistics Yearbook (2008 Edition).*

Organisation for Economic Cooperation and Development (OECD), 2 rue Andre Pascal, F-75775 Paris Cedex 16, France, (Telephone in U.S. (202) 785-6323), (Fax in U.S. (202) 785-0350), www.oecd.org; *Geographical Distribution of Financial Flows to Aid Recipients 2002-2006.*

FRANCE - GREEN PEPPER AND CHILIE PRODUCTION

See FRANCE - CROPS

FRANCE - GROSS DOMESTIC PRODUCT

Economist Intelligence Unit, 111 West 57th Street, New York, NY 10019, (212) 554-0600, Fax: (212) 586-1181, www.eiu.com; *France Country Report.*

Euromonitor International, Inc., 224 S. Michigan Avenue, Suite 1500, Chicago, IL 60604, (312) 922-1115, Fax: (312) 922-1157, www.euromonitor.com; *The World Economic Factbook 2008.*

European Union, Delegation of the European Commission to the United States, 2300 M Street, NW, Washington, DC 20037, (202) 862-9500, Fax: (202) 429-1766, www.eurunion.org; *Eurostatistics: Data for Short-Term Economic Analysis (2007 edition); Iron and Steel;* and *RD Expenditure in Europe (2006 edition).*

Eurostat, Batiment Jean Monnet, Rue Alcide de Gasperi, L-2920 Luxembourg, http://epp.eurostat.ec.europa.eu; *Eurostat Yearbook 2006-2007.*

International Monetary Fund (IMF), 700 Nineteenth Street, NW, Washington, DC 20431, (202) 623-7000, Fax: (202) 623-4661, www.imf.org; *International Financial Statistics Yearbook 2007.*

M.E. Sharpe, 80 Business Park Drive, Armonk, NY 10504, (800) 541-6563, Fax: (914) 273-2106, www.mesharpe.com; *The Illustrated Book of World Rankings.*

Organisation for Economic Cooperation and Development (OECD), 2 rue Andre Pascal, F-75775 Paris Cedex 16, France, (Telephone in U.S. (202) 785-6323), (Fax in U.S. (202) 785-0350), www.oecd.org; *Comparison of Gross Domestic Product (GDP) for OECD Countries; Geographical Distribution of Financial Flows to Aid Recipients 2002-2006; OECD Economic Outlook 2008;* and *Revenue Statistics 1965-2006 - 2007 Edition.*

Taylor and Francis Group, An Informa Business, 2 Park Square, Milton Park, Abingdon, Oxford OX14 4RN, United Kingdom, (Dial from U.S. (212) 216-7800), (Fax from U.S. (212) 564-7854), www.tandf.co.uk; *The Europa World Year Book.*

United Nations Statistics Division, New York, NY 10017, (800) 253-9646, Fax: (212) 963-4116, http://unstats.un.org; *Human Development Report 2006; National Accounts Statistics: Compendium of Income Distribution Statistics; Statistical Yearbook;* and *Trends in Europe and North America: The Statistical Yearbook of the ECE 2005.*

The World Bank, 1818 H Street, NW, Washington, DC 20433, (202) 473-1000, Fax: (202) 477-6391, www.worldbank.org; *World Development Indicators (WDI) 2008* and *World Development Report 2008.*

FRANCE - GROSS NATIONAL PRODUCT

European Union, Delegation of the European Commission to the United States, 2300 M Street, NW, Washington, DC 20037, (202) 862-9500, Fax: (202) 429-1766, www.eurunion.org; *The EU Economy, 2007 Review: Moving Europe's Productivity Frontier.*

Eurostat, Batiment Jean Monnet, Rue Alcide de Gasperi, L-2920 Luxembourg, http://epp.eurostat.ec.europa.eu; *Eurostat Yearbook 2006-2007.*

M.E. Sharpe, 80 Business Park Drive, Armonk, NY 10504, (800) 541-6563, Fax: (914) 273-2106, www.mesharpe.com; *The Illustrated Book of World Rankings.*

Organisation for Economic Cooperation and Development (OECD), 2 rue Andre Pascal, F-75775 Paris Cedex 16, France, (Telephone in U.S. (202) 785-6323), (Fax in U.S. (202) 785-0350), www.oecd.org; *Geographical Distribution of Financial Flows to Aid Recipients 2002-2006; OECD Composite Leading Indicators (CLIs), Updated September 2007;* and *OECD Economic Outlook 2008.*

Palgrave Macmillan Ltd., Houndmills, Basingstoke, Hampshire, RG21 6XS, England, (Telephone in U.S. (888) 330-8477), (Fax in U.S. (800) 672-2054), www.palgrave.com; *The Statesman's Yearbook 2008.*

Taylor and Francis Group, An Informa Business, 2 Park Square, Milton Park, Abingdon, Oxford OX14 4RN, United Kingdom, (Dial from U.S. (212) 216-7800), (Fax from U.S. (212) 564-7854), www.tandf.co.uk; *The Europa World Year Book.*

U.S. Department of State (DOS), 2201 C Street NW, Washington, DC 20520, (202) 647-4000, www.state.gov; *World Military Expenditures and Arms Transfers (WMEAT).*

United Nations Statistics Division, New York, NY 10017, (800) 253-9646, Fax: (212) 963-4116, http://unstats.un.org; *Statistical Yearbook.*

The World Bank, 1818 H Street, NW, Washington, DC 20433, (202) 473-1000, Fax: (202) 477-6391, www.worldbank.org; *The World Bank Atlas 2003-2004; World Development Indicators (WDI) 2008;* and *World Development Report 2008.*

FRANCE - HAY PRODUCTION

See FRANCE - CROPS

FRANCE - HAZELNUT PRODUCTION

See FRANCE - CROPS

FRANCE - HEALTH

See FRANCE - PUBLIC HEALTH

FRANCE - HEMP FIBRE PRODUCTION

See FRANCE - TEXTILE INDUSTRY

FRANCE - HIDES AND SKINS INDUSTRY

Organisation for Economic Cooperation and Development (OECD), 2 rue Andre Pascal, F-75775 Paris Cedex 16, France, (Telephone in U.S. (202) 785-6323), (Fax in U.S. (202) 785-0350), www.oecd.org; *Indicators of Industrial Activity* and *International Trade by Commodity Statistics (ITCS).*

United Nations Food and Agricultural Organization (FAO), Viale delle Terme di Caracalla, 00100 Rome, Italy, (Dial from U.S. (202) 653-2400), (Fax from U.S. (202) 653 5760), www.fao.org; *FAO Production Yearbook 2002.*

FRANCE - HOPS PRODUCTION

See FRANCE - CROPS

FRANCE - HOUSING

Euromonitor International, Inc., 224 S. Michigan Avenue, Suite 1500, Chicago, IL 60604, (312) 922-1115, Fax: (312) 922-1157, www.euromonitor.com; *World Marketing Data and Statistics.*

European Union, Delegation of the European Commission to the United States, 2300 M Street, NW, Washington, DC 20037, (202) 862-9500, Fax: (202) 429-1766, www.eurunion.org; *European Union Labour Force Survey* and *Regions - Statistical Yearbook 2006.*

Eurostat, Batiment Jean Monnet, Rue Alcide de Gasperi, L-2920 Luxembourg, http://epp.eurostat.ec.europa.eu; *Eurostat Yearbook 2006-2007.*

M.E. Sharpe, 80 Business Park Drive, Armonk, NY 10504, (800) 541-6563, Fax: (914) 273-2106, www.mesharpe.com; *The Illustrated Book of World Rankings.*

United Nations Statistics Division, New York, NY 10017, (800) 253-9646, Fax: (212) 963-4116, http://unstats.un.org; *Statistical Yearbook* and *Trends in Europe and North America: The Statistical Yearbook of the ECE 2005.*

FRANCE - HOUSING CONSTRUCTION

See FRANCE - CONSTRUCTION INDUSTRY

FRANCE - ILLITERATE PERSONS

Euromonitor International, Inc., 224 S. Michigan Avenue, Suite 1500, Chicago, IL 60604, (312) 922-1115, Fax: (312) 922-1157, www.euromonitor.com; *The World Economic Factbook 2008.*

Palgrave Macmillan Ltd., Houndmills, Basingstoke, Hampshire, RG21 6XS, England, (Telephone in U.S. (888) 330-8477), (Fax in U.S. (800) 672-2054), www.palgrave.com; *The Statesman's Yearbook 2008.*

UNESCO Institute for Statistics, C.P. 6128 Succursale Centre-Ville, Montreal, Quebec, H3C 3J7 Canada, (Dial from U.S. (514) 343-6880), (Fax from U.S. (514) 343 6882), www.uis.unesco.org; *Statistical Tables.*

United Nations Statistics Division, New York, NY 10017, (800) 253-9646, Fax: (212) 963-4116, http://unstats.un.org; *Human Development Report 2006.*

FRANCE - IMPORTS

Central Intelligence Agency, Office of Public Affairs, Washington, DC 20505, (703) 482-0623, Fax: (703) 482-1739, www.cia.gov; *The World Factbook.*

Economist Intelligence Unit, 111 West 57th Street, New York, NY 10019, (212) 554-0600, Fax: (212) 586-1181, www.eiu.com; *France Country Report.*

Euromonitor International, Inc., 224 S. Michigan Avenue, Suite 1500, Chicago, IL 60604, (312) 922-1115, Fax: (312) 922-1157, www.euromonitor.com; *The World Economic Factbook 2008.*

European Union, Delegation of the European Commission to the United States, 2300 M Street, NW, Washington, DC 20037, (202) 862-9500, Fax: (202) 429-1766, www.eurunion.org; *European Union Energy Transport in Figures 2006; Eurostatistics: Data for Short-Term Economic Analysis (2007 edition); External and Intra-European Union Trade: Data 1958-2002; External and Intra-European Union Trade: Data 1999-2004;* and *Fishery Statistics - 1990-2006.*

Eurostat, Batiment Jean Monnet, Rue Alcide de Gasperi, L-2920 Luxembourg, http://epp.eurostat.ec.europa.eu; *Eurostat Yearbook 2006-2007.*

International Iron and Steel Institute (IISI), Rue Colonel Bourg 120, B-1140 Brussels, Belgium, www.worldsteel.org; *Steel Statistical Yearbook 2006.*

International Lead and Zinc Study Group (ILZSG), Rua Almirante Barroso 38, 5th Floor, Lisbon 1000 - 013, Portugal, www.ilzsg.org; Interactive Statistical Database.

International Monetary Fund (IMF), 700 Nineteenth Street, NW, Washington, DC 20431, (202) 623-7000, Fax: (202) 623-4661, www.imf.org; *Direction of Trade Statistics Yearbook 2007; Government Finance Statistics Yearbook (2008 Edition);* and *International Financial Statistics Yearbook 2007.*

Organisation for Economic Cooperation and Development (OECD), 2 rue Andre Pascal, F-75775 Paris Cedex 16, France, (Telephone in U.S. (202) 785-6323), (Fax in U.S. (202) 785-0350), www.oecd.org; *Iron and Steel Industry in 2004 (2006 Edition); 2005 OECD Agricultural Outlook Tables, 1970-2014; OECD Economic Outlook 2008; OECD Economic Survey - France 2007; Review of Fisheries in OECD Countries: Country Statistics 2001 to 2003 - 2005 Edition;* and STructural ANalysis (STAN) database.

Palgrave Macmillan Ltd., Houndmills, Basingstoke, Hampshire, RG21 6XS, England, (Telephone in U.S. (888) 330-8477), (Fax in U.S. (800) 672-2054), www.palgrave.com; *The Statesman's Yearbook 2008.*

Platts, 2 Penn Plaza, 25th Floor, New York, NY 10121-2298, (212) 904-3070, www.platts.com; *Energy Economist.*

Taylor and Francis Group, An Informa Business, 2 Park Square, Milton Park, Abingdon, Oxford OX14 4RN, United Kingdom, (Dial from U.S. (212) 216-7800), (Fax from U.S. (212) 564-7854), www.tandf.co.uk; *The Europa World Year Book.*

Technical Association of the Pulp and Paper Industry (TAPPI), 15 Technology Parkway South, Norcross, GA 30092, (770) 446-1400, Fax: (770) 446-6947, www.tappi.org; *TAPPI Annual Report.*

United Nations Conference on Trade and Development (UNCTAD), DC2-1120, United Nations, New York, NY 10017, (212) 963-0027, www.unctad.org; *Handbook of Statistics 2005.*

United Nations Food and Agricultural Organization (FAO), Viale delle Terme di Caracalla, 00100 Rome, Italy, (Dial from U.S. (202) 653-2400), (Fax from U.S. (202) 653 5760), www.fao.org; *The State of Food and Agriculture (SOFA) 2006.*

United Nations Statistics Division, New York, NY 10017, (800) 253-9646, Fax: (212) 963-4116, http://unstats.un.org; *Energy Statistics Yearbook 2003* and *Trends in Europe and North America: The Statistical Yearbook of the ECE 2005.*

The World Bank, 1818 H Street, NW, Washington, DC 20433, (202) 473-1000, Fax: (202) 477-6391, www.worldbank.org; *World Development Indicators (WDI) 2008* and *World Development Report 2008.*

FRANCE - INCOME TAXES

See FRANCE - TAXATION

FRANCE - INDUSTRIAL METALS PRODUCTION

See FRANCE - MINERAL INDUSTRIES

FRANCE - INDUSTRIAL PRODUCTIVITY

European Union, Delegation of the European Commission to the United States, 2300 M Street, NW, Washington, DC 20037, (202) 862-9500, Fax: (202) 429-1766, www.eurunion.org; *Eurostatistics: Data for Short-Term Economic Analysis (2007 edition); Fishery Statistics - 1990-2006;* and *RD Expenditure in Europe (2006 edition).*

Eurostat, Batiment Jean Monnet, Rue Alcide de Gasperi, L-2920 Luxembourg, http://epp.eurostat.ec.europa.eu; *Eurostat Yearbook 2006-2007.*

International Iron and Steel Institute (IISI), Rue Colonel Bourg 120, B-1140 Brussels, Belgium, www.worldsteel.org; *Steel Statistical Yearbook 2006.*

International Lead and Zinc Study Group (ILZSG), Rua Almirante Barroso 38, 5th Floor, Lisbon 1000 - 013, Portugal, www.ilzsg.org; Interactive Statistical Database.

M.E. Sharpe, 80 Business Park Drive, Armonk, NY 10504, (800) 541-6563, Fax: (914) 273-2106, www.mesharpe.com; *The Illustrated Book of World Rankings.*

Organisation for Economic Cooperation and Development (OECD), 2 rue Andre Pascal, F-75775 Paris Cedex 16, France, (Telephone in U.S. (202) 785-6323), (Fax in U.S. (202) 785-0350), www.oecd.org; *Environmental Impacts of Foreign Direct Investment in the Mining Sector in the Newly Independent States (NIS); Indicators of Industrial Activity; Iron and Steel Industry in 2004 (2006 Edition); A New World Map in Textiles and Clothing: Adjusting to Change; 2005 OECD Agricultural Outlook Tables, 1970-2014; OECD Economic Outlook 2008;* and STructural ANalysis (STAN) database.

Technical Association of the Pulp and Paper Industry (TAPPI), 15 Technology Parkway South, Norcross, GA 30092, (770) 446-1400, Fax: (770) 446-6947, www.tappi.org; *TAPPI Annual Report.*

FRANCE - INDUSTRIAL PROPERTY

United Nations Statistics Division, New York, NY 10017, (800) 253-9646, Fax: (212) 963-4116, http://unstats.un.org; *Statistical Yearbook.*

World Intellectual Property Organization (WIPO), PO Box 18, CH-1211 Geneva 20, Switzerland, www.wipo.int; *Industrial Property Statistics* and *Industrial Property Statistics Online Directory.*

FRANCE - INDUSTRIES

Central Intelligence Agency, Office of Public Affairs, Washington, DC 20505, (703) 482-0623, Fax: (703) 482-1739, www.cia.gov; *The World Factbook.*

Economist Intelligence Unit, 111 West 57th Street, New York, NY 10019, (212) 554-0600, Fax: (212) 586-1181, www.eiu.com; *France Country Report.*

Euromonitor International, Inc., 224 S. Michigan Avenue, Suite 1500, Chicago, IL 60604, (312) 922-1115, Fax: (312) 922-1157, www.euromonitor.com; *The World Economic Factbook 2008* and *World Marketing Data and Statistics.*

European Union, Delegation of the European Commission to the United States, 2300 M Street, NW, Washington, DC 20037, (202) 862-9500, Fax: (202) 429-1766, www.eurunion.org; *European Union Labour Force Survey* and *Eurostatistics: Data for Short-Term Economic Analysis (2007 edition).*

Eurostat, Batiment Jean Monnet, Rue Alcide de Gasperi, L-2920 Luxembourg, http://epp.eurostat.ec.europa.eu; *Eurostat Yearbook 2006-2007.*

International Labour Office, I.L.O. Publications, 4 route des Morillons, CH-1211 Geneva 22, Switzerland, (Telephone in U.S. (202) 653-7652), (Fax in U.S. (202) 653-7687), www.ilo.org; *Yearbook of Labour Statistics 2006.*

M.E. Sharpe, 80 Business Park Drive, Armonk, NY 10504, (800) 541-6563, Fax: (914) 273-2106, www.mesharpe.com; *The Illustrated Book of World Rankings.*

Organisation for Economic Cooperation and Development (OECD), 2 rue Andre Pascal, F-75775 Paris Cedex 16, France, (Telephone in U.S. (202) 785-6323), (Fax in U.S. (202) 785-0350), www.oecd.org; *Indicators of Industrial Activity; Key Environmental Indicators 2004; OECD Economic Outlook 2008;* and STructural ANalysis (STAN) database.

Palgrave Macmillan Ltd., Houndmills, Basingstoke, Hampshire, RG21 6XS, England, (Telephone in U.S. (888) 330-8477), (Fax in U.S. (800) 672-2054), www.palgrave.com; *The Statesman's Yearbook 2008.*

Taylor and Francis Group, An Informa Business, 2 Park Square, Milton Park, Abingdon, Oxford OX14 4RN, United Kingdom, (Dial from U.S. (212) 216-7800), (Fax from U.S. (212) 564-7854), www.tandf.co.uk; *The Europa World Year Book.*

United Nations Industrial Development Organization (UNIDO), 1 United Nations Plaza, New York, NY 10017, (212) 963 6890, Fax: (212) 963-7904, http://unido.org; Industrial Statistics Database 2008 (INDSTAT) and *The International Yearbook of Industrial Statistics 2008.*

United Nations Statistics Division, New York, NY 10017, (800) 253-9646, Fax: (212) 963-4116, http://unstats.un.org; *2004 Industrial Commodity Statistics Yearbook; Statistical Yearbook;* and *Trends in Europe and North America: The Statistical Yearbook of the ECE 2005.*

The World Bank, 1818 H Street, NW, Washington, DC 20433, (202) 473-1000, Fax: (202) 477-6391, www.worldbank.org; *France* and *World Development Indicators (WDI) 2008.*

FRANCE - INFANT AND MATERNAL MORTALITY

See FRANCE - MORTALITY

FRANCE - INORGANIC ACIDS

Eurostat, Batiment Jean Monnet, Rue Alcide de Gasperi, L-2920 Luxembourg, http://epp.eurostat.ec.europa.eu; *Eurostat Yearbook 2006-2007.*

Organisation for Economic Cooperation and Development (OECD), 2 rue Andre Pascal, F-75775 Paris Cedex 16, France, (Telephone in U.S. (202) 785-6323), (Fax in U.S. (202) 785-0350), www.oecd.org; *Indicators of Industrial Activity.*

United Nations Statistics Division, New York, NY 10017, (800) 253-9646, Fax: (212) 963-4116, http://unstats.un.org; *Statistical Yearbook.*

FRANCE - INTEREST RATES

Eurostat, Batiment Jean Monnet, Rue Alcide de Gasperi, L-2920 Luxembourg, http://epp.eurostat.ec.europa.eu; *Eurostat Yearbook 2006-2007.*

Organisation for Economic Cooperation and Development (OECD), 2 rue Andre Pascal, F-75775 Paris Cedex 16, France, (Telephone in U.S. (202) 785-6323), (Fax in U.S. (202) 785-0350), www.oecd.org; *Financial Market Trends: OECD Periodical* and *OECD Economic Outlook 2008.*

United Nations Statistics Division, New York, NY 10017, (800) 253-9646, Fax: (212) 963-4116, http://unstats.un.org; *Statistical Yearbook.*

FRANCE - INTERNAL REVENUE

Organisation for Economic Cooperation and Development (OECD), 2 rue Andre Pascal, F-75775 Paris Cedex 16, France, (Telephone in U.S. (202) 785-6323), (Fax in U.S. (202) 785-0350), www.oecd.org; *Revenue Statistics 1965-2006 - 2007 Edition.*

FRANCE - INTERNATIONAL FINANCE

Eurostat, Batiment Jean Monnet, Rue Alcide de Gasperi, L-2920 Luxembourg, http://epp.eurostat.ec.europa.eu; *Eurostat Yearbook 2006-2007.*

International Finance Corporation (IFC), 2121 Pennsylvania Avenue, NW, Washington, DC 20433 USA, (202) 473-1000, Fax: (202) 974-4384, www.ifc.org; *Annual Report 2007.*

Organisation for Economic Cooperation and Development (OECD), 2 rue Andre Pascal, F-75775 Paris Cedex 16, France, (Telephone in U.S. (202) 785-6323), (Fax in U.S. (202) 785-0350), www.oecd.org; *Financial Market Trends: OECD Periodical* and *OECD Economic Outlook 2008.*

FRANCE - INTERNATIONAL LIQUIDITY

International Monetary Fund (IMF), 700 Nineteenth Street, NW, Washington, DC 20431, (202) 623-7000, Fax: (202) 623-4661, www.imf.org; *International Financial Statistics Yearbook 2007.*

Organisation for Economic Cooperation and Development (OECD), 2 rue Andre Pascal, F-75775 Paris Cedex 16, France, (Telephone in U.S. (202) 785-6323), (Fax in U.S. (202) 785-0350), www.oecd.org; *Financial Market Trends: OECD Periodical* and *OECD Economic Outlook 2008.*

FRANCE - INTERNATIONAL STATISTICS

Organisation for Economic Cooperation and Development (OECD), 2 rue Andre Pascal, F-75775 Paris Cedex 16, France, (Telephone in U.S. (202) 785-6323), (Fax in U.S. (202) 785-0350), www.oecd.org; *Financial Market Trends: OECD Periodical* and *Household, Tourism, Travel: Trends, Environmental Impacts and Policy Responses.*

FRANCE - INTERNATIONAL TRADE

Banque de France, 48 rue Croix des Petits champs, 75001 Paris, France, www.banque-france.fr/home.htm; *Monthly Business Survey Overview.*

Bernan Essential Government Publications, 4611-F Assembly Drive, Lanham MD, 20706-4391, (301) 459-2255, Fax: (800) 865-3450, www.bernan.com; *OECD Factbook 2006.*

Economist Intelligence Unit, 111 West 57th Street, New York, NY 10019, (212) 554-0600, Fax: (212) 586-1181, www.eiu.com; *France Country Report.*

Euromonitor International, Inc., 224 S. Michigan Avenue, Suite 1500, Chicago, IL 60604, (312) 922-1115, Fax: (312) 922-1157, www.euromonitor.com; *European Marketing Data and Statistics 2008; The World Economic Factbook 2008;* and *World Marketing Data and Statistics.*

European Union, Delegation of the European Commission to the United States, 2300 M Street, NW, Washington, DC 20037, (202) 862-9500, Fax: (202) 429-1766, www.eurunion.org; *Eurostatistics: Data for Short-Term Economic Analysis (2007 edition); External and Intra-European Union Trade: Data 1958-2002; External and Intra-European Union Trade: Data 1999-2004;* and *Iron and Steel.*

Eurostat, Batiment Jean Monnet, Rue Alcide de Gasperi, L-2920 Luxembourg, http://epp.eurostat.ec.europa.eu; *Eurostat Yearbook 2006-2007* and Intra- and Extra-EU Trade.

Federal Statistical Office Germany, D-65180 Wiesbaden, Germany, www.destatis.de; *France 2005.*

International Iron and Steel Institute (IISI), Rue Colonel Bourg 120, B-1140 Brussels, Belgium, www.worldsteel.org; *Steel Statistical Yearbook 2006.*

International Monetary Fund (IMF), 700 Nineteenth Street, NW, Washington, DC 20431, (202) 623-7000, Fax: (202) 623-4661, www.imf.org; *International Financial Statistics Yearbook 2007.*

M.E. Sharpe, 80 Business Park Drive, Armonk, NY 10504, (800) 541-6563, Fax: (914) 273-2106, www.mesharpe.com; *The Illustrated Book of World Rankings.*

Organisation for Economic Cooperation and Development (OECD), 2 rue Andre Pascal, F-75775 Paris Cedex 16, France, (Telephone in U.S. (202) 785-6323), (Fax in U.S. (202) 785-0350), www.oecd.org; *International Trade by Commodity Statistics (ITCS); 2005 OECD Agricultural Outlook Tables, 1970-2014; OECD Economic Outlook 2008; OECD in Figures 2007; OECD Main Economic Indicators (MEI);* and *Statistics on Ship Production, Exports and Orders in 2004.*

Palgrave Macmillan Ltd., Houndmills, Basingstoke, Hampshire, RG21 6XS, England, (Telephone in U.S. (888) 330-8477), (Fax in U.S. (800) 672-2054), www.palgrave.com; *The Statesman's Yearbook 2008.*

Taylor and Francis Group, An Informa Business, 2 Park Square, Milton Park, Abingdon, Oxford OX14 4RN, United Kingdom, (Dial from U.S. (212) 216-7800), (Fax from U.S. (212) 564-7854), www.tandf.co.uk; *The Europa World Year Book.*

United Nations Conference on Trade and Development (UNCTAD), DC2-1120, United Nations, New York, NY 10017, (212) 963-0027, www.unctad.org; *UNCTAD Commodity Yearbook.*

United Nations Food and Agricultural Organization (FAO), Viale delle Terme di Caracalla, 00100 Rome, Italy, (Dial from U.S. (202) 653-2400), (Fax from U.S. (202) 653 5760), www.fao.org; *FAO Trade Yearbook* and *The State of Food and Agriculture (SOFA) 2006.*

United Nations Statistics Division, New York, NY 10017, (800) 253-9646, Fax: (212) 963-4116, http://unstats.un.org; *International Trade Statistics Yearbook* and *Statistical Yearbook.*

The World Bank, 1818 H Street, NW, Washington, DC 20433, (202) 473-1000, Fax: (202) 477-6391, www.worldbank.org; *France; World Development Indicators (WDI) 2008;* and *World Development Report 2008.*

World Bureau of Metal Statistics (WBMS), 27a High Street, Ware, Hertfordshire, SG12 9BA, United Kingdom, www.world-bureau.com; *World Flow Charts* and *World Metal Statistics.*

World Trade Organization (WTO), Centre William Rappard, Rue de Lausanne 154, CH-1211 Geneva 21, Switzerland, www.wto.org; *International Trade Statistics 2006.*

FRANCE - INTERNET USERS

Eurostat, Batiment Jean Monnet, Rue Alcide de Gasperi, L-2920 Luxembourg, http://epp.eurostat.ec.europa.eu; *Internet Usage by Enterprises 2007.*

International Telecommunication Union (ITU), Place des Nations, 1211 Geneva 20, Switzerland, www.itu.int; *World Telecommunication/ICT Indicators Database on CD-ROM; World Telecommunication/ICT Indicators Database Online;* and *Yearbook of Statistics - Telecommunication Services (Chronological Time Series 1997-2006).*

The World Bank, 1818 H Street, NW, Washington, DC 20433, (202) 473-1000, Fax: (202) 477-6391, www.worldbank.org; *France.*

FRANCE - INVESTMENTS

International Monetary Fund (IMF), 700 Nineteenth Street, NW, Washington, DC 20431, (202) 623-7000, Fax: (202) 623-4661, www.imf.org; *International Financial Statistics Yearbook 2007.*

Organisation for Economic Cooperation and Development (OECD), 2 rue Andre Pascal, F-75775 Paris Cedex 16, France, (Telephone in U.S. (202) 785-6323), (Fax in U.S. (202) 785-0350), www.oecd.org; *Financial Market Trends: OECD Periodical; Iron and Steel Industry in 2004 (2006 Edition); A New World Map in Textiles and Clothing: Adjusting to Change; OECD Economic Outlook 2008;* and STructural ANalysis (STAN) database.

FRANCE - IRON AND IRON ORE PRODUCTION

See FRANCE - MINERAL INDUSTRIES

FRANCE - JUTE PRODUCTION

See FRANCE - CROPS

FRANCE - LABOR

Central Intelligence Agency, Office of Public Affairs, Washington, DC 20505, (703) 482-0623, Fax: (703) 482-1739, www.cia.gov; *The World Factbook.*

Euromonitor International, Inc., 224 S. Michigan Avenue, Suite 1500, Chicago, IL 60604, (312) 922-1115, Fax: (312) 922-1157, www.euromonitor.com; *World Marketing Data and Statistics.*

European Union, Delegation of the European Commission to the United States, 2300 M Street, NW, Washington, DC 20037, (202) 862-9500, Fax: (202) 429-1766, www.eurunion.org; *European Union Labour Force Survey* and *Regions - Statistical Yearbook 2006.*

Eurostat, Batiment Jean Monnet, Rue Alcide de Gasperi, L-2920 Luxembourg, http://epp.eurostat.ec.europa.eu; *Eurostat Yearbook 2006-2007.*

International Labour Office, I.L.O. Publications, 4 route des Morillons, CH-1211 Geneva 22, Switzerland, (Telephone in U.S. (202) 653-7652), (Fax in U.S. (202) 653-7687), www.ilo.org; *Yearbook of Labour Statistics 2006.*

M.E. Sharpe, 80 Business Park Drive, Armonk, NY 10504, (800) 541-6563, Fax: (914) 273-2106, www.mesharpe.com; *The Illustrated Book of World Rankings.*

Organisation for Economic Cooperation and Development (OECD), 2 rue Andre Pascal, F-75775 Paris Cedex 16, France, (Telephone in U.S. (202) 785-6323), (Fax in U.S. (202) 785-0350), www.oecd.org; *Iron and Steel Industry in 2004 (2006 Edition); A New World Map in Textiles and Clothing: Adjusting to Change; OECD Economic Outlook 2008; OECD Economic Survey - France 2007; OECD Employment Outlook 2007; OECD Main Economic Indicators (MEI);* and *Statistics on Ship Production, Exports and Orders in 2004.*

Palgrave Macmillan Ltd., Houndmills, Basingstoke, Hampshire, RG21 6XS, England, (Telephone in U.S. (888) 330-8477), (Fax in U.S. (800) 672-2054), www.palgrave.com; *The Statesman's Yearbook 2008.*

Taylor and Francis Group, An Informa Business, 2 Park Square, Milton Park, Abingdon, Oxford OX14 4RN, United Kingdom, (Dial from U.S. (212) 216-7800), (Fax from U.S. (212) 564-7854), www.tandf.co.uk; *The Europa World Year Book.*

United Nations Food and Agricultural Organization (FAO), Viale delle Terme di Caracalla, 00100 Rome, Italy, (Dial from U.S. (202) 653-2400), (Fax from U.S. (202) 653 5760), www.fao.org; *The State of Food and Agriculture (SOFA) 2006.*

United Nations Statistics Division, New York, NY 10017, (800) 253-9646, Fax: (212) 963-4116, http://unstats.un.org; *Human Development Report 2006.*

The World Bank, 1818 H Street, NW, Washington, DC 20433, (202) 473-1000, Fax: (202) 477-6391, www.worldbank.org; *The World Bank Atlas 2003-2004; World Development Indicators (WDI) 2008;* and *World Development Report 2008.*

FRANCE - LAND USE

Central Intelligence Agency, Office of Public Affairs, Washington, DC 20505, (703) 482-0623, Fax: (703) 482-1739, www.cia.gov; *The World Factbook.*

Euromonitor International, Inc., 224 S. Michigan Avenue, Suite 1500, Chicago, IL 60604, (312) 922-1115, Fax: (312) 922-1157, www.euromonitor.com; *European Marketing Data and Statistics 2008.*

European Union, Delegation of the European Commission to the United States, 2300 M Street, NW, Washington, DC 20037, (202) 862-9500, Fax: (202) 429-1766, www.eurunion.org; *Agricultural Statistics: Data 1995-2005; Agriculture in the European Union: Statistical and Economic Information 2006;* and *Regions - Statistical Yearbook 2006.*

Eurostat, Batiment Jean Monnet, Rue Alcide de Gasperi, L-2920 Luxembourg, http://epp.eurostat.ec.europa.eu; *Eurostat Yearbook 2006-2007.*

United Nations Food and Agricultural Organization (FAO), Viale delle Terme di Caracalla, 00100 Rome, Italy, (Dial from U.S. (202) 653-2400), (Fax from U.S. (202) 653 5760), www.fao.org; *FAO Production Yearbook 2002.*

The World Bank, 1818 H Street, NW, Washington, DC 20433, (202) 473-1000, Fax: (202) 477-6391, www.worldbank.org; *World Development Report 2008.*

FRANCE - LEATHER INDUSTRY AND TRADE

Eurostat, Batiment Jean Monnet, Rue Alcide de Gasperi, L-2920 Luxembourg, http://epp.eurostat.ec.europa.eu; *Eurostat Yearbook 2006-2007.*

Organisation for Economic Cooperation and Development (OECD), 2 rue Andre Pascal, F-75775 Paris Cedex 16, France, (Telephone in U.S. (202) 785-6323), (Fax in U.S. (202) 785-0350), www.oecd.org; *Indicators of Industrial Activity.*

FRANCE - LIBRARIES

M.E. Sharpe, 80 Business Park Drive, Armonk, NY 10504, (800) 541-6563, Fax: (914) 273-2106, www.mesharpe.com; *The Illustrated Book of World Rankings.*

UNESCO Institute for Statistics, C.P. 6128 Succursale Centre-Ville, Montreal, Quebec, H3C 3J7 Canada, (Dial from U.S. (514) 343-6880), (Fax from U.S. (514) 343 6882), www.uis.unesco.org; *Statistical Tables.*

United Nations Statistics Division, New York, NY 10017, (800) 253-9646, Fax: (212) 963-4116, http://unstats.un.org; *Trends in Europe and North America: The Statistical Yearbook of the ECE 2005.*

FRANCE - LICENSES

International Monetary Fund (IMF), 700 Nineteenth Street, NW, Washington, DC 20431, (202) 623-7000, Fax: (202) 623-4661, www.imf.org; *Government Finance Statistics Yearbook (2008 Edition).*

FRANCE - LIFE EXPECTANCY

Central Intelligence Agency, Office of Public Affairs, Washington, DC 20505, (703) 482-0623, Fax: (703) 482-1739, www.cia.gov; *The World Factbook.*

Euromonitor International, Inc., 224 S. Michigan Avenue, Suite 1500, Chicago, IL 60604, (312) 922-1115, Fax: (312) 922-1157, www.euromonitor.com; *The World Economic Factbook 2008.*

Organisation for Economic Cooperation and Development (OECD), 2 rue Andre Pascal, F-75775 Paris Cedex 16, France, (Telephone in U.S. (202) 785-6323), (Fax in U.S. (202) 785-0350), www.oecd.org; *OECD Economic Outlook 2008.*

Palgrave Macmillan Ltd., Houndmills, Basingstoke, Hampshire, RG21 6XS, England, (Telephone in U.S. (888) 330-8477), (Fax in U.S. (800) 672-2054), www.palgrave.com; *The Statesman's Yearbook 2008.*

United Nations Statistics Division, New York, NY 10017, (800) 253-9646, Fax: (212) 963-4116, http://unstats.un.org; *Human Development Report 2006; Trends in Europe and North America: The Statistical Yearbook of the ECE 2005;* and *World Statistics Pocketbook.*

The World Bank, 1818 H Street, NW, Washington, DC 20433, (202) 473-1000, Fax: (202) 477-6391, www.worldbank.org; *The World Bank Atlas 2003-2004* and *World Development Report 2008.*

FRANCE - LITERACY

Euromonitor International, Inc., 224 S. Michigan Avenue, Suite 1500, Chicago, IL 60604, (312) 922-1115, Fax: (312) 922-1157, www.euromonitor.com; *World Marketing Data and Statistics.*

FRANCE - LIVESTOCK

Euromonitor International, Inc., 224 S. Michigan Avenue, Suite 1500, Chicago, IL 60604, (312) 922-1115, Fax: (312) 922-1157, www.euromonitor.com; *European Marketing Data and Statistics 2008.*

European Union, Delegation of the European Commission to the United States, 2300 M Street, NW, Washington, DC 20037, (202) 862-9500, Fax: (202) 429-1766, www.eurunion.org; *Agricultural Statistics: Data 1995-2005; Eurostatistics: Data for Short-Term Economic Analysis (2007 edition);* and *Regions - Statistical Yearbook 2006.*

Eurostat, Batiment Jean Monnet, Rue Alcide de Gasperi, L-2920 Luxembourg, http://epp.eurostat.ec.europa.eu; *Eurostat Yearbook 2006-2007.*

M.E. Sharpe, 80 Business Park Drive, Armonk, NY 10504, (800) 541-6563, Fax: (914) 273-2106, www.mesharpe.com; *The Illustrated Book of World Rankings.*

Organisation for Economic Cooperation and Development (OECD), 2 rue Andre Pascal, F-75775 Paris Cedex 16, France, (Telephone in U.S. (202) 785-6323), (Fax in U.S. (202) 785-0350), www.oecd.org; *2005 OECD Agricultural Outlook Tables, 1970-2014.*

Palgrave Macmillan Ltd., Houndmills, Basingstoke, Hampshire, RG21 6XS, England, (Telephone in U.S. (888) 330-8477), (Fax in U.S. (800) 672-2054), www.palgrave.com; *The Statesman's Yearbook 2008.*

Taylor and Francis Group, An Informa Business, 2 Park Square, Milton Park, Abingdon, Oxford OX14 4RN, United Kingdom, (Dial from U.S. (212) 216-7800), (Fax from U.S. (212) 564-7854), www.tandf.co.uk; *The Europa World Year Book.*

United Nations Conference on Trade and Development (UNCTAD), DC2-1120, United Nations, New York, NY 10017, (212) 963-0027, www.unctad.org; *UNCTAD Commodity Yearbook.*

United Nations Food and Agricultural Organization (FAO), Viale delle Terme di Caracalla, 00100 Rome, Italy, (Dial from U.S. (202) 653-2400), (Fax from U.S. (202) 653 5760), www.fao.org; *FAO Production Yearbook 2002* and *The State of Food and Agriculture (SOFA) 2006.*

United Nations Statistics Division, New York, NY 10017, (800) 253-9646, Fax: (212) 963-4116, http://unstats.un.org; *Statistical Yearbook.*

FRANCE - MACHINERY

Organisation for Economic Cooperation and Development (OECD), 2 rue Andre Pascal, F-75775 Paris Cedex 16, France, (Telephone in U.S. (202) 785-6323), (Fax in U.S. (202) 785-0350), www.oecd.org; *Indicators of Industrial Activity.*

FRANCE - MAGNESIUM PRODUCTION AND CONSUMPTION

See FRANCE - MINERAL INDUSTRIES

FRANCE - MANUFACTURES

European Union, Delegation of the European Commission to the United States, 2300 M Street, NW, Washington, DC 20037, (202) 862-9500, Fax: (202) 429-1766, www.eurunion.org; *European Union Labour Force Survey; Eurostatistics: Data for Short-Term Economic Analysis (2007 edition);* and *The Textile Industry in the EU.*

Eurostat, Batiment Jean Monnet, Rue Alcide de Gasperi, L-2920 Luxembourg, http://epp.eurostat.ec.europa.eu; *Eurostat Yearbook 2006-2007.*

M.E. Sharpe, 80 Business Park Drive, Armonk, NY 10504, (800) 541-6563, Fax: (914) 273-2106, www.mesharpe.com; *The Illustrated Book of World Rankings.*

Organisation for Economic Cooperation and Development (OECD), 2 rue Andre Pascal, F-75775 Paris Cedex 16, France, (Telephone in U.S. (202) 785-6323), (Fax in U.S. (202) 785-0350), www.oecd.org; *Indicators of Industrial Activity; International Trade by Commodity Statistics (ITCS); OECD Economic Survey - France 2007;* and STructural ANalysis (STAN) database.

United Nations Statistics Division, New York, NY 10017, (800) 253-9646, Fax: (212) 963-4116, http://unstats.un.org; *Statistical Yearbook.*

The World Bank, 1818 H Street, NW, Washington, DC 20433, (202) 473-1000, Fax: (202) 477-6391, www.worldbank.org; *World Development Indicators (WDI) 2008.*

FRANCE - MARRIAGE

Eurostat, Batiment Jean Monnet, Rue Alcide de Gasperi, L-2920 Luxembourg, http://epp.eurostat.ec.europa.eu; *Eurostat Yearbook 2006-2007.*

M.E. Sharpe, 80 Business Park Drive, Armonk, NY 10504, (800) 541-6563, Fax: (914) 273-2106, www.mesharpe.com; *The Illustrated Book of World Rankings.*

Taylor and Francis Group, An Informa Business, 2 Park Square, Milton Park, Abingdon, Oxford OX14 4RN, United Kingdom, (Dial from U.S. (212) 216-7800), (Fax from U.S. (212) 564-7854), www.tandf.co.uk; *The Europa World Year Book.*

United Nations Statistics Division, New York, NY 10017, (800) 253-9646, Fax: (212) 963-4116, http://unstats.un.org; *Demographic Yearbook; Statistical Yearbook;* and *Trends in Europe and North America: The Statistical Yearbook of the ECE 2005.*

FRANCE - MERCURY PRODUCTION

See FRANCE - MINERAL INDUSTRIES

FRANCE - METAL PRODUCTS

Eurostat, Batiment Jean Monnet, Rue Alcide de Gasperi, L-2920 Luxembourg, http://epp.eurostat.ec.europa.eu; *Eurostat Yearbook 2006-2007.*

FRANCE - MILK PRODUCTION

See FRANCE - DAIRY PROCESSING

FRANCE - MINERAL INDUSTRIES

Commodity Research Bureau, 330 South Wells Street, Suite 612, Chicago, IL 60606-7110, (800) 621-5271, Fax: (312) 939-4135, www.crbtrader.com; *2006 CRB Commodity Yearbook and CD.*

European Union, Delegation of the European Commission to the United States, 2300 M Street, NW, Washington, DC 20037, (202) 862-9500, Fax: (202) 429-1766, www.eurunion.org; *European Union Energy Transport in Figures 2006; Eurostatistics: Data for Short-Term Economic Analysis (2007 edition);* and *Regions - Statistical Yearbook 2006.*

Eurostat, Batiment Jean Monnet, Rue Alcide de Gasperi, L-2920 Luxembourg, http://epp.eurostat.ec.europa.eu; *Energy - Monthly Statistics; Eurostat Yearbook 2006-2007;* and *Panorama of Energy - 2007 Edition.*

International Energy Agency (IEA), 9, rue de la Federation, 75739 Paris Cedex 15, France, www.iea.org; *Key World Energy Statistics 2007.*

International Iron and Steel Institute (IISI), Rue Colonel Bourg 120, B-1140 Brussels, Belgium, www.worldsteel.org; *Steel Statistical Yearbook 2006.*

International Labour Office, I.L.O. Publications, 4 route des Morillons, CH-1211 Geneva 22, Switzerland, (Telephone in U.S. (202) 653-7652), (Fax in U.S. (202) 653-7687), www.ilo.org; *Yearbook of Labour Statistics 2006.*

International Lead and Zinc Study Group (ILZSG), Rua Almirante Barroso 38, 5th Floor, Lisbon 1000 - 013, Portugal, www.ilzsg.org; Interactive Statistical Database.

M.E. Sharpe, 80 Business Park Drive, Armonk, NY 10504, (800) 541-6563, Fax: (914) 273-2106, www.mesharpe.com; *The Illustrated Book of World Rankings.*

Organisation for Economic Cooperation and Development (OECD), 2 rue Andre Pascal, F-75775 Paris Cedex 16, France, (Telephone in U.S. (202) 785-6323), (Fax in U.S. (202) 785-0350), www.oecd.org; *Energy Statistics of OECD Countries* (2007 Edition); *Environmental Impacts of Foreign Direct Investment in the Mining Sector in the Newly Independent States (NIS); Indicators of Industrial Activity; International Trade by Commodity Statistics (ITCS); Iron and Steel Industry in 2004 (2006 Edition); OECD Economic Survey - France 2007;* STructural ANalysis (STAN) database; and *World Energy Outlook 2007.*

Palgrave Macmillan Ltd., Houndmills, Basingstoke, Hampshire, RG21 6XS, England, (Telephone in U.S. (888) 330-8477), (Fax in U.S. (800) 672-2054), www.palgrave.com; *The Statesman's Yearbook 2008.*

Platts, 2 Penn Plaza, 25th Floor, New York, NY 10121-2298, (212) 904-3070, www.platts.com; *Energy Economist* and *EU Energy.*

Taylor and Francis Group, An Informa Business, 2 Park Square, Milton Park, Abingdon, Oxford OX14 4RN, United Kingdom, (Dial from U.S. (212) 216-7800), (Fax from U.S. (212) 564-7854), www.tandf.co.uk; *The Europa World Year Book.*

United Nations Conference on Trade and Development (UNCTAD), DC2-1120, United Nations, New York, NY 10017, (212) 963-0027, www.unctad.org; *UNCTAD Commodity Yearbook.*

United Nations Statistics Division, New York, NY 10017, (800) 253-9646, Fax: (212) 963-4116, http://unstats.un.org; *Energy Statistics Yearbook 2003* and *Statistical Yearbook.*

World Bureau of Metal Statistics (WBMS), 27a High Street, Ware, Hertfordshire, SG12 9BA, United Kingdom, www.world-bureau.com; *Annual Stainless Steel Statistics; World Flow Charts; World Metal Statistics; World Nickel Statistics;* and *World Tin Statistics.*

FRANCE - MOLASSES PRODUCTION

See FRANCE - CROPS

FRANCE - MONEY

Banque de France, 48 rue Croix des Petits champs, 75001 Paris, France, www.banque-france.fr/home.htm; Money and Banking Statistics.

European Central Bank (ECB), Postfach 160319, D-60066 Frankfurt am Main, Germany, www.ecb.int; *Monetary Developments in the Euro Area; Monthly Bulletin;* and *Statistics Pocket Book.*

Organisation for Economic Cooperation and Development (OECD), 2 rue Andre Pascal, F-75775 Paris Cedex 16, France, (Telephone in U.S. (202) 785-6323), (Fax in U.S. (202) 785-0350), www.oecd.org; *OECD Economic Survey - France 2007.*

FRANCE - MONEY EXCHANGE RATES

See FRANCE - FOREIGN EXCHANGE RATES

FRANCE - MONEY SUPPLY

Banque de France, 48 rue Croix des Petits champs, 75001 Paris, France, www.banque-france.fr/home.htm; Money and Banking Statistics.

Economist Intelligence Unit, 111 West 57th Street, New York, NY 10019, (212) 554-0600, Fax: (212) 586-1181, www.eiu.com; *France Country Report.*

European Union, Delegation of the European Commission to the United States, 2300 M Street, NW, Washington, DC 20037, (202) 862-9500, Fax: (202) 429-1766, www.eurunion.org; *Eurostatistics: Data for Short-Term Economic Analysis (2007 edition).*

Eurostat, Batiment Jean Monnet, Rue Alcide de Gasperi, L-2920 Luxembourg, http://epp.eurostat.ec.europa.eu; *Eurostat Yearbook 2006-2007.*

International Monetary Fund (IMF), 700 Nineteenth Street, NW, Washington, DC 20431, (202) 623-7000, Fax: (202) 623-4661, www.imf.org; *International Financial Statistics Yearbook 2007.*

Organisation for Economic Cooperation and Development (OECD), 2 rue Andre Pascal, F-75775 Paris Cedex 16, France, (Telephone in U.S. (202) 785-6323), (Fax in U.S. (202) 785-0350), www.oecd.org; *OECD Economic Outlook 2008.*

Taylor and Francis Group, An Informa Business, 2 Park Square, Milton Park, Abingdon, Oxford OX14 4RN, United Kingdom, (Dial from U.S. (212) 216-7800), (Fax from U.S. (212) 564-7854), www.tandf.co.uk; *The Europa World Year Book.*

United Nations Statistics Division, New York, NY 10017, (800) 253-9646, Fax: (212) 963-4116, http://unstats.un.org; *Statistical Yearbook.*

The World Bank, 1818 H Street, NW, Washington, DC 20433, (202) 473-1000, Fax: (202) 477-6391, www.worldbank.org; *France* and *World Development Indicators (WDI) 2008.*

FRANCE - MORTALITY

Central Intelligence Agency, Office of Public Affairs, Washington, DC 20505, (703) 482-0623, Fax: (703) 482-1739, www.cia.gov; *The World Factbook.*

Euromonitor International, Inc., 224 S. Michigan Avenue, Suite 1500, Chicago, IL 60604, (312) 922-1115, Fax: (312) 922-1157, www.euromonitor.com; *The World Economic Factbook 2008.*

European Union, Delegation of the European Commission to the United States, 2300 M Street, NW, Washington, DC 20037, (202) 862-9500, Fax: (202) 429-1766, www.eurunion.org; *First Demographic Estimates for 2006.*

Eurostat, Batiment Jean Monnet, Rue Alcide de Gasperi, L-2920 Luxembourg, http://epp.eurostat.ec.europa.eu; *Eurostat Yearbook 2006-2007.*

Palgrave Macmillan Ltd., Houndmills, Basingstoke, Hampshire, RG21 6XS, England, (Telephone in U.S. (888) 330-8477), (Fax in U.S. (800) 672-2054), www.palgrave.com; *The Statesman's Yearbook 2008.*

Taylor and Francis Group, An Informa Business, 2 Park Square, Milton Park, Abingdon, Oxford OX14 4RN, United Kingdom, (Dial from U.S. (212) 216-7800), (Fax from U.S. (212) 564-7854), www.tandf.co.uk; *The Europa World Year Book.*

UNICEF, 3 United Nations Plaza, New York, NY 10017, (800) 253-9646, Fax: (212) 887-7465, www.unicef.org; *The State of the World's Children 2008.*

United Nations Statistics Division, New York, NY 10017, (800) 253-9646, Fax: (212) 963-4116, http://unstats.un.org; *Demographic Yearbook; Human Development Report 2006; Statistical Yearbook; Trends in Europe and North America: The Statistical Yearbook of the ECE 2005;* and *World Statistics Pocketbook.*

The World Bank, 1818 H Street, NW, Washington, DC 20433, (202) 473-1000, Fax: (202) 477-6391, www.worldbank.org; *The World Bank Atlas 2003-2004; World Development Indicators (WDI) 2008;* and *World Development Report 2008.*

World Health Organization (WHO), Avenue Appia 20, 1211 Geneve 27, Switzerland, (Telephone in U.S. (212) 331-9081), www.who.int; *The WHO Global Atlas of Infectious Diseases* and *World Health Report 2006.*

FRANCE - MOTION PICTURES

Palgrave Macmillan Ltd., Houndmills, Basingstoke, Hampshire, RG21 6XS, England, (Telephone in U.S. (888) 330-8477), (Fax in U.S. (800) 672-2054), www.palgrave.com; *The Statesman's Yearbook 2008.*

UNESCO Institute for Statistics, C.P. 6128 Succursale Centre-Ville, Montreal, Quebec, H3C 3J7 Canada, (Dial from U.S. (514) 343-6880), (Fax from U.S. (514) 343 6882), www.uis.unesco.org; *Statistical Tables.*

United Nations Statistics Division, New York, NY 10017, (800) 253-9646, Fax: (212) 963-4116, http://unstats.un.org; *Statistical Yearbook.*

FRANCE - MOTOR VEHICLES

European Union, Delegation of the European Commission to the United States, 2300 M Street, NW, Washington, DC 20037, (202) 862-9500, Fax: (202) 429-1766, www.eurunion.org; *Statistical Overview of Transport in the European Union (Data 1970-2001).*

Eurostat, Batiment Jean Monnet, Rue Alcide de Gasperi, L-2920 Luxembourg, http://epp.eurostat.ec.europa.eu; *Eurostat Yearbook 2006-2007.*

International Road Federation (IFR), Madison Place, 500 Montgomery Street, 5th Floor, Alexandria, VA 22314, (703) 535-1001, Fax: (703) 535-1007, www.irfnet.org; *World Road Statistics 2006.*

Taylor and Francis Group, An Informa Business, 2 Park Square, Milton Park, Abingdon, Oxford OX14 4RN, United Kingdom, (Dial from U.S. (212) 216-

7800), (Fax from U.S. (212) 564-7854), www.tandf.co.uk; *The Europa World Year Book.*

United Nations Statistics Division, New York, NY 10017, (800) 253-9646, Fax: (212) 963-4116, http://unstats.un.org; *Statistical Yearbook.*

FRANCE - MUSEUMS

M.E. Sharpe, 80 Business Park Drive, Armonk, NY 10504, (800) 541-6563, Fax: (914) 273-2106, www.mesharpe.com; *The Illustrated Book of World Rankings.*

UNESCO Institute for Statistics, C.P. 6128 Succursale Centre-Ville, Montreal, Quebec, H3C 3J7 Canada, (Dial from U.S. (514) 343-6880), (Fax from U.S. (514) 343 6882), www.uis.unesco.org; *Statistical Tables.*

FRANCE - NATURAL GAS PRODUCTION

See FRANCE - MINERAL INDUSTRIES

FRANCE - NICKEL AND NICKEL ORE

See FRANCE - MINERAL INDUSTRIES

FRANCE - NUTRITION

United Nations Food and Agricultural Organization (FAO), Viale delle Terme di Caracalla, 00100 Rome, Italy, (Dial from U.S. (202) 653-2400), (Fax from U.S. (202) 653 5760), www.fao.org; *The State of Food and Agriculture (SOFA) 2006.*

FRANCE - OATS PRODUCTION

See FRANCE - CROPS

FRANCE - OILSEED PLANTS

Eurostat, Batiment Jean Monnet, Rue Alcide de Gasperi, L-2920 Luxembourg, http://epp.eurostat.ec.europa.eu; *Eurostat Yearbook 2006-2007.*

Organisation for Economic Cooperation and Development (OECD), 2 rue Andre Pascal, F-75775 Paris Cedex 16, France, (Telephone in U.S. (202) 785-6323), (Fax in U.S. (202) 785-0350), www.oecd.org; *International Trade by Commodity Statistics (ITCS).*

FRANCE - OLDER PEOPLE

M.E. Sharpe, 80 Business Park Drive, Armonk, NY 10504, (800) 541-6563, Fax: (914) 273-2106, www.mesharpe.com; *The Illustrated Book of World Rankings.*

FRANCE - ONION PRODUCTION

See FRANCE - CROPS

FRANCE - PALM OIL PRODUCTION

See FRANCE - CROPS

FRANCE - PAPER

See FRANCE - FORESTS AND FORESTRY

FRANCE - PEANUT PRODUCTION

See FRANCE - CROPS

FRANCE - PEPPER PRODUCTION

See FRANCE - CROPS

FRANCE - PERIODICALS

UNESCO Institute for Statistics, C.P. 6128 Succursale Centre-Ville, Montreal, Quebec, H3C 3J7 Canada, (Dial from U.S. (514) 343-6880), (Fax from U.S. (514) 343 6882), www.uis.unesco.org; *Statistical Tables.*

FRANCE - PESTICIDES

United Nations Food and Agricultural Organization (FAO), Viale delle Terme di Caracalla, 00100 Rome, Italy, (Dial from U.S. (202) 653-2400), (Fax from U.S. (202) 653 5760), www.fao.org; *The State of Food and Agriculture (SOFA) 2006.*

FRANCE - PETROLEUM INDUSTRY AND TRADE

Euromonitor International, Inc., 224 S. Michigan Avenue, Suite 1500, Chicago, IL 60604, (312) 922-1115, Fax: (312) 922-1157, www.euromonitor.com; *European Marketing Data and Statistics 2008.*

Eurostat, Batiment Jean Monnet, Rue Alcide de Gasperi, L-2920 Luxembourg, http://epp.eurostat.ec.europa.eu; *Eurostat Yearbook 2006-2007.*

International Energy Agency (IEA), 9, rue de la Federation, 75739 Paris Cedex 15, France, www.iea.org; *Key World Energy Statistics 2007.*

M.E. Sharpe, 80 Business Park Drive, Armonk, NY 10504, (800) 541-6563, Fax: (914) 273-2106, www.mesharpe.com; *The Illustrated Book of World Rankings.*

Organisation for Economic Cooperation and Development (OECD), 2 rue Andre Pascal, F-75775 Paris Cedex 16, France, (Telephone in U.S. (202) 785-6323), (Fax in U.S. (202) 785-0350), www.oecd.org; *Energy Statistics of OECD Countries* (2007 Edition); *Indicators of Industrial Activity; International Trade by Commodity Statistics (ITCS); Oil Information 2006 Edition;* and *World Energy Outlook 2007.*

Palgrave Macmillan Ltd., Houndmills, Basingstoke, Hampshire, RG21 6XS, England, (Telephone in U.S. (888) 330-8477), (Fax in U.S. (800) 672-2054), www.palgrave.com; *The Statesman's Yearbook 2008.*

PennWell Corporation, 1421 South Sheridan Road, Tulsa, OK 74112, (918) 835-3161, www.pennwell.com; *International Petroleum Encyclopedia 2007.*

Platts, 2 Penn Plaza, 25th Floor, New York, NY 10121-2298, (212) 904-3070, www.platts.com; *Energy Economist.*

U.S. Department of Energy (DOE), Energy Information Administration (EIA), 1000 Independence Avenue, SW, Washington, DC 20585, (202) 586-8800, www.eia.doe.gov; *International Energy Annual 2004* and *International Energy Outlook 2006.*

United Nations Conference on Trade and Development (UNCTAD), DC2-1120, United Nations, New York, NY 10017, (212) 963-0027, www.unctad.org; *UNCTAD Commodity Yearbook.*

United Nations Statistics Division, New York, NY 10017, (800) 253-9646, Fax: (212) 963-4116, http://unstats.un.org; *Energy Statistics Yearbook 2003; Statistical Yearbook;* and *Trends in Europe and North America: The Statistical Yearbook of the ECE 2005.*

FRANCE - PHOSPHATES PRODUCTION

See FRANCE - MINERAL INDUSTRIES

FRANCE - PIPELINES

European Union, Delegation of the European Commission to the United States, 2300 M Street, NW, Washington, DC 20037, (202) 862-9500, Fax: (202) 429-1766, www.eurunion.org; *Statistical Overview of Transport in the European Union (Data 1970-2001).*

United Nations Statistics Division, New York, NY 10017, (800) 253-9646, Fax: (212) 963-4116, http://unstats.un.org; *Annual Bulletin of Transport Statistics for Europe and North America 2004.*

FRANCE - PLASTICS INDUSTRY AND TRADE

Eurostat, Batiment Jean Monnet, Rue Alcide de Gasperi, L-2920 Luxembourg, http://epp.eurostat.ec.europa.eu; *Eurostat Yearbook 2006-2007.*

Organisation for Economic Cooperation and Development (OECD), 2 rue Andre Pascal, F-75775 Paris Cedex 16, France, (Telephone in U.S. (202) 785-6323), (Fax in U.S. (202) 785-0350), www.oecd.org; *International Trade by Commodity Statistics (ITCS).*

United Nations Statistics Division, New York, NY 10017, (800) 253-9646, Fax: (212) 963-4116, http://unstats.un.org; *Statistical Yearbook.*

FRANCE - PLATINUM PRODUCTION

See FRANCE - MINERAL INDUSTRIES

FRANCE - POLITICAL SCIENCE

Central Intelligence Agency, Office of Public Affairs, Washington, DC 20505, (703) 482-0623, Fax: (703) 482-1739, www.cia.gov; *The World Factbook.*

European Union, Delegation of the European Commission to the United States, 2300 M Street, NW, Washington, DC 20037, (202) 862-9500, Fax: (202) 429-1766, www.eurunion.org; *RD Expenditure in Europe (2006 edition).*

Eurostat, Batiment Jean Monnet, Rue Alcide de Gasperi, L-2920 Luxembourg, http://epp.eurostat.ec.europa.eu; *Eurostat Yearbook 2006-2007.*

International Monetary Fund (IMF), 700 Nineteenth Street, NW, Washington, DC 20431, (202) 623-7000, Fax: (202) 623-4661, www.imf.org; *Government Finance Statistics Yearbook (2008 Edition)* and *International Financial Statistics Yearbook 2007.*

Organisation for Economic Cooperation and Development (OECD), 2 rue Andre Pascal, F-75775 Paris Cedex 16, France, (Telephone in U.S. (202) 785-6323), (Fax in U.S. (202) 785-0350), www.oecd.org; *OECD Economic Outlook 2008* and *Revenue Statistics 1965-2006 - 2007 Edition.*

Palgrave Macmillan Ltd., Houndmills, Basingstoke, Hampshire, RG21 6XS, England, (Telephone in U.S. (888) 330-8477), (Fax in U.S. (800) 672-2054), www.palgrave.com; *The Statesman's Yearbook 2008.*

Taylor and Francis Group, An Informa Business, 2 Park Square, Milton Park, Abingdon, Oxford OX14 4RN, United Kingdom, (Dial from U.S. (212) 216-7800), (Fax from U.S. (212) 564-7854), www.tandf.co.uk; *The Europa World Year Book.*

United Nations Statistics Division, New York, NY 10017, (800) 253-9646, Fax: (212) 963-4116, http://unstats.un.org; *National Accounts Statistics: Compendium of Income Distribution Statistics* and *Statistical Yearbook.*

The World Bank, 1818 H Street, NW, Washington, DC 20433, (202) 473-1000, Fax: (202) 477-6391, www.worldbank.org; *World Development Indicators (WDI) 2008* and *World Development Report 2008.*

FRANCE - POPULATION

Banque de France, 48 rue Croix des Petits champs, 75001 Paris, France, www.banque-france.fr/home.htm; *Key Data for the Euro Area.*

Central Intelligence Agency, Office of Public Affairs, Washington, DC 20505, (703) 482-0623, Fax: (703) 482-1739, www.cia.gov; *The World Factbook.*

Economist Intelligence Unit, 111 West 57th Street, New York, NY 10019, (212) 554-0600, Fax: (212) 586-1181, www.eiu.com; *France Country Report.*

Euromonitor International, Inc., 224 S. Michigan Avenue, Suite 1500, Chicago, IL 60604, (312) 922-1115, Fax: (312) 922-1157, www.euromonitor.com; *European Marketing Data and Statistics 2008* and *The World Economic Factbook 2008.*

European Union, Delegation of the European Commission to the United States, 2300 M Street, NW, Washington, DC 20037, (202) 862-9500, Fax: (202) 429-1766, www.eurunion.org; *European Union Labour Force Survey; First Demographic Estimates for 2006;* and *Regions - Statistical Yearbook 2006.*

Eurostat, Batiment Jean Monnet, Rue Alcide de Gasperi, L-2920 Luxembourg, http://epp.eurostat.ec.europa.eu; *Eurostat Yearbook 2006-2007* and *The Life of Women and Men in Europe - A Statistical Portrait.*

Federal Statistical Office Germany, D-65180 Wiesbaden, Germany, www.destatis.de; *France 2005.*

International Labour Office, I.L.O. Publications, 4 route des Morillons, CH-1211 Geneva 22, Switzerland, (Telephone in U.S. (202) 653-7652), (Fax in U.S. (202) 653-7687), www.ilo.org; *Yearbook of Labour Statistics 2006.*

M.E. Sharpe, 80 Business Park Drive, Armonk, NY 10504, (800) 541-6563, Fax: (914) 273-2106, www.mesharpe.com; *The Illustrated Book of World Rankings.*

Organisation for Economic Cooperation and Development (OECD), 2 rue Andre Pascal, F-75775 Paris Cedex 16, France, (Telephone in U.S. (202) 785-6323), (Fax in U.S. (202) 785-0350), www.oecd.org; *Labour Force Statistics: 1986-2005, 2007 Edition.*

Palgrave Macmillan Ltd., Houndmills, Basingstoke, Hampshire, RG21 6XS, England, (Telephone in U.S. (888) 330-8477), (Fax in U.S. (800) 672-2054), www.palgrave.com; *The Statesman's Yearbook 2008.*

Taylor and Francis Group, An Informa Business, 2 Park Square, Milton Park, Abingdon, Oxford OX14 4RN, United Kingdom, (Dial from U.S. (212) 216-7800), (Fax from U.S. (212) 564-7854), www.tandf.co.uk; *The Europa World Year Book.*

U.S. Department of State (DOS), 2201 C Street NW, Washington, DC 20520, (202) 647-4000, www.state.gov; *World Military Expenditures and Arms Transfers (WMEAT).*

UNESCO Institute for Statistics, C.P. 6128 Succursale Centre-Ville, Montreal, Quebec, H3C 3J7 Canada, (Dial from U.S. (514) 343-6880), (Fax from U.S. (514) 343 6882), www.uis.unesco.org; *Statistical Tables.*

United Nations Food and Agricultural Organization (FAO), Viale delle Terme di Caracalla, 00100 Rome, Italy, (Dial from U.S. (202) 653-2400), (Fax from U.S. (202) 653 5760), www.fao.org; *FAO Production Yearbook 2002.*

United Nations Statistics Division, New York, NY 10017, (800) 253-9646, Fax: (212) 963-4116, http://unstats.un.org; *Demographic Yearbook; Human Development Report 2006; Statistical Yearbook; Trends in Europe and North America: The Statistical Yearbook of the ECE 2005;* and *World Statistics Pocketbook.*

The World Bank, 1818 H Street, NW, Washington, DC 20433, (202) 473-1000, Fax: (202) 477-6391, www.worldbank.org; *France; The World Bank Atlas 2003-2004;* and *World Development Report 2008.*

World Health Organization (WHO), Avenue Appia 20, 1211 Geneve 27, Switzerland, (Telephone in U.S. (212) 331-9081), www.who.int; *World Health Report 2006.*

FRANCE - POPULATION DENSITY

Central Intelligence Agency, Office of Public Affairs, Washington, DC 20505, (703) 482-0623, Fax: (703) 482-1739, www.cia.gov; *The World Factbook.*

Euromonitor International, Inc., 224 S. Michigan Avenue, Suite 1500, Chicago, IL 60604, (312) 922-1115, Fax: (312) 922-1157, www.euromonitor.com; *The World Economic Factbook 2008.*

European Union, Delegation of the European Commission to the United States, 2300 M Street, NW, Washington, DC 20037, (202) 862-9500, Fax: (202) 429-1766, www.eurunion.org; *First Demographic Estimates for 2006.*

Eurostat, Batiment Jean Monnet, Rue Alcide de Gasperi, L-2920 Luxembourg, http://epp.eurostat.ec.europa.eu; *Eurostat Yearbook 2006-2007.*

M.E. Sharpe, 80 Business Park Drive, Armonk, NY 10504, (800) 541-6563, Fax: (914) 273-2106, www.mesharpe.com; *The Illustrated Book of World Rankings.*

Palgrave Macmillan Ltd., Houndmills, Basingstoke, Hampshire, RG21 6XS, England, (Telephone in U.S. (888) 330-8477), (Fax in U.S. (800) 672-2054), www.palgrave.com; *The Statesman's Yearbook 2008.*

Taylor and Francis Group, An Informa Business, 2 Park Square, Milton Park, Abingdon, Oxford OX14 4RN, United Kingdom, (Dial from U.S. (212) 216-7800), (Fax from U.S. (212) 564-7854), www.tandf.co.uk; *The Europa World Year Book.*

UNESCO Institute for Statistics, C.P. 6128 Succursale Centre-Ville, Montreal, Quebec, H3C 3J7 Canada, (Dial from U.S. (514) 343-6880), (Fax from U.S. (514) 343 6882), www.uis.unesco.org; *Statistical Tables.*

United Nations Food and Agricultural Organization (FAO), Viale delle Terme di Caracalla, 00100 Rome, Italy, (Dial from U.S. (202) 653-2400), (Fax from U.S. (202) 653 5760), www.fao.org; *The State of Food and Agriculture (SOFA) 2006.*

United Nations Statistics Division, New York, NY 10017, (800) 253-9646, Fax: (212) 963-4116, http://unstats.un.org; *Statistical Yearbook* and *Trends in Europe and North America: The Statistical Yearbook of the ECE 2005.*

The World Bank, 1818 H Street, NW, Washington, DC 20433, (202) 473-1000, Fax: (202) 477-6391, www.worldbank.org; *France* and *World Development Report 2008.*

FRANCE - POSTAL SERVICE

European Union, Delegation of the European Commission to the United States, 2300 M Street, NW, Washington, DC 20037, (202) 862-9500, Fax: (202) 429-1766, www.eurunion.org; *Statistical Overview of Transport in the European Union (Data 1970-2001).*

M.E. Sharpe, 80 Business Park Drive, Armonk, NY 10504, (800) 541-6563, Fax: (914) 273-2106, www.mesharpe.com; *The Illustrated Book of World Rankings.*

Palgrave Macmillan Ltd., Houndmills, Basingstoke, Hampshire, RG21 6XS, England, (Telephone in U.S. (888) 330-8477), (Fax in U.S. (800) 672-2054), www.palgrave.com; *The Statesman's Yearbook 2008.*

United Nations Statistics Division, New York, NY 10017, (800) 253-9646, Fax: (212) 963-4116, http://unstats.un.org; *Statistical Yearbook* and *Trends in Europe and North America: The Statistical Yearbook of the ECE 2005.*

FRANCE - POWER RESOURCES

Euromonitor International, Inc., 224 S. Michigan Avenue, Suite 1500, Chicago, IL 60604, (312) 922-1115, Fax: (312) 922-1157, www.euromonitor.com; *European Marketing Data and Statistics 2008; The World Economic Factbook 2008;* and *World Marketing Data and Statistics.*

European Union, Delegation of the European Commission to the United States, 2300 M Street, NW, Washington, DC 20037, (202) 862-9500, Fax: (202) 429-1766, www.eurunion.org; *European Union Energy Transport in Figures 2006; Regions - Statistical Yearbook 2006;* and *Statistical Overview of Transport in the European Union (Data 1970-2001).*

Eurostat, Batiment Jean Monnet, Rue Alcide de Gasperi, L-2920 Luxembourg, http://epp.eurostat.ec.europa.eu; *Eurostat Yearbook 2006-2007.*

M.E. Sharpe, 80 Business Park Drive, Armonk, NY 10504, (800) 541-6563, Fax: (914) 273-2106, www.mesharpe.com; *The Illustrated Book of World Rankings.*

Organisation for Economic Cooperation and Development (OECD), 2 rue Andre Pascal, F-75775 Paris Cedex 16, France, (Telephone in U.S. (202) 785-6323), (Fax in U.S. (202) 785-0350), www.oecd.org; *Coal Information: 2007 Edition; Energy Statistics of OECD Countries* (2007 Edition); *Key Environmental Indicators 2004; Oil Information 2006 Edition;* and *World Energy Outlook 2007.*

Palgrave Macmillan Ltd., Houndmills, Basingstoke, Hampshire, RG21 6XS, England, (Telephone in U.S. (888) 330-8477), (Fax in U.S. (800) 672-2054), www.palgrave.com; *The Statesman's Yearbook 2008.*

Platts, 2 Penn Plaza, 25th Floor, New York, NY 10121-2298, (212) 904-3070, www.platts.com; *Energy Economist* and *European Power Daily.*

U.S. Department of Energy (DOE), Energy Information Administration (EIA), 1000 Independence Avenue, SW, Washington, DC 20585, (202) 586-8800, www.eia.doe.gov; *International Energy Annual 2004* and *International Energy Outlook 2006.*

United Nations Food and Agricultural Organization (FAO), Viale delle Terme di Caracalla, 00100 Rome, Italy, (Dial from U.S. (202) 653-2400), (Fax from U.S. (202) 653 5760), www.fao.org; *The State of Food and Agriculture (SOFA) 2006.*

United Nations Statistics Division, New York, NY 10017, (800) 253-9646, Fax: (212) 963-4116, http://unstats.un.org; *Energy Statistics Yearbook 2003; Human Development Report 2006; Statistical Yearbook; Trends in Europe and North America: The Statistical Yearbook of the ECE 2005;* and *World Statistics Pocketbook.*

The World Bank, 1818 H Street, NW, Washington, DC 20433, (202) 473-1000, Fax: (202) 477-6391, www.worldbank.org; *The World Bank Atlas 2003-2004* and *World Development Report 2008.*

FRANCE - PRICES

Euromonitor International, Inc., 224 S. Michigan Avenue, Suite 1500, Chicago, IL 60604, (312) 922-1115, Fax: (312) 922-1157, www.euromonitor.com; *European Marketing Data and Statistics 2008* and *World Marketing Data and Statistics.*

European Union, Delegation of the European Commission to the United States, 2300 M Street, NW, Washington, DC 20037, (202) 862-9500, Fax: (202) 429-1766, www.eurunion.org; *Eurostatistics: Data for Short-Term Economic Analysis (2007 edition).*

Eurostat, Batiment Jean Monnet, Rue Alcide de Gasperi, L-2920 Luxembourg, http://epp.eurostat.ec.europa.eu; *Eurostat Yearbook 2006-2007.*

International Labour Office, I.L.O. Publications, 4 route des Morillons, CH-1211 Geneva 22, Switzerland, (Telephone in U.S. (202) 653-7652), (Fax in U.S. (202) 653-7687), www.ilo.org; *Yearbook of Labour Statistics 2006.*

International Lead and Zinc Study Group (ILZSG), Rua Almirante Barroso 38, 5th Floor, Lisbon 1000 - 013, Portugal, www.ilzsg.org; Interactive Statistical Database.

International Monetary Fund (IMF), 700 Nineteenth Street, NW, Washington, DC 20431, (202) 623-7000, Fax: (202) 623-4661, www.imf.org; *International Financial Statistics Yearbook 2007.*

M.E. Sharpe, 80 Business Park Drive, Armonk, NY 10504, (800) 541-6563, Fax: (914) 273-2106, www.mesharpe.com; *The Illustrated Book of World Rankings.*

Organisation for Economic Cooperation and Development (OECD), 2 rue Andre Pascal, F-75775 Paris Cedex 16, France, (Telephone in U.S. (202) 785-6323), (Fax in U.S. (202) 785-0350), www.oecd.org; *Indicators of Industrial Activity; Iron and Steel Industry in 2004 (2006 Edition); OECD Economic Outlook 2008;* and *OECD Main Economic Indicators (MEI).*

Technical Association of the Pulp and Paper Industry (TAPPI), 15 Technology Parkway South, Norcross, GA 30092, (770) 446-1400, Fax: (770) 446-6947, www.tappi.org; *TAPPI Annual Report.*

United Nations Food and Agricultural Organization (FAO), Viale delle Terme di Caracalla, 00100 Rome, Italy, (Dial from U.S. (202) 653-2400), (Fax from U.S. (202) 653 5760), www.fao.org; *FAO Production Yearbook 2002* and *The State of Food and Agriculture (SOFA) 2006.*

The World Bank, 1818 H Street, NW, Washington, DC 20433, (202) 473-1000, Fax: (202) 477-6391, www.worldbank.org; *France.*

World Bureau of Metal Statistics (WBMS), 27a High Street, Ware, Hertfordshire, SG12 9BA, United Kingdom, www.world-bureau.com; *World Flow Charts* and *World Metal Statistics.*

FRANCE - PROFESSIONS

Eurostat, Batiment Jean Monnet, Rue Alcide de Gasperi, L-2920 Luxembourg, http://epp.eurostat.ec.europa.eu; *Eurostat Yearbook 2006-2007.*

UNESCO Institute for Statistics, C.P. 6128 Succursale Centre-Ville, Montreal, Quebec, H3C 3J7 Canada, (Dial from U.S. (514) 343-6880), (Fax from U.S. (514) 343 6882), www.uis.unesco.org; *Statistical Tables.*

United Nations Statistics Division, New York, NY 10017, (800) 253-9646, Fax: (212) 963-4116, http://unstats.un.org; *Statistical Yearbook.*

FRANCE - PUBLIC HEALTH

Euromonitor International, Inc., 224 S. Michigan Avenue, Suite 1500, Chicago, IL 60604, (312) 922-1115, Fax: (312) 922-1157, www.euromonitor.com; *World Health Databook 2007/2008* and *World Marketing Data and Statistics.*

European Centre for Disease Prevention and Control (ECDC), 171 83 Stockholm, Sweden, www.ecdc.europa.eu; *Eurosurveillance.*

European Union, Delegation of the European Commission to the United States, 2300 M Street, NW, Washington, DC 20037, (202) 862-9500, Fax: (202) 429-1766, www.eurunion.org; *Regions - Statistical Yearbook 2006.*

Eurostat, Batiment Jean Monnet, Rue Alcide de Gasperi, L-2920 Luxembourg, http://epp.eurostat.ec.europa.eu; *Eurostat Yearbook 2006-2007.*

Health and Consumer Protection Directorate-General, European Commission, B-1049 Brussels, Belgium, http://ec.europa.eu/dgs/health_consumer/index_en.htm; *Injuries in the European Union: Statistics Summary 2002-2004.*

International Monetary Fund (IMF), 700 Nineteenth Street, NW, Washington, DC 20431, (202) 623-7000, Fax: (202) 623-4661, www.imf.org; *Government Finance Statistics Yearbook (2008 Edition).*

M.E. Sharpe, 80 Business Park Drive, Armonk, NY 10504, (800) 541-6563, Fax: (914) 273-2106, www.mesharpe.com; *The Illustrated Book of World Rankings.*

Organisation for Economic Cooperation and Development (OECD), 2 rue Andre Pascal, F-75775 Paris Cedex 16, France, (Telephone in U.S. (202) 785-6323), (Fax in U.S. (202) 785-0350), www.oecd.org; *Health at a Glance 2007 - OECD Indicators.*

Palgrave Macmillan Ltd., Houndmills, Basingstoke, Hampshire, RG21 6XS, England, (Telephone in U.S. (888) 330-8477), (Fax in U.S. (800) 672-2054), www.palgrave.com; *The Statesman's Yearbook 2008.*

Robert Koch Institute, Nordufer 20, D 13353 Berlin, Germany, www.rki.de; *EUVAC-NET Report: Pertussis-Surveillance 1998-2002.*

UNICEF, 3 United Nations Plaza, New York, NY 10017, (800) 253-9646, Fax: (212) 887-7465, www.unicef.org; *The State of the World's Children 2008.*

United Nations Statistics Division, New York, NY 10017, (800) 253-9646, Fax: (212) 963-4116, http://unstats.un.org; *Human Development Report 2006; Statistical Yearbook;* and *Trends in Europe and North America: The Statistical Yearbook of the ECE 2005.*

The World Bank, 1818 H Street, NW, Washington, DC 20433, (202) 473-1000, Fax: (202) 477-6391, www.worldbank.org; *France* and *World Development Report 2008.*

World Health Organization (WHO), Avenue Appia 20, 1211 Geneve 27, Switzerland, (Telephone in U.S. (212) 331-9081), www.who.int; The WHO Global Atlas of Infectious Diseases and *World Health Report 2006.*

FRANCE - PUBLISHERS AND PUBLISHING

Organisation for Economic Cooperation and Development (OECD), 2 rue Andre Pascal, F-75775 Paris Cedex 16, France, (Telephone in U.S. (202) 785-6323), (Fax in U.S. (202) 785-0350), www.oecd.org; *Indicators of Industrial Activity.*

Taylor and Francis Group, An Informa Business, 2 Park Square, Milton Park, Abingdon, Oxford OX14 4RN, United Kingdom, (Dial from U.S. (212) 216-7800), (Fax from U.S. (212) 564-7854), www.tandf.co.uk; *The Europa World Year Book.*

United Nations Statistics Division, New York, NY 10017, (800) 253-9646, Fax: (212) 963-4116, http://unstats.un.org; *Trends in Europe and North America: The Statistical Yearbook of the ECE 2005.*

FRANCE - RADIO - RECEIVERS AND RECEPTION

Palgrave Macmillan Ltd., Houndmills, Basingstoke, Hampshire, RG21 6XS, England, (Telephone in U.S. (888) 330-8477), (Fax in U.S. (800) 672-2054), www.palgrave.com; *The Statesman's Yearbook 2008.*

United Nations Statistics Division, New York, NY 10017, (800) 253-9646, Fax: (212) 963-4116, http://unstats.un.org; *Statistical Yearbook.*

FRANCE - RAILROADS

Euromonitor International, Inc., 224 S. Michigan Avenue, Suite 1500, Chicago, IL 60604, (312) 922-1115, Fax: (312) 922-1157, www.euromonitor.com; *European Marketing Data and Statistics 2008.*

European Union, Delegation of the European Commission to the United States, 2300 M Street, NW, Washington, DC 20037, (202) 862-9500, Fax: (202) 429-1766, www.eurunion.org; *Regions - Statistical Yearbook 2006* and *Statistical Overview of Transport in the European Union (Data 1970-2001).*

Eurostat, Batiment Jean Monnet, Rue Alcide de Gasperi, L-2920 Luxembourg, http://epp.eurostat.ec.europa.eu; *Eurostat Yearbook 2006-2007.*

Jane's Information Group, 110 North Royal Street, Suite 200, Alexandria, VA 22314, (703) 683-3700, Fax: (800) 836-0297, www.janes.com; *Jane's World Railways.*

Palgrave Macmillan Ltd., Houndmills, Basingstoke, Hampshire, RG21 6XS, England, (Telephone in U.S. (888) 330-8477), (Fax in U.S. (800) 672-2054), www.palgrave.com; *The Statesman's Yearbook 2008.*

Taylor and Francis Group, An Informa Business, 2 Park Square, Milton Park, Abingdon, Oxford OX14 4RN, United Kingdom, (Dial from U.S. (212) 216-7800), (Fax from U.S. (212) 564-7854), www.tandf.co.uk; *The Europa World Year Book.*

United Nations Statistics Division, New York, NY 10017, (800) 253-9646, Fax: (212) 963-4116, http://unstats.un.org; *Annual Bulletin of Transport Statistics for Europe and North America 2004; Statistical Yearbook;* and *Trends in Europe and North America: The Statistical Yearbook of the ECE 2005.*

FRANCE - RANCHING

Eurostat, Batiment Jean Monnet, Rue Alcide de Gasperi, L-2920 Luxembourg, http://epp.eurostat.ec.europa.eu; *Eurostat Yearbook 2006-2007.*

FRANCE - RELIGION

Central Intelligence Agency, Office of Public Affairs, Washington, DC 20505, (703) 482-0623, Fax: (703) 482-1739, www.cia.gov; *The World Factbook.*

M.E. Sharpe, 80 Business Park Drive, Armonk, NY 10504, (800) 541-6563, Fax: (914) 273-2106, www.mesharpe.com; *The Illustrated Book of World Rankings.*

Palgrave Macmillan Ltd., Houndmills, Basingstoke, Hampshire, RG21 6XS, England, (Telephone in U.S. (888) 330-8477), (Fax in U.S. (800) 672-2054), www.palgrave.com; *The Statesman's Yearbook 2008.*

FRANCE - RESERVES (ACCOUNTING)

Eurostat, Batiment Jean Monnet, Rue Alcide de Gasperi, L-2920 Luxembourg, http://epp.eurostat.ec.europa.eu; *Eurostat Yearbook 2006-2007.*

Organisation for Economic Cooperation and Development (OECD), 2 rue Andre Pascal, F-75775 Paris Cedex 16, France, (Telephone in U.S. (202) 785-6323), (Fax in U.S. (202) 785-0350), www.oecd.org; *Financial Market Trends: OECD Periodical* and *OECD Economic Outlook 2008.*

United Nations Statistics Division, New York, NY 10017, (800) 253-9646, Fax: (212) 963-4116, http://unstats.un.org; *Statistical Yearbook.*

The World Bank, 1818 H Street, NW, Washington, DC 20433, (202) 473-1000, Fax: (202) 477-6391, www.worldbank.org; *World Development Indicators (WDI) 2008.*

FRANCE - RETAIL TRADE

Banque de France, 48 rue Croix des Petits champs, 75001 Paris, France, www.banque-france.fr/home.htm; *Monthly Business Survey Overview.*

Euromonitor International, Inc., 224 S. Michigan Avenue, Suite 1500, Chicago, IL 60604, (312) 922-1115, Fax: (312) 922-1157, www.euromonitor.com; *World Marketing Data and Statistics.*

European Union, Delegation of the European Commission to the United States, 2300 M Street, NW, Washington, DC 20037, (202) 862-9500, Fax: (202) 429-1766, www.eurunion.org; *Eurostatistics: Data for Short-Term Economic Analysis (2007 edition).*

Eurostat, Batiment Jean Monnet, Rue Alcide de Gasperi, L-2920 Luxembourg, http://epp.eurostat.ec.europa.eu; *Eurostat Yearbook 2006-2007.*

United Nations Statistics Division, New York, NY 10017, (800) 253-9646, Fax: (212) 963-4116, http://unstats.un.org; *Statistical Yearbook.*

FRANCE - RICE PRODUCTION

See FRANCE - CROPS

FRANCE - ROADS

Central Intelligence Agency, Office of Public Affairs, Washington, DC 20505, (703) 482-0623, Fax: (703) 482-1739, www.cia.gov; *The World Factbook.*

European Union, Delegation of the European Commission to the United States, 2300 M Street, NW, Washington, DC 20037, (202) 862-9500, Fax: (202) 429-1766, www.eurunion.org; *Statistical Overview of Transport in the European Union (Data 1970-2001).*

Eurostat, Batiment Jean Monnet, Rue Alcide de Gasperi, L-2920 Luxembourg, http://epp.eurostat.ec.europa.eu; *Eurostat Yearbook 2006-2007.*

International Road Federation (IFR), Madison Place, 500 Montgomery Street, 5th Floor, Alexandria, VA 22314, (703) 535-1001, Fax: (703) 535-1007, www.irfnet.org; *World Road Statistics 2006.*

Palgrave Macmillan Ltd., Houndmills, Basingstoke, Hampshire, RG21 6XS, England, (Telephone in U.S. (888) 330-8477), (Fax in U.S. (800) 672-2054), www.palgrave.com; *The Statesman's Yearbook 2008.*

United Nations Statistics Division, New York, NY 10017, (800) 253-9646, Fax: (212) 963-4116, http://unstats.un.org; *Annual Bulletin of Transport Statistics for Europe and North America 2004* and *Trends in Europe and North America: The Statistical Yearbook of the ECE 2005.*

FRANCE - RUBBER INDUSTRY AND TRADE

Eurostat, Batiment Jean Monnet, Rue Alcide de Gasperi, L-2920 Luxembourg, http://epp.eurostat.ec.europa.eu; *Eurostat Yearbook 2006-2007.*

International Rubber Study Group (IRSG), 1st Floor, Heron House, 109/115 Wembley Hill Road, Wembley, Middlesex HA9 8DA, United Kingdom, www.rubberstudy.com; *Rubber Statistical Bulletin; Summary of World Rubber Statistics 2005; World Rubber Statistics Handbook (Volume 6, 1975-2001);* and *World Rubber Statistics Historic Handbook.*

M.E. Sharpe, 80 Business Park Drive, Armonk, NY 10504, (800) 541-6563, Fax: (914) 273-2106, www.mesharpe.com; *The Illustrated Book of World Rankings.*

Organisation for Economic Cooperation and Development (OECD), 2 rue Andre Pascal, F-75775 Paris Cedex 16, France, (Telephone in U.S. (202) 785-6323), (Fax in U.S. (202) 785-0350), www.oecd.org; *International Trade by Commodity Statistics (ITCS).*

United Nations Statistics Division, New York, NY 10017, (800) 253-9646, Fax: (212) 963-4116, http://unstats.un.org; *Statistical Yearbook.*

FRANCE - RYE PRODUCTION

See FRANCE - CROPS

FRANCE - SAFFLOWER SEED PRODUCTION

See FRANCE - CROPS

FRANCE - SALT PRODUCTION

See FRANCE - MINERAL INDUSTRIES

FRANCE - SAVINGS ACCOUNT DEPOSITS

See FRANCE - BANKS AND BANKING

FRANCE - SHEEP

See FRANCE - LIVESTOCK

FRANCE - SHIPBUILDING

Organisation for Economic Cooperation and Development (OECD), 2 rue Andre Pascal, F-75775 Paris Cedex 16, France, (Telephone in U.S. (202) 785-6323), (Fax in U.S. (202) 785-0350), www.oecd.org; *Indicators of Industrial Activity.*

FRANCE - SHIPPING

European Union, Delegation of the European Commission to the United States, 2300 M Street, NW, Washington, DC 20037, (202) 862-9500, Fax: (202) 429-1766, www.eurunion.org; *Fishery Statistics - 1990-2006; Regions - Statistical Yearbook 2006;* and *Statistical Overview of Transport in the European Union (Data 1970-2001).*

Eurostat, Batiment Jean Monnet, Rue Alcide de Gasperi, L-2920 Luxembourg, http://epp.eurostat.ec.europa.eu; *Eurostat Yearbook 2006-2007.*

Lloyd's Register - Fairplay, 8410 N.W. 53rd Terrace, Suite 207, Miami FL 33166, (305) 718-9929, Fax: (305) 718-9663, www.lrfairplay.com; *Register of Ships 2007-2008; World Casualty Statistics 2007; World Fleet Statistics 2006; World Marine Propulsion Report 2006-2010; World Shipbuilding Statistics 2007;* and The World Shipping Encyclopaedia.

Organisation for Economic Cooperation and Development (OECD), 2 rue Andre Pascal, F-75775 Paris Cedex 16, France, (Telephone in U.S. (202) 785-6323), (Fax in U.S. (202) 785-0350), www.oecd.org; *Statistics on Ship Production, Exports and Orders in 2004.*

Palgrave Macmillan Ltd., Houndmills, Basingstoke, Hampshire, RG21 6XS, England, (Telephone in U.S. (888) 330-8477), (Fax in U.S. (800) 672-2054), www.palgrave.com; *The Statesman's Yearbook 2008.*

Taylor and Francis Group, An Informa Business, 2 Park Square, Milton Park, Abingdon, Oxford OX14 4RN, United Kingdom, (Dial from U.S. (212) 216-7800), (Fax from U.S. (212) 564-7854), www.tandf.co.uk; *The Europa World Year Book.*

U.S. Department of Transportation (DOT), Maritime Administration (MARAD), West Building, Southeast Federal Center, 1200 New Jersey Avenue, SE, Washington, DC 20590, (800) 99-MARAD, www.marad.dot.gov; *World Merchant Fleet 2005.*

United Nations Statistics Division, New York, NY 10017, (800) 253-9646, Fax: (212) 963-4116, http://unstats.un.org; *Annual Bulletin of Transport Statistics for Europe and North America 2004* and *Statistical Yearbook.*

FRANCE - SILVER PRODUCTION

See FRANCE - MINERAL INDUSTRIES

FRANCE - SOCIAL CLASSES

European Union, Delegation of the European Commission to the United States, 2300 M Street, NW, Washington, DC 20037, (202) 862-9500, Fax: (202) 429-1766, www.eurunion.org; *European Union Labour Force Survey.*

Eurostat, Batiment Jean Monnet, Rue Alcide de Gasperi, L-2920 Luxembourg, http://epp.eurostat.ec.europa.eu; *Eurostat Yearbook 2006-2007.*

FRANCE - SOCIAL ECOLOGY

Eurostat, Batiment Jean Monnet, Rue Alcide de Gasperi, L-2920 Luxembourg, http://epp.eurostat.ec.europa.eu; *Eurostat Yearbook 2006-2007.*

M.E. Sharpe, 80 Business Park Drive, Armonk, NY 10504, (800) 541-6563, Fax: (914) 273-2106, www.mesharpe.com; *The Illustrated Book of World Rankings.*

United Nations Statistics Division, New York, NY 10017, (800) 253-9646, Fax: (212) 963-4116, http://unstats.un.org; *World Statistics Pocketbook.*

FRANCE - SOCIAL SECURITY

Eurostat, Batiment Jean Monnet, Rue Alcide de Gasperi, L-2920 Luxembourg, http://epp.eurostat.ec.europa.eu; *Eurostat Yearbook 2006-2007.*

International Monetary Fund (IMF), 700 Nineteenth Street, NW, Washington, DC 20431, (202) 623-7000, Fax: (202) 623-4661, www.imf.org; *Government Finance Statistics Yearbook (2008 Edition).*

Organisation for Economic Cooperation and Development (OECD), 2 rue Andre Pascal, F-75775 Paris Cedex 16, France, (Telephone in U.S. (202) 785-6323), (Fax in U.S. (202) 785-0350), www.oecd.org; *Revenue Statistics 1965-2006 - 2007 Edition.*

Palgrave Macmillan Ltd., Houndmills, Basingstoke, Hampshire, RG21 6XS, England, (Telephone in U.S. (888) 330-8477), (Fax in U.S. (800) 672-2054), www.palgrave.com; *The Statesman's Yearbook 2008.*

United Nations Statistics Division, New York, NY 10017, (800) 253-9646, Fax: (212) 963-4116, http://unstats.un.org; *National Accounts Statistics: Compendium of Income Distribution Statistics.*

FRANCE - SOYBEAN PRODUCTION

See FRANCE - CROPS

FRANCE - STEEL PRODUCTION

See FRANCE - MINERAL INDUSTRIES

FRANCE - STRAW PRODUCTION

See FRANCE - CROPS

FRANCE - SUGAR PRODUCTION

See FRANCE - CROPS

FRANCE - SULPHUR PRODUCTION

See FRANCE - MINERAL INDUSTRIES

FRANCE - SUNFLOWER PRODUCTION

See FRANCE - CROPS

FRANCE - TAXATION

Eurostat, Batiment Jean Monnet, Rue Alcide de Gasperi, L-2920 Luxembourg, http://epp.eurostat.ec.europa.eu; *Eurostat Yearbook 2006-2007* and *Taxation Trends in the European Union - Data for the EU Member States and Norway.*

International Monetary Fund (IMF), 700 Nineteenth Street, NW, Washington, DC 20431, (202) 623-7000, Fax: (202) 623-4661, www.imf.org; *Government Finance Statistics Yearbook (2008 Edition).*

International Road Federation (IFR), Madison Place, 500 Montgomery Street, 5th Floor, Alexandria, VA 22314, (703) 535-1001, Fax: (703) 535-1007, www.irfnet.org; *World Road Statistics 2006.*

Organisation for Economic Cooperation and Development (OECD), 2 rue Andre Pascal, F-75775 Paris Cedex 16, France, (Telephone in U.S. (202) 785-6323), (Fax in U.S. (202) 785-0350), www.oecd.org; *Revenue Statistics 1965-2006 - 2007 Edition.*

Palgrave Macmillan Ltd., Houndmills, Basingstoke, Hampshire, RG21 6XS, England, (Telephone in U.S. (888) 330-8477), (Fax in U.S. (800) 672-2054), www.palgrave.com; *The Statesman's Yearbook 2008.*

Taylor and Francis Group, An Informa Business, 2 Park Square, Milton Park, Abingdon, Oxford OX14 4RN, United Kingdom, (Dial from U.S. (212) 216-7800), (Fax from U.S. (212) 564-7854), www.tandf.co.uk; *The Europa World Year Book.*

The World Bank, 1818 H Street, NW, Washington, DC 20433, (202) 473-1000, Fax: (202) 477-6391, www.worldbank.org; *World Development Indicators (WDI) 2008.*

FRANCE - TEA PRODUCTION

See FRANCE - CROPS

FRANCE - TELEPHONE

European Union, Delegation of the European Commission to the United States, 2300 M Street, NW, Washington, DC 20037, (202) 862-9500, Fax: (202) 429-1766, www.eurunion.org; *Statistical Overview of Transport in the European Union (Data 1970-2001).*

Eurostat, Batiment Jean Monnet, Rue Alcide de Gasperi, L-2920 Luxembourg, http://epp.eurostat.ec.europa.eu; *Eurostat Yearbook 2006-2007.*

International Telecommunication Union (ITU), Place des Nations, 1211 Geneva 20, Switzerland, www.itu.int; World Telecommunication Indicators Database.

Palgrave Macmillan Ltd., Houndmills, Basingstoke, Hampshire, RG21 6XS, England, (Telephone in U.S. (888) 330-8477), (Fax in U.S. (800) 672-2054), www.palgrave.com; *The Statesman's Yearbook 2008.*

Taylor and Francis Group, An Informa Business, 2 Park Square, Milton Park, Abingdon, Oxford OX14 4RN, United Kingdom, (Dial from U.S. (212) 216-7800), (Fax from U.S. (212) 564-7854), www.tandf.co.uk; *The Europa World Year Book.*

United Nations Statistics Division, New York, NY 10017, (800) 253-9646, Fax: (212) 963-4116, http://unstats.un.org; *Statistical Yearbook; Trends in Europe and North America: The Statistical Yearbook of the ECE 2005;* and *World Statistics Pocketbook.*

FRANCE - TELEVISION - RECEIVERS AND RECEPTION

Eurostat, Batiment Jean Monnet, Rue Alcide de Gasperi, L-2920 Luxembourg, http://epp.eurostat.ec.europa.eu; *Eurostat Yearbook 2006-2007.*

United Nations Statistics Division, New York, NY 10017, (800) 253-9646, Fax: (212) 963-4116, http://unstats.un.org; *Statistical Yearbook.*

FRANCE - TEXTILE INDUSTRY

CTCOE (Centre Textile de Conjoncture et d'Observation Economique), 37/39 rue de Neuilly, BP 249, F-92113 Cedex, France; unpublished data.

Euromonitor International, Inc., 224 S. Michigan Avenue, Suite 1500, Chicago, IL 60604, (312) 922-1115, Fax: (312) 922-1157, www.euromonitor.com; *World Marketing Data and Statistics.*

European Union, Delegation of the European Commission to the United States, 2300 M Street, NW, Washington, DC 20037, (202) 862-9500, Fax: (202) 429-1766, www.eurunion.org; *Eurostatistics: Data for Short-Term Economic Analysis (2007 edition)* and *The Textile Industry in the EU.*

Eurostat, Batiment Jean Monnet, Rue Alcide de Gasperi, L-2920 Luxembourg, http://epp.eurostat.ec.europa.eu; *Eurostat Yearbook 2006-2007.*

M.E. Sharpe, 80 Business Park Drive, Armonk, NY 10504, (800) 541-6563, Fax: (914) 273-2106, www.mesharpe.com; *The Illustrated Book of World Rankings.*

Organisation for Economic Cooperation and Development (OECD), 2 rue Andre Pascal, F-75775 Paris Cedex 16, France, (Telephone in U.S. (202) 785-6323), (Fax in U.S. (202) 785-0350), www.oecd.org; *Indicators of Industrial Activity; International Trade by Commodity Statistics (ITCS); A New World Map in Textiles and Clothing: Adjusting to Change; 2005 OECD Agricultural Outlook Tables, 1970-2014;* and STructural ANalysis (STAN) database.

United Nations Conference on Trade and Development (UNCTAD), DC2-1120, United Nations, New York, NY 10017, (212) 963-0027, www.unctad.org; *UNCTAD Commodity Yearbook.*

United Nations Statistics Division, New York, NY 10017, (800) 253-9646, Fax: (212) 963-4116, http://unstats.un.org; *Statistical Yearbook.*

FRANCE - THEATER

UNESCO Institute for Statistics, C.P. 6128 Succursale Centre-Ville, Montreal, Quebec, H3C 3J7 Canada, (Dial from U.S. (514) 343-6880), (Fax from U.S. (514) 343 6882), www.uis.unesco.org; *Statistical Tables.*

FRANCE - TIMBER

See FRANCE - FORESTS AND FORESTRY

FRANCE - TIN PRODUCTION

See FRANCE - MINERAL INDUSTRIES

FRANCE - TIRE INDUSTRY

United Nations Statistics Division, New York, NY 10017, (800) 253-9646, Fax: (212) 963-4116, http://unstats.un.org; *Statistical Yearbook.*

FRANCE - TOBACCO INDUSTRY

Euromonitor International, Inc., 224 S. Michigan Avenue, Suite 1500, Chicago, IL 60604, (312) 922-1115, Fax: (312) 922-1157, www.euromonitor.com; *European Marketing Data and Statistics 2008.*

Eurostat, Batiment Jean Monnet, Rue Alcide de Gasperi, L-2920 Luxembourg, http://epp.eurostat.ec.europa.eu; *Eurostat Yearbook 2006-2007.*

Foreign Agricultural Service (FAS), U.S. Department of Agriculture (USDA), 1400 Independence Avenue, SW, Washington, DC 20250, (202) 720-3935, www.fas.usda.gov; *Tobacco: World Markets and Trade.*

M.E. Sharpe, 80 Business Park Drive, Armonk, NY 10504, (800) 541-6563, Fax: (914) 273-2106, www.mesharpe.com; *The Illustrated Book of World Rankings.*

Organisation for Economic Cooperation and Development (OECD), 2 rue Andre Pascal, F-75775 Paris Cedex 16, France, (Telephone in U.S. (202) 785-6323), (Fax in U.S. (202) 785-0350), www.oecd.org; *Indicators of Industrial Activity; International Trade by Commodity Statistics (ITCS);* and STructural ANalysis (STAN) database.

United Nations Statistics Division, New York, NY 10017, (800) 253-9646, Fax: (212) 963-4116, http://unstats.un.org; *Statistical Yearbook.*

FRANCE - TOURISM

Euromonitor International, Inc., 224 S. Michigan Avenue, Suite 1500, Chicago, IL 60604, (312) 922-1115, Fax: (312) 922-1157, www.euromonitor.com; *European Marketing Data and Statistics 2008* and *The World Economic Factbook 2008.*

European Union, Delegation of the European Commission to the United States, 2300 M Street, NW, Washington, DC 20037, (202) 862-9500, Fax: (202) 429-1766, www.eurunion.org; *Statistical Overview of Transport in the European Union (Data 1970-2001).*

Eurostat, Batiment Jean Monnet, Rue Alcide de Gasperi, L-2920 Luxembourg, http://epp.eurostat.ec.europa.eu; *Tourism in Europe: First Results for 2007.*

International Road Federation (IFR), Madison Place, 500 Montgomery Street, 5th Floor, Alexandria, VA 22314, (703) 535-1001, Fax: (703) 535-1007, www.irfnet.org; *World Road Statistics 2006.*

M.E. Sharpe, 80 Business Park Drive, Armonk, NY 10504, (800) 541-6563, Fax: (914) 273-2106, www.mesharpe.com; *The Illustrated Book of World Rankings.*

Organisation for Economic Cooperation and Development (OECD), 2 rue Andre Pascal, F-75775 Paris Cedex 16, France, (Telephone in U.S. (202) 785-6323), (Fax in U.S. (202) 785-0350), www.oecd.org; *Household, Tourism, Travel: Trends, Environmental Impacts and Policy Responses.*

Palgrave Macmillan Ltd., Houndmills, Basingstoke, Hampshire, RG21 6XS, England, (Telephone in U.S. (888) 330-8477), (Fax in U.S. (800) 672-2054), www.palgrave.com; *The Statesman's Yearbook 2008.*

Taylor and Francis Group, An Informa Business, 2 Park Square, Milton Park, Abingdon, Oxford OX14 4RN, United Kingdom, (Dial from U.S. (212) 216-7800), (Fax from U.S. (212) 564-7854), www.tandf.co.uk; *The Europa World Year Book.*

United Nations Statistics Division, New York, NY 10017, (800) 253-9646, Fax: (212) 963-4116, http://unstats.un.org; *Statistical Yearbook* and *Trends in Europe and North America: The Statistical Yearbook of the ECE 2005.*

United Nations World Tourism Organization (UNWTO), Capitan Haya 42, 28020 Madrid, Spain, www.world-tourism.org; *The French Ecotourism Market; Tourism Market Trends 2004 - Europe;* and *Yearbook of Tourism Statistics.*

The World Bank, 1818 H Street, NW, Washington, DC 20433, (202) 473-1000, Fax: (202) 477-6391, www.worldbank.org; *France.*

FRANCE - TRADE

See FRANCE - INTERNATIONAL TRADE

FRANCE - TRANSPORTATION

Central Intelligence Agency, Office of Public Affairs, Washington, DC 20505, (703) 482-0623, Fax: (703) 482-1739, www.cia.gov; *The World Factbook.*

Euromonitor International, Inc., 224 S. Michigan Avenue, Suite 1500, Chicago, IL 60604, (312) 922-1115, Fax: (312) 922-1157, www.euromonitor.com; *World Marketing Data and Statistics.*

European Union, Delegation of the European Commission to the United States, 2300 M Street, NW, Washington, DC 20037, (202) 862-9500, Fax: (202) 429-1766, www.eurunion.org; *Regions - Statistical Yearbook 2006* and *Statistical Overview of Transport in the European Union (Data 1970-2001).*

Eurostat, Batiment Jean Monnet, Rue Alcide de Gasperi, L-2920 Luxembourg, http://epp.eurostat.ec.europa.eu; *Eurostat Yearbook 2006-2007; Regional Passenger and Freight Air Transport in Europe in 2006;* and *Regional Road and Rail Transport Networks.*

M.E. Sharpe, 80 Business Park Drive, Armonk, NY 10504, (800) 541-6563, Fax: (914) 273-2106, www.mesharpe.com; *The Illustrated Book of World Rankings.*

Palgrave Macmillan Ltd., Houndmills, Basingstoke, Hampshire, RG21 6XS, England, (Telephone in U.S. (888) 330-8477), (Fax in U.S. (800) 672-2054), www.palgrave.com; *The Statesman's Yearbook 2008.*

Platts, 2 Penn Plaza, 25th Floor, New York, NY 10121-2298, (212) 904-3070, www.platts.com; *Energy Economist.*

Taylor and Francis Group, An Informa Business, 2 Park Square, Milton Park, Abingdon, Oxford OX14 4RN, United Kingdom, (Dial from U.S. (212) 216-7800), (Fax from U.S. (212) 564-7854), www.tandf.co.uk; *The Europa World Year Book.*

United Nations Statistics Division, New York, NY 10017, (800) 253-9646, Fax: (212) 963-4116, http://unstats.un.org; *Energy Statistics Yearbook 2003; Human Development Report 2006;* and *Trends in Europe and North America: The Statistical Yearbook of the ECE 2005.*

The World Bank, 1818 H Street, NW, Washington, DC 20433, (202) 473-1000, Fax: (202) 477-6391, www.worldbank.org; *France.*

FRANCE - TURKEYS

See FRANCE - LIVESTOCK

FRANCE - UNEMPLOYMENT

Central Intelligence Agency, Office of Public Affairs, Washington, DC 20505, (703) 482-0623, Fax: (703) 482-1739, www.cia.gov; *The World Factbook.*

Euromonitor International, Inc., 224 S. Michigan Avenue, Suite 1500, Chicago, IL 60604, (312) 922-1115, Fax: (312) 922-1157, www.euromonitor.com; *European Marketing Data and Statistics 2008.*

European Union, Delegation of the European Commission to the United States, 2300 M Street, NW, Washington, DC 20037, (202) 862-9500, Fax: (202) 429-1766, www.eurunion.org; *European Union Labour Force Survey; Eurostatistics: Data for Short-Term Economic Analysis (2007 edition);* and *Regions - Statistical Yearbook 2006.*

Eurostat, Batiment Jean Monnet, Rue Alcide de Gasperi, L-2920 Luxembourg, http://epp.eurostat.ec.europa.eu; *Eurostat Yearbook 2006-2007.*

International Labour Office, I.L.O. Publications, 4 route des Morillons, CH-1211 Geneva 22, Switzerland, (Telephone in U.S. (202) 653-7652), (Fax in U.S. (202) 653-7687), www.ilo.org; *Yearbook of Labour Statistics 2006.*

Organisation for Economic Cooperation and Development (OECD), 2 rue Andre Pascal, F-75775 Paris Cedex 16, France, (Telephone in U.S. (202) 785-6323), (Fax in U.S. (202) 785-0350), www.oecd.org; *Labour Force Statistics: 1986-2005, 2007 Edition; OECD Composite Leading Indicators (CLIs), Updated September 2007; OECD Economic Outlook 2008; OECD Economic Survey - France 2007;* and *OECD Employment Outlook 2007.*

Palgrave Macmillan Ltd., Houndmills, Basingstoke, Hampshire, RG21 6XS, England, (Telephone in U.S. (888) 330-8477), (Fax in U.S. (800) 672-2054), www.palgrave.com; *The Statesman's Yearbook 2008.*

United Nations Statistics Division, New York, NY 10017, (800) 253-9646, Fax: (212) 963-4116, http://unstats.un.org; *Statistical Yearbook* and *Trends in Europe and North America: The Statistical Yearbook of the ECE 2005.*

FRANCE - URANIUM PRODUCTION AND CONSUMPTION

See FRANCE - MINERAL INDUSTRIES

FRANCE - VITAL STATISTICS

Eurostat, Batiment Jean Monnet, Rue Alcide de Gasperi, L-2920 Luxembourg, http://epp.eurostat.ec.europa.eu; *Eurostat Yearbook 2006-2007.*

Palgrave Macmillan Ltd., Houndmills, Basingstoke, Hampshire, RG21 6XS, England, (Telephone in U.S. (888) 330-8477), (Fax in U.S. (800) 672-2054), www.palgrave.com; *The Statesman's Yearbook 2008.*

United Nations Statistics Division, New York, NY 10017, (800) 253-9646, Fax: (212) 963-4116, http://unstats.un.org; *Statistical Yearbook.*

World Health Organization (WHO), Avenue Appia 20, 1211 Geneve 27, Switzerland, (Telephone in U.S. (212) 331-9081), www.who.int; *World Health Report 2006.*

FRANCE - WAGES

Euromonitor International, Inc., 224 S. Michigan Avenue, Suite 1500, Chicago, IL 60604, (312) 922-1115, Fax: (312) 922-1157, www.euromonitor.com; *European Marketing Data and Statistics 2008.*

European Union, Delegation of the European Commission to the United States, 2300 M Street, NW, Washington, DC 20037, (202) 862-9500, Fax: (202) 429-1766, www.eurunion.org; *Agriculture in the European Union: Statistical and Economic Information 2006* and *Eurostatistics: Data for Short-Term Economic Analysis (2007 edition).*

Eurostat, Batiment Jean Monnet, Rue Alcide de Gasperi, L-2920 Luxembourg, http://epp.eurostat.ec.europa.eu; *Eurostat Yearbook 2006-2007.*

International Labour Office, I.L.O. Publications, 4 route des Morillons, CH-1211 Geneva 22, Switzerland, (Telephone in U.S. (202) 653-7652), (Fax in U.S. (202) 653-7687), www.ilo.org; *Yearbook of Labour Statistics 2006.*

Organisation for Economic Cooperation and Development (OECD), 2 rue Andre Pascal, F-75775 Paris Cedex 16, France, (Telephone in U.S. (202) 785-6323), (Fax in U.S. (202) 785-0350), www.oecd.org; *ICT Sector Data and Metadata by Country; OECD Economic Outlook 2008; OECD Main Economic Indicators (MEI);* and STructural ANalysis (STAN) database.

United Nations Statistics Division, New York, NY 10017, (800) 253-9646, Fax: (212) 963-4116, http://unstats.un.org; *Statistical Yearbook.*

The World Bank, 1818 H Street, NW, Washington, DC 20433, (202) 473-1000, Fax: (202) 477-6391, www.worldbank.org; *France.*

FRANCE - WALNUT PRODUCTION

See FRANCE - CROPS

FRANCE - WEATHER

See FRANCE - CLIMATE

FRANCE - WELFARE STATE

Eurostat, Batiment Jean Monnet, Rue Alcide de Gasperi, L-2920 Luxembourg, http://epp.eurostat.ec.europa.eu; *Eurostat Yearbook 2006-2007.*

International Monetary Fund (IMF), 700 Nineteenth Street, NW, Washington, DC 20431, (202) 623-7000, Fax: (202) 623-4661, www.imf.org; *Government Finance Statistics Yearbook (2008 Edition).*

Palgrave Macmillan Ltd., Houndmills, Basingstoke, Hampshire, RG21 6XS, England, (Telephone in U.S. (888) 330-8477), (Fax in U.S. (800) 672-2054), www.palgrave.com; *The Statesman's Yearbook 2008.*

FRANCE - WHEAT PRODUCTION

See FRANCE - CROPS

FRANCE - WHOLESALE PRICE INDEXES

Eurostat, Batiment Jean Monnet, Rue Alcide de Gasperi, L-2920 Luxembourg, http://epp.eurostat.ec.europa.eu; *Eurostat Yearbook 2006-2007.*

United Nations Statistics Division, New York, NY 10017, (800) 253-9646, Fax: (212) 963-4116, http://unstats.un.org; *Statistical Yearbook.*

FRANCE - WHOLESALE TRADE

Eurostat, Batiment Jean Monnet, Rue Alcide de Gasperi, L-2920 Luxembourg, http://epp.eurostat.ec.europa.eu; *Eurostat Yearbook 2006-2007.*

United Nations Statistics Division, New York, NY 10017, (800) 253-9646, Fax: (212) 963-4116, http://unstats.un.org; *Statistical Yearbook.*

FRANCE - WINE PRODUCTION

See FRANCE - BEVERAGE INDUSTRY

FRANCE - WOOD AND WOOD PULP

See FRANCE - FORESTS AND FORESTRY

FRANCE - WOOD PRODUCTS

Eurostat, Batiment Jean Monnet, Rue Alcide de Gasperi, L-2920 Luxembourg, http://epp.eurostat.ec.europa.eu; *Eurostat Yearbook 2006-2007.*

Organisation for Economic Cooperation and Development (OECD), 2 rue Andre Pascal, F-75775 Paris Cedex 16, France, (Telephone in U.S. (202) 785-6323), (Fax in U.S. (202) 785-0350), www.oecd.org; *International Trade by Commodity Statistics (ITCS)* and STructural ANalysis (STAN) database.

FRANCE - WOOL PRODUCTION

See FRANCE - TEXTILE INDUSTRY

FRANCE - YARN PRODUCTION

See FRANCE - TEXTILE INDUSTRY

FRANCE - ZINC AND ZINC ORE

See FRANCE - MINERAL INDUSTRIES

FRATERNAL ASSOCIATIONS

Thomson Gale, 27500 Drake Road, Farmington Hills, MI 48331, (248) 699-4253, www.galegroup.com; *Encyclopedia of Associations.*

FRATERNITIES

Thomson Gale, 27500 Drake Road, Farmington Hills, MI 48331, (248) 699-4253, www.galegroup.com; *Encyclopedia of Associations.*

FRAUD

Federal Trade Commission (FTC), 600 Pennsylvania Avenue, NW, Washington, DC 20580, (202) 326-2222, www.ftc.gov; *National and State Trends in Fraud and Identity Theft, January-December 2004.*

U.S. Library of Congress (LOC), Congressional Research Service (CRS), The Library of Congress, 101 Independence Avenue, SE, Washington, DC 20540-7500, (202) 707-5700, www.loc.gov/crsinfo; *Immigration Fraud: Policies, Investigations, and Issues.*

FREE TRADE

International Trade Administration (ITA), U.S. Department of Commerce (DOC), 1401 Constitution Avenue, NW, Washington, DC 20230, (800) USA-TRAD(E), Fax: (202) 482-4473, www.ita.doc.gov; *CAFTA-DR: A State Export Overview, 2000-2004* and *NAFTA - 10 Years Later.*

FREEWAYS AND EXPRESSWAYS - CONDITIONS

U.S. Department of Transportation (DOT), Federal Highway Administration (FHA), 1200 New Jersey Avenue, SE, Washington, DC 20590, (202) 366-0660, www.fhwa.dot.gov; *Highway Statistics 2006.*

FREIGHT TRAFFIC

See TRANSPORTATION - FREIGHT

FRENCH GUIANA - PRIMARY STATISTICS SOURCES

National Institute for Statistics and Economic Studies (Institut National de la Statistique et des Etudes Economiques (INSEE)), Tour "Gamma A", 195 Rue de Bercy, 75582, Paris Cedex 12, France, www.insee.fr; *La population des departements d'outre-mer - Recensement de la population de 1999.*

FRENCH GUIANA - AGRICULTURAL MACHINERY

United Nations Statistics Division, New York, NY 10017, (800) 253-9646, Fax: (212) 963-4116, http://unstats.un.org; *Statistical Yearbook.*

FRENCH GUIANA - AGRICULTURE

Euromonitor International, Inc., 224 S. Michigan Avenue, Suite 1500, Chicago, IL 60604, (312) 922-1115, Fax: (312) 922-1157, www.euromonitor.com; *World Marketing Data and Statistics.*

M.E. Sharpe, 80 Business Park Drive, Armonk, NY 10504, (800) 541-6563, Fax: (914) 273-2106, www.mesharpe.com; *The Illustrated Book of World Rankings.*

Palgrave Macmillan Ltd., Houndmills, Basingstoke, Hampshire, RG21 6XS, England, (Telephone in U.S. (888) 330-8477), (Fax in U.S. (800) 672-2054), www.palgrave.com; *The Statesman's Yearbook 2008.*

Taylor and Francis Group, An Informa Business, 2 Park Square, Milton Park, Abingdon, Oxford OX14 4RN, United Kingdom, (Dial from U.S. (212) 216-7800), (Fax from U.S. (212) 564-7854), www.tandf.co.uk; *The Europa World Year Book.*

United Nations Conference on Trade and Development (UNCTAD), DC2-1120, United Nations, New York, NY 10017, (212) 963-0027, www.unctad.org; *UNCTAD Commodity Yearbook.*

United Nations Food and Agricultural Organization (FAO), Viale delle Terme di Caracalla, 00100 Rome, Italy, (Dial from U.S. (202) 653-2400), (Fax from U.S. (202) 653 5760), www.fao.org; AQUASTAT; *FAO Production Yearbook 2002; FAO Trade Yearbook;* and *The State of Food and Agriculture (SOFA) 2006.*

United Nations Statistics Division, New York, NY 10017, (800) 253-9646, Fax: (212) 963-4116, http://unstats.un.org; *Statistical Yearbook.*

FRENCH GUIANA - AIRLINES

M.E. Sharpe, 80 Business Park Drive, Armonk, NY 10504, (800) 541-6563, Fax: (914) 273-2106, www.mesharpe.com; *The Illustrated Book of World Rankings.*

Palgrave Macmillan Ltd., Houndmills, Basingstoke, Hampshire, RG21 6XS, England, (Telephone in U.S. (888) 330-8477), (Fax in U.S. (800) 672-2054), www.palgrave.com; *The Statesman's Yearbook 2008.*

Taylor and Francis Group, An Informa Business, 2 Park Square, Milton Park, Abingdon, Oxford OX14 4RN, United Kingdom, (Dial from U.S. (212) 216-7800), (Fax from U.S. (212) 564-7854), www.tandf.co.uk; *The Europa World Year Book.*

FRENCH GUIANA - AIRPORTS

Central Intelligence Agency, Office of Public Affairs, Washington, DC 20505, (703) 482-0623, Fax: (703) 482-1739, www.cia.gov; *The World Factbook.*

FRENCH GUIANA - ALUMINUM PRODUCTION

See FRENCH GUIANA - MINERAL INDUSTRIES

FRENCH GUIANA - ARMED FORCES

Central Intelligence Agency, Office of Public Affairs, Washington, DC 20505, (703) 482-0623, Fax: (703) 482-1739, www.cia.gov; *The World Factbook.*

Euromonitor International, Inc., 224 S. Michigan Avenue, Suite 1500, Chicago, IL 60604, (312) 922-1115, Fax: (312) 922-1157, www.euromonitor.com; *World Marketing Data and Statistics.*

FRENCH GUIANA - BANKS AND BANKING

Euromonitor International, Inc., 224 S. Michigan Avenue, Suite 1500, Chicago, IL 60604, (312) 922-1115, Fax: (312) 922-1157, www.euromonitor.com; *World Marketing Data and Statistics.*

M.E. Sharpe, 80 Business Park Drive, Armonk, NY 10504, (800) 541-6563, Fax: (914) 273-2106, www.mesharpe.com; *The Illustrated Book of World Rankings.*

Palgrave Macmillan Ltd., Houndmills, Basingstoke, Hampshire, RG21 6XS, England, (Telephone in U.S. (888) 330-8477), (Fax in U.S. (800) 672-2054), www.palgrave.com; *The Statesman's Yearbook 2008.*

FRENCH GUIANA - BARLEY PRODUCTION

See FRENCH GUIANA - CROPS

FRENCH GUIANA - BEVERAGE INDUSTRY

M.E. Sharpe, 80 Business Park Drive, Armonk, NY 10504, (800) 541-6563, Fax: (914) 273-2106, www.mesharpe.com; *The Illustrated Book of World Rankings.*

FRENCH GUIANA - BROADCASTING

Central Intelligence Agency, Office of Public Affairs, Washington, DC 20505, (703) 482-0623, Fax: (703) 482-1739, www.cia.gov; *The World Factbook.*

Euromonitor International, Inc., 224 S. Michigan Avenue, Suite 1500, Chicago, IL 60604, (312) 922-1115, Fax: (312) 922-1157, www.euromonitor.com; *World Marketing Data and Statistics.*

M.E. Sharpe, 80 Business Park Drive, Armonk, NY 10504, (800) 541-6563, Fax: (914) 273-2106, www.mesharpe.com; *The Illustrated Book of World Rankings.*

Palgrave Macmillan Ltd., Houndmills, Basingstoke, Hampshire, RG21 6XS, England, (Telephone in U.S. (888) 330-8477), (Fax in U.S. (800) 672-2054), www.palgrave.com; *The Statesman's Yearbook 2008.*

WRTH Publications Limited, PO Box 290, Oxford OX2 7FT, UK, www.wrth.com; *World Radio TV Handbook 2007.*

FRENCH GUIANA - BUDGET

Central Intelligence Agency, Office of Public Affairs, Washington, DC 20505, (703) 482-0623, Fax: (703) 482-1739, www.cia.gov; *The World Factbook.*

FRENCH GUIANA - CATTLE

See FRENCH GUIANA - LIVESTOCK

FRENCH GUIANA - CHILDBIRTH - STATISTICS

Central Intelligence Agency, Office of Public Affairs, Washington, DC 20505, (703) 482-0623, Fax: (703) 482-1739, www.cia.gov; *The World Factbook.*

Euromonitor International, Inc., 224 S. Michigan Avenue, Suite 1500, Chicago, IL 60604, (312) 922-1115, Fax: (312) 922-1157, www.euromonitor.com; *International Marketing Data and Statistics 2008* and *The World Economic Factbook 2008.*

M.E. Sharpe, 80 Business Park Drive, Armonk, NY 10504, (800) 541-6563, Fax: (914) 273-2106, www.mesharpe.com; *The Illustrated Book of World Rankings.*

Palgrave Macmillan Ltd., Houndmills, Basingstoke, Hampshire, RG21 6XS, England, (Telephone in U.S. (888) 330-8477), (Fax in U.S. (800) 672-2054), www.palgrave.com; *The Statesman's Yearbook 2008.*

Taylor and Francis Group, An Informa Business, 2 Park Square, Milton Park, Abingdon, Oxford OX14 4RN, United Kingdom, (Dial from U.S. (212) 216-7800), (Fax from U.S. (212) 564-7854), www.tandf.co.uk; *The Europa World Year Book.*

United Nations Statistics Division, New York, NY 10017, (800) 253-9646, Fax: (212) 963-4116, http://unstats.un.org; *Demographic Yearbook* and *Statistical Yearbook.*

World Health Organization (WHO), Avenue Appia 20, 1211 Geneve 27, Switzerland, (Telephone in U.S. (212) 331-9081), www.who.int; *World Health Report 2006.*

FRENCH GUIANA - CLIMATE

M.E. Sharpe, 80 Business Park Drive, Armonk, NY 10504, (800) 541-6563, Fax: (914) 273-2106, www.mesharpe.com; *The Illustrated Book of World Rankings.*

FRENCH GUIANA - COAL PRODUCTION

See FRENCH GUIANA - MINERAL INDUSTRIES

FRENCH GUIANA - COFFEE

See FRENCH GUIANA - CROPS

FRENCH GUIANA - COMMERCE

Palgrave Macmillan Ltd., Houndmills, Basingstoke, Hampshire, RG21 6XS, England, (Telephone in U.S. (888) 330-8477), (Fax in U.S. (800) 672-2054), www.palgrave.com; *The Statesman's Yearbook 2008.*

FRENCH GUIANA - COMMODITY EXCHANGES

Commodity Research Bureau, 330 South Wells Street, Suite 612, Chicago, IL 60606-7110, (800) 621-5271, Fax: (312) 939-4135, www.crbtrader.com; *2006 CRB Commodity Yearbook and CD.*

International Monetary Fund (IMF), 700 Nineteenth Street, NW, Washington, DC 20431, (202) 623-7000, Fax: (202) 623-4661, www.imf.org; *IMF Primary Commodity Prices.*

United Nations Food and Agricultural Organization (FAO), Viale delle Terme di Caracalla, 00100 Rome, Italy, (Dial from U.S. (202) 653-2400), (Fax from U.S. (202) 653 5760), www.fao.org; *The State of Food and Agriculture (SOFA) 2006.*

FRENCH GUIANA - CONSTRUCTION INDUSTRY

M.E. Sharpe, 80 Business Park Drive, Armonk, NY 10504, (800) 541-6563, Fax: (914) 273-2106, www.mesharpe.com; *The Illustrated Book of World Rankings.*

United Nations Statistics Division, New York, NY 10017, (800) 253-9646, Fax: (212) 963-4116, http://unstats.un.org; *Statistical Yearbook.*

FRENCH GUIANA - CONSUMER PRICE INDEXES

Taylor and Francis Group, An Informa Business, 2 Park Square, Milton Park, Abingdon, Oxford OX14 4RN, United Kingdom, (Dial from U.S. (212) 216-7800), (Fax from U.S. (212) 564-7854), www.tandf.co.uk; *The Europa World Year Book.*

United Nations Statistics Division, New York, NY 10017, (800) 253-9646, Fax: (212) 963-4116, http://unstats.un.org; *Statistical Yearbook.*

FRENCH GUIANA - COPPER INDUSTRY AND TRADE

See FRENCH GUIANA - MINERAL INDUSTRIES

FRENCH GUIANA - CORN INDUSTRY

See FRENCH GUIANA - CROPS

FRENCH GUIANA - COTTON

See FRENCH GUIANA - CROPS

FRENCH GUIANA - CROPS

M.E. Sharpe, 80 Business Park Drive, Armonk, NY 10504, (800) 541-6563, Fax: (914) 273-2106, www.mesharpe.com; *The Illustrated Book of World Rankings.*

Palgrave Macmillan Ltd., Houndmills, Basingstoke, Hampshire, RG21 6XS, England, (Telephone in U.S. (888) 330-8477), (Fax in U.S. (800) 672-2054), www.palgrave.com; *The Statesman's Yearbook 2008.*

Taylor and Francis Group, An Informa Business, 2 Park Square, Milton Park, Abingdon, Oxford OX14 4RN, United Kingdom, (Dial from U.S. (212) 216-7800), (Fax from U.S. (212) 564-7854), www.tandf.co.uk; *The Europa World Year Book.*

United Nations Conference on Trade and Development (UNCTAD), DC2-1120, United Nations, New York, NY 10017, (212) 963-0027, www.unctad.org; *UNCTAD Commodity Yearbook.*

United Nations Food and Agricultural Organization (FAO), Viale delle Terme di Caracalla, 00100 Rome, Italy, (Dial from U.S. (202) 653-2400), (Fax from U.S. (202) 653 5760), www.fao.org; *FAO Production Yearbook 2002* and *The State of Food and Agriculture (SOFA) 2006.*

FRENCH GUIANA - CUSTOMS ADMINISTRATION

Palgrave Macmillan Ltd., Houndmills, Basingstoke, Hampshire, RG21 6XS, England, (Telephone in U.S. (888) 330-8477), (Fax in U.S. (800) 672-2054), www.palgrave.com; *The Statesman's Yearbook 2008.*

FRENCH GUIANA - DAIRY PROCESSING

M.E. Sharpe, 80 Business Park Drive, Armonk, NY 10504, (800) 541-6563, Fax: (914) 273-2106, www.mesharpe.com; *The Illustrated Book of World Rankings.*

Palgrave Macmillan Ltd., Houndmills, Basingstoke, Hampshire, RG21 6XS, England, (Telephone in U.S. (888) 330-8477), (Fax in U.S. (800) 672-2054), www.palgrave.com; *The Statesman's Yearbook 2008.*

Taylor and Francis Group, An Informa Business, 2 Park Square, Milton Park, Abingdon, Oxford OX14 4RN, United Kingdom, (Dial from U.S. (212) 216-7800), (Fax from U.S. (212) 564-7854), www.tandf.co.uk; *The Europa World Year Book.*

United Nations Food and Agricultural Organization (FAO), Viale delle Terme di Caracalla, 00100 Rome, Italy, (Dial from U.S. (202) 653-2400), (Fax from U.S. (202) 653 5760), www.fao.org; *The State of Food and Agriculture (SOFA) 2006.*

FRENCH GUIANA - DEATH RATES

See FRENCH GUIANA - MORTALITY

FRENCH GUIANA - DEMOGRAPHY

Euromonitor International, Inc., 224 S. Michigan Avenue, Suite 1500, Chicago, IL 60604, (312) 922-1115, Fax: (312) 922-1157, www.euromonitor.com; *International Marketing Data and Statistics 2008; The World Economic Factbook 2008;* and *World Marketing Data and Statistics.*

M.E. Sharpe, 80 Business Park Drive, Armonk, NY 10504, (800) 541-6563, Fax: (914) 273-2106, www.mesharpe.com; *The Illustrated Book of World Rankings.*

FRENCH GUIANA - DIAMONDS

See FRENCH GUIANA - MINERAL INDUSTRIES

FRENCH GUIANA - DISPOSABLE INCOME

M.E. Sharpe, 80 Business Park Drive, Armonk, NY 10504, (800) 541-6563, Fax: (914) 273-2106, www.mesharpe.com; *The Illustrated Book of World Rankings.*

FRENCH GUIANA - DIVORCE

M.E. Sharpe, 80 Business Park Drive, Armonk, NY 10504, (800) 541-6563, Fax: (914) 273-2106, www.mesharpe.com; *The Illustrated Book of World Rankings.*

United Nations Statistics Division, New York, NY 10017, (800) 253-9646, Fax: (212) 963-4116, http://unstats.un.org; *Demographic Yearbook* and *Statistical Yearbook.*

FRENCH GUIANA - ECONOMIC ASSISTANCE

United Nations Statistics Division, New York, NY 10017, (800) 253-9646, Fax: (212) 963-4116, http://unstats.un.org; *Statistical Yearbook.*

FRENCH GUIANA - ECONOMIC CONDITIONS

Center for International Business Education Research (CIBER), Columbia Business School and School of International and Public Affairs, Uris Hall, Room 212, 3022 Broadway, New York, NY 10027-6902, Mr. Joshua Safier, (212) 854-4750, Fax: (212) 222-9821, www.columbia.edu/cu/ciber/; Datastream International.

Central Intelligence Agency, Office of Public Affairs, Washington, DC 20505, (703) 482-0623, Fax: (703) 482-1739, www.cia.gov; *The World Factbook.*

DSI Data Service Information, Xantener Strasse 51a, D-47495 Rheinberg, Germany, www.dsidata.com; *Campus Solution.*

Dun and Bradstreet (DB) Corporation, 103 JFK Parkway, Short Hills, NJ 07078, (973) 921-5500, www.dnb.com; *Country Report.*

Euromonitor International, Inc., 224 S. Michigan Avenue, Suite 1500, Chicago, IL 60604, (312) 922-1115, Fax: (312) 922-1157, www.euromonitor.com; *The World Economic Factbook 2008* and *World Marketing Data and Statistics.*

International Monetary Fund (IMF), 700 Nineteenth Street, NW, Washington, DC 20431, (202) 623-7000, Fax: (202) 623-4661, www.imf.org; *World Economic Outlook Reports.*

M.E. Sharpe, 80 Business Park Drive, Armonk, NY 10504, (800) 541-6563, Fax: (914) 273-2106, www.mesharpe.com; *The Illustrated Book of World Rankings.*

Palgrave Macmillan Ltd., Houndmills, Basingstoke, Hampshire, RG21 6XS, England, (Telephone in U.S. (888) 330-8477), (Fax in U.S. (800) 672-2054), www.palgrave.com; *The Statesman's Yearbook 2008.*

Taylor and Francis Group, An Informa Business, 2 Park Square, Milton Park, Abingdon, Oxford OX14 4RN, United Kingdom, (Dial from U.S. (212) 216-7800), (Fax from U.S. (212) 564-7854), www.tandf.co.uk; *The Europa World Year Book.*

United Nations Statistics Division, New York, NY 10017, (800) 253-9646, Fax: (212) 963-4116, http://unstats.un.org; *World Statistics Pocketbook.*

The World Bank, 1818 H Street, NW, Washington, DC 20433, (202) 473-1000, Fax: (202) 477-6391, www.worldbank.org; *Global Economic Monitor (GEM); Global Economic Prospects 2008;* and *The World Bank Atlas 2003-2004.*

FRENCH GUIANA - EDUCATION

Euromonitor International, Inc., 224 S. Michigan Avenue, Suite 1500, Chicago, IL 60604, (312) 922-

1115, Fax: (312) 922-1157, www.euromonitor.com; *International Marketing Data and Statistics 2008* and *World Marketing Data and Statistics.*

M.E. Sharpe, 80 Business Park Drive, Armonk, NY 10504, (800) 541-6563, Fax: (914) 273-2106, www.mesharpe.com; *The Illustrated Book of World Rankings.*

Palgrave Macmillan Ltd., Houndmills, Basingstoke, Hampshire, RG21 6XS, England, (Telephone in U.S. (888) 330-8477), (Fax in U.S. (800) 672-2054), www.palgrave.com; *The Statesman's Yearbook 2008.*

Taylor and Francis Group, An Informa Business, 2 Park Square, Milton Park, Abingdon, Oxford OX14 4RN, United Kingdom, (Dial from U.S. (212) 216-7800), (Fax from U.S. (212) 564-7854), www.tandf.co.uk; *The Europa World Year Book.*

FRENCH GUIANA - ELECTRICITY

M.E. Sharpe, 80 Business Park Drive, Armonk, NY 10504, (800) 541-6563, Fax: (914) 273-2106, www.mesharpe.com; *The Illustrated Book of World Rankings.*

Palgrave Macmillan Ltd., Houndmills, Basingstoke, Hampshire, RG21 6XS, England, (Telephone in U.S. (888) 330-8477), (Fax in U.S. (800) 672-2054), www.palgrave.com; *The Statesman's Yearbook 2008.*

United Nations Statistics Division, New York, NY 10017, (800) 253-9646, Fax: (212) 963-4116, http://unstats.un.org; *Statistical Yearbook.*

FRENCH GUIANA - EMPLOYMENT

Euromonitor International, Inc., 224 S. Michigan Avenue, Suite 1500, Chicago, IL 60604, (312) 922-1115, Fax: (312) 922-1157, www.euromonitor.com; *International Marketing Data and Statistics 2008.*

International Labour Office, I.L.O. Publications, 4 route des Morillons, CH-1211 Geneva 22, Switzerland, (Telephone in U.S. (202) 653-7652), (Fax in U.S. (202) 653-7687), www.ilo.org; *Yearbook of Labour Statistics 2006.*

M.E. Sharpe, 80 Business Park Drive, Armonk, NY 10504, (800) 541-6563, Fax: (914) 273-2106, www.mesharpe.com; *The Illustrated Book of World Rankings.*

United Nations Food and Agricultural Organization (FAO), Viale delle Terme di Caracalla, 00100 Rome, Italy, (Dial from U.S. (202) 653-2400), (Fax from U.S. (202) 653 5760), www.fao.org; *The State of Food and Agriculture (SOFA) 2006.*

FRENCH GUIANA - ENVIRONMENTAL CONDITIONS

DSI Data Service Information, Xantener Strasse 51a, D-47495 Rheinberg, Germany, www.dsidata.com; *Campus Solution* and *DSI's Global Environmental Database.*

United Nations Statistics Division, New York, NY 10017, (800) 253-9646, Fax: (212) 963-4116, http://unstats.un.org; *World Statistics Pocketbook.*

FRENCH GUIANA - EXPORTS

Central Intelligence Agency, Office of Public Affairs, Washington, DC 20505, (703) 482-0623, Fax: (703) 482-1739, www.cia.gov; *The World Factbook.*

Euromonitor International, Inc., 224 S. Michigan Avenue, Suite 1500, Chicago, IL 60604, (312) 922-1115, Fax: (312) 922-1157, www.euromonitor.com; *International Marketing Data and Statistics 2008* and *The World Economic Factbook 2008.*

International Monetary Fund (IMF), 700 Nineteenth Street, NW, Washington, DC 20431, (202) 623-7000, Fax: (202) 623-4661, www.imf.org; *Direction of Trade Statistics Yearbook 2007.*

Palgrave Macmillan Ltd., Houndmills, Basingstoke, Hampshire, RG21 6XS, England, (Telephone in U.S. (888) 330-8477), (Fax in U.S. (800) 672-2054), www.palgrave.com; *The Statesman's Yearbook 2008.*

Taylor and Francis Group, An Informa Business, 2 Park Square, Milton Park, Abingdon, Oxford OX14 4RN, United Kingdom, (Dial from U.S. (212) 216-7800), (Fax from U.S. (212) 564-7854), www.tandf.co.uk; *The Europa World Year Book.*

United Nations Food and Agricultural Organization (FAO), Viale delle Terme di Caracalla, 00100 Rome, Italy, (Dial from U.S. (202) 653-2400), (Fax from U.S. (202) 653 5760), www.fao.org; *The State of Food and Agriculture (SOFA) 2006.*

FRENCH GUIANA - FERTILITY, HUMAN

Central Intelligence Agency, Office of Public Affairs, Washington, DC 20505, (703) 482-0623, Fax: (703) 482-1739, www.cia.gov; *The World Factbook.*

M.E. Sharpe, 80 Business Park Drive, Armonk, NY 10504, (800) 541-6563, Fax: (914) 273-2106, www.mesharpe.com; *The Illustrated Book of World Rankings.*

The World Bank, 1818 H Street, NW, Washington, DC 20433, (202) 473-1000, Fax: (202) 477-6391, www.worldbank.org; *The World Bank Atlas 2003-2004.*

FRENCH GUIANA - FERTILIZER INDUSTRY

United Nations Food and Agricultural Organization (FAO), Viale delle Terme di Caracalla, 00100 Rome, Italy, (Dial from U.S. (202) 653-2400), (Fax from U.S. (202) 653 5760), www.fao.org; *The State of Food and Agriculture (SOFA) 2006.*

FRENCH GUIANA - FETAL MORTALITY

See FRENCH GUIANA - MORTALITY

FRENCH GUIANA - FINANCE, PUBLIC

Bernan Essential Government Publications, 4611-F Assembly Drive, Lanham MD, 20706-4391, (301) 459-2255, Fax: (800) 865-3450, www.bernan.com; *National Accounts Statistics.*

International Monetary Fund (IMF), 700 Nineteenth Street, NW, Washington, DC 20431, (202) 623-7000, Fax: (202) 623-4661, www.imf.org; *International Financial Statistics* and *International Financial Statistics Online Service.*

M.E. Sharpe, 80 Business Park Drive, Armonk, NY 10504, (800) 541-6563, Fax: (914) 273-2106, www.mesharpe.com; *The Illustrated Book of World Rankings.*

Taylor and Francis Group, An Informa Business, 2 Park Square, Milton Park, Abingdon, Oxford OX14 4RN, United Kingdom, (Dial from U.S. (212) 216-7800), (Fax from U.S. (212) 564-7854), www.tandf.co.uk; *The Europa World Year Book.*

FRENCH GUIANA - FISHERIES

M.E. Sharpe, 80 Business Park Drive, Armonk, NY 10504, (800) 541-6563, Fax: (914) 273-2106, www.mesharpe.com; *The Illustrated Book of World Rankings.*

Palgrave Macmillan Ltd., Houndmills, Basingstoke, Hampshire, RG21 6XS, England, (Telephone in U.S. (888) 330-8477), (Fax in U.S. (800) 672-2054), www.palgrave.com; *The Statesman's Yearbook 2008.*

Taylor and Francis Group, An Informa Business, 2 Park Square, Milton Park, Abingdon, Oxford OX14 4RN, United Kingdom, (Dial from U.S. (212) 216-7800), (Fax from U.S. (212) 564-7854), www.tandf.co.uk; *The Europa World Year Book.*

United Nations Conference on Trade and Development (UNCTAD), DC2-1120, United Nations, New York, NY 10017, (212) 963-0027, www.unctad.org; *UNCTAD Commodity Yearbook.*

United Nations Food and Agricultural Organization (FAO), Viale delle Terme di Caracalla, 00100 Rome, Italy, (Dial from U.S. (202) 653-2400), (Fax from U.S. (202) 653 5760), www.fao.org; *FAO Yearbook of Fishery Statistics;* Fishery Databases; FISHSTAT Database. Subjects covered include: Aquaculture production, capture production, fishery commodities; and *The State of Food and Agriculture (SOFA) 2006.*

United Nations Statistics Division, New York, NY 10017, (800) 253-9646, Fax: (212) 963-4116, http://unstats.un.org; *Statistical Yearbook.*

FRENCH GUIANA - FOOD

United Nations Conference on Trade and Development (UNCTAD), DC2-1120, United Nations, New York, NY 10017, (212) 963-0027, www.unctad.org; *UNCTAD Commodity Yearbook.*

United Nations Food and Agricultural Organization (FAO), Viale delle Terme di Caracalla, 00100 Rome, Italy, (Dial from U.S. (202) 653-2400), (Fax from U.S. (202) 653 5760), www.fao.org; *FAO Production Yearbook 2002* and *The State of Food and Agriculture (SOFA) 2006.*

FRENCH GUIANA - FOREIGN EXCHANGE RATES

Central Intelligence Agency, Office of Public Affairs, Washington, DC 20505, (703) 482-0623, Fax: (703) 482-1739, www.cia.gov; *The World Factbook.*

Euromonitor International, Inc., 224 S. Michigan Avenue, Suite 1500, Chicago, IL 60604, (312) 922-1115, Fax: (312) 922-1157, www.euromonitor.com; *International Marketing Data and Statistics 2008* and *The World Economic Factbook 2008.*

Taylor and Francis Group, An Informa Business, 2 Park Square, Milton Park, Abingdon, Oxford OX14 4RN, United Kingdom, (Dial from U.S. (212) 216-7800), (Fax from U.S. (212) 564-7854), www.tandf.co.uk; *The Europa World Year Book.*

United Nations Statistics Division, New York, NY 10017, (800) 253-9646, Fax: (212) 963-4116, http://unstats.un.org; *World Statistics Pocketbook.*

FRENCH GUIANA - FORESTS AND FORESTRY

M.E. Sharpe, 80 Business Park Drive, Armonk, NY 10504, (800) 541-6563, Fax: (914) 273-2106, www.mesharpe.com; *The Illustrated Book of World Rankings.*

Palgrave Macmillan Ltd., Houndmills, Basingstoke, Hampshire, RG21 6XS, England, (Telephone in U.S. (888) 330-8477), (Fax in U.S. (800) 672-2054), www.palgrave.com; *The Statesman's Yearbook 2008.*

Taylor and Francis Group, An Informa Business, 2 Park Square, Milton Park, Abingdon, Oxford OX14 4RN, United Kingdom, (Dial from U.S. (212) 216-7800), (Fax from U.S. (212) 564-7854), www.tandf.co.uk; *The Europa World Year Book.*

UNESCO Institute for Statistics, C.P. 6128 Succursale Centre-Ville, Montreal, Quebec, H3C 3J7 Canada, (Dial from U.S. (514) 343-6880), (Fax from U.S. (514) 343 6882), www.uis.unesco.org; *Statistical Tables.*

United Nations Conference on Trade and Development (UNCTAD), DC2-1120, United Nations, New York, NY 10017, (212) 963-0027, www.unctad.org; *UNCTAD Commodity Yearbook.*

United Nations Food and Agricultural Organization (FAO), Viale delle Terme di Caracalla, 00100 Rome, Italy, (Dial from U.S. (202) 653-2400), (Fax from U.S. (202) 653 5760), www.fao.org; *FAO Yearbook of Forest Products* and *The State of Food and Agriculture (SOFA) 2006.*

United Nations Statistics Division, New York, NY 10017, (800) 253-9646, Fax: (212) 963-4116, http://unstats.un.org; *Statistical Yearbook.*

FRENCH GUIANA - GAS PRODUCTION

See FRENCH GUIANA - MINERAL INDUSTRIES

FRENCH GUIANA - GEOGRAPHIC INFORMATION SYSTEMS

M.E. Sharpe, 80 Business Park Drive, Armonk, NY 10504, (800) 541-6563, Fax: (914) 273-2106, www.mesharpe.com; *The Illustrated Book of World Rankings.*

FRENCH GUIANA - GOLD PRODUCTION

See FRENCH GUIANA - MINERAL INDUSTRIES

FRENCH GUIANA - GROSS DOMESTIC PRODUCT

Euromonitor International, Inc., 224 S. Michigan Avenue, Suite 1500, Chicago, IL 60604, (312) 922-

1115, Fax: (312) 922-1157, www.euromonitor.com; *International Marketing Data and Statistics 2008* and *The World Economic Factbook 2008.*

M.E. Sharpe, 80 Business Park Drive, Armonk, NY 10504, (800) 541-6563, Fax: (914) 273-2106, www.mesharpe.com; *The Illustrated Book of World Rankings.*

Taylor and Francis Group, An Informa Business, 2 Park Square, Milton Park, Abingdon, Oxford OX14 4RN, United Kingdom, (Dial from U.S. (212) 216-7800), (Fax from U.S. (212) 564-7854), www.tandf.co.uk; *The Europa World Year Book.*

FRENCH GUIANA - GROSS NATIONAL PRODUCT

M.E. Sharpe, 80 Business Park Drive, Armonk, NY 10504, (800) 541-6563, Fax: (914) 273-2106, www.mesharpe.com; *The Illustrated Book of World Rankings.*

The World Bank, 1818 H Street, NW, Washington, DC 20433, (202) 473-1000, Fax: (202) 477-6391, www.worldbank.org; *The World Bank Atlas 2003-2004.*

FRENCH GUIANA - HIDES AND SKINS INDUSTRY

United Nations Food and Agricultural Organization (FAO), Viale delle Terme di Caracalla, 00100 Rome, Italy, (Dial from U.S. (202) 653-2400), (Fax from U.S. (202) 653 5760), www.fao.org; *FAO Production Yearbook 2002.*

FRENCH GUIANA - HOUSING

Euromonitor International, Inc., 224 S. Michigan Avenue, Suite 1500, Chicago, IL 60604, (312) 922-1115, Fax: (312) 922-1157, www.euromonitor.com; *World Marketing Data and Statistics.*

M.E. Sharpe, 80 Business Park Drive, Armonk, NY 10504, (800) 541-6563, Fax: (914) 273-2106, www.mesharpe.com; *The Illustrated Book of World Rankings.*

FRENCH GUIANA - ILLITERATE PERSONS

Central Intelligence Agency, Office of Public Affairs, Washington, DC 20505, (703) 482-0623, Fax: (703) 482-1739, www.cia.gov; *The World Factbook.*

Euromonitor International, Inc., 224 S. Michigan Avenue, Suite 1500, Chicago, IL 60604, (312) 922-1115, Fax: (312) 922-1157, www.euromonitor.com; *The World Economic Factbook 2008.*

UNESCO Institute for Statistics, C.P. 6128 Succursale Centre-Ville, Montreal, Quebec, H3C 3J7 Canada, (Dial from U.S. (514) 343-6880), (Fax from U.S. (514) 343 6882), www.uis.unesco.org; *Statistical Tables.*

FRENCH GUIANA - IMPORTS

Central Intelligence Agency, Office of Public Affairs, Washington, DC 20505, (703) 482-0623, Fax: (703) 482-1739, www.cia.gov; *The World Factbook.*

Euromonitor International, Inc., 224 S. Michigan Avenue, Suite 1500, Chicago, IL 60604, (312) 922-1115, Fax: (312) 922-1157, www.euromonitor.com; *International Marketing Data and Statistics 2008* and *The World Economic Factbook 2008.*

International Monetary Fund (IMF), 700 Nineteenth Street, NW, Washington, DC 20431, (202) 623-7000, Fax: (202) 623-4661, www.imf.org; *Direction of Trade Statistics Yearbook 2007.*

Palgrave Macmillan Ltd., Houndmills, Basingstoke, Hampshire, RG21 6XS, England, (Telephone in U.S. (888) 330-8477), (Fax in U.S. (800) 672-2054), www.palgrave.com; *The Statesman's Yearbook 2008.*

Taylor and Francis Group, An Informa Business, 2 Park Square, Milton Park, Abingdon, Oxford OX14 4RN, United Kingdom, (Dial from U.S. (212) 216-7800), (Fax from U.S. (212) 564-7854), www.tandf.co.uk; *The Europa World Year Book.*

United Nations Food and Agricultural Organization (FAO), Viale delle Terme di Caracalla, 00100 Rome, Italy, (Dial from U.S. (202) 653-2400), (Fax from U.S. (202) 653 5760), www.fao.org; *The State of Food and Agriculture (SOFA) 2006.*

FRENCH GUIANA - INDUSTRIAL PRODUCTIVITY

M.E. Sharpe, 80 Business Park Drive, Armonk, NY 10504, (800) 541-6563, Fax: (914) 273-2106, www.mesharpe.com; *The Illustrated Book of World Rankings.*

FRENCH GUIANA - INDUSTRIES

Central Intelligence Agency, Office of Public Affairs, Washington, DC 20505, (703) 482-0623, Fax: (703) 482-1739, www.cia.gov; *The World Factbook.*

Euromonitor International, Inc., 224 S. Michigan Avenue, Suite 1500, Chicago, IL 60604, (312) 922-1115, Fax: (312) 922-1157, www.euromonitor.com; *The World Economic Factbook 2008* and *World Marketing Data and Statistics.*

International Labour Office, I.L.O. Publications, 4 route des Morillons, CH-1211 Geneva 22, Switzerland, (Telephone in U.S. (202) 653-7652), (Fax in U.S. (202) 653-7687), www.ilo.org; *Yearbook of Labour Statistics 2006.*

M.E. Sharpe, 80 Business Park Drive, Armonk, NY 10504, (800) 541-6563, Fax: (914) 273-2106, www.mesharpe.com; *The Illustrated Book of World Rankings.*

Palgrave Macmillan Ltd., Houndmills, Basingstoke, Hampshire, RG21 6XS, England, (Telephone in U.S. (888) 330-8477), (Fax in U.S. (800) 672-2054), www.palgrave.com; *The Statesman's Yearbook 2008.*

Taylor and Francis Group, An Informa Business, 2 Park Square, Milton Park, Abingdon, Oxford OX14 4RN, United Kingdom, (Dial from U.S. (212) 216-7800), (Fax from U.S. (212) 564-7854), www.tandf.co.uk; *The Europa World Year Book.*

United Nations Industrial Development Organization (UNIDO), 1 United Nations Plaza, New York, NY 10017, (212) 963 6890, Fax: (212) 963-7904, http://unido.org; Industrial Statistics Database 2008 (INDSTAT) and *The International Yearbook of Industrial Statistics 2008.*

FRENCH GUIANA - INFANT AND MATERNAL MORTALITY

See FRENCH GUIANA - MORTALITY

FRENCH GUIANA - INTERNATIONAL TRADE

Euromonitor International, Inc., 224 S. Michigan Avenue, Suite 1500, Chicago, IL 60604, (312) 922-1115, Fax: (312) 922-1157, www.euromonitor.com; *The World Economic Factbook 2008* and *World Marketing Data and Statistics.*

M.E. Sharpe, 80 Business Park Drive, Armonk, NY 10504, (800) 541-6563, Fax: (914) 273-2106, www.mesharpe.com; *The Illustrated Book of World Rankings.*

Palgrave Macmillan Ltd., Houndmills, Basingstoke, Hampshire, RG21 6XS, England, (Telephone in U.S. (888) 330-8477), (Fax in U.S. (800) 672-2054), www.palgrave.com; *The Statesman's Yearbook 2008.*

Taylor and Francis Group, An Informa Business, 2 Park Square, Milton Park, Abingdon, Oxford OX14 4RN, United Kingdom, (Dial from U.S. (212) 216-7800), (Fax from U.S. (212) 564-7854), www.tandf.co.uk; *The Europa World Year Book.*

United Nations Conference on Trade and Development (UNCTAD), DC2-1120, United Nations, New York, NY 10017, (212) 963-0027, www.unctad.org; *UNCTAD Commodity Yearbook.*

United Nations Food and Agricultural Organization (FAO), Viale delle Terme di Caracalla, 00100 Rome, Italy, (Dial from U.S. (202) 653-2400), (Fax from U.S. (202) 653 5760), www.fao.org; *FAO Trade Yearbook* and *The State of Food and Agriculture (SOFA) 2006.*

United Nations Statistics Division, New York, NY 10017, (800) 253-9646, Fax: (212) 963-4116, http://unstats.un.org; *International Trade Statistics Yearbook* and *Statistical Yearbook.*

World Trade Organization (WTO), Centre William Rappard, Rue de Lausanne 154, CH-1211 Geneva 21, Switzerland, www.wto.org; *International Trade Statistics 2006.*

FRENCH GUIANA - INTERNET USERS

International Telecommunication Union (ITU), Place des Nations, 1211 Geneva 20, Switzerland, www.itu.int; *World Telecommunication/ICT Indicators Database on CD-ROM; World Telecommunication/ICT Indicators Database Online;* and *Yearbook of Statistics - Telecommunication Services (Chronological Time Series 1997-2006).*

FRENCH GUIANA - IRON AND IRON ORE PRODUCTION

See FRENCH GUIANA - MINERAL INDUSTRIES

FRENCH GUIANA - LABOR

Central Intelligence Agency, Office of Public Affairs, Washington, DC 20505, (703) 482-0623, Fax: (703) 482-1739, www.cia.gov; *The World Factbook.*

Euromonitor International, Inc., 224 S. Michigan Avenue, Suite 1500, Chicago, IL 60604, (312) 922-1115, Fax: (312) 922-1157, www.euromonitor.com; *International Marketing Data and Statistics 2008* and *World Marketing Data and Statistics.*

International Labour Office, I.L.O. Publications, 4 route des Morillons, CH-1211 Geneva 22, Switzerland, (Telephone in U.S. (202) 653-7652), (Fax in U.S. (202) 653-7687), www.ilo.org; *Yearbook of Labour Statistics 2006.*

M.E. Sharpe, 80 Business Park Drive, Armonk, NY 10504, (800) 541-6563, Fax: (914) 273-2106, www.mesharpe.com; *The Illustrated Book of World Rankings.*

Palgrave Macmillan Ltd., Houndmills, Basingstoke, Hampshire, RG21 6XS, England, (Telephone in U.S. (888) 330-8477), (Fax in U.S. (800) 672-2054), www.palgrave.com; *The Statesman's Yearbook 2008.*

Taylor and Francis Group, An Informa Business, 2 Park Square, Milton Park, Abingdon, Oxford OX14 4RN, United Kingdom, (Dial from U.S. (212) 216-7800), (Fax from U.S. (212) 564-7854), www.tandf.co.uk; *The Europa World Year Book.*

United Nations Food and Agricultural Organization (FAO), Viale delle Terme di Caracalla, 00100 Rome, Italy, (Dial from U.S. (202) 653-2400), (Fax from U.S. (202) 653 5760), www.fao.org; *The State of Food and Agriculture (SOFA) 2006.*

The World Bank, 1818 H Street, NW, Washington, DC 20433, (202) 473-1000, Fax: (202) 477-6391, www.worldbank.org; *The World Bank Atlas 2003-2004.*

FRENCH GUIANA - LAND USE

Central Intelligence Agency, Office of Public Affairs, Washington, DC 20505, (703) 482-0623, Fax: (703) 482-1739, www.cia.gov; *The World Factbook.*

Euromonitor International, Inc., 224 S. Michigan Avenue, Suite 1500, Chicago, IL 60604, (312) 922-1115, Fax: (312) 922-1157, www.euromonitor.com; *International Marketing Data and Statistics 2008.*

United Nations Food and Agricultural Organization (FAO), Viale delle Terme di Caracalla, 00100 Rome, Italy, (Dial from U.S. (202) 653-2400), (Fax from U.S. (202) 653 5760), www.fao.org; *FAO Production Yearbook 2002.*

FRENCH GUIANA - LIBRARIES

M.E. Sharpe, 80 Business Park Drive, Armonk, NY 10504, (800) 541-6563, Fax: (914) 273-2106, www.mesharpe.com; *The Illustrated Book of World Rankings.*

FRENCH GUIANA - LIFE EXPECTANCY

Central Intelligence Agency, Office of Public Affairs, Washington, DC 20505, (703) 482-0623, Fax: (703) 482-1739, www.cia.gov; *The World Factbook.*

Euromonitor International, Inc., 224 S. Michigan Avenue, Suite 1500, Chicago, IL 60604, (312) 922-1115, Fax: (312) 922-1157, www.euromonitor.com; *The World Economic Factbook 2008.*

United Nations Statistics Division, New York, NY 10017, (800) 253-9646, Fax: (212) 963-4116, http://unstats.un.org; *World Statistics Pocketbook.*

The World Bank, 1818 H Street, NW, Washington, DC 20433, (202) 473-1000, Fax: (202) 477-6391, www.worldbank.org; *The World Bank Atlas 2003-2004.*

FRENCH GUIANA - LITERACY

Euromonitor International, Inc., 224 S. Michigan Avenue, Suite 1500, Chicago, IL 60604, (312) 922-1115, Fax: (312) 922-1157, www.euromonitor.com; *World Marketing Data and Statistics.*

FRENCH GUIANA - LIVESTOCK

M.E. Sharpe, 80 Business Park Drive, Armonk, NY 10504, (800) 541-6563, Fax: (914) 273-2106, www.mesharpe.com; *The Illustrated Book of World Rankings.*

Palgrave Macmillan Ltd., Houndmills, Basingstoke, Hampshire, RG21 6XS, England, (Telephone in U.S. (888) 330-8477), (Fax in U.S. (800) 672-2054), www.palgrave.com; *The Statesman's Yearbook 2008.*

Taylor and Francis Group, An Informa Business, 2 Park Square, Milton Park, Abingdon, Oxford OX14 4RN, United Kingdom, (Dial from U.S. (212) 216-7800), (Fax from U.S. (212) 564-7854), www.tandf.co.uk; *The Europa World Year Book.*

United Nations Conference on Trade and Development (UNCTAD), DC2-1120, United Nations, New York, NY 10017, (212) 963-0027, www.unctad.org; *UNCTAD Commodity Yearbook.*

United Nations Food and Agricultural Organization (FAO), Viale delle Terme di Caracalla, 00100 Rome, Italy, (Dial from U.S. (202) 653-2400), (Fax from U.S. (202) 653 5760), www.fao.org; *FAO Production Yearbook 2002* and *The State of Food and Agriculture (SOFA) 2006.*

United Nations Statistics Division, New York, NY 10017, (800) 253-9646, Fax: (212) 963-4116, http://unstats.un.org; *Statistical Yearbook.*

FRENCH GUIANA - MANUFACTURES

M.E. Sharpe, 80 Business Park Drive, Armonk, NY 10504, (800) 541-6563, Fax: (914) 273-2106, www.mesharpe.com; *The Illustrated Book of World Rankings.*

FRENCH GUIANA - MARRIAGE

M.E. Sharpe, 80 Business Park Drive, Armonk, NY 10504, (800) 541-6563, Fax: (914) 273-2106, www.mesharpe.com; *The Illustrated Book of World Rankings.*

United Nations Statistics Division, New York, NY 10017, (800) 253-9646, Fax: (212) 963-4116, http://unstats.un.org; *Demographic Yearbook* and *Statistical Yearbook.*

FRENCH GUIANA - MILK PRODUCTION

See FRENCH GUIANA - DAIRY PROCESSING

FRENCH GUIANA - MINERAL INDUSTRIES

M.E. Sharpe, 80 Business Park Drive, Armonk, NY 10504, (800) 541-6563, Fax: (914) 273-2106, www.mesharpe.com; *The Illustrated Book of World Rankings.*

Palgrave Macmillan Ltd., Houndmills, Basingstoke, Hampshire, RG21 6XS, England, (Telephone in U.S. (888) 330-8477), (Fax in U.S. (800) 672-2054), www.palgrave.com; *The Statesman's Yearbook 2008.*

Taylor and Francis Group, An Informa Business, 2 Park Square, Milton Park, Abingdon, Oxford OX14 4RN, United Kingdom, (Dial from U.S. (212) 216-7800), (Fax from U.S. (212) 564-7854), www.tandf.co.uk; *The Europa World Year Book.*

United Nations Conference on Trade and Development (UNCTAD), DC2-1120, United Nations, New York, NY 10017, (212) 963-0027, www.unctad.org; *UNCTAD Commodity Yearbook.*

FRENCH GUIANA - MONEY SUPPLY

Taylor and Francis Group, An Informa Business, 2 Park Square, Milton Park, Abingdon, Oxford OX14 4RN, United Kingdom, (Dial from U.S. (212) 216-7800), (Fax from U.S. (212) 564-7854), www.tandf.co.uk; *The Europa World Year Book.*

FRENCH GUIANA - MORTALITY

Central Intelligence Agency, Office of Public Affairs, Washington, DC 20505, (703) 482-0623, Fax: (703) 482-1739, www.cia.gov; *The World Factbook.*

Euromonitor International, Inc., 224 S. Michigan Avenue, Suite 1500, Chicago, IL 60604, (312) 922-1115, Fax: (312) 922-1157, www.euromonitor.com; *International Marketing Data and Statistics 2008* and *The World Economic Factbook 2008.*

Palgrave Macmillan Ltd., Houndmills, Basingstoke, Hampshire, RG21 6XS, England, (Telephone in U.S. (888) 330-8477), (Fax in U.S. (800) 672-2054), www.palgrave.com; *The Statesman's Yearbook 2008.*

Taylor and Francis Group, An Informa Business, 2 Park Square, Milton Park, Abingdon, Oxford OX14 4RN, United Kingdom, (Dial from U.S. (212) 216-7800), (Fax from U.S. (212) 564-7854), www.tandf.co.uk; *The Europa World Year Book.*

United Nations Statistics Division, New York, NY 10017, (800) 253-9646, Fax: (212) 963-4116, http://unstats.un.org; *Demographic Yearbook; Statistical Yearbook;* and *World Statistics Pocketbook.*

The World Bank, 1818 H Street, NW, Washington, DC 20433, (202) 473-1000, Fax: (202) 477-6391, www.worldbank.org; *The World Bank Atlas 2003-2004.*

World Health Organization (WHO), Avenue Appia 20, 1211 Geneve 27, Switzerland, (Telephone in U.S. (212) 331-9081), www.who.int; *The WHO Global Atlas of Infectious Diseases* and *World Health Report 2006.*

FRENCH GUIANA - MOTOR VEHICLES

Taylor and Francis Group, An Informa Business, 2 Park Square, Milton Park, Abingdon, Oxford OX14 4RN, United Kingdom, (Dial from U.S. (212) 216-7800), (Fax from U.S. (212) 564-7854), www.tandf.co.uk; *The Europa World Year Book.*

United Nations Statistics Division, New York, NY 10017, (800) 253-9646, Fax: (212) 963-4116, http://unstats.un.org; *Statistical Yearbook.*

FRENCH GUIANA - MUSEUMS

M.E. Sharpe, 80 Business Park Drive, Armonk, NY 10504, (800) 541-6563, Fax: (914) 273-2106, www.mesharpe.com; *The Illustrated Book of World Rankings.*

UNESCO Institute for Statistics, C.P. 6128 Succursale Centre-Ville, Montreal, Quebec, H3C 3J7 Canada, (Dial from U.S. (514) 343-6880), (Fax from U.S. (514) 343 6882), www.uis.unesco.org; *Statistical Tables.*

FRENCH GUIANA - NATURAL GAS PRODUCTION

See FRENCH GUIANA - MINERAL INDUSTRIES

FRENCH GUIANA - NUTRITION

United Nations Food and Agricultural Organization (FAO), Viale delle Terme di Caracalla, 00100 Rome, Italy, (Dial from U.S. (202) 653-2400), (Fax from U.S. (202) 653 5760), www.fao.org; *The State of Food and Agriculture (SOFA) 2006.*

FRENCH GUIANA - OLDER PEOPLE

M.E. Sharpe, 80 Business Park Drive, Armonk, NY 10504, (800) 541-6563, Fax: (914) 273-2106, www.mesharpe.com; *The Illustrated Book of World Rankings.*

FRENCH GUIANA - PEANUT PRODUCTION

See FRENCH GUIANA - CROPS

FRENCH GUIANA - PESTICIDES

United Nations Food and Agricultural Organization (FAO), Viale delle Terme di Caracalla, 00100 Rome, Italy, (Dial from U.S. (202) 653-2400), (Fax from U.S. (202) 653 5760), www.fao.org; *The State of Food and Agriculture (SOFA) 2006.*

FRENCH GUIANA - PETROLEUM INDUSTRY AND TRADE

M.E. Sharpe, 80 Business Park Drive, Armonk, NY 10504, (800) 541-6563, Fax: (914) 273-2106, www.mesharpe.com; *The Illustrated Book of World Rankings.*

PennWell Corporation, 1421 South Sheridan Road, Tulsa, OK 74112, (918) 835-3161, www.pennwell.com; *International Petroleum Encyclopedia 2007.*

United Nations Conference on Trade and Development (UNCTAD), DC2-1120, United Nations, New York, NY 10017, (212) 963-0027, www.unctad.org; *UNCTAD Commodity Yearbook.*

United Nations Food and Agricultural Organization (FAO), Viale delle Terme di Caracalla, 00100 Rome, Italy, (Dial from U.S. (202) 653-2400), (Fax from U.S. (202) 653 5760), www.fao.org; *The State of Food and Agriculture (SOFA) 2006.*

FRENCH GUIANA - POLITICAL SCIENCE

Central Intelligence Agency, Office of Public Affairs, Washington, DC 20505, (703) 482-0623, Fax: (703) 482-1739, www.cia.gov; *The World Factbook.*

Palgrave Macmillan Ltd., Houndmills, Basingstoke, Hampshire, RG21 6XS, England, (Telephone in U.S. (888) 330-8477), (Fax in U.S. (800) 672-2054), www.palgrave.com; *The Statesman's Yearbook 2008.*

Taylor and Francis Group, An Informa Business, 2 Park Square, Milton Park, Abingdon, Oxford OX14 4RN, United Kingdom, (Dial from U.S. (212) 216-7800), (Fax from U.S. (212) 564-7854), www.tandf.co.uk; *The Europa World Year Book.*

FRENCH GUIANA - POPULATION

Central Intelligence Agency, Office of Public Affairs, Washington, DC 20505, (703) 482-0623, Fax: (703) 482-1739, www.cia.gov; *The World Factbook.*

Euromonitor International, Inc., 224 S. Michigan Avenue, Suite 1500, Chicago, IL 60604, (312) 922-1115, Fax: (312) 922-1157, www.euromonitor.com; *International Marketing Data and Statistics 2008* and *The World Economic Factbook 2008.*

International Labour Office, I.L.O. Publications, 4 route des Morillons, CH-1211 Geneva 22, Switzerland, (Telephone in U.S. (202) 653-7652), (Fax in U.S. (202) 653-7687), www.ilo.org; *Yearbook of Labour Statistics 2006.*

M.E. Sharpe, 80 Business Park Drive, Armonk, NY 10504, (800) 541-6563, Fax: (914) 273-2106, www.mesharpe.com; *The Illustrated Book of World Rankings.*

Palgrave Macmillan Ltd., Houndmills, Basingstoke, Hampshire, RG21 6XS, England, (Telephone in U.S. (888) 330-8477), (Fax in U.S. (800) 672-2054), www.palgrave.com; *The Statesman's Yearbook 2008.*

Taylor and Francis Group, An Informa Business, 2 Park Square, Milton Park, Abingdon, Oxford OX14 4RN, United Kingdom, (Dial from U.S. (212) 216-7800), (Fax from U.S. (212) 564-7854), www.tandf.co.uk; *The Europa World Year Book.*

United Nations Food and Agricultural Organization (FAO), Viale delle Terme di Caracalla, 00100 Rome, Italy, (Dial from U.S. (202) 653-2400), (Fax from U.S. (202) 653 5760), www.fao.org; *FAO Production Yearbook 2002.*

United Nations Statistics Division, New York, NY 10017, (800) 253-9646, Fax: (212) 963-4116, http://unstats.un.org; *Demographic Yearbook; Statistical Yearbook;* and *World Statistics Pocketbook.*

The World Bank, 1818 H Street, NW, Washington, DC 20433, (202) 473-1000, Fax: (202) 477-6391, www.worldbank.org; *The World Bank Atlas 2003-2004.*

World Health Organization (WHO), Avenue Appia 20, 1211 Geneve 27, Switzerland, (Telephone in U.S. (212) 331-9081), www.who.int; *World Health Report 2006.*

FRENCH GUIANA - POPULATION DENSITY

Central Intelligence Agency, Office of Public Affairs, Washington, DC 20505, (703) 482-0623, Fax: (703) 482-1739, www.cia.gov; *The World Factbook.*

Euromonitor International, Inc., 224 S. Michigan Avenue, Suite 1500, Chicago, IL 60604, (312) 922-1115, Fax: (312) 922-1157, www.euromonitor.com; *The World Economic Factbook 2008.*

M.E. Sharpe, 80 Business Park Drive, Armonk, NY 10504, (800) 541-6563, Fax: (914) 273-2106, www.mesharpe.com; *The Illustrated Book of World Rankings.*

Palgrave Macmillan Ltd., Houndmills, Basingstoke, Hampshire, RG21 6XS, England, (Telephone in U.S. (888) 330-8477), (Fax in U.S. (800) 672-2054), www.palgrave.com; *The Statesman's Yearbook 2008.*

Taylor and Francis Group, An Informa Business, 2 Park Square, Milton Park, Abingdon, Oxford OX14 4RN, United Kingdom, (Dial from U.S. (212) 216-7800), (Fax from U.S. (212) 564-7854), www.tandf.co.uk; *The Europa World Year Book.*

United Nations Food and Agricultural Organization (FAO), Viale delle Terme di Caracalla, 00100 Rome, Italy, (Dial from U.S. (202) 653-2400), (Fax from U.S. (202) 653 5760), www.fao.org; *The State of Food and Agriculture (SOFA) 2006.*

United Nations Statistics Division, New York, NY 10017, (800) 253-9646, Fax: (212) 963-4116, http://unstats.un.org; *Statistical Yearbook.*

FRENCH GUIANA - POSTAL SERVICE

M.E. Sharpe, 80 Business Park Drive, Armonk, NY 10504, (800) 541-6563, Fax: (914) 273-2106, www.mesharpe.com; *The Illustrated Book of World Rankings.*

FRENCH GUIANA - POWER RESOURCES

Euromonitor International, Inc., 224 S. Michigan Avenue, Suite 1500, Chicago, IL 60604, (312) 922-1115, Fax: (312) 922-1157, www.euromonitor.com; *International Marketing Data and Statistics 2008; The World Economic Factbook 2008;* and *World Marketing Data and Statistics.*

M.E. Sharpe, 80 Business Park Drive, Armonk, NY 10504, (800) 541-6563, Fax: (914) 273-2106, www.mesharpe.com; *The Illustrated Book of World Rankings.*

Palgrave Macmillan Ltd., Houndmills, Basingstoke, Hampshire, RG21 6XS, England, (Telephone in U.S. (888) 330-8477), (Fax in U.S. (800) 672-2054), www.palgrave.com; *The Statesman's Yearbook 2008.*

Platts, 2 Penn Plaza, 25th Floor, New York, NY 10121-2298, (212) 904-3070, www.platts.com; *Energy Economist.*

United Nations Food and Agricultural Organization (FAO), Viale delle Terme di Caracalla, 00100 Rome, Italy, (Dial from U.S. (202) 653-2400), (Fax from U.S. (202) 653 5760), www.fao.org; *The State of Food and Agriculture (SOFA) 2006.*

United Nations Statistics Division, New York, NY 10017, (800) 253-9646, Fax: (212) 963-4116, http://unstats.un.org; *Energy Statistics Yearbook 2003; Statistical Yearbook;* and *World Statistics Pocketbook.*

The World Bank, 1818 H Street, NW, Washington, DC 20433, (202) 473-1000, Fax: (202) 477-6391, www.worldbank.org; *The World Bank Atlas 2003-2004.*

FRENCH GUIANA - PRICES

Euromonitor International, Inc., 224 S. Michigan Avenue, Suite 1500, Chicago, IL 60604, (312) 922-1115, Fax: (312) 922-1157, www.euromonitor.com; *World Marketing Data and Statistics.*

International Labour Office, I.L.O. Publications, 4 route des Morillons, CH-1211 Geneva 22, Switzerland, (Telephone in U.S. (202) 653-7652), (Fax in U.S. (202) 653-7687), www.ilo.org; *Yearbook of Labour Statistics 2006.*

M.E. Sharpe, 80 Business Park Drive, Armonk, NY 10504, (800) 541-6563, Fax: (914) 273-2106, www.mesharpe.com; *The Illustrated Book of World Rankings.*

United Nations Food and Agricultural Organization (FAO), Viale delle Terme di Caracalla, 00100 Rome, Italy, (Dial from U.S. (202) 653-2400), (Fax from U.S. (202) 653 5760), www.fao.org; *FAO Production Yearbook 2002* and *The State of Food and Agriculture (SOFA) 2006.*

FRENCH GUIANA - PUBLIC HEALTH

Euromonitor International, Inc., 224 S. Michigan Avenue, Suite 1500, Chicago, IL 60604, (312) 922-1115, Fax: (312) 922-1157, www.euromonitor.com; *World Marketing Data and Statistics.*

M.E. Sharpe, 80 Business Park Drive, Armonk, NY 10504, (800) 541-6563, Fax: (914) 273-2106, www.mesharpe.com; *The Illustrated Book of World Rankings.*

Palgrave Macmillan Ltd., Houndmills, Basingstoke, Hampshire, RG21 6XS, England, (Telephone in U.S. (888) 330-8477), (Fax in U.S. (800) 672-2054), www.palgrave.com; *The Statesman's Yearbook 2008.*

United Nations Statistics Division, New York, NY 10017, (800) 253-9646, Fax: (212) 963-4116, http://unstats.un.org; *Statistical Yearbook.*

World Health Organization (WHO), Avenue Appia 20, 1211 Geneve 27, Switzerland, (Telephone in U.S. (212) 331-9081), www.who.int; The WHO Global Atlas of Infectious Diseases and *World Health Report 2006.*

FRENCH GUIANA - RADIO BROADCASTING

Palgrave Macmillan Ltd., Houndmills, Basingstoke, Hampshire, RG21 6XS, England, (Telephone in U.S. (888) 330-8477), (Fax in U.S. (800) 672-2054), www.palgrave.com; *The Statesman's Yearbook 2008.*

FRENCH GUIANA - RELIGION

Central Intelligence Agency, Office of Public Affairs, Washington, DC 20505, (703) 482-0623, Fax: (703) 482-1739, www.cia.gov; *The World Factbook.*

M.E. Sharpe, 80 Business Park Drive, Armonk, NY 10504, (800) 541-6563, Fax: (914) 273-2106, www.mesharpe.com; *The Illustrated Book of World Rankings.*

Palgrave Macmillan Ltd., Houndmills, Basingstoke, Hampshire, RG21 6XS, England, (Telephone in U.S. (888) 330-8477), (Fax in U.S. (800) 672-2054), www.palgrave.com; *The Statesman's Yearbook 2008.*

FRENCH GUIANA - RENT CHARGES

International Labour Office, I.L.O. Publications, 4 route des Morillons, CH-1211 Geneva 22, Switzerland, (Telephone in U.S. (202) 653-7652), (Fax in U.S. (202) 653-7687), www.ilo.org; *Yearbook of Labour Statistics 2006.*

FRENCH GUIANA - RETAIL TRADE

Euromonitor International, Inc., 224 S. Michigan Avenue, Suite 1500, Chicago, IL 60604, (312) 922-1115, Fax: (312) 922-1157, www.euromonitor.com; *World Marketing Data and Statistics.*

FRENCH GUIANA - RICE PRODUCTION

See FRENCH GUIANA - CROPS

FRENCH GUIANA - ROADS

Central Intelligence Agency, Office of Public Affairs, Washington, DC 20505, (703) 482-0623, Fax: (703) 482-1739, www.cia.gov; *The World Factbook.*

Palgrave Macmillan Ltd., Houndmills, Basingstoke, Hampshire, RG21 6XS, England, (Telephone in U.S. (888) 330-8477), (Fax in U.S. (800) 672-2054), www.palgrave.com; *The Statesman's Yearbook 2008.*

FRENCH GUIANA - RUBBER INDUSTRY AND TRADE

International Rubber Study Group (IRSG), 1st Floor, Heron House, 109/115 Wembley Hill Road, Wembley, Middlesex HA9 8DA, United Kingdom, www.rubberstudy.com; *Rubber Statistical Bulletin; Summary of World Rubber Statistics 2005; World Rubber Statistics Handbook (Volume 6, 1975-2001);* and *World Rubber Statistics Historic Handbook.*

M.E. Sharpe, 80 Business Park Drive, Armonk, NY 10504, (800) 541-6563, Fax: (914) 273-2106, www.mesharpe.com; *The Illustrated Book of World Rankings.*

FRENCH GUIANA - SHEEP

See FRENCH GUIANA - LIVESTOCK

FRENCH GUIANA - SHIPPING

Palgrave Macmillan Ltd., Houndmills, Basingstoke, Hampshire, RG21 6XS, England, (Telephone in U.S. (888) 330-8477), (Fax in U.S. (800) 672-2054), www.palgrave.com; *The Statesman's Yearbook 2008.*

Taylor and Francis Group, An Informa Business, 2 Park Square, Milton Park, Abingdon, Oxford OX14 4RN, United Kingdom, (Dial from U.S. (212) 216-7800), (Fax from U.S. (212) 564-7854), www.tandf.co.uk; *The Europa World Year Book.*

United Nations Statistics Division, New York, NY 10017, (800) 253-9646, Fax: (212) 963-4116, http://unstats.un.org; *Statistical Yearbook.*

FRENCH GUIANA - SILVER PRODUCTION

See FRENCH GUIANA - MINERAL INDUSTRIES

FRENCH GUIANA - SOCIAL ECOLOGY

M.E. Sharpe, 80 Business Park Drive, Armonk, NY 10504, (800) 541-6563, Fax: (914) 273-2106, www.mesharpe.com; *The Illustrated Book of World Rankings.*

United Nations Statistics Division, New York, NY 10017, (800) 253-9646, Fax: (212) 963-4116, http://unstats.un.org; *World Statistics Pocketbook.*

FRENCH GUIANA - SOCIAL SECURITY

Palgrave Macmillan Ltd., Houndmills, Basingstoke, Hampshire, RG21 6XS, England, (Telephone in U.S. (888) 330-8477), (Fax in U.S. (800) 672-2054), www.palgrave.com; *The Statesman's Yearbook 2008.*

FRENCH GUIANA - STEEL PRODUCTION

See FRENCH GUIANA - MINERAL INDUSTRIES

FRENCH GUIANA - SUGAR PRODUCTION

See FRENCH GUIANA - CROPS

FRENCH GUIANA - TELEPHONE

International Telecommunication Union (ITU), Place des Nations, 1211 Geneva 20, Switzerland, www.itu.int; World Telecommunication Indicators Database.

Palgrave Macmillan Ltd., Houndmills, Basingstoke, Hampshire, RG21 6XS, England, (Telephone in U.S. (888) 330-8477), (Fax in U.S. (800) 672-2054), www.palgrave.com; *The Statesman's Yearbook 2008.*

United Nations Statistics Division, New York, NY 10017, (800) 253-9646, Fax: (212) 963-4116, http://unstats.un.org; *Statistical Yearbook* and *World Statistics Pocketbook.*

FRENCH GUIANA - TELEVISION - RECEIVERS AND RECEPTION

United Nations Statistics Division, New York, NY 10017, (800) 253-9646, Fax: (212) 963-4116, http://unstats.un.org; *Statistical Yearbook.*

FRENCH GUIANA - TEXTILE INDUSTRY

United Nations Conference on Trade and Development (UNCTAD), DC2-1120, United Nations, New York, NY 10017, (212) 963-0027, www.unctad.org; *UNCTAD Commodity Yearbook.*

FRENCH GUIANA - TOBACCO INDUSTRY

Foreign Agricultural Service (FAS), U.S. Department of Agriculture (USDA), 1400 Independence Avenue, SW, Washington, DC 20250, (202) 720-3935, www.fas.usda.gov; *Tobacco: World Markets and Trade.*

M.E. Sharpe, 80 Business Park Drive, Armonk, NY 10504, (800) 541-6563, Fax: (914) 273-2106, www.mesharpe.com; *The Illustrated Book of World Rankings.*

FRENCH GUIANA - TOURISM

Euromonitor International, Inc., 224 S. Michigan Avenue, Suite 1500, Chicago, IL 60604, (312) 922-1115, Fax: (312) 922-1157, www.euromonitor.com; *The World Economic Factbook 2008* and *World Marketing Data and Statistics.*

M.E. Sharpe, 80 Business Park Drive, Armonk, NY 10504, (800) 541-6563, Fax: (914) 273-2106, www.mesharpe.com; *The Illustrated Book of World Rankings.*

Palgrave Macmillan Ltd., Houndmills, Basingstoke, Hampshire, RG21 6XS, England, (Telephone in U.S. (888) 330-8477), (Fax in U.S. (800) 672-2054), www.palgrave.com; *The Statesman's Yearbook 2008.*

FRENCH GUIANA - TRADE

See FRENCH GUIANA - INTERNATIONAL TRADE

FRENCH GUIANA - TRANSPORTATION

Central Intelligence Agency, Office of Public Affairs, Washington, DC 20505, (703) 482-0623, Fax: (703) 482-1739, www.cia.gov; *The World Factbook.*

Euromonitor International, Inc., 224 S. Michigan Avenue, Suite 1500, Chicago, IL 60604, (312) 922-1115, Fax: (312) 922-1157, www.euromonitor.com; *International Marketing Data and Statistics 2008* and *World Marketing Data and Statistics.*

M.E. Sharpe, 80 Business Park Drive, Armonk, NY 10504, (800) 541-6563, Fax: (914) 273-2106, www.mesharpe.com; *The Illustrated Book of World Rankings.*

Palgrave Macmillan Ltd., Houndmills, Basingstoke, Hampshire, RG21 6XS, England, (Telephone in U.S. (888) 330-8477), (Fax in U.S. (800) 672-2054), www.palgrave.com; *The Statesman's Yearbook 2008.*

Taylor and Francis Group, An Informa Business, 2 Park Square, Milton Park, Abingdon, Oxford OX14 4RN, United Kingdom, (Dial from U.S. (212) 216-7800), (Fax from U.S. (212) 564-7854), www.tandf.co.uk; *The Europa World Year Book.*

FRENCH GUIANA - UNEMPLOYMENT

Central Intelligence Agency, Office of Public Affairs, Washington, DC 20505, (703) 482-0623, Fax: (703) 482-1739, www.cia.gov; *The World Factbook.*

International Labour Office, I.L.O. Publications, 4 route des Morillons, CH-1211 Geneva 22, Switzerland, (Telephone in U.S. (202) 653-7652), (Fax in U.S. (202) 653-7687), www.ilo.org; *Yearbook of Labour Statistics 2006.*

Palgrave Macmillan Ltd., Houndmills, Basingstoke, Hampshire, RG21 6XS, England, (Telephone in U.S. (888) 330-8477), (Fax in U.S. (800) 672-2054), www.palgrave.com; *The Statesman's Yearbook 2008.*

United Nations Statistics Division, New York, NY 10017, (800) 253-9646, Fax: (212) 963-4116, http://unstats.un.org; *Statistical Yearbook.*

FRENCH GUIANA - VITAL STATISTICS

Palgrave Macmillan Ltd., Houndmills, Basingstoke, Hampshire, RG21 6XS, England, (Telephone in U.S. (888) 330-8477), (Fax in U.S. (800) 672-2054), www.palgrave.com; *The Statesman's Yearbook 2008.*

United Nations Statistics Division, New York, NY 10017, (800) 253-9646, Fax: (212) 963-4116, http://unstats.un.org; *Statistical Yearbook.*

World Health Organization (WHO), Avenue Appia 20, 1211 Geneve 27, Switzerland, (Telephone in U.S. (212) 331-9081), www.who.int; *World Health Report 2006.*

FRENCH GUIANA - WAGES

International Labour Office, I.L.O. Publications, 4 route des Morillons, CH-1211 Geneva 22, Switzerland, (Telephone in U.S. (202) 653-7652), (Fax in U.S. (202) 653-7687), www.ilo.org; *Yearbook of Labour Statistics 2006.*

FRENCH GUIANA - WHEAT PRODUCTION

See FRENCH GUIANA - CROPS

FRENCH GUIANA - WINE AND WINE MAKING

M.E. Sharpe, 80 Business Park Drive, Armonk, NY 10504, (800) 541-6563, Fax: (914) 273-2106, www.mesharpe.com; *The Illustrated Book of World Rankings.*

FRENCH GUIANA - WOOL INDUSTRY

M.E. Sharpe, 80 Business Park Drive, Armonk, NY 10504, (800) 541-6563, Fax: (914) 273-2106, www.mesharpe.com; *The Illustrated Book of World Rankings.*

FRENCH POLYNESIA - NATIONAL STATISTICAL OFFICE

Institut Statistique de Polynesie Francaise (ISPF), BP 395, 98713 Papeete, French Polynesia, www.ispf.pf; National Data Center.

FRENCH POLYNESIA - PRIMARY STATISTICS SOURCES

Institut Statistique de Polynesie Francaise (ISPF), BP 395, 98713 Papeete, French Polynesia, www.ispf.pf; *La Polynesie en Bref 2006.*

FRENCH POLYNESIA - AGRICULTURAL MACHINERY

United Nations Statistics Division, New York, NY 10017, (800) 253-9646, Fax: (212) 963-4116, http://unstats.un.org; *Statistical Yearbook.*

FRENCH POLYNESIA - AGRICULTURE

Euromonitor International, Inc., 224 S. Michigan Avenue, Suite 1500, Chicago, IL 60604, (312) 922-1115, Fax: (312) 922-1157, www.euromonitor.com; *World Marketing Data and Statistics.*

Palgrave Macmillan Ltd., Houndmills, Basingstoke, Hampshire, RG21 6XS, England, (Telephone in U.S. (888) 330-8477), (Fax in U.S. (800) 672-2054), www.palgrave.com; *The Statesman's Yearbook 2008.*

Taylor and Francis Group, An Informa Business, 2 Park Square, Milton Park, Abingdon, Oxford OX14 4RN, United Kingdom, (Dial from U.S. (212) 216-7800), (Fax from U.S. (212) 564-7854), www.tandf.co.uk; *The Europa World Year Book.*

United Nations Conference on Trade and Development (UNCTAD), DC2-1120, United Nations, New York, NY 10017, (212) 963-0027, www.unctad.org; *UNCTAD Commodity Yearbook.*

United Nations Food and Agricultural Organization (FAO), Viale delle Terme di Caracalla, 00100 Rome, Italy, (Dial from U.S. (202) 653-2400), (Fax from U.S. (202) 653 5760), www.fao.org; AQUASTAT; *FAO Production Yearbook 2002; FAO Trade Yearbook;* and *The State of Food and Agriculture (SOFA) 2006.*

United Nations Statistics Division, New York, NY 10017, (800) 253-9646, Fax: (212) 963-4116, http://unstats.un.org; *Statistical Yearbook.*

The World Bank, 1818 H Street, NW, Washington, DC 20433, (202) 473-1000, Fax: (202) 477-6391, www.worldbank.org; *French Polynesia.*

FRENCH POLYNESIA - AIRLINES

Palgrave Macmillan Ltd., Houndmills, Basingstoke, Hampshire, RG21 6XS, England, (Telephone in U.S. (888) 330-8477), (Fax in U.S. (800) 672-2054), www.palgrave.com; *The Statesman's Yearbook 2008.*

Taylor and Francis Group, An Informa Business, 2 Park Square, Milton Park, Abingdon, Oxford OX14 4RN, United Kingdom, (Dial from U.S. (212) 216-7800), (Fax from U.S. (212) 564-7854), www.tandf.co.uk; *The Europa World Year Book.*

FRENCH POLYNESIA - AIRPORTS

Central Intelligence Agency, Office of Public Affairs, Washington, DC 20505, (703) 482-0623, Fax: (703) 482-1739, www.cia.gov; *The World Factbook.*

FRENCH POLYNESIA - ARMED FORCES

Central Intelligence Agency, Office of Public Affairs, Washington, DC 20505, (703) 482-0623, Fax: (703) 482-1739, www.cia.gov; *The World Factbook.*

Euromonitor International, Inc., 224 S. Michigan Avenue, Suite 1500, Chicago, IL 60604, (312) 922-1115, Fax: (312) 922-1157, www.euromonitor.com; *World Marketing Data and Statistics.*

FRENCH POLYNESIA - BANKS AND BANKING

Euromonitor International, Inc., 224 S. Michigan Avenue, Suite 1500, Chicago, IL 60604, (312) 922-1115, Fax: (312) 922-1157, www.euromonitor.com; *World Marketing Data and Statistics.*

Palgrave Macmillan Ltd., Houndmills, Basingstoke, Hampshire, RG21 6XS, England, (Telephone in U.S. (888) 330-8477), (Fax in U.S. (800) 672-2054), www.palgrave.com; *The Statesman's Yearbook 2008.*

FRENCH POLYNESIA - BEVERAGE INDUSTRY

United Nations Statistics Division, New York, NY 10017, (800) 253-9646, Fax: (212) 963-4116, http://unstats.un.org; *Statistical Yearbook.*

FRENCH POLYNESIA - BROADCASTING

Central Intelligence Agency, Office of Public Affairs, Washington, DC 20505, (703) 482-0623, Fax: (703) 482-1739, www.cia.gov; *The World Factbook.*

Euromonitor International, Inc., 224 S. Michigan Avenue, Suite 1500, Chicago, IL 60604, (312) 922-1115, Fax: (312) 922-1157, www.euromonitor.com; *World Marketing Data and Statistics.*

Palgrave Macmillan Ltd., Houndmills, Basingstoke, Hampshire, RG21 6XS, England, (Telephone in U.S. (888) 330-8477), (Fax in U.S. (800) 672-2054), www.palgrave.com; *The Statesman's Yearbook 2008.*

FRENCH POLYNESIA - BUDGET

Central Intelligence Agency, Office of Public Affairs, Washington, DC 20505, (703) 482-0623, Fax: (703) 482-1739, www.cia.gov; *The World Factbook.*

FRENCH POLYNESIA - CATTLE

See FRENCH POLYNESIA - LIVESTOCK

FRENCH POLYNESIA - CHILDBIRTH - STATISTICS

Central Intelligence Agency, Office of Public Affairs, Washington, DC 20505, (703) 482-0623, Fax: (703) 482-1739, www.cia.gov; *The World Factbook.*

Euromonitor International, Inc., 224 S. Michigan Avenue, Suite 1500, Chicago, IL 60604, (312) 922-1115, Fax: (312) 922-1157, www.euromonitor.com; *International Marketing Data and Statistics 2008* and *The World Economic Factbook 2008.*

Palgrave Macmillan Ltd., Houndmills, Basingstoke, Hampshire, RG21 6XS, England, (Telephone in U.S. (888) 330-8477), (Fax in U.S. (800) 672-2054), www.palgrave.com; *The Statesman's Yearbook 2008.*

Taylor and Francis Group, An Informa Business, 2 Park Square, Milton Park, Abingdon, Oxford OX14 4RN, United Kingdom, (Dial from U.S. (212) 216-7800), (Fax from U.S. (212) 564-7854), www.tandf.co.uk; *The Europa World Year Book.*

United Nations Statistics Division, New York, NY 10017, (800) 253-9646, Fax: (212) 963-4116, http://unstats.un.org; *Demographic Yearbook* and *Statistical Yearbook.*

FRENCH POLYNESIA - CLIMATE

Palgrave Macmillan Ltd., Houndmills, Basingstoke, Hampshire, RG21 6XS, England, (Telephone in U.S. (888) 330-8477), (Fax in U.S. (800) 672-2054), www.palgrave.com; *The Statesman's Yearbook 2008.*

FRENCH POLYNESIA - CLOTHING EXPORTS AND IMPORTS

See FRENCH POLYNESIA - TEXTILE INDUSTRY

FRENCH POLYNESIA - COMMERCE

Palgrave Macmillan Ltd., Houndmills, Basingstoke, Hampshire, RG21 6XS, England, (Telephone in U.S. (888) 330-8477), (Fax in U.S. (800) 672-2054), www.palgrave.com; *The Statesman's Yearbook 2008.*

FRENCH POLYNESIA - COMMODITY EXCHANGES

Commodity Research Bureau, 330 South Wells Street, Suite 612, Chicago, IL 60606-7110, (800) 621-5271, Fax: (312) 939-4135, www.crbtrader.com; *2006 CRB Commodity Yearbook and CD.*

International Monetary Fund (IMF), 700 Nineteenth Street, NW, Washington, DC 20431, (202) 623-7000, Fax: (202) 623-4661, www.imf.org; *IMF Primary Commodity Prices.*

United Nations Food and Agricultural Organization (FAO), Viale delle Terme di Caracalla, 00100 Rome, Italy, (Dial from U.S. (202) 653-2400), (Fax from U.S. (202) 653 5760), www.fao.org; *The State of Food and Agriculture (SOFA) 2006.*

FRENCH POLYNESIA - COMMUNICATION AND TRAFFIC

United Nations Statistics Division, New York, NY 10017, (800) 253-9646, Fax: (212) 963-4116, http://unstats.un.org; *Statistical Yearbook.*

FRENCH POLYNESIA - CONSTRUCTION INDUSTRY

United Nations Statistics Division, New York, NY 10017, (800) 253-9646, Fax: (212) 963-4116, http://unstats.un.org; *Statistical Yearbook.*

FRENCH POLYNESIA - CONSUMER PRICE INDEXES

Taylor and Francis Group, An Informa Business, 2 Park Square, Milton Park, Abingdon, Oxford OX14 4RN, United Kingdom, (Dial from U.S. (212) 216-7800), (Fax from U.S. (212) 564-7854), www.tandf.co.uk; *The Europa World Year Book.*

United Nations Statistics Division, New York, NY 10017, (800) 253-9646, Fax: (212) 963-4116, http://unstats.un.org; *Statistical Yearbook.*

The World Bank, 1818 H Street, NW, Washington, DC 20433, (202) 473-1000, Fax: (202) 477-6391, www.worldbank.org; *French Polynesia.*

FRENCH POLYNESIA - CONSUMPTION (ECONOMICS)

Secretariat of the Pacific Community (SPC), BP D5, 98848 Noumea Cedex, New Caledonia, www.spc.int/corp; *Selected Pacific Economies - a Statistical Summary (SPESS).*

FRENCH POLYNESIA - CORN INDUSTRY

See FRENCH POLYNESIA - CROPS

FRENCH POLYNESIA - COST AND STANDARD OF LIVING

Secretariat of the Pacific Community (SPC), BP D5, 98848 Noumea Cedex, New Caledonia, www.spc.int/corp; *Selected Pacific Economies - a Statistical Summary (SPESS).*

FRENCH POLYNESIA - CROPS

Palgrave Macmillan Ltd., Houndmills, Basingstoke, Hampshire, RG21 6XS, England, (Telephone in U.S. (888) 330-8477), (Fax in U.S. (800) 672-2054), www.palgrave.com; *The Statesman's Yearbook 2008.*

Taylor and Francis Group, An Informa Business, 2 Park Square, Milton Park, Abingdon, Oxford OX14 4RN, United Kingdom, (Dial from U.S. (212) 216-7800), (Fax from U.S. (212) 564-7854), www.tandf.co.uk; *The Europa World Year Book.*

United Nations Conference on Trade and Development (UNCTAD), DC2-1120, United Nations, New York, NY 10017, (212) 963-0027, www.unctad.org; *UNCTAD Commodity Yearbook.*

United Nations Food and Agricultural Organization (FAO), Viale delle Terme di Caracalla, 00100 Rome, Italy, (Dial from U.S. (202) 653-2400), (Fax from U.S. (202) 653 5760), www.fao.org; *FAO Production Yearbook 2002* and *The State of Food and Agriculture (SOFA) 2006.*

FRENCH POLYNESIA - CUSTOMS ADMINISTRATION

Palgrave Macmillan Ltd., Houndmills, Basingstoke, Hampshire, RG21 6XS, England, (Telephone in U.S. (888) 330-8477), (Fax in U.S. (800) 672-2054), www.palgrave.com; *The Statesman's Yearbook 2008.*

FRENCH POLYNESIA - DAIRY PROCESSING

Palgrave Macmillan Ltd., Houndmills, Basingstoke, Hampshire, RG21 6XS, England, (Telephone in U.S. (888) 330-8477), (Fax in U.S. (800) 672-2054), www.palgrave.com; *The Statesman's Yearbook 2008.*

Taylor and Francis Group, An Informa Business, 2 Park Square, Milton Park, Abingdon, Oxford OX14 4RN, United Kingdom, (Dial from U.S. (212) 216-7800), (Fax from U.S. (212) 564-7854), www.tandf.co.uk; *The Europa World Year Book.*

United Nations Food and Agricultural Organization (FAO), Viale delle Terme di Caracalla, 00100 Rome, Italy, (Dial from U.S. (202) 653-2400), (Fax from U.S. (202) 653 5760), www.fao.org; *FAO Production Yearbook 2002* and *The State of Food and Agriculture (SOFA) 2006.*

FRENCH POLYNESIA - DEATH RATES

See FRENCH POLYNESIA - MORTALITY

FRENCH POLYNESIA - DEBTS, EXTERNAL

The World Bank, 1818 H Street, NW, Washington, DC 20433, (202) 473-1000, Fax: (202) 477-6391, www.worldbank.org; *Global Development Finance 2007.*

Worldinformation.com, 2 Market Street, Saffron Walden, Essex CB10 1HZ, United Kingdom, www.worldinformation.com; The World of Information (www.worldinformation.com).

FRENCH POLYNESIA - DEMOGRAPHY

Euromonitor International, Inc., 224 S. Michigan Avenue, Suite 1500, Chicago, IL 60604, (312) 922-1115, Fax: (312) 922-1157, www.euromonitor.com; *International Marketing Data and Statistics 2008; The World Economic Factbook 2008;* and *World Marketing Data and Statistics.*

The World Bank, 1818 H Street, NW, Washington, DC 20433, (202) 473-1000, Fax: (202) 477-6391, www.worldbank.org; *French Polynesia.*

FRENCH POLYNESIA - DISPOSABLE INCOME

United Nations Statistics Division, New York, NY 10017, (800) 253-9646, Fax: (212) 963-4116, http://unstats.un.org; *National Accounts Statistics: Compendium of Income Distribution Statistics* and *Statistical Yearbook.*

FRENCH POLYNESIA - DIVORCE

United Nations Statistics Division, New York, NY 10017, (800) 253-9646, Fax: (212) 963-4116, http://unstats.un.org; *Demographic Yearbook* and *Statistical Yearbook.*

FRENCH POLYNESIA - ECONOMIC ASSISTANCE

United Nations Statistics Division, New York, NY 10017, (800) 253-9646, Fax: (212) 963-4116, http://unstats.un.org; *Statistical Yearbook.*

FRENCH POLYNESIA - ECONOMIC CONDITIONS

Center for International Business Education Research (CIBER), Columbia Business School and School of International and Public Affairs, Uris Hall, Room 212, 3022 Broadway, New York, NY 10027-6902, Mr. Joshua Safier, (212) 854-4750, Fax: (212) 222-9821, www.columbia.edu/cu/ciber/; Datastream International.

Central Intelligence Agency, Office of Public Affairs, Washington, DC 20505, (703) 482-0623, Fax: (703) 482-1739, www.cia.gov; *The World Factbook.*

DSI Data Service Information, Xantener Strasse 51a, D-47495 Rheinberg, Germany, www.dsidata.com; *Campus Solution.*

Dun and Bradstreet (DB) Corporation, 103 JFK Parkway, Short Hills, NJ 07078, (973) 921-5500, www.dnb.com; *Country Report.*

Euromonitor International, Inc., 224 S. Michigan Avenue, Suite 1500, Chicago, IL 60604, (312) 922-1115, Fax: (312) 922-1157, www.euromonitor.com; *The World Economic Factbook 2008* and *World Marketing Data and Statistics.*

International Monetary Fund (IMF), 700 Nineteenth Street, NW, Washington, DC 20431, (202) 623-7000, Fax: (202) 623-4661, www.imf.org; *World Economic Outlook Reports.*

Palgrave Macmillan Ltd., Houndmills, Basingstoke, Hampshire, RG21 6XS, England, (Telephone in U.S. (888) 330-8477), (Fax in U.S. (800) 672-2054), www.palgrave.com; *The Statesman's Yearbook 2008.*

Secretariat of the Pacific Community (SPC), BP D5, 98848 Noumea Cedex, New Caledonia, www.spc.int/corp; PRISM (Pacific Regional Information System).

Taylor and Francis Group, An Informa Business, 2 Park Square, Milton Park, Abingdon, Oxford OX14 4RN, United Kingdom, (Dial from U.S. (212) 216-7800), (Fax from U.S. (212) 564-7854), www.tandf.co.uk; *The Europa World Year Book.*

United Nations Statistics Division, New York, NY 10017, (800) 253-9646, Fax: (212) 963-4116, http://unstats.un.org; *World Statistics Pocketbook.*

The World Bank, 1818 H Street, NW, Washington, DC 20433, (202) 473-1000, Fax: (202) 477-6391, www.worldbank.org; *French Polynesia; Global Economic Monitor (GEM); Global Economic Prospects 2008;* and *The World Bank Atlas 2003-2004.*

FRENCH POLYNESIA - EDUCATION

Euromonitor International, Inc., 224 S. Michigan Avenue, Suite 1500, Chicago, IL 60604, (312) 922-1115, Fax: (312) 922-1157, www.euromonitor.com; *International Marketing Data and Statistics 2008* and *World Marketing Data and Statistics.*

Palgrave Macmillan Ltd., Houndmills, Basingstoke, Hampshire, RG21 6XS, England, (Telephone in U.S. (888) 330-8477), (Fax in U.S. (800) 672-2054), www.palgrave.com; *The Statesman's Yearbook 2008.*

Taylor and Francis Group, An Informa Business, 2 Park Square, Milton Park, Abingdon, Oxford OX14 4RN, United Kingdom, (Dial from U.S. (212) 216-7800), (Fax from U.S. (212) 564-7854), www.tandf.co.uk; *The Europa World Year Book.*

UNESCO Institute for Statistics, C.P. 6128 Succursale Centre-Ville, Montreal, Quebec, H3C 3J7 Canada, (Dial from U.S. (514) 343-6880), (Fax from U.S. (514) 343 6882), www.uis.unesco.org; *Statistical Tables.*

The World Bank, 1818 H Street, NW, Washington, DC 20433, (202) 473-1000, Fax: (202) 477-6391, www.worldbank.org; *French Polynesia.*

FRENCH POLYNESIA - ELECTRICITY

Palgrave Macmillan Ltd., Houndmills, Basingstoke, Hampshire, RG21 6XS, England, (Telephone in U.S. (888) 330-8477), (Fax in U.S. (800) 672-2054), www.palgrave.com; *The Statesman's Yearbook 2008.*

United Nations Statistics Division, New York, NY 10017, (800) 253-9646, Fax: (212) 963-4116, http://unstats.un.org; *Statistical Yearbook.*

FRENCH POLYNESIA - EMPLOYMENT

Euromonitor International, Inc., 224 S. Michigan Avenue, Suite 1500, Chicago, IL 60604, (312) 922-1115, Fax: (312) 922-1157, www.euromonitor.com; *International Marketing Data and Statistics 2008.*

The World Bank, 1818 H Street, NW, Washington, DC 20433, (202) 473-1000, Fax: (202) 477-6391, www.worldbank.org; *French Polynesia.*

FRENCH POLYNESIA - ENVIRONMENTAL CONDITIONS

DSI Data Service Information, Xantener Strasse 51a, D-47495 Rheinberg, Germany, www.dsidata.com; *Campus Solution* and *DSI's Global Environmental Database.*

United Nations Statistics Division, New York, NY 10017, (800) 253-9646, Fax: (212) 963-4116, http://unstats.un.org; *World Statistics Pocketbook.*

FRENCH POLYNESIA - EXPORTS

Central Intelligence Agency, Office of Public Affairs, Washington, DC 20505, (703) 482-0623, Fax: (703) 482-1739, www.cia.gov; *The World Factbook.*

Euromonitor International, Inc., 224 S. Michigan Avenue, Suite 1500, Chicago, IL 60604, (312) 922-1115, Fax: (312) 922-1157, www.euromonitor.com; *International Marketing Data and Statistics 2008* and *The World Economic Factbook 2008.*

International Monetary Fund (IMF), 700 Nineteenth Street, NW, Washington, DC 20431, (202) 623-7000, Fax: (202) 623-4661, www.imf.org; *Direction of Trade Statistics Yearbook 2007.*

Palgrave Macmillan Ltd., Houndmills, Basingstoke, Hampshire, RG21 6XS, England, (Telephone in U.S. (888) 330-8477), (Fax in U.S. (800) 672-2054), www.palgrave.com; *The Statesman's Yearbook 2008.*

Secretariat of the Pacific Community (SPC), BP D5, 98848 Noumea Cedex, New Caledonia, www.spc.int/corp; *Selected Pacific Economies - a Statistical Summary (SPESS).*

Taylor and Francis Group, An Informa Business, 2 Park Square, Milton Park, Abingdon, Oxford OX14 4RN, United Kingdom, (Dial from U.S. (212) 216-7800), (Fax from U.S. (212) 564-7854), www.tandf.co.uk; *The Europa World Year Book.*

United Nations Food and Agricultural Organization (FAO), Viale delle Terme di Caracalla, 00100 Rome, Italy, (Dial from U.S. (202) 653-2400), (Fax from U.S. (202) 653 5760), www.fao.org; *The State of Food and Agriculture (SOFA) 2006.*

Worldinformation.com, 2 Market Street, Saffron Walden, Essex CB10 1HZ, United Kingdom, www.worldinformation.com; The World of Information (www.worldinformation.com).

FRENCH POLYNESIA - FERTILITY, HUMAN

Central Intelligence Agency, Office of Public Affairs, Washington, DC 20505, (703) 482-0623, Fax: (703) 482-1739, www.cia.gov; *The World Factbook.*

The World Bank, 1818 H Street, NW, Washington, DC 20433, (202) 473-1000, Fax: (202) 477-6391, www.worldbank.org; *The World Bank Atlas 2003-2004.*

FRENCH POLYNESIA - FERTILIZER INDUSTRY

United Nations Food and Agricultural Organization (FAO), Viale delle Terme di Caracalla, 00100 Rome, Italy, (Dial from U.S. (202) 653-2400), (Fax from U.S. (202) 653 5760), www.fao.org; *The State of Food and Agriculture (SOFA) 2006.*

FRENCH POLYNESIA - FETAL MORTALITY

See FRENCH POLYNESIA - MORTALITY

FRENCH POLYNESIA - FINANCE

United Nations Statistics Division, New York, NY 10017, (800) 253-9646, Fax: (212) 963-4116, http://unstats.un.org; *National Accounts Statistics: Analysis of Main Aggregates.*

The World Bank, 1818 H Street, NW, Washington, DC 20433, (202) 473-1000, Fax: (202) 477-6391, www.worldbank.org; *French Polynesia.*

FRENCH POLYNESIA - FINANCE, PUBLIC

Bernan Essential Government Publications, 4611-F Assembly Drive, Lanham MD, 20706-4391, (301) 459-2255, Fax: (800) 865-3450, www.bernan.com; *National Accounts Statistics.*

International Monetary Fund (IMF), 700 Nineteenth Street, NW, Washington, DC 20431, (202) 623-7000, Fax: (202) 623-4661, www.imf.org; *International Financial Statistics* and *International Financial Statistics Online Service.*

Palgrave Macmillan Ltd., Houndmills, Basingstoke, Hampshire, RG21 6XS, England, (Telephone in U.S. (888) 330-8477), (Fax in U.S. (800) 672-2054), www.palgrave.com; *The Statesman's Yearbook 2008.*

Taylor and Francis Group, An Informa Business, 2 Park Square, Milton Park, Abingdon, Oxford OX14 4RN, United Kingdom, (Dial from U.S. (212) 216-7800), (Fax from U.S. (212) 564-7854), www.tandf.co.uk; *The Europa World Year Book.*

The World Bank, 1818 H Street, NW, Washington, DC 20433, (202) 473-1000, Fax: (202) 477-6391, www.worldbank.org; *French Polynesia.*

FRENCH POLYNESIA - FISHERIES

Palgrave Macmillan Ltd., Houndmills, Basingstoke, Hampshire, RG21 6XS, England, (Telephone in U.S. (888) 330-8477), (Fax in U.S. (800) 672-2054), www.palgrave.com; *The Statesman's Yearbook 2008.*

Taylor and Francis Group, An Informa Business, 2 Park Square, Milton Park, Abingdon, Oxford OX14 4RN, United Kingdom, (Dial from U.S. (212) 216-7800), (Fax from U.S. (212) 564-7854), www.tandf.co.uk; *The Europa World Year Book.*

United Nations Conference on Trade and Development (UNCTAD), DC2-1120, United Nations, New York, NY 10017, (212) 963-0027, www.unctad.org; *UNCTAD Commodity Yearbook.*

United Nations Food and Agricultural Organization (FAO), Viale delle Terme di Caracalla, 00100 Rome, Italy, (Dial from U.S. (202) 653-2400), (Fax from U.S. (202) 653 5760), www.fao.org; *FAO Yearbook of Fishery Statistics;* Fishery Databases; FISHSTAT Database. Subjects covered include: Aquaculture production, capture production, fishery commodities; and *The State of Food and Agriculture (SOFA) 2006.*

United Nations Statistics Division, New York, NY 10017, (800) 253-9646, Fax: (212) 963-4116, http://unstats.un.org; *Statistical Yearbook.*

The World Bank, 1818 H Street, NW, Washington, DC 20433, (202) 473-1000, Fax: (202) 477-6391, www.worldbank.org; *French Polynesia.*

FRENCH POLYNESIA - FOOD

Secretariat of the Pacific Community (SPC), BP D5, 98848 Noumea Cedex, New Caledonia, www.spc.int/corp; *Selected Pacific Economies - a Statistical Summary (SPESS).*

United Nations Conference on Trade and Development (UNCTAD), DC2-1120, United Nations, New York, NY 10017, (212) 963-0027, www.unctad.org; *UNCTAD Commodity Yearbook.*

United Nations Food and Agricultural Organization (FAO), Viale delle Terme di Caracalla, 00100 Rome, Italy, (Dial from U.S. (202) 653-2400), (Fax from U.S. (202) 653 5760), www.fao.org; *FAO Production Yearbook 2002* and *The State of Food and Agriculture (SOFA) 2006.*

FRENCH POLYNESIA - FOREIGN EXCHANGE RATES

Central Intelligence Agency, Office of Public Affairs, Washington, DC 20505, (703) 482-0623, Fax: (703) 482-1739, www.cia.gov; *The World Factbook.*

Euromonitor International, Inc., 224 S. Michigan Avenue, Suite 1500, Chicago, IL 60604, (312) 922-1115, Fax: (312) 922-1157, www.euromonitor.com; *International Marketing Data and Statistics 2008* and *The World Economic Factbook 2008.*

Taylor and Francis Group, An Informa Business, 2 Park Square, Milton Park, Abingdon, Oxford OX14 4RN, United Kingdom, (Dial from U.S. (212) 216-7800), (Fax from U.S. (212) 564-7854), www.tandf.co.uk; *The Europa World Year Book.*

United Nations Statistics Division, New York, NY 10017, (800) 253-9646, Fax: (212) 963-4116, http://unstats.un.org; *World Statistics Pocketbook.*

Worldinformation.com, 2 Market Street, Saffron Walden, Essex CB10 1HZ, United Kingdom, www.worldinformation.com; The World of Information (www.worldinformation.com).

FRENCH POLYNESIA - FORESTS AND FORESTRY

UNESCO Institute for Statistics, C.P. 6128 Succursale Centre-Ville, Montreal, Quebec, H3C 3J7 Canada, (Dial from U.S. (514) 343-6880), (Fax from U.S. (514) 343 6882), www.uis.unesco.org; *Statistical Tables.*

United Nations Conference on Trade and Development (UNCTAD), DC2-1120, United Nations, New York, NY 10017, (212) 963-0027, www.unctad.org; *UNCTAD Commodity Yearbook.*

United Nations Food and Agricultural Organization (FAO), Viale delle Terme di Caracalla, 00100 Rome, Italy, (Dial from U.S. (202) 653-2400), (Fax from U.S. (202) 653 5760), www.fao.org; *FAO Yearbook of Forest Products* and *The State of Food and Agriculture (SOFA) 2006.*

United Nations Statistics Division, New York, NY 10017, (800) 253-9646, Fax: (212) 963-4116, http://unstats.un.org; *Statistical Yearbook.*

The World Bank, 1818 H Street, NW, Washington, DC 20433, (202) 473-1000, Fax: (202) 477-6391, www.worldbank.org; *French Polynesia.*

FRENCH POLYNESIA - GROSS DOMESTIC PRODUCT

Euromonitor International, Inc., 224 S. Michigan Avenue, Suite 1500, Chicago, IL 60604, (312) 922-1115, Fax: (312) 922-1157, www.euromonitor.com; *International Marketing Data and Statistics 2008* and *The World Economic Factbook 2008.*

Taylor and Francis Group, An Informa Business, 2 Park Square, Milton Park, Abingdon, Oxford OX14 4RN, United Kingdom, (Dial from U.S. (212) 216-7800), (Fax from U.S. (212) 564-7854), www.tandf.co.uk; *The Europa World Year Book.*

United Nations Statistics Division, New York, NY 10017, (800) 253-9646, Fax: (212) 963-4116, http://unstats.un.org; *National Accounts Statistics: Compendium of Income Distribution Statistics* and *Statistical Yearbook.*

FRENCH POLYNESIA - GROSS NATIONAL PRODUCT

The World Bank, 1818 H Street, NW, Washington, DC 20433, (202) 473-1000, Fax: (202) 477-6391, www.worldbank.org; *The World Bank Atlas 2003-2004.*

Worldinformation.com, 2 Market Street, Saffron Walden, Essex CB10 1HZ, United Kingdom, www.

worldinformation.com; The World of Information (www.worldinformation.com).

FRENCH POLYNESIA - HIDES AND SKINS INDUSTRY

United Nations Food and Agricultural Organization (FAO), Viale delle Terme di Caracalla, 00100 Rome, Italy, (Dial from U.S. (202) 653-2400), (Fax from U.S. (202) 653 5760), www.fao.org; *FAO Production Yearbook 2002.*

FRENCH POLYNESIA - HOUSING

Euromonitor International, Inc., 224 S. Michigan Avenue, Suite 1500, Chicago, IL 60604, (312) 922-1115, Fax: (312) 922-1157, www.euromonitor.com; *World Marketing Data and Statistics.*

Secretariat of the Pacific Community (SPC), BP D5, 98848 Noumea Cedex, New Caledonia, www.spc.int/corp; *Selected Pacific Economies - a Statistical Summary (SPESS).*

FRENCH POLYNESIA - ILLITERATE PERSONS

Euromonitor International, Inc., 224 S. Michigan Avenue, Suite 1500, Chicago, IL 60604, (312) 922-1115, Fax: (312) 922-1157, www.euromonitor.com; *The World Economic Factbook 2008.*

UNESCO Institute for Statistics, C.P. 6128 Succursale Centre-Ville, Montreal, Quebec, H3C 3J7 Canada, (Dial from U.S. (514) 343-6880), (Fax from U.S. (514) 343 6882), www.uis.unesco.org; *Statistical Tables.*

FRENCH POLYNESIA - IMPORTS

Central Intelligence Agency, Office of Public Affairs, Washington, DC 20505, (703) 482-0623, Fax: (703) 482-1739, www.cia.gov; *The World Factbook.*

Euromonitor International, Inc., 224 S. Michigan Avenue, Suite 1500, Chicago, IL 60604, (312) 922-1115, Fax: (312) 922-1157, www.euromonitor.com; *International Marketing Data and Statistics 2008* and *The World Economic Factbook 2008.*

International Monetary Fund (IMF), 700 Nineteenth Street, NW, Washington, DC 20431, (202) 623-7000, Fax: (202) 623-4661, www.imf.org; *Direction of Trade Statistics Yearbook 2007.*

Palgrave Macmillan Ltd., Houndmills, Basingstoke, Hampshire, RG21 6XS, England, (Telephone in U.S. (888) 330-8477), (Fax in U.S. (800) 672-2054), www.palgrave.com; *The Statesman's Yearbook 2008.*

Secretariat of the Pacific Community (SPC), BP D5, 98848 Noumea Cedex, New Caledonia, www.spc.int/corp; *Selected Pacific Economies - a Statistical Summary (SPESS).*

Taylor and Francis Group, An Informa Business, 2 Park Square, Milton Park, Abingdon, Oxford OX14 4RN, United Kingdom, (Dial from U.S. (212) 216-7800), (Fax from U.S. (212) 564-7854), www.tandf.co.uk; *The Europa World Year Book.*

United Nations Food and Agricultural Organization (FAO), Viale delle Terme di Caracalla, 00100 Rome, Italy, (Dial from U.S. (202) 653-2400), (Fax from U.S. (202) 653 5760), www.fao.org; *The State of Food and Agriculture (SOFA) 2006.*

Worldinformation.com, 2 Market Street, Saffron Walden, Essex CB10 1HZ, United Kingdom, www.worldinformation.com; The World of Information (www.worldinformation.com).

FRENCH POLYNESIA - INDUSTRIES

Central Intelligence Agency, Office of Public Affairs, Washington, DC 20505, (703) 482-0623, Fax: (703) 482-1739, www.cia.gov; *The World Factbook.*

Euromonitor International, Inc., 224 S. Michigan Avenue, Suite 1500, Chicago, IL 60604, (312) 922-1115, Fax: (312) 922-1157, www.euromonitor.com; *The World Economic Factbook 2008* and *World Marketing Data and Statistics.*

Palgrave Macmillan Ltd., Houndmills, Basingstoke, Hampshire, RG21 6XS, England, (Telephone in U.S. (888) 330-8477), (Fax in U.S. (800) 672-2054), www.palgrave.com; *The Statesman's Yearbook 2008.*

Taylor and Francis Group, An Informa Business, 2 Park Square, Milton Park, Abingdon, Oxford OX14 4RN, United Kingdom, (Dial from U.S. (212) 216-7800), (Fax from U.S. (212) 564-7854), www.tandf.co.uk; *The Europa World Year Book.*

United Nations Industrial Development Organization (UNIDO), 1 United Nations Plaza, New York, NY 10017, (212) 963 6890, Fax: (212) 963-7904, http://unido.org; Industrial Statistics Database 2008 (INDSTAT) and *The International Yearbook of Industrial Statistics 2008.*

The World Bank, 1818 H Street, NW, Washington, DC 20433, (202) 473-1000, Fax: (202) 477-6391, www.worldbank.org; *French Polynesia.*

FRENCH POLYNESIA - INFANT AND MATERNAL MORTALITY

See FRENCH POLYNESIA - MORTALITY

FRENCH POLYNESIA - INTERNATIONAL TRADE

Euromonitor International, Inc., 224 S. Michigan Avenue, Suite 1500, Chicago, IL 60604, (312) 922-1115, Fax: (312) 922-1157, www.euromonitor.com; *The World Economic Factbook 2008* and *World Marketing Data and Statistics.*

Palgrave Macmillan Ltd., Houndmills, Basingstoke, Hampshire, RG21 6XS, England, (Telephone in U.S. (888) 330-8477), (Fax in U.S. (800) 672-2054), www.palgrave.com; *The Statesman's Yearbook 2008.*

Secretariat of the Pacific Community (SPC), BP D5, 98848 Noumea Cedex, New Caledonia, www.spc.int/corp; *Selected Pacific Economies - a Statistical Summary (SPESS).*

Taylor and Francis Group, An Informa Business, 2 Park Square, Milton Park, Abingdon, Oxford OX14 4RN, United Kingdom, (Dial from U.S. (212) 216-7800), (Fax from U.S. (212) 564-7854), www.tandf.co.uk; *The Europa World Year Book.*

United Nations Conference on Trade and Development (UNCTAD), DC2-1120, United Nations, New York, NY 10017, (212) 963-0027, www.unctad.org; *UNCTAD Commodity Yearbook.*

United Nations Food and Agricultural Organization (FAO), Viale delle Terme di Caracalla, 00100 Rome, Italy, (Dial from U.S. (202) 653-2400), (Fax from U.S. (202) 653 5760), www.fao.org; *FAO Trade Yearbook* and *The State of Food and Agriculture (SOFA) 2006.*

United Nations Statistics Division, New York, NY 10017, (800) 253-9646, Fax: (212) 963-4116, http://unstats.un.org; *International Trade Statistics Yearbook* and *Statistical Yearbook.*

The World Bank, 1818 H Street, NW, Washington, DC 20433, (202) 473-1000, Fax: (202) 477-6391, www.worldbank.org; *French Polynesia.*

World Trade Organization (WTO), Centre William Rappard, Rue de Lausanne 154, CH-1211 Geneva 21, Switzerland, www.wto.org; *International Trade Statistics 2006.*

FRENCH POLYNESIA - INTERNET USERS

International Telecommunication Union (ITU), Place des Nations, 1211 Geneva 20, Switzerland, www.itu.int; *World Telecommunication/ICT Indicators Database on CD-ROM; World Telecommunication/ICT Indicators Database Online;* and *Yearbook of Statistics - Telecommunication Services (Chronological Time Series 1997-2006).*

The World Bank, 1818 H Street, NW, Washington, DC 20433, (202) 473-1000, Fax: (202) 477-6391, www.worldbank.org; *French Polynesia.*

FRENCH POLYNESIA - LABOR

Central Intelligence Agency, Office of Public Affairs, Washington, DC 20505, (703) 482-0623, Fax: (703) 482-1739, www.cia.gov; *The World Factbook.*

Euromonitor International, Inc., 224 S. Michigan Avenue, Suite 1500, Chicago, IL 60604, (312) 922-1115, Fax: (312) 922-1157, www.euromonitor.com; *International Marketing Data and Statistics 2008* and *World Marketing Data and Statistics.*

Palgrave Macmillan Ltd., Houndmills, Basingstoke, Hampshire, RG21 6XS, England, (Telephone in U.S. (888) 330-8477), (Fax in U.S. (800) 672-2054), www.palgrave.com; *The Statesman's Yearbook 2008.*

Taylor and Francis Group, An Informa Business, 2 Park Square, Milton Park, Abingdon, Oxford OX14 4RN, United Kingdom, (Dial from U.S. (212) 216-7800), (Fax from U.S. (212) 564-7854), www.tandf.co.uk; *The Europa World Year Book.*

United Nations Food and Agricultural Organization (FAO), Viale delle Terme di Caracalla, 00100 Rome, Italy, (Dial from U.S. (202) 653-2400), (Fax from U.S. (202) 653 5760), www.fao.org; *The State of Food and Agriculture (SOFA) 2006.*

The World Bank, 1818 H Street, NW, Washington, DC 20433, (202) 473-1000, Fax: (202) 477-6391, www.worldbank.org; *The World Bank Atlas 2003-2004.*

FRENCH POLYNESIA - LAND USE

Central Intelligence Agency, Office of Public Affairs, Washington, DC 20505, (703) 482-0623, Fax: (703) 482-1739, www.cia.gov; *The World Factbook.*

Euromonitor International, Inc., 224 S. Michigan Avenue, Suite 1500, Chicago, IL 60604, (312) 922-1115, Fax: (312) 922-1157, www.euromonitor.com; *International Marketing Data and Statistics 2008.*

United Nations Food and Agricultural Organization (FAO), Viale delle Terme di Caracalla, 00100 Rome, Italy, (Dial from U.S. (202) 653-2400), (Fax from U.S. (202) 653 5760), www.fao.org; *FAO Production Yearbook 2002.*

FRENCH POLYNESIA - LIBRARIES

UNESCO Institute for Statistics, C.P. 6128 Succursale Centre-Ville, Montreal, Quebec, H3C 3J7 Canada, (Dial from U.S. (514) 343-6880), (Fax from U.S. (514) 343 6882), www.uis.unesco.org; *Statistical Tables.*

FRENCH POLYNESIA - LIFE EXPECTANCY

Central Intelligence Agency, Office of Public Affairs, Washington, DC 20505, (703) 482-0623, Fax: (703) 482-1739, www.cia.gov; *The World Factbook.*

Euromonitor International, Inc., 224 S. Michigan Avenue, Suite 1500, Chicago, IL 60604, (312) 922-1115, Fax: (312) 922-1157, www.euromonitor.com; *The World Economic Factbook 2008.*

United Nations Statistics Division, New York, NY 10017, (800) 253-9646, Fax: (212) 963-4116, http://unstats.un.org; *World Statistics Pocketbook.*

The World Bank, 1818 H Street, NW, Washington, DC 20433, (202) 473-1000, Fax: (202) 477-6391, www.worldbank.org; *The World Bank Atlas 2003-2004.*

FRENCH POLYNESIA - LITERACY

Euromonitor International, Inc., 224 S. Michigan Avenue, Suite 1500, Chicago, IL 60604, (312) 922-1115, Fax: (312) 922-1157, www.euromonitor.com; *World Marketing Data and Statistics.*

FRENCH POLYNESIA - LIVESTOCK

Palgrave Macmillan Ltd., Houndmills, Basingstoke, Hampshire, RG21 6XS, England, (Telephone in U.S. (888) 330-8477), (Fax in U.S. (800) 672-2054), www.palgrave.com; *The Statesman's Yearbook 2008.*

Taylor and Francis Group, An Informa Business, 2 Park Square, Milton Park, Abingdon, Oxford OX14 4RN, United Kingdom, (Dial from U.S. (212) 216-7800), (Fax from U.S. (212) 564-7854), www.tandf.co.uk; *The Europa World Year Book.*

United Nations Conference on Trade and Development (UNCTAD), DC2-1120, United Nations, New York, NY 10017, (212) 963-0027, www.unctad.org; *UNCTAD Commodity Yearbook.*

United Nations Food and Agricultural Organization (FAO), Viale delle Terme di Caracalla, 00100 Rome, Italy, (Dial from U.S. (202) 653-2400), (Fax from U.S. (202) 653 5760), www.fao.org; *FAO Production Yearbook 2002* and *The State of Food and Agriculture (SOFA) 2006.*

United Nations Statistics Division, New York, NY 10017, (800) 253-9646, Fax: (212) 963-4116, http://unstats.un.org; *Statistical Yearbook.*

FRENCH POLYNESIA - MARRIAGE

Taylor and Francis Group, An Informa Business, 2 Park Square, Milton Park, Abingdon, Oxford OX14 4RN, United Kingdom, (Dial from U.S. (212) 216-7800), (Fax from U.S. (212) 564-7854), www.tandf.co.uk; *The Europa World Year Book.*

United Nations Statistics Division, New York, NY 10017, (800) 253-9646, Fax: (212) 963-4116, http://unstats.un.org; *Demographic Yearbook* and *Statistical Yearbook.*

FRENCH POLYNESIA - MINERAL INDUSTRIES

United Nations Conference on Trade and Development (UNCTAD), DC2-1120, United Nations, New York, NY 10017, (212) 963-0027, www.unctad.org; *UNCTAD Commodity Yearbook.*

FRENCH POLYNESIA - MONEY SUPPLY

Taylor and Francis Group, An Informa Business, 2 Park Square, Milton Park, Abingdon, Oxford OX14 4RN, United Kingdom, (Dial from U.S. (212) 216-7800), (Fax from U.S. (212) 564-7854), www.tandf.co.uk; *The Europa World Year Book.*

The World Bank, 1818 H Street, NW, Washington, DC 20433, (202) 473-1000, Fax: (202) 477-6391, www.worldbank.org; *French Polynesia.*

FRENCH POLYNESIA - MORTALITY

Central Intelligence Agency, Office of Public Affairs, Washington, DC 20505, (703) 482-0623, Fax: (703) 482-1739, www.cia.gov; *The World Factbook.*

Euromonitor International, Inc., 224 S. Michigan Avenue, Suite 1500, Chicago, IL 60604, (312) 922-1115, Fax: (312) 922-1157, www.euromonitor.com; *International Marketing Data and Statistics 2008* and *The World Economic Factbook 2008.*

Palgrave Macmillan Ltd., Houndmills, Basingstoke, Hampshire, RG21 6XS, England, (Telephone in U.S. (888) 330-8477), (Fax in U.S. (800) 672-2054), www.palgrave.com; *The Statesman's Yearbook 2008.*

Taylor and Francis Group, An Informa Business, 2 Park Square, Milton Park, Abingdon, Oxford OX14 4RN, United Kingdom, (Dial from U.S. (212) 216-7800), (Fax from U.S. (212) 564-7854), www.tandf.co.uk; *The Europa World Year Book.*

United Nations Statistics Division, New York, NY 10017, (800) 253-9646, Fax: (212) 963-4116, http://unstats.un.org; *Demographic Yearbook; Statistical Yearbook;* and *World Statistics Pocketbook.*

The World Bank, 1818 H Street, NW, Washington, DC 20433, (202) 473-1000, Fax: (202) 477-6391, www.worldbank.org; *The World Bank Atlas 2003-2004.*

World Health Organization (WHO), Avenue Appia 20, 1211 Geneve 27, Switzerland, (Telephone in U.S. (212) 331-9081), www.who.int; The WHO Global Atlas of Infectious Diseases.

FRENCH POLYNESIA - MOTION PICTURES

Palgrave Macmillan Ltd., Houndmills, Basingstoke, Hampshire, RG21 6XS, England, (Telephone in U.S. (888) 330-8477), (Fax in U.S. (800) 672-2054), www.palgrave.com; *The Statesman's Yearbook 2008.*

United Nations Statistics Division, New York, NY 10017, (800) 253-9646, Fax: (212) 963-4116, http://unstats.un.org; *Statistical Yearbook.*

FRENCH POLYNESIA - MOTOR VEHICLES

Taylor and Francis Group, An Informa Business, 2 Park Square, Milton Park, Abingdon, Oxford OX14 4RN, United Kingdom, (Dial from U.S. (212) 216-7800), (Fax from U.S. (212) 564-7854), www.tandf.co.uk; *The Europa World Year Book.*

United Nations Statistics Division, New York, NY 10017, (800) 253-9646, Fax: (212) 963-4116, http://unstats.un.org; *Statistical Yearbook.*

FRENCH POLYNESIA - MUSEUMS

UNESCO Institute for Statistics, C.P. 6128 Succursale Centre-Ville, Montreal, Quebec, H3C 3J7 Canada, (Dial from U.S. (514) 343-6880), (Fax from U.S. (514) 343 6882), www.uis.unesco.org; *Statistical Tables.*

FRENCH POLYNESIA - NUTRITION

United Nations Food and Agricultural Organization (FAO), Viale delle Terme di Caracalla, 00100 Rome, Italy, (Dial from U.S. (202) 653-2400), (Fax from U.S. (202) 653 5760), www.fao.org; *The State of Food and Agriculture (SOFA) 2006.*

FRENCH POLYNESIA - PERIODICALS

UNESCO Institute for Statistics, C.P. 6128 Succursale Centre-Ville, Montreal, Quebec, H3C 3J7 Canada, (Dial from U.S. (514) 343-6880), (Fax from U.S. (514) 343 6882), www.uis.unesco.org; *Statistical Tables.*

FRENCH POLYNESIA - PESTICIDES

United Nations Food and Agricultural Organization (FAO), Viale delle Terme di Caracalla, 00100 Rome, Italy, (Dial from U.S. (202) 653-2400), (Fax from U.S. (202) 653 5760), www.fao.org; *The State of Food and Agriculture (SOFA) 2006.*

FRENCH POLYNESIA - PETROLEUM INDUSTRY AND TRADE

PennWell Corporation, 1421 South Sheridan Road, Tulsa, OK 74112, (918) 835-3161, www.pennwell.com; *International Petroleum Encyclopedia 2007.*

United Nations Conference on Trade and Development (UNCTAD), DC2-1120, United Nations, New York, NY 10017, (212) 963-0027, www.unctad.org; *UNCTAD Commodity Yearbook.*

United Nations Food and Agricultural Organization (FAO), Viale delle Terme di Caracalla, 00100 Rome, Italy, (Dial from U.S. (202) 653-2400), (Fax from U.S. (202) 653 5760), www.fao.org; *The State of Food and Agriculture (SOFA) 2006.*

FRENCH POLYNESIA - POLITICAL SCIENCE

Central Intelligence Agency, Office of Public Affairs, Washington, DC 20505, (703) 482-0623, Fax: (703) 482-1739, www.cia.gov; *The World Factbook.*

Palgrave Macmillan Ltd., Houndmills, Basingstoke, Hampshire, RG21 6XS, England, (Telephone in U.S. (888) 330-8477), (Fax in U.S. (800) 672-2054), www.palgrave.com; *The Statesman's Yearbook 2008.*

Taylor and Francis Group, An Informa Business, 2 Park Square, Milton Park, Abingdon, Oxford OX14 4RN, United Kingdom, (Dial from U.S. (212) 216-7800), (Fax from U.S. (212) 564-7854), www.tandf.co.uk; *The Europa World Year Book.*

United Nations Statistics Division, New York, NY 10017, (800) 253-9646, Fax: (212) 963-4116, http://unstats.un.org; *National Accounts Statistics: Compendium of Income Distribution Statistics.*

FRENCH POLYNESIA - POPULATION

Central Intelligence Agency, Office of Public Affairs, Washington, DC 20505, (703) 482-0623, Fax: (703) 482-1739, www.cia.gov; *The World Factbook.*

Euromonitor International, Inc., 224 S. Michigan Avenue, Suite 1500, Chicago, IL 60604, (312) 922-1115, Fax: (312) 922-1157, www.euromonitor.com; *International Marketing Data and Statistics 2008* and *The World Economic Factbook 2008.*

Palgrave Macmillan Ltd., Houndmills, Basingstoke, Hampshire, RG21 6XS, England, (Telephone in U.S. (888) 330-8477), (Fax in U.S. (800) 672-2054), www.palgrave.com; *The Statesman's Yearbook 2008.*

Taylor and Francis Group, An Informa Business, 2 Park Square, Milton Park, Abingdon, Oxford OX14 4RN, United Kingdom, (Dial from U.S. (212) 216-7800), (Fax from U.S. (212) 564-7854), www.tandf.co.uk; *The Europa World Year Book.*

United Nations Food and Agricultural Organization (FAO), Viale delle Terme di Caracalla, 00100 Rome, Italy, (Dial from U.S. (202) 653-2400), (Fax from U.S. (202) 653 5760), www.fao.org; *FAO Production Yearbook 2002.*

United Nations Statistics Division, New York, NY 10017, (800) 253-9646, Fax: (212) 963-4116, http://unstats.un.org; *Demographic Yearbook; Statistical Yearbook;* and *World Statistics Pocketbook.*

The World Bank, 1818 H Street, NW, Washington, DC 20433, (202) 473-1000, Fax: (202) 477-6391, www.worldbank.org; *French Polynesia* and *The World Bank Atlas 2003-2004.*

World Health Organization (WHO), Avenue Appia 20, 1211 Geneve 27, Switzerland, (Telephone in U.S. (212) 331-9081), www.who.int; *World Health Report 2006.*

Worldinformation.com, 2 Market Street, Saffron Walden, Essex CB10 1HZ, United Kingdom, www.worldinformation.com; The World of Information (www.worldinformation.com).

FRENCH POLYNESIA - POPULATION DENSITY

Central Intelligence Agency, Office of Public Affairs, Washington, DC 20505, (703) 482-0623, Fax: (703) 482-1739, www.cia.gov; *The World Factbook.*

Euromonitor International, Inc., 224 S. Michigan Avenue, Suite 1500, Chicago, IL 60604, (312) 922-1115, Fax: (312) 922-1157, www.euromonitor.com; *The World Economic Factbook 2008.*

Palgrave Macmillan Ltd., Houndmills, Basingstoke, Hampshire, RG21 6XS, England, (Telephone in U.S. (888) 330-8477), (Fax in U.S. (800) 672-2054), www.palgrave.com; *The Statesman's Yearbook 2008.*

Taylor and Francis Group, An Informa Business, 2 Park Square, Milton Park, Abingdon, Oxford OX14 4RN, United Kingdom, (Dial from U.S. (212) 216-7800), (Fax from U.S. (212) 564-7854), www.tandf.co.uk; *The Europa World Year Book.*

United Nations Food and Agricultural Organization (FAO), Viale delle Terme di Caracalla, 00100 Rome, Italy, (Dial from U.S. (202) 653-2400), (Fax from U.S. (202) 653 5760), www.fao.org; *The State of Food and Agriculture (SOFA) 2006.*

United Nations Statistics Division, New York, NY 10017, (800) 253-9646, Fax: (212) 963-4116, http://unstats.un.org; *Statistical Yearbook.*

The World Bank, 1818 H Street, NW, Washington, DC 20433, (202) 473-1000, Fax: (202) 477-6391, www.worldbank.org; *French Polynesia* and *French Polynesia.*

FRENCH POLYNESIA - POSTAL SERVICE

United Nations Statistics Division, New York, NY 10017, (800) 253-9646, Fax: (212) 963-4116, http://unstats.un.org; *Statistical Yearbook.*

FRENCH POLYNESIA - POWER RESOURCES

Euromonitor International, Inc., 224 S. Michigan Avenue, Suite 1500, Chicago, IL 60604, (312) 922-1115, Fax: (312) 922-1157, www.euromonitor.com; *International Marketing Data and Statistics 2008; The World Economic Factbook 2008;* and *World Marketing Data and Statistics.*

Palgrave Macmillan Ltd., Houndmills, Basingstoke, Hampshire, RG21 6XS, England, (Telephone in U.S. (888) 330-8477), (Fax in U.S. (800) 672-2054), www.palgrave.com; *The Statesman's Yearbook 2008.*

Platts, 2 Penn Plaza, 25th Floor, New York, NY 10121-2298, (212) 904-3070, www.platts.com; *Energy Economist.*

United Nations Food and Agricultural Organization (FAO), Viale delle Terme di Caracalla, 00100 Rome, Italy, (Dial from U.S. (202) 653-2400), (Fax from U.S. (202) 653 5760), www.fao.org; *The State of Food and Agriculture (SOFA) 2006.*

United Nations Statistics Division, New York, NY 10017, (800) 253-9646, Fax: (212) 963-4116, http://unstats.un.org; *Energy Statistics Yearbook 2003; Statistical Yearbook;* and *World Statistics Pocketbook.*

The World Bank, 1818 H Street, NW, Washington, DC 20433, (202) 473-1000, Fax: (202) 477-6391, www.worldbank.org; *The World Bank Atlas 2003-2004.*

FRENCH POLYNESIA - PRICES

Euromonitor International, Inc., 224 S. Michigan Avenue, Suite 1500, Chicago, IL 60604, (312) 922-1115, Fax: (312) 922-1157, www.euromonitor.com; *World Marketing Data and Statistics.*

Secretariat of the Pacific Community (SPC), BP D5, 98848 Noumea Cedex, New Caledonia, www.spc.int/corp; *Selected Pacific Economies - a Statistical Summary (SPESS).*

United Nations Food and Agricultural Organization (FAO), Viale delle Terme di Caracalla, 00100 Rome, Italy, (Dial from U.S. (202) 653-2400), (Fax from U.S. (202) 653 5760), www.fao.org; *FAO Production Yearbook 2002* and *The State of Food and Agriculture (SOFA) 2006.*

The World Bank, 1818 H Street, NW, Washington, DC 20433, (202) 473-1000, Fax: (202) 477-6391, www.worldbank.org; *French Polynesia.*

FRENCH POLYNESIA - PROFESSIONS

United Nations Statistics Division, New York, NY 10017, (800) 253-9646, Fax: (212) 963-4116, http://unstats.un.org; *Statistical Yearbook.*

FRENCH POLYNESIA - PUBLIC HEALTH

Euromonitor International, Inc., 224 S. Michigan Avenue, Suite 1500, Chicago, IL 60604, (312) 922-1115, Fax: (312) 922-1157, www.euromonitor.com; *World Marketing Data and Statistics.*

Palgrave Macmillan Ltd., Houndmills, Basingstoke, Hampshire, RG21 6XS, England, (Telephone in U.S. (888) 330-8477), (Fax in U.S. (800) 672-2054), www.palgrave.com; *The Statesman's Yearbook 2008.*

Secretariat of the Pacific Community (SPC), BP D5, 98848 Noumea Cedex, New Caledonia, www.spc.int/corp; *Selected Pacific Economies - a Statistical Summary (SPESS).*

United Nations Statistics Division, New York, NY 10017, (800) 253-9646, Fax: (212) 963-4116, http://unstats.un.org; *Statistical Yearbook.*

World Health Organization (WHO), Avenue Appia 20, 1211 Geneve 27, Switzerland, (Telephone in U.S. (212) 331-9081), www.who.int; The WHO Global Atlas of Infectious Diseases and *World Health Report 2006.*

FRENCH POLYNESIA - PUBLISHERS AND PUBLISHING

UNESCO Institute for Statistics, C.P. 6128 Succursale Centre-Ville, Montreal, Quebec, H3C 3J7 Canada, (Dial from U.S. (514) 343-6880), (Fax from U.S. (514) 343 6882), www.uis.unesco.org; *Statistical Tables.*

FRENCH POLYNESIA - RADIO BROADCASTING

Palgrave Macmillan Ltd., Houndmills, Basingstoke, Hampshire, RG21 6XS, England, (Telephone in U.S. (888) 330-8477), (Fax in U.S. (800) 672-2054), www.palgrave.com; *The Statesman's Yearbook 2008.*

FRENCH POLYNESIA - RELIGION

Central Intelligence Agency, Office of Public Affairs, Washington, DC 20505, (703) 482-0623, Fax: (703) 482-1739, www.cia.gov; *The World Factbook.*

Palgrave Macmillan Ltd., Houndmills, Basingstoke, Hampshire, RG21 6XS, England, (Telephone in U.S. (888) 330-8477), (Fax in U.S. (800) 672-2054), www.palgrave.com; *The Statesman's Yearbook 2008.*

FRENCH POLYNESIA - RETAIL TRADE

Euromonitor International, Inc., 224 S. Michigan Avenue, Suite 1500, Chicago, IL 60604, (312) 922-1115, Fax: (312) 922-1157, www.euromonitor.com; *World Marketing Data and Statistics.*

FRENCH POLYNESIA - ROADS

Central Intelligence Agency, Office of Public Affairs, Washington, DC 20505, (703) 482-0623, Fax: (703) 482-1739, www.cia.gov; *The World Factbook.*

Palgrave Macmillan Ltd., Houndmills, Basingstoke, Hampshire, RG21 6XS, England, (Telephone in U.S. (888) 330-8477), (Fax in U.S. (800) 672-2054), www.palgrave.com; *The Statesman's Yearbook 2008.*

FRENCH POLYNESIA - SHEEP

See FRENCH POLYNESIA - LIVESTOCK

FRENCH POLYNESIA - SHIPPING

Palgrave Macmillan Ltd., Houndmills, Basingstoke, Hampshire, RG21 6XS, England, (Telephone in U.S. (888) 330-8477), (Fax in U.S. (800) 672-2054), www.palgrave.com; *The Statesman's Yearbook 2008.*

Taylor and Francis Group, An Informa Business, 2 Park Square, Milton Park, Abingdon, Oxford OX14 4RN, United Kingdom, (Dial from U.S. (212) 216-7800), (Fax from U.S. (212) 564-7854), www.tandf.co.uk; *The Europa World Year Book.*

United Nations Statistics Division, New York, NY 10017, (800) 253-9646, Fax: (212) 963-4116, http://unstats.un.org; *Statistical Yearbook.*

FRENCH POLYNESIA - SOCIAL ECOLOGY

United Nations Statistics Division, New York, NY 10017, (800) 253-9646, Fax: (212) 963-4116, http://unstats.un.org; *World Statistics Pocketbook.*

FRENCH POLYNESIA - SOCIAL SECURITY

United Nations Statistics Division, New York, NY 10017, (800) 253-9646, Fax: (212) 963-4116, http://unstats.un.org; *National Accounts Statistics: Compendium of Income Distribution Statistics.*

FRENCH POLYNESIA - TELEPHONE

International Telecommunication Union (ITU), Place des Nations, 1211 Geneva 20, Switzerland, www.itu.int; World Telecommunication Indicators Database.

Palgrave Macmillan Ltd., Houndmills, Basingstoke, Hampshire, RG21 6XS, England, (Telephone in U.S. (888) 330-8477), (Fax in U.S. (800) 672-2054), www.palgrave.com; *The Statesman's Yearbook 2008.*

Taylor and Francis Group, An Informa Business, 2 Park Square, Milton Park, Abingdon, Oxford OX14 4RN, United Kingdom, (Dial from U.S. (212) 216-7800), (Fax from U.S. (212) 564-7854), www.tandf.co.uk; *The Europa World Year Book.*

United Nations Statistics Division, New York, NY 10017, (800) 253-9646, Fax: (212) 963-4116, http://unstats.un.org; *Statistical Yearbook* and *World Statistics Pocketbook.*

FRENCH POLYNESIA - TEXTILE INDUSTRY

Secretariat of the Pacific Community (SPC), BP D5, 98848 Noumea Cedex, New Caledonia, www.spc.int/corp; *Selected Pacific Economies - a Statistical Summary (SPESS).*

United Nations Conference on Trade and Development (UNCTAD), DC2-1120, United Nations, New York, NY 10017, (212) 963-0027, www.unctad.org; *UNCTAD Commodity Yearbook.*

FRENCH POLYNESIA - THEATER

UNESCO Institute for Statistics, C.P. 6128 Succursale Centre-Ville, Montreal, Quebec, H3C 3J7 Canada, (Dial from U.S. (514) 343-6880), (Fax from U.S. (514) 343 6882), www.uis.unesco.org; *Statistical Tables.*

FRENCH POLYNESIA - TOBACCO INDUSTRY

Foreign Agricultural Service (FAS), U.S. Department of Agriculture (USDA), 1400 Independence Avenue, SW, Washington, DC 20250, (202) 720-3935, www.fas.usda.gov; *Tobacco: World Markets and Trade.*

Secretariat of the Pacific Community (SPC), BP D5, 98848 Noumea Cedex, New Caledonia, www.spc.int/corp; *Selected Pacific Economies - a Statistical Summary (SPESS).*

FRENCH POLYNESIA - TOURISM

Euromonitor International, Inc., 224 S. Michigan Avenue, Suite 1500, Chicago, IL 60604, (312) 922-1115, Fax: (312) 922-1157, www.euromonitor.com; *The World Economic Factbook 2008* and *World Marketing Data and Statistics.*

Palgrave Macmillan Ltd., Houndmills, Basingstoke, Hampshire, RG21 6XS, England, (Telephone in U.S. (888) 330-8477), (Fax in U.S. (800) 672-2054), www.palgrave.com; *The Statesman's Yearbook 2008.*

Taylor and Francis Group, An Informa Business, 2 Park Square, Milton Park, Abingdon, Oxford OX14 4RN, United Kingdom, (Dial from U.S. (212) 216-7800), (Fax from U.S. (212) 564-7854), www.tandf.co.uk; *The Europa World Year Book.*

United Nations Statistics Division, New York, NY 10017, (800) 253-9646, Fax: (212) 963-4116, http://unstats.un.org; *Statistical Yearbook.*

United Nations World Tourism Organization (UNWTO), Capitan Haya 42, 28020 Madrid, Spain, www.world-tourism.org; *Yearbook of Tourism Statistics.*

The World Bank, 1818 H Street, NW, Washington, DC 20433, (202) 473-1000, Fax: (202) 477-6391, www.worldbank.org; *French Polynesia.*

FRENCH POLYNESIA - TRADE

See FRENCH POLYNESIA - INTERNATIONAL TRADE

FRENCH POLYNESIA - TRANSPORTATION

Central Intelligence Agency, Office of Public Affairs, Washington, DC 20505, (703) 482-0623, Fax: (703) 482-1739, www.cia.gov; *The World Factbook.*

Euromonitor International, Inc., 224 S. Michigan Avenue, Suite 1500, Chicago, IL 60604, (312) 922-1115, Fax: (312) 922-1157, www.euromonitor.com; *International Marketing Data and Statistics 2008* and *World Marketing Data and Statistics.*

Palgrave Macmillan Ltd., Houndmills, Basingstoke, Hampshire, RG21 6XS, England, (Telephone in U.S. (888) 330-8477), (Fax in U.S. (800) 672-2054), www.palgrave.com; *The Statesman's Yearbook 2008.*

Secretariat of the Pacific Community (SPC), BP D5, 98848 Noumea Cedex, New Caledonia, www.spc.int/corp; *Selected Pacific Economies - a Statistical Summary (SPESS).*

Taylor and Francis Group, An Informa Business, 2 Park Square, Milton Park, Abingdon, Oxford OX14 4RN, United Kingdom, (Dial from U.S. (212) 216-7800), (Fax from U.S. (212) 564-7854), www.tandf.co.uk; *The Europa World Year Book.*

The World Bank, 1818 H Street, NW, Washington, DC 20433, (202) 473-1000, Fax: (202) 477-6391, www.worldbank.org; *French Polynesia* and *French Polynesia.*

FRENCH POLYNESIA - UNEMPLOYMENT

Central Intelligence Agency, Office of Public Affairs, Washington, DC 20505, (703) 482-0623, Fax: (703) 482-1739, www.cia.gov; *The World Factbook.*

FRENCH POLYNESIA - VITAL STATISTICS

Palgrave Macmillan Ltd., Houndmills, Basingstoke, Hampshire, RG21 6XS, England, (Telephone in U.S.

(888) 330-8477), (Fax in U.S. (800) 672-2054), www.palgrave.com; *The Statesman's Yearbook 2008.*

United Nations Statistics Division, New York, NY 10017, (800) 253-9646, Fax: (212) 963-4116, http://unstats.un.org; *Statistical Yearbook.*

World Health Organization (WHO), Avenue Appia 20, 1211 Geneve 27, Switzerland, (Telephone in U.S. (212) 331-9081), www.who.int; *World Health Report 2006.*

FRUITS - CONSUMER EXPENDITURES

U.S. Bureau of Labor Statistics (BLS), Postal Square Building, 2 Massachusetts Avenue, NE, Washington, DC 20212-0001, (202) 691-5200, Fax: (202) 691-6325, www.bls.gov; *Consumer Expenditures in 2006.*

FRUITS - CONSUMPTION

Center for Nutrition Policy and Promotion (CNPP), U.S. Department of Agriculture (USDA), 3101 Park Center Drive, 10th Floor, Alexandria, VA 22302-1594, (703) 305-7600, Fax: (703) 305-3300, www.usda.gov/cnpp; *The Healthy Eating Index.*

Economic Research Service (ERS), U.S. Department of Agriculture (USDA), 1800 M Street, NW, Washington, DC 20036-5831, (202) 694-5050, Fax: (202) 694-5689, www.ers.usda.gov; *Agricultural Outlook; Food CPI, Prices, and Expenditures;* and *Fruit and Tree Nuts Outlook.*

FRUITS - FARM MARKETINGS AND SALES

Economic Research Service (ERS), U.S. Department of Agriculture (USDA), 1800 M Street, NW, Washington, DC 20036-5831, (202) 694-5050, Fax: (202) 694-5689, www.ers.usda.gov; *Agricultural Income and Finance Outlook* and *Farm Income: Data Files.*

FRUITS - INTERNATIONAL TRADE

Economic Research Service (ERS), U.S. Department of Agriculture (USDA), 1800 M Street, NW, Washington, DC 20036-5831, (202) 694-5050, Fax: (202) 694-5689, www.ers.usda.gov; *Agricultural Statistics; Food CPI, Prices, and Expenditures; Foreign Agricultural Trade of the United States (FATUS);* and *Fruit and Tree Nuts Outlook.*

National Agricultural Statistics Service (NASS), U.S. Department of Agriculture (USDA), 1400 Independence Avenue, SW, Washington, DC 20250, (800) 727-9540, Fax: (202) 690-2090, www.nass.usda.gov; *2006 Agricultural Statistics.*

U.S. Census Bureau, Foreign Trade Division, 4700 Silver Hill Road, Washington DC 20233-0001, (301) 763-3030, www.census.gov/foreign-trade/www/; *U.S. International Trade in Goods and Services.*

FRUITS - IRON (DIETARY) SOURCE

Center for Nutrition Policy and Promotion (CNPP), U.S. Department of Agriculture (USDA), 3101 Park Center Drive, 10th Floor, Alexandria, VA 22302-1594, (703) 305-7600, Fax: (703) 305-3300, www.usda.gov/cnpp; *Nutrient Content of the U.S. Food Supply Summary Report 2005.*

FRUITS - PESTICIDES

Foreign Agricultural Service (FAS), U.S. Department of Agriculture (USDA), 1400 Independence Avenue, SW, Washington, DC 20250, (202) 720-3935, www.fas.usda.gov; Production, Supply and Distribution Online (PSD) Online.

FRUITS - PRICES

National Agricultural Statistics Service (NASS), U.S. Department of Agriculture (USDA), 1400 Independence Avenue, SW, Washington, DC 20250, (800) 727-9540, Fax: (202) 690-2090, www.nass.usda.gov; *Agricultural Prices.*

U.S. Bureau of Labor Statistics (BLS), Postal Square Building, 2 Massachusetts Avenue, NE, Washington, DC 20212-0001, (202) 691-5200, Fax: (202) 691-6325, www.bls.gov; *Consumer Price Index Detailed Report; Monthly Labor Review (MLR);* and unpublished data.

FRUITS - PRODUCTION

Economic Research Service (ERS), U.S. Department of Agriculture (USDA), 1800 M Street, NW, Washington, DC 20036-5831, (202) 694-5050, Fax: (202) 694-5689, www.ers.usda.gov; *Agricultural Outlook* and *Fruit and Tree Nuts Outlook.*

National Agricultural Statistics Service (NASS), U.S. Department of Agriculture (USDA), 1400 Independence Avenue, SW, Washington, DC 20250, (800) 727-9540, Fax: (202) 690-2090, www.nass.usda.gov; *Citrus Fruits; Cold Storage;* and *Noncitrus Fruits and Nuts: Final Estimates 1998-2003.*

FUEL

International Food Policy Research Institute (IFPRI), 2033 K Street, NW, Washington, D.C., 2006, (202) 862-5600, www.ifpri.org; *Food Prices, Biofuels, and Climate Change.*

PennWell Corporation, 1421 South Sheridan Road, Tulsa, OK 74112, (918) 835-3161, www.pennwell.com; *International Petroleum Encyclopedia 2007; Oil and Gas Financial Journal;* and *Oil and Gas Journal.*

FUEL - COMMERCIAL BUILDING USE

U.S. Department of Energy (DOE), Energy Information Administration (EIA), 1000 Independence Avenue, SW, Washington, DC 20585, (202) 586-8800, www.eia.doe.gov; *Commercial Buildings Energy Consumption Survey (CBECS).*

FUEL - CONSUMER EXPENDITURES

U.S. Bureau of Labor Statistics (BLS), Postal Square Building, 2 Massachusetts Avenue, NE, Washington, DC 20212-0001, (202) 691-5200, Fax: (202) 691-6325, www.bls.gov; *Consumer Expenditures in 2006.*

FUEL - CONSUMPTION - AIRPLANES

Federal Aviation Administration (FAA), 800 Independence Avenue, SW, Washington, DC 20591, (866) 835-5322, www.faa.gov; *FAA Aerospace Forecasts - Fiscal Years 2007-2020* and unpublished data.

United Nations Environment Programme (UNEP), PO Box 30552, Nairobi, Kenya, www.unep.org; *Climate Action.*

FUEL - CONSUMPTION - MOTOR VEHICLES

U.S. Department of Transportation (DOT), Federal Highway Administration (FHA), 1200 New Jersey Avenue, SE, Washington, DC 20590, (202) 366-0660, www.fhwa.dot.gov; *Highway Statistics 2006.*

United Nations Environment Programme (UNEP), PO Box 30552, Nairobi, Kenya, www.unep.org; *Climate Action.*

FUEL - CONSUMPTION - UTILITIES

Edison Electric Institute (EEI), 701 Pennsylvania Avenue, NW, Washington, DC 20004-2696, (202) 508-5000, www.eei.org; *Historical Statistics of the Electric Utility Industry through 1992.*

U.S. Department of Energy (DOE), Energy Information Administration (EIA), 1000 Independence Avenue, SW, Washington, DC 20585, (202) 586-8800, www.eia.doe.gov; *Annual Energy Review 2005; Electric Power Annual;* and unpublished data.

United Nations Environment Programme (UNEP), PO Box 30552, Nairobi, Kenya, www.unep.org; *Climate Action.*

FUEL - ELECTRICITY GENERATED BY

Edison Electric Institute (EEI), 701 Pennsylvania Avenue, NW, Washington, DC 20004-2696, (202) 508-5000, www.eei.org; *Historical Statistics of the Electric Utility Industry through 1992.*

U.S. Department of Energy (DOE), Energy Information Administration (EIA), 1000 Independence Avenue, SW, Washington, DC 20585, (202) 586-8800, www.eia.doe.gov; *Annual Energy Review 2005; Electric Power Annual; Electric Power Monthly (EPM); Inventory of Electric Utility Power Plants in the United States 2000;* and unpublished data.

FUEL - PRICES

U.S. Bureau of Labor Statistics (BLS), Postal Square Building, 2 Massachusetts Avenue, NE, Washington, DC 20212-0001, (202) 691-5200, Fax: (202) 691-6325, www.bls.gov; *Consumer Price Index Detailed Report; Monthly Labor Review (MLR); Producer Price Indexes (PPI); U.S. Import and Export Price Indexes;* and unpublished data.

U.S. Department of Energy (DOE), Energy Information Administration (EIA), 1000 Independence Avenue, SW, Washington, DC 20585, (202) 586-8800, www.eia.doe.gov; *Annual Energy Review 2005; Monthly Energy Review (MER); Petroleum Marketing Monthly;* and *State Energy Data 2003 Price and Expenditure Data.*

FUEL - PRICES - RETAIL

U.S. Department of Energy (DOE), Energy Information Administration (EIA), 1000 Independence Avenue, SW, Washington, DC 20585, (202) 586-8800, www.eia.doe.gov; *Monthly Energy Review (MER).*

FUEL - PRODUCTION AND VALUE

U.S. Department of Energy (DOE), Energy Information Administration (EIA), 1000 Independence Avenue, SW, Washington, DC 20585, (202) 586-8800, www.eia.doe.gov; *Annual Energy Review 2005* and *Monthly Energy Review (MER).*

World Resources Institute (WRI), 10 G Street, NE, Suite 800 Washington, DC 20002, (202) 729-7600, www.wri.org; *Thirst for Corn: What 2007 Plantings Could Mean for the Environment.*

FUEL - RESIDENTIAL USE

American Gas Association, 400 North Capitol Street, NW, Washington, DC 20001-1535, (202) 824-7000, www.aga.org; *Gas Facts.*

U.S. Department of Energy (DOE), Energy Information Administration (EIA), 1000 Independence Avenue, SW, Washington, DC 20585, (202) 586-8800, www.eia.doe.gov; *Renewable Energy Annual 2004.*

FUEL - WORLD PRODUCTION

U.S. Department of Energy (DOE), Energy Information Administration (EIA), 1000 Independence Avenue, SW, Washington, DC 20585, (202) 586-8800, www.eia.doe.gov; *Annual Energy Review 2005.*

FUNERAL SERVICES AND CREMATORIES

U.S. Census Bureau, 4700 Silver Hill Road, Washington DC 20233-0001, (301) 763-3030, www.census.gov; unpublished data.

U.S. Census Bureau, Company Statistics Division, 4700 Silver Hill Road, Washington DC 20233-0001, (301) 763-3030, www.census.gov/csd/; *County Business Patterns 2004* and *Current Business Reports.*

U.S. Census Bureau, Service Sector Statistics Division, 4700 Silver Hill Road, Washington DC 20233-0001, (301) 763-3030, www.census.gov/svsd/www/economic.html; *2004 Service Annual Survey.*

FURNITURE

Bureau of Economic Analysis (BEA), U.S. Department of Commerce (DOC), 1441 L Street NW, Washington, DC 20230, (202) 606-9900, www.bea.gov; *2007 Annual Revision of the National Income and Product Accounts (NIPA)* and *Survey of Current Business (SCB).*

The NPD Group, Port Washington, 900 West Shore Road, Port Washington, NY 11050, (866) 444-1411, www.npd.com; *Market Research for the Appliances, Home Improvement, Home Textiles, and Housewares Industries.*

U.S. Bureau of Labor Statistics (BLS), Postal Square Building, 2 Massachusetts Avenue, NE, Washington, DC 20212-0001, (202) 691-5200, Fax: (202) 691-6325, www.bls.gov; *Consumer Expenditures in 2006; Consumer Price Index Detailed Report;* and *Monthly Labor Review (MLR).*

U.S. Census Bureau, Foreign Trade Division, 4700 Silver Hill Road, Washington DC 20233-0001, (301) 763-3030, www.census.gov/foreign-trade/www/; *U.S. International Trade in Goods and Services.*

FURNITURE AND HOME FURNISHING STORES

The NPD Group, Port Washington, 900 West Shore Road, Port Washington, NY 11050, (866) 444-1411, www.npd.com; *Market Research for the Appliances, Home Improvement, Home Textiles, and Housewares Industries.*

Office of Trade and Industry Information (OTII), Manufacturing and Services, International Trade Administration, U.S. Department of Commerce, 1401 Constitution Ave, NW, Washington, DC 20230, (800) USA TRAD(E), http://trade.gov/index.asp; *TradeStats Express.*

U.S. Census Bureau, Center for Economic Studies, 4600 Silver Hill Road, Washington DC 20233, (301) 457-1235, www.ces.census.gov; *2002 Economic Census, Retail Trade* and *2002 Economic Census, Wholesale Trade.*

U.S. Census Bureau, Company Statistics Division, 4700 Silver Hill Road, Washington DC 20233-0001, (301) 763-3030, www.census.gov/csd/; *County Business Patterns 2004.*

FURNITURE AND HOME FURNISHING STORES - EARNINGS

Office of Trade and Industry Information (OTII), Manufacturing and Services, International Trade Administration, U.S. Department of Commerce, 1401 Constitution Ave, NW, Washington, DC 20230, (800) USA TRAD(E), http://trade.gov/index.asp; *TradeStats Express.*

U.S. Bureau of Labor Statistics (BLS), Postal Square Building, 2 Massachusetts Avenue, NE, Washington, DC 20212-0001, (202) 691-5200, Fax: (202) 691-6325, www.bls.gov; *Current Employment Statistics Survey (CES)* and *Employment and Earnings (EE).*

U.S. Census Bureau, Center for Economic Studies, 4600 Silver Hill Road, Washington DC 20233, (301) 457-1235, www.ces.census.gov; *2002 Economic Census, Retail Trade.*

U.S. Census Bureau, Company Statistics Division, 4700 Silver Hill Road, Washington DC 20233-0001, (301) 763-3030, www.census.gov/csd/; *County Business Patterns 2004.*

FURNITURE AND HOME FURNISHING STORES - ELECTRONIC COMMERCE

U.S. Census Bureau, 4700 Silver Hill Road, Washington DC 20233-0001, (301) 763-3030, www.census.gov; *2006 E-Commerce Multi-Sector Report* and *E-Stats - Measuring the Electronic Economy.*

FURNITURE AND HOME FURNISHING STORES - EMPLOYEES

U.S. Bureau of Labor Statistics (BLS), Postal Square Building, 2 Massachusetts Avenue, NE, Washington, DC 20212-0001, (202) 691-5200, Fax: (202) 691-6325, www.bls.gov; *Current Employment Statistics Survey (CES)* and *Employment and Earnings (EE).*

U.S. Census Bureau, Center for Economic Studies, 4600 Silver Hill Road, Washington DC 20233, (301) 457-1235, www.ces.census.gov; *2002 Economic Census, Retail Trade.*

U.S. Census Bureau, Company Statistics Division, 4700 Silver Hill Road, Washington DC 20233-0001, (301) 763-3030, www.census.gov/csd/; *County Business Patterns 2004.*

FURNITURE AND HOME FURNISHING STORES - INVENTORIES

U.S. Census Bureau, 4700 Silver Hill Road, Washington DC 20233-0001, (301) 763-3030, www.census.gov; unpublished data.

U.S. Census Bureau, Company Statistics Division, 4700 Silver Hill Road, Washington DC 20233-0001, (301) 763-3030, www.census.gov/csd/; *Current Business Reports.*

U.S. Census Bureau, Service Sector Statistics Division, 4700 Silver Hill Road, Washington DC 20233-0001, (301) 763-3030, www.census.gov/svsd/www/economic.html; *Annual Benchmark Report for Wholesale Trade.*

FURNITURE AND HOME FURNISHING STORES - NONEMPLOYERS

U.S. Census Bureau, 4700 Silver Hill Road, Washington DC 20233-0001, (301) 763-3030, www.census.gov; *2002 Economic Census, Nonemployer Statistics.*

FURNITURE AND HOME FURNISHING STORES - PRODUCTIVITY

U.S. Bureau of Labor Statistics (BLS), Postal Square Building, 2 Massachusetts Avenue, NE, Washington, DC 20212-0001, (202) 691-5200, Fax: (202) 691-6325, www.bls.gov; *Industry Productivity and Costs.*

FURNITURE AND HOME FURNISHING STORES - PURCHASES

Office of Trade and Industry Information (OTII), Manufacturing and Services, International Trade Administration, U.S. Department of Commerce, 1401 Constitution Ave, NW, Washington, DC 20230, (800) USA TRAD(E), http://trade.gov/index.asp; *TradeStats Express.*

U.S. Census Bureau, 4700 Silver Hill Road, Washington DC 20233-0001, (301) 763-3030, www.census.gov; unpublished data.

U.S. Census Bureau, Center for Economic Studies, 4600 Silver Hill Road, Washington DC 20233, (301) 457-1235, www.ces.census.gov; *2002 Economic Census, Retail Trade.*

U.S. Census Bureau, Company Statistics Division, 4700 Silver Hill Road, Washington DC 20233-0001, (301) 763-3030, www.census.gov/csd/; *Current Business Reports.*

FURNITURE AND HOME FURNISHING STORES - SALES

The NPD Group, Port Washington, 900 West Shore Road, Port Washington, NY 11050, (866) 444-1411, www.npd.com; *Market Research for the Appliances, Home Improvement, Home Textiles, and Housewares Industries.*

Office of Trade and Industry Information (OTII), Manufacturing and Services, International Trade Administration, U.S. Department of Commerce, 1401 Constitution Ave, NW, Washington, DC 20230, (800) USA TRAD(E), http://trade.gov/index.asp; *TradeStats Express.*

U.S. Census Bureau, 4700 Silver Hill Road, Washington DC 20233-0001, (301) 763-3030, www.census.gov; unpublished data.

U.S. Census Bureau, Center for Economic Studies, 4600 Silver Hill Road, Washington DC 20233, (301) 457-1235, www.ces.census.gov; *2002 Economic Census, Health Care and Social Assistance* and *2002 Economic Census, Retail Trade.*

FURNITURE AND RELATED PRODUCTS - MANUFACTURING - EARNINGS

The NPD Group, Port Washington, 900 West Shore Road, Port Washington, NY 11050, (866) 444-1411, www.npd.com; *Market Research for the Appliances, Home Improvement, Home Textiles, and Housewares Industries.*

U.S. Bureau of Labor Statistics (BLS), Postal Square Building, 2 Massachusetts Avenue, NE, Washington, DC 20212-0001, (202) 691-5200, Fax: (202) 691-6325, www.bls.gov; *Current Employment Statistics Survey (CES)* and *Employment and Earnings (EE).*

U.S. Census Bureau, Foreign Trade Division, 4700 Silver Hill Road, Washington DC 20233-0001, (301) 763-3030, www.census.gov/foreign-trade/www/; *U.S. International Trade in Goods and Services.*

U.S. Census Bureau, Manufacturing and Construction Division, 4600 Silver Hill Road, Washington DC 20233, (301) 763-4673, www.census.gov/mcd; *Annual Survey of Manufactures (ASM)* and *Census of Manufactures.*

FURNITURE AND RELATED PRODUCTS - MANUFACTURING - ELECTRONIC COMMERCE

U.S. Census Bureau, 4700 Silver Hill Road, Washington DC 20233-0001, (301) 763-3030, www.census.gov; *E-Stats - Measuring the Electronic Economy.*

FURNITURE AND RELATED PRODUCTS - MANUFACTURING - EMPLOYEES

U.S. Bureau of Labor Statistics (BLS), Postal Square Building, 2 Massachusetts Avenue, NE, Washington, DC 20212-0001, (202) 691-5200, Fax: (202) 691-6325, www.bls.gov; *Current Employment Statistics Survey (CES); Employment and Earnings (EE); Monthly Labor Review (MLR);* and unpublished data.

U.S. Census Bureau, Foreign Trade Division, 4700 Silver Hill Road, Washington DC 20233-0001, (301) 763-3030, www.census.gov/foreign-trade/www/; *U.S. International Trade in Goods and Services.*

U.S. Census Bureau, Manufacturing and Construction Division, 4600 Silver Hill Road, Washington DC 20233, (301) 763-4673, www.census.gov/mcd; *Annual Survey of Manufactures (ASM)* and *Census of Manufactures.*

FURNITURE AND RELATED PRODUCTS - MANUFACTURING - ENERGY CONSUMPTION

U.S. Department of Energy (DOE), Energy Information Administration (EIA), 1000 Independence Avenue, SW, Washington, DC 20585, (202) 586-8800, www.eia.doe.gov; *Manufacturing Energy Consumption Survey (MECS) 2002.*

FURNITURE AND RELATED PRODUCTS - MANUFACTURING - ESTABLISHMENTS

U.S. Census Bureau, Center for Economic Studies, 4600 Silver Hill Road, Washington DC 20233, (301) 457-1235, www.ces.census.gov; *2002 Economic Census, Transportation and Warehousing.*

FURNITURE AND RELATED PRODUCTS - MANUFACTURING - GROSS DOMESTIC PRODUCT

Bureau of Economic Analysis (BEA), U.S. Department of Commerce (DOC), 1441 L Street NW, Washington, DC 20230, (202) 606-9900, www.bea.gov; *Survey of Current Business (SCB).*

FURNITURE AND RELATED PRODUCTS - MANUFACTURING - INTERNATIONAL TRADE

The NPD Group, Port Washington, 900 West Shore Road, Port Washington, NY 11050, (866) 444-1411, www.npd.com; *Market Research for the Appliances, Home Improvement, Home Textiles, and Housewares Industries.*

U.S. Census Bureau, Foreign Trade Division, 4700 Silver Hill Road, Washington DC 20233-0001, (301) 763-3030, www.census.gov/foreign-trade/www/; *U.S. International Trade in Goods and Services.*

FURNITURE AND RELATED PRODUCTS - MANUFACTURING - MERGERS AND ACQUISITIONS

Thomson Financial, 195 Broadway, New York, NY 10007, (646) 822-2000, www.thomson.com; Thomson Research.

FURNITURE AND RELATED PRODUCTS - MANUFACTURING - OCCUPATIONAL SAFETY

U.S. Bureau of Labor Statistics (BLS), Postal Square Building, 2 Massachusetts Avenue, NE, Washington, DC 20212-0001, (202) 691-5200, Fax: (202) 691-6325, www.bls.gov; *Injuries, Illnesses, and Fatalities (IIF).*

FURNITURE AND RELATED PRODUCTS - MANUFACTURING - PRODUCTIVITY

Board of Governors of the Federal Reserve System, Constitution Avenue, NW, Washington, DC 20551, (202) 452-3000, www.federalreserve.gov; *Federal Reserve Bulletin* and *Industrial Production and Capacity Utilization.*

U.S. Bureau of Labor Statistics (BLS), Postal Square Building, 2 Massachusetts Avenue, NE, Washington, DC 20212-0001, (202) 691-5200, Fax: (202) 691-6325, www.bls.gov; *Industry Productivity and Costs.*

FURNITURE AND RELATED PRODUCTS - MANUFACTURING - SHIPMENTS

U.S. Census Bureau, Center for Economic Studies, 4600 Silver Hill Road, Washington DC 20233, (301) 457-1235, www.ces.census.gov; *2002 Economic Census, Manufacturing.*

U.S. Census Bureau, Manufacturing and Construction Division, 4600 Silver Hill Road, Washington DC 20233, (301) 763-4673, www.census.gov/mcd; *Annual Survey of Manufactures (ASM)* and *Census of Manufactures.*

FURNITURE AND RELATED PRODUCTS - MANUFACTURING - TOXIC CHEMICAL RELEASES

U.S. Environmental Protection Agency (EPA), Ariel Rios Building, 1200 Pennsylvania Avenue, NW, Washington, DC 20460, (202) 272-0167, www.epa.gov; Toxics Release Inventory (TRI) Database.

FUTURES PRICE INDEXES - SELECTED COMMODITIES

Commodity Research Bureau, 330 South Wells Street, Suite 612, Chicago, IL 60606-7110, (800) 621-5271, Fax: (312) 939-4135, www.crbtrader.com; *CRB Commodity Index Report* and *2006 CRB Commodity Yearbook and CD.*STATISTICS SOURCES, Thirty-second Edition - 2009STATISTICS SOURCES, Thirty-second Edition - 2009

GABON - NATIONAL STATISTICAL OFFICE

Direction Generale de la Statistique et des Etudes Economiques (DGSEE), BP 2119, Libreville, Gabon, www.stat-gabon.ga; National Data Center.

GABON - PRIMARY STATISTICS SOURCES

Direction Generale de la Statistique et des Etudes Economiques (DGSEE), BP 2119, Libreville, Gabon, www.stat-gabon.ga; *Annuaire Statistique du Gabon* (Statistical Yearbook of Gabon); *Le Gabon en quelques chiffres*; and *Situation Economique et Financiere des Entreprises du Secteur Moderne du Gabon en 1999.*

GABON - AGRICULTURAL MACHINERY

United Nations Statistics Division, New York, NY 10017, (800) 253-9646, Fax: (212) 963-4116, http://unstats.un.org; *Statistical Yearbook.*

GABON - AGRICULTURE

Economist Intelligence Unit, 111 West 57th Street, New York, NY 10019, (212) 554-0600, Fax: (212) 586-1181, www.eiu.com; *Gabon Country Report.*

Euromonitor International, Inc., 224 S. Michigan Avenue, Suite 1500, Chicago, IL 60604, (312) 922-1115, Fax: (312) 922-1157, www.euromonitor.com; *World Marketing Data and Statistics.*

M.E. Sharpe, 80 Business Park Drive, Armonk, NY 10504, (800) 541-6563, Fax: (914) 273-2106, www.mesharpe.com; *The Illustrated Book of World Rankings.*

Palgrave Macmillan Ltd., Houndmills, Basingstoke, Hampshire, RG21 6XS, England, (Telephone in U.S. (888) 330-8477), (Fax in U.S. (800) 672-2054), www.palgrave.com; *The Statesman's Yearbook 2008.*

Taylor and Francis Group, An Informa Business, 2 Park Square, Milton Park, Abingdon, Oxford OX14 4RN, United Kingdom, (Dial from U.S. (212) 216-7800), (Fax from U.S. (212) 564-7854), www.tandf.co.uk; *The Europa World Year Book.*

United Nations Conference on Trade and Development (UNCTAD), DC2-1120, United Nations, New York, NY 10017, (212) 963-0027, www.unctad.org; *UNCTAD Commodity Yearbook.*

United Nations Economic Commission for Africa (ECA), PO Box 3001, Addis Ababa, Ethiopia, (Telephone in U.S. (212) 963-4957), www.uneca.org; *African Statistical Yearbook 2006.*

United Nations Food and Agricultural Organization (FAO), Viale delle Terme di Caracalla, 00100 Rome, Italy, (Dial from U.S. (202) 653-2400), (Fax from U.S. (202) 653 5760), www.fao.org; AQUASTAT; *FAO Production Yearbook 2002; FAO Trade Yearbook;* and *The State of Food and Agriculture (SOFA) 2006.*

United Nations Statistics Division, New York, NY 10017, (800) 253-9646, Fax: (212) 963-4116, http://unstats.un.org; *Statistical Yearbook* and *Survey of Economic and Social Conditions in Africa 2005.*

The World Bank, 1818 H Street, NW, Washington, DC 20433, (202) 473-1000, Fax: (202) 477-6391, www.worldbank.org; *Africa Live Database (LDB); African Development Indicators (ADI) 2007; Gabon;* and *World Development Indicators (WDI) 2008.*

GABON - AIRLINES

International Civil Aviation Organization (ICAO), External Relations and Public Information Office (EPO), 999 University Street, Montreal, Quebec H3C 5H7, Canada, (Dial from U.S. (514) 954-8219), (Fax from U.S. (514) 954-6077), www.icao.int; *Civil Aviation Statistics of the World.*

M.E. Sharpe, 80 Business Park Drive, Armonk, NY 10504, (800) 541-6563, Fax: (914) 273-2106, www.mesharpe.com; *The Illustrated Book of World Rankings.*

Palgrave Macmillan Ltd., Houndmills, Basingstoke, Hampshire, RG21 6XS, England, (Telephone in U.S. (888) 330-8477), (Fax in U.S. (800) 672-2054), www.palgrave.com; *The Statesman's Yearbook 2008.*

Taylor and Francis Group, An Informa Business, 2 Park Square, Milton Park, Abingdon, Oxford OX14 4RN, United Kingdom, (Dial from U.S. (212) 216-7800), (Fax from U.S. (212) 564-7854), www.tandf.co.uk; *The Europa World Year Book.*

United Nations Economic Commission for Africa (ECA), PO Box 3001, Addis Ababa, Ethiopia, (Telephone in U.S. (212) 963-4957), www.uneca.org; *African Statistical Yearbook 2006.*

United Nations Statistics Division, New York, NY 10017, (800) 253-9646, Fax: (212) 963-4116, http://unstats.un.org; *Statistical Yearbook.*

GABON - AIRPORTS

Central Intelligence Agency, Office of Public Affairs, Washington, DC 20505, (703) 482-0623, Fax: (703) 482-1739, www.cia.gov; *The World Factbook.*

GABON - ALUMINUM PRODUCTION

See GABON - MINERAL INDUSTRIES

GABON - ARMED FORCES

Central Intelligence Agency, Office of Public Affairs, Washington, DC 20505, (703) 482-0623, Fax: (703) 482-1739, www.cia.gov; *The World Factbook.*

Euromonitor International, Inc., 224 S. Michigan Avenue, Suite 1500, Chicago, IL 60604, (312) 922-1115, Fax: (312) 922-1157, www.euromonitor.com; *World Marketing Data and Statistics.*

International Institute for Strategic Studies (IISS), Arundel House, 13-15 Arundel Street, Temple Place, London WC2R 3DX, England, www.iiss.org; *The Military Balance 2007.*

Palgrave Macmillan Ltd., Houndmills, Basingstoke, Hampshire, RG21 6XS, England, (Telephone in U.S. (888) 330-8477), (Fax in U.S. (800) 672-2054), www.palgrave.com; *The Statesman's Yearbook 2008.*

U.S. Department of State (DOS), 2201 C Street NW, Washington, DC 20520, (202) 647-4000, www.state.gov; *World Military Expenditures and Arms Transfers (WMEAT).*

United Nations Statistics Division, New York, NY 10017, (800) 253-9646, Fax: (212) 963-4116, http://unstats.un.org; *Human Development Report 2006.*

GABON - BALANCE OF PAYMENTS

African Development Bank Group, Rue Joseph Anoma, 01 BP 1387 Abidjan 01, Cote d'Ivoire, www.afdb.org; *Statistics Pocketbook 2008.*

International Monetary Fund (IMF), 700 Nineteenth Street, NW, Washington, DC 20431, (202) 623-7000, Fax: (202) 623-4661, www.imf.org; *Balance of Payments Statistics Newsletter* and *Balance of Payments Statistics Yearbook 2007.*

Taylor and Francis Group, An Informa Business, 2 Park Square, Milton Park, Abingdon, Oxford OX14 4RN, United Kingdom, (Dial from U.S. (212) 216-7800), (Fax from U.S. (212) 564-7854), www.tandf.co.uk; *The Europa World Year Book.*

United Nations Conference on Trade and Development (UNCTAD), DC2-1120, United Nations, New York, NY 10017, (212) 963-0027, www.unctad.org; *Handbook of Statistics 2005.*

United Nations Economic Commission for Africa (ECA), PO Box 3001, Addis Ababa, Ethiopia, (Telephone in U.S. (212) 963-4957), www.uneca.org; *African Statistical Yearbook 2006.*

The World Bank, 1818 H Street, NW, Washington, DC 20433, (202) 473-1000, Fax: (202) 477-6391, www.worldbank.org; *Gabon; World Development Indicators (WDI) 2008;* and *World Development Report 2008.*

GABON - BANKS AND BANKING

Euromonitor International, Inc., 224 S. Michigan Avenue, Suite 1500, Chicago, IL 60604, (312) 922-1115, Fax: (312) 922-1157, www.euromonitor.com; *World Marketing Data and Statistics.*

International Monetary Fund (IMF), 700 Nineteenth Street, NW, Washington, DC 20431, (202) 623-7000, Fax: (202) 623-4661, www.imf.org; *International Financial Statistics Yearbook 2007.*

M.E. Sharpe, 80 Business Park Drive, Armonk, NY 10504, (800) 541-6563, Fax: (914) 273-2106, www.mesharpe.com; *The Illustrated Book of World Rankings.*

Palgrave Macmillan Ltd., Houndmills, Basingstoke, Hampshire, RG21 6XS, England, (Telephone in U.S. (888) 330-8477), (Fax in U.S. (800) 672-2054), www.palgrave.com; *The Statesman's Yearbook 2008.*

Taylor and Francis Group, An Informa Business, 2 Park Square, Milton Park, Abingdon, Oxford OX14 4RN, United Kingdom, (Dial from U.S. (212) 216-7800), (Fax from U.S. (212) 564-7854), www.tandf.co.uk; *The Europa World Year Book.*

United Nations Economic Commission for Africa (ECA), PO Box 3001, Addis Ababa, Ethiopia, (Telephone in U.S. (212) 963-4957), www.uneca.org; *African Statistical Yearbook 2006.*

GABON - BARLEY PRODUCTION

See GABON - CROPS

GABON - BEVERAGE INDUSTRY

M.E. Sharpe, 80 Business Park Drive, Armonk, NY 10504, (800) 541-6563, Fax: (914) 273-2106, www.mesharpe.com; *The Illustrated Book of World Rankings.*

United Nations Statistics Division, New York, NY 10017, (800) 253-9646, Fax: (212) 963-4116, http://unstats.un.org; *Statistical Yearbook.*

GABON - BONDS

International Monetary Fund (IMF), 700 Nineteenth Street, NW, Washington, DC 20431, (202) 623-7000, Fax: (202) 623-4661, www.imf.org; *Government Finance Statistics Yearbook (2008 Edition).*

GABON - BROADCASTING

Central Intelligence Agency, Office of Public Affairs, Washington, DC 20505, (703) 482-0623, Fax: (703) 482-1739, www.cia.gov; *The World Factbook.*

Euromonitor International, Inc., 224 S. Michigan Avenue, Suite 1500, Chicago, IL 60604, (312) 922-1115, Fax: (312) 922-1157, www.euromonitor.com; *World Marketing Data and Statistics.*

M.E. Sharpe, 80 Business Park Drive, Armonk, NY 10504, (800) 541-6563, Fax: (914) 273-2106, www.mesharpe.com; *The Illustrated Book of World Rankings.*

Palgrave Macmillan Ltd., Houndmills, Basingstoke, Hampshire, RG21 6XS, England, (Telephone in U.S. (888) 330-8477), (Fax in U.S. (800) 672-2054), www.palgrave.com; *The Statesman's Yearbook 2008.*

WRTH Publications Limited, PO Box 290, Oxford OX2 7FT, UK, www.wrth.com; *World Radio TV Handbook 2007.*

GABON - BUDGET

Central Intelligence Agency, Office of Public Affairs, Washington, DC 20505, (703) 482-0623, Fax: (703) 482-1739, www.cia.gov; *The World Factbook.*

GABON - CAPITAL LEVY

International Monetary Fund (IMF), 700 Nineteenth Street, NW, Washington, DC 20431, (202) 623-7000, Fax: (202) 623-4661, www.imf.org; *Government Finance Statistics Yearbook (2008 Edition).*

GABON - CATTLE

See GABON - LIVESTOCK

GABON - CHICKENS

See GABON - LIVESTOCK

GABON - CHILDBIRTH - STATISTICS

Central Intelligence Agency, Office of Public Affairs, Washington, DC 20505, (703) 482-0623, Fax: (703) 482-1739, www.cia.gov; *The World Factbook.*

Euromonitor International, Inc., 224 S. Michigan Avenue, Suite 1500, Chicago, IL 60604, (312) 922-1115, Fax: (312) 922-1157, www.euromonitor.com; *International Marketing Data and Statistics 2008* and *The World Economic Factbook 2008.*

M.E. Sharpe, 80 Business Park Drive, Armonk, NY 10504, (800) 541-6563, Fax: (914) 273-2106, www.mesharpe.com; *The Illustrated Book of World Rankings.*

Palgrave Macmillan Ltd., Houndmills, Basingstoke, Hampshire, RG21 6XS, England, (Telephone in U.S. (888) 330-8477), (Fax in U.S. (800) 672-2054), www.palgrave.com; *The Statesman's Yearbook 2008.*

Taylor and Francis Group, An Informa Business, 2 Park Square, Milton Park, Abingdon, Oxford OX14 4RN, United Kingdom, (Dial from U.S. (212) 216-7800), (Fax from U.S. (212) 564-7854), www.tandf.co.uk; *The Europa World Year Book.*

United Nations Statistics Division, New York, NY 10017, (800) 253-9646, Fax: (212) 963-4116, http://unstats.un.org; *Demographic Yearbook; Statistical Yearbook;* and *Survey of Economic and Social Conditions in Africa 2005.*

The World Bank, 1818 H Street, NW, Washington, DC 20433, (202) 473-1000, Fax: (202) 477-6391, www.worldbank.org; *World Development Indicators (WDI) 2008.*

GABON - CLIMATE

International Institute for Environment and Development (IIED), 3 Endsleigh Street, London, England, WC1H 0DD, United Kingdom, www.iied.org; *Environment Urbanization* and *Haramata - Bulletin of the Drylands.*

M.E. Sharpe, 80 Business Park Drive, Armonk, NY 10504, (800) 541-6563, Fax: (914) 273-2106, www.mesharpe.com; *The Illustrated Book of World Rankings.*

Palgrave Macmillan Ltd., Houndmills, Basingstoke, Hampshire, RG21 6XS, England, (Telephone in U.S. (888) 330-8477), (Fax in U.S. (800) 672-2054), www.palgrave.com; *The Statesman's Yearbook 2008.*

GABON - COAL PRODUCTION

See GABON - MINERAL INDUSTRIES

GABON - COCOA PRODUCTION

See GABON - CROPS

GABON - COFFEE

See GABON - CROPS

GABON - COMMERCE

Palgrave Macmillan Ltd., Houndmills, Basingstoke, Hampshire, RG21 6XS, England, (Telephone in U.S. (888) 330-8477), (Fax in U.S. (800) 672-2054), www.palgrave.com; *The Statesman's Yearbook 2008.*

GABON - COMMODITY EXCHANGES

Commodity Research Bureau, 330 South Wells Street, Suite 612, Chicago, IL 60606-7110, (800) 621-5271, Fax: (312) 939-4135, www.crbtrader.com; *2006 CRB Commodity Yearbook and CD.*

International Monetary Fund (IMF), 700 Nineteenth Street, NW, Washington, DC 20431, (202) 623-7000, Fax: (202) 623-4661, www.imf.org; *IMF Primary Commodity Prices.*

United Nations Food and Agricultural Organization (FAO), Viale delle Terme di Caracalla, 00100 Rome, Italy, (Dial from U.S. (202) 653-2400), (Fax from U.S. (202) 653 5760), www.fao.org; *The State of Food and Agriculture (SOFA) 2006.*

GABON - CONSTRUCTION INDUSTRY

M.E. Sharpe, 80 Business Park Drive, Armonk, NY 10504, (800) 541-6563, Fax: (914) 273-2106, www.mesharpe.com; *The Illustrated Book of World Rankings.*

United Nations Economic Commission for Africa (ECA), PO Box 3001, Addis Ababa, Ethiopia, (Telephone in U.S. (212) 963-4957), www.uneca.org; *African Statistical Yearbook 2006.*

United Nations Statistics Division, New York, NY 10017, (800) 253-9646, Fax: (212) 963-4116, http://unstats.un.org; *Statistical Yearbook.*

GABON - CONSUMER PRICE INDEXES

Taylor and Francis Group, An Informa Business, 2 Park Square, Milton Park, Abingdon, Oxford OX14 4RN, United Kingdom, (Dial from U.S. (212) 216-7800), (Fax from U.S. (212) 564-7854), www.tandf.co.uk; *The Europa World Year Book.*

United Nations Economic Commission for Africa (ECA), PO Box 3001, Addis Ababa, Ethiopia, (Telephone in U.S. (212) 963-4957), www.uneca.org; *African Statistical Yearbook 2006.*

United Nations Statistics Division, New York, NY 10017, (800) 253-9646, Fax: (212) 963-4116, http://unstats.un.org; *Statistical Yearbook* and *Survey of Economic and Social Conditions in Africa 2005.*

The World Bank, 1818 H Street, NW, Washington, DC 20433, (202) 473-1000, Fax: (202) 477-6391, www.worldbank.org; *Gabon.*

GABON - CONSUMPTION (ECONOMICS)

African Development Bank Group, Rue Joseph Anoma, 01 BP 1387 Abidjan 01, Cote d'Ivoire, www.afdb.org; *Statistics Pocketbook 2008.*

United Nations Statistics Division, New York, NY 10017, (800) 253-9646, Fax: (212) 963-4116, http://unstats.un.org; *Survey of Economic and Social Conditions in Africa 2005.*

The World Bank, 1818 H Street, NW, Washington, DC 20433, (202) 473-1000, Fax: (202) 477-6391, www.worldbank.org; *World Development Report 2008.*

GABON - COPPER INDUSTRY AND TRADE

See GABON - MINERAL INDUSTRIES

GABON - CORN INDUSTRY

See GABON - CROPS

GABON - COTTON

See GABON - CROPS

GABON - CROPS

M.E. Sharpe, 80 Business Park Drive, Armonk, NY 10504, (800) 541-6563, Fax: (914) 273-2106, www.mesharpe.com; *The Illustrated Book of World Rankings.*

Palgrave Macmillan Ltd., Houndmills, Basingstoke, Hampshire, RG21 6XS, England, (Telephone in U.S. (888) 330-8477), (Fax in U.S. (800) 672-2054), www.palgrave.com; *The Statesman's Yearbook 2008.*

Taylor and Francis Group, An Informa Business, 2 Park Square, Milton Park, Abingdon, Oxford OX14 4RN, United Kingdom, (Dial from U.S. (212) 216-7800), (Fax from U.S. (212) 564-7854), www.tandf.co.uk; *The Europa World Year Book.*

United Nations Conference on Trade and Development (UNCTAD), DC2-1120, United Nations, New York, NY 10017, (212) 963-0027, www.unctad.org; *UNCTAD Commodity Yearbook.*

United Nations Economic Commission for Africa (ECA), PO Box 3001, Addis Ababa, Ethiopia, (Telephone in U.S. (212) 963-4957), www.uneca.org; *African Statistical Yearbook 2006.*

United Nations Food and Agricultural Organization (FAO), Viale delle Terme di Caracalla, 00100 Rome, Italy, (Dial from U.S. (202) 653-2400), (Fax from U.S. (202) 653 5760), www.fao.org; *FAO Production Yearbook 2002* and *The State of Food and Agriculture (SOFA) 2006.*

United Nations Statistics Division, New York, NY 10017, (800) 253-9646, Fax: (212) 963-4116, http://unstats.un.org; *Statistical Yearbook.*

GABON - CUSTOMS ADMINISTRATION

International Monetary Fund (IMF), 700 Nineteenth Street, NW, Washington, DC 20431, (202) 623-7000, Fax: (202) 623-4661, www.imf.org; *Government Finance Statistics Yearbook (2008 Edition).*

Palgrave Macmillan Ltd., Houndmills, Basingstoke, Hampshire, RG21 6XS, England, (Telephone in U.S. (888) 330-8477), (Fax in U.S. (800) 672-2054), www.palgrave.com; *The Statesman's Yearbook 2008.*

GABON - DAIRY PROCESSING

M.E. Sharpe, 80 Business Park Drive, Armonk, NY 10504, (800) 541-6563, Fax: (914) 273-2106, www.mesharpe.com; *The Illustrated Book of World Rankings.*

Palgrave Macmillan Ltd., Houndmills, Basingstoke, Hampshire, RG21 6XS, England, (Telephone in U.S. (888) 330-8477), (Fax in U.S. (800) 672-2054), www.palgrave.com; *The Statesman's Yearbook 2008.*

United Nations Food and Agricultural Organization (FAO), Viale delle Terme di Caracalla, 00100 Rome, Italy, (Dial from U.S. (202) 653-2400), (Fax from U.S. (202) 653 5760), www.fao.org; *The State of Food and Agriculture (SOFA) 2006.*

GABON - DEATH RATES

See GABON - MORTALITY

GABON - DEBTS, EXTERNAL

African Development Bank Group, Rue Joseph Anoma, 01 BP 1387 Abidjan 01, Cote d'Ivoire, www.afdb.org; *Statistics Pocketbook 2008.*

Palgrave Macmillan Ltd., Houndmills, Basingstoke, Hampshire, RG21 6XS, England, (Telephone in U.S. (888) 330-8477), (Fax in U.S. (800) 672-2054), www.palgrave.com; *The Statesman's Yearbook 2008.*

United Nations Statistics Division, New York, NY 10017, (800) 253-9646, Fax: (212) 963-4116, http://unstats.un.org; *Survey of Economic and Social Conditions in Africa 2005.*

The World Bank, 1818 H Street, NW, Washington, DC 20433, (202) 473-1000, Fax: (202) 477-6391, www.worldbank.org; *Africa Live Database (LDB); African Development Indicators (ADI) 2007; Global Development Finance 2007; World Development Indicators (WDI) 2008;* and *World Development Report 2008.*

GABON - DEFENSE EXPENDITURES

See GABON - ARMED FORCES

GABON - DEMOGRAPHY

Euromonitor International, Inc., 224 S. Michigan Avenue, Suite 1500, Chicago, IL 60604, (312) 922-1115, Fax: (312) 922-1157, www.euromonitor.com; *International Marketing Data and Statistics 2008; The World Economic Factbook 2008;* and *World Marketing Data and Statistics.*

M.E. Sharpe, 80 Business Park Drive, Armonk, NY 10504, (800) 541-6563, Fax: (914) 273-2106, www.mesharpe.com; *The Illustrated Book of World Rankings.*

United Nations Statistics Division, New York, NY 10017, (800) 253-9646, Fax: (212) 963-4116, http://unstats.un.org; *Human Development Report 2006* and *Survey of Economic and Social Conditions in Africa 2005.*

The World Bank, 1818 H Street, NW, Washington, DC 20433, (202) 473-1000, Fax: (202) 477-6391, www.worldbank.org; *Gabon.*

GABON - DIAMONDS

See GABON - MINERAL INDUSTRIES

GABON - DISPOSABLE INCOME

M.E. Sharpe, 80 Business Park Drive, Armonk, NY 10504, (800) 541-6563, Fax: (914) 273-2106, www.mesharpe.com; *The Illustrated Book of World Rankings.*

United Nations Statistics Division, New York, NY 10017, (800) 253-9646, Fax: (212) 963-4116, http://unstats.un.org; *National Accounts Statistics: Compendium of Income Distribution Statistics* and *Statistical Yearbook.*

GABON - DIVORCE

M.E. Sharpe, 80 Business Park Drive, Armonk, NY 10504, (800) 541-6563, Fax: (914) 273-2106, www.mesharpe.com; *The Illustrated Book of World Rankings.*

United Nations Statistics Division, New York, NY 10017, (800) 253-9646, Fax: (212) 963-4116, http://unstats.un.org; *Demographic Yearbook.*

GABON - ECONOMIC ASSISTANCE

United Nations Statistics Division, New York, NY 10017, (800) 253-9646, Fax: (212) 963-4116, http://unstats.un.org; *Statistical Yearbook.*

GABON - ECONOMIC CONDITIONS

African Development Bank Group, Rue Joseph Anoma, 01 BP 1387 Abidjan 01, Cote d'Ivoire, www.afdb.org; *The African Statistical Journal; Gender, Poverty and Environmental Indicators on African Countries 2007; Selected Statistics on African Countries 2007;* and *Statistics Pocketbook 2008.*

Center for International Business Education Research (CIBER), Columbia Business School and School of International and Public Affairs, Uris Hall, Room 212, 3022 Broadway, New York, NY 10027-6902, Mr. Joshua Safier, (212) 854-4750, Fax: (212) 222-9821, www.columbia.edu/cu/ciber/; Datastream International.

Central Intelligence Agency, Office of Public Affairs, Washington, DC 20505, (703) 482-0623, Fax: (703) 482-1739, www.cia.gov; *The World Factbook.*

DSI Data Service Information, Xantener Strasse 51a, D-47495 Rheinberg, Germany, www.dsidata.com; *Campus Solution.*

Dun and Bradstreet (DB) Corporation, 103 JFK Parkway, Short Hills, NJ 07078, (973) 921-5500, www.dnb.com; *Country Report.*

Economist Intelligence Unit, 111 West 57th Street, New York, NY 10019, (212) 554-0600, Fax: (212) 586-1181, www.eiu.com; *Business Africa* and *Gabon Country Report.*

Euromonitor International, Inc., 224 S. Michigan Avenue, Suite 1500, Chicago, IL 60604, (312) 922-1115, Fax: (312) 922-1157, www.euromonitor.com; *The World Economic Factbook 2008* and *World Marketing Data and Statistics.*

International Monetary Fund (IMF), 700 Nineteenth Street, NW, Washington, DC 20431, (202) 623-7000, Fax: (202) 623-4661, www.imf.org; *World Economic Outlook Reports.*

M.E. Sharpe, 80 Business Park Drive, Armonk, NY 10504, (800) 541-6563, Fax: (914) 273-2106, www.mesharpe.com; *The Illustrated Book of World Rankings.*

Palgrave Macmillan Ltd., Houndmills, Basingstoke, Hampshire, RG21 6XS, England, (Telephone in U.S. (888) 330-8477), (Fax in U.S. (800) 672-2054), www.palgrave.com; *The Statesman's Yearbook 2008.*

Taylor and Francis Group, An Informa Business, 2 Park Square, Milton Park, Abingdon, Oxford OX14 4RN, United Kingdom, (Dial from U.S. (212) 216-7800), (Fax from U.S. (212) 564-7854), www.tandf.co.uk; *The Europa World Year Book.*

United Nations Statistics Division, New York, NY 10017, (800) 253-9646, Fax: (212) 963-4116, http://unstats.un.org; *Compendium of Intra-African and Related Foreign Trade Statistics 2003* and *World Statistics Pocketbook.*

The World Bank, 1818 H Street, NW, Washington, DC 20433, (202) 473-1000, Fax: (202) 477-6391, www.worldbank.org; *Africa Household Survey Databank; Africa Live Database (LDB); Africa Standardized Files and Indicators; African Development Indicators (ADI) 2007; Gabon; Global Economic Monitor (GEM); Global Economic Prospects 2008; The World Bank Atlas 2003-2004;* and *World Development Report 2008.*

GABON - EDUCATION

African Development Bank Group, Rue Joseph Anoma, 01 BP 1387 Abidjan 01, Cote d'Ivoire, www.afdb.org; *Statistics Pocketbook 2008.*

Euromonitor International, Inc., 224 S. Michigan Avenue, Suite 1500, Chicago, IL 60604, (312) 922-1115, Fax: (312) 922-1157, www.euromonitor.com; *International Marketing Data and Statistics 2008* and *World Marketing Data and Statistics.*

M.E. Sharpe, 80 Business Park Drive, Armonk, NY 10504, (800) 541-6563, Fax: (914) 273-2106, www.mesharpe.com; *The Illustrated Book of World Rankings.*

Palgrave Macmillan Ltd., Houndmills, Basingstoke, Hampshire, RG21 6XS, England, (Telephone in U.S. (888) 330-8477), (Fax in U.S. (800) 672-2054), www.palgrave.com; *The Statesman's Yearbook 2008.*

Taylor and Francis Group, An Informa Business, 2 Park Square, Milton Park, Abingdon, Oxford OX14 4RN, United Kingdom, (Dial from U.S. (212) 216-7800), (Fax from U.S. (212) 564-7854), www.tandf.co.uk; *The Europa World Year Book.*

UNESCO Institute for Statistics, C.P. 6128 Succursale Centre-Ville, Montreal, Quebec, H3C 3J7 Canada, (Dial from U.S. (514) 343-6880), (Fax from U.S. (514) 343 6882), www.uis.unesco.org; *Statistical Tables.*

United Nations Economic Commission for Africa (ECA), PO Box 3001, Addis Ababa, Ethiopia, (Telephone in U.S. (212) 963-4957), www.uneca.org; *African Statistical Yearbook 2006.*

United Nations Statistics Division, New York, NY 10017, (800) 253-9646, Fax: (212) 963-4116, http://unstats.un.org; *Human Development Report 2006* and *Survey of Economic and Social Conditions in Africa 2005.*

The World Bank, 1818 H Street, NW, Washington, DC 20433, (202) 473-1000, Fax: (202) 477-6391, www.worldbank.org; *Gabon; World Development Indicators (WDI) 2008;* and *World Development Report 2008.*

GABON - ELECTRICITY

M.E. Sharpe, 80 Business Park Drive, Armonk, NY 10504, (800) 541-6563, Fax: (914) 273-2106, www.mesharpe.com; *The Illustrated Book of World Rankings.*

Organisation for Economic Cooperation and Development (OECD), 2 rue Andre Pascal, F-75775 Paris Cedex 16, France, (Telephone in U.S. (202) 785-6323), (Fax in U.S. (202) 785-0350), www.oecd.org; *World Energy Outlook 2007.*

Palgrave Macmillan Ltd., Houndmills, Basingstoke, Hampshire, RG21 6XS, England, (Telephone in U.S. (888) 330-8477), (Fax in U.S. (800) 672-2054), www.palgrave.com; *The Statesman's Yearbook 2008.*

U.S. Department of Energy (DOE), Energy Information Administration (EIA), 1000 Independence Avenue, SW, Washington, DC 20585, (202) 586-8800, www.eia.doe.gov; *International Energy Annual 2004* and *International Energy Outlook 2006.*

United Nations Economic Commission for Africa (ECA), PO Box 3001, Addis Ababa, Ethiopia, (Telephone in U.S. (212) 963-4957), www.uneca.org; *African Statistical Yearbook 2006.*

United Nations Statistics Division, New York, NY 10017, (800) 253-9646, Fax: (212) 963-4116, http://unstats.un.org; *Human Development Report 2006; Statistical Yearbook;* and *Survey of Economic and Social Conditions in Africa 2005.*

GABON - EMPLOYMENT

Euromonitor International, Inc., 224 S. Michigan Avenue, Suite 1500, Chicago, IL 60604, (312) 922-1115, Fax: (312) 922-1157, www.euromonitor.com; *International Marketing Data and Statistics 2008.*

International Labour Office, I.L.O. Publications, 4 route des Morillons, CH-1211 Geneva 22, Switzerland, (Telephone in U.S. (202) 653-7652), (Fax in U.S. (202) 653-7687), www.ilo.org; *Yearbook of Labour Statistics 2006.*

M.E. Sharpe, 80 Business Park Drive, Armonk, NY 10504, (800) 541-6563, Fax: (914) 273-2106, www.mesharpe.com; *The Illustrated Book of World Rankings.*

United Nations Economic Commission for Africa (ECA), PO Box 3001, Addis Ababa, Ethiopia, (Telephone in U.S. (212) 963-4957), www.uneca.org; *African Statistical Yearbook 2006.*

United Nations Statistics Division, New York, NY 10017, (800) 253-9646, Fax: (212) 963-4116, http://unstats.un.org; *Statistical Yearbook* and *Survey of Economic and Social Conditions in Africa 2005.*

The World Bank, 1818 H Street, NW, Washington, DC 20433, (202) 473-1000, Fax: (202) 477-6391, www.worldbank.org; *Gabon.*

GABON - ENVIRONMENTAL CONDITIONS

DSI Data Service Information, Xantener Strasse 51a, D-47495 Rheinberg, Germany, www.dsidata.com; *Campus Solution* and *DSI's Global Environmental Database*.

Economist Intelligence Unit, 111 West 57th Street, New York, NY 10019, (212) 554-0600, Fax: (212) 586-1181, www.eiu.com; *Gabon Country Report*.

International Institute for Environment and Development (IIED), 3 Endsleigh Street, London, England, WC1H 0DD, United Kingdom, www.iied.org; *Environment Urbanization* and *Haramata - Bulletin of the Drylands*.

United Nations Statistics Division, New York, NY 10017, (800) 253-9646, Fax: (212) 963-4116, http://unstats.un.org; *World Statistics Pocketbook*.

GABON - EXPORTS

African Development Bank Group, Rue Joseph Anoma, 01 BP 1387 Abidjan 01, Cote d'Ivoire, www.afdb.org; *Statistics Pocketbook 2008*.

Central Intelligence Agency, Office of Public Affairs, Washington, DC 20505, (703) 482-0623, Fax: (703) 482-1739, www.cia.gov; *The World Factbook*.

Economist Intelligence Unit, 111 West 57th Street, New York, NY 10019, (212) 554-0600, Fax: (212) 586-1181, www.eiu.com; *Gabon Country Report*.

Euromonitor International, Inc., 224 S. Michigan Avenue, Suite 1500, Chicago, IL 60604, (312) 922-1115, Fax: (312) 922-1157, www.euromonitor.com; *International Marketing Data and Statistics 2008* and *The World Economic Factbook 2008*.

International Monetary Fund (IMF), 700 Nineteenth Street, NW, Washington, DC 20431, (202) 623-7000, Fax: (202) 623-4661, www.imf.org; *Direction of Trade Statistics Yearbook 2007* and *International Financial Statistics Yearbook 2007*.

Palgrave Macmillan Ltd., Houndmills, Basingstoke, Hampshire, RG21 6XS, England, (Telephone in U.S. (888) 330-8477), (Fax in U.S. (800) 672-2054), www.palgrave.com; *The Statesman's Yearbook 2008*.

Taylor and Francis Group, An Informa Business, 2 Park Square, Milton Park, Abingdon, Oxford OX14 4RN, United Kingdom, (Dial from U.S. (212) 216-7800), (Fax from U.S. (212) 564-7854), www.tandf.co.uk; *The Europa World Year Book*.

United Nations Conference on Trade and Development (UNCTAD), DC2-1120, United Nations, New York, NY 10017, (212) 963-0027, www.unctad.org; *Handbook of Statistics 2005*.

United Nations Economic Commission for Africa (ECA), PO Box 3001, Addis Ababa, Ethiopia, (Telephone in U.S. (212) 963-4957), www.uneca.org; *African Statistical Yearbook 2006*.

United Nations Food and Agricultural Organization (FAO), Viale delle Terme di Caracalla, 00100 Rome, Italy, (Dial from U.S. (202) 653-2400), (Fax from U.S. (202) 653 5760), www.fao.org; *The State of Food and Agriculture (SOFA) 2006*.

United Nations Statistics Division, New York, NY 10017, (800) 253-9646, Fax: (212) 963-4116, http://unstats.un.org; *Compendium of Intra-African and Related Foreign Trade Statistics 2003* and *Survey of Economic and Social Conditions in Africa 2005*.

The World Bank, 1818 H Street, NW, Washington, DC 20433, (202) 473-1000, Fax: (202) 477-6391, www.worldbank.org; *World Development Indicators (WDI) 2008* and *World Development Report 2008*.

GABON - FERTILITY, HUMAN

Central Intelligence Agency, Office of Public Affairs, Washington, DC 20505, (703) 482-0623, Fax: (703) 482-1739, www.cia.gov; *The World Factbook*.

M.E. Sharpe, 80 Business Park Drive, Armonk, NY 10504, (800) 541-6563, Fax: (914) 273-2106, www.mesharpe.com; *The Illustrated Book of World Rankings*.

United Nations Statistics Division, New York, NY 10017, (800) 253-9646, Fax: (212) 963-4116, http://unstats.un.org; *Human Development Report 2006* and *Survey of Economic and Social Conditions in Africa 2005*.

The World Bank, 1818 H Street, NW, Washington, DC 20433, (202) 473-1000, Fax: (202) 477-6391, www.worldbank.org; *The World Bank Atlas 2003-2004; World Development Indicators (WDI) 2008*; and *World Development Report 2008*.

GABON - FERTILIZER INDUSTRY

United Nations Food and Agricultural Organization (FAO), Viale delle Terme di Caracalla, 00100 Rome, Italy, (Dial from U.S. (202) 653-2400), (Fax from U.S. (202) 653 5760), www.fao.org; *FAO Fertilizer Yearbook* and *The State of Food and Agriculture (SOFA) 2006*.

GABON - FETAL MORTALITY

See GABON - MORTALITY

GABON - FINANCE

International Monetary Fund (IMF), 700 Nineteenth Street, NW, Washington, DC 20431, (202) 623-7000, Fax: (202) 623-4661, www.imf.org; *International Financial Statistics Yearbook 2007*.

Taylor and Francis Group, An Informa Business, 2 Park Square, Milton Park, Abingdon, Oxford OX14 4RN, United Kingdom, (Dial from U.S. (212) 216-7800), (Fax from U.S. (212) 564-7854), www.tandf.co.uk; *The Europa World Year Book*.

United Nations Economic Commission for Africa (ECA), PO Box 3001, Addis Ababa, Ethiopia, (Telephone in U.S. (212) 963-4957), www.uneca.org; *African Statistical Yearbook 2006*.

United Nations Statistics Division, New York, NY 10017, (800) 253-9646, Fax: (212) 963-4116, http://unstats.un.org; *National Accounts Statistics: Compendium of Income Distribution Statistics* and *Statistical Yearbook*.

The World Bank, 1818 H Street, NW, Washington, DC 20433, (202) 473-1000, Fax: (202) 477-6391, www.worldbank.org; *Gabon*.

GABON - FINANCE, PUBLIC

African Development Bank Group, Rue Joseph Anoma, 01 BP 1387 Abidjan 01, Cote d'Ivoire, www.afdb.org; *Statistics Pocketbook 2008*.

Bernan Essential Government Publications, 4611-F Assembly Drive, Lanham MD, 20706-4391, (301) 459-2255, Fax: (800) 865-3450, www.bernan.com; *National Accounts Statistics*.

Economist Intelligence Unit, 111 West 57th Street, New York, NY 10019, (212) 554-0600, Fax: (212) 586-1181, www.eiu.com; *Gabon Country Report*.

International Monetary Fund (IMF), 700 Nineteenth Street, NW, Washington, DC 20431, (202) 623-7000, Fax: (202) 623-4661, www.imf.org; *International Financial Statistics* and *International Financial Statistics Online Service*.

M.E. Sharpe, 80 Business Park Drive, Armonk, NY 10504, (800) 541-6563, Fax: (914) 273-2106, www.mesharpe.com; *The Illustrated Book of World Rankings*.

Palgrave Macmillan Ltd., Houndmills, Basingstoke, Hampshire, RG21 6XS, England, (Telephone in U.S. (888) 330-8477), (Fax in U.S. (800) 672-2054), www.palgrave.com; *The Statesman's Yearbook 2008*.

Taylor and Francis Group, An Informa Business, 2 Park Square, Milton Park, Abingdon, Oxford OX14 4RN, United Kingdom, (Dial from U.S. (212) 216-7800), (Fax from U.S. (212) 564-7854), www.tandf.co.uk; *The Europa World Year Book*.

United Nations Economic Commission for Africa (ECA), PO Box 3001, Addis Ababa, Ethiopia, (Telephone in U.S. (212) 963-4957), www.uneca.org; *African Statistical Yearbook 2006*.

The World Bank, 1818 H Street, NW, Washington, DC 20433, (202) 473-1000, Fax: (202) 477-6391, www.worldbank.org; *Gabon*.

GABON - FISHERIES

M.E. Sharpe, 80 Business Park Drive, Armonk, NY 10504, (800) 541-6563, Fax: (914) 273-2106, www.mesharpe.com; *The Illustrated Book of World Rankings*.

Palgrave Macmillan Ltd., Houndmills, Basingstoke, Hampshire, RG21 6XS, England, (Telephone in U.S. (888) 330-8477), (Fax in U.S. (800) 672-2054), www.palgrave.com; *The Statesman's Yearbook 2008*.

Taylor and Francis Group, An Informa Business, 2 Park Square, Milton Park, Abingdon, Oxford OX14 4RN, United Kingdom, (Dial from U.S. (212) 216-7800), (Fax from U.S. (212) 564-7854), www.tandf.co.uk; *The Europa World Year Book*.

United Nations Conference on Trade and Development (UNCTAD), DC2-1120, United Nations, New York, NY 10017, (212) 963-0027, www.unctad.org; *UNCTAD Commodity Yearbook*.

United Nations Economic Commission for Africa (ECA), PO Box 3001, Addis Ababa, Ethiopia, (Telephone in U.S. (212) 963-4957), www.uneca.org; *African Statistical Yearbook 2006*.

United Nations Food and Agricultural Organization (FAO), Viale delle Terme di Caracalla, 00100 Rome, Italy, (Dial from U.S. (202) 653-2400), (Fax from U.S. (202) 653 5760), www.fao.org; *FAO Yearbook of Fishery Statistics;* Fishery Databases; FISHSTAT Database. Subjects covered include: Aquaculture production, capture production, fishery commodities; and *The State of Food and Agriculture (SOFA) 2006*.

United Nations Statistics Division, New York, NY 10017, (800) 253-9646, Fax: (212) 963-4116, http://unstats.un.org; *Statistical Yearbook* and *Survey of Economic and Social Conditions in Africa 2005*.

The World Bank, 1818 H Street, NW, Washington, DC 20433, (202) 473-1000, Fax: (202) 477-6391, www.worldbank.org; *Gabon*.

GABON - FLOUR INDUSTRY

United Nations Statistics Division, New York, NY 10017, (800) 253-9646, Fax: (212) 963-4116, http://unstats.un.org; *Statistical Yearbook*.

GABON - FOOD

African Development Bank Group, Rue Joseph Anoma, 01 BP 1387 Abidjan 01, Cote d'Ivoire, www.afdb.org; *Statistics Pocketbook 2008*.

United Nations Conference on Trade and Development (UNCTAD), DC2-1120, United Nations, New York, NY 10017, (212) 963-0027, www.unctad.org; *UNCTAD Commodity Yearbook*.

United Nations Food and Agricultural Organization (FAO), Viale delle Terme di Caracalla, 00100 Rome, Italy, (Dial from U.S. (202) 653-2400), (Fax from U.S. (202) 653 5760), www.fao.org; *FAO Production Yearbook 2002* and *The State of Food and Agriculture (SOFA) 2006*.

United Nations Statistics Division, New York, NY 10017, (800) 253-9646, Fax: (212) 963-4116, http://unstats.un.org; *Human Development Report 2006*.

GABON - FOREIGN EXCHANGE RATES

African Development Bank Group, Rue Joseph Anoma, 01 BP 1387 Abidjan 01, Cote d'Ivoire, www.afdb.org; *Statistics Pocketbook 2008*.

Central Intelligence Agency, Office of Public Affairs, Washington, DC 20505, (703) 482-0623, Fax: (703) 482-1739, www.cia.gov; *The World Factbook*.

Euromonitor International, Inc., 224 S. Michigan Avenue, Suite 1500, Chicago, IL 60604, (312) 922-1115, Fax: (312) 922-1157, www.euromonitor.com; *International Marketing Data and Statistics 2008* and *The World Economic Factbook 2008*.

International Civil Aviation Organization (ICAO), External Relations and Public Information Office (EPO), 999 University Street, Montreal, Quebec H3C 5H7, Canada, (Dial from U.S. (514) 954-8219), (Fax from U.S. (514) 954-6077), www.icao.int; *Civil Aviation Statistics of the World*.

International Monetary Fund (IMF), 700 Nineteenth Street, NW, Washington, DC 20431, (202) 623-7000, Fax: (202) 623-4661, www.imf.org; *International Financial Statistics Yearbook 2007.*

Taylor and Francis Group, An Informa Business, 2 Park Square, Milton Park, Abingdon, Oxford OX14 4RN, United Kingdom, (Dial from U.S. (212) 216-7800), (Fax from U.S. (212) 564-7854), www.tandf.co.uk; *The Europa World Year Book.*

United Nations Statistics Division, New York, NY 10017, (800) 253-9646, Fax: (212) 963-4116, http://unstats.un.org; *Compendium of Intra-African and Related Foreign Trade Statistics 2003; Statistical Yearbook;* and *World Statistics Pocketbook.*

GABON - FORESTS AND FORESTRY

International Monetary Fund (IMF), 700 Nineteenth Street, NW, Washington, DC 20431, (202) 623-7000, Fax: (202) 623-4661, www.imf.org; *International Financial Statistics Yearbook 2007.*

M.E. Sharpe, 80 Business Park Drive, Armonk, NY 10504, (800) 541-6563, Fax: (914) 273-2106, www.mesharpe.com; *The Illustrated Book of World Rankings.*

Palgrave Macmillan Ltd., Houndmills, Basingstoke, Hampshire, RG21 6XS, England, (Telephone in U.S. (888) 330-8477), (Fax in U.S. (800) 672-2054), www.palgrave.com; *The Statesman's Yearbook 2008.*

Taylor and Francis Group, An Informa Business, 2 Park Square, Milton Park, Abingdon, Oxford OX14 4RN, United Kingdom, (Dial from U.S. (212) 216-7800), (Fax from U.S. (212) 564-7854), www.tandf.co.uk; *The Europa World Year Book.*

UNESCO Institute for Statistics, C.P. 6128 Succursale Centre-Ville, Montreal, Quebec, H3C 3J7 Canada, (Dial from U.S. (514) 343-6880), (Fax from U.S. (514) 343 6882), www.uis.unesco.org; *Statistical Tables.*

United Nations Conference on Trade and Development (UNCTAD), DC2-1120, United Nations, New York, NY 10017, (212) 963-0027, www.unctad.org; *UNCTAD Commodity Yearbook.*

United Nations Economic Commission for Africa (ECA), PO Box 3001, Addis Ababa, Ethiopia, (Telephone in U.S. (212) 963-4957), www.uneca.org; *African Statistical Yearbook 2006.*

United Nations Food and Agricultural Organization (FAO), Viale delle Terme di Caracalla, 00100 Rome, Italy, (Dial from U.S. (202) 653-2400), (Fax from U.S. (202) 653 5760), www.fao.org; *FAO Yearbook of Forest Products* and *The State of Food and Agriculture (SOFA) 2006.*

United Nations Statistics Division, New York, NY 10017, (800) 253-9646, Fax: (212) 963-4116, http://unstats.un.org; *Statistical Yearbook.*

The World Bank, 1818 H Street, NW, Washington, DC 20433, (202) 473-1000, Fax: (202) 477-6391, www.worldbank.org; *Gabon* and *World Development Report 2008.*

GABON - GAS PRODUCTION

See GABON - MINERAL INDUSTRIES

GABON - GEOGRAPHIC INFORMATION SYSTEMS

M.E. Sharpe, 80 Business Park Drive, Armonk, NY 10504, (800) 541-6563, Fax: (914) 273-2106, www.mesharpe.com; *The Illustrated Book of World Rankings.*

The World Bank, 1818 H Street, NW, Washington, DC 20433, (202) 473-1000, Fax: (202) 477-6391, www.worldbank.org; *Gabon.*

GABON - GOLD INDUSTRY

International Monetary Fund (IMF), 700 Nineteenth Street, NW, Washington, DC 20431, (202) 623-7000, Fax: (202) 623-4661, www.imf.org; *International Financial Statistics Yearbook 2007.*

M.E. Sharpe, 80 Business Park Drive, Armonk, NY 10504, (800) 541-6563, Fax: (914) 273-2106, www.mesharpe.com; *The Illustrated Book of World Rankings.*

United Nations Statistics Division, New York, NY 10017, (800) 253-9646, Fax: (212) 963-4116, http://unstats.un.org; *Statistical Yearbook.*

The World Bank, 1818 H Street, NW, Washington, DC 20433, (202) 473-1000, Fax: (202) 477-6391, www.worldbank.org; *World Development Indicators (WDI) 2008.*

GABON - GOLD PRODUCTION

See GABON - MINERAL INDUSTRIES

GABON - GRANTS-IN-AID

International Monetary Fund (IMF), 700 Nineteenth Street, NW, Washington, DC 20431, (202) 623-7000, Fax: (202) 623-4661, www.imf.org; *Government Finance Statistics Yearbook (2008 Edition).*

GABON - GROSS DOMESTIC PRODUCT

African Development Bank Group, Rue Joseph Anoma, 01 BP 1387 Abidjan 01, Cote d'Ivoire, www.afdb.org; *Statistics Pocketbook 2008.*

Economist Intelligence Unit, 111 West 57th Street, New York, NY 10019, (212) 554-0600, Fax: (212) 586-1181, www.eiu.com; *Gabon Country Report.*

Euromonitor International, Inc., 224 S. Michigan Avenue, Suite 1500, Chicago, IL 60604, (312) 922-1115, Fax: (312) 922-1157, www.euromonitor.com; *International Marketing Data and Statistics 2008* and *The World Economic Factbook 2008.*

M.E. Sharpe, 80 Business Park Drive, Armonk, NY 10504, (800) 541-6563, Fax: (914) 273-2106, www.mesharpe.com; *The Illustrated Book of World Rankings.*

Taylor and Francis Group, An Informa Business, 2 Park Square, Milton Park, Abingdon, Oxford OX14 4RN, United Kingdom, (Dial from U.S. (212) 216-7800), (Fax from U.S. (212) 564-7854), www.tandf.co.uk; *The Europa World Year Book.*

United Nations Economic Commission for Africa (ECA), PO Box 3001, Addis Ababa, Ethiopia, (Telephone in U.S. (212) 963-4957), www.uneca.org; *African Statistical Yearbook 2006.*

United Nations Statistics Division, New York, NY 10017, (800) 253-9646, Fax: (212) 963-4116, http://unstats.un.org; *Human Development Report 2006; National Accounts Statistics: Compendium of Income Distribution Statistics; Statistical Yearbook;* and *Survey of Economic and Social Conditions in Africa 2005.*

The World Bank, 1818 H Street, NW, Washington, DC 20433, (202) 473-1000, Fax: (202) 477-6391, www.worldbank.org; *World Development Indicators (WDI) 2008* and *World Development Report 2008.*

GABON - GROSS NATIONAL PRODUCT

M.E. Sharpe, 80 Business Park Drive, Armonk, NY 10504, (800) 541-6563, Fax: (914) 273-2106, www.mesharpe.com; *The Illustrated Book of World Rankings.*

Palgrave Macmillan Ltd., Houndmills, Basingstoke, Hampshire, RG21 6XS, England, (Telephone in U.S. (888) 330-8477), (Fax in U.S. (800) 672-2054), www.palgrave.com; *The Statesman's Yearbook 2008.*

U.S. Department of State (DOS), 2201 C Street NW, Washington, DC 20520, (202) 647-4000, www.state.gov; *World Military Expenditures and Arms Transfers (WMEAT).*

The World Bank, 1818 H Street, NW, Washington, DC 20433, (202) 473-1000, Fax: (202) 477-6391, www.worldbank.org; *The World Bank Atlas 2003-2004; World Development Indicators (WDI) 2008;* and *World Development Report 2008.*

GABON - HIDES AND SKINS INDUSTRY

United Nations Food and Agricultural Organization (FAO), Viale delle Terme di Caracalla, 00100 Rome, Italy, (Dial from U.S. (202) 653-2400), (Fax from U.S. (202) 653 5760), www.fao.org; *FAO Production Yearbook 2002.*

GABON - HOUSING

Euromonitor International, Inc., 224 S. Michigan Avenue, Suite 1500, Chicago, IL 60604, (312) 922-1115, Fax: (312) 922-1157, www.euromonitor.com; *World Marketing Data and Statistics.*

The World Bank, 1818 H Street, NW, Washington, DC 20433, (202) 473-1000, Fax: (202) 477-6391, www.worldbank.org; *World Development Indicators (WDI) 2008.*

GABON - ILLITERATE PERSONS

Euromonitor International, Inc., 224 S. Michigan Avenue, Suite 1500, Chicago, IL 60604, (312) 922-1115, Fax: (312) 922-1157, www.euromonitor.com; *The World Economic Factbook 2008.*

UNESCO Institute for Statistics, C.P. 6128 Succursale Centre-Ville, Montreal, Quebec, H3C 3J7 Canada, (Dial from U.S. (514) 343-6880), (Fax from U.S. (514) 343 6882), www.uis.unesco.org; *Statistical Tables.*

United Nations Statistics Division, New York, NY 10017, (800) 253-9646, Fax: (212) 963-4116, http://unstats.un.org; *Human Development Report 2006.*

GABON - IMPORTS

Central Intelligence Agency, Office of Public Affairs, Washington, DC 20505, (703) 482-0623, Fax: (703) 482-1739, www.cia.gov; *The World Factbook.*

Economist Intelligence Unit, 111 West 57th Street, New York, NY 10019, (212) 554-0600, Fax: (212) 586-1181, www.eiu.com; *Gabon Country Report.*

Euromonitor International, Inc., 224 S. Michigan Avenue, Suite 1500, Chicago, IL 60604, (312) 922-1115, Fax: (312) 922-1157, www.euromonitor.com; *International Marketing Data and Statistics 2008* and *The World Economic Factbook 2008.*

International Monetary Fund (IMF), 700 Nineteenth Street, NW, Washington, DC 20431, (202) 623-7000, Fax: (202) 623-4661, www.imf.org; *Direction of Trade Statistics Yearbook 2007; Government Finance Statistics Yearbook (2008 Edition);* and *International Financial Statistics Yearbook 2007.*

Palgrave Macmillan Ltd., Houndmills, Basingstoke, Hampshire, RG21 6XS, England, (Telephone in U.S. (888) 330-8477), (Fax in U.S. (800) 672-2054), www.palgrave.com; *The Statesman's Yearbook 2008.*

Taylor and Francis Group, An Informa Business, 2 Park Square, Milton Park, Abingdon, Oxford OX14 4RN, United Kingdom, (Dial from U.S. (212) 216-7800), (Fax from U.S. (212) 564-7854), www.tandf.co.uk; *The Europa World Year Book.*

United Nations Conference on Trade and Development (UNCTAD), DC2-1120, United Nations, New York, NY 10017, (212) 963-0027, www.unctad.org; *Handbook of Statistics 2005.*

United Nations Economic Commission for Africa (ECA), PO Box 3001, Addis Ababa, Ethiopia, (Telephone in U.S. (212) 963-4957), www.uneca.org; *African Statistical Yearbook 2006.*

United Nations Food and Agricultural Organization (FAO), Viale delle Terme di Caracalla, 00100 Rome, Italy, (Dial from U.S. (202) 653-2400), (Fax from U.S. (202) 653 5760), www.fao.org; *The State of Food and Agriculture (SOFA) 2006.*

United Nations Statistics Division, New York, NY 10017, (800) 253-9646, Fax: (212) 963-4116, http://unstats.un.org; *Compendium of Intra-African and Related Foreign Trade Statistics 2003* and *Survey of Economic and Social Conditions in Africa 2005.*

The World Bank, 1818 H Street, NW, Washington, DC 20433, (202) 473-1000, Fax: (202) 477-6391, www.worldbank.org; *World Development Indicators (WDI) 2008* and *World Development Report 2008.*

GABON - INCOME TAXES

See GABON - TAXATION

GABON - INDUSTRIAL PRODUCTIVITY

M.E. Sharpe, 80 Business Park Drive, Armonk, NY 10504, (800) 541-6563, Fax: (914) 273-2106, www.mesharpe.com; *The Illustrated Book of World Rankings.*

GABON - INDUSTRIES

Central Intelligence Agency, Office of Public Affairs, Washington, DC 20505, (703) 482-0623, Fax: (703) 482-1739, www.cia.gov; *The World Factbook.*

Economist Intelligence Unit, 111 West 57th Street, New York, NY 10019, (212) 554-0600, Fax: (212) 586-1181, www.eiu.com; *Gabon Country Report.*

Euromonitor International, Inc., 224 S. Michigan Avenue, Suite 1500, Chicago, IL 60604, (312) 922-1115, Fax: (312) 922-1157, www.euromonitor.com; *The World Economic Factbook 2008* and *World Marketing Data and Statistics.*

International Labour Office, I.L.O. Publications, 4 route des Morillons, CH-1211 Geneva 22, Switzerland, (Telephone in U.S. (202) 653-7652), (Fax in U.S. (202) 653-7687), www.ilo.org; *Yearbook of Labour Statistics 2006.*

M.E. Sharpe, 80 Business Park Drive, Armonk, NY 10504, (800) 541-6563, Fax: (914) 273-2106, www.mesharpe.com; *The Illustrated Book of World Rankings.*

Palgrave Macmillan Ltd., Houndmills, Basingstoke, Hampshire, RG21 6XS, England, (Telephone in U.S. (888) 330-8477), (Fax in U.S. (800) 672-2054), www.palgrave.com; *The Statesman's Yearbook 2008.*

Taylor and Francis Group, An Informa Business, 2 Park Square, Milton Park, Abingdon, Oxford OX14 4RN, United Kingdom, (Dial from U.S. (212) 216-7800), (Fax from U.S. (212) 564-7854), www.tandf.co.uk; *The Europa World Year Book.*

United Nations Economic Commission for Africa (ECA), PO Box 3001, Addis Ababa, Ethiopia, (Telephone in U.S. (212) 963-4957), www.uneca.org; *African Statistical Yearbook 2006.*

United Nations Industrial Development Organization (UNIDO), 1 United Nations Plaza, New York, NY 10017, (212) 963 6890, Fax: (212) 963-7904, http://unido.org; Industrial Statistics Database 2008 (INDSTAT) and *The International Yearbook of Industrial Statistics 2008.*

United Nations Statistics Division, New York, NY 10017, (800) 253-9646, Fax: (212) 963-4116, http://unstats.un.org; *Survey of Economic and Social Conditions in Africa 2005.*

The World Bank, 1818 H Street, NW, Washington, DC 20433, (202) 473-1000, Fax: (202) 477-6391, www.worldbank.org; *Gabon* and *World Development Indicators (WDI) 2008.*

GABON - INFANT AND MATERNAL MORTALITY

See GABON - MORTALITY

GABON - INTERNATIONAL LIQUIDITY

International Monetary Fund (IMF), 700 Nineteenth Street, NW, Washington, DC 20431, (202) 623-7000, Fax: (202) 623-4661, www.imf.org; *International Financial Statistics Yearbook 2007.*

GABON - INTERNATIONAL TRADE

African Development Bank Group, Rue Joseph Anoma, 01 BP 1387 Abidjan 01, Cote d'Ivoire, www.afdb.org; *Statistics Pocketbook 2008.*

Economist Intelligence Unit, 111 West 57th Street, New York, NY 10019, (212) 554-0600, Fax: (212) 586-1181, www.eiu.com; *Gabon Country Report.*

Euromonitor International, Inc., 224 S. Michigan Avenue, Suite 1500, Chicago, IL 60604, (312) 922-1115, Fax: (312) 922-1157, www.euromonitor.com; *The World Economic Factbook 2008* and *World Marketing Data and Statistics.*

M.E. Sharpe, 80 Business Park Drive, Armonk, NY 10504, (800) 541-6563, Fax: (914) 273-2106, www.mesharpe.com; *The Illustrated Book of World Rankings.*

Organisation for Economic Cooperation and Development (OECD), 2 rue Andre Pascal, F-75775 Paris Cedex 16, France, (Telephone in U.S. (202) 785-6323), (Fax in U.S. (202) 785-0350), www.oecd.org; *International Trade by Commodity Statistics (ITCS).*

Palgrave Macmillan Ltd., Houndmills, Basingstoke, Hampshire, RG21 6XS, England, (Telephone in U.S. (888) 330-8477), (Fax in U.S. (800) 672-2054), www.palgrave.com; *The Statesman's Yearbook 2008.*

Taylor and Francis Group, An Informa Business, 2 Park Square, Milton Park, Abingdon, Oxford OX14 4RN, United Kingdom, (Dial from U.S. (212) 216-7800), (Fax from U.S. (212) 564-7854), www.tandf.co.uk; *The Europa World Year Book.*

United Nations Conference on Trade and Development (UNCTAD), DC2-1120, United Nations, New York, NY 10017, (212) 963-0027, www.unctad.org; *UNCTAD Commodity Yearbook.*

United Nations Economic Commission for Africa (ECA), PO Box 3001, Addis Ababa, Ethiopia, (Telephone in U.S. (212) 963-4957), www.uneca.org; *African Statistical Yearbook 2006.*

United Nations Food and Agricultural Organization (FAO), Viale delle Terme di Caracalla, 00100 Rome, Italy, (Dial from U.S. (202) 653-2400), (Fax from U.S. (202) 653 5760), www.fao.org; *FAO Trade Yearbook* and *The State of Food and Agriculture (SOFA) 2006.*

United Nations Statistics Division, New York, NY 10017, (800) 253-9646, Fax: (212) 963-4116, http://unstats.un.org; *Compendium of Intra-African and Related Foreign Trade Statistics 2003; International Trade Statistics Yearbook;* and *Statistical Yearbook.*

The World Bank, 1818 H Street, NW, Washington, DC 20433, (202) 473-1000, Fax: (202) 477-6391, www.worldbank.org; *Gabon; World Development Indicators (WDI) 2008;* and *World Development Report 2008.*

World Trade Organization (WTO), Centre William Rappard, Rue de Lausanne 154, CH-1211 Geneva 21, Switzerland, www.wto.org; *International Trade Statistics 2006.*

GABON - INTERNET USERS

International Telecommunication Union (ITU), Place des Nations, 1211 Geneva 20, Switzerland, www.itu.int; *World Telecommunication/ICT Indicators Database on CD-ROM; World Telecommunication/ICT Indicators Database Online;* and *Yearbook of Statistics - Telecommunication Services (Chronological Time Series 1997-2006).*

The World Bank, 1818 H Street, NW, Washington, DC 20433, (202) 473-1000, Fax: (202) 477-6391, www.worldbank.org; *Gabon.*

GABON - IRON AND IRON ORE PRODUCTION

See GABON - MINERAL INDUSTRIES

GABON - LABOR

African Development Bank Group, Rue Joseph Anoma, 01 BP 1387 Abidjan 01, Cote d'Ivoire, www.afdb.org; *Statistics Pocketbook 2008.*

Central Intelligence Agency, Office of Public Affairs, Washington, DC 20505, (703) 482-0623, Fax: (703) 482-1739, www.cia.gov; *The World Factbook.*

Euromonitor International, Inc., 224 S. Michigan Avenue, Suite 1500, Chicago, IL 60604, (312) 922-1115, Fax: (312) 922-1157, www.euromonitor.com; *International Marketing Data and Statistics 2008* and *World Marketing Data and Statistics.*

International Labour Office, I.L.O. Publications, 4 route des Morillons, CH-1211 Geneva 22, Switzerland, (Telephone in U.S. (202) 653-7652), (Fax in U.S. (202) 653-7687), www.ilo.org; *Yearbook of Labour Statistics 2006.*

M.E. Sharpe, 80 Business Park Drive, Armonk, NY 10504, (800) 541-6563, Fax: (914) 273-2106, www.mesharpe.com; *The Illustrated Book of World Rankings.*

Palgrave Macmillan Ltd., Houndmills, Basingstoke, Hampshire, RG21 6XS, England, (Telephone in U.S. (888) 330-8477), (Fax in U.S. (800) 672-2054), www.palgrave.com; *The Statesman's Yearbook 2008.*

Taylor and Francis Group, An Informa Business, 2 Park Square, Milton Park, Abingdon, Oxford OX14 4RN, United Kingdom, (Dial from U.S. (212) 216-7800), (Fax from U.S. (212) 564-7854), www.tandf.co.uk; *The Europa World Year Book.*

United Nations Food and Agricultural Organization (FAO), Viale delle Terme di Caracalla, 00100 Rome, Italy, (Dial from U.S. (202) 653-2400), (Fax from U.S. (202) 653 5760), www.fao.org; *The State of Food and Agriculture (SOFA) 2006.*

United Nations Statistics Division, New York, NY 10017, (800) 253-9646, Fax: (212) 963-4116, http://unstats.un.org; *Human Development Report 2006.*

The World Bank, 1818 H Street, NW, Washington, DC 20433, (202) 473-1000, Fax: (202) 477-6391, www.worldbank.org; *The World Bank Atlas 2003-2004; World Development Indicators (WDI) 2008;* and *World Development Report 2008.*

GABON - LAND USE

Central Intelligence Agency, Office of Public Affairs, Washington, DC 20505, (703) 482-0623, Fax: (703) 482-1739, www.cia.gov; *The World Factbook.*

Euromonitor International, Inc., 224 S. Michigan Avenue, Suite 1500, Chicago, IL 60604, (312) 922-1115, Fax: (312) 922-1157, www.euromonitor.com; *International Marketing Data and Statistics 2008.*

United Nations Food and Agricultural Organization (FAO), Viale delle Terme di Caracalla, 00100 Rome, Italy, (Dial from U.S. (202) 653-2400), (Fax from U.S. (202) 653 5760), www.fao.org; *FAO Production Yearbook 2002.*

The World Bank, 1818 H Street, NW, Washington, DC 20433, (202) 473-1000, Fax: (202) 477-6391, www.worldbank.org; *World Development Report 2008.*

GABON - LIBRARIES

M.E. Sharpe, 80 Business Park Drive, Armonk, NY 10504, (800) 541-6563, Fax: (914) 273-2106, www.mesharpe.com; *The Illustrated Book of World Rankings.*

GABON - LIFE EXPECTANCY

African Development Bank Group, Rue Joseph Anoma, 01 BP 1387 Abidjan 01, Cote d'Ivoire, www.afdb.org; *Statistics Pocketbook 2008.*

Central Intelligence Agency, Office of Public Affairs, Washington, DC 20505, (703) 482-0623, Fax: (703) 482-1739, www.cia.gov; *The World Factbook.*

Euromonitor International, Inc., 224 S. Michigan Avenue, Suite 1500, Chicago, IL 60604, (312) 922-1115, Fax: (312) 922-1157, www.euromonitor.com; *The World Economic Factbook 2008.*

Palgrave Macmillan Ltd., Houndmills, Basingstoke, Hampshire, RG21 6XS, England, (Telephone in U.S. (888) 330-8477), (Fax in U.S. (800) 672-2054), www.palgrave.com; *The Statesman's Yearbook 2008.*

United Nations Statistics Division, New York, NY 10017, (800) 253-9646, Fax: (212) 963-4116, http://unstats.un.org; *Human Development Report 2006* and *World Statistics Pocketbook.*

The World Bank, 1818 H Street, NW, Washington, DC 20433, (202) 473-1000, Fax: (202) 477-6391, www.worldbank.org; *The World Bank Atlas 2003-2004* and *World Development Report 2008.*

GABON - LITERACY

Euromonitor International, Inc., 224 S. Michigan Avenue, Suite 1500, Chicago, IL 60604, (312) 922-1115, Fax: (312) 922-1157, www.euromonitor.com; *World Marketing Data and Statistics.*

United Nations Statistics Division, New York, NY 10017, (800) 253-9646, Fax: (212) 963-4116, http://unstats.un.org; *Survey of Economic and Social Conditions in Africa 2005.*

GABON - LIVESTOCK

M.E. Sharpe, 80 Business Park Drive, Armonk, NY 10504, (800) 541-6563, Fax: (914) 273-2106, www.mesharpe.com; *The Illustrated Book of World Rankings.*

Palgrave Macmillan Ltd., Houndmills, Basingstoke, Hampshire, RG21 6XS, England, (Telephone in U.S. (888) 330-8477), (Fax in U.S. (800) 672-2054), www.palgrave.com; *The Statesman's Yearbook 2008.*

Taylor and Francis Group, An Informa Business, 2 Park Square, Milton Park, Abingdon, Oxford OX14 4RN, United Kingdom, (Dial from U.S. (212) 216-7800), (Fax from U.S. (212) 564-7854), www.tandf.co.uk; *The Europa World Year Book.*

United Nations Conference on Trade and Development (UNCTAD), DC2-1120, United Nations, New York, NY 10017, (212) 963-0027, www.unctad.org; *UNCTAD Commodity Yearbook.*

United Nations Economic Commission for Africa (ECA), PO Box 3001, Addis Ababa, Ethiopia, (Telephone in U.S. (212) 963-4957), www.uneca.org; *African Statistical Yearbook 2006.*

United Nations Food and Agricultural Organization (FAO), Viale delle Terme di Caracalla, 00100 Rome, Italy, (Dial from U.S. (202) 653-2400), (Fax from U.S. (202) 653 5760), www.fao.org; *FAO Production Yearbook 2002* and *The State of Food and Agriculture (SOFA) 2006.*

United Nations Statistics Division, New York, NY 10017, (800) 253-9646, Fax: (212) 963-4116, http://unstats.un.org; *Statistical Yearbook* and *Survey of Economic and Social Conditions in Africa 2005.*

GABON - MANUFACTURES

M.E. Sharpe, 80 Business Park Drive, Armonk, NY 10504, (800) 541-6563, Fax: (914) 273-2106, www.mesharpe.com; *The Illustrated Book of World Rankings.*

United Nations Economic Commission for Africa (ECA), PO Box 3001, Addis Ababa, Ethiopia, (Telephone in U.S. (212) 963-4957), www.uneca.org; *African Statistical Yearbook 2006.*

United Nations Statistics Division, New York, NY 10017, (800) 253-9646, Fax: (212) 963-4116, http://unstats.un.org; *Survey of Economic and Social Conditions in Africa 2005.*

The World Bank, 1818 H Street, NW, Washington, DC 20433, (202) 473-1000, Fax: (202) 477-6391, www.worldbank.org; *World Development Indicators (WDI) 2008.*

GABON - MARRIAGE

M.E. Sharpe, 80 Business Park Drive, Armonk, NY 10504, (800) 541-6563, Fax: (914) 273-2106, www.mesharpe.com; *The Illustrated Book of World Rankings.*

United Nations Statistics Division, New York, NY 10017, (800) 253-9646, Fax: (212) 963-4116, http://unstats.un.org; *Demographic Yearbook.*

GABON - MEAT PRODUCTION

See GABON - LIVESTOCK

GABON - MILK PRODUCTION

See GABON - DAIRY PROCESSING

GABON - MINERAL INDUSTRIES

Commodity Research Bureau, 330 South Wells Street, Suite 612, Chicago, IL 60606-7110, (800) 621-5271, Fax: (312) 939-4135, www.crbtrader.com; *2006 CRB Commodity Yearbook and CD.*

International Monetary Fund (IMF), 700 Nineteenth Street, NW, Washington, DC 20431, (202) 623-7000, Fax: (202) 623-4661, www.imf.org; *International Financial Statistics Yearbook 2007.*

M.E. Sharpe, 80 Business Park Drive, Armonk, NY 10504, (800) 541-6563, Fax: (914) 273-2106, www.mesharpe.com; *The Illustrated Book of World Rankings.*

Organisation for Economic Cooperation and Development (OECD), 2 rue Andre Pascal, F-75775 Paris Cedex 16, France, (Telephone in U.S. (202) 785-6323), (Fax in U.S. (202) 785-0350), www.oecd.org; *World Energy Outlook 2007.*

Palgrave Macmillan Ltd., Houndmills, Basingstoke, Hampshire, RG21 6XS, England, (Telephone in U.S. (888) 330-8477), (Fax in U.S. (800) 672-2054), www.palgrave.com; *The Statesman's Yearbook 2008.*

Taylor and Francis Group, An Informa Business, 2 Park Square, Milton Park, Abingdon, Oxford OX14 4RN, United Kingdom, (Dial from U.S. (212) 216-7800), (Fax from U.S. (212) 564-7854), www.tandf.co.uk; *The Europa World Year Book.*

United Nations Conference on Trade and Development (UNCTAD), DC2-1120, United Nations, New York, NY 10017, (212) 963-0027, www.unctad.org; *UNCTAD Commodity Yearbook.*

United Nations Economic Commission for Africa (ECA), PO Box 3001, Addis Ababa, Ethiopia, (Telephone in U.S. (212) 963-4957), www.uneca.org; *African Statistical Yearbook 2006.*

United Nations Statistics Division, New York, NY 10017, (800) 253-9646, Fax: (212) 963-4116, http://unstats.un.org; *Statistical Yearbook.*

GABON - MONEY EXCHANGE RATES

See GABON - FOREIGN EXCHANGE RATES

GABON - MONEY SUPPLY

African Development Bank Group, Rue Joseph Anoma, 01 BP 1387 Abidjan 01, Cote d'Ivoire, www.afdb.org; *Statistics Pocketbook 2008.*

Economist Intelligence Unit, 111 West 57th Street, New York, NY 10019, (212) 554-0600, Fax: (212) 586-1181, www.eiu.com; *Gabon Country Report.*

International Monetary Fund (IMF), 700 Nineteenth Street, NW, Washington, DC 20431, (202) 623-7000, Fax: (202) 623-4661, www.imf.org; *International Financial Statistics Yearbook 2007.*

Taylor and Francis Group, An Informa Business, 2 Park Square, Milton Park, Abingdon, Oxford OX14 4RN, United Kingdom, (Dial from U.S. (212) 216-7800), (Fax from U.S. (212) 564-7854), www.tandf.co.uk; *The Europa World Year Book.*

United Nations Statistics Division, New York, NY 10017, (800) 253-9646, Fax: (212) 963-4116, http://unstats.un.org; *Statistical Yearbook.*

The World Bank, 1818 H Street, NW, Washington, DC 20433, (202) 473-1000, Fax: (202) 477-6391, www.worldbank.org; *Gabon* and *World Development Indicators (WDI) 2008.*

GABON - MORTALITY

Central Intelligence Agency, Office of Public Affairs, Washington, DC 20505, (703) 482-0623, Fax: (703) 482-1739, www.cia.gov; *The World Factbook.*

Euromonitor International, Inc., 224 S. Michigan Avenue, Suite 1500, Chicago, IL 60604, (312) 922-1115, Fax: (312) 922-1157, www.euromonitor.com; *International Marketing Data and Statistics 2008* and *The World Economic Factbook 2008.*

Palgrave Macmillan Ltd., Houndmills, Basingstoke, Hampshire, RG21 6XS, England, (Telephone in U.S. (888) 330-8477), (Fax in U.S. (800) 672-2054), www.palgrave.com; *The Statesman's Yearbook 2008.*

Taylor and Francis Group, An Informa Business, 2 Park Square, Milton Park, Abingdon, Oxford OX14 4RN, United Kingdom, (Dial from U.S. (212) 216-7800), (Fax from U.S. (212) 564-7854), www.tandf.co.uk; *The Europa World Year Book.*

UNICEF, 3 United Nations Plaza, New York, NY 10017, (800) 253-9646, Fax: (212) 887-7465, www.unicef.org; *The State of the World's Children 2008.*

United Nations Statistics Division, New York, NY 10017, (800) 253-9646, Fax: (212) 963-4116, http://unstats.un.org; *Demographic Yearbook; Human Development Report 2006; Statistical Yearbook; Survey of Economic and Social Conditions in Africa 2005;* and *World Statistics Pocketbook.*

The World Bank, 1818 H Street, NW, Washington, DC 20433, (202) 473-1000, Fax: (202) 477-6391, www.worldbank.org; *The World Bank Atlas 2003-2004* and *World Development Report 2008.*

World Health Organization (WHO), Avenue Appia 20, 1211 Geneve 27, Switzerland, (Telephone in U.S. (212) 331-9081), www.who.int; *The WHO Global Atlas of Infectious Diseases* and *World Health Report 2006.*

GABON - MOTOR VEHICLES

International Road Federation (IFR), Madison Place, 500 Montgomery Street, 5th Floor, Alexandria, VA 22314, (703) 535-1001, Fax: (703) 535-1007, www.irfnet.org; *World Road Statistics 2006.*

Taylor and Francis Group, An Informa Business, 2 Park Square, Milton Park, Abingdon, Oxford OX14 4RN, United Kingdom, (Dial from U.S. (212) 216-7800), (Fax from U.S. (212) 564-7854), www.tandf.co.uk; *The Europa World Year Book.*

United Nations Statistics Division, New York, NY 10017, (800) 253-9646, Fax: (212) 963-4116, http://unstats.un.org; *Statistical Yearbook* and *Survey of Economic and Social Conditions in Africa 2005.*

GABON - MUSEUMS

M.E. Sharpe, 80 Business Park Drive, Armonk, NY 10504, (800) 541-6563, Fax: (914) 273-2106, www.mesharpe.com; *The Illustrated Book of World Rankings.*

UNESCO Institute for Statistics, C.P. 6128 Succursale Centre-Ville, Montreal, Quebec, H3C 3J7 Canada, (Dial from U.S. (514) 343-6880), (Fax from U.S. (514) 343 6882), www.uis.unesco.org; *Statistical Tables.*

GABON - NATURAL GAS PRODUCTION

See GABON - MINERAL INDUSTRIES

GABON - NUTRITION

African Development Bank Group, Rue Joseph Anoma, 01 BP 1387 Abidjan 01, Cote d'Ivoire, www.afdb.org; *Statistics Pocketbook 2008.*

United Nations Food and Agricultural Organization (FAO), Viale delle Terme di Caracalla, 00100 Rome, Italy, (Dial from U.S. (202) 653-2400), (Fax from U.S. (202) 653 5760), www.fao.org; *The State of Food and Agriculture (SOFA) 2006.*

GABON - OLDER PEOPLE

M.E. Sharpe, 80 Business Park Drive, Armonk, NY 10504, (800) 541-6563, Fax: (914) 273-2106, www.mesharpe.com; *The Illustrated Book of World Rankings.*

GABON - PALM OIL PRODUCTION

See GABON - CROPS

GABON - PAPER

See GABON - FORESTS AND FORESTRY

GABON - PEANUT PRODUCTION

See GABON - CROPS

GABON - PESTICIDES

United Nations Food and Agricultural Organization (FAO), Viale delle Terme di Caracalla, 00100 Rome, Italy, (Dial from U.S. (202) 653-2400), (Fax from U.S. (202) 653 5760), www.fao.org; *The State of Food and Agriculture (SOFA) 2006.*

GABON - PETROLEUM INDUSTRY AND TRADE

M.E. Sharpe, 80 Business Park Drive, Armonk, NY 10504, (800) 541-6563, Fax: (914) 273-2106, www.mesharpe.com; *The Illustrated Book of World Rankings.*

Organisation for Economic Cooperation and Development (OECD), 2 rue Andre Pascal, F-75775 Paris Cedex 16, France, (Telephone in U.S. (202) 785-6323), (Fax in U.S. (202) 785-0350), www.oecd.org; *World Energy Outlook 2007.*

Palgrave Macmillan Ltd., Houndmills, Basingstoke, Hampshire, RG21 6XS, England, (Telephone in U.S. (888) 330-8477), (Fax in U.S. (800) 672-2054), www.palgrave.com; *The Statesman's Yearbook 2008.*

PennWell Corporation, 1421 South Sheridan Road, Tulsa, OK 74112, (918) 835-3161, www.pennwell.com; *International Petroleum Encyclopedia 2007.*

U.S. Department of Energy (DOE), Energy Information Administration (EIA), 1000 Independence Avenue, SW, Washington, DC 20585, (202) 586-8800, www.eia.doe.gov; *International Energy Annual 2004* and *International Energy Outlook 2006.*

United Nations Conference on Trade and Development (UNCTAD), DC2-1120, United Nations, New York, NY 10017, (212) 963-0027, www.unctad.org; *UNCTAD Commodity Yearbook.*

United Nations Food and Agricultural Organization (FAO), Viale delle Terme di Caracalla, 00100 Rome, Italy, (Dial from U.S. (202) 653-2400), (Fax from U.S. (202) 653 5760), www.fao.org; *The State of Food and Agriculture (SOFA) 2006.*

United Nations Statistics Division, New York, NY 10017, (800) 253-9646, Fax: (212) 963-4116, http://unstats.un.org; *Statistical Yearbook.*

GABON - POLITICAL SCIENCE

Central Intelligence Agency, Office of Public Affairs, Washington, DC 20505, (703) 482-0623, Fax: (703) 482-1739, www.cia.gov; *The World Factbook.*

International Monetary Fund (IMF), 700 Nineteenth Street, NW, Washington, DC 20431, (202) 623-7000, Fax: (202) 623-4661, www.imf.org; *Government Finance Statistics Yearbook (2008 Edition)* and *International Financial Statistics Yearbook 2007.*

Palgrave Macmillan Ltd., Houndmills, Basingstoke, Hampshire, RG21 6XS, England, (Telephone in U.S. (888) 330-8477), (Fax in U.S. (800) 672-2054), www.palgrave.com; *The Statesman's Yearbook 2008.*

Taylor and Francis Group, An Informa Business, 2 Park Square, Milton Park, Abingdon, Oxford OX14 4RN, United Kingdom, (Dial from U.S. (212) 216-7800), (Fax from U.S. (212) 564-7854), www.tandf.co.uk; *The Europa World Year Book.*

United Nations Statistics Division, New York, NY 10017, (800) 253-9646, Fax: (212) 963-4116, http://unstats.un.org; *National Accounts Statistics: Compendium of Income Distribution Statistics* and *Survey of Economic and Social Conditions in Africa 2005.*

The World Bank, 1818 H Street, NW, Washington, DC 20433, (202) 473-1000, Fax: (202) 477-6391, www.worldbank.org; *World Development Indicators (WDI) 2008* and *World Development Report 2008.*

GABON - POPULATION

African Development Bank Group, Rue Joseph Anoma, 01 BP 1387 Abidjan 01, Cote d'Ivoire, www.afdb.org; *The African Statistical Journal; Gender, Poverty and Environmental Indicators on African Countries 2007; Selected Statistics on African Countries 2007;* and *Statistics Pocketbook 2008.*

Central Intelligence Agency, Office of Public Affairs, Washington, DC 20505, (703) 482-0623, Fax: (703) 482-1739, www.cia.gov; *The World Factbook.*

Economist Intelligence Unit, 111 West 57th Street, New York, NY 10019, (212) 554-0600, Fax: (212) 586-1181, www.eiu.com; *Gabon Country Report.*

Euromonitor International, Inc., 224 S. Michigan Avenue, Suite 1500, Chicago, IL 60604, (312) 922-1115, Fax: (312) 922-1157, www.euromonitor.com; *International Marketing Data and Statistics 2008* and *The World Economic Factbook 2008.*

Eurostat, Batiment Jean Monnet, Rue Alcide de Gasperi, L-2920 Luxembourg, http://epp.eurostat.ec.europa.eu; *Demographic Indicators - Population by Age-Classes.*

International Labour Office, I.L.O. Publications, 4 route des Morillons, CH-1211 Geneva 22, Switzerland, (Telephone in U.S. (202) 653-7652), (Fax in U.S. (202) 653-7687), www.ilo.org; *Yearbook of Labour Statistics 2006.*

M.E. Sharpe, 80 Business Park Drive, Armonk, NY 10504, (800) 541-6563, Fax: (914) 273-2106, www.mesharpe.com; *The Illustrated Book of World Rankings.*

Palgrave Macmillan Ltd., Houndmills, Basingstoke, Hampshire, RG21 6XS, England, (Telephone in U.S. (888) 330-8477), (Fax in U.S. (800) 672-2054), www.palgrave.com; *The Statesman's Yearbook 2008.*

Taylor and Francis Group, An Informa Business, 2 Park Square, Milton Park, Abingdon, Oxford OX14 4RN, United Kingdom, (Dial from U.S. (212) 216-7800), (Fax from U.S. (212) 564-7854), www.tandf.co.uk; *The Europa World Year Book.*

U.S. Department of State (DOS), 2201 C Street NW, Washington, DC 20520, (202) 647-4000, www.state.gov; *World Military Expenditures and Arms Transfers (WMEAT).*

United Nations Food and Agricultural Organization (FAO), Viale delle Terme di Caracalla, 00100 Rome, Italy, (Dial from U.S. (202) 653-2400), (Fax from U.S. (202) 653 5760), www.fao.org; *FAO Production Yearbook 2002.*

United Nations Statistics Division, New York, NY 10017, (800) 253-9646, Fax: (212) 963-4116, http://unstats.un.org; *Demographic Yearbook; Human Development Report 2006; Statistical Yearbook; Survey of Economic and Social Conditions in Africa 2005;* and *World Statistics Pocketbook.*

The World Bank, 1818 H Street, NW, Washington, DC 20433, (202) 473-1000, Fax: (202) 477-6391, www.worldbank.org; *Gabon; The World Bank Atlas 2003-2004;* and *World Development Report 2008.*

World Health Organization (WHO), Avenue Appia 20, 1211 Geneve 27, Switzerland, (Telephone in U.S. (212) 331-9081), www.who.int; *World Health Report 2006.*

GABON - POPULATION DENSITY

African Development Bank Group, Rue Joseph Anoma, 01 BP 1387 Abidjan 01, Cote d'Ivoire, www.afdb.org; *Statistics Pocketbook 2008.*

Central Intelligence Agency, Office of Public Affairs, Washington, DC 20505, (703) 482-0623, Fax: (703) 482-1739, www.cia.gov; *The World Factbook.*

Euromonitor International, Inc., 224 S. Michigan Avenue, Suite 1500, Chicago, IL 60604, (312) 922-1115, Fax: (312) 922-1157, www.euromonitor.com; *The World Economic Factbook 2008.*

M.E. Sharpe, 80 Business Park Drive, Armonk, NY 10504, (800) 541-6563, Fax: (914) 273-2106, www.mesharpe.com; *The Illustrated Book of World Rankings.*

Palgrave Macmillan Ltd., Houndmills, Basingstoke, Hampshire, RG21 6XS, England, (Telephone in U.S. (888) 330-8477), (Fax in U.S. (800) 672-2054), www.palgrave.com; *The Statesman's Yearbook 2008.*

Taylor and Francis Group, An Informa Business, 2 Park Square, Milton Park, Abingdon, Oxford OX14 4RN, United Kingdom, (Dial from U.S. (212) 216-7800), (Fax from U.S. (212) 564-7854), www.tandf.co.uk; *The Europa World Year Book.*

UNESCO Institute for Statistics, C.P. 6128 Succursale Centre-Ville, Montreal, Quebec, H3C 3J7 Canada, (Dial from U.S. (514) 343-6880), (Fax from U.S. (514) 343 6882), www.uis.unesco.org; *Statistical Tables.*

United Nations Food and Agricultural Organization (FAO), Viale delle Terme di Caracalla, 00100 Rome, Italy, (Dial from U.S. (202) 653-2400), (Fax from U.S. (202) 653 5760), www.fao.org; *The State of Food and Agriculture (SOFA) 2006.*

United Nations Statistics Division, New York, NY 10017, (800) 253-9646, Fax: (212) 963-4116, http://unstats.un.org; *Statistical Yearbook* and *Survey of Economic and Social Conditions in Africa 2005.*

The World Bank, 1818 H Street, NW, Washington, DC 20433, (202) 473-1000, Fax: (202) 477-6391, www.worldbank.org; *Gabon* and *World Development Report 2008.*

GABON - POSTAL SERVICE

M.E. Sharpe, 80 Business Park Drive, Armonk, NY 10504, (800) 541-6563, Fax: (914) 273-2106, www.mesharpe.com; *The Illustrated Book of World Rankings.*

United Nations Statistics Division, New York, NY 10017, (800) 253-9646, Fax: (212) 963-4116, http://unstats.un.org; *Statistical Yearbook.*

GABON - POWER RESOURCES

Euromonitor International, Inc., 224 S. Michigan Avenue, Suite 1500, Chicago, IL 60604, (312) 922-1115, Fax: (312) 922-1157, www.euromonitor.com; *International Marketing Data and Statistics 2008; The World Economic Factbook 2008;* and *World Marketing Data and Statistics.*

M.E. Sharpe, 80 Business Park Drive, Armonk, NY 10504, (800) 541-6563, Fax: (914) 273-2106, www.mesharpe.com; *The Illustrated Book of World Rankings.*

Organisation for Economic Cooperation and Development (OECD), 2 rue Andre Pascal, F-75775 Paris Cedex 16, France, (Telephone in U.S. (202) 785-6323), (Fax in U.S. (202) 785-0350), www.oecd.org; *World Energy Outlook 2007.*

Palgrave Macmillan Ltd., Houndmills, Basingstoke, Hampshire, RG21 6XS, England, (Telephone in U.S. (888) 330-8477), (Fax in U.S. (800) 672-2054), www.palgrave.com; *The Statesman's Yearbook 2008.*

Platts, 2 Penn Plaza, 25th Floor, New York, NY 10121-2298, (212) 904-3070, www.platts.com; *Energy Economist.*

U.S. Department of Energy (DOE), Energy Information Administration (EIA), 1000 Independence Avenue, SW, Washington, DC 20585, (202) 586-8800, www.eia.doe.gov; *International Energy Annual 2004* and *International Energy Outlook 2006.*

United Nations Economic Commission for Africa (ECA), PO Box 3001, Addis Ababa, Ethiopia, (Telephone in U.S. (212) 963-4957), www.uneca.org; *African Statistical Yearbook 2006.*

United Nations Food and Agricultural Organization (FAO), Viale delle Terme di Caracalla, 00100 Rome, Italy, (Dial from U.S. (202) 653-2400), (Fax from U.S. (202) 653 5760), www.fao.org; *The State of Food and Agriculture (SOFA) 2006.*

United Nations Statistics Division, New York, NY 10017, (800) 253-9646, Fax: (212) 963-4116, http://unstats.un.org; *Energy Statistics Yearbook 2003; Human Development Report 2006; Statistical Yearbook;* and *World Statistics Pocketbook.*

The World Bank, 1818 H Street, NW, Washington, DC 20433, (202) 473-1000, Fax: (202) 477-6391, www.worldbank.org; *The World Bank Atlas 2003-2004* and *World Development Report 2008.*

GABON - PRICES

Euromonitor International, Inc., 224 S. Michigan Avenue, Suite 1500, Chicago, IL 60604, (312) 922-1115, Fax: (312) 922-1157, www.euromonitor.com; *World Marketing Data and Statistics.*

International Labour Office, I.L.O. Publications, 4 route des Morillons, CH-1211 Geneva 22, Switzerland, (Telephone in U.S. (202) 653-7652), (Fax in U.S. (202) 653-7687), www.ilo.org; *Yearbook of Labour Statistics 2006.*

International Monetary Fund (IMF), 700 Nineteenth Street, NW, Washington, DC 20431, (202) 623-7000, Fax: (202) 623-4661, www.imf.org; *International Financial Statistics Yearbook 2007.*

M.E. Sharpe, 80 Business Park Drive, Armonk, NY 10504, (800) 541-6563, Fax: (914) 273-2106, www.mesharpe.com; *The Illustrated Book of World Rankings.*

United Nations Economic Commission for Africa (ECA), PO Box 3001, Addis Ababa, Ethiopia, (Telephone in U.S. (212) 963-4957), www.uneca.org; *African Statistical Yearbook 2006.*

United Nations Food and Agricultural Organization (FAO), Viale delle Terme di Caracalla, 00100 Rome, Italy, (Dial from U.S. (202) 653-2400), (Fax from U.S. (202) 653 5760), www.fao.org; *FAO Production Yearbook 2002* and *The State of Food and Agriculture (SOFA) 2006.*

The World Bank, 1818 H Street, NW, Washington, DC 20433, (202) 473-1000, Fax: (202) 477-6391, www.worldbank.org; *Gabon.*

GABON - PROFESSIONS

UNESCO Institute for Statistics, C.P. 6128 Succursale Centre-Ville, Montreal, Quebec, H3C 3J7 Canada, (Dial from U.S. (514) 343-6880), (Fax from U.S. (514) 343 6882), www.uis.unesco.org; *Statistical Tables.*

United Nations Statistics Division, New York, NY 10017, (800) 253-9646, Fax: (212) 963-4116, http://unstats.un.org; *Statistical Yearbook.*

GABON - PUBLIC HEALTH

African Development Bank Group, Rue Joseph Anoma, 01 BP 1387 Abidjan 01, Cote d'Ivoire, www.afdb.org; *Statistics Pocketbook 2008.*

Euromonitor International, Inc., 224 S. Michigan Avenue, Suite 1500, Chicago, IL 60604, (312) 922-1115, Fax: (312) 922-1157, www.euromonitor.com; *World Marketing Data and Statistics.*

M.E. Sharpe, 80 Business Park Drive, Armonk, NY 10504, (800) 541-6563, Fax: (914) 273-2106, www.mesharpe.com; *The Illustrated Book of World Rankings.*

Palgrave Macmillan Ltd., Houndmills, Basingstoke, Hampshire, RG21 6XS, England, (Telephone in U.S. (888) 330-8477), (Fax in U.S. (800) 672-2054), www.palgrave.com; *The Statesman's Yearbook 2008.*

UNICEF, 3 United Nations Plaza, New York, NY 10017, (800) 253-9646, Fax: (212) 887-7465, www.unicef.org; *The State of the World's Children 2008.*

United Nations Economic Commission for Africa (ECA), PO Box 3001, Addis Ababa, Ethiopia, (Telephone in U.S. (212) 963-4957), www.uneca.org; *African Statistical Yearbook 2006.*

United Nations Statistics Division, New York, NY 10017, (800) 253-9646, Fax: (212) 963-4116, http://unstats.un.org; *Human Development Report 2006* and *Statistical Yearbook.*

The World Bank, 1818 H Street, NW, Washington, DC 20433, (202) 473-1000, Fax: (202) 477-6391, www.worldbank.org; *Gabon* and *World Development Report 2008.*

World Health Organization (WHO), Avenue Appia 20, 1211 Geneve 27, Switzerland, (Telephone in U.S. (212) 331-9081), www.who.int; The WHO Global Atlas of Infectious Diseases and *World Health Report 2006.*

GABON - RADIO BROADCASTING

Palgrave Macmillan Ltd., Houndmills, Basingstoke, Hampshire, RG21 6XS, England, (Telephone in U.S. (888) 330-8477), (Fax in U.S. (800) 672-2054), www.palgrave.com; *The Statesman's Yearbook 2008.*

GABON - RAILROADS

Jane's Information Group, 110 North Royal Street, Suite 200, Alexandria, VA 22314, (703) 683-3700, Fax: (800) 836-0297, www.janes.com; *Jane's World Railways.*

Palgrave Macmillan Ltd., Houndmills, Basingstoke, Hampshire, RG21 6XS, England, (Telephone in U.S. (888) 330-8477), (Fax in U.S. (800) 672-2054), www.palgrave.com; *The Statesman's Yearbook 2008.*

Taylor and Francis Group, An Informa Business, 2 Park Square, Milton Park, Abingdon, Oxford OX14 4RN, United Kingdom, (Dial from U.S. (212) 216-7800), (Fax from U.S. (212) 564-7854), www.tandf.co.uk; *The Europa World Year Book.*

United Nations Economic Commission for Africa (ECA), PO Box 3001, Addis Ababa, Ethiopia, (Telephone in U.S. (212) 963-4957), www.uneca.org; *African Statistical Yearbook 2006.*

United Nations Statistics Division, New York, NY 10017, (800) 253-9646, Fax: (212) 963-4116, http://unstats.un.org; *Survey of Economic and Social Conditions in Africa 2005.*

GABON - RELIGION

Central Intelligence Agency, Office of Public Affairs, Washington, DC 20505, (703) 482-0623, Fax: (703) 482-1739, www.cia.gov; *The World Factbook.*

M.E. Sharpe, 80 Business Park Drive, Armonk, NY 10504, (800) 541-6563, Fax: (914) 273-2106, www.mesharpe.com; *The Illustrated Book of World Rankings.*

Palgrave Macmillan Ltd., Houndmills, Basingstoke, Hampshire, RG21 6XS, England, (Telephone in U.S. (888) 330-8477), (Fax in U.S. (800) 672-2054), www.palgrave.com; *The Statesman's Yearbook 2008.*

GABON - RESERVES (ACCOUNTING)

African Development Bank Group, Rue Joseph Anoma, 01 BP 1387 Abidjan 01, Cote d'Ivoire, www.afdb.org; *Statistics Pocketbook 2008.*

United Nations Statistics Division, New York, NY 10017, (800) 253-9646, Fax: (212) 963-4116, http://unstats.un.org; *Statistical Yearbook.*

The World Bank, 1818 H Street, NW, Washington, DC 20433, (202) 473-1000, Fax: (202) 477-6391, www.worldbank.org; *World Development Indicators (WDI) 2008.*

GABON - RETAIL TRADE

Euromonitor International, Inc., 224 S. Michigan Avenue, Suite 1500, Chicago, IL 60604, (312) 922-1115, Fax: (312) 922-1157, www.euromonitor.com; *World Marketing Data and Statistics.*

GABON - RICE PRODUCTION

See GABON - CROPS

GABON - ROADS

Central Intelligence Agency, Office of Public Affairs, Washington, DC 20505, (703) 482-0623, Fax: (703) 482-1739, www.cia.gov; *The World Factbook.*

International Road Federation (IFR), Madison Place, 500 Montgomery Street, 5th Floor, Alexandria, VA 22314, (703) 535-1001, Fax: (703) 535-1007, www.irfnet.org; *World Road Statistics 2006.*

Palgrave Macmillan Ltd., Houndmills, Basingstoke, Hampshire, RG21 6XS, England, (Telephone in U.S. (888) 330-8477), (Fax in U.S. (800) 672-2054), www.palgrave.com; *The Statesman's Yearbook 2008.*

United Nations Economic Commission for Africa (ECA), PO Box 3001, Addis Ababa, Ethiopia, (Telephone in U.S. (212) 963-4957), www.uneca.org; *African Statistical Yearbook 2006.*

United Nations Statistics Division, New York, NY 10017, (800) 253-9646, Fax: (212) 963-4116, http://unstats.un.org; *Survey of Economic and Social Conditions in Africa 2005.*

GABON - RUBBER INDUSTRY AND TRADE

International Rubber Study Group (IRSG), 1st Floor, Heron House, 109/115 Wembley Hill Road, Wembley, Middlesex HA9 8DA, United Kingdom, www.rubberstudy.com; *Rubber Statistical Bulletin; Summary of World Rubber Statistics 2005; World Rubber Statistics Handbook (Volume 6, 1975-2001);* and *World Rubber Statistics Historic Handbook.*

M.E. Sharpe, 80 Business Park Drive, Armonk, NY 10504, (800) 541-6563, Fax: (914) 273-2106, www.mesharpe.com; *The Illustrated Book of World Rankings.*

GABON - SHEEP

See GABON - LIVESTOCK

GABON - SHIPPING

Lloyd's Register - Fairplay, 8410 N.W. 53rd Terrace, Suite 207, Miami FL 33166, (305) 718-9929, Fax: (305) 718-9663, www.lrfairplay.com; *Register of Ships 2007-2008; World Casualty Statistics 2007; World Fleet Statistics 2006; World Marine Propulsion Report 2006-2010; World Shipbuilding Statistics 2007;* and The World Shipping Encyclopaedia.

Palgrave Macmillan Ltd., Houndmills, Basingstoke, Hampshire, RG21 6XS, England, (Telephone in U.S. (888) 330-8477), (Fax in U.S. (800) 672-2054), www.palgrave.com; *The Statesman's Yearbook 2008.*

Taylor and Francis Group, An Informa Business, 2 Park Square, Milton Park, Abingdon, Oxford OX14 4RN, United Kingdom, (Dial from U.S. (212) 216-7800), (Fax from U.S. (212) 564-7854), www.tandf.co.uk; *The Europa World Year Book.*

U.S. Department of Transportation (DOT), Maritime Administration (MARAD), West Building, Southeast Federal Center, 1200 New Jersey Avenue, SE, Washington, DC 20590, (800) 99-MARAD, www.marad.dot.gov; *World Merchant Fleet 2005.*

United Nations Economic Commission for Africa (ECA), PO Box 3001, Addis Ababa, Ethiopia, (Telephone in U.S. (212) 963-4957), www.uneca.org; *African Statistical Yearbook 2006.*

United Nations Statistics Division, New York, NY 10017, (800) 253-9646, Fax: (212) 963-4116, http://unstats.un.org; *Statistical Yearbook.*

GABON - SILVER PRODUCTION

See GABON - MINERAL INDUSTRIES

GABON - SOCIAL ECOLOGY

M.E. Sharpe, 80 Business Park Drive, Armonk, NY 10504, (800) 541-6563, Fax: (914) 273-2106, www.mesharpe.com; *The Illustrated Book of World Rankings.*

United Nations Statistics Division, New York, NY 10017, (800) 253-9646, Fax: (212) 963-4116, http://unstats.un.org; *World Statistics Pocketbook.*

GABON - SOCIAL SECURITY

United Nations Statistics Division, New York, NY 10017, (800) 253-9646, Fax: (212) 963-4116, http://unstats.un.org; *National Accounts Statistics: Compendium of Income Distribution Statistics.*

GABON - STEEL PRODUCTION

See GABON - MINERAL INDUSTRIES

GABON - SUGAR PRODUCTION

See GABON - CROPS

GABON - TAXATION

International Monetary Fund (IMF), 700 Nineteenth Street, NW, Washington, DC 20431, (202) 623-7000, Fax: (202) 623-4661, www.imf.org; *Government Finance Statistics Yearbook (2008 Edition).*

International Road Federation (IFR), Madison Place, 500 Montgomery Street, 5th Floor, Alexandria, VA 22314, (703) 535-1001, Fax: (703) 535-1007, www.irfnet.org; *World Road Statistics 2006.*

Taylor and Francis Group, An Informa Business, 2 Park Square, Milton Park, Abingdon, Oxford OX14 4RN, United Kingdom, (Dial from U.S. (212) 216-7800), (Fax from U.S. (212) 564-7854), www.tandf.co.uk; *The Europa World Year Book.*

The World Bank, 1818 H Street, NW, Washington, DC 20433, (202) 473-1000, Fax: (202) 477-6391, www.worldbank.org; *World Development Indicators (WDI) 2008.*

GABON - TELEPHONE

Central Intelligence Agency, Office of Public Affairs, Washington, DC 20505, (703) 482-0623, Fax: (703) 482-1739, www.cia.gov; *The World Factbook.*

International Telecommunication Union (ITU), Place des Nations, 1211 Geneva 20, Switzerland, www.itu.int; World Telecommunication Indicators Database.

Palgrave Macmillan Ltd., Houndmills, Basingstoke, Hampshire, RG21 6XS, England, (Telephone in U.S. (888) 330-8477), (Fax in U.S. (800) 672-2054), www.palgrave.com; *The Statesman's Yearbook 2008.*

Taylor and Francis Group, An Informa Business, 2 Park Square, Milton Park, Abingdon, Oxford OX14

4RN, United Kingdom, (Dial from U.S. (212) 216-7800), (Fax from U.S. (212) 564-7854), www.tandf.co.uk; *The Europa World Year Book.*

United Nations Statistics Division, New York, NY 10017, (800) 253-9646, Fax: (212) 963-4116, http://unstats.un.org; *Statistical Yearbook* and *World Statistics Pocketbook.*

GABON - TEXTILE INDUSTRY

M.E. Sharpe, 80 Business Park Drive, Armonk, NY 10504, (800) 541-6563, Fax: (914) 273-2106, www.mesharpe.com; *The Illustrated Book of World Rankings.*

United Nations Conference on Trade and Development (UNCTAD), DC2-1120, United Nations, New York, NY 10017, (212) 963-0027, www.unctad.org; *UNCTAD Commodity Yearbook.*

GABON - TOBACCO INDUSTRY

Foreign Agricultural Service (FAS), U.S. Department of Agriculture (USDA), 1400 Independence Avenue, SW, Washington, DC 20250, (202) 720-3935, www.fas.usda.gov; *Tobacco: World Markets and Trade.*

M.E. Sharpe, 80 Business Park Drive, Armonk, NY 10504, (800) 541-6563, Fax: (914) 273-2106, www.mesharpe.com; *The Illustrated Book of World Rankings.*

United Nations Statistics Division, New York, NY 10017, (800) 253-9646, Fax: (212) 963-4116, http://unstats.un.org; *Statistical Yearbook.*

GABON - TOURISM

Euromonitor International, Inc., 224 S. Michigan Avenue, Suite 1500, Chicago, IL 60604, (312) 922-1115, Fax: (312) 922-1157, www.euromonitor.com; *The World Economic Factbook 2008* and *World Marketing Data and Statistics.*

M.E. Sharpe, 80 Business Park Drive, Armonk, NY 10504, (800) 541-6563, Fax: (914) 273-2106, www.mesharpe.com; *The Illustrated Book of World Rankings.*

Taylor and Francis Group, An Informa Business, 2 Park Square, Milton Park, Abingdon, Oxford OX14 4RN, United Kingdom, (Dial from U.S. (212) 216-7800), (Fax from U.S. (212) 564-7854), www.tandf.co.uk; *The Europa World Year Book.*

United Nations Economic Commission for Africa (ECA), PO Box 3001, Addis Ababa, Ethiopia, (Telephone in U.S. (212) 963-4957), www.uneca.org; *African Statistical Yearbook 2006.*

United Nations Statistics Division, New York, NY 10017, (800) 253-9646, Fax: (212) 963-4116, http://unstats.un.org; *Statistical Yearbook.*

The World Bank, 1818 H Street, NW, Washington, DC 20433, (202) 473-1000, Fax: (202) 477-6391, www.worldbank.org; *Gabon.*

GABON - TRADE

See GABON - INTERNATIONAL TRADE

GABON - TRANSPORTATION

Central Intelligence Agency, Office of Public Affairs, Washington, DC 20505, (703) 482-0623, Fax: (703) 482-1739, www.cia.gov; *The World Factbook.*

Euromonitor International, Inc., 224 S. Michigan Avenue, Suite 1500, Chicago, IL 60604, (312) 922-1115, Fax: (312) 922-1157, www.euromonitor.com; *International Marketing Data and Statistics 2008* and *World Marketing Data and Statistics.*

M.E. Sharpe, 80 Business Park Drive, Armonk, NY 10504, (800) 541-6563, Fax: (914) 273-2106, www.mesharpe.com; *The Illustrated Book of World Rankings.*

Palgrave Macmillan Ltd., Houndmills, Basingstoke, Hampshire, RG21 6XS, England, (Telephone in U.S. (888) 330-8477), (Fax in U.S. (800) 672-2054), www.palgrave.com; *The Statesman's Yearbook 2008.*

Taylor and Francis Group, An Informa Business, 2 Park Square, Milton Park, Abingdon, Oxford OX14 4RN, United Kingdom, (Dial from U.S. (212) 216-7800), (Fax from U.S. (212) 564-7854), www.tandf.co.uk; *The Europa World Year Book.*

United Nations Economic Commission for Africa (ECA), PO Box 3001, Addis Ababa, Ethiopia, (Telephone in U.S. (212) 963-4957), www.uneca.org; *African Statistical Yearbook 2006.*

United Nations Statistics Division, New York, NY 10017, (800) 253-9646, Fax: (212) 963-4116, http://unstats.un.org; *Human Development Report 2006.*

The World Bank, 1818 H Street, NW, Washington, DC 20433, (202) 473-1000, Fax: (202) 477-6391, www.worldbank.org; *Africa Live Database (LDB)* and *Gabon.*

GABON - UNEMPLOYMENT

Central Intelligence Agency, Office of Public Affairs, Washington, DC 20505, (703) 482-0623, Fax: (703) 482-1739, www.cia.gov; *The World Factbook.*

International Labour Office, I.L.O. Publications, 4 route des Morillons, CH-1211 Geneva 22, Switzerland, (Telephone in U.S. (202) 653-7652), (Fax in U.S. (202) 653-7687), www.ilo.org; *Yearbook of Labour Statistics 2006.*

GABON - URANIUM PRODUCTION AND CONSUMPTION

See GABON - MINERAL INDUSTRIES

GABON - VITAL STATISTICS

Palgrave Macmillan Ltd., Houndmills, Basingstoke, Hampshire, RG21 6XS, England, (Telephone in U.S. (888) 330-8477), (Fax in U.S. (800) 672-2054), www.palgrave.com; *The Statesman's Yearbook 2008.*

United Nations Statistics Division, New York, NY 10017, (800) 253-9646, Fax: (212) 963-4116, http://unstats.un.org; *Statistical Yearbook.*

World Health Organization (WHO), Avenue Appia 20, 1211 Geneve 27, Switzerland, (Telephone in U.S. (212) 331-9081), www.who.int; *World Health Report 2006.*

GABON - WAGES

International Labour Office, I.L.O. Publications, 4 route des Morillons, CH-1211 Geneva 22, Switzerland, (Telephone in U.S. (202) 653-7652), (Fax in U.S. (202) 653-7687), www.ilo.org; *Yearbook of Labour Statistics 2006.*

The World Bank, 1818 H Street, NW, Washington, DC 20433, (202) 473-1000, Fax: (202) 477-6391, www.worldbank.org; *Gabon.*

GABON - WEATHER

See GABON - CLIMATE

GABON - WHEAT PRODUCTION

See GABON - CROPS

GABON - WHOLESALE PRICE INDEXES

International Monetary Fund (IMF), 700 Nineteenth Street, NW, Washington, DC 20431, (202) 623-7000, Fax: (202) 623-4661, www.imf.org; *International Financial Statistics Yearbook 2007.*

United Nations Statistics Division, New York, NY 10017, (800) 253-9646, Fax: (212) 963-4116, http://unstats.un.org; *Statistical Yearbook.*

GABON - WINE PRODUCTION

See GABON - BEVERAGE INDUSTRY

GABON - WOOD AND WOOD PULP

See GABON - FORESTS AND FORESTRY

GABON - WOOL PRODUCTION

See GABON - TEXTILE INDUSTRY

GALLBLADDER DISORDERS - DEATHS

Bernan Essential Government Publications, 4611-F Assembly Drive, Lanham MD, 20706-4391, (301) 459-2255, Fax: (800) 865-3450, www.bernan.com; *Vital Statistics of the United States: Births, Life Expectancy, Deaths, and Selected Health Data.*

National Center for Health Statistics (NCHS), Centers for Disease Control and Prevention (CDC), U.S. Department of Health and Human Services (HHS), 3311 Toledo Road, Hyattsville, MD 20782, (866) 232-4636, www.cdc.gov/nchs; *National Vital Statistics Reports (NVSR); Vital Statistics of the United States (VSUS);* and unpublished data.

GALLIUM

U.S. Department of the Interior (DOI), U.S. Geological Survey (USGS), Office of Minerals Information, 12201 Sunrise Valley Drive, Reston, VA 20192, Mr. Kenneth A. Beckman, (703) 648-4916, Fax: (703) 648-4995, http://minerals.usgs.gov/minerals; *Mineral Commodity Summaries.*

GAMBIA, THE - NATIONAL STATISTICAL OFFICE

Central Statistics Department, The Gambia, Central Bank Building, 1/2 Ecowas Avenue, Banjul, The Gambia, www.gambia.gm/Statistics/; various fact sheets.

GAMBIA, THE - PRIMARY STATISTICS SOURCES

Central Statistics Department, The Gambia, Central Bank Building, 1/2 Ecowas Avenue, Banjul, The Gambia, www.gambia.gm/Statistics/; *Direction of Trade from Africa.*

GAMBIA, THE - AGRICULTURAL MACHINERY

United Nations Statistics Division, New York, NY 10017, (800) 253-9646, Fax: (212) 963-4116, http://unstats.un.org; *Statistical Yearbook.*

GAMBIA, THE - AGRICULTURE

Economist Intelligence Unit, 111 West 57th Street, New York, NY 10019, (212) 554-0600, Fax: (212) 586-1181, www.eiu.com; *The Gambia Country Report.*

Euromonitor International, Inc., 224 S. Michigan Avenue, Suite 1500, Chicago, IL 60604, (312) 922-1115, Fax: (312) 922-1157, www.euromonitor.com; *World Marketing Data and Statistics.*

M.E. Sharpe, 80 Business Park Drive, Armonk, NY 10504, (800) 541-6563, Fax: (914) 273-2106, www.mesharpe.com; *The Illustrated Book of World Rankings.*

Palgrave Macmillan Ltd., Houndmills, Basingstoke, Hampshire, RG21 6XS, England, (Telephone in U.S. (888) 330-8477), (Fax in U.S. (800) 672-2054), www.palgrave.com; *The Statesman's Yearbook 2008.*

Taylor and Francis Group, An Informa Business, 2 Park Square, Milton Park, Abingdon, Oxford OX14 4RN, United Kingdom, (Dial from U.S. (212) 216-7800), (Fax from U.S. (212) 564-7854), www.tandf.co.uk; *The Europa World Year Book.*

United Nations Conference on Trade and Development (UNCTAD), DC2-1120, United Nations, New York, NY 10017, (212) 963-0027, www.unctad.org; *UNCTAD Commodity Yearbook.*

United Nations Economic Commission for Africa (ECA), PO Box 3001, Addis Ababa, Ethiopia, (Telephone in U.S. (212) 963-4957), www.uneca.org; *African Statistical Yearbook 2006.*

United Nations Food and Agricultural Organization (FAO), Viale delle Terme di Caracalla, 00100 Rome, Italy, (Dial from U.S. (202) 653-2400), (Fax from U.S. (202) 653 5760), www.fao.org; AQUASTAT; *FAO Production Yearbook 2002; FAO Trade Yearbook;* and *The State of Food and Agriculture (SOFA) 2006.*

United Nations Statistics Division, New York, NY 10017, (800) 253-9646, Fax: (212) 963-4116, http://

unstats.un.org; *Statistical Yearbook* and *Survey of Economic and Social Conditions in Africa 2005.*

The World Bank, 1818 H Street, NW, Washington, DC 20433, (202) 473-1000, Fax: (202) 477-6391, www.worldbank.org; *Africa Live Database (LDB); African Development Indicators (ADI) 2007; Gambia;* and *World Development Indicators (WDI) 2008.*

GAMBIA, THE - AIRLINES

M.E. Sharpe, 80 Business Park Drive, Armonk, NY 10504, (800) 541-6563, Fax: (914) 273-2106, www.mesharpe.com; *The Illustrated Book of World Rankings.*

Palgrave Macmillan Ltd., Houndmills, Basingstoke, Hampshire, RG21 6XS, England, (Telephone in U.S. (888) 330-8477), (Fax in U.S. (800) 672-2054), www.palgrave.com; *The Statesman's Yearbook 2008.*

Taylor and Francis Group, An Informa Business, 2 Park Square, Milton Park, Abingdon, Oxford OX14 4RN, United Kingdom, (Dial from U.S. (212) 216-7800), (Fax from U.S. (212) 564-7854), www.tandf.co.uk; *The Europa World Year Book.*

United Nations Economic Commission for Africa (ECA), PO Box 3001, Addis Ababa, Ethiopia, (Telephone in U.S. (212) 963-4957), www.uneca.org; *African Statistical Yearbook 2006.*

GAMBIA, THE - AIRPORTS

Central Intelligence Agency, Office of Public Affairs, Washington, DC 20505, (703) 482-0623, Fax: (703) 482-1739, www.cia.gov; *The World Factbook.*

GAMBIA, THE - ALUMINUM PRODUCTION

See GAMBIA, THE - MINERAL INDUSTRIES

GAMBIA, THE - ARMED FORCES

Central Intelligence Agency, Office of Public Affairs, Washington, DC 20505, (703) 482-0623, Fax: (703) 482-1739, www.cia.gov; *The World Factbook.*

Euromonitor International, Inc., 224 S. Michigan Avenue, Suite 1500, Chicago, IL 60604, (312) 922-1115, Fax: (312) 922-1157, www.euromonitor.com; *World Marketing Data and Statistics.*

International Institute for Strategic Studies (IISS), Arundel House, 13-15 Arundel Street, Temple Place, London WC2R 3DX, England, www.iiss.org; *The Military Balance 2007.*

International Monetary Fund (IMF), 700 Nineteenth Street, NW, Washington, DC 20431, (202) 623-7000, Fax: (202) 623-4661, www.imf.org; *Government Finance Statistics Yearbook (2008 Edition).*

Palgrave Macmillan Ltd., Houndmills, Basingstoke, Hampshire, RG21 6XS, England, (Telephone in U.S. (888) 330-8477), (Fax in U.S. (800) 672-2054), www.palgrave.com; *The Statesman's Yearbook 2008.*

U.S. Department of State (DOS), 2201 C Street NW, Washington, DC 20520, (202) 647-4000, www.state.gov; *World Military Expenditures and Arms Transfers (WMEAT).*

United Nations Statistics Division, New York, NY 10017, (800) 253-9646, Fax: (212) 963-4116, http://unstats.un.org; *Human Development Report 2006.*

GAMBIA, THE - BALANCE OF PAYMENTS

African Development Bank Group, Rue Joseph Anoma, 01 BP 1387 Abidjan 01, Cote d'Ivoire, www.afdb.org; *Statistics Pocketbook 2008.*

International Monetary Fund (IMF), 700 Nineteenth Street, NW, Washington, DC 20431, (202) 623-7000, Fax: (202) 623-4661, www.imf.org; *Balance of Payments Statistics Newsletter* and *Balance of Payments Statistics Yearbook 2007.*

Taylor and Francis Group, An Informa Business, 2 Park Square, Milton Park, Abingdon, Oxford OX14 4RN, United Kingdom, (Dial from U.S. (212) 216-7800), (Fax from U.S. (212) 564-7854), www.tandf.co.uk; *The Europa World Year Book.*

United Nations Conference on Trade and Development (UNCTAD), DC2-1120, United Nations, New York, NY 10017, (212) 963-0027, www.unctad.org; *Handbook of Statistics 2005.*

United Nations Economic Commission for Africa (ECA), PO Box 3001, Addis Ababa, Ethiopia, (Telephone in U.S. (212) 963-4957), www.uneca.org; *African Statistical Yearbook 2006.*

The World Bank, 1818 H Street, NW, Washington, DC 20433, (202) 473-1000, Fax: (202) 477-6391, www.worldbank.org; *Gambia; World Development Indicators (WDI) 2008;* and *World Development Report 2008.*

GAMBIA, THE - BANKS AND BANKING

Euromonitor International, Inc., 224 S. Michigan Avenue, Suite 1500, Chicago, IL 60604, (312) 922-1115, Fax: (312) 922-1157, www.euromonitor.com; *World Marketing Data and Statistics.*

International Monetary Fund (IMF), 700 Nineteenth Street, NW, Washington, DC 20431, (202) 623-7000, Fax: (202) 623-4661, www.imf.org; *International Financial Statistics Yearbook 2007.*

M.E. Sharpe, 80 Business Park Drive, Armonk, NY 10504, (800) 541-6563, Fax: (914) 273-2106, www.mesharpe.com; *The Illustrated Book of World Rankings.*

Palgrave Macmillan Ltd., Houndmills, Basingstoke, Hampshire, RG21 6XS, England, (Telephone in U.S. (888) 330-8477), (Fax in U.S. (800) 672-2054), www.palgrave.com; *The Statesman's Yearbook 2008.*

Taylor and Francis Group, An Informa Business, 2 Park Square, Milton Park, Abingdon, Oxford OX14 4RN, United Kingdom, (Dial from U.S. (212) 216-7800), (Fax from U.S. (212) 564-7854), www.tandf.co.uk; *The Europa World Year Book.*

United Nations Economic Commission for Africa (ECA), PO Box 3001, Addis Ababa, Ethiopia, (Telephone in U.S. (212) 963-4957), www.uneca.org; *African Statistical Yearbook 2006.*

GAMBIA, THE - BARLEY PRODUCTION

See GAMBIA, THE - CROPS

GAMBIA, THE - BEVERAGE INDUSTRY

M.E. Sharpe, 80 Business Park Drive, Armonk, NY 10504, (800) 541-6563, Fax: (914) 273-2106, www.mesharpe.com; *The Illustrated Book of World Rankings.*

GAMBIA, THE - BONDS

International Monetary Fund (IMF), 700 Nineteenth Street, NW, Washington, DC 20431, (202) 623-7000, Fax: (202) 623-4661, www.imf.org; *Government Finance Statistics Yearbook (2008 Edition).*

GAMBIA, THE - BROADCASTING

Central Intelligence Agency, Office of Public Affairs, Washington, DC 20505, (703) 482-0623, Fax: (703) 482-1739, www.cia.gov; *The World Factbook.*

Euromonitor International, Inc., 224 S. Michigan Avenue, Suite 1500, Chicago, IL 60604, (312) 922-1115, Fax: (312) 922-1157, www.euromonitor.com; *World Marketing Data and Statistics.*

M.E. Sharpe, 80 Business Park Drive, Armonk, NY 10504, (800) 541-6563, Fax: (914) 273-2106, www.mesharpe.com; *The Illustrated Book of World Rankings.*

Palgrave Macmillan Ltd., Houndmills, Basingstoke, Hampshire, RG21 6XS, England, (Telephone in U.S. (888) 330-8477), (Fax in U.S. (800) 672-2054), www.palgrave.com; *The Statesman's Yearbook 2008.*

WRTH Publications Limited, PO Box 290, Oxford OX2 7FT, UK, www.wrth.com; *World Radio TV Handbook 2007.*

GAMBIA, THE - BUDGET

Central Intelligence Agency, Office of Public Affairs, Washington, DC 20505, (703) 482-0623, Fax: (703) 482-1739, www.cia.gov; *The World Factbook.*

GAMBIA, THE - CAPITAL LEVY

International Monetary Fund (IMF), 700 Nineteenth Street, NW, Washington, DC 20431, (202) 623-7000, Fax: (202) 623-4661, www.imf.org; *Government Finance Statistics Yearbook (2008 Edition).*

GAMBIA, THE - CATTLE

See GAMBIA, THE - LIVESTOCK

GAMBIA, THE - CHILDBIRTH - STATISTICS

Central Intelligence Agency, Office of Public Affairs, Washington, DC 20505, (703) 482-0623, Fax: (703) 482-1739, www.cia.gov; *The World Factbook.*

Euromonitor International, Inc., 224 S. Michigan Avenue, Suite 1500, Chicago, IL 60604, (312) 922-1115, Fax: (312) 922-1157, www.euromonitor.com; *International Marketing Data and Statistics 2008* and *The World Economic Factbook 2008.*

M.E. Sharpe, 80 Business Park Drive, Armonk, NY 10504, (800) 541-6563, Fax: (914) 273-2106, www.mesharpe.com; *The Illustrated Book of World Rankings.*

Palgrave Macmillan Ltd., Houndmills, Basingstoke, Hampshire, RG21 6XS, England, (Telephone in U.S. (888) 330-8477), (Fax in U.S. (800) 672-2054), www.palgrave.com; *The Statesman's Yearbook 2008.*

Taylor and Francis Group, An Informa Business, 2 Park Square, Milton Park, Abingdon, Oxford OX14 4RN, United Kingdom, (Dial from U.S. (212) 216-7800), (Fax from U.S. (212) 564-7854), www.tandf.co.uk; *The Europa World Year Book.*

United Nations Statistics Division, New York, NY 10017, (800) 253-9646, Fax: (212) 963-4116, http://unstats.un.org; *Demographic Yearbook; Statistical Yearbook;* and *Survey of Economic and Social Conditions in Africa 2005.*

The World Bank, 1818 H Street, NW, Washington, DC 20433, (202) 473-1000, Fax: (202) 477-6391, www.worldbank.org; *World Development Indicators (WDI) 2008.*

GAMBIA, THE - CLIMATE

International Institute for Environment and Development (IIED), 3 Endsleigh Street, London, England, WC1H 0DD, United Kingdom, www.iied.org; *Environment Urbanization* and *Haramata - Bulletin of the Drylands.*

M.E. Sharpe, 80 Business Park Drive, Armonk, NY 10504, (800) 541-6563, Fax: (914) 273-2106, www.mesharpe.com; *The Illustrated Book of World Rankings.*

Palgrave Macmillan Ltd., Houndmills, Basingstoke, Hampshire, RG21 6XS, England, (Telephone in U.S. (888) 330-8477), (Fax in U.S. (800) 672-2054), www.palgrave.com; *The Statesman's Yearbook 2008.*

GAMBIA, THE - COAL PRODUCTION

See GAMBIA, THE - MINERAL INDUSTRIES

GAMBIA, THE - COFFEE

See GAMBIA, THE - CROPS

GAMBIA, THE - COMMERCE

Palgrave Macmillan Ltd., Houndmills, Basingstoke, Hampshire, RG21 6XS, England, (Telephone in U.S. (888) 330-8477), (Fax in U.S. (800) 672-2054), www.palgrave.com; *The Statesman's Yearbook 2008.*

GAMBIA, THE - COMMODITY EXCHANGES

United Nations Food and Agricultural Organization (FAO), Viale delle Terme di Caracalla, 00100 Rome, Italy, (Dial from U.S. (202) 653-2400), (Fax from U.S. (202) 653 5760), www.fao.org; *The State of Food and Agriculture (SOFA) 2006.*

GAMBIA, THE - CONSTRUCTION INDUSTRY

M.E. Sharpe, 80 Business Park Drive, Armonk, NY 10504, (800) 541-6563, Fax: (914) 273-2106, www.mesharpe.com; *The Illustrated Book of World Rankings.*

United Nations Economic Commission for Africa (ECA), PO Box 3001, Addis Ababa, Ethiopia, (Telephone in U.S. (212) 963-4957), www.uneca.org; *African Statistical Yearbook 2006.*

United Nations Statistics Division, New York, NY 10017, (800) 253-9646, Fax: (212) 963-4116, http://unstats.un.org; *Statistical Yearbook.*

GAMBIA, THE - CONSUMER PRICE INDEXES

Taylor and Francis Group, An Informa Business, 2 Park Square, Milton Park, Abingdon, Oxford OX14 4RN, United Kingdom, (Dial from U.S. (212) 216-7800), (Fax from U.S. (212) 564-7854), www.tandf.co.uk; *The Europa World Year Book.*

United Nations Economic Commission for Africa (ECA), PO Box 3001, Addis Ababa, Ethiopia, (Telephone in U.S. (212) 963-4957), www.uneca.org; *African Statistical Yearbook 2006.*

United Nations Statistics Division, New York, NY 10017, (800) 253-9646, Fax: (212) 963-4116, http://unstats.un.org; *Statistical Yearbook* and *Survey of Economic and Social Conditions in Africa 2005.*

The World Bank, 1818 H Street, NW, Washington, DC 20433, (202) 473-1000, Fax: (202) 477-6391, www.worldbank.org; *Gambia.*

GAMBIA, THE - CONSUMPTION (ECONOMICS)

African Development Bank Group, Rue Joseph Anoma, 01 BP 1387 Abidjan 01, Cote d'Ivoire, www.afdb.org; *Statistics Pocketbook 2008.*

United Nations Statistics Division, New York, NY 10017, (800) 253-9646, Fax: (212) 963-4116, http://unstats.un.org; *Survey of Economic and Social Conditions in Africa 2005.*

The World Bank, 1818 H Street, NW, Washington, DC 20433, (202) 473-1000, Fax: (202) 477-6391, www.worldbank.org; *World Development Report 2008.*

GAMBIA, THE - COPPER INDUSTRY AND TRADE

See GAMBIA, THE - MINERAL INDUSTRIES

GAMBIA, THE - CORN INDUSTRY

See GAMBIA, THE - CROPS

GAMBIA, THE - COST AND STANDARD OF LIVING

International Monetary Fund (IMF), 700 Nineteenth Street, NW, Washington, DC 20431, (202) 623-7000, Fax: (202) 623-4661, www.imf.org; *Government Finance Statistics Yearbook (2008 Edition).*

GAMBIA, THE - COTTON

See GAMBIA, THE - CROPS

GAMBIA, THE - CROPS

International Monetary Fund (IMF), 700 Nineteenth Street, NW, Washington, DC 20431, (202) 623-7000, Fax: (202) 623-4661, www.imf.org; *International Financial Statistics Yearbook 2007.*

M.E. Sharpe, 80 Business Park Drive, Armonk, NY 10504, (800) 541-6563, Fax: (914) 273-2106, www.mesharpe.com; *The Illustrated Book of World Rankings.*

Palgrave Macmillan Ltd., Houndmills, Basingstoke, Hampshire, RG21 6XS, England, (Telephone in U.S. (888) 330-8477), (Fax in U.S. (800) 672-2054), www.palgrave.com; *The Statesman's Yearbook 2008.*

Taylor and Francis Group, An Informa Business, 2 Park Square, Milton Park, Abingdon, Oxford OX14 4RN, United Kingdom, (Dial from U.S. (212) 216-7800), (Fax from U.S. (212) 564-7854), www.tandf.co.uk; *The Europa World Year Book.*

United Nations Conference on Trade and Development (UNCTAD), DC2-1120, United Nations, New York, NY 10017, (212) 963-0027, www.unctad.org; *UNCTAD Commodity Yearbook.*

United Nations Economic Commission for Africa (ECA), PO Box 3001, Addis Ababa, Ethiopia, (Telephone in U.S. (212) 963-4957), www.uneca.org; *African Statistical Yearbook 2006.*

United Nations Food and Agricultural Organization (FAO), Viale delle Terme di Caracalla, 00100 Rome, Italy, (Dial from U.S. (202) 653-2400), (Fax from U.S. (202) 653 5760), www.fao.org; *FAO Production Yearbook 2002* and *The State of Food and Agriculture (SOFA) 2006.*

United Nations Statistics Division, New York, NY 10017, (800) 253-9646, Fax: (212) 963-4116, http://unstats.un.org; *Statistical Yearbook.*

GAMBIA, THE - CUSTOMS ADMINISTRATION

International Monetary Fund (IMF), 700 Nineteenth Street, NW, Washington, DC 20431, (202) 623-7000, Fax: (202) 623-4661, www.imf.org; *Government Finance Statistics Yearbook (2008 Edition).*

GAMBIA, THE - DAIRY PROCESSING

M.E. Sharpe, 80 Business Park Drive, Armonk, NY 10504, (800) 541-6563, Fax: (914) 273-2106, www.mesharpe.com; *The Illustrated Book of World Rankings.*

Palgrave Macmillan Ltd., Houndmills, Basingstoke, Hampshire, RG21 6XS, England, (Telephone in U.S. (888) 330-8477), (Fax in U.S. (800) 672-2054), www.palgrave.com; *The Statesman's Yearbook 2008.*

Taylor and Francis Group, An Informa Business, 2 Park Square, Milton Park, Abingdon, Oxford OX14 4RN, United Kingdom, (Dial from U.S. (212) 216-7800), (Fax from U.S. (212) 564-7854), www.tandf.co.uk; *The Europa World Year Book.*

United Nations Food and Agricultural Organization (FAO), Viale delle Terme di Caracalla, 00100 Rome, Italy, (Dial from U.S. (202) 653-2400), (Fax from U.S. (202) 653 5760), www.fao.org; *The State of Food and Agriculture (SOFA) 2006.*

GAMBIA, THE - DEATH RATES

See GAMBIA, THE - MORTALITY

GAMBIA, THE - DEBTS, EXTERNAL

African Development Bank Group, Rue Joseph Anoma, 01 BP 1387 Abidjan 01, Cote d'Ivoire, www.afdb.org; *Statistics Pocketbook 2008.*

International Monetary Fund (IMF), 700 Nineteenth Street, NW, Washington, DC 20431, (202) 623-7000, Fax: (202) 623-4661, www.imf.org; *Government Finance Statistics Yearbook (2008 Edition).*

United Nations Statistics Division, New York, NY 10017, (800) 253-9646, Fax: (212) 963-4116, http://unstats.un.org; *Survey of Economic and Social Conditions in Africa 2005.*

The World Bank, 1818 H Street, NW, Washington, DC 20433, (202) 473-1000, Fax: (202) 477-6391, www.worldbank.org; *Africa Live Database (LDB); African Development Indicators (ADI) 2007; World Development Indicators (WDI) 2008;* and *World Development Report 2008.*

GAMBIA, THE - DEFENSE EXPENDITURES

See GAMBIA, THE - ARMED FORCES

GAMBIA, THE - DEMOGRAPHY

Euromonitor International, Inc., 224 S. Michigan Avenue, Suite 1500, Chicago, IL 60604, (312) 922-1115, Fax: (312) 922-1157, www.euromonitor.com; *International Marketing Data and Statistics 2008; The World Economic Factbook 2008;* and *World Marketing Data and Statistics.*

M.E. Sharpe, 80 Business Park Drive, Armonk, NY 10504, (800) 541-6563, Fax: (914) 273-2106, www.mesharpe.com; *The Illustrated Book of World Rankings.*

United Nations Statistics Division, New York, NY 10017, (800) 253-9646, Fax: (212) 963-4116, http://unstats.un.org; *Human Development Report 2006* and *Survey of Economic and Social Conditions in Africa 2005.*

The World Bank, 1818 H Street, NW, Washington, DC 20433, (202) 473-1000, Fax: (202) 477-6391, www.worldbank.org; *Gambia.*

GAMBIA, THE - DIAMONDS

See GAMBIA, THE - MINERAL INDUSTRIES

GAMBIA, THE - DISPOSABLE INCOME

M.E. Sharpe, 80 Business Park Drive, Armonk, NY 10504, (800) 541-6563, Fax: (914) 273-2106, www.mesharpe.com; *The Illustrated Book of World Rankings.*

United Nations Statistics Division, New York, NY 10017, (800) 253-9646, Fax: (212) 963-4116, http://unstats.un.org; *National Accounts Statistics: Compendium of Income Distribution Statistics* and *Statistical Yearbook.*

GAMBIA, THE - DIVORCE

M.E. Sharpe, 80 Business Park Drive, Armonk, NY 10504, (800) 541-6563, Fax: (914) 273-2106, www.mesharpe.com; *The Illustrated Book of World Rankings.*

United Nations Statistics Division, New York, NY 10017, (800) 253-9646, Fax: (212) 963-4116, http://unstats.un.org; *Demographic Yearbook.*

GAMBIA, THE - ECONOMIC ASSISTANCE

United Nations Statistics Division, New York, NY 10017, (800) 253-9646, Fax: (212) 963-4116, http://unstats.un.org; *Statistical Yearbook.*

GAMBIA, THE - ECONOMIC CONDITIONS

African Development Bank Group, Rue Joseph Anoma, 01 BP 1387 Abidjan 01, Cote d'Ivoire, www.afdb.org; *The African Statistical Journal; Gender, Poverty and Environmental Indicators on African Countries 2007; Selected Statistics on African Countries 2007;* and *Statistics Pocketbook 2008.*

Central Intelligence Agency, Office of Public Affairs, Washington, DC 20505, (703) 482-0623, Fax: (703) 482-1739, www.cia.gov; *The World Factbook.*

Economist Intelligence Unit, 111 West 57th Street, New York, NY 10019, (212) 554-0600, Fax: (212) 586-1181, www.eiu.com; *Business Africa* and *The Gambia Country Report.*

Euromonitor International, Inc., 224 S. Michigan Avenue, Suite 1500, Chicago, IL 60604, (312) 922-1115, Fax: (312) 922-1157, www.euromonitor.com; *The World Economic Factbook 2008* and *World Marketing Data and Statistics.*

M.E. Sharpe, 80 Business Park Drive, Armonk, NY 10504, (800) 541-6563, Fax: (914) 273-2106, www.mesharpe.com; *The Illustrated Book of World Rankings.*

Palgrave Macmillan Ltd., Houndmills, Basingstoke, Hampshire, RG21 6XS, England, (Telephone in U.S. (888) 330-8477), (Fax in U.S. (800) 672-2054), www.palgrave.com; *The Statesman's Yearbook 2008.*

Taylor and Francis Group, An Informa Business, 2 Park Square, Milton Park, Abingdon, Oxford OX14 4RN, United Kingdom, (Dial from U.S. (212) 216-7800), (Fax from U.S. (212) 564-7854), www.tandf.co.uk; *The Europa World Year Book.*

United Nations Statistics Division, New York, NY 10017, (800) 253-9646, Fax: (212) 963-4116, http://unstats.un.org; *Compendium of Intra-African and Related Foreign Trade Statistics 2003* and *World Statistics Pocketbook.*

The World Bank, 1818 H Street, NW, Washington, DC 20433, (202) 473-1000, Fax: (202) 477-6391, www.worldbank.org; *Africa Household Survey Databank; Africa Live Database (LDB); Africa Standardized Files and Indicators; African Development Indicators (ADI) 2007; Gambia; The World Bank Atlas 2003-2004;* and *World Development Report 2008.*

GAMBIA, THE - EDUCATION

African Development Bank Group, Rue Joseph Anoma, 01 BP 1387 Abidjan 01, Cote d'Ivoire, www.afdb.org; *Statistics Pocketbook 2008.*

Euromonitor International, Inc., 224 S. Michigan Avenue, Suite 1500, Chicago, IL 60604, (312) 922-1115, Fax: (312) 922-1157, www.euromonitor.com; *International Marketing Data and Statistics 2008* and *World Marketing Data and Statistics.*

International Monetary Fund (IMF), 700 Nineteenth Street, NW, Washington, DC 20431, (202) 623-7000, Fax: (202) 623-4661, www.imf.org; *Government Finance Statistics Yearbook (2008 Edition).*

M.E. Sharpe, 80 Business Park Drive, Armonk, NY 10504, (800) 541-6563, Fax: (914) 273-2106, www.mesharpe.com; *The Illustrated Book of World Rankings.*

Palgrave Macmillan Ltd., Houndmills, Basingstoke, Hampshire, RG21 6XS, England, (Telephone in U.S. (888) 330-8477), (Fax in U.S. (800) 672-2054), www.palgrave.com; *The Statesman's Yearbook 2008.*

Taylor and Francis Group, An Informa Business, 2 Park Square, Milton Park, Abingdon, Oxford OX14 4RN, United Kingdom, (Dial from U.S. (212) 216-7800), (Fax from U.S. (212) 564-7854), www.tandf.co.uk; *The Europa World Year Book.*

UNESCO Institute for Statistics, C.P. 6128 Succursale Centre-Ville, Montreal, Quebec, H3C 3J7 Canada, (Dial from U.S. (514) 343-6880), (Fax from U.S. (514) 343 6882), www.uis.unesco.org; *Statistical Tables.*

United Nations Economic Commission for Africa (ECA), PO Box 3001, Addis Ababa, Ethiopia, (Telephone in U.S. (212) 963-4957), www.uneca.org; *African Statistical Yearbook 2006.*

United Nations Statistics Division, New York, NY 10017, (800) 253-9646, Fax: (212) 963-4116, http://unstats.un.org; *Human Development Report 2006* and *Survey of Economic and Social Conditions in Africa 2005.*

The World Bank, 1818 H Street, NW, Washington, DC 20433, (202) 473-1000, Fax: (202) 477-6391, www.worldbank.org; *Gambia; World Development Indicators (WDI) 2008;* and *World Development Report 2008.*

GAMBIA, THE - ELECTRICITY

M.E. Sharpe, 80 Business Park Drive, Armonk, NY 10504, (800) 541-6563, Fax: (914) 273-2106, www.mesharpe.com; *The Illustrated Book of World Rankings.*

Palgrave Macmillan Ltd., Houndmills, Basingstoke, Hampshire, RG21 6XS, England, (Telephone in U.S. (888) 330-8477), (Fax in U.S. (800) 672-2054), www.palgrave.com; *The Statesman's Yearbook 2008.*

United Nations Economic Commission for Africa (ECA), PO Box 3001, Addis Ababa, Ethiopia, (Telephone in U.S. (212) 963-4957), www.uneca.org; *African Statistical Yearbook 2006.*

United Nations Statistics Division, New York, NY 10017, (800) 253-9646, Fax: (212) 963-4116, http://unstats.un.org; *Human Development Report 2006; Statistical Yearbook;* and *Survey of Economic and Social Conditions in Africa 2005.*

GAMBIA, THE - EMPLOYMENT

Euromonitor International, Inc., 224 S. Michigan Avenue, Suite 1500, Chicago, IL 60604, (312) 922-1115, Fax: (312) 922-1157, www.euromonitor.com; *International Marketing Data and Statistics 2008.*

International Labour Office, I.L.O. Publications, 4 route des Morillons, CH-1211 Geneva 22, Switzerland, (Telephone in U.S. (202) 653-7652), (Fax in U.S. (202) 653-7687), www.ilo.org; *Yearbook of Labour Statistics 2006.*

M.E. Sharpe, 80 Business Park Drive, Armonk, NY 10504, (800) 541-6563, Fax: (914) 273-2106, www.mesharpe.com; *The Illustrated Book of World Rankings.*

United Nations Economic Commission for Africa (ECA), PO Box 3001, Addis Ababa, Ethiopia, (Telephone in U.S. (212) 963-4957), www.uneca.org; *African Statistical Yearbook 2006.*

United Nations Statistics Division, New York, NY 10017, (800) 253-9646, Fax: (212) 963-4116, http://unstats.un.org; *Statistical Yearbook* and *Survey of Economic and Social Conditions in Africa 2005.*

The World Bank, 1818 H Street, NW, Washington, DC 20433, (202) 473-1000, Fax: (202) 477-6391, www.worldbank.org; *Gambia.*

GAMBIA, THE - ENVIRONMENTAL CONDITIONS

DSI Data Service Information, Xantener Strasse 51a, D-47495 Rheinberg, Germany, www.dsidata.com; *Campus Solution.*

Economist Intelligence Unit, 111 West 57th Street, New York, NY 10019, (212) 554-0600, Fax: (212) 586-1181, www.eiu.com; *The Gambia Country Report.*

International Institute for Environment and Development (IIED), 3 Endsleigh Street, London, England, WC1H 0DD, United Kingdom, www.iied.org; *Environment Urbanization* and *Haramata - Bulletin of the Drylands.*

United Nations Statistics Division, New York, NY 10017, (800) 253-9646, Fax: (212) 963-4116, http://unstats.un.org; *World Statistics Pocketbook.*

GAMBIA, THE - EXPORTS

African Development Bank Group, Rue Joseph Anoma, 01 BP 1387 Abidjan 01, Cote d'Ivoire, www.afdb.org; *Statistics Pocketbook 2008.*

Central Intelligence Agency, Office of Public Affairs, Washington, DC 20505, (703) 482-0623, Fax: (703) 482-1739, www.cia.gov; *The World Factbook.*

Economist Intelligence Unit, 111 West 57th Street, New York, NY 10019, (212) 554-0600, Fax: (212) 586-1181, www.eiu.com; *The Gambia Country Report.*

Euromonitor International, Inc., 224 S. Michigan Avenue, Suite 1500, Chicago, IL 60604, (312) 922-1115, Fax: (312) 922-1157, www.euromonitor.com; *International Marketing Data and Statistics 2008* and *The World Economic Factbook 2008.*

International Monetary Fund (IMF), 700 Nineteenth Street, NW, Washington, DC 20431, (202) 623-7000, Fax: (202) 623-4661, www.imf.org; *Direction of Trade Statistics Yearbook 2007; Government Finance Statistics Yearbook (2008 Edition);* and *International Financial Statistics Yearbook 2007.*

Palgrave Macmillan Ltd., Houndmills, Basingstoke, Hampshire, RG21 6XS, England, (Telephone in U.S. (888) 330-8477), (Fax in U.S. (800) 672-2054), www.palgrave.com; *The Statesman's Yearbook 2008.*

Taylor and Francis Group, An Informa Business, 2 Park Square, Milton Park, Abingdon, Oxford OX14 4RN, United Kingdom, (Dial from U.S. (212) 216-7800), (Fax from U.S. (212) 564-7854), www.tandf.co.uk; *The Europa World Year Book.*

United Nations Conference on Trade and Development (UNCTAD), DC2-1120, United Nations, New York, NY 10017, (212) 963-0027, www.unctad.org; *Handbook of Statistics 2005.*

United Nations Economic Commission for Africa (ECA), PO Box 3001, Addis Ababa, Ethiopia, (Telephone in U.S. (212) 963-4957), www.uneca.org; *African Statistical Yearbook 2006.*

United Nations Food and Agricultural Organization (FAO), Viale delle Terme di Caracalla, 00100 Rome, Italy, (Dial from U.S. (202) 653-2400), (Fax from U.S. (202) 653 5760), www.fao.org; *The State of Food and Agriculture (SOFA) 2006.*

United Nations Statistics Division, New York, NY 10017, (800) 253-9646, Fax: (212) 963-4116, http://unstats.un.org; *Compendium of Intra-African and Related Foreign Trade Statistics 2003* and *Survey of Economic and Social Conditions in Africa 2005.*

The World Bank, 1818 H Street, NW, Washington, DC 20433, (202) 473-1000, Fax: (202) 477-6391, www.worldbank.org; *World Development Indicators (WDI) 2008* and *World Development Report 2008.*

GAMBIA, THE - FERTILITY, HUMAN

Central Intelligence Agency, Office of Public Affairs, Washington, DC 20505, (703) 482-0623, Fax: (703) 482-1739, www.cia.gov; *The World Factbook.*

M.E. Sharpe, 80 Business Park Drive, Armonk, NY 10504, (800) 541-6563, Fax: (914) 273-2106, www.mesharpe.com; *The Illustrated Book of World Rankings.*

United Nations Statistics Division, New York, NY 10017, (800) 253-9646, Fax: (212) 963-4116, http://unstats.un.org; *Human Development Report 2006* and *Survey of Economic and Social Conditions in Africa 2005.*

The World Bank, 1818 H Street, NW, Washington, DC 20433, (202) 473-1000, Fax: (202) 477-6391, www.worldbank.org; *The World Bank Atlas 2003-2004; World Development Indicators (WDI) 2008;* and *World Development Report 2008.*

GAMBIA, THE - FERTILIZER INDUSTRY

United Nations Food and Agricultural Organization (FAO), Viale delle Terme di Caracalla, 00100 Rome, Italy, (Dial from U.S. (202) 653-2400), (Fax from U.S. (202) 653 5760), www.fao.org; *FAO Fertilizer Yearbook* and *The State of Food and Agriculture (SOFA) 2006.*

United Nations Statistics Division, New York, NY 10017, (800) 253-9646, Fax: (212) 963-4116, http://unstats.un.org; *Statistical Yearbook.*

GAMBIA, THE - FETAL MORTALITY

See GAMBIA, THE - MORTALITY

GAMBIA, THE - FINANCE

International Monetary Fund (IMF), 700 Nineteenth Street, NW, Washington, DC 20431, (202) 623-7000, Fax: (202) 623-4661, www.imf.org; *International Financial Statistics Yearbook 2007.*

United Nations Economic Commission for Africa (ECA), PO Box 3001, Addis Ababa, Ethiopia, (Telephone in U.S. (212) 963-4957), www.uneca.org; *African Statistical Yearbook 2006.*

United Nations Statistics Division, New York, NY 10017, (800) 253-9646, Fax: (212) 963-4116, http://unstats.un.org; *Statistical Yearbook.*

The World Bank, 1818 H Street, NW, Washington, DC 20433, (202) 473-1000, Fax: (202) 477-6391, www.worldbank.org; *Gambia.*

GAMBIA, THE - FINANCE, PUBLIC

African Development Bank Group, Rue Joseph Anoma, 01 BP 1387 Abidjan 01, Cote d'Ivoire, www.afdb.org; *Statistics Pocketbook 2008.*

Economist Intelligence Unit, 111 West 57th Street, New York, NY 10019, (212) 554-0600, Fax: (212) 586-1181, www.eiu.com; *The Gambia Country Report.*

International Monetary Fund (IMF), 700 Nineteenth Street, NW, Washington, DC 20431, (202) 623-7000, Fax: (202) 623-4661, www.imf.org; *Government Finance Statistics Yearbook (2008 Edition).*

M.E. Sharpe, 80 Business Park Drive, Armonk, NY 10504, (800) 541-6563, Fax: (914) 273-2106, www.mesharpe.com; *The Illustrated Book of World Rankings.*

Palgrave Macmillan Ltd., Houndmills, Basingstoke, Hampshire, RG21 6XS, England, (Telephone in U.S. (888) 330-8477), (Fax in U.S. (800) 672-2054), www.palgrave.com; *The Statesman's Yearbook 2008.*

Taylor and Francis Group, An Informa Business, 2 Park Square, Milton Park, Abingdon, Oxford OX14 4RN, United Kingdom, (Dial from U.S. (212) 216-7800), (Fax from U.S. (212) 564-7854), www.tandf.co.uk; *The Europa World Year Book.*

United Nations Economic Commission for Africa (ECA), PO Box 3001, Addis Ababa, Ethiopia, (Telephone in U.S. (212) 963-4957), www.uneca.org; *African Statistical Yearbook 2006.*

The World Bank, 1818 H Street, NW, Washington, DC 20433, (202) 473-1000, Fax: (202) 477-6391, www.worldbank.org; *Gambia.*

GAMBIA, THE - FISHERIES

M.E. Sharpe, 80 Business Park Drive, Armonk, NY 10504, (800) 541-6563, Fax: (914) 273-2106, www.mesharpe.com; *The Illustrated Book of World Rankings.*

Palgrave Macmillan Ltd., Houndmills, Basingstoke, Hampshire, RG21 6XS, England, (Telephone in U.S. (888) 330-8477), (Fax in U.S. (800) 672-2054), www.palgrave.com; *The Statesman's Yearbook 2008.*

Taylor and Francis Group, An Informa Business, 2 Park Square, Milton Park, Abingdon, Oxford OX14 4RN, United Kingdom, (Dial from U.S. (212) 216-7800), (Fax from U.S. (212) 564-7854), www.tandf.co.uk; *The Europa World Year Book.*

United Nations Conference on Trade and Development (UNCTAD), DC2-1120, United Nations, New York, NY 10017, (212) 963-0027, www.unctad.org; *UNCTAD Commodity Yearbook.*

United Nations Economic Commission for Africa (ECA), PO Box 3001, Addis Ababa, Ethiopia, (Telephone in U.S. (212) 963-4957), www.uneca.org; *African Statistical Yearbook 2006.*

United Nations Food and Agricultural Organization (FAO), Viale delle Terme di Caracalla, 00100 Rome, Italy, (Dial from U.S. (202) 653-2400), (Fax from U.S. (202) 653 5760), www.fao.org; *FAO Yearbook of Fishery Statistics;* Fishery Databases; FISHSTAT Database. Subjects covered include: Aquaculture production, capture production, fishery commodities; and *The State of Food and Agriculture (SOFA) 2006.*

United Nations Statistics Division, New York, NY 10017, (800) 253-9646, Fax: (212) 963-4116, http://unstats.un.org; *Statistical Yearbook* and *Survey of Economic and Social Conditions in Africa 2005.*

The World Bank, 1818 H Street, NW, Washington, DC 20433, (202) 473-1000, Fax: (202) 477-6391, www.worldbank.org; *Gambia.*

GAMBIA, THE - FOOD

African Development Bank Group, Rue Joseph Anoma, 01 BP 1387 Abidjan 01, Cote d'Ivoire, www.afdb.org; *Statistics Pocketbook 2008.*

United Nations Conference on Trade and Development (UNCTAD), DC2-1120, United Nations, New York, NY 10017, (212) 963-0027, www.unctad.org; *UNCTAD Commodity Yearbook.*

United Nations Food and Agricultural Organization (FAO), Viale delle Terme di Caracalla, 00100 Rome, Italy, (Dial from U.S. (202) 653-2400), (Fax from U.S. (202) 653 5760), www.fao.org; *FAO Production Yearbook 2002* and *The State of Food and Agriculture (SOFA) 2006.*

United Nations Statistics Division, New York, NY 10017, (800) 253-9646, Fax: (212) 963-4116, http://unstats.un.org; *Human Development Report 2006.*

GAMBIA, THE - FOREIGN EXCHANGE RATES

African Development Bank Group, Rue Joseph Anoma, 01 BP 1387 Abidjan 01, Cote d'Ivoire, www.afdb.org; *Statistics Pocketbook 2008.*

Central Intelligence Agency, Office of Public Affairs, Washington, DC 20505, (703) 482-0623, Fax: (703) 482-1739, www.cia.gov; *The World Factbook.*

Euromonitor International, Inc., 224 S. Michigan Avenue, Suite 1500, Chicago, IL 60604, (312) 922-1115, Fax: (312) 922-1157, www.euromonitor.com; *International Marketing Data and Statistics 2008* and *The World Economic Factbook 2008.*

International Monetary Fund (IMF), 700 Nineteenth Street, NW, Washington, DC 20431, (202) 623-7000, Fax: (202) 623-4661, www.imf.org; *International Financial Statistics Yearbook 2007.*

Taylor and Francis Group, An Informa Business, 2 Park Square, Milton Park, Abingdon, Oxford OX14 4RN, United Kingdom, (Dial from U.S. (212) 216-7800), (Fax from U.S. (212) 564-7854), www.tandf.co.uk; *The Europa World Year Book.*

United Nations Statistics Division, New York, NY 10017, (800) 253-9646, Fax: (212) 963-4116, http://unstats.un.org; *Compendium of Intra-African and Related Foreign Trade Statistics 2003; Statistical Yearbook;* and *World Statistics Pocketbook.*

GAMBIA, THE - FORESTS AND FORESTRY

M.E. Sharpe, 80 Business Park Drive, Armonk, NY 10504, (800) 541-6563, Fax: (914) 273-2106, www.mesharpe.com; *The Illustrated Book of World Rankings.*

Palgrave Macmillan Ltd., Houndmills, Basingstoke, Hampshire, RG21 6XS, England, (Telephone in U.S. (888) 330-8477), (Fax in U.S. (800) 672-2054), www.palgrave.com; *The Statesman's Yearbook 2008.*

Taylor and Francis Group, An Informa Business, 2 Park Square, Milton Park, Abingdon, Oxford OX14 4RN, United Kingdom, (Dial from U.S. (212) 216-7800), (Fax from U.S. (212) 564-7854), www.tandf.co.uk; *The Europa World Year Book.*

United Nations Conference on Trade and Development (UNCTAD), DC2-1120, United Nations, New York, NY 10017, (212) 963-0027, www.unctad.org; *UNCTAD Commodity Yearbook.*

United Nations Economic Commission for Africa (ECA), PO Box 3001, Addis Ababa, Ethiopia, (Telephone in U.S. (212) 963-4957), www.uneca.org; *African Statistical Yearbook 2006.*

United Nations Food and Agricultural Organization (FAO), Viale delle Terme di Caracalla, 00100 Rome, Italy, (Dial from U.S. (202) 653-2400), (Fax from U.S. (202) 653 5760), www.fao.org; *FAO Yearbook of Forest Products* and *The State of Food and Agriculture (SOFA) 2006.*

United Nations Statistics Division, New York, NY 10017, (800) 253-9646, Fax: (212) 963-4116, http://unstats.un.org; *Statistical Yearbook.*

The World Bank, 1818 H Street, NW, Washington, DC 20433, (202) 473-1000, Fax: (202) 477-6391, www.worldbank.org; *Gambia* and *World Development Report 2008.*

GAMBIA, THE - GAS PRODUCTION

See GAMBIA, THE - MINERAL INDUSTRIES

GAMBIA, THE - GEOGRAPHIC INFORMATION SYSTEMS

M.E. Sharpe, 80 Business Park Drive, Armonk, NY 10504, (800) 541-6563, Fax: (914) 273-2106, www.mesharpe.com; *The Illustrated Book of World Rankings.*

The World Bank, 1818 H Street, NW, Washington, DC 20433, (202) 473-1000, Fax: (202) 477-6391, www.worldbank.org; *Gambia.*

GAMBIA, THE - GOLD INDUSTRY

International Monetary Fund (IMF), 700 Nineteenth Street, NW, Washington, DC 20431, (202) 623-7000, Fax: (202) 623-4661, www.imf.org; *International Financial Statistics Yearbook 2007.*

United Nations Statistics Division, New York, NY 10017, (800) 253-9646, Fax: (212) 963-4116, http://unstats.un.org; *Statistical Yearbook.*

The World Bank, 1818 H Street, NW, Washington, DC 20433, (202) 473-1000, Fax: (202) 477-6391, www.worldbank.org; *World Development Indicators (WDI) 2008.*

GAMBIA, THE - GOLD PRODUCTION

See GAMBIA, THE - MINERAL INDUSTRIES

GAMBIA, THE - GRANTS-IN-AID

International Monetary Fund (IMF), 700 Nineteenth Street, NW, Washington, DC 20431, (202) 623-7000, Fax: (202) 623-4661, www.imf.org; *Government Finance Statistics Yearbook (2008 Edition).*

GAMBIA, THE - GROSS DOMESTIC PRODUCT

African Development Bank Group, Rue Joseph Anoma, 01 BP 1387 Abidjan 01, Cote d'Ivoire, www.afdb.org; *Statistics Pocketbook 2008.*

Economist Intelligence Unit, 111 West 57th Street, New York, NY 10019, (212) 554-0600, Fax: (212) 586-1181, www.eiu.com; *The Gambia Country Report.*

Euromonitor International, Inc., 224 S. Michigan Avenue, Suite 1500, Chicago, IL 60604, (312) 922-1115, Fax: (312) 922-1157, www.euromonitor.com; *International Marketing Data and Statistics 2008* and *The World Economic Factbook 2008.*

M.E. Sharpe, 80 Business Park Drive, Armonk, NY 10504, (800) 541-6563, Fax: (914) 273-2106, www.mesharpe.com; *The Illustrated Book of World Rankings.*

Taylor and Francis Group, An Informa Business, 2 Park Square, Milton Park, Abingdon, Oxford OX14 4RN, United Kingdom, (Dial from U.S. (212) 216-7800), (Fax from U.S. (212) 564-7854), www.tandf.co.uk; *The Europa World Year Book.*

United Nations Economic Commission for Africa (ECA), PO Box 3001, Addis Ababa, Ethiopia, (Telephone in U.S. (212) 963-4957), www.uneca.org; *African Statistical Yearbook 2006.*

United Nations Statistics Division, New York, NY 10017, (800) 253-9646, Fax: (212) 963-4116, http://unstats.un.org; *Human Development Report 2006; National Accounts Statistics: Compendium of Income Distribution Statistics; Statistical Yearbook;* and *Survey of Economic and Social Conditions in Africa 2005.*

The World Bank, 1818 H Street, NW, Washington, DC 20433, (202) 473-1000, Fax: (202) 477-6391, www.worldbank.org; *World Development Indicators (WDI) 2008* and *World Development Report 2008.*

GAMBIA, THE - GROSS NATIONAL PRODUCT

M.E. Sharpe, 80 Business Park Drive, Armonk, NY 10504, (800) 541-6563, Fax: (914) 273-2106, www.mesharpe.com; *The Illustrated Book of World Rankings.*

Palgrave Macmillan Ltd., Houndmills, Basingstoke, Hampshire, RG21 6XS, England, (Telephone in U.S. (888) 330-8477), (Fax in U.S. (800) 672-2054), www.palgrave.com; *The Statesman's Yearbook 2008.*

U.S. Department of State (DOS), 2201 C Street NW, Washington, DC 20520, (202) 647-4000, www.state.gov; *World Military Expenditures and Arms Transfers (WMEAT).*

The World Bank, 1818 H Street, NW, Washington, DC 20433, (202) 473-1000, Fax: (202) 477-6391, www.worldbank.org; *The World Bank Atlas 2003-2004; World Development Indicators (WDI) 2008;* and *World Development Report 2008.*

GAMBIA, THE - HARDWOOD INDUSTRY

M.E. Sharpe, 80 Business Park Drive, Armonk, NY 10504, (800) 541-6563, Fax: (914) 273-2106, www.mesharpe.com; *The Illustrated Book of World Rankings.*

GAMBIA, THE - HIDES AND SKINS INDUSTRY

United Nations Food and Agricultural Organization (FAO), Viale delle Terme di Caracalla, 00100 Rome, Italy, (Dial from U.S. (202) 653-2400), (Fax from U.S. (202) 653 5760), www.fao.org; *FAO Production Yearbook 2002.*

GAMBIA, THE - HOUSING

Euromonitor International, Inc., 224 S. Michigan Avenue, Suite 1500, Chicago, IL 60604, (312) 922-1115, Fax: (312) 922-1157, www.euromonitor.com; *World Marketing Data and Statistics.*

M.E. Sharpe, 80 Business Park Drive, Armonk, NY 10504, (800) 541-6563, Fax: (914) 273-2106, www.mesharpe.com; *The Illustrated Book of World Rankings.*

GAMBIA, THE - ILLITERATE PERSONS

Euromonitor International, Inc., 224 S. Michigan Avenue, Suite 1500, Chicago, IL 60604, (312) 922-

1115, Fax: (312) 922-1157, www.euromonitor.com; *The World Economic Factbook 2008.*

Palgrave Macmillan Ltd., Houndmills, Basingstoke, Hampshire, RG21 6XS, England, (Telephone in U.S. (888) 330-8477), (Fax in U.S. (800) 672-2054), www.palgrave.com; *The Statesman's Yearbook 2008.*

UNESCO Institute for Statistics, C.P. 6128 Succursale Centre-Ville, Montreal, Quebec, H3C 3J7 Canada, (Dial from U.S. (514) 343-6880), (Fax from U.S. (514) 343 6882), www.uis.unesco.org; *Statistical Tables.*

United Nations Statistics Division, New York, NY 10017, (800) 253-9646, Fax: (212) 963-4116, http://unstats.un.org; *Human Development Report 2006.*

GAMBIA, THE - IMPORTS

Central Intelligence Agency, Office of Public Affairs, Washington, DC 20505, (703) 482-0623, Fax: (703) 482-1739, www.cia.gov; *The World Factbook.*

Economist Intelligence Unit, 111 West 57th Street, New York, NY 10019, (212) 554-0600, Fax: (212) 586-1181, www.eiu.com; *The Gambia Country Report.*

Euromonitor International, Inc., 224 S. Michigan Avenue, Suite 1500, Chicago, IL 60604, (312) 922-1115, Fax: (312) 922-1157, www.euromonitor.com; *International Marketing Data and Statistics 2008* and *The World Economic Factbook 2008.*

International Monetary Fund (IMF), 700 Nineteenth Street, NW, Washington, DC 20431, (202) 623-7000, Fax: (202) 623-4661, www.imf.org; *Direction of Trade Statistics Yearbook 2007; Government Finance Statistics Yearbook (2008 Edition);* and *International Financial Statistics Yearbook 2007.*

Palgrave Macmillan Ltd., Houndmills, Basingstoke, Hampshire, RG21 6XS, England, (Telephone in U.S. (888) 330-8477), (Fax in U.S. (800) 672-2054), www.palgrave.com; *The Statesman's Yearbook 2008.*

Taylor and Francis Group, An Informa Business, 2 Park Square, Milton Park, Abingdon, Oxford OX14 4RN, United Kingdom, (Dial from U.S. (212) 216-7800), (Fax from U.S. (212) 564-7854), www.tandf.co.uk; *The Europa World Year Book.*

United Nations Conference on Trade and Development (UNCTAD), DC2-1120, United Nations, New York, NY 10017, (212) 963-0027, www.unctad.org; *Handbook of Statistics 2005.*

United Nations Economic Commission for Africa (ECA), PO Box 3001, Addis Ababa, Ethiopia, (Telephone in U.S. (212) 963-4957), www.uneca.org; *African Statistical Yearbook 2006.*

United Nations Food and Agricultural Organization (FAO), Viale delle Terme di Caracalla, 00100 Rome, Italy, (Dial from U.S. (202) 653-2400), (Fax from U.S. (202) 653 5760), www.fao.org; *The State of Food and Agriculture (SOFA) 2006.*

United Nations Statistics Division, New York, NY 10017, (800) 253-9646, Fax: (212) 963-4116, http://unstats.un.org; *Compendium of Intra-African and Related Foreign Trade Statistics 2003* and *Survey of Economic and Social Conditions in Africa 2005.*

The World Bank, 1818 H Street, NW, Washington, DC 20433, (202) 473-1000, Fax: (202) 477-6391, www.worldbank.org; *World Development Indicators (WDI) 2008* and *World Development Report 2008.*

GAMBIA, THE - INCOME TAXES

See GAMBIA, THE - TAXATION

GAMBIA, THE - INDUSTRIAL PRODUCTIVITY

M.E. Sharpe, 80 Business Park Drive, Armonk, NY 10504, (800) 541-6563, Fax: (914) 273-2106, www.mesharpe.com; *The Illustrated Book of World Rankings.*

GAMBIA, THE - INDUSTRIAL PROPERTY

World Intellectual Property Organization (WIPO), PO Box 18, CH-1211 Geneva 20, Switzerland, www.wipo.int; *Industrial Property Statistics* and *Industrial Property Statistics Online Directory.*

GAMBIA, THE - INDUSTRIES

Central Intelligence Agency, Office of Public Affairs, Washington, DC 20505, (703) 482-0623, Fax: (703) 482-1739, www.cia.gov; *The World Factbook.*

Economist Intelligence Unit, 111 West 57th Street, New York, NY 10019, (212) 554-0600, Fax: (212) 586-1181, www.eiu.com; *The Gambia Country Report.*

Euromonitor International, Inc., 224 S. Michigan Avenue, Suite 1500, Chicago, IL 60604, (312) 922-1115, Fax: (312) 922-1157, www.euromonitor.com; *The World Economic Factbook 2008* and *World Marketing Data and Statistics.*

International Labour Office, I.L.O. Publications, 4 route des Morillons, CH-1211 Geneva 22, Switzerland, (Telephone in U.S. (202) 653-7652), (Fax in U.S. (202) 653-7687), www.ilo.org; *Yearbook of Labour Statistics 2006.*

M.E. Sharpe, 80 Business Park Drive, Armonk, NY 10504, (800) 541-6563, Fax: (914) 273-2106, www.mesharpe.com; *The Illustrated Book of World Rankings.*

Palgrave Macmillan Ltd., Houndmills, Basingstoke, Hampshire, RG21 6XS, England, (Telephone in U.S. (888) 330-8477), (Fax in U.S. (800) 672-2054), www.palgrave.com; *The Statesman's Yearbook 2008.*

Taylor and Francis Group, An Informa Business, 2 Park Square, Milton Park, Abingdon, Oxford OX14 4RN, United Kingdom, (Dial from U.S. (212) 216-7800), (Fax from U.S. (212) 564-7854), www.tandf.co.uk; *The Europa World Year Book.*

United Nations Economic Commission for Africa (ECA), PO Box 3001, Addis Ababa, Ethiopia, (Telephone in U.S. (212) 963-4957), www.uneca.org; *African Statistical Yearbook 2006.*

United Nations Statistics Division, New York, NY 10017, (800) 253-9646, Fax: (212) 963-4116, http://unstats.un.org; *2004 Industrial Commodity Statistics Yearbook* and *Survey of Economic and Social Conditions in Africa 2005.*

The World Bank, 1818 H Street, NW, Washington, DC 20433, (202) 473-1000, Fax: (202) 477-6391, www.worldbank.org; *Gambia* and *World Development Indicators (WDI) 2008.*

GAMBIA, THE - INFANT AND MATERNAL MORTALITY

See GAMBIA, THE - MORTALITY

GAMBIA, THE - INTERNATIONAL LIQUIDITY

International Monetary Fund (IMF), 700 Nineteenth Street, NW, Washington, DC 20431, (202) 623-7000, Fax: (202) 623-4661, www.imf.org; *International Financial Statistics Yearbook 2007.*

GAMBIA, THE - INTERNATIONAL TRADE

African Development Bank Group, Rue Joseph Anoma, 01 BP 1387 Abidjan 01, Cote d'Ivoire, www.afdb.org; *Statistics Pocketbook 2008.*

Economist Intelligence Unit, 111 West 57th Street, New York, NY 10019, (212) 554-0600, Fax: (212) 586-1181, www.eiu.com; *The Gambia Country Report.*

Euromonitor International, Inc., 224 S. Michigan Avenue, Suite 1500, Chicago, IL 60604, (312) 922-1115, Fax: (312) 922-1157, www.euromonitor.com; *The World Economic Factbook 2008* and *World Marketing Data and Statistics.*

International Monetary Fund (IMF), 700 Nineteenth Street, NW, Washington, DC 20431, (202) 623-7000, Fax: (202) 623-4661, www.imf.org; *International Financial Statistics Yearbook 2007.*

M.E. Sharpe, 80 Business Park Drive, Armonk, NY 10504, (800) 541-6563, Fax: (914) 273-2106, www.mesharpe.com; *The Illustrated Book of World Rankings.*

Organisation for Economic Cooperation and Development (OECD), 2 rue Andre Pascal, F-75775 Paris Cedex 16, France, (Telephone in U.S. (202) 785-6323), (Fax in U.S. (202) 785-0350), www.oecd.org; *International Trade by Commodity Statistics (ITCS).*

Palgrave Macmillan Ltd., Houndmills, Basingstoke, Hampshire, RG21 6XS, England, (Telephone in U.S. (888) 330-8477), (Fax in U.S. (800) 672-2054), www.palgrave.com; *The Statesman's Yearbook 2008.*

Taylor and Francis Group, An Informa Business, 2 Park Square, Milton Park, Abingdon, Oxford OX14 4RN, United Kingdom, (Dial from U.S. (212) 216-7800), (Fax from U.S. (212) 564-7854), www.tandf.co.uk; *The Europa World Year Book.*

United Nations Conference on Trade and Development (UNCTAD), DC2-1120, United Nations, New York, NY 10017, (212) 963-0027, www.unctad.org; *UNCTAD Commodity Yearbook.*

United Nations Economic Commission for Africa (ECA), PO Box 3001, Addis Ababa, Ethiopia, (Telephone in U.S. (212) 963-4957), www.uneca.org; *African Statistical Yearbook 2006.*

United Nations Food and Agricultural Organization (FAO), Viale delle Terme di Caracalla, 00100 Rome, Italy, (Dial from U.S. (202) 653-2400), (Fax from U.S. (202) 653 5760), www.fao.org; *FAO Trade Yearbook* and *The State of Food and Agriculture (SOFA) 2006.*

United Nations Statistics Division, New York, NY 10017, (800) 253-9646, Fax: (212) 963-4116, http://unstats.un.org; *Compendium of Intra-African and Related Foreign Trade Statistics 2003; International Trade Statistics Yearbook;* and *Statistical Yearbook.*

The World Bank, 1818 H Street, NW, Washington, DC 20433, (202) 473-1000, Fax: (202) 477-6391, www.worldbank.org; *Gambia; World Development Indicators (WDI) 2008;* and *World Development Report 2008.*

World Trade Organization (WTO), Centre William Rappard, Rue de Lausanne 154, CH-1211 Geneva 21, Switzerland, www.wto.org; *International Trade Statistics 2006.*

GAMBIA, THE - IRON AND IRON ORE PRODUCTION

See GAMBIA, THE - MINERAL INDUSTRIES

GAMBIA, THE - LABOR

African Development Bank Group, Rue Joseph Anoma, 01 BP 1387 Abidjan 01, Cote d'Ivoire, www.afdb.org; *Statistics Pocketbook 2008.*

Central Intelligence Agency, Office of Public Affairs, Washington, DC 20505, (703) 482-0623, Fax: (703) 482-1739, www.cia.gov; *The World Factbook.*

Euromonitor International, Inc., 224 S. Michigan Avenue, Suite 1500, Chicago, IL 60604, (312) 922-1115, Fax: (312) 922-1157, www.euromonitor.com; *International Marketing Data and Statistics 2008* and *World Marketing Data and Statistics.*

International Labour Office, I.L.O. Publications, 4 route des Morillons, CH-1211 Geneva 22, Switzerland, (Telephone in U.S. (202) 653-7652), (Fax in U.S. (202) 653-7687), www.ilo.org; *Yearbook of Labour Statistics 2006.*

M.E. Sharpe, 80 Business Park Drive, Armonk, NY 10504, (800) 541-6563, Fax: (914) 273-2106, www.mesharpe.com; *The Illustrated Book of World Rankings.*

Taylor and Francis Group, An Informa Business, 2 Park Square, Milton Park, Abingdon, Oxford OX14 4RN, United Kingdom, (Dial from U.S. (212) 216-7800), (Fax from U.S. (212) 564-7854), www.tandf.co.uk; *The Europa World Year Book.*

United Nations Food and Agricultural Organization (FAO), Viale delle Terme di Caracalla, 00100 Rome, Italy, (Dial from U.S. (202) 653-2400), (Fax from U.S. (202) 653 5760), www.fao.org; *The State of Food and Agriculture (SOFA) 2006.*

United Nations Statistics Division, New York, NY 10017, (800) 253-9646, Fax: (212) 963-4116, http://unstats.un.org; *Human Development Report 2006.*

The World Bank, 1818 H Street, NW, Washington, DC 20433, (202) 473-1000, Fax: (202) 477-6391,

www.worldbank.org; *The World Bank Atlas 2003-2004; World Development Indicators (WDI) 2008;* and *World Development Report 2008.*

GAMBIA, THE - LAND USE

Central Intelligence Agency, Office of Public Affairs, Washington, DC 20505, (703) 482-0623, Fax: (703) 482-1739, www.cia.gov; *The World Factbook.*

Euromonitor International, Inc., 224 S. Michigan Avenue, Suite 1500, Chicago, IL 60604, (312) 922-1115, Fax: (312) 922-1157, www.euromonitor.com; *International Marketing Data and Statistics 2008.*

United Nations Food and Agricultural Organization (FAO), Viale delle Terme di Caracalla, 00100 Rome, Italy, (Dial from U.S. (202) 653-2400), (Fax from U.S. (202) 653 5760), www.fao.org; *FAO Production Yearbook 2002.*

The World Bank, 1818 H Street, NW, Washington, DC 20433, (202) 473-1000, Fax: (202) 477-6391, www.worldbank.org; *World Development Report 2008.*

GAMBIA, THE - LIBRARIES

M.E. Sharpe, 80 Business Park Drive, Armonk, NY 10504, (800) 541-6563, Fax: (914) 273-2106, www.mesharpe.com; *The Illustrated Book of World Rankings.*

UNESCO Institute for Statistics, C.P. 6128 Succursale Centre-Ville, Montreal, Quebec, H3C 3J7 Canada, (Dial from U.S. (514) 343-6880), (Fax from U.S. (514) 343 6882), www.uis.unesco.org; *Statistical Tables.*

GAMBIA, THE - LIFE EXPECTANCY

African Development Bank Group, Rue Joseph Anoma, 01 BP 1387 Abidjan 01, Cote d'Ivoire, www.afdb.org; *Statistics Pocketbook 2008.*

Central Intelligence Agency, Office of Public Affairs, Washington, DC 20505, (703) 482-0623, Fax: (703) 482-1739, www.cia.gov; *The World Factbook.*

Euromonitor International, Inc., 224 S. Michigan Avenue, Suite 1500, Chicago, IL 60604, (312) 922-1115, Fax: (312) 922-1157, www.euromonitor.com; *The World Economic Factbook 2008.*

Palgrave Macmillan Ltd., Houndmills, Basingstoke, Hampshire, RG21 6XS, England, (Telephone in U.S. (888) 330-8477), (Fax in U.S. (800) 672-2054), www.palgrave.com; *The Statesman's Yearbook 2008.*

United Nations Statistics Division, New York, NY 10017, (800) 253-9646, Fax: (212) 963-4116, http://unstats.un.org; *Human Development Report 2006* and *World Statistics Pocketbook.*

The World Bank, 1818 H Street, NW, Washington, DC 20433, (202) 473-1000, Fax: (202) 477-6391, www.worldbank.org; *The World Bank Atlas 2003-2004* and *World Development Report 2008.*

GAMBIA, THE - LITERACY

Euromonitor International, Inc., 224 S. Michigan Avenue, Suite 1500, Chicago, IL 60604, (312) 922-1115, Fax: (312) 922-1157, www.euromonitor.com; *World Marketing Data and Statistics.*

United Nations Statistics Division, New York, NY 10017, (800) 253-9646, Fax: (212) 963-4116, http://unstats.un.org; *Survey of Economic and Social Conditions in Africa 2005.*

GAMBIA, THE - LIVESTOCK

M.E. Sharpe, 80 Business Park Drive, Armonk, NY 10504, (800) 541-6563, Fax: (914) 273-2106, www.mesharpe.com; *The Illustrated Book of World Rankings.*

Palgrave Macmillan Ltd., Houndmills, Basingstoke, Hampshire, RG21 6XS, England, (Telephone in U.S. (888) 330-8477), (Fax in U.S. (800) 672-2054), www.palgrave.com; *The Statesman's Yearbook 2008.*

Taylor and Francis Group, An Informa Business, 2 Park Square, Milton Park, Abingdon, Oxford OX14 4RN, United Kingdom, (Dial from U.S. (212) 216-7800), (Fax from U.S. (212) 564-7854), www.tandf.co.uk; *The Europa World Year Book.*

United Nations Conference on Trade and Development (UNCTAD), DC2-1120, United Nations, New York, NY 10017, (212) 963-0027, www.unctad.org; *UNCTAD Commodity Yearbook.*

United Nations Economic Commission for Africa (ECA), PO Box 3001, Addis Ababa, Ethiopia, (Telephone in U.S. (212) 963-4957), www.uneca.org; *African Statistical Yearbook 2006.*

United Nations Food and Agricultural Organization (FAO), Viale delle Terme di Caracalla, 00100 Rome, Italy, (Dial from U.S. (202) 653-2400), (Fax from U.S. (202) 653 5760), www.fao.org; *FAO Production Yearbook 2002* and *The State of Food and Agriculture (SOFA) 2006.*

United Nations Statistics Division, New York, NY 10017, (800) 253-9646, Fax: (212) 963-4116, http://unstats.un.org; *Statistical Yearbook* and *Survey of Economic and Social Conditions in Africa 2005.*

GAMBIA, THE - MANUFACTURES

M.E. Sharpe, 80 Business Park Drive, Armonk, NY 10504, (800) 541-6563, Fax: (914) 273-2106, www.mesharpe.com; *The Illustrated Book of World Rankings.*

United Nations Economic Commission for Africa (ECA), PO Box 3001, Addis Ababa, Ethiopia, (Telephone in U.S. (212) 963-4957), www.uneca.org; *African Statistical Yearbook 2006.*

United Nations Statistics Division, New York, NY 10017, (800) 253-9646, Fax: (212) 963-4116, http://unstats.un.org; *Survey of Economic and Social Conditions in Africa 2005.*

The World Bank, 1818 H Street, NW, Washington, DC 20433, (202) 473-1000, Fax: (202) 477-6391, www.worldbank.org; *World Development Indicators (WDI) 2008.*

GAMBIA, THE - MARRIAGE

M.E. Sharpe, 80 Business Park Drive, Armonk, NY 10504, (800) 541-6563, Fax: (914) 273-2106, www.mesharpe.com; *The Illustrated Book of World Rankings.*

United Nations Statistics Division, New York, NY 10017, (800) 253-9646, Fax: (212) 963-4116, http://unstats.un.org; *Demographic Yearbook.*

GAMBIA, THE - MEAT PRODUCTION

See GAMBIA, THE - LIVESTOCK

GAMBIA, THE - MEDICAL CARE, COST OF

International Monetary Fund (IMF), 700 Nineteenth Street, NW, Washington, DC 20431, (202) 623-7000, Fax: (202) 623-4661, www.imf.org; *Government Finance Statistics Yearbook (2008 Edition).*

GAMBIA, THE - MILK PRODUCTION

See GAMBIA, THE - DAIRY PROCESSING

GAMBIA, THE - MINERAL INDUSTRIES

M.E. Sharpe, 80 Business Park Drive, Armonk, NY 10504, (800) 541-6563, Fax: (914) 273-2106, www.mesharpe.com; *The Illustrated Book of World Rankings.*

Palgrave Macmillan Ltd., Houndmills, Basingstoke, Hampshire, RG21 6XS, England, (Telephone in U.S. (888) 330-8477), (Fax in U.S. (800) 672-2054), www.palgrave.com; *The Statesman's Yearbook 2008.*

Taylor and Francis Group, An Informa Business, 2 Park Square, Milton Park, Abingdon, Oxford OX14 4RN, United Kingdom, (Dial from U.S. (212) 216-7800), (Fax from U.S. (212) 564-7854), www.tandf.co.uk; *The Europa World Year Book.*

United Nations Conference on Trade and Development (UNCTAD), DC2-1120, United Nations, New York, NY 10017, (212) 963-0027, www.unctad.org; *UNCTAD Commodity Yearbook.*

United Nations Economic Commission for Africa (ECA), PO Box 3001, Addis Ababa, Ethiopia, (Telephone in U.S. (212) 963-4957), www.uneca.org; *African Statistical Yearbook 2006.*

GAMBIA, THE - MONEY EXCHANGE RATES

See GAMBIA, THE - FOREIGN EXCHANGE RATES

GAMBIA, THE - MONEY SUPPLY

African Development Bank Group, Rue Joseph Anoma, 01 BP 1387 Abidjan 01, Cote d'Ivoire, www.afdb.org; *Statistics Pocketbook 2008.*

Economist Intelligence Unit, 111 West 57th Street, New York, NY 10019, (212) 554-0600, Fax: (212) 586-1181, www.eiu.com; *The Gambia Country Report.*

International Monetary Fund (IMF), 700 Nineteenth Street, NW, Washington, DC 20431, (202) 623-7000, Fax: (202) 623-4661, www.imf.org; *International Financial Statistics Yearbook 2007.*

Taylor and Francis Group, An Informa Business, 2 Park Square, Milton Park, Abingdon, Oxford OX14 4RN, United Kingdom, (Dial from U.S. (212) 216-7800), (Fax from U.S. (212) 564-7854), www.tandf.co.uk; *The Europa World Year Book.*

United Nations Statistics Division, New York, NY 10017, (800) 253-9646, Fax: (212) 963-4116, http://unstats.un.org; *Statistical Yearbook.*

The World Bank, 1818 H Street, NW, Washington, DC 20433, (202) 473-1000, Fax: (202) 477-6391, www.worldbank.org; *Gambia* and *World Development Indicators (WDI) 2008.*

GAMBIA, THE - MORTALITY

Central Intelligence Agency, Office of Public Affairs, Washington, DC 20505, (703) 482-0623, Fax: (703) 482-1739, www.cia.gov; *The World Factbook.*

Euromonitor International, Inc., 224 S. Michigan Avenue, Suite 1500, Chicago, IL 60604, (312) 922-1115, Fax: (312) 922-1157, www.euromonitor.com; *International Marketing Data and Statistics 2008* and *The World Economic Factbook 2008.*

Palgrave Macmillan Ltd., Houndmills, Basingstoke, Hampshire, RG21 6XS, England, (Telephone in U.S. (888) 330-8477), (Fax in U.S. (800) 672-2054), www.palgrave.com; *The Statesman's Yearbook 2008.*

Taylor and Francis Group, An Informa Business, 2 Park Square, Milton Park, Abingdon, Oxford OX14 4RN, United Kingdom, (Dial from U.S. (212) 216-7800), (Fax from U.S. (212) 564-7854), www.tandf.co.uk; *The Europa World Year Book.*

UNICEF, 3 United Nations Plaza, New York, NY 10017, (800) 253-9646, Fax: (212) 887-7465, www.unicef.org; *The State of the World's Children 2008.*

United Nations Statistics Division, New York, NY 10017, (800) 253-9646, Fax: (212) 963-4116, http://unstats.un.org; *Demographic Yearbook; Human Development Report 2006; Statistical Yearbook; Survey of Economic and Social Conditions in Africa 2005;* and *World Statistics Pocketbook.*

The World Bank, 1818 H Street, NW, Washington, DC 20433, (202) 473-1000, Fax: (202) 477-6391, www.worldbank.org; *The World Bank Atlas 2003-2004; World Development Indicators (WDI) 2008;* and *World Development Report 2008.*

World Health Organization (WHO), Avenue Appia 20, 1211 Geneve 27, Switzerland, (Telephone in U.S. (212) 331-9081), www.who.int; *World Health Report 2006.*

GAMBIA, THE - MOTION PICTURES

Palgrave Macmillan Ltd., Houndmills, Basingstoke, Hampshire, RG21 6XS, England, (Telephone in U.S. (888) 330-8477), (Fax in U.S. (800) 672-2054), www.palgrave.com; *The Statesman's Yearbook 2008.*

United Nations Statistics Division, New York, NY 10017, (800) 253-9646, Fax: (212) 963-4116, http://unstats.un.org; *Statistical Yearbook.*

GAMBIA, THE - MOTOR VEHICLES

Taylor and Francis Group, An Informa Business, 2 Park Square, Milton Park, Abingdon, Oxford OX14 4RN, United Kingdom, (Dial from U.S. (212) 216-7800), (Fax from U.S. (212) 564-7854), www.tandf.co.uk; *The Europa World Year Book.*

United Nations Statistics Division, New York, NY 10017, (800) 253-9646, Fax: (212) 963-4116, http://unstats.un.org; *Statistical Yearbook* and *Survey of Economic and Social Conditions in Africa 2005.*

GAMBIA, THE - MUSEUMS

M.E. Sharpe, 80 Business Park Drive, Armonk, NY 10504, (800) 541-6563, Fax: (914) 273-2106, www.mesharpe.com; *The Illustrated Book of World Rankings.*

GAMBIA, THE - NATURAL GAS PRODUCTION

See GAMBIA, THE - MINERAL INDUSTRIES

GAMBIA, THE - NUTRITION

African Development Bank Group, Rue Joseph Anoma, 01 BP 1387 Abidjan 01, Cote d'Ivoire, www.afdb.org; *Statistics Pocketbook 2008.*

United Nations Food and Agricultural Organization (FAO), Viale delle Terme di Caracalla, 00100 Rome, Italy, (Dial from U.S. (202) 653-2400), (Fax from U.S. (202) 653 5760), www.fao.org; *The State of Food and Agriculture (SOFA) 2006.*

GAMBIA, THE - PALM OIL PRODUCTION

See GAMBIA, THE - CROPS

GAMBIA, THE - PEANUT PRODUCTION

See GAMBIA, THE - CROPS

GAMBIA, THE - PERIODICALS

UNESCO Institute for Statistics, C.P. 6128 Succursale Centre-Ville, Montreal, Quebec, H3C 3J7 Canada, (Dial from U.S. (514) 343-6880), (Fax from U.S. (514) 343 6882), www.uis.unesco.org; *Statistical Tables.*

GAMBIA, THE - PESTICIDES

United Nations Food and Agricultural Organization (FAO), Viale delle Terme di Caracalla, 00100 Rome, Italy, (Dial from U.S. (202) 653-2400), (Fax from U.S. (202) 653 5760), www.fao.org; *The State of Food and Agriculture (SOFA) 2006.*

GAMBIA, THE - PETROLEUM INDUSTRY AND TRADE

M.E. Sharpe, 80 Business Park Drive, Armonk, NY 10504, (800) 541-6563, Fax: (914) 273-2106, www.mesharpe.com; *The Illustrated Book of World Rankings.*

Palgrave Macmillan Ltd., Houndmills, Basingstoke, Hampshire, RG21 6XS, England, (Telephone in U.S. (888) 330-8477), (Fax in U.S. (800) 672-2054), www.palgrave.com; *The Statesman's Yearbook 2008.*

PennWell Corporation, 1421 South Sheridan Road, Tulsa, OK 74112, (918) 835-3161, www.pennwell.com; *International Petroleum Encyclopedia 2007.*

United Nations Conference on Trade and Development (UNCTAD), DC2-1120, United Nations, New York, NY 10017, (212) 963-0027, www.unctad.org; *UNCTAD Commodity Yearbook.*

United Nations Food and Agricultural Organization (FAO), Viale delle Terme di Caracalla, 00100 Rome, Italy, (Dial from U.S. (202) 653-2400), (Fax from U.S. (202) 653 5760), www.fao.org; *The State of Food and Agriculture (SOFA) 2006.*

GAMBIA, THE - POLITICAL SCIENCE

Central Intelligence Agency, Office of Public Affairs, Washington, DC 20505, (703) 482-0623, Fax: (703) 482-1739, www.cia.gov; *The World Factbook.*

International Monetary Fund (IMF), 700 Nineteenth Street, NW, Washington, DC 20431, (202) 623-7000, Fax: (202) 623-4661, www.imf.org; *Government Finance Statistics Yearbook (2008 Edition)* and *International Financial Statistics Yearbook 2007.*

Palgrave Macmillan Ltd., Houndmills, Basingstoke, Hampshire, RG21 6XS, England, (Telephone in U.S. (888) 330-8477), (Fax in U.S. (800) 672-2054), www.palgrave.com; *The Statesman's Yearbook 2008.*

Taylor and Francis Group, An Informa Business, 2 Park Square, Milton Park, Abingdon, Oxford OX14 4RN, United Kingdom, (Dial from U.S. (212) 216-7800), (Fax from U.S. (212) 564-7854), www.tandf.co.uk; *The Europa World Year Book.*

United Nations Statistics Division, New York, NY 10017, (800) 253-9646, Fax: (212) 963-4116, http://unstats.un.org; *National Accounts Statistics: Compendium of Income Distribution Statistics* and *Survey of Economic and Social Conditions in Africa 2005.*

The World Bank, 1818 H Street, NW, Washington, DC 20433, (202) 473-1000, Fax: (202) 477-6391, www.worldbank.org; *World Development Indicators (WDI) 2008* and *World Development Report 2008.*

GAMBIA, THE - POPULATION

African Development Bank Group, Rue Joseph Anoma, 01 BP 1387 Abidjan 01, Cote d'Ivoire, www.afdb.org; *The African Statistical Journal; Gender, Poverty and Environmental Indicators on African Countries 2007; Selected Statistics on African Countries 2007;* and *Statistics Pocketbook 2008.*

Central Intelligence Agency, Office of Public Affairs, Washington, DC 20505, (703) 482-0623, Fax: (703) 482-1739, www.cia.gov; *The World Factbook.*

Economist Intelligence Unit, 111 West 57th Street, New York, NY 10019, (212) 554-0600, Fax: (212) 586-1181, www.eiu.com; *The Gambia Country Report.*

Euromonitor International, Inc., 224 S. Michigan Avenue, Suite 1500, Chicago, IL 60604, (312) 922-1115, Fax: (312) 922-1157, www.euromonitor.com; *International Marketing Data and Statistics 2008* and *The World Economic Factbook 2008.*

Eurostat, Batiment Jean Monnet, Rue Alcide de Gasperi, L-2920 Luxembourg, http://epp.eurostat.ec.europa.eu; *Demographic Indicators - Population by Age-Classes.*

International Labour Office, I.L.O. Publications, 4 route des Morillons, CH-1211 Geneva 22, Switzerland, (Telephone in U.S. (202) 653-7652), (Fax in U.S. (202) 653-7687), www.ilo.org; *Yearbook of Labour Statistics 2006.*

M.E. Sharpe, 80 Business Park Drive, Armonk, NY 10504, (800) 541-6563, Fax: (914) 273-2106, www.mesharpe.com; *The Illustrated Book of World Rankings.*

Palgrave Macmillan Ltd., Houndmills, Basingstoke, Hampshire, RG21 6XS, England, (Telephone in U.S. (888) 330-8477), (Fax in U.S. (800) 672-2054), www.palgrave.com; *The Statesman's Yearbook 2008.*

Taylor and Francis Group, An Informa Business, 2 Park Square, Milton Park, Abingdon, Oxford OX14 4RN, United Kingdom, (Dial from U.S. (212) 216-7800), (Fax from U.S. (212) 564-7854), www.tandf.co.uk; *The Europa World Year Book.*

U.S. Department of State (DOS), 2201 C Street NW, Washington, DC 20520, (202) 647-4000, www.state.gov; *World Military Expenditures and Arms Transfers (WMEAT).*

United Nations Food and Agricultural Organization (FAO), Viale delle Terme di Caracalla, 00100 Rome, Italy, (Dial from U.S. (202) 653-2400), (Fax from U.S. (202) 653 5760), www.fao.org; *FAO Production Yearbook 2002.*

United Nations Statistics Division, New York, NY 10017, (800) 253-9646, Fax: (212) 963-4116, http://unstats.un.org; *Demographic Yearbook; Human Development Report 2006; Statistical Yearbook; Survey of Economic and Social Conditions in Africa 2005;* and *World Statistics Pocketbook.*

The World Bank, 1818 H Street, NW, Washington, DC 20433, (202) 473-1000, Fax: (202) 477-6391, www.worldbank.org; *Gambia; The World Bank Atlas 2003-2004;* and *World Development Report 2008.*

World Health Organization (WHO), Avenue Appia 20, 1211 Geneve 27, Switzerland, (Telephone in U.S. (212) 331-9081), www.who.int; *World Health Report 2006.*

GAMBIA, THE - POPULATION DENSITY

African Development Bank Group, Rue Joseph Anoma, 01 BP 1387 Abidjan 01, Cote d'Ivoire, www.afdb.org; *Statistics Pocketbook 2008.*

Central Intelligence Agency, Office of Public Affairs, Washington, DC 20505, (703) 482-0623, Fax: (703) 482-1739, www.cia.gov; *The World Factbook.*

Euromonitor International, Inc., 224 S. Michigan Avenue, Suite 1500, Chicago, IL 60604, (312) 922-1115, Fax: (312) 922-1157, www.euromonitor.com; *The World Economic Factbook 2008.*

M.E. Sharpe, 80 Business Park Drive, Armonk, NY 10504, (800) 541-6563, Fax: (914) 273-2106, www.mesharpe.com; *The Illustrated Book of World Rankings.*

Palgrave Macmillan Ltd., Houndmills, Basingstoke, Hampshire, RG21 6XS, England, (Telephone in U.S. (888) 330-8477), (Fax in U.S. (800) 672-2054), www.palgrave.com; *The Statesman's Yearbook 2008.*

Taylor and Francis Group, An Informa Business, 2 Park Square, Milton Park, Abingdon, Oxford OX14 4RN, United Kingdom, (Dial from U.S. (212) 216-7800), (Fax from U.S. (212) 564-7854), www.tandf.co.uk; *The Europa World Year Book.*

United Nations Food and Agricultural Organization (FAO), Viale delle Terme di Caracalla, 00100 Rome, Italy, (Dial from U.S. (202) 653-2400), (Fax from U.S. (202) 653 5760), www.fao.org; *The State of Food and Agriculture (SOFA) 2006.*

United Nations Statistics Division, New York, NY 10017, (800) 253-9646, Fax: (212) 963-4116, http://unstats.un.org; *Survey of Economic and Social Conditions in Africa 2005.*

The World Bank, 1818 H Street, NW, Washington, DC 20433, (202) 473-1000, Fax: (202) 477-6391, www.worldbank.org; *Gambia* and *World Development Report 2008.*

GAMBIA, THE - POSTAL SERVICE

M.E. Sharpe, 80 Business Park Drive, Armonk, NY 10504, (800) 541-6563, Fax: (914) 273-2106, www.mesharpe.com; *The Illustrated Book of World Rankings.*

Palgrave Macmillan Ltd., Houndmills, Basingstoke, Hampshire, RG21 6XS, England, (Telephone in U.S. (888) 330-8477), (Fax in U.S. (800) 672-2054), www.palgrave.com; *The Statesman's Yearbook 2008.*

GAMBIA, THE - POWER RESOURCES

Euromonitor International, Inc., 224 S. Michigan Avenue, Suite 1500, Chicago, IL 60604, (312) 922-1115, Fax: (312) 922-1157, www.euromonitor.com; *International Marketing Data and Statistics 2008; The World Economic Factbook 2008;* and *World Marketing Data and Statistics.*

M.E. Sharpe, 80 Business Park Drive, Armonk, NY 10504, (800) 541-6563, Fax: (914) 273-2106, www.mesharpe.com; *The Illustrated Book of World Rankings.*

Palgrave Macmillan Ltd., Houndmills, Basingstoke, Hampshire, RG21 6XS, England, (Telephone in U.S. (888) 330-8477), (Fax in U.S. (800) 672-2054), www.palgrave.com; *The Statesman's Yearbook 2008.*

Platts, 2 Penn Plaza, 25th Floor, New York, NY 10121-2298, (212) 904-3070, www.platts.com; *Energy Economist.*

United Nations Economic Commission for Africa (ECA), PO Box 3001, Addis Ababa, Ethiopia, (Telephone in U.S. (212) 963-4957), www.uneca.org; *African Statistical Yearbook 2006.*

United Nations Food and Agricultural Organization (FAO), Viale delle Terme di Caracalla, 00100 Rome, Italy, (Dial from U.S. (202) 653-2400), (Fax from

U.S. (202) 653 5760), www.fao.org; *The State of Food and Agriculture (SOFA) 2006.*

United Nations Statistics Division, New York, NY 10017, (800) 253-9646, Fax: (212) 963-4116, http://unstats.un.org; *Energy Statistics Yearbook 2003; Human Development Report 2006; Statistical Yearbook;* and *World Statistics Pocketbook.*

The World Bank, 1818 H Street, NW, Washington, DC 20433, (202) 473-1000, Fax: (202) 477-6391, www.worldbank.org; *The World Bank Atlas 2003-2004* and *World Development Report 2008.*

GAMBIA, THE - PRICES

Euromonitor International, Inc., 224 S. Michigan Avenue, Suite 1500, Chicago, IL 60604, (312) 922-1115, Fax: (312) 922-1157, www.euromonitor.com; *World Marketing Data and Statistics.*

International Labour Office, I.L.O. Publications, 4 route des Morillons, CH-1211 Geneva 22, Switzerland, (Telephone in U.S. (202) 653-7652), (Fax in U.S. (202) 653-7687), www.ilo.org; *Yearbook of Labour Statistics 2006.*

International Monetary Fund (IMF), 700 Nineteenth Street, NW, Washington, DC 20431, (202) 623-7000, Fax: (202) 623-4661, www.imf.org; *International Financial Statistics Yearbook 2007.*

M.E. Sharpe, 80 Business Park Drive, Armonk, NY 10504, (800) 541-6563, Fax: (914) 273-2106, www.mesharpe.com; *The Illustrated Book of World Rankings.*

United Nations Economic Commission for Africa (ECA), PO Box 3001, Addis Ababa, Ethiopia, (Telephone in U.S. (212) 963-4957), www.uneca.org; *African Statistical Yearbook 2006.*

United Nations Food and Agricultural Organization (FAO), Viale delle Terme di Caracalla, 00100 Rome, Italy, (Dial from U.S. (202) 653-2400), (Fax from U.S. (202) 653 5760), www.fao.org; *FAO Production Yearbook 2002* and *The State of Food and Agriculture (SOFA) 2006.*

The World Bank, 1818 H Street, NW, Washington, DC 20433, (202) 473-1000, Fax: (202) 477-6391, www.worldbank.org; *Gambia.*

GAMBIA, THE - PUBLIC HEALTH

African Development Bank Group, Rue Joseph Anoma, 01 BP 1387 Abidjan 01, Cote d'Ivoire, www.afdb.org; *Statistics Pocketbook 2008.*

Euromonitor International, Inc., 224 S. Michigan Avenue, Suite 1500, Chicago, IL 60604, (312) 922-1115, Fax: (312) 922-1157, www.euromonitor.com; *World Marketing Data and Statistics.*

M.E. Sharpe, 80 Business Park Drive, Armonk, NY 10504, (800) 541-6563, Fax: (914) 273-2106, www.mesharpe.com; *The Illustrated Book of World Rankings.*

Palgrave Macmillan Ltd., Houndmills, Basingstoke, Hampshire, RG21 6XS, England, (Telephone in U.S. (888) 330-8477), (Fax in U.S. (800) 672-2054), www.palgrave.com; *The Statesman's Yearbook 2008.*

UNICEF, 3 United Nations Plaza, New York, NY 10017, (800) 253-9646, Fax: (212) 887-7465, www.unicef.org; *The State of the World's Children 2008.*

United Nations Economic Commission for Africa (ECA), PO Box 3001, Addis Ababa, Ethiopia, (Telephone in U.S. (212) 963-4957), www.uneca.org; *African Statistical Yearbook 2006.*

United Nations Statistics Division, New York, NY 10017, (800) 253-9646, Fax: (212) 963-4116, http://unstats.un.org; *Human Development Report 2006* and *Statistical Yearbook.*

The World Bank, 1818 H Street, NW, Washington, DC 20433, (202) 473-1000, Fax: (202) 477-6391, www.worldbank.org; *Gambia* and *World Development Report 2008.*

World Health Organization (WHO), Avenue Appia 20, 1211 Geneve 27, Switzerland, (Telephone in U.S. (212) 331-9081), www.who.int; *World Health Report 2006.*

GAMBIA, THE - PUBLISHERS AND PUBLISHING

UNESCO Institute for Statistics, C.P. 6128 Succursale Centre-Ville, Montreal, Quebec, H3C 3J7 Canada, (Dial from U.S. (514) 343-6880), (Fax from U.S. (514) 343 6882), www.uis.unesco.org; *Statistical Tables.*

GAMBIA, THE - RADIO BROADCASTING

Palgrave Macmillan Ltd., Houndmills, Basingstoke, Hampshire, RG21 6XS, England, (Telephone in U.S. (888) 330-8477), (Fax in U.S. (800) 672-2054), www.palgrave.com; *The Statesman's Yearbook 2008.*

GAMBIA, THE - RAILROADS

United Nations Economic Commission for Africa (ECA), PO Box 3001, Addis Ababa, Ethiopia, (Telephone in U.S. (212) 963-4957), www.uneca.org; *African Statistical Yearbook 2006.*

GAMBIA, THE - RELIGION

Central Intelligence Agency, Office of Public Affairs, Washington, DC 20505, (703) 482-0623, Fax: (703) 482-1739, www.cia.gov; *The World Factbook.*

M.E. Sharpe, 80 Business Park Drive, Armonk, NY 10504, (800) 541-6563, Fax: (914) 273-2106, www.mesharpe.com; *The Illustrated Book of World Rankings.*

Palgrave Macmillan Ltd., Houndmills, Basingstoke, Hampshire, RG21 6XS, England, (Telephone in U.S. (888) 330-8477), (Fax in U.S. (800) 672-2054), www.palgrave.com; *The Statesman's Yearbook 2008.*

GAMBIA, THE - RENT CHARGES

International Labour Office, I.L.O. Publications, 4 route des Morillons, CH-1211 Geneva 22, Switzerland, (Telephone in U.S. (202) 653-7652), (Fax in U.S. (202) 653-7687), www.ilo.org; *Yearbook of Labour Statistics 2006.*

GAMBIA, THE - RESERVES (ACCOUNTING)

African Development Bank Group, Rue Joseph Anoma, 01 BP 1387 Abidjan 01, Cote d'Ivoire, www.afdb.org; *Statistics Pocketbook 2008.*

United Nations Statistics Division, New York, NY 10017, (800) 253-9646, Fax: (212) 963-4116, http://unstats.un.org; *Statistical Yearbook.*

The World Bank, 1818 H Street, NW, Washington, DC 20433, (202) 473-1000, Fax: (202) 477-6391, www.worldbank.org; *World Development Indicators (WDI) 2008.*

GAMBIA, THE - RETAIL TRADE

Euromonitor International, Inc., 224 S. Michigan Avenue, Suite 1500, Chicago, IL 60604, (312) 922-1115, Fax: (312) 922-1157, www.euromonitor.com; *World Marketing Data and Statistics.*

GAMBIA, THE - RICE PRODUCTION

See GAMBIA, THE - CROPS

GAMBIA, THE - ROADS

Central Intelligence Agency, Office of Public Affairs, Washington, DC 20505, (703) 482-0623, Fax: (703) 482-1739, www.cia.gov; *The World Factbook.*

Palgrave Macmillan Ltd., Houndmills, Basingstoke, Hampshire, RG21 6XS, England, (Telephone in U.S. (888) 330-8477), (Fax in U.S. (800) 672-2054), www.palgrave.com; *The Statesman's Yearbook 2008.*

United Nations Economic Commission for Africa (ECA), PO Box 3001, Addis Ababa, Ethiopia, (Telephone in U.S. (212) 963-4957), www.uneca.org; *African Statistical Yearbook 2006.*

United Nations Statistics Division, New York, NY 10017, (800) 253-9646, Fax: (212) 963-4116, http://unstats.un.org; *Survey of Economic and Social Conditions in Africa 2005.*

GAMBIA, THE - RUBBER INDUSTRY AND TRADE

International Rubber Study Group (IRSG), 1st Floor, Heron House, 109/115 Wembley Hill Road, Wembley, Middlesex HA9 8DA, United Kingdom, www.rubberstudy.com; *Rubber Statistical Bulletin; Summary of World Rubber Statistics 2005; World Rubber Statistics Handbook (Volume 6, 1975-2001);* and *World Rubber Statistics Historic Handbook.*

M.E. Sharpe, 80 Business Park Drive, Armonk, NY 10504, (800) 541-6563, Fax: (914) 273-2106, www.mesharpe.com; *The Illustrated Book of World Rankings.*

GAMBIA, THE - SHEEP

See GAMBIA, THE - LIVESTOCK

GAMBIA, THE - SHIPPING

Palgrave Macmillan Ltd., Houndmills, Basingstoke, Hampshire, RG21 6XS, England, (Telephone in U.S. (888) 330-8477), (Fax in U.S. (800) 672-2054), www.palgrave.com; *The Statesman's Yearbook 2008.*

Taylor and Francis Group, An Informa Business, 2 Park Square, Milton Park, Abingdon, Oxford OX14 4RN, United Kingdom, (Dial from U.S. (212) 216-7800), (Fax from U.S. (212) 564-7854), www.tandf.co.uk; *The Europa World Year Book.*

United Nations Economic Commission for Africa (ECA), PO Box 3001, Addis Ababa, Ethiopia, (Telephone in U.S. (212) 963-4957), www.uneca.org; *African Statistical Yearbook 2006.*

United Nations Statistics Division, New York, NY 10017, (800) 253-9646, Fax: (212) 963-4116, http://unstats.un.org; *Statistical Yearbook.*

GAMBIA, THE - SILVER PRODUCTION

See GAMBIA, THE - MINERAL INDUSTRIES

GAMBIA, THE - SOCIAL ECOLOGY

M.E. Sharpe, 80 Business Park Drive, Armonk, NY 10504, (800) 541-6563, Fax: (914) 273-2106, www.mesharpe.com; *The Illustrated Book of World Rankings.*

United Nations Statistics Division, New York, NY 10017, (800) 253-9646, Fax: (212) 963-4116, http://unstats.un.org; *World Statistics Pocketbook.*

GAMBIA, THE - SOCIAL SECURITY

International Monetary Fund (IMF), 700 Nineteenth Street, NW, Washington, DC 20431, (202) 623-7000, Fax: (202) 623-4661, www.imf.org; *Government Finance Statistics Yearbook (2008 Edition).*

United Nations Statistics Division, New York, NY 10017, (800) 253-9646, Fax: (212) 963-4116, http://unstats.un.org; *National Accounts Statistics: Compendium of Income Distribution Statistics.*

GAMBIA, THE - STEEL PRODUCTION

See GAMBIA, THE - MINERAL INDUSTRIES

GAMBIA, THE - SUGAR PRODUCTION

See GAMBIA, THE - CROPS

GAMBIA, THE - TAXATION

International Monetary Fund (IMF), 700 Nineteenth Street, NW, Washington, DC 20431, (202) 623-7000, Fax: (202) 623-4661, www.imf.org; *Government Finance Statistics Yearbook (2008 Edition).*

Taylor and Francis Group, An Informa Business, 2 Park Square, Milton Park, Abingdon, Oxford OX14 4RN, United Kingdom, (Dial from U.S. (212) 216-7800), (Fax from U.S. (212) 564-7854), www.tandf.co.uk; *The Europa World Year Book.*

The World Bank, 1818 H Street, NW, Washington, DC 20433, (202) 473-1000, Fax: (202) 477-6391, www.worldbank.org; *World Development Indicators (WDI) 2008.*

GAMBIA, THE - TELEPHONE

International Telecommunication Union (ITU), Place des Nations, 1211 Geneva 20, Switzerland, www.itu.int; World Telecommunication Indicators Database.

Palgrave Macmillan Ltd., Houndmills, Basingstoke, Hampshire, RG21 6XS, England, (Telephone in U.S. (888) 330-8477), (Fax in U.S. (800) 672-2054), www.palgrave.com; *The Statesman's Yearbook 2008.*

United Nations Statistics Division, New York, NY 10017, (800) 253-9646, Fax: (212) 963-4116, http://unstats.un.org; *Statistical Yearbook* and *World Statistics Pocketbook.*

GAMBIA, THE - TEXTILE INDUSTRY

M.E. Sharpe, 80 Business Park Drive, Armonk, NY 10504, (800) 541-6563, Fax: (914) 273-2106, www.mesharpe.com; *The Illustrated Book of World Rankings.*

Palgrave Macmillan Ltd., Houndmills, Basingstoke, Hampshire, RG21 6XS, England, (Telephone in U.S. (888) 330-8477), (Fax in U.S. (800) 672-2054), www.palgrave.com; *The Statesman's Yearbook 2008.*

United Nations Conference on Trade and Development (UNCTAD), DC2-1120, United Nations, New York, NY 10017, (212) 963-0027, www.unctad.org; *UNCTAD Commodity Yearbook.*

GAMBIA, THE - TOBACCO INDUSTRY

Foreign Agricultural Service (FAS), U.S. Department of Agriculture (USDA), 1400 Independence Avenue, SW, Washington, DC 20250, (202) 720-3935, www.fas.usda.gov; *Tobacco: World Markets and Trade.*

M.E. Sharpe, 80 Business Park Drive, Armonk, NY 10504, (800) 541-6563, Fax: (914) 273-2106, www.mesharpe.com; *The Illustrated Book of World Rankings.*

GAMBIA, THE - TOURISM

Euromonitor International, Inc., 224 S. Michigan Avenue, Suite 1500, Chicago, IL 60604, (312) 922-1115, Fax: (312) 922-1157, www.euromonitor.com; *The World Economic Factbook 2008* and *World Marketing Data and Statistics.*

M.E. Sharpe, 80 Business Park Drive, Armonk, NY 10504, (800) 541-6563, Fax: (914) 273-2106, www.mesharpe.com; *The Illustrated Book of World Rankings.*

Palgrave Macmillan Ltd., Houndmills, Basingstoke, Hampshire, RG21 6XS, England, (Telephone in U.S. (888) 330-8477), (Fax in U.S. (800) 672-2054), www.palgrave.com; *The Statesman's Yearbook 2008.*

Taylor and Francis Group, An Informa Business, 2 Park Square, Milton Park, Abingdon, Oxford OX14 4RN, United Kingdom, (Dial from U.S. (212) 216-7800), (Fax from U.S. (212) 564-7854), www.tandf.co.uk; *The Europa World Year Book.*

United Nations Economic Commission for Africa (ECA), PO Box 3001, Addis Ababa, Ethiopia, (Telephone in U.S. (212) 963-4957), www.uneca.org; *African Statistical Yearbook 2006.*

United Nations Statistics Division, New York, NY 10017, (800) 253-9646, Fax: (212) 963-4116, http://unstats.un.org; *Statistical Yearbook.*

The World Bank, 1818 H Street, NW, Washington, DC 20433, (202) 473-1000, Fax: (202) 477-6391, www.worldbank.org; *Gambia.*

GAMBIA, THE - TRADE

See GAMBIA, THE - INTERNATIONAL TRADE

GAMBIA, THE - TRANSPORTATION

Central Intelligence Agency, Office of Public Affairs, Washington, DC 20505, (703) 482-0623, Fax: (703) 482-1739, www.cia.gov; *The World Factbook.*

Euromonitor International, Inc., 224 S. Michigan Avenue, Suite 1500, Chicago, IL 60604, (312) 922-1115, Fax: (312) 922-1157, www.euromonitor.com; *International Marketing Data and Statistics 2008* and *World Marketing Data and Statistics.*

M.E. Sharpe, 80 Business Park Drive, Armonk, NY 10504, (800) 541-6563, Fax: (914) 273-2106, www.mesharpe.com; *The Illustrated Book of World Rankings.*

Palgrave Macmillan Ltd., Houndmills, Basingstoke, Hampshire, RG21 6XS, England, (Telephone in U.S. (888) 330-8477), (Fax in U.S. (800) 672-2054), www.palgrave.com; *The Statesman's Yearbook 2008.*

Taylor and Francis Group, An Informa Business, 2 Park Square, Milton Park, Abingdon, Oxford OX14 4RN, United Kingdom, (Dial from U.S. (212) 216-7800), (Fax from U.S. (212) 564-7854), www.tandf.co.uk; *The Europa World Year Book.*

United Nations Economic Commission for Africa (ECA), PO Box 3001, Addis Ababa, Ethiopia, (Telephone in U.S. (212) 963-4957), www.uneca.org; *African Statistical Yearbook 2006.*

United Nations Statistics Division, New York, NY 10017, (800) 253-9646, Fax: (212) 963-4116, http://unstats.un.org; *Human Development Report 2006.*

The World Bank, 1818 H Street, NW, Washington, DC 20433, (202) 473-1000, Fax: (202) 477-6391, www.worldbank.org; *Africa Live Database (LDB)* and *Gambia.*

GAMBIA, THE - UNEMPLOYMENT

Central Intelligence Agency, Office of Public Affairs, Washington, DC 20505, (703) 482-0623, Fax: (703) 482-1739, www.cia.gov; *The World Factbook.*

International Labour Office, I.L.O. Publications, 4 route des Morillons, CH-1211 Geneva 22, Switzerland, (Telephone in U.S. (202) 653-7652), (Fax in U.S. (202) 653-7687), www.ilo.org; *Yearbook of Labour Statistics 2006.*

GAMBIA, THE - VITAL STATISTICS

Palgrave Macmillan Ltd., Houndmills, Basingstoke, Hampshire, RG21 6XS, England, (Telephone in U.S. (888) 330-8477), (Fax in U.S. (800) 672-2054), www.palgrave.com; *The Statesman's Yearbook 2008.*

United Nations Statistics Division, New York, NY 10017, (800) 253-9646, Fax: (212) 963-4116, http://unstats.un.org; *Statistical Yearbook.*

World Health Organization (WHO), Avenue Appia 20, 1211 Geneve 27, Switzerland, (Telephone in U.S. (212) 331-9081), www.who.int; *World Health Report 2006.*

GAMBIA, THE - WAGES

International Labour Office, I.L.O. Publications, 4 route des Morillons, CH-1211 Geneva 22, Switzerland, (Telephone in U.S. (202) 653-7652), (Fax in U.S. (202) 653-7687), www.ilo.org; *Yearbook of Labour Statistics 2006.*

The World Bank, 1818 H Street, NW, Washington, DC 20433, (202) 473-1000, Fax: (202) 477-6391, www.worldbank.org; *Gambia.*

GAMBIA, THE - WEATHER

See GAMBIA, THE - CLIMATE

GAMBIA, THE - WELFARE STATE

International Monetary Fund (IMF), 700 Nineteenth Street, NW, Washington, DC 20431, (202) 623-7000, Fax: (202) 623-4661, www.imf.org; *Government Finance Statistics Yearbook (2008 Edition).*

GAMBIA, THE - WHEAT PRODUCTION

See GAMBIA, THE - CROPS

GAMBIA, THE - WINE PRODUCTION

See GAMBIA, THE - BEVERAGE INDUSTRY

GAMBIA, THE - WOOL PRODUCTION

See GAMBIA, THE - TEXTILE INDUSTRY

GAMBLING - ARRESTS

Federal Bureau of Investigation (FBI), J. Edgar Hoover Building, 935 Pennsylvania Avenue, NW, Washington, DC 20535-0001, (202) 324-3000, www.fbi.gov; *Crime in the United States (CIUS) 2007 (Preliminary).*

Justice Research and Statistics Association (JRSA), 777 N. Capitol Street, NE, Suite 801, Washington, DC 20002, (202) 842-9330, Fax: (202) 842-9329, www.jrsa.org; *Crime and Justice Atlas 2001.*

GANGS

Federal Bureau of Investigation (FBI), J. Edgar Hoover Building, 935 Pennsylvania Avenue, NW, Washington, DC 20535-0001, (202) 324-3000, www.fbi.gov; *Crime in the United States (CIUS) 2007 (Preliminary).*

Justice Research and Statistics Association (JRSA), 777 N. Capitol Street, NE, Suite 801, Washington, DC 20002, (202) 842-9330, Fax: (202) 842-9329, www.jrsa.org; *Crime and Justice Atlas 2001.*

U.S. Department of Justice (DOJ), Bureau of Justice Statistics, 810 Seventh Street, NW, Washington, DC 20531, (202) 307-0765, www.ojp.usdoj.gov/bjs/; *Violence by Gang Members, 1993-2003.*

U.S. Department of Justice (DOJ), National Institute of Justice (NIJ), 810 Seventh Street, NW, Washington, DC 20531, (202) 307-2942, Fax: (202) 616-0275, www.ojp.usdoj.gov/nij/; *Responding to Gangs: Evaluation and Research.*

GARAGES

See GASOLINE STATIONS - RETAIL

GARDEN ACTIVITIES AND EQUIPMENT

National Gardening Association, 1100 Dorset Street, South Burlington, VT 05403, (802) 863-5251, http://garden.org; *2007 National Gardening Survey.*

GARDEN SUPPLIES

See BUILDING MATERIALS AND GARDEN SUPPLIES

GARNET (ABRASIVE) - PRODUCTION AND VALUE

U.S. Department of the Interior (DOI), U.S. Geological Survey (USGS), Office of Minerals Information, 12201 Sunrise Valley Drive, Reston, VA 20192, Mr. Kenneth A. Beckman, (703) 648-4916, Fax: (703) 648-4995, http://minerals.usgs.gov/minerals; *Mineral Commodity Summaries* and *Minerals Yearbook.*

GARNET - INDUSTRIAL

U.S. Department of the Interior (DOI), U.S. Geological Survey (USGS), Office of Minerals Information, 12201 Sunrise Valley Drive, Reston, VA 20192, Mr. Kenneth A. Beckman, (703) 648-4916, Fax: (703) 648-4995, http://minerals.usgs.gov/minerals; *Mineral Commodity Summaries.*

GAS

See also GASOLINE and PETROLEUM INDUSTRY AND TRADE

American Petroleum Institute (API), 1220 L Street, NW, Washington, DC 20005-4070, (202) 682-8000, http://api-ec.api.org; *Petroleum Facts at a Glance.*

Lundberg Survey, Incorporated (LSI), 911 Via Alondra, Camarillo, CA 93012, (805) 383-2400, Fax: (805) 383-2424, www.lundbergsurvey.com; *Energy Detente; Lundberg Letter; National Retail Gasoline and Diesel Price Survey;* and *National Share of Market Report.*

PennWell Corporation, 1421 South Sheridan Road, Tulsa, OK 74112, (918) 835-3161, www.pennwell.com; *Oil and Gas Financial Journal* and *Oil and Gas Journal.*

GAS - LIQUIFIED PETROLEUM GASES

U.S. Department of Energy (DOE), Energy Information Administration (EIA), 1000 Independence Avenue, SW, Washington, DC 20585, (202) 586-8800, www.eia.doe.gov; *Petroleum Supply Annual 2004.*

GAS - NATURAL

U.S. Bureau of Labor Statistics (BLS), Postal Square Building, 2 Massachusetts Avenue, NE,

Washington, DC 20212-0001, (202) 691-5200, Fax: (202) 691-6325, www.bls.gov; *Current Employment Statistics Survey (CES)* and *Employment and Earnings (EE).*

U.S. Department of Energy (DOE), Energy Information Administration (EIA), 1000 Independence Avenue, SW, Washington, DC 20585, (202) 586-8800, www.eia.doe.gov; *Annual Energy Review 2005; International Energy Annual 2004; International Energy Outlook 2006; Monthly Energy Review (MER);* and *Natural Gas Annual 2004.*

GAS - NATURAL - CONSUMPTION

PennWell Corporation, 1421 South Sheridan Road, Tulsa, OK 74112, (918) 835-3161, www.pennwell.com; *Oil and Gas Financial Journal* and *Oil and Gas Journal.*

U.S. Department of Energy (DOE), Energy Information Administration (EIA), 1000 Independence Avenue, SW, Washington, DC 20585, (202) 586-8800, www.eia.doe.gov; *Annual Energy Review 2005; International Energy Annual 2004; International Energy Outlook 2006; Natural Gas Annual 2004; Residential Energy Consumption Survey (RECS); State Energy Data Report;* and *U.S. Crude Oil, Natural Gas, and Natural Gas Liquids Reserves, 2005 Annual Report.*

GAS - NATURAL - ENERGY EXPENDITURES

U.S. Department of Energy (DOE), Energy Information Administration (EIA), 1000 Independence Avenue, SW, Washington, DC 20585, (202) 586-8800, www.eia.doe.gov; *Residential Energy Consumption Survey (RECS)* and *State Energy Data 2003 Price and Expenditure Data.*

GAS - NATURAL - INTERNATIONAL TRADE

PennWell Corporation, 1421 South Sheridan Road, Tulsa, OK 74112, (918) 835-3161, www.pennwell.com; *Oil and Gas Financial Journal* and *Oil and Gas Journal.*

U.S. Census Bureau, Foreign Trade Division, 4700 Silver Hill Road, Washington DC 20233-0001, (301) 763-3030, www.census.gov/foreign-trade/www/; *U.S. International Trade in Goods and Services.*

U.S. Department of Energy (DOE), Energy Information Administration (EIA), 1000 Independence Avenue, SW, Washington, DC 20585, (202) 586-8800, www.eia.doe.gov; *Annual Energy Outlook 2006; Annual Energy Review 2005;* and *Natural Gas Monthly.*

GAS - NATURAL - OFFSHORE LEASE REVENUES

U.S. Department of Energy (DOE), Energy Information Administration (EIA), 1000 Independence Avenue, SW, Washington, DC 20585, (202) 586-8800, www.eia.doe.gov; *Petroleum Supply Annual 2004.*

GAS - NATURAL - PRICES

PennWell Corporation, 1421 South Sheridan Road, Tulsa, OK 74112, (918) 835-3161, www.pennwell.com; *Oil and Gas Financial Journal* and *Oil and Gas Journal.*

U.S. Department of Commerce (DOC), Economics and Statistics Administration (ESA), 1401 Constitution Avenue, NW, Washington, DC 20230, (800) 782-8872, www.esa.doc.gov; *Impact of Increased Natural Gas Prices on U.S. Economy and Industries: Report to Congress.*

U.S. Department of Energy (DOE), Energy Information Administration (EIA), 1000 Independence Avenue, SW, Washington, DC 20585, (202) 586-8800, www.eia.doe.gov; *Annual Energy Review 2005; International Energy Annual 2004; International Energy Outlook 2006;* and *Monthly Energy Review (MER).*

U.S. Department of the Interior (DOI), U.S. Geological Survey (USGS), Office of Minerals Information, 12201 Sunrise Valley Drive, Reston, VA 20192, Mr. Kenneth A. Beckman, (703) 648-4916, Fax: (703) 648-4995, http://minerals.usgs.gov/minerals; *Mineral Commodity Summaries.*

GAS - NATURAL - PRODUCTION AND VALUE

PennWell Corporation, 1421 South Sheridan Road, Tulsa, OK 74112, (918) 835-3161, www.pennwell.com; *Oil and Gas Financial Journal* and *Oil and Gas Journal.*

U.S. Department of Energy (DOE), Energy Information Administration (EIA), 1000 Independence Avenue, SW, Washington, DC 20585, (202) 586-8800, www.eia.doe.gov; *Annual Energy Review 2005; International Energy Annual 2004; International Energy Outlook 2006; Monthly Energy Review (MER); Natural Gas Annual 2004; Natural Gas Monthly; Petroleum Supply Annual 2004; U.S. Crude Oil, Natural Gas, and Natural Gas Liquids Reserves, 2005 Annual Report;* and unpublished data.

GAS - NATURAL - PRODUCTION AND VALUE - FOREIGN COUNTRIES

Platts, 2 Penn Plaza, 25th Floor, New York, NY 10121-2298, (212) 904-3070, www.platts.com; *Energy Economist.*

U.S. Department of the Interior (DOI), U.S. Geological Survey (USGS), Office of Minerals Information, 12201 Sunrise Valley Drive, Reston, VA 20192, Mr. Kenneth A. Beckman, (703) 648-4916, Fax: (703) 648-4995, http://minerals.usgs.gov/minerals; *Mineral Commodity Summaries.*

United Nations Statistics Division, New York, NY 10017, (800) 253-9646, Fax: (212) 963-4116, http://unstats.un.org; *Energy Statistics Yearbook 2003.*

GAS - NATURAL - PRODUCTION AND VALUE - INDEXES

Board of Governors of the Federal Reserve System, Constitution Avenue, NW, Washington, DC 20551, (202) 452-3000, www.federalreserve.gov; *Federal Reserve Bulletin* and *Industrial Production and Capacity Utilization.*

GAS - NATURAL - RESERVES

U.S. Department of Energy (DOE), Energy Information Administration (EIA), 1000 Independence Avenue, SW, Washington, DC 20585, (202) 586-8800, www.eia.doe.gov; *Annual Energy Review 2005; International Energy Annual 2004; International Energy Outlook 2006; Monthly Energy Review (MER);* and *Natural Gas Annual 2004.*

GAS - NATURAL - RESIDENTIAL

U.S. Department of Energy (DOE), Energy Information Administration (EIA), 1000 Independence Avenue, SW, Washington, DC 20585, (202) 586-8800, www.eia.doe.gov; *Residential Energy Consumption Survey (RECS).*

GAS - NATURAL - WORLD PRODUCTION

PennWell Corporation, 1421 South Sheridan Road, Tulsa, OK 74112, (918) 835-3161, www.pennwell.com; *Oil and Gas Financial Journal; Oil and Gas Journal;* and *Oil Gas Journal Latinoamericana.*

U.S. Department of Energy (DOE), Energy Information Administration (EIA), 1000 Independence Avenue, SW, Washington, DC 20585, (202) 586-8800, www.eia.doe.gov; *International Energy Annual 2004* and *International Energy Outlook 2006.*

GAS - NATURAL GAS PLANT LIQUIDS

U.S. Department of Energy (DOE), Energy Information Administration (EIA), 1000 Independence Avenue, SW, Washington, DC 20585, (202) 586-8800, www.eia.doe.gov; *Annual Energy Outlook 2006; Natural Gas Annual 2004; Natural Gas Monthly;* and *Petroleum Supply Annual 2004.*

GAS - PRICE INDEXES

Bureau of Economic Analysis (BEA), U.S. Department of Commerce (DOC), 1441 L Street NW, Washington, DC 20230, (202) 606-9900, www.bea.gov; *Survey of Current Business (SCB).*

U.S. Bureau of Labor Statistics (BLS), Postal Square Building, 2 Massachusetts Avenue, NE, Washington, DC 20212-0001, (202) 691-5200, Fax: (202) 691-6325, www.bls.gov; *Consumer Price Index Detailed Report.*

GAS - PRODUCTION AND DISTRIBUTION

U.S. Bureau of Labor Statistics (BLS), Postal Square Building, 2 Massachusetts Avenue, NE, Washington, DC 20212-0001, (202) 691-5200, Fax: (202) 691-6325, www.bls.gov; *Current Employment Statistics Survey (CES)* and *Employment and Earnings (EE).*

GAS AND ELECTRIC UTILITIES

See GAS UTILITY INDUSTRY

GAS UTILITY INDUSTRY - ACCIDENTS

U.S. Department of Labor (DOL), Bureau of Labor Statistics (BLS), Postal Square Building, 2 Massachusetts Avenue, NE, Washington, DC 20212-0001, (202) 691-5200, Fax: (202) 691-6325, www.bls.gov; *Injuries, Illnesses, and Fatalities (IIF).*

U.S. Department of Transportation (DOT), Research and Innovative Technology Administration (RITA), Bureau of Transportation Statistics (BTS), 1200 New Jersey Avenue, SE, Washington, DC 20590, (800) 853-1351, www.bts.gov; *TranStats.*

GAS UTILITY INDUSTRY - CAPITAL EXPENDITURES

U.S. Census Bureau, Company Statistics Division, 4700 Silver Hill Road, Washington DC 20233-0001, (301) 763-3030, www.census.gov/csd/; *Annual Capital Expenditures Survey (ACES).*

GAS UTILITY INDUSTRY - CONSTRUCTION EXPENDITURES

American Gas Association, 400 North Capitol Street, NW, Washington, DC 20001-1535, (202) 824-7000, www.aga.org; *Gas Facts.*

GAS UTILITY INDUSTRY - CUSTOMERS

American Gas Association, 400 North Capitol Street, NW, Washington, DC 20001-1535, (202) 824-7000, www.aga.org; *Gas Facts.*

GAS UTILITY INDUSTRY - END USERS

American Gas Association, 400 North Capitol Street, NW, Washington, DC 20001-1535, (202) 824-7000, www.aga.org; *Gas Facts.*

GAS UTILITY INDUSTRY - FINANCES

American Gas Association, 400 North Capitol Street, NW, Washington, DC 20001-1535, (202) 824-7000, www.aga.org; *Gas Facts.*

GAS UTILITY INDUSTRY - PRICES

American Gas Association, 400 North Capitol Street, NW, Washington, DC 20001-1535, (202) 824-7000, www.aga.org; *Gas Facts.*

GAS UTILITY INDUSTRY - REVENUES

American Gas Association, 400 North Capitol Street, NW, Washington, DC 20001-1535, (202) 824-7000, www.aga.org; *Gas Facts.*

GAS UTILITY INDUSTRY - SALES

American Gas Association, 400 North Capitol Street, NW, Washington, DC 20001-1535, (202) 824-7000, www.aga.org; *Gas Facts.*

GASOLINE - BLENDING COMPONENTS

U.S. Department of Energy (DOE), Energy Information Administration (EIA), 1000 Independence Avenue, SW, Washington, DC 20585, (202) 586-8800, www.eia.doe.gov; *Annual Energy Review 2005; Petroleum Supply Annual 2004;* and *U.S.*

Crude Oil, Natural Gas, and Natural Gas Liquids Reserves, 2005 Annual Report.

GASOLINE - EXCISE TAXES

U.S. Department of Energy (DOE), Energy Information Administration (EIA), 1000 Independence Avenue, SW, Washington, DC 20585, (202) 586-8800, www.eia.doe.gov; *Petroleum Marketing Monthly.*

U.S. Department of Transportation (DOT), Federal Highway Administration (FHA), 1200 New Jersey Avenue, SE, Washington, DC 20590, (202) 366-0660, www.fhwa.dot.gov; *Highway Statistics 2006.*

GASOLINE - FINISHED MOTOR GASOLINE

U.S. Department of Energy (DOE), Energy Information Administration (EIA), 1000 Independence Avenue, SW, Washington, DC 20585, (202) 586-8800, www.eia.doe.gov; *Annual Energy Review 2005* and *Petroleum Supply Annual 2004.*

GASOLINE - PRICES

Lundberg Survey, Incorporated (LSI), 911 Via Alondra, Camarillo, CA 93012, (805) 383-2400, Fax: (805) 383-2424, www.lundbergsurvey.com; *Energy Detente; Lundberg Letter; National Retail Gasoline and Diesel Price Survey;* and *National Share of Market Report.*

U.S. Department of Energy (DOE), Energy Information Administration (EIA), 1000 Independence Avenue, SW, Washington, DC 20585, (202) 586-8800, www.eia.doe.gov; *Petroleum Marketing Monthly.*

GASOLINE - SUPPLY

Lundberg Survey, Incorporated (LSI), 911 Via Alondra, Camarillo, CA 93012, (805) 383-2400, Fax: (805) 383-2424, www.lundbergsurvey.com; *Energy Detente; Lundberg Letter; National Retail Gasoline and Diesel Price Survey;* and *National Share of Market Report.*

U.S. Department of Energy (DOE), Energy Information Administration (EIA), 1000 Independence Avenue, SW, Washington, DC 20585, (202) 586-8800, www.eia.doe.gov; *Monthly Energy Review (MER).*

GASOLINE STATIONS - RETAIL

Office of Trade and Industry Information (OTII), Manufacturing and Services, International Trade Administration, U.S. Department of Commerce, 1401 Constitution Ave, NW, Washington, DC 20230, (800) USA TRAD(E), http://trade.gov/index.asp; *TradeStats Express.*

U.S. Census Bureau, Center for Economic Studies, 4600 Silver Hill Road, Washington DC 20233, (301) 457-1235, www.ces.census.gov; *2002 Economic Census, Retail Trade* and *2002 Economic Census, Wholesale Trade.*

U.S. Census Bureau, Company Statistics Division, 4700 Silver Hill Road, Washington DC 20233-0001, (301) 763-3030, www.census.gov/csd/; *County Business Patterns 2004.*

GASOLINE STATIONS - RETAIL - EARNINGS

Office of Trade and Industry Information (OTII), Manufacturing and Services, International Trade Administration, U.S. Department of Commerce, 1401 Constitution Ave, NW, Washington, DC 20230, (800) USA TRAD(E), http://trade.gov/index.asp; *TradeStats Express.*

U.S. Census Bureau, Center for Economic Studies, 4600 Silver Hill Road, Washington DC 20233, (301) 457-1235, www.ces.census.gov; *2002 Economic Census, Retail Trade.*

U.S. Census Bureau, Company Statistics Division, 4700 Silver Hill Road, Washington DC 20233-0001, (301) 763-3030, www.census.gov/csd/; *County Business Patterns 2004.*

GASOLINE STATIONS - RETAIL - ELECTRONIC COMMERCE

U.S. Census Bureau, 4700 Silver Hill Road, Washington DC 20233-0001, (301) 763-3030, www.census.gov; *2006 E-Commerce Multi-Sector Report* and *E-Stats - Measuring the Electronic Economy.*

GASOLINE STATIONS - RETAIL - EMPLOYEES

U.S. Census Bureau, Center for Economic Studies, 4600 Silver Hill Road, Washington DC 20233, (301) 457-1235, www.ces.census.gov; *2002 Economic Census, Retail Trade.*

U.S. Census Bureau, Company Statistics Division, 4700 Silver Hill Road, Washington DC 20233-0001, (301) 763-3030, www.census.gov/csd/; *County Business Patterns 2004.*

GASOLINE STATIONS - RETAIL - FINANCES

U.S. Department of the Treasury (DOT), Internal Revenue Service (IRS), Statistics of Income Division (SIS), PO Box 2608, Washington, DC, 20013-2608, (202) 874-0410, Fax: (202) 874-0964, www.irs.ustreas.gov; *Statistics of Income Bulletin.*

GASOLINE STATIONS - RETAIL - NONEMPLOYERS

U.S. Census Bureau, 4700 Silver Hill Road, Washington DC 20233-0001, (301) 763-3030, www.census.gov; *2002 Economic Census, Nonemployer Statistics.*

GASOLINE STATIONS - RETAIL - PRODUCTIVITY

U.S. Bureau of Labor Statistics (BLS), Postal Square Building, 2 Massachusetts Avenue, NE, Washington, DC 20212-0001, (202) 691-5200, Fax: (202) 691-6325, www.bls.gov; *Industry Productivity and Costs.*

GASOLINE STATIONS - RETAIL - PURCHASES

U.S. Department of the Treasury (DOT), Internal Revenue Service (IRS), Statistics of Income Division (SIS), PO Box 2608, Washington, DC, 20013-2608, (202) 874-0410, Fax: (202) 874-0964, www.irs.ustreas.gov; *Statistics of Income Bulletin.*

GASOLINE STATIONS - RETAIL - SALES

Claritas, 5375 Mira Sorrento Place, Suite 400, San Diego, CA 92121, (800) 866-6520, Fax: (858) 550-5800, www.claritas.com; *Consumer Buying Power.*

Office of Trade and Industry Information (OTII), Manufacturing and Services, International Trade Administration, U.S. Department of Commerce, 1401 Constitution Ave, NW, Washington, DC 20230, (800) USA TRAD(E), http://trade.gov/index.asp; *TradeStats Express.*

U.S. Census Bureau, 4700 Silver Hill Road, Washington DC 20233-0001, (301) 763-3030, www.census.gov; unpublished data.

U.S. Census Bureau, Center for Economic Studies, 4600 Silver Hill Road, Washington DC 20233, (301) 457-1235, www.ces.census.gov; *2002 Economic Census, Retail Trade.*

U.S. Census Bureau, Company Statistics Division, 4700 Silver Hill Road, Washington DC 20233-0001, (301) 763-3030, www.census.gov/csd/; *Current Business Reports.*

GASTROENTEROLOGY

American Medical Association, 515 North State Street, Chicago, IL 60610, (800) 621-8335, www.ama-assn.org; *Physician Characteristics and Distribution in the United States, 2008* and *Physician Compensation and Production Survey: 2007 Report Based on 2006 Data.*

Health Protection Surveillance Centre (HPSC), 25-27 Middle Gardiner Street, Dublin 1, Ireland, www.ndsc.ie/hpsc; *Acute Gastroenteritis in Ireland, North and South: A Telephone Survey.*

GAZA STRIP - PRIMARY STATISTICS SOURCES

Municipality of Gaza, PO Box 16, Gaza City, Palestine, www.mogaza.org; *Statistics about Gaza Strip.*

Palestinian Central Bureau of Statistics (PCBS), PO Box 1647, Ramallah, West Bank, Palestine, www.pcbs.gov.ps; *Agricultural Statistics 2005/2006* and *Statistical Atlas of Palestine.*

GEM STONES

U.S. Department of the Interior (DOI), U.S. Geological Survey (USGS), Office of Minerals Information, 12201 Sunrise Valley Drive, Reston, VA 20192, Mr. Kenneth A. Beckman, (703) 648-4916, Fax: (703) 648-4995, http://minerals.usgs.gov/minerals; *Mineral Commodity Summaries* and *Minerals Yearbook.*

GENERAL MERCHANDISE STORES - EARNINGS

Office of Trade and Industry Information (OTII), Manufacturing and Services, International Trade Administration, U.S. Department of Commerce, 1401 Constitution Ave, NW, Washington, DC 20230, (800) USA TRAD(E), http://trade.gov/index.asp; *TradeStats Express.*

U.S. Bureau of Labor Statistics (BLS), Postal Square Building, 2 Massachusetts Avenue, NE, Washington, DC 20212-0001, (202) 691-5200, Fax: (202) 691-6325, www.bls.gov; *Current Employment Statistics Survey (CES)* and *Employment and Earnings (EE).*

U.S. Census Bureau, Center for Economic Studies, 4600 Silver Hill Road, Washington DC 20233, (301) 457-1235, www.ces.census.gov; *2002 Economic Census, Retail Trade* and *2002 Economic Census, Wholesale Trade.*

GENERAL MERCHANDISE STORES - ELECTRONIC COMMERCE

U.S. Census Bureau, 4700 Silver Hill Road, Washington DC 20233-0001, (301) 763-3030, www.census.gov; *2006 E-Commerce Multi-Sector Report* and *E-Stats - Measuring the Electronic Economy.*

GENERAL MERCHANDISE STORES - EMPLOYEES

U.S. Bureau of Labor Statistics (BLS), Postal Square Building, 2 Massachusetts Avenue, NE, Washington, DC 20212-0001, (202) 691-5200, Fax: (202) 691-6325, www.bls.gov; *Current Employment Statistics Survey (CES)* and *Employment and Earnings (EE).*

GENERAL MERCHANDISE STORES - ESTABLISHMENTS

Office of Trade and Industry Information (OTII), Manufacturing and Services, International Trade Administration, U.S. Department of Commerce, 1401 Constitution Ave, NW, Washington, DC 20230, (800) USA TRAD(E), http://trade.gov/index.asp; *TradeStats Express.*

U.S. Census Bureau, Center for Economic Studies, 4600 Silver Hill Road, Washington DC 20233, (301) 457-1235, www.ces.census.gov; *2002 Economic Census, Retail Trade.*

U.S. Census Bureau, Company Statistics Division, 4700 Silver Hill Road, Washington DC 20233-0001, (301) 763-3030, www.census.gov/csd/; *County Business Patterns 2004.*

GENERAL MERCHANDISE STORES - INVENTORIES

Office of Trade and Industry Information (OTII), Manufacturing and Services, International Trade Administration, U.S. Department of Commerce,

1401 Constitution Ave, NW, Washington, DC 20230, (800) USA TRAD(E), http://trade.gov/index.asp; *TradeStats Express*.

U.S. Census Bureau, Center for Economic Studies, 4600 Silver Hill Road, Washington DC 20233, (301) 457-1235, www.ces.census.gov; *2002 Economic Census, Retail Trade*.

U.S. Census Bureau, Company Statistics Division, 4700 Silver Hill Road, Washington DC 20233-0001, (301) 763-3030, www.census.gov/csd/; *Current Business Reports*.

GENERAL MERCHANDISE STORES - MERGERS AND ACQUISITIONS

Thomson Financial, 195 Broadway, New York, NY 10007, (646) 822-2000, www.thomson.com; Thomson Research.

GENERAL MERCHANDISE STORES - NONEMPLOYERS

U.S. Census Bureau, 4700 Silver Hill Road, Washington DC 20233-0001, (301) 763-3030, www.census.gov; *2002 Economic Census, Nonemployer Statistics*.

GENERAL MERCHANDISE STORES - PRODUCTIVITY

U.S. Bureau of Labor Statistics (BLS), Postal Square Building, 2 Massachusetts Avenue, NE, Washington, DC 20212-0001, (202) 691-5200, Fax: (202) 691-6325, www.bls.gov; *Industry Productivity and Costs*.

GENERAL MERCHANDISE STORES - PURCHASES

U.S. Department of the Treasury (DOT), Internal Revenue Service (IRS), Statistics of Income Division (SIS), PO Box 2608, Washington, DC, 20013-2608, (202) 874-0410, Fax: (202) 874-0964, www.irs.ustreas.gov; *Statistics of Income Bulletin*.

GENERAL MERCHANDISE STORES - SALES

Claritas, 5375 Mira Sorrento Place, Suite 400, San Diego, CA 92121, (800) 866-6520, Fax: (858) 550-5800, www.claritas.com; *Consumer Buying Power*.

Office of Trade and Industry Information (OTII), Manufacturing and Services, International Trade Administration, U.S. Department of Commerce, 1401 Constitution Ave, NW, Washington, DC 20230, (800) USA TRAD(E), http://trade.gov/index.asp; *TradeStats Express*.

U.S. Census Bureau, Center for Economic Studies, 4600 Silver Hill Road, Washington DC 20233, (301) 457-1235, www.ces.census.gov; *2002 Economic Census, Retail Trade*.

U.S. Census Bureau, Company Statistics Division, 4700 Silver Hill Road, Washington DC 20233-0001, (301) 763-3030, www.census.gov/csd/; *County Business Patterns 2004*.

GENETICALLY MODIFIED SEED PLANTINGS

National Agricultural Statistics Service (NASS), U.S. Department of Agriculture (USDA), 1400 Independence Avenue, SW, Washington, DC 20250, (800) 727-9540, Fax: (202) 690-2090, www.nass.usda.gov; *Acreage*.

GEOGRAPHY AND CARTOGRAPHY

See LAND - AREA

GEORGIA

See also - STATE DATA (FOR INDIVIDUAL STATES)

Selig Center for Economic Growth, Terry College of Business, University of Georgia, Athens, GA 30602-6269, Mr. Jeffrey M. Humphreys, Director, (706) 425-2962, www.selig.uga.edu; *Georgia Business and Economic Conditions (GBEC); Georgia Economic Outlook;* and *The Multicultural Economy: Minority Buying Power in 2006*.

GEORGIA - STATE DATA CENTERS

Georgia Institute of Technology Library and Information Center, Government Information Department, 1st Floor West, 704 Cherry Street, Atlanta, GA 30332-0900, (404) 894-4530, www.library.gatech.edu; State Data Center.

Planning, Research, and Evaluation Division, Governor's Office of Planning and Budget, 270 Washington Street, SW, Suite 8100, Atlanta, GA 30334, (404) 656-6505, Fax: (404) 656-7916, http://www.gadata.org; State Data Center.

University of Georgia Libraries, Government Documents Department, University of Georgia, Athens, GA 30602-1641, Mr. John Prechtel, (706) 542-3472, www.libs.uga.edu/govdocs; State Data Center.

GEORGIA - PRIMARY STATISTICS SOURCES

Center for Agribusiness and Economic Development, University of Georgia, 301 Lumpkin House, Athens, GA 30602-7509, (706) 542-2434, Fax: (706) 542-0770, www.caed.uga.edu; *2007 Georgia County Guide*.

Selig Center for Economic Growth, Terry College of Business, University of Georgia, Athens, GA 30602-6269, Mr. Jeffrey M. Humphreys, Director, (706) 425-2962, www.selig.uga.edu; *Georgia Statistical Abstract 2004-2005*.

GEORGIA (REPUBLIC) - NATIONAL STATISTICAL OFFICE

State Department for Statistics (SDS) of Georgia, 4 Beijing Str., Tbilisi 0115, Georgia, www.statistics.ge; National Data Center.

GEORGIA (REPUBLIC) - PRIMARY STATISTICS SOURCES

State Department for Statistics (SDS) of Georgia, 4 Beijing Str., Tbilisi 0115, Georgia, www.statistics.ge; *Industry in Georgia 2006* and *Statistical Yearbook of Georgia 2007*.

Turkish Statistical Institute (Turkstat), Prime Ministry State Institute of Statistics (SIS), Information Dissemination Division, Necatibey Caddesi No. 114, 06100 Bakanliklar, Ankara, Turkey, www.die.gov.tr/ENGLISH; *Statistical Indicators 1923-2004*.

GEORGIA (REPUBLIC) - ABORTION

United Nations Statistics Division, New York, NY 10017, (800) 253-9646, Fax: (212) 963-4116, http://unstats.un.org; *Trends in Europe and North America: The Statistical Yearbook of the ECE 2005*.

GEORGIA (REPUBLIC) - AGRICULTURE

Academic International Press, PO Box 1111, Gulf Breeze, FL 32562-1111, Fax: (850) 934-0953, www.ai-press.com; *Russia and Eurasia Facts and Figures Annual*.

Economist Intelligence Unit, 111 West 57th Street, New York, NY 10019, (212) 554-0600, Fax: (212) 586-1181, www.eiu.com; *Georgia Country Report*.

Euromonitor International, Inc., 224 S. Michigan Avenue, Suite 1500, Chicago, IL 60604, (312) 922-1115, Fax: (312) 922-1157, www.euromonitor.com; *World Marketing Data and Statistics*.

Palgrave Macmillan Ltd., Houndmills, Basingstoke, Hampshire, RG21 6XS, England, (Telephone in U.S. (888) 330-8477), (Fax in U.S. (800) 672-2054), www.palgrave.com; *The Statesman's Yearbook 2008*.

Taylor and Francis Group, An Informa Business, 2 Park Square, Milton Park, Abingdon, Oxford OX14 4RN, United Kingdom, (Dial from U.S. (212) 216-7800), (Fax from U.S. (212) 564-7854), www.tandf.co.uk; *The Europa World Year Book*.

United Nations Food and Agricultural Organization (FAO), Viale delle Terme di Caracalla, 00100 Rome, Italy, (Dial from U.S. (202) 653-2400), (Fax from U.S. (202) 653 5760), www.fao.org; AQUASTAT; *FAO Production Yearbook 2002; FAO Trade Yearbook;* and *The State of Food and Agriculture (SOFA) 2006*.

United Nations Statistics Division, New York, NY 10017, (800) 253-9646, Fax: (212) 963-4116, http://unstats.un.org; *2004 Industrial Commodity Statistics Yearbook* and *Statistical Yearbook*.

The World Bank, 1818 H Street, NW, Washington, DC 20433, (202) 473-1000, Fax: (202) 477-6391, www.worldbank.org; *Georgia* and *Statistical Handbook: States of the Former USSR*.

GEORGIA (REPUBLIC) - AIRLINES

International Civil Aviation Organization (ICAO), External Relations and Public Information Office (EPO), 999 University Street, Montreal, Quebec H3C 5H7, Canada, (Dial from U.S. (514) 954-8219), (Fax from U.S. (514) 954-6077), www.icao.int; *Civil Aviation Statistics of the World*.

Palgrave Macmillan Ltd., Houndmills, Basingstoke, Hampshire, RG21 6XS, England, (Telephone in U.S. (888) 330-8477), (Fax in U.S. (800) 672-2054), www.palgrave.com; *The Statesman's Yearbook 2008*.

United Nations Statistics Division, New York, NY 10017, (800) 253-9646, Fax: (212) 963-4116, http://unstats.un.org; *Statistical Yearbook*.

GEORGIA (REPUBLIC) - AIRPORTS

Central Intelligence Agency, Office of Public Affairs, Washington, DC 20505, (703) 482-0623, Fax: (703) 482-1739, www.cia.gov; *The World Factbook*.

GEORGIA (REPUBLIC) - ARMED FORCES

Academic International Press, PO Box 1111, Gulf Breeze, FL 32562-1111, Fax: (850) 934-0953, www.ai-press.com; *Russia and Eurasia Facts and Figures Annual*.

Central Intelligence Agency, Office of Public Affairs, Washington, DC 20505, (703) 482-0623, Fax: (703) 482-1739, www.cia.gov; *The World Factbook*.

Euromonitor International, Inc., 224 S. Michigan Avenue, Suite 1500, Chicago, IL 60604, (312) 922-1115, Fax: (312) 922-1157, www.euromonitor.com; *World Marketing Data and Statistics*.

International Institute for Strategic Studies (IISS), Arundel House, 13-15 Arundel Street, Temple Place, London WC2R 3DX, England, www.iiss.org; *The Military Balance 2007*.

Palgrave Macmillan Ltd., Houndmills, Basingstoke, Hampshire, RG21 6XS, England, (Telephone in U.S. (888) 330-8477), (Fax in U.S. (800) 672-2054), www.palgrave.com; *The Statesman's Yearbook 2008*.

United Nations Statistics Division, New York, NY 10017, (800) 253-9646, Fax: (212) 963-4116, http://unstats.un.org; *Human Development Report 2006*.

GEORGIA (REPUBLIC) - BALANCE OF PAYMENTS

Taylor and Francis Group, An Informa Business, 2 Park Square, Milton Park, Abingdon, Oxford OX14 4RN, United Kingdom, (Dial from U.S. (212) 216-7800), (Fax from U.S. (212) 564-7854), www.tandf.co.uk; *The Europa World Year Book*.

United Nations Conference on Trade and Development (UNCTAD), DC2-1120, United Nations, New York, NY 10017, (212) 963-0027, www.unctad.org; *Handbook of Statistics 2005*.

The World Bank, 1818 H Street, NW, Washington, DC 20433, (202) 473-1000, Fax: (202) 477-6391, www.worldbank.org; *Georgia* and *World Development Report 2008*.

GEORGIA (REPUBLIC) - BANKS AND BANKING

Euromonitor International, Inc., 224 S. Michigan Avenue, Suite 1500, Chicago, IL 60604, (312) 922-1115, Fax: (312) 922-1157, www.euromonitor.com; *World Marketing Data and Statistics.*

GEORGIA (REPUBLIC) - BEVERAGE INDUSTRY

United Nations Statistics Division, New York, NY 10017, (800) 253-9646, Fax: (212) 963-4116, http://unstats.un.org; *Statistical Yearbook.*

GEORGIA (REPUBLIC) - BROADCASTING

Central Intelligence Agency, Office of Public Affairs, Washington, DC 20505, (703) 482-0623, Fax: (703) 482-1739, www.cia.gov; *The World Factbook.*

Euromonitor International, Inc., 224 S. Michigan Avenue, Suite 1500, Chicago, IL 60604, (312) 922-1115, Fax: (312) 922-1157, www.euromonitor.com; *World Marketing Data and Statistics.*

Palgrave Macmillan Ltd., Houndmills, Basingstoke, Hampshire, RG21 6XS, England, (Telephone in U.S. (888) 330-8477), (Fax in U.S. (800) 672-2054), www.palgrave.com; *The Statesman's Yearbook 2008.*

UNESCO Institute for Statistics, C.P. 6128 Succursale Centre-Ville, Montreal, Quebec, H3C 3J7 Canada, (Dial from U.S. (514) 343-6880), (Fax from U.S. (514) 343 6882), www.uis.unesco.org; *Statistical Tables.*

United Nations Statistics Division, New York, NY 10017, (800) 253-9646, Fax: (212) 963-4116, http://unstats.un.org; *Trends in Europe and North America: The Statistical Yearbook of the ECE 2005.*

GEORGIA (REPUBLIC) - BUDGET

Central Intelligence Agency, Office of Public Affairs, Washington, DC 20505, (703) 482-0623, Fax: (703) 482-1739, www.cia.gov; *The World Factbook.*

GEORGIA (REPUBLIC) - BUSINESS

United Nations Statistics Division, New York, NY 10017, (800) 253-9646, Fax: (212) 963-4116, http://unstats.un.org; *Statistical Yearbook.*

GEORGIA (REPUBLIC) - CAPITAL INVESTMENTS

The World Bank, 1818 H Street, NW, Washington, DC 20433, (202) 473-1000, Fax: (202) 477-6391, www.worldbank.org; *Statistical Handbook: States of the Former USSR.*

GEORGIA (REPUBLIC) - CATTLE

See GEORGIA (REPUBLIC) - LIVESTOCK

GEORGIA (REPUBLIC) - CHILDBIRTH - STATISTICS

Central Intelligence Agency, Office of Public Affairs, Washington, DC 20505, (703) 482-0623, Fax: (703) 482-1739, www.cia.gov; *The World Factbook.*

Euromonitor International, Inc., 224 S. Michigan Avenue, Suite 1500, Chicago, IL 60604, (312) 922-1115, Fax: (312) 922-1157, www.euromonitor.com; *The World Economic Factbook 2008.*

Taylor and Francis Group, An Informa Business, 2 Park Square, Milton Park, Abingdon, Oxford OX14 4RN, United Kingdom, (Dial from U.S. (212) 216-7800), (Fax from U.S. (212) 564-7854), www.tandf.co.uk; *The Europa World Year Book.*

United Nations Statistics Division, New York, NY 10017, (800) 253-9646, Fax: (212) 963-4116, http://unstats.un.org; *Statistical Yearbook.*

World Health Organization (WHO), Avenue Appia 20, 1211 Geneve 27, Switzerland, (Telephone in U.S. (212) 331-9081), www.who.int; *World Health Report 2006.*

GEORGIA (REPUBLIC) - COAL PRODUCTION

See GEORGIA (REPUBLIC) - MINERAL INDUSTRIES

GEORGIA (REPUBLIC) - CONSTRUCTION INDUSTRY

Academic International Press, PO Box 1111, Gulf Breeze, FL 32562-1111, Fax: (850) 934-0953, www.ai-press.com; *Russia and Eurasia Facts and Figures Annual.*

United Nations Statistics Division, New York, NY 10017, (800) 253-9646, Fax: (212) 963-4116, http://unstats.un.org; *Statistical Yearbook.*

GEORGIA (REPUBLIC) - CONSUMER PRICE INDEXES

Taylor and Francis Group, An Informa Business, 2 Park Square, Milton Park, Abingdon, Oxford OX14 4RN, United Kingdom, (Dial from U.S. (212) 216-7800), (Fax from U.S. (212) 564-7854), www.tandf.co.uk; *The Europa World Year Book.*

United Nations Statistics Division, New York, NY 10017, (800) 253-9646, Fax: (212) 963-4116, http://unstats.un.org; *Statistical Yearbook* and *Trends in Europe and North America: The Statistical Yearbook of the ECE 2005.*

The World Bank, 1818 H Street, NW, Washington, DC 20433, (202) 473-1000, Fax: (202) 477-6391, www.worldbank.org; *Georgia.*

GEORGIA (REPUBLIC) - CONSUMPTION (ECONOMICS)

The World Bank, 1818 H Street, NW, Washington, DC 20433, (202) 473-1000, Fax: (202) 477-6391, www.worldbank.org; *Statistical Handbook: States of the Former USSR* and *World Development Report 2008.*

GEORGIA (REPUBLIC) - COTTON

See GEORGIA (REPUBLIC) - CROPS

GEORGIA (REPUBLIC) - CRIME

Academic International Press, PO Box 1111, Gulf Breeze, FL 32562-1111, Fax: (850) 934-0953, www.ai-press.com; *Russia and Eurasia Facts and Figures Annual.*

United Nations Statistics Division, New York, NY 10017, (800) 253-9646, Fax: (212) 963-4116, http://unstats.un.org; *Trends in Europe and North America: The Statistical Yearbook of the ECE 2005.*

GEORGIA (REPUBLIC) - CROPS

Academic International Press, PO Box 1111, Gulf Breeze, FL 32562-1111, Fax: (850) 934-0953, www.ai-press.com; *Russia and Eurasia Facts and Figures Annual.*

Palgrave Macmillan Ltd., Houndmills, Basingstoke, Hampshire, RG21 6XS, England, (Telephone in U.S. (888) 330-8477), (Fax in U.S. (800) 672-2054), www.palgrave.com; *The Statesman's Yearbook 2008.*

Taylor and Francis Group, An Informa Business, 2 Park Square, Milton Park, Abingdon, Oxford OX14 4RN, United Kingdom, (Dial from U.S. (212) 216-7800), (Fax from U.S. (212) 564-7854), www.tandf.co.uk; *The Europa World Year Book.*

United Nations Food and Agricultural Organization (FAO), Viale delle Terme di Caracalla, 00100 Rome, Italy, (Dial from U.S. (202) 653-2400), (Fax from U.S. (202) 653 5760), www.fao.org; *FAO Production Yearbook 2002* and *The State of Food and Agriculture (SOFA) 2006.*

United Nations Statistics Division, New York, NY 10017, (800) 253-9646, Fax: (212) 963-4116, http://unstats.un.org; *2004 Industrial Commodity Statistics Yearbook* and *Statistical Yearbook.*

The World Bank, 1818 H Street, NW, Washington, DC 20433, (202) 473-1000, Fax: (202) 477-6391, www.worldbank.org; *Statistical Handbook: States of the Former USSR.*

GEORGIA (REPUBLIC) - DAIRY PROCESSING

Palgrave Macmillan Ltd., Houndmills, Basingstoke, Hampshire, RG21 6XS, England, (Telephone in U.S. (888) 330-8477), (Fax in U.S. (800) 672-2054), www.palgrave.com; *The Statesman's Yearbook 2008.*

Taylor and Francis Group, An Informa Business, 2 Park Square, Milton Park, Abingdon, Oxford OX14 4RN, United Kingdom, (Dial from U.S. (212) 216-7800), (Fax from U.S. (212) 564-7854), www.tandf.co.uk; *The Europa World Year Book.*

United Nations Food and Agricultural Organization (FAO), Viale delle Terme di Caracalla, 00100 Rome, Italy, (Dial from U.S. (202) 653-2400), (Fax from U.S. (202) 653 5760), www.fao.org; *FAO Production Yearbook 2002* and *The State of Food and Agriculture (SOFA) 2006.*

United Nations Statistics Division, New York, NY 10017, (800) 253-9646, Fax: (212) 963-4116, http://unstats.un.org; *2004 Industrial Commodity Statistics Yearbook* and *Statistical Yearbook.*

GEORGIA (REPUBLIC) - DEATH RATES

See GEORGIA (REPUBLIC) - MORTALITY

GEORGIA (REPUBLIC) - DEBTS, EXTERNAL

The World Bank, 1818 H Street, NW, Washington, DC 20433, (202) 473-1000, Fax: (202) 477-6391, www.worldbank.org; *World Development Indicators (WDI) 2008* and *World Development Report 2008.*

GEORGIA (REPUBLIC) - DEMOGRAPHY

Euromonitor International, Inc., 224 S. Michigan Avenue, Suite 1500, Chicago, IL 60604, (312) 922-1115, Fax: (312) 922-1157, www.euromonitor.com; *The World Economic Factbook 2008* and *World Marketing Data and Statistics.*

United Nations Statistics Division, New York, NY 10017, (800) 253-9646, Fax: (212) 963-4116, http://unstats.un.org; *Demographic Yearbook* and *Human Development Report 2006.*

The World Bank, 1818 H Street, NW, Washington, DC 20433, (202) 473-1000, Fax: (202) 477-6391, www.worldbank.org; *Georgia* and *Statistical Handbook: States of the Former USSR.*

GEORGIA (REPUBLIC) - DISPOSABLE INCOME

United Nations Statistics Division, New York, NY 10017, (800) 253-9646, Fax: (212) 963-4116, http://unstats.un.org; *Statistical Yearbook.*

GEORGIA (REPUBLIC) - DIVORCE

United Nations Statistics Division, New York, NY 10017, (800) 253-9646, Fax: (212) 963-4116, http://unstats.un.org; *Demographic Yearbook; Statistical Yearbook;* and *Trends in Europe and North America: The Statistical Yearbook of the ECE 2005.*

GEORGIA (REPUBLIC) - ECONOMIC CONDITIONS

Academic International Press, PO Box 1111, Gulf Breeze, FL 32562-1111, Fax: (850) 934-0953, www.ai-press.com; *Russia and Eurasia Facts and Figures Annual.*

Central Intelligence Agency, Office of Public Affairs, Washington, DC 20505, (703) 482-0623, Fax: (703) 482-1739, www.cia.gov; *The World Factbook.*

Economist Intelligence Unit, 111 West 57th Street, New York, NY 10019, (212) 554-0600, Fax: (212) 586-1181, www.eiu.com; *Georgia Country Report.*

Euromonitor International, Inc., 224 S. Michigan Avenue, Suite 1500, Chicago, IL 60604, (312) 922-1115, Fax: (312) 922-1157, www.euromonitor.com; *The World Economic Factbook 2008* and *World Marketing Data and Statistics.*

Taylor and Francis Group, An Informa Business, 2 Park Square, Milton Park, Abingdon, Oxford OX14 4RN, United Kingdom, (Dial from U.S. (212) 216-7800), (Fax from U.S. (212) 564-7854), www.tandf.co.uk; *The Europa World Year Book.*

United Nations Statistics Division, New York, NY 10017, (800) 253-9646, Fax: (212) 963-4116, http://unstats.un.org; *World Statistics Pocketbook.*

The World Bank, 1818 H Street, NW, Washington, DC 20433, (202) 473-1000, Fax: (202) 477-6391, www.worldbank.org; *Georgia; The World Bank Atlas 2003-2004;* and *World Development Report 2008.*

GEORGIA (REPUBLIC) - EDUCATION

Academic International Press, PO Box 1111, Gulf Breeze, FL 32562-1111, Fax: (850) 934-0953, www.ai-press.com; *Russia and Eurasia Facts and Figures Annual.*

Euromonitor International, Inc., 224 S. Michigan Avenue, Suite 1500, Chicago, IL 60604, (312) 922-1115, Fax: (312) 922-1157, www.euromonitor.com; *World Marketing Data and Statistics.*

Palgrave Macmillan Ltd., Houndmills, Basingstoke, Hampshire, RG21 6XS, England, (Telephone in U.S. (888) 330-8477), (Fax in U.S. (800) 672-2054), www.palgrave.com; *The Statesman's Yearbook 2008.*

Taylor and Francis Group, An Informa Business, 2 Park Square, Milton Park, Abingdon, Oxford OX14 4RN, United Kingdom, (Dial from U.S. (212) 216-7800), (Fax from U.S. (212) 564-7854), www.tandf.co.uk; *The Europa World Year Book.*

UNESCO Institute for Statistics, C.P. 6128 Succursale Centre-Ville, Montreal, Quebec, H3C 3J7 Canada, (Dial from U.S. (514) 343-6880), (Fax from U.S. (514) 343 6882), www.uis.unesco.org; *Statistical Tables.*

United Nations Statistics Division, New York, NY 10017, (800) 253-9646, Fax: (212) 963-4116, http://unstats.un.org; *Human Development Report 2006* and *Trends in Europe and North America: The Statistical Yearbook of the ECE 2005.*

The World Bank, 1818 H Street, NW, Washington, DC 20433, (202) 473-1000, Fax: (202) 477-6391, www.worldbank.org; *Georgia* and *World Development Report 2008.*

GEORGIA (REPUBLIC) - ELECTRICITY

Palgrave Macmillan Ltd., Houndmills, Basingstoke, Hampshire, RG21 6XS, England, (Telephone in U.S. (888) 330-8477), (Fax in U.S. (800) 672-2054), www.palgrave.com; *The Statesman's Yearbook 2008.*

Platts, 2 Penn Plaza, 25th Floor, New York, NY 10121-2298, (212) 904-3070, www.platts.com; *Energy Economist.*

U.S. Department of Energy (DOE), Energy Information Administration (EIA), 1000 Independence Avenue, SW, Washington, DC 20585, (202) 586-8800, www.eia.doe.gov; *International Energy Annual 2004* and *International Energy Outlook 2006.*

United Nations Statistics Division, New York, NY 10017, (800) 253-9646, Fax: (212) 963-4116, http://unstats.un.org; *Energy Statistics Yearbook 2003; Human Development Report 2006; Statistical Yearbook;* and *Trends in Europe and North America: The Statistical Yearbook of the ECE 2005.*

The World Bank, 1818 H Street, NW, Washington, DC 20433, (202) 473-1000, Fax: (202) 477-6391, www.worldbank.org; *Statistical Handbook: States of the Former USSR.*

GEORGIA (REPUBLIC) - EMPLOYMENT

International Labour Office, I.L.O. Publications, 4 route des Morillons, CH-1211 Geneva 22, Switzerland, (Telephone in U.S. (202) 653-7652), (Fax in U.S. (202) 653-7687), www.ilo.org; *Yearbook of Labour Statistics 2006.*

United Nations Statistics Division, New York, NY 10017, (800) 253-9646, Fax: (212) 963-4116, http://unstats.un.org; *Statistical Yearbook* and *Trends in Europe and North America: The Statistical Yearbook of the ECE 2005.*

The World Bank, 1818 H Street, NW, Washington, DC 20433, (202) 473-1000, Fax: (202) 477-6391, www.worldbank.org; *Georgia* and *Statistical Handbook: States of the Former USSR.*

GEORGIA (REPUBLIC) - ENVIRONMENTAL CONDITIONS

DSI Data Service Information, Xantener Strasse 51a, D-47495 Rheinberg, Germany, www.dsidata.com; *Campus Solution.*

Economist Intelligence Unit, 111 West 57th Street, New York, NY 10019, (212) 554-0600, Fax: (212) 586-1181, www.eiu.com; *Georgia Country Report.*

United Nations Environment Programme (UNEP), PO Box 30552, Nairobi, Kenya, www.unep.org; *Tiblisi Environmental Atlas.*

United Nations Statistics Division, New York, NY 10017, (800) 253-9646, Fax: (212) 963-4116, http://unstats.un.org; *Statistical Yearbook; Trends in Europe and North America: The Statistical Yearbook of the ECE 2005;* and *World Statistics Pocketbook.*

GEORGIA (REPUBLIC) - EXPORTS

Academic International Press, PO Box 1111, Gulf Breeze, FL 32562-1111, Fax: (850) 934-0953, www.ai-press.com; *Russia and Eurasia Facts and Figures Annual.*

Central Intelligence Agency, Office of Public Affairs, Washington, DC 20505, (703) 482-0623, Fax: (703) 482-1739, www.cia.gov; *The World Factbook.*

Economist Intelligence Unit, 111 West 57th Street, New York, NY 10019, (212) 554-0600, Fax: (212) 586-1181, www.eiu.com; *Georgia Country Report.*

Euromonitor International, Inc., 224 S. Michigan Avenue, Suite 1500, Chicago, IL 60604, (312) 922-1115, Fax: (312) 922-1157, www.euromonitor.com; *The World Economic Factbook 2008.*

International Monetary Fund (IMF), 700 Nineteenth Street, NW, Washington, DC 20431, (202) 623-7000, Fax: (202) 623-4661, www.imf.org; *Direction of Trade Statistics Yearbook 2007.*

Taylor and Francis Group, An Informa Business, 2 Park Square, Milton Park, Abingdon, Oxford OX14 4RN, United Kingdom, (Dial from U.S. (212) 216-7800), (Fax from U.S. (212) 564-7854), www.tandf.co.uk; *The Europa World Year Book.*

UNICEF, 3 United Nations Plaza, New York, NY 10017, (800) 253-9646, Fax: (212) 887-7465, www.unicef.org; *The State of the World's Children 2008.*

United Nations Statistics Division, New York, NY 10017, (800) 253-9646, Fax: (212) 963-4116, http://unstats.un.org; *International Trade Statistics Yearbook* and *Trends in Europe and North America: The Statistical Yearbook of the ECE 2005.*

The World Bank, 1818 H Street, NW, Washington, DC 20433, (202) 473-1000, Fax: (202) 477-6391, www.worldbank.org; *Statistical Handbook: States of the Former USSR; World Development Indicators (WDI) 2008;* and *World Development Report 2008.*

GEORGIA (REPUBLIC) - FERTILITY, HUMAN

Central Intelligence Agency, Office of Public Affairs, Washington, DC 20505, (703) 482-0623, Fax: (703) 482-1739, www.cia.gov; *The World Factbook.*

United Nations Statistics Division, New York, NY 10017, (800) 253-9646, Fax: (212) 963-4116, http://unstats.un.org; *Human Development Report 2006* and *Trends in Europe and North America: The Statistical Yearbook of the ECE 2005.*

The World Bank, 1818 H Street, NW, Washington, DC 20433, (202) 473-1000, Fax: (202) 477-6391, www.worldbank.org; *Statistical Handbook: States of the Former USSR; The World Bank Atlas 2003-2004; World Development Indicators (WDI) 2008;* and *World Development Report 2008.*

World Health Organization (WHO), Avenue Appia 20, 1211 Geneve 27, Switzerland, (Telephone in U.S. (212) 331-9081), www.who.int; *World Health Report 2006.*

GEORGIA (REPUBLIC) - FERTILIZER INDUSTRY

United Nations Food and Agricultural Organization (FAO), Viale delle Terme di Caracalla, 00100 Rome, Italy, (Dial from U.S. (202) 653-2400), (Fax from U.S. (202) 653 5760), www.fao.org; *FAO Fertilizer Yearbook.*

United Nations Statistics Division, New York, NY 10017, (800) 253-9646, Fax: (212) 963-4116, http://unstats.un.org; *2004 Industrial Commodity Statistics Yearbook* and *Statistical Yearbook.*

GEORGIA (REPUBLIC) - FINANCE

Taylor and Francis Group, An Informa Business, 2 Park Square, Milton Park, Abingdon, Oxford OX14 4RN, United Kingdom, (Dial from U.S. (212) 216-7800), (Fax from U.S. (212) 564-7854), www.tandf.co.uk; *The Europa World Year Book.*

United Nations Statistics Division, New York, NY 10017, (800) 253-9646, Fax: (212) 963-4116, http://unstats.un.org; *National Accounts Statistics: Compendium of Income Distribution Statistics* and *Statistical Yearbook.*

The World Bank, 1818 H Street, NW, Washington, DC 20433, (202) 473-1000, Fax: (202) 477-6391, www.worldbank.org; *Georgia* and *Statistical Handbook: States of the Former USSR.*

GEORGIA (REPUBLIC) - FINANCE, PUBLIC

Economist Intelligence Unit, 111 West 57th Street, New York, NY 10019, (212) 554-0600, Fax: (212) 586-1181, www.eiu.com; *Georgia Country Report.*

Taylor and Francis Group, An Informa Business, 2 Park Square, Milton Park, Abingdon, Oxford OX14 4RN, United Kingdom, (Dial from U.S. (212) 216-7800), (Fax from U.S. (212) 564-7854), www.tandf.co.uk; *The Europa World Year Book.*

The World Bank, 1818 H Street, NW, Washington, DC 20433, (202) 473-1000, Fax: (202) 477-6391, www.worldbank.org; *Georgia* and *Statistical Handbook: States of the Former USSR.*

GEORGIA (REPUBLIC) - FISHERIES

Taylor and Francis Group, An Informa Business, 2 Park Square, Milton Park, Abingdon, Oxford OX14 4RN, United Kingdom, (Dial from U.S. (212) 216-7800), (Fax from U.S. (212) 564-7854), www.tandf.co.uk; *The Europa World Year Book.*

United Nations Environment Programme (UNEP), PO Box 30552, Nairobi, Kenya, www.unep.org; *Tiblisi Environmental Atlas.*

United Nations Food and Agricultural Organization (FAO), Viale delle Terme di Caracalla, 00100 Rome, Italy, (Dial from U.S. (202) 653-2400), (Fax from U.S. (202) 653 5760), www.fao.org; *FAO Yearbook of Fishery Statistics;* Fishery Databases; FISHSTAT Database. Subjects covered include: Aquaculture production, capture production, fishery commodities; and *The State of Food and Agriculture (SOFA) 2006.*

United Nations Statistics Division, New York, NY 10017, (800) 253-9646, Fax: (212) 963-4116, http://unstats.un.org; *2004 Industrial Commodity Statistics Yearbook* and *Statistical Yearbook.*

The World Bank, 1818 H Street, NW, Washington, DC 20433, (202) 473-1000, Fax: (202) 477-6391, www.worldbank.org; *Georgia.*

GEORGIA (REPUBLIC) - FOOD

United Nations Food and Agricultural Organization (FAO), Viale delle Terme di Caracalla, 00100 Rome, Italy, (Dial from U.S. (202) 653-2400), (Fax from U.S. (202) 653 5760), www.fao.org; *FAO Production Yearbook 2002* and *The State of Food and Agriculture (SOFA) 2006.*

United Nations Statistics Division, New York, NY 10017, (800) 253-9646, Fax: (212) 963-4116, http://unstats.un.org; *Human Development Report 2006* and *2004 Industrial Commodity Statistics Yearbook.*

GEORGIA (REPUBLIC) - FOREIGN EXCHANGE RATES

Central Intelligence Agency, Office of Public Affairs, Washington, DC 20505, (703) 482-0623, Fax: (703) 482-1739, www.cia.gov; *The World Factbook.*

Euromonitor International, Inc., 224 S. Michigan Avenue, Suite 1500, Chicago, IL 60604, (312) 922-1115, Fax: (312) 922-1157, www.euromonitor.com; *The World Economic Factbook 2008.*

Taylor and Francis Group, An Informa Business, 2 Park Square, Milton Park, Abingdon, Oxford OX14 4RN, United Kingdom, (Dial from U.S. (212) 216-7800), (Fax from U.S. (212) 564-7854), www.tandf.co.uk; *The Europa World Year Book.*

United Nations Statistics Division, New York, NY 10017, (800) 253-9646, Fax: (212) 963-4116, http://unstats.un.org; *Statistical Yearbook; Trends in Europe and North America: The Statistical Yearbook of the ECE 2005;* and *World Statistics Pocketbook.*

GEORGIA (REPUBLIC) - FORESTS AND FORESTRY

Academic International Press, PO Box 1111, Gulf Breeze, FL 32562-1111, Fax: (850) 934-0953, www.ai-press.com; *Russia and Eurasia Facts and Figures Annual.*

Palgrave Macmillan Ltd., Houndmills, Basingstoke, Hampshire, RG21 6XS, England, (Telephone in U.S. (888) 330-8477), (Fax in U.S. (800) 672-2054), www.palgrave.com; *The Statesman's Yearbook 2008.*

UNESCO Institute for Statistics, C.P. 6128 Succursale Centre-Ville, Montreal, Quebec, H3C 3J7 Canada, (Dial from U.S. (514) 343-6880), (Fax from U.S. (514) 343 6882), www.uis.unesco.org; *Statistical Tables.*

United Nations Environment Programme (UNEP), PO Box 30552, Nairobi, Kenya, www.unep.org; *Tiblisi Environmental Atlas.*

United Nations Food and Agricultural Organization (FAO), Viale delle Terme di Caracalla, 00100 Rome, Italy, (Dial from U.S. (202) 653-2400), (Fax from U.S. (202) 653 5760), www.fao.org; *FAO Yearbook of Forest Products* and *The State of Food and Agriculture (SOFA) 2006.*

United Nations Statistics Division, New York, NY 10017, (800) 253-9646, Fax: (212) 963-4116, http://unstats.un.org; *2004 Industrial Commodity Statistics Yearbook; Statistical Yearbook;* and *Trends in Europe and North America: The Statistical Yearbook of the ECE 2005.*

The World Bank, 1818 H Street, NW, Washington, DC 20433, (202) 473-1000, Fax: (202) 477-6391, www.worldbank.org; *Georgia* and *World Development Report 2008.*

GEORGIA (REPUBLIC) - GROSS DOMESTIC PRODUCT

Academic International Press, PO Box 1111, Gulf Breeze, FL 32562-1111, Fax: (850) 934-0953, www.ai-press.com; *Russia and Eurasia Facts and Figures Annual.*

Economist Intelligence Unit, 111 West 57th Street, New York, NY 10019, (212) 554-0600, Fax: (212) 586-1181, www.eiu.com; *Georgia Country Report.*

Euromonitor International, Inc., 224 S. Michigan Avenue, Suite 1500, Chicago, IL 60604, (312) 922-1115, Fax: (312) 922-1157, www.euromonitor.com; *The World Economic Factbook 2008.*

United Nations Statistics Division, New York, NY 10017, (800) 253-9646, Fax: (212) 963-4116, http://unstats.un.org; *Human Development Report 2006; National Accounts Statistics: Compendium of Income Distribution Statistics; Statistical Yearbook;* and *Trends in Europe and North America: The Statistical Yearbook of the ECE 2005.*

The World Bank, 1818 H Street, NW, Washington, DC 20433, (202) 473-1000, Fax: (202) 477-6391, www.worldbank.org; *Statistical Handbook: States of the Former USSR; World Development Indicators (WDI) 2008;* and *World Development Report 2008.*

GEORGIA (REPUBLIC) - GROSS NATIONAL PRODUCT

Palgrave Macmillan Ltd., Houndmills, Basingstoke, Hampshire, RG21 6XS, England, (Telephone in U.S. (888) 330-8477), (Fax in U.S. (800) 672-2054), www.palgrave.com; *The Statesman's Yearbook 2008.*

United Nations Statistics Division, New York, NY 10017, (800) 253-9646, Fax: (212) 963-4116, http://unstats.un.org; *Statistical Yearbook.*

The World Bank, 1818 H Street, NW, Washington, DC 20433, (202) 473-1000, Fax: (202) 477-6391, www.worldbank.org; *The World Bank Atlas 2003-2004; World Development Indicators (WDI) 2008;* and *World Development Report 2008.*

GEORGIA (REPUBLIC) - HOUSING

Euromonitor International, Inc., 224 S. Michigan Avenue, Suite 1500, Chicago, IL 60604, (312) 922-1115, Fax: (312) 922-1157, www.euromonitor.com; *World Marketing Data and Statistics.*

United Nations Statistics Division, New York, NY 10017, (800) 253-9646, Fax: (212) 963-4116, http://unstats.un.org; *Trends in Europe and North America: The Statistical Yearbook of the ECE 2005.*

GEORGIA (REPUBLIC) - ILLITERATE PERSONS

Euromonitor International, Inc., 224 S. Michigan Avenue, Suite 1500, Chicago, IL 60604, (312) 922-1115, Fax: (312) 922-1157, www.euromonitor.com; *The World Economic Factbook 2008.*

UNESCO Institute for Statistics, C.P. 6128 Succursale Centre-Ville, Montreal, Quebec, H3C 3J7 Canada, (Dial from U.S. (514) 343-6880), (Fax from U.S. (514) 343 6882), www.uis.unesco.org; *Statistical Tables.*

United Nations Statistics Division, New York, NY 10017, (800) 253-9646, Fax: (212) 963-4116, http://unstats.un.org; *Human Development Report 2006.*

GEORGIA (REPUBLIC) - IMPORTS

Academic International Press, PO Box 1111, Gulf Breeze, FL 32562-1111, Fax: (850) 934-0953, www.ai-press.com; *Russia and Eurasia Facts and Figures Annual.*

Central Intelligence Agency, Office of Public Affairs, Washington, DC 20505, (703) 482-0623, Fax: (703) 482-1739, www.cia.gov; *The World Factbook.*

Economist Intelligence Unit, 111 West 57th Street, New York, NY 10019, (212) 554-0600, Fax: (212) 586-1181, www.eiu.com; *Georgia Country Report.*

Euromonitor International, Inc., 224 S. Michigan Avenue, Suite 1500, Chicago, IL 60604, (312) 922-1115, Fax: (312) 922-1157, www.euromonitor.com; *The World Economic Factbook 2008.*

International Monetary Fund (IMF), 700 Nineteenth Street, NW, Washington, DC 20431, (202) 623-7000, Fax: (202) 623-4661, www.imf.org; *Direction of Trade Statistics Yearbook 2007.*

Taylor and Francis Group, An Informa Business, 2 Park Square, Milton Park, Abingdon, Oxford OX14 4RN, United Kingdom, (Dial from U.S. (212) 216-7800), (Fax from U.S. (212) 564-7854), www.tandf.co.uk; *The Europa World Year Book.*

United Nations Statistics Division, New York, NY 10017, (800) 253-9646, Fax: (212) 963-4116, http://unstats.un.org; *International Trade Statistics Yearbook* and *Trends in Europe and North America: The Statistical Yearbook of the ECE 2005.*

The World Bank, 1818 H Street, NW, Washington, DC 20433, (202) 473-1000, Fax: (202) 477-6391, www.worldbank.org; *Statistical Handbook: States of the Former USSR; World Development Indicators (WDI) 2008;* and *World Development Report 2008.*

GEORGIA (REPUBLIC) - INDUSTRIAL PRODUCTIVITY

The World Bank, 1818 H Street, NW, Washington, DC 20433, (202) 473-1000, Fax: (202) 477-6391, www.worldbank.org; *Statistical Handbook: States of the Former USSR.*

GEORGIA (REPUBLIC) - INDUSTRIAL PROPERTY

United Nations Statistics Division, New York, NY 10017, (800) 253-9646, Fax: (212) 963-4116, http://unstats.un.org; *Statistical Yearbook.*

GEORGIA (REPUBLIC) - INDUSTRIES

Academic International Press, PO Box 1111, Gulf Breeze, FL 32562-1111, Fax: (850) 934-0953, www.ai-press.com; *Russia and Eurasia Facts and Figures Annual.*

Central Intelligence Agency, Office of Public Affairs, Washington, DC 20505, (703) 482-0623, Fax: (703) 482-1739, www.cia.gov; *The World Factbook.*

Economist Intelligence Unit, 111 West 57th Street, New York, NY 10019, (212) 554-0600, Fax: (212) 586-1181, www.eiu.com; *Georgia Country Report.*

Euromonitor International, Inc., 224 S. Michigan Avenue, Suite 1500, Chicago, IL 60604, (312) 922-1115, Fax: (312) 922-1157, www.euromonitor.com; *The World Economic Factbook 2008* and *World Marketing Data and Statistics.*

International Labour Office, I.L.O. Publications, 4 route des Morillons, CH-1211 Geneva 22, Switzerland, (Telephone in U.S. (202) 653-7652), (Fax in U.S. (202) 653-7687), www.ilo.org; *Yearbook of Labour Statistics 2006.*

Palgrave Macmillan Ltd., Houndmills, Basingstoke, Hampshire, RG21 6XS, England, (Telephone in U.S. (888) 330-8477), (Fax in U.S. (800) 672-2054), www.palgrave.com; *The Statesman's Yearbook 2008.*

Taylor and Francis Group, An Informa Business, 2 Park Square, Milton Park, Abingdon, Oxford OX14 4RN, United Kingdom, (Dial from U.S. (212) 216-7800), (Fax from U.S. (212) 564-7854), www.tandf.co.uk; *The Europa World Year Book.*

United Nations Statistics Division, New York, NY 10017, (800) 253-9646, Fax: (212) 963-4116, http://unstats.un.org; *2004 Industrial Commodity Statistics Yearbook; Statistical Yearbook;* and *Trends in Europe and North America: The Statistical Yearbook of the ECE 2005.*

The World Bank, 1818 H Street, NW, Washington, DC 20433, (202) 473-1000, Fax: (202) 477-6391, www.worldbank.org; *Georgia; Statistical Handbook: States of the Former USSR;* and *World Development Indicators (WDI) 2008.*

GEORGIA (REPUBLIC) - INFANT AND MATERNAL MORTALITY

See GEORGIA (REPUBLIC) - MORTALITY

GEORGIA (REPUBLIC) - INTERNATIONAL TRADE

Academic International Press, PO Box 1111, Gulf Breeze, FL 32562-1111, Fax: (850) 934-0953, www.ai-press.com; *Russia and Eurasia Facts and Figures Annual.*

Economist Intelligence Unit, 111 West 57th Street, New York, NY 10019, (212) 554-0600, Fax: (212) 586-1181, www.eiu.com; *Georgia Country Report.*

Euromonitor International, Inc., 224 S. Michigan Avenue, Suite 1500, Chicago, IL 60604, (312) 922-1115, Fax: (312) 922-1157, www.euromonitor.com; *The World Economic Factbook 2008* and *World Marketing Data and Statistics.*

International Monetary Fund (IMF), 700 Nineteenth Street, NW, Washington, DC 20431, (202) 623-7000, Fax: (202) 623-4661, www.imf.org; *Direction of Trade Statistics Yearbook 2007.*

Taylor and Francis Group, An Informa Business, 2 Park Square, Milton Park, Abingdon, Oxford OX14 4RN, United Kingdom, (Dial from U.S. (212) 216-7800), (Fax from U.S. (212) 564-7854), www.tandf.co.uk; *The Europa World Year Book.*

United Nations Food and Agricultural Organization (FAO), Viale delle Terme di Caracalla, 00100 Rome, Italy, (Dial from U.S. (202) 653-2400), (Fax from U.S. (202) 653 5760), www.fao.org; *FAO Trade Yearbook.*

United Nations Statistics Division, New York, NY 10017, (800) 253-9646, Fax: (212) 963-4116, http://unstats.un.org; *International Trade Statistics Yearbook* and *Statistical Yearbook.*

The World Bank, 1818 H Street, NW, Washington, DC 20433, (202) 473-1000, Fax: (202) 477-6391, www.worldbank.org; *Georgia; Statistical Handbook: States of the Former USSR; World Development Indicators (WDI) 2008;* and *World Development Report 2008.*

World Trade Organization (WTO), Centre William Rappard, Rue de Lausanne 154, CH-1211 Geneva 21, Switzerland, www.wto.org; *International Trade Statistics 2006.*

GEORGIA (REPUBLIC) - LABOR

Academic International Press, PO Box 1111, Gulf Breeze, FL 32562-1111, Fax: (850) 934-0953, www.ai-press.com; *Russia and Eurasia Facts and Figures Annual.*

Central Intelligence Agency, Office of Public Affairs, Washington, DC 20505, (703) 482-0623, Fax: (703) 482-1739, www.cia.gov; *The World Factbook.*

Euromonitor International, Inc., 224 S. Michigan Avenue, Suite 1500, Chicago, IL 60604, (312) 922-1115, Fax: (312) 922-1157, www.euromonitor.com; *World Marketing Data and Statistics.*

International Labour Office, I.L.O. Publications, 4 route des Morillons, CH-1211 Geneva 22, Switzerland, (Telephone in U.S. (202) 653-7652), (Fax in U.S. (202) 653-7687), www.ilo.org; *Yearbook of Labour Statistics 2006.*

Palgrave Macmillan Ltd., Houndmills, Basingstoke, Hampshire, RG21 6XS, England, (Telephone in U.S. (888) 330-8477), (Fax in U.S. (800) 672-2054), www.palgrave.com; *The Statesman's Yearbook 2008.*

State Department for Statistics (SDS) of Georgia, 4 Beijing Str., Tbilisi 0115, Georgia, www.statistics.ge; *Labour Market in Georgia 2003-2005.*

United Nations Statistics Division, New York, NY 10017, (800) 253-9646, Fax: (212) 963-4116, http://unstats.un.org; *Human Development Report 2006* and *Statistical Yearbook.*

The World Bank, 1818 H Street, NW, Washington, DC 20433, (202) 473-1000, Fax: (202) 477-6391, www.worldbank.org; *The World Bank Atlas 2003-2004; World Development Indicators (WDI) 2008;* and *World Development Report 2008.*

GEORGIA (REPUBLIC) - LAND USE

Central Intelligence Agency, Office of Public Affairs, Washington, DC 20505, (703) 482-0623, Fax: (703) 482-1739, www.cia.gov; *The World Factbook.*

United Nations Environment Programme (UNEP), PO Box 30552, Nairobi, Kenya, www.unep.org; *Tiblisi Environmental Atlas.*

United Nations Food and Agricultural Organization (FAO), Viale delle Terme di Caracalla, 00100 Rome, Italy, (Dial from U.S. (202) 653-2400), (Fax from U.S. (202) 653 5760), www.fao.org; *FAO Production Yearbook 2002.*

The World Bank, 1818 H Street, NW, Washington, DC 20433, (202) 473-1000, Fax: (202) 477-6391, www.worldbank.org; *World Development Report 2008.*

GEORGIA (REPUBLIC) - LIBRARIES

UNESCO Institute for Statistics, C.P. 6128 Succursale Centre-Ville, Montreal, Quebec, H3C 3J7 Canada, (Dial from U.S. (514) 343-6880), (Fax from U.S. (514) 343 6882), www.uis.unesco.org; *Statistical Tables.*

United Nations Statistics Division, New York, NY 10017, (800) 253-9646, Fax: (212) 963-4116, http://unstats.un.org; *Trends in Europe and North America: The Statistical Yearbook of the ECE 2005.*

GEORGIA (REPUBLIC) - LIFE EXPECTANCY

Central Intelligence Agency, Office of Public Affairs, Washington, DC 20505, (703) 482-0623, Fax: (703) 482-1739, www.cia.gov; *The World Factbook.*

Euromonitor International, Inc., 224 S. Michigan Avenue, Suite 1500, Chicago, IL 60604, (312) 922-1115, Fax: (312) 922-1157, www.euromonitor.com; *The World Economic Factbook 2008.*

United Nations Statistics Division, New York, NY 10017, (800) 253-9646, Fax: (212) 963-4116, http://unstats.un.org; *Demographic Yearbook; Human Development Report 2006; Trends in Europe and North America: The Statistical Yearbook of the ECE 2005;* and *World Statistics Pocketbook.*

The World Bank, 1818 H Street, NW, Washington, DC 20433, (202) 473-1000, Fax: (202) 477-6391, www.worldbank.org; *The World Bank Atlas 2003-2004; World Development Indicators (WDI) 2008;* and *World Development Report 2008.*

World Health Organization (WHO), Avenue Appia 20, 1211 Geneve 27, Switzerland, (Telephone in U.S. (212) 331-9081), www.who.int; *World Health Report 2006.*

GEORGIA (REPUBLIC) - LITERACY

Euromonitor International, Inc., 224 S. Michigan Avenue, Suite 1500, Chicago, IL 60604, (312) 922-1115, Fax: (312) 922-1157, www.euromonitor.com; *World Marketing Data and Statistics.*

GEORGIA (REPUBLIC) - LIVESTOCK

Academic International Press, PO Box 1111, Gulf Breeze, FL 32562-1111, Fax: (850) 934-0953, www.ai-press.com; *Russia and Eurasia Facts and Figures Annual.*

Palgrave Macmillan Ltd., Houndmills, Basingstoke, Hampshire, RG21 6XS, England, (Telephone in U.S. (888) 330-8477), (Fax in U.S. (800) 672-2054), www.palgrave.com; *The Statesman's Yearbook 2008.*

Taylor and Francis Group, An Informa Business, 2 Park Square, Milton Park, Abingdon, Oxford OX14 4RN, United Kingdom, (Dial from U.S. (212) 216-7800), (Fax from U.S. (212) 564-7854), www.tandf.co.uk; *The Europa World Year Book.*

United Nations Food and Agricultural Organization (FAO), Viale delle Terme di Caracalla, 00100 Rome, Italy, (Dial from U.S. (202) 653-2400), (Fax from U.S. (202) 653 5760), www.fao.org; *FAO Production Yearbook 2002* and *The State of Food and Agriculture (SOFA) 2006.*

United Nations Statistics Division, New York, NY 10017, (800) 253-9646, Fax: (212) 963-4116, http://unstats.un.org; *2004 Industrial Commodity Statistics Yearbook* and *Statistical Yearbook.*

GEORGIA (REPUBLIC) - MACHINERY

United Nations Statistics Division, New York, NY 10017, (800) 253-9646, Fax: (212) 963-4116, http://unstats.un.org; *2004 Industrial Commodity Statistics Yearbook.*

GEORGIA (REPUBLIC) - MANUFACTURES

United Nations Statistics Division, New York, NY 10017, (800) 253-9646, Fax: (212) 963-4116, http://unstats.un.org; *2004 Industrial Commodity Statistics Yearbook* and *Statistical Yearbook.*

The World Bank, 1818 H Street, NW, Washington, DC 20433, (202) 473-1000, Fax: (202) 477-6391, www.worldbank.org; *World Development Indicators (WDI) 2008.*

GEORGIA (REPUBLIC) - MARRIAGE

Academic International Press, PO Box 1111, Gulf Breeze, FL 32562-1111, Fax: (850) 934-0953, www.ai-press.com; *Russia and Eurasia Facts and Figures Annual.*

Taylor and Francis Group, An Informa Business, 2 Park Square, Milton Park, Abingdon, Oxford OX14 4RN, United Kingdom, (Dial from U.S. (212) 216-7800), (Fax from U.S. (212) 564-7854), www.tandf.co.uk; *The Europa World Year Book.*

United Nations Statistics Division, New York, NY 10017, (800) 253-9646, Fax: (212) 963-4116, http://unstats.un.org; *Demographic Yearbook; Statistical Yearbook;* and *Trends in Europe and North America: The Statistical Yearbook of the ECE 2005.*

GEORGIA (REPUBLIC) - MINERAL INDUSTRIES

Academic International Press, PO Box 1111, Gulf Breeze, FL 32562-1111, Fax: (850) 934-0953, www.ai-press.com; *Russia and Eurasia Facts and Figures Annual.*

Palgrave Macmillan Ltd., Houndmills, Basingstoke, Hampshire, RG21 6XS, England, (Telephone in U.S. (888) 330-8477), (Fax in U.S. (800) 672-2054), www.palgrave.com; *The Statesman's Yearbook 2008.*

Platts, 2 Penn Plaza, 25th Floor, New York, NY 10121-2298, (212) 904-3070, www.platts.com; *Energy Economist.*

Taylor and Francis Group, An Informa Business, 2 Park Square, Milton Park, Abingdon, Oxford OX14 4RN, United Kingdom, (Dial from U.S. (212) 216-7800), (Fax from U.S. (212) 564-7854), www.tandf.co.uk; *The Europa World Year Book.*

United Nations Environment Programme (UNEP), PO Box 30552, Nairobi, Kenya, www.unep.org; *Tiblisi Environmental Atlas.*

United Nations Statistics Division, New York, NY 10017, (800) 253-9646, Fax: (212) 963-4116, http://unstats.un.org; *Energy Statistics Yearbook 2003; 2004 Industrial Commodity Statistics Yearbook;* and *Statistical Yearbook.*

The World Bank, 1818 H Street, NW, Washington, DC 20433, (202) 473-1000, Fax: (202) 477-6391, www.worldbank.org; *Georgia.*

GEORGIA (REPUBLIC) - MONEY SUPPLY

Economist Intelligence Unit, 111 West 57th Street, New York, NY 10019, (212) 554-0600, Fax: (212) 586-1181, www.eiu.com; *Georgia Country Report.*

Taylor and Francis Group, An Informa Business, 2 Park Square, Milton Park, Abingdon, Oxford OX14 4RN, United Kingdom, (Dial from U.S. (212) 216-7800), (Fax from U.S. (212) 564-7854), www.tandf.co.uk; *The Europa World Year Book.*

The World Bank, 1818 H Street, NW, Washington, DC 20433, (202) 473-1000, Fax: (202) 477-6391, www.worldbank.org; *Georgia.*

GEORGIA (REPUBLIC) - MONUMENTS AND HISTORIC SITES

UNESCO Institute for Statistics, C.P. 6128 Succursale Centre-Ville, Montreal, Quebec, H3C 3J7 Canada, (Dial from U.S. (514) 343-6880), (Fax from U.S. (514) 343 6882), www.uis.unesco.org; *Statistical Tables.*

GEORGIA (REPUBLIC) - MORTALITY

Central Intelligence Agency, Office of Public Affairs, Washington, DC 20505, (703) 482-0623, Fax: (703) 482-1739, www.cia.gov; *The World Factbook.*

Euromonitor International, Inc., 224 S. Michigan Avenue, Suite 1500, Chicago, IL 60604, (312) 922-1115, Fax: (312) 922-1157, www.euromonitor.com; *The World Economic Factbook 2008.*

Taylor and Francis Group, An Informa Business, 2 Park Square, Milton Park, Abingdon, Oxford OX14 4RN, United Kingdom, (Dial from U.S. (212) 216-7800), (Fax from U.S. (212) 564-7854), www.tandf.co.uk; *The Europa World Year Book.*

UNICEF, 3 United Nations Plaza, New York, NY 10017, (800) 253-9646, Fax: (212) 887-7465, www.unicef.org; *The State of the World's Children 2008.*

United Nations Statistics Division, New York, NY 10017, (800) 253-9646, Fax: (212) 963-4116, http://unstats.un.org; *Demographic Yearbook; Human Development Report 2006; Statistical Yearbook; Trends in Europe and North America: The Statistical Yearbook of the ECE 2005;* and *World Statistics Pocketbook.*

The World Bank, 1818 H Street, NW, Washington, DC 20433, (202) 473-1000, Fax: (202) 477-6391, www.worldbank.org; *The World Bank Atlas 2003-2004; World Development Indicators (WDI) 2008;* and *World Development Report 2008.*

World Health Organization (WHO), Avenue Appia 20, 1211 Geneve 27, Switzerland, (Telephone in U.S. (212) 331-9081), www.who.int; *World Health Report 2006.*

GEORGIA (REPUBLIC) - MOTION PICTURES

UNESCO Institute for Statistics, C.P. 6128 Succursale Centre-Ville, Montreal, Quebec, H3C 3J7

Canada, (Dial from U.S. (514) 343-6880), (Fax from U.S. (514) 343 6882), www.uis.unesco.org; *Statistical Tables.*

United Nations Statistics Division, New York, NY 10017, (800) 253-9646, Fax: (212) 963-4116, http://unstats.un.org; *Statistical Yearbook.*

GEORGIA (REPUBLIC) - MOTOR VEHICLES

United Nations Statistics Division, New York, NY 10017, (800) 253-9646, Fax: (212) 963-4116, http://unstats.un.org; *Statistical Yearbook.*

GEORGIA (REPUBLIC) - MUSEUMS

UNESCO Institute for Statistics, C.P. 6128 Succursale Centre-Ville, Montreal, Quebec, H3C 3J7 Canada, (Dial from U.S. (514) 343-6880), (Fax from U.S. (514) 343 6882), www.uis.unesco.org; *Statistical Tables.*

GEORGIA (REPUBLIC) - PERIODICALS

UNESCO Institute for Statistics, C.P. 6128 Succursale Centre-Ville, Montreal, Quebec, H3C 3J7 Canada, (Dial from U.S. (514) 343-6880), (Fax from U.S. (514) 343 6882), www.uis.unesco.org; *Statistical Tables.*

GEORGIA (REPUBLIC) - PETROLEUM INDUSTRY AND TRADE

Palgrave Macmillan Ltd., Houndmills, Basingstoke, Hampshire, RG21 6XS, England, (Telephone in U.S. (888) 330-8477), (Fax in U.S. (800) 672-2054), www.palgrave.com; *The Statesman's Yearbook 2008.*

PennWell Corporation, 1421 South Sheridan Road, Tulsa, OK 74112, (918) 835-3161, www.pennwell.com; *International Petroleum Encyclopedia 2007.*

Platts, 2 Penn Plaza, 25th Floor, New York, NY 10121-2298, (212) 904-3070, www.platts.com; *Energy Economist.*

U.S. Department of Energy (DOE), Energy Information Administration (EIA), 1000 Independence Avenue, SW, Washington, DC 20585, (202) 586-8800, www.eia.doe.gov; *International Energy Annual 2004* and *International Energy Outlook 2006.*

United Nations Food and Agricultural Organization (FAO), Viale delle Terme di Caracalla, 00100 Rome, Italy, (Dial from U.S. (202) 653-2400), (Fax from U.S. (202) 653 5760), www.fao.org; *The State of Food and Agriculture (SOFA) 2006.*

United Nations Statistics Division, New York, NY 10017, (800) 253-9646, Fax: (212) 963-4116, http://unstats.un.org; *Energy Statistics Yearbook 2003; 2004 Industrial Commodity Statistics Yearbook; Statistical Yearbook;* and *Trends in Europe and North America: The Statistical Yearbook of the ECE 2005.*

GEORGIA (REPUBLIC) - POLITICAL SCIENCE

Academic International Press, PO Box 1111, Gulf Breeze, FL 32562-1111, Fax: (850) 934-0953, www.ai-press.com; *Russia and Eurasia Facts and Figures Annual.*

Central Intelligence Agency, Office of Public Affairs, Washington, DC 20505, (703) 482-0623, Fax: (703) 482-1739, www.cia.gov; *The World Factbook.*

Palgrave Macmillan Ltd., Houndmills, Basingstoke, Hampshire, RG21 6XS, England, (Telephone in U.S. (888) 330-8477), (Fax in U.S. (800) 672-2054), www.palgrave.com; *The Statesman's Yearbook 2008.*

Taylor and Francis Group, An Informa Business, 2 Park Square, Milton Park, Abingdon, Oxford OX14 4RN, United Kingdom, (Dial from U.S. (212) 216-7800), (Fax from U.S. (212) 564-7854), www.tandf.co.uk; *The Europa World Year Book.*

United Nations Statistics Division, New York, NY 10017, (800) 253-9646, Fax: (212) 963-4116, http://unstats.un.org; *Statistical Yearbook.*

The World Bank, 1818 H Street, NW, Washington, DC 20433, (202) 473-1000, Fax: (202) 477-6391, www.worldbank.org; *Statistical Handbook: States of the Former USSR* and *World Development Report 2008.*

GEORGIA (REPUBLIC) - POPULATION

Academic International Press, PO Box 1111, Gulf Breeze, FL 32562-1111, Fax: (850) 934-0953, www.ai-press.com; *Russia and Eurasia Facts and Figures Annual.*

Central Intelligence Agency, Office of Public Affairs, Washington, DC 20505, (703) 482-0623, Fax: (703) 482-1739, www.cia.gov; *The World Factbook.*

Economist Intelligence Unit, 111 West 57th Street, New York, NY 10019, (212) 554-0600, Fax: (212) 586-1181, www.eiu.com; *Georgia Country Report.*

Euromonitor International, Inc., 224 S. Michigan Avenue, Suite 1500, Chicago, IL 60604, (312) 922-1115, Fax: (312) 922-1157, www.euromonitor.com; *The World Economic Factbook 2008.*

International Labour Office, I.L.O. Publications, 4 route des Morillons, CH-1211 Geneva 22, Switzerland, (Telephone in U.S. (202) 653-7652), (Fax in U.S. (202) 653-7687), www.ilo.org; *Yearbook of Labour Statistics 2006.*

Palgrave Macmillan Ltd., Houndmills, Basingstoke, Hampshire, RG21 6XS, England, (Telephone in U.S. (888) 330-8477), (Fax in U.S. (800) 672-2054), www.palgrave.com; *The Statesman's Yearbook 2008.*

Taylor and Francis Group, An Informa Business, 2 Park Square, Milton Park, Abingdon, Oxford OX14 4RN, United Kingdom, (Dial from U.S. (212) 216-7800), (Fax from U.S. (212) 564-7854), www.tandf.co.uk; *The Europa World Year Book.*

UNESCO Institute for Statistics, C.P. 6128 Succursale Centre-Ville, Montreal, Quebec, H3C 3J7 Canada, (Dial from U.S. (514) 343-6880), (Fax from U.S. (514) 343 6882), www.uis.unesco.org; *Statistical Tables.*

United Nations Food and Agricultural Organization (FAO), Viale delle Terme di Caracalla, 00100 Rome, Italy, (Dial from U.S. (202) 653-2400), (Fax from U.S. (202) 653 5760), www.fao.org; *FAO Production Yearbook 2002.*

United Nations Statistics Division, New York, NY 10017, (800) 253-9646, Fax: (212) 963-4116, http://unstats.un.org; *Demographic Yearbook; Human Development Report 2006; Statistical Yearbook; Trends in Europe and North America: The Statistical Yearbook of the ECE 2005;* and *World Statistics Pocketbook.*

The World Bank, 1818 H Street, NW, Washington, DC 20433, (202) 473-1000, Fax: (202) 477-6391, www.worldbank.org; *Georgia; Statistical Handbook: States of the Former USSR; The World Bank Atlas 2003-2004; World Development Indicators (WDI) 2008;* and *World Development Report 2008.*

World Health Organization (WHO), Avenue Appia 20, 1211 Geneve 27, Switzerland, (Telephone in U.S. (212) 331-9081), www.who.int; *World Health Report 2006.*

GEORGIA (REPUBLIC) - POPULATION DENSITY

Central Intelligence Agency, Office of Public Affairs, Washington, DC 20505, (703) 482-0623, Fax: (703) 482-1739, www.cia.gov; *The World Factbook.*

Euromonitor International, Inc., 224 S. Michigan Avenue, Suite 1500, Chicago, IL 60604, (312) 922-1115, Fax: (312) 922-1157, www.euromonitor.com; *The World Economic Factbook 2008.*

Palgrave Macmillan Ltd., Houndmills, Basingstoke, Hampshire, RG21 6XS, England, (Telephone in U.S. (888) 330-8477), (Fax in U.S. (800) 672-2054), www.palgrave.com; *The Statesman's Yearbook 2008.*

Taylor and Francis Group, An Informa Business, 2 Park Square, Milton Park, Abingdon, Oxford OX14 4RN, United Kingdom, (Dial from U.S. (212) 216-7800), (Fax from U.S. (212) 564-7854), www.tandf.co.uk; *The Europa World Year Book.*

UNESCO Institute for Statistics, C.P. 6128 Succursale Centre-Ville, Montreal, Quebec, H3C 3J7 Canada, (Dial from U.S. (514) 343-6880), (Fax from U.S. (514) 343 6882), www.uis.unesco.org; *Statistical Tables.*

United Nations Statistics Division, New York, NY 10017, (800) 253-9646, Fax: (212) 963-4116, http://unstats.un.org; *Statistical Yearbook* and *Trends in Europe and North America: The Statistical Yearbook of the ECE 2005.*

The World Bank, 1818 H Street, NW, Washington, DC 20433, (202) 473-1000, Fax: (202) 477-6391, www.worldbank.org; *Georgia* and *World Development Report 2008.*

GEORGIA (REPUBLIC) - POSTAL SERVICE

United Nations Statistics Division, New York, NY 10017, (800) 253-9646, Fax: (212) 963-4116, http://unstats.un.org; *Statistical Yearbook* and *Trends in Europe and North America: The Statistical Yearbook of the ECE 2005.*

GEORGIA (REPUBLIC) - POULTRY

See GEORGIA (REPUBLIC) - LIVESTOCK

GEORGIA (REPUBLIC) - POWER RESOURCES

Academic International Press, PO Box 1111, Gulf Breeze, FL 32562-1111, Fax: (850) 934-0953, www.ai-press.com; *Russia and Eurasia Facts and Figures Annual.*

Euromonitor International, Inc., 224 S. Michigan Avenue, Suite 1500, Chicago, IL 60604, (312) 922-1115, Fax: (312) 922-1157, www.euromonitor.com; *The World Economic Factbook 2008* and *World Marketing Data and Statistics.*

Palgrave Macmillan Ltd., Houndmills, Basingstoke, Hampshire, RG21 6XS, England, (Telephone in U.S. (888) 330-8477), (Fax in U.S. (800) 672-2054), www.palgrave.com; *The Statesman's Yearbook 2008.*

Platts, 2 Penn Plaza, 25th Floor, New York, NY 10121-2298, (212) 904-3070, www.platts.com; *Energy Economist.*

U.S. Department of Energy (DOE), Energy Information Administration (EIA), 1000 Independence Avenue, SW, Washington, DC 20585, (202) 586-8800, www.eia.doe.gov; *International Energy Annual 2004* and *International Energy Outlook 2006.*

United Nations Statistics Division, New York, NY 10017, (800) 253-9646, Fax: (212) 963-4116, http://unstats.un.org; *Energy Statistics Yearbook 2003; Human Development Report 2006; Statistical Yearbook; Trends in Europe and North America: The Statistical Yearbook of the ECE 2005;* and *World Statistics Pocketbook.*

The World Bank, 1818 H Street, NW, Washington, DC 20433, (202) 473-1000, Fax: (202) 477-6391, www.worldbank.org; *Statistical Handbook: States of the Former USSR; The World Bank Atlas 2003-2004;* and *World Development Report 2008.*

GEORGIA (REPUBLIC) - PRICES

Euromonitor International, Inc., 224 S. Michigan Avenue, Suite 1500, Chicago, IL 60604, (312) 922-1115, Fax: (312) 922-1157, www.euromonitor.com; *World Marketing Data and Statistics.*

International Labour Office, I.L.O. Publications, 4 route des Morillons, CH-1211 Geneva 22, Switzerland, (Telephone in U.S. (202) 653-7652), (Fax in U.S. (202) 653-7687), www.ilo.org; *Yearbook of Labour Statistics 2006.*

United Nations Food and Agricultural Organization (FAO), Viale delle Terme di Caracalla, 00100 Rome, Italy, (Dial from U.S. (202) 653-2400), (Fax from U.S. (202) 653 5760), www.fao.org; *FAO Production Yearbook 2002.*

The World Bank, 1818 H Street, NW, Washington, DC 20433, (202) 473-1000, Fax: (202) 477-6391, www.worldbank.org; *Georgia* and *Statistical Handbook: States of the Former USSR.*

GEORGIA (REPUBLIC) - PROFESSIONS

United Nations Statistics Division, New York, NY 10017, (800) 253-9646, Fax: (212) 963-4116, http://unstats.un.org; *Statistical Yearbook.*

GEORGIA (REPUBLIC) - PUBLIC HEALTH

Academic International Press, PO Box 1111, Gulf Breeze, FL 32562-1111, Fax: (850) 934-0953, www.ai-press.com; *Russia and Eurasia Facts and Figures Annual.*

Euromonitor International, Inc., 224 S. Michigan Avenue, Suite 1500, Chicago, IL 60604, (312) 922-1115, Fax: (312) 922-1157, www.euromonitor.com; *World Marketing Data and Statistics.*

Palgrave Macmillan Ltd., Houndmills, Basingstoke, Hampshire, RG21 6XS, England, (Telephone in U.S. (888) 330-8477), (Fax in U.S. (800) 672-2054), www.palgrave.com; *The Statesman's Yearbook 2008.*

UNICEF, 3 United Nations Plaza, New York, NY 10017, (800) 253-9646, Fax: (212) 887-7465, www.unicef.org; *The State of the World's Children 2008.*

United Nations Statistics Division, New York, NY 10017, (800) 253-9646, Fax: (212) 963-4116, http://unstats.un.org; *Human Development Report 2006; Statistical Yearbook;* and *Trends in Europe and North America: The Statistical Yearbook of the ECE 2005.*

The World Bank, 1818 H Street, NW, Washington, DC 20433, (202) 473-1000, Fax: (202) 477-6391, www.worldbank.org; *Georgia* and *World Development Report 2008.*

World Health Organization (WHO), Avenue Appia 20, 1211 Geneve 27, Switzerland, (Telephone in U.S. (212) 331-9081), www.who.int; *World Health Report 2006.*

GEORGIA (REPUBLIC) - PUBLISHERS AND PUBLISHING

UNESCO Institute for Statistics, C.P. 6128 Succursale Centre-Ville, Montreal, Quebec, H3C 3J7 Canada, (Dial from U.S. (514) 343-6880), (Fax from U.S. (514) 343 6882), www.uis.unesco.org; *Statistical Tables.*

United Nations Statistics Division, New York, NY 10017, (800) 253-9646, Fax: (212) 963-4116, http://unstats.un.org; *Trends in Europe and North America: The Statistical Yearbook of the ECE 2005.*

GEORGIA (REPUBLIC) - RADIO BROADCASTING

Palgrave Macmillan Ltd., Houndmills, Basingstoke, Hampshire, RG21 6XS, England, (Telephone in U.S. (888) 330-8477), (Fax in U.S. (800) 672-2054), www.palgrave.com; *The Statesman's Yearbook 2008.*

United Nations Statistics Division, New York, NY 10017, (800) 253-9646, Fax: (212) 963-4116, http://unstats.un.org; *Statistical Yearbook.*

GEORGIA (REPUBLIC) - RAILROADS

Palgrave Macmillan Ltd., Houndmills, Basingstoke, Hampshire, RG21 6XS, England, (Telephone in U.S. (888) 330-8477), (Fax in U.S. (800) 672-2054), www.palgrave.com; *The Statesman's Yearbook 2008.*

United Nations Statistics Division, New York, NY 10017, (800) 253-9646, Fax: (212) 963-4116, http://unstats.un.org; *Statistical Yearbook* and *Trends in Europe and North America: The Statistical Yearbook of the ECE 2005.*

GEORGIA (REPUBLIC) - RELIGION

Academic International Press, PO Box 1111, Gulf Breeze, FL 32562-1111, Fax: (850) 934-0953, www.ai-press.com; *Russia and Eurasia Facts and Figures Annual.*

Central Intelligence Agency, Office of Public Affairs, Washington, DC 20505, (703) 482-0623, Fax: (703) 482-1739, www.cia.gov; *The World Factbook.*

Palgrave Macmillan Ltd., Houndmills, Basingstoke, Hampshire, RG21 6XS, England, (Telephone in U.S. (888) 330-8477), (Fax in U.S. (800) 672-2054), www.palgrave.com; *The Statesman's Yearbook 2008.*

GEORGIA (REPUBLIC) - RENT CHARGES

International Labour Office, I.L.O. Publications, 4 route des Morillons, CH-1211 Geneva 22, Switzerland, (Telephone in U.S. (202) 653-7652), (Fax in U.S. (202) 653-7687), www.ilo.org; *Yearbook of Labour Statistics 2006.*

GEORGIA (REPUBLIC) - RETAIL TRADE

Euromonitor International, Inc., 224 S. Michigan Avenue, Suite 1500, Chicago, IL 60604, (312) 922-1115, Fax: (312) 922-1157, www.euromonitor.com; *World Marketing Data and Statistics.*

United Nations Statistics Division, New York, NY 10017, (800) 253-9646, Fax: (212) 963-4116, http://unstats.un.org; *Statistical Yearbook.*

GEORGIA (REPUBLIC) - ROADS

Central Intelligence Agency, Office of Public Affairs, Washington, DC 20505, (703) 482-0623, Fax: (703) 482-1739, www.cia.gov; *The World Factbook.*

Palgrave Macmillan Ltd., Houndmills, Basingstoke, Hampshire, RG21 6XS, England, (Telephone in U.S. (888) 330-8477), (Fax in U.S. (800) 672-2054), www.palgrave.com; *The Statesman's Yearbook 2008.*

United Nations Statistics Division, New York, NY 10017, (800) 253-9646, Fax: (212) 963-4116, http://unstats.un.org; *Trends in Europe and North America: The Statistical Yearbook of the ECE 2005.*

GEORGIA (REPUBLIC) - RUBBER INDUSTRY AND TRADE

International Rubber Study Group (IRSG), 1st Floor, Heron House, 109/115 Wembley Hill Road, Wembley, Middlesex HA9 8DA, United Kingdom, www.rubberstudy.com; *Rubber Statistical Bulletin; Summary of World Rubber Statistics 2005; World Rubber Statistics Handbook (Volume 6, 1975-2001);* and *World Rubber Statistics Historic Handbook.*

United Nations Statistics Division, New York, NY 10017, (800) 253-9646, Fax: (212) 963-4116, http://unstats.un.org; *Statistical Yearbook.*

GEORGIA (REPUBLIC) - SHEEP

See GEORGIA (REPUBLIC) - LIVESTOCK

GEORGIA (REPUBLIC) - SHIPPING

United Nations Statistics Division, New York, NY 10017, (800) 253-9646, Fax: (212) 963-4116, http://unstats.un.org; *Statistical Yearbook.*

GEORGIA (REPUBLIC) - SOCIAL ECOLOGY

United Nations Statistics Division, New York, NY 10017, (800) 253-9646, Fax: (212) 963-4116, http://unstats.un.org; *World Statistics Pocketbook.*

GEORGIA (REPUBLIC) - STEEL PRODUCTION

See GEORGIA (REPUBLIC) - MINERAL INDUSTRIES

GEORGIA (REPUBLIC) - TAXATION

Taylor and Francis Group, An Informa Business, 2 Park Square, Milton Park, Abingdon, Oxford OX14 4RN, United Kingdom, (Dial from U.S. (212) 216-7800), (Fax from U.S. (212) 564-7854), www.tandf.co.uk; *The Europa World Year Book.*

GEORGIA (REPUBLIC) - TELEPHONE

Central Intelligence Agency, Office of Public Affairs, Washington, DC 20505, (703) 482-0623, Fax: (703) 482-1739, www.cia.gov; *The World Factbook.*

United Nations Statistics Division, New York, NY 10017, (800) 253-9646, Fax: (212) 963-4116, http://unstats.un.org; *Statistical Yearbook; Trends in Europe and North America: The Statistical Yearbook of the ECE 2005;* and *World Statistics Pocketbook.*

GEORGIA (REPUBLIC) - TEXTILE INDUSTRY

Palgrave Macmillan Ltd., Houndmills, Basingstoke, Hampshire, RG21 6XS, England, (Telephone in U.S. (888) 330-8477), (Fax in U.S. (800) 672-2054), www.palgrave.com; *The Statesman's Yearbook 2008.*

United Nations Statistics Division, New York, NY 10017, (800) 253-9646, Fax: (212) 963-4116, http://unstats.un.org; *2004 Industrial Commodity Statistics Yearbook* and *Statistical Yearbook.*

GEORGIA (REPUBLIC) - THEATER

UNESCO Institute for Statistics, C.P. 6128 Succursale Centre-Ville, Montreal, Quebec, H3C 3J7 Canada, (Dial from U.S. (514) 343-6880), (Fax from U.S. (514) 343 6882), www.uis.unesco.org; *Statistical Tables.*

GEORGIA (REPUBLIC) - TIRE INDUSTRY

United Nations Statistics Division, New York, NY 10017, (800) 253-9646, Fax: (212) 963-4116, http://unstats.un.org; *Statistical Yearbook.*

GEORGIA (REPUBLIC) - TOBACCO INDUSTRY

Foreign Agricultural Service (FAS), U.S. Department of Agriculture (USDA), 1400 Independence Avenue, SW, Washington, DC 20250, (202) 720-3935, www.fas.usda.gov; *Tobacco: World Markets and Trade.*

United Nations Statistics Division, New York, NY 10017, (800) 253-9646, Fax: (212) 963-4116, http://unstats.un.org; *Statistical Yearbook.*

GEORGIA (REPUBLIC) - TOURISM

Euromonitor International, Inc., 224 S. Michigan Avenue, Suite 1500, Chicago, IL 60604, (312) 922-1115, Fax: (312) 922-1157, www.euromonitor.com; *The World Economic Factbook 2008* and *World Marketing Data and Statistics.*

United Nations Statistics Division, New York, NY 10017, (800) 253-9646, Fax: (212) 963-4116, http://unstats.un.org; *Statistical Yearbook* and *Trends in Europe and North America: The Statistical Yearbook of the ECE 2005.*

The World Bank, 1818 H Street, NW, Washington, DC 20433, (202) 473-1000, Fax: (202) 477-6391, www.worldbank.org; *Georgia.*

GEORGIA (REPUBLIC) - TRANSPORTATION

Academic International Press, PO Box 1111, Gulf Breeze, FL 32562-1111, Fax: (850) 934-0953, www.ai-press.com; *Russia and Eurasia Facts and Figures Annual.*

Central Intelligence Agency, Office of Public Affairs, Washington, DC 20505, (703) 482-0623, Fax: (703) 482-1739, www.cia.gov; *The World Factbook.*

Euromonitor International, Inc., 224 S. Michigan Avenue, Suite 1500, Chicago, IL 60604, (312) 922-1115, Fax: (312) 922-1157, www.euromonitor.com; *World Marketing Data and Statistics.*

Palgrave Macmillan Ltd., Houndmills, Basingstoke, Hampshire, RG21 6XS, England, (Telephone in U.S. (888) 330-8477), (Fax in U.S. (800) 672-2054), www.palgrave.com; *The Statesman's Yearbook 2008.*

United Nations Statistics Division, New York, NY 10017, (800) 253-9646, Fax: (212) 963-4116, http://unstats.un.org; *Human Development Report 2006* and *Trends in Europe and North America: The Statistical Yearbook of the ECE 2005.*

The World Bank, 1818 H Street, NW, Washington, DC 20433, (202) 473-1000, Fax: (202) 477-6391, www.worldbank.org; *Georgia.*

GEORGIA (REPUBLIC) - UNEMPLOYMENT

Central Intelligence Agency, Office of Public Affairs, Washington, DC 20505, (703) 482-0623, Fax: (703) 482-1739, www.cia.gov; *The World Factbook.*

International Labour Office, I.L.O. Publications, 4 route des Morillons, CH-1211 Geneva 22, Switzerland, (Telephone in U.S. (202) 653-7652), (Fax in U.S. (202) 653-7687), www.ilo.org; *Yearbook of Labour Statistics 2006.*

United Nations Statistics Division, New York, NY 10017, (800) 253-9646, Fax: (212) 963-4116, http://

unstats.un.org; *Statistical Yearbook* and *Trends in Europe and North America: The Statistical Yearbook of the ECE 2005.*

The World Bank, 1818 H Street, NW, Washington, DC 20433, (202) 473-1000, Fax: (202) 477-6391, www.worldbank.org; *Georgia.*

GEORGIA (REPUBLIC) - VITAL STATISTICS

Palgrave Macmillan Ltd., Houndmills, Basingstoke, Hampshire, RG21 6XS, England, (Telephone in U.S. (888) 330-8477), (Fax in U.S. (800) 672-2054), www.palgrave.com; *The Statesman's Yearbook 2008.*

United Nations Environment Programme (UNEP), PO Box 30552, Nairobi, Kenya, www.unep.org; *Tiblisi Environmental Atlas.*

United Nations Statistics Division, New York, NY 10017, (800) 253-9646, Fax: (212) 963-4116, http://unstats.un.org; *Statistical Yearbook.*

World Health Organization (WHO), Avenue Appia 20, 1211 Geneve 27, Switzerland, (Telephone in U.S. (212) 331-9081), www.who.int; *World Health Report 2006.*

GEORGIA (REPUBLIC) - WAGES

International Labour Office, I.L.O. Publications, 4 route des Morillons, CH-1211 Geneva 22, Switzerland, (Telephone in U.S. (202) 653-7652), (Fax in U.S. (202) 653-7687), www.ilo.org; *Yearbook of Labour Statistics 2006.*

United Nations Statistics Division, New York, NY 10017, (800) 253-9646, Fax: (212) 963-4116, http://unstats.un.org; *Statistical Yearbook.*

The World Bank, 1818 H Street, NW, Washington, DC 20433, (202) 473-1000, Fax: (202) 477-6391, www.worldbank.org; *Georgia* and *Statistical Handbook: States of the Former USSR.*

GEORGIA (REPUBLIC) - WHOLESALE PRICE INDEXES

United Nations Statistics Division, New York, NY 10017, (800) 253-9646, Fax: (212) 963-4116, http://unstats.un.org; *Statistical Yearbook.*

GEORGIA (REPUBLIC) - WHOLESALE TRADE

United Nations Statistics Division, New York, NY 10017, (800) 253-9646, Fax: (212) 963-4116, http://unstats.un.org; *Statistical Yearbook.*

GEORGIA (REPUBLIC) - WOOL PRODUCTION

See GEORGIA (REPUBLIC) - TEXTILE INDUSTRY

GEOTHERMAL ENERGY

Environmental Business International, Inc., 4452 Park Boulevard, Suite 306, San Diego, CA 92116, (619) 295-7685, Fax: (619) 295-5743, www.ebiusa.com; *Environmental Business Journal (EBJ) 2006; Environmental Market Reports;* and *U.S. and Global Environmental Market Data.*

U.S. Department of Energy (DOE), Energy Information Administration (EIA), 1000 Independence Avenue, SW, Washington, DC 20585, (202) 586-8800, www.eia.doe.gov; *Annual Energy Review 2005* and *Monthly Energy Review (MER).*

GERMANIUM

U.S. Department of the Interior (DOI), U.S. Geological Survey (USGS), Office of Minerals Information, 12201 Sunrise Valley Drive, Reston, VA 20192, Mr. Kenneth A. Beckman, (703) 648-4916, Fax: (703) 648-4995, http://minerals.usgs.gov/minerals; *Mineral Commodity Summaries.*

GERMANY - NATIONAL STATISTICAL OFFICE

Federal Statistical Office, Statistical Information Service, Gustav - Stresemann - Ring 11, 65189 Wiesbaden, Germany, www.destatis.de/e_home.htm; National Data Center.

GERMANY - PRIMARY STATISTICS SOURCES

Eurostat, Batiment Jean Monnet, Rue Alcide de Gasperi, L-2920 Luxembourg, http://epp.eurostat.ec.europa.eu; *Pocketbook on Candidate and Potential Candidate Countries.*

Federal Statistical Office, Statistical Information Service, Gustav - Stresemann - Ring 11, 65189 Wiesbaden, Germany, www.destatis.de/e_home.htm; *Key data on Germany 2007* and *Statistisches Jahrbuch 2007* (Statistical Yearbook of Germany 2007).

GERMANY - DATABASES

BBE Unternehmensberatung GmbH, Kap am Sudkai, Agrippinawerft 30, 50678 Cologne, Germany, www.bbeberatung.com/bbe_eng; BBE Research-Plus.

Deutsche Bundesbank Statistics Department, Wilhelm-Epstein-Strasse 14, 60431 Frankfurt am Main, Germany, www.bundesbank.de/statistik/statistik.en.php; Database: Subject coverage: Statistics on banking, securities, balance of payments, and seasonally adjusted economic data.

German Institute for Economic Research (Deutsches Institut fuer Wirtschaftsforschung - DIW Berlin), 14191 Berlin, Germany, www.diw.de/english; Databases. Subject coverage: Economy, including gross national product, business trends, income, employment, and capital.

Haver Analytics, 49 East 41st Street, New York, NY 10165-6200, (212) 986-9300, www.haver.com; Databases: Economic and financial information.

TNS Infratest - Business Intelligence, Landsberger Strasse 338, 80687 Munich, Germany, www.tns-infratest.com/00_En/index.asp; FAKT Database. Subject coverage: General economic factors, top companies, Internet/electronic commerce, information technology and telecommunication, media research, advertising, financial market, health care, society and public life.

GERMANY - ABORTION

European Union, Delegation of the European Commission to the United States, 2300 M Street, NW, Washington, DC 20037, (202) 862-9500, Fax: (202) 429-1766, www.eurunion.org; *First Demographic Estimates for 2006.*

United Nations Statistics Division, New York, NY 10017, (800) 253-9646, Fax: (212) 963-4116, http://unstats.un.org; *Trends in Europe and North America: The Statistical Yearbook of the ECE 2005.*

GERMANY - AGRICULTURAL MACHINERY

European Union, Delegation of the European Commission to the United States, 2300 M Street, NW, Washington, DC 20037, (202) 862-9500, Fax: (202) 429-1766, www.eurunion.org; *Statistical Overview of Transport in the European Union (Data 1970-2001).*

United Nations Statistics Division, New York, NY 10017, (800) 253-9646, Fax: (212) 963-4116, http://unstats.un.org; *Statistical Yearbook.*

GERMANY - AGRICULTURE

Economist Intelligence Unit, 111 West 57th Street, New York, NY 10019, (212) 554-0600, Fax: (212) 586-1181, www.eiu.com; *Germany Country Report.*

Euromonitor International, Inc., 224 S. Michigan Avenue, Suite 1500, Chicago, IL 60604, (312) 922-1115, Fax: (312) 922-1157, www.euromonitor.com; *World Marketing Data and Statistics.*

European Union, Delegation of the European Commission to the United States, 2300 M Street, NW, Washington, DC 20037, (202) 862-9500, Fax: (202) 429-1766, www.eurunion.org; *Agricultural Statistics: Data 1995-2005; Agriculture in the European Union: Statistical and Economic Information 2006; European Union Labour Force Survey;* and *Eurostatistics: Data for Short-Term Economic Analysis (2007 edition).*

Eurostat, Batiment Jean Monnet, Rue Alcide de Gasperi, L-2920 Luxembourg, http://epp.eurostat.ec.europa.eu; *EU Agricultural Prices in 2007* and *Eurostat Yearbook 2006-2007.*

M.E. Sharpe, 80 Business Park Drive, Armonk, NY 10504, (800) 541-6563, Fax: (914) 273-2106, www.mesharpe.com; *The Illustrated Book of World Rankings.*

Organisation for Economic Cooperation and Development (OECD), 2 rue Andre Pascal, F-75775 Paris Cedex 16, France, (Telephone in U.S. (202) 785-6323), (Fax in U.S. (202) 785-0350), www.oecd.org; *Indicators of Industrial Activity; 2005 OECD Agricultural Outlook Tables, 1970-2014; OECD Agricultural Outlook: 2007-2016; OECD Economic Survey - Germany 2008;* and STructural ANalysis (STAN) database.

Palgrave Macmillan Ltd., Houndmills, Basingstoke, Hampshire, RG21 6XS, England, (Telephone in U.S. (888) 330-8477), (Fax in U.S. (800) 672-2054), www.palgrave.com; *The Statesman's Yearbook 2008.*

Taylor and Francis Group, An Informa Business, 2 Park Square, Milton Park, Abingdon, Oxford OX14 4RN, United Kingdom, (Dial from U.S. (212) 216-7800), (Fax from U.S. (212) 564-7854), www.tandf.co.uk; *The Europa World Year Book.*

United Nations Conference on Trade and Development (UNCTAD), DC2-1120, United Nations, New York, NY 10017, (212) 963-0027, www.unctad.org; *UNCTAD Commodity Yearbook.*

United Nations Food and Agricultural Organization (FAO), Viale delle Terme di Caracalla, 00100 Rome, Italy, (Dial from U.S. (202) 653-2400), (Fax from U.S. (202) 653 5760), www.fao.org; AQUASTAT; *FAO Production Yearbook 2002; FAO Trade Yearbook;* and *The State of Food and Agriculture (SOFA) 2006.*

United Nations Statistics Division, New York, NY 10017, (800) 253-9646, Fax: (212) 963-4116, http://unstats.un.org; *Statistical Yearbook.*

The World Bank, 1818 H Street, NW, Washington, DC 20433, (202) 473-1000, Fax: (202) 477-6391, www.worldbank.org; *Germany* and *World Development Indicators (WDI) 2008.*

GERMANY - AIRLINES

European Union, Delegation of the European Commission to the United States, 2300 M Street, NW, Washington, DC 20037, (202) 862-9500, Fax: (202) 429-1766, www.eurunion.org; *Regions - Statistical Yearbook 2006* and *Statistical Overview of Transport in the European Union (Data 1970-2001).*

Eurostat, Batiment Jean Monnet, Rue Alcide de Gasperi, L-2920 Luxembourg, http://epp.eurostat.ec.europa.eu; *Eurostat Yearbook 2006-2007* and *Regional Passenger and Freight Air Transport in Europe in 2006.*

International Civil Aviation Organization (ICAO), External Relations and Public Information Office (EPO), 999 University Street, Montreal, Quebec H3C 5H7, Canada, (Dial from U.S. (514) 954-8219), (Fax from U.S. (514) 954-6077), www.icao.int; *Civil Aviation Statistics of the World.*

M.E. Sharpe, 80 Business Park Drive, Armonk, NY 10504, (800) 541-6563, Fax: (914) 273-2106, www.mesharpe.com; *The Illustrated Book of World Rankings.*

Organisation for Economic Cooperation and Development (OECD), 2 rue Andre Pascal, F-75775 Paris Cedex 16, France, (Telephone in U.S. (202) 785-6323), (Fax in U.S. (202) 785-0350), www.oecd.org; *Household, Tourism, Travel: Trends, Environmental Impacts and Policy Responses.*

Palgrave Macmillan Ltd., Houndmills, Basingstoke, Hampshire, RG21 6XS, England, (Telephone in U.S.

(888) 330-8477), (Fax in U.S. (800) 672-2054), www.palgrave.com; *The Statesman's Yearbook 2008.*

Taylor and Francis Group, An Informa Business, 2 Park Square, Milton Park, Abingdon, Oxford OX14 4RN, United Kingdom, (Dial from U.S. (212) 216-7800), (Fax from U.S. (212) 564-7854), www.tandf.co.uk; *The Europa World Year Book.*

United Nations Statistics Division, New York, NY 10017, (800) 253-9646, Fax: (212) 963-4116, http://unstats.un.org; *Statistical Yearbook.*

GERMANY - AIRPORTS

Central Intelligence Agency, Office of Public Affairs, Washington, DC 20505, (703) 482-0623, Fax: (703) 482-1739, www.cia.gov; *The World Factbook.*

GERMANY - ALMOND PRODUCTION

See GERMANY - CROPS

GERMANY - ALUMINUM PRODUCTION

See GERMANY - MINERAL INDUSTRIES

GERMANY - ANIMAL FEEDING

Organisation for Economic Cooperation and Development (OECD), 2 rue Andre Pascal, F-75775 Paris Cedex 16, France, (Telephone in U.S. (202) 785-6323), (Fax in U.S. (202) 785-0350), www.oecd.org; *International Trade by Commodity Statistics (ITCS).*

United Nations Statistics Division, New York, NY 10017, (800) 253-9646, Fax: (212) 963-4116, http://unstats.un.org; *Statistical Yearbook.*

GERMANY - APPLE PRODUCTION

See GERMANY - CROPS

GERMANY - ARMED FORCES

Central Intelligence Agency, Office of Public Affairs, Washington, DC 20505, (703) 482-0623, Fax: (703) 482-1739, www.cia.gov; *The World Factbook.*

Euromonitor International, Inc., 224 S. Michigan Avenue, Suite 1500, Chicago, IL 60604, (312) 922-1115, Fax: (312) 922-1157, www.euromonitor.com; *World Marketing Data and Statistics.*

European Union, Delegation of the European Commission to the United States, 2300 M Street, NW, Washington, DC 20037, (202) 862-9500, Fax: (202) 429-1766, www.eurunion.org; *RD Expenditure in Europe (2006 edition).*

International Institute for Strategic Studies (IISS), Arundel House, 13-15 Arundel Street, Temple Place, London WC2R 3DX, England, www.iiss.org; *The Military Balance 2007.*

Palgrave Macmillan Ltd., Houndmills, Basingstoke, Hampshire, RG21 6XS, England, (Telephone in U.S. (888) 330-8477), (Fax in U.S. (800) 672-2054), www.palgrave.com; *The Statesman's Yearbook 2008.*

U.S. Department of State (DOS), 2201 C Street NW, Washington, DC 20520, (202) 647-4000, www.state.gov; *World Military Expenditures and Arms Transfers (WMEAT).*

United Nations Statistics Division, New York, NY 10017, (800) 253-9646, Fax: (212) 963-4116, http://unstats.un.org; *Human Development Report 2006.*

GERMANY - AUTOMOBILE INDUSTRY AND TRADE

European Union, Delegation of the European Commission to the United States, 2300 M Street, NW, Washington, DC 20037, (202) 862-9500, Fax: (202) 429-1766, www.eurunion.org; *Eurostatistics: Data for Short-Term Economic Analysis (2007 edition).*

Eurostat, Batiment Jean Monnet, Rue Alcide de Gasperi, L-2920 Luxembourg, http://epp.eurostat.ec.europa.eu; *Eurostat Yearbook 2006-2007.*

International Road Federation (IFR), Madison Place, 500 Montgomery Street, 5th Floor, Alexandria, VA 22314, (703) 535-1001, Fax: (703) 535-1007, www.irfnet.org; *World Road Statistics 2006.*

Organisation for Economic Cooperation and Development (OECD), 2 rue Andre Pascal, F-75775 Paris Cedex 16, France, (Telephone in U.S. (202) 785-6323), (Fax in U.S. (202) 785-0350), www.oecd.org; *Indicators of Industrial Activity* and *International Trade by Commodity Statistics (ITCS).*

United Nations Statistics Division, New York, NY 10017, (800) 253-9646, Fax: (212) 963-4116, http://unstats.un.org; *Statistical Yearbook.*

GERMANY - BALANCE OF PAYMENTS

European Union, Delegation of the European Commission to the United States, 2300 M Street, NW, Washington, DC 20037, (202) 862-9500, Fax: (202) 429-1766, www.eurunion.org; *Eurostatistics: Data for Short-Term Economic Analysis (2007 edition).*

Eurostat, Batiment Jean Monnet, Rue Alcide de Gasperi, L-2920 Luxembourg, http://epp.eurostat.ec.europa.eu; *Eurostat Yearbook 2006-2007.*

International Monetary Fund (IMF), 700 Nineteenth Street, NW, Washington, DC 20431, (202) 623-7000, Fax: (202) 623-4661, www.imf.org; *Balance of Payments Statistics Newsletter; Balance of Payments Statistics Yearbook 2007;* and *International Financial Statistics Yearbook 2007.*

Organisation for Economic Cooperation and Development (OECD), 2 rue Andre Pascal, F-75775 Paris Cedex 16, France, (Telephone in U.S. (202) 785-6323), (Fax in U.S. (202) 785-0350), www.oecd.org; *Geographical Distribution of Financial Flows to Aid Recipients 2002-2006; OECD Economic Outlook 2008; OECD Economic Survey - Germany 2008;* and *OECD Main Economic Indicators (MEI).*

Platts, 2 Penn Plaza, 25th Floor, New York, NY 10121-2298, (212) 904-3070, www.platts.com; *Energy Economist.*

Taylor and Francis Group, An Informa Business, 2 Park Square, Milton Park, Abingdon, Oxford OX14 4RN, United Kingdom, (Dial from U.S. (212) 216-7800), (Fax from U.S. (212) 564-7854), www.tandf.co.uk; *The Europa World Year Book.*

UNICEF, 3 United Nations Plaza, New York, NY 10017, (800) 253-9646, Fax: (212) 887-7465, www.unicef.org; *The State of the World's Children 2008.*

United Nations Statistics Division, New York, NY 10017, (800) 253-9646, Fax: (212) 963-4116, http://unstats.un.org; *Energy Statistics Yearbook 2003.*

The World Bank, 1818 H Street, NW, Washington, DC 20433, (202) 473-1000, Fax: (202) 477-6391, www.worldbank.org; *Germany; World Development Indicators (WDI) 2008;* and *World Development Report 2008.*

GERMANY - BANANAS

See GERMANY - CROPS

GERMANY - BANKS AND BANKING

Euromonitor International, Inc., 224 S. Michigan Avenue, Suite 1500, Chicago, IL 60604, (312) 922-1115, Fax: (312) 922-1157, www.euromonitor.com; *World Marketing Data and Statistics.*

European Union, Delegation of the European Commission to the United States, 2300 M Street, NW, Washington, DC 20037, (202) 862-9500, Fax: (202) 429-1766, www.eurunion.org; *The EU Economy, 2007 Review: Moving Europe's Productivity Frontier* and *Eurostatistics: Data for Short-Term Economic Analysis (2007 edition).*

Eurostat, Batiment Jean Monnet, Rue Alcide de Gasperi, L-2920 Luxembourg, http://epp.eurostat.ec.europa.eu; *Eurostat Yearbook 2006-2007.*

International Monetary Fund (IMF), 700 Nineteenth Street, NW, Washington, DC 20431, (202) 623-7000, Fax: (202) 623-4661, www.imf.org; *International Financial Statistics Yearbook 2007.*

M.E. Sharpe, 80 Business Park Drive, Armonk, NY 10504, (800) 541-6563, Fax: (914) 273-2106, www.mesharpe.com; *The Illustrated Book of World Rankings.*

Organisation for Economic Cooperation and Development (OECD), 2 rue Andre Pascal, F-75775 Paris Cedex 16, France, (Telephone in U.S. (202) 785-6323), (Fax in U.S. (202) 785-0350), www.oecd.org; *Financial Market Trends: OECD Periodical; OECD Economic Outlook 2008;* and *OECD Economic Survey - Germany 2008.*

Palgrave Macmillan Ltd., Houndmills, Basingstoke, Hampshire, RG21 6XS, England, (Telephone in U.S. (888) 330-8477), (Fax in U.S. (800) 672-2054), www.palgrave.com; *The Statesman's Yearbook 2008.*

Taylor and Francis Group, An Informa Business, 2 Park Square, Milton Park, Abingdon, Oxford OX14 4RN, United Kingdom, (Dial from U.S. (212) 216-7800), (Fax from U.S. (212) 564-7854), www.tandf.co.uk; *The Europa World Year Book.*

United Nations Statistics Division, New York, NY 10017, (800) 253-9646, Fax: (212) 963-4116, http://unstats.un.org; *Statistical Yearbook.*

GERMANY - BARLEY PRODUCTION

See GERMANY - CROPS

GERMANY - BEVERAGE INDUSTRY

Eurostat, Batiment Jean Monnet, Rue Alcide de Gasperi, L-2920 Luxembourg, http://epp.eurostat.ec.europa.eu; *Eurostat Yearbook 2006-2007.*

M.E. Sharpe, 80 Business Park Drive, Armonk, NY 10504, (800) 541-6563, Fax: (914) 273-2106, www.mesharpe.com; *The Illustrated Book of World Rankings.*

Organisation for Economic Cooperation and Development (OECD), 2 rue Andre Pascal, F-75775 Paris Cedex 16, France, (Telephone in U.S. (202) 785-6323), (Fax in U.S. (202) 785-0350), www.oecd.org; *Indicators of Industrial Activity.*

United Nations Statistics Division, New York, NY 10017, (800) 253-9646, Fax: (212) 963-4116, http://unstats.un.org; *Statistical Yearbook.*

GERMANY - BONDS

Eurostat, Batiment Jean Monnet, Rue Alcide de Gasperi, L-2920 Luxembourg, http://epp.eurostat.ec.europa.eu; *Eurostat Yearbook 2006-2007.*

Organisation for Economic Cooperation and Development (OECD), 2 rue Andre Pascal, F-75775 Paris Cedex 16, France, (Telephone in U.S. (202) 785-6323), (Fax in U.S. (202) 785-0350), www.oecd.org; *Financial Market Trends: OECD Periodical.*

United Nations Statistics Division, New York, NY 10017, (800) 253-9646, Fax: (212) 963-4116, http://unstats.un.org; *Statistical Yearbook.*

GERMANY - BROADCASTING

Central Intelligence Agency, Office of Public Affairs, Washington, DC 20505, (703) 482-0623, Fax: (703) 482-1739, www.cia.gov; *The World Factbook.*

Euromonitor International, Inc., 224 S. Michigan Avenue, Suite 1500, Chicago, IL 60604, (312) 922-1115, Fax: (312) 922-1157, www.euromonitor.com; *World Marketing Data and Statistics.*

Eurostat, Batiment Jean Monnet, Rue Alcide de Gasperi, L-2920 Luxembourg, http://epp.eurostat.ec.europa.eu; *Eurostat Yearbook 2006-2007.*

M.E. Sharpe, 80 Business Park Drive, Armonk, NY 10504, (800) 541-6563, Fax: (914) 273-2106, www.mesharpe.com; *The Illustrated Book of World Rankings.*

Palgrave Macmillan Ltd., Houndmills, Basingstoke, Hampshire, RG21 6XS, England, (Telephone in U.S. (888) 330-8477), (Fax in U.S. (800) 672-2054), www.palgrave.com; *The Statesman's Yearbook 2008.*

United Nations Statistics Division, New York, NY 10017, (800) 253-9646, Fax: (212) 963-4116, http://unstats.un.org; *Trends in Europe and North America: The Statistical Yearbook of the ECE 2005.*

WRTH Publications Limited, PO Box 290, Oxford OX2 7FT, UK, www.wrth.com; *World Radio TV Handbook 2007.*

GERMANY - BUDGET

Central Intelligence Agency, Office of Public Affairs, Washington, DC 20505, (703) 482-0623, Fax: (703) 482-1739, www.cia.gov; *The World Factbook.*

Eurostat, Batiment Jean Monnet, Rue Alcide de Gasperi, L-2920 Luxembourg, http://epp.eurostat.ec.europa.eu; *Government Budgets.*

GERMANY - BUSINESS

Eurostat, Batiment Jean Monnet, Rue Alcide de Gasperi, L-2920 Luxembourg, http://epp.eurostat.ec.europa.eu; *Eurostat Yearbook 2006-2007.*

Organisation for Economic Cooperation and Development (OECD), 2 rue Andre Pascal, F-75775 Paris Cedex 16, France, (Telephone in U.S. (202) 785-6323), (Fax in U.S. (202) 785-0350), www.oecd.org; *OECD Main Economic Indicators (MEI).*

United Nations Statistics Division, New York, NY 10017, (800) 253-9646, Fax: (212) 963-4116, http://unstats.un.org; *Statistical Yearbook.*

GERMANY - CADMIUM PRODUCTION

See GERMANY - MINERAL INDUSTRIES

GERMANY - CAPITAL INVESTMENTS

Organisation for Economic Cooperation and Development (OECD), 2 rue Andre Pascal, F-75775 Paris Cedex 16, France, (Telephone in U.S. (202) 785-6323), (Fax in U.S. (202) 785-0350), www.oecd.org; *Financial Market Trends: OECD Periodical* and *OECD Economic Outlook 2008.*

GERMANY - CAPITAL LEVY

Organisation for Economic Cooperation and Development (OECD), 2 rue Andre Pascal, F-75775 Paris Cedex 16, France, (Telephone in U.S. (202) 785-6323), (Fax in U.S. (202) 785-0350), www.oecd.org; *Financial Market Trends: OECD Periodical* and *OECD Economic Outlook 2008.*

GERMANY - CATTLE

See GERMANY - LIVESTOCK

GERMANY - CHESTNUT PRODUCTION

See GERMANY - CROPS

GERMANY - CHICKENS

See GERMANY - LIVESTOCK

GERMANY - CHILDBIRTH - STATISTICS

Central Intelligence Agency, Office of Public Affairs, Washington, DC 20505, (703) 482-0623, Fax: (703) 482-1739, www.cia.gov; *The World Factbook.*

Euromonitor International, Inc., 224 S. Michigan Avenue, Suite 1500, Chicago, IL 60604, (312) 922-1115, Fax: (312) 922-1157, www.euromonitor.com; *The World Economic Factbook 2008.*

European Union, Delegation of the European Commission to the United States, 2300 M Street, NW, Washington, DC 20037, (202) 862-9500, Fax: (202) 429-1766, www.eurunion.org; *First Demographic Estimates for 2006.*

Eurostat, Batiment Jean Monnet, Rue Alcide de Gasperi, L-2920 Luxembourg, http://epp.eurostat.ec.europa.eu; *Eurostat Yearbook 2006-2007.*

M.E. Sharpe, 80 Business Park Drive, Armonk, NY 10504, (800) 541-6563, Fax: (914) 273-2106, www.mesharpe.com; *The Illustrated Book of World Rankings.*

Palgrave Macmillan Ltd., Houndmills, Basingstoke, Hampshire, RG21 6XS, England, (Telephone in U.S. (888) 330-8477), (Fax in U.S. (800) 672-2054), www.palgrave.com; *The Statesman's Yearbook 2008.*

Taylor and Francis Group, An Informa Business, 2 Park Square, Milton Park, Abingdon, Oxford OX14 4RN, United Kingdom, (Dial from U.S. (212) 216-7800), (Fax from U.S. (212) 564-7854), www.tandf.co.uk; *The Europa World Year Book.*

United Nations Statistics Division, New York, NY 10017, (800) 253-9646, Fax: (212) 963-4116, http://unstats.un.org; *Demographic Yearbook* and *Statistical Yearbook.*

The World Bank, 1818 H Street, NW, Washington, DC 20433, (202) 473-1000, Fax: (202) 477-6391, www.worldbank.org; *World Development Indicators (WDI) 2008.*

World Health Organization (WHO), Avenue Appia 20, 1211 Geneve 27, Switzerland, (Telephone in U.S. (212) 331-9081), www.who.int; *World Health Report 2006.*

GERMANY - CLIMATE

M.E. Sharpe, 80 Business Park Drive, Armonk, NY 10504, (800) 541-6563, Fax: (914) 273-2106, www.mesharpe.com; *The Illustrated Book of World Rankings.*

Palgrave Macmillan Ltd., Houndmills, Basingstoke, Hampshire, RG21 6XS, England, (Telephone in U.S. (888) 330-8477), (Fax in U.S. (800) 672-2054), www.palgrave.com; *The Statesman's Yearbook 2008.*

GERMANY - CLOTHING EXPORTS AND IMPORTS

See GERMANY - TEXTILE INDUSTRY

GERMANY - COAL PRODUCTION

See GERMANY - MINERAL INDUSTRIES

GERMANY - COBALT PRODUCTION

See GERMANY - MINERAL INDUSTRIES

GERMANY - COCOA PRODUCTION

See GERMANY - CROPS

GERMANY - COFFEE

See GERMANY - CROPS

GERMANY - COMMERCE

Palgrave Macmillan Ltd., Houndmills, Basingstoke, Hampshire, RG21 6XS, England, (Telephone in U.S. (888) 330-8477), (Fax in U.S. (800) 672-2054), www.palgrave.com; *The Statesman's Yearbook 2008.*

GERMANY - COMMODITY EXCHANGES

Commodity Research Bureau, 330 South Wells Street, Suite 612, Chicago, IL 60606-7110, (800) 621-5271, Fax: (312) 939-4135, www.crbtrader.com; *2006 CRB Commodity Yearbook and CD.*

Global Financial Data, Inc., 784 Fremont Villas, Los Angeles, CA 90042, (323) 924-1016, www.globalfindata.com; unpublished data.

International Lead and Zinc Study Group (ILZSG), Rua Almirante Barroso 38, 5th Floor, Lisbon 1000 - 013, Portugal, www.ilzsg.org; Interactive Statistical Database.

International Monetary Fund (IMF), 700 Nineteenth Street, NW, Washington, DC 20431, (202) 623-7000, Fax: (202) 623-4661, www.imf.org; *IMF Primary Commodity Prices.*

United Nations Food and Agricultural Organization (FAO), Viale delle Terme di Caracalla, 00100 Rome, Italy, (Dial from U.S. (202) 653-2400), (Fax from U.S. (202) 653 5760), www.fao.org; *The State of Food and Agriculture (SOFA) 2006.*

United Nations Statistics Division, New York, NY 10017, (800) 253-9646, Fax: (212) 963-4116, http://unstats.un.org; *Statistical Yearbook.*

World Bureau of Metal Statistics (WBMS), 27a High Street, Ware, Hertfordshire, SG12 9BA, United Kingdom, www.world-bureau.com; *Annual Stainless Steel Statistics; World Flow Charts; World Metal Statistics; World Nickel Statistics;* and *World Tin Statistics.*

GERMANY - COMMUNICATION AND TRAFFIC

European Union, Delegation of the European Commission to the United States, 2300 M Street, NW, Washington, DC 20037, (202) 862-9500, Fax: (202) 429-1766, www.eurunion.org; *Statistical Overview of Transport in the European Union (Data 1970-2001).*

United Nations Statistics Division, New York, NY 10017, (800) 253-9646, Fax: (212) 963-4116, http://unstats.un.org; *Statistical Yearbook.*

GERMANY - CONSTRUCTION INDUSTRY

European Union, Delegation of the European Commission to the United States, 2300 M Street, NW, Washington, DC 20037, (202) 862-9500, Fax: (202) 429-1766, www.eurunion.org; *European Union Labour Force Survey.*

Eurostat, Batiment Jean Monnet, Rue Alcide de Gasperi, L-2920 Luxembourg, http://epp.eurostat.ec.europa.eu; *Eurostat Yearbook 2006-2007.*

M.E. Sharpe, 80 Business Park Drive, Armonk, NY 10504, (800) 541-6563, Fax: (914) 273-2106, www.mesharpe.com; *The Illustrated Book of World Rankings.*

Organisation for Economic Cooperation and Development (OECD), 2 rue Andre Pascal, F-75775 Paris Cedex 16, France, (Telephone in U.S. (202) 785-6323), (Fax in U.S. (202) 785-0350), www.oecd.org; *Iron and Steel Industry in 2004 (2006 Edition); OECD Economic Survey - Germany 2008; OECD Main Economic Indicators (MEI);* and STructural ANalysis (STAN) database.

Palgrave Macmillan Ltd., Houndmills, Basingstoke, Hampshire, RG21 6XS, England, (Telephone in U.S. (888) 330-8477), (Fax in U.S. (800) 672-2054), www.palgrave.com; *The Statesman's Yearbook 2008.*

United Nations Statistics Division, New York, NY 10017, (800) 253-9646, Fax: (212) 963-4116, http://unstats.un.org; *Statistical Yearbook.*

GERMANY - CONSUMER PRICE INDEXES

Eurostat, Batiment Jean Monnet, Rue Alcide de Gasperi, L-2920 Luxembourg, http://epp.eurostat.ec.europa.eu; *Eurostat Yearbook 2006-2007.*

International Labour Office, I.L.O. Publications, 4 route des Morillons, CH-1211 Geneva 22, Switzerland, (Telephone in U.S. (202) 653-7652), (Fax in U.S. (202) 653-7687), www.ilo.org; *Yearbook of Labour Statistics 2006.*

Organisation for Economic Cooperation and Development (OECD), 2 rue Andre Pascal, F-75775 Paris Cedex 16, France, (Telephone in U.S. (202) 785-6323), (Fax in U.S. (202) 785-0350), www.oecd.org; *OECD Economic Outlook 2008.*

Taylor and Francis Group, An Informa Business, 2 Park Square, Milton Park, Abingdon, Oxford OX14 4RN, United Kingdom, (Dial from U.S. (212) 216-7800), (Fax from U.S. (212) 564-7854), www.tandf.co.uk; *The Europa World Year Book.*

United Nations Statistics Division, New York, NY 10017, (800) 253-9646, Fax: (212) 963-4116, http://unstats.un.org; *Statistical Yearbook* and *Trends in Europe and North America: The Statistical Yearbook of the ECE 2005.*

The World Bank, 1818 H Street, NW, Washington, DC 20433, (202) 473-1000, Fax: (202) 477-6391, www.worldbank.org; *Germany.*

GERMANY - CONSUMPTION (ECONOMICS)

Eurostat, Batiment Jean Monnet, Rue Alcide de Gasperi, L-2920 Luxembourg, http://epp.eurostat.ec.europa.eu; *Eurostat Yearbook 2006-2007.*

International Iron and Steel Institute (IISI), Rue Colonel Bourg 120, B-1140 Brussels, Belgium, www.worldsteel.org; *Steel Statistical Yearbook 2006.*

International Lead and Zinc Study Group (ILZSG), Rua Almirante Barroso 38, 5th Floor, Lisbon 1000 - 013, Portugal, www.ilzsg.org; Interactive Statistical Database.

Organisation for Economic Cooperation and Development (OECD), 2 rue Andre Pascal, F-75775 Paris Cedex 16, France, (Telephone in U.S. (202) 785-6323), (Fax in U.S. (202) 785-0350), www.oecd.org; *Environmental Impacts of Foreign Direct Investment in the Mining Sector in the Newly Independent States (NIS); Iron and Steel Industry in 2004 (2006 Edition); A New World Map in Textiles and Clothing:*

Adjusting to Change; 2005 OECD Agricultural Outlook Tables, 1970-2014; Revenue Statistics 1965-2006 - 2007 Edition; and *Towards Sustainable Household Consumption?: Trends and Policies in OECD Countries.*

Technical Association of the Pulp and Paper Industry (TAPPI), 15 Technology Parkway South, Norcross, GA 30092, (770) 446-1400, Fax: (770) 446-6947, www.tappi.org; *TAPPI Annual Report.*

The World Bank, 1818 H Street, NW, Washington, DC 20433, (202) 473-1000, Fax: (202) 477-6391, www.worldbank.org; *World Development Report 2008.*

GERMANY - COPPER INDUSTRY AND TRADE

See GERMANY - MINERAL INDUSTRIES

GERMANY - CORN INDUSTRY

See GERMANY - CROPS

GERMANY - COST AND STANDARD OF LIVING

Eurostat, Batiment Jean Monnet, Rue Alcide de Gasperi, L-2920 Luxembourg, http://epp.eurostat.ec.europa.eu; *Eurostat Yearbook 2006-2007.*

GERMANY - COTTON

See GERMANY - CROPS

GERMANY - CRIME

Eurostat, Batiment Jean Monnet, Rue Alcide de Gasperi, L-2920 Luxembourg, http://epp.eurostat.ec.europa.eu; *Crime and Criminal Justice; General Government Expenditure and Revenue in the EU, 2006;* and *Study on Crime Victimisation.*

International Criminal Police Organization (INTERPOL), General Secretariat, 200 quai Charles de Gaulle, 69006 Lyon, France, www.interpol.int; *International Crime Statistics.*

International Organization for Migration (IOM), 17, Route des Morillons, CH-1211 Geneva 19, Switzerland, www.iom.int; *Trafficking in Human Beings and the 2006 World Cup in Germany.*

U.S. Department of Justice (DOJ), Bureau of Justice Statistics, 810 Seventh Street, NW, Washington, DC 20531, (202) 307-0765, www.ojp.usdoj.gov/bjs/; *The World Factbook of Criminal Justice Systems.*

United Nations Statistics Division, New York, NY 10017, (800) 253-9646, Fax: (212) 963-4116, http://unstats.un.org; *Trends in Europe and North America: The Statistical Yearbook of the ECE 2005.*

Yale University Press, PO Box 209040, New Haven, CT 06520-9040, (203) 432-0960, Fax: (203) 432-0948, http://yalepress.yale.edu/yupbooks; *Violence and Crime in Cross-National Perspective.*

GERMANY - CROPS

Euromonitor International, Inc., 224 S. Michigan Avenue, Suite 1500, Chicago, IL 60604, (312) 922-1115, Fax: (312) 922-1157, www.euromonitor.com; *European Marketing Data and Statistics 2008.*

European Union, Delegation of the European Commission to the United States, 2300 M Street, NW, Washington, DC 20037, (202) 862-9500, Fax: (202) 429-1766, www.eurunion.org; *Agricultural Statistics: Data 1995-2005; Eurostatistics: Data for Short-Term Economic Analysis (2007 edition);* and *Regions - Statistical Yearbook 2006.*

Eurostat, Batiment Jean Monnet, Rue Alcide de Gasperi, L-2920 Luxembourg, http://epp.eurostat.ec.europa.eu; *Eurostat Yearbook 2006-2007.*

M.E. Sharpe, 80 Business Park Drive, Armonk, NY 10504, (800) 541-6563, Fax: (914) 273-2106, www.mesharpe.com; *The Illustrated Book of World Rankings.*

Organisation for Economic Cooperation and Development (OECD), 2 rue Andre Pascal, F-75775 Paris Cedex 16, France, (Telephone in U.S. (202) 785-6323), (Fax in U.S. (202) 785-0350), www.oecd.org; *International Trade by Commodity Statistics (ITCS)* and *2005 OECD Agricultural Outlook Tables, 1970-2014.*

Palgrave Macmillan Ltd., Houndmills, Basingstoke, Hampshire, RG21 6XS, England, (Telephone in U.S. (888) 330-8477), (Fax in U.S. (800) 672-2054), www.palgrave.com; *The Statesman's Yearbook 2008.*

Taylor and Francis Group, An Informa Business, 2 Park Square, Milton Park, Abingdon, Oxford OX14 4RN, United Kingdom, (Dial from U.S. (212) 216-7800), (Fax from U.S. (212) 564-7854), www.tandf.co.uk; *The Europa World Year Book.*

United Nations Conference on Trade and Development (UNCTAD), DC2-1120, United Nations, New York, NY 10017, (212) 963-0027, www.unctad.org; *UNCTAD Commodity Yearbook.*

United Nations Food and Agricultural Organization (FAO), Viale delle Terme di Caracalla, 00100 Rome, Italy, (Dial from U.S. (202) 653-2400), (Fax from U.S. (202) 653 5760), www.fao.org; *FAO Production Yearbook 2002* and *The State of Food and Agriculture (SOFA) 2006.*

United Nations Statistics Division, New York, NY 10017, (800) 253-9646, Fax: (212) 963-4116, http://unstats.un.org; *Statistical Yearbook.*

GERMANY - CUSTOMS ADMINISTRATION

Eurostat, Batiment Jean Monnet, Rue Alcide de Gasperi, L-2920 Luxembourg, http://epp.eurostat.ec.europa.eu; *Eurostat Yearbook 2006-2007.*

Organisation for Economic Cooperation and Development (OECD), 2 rue Andre Pascal, F-75775 Paris Cedex 16, France, (Telephone in U.S. (202) 785-6323), (Fax in U.S. (202) 785-0350), www.oecd.org; *Environmental Impacts of Foreign Direct Investment in the Mining Sector in the Newly Independent States (NIS).*

Palgrave Macmillan Ltd., Houndmills, Basingstoke, Hampshire, RG21 6XS, England, (Telephone in U.S. (888) 330-8477), (Fax in U.S. (800) 672-2054), www.palgrave.com; *The Statesman's Yearbook 2008.*

GERMANY - DAIRY PROCESSING

European Union, Delegation of the European Commission to the United States, 2300 M Street, NW, Washington, DC 20037, (202) 862-9500, Fax: (202) 429-1766, www.eurunion.org; *Eurostatistics: Data for Short-Term Economic Analysis (2007 edition).*

Eurostat, Batiment Jean Monnet, Rue Alcide de Gasperi, L-2920 Luxembourg, http://epp.eurostat.ec.europa.eu; *Eurostat Yearbook 2006-2007.*

M.E. Sharpe, 80 Business Park Drive, Armonk, NY 10504, (800) 541-6563, Fax: (914) 273-2106, www.mesharpe.com; *The Illustrated Book of World Rankings.*

Organisation for Economic Cooperation and Development (OECD), 2 rue Andre Pascal, F-75775 Paris Cedex 16, France, (Telephone in U.S. (202) 785-6323), (Fax in U.S. (202) 785-0350), www.oecd.org; *2005 OECD Agricultural Outlook Tables, 1970-2014.*

Palgrave Macmillan Ltd., Houndmills, Basingstoke, Hampshire, RG21 6XS, England, (Telephone in U.S. (888) 330-8477), (Fax in U.S. (800) 672-2054), www.palgrave.com; *The Statesman's Yearbook 2008.*

Taylor and Francis Group, An Informa Business, 2 Park Square, Milton Park, Abingdon, Oxford OX14 4RN, United Kingdom, (Dial from U.S. (212) 216-7800), (Fax from U.S. (212) 564-7854), www.tandf.co.uk; *The Europa World Year Book.*

United Nations Food and Agricultural Organization (FAO), Viale delle Terme di Caracalla, 00100 Rome, Italy, (Dial from U.S. (202) 653-2400), (Fax from U.S. (202) 653 5760), www.fao.org; *FAO Production Yearbook 2002* and *The State of Food and Agriculture (SOFA) 2006.*

United Nations Statistics Division, New York, NY 10017, (800) 253-9646, Fax: (212) 963-4116, http://unstats.un.org; *Statistical Yearbook.*

GERMANY - DEATH RATES

See GERMANY - MORTALITY

GERMANY - DEBTS, EXTERNAL

Organisation for Economic Cooperation and Development (OECD), 2 rue Andre Pascal, F-75775 Paris Cedex 16, France, (Telephone in U.S. (202) 785-6323), (Fax in U.S. (202) 785-0350), www.oecd.org; *Financial Market Trends: OECD Periodical; Geographical Distribution of Financial Flows to Aid Recipients 2002-2006;* and *OECD Economic Outlook 2008.*

Palgrave Macmillan Ltd., Houndmills, Basingstoke, Hampshire, RG21 6XS, England, (Telephone in U.S. (888) 330-8477), (Fax in U.S. (800) 672-2054), www.palgrave.com; *The Statesman's Yearbook 2008.*

The World Bank, 1818 H Street, NW, Washington, DC 20433, (202) 473-1000, Fax: (202) 477-6391, www.worldbank.org; *Global Development Finance 2007; World Development Indicators (WDI) 2008;* and *World Development Report 2008.*

GERMANY - DEFENSE EXPENDITURES

See GERMANY - ARMED FORCES

GERMANY - DEMOGRAPHY

Euromonitor International, Inc., 224 S. Michigan Avenue, Suite 1500, Chicago, IL 60604, (312) 922-1115, Fax: (312) 922-1157, www.euromonitor.com; *The World Economic Factbook 2008* and *World Marketing Data and Statistics.*

European Union, Delegation of the European Commission to the United States, 2300 M Street, NW, Washington, DC 20037, (202) 862-9500, Fax: (202) 429-1766, www.eurunion.org; *First Demographic Estimates for 2006* and *Regions - Statistical Yearbook 2006.*

Eurostat, Batiment Jean Monnet, Rue Alcide de Gasperi, L-2920 Luxembourg, http://epp.eurostat.ec.europa.eu; *Demographic Outlook - National Reports on the Demographic Developments in 2006* and *Eurostat Yearbook 2006-2007.*

M.E. Sharpe, 80 Business Park Drive, Armonk, NY 10504, (800) 541-6563, Fax: (914) 273-2106, www.mesharpe.com; *The Illustrated Book of World Rankings.*

United Nations Statistics Division, New York, NY 10017, (800) 253-9646, Fax: (212) 963-4116, http://unstats.un.org; *Human Development Report 2006.*

The World Bank, 1818 H Street, NW, Washington, DC 20433, (202) 473-1000, Fax: (202) 477-6391, www.worldbank.org; *Germany.*

GERMANY - DIAMONDS

See GERMANY - MINERAL INDUSTRIES

GERMANY - DISPOSABLE INCOME

M.E. Sharpe, 80 Business Park Drive, Armonk, NY 10504, (800) 541-6563, Fax: (914) 273-2106, www.mesharpe.com; *The Illustrated Book of World Rankings.*

Organisation for Economic Cooperation and Development (OECD), 2 rue Andre Pascal, F-75775 Paris Cedex 16, France, (Telephone in U.S. (202) 785-6323), (Fax in U.S. (202) 785-0350), www.oecd.org; *OECD Economic Outlook 2008.*

United Nations Statistics Division, New York, NY 10017, (800) 253-9646, Fax: (212) 963-4116, http://unstats.un.org; *National Accounts Statistics: Compendium of Income Distribution Statistics* and *Statistical Yearbook.*

GERMANY - DIVORCE

European Union, Delegation of the European Commission to the United States, 2300 M Street, NW, Washington, DC 20037, (202) 862-9500, Fax: (202) 429-1766, www.eurunion.org; *First Demographic Estimates for 2006.*

M.E. Sharpe, 80 Business Park Drive, Armonk, NY 10504, (800) 541-6563, Fax: (914) 273-2106, www.mesharpe.com; *The Illustrated Book of World Rankings.*

United Nations Statistics Division, New York, NY 10017, (800) 253-9646, Fax: (212) 963-4116, http://

unstats.un.org; *Demographic Yearbook; Statistical Yearbook;* and *Trends in Europe and North America: The Statistical Yearbook of the ECE 2005.*

GERMANY - ECONOMIC ASSISTANCE

European Union, Delegation of the European Commission to the United States, 2300 M Street, NW, Washington, DC 20037, (202) 862-9500, Fax: (202) 429-1766, www.eurunion.org; *RD Expenditure in Europe (2006 edition).*

Eurostat, Batiment Jean Monnet, Rue Alcide de Gasperi, L-2920 Luxembourg, http://epp.eurostat.ec.europa.eu; *Eurostat Yearbook 2006-2007.*

Organisation for Economic Cooperation and Development (OECD), 2 rue Andre Pascal, F-75775 Paris Cedex 16, France, (Telephone in U.S. (202) 785-6323), (Fax in U.S. (202) 785-0350), www.oecd.org; *Geographical Distribution of Financial Flows to Aid Recipients 2002-2006.*

United Nations Statistics Division, New York, NY 10017, (800) 253-9646, Fax: (212) 963-4116, http://unstats.un.org; *Statistical Yearbook.*

The World Bank, 1818 H Street, NW, Washington, DC 20433, (202) 473-1000, Fax: (202) 477-6391, www.worldbank.org; *Germany.*

GERMANY - ECONOMIC CONDITIONS

Banque de France, 48 rue Croix des Petits champs, 75001 Paris, France, www.banque-france.fr/home.htm; *Key Data for the Euro Area.*

Center for International Business Education Research (CIBER), Columbia Business School and School of International and Public Affairs, Uris Hall, Room 212, 3022 Broadway, New York, NY 10027-6902, Mr. Joshua Safier, (212) 854-4750, Fax: (212) 222-9821, www.columbia.edu/cu/ciber/; Datastream International.

Central Intelligence Agency, Office of Public Affairs, Washington, DC 20505, (703) 482-0623, Fax: (703) 482-1739, www.cia.gov; *The World Factbook.*

DSI Data Service Information, Xantener Strasse 51a, D-47495 Rheinberg, Germany, www.dsidata.com; *Campus Solution.*

Dun and Bradstreet (DB) Corporation, 103 JFK Parkway, Short Hills, NJ 07078, (973) 921-5500, www.dnb.com; *Country Report.*

Economist Intelligence Unit, 111 West 57th Street, New York, NY 10019, (212) 554-0600, Fax: (212) 586-1181, www.eiu.com; *Germany Country Report.*

Euromonitor International, Inc., 224 S. Michigan Avenue, Suite 1500, Chicago, IL 60604, (312) 922-1115, Fax: (312) 922-1157, www.euromonitor.com; *European Marketing Data and Statistics 2008; The World Economic Factbook 2008;* and *World Marketing Data and Statistics.*

European Union, Delegation of the European Commission to the United States, 2300 M Street, NW, Washington, DC 20037, (202) 862-9500, Fax: (202) 429-1766, www.eurunion.org; *The EU Economy, 2007 Review: Moving Europe's Productivity Frontier* and *European Union Labour Force Survey.*

Eurostat, Batiment Jean Monnet, Rue Alcide de Gasperi, L-2920 Luxembourg, http://epp.eurostat.ec.europa.eu; *Consumers in Europe - Facts and Figures on Services of General Interest; EU Economic Data Pocketbook;* and *Eurostat Yearbook 2006-2007.*

International Monetary Fund (IMF), 700 Nineteenth Street, NW, Washington, DC 20431, (202) 623-7000, Fax: (202) 623-4661, www.imf.org; *World Economic Outlook Reports.*

M.E. Sharpe, 80 Business Park Drive, Armonk, NY 10504, (800) 541-6563, Fax: (914) 273-2106, www.mesharpe.com; *The Illustrated Book of World Rankings.*

Organisation for Economic Cooperation and Development (OECD), 2 rue Andre Pascal, F-75775 Paris Cedex 16, France, (Telephone in U.S. (202) 785-6323), (Fax in U.S. (202) 785-0350), www.oecd.org; *Geographical Distribution of Financial Flows to Aid Recipients 2002-2006; ICT Sector Data and Metadata by Country; Labour Force Statistics: 1986-2005, 2007 Edition; OECD Composite Leading Indicators (CLIs), Updated September 2007; OECD Economic Outlook 2008; OECD Economic Survey - Germany 2008; OECD Employment Outlook 2007; OECD in Figures 2007;* and *OECD Main Economic Indicators (MEI).*

Palgrave Macmillan Ltd., Houndmills, Basingstoke, Hampshire, RG21 6XS, England, (Telephone in U.S. (888) 330-8477), (Fax in U.S. (800) 672-2054), www.palgrave.com; *The Statesman's Yearbook 2008.*

Platts, 2 Penn Plaza, 25th Floor, New York, NY 10121-2298, (212) 904-3070, www.platts.com; *Energy Economist.*

Taylor and Francis Group, An Informa Business, 2 Park Square, Milton Park, Abingdon, Oxford OX14 4RN, United Kingdom, (Dial from U.S. (212) 216-7800), (Fax from U.S. (212) 564-7854), www.tandf.co.uk; *The Europa World Year Book.*

United Nations Statistics Division, New York, NY 10017, (800) 253-9646, Fax: (212) 963-4116, http://unstats.un.org; *Energy Statistics Yearbook 2003* and *World Statistics Pocketbook.*

The World Bank, 1818 H Street, NW, Washington, DC 20433, (202) 473-1000, Fax: (202) 477-6391, www.worldbank.org; *Global Economic Monitor (GEM); Global Economic Prospects 2008; The World Bank Atlas 2003-2004;* and *World Development Report 2008.*

GERMANY - ECONOMICS - SOCIOLOGICAL ASPECTS

Eurostat, Batiment Jean Monnet, Rue Alcide de Gasperi, L-2920 Luxembourg, http://epp.eurostat.ec.europa.eu; *Eurostat Yearbook 2006-2007.*

Organisation for Economic Cooperation and Development (OECD), 2 rue Andre Pascal, F-75775 Paris Cedex 16, France, (Telephone in U.S. (202) 785-6323), (Fax in U.S. (202) 785-0350), www.oecd.org; *OECD Economic Outlook 2008.*

GERMANY - EDUCATION

Euromonitor International, Inc., 224 S. Michigan Avenue, Suite 1500, Chicago, IL 60604, (312) 922-1115, Fax: (312) 922-1157, www.euromonitor.com; *European Marketing Data and Statistics 2008* and *World Marketing Data and Statistics.*

European Union, Delegation of the European Commission to the United States, 2300 M Street, NW, Washington, DC 20037, (202) 862-9500, Fax: (202) 429-1766, www.eurunion.org; *Education across Europe 2003* and *Regions - Statistical Yearbook 2006.*

Eurostat, Batiment Jean Monnet, Rue Alcide de Gasperi, L-2920 Luxembourg, http://epp.eurostat.ec.europa.eu; *Education, Science and Culture Statistics* and *Eurostat Yearbook 2006-2007.*

M.E. Sharpe, 80 Business Park Drive, Armonk, NY 10504, (800) 541-6563, Fax: (914) 273-2106, www.mesharpe.com; *The Illustrated Book of World Rankings.*

Organisation for Economic Cooperation and Development (OECD), 2 rue Andre Pascal, F-75775 Paris Cedex 16, France, (Telephone in U.S. (202) 785-6323), (Fax in U.S. (202) 785-0350), www.oecd.org; *Education at a Glance* (2007 Edition).

Taylor and Francis Group, An Informa Business, 2 Park Square, Milton Park, Abingdon, Oxford OX14 4RN, United Kingdom, (Dial from U.S. (212) 216-7800), (Fax from U.S. (212) 564-7854), www.tandf.co.uk; *The Europa World Year Book.*

UNESCO Institute for Statistics, C.P. 6128 Succursale Centre-Ville, Montreal, Quebec, H3C 3J7 Canada, (Dial from U.S. (514) 343-6880), (Fax from U.S. (514) 343 6882), www.uis.unesco.org; *Statistical Tables.*

United Nations Statistics Division, New York, NY 10017, (800) 253-9646, Fax: (212) 963-4116, http://unstats.un.org; *Human Development Report 2006* and *Trends in Europe and North America: The Statistical Yearbook of the ECE 2005.*

The World Bank, 1818 H Street, NW, Washington, DC 20433, (202) 473-1000, Fax: (202) 477-6391, www.worldbank.org; *Germany; World Development Indicators (WDI) 2008;* and *World Development Report 2008.*

GERMANY - ELECTRICITY

European Union, Delegation of the European Commission to the United States, 2300 M Street, NW, Washington, DC 20037, (202) 862-9500, Fax: (202) 429-1766, www.eurunion.org; *European Union Energy Transport in Figures 2006; Eurostatistics: Data for Short-Term Economic Analysis (2007 edition);* and *Regions - Statistical Yearbook 2006.*

Eurostat, Batiment Jean Monnet, Rue Alcide de Gasperi, L-2920 Luxembourg, http://epp.eurostat.ec.europa.eu; *Energy - Monthly Statistics; Eurostat Yearbook 2006-2007;* and *Panorama of Energy - 2007 Edition.*

M.E. Sharpe, 80 Business Park Drive, Armonk, NY 10504, (800) 541-6563, Fax: (914) 273-2106, www.mesharpe.com; *The Illustrated Book of World Rankings.*

Organisation for Economic Cooperation and Development (OECD), 2 rue Andre Pascal, F-75775 Paris Cedex 16, France, (Telephone in U.S. (202) 785-6323), (Fax in U.S. (202) 785-0350), www.oecd.org; *Coal Information: 2007 Edition; Energy Statistics of OECD Countries* (2007 Edition); *Indicators of Industrial Activity;* STructural ANalysis (STAN) database; and *World Energy Outlook 2007.*

Palgrave Macmillan Ltd., Houndmills, Basingstoke, Hampshire, RG21 6XS, England, (Telephone in U.S. (888) 330-8477), (Fax in U.S. (800) 672-2054), www.palgrave.com; *The Statesman's Yearbook 2008.*

Platts, 2 Penn Plaza, 25th Floor, New York, NY 10121-2298, (212) 904-3070, www.platts.com; *Energy Economist; EU Energy;* and *European Electricity Review 2004.*

U.S. Department of Energy (DOE), Energy Information Administration (EIA), 1000 Independence Avenue, SW, Washington, DC 20585, (202) 586-8800, www.eia.doe.gov; *International Energy Annual 2004* and *International Energy Outlook 2006.*

United Nations Statistics Division, New York, NY 10017, (800) 253-9646, Fax: (212) 963-4116, http://unstats.un.org; *Energy Statistics Yearbook 2003; Human Development Report 2006; Statistical Yearbook;* and *Trends in Europe and North America: The Statistical Yearbook of the ECE 2005.*

GERMANY - EMPLOYMENT

Bernan Essential Government Publications, 4611-F Assembly Drive, Lanham MD, 20706-4391, (301) 459-2255, Fax: (800) 865-3450, www.bernan.com; *OECD Factbook 2006.*

Euromonitor International, Inc., 224 S. Michigan Avenue, Suite 1500, Chicago, IL 60604, (312) 922-1115, Fax: (312) 922-1157, www.euromonitor.com; *European Marketing Data and Statistics 2008.*

European Union, Delegation of the European Commission to the United States, 2300 M Street, NW, Washington, DC 20037, (202) 862-9500, Fax: (202) 429-1766, www.eurunion.org; *Agriculture in the European Union: Statistical and Economic Information 2006; European Union Labour Force Survey; Eurostatistics: Data for Short-Term Economic Analysis (2007 edition); Iron and Steel;* and *Statistical Overview of Transport in the European Union (Data 1970-2001).*

Eurostat, Batiment Jean Monnet, Rue Alcide de Gasperi, L-2920 Luxembourg, http://epp.eurostat.ec.europa.eu; *Eurostat Yearbook 2006-2007.*

International Labour Office, I.L.O. Publications, 4 route des Morillons, CH-1211 Geneva 22, Switzerland, (Telephone in U.S. (202) 653-7652), (Fax in U.S. (202) 653-7687), www.ilo.org; *Yearbook of Labour Statistics 2006.*

M.E. Sharpe, 80 Business Park Drive, Armonk, NY 10504, (800) 541-6563, Fax: (914) 273-2106, www.mesharpe.com; *The Illustrated Book of World Rankings.*

Organisation for Economic Cooperation and Development (OECD), 2 rue Andre Pascal, F-75775 Paris Cedex 16, France, (Telephone in U.S. (202) 785-6323), (Fax in U.S. (202) 785-0350), www.oecd.org; *ICT Sector Data and Metadata by Country; Iron and Steel Industry in 2004 (2006 Edition); Labour Force Statistics: 1986-2005, 2007 Edition; OECD Composite Leading Indicators (CLIs), Updated September 2007; OECD Economic Outlook 2008; OECD Economic Survey - Germany 2008; OECD Employment Outlook 2007;* and *OECD in Figures 2007.*

United Nations Statistics Division, New York, NY 10017, (800) 253-9646, Fax: (212) 963-4116, http://unstats.un.org; *Statistical Yearbook* and *Trends in Europe and North America: The Statistical Yearbook of the ECE 2005.*

The World Bank, 1818 H Street, NW, Washington, DC 20433, (202) 473-1000, Fax: (202) 477-6391, www.worldbank.org; *Germany.*

GERMANY - ENERGY INDUSTRIES

Enerdata, 10 Rue Royale, 75008 Paris, France, www.enerdata.fr; *Global Energy Market Data.*

Eurostat, Batiment Jean Monnet, Rue Alcide de Gasperi, L-2920 Luxembourg, http://epp.eurostat.ec.europa.eu; *Energy - Monthly Statistics; Eurostat Yearbook 2006-2007;* and *Panorama of Energy - 2007 Edition.*

International Energy Agency (IEA), 9, rue de la Federation, 75739 Paris Cedex 15, France, www.iea.org; *Key World Energy Statistics 2007.*

Organisation for Economic Cooperation and Development (OECD), 2 rue Andre Pascal, F-75775 Paris Cedex 16, France, (Telephone in U.S. (202) 785-6323), (Fax in U.S. (202) 785-0350), www.oecd.org; *Towards Sustainable Household Consumption?: Trends and Policies in OECD Countries.*

Platts, 2 Penn Plaza, 25th Floor, New York, NY 10121-2298, (212) 904-3070, www.platts.com; *EU Energy* and *European Power Daily.*

United Nations Statistics Division, New York, NY 10017, (800) 253-9646, Fax: (212) 963-4116, http://unstats.un.org; *Statistical Yearbook.*

GERMANY - ENVIRONMENTAL CONDITIONS

Center for Research on the Epidemiology of Disasters (CRED), Universite Catholique de Louvain, Ecole de Sante Publique, 30.94 Clos Chapelle-aux-Champs, 1200 Brussels, Belgium, www.cred.be; *Three Decades of Floods in Europe: A Preliminary Analysis of EMDAT Data.*

DSI Data Service Information, Xantener Strasse 51a, D-47495 Rheinberg, Germany, www.dsidata.com; *Campus Solution* and *DSI's Global Environmental Database.*

Economist Intelligence Unit, 111 West 57th Street, New York, NY 10019, (212) 554-0600, Fax: (212) 586-1181, www.eiu.com; *Germany Country Report.*

Eurostat, Batiment Jean Monnet, Rue Alcide de Gasperi, L-2920 Luxembourg, http://epp.eurostat.ec.europa.eu; *Environmental Protection Expenditure in Europe.*

Organisation for Economic Cooperation and Development (OECD), 2 rue Andre Pascal, F-75775 Paris Cedex 16, France, (Telephone in U.S. (202) 785-6323), (Fax in U.S. (202) 785-0350), www.oecd.org; *Key Environmental Indicators 2004.*

Platts, 2 Penn Plaza, 25th Floor, New York, NY 10121-2298, (212) 904-3070, www.platts.com; *Emissions Daily.*

United Nations Statistics Division, New York, NY 10017, (800) 253-9646, Fax: (212) 963-4116, http://unstats.un.org; *Trends in Europe and North America: The Statistical Yearbook of the ECE 2005* and *World Statistics Pocketbook.*

GERMANY - EXPENDITURES, PUBLIC

Eurostat, Batiment Jean Monnet, Rue Alcide de Gasperi, L-2920 Luxembourg, http://epp.eurostat.ec.europa.eu; *European Social Statistics - Social Protection Expenditure and Receipts - Data 1997-2005* and *Eurostat Yearbook 2006-2007.*

Organisation for Economic Cooperation and Development (OECD), 2 rue Andre Pascal, F-75775 Paris Cedex 16, France, (Telephone in U.S. (202) 785-6323), (Fax in U.S. (202) 785-0350), www.oecd.org; *Revenue Statistics 1965-2006 - 2007 Edition.*

GERMANY - EXPORTS

Central Intelligence Agency, Office of Public Affairs, Washington, DC 20505, (703) 482-0623, Fax: (703) 482-1739, www.cia.gov; *The World Factbook.*

Economist Intelligence Unit, 111 West 57th Street, New York, NY 10019, (212) 554-0600, Fax: (212) 586-1181, www.eiu.com; *Germany Country Report.*

Euromonitor International, Inc., 224 S. Michigan Avenue, Suite 1500, Chicago, IL 60604, (312) 922-1115, Fax: (312) 922-1157, www.euromonitor.com; *The World Economic Factbook 2008.*

European Union, Delegation of the European Commission to the United States, 2300 M Street, NW, Washington, DC 20037, (202) 862-9500, Fax: (202) 429-1766, www.eurunion.org; *European Union Energy Transport in Figures 2006; Eurostatistics: Data for Short-Term Economic Analysis (2007 edition); External and Intra-European Union Trade: Data 1958-2002; External and Intra-European Union Trade: Data 1999-2004;* and *Fishery Statistics - 1990-2006.*

Eurostat, Batiment Jean Monnet, Rue Alcide de Gasperi, L-2920 Luxembourg, http://epp.eurostat.ec.europa.eu; *Eurostat Yearbook 2006-2007.*

International Iron and Steel Institute (IISI), Rue Colonel Bourg 120, B-1140 Brussels, Belgium, www.worldsteel.org; *Steel Statistical Yearbook 2006.*

International Lead and Zinc Study Group (ILZSG), Rua Almirante Barroso 38, 5th Floor, Lisbon 1000 - 013, Portugal, www.ilzsg.org; Interactive Statistical Database.

International Monetary Fund (IMF), 700 Nineteenth Street, NW, Washington, DC 20431, (202) 623-7000, Fax: (202) 623-4661, www.imf.org; *Direction of Trade Statistics Yearbook 2007.*

Organisation for Economic Cooperation and Development (OECD), 2 rue Andre Pascal, F-75775 Paris Cedex 16, France, (Telephone in U.S. (202) 785-6323), (Fax in U.S. (202) 785-0350), www.oecd.org; *Geographical Distribution of Financial Flows to Aid Recipients 2002-2006; International Trade by Commodity Statistics (ITCS); Iron and Steel Industry in 2004 (2006 Edition); 2005 OECD Agricultural Outlook Tables, 1970-2014; OECD Economic Outlook 2008; OECD Economic Survey - Germany 2008; Review of Fisheries in OECD Countries: Country Statistics 2001 to 2003 - 2005 Edition;* and STructural ANalysis (STAN) database.

Palgrave Macmillan Ltd., Houndmills, Basingstoke, Hampshire, RG21 6XS, England, (Telephone in U.S. (888) 330-8477), (Fax in U.S. (800) 672-2054), www.palgrave.com; *The Statesman's Yearbook 2008.*

Platts, 2 Penn Plaza, 25th Floor, New York, NY 10121-2298, (212) 904-3070, www.platts.com; *Energy Economist.*

Taylor and Francis Group, An Informa Business, 2 Park Square, Milton Park, Abingdon, Oxford OX14 4RN, United Kingdom, (Dial from U.S. (212) 216-7800), (Fax from U.S. (212) 564-7854), www.tandf.co.uk; *The Europa World Year Book.*

Technical Association of the Pulp and Paper Industry (TAPPI), 15 Technology Parkway South, Norcross, GA 30092, (770) 446-1400, Fax: (770) 446-6947, www.tappi.org; *TAPPI Annual Report.*

UNICEF, 3 United Nations Plaza, New York, NY 10017, (800) 253-9646, Fax: (212) 887-7465, www.unicef.org; *The State of the World's Children 2008.*

United Nations Food and Agricultural Organization (FAO), Viale delle Terme di Caracalla, 00100 Rome, Italy, (Dial from U.S. (202) 653-2400), (Fax from U.S. (202) 653 5760), www.fao.org; *The State of Food and Agriculture (SOFA) 2006.*

United Nations Statistics Division, New York, NY 10017, (800) 253-9646, Fax: (212) 963-4116, http://unstats.un.org; *Energy Statistics Yearbook 2003* and *Trends in Europe and North America: The Statistical Yearbook of the ECE 2005.*

The World Bank, 1818 H Street, NW, Washington, DC 20433, (202) 473-1000, Fax: (202) 477-6391, www.worldbank.org; *World Development Indicators (WDI) 2008* and *World Development Report 2008.*

GERMANY - FEMALE WORKING POPULATION

See GERMANY - EMPLOYMENT

GERMANY - FERTILITY, HUMAN

Central Intelligence Agency, Office of Public Affairs, Washington, DC 20505, (703) 482-0623, Fax: (703) 482-1739, www.cia.gov; *The World Factbook.*

European Union, Delegation of the European Commission to the United States, 2300 M Street, NW, Washington, DC 20037, (202) 862-9500, Fax: (202) 429-1766, www.eurunion.org; *First Demographic Estimates for 2006.*

M.E. Sharpe, 80 Business Park Drive, Armonk, NY 10504, (800) 541-6563, Fax: (914) 273-2106, www.mesharpe.com; *The Illustrated Book of World Rankings.*

United Nations Statistics Division, New York, NY 10017, (800) 253-9646, Fax: (212) 963-4116, http://unstats.un.org; *Human Development Report 2006* and *Trends in Europe and North America: The Statistical Yearbook of the ECE 2005.*

The World Bank, 1818 H Street, NW, Washington, DC 20433, (202) 473-1000, Fax: (202) 477-6391, www.worldbank.org; *The World Bank Atlas 2003-2004; World Development Indicators (WDI) 2008;* and *World Development Report 2008.*

GERMANY - FERTILIZER INDUSTRY

Eurostat, Batiment Jean Monnet, Rue Alcide de Gasperi, L-2920 Luxembourg, http://epp.eurostat.ec.europa.eu; *Eurostat Yearbook 2006-2007.*

Organisation for Economic Cooperation and Development (OECD), 2 rue Andre Pascal, F-75775 Paris Cedex 16, France, (Telephone in U.S. (202) 785-6323), (Fax in U.S. (202) 785-0350), www.oecd.org; *International Trade by Commodity Statistics (ITCS)* and *2005 OECD Agricultural Outlook Tables, 1970-2014.*

United Nations Food and Agricultural Organization (FAO), Viale delle Terme di Caracalla, 00100 Rome, Italy, (Dial from U.S. (202) 653-2400), (Fax from U.S. (202) 653 5760), www.fao.org; *The State of Food and Agriculture (SOFA) 2006.*

United Nations Statistics Division, New York, NY 10017, (800) 253-9646, Fax: (212) 963-4116, http://unstats.un.org; *Statistical Yearbook.*

GERMANY - FETAL MORTALITY

See GERMANY - MORTALITY

GERMANY - FILM

See GERMANY - MOTION PICTURES

GERMANY - FINANCE

European Union, Delegation of the European Commission to the United States, 2300 M Street, NW, Washington, DC 20037, (202) 862-9500, Fax: (202) 429-1766, www.eurunion.org; *Eurostatistics: Data for Short-Term Economic Analysis (2007 edition).*

Eurostat, Batiment Jean Monnet, Rue Alcide de Gasperi, L-2920 Luxembourg, http://epp.eurostat.ec.europa.eu; *Eurostat Yearbook 2006-2007.*

International Monetary Fund (IMF), 700 Nineteenth Street, NW, Washington, DC 20431, (202) 623-7000, Fax: (202) 623-4661, www.imf.org; *International Financial Statistics Yearbook 2007.*

Organisation for Economic Cooperation and Development (OECD), 2 rue Andre Pascal, F-75775 Paris Cedex 16, France, (Telephone in U.S. (202) 785-

6323), (Fax in U.S. (202) 785-0350), www.oecd.org; *OECD Economic Outlook 2008.*

Taylor and Francis Group, An Informa Business, 2 Park Square, Milton Park, Abingdon, Oxford OX14 4RN, United Kingdom, (Dial from U.S. (212) 216-7800), (Fax from U.S. (212) 564-7854), www.tandf.co.uk; *The Europa World Year Book.*

United Nations Statistics Division, New York, NY 10017, (800) 253-9646, Fax: (212) 963-4116, http://unstats.un.org; *National Accounts Statistics: Compendium of Income Distribution Statistics* and *Statistical Yearbook.*

The World Bank, 1818 H Street, NW, Washington, DC 20433, (202) 473-1000, Fax: (202) 477-6391, www.worldbank.org; *Germany.*

GERMANY - FINANCE, PUBLIC

Banque de France, 48 rue Croix des Petits champs, 75001 Paris, France, www.banque-france.fr/home.htm; *Key Data for the Euro Area* and *Public Finance.*

Bernan Essential Government Publications, 4611-F Assembly Drive, Lanham MD, 20706-4391, (301) 459-2255, Fax: (800) 865-3450, www.bernan.com; *National Accounts Statistics.*

Economist Intelligence Unit, 111 West 57th Street, New York, NY 10019, (212) 554-0600, Fax: (212) 586-1181, www.eiu.com; *Germany Country Report.*

European Union, Delegation of the European Commission to the United States, 2300 M Street, NW, Washington, DC 20037, (202) 862-9500, Fax: (202) 429-1766, www.eurunion.org; *Eurostatistics: Data for Short-Term Economic Analysis (2007 edition).*

Eurostat, Batiment Jean Monnet, Rue Alcide de Gasperi, L-2920 Luxembourg, http://epp.eurostat.ec.europa.eu; *Eurostat Yearbook 2006-2007.*

International Monetary Fund (IMF), 700 Nineteenth Street, NW, Washington, DC 20431, (202) 623-7000, Fax: (202) 623-4661, www.imf.org; *International Financial Statistics* and *International Financial Statistics Online Service.*

M.E. Sharpe, 80 Business Park Drive, Armonk, NY 10504, (800) 541-6563, Fax: (914) 273-2106, www.mesharpe.com; *The Illustrated Book of World Rankings.*

Organisation for Economic Cooperation and Development (OECD), 2 rue Andre Pascal, F-75775 Paris Cedex 16, France, (Telephone in U.S. (202) 785-6323), (Fax in U.S. (202) 785-0350), www.oecd.org; *Financial Market Trends: OECD Periodical; Geographical Distribution of Financial Flows to Aid Recipients 2002-2006; OECD Economic Outlook 2008; OECD Main Economic Indicators (MEI);* and *Revenue Statistics 1965-2006 - 2007 Edition.*

Palgrave Macmillan Ltd., Houndmills, Basingstoke, Hampshire, RG21 6XS, England, (Telephone in U.S. (888) 330-8477), (Fax in U.S. (800) 672-2054), www.palgrave.com; *The Statesman's Yearbook 2008.*

Taylor and Francis Group, An Informa Business, 2 Park Square, Milton Park, Abingdon, Oxford OX14 4RN, United Kingdom, (Dial from U.S. (212) 216-7800), (Fax from U.S. (212) 564-7854), www.tandf.co.uk; *The Europa World Year Book.*

GERMANY - FISHERIES

Euromonitor International, Inc., 224 S. Michigan Avenue, Suite 1500, Chicago, IL 60604, (312) 922-1115, Fax: (312) 922-1157, www.euromonitor.com; *European Marketing Data and Statistics 2008.*

European Union, Delegation of the European Commission to the United States, 2300 M Street, NW, Washington, DC 20037, (202) 862-9500, Fax: (202) 429-1766, www.eurunion.org; *Agricultural Statistics: Data 1995-2005* and *Fishery Statistics - 1990-2006.*

Eurostat, Batiment Jean Monnet, Rue Alcide de Gasperi, L-2920 Luxembourg, http://epp.eurostat.ec.europa.eu; *Eurostat Yearbook 2006-2007.*

M.E. Sharpe, 80 Business Park Drive, Armonk, NY 10504, (800) 541-6563, Fax: (914) 273-2106, www.mesharpe.com; *The Illustrated Book of World Rankings.*

Organisation for Economic Cooperation and Development (OECD), 2 rue Andre Pascal, F-75775 Paris Cedex 16, France, (Telephone in U.S. (202) 785-6323), (Fax in U.S. (202) 785-0350), www.oecd.org; *International Trade by Commodity Statistics (ITCS); Review of Fisheries in OECD Countries: Country Statistics 2001 to 2003 - 2005 Edition;* and STructural ANalysis (STAN) database.

Palgrave Macmillan Ltd., Houndmills, Basingstoke, Hampshire, RG21 6XS, England, (Telephone in U.S. (888) 330-8477), (Fax in U.S. (800) 672-2054), www.palgrave.com; *The Statesman's Yearbook 2008.*

Taylor and Francis Group, An Informa Business, 2 Park Square, Milton Park, Abingdon, Oxford OX14 4RN, United Kingdom, (Dial from U.S. (212) 216-7800), (Fax from U.S. (212) 564-7854), www.tandf.co.uk; *The Europa World Year Book.*

United Nations Conference on Trade and Development (UNCTAD), DC2-1120, United Nations, New York, NY 10017, (212) 963-0027, www.unctad.org; *UNCTAD Commodity Yearbook.*

United Nations Food and Agricultural Organization (FAO), Viale delle Terme di Caracalla, 00100 Rome, Italy, (Dial from U.S. (202) 653-2400), (Fax from U.S. (202) 653 5760), www.fao.org; *FAO Yearbook of Fishery Statistics;* Fishery Databases; FISHSTAT Database. Subjects covered include: Aquaculture production, capture production, fishery commodities; and *The State of Food and Agriculture (SOFA) 2006.*

United Nations Statistics Division, New York, NY 10017, (800) 253-9646, Fax: (212) 963-4116, http://unstats.un.org; *Statistical Yearbook.*

The World Bank, 1818 H Street, NW, Washington, DC 20433, (202) 473-1000, Fax: (202) 477-6391, www.worldbank.org; *Germany.*

GERMANY - FLOUR INDUSTRY

Eurostat, Batiment Jean Monnet, Rue Alcide de Gasperi, L-2920 Luxembourg, http://epp.eurostat.ec.europa.eu; *Eurostat Yearbook 2006-2007.*

United Nations Statistics Division, New York, NY 10017, (800) 253-9646, Fax: (212) 963-4116, http://unstats.un.org; *Statistical Yearbook.*

GERMANY - FOOD

Euromonitor International, Inc., 224 S. Michigan Avenue, Suite 1500, Chicago, IL 60604, (312) 922-1115, Fax: (312) 922-1157, www.euromonitor.com; *Retail Trade International 2007.*

Eurostat, Batiment Jean Monnet, Rue Alcide de Gasperi, L-2920 Luxembourg, http://epp.eurostat.ec.europa.eu; *Eurostat Yearbook 2006-2007.*

Organisation for Economic Cooperation and Development (OECD), 2 rue Andre Pascal, F-75775 Paris Cedex 16, France, (Telephone in U.S. (202) 785-6323), (Fax in U.S. (202) 785-0350), www.oecd.org; *International Trade by Commodity Statistics (ITCS)* and *Towards Sustainable Household Consumption?: Trends and Policies in OECD Countries.*

United Nations Conference on Trade and Development (UNCTAD), DC2-1120, United Nations, New York, NY 10017, (212) 963-0027, www.unctad.org; *UNCTAD Commodity Yearbook.*

United Nations Food and Agricultural Organization (FAO), Viale delle Terme di Caracalla, 00100 Rome, Italy, (Dial from U.S. (202) 653-2400), (Fax from U.S. (202) 653 5760), www.fao.org; *FAO Production Yearbook 2002* and *The State of Food and Agriculture (SOFA) 2006.*

United Nations Statistics Division, New York, NY 10017, (800) 253-9646, Fax: (212) 963-4116, http://unstats.un.org; *Human Development Report 2006.*

GERMANY - FOOTWEAR

Organisation for Economic Cooperation and Development (OECD), 2 rue Andre Pascal, F-75775 Paris Cedex 16, France, (Telephone in U.S. (202) 785-6323), (Fax in U.S. (202) 785-0350), www.oecd.org; *Indicators of Industrial Activity.*

GERMANY - FOREIGN EXCHANGE RATES

Central Intelligence Agency, Office of Public Affairs, Washington, DC 20505, (703) 482-0623, Fax: (703) 482-1739, www.cia.gov; *The World Factbook.*

Euromonitor International, Inc., 224 S. Michigan Avenue, Suite 1500, Chicago, IL 60604, (312) 922-1115, Fax: (312) 922-1157, www.euromonitor.com; *The World Economic Factbook 2008.*

European Union, Delegation of the European Commission to the United States, 2300 M Street, NW, Washington, DC 20037, (202) 862-9500, Fax: (202) 429-1766, www.eurunion.org; *Eurostatistics: Data for Short-Term Economic Analysis (2007 edition).*

Eurostat, Batiment Jean Monnet, Rue Alcide de Gasperi, L-2920 Luxembourg, http://epp.eurostat.ec.europa.eu; *Eurostat Yearbook 2006-2007.*

International Civil Aviation Organization (ICAO), External Relations and Public Information Office (EPO), 999 University Street, Montreal, Quebec H3C 5H7, Canada, (Dial from U.S. (514) 954-8219), (Fax from U.S. (514) 954-6077), www.icao.int; *Civil Aviation Statistics of the World.*

International Monetary Fund (IMF), 700 Nineteenth Street, NW, Washington, DC 20431, (202) 623-7000, Fax: (202) 623-4661, www.imf.org; *International Financial Statistics Yearbook 2007.*

Organisation for Economic Cooperation and Development (OECD), 2 rue Andre Pascal, F-75775 Paris Cedex 16, France, (Telephone in U.S. (202) 785-6323), (Fax in U.S. (202) 785-0350), www.oecd.org; *Financial Market Trends: OECD Periodical; Household, Tourism, Travel: Trends, Environmental Impacts and Policy Responses; OECD Economic Outlook 2008;* and *Revenue Statistics 1965-2006 - 2007 Edition.*

Taylor and Francis Group, An Informa Business, 2 Park Square, Milton Park, Abingdon, Oxford OX14 4RN, United Kingdom, (Dial from U.S. (212) 216-7800), (Fax from U.S. (212) 564-7854), www.tandf.co.uk; *The Europa World Year Book.*

United Nations Statistics Division, New York, NY 10017, (800) 253-9646, Fax: (212) 963-4116, http://unstats.un.org; *Statistical Yearbook; Trends in Europe and North America: The Statistical Yearbook of the ECE 2005;* and *World Statistics Pocketbook.*

GERMANY - FORESTS AND FORESTRY

American Forest Paper Association (AFPA), 1111 Nineteenth Street, NW, Suite 800, Washington, DC 20036, (800) 878-8878, www.afandpa.org; *2007 Annual Statistics of Paper, Paperboard, and Wood Pulp.*

Euromonitor International, Inc., 224 S. Michigan Avenue, Suite 1500, Chicago, IL 60604, (312) 922-1115, Fax: (312) 922-1157, www.euromonitor.com; *European Marketing Data and Statistics 2008.*

European Union, Delegation of the European Commission to the United States, 2300 M Street, NW, Washington, DC 20037, (202) 862-9500, Fax: (202) 429-1766, www.eurunion.org; *Agricultural Statistics: Data 1995-2005.*

Eurostat, Batiment Jean Monnet, Rue Alcide de Gasperi, L-2920 Luxembourg, http://epp.eurostat.ec.europa.eu; *Eurostat Yearbook 2006-2007.*

M.E. Sharpe, 80 Business Park Drive, Armonk, NY 10504, (800) 541-6563, Fax: (914) 273-2106, www.mesharpe.com; *The Illustrated Book of World Rankings.*

Organisation for Economic Cooperation and Development (OECD), 2 rue Andre Pascal, F-75775 Paris Cedex 16, France, (Telephone in U.S. (202) 785-6323), (Fax in U.S. (202) 785-0350), www.oecd.org; *Indicators of Industrial Activity; International Trade by Commodity Statistics (ITCS);* and STructural ANalysis (STAN) database.

Palgrave Macmillan Ltd., Houndmills, Basingstoke, Hampshire, RG21 6XS, England, (Telephone in U.S. (888) 330-8477), (Fax in U.S. (800) 672-2054), www.palgrave.com; *The Statesman's Yearbook 2008.*

Taylor and Francis Group, An Informa Business, 2 Park Square, Milton Park, Abingdon, Oxford OX14 4RN, United Kingdom, (Dial from U.S. (212) 216-7800), (Fax from U.S. (212) 564-7854), www.tandf.co.uk; *The Europa World Year Book.*

Technical Association of the Pulp and Paper Industry (TAPPI), 15 Technology Parkway South, Norcross, GA 30092, (770) 446-1400, Fax: (770) 446-6947, www.tappi.org; *TAPPI Annual Report.*

UNESCO Institute for Statistics, C.P. 6128 Succursale Centre-Ville, Montreal, Quebec, H3C 3J7 Canada, (Dial from U.S. (514) 343-6880), (Fax from U.S. (514) 343 6882), www.uis.unesco.org; *Statistical Tables.*

United Nations Conference on Trade and Development (UNCTAD), DC2-1120, United Nations, New York, NY 10017, (212) 963-0027, www.unctad.org; *UNCTAD Commodity Yearbook.*

United Nations Food and Agricultural Organization (FAO), Viale delle Terme di Caracalla, 00100 Rome, Italy, (Dial from U.S. (202) 653-2400), (Fax from U.S. (202) 653 5760), www.fao.org; *FAO Yearbook of Forest Products* and *The State of Food and Agriculture (SOFA) 2006.*

United Nations Statistics Division, New York, NY 10017, (800) 253-9646, Fax: (212) 963-4116, http://unstats.un.org; *Statistical Yearbook* and *Trends in Europe and North America: The Statistical Yearbook of the ECE 2005.*

The World Bank, 1818 H Street, NW, Washington, DC 20433, (202) 473-1000, Fax: (202) 477-6391, www.worldbank.org; *Germany* and *World Development Report 2008.*

GERMANY - FRUIT PRODUCTION

See GERMANY - CROPS

GERMANY - GAS PRODUCTION

See GERMANY - MINERAL INDUSTRIES

GERMANY - GEOGRAPHIC INFORMATION SYSTEMS

Eurostat, Batiment Jean Monnet, Rue Alcide de Gasperi, L-2920 Luxembourg, http://epp.eurostat.ec.europa.eu; *Eurostat Yearbook 2006-2007.*

M.E. Sharpe, 80 Business Park Drive, Armonk, NY 10504, (800) 541-6563, Fax: (914) 273-2106, www.mesharpe.com; *The Illustrated Book of World Rankings.*

GERMANY - GLASS TRADE

Organisation for Economic Cooperation and Development (OECD), 2 rue Andre Pascal, F-75775 Paris Cedex 16, France, (Telephone in U.S. (202) 785-6323), (Fax in U.S. (202) 785-0350), www.oecd.org; *Indicators of Industrial Activity.*

GERMANY - GOLD INDUSTRY

International Monetary Fund (IMF), 700 Nineteenth Street, NW, Washington, DC 20431, (202) 623-7000, Fax: (202) 623-4661, www.imf.org; *International Financial Statistics Yearbook 2007.*

United Nations Statistics Division, New York, NY 10017, (800) 253-9646, Fax: (212) 963-4116, http://unstats.un.org; *Statistical Yearbook.*

The World Bank, 1818 H Street, NW, Washington, DC 20433, (202) 473-1000, Fax: (202) 477-6391, www.worldbank.org; *World Development Indicators (WDI) 2008.*

GERMANY - GOLD PRODUCTION

See GERMANY - MINERAL INDUSTRIES

GERMANY - GRANTS-IN-AID

Organisation for Economic Cooperation and Development (OECD), 2 rue Andre Pascal, F-75775 Paris Cedex 16, France, (Telephone in U.S. (202) 785-6323), (Fax in U.S. (202) 785-0350), www.oecd.org; *Geographical Distribution of Financial Flows to Aid Recipients 2002-2006.*

GERMANY - GREEN PEPPER AND CHILIE PRODUCTION

See GERMANY - CROPS

GERMANY - GROSS DOMESTIC PRODUCT

Economist Intelligence Unit, 111 West 57th Street, New York, NY 10019, (212) 554-0600, Fax: (212) 586-1181, www.eiu.com; *Germany Country Report.*

Euromonitor International, Inc., 224 S. Michigan Avenue, Suite 1500, Chicago, IL 60604, (312) 922-1115, Fax: (312) 922-1157, www.euromonitor.com; *The World Economic Factbook 2008.*

European Union, Delegation of the European Commission to the United States, 2300 M Street, NW, Washington, DC 20037, (202) 862-9500, Fax: (202) 429-1766, www.eurunion.org; *Eurostatistics: Data for Short-Term Economic Analysis (2007 edition); Iron and Steel;* and *RD Expenditure in Europe (2006 edition).*

Eurostat, Batiment Jean Monnet, Rue Alcide de Gasperi, L-2920 Luxembourg, http://epp.eurostat.ec.europa.eu; *Eurostat Yearbook 2006-2007.*

M.E. Sharpe, 80 Business Park Drive, Armonk, NY 10504, (800) 541-6563, Fax: (914) 273-2106, www.mesharpe.com; *The Illustrated Book of World Rankings.*

Organisation for Economic Cooperation and Development (OECD), 2 rue Andre Pascal, F-75775 Paris Cedex 16, France, (Telephone in U.S. (202) 785-6323), (Fax in U.S. (202) 785-0350), www.oecd.org; *Comparison of Gross Domestic Product (GDP) for OECD Countries; Geographical Distribution of Financial Flows to Aid Recipients 2002-2006; OECD Economic Outlook 2008;* and *Revenue Statistics 1965-2006 - 2007 Edition.*

Taylor and Francis Group, An Informa Business, 2 Park Square, Milton Park, Abingdon, Oxford OX14 4RN, United Kingdom, (Dial from U.S. (212) 216-7800), (Fax from U.S. (212) 564-7854), www.tandf.co.uk; *The Europa World Year Book.*

United Nations Statistics Division, New York, NY 10017, (800) 253-9646, Fax: (212) 963-4116, http://unstats.un.org; *Human Development Report 2006; National Accounts Statistics: Compendium of Income Distribution Statistics; Statistical Yearbook;* and *Trends in Europe and North America: The Statistical Yearbook of the ECE 2005.*

The World Bank, 1818 H Street, NW, Washington, DC 20433, (202) 473-1000, Fax: (202) 477-6391, www.worldbank.org; *World Development Indicators (WDI) 2008* and *World Development Report 2008.*

GERMANY - GROSS NATIONAL PRODUCT

European Union, Delegation of the European Commission to the United States, 2300 M Street, NW, Washington, DC 20037, (202) 862-9500, Fax: (202) 429-1766, www.eurunion.org; *The EU Economy, 2007 Review: Moving Europe's Productivity Frontier.*

Eurostat, Batiment Jean Monnet, Rue Alcide de Gasperi, L-2920 Luxembourg, http://epp.eurostat.ec.europa.eu; *Eurostat Yearbook 2006-2007.*

M.E. Sharpe, 80 Business Park Drive, Armonk, NY 10504, (800) 541-6563, Fax: (914) 273-2106, www.mesharpe.com; *The Illustrated Book of World Rankings.*

Organisation for Economic Cooperation and Development (OECD), 2 rue Andre Pascal, F-75775 Paris Cedex 16, France, (Telephone in U.S. (202) 785-6323), (Fax in U.S. (202) 785-0350), www.oecd.org; *Geographical Distribution of Financial Flows to Aid Recipients 2002-2006; OECD Composite Leading Indicators (CLIs), Updated September 2007; OECD Economic Outlook 2008;* and *OECD Main Economic Indicators (MEI).*

Palgrave Macmillan Ltd., Houndmills, Basingstoke, Hampshire, RG21 6XS, England, (Telephone in U.S. (888) 330-8477), (Fax in U.S. (800) 672-2054), www.palgrave.com; *The Statesman's Yearbook 2008.*

Taylor and Francis Group, An Informa Business, 2 Park Square, Milton Park, Abingdon, Oxford OX14 4RN, United Kingdom, (Dial from U.S. (212) 216-7800), (Fax from U.S. (212) 564-7854), www.tandf.co.uk; *The Europa World Year Book.*

U.S. Department of State (DOS), 2201 C Street NW, Washington, DC 20520, (202) 647-4000, www.state.gov; *World Military Expenditures and Arms Transfers (WMEAT).*

United Nations Statistics Division, New York, NY 10017, (800) 253-9646, Fax: (212) 963-4116, http://unstats.un.org; *Statistical Yearbook.*

The World Bank, 1818 H Street, NW, Washington, DC 20433, (202) 473-1000, Fax: (202) 477-6391, www.worldbank.org; *The World Bank Atlas 2003-2004; World Development Indicators (WDI) 2008;* and *World Development Report 2008.*

GERMANY - HAY PRODUCTION

See GERMANY - CROPS

GERMANY - HAZELNUT PRODUCTION

See GERMANY - CROPS

GERMANY - HEALTH

See GERMANY - PUBLIC HEALTH

GERMANY - HEMP FIBRE PRODUCTION

See GERMANY - TEXTILE INDUSTRY

GERMANY - HIDES AND SKINS INDUSTRY

Organisation for Economic Cooperation and Development (OECD), 2 rue Andre Pascal, F-75775 Paris Cedex 16, France, (Telephone in U.S. (202) 785-6323), (Fax in U.S. (202) 785-0350), www.oecd.org; *Indicators of Industrial Activity* and *International Trade by Commodity Statistics (ITCS).*

United Nations Food and Agricultural Organization (FAO), Viale delle Terme di Caracalla, 00100 Rome, Italy, (Dial from U.S. (202) 653-2400), (Fax from U.S. (202) 653 5760), www.fao.org; *FAO Production Yearbook 2002.*

GERMANY - HOPS PRODUCTION

See GERMANY - CROPS

GERMANY - HOUSING

Euromonitor International, Inc., 224 S. Michigan Avenue, Suite 1500, Chicago, IL 60604, (312) 922-1115, Fax: (312) 922-1157, www.euromonitor.com; *World Marketing Data and Statistics.*

European Union, Delegation of the European Commission to the United States, 2300 M Street, NW, Washington, DC 20037, (202) 862-9500, Fax: (202) 429-1766, www.eurunion.org; *European Union Labour Force Survey* and *Regions - Statistical Yearbook 2006.*

Eurostat, Batiment Jean Monnet, Rue Alcide de Gasperi, L-2920 Luxembourg, http://epp.eurostat.ec.europa.eu; *Eurostat Yearbook 2006-2007.*

M.E. Sharpe, 80 Business Park Drive, Armonk, NY 10504, (800) 541-6563, Fax: (914) 273-2106, www.mesharpe.com; *The Illustrated Book of World Rankings.*

United Nations Statistics Division, New York, NY 10017, (800) 253-9646, Fax: (212) 963-4116, http://unstats.un.org; *Trends in Europe and North America: The Statistical Yearbook of the ECE 2005.*

GERMANY - HOUSING CONSTRUCTION

See GERMANY - CONSTRUCTION INDUSTRY

GERMANY - ILLITERATE PERSONS

Euromonitor International, Inc., 224 S. Michigan Avenue, Suite 1500, Chicago, IL 60604, (312) 922-1115, Fax: (312) 922-1157, www.euromonitor.com; *The World Economic Factbook 2008.*

United Nations Statistics Division, New York, NY 10017, (800) 253-9646, Fax: (212) 963-4116, http://unstats.un.org; *Human Development Report 2006.*

GERMANY - IMPORTS

Central Intelligence Agency, Office of Public Affairs, Washington, DC 20505, (703) 482-0623, Fax: (703) 482-1739, www.cia.gov; *The World Factbook.*

Economist Intelligence Unit, 111 West 57th Street, New York, NY 10019, (212) 554-0600, Fax: (212) 586-1181, www.eiu.com; *Germany Country Report.*

Euromonitor International, Inc., 224 S. Michigan Avenue, Suite 1500, Chicago, IL 60604, (312) 922-1115, Fax: (312) 922-1157, www.euromonitor.com; *The World Economic Factbook 2008.*

European Union, Delegation of the European Commission to the United States, 2300 M Street, NW, Washington, DC 20037, (202) 862-9500, Fax: (202) 429-1766, www.eurunion.org; *European Union Energy Transport in Figures 2006; Eurostatistics: Data for Short-Term Economic Analysis (2007 edition); External and Intra-European Union Trade: Data 1958-2002; External and Intra-European Union Trade: Data 1999-2004;* and *Fishery Statistics - 1990-2006.*

Eurostat, Batiment Jean Monnet, Rue Alcide de Gasperi, L-2920 Luxembourg, http://epp.eurostat.ec.europa.eu; *Eurostat Yearbook 2006-2007.*

International Iron and Steel Institute (IISI), Rue Colonel Bourg 120, B-1140 Brussels, Belgium, www.worldsteel.org; *Steel Statistical Yearbook 2006.*

International Lead and Zinc Study Group (ILZSG), Rua Almirante Barroso 38, 5th Floor, Lisbon 1000 - 013, Portugal, www.ilzsg.org; Interactive Statistical Database.

International Monetary Fund (IMF), 700 Nineteenth Street, NW, Washington, DC 20431, (202) 623-7000, Fax: (202) 623-4661, www.imf.org; *Direction of Trade Statistics Yearbook 2007.*

Organisation for Economic Cooperation and Development (OECD), 2 rue Andre Pascal, F-75775 Paris Cedex 16, France, (Telephone in U.S. (202) 785-6323), (Fax in U.S. (202) 785-0350), www.oecd.org; *Iron and Steel Industry in 2004 (2006 Edition); 2005 OECD Agricultural Outlook Tables, 1970-2014; OECD Economic Outlook 2008; OECD Economic Survey - Germany 2008; Review of Fisheries in OECD Countries: Country Statistics 2001 to 2003 - 2005 Edition;* and STructural ANalysis (STAN) database.

Palgrave Macmillan Ltd., Houndmills, Basingstoke, Hampshire, RG21 6XS, England, (Telephone in U.S. (888) 330-8477), (Fax in U.S. (800) 672-2054), www.palgrave.com; *The Statesman's Yearbook 2008.*

Platts, 2 Penn Plaza, 25th Floor, New York, NY 10121-2298, (212) 904-3070, www.platts.com; *Energy Economist.*

Taylor and Francis Group, An Informa Business, 2 Park Square, Milton Park, Abingdon, Oxford OX14 4RN, United Kingdom, (Dial from U.S. (212) 216-7800), (Fax from U.S. (212) 564-7854), www.tandf.co.uk; *The Europa World Year Book.*

Technical Association of the Pulp and Paper Industry (TAPPI), 15 Technology Parkway South, Norcross, GA 30092, (770) 446-1400, Fax: (770) 446-6947, www.tappi.org; *TAPPI Annual Report.*

UNICEF, 3 United Nations Plaza, New York, NY 10017, (800) 253-9646, Fax: (212) 887-7465, www.unicef.org; *The State of the World's Children 2008.*

United Nations Food and Agricultural Organization (FAO), Viale delle Terme di Caracalla, 00100 Rome, Italy, (Dial from U.S. (202) 653-2400), (Fax from U.S. (202) 653 5760), www.fao.org; *The State of Food and Agriculture (SOFA) 2006.*

United Nations Statistics Division, New York, NY 10017, (800) 253-9646, Fax: (212) 963-4116, http://unstats.un.org; *Energy Statistics Yearbook 2003* and *Trends in Europe and North America: The Statistical Yearbook of the ECE 2005.*

The World Bank, 1818 H Street, NW, Washington, DC 20433, (202) 473-1000, Fax: (202) 477-6391, www.worldbank.org; *World Development Indicators (WDI) 2008* and *World Development Report 2008.*

GERMANY - INCOME TAXES

See GERMANY - TAXATION

GERMANY - INDUSTRIAL PRODUCTIVITY

European Union, Delegation of the European Commission to the United States, 2300 M Street, NW, Washington, DC 20037, (202) 862-9500, Fax: (202) 429-1766, www.eurunion.org; *Eurostatistics: Data for Short-Term Economic Analysis (2007 edition); Fishery Statistics - 1990-2006;* and *RD Expenditure in Europe (2006 edition).*

Eurostat, Batiment Jean Monnet, Rue Alcide de Gasperi, L-2920 Luxembourg, http://epp.eurostat.ec.europa.eu; *Eurostat Yearbook 2006-2007.*

International Iron and Steel Institute (IISI), Rue Colonel Bourg 120, B-1140 Brussels, Belgium, www.worldsteel.org; *Steel Statistical Yearbook 2006.*

International Lead and Zinc Study Group (ILZSG), Rua Almirante Barroso 38, 5th Floor, Lisbon 1000 - 013, Portugal, www.ilzsg.org; Interactive Statistical Database.

M.E. Sharpe, 80 Business Park Drive, Armonk, NY 10504, (800) 541-6563, Fax: (914) 273-2106, www.mesharpe.com; *The Illustrated Book of World Rankings.*

Organisation for Economic Cooperation and Development (OECD), 2 rue Andre Pascal, F-75775 Paris Cedex 16, France, (Telephone in U.S. (202) 785-6323), (Fax in U.S. (202) 785-0350), www.oecd.org; *Environmental Impacts of Foreign Direct Investment in the Mining Sector in the Newly Independent States (NIS); Indicators of Industrial Activity; Iron and Steel Industry in 2004 (2006 Edition); A New World Map in Textiles and Clothing: Adjusting to Change; 2005 OECD Agricultural Outlook Tables, 1970-2014; OECD Economic Outlook 2008;* and STructural ANalysis (STAN) database.

Technical Association of the Pulp and Paper Industry (TAPPI), 15 Technology Parkway South, Norcross, GA 30092, (770) 446-1400, Fax: (770) 446-6947, www.tappi.org; *TAPPI Annual Report.*

GERMANY - INDUSTRIAL PROPERTY

United Nations Statistics Division, New York, NY 10017, (800) 253-9646, Fax: (212) 963-4116, http://unstats.un.org; *Statistical Yearbook.*

World Intellectual Property Organization (WIPO), PO Box 18, CH-1211 Geneva 20, Switzerland, www.wipo.int; *Industrial Property Statistics* and *Industrial Property Statistics Online Directory.*

GERMANY - INDUSTRIES

Central Intelligence Agency, Office of Public Affairs, Washington, DC 20505, (703) 482-0623, Fax: (703) 482-1739, www.cia.gov; *The World Factbook.*

Economist Intelligence Unit, 111 West 57th Street, New York, NY 10019, (212) 554-0600, Fax: (212) 586-1181, www.eiu.com; *Germany Country Report.*

Euromonitor International, Inc., 224 S. Michigan Avenue, Suite 1500, Chicago, IL 60604, (312) 922-1115, Fax: (312) 922-1157, www.euromonitor.com; *The World Economic Factbook 2008* and *World Marketing Data and Statistics.*

European Union, Delegation of the European Commission to the United States, 2300 M Street, NW, Washington, DC 20037, (202) 862-9500, Fax: (202) 429-1766, www.eurunion.org; *European Union Labour Force Survey* and *Eurostatistics: Data for Short-Term Economic Analysis (2007 edition).*

Eurostat, Batiment Jean Monnet, Rue Alcide de Gasperi, L-2920 Luxembourg, http://epp.eurostat.ec.europa.eu; *Eurostat Yearbook 2006-2007.*

International Labour Office, I.L.O. Publications, 4 route des Morillons, CH-1211 Geneva 22, Switzerland, (Telephone in U.S. (202) 653-7652), (Fax in U.S. (202) 653-7687), www.ilo.org; *Yearbook of Labour Statistics 2006.*

M.E. Sharpe, 80 Business Park Drive, Armonk, NY 10504, (800) 541-6563, Fax: (914) 273-2106, www.mesharpe.com; *The Illustrated Book of World Rankings.*

Organisation for Economic Cooperation and Development (OECD), 2 rue Andre Pascal, F-75775 Paris Cedex 16, France, (Telephone in U.S. (202) 785-6323), (Fax in U.S. (202) 785-0350), www.oecd.org; *Indicators of Industrial Activity; Key Environmental Indicators 2004; OECD Economic Outlook 2008; OECD Main Economic Indicators (MEI);* and STructural ANalysis (STAN) database.

Palgrave Macmillan Ltd., Houndmills, Basingstoke, Hampshire, RG21 6XS, England, (Telephone in U.S. (888) 330-8477), (Fax in U.S. (800) 672-2054), www.palgrave.com; *The Statesman's Yearbook 2008.*

Taylor and Francis Group, An Informa Business, 2 Park Square, Milton Park, Abingdon, Oxford OX14 4RN, United Kingdom, (Dial from U.S. (212) 216-7800), (Fax from U.S. (212) 564-7854), www.tandf.co.uk; *The Europa World Year Book.*

United Nations Industrial Development Organization (UNIDO), 1 United Nations Plaza, New York, NY 10017, (212) 963 6890, Fax: (212) 963-7904, http://unido.org; Industrial Statistics Database 2008 (INDSTAT) and *The International Yearbook of Industrial Statistics 2008.*

United Nations Statistics Division, New York, NY 10017, (800) 253-9646, Fax: (212) 963-4116, http://unstats.un.org; *2004 Industrial Commodity Statistics Yearbook; Statistical Yearbook;* and *Trends in Europe and North America: The Statistical Yearbook of the ECE 2005.*

The World Bank, 1818 H Street, NW, Washington, DC 20433, (202) 473-1000, Fax: (202) 477-6391, www.worldbank.org; *Germany* and *World Development Indicators (WDI) 2008.*

GERMANY - INFANT AND MATERNAL MORTALITY

See GERMANY - MORTALITY

GERMANY - INORGANIC ACIDS

Eurostat, Batiment Jean Monnet, Rue Alcide de Gasperi, L-2920 Luxembourg, http://epp.eurostat.ec.europa.eu; *Eurostat Yearbook 2006-2007.*

Organisation for Economic Cooperation and Development (OECD), 2 rue Andre Pascal, F-75775 Paris Cedex 16, France, (Telephone in U.S. (202) 785-6323), (Fax in U.S. (202) 785-0350), www.oecd.org; *Indicators of Industrial Activity.*

United Nations Statistics Division, New York, NY 10017, (800) 253-9646, Fax: (212) 963-4116, http://unstats.un.org; *Statistical Yearbook.*

GERMANY - INTEREST RATES

Eurostat, Batiment Jean Monnet, Rue Alcide de Gasperi, L-2920 Luxembourg, http://epp.eurostat.ec.europa.eu; *Eurostat Yearbook 2006-2007.*

Organisation for Economic Cooperation and Development (OECD), 2 rue Andre Pascal, F-75775 Paris Cedex 16, France, (Telephone in U.S. (202) 785-6323), (Fax in U.S. (202) 785-0350), www.oecd.org; *Financial Market Trends: OECD Periodical; OECD Economic Outlook 2008;* and *OECD Main Economic Indicators (MEI).*

United Nations Statistics Division, New York, NY 10017, (800) 253-9646, Fax: (212) 963-4116, http://unstats.un.org; *Statistical Yearbook.*

GERMANY - INTERNAL REVENUE

Organisation for Economic Cooperation and Development (OECD), 2 rue Andre Pascal, F-75775 Paris Cedex 16, France, (Telephone in U.S. (202) 785-6323), (Fax in U.S. (202) 785-0350), www.oecd.org; *Revenue Statistics 1965-2006 - 2007 Edition.*

GERMANY - INTERNATIONAL FINANCE

Eurostat, Batiment Jean Monnet, Rue Alcide de Gasperi, L-2920 Luxembourg, http://epp.eurostat.ec.europa.eu; *Eurostat Yearbook 2006-2007.*

International Finance Corporation (IFC), 2121 Pennsylvania Avenue, NW, Washington, DC 20433 USA, (202) 473-1000, Fax: (202) 974-4384, www.ifc.org; *Annual Report 2007.*

Organisation for Economic Cooperation and Development (OECD), 2 rue Andre Pascal, F-75775 Paris Cedex 16, France, (Telephone in U.S. (202) 785-6323), (Fax in U.S. (202) 785-0350), www.oecd.org; *Financial Market Trends: OECD Periodical* and *OECD Economic Outlook 2008.*

GERMANY - INTERNATIONAL LIQUIDITY

Organisation for Economic Cooperation and Development (OECD), 2 rue Andre Pascal, F-75775 Paris Cedex 16, France, (Telephone in U.S. (202) 785-6323), (Fax in U.S. (202) 785-0350), www.oecd.org; *Financial Market Trends: OECD Periodical* and *OECD Economic Outlook 2008.*

GERMANY - INTERNATIONAL STATISTICS

Organisation for Economic Cooperation and Development (OECD), 2 rue Andre Pascal, F-75775 Paris Cedex 16, France, (Telephone in U.S. (202) 785-6323), (Fax in U.S. (202) 785-0350), www.oecd.org; *Financial Market Trends: OECD Periodical* and *Household, Tourism, Travel: Trends, Environmental Impacts and Policy Responses.*

GERMANY - INTERNATIONAL TRADE

Banque de France, 48 rue Croix des Petits champs, 75001 Paris, France, www.banque-france.fr/home.htm; *Monthly Business Survey Overview.*

Bernan Essential Government Publications, 4611-F Assembly Drive, Lanham MD, 20706-4391, (301) 459-2255, Fax: (800) 865-3450, www.bernan.com; *OECD Factbook 2006.*

Economist Intelligence Unit, 111 West 57th Street, New York, NY 10019, (212) 554-0600, Fax: (212) 586-1181, www.eiu.com; *Germany Country Report.*

Euromonitor International, Inc., 224 S. Michigan Avenue, Suite 1500, Chicago, IL 60604, (312) 922-1115, Fax: (312) 922-1157, www.euromonitor.com; *European Marketing Data and Statistics 2008; The World Economic Factbook 2008;* and *World Marketing Data and Statistics.*

European Union, Delegation of the European Commission to the United States, 2300 M Street, NW, Washington, DC 20037, (202) 862-9500, Fax: (202) 429-1766, www.eurunion.org; *Eurostatistics: Data for Short-Term Economic Analysis (2007 edition); External and Intra-European Union Trade: Data 1958-2002; External and Intra-European Union Trade: Data 1999-2004;* and *Iron and Steel.*

Eurostat, Batiment Jean Monnet, Rue Alcide de Gasperi, L-2920 Luxembourg, http://epp.eurostat.ec.europa.eu; *Eurostat Yearbook 2006-2007* and Intra- and Extra-EU Trade.

International Iron and Steel Institute (IISI), Rue Colonel Bourg 120, B-1140 Brussels, Belgium, www.worldsteel.org; *Steel Statistical Yearbook 2006.*

International Monetary Fund (IMF), 700 Nineteenth Street, NW, Washington, DC 20431, (202) 623-7000, Fax: (202) 623-4661, www.imf.org; *International Financial Statistics Yearbook 2007.*

M.E. Sharpe, 80 Business Park Drive, Armonk, NY 10504, (800) 541-6563, Fax: (914) 273-2106, www.mesharpe.com; *The Illustrated Book of World Rankings.*

Organisation for Economic Cooperation and Development (OECD), 2 rue Andre Pascal, F-75775 Paris Cedex 16, France, (Telephone in U.S. (202) 785-6323), (Fax in U.S. (202) 785-0350), www.oecd.org; *International Trade by Commodity Statistics (ITCS); 2005 OECD Agricultural Outlook Tables, 1970-2014; OECD Economic Outlook 2008; OECD Economic Survey - Germany 2008; OECD in Figures 2007; OECD Main Economic Indicators (MEI);* and *Statistics on Ship Production, Exports and Orders in 2004.*

Palgrave Macmillan Ltd., Houndmills, Basingstoke, Hampshire, RG21 6XS, England, (Telephone in U.S. (888) 330-8477), (Fax in U.S. (800) 672-2054), www.palgrave.com; *The Statesman's Yearbook 2008.*

Platts, 2 Penn Plaza, 25th Floor, New York, NY 10121-2298, (212) 904-3070, www.platts.com; *Energy Economist.*

Taylor and Francis Group, An Informa Business, 2 Park Square, Milton Park, Abingdon, Oxford OX14 4RN, United Kingdom, (Dial from U.S. (212) 216-7800), (Fax from U.S. (212) 564-7854), www.tandf.co.uk; *The Europa World Year Book.*

United Nations Conference on Trade and Development (UNCTAD), DC2-1120, United Nations, New York, NY 10017, (212) 963-0027, www.unctad.org; *UNCTAD Commodity Yearbook.*

United Nations Food and Agricultural Organization (FAO), Viale delle Terme di Caracalla, 00100 Rome, Italy, (Dial from U.S. (202) 653-2400), (Fax from U.S. (202) 653 5760), www.fao.org; *FAO Trade Yearbook* and *The State of Food and Agriculture (SOFA) 2006.*

United Nations Statistics Division, New York, NY 10017, (800) 253-9646, Fax: (212) 963-4116, http://unstats.un.org; *Energy Statistics Yearbook 2003; International Trade Statistics Yearbook;* and *Statistical Yearbook.*

The World Bank, 1818 H Street, NW, Washington, DC 20433, (202) 473-1000, Fax: (202) 477-6391, www.worldbank.org; *Germany; World Development Indicators (WDI) 2008;* and *World Development Report 2008.*

World Bureau of Metal Statistics (WBMS), 27a High Street, Ware, Hertfordshire, SG12 9BA, United Kingdom, www.world-bureau.com; *World Flow Charts* and *World Metal Statistics.*

World Trade Organization (WTO), Centre William Rappard, Rue de Lausanne 154, CH-1211 Geneva 21, Switzerland, www.wto.org; *International Trade Statistics 2006.*

GERMANY - INTERNET USERS

Eurostat, Batiment Jean Monnet, Rue Alcide de Gasperi, L-2920 Luxembourg, http://epp.eurostat.ec.europa.eu; *Internet Usage by Enterprises 2007.*

International Telecommunication Union (ITU), Place des Nations, 1211 Geneva 20, Switzerland, www.itu.int; *World Telecommunication/ICT Indicators Database on CD-ROM; World Telecommunication/ICT Indicators Database Online;* and *Yearbook of Statistics - Telecommunication Services (Chronological Time Series 1997-2006).*

The World Bank, 1818 H Street, NW, Washington, DC 20433, (202) 473-1000, Fax: (202) 477-6391, www.worldbank.org; *Germany.*

GERMANY - INVESTMENTS

Organisation for Economic Cooperation and Development (OECD), 2 rue Andre Pascal, F-75775 Paris Cedex 16, France, (Telephone in U.S. (202) 785-6323), (Fax in U.S. (202) 785-0350), www.oecd.org; *Financial Market Trends: OECD Periodical; Iron and Steel Industry in 2004 (2006 Edition); A New World Map in Textiles and Clothing: Adjusting to Change; OECD Economic Outlook 2008;* and STructural ANalysis (STAN) database.

GERMANY - IRON AND IRON ORE PRODUCTION

See GERMANY - MINERAL INDUSTRIES

GERMANY - JUTE PRODUCTION

See GERMANY - CROPS

GERMANY - LABOR

Central Intelligence Agency, Office of Public Affairs, Washington, DC 20505, (703) 482-0623, Fax: (703) 482-1739, www.cia.gov; *The World Factbook.*

Euromonitor International, Inc., 224 S. Michigan Avenue, Suite 1500, Chicago, IL 60604, (312) 922-1115, Fax: (312) 922-1157, www.euromonitor.com; *World Marketing Data and Statistics.*

European Union, Delegation of the European Commission to the United States, 2300 M Street, NW, Washington, DC 20037, (202) 862-9500, Fax: (202) 429-1766, www.eurunion.org; *European Union Labour Force Survey* and *Regions - Statistical Yearbook 2006.*

Eurostat, Batiment Jean Monnet, Rue Alcide de Gasperi, L-2920 Luxembourg, http://epp.eurostat.ec.europa.eu; *Eurostat Yearbook 2006-2007.*

International Labour Office, I.L.O. Publications, 4 route des Morillons, CH-1211 Geneva 22, Switzerland, (Telephone in U.S. (202) 653-7652), (Fax in U.S. (202) 653-7687), www.ilo.org; *Yearbook of Labour Statistics 2006.*

M.E. Sharpe, 80 Business Park Drive, Armonk, NY 10504, (800) 541-6563, Fax: (914) 273-2106, www.mesharpe.com; *The Illustrated Book of World Rankings.*

Organisation for Economic Cooperation and Development (OECD), 2 rue Andre Pascal, F-75775 Paris Cedex 16, France, (Telephone in U.S. (202) 785-6323), (Fax in U.S. (202) 785-0350), www.oecd.org; *Iron and Steel Industry in 2004 (2006 Edition); A New World Map in Textiles and Clothing: Adjusting to Change; OECD Economic Outlook 2008; OECD Economic Survey - Germany 2008; OECD Employment Outlook 2007; OECD Main Economic Indicators (MEI);* and *Statistics on Ship Production, Exports and Orders in 2004.*

Palgrave Macmillan Ltd., Houndmills, Basingstoke, Hampshire, RG21 6XS, England, (Telephone in U.S. (888) 330-8477), (Fax in U.S. (800) 672-2054), www.palgrave.com; *The Statesman's Yearbook 2008.*

Taylor and Francis Group, An Informa Business, 2 Park Square, Milton Park, Abingdon, Oxford OX14 4RN, United Kingdom, (Dial from U.S. (212) 216-7800), (Fax from U.S. (212) 564-7854), www.tandf.co.uk; *The Europa World Year Book.*

United Nations Food and Agricultural Organization (FAO), Viale delle Terme di Caracalla, 00100 Rome, Italy, (Dial from U.S. (202) 653-2400), (Fax from U.S. (202) 653 5760), www.fao.org; *The State of Food and Agriculture (SOFA) 2006.*

United Nations Statistics Division, New York, NY 10017, (800) 253-9646, Fax: (212) 963-4116, http://unstats.un.org; *Human Development Report 2006.*

The World Bank, 1818 H Street, NW, Washington, DC 20433, (202) 473-1000, Fax: (202) 477-6391, www.worldbank.org; *The World Bank Atlas 2003-2004; World Development Indicators (WDI) 2008;* and *World Development Report 2008.*

GERMANY - LAND USE

Central Intelligence Agency, Office of Public Affairs, Washington, DC 20505, (703) 482-0623, Fax: (703) 482-1739, www.cia.gov; *The World Factbook.*

Euromonitor International, Inc., 224 S. Michigan Avenue, Suite 1500, Chicago, IL 60604, (312) 922-1115, Fax: (312) 922-1157, www.euromonitor.com; *European Marketing Data and Statistics 2008.*

European Union, Delegation of the European Commission to the United States, 2300 M Street, NW, Washington, DC 20037, (202) 862-9500, Fax: (202) 429-1766, www.eurunion.org; *Agricultural Statistics: Data 1995-2005; Agriculture in the European Union: Statistical and Economic Information 2006;* and *Regions - Statistical Yearbook 2006.*

Eurostat, Batiment Jean Monnet, Rue Alcide de Gasperi, L-2920 Luxembourg, http://epp.eurostat.ec.europa.eu; *Eurostat Yearbook 2006-2007.*

United Nations Food and Agricultural Organization (FAO), Viale delle Terme di Caracalla, 00100 Rome, Italy, (Dial from U.S. (202) 653-2400), (Fax from U.S. (202) 653 5760), www.fao.org; *FAO Production Yearbook 2002.*

The World Bank, 1818 H Street, NW, Washington, DC 20433, (202) 473-1000, Fax: (202) 477-6391, www.worldbank.org; *World Development Report 2008.*

GERMANY - LEATHER INDUSTRY AND TRADE

Eurostat, Batiment Jean Monnet, Rue Alcide de Gasperi, L-2920 Luxembourg, http://epp.eurostat.ec.europa.eu; *Eurostat Yearbook 2006-2007.*

Organisation for Economic Cooperation and Development (OECD), 2 rue Andre Pascal, F-75775 Paris

Cedex 16, France, (Telephone in U.S. (202) 785-6323), (Fax in U.S. (202) 785-0350), www.oecd.org; *Indicators of Industrial Activity.*

GERMANY - LIBRARIES

M.E. Sharpe, 80 Business Park Drive, Armonk, NY 10504, (800) 541-6563, Fax: (914) 273-2106, www.mesharpe.com; *The Illustrated Book of World Rankings.*

UNESCO Institute for Statistics, C.P. 6128 Succursale Centre-Ville, Montreal, Quebec, H3C 3J7 Canada, (Dial from U.S. (514) 343-6880), (Fax from U.S. (514) 343 6882), www.uis.unesco.org; *Statistical Tables.*

United Nations Statistics Division, New York, NY 10017, (800) 253-9646, Fax: (212) 963-4116, http://unstats.un.org; *Trends in Europe and North America: The Statistical Yearbook of the ECE 2005.*

GERMANY - LIFE EXPECTANCY

Central Intelligence Agency, Office of Public Affairs, Washington, DC 20505, (703) 482-0623, Fax: (703) 482-1739, www.cia.gov; *The World Factbook.*

Euromonitor International, Inc., 224 S. Michigan Avenue, Suite 1500, Chicago, IL 60604, (312) 922-1115, Fax: (312) 922-1157, www.euromonitor.com; *The World Economic Factbook 2008.*

Organisation for Economic Cooperation and Development (OECD), 2 rue Andre Pascal, F-75775 Paris Cedex 16, France, (Telephone in U.S. (202) 785-6323), (Fax in U.S. (202) 785-0350), www.oecd.org; *OECD Economic Outlook 2008.*

Palgrave Macmillan Ltd., Houndmills, Basingstoke, Hampshire, RG21 6XS, England, (Telephone in U.S. (888) 330-8477), (Fax in U.S. (800) 672-2054), www.palgrave.com; *The Statesman's Yearbook 2008.*

United Nations Statistics Division, New York, NY 10017, (800) 253-9646, Fax: (212) 963-4116, http://unstats.un.org; *Human Development Report 2006; Trends in Europe and North America: The Statistical Yearbook of the ECE 2005;* and *World Statistics Pocketbook.*

The World Bank, 1818 H Street, NW, Washington, DC 20433, (202) 473-1000, Fax: (202) 477-6391, www.worldbank.org; *The World Bank Atlas 2003-2004* and *World Development Report 2008.*

GERMANY - LITERACY

Euromonitor International, Inc., 224 S. Michigan Avenue, Suite 1500, Chicago, IL 60604, (312) 922-1115, Fax: (312) 922-1157, www.euromonitor.com; *World Marketing Data and Statistics.*

GERMANY - LIVESTOCK

Euromonitor International, Inc., 224 S. Michigan Avenue, Suite 1500, Chicago, IL 60604, (312) 922-1115, Fax: (312) 922-1157, www.euromonitor.com; *European Marketing Data and Statistics 2008.*

European Union, Delegation of the European Commission to the United States, 2300 M Street, NW, Washington, DC 20037, (202) 862-9500, Fax: (202) 429-1766, www.eurunion.org; *Agricultural Statistics: Data 1995-2005; Eurostatistics: Data for Short-Term Economic Analysis (2007 edition);* and *Regions - Statistical Yearbook 2006.*

Eurostat, Batiment Jean Monnet, Rue Alcide de Gasperi, L-2920 Luxembourg, http://epp.eurostat.ec.europa.eu; *Eurostat Yearbook 2006-2007.*

M.E. Sharpe, 80 Business Park Drive, Armonk, NY 10504, (800) 541-6563, Fax: (914) 273-2106, www.mesharpe.com; *The Illustrated Book of World Rankings.*

Organisation for Economic Cooperation and Development (OECD), 2 rue Andre Pascal, F-75775 Paris Cedex 16, France, (Telephone in U.S. (202) 785-6323), (Fax in U.S. (202) 785-0350), www.oecd.org; *2005 OECD Agricultural Outlook Tables, 1970-2014.*

Palgrave Macmillan Ltd., Houndmills, Basingstoke, Hampshire, RG21 6XS, England, (Telephone in U.S. (888) 330-8477), (Fax in U.S. (800) 672-2054), www.palgrave.com; *The Statesman's Yearbook 2008.*

Taylor and Francis Group, An Informa Business, 2 Park Square, Milton Park, Abingdon, Oxford OX14 4RN, United Kingdom, (Dial from U.S. (212) 216-7800), (Fax from U.S. (212) 564-7854), www.tandf.co.uk; *The Europa World Year Book.*

United Nations Conference on Trade and Development (UNCTAD), DC2-1120, United Nations, New York, NY 10017, (212) 963-0027, www.unctad.org; *UNCTAD Commodity Yearbook.*

United Nations Food and Agricultural Organization (FAO), Viale delle Terme di Caracalla, 00100 Rome, Italy, (Dial from U.S. (202) 653-2400), (Fax from U.S. (202) 653 5760), www.fao.org; *FAO Production Yearbook 2002* and *The State of Food and Agriculture (SOFA) 2006.*

United Nations Statistics Division, New York, NY 10017, (800) 253-9646, Fax: (212) 963-4116, http://unstats.un.org; *Statistical Yearbook.*

GERMANY - MACHINERY

Organisation for Economic Cooperation and Development (OECD), 2 rue Andre Pascal, F-75775 Paris Cedex 16, France, (Telephone in U.S. (202) 785-6323), (Fax in U.S. (202) 785-0350), www.oecd.org; *Indicators of Industrial Activity.*

GERMANY - MAGNESIUM PRODUCTION AND CONSUMPTION

See GERMANY - MINERAL INDUSTRIES

GERMANY - MANUFACTURES

European Union, Delegation of the European Commission to the United States, 2300 M Street, NW, Washington, DC 20037, (202) 862-9500, Fax: (202) 429-1766, www.eurunion.org; *European Union Labour Force Survey; Eurostatistics: Data for Short-Term Economic Analysis (2007 edition);* and *The Textile Industry in the EU.*

Eurostat, Batiment Jean Monnet, Rue Alcide de Gasperi, L-2920 Luxembourg, http://epp.eurostat.ec.europa.eu; *Eurostat Yearbook 2006-2007.*

M.E. Sharpe, 80 Business Park Drive, Armonk, NY 10504, (800) 541-6563, Fax: (914) 273-2106, www.mesharpe.com; *The Illustrated Book of World Rankings.*

Organisation for Economic Cooperation and Development (OECD), 2 rue Andre Pascal, F-75775 Paris Cedex 16, France, (Telephone in U.S. (202) 785-6323), (Fax in U.S. (202) 785-0350), www.oecd.org; *Indicators of Industrial Activity; International Trade by Commodity Statistics (ITCS); OECD Economic Survey - Germany 2008; OECD Main Economic Indicators (MEI);* and STructural ANalysis (STAN) database.

United Nations Statistics Division, New York, NY 10017, (800) 253-9646, Fax: (212) 963-4116, http://unstats.un.org; *Statistical Yearbook.*

The World Bank, 1818 H Street, NW, Washington, DC 20433, (202) 473-1000, Fax: (202) 477-6391, www.worldbank.org; *World Development Indicators (WDI) 2008.*

GERMANY - MARRIAGE

Eurostat, Batiment Jean Monnet, Rue Alcide de Gasperi, L-2920 Luxembourg, http://epp.eurostat.ec.europa.eu; *Eurostat Yearbook 2006-2007.*

M.E. Sharpe, 80 Business Park Drive, Armonk, NY 10504, (800) 541-6563, Fax: (914) 273-2106, www.mesharpe.com; *The Illustrated Book of World Rankings.*

Taylor and Francis Group, An Informa Business, 2 Park Square, Milton Park, Abingdon, Oxford OX14 4RN, United Kingdom, (Dial from U.S. (212) 216-7800), (Fax from U.S. (212) 564-7854), www.tandf.co.uk; *The Europa World Year Book.*

United Nations Statistics Division, New York, NY 10017, (800) 253-9646, Fax: (212) 963-4116, http://unstats.un.org; *Demographic Yearbook; Statistical Yearbook;* and *Trends in Europe and North America: The Statistical Yearbook of the ECE 2005.*

GERMANY - MEAT PRODUCTION

See GERMANY - LIVESTOCK

GERMANY - MERCURY PRODUCTION

See GERMANY - MINERAL INDUSTRIES

GERMANY - METAL PRODUCTS

Eurostat, Batiment Jean Monnet, Rue Alcide de Gasperi, L-2920 Luxembourg, http://epp.eurostat.ec.europa.eu; *Eurostat Yearbook 2006-2007.*

Organisation for Economic Cooperation and Development (OECD), 2 rue Andre Pascal, F-75775 Paris Cedex 16, France, (Telephone in U.S. (202) 785-6323), (Fax in U.S. (202) 785-0350), www.oecd.org; *Indicators of Industrial Activity.*

United Nations Statistics Division, New York, NY 10017, (800) 253-9646, Fax: (212) 963-4116, http://unstats.un.org; *Statistical Yearbook.*

GERMANY - MILK PRODUCTION

See GERMANY - DAIRY PROCESSING

GERMANY - MINERAL INDUSTRIES

Commodity Research Bureau, 330 South Wells Street, Suite 612, Chicago, IL 60606-7110, (800) 621-5271, Fax: (312) 939-4135, www.crbtrader.com; *2006 CRB Commodity Yearbook and CD.*

European Union, Delegation of the European Commission to the United States, 2300 M Street, NW, Washington, DC 20037, (202) 862-9500, Fax: (202) 429-1766, www.eurunion.org; *European Union Energy Transport in Figures 2006; Eurostatistics: Data for Short-Term Economic Analysis (2007 edition); Iron and Steel;* and *Regions - Statistical Yearbook 2006.*

Eurostat, Batiment Jean Monnet, Rue Alcide de Gasperi, L-2920 Luxembourg, http://epp.eurostat.ec.europa.eu; *Energy - Monthly Statistics; Eurostat Yearbook 2006-2007;* and *Panorama of Energy - 2007 Edition.*

International Energy Agency (IEA), 9, rue de la Federation, 75739 Paris Cedex 15, France, www.iea.org; *Key World Energy Statistics 2007.*

International Iron and Steel Institute (IISI), Rue Colonel Bourg 120, B-1140 Brussels, Belgium, www.worldsteel.org; *Steel Statistical Yearbook 2006.*

International Lead and Zinc Study Group (ILZSG), Rua Almirante Barroso 38, 5th Floor, Lisbon 1000 - 013, Portugal, www.ilzsg.org; Interactive Statistical Database.

M.E. Sharpe, 80 Business Park Drive, Armonk, NY 10504, (800) 541-6563, Fax: (914) 273-2106, www.mesharpe.com; *The Illustrated Book of World Rankings.*

Organisation for Economic Cooperation and Development (OECD), 2 rue Andre Pascal, F-75775 Paris Cedex 16, France, (Telephone in U.S. (202) 785-6323), (Fax in U.S. (202) 785-0350), www.oecd.org; *Energy Statistics of OECD Countries* (2007 Edition); *Indicators of Industrial Activity; International Trade by Commodity Statistics (ITCS); OECD Economic Survey - Germany 2008;* STructural ANalysis (STAN) database; and *World Energy Outlook 2007.*

Palgrave Macmillan Ltd., Houndmills, Basingstoke, Hampshire, RG21 6XS, England, (Telephone in U.S. (888) 330-8477), (Fax in U.S. (800) 672-2054), www.palgrave.com; *The Statesman's Yearbook 2008.*

Platts, 2 Penn Plaza, 25th Floor, New York, NY 10121-2298, (212) 904-3070, www.platts.com; *Energy Economist* and *EU Energy.*

Taylor and Francis Group, An Informa Business, 2 Park Square, Milton Park, Abingdon, Oxford OX14 4RN, United Kingdom, (Dial from U.S. (212) 216-7800), (Fax from U.S. (212) 564-7854), www.tandf.co.uk; *The Europa World Year Book.*

United Nations Conference on Trade and Development (UNCTAD), DC2-1120, United Nations, New York, NY 10017, (212) 963-0027, www.unctad.org; *UNCTAD Commodity Yearbook.*

United Nations Statistics Division, New York, NY 10017, (800) 253-9646, Fax: (212) 963-4116, http://unstats.un.org; *Energy Statistics Yearbook 2003* and *Statistical Yearbook.*

World Bureau of Metal Statistics (WBMS), 27a High Street, Ware, Hertfordshire, SG12 9BA, United Kingdom, www.world-bureau.com; *Annual Stainless Steel Statistics; World Flow Charts; World Metal Statistics; World Nickel Statistics;* and *World Tin Statistics.*

GERMANY - MOLASSES PRODUCTION

See GERMANY - CROPS

GERMANY - MONEY

European Central Bank (ECB), Postfach 160319, D-60066 Frankfurt am Main, Germany, www.ecb.int; *Monetary Developments in the Euro Area; Monthly Bulletin;* and *Statistics Pocket Book.*

Organisation for Economic Cooperation and Development (OECD), 2 rue Andre Pascal, F-75775 Paris Cedex 16, France, (Telephone in U.S. (202) 785-6323), (Fax in U.S. (202) 785-0350), www.oecd.org; *OECD Economic Survey - Germany 2008.*

The World Bank, 1818 H Street, NW, Washington, DC 20433, (202) 473-1000, Fax: (202) 477-6391, www.worldbank.org; *Germany.*

GERMANY - MONEY EXCHANGE RATES

See GERMANY - FOREIGN EXCHANGE RATES

GERMANY - MONEY SUPPLY

Economist Intelligence Unit, 111 West 57th Street, New York, NY 10019, (212) 554-0600, Fax: (212) 586-1181, www.eiu.com; *Germany Country Report.*

European Union, Delegation of the European Commission to the United States, 2300 M Street, NW, Washington, DC 20037, (202) 862-9500, Fax: (202) 429-1766, www.eurunion.org; *Eurostatistics: Data for Short-Term Economic Analysis (2007 edition).*

Eurostat, Batiment Jean Monnet, Rue Alcide de Gasperi, L-2920 Luxembourg, http://epp.eurostat.ec.europa.eu; *Eurostat Yearbook 2006-2007.*

International Monetary Fund (IMF), 700 Nineteenth Street, NW, Washington, DC 20431, (202) 623-7000, Fax: (202) 623-4661, www.imf.org; *International Financial Statistics Yearbook 2007.*

Organisation for Economic Cooperation and Development (OECD), 2 rue Andre Pascal, F-75775 Paris Cedex 16, France, (Telephone in U.S. (202) 785-6323), (Fax in U.S. (202) 785-0350), www.oecd.org; *OECD Economic Outlook 2008.*

Taylor and Francis Group, An Informa Business, 2 Park Square, Milton Park, Abingdon, Oxford OX14 4RN, United Kingdom, (Dial from U.S. (212) 216-7800), (Fax from U.S. (212) 564-7854), www.tandf.co.uk; *The Europa World Year Book.*

United Nations Statistics Division, New York, NY 10017, (800) 253-9646, Fax: (212) 963-4116, http://unstats.un.org; *Statistical Yearbook.*

The World Bank, 1818 H Street, NW, Washington, DC 20433, (202) 473-1000, Fax: (202) 477-6391, www.worldbank.org; *World Development Indicators (WDI) 2008.*

GERMANY - MORTALITY

Central Intelligence Agency, Office of Public Affairs, Washington, DC 20505, (703) 482-0623, Fax: (703) 482-1739, www.cia.gov; *The World Factbook.*

Euromonitor International, Inc., 224 S. Michigan Avenue, Suite 1500, Chicago, IL 60604, (312) 922-1115, Fax: (312) 922-1157, www.euromonitor.com; *The World Economic Factbook 2008.*

European Union, Delegation of the European Commission to the United States, 2300 M Street, NW, Washington, DC 20037, (202) 862-9500, Fax: (202) 429-1766, www.eurunion.org; *First Demographic Estimates for 2006.*

Eurostat, Batiment Jean Monnet, Rue Alcide de Gasperi, L-2920 Luxembourg, http://epp.eurostat.ec.europa.eu; *Eurostat Yearbook 2006-2007.*

Taylor and Francis Group, An Informa Business, 2 Park Square, Milton Park, Abingdon, Oxford OX14 4RN, United Kingdom, (Dial from U.S. (212) 216-7800), (Fax from U.S. (212) 564-7854), www.tandf.co.uk; *The Europa World Year Book.*

UNICEF, 3 United Nations Plaza, New York, NY 10017, (800) 253-9646, Fax: (212) 887-7465, www.unicef.org; *The State of the World's Children 2008.*

United Nations Statistics Division, New York, NY 10017, (800) 253-9646, Fax: (212) 963-4116, http://unstats.un.org; *Demographic Yearbook; Human Development Report 2006; Statistical Yearbook; Trends in Europe and North America: The Statistical Yearbook of the ECE 2005;* and *World Statistics Pocketbook.*

The World Bank, 1818 H Street, NW, Washington, DC 20433, (202) 473-1000, Fax: (202) 477-6391, www.worldbank.org; *The World Bank Atlas 2003-2004; World Development Indicators (WDI) 2008;* and *World Development Report 2008.*

World Health Organization (WHO), Avenue Appia 20, 1211 Geneve 27, Switzerland, (Telephone in U.S. (212) 331-9081), www.who.int; The WHO Global Atlas of Infectious Diseases and *World Health Report 2006.*

GERMANY - MOTION PICTURES

Palgrave Macmillan Ltd., Houndmills, Basingstoke, Hampshire, RG21 6XS, England, (Telephone in U.S. (888) 330-8477), (Fax in U.S. (800) 672-2054), www.palgrave.com; *The Statesman's Yearbook 2008.*

UNESCO Institute for Statistics, C.P. 6128 Succursale Centre-Ville, Montreal, Quebec, H3C 3J7 Canada, (Dial from U.S. (514) 343-6880), (Fax from U.S. (514) 343 6882), www.uis.unesco.org; *Statistical Tables.*

United Nations Statistics Division, New York, NY 10017, (800) 253-9646, Fax: (212) 963-4116, http://unstats.un.org; *Statistical Yearbook.*

GERMANY - MOTOR VEHICLES

European Union, Delegation of the European Commission to the United States, 2300 M Street, NW, Washington, DC 20037, (202) 862-9500, Fax: (202) 429-1766, www.eurunion.org; *Statistical Overview of Transport in the European Union (Data 1970-2001).*

Eurostat, Batiment Jean Monnet, Rue Alcide de Gasperi, L-2920 Luxembourg, http://epp.eurostat.ec.europa.eu; *Eurostat Yearbook 2006-2007.*

Taylor and Francis Group, An Informa Business, 2 Park Square, Milton Park, Abingdon, Oxford OX14 4RN, United Kingdom, (Dial from U.S. (212) 216-7800), (Fax from U.S. (212) 564-7854), www.tandf.co.uk; *The Europa World Year Book.*

United Nations Statistics Division, New York, NY 10017, (800) 253-9646, Fax: (212) 963-4116, http://unstats.un.org; *Statistical Yearbook.*

GERMANY - MUSEUMS

M.E. Sharpe, 80 Business Park Drive, Armonk, NY 10504, (800) 541-6563, Fax: (914) 273-2106, www.mesharpe.com; *The Illustrated Book of World Rankings.*

UNESCO Institute for Statistics, C.P. 6128 Succursale Centre-Ville, Montreal, Quebec, H3C 3J7 Canada, (Dial from U.S. (514) 343-6880), (Fax from U.S. (514) 343 6882), www.uis.unesco.org; *Statistical Tables.*

GERMANY - NATIONAL INCOME

United Nations Statistics Division, New York, NY 10017, (800) 253-9646, Fax: (212) 963-4116, http://unstats.un.org; *Statistical Yearbook.*

GERMANY - NATURAL GAS PRODUCTION

See GERMANY - MINERAL INDUSTRIES

GERMANY - NICKEL AND NICKEL ORE

See GERMANY - MINERAL INDUSTRIES

GERMANY - NUTRITION

United Nations Food and Agricultural Organization (FAO), Viale delle Terme di Caracalla, 00100 Rome, Italy, (Dial from U.S. (202) 653-2400), (Fax from U.S. (202) 653 5760), www.fao.org; *The State of Food and Agriculture (SOFA) 2006.*

GERMANY - OATS PRODUCTION

See GERMANY - CROPS

GERMANY - OIL PRODUCING CROPS

See GERMANY - CROPS

GERMANY - OLDER PEOPLE

M.E. Sharpe, 80 Business Park Drive, Armonk, NY 10504, (800) 541-6563, Fax: (914) 273-2106, www.mesharpe.com; *The Illustrated Book of World Rankings.*

GERMANY - ONION PRODUCTION

See GERMANY - CROPS

GERMANY - PALM OIL PRODUCTION

See GERMANY - CROPS

GERMANY - PAPER

See GERMANY - FORESTS AND FORESTRY

GERMANY - PEANUT PRODUCTION

See GERMANY - CROPS

GERMANY - PEPPER PRODUCTION

See GERMANY - CROPS

GERMANY - PERIODICALS

UNESCO Institute for Statistics, C.P. 6128 Succursale Centre-Ville, Montreal, Quebec, H3C 3J7 Canada, (Dial from U.S. (514) 343-6880), (Fax from U.S. (514) 343 6882), www.uis.unesco.org; *Statistical Tables.*

GERMANY - PESTICIDES

United Nations Food and Agricultural Organization (FAO), Viale delle Terme di Caracalla, 00100 Rome, Italy, (Dial from U.S. (202) 653-2400), (Fax from U.S. (202) 653 5760), www.fao.org; *The State of Food and Agriculture (SOFA) 2006.*

GERMANY - PETROLEUM INDUSTRY AND TRADE

Euromonitor International, Inc., 224 S. Michigan Avenue, Suite 1500, Chicago, IL 60604, (312) 922-1115, Fax: (312) 922-1157, www.euromonitor.com; *European Marketing Data and Statistics 2008.*

Eurostat, Batiment Jean Monnet, Rue Alcide de Gasperi, L-2920 Luxembourg, http://epp.eurostat.ec.europa.eu; *Eurostat Yearbook 2006-2007.*

International Energy Agency (IEA), 9, rue de la Federation, 75739 Paris Cedex 15, France, www.iea.org; *Key World Energy Statistics 2007.*

M.E. Sharpe, 80 Business Park Drive, Armonk, NY 10504, (800) 541-6563, Fax: (914) 273-2106, www.mesharpe.com; *The Illustrated Book of World Rankings.*

Organisation for Economic Cooperation and Development (OECD), 2 rue Andre Pascal, F-75775 Paris Cedex 16, France, (Telephone in U.S. (202) 785-6323), (Fax in U.S. (202) 785-0350), www.oecd.org; *Energy Statistics of OECD Countries* (2007 Edition); *Indicators of Industrial Activity; International Trade by Commodity Statistics (ITCS); Oil Information 2006 Edition;* and *World Energy Outlook 2007.*

Palgrave Macmillan Ltd., Houndmills, Basingstoke, Hampshire, RG21 6XS, England, (Telephone in U.S. (888) 330-8477), (Fax in U.S. (800) 672-2054), www.palgrave.com; *The Statesman's Yearbook 2008.*

PennWell Corporation, 1421 South Sheridan Road, Tulsa, OK 74112, (918) 835-3161, www.pennwell.com; *International Petroleum Encyclopedia 2007.*

Platts, 2 Penn Plaza, 25th Floor, New York, NY 10121-2298, (212) 904-3070, www.platts.com; *Energy Economist.*

U.S. Department of Energy (DOE), Energy Information Administration (EIA), 1000 Independence Avenue, SW, Washington, DC 20585, (202) 586-8800, www.eia.doe.gov; *International Energy Annual 2004* and *International Energy Outlook 2006*.

United Nations Conference on Trade and Development (UNCTAD), DC2-1120, United Nations, New York, NY 10017, (212) 963-0027, www.unctad.org; *UNCTAD Commodity Yearbook*.

United Nations Food and Agricultural Organization (FAO), Viale delle Terme di Caracalla, 00100 Rome, Italy, (Dial from U.S. (202) 653-2400), (Fax from U.S. (202) 653 5760), www.fao.org; *The State of Food and Agriculture (SOFA) 2006*.

United Nations Statistics Division, New York, NY 10017, (800) 253-9646, Fax: (212) 963-4116, http://unstats.un.org; *Energy Statistics Yearbook 2003; Statistical Yearbook;* and *Trends in Europe and North America: The Statistical Yearbook of the ECE 2005*.

GERMANY - PHOSPHATES PRODUCTION

See GERMANY - MINERAL INDUSTRIES

GERMANY - PIPELINES

European Union, Delegation of the European Commission to the United States, 2300 M Street, NW, Washington, DC 20037, (202) 862-9500, Fax: (202) 429-1766, www.eurunion.org; *Statistical Overview of Transport in the European Union (Data 1970-2001)*.

United Nations Statistics Division, New York, NY 10017, (800) 253-9646, Fax: (212) 963-4116, http://unstats.un.org; *Annual Bulletin of Transport Statistics for Europe and North America 2004*.

GERMANY - PLASTICS INDUSTRY AND TRADE

Eurostat, Batiment Jean Monnet, Rue Alcide de Gasperi, L-2920 Luxembourg, http://epp.eurostat.ec.europa.eu; *Eurostat Yearbook 2006-2007*.

Organisation for Economic Cooperation and Development (OECD), 2 rue Andre Pascal, F-75775 Paris Cedex 16, France, (Telephone in U.S. (202) 785-6323), (Fax in U.S. (202) 785-0350), www.oecd.org; *International Trade by Commodity Statistics (ITCS)*.

United Nations Statistics Division, New York, NY 10017, (800) 253-9646, Fax: (212) 963-4116, http://unstats.un.org; *Statistical Yearbook*.

GERMANY - PLATINUM PRODUCTION

See GERMANY - MINERAL INDUSTRIES

GERMANY - POLITICAL SCIENCE

Central Intelligence Agency, Office of Public Affairs, Washington, DC 20505, (703) 482-0623, Fax: (703) 482-1739, www.cia.gov; *The World Factbook*.

European Union, Delegation of the European Commission to the United States, 2300 M Street, NW, Washington, DC 20037, (202) 862-9500, Fax: (202) 429-1766, www.eurunion.org; *RD Expenditure in Europe (2006 edition)*.

Eurostat, Batiment Jean Monnet, Rue Alcide de Gasperi, L-2920 Luxembourg, http://epp.eurostat.ec.europa.eu; *Eurostat Yearbook 2006-2007*.

Organisation for Economic Cooperation and Development (OECD), 2 rue Andre Pascal, F-75775 Paris Cedex 16, France, (Telephone in U.S. (202) 785-6323), (Fax in U.S. (202) 785-0350), www.oecd.org; *OECD Economic Outlook 2008* and *Revenue Statistics 1965-2006 - 2007 Edition*.

Palgrave Macmillan Ltd., Houndmills, Basingstoke, Hampshire, RG21 6XS, England, (Telephone in U.S. (888) 330-8477), (Fax in U.S. (800) 672-2054), www.palgrave.com; *The Statesman's Yearbook 2008*.

Taylor and Francis Group, An Informa Business, 2 Park Square, Milton Park, Abingdon, Oxford OX14 4RN, United Kingdom, (Dial from U.S. (212) 216-7800), (Fax from U.S. (212) 564-7854), www.tandf.co.uk; *The Europa World Year Book*.

United Nations Statistics Division, New York, NY 10017, (800) 253-9646, Fax: (212) 963-4116, http://unstats.un.org; *National Accounts Statistics: Compendium of Income Distribution Statistics* and *Statistical Yearbook*.

The World Bank, 1818 H Street, NW, Washington, DC 20433, (202) 473-1000, Fax: (202) 477-6391, www.worldbank.org; *World Development Indicators (WDI) 2008* and *World Development Report 2008*.

GERMANY - POPULATION

Banque de France, 48 rue Croix des Petits champs, 75001 Paris, France, www.banque-france.fr/home.htm; *Key Data for the Euro Area*.

Central Intelligence Agency, Office of Public Affairs, Washington, DC 20505, (703) 482-0623, Fax: (703) 482-1739, www.cia.gov; *The World Factbook*.

Economist Intelligence Unit, 111 West 57th Street, New York, NY 10019, (212) 554-0600, Fax: (212) 586-1181, www.eiu.com; *Germany Country Report*.

Euromonitor International, Inc., 224 S. Michigan Avenue, Suite 1500, Chicago, IL 60604, (312) 922-1115, Fax: (312) 922-1157, www.euromonitor.com; *European Marketing Data and Statistics 2008* and *The World Economic Factbook 2008*.

European Union, Delegation of the European Commission to the United States, 2300 M Street, NW, Washington, DC 20037, (202) 862-9500, Fax: (202) 429-1766, www.eurunion.org; *European Union Labour Force Survey; First Demographic Estimates for 2006;* and *Regions - Statistical Yearbook 2006*.

Eurostat, Batiment Jean Monnet, Rue Alcide de Gasperi, L-2920 Luxembourg, http://epp.eurostat.ec.europa.eu; *Eurostat Yearbook 2006-2007*.

International Labour Office, I.L.O. Publications, 4 route des Morillons, CH-1211 Geneva 22, Switzerland, (Telephone in U.S. (202) 653-7652), (Fax in U.S. (202) 653-7687), www.ilo.org; *Yearbook of Labour Statistics 2006*.

International Organization for Migration (IOM), 17, Route des Morillons, CH-1211 Geneva 19, Switzerland, www.iom.int; *Trafficking in Human Beings and the 2006 World Cup in Germany*.

M.E. Sharpe, 80 Business Park Drive, Armonk, NY 10504, (800) 541-6563, Fax: (914) 273-2106, www.mesharpe.com; *The Illustrated Book of World Rankings*.

Organisation for Economic Cooperation and Development (OECD), 2 rue Andre Pascal, F-75775 Paris Cedex 16, France, (Telephone in U.S. (202) 785-6323), (Fax in U.S. (202) 785-0350), www.oecd.org; *Labour Force Statistics: 1986-2005, 2007 Edition*.

Palgrave Macmillan Ltd., Houndmills, Basingstoke, Hampshire, RG21 6XS, England, (Telephone in U.S. (888) 330-8477), (Fax in U.S. (800) 672-2054), www.palgrave.com; *The Statesman's Yearbook 2008*.

Taylor and Francis Group, An Informa Business, 2 Park Square, Milton Park, Abingdon, Oxford OX14 4RN, United Kingdom, (Dial from U.S. (212) 216-7800), (Fax from U.S. (212) 564-7854), www.tandf.co.uk; *The Europa World Year Book*.

U.S. Department of State (DOS), 2201 C Street NW, Washington, DC 20520, (202) 647-4000, www.state.gov; *World Military Expenditures and Arms Transfers (WMEAT)*.

UNESCO Institute for Statistics, C.P. 6128 Succursale Centre-Ville, Montreal, Quebec, H3C 3J7 Canada, (Dial from U.S. (514) 343-6880), (Fax from U.S. (514) 343 6882), www.uis.unesco.org; *Statistical Tables*.

United Nations Food and Agricultural Organization (FAO), Viale delle Terme di Caracalla, 00100 Rome, Italy, (Dial from U.S. (202) 653-2400), (Fax from U.S. (202) 653 5760), www.fao.org; *FAO Production Yearbook 2002*.

United Nations Statistics Division, New York, NY 10017, (800) 253-9646, Fax: (212) 963-4116, http://unstats.un.org; *Demographic Yearbook; Human Development Report 2006; Statistical Yearbook; Trends in Europe and North America: The Statistical Yearbook of the ECE 2005;* and *World Statistics Pocketbook*.

The World Bank, 1818 H Street, NW, Washington, DC 20433, (202) 473-1000, Fax: (202) 477-6391, www.worldbank.org; *Germany; The World Bank Atlas 2003-2004;* and *World Development Report 2008*.

World Health Organization (WHO), Avenue Appia 20, 1211 Geneve 27, Switzerland, (Telephone in U.S. (212) 331-9081), www.who.int; *World Health Report 2006*.

GERMANY - POPULATION DENSITY

Central Intelligence Agency, Office of Public Affairs, Washington, DC 20505, (703) 482-0623, Fax: (703) 482-1739, www.cia.gov; *The World Factbook*.

Euromonitor International, Inc., 224 S. Michigan Avenue, Suite 1500, Chicago, IL 60604, (312) 922-1115, Fax: (312) 922-1157, www.euromonitor.com; *The World Economic Factbook 2008*.

European Union, Delegation of the European Commission to the United States, 2300 M Street, NW, Washington, DC 20037, (202) 862-9500, Fax: (202) 429-1766, www.eurunion.org; *First Demographic Estimates for 2006*.

Eurostat, Batiment Jean Monnet, Rue Alcide de Gasperi, L-2920 Luxembourg, http://epp.eurostat.ec.europa.eu; *Eurostat Yearbook 2006-2007*.

M.E. Sharpe, 80 Business Park Drive, Armonk, NY 10504, (800) 541-6563, Fax: (914) 273-2106, www.mesharpe.com; *The Illustrated Book of World Rankings*.

Palgrave Macmillan Ltd., Houndmills, Basingstoke, Hampshire, RG21 6XS, England, (Telephone in U.S. (888) 330-8477), (Fax in U.S. (800) 672-2054), www.palgrave.com; *The Statesman's Yearbook 2008*.

Taylor and Francis Group, An Informa Business, 2 Park Square, Milton Park, Abingdon, Oxford OX14 4RN, United Kingdom, (Dial from U.S. (212) 216-7800), (Fax from U.S. (212) 564-7854), www.tandf.co.uk; *The Europa World Year Book*.

UNESCO Institute for Statistics, C.P. 6128 Succursale Centre-Ville, Montreal, Quebec, H3C 3J7 Canada, (Dial from U.S. (514) 343-6880), (Fax from U.S. (514) 343 6882), www.uis.unesco.org; *Statistical Tables*.

United Nations Food and Agricultural Organization (FAO), Viale delle Terme di Caracalla, 00100 Rome, Italy, (Dial from U.S. (202) 653-2400), (Fax from U.S. (202) 653 5760), www.fao.org; *The State of Food and Agriculture (SOFA) 2006*.

United Nations Statistics Division, New York, NY 10017, (800) 253-9646, Fax: (212) 963-4116, http://unstats.un.org; *Statistical Yearbook* and *Trends in Europe and North America: The Statistical Yearbook of the ECE 2005*.

The World Bank, 1818 H Street, NW, Washington, DC 20433, (202) 473-1000, Fax: (202) 477-6391, www.worldbank.org; *Germany* and *World Development Report 2008*.

GERMANY - POSTAL SERVICE

European Union, Delegation of the European Commission to the United States, 2300 M Street, NW, Washington, DC 20037, (202) 862-9500, Fax: (202) 429-1766, www.eurunion.org; *Statistical Overview of Transport in the European Union (Data 1970-2001)*.

M.E. Sharpe, 80 Business Park Drive, Armonk, NY 10504, (800) 541-6563, Fax: (914) 273-2106, www.mesharpe.com; *The Illustrated Book of World Rankings*.

Palgrave Macmillan Ltd., Houndmills, Basingstoke, Hampshire, RG21 6XS, England, (Telephone in U.S. (888) 330-8477), (Fax in U.S. (800) 672-2054), www.palgrave.com; *The Statesman's Yearbook 2008*.

United Nations Statistics Division, New York, NY 10017, (800) 253-9646, Fax: (212) 963-4116, http://

unstats.un.org; *Statistical Yearbook* and *Trends in Europe and North America: The Statistical Yearbook of the ECE 2005.*

GERMANY - POWER RESOURCES

Euromonitor International, Inc., 224 S. Michigan Avenue, Suite 1500, Chicago, IL 60604, (312) 922-1115, Fax: (312) 922-1157, www.euromonitor.com; *European Marketing Data and Statistics 2008; The World Economic Factbook 2008;* and *World Marketing Data and Statistics.*

European Union, Delegation of the European Commission to the United States, 2300 M Street, NW, Washington, DC 20037, (202) 862-9500, Fax: (202) 429-1766, www.eurunion.org; *European Union Energy Transport in Figures 2006; Regions - Statistical Yearbook 2006;* and *Statistical Overview of Transport in the European Union (Data 1970-2001).*

Eurostat, Batiment Jean Monnet, Rue Alcide de Gasperi, L-2920 Luxembourg, http://epp.eurostat.ec.europa.eu; *Eurostat Yearbook 2006-2007.*

M.E. Sharpe, 80 Business Park Drive, Armonk, NY 10504, (800) 541-6563, Fax: (914) 273-2106, www.mesharpe.com; *The Illustrated Book of World Rankings.*

Organisation for Economic Cooperation and Development (OECD), 2 rue Andre Pascal, F-75775 Paris Cedex 16, France, (Telephone in U.S. (202) 785-6323), (Fax in U.S. (202) 785-0350), www.oecd.org; *Coal Information: 2007 Edition; Energy Statistics of OECD Countries* (2007 Edition); *Key Environmental Indicators 2004; Oil Information 2006 Edition;* and *World Energy Outlook 2007.*

Palgrave Macmillan Ltd., Houndmills, Basingstoke, Hampshire, RG21 6XS, England, (Telephone in U.S. (888) 330-8477), (Fax in U.S. (800) 672-2054), www.palgrave.com; *The Statesman's Yearbook 2008.*

Platts, 2 Penn Plaza, 25th Floor, New York, NY 10121-2298, (212) 904-3070, www.platts.com; *Energy Economist* and *European Power Daily.*

U.S. Department of Energy (DOE), Energy Information Administration (EIA), 1000 Independence Avenue, SW, Washington, DC 20585, (202) 586-8800, www.eia.doe.gov; *International Energy Annual 2004* and *International Energy Outlook 2006.*

United Nations Food and Agricultural Organization (FAO), Viale delle Terme di Caracalla, 00100 Rome, Italy, (Dial from U.S. (202) 653-2400), (Fax from U.S. (202) 653 5760), www.fao.org; *The State of Food and Agriculture (SOFA) 2006.*

United Nations Statistics Division, New York, NY 10017, (800) 253-9646, Fax: (212) 963-4116, http://unstats.un.org; *Energy Statistics Yearbook 2003; Human Development Report 2006; Statistical Yearbook; Trends in Europe and North America: The Statistical Yearbook of the ECE 2005;* and *World Statistics Pocketbook.*

The World Bank, 1818 H Street, NW, Washington, DC 20433, (202) 473-1000, Fax: (202) 477-6391, www.worldbank.org; *The World Bank Atlas 2003-2004* and *World Development Report 2008.*

GERMANY - PRICES

Euromonitor International, Inc., 224 S. Michigan Avenue, Suite 1500, Chicago, IL 60604, (312) 922-1115, Fax: (312) 922-1157, www.euromonitor.com; *European Marketing Data and Statistics 2008* and *World Marketing Data and Statistics.*

European Union, Delegation of the European Commission to the United States, 2300 M Street, NW, Washington, DC 20037, (202) 862-9500, Fax: (202) 429-1766, www.eurunion.org; *Eurostatistics: Data for Short-Term Economic Analysis (2007 edition).*

Eurostat, Batiment Jean Monnet, Rue Alcide de Gasperi, L-2920 Luxembourg, http://epp.eurostat.ec.europa.eu; *Eurostat Yearbook 2006-2007.*

International Labour Office, I.L.O. Publications, 4 route des Morillons, CH-1211 Geneva 22, Switzerland, (Telephone in U.S. (202) 653-7652), (Fax in U.S. (202) 653-7687), www.ilo.org; *Yearbook of Labour Statistics 2006.*

International Lead and Zinc Study Group (ILZSG), Rua Almirante Barroso 38, 5th Floor, Lisbon 1000 - 013, Portugal, www.ilzsg.org; Interactive Statistical Database.

M.E. Sharpe, 80 Business Park Drive, Armonk, NY 10504, (800) 541-6563, Fax: (914) 273-2106, www.mesharpe.com; *The Illustrated Book of World Rankings.*

Organisation for Economic Cooperation and Development (OECD), 2 rue Andre Pascal, F-75775 Paris Cedex 16, France, (Telephone in U.S. (202) 785-6323), (Fax in U.S. (202) 785-0350), www.oecd.org; *Indicators of Industrial Activity; Iron and Steel Industry in 2004 (2006 Edition); OECD Economic Outlook 2008;* and *OECD Main Economic Indicators (MEI).*

Technical Association of the Pulp and Paper Industry (TAPPI), 15 Technology Parkway South, Norcross, GA 30092, (770) 446-1400, Fax: (770) 446-6947, www.tappi.org; *TAPPI Annual Report.*

United Nations Food and Agricultural Organization (FAO), Viale delle Terme di Caracalla, 00100 Rome, Italy, (Dial from U.S. (202) 653-2400), (Fax from U.S. (202) 653 5760), www.fao.org; *FAO Production Yearbook 2002* and *The State of Food and Agriculture (SOFA) 2006.*

The World Bank, 1818 H Street, NW, Washington, DC 20433, (202) 473-1000, Fax: (202) 477-6391, www.worldbank.org; *Germany.*

World Bureau of Metal Statistics (WBMS), 27a High Street, Ware, Hertfordshire, SG12 9BA, United Kingdom, www.world-bureau.com; *World Flow Charts* and *World Metal Statistics.*

GERMANY - PROFESSIONS

Eurostat, Batiment Jean Monnet, Rue Alcide de Gasperi, L-2920 Luxembourg, http://epp.eurostat.ec.europa.eu; *Eurostat Yearbook 2006-2007.*

United Nations Statistics Division, New York, NY 10017, (800) 253-9646, Fax: (212) 963-4116, http://unstats.un.org; *Statistical Yearbook.*

GERMANY - PUBLIC HEALTH

Euromonitor International, Inc., 224 S. Michigan Avenue, Suite 1500, Chicago, IL 60604, (312) 922-1115, Fax: (312) 922-1157, www.euromonitor.com; *World Health Databook 2007/2008* and *World Marketing Data and Statistics.*

European Centre for Disease Prevention and Control (ECDC), 171 83 Stockholm, Sweden, www.ecdc.europa.eu; *Eurosurveillance.*

European Union, Delegation of the European Commission to the United States, 2300 M Street, NW, Washington, DC 20037, (202) 862-9500, Fax: (202) 429-1766, www.eurunion.org; *Regions - Statistical Yearbook 2006.*

Eurostat, Batiment Jean Monnet, Rue Alcide de Gasperi, L-2920 Luxembourg, http://epp.eurostat.ec.europa.eu; *Eurostat Yearbook 2006-2007.*

Health and Consumer Protection Directorate-General, European Commission, B-1049 Brussels, Belgium, http://ec.europa.eu/dgs/health_consumer/index_en.htm; *Injuries in the European Union: Statistics Summary 2002-2004.*

M.E. Sharpe, 80 Business Park Drive, Armonk, NY 10504, (800) 541-6563, Fax: (914) 273-2106, www.mesharpe.com; *The Illustrated Book of World Rankings.*

Organisation for Economic Cooperation and Development (OECD), 2 rue Andre Pascal, F-75775 Paris Cedex 16, France, (Telephone in U.S. (202) 785-6323), (Fax in U.S. (202) 785-0350), www.oecd.org; *Health at a Glance 2007 - OECD Indicators.*

Palgrave Macmillan Ltd., Houndmills, Basingstoke, Hampshire, RG21 6XS, England, (Telephone in U.S. (888) 330-8477), (Fax in U.S. (800) 672-2054), www.palgrave.com; *The Statesman's Yearbook 2008.*

Robert Koch Institute, Nordufer 20, D 13353 Berlin, Germany, www.rki.de; *EUVAC-NET Report: Pertussis-Surveillance 1998-2002* and *Health in Germany 2006.*

UNICEF, 3 United Nations Plaza, New York, NY 10017, (800) 253-9646, Fax: (212) 887-7465, www.unicef.org; *The State of the World's Children 2008.*

United Nations Statistics Division, New York, NY 10017, (800) 253-9646, Fax: (212) 963-4116, http://unstats.un.org; *Human Development Report 2006; Statistical Yearbook;* and *Trends in Europe and North America: The Statistical Yearbook of the ECE 2005.*

The World Bank, 1818 H Street, NW, Washington, DC 20433, (202) 473-1000, Fax: (202) 477-6391, www.worldbank.org; *Germany* and *World Development Report 2008.*

World Health Organization (WHO), Avenue Appia 20, 1211 Geneve 27, Switzerland, (Telephone in U.S. (212) 331-9081), www.who.int; *The WHO Global Atlas of Infectious Diseases* and *World Health Report 2006.*

GERMANY - PUBLIC UTILITIES

Eurostat, Batiment Jean Monnet, Rue Alcide de Gasperi, L-2920 Luxembourg, http://epp.eurostat.ec.europa.eu; *Eurostat Yearbook 2006-2007.*

GERMANY - PUBLISHERS AND PUBLISHING

Organisation for Economic Cooperation and Development (OECD), 2 rue Andre Pascal, F-75775 Paris Cedex 16, France, (Telephone in U.S. (202) 785-6323), (Fax in U.S. (202) 785-0350), www.oecd.org; *Indicators of Industrial Activity.*

Palgrave Macmillan Ltd., Houndmills, Basingstoke, Hampshire, RG21 6XS, England, (Telephone in U.S. (888) 330-8477), (Fax in U.S. (800) 672-2054), www.palgrave.com; *The Statesman's Yearbook 2008.*

Taylor and Francis Group, An Informa Business, 2 Park Square, Milton Park, Abingdon, Oxford OX14 4RN, United Kingdom, (Dial from U.S. (212) 216-7800), (Fax from U.S. (212) 564-7854), www.tandf.co.uk; *The Europa World Year Book.*

UNESCO Institute for Statistics, C.P. 6128 Succursale Centre-Ville, Montreal, Quebec, H3C 3J7 Canada, (Dial from U.S. (514) 343-6880), (Fax from U.S. (514) 343 6882), www.uis.unesco.org; *Statistical Tables.*

United Nations Statistics Division, New York, NY 10017, (800) 253-9646, Fax: (212) 963-4116, http://unstats.un.org; *Trends in Europe and North America: The Statistical Yearbook of the ECE 2005.*

GERMANY - RADIO - RECEIVERS AND RECEPTION

Palgrave Macmillan Ltd., Houndmills, Basingstoke, Hampshire, RG21 6XS, England, (Telephone in U.S. (888) 330-8477), (Fax in U.S. (800) 672-2054), www.palgrave.com; *The Statesman's Yearbook 2008.*

United Nations Statistics Division, New York, NY 10017, (800) 253-9646, Fax: (212) 963-4116, http://unstats.un.org; *Statistical Yearbook.*

GERMANY - RAILROADS

Euromonitor International, Inc., 224 S. Michigan Avenue, Suite 1500, Chicago, IL 60604, (312) 922-1115, Fax: (312) 922-1157, www.euromonitor.com; *European Marketing Data and Statistics 2008.*

European Union, Delegation of the European Commission to the United States, 2300 M Street, NW, Washington, DC 20037, (202) 862-9500, Fax: (202) 429-1766, www.eurunion.org; *Regions - Statistical Yearbook 2006* and *Statistical Overview of Transport in the European Union (Data 1970-2001).*

Eurostat, Batiment Jean Monnet, Rue Alcide de Gasperi, L-2920 Luxembourg, http://epp.eurostat.ec.europa.eu; *Eurostat Yearbook 2006-2007.*

Jane's Information Group, 110 North Royal Street, Suite 200, Alexandria, VA 22314, (703) 683-3700, Fax: (800) 836-0297, www.janes.com; *Jane's World Railways.*

Palgrave Macmillan Ltd., Houndmills, Basingstoke, Hampshire, RG21 6XS, England, (Telephone in U.S.

(888) 330-8477), (Fax in U.S. (800) 672-2054), www.palgrave.com; *The Statesman's Yearbook 2008.*

Taylor and Francis Group, An Informa Business, 2 Park Square, Milton Park, Abingdon, Oxford OX14 4RN, United Kingdom, (Dial from U.S. (212) 216-7800), (Fax from U.S. (212) 564-7854), www.tandf.co.uk; *The Europa World Year Book.*

United Nations Statistics Division, New York, NY 10017, (800) 253-9646, Fax: (212) 963-4116, http://unstats.un.org; *Annual Bulletin of Transport Statistics for Europe and North America 2004; Statistical Yearbook;* and *Trends in Europe and North America: The Statistical Yearbook of the ECE 2005.*

GERMANY - RELIGION

Central Intelligence Agency, Office of Public Affairs, Washington, DC 20505, (703) 482-0623, Fax: (703) 482-1739, www.cia.gov; *The World Factbook.*

M.E. Sharpe, 80 Business Park Drive, Armonk, NY 10504, (800) 541-6563, Fax: (914) 273-2106, www.mesharpe.com; *The Illustrated Book of World Rankings.*

Palgrave Macmillan Ltd., Houndmills, Basingstoke, Hampshire, RG21 6XS, England, (Telephone in U.S. (888) 330-8477), (Fax in U.S. (800) 672-2054), www.palgrave.com; *The Statesman's Yearbook 2008.*

GERMANY - RENT CHARGES

International Labour Office, I.L.O. Publications, 4 route des Morillons, CH-1211 Geneva 22, Switzerland, (Telephone in U.S. (202) 653-7652), (Fax in U.S. (202) 653-7687), www.ilo.org; *Yearbook of Labour Statistics 2006.*

GERMANY - RESERVES (ACCOUNTING)

Eurostat, Batiment Jean Monnet, Rue Alcide de Gasperi, L-2920 Luxembourg, http://epp.eurostat.ec.europa.eu; *Eurostat Yearbook 2006-2007.*

Organisation for Economic Cooperation and Development (OECD), 2 rue Andre Pascal, F-75775 Paris Cedex 16, France, (Telephone in U.S. (202) 785-6323), (Fax in U.S. (202) 785-0350), www.oecd.org; *Financial Market Trends: OECD Periodical* and *OECD Economic Outlook 2008.*

United Nations Statistics Division, New York, NY 10017, (800) 253-9646, Fax: (212) 963-4116, http://unstats.un.org; *Statistical Yearbook.*

The World Bank, 1818 H Street, NW, Washington, DC 20433, (202) 473-1000, Fax: (202) 477-6391, www.worldbank.org; *World Development Indicators (WDI) 2008.*

GERMANY - RETAIL TRADE

Banque de France, 48 rue Croix des Petits champs, 75001 Paris, France, www.banque-france.fr/home.htm; *Monthly Business Survey Overview.*

Euromonitor International, Inc., 224 S. Michigan Avenue, Suite 1500, Chicago, IL 60604, (312) 922-1115, Fax: (312) 922-1157, www.euromonitor.com; *Retail Trade International 2007* and *World Marketing Data and Statistics.*

European Union, Delegation of the European Commission to the United States, 2300 M Street, NW, Washington, DC 20037, (202) 862-9500, Fax: (202) 429-1766, www.eurunion.org; *Eurostatistics: Data for Short-Term Economic Analysis (2007 edition).*

Eurostat, Batiment Jean Monnet, Rue Alcide de Gasperi, L-2920 Luxembourg, http://epp.eurostat.ec.europa.eu; *Eurostat Yearbook 2006-2007.*

United Nations Statistics Division, New York, NY 10017, (800) 253-9646, Fax: (212) 963-4116, http://unstats.un.org; *Statistical Yearbook.*

GERMANY - RICE PRODUCTION

See GERMANY - CROPS

GERMANY - ROADS

Central Intelligence Agency, Office of Public Affairs, Washington, DC 20505, (703) 482-0623, Fax: (703) 482-1739, www.cia.gov; *The World Factbook.*

European Union, Delegation of the European Commission to the United States, 2300 M Street, NW, Washington, DC 20037, (202) 862-9500, Fax: (202) 429-1766, www.eurunion.org; *Statistical Overview of Transport in the European Union (Data 1970-2001).*

Eurostat, Batiment Jean Monnet, Rue Alcide de Gasperi, L-2920 Luxembourg, http://epp.eurostat.ec.europa.eu; *Eurostat Yearbook 2006-2007.*

International Road Federation (IFR), Madison Place, 500 Montgomery Street, 5th Floor, Alexandria, VA 22314, (703) 535-1001, Fax: (703) 535-1007, www.irfnet.org; *World Road Statistics 2006.*

Palgrave Macmillan Ltd., Houndmills, Basingstoke, Hampshire, RG21 6XS, England, (Telephone in U.S. (888) 330-8477), (Fax in U.S. (800) 672-2054), www.palgrave.com; *The Statesman's Yearbook 2008.*

United Nations Statistics Division, New York, NY 10017, (800) 253-9646, Fax: (212) 963-4116, http://unstats.un.org; *Annual Bulletin of Transport Statistics for Europe and North America 2004* and *Trends in Europe and North America: The Statistical Yearbook of the ECE 2005.*

GERMANY - RUBBER INDUSTRY AND TRADE

Eurostat, Batiment Jean Monnet, Rue Alcide de Gasperi, L-2920 Luxembourg, http://epp.eurostat.ec.europa.eu; *Eurostat Yearbook 2006-2007.*

International Rubber Study Group (IRSG), 1st Floor, Heron House, 109/115 Wembley Hill Road, Wembley, Middlesex HA9 8DA, United Kingdom, www.rubberstudy.com; *Rubber Statistical Bulletin; Summary of World Rubber Statistics 2005; World Rubber Statistics Handbook (Volume 6, 1975-2001);* and *World Rubber Statistics Historic Handbook.*

M.E. Sharpe, 80 Business Park Drive, Armonk, NY 10504, (800) 541-6563, Fax: (914) 273-2106, www.mesharpe.com; *The Illustrated Book of World Rankings.*

Organisation for Economic Cooperation and Development (OECD), 2 rue Andre Pascal, F-75775 Paris Cedex 16, France, (Telephone in U.S. (202) 785-6323), (Fax in U.S. (202) 785-0350), www.oecd.org; *International Trade by Commodity Statistics (ITCS).*

United Nations Statistics Division, New York, NY 10017, (800) 253-9646, Fax: (212) 963-4116, http://unstats.un.org; *Statistical Yearbook.*

GERMANY - RYE PRODUCTION

See GERMANY - CROPS

GERMANY - SAFFLOWER SEED PRODUCTION

See GERMANY - CROPS

GERMANY - SALT PRODUCTION

See GERMANY - MINERAL INDUSTRIES

GERMANY - SAVINGS ACCOUNT DEPOSITS

See GERMANY - BANKS AND BANKING

GERMANY - SHEEP

See GERMANY - LIVESTOCK

GERMANY - SHIPBUILDING

Organisation for Economic Cooperation and Development (OECD), 2 rue Andre Pascal, F-75775 Paris Cedex 16, France, (Telephone in U.S. (202) 785-6323), (Fax in U.S. (202) 785-0350), www.oecd.org; *Indicators of Industrial Activity.*

GERMANY - SHIPPING

European Union, Delegation of the European Commission to the United States, 2300 M Street, NW, Washington, DC 20037, (202) 862-9500, Fax: (202) 429-1766, www.eurunion.org; *Fishery Statistics - 1990-2006; Regions - Statistical Yearbook 2006;* and *Statistical Overview of Transport in the European Union (Data 1970-2001).*

Eurostat, Batiment Jean Monnet, Rue Alcide de Gasperi, L-2920 Luxembourg, http://epp.eurostat.ec.europa.eu; *Eurostat Yearbook 2006-2007.*

Lloyd's Register - Fairplay, 8410 N.W. 53rd Terrace, Suite 207, Miami FL 33166, (305) 718-9929, Fax: (305) 718-9663, www.lrfairplay.com; *Register of Ships 2007-2008; World Casualty Statistics 2007; World Fleet Statistics 2006; World Marine Propulsion Report 2006-2010; World Shipbuilding Statistics 2007;* and The World Shipping Encyclopaedia.

Organisation for Economic Cooperation and Development (OECD), 2 rue Andre Pascal, F-75775 Paris Cedex 16, France, (Telephone in U.S. (202) 785-6323), (Fax in U.S. (202) 785-0350), www.oecd.org; *Statistics on Ship Production, Exports and Orders in 2004.*

Palgrave Macmillan Ltd., Houndmills, Basingstoke, Hampshire, RG21 6XS, England, (Telephone in U.S. (888) 330-8477), (Fax in U.S. (800) 672-2054), www.palgrave.com; *The Statesman's Yearbook 2008.*

Taylor and Francis Group, An Informa Business, 2 Park Square, Milton Park, Abingdon, Oxford OX14 4RN, United Kingdom, (Dial from U.S. (212) 216-7800), (Fax from U.S. (212) 564-7854), www.tandf.co.uk; *The Europa World Year Book.*

U.S. Department of Transportation (DOT), Maritime Administration (MARAD), West Building, Southeast Federal Center, 1200 New Jersey Avenue, SE, Washington, DC 20590, (800) 99-MARAD, www.marad.dot.gov; *World Merchant Fleet 2005.*

United Nations Statistics Division, New York, NY 10017, (800) 253-9646, Fax: (212) 963-4116, http://unstats.un.org; *Annual Bulletin of Transport Statistics for Europe and North America 2004* and *Statistical Yearbook.*

GERMANY - SILVER PRODUCTION

See GERMANY - MINERAL INDUSTRIES

GERMANY - SOCIAL CLASSES

European Union, Delegation of the European Commission to the United States, 2300 M Street, NW, Washington, DC 20037, (202) 862-9500, Fax: (202) 429-1766, www.eurunion.org; *European Union Labour Force Survey.*

Eurostat, Batiment Jean Monnet, Rue Alcide de Gasperi, L-2920 Luxembourg, http://epp.eurostat.ec.europa.eu; *Eurostat Yearbook 2006-2007.*

GERMANY - SOCIAL ECOLOGY

Eurostat, Batiment Jean Monnet, Rue Alcide de Gasperi, L-2920 Luxembourg, http://epp.eurostat.ec.europa.eu; *Eurostat Yearbook 2006-2007.*

M.E. Sharpe, 80 Business Park Drive, Armonk, NY 10504, (800) 541-6563, Fax: (914) 273-2106, www.mesharpe.com; *The Illustrated Book of World Rankings.*

United Nations Statistics Division, New York, NY 10017, (800) 253-9646, Fax: (212) 963-4116, http://unstats.un.org; *World Statistics Pocketbook.*

GERMANY - SOCIAL SECURITY

Eurostat, Batiment Jean Monnet, Rue Alcide de Gasperi, L-2920 Luxembourg, http://epp.eurostat.ec.europa.eu; *Eurostat Yearbook 2006-2007.*

Organisation for Economic Cooperation and Development (OECD), 2 rue Andre Pascal, F-75775 Paris Cedex 16, France, (Telephone in U.S. (202) 785-6323), (Fax in U.S. (202) 785-0350), www.oecd.org; *Revenue Statistics 1965-2006 - 2007 Edition.*

Palgrave Macmillan Ltd., Houndmills, Basingstoke, Hampshire, RG21 6XS, England, (Telephone in U.S. (888) 330-8477), (Fax in U.S. (800) 672-2054), www.palgrave.com; *The Statesman's Yearbook 2008.*

United Nations Statistics Division, New York, NY 10017, (800) 253-9646, Fax: (212) 963-4116, http://unstats.un.org; *National Accounts Statistics: Compendium of Income Distribution Statistics.*

GERMANY - SOYBEAN PRODUCTION

See GERMANY - CROPS

GERMANY - STATE AFFORESTATION

See GERMANY - FORESTS AND FORESTRY

GERMANY - STEEL PRODUCTION

See GERMANY - MINERAL INDUSTRIES

GERMANY - STRAW PRODUCTION

See GERMANY - CROPS

GERMANY - SUGAR PRODUCTION

See GERMANY - CROPS

GERMANY - SULPHUR PRODUCTION

See GERMANY - MINERAL INDUSTRIES

GERMANY - SUNFLOWER PRODUCTION

See GERMANY - CROPS

GERMANY - TAXATION

Eurostat, Batiment Jean Monnet, Rue Alcide de Gasperi, L-2920 Luxembourg, http://epp.eurostat.ec.europa.eu; *Eurostat Yearbook 2006-2007* and *Taxation Trends in the European Union - Data for the EU Member States and Norway.*

International Institute for Strategic Studies (IISS), Arundel House, 13-15 Arundel Street, Temple Place, London WC2R 3DX, England, www.iiss.org; *The Military Balance 2007.*

Organisation for Economic Cooperation and Development (OECD), 2 rue Andre Pascal, F-75775 Paris Cedex 16, France, (Telephone in U.S. (202) 785-6323), (Fax in U.S. (202) 785-0350), www.oecd.org; *Revenue Statistics 1965-2006 - 2007 Edition.*

Palgrave Macmillan Ltd., Houndmills, Basingstoke, Hampshire, RG21 6XS, England, (Telephone in U.S. (888) 330-8477), (Fax in U.S. (800) 672-2054), www.palgrave.com; *The Statesman's Yearbook 2008.*

Taylor and Francis Group, An Informa Business, 2 Park Square, Milton Park, Abingdon, Oxford OX14 4RN, United Kingdom, (Dial from U.S. (212) 216-7800), (Fax from U.S. (212) 564-7854), www.tandf.co.uk; *The Europa World Year Book.*

The World Bank, 1818 H Street, NW, Washington, DC 20433, (202) 473-1000, Fax: (202) 477-6391, www.worldbank.org; *World Development Indicators (WDI) 2008.*

GERMANY - TEA PRODUCTION

See GERMANY - CROPS

GERMANY - TELEPHONE

European Union, Delegation of the European Commission to the United States, 2300 M Street, NW, Washington, DC 20037, (202) 862-9500, Fax: (202) 429-1766, www.eurunion.org; *Statistical Overview of Transport in the European Union (Data 1970-2001).*

Eurostat, Batiment Jean Monnet, Rue Alcide de Gasperi, L-2920 Luxembourg, http://epp.eurostat.ec.europa.eu; *Eurostat Yearbook 2006-2007.*

International Telecommunication Union (ITU), Place des Nations, 1211 Geneva 20, Switzerland, www.itu.int; World Telecommunication Indicators Database.

Palgrave Macmillan Ltd., Houndmills, Basingstoke, Hampshire, RG21 6XS, England, (Telephone in U.S. (888) 330-8477), (Fax in U.S. (800) 672-2054), www.palgrave.com; *The Statesman's Yearbook 2008.*

Taylor and Francis Group, An Informa Business, 2 Park Square, Milton Park, Abingdon, Oxford OX14 4RN, United Kingdom, (Dial from U.S. (212) 216-7800), (Fax from U.S. (212) 564-7854), www.tandf.co.uk; *The Europa World Year Book.*

United Nations Statistics Division, New York, NY 10017, (800) 253-9646, Fax: (212) 963-4116, http://unstats.un.org; *Statistical Yearbook; Trends in Europe and North America: The Statistical Yearbook of the ECE 2005;* and *World Statistics Pocketbook.*

GERMANY - TELEVISION BROADCASTING

Eurostat, Batiment Jean Monnet, Rue Alcide de Gasperi, L-2920 Luxembourg, http://epp.eurostat.ec.europa.eu; *Eurostat Yearbook 2006-2007.*

United Nations Statistics Division, New York, NY 10017, (800) 253-9646, Fax: (212) 963-4116, http://unstats.un.org; *Statistical Yearbook.*

GERMANY - TEXTILE INDUSTRY

Euromonitor International, Inc., 224 S. Michigan Avenue, Suite 1500, Chicago, IL 60604, (312) 922-1115, Fax: (312) 922-1157, www.euromonitor.com; *Retail Trade International 2007.*

European Union, Delegation of the European Commission to the United States, 2300 M Street, NW, Washington, DC 20037, (202) 862-9500, Fax: (202) 429-1766, www.eurunion.org; *Eurostatistics: Data for Short-Term Economic Analysis (2007 edition)* and *The Textile Industry in the EU.*

Eurostat, Batiment Jean Monnet, Rue Alcide de Gasperi, L-2920 Luxembourg, http://epp.eurostat.ec.europa.eu; *Eurostat Yearbook 2006-2007.*

M.E. Sharpe, 80 Business Park Drive, Armonk, NY 10504, (800) 541-6563, Fax: (914) 273-2106, www.mesharpe.com; *The Illustrated Book of World Rankings.*

Organisation for Economic Cooperation and Development (OECD), 2 rue Andre Pascal, F-75775 Paris Cedex 16, France, (Telephone in U.S. (202) 785-6323), (Fax in U.S. (202) 785-0350), www.oecd.org; *Indicators of Industrial Activity; International Trade by Commodity Statistics (ITCS); A New World Map in Textiles and Clothing: Adjusting to Change; 2005 OECD Agricultural Outlook Tables, 1970-2014;* and STructural ANalysis (STAN) database.

Palgrave Macmillan Ltd., Houndmills, Basingstoke, Hampshire, RG21 6XS, England, (Telephone in U.S. (888) 330-8477), (Fax in U.S. (800) 672-2054), www.palgrave.com; *The Statesman's Yearbook 2008.*

United Nations Conference on Trade and Development (UNCTAD), DC2-1120, United Nations, New York, NY 10017, (212) 963-0027, www.unctad.org; *UNCTAD Commodity Yearbook.*

United Nations Food and Agricultural Organization (FAO), Viale delle Terme di Caracalla, 00100 Rome, Italy, (Dial from U.S. (202) 653-2400), (Fax from U.S. (202) 653 5760), www.fao.org; *The State of Food and Agriculture (SOFA) 2006.*

United Nations Statistics Division, New York, NY 10017, (800) 253-9646, Fax: (212) 963-4116, http://unstats.un.org; *Statistical Yearbook.*

GERMANY - THEATER

UNESCO Institute for Statistics, C.P. 6128 Succursale Centre-Ville, Montreal, Quebec, H3C 3J7 Canada, (Dial from U.S. (514) 343-6880), (Fax from U.S. (514) 343 6882), www.uis.unesco.org; *Statistical Tables.*

GERMANY - TIMBER

See GERMANY - FORESTS AND FORESTRY

GERMANY - TIN PRODUCTION

See GERMANY - MINERAL INDUSTRIES

GERMANY - TIRE INDUSTRY

United Nations Statistics Division, New York, NY 10017, (800) 253-9646, Fax: (212) 963-4116, http://unstats.un.org; *Statistical Yearbook.*

GERMANY - TOBACCO INDUSTRY

Euromonitor International, Inc., 224 S. Michigan Avenue, Suite 1500, Chicago, IL 60604, (312) 922-1115, Fax: (312) 922-1157, www.euromonitor.com; *European Marketing Data and Statistics 2008.*

Eurostat, Batiment Jean Monnet, Rue Alcide de Gasperi, L-2920 Luxembourg, http://epp.eurostat.ec.europa.eu; *Eurostat Yearbook 2006-2007.*

Foreign Agricultural Service (FAS), U.S. Department of Agriculture (USDA), 1400 Independence Avenue, SW, Washington, DC 20250, (202) 720-3935, www.fas.usda.gov; *Tobacco: World Markets and Trade.*

M.E. Sharpe, 80 Business Park Drive, Armonk, NY 10504, (800) 541-6563, Fax: (914) 273-2106, www.mesharpe.com; *The Illustrated Book of World Rankings.*

Organisation for Economic Cooperation and Development (OECD), 2 rue Andre Pascal, F-75775 Paris Cedex 16, France, (Telephone in U.S. (202) 785-6323), (Fax in U.S. (202) 785-0350), www.oecd.org; *Indicators of Industrial Activity; International Trade by Commodity Statistics (ITCS);* and STructural ANalysis (STAN) database.

United Nations Statistics Division, New York, NY 10017, (800) 253-9646, Fax: (212) 963-4116, http://unstats.un.org; *Statistical Yearbook.*

GERMANY - TOURISM

Euromonitor International, Inc., 224 S. Michigan Avenue, Suite 1500, Chicago, IL 60604, (312) 922-1115, Fax: (312) 922-1157, www.euromonitor.com; *European Marketing Data and Statistics 2008; The World Economic Factbook 2008;* and *World Marketing Data and Statistics.*

European Union, Delegation of the European Commission to the United States, 2300 M Street, NW, Washington, DC 20037, (202) 862-9500, Fax: (202) 429-1766, www.eurunion.org; *Statistical Overview of Transport in the European Union (Data 1970-2001).*

Eurostat, Batiment Jean Monnet, Rue Alcide de Gasperi, L-2920 Luxembourg, http://epp.eurostat.ec.europa.eu; *Tourism in Europe: First Results for 2007.*

M.E. Sharpe, 80 Business Park Drive, Armonk, NY 10504, (800) 541-6563, Fax: (914) 273-2106, www.mesharpe.com; *The Illustrated Book of World Rankings.*

Organisation for Economic Cooperation and Development (OECD), 2 rue Andre Pascal, F-75775 Paris Cedex 16, France, (Telephone in U.S. (202) 785-6323), (Fax in U.S. (202) 785-0350), www.oecd.org; *Household, Tourism, Travel: Trends, Environmental Impacts and Policy Responses.*

Palgrave Macmillan Ltd., Houndmills, Basingstoke, Hampshire, RG21 6XS, England, (Telephone in U.S. (888) 330-8477), (Fax in U.S. (800) 672-2054), www.palgrave.com; *The Statesman's Yearbook 2008.*

Taylor and Francis Group, An Informa Business, 2 Park Square, Milton Park, Abingdon, Oxford OX14 4RN, United Kingdom, (Dial from U.S. (212) 216-7800), (Fax from U.S. (212) 564-7854), www.tandf.co.uk; *The Europa World Year Book.*

United Nations Statistics Division, New York, NY 10017, (800) 253-9646, Fax: (212) 963-4116, http://unstats.un.org; *Statistical Yearbook* and *Trends in Europe and North America: The Statistical Yearbook of the ECE 2005.*

United Nations World Tourism Organization (UNWTO), Capitan Haya 42, 28020 Madrid, Spain, www.world-tourism.org; *The German Ecotourism Market; Tourism Market Trends 2004 - Europe;* and *Yearbook of Tourism Statistics.*

The World Bank, 1818 H Street, NW, Washington, DC 20433, (202) 473-1000, Fax: (202) 477-6391, www.worldbank.org; *Germany.*

GERMANY - TRADE

See GERMANY - INTERNATIONAL TRADE

GERMANY - TRANSPORTATION

Euromonitor International, Inc., 224 S. Michigan Avenue, Suite 1500, Chicago, IL 60604, (312) 922-1115, Fax: (312) 922-1157, www.euromonitor.com; *World Marketing Data and Statistics.*

European Union, Delegation of the European Commission to the United States, 2300 M Street, NW,

Washington, DC 20037, (202) 862-9500, Fax: (202) 429-1766, www.eurunion.org; *Statistical Overview of Transport in the European Union (Data 1970-2001).*

Eurostat, Batiment Jean Monnet, Rue Alcide de Gasperi, L-2920 Luxembourg, http://epp.eurostat.ec.europa.eu; *Eurostat Yearbook 2006-2007; Regional Passenger and Freight Air Transport in Europe in 2006;* and *Regional Road and Rail Transport Networks.*

M.E. Sharpe, 80 Business Park Drive, Armonk, NY 10504, (800) 541-6563, Fax: (914) 273-2106, www.mesharpe.com; *The Illustrated Book of World Rankings.*

Palgrave Macmillan Ltd., Houndmills, Basingstoke, Hampshire, RG21 6XS, England, (Telephone in U.S. (888) 330-8477), (Fax in U.S. (800) 672-2054), www.palgrave.com; *The Statesman's Yearbook 2008.*

Platts, 2 Penn Plaza, 25th Floor, New York, NY 10121-2298, (212) 904-3070, www.platts.com; *Energy Economist.*

Taylor and Francis Group, An Informa Business, 2 Park Square, Milton Park, Abingdon, Oxford OX14 4RN, United Kingdom, (Dial from U.S. (212) 216-7800), (Fax from U.S. (212) 564-7854), www.tandf.co.uk; *The Europa World Year Book.*

United Nations Statistics Division, New York, NY 10017, (800) 253-9646, Fax: (212) 963-4116, http://unstats.un.org; *Energy Statistics Yearbook 2003; Human Development Report 2006;* and *Trends in Europe and North America: The Statistical Yearbook of the ECE 2005.*

The World Bank, 1818 H Street, NW, Washington, DC 20433, (202) 473-1000, Fax: (202) 477-6391, www.worldbank.org; *Germany* and *Germany.*

GERMANY - TURKEYS

See GERMANY - LIVESTOCK

GERMANY - UNEMPLOYMENT

Euromonitor International, Inc., 224 S. Michigan Avenue, Suite 1500, Chicago, IL 60604, (312) 922-1115, Fax: (312) 922-1157, www.euromonitor.com; *European Marketing Data and Statistics 2008.*

European Union, Delegation of the European Commission to the United States, 2300 M Street, NW, Washington, DC 20037, (202) 862-9500, Fax: (202) 429-1766, www.eurunion.org; *European Union Labour Force Survey; Eurostatistics: Data for Short-Term Economic Analysis (2007 edition);* and *Regions - Statistical Yearbook 2006.*

International Labour Office, I.L.O. Publications, 4 route des Morillons, CH-1211 Geneva 22, Switzerland, (Telephone in U.S. (202) 653-7652), (Fax in U.S. (202) 653-7687), www.ilo.org; *Yearbook of Labour Statistics 2006.*

Organisation for Economic Cooperation and Development (OECD), 2 rue Andre Pascal, F-75775 Paris Cedex 16, France, (Telephone in U.S. (202) 785-6323), (Fax in U.S. (202) 785-0350), www.oecd.org; *Labour Force Statistics: 1986-2005, 2007 Edition; OECD Composite Leading Indicators (CLIs), Updated September 2007; OECD Economic Outlook 2008; OECD Economic Survey - Germany 2008;* and *OECD Employment Outlook 2007.*

Palgrave Macmillan Ltd., Houndmills, Basingstoke, Hampshire, RG21 6XS, England, (Telephone in U.S. (888) 330-8477), (Fax in U.S. (800) 672-2054), www.palgrave.com; *The Statesman's Yearbook 2008.*

United Nations Statistics Division, New York, NY 10017, (800) 253-9646, Fax: (212) 963-4116, http://unstats.un.org; *Statistical Yearbook* and *Trends in Europe and North America: The Statistical Yearbook of the ECE 2005.*

GERMANY - URANIUM PRODUCTION AND CONSUMPTION

See GERMANY - MINERAL INDUSTRIES

GERMANY - VITAL STATISTICS

Eurostat, Batiment Jean Monnet, Rue Alcide de Gasperi, L-2920 Luxembourg, http://epp.eurostat.ec.europa.eu; *Eurostat Yearbook 2006-2007.*

Palgrave Macmillan Ltd., Houndmills, Basingstoke, Hampshire, RG21 6XS, England, (Telephone in U.S. (888) 330-8477), (Fax in U.S. (800) 672-2054), www.palgrave.com; *The Statesman's Yearbook 2008.*

United Nations Statistics Division, New York, NY 10017, (800) 253-9646, Fax: (212) 963-4116, http://unstats.un.org; *Statistical Yearbook.*

World Health Organization (WHO), Avenue Appia 20, 1211 Geneve 27, Switzerland, (Telephone in U.S. (212) 331-9081), www.who.int; *World Health Report 2006.*

GERMANY - WAGES

Euromonitor International, Inc., 224 S. Michigan Avenue, Suite 1500, Chicago, IL 60604, (312) 922-1115, Fax: (312) 922-1157, www.euromonitor.com; *European Marketing Data and Statistics 2008.*

European Union, Delegation of the European Commission to the United States, 2300 M Street, NW, Washington, DC 20037, (202) 862-9500, Fax: (202) 429-1766, www.eurunion.org; *Agriculture in the European Union: Statistical and Economic Information 2006* and *Eurostatistics: Data for Short-Term Economic Analysis (2007 edition).*

Eurostat, Batiment Jean Monnet, Rue Alcide de Gasperi, L-2920 Luxembourg, http://epp.eurostat.ec.europa.eu; *Eurostat Yearbook 2006-2007.*

International Labour Office, I.L.O. Publications, 4 route des Morillons, CH-1211 Geneva 22, Switzerland, (Telephone in U.S. (202) 653-7652), (Fax in U.S. (202) 653-7687), www.ilo.org; *Yearbook of Labour Statistics 2006.*

Organisation for Economic Cooperation and Development (OECD), 2 rue Andre Pascal, F-75775 Paris Cedex 16, France, (Telephone in U.S. (202) 785-6323), (Fax in U.S. (202) 785-0350), www.oecd.org; *ICT Sector Data and Metadata by Country; OECD Economic Outlook 2008; OECD Main Economic Indicators (MEI);* and STructural ANalysis (STAN) database.

United Nations Statistics Division, New York, NY 10017, (800) 253-9646, Fax: (212) 963-4116, http://unstats.un.org; *Statistical Yearbook.*

The World Bank, 1818 H Street, NW, Washington, DC 20433, (202) 473-1000, Fax: (202) 477-6391, www.worldbank.org; *Germany.*

GERMANY - WALNUT PRODUCTION

See GERMANY - CROPS

GERMANY - WEATHER

See GERMANY - CLIMATE

GERMANY - WELFARE STATE

Eurostat, Batiment Jean Monnet, Rue Alcide de Gasperi, L-2920 Luxembourg, http://epp.eurostat.ec.europa.eu; *Eurostat Yearbook 2006-2007.*

Palgrave Macmillan Ltd., Houndmills, Basingstoke, Hampshire, RG21 6XS, England, (Telephone in U.S. (888) 330-8477), (Fax in U.S. (800) 672-2054), www.palgrave.com; *The Statesman's Yearbook 2008.*

GERMANY - WHEAT PRODUCTION

See GERMANY - CROPS

GERMANY - WHOLESALE PRICE INDEXES

Eurostat, Batiment Jean Monnet, Rue Alcide de Gasperi, L-2920 Luxembourg, http://epp.eurostat.ec.europa.eu; *Eurostat Yearbook 2006-2007.*

United Nations Statistics Division, New York, NY 10017, (800) 253-9646, Fax: (212) 963-4116, http://unstats.un.org; *Statistical Yearbook.*

GERMANY - WHOLESALE TRADE

Eurostat, Batiment Jean Monnet, Rue Alcide de Gasperi, L-2920 Luxembourg, http://epp.eurostat.ec.europa.eu; *Eurostat Yearbook 2006-2007.*

United Nations Statistics Division, New York, NY 10017, (800) 253-9646, Fax: (212) 963-4116, http://unstats.un.org; *Statistical Yearbook.*

GERMANY - WINE PRODUCTION

See GERMANY - BEVERAGE INDUSTRY

GERMANY - WOOD AND WOOD PULP

See GERMANY - FORESTS AND FORESTRY

GERMANY - WOOD PRODUCTS

Eurostat, Batiment Jean Monnet, Rue Alcide de Gasperi, L-2920 Luxembourg, http://epp.eurostat.ec.europa.eu; *Eurostat Yearbook 2006-2007.*

Organisation for Economic Cooperation and Development (OECD), 2 rue Andre Pascal, F-75775 Paris Cedex 16, France, (Telephone in U.S. (202) 785-6323), (Fax in U.S. (202) 785-0350), www.oecd.org; *International Trade by Commodity Statistics (ITCS)* and STructural ANalysis (STAN) database.

GERMANY - WOOL PRODUCTION

See GERMANY - TEXTILE INDUSTRY

GERMANY - YARN PRODUCTION

See GERMANY - TEXTILE INDUSTRY

GERMANY - ZINC AND ZINC ORE

See GERMANY - MINERAL INDUSTRIES

GHANA - NATIONAL STATISTICAL OFFICE

Ghana Statistical Service, PO Box 1098, Accra, Ghana; National Data Center.

GHANA - PRIMARY STATISTICS SOURCES

Ghana Statistical Service, PO Box 1098, Accra, Ghana; *Quarterly Digest of Statistics.*

GHANA - AGRICULTURAL MACHINERY

United Nations Statistics Division, New York, NY 10017, (800) 253-9646, Fax: (212) 963-4116, http://unstats.un.org; *Statistical Yearbook.*

GHANA - AGRICULTURE

Economist Intelligence Unit, 111 West 57th Street, New York, NY 10019, (212) 554-0600, Fax: (212) 586-1181, www.eiu.com; *Ghana Country Report.*

Euromonitor International, Inc., 224 S. Michigan Avenue, Suite 1500, Chicago, IL 60604, (312) 922-1115, Fax: (312) 922-1157, www.euromonitor.com; *International Marketing Data and Statistics 2008* and *World Marketing Data and Statistics.*

M.E. Sharpe, 80 Business Park Drive, Armonk, NY 10504, (800) 541-6563, Fax: (914) 273-2106, www.mesharpe.com; *The Illustrated Book of World Rankings.*

Palgrave Macmillan Ltd., Houndmills, Basingstoke, Hampshire, RG21 6XS, England, (Telephone in U.S. (888) 330-8477), (Fax in U.S. (800) 672-2054), www.palgrave.com; *The Statesman's Yearbook 2008.*

Taylor and Francis Group, An Informa Business, 2 Park Square, Milton Park, Abingdon, Oxford OX14 4RN, United Kingdom, (Dial from U.S. (212) 216-7800), (Fax from U.S. (212) 564-7854), www.tandf.co.uk; *The Europa World Year Book.*

United Nations Conference on Trade and Development (UNCTAD), DC2-1120, United Nations, New York, NY 10017, (212) 963-0027, www.unctad.org; *UNCTAD Commodity Yearbook.*

United Nations Economic Commission for Africa (ECA), PO Box 3001, Addis Ababa, Ethiopia, (Telephone in U.S. (212) 963-4957), www.uneca.org; *African Statistical Yearbook 2006.*

United Nations Food and Agricultural Organization (FAO), Viale delle Terme di Caracalla, 00100 Rome, Italy, (Dial from U.S. (202) 653-2400), (Fax from U.S. (202) 653 5760), www.fao.org; AQUASTAT;

FAO Production Yearbook 2002; FAO Trade Yearbook; and *The State of Food and Agriculture (SOFA) 2006.*

United Nations Statistics Division, New York, NY 10017, (800) 253-9646, Fax: (212) 963-4116, http://unstats.un.org; *Statistical Yearbook* and *Survey of Economic and Social Conditions in Africa 2005.*

The World Bank, 1818 H Street, NW, Washington, DC 20433, (202) 473-1000, Fax: (202) 477-6391, www.worldbank.org; *Africa Live Database (LDB); African Development Indicators (ADI) 2007; Ghana;* and *World Development Indicators (WDI) 2008.*

GHANA - AIRLINES

International Civil Aviation Organization (ICAO), External Relations and Public Information Office (EPO), 999 University Street, Montreal, Quebec H3C 5H7, Canada, (Dial from U.S. (514) 954-8219), (Fax from U.S. (514) 954-6077), www.icao.int; *Civil Aviation Statistics of the World.*

M.E. Sharpe, 80 Business Park Drive, Armonk, NY 10504, (800) 541-6563, Fax: (914) 273-2106, www.mesharpe.com; *The Illustrated Book of World Rankings.*

Palgrave Macmillan Ltd., Houndmills, Basingstoke, Hampshire, RG21 6XS, England, (Telephone in U.S. (888) 330-8477), (Fax in U.S. (800) 672-2054), www.palgrave.com; *The Statesman's Yearbook 2008.*

Taylor and Francis Group, An Informa Business, 2 Park Square, Milton Park, Abingdon, Oxford OX14 4RN, United Kingdom, (Dial from U.S. (212) 216-7800), (Fax from U.S. (212) 564-7854), www.tandf.co.uk; *The Europa World Year Book.*

United Nations Economic Commission for Africa (ECA), PO Box 3001, Addis Ababa, Ethiopia, (Telephone in U.S. (212) 963-4957), www.uneca.org; *African Statistical Yearbook 2006.*

United Nations Statistics Division, New York, NY 10017, (800) 253-9646, Fax: (212) 963-4116, http://unstats.un.org; *Statistical Yearbook.*

GHANA - AIRPORTS

Central Intelligence Agency, Office of Public Affairs, Washington, DC 20505, (703) 482-0623, Fax: (703) 482-1739, www.cia.gov; *The World Factbook.*

GHANA - ALUMINUM PRODUCTION

See GHANA - MINERAL INDUSTRIES

GHANA - ARMED FORCES

Central Intelligence Agency, Office of Public Affairs, Washington, DC 20505, (703) 482-0623, Fax: (703) 482-1739, www.cia.gov; *The World Factbook.*

Euromonitor International, Inc., 224 S. Michigan Avenue, Suite 1500, Chicago, IL 60604, (312) 922-1115, Fax: (312) 922-1157, www.euromonitor.com; *World Marketing Data and Statistics.*

International Institute for Strategic Studies (IISS), Arundel House, 13-15 Arundel Street, Temple Place, London WC2R 3DX, England, www.iiss.org; *The Military Balance 2007.*

International Monetary Fund (IMF), 700 Nineteenth Street, NW, Washington, DC 20431, (202) 623-7000, Fax: (202) 623-4661, www.imf.org; *Government Finance Statistics Yearbook (2008 Edition).*

Palgrave Macmillan Ltd., Houndmills, Basingstoke, Hampshire, RG21 6XS, England, (Telephone in U.S. (888) 330-8477), (Fax in U.S. (800) 672-2054), www.palgrave.com; *The Statesman's Yearbook 2008.*

U.S. Department of State (DOS), 2201 C Street NW, Washington, DC 20520, (202) 647-4000, www.state.gov; *World Military Expenditures and Arms Transfers (WMEAT).*

United Nations Statistics Division, New York, NY 10017, (800) 253-9646, Fax: (212) 963-4116, http://unstats.un.org; *Human Development Report 2006.*

GHANA - AUTOMOBILE INDUSTRY AND TRADE

United Nations Statistics Division, New York, NY 10017, (800) 253-9646, Fax: (212) 963-4116, http://unstats.un.org; *Statistical Yearbook.*

GHANA - BALANCE OF PAYMENTS

African Development Bank Group, Rue Joseph Anoma, 01 BP 1387 Abidjan 01, Cote d'Ivoire, www.afdb.org; *Statistics Pocketbook 2008.*

International Monetary Fund (IMF), 700 Nineteenth Street, NW, Washington, DC 20431, (202) 623-7000, Fax: (202) 623-4661, www.imf.org; *Balance of Payments Statistics Newsletter; Balance of Payments Statistics Yearbook 2007;* and *International Financial Statistics Yearbook 2007.*

Taylor and Francis Group, An Informa Business, 2 Park Square, Milton Park, Abingdon, Oxford OX14 4RN, United Kingdom, (Dial from U.S. (212) 216-7800), (Fax from U.S. (212) 564-7854), www.tandf.co.uk; *The Europa World Year Book.*

United Nations Conference on Trade and Development (UNCTAD), DC2-1120, United Nations, New York, NY 10017, (212) 963-0027, www.unctad.org; *Handbook of Statistics 2005.*

United Nations Economic Commission for Africa (ECA), PO Box 3001, Addis Ababa, Ethiopia, (Telephone in U.S. (212) 963-4957), www.uneca.org; *African Statistical Yearbook 2006.*

The World Bank, 1818 H Street, NW, Washington, DC 20433, (202) 473-1000, Fax: (202) 477-6391, www.worldbank.org; *Ghana; World Development Indicators (WDI) 2008;* and *World Development Report 2008.*

GHANA - BANKS AND BANKING

Euromonitor International, Inc., 224 S. Michigan Avenue, Suite 1500, Chicago, IL 60604, (312) 922-1115, Fax: (312) 922-1157, www.euromonitor.com; *World Marketing Data and Statistics.*

International Monetary Fund (IMF), 700 Nineteenth Street, NW, Washington, DC 20431, (202) 623-7000, Fax: (202) 623-4661, www.imf.org; *Government Finance Statistics Yearbook (2008 Edition)* and *International Financial Statistics Yearbook 2007.*

M.E. Sharpe, 80 Business Park Drive, Armonk, NY 10504, (800) 541-6563, Fax: (914) 273-2106, www.mesharpe.com; *The Illustrated Book of World Rankings.*

Palgrave Macmillan Ltd., Houndmills, Basingstoke, Hampshire, RG21 6XS, England, (Telephone in U.S. (888) 330-8477), (Fax in U.S. (800) 672-2054), www.palgrave.com; *The Statesman's Yearbook 2008.*

Taylor and Francis Group, An Informa Business, 2 Park Square, Milton Park, Abingdon, Oxford OX14 4RN, United Kingdom, (Dial from U.S. (212) 216-7800), (Fax from U.S. (212) 564-7854), www.tandf.co.uk; *The Europa World Year Book.*

United Nations Economic Commission for Africa (ECA), PO Box 3001, Addis Ababa, Ethiopia, (Telephone in U.S. (212) 963-4957), www.uneca.org; *African Statistical Yearbook 2006.*

United Nations Statistics Division, New York, NY 10017, (800) 253-9646, Fax: (212) 963-4116, http://unstats.un.org; *Statistical Yearbook.*

GHANA - BARLEY PRODUCTION

See GHANA - CROPS

GHANA - BEVERAGE INDUSTRY

M.E. Sharpe, 80 Business Park Drive, Armonk, NY 10504, (800) 541-6563, Fax: (914) 273-2106, www.mesharpe.com; *The Illustrated Book of World Rankings.*

United Nations Statistics Division, New York, NY 10017, (800) 253-9646, Fax: (212) 963-4116, http://unstats.un.org; *Statistical Yearbook.*

GHANA - BONDS

International Monetary Fund (IMF), 700 Nineteenth Street, NW, Washington, DC 20431, (202) 623-7000, Fax: (202) 623-4661, www.imf.org; *Government Finance Statistics Yearbook (2008 Edition).*

GHANA - BROADCASTING

Central Intelligence Agency, Office of Public Affairs, Washington, DC 20505, (703) 482-0623, Fax: (703) 482-1739, www.cia.gov; *The World Factbook.*

Euromonitor International, Inc., 224 S. Michigan Avenue, Suite 1500, Chicago, IL 60604, (312) 922-1115, Fax: (312) 922-1157, www.euromonitor.com; *World Marketing Data and Statistics.*

M.E. Sharpe, 80 Business Park Drive, Armonk, NY 10504, (800) 541-6563, Fax: (914) 273-2106, www.mesharpe.com; *The Illustrated Book of World Rankings.*

Palgrave Macmillan Ltd., Houndmills, Basingstoke, Hampshire, RG21 6XS, England, (Telephone in U.S. (888) 330-8477), (Fax in U.S. (800) 672-2054), www.palgrave.com; *The Statesman's Yearbook 2008.*

WRTH Publications Limited, PO Box 290, Oxford OX2 7FT, UK, www.wrth.com; *World Radio TV Handbook 2007.*

GHANA - BUDGET

Central Intelligence Agency, Office of Public Affairs, Washington, DC 20505, (703) 482-0623, Fax: (703) 482-1739, www.cia.gov; *The World Factbook.*

GHANA - BUSINESS

Economist Intelligence Unit, 111 West 57th Street, New York, NY 10019, (212) 554-0600, Fax: (212) 586-1181, www.eiu.com; *Business Africa.*

United Nations Statistics Division, New York, NY 10017, (800) 253-9646, Fax: (212) 963-4116, http://unstats.un.org; *Statistical Yearbook.*

GHANA - CACAO

See GHANA - CROPS

GHANA - CAPITAL LEVY

International Monetary Fund (IMF), 700 Nineteenth Street, NW, Washington, DC 20431, (202) 623-7000, Fax: (202) 623-4661, www.imf.org; *Government Finance Statistics Yearbook (2008 Edition).*

GHANA - CATTLE

See GHANA - LIVESTOCK

GHANA - CHICKENS

See GHANA - LIVESTOCK

GHANA - CHILDBIRTH - STATISTICS

Central Intelligence Agency, Office of Public Affairs, Washington, DC 20505, (703) 482-0623, Fax: (703) 482-1739, www.cia.gov; *The World Factbook.*

Euromonitor International, Inc., 224 S. Michigan Avenue, Suite 1500, Chicago, IL 60604, (312) 922-1115, Fax: (312) 922-1157, www.euromonitor.com; *International Marketing Data and Statistics 2008* and *The World Economic Factbook 2008.*

M.E. Sharpe, 80 Business Park Drive, Armonk, NY 10504, (800) 541-6563, Fax: (914) 273-2106, www.mesharpe.com; *The Illustrated Book of World Rankings.*

Palgrave Macmillan Ltd., Houndmills, Basingstoke, Hampshire, RG21 6XS, England, (Telephone in U.S. (888) 330-8477), (Fax in U.S. (800) 672-2054), www.palgrave.com; *The Statesman's Yearbook 2008.*

Taylor and Francis Group, An Informa Business, 2 Park Square, Milton Park, Abingdon, Oxford OX14 4RN, United Kingdom, (Dial from U.S. (212) 216-7800), (Fax from U.S. (212) 564-7854), www.tandf.co.uk; *The Europa World Year Book.*

United Nations Statistics Division, New York, NY 10017, (800) 253-9646, Fax: (212) 963-4116, http://unstats.un.org; *Demographic Yearbook; Statistical Yearbook;* and *Survey of Economic and Social Conditions in Africa 2005.*

The World Bank, 1818 H Street, NW, Washington, DC 20433, (202) 473-1000, Fax: (202) 477-6391, www.worldbank.org; *World Development Indicators (WDI) 2008.*

GHANA - CLIMATE

International Institute for Environment and Development (IIED), 3 Endsleigh Street, London, England,

WC1H 0DD, United Kingdom, www.iied.org; *Environment Urbanization* and *Haramata - Bulletin of the Drylands.*

M.E. Sharpe, 80 Business Park Drive, Armonk, NY 10504, (800) 541-6563, Fax: (914) 273-2106, www.mesharpe.com; *The Illustrated Book of World Rankings.*

Palgrave Macmillan Ltd., Houndmills, Basingstoke, Hampshire, RG21 6XS, England, (Telephone in U.S. (888) 330-8477), (Fax in U.S. (800) 672-2054), www.palgrave.com; *The Statesman's Yearbook 2008.*

GHANA - COAL PRODUCTION

See GHANA - MINERAL INDUSTRIES

GHANA - COCOA PRODUCTION

See GHANA - CROPS

GHANA - COFFEE

See GHANA - CROPS

GHANA - COMMERCE

Palgrave Macmillan Ltd., Houndmills, Basingstoke, Hampshire, RG21 6XS, England, (Telephone in U.S. (888) 330-8477), (Fax in U.S. (800) 672-2054), www.palgrave.com; *The Statesman's Yearbook 2008.*

GHANA - COMMODITY EXCHANGES

Commodity Research Bureau, 330 South Wells Street, Suite 612, Chicago, IL 60606-7110, (800) 621-5271, Fax: (312) 939-4135, www.crbtrader.com; *2006 CRB Commodity Yearbook and CD.*

International Monetary Fund (IMF), 700 Nineteenth Street, NW, Washington, DC 20431, (202) 623-7000, Fax: (202) 623-4661, www.imf.org; *IMF Primary Commodity Prices.*

United Nations Food and Agricultural Organization (FAO), Viale delle Terme di Caracalla, 00100 Rome, Italy, (Dial from U.S. (202) 653-2400), (Fax from U.S. (202) 653 5760), www.fao.org; *The State of Food and Agriculture (SOFA) 2006.*

GHANA - COMMUNICATION AND TRAFFIC

United Nations Statistics Division, New York, NY 10017, (800) 253-9646, Fax: (212) 963-4116, http://unstats.un.org; *Statistical Yearbook.*

GHANA - CONSTRUCTION INDUSTRY

M.E. Sharpe, 80 Business Park Drive, Armonk, NY 10504, (800) 541-6563, Fax: (914) 273-2106, www.mesharpe.com; *The Illustrated Book of World Rankings.*

United Nations Economic Commission for Africa (ECA), PO Box 3001, Addis Ababa, Ethiopia, (Telephone in U.S. (212) 963-4957), www.uneca.org; *African Statistical Yearbook 2006.*

United Nations Statistics Division, New York, NY 10017, (800) 253-9646, Fax: (212) 963-4116, http://unstats.un.org; *Statistical Yearbook.*

GHANA - CONSUMER PRICE INDEXES

Taylor and Francis Group, An Informa Business, 2 Park Square, Milton Park, Abingdon, Oxford OX14 4RN, United Kingdom, (Dial from U.S. (212) 216-7800), (Fax from U.S. (212) 564-7854), www.tandf.co.uk; *The Europa World Year Book.*

United Nations Economic Commission for Africa (ECA), PO Box 3001, Addis Ababa, Ethiopia, (Telephone in U.S. (212) 963-4957), www.uneca.org; *African Statistical Yearbook 2006.*

United Nations Statistics Division, New York, NY 10017, (800) 253-9646, Fax: (212) 963-4116, http://unstats.un.org; *Statistical Yearbook* and *Survey of Economic and Social Conditions in Africa 2005.*

The World Bank, 1818 H Street, NW, Washington, DC 20433, (202) 473-1000, Fax: (202) 477-6391, www.worldbank.org; *Ghana.*

GHANA - CONSUMPTION (ECONOMICS)

African Development Bank Group, Rue Joseph Anoma, 01 BP 1387 Abidjan 01, Cote d'Ivoire, www.afdb.org; *Statistics Pocketbook 2008.*

United Nations Statistics Division, New York, NY 10017, (800) 253-9646, Fax: (212) 963-4116, http://unstats.un.org; *Survey of Economic and Social Conditions in Africa 2005.*

The World Bank, 1818 H Street, NW, Washington, DC 20433, (202) 473-1000, Fax: (202) 477-6391, www.worldbank.org; *World Development Report 2008.*

GHANA - COPPER INDUSTRY AND TRADE

See GHANA - MINERAL INDUSTRIES

GHANA - CORN INDUSTRY

See GHANA - CROPS

GHANA - COST AND STANDARD OF LIVING

International Monetary Fund (IMF), 700 Nineteenth Street, NW, Washington, DC 20431, (202) 623-7000, Fax: (202) 623-4661, www.imf.org; *Government Finance Statistics Yearbook (2008 Edition).*

GHANA - COTTON

See GHANA - CROPS

GHANA - CRIME

U.S. Department of Justice (DOJ), Bureau of Justice Statistics, 810 Seventh Street, NW, Washington, DC 20531, (202) 307-0765, www.ojp.usdoj.gov/bjs/; *The World Factbook of Criminal Justice Systems.*

Yale University Press, PO Box 209040, New Haven, CT 06520-9040, (203) 432-0960, Fax: (203) 432-0948, http://yalepress.yale.edu/yupbooks; *Violence and Crime in Cross-National Perspective.*

GHANA - CROPS

International Monetary Fund (IMF), 700 Nineteenth Street, NW, Washington, DC 20431, (202) 623-7000, Fax: (202) 623-4661, www.imf.org; *International Financial Statistics Yearbook 2007.*

M.E. Sharpe, 80 Business Park Drive, Armonk, NY 10504, (800) 541-6563, Fax: (914) 273-2106, www.mesharpe.com; *The Illustrated Book of World Rankings.*

Palgrave Macmillan Ltd., Houndmills, Basingstoke, Hampshire, RG21 6XS, England, (Telephone in U.S. (888) 330-8477), (Fax in U.S. (800) 672-2054), www.palgrave.com; *The Statesman's Yearbook 2008.*

Taylor and Francis Group, An Informa Business, 2 Park Square, Milton Park, Abingdon, Oxford OX14 4RN, United Kingdom, (Dial from U.S. (212) 216-7800), (Fax from U.S. (212) 564-7854), www.tandf.co.uk; *The Europa World Year Book.*

United Nations Conference on Trade and Development (UNCTAD), DC2-1120, United Nations, New York, NY 10017, (212) 963-0027, www.unctad.org; *UNCTAD Commodity Yearbook.*

United Nations Economic Commission for Africa (ECA), PO Box 3001, Addis Ababa, Ethiopia, (Telephone in U.S. (212) 963-4957), www.uneca.org; *African Statistical Yearbook 2006.*

United Nations Food and Agricultural Organization (FAO), Viale delle Terme di Caracalla, 00100 Rome, Italy, (Dial from U.S. (202) 653-2400), (Fax from U.S. (202) 653 5760), www.fao.org; *FAO Production Yearbook 2002* and *The State of Food and Agriculture (SOFA) 2006.*

United Nations Statistics Division, New York, NY 10017, (800) 253-9646, Fax: (212) 963-4116, http://unstats.un.org; *Statistical Yearbook.*

GHANA - CUSTOMS ADMINISTRATION

International Monetary Fund (IMF), 700 Nineteenth Street, NW, Washington, DC 20431, (202) 623-7000, Fax: (202) 623-4661, www.imf.org; *Government Finance Statistics Yearbook (2008 Edition).*

Palgrave Macmillan Ltd., Houndmills, Basingstoke, Hampshire, RG21 6XS, England, (Telephone in U.S. (888) 330-8477), (Fax in U.S. (800) 672-2054), www.palgrave.com; *The Statesman's Yearbook 2008.*

GHANA - DAIRY PROCESSING

M.E. Sharpe, 80 Business Park Drive, Armonk, NY 10504, (800) 541-6563, Fax: (914) 273-2106, www.mesharpe.com; *The Illustrated Book of World Rankings.*

Palgrave Macmillan Ltd., Houndmills, Basingstoke, Hampshire, RG21 6XS, England, (Telephone in U.S. (888) 330-8477), (Fax in U.S. (800) 672-2054), www.palgrave.com; *The Statesman's Yearbook 2008.*

Taylor and Francis Group, An Informa Business, 2 Park Square, Milton Park, Abingdon, Oxford OX14 4RN, United Kingdom, (Dial from U.S. (212) 216-7800), (Fax from U.S. (212) 564-7854), www.tandf.co.uk; *The Europa World Year Book.*

United Nations Food and Agricultural Organization (FAO), Viale delle Terme di Caracalla, 00100 Rome, Italy, (Dial from U.S. (202) 653-2400), (Fax from U.S. (202) 653 5760), www.fao.org; *The State of Food and Agriculture (SOFA) 2006.*

United Nations Statistics Division, New York, NY 10017, (800) 253-9646, Fax: (212) 963-4116, http://unstats.un.org; *Statistical Yearbook.*

GHANA - DEATH RATES

See GHANA - MORTALITY

GHANA - DEBTS, EXTERNAL

African Development Bank Group, Rue Joseph Anoma, 01 BP 1387 Abidjan 01, Cote d'Ivoire, www.afdb.org; *Statistics Pocketbook 2008.*

International Monetary Fund (IMF), 700 Nineteenth Street, NW, Washington, DC 20431, (202) 623-7000, Fax: (202) 623-4661, www.imf.org; *Government Finance Statistics Yearbook (2008 Edition).*

Palgrave Macmillan Ltd., Houndmills, Basingstoke, Hampshire, RG21 6XS, England, (Telephone in U.S. (888) 330-8477), (Fax in U.S. (800) 672-2054), www.palgrave.com; *The Statesman's Yearbook 2008.*

United Nations Statistics Division, New York, NY 10017, (800) 253-9646, Fax: (212) 963-4116, http://unstats.un.org; *Survey of Economic and Social Conditions in Africa 2005.*

The World Bank, 1818 H Street, NW, Washington, DC 20433, (202) 473-1000, Fax: (202) 477-6391, www.worldbank.org; *Africa Live Database (LDB); African Development Indicators (ADI) 2007; Global Development Finance 2007;* and *World Development Report 2008.*

GHANA - DEFENSE EXPENDITURES

See GHANA - ARMED FORCES

GHANA - DEMOGRAPHY

Euromonitor International, Inc., 224 S. Michigan Avenue, Suite 1500, Chicago, IL 60604, (312) 922-1115, Fax: (312) 922-1157, www.euromonitor.com; *International Marketing Data and Statistics 2008; The World Economic Factbook 2008;* and *World Marketing Data and Statistics.*

M.E. Sharpe, 80 Business Park Drive, Armonk, NY 10504, (800) 541-6563, Fax: (914) 273-2106, www.mesharpe.com; *The Illustrated Book of World Rankings.*

United Nations Statistics Division, New York, NY 10017, (800) 253-9646, Fax: (212) 963-4116, http://unstats.un.org; *Human Development Report 2006* and *Survey of Economic and Social Conditions in Africa 2005.*

The World Bank, 1818 H Street, NW, Washington, DC 20433, (202) 473-1000, Fax: (202) 477-6391, www.worldbank.org; *Ghana.*

GHANA - DIAMONDS

See GHANA - MINERAL INDUSTRIES

GHANA - DISPOSABLE INCOME

M.E. Sharpe, 80 Business Park Drive, Armonk, NY 10504, (800) 541-6563, Fax: (914) 273-2106, www.mesharpe.com; *The Illustrated Book of World Rankings.*

United Nations Statistics Division, New York, NY 10017, (800) 253-9646, Fax: (212) 963-4116, http://unstats.un.org; *National Accounts Statistics: Compendium of Income Distribution Statistics* and *Statistical Yearbook.*

GHANA - DIVORCE

M.E. Sharpe, 80 Business Park Drive, Armonk, NY 10504, (800) 541-6563, Fax: (914) 273-2106, www.mesharpe.com; *The Illustrated Book of World Rankings.*

United Nations Statistics Division, New York, NY 10017, (800) 253-9646, Fax: (212) 963-4116, http://unstats.un.org; *Demographic Yearbook.*

GHANA - ECONOMIC ASSISTANCE

United Nations Statistics Division, New York, NY 10017, (800) 253-9646, Fax: (212) 963-4116, http://unstats.un.org; *Statistical Yearbook.*

GHANA - ECONOMIC CONDITIONS

African Development Bank Group, Rue Joseph Anoma, 01 BP 1387 Abidjan 01, Cote d'Ivoire, www.afdb.org; *The African Statistical Journal; Gender, Poverty and Environmental Indicators on African Countries 2007; Selected Statistics on African Countries 2007;* and *Statistics Pocketbook 2008.*

Center for International Business Education Research (CIBER), Columbia Business School and School of International and Public Affairs, Uris Hall, Room 212, 3022 Broadway, New York, NY 10027-6902, Mr. Joshua Safier, (212) 854-4750, Fax: (212) 222-9821, www.columbia.edu/cu/ciber/; Datastream International.

Central Intelligence Agency, Office of Public Affairs, Washington, DC 20505, (703) 482-0623, Fax: (703) 482-1739, www.cia.gov; *The World Factbook.*

DSI Data Service Information, Xantener Strasse 51a, D-47495 Rheinberg, Germany, www.dsidata.com; *Campus Solution.*

Dun and Bradstreet (DB) Corporation, 103 JFK Parkway, Short Hills, NJ 07078, (973) 921-5500, www.dnb.com; *Country Report.*

Economist Intelligence Unit, 111 West 57th Street, New York, NY 10019, (212) 554-0600, Fax: (212) 586-1181, www.eiu.com; *Business Africa* and *Ghana Country Report.*

Euromonitor International, Inc., 224 S. Michigan Avenue, Suite 1500, Chicago, IL 60604, (312) 922-1115, Fax: (312) 922-1157, www.euromonitor.com; *International Marketing Data and Statistics 2008; The World Economic Factbook 2008;* and *World Marketing Data and Statistics.*

International Monetary Fund (IMF), 700 Nineteenth Street, NW, Washington, DC 20431, (202) 623-7000, Fax: (202) 623-4661, www.imf.org; *World Economic Outlook Reports.*

M.E. Sharpe, 80 Business Park Drive, Armonk, NY 10504, (800) 541-6563, Fax: (914) 273-2106, www.mesharpe.com; *The Illustrated Book of World Rankings.*

Taylor and Francis Group, An Informa Business, 2 Park Square, Milton Park, Abingdon, Oxford OX14 4RN, United Kingdom, (Dial from U.S. (212) 216-7800), (Fax from U.S. (212) 564-7854), www.tandf.co.uk; *The Europa World Year Book.*

United Nations Statistics Division, New York, NY 10017, (800) 253-9646, Fax: (212) 963-4116, http://unstats.un.org; *Compendium of Intra-African and Related Foreign Trade Statistics 2003* and *World Statistics Pocketbook.*

The World Bank, 1818 H Street, NW, Washington, DC 20433, (202) 473-1000, Fax: (202) 477-6391, www.worldbank.org; *Africa Household Survey Databank; Africa Live Database (LDB); Africa Standardized Files and Indicators; African Development Indicators (ADI) 2007; Ghana; Global Economic Monitor (GEM); Global Economic Prospects 2008; The World Bank Atlas 2003-2004;* and *World Development Report 2008.*

GHANA - EDUCATION

African Development Bank Group, Rue Joseph Anoma, 01 BP 1387 Abidjan 01, Cote d'Ivoire, www.afdb.org; *Statistics Pocketbook 2008.*

Euromonitor International, Inc., 224 S. Michigan Avenue, Suite 1500, Chicago, IL 60604, (312) 922-1115, Fax: (312) 922-1157, www.euromonitor.com; *International Marketing Data and Statistics 2008* and *World Marketing Data and Statistics.*

International Monetary Fund (IMF), 700 Nineteenth Street, NW, Washington, DC 20431, (202) 623-7000, Fax: (202) 623-4661, www.imf.org; *Government Finance Statistics Yearbook (2008 Edition).*

M.E. Sharpe, 80 Business Park Drive, Armonk, NY 10504, (800) 541-6563, Fax: (914) 273-2106, www.mesharpe.com; *The Illustrated Book of World Rankings.*

Palgrave Macmillan Ltd., Houndmills, Basingstoke, Hampshire, RG21 6XS, England, (Telephone in U.S. (888) 330-8477), (Fax in U.S. (800) 672-2054), www.palgrave.com; *The Statesman's Yearbook 2008.*

Taylor and Francis Group, An Informa Business, 2 Park Square, Milton Park, Abingdon, Oxford OX14 4RN, United Kingdom, (Dial from U.S. (212) 216-7800), (Fax from U.S. (212) 564-7854), www.tandf.co.uk; *The Europa World Year Book.*

UNESCO Institute for Statistics, C.P. 6128 Succursale Centre-Ville, Montreal, Quebec, H3C 3J7 Canada, (Dial from U.S. (514) 343-6880), (Fax from U.S. (514) 343 6882), www.uis.unesco.org; *Statistical Tables.*

United Nations Economic Commission for Africa (ECA), PO Box 3001, Addis Ababa, Ethiopia, (Telephone in U.S. (212) 963-4957), www.uneca.org; *African Statistical Yearbook 2006.*

United Nations Statistics Division, New York, NY 10017, (800) 253-9646, Fax: (212) 963-4116, http://unstats.un.org; *Human Development Report 2006* and *Survey of Economic and Social Conditions in Africa 2005.*

The World Bank, 1818 H Street, NW, Washington, DC 20433, (202) 473-1000, Fax: (202) 477-6391, www.worldbank.org; *Ghana; World Development Indicators (WDI) 2008;* and *World Development Report 2008.*

GHANA - EGGPLANT PRODUCTION

See GHANA - CROPS

GHANA - ELECTRICITY

M.E. Sharpe, 80 Business Park Drive, Armonk, NY 10504, (800) 541-6563, Fax: (914) 273-2106, www.mesharpe.com; *The Illustrated Book of World Rankings.*

Organisation for Economic Cooperation and Development (OECD), 2 rue Andre Pascal, F-75775 Paris Cedex 16, France, (Telephone in U.S. (202) 785-6323), (Fax in U.S. (202) 785-0350), www.oecd.org; *World Energy Outlook 2007.*

Palgrave Macmillan Ltd., Houndmills, Basingstoke, Hampshire, RG21 6XS, England, (Telephone in U.S. (888) 330-8477), (Fax in U.S. (800) 672-2054), www.palgrave.com; *The Statesman's Yearbook 2008.*

U.S. Department of Energy (DOE), Energy Information Administration (EIA), 1000 Independence Avenue, SW, Washington, DC 20585, (202) 586-8800, www.eia.doe.gov; *International Energy Annual 2004* and *International Energy Outlook 2006.*

United Nations Economic Commission for Africa (ECA), PO Box 3001, Addis Ababa, Ethiopia, (Telephone in U.S. (212) 963-4957), www.uneca.org; *African Statistical Yearbook 2006.*

United Nations Statistics Division, New York, NY 10017, (800) 253-9646, Fax: (212) 963-4116, http://unstats.un.org; *Human Development Report 2006; Statistical Yearbook;* and *Survey of Economic and Social Conditions in Africa 2005.*

GHANA - EMPLOYMENT

Euromonitor International, Inc., 224 S. Michigan Avenue, Suite 1500, Chicago, IL 60604, (312) 922-1115, Fax: (312) 922-1157, www.euromonitor.com; *International Marketing Data and Statistics 2008.*

International Labour Office, I.L.O. Publications, 4 route des Morillons, CH-1211 Geneva 22, Switzerland, (Telephone in U.S. (202) 653-7652), (Fax in U.S. (202) 653-7687), www.ilo.org; *Yearbook of Labour Statistics 2006.*

M.E. Sharpe, 80 Business Park Drive, Armonk, NY 10504, (800) 541-6563, Fax: (914) 273-2106, www.mesharpe.com; *The Illustrated Book of World Rankings.*

United Nations Economic Commission for Africa (ECA), PO Box 3001, Addis Ababa, Ethiopia, (Telephone in U.S. (212) 963-4957), www.uneca.org; *African Statistical Yearbook 2006.*

United Nations Statistics Division, New York, NY 10017, (800) 253-9646, Fax: (212) 963-4116, http://unstats.un.org; *Statistical Yearbook* and *Survey of Economic and Social Conditions in Africa 2005.*

The World Bank, 1818 H Street, NW, Washington, DC 20433, (202) 473-1000, Fax: (202) 477-6391, www.worldbank.org; *Ghana.*

GHANA - ENERGY INDUSTRIES

Enerdata, 10 Rue Royale, 75008 Paris, France, www.enerdata.fr; *Global Energy Market Data.*

United Nations Statistics Division, New York, NY 10017, (800) 253-9646, Fax: (212) 963-4116, http://unstats.un.org; *Statistical Yearbook.*

GHANA - ENVIRONMENTAL CONDITIONS

DSI Data Service Information, Xantener Strasse 51a, D-47495 Rheinberg, Germany, www.dsidata.com; *Campus Solution* and *DSI's Global Environmental Database.*

Economist Intelligence Unit, 111 West 57th Street, New York, NY 10019, (212) 554-0600, Fax: (212) 586-1181, www.eiu.com; *Ghana Country Report.*

International Institute for Environment and Development (IIED), 3 Endsleigh Street, London, England, WC1H 0DD, United Kingdom, www.iied.org; *Environment Urbanization* and *Haramata - Bulletin of the Drylands.*

United Nations Statistics Division, New York, NY 10017, (800) 253-9646, Fax: (212) 963-4116, http://unstats.un.org; *World Statistics Pocketbook.*

GHANA - EXPORTS

African Development Bank Group, Rue Joseph Anoma, 01 BP 1387 Abidjan 01, Cote d'Ivoire, www.afdb.org; *Statistics Pocketbook 2008.*

Central Intelligence Agency, Office of Public Affairs, Washington, DC 20505, (703) 482-0623, Fax: (703) 482-1739, www.cia.gov; *The World Factbook.*

Economist Intelligence Unit, 111 West 57th Street, New York, NY 10019, (212) 554-0600, Fax: (212) 586-1181, www.eiu.com; *Ghana Country Report.*

Euromonitor International, Inc., 224 S. Michigan Avenue, Suite 1500, Chicago, IL 60604, (312) 922-1115, Fax: (312) 922-1157, www.euromonitor.com; *International Marketing Data and Statistics 2008* and *The World Economic Factbook 2008.*

International Monetary Fund (IMF), 700 Nineteenth Street, NW, Washington, DC 20431, (202) 623-7000, Fax: (202) 623-4661, www.imf.org; *Direction of Trade Statistics Yearbook 2007; Government Finance Statistics Yearbook (2008 Edition);* and *International Financial Statistics Yearbook 2007.*

Palgrave Macmillan Ltd., Houndmills, Basingstoke, Hampshire, RG21 6XS, England, (Telephone in U.S. (888) 330-8477), (Fax in U.S. (800) 672-2054), www.palgrave.com; *The Statesman's Yearbook 2008.*

Taylor and Francis Group, An Informa Business, 2 Park Square, Milton Park, Abingdon, Oxford OX14 4RN, United Kingdom, (Dial from U.S. (212) 216-7800), (Fax from U.S. (212) 564-7854), www.tandf.co.uk; *The Europa World Year Book.*

United Nations Conference on Trade and Development (UNCTAD), DC2-1120, United Nations, New York, NY 10017, (212) 963-0027, www.unctad.org; *Handbook of Statistics 2005.*

United Nations Economic Commission for Africa (ECA), PO Box 3001, Addis Ababa, Ethiopia, (Telephone in U.S. (212) 963-4957), www.uneca.org; *African Statistical Yearbook 2006.*

United Nations Food and Agricultural Organization (FAO), Viale delle Terme di Caracalla, 00100 Rome, Italy, (Dial from U.S. (202) 653-2400), (Fax from U.S. (202) 653 5760), www.fao.org; *The State of Food and Agriculture (SOFA) 2006.*

United Nations Statistics Division, New York, NY 10017, (800) 253-9646, Fax: (212) 963-4116, http://unstats.un.org; *Compendium of Intra-African and Related Foreign Trade Statistics 2003* and *Survey of Economic and Social Conditions in Africa 2005.*

The World Bank, 1818 H Street, NW, Washington, DC 20433, (202) 473-1000, Fax: (202) 477-6391, www.worldbank.org; *World Development Indicators (WDI) 2008* and *World Development Report 2008.*

GHANA - FEMALE WORKING POPULATION

See GHANA - EMPLOYMENT

GHANA - FERTILITY, HUMAN

Central Intelligence Agency, Office of Public Affairs, Washington, DC 20505, (703) 482-0623, Fax: (703) 482-1739, www.cia.gov; *The World Factbook.*

M.E. Sharpe, 80 Business Park Drive, Armonk, NY 10504, (800) 541-6563, Fax: (914) 273-2106, www.mesharpe.com; *The Illustrated Book of World Rankings.*

United Nations Statistics Division, New York, NY 10017, (800) 253-9646, Fax: (212) 963-4116, http://unstats.un.org; *Human Development Report 2006* and *Survey of Economic and Social Conditions in Africa 2005.*

The World Bank, 1818 H Street, NW, Washington, DC 20433, (202) 473-1000, Fax: (202) 477-6391, www.worldbank.org; *The World Bank Atlas 2003-2004; World Development Indicators (WDI) 2008;* and *World Development Report 2008.*

GHANA - FERTILIZER INDUSTRY

United Nations Food and Agricultural Organization (FAO), Viale delle Terme di Caracalla, 00100 Rome, Italy, (Dial from U.S. (202) 653-2400), (Fax from U.S. (202) 653 5760), www.fao.org; *FAO Fertilizer Yearbook* and *The State of Food and Agriculture (SOFA) 2006.*

United Nations Statistics Division, New York, NY 10017, (800) 253-9646, Fax: (212) 963-4116, http://unstats.un.org; *Statistical Yearbook.*

GHANA - FETAL MORTALITY

See GHANA - MORTALITY

GHANA - FILM

See GHANA - MOTION PICTURES

GHANA - FINANCE

International Monetary Fund (IMF), 700 Nineteenth Street, NW, Washington, DC 20431, (202) 623-7000, Fax: (202) 623-4661, www.imf.org; *International Financial Statistics Yearbook 2007.*

Taylor and Francis Group, An Informa Business, 2 Park Square, Milton Park, Abingdon, Oxford OX14 4RN, United Kingdom, (Dial from U.S. (212) 216-7800), (Fax from U.S. (212) 564-7854), www.tandf.co.uk; *The Europa World Year Book.*

United Nations Economic Commission for Africa (ECA), PO Box 3001, Addis Ababa, Ethiopia, (Telephone in U.S. (212) 963-4957), www.uneca.org; *African Statistical Yearbook 2006.*

United Nations Statistics Division, New York, NY 10017, (800) 253-9646, Fax: (212) 963-4116, http://unstats.un.org; *National Accounts Statistics: Compendium of Income Distribution Statistics* and *Statistical Yearbook.*

The World Bank, 1818 H Street, NW, Washington, DC 20433, (202) 473-1000, Fax: (202) 477-6391, www.worldbank.org; *Ghana.*

GHANA - FINANCE, PUBLIC

African Development Bank Group, Rue Joseph Anoma, 01 BP 1387 Abidjan 01, Cote d'Ivoire, www.afdb.org; *Statistics Pocketbook 2008.*

Bernan Essential Government Publications, 4611-F Assembly Drive, Lanham MD, 20706-4391, (301) 459-2255, Fax: (800) 865-3450, www.bernan.com; *National Accounts Statistics.*

Economist Intelligence Unit, 111 West 57th Street, New York, NY 10019, (212) 554-0600, Fax: (212) 586-1181, www.eiu.com; *Ghana Country Report.*

International Monetary Fund (IMF), 700 Nineteenth Street, NW, Washington, DC 20431, (202) 623-7000, Fax: (202) 623-4661, www.imf.org; *Government Finance Statistics Yearbook (2008 Edition); International Financial Statistics;* and *International Financial Statistics Online Service.*

M.E. Sharpe, 80 Business Park Drive, Armonk, NY 10504, (800) 541-6563, Fax: (914) 273-2106, www.mesharpe.com; *The Illustrated Book of World Rankings.*

Palgrave Macmillan Ltd., Houndmills, Basingstoke, Hampshire, RG21 6XS, England, (Telephone in U.S. (888) 330-8477), (Fax in U.S. (800) 672-2054), www.palgrave.com; *The Statesman's Yearbook 2008.*

Taylor and Francis Group, An Informa Business, 2 Park Square, Milton Park, Abingdon, Oxford OX14 4RN, United Kingdom, (Dial from U.S. (212) 216-7800), (Fax from U.S. (212) 564-7854), www.tandf.co.uk; *The Europa World Year Book.*

United Nations Economic Commission for Africa (ECA), PO Box 3001, Addis Ababa, Ethiopia, (Telephone in U.S. (212) 963-4957), www.uneca.org; *African Statistical Yearbook 2006.*

The World Bank, 1818 H Street, NW, Washington, DC 20433, (202) 473-1000, Fax: (202) 477-6391, www.worldbank.org; *Ghana.*

GHANA - FISHERIES

M.E. Sharpe, 80 Business Park Drive, Armonk, NY 10504, (800) 541-6563, Fax: (914) 273-2106, www.mesharpe.com; *The Illustrated Book of World Rankings.*

Palgrave Macmillan Ltd., Houndmills, Basingstoke, Hampshire, RG21 6XS, England, (Telephone in U.S. (888) 330-8477), (Fax in U.S. (800) 672-2054), www.palgrave.com; *The Statesman's Yearbook 2008.*

Taylor and Francis Group, An Informa Business, 2 Park Square, Milton Park, Abingdon, Oxford OX14 4RN, United Kingdom, (Dial from U.S. (212) 216-7800), (Fax from U.S. (212) 564-7854), www.tandf.co.uk; *The Europa World Year Book.*

United Nations Conference on Trade and Development (UNCTAD), DC2-1120, United Nations, New York, NY 10017, (212) 963-0027, www.unctad.org; *UNCTAD Commodity Yearbook.*

United Nations Economic Commission for Africa (ECA), PO Box 3001, Addis Ababa, Ethiopia, (Telephone in U.S. (212) 963-4957), www.uneca.org; *African Statistical Yearbook 2006.*

United Nations Food and Agricultural Organization (FAO), Viale delle Terme di Caracalla, 00100 Rome, Italy, (Dial from U.S. (202) 653-2400), (Fax from U.S. (202) 653 5760), www.fao.org; *FAO Yearbook of Fishery Statistics;* Fishery Databases; FISHSTAT Database. Subjects covered include: Aquaculture production, capture production, fishery commodities; and *The State of Food and Agriculture (SOFA) 2006.*

United Nations Statistics Division, New York, NY 10017, (800) 253-9646, Fax: (212) 963-4116, http://unstats.un.org; *Statistical Yearbook* and *Survey of Economic and Social Conditions in Africa 2005.*

The World Bank, 1818 H Street, NW, Washington, DC 20433, (202) 473-1000, Fax: (202) 477-6391, www.worldbank.org; *Ghana.*

GHANA - FLOUR INDUSTRY

United Nations Statistics Division, New York, NY 10017, (800) 253-9646, Fax: (212) 963-4116, http://unstats.un.org; *Statistical Yearbook.*

GHANA - FOOD

African Development Bank Group, Rue Joseph Anoma, 01 BP 1387 Abidjan 01, Cote d'Ivoire, www.afdb.org; *Statistics Pocketbook 2008.*

United Nations Conference on Trade and Development (UNCTAD), DC2-1120, United Nations, New York, NY 10017, (212) 963-0027, www.unctad.org; *UNCTAD Commodity Yearbook.*

United Nations Food and Agricultural Organization (FAO), Viale delle Terme di Caracalla, 00100 Rome, Italy, (Dial from U.S. (202) 653-2400), (Fax from U.S. (202) 653 5760), www.fao.org; *FAO Production Yearbook 2002* and *The State of Food and Agriculture (SOFA) 2006.*

United Nations Statistics Division, New York, NY 10017, (800) 253-9646, Fax: (212) 963-4116, http://unstats.un.org; *Human Development Report 2006.*

GHANA - FOREIGN EXCHANGE RATES

African Development Bank Group, Rue Joseph Anoma, 01 BP 1387 Abidjan 01, Cote d'Ivoire, www.afdb.org; *Statistics Pocketbook 2008.*

Central Intelligence Agency, Office of Public Affairs, Washington, DC 20505, (703) 482-0623, Fax: (703) 482-1739, www.cia.gov; *The World Factbook.*

Euromonitor International, Inc., 224 S. Michigan Avenue, Suite 1500, Chicago, IL 60604, (312) 922-1115, Fax: (312) 922-1157, www.euromonitor.com; *International Marketing Data and Statistics 2008* and *The World Economic Factbook 2008.*

International Civil Aviation Organization (ICAO), External Relations and Public Information Office (EPO), 999 University Street, Montreal, Quebec H3C 5H7, Canada, (Dial from U.S. (514) 954-8219), (Fax from U.S. (514) 954-6077), www.icao.int; *Civil Aviation Statistics of the World.*

International Monetary Fund (IMF), 700 Nineteenth Street, NW, Washington, DC 20431, (202) 623-7000, Fax: (202) 623-4661, www.imf.org; *International Financial Statistics Yearbook 2007.*

Taylor and Francis Group, An Informa Business, 2 Park Square, Milton Park, Abingdon, Oxford OX14 4RN, United Kingdom, (Dial from U.S. (212) 216-7800), (Fax from U.S. (212) 564-7854), www.tandf.co.uk; *The Europa World Year Book.*

United Nations Statistics Division, New York, NY 10017, (800) 253-9646, Fax: (212) 963-4116, http://unstats.un.org; *Compendium of Intra-African and Related Foreign Trade Statistics 2003; Statistical Yearbook;* and *World Statistics Pocketbook.*

GHANA - FORESTS AND FORESTRY

International Monetary Fund (IMF), 700 Nineteenth Street, NW, Washington, DC 20431, (202) 623-7000, Fax: (202) 623-4661, www.imf.org; *International Financial Statistics Yearbook 2007.*

M.E. Sharpe, 80 Business Park Drive, Armonk, NY 10504, (800) 541-6563, Fax: (914) 273-2106, www.mesharpe.com; *The Illustrated Book of World Rankings.*

Palgrave Macmillan Ltd., Houndmills, Basingstoke, Hampshire, RG21 6XS, England, (Telephone in U.S. (888) 330-8477), (Fax in U.S. (800) 672-2054), www.palgrave.com; *The Statesman's Yearbook 2008.*

Taylor and Francis Group, An Informa Business, 2 Park Square, Milton Park, Abingdon, Oxford OX14 4RN, United Kingdom, (Dial from U.S. (212) 216-

7800), (Fax from U.S. (212) 564-7854), www.tandf.co.uk; *The Europa World Year Book.*

UNESCO Institute for Statistics, C.P. 6128 Succursale Centre-Ville, Montreal, Quebec, H3C 3J7 Canada, (Dial from U.S. (514) 343-6880), (Fax from U.S. (514) 343 6882), www.uis.unesco.org; *Statistical Tables.*

United Nations Conference on Trade and Development (UNCTAD), DC2-1120, United Nations, New York, NY 10017, (212) 963-0027, www.unctad.org; *UNCTAD Commodity Yearbook.*

United Nations Economic Commission for Africa (ECA), PO Box 3001, Addis Ababa, Ethiopia, (Telephone in U.S. (212) 963-4957), www.uneca.org; *African Statistical Yearbook 2006.*

United Nations Food and Agricultural Organization (FAO), Viale delle Terme di Caracalla, 00100 Rome, Italy, (Dial from U.S. (202) 653-2400), (Fax from U.S. (202) 653 5760), www.fao.org; *FAO Yearbook of Forest Products* and *The State of Food and Agriculture (SOFA) 2006.*

United Nations Statistics Division, New York, NY 10017, (800) 253-9646, Fax: (212) 963-4116, http://unstats.un.org; *Statistical Yearbook.*

The World Bank, 1818 H Street, NW, Washington, DC 20433, (202) 473-1000, Fax: (202) 477-6391, www.worldbank.org; *Ghana* and *World Development Report 2008.*

GHANA - GAS PRODUCTION

See GHANA - MINERAL INDUSTRIES

GHANA - GEOGRAPHIC INFORMATION SYSTEMS

M.E. Sharpe, 80 Business Park Drive, Armonk, NY 10504, (800) 541-6563, Fax: (914) 273-2106, www.mesharpe.com; *The Illustrated Book of World Rankings.*

The World Bank, 1818 H Street, NW, Washington, DC 20433, (202) 473-1000, Fax: (202) 477-6391, www.worldbank.org; *Ghana.*

GHANA - GOLD INDUSTRY

International Monetary Fund (IMF), 700 Nineteenth Street, NW, Washington, DC 20431, (202) 623-7000, Fax: (202) 623-4661, www.imf.org; *International Financial Statistics Yearbook 2007.*

United Nations Statistics Division, New York, NY 10017, (800) 253-9646, Fax: (212) 963-4116, http://unstats.un.org; *Statistical Yearbook.*

The World Bank, 1818 H Street, NW, Washington, DC 20433, (202) 473-1000, Fax: (202) 477-6391, www.worldbank.org; *World Development Indicators (WDI) 2008.*

GHANA - GOLD PRODUCTION

See GHANA - MINERAL INDUSTRIES

GHANA - GRANTS-IN-AID

International Monetary Fund (IMF), 700 Nineteenth Street, NW, Washington, DC 20431, (202) 623-7000, Fax: (202) 623-4661, www.imf.org; *Government Finance Statistics Yearbook (2008 Edition).*

GHANA - GREEN PEPPER AND CHILIE PRODUCTION

See GHANA - CROPS

GHANA - GROSS DOMESTIC PRODUCT

African Development Bank Group, Rue Joseph Anoma, 01 BP 1387 Abidjan 01, Cote d'Ivoire, www.afdb.org; *Statistics Pocketbook 2008.*

Economist Intelligence Unit, 111 West 57th Street, New York, NY 10019, (212) 554-0600, Fax: (212) 586-1181, www.eiu.com; *Ghana Country Report.*

Euromonitor International, Inc., 224 S. Michigan Avenue, Suite 1500, Chicago, IL 60604, (312) 922-1115, Fax: (312) 922-1157, www.euromonitor.com; *International Marketing Data and Statistics 2008* and *The World Economic Factbook 2008.*

M.E. Sharpe, 80 Business Park Drive, Armonk, NY 10504, (800) 541-6563, Fax: (914) 273-2106, www.mesharpe.com; *The Illustrated Book of World Rankings.*

Taylor and Francis Group, An Informa Business, 2 Park Square, Milton Park, Abingdon, Oxford OX14 4RN, United Kingdom, (Dial from U.S. (212) 216-7800), (Fax from U.S. (212) 564-7854), www.tandf.co.uk; *The Europa World Year Book.*

United Nations Economic Commission for Africa (ECA), PO Box 3001, Addis Ababa, Ethiopia, (Telephone in U.S. (212) 963-4957), www.uneca.org; *African Statistical Yearbook 2006.*

United Nations Statistics Division, New York, NY 10017, (800) 253-9646, Fax: (212) 963-4116, http://unstats.un.org; *Human Development Report 2006; National Accounts Statistics: Compendium of Income Distribution Statistics; Statistical Yearbook;* and *Survey of Economic and Social Conditions in Africa 2005.*

The World Bank, 1818 H Street, NW, Washington, DC 20433, (202) 473-1000, Fax: (202) 477-6391, www.worldbank.org; *World Development Indicators (WDI) 2008* and *World Development Report 2008.*

GHANA - GROSS NATIONAL PRODUCT

Euromonitor International, Inc., 224 S. Michigan Avenue, Suite 1500, Chicago, IL 60604, (312) 922-1115, Fax: (312) 922-1157, www.euromonitor.com; *International Marketing Data and Statistics 2008.*

M.E. Sharpe, 80 Business Park Drive, Armonk, NY 10504, (800) 541-6563, Fax: (914) 273-2106, www.mesharpe.com; *The Illustrated Book of World Rankings.*

Palgrave Macmillan Ltd., Houndmills, Basingstoke, Hampshire, RG21 6XS, England, (Telephone in U.S. (888) 330-8477), (Fax in U.S. (800) 672-2054), www.palgrave.com; *The Statesman's Yearbook 2008.*

Taylor and Francis Group, An Informa Business, 2 Park Square, Milton Park, Abingdon, Oxford OX14 4RN, United Kingdom, (Dial from U.S. (212) 216-7800), (Fax from U.S. (212) 564-7854), www.tandf.co.uk; *The Europa World Year Book.*

U.S. Department of State (DOS), 2201 C Street NW, Washington, DC 20520, (202) 647-4000, www.state.gov; *World Military Expenditures and Arms Transfers (WMEAT).*

United Nations Statistics Division, New York, NY 10017, (800) 253-9646, Fax: (212) 963-4116, http://unstats.un.org; *Statistical Yearbook.*

The World Bank, 1818 H Street, NW, Washington, DC 20433, (202) 473-1000, Fax: (202) 477-6391, www.worldbank.org; *The World Bank Atlas 2003-2004; World Development Indicators (WDI) 2008;* and *World Development Report 2008.*

GHANA - HIDES AND SKINS INDUSTRY

United Nations Food and Agricultural Organization (FAO), Viale delle Terme di Caracalla, 00100 Rome, Italy, (Dial from U.S. (202) 653-2400), (Fax from U.S. (202) 653 5760), www.fao.org; *FAO Production Yearbook 2002.*

GHANA - HOUSING

Euromonitor International, Inc., 224 S. Michigan Avenue, Suite 1500, Chicago, IL 60604, (312) 922-1115, Fax: (312) 922-1157, www.euromonitor.com; *World Marketing Data and Statistics.*

M.E. Sharpe, 80 Business Park Drive, Armonk, NY 10504, (800) 541-6563, Fax: (914) 273-2106, www.mesharpe.com; *The Illustrated Book of World Rankings.*

GHANA - ILLITERATE PERSONS

Euromonitor International, Inc., 224 S. Michigan Avenue, Suite 1500, Chicago, IL 60604, (312) 922-1115, Fax: (312) 922-1157, www.euromonitor.com; *The World Economic Factbook 2008.*

UNESCO Institute for Statistics, C.P. 6128 Succursale Centre-Ville, Montreal, Quebec, H3C 3J7 Canada, (Dial from U.S. (514) 343-6880), (Fax from U.S. (514) 343 6882), www.uis.unesco.org; *Statistical Tables.*

United Nations Statistics Division, New York, NY 10017, (800) 253-9646, Fax: (212) 963-4116, http://unstats.un.org; *Human Development Report 2006.*

GHANA - IMPORTS

Central Intelligence Agency, Office of Public Affairs, Washington, DC 20505, (703) 482-0623, Fax: (703) 482-1739, www.cia.gov; *The World Factbook.*

Economist Intelligence Unit, 111 West 57th Street, New York, NY 10019, (212) 554-0600, Fax: (212) 586-1181, www.eiu.com; *Ghana Country Report.*

Euromonitor International, Inc., 224 S. Michigan Avenue, Suite 1500, Chicago, IL 60604, (312) 922-1115, Fax: (312) 922-1157, www.euromonitor.com; *International Marketing Data and Statistics 2008* and *The World Economic Factbook 2008.*

International Monetary Fund (IMF), 700 Nineteenth Street, NW, Washington, DC 20431, (202) 623-7000, Fax: (202) 623-4661, www.imf.org; *Direction of Trade Statistics Yearbook 2007; Government Finance Statistics Yearbook (2008 Edition);* and *International Financial Statistics Yearbook 2007.*

Palgrave Macmillan Ltd., Houndmills, Basingstoke, Hampshire, RG21 6XS, England, (Telephone in U.S. (888) 330-8477), (Fax in U.S. (800) 672-2054), www.palgrave.com; *The Statesman's Yearbook 2008.*

Taylor and Francis Group, An Informa Business, 2 Park Square, Milton Park, Abingdon, Oxford OX14 4RN, United Kingdom, (Dial from U.S. (212) 216-7800), (Fax from U.S. (212) 564-7854), www.tandf.co.uk; *The Europa World Year Book.*

U.S. Department of State (DOS), 2201 C Street NW, Washington, DC 20520, (202) 647-4000, www.state.gov; *World Military Expenditures and Arms Transfers (WMEAT).*

United Nations Conference on Trade and Development (UNCTAD), DC2-1120, United Nations, New York, NY 10017, (212) 963-0027, www.unctad.org; *Handbook of Statistics 2005.*

United Nations Food and Agricultural Organization (FAO), Viale delle Terme di Caracalla, 00100 Rome, Italy, (Dial from U.S. (202) 653-2400), (Fax from U.S. (202) 653 5760), www.fao.org; *The State of Food and Agriculture (SOFA) 2006.*

United Nations Statistics Division, New York, NY 10017, (800) 253-9646, Fax: (212) 963-4116, http://unstats.un.org; *Compendium of Intra-African and Related Foreign Trade Statistics 2003* and *Survey of Economic and Social Conditions in Africa 2005.*

The World Bank, 1818 H Street, NW, Washington, DC 20433, (202) 473-1000, Fax: (202) 477-6391, www.worldbank.org; *World Development Indicators (WDI) 2008* and *World Development Report 2008.*

GHANA - INCOME TAXES

See GHANA - TAXATION

GHANA - INDUSTRIAL METALS PRODUCTION

See GHANA - MINERAL INDUSTRIES

GHANA - INDUSTRIAL PRODUCTIVITY

Euromonitor International, Inc., 224 S. Michigan Avenue, Suite 1500, Chicago, IL 60604, (312) 922-1115, Fax: (312) 922-1157, www.euromonitor.com; *International Marketing Data and Statistics 2008.*

M.E. Sharpe, 80 Business Park Drive, Armonk, NY 10504, (800) 541-6563, Fax: (914) 273-2106, www.mesharpe.com; *The Illustrated Book of World Rankings.*

GHANA - INDUSTRIAL PROPERTY

United Nations Statistics Division, New York, NY 10017, (800) 253-9646, Fax: (212) 963-4116, http://unstats.un.org; *Statistical Yearbook.*

World Intellectual Property Organization (WIPO), PO Box 18, CH-1211 Geneva 20, Switzerland, www.wipo.int; *Industrial Property Statistics* and *Industrial Property Statistics Online Directory.*

GHANA - INDUSTRIES

Central Intelligence Agency, Office of Public Affairs, Washington, DC 20505, (703) 482-0623, Fax: (703) 482-1739, www.cia.gov; *The World Factbook.*

Economist Intelligence Unit, 111 West 57th Street, New York, NY 10019, (212) 554-0600, Fax: (212) 586-1181, www.eiu.com; *Ghana Country Report.*

Euromonitor International, Inc., 224 S. Michigan Avenue, Suite 1500, Chicago, IL 60604, (312) 922-1115, Fax: (312) 922-1157, www.euromonitor.com; *The World Economic Factbook 2008* and *World Marketing Data and Statistics.*

International Labour Office, I.L.O. Publications, 4 route des Morillons, CH-1211 Geneva 22, Switzerland, (Telephone in U.S. (202) 653-7652), (Fax in U.S. (202) 653-7687), www.ilo.org; *Yearbook of Labour Statistics 2006.*

M.E. Sharpe, 80 Business Park Drive, Armonk, NY 10504, (800) 541-6563, Fax: (914) 273-2106, www.mesharpe.com; *The Illustrated Book of World Rankings.*

Palgrave Macmillan Ltd., Houndmills, Basingstoke, Hampshire, RG21 6XS, England, (Telephone in U.S. (888) 330-8477), (Fax in U.S. (800) 672-2054), www.palgrave.com; *The Statesman's Yearbook 2008.*

Taylor and Francis Group, An Informa Business, 2 Park Square, Milton Park, Abingdon, Oxford OX14 4RN, United Kingdom, (Dial from U.S. (212) 216-7800), (Fax from U.S. (212) 564-7854), www.tandf.co.uk; *The Europa World Year Book.*

United Nations Economic Commission for Africa (ECA), PO Box 3001, Addis Ababa, Ethiopia, (Telephone in U.S. (212) 963-4957), www.uneca.org; *African Statistical Yearbook 2006.*

United Nations Industrial Development Organization (UNIDO), 1 United Nations Plaza, New York, NY 10017, (212) 963 6890, Fax: (212) 963-7904, http://unido.org; Industrial Statistics Database 2008 (INDSTAT) and *The International Yearbook of Industrial Statistics 2008.*

United Nations Statistics Division, New York, NY 10017, (800) 253-9646, Fax: (212) 963-4116, http://unstats.un.org; *2004 Industrial Commodity Statistics Yearbook; Statistical Yearbook;* and *Survey of Economic and Social Conditions in Africa 2005.*

The World Bank, 1818 H Street, NW, Washington, DC 20433, (202) 473-1000, Fax: (202) 477-6391, www.worldbank.org; *Ghana* and *World Development Indicators (WDI) 2008.*

GHANA - INFANT AND MATERNAL MORTALITY

See GHANA - MORTALITY

GHANA - INTERNATIONAL LIQUIDITY

International Monetary Fund (IMF), 700 Nineteenth Street, NW, Washington, DC 20431, (202) 623-7000, Fax: (202) 623-4661, www.imf.org; *International Financial Statistics Yearbook 2007.*

GHANA - INTERNATIONAL TRADE

African Development Bank Group, Rue Joseph Anoma, 01 BP 1387 Abidjan 01, Cote d'Ivoire, www.afdb.org; *Statistics Pocketbook 2008.*

Economist Intelligence Unit, 111 West 57th Street, New York, NY 10019, (212) 554-0600, Fax: (212) 586-1181, www.eiu.com; *Ghana Country Report.*

Euromonitor International, Inc., 224 S. Michigan Avenue, Suite 1500, Chicago, IL 60604, (312) 922-1115, Fax: (312) 922-1157, www.euromonitor.com; *International Marketing Data and Statistics 2008; The World Economic Factbook 2008;* and *World Marketing Data and Statistics.*

International Monetary Fund (IMF), 700 Nineteenth Street, NW, Washington, DC 20431, (202) 623-7000, Fax: (202) 623-4661, www.imf.org; *International Financial Statistics Yearbook 2007.*

M.E. Sharpe, 80 Business Park Drive, Armonk, NY 10504, (800) 541-6563, Fax: (914) 273-2106, www.mesharpe.com; *The Illustrated Book of World Rankings.*

Palgrave Macmillan Ltd., Houndmills, Basingstoke, Hampshire, RG21 6XS, England, (Telephone in U.S. (888) 330-8477), (Fax in U.S. (800) 672-2054), www.palgrave.com; *The Statesman's Yearbook 2008.*

Taylor and Francis Group, An Informa Business, 2 Park Square, Milton Park, Abingdon, Oxford OX14 4RN, United Kingdom, (Dial from U.S. (212) 216-7800), (Fax from U.S. (212) 564-7854), www.tandf.co.uk; *The Europa World Year Book.*

United Nations Conference on Trade and Development (UNCTAD), DC2-1120, United Nations, New York, NY 10017, (212) 963-0027, www.unctad.org; *UNCTAD Commodity Yearbook.*

United Nations Economic Commission for Africa (ECA), PO Box 3001, Addis Ababa, Ethiopia, (Telephone in U.S. (212) 963-4957), www.uneca.org; *African Statistical Yearbook 2006.*

United Nations Food and Agricultural Organization (FAO), Viale delle Terme di Caracalla, 00100 Rome, Italy, (Dial from U.S. (202) 653-2400), (Fax from U.S. (202) 653 5760), www.fao.org; *FAO Trade Yearbook* and *The State of Food and Agriculture (SOFA) 2006.*

United Nations Statistics Division, New York, NY 10017, (800) 253-9646, Fax: (212) 963-4116, http://unstats.un.org; *Compendium of Intra-African and Related Foreign Trade Statistics 2003; International Trade Statistics Yearbook;* and *Statistical Yearbook.*

The World Bank, 1818 H Street, NW, Washington, DC 20433, (202) 473-1000, Fax: (202) 477-6391, www.worldbank.org; *Ghana; World Development Indicators (WDI) 2008;* and *World Development Report 2008.*

World Trade Organization (WTO), Centre William Rappard, Rue de Lausanne 154, CH-1211 Geneva 21, Switzerland, www.wto.org; *International Trade Statistics 2006.*

GHANA - INTERNET USERS

International Telecommunication Union (ITU), Place des Nations, 1211 Geneva 20, Switzerland, www.itu.int; *World Telecommunication/ICT Indicators Database on CD-ROM; World Telecommunication/ICT Indicators Database Online;* and *Yearbook of Statistics - Telecommunication Services (Chronological Time Series 1997-2006).*

The World Bank, 1818 H Street, NW, Washington, DC 20433, (202) 473-1000, Fax: (202) 477-6391, www.worldbank.org; *Ghana.*

GHANA - IRON AND IRON ORE PRODUCTION

See GHANA - MINERAL INDUSTRIES

GHANA - IRRIGATION

Euromonitor International, Inc., 224 S. Michigan Avenue, Suite 1500, Chicago, IL 60604, (312) 922-1115, Fax: (312) 922-1157, www.euromonitor.com; *International Marketing Data and Statistics 2008.*

GHANA - LABOR

African Development Bank Group, Rue Joseph Anoma, 01 BP 1387 Abidjan 01, Cote d'Ivoire, www.afdb.org; *Statistics Pocketbook 2008.*

Central Intelligence Agency, Office of Public Affairs, Washington, DC 20505, (703) 482-0623, Fax: (703) 482-1739, www.cia.gov; *The World Factbook.*

Euromonitor International, Inc., 224 S. Michigan Avenue, Suite 1500, Chicago, IL 60604, (312) 922-1115, Fax: (312) 922-1157, www.euromonitor.com; *International Marketing Data and Statistics 2008* and *World Marketing Data and Statistics.*

International Labour Office, I.L.O. Publications, 4 route des Morillons, CH-1211 Geneva 22, Switzerland, (Telephone in U.S. (202) 653-7652), (Fax in U.S. (202) 653-7687), www.ilo.org; *Yearbook of Labour Statistics 2006.*

M.E. Sharpe, 80 Business Park Drive, Armonk, NY 10504, (800) 541-6563, Fax: (914) 273-2106, www.mesharpe.com; *The Illustrated Book of World Rankings.*

Palgrave Macmillan Ltd., Houndmills, Basingstoke, Hampshire, RG21 6XS, England, (Telephone in U.S. (888) 330-8477), (Fax in U.S. (800) 672-2054), www.palgrave.com; *The Statesman's Yearbook 2008.*

Taylor and Francis Group, An Informa Business, 2 Park Square, Milton Park, Abingdon, Oxford OX14 4RN, United Kingdom, (Dial from U.S. (212) 216-7800), (Fax from U.S. (212) 564-7854), www.tandf.co.uk; *The Europa World Year Book.*

United Nations Food and Agricultural Organization (FAO), Viale delle Terme di Caracalla, 00100 Rome, Italy, (Dial from U.S. (202) 653-2400), (Fax from U.S. (202) 653 5760), www.fao.org; *The State of Food and Agriculture (SOFA) 2006.*

United Nations Statistics Division, New York, NY 10017, (800) 253-9646, Fax: (212) 963-4116, http://unstats.un.org; *Human Development Report 2006.*

The World Bank, 1818 H Street, NW, Washington, DC 20433, (202) 473-1000, Fax: (202) 477-6391, www.worldbank.org; *The World Bank Atlas 2003-2004; World Development Indicators (WDI) 2008;* and *World Development Report 2008.*

GHANA - LAND USE

Central Intelligence Agency, Office of Public Affairs, Washington, DC 20505, (703) 482-0623, Fax: (703) 482-1739, www.cia.gov; *The World Factbook.*

Euromonitor International, Inc., 224 S. Michigan Avenue, Suite 1500, Chicago, IL 60604, (312) 922-1115, Fax: (312) 922-1157, www.euromonitor.com; *International Marketing Data and Statistics 2008.*

United Nations Food and Agricultural Organization (FAO), Viale delle Terme di Caracalla, 00100 Rome, Italy, (Dial from U.S. (202) 653-2400), (Fax from U.S. (202) 653 5760), www.fao.org; *FAO Production Yearbook 2002.*

The World Bank, 1818 H Street, NW, Washington, DC 20433, (202) 473-1000, Fax: (202) 477-6391, www.worldbank.org; *World Development Report 2008.*

GHANA - LIBRARIES

M.E. Sharpe, 80 Business Park Drive, Armonk, NY 10504, (800) 541-6563, Fax: (914) 273-2106, www.mesharpe.com; *The Illustrated Book of World Rankings.*

UNESCO Institute for Statistics, C.P. 6128 Succursale Centre-Ville, Montreal, Quebec, H3C 3J7 Canada, (Dial from U.S. (514) 343-6880), (Fax from U.S. (514) 343 6882), www.uis.unesco.org; *Statistical Tables.*

GHANA - LICENSES

International Monetary Fund (IMF), 700 Nineteenth Street, NW, Washington, DC 20431, (202) 623-7000, Fax: (202) 623-4661, www.imf.org; *Government Finance Statistics Yearbook (2008 Edition).*

GHANA - LIFE EXPECTANCY

African Development Bank Group, Rue Joseph Anoma, 01 BP 1387 Abidjan 01, Cote d'Ivoire, www.afdb.org; *Statistics Pocketbook 2008.*

Central Intelligence Agency, Office of Public Affairs, Washington, DC 20505, (703) 482-0623, Fax: (703) 482-1739, www.cia.gov; *The World Factbook.*

Euromonitor International, Inc., 224 S. Michigan Avenue, Suite 1500, Chicago, IL 60604, (312) 922-1115, Fax: (312) 922-1157, www.euromonitor.com; *The World Economic Factbook 2008.*

Palgrave Macmillan Ltd., Houndmills, Basingstoke, Hampshire, RG21 6XS, England, (Telephone in U.S. (888) 330-8477), (Fax in U.S. (800) 672-2054), www.palgrave.com; *The Statesman's Yearbook 2008.*

United Nations Statistics Division, New York, NY 10017, (800) 253-9646, Fax: (212) 963-4116, http://unstats.un.org; *Human Development Report 2006* and *World Statistics Pocketbook*.

The World Bank, 1818 H Street, NW, Washington, DC 20433, (202) 473-1000, Fax: (202) 477-6391, www.worldbank.org; *The World Bank Atlas 2003-2004* and *World Development Report 2008*.

GHANA - LITERACY

Euromonitor International, Inc., 224 S. Michigan Avenue, Suite 1500, Chicago, IL 60604, (312) 922-1115, Fax: (312) 922-1157, www.euromonitor.com; *World Marketing Data and Statistics*.

United Nations Statistics Division, New York, NY 10017, (800) 253-9646, Fax: (212) 963-4116, http://unstats.un.org; *Survey of Economic and Social Conditions in Africa 2005*.

GHANA - LIVESTOCK

Euromonitor International, Inc., 224 S. Michigan Avenue, Suite 1500, Chicago, IL 60604, (312) 922-1115, Fax: (312) 922-1157, www.euromonitor.com; *International Marketing Data and Statistics 2008*.

M.E. Sharpe, 80 Business Park Drive, Armonk, NY 10504, (800) 541-6563, Fax: (914) 273-2106, www.mesharpe.com; *The Illustrated Book of World Rankings*.

Palgrave Macmillan Ltd., Houndmills, Basingstoke, Hampshire, RG21 6XS, England, (Telephone in U.S. (888) 330-8477), (Fax in U.S. (800) 672-2054), www.palgrave.com; *The Statesman's Yearbook 2008*.

Taylor and Francis Group, An Informa Business, 2 Park Square, Milton Park, Abingdon, Oxford OX14 4RN, United Kingdom, (Dial from U.S. (212) 216-7800), (Fax from U.S. (212) 564-7854), www.tandf.co.uk; *The Europa World Year Book*.

United Nations Conference on Trade and Development (UNCTAD), DC2-1120, United Nations, New York, NY 10017, (212) 963-0027, www.unctad.org; *UNCTAD Commodity Yearbook*.

United Nations Economic Commission for Africa (ECA), PO Box 3001, Addis Ababa, Ethiopia, (Telephone in U.S. (212) 963-4957), www.uneca.org; *African Statistical Yearbook 2006*.

United Nations Food and Agricultural Organization (FAO), Viale delle Terme di Caracalla, 00100 Rome, Italy, (Dial from U.S. (202) 653-2400), (Fax from U.S. (202) 653 5760), www.fao.org; *FAO Production Yearbook 2002* and *The State of Food and Agriculture (SOFA) 2006*.

United Nations Statistics Division, New York, NY 10017, (800) 253-9646, Fax: (212) 963-4116, http://unstats.un.org; *Statistical Yearbook* and *Survey of Economic and Social Conditions in Africa 2005*.

GHANA - LOCAL TAXATION

Euromonitor International, Inc., 224 S. Michigan Avenue, Suite 1500, Chicago, IL 60604, (312) 922-1115, Fax: (312) 922-1157, www.euromonitor.com; *International Marketing Data and Statistics 2008*.

GHANA - MANUFACTURES

M.E. Sharpe, 80 Business Park Drive, Armonk, NY 10504, (800) 541-6563, Fax: (914) 273-2106, www.mesharpe.com; *The Illustrated Book of World Rankings*.

United Nations Economic Commission for Africa (ECA), PO Box 3001, Addis Ababa, Ethiopia, (Telephone in U.S. (212) 963-4957), www.uneca.org; *African Statistical Yearbook 2006*.

United Nations Statistics Division, New York, NY 10017, (800) 253-9646, Fax: (212) 963-4116, http://unstats.un.org; *Statistical Yearbook* and *Survey of Economic and Social Conditions in Africa 2005*.

The World Bank, 1818 H Street, NW, Washington, DC 20433, (202) 473-1000, Fax: (202) 477-6391, www.worldbank.org; *World Development Indicators (WDI) 2008*.

GHANA - MARRIAGE

M.E. Sharpe, 80 Business Park Drive, Armonk, NY 10504, (800) 541-6563, Fax: (914) 273-2106, www.mesharpe.com; *The Illustrated Book of World Rankings*.

United Nations Statistics Division, New York, NY 10017, (800) 253-9646, Fax: (212) 963-4116, http://unstats.un.org; *Demographic Yearbook*.

GHANA - MEAT PRODUCTION

See GHANA - LIVESTOCK

GHANA - MEDICAL CARE, COST OF

International Monetary Fund (IMF), 700 Nineteenth Street, NW, Washington, DC 20431, (202) 623-7000, Fax: (202) 623-4661, www.imf.org; *Government Finance Statistics Yearbook (2008 Edition)*.

GHANA - MILK PRODUCTION

See GHANA - DAIRY PROCESSING

GHANA - MINERAL INDUSTRIES

Commodity Research Bureau, 330 South Wells Street, Suite 612, Chicago, IL 60606-7110, (800) 621-5271, Fax: (312) 939-4135, www.crbtrader.com; *2006 CRB Commodity Yearbook and CD*.

M.E. Sharpe, 80 Business Park Drive, Armonk, NY 10504, (800) 541-6563, Fax: (914) 273-2106, www.mesharpe.com; *The Illustrated Book of World Rankings*.

Organisation for Economic Cooperation and Development (OECD), 2 rue Andre Pascal, F-75775 Paris Cedex 16, France, (Telephone in U.S. (202) 785-6323), (Fax in U.S. (202) 785-0350), www.oecd.org; *World Energy Outlook 2007*.

Palgrave Macmillan Ltd., Houndmills, Basingstoke, Hampshire, RG21 6XS, England, (Telephone in U.S. (888) 330-8477), (Fax in U.S. (800) 672-2054), www.palgrave.com; *The Statesman's Yearbook 2008*.

Taylor and Francis Group, An Informa Business, 2 Park Square, Milton Park, Abingdon, Oxford OX14 4RN, United Kingdom, (Dial from U.S. (212) 216-7800), (Fax from U.S. (212) 564-7854), www.tandf.co.uk; *The Europa World Year Book*.

United Nations Conference on Trade and Development (UNCTAD), DC2-1120, United Nations, New York, NY 10017, (212) 963-0027, www.unctad.org; *UNCTAD Commodity Yearbook*.

United Nations Statistics Division, New York, NY 10017, (800) 253-9646, Fax: (212) 963-4116, http://unstats.un.org; *Statistical Yearbook*.

GHANA - MONEY EXCHANGE RATES

See GHANA - FOREIGN EXCHANGE RATES

GHANA - MONEY SUPPLY

African Development Bank Group, Rue Joseph Anoma, 01 BP 1387 Abidjan 01, Cote d'Ivoire, www.afdb.org; *Statistics Pocketbook 2008*.

Economist Intelligence Unit, 111 West 57th Street, New York, NY 10019, (212) 554-0600, Fax: (212) 586-1181, www.eiu.com; *Ghana Country Report*.

Euromonitor International, Inc., 224 S. Michigan Avenue, Suite 1500, Chicago, IL 60604, (312) 922-1115, Fax: (312) 922-1157, www.euromonitor.com; *International Marketing Data and Statistics 2008*.

International Monetary Fund (IMF), 700 Nineteenth Street, NW, Washington, DC 20431, (202) 623-7000, Fax: (202) 623-4661, www.imf.org; *International Financial Statistics Yearbook 2007*.

Taylor and Francis Group, An Informa Business, 2 Park Square, Milton Park, Abingdon, Oxford OX14 4RN, United Kingdom, (Dial from U.S. (212) 216-7800), (Fax from U.S. (212) 564-7854), www.tandf.co.uk; *The Europa World Year Book*.

United Nations Statistics Division, New York, NY 10017, (800) 253-9646, Fax: (212) 963-4116, http://unstats.un.org; *Statistical Yearbook*.

The World Bank, 1818 H Street, NW, Washington, DC 20433, (202) 473-1000, Fax: (202) 477-6391, www.worldbank.org; *Ghana* and *World Development Indicators (WDI) 2008*.

GHANA - MORTALITY

Central Intelligence Agency, Office of Public Affairs, Washington, DC 20505, (703) 482-0623, Fax: (703) 482-1739, www.cia.gov; *The World Factbook*.

Euromonitor International, Inc., 224 S. Michigan Avenue, Suite 1500, Chicago, IL 60604, (312) 922-1115, Fax: (312) 922-1157, www.euromonitor.com; *International Marketing Data and Statistics 2008* and *The World Economic Factbook 2008*.

Palgrave Macmillan Ltd., Houndmills, Basingstoke, Hampshire, RG21 6XS, England, (Telephone in U.S. (888) 330-8477), (Fax in U.S. (800) 672-2054), www.palgrave.com; *The Statesman's Yearbook 2008*.

Taylor and Francis Group, An Informa Business, 2 Park Square, Milton Park, Abingdon, Oxford OX14 4RN, United Kingdom, (Dial from U.S. (212) 216-7800), (Fax from U.S. (212) 564-7854), www.tandf.co.uk; *The Europa World Year Book*.

UNICEF, 3 United Nations Plaza, New York, NY 10017, (800) 253-9646, Fax: (212) 887-7465, www.unicef.org; *The State of the World's Children 2008*.

United Nations Statistics Division, New York, NY 10017, (800) 253-9646, Fax: (212) 963-4116, http://unstats.un.org; *Demographic Yearbook; Human Development Report 2006; Statistical Yearbook; Survey of Economic and Social Conditions in Africa 2005;* and *World Statistics Pocketbook*.

The World Bank, 1818 H Street, NW, Washington, DC 20433, (202) 473-1000, Fax: (202) 477-6391, www.worldbank.org; *The World Bank Atlas 2003-2004; World Development Indicators (WDI) 2008;* and *World Development Report 2008*.

World Health Organization (WHO), Avenue Appia 20, 1211 Geneve 27, Switzerland, (Telephone in U.S. (212) 331-9081), www.who.int; The WHO Global Atlas of Infectious Diseases and *World Health Report 2006*.

GHANA - MOTION PICTURES

Palgrave Macmillan Ltd., Houndmills, Basingstoke, Hampshire, RG21 6XS, England, (Telephone in U.S. (888) 330-8477), (Fax in U.S. (800) 672-2054), www.palgrave.com; *The Statesman's Yearbook 2008*.

UNESCO Institute for Statistics, C.P. 6128 Succursale Centre-Ville, Montreal, Quebec, H3C 3J7 Canada, (Dial from U.S. (514) 343-6880), (Fax from U.S. (514) 343 6882), www.uis.unesco.org; *Statistical Tables*.

United Nations Statistics Division, New York, NY 10017, (800) 253-9646, Fax: (212) 963-4116, http://unstats.un.org; *Statistical Yearbook*.

GHANA - MOTOR VEHICLES

International Road Federation (IFR), Madison Place, 500 Montgomery Street, 5th Floor, Alexandria, VA 22314, (703) 535-1001, Fax: (703) 535-1007, www.irfnet.org; *World Road Statistics 2006*.

Taylor and Francis Group, An Informa Business, 2 Park Square, Milton Park, Abingdon, Oxford OX14 4RN, United Kingdom, (Dial from U.S. (212) 216-7800), (Fax from U.S. (212) 564-7854), www.tandf.co.uk; *The Europa World Year Book*.

United Nations Statistics Division, New York, NY 10017, (800) 253-9646, Fax: (212) 963-4116, http://unstats.un.org; *Statistical Yearbook* and *Survey of Economic and Social Conditions in Africa 2005*.

GHANA - MUSEUMS

M.E. Sharpe, 80 Business Park Drive, Armonk, NY 10504, (800) 541-6563, Fax: (914) 273-2106, www.mesharpe.com; *The Illustrated Book of World Rankings*.

UNESCO Institute for Statistics, C.P. 6128 Succursale Centre-Ville, Montreal, Quebec, H3C 3J7 Canada, (Dial from U.S. (514) 343-6880), (Fax from U.S. (514) 343 6882), www.uis.unesco.org; *Statistical Tables*.

GHANA - NATURAL GAS PRODUCTION

See GHANA - MINERAL INDUSTRIES

GHANA - NUTRITION

African Development Bank Group, Rue Joseph Anoma, 01 BP 1387 Abidjan 01, Cote d'Ivoire, www.afdb.org; *Statistics Pocketbook 2008.*

United Nations Food and Agricultural Organization (FAO), Viale delle Terme di Caracalla, 00100 Rome, Italy, (Dial from U.S. (202) 653-2400), (Fax from U.S. (202) 653 5760), www.fao.org; *The State of Food and Agriculture (SOFA) 2006.*

GHANA - OLDER PEOPLE

M.E. Sharpe, 80 Business Park Drive, Armonk, NY 10504, (800) 541-6563, Fax: (914) 273-2106, www.mesharpe.com; *The Illustrated Book of World Rankings.*

GHANA - PALM OIL PRODUCTION

See GHANA - CROPS

GHANA - PAPER

See GHANA - FORESTS AND FORESTRY

GHANA - PEANUT PRODUCTION

See GHANA - CROPS

GHANA - PERIODICALS

UNESCO Institute for Statistics, C.P. 6128 Succursale Centre-Ville, Montreal, Quebec, H3C 3J7 Canada, (Dial from U.S. (514) 343-6880), (Fax from U.S. (514) 343 6882), www.uis.unesco.org; *Statistical Tables.*

GHANA - PESTICIDES

United Nations Food and Agricultural Organization (FAO), Viale delle Terme di Caracalla, 00100 Rome, Italy, (Dial from U.S. (202) 653-2400), (Fax from U.S. (202) 653 5760), www.fao.org; *The State of Food and Agriculture (SOFA) 2006.*

GHANA - PETROLEUM INDUSTRY AND TRADE

M.E. Sharpe, 80 Business Park Drive, Armonk, NY 10504, (800) 541-6563, Fax: (914) 273-2106, www.mesharpe.com; *The Illustrated Book of World Rankings.*

Organisation for Economic Cooperation and Development (OECD), 2 rue Andre Pascal, F-75775 Paris Cedex 16, France, (Telephone in U.S. (202) 785-6323), (Fax in U.S. (202) 785-0350), www.oecd.org; *World Energy Outlook 2007.*

Palgrave Macmillan Ltd., Houndmills, Basingstoke, Hampshire, RG21 6XS, England, (Telephone in U.S. (888) 330-8477), (Fax in U.S. (800) 672-2054), www.palgrave.com; *The Statesman's Yearbook 2008.*

PennWell Corporation, 1421 South Sheridan Road, Tulsa, OK 74112, (918) 835-3161, www.pennwell.com; *International Petroleum Encyclopedia 2007.*

U.S. Department of Energy (DOE), Energy Information Administration (EIA), 1000 Independence Avenue, SW, Washington, DC 20585, (202) 586-8800, www.eia.doe.gov; *International Energy Annual 2004* and *International Energy Outlook 2006.*

United Nations Conference on Trade and Development (UNCTAD), DC2-1120, United Nations, New York, NY 10017, (212) 963-0027, www.unctad.org; *UNCTAD Commodity Yearbook.*

United Nations Food and Agricultural Organization (FAO), Viale delle Terme di Caracalla, 00100 Rome, Italy, (Dial from U.S. (202) 653-2400), (Fax from U.S. (202) 653 5760), www.fao.org; *The State of Food and Agriculture (SOFA) 2006.*

United Nations Statistics Division, New York, NY 10017, (800) 253-9646, Fax: (212) 963-4116, http://unstats.un.org; *Statistical Yearbook.*

GHANA - POLITICAL SCIENCE

Central Intelligence Agency, Office of Public Affairs, Washington, DC 20505, (703) 482-0623, Fax: (703) 482-1739, www.cia.gov; *The World Factbook.*

International Monetary Fund (IMF), 700 Nineteenth Street, NW, Washington, DC 20431, (202) 623-7000, Fax: (202) 623-4661, www.imf.org; *Government Finance Statistics Yearbook (2008 Edition)* and *International Financial Statistics Yearbook 2007.*

Palgrave Macmillan Ltd., Houndmills, Basingstoke, Hampshire, RG21 6XS, England, (Telephone in U.S. (888) 330-8477), (Fax in U.S. (800) 672-2054), www.palgrave.com; *The Statesman's Yearbook 2008.*

Taylor and Francis Group, An Informa Business, 2 Park Square, Milton Park, Abingdon, Oxford OX14 4RN, United Kingdom, (Dial from U.S. (212) 216-7800), (Fax from U.S. (212) 564-7854), www.tandf.co.uk; *The Europa World Year Book.*

United Nations Statistics Division, New York, NY 10017, (800) 253-9646, Fax: (212) 963-4116, http://unstats.un.org; *National Accounts Statistics: Compendium of Income Distribution Statistics; Statistical Yearbook;* and *Survey of Economic and Social Conditions in Africa 2005.*

The World Bank, 1818 H Street, NW, Washington, DC 20433, (202) 473-1000, Fax: (202) 477-6391, www.worldbank.org; *World Development Indicators (WDI) 2008* and *World Development Report 2008.*

GHANA - POPULATION

African Development Bank Group, Rue Joseph Anoma, 01 BP 1387 Abidjan 01, Cote d'Ivoire, www.afdb.org; *The African Statistical Journal; Gender, Poverty and Environmental Indicators on African Countries 2007; Selected Statistics on African Countries 2007;* and *Statistics Pocketbook 2008.*

Central Intelligence Agency, Office of Public Affairs, Washington, DC 20505, (703) 482-0623, Fax: (703) 482-1739, www.cia.gov; *The World Factbook.*

Economist Intelligence Unit, 111 West 57th Street, New York, NY 10019, (212) 554-0600, Fax: (212) 586-1181, www.eiu.com; *Ghana Country Report.*

Euromonitor International, Inc., 224 S. Michigan Avenue, Suite 1500, Chicago, IL 60604, (312) 922-1115, Fax: (312) 922-1157, www.euromonitor.com; *International Marketing Data and Statistics 2008* and *The World Economic Factbook 2008.*

Eurostat, Batiment Jean Monnet, Rue Alcide de Gasperi, L-2920 Luxembourg, http://epp.eurostat.ec.europa.eu; *Demographic Indicators - Population by Age-Classes.*

International Labour Office, I.L.O. Publications, 4 route des Morillons, CH-1211 Geneva 22, Switzerland, (Telephone in U.S. (202) 653-7652), (Fax in U.S. (202) 653-7687), www.ilo.org; *Yearbook of Labour Statistics 2006.*

M.E. Sharpe, 80 Business Park Drive, Armonk, NY 10504, (800) 541-6563, Fax: (914) 273-2106, www.mesharpe.com; *The Illustrated Book of World Rankings.*

Palgrave Macmillan Ltd., Houndmills, Basingstoke, Hampshire, RG21 6XS, England, (Telephone in U.S. (888) 330-8477), (Fax in U.S. (800) 672-2054), www.palgrave.com; *The Statesman's Yearbook 2008.*

Taylor and Francis Group, An Informa Business, 2 Park Square, Milton Park, Abingdon, Oxford OX14 4RN, United Kingdom, (Dial from U.S. (212) 216-7800), (Fax from U.S. (212) 564-7854), www.tandf.co.uk; *The Europa World Year Book.*

U.S. Department of State (DOS), 2201 C Street NW, Washington, DC 20520, (202) 647-4000, www.state.gov; *World Military Expenditures and Arms Transfers (WMEAT).*

UNESCO Institute for Statistics, C.P. 6128 Succursale Centre-Ville, Montreal, Quebec, H3C 3J7 Canada, (Dial from U.S. (514) 343-6880), (Fax from U.S. (514) 343 6882), www.uis.unesco.org; *Statistical Tables.*

United Nations Food and Agricultural Organization (FAO), Viale delle Terme di Caracalla, 00100 Rome, Italy, (Dial from U.S. (202) 653-2400), (Fax from U.S. (202) 653 5760), www.fao.org; *FAO Production Yearbook 2002.*

United Nations Statistics Division, New York, NY 10017, (800) 253-9646, Fax: (212) 963-4116, http://unstats.un.org; *Demographic Yearbook; Human Development Report 2006; Statistical Yearbook; Survey of Economic and Social Conditions in Africa 2005;* and *World Statistics Pocketbook.*

The World Bank, 1818 H Street, NW, Washington, DC 20433, (202) 473-1000, Fax: (202) 477-6391, www.worldbank.org; *Ghana; The World Bank Atlas 2003-2004;* and *World Development Report 2008.*

World Health Organization (WHO), Avenue Appia 20, 1211 Geneve 27, Switzerland, (Telephone in U.S. (212) 331-9081), www.who.int; *World Health Report 2006.*

GHANA - POPULATION DENSITY

African Development Bank Group, Rue Joseph Anoma, 01 BP 1387 Abidjan 01, Cote d'Ivoire, www.afdb.org; *Statistics Pocketbook 2008.*

Central Intelligence Agency, Office of Public Affairs, Washington, DC 20505, (703) 482-0623, Fax: (703) 482-1739, www.cia.gov; *The World Factbook.*

Euromonitor International, Inc., 224 S. Michigan Avenue, Suite 1500, Chicago, IL 60604, (312) 922-1115, Fax: (312) 922-1157, www.euromonitor.com; *International Marketing Data and Statistics 2008* and *The World Economic Factbook 2008.*

M.E. Sharpe, 80 Business Park Drive, Armonk, NY 10504, (800) 541-6563, Fax: (914) 273-2106, www.mesharpe.com; *The Illustrated Book of World Rankings.*

Palgrave Macmillan Ltd., Houndmills, Basingstoke, Hampshire, RG21 6XS, England, (Telephone in U.S. (888) 330-8477), (Fax in U.S. (800) 672-2054), www.palgrave.com; *The Statesman's Yearbook 2008.*

Taylor and Francis Group, An Informa Business, 2 Park Square, Milton Park, Abingdon, Oxford OX14 4RN, United Kingdom, (Dial from U.S. (212) 216-7800), (Fax from U.S. (212) 564-7854), www.tandf.co.uk; *The Europa World Year Book.*

UNESCO Institute for Statistics, C.P. 6128 Succursale Centre-Ville, Montreal, Quebec, H3C 3J7 Canada, (Dial from U.S. (514) 343-6880), (Fax from U.S. (514) 343 6882), www.uis.unesco.org; *Statistical Tables.*

United Nations Food and Agricultural Organization (FAO), Viale delle Terme di Caracalla, 00100 Rome, Italy, (Dial from U.S. (202) 653-2400), (Fax from U.S. (202) 653 5760), www.fao.org; *The State of Food and Agriculture (SOFA) 2006.*

United Nations Statistics Division, New York, NY 10017, (800) 253-9646, Fax: (212) 963-4116, http://unstats.un.org; *Statistical Yearbook* and *Survey of Economic and Social Conditions in Africa 2005.*

The World Bank, 1818 H Street, NW, Washington, DC 20433, (202) 473-1000, Fax: (202) 477-6391, www.worldbank.org; *Ghana* and *World Development Report 2008.*

GHANA - POSTAL SERVICE

M.E. Sharpe, 80 Business Park Drive, Armonk, NY 10504, (800) 541-6563, Fax: (914) 273-2106, www.mesharpe.com; *The Illustrated Book of World Rankings.*

United Nations Statistics Division, New York, NY 10017, (800) 253-9646, Fax: (212) 963-4116, http://unstats.un.org; *Statistical Yearbook.*

GHANA - POWER RESOURCES

Euromonitor International, Inc., 224 S. Michigan Avenue, Suite 1500, Chicago, IL 60604, (312) 922-1115, Fax: (312) 922-1157, www.euromonitor.com; *International Marketing Data and Statistics 2008; The World Economic Factbook 2008;* and *World Marketing Data and Statistics.*

M.E. Sharpe, 80 Business Park Drive, Armonk, NY 10504, (800) 541-6563, Fax: (914) 273-2106, www.mesharpe.com; *The Illustrated Book of World Rankings.*

Organisation for Economic Cooperation and Development (OECD), 2 rue Andre Pascal, F-75775 Paris Cedex 16, France, (Telephone in U.S. (202) 785-

6323), (Fax in U.S. (202) 785-0350), www.oecd.org; *World Energy Outlook 2007.*

Palgrave Macmillan Ltd., Houndmills, Basingstoke, Hampshire, RG21 6XS, England, (Telephone in U.S. (888) 330-8477), (Fax in U.S. (800) 672-2054), www.palgrave.com; *The Statesman's Yearbook 2008.*

Platts, 2 Penn Plaza, 25th Floor, New York, NY 10121-2298, (212) 904-3070, www.platts.com; *Energy Economist.*

U.S. Department of Energy (DOE), Energy Information Administration (EIA), 1000 Independence Avenue, SW, Washington, DC 20585, (202) 586-8800, www.eia.doe.gov; *International Energy Annual 2004* and *International Energy Outlook 2006.*

United Nations Economic Commission for Africa (ECA), PO Box 3001, Addis Ababa, Ethiopia, (Telephone in U.S. (212) 963-4957), www.uneca.org; *African Statistical Yearbook 2006.*

United Nations Food and Agricultural Organization (FAO), Viale delle Terme di Caracalla, 00100 Rome, Italy, (Dial from U.S. (202) 653-2400), (Fax from U.S. (202) 653 5760), www.fao.org; *The State of Food and Agriculture (SOFA) 2006.*

United Nations Statistics Division, New York, NY 10017, (800) 253-9646, Fax: (212) 963-4116, http://unstats.un.org; *Energy Statistics Yearbook 2003; Human Development Report 2006; Statistical Yearbook;* and *World Statistics Pocketbook.*

The World Bank, 1818 H Street, NW, Washington, DC 20433, (202) 473-1000, Fax: (202) 477-6391, www.worldbank.org; *The World Bank Atlas 2003-2004* and *World Development Report 2008.*

GHANA - PRICES

Euromonitor International, Inc., 224 S. Michigan Avenue, Suite 1500, Chicago, IL 60604, (312) 922-1115, Fax: (312) 922-1157, www.euromonitor.com; *World Marketing Data and Statistics.*

International Labour Office, I.L.O. Publications, 4 route des Morillons, CH-1211 Geneva 22, Switzerland, (Telephone in U.S. (202) 653-7652), (Fax in U.S. (202) 653-7687), www.ilo.org; *Yearbook of Labour Statistics 2006.*

International Monetary Fund (IMF), 700 Nineteenth Street, NW, Washington, DC 20431, (202) 623-7000, Fax: (202) 623-4661, www.imf.org; *International Financial Statistics Yearbook 2007.*

M.E. Sharpe, 80 Business Park Drive, Armonk, NY 10504, (800) 541-6563, Fax: (914) 273-2106, www.mesharpe.com; *The Illustrated Book of World Rankings.*

United Nations Economic Commission for Africa (ECA), PO Box 3001, Addis Ababa, Ethiopia, (Telephone in U.S. (212) 963-4957), www.uneca.org; *African Statistical Yearbook 2006.*

United Nations Food and Agricultural Organization (FAO), Viale delle Terme di Caracalla, 00100 Rome, Italy, (Dial from U.S. (202) 653-2400), (Fax from U.S. (202) 653 5760), www.fao.org; *FAO Production Yearbook 2002* and *The State of Food and Agriculture (SOFA) 2006.*

The World Bank, 1818 H Street, NW, Washington, DC 20433, (202) 473-1000, Fax: (202) 477-6391, www.worldbank.org; *Ghana.*

GHANA - PROFESSIONS

UNESCO Institute for Statistics, C.P. 6128 Succursale Centre-Ville, Montreal, Quebec, H3C 3J7 Canada, (Dial from U.S. (514) 343-6880), (Fax from U.S. (514) 343 6882), www.uis.unesco.org; *Statistical Tables.*

United Nations Statistics Division, New York, NY 10017, (800) 253-9646, Fax: (212) 963-4116, http://unstats.un.org; *Statistical Yearbook.*

GHANA - PUBLIC HEALTH

African Development Bank Group, Rue Joseph Anoma, 01 BP 1387 Abidjan 01, Cote d'Ivoire, www.afdb.org; *Statistics Pocketbook 2008.*

Euromonitor International, Inc., 224 S. Michigan Avenue, Suite 1500, Chicago, IL 60604, (312) 922-1115, Fax: (312) 922-1157, www.euromonitor.com; *World Marketing Data and Statistics.*

M.E. Sharpe, 80 Business Park Drive, Armonk, NY 10504, (800) 541-6563, Fax: (914) 273-2106, www.mesharpe.com; *The Illustrated Book of World Rankings.*

Palgrave Macmillan Ltd., Houndmills, Basingstoke, Hampshire, RG21 6XS, England, (Telephone in U.S. (888) 330-8477), (Fax in U.S. (800) 672-2054), www.palgrave.com; *The Statesman's Yearbook 2008.*

UNICEF, 3 United Nations Plaza, New York, NY 10017, (800) 253-9646, Fax: (212) 887-7465, www.unicef.org; *The State of the World's Children 2008.*

United Nations Economic Commission for Africa (ECA), PO Box 3001, Addis Ababa, Ethiopia, (Telephone in U.S. (212) 963-4957), www.uneca.org; *African Statistical Yearbook 2006.*

United Nations Statistics Division, New York, NY 10017, (800) 253-9646, Fax: (212) 963-4116, http://unstats.un.org; *Human Development Report 2006* and *Statistical Yearbook.*

The World Bank, 1818 H Street, NW, Washington, DC 20433, (202) 473-1000, Fax: (202) 477-6391, www.worldbank.org; *Ghana* and *World Development Report 2008.*

World Health Organization (WHO), Avenue Appia 20, 1211 Geneve 27, Switzerland, (Telephone in U.S. (212) 331-9081), www.who.int; The WHO Global Atlas of Infectious Diseases and *World Health Report 2006.*

GHANA - PUBLISHERS AND PUBLISHING

UNESCO Institute for Statistics, C.P. 6128 Succursale Centre-Ville, Montreal, Quebec, H3C 3J7 Canada, (Dial from U.S. (514) 343-6880), (Fax from U.S. (514) 343 6882), www.uis.unesco.org; *Statistical Tables.*

GHANA - RADIO - RECEIVERS AND RECEPTION

Palgrave Macmillan Ltd., Houndmills, Basingstoke, Hampshire, RG21 6XS, England, (Telephone in U.S. (888) 330-8477), (Fax in U.S. (800) 672-2054), www.palgrave.com; *The Statesman's Yearbook 2008.*

United Nations Statistics Division, New York, NY 10017, (800) 253-9646, Fax: (212) 963-4116, http://unstats.un.org; *Statistical Yearbook.*

GHANA - RAILROADS

Jane's Information Group, 110 North Royal Street, Suite 200, Alexandria, VA 22314, (703) 683-3700, Fax: (800) 836-0297, www.janes.com; *Jane's World Railways.*

Palgrave Macmillan Ltd., Houndmills, Basingstoke, Hampshire, RG21 6XS, England, (Telephone in U.S. (888) 330-8477), (Fax in U.S. (800) 672-2054), www.palgrave.com; *The Statesman's Yearbook 2008.*

Taylor and Francis Group, An Informa Business, 2 Park Square, Milton Park, Abingdon, Oxford OX14 4RN, United Kingdom, (Dial from U.S. (212) 216-7800), (Fax from U.S. (212) 564-7854), www.tandf.co.uk; *The Europa World Year Book.*

United Nations Economic Commission for Africa (ECA), PO Box 3001, Addis Ababa, Ethiopia, (Telephone in U.S. (212) 963-4957), www.uneca.org; *African Statistical Yearbook 2006.*

United Nations Statistics Division, New York, NY 10017, (800) 253-9646, Fax: (212) 963-4116, http://unstats.un.org; *Statistical Yearbook* and *Survey of Economic and Social Conditions in Africa 2005.*

GHANA - RELIGION

Central Intelligence Agency, Office of Public Affairs, Washington, DC 20505, (703) 482-0623, Fax: (703) 482-1739, www.cia.gov; *The World Factbook.*

M.E. Sharpe, 80 Business Park Drive, Armonk, NY 10504, (800) 541-6563, Fax: (914) 273-2106, www.mesharpe.com; *The Illustrated Book of World Rankings.*

Palgrave Macmillan Ltd., Houndmills, Basingstoke, Hampshire, RG21 6XS, England, (Telephone in U.S. (888) 330-8477), (Fax in U.S. (800) 672-2054), www.palgrave.com; *The Statesman's Yearbook 2008.*

GHANA - RENT CHARGES

International Labour Office, I.L.O. Publications, 4 route des Morillons, CH-1211 Geneva 22, Switzerland, (Telephone in U.S. (202) 653-7652), (Fax in U.S. (202) 653-7687), www.ilo.org; *Yearbook of Labour Statistics 2006.*

GHANA - RESERVES (ACCOUNTING)

African Development Bank Group, Rue Joseph Anoma, 01 BP 1387 Abidjan 01, Cote d'Ivoire, www.afdb.org; *Statistics Pocketbook 2008.*

Euromonitor International, Inc., 224 S. Michigan Avenue, Suite 1500, Chicago, IL 60604, (312) 922-1115, Fax: (312) 922-1157, www.euromonitor.com; *International Marketing Data and Statistics 2008.*

International Monetary Fund (IMF), 700 Nineteenth Street, NW, Washington, DC 20431, (202) 623-7000, Fax: (202) 623-4661, www.imf.org; *International Financial Statistics Yearbook 2007.*

United Nations Statistics Division, New York, NY 10017, (800) 253-9646, Fax: (212) 963-4116, http://unstats.un.org; *Statistical Yearbook.*

The World Bank, 1818 H Street, NW, Washington, DC 20433, (202) 473-1000, Fax: (202) 477-6391, www.worldbank.org; *World Development Indicators (WDI) 2008.*

GHANA - RETAIL TRADE

Euromonitor International, Inc., 224 S. Michigan Avenue, Suite 1500, Chicago, IL 60604, (312) 922-1115, Fax: (312) 922-1157, www.euromonitor.com; *World Marketing Data and Statistics.*

United Nations Statistics Division, New York, NY 10017, (800) 253-9646, Fax: (212) 963-4116, http://unstats.un.org; *Statistical Yearbook.*

GHANA - RICE PRODUCTION

See GHANA - CROPS

GHANA - ROADS

Central Intelligence Agency, Office of Public Affairs, Washington, DC 20505, (703) 482-0623, Fax: (703) 482-1739, www.cia.gov; *The World Factbook.*

International Road Federation (IFR), Madison Place, 500 Montgomery Street, 5th Floor, Alexandria, VA 22314, (703) 535-1001, Fax: (703) 535-1007, www.irfnet.org; *World Road Statistics 2006.*

Palgrave Macmillan Ltd., Houndmills, Basingstoke, Hampshire, RG21 6XS, England, (Telephone in U.S. (888) 330-8477), (Fax in U.S. (800) 672-2054), www.palgrave.com; *The Statesman's Yearbook 2008.*

United Nations Economic Commission for Africa (ECA), PO Box 3001, Addis Ababa, Ethiopia, (Telephone in U.S. (212) 963-4957), www.uneca.org; *African Statistical Yearbook 2006.*

United Nations Statistics Division, New York, NY 10017, (800) 253-9646, Fax: (212) 963-4116, http://unstats.un.org; *Survey of Economic and Social Conditions in Africa 2005.*

GHANA - RUBBER INDUSTRY AND TRADE

International Rubber Study Group (IRSG), 1st Floor, Heron House, 109/115 Wembley Hill Road, Wembley, Middlesex HA9 8DA, United Kingdom, www.rubberstudy.com; *Rubber Statistical Bulletin; Summary of World Rubber Statistics 2005; World Rubber Statistics Handbook (Volume 6, 1975-2001);* and *World Rubber Statistics Historic Handbook.*

M.E. Sharpe, 80 Business Park Drive, Armonk, NY 10504, (800) 541-6563, Fax: (914) 273-2106, www.mesharpe.com; *The Illustrated Book of World Rankings.*

United Nations Statistics Division, New York, NY 10017, (800) 253-9646, Fax: (212) 963-4116, http://unstats.un.org; *Statistical Yearbook.*

GHANA - SALT PRODUCTION

See GHANA - MINERAL INDUSTRIES

GHANA - SHEEP

See GHANA - LIVESTOCK

GHANA - SHIPPING

Palgrave Macmillan Ltd., Houndmills, Basingstoke, Hampshire, RG21 6XS, England, (Telephone in U.S. (888) 330-8477), (Fax in U.S. (800) 672-2054), www.palgrave.com; *The Statesman's Yearbook 2008.*

Taylor and Francis Group, An Informa Business, 2 Park Square, Milton Park, Abingdon, Oxford OX14 4RN, United Kingdom, (Dial from U.S. (212) 216-7800), (Fax from U.S. (212) 564-7854), www.tandf.co.uk; *The Europa World Year Book.*

U.S. Department of Transportation (DOT), Maritime Administration (MARAD), West Building, Southeast Federal Center, 1200 New Jersey Avenue, SE, Washington, DC 20590, (800) 99-MARAD, www.marad.dot.gov; *World Merchant Fleet 2005.*

United Nations Economic Commission for Africa (ECA), PO Box 3001, Addis Ababa, Ethiopia, (Telephone in U.S. (212) 963-4957), www.uneca.org; *African Statistical Yearbook 2006.*

United Nations Statistics Division, New York, NY 10017, (800) 253-9646, Fax: (212) 963-4116, http://unstats.un.org; *Statistical Yearbook.*

GHANA - SILVER PRODUCTION

See GHANA - MINERAL INDUSTRIES

GHANA - SOCIAL ECOLOGY

M.E. Sharpe, 80 Business Park Drive, Armonk, NY 10504, (800) 541-6563, Fax: (914) 273-2106, www.mesharpe.com; *The Illustrated Book of World Rankings.*

United Nations Statistics Division, New York, NY 10017, (800) 253-9646, Fax: (212) 963-4116, http://unstats.un.org; *World Statistics Pocketbook.*

GHANA - SOCIAL SECURITY

International Monetary Fund (IMF), 700 Nineteenth Street, NW, Washington, DC 20431, (202) 623-7000, Fax: (202) 623-4661, www.imf.org; *Government Finance Statistics Yearbook (2008 Edition).*

United Nations Statistics Division, New York, NY 10017, (800) 253-9646, Fax: (212) 963-4116, http://unstats.un.org; *National Accounts Statistics: Compendium of Income Distribution Statistics.*

GHANA - STEEL PRODUCTION

See GHANA - MINERAL INDUSTRIES

GHANA - SUGAR PRODUCTION

See GHANA - CROPS

GHANA - TAXATION

International Monetary Fund (IMF), 700 Nineteenth Street, NW, Washington, DC 20431, (202) 623-7000, Fax: (202) 623-4661, www.imf.org; *Government Finance Statistics Yearbook (2008 Edition).*

International Road Federation (IFR), Madison Place, 500 Montgomery Street, 5th Floor, Alexandria, VA 22314, (703) 535-1001, Fax: (703) 535-1007, www.irfnet.org; *World Road Statistics 2006.*

Taylor and Francis Group, An Informa Business, 2 Park Square, Milton Park, Abingdon, Oxford OX14 4RN, United Kingdom, (Dial from U.S. (212) 216-7800), (Fax from U.S. (212) 564-7854), www.tandf.co.uk; *The Europa World Year Book.*

The World Bank, 1818 H Street, NW, Washington, DC 20433, (202) 473-1000, Fax: (202) 477-6391, www.worldbank.org; *World Development Indicators (WDI) 2008.*

GHANA - TELEPHONE

International Telecommunication Union (ITU), Place des Nations, 1211 Geneva 20, Switzerland, www.itu.int; World Telecommunication Indicators Database.

Palgrave Macmillan Ltd., Houndmills, Basingstoke, Hampshire, RG21 6XS, England, (Telephone in U.S. (888) 330-8477), (Fax in U.S. (800) 672-2054), www.palgrave.com; *The Statesman's Yearbook 2008.*

Taylor and Francis Group, An Informa Business, 2 Park Square, Milton Park, Abingdon, Oxford OX14 4RN, United Kingdom, (Dial from U.S. (212) 216-7800), (Fax from U.S. (212) 564-7854), www.tandf.co.uk; *The Europa World Year Book.*

United Nations Statistics Division, New York, NY 10017, (800) 253-9646, Fax: (212) 963-4116, http://unstats.un.org; *Statistical Yearbook* and *World Statistics Pocketbook.*

GHANA - TELEVISION - RECEIVERS AND RECEPTION

United Nations Statistics Division, New York, NY 10017, (800) 253-9646, Fax: (212) 963-4116, http://unstats.un.org; *Statistical Yearbook.*

GHANA - TEXTILE INDUSTRY

M.E. Sharpe, 80 Business Park Drive, Armonk, NY 10504, (800) 541-6563, Fax: (914) 273-2106, www.mesharpe.com; *The Illustrated Book of World Rankings.*

United Nations Conference on Trade and Development (UNCTAD), DC2-1120, United Nations, New York, NY 10017, (212) 963-0027, www.unctad.org; *UNCTAD Commodity Yearbook.*

GHANA - THEATER

UNESCO Institute for Statistics, C.P. 6128 Succursale Centre-Ville, Montreal, Quebec, H3C 3J7 Canada, (Dial from U.S. (514) 343-6880), (Fax from U.S. (514) 343 6882), www.uis.unesco.org; *Statistical Tables.*

GHANA - TIRE INDUSTRY

United Nations Statistics Division, New York, NY 10017, (800) 253-9646, Fax: (212) 963-4116, http://unstats.un.org; *Statistical Yearbook.*

GHANA - TOBACCO INDUSTRY

Foreign Agricultural Service (FAS), U.S. Department of Agriculture (USDA), 1400 Independence Avenue, SW, Washington, DC 20250, (202) 720-3935, www.fas.usda.gov; *Tobacco: World Markets and Trade.*

M.E. Sharpe, 80 Business Park Drive, Armonk, NY 10504, (800) 541-6563, Fax: (914) 273-2106, www.mesharpe.com; *The Illustrated Book of World Rankings.*

United Nations Statistics Division, New York, NY 10017, (800) 253-9646, Fax: (212) 963-4116, http://unstats.un.org; *Statistical Yearbook.*

GHANA - TOURISM

Euromonitor International, Inc., 224 S. Michigan Avenue, Suite 1500, Chicago, IL 60604, (312) 922-1115, Fax: (312) 922-1157, www.euromonitor.com; *The World Economic Factbook 2008* and *World Marketing Data and Statistics.*

M.E. Sharpe, 80 Business Park Drive, Armonk, NY 10504, (800) 541-6563, Fax: (914) 273-2106, www.mesharpe.com; *The Illustrated Book of World Rankings.*

Palgrave Macmillan Ltd., Houndmills, Basingstoke, Hampshire, RG21 6XS, England, (Telephone in U.S. (888) 330-8477), (Fax in U.S. (800) 672-2054), www.palgrave.com; *The Statesman's Yearbook 2008.*

Taylor and Francis Group, An Informa Business, 2 Park Square, Milton Park, Abingdon, Oxford OX14 4RN, United Kingdom, (Dial from U.S. (212) 216-7800), (Fax from U.S. (212) 564-7854), www.tandf.co.uk; *The Europa World Year Book.*

United Nations Economic Commission for Africa (ECA), PO Box 3001, Addis Ababa, Ethiopia, (Telephone in U.S. (212) 963-4957), www.uneca.org; *African Statistical Yearbook 2006.*

United Nations Statistics Division, New York, NY 10017, (800) 253-9646, Fax: (212) 963-4116, http://unstats.un.org; *Statistical Yearbook.*

The World Bank, 1818 H Street, NW, Washington, DC 20433, (202) 473-1000, Fax: (202) 477-6391, www.worldbank.org; *Ghana.*

GHANA - TRADE

See GHANA - INTERNATIONAL TRADE

GHANA - TRANSPORTATION

Central Intelligence Agency, Office of Public Affairs, Washington, DC 20505, (703) 482-0623, Fax: (703) 482-1739, www.cia.gov; *The World Factbook.*

Euromonitor International, Inc., 224 S. Michigan Avenue, Suite 1500, Chicago, IL 60604, (312) 922-1115, Fax: (312) 922-1157, www.euromonitor.com; *International Marketing Data and Statistics 2008* and *World Marketing Data and Statistics.*

M.E. Sharpe, 80 Business Park Drive, Armonk, NY 10504, (800) 541-6563, Fax: (914) 273-2106, www.mesharpe.com; *The Illustrated Book of World Rankings.*

Palgrave Macmillan Ltd., Houndmills, Basingstoke, Hampshire, RG21 6XS, England, (Telephone in U.S. (888) 330-8477), (Fax in U.S. (800) 672-2054), www.palgrave.com; *The Statesman's Yearbook 2008.*

Taylor and Francis Group, An Informa Business, 2 Park Square, Milton Park, Abingdon, Oxford OX14 4RN, United Kingdom, (Dial from U.S. (212) 216-7800), (Fax from U.S. (212) 564-7854), www.tandf.co.uk; *The Europa World Year Book.*

United Nations Economic Commission for Africa (ECA), PO Box 3001, Addis Ababa, Ethiopia, (Telephone in U.S. (212) 963-4957), www.uneca.org; *African Statistical Yearbook 2006.*

United Nations Statistics Division, New York, NY 10017, (800) 253-9646, Fax: (212) 963-4116, http://unstats.un.org; *Human Development Report 2006.*

The World Bank, 1818 H Street, NW, Washington, DC 20433, (202) 473-1000, Fax: (202) 477-6391, www.worldbank.org; *Africa Live Database (LDB)* and *Ghana.*

GHANA - UNEMPLOYMENT

Central Intelligence Agency, Office of Public Affairs, Washington, DC 20505, (703) 482-0623, Fax: (703) 482-1739, www.cia.gov; *The World Factbook.*

Euromonitor International, Inc., 224 S. Michigan Avenue, Suite 1500, Chicago, IL 60604, (312) 922-1115, Fax: (312) 922-1157, www.euromonitor.com; *International Marketing Data and Statistics 2008.*

International Labour Office, I.L.O. Publications, 4 route des Morillons, CH-1211 Geneva 22, Switzerland, (Telephone in U.S. (202) 653-7652), (Fax in U.S. (202) 653-7687), www.ilo.org; *Yearbook of Labour Statistics 2006.*

United Nations Statistics Division, New York, NY 10017, (800) 253-9646, Fax: (212) 963-4116, http://unstats.un.org; *Statistical Yearbook.*

GHANA - VITAL STATISTICS

Euromonitor International, Inc., 224 S. Michigan Avenue, Suite 1500, Chicago, IL 60604, (312) 922-1115, Fax: (312) 922-1157, www.euromonitor.com; *International Marketing Data and Statistics 2008.*

Palgrave Macmillan Ltd., Houndmills, Basingstoke, Hampshire, RG21 6XS, England, (Telephone in U.S. (888) 330-8477), (Fax in U.S. (800) 672-2054), www.palgrave.com; *The Statesman's Yearbook 2008.*

United Nations Statistics Division, New York, NY 10017, (800) 253-9646, Fax: (212) 963-4116, http://unstats.un.org; *Statistical Yearbook.*

World Health Organization (WHO), Avenue Appia 20, 1211 Geneve 27, Switzerland, (Telephone in U.S. (212) 331-9081), www.who.int; *World Health Report 2006.*

GHANA - WAGES

International Labour Office, I.L.O. Publications, 4 route des Morillons, CH-1211 Geneva 22, Switzerland, (Telephone in U.S. (202) 653-7652), (Fax in U.S. (202) 653-7687), www.ilo.org; *Yearbook of Labour Statistics 2006.*

United Nations Statistics Division, New York, NY 10017, (800) 253-9646, Fax: (212) 963-4116, http://unstats.un.org; *Statistical Yearbook.*

The World Bank, 1818 H Street, NW, Washington, DC 20433, (202) 473-1000, Fax: (202) 477-6391, www.worldbank.org; *Ghana.*

GHANA - WEATHER

See GHANA - CLIMATE

GHANA - WELFARE STATE

International Monetary Fund (IMF), 700 Nineteenth Street, NW, Washington, DC 20431, (202) 623-7000, Fax: (202) 623-4661, www.imf.org; *Government Finance Statistics Yearbook (2008 Edition).*

GHANA - WHEAT PRODUCTION

See GHANA - CROPS

GHANA - WHOLESALE PRICE INDEXES

International Monetary Fund (IMF), 700 Nineteenth Street, NW, Washington, DC 20431, (202) 623-7000, Fax: (202) 623-4661, www.imf.org; *International Financial Statistics Yearbook 2007.*

United Nations Statistics Division, New York, NY 10017, (800) 253-9646, Fax: (212) 963-4116, http://unstats.un.org; *Statistical Yearbook.*

GHANA - WHOLESALE TRADE

United Nations Statistics Division, New York, NY 10017, (800) 253-9646, Fax: (212) 963-4116, http://unstats.un.org; *Statistical Yearbook.*

GHANA - WINE PRODUCTION

See GHANA - BEVERAGE INDUSTRY

GHANA - WOOD AND WOOD PULP

See GHANA - FORESTS AND FORESTRY

GHANA - WOOL PRODUCTION

See GHANA - TEXTILE INDUSTRY

GIBRALTAR - NATIONAL STATISTICAL OFFICE

Statistics Office, 99 Harbours Walk, The New Harbours, Gibraltar, www.gibraltar.gov.gi; National Data Center.

GIBRALTAR - PRIMARY STATISTICS SOURCES

Statistics Office, 99 Harbours Walk, The New Harbours, Gibraltar, www.gibraltar.gov.gi; *Abstract of Statistics 2005.*

GIBRALTAR - AGRICULTURE

Economist Intelligence Unit, 111 West 57th Street, New York, NY 10019, (212) 554-0600, Fax: (212) 586-1181, www.eiu.com; *Gibraltar.*

Euromonitor International, Inc., 224 S. Michigan Avenue, Suite 1500, Chicago, IL 60604, (312) 922-1115, Fax: (312) 922-1157, www.euromonitor.com; *World Marketing Data and Statistics.*

United Nations Food and Agricultural Organization (FAO), Viale delle Terme di Caracalla, 00100 Rome, Italy, (Dial from U.S. (202) 653-2400), (Fax from U.S. (202) 653 5760), www.fao.org; AQUASTAT; *FAO Production Yearbook 2002; FAO Trade Yearbook;* and *The State of Food and Agriculture (SOFA) 2006.*

GIBRALTAR - AIRLINES

Palgrave Macmillan Ltd., Houndmills, Basingstoke, Hampshire, RG21 6XS, England, (Telephone in U.S. (888) 330-8477), (Fax in U.S. (800) 672-2054), www.palgrave.com; *The Statesman's Yearbook 2008.*

Statistics Office, 99 Harbours Walk, The New Harbours, Gibraltar, www.gibraltar.gov.gi; *Air Traffic Survey 2005.*

Taylor and Francis Group, An Informa Business, 2 Park Square, Milton Park, Abingdon, Oxford OX14 4RN, United Kingdom, (Dial from U.S. (212) 216-7800), (Fax from U.S. (212) 564-7854), www.tandf.co.uk; *The Europa World Year Book.*

GIBRALTAR - AIRPORTS

Central Intelligence Agency, Office of Public Affairs, Washington, DC 20505, (703) 482-0623, Fax: (703) 482-1739, www.cia.gov; *The World Factbook.*

Statistics Office, 99 Harbours Walk, The New Harbours, Gibraltar, www.gibraltar.gov.gi; *Air Traffic Survey 2005.*

GIBRALTAR - ARMED FORCES

Central Intelligence Agency, Office of Public Affairs, Washington, DC 20505, (703) 482-0623, Fax: (703) 482-1739, www.cia.gov; *The World Factbook.*

Euromonitor International, Inc., 224 S. Michigan Avenue, Suite 1500, Chicago, IL 60604, (312) 922-1115, Fax: (312) 922-1157, www.euromonitor.com; *World Marketing Data and Statistics.*

Palgrave Macmillan Ltd., Houndmills, Basingstoke, Hampshire, RG21 6XS, England, (Telephone in U.S. (888) 330-8477), (Fax in U.S. (800) 672-2054), www.palgrave.com; *The Statesman's Yearbook 2008.*

GIBRALTAR - BANKS AND BANKING

Euromonitor International, Inc., 224 S. Michigan Avenue, Suite 1500, Chicago, IL 60604, (312) 922-1115, Fax: (312) 922-1157, www.euromonitor.com; *World Marketing Data and Statistics.*

Palgrave Macmillan Ltd., Houndmills, Basingstoke, Hampshire, RG21 6XS, England, (Telephone in U.S. (888) 330-8477), (Fax in U.S. (800) 672-2054), www.palgrave.com; *The Statesman's Yearbook 2008.*

GIBRALTAR - BROADCASTING

Central Intelligence Agency, Office of Public Affairs, Washington, DC 20505, (703) 482-0623, Fax: (703) 482-1739, www.cia.gov; *The World Factbook.*

Euromonitor International, Inc., 224 S. Michigan Avenue, Suite 1500, Chicago, IL 60604, (312) 922-1115, Fax: (312) 922-1157, www.euromonitor.com; *World Marketing Data and Statistics.*

Palgrave Macmillan Ltd., Houndmills, Basingstoke, Hampshire, RG21 6XS, England, (Telephone in U.S. (888) 330-8477), (Fax in U.S. (800) 672-2054), www.palgrave.com; *The Statesman's Yearbook 2008.*

UNESCO Institute for Statistics, C.P. 6128 Succursale Centre-Ville, Montreal, Quebec, H3C 3J7 Canada, (Dial from U.S. (514) 343-6880), (Fax from U.S. (514) 343 6882), www.uis.unesco.org; *Statistical Tables.*

WRTH Publications Limited, PO Box 290, Oxford OX2 7FT, UK, www.wrth.com; *World Radio TV Handbook 2007.*

GIBRALTAR - BUDGET

Central Intelligence Agency, Office of Public Affairs, Washington, DC 20505, (703) 482-0623, Fax: (703) 482-1739, www.cia.gov; *The World Factbook.*

GIBRALTAR - CHILDBIRTH - STATISTICS

Central Intelligence Agency, Office of Public Affairs, Washington, DC 20505, (703) 482-0623, Fax: (703) 482-1739, www.cia.gov; *The World Factbook.*

Euromonitor International, Inc., 224 S. Michigan Avenue, Suite 1500, Chicago, IL 60604, (312) 922-1115, Fax: (312) 922-1157, www.euromonitor.com; *The World Economic Factbook 2008.*

Palgrave Macmillan Ltd., Houndmills, Basingstoke, Hampshire, RG21 6XS, England, (Telephone in U.S. (888) 330-8477), (Fax in U.S. (800) 672-2054), www.palgrave.com; *The Statesman's Yearbook 2008.*

Taylor and Francis Group, An Informa Business, 2 Park Square, Milton Park, Abingdon, Oxford OX14 4RN, United Kingdom, (Dial from U.S. (212) 216-7800), (Fax from U.S. (212) 564-7854), www.tandf.co.uk; *The Europa World Year Book.*

United Nations Statistics Division, New York, NY 10017, (800) 253-9646, Fax: (212) 963-4116, http://unstats.un.org; *Demographic Yearbook* and *Statistical Yearbook.*

World Health Organization (WHO), Avenue Appia 20, 1211 Geneve 27, Switzerland, (Telephone in U.S. (212) 331-9081), www.who.int; *World Health Report 2006.*

GIBRALTAR - CLIMATE

Palgrave Macmillan Ltd., Houndmills, Basingstoke, Hampshire, RG21 6XS, England, (Telephone in U.S. (888) 330-8477), (Fax in U.S. (800) 672-2054), www.palgrave.com; *The Statesman's Yearbook 2008.*

GIBRALTAR - COMMERCE

Palgrave Macmillan Ltd., Houndmills, Basingstoke, Hampshire, RG21 6XS, England, (Telephone in U.S. (888) 330-8477), (Fax in U.S. (800) 672-2054), www.palgrave.com; *The Statesman's Yearbook 2008.*

GIBRALTAR - COMMODITY EXCHANGES

Commodity Research Bureau, 330 South Wells Street, Suite 612, Chicago, IL 60606-7110, (800) 621-5271, Fax: (312) 939-4135, www.crbtrader.com; *2006 CRB Commodity Yearbook and CD.*

International Monetary Fund (IMF), 700 Nineteenth Street, NW, Washington, DC 20431, (202) 623-7000, Fax: (202) 623-4661, www.imf.org; *IMF Primary Commodity Prices.*

United Nations Food and Agricultural Organization (FAO), Viale delle Terme di Caracalla, 00100 Rome, Italy, (Dial from U.S. (202) 653-2400), (Fax from U.S. (202) 653 5760), www.fao.org; *The State of Food and Agriculture (SOFA) 2006.*

GIBRALTAR - CONSTRUCTION INDUSTRY

Palgrave Macmillan Ltd., Houndmills, Basingstoke, Hampshire, RG21 6XS, England, (Telephone in U.S. (888) 330-8477), (Fax in U.S. (800) 672-2054), www.palgrave.com; *The Statesman's Yearbook 2008.*

GIBRALTAR - CONSUMER PRICE INDEXES

International Labour Office, I.L.O. Publications, 4 route des Morillons, CH-1211 Geneva 22, Switzerland, (Telephone in U.S. (202) 653-7652), (Fax in U.S. (202) 653-7687), www.ilo.org; *Yearbook of Labour Statistics 2006.*

Taylor and Francis Group, An Informa Business, 2 Park Square, Milton Park, Abingdon, Oxford OX14 4RN, United Kingdom, (Dial from U.S. (212) 216-7800), (Fax from U.S. (212) 564-7854), www.tandf.co.uk; *The Europa World Year Book.*

United Nations Statistics Division, New York, NY 10017, (800) 253-9646, Fax: (212) 963-4116, http://unstats.un.org; *Statistical Yearbook.*

GIBRALTAR - CORN INDUSTRY

See GIBRALTAR - CROPS

GIBRALTAR - CROPS

United Nations Food and Agricultural Organization (FAO), Viale delle Terme di Caracalla, 00100 Rome, Italy, (Dial from U.S. (202) 653-2400), (Fax from U.S. (202) 653 5760), www.fao.org; *The State of Food and Agriculture (SOFA) 2006.*

GIBRALTAR - CUSTOMS ADMINISTRATION

Palgrave Macmillan Ltd., Houndmills, Basingstoke, Hampshire, RG21 6XS, England, (Telephone in U.S. (888) 330-8477), (Fax in U.S. (800) 672-2054), www.palgrave.com; *The Statesman's Yearbook 2008.*

GIBRALTAR - DAIRY PROCESSING

United Nations Food and Agricultural Organization (FAO), Viale delle Terme di Caracalla, 00100 Rome,

Italy, (Dial from U.S. (202) 653-2400), (Fax from U.S. (202) 653 5760), www.fao.org; *The State of Food and Agriculture (SOFA) 2006.*

GIBRALTAR - DEATH RATES

See GIBRALTAR - MORTALITY

GIBRALTAR - DEMOGRAPHY

Euromonitor International, Inc., 224 S. Michigan Avenue, Suite 1500, Chicago, IL 60604, (312) 922-1115, Fax: (312) 922-1157, www.euromonitor.com; *The World Economic Factbook 2008* and *World Marketing Data and Statistics.*

GIBRALTAR - DIVORCE

United Nations Statistics Division, New York, NY 10017, (800) 253-9646, Fax: (212) 963-4116, http://unstats.un.org; *Demographic Yearbook* and *Statistical Yearbook.*

GIBRALTAR - ECONOMIC CONDITIONS

Center for International Business Education Research (CIBER), Columbia Business School and School of International and Public Affairs, Uris Hall, Room 212, 3022 Broadway, New York, NY 10027-6902, Mr. Joshua Safier, (212) 854-4750, Fax: (212) 222-9821, www.columbia.edu/cu/ciber/; Datastream International.

Central Intelligence Agency, Office of Public Affairs, Washington, DC 20505, (703) 482-0623, Fax: (703) 482-1739, www.cia.gov; *The World Factbook.*

DSI Data Service Information, Xantener Strasse 51a, D-47495 Rheinberg, Germany, www.dsidata.com; *Campus Solution.*

Dun and Bradstreet (DB) Corporation, 103 JFK Parkway, Short Hills, NJ 07078, (973) 921-5500, www.dnb.com; *Country Report.*

Economist Intelligence Unit, 111 West 57th Street, New York, NY 10019, (212) 554-0600, Fax: (212) 586-1181, www.eiu.com; *Gibraltar.*

Euromonitor International, Inc., 224 S. Michigan Avenue, Suite 1500, Chicago, IL 60604, (312) 922-1115, Fax: (312) 922-1157, www.euromonitor.com; *The World Economic Factbook 2008* and *World Marketing Data and Statistics.*

International Monetary Fund (IMF), 700 Nineteenth Street, NW, Washington, DC 20431, (202) 623-7000, Fax: (202) 623-4661, www.imf.org; *World Economic Outlook Reports.*

Palgrave Macmillan Ltd., Houndmills, Basingstoke, Hampshire, RG21 6XS, England, (Telephone in U.S. (888) 330-8477), (Fax in U.S. (800) 672-2054), www.palgrave.com; *The Statesman's Yearbook 2008.*

Taylor and Francis Group, An Informa Business, 2 Park Square, Milton Park, Abingdon, Oxford OX14 4RN, United Kingdom, (Dial from U.S. (212) 216-7800), (Fax from U.S. (212) 564-7854), www.tandf.co.uk; *The Europa World Year Book.*

The World Bank, 1818 H Street, NW, Washington, DC 20433, (202) 473-1000, Fax: (202) 477-6391, www.worldbank.org; *Global Economic Monitor (GEM); Global Economic Prospects 2008;* and *The World Bank Atlas 2003-2004.*

GIBRALTAR - EDUCATION

Euromonitor International, Inc., 224 S. Michigan Avenue, Suite 1500, Chicago, IL 60604, (312) 922-1115, Fax: (312) 922-1157, www.euromonitor.com; *World Marketing Data and Statistics.*

Palgrave Macmillan Ltd., Houndmills, Basingstoke, Hampshire, RG21 6XS, England, (Telephone in U.S. (888) 330-8477), (Fax in U.S. (800) 672-2054), www.palgrave.com; *The Statesman's Yearbook 2008.*

Taylor and Francis Group, An Informa Business, 2 Park Square, Milton Park, Abingdon, Oxford OX14 4RN, United Kingdom, (Dial from U.S. (212) 216-7800), (Fax from U.S. (212) 564-7854), www.tandf.co.uk; *The Europa World Year Book.*

UNESCO Institute for Statistics, C.P. 6128 Succursale Centre-Ville, Montreal, Quebec, H3C 3J7 Canada, (Dial from U.S. (514) 343-6880), (Fax from U.S. (514) 343 6882), www.uis.unesco.org; *Statistical Tables.*

GIBRALTAR - ELECTRICITY

United Nations Statistics Division, New York, NY 10017, (800) 253-9646, Fax: (212) 963-4116, http://unstats.un.org; *Statistical Yearbook.*

GIBRALTAR - EMPLOYMENT

International Labour Office, I.L.O. Publications, 4 route des Morillons, CH-1211 Geneva 22, Switzerland, (Telephone in U.S. (202) 653-7652), (Fax in U.S. (202) 653-7687), www.ilo.org; *Yearbook of Labour Statistics 2006.*

United Nations Statistics Division, New York, NY 10017, (800) 253-9646, Fax: (212) 963-4116, http://unstats.un.org; *Statistical Yearbook.*

GIBRALTAR - ENVIRONMENTAL CONDITIONS

DSI Data Service Information, Xantener Strasse 51a, D-47495 Rheinberg, Germany, www.dsidata.com; *Campus Solution* and *DSI's Global Environmental Database.*

Economist Intelligence Unit, 111 West 57th Street, New York, NY 10019, (212) 554-0600, Fax: (212) 586-1181, www.eiu.com; *Gibraltar.*

GIBRALTAR - EXPORTS

Central Intelligence Agency, Office of Public Affairs, Washington, DC 20505, (703) 482-0623, Fax: (703) 482-1739, www.cia.gov; *The World Factbook.*

Economist Intelligence Unit, 111 West 57th Street, New York, NY 10019, (212) 554-0600, Fax: (212) 586-1181, www.eiu.com; *Gibraltar.*

Euromonitor International, Inc., 224 S. Michigan Avenue, Suite 1500, Chicago, IL 60604, (312) 922-1115, Fax: (312) 922-1157, www.euromonitor.com; *The World Economic Factbook 2008.*

International Monetary Fund (IMF), 700 Nineteenth Street, NW, Washington, DC 20431, (202) 623-7000, Fax: (202) 623-4661, www.imf.org; *Direction of Trade Statistics Yearbook 2007.*

Palgrave Macmillan Ltd., Houndmills, Basingstoke, Hampshire, RG21 6XS, England, (Telephone in U.S. (888) 330-8477), (Fax in U.S. (800) 672-2054), www.palgrave.com; *The Statesman's Yearbook 2008.*

Taylor and Francis Group, An Informa Business, 2 Park Square, Milton Park, Abingdon, Oxford OX14 4RN, United Kingdom, (Dial from U.S. (212) 216-7800), (Fax from U.S. (212) 564-7854), www.tandf.co.uk; *The Europa World Year Book.*

United Nations Food and Agricultural Organization (FAO), Viale delle Terme di Caracalla, 00100 Rome, Italy, (Dial from U.S. (202) 653-2400), (Fax from U.S. (202) 653 5760), www.fao.org; *The State of Food and Agriculture (SOFA) 2006.*

GIBRALTAR - FERTILITY, HUMAN

Central Intelligence Agency, Office of Public Affairs, Washington, DC 20505, (703) 482-0623, Fax: (703) 482-1739, www.cia.gov; *The World Factbook.*

The World Bank, 1818 H Street, NW, Washington, DC 20433, (202) 473-1000, Fax: (202) 477-6391, www.worldbank.org; *The World Bank Atlas 2003-2004.*

GIBRALTAR - FERTILIZER INDUSTRY

United Nations Food and Agricultural Organization (FAO), Viale delle Terme di Caracalla, 00100 Rome, Italy, (Dial from U.S. (202) 653-2400), (Fax from U.S. (202) 653 5760), www.fao.org; *The State of Food and Agriculture (SOFA) 2006.*

GIBRALTAR - FETAL MORTALITY

See GIBRALTAR - MORTALITY

GIBRALTAR - FINANCE, PUBLIC

Banque de France, 48 rue Croix des Petits champs, 75001 Paris, France, www.banque-france.fr/home.htm; *Public Finance.*

Bernan Essential Government Publications, 4611-F Assembly Drive, Lanham MD, 20706-4391, (301) 459-2255, Fax: (800) 865-3450, www.bernan.com; *National Accounts Statistics.*

Economist Intelligence Unit, 111 West 57th Street, New York, NY 10019, (212) 554-0600, Fax: (212) 586-1181, www.eiu.com; *Gibraltar.*

International Monetary Fund (IMF), 700 Nineteenth Street, NW, Washington, DC 20431, (202) 623-7000, Fax: (202) 623-4661, www.imf.org; *International Financial Statistics* and *International Financial Statistics Online Service.*

Palgrave Macmillan Ltd., Houndmills, Basingstoke, Hampshire, RG21 6XS, England, (Telephone in U.S. (888) 330-8477), (Fax in U.S. (800) 672-2054), www.palgrave.com; *The Statesman's Yearbook 2008.*

Taylor and Francis Group, An Informa Business, 2 Park Square, Milton Park, Abingdon, Oxford OX14 4RN, United Kingdom, (Dial from U.S. (212) 216-7800), (Fax from U.S. (212) 564-7854), www.tandf.co.uk; *The Europa World Year Book.*

GIBRALTAR - FISHERIES

United Nations Food and Agricultural Organization (FAO), Viale delle Terme di Caracalla, 00100 Rome, Italy, (Dial from U.S. (202) 653-2400), (Fax from U.S. (202) 653 5760), www.fao.org; *FAO Yearbook of Fishery Statistics;* Fishery Databases; FISHSTAT Database. Subjects covered include: Aquaculture production, capture production, fishery commodities; and *The State of Food and Agriculture (SOFA) 2006.*

GIBRALTAR - FOOD

United Nations Food and Agricultural Organization (FAO), Viale delle Terme di Caracalla, 00100 Rome, Italy, (Dial from U.S. (202) 653-2400), (Fax from U.S. (202) 653 5760), www.fao.org; *FAO Production Yearbook 2002* and *The State of Food and Agriculture (SOFA) 2006.*

GIBRALTAR - FOREIGN EXCHANGE RATES

Central Intelligence Agency, Office of Public Affairs, Washington, DC 20505, (703) 482-0623, Fax: (703) 482-1739, www.cia.gov; *The World Factbook.*

Euromonitor International, Inc., 224 S. Michigan Avenue, Suite 1500, Chicago, IL 60604, (312) 922-1115, Fax: (312) 922-1157, www.euromonitor.com; *The World Economic Factbook 2008.*

Taylor and Francis Group, An Informa Business, 2 Park Square, Milton Park, Abingdon, Oxford OX14 4RN, United Kingdom, (Dial from U.S. (212) 216-7800), (Fax from U.S. (212) 564-7854), www.tandf.co.uk; *The Europa World Year Book.*

GIBRALTAR - FORESTS AND FORESTRY

UNESCO Institute for Statistics, C.P. 6128 Succursale Centre-Ville, Montreal, Quebec, H3C 3J7 Canada, (Dial from U.S. (514) 343-6880), (Fax from U.S. (514) 343 6882), www.uis.unesco.org; *Statistical Tables.*

United Nations Food and Agricultural Organization (FAO), Viale delle Terme di Caracalla, 00100 Rome, Italy, (Dial from U.S. (202) 653-2400), (Fax from U.S. (202) 653 5760), www.fao.org; *The State of Food and Agriculture (SOFA) 2006.*

United Nations Statistics Division, New York, NY 10017, (800) 253-9646, Fax: (212) 963-4116, http://unstats.un.org; *Statistical Yearbook.*

GIBRALTAR - GROSS DOMESTIC PRODUCT

Economist Intelligence Unit, 111 West 57th Street, New York, NY 10019, (212) 554-0600, Fax: (212) 586-1181, www.eiu.com; *Gibraltar.*

Euromonitor International, Inc., 224 S. Michigan Avenue, Suite 1500, Chicago, IL 60604, (312) 922-1115, Fax: (312) 922-1157, www.euromonitor.com; *The World Economic Factbook 2008.*

GIBRALTAR - GROSS NATIONAL PRODUCT

Palgrave Macmillan Ltd., Houndmills, Basingstoke, Hampshire, RG21 6XS, England, (Telephone in U.S. (888) 330-8477), (Fax in U.S. (800) 672-2054), www.palgrave.com; *The Statesman's Yearbook 2008.*

The World Bank, 1818 H Street, NW, Washington, DC 20433, (202) 473-1000, Fax: (202) 477-6391, www.worldbank.org; *The World Bank Atlas 2003-2004.*

GIBRALTAR - HOUSING

Euromonitor International, Inc., 224 S. Michigan Avenue, Suite 1500, Chicago, IL 60604, (312) 922-1115, Fax: (312) 922-1157, www.euromonitor.com; *World Marketing Data and Statistics.*

GIBRALTAR - ILLITERATE PERSONS

Euromonitor International, Inc., 224 S. Michigan Avenue, Suite 1500, Chicago, IL 60604, (312) 922-1115, Fax: (312) 922-1157, www.euromonitor.com; *The World Economic Factbook 2008.*

UNESCO Institute for Statistics, C.P. 6128 Succursale Centre-Ville, Montreal, Quebec, H3C 3J7 Canada, (Dial from U.S. (514) 343-6880), (Fax from U.S. (514) 343 6882), www.uis.unesco.org; *Statistical Tables.*

GIBRALTAR - IMPORTS

Central Intelligence Agency, Office of Public Affairs, Washington, DC 20505, (703) 482-0623, Fax: (703) 482-1739, www.cia.gov; *The World Factbook.*

Economist Intelligence Unit, 111 West 57th Street, New York, NY 10019, (212) 554-0600, Fax: (212) 586-1181, www.eiu.com; *Gibraltar.*

Euromonitor International, Inc., 224 S. Michigan Avenue, Suite 1500, Chicago, IL 60604, (312) 922-1115, Fax: (312) 922-1157, www.euromonitor.com; *The World Economic Factbook 2008.*

International Monetary Fund (IMF), 700 Nineteenth Street, NW, Washington, DC 20431, (202) 623-7000, Fax: (202) 623-4661, www.imf.org; *Direction of Trade Statistics Yearbook 2007.*

Palgrave Macmillan Ltd., Houndmills, Basingstoke, Hampshire, RG21 6XS, England, (Telephone in U.S. (888) 330-8477), (Fax in U.S. (800) 672-2054), www.palgrave.com; *The Statesman's Yearbook 2008.*

Taylor and Francis Group, An Informa Business, 2 Park Square, Milton Park, Abingdon, Oxford OX14 4RN, United Kingdom, (Dial from U.S. (212) 216-7800), (Fax from U.S. (212) 564-7854), www.tandf.co.uk; *The Europa World Year Book.*

United Nations Food and Agricultural Organization (FAO), Viale delle Terme di Caracalla, 00100 Rome, Italy, (Dial from U.S. (202) 653-2400), (Fax from U.S. (202) 653 5760), www.fao.org; *The State of Food and Agriculture (SOFA) 2006.*

GIBRALTAR - INDUSTRIES

Central Intelligence Agency, Office of Public Affairs, Washington, DC 20505, (703) 482-0623, Fax: (703) 482-1739, www.cia.gov; *The World Factbook.*

Economist Intelligence Unit, 111 West 57th Street, New York, NY 10019, (212) 554-0600, Fax: (212) 586-1181, www.eiu.com; *Gibraltar.*

Euromonitor International, Inc., 224 S. Michigan Avenue, Suite 1500, Chicago, IL 60604, (312) 922-1115, Fax: (312) 922-1157, www.euromonitor.com; *The World Economic Factbook 2008* and *World Marketing Data and Statistics.*

International Labour Office, I.L.O. Publications, 4 route des Morillons, CH-1211 Geneva 22, Switzerland, (Telephone in U.S. (202) 653-7652), (Fax in U.S. (202) 653-7687), www.ilo.org; *Yearbook of Labour Statistics 2006.*

Palgrave Macmillan Ltd., Houndmills, Basingstoke, Hampshire, RG21 6XS, England, (Telephone in U.S. (888) 330-8477), (Fax in U.S. (800) 672-2054), www.palgrave.com; *The Statesman's Yearbook 2008.*

United Nations Industrial Development Organization (UNIDO), 1 United Nations Plaza, New York, NY 10017, (212) 963 6890, Fax: (212) 963-7904, http://unido.org; Industrial Statistics Database 2008 (INDSTAT) and *The International Yearbook of Industrial Statistics 2008.*

GIBRALTAR - INFANT AND MATERNAL MORTALITY

See GIBRALTAR - MORTALITY

GIBRALTAR - INTERNATIONAL TRADE

Banque de France, 48 rue Croix des Petits champs, 75001 Paris, France, www.banque-france.fr/home.htm; *Monthly Business Survey Overview.*

Economist Intelligence Unit, 111 West 57th Street, New York, NY 10019, (212) 554-0600, Fax: (212) 586-1181, www.eiu.com; *Gibraltar.*

Euromonitor International, Inc., 224 S. Michigan Avenue, Suite 1500, Chicago, IL 60604, (312) 922-1115, Fax: (312) 922-1157, www.euromonitor.com; *The World Economic Factbook 2008* and *World Marketing Data and Statistics.*

Palgrave Macmillan Ltd., Houndmills, Basingstoke, Hampshire, RG21 6XS, England, (Telephone in U.S. (888) 330-8477), (Fax in U.S. (800) 672-2054), www.palgrave.com; *The Statesman's Yearbook 2008.*

Taylor and Francis Group, An Informa Business, 2 Park Square, Milton Park, Abingdon, Oxford OX14 4RN, United Kingdom, (Dial from U.S. (212) 216-7800), (Fax from U.S. (212) 564-7854), www.tandf.co.uk; *The Europa World Year Book.*

United Nations Food and Agricultural Organization (FAO), Viale delle Terme di Caracalla, 00100 Rome, Italy, (Dial from U.S. (202) 653-2400), (Fax from U.S. (202) 653 5760), www.fao.org; *FAO Trade Yearbook* and *The State of Food and Agriculture (SOFA) 2006.*

United Nations Statistics Division, New York, NY 10017, (800) 253-9646, Fax: (212) 963-4116, http://unstats.un.org; *Statistical Yearbook.*

World Trade Organization (WTO), Centre William Rappard, Rue de Lausanne 154, CH-1211 Geneva 21, Switzerland, www.wto.org; *International Trade Statistics 2006.*

GIBRALTAR - INTERNET USERS

International Telecommunication Union (ITU), Place des Nations, 1211 Geneva 20, Switzerland, www.itu.int; *World Telecommunication/ICT Indicators Database on CD-ROM; World Telecommunication/ICT Indicators Database Online;* and *Yearbook of Statistics - Telecommunication Services (Chronological Time Series 1997-2006).*

GIBRALTAR - LABOR

Central Intelligence Agency, Office of Public Affairs, Washington, DC 20505, (703) 482-0623, Fax: (703) 482-1739, www.cia.gov; *The World Factbook.*

Euromonitor International, Inc., 224 S. Michigan Avenue, Suite 1500, Chicago, IL 60604, (312) 922-1115, Fax: (312) 922-1157, www.euromonitor.com; *World Marketing Data and Statistics.*

International Labour Office, I.L.O. Publications, 4 route des Morillons, CH-1211 Geneva 22, Switzerland, (Telephone in U.S. (202) 653-7652), (Fax in U.S. (202) 653-7687), www.ilo.org; *Yearbook of Labour Statistics 2006.*

Palgrave Macmillan Ltd., Houndmills, Basingstoke, Hampshire, RG21 6XS, England, (Telephone in U.S. (888) 330-8477), (Fax in U.S. (800) 672-2054), www.palgrave.com; *The Statesman's Yearbook 2008.*

Statistics Office, 99 Harbours Walk, The New Harbours, Gibraltar, www.gibraltar.gov.gi; *Employment Survey 2005.*

United Nations Food and Agricultural Organization (FAO), Viale delle Terme di Caracalla, 00100 Rome, Italy, (Dial from U.S. (202) 653-2400), (Fax from U.S. (202) 653 5760), www.fao.org; *The State of Food and Agriculture (SOFA) 2006.*

The World Bank, 1818 H Street, NW, Washington, DC 20433, (202) 473-1000, Fax: (202) 477-6391, www.worldbank.org; *The World Bank Atlas 2003-2004.*

GIBRALTAR - LAND USE

Central Intelligence Agency, Office of Public Affairs, Washington, DC 20505, (703) 482-0623, Fax: (703) 482-1739, www.cia.gov; *The World Factbook.*

United Nations Food and Agricultural Organization (FAO), Viale delle Terme di Caracalla, 00100 Rome, Italy, (Dial from U.S. (202) 653-2400), (Fax from U.S. (202) 653 5760), www.fao.org; *FAO Production Yearbook 2002.*

GIBRALTAR - LIBRARIES

UNESCO Institute for Statistics, C.P. 6128 Succursale Centre-Ville, Montreal, Quebec, H3C 3J7 Canada, (Dial from U.S. (514) 343-6880), (Fax from U.S. (514) 343 6882), www.uis.unesco.org; *Statistical Tables.*

GIBRALTAR - LIFE EXPECTANCY

Central Intelligence Agency, Office of Public Affairs, Washington, DC 20505, (703) 482-0623, Fax: (703) 482-1739, www.cia.gov; *The World Factbook.*

Euromonitor International, Inc., 224 S. Michigan Avenue, Suite 1500, Chicago, IL 60604, (312) 922-1115, Fax: (312) 922-1157, www.euromonitor.com; *The World Economic Factbook 2008.*

The World Bank, 1818 H Street, NW, Washington, DC 20433, (202) 473-1000, Fax: (202) 477-6391, www.worldbank.org; *The World Bank Atlas 2003-2004.*

GIBRALTAR - LITERACY

Euromonitor International, Inc., 224 S. Michigan Avenue, Suite 1500, Chicago, IL 60604, (312) 922-1115, Fax: (312) 922-1157, www.euromonitor.com; *World Marketing Data and Statistics.*

GIBRALTAR - LIVESTOCK

United Nations Food and Agricultural Organization (FAO), Viale delle Terme di Caracalla, 00100 Rome, Italy, (Dial from U.S. (202) 653-2400), (Fax from U.S. (202) 653 5760), www.fao.org; *FAO Production Yearbook 2002* and *The State of Food and Agriculture (SOFA) 2006.*

GIBRALTAR - MARRIAGE

Taylor and Francis Group, An Informa Business, 2 Park Square, Milton Park, Abingdon, Oxford OX14 4RN, United Kingdom, (Dial from U.S. (212) 216-7800), (Fax from U.S. (212) 564-7854), www.tandf.co.uk; *The Europa World Year Book.*

United Nations Statistics Division, New York, NY 10017, (800) 253-9646, Fax: (212) 963-4116, http://unstats.un.org; *Demographic Yearbook* and *Statistical Yearbook.*

GIBRALTAR - MEAT PRODUCTION

See GIBRALTAR - LIVESTOCK

GIBRALTAR - MONEY SUPPLY

Economist Intelligence Unit, 111 West 57th Street, New York, NY 10019, (212) 554-0600, Fax: (212) 586-1181, www.eiu.com; *Gibraltar.*

GIBRALTAR - MORTALITY

Central Intelligence Agency, Office of Public Affairs, Washington, DC 20505, (703) 482-0623, Fax: (703) 482-1739, www.cia.gov; *The World Factbook.*

Euromonitor International, Inc., 224 S. Michigan Avenue, Suite 1500, Chicago, IL 60604, (312) 922-1115, Fax: (312) 922-1157, www.euromonitor.com; *The World Economic Factbook 2008.*

Palgrave Macmillan Ltd., Houndmills, Basingstoke, Hampshire, RG21 6XS, England, (Telephone in U.S. (888) 330-8477), (Fax in U.S. (800) 672-2054), www.palgrave.com; *The Statesman's Yearbook 2008.*

Taylor and Francis Group, An Informa Business, 2 Park Square, Milton Park, Abingdon, Oxford OX14 4RN, United Kingdom, (Dial from U.S. (212) 216-7800), (Fax from U.S. (212) 564-7854), www.tandf.co.uk; *The Europa World Year Book.*

United Nations Statistics Division, New York, NY 10017, (800) 253-9646, Fax: (212) 963-4116, http://unstats.un.org; *Demographic Yearbook* and *Statistical Yearbook.*

The World Bank, 1818 H Street, NW, Washington, DC 20433, (202) 473-1000, Fax: (202) 477-6391, www.worldbank.org; *The World Bank Atlas 2003-2004.*

World Health Organization (WHO), Avenue Appia 20, 1211 Geneve 27, Switzerland, (Telephone in U.S. (212) 331-9081), www.who.int; The WHO Global Atlas of Infectious Diseases and *World Health Report 2006.*

GIBRALTAR - MOTION PICTURES

United Nations Statistics Division, New York, NY 10017, (800) 253-9646, Fax: (212) 963-4116, http://unstats.un.org; *Statistical Yearbook.*

GIBRALTAR - MOTOR VEHICLES

Taylor and Francis Group, An Informa Business, 2 Park Square, Milton Park, Abingdon, Oxford OX14 4RN, United Kingdom, (Dial from U.S. (212) 216-7800), (Fax from U.S. (212) 564-7854), www.tandf.co.uk; *The Europa World Year Book.*

United Nations Statistics Division, New York, NY 10017, (800) 253-9646, Fax: (212) 963-4116, http://unstats.un.org; *Statistical Yearbook.*

GIBRALTAR - MUSEUMS

UNESCO Institute for Statistics, C.P. 6128 Succursale Centre-Ville, Montreal, Quebec, H3C 3J7 Canada, (Dial from U.S. (514) 343-6880), (Fax from U.S. (514) 343 6882), www.uis.unesco.org; *Statistical Tables.*

GIBRALTAR - NUTRITION

United Nations Food and Agricultural Organization (FAO), Viale delle Terme di Caracalla, 00100 Rome, Italy, (Dial from U.S. (202) 653-2400), (Fax from U.S. (202) 653 5760), www.fao.org; *The State of Food and Agriculture (SOFA) 2006.*

GIBRALTAR - PERIODICALS

UNESCO Institute for Statistics, C.P. 6128 Succursale Centre-Ville, Montreal, Quebec, H3C 3J7 Canada, (Dial from U.S. (514) 343-6880), (Fax from U.S. (514) 343 6882), www.uis.unesco.org; *Statistical Tables.*

GIBRALTAR - PESTICIDES

United Nations Food and Agricultural Organization (FAO), Viale delle Terme di Caracalla, 00100 Rome, Italy, (Dial from U.S. (202) 653-2400), (Fax from U.S. (202) 653 5760), www.fao.org; *The State of Food and Agriculture (SOFA) 2006.*

GIBRALTAR - PETROLEUM INDUSTRY AND TRADE

PennWell Corporation, 1421 South Sheridan Road, Tulsa, OK 74112, (918) 835-3161, www.pennwell.com; *International Petroleum Encyclopedia 2007.*

United Nations Food and Agricultural Organization (FAO), Viale delle Terme di Caracalla, 00100 Rome, Italy, (Dial from U.S. (202) 653-2400), (Fax from U.S. (202) 653 5760), www.fao.org; *The State of Food and Agriculture (SOFA) 2006.*

GIBRALTAR - POLITICAL SCIENCE

Central Intelligence Agency, Office of Public Affairs, Washington, DC 20505, (703) 482-0623, Fax: (703) 482-1739, www.cia.gov; *The World Factbook.*

Palgrave Macmillan Ltd., Houndmills, Basingstoke, Hampshire, RG21 6XS, England, (Telephone in U.S. (888) 330-8477), (Fax in U.S. (800) 672-2054), www.palgrave.com; *The Statesman's Yearbook 2008.*

Taylor and Francis Group, An Informa Business, 2 Park Square, Milton Park, Abingdon, Oxford OX14 4RN, United Kingdom, (Dial from U.S. (212) 216-7800), (Fax from U.S. (212) 564-7854), www.tandf.co.uk; *The Europa World Year Book.*

GIBRALTAR - POPULATION

Central Intelligence Agency, Office of Public Affairs, Washington, DC 20505, (703) 482-0623, Fax: (703) 482-1739, www.cia.gov; *The World Factbook.*

Economist Intelligence Unit, 111 West 57th Street, New York, NY 10019, (212) 554-0600, Fax: (212) 586-1181, www.eiu.com; *Gibraltar.*

Euromonitor International, Inc., 224 S. Michigan Avenue, Suite 1500, Chicago, IL 60604, (312) 922-1115, Fax: (312) 922-1157, www.euromonitor.com; *The World Economic Factbook 2008.*

International Labour Office, I.L.O. Publications, 4 route des Morillons, CH-1211 Geneva 22, Switzerland, (Telephone in U.S. (202) 653-7652), (Fax in U.S. (202) 653-7687), www.ilo.org; *Yearbook of Labour Statistics 2006.*

Palgrave Macmillan Ltd., Houndmills, Basingstoke, Hampshire, RG21 6XS, England, (Telephone in U.S. (888) 330-8477), (Fax in U.S. (800) 672-2054), www.palgrave.com; *The Statesman's Yearbook 2008.*

Taylor and Francis Group, An Informa Business, 2 Park Square, Milton Park, Abingdon, Oxford OX14 4RN, United Kingdom, (Dial from U.S. (212) 216-7800), (Fax from U.S. (212) 564-7854), www.tandf.co.uk; *The Europa World Year Book.*

United Nations Food and Agricultural Organization (FAO), Viale delle Terme di Caracalla, 00100 Rome, Italy, (Dial from U.S. (202) 653-2400), (Fax from U.S. (202) 653 5760), www.fao.org; *FAO Production Yearbook 2002.*

United Nations Statistics Division, New York, NY 10017, (800) 253-9646, Fax: (212) 963-4116, http://unstats.un.org; *Demographic Yearbook* and *Statistical Yearbook.*

The World Bank, 1818 H Street, NW, Washington, DC 20433, (202) 473-1000, Fax: (202) 477-6391, www.worldbank.org; *The World Bank Atlas 2003-2004.*

World Health Organization (WHO), Avenue Appia 20, 1211 Geneve 27, Switzerland, (Telephone in U.S. (212) 331-9081), www.who.int; *World Health Report 2006.*

GIBRALTAR - POPULATION DENSITY

Central Intelligence Agency, Office of Public Affairs, Washington, DC 20505, (703) 482-0623, Fax: (703) 482-1739, www.cia.gov; *The World Factbook.*

Euromonitor International, Inc., 224 S. Michigan Avenue, Suite 1500, Chicago, IL 60604, (312) 922-1115, Fax: (312) 922-1157, www.euromonitor.com; *The World Economic Factbook 2008.*

Palgrave Macmillan Ltd., Houndmills, Basingstoke, Hampshire, RG21 6XS, England, (Telephone in U.S. (888) 330-8477), (Fax in U.S. (800) 672-2054), www.palgrave.com; *The Statesman's Yearbook 2008.*

Taylor and Francis Group, An Informa Business, 2 Park Square, Milton Park, Abingdon, Oxford OX14 4RN, United Kingdom, (Dial from U.S. (212) 216-7800), (Fax from U.S. (212) 564-7854), www.tandf.co.uk; *The Europa World Year Book.*

United Nations Food and Agricultural Organization (FAO), Viale delle Terme di Caracalla, 00100 Rome, Italy, (Dial from U.S. (202) 653-2400), (Fax from U.S. (202) 653 5760), www.fao.org; *The State of Food and Agriculture (SOFA) 2006.*

United Nations Statistics Division, New York, NY 10017, (800) 253-9646, Fax: (212) 963-4116, http://unstats.un.org; *Statistical Yearbook.*

GIBRALTAR - POSTAL SERVICE

Palgrave Macmillan Ltd., Houndmills, Basingstoke, Hampshire, RG21 6XS, England, (Telephone in U.S. (888) 330-8477), (Fax in U.S. (800) 672-2054), www.palgrave.com; *The Statesman's Yearbook 2008.*

United Nations Statistics Division, New York, NY 10017, (800) 253-9646, Fax: (212) 963-4116, http://unstats.un.org; *Statistical Yearbook.*

GIBRALTAR - POWER RESOURCES

Euromonitor International, Inc., 224 S. Michigan Avenue, Suite 1500, Chicago, IL 60604, (312) 922-1115, Fax: (312) 922-1157, www.euromonitor.com; *The World Economic Factbook 2008* and *World Marketing Data and Statistics.*

Platts, 2 Penn Plaza, 25th Floor, New York, NY 10121-2298, (212) 904-3070, www.platts.com; *Energy Economist.*

United Nations Food and Agricultural Organization (FAO), Viale delle Terme di Caracalla, 00100 Rome, Italy, (Dial from U.S. (202) 653-2400), (Fax from U.S. (202) 653 5760), www.fao.org; *The State of Food and Agriculture (SOFA) 2006.*

United Nations Statistics Division, New York, NY 10017, (800) 253-9646, Fax: (212) 963-4116, http://unstats.un.org; *Energy Statistics Yearbook 2003* and *Statistical Yearbook.*

The World Bank, 1818 H Street, NW, Washington, DC 20433, (202) 473-1000, Fax: (202) 477-6391, www.worldbank.org; *The World Bank Atlas 2003-2004.*

GIBRALTAR - PRICES

Euromonitor International, Inc., 224 S. Michigan Avenue, Suite 1500, Chicago, IL 60604, (312) 922-1115, Fax: (312) 922-1157, www.euromonitor.com; *World Marketing Data and Statistics.*

International Labour Office, I.L.O. Publications, 4 route des Morillons, CH-1211 Geneva 22, Switzerland, (Telephone in U.S. (202) 653-7652), (Fax in U.S. (202) 653-7687), www.ilo.org; *Yearbook of Labour Statistics 2006.*

United Nations Food and Agricultural Organization (FAO), Viale delle Terme di Caracalla, 00100 Rome, Italy, (Dial from U.S. (202) 653-2400), (Fax from U.S. (202) 653 5760), www.fao.org; *FAO Production Yearbook 2002* and *The State of Food and Agriculture (SOFA) 2006.*

GIBRALTAR - PROFESSIONS

United Nations Statistics Division, New York, NY 10017, (800) 253-9646, Fax: (212) 963-4116, http://unstats.un.org; *Statistical Yearbook.*

GIBRALTAR - PUBLIC HEALTH

Euromonitor International, Inc., 224 S. Michigan Avenue, Suite 1500, Chicago, IL 60604, (312) 922-1115, Fax: (312) 922-1157, www.euromonitor.com; *World Marketing Data and Statistics.*

Palgrave Macmillan Ltd., Houndmills, Basingstoke, Hampshire, RG21 6XS, England, (Telephone in U.S. (888) 330-8477), (Fax in U.S. (800) 672-2054), www.palgrave.com; *The Statesman's Yearbook 2008.*

United Nations Statistics Division, New York, NY 10017, (800) 253-9646, Fax: (212) 963-4116, http://unstats.un.org; *Statistical Yearbook.*

World Health Organization (WHO), Avenue Appia 20, 1211 Geneve 27, Switzerland, (Telephone in U.S. (212) 331-9081), www.who.int; The WHO Global Atlas of Infectious Diseases.

GIBRALTAR - RADIO BROADCASTING

Palgrave Macmillan Ltd., Houndmills, Basingstoke, Hampshire, RG21 6XS, England, (Telephone in U.S. (888) 330-8477), (Fax in U.S. (800) 672-2054), www.palgrave.com; *The Statesman's Yearbook 2008.*

GIBRALTAR - RELIGION

Central Intelligence Agency, Office of Public Affairs, Washington, DC 20505, (703) 482-0623, Fax: (703) 482-1739, www.cia.gov; *The World Factbook.*

Palgrave Macmillan Ltd., Houndmills, Basingstoke, Hampshire, RG21 6XS, England, (Telephone in U.S. (888) 330-8477), (Fax in U.S. (800) 672-2054), www.palgrave.com; *The Statesman's Yearbook 2008.*

GIBRALTAR - RENT CHARGES

International Labour Office, I.L.O. Publications, 4 route des Morillons, CH-1211 Geneva 22, Switzerland, (Telephone in U.S. (202) 653-7652), (Fax in U.S. (202) 653-7687), www.ilo.org; *Yearbook of Labour Statistics 2006.*

GIBRALTAR - RETAIL TRADE

Banque de France, 48 rue Croix des Petits champs, 75001 Paris, France, www.banque-france.fr/home.htm; *Monthly Business Survey Overview.*

Euromonitor International, Inc., 224 S. Michigan Avenue, Suite 1500, Chicago, IL 60604, (312) 922-1115, Fax: (312) 922-1157, www.euromonitor.com; *World Marketing Data and Statistics.*

GIBRALTAR - ROADS

Central Intelligence Agency, Office of Public Affairs, Washington, DC 20505, (703) 482-0623, Fax: (703) 482-1739, www.cia.gov; *The World Factbook.*

Palgrave Macmillan Ltd., Houndmills, Basingstoke, Hampshire, RG21 6XS, England, (Telephone in U.S. (888) 330-8477), (Fax in U.S. (800) 672-2054), www.palgrave.com; *The Statesman's Yearbook 2008.*

GIBRALTAR - SHIPPING

Palgrave Macmillan Ltd., Houndmills, Basingstoke, Hampshire, RG21 6XS, England, (Telephone in U.S. (888) 330-8477), (Fax in U.S. (800) 672-2054), www.palgrave.com; *The Statesman's Yearbook 2008.*

Taylor and Francis Group, An Informa Business, 2 Park Square, Milton Park, Abingdon, Oxford OX14 4RN, United Kingdom, (Dial from U.S. (212) 216-7800), (Fax from U.S. (212) 564-7854), www.tandf.co.uk; *The Europa World Year Book.*

United Nations Statistics Division, New York, NY 10017, (800) 253-9646, Fax: (212) 963-4116, http://unstats.un.org; *Statistical Yearbook.*

GIBRALTAR - SOCIAL SECURITY

Palgrave Macmillan Ltd., Houndmills, Basingstoke, Hampshire, RG21 6XS, England, (Telephone in U.S. (888) 330-8477), (Fax in U.S. (800) 672-2054), www.palgrave.com; *The Statesman's Yearbook 2008.*

GIBRALTAR - TAXATION

Taylor and Francis Group, An Informa Business, 2 Park Square, Milton Park, Abingdon, Oxford OX14 4RN, United Kingdom, (Dial from U.S. (212) 216-7800), (Fax from U.S. (212) 564-7854), www.tandf.co.uk; *The Europa World Year Book.*

GIBRALTAR - TELEPHONE

International Telecommunication Union (ITU), Place des Nations, 1211 Geneva 20, Switzerland, www.itu.int; World Telecommunication Indicators Database.

Palgrave Macmillan Ltd., Houndmills, Basingstoke, Hampshire, RG21 6XS, England, (Telephone in U.S. (888) 330-8477), (Fax in U.S. (800) 672-2054), www.palgrave.com; *The Statesman's Yearbook 2008.*

Taylor and Francis Group, An Informa Business, 2 Park Square, Milton Park, Abingdon, Oxford OX14 4RN, United Kingdom, (Dial from U.S. (212) 216-7800), (Fax from U.S. (212) 564-7854), www.tandf.co.uk; *The Europa World Year Book.*

United Nations Statistics Division, New York, NY 10017, (800) 253-9646, Fax: (212) 963-4116, http://unstats.un.org; *Statistical Yearbook.*

GIBRALTAR - THEATER

UNESCO Institute for Statistics, C.P. 6128 Succursale Centre-Ville, Montreal, Quebec, H3C 3J7 Canada, (Dial from U.S. (514) 343-6880), (Fax from U.S. (514) 343 6882), www.uis.unesco.org; *Statistical Tables.*

GIBRALTAR - TOURISM

Euromonitor International, Inc., 224 S. Michigan Avenue, Suite 1500, Chicago, IL 60604, (312) 922-1115, Fax: (312) 922-1157, www.euromonitor.com; *The World Economic Factbook 2008* and *World Marketing Data and Statistics.*

Palgrave Macmillan Ltd., Houndmills, Basingstoke, Hampshire, RG21 6XS, England, (Telephone in U.S. (888) 330-8477), (Fax in U.S. (800) 672-2054), www.palgrave.com; *The Statesman's Yearbook 2008.*

Statistics Office, 99 Harbours Walk, The New Harbours, Gibraltar, www.gibraltar.gov.gi; *Hotel Occupancy Survey 2005* and *Tourist Survey 2005.*

Taylor and Francis Group, An Informa Business, 2 Park Square, Milton Park, Abingdon, Oxford OX14 4RN, United Kingdom, (Dial from U.S. (212) 216-7800), (Fax from U.S. (212) 564-7854), www.tandf.co.uk; *The Europa World Year Book.*

United Nations Statistics Division, New York, NY 10017, (800) 253-9646, Fax: (212) 963-4116, http://unstats.un.org; *Statistical Yearbook.*

GIBRALTAR - TRADE

See GIBRALTAR - INTERNATIONAL TRADE

GIBRALTAR - TRANSPORTATION

Central Intelligence Agency, Office of Public Affairs, Washington, DC 20505, (703) 482-0623, Fax: (703) 482-1739, www.cia.gov; *The World Factbook.*

Euromonitor International, Inc., 224 S. Michigan Avenue, Suite 1500, Chicago, IL 60604, (312) 922-1115, Fax: (312) 922-1157, www.euromonitor.com; *World Marketing Data and Statistics.*

Palgrave Macmillan Ltd., Houndmills, Basingstoke, Hampshire, RG21 6XS, England, (Telephone in U.S. (888) 330-8477), (Fax in U.S. (800) 672-2054), www.palgrave.com; *The Statesman's Yearbook 2008.*

Taylor and Francis Group, An Informa Business, 2 Park Square, Milton Park, Abingdon, Oxford OX14 4RN, United Kingdom, (Dial from U.S. (212) 216-7800), (Fax from U.S. (212) 564-7854), www.tandf.co.uk; *The Europa World Year Book.*

GIBRALTAR - UNEMPLOYMENT

Central Intelligence Agency, Office of Public Affairs, Washington, DC 20505, (703) 482-0623, Fax: (703) 482-1739, www.cia.gov; *The World Factbook.*

International Labour Office, I.L.O. Publications, 4 route des Morillons, CH-1211 Geneva 22, Switzerland, (Telephone in U.S. (202) 653-7652), (Fax in U.S. (202) 653-7687), www.ilo.org; *Yearbook of Labour Statistics 2006.*

United Nations Statistics Division, New York, NY 10017, (800) 253-9646, Fax: (212) 963-4116, http://unstats.un.org; *Statistical Yearbook.*

GIBRALTAR - VITAL STATISTICS

Palgrave Macmillan Ltd., Houndmills, Basingstoke, Hampshire, RG21 6XS, England, (Telephone in U.S. (888) 330-8477), (Fax in U.S. (800) 672-2054), www.palgrave.com; *The Statesman's Yearbook 2008.*

United Nations Statistics Division, New York, NY 10017, (800) 253-9646, Fax: (212) 963-4116, http://unstats.un.org; *Statistical Yearbook.*

World Health Organization (WHO), Avenue Appia 20, 1211 Geneve 27, Switzerland, (Telephone in U.S. (212) 331-9081), www.who.int; *World Health Report 2006.*

GIBRALTAR - WAGES

International Labour Office, I.L.O. Publications, 4 route des Morillons, CH-1211 Geneva 22, Switzerland, (Telephone in U.S. (202) 653-7652), (Fax in U.S. (202) 653-7687), www.ilo.org; *Yearbook of Labour Statistics 2006.*

United Nations Statistics Division, New York, NY 10017, (800) 253-9646, Fax: (212) 963-4116, http://unstats.un.org; *Statistical Yearbook.*

GIFT AND ESTATE TAXES

U.S. Census Bureau, Governments Division, 4600 Silver Hill Road, Washington DC 20233, (800) 242-2184, www.census.gov/govs/www; *2002 Census of Governments* and *2002 Census of Governments, Government Finances.*

U.S. Department of the Treasury (DOT), Internal Revenue Service (IRS), Statistics of Income Division (SIS), PO Box 2608, Washington, DC, 20013-2608, (202) 874-0410, Fax: (202) 874-0964, www.irs.ustreas.gov; *IRS Data Book 2004-2005.*

GIFT, NOVELTY, AND SOUVENIR SHOPS

Office of Trade and Industry Information (OTII), Manufacturing and Services, International Trade Administration, U.S. Department of Commerce, 1401 Constitution Ave, NW, Washington, DC 20230, (800) USA TRAD(E), http://trade.gov/index.asp; *TradeStats Express.*

U.S. Census Bureau, 4700 Silver Hill Road, Washington DC 20233-0001, (301) 763-3030, www.census.gov; unpublished data.

U.S. Census Bureau, Center for Economic Studies, 4600 Silver Hill Road, Washington DC 20233, (301) 457-1235, www.ces.census.gov; *2002 Economic Census, Retail Trade* and *2002 Economic Census, Wholesale Trade.*

U.S. Census Bureau, Company Statistics Division, 4700 Silver Hill Road, Washington DC 20233-0001, (301) 763-3030, www.census.gov/csd/; *County Business Patterns 2004.*

GOLD - CONSUMPTION

U.S. Department of the Interior (DOI), U.S. Geological Survey (USGS), Office of Minerals Information, 12201 Sunrise Valley Drive, Reston, VA 20192, Mr. Kenneth A. Beckman, (703) 648-4916, Fax: (703) 648-4995, http://minerals.usgs.gov/minerals; *Mineral Commodity Summaries.*

GOLD - EMPLOYMENT

U.S. Bureau of Labor Statistics (BLS), Postal Square Building, 2 Massachusetts Avenue, NE, Washington, DC 20212-0001, (202) 691-5200, Fax: (202) 691-6325, www.bls.gov; *Current Employment Statistics Survey (CES)* and *Employment and Earnings (EE).*

U.S. Department of the Interior (DOI), U.S. Geological Survey (USGS), Office of Minerals Information, 12201 Sunrise Valley Drive, Reston, VA 20192, Mr. Kenneth A. Beckman, (703) 648-4916, Fax: (703) 648-4995, http://minerals.usgs.gov/minerals; *Mineral Commodity Summaries.*

GOLD - INTERNATIONAL TRADE

U.S. Census Bureau, Foreign Trade Division, 4700 Silver Hill Road, Washington DC 20233-0001, (301) 763-3030, www.census.gov/foreign-trade/www/; *U.S. International Trade in Goods and Services.*

U.S. Department of the Interior (DOI), U.S. Geological Survey (USGS), Office of Minerals Information, 12201 Sunrise Valley Drive, Reston, VA 20192, Mr. Kenneth A. Beckman, (703) 648-4916, Fax: (703) 648-4995, http://minerals.usgs.gov/minerals; *Mineral Commodity Summaries.*

GOLD - MINING INDUSTRY

U.S. Census Bureau, Center for Economic Studies, 4600 Silver Hill Road, Washington DC 20233, (301) 457-1235, www.ces.census.gov; *2002 Economic Census, Mining.*

GOLD - PRICES

U.S. Department of the Interior (DOI), U.S. Geological Survey (USGS), Office of Minerals Information, 12201 Sunrise Valley Drive, Reston, VA 20192, Mr. Kenneth A. Beckman, (703) 648-4916, Fax: (703) 648-4995, http://minerals.usgs.gov/minerals; *Mineral Commodity Summaries.*

GOLD - PRODUCTION AND VALUE

U.S. Department of the Interior (DOI), U.S. Geological Survey (USGS), Office of Minerals Information, 12201 Sunrise Valley Drive, Reston, VA 20192, Mr. Kenneth A. Beckman, (703) 648-4916, Fax: (703) 648-4995, http://minerals.usgs.gov/minerals; *Mineral Commodity Summaries* and *Minerals Yearbook.*

GOLD - PRODUCTION AND VALUE - WORLD

U.S. Department of the Interior (DOI), U.S. Geological Survey (USGS), Office of Minerals Information, 12201 Sunrise Valley Drive, Reston, VA 20192, Mr. Kenneth A. Beckman, (703) 648-4916, Fax: (703)

648-4995, http://minerals.usgs.gov/minerals; *Mineral Commodity Summaries* and *Minerals Yearbook.*

GOLD - RESERVES

Board of Governors of the Federal Reserve System, Constitution Avenue, NW, Washington, DC 20551, (202) 452-3000, www.federalreserve.gov; *Federal Reserve Bulletin.*

U.S. Department of the Treasury (DOT), 1500 Pennsylvania Avenue, NW, Washington, DC 20220, (202) 622-2000, Fax: (202) 622-6415, www.ustreas.gov; *Treasury Bulletin.*

GOLF

National Golf Foundation (NGF), 1150 South U.S. Highway One, Suite 401, Jupiter, FL 33477, (888) 275-4643, Fax: (561) 744-6107, www.ngf.org; *The Golf Consumer Research Program.*

National Sporting Goods Association (NSGA), 1601 Feehanville Drive, Suite 300, Mount Prospect, IL 60056, (847) 296-6742, Fax: (847) 391-9827, www.nsga.org; *2006 Sports Participation* and *Ten-Year History of Selected Sports Participation, 1996-2006.*

U.S. Census Bureau, Center for Economic Studies, 4600 Silver Hill Road, Washington DC 20233, (301) 457-1235, www.ces.census.gov; *2002 Economic Census, Arts, Entertainment and Recreation.*

GOLF COURSE INDUSTRY RECEIPTS

U.S. Census Bureau, Company Statistics Division, 4700 Silver Hill Road, Washington DC 20233-0001, (301) 763-3030, www.census.gov/csd/; *Current Business Reports.*

GONORRHEA

Centers for Disease Control and Prevention (CDC), U.S. Department of Health and Human Services (HHS), 1600 Clifton Road, Atlanta, GA 30333, (800) 311-3435, www.cdc.gov; *Morbidity and Mortality Weekly Report (MMWR)* and *Summary of Notifiable Diseases, United States, 2006.*

GOVERNMENT

See also EXPENDITURES OF UNITED STATES GOVERNMENT

Congressional Quarterly, Inc., 1255 22nd Street, NW, Washington, DC 20037, (202) 419-8500, www.cq.com; *Supreme Court Compendium.*

Federal Bureau of Investigation (FBI), J. Edgar Hoover Building, 935 Pennsylvania Avenue, NW, Washington, DC 20535-0001, (202) 324-3000, www.fbi.gov; *Facts and Figures 2003.*

Population Reference Bureau, 1875 Connecticut Avenue, NW, Suite 520, Washington, DC, 20009-5728, (800) 877-9881, Fax: (202) 328-3937, www.prb.org; *Government Spending in an Older America.*

U.S. Bureau of Labor Statistics (BLS), Postal Square Building, 2 Massachusetts Avenue, NE, Washington, DC 20212-0001, (202) 691-5200, Fax: (202) 691-6325, www.bls.gov; *Industries at a Glance.*

U.S. National Archives and Records Administration, 8601 Adelphi Road, College Park, MD 20740-6001, (866) 272-6272, Fax: (301) 837-0483, www.archives.gov; unpublished data.

University of Michigan Library Documents Center, 203 Hatcher Graduate Library North, Ann Arbor, MI 48109-1205, (734) 764-0410, Fax: (734) 764-0259, www.lib.umich.edu/govdocs; *Statistical Universe: Index to Federal, State, International and Business Statistics.*

GOVERNMENT - CAPITAL STOCKS

Bureau of Economic Analysis (BEA), U.S. Department of Commerce (DOC), 1441 L Street NW, Washington, DC 20230, (202) 606-9900, www.bea.gov; *Survey of Current Business (SCB).*

GOVERNMENT - CONSTRUCTION VALUE OF BUILDINGS

U.S. Census Bureau, Manufacturing and Construction Division, 4600 Silver Hill Road, Washington DC 20233, (301) 763-4673, www.census.gov/mcd; *Current Construction Reports.*

GOVERNMENT - EARNINGS

Bureau of Economic Analysis (BEA), U.S. Department of Commerce (DOC), 1441 L Street NW, Washington, DC 20230, (202) 606-9900, www.bea.gov; *2007 Annual Revision of the National Income and Product Accounts (NIPA)* and *Survey of Current Business (SCB).*

U.S. Bureau of Labor Statistics (BLS), Postal Square Building, 2 Massachusetts Avenue, NE, Washington, DC 20212-0001, (202) 691-5200, Fax: (202) 691-6325, www.bls.gov; *Current Employment Statistics Survey (CES)* and *Employment and Earnings (EE).*

U.S. Census Bureau, Governments Division, 4600 Silver Hill Road, Washington DC 20233, (800) 242-2184, www.census.gov/govs/www; *2002 Census of Governments, Public Employment and Payroll.*

GOVERNMENT - EMPLOYEES

National Science Foundation, Division of Science Resources Statistics (SRS), 4201 Wilson Boulevard, Arlington, VA 22230, (703) 292-8780, Fax: (703) 292-9092, www.nsf.gov; *National Patterns of Research and Development Resources: 2006 Data Update.*

U.S. Bureau of Labor Statistics (BLS), Postal Square Building, 2 Massachusetts Avenue, NE, Washington, DC 20212-0001, (202) 691-5200, Fax: (202) 691-6325, www.bls.gov; *Current Employment Statistics Survey (CES); Employment and Earnings (EE); Monthly Labor Review (MLR);* and unpublished data.

U.S. Department of Justice (DOJ), Bureau of Justice Statistics, 810 Seventh Street, NW, Washington, DC 20531, (202) 307-0765, www.ojp.usdoj.gov/bjs/; *Justice Expenditure and Employment in the United States 2003.*

U.S. Office of Personnel Management (OPM), 1900 E Street, NW, Washington, DC 20415-1000, (202) 606-1800, www.opm.gov; *The Fact Book: 2005 Edition.*

United States Office of Personnel Management (OMB), 1900 E Street, NW, Washington, DC 20415-1000, (202) 606-1800, www.opm.gov; *Central Personnel Data File (CPDF).*

GOVERNMENT - EMPLOYEES - BENEFITS

U.S. Bureau of Labor Statistics (BLS), Postal Square Building, 2 Massachusetts Avenue, NE, Washington, DC 20212-0001, (202) 691-5200, Fax: (202) 691-6325, www.bls.gov; *Employee Benefits in State and Local Governments* and *Employer Costs for Employee Compensation.*

GOVERNMENT - EMPLOYEES - CITY GOVERNMENT

U.S. Census Bureau, 4700 Silver Hill Road, Washington DC 20233-0001, (301) 763-3030, www.census.gov; unpublished data.

U.S. Census Bureau, Governments Division, 4600 Silver Hill Road, Washington DC 20233, (800) 242-2184, www.census.gov/govs/www; *2002 Census of Governments, Public Employment and Payroll.*

GOVERNMENT - EMPLOYEES - FEDERAL - CIVILIAN

U.S. Bureau of Labor Statistics (BLS), Postal Square Building, 2 Massachusetts Avenue, NE, Washington, DC 20212-0001, (202) 691-5200, Fax: (202) 691-6325, www.bls.gov; *Employment and Earnings (EE)* and *Monthly Labor Review (MLR).*

U.S. Census Bureau, Governments Division, 4600 Silver Hill Road, Washington DC 20233, (800) 242-2184, www.census.gov/govs/www; *2002 Census of Governments, Government Finances* and *2002 Census of Governments, Public Employment and Payroll.*

U.S. Library of Congress (LOC), Congressional Research Service (CRS), The Library of Congress, 101 Independence Avenue, SE, Washington, DC 20540-7500, (202) 707-5700, www.loc.gov/crsinfo; *Federal Employees: Pay and Pension Increases Since 1969.*

U.S. Office of Personnel Management (OPM), 1900 E Street, NW, Washington, DC 20415-1000, (202) 606-1800, www.opm.gov; *Biennial Report of Employment by Geographic Area; 2004 Demographic Profile of the Federal Workforce;* and *Employment and Trends.*

United States Office of Personnel Management (OMB), 1900 E Street, NW, Washington, DC 20415-1000, (202) 606-1800, www.opm.gov; *Central Personnel Data File (CPDF); Employment and Trends of Federal Civilian Workforce Statistics;* and *Pay Structure of the Federal Civil Service.*

GOVERNMENT - EMPLOYEES - LAW ENFORCEMENT

U.S. Department of Justice (DOJ), Bureau of Justice Statistics, 810 Seventh Street, NW, Washington, DC 20531, (202) 307-0765, www.ojp.usdoj.gov/bjs/; *Assessing Measurement Techniques for Identifying Race, Ethnicity, and Gender: Observation-Based Data Collection in Airports and at Immigration Checkpoints; Federal Law Enforcement Officers, 2004; Justice Expenditure and Employment in the United States 2003; Sheriffs' Offices, 2003;* and *The Sourcebook of Criminal Justice Statistics, 2003.*

GOVERNMENT - EMPLOYEES - LOCAL GOVERNMENT

U.S. Census Bureau, 4700 Silver Hill Road, Washington DC 20233-0001, (301) 763-3030, www.census.gov; unpublished data.

U.S. Census Bureau, Governments Division, 4600 Silver Hill Road, Washington DC 20233, (800) 242-2184, www.census.gov/govs/www; *2002 Census of Governments, Public Employment and Payroll.*

GOVERNMENT - EMPLOYEES - RETIREMENT SYSTEMS

Employee Benefit Research Institute (EBRI), Suite 600, 2121 K Street, NW, Washington, DC 20037-1896, (202) 659-0670, Fax: (202) 775-6312, www.ebri.org; *EBRI Databook on Employee Benefits.*

Social Security Administration (SSA), Office of Public Inquiries, Windsor Park Building, 6401 Security Boulevard, Baltimore, MD 21235, (800) 772-1213, www.ssa.gov; *Social Security Bulletin* and unpublished data.

United States Office of Personnel Management (OMB), 1900 E Street, NW, Washington, DC 20415-1000, (202) 606-1800, www.opm.gov; *Retirement Statistics.*

GOVERNMENT - EMPLOYEES - STATE GOVERNMENT

U.S. Census Bureau, 4700 Silver Hill Road, Washington DC 20233-0001, (301) 763-3030, www.census.gov; unpublished data.

U.S. Census Bureau, Governments Division, 4600 Silver Hill Road, Washington DC 20233, (800) 242-2184, www.census.gov/govs/www; *2002 Census of Governments, Public Employment and Payroll.*

GOVERNMENT - EMPLOYEES - STATES

U.S. Bureau of Labor Statistics (BLS), Postal Square Building, 2 Massachusetts Avenue, NE, Washington, DC 20212-0001, (202) 691-5200, Fax: (202) 691-6325, www.bls.gov; *Employment and Earnings (EE).*

U.S. Census Bureau, 4700 Silver Hill Road, Washington DC 20233-0001, (301) 763-3030, www.census.gov; unpublished data.

U.S. Census Bureau, Governments Division, 4600 Silver Hill Road, Washington DC 20233, (800) 242-2184, www.census.gov/govs/www; *2002 Census of Governments, Public Employment and Payroll.*

GOVERNMENT - EMPLOYMENT COST INDEX

U.S. Bureau of Labor Statistics (BLS), Postal Square Building, 2 Massachusetts Avenue, NE,

Washington, DC 20212-0001, (202) 691-5200, Fax: (202) 691-6325, www.bls.gov; *Current Employment Statistics Survey (CES); Employment Cost Index;* and unpublished data.

GOVERNMENT - EXPENDITURES - CAPITAL OUTLAY

U.S. Census Bureau, 4700 Silver Hill Road, Washington DC 20233-0001, (301) 763-3030, www.census.gov; unpublished data.

U.S. Census Bureau, Governments Division, 4600 Silver Hill Road, Washington DC 20233, (800) 242-2184, www.census.gov/govs/www; *2002 Census of Governments* and *2002 Census of Governments, Government Finances.*

GOVERNMENT - EXPENDITURES - CITY GOVERNMENT

National Education Association (NEA), 1201 Sixteenth Street, NW, Washington, DC 20036-3290, (202) 833-4000, Fax: (202) 822-7974, www.nea.org; *Rankings and Estimates: Rankings of the States 2006 and Estimates of School Statistics 2007.*

U.S. Census Bureau, 4700 Silver Hill Road, Washington DC 20233-0001, (301) 763-3030, www.census.gov; *State and County QuickFacts.*

U.S. Census Bureau, Governments Division, 4600 Silver Hill Road, Washington DC 20233, (800) 242-2184, www.census.gov/govs/www; *2002 Census of Governments, Government Finances.*

U.S. Department of Justice (DOJ), Bureau of Justice Statistics, 810 Seventh Street, NW, Washington, DC 20531, (202) 307-0765, www.ojp.usdoj.gov/bjs/; *Justice Expenditure and Employment in the United States 2003.*

GOVERNMENT - EXPENDITURES - CONSUMPTION

Bureau of Economic Analysis (BEA), U.S. Department of Commerce (DOC), 1441 L Street NW, Washington, DC 20230, (202) 606-9900, www.bea.gov; National Income and Product Accounts (NIPA) Tables (web app) and *Survey of Current Business (SCB).*

GOVERNMENT - EXPENDITURES - COUNTY GOVERNMENT

National Education Association (NEA), 1201 Sixteenth Street, NW, Washington, DC 20036-3290, (202) 833-4000, Fax: (202) 822-7974, www.nea.org; *Rankings and Estimates: Rankings of the States 2006 and Estimates of School Statistics 2007.*

U.S. Census Bureau, 4700 Silver Hill Road, Washington DC 20233-0001, (301) 763-3030, www.census.gov; *State and County QuickFacts.*

U.S. Census Bureau, Governments Division, 4600 Silver Hill Road, Washington DC 20233, (800) 242-2184, www.census.gov/govs/www; *2002 Census of Governments, Government Finances.*

U.S. Department of Justice (DOJ), Bureau of Justice Statistics, 810 Seventh Street, NW, Washington, DC 20531, (202) 307-0765, www.ojp.usdoj.gov/bjs/; *Justice Expenditure and Employment in the United States 2003.*

GOVERNMENT - EXPENDITURES - FEDERAL

American Enterprise Institute (AEI), 1150 Seventeenth Street, NW, Washington, DC 20036, (202) 862-5800, Fax: (202) 862-7177, www.aei.org; unpublished data.

National Education Association (NEA), 1201 Sixteenth Street, NW, Washington, DC 20036-3290, (202) 833-4000, Fax: (202) 822-7974, www.nea.org; *Rankings and Estimates: Rankings of the States 2006 and Estimates of School Statistics 2007.*

The Office of Management and Budget (OMB), 725 17th Street, NW, Washington, DC 20503, (202) 395-3080, Fax: (202) 395-3888, www.whitehouse.gov/omb; *Analytical Perspectives, Budget of the United States Government, Fiscal Year 2009* and *Budget of the United States Government, Federal Year 2009.*

U.S. Census Bureau, Governments Division, 4600 Silver Hill Road, Washington DC 20233, (800) 242-2184, www.census.gov/govs/www; *2002 Census of Governments* and *2002 Census of Governments, Government Finances.*

U.S. Department of Justice (DOJ), Bureau of Justice Statistics, 810 Seventh Street, NW, Washington, DC 20531, (202) 307-0765, www.ojp.usdoj.gov/bjs/; *Justice Expenditure and Employment in the United States 2003.*

U.S. Library of Congress (LOC), Congressional Research Service (CRS), The Library of Congress, 101 Independence Avenue, SE, Washington, DC 20540-7500, (202) 707-5700, www.loc.gov/crsinfo; *Federal Employees: Pay and Pension Increases Since 1969.*

GOVERNMENT - EXPENDITURES - FEDERAL - AID TO STATE AND LOCAL GOVERNMENTS

The Office of Management and Budget (OMB), 725 17th Street, NW, Washington, DC 20503, (202) 395-3080, Fax: (202) 395-3888, www.whitehouse.gov/omb; *Historical Tables.*

GOVERNMENT - EXPENDITURES - FEDERAL - CAPITAL OUTLAY

U.S. Census Bureau, Governments Division, 4600 Silver Hill Road, Washington DC 20233, (800) 242-2184, www.census.gov/govs/www; *2002 Census of Governments* and *2002 Census of Governments, Government Finances.*

GOVERNMENT - EXPENDITURES - FEDERAL - PUBLIC ASSISTANCE PROGRAMS

Economic Policy Institute (EPI), 1333 H Street, NW, Suite 300, East Tower, Washington, DC 20005-4707, (202) 775-8810, www.epi.org; *The End of Welfare? Consequences of Federal Devolution for the Nation.*

U.S. Library of Congress (LOC), Congressional Research Service (CRS), The Library of Congress, 101 Independence Avenue, SE, Washington, DC 20540-7500, (202) 707-5700, www.loc.gov/crsinfo; *Cash and Non-cash Benefits for Persons With Limited Income: Eligibility Rules, Recipient and Expenditure Data.*

GOVERNMENT - EXPENDITURES - STATE AND LOCAL GOVERNMENT

National Education Association (NEA), 1201 Sixteenth Street, NW, Washington, DC 20036-3290, (202) 833-4000, Fax: (202) 822-7974, www.nea.org; *Rankings and Estimates: Rankings of the States 2006 and Estimates of School Statistics 2007.*

U.S. Census Bureau, Governments Division, 4600 Silver Hill Road, Washington DC 20233, (800) 242-2184, www.census.gov/govs/www; *2002 Census of Governments, Government Finances.*

U.S. Department of Justice (DOJ), Bureau of Justice Statistics, 810 Seventh Street, NW, Washington, DC 20531, (202) 307-0765, www.ojp.usdoj.gov/bjs/; *Justice Expenditure and Employment in the United States 2003.*

GOVERNMENT - EXPENDITURES - STATE GOVERNMENT

National Association of State Budget Officers (NASBO), Hall of the States Building - Suite 642, 444 North Capitol Street, NW, Washington, DC 20001-1511, (202) 624-5382, Fax: (202) 624-7745, www.nasbo.org; *Fiscal Survey of the States, Fall 2007* and *State Expenditure Report, Fiscal Year 2006.*

U.S. Census Bureau, Governments Division, 4600 Silver Hill Road, Washington DC 20233, (800) 242-2184, www.census.gov/govs/www; *2002 Census of Governments; 2002 Census of Governments, Government Finances;* and *Federal, State, and Local Governments: State Government Tax Collections (STC).*

GOVERNMENT - FEDERALLY OWNED LAND

General Services Administration (GSA), 1800 F Street, NW, Washington, DC 20405, (202) 708-5082, www.gsa.gov; *Federal Real Property Profile 2004 (FRPP).*

GOVERNMENT - FLOW OF FUNDS

American Enterprise Institute (AEI), 1150 Seventeenth Street, NW, Washington, DC 20036, (202) 862-5800, Fax: (202) 862-7177, www.aei.org; unpublished data.

Board of Governors of the Federal Reserve System, Constitution Avenue, NW, Washington, DC 20551, (202) 452-3000, www.federalreserve.gov; *Flow of Funds Accounts of the United States.*

GOVERNMENT - GROSS DOMESTIC PRODUCT

Bureau of Economic Analysis (BEA), U.S. Department of Commerce (DOC), 1441 L Street NW, Washington, DC 20230, (202) 606-9900, www.bea.gov; *2007 Annual Revision of the National Income and Product Accounts (NIPA)* and *Survey of Current Business (SCB).*

GOVERNMENT - HOSPITALS

American Hospital Association (AHA), One North Franklin, Chicago, IL 60606-3421, (312) 422-3000, www.aha.org; *Hospital Statistics 2008.*

GOVERNMENT - INDUSTRIAL SAFETY

National Safety Council (NSC), 1121 Spring Lake Drive, Itasca, IL 60143-3201, (630) 285-1121, www.nsc.org; *Injury Facts.*

GOVERNMENT - LOCAL GOVERNMENT - CITIES - EMPLOYEES, EARNINGS, AND PAYROLL

U.S. Census Bureau, Governments Division, 4600 Silver Hill Road, Washington DC 20233, (800) 242-2184, www.census.gov/govs/www; *2002 Census of Governments, Public Employment and Payroll.*

GOVERNMENT - LOCAL GOVERNMENT - CITIES - FINANCES

U.S. Census Bureau, Governments Division, 4600 Silver Hill Road, Washington DC 20233, (800) 242-2184, www.census.gov/govs/www; *2002 Census of Governments, Government Finances.*

GOVERNMENT - LOCAL GOVERNMENT - COUNTIES - EMPLOYEES, EARNINGS, AND PAYROLL

U.S. Census Bureau, Governments Division, 4600 Silver Hill Road, Washington DC 20233, (800) 242-2184, www.census.gov/govs/www; *2002 Census of Governments, Public Employment and Payroll.*

GOVERNMENT - LOCAL GOVERNMENT - COUNTIES - FINANCES

U.S. Census Bureau, Governments Division, 4600 Silver Hill Road, Washington DC 20233, (800) 242-2184, www.census.gov/govs/www; *2002 Census of Governments, Government Finances.*

GOVERNMENT - LOCAL GOVERNMENT - EARNINGS

U.S. Census Bureau, 4700 Silver Hill Road, Washington DC 20233-0001, (301) 763-3030, www.census.gov; unpublished data.

U.S. Census Bureau, Governments Division, 4600 Silver Hill Road, Washington DC 20233, (800) 242-2184, www.census.gov/govs/www; *2002 Census of Governments, Public Employment and Payroll.*

GOVERNMENT - LOCAL GOVERNMENT - EMPLOYEES

U.S. Census Bureau, Governments Division, 4600 Silver Hill Road, Washington DC 20233, (800) 242-2184, www.census.gov/govs/www; *2002 Census of Governments, Public Employment and Payroll.*

GOVERNMENT - LOCAL GOVERNMENT - NUMBER, BY TYPE

U.S. Census Bureau, Governments Division, 4600 Silver Hill Road, Washington DC 20233, (800) 242-2184, www.census.gov/govs/www; *2002 Census of Governments, Government Finances* and *2002 Census of Governments, Government Organization.*

GOVERNMENT - LOCAL GOVERNMENT - PAYROLL

U.S. Census Bureau, Governments Division, 4600 Silver Hill Road, Washington DC 20233, (800) 242-2184, www.census.gov/govs/www; *2002 Census of Governments, Public Employment and Payroll.*

GOVERNMENT - LOCAL GOVERNMENT - POPULATION, BY SIZE - GROUP

U.S. Census Bureau, Governments Division, 4600 Silver Hill Road, Washington DC 20233, (800) 242-2184, www.census.gov/govs/www; *2002 Census of Governments, Government Organization.*

GOVERNMENT - NUMBER OF UNITS BY TYPE OF GOVERNMENT

U.S. Census Bureau, Governments Division, 4600 Silver Hill Road, Washington DC 20233, (800) 242-2184, www.census.gov/govs/www; *2002 Census of Governments, Government Organization.*

GOVERNMENT - PAYROLLS

U.S. Census Bureau, 4700 Silver Hill Road, Washington DC 20233-0001, (301) 763-3030, www.census.gov; unpublished data.

U.S. Census Bureau, Governments Division, 4600 Silver Hill Road, Washington DC 20233, (800) 242-2184, www.census.gov/govs/www; *2002 Census of Governments, Public Employment and Payroll.*

U.S. Department of Justice (DOJ), Bureau of Justice Statistics, 810 Seventh Street, NW, Washington, DC 20531, (202) 307-0765, www.ojp.usdoj.gov/bjs/; *Justice Expenditure and Employment in the United States 2003.*

U.S. Library of Congress (LOC), Congressional Research Service (CRS), The Library of Congress, 101 Independence Avenue, SE, Washington, DC 20540-7500, (202) 707-5700, www.loc.gov/crsinfo; *Federal Employees: Pay and Pension Increases Since 1969.*

GOVERNMENT - PURCHASES OF GOODS AND SERVICES

Bureau of Economic Analysis (BEA), U.S. Department of Commerce (DOC), 1441 L Street NW, Washington, DC 20230, (202) 606-9900, www.bea.gov; *2007 Annual Revision of the National Income and Product Accounts (NIPA)* and *Survey of Current Business (SCB).*

GOVERNMENT - ROADS

U.S. Department of Transportation (DOT), Federal Highway Administration (FHA), 1200 New Jersey Avenue, SE, Washington, DC 20590, (202) 366-0660, www.fhwa.dot.gov; *Highway Statistics 2006.*

GOVERNMENT - SALARIES AND WAGES - FEDERAL

U.S. Library of Congress (LOC), Congressional Research Service (CRS), The Library of Congress, 101 Independence Avenue, SE, Washington, DC 20540-7500, (202) 707-5700, www.loc.gov/crsinfo; *Federal Employees: Pay and Pension Increases Since 1969.*

United States Office of Personnel Management (OMB), 1900 E Street, NW, Washington, DC 20415-1000, (202) 606-1800, www.opm.gov; *Pay Structure of the Federal Civil Service.*

GOVERNMENT - SALARIES AND WAGES - NATIONAL INCOME COMPONENT

Bureau of Economic Analysis (BEA), U.S. Department of Commerce (DOC), 1441 L Street NW, Washington, DC 20230, (202) 606-9900, www.bea.gov; *2007 Annual Revision of the National Income and Product Accounts (NIPA)* and *Survey of Current Business (SCB).*

GOVERNMENT - SALARIES AND WAGES - STATE AND LOCAL GOVERNMENT EMPLOYEES

U.S. Census Bureau, Governments Division, 4600 Silver Hill Road, Washington DC 20233, (800) 242-2184, www.census.gov/govs/www; *2002 Census of Governments, Public Employment and Payroll.*

GOVERNMENT - SECURITIES

Board of Governors of the Federal Reserve System, Constitution Avenue, NW, Washington, DC 20551, (202) 452-3000, www.federalreserve.gov; *Federal Reserve Bulletin* and *Statistical Digest.*

U.S. Department of the Treasury (DOT), 1500 Pennsylvania Avenue, NW, Washington, DC 20220, (202) 622-2000, Fax: (202) 622-6415, www.ustreas.gov; *Treasury Bulletin.*

GOVERNMENT - STATE AND LOCAL GOVERNMENTS - BENEFITS

U.S. Bureau of Labor Statistics (BLS), Postal Square Building, 2 Massachusetts Avenue, NE, Washington, DC 20212-0001, (202) 691-5200, Fax: (202) 691-6325, www.bls.gov; *Employer Costs for Employee Compensation* and unpublished data.

GOVERNMENT - STATE AND LOCAL GOVERNMENTS - BOND RATINGS

Moody's Investors Service, 99 Church Street, New York, NY 10007, (212) 553-0300, www.moodys.com; unpublished data.

Standard and Poor's Corporation, 55 Water Street, New York, NY 10041, (212) 438-1000, www.standardandpoors.com; unpublished data.

GOVERNMENT - STATE AND LOCAL GOVERNMENTS - EMPLOYEES

U.S. Census Bureau, Governments Division, 4600 Silver Hill Road, Washington DC 20233, (800) 242-2184, www.census.gov/govs/www; *2002 Census of Governments, Public Employment and Payroll.*

U.S. Department of Justice (DOJ), Bureau of Justice Statistics, 810 Seventh Street, NW, Washington, DC 20531, (202) 307-0765, www.ojp.usdoj.gov/bjs/; *Justice Expenditure and Employment in the United States 2003.*

GOVERNMENT - STATE AND LOCAL GOVERNMENTS - FEDERAL AID

Executive Office of the President, Council of Economic Advisors, The White House, 1600 Pennsylvania Avenue NW, Washington, DC 20500, (202) 456-1414, www.whitehouse.gov/cea; *2007 Economic Report of the President.*

U.S. Census Bureau, Governments Division, 4600 Silver Hill Road, Washington DC 20233, (800) 242-2184, www.census.gov/govs/www; *Federal Aid to States for Fiscal Year 2004.*

GOVERNMENT - STATE AND LOCAL GOVERNMENTS - FINANCES

Bureau of Economic Analysis (BEA), U.S. Department of Commerce (DOC), 1441 L Street NW, Washington, DC 20230, (202) 606-9900, www.bea.gov; *2007 Annual Revision of the National Income and Product Accounts (NIPA)* and *Survey of Current Business (SCB).*

U.S. Census Bureau, Governments Division, 4600 Silver Hill Road, Washington DC 20233, (800) 242-2184, www.census.gov/govs/www; *2002 Census of Governments* and *2002 Census of Governments, Government Finances.*

U.S. Library of Congress (LOC), Congressional Research Service (CRS), The Library of Congress, 101 Independence Avenue, SE, Washington, DC 20540-7500, (202) 707-5700, www.loc.gov/crsinfo; *FY2006 Appropriations for State and Local Homeland Security.*

GOVERNMENT - STATE AND LOCAL GOVERNMENTS - PAYROLL

U.S. Census Bureau, Governments Division, 4600 Silver Hill Road, Washington DC 20233, (800) 242-2184, www.census.gov/govs/www; *2002 Census of Governments, Government Finances* and *2002 Census of Governments, Public Employment and Payroll.*

U.S. Department of Justice (DOJ), Bureau of Justice Statistics, 810 Seventh Street, NW, Washington, DC 20531, (202) 307-0765, www.ojp.usdoj.gov/bjs/; *Justice Expenditure and Employment in the United States 2003.*

GOVERNMENT - STRATEGIC AND CRITICAL MATERIALS - SUMMARY

U.S. Department of Defense (DOD), Defense Logistics Agency (DLA), 8725 John J. Kingman Road, Fort Belvoir, VA 22060, (703) 767-6666, www.dla.mil; *Stockpile Report to the Congress 2002.*

GOVERNMENT INSURANCE

See SOCIAL INSURANCE

GOVERNMENT LAND

See PUBLIC LANDS

GOVERNMENT NATIONAL MORTGAGE ASSOCIATION LOANS

Board of Governors of the Federal Reserve System, Constitution Avenue, NW, Washington, DC 20551, (202) 452-3000, www.federalreserve.gov; *Federal Reserve Bulletin.*

GOVERNORS - NUMBER AND VOTE CAST

Congressional Quarterly, Inc., 1255 22nd Street, NW, Washington, DC 20037, (202) 419-8500, www.cq.com; *America Votes 27: Election Returns by State, 2005-2006; Statistical History of the American Electorate;* and unpublished data.

National Governors Association (NGA), Hall of the States, Suite 267, 444 North Capitol Street, NW, Washington, DC 20001-1512, (202) 624-5300, Fax: (202) 624-5313, www.nga.org; *Governors Database.*

GRADUATE STUDENTS

Council of Graduate Schools, One Dupont Circle NW, Suite 230, Washington, DC 20036, (202) 223-3791, www.cgsnet.org; *Findings from the 2007 CGS International Graduate Admissions Survey: Phase I - Applications; Findings from the 2007 CGS International Graduate Admissions Survey: Phase II - Final Applications and Initial Offers of Acceptance; Findings from the 2007 CGS International Graduate Amissions Survey: Phase III - Admissions and Enrollment; Graduate Enrollment and Degrees Report;* and *Graduate Enrollment and Degrees: 1996 to 2006.*

Institute of International Education (IIE), 809 United Nations Plaza, New York, NY 10017-3580, (212) 883-8200, Fax: (212) 984-5452, www.iie.org; *International Student Enrollment Survey: Survey Report Fall 2007* and *Open Doors 1948-2004: CD-ROM.*

GRADUATES - COLLEGE

National Center for Education Statistics (NCES), 1990 K Street, NW, Washington, DC 20006, (202) 502-7300, http://nces.ed.gov; *Digest of Education Statistics 2007* and *Projections of Education Statistics to 2016.*

GRADUATES - HIGH SCHOOL

National Center for Education Statistics (NCES), 1990 K Street, NW, Washington, DC 20006, (202) 502-7300, http://nces.ed.gov; *Digest of Education Statistics 2007* and *Projections of Education Statistics to 2016.*

U.S. Census Bureau, 4700 Silver Hill Road, Washington DC 20233-0001, (301) 763-3030, www.census.gov; unpublished data.

U.S. Census Bureau, Population Division, 4700 Silver Hill Road, Washington DC 20233-0001, (301) 763-3030, www.census.gov/population/www/; *Current Population Reports.*

GRAIN - CAR LOADINGS

Association of American Railroads (AAR), 50 F Street, NW, Washington, DC 20001-1564, (202) 639-2100, www.aar.org; *Weekly Railroad Traffic.*

GRAIN - CONSUMPTION

Economic Research Service (ERS), U.S. Department of Agriculture (USDA), 1800 M Street, NW, Washington, DC 20036-5831, (202) 694-5050, Fax: (202) 694-5689, www.ers.usda.gov; *Agricultural Outlook* and *Food CPI, Prices, and Expenditures.*

GRAIN - FARM MARKETINGS - SALES

Economic Research Service (ERS), U.S. Department of Agriculture (USDA), 1800 M Street, NW, Washington, DC 20036-5831, (202) 694-5050, Fax: (202) 694-5689, www.ers.usda.gov; *Agricultural Income and Finance Outlook* and *Farm Income: Data Files.*

GRAIN - INTERNATIONAL TRADE

Economic Research Service (ERS), U.S. Department of Agriculture (USDA), 1800 M Street, NW, Washington, DC 20036-5831, (202) 694-5050, Fax: (202) 694-5689, www.ers.usda.gov; *Agricultural Statistics* and *Foreign Agricultural Trade of the United States (FATUS).*

International Grains Council (IGC), 1 Canada Square, Canary Wharf, London E14 5AE, England, www.igc.org.uk; *World Grain Statistics 2005.*

National Agricultural Statistics Service (NASS), U.S. Department of Agriculture (USDA), 1400 Independence Avenue, SW, Washington, DC 20250, (800) 727-9540, Fax: (202) 690-2090, www.nass.usda.gov; *2006 Agricultural Statistics.*

GRAIN - IRON (DIETARY) SOURCE

Center for Nutrition Policy and Promotion (CNPP), U.S. Department of Agriculture (USDA), 3101 Park Center Drive, 10th Floor, Alexandria, VA 22302-1594, (703) 305-7600, Fax: (703) 305-3300, www.usda.gov/cnpp; *Nutrient Content of the U.S. Food Supply Summary Report 2005.*

GRAIN - PRICES

National Agricultural Statistics Service (NASS), U.S. Department of Agriculture (USDA), 1400 Independence Avenue, SW, Washington, DC 20250, (800) 727-9540, Fax: (202) 690-2090, www.nass.usda.gov; *Agricultural Prices.*

GRAIN - PRODUCTION

Economic Research Service (ERS), U.S. Department of Agriculture (USDA), 1800 M Street, NW, Washington, DC 20036-5831, (202) 694-5050, Fax: (202) 694-5689, www.ers.usda.gov; *Agricultural Outlook.*

National Agricultural Statistics Service (NASS), U.S. Department of Agriculture (USDA), 1400 Independence Avenue, SW, Washington, DC 20250, (800) 727-9540, Fax: (202) 690-2090, www.nass.usda.gov; *Grain Stocks* and *Rice Stocks.*

GRAIN - SHIPMENTS

Association of American Railroads (AAR), 50 F Street, NW, Washington, DC 20001-1564, (202) 639-2100, www.aar.org; *Rail Transportation of Grain.*

GRANDPARENTS

Population Reference Bureau, 1875 Connecticut Avenue, NW, Suite 520, Washington, DC, 20009-5728, (800) 877-9881, Fax: (202) 328-3937, www.prb.org; *The American People Series.*

U.S. Census Bureau, Population Division, 4700 Silver Hill Road, Washington DC 20233-0001, (301) 763-3030, www.census.gov/population/www/; *Census 2000 Profiles of General Demographic Characteristics.*

GRANTS - BY FOUNDATIONS

The Foundation Center, 79 Fifth Avenue, New York, NY 10003-3076, (212) 620-4230, Fax: (212) 807-3677, www.fdncenter.org; *FC Stats - Grantmaker; FC Stats - Grants; Foundation Growth and Giving Estimates: Current Outlook (2008 Edition);* and *Top Funders: Top 100 U.S. Foundations by Asset Size.*

GRAPEFRUIT

Economic Research Service (ERS), U.S. Department of Agriculture (USDA), 1800 M Street, NW, Washington, DC 20036-5831, (202) 694-5050, Fax: (202) 694-5689, www.ers.usda.gov; *Agricultural Income and Finance Outlook; Agricultural Outlook; Farm Income: Data Files;* and *Food CPI, Prices, and Expenditures.*

National Agricultural Statistics Service (NASS), U.S. Department of Agriculture (USDA), 1400 Independence Avenue, SW, Washington, DC 20250, (800) 727-9540, Fax: (202) 690-2090, www.nass.usda.gov; *Citrus Fruits.*

GRAPES

Economic Research Service (ERS), U.S. Department of Agriculture (USDA), 1800 M Street, NW, Washington, DC 20036-5831, (202) 694-5050, Fax: (202) 694-5689, www.ers.usda.gov; *Agricultural Income and Finance Outlook; Agricultural Outlook; Farm Income: Data Files;* and *Food CPI, Prices, and Expenditures.*

National Agricultural Statistics Service (NASS), U.S. Department of Agriculture (USDA), 1400 Independence Avenue, SW, Washington, DC 20250, (800) 727-9540, Fax: (202) 690-2090, www.nass.usda.gov; *Noncitrus Fruits and Nuts: Final Estimates 1998-2003.*

GRAPHITE

U.S. Department of the Interior (DOI), U.S. Geological Survey (USGS), Office of Minerals Information, 12201 Sunrise Valley Drive, Reston, VA 20192, Mr. Kenneth A. Beckman, (703) 648-4916, Fax: (703) 648-4995, http://minerals.usgs.gov/minerals; *Mineral Commodity Summaries.*

GRAZING - NATIONAL FORESTS - LIVESTOCK AND RECEIPTS

USDA Forest Service, 1400 Independence Ave, SW, Washington, DC 20250-0003, (202) 205-8333, www.fs.fed.us; *Land Areas of the National Forest System 2006.*

GRAZING - PUBLIC LANDS - LEASES

General Services Administration (GSA), 1800 F Street, NW, Washington, DC 20405, (202) 708-5082, www.gsa.gov; *Federal Real Property Profile 2004 (FRPP).*

GREAT BRITAIN

See UNITED KINGDOM

GREAT LAKES - AREA

U.S. Census Bureau, 4700 Silver Hill Road, Washington DC 20233-0001, (301) 763-3030, www.census.gov; TIGER Map Service (web app).

GREAT LAKES - COMMERCE

Waterborne Commerce Statistics Center (WCSC), Navigation Data Center (NDC), U.S. Army Corps of Engineers, PO Box 61280, New Orleans, LA 70161-1280, (504) 862-1426, www.iwr.usace.army.mil/ndc/wcsc/wcsc.htm; *2006 Waterborne Commerce of the United States (WCUS).*

GREAT LAKES - WATER QUALITY

U.S. Environmental Protection Agency (EPA), Ariel Rios Building, 1200 Pennsylvania Avenue, NW, Washington, DC 20460, (202) 272-0167, www.epa.gov; National Water Quality Standards Database (WQSDB).

GREECE - NATIONAL STATISTICAL OFFICE

National Statistical Service of Greece (NSSG), 14-16 Lycourgou Street, 10166, Athens, Greece, www.statistics.gr; National Data Center.

GREECE - PRIMARY STATISTICS SOURCES

Eurostat, Batiment Jean Monnet, Rue Alcide de Gasperi, L-2920 Luxembourg, http://epp.eurostat.ec.europa.eu; *Euro-Mediterranean Statistics 2007* and *Pocketbook on Candidate and Potential Candidate Countries.*

National Statistical Service of Greece (NSSG), 14-16 Lycourgou Street, 10166, Athens, Greece, www.statistics.gr; *Monthly Statistical Bulletin* and *Statistical Yearbook of Greece 2004.*

GREECE - ABORTION

European Union, Delegation of the European Commission to the United States, 2300 M Street, NW, Washington, DC 20037, (202) 862-9500, Fax: (202) 429-1766, www.eurunion.org; *First Demographic Estimates for 2006.*

United Nations Statistics Division, New York, NY 10017, (800) 253-9646, Fax: (212) 963-4116, http://unstats.un.org; *Demographic Yearbook* and *Trends in Europe and North America: The Statistical Yearbook of the ECE 2005.*

GREECE - AGRICULTURAL MACHINERY

European Union, Delegation of the European Commission to the United States, 2300 M Street, NW, Washington, DC 20037, (202) 862-9500, Fax: (202) 429-1766, www.eurunion.org; *Statistical Overview of Transport in the European Union (Data 1970-2001).*

United Nations Statistics Division, New York, NY 10017, (800) 253-9646, Fax: (212) 963-4116, http://unstats.un.org; *Statistical Yearbook.*

GREECE - AGRICULTURE

Economist Intelligence Unit, 111 West 57th Street, New York, NY 10019, (212) 554-0600, Fax: (212) 586-1181, www.eiu.com; *Greece Country Report.*

Euromonitor International, Inc., 224 S. Michigan Avenue, Suite 1500, Chicago, IL 60604, (312) 922-1115, Fax: (312) 922-1157, www.euromonitor.com; *World Marketing Data and Statistics.*

European Union, Delegation of the European Commission to the United States, 2300 M Street, NW, Washington, DC 20037, (202) 862-9500, Fax: (202) 429-1766, www.eurunion.org; *Agricultural Statistics: Data 1995-2005; European Union Labour Force Survey; Eurostatistics: Data for Short-Term Economic Analysis (2007 edition);* and *Regions - Statistical Yearbook 2006.*

Eurostat, Batiment Jean Monnet, Rue Alcide de Gasperi, L-2920 Luxembourg, http://epp.eurostat.ec.europa.eu; *EU Agricultural Prices in 2007* and *Eurostat Yearbook 2006-2007.*

M.E. Sharpe, 80 Business Park Drive, Armonk, NY 10504, (800) 541-6563, Fax: (914) 273-2106, www.mesharpe.com; *The Illustrated Book of World Rankings.*

Organisation for Economic Cooperation and Development (OECD), 2 rue Andre Pascal, F-75775 Paris Cedex 16, France, (Telephone in U.S. (202) 785-6323), (Fax in U.S. (202) 785-0350), www.oecd.org; *2005 OECD Agricultural Outlook Tables, 1970-2014; OECD Agricultural Outlook: 2007-2016; OECD Economic Survey - Greece 2007;* and STructural ANalysis (STAN) database.

Palgrave Macmillan Ltd., Houndmills, Basingstoke, Hampshire, RG21 6XS, England, (Telephone in U.S. (888) 330-8477), (Fax in U.S. (800) 672-2054), www.palgrave.com; *The Statesman's Yearbook 2008.*

Taylor and Francis Group, An Informa Business, 2 Park Square, Milton Park, Abingdon, Oxford OX14 4RN, United Kingdom, (Dial from U.S. (212) 216-7800), (Fax from U.S. (212) 564-7854), www.tandf.co.uk; *The Europa World Year Book.*

United Nations Conference on Trade and Development (UNCTAD), DC2-1120, United Nations, New York, NY 10017, (212) 963-0027, www.unctad.org; *UNCTAD Commodity Yearbook.*

United Nations Food and Agricultural Organization (FAO), Viale delle Terme di Caracalla, 00100 Rome, Italy, (Dial from U.S. (202) 653-2400), (Fax from U.S. (202) 653 5760), www.fao.org; AQUASTAT; *FAO Production Yearbook 2002; FAO Trade Yearbook;* and *The State of Food and Agriculture (SOFA) 2006.*

United Nations Statistics Division, New York, NY 10017, (800) 253-9646, Fax: (212) 963-4116, http://unstats.un.org; *Statistical Yearbook.*

The World Bank, 1818 H Street, NW, Washington, DC 20433, (202) 473-1000, Fax: (202) 477-6391, www.worldbank.org; *Greece* and *World Development Indicators (WDI) 2008.*

GREECE - AIRLINES

European Union, Delegation of the European Commission to the United States, 2300 M Street, NW, Washington, DC 20037, (202) 862-9500, Fax: (202) 429-1766, www.eurunion.org; *Regions - Statistical Yearbook 2006* and *Statistical Overview of Transport in the European Union (Data 1970-2001).*

Eurostat, Batiment Jean Monnet, Rue Alcide de Gasperi, L-2920 Luxembourg, http://epp.eurostat.ec.europa.eu; *Eurostat Yearbook 2006-2007* and *Regional Passenger and Freight Air Transport in Europe in 2006.*

International Civil Aviation Organization (ICAO), External Relations and Public Information Office (EPO), 999 University Street, Montreal, Quebec H3C 5H7, Canada, (Dial from U.S. (514) 954-8219), (Fax from U.S. (514) 954-6077), www.icao.int; *Civil Aviation Statistics of the World.*

M.E. Sharpe, 80 Business Park Drive, Armonk, NY 10504, (800) 541-6563, Fax: (914) 273-2106, www.mesharpe.com; *The Illustrated Book of World Rankings.*

Organisation for Economic Cooperation and Development (OECD), 2 rue Andre Pascal, F-75775 Paris Cedex 16, France, (Telephone in U.S. (202) 785-6323), (Fax in U.S. (202) 785-0350), www.oecd.org; *Household, Tourism, Travel: Trends, Environmental Impacts and Policy Responses.*

Palgrave Macmillan Ltd., Houndmills, Basingstoke, Hampshire, RG21 6XS, England, (Telephone in U.S. (888) 330-8477), (Fax in U.S. (800) 672-2054), www.palgrave.com; *The Statesman's Yearbook 2008.*

Taylor and Francis Group, An Informa Business, 2 Park Square, Milton Park, Abingdon, Oxford OX14 4RN, United Kingdom, (Dial from U.S. (212) 216-7800), (Fax from U.S. (212) 564-7854), www.tandf.co.uk; *The Europa World Year Book.*

United Nations Statistics Division, New York, NY 10017, (800) 253-9646, Fax: (212) 963-4116, http://unstats.un.org; *Statistical Yearbook.*

GREECE - AIRPORTS

Central Intelligence Agency, Office of Public Affairs, Washington, DC 20505, (703) 482-0623, Fax: (703) 482-1739, www.cia.gov; *The World Factbook.*

GREECE - ALMOND PRODUCTION

See GREECE - CROPS

GREECE - ALUMINUM PRODUCTION

See GREECE - MINERAL INDUSTRIES

GREECE - ANIMAL FEEDING

Organisation for Economic Cooperation and Development (OECD), 2 rue Andre Pascal, F-75775 Paris Cedex 16, France, (Telephone in U.S. (202) 785-6323), (Fax in U.S. (202) 785-0350), www.oecd.org; *International Trade by Commodity Statistics (ITCS).*

GREECE - APPLE PRODUCTION

See GREECE - CROPS

GREECE - ARMED FORCES

Central Intelligence Agency, Office of Public Affairs, Washington, DC 20505, (703) 482-0623, Fax: (703) 482-1739, www.cia.gov; *The World Factbook.*

Euromonitor International, Inc., 224 S. Michigan Avenue, Suite 1500, Chicago, IL 60604, (312) 922-1115, Fax: (312) 922-1157, www.euromonitor.com; *World Marketing Data and Statistics.*

European Union, Delegation of the European Commission to the United States, 2300 M Street, NW, Washington, DC 20037, (202) 862-9500, Fax: (202) 429-1766, www.eurunion.org; *RD Expenditure in Europe (2006 edition).*

International Institute for Strategic Studies (IISS), Arundel House, 13-15 Arundel Street, Temple Place, London WC2R 3DX, England, www.iiss.org; *The Military Balance 2007.*

International Monetary Fund (IMF), 700 Nineteenth Street, NW, Washington, DC 20431, (202) 623-7000, Fax: (202) 623-4661, www.imf.org; *Government Finance Statistics Yearbook (2008 Edition).*

Palgrave Macmillan Ltd., Houndmills, Basingstoke, Hampshire, RG21 6XS, England, (Telephone in U.S. (888) 330-8477), (Fax in U.S. (800) 672-2054), www.palgrave.com; *The Statesman's Yearbook 2008.*

U.S. Department of State (DOS), 2201 C Street NW, Washington, DC 20520, (202) 647-4000, www.state.gov; *World Military Expenditures and Arms Transfers (WMEAT).*

United Nations Statistics Division, New York, NY 10017, (800) 253-9646, Fax: (212) 963-4116, http://unstats.un.org; *Human Development Report 2006.*

GREECE - ARTICHOKE PRODUCTION

See GREECE - CROPS

GREECE - AUTOMOBILE INDUSTRY AND TRADE

European Union, Delegation of the European Commission to the United States, 2300 M Street, NW, Washington, DC 20037, (202) 862-9500, Fax: (202) 429-1766, www.eurunion.org; *Eurostatistics: Data for Short-Term Economic Analysis (2007 edition).*

Eurostat, Batiment Jean Monnet, Rue Alcide de Gasperi, L-2920 Luxembourg, http://epp.eurostat.ec.europa.eu; *Eurostat Yearbook 2006-2007.*

Organisation for Economic Cooperation and Development (OECD), 2 rue Andre Pascal, F-75775 Paris Cedex 16, France, (Telephone in U.S. (202) 785-6323), (Fax in U.S. (202) 785-0350), www.oecd.org; *International Trade by Commodity Statistics (ITCS).*

United Nations Statistics Division, New York, NY 10017, (800) 253-9646, Fax: (212) 963-4116, http://unstats.un.org; *Statistical Yearbook.*

GREECE - BALANCE OF PAYMENTS

European Union, Delegation of the European Commission to the United States, 2300 M Street, NW, Washington, DC 20037, (202) 862-9500, Fax: (202) 429-1766, www.eurunion.org; *Eurostatistics: Data for Short-Term Economic Analysis (2007 edition).*

Eurostat, Batiment Jean Monnet, Rue Alcide de Gasperi, L-2920 Luxembourg, http://epp.eurostat.ec.europa.eu; *Eurostat Yearbook 2006-2007.*

International Monetary Fund (IMF), 700 Nineteenth Street, NW, Washington, DC 20431, (202) 623-7000, Fax: (202) 623-4661, www.imf.org; *Balance of Payments Statistics Newsletter; Balance of Payments Statistics Yearbook 2007;* and *International Financial Statistics Yearbook 2007.*

Organisation for Economic Cooperation and Development (OECD), 2 rue Andre Pascal, F-75775 Paris Cedex 16, France, (Telephone in U.S. (202) 785-6323), (Fax in U.S. (202) 785-0350), www.oecd.org; *Geographical Distribution of Financial Flows to Aid Recipients 2002-2006; OECD Economic Outlook 2008; OECD Economic Survey - Greece 2007;* and *OECD Main Economic Indicators (MEI).*

Platts, 2 Penn Plaza, 25th Floor, New York, NY 10121-2298, (212) 904-3070, www.platts.com; *Energy Economist.*

Taylor and Francis Group, An Informa Business, 2 Park Square, Milton Park, Abingdon, Oxford OX14 4RN, United Kingdom, (Dial from U.S. (212) 216-7800), (Fax from U.S. (212) 564-7854), www.tandf.co.uk; *The Europa World Year Book.*

United Nations Conference on Trade and Development (UNCTAD), DC2-1120, United Nations, New York, NY 10017, (212) 963-0027, www.unctad.org; *Handbook of Statistics 2005.*

United Nations Statistics Division, New York, NY 10017, (800) 253-9646, Fax: (212) 963-4116, http://unstats.un.org; *Energy Statistics Yearbook 2003.*

The World Bank, 1818 H Street, NW, Washington, DC 20433, (202) 473-1000, Fax: (202) 477-6391, www.worldbank.org; *Greece; World Development Indicators (WDI) 2008;* and *World Development Report 2008.*

GREECE - BANANAS

See GREECE - CROPS

GREECE - BANKS AND BANKING

Euromonitor International, Inc., 224 S. Michigan Avenue, Suite 1500, Chicago, IL 60604, (312) 922-1115, Fax: (312) 922-1157, www.euromonitor.com; *World Marketing Data and Statistics.*

European Union, Delegation of the European Commission to the United States, 2300 M Street, NW, Washington, DC 20037, (202) 862-9500, Fax: (202) 429-1766, www.eurunion.org; *The EU Economy, 2007 Review: Moving Europe's Productivity Frontier* and *Eurostatistics: Data for Short-Term Economic Analysis (2007 edition).*

Eurostat, Batiment Jean Monnet, Rue Alcide de Gasperi, L-2920 Luxembourg, http://epp.eurostat.ec.europa.eu; *Eurostat Yearbook 2006-2007.*

International Monetary Fund (IMF), 700 Nineteenth Street, NW, Washington, DC 20431, (202) 623-7000, Fax: (202) 623-4661, www.imf.org; *Government Finance Statistics Yearbook (2008 Edition)* and *International Financial Statistics Yearbook 2007.*

M.E. Sharpe, 80 Business Park Drive, Armonk, NY 10504, (800) 541-6563, Fax: (914) 273-2106, www.mesharpe.com; *The Illustrated Book of World Rankings.*

Organisation for Economic Cooperation and Development (OECD), 2 rue Andre Pascal, F-75775 Paris Cedex 16, France, (Telephone in U.S. (202) 785-6323), (Fax in U.S. (202) 785-0350), www.oecd.org; *Financial Market Trends: OECD Periodical; OECD Economic Outlook 2008;* and *OECD Economic Survey - Greece 2007.*

Palgrave Macmillan Ltd., Houndmills, Basingstoke, Hampshire, RG21 6XS, England, (Telephone in U.S. (888) 330-8477), (Fax in U.S. (800) 672-2054), www.palgrave.com; *The Statesman's Yearbook 2008.*

Taylor and Francis Group, An Informa Business, 2 Park Square, Milton Park, Abingdon, Oxford OX14 4RN, United Kingdom, (Dial from U.S. (212) 216-7800), (Fax from U.S. (212) 564-7854), www.tandf.co.uk; *The Europa World Year Book.*

United Nations Statistics Division, New York, NY 10017, (800) 253-9646, Fax: (212) 963-4116, http://unstats.un.org; *Statistical Yearbook.*

GREECE - BARLEY PRODUCTION

See GREECE - CROPS

GREECE - BEVERAGE INDUSTRY

Eurostat, Batiment Jean Monnet, Rue Alcide de Gasperi, L-2920 Luxembourg, http://epp.eurostat.ec.europa.eu; *Eurostat Yearbook 2006-2007.*

M.E. Sharpe, 80 Business Park Drive, Armonk, NY 10504, (800) 541-6563, Fax: (914) 273-2106, www.mesharpe.com; *The Illustrated Book of World Rankings.*

United Nations Statistics Division, New York, NY 10017, (800) 253-9646, Fax: (212) 963-4116, http://unstats.un.org; *Statistical Yearbook.*

GREECE - BONDS

Eurostat, Batiment Jean Monnet, Rue Alcide de Gasperi, L-2920 Luxembourg, http://epp.eurostat.ec.europa.eu; *Eurostat Yearbook 2006-2007.*

International Monetary Fund (IMF), 700 Nineteenth Street, NW, Washington, DC 20431, (202) 623-7000, Fax: (202) 623-4661, www.imf.org; *Government Finance Statistics Yearbook (2008 Edition).*

Organisation for Economic Cooperation and Development (OECD), 2 rue Andre Pascal, F-75775 Paris Cedex 16, France, (Telephone in U.S. (202) 785-6323), (Fax in U.S. (202) 785-0350), www.oecd.org; *Financial Market Trends: OECD Periodical.*

GREECE - BROADCASTING

Central Intelligence Agency, Office of Public Affairs, Washington, DC 20505, (703) 482-0623, Fax: (703) 482-1739, www.cia.gov; *The World Factbook.*

Euromonitor International, Inc., 224 S. Michigan Avenue, Suite 1500, Chicago, IL 60604, (312) 922-1115, Fax: (312) 922-1157, www.euromonitor.com; *World Marketing Data and Statistics.*

Eurostat, Batiment Jean Monnet, Rue Alcide de Gasperi, L-2920 Luxembourg, http://epp.eurostat.ec.europa.eu; *Eurostat Yearbook 2006-2007.*

M.E. Sharpe, 80 Business Park Drive, Armonk, NY 10504, (800) 541-6563, Fax: (914) 273-2106, www.mesharpe.com; *The Illustrated Book of World Rankings.*

Palgrave Macmillan Ltd., Houndmills, Basingstoke, Hampshire, RG21 6XS, England, (Telephone in U.S. (888) 330-8477), (Fax in U.S. (800) 672-2054), www.palgrave.com; *The Statesman's Yearbook 2008.*

UNESCO Institute for Statistics, C.P. 6128 Succursale Centre-Ville, Montreal, Quebec, H3C 3J7 Canada, (Dial from U.S. (514) 343-6880), (Fax from U.S. (514) 343 6882), www.uis.unesco.org; *Statistical Tables.*

United Nations Statistics Division, New York, NY 10017, (800) 253-9646, Fax: (212) 963-4116, http://unstats.un.org; *Trends in Europe and North America: The Statistical Yearbook of the ECE 2005.*

WRTH Publications Limited, PO Box 290, Oxford OX2 7FT, UK, www.wrth.com; *World Radio TV Handbook 2007.*

GREECE - BUDGET

Central Intelligence Agency, Office of Public Affairs, Washington, DC 20505, (703) 482-0623, Fax: (703) 482-1739, www.cia.gov; *The World Factbook.*

Eurostat, Batiment Jean Monnet, Rue Alcide de Gasperi, L-2920 Luxembourg, http://epp.eurostat.ec.europa.eu; *Government Budgets.*

GREECE - BUSINESS

Eurostat, Batiment Jean Monnet, Rue Alcide de Gasperi, L-2920 Luxembourg, http://epp.eurostat.ec.europa.eu; *Eurostat Yearbook 2006-2007.*

United Nations Statistics Division, New York, NY 10017, (800) 253-9646, Fax: (212) 963-4116, http://unstats.un.org; *Statistical Yearbook.*

GREECE - CADMIUM PRODUCTION

See GREECE - MINERAL INDUSTRIES

GREECE - CAPITAL INVESTMENTS

Organisation for Economic Cooperation and Development (OECD), 2 rue Andre Pascal, F-75775 Paris Cedex 16, France, (Telephone in U.S. (202) 785-6323), (Fax in U.S. (202) 785-0350), www.oecd.org; *Financial Market Trends: OECD Periodical* and *OECD Economic Outlook 2008.*

GREECE - CAPITAL LEVY

International Monetary Fund (IMF), 700 Nineteenth Street, NW, Washington, DC 20431, (202) 623-7000, Fax: (202) 623-4661, www.imf.org; *Government Finance Statistics Yearbook (2008 Edition).*

Organisation for Economic Cooperation and Development (OECD), 2 rue Andre Pascal, F-75775 Paris Cedex 16, France, (Telephone in U.S. (202) 785-6323), (Fax in U.S. (202) 785-0350), www.oecd.org; *Financial Market Trends: OECD Periodical* and *OECD Economic Outlook 2008.*

GREECE - CATTLE

See GREECE - LIVESTOCK

GREECE - CHESTNUT PRODUCTION

See GREECE - CROPS

GREECE - CHICK PEA PRODUCTION

See GREECE - CROPS

GREECE - CHICKENS

See GREECE - LIVESTOCK

GREECE - CHILDBIRTH - STATISTICS

Central Intelligence Agency, Office of Public Affairs, Washington, DC 20505, (703) 482-0623, Fax: (703) 482-1739, www.cia.gov; *The World Factbook.*

Euromonitor International, Inc., 224 S. Michigan Avenue, Suite 1500, Chicago, IL 60604, (312) 922-1115, Fax: (312) 922-1157, www.euromonitor.com; *The World Economic Factbook 2008.*

European Union, Delegation of the European Commission to the United States, 2300 M Street, NW, Washington, DC 20037, (202) 862-9500, Fax: (202) 429-1766, www.eurunion.org; *First Demographic Estimates for 2006.*

Eurostat, Batiment Jean Monnet, Rue Alcide de Gasperi, L-2920 Luxembourg, http://epp.eurostat.ec.europa.eu; *Eurostat Yearbook 2006-2007.*

M.E. Sharpe, 80 Business Park Drive, Armonk, NY 10504, (800) 541-6563, Fax: (914) 273-2106, www.mesharpe.com; *The Illustrated Book of World Rankings.*

Palgrave Macmillan Ltd., Houndmills, Basingstoke, Hampshire, RG21 6XS, England, (Telephone in U.S. (888) 330-8477), (Fax in U.S. (800) 672-2054), www.palgrave.com; *The Statesman's Yearbook 2008.*

Taylor and Francis Group, An Informa Business, 2 Park Square, Milton Park, Abingdon, Oxford OX14 4RN, United Kingdom, (Dial from U.S. (212) 216-7800), (Fax from U.S. (212) 564-7854), www.tandf.co.uk; *The Europa World Year Book.*

United Nations Statistics Division, New York, NY 10017, (800) 253-9646, Fax: (212) 963-4116, http://unstats.un.org; *Demographic Yearbook* and *Statistical Yearbook.*

The World Bank, 1818 H Street, NW, Washington, DC 20433, (202) 473-1000, Fax: (202) 477-6391, www.worldbank.org; *World Development Indicators (WDI) 2008.*

World Health Organization (WHO), Avenue Appia 20, 1211 Geneve 27, Switzerland, (Telephone in U.S. (212) 331-9081), www.who.int; *World Health Report 2006.*

GREECE - CLIMATE

M.E. Sharpe, 80 Business Park Drive, Armonk, NY 10504, (800) 541-6563, Fax: (914) 273-2106, www.mesharpe.com; *The Illustrated Book of World Rankings.*

Palgrave Macmillan Ltd., Houndmills, Basingstoke, Hampshire, RG21 6XS, England, (Telephone in U.S. (888) 330-8477), (Fax in U.S. (800) 672-2054), www.palgrave.com; *The Statesman's Yearbook 2008.*

GREECE - CLOTHING EXPORTS AND IMPORTS

See GREECE - TEXTILE INDUSTRY

GREECE - COAL PRODUCTION

See GREECE - MINERAL INDUSTRIES

GREECE - COBALT PRODUCTION

See GREECE - MINERAL INDUSTRIES

GREECE - COCOA PRODUCTION

See GREECE - CROPS

GREECE - COFFEE

See GREECE - CROPS

GREECE - COMMERCE

Palgrave Macmillan Ltd., Houndmills, Basingstoke, Hampshire, RG21 6XS, England, (Telephone in U.S. (888) 330-8477), (Fax in U.S. (800) 672-2054), www.palgrave.com; *The Statesman's Yearbook 2008.*

GREECE - COMMODITY EXCHANGES

Commodity Research Bureau, 330 South Wells Street, Suite 612, Chicago, IL 60606-7110, (800) 621-5271, Fax: (312) 939-4135, www.crbtrader.com; *2006 CRB Commodity Yearbook and CD.*

International Monetary Fund (IMF), 700 Nineteenth Street, NW, Washington, DC 20431, (202) 623-7000, Fax: (202) 623-4661, www.imf.org; *IMF Primary Commodity Prices.*

United Nations Food and Agricultural Organization (FAO), Viale delle Terme di Caracalla, 00100 Rome, Italy, (Dial from U.S. (202) 653-2400), (Fax from U.S. (202) 653 5760), www.fao.org; *The State of Food and Agriculture (SOFA) 2006.*

GREECE - COMMUNICATION AND TRAFFIC

European Union, Delegation of the European Commission to the United States, 2300 M Street, NW, Washington, DC 20037, (202) 862-9500, Fax: (202) 429-1766, www.eurunion.org; *Statistical Overview of Transport in the European Union (Data 1970-2001).*

United Nations Statistics Division, New York, NY 10017, (800) 253-9646, Fax: (212) 963-4116, http://unstats.un.org; *Statistical Yearbook.*

GREECE - CONSTRUCTION INDUSTRY

European Union, Delegation of the European Commission to the United States, 2300 M Street, NW, Washington, DC 20037, (202) 862-9500, Fax: (202) 429-1766, www.eurunion.org; *European Union Labour Force Survey.*

Eurostat, Batiment Jean Monnet, Rue Alcide de Gasperi, L-2920 Luxembourg, http://epp.eurostat.ec.europa.eu; *Eurostat Yearbook 2006-2007.*

M.E. Sharpe, 80 Business Park Drive, Armonk, NY 10504, (800) 541-6563, Fax: (914) 273-2106, www.mesharpe.com; *The Illustrated Book of World Rankings.*

Organisation for Economic Cooperation and Development (OECD), 2 rue Andre Pascal, F-75775 Paris Cedex 16, France, (Telephone in U.S. (202) 785-6323), (Fax in U.S. (202) 785-0350), www.oecd.org; *Iron and Steel Industry in 2004 (2006 Edition); OECD Economic Survey - Greece 2007; OECD Main Economic Indicators (MEI);* and STructural ANalysis (STAN) database.

Palgrave Macmillan Ltd., Houndmills, Basingstoke, Hampshire, RG21 6XS, England, (Telephone in U.S. (888) 330-8477), (Fax in U.S. (800) 672-2054), www.palgrave.com; *The Statesman's Yearbook 2008.*

United Nations Statistics Division, New York, NY 10017, (800) 253-9646, Fax: (212) 963-4116, http://unstats.un.org; *Statistical Yearbook.*

GREECE - CONSUMER PRICE INDEXES

Eurostat, Batiment Jean Monnet, Rue Alcide de Gasperi, L-2920 Luxembourg, http://epp.eurostat.ec.europa.eu; *Eurostat Yearbook 2006-2007.*

International Labour Office, I.L.O. Publications, 4 route des Morillons, CH-1211 Geneva 22, Switzerland, (Telephone in U.S. (202) 653-7652), (Fax in U.S. (202) 653-7687), www.ilo.org; *Yearbook of Labour Statistics 2006.*

Organisation for Economic Cooperation and Development (OECD), 2 rue Andre Pascal, F-75775 Paris Cedex 16, France, (Telephone in U.S. (202) 785-6323), (Fax in U.S. (202) 785-0350), www.oecd.org; *OECD Economic Outlook 2008.*

Taylor and Francis Group, An Informa Business, 2 Park Square, Milton Park, Abingdon, Oxford OX14 4RN, United Kingdom, (Dial from U.S. (212) 216-7800), (Fax from U.S. (212) 564-7854), www.tandf.co.uk; *The Europa World Year Book.*

United Nations Statistics Division, New York, NY 10017, (800) 253-9646, Fax: (212) 963-4116, http://unstats.un.org; *Statistical Yearbook* and *Trends in Europe and North America: The Statistical Yearbook of the ECE 2005.*

The World Bank, 1818 H Street, NW, Washington, DC 20433, (202) 473-1000, Fax: (202) 477-6391, www.worldbank.org; *Greece.*

GREECE - CONSUMPTION (ECONOMICS)

Eurostat, Batiment Jean Monnet, Rue Alcide de Gasperi, L-2920 Luxembourg, http://epp.eurostat.ec.europa.eu; *Eurostat Yearbook 2006-2007.*

Organisation for Economic Cooperation and Development (OECD), 2 rue Andre Pascal, F-75775 Paris Cedex 16, France, (Telephone in U.S. (202) 785-6323), (Fax in U.S. (202) 785-0350), www.oecd.org; *Environmental Impacts of Foreign Direct Investment in the Mining Sector in the Newly Independent States (NIS); Iron and Steel Industry in 2004 (2006 Edition); A New World Map in Textiles and Clothing: Adjusting to Change; 2005 OECD Agricultural Outlook Tables, 1970-2014; Revenue Statistics 1965-2006 - 2007 Edition;* and *Towards Sustainable Household Consumption?: Trends and Policies in OECD Countries.*

Technical Association of the Pulp and Paper Industry (TAPPI), 15 Technology Parkway South, Norcross, GA 30092, (770) 446-1400, Fax: (770) 446-6947, www.tappi.org; *TAPPI Annual Report.*

The World Bank, 1818 H Street, NW, Washington, DC 20433, (202) 473-1000, Fax: (202) 477-6391, www.worldbank.org; *World Development Report 2008.*

GREECE - COPPER INDUSTRY AND TRADE

See GREECE - MINERAL INDUSTRIES

GREECE - CORN INDUSTRY

See GREECE - CROPS

GREECE - COST AND STANDARD OF LIVING

Eurostat, Batiment Jean Monnet, Rue Alcide de Gasperi, L-2920 Luxembourg, http://epp.eurostat.ec.europa.eu; *Eurostat Yearbook 2006-2007.*

International Monetary Fund (IMF), 700 Nineteenth Street, NW, Washington, DC 20431, (202) 623-7000, Fax: (202) 623-4661, www.imf.org; *Government Finance Statistics Yearbook (2008 Edition).*

GREECE - COTTON

See GREECE - CROPS

GREECE - CRIME

Eurostat, Batiment Jean Monnet, Rue Alcide de Gasperi, L-2920 Luxembourg, http://epp.eurostat.ec.europa.eu; *Crime and Criminal Justice; General Government Expenditure and Revenue in the EU, 2006;* and *Study on Crime Victimisation.*

International Criminal Police Organization (INTERPOL), General Secretariat, 200 quai Charles de Gaulle, 69006 Lyon, France, www.interpol.int; *International Crime Statistics.*

United Nations Statistics Division, New York, NY 10017, (800) 253-9646, Fax: (212) 963-4116, http://unstats.un.org; *Trends in Europe and North America: The Statistical Yearbook of the ECE 2005.*

Yale University Press, PO Box 209040, New Haven, CT 06520-9040, (203) 432-0960, Fax: (203) 432-0948, http://yalepress.yale.edu/yupbooks; *Violence and Crime in Cross-National Perspective.*

GREECE - CROPS

Euromonitor International, Inc., 224 S. Michigan Avenue, Suite 1500, Chicago, IL 60604, (312) 922-1115, Fax: (312) 922-1157, www.euromonitor.com; *European Marketing Data and Statistics 2008.*

European Union, Delegation of the European Commission to the United States, 2300 M Street, NW, Washington, DC 20037, (202) 862-9500, Fax: (202) 429-1766, www.eurunion.org; *Agricultural Statistics: Data 1995-2005; Agriculture in the European Union: Statistical and Economic Information 2006; Eurostatistics: Data for Short-Term Economic Analysis (2007 edition);* and *Regions - Statistical Yearbook 2006.*

Eurostat, Batiment Jean Monnet, Rue Alcide de Gasperi, L-2920 Luxembourg, http://epp.eurostat.ec.europa.eu; *Eurostat Yearbook 2006-2007.*

M.E. Sharpe, 80 Business Park Drive, Armonk, NY 10504, (800) 541-6563, Fax: (914) 273-2106, www.mesharpe.com; *The Illustrated Book of World Rankings.*

Organisation for Economic Cooperation and Development (OECD), 2 rue Andre Pascal, F-75775 Paris Cedex 16, France, (Telephone in U.S. (202) 785-6323), (Fax in U.S. (202) 785-0350), www.oecd.org; *International Trade by Commodity Statistics (ITCS)* and *2005 OECD Agricultural Outlook Tables, 1970-2014.*

Palgrave Macmillan Ltd., Houndmills, Basingstoke, Hampshire, RG21 6XS, England, (Telephone in U.S. (888) 330-8477), (Fax in U.S. (800) 672-2054), www.palgrave.com; *The Statesman's Yearbook 2008.*

Taylor and Francis Group, An Informa Business, 2 Park Square, Milton Park, Abingdon, Oxford OX14 4RN, United Kingdom, (Dial from U.S. (212) 216-7800), (Fax from U.S. (212) 564-7854), www.tandf.co.uk; *The Europa World Year Book.*

United Nations Conference on Trade and Development (UNCTAD), DC2-1120, United Nations, New York, NY 10017, (212) 963-0027, www.unctad.org; *UNCTAD Commodity Yearbook.*

United Nations Food and Agricultural Organization (FAO), Viale delle Terme di Caracalla, 00100 Rome, Italy, (Dial from U.S. (202) 653-2400), (Fax from U.S. (202) 653 5760), www.fao.org; *FAO Production Yearbook 2002* and *The State of Food and Agriculture (SOFA) 2006.*

United Nations Statistics Division, New York, NY 10017, (800) 253-9646, Fax: (212) 963-4116, http://unstats.un.org; *Statistical Yearbook.*

GREECE - CUSTOMS ADMINISTRATION

Eurostat, Batiment Jean Monnet, Rue Alcide de Gasperi, L-2920 Luxembourg, http://epp.eurostat.ec.europa.eu; *Eurostat Yearbook 2006-2007.*

International Monetary Fund (IMF), 700 Nineteenth Street, NW, Washington, DC 20431, (202) 623-7000, Fax: (202) 623-4661, www.imf.org; *Government Finance Statistics Yearbook (2008 Edition).*

Organisation for Economic Cooperation and Development (OECD), 2 rue Andre Pascal, F-75775 Paris Cedex 16, France, (Telephone in U.S. (202) 785-6323), (Fax in U.S. (202) 785-0350), www.oecd.org; *Environmental Impacts of Foreign Direct Investment in the Mining Sector in the Newly Independent States (NIS).*

Palgrave Macmillan Ltd., Houndmills, Basingstoke, Hampshire, RG21 6XS, England, (Telephone in U.S. (888) 330-8477), (Fax in U.S. (800) 672-2054), www.palgrave.com; *The Statesman's Yearbook 2008.*

GREECE - DAIRY PROCESSING

European Union, Delegation of the European Commission to the United States, 2300 M Street, NW, Washington, DC 20037, (202) 862-9500, Fax: (202) 429-1766, www.eurunion.org; *Eurostatistics: Data for Short-Term Economic Analysis (2007 edition).*

Eurostat, Batiment Jean Monnet, Rue Alcide de Gasperi, L-2920 Luxembourg, http://epp.eurostat.ec.europa.eu; *Eurostat Yearbook 2006-2007.*

M.E. Sharpe, 80 Business Park Drive, Armonk, NY 10504, (800) 541-6563, Fax: (914) 273-2106, www.mesharpe.com; *The Illustrated Book of World Rankings.*

Organisation for Economic Cooperation and Development (OECD), 2 rue Andre Pascal, F-75775 Paris Cedex 16, France, (Telephone in U.S. (202) 785-6323), (Fax in U.S. (202) 785-0350), www.oecd.org; *2005 OECD Agricultural Outlook Tables, 1970-2014.*

Palgrave Macmillan Ltd., Houndmills, Basingstoke, Hampshire, RG21 6XS, England, (Telephone in U.S. (888) 330-8477), (Fax in U.S. (800) 672-2054), www.palgrave.com; *The Statesman's Yearbook 2008.*

Taylor and Francis Group, An Informa Business, 2 Park Square, Milton Park, Abingdon, Oxford OX14 4RN, United Kingdom, (Dial from U.S. (212) 216-7800), (Fax from U.S. (212) 564-7854), www.tandf.co.uk; *The Europa World Year Book.*

United Nations Food and Agricultural Organization (FAO), Viale delle Terme di Caracalla, 00100 Rome, Italy, (Dial from U.S. (202) 653-2400), (Fax from U.S. (202) 653 5760), www.fao.org; *FAO Production Yearbook 2002* and *The State of Food and Agriculture (SOFA) 2006.*

United Nations Statistics Division, New York, NY 10017, (800) 253-9646, Fax: (212) 963-4116, http://unstats.un.org; *Statistical Yearbook.*

GREECE - DEATH RATES

See GREECE - MORTALITY

GREECE - DEBTS, EXTERNAL

International Monetary Fund (IMF), 700 Nineteenth Street, NW, Washington, DC 20431, (202) 623-7000, Fax: (202) 623-4661, www.imf.org; *Government Finance Statistics Yearbook (2008 Edition).*

Organisation for Economic Cooperation and Development (OECD), 2 rue Andre Pascal, F-75775 Paris Cedex 16, France, (Telephone in U.S. (202) 785-6323), (Fax in U.S. (202) 785-0350), www.oecd.org; *Financial Market Trends: OECD Periodical; Geographical Distribution of Financial Flows to Aid Recipients 2002-2006;* and *OECD Economic Outlook 2008.*

The World Bank, 1818 H Street, NW, Washington, DC 20433, (202) 473-1000, Fax: (202) 477-6391, www.worldbank.org; *Global Development Finance 2007; World Development Indicators (WDI) 2008;* and *World Development Report 2008.*

GREECE - DEFENSE EXPENDITURES

See GREECE - ARMED FORCES

GREECE - DEMOGRAPHY

Euromonitor International, Inc., 224 S. Michigan Avenue, Suite 1500, Chicago, IL 60604, (312) 922-1115, Fax: (312) 922-1157, www.euromonitor.com; *The World Economic Factbook 2008* and *World Marketing Data and Statistics.*

European Union, Delegation of the European Commission to the United States, 2300 M Street, NW, Washington, DC 20037, (202) 862-9500, Fax: (202) 429-1766, www.eurunion.org; *First Demographic Estimates for 2006* and *Regions - Statistical Yearbook 2006.*

Eurostat, Batiment Jean Monnet, Rue Alcide de Gasperi, L-2920 Luxembourg, http://epp.eurostat.ec.europa.eu; *Demographic Outlook - National Reports on the Demographic Developments in 2006* and *Eurostat Yearbook 2006-2007.*

M.E. Sharpe, 80 Business Park Drive, Armonk, NY 10504, (800) 541-6563, Fax: (914) 273-2106, www.mesharpe.com; *The Illustrated Book of World Rankings.*

United Nations Statistics Division, New York, NY 10017, (800) 253-9646, Fax: (212) 963-4116, http://unstats.un.org; *Human Development Report 2006.*

The World Bank, 1818 H Street, NW, Washington, DC 20433, (202) 473-1000, Fax: (202) 477-6391, www.worldbank.org; *Greece.*

GREECE - DIAMONDS

See GREECE - MINERAL INDUSTRIES

GREECE - DISPOSABLE INCOME

M.E. Sharpe, 80 Business Park Drive, Armonk, NY 10504, (800) 541-6563, Fax: (914) 273-2106, www.mesharpe.com; *The Illustrated Book of World Rankings.*

Organisation for Economic Cooperation and Development (OECD), 2 rue Andre Pascal, F-75775 Paris Cedex 16, France, (Telephone in U.S. (202) 785-6323), (Fax in U.S. (202) 785-0350), www.oecd.org; *OECD Economic Outlook 2008.*

United Nations Statistics Division, New York, NY 10017, (800) 253-9646, Fax: (212) 963-4116, http://unstats.un.org; *National Accounts Statistics: Compendium of Income Distribution Statistics* and *Statistical Yearbook.*

GREECE - DIVORCE

European Union, Delegation of the European Commission to the United States, 2300 M Street, NW, Washington, DC 20037, (202) 862-9500, Fax: (202) 429-1766, www.eurunion.org; *First Demographic Estimates for 2006.*

M.E. Sharpe, 80 Business Park Drive, Armonk, NY 10504, (800) 541-6563, Fax: (914) 273-2106, www.mesharpe.com; *The Illustrated Book of World Rankings.*

United Nations Statistics Division, New York, NY 10017, (800) 253-9646, Fax: (212) 963-4116, http://unstats.un.org; *Demographic Yearbook; Statistical Yearbook;* and *Trends in Europe and North America: The Statistical Yearbook of the ECE 2005.*

GREECE - ECONOMIC ASSISTANCE

European Union, Delegation of the European Commission to the United States, 2300 M Street, NW, Washington, DC 20037, (202) 862-9500, Fax: (202) 429-1766, www.eurunion.org; *RD Expenditure in Europe (2006 edition).*

Eurostat, Batiment Jean Monnet, Rue Alcide de Gasperi, L-2920 Luxembourg, http://epp.eurostat.ec.europa.eu; *Eurostat Yearbook 2006-2007.*

Organisation for Economic Cooperation and Development (OECD), 2 rue Andre Pascal, F-75775 Paris Cedex 16, France, (Telephone in U.S. (202) 785-6323), (Fax in U.S. (202) 785-0350), www.oecd.org; *Geographical Distribution of Financial Flows to Aid Recipients 2002-2006.*

GREECE - ECONOMIC CONDITIONS

Banque de France, 48 rue Croix des Petits champs, 75001 Paris, France, www.banque-france.fr/home.htm; *Key Data for the Euro Area.*

Center for International Business Education Research (CIBER), Columbia Business School and School of International and Public Affairs, Uris Hall, Room 212, 3022 Broadway, New York, NY 10027-6902, Mr. Joshua Safier, (212) 854-4750, Fax: (212) 222-9821, www.columbia.edu/cu/ciber/; Datastream International.

Central Intelligence Agency, Office of Public Affairs, Washington, DC 20505, (703) 482-0623, Fax: (703) 482-1739, www.cia.gov; *The World Factbook.*

DSI Data Service Information, Xantener Strasse 51a, D-47495 Rheinberg, Germany, www.dsidata.com; *Campus Solution.*

Dun and Bradstreet (DB) Corporation, 103 JFK Parkway, Short Hills, NJ 07078, (973) 921-5500, www.dnb.com; *Country Report.*

Economist Intelligence Unit, 111 West 57th Street, New York, NY 10019, (212) 554-0600, Fax: (212) 586-1181, www.eiu.com; *Greece Country Report.*

Euromonitor International, Inc., 224 S. Michigan Avenue, Suite 1500, Chicago, IL 60604, (312) 922-1115, Fax: (312) 922-1157, www.euromonitor.com; *European Marketing Data and Statistics 2008; The World Economic Factbook 2008;* and *World Marketing Data and Statistics.*

European Union, Delegation of the European Commission to the United States, 2300 M Street, NW, Washington, DC 20037, (202) 862-9500, Fax: (202) 429-1766, www.eurunion.org; *The EU Economy, 2007 Review: Moving Europe's Productivity Frontier* and *European Union Labour Force Survey.*

Eurostat, Batiment Jean Monnet, Rue Alcide de Gasperi, L-2920 Luxembourg, http://epp.eurostat.ec.europa.eu; *Consumers in Europe - Facts and Figures on Services of General Interest; EU Economic Data Pocketbook;* and *Eurostat Yearbook 2006-2007.*

International Monetary Fund (IMF), 700 Nineteenth Street, NW, Washington, DC 20431, (202) 623-7000, Fax: (202) 623-4661, www.imf.org; *World Economic Outlook Reports.*

M.E. Sharpe, 80 Business Park Drive, Armonk, NY 10504, (800) 541-6563, Fax: (914) 273-2106, www.mesharpe.com; *The Illustrated Book of World Rankings.*

Organisation for Economic Cooperation and Development (OECD), 2 rue Andre Pascal, F-75775 Paris Cedex 16, France, (Telephone in U.S. (202) 785-6323), (Fax in U.S. (202) 785-0350), www.oecd.org; *Geographical Distribution of Financial Flows to Aid Recipients 2002-2006; ICT Sector Data and Metadata by Country; Labour Force Statistics: 1986-2005, 2007 Edition; OECD Composite Leading Indicators (CLIs), Updated September 2007; OECD Economic Outlook 2008; OECD Economic Survey - Greece 2007; OECD Employment Outlook 2007; OECD in Figures 2007;* and *OECD Main Economic Indicators (MEI).*

Palgrave Macmillan Ltd., Houndmills, Basingstoke, Hampshire, RG21 6XS, England, (Telephone in U.S. (888) 330-8477), (Fax in U.S. (800) 672-2054), www.palgrave.com; *The Statesman's Yearbook 2008.*

Platts, 2 Penn Plaza, 25th Floor, New York, NY 10121-2298, (212) 904-3070, www.platts.com; *Energy Economist.*

Taylor and Francis Group, An Informa Business, 2 Park Square, Milton Park, Abingdon, Oxford OX14 4RN, United Kingdom, (Dial from U.S. (212) 216-7800), (Fax from U.S. (212) 564-7854), www.tandf.co.uk; *The Europa World Year Book.*

United Nations Statistics Division, New York, NY 10017, (800) 253-9646, Fax: (212) 963-4116, http://unstats.un.org; *Energy Statistics Yearbook 2003* and *World Statistics Pocketbook.*

The World Bank, 1818 H Street, NW, Washington, DC 20433, (202) 473-1000, Fax: (202) 477-6391, www.worldbank.org; *Global Economic Monitor (GEM); Global Economic Prospects 2008; Greece; The World Bank Atlas 2003-2004;* and *World Development Report 2008.*

GREECE - ECONOMICS - SOCIOLOGICAL ASPECTS

Eurostat, Batiment Jean Monnet, Rue Alcide de Gasperi, L-2920 Luxembourg, http://epp.eurostat.ec.europa.eu; *Eurostat Yearbook 2006-2007.*

Organisation for Economic Cooperation and Development (OECD), 2 rue Andre Pascal, F-75775 Paris Cedex 16, France, (Telephone in U.S. (202) 785-6323), (Fax in U.S. (202) 785-0350), www.oecd.org; *OECD Economic Outlook 2008.*

GREECE - EDUCATION

Euromonitor International, Inc., 224 S. Michigan Avenue, Suite 1500, Chicago, IL 60604, (312) 922-1115, Fax: (312) 922-1157, www.euromonitor.com; *European Marketing Data and Statistics 2008* and *World Marketing Data and Statistics.*

European Union, Delegation of the European Commission to the United States, 2300 M Street, NW, Washington, DC 20037, (202) 862-9500, Fax: (202) 429-1766, www.eurunion.org; *Education across Europe 2003* and *Regions - Statistical Yearbook 2006.*

Eurostat, Batiment Jean Monnet, Rue Alcide de Gasperi, L-2920 Luxembourg, http://epp.eurostat.ec.europa.eu; *Education, Science and Culture Statistics* and *Eurostat Yearbook 2006-2007.*

International Monetary Fund (IMF), 700 Nineteenth Street, NW, Washington, DC 20431, (202) 623-7000, Fax: (202) 623-4661, www.imf.org; *Government Finance Statistics Yearbook (2008 Edition).*

M.E. Sharpe, 80 Business Park Drive, Armonk, NY 10504, (800) 541-6563, Fax: (914) 273-2106, www.mesharpe.com; *The Illustrated Book of World Rankings.*

Organisation for Economic Cooperation and Development (OECD), 2 rue Andre Pascal, F-75775 Paris Cedex 16, France, (Telephone in U.S. (202) 785-6323), (Fax in U.S. (202) 785-0350), www.oecd.org; *Education at a Glance* (2007 Edition).

Palgrave Macmillan Ltd., Houndmills, Basingstoke, Hampshire, RG21 6XS, England, (Telephone in U.S. (888) 330-8477), (Fax in U.S. (800) 672-2054), www.palgrave.com; *The Statesman's Yearbook 2008.*

Taylor and Francis Group, An Informa Business, 2 Park Square, Milton Park, Abingdon, Oxford OX14 4RN, United Kingdom, (Dial from U.S. (212) 216-7800), (Fax from U.S. (212) 564-7854), www.tandf.co.uk; *The Europa World Year Book.*

UNESCO Institute for Statistics, C.P. 6128 Succursale Centre-Ville, Montreal, Quebec, H3C 3J7 Canada, (Dial from U.S. (514) 343-6880), (Fax from U.S. (514) 343 6882), www.uis.unesco.org; *Statistical Tables.*

United Nations Statistics Division, New York, NY 10017, (800) 253-9646, Fax: (212) 963-4116, http://unstats.un.org; *Human Development Report 2006* and *Trends in Europe and North America: The Statistical Yearbook of the ECE 2005.*

The World Bank, 1818 H Street, NW, Washington, DC 20433, (202) 473-1000, Fax: (202) 477-6391, www.worldbank.org; *Greece; World Development Indicators (WDI) 2008;* and *World Development Report 2008.*

GREECE - EGGPLANT PRODUCTION

See GREECE - CROPS

GREECE - ELECTRICITY

European Union, Delegation of the European Commission to the United States, 2300 M Street, NW, Washington, DC 20037, (202) 862-9500, Fax: (202) 429-1766, www.eurunion.org; *European Union Energy Transport in Figures 2006; Eurostatistics: Data for Short-Term Economic Analysis (2007 edition);* and *Regions - Statistical Yearbook 2006.*

Eurostat, Batiment Jean Monnet, Rue Alcide de Gasperi, L-2920 Luxembourg, http://epp.eurostat.ec.europa.eu; *Energy - Monthly Statistics; Eurostat Yearbook 2006-2007;* and *Panorama of Energy - 2007 Edition.*

M.E. Sharpe, 80 Business Park Drive, Armonk, NY 10504, (800) 541-6563, Fax: (914) 273-2106, www.mesharpe.com; *The Illustrated Book of World Rankings.*

Organisation for Economic Cooperation and Development (OECD), 2 rue Andre Pascal, F-75775 Paris Cedex 16, France, (Telephone in U.S. (202) 785-6323), (Fax in U.S. (202) 785-0350), www.oecd.org; *Coal Information: 2007 Edition; Energy Statistics of OECD Countries* (2007 Edition); STructural ANalysis (STAN) database; and *World Energy Outlook 2007.*

Palgrave Macmillan Ltd., Houndmills, Basingstoke, Hampshire, RG21 6XS, England, (Telephone in U.S. (888) 330-8477), (Fax in U.S. (800) 672-2054), www.palgrave.com; *The Statesman's Yearbook 2008.*

Platts, 2 Penn Plaza, 25th Floor, New York, NY 10121-2298, (212) 904-3070, www.platts.com; *Energy Economist; EU Energy;* and *European Electricity Review 2004.*

U.S. Department of Energy (DOE), Energy Information Administration (EIA), 1000 Independence Avenue, SW, Washington, DC 20585, (202) 586-8800, www.eia.doe.gov; *International Energy Annual 2004* and *International Energy Outlook 2006.*

United Nations Statistics Division, New York, NY 10017, (800) 253-9646, Fax: (212) 963-4116, http://unstats.un.org; *Energy Statistics Yearbook 2003; Human Development Report 2006; Statistical Yearbook;* and *Trends in Europe and North America: The Statistical Yearbook of the ECE 2005.*

GREECE - EMPLOYMENT

Bernan Essential Government Publications, 4611-F Assembly Drive, Lanham MD, 20706-4391, (301) 459-2255, Fax: (800) 865-3450, www.bernan.com; *OECD Factbook 2006.*

Euromonitor International, Inc., 224 S. Michigan Avenue, Suite 1500, Chicago, IL 60604, (312) 922-1115, Fax: (312) 922-1157, www.euromonitor.com; *European Marketing Data and Statistics 2008.*

European Union, Delegation of the European Commission to the United States, 2300 M Street, NW, Washington, DC 20037, (202) 862-9500, Fax: (202) 429-1766, www.eurunion.org; *Agriculture in the European Union: Statistical and Economic Information 2006; European Union Labour Force Survey; Eurostatistics: Data for Short-Term Economic Analysis (2007 edition); Iron and Steel;* and *Statistical Overview of Transport in the European Union (Data 1970-2001).*

Eurostat, Batiment Jean Monnet, Rue Alcide de Gasperi, L-2920 Luxembourg, http://epp.eurostat.ec.europa.eu; *Eurostat Yearbook 2006-2007.*

International Labour Office, I.L.O. Publications, 4 route des Morillons, CH-1211 Geneva 22, Switzerland, (Telephone in U.S. (202) 653-7652), (Fax in U.S. (202) 653-7687), www.ilo.org; *Yearbook of Labour Statistics 2006.*

M.E. Sharpe, 80 Business Park Drive, Armonk, NY 10504, (800) 541-6563, Fax: (914) 273-2106, www.mesharpe.com; *The Illustrated Book of World Rankings.*

Organisation for Economic Cooperation and Development (OECD), 2 rue Andre Pascal, F-75775 Paris Cedex 16, France, (Telephone in U.S. (202) 785-6323), (Fax in U.S. (202) 785-0350), www.oecd.org; *ICT Sector Data and Metadata by Country; Iron and Steel Industry in 2004 (2006 Edition); Labour Force Statistics: 1986-2005, 2007 Edition; A New World Map in Textiles and Clothing: Adjusting to Change; OECD Composite Leading Indicators (CLIs), Updated September 2007; OECD Economic Outlook 2008; OECD Economic Survey - Greece 2007; OECD Employment Outlook 2007;* and *OECD in Figures 2007.*

United Nations Statistics Division, New York, NY 10017, (800) 253-9646, Fax: (212) 963-4116, http://unstats.un.org; *Statistical Yearbook* and *Trends in Europe and North America: The Statistical Yearbook of the ECE 2005.*

The World Bank, 1818 H Street, NW, Washington, DC 20433, (202) 473-1000, Fax: (202) 477-6391, www.worldbank.org; *Greece.*

GREECE - ENERGY INDUSTRIES

Enerdata, 10 Rue Royale, 75008 Paris, France, www.enerdata.fr; *Global Energy Market Data.*

Eurostat, Batiment Jean Monnet, Rue Alcide de Gasperi, L-2920 Luxembourg, http://epp.eurostat.ec.europa.eu; *Energy - Monthly Statistics; Eurostat Yearbook 2006-2007;* and *Panorama of Energy - 2007 Edition.*

International Energy Agency (IEA), 9, rue de la Federation, 75739 Paris Cedex 15, France, www.iea.org; *Key World Energy Statistics 2007.*

Organisation for Economic Cooperation and Development (OECD), 2 rue Andre Pascal, F-75775 Paris Cedex 16, France, (Telephone in U.S. (202) 785-6323), (Fax in U.S. (202) 785-0350), www.oecd.org; *Towards Sustainable Household Consumption?: Trends and Policies in OECD Countries.*

Platts, 2 Penn Plaza, 25th Floor, New York, NY 10121-2298, (212) 904-3070, www.platts.com; *Energy in East Europe; EU Energy;* and *European Power Daily.*

United Nations Statistics Division, New York, NY 10017, (800) 253-9646, Fax: (212) 963-4116, http://unstats.un.org; *Statistical Yearbook.*

GREECE - ENVIRONMENTAL CONDITIONS

Center for Research on the Epidemiology of Disasters (CRED), Universite Catholique de Louvain, Ecole de Sante Publique, 30.94 Clos Chapelle-aux-Champs, 1200 Brussels, Belgium, www.cred.be; *Three Decades of Floods in Europe: A Preliminary Analysis of EMDAT Data.*

DSI Data Service Information, Xantener Strasse 51a, D-47495 Rheinberg, Germany, www.dsidata.com; *Campus Solution* and *DSI's Global Environmental Database.*

Economist Intelligence Unit, 111 West 57th Street, New York, NY 10019, (212) 554-0600, Fax: (212) 586-1181, www.eiu.com; *Greece Country Report.*

Eurostat, Batiment Jean Monnet, Rue Alcide de Gasperi, L-2920 Luxembourg, http://epp.eurostat.ec.europa.eu; *Environmental Protection Expenditure in Europe.*

Organisation for Economic Cooperation and Development (OECD), 2 rue Andre Pascal, F-75775 Paris Cedex 16, France, (Telephone in U.S. (202) 785-6323), (Fax in U.S. (202) 785-0350), www.oecd.org; *Key Environmental Indicators 2004.*

Platts, 2 Penn Plaza, 25th Floor, New York, NY 10121-2298, (212) 904-3070, www.platts.com; *Emissions Daily.*

United Nations Statistics Division, New York, NY 10017, (800) 253-9646, Fax: (212) 963-4116, http://unstats.un.org; *Trends in Europe and North America: The Statistical Yearbook of the ECE 2005* and *World Statistics Pocketbook.*

GREECE - EXPENDITURES, PUBLIC

Eurostat, Batiment Jean Monnet, Rue Alcide de Gasperi, L-2920 Luxembourg, http://epp.eurostat.ec.europa.eu; *European Social Statistics - Social Protection Expenditure and Receipts - Data 1997-2005* and *Eurostat Yearbook 2006-2007.*

Organisation for Economic Cooperation and Development (OECD), 2 rue Andre Pascal, F-75775 Paris Cedex 16, France, (Telephone in U.S. (202) 785-6323), (Fax in U.S. (202) 785-0350), www.oecd.org; *Revenue Statistics 1965-2006 - 2007 Edition.*

GREECE - EXPORTS

Central Intelligence Agency, Office of Public Affairs, Washington, DC 20505, (703) 482-0623, Fax: (703) 482-1739, www.cia.gov; *The World Factbook.*

Economist Intelligence Unit, 111 West 57th Street, New York, NY 10019, (212) 554-0600, Fax: (212) 586-1181, www.eiu.com; *Greece Country Report.*

Euromonitor International, Inc., 224 S. Michigan Avenue, Suite 1500, Chicago, IL 60604, (312) 922-1115, Fax: (312) 922-1157, www.euromonitor.com; *The World Economic Factbook 2008.*

European Union, Delegation of the European Commission to the United States, 2300 M Street, NW, Washington, DC 20037, (202) 862-9500, Fax: (202) 429-1766, www.eurunion.org; *European Union Energy Transport in Figures 2006; Eurostatistics: Data for Short-Term Economic Analysis (2007 edition); External and Intra-European Union Trade: Data 1958-2002; External and Intra-European Union Trade: Data 1999-2004;* and *Fishery Statistics - 1990-2006.*

Eurostat, Batiment Jean Monnet, Rue Alcide de Gasperi, L-2920 Luxembourg, http://epp.eurostat.ec.europa.eu; *Eurostat Yearbook 2006-2007.*

International Monetary Fund (IMF), 700 Nineteenth Street, NW, Washington, DC 20431, (202) 623-7000, Fax: (202) 623-4661, www.imf.org; *Direction of Trade Statistics Yearbook 2007; Government Finance Statistics Yearbook (2008 Edition);* and *International Financial Statistics Yearbook 2007.*

Organisation for Economic Cooperation and Development (OECD), 2 rue Andre Pascal, F-75775 Paris Cedex 16, France, (Telephone in U.S. (202) 785-6323), (Fax in U.S. (202) 785-0350), www.oecd.org; *Geographical Distribution of Financial Flows to Aid Recipients 2002-2006; International Trade by Commodity Statistics (ITCS); Iron and Steel Industry in 2004 (2006 Edition); 2005 OECD Agricultural Outlook Tables, 1970-2014; OECD Economic Outlook 2008; OECD Economic Survey - Greece 2007; Review of Fisheries in OECD Countries: Country Statistics 2001 to 2003 - 2005 Edition;* and STructural ANalysis (STAN) database.

Palgrave Macmillan Ltd., Houndmills, Basingstoke, Hampshire, RG21 6XS, England, (Telephone in U.S. (888) 330-8477), (Fax in U.S. (800) 672-2054), www.palgrave.com; *The Statesman's Yearbook 2008.*

Platts, 2 Penn Plaza, 25th Floor, New York, NY 10121-2298, (212) 904-3070, www.platts.com; *Energy Economist.*

Taylor and Francis Group, An Informa Business, 2 Park Square, Milton Park, Abingdon, Oxford OX14 4RN, United Kingdom, (Dial from U.S. (212) 216-7800), (Fax from U.S. (212) 564-7854), www.tandf.co.uk; *The Europa World Year Book.*

Technical Association of the Pulp and Paper Industry (TAPPI), 15 Technology Parkway South, Norcross, GA 30092, (770) 446-1400, Fax: (770) 446-6947, www.tappi.org; *TAPPI Annual Report.*

United Nations Conference on Trade and Development (UNCTAD), DC2-1120, United Nations, New York, NY 10017, (212) 963-0027, www.unctad.org; *Handbook of Statistics 2005.*

United Nations Food and Agricultural Organization (FAO), Viale delle Terme di Caracalla, 00100 Rome, Italy, (Dial from U.S. (202) 653-2400), (Fax from U.S. (202) 653 5760), www.fao.org; *The State of Food and Agriculture (SOFA) 2006.*

United Nations Statistics Division, New York, NY 10017, (800) 253-9646, Fax: (212) 963-4116, http://unstats.un.org; *Energy Statistics Yearbook 2003* and *Trends in Europe and North America: The Statistical Yearbook of the ECE 2005.*

The World Bank, 1818 H Street, NW, Washington, DC 20433, (202) 473-1000, Fax: (202) 477-6391, www.worldbank.org; *World Development Indicators (WDI) 2008* and *World Development Report 2008.*

GREECE - FEMALE WORKING POPULATION

See GREECE - EMPLOYMENT

GREECE - FERTILITY, HUMAN

Central Intelligence Agency, Office of Public Affairs, Washington, DC 20505, (703) 482-0623, Fax: (703) 482-1739, www.cia.gov; *The World Factbook.*

European Union, Delegation of the European Commission to the United States, 2300 M Street, NW, Washington, DC 20037, (202) 862-9500, Fax: (202) 429-1766, www.eurunion.org; *First Demographic Estimates for 2006.*

M.E. Sharpe, 80 Business Park Drive, Armonk, NY 10504, (800) 541-6563, Fax: (914) 273-2106, www.mesharpe.com; *The Illustrated Book of World Rankings.*

United Nations Statistics Division, New York, NY 10017, (800) 253-9646, Fax: (212) 963-4116, http://unstats.un.org; *Human Development Report 2006* and *Trends in Europe and North America: The Statistical Yearbook of the ECE 2005.*

The World Bank, 1818 H Street, NW, Washington, DC 20433, (202) 473-1000, Fax: (202) 477-6391, www.worldbank.org; *The World Bank Atlas 2003-2004; World Development Indicators (WDI) 2008;* and *World Development Report 2008.*

GREECE - FERTILIZER INDUSTRY

Eurostat, Batiment Jean Monnet, Rue Alcide de Gasperi, L-2920 Luxembourg, http://epp.eurostat.ec.europa.eu; *Eurostat Yearbook 2006-2007.*

Organisation for Economic Cooperation and Development (OECD), 2 rue Andre Pascal, F-75775 Paris Cedex 16, France, (Telephone in U.S. (202) 785-6323), (Fax in U.S. (202) 785-0350), www.oecd.org; *International Trade by Commodity Statistics (ITCS)* and *2005 OECD Agricultural Outlook Tables, 1970-2014.*

United Nations Food and Agricultural Organization (FAO), Viale delle Terme di Caracalla, 00100 Rome, Italy, (Dial from U.S. (202) 653-2400), (Fax from U.S. (202) 653 5760), www.fao.org; *The State of Food and Agriculture (SOFA) 2006.*

United Nations Statistics Division, New York, NY 10017, (800) 253-9646, Fax: (212) 963-4116, http://unstats.un.org; *Statistical Yearbook.*

GREECE - FETAL MORTALITY

See GREECE - MORTALITY

GREECE - FILM

See GREECE - MOTION PICTURES

GREECE - FINANCE

European Union, Delegation of the European Commission to the United States, 2300 M Street, NW, Washington, DC 20037, (202) 862-9500, Fax: (202) 429-1766, www.eurunion.org; *Eurostatistics: Data for Short-Term Economic Analysis (2007 edition).*

Eurostat, Batiment Jean Monnet, Rue Alcide de Gasperi, L-2920 Luxembourg, http://epp.eurostat.ec.europa.eu; *Eurostat Yearbook 2006-2007.*

International Monetary Fund (IMF), 700 Nineteenth Street, NW, Washington, DC 20431, (202) 623-7000, Fax: (202) 623-4661, www.imf.org; *International Financial Statistics Yearbook 2007.*

Organisation for Economic Cooperation and Development (OECD), 2 rue Andre Pascal, F-75775 Paris Cedex 16, France, (Telephone in U.S. (202) 785-6323), (Fax in U.S. (202) 785-0350), www.oecd.org; *OECD Economic Outlook 2008.*

Taylor and Francis Group, An Informa Business, 2 Park Square, Milton Park, Abingdon, Oxford OX14 4RN, United Kingdom, (Dial from U.S. (212) 216-7800), (Fax from U.S. (212) 564-7854), www.tandf.co.uk; *The Europa World Year Book.*

United Nations Statistics Division, New York, NY 10017, (800) 253-9646, Fax: (212) 963-4116, http://unstats.un.org; *National Accounts Statistics: Compendium of Income Distribution Statistics* and *Statistical Yearbook.*

The World Bank, 1818 H Street, NW, Washington, DC 20433, (202) 473-1000, Fax: (202) 477-6391, www.worldbank.org; *Greece.*

GREECE - FINANCE, PUBLIC

Banque de France, 48 rue Croix des Petits champs, 75001 Paris, France, www.banque-france.fr/home.htm; *Key Data for the Euro Area* and *Public Finance.*

Bernan Essential Government Publications, 4611-F Assembly Drive, Lanham MD, 20706-4391, (301) 459-2255, Fax: (800) 865-3450, www.bernan.com; *National Accounts Statistics.*

Economist Intelligence Unit, 111 West 57th Street, New York, NY 10019, (212) 554-0600, Fax: (212) 586-1181, www.eiu.com; *Greece Country Report.*

European Union, Delegation of the European Commission to the United States, 2300 M Street, NW, Washington, DC 20037, (202) 862-9500, Fax: (202) 429-1766, www.eurunion.org; *Eurostatistics: Data for Short-Term Economic Analysis (2007 edition).*

Eurostat, Batiment Jean Monnet, Rue Alcide de Gasperi, L-2920 Luxembourg, http://epp.eurostat.ec.europa.eu; *Eurostat Yearbook 2006-2007.*

International Monetary Fund (IMF), 700 Nineteenth Street, NW, Washington, DC 20431, (202) 623-7000, Fax: (202) 623-4661, www.imf.org; *Government Finance Statistics Yearbook (2008 Edition); International Financial Statistics;* and *International Financial Statistics Online Service.*

M.E. Sharpe, 80 Business Park Drive, Armonk, NY 10504, (800) 541-6563, Fax: (914) 273-2106, www.mesharpe.com; *The Illustrated Book of World Rankings.*

Organisation for Economic Cooperation and Development (OECD), 2 rue Andre Pascal, F-75775 Paris Cedex 16, France, (Telephone in U.S. (202) 785-6323), (Fax in U.S. (202) 785-0350), www.oecd.org; *Financial Market Trends: OECD Periodical; Geographical Distribution of Financial Flows to Aid Recipients 2002-2006; OECD Economic Outlook 2008;* and *Revenue Statistics 1965-2006 - 2007 Edition.*

Palgrave Macmillan Ltd., Houndmills, Basingstoke, Hampshire, RG21 6XS, England, (Telephone in U.S. (888) 330-8477), (Fax in U.S. (800) 672-2054), www.palgrave.com; *The Statesman's Yearbook 2008.*

Taylor and Francis Group, An Informa Business, 2 Park Square, Milton Park, Abingdon, Oxford OX14 4RN, United Kingdom, (Dial from U.S. (212) 216-7800), (Fax from U.S. (212) 564-7854), www.tandf.co.uk; *The Europa World Year Book.*

The World Bank, 1818 H Street, NW, Washington, DC 20433, (202) 473-1000, Fax: (202) 477-6391, www.worldbank.org; *Greece.*

GREECE - FISHERIES

Euromonitor International, Inc., 224 S. Michigan Avenue, Suite 1500, Chicago, IL 60604, (312) 922-1115, Fax: (312) 922-1157, www.euromonitor.com; *European Marketing Data and Statistics 2008.*

European Union, Delegation of the European Commission to the United States, 2300 M Street, NW, Washington, DC 20037, (202) 862-9500, Fax: (202) 429-1766, www.eurunion.org; *Agricultural Statistics: Data 1995-2005* and *Fishery Statistics - 1990-2006.*

Eurostat, Batiment Jean Monnet, Rue Alcide de Gasperi, L-2920 Luxembourg, http://epp.eurostat.ec.europa.eu; *Eurostat Yearbook 2006-2007.*

M.E. Sharpe, 80 Business Park Drive, Armonk, NY 10504, (800) 541-6563, Fax: (914) 273-2106, www.mesharpe.com; *The Illustrated Book of World Rankings.*

Organisation for Economic Cooperation and Development (OECD), 2 rue Andre Pascal, F-75775 Paris Cedex 16, France, (Telephone in U.S. (202) 785-6323), (Fax in U.S. (202) 785-0350), www.oecd.org; *International Trade by Commodity Statistics (ITCS); Review of Fisheries in OECD Countries: Country Statistics 2001 to 2003 - 2005 Edition;* and STructural ANalysis (STAN) database.

Palgrave Macmillan Ltd., Houndmills, Basingstoke, Hampshire, RG21 6XS, England, (Telephone in U.S. (888) 330-8477), (Fax in U.S. (800) 672-2054), www.palgrave.com; *The Statesman's Yearbook 2008.*

Taylor and Francis Group, An Informa Business, 2 Park Square, Milton Park, Abingdon, Oxford OX14 4RN, United Kingdom, (Dial from U.S. (212) 216-7800), (Fax from U.S. (212) 564-7854), www.tandf.co.uk; *The Europa World Year Book.*

United Nations Conference on Trade and Development (UNCTAD), DC2-1120, United Nations, New York, NY 10017, (212) 963-0027, www.unctad.org; *UNCTAD Commodity Yearbook.*

United Nations Food and Agricultural Organization (FAO), Viale delle Terme di Caracalla, 00100 Rome, Italy, (Dial from U.S. (202) 653-2400), (Fax from U.S. (202) 653 5760), www.fao.org; *FAO Yearbook of Fishery Statistics;* Fishery Databases; FISHSTAT Database. Subjects covered include: Aquaculture production, capture production, fishery commodities; and *The State of Food and Agriculture (SOFA) 2006.*

United Nations Statistics Division, New York, NY 10017, (800) 253-9646, Fax: (212) 963-4116, http://unstats.un.org; *Statistical Yearbook.*

The World Bank, 1818 H Street, NW, Washington, DC 20433, (202) 473-1000, Fax: (202) 477-6391, www.worldbank.org; *Greece.*

GREECE - FLOUR INDUSTRY

Eurostat, Batiment Jean Monnet, Rue Alcide de Gasperi, L-2920 Luxembourg, http://epp.eurostat.ec.europa.eu; *Eurostat Yearbook 2006-2007.*

United Nations Statistics Division, New York, NY 10017, (800) 253-9646, Fax: (212) 963-4116, http://unstats.un.org; *Statistical Yearbook.*

GREECE - FOOD

Euromonitor International, Inc., 224 S. Michigan Avenue, Suite 1500, Chicago, IL 60604, (312) 922-1115, Fax: (312) 922-1157, www.euromonitor.com; *Retail Trade International 2007.*

Eurostat, Batiment Jean Monnet, Rue Alcide de Gasperi, L-2920 Luxembourg, http://epp.eurostat.ec.europa.eu; *Eurostat Yearbook 2006-2007.*

Organisation for Economic Cooperation and Development (OECD), 2 rue Andre Pascal, F-75775 Paris Cedex 16, France, (Telephone in U.S. (202) 785-6323), (Fax in U.S. (202) 785-0350), www.oecd.org; *International Trade by Commodity Statistics (ITCS).*

United Nations Conference on Trade and Development (UNCTAD), DC2-1120, United Nations, New York, NY 10017, (212) 963-0027, www.unctad.org; *UNCTAD Commodity Yearbook.*

United Nations Food and Agricultural Organization (FAO), Viale delle Terme di Caracalla, 00100 Rome, Italy, (Dial from U.S. (202) 653-2400), (Fax from U.S. (202) 653 5760), www.fao.org; *FAO Production Yearbook 2002* and *The State of Food and Agriculture (SOFA) 2006.*

United Nations Statistics Division, New York, NY 10017, (800) 253-9646, Fax: (212) 963-4116, http://unstats.un.org; *Human Development Report 2006.*

GREECE - FOREIGN EXCHANGE RATES

Central Intelligence Agency, Office of Public Affairs, Washington, DC 20505, (703) 482-0623, Fax: (703) 482-1739, www.cia.gov; *The World Factbook.*

Euromonitor International, Inc., 224 S. Michigan Avenue, Suite 1500, Chicago, IL 60604, (312) 922-1115, Fax: (312) 922-1157, www.euromonitor.com; *The World Economic Factbook 2008.*

European Union, Delegation of the European Commission to the United States, 2300 M Street, NW, Washington, DC 20037, (202) 862-9500, Fax: (202) 429-1766, www.eurunion.org; *Eurostatistics: Data for Short-Term Economic Analysis (2007 edition).*

Eurostat, Batiment Jean Monnet, Rue Alcide de Gasperi, L-2920 Luxembourg, http://epp.eurostat.ec.europa.eu; *Eurostat Yearbook 2006-2007.*

International Civil Aviation Organization (ICAO), External Relations and Public Information Office (EPO), 999 University Street, Montreal, Quebec H3C 5H7, Canada, (Dial from U.S. (514) 954-8219), (Fax from U.S. (514) 954-6077), www.icao.int; *Civil Aviation Statistics of the World.*

International Monetary Fund (IMF), 700 Nineteenth Street, NW, Washington, DC 20431, (202) 623-7000, Fax: (202) 623-4661, www.imf.org; *International Financial Statistics Yearbook 2007.*

Organisation for Economic Cooperation and Development (OECD), 2 rue Andre Pascal, F-75775 Paris Cedex 16, France, (Telephone in U.S. (202) 785-6323), (Fax in U.S. (202) 785-0350), www.oecd.org; *Financial Market Trends: OECD Periodical; Household, Tourism, Travel: Trends, Environmental Impacts and Policy Responses; OECD Economic Outlook 2008;* and *Revenue Statistics 1965-2006 - 2007 Edition.*

Taylor and Francis Group, An Informa Business, 2 Park Square, Milton Park, Abingdon, Oxford OX14 4RN, United Kingdom, (Dial from U.S. (212) 216-7800), (Fax from U.S. (212) 564-7854), www.tandf.co.uk; *The Europa World Year Book.*

United Nations Statistics Division, New York, NY 10017, (800) 253-9646, Fax: (212) 963-4116, http://

unstats.un.org; *Statistical Yearbook; Trends in Europe and North America: The Statistical Yearbook of the ECE 2005;* and *World Statistics Pocketbook.*

GREECE - FORESTS AND FORESTRY

American Forest Paper Association (AFPA), 1111 Nineteenth Street, NW, Suite 800, Washington, DC 20036, (800) 878-8878, www.afandpa.org; *2007 Annual Statistics of Paper, Paperboard, and Wood Pulp.*

Euromonitor International, Inc., 224 S. Michigan Avenue, Suite 1500, Chicago, IL 60604, (312) 922-1115, Fax: (312) 922-1157, www.euromonitor.com; *European Marketing Data and Statistics 2008.*

European Union, Delegation of the European Commission to the United States, 2300 M Street, NW, Washington, DC 20037, (202) 862-9500, Fax: (202) 429-1766, www.eurunion.org; *Agricultural Statistics: Data 1995-2005.*

Eurostat, Batiment Jean Monnet, Rue Alcide de Gasperi, L-2920 Luxembourg, http://epp.eurostat.ec.europa.eu; *Eurostat Yearbook 2006-2007.*

M.E. Sharpe, 80 Business Park Drive, Armonk, NY 10504, (800) 541-6563, Fax: (914) 273-2106, www.mesharpe.com; *The Illustrated Book of World Rankings.*

Organisation for Economic Cooperation and Development (OECD), 2 rue Andre Pascal, F-75775 Paris Cedex 16, France, (Telephone in U.S. (202) 785-6323), (Fax in U.S. (202) 785-0350), www.oecd.org; *International Trade by Commodity Statistics (ITCS)* and STructural ANalysis (STAN) database.

Palgrave Macmillan Ltd., Houndmills, Basingstoke, Hampshire, RG21 6XS, England, (Telephone in U.S. (888) 330-8477), (Fax in U.S. (800) 672-2054), www.palgrave.com; *The Statesman's Yearbook 2008.*

Taylor and Francis Group, An Informa Business, 2 Park Square, Milton Park, Abingdon, Oxford OX14 4RN, United Kingdom, (Dial from U.S. (212) 216-7800), (Fax from U.S. (212) 564-7854), www.tandf.co.uk; *The Europa World Year Book.*

Technical Association of the Pulp and Paper Industry (TAPPI), 15 Technology Parkway South, Norcross, GA 30092, (770) 446-1400, Fax: (770) 446-6947, www.tappi.org; *TAPPI Annual Report.*

UNESCO Institute for Statistics, C.P. 6128 Succursale Centre-Ville, Montreal, Quebec, H3C 3J7 Canada, (Dial from U.S. (514) 343-6880), (Fax from U.S. (514) 343 6882), www.uis.unesco.org; *Statistical Tables.*

United Nations Conference on Trade and Development (UNCTAD), DC2-1120, United Nations, New York, NY 10017, (212) 963-0027, www.unctad.org; *UNCTAD Commodity Yearbook.*

United Nations Food and Agricultural Organization (FAO), Viale delle Terme di Caracalla, 00100 Rome, Italy, (Dial from U.S. (202) 653-2400), (Fax from U.S. (202) 653 5760), www.fao.org; *FAO Yearbook of Forest Products* and *The State of Food and Agriculture (SOFA) 2006.*

United Nations Statistics Division, New York, NY 10017, (800) 253-9646, Fax: (212) 963-4116, http://unstats.un.org; *Statistical Yearbook* and *Trends in Europe and North America: The Statistical Yearbook of the ECE 2005.*

The World Bank, 1818 H Street, NW, Washington, DC 20433, (202) 473-1000, Fax: (202) 477-6391, www.worldbank.org; *Greece* and *World Development Report 2008.*

GREECE - FRUIT PRODUCTION

See GREECE - CROPS

GREECE - GAS PRODUCTION

See GREECE - MINERAL INDUSTRIES

GREECE - GEOGRAPHIC INFORMATION SYSTEMS

Eurostat, Batiment Jean Monnet, Rue Alcide de Gasperi, L-2920 Luxembourg, http://epp.eurostat.ec.europa.eu; *Eurostat Yearbook 2006-2007.*

M.E. Sharpe, 80 Business Park Drive, Armonk, NY 10504, (800) 541-6563, Fax: (914) 273-2106, www.mesharpe.com; *The Illustrated Book of World Rankings.*

The World Bank, 1818 H Street, NW, Washington, DC 20433, (202) 473-1000, Fax: (202) 477-6391, www.worldbank.org; *Greece.*

GREECE - GOLD INDUSTRY

International Monetary Fund (IMF), 700 Nineteenth Street, NW, Washington, DC 20431, (202) 623-7000, Fax: (202) 623-4661, www.imf.org; *International Financial Statistics Yearbook 2007.*

United Nations Statistics Division, New York, NY 10017, (800) 253-9646, Fax: (212) 963-4116, http://unstats.un.org; *Statistical Yearbook.*

The World Bank, 1818 H Street, NW, Washington, DC 20433, (202) 473-1000, Fax: (202) 477-6391, www.worldbank.org; *World Development Indicators (WDI) 2008.*

GREECE - GOLD PRODUCTION

See GREECE - MINERAL INDUSTRIES

GREECE - GRANTS-IN-AID

International Monetary Fund (IMF), 700 Nineteenth Street, NW, Washington, DC 20431, (202) 623-7000, Fax: (202) 623-4661, www.imf.org; *Government Finance Statistics Yearbook (2008 Edition).*

Organisation for Economic Cooperation and Development (OECD), 2 rue Andre Pascal, F-75775 Paris Cedex 16, France, (Telephone in U.S. (202) 785-6323), (Fax in U.S. (202) 785-0350), www.oecd.org; *Geographical Distribution of Financial Flows to Aid Recipients 2002-2006.*

GREECE - GREEN PEPPER AND CHILIE PRODUCTION

See GREECE - CROPS

GREECE - GROSS DOMESTIC PRODUCT

Economist Intelligence Unit, 111 West 57th Street, New York, NY 10019, (212) 554-0600, Fax: (212) 586-1181, www.eiu.com; *Greece Country Report.*

Euromonitor International, Inc., 224 S. Michigan Avenue, Suite 1500, Chicago, IL 60604, (312) 922-1115, Fax: (312) 922-1157, www.euromonitor.com; *The World Economic Factbook 2008.*

European Union, Delegation of the European Commission to the United States, 2300 M Street, NW, Washington, DC 20037, (202) 862-9500, Fax: (202) 429-1766, www.eurunion.org; *Eurostatistics: Data for Short-Term Economic Analysis (2007 edition); Iron and Steel;* and *RD Expenditure in Europe (2006 edition).*

Eurostat, Batiment Jean Monnet, Rue Alcide de Gasperi, L-2920 Luxembourg, http://epp.eurostat.ec.europa.eu; *Eurostat Yearbook 2006-2007.*

M.E. Sharpe, 80 Business Park Drive, Armonk, NY 10504, (800) 541-6563, Fax: (914) 273-2106, www.mesharpe.com; *The Illustrated Book of World Rankings.*

Organisation for Economic Cooperation and Development (OECD), 2 rue Andre Pascal, F-75775 Paris Cedex 16, France, (Telephone in U.S. (202) 785-6323), (Fax in U.S. (202) 785-0350), www.oecd.org; *Comparison of Gross Domestic Product (GDP) for OECD Countries; Geographical Distribution of Financial Flows to Aid Recipients 2002-2006; OECD Economic Outlook 2008;* and *Revenue Statistics 1965-2006 - 2007 Edition.*

Taylor and Francis Group, An Informa Business, 2 Park Square, Milton Park, Abingdon, Oxford OX14 4RN, United Kingdom, (Dial from U.S. (212) 216-7800), (Fax from U.S. (212) 564-7854), www.tandf.co.uk; *The Europa World Year Book.*

United Nations Statistics Division, New York, NY 10017, (800) 253-9646, Fax: (212) 963-4116, http://unstats.un.org; *Human Development Report 2006; National Accounts Statistics: Compendium of Income Distribution Statistics; Statistical Yearbook;* and *Trends in Europe and North America: The Statistical Yearbook of the ECE 2005.*

The World Bank, 1818 H Street, NW, Washington, DC 20433, (202) 473-1000, Fax: (202) 477-6391, www.worldbank.org; *World Development Indicators (WDI) 2008* and *World Development Report 2008.*

GREECE - GROSS NATIONAL PRODUCT

European Union, Delegation of the European Commission to the United States, 2300 M Street, NW, Washington, DC 20037, (202) 862-9500, Fax: (202) 429-1766, www.eurunion.org; *The EU Economy, 2007 Review: Moving Europe's Productivity Frontier.*

Eurostat, Batiment Jean Monnet, Rue Alcide de Gasperi, L-2920 Luxembourg, http://epp.eurostat.ec.europa.eu; *Eurostat Yearbook 2006-2007.*

M.E. Sharpe, 80 Business Park Drive, Armonk, NY 10504, (800) 541-6563, Fax: (914) 273-2106, www.mesharpe.com; *The Illustrated Book of World Rankings.*

Organisation for Economic Cooperation and Development (OECD), 2 rue Andre Pascal, F-75775 Paris Cedex 16, France, (Telephone in U.S. (202) 785-6323), (Fax in U.S. (202) 785-0350), www.oecd.org; *Geographical Distribution of Financial Flows to Aid Recipients 2002-2006; OECD Composite Leading Indicators (CLIs), Updated September 2007;* and *OECD Economic Outlook 2008.*

Palgrave Macmillan Ltd., Houndmills, Basingstoke, Hampshire, RG21 6XS, England, (Telephone in U.S. (888) 330-8477), (Fax in U.S. (800) 672-2054), www.palgrave.com; *The Statesman's Yearbook 2008.*

U.S. Department of State (DOS), 2201 C Street NW, Washington, DC 20520, (202) 647-4000, www.state.gov; *World Military Expenditures and Arms Transfers (WMEAT).*

United Nations Statistics Division, New York, NY 10017, (800) 253-9646, Fax: (212) 963-4116, http://unstats.un.org; *Statistical Yearbook.*

The World Bank, 1818 H Street, NW, Washington, DC 20433, (202) 473-1000, Fax: (202) 477-6391, www.worldbank.org; *The World Bank Atlas 2003-2004; World Development Indicators (WDI) 2008;* and *World Development Report 2008.*

GREECE - HAY PRODUCTION

See GREECE - CROPS

GREECE - HAZELNUT PRODUCTION

See GREECE - CROPS

GREECE - HEALTH

See GREECE - PUBLIC HEALTH

GREECE - HEMP FIBRE PRODUCTION

See GREECE - TEXTILE INDUSTRY

GREECE - HIDES AND SKINS INDUSTRY

Organisation for Economic Cooperation and Development (OECD), 2 rue Andre Pascal, F-75775 Paris Cedex 16, France, (Telephone in U.S. (202) 785-6323), (Fax in U.S. (202) 785-0350), www.oecd.org; *International Trade by Commodity Statistics (ITCS).*

United Nations Food and Agricultural Organization (FAO), Viale delle Terme di Caracalla, 00100 Rome, Italy, (Dial from U.S. (202) 653-2400), (Fax from U.S. (202) 653 5760), www.fao.org; *FAO Production Yearbook 2002.*

GREECE - HOPS PRODUCTION

See GREECE - CROPS

GREECE - HOUSING

Euromonitor International, Inc., 224 S. Michigan Avenue, Suite 1500, Chicago, IL 60604, (312) 922-1115, Fax: (312) 922-1157, www.euromonitor.com; *World Marketing Data and Statistics.*

European Union, Delegation of the European Commission to the United States, 2300 M Street, NW, Washington, DC 20037, (202) 862-9500, Fax: (202) 429-1766, www.eurunion.org; *European Union Labour Force Survey* and *Regions - Statistical Yearbook 2006*.

Eurostat, Batiment Jean Monnet, Rue Alcide de Gasperi, L-2920 Luxembourg, http://epp.eurostat.ec.europa.eu; *Eurostat Yearbook 2006-2007*.

M.E. Sharpe, 80 Business Park Drive, Armonk, NY 10504, (800) 541-6563, Fax: (914) 273-2106, www.mesharpe.com; *The Illustrated Book of World Rankings*.

United Nations Statistics Division, New York, NY 10017, (800) 253-9646, Fax: (212) 963-4116, http://unstats.un.org; *Trends in Europe and North America: The Statistical Yearbook of the ECE 2005*.

GREECE - HOUSING CONSTRUCTION

See GREECE - CONSTRUCTION INDUSTRY

GREECE - ILLITERATE PERSONS

Euromonitor International, Inc., 224 S. Michigan Avenue, Suite 1500, Chicago, IL 60604, (312) 922-1115, Fax: (312) 922-1157, www.euromonitor.com; *The World Economic Factbook 2008*.

UNESCO Institute for Statistics, C.P. 6128 Succursale Centre-Ville, Montreal, Quebec, H3C 3J7 Canada, (Dial from U.S. (514) 343-6880), (Fax from U.S. (514) 343 6882), www.uis.unesco.org; *Statistical Tables*.

United Nations Statistics Division, New York, NY 10017, (800) 253-9646, Fax: (212) 963-4116, http://unstats.un.org; *Human Development Report 2006*.

GREECE - IMPORTS

Central Intelligence Agency, Office of Public Affairs, Washington, DC 20505, (703) 482-0623, Fax: (703) 482-1739, www.cia.gov; *The World Factbook*.

Economist Intelligence Unit, 111 West 57th Street, New York, NY 10019, (212) 554-0600, Fax: (212) 586-1181, www.eiu.com; *Greece Country Report*.

Euromonitor International, Inc., 224 S. Michigan Avenue, Suite 1500, Chicago, IL 60604, (312) 922-1115, Fax: (312) 922-1157, www.euromonitor.com; *The World Economic Factbook 2008*.

European Union, Delegation of the European Commission to the United States, 2300 M Street, NW, Washington, DC 20037, (202) 862-9500, Fax: (202) 429-1766, www.eurunion.org; *European Union Energy Transport in Figures 2006; Eurostatistics: Data for Short-Term Economic Analysis (2007 edition); External and Intra-European Union Trade: Data 1958-2002; External and Intra-European Union Trade: Data 1999-2004;* and *Fishery Statistics - 1990-2006*.

Eurostat, Batiment Jean Monnet, Rue Alcide de Gasperi, L-2920 Luxembourg, http://epp.eurostat.ec.europa.eu; *Eurostat Yearbook 2006-2007*.

International Monetary Fund (IMF), 700 Nineteenth Street, NW, Washington, DC 20431, (202) 623-7000, Fax: (202) 623-4661, www.imf.org; *Direction of Trade Statistics Yearbook 2007; Government Finance Statistics Yearbook (2008 Edition);* and *International Financial Statistics Yearbook 2007*.

Organisation for Economic Cooperation and Development (OECD), 2 rue Andre Pascal, F-75775 Paris Cedex 16, France, (Telephone in U.S. (202) 785-6323), (Fax in U.S. (202) 785-0350), www.oecd.org; *Iron and Steel Industry in 2004 (2006 Edition); 2005 OECD Agricultural Outlook Tables, 1970-2014; OECD Economic Outlook 2008; OECD Economic Survey - Greece 2007; Review of Fisheries in OECD Countries: Country Statistics 2001 to 2003 - 2005 Edition;* and STructural ANalysis (STAN) database.

Palgrave Macmillan Ltd., Houndmills, Basingstoke, Hampshire, RG21 6XS, England, (Telephone in U.S. (888) 330-8477), (Fax in U.S. (800) 672-2054), www.palgrave.com; *The Statesman's Yearbook 2008*.

Platts, 2 Penn Plaza, 25th Floor, New York, NY 10121-2298, (212) 904-3070, www.platts.com; *Energy Economist*.

Taylor and Francis Group, An Informa Business, 2 Park Square, Milton Park, Abingdon, Oxford OX14 4RN, United Kingdom, (Dial from U.S. (212) 216-7800), (Fax from U.S. (212) 564-7854), www.tandf.co.uk; *The Europa World Year Book*.

Technical Association of the Pulp and Paper Industry (TAPPI), 15 Technology Parkway South, Norcross, GA 30092, (770) 446-1400, Fax: (770) 446-6947, www.tappi.org; *TAPPI Annual Report*.

United Nations Conference on Trade and Development (UNCTAD), DC2-1120, United Nations, New York, NY 10017, (212) 963-0027, www.unctad.org; *Handbook of Statistics 2005*.

United Nations Food and Agricultural Organization (FAO), Viale delle Terme di Caracalla, 00100 Rome, Italy, (Dial from U.S. (202) 653-2400), (Fax from U.S. (202) 653 5760), www.fao.org; *The State of Food and Agriculture (SOFA) 2006*.

United Nations Statistics Division, New York, NY 10017, (800) 253-9646, Fax: (212) 963-4116, http://unstats.un.org; *Energy Statistics Yearbook 2003* and *Trends in Europe and North America: The Statistical Yearbook of the ECE 2005*.

The World Bank, 1818 H Street, NW, Washington, DC 20433, (202) 473-1000, Fax: (202) 477-6391, www.worldbank.org; *World Development Indicators (WDI) 2008* and *World Development Report 2008*.

GREECE - INCOME TAXES

See GREECE - TAXATION

GREECE - INDUSTRIAL METALS PRODUCTION

See GREECE - MINERAL INDUSTRIES

GREECE - INDUSTRIAL PRODUCTIVITY

European Union, Delegation of the European Commission to the United States, 2300 M Street, NW, Washington, DC 20037, (202) 862-9500, Fax: (202) 429-1766, www.eurunion.org; *Eurostatistics: Data for Short-Term Economic Analysis (2007 edition); Fishery Statistics - 1990-2006;* and *RD Expenditure in Europe (2006 edition)*.

Eurostat, Batiment Jean Monnet, Rue Alcide de Gasperi, L-2920 Luxembourg, http://epp.eurostat.ec.europa.eu; *Eurostat Yearbook 2006-2007*.

M.E. Sharpe, 80 Business Park Drive, Armonk, NY 10504, (800) 541-6563, Fax: (914) 273-2106, www.mesharpe.com; *The Illustrated Book of World Rankings*.

Organisation for Economic Cooperation and Development (OECD), 2 rue Andre Pascal, F-75775 Paris Cedex 16, France, (Telephone in U.S. (202) 785-6323), (Fax in U.S. (202) 785-0350), www.oecd.org; *Environmental Impacts of Foreign Direct Investment in the Mining Sector in the Newly Independent States (NIS); Iron and Steel Industry in 2004 (2006 Edition); A New World Map in Textiles and Clothing: Adjusting to Change; 2005 OECD Agricultural Outlook Tables, 1970-2014; OECD Economic Outlook 2008;* and STructural ANalysis (STAN) database.

Technical Association of the Pulp and Paper Industry (TAPPI), 15 Technology Parkway South, Norcross, GA 30092, (770) 446-1400, Fax: (770) 446-6947, www.tappi.org; *TAPPI Annual Report*.

GREECE - INDUSTRIAL PROPERTY

United Nations Statistics Division, New York, NY 10017, (800) 253-9646, Fax: (212) 963-4116, http://unstats.un.org; *Statistical Yearbook*.

GREECE - INDUSTRIES

Central Intelligence Agency, Office of Public Affairs, Washington, DC 20505, (703) 482-0623, Fax: (703) 482-1739, www.cia.gov; *The World Factbook*.

Economist Intelligence Unit, 111 West 57th Street, New York, NY 10019, (212) 554-0600, Fax: (212) 586-1181, www.eiu.com; *Greece Country Report*.

Euromonitor International, Inc., 224 S. Michigan Avenue, Suite 1500, Chicago, IL 60604, (312) 922-1115, Fax: (312) 922-1157, www.euromonitor.com; *The World Economic Factbook 2008* and *World Marketing Data and Statistics*.

European Union, Delegation of the European Commission to the United States, 2300 M Street, NW, Washington, DC 20037, (202) 862-9500, Fax: (202) 429-1766, www.eurunion.org; *European Union Labour Force Survey* and *Eurostatistics: Data for Short-Term Economic Analysis (2007 edition)*.

Eurostat, Batiment Jean Monnet, Rue Alcide de Gasperi, L-2920 Luxembourg, http://epp.eurostat.ec.europa.eu; *Eurostat Yearbook 2006-2007*.

International Labour Office, I.L.O. Publications, 4 route des Morillons, CH-1211 Geneva 22, Switzerland, (Telephone in U.S. (202) 653-7652), (Fax in U.S. (202) 653-7687), www.ilo.org; *Yearbook of Labour Statistics 2006*.

M.E. Sharpe, 80 Business Park Drive, Armonk, NY 10504, (800) 541-6563, Fax: (914) 273-2106, www.mesharpe.com; *The Illustrated Book of World Rankings*.

Organisation for Economic Cooperation and Development (OECD), 2 rue Andre Pascal, F-75775 Paris Cedex 16, France, (Telephone in U.S. (202) 785-6323), (Fax in U.S. (202) 785-0350), www.oecd.org; *Key Environmental Indicators 2004; OECD Economic Outlook 2008; OECD Main Economic Indicators (MEI);* and STructural ANalysis (STAN) database.

Palgrave Macmillan Ltd., Houndmills, Basingstoke, Hampshire, RG21 6XS, England, (Telephone in U.S. (888) 330-8477), (Fax in U.S. (800) 672-2054), www.palgrave.com; *The Statesman's Yearbook 2008*.

Taylor and Francis Group, An Informa Business, 2 Park Square, Milton Park, Abingdon, Oxford OX14 4RN, United Kingdom, (Dial from U.S. (212) 216-7800), (Fax from U.S. (212) 564-7854), www.tandf.co.uk; *The Europa World Year Book*.

United Nations Industrial Development Organization (UNIDO), 1 United Nations Plaza, New York, NY 10017, (212) 963 6890, Fax: (212) 963-7904, http://unido.org; Industrial Statistics Database 2008 (INDSTAT) and *The International Yearbook of Industrial Statistics 2008*.

United Nations Statistics Division, New York, NY 10017, (800) 253-9646, Fax: (212) 963-4116, http://unstats.un.org; *2004 Industrial Commodity Statistics Yearbook; Statistical Yearbook;* and *Trends in Europe and North America: The Statistical Yearbook of the ECE 2005*.

The World Bank, 1818 H Street, NW, Washington, DC 20433, (202) 473-1000, Fax: (202) 477-6391, www.worldbank.org; *Greece* and *World Development Indicators (WDI) 2008*.

GREECE - INFANT AND MATERNAL MORTALITY

See GREECE - MORTALITY

GREECE - INORGANIC ACIDS

Eurostat, Batiment Jean Monnet, Rue Alcide de Gasperi, L-2920 Luxembourg, http://epp.eurostat.ec.europa.eu; *Eurostat Yearbook 2006-2007*.

United Nations Statistics Division, New York, NY 10017, (800) 253-9646, Fax: (212) 963-4116, http://unstats.un.org; *Statistical Yearbook*.

GREECE - INTEREST RATES

Eurostat, Batiment Jean Monnet, Rue Alcide de Gasperi, L-2920 Luxembourg, http://epp.eurostat.ec.europa.eu; *Eurostat Yearbook 2006-2007*.

Organisation for Economic Cooperation and Development (OECD), 2 rue Andre Pascal, F-75775 Paris Cedex 16, France, (Telephone in U.S. (202) 785-6323), (Fax in U.S. (202) 785-0350), www.oecd.org; *Financial Market Trends: OECD Periodical* and *OECD Economic Outlook 2008*.

GREECE - INTERNAL REVENUE

Organisation for Economic Cooperation and Development (OECD), 2 rue Andre Pascal, F-75775 Paris

Cedex 16, France, (Telephone in U.S. (202) 785-6323), (Fax in U.S. (202) 785-0350), www.oecd.org; *Revenue Statistics 1965-2006 - 2007 Edition.*

GREECE - INTERNATIONAL FINANCE

Eurostat, Batiment Jean Monnet, Rue Alcide de Gasperi, L-2920 Luxembourg, http://epp.eurostat.ec.europa.eu; *Eurostat Yearbook 2006-2007.*

International Finance Corporation (IFC), 2121 Pennsylvania Avenue, NW, Washington, DC 20433 USA, (202) 473-1000, Fax: (202) 974-4384, www.ifc.org; *Annual Report 2007.*

Organisation for Economic Cooperation and Development (OECD), 2 rue Andre Pascal, F-75775 Paris Cedex 16, France, (Telephone in U.S. (202) 785-6323), (Fax in U.S. (202) 785-0350), www.oecd.org; *Financial Market Trends: OECD Periodical; OECD Economic Outlook 2008;* and *OECD Main Economic Indicators (MEI).*

GREECE - INTERNATIONAL LIQUIDITY

International Monetary Fund (IMF), 700 Nineteenth Street, NW, Washington, DC 20431, (202) 623-7000, Fax: (202) 623-4661, www.imf.org; *International Financial Statistics Yearbook 2007.*

Organisation for Economic Cooperation and Development (OECD), 2 rue Andre Pascal, F-75775 Paris Cedex 16, France, (Telephone in U.S. (202) 785-6323), (Fax in U.S. (202) 785-0350), www.oecd.org; *Financial Market Trends: OECD Periodical* and *OECD Economic Outlook 2008.*

GREECE - INTERNATIONAL STATISTICS

Organisation for Economic Cooperation and Development (OECD), 2 rue Andre Pascal, F-75775 Paris Cedex 16, France, (Telephone in U.S. (202) 785-6323), (Fax in U.S. (202) 785-0350), www.oecd.org; *Financial Market Trends: OECD Periodical* and *Household, Tourism, Travel: Trends, Environmental Impacts and Policy Responses.*

GREECE - INTERNATIONAL TRADE

Banque de France, 48 rue Croix des Petits champs, 75001 Paris, France, www.banque-france.fr/home.htm; *Monthly Business Survey Overview.*

Bernan Essential Government Publications, 4611-F Assembly Drive, Lanham MD, 20706-4391, (301) 459-2255, Fax: (800) 865-3450, www.bernan.com; *OECD Factbook 2006.*

Economist Intelligence Unit, 111 West 57th Street, New York, NY 10019, (212) 554-0600, Fax: (212) 586-1181, www.eiu.com; *Greece Country Report.*

Euromonitor International, Inc., 224 S. Michigan Avenue, Suite 1500, Chicago, IL 60604, (312) 922-1115, Fax: (312) 922-1157, www.euromonitor.com; *European Marketing Data and Statistics 2008; The World Economic Factbook 2008;* and *World Marketing Data and Statistics.*

European Union, Delegation of the European Commission to the United States, 2300 M Street, NW, Washington, DC 20037, (202) 862-9500, Fax: (202) 429-1766, www.eurunion.org; *Eurostatistics: Data for Short-Term Economic Analysis (2007 edition); External and Intra-European Union Trade: Data 1958-2002; External and Intra-European Union Trade: Data 1999-2004;* and *Iron and Steel.*

Eurostat, Batiment Jean Monnet, Rue Alcide de Gasperi, L-2920 Luxembourg, http://epp.eurostat.ec.europa.eu; *Eurostat Yearbook 2006-2007* and Intra- and Extra-EU Trade.

International Monetary Fund (IMF), 700 Nineteenth Street, NW, Washington, DC 20431, (202) 623-7000, Fax: (202) 623-4661, www.imf.org; *International Financial Statistics Yearbook 2007.*

M.E. Sharpe, 80 Business Park Drive, Armonk, NY 10504, (800) 541-6563, Fax: (914) 273-2106, www.mesharpe.com; *The Illustrated Book of World Rankings.*

Organisation for Economic Cooperation and Development (OECD), 2 rue Andre Pascal, F-75775 Paris Cedex 16, France, (Telephone in U.S. (202) 785-6323), (Fax in U.S. (202) 785-0350), www.oecd.org; *International Trade by Commodity Statistics (ITCS); 2005 OECD Agricultural Outlook Tables, 1970-2014; OECD Economic Outlook 2008; OECD Economic Survey - Greece 2007; OECD in Figures 2007; OECD Main Economic Indicators (MEI);* and *Statistics on Ship Production, Exports and Orders in 2004.*

Palgrave Macmillan Ltd., Houndmills, Basingstoke, Hampshire, RG21 6XS, England, (Telephone in U.S. (888) 330-8477), (Fax in U.S. (800) 672-2054), www.palgrave.com; *The Statesman's Yearbook 2008.*

Platts, 2 Penn Plaza, 25th Floor, New York, NY 10121-2298, (212) 904-3070, www.platts.com; *Energy Economist.*

Taylor and Francis Group, An Informa Business, 2 Park Square, Milton Park, Abingdon, Oxford OX14 4RN, United Kingdom, (Dial from U.S. (212) 216-7800), (Fax from U.S. (212) 564-7854), www.tandf.co.uk; *The Europa World Year Book.*

United Nations Conference on Trade and Development (UNCTAD), DC2-1120, United Nations, New York, NY 10017, (212) 963-0027, www.unctad.org; *UNCTAD Commodity Yearbook.*

United Nations Food and Agricultural Organization (FAO), Viale delle Terme di Caracalla, 00100 Rome, Italy, (Dial from U.S. (202) 653-2400), (Fax from U.S. (202) 653 5760), www.fao.org; *FAO Trade Yearbook* and *The State of Food and Agriculture (SOFA) 2006.*

United Nations Statistics Division, New York, NY 10017, (800) 253-9646, Fax: (212) 963-4116, http://unstats.un.org; *Energy Statistics Yearbook 2003; International Trade Statistics Yearbook;* and *Statistical Yearbook.*

The World Bank, 1818 H Street, NW, Washington, DC 20433, (202) 473-1000, Fax: (202) 477-6391, www.worldbank.org; *Greece; World Development Indicators (WDI) 2008;* and *World Development Report 2008.*

World Trade Organization (WTO), Centre William Rappard, Rue de Lausanne 154, CH-1211 Geneva 21, Switzerland, www.wto.org; *International Trade Statistics 2006.*

GREECE - INTERNET USERS

Eurostat, Batiment Jean Monnet, Rue Alcide de Gasperi, L-2920 Luxembourg, http://epp.eurostat.ec.europa.eu; *Internet Usage by Enterprises 2007.*

International Telecommunication Union (ITU), Place des Nations, 1211 Geneva 20, Switzerland, www.itu.int; *World Telecommunication/ICT Indicators Database on CD-ROM; World Telecommunication/ICT Indicators Database Online;* and *Yearbook of Statistics - Telecommunication Services (Chronological Time Series 1997-2006).*

The World Bank, 1818 H Street, NW, Washington, DC 20433, (202) 473-1000, Fax: (202) 477-6391, www.worldbank.org; *Greece.*

GREECE - INVESTMENTS

International Monetary Fund (IMF), 700 Nineteenth Street, NW, Washington, DC 20431, (202) 623-7000, Fax: (202) 623-4661, www.imf.org; *International Financial Statistics Yearbook 2007.*

Organisation for Economic Cooperation and Development (OECD), 2 rue Andre Pascal, F-75775 Paris Cedex 16, France, (Telephone in U.S. (202) 785-6323), (Fax in U.S. (202) 785-0350), www.oecd.org; *Financial Market Trends: OECD Periodical; Iron and Steel Industry in 2004 (2006 Edition); A New World Map in Textiles and Clothing: Adjusting to Change; OECD Economic Outlook 2008;* and STructural ANalysis (STAN) database.

GREECE - IRON AND IRON ORE PRODUCTION

See GREECE - MINERAL INDUSTRIES

GREECE - JUTE PRODUCTION

See GREECE - CROPS

GREECE - LABOR

Central Intelligence Agency, Office of Public Affairs, Washington, DC 20505, (703) 482-0623, Fax: (703) 482-1739, www.cia.gov; *The World Factbook.*

Euromonitor International, Inc., 224 S. Michigan Avenue, Suite 1500, Chicago, IL 60604, (312) 922-1115, Fax: (312) 922-1157, www.euromonitor.com; *World Marketing Data and Statistics.*

European Union, Delegation of the European Commission to the United States, 2300 M Street, NW, Washington, DC 20037, (202) 862-9500, Fax: (202) 429-1766, www.eurunion.org; *European Union Labour Force Survey* and *Regions - Statistical Yearbook 2006.*

Eurostat, Batiment Jean Monnet, Rue Alcide de Gasperi, L-2920 Luxembourg, http://epp.eurostat.ec.europa.eu; *Eurostat Yearbook 2006-2007.*

International Labour Office, I.L.O. Publications, 4 route des Morillons, CH-1211 Geneva 22, Switzerland, (Telephone in U.S. (202) 653-7652), (Fax in U.S. (202) 653-7687), www.ilo.org; *Yearbook of Labour Statistics 2006.*

M.E. Sharpe, 80 Business Park Drive, Armonk, NY 10504, (800) 541-6563, Fax: (914) 273-2106, www.mesharpe.com; *The Illustrated Book of World Rankings.*

Organisation for Economic Cooperation and Development (OECD), 2 rue Andre Pascal, F-75775 Paris Cedex 16, France, (Telephone in U.S. (202) 785-6323), (Fax in U.S. (202) 785-0350), www.oecd.org; *Iron and Steel Industry in 2004 (2006 Edition); A New World Map in Textiles and Clothing: Adjusting to Change; OECD Economic Outlook 2008; OECD Economic Survey - Greece 2007; OECD Employment Outlook 2007; OECD Main Economic Indicators (MEI);* and *Statistics on Ship Production, Exports and Orders in 2004.*

Palgrave Macmillan Ltd., Houndmills, Basingstoke, Hampshire, RG21 6XS, England, (Telephone in U.S. (888) 330-8477), (Fax in U.S. (800) 672-2054), www.palgrave.com; *The Statesman's Yearbook 2008.*

Taylor and Francis Group, An Informa Business, 2 Park Square, Milton Park, Abingdon, Oxford OX14 4RN, United Kingdom, (Dial from U.S. (212) 216-7800), (Fax from U.S. (212) 564-7854), www.tandf.co.uk; *The Europa World Year Book.*

United Nations Food and Agricultural Organization (FAO), Viale delle Terme di Caracalla, 00100 Rome, Italy, (Dial from U.S. (202) 653-2400), (Fax from U.S. (202) 653 5760), www.fao.org; *The State of Food and Agriculture (SOFA) 2006.*

United Nations Statistics Division, New York, NY 10017, (800) 253-9646, Fax: (212) 963-4116, http://unstats.un.org; *Human Development Report 2006.*

The World Bank, 1818 H Street, NW, Washington, DC 20433, (202) 473-1000, Fax: (202) 477-6391, www.worldbank.org; *The World Bank Atlas 2003-2004; World Development Indicators (WDI) 2008;* and *World Development Report 2008.*

GREECE - LAND USE

Central Intelligence Agency, Office of Public Affairs, Washington, DC 20505, (703) 482-0623, Fax: (703) 482-1739, www.cia.gov; *The World Factbook.*

Euromonitor International, Inc., 224 S. Michigan Avenue, Suite 1500, Chicago, IL 60604, (312) 922-1115, Fax: (312) 922-1157, www.euromonitor.com; *European Marketing Data and Statistics 2008.*

European Union, Delegation of the European Commission to the United States, 2300 M Street, NW, Washington, DC 20037, (202) 862-9500, Fax: (202) 429-1766, www.eurunion.org; *Agricultural Statistics: Data 1995-2005; Agriculture in the European Union: Statistical and Economic Information 2006;* and *Regions - Statistical Yearbook 2006.*

Eurostat, Batiment Jean Monnet, Rue Alcide de Gasperi, L-2920 Luxembourg, http://epp.eurostat.ec.europa.eu; *Eurostat Yearbook 2006-2007.*

United Nations Food and Agricultural Organization (FAO), Viale delle Terme di Caracalla, 00100 Rome,

Italy, (Dial from U.S. (202) 653-2400), (Fax from U.S. (202) 653 5760), www.fao.org; *FAO Production Yearbook 2002.*

The World Bank, 1818 H Street, NW, Washington, DC 20433, (202) 473-1000, Fax: (202) 477-6391, www.worldbank.org; *World Development Report 2008.*

GREECE - LEATHER INDUSTRY AND TRADE

Eurostat, Batiment Jean Monnet, Rue Alcide de Gasperi, L-2920 Luxembourg, http://epp.eurostat.ec.europa.eu; *Eurostat Yearbook 2006-2007.*

GREECE - LIBRARIES

Euromonitor International, Inc., 224 S. Michigan Avenue, Suite 1500, Chicago, IL 60604, (312) 922-1115, Fax: (312) 922-1157, www.euromonitor.com; *European Marketing Data and Statistics 2008.*

M.E. Sharpe, 80 Business Park Drive, Armonk, NY 10504, (800) 541-6563, Fax: (914) 273-2106, www.mesharpe.com; *The Illustrated Book of World Rankings.*

United Nations Statistics Division, New York, NY 10017, (800) 253-9646, Fax: (212) 963-4116, http://unstats.un.org; *Trends in Europe and North America: The Statistical Yearbook of the ECE 2005.*

GREECE - LICENSES

International Monetary Fund (IMF), 700 Nineteenth Street, NW, Washington, DC 20431, (202) 623-7000, Fax: (202) 623-4661, www.imf.org; *Government Finance Statistics Yearbook (2008 Edition).*

GREECE - LIFE EXPECTANCY

Central Intelligence Agency, Office of Public Affairs, Washington, DC 20505, (703) 482-0623, Fax: (703) 482-1739, www.cia.gov; *The World Factbook.*

Euromonitor International, Inc., 224 S. Michigan Avenue, Suite 1500, Chicago, IL 60604, (312) 922-1115, Fax: (312) 922-1157, www.euromonitor.com; *The World Economic Factbook 2008.*

Organisation for Economic Cooperation and Development (OECD), 2 rue Andre Pascal, F-75775 Paris Cedex 16, France, (Telephone in U.S. (202) 785-6323), (Fax in U.S. (202) 785-0350), www.oecd.org; *OECD Economic Outlook 2008.*

United Nations Statistics Division, New York, NY 10017, (800) 253-9646, Fax: (212) 963-4116, http://unstats.un.org; *Human Development Report 2006; Trends in Europe and North America: The Statistical Yearbook of the ECE 2005;* and *World Statistics Pocketbook.*

The World Bank, 1818 H Street, NW, Washington, DC 20433, (202) 473-1000, Fax: (202) 477-6391, www.worldbank.org; *The World Bank Atlas 2003-2004* and *World Development Report 2008.*

GREECE - LITERACY

Euromonitor International, Inc., 224 S. Michigan Avenue, Suite 1500, Chicago, IL 60604, (312) 922-1115, Fax: (312) 922-1157, www.euromonitor.com; *World Marketing Data and Statistics.*

GREECE - LIVESTOCK

Euromonitor International, Inc., 224 S. Michigan Avenue, Suite 1500, Chicago, IL 60604, (312) 922-1115, Fax: (312) 922-1157, www.euromonitor.com; *European Marketing Data and Statistics 2008.*

European Union, Delegation of the European Commission to the United States, 2300 M Street, NW, Washington, DC 20037, (202) 862-9500, Fax: (202) 429-1766, www.eurunion.org; *Agricultural Statistics: Data 1995-2005; Eurostatistics: Data for Short-Term Economic Analysis (2007 edition);* and *Regions - Statistical Yearbook 2006.*

Eurostat, Batiment Jean Monnet, Rue Alcide de Gasperi, L-2920 Luxembourg, http://epp.eurostat.ec.europa.eu; *Eurostat Yearbook 2006-2007.*

M.E. Sharpe, 80 Business Park Drive, Armonk, NY 10504, (800) 541-6563, Fax: (914) 273-2106, www.mesharpe.com; *The Illustrated Book of World Rankings.*

Organisation for Economic Cooperation and Development (OECD), 2 rue Andre Pascal, F-75775 Paris Cedex 16, France, (Telephone in U.S. (202) 785-6323), (Fax in U.S. (202) 785-0350), www.oecd.org; *2005 OECD Agricultural Outlook Tables, 1970-2014.*

Palgrave Macmillan Ltd., Houndmills, Basingstoke, Hampshire, RG21 6XS, England, (Telephone in U.S. (888) 330-8477), (Fax in U.S. (800) 672-2054), www.palgrave.com; *The Statesman's Yearbook 2008.*

Taylor and Francis Group, An Informa Business, 2 Park Square, Milton Park, Abingdon, Oxford OX14 4RN, United Kingdom, (Dial from U.S. (212) 216-7800), (Fax from U.S. (212) 564-7854), www.tandf.co.uk; *The Europa World Year Book.*

United Nations Conference on Trade and Development (UNCTAD), DC2-1120, United Nations, New York, NY 10017, (212) 963-0027, www.unctad.org; *UNCTAD Commodity Yearbook.*

United Nations Food and Agricultural Organization (FAO), Viale delle Terme di Caracalla, 00100 Rome, Italy, (Dial from U.S. (202) 653-2400), (Fax from U.S. (202) 653 5760), www.fao.org; *FAO Production Yearbook 2002* and *The State of Food and Agriculture (SOFA) 2006.*

United Nations Statistics Division, New York, NY 10017, (800) 253-9646, Fax: (212) 963-4116, http://unstats.un.org; *Statistical Yearbook.*

GREECE - MAGNESIUM PRODUCTION AND CONSUMPTION

See GREECE - MINERAL INDUSTRIES

GREECE - MANUFACTURES

European Union, Delegation of the European Commission to the United States, 2300 M Street, NW, Washington, DC 20037, (202) 862-9500, Fax: (202) 429-1766, www.eurunion.org; *European Union Labour Force Survey; Eurostatistics: Data for Short-Term Economic Analysis (2007 edition);* and *The Textile Industry in the EU.*

Eurostat, Batiment Jean Monnet, Rue Alcide de Gasperi, L-2920 Luxembourg, http://epp.eurostat.ec.europa.eu; *Eurostat Yearbook 2006-2007.*

International Monetary Fund (IMF), 700 Nineteenth Street, NW, Washington, DC 20431, (202) 623-7000, Fax: (202) 623-4661, www.imf.org; *International Financial Statistics Yearbook 2007.*

M.E. Sharpe, 80 Business Park Drive, Armonk, NY 10504, (800) 541-6563, Fax: (914) 273-2106, www.mesharpe.com; *The Illustrated Book of World Rankings.*

Organisation for Economic Cooperation and Development (OECD), 2 rue Andre Pascal, F-75775 Paris Cedex 16, France, (Telephone in U.S. (202) 785-6323), (Fax in U.S. (202) 785-0350), www.oecd.org; *International Trade by Commodity Statistics (ITCS); OECD Economic Survey - Greece 2007;* and STructural ANalysis (STAN) database.

United Nations Statistics Division, New York, NY 10017, (800) 253-9646, Fax: (212) 963-4116, http://unstats.un.org; *Statistical Yearbook.*

The World Bank, 1818 H Street, NW, Washington, DC 20433, (202) 473-1000, Fax: (202) 477-6391, www.worldbank.org; *World Development Indicators (WDI) 2008.*

GREECE - MARRIAGE

Eurostat, Batiment Jean Monnet, Rue Alcide de Gasperi, L-2920 Luxembourg, http://epp.eurostat.ec.europa.eu; *Eurostat Yearbook 2006-2007.*

M.E. Sharpe, 80 Business Park Drive, Armonk, NY 10504, (800) 541-6563, Fax: (914) 273-2106, www.mesharpe.com; *The Illustrated Book of World Rankings.*

Taylor and Francis Group, An Informa Business, 2 Park Square, Milton Park, Abingdon, Oxford OX14 4RN, United Kingdom, (Dial from U.S. (212) 216-7800), (Fax from U.S. (212) 564-7854), www.tandf.co.uk; *The Europa World Year Book.*

United Nations Statistics Division, New York, NY 10017, (800) 253-9646, Fax: (212) 963-4116, http://unstats.un.org; *Demographic Yearbook; Statistical Yearbook;* and *Trends in Europe and North America: The Statistical Yearbook of the ECE 2005.*

GREECE - MEAT PRODUCTION

See GREECE - LIVESTOCK

GREECE - MERCURY PRODUCTION

See GREECE - MINERAL INDUSTRIES

GREECE - METAL PRODUCTS

Eurostat, Batiment Jean Monnet, Rue Alcide de Gasperi, L-2920 Luxembourg, http://epp.eurostat.ec.europa.eu; *Eurostat Yearbook 2006-2007.*

GREECE - MILK PRODUCTION

See GREECE - DAIRY PROCESSING

GREECE - MINERAL INDUSTRIES

Commodity Research Bureau, 330 South Wells Street, Suite 612, Chicago, IL 60606-7110, (800) 621-5271, Fax: (312) 939-4135, www.crbtrader.com; *2006 CRB Commodity Yearbook and CD.*

European Union, Delegation of the European Commission to the United States, 2300 M Street, NW, Washington, DC 20037, (202) 862-9500, Fax: (202) 429-1766, www.eurunion.org; *European Union Energy Transport in Figures 2006; Eurostatistics: Data for Short-Term Economic Analysis (2007 edition); Iron and Steel;* and *Regions - Statistical Yearbook 2006.*

Eurostat, Batiment Jean Monnet, Rue Alcide de Gasperi, L-2920 Luxembourg, http://epp.eurostat.ec.europa.eu; *Energy - Monthly Statistics; Eurostat Yearbook 2006-2007;* and *Panorama of Energy - 2007 Edition.*

International Energy Agency (IEA), 9, rue de la Federation, 75739 Paris Cedex 15, France, www.iea.org; *Key World Energy Statistics 2007.*

International Labour Office, I.L.O. Publications, 4 route des Morillons, CH-1211 Geneva 22, Switzerland, (Telephone in U.S. (202) 653-7652), (Fax in U.S. (202) 653-7687), www.ilo.org; *Yearbook of Labour Statistics 2006.*

M.E. Sharpe, 80 Business Park Drive, Armonk, NY 10504, (800) 541-6563, Fax: (914) 273-2106, www.mesharpe.com; *The Illustrated Book of World Rankings.*

Organisation for Economic Cooperation and Development (OECD), 2 rue Andre Pascal, F-75775 Paris Cedex 16, France, (Telephone in U.S. (202) 785-6323), (Fax in U.S. (202) 785-0350), www.oecd.org; *Energy Statistics of OECD Countries* (2007 Edition); *Environmental Impacts of Foreign Direct Investment in the Mining Sector in the Newly Independent States (NIS); International Trade by Commodity Statistics (ITCS); Iron and Steel Industry in 2004 (2006 Edition); OECD Economic Survey - Greece 2007;* STructural ANalysis (STAN) database; and *World Energy Outlook 2007.*

Palgrave Macmillan Ltd., Houndmills, Basingstoke, Hampshire, RG21 6XS, England, (Telephone in U.S. (888) 330-8477), (Fax in U.S. (800) 672-2054), www.palgrave.com; *The Statesman's Yearbook 2008.*

Platts, 2 Penn Plaza, 25th Floor, New York, NY 10121-2298, (212) 904-3070, www.platts.com; *Energy in East Europe* and *EU Energy.*

Taylor and Francis Group, An Informa Business, 2 Park Square, Milton Park, Abingdon, Oxford OX14 4RN, United Kingdom, (Dial from U.S. (212) 216-7800), (Fax from U.S. (212) 564-7854), www.tandf.co.uk; *The Europa World Year Book.*

United Nations Conference on Trade and Development (UNCTAD), DC2-1120, United Nations, New York, NY 10017, (212) 963-0027, www.unctad.org; *UNCTAD Commodity Yearbook.*

United Nations Statistics Division, New York, NY 10017, (800) 253-9646, Fax: (212) 963-4116, http://unstats.un.org; *Statistical Yearbook.*

GREECE - MONEY

European Central Bank (ECB), Postfach 160319, D-60066 Frankfurt am Main, Germany, www.ecb.int;

Monetary Developments in the Euro Area; Monthly Bulletin; and *Statistics Pocket Book.*

Organisation for Economic Cooperation and Development (OECD), 2 rue Andre Pascal, F-75775 Paris Cedex 16, France, (Telephone in U.S. (202) 785-6323), (Fax in U.S. (202) 785-0350), www.oecd.org; *OECD Economic Survey - Greece 2007.*

GREECE - MONEY EXCHANGE RATES

See GREECE - FOREIGN EXCHANGE RATES

GREECE - MONEY SUPPLY

Economist Intelligence Unit, 111 West 57th Street, New York, NY 10019, (212) 554-0600, Fax: (212) 586-1181, www.eiu.com; *Greece Country Report.*

European Union, Delegation of the European Commission to the United States, 2300 M Street, NW, Washington, DC 20037, (202) 862-9500, Fax: (202) 429-1766, www.eurunion.org; *Eurostatistics: Data for Short-Term Economic Analysis (2007 edition).*

Eurostat, Batiment Jean Monnet, Rue Alcide de Gasperi, L-2920 Luxembourg, http://epp.eurostat.ec.europa.eu; *Eurostat Yearbook 2006-2007.*

International Monetary Fund (IMF), 700 Nineteenth Street, NW, Washington, DC 20431, (202) 623-7000, Fax: (202) 623-4661, www.imf.org; *International Financial Statistics Yearbook 2007.*

Organisation for Economic Cooperation and Development (OECD), 2 rue Andre Pascal, F-75775 Paris Cedex 16, France, (Telephone in U.S. (202) 785-6323), (Fax in U.S. (202) 785-0350), www.oecd.org; *OECD Economic Outlook 2008.*

Taylor and Francis Group, An Informa Business, 2 Park Square, Milton Park, Abingdon, Oxford OX14 4RN, United Kingdom, (Dial from U.S. (212) 216-7800), (Fax from U.S. (212) 564-7854), www.tandf.co.uk; *The Europa World Year Book.*

United Nations Statistics Division, New York, NY 10017, (800) 253-9646, Fax: (212) 963-4116, http://unstats.un.org; *Statistical Yearbook.*

The World Bank, 1818 H Street, NW, Washington, DC 20433, (202) 473-1000, Fax: (202) 477-6391, www.worldbank.org; *Greece* and *World Development Indicators (WDI) 2008.*

GREECE - MONUMENTS AND HISTORIC SITES

UNESCO Institute for Statistics, C.P. 6128 Succursale Centre-Ville, Montreal, Quebec, H3C 3J7 Canada, (Dial from U.S. (514) 343-6880), (Fax from U.S. (514) 343 6882), www.uis.unesco.org; *Statistical Tables.*

GREECE - MORTALITY

Central Intelligence Agency, Office of Public Affairs, Washington, DC 20505, (703) 482-0623, Fax: (703) 482-1739, www.cia.gov; *The World Factbook.*

Euromonitor International, Inc., 224 S. Michigan Avenue, Suite 1500, Chicago, IL 60604, (312) 922-1115, Fax: (312) 922-1157, www.euromonitor.com; *The World Economic Factbook 2008.*

European Union, Delegation of the European Commission to the United States, 2300 M Street, NW, Washington, DC 20037, (202) 862-9500, Fax: (202) 429-1766, www.eurunion.org; *First Demographic Estimates for 2006.*

Eurostat, Batiment Jean Monnet, Rue Alcide de Gasperi, L-2920 Luxembourg, http://epp.eurostat.ec.europa.eu; *Eurostat Yearbook 2006-2007.*

Palgrave Macmillan Ltd., Houndmills, Basingstoke, Hampshire, RG21 6XS, England, (Telephone in U.S. (888) 330-8477), (Fax in U.S. (800) 672-2054), www.palgrave.com; *The Statesman's Yearbook 2008.*

Taylor and Francis Group, An Informa Business, 2 Park Square, Milton Park, Abingdon, Oxford OX14 4RN, United Kingdom, (Dial from U.S. (212) 216-7800), (Fax from U.S. (212) 564-7854), www.tandf.co.uk; *The Europa World Year Book.*

UNICEF, 3 United Nations Plaza, New York, NY 10017, (800) 253-9646, Fax: (212) 887-7465, www.unicef.org; *The State of the World's Children 2008.*

United Nations Statistics Division, New York, NY 10017, (800) 253-9646, Fax: (212) 963-4116, http://unstats.un.org; *Demographic Yearbook; Human Development Report 2006; Statistical Yearbook; Trends in Europe and North America: The Statistical Yearbook of the ECE 2005;* and *World Statistics Pocketbook.*

The World Bank, 1818 H Street, NW, Washington, DC 20433, (202) 473-1000, Fax: (202) 477-6391, www.worldbank.org; *The World Bank Atlas 2003-2004; World Development Indicators (WDI) 2008;* and *World Development Report 2008.*

World Health Organization (WHO), Avenue Appia 20, 1211 Geneve 27, Switzerland, (Telephone in U.S. (212) 331-9081), www.who.int; The WHO Global Atlas of Infectious Diseases and *World Health Report 2006.*

GREECE - MOTION PICTURES

Palgrave Macmillan Ltd., Houndmills, Basingstoke, Hampshire, RG21 6XS, England, (Telephone in U.S. (888) 330-8477), (Fax in U.S. (800) 672-2054), www.palgrave.com; *The Statesman's Yearbook 2008.*

UNESCO Institute for Statistics, C.P. 6128 Succursale Centre-Ville, Montreal, Quebec, H3C 3J7 Canada, (Dial from U.S. (514) 343-6880), (Fax from U.S. (514) 343 6882), www.uis.unesco.org; *Statistical Tables.*

GREECE - MOTOR VEHICLES

European Union, Delegation of the European Commission to the United States, 2300 M Street, NW, Washington, DC 20037, (202) 862-9500, Fax: (202) 429-1766, www.eurunion.org; *Statistical Overview of Transport in the European Union (Data 1970-2001).*

Eurostat, Batiment Jean Monnet, Rue Alcide de Gasperi, L-2920 Luxembourg, http://epp.eurostat.ec.europa.eu; *Eurostat Yearbook 2006-2007.*

International Road Federation (IFR), Madison Place, 500 Montgomery Street, 5th Floor, Alexandria, VA 22314, (703) 535-1001, Fax: (703) 535-1007, www.irfnet.org; *World Road Statistics 2006.*

Taylor and Francis Group, An Informa Business, 2 Park Square, Milton Park, Abingdon, Oxford OX14 4RN, United Kingdom, (Dial from U.S. (212) 216-7800), (Fax from U.S. (212) 564-7854), www.tandf.co.uk; *The Europa World Year Book.*

United Nations Statistics Division, New York, NY 10017, (800) 253-9646, Fax: (212) 963-4116, http://unstats.un.org; *Statistical Yearbook.*

GREECE - MUSEUMS

M.E. Sharpe, 80 Business Park Drive, Armonk, NY 10504, (800) 541-6563, Fax: (914) 273-2106, www.mesharpe.com; *The Illustrated Book of World Rankings.*

UNESCO Institute for Statistics, C.P. 6128 Succursale Centre-Ville, Montreal, Quebec, H3C 3J7 Canada, (Dial from U.S. (514) 343-6880), (Fax from U.S. (514) 343 6882), www.uis.unesco.org; *Statistical Tables.*

GREECE - NATURAL GAS PRODUCTION

See GREECE - MINERAL INDUSTRIES

GREECE - NICKEL AND NICKEL ORE

See GREECE - MINERAL INDUSTRIES

GREECE - NUTRITION

United Nations Food and Agricultural Organization (FAO), Viale delle Terme di Caracalla, 00100 Rome, Italy, (Dial from U.S. (202) 653-2400), (Fax from U.S. (202) 653 5760), www.fao.org; *The State of Food and Agriculture (SOFA) 2006.*

GREECE - OATS PRODUCTION

See GREECE - CROPS

GREECE - OILSEED PLANTS

Eurostat, Batiment Jean Monnet, Rue Alcide de Gasperi, L-2920 Luxembourg, http://epp.eurostat.ec.europa.eu; *Eurostat Yearbook 2006-2007.*

Organisation for Economic Cooperation and Development (OECD), 2 rue Andre Pascal, F-75775 Paris Cedex 16, France, (Telephone in U.S. (202) 785-6323), (Fax in U.S. (202) 785-0350), www.oecd.org; *International Trade by Commodity Statistics (ITCS).*

GREECE - OLDER PEOPLE

M.E. Sharpe, 80 Business Park Drive, Armonk, NY 10504, (800) 541-6563, Fax: (914) 273-2106, www.mesharpe.com; *The Illustrated Book of World Rankings.*

GREECE - ONION PRODUCTION

See GREECE - CROPS

GREECE - ORANGES PRODUCTION

See GREECE - CROPS

GREECE - PALM OIL PRODUCTION

See GREECE - CROPS

GREECE - PAPER

See GREECE - FORESTS AND FORESTRY

GREECE - PEANUT PRODUCTION

See GREECE - CROPS

GREECE - PEPPER PRODUCTION

See GREECE - CROPS

GREECE - PERIODICALS

UNESCO Institute for Statistics, C.P. 6128 Succursale Centre-Ville, Montreal, Quebec, H3C 3J7 Canada, (Dial from U.S. (514) 343-6880), (Fax from U.S. (514) 343 6882), www.uis.unesco.org; *Statistical Tables.*

GREECE - PESTICIDES

United Nations Food and Agricultural Organization (FAO), Viale delle Terme di Caracalla, 00100 Rome, Italy, (Dial from U.S. (202) 653-2400), (Fax from U.S. (202) 653 5760), www.fao.org; *The State of Food and Agriculture (SOFA) 2006.*

GREECE - PETROLEUM INDUSTRY AND TRADE

Eurostat, Batiment Jean Monnet, Rue Alcide de Gasperi, L-2920 Luxembourg, http://epp.eurostat.ec.europa.eu; *Eurostat Yearbook 2006-2007.*

International Energy Agency (IEA), 9, rue de la Federation, 75739 Paris Cedex 15, France, www.iea.org; *Key World Energy Statistics 2007.*

M.E. Sharpe, 80 Business Park Drive, Armonk, NY 10504, (800) 541-6563, Fax: (914) 273-2106, www.mesharpe.com; *The Illustrated Book of World Rankings.*

Organisation for Economic Cooperation and Development (OECD), 2 rue Andre Pascal, F-75775 Paris Cedex 16, France, (Telephone in U.S. (202) 785-6323), (Fax in U.S. (202) 785-0350), www.oecd.org; *Energy Statistics of OECD Countries* (2007 Edition); *International Trade by Commodity Statistics (ITCS); Oil Information 2006 Edition;* and *World Energy Outlook 2007.*

Palgrave Macmillan Ltd., Houndmills, Basingstoke, Hampshire, RG21 6XS, England, (Telephone in U.S. (888) 330-8477), (Fax in U.S. (800) 672-2054), www.palgrave.com; *The Statesman's Yearbook 2008.*

PennWell Corporation, 1421 South Sheridan Road, Tulsa, OK 74112, (918) 835-3161, www.pennwell.com; *International Petroleum Encyclopedia 2007.*

Platts, 2 Penn Plaza, 25th Floor, New York, NY 10121-2298, (212) 904-3070, www.platts.com; *Energy Economist.*

U.S. Department of Energy (DOE), Energy Information Administration (EIA), 1000 Independence Avenue, SW, Washington, DC 20585, (202) 586-8800, www.eia.doe.gov; *International Energy Annual 2004* and *International Energy Outlook 2006.*

United Nations Conference on Trade and Development (UNCTAD), DC2-1120, United Nations, New York, NY 10017, (212) 963-0027, www.unctad.org; *UNCTAD Commodity Yearbook.*

United Nations Food and Agricultural Organization (FAO), Viale delle Terme di Caracalla, 00100 Rome, Italy, (Dial from U.S. (202) 653-2400), (Fax from U.S. (202) 653 5760), www.fao.org; *The State of Food and Agriculture (SOFA) 2006.*

United Nations Statistics Division, New York, NY 10017, (800) 253-9646, Fax: (212) 963-4116, http://unstats.un.org; *Energy Statistics Yearbook 2003; Statistical Yearbook;* and *Trends in Europe and North America: The Statistical Yearbook of the ECE 2005.*

GREECE - PHOSPHATES PRODUCTION

See GREECE - MINERAL INDUSTRIES

GREECE - PIPELINES

European Union, Delegation of the European Commission to the United States, 2300 M Street, NW, Washington, DC 20037, (202) 862-9500, Fax: (202) 429-1766, www.eurunion.org; *Statistical Overview of Transport in the European Union (Data 1970-2001).*

GREECE - PISTACHIO PRODUCTION

See GREECE - CROPS

GREECE - PLASTICS INDUSTRY AND TRADE

Eurostat, Batiment Jean Monnet, Rue Alcide de Gasperi, L-2920 Luxembourg, http://epp.eurostat.ec.europa.eu; *Eurostat Yearbook 2006-2007.*

Organisation for Economic Cooperation and Development (OECD), 2 rue Andre Pascal, F-75775 Paris Cedex 16, France, (Telephone in U.S. (202) 785-6323), (Fax in U.S. (202) 785-0350), www.oecd.org; *International Trade by Commodity Statistics (ITCS).*

United Nations Statistics Division, New York, NY 10017, (800) 253-9646, Fax: (212) 963-4116, http://unstats.un.org; *Statistical Yearbook.*

GREECE - PLATINUM PRODUCTION

See GREECE - MINERAL INDUSTRIES

GREECE - POLITICAL SCIENCE

Central Intelligence Agency, Office of Public Affairs, Washington, DC 20505, (703) 482-0623, Fax: (703) 482-1739, www.cia.gov; *The World Factbook.*

European Union, Delegation of the European Commission to the United States, 2300 M Street, NW, Washington, DC 20037, (202) 862-9500, Fax: (202) 429-1766, www.eurunion.org; *RD Expenditure in Europe (2006 edition).*

Eurostat, Batiment Jean Monnet, Rue Alcide de Gasperi, L-2920 Luxembourg, http://epp.eurostat.ec.europa.eu; *Eurostat Yearbook 2006-2007.*

International Monetary Fund (IMF), 700 Nineteenth Street, NW, Washington, DC 20431, (202) 623-7000, Fax: (202) 623-4661, www.imf.org; *Government Finance Statistics Yearbook (2008 Edition)* and *International Financial Statistics Yearbook 2007.*

Organisation for Economic Cooperation and Development (OECD), 2 rue Andre Pascal, F-75775 Paris Cedex 16, France, (Telephone in U.S. (202) 785-6323), (Fax in U.S. (202) 785-0350), www.oecd.org; *OECD Economic Outlook 2008* and *Revenue Statistics 1965-2006 - 2007 Edition.*

Palgrave Macmillan Ltd., Houndmills, Basingstoke, Hampshire, RG21 6XS, England, (Telephone in U.S. (888) 330-8477), (Fax in U.S. (800) 672-2054), www.palgrave.com; *The Statesman's Yearbook 2008.*

Taylor and Francis Group, An Informa Business, 2 Park Square, Milton Park, Abingdon, Oxford OX14 4RN, United Kingdom, (Dial from U.S. (212) 216-7800), (Fax from U.S. (212) 564-7854), www.tandf.co.uk; *The Europa World Year Book.*

United Nations Statistics Division, New York, NY 10017, (800) 253-9646, Fax: (212) 963-4116, http://unstats.un.org; *National Accounts Statistics: Compendium of Income Distribution Statistics* and *Statistical Yearbook.*

The World Bank, 1818 H Street, NW, Washington, DC 20433, (202) 473-1000, Fax: (202) 477-6391, www.worldbank.org; *World Development Indicators (WDI) 2008* and *World Development Report 2008.*

GREECE - POPULATION

Banque de France, 48 rue Croix des Petits champs, 75001 Paris, France, www.banque-france.fr/home.htm; *Key Data for the Euro Area.*

Central Intelligence Agency, Office of Public Affairs, Washington, DC 20505, (703) 482-0623, Fax: (703) 482-1739, www.cia.gov; *The World Factbook.*

Economist Intelligence Unit, 111 West 57th Street, New York, NY 10019, (212) 554-0600, Fax: (212) 586-1181, www.eiu.com; *Greece Country Report.*

Euromonitor International, Inc., 224 S. Michigan Avenue, Suite 1500, Chicago, IL 60604, (312) 922-1115, Fax: (312) 922-1157, www.euromonitor.com; *European Marketing Data and Statistics 2008* and *The World Economic Factbook 2008.*

European Union, Delegation of the European Commission to the United States, 2300 M Street, NW, Washington, DC 20037, (202) 862-9500, Fax: (202) 429-1766, www.eurunion.org; *European Union Labour Force Survey; First Demographic Estimates for 2006; Iron and Steel;* and *Regions - Statistical Yearbook 2006.*

Eurostat, Batiment Jean Monnet, Rue Alcide de Gasperi, L-2920 Luxembourg, http://epp.eurostat.ec.europa.eu; *Eurostat Yearbook 2006-2007* and *The Life of Women and Men in Europe - A Statistical Portrait.*

International Labour Office, I.L.O. Publications, 4 route des Morillons, CH-1211 Geneva 22, Switzerland, (Telephone in U.S. (202) 653-7652), (Fax in U.S. (202) 653-7687), www.ilo.org; *Yearbook of Labour Statistics 2006.*

M.E. Sharpe, 80 Business Park Drive, Armonk, NY 10504, (800) 541-6563, Fax: (914) 273-2106, www.mesharpe.com; *The Illustrated Book of World Rankings.*

Organisation for Economic Cooperation and Development (OECD), 2 rue Andre Pascal, F-75775 Paris Cedex 16, France, (Telephone in U.S. (202) 785-6323), (Fax in U.S. (202) 785-0350), www.oecd.org; *Labour Force Statistics: 1986-2005, 2007 Edition.*

Palgrave Macmillan Ltd., Houndmills, Basingstoke, Hampshire, RG21 6XS, England, (Telephone in U.S. (888) 330-8477), (Fax in U.S. (800) 672-2054), www.palgrave.com; *The Statesman's Yearbook 2008.*

Taylor and Francis Group, An Informa Business, 2 Park Square, Milton Park, Abingdon, Oxford OX14 4RN, United Kingdom, (Dial from U.S. (212) 216-7800), (Fax from U.S. (212) 564-7854), www.tandf.co.uk; *The Europa World Year Book.*

U.S. Department of State (DOS), 2201 C Street NW, Washington, DC 20520, (202) 647-4000, www.state.gov; *World Military Expenditures and Arms Transfers (WMEAT).*

UNESCO Institute for Statistics, C.P. 6128 Succursale Centre-Ville, Montreal, Quebec, H3C 3J7 Canada, (Dial from U.S. (514) 343-6880), (Fax from U.S. (514) 343 6882), www.uis.unesco.org; *Statistical Tables.*

United Nations Food and Agricultural Organization (FAO), Viale delle Terme di Caracalla, 00100 Rome, Italy, (Dial from U.S. (202) 653-2400), (Fax from U.S. (202) 653 5760), www.fao.org; *FAO Production Yearbook 2002.*

United Nations Statistics Division, New York, NY 10017, (800) 253-9646, Fax: (212) 963-4116, http://unstats.un.org; *Demographic Yearbook; Human Development Report 2006; Statistical Yearbook; Trends in Europe and North America: The Statistical Yearbook of the ECE 2005;* and *World Statistics Pocketbook.*

The World Bank, 1818 H Street, NW, Washington, DC 20433, (202) 473-1000, Fax: (202) 477-6391, www.worldbank.org; *Greece; The World Bank Atlas 2003-2004;* and *World Development Report 2008.*

World Health Organization (WHO), Avenue Appia 20, 1211 Geneve 27, Switzerland, (Telephone in U.S. (212) 331-9081), www.who.int; *World Health Report 2006.*

GREECE - POPULATION DENSITY

Central Intelligence Agency, Office of Public Affairs, Washington, DC 20505, (703) 482-0623, Fax: (703) 482-1739, www.cia.gov; *The World Factbook.*

Euromonitor International, Inc., 224 S. Michigan Avenue, Suite 1500, Chicago, IL 60604, (312) 922-1115, Fax: (312) 922-1157, www.euromonitor.com; *The World Economic Factbook 2008.*

European Union, Delegation of the European Commission to the United States, 2300 M Street, NW, Washington, DC 20037, (202) 862-9500, Fax: (202) 429-1766, www.eurunion.org; *First Demographic Estimates for 2006.*

Eurostat, Batiment Jean Monnet, Rue Alcide de Gasperi, L-2920 Luxembourg, http://epp.eurostat.ec.europa.eu; *Eurostat Yearbook 2006-2007.*

M.E. Sharpe, 80 Business Park Drive, Armonk, NY 10504, (800) 541-6563, Fax: (914) 273-2106, www.mesharpe.com; *The Illustrated Book of World Rankings.*

Palgrave Macmillan Ltd., Houndmills, Basingstoke, Hampshire, RG21 6XS, England, (Telephone in U.S. (888) 330-8477), (Fax in U.S. (800) 672-2054), www.palgrave.com; *The Statesman's Yearbook 2008.*

Taylor and Francis Group, An Informa Business, 2 Park Square, Milton Park, Abingdon, Oxford OX14 4RN, United Kingdom, (Dial from U.S. (212) 216-7800), (Fax from U.S. (212) 564-7854), www.tandf.co.uk; *The Europa World Year Book.*

UNESCO Institute for Statistics, C.P. 6128 Succursale Centre-Ville, Montreal, Quebec, H3C 3J7 Canada, (Dial from U.S. (514) 343-6880), (Fax from U.S. (514) 343 6882), www.uis.unesco.org; *Statistical Tables.*

United Nations Food and Agricultural Organization (FAO), Viale delle Terme di Caracalla, 00100 Rome, Italy, (Dial from U.S. (202) 653-2400), (Fax from U.S. (202) 653 5760), www.fao.org; *The State of Food and Agriculture (SOFA) 2006.*

United Nations Statistics Division, New York, NY 10017, (800) 253-9646, Fax: (212) 963-4116, http://unstats.un.org; *Statistical Yearbook* and *Trends in Europe and North America: The Statistical Yearbook of the ECE 2005.*

The World Bank, 1818 H Street, NW, Washington, DC 20433, (202) 473-1000, Fax: (202) 477-6391, www.worldbank.org; *Greece* and *World Development Report 2008.*

GREECE - POSTAL SERVICE

European Union, Delegation of the European Commission to the United States, 2300 M Street, NW, Washington, DC 20037, (202) 862-9500, Fax: (202) 429-1766, www.eurunion.org; *Statistical Overview of Transport in the European Union (Data 1970-2001).*

M.E. Sharpe, 80 Business Park Drive, Armonk, NY 10504, (800) 541-6563, Fax: (914) 273-2106, www.mesharpe.com; *The Illustrated Book of World Rankings.*

United Nations Statistics Division, New York, NY 10017, (800) 253-9646, Fax: (212) 963-4116, http://unstats.un.org; *Statistical Yearbook* and *Trends in Europe and North America: The Statistical Yearbook of the ECE 2005.*

GREECE - POWER RESOURCES

Euromonitor International, Inc., 224 S. Michigan Avenue, Suite 1500, Chicago, IL 60604, (312) 922-1115, Fax: (312) 922-1157, www.euromonitor.com; *European Marketing Data and Statistics 2008; The World Economic Factbook 2008;* and *World Marketing Data and Statistics.*

European Union, Delegation of the European Commission to the United States, 2300 M Street, NW,

Washington, DC 20037, (202) 862-9500, Fax: (202) 429-1766, www.eurunion.org; *European Union Energy Transport in Figures 2006; Regions - Statistical Yearbook 2006;* and *Statistical Overview of Transport in the European Union (Data 1970-2001).*

Eurostat, Batiment Jean Monnet, Rue Alcide de Gasperi, L-2920 Luxembourg, http://epp.eurostat.ec.europa.eu; *Eurostat Yearbook 2006-2007.*

M.E. Sharpe, 80 Business Park Drive, Armonk, NY 10504, (800) 541-6563, Fax: (914) 273-2106, www.mesharpe.com; *The Illustrated Book of World Rankings.*

Organisation for Economic Cooperation and Development (OECD), 2 rue Andre Pascal, F-75775 Paris Cedex 16, France, (Telephone in U.S. (202) 785-6323), (Fax in U.S. (202) 785-0350), www.oecd.org; *Coal Information: 2007 Edition; Energy Statistics of OECD Countries* (2007 Edition); *Key Environmental Indicators 2004; Oil Information 2006 Edition;* and *World Energy Outlook 2007.*

Palgrave Macmillan Ltd., Houndmills, Basingstoke, Hampshire, RG21 6XS, England, (Telephone in U.S. (888) 330-8477), (Fax in U.S. (800) 672-2054), www.palgrave.com; *The Statesman's Yearbook 2008.*

Platts, 2 Penn Plaza, 25th Floor, New York, NY 10121-2298, (212) 904-3070, www.platts.com; *Energy Economist* and *European Power Daily.*

U.S. Department of Energy (DOE), Energy Information Administration (EIA), 1000 Independence Avenue, SW, Washington, DC 20585, (202) 586-8800, www.eia.doe.gov; *International Energy Annual 2004* and *International Energy Outlook 2006.*

United Nations Food and Agricultural Organization (FAO), Viale delle Terme di Caracalla, 00100 Rome, Italy, (Dial from U.S. (202) 653-2400), (Fax from U.S. (202) 653 5760), www.fao.org; *The State of Food and Agriculture (SOFA) 2006.*

United Nations Statistics Division, New York, NY 10017, (800) 253-9646, Fax: (212) 963-4116, http://unstats.un.org; *Energy Statistics Yearbook 2003; Human Development Report 2006; Statistical Yearbook; Trends in Europe and North America: The Statistical Yearbook of the ECE 2005;* and *World Statistics Pocketbook.*

The World Bank, 1818 H Street, NW, Washington, DC 20433, (202) 473-1000, Fax: (202) 477-6391, www.worldbank.org; *The World Bank Atlas 2003-2004* and *World Development Report 2008.*

GREECE - PRICES

Euromonitor International, Inc., 224 S. Michigan Avenue, Suite 1500, Chicago, IL 60604, (312) 922-1115, Fax: (312) 922-1157, www.euromonitor.com; *European Marketing Data and Statistics 2008* and *World Marketing Data and Statistics.*

European Union, Delegation of the European Commission to the United States, 2300 M Street, NW, Washington, DC 20037, (202) 862-9500, Fax: (202) 429-1766, www.eurunion.org; *Eurostatistics: Data for Short-Term Economic Analysis (2007 edition).*

Eurostat, Batiment Jean Monnet, Rue Alcide de Gasperi, L-2920 Luxembourg, http://epp.eurostat.ec.europa.eu; *Eurostat Yearbook 2006-2007.*

International Labour Office, I.L.O. Publications, 4 route des Morillons, CH-1211 Geneva 22, Switzerland, (Telephone in U.S. (202) 653-7652), (Fax in U.S. (202) 653-7687), www.ilo.org; *Yearbook of Labour Statistics 2006.*

International Monetary Fund (IMF), 700 Nineteenth Street, NW, Washington, DC 20431, (202) 623-7000, Fax: (202) 623-4661, www.imf.org; *International Financial Statistics Yearbook 2007.*

M.E. Sharpe, 80 Business Park Drive, Armonk, NY 10504, (800) 541-6563, Fax: (914) 273-2106, www.mesharpe.com; *The Illustrated Book of World Rankings.*

Organisation for Economic Cooperation and Development (OECD), 2 rue Andre Pascal, F-75775 Paris Cedex 16, France, (Telephone in U.S. (202) 785-6323), (Fax in U.S. (202) 785-0350), www.oecd.org; *Iron and Steel Industry in 2004 (2006 Edition); OECD Economic Outlook 2008;* and *OECD Main Economic Indicators (MEI).*

Technical Association of the Pulp and Paper Industry (TAPPI), 15 Technology Parkway South, Norcross, GA 30092, (770) 446-1400, Fax: (770) 446-6947, www.tappi.org; *TAPPI Annual Report.*

United Nations Food and Agricultural Organization (FAO), Viale delle Terme di Caracalla, 00100 Rome, Italy, (Dial from U.S. (202) 653-2400), (Fax from U.S. (202) 653 5760), www.fao.org; *FAO Production Yearbook 2002* and *The State of Food and Agriculture (SOFA) 2006.*

The World Bank, 1818 H Street, NW, Washington, DC 20433, (202) 473-1000, Fax: (202) 477-6391, www.worldbank.org; *Greece.*

GREECE - PROFESSIONS

Eurostat, Batiment Jean Monnet, Rue Alcide de Gasperi, L-2920 Luxembourg, http://epp.eurostat.ec.europa.eu; *Eurostat Yearbook 2006-2007.*

United Nations Statistics Division, New York, NY 10017, (800) 253-9646, Fax: (212) 963-4116, http://unstats.un.org; *Statistical Yearbook.*

GREECE - PUBLIC HEALTH

Euromonitor International, Inc., 224 S. Michigan Avenue, Suite 1500, Chicago, IL 60604, (312) 922-1115, Fax: (312) 922-1157, www.euromonitor.com; *World Health Databook 2007/2008* and *World Marketing Data and Statistics.*

European Union, Delegation of the European Commission to the United States, 2300 M Street, NW, Washington, DC 20037, (202) 862-9500, Fax: (202) 429-1766, www.eurunion.org; *Regions - Statistical Yearbook 2006.*

Eurostat, Batiment Jean Monnet, Rue Alcide de Gasperi, L-2920 Luxembourg, http://epp.eurostat.ec.europa.eu; *Eurostat Yearbook 2006-2007.*

Health and Consumer Protection Directorate-General, European Commission, B-1049 Brussels, Belgium, http://ec.europa.eu/dgs/health_consumer/index_en.htm; *Injuries in the European Union: Statistics Summary 2002-2004.*

International Monetary Fund (IMF), 700 Nineteenth Street, NW, Washington, DC 20431, (202) 623-7000, Fax: (202) 623-4661, www.imf.org; *Government Finance Statistics Yearbook (2008 Edition).*

M.E. Sharpe, 80 Business Park Drive, Armonk, NY 10504, (800) 541-6563, Fax: (914) 273-2106, www.mesharpe.com; *The Illustrated Book of World Rankings.*

Organisation for Economic Cooperation and Development (OECD), 2 rue Andre Pascal, F-75775 Paris Cedex 16, France, (Telephone in U.S. (202) 785-6323), (Fax in U.S. (202) 785-0350), www.oecd.org; *Health at a Glance 2007 - OECD Indicators.*

Palgrave Macmillan Ltd., Houndmills, Basingstoke, Hampshire, RG21 6XS, England, (Telephone in U.S. (888) 330-8477), (Fax in U.S. (800) 672-2054), www.palgrave.com; *The Statesman's Yearbook 2008.*

Robert Koch Institute, Nordufer 20, D 13353 Berlin, Germany, www.rki.de; *EUVAC-NET Report: Pertussis-Surveillance 1998-2002.*

UNICEF, 3 United Nations Plaza, New York, NY 10017, (800) 253-9646, Fax: (212) 887-7465, www.unicef.org; *The State of the World's Children 2008.*

United Nations Statistics Division, New York, NY 10017, (800) 253-9646, Fax: (212) 963-4116, http://unstats.un.org; *Human Development Report 2006; Statistical Yearbook;* and *Trends in Europe and North America: The Statistical Yearbook of the ECE 2005.*

The World Bank, 1818 H Street, NW, Washington, DC 20433, (202) 473-1000, Fax: (202) 477-6391, www.worldbank.org; *Greece* and *World Development Report 2008.*

World Health Organization (WHO), Avenue Appia 20, 1211 Geneve 27, Switzerland, (Telephone in U.S. (212) 331-9081), www.who.int; The WHO Global Atlas of Infectious Diseases and *World Health Report 2006.*

GREECE - PUBLIC UTILITIES

Eurostat, Batiment Jean Monnet, Rue Alcide de Gasperi, L-2920 Luxembourg, http://epp.eurostat.ec.europa.eu; *Eurostat Yearbook 2006-2007.*

GREECE - PUBLISHERS AND PUBLISHING

Taylor and Francis Group, An Informa Business, 2 Park Square, Milton Park, Abingdon, Oxford OX14 4RN, United Kingdom, (Dial from U.S. (212) 216-7800), (Fax from U.S. (212) 564-7854), www.tandf.co.uk; *The Europa World Year Book.*

UNESCO Institute for Statistics, C.P. 6128 Succursale Centre-Ville, Montreal, Quebec, H3C 3J7 Canada, (Dial from U.S. (514) 343-6880), (Fax from U.S. (514) 343 6882), www.uis.unesco.org; *Statistical Tables.*

United Nations Statistics Division, New York, NY 10017, (800) 253-9646, Fax: (212) 963-4116, http://unstats.un.org; *Trends in Europe and North America: The Statistical Yearbook of the ECE 2005.*

GREECE - RADIO BROADCASTING

Palgrave Macmillan Ltd., Houndmills, Basingstoke, Hampshire, RG21 6XS, England, (Telephone in U.S. (888) 330-8477), (Fax in U.S. (800) 672-2054), www.palgrave.com; *The Statesman's Yearbook 2008.*

GREECE - RAILROADS

Euromonitor International, Inc., 224 S. Michigan Avenue, Suite 1500, Chicago, IL 60604, (312) 922-1115, Fax: (312) 922-1157, www.euromonitor.com; *European Marketing Data and Statistics 2008.*

European Union, Delegation of the European Commission to the United States, 2300 M Street, NW, Washington, DC 20037, (202) 862-9500, Fax: (202) 429-1766, www.eurunion.org; *Regions - Statistical Yearbook 2006* and *Statistical Overview of Transport in the European Union (Data 1970-2001).*

Eurostat, Batiment Jean Monnet, Rue Alcide de Gasperi, L-2920 Luxembourg, http://epp.eurostat.ec.europa.eu; *Eurostat Yearbook 2006-2007.*

Jane's Information Group, 110 North Royal Street, Suite 200, Alexandria, VA 22314, (703) 683-3700, Fax: (800) 836-0297, www.janes.com; *Jane's World Railways.*

Palgrave Macmillan Ltd., Houndmills, Basingstoke, Hampshire, RG21 6XS, England, (Telephone in U.S. (888) 330-8477), (Fax in U.S. (800) 672-2054), www.palgrave.com; *The Statesman's Yearbook 2008.*

Taylor and Francis Group, An Informa Business, 2 Park Square, Milton Park, Abingdon, Oxford OX14 4RN, United Kingdom, (Dial from U.S. (212) 216-7800), (Fax from U.S. (212) 564-7854), www.tandf.co.uk; *The Europa World Year Book.*

United Nations Statistics Division, New York, NY 10017, (800) 253-9646, Fax: (212) 963-4116, http://unstats.un.org; *Annual Bulletin of Transport Statistics for Europe and North America 2004; Statistical Yearbook;* and *Trends in Europe and North America: The Statistical Yearbook of the ECE 2005.*

GREECE - RANCHING

Eurostat, Batiment Jean Monnet, Rue Alcide de Gasperi, L-2920 Luxembourg, http://epp.eurostat.ec.europa.eu; *Eurostat Yearbook 2006-2007.*

GREECE - RELIGION

Central Intelligence Agency, Office of Public Affairs, Washington, DC 20505, (703) 482-0623, Fax: (703) 482-1739, www.cia.gov; *The World Factbook.*

M.E. Sharpe, 80 Business Park Drive, Armonk, NY 10504, (800) 541-6563, Fax: (914) 273-2106, www.mesharpe.com; *The Illustrated Book of World Rankings.*

Palgrave Macmillan Ltd., Houndmills, Basingstoke, Hampshire, RG21 6XS, England, (Telephone in U.S. (888) 330-8477), (Fax in U.S. (800) 672-2054), www.palgrave.com; *The Statesman's Yearbook 2008.*

GREECE - RENT CHARGES

International Labour Office, I.L.O. Publications, 4 route des Morillons, CH-1211 Geneva 22, Switzerland, (Telephone in U.S. (202) 653-7652), (Fax in U.S. (202) 653-7687), www.ilo.org; *Yearbook of Labour Statistics 2006.*

GREECE - RESERVES (ACCOUNTING)

Eurostat, Batiment Jean Monnet, Rue Alcide de Gasperi, L-2920 Luxembourg, http://epp.eurostat.ec.europa.eu; *Eurostat Yearbook 2006-2007.*

Organisation for Economic Cooperation and Development (OECD), 2 rue Andre Pascal, F-75775 Paris Cedex 16, France, (Telephone in U.S. (202) 785-6323), (Fax in U.S. (202) 785-0350), www.oecd.org; *Financial Market Trends: OECD Periodical* and *OECD Economic Outlook 2008.*

United Nations Statistics Division, New York, NY 10017, (800) 253-9646, Fax: (212) 963-4116, http://unstats.un.org; *Statistical Yearbook.*

The World Bank, 1818 H Street, NW, Washington, DC 20433, (202) 473-1000, Fax: (202) 477-6391, www.worldbank.org; *World Development Indicators (WDI) 2008.*

GREECE - RETAIL TRADE

Banque de France, 48 rue Croix des Petits champs, 75001 Paris, France, www.banque-france.fr/home.htm; *Monthly Business Survey Overview.*

Euromonitor International, Inc., 224 S. Michigan Avenue, Suite 1500, Chicago, IL 60604, (312) 922-1115, Fax: (312) 922-1157, www.euromonitor.com; *Retail Trade International 2007.*

European Union, Delegation of the European Commission to the United States, 2300 M Street, NW, Washington, DC 20037, (202) 862-9500, Fax: (202) 429-1766, www.eurunion.org; *Eurostatistics: Data for Short-Term Economic Analysis (2007 edition).*

Eurostat, Batiment Jean Monnet, Rue Alcide de Gasperi, L-2920 Luxembourg, http://epp.eurostat.ec.europa.eu; *Eurostat Yearbook 2006-2007.*

GREECE - RICE PRODUCTION

See GREECE - CROPS

GREECE - ROADS

Central Intelligence Agency, Office of Public Affairs, Washington, DC 20505, (703) 482-0623, Fax: (703) 482-1739, www.cia.gov; *The World Factbook.*

European Union, Delegation of the European Commission to the United States, 2300 M Street, NW, Washington, DC 20037, (202) 862-9500, Fax: (202) 429-1766, www.eurunion.org; *Statistical Overview of Transport in the European Union (Data 1970-2001).*

Eurostat, Batiment Jean Monnet, Rue Alcide de Gasperi, L-2920 Luxembourg, http://epp.eurostat.ec.europa.eu; *Eurostat Yearbook 2006-2007.*

International Road Federation (IFR), Madison Place, 500 Montgomery Street, 5th Floor, Alexandria, VA 22314, (703) 535-1001, Fax: (703) 535-1007, www.irfnet.org; *World Road Statistics 2006.*

Palgrave Macmillan Ltd., Houndmills, Basingstoke, Hampshire, RG21 6XS, England, (Telephone in U.S. (888) 330-8477), (Fax in U.S. (800) 672-2054), www.palgrave.com; *The Statesman's Yearbook 2008.*

United Nations Statistics Division, New York, NY 10017, (800) 253-9646, Fax: (212) 963-4116, http://unstats.un.org; *Trends in Europe and North America: The Statistical Yearbook of the ECE 2005.*

GREECE - RUBBER INDUSTRY AND TRADE

Eurostat, Batiment Jean Monnet, Rue Alcide de Gasperi, L-2920 Luxembourg, http://epp.eurostat.ec.europa.eu; *Eurostat Yearbook 2006-2007.*

International Rubber Study Group (IRSG), 1st Floor, Heron House, 109/115 Wembley Hill Road, Wembley, Middlesex HA9 8DA, United Kingdom, www.rubberstudy.com; *Rubber Statistical Bulletin; Summary of World Rubber Statistics 2005; World Rubber Statistics Handbook (Volume 6, 1975-2001);* and *World Rubber Statistics Historic Handbook.*

M.E. Sharpe, 80 Business Park Drive, Armonk, NY 10504, (800) 541-6563, Fax: (914) 273-2106, www.mesharpe.com; *The Illustrated Book of World Rankings.*

Organisation for Economic Cooperation and Development (OECD), 2 rue Andre Pascal, F-75775 Paris Cedex 16, France, (Telephone in U.S. (202) 785-6323), (Fax in U.S. (202) 785-0350), www.oecd.org; *International Trade by Commodity Statistics (ITCS).*

GREECE - RYE PRODUCTION

See GREECE - CROPS

GREECE - SAFFLOWER SEED PRODUCTION

See GREECE - CROPS

GREECE - SALT PRODUCTION

See GREECE - MINERAL INDUSTRIES

GREECE - SAVINGS ACCOUNT DEPOSITS

See GREECE - BANKS AND BANKING

GREECE - SHEEP

See GREECE - LIVESTOCK

GREECE - SHIPPING

European Union, Delegation of the European Commission to the United States, 2300 M Street, NW, Washington, DC 20037, (202) 862-9500, Fax: (202) 429-1766, www.eurunion.org; *Fishery Statistics - 1990-2006; Regions - Statistical Yearbook 2006;* and *Statistical Overview of Transport in the European Union (Data 1970-2001).*

Eurostat, Batiment Jean Monnet, Rue Alcide de Gasperi, L-2920 Luxembourg, http://epp.eurostat.ec.europa.eu; *Eurostat Yearbook 2006-2007.*

Lloyd's Register - Fairplay, 8410 N.W. 53rd Terrace, Suite 207, Miami FL 33166, (305) 718-9929, Fax: (305) 718-9663, www.lrfairplay.com; *Register of Ships 2007-2008; World Casualty Statistics 2007; World Fleet Statistics 2006; World Marine Propulsion Report 2006-2010; World Shipbuilding Statistics 2007;* and The World Shipping Encyclopaedia.

Organisation for Economic Cooperation and Development (OECD), 2 rue Andre Pascal, F-75775 Paris Cedex 16, France, (Telephone in U.S. (202) 785-6323), (Fax in U.S. (202) 785-0350), www.oecd.org; *Statistics on Ship Production, Exports and Orders in 2004.*

Palgrave Macmillan Ltd., Houndmills, Basingstoke, Hampshire, RG21 6XS, England, (Telephone in U.S. (888) 330-8477), (Fax in U.S. (800) 672-2054), www.palgrave.com; *The Statesman's Yearbook 2008.*

Taylor and Francis Group, An Informa Business, 2 Park Square, Milton Park, Abingdon, Oxford OX14 4RN, United Kingdom, (Dial from U.S. (212) 216-7800), (Fax from U.S. (212) 564-7854), www.tandf.co.uk; *The Europa World Year Book.*

U.S. Department of Transportation (DOT), Maritime Administration (MARAD), West Building, Southeast Federal Center, 1200 New Jersey Avenue, SE, Washington, DC 20590, (800) 99-MARAD, www.marad.dot.gov; *World Merchant Fleet 2005.*

United Nations Statistics Division, New York, NY 10017, (800) 253-9646, Fax: (212) 963-4116, http://unstats.un.org; *Statistical Yearbook.*

GREECE - SILVER PRODUCTION

See GREECE - MINERAL INDUSTRIES

GREECE - SOCIAL CLASSES

European Union, Delegation of the European Commission to the United States, 2300 M Street, NW, Washington, DC 20037, (202) 862-9500, Fax: (202) 429-1766, www.eurunion.org; *European Union Labour Force Survey.*

Eurostat, Batiment Jean Monnet, Rue Alcide de Gasperi, L-2920 Luxembourg, http://epp.eurostat.ec.europa.eu; *Eurostat Yearbook 2006-2007.*

GREECE - SOCIAL ECOLOGY

Eurostat, Batiment Jean Monnet, Rue Alcide de Gasperi, L-2920 Luxembourg, http://epp.eurostat.ec.europa.eu; *Eurostat Yearbook 2006-2007.*

M.E. Sharpe, 80 Business Park Drive, Armonk, NY 10504, (800) 541-6563, Fax: (914) 273-2106, www.mesharpe.com; *The Illustrated Book of World Rankings.*

United Nations Statistics Division, New York, NY 10017, (800) 253-9646, Fax: (212) 963-4116, http://unstats.un.org; *World Statistics Pocketbook.*

GREECE - SOCIAL SECURITY

Eurostat, Batiment Jean Monnet, Rue Alcide de Gasperi, L-2920 Luxembourg, http://epp.eurostat.ec.europa.eu; *Eurostat Yearbook 2006-2007.*

International Monetary Fund (IMF), 700 Nineteenth Street, NW, Washington, DC 20431, (202) 623-7000, Fax: (202) 623-4661, www.imf.org; *Government Finance Statistics Yearbook (2008 Edition).*

Organisation for Economic Cooperation and Development (OECD), 2 rue Andre Pascal, F-75775 Paris Cedex 16, France, (Telephone in U.S. (202) 785-6323), (Fax in U.S. (202) 785-0350), www.oecd.org; *Revenue Statistics 1965-2006 - 2007 Edition.*

United Nations Statistics Division, New York, NY 10017, (800) 253-9646, Fax: (212) 963-4116, http://unstats.un.org; *National Accounts Statistics: Compendium of Income Distribution Statistics.*

GREECE - SOYBEAN PRODUCTION

See GREECE - CROPS

GREECE - STATE AFFORESTATION

See GREECE - FORESTS AND FORESTRY

GREECE - STEEL PRODUCTION

See GREECE - MINERAL INDUSTRIES

GREECE - STRAW PRODUCTION

See GREECE - CROPS

GREECE - SUGAR PRODUCTION

See GREECE - CROPS

GREECE - SULPHUR PRODUCTION

See GREECE - MINERAL INDUSTRIES

GREECE - SUNFLOWER PRODUCTION

See GREECE - CROPS

GREECE - TAXATION

Eurostat, Batiment Jean Monnet, Rue Alcide de Gasperi, L-2920 Luxembourg, http://epp.eurostat.ec.europa.eu; *Eurostat Yearbook 2006-2007* and *Taxation Trends in the European Union - Data for the EU Member States and Norway.*

International Monetary Fund (IMF), 700 Nineteenth Street, NW, Washington, DC 20431, (202) 623-7000, Fax: (202) 623-4661, www.imf.org; *Government Finance Statistics Yearbook (2008 Edition).*

International Road Federation (IFR), Madison Place, 500 Montgomery Street, 5th Floor, Alexandria, VA 22314, (703) 535-1001, Fax: (703) 535-1007, www.irfnet.org; *World Road Statistics 2006.*

Organisation for Economic Cooperation and Development (OECD), 2 rue Andre Pascal, F-75775 Paris Cedex 16, France, (Telephone in U.S. (202) 785-6323), (Fax in U.S. (202) 785-0350), www.oecd.org; *Revenue Statistics 1965-2006 - 2007 Edition.*

Taylor and Francis Group, An Informa Business, 2 Park Square, Milton Park, Abingdon, Oxford OX14 4RN, United Kingdom, (Dial from U.S. (212) 216-7800), (Fax from U.S. (212) 564-7854), www.tandf.co.uk; *The Europa World Year Book.*

The World Bank, 1818 H Street, NW, Washington, DC 20433, (202) 473-1000, Fax: (202) 477-6391, www.worldbank.org; *World Development Indicators (WDI) 2008.*

GREECE - TEA PRODUCTION

See GREECE - CROPS

GREECE - TELEPHONE

European Union, Delegation of the European Commission to the United States, 2300 M Street, NW, Washington, DC 20037, (202) 862-9500, Fax: (202) 429-1766, www.eurunion.org; *Statistical Overview of Transport in the European Union (Data 1970-2001).*

Eurostat, Batiment Jean Monnet, Rue Alcide de Gasperi, L-2920 Luxembourg, http://epp.eurostat.ec.europa.eu; *Eurostat Yearbook 2006-2007.*

International Telecommunication Union (ITU), Place des Nations, 1211 Geneva 20, Switzerland, www.itu.int; World Telecommunication Indicators Database.

Palgrave Macmillan Ltd., Houndmills, Basingstoke, Hampshire, RG21 6XS, England, (Telephone in U.S. (888) 330-8477), (Fax in U.S. (800) 672-2054), www.palgrave.com; *The Statesman's Yearbook 2008.*

Taylor and Francis Group, An Informa Business, 2 Park Square, Milton Park, Abingdon, Oxford OX14 4RN, United Kingdom, (Dial from U.S. (212) 216-7800), (Fax from U.S. (212) 564-7854), www.tandf.co.uk; *The Europa World Year Book.*

United Nations Statistics Division, New York, NY 10017, (800) 253-9646, Fax: (212) 963-4116, http://unstats.un.org; *Statistical Yearbook; Trends in Europe and North America: The Statistical Yearbook of the ECE 2005;* and *World Statistics Pocketbook.*

GREECE - TELEVISION - RECEIVERS AND RECEPTION

Eurostat, Batiment Jean Monnet, Rue Alcide de Gasperi, L-2920 Luxembourg, http://epp.eurostat.ec.europa.eu; *Eurostat Yearbook 2006-2007.*

United Nations Statistics Division, New York, NY 10017, (800) 253-9646, Fax: (212) 963-4116, http://unstats.un.org; *Statistical Yearbook.*

GREECE - TEXTILE INDUSTRY

Euromonitor International, Inc., 224 S. Michigan Avenue, Suite 1500, Chicago, IL 60604, (312) 922-1115, Fax: (312) 922-1157, www.euromonitor.com; *Retail Trade International 2007.*

European Union, Delegation of the European Commission to the United States, 2300 M Street, NW, Washington, DC 20037, (202) 862-9500, Fax: (202) 429-1766, www.eurunion.org; *Agriculture in the European Union: Statistical and Economic Information 2006; Eurostatistics: Data for Short-Term Economic Analysis (2007 edition);* and *The Textile Industry in the EU.*

Eurostat, Batiment Jean Monnet, Rue Alcide de Gasperi, L-2920 Luxembourg, http://epp.eurostat.ec.europa.eu; *Eurostat Yearbook 2006-2007.*

M.E. Sharpe, 80 Business Park Drive, Armonk, NY 10504, (800) 541-6563, Fax: (914) 273-2106, www.mesharpe.com; *The Illustrated Book of World Rankings.*

Organisation for Economic Cooperation and Development (OECD), 2 rue Andre Pascal, F-75775 Paris Cedex 16, France, (Telephone in U.S. (202) 785-6323), (Fax in U.S. (202) 785-0350), www.oecd.org; *International Trade by Commodity Statistics (ITCS); A New World Map in Textiles and Clothing: Adjusting to Change;* and STructural ANalysis (STAN) database.

Palgrave Macmillan Ltd., Houndmills, Basingstoke, Hampshire, RG21 6XS, England, (Telephone in U.S. (888) 330-8477), (Fax in U.S. (800) 672-2054), www.palgrave.com; *The Statesman's Yearbook 2008.*

United Nations Statistics Division, New York, NY 10017, (800) 253-9646, Fax: (212) 963-4116, http://unstats.un.org; *Statistical Yearbook.*

GREECE - THEATER

UNESCO Institute for Statistics, C.P. 6128 Succursale Centre-Ville, Montreal, Quebec, H3C 3J7 Canada, (Dial from U.S. (514) 343-6880), (Fax from U.S. (514) 343 6882), www.uis.unesco.org; *Statistical Tables.*

GREECE - TIMBER

See GREECE - FORESTS AND FORESTRY

GREECE - TIN INDUSTRY

Euromonitor International, Inc., 224 S. Michigan Avenue, Suite 1500, Chicago, IL 60604, (312) 922-1115, Fax: (312) 922-1157, www.euromonitor.com; *European Marketing Data and Statistics 2008.*

Eurostat, Batiment Jean Monnet, Rue Alcide de Gasperi, L-2920 Luxembourg, http://epp.eurostat.ec.europa.eu; *Eurostat Yearbook 2006-2007.*

M.E. Sharpe, 80 Business Park Drive, Armonk, NY 10504, (800) 541-6563, Fax: (914) 273-2106, www.mesharpe.com; *The Illustrated Book of World Rankings.*

Organisation for Economic Cooperation and Development (OECD), 2 rue Andre Pascal, F-75775 Paris Cedex 16, France, (Telephone in U.S. (202) 785-6323), (Fax in U.S. (202) 785-0350), www.oecd.org; *International Trade by Commodity Statistics (ITCS)* and STructural ANalysis (STAN) database.

United Nations Statistics Division, New York, NY 10017, (800) 253-9646, Fax: (212) 963-4116, http://unstats.un.org; *Statistical Yearbook.*

GREECE - TIN PRODUCTION

See GREECE - MINERAL INDUSTRIES

GREECE - TOURISM

Euromonitor International, Inc., 224 S. Michigan Avenue, Suite 1500, Chicago, IL 60604, (312) 922-1115, Fax: (312) 922-1157, www.euromonitor.com; *European Marketing Data and Statistics 2008; The World Economic Factbook 2008;* and *World Marketing Data and Statistics.*

European Union, Delegation of the European Commission to the United States, 2300 M Street, NW, Washington, DC 20037, (202) 862-9500, Fax: (202) 429-1766, www.eurunion.org; *Statistical Overview of Transport in the European Union (Data 1970-2001).*

Eurostat, Batiment Jean Monnet, Rue Alcide de Gasperi, L-2920 Luxembourg, http://epp.eurostat.ec.europa.eu; *Tourism in Europe: First Results for 2007.*

M.E. Sharpe, 80 Business Park Drive, Armonk, NY 10504, (800) 541-6563, Fax: (914) 273-2106, www.mesharpe.com; *The Illustrated Book of World Rankings.*

Organisation for Economic Cooperation and Development (OECD), 2 rue Andre Pascal, F-75775 Paris Cedex 16, France, (Telephone in U.S. (202) 785-6323), (Fax in U.S. (202) 785-0350), www.oecd.org; *Household, Tourism, Travel: Trends, Environmental Impacts and Policy Responses.*

Palgrave Macmillan Ltd., Houndmills, Basingstoke, Hampshire, RG21 6XS, England, (Telephone in U.S. (888) 330-8477), (Fax in U.S. (800) 672-2054), www.palgrave.com; *The Statesman's Yearbook 2008.*

Taylor and Francis Group, An Informa Business, 2 Park Square, Milton Park, Abingdon, Oxford OX14 4RN, United Kingdom, (Dial from U.S. (212) 216-7800), (Fax from U.S. (212) 564-7854), www.tandf.co.uk; *The Europa World Year Book.*

United Nations Statistics Division, New York, NY 10017, (800) 253-9646, Fax: (212) 963-4116, http://unstats.un.org; *Statistical Yearbook* and *Trends in Europe and North America: The Statistical Yearbook of the ECE 2005.*

United Nations World Tourism Organization (UNWTO), Capitan Haya 42, 28020 Madrid, Spain, www.world-tourism.org; *Tourism Market Trends 2004 - Europe* and *Yearbook of Tourism Statistics.*

The World Bank, 1818 H Street, NW, Washington, DC 20433, (202) 473-1000, Fax: (202) 477-6391, www.worldbank.org; *Greece.*

GREECE - TRADE

See GREECE - INTERNATIONAL TRADE

GREECE - TRANSPORTATION

Central Intelligence Agency, Office of Public Affairs, Washington, DC 20505, (703) 482-0623, Fax: (703) 482-1739, www.cia.gov; *The World Factbook.*

Euromonitor International, Inc., 224 S. Michigan Avenue, Suite 1500, Chicago, IL 60604, (312) 922-1115, Fax: (312) 922-1157, www.euromonitor.com; *World Marketing Data and Statistics.*

European Union, Delegation of the European Commission to the United States, 2300 M Street, NW, Washington, DC 20037, (202) 862-9500, Fax: (202) 429-1766, www.eurunion.org; *Regions - Statistical Yearbook 2006* and *Statistical Overview of Transport in the European Union (Data 1970-2001).*

Eurostat, Batiment Jean Monnet, Rue Alcide de Gasperi, L-2920 Luxembourg, http://epp.eurostat.ec.europa.eu; *Eurostat Yearbook 2006-2007; Regional Passenger and Freight Air Transport in Europe in 2006;* and *Regional Road and Rail Transport Networks.*

M.E. Sharpe, 80 Business Park Drive, Armonk, NY 10504, (800) 541-6563, Fax: (914) 273-2106, www.mesharpe.com; *The Illustrated Book of World Rankings.*

Palgrave Macmillan Ltd., Houndmills, Basingstoke, Hampshire, RG21 6XS, England, (Telephone in U.S. (888) 330-8477), (Fax in U.S. (800) 672-2054), www.palgrave.com; *The Statesman's Yearbook 2008.*

Platts, 2 Penn Plaza, 25th Floor, New York, NY 10121-2298, (212) 904-3070, www.platts.com; *Energy Economist.*

Taylor and Francis Group, An Informa Business, 2 Park Square, Milton Park, Abingdon, Oxford OX14 4RN, United Kingdom, (Dial from U.S. (212) 216-7800), (Fax from U.S. (212) 564-7854), www.tandf.co.uk; *The Europa World Year Book.*

United Nations Statistics Division, New York, NY 10017, (800) 253-9646, Fax: (212) 963-4116, http://unstats.un.org; *Energy Statistics Yearbook 2003; Human Development Report 2006;* and *Trends in Europe and North America: The Statistical Yearbook of the ECE 2005.*

The World Bank, 1818 H Street, NW, Washington, DC 20433, (202) 473-1000, Fax: (202) 477-6391, www.worldbank.org; *Greece.*

GREECE - TURKEYS

See GREECE - LIVESTOCK

GREECE - UNEMPLOYMENT

Central Intelligence Agency, Office of Public Affairs, Washington, DC 20505, (703) 482-0623, Fax: (703) 482-1739, www.cia.gov; *The World Factbook.*

Euromonitor International, Inc., 224 S. Michigan Avenue, Suite 1500, Chicago, IL 60604, (312) 922-1115, Fax: (312) 922-1157, www.euromonitor.com; *European Marketing Data and Statistics 2008.*

European Union, Delegation of the European Commission to the United States, 2300 M Street, NW, Washington, DC 20037, (202) 862-9500, Fax: (202) 429-1766, www.eurunion.org; *European Union Labour Force Survey.*

Eurostat, Batiment Jean Monnet, Rue Alcide de Gasperi, L-2920 Luxembourg, http://epp.eurostat.ec.europa.eu; *Eurostat Yearbook 2006-2007.*

International Labour Office, I.L.O. Publications, 4 route des Morillons, CH-1211 Geneva 22, Switzerland, (Telephone in U.S. (202) 653-7652), (Fax in U.S. (202) 653-7687), www.ilo.org; *Yearbook of Labour Statistics 2006.*

Organisation for Economic Cooperation and Development (OECD), 2 rue Andre Pascal, F-75775 Paris Cedex 16, France, (Telephone in U.S. (202) 785-6323), (Fax in U.S. (202) 785-0350), www.oecd.org; *Labour Force Statistics: 1986-2005, 2007 Edition; OECD Composite Leading Indicators (CLIs), Updated September 2007; OECD Economic Outlook 2008;* and *OECD Employment Outlook 2007.*

Palgrave Macmillan Ltd., Houndmills, Basingstoke, Hampshire, RG21 6XS, England, (Telephone in U.S. (888) 330-8477), (Fax in U.S. (800) 672-2054), www.palgrave.com; *The Statesman's Yearbook 2008.*

United Nations Statistics Division, New York, NY 10017, (800) 253-9646, Fax: (212) 963-4116, http://unstats.un.org; *Statistical Yearbook* and *Trends in Europe and North America: The Statistical Yearbook of the ECE 2005.*

GREECE - URANIUM PRODUCTION AND CONSUMPTION

See GREECE - MINERAL INDUSTRIES

GREECE - VITAL STATISTICS

Eurostat, Batiment Jean Monnet, Rue Alcide de Gasperi, L-2920 Luxembourg, http://epp.eurostat.ec.europa.eu; *Eurostat Yearbook 2006-2007.*

Palgrave Macmillan Ltd., Houndmills, Basingstoke, Hampshire, RG21 6XS, England, (Telephone in U.S. (888) 330-8477), (Fax in U.S. (800) 672-2054), www.palgrave.com; *The Statesman's Yearbook 2008.*

United Nations Statistics Division, New York, NY 10017, (800) 253-9646, Fax: (212) 963-4116, http://unstats.un.org; *Statistical Yearbook.*

World Health Organization (WHO), Avenue Appia 20, 1211 Geneve 27, Switzerland, (Telephone in U.S. (212) 331-9081), www.who.int; *World Health Report 2006.*

GREECE - WAGES

Euromonitor International, Inc., 224 S. Michigan Avenue, Suite 1500, Chicago, IL 60604, (312) 922-1115, Fax: (312) 922-1157, www.euromonitor.com; *European Marketing Data and Statistics 2008.*

European Union, Delegation of the European Commission to the United States, 2300 M Street, NW, Washington, DC 20037, (202) 862-9500, Fax: (202) 429-1766, www.eurunion.org; *Agriculture in the European Union: Statistical and Economic Information 2006.*

Eurostat, Batiment Jean Monnet, Rue Alcide de Gasperi, L-2920 Luxembourg, http://epp.eurostat.ec.europa.eu; *Eurostat Yearbook 2006-2007.*

International Labour Office, I.L.O. Publications, 4 route des Morillons, CH-1211 Geneva 22, Switzerland, (Telephone in U.S. (202) 653-7652), (Fax in U.S. (202) 653-7687), www.ilo.org; *Yearbook of Labour Statistics 2006.*

Organisation for Economic Cooperation and Development (OECD), 2 rue Andre Pascal, F-75775 Paris Cedex 16, France, (Telephone in U.S. (202) 785-6323), (Fax in U.S. (202) 785-0350), www.oecd.org; *ICT Sector Data and Metadata by Country; OECD Economic Outlook 2008; OECD Main Economic Indicators (MEI);* and STructural ANalysis (STAN) database.

United Nations Statistics Division, New York, NY 10017, (800) 253-9646, Fax: (212) 963-4116, http://unstats.un.org; *Statistical Yearbook.*

The World Bank, 1818 H Street, NW, Washington, DC 20433, (202) 473-1000, Fax: (202) 477-6391, www.worldbank.org; *Greece.*

GREECE - WALNUT PRODUCTION

See GREECE - CROPS

GREECE - WEATHER

See GREECE - CLIMATE

GREECE - WELFARE STATE

Eurostat, Batiment Jean Monnet, Rue Alcide de Gasperi, L-2920 Luxembourg, http://epp.eurostat.ec.europa.eu; *Eurostat Yearbook 2006-2007.*

International Monetary Fund (IMF), 700 Nineteenth Street, NW, Washington, DC 20431, (202) 623-7000, Fax: (202) 623-4661, www.imf.org; *Government Finance Statistics Yearbook (2008 Edition).*

GREECE - WHEAT PRODUCTION

See GREECE - CROPS

GREECE - WHOLESALE PRICE INDEXES

Eurostat, Batiment Jean Monnet, Rue Alcide de Gasperi, L-2920 Luxembourg, http://epp.eurostat.ec.europa.eu; *Eurostat Yearbook 2006-2007.*

International Monetary Fund (IMF), 700 Nineteenth Street, NW, Washington, DC 20431, (202) 623-7000, Fax: (202) 623-4661, www.imf.org; *International Financial Statistics Yearbook 2007.*

United Nations Statistics Division, New York, NY 10017, (800) 253-9646, Fax: (212) 963-4116, http://unstats.un.org; *Statistical Yearbook.*

GREECE - WHOLESALE TRADE

Eurostat, Batiment Jean Monnet, Rue Alcide de Gasperi, L-2920 Luxembourg, http://epp.eurostat.ec.europa.eu; *Eurostat Yearbook 2006-2007.*

United Nations Statistics Division, New York, NY 10017, (800) 253-9646, Fax: (212) 963-4116, http://unstats.un.org; *Statistical Yearbook.*

GREECE - WINE PRODUCTION

See GREECE - BEVERAGE INDUSTRY

GREECE - WOOD AND WOOD PULP

See GREECE - FORESTS AND FORESTRY

GREECE - WOOD PRODUCTS

Eurostat, Batiment Jean Monnet, Rue Alcide de Gasperi, L-2920 Luxembourg, http://epp.eurostat.ec.europa.eu; *Eurostat Yearbook 2006-2007.*

Organisation for Economic Cooperation and Development (OECD), 2 rue Andre Pascal, F-75775 Paris Cedex 16, France, (Telephone in U.S. (202) 785-6323), (Fax in U.S. (202) 785-0350), www.oecd.org; *International Trade by Commodity Statistics (ITCS)* and STructural ANalysis (STAN) database.

GREECE - WOOL PRODUCTION

See GREECE - TEXTILE INDUSTRY

GREECE - YARN PRODUCTION

See GREECE - TEXTILE INDUSTRY

GREECE - ZINC AND ZINC ORE

See GREECE - MINERAL INDUSTRIES

GREECE - ZOOS

UNESCO Institute for Statistics, C.P. 6128 Succursale Centre-Ville, Montreal, Quebec, H3C 3J7 Canada, (Dial from U.S. (514) 343-6880), (Fax from U.S. (514) 343 6882), www.uis.unesco.org; *Statistical Tables.*

GREENHOUSE AND NURSERY CROPS

Economic Research Service (ERS), U.S. Department of Agriculture (USDA), 1800 M Street, NW, Washington, DC 20036-5831, (202) 694-5050, Fax: (202) 694-5689, www.ers.usda.gov; *Agricultural Income and Finance Outlook; Farm Income: Data Files;* and *Floriculture and Nursery Crops: 2007.*

GREENHOUSE GASES

U.S. Department of Energy (DOE), Energy Information Administration (EIA), 1000 Independence Avenue, SW, Washington, DC 20585, (202) 586-8800, www.eia.doe.gov; *Emissions of Greenhouse Gases in the United States 2005.*

World Resources Institute (WRI), 10 G Street, NE, Suite 800 Washington, DC 20002, (202) 729-7600, www.wri.org; *Charting the Midwest: An Inventory and Analysis of Greenhouse Gas Emissions in America's Heartland.*

GREENLAND - NATIONAL STATISTICAL OFFICE

Statistics Greenland, PO Box 1025, 3900 Nuuk, Greenland, www.statgreen.gl/english; National Data Center.

GREENLAND - PRIMARY STATISTICS SOURCES

Statistics Greenland, PO Box 1025, 3900 Nuuk, Greenland, www.statgreen.gl/english; Statbank Greenland.

GREENLAND - ABORTION

United Nations Statistics Division, New York, NY 10017, (800) 253-9646, Fax: (212) 963-4116, http://unstats.un.org; *Demographic Yearbook.*

GREENLAND - AGRICULTURAL MACHINERY

United Nations Statistics Division, New York, NY 10017, (800) 253-9646, Fax: (212) 963-4116, http://unstats.un.org; *Statistical Yearbook.*

GREENLAND - AGRICULTURE

Palgrave Macmillan Ltd., Houndmills, Basingstoke, Hampshire, RG21 6XS, England, (Telephone in U.S. (888) 330-8477), (Fax in U.S. (800) 672-2054), www.palgrave.com; *The Statesman's Yearbook 2008.*

Statistics Greenland, PO Box 1025, 3900 Nuuk, Greenland, www.statgreen.gl/english; *Greenland in Figures 2007.*

Taylor and Francis Group, An Informa Business, 2 Park Square, Milton Park, Abingdon, Oxford OX14 4RN, United Kingdom, (Dial from U.S. (212) 216-7800), (Fax from U.S. (212) 564-7854), www.tandf.co.uk; *The Europa World Year Book.*

United Nations Conference on Trade and Development (UNCTAD), DC2-1120, United Nations, New York, NY 10017, (212) 963-0027, www.unctad.org; *UNCTAD Commodity Yearbook.*

United Nations Food and Agricultural Organization (FAO), Viale delle Terme di Caracalla, 00100 Rome, Italy, (Dial from U.S. (202) 653-2400), (Fax from U.S. (202) 653 5760), www.fao.org; AQUASTAT; *FAO Production Yearbook 2002; FAO Trade Yearbook;* and *The State of Food and Agriculture (SOFA) 2006.*

United Nations Statistics Division, New York, NY 10017, (800) 253-9646, Fax: (212) 963-4116, http://unstats.un.org; *Statistical Yearbook.*

The World Bank, 1818 H Street, NW, Washington, DC 20433, (202) 473-1000, Fax: (202) 477-6391, www.worldbank.org; *Greenland.*

GREENLAND - AIRLINES

Palgrave Macmillan Ltd., Houndmills, Basingstoke, Hampshire, RG21 6XS, England, (Telephone in U.S. (888) 330-8477), (Fax in U.S. (800) 672-2054), www.palgrave.com; *The Statesman's Yearbook 2008.*

Taylor and Francis Group, An Informa Business, 2 Park Square, Milton Park, Abingdon, Oxford OX14 4RN, United Kingdom, (Dial from U.S. (212) 216-7800), (Fax from U.S. (212) 564-7854), www.tandf.co.uk; *The Europa World Year Book.*

GREENLAND - AIRPORTS

Central Intelligence Agency, Office of Public Affairs, Washington, DC 20505, (703) 482-0623, Fax: (703) 482-1739, www.cia.gov; *The World Factbook.*

GREENLAND - ARMED FORCES

Central Intelligence Agency, Office of Public Affairs, Washington, DC 20505, (703) 482-0623, Fax: (703) 482-1739, www.cia.gov; *The World Factbook.*

GREENLAND - BALANCE OF PAYMENTS

Statistics Greenland, PO Box 1025, 3900 Nuuk, Greenland, www.statgreen.gl/english; *Greenland in Figures 2007.*

The World Bank, 1818 H Street, NW, Washington, DC 20433, (202) 473-1000, Fax: (202) 477-6391, www.worldbank.org; *Greenland.*

GREENLAND - BANKS AND BANKING

Palgrave Macmillan Ltd., Houndmills, Basingstoke, Hampshire, RG21 6XS, England, (Telephone in U.S.

(888) 330-8477), (Fax in U.S. (800) 672-2054), www.palgrave.com; *The Statesman's Yearbook 2008.*

GREENLAND - BROADCASTING

Central Intelligence Agency, Office of Public Affairs, Washington, DC 20505, (703) 482-0623, Fax: (703) 482-1739, www.cia.gov; *The World Factbook.*

Palgrave Macmillan Ltd., Houndmills, Basingstoke, Hampshire, RG21 6XS, England, (Telephone in U.S. (888) 330-8477), (Fax in U.S. (800) 672-2054), www.palgrave.com; *The Statesman's Yearbook 2008.*

GREENLAND - BUDGET

Central Intelligence Agency, Office of Public Affairs, Washington, DC 20505, (703) 482-0623, Fax: (703) 482-1739, www.cia.gov; *The World Factbook.*

GREENLAND - CHILDBIRTH - STATISTICS

Central Intelligence Agency, Office of Public Affairs, Washington, DC 20505, (703) 482-0623, Fax: (703) 482-1739, www.cia.gov; *The World Factbook.*

Taylor and Francis Group, An Informa Business, 2 Park Square, Milton Park, Abingdon, Oxford OX14 4RN, United Kingdom, (Dial from U.S. (212) 216-7800), (Fax from U.S. (212) 564-7854), www.tandf.co.uk; *The Europa World Year Book.*

United Nations Statistics Division, New York, NY 10017, (800) 253-9646, Fax: (212) 963-4116, http://unstats.un.org; *Demographic Yearbook* and *Statistical Yearbook.*

GREENLAND - CLIMATE

Palgrave Macmillan Ltd., Houndmills, Basingstoke, Hampshire, RG21 6XS, England, (Telephone in U.S. (888) 330-8477), (Fax in U.S. (800) 672-2054), www.palgrave.com; *The Statesman's Yearbook 2008.*

GREENLAND - COCOA PRODUCTION

See GREENLAND - CROPS

GREENLAND - COMMERCE

Palgrave Macmillan Ltd., Houndmills, Basingstoke, Hampshire, RG21 6XS, England, (Telephone in U.S. (888) 330-8477), (Fax in U.S. (800) 672-2054), www.palgrave.com; *The Statesman's Yearbook 2008.*

GREENLAND - COMMODITY EXCHANGES

Commodity Research Bureau, 330 South Wells Street, Suite 612, Chicago, IL 60606-7110, (800) 621-5271, Fax: (312) 939-4135, www.crbtrader.com; *2006 CRB Commodity Yearbook and CD.*

International Monetary Fund (IMF), 700 Nineteenth Street, NW, Washington, DC 20431, (202) 623-7000, Fax: (202) 623-4661, www.imf.org; *IMF Primary Commodity Prices.*

United Nations Food and Agricultural Organization (FAO), Viale delle Terme di Caracalla, 00100 Rome, Italy, (Dial from U.S. (202) 653-2400), (Fax from U.S. (202) 653 5760), www.fao.org; *The State of Food and Agriculture (SOFA) 2006.*

GREENLAND - CONSUMER PRICE INDEXES

International Labour Office, I.L.O. Publications, 4 route des Morillons, CH-1211 Geneva 22, Switzerland, (Telephone in U.S. (202) 653-7652), (Fax in U.S. (202) 653-7687), www.ilo.org; *Yearbook of Labour Statistics 2006.*

Taylor and Francis Group, An Informa Business, 2 Park Square, Milton Park, Abingdon, Oxford OX14 4RN, United Kingdom, (Dial from U.S. (212) 216-7800), (Fax from U.S. (212) 564-7854), www.tandf.co.uk; *The Europa World Year Book.*

United Nations Statistics Division, New York, NY 10017, (800) 253-9646, Fax: (212) 963-4116, http://unstats.un.org; *Statistical Yearbook.*

The World Bank, 1818 H Street, NW, Washington, DC 20433, (202) 473-1000, Fax: (202) 477-6391, www.worldbank.org; *Greenland.*

GREENLAND - CORN INDUSTRY

See GREENLAND - CROPS

GREENLAND - CROPS

United Nations Conference on Trade and Development (UNCTAD), DC2-1120, United Nations, New York, NY 10017, (212) 963-0027, www.unctad.org; *UNCTAD Commodity Yearbook.*

United Nations Food and Agricultural Organization (FAO), Viale delle Terme di Caracalla, 00100 Rome, Italy, (Dial from U.S. (202) 653-2400), (Fax from U.S. (202) 653 5760), www.fao.org; *The State of Food and Agriculture (SOFA) 2006.*

United Nations Statistics Division, New York, NY 10017, (800) 253-9646, Fax: (212) 963-4116, http://unstats.un.org; *Statistical Yearbook.*

GREENLAND - DEATH RATES

See GREENLAND - MORTALITY

GREENLAND - DIVORCE

United Nations Statistics Division, New York, NY 10017, (800) 253-9646, Fax: (212) 963-4116, http://unstats.un.org; *Demographic Yearbook* and *Statistical Yearbook.*

GREENLAND - ECONOMIC CONDITIONS

Center for International Business Education Research (CIBER), Columbia Business School and School of International and Public Affairs, Uris Hall, Room 212, 3022 Broadway, New York, NY 10027-6902, Mr. Joshua Safier, (212) 854-4750, Fax: (212) 222-9821, www.columbia.edu/cu/ciber/; Datastream International.

Central Intelligence Agency, Office of Public Affairs, Washington, DC 20505, (703) 482-0623, Fax: (703) 482-1739, www.cia.gov; *The World Factbook.*

DSI Data Service Information, Xantener Strasse 51a, D-47495 Rheinberg, Germany, www.dsidata.com; *Campus Solution.*

Dun and Bradstreet (DB) Corporation, 103 JFK Parkway, Short Hills, NJ 07078, (973) 921-5500, www.dnb.com; *Country Report.*

International Monetary Fund (IMF), 700 Nineteenth Street, NW, Washington, DC 20431, (202) 623-7000, Fax: (202) 623-4661, www.imf.org; *World Economic Outlook Reports.*

Palgrave Macmillan Ltd., Houndmills, Basingstoke, Hampshire, RG21 6XS, England, (Telephone in U.S. (888) 330-8477), (Fax in U.S. (800) 672-2054), www.palgrave.com; *The Statesman's Yearbook 2008.*

The World Bank, 1818 H Street, NW, Washington, DC 20433, (202) 473-1000, Fax: (202) 477-6391, www.worldbank.org; *Global Economic Monitor (GEM); Global Economic Prospects 2008; Greenland;* and *The World Bank Atlas 2003-2004.*

GREENLAND - EDUCATION

Palgrave Macmillan Ltd., Houndmills, Basingstoke, Hampshire, RG21 6XS, England, (Telephone in U.S. (888) 330-8477), (Fax in U.S. (800) 672-2054), www.palgrave.com; *The Statesman's Yearbook 2008.*

Statistics Greenland, PO Box 1025, 3900 Nuuk, Greenland, www.statgreen.gl/english; *Greenland in Figures 2007.*

The World Bank, 1818 H Street, NW, Washington, DC 20433, (202) 473-1000, Fax: (202) 477-6391, www.worldbank.org; *Greenland.*

GREENLAND - ELECTRICITY

Palgrave Macmillan Ltd., Houndmills, Basingstoke, Hampshire, RG21 6XS, England, (Telephone in U.S. (888) 330-8477), (Fax in U.S. (800) 672-2054), www.palgrave.com; *The Statesman's Yearbook 2008.*

United Nations Statistics Division, New York, NY 10017, (800) 253-9646, Fax: (212) 963-4116, http://unstats.un.org; *Statistical Yearbook.*

GREENLAND - EMPLOYMENT

International Labour Office, I.L.O. Publications, 4 route des Morillons, CH-1211 Geneva 22, Switzerland, (Telephone in U.S. (202) 653-7652), (Fax in U.S. (202) 653-7687), www.ilo.org; *Yearbook of Labour Statistics 2006.*

Statistics Greenland, PO Box 1025, 3900 Nuuk, Greenland, www.statgreen.gl/english; *Greenland in Figures 2007.*

The World Bank, 1818 H Street, NW, Washington, DC 20433, (202) 473-1000, Fax: (202) 477-6391, www.worldbank.org; *Greenland.*

GREENLAND - EXPORTS

Central Intelligence Agency, Office of Public Affairs, Washington, DC 20505, (703) 482-0623, Fax: (703) 482-1739, www.cia.gov; *The World Factbook.*

International Monetary Fund (IMF), 700 Nineteenth Street, NW, Washington, DC 20431, (202) 623-7000, Fax: (202) 623-4661, www.imf.org; *Direction of Trade Statistics Yearbook 2007.*

Organisation for Economic Cooperation and Development (OECD), 2 rue Andre Pascal, F-75775 Paris Cedex 16, France, (Telephone in U.S. (202) 785-6323), (Fax in U.S. (202) 785-0350), www.oecd.org; *Review of Fisheries in OECD Countries: Country Statistics 2001 to 2003 - 2005 Edition.*

Palgrave Macmillan Ltd., Houndmills, Basingstoke, Hampshire, RG21 6XS, England, (Telephone in U.S. (888) 330-8477), (Fax in U.S. (800) 672-2054), www.palgrave.com; *The Statesman's Yearbook 2008.*

Taylor and Francis Group, An Informa Business, 2 Park Square, Milton Park, Abingdon, Oxford OX14 4RN, United Kingdom, (Dial from U.S. (212) 216-7800), (Fax from U.S. (212) 564-7854), www.tandf.co.uk; *The Europa World Year Book.*

United Nations Food and Agricultural Organization (FAO), Viale delle Terme di Caracalla, 00100 Rome, Italy, (Dial from U.S. (202) 653-2400), (Fax from U.S. (202) 653 5760), www.fao.org; *The State of Food and Agriculture (SOFA) 2006.*

GREENLAND - FERTILITY, HUMAN

Central Intelligence Agency, Office of Public Affairs, Washington, DC 20505, (703) 482-0623, Fax: (703) 482-1739, www.cia.gov; *The World Factbook.*

United Nations Statistics Division, New York, NY 10017, (800) 253-9646, Fax: (212) 963-4116, http://unstats.un.org; *Demographic Yearbook.*

The World Bank, 1818 H Street, NW, Washington, DC 20433, (202) 473-1000, Fax: (202) 477-6391, www.worldbank.org; *The World Bank Atlas 2003-2004.*

World Health Organization (WHO), Avenue Appia 20, 1211 Geneve 27, Switzerland, (Telephone in U.S. (212) 331-9081), www.who.int; *World Health Report 2006.*

GREENLAND - FERTILIZER INDUSTRY

United Nations Food and Agricultural Organization (FAO), Viale delle Terme di Caracalla, 00100 Rome, Italy, (Dial from U.S. (202) 653-2400), (Fax from U.S. (202) 653 5760), www.fao.org; *The State of Food and Agriculture (SOFA) 2006.*

GREENLAND - FETAL MORTALITY

See GREENLAND - MORTALITY

GREENLAND - FINANCE

Statistics Greenland, PO Box 1025, 3900 Nuuk, Greenland, www.statgreen.gl/english; *Greenland in Figures 2007.*

The World Bank, 1818 H Street, NW, Washington, DC 20433, (202) 473-1000, Fax: (202) 477-6391, www.worldbank.org; *Greenland.*

GREENLAND - FINANCE, PUBLIC

Bernan Essential Government Publications, 4611-F Assembly Drive, Lanham MD, 20706-4391, (301) 459-2255, Fax: (800) 865-3450, www.bernan.com; *National Accounts Statistics.*

International Monetary Fund (IMF), 700 Nineteenth Street, NW, Washington, DC 20431, (202) 623-

7000, Fax: (202) 623-4661, www.imf.org; *International Financial Statistics* and *International Financial Statistics Online Service.*

Palgrave Macmillan Ltd., Houndmills, Basingstoke, Hampshire, RG21 6XS, England, (Telephone in U.S. (888) 330-8477), (Fax in U.S. (800) 672-2054), www.palgrave.com; *The Statesman's Yearbook 2008.*

Statistics Greenland, PO Box 1025, 3900 Nuuk, Greenland, www.statgreen.gl/english; *Greenland in Figures 2007.*

Taylor and Francis Group, An Informa Business, 2 Park Square, Milton Park, Abingdon, Oxford OX14 4RN, United Kingdom, (Dial from U.S. (212) 216-7800), (Fax from U.S. (212) 564-7854), www.tandf.co.uk; *The Europa World Year Book.*

The World Bank, 1818 H Street, NW, Washington, DC 20433, (202) 473-1000, Fax: (202) 477-6391, www.worldbank.org; *Greenland.*

GREENLAND - FISHERIES

Organisation for Economic Cooperation and Development (OECD), 2 rue Andre Pascal, F-75775 Paris Cedex 16, France, (Telephone in U.S. (202) 785-6323), (Fax in U.S. (202) 785-0350), www.oecd.org; *Review of Fisheries in OECD Countries: Country Statistics 2001 to 2003 - 2005 Edition.*

Palgrave Macmillan Ltd., Houndmills, Basingstoke, Hampshire, RG21 6XS, England, (Telephone in U.S. (888) 330-8477), (Fax in U.S. (800) 672-2054), www.palgrave.com; *The Statesman's Yearbook 2008.*

Statistics Greenland, PO Box 1025, 3900 Nuuk, Greenland, www.statgreen.gl/english; *Greenland in Figures 2007.*

Taylor and Francis Group, An Informa Business, 2 Park Square, Milton Park, Abingdon, Oxford OX14 4RN, United Kingdom, (Dial from U.S. (212) 216-7800), (Fax from U.S. (212) 564-7854), www.tandf.co.uk; *The Europa World Year Book.*

United Nations Conference on Trade and Development (UNCTAD), DC2-1120, United Nations, New York, NY 10017, (212) 963-0027, www.unctad.org; *UNCTAD Commodity Yearbook.*

United Nations Food and Agricultural Organization (FAO), Viale delle Terme di Caracalla, 00100 Rome, Italy, (Dial from U.S. (202) 653-2400), (Fax from U.S. (202) 653 5760), www.fao.org; *FAO Yearbook of Fishery Statistics;* Fishery Databases; FISHSTAT Database. Subjects covered include: Aquaculture production, capture production, fishery commodities; and *The State of Food and Agriculture (SOFA) 2006.*

United Nations Statistics Division, New York, NY 10017, (800) 253-9646, Fax: (212) 963-4116, http://unstats.un.org; *Statistical Yearbook.*

The World Bank, 1818 H Street, NW, Washington, DC 20433, (202) 473-1000, Fax: (202) 477-6391, www.worldbank.org; *Greenland.*

GREENLAND - FOOD

United Nations Conference on Trade and Development (UNCTAD), DC2-1120, United Nations, New York, NY 10017, (212) 963-0027, www.unctad.org; *UNCTAD Commodity Yearbook.*

United Nations Food and Agricultural Organization (FAO), Viale delle Terme di Caracalla, 00100 Rome, Italy, (Dial from U.S. (202) 653-2400), (Fax from U.S. (202) 653 5760), www.fao.org; *FAO Production Yearbook 2002* and *The State of Food and Agriculture (SOFA) 2006.*

GREENLAND - FOREIGN EXCHANGE RATES

Central Intelligence Agency, Office of Public Affairs, Washington, DC 20505, (703) 482-0623, Fax: (703) 482-1739, www.cia.gov; *The World Factbook.*

Taylor and Francis Group, An Informa Business, 2 Park Square, Milton Park, Abingdon, Oxford OX14 4RN, United Kingdom, (Dial from U.S. (212) 216-7800), (Fax from U.S. (212) 564-7854), www.tandf.co.uk; *The Europa World Year Book.*

GREENLAND - FORESTS AND FORESTRY

Statistics Greenland, PO Box 1025, 3900 Nuuk, Greenland, www.statgreen.gl/english; *Greenland in Figures 2007.*

United Nations Conference on Trade and Development (UNCTAD), DC2-1120, United Nations, New York, NY 10017, (212) 963-0027, www.unctad.org; *UNCTAD Commodity Yearbook.*

United Nations Food and Agricultural Organization (FAO), Viale delle Terme di Caracalla, 00100 Rome, Italy, (Dial from U.S. (202) 653-2400), (Fax from U.S. (202) 653 5760), www.fao.org; *The State of Food and Agriculture (SOFA) 2006.*

The World Bank, 1818 H Street, NW, Washington, DC 20433, (202) 473-1000, Fax: (202) 477-6391, www.worldbank.org; *Greenland.*

GREENLAND - GROSS DOMESTIC PRODUCT

Taylor and Francis Group, An Informa Business, 2 Park Square, Milton Park, Abingdon, Oxford OX14 4RN, United Kingdom, (Dial from U.S. (212) 216-7800), (Fax from U.S. (212) 564-7854), www.tandf.co.uk; *The Europa World Year Book.*

GREENLAND - GROSS NATIONAL PRODUCT

The World Bank, 1818 H Street, NW, Washington, DC 20433, (202) 473-1000, Fax: (202) 477-6391, www.worldbank.org; *The World Bank Atlas 2003-2004.*

GREENLAND - IMPORTS

Central Intelligence Agency, Office of Public Affairs, Washington, DC 20505, (703) 482-0623, Fax: (703) 482-1739, www.cia.gov; *The World Factbook.*

International Monetary Fund (IMF), 700 Nineteenth Street, NW, Washington, DC 20431, (202) 623-7000, Fax: (202) 623-4661, www.imf.org; *Direction of Trade Statistics Yearbook 2007.*

Organisation for Economic Cooperation and Development (OECD), 2 rue Andre Pascal, F-75775 Paris Cedex 16, France, (Telephone in U.S. (202) 785-6323), (Fax in U.S. (202) 785-0350), www.oecd.org; *Review of Fisheries in OECD Countries: Country Statistics 2001 to 2003 - 2005 Edition.*

Palgrave Macmillan Ltd., Houndmills, Basingstoke, Hampshire, RG21 6XS, England, (Telephone in U.S. (888) 330-8477), (Fax in U.S. (800) 672-2054), www.palgrave.com; *The Statesman's Yearbook 2008.*

Taylor and Francis Group, An Informa Business, 2 Park Square, Milton Park, Abingdon, Oxford OX14 4RN, United Kingdom, (Dial from U.S. (212) 216-7800), (Fax from U.S. (212) 564-7854), www.tandf.co.uk; *The Europa World Year Book.*

United Nations Food and Agricultural Organization (FAO), Viale delle Terme di Caracalla, 00100 Rome, Italy, (Dial from U.S. (202) 653-2400), (Fax from U.S. (202) 653 5760), www.fao.org; *The State of Food and Agriculture (SOFA) 2006.*

GREENLAND - INDUSTRIES

Central Intelligence Agency, Office of Public Affairs, Washington, DC 20505, (703) 482-0623, Fax: (703) 482-1739, www.cia.gov; *The World Factbook.*

International Labour Office, I.L.O. Publications, 4 route des Morillons, CH-1211 Geneva 22, Switzerland, (Telephone in U.S. (202) 653-7652), (Fax in U.S. (202) 653-7687), www.ilo.org; *Yearbook of Labour Statistics 2006.*

Palgrave Macmillan Ltd., Houndmills, Basingstoke, Hampshire, RG21 6XS, England, (Telephone in U.S. (888) 330-8477), (Fax in U.S. (800) 672-2054), www.palgrave.com; *The Statesman's Yearbook 2008.*

Statistics Greenland, PO Box 1025, 3900 Nuuk, Greenland, www.statgreen.gl/english; *Greenland in Figures 2007.*

Taylor and Francis Group, An Informa Business, 2 Park Square, Milton Park, Abingdon, Oxford OX14 4RN, United Kingdom, (Dial from U.S. (212) 216-7800), (Fax from U.S. (212) 564-7854), www.tandf.co.uk; *The Europa World Year Book.*

United Nations Industrial Development Organization (UNIDO), 1 United Nations Plaza, New York, NY 10017, (212) 963 6890, Fax: (212) 963-7904, http://unido.org; Industrial Statistics Database 2008 (INDSTAT) and *The International Yearbook of Industrial Statistics 2008.*

The World Bank, 1818 H Street, NW, Washington, DC 20433, (202) 473-1000, Fax: (202) 477-6391, www.worldbank.org; *Greenland.*

GREENLAND - INFANT AND MATERNAL MORTALITY

See GREENLAND - MORTALITY

GREENLAND - INTERNATIONAL TRADE

Palgrave Macmillan Ltd., Houndmills, Basingstoke, Hampshire, RG21 6XS, England, (Telephone in U.S. (888) 330-8477), (Fax in U.S. (800) 672-2054), www.palgrave.com; *The Statesman's Yearbook 2008.*

Statistics Greenland, PO Box 1025, 3900 Nuuk, Greenland, www.statgreen.gl/english; *Greenland in Figures 2007.*

Taylor and Francis Group, An Informa Business, 2 Park Square, Milton Park, Abingdon, Oxford OX14 4RN, United Kingdom, (Dial from U.S. (212) 216-7800), (Fax from U.S. (212) 564-7854), www.tandf.co.uk; *The Europa World Year Book.*

United Nations Conference on Trade and Development (UNCTAD), DC2-1120, United Nations, New York, NY 10017, (212) 963-0027, www.unctad.org; *UNCTAD Commodity Yearbook.*

United Nations Food and Agricultural Organization (FAO), Viale delle Terme di Caracalla, 00100 Rome, Italy, (Dial from U.S. (202) 653-2400), (Fax from U.S. (202) 653 5760), www.fao.org; *FAO Trade Yearbook* and *The State of Food and Agriculture (SOFA) 2006.*

United Nations Statistics Division, New York, NY 10017, (800) 253-9646, Fax: (212) 963-4116, http://unstats.un.org; *International Trade Statistics Yearbook* and *Statistical Yearbook.*

The World Bank, 1818 H Street, NW, Washington, DC 20433, (202) 473-1000, Fax: (202) 477-6391, www.worldbank.org; *Greenland.*

World Trade Organization (WTO), Centre William Rappard, Rue de Lausanne 154, CH-1211 Geneva 21, Switzerland, www.wto.org; *International Trade Statistics 2006.*

GREENLAND - INTERNET USERS

International Telecommunication Union (ITU), Place des Nations, 1211 Geneva 20, Switzerland, www.itu.int; *World Telecommunication/ICT Indicators Database on CD-ROM; World Telecommunication/ICT Indicators Database Online;* and *Yearbook of Statistics - Telecommunication Services (Chronological Time Series 1997-2006).*

The World Bank, 1818 H Street, NW, Washington, DC 20433, (202) 473-1000, Fax: (202) 477-6391, www.worldbank.org; *Greenland.*

GREENLAND - LABOR

Central Intelligence Agency, Office of Public Affairs, Washington, DC 20505, (703) 482-0623, Fax: (703) 482-1739, www.cia.gov; *The World Factbook.*

International Labour Office, I.L.O. Publications, 4 route des Morillons, CH-1211 Geneva 22, Switzerland, (Telephone in U.S. (202) 653-7652), (Fax in U.S. (202) 653-7687), www.ilo.org; *Yearbook of Labour Statistics 2006.*

Taylor and Francis Group, An Informa Business, 2 Park Square, Milton Park, Abingdon, Oxford OX14 4RN, United Kingdom, (Dial from U.S. (212) 216-7800), (Fax from U.S. (212) 564-7854), www.tandf.co.uk; *The Europa World Year Book.*

United Nations Food and Agricultural Organization (FAO), Viale delle Terme di Caracalla, 00100 Rome,

Italy, (Dial from U.S. (202) 653-2400), (Fax from U.S. (202) 653 5760), www.fao.org; *The State of Food and Agriculture (SOFA) 2006.*

The World Bank, 1818 H Street, NW, Washington, DC 20433, (202) 473-1000, Fax: (202) 477-6391, www.worldbank.org; *The World Bank Atlas 2003-2004.*

GREENLAND - LAND USE

Central Intelligence Agency, Office of Public Affairs, Washington, DC 20505, (703) 482-0623, Fax: (703) 482-1739, www.cia.gov; *The World Factbook.*

United Nations Food and Agricultural Organization (FAO), Viale delle Terme di Caracalla, 00100 Rome, Italy, (Dial from U.S. (202) 653-2400), (Fax from U.S. (202) 653 5760), www.fao.org; *FAO Production Yearbook 2002.*

GREENLAND - LIBRARIES

UNESCO Institute for Statistics, C.P. 6128 Succursale Centre-Ville, Montreal, Quebec, H3C 3J7 Canada, (Dial from U.S. (514) 343-6880), (Fax from U.S. (514) 343 6882), www.uis.unesco.org; *Statistical Tables.*

GREENLAND - LIFE EXPECTANCY

Central Intelligence Agency, Office of Public Affairs, Washington, DC 20505, (703) 482-0623, Fax: (703) 482-1739, www.cia.gov; *The World Factbook.*

The World Bank, 1818 H Street, NW, Washington, DC 20433, (202) 473-1000, Fax: (202) 477-6391, www.worldbank.org; *The World Bank Atlas 2003-2004.*

GREENLAND - LIVESTOCK

Palgrave Macmillan Ltd., Houndmills, Basingstoke, Hampshire, RG21 6XS, England, (Telephone in U.S. (888) 330-8477), (Fax in U.S. (800) 672-2054), www.palgrave.com; *The Statesman's Yearbook 2008.*

Taylor and Francis Group, An Informa Business, 2 Park Square, Milton Park, Abingdon, Oxford OX14 4RN, United Kingdom, (Dial from U.S. (212) 216-7800), (Fax from U.S. (212) 564-7854), www.tandf.co.uk; *The Europa World Year Book.*

United Nations Conference on Trade and Development (UNCTAD), DC2-1120, United Nations, New York, NY 10017, (212) 963-0027, www.unctad.org; *UNCTAD Commodity Yearbook.*

United Nations Food and Agricultural Organization (FAO), Viale delle Terme di Caracalla, 00100 Rome, Italy, (Dial from U.S. (202) 653-2400), (Fax from U.S. (202) 653 5760), www.fao.org; *FAO Production Yearbook 2002* and *The State of Food and Agriculture (SOFA) 2006.*

United Nations Statistics Division, New York, NY 10017, (800) 253-9646, Fax: (212) 963-4116, http://unstats.un.org; *Statistical Yearbook.*

GREENLAND - MARRIAGE

Taylor and Francis Group, An Informa Business, 2 Park Square, Milton Park, Abingdon, Oxford OX14 4RN, United Kingdom, (Dial from U.S. (212) 216-7800), (Fax from U.S. (212) 564-7854), www.tandf.co.uk; *The Europa World Year Book.*

United Nations Statistics Division, New York, NY 10017, (800) 253-9646, Fax: (212) 963-4116, http://unstats.un.org; *Demographic Yearbook* and *Statistical Yearbook.*

GREENLAND - MEAT PRODUCTION

See GREENLAND - LIVESTOCK

GREENLAND - MINERAL INDUSTRIES

Taylor and Francis Group, An Informa Business, 2 Park Square, Milton Park, Abingdon, Oxford OX14 4RN, United Kingdom, (Dial from U.S. (212) 216-7800), (Fax from U.S. (212) 564-7854), www.tandf.co.uk; *The Europa World Year Book.*

United Nations Conference on Trade and Development (UNCTAD), DC2-1120, United Nations, New York, NY 10017, (212) 963-0027, www.unctad.org; *UNCTAD Commodity Yearbook.*

GREENLAND - MORTALITY

Central Intelligence Agency, Office of Public Affairs, Washington, DC 20505, (703) 482-0623, Fax: (703) 482-1739, www.cia.gov; *The World Factbook.*

Taylor and Francis Group, An Informa Business, 2 Park Square, Milton Park, Abingdon, Oxford OX14 4RN, United Kingdom, (Dial from U.S. (212) 216-7800), (Fax from U.S. (212) 564-7854), www.tandf.co.uk; *The Europa World Year Book.*

United Nations Statistics Division, New York, NY 10017, (800) 253-9646, Fax: (212) 963-4116, http://unstats.un.org; *Demographic Yearbook* and *Statistical Yearbook.*

The World Bank, 1818 H Street, NW, Washington, DC 20433, (202) 473-1000, Fax: (202) 477-6391, www.worldbank.org; *The World Bank Atlas 2003-2004.*

World Health Organization (WHO), Avenue Appia 20, 1211 Geneve 27, Switzerland, (Telephone in U.S. (212) 331-9081), www.who.int; The WHO Global Atlas of Infectious Diseases and *World Health Report 2006.*

GREENLAND - MOTOR VEHICLES

Taylor and Francis Group, An Informa Business, 2 Park Square, Milton Park, Abingdon, Oxford OX14 4RN, United Kingdom, (Dial from U.S. (212) 216-7800), (Fax from U.S. (212) 564-7854), www.tandf.co.uk; *The Europa World Year Book.*

United Nations Statistics Division, New York, NY 10017, (800) 253-9646, Fax: (212) 963-4116, http://unstats.un.org; *Statistical Yearbook.*

GREENLAND - NUTRITION

United Nations Food and Agricultural Organization (FAO), Viale delle Terme di Caracalla, 00100 Rome, Italy, (Dial from U.S. (202) 653-2400), (Fax from U.S. (202) 653 5760), www.fao.org; *The State of Food and Agriculture (SOFA) 2006.*

GREENLAND - PESTICIDES

United Nations Food and Agricultural Organization (FAO), Viale delle Terme di Caracalla, 00100 Rome, Italy, (Dial from U.S. (202) 653-2400), (Fax from U.S. (202) 653 5760), www.fao.org; *The State of Food and Agriculture (SOFA) 2006.*

GREENLAND - PETROLEUM INDUSTRY AND TRADE

PennWell Corporation, 1421 South Sheridan Road, Tulsa, OK 74112, (918) 835-3161, www.pennwell.com; *International Petroleum Encyclopedia 2007.*

United Nations Conference on Trade and Development (UNCTAD), DC2-1120, United Nations, New York, NY 10017, (212) 963-0027, www.unctad.org; *UNCTAD Commodity Yearbook.*

United Nations Food and Agricultural Organization (FAO), Viale delle Terme di Caracalla, 00100 Rome, Italy, (Dial from U.S. (202) 653-2400), (Fax from U.S. (202) 653 5760), www.fao.org; *The State of Food and Agriculture (SOFA) 2006.*

GREENLAND - POLITICAL SCIENCE

Central Intelligence Agency, Office of Public Affairs, Washington, DC 20505, (703) 482-0623, Fax: (703) 482-1739, www.cia.gov; *The World Factbook.*

Palgrave Macmillan Ltd., Houndmills, Basingstoke, Hampshire, RG21 6XS, England, (Telephone in U.S. (888) 330-8477), (Fax in U.S. (800) 672-2054), www.palgrave.com; *The Statesman's Yearbook 2008.*

Taylor and Francis Group, An Informa Business, 2 Park Square, Milton Park, Abingdon, Oxford OX14 4RN, United Kingdom, (Dial from U.S. (212) 216-7800), (Fax from U.S. (212) 564-7854), www.tandf.co.uk; *The Europa World Year Book.*

GREENLAND - POPULATION

Central Intelligence Agency, Office of Public Affairs, Washington, DC 20505, (703) 482-0623, Fax: (703) 482-1739, www.cia.gov; *The World Factbook.*

International Labour Office, I.L.O. Publications, 4 route des Morillons, CH-1211 Geneva 22, Switzerland, (Telephone in U.S. (202) 653-7652), (Fax in U.S. (202) 653-7687), www.ilo.org; *Yearbook of Labour Statistics 2006.*

Palgrave Macmillan Ltd., Houndmills, Basingstoke, Hampshire, RG21 6XS, England, (Telephone in U.S. (888) 330-8477), (Fax in U.S. (800) 672-2054), www.palgrave.com; *The Statesman's Yearbook 2008.*

Statistics Greenland, PO Box 1025, 3900 Nuuk, Greenland, www.statgreen.gl/english; *Greenland in Figures 2007.*

Taylor and Francis Group, An Informa Business, 2 Park Square, Milton Park, Abingdon, Oxford OX14 4RN, United Kingdom, (Dial from U.S. (212) 216-7800), (Fax from U.S. (212) 564-7854), www.tandf.co.uk; *The Europa World Year Book.*

UNESCO Institute for Statistics, C.P. 6128 Succursale Centre-Ville, Montreal, Quebec, H3C 3J7 Canada, (Dial from U.S. (514) 343-6880), (Fax from U.S. (514) 343 6882), www.uis.unesco.org; *Statistical Tables.*

United Nations Food and Agricultural Organization (FAO), Viale delle Terme di Caracalla, 00100 Rome, Italy, (Dial from U.S. (202) 653-2400), (Fax from U.S. (202) 653 5760), www.fao.org; *FAO Production Yearbook 2002.*

United Nations Statistics Division, New York, NY 10017, (800) 253-9646, Fax: (212) 963-4116, http://unstats.un.org; *Demographic Yearbook* and *Statistical Yearbook.*

The World Bank, 1818 H Street, NW, Washington, DC 20433, (202) 473-1000, Fax: (202) 477-6391, www.worldbank.org; *Greenland* and *The World Bank Atlas 2003-2004.*

World Health Organization (WHO), Avenue Appia 20, 1211 Geneve 27, Switzerland, (Telephone in U.S. (212) 331-9081), www.who.int; *World Health Report 2006.*

GREENLAND - POPULATION DENSITY

Central Intelligence Agency, Office of Public Affairs, Washington, DC 20505, (703) 482-0623, Fax: (703) 482-1739, www.cia.gov; *The World Factbook.*

Palgrave Macmillan Ltd., Houndmills, Basingstoke, Hampshire, RG21 6XS, England, (Telephone in U.S. (888) 330-8477), (Fax in U.S. (800) 672-2054), www.palgrave.com; *The Statesman's Yearbook 2008.*

Statistics Greenland, PO Box 1025, 3900 Nuuk, Greenland, www.statgreen.gl/english; *Greenland in Figures 2007.*

Taylor and Francis Group, An Informa Business, 2 Park Square, Milton Park, Abingdon, Oxford OX14 4RN, United Kingdom, (Dial from U.S. (212) 216-7800), (Fax from U.S. (212) 564-7854), www.tandf.co.uk; *The Europa World Year Book.*

UNESCO Institute for Statistics, C.P. 6128 Succursale Centre-Ville, Montreal, Quebec, H3C 3J7 Canada, (Dial from U.S. (514) 343-6880), (Fax from U.S. (514) 343 6882), www.uis.unesco.org; *Statistical Tables.*

United Nations Food and Agricultural Organization (FAO), Viale delle Terme di Caracalla, 00100 Rome, Italy, (Dial from U.S. (202) 653-2400), (Fax from U.S. (202) 653 5760), www.fao.org; *The State of Food and Agriculture (SOFA) 2006.*

United Nations Statistics Division, New York, NY 10017, (800) 253-9646, Fax: (212) 963-4116, http://unstats.un.org; *Statistical Yearbook.*

The World Bank, 1818 H Street, NW, Washington, DC 20433, (202) 473-1000, Fax: (202) 477-6391, www.worldbank.org; *Greenland.*

GREENLAND - POWER RESOURCES

Palgrave Macmillan Ltd., Houndmills, Basingstoke, Hampshire, RG21 6XS, England, (Telephone in U.S. (888) 330-8477), (Fax in U.S. (800) 672-2054), www.palgrave.com; *The Statesman's Yearbook 2008.*

United Nations Food and Agricultural Organization (FAO), Viale delle Terme di Caracalla, 00100 Rome,

Italy, (Dial from U.S. (202) 653-2400), (Fax from U.S. (202) 653 5760), www.fao.org; *The State of Food and Agriculture (SOFA) 2006.*

United Nations Statistics Division, New York, NY 10017, (800) 253-9646, Fax: (212) 963-4116, http://unstats.un.org; *Statistical Yearbook.*

The World Bank, 1818 H Street, NW, Washington, DC 20433, (202) 473-1000, Fax: (202) 477-6391, www.worldbank.org; *The World Bank Atlas 2003-2004.*

GREENLAND - PRICES

International Labour Office, I.L.O. Publications, 4 route des Morillons, CH-1211 Geneva 22, Switzerland, (Telephone in U.S. (202) 653-7652), (Fax in U.S. (202) 653-7687), www.ilo.org; *Yearbook of Labour Statistics 2006.*

Statistics Greenland, PO Box 1025, 3900 Nuuk, Greenland, www.statgreen.gl/english; *Greenland in Figures 2007.*

United Nations Food and Agricultural Organization (FAO), Viale delle Terme di Caracalla, 00100 Rome, Italy, (Dial from U.S. (202) 653-2400), (Fax from U.S. (202) 653 5760), www.fao.org; *FAO Production Yearbook 2002* and *The State of Food and Agriculture (SOFA) 2006.*

The World Bank, 1818 H Street, NW, Washington, DC 20433, (202) 473-1000, Fax: (202) 477-6391, www.worldbank.org; *Greenland.*

GREENLAND - PUBLIC HEALTH

Palgrave Macmillan Ltd., Houndmills, Basingstoke, Hampshire, RG21 6XS, England, (Telephone in U.S. (888) 330-8477), (Fax in U.S. (800) 672-2054), www.palgrave.com; *The Statesman's Yearbook 2008.*

Statistics Greenland, PO Box 1025, 3900 Nuuk, Greenland, www.statgreen.gl/english; *Greenland in Figures 2007.*

United Nations Statistics Division, New York, NY 10017, (800) 253-9646, Fax: (212) 963-4116, http://unstats.un.org; *Statistical Yearbook.*

The World Bank, 1818 H Street, NW, Washington, DC 20433, (202) 473-1000, Fax: (202) 477-6391, www.worldbank.org; *Greenland.*

World Health Organization (WHO), Avenue Appia 20, 1211 Geneve 27, Switzerland, (Telephone in U.S. (212) 331-9081), www.who.int; The WHO Global Atlas of Infectious Diseases and *World Health Report 2006.*

GREENLAND - RADIO BROADCASTING

Palgrave Macmillan Ltd., Houndmills, Basingstoke, Hampshire, RG21 6XS, England, (Telephone in U.S. (888) 330-8477), (Fax in U.S. (800) 672-2054), www.palgrave.com; *The Statesman's Yearbook 2008.*

GREENLAND - RELIGION

Central Intelligence Agency, Office of Public Affairs, Washington, DC 20505, (703) 482-0623, Fax: (703) 482-1739, www.cia.gov; *The World Factbook.*

Palgrave Macmillan Ltd., Houndmills, Basingstoke, Hampshire, RG21 6XS, England, (Telephone in U.S. (888) 330-8477), (Fax in U.S. (800) 672-2054), www.palgrave.com; *The Statesman's Yearbook 2008.*

GREENLAND - RENT CHARGES

International Labour Office, I.L.O. Publications, 4 route des Morillons, CH-1211 Geneva 22, Switzerland, (Telephone in U.S. (202) 653-7652), (Fax in U.S. (202) 653-7687), www.ilo.org; *Yearbook of Labour Statistics 2006.*

GREENLAND - ROADS

Central Intelligence Agency, Office of Public Affairs, Washington, DC 20505, (703) 482-0623, Fax: (703) 482-1739, www.cia.gov; *The World Factbook.*

GREENLAND - SHEEP

See GREENLAND - LIVESTOCK

GREENLAND - SHIPPING

Palgrave Macmillan Ltd., Houndmills, Basingstoke, Hampshire, RG21 6XS, England, (Telephone in U.S. (888) 330-8477), (Fax in U.S. (800) 672-2054), www.palgrave.com; *The Statesman's Yearbook 2008.*

Taylor and Francis Group, An Informa Business, 2 Park Square, Milton Park, Abingdon, Oxford OX14 4RN, United Kingdom, (Dial from U.S. (212) 216-7800), (Fax from U.S. (212) 564-7854), www.tandf.co.uk; *The Europa World Year Book.*

United Nations Statistics Division, New York, NY 10017, (800) 253-9646, Fax: (212) 963-4116, http://unstats.un.org; *Statistical Yearbook.*

GREENLAND - SOCIAL SECURITY

Palgrave Macmillan Ltd., Houndmills, Basingstoke, Hampshire, RG21 6XS, England, (Telephone in U.S. (888) 330-8477), (Fax in U.S. (800) 672-2054), www.palgrave.com; *The Statesman's Yearbook 2008.*

GREENLAND - TELEPHONE

Palgrave Macmillan Ltd., Houndmills, Basingstoke, Hampshire, RG21 6XS, England, (Telephone in U.S. (888) 330-8477), (Fax in U.S. (800) 672-2054), www.palgrave.com; *The Statesman's Yearbook 2008.*

GREENLAND - TEXTILE INDUSTRY

United Nations Conference on Trade and Development (UNCTAD), DC2-1120, United Nations, New York, NY 10017, (212) 963-0027, www.unctad.org; *UNCTAD Commodity Yearbook.*

GREENLAND - TOURISM

Statistics Greenland, PO Box 1025, 3900 Nuuk, Greenland, www.statgreen.gl/english; *Greenland in Figures 2007.*

The World Bank, 1818 H Street, NW, Washington, DC 20433, (202) 473-1000, Fax: (202) 477-6391, www.worldbank.org; *Greenland.*

GREENLAND - TRADE

See GREENLAND - INTERNATIONAL TRADE

GREENLAND - TRANSPORTATION

Central Intelligence Agency, Office of Public Affairs, Washington, DC 20505, (703) 482-0623, Fax: (703) 482-1739, www.cia.gov; *The World Factbook.*

Palgrave Macmillan Ltd., Houndmills, Basingstoke, Hampshire, RG21 6XS, England, (Telephone in U.S. (888) 330-8477), (Fax in U.S. (800) 672-2054), www.palgrave.com; *The Statesman's Yearbook 2008.*

Statistics Greenland, PO Box 1025, 3900 Nuuk, Greenland, www.statgreen.gl/english; *Greenland in Figures 2007.*

Taylor and Francis Group, An Informa Business, 2 Park Square, Milton Park, Abingdon, Oxford OX14 4RN, United Kingdom, (Dial from U.S. (212) 216-7800), (Fax from U.S. (212) 564-7854), www.tandf.co.uk; *The Europa World Year Book.*

The World Bank, 1818 H Street, NW, Washington, DC 20433, (202) 473-1000, Fax: (202) 477-6391, www.worldbank.org; *Greenland.*

GREENLAND - UNEMPLOYMENT

Central Intelligence Agency, Office of Public Affairs, Washington, DC 20505, (703) 482-0623, Fax: (703) 482-1739, www.cia.gov; *The World Factbook.*

International Labour Office, I.L.O. Publications, 4 route des Morillons, CH-1211 Geneva 22, Switzerland, (Telephone in U.S. (202) 653-7652), (Fax in U.S. (202) 653-7687), www.ilo.org; *Yearbook of Labour Statistics 2006.*

GREENLAND - VITAL STATISTICS

United Nations Statistics Division, New York, NY 10017, (800) 253-9646, Fax: (212) 963-4116, http://unstats.un.org; *Statistical Yearbook.*

World Health Organization (WHO), Avenue Appia 20, 1211 Geneve 27, Switzerland, (Telephone in U.S. (212) 331-9081), www.who.int; *World Health Report 2006.*

GREENLAND - WAGES

International Labour Office, I.L.O. Publications, 4 route des Morillons, CH-1211 Geneva 22, Switzerland, (Telephone in U.S. (202) 653-7652), (Fax in U.S. (202) 653-7687), www.ilo.org; *Yearbook of Labour Statistics 2006.*

Statistics Greenland, PO Box 1025, 3900 Nuuk, Greenland, www.statgreen.gl/english; *Greenland in Figures 2007.*

The World Bank, 1818 H Street, NW, Washington, DC 20433, (202) 473-1000, Fax: (202) 477-6391, www.worldbank.org; *Greenland.*

GRENADA - NATIONAL STATISTICAL OFFICE

Central Statistical Office, The Financial Complex, Ministry of Finance, The Carenage, St George's, Grenada, (Dial from U.S. (473) 440-1369), (Fax from U.S. (473) 440-4115), http://finance.gov.gd/subdepts/cstl.aspx; National Data Center.

GRENADA - PRIMARY STATISTICS SOURCES

TSO (The Stationery Office), PO Box 29, Norwich, NR3 1GN, United Kingdom, www.tso.co.uk; *Grenada: Statistical Appendix.*

GRENADA - AGRICULTURAL MACHINERY

United Nations Statistics Division, New York, NY 10017, (800) 253-9646, Fax: (212) 963-4116, http://unstats.un.org; *Statistical Yearbook.*

GRENADA - AGRICULTURE

Economist Intelligence Unit, 111 West 57th Street, New York, NY 10019, (212) 554-0600, Fax: (212) 586-1181, www.eiu.com; *Organisation of Eastern Caribbean States.*

Euromonitor International, Inc., 224 S. Michigan Avenue, Suite 1500, Chicago, IL 60604, (312) 922-1115, Fax: (312) 922-1157, www.euromonitor.com; *World Marketing Data and Statistics.*

Palgrave Macmillan Ltd., Houndmills, Basingstoke, Hampshire, RG21 6XS, England, (Telephone in U.S. (888) 330-8477), (Fax in U.S. (800) 672-2054), www.palgrave.com; *The Statesman's Yearbook 2008.*

Taylor and Francis Group, An Informa Business, 2 Park Square, Milton Park, Abingdon, Oxford OX14 4RN, United Kingdom, (Dial from U.S. (212) 216-7800), (Fax from U.S. (212) 564-7854), www.tandf.co.uk; *The Europa World Year Book.*

United Nations Conference on Trade and Development (UNCTAD), DC2-1120, United Nations, New York, NY 10017, (212) 963-0027, www.unctad.org; *UNCTAD Commodity Yearbook.*

United Nations Food and Agricultural Organization (FAO), Viale delle Terme di Caracalla, 00100 Rome, Italy, (Dial from U.S. (202) 653-2400), (Fax from U.S. (202) 653 5760), www.fao.org; AQUASTAT; *FAO Production Yearbook 2002; FAO Trade Yearbook;* and *The State of Food and Agriculture (SOFA) 2006.*

United Nations Statistics Division, New York, NY 10017, (800) 253-9646, Fax: (212) 963-4116, http://unstats.un.org; *Statistical Yearbook.*

The World Bank, 1818 H Street, NW, Washington, DC 20433, (202) 473-1000, Fax: (202) 477-6391, www.worldbank.org; *Grenada* and *World Development Indicators (WDI) 2008.*

GRENADA - AIRLINES

Palgrave Macmillan Ltd., Houndmills, Basingstoke, Hampshire, RG21 6XS, England, (Telephone in U.S. (888) 330-8477), (Fax in U.S. (800) 672-2054), www.palgrave.com; *The Statesman's Yearbook 2008.*

Taylor and Francis Group, An Informa Business, 2 Park Square, Milton Park, Abingdon, Oxford OX14

4RN, United Kingdom, (Dial from U.S. (212) 216-7800), (Fax from U.S. (212) 564-7854), www.tandf.co.uk; *The Europa World Year Book.*

GRENADA - AIRPORTS

Central Intelligence Agency, Office of Public Affairs, Washington, DC 20505, (703) 482-0623, Fax: (703) 482-1739, www.cia.gov; *The World Factbook.*

GRENADA - ARMED FORCES

Central Intelligence Agency, Office of Public Affairs, Washington, DC 20505, (703) 482-0623, Fax: (703) 482-1739, www.cia.gov; *The World Factbook.*

Euromonitor International, Inc., 224 S. Michigan Avenue, Suite 1500, Chicago, IL 60604, (312) 922-1115, Fax: (312) 922-1157, www.euromonitor.com; *World Marketing Data and Statistics.*

International Monetary Fund (IMF), 700 Nineteenth Street, NW, Washington, DC 20431, (202) 623-7000, Fax: (202) 623-4661, www.imf.org; *Government Finance Statistics Yearbook (2008 Edition).*

Palgrave Macmillan Ltd., Houndmills, Basingstoke, Hampshire, RG21 6XS, England, (Telephone in U.S. (888) 330-8477), (Fax in U.S. (800) 672-2054), www.palgrave.com; *The Statesman's Yearbook 2008.*

United Nations Statistics Division, New York, NY 10017, (800) 253-9646, Fax: (212) 963-4116, http://unstats.un.org; *Human Development Report 2006.*

GRENADA - BALANCE OF PAYMENTS

International Monetary Fund (IMF), 700 Nineteenth Street, NW, Washington, DC 20431, (202) 623-7000, Fax: (202) 623-4661, www.imf.org; *Balance of Payments Statistics Newsletter* and *Balance of Payments Statistics Yearbook 2007.*

Taylor and Francis Group, An Informa Business, 2 Park Square, Milton Park, Abingdon, Oxford OX14 4RN, United Kingdom, (Dial from U.S. (212) 216-7800), (Fax from U.S. (212) 564-7854), www.tandf.co.uk; *The Europa World Year Book.*

United Nations Conference on Trade and Development (UNCTAD), DC2-1120, United Nations, New York, NY 10017, (212) 963-0027, www.unctad.org; *Handbook of Statistics 2005.*

United Nations Statistics Division, New York, NY 10017, (800) 253-9646, Fax: (212) 963-4116, http://unstats.un.org; *Economic Survey of Latin America and the Caribbean 2004-2005.*

The World Bank, 1818 H Street, NW, Washington, DC 20433, (202) 473-1000, Fax: (202) 477-6391, www.worldbank.org; *Grenada* and *World Development Indicators (WDI) 2008.*

GRENADA - BANANAS

See GRENADA - CROPS

GRENADA - BANKS AND BANKING

Euromonitor International, Inc., 224 S. Michigan Avenue, Suite 1500, Chicago, IL 60604, (312) 922-1115, Fax: (312) 922-1157, www.euromonitor.com; *World Marketing Data and Statistics.*

International Monetary Fund (IMF), 700 Nineteenth Street, NW, Washington, DC 20431, (202) 623-7000, Fax: (202) 623-4661, www.imf.org; *International Financial Statistics Yearbook 2007.*

Palgrave Macmillan Ltd., Houndmills, Basingstoke, Hampshire, RG21 6XS, England, (Telephone in U.S. (888) 330-8477), (Fax in U.S. (800) 672-2054), www.palgrave.com; *The Statesman's Yearbook 2008.*

Taylor and Francis Group, An Informa Business, 2 Park Square, Milton Park, Abingdon, Oxford OX14 4RN, United Kingdom, (Dial from U.S. (212) 216-7800), (Fax from U.S. (212) 564-7854), www.tandf.co.uk; *The Europa World Year Book.*

GRENADA - BONDS

International Monetary Fund (IMF), 700 Nineteenth Street, NW, Washington, DC 20431, (202) 623-7000, Fax: (202) 623-4661, www.imf.org; *Government Finance Statistics Yearbook (2008 Edition).*

GRENADA - BROADCASTING

Central Intelligence Agency, Office of Public Affairs, Washington, DC 20505, (703) 482-0623, Fax: (703) 482-1739, www.cia.gov; *The World Factbook.*

Euromonitor International, Inc., 224 S. Michigan Avenue, Suite 1500, Chicago, IL 60604, (312) 922-1115, Fax: (312) 922-1157, www.euromonitor.com; *World Marketing Data and Statistics.*

Palgrave Macmillan Ltd., Houndmills, Basingstoke, Hampshire, RG21 6XS, England, (Telephone in U.S. (888) 330-8477), (Fax in U.S. (800) 672-2054), www.palgrave.com; *The Statesman's Yearbook 2008.*

GRENADA - BUDGET

Central Intelligence Agency, Office of Public Affairs, Washington, DC 20505, (703) 482-0623, Fax: (703) 482-1739, www.cia.gov; *The World Factbook.*

GRENADA - CACAO

See GRENADA - CROPS

GRENADA - CAPITAL LEVY

International Monetary Fund (IMF), 700 Nineteenth Street, NW, Washington, DC 20431, (202) 623-7000, Fax: (202) 623-4661, www.imf.org; *Government Finance Statistics Yearbook (2008 Edition).*

GRENADA - CATTLE

See GRENADA - LIVESTOCK

GRENADA - CHILDBIRTH - STATISTICS

Central Intelligence Agency, Office of Public Affairs, Washington, DC 20505, (703) 482-0623, Fax: (703) 482-1739, www.cia.gov; *The World Factbook.*

Euromonitor International, Inc., 224 S. Michigan Avenue, Suite 1500, Chicago, IL 60604, (312) 922-1115, Fax: (312) 922-1157, www.euromonitor.com; *International Marketing Data and Statistics 2008* and *The World Economic Factbook 2008.*

Palgrave Macmillan Ltd., Houndmills, Basingstoke, Hampshire, RG21 6XS, England, (Telephone in U.S. (888) 330-8477), (Fax in U.S. (800) 672-2054), www.palgrave.com; *The Statesman's Yearbook 2008.*

Taylor and Francis Group, An Informa Business, 2 Park Square, Milton Park, Abingdon, Oxford OX14 4RN, United Kingdom, (Dial from U.S. (212) 216-7800), (Fax from U.S. (212) 564-7854), www.tandf.co.uk; *The Europa World Year Book.*

United Nations Statistics Division, New York, NY 10017, (800) 253-9646, Fax: (212) 963-4116, http://unstats.un.org; *Demographic Yearbook.*

The World Bank, 1818 H Street, NW, Washington, DC 20433, (202) 473-1000, Fax: (202) 477-6391, www.worldbank.org; *World Development Indicators (WDI) 2008.*

GRENADA - CLIMATE

Palgrave Macmillan Ltd., Houndmills, Basingstoke, Hampshire, RG21 6XS, England, (Telephone in U.S. (888) 330-8477), (Fax in U.S. (800) 672-2054), www.palgrave.com; *The Statesman's Yearbook 2008.*

GRENADA - COCOA PRODUCTION

See GRENADA - CROPS

GRENADA - COMMERCE

Palgrave Macmillan Ltd., Houndmills, Basingstoke, Hampshire, RG21 6XS, England, (Telephone in U.S. (888) 330-8477), (Fax in U.S. (800) 672-2054), www.palgrave.com; *The Statesman's Yearbook 2008.*

GRENADA - COMMODITY EXCHANGES

Commodity Research Bureau, 330 South Wells Street, Suite 612, Chicago, IL 60606-7110, (800) 621-5271, Fax: (312) 939-4135, www.crbtrader.com; *2006 CRB Commodity Yearbook and CD.*

International Monetary Fund (IMF), 700 Nineteenth Street, NW, Washington, DC 20431, (202) 623-7000, Fax: (202) 623-4661, www.imf.org; *IMF Primary Commodity Prices.*

United Nations Food and Agricultural Organization (FAO), Viale delle Terme di Caracalla, 00100 Rome, Italy, (Dial from U.S. (202) 653-2400), (Fax from U.S. (202) 653 5760), www.fao.org; *The State of Food and Agriculture (SOFA) 2006.*

GRENADA - CONSUMER PRICE INDEXES

Taylor and Francis Group, An Informa Business, 2 Park Square, Milton Park, Abingdon, Oxford OX14 4RN, United Kingdom, (Dial from U.S. (212) 216-7800), (Fax from U.S. (212) 564-7854), www.tandf.co.uk; *The Europa World Year Book.*

The World Bank, 1818 H Street, NW, Washington, DC 20433, (202) 473-1000, Fax: (202) 477-6391, www.worldbank.org; *Grenada.*

GRENADA - CORN INDUSTRY

See GRENADA - CROPS

GRENADA - COST AND STANDARD OF LIVING

International Monetary Fund (IMF), 700 Nineteenth Street, NW, Washington, DC 20431, (202) 623-7000, Fax: (202) 623-4661, www.imf.org; *Government Finance Statistics Yearbook (2008 Edition).*

GRENADA - CROPS

International Monetary Fund (IMF), 700 Nineteenth Street, NW, Washington, DC 20431, (202) 623-7000, Fax: (202) 623-4661, www.imf.org; *International Financial Statistics Yearbook 2007.*

Organization of American States (OAS), 17th Street Constitution Avenue NW, Washington, DC 20006, (202) 458-3000, www.oas.org; *The OAS in Transition: 1994-2004.*

Palgrave Macmillan Ltd., Houndmills, Basingstoke, Hampshire, RG21 6XS, England, (Telephone in U.S. (888) 330-8477), (Fax in U.S. (800) 672-2054), www.palgrave.com; *The Statesman's Yearbook 2008.*

Taylor and Francis Group, An Informa Business, 2 Park Square, Milton Park, Abingdon, Oxford OX14 4RN, United Kingdom, (Dial from U.S. (212) 216-7800), (Fax from U.S. (212) 564-7854), www.tandf.co.uk; *The Europa World Year Book.*

United Nations Conference on Trade and Development (UNCTAD), DC2-1120, United Nations, New York, NY 10017, (212) 963-0027, www.unctad.org; *UNCTAD Commodity Yearbook.*

United Nations Food and Agricultural Organization (FAO), Viale delle Terme di Caracalla, 00100 Rome, Italy, (Dial from U.S. (202) 653-2400), (Fax from U.S. (202) 653 5760), www.fao.org; *FAO Production Yearbook 2002* and *The State of Food and Agriculture (SOFA) 2006.*

United Nations Statistics Division, New York, NY 10017, (800) 253-9646, Fax: (212) 963-4116, http://unstats.un.org; *Statistical Yearbook.*

GRENADA - CUSTOMS ADMINISTRATION

International Monetary Fund (IMF), 700 Nineteenth Street, NW, Washington, DC 20431, (202) 623-7000, Fax: (202) 623-4661, www.imf.org; *Government Finance Statistics Yearbook (2008 Edition).*

Palgrave Macmillan Ltd., Houndmills, Basingstoke, Hampshire, RG21 6XS, England, (Telephone in U.S. (888) 330-8477), (Fax in U.S. (800) 672-2054), www.palgrave.com; *The Statesman's Yearbook 2008.*

GRENADA - DAIRY PROCESSING

Palgrave Macmillan Ltd., Houndmills, Basingstoke, Hampshire, RG21 6XS, England, (Telephone in U.S. (888) 330-8477), (Fax in U.S. (800) 672-2054), www.palgrave.com; *The Statesman's Yearbook 2008.*

GRENADA - DEATH RATES

See GRENADA - MORTALITY

GRENADA - DEBTS, EXTERNAL

United Nations Statistics Division, New York, NY 10017, (800) 253-9646, Fax: (212) 963-4116, http://

unstats.un.org; *Economic Survey of Latin America and the Caribbean 2004-2005.*

The World Bank, 1818 H Street, NW, Washington, DC 20433, (202) 473-1000, Fax: (202) 477-6391, www.worldbank.org; *Global Development Finance 2007* and *World Development Indicators (WDI) 2008.*

GRENADA - DEFENSE EXPENDITURES

See GRENADA - ARMED FORCES

GRENADA - DEMOGRAPHY

Euromonitor International, Inc., 224 S. Michigan Avenue, Suite 1500, Chicago, IL 60604, (312) 922-1115, Fax: (312) 922-1157, www.euromonitor.com; *International Marketing Data and Statistics 2008; The World Economic Factbook 2008;* and *World Marketing Data and Statistics.*

United Nations Statistics Division, New York, NY 10017, (800) 253-9646, Fax: (212) 963-4116, http://unstats.un.org; *Human Development Report 2006.*

The World Bank, 1818 H Street, NW, Washington, DC 20433, (202) 473-1000, Fax: (202) 477-6391, www.worldbank.org; *Grenada.*

GRENADA - DISPOSABLE INCOME

United Nations Statistics Division, New York, NY 10017, (800) 253-9646, Fax: (212) 963-4116, http://unstats.un.org; *National Accounts Statistics: Compendium of Income Distribution Statistics* and *Statistical Yearbook.*

GRENADA - DIVORCE

United Nations Statistics Division, New York, NY 10017, (800) 253-9646, Fax: (212) 963-4116, http://unstats.un.org; *Demographic Yearbook* and *Statistical Yearbook.*

GRENADA - ECONOMIC CONDITIONS

Center for International Business Education Research (CIBER), Columbia Business School and School of International and Public Affairs, Uris Hall, Room 212, 3022 Broadway, New York, NY 10027-6902, Mr. Joshua Safier, (212) 854-4750, Fax: (212) 222-9821, www.columbia.edu/cu/ciber/; Datastream International.

Central Intelligence Agency, Office of Public Affairs, Washington, DC 20505, (703) 482-0623, Fax: (703) 482-1739, www.cia.gov; *The World Factbook.*

DSI Data Service Information, Xantener Strasse 51a, D-47495 Rheinberg, Germany, www.dsidata.com; *Campus Solution.*

Dun and Bradstreet (DB) Corporation, 103 JFK Parkway, Short Hills, NJ 07078, (973) 921-5500, www.dnb.com; *Country Report.*

Economist Intelligence Unit, 111 West 57th Street, New York, NY 10019, (212) 554-0600, Fax: (212) 586-1181, www.eiu.com; *Organisation of Eastern Caribbean States.*

Euromonitor International, Inc., 224 S. Michigan Avenue, Suite 1500, Chicago, IL 60604, (312) 922-1115, Fax: (312) 922-1157, www.euromonitor.com; *The World Economic Factbook 2008* and *World Marketing Data and Statistics.*

International Monetary Fund (IMF), 700 Nineteenth Street, NW, Washington, DC 20431, (202) 623-7000, Fax: (202) 623-4661, www.imf.org; *World Economic Outlook Reports.*

Organization of American States (OAS), 17th Street Constitution Avenue NW, Washington, DC 20006, (202) 458-3000, www.oas.org; *The OAS in Transition: 1994-2004.*

Palgrave Macmillan Ltd., Houndmills, Basingstoke, Hampshire, RG21 6XS, England, (Telephone in U.S. (888) 330-8477), (Fax in U.S. (800) 672-2054), www.palgrave.com; *The Statesman's Yearbook 2008.*

Taylor and Francis Group, An Informa Business, 2 Park Square, Milton Park, Abingdon, Oxford OX14 4RN, United Kingdom, (Dial from U.S. (212) 216-7800), (Fax from U.S. (212) 564-7854), www.tandf.co.uk; *The Europa World Year Book.*

United Nations Statistics Division, New York, NY 10017, (800) 253-9646, Fax: (212) 963-4116, http://unstats.un.org; *Economic Survey of Latin America and the Caribbean 2004-2005* and *World Statistics Pocketbook.*

The World Bank, 1818 H Street, NW, Washington, DC 20433, (202) 473-1000, Fax: (202) 477-6391, www.worldbank.org; *Global Economic Monitor (GEM); Global Economic Prospects 2008; Grenada;* and *The World Bank Atlas 2003-2004.*

GRENADA - EDUCATION

Euromonitor International, Inc., 224 S. Michigan Avenue, Suite 1500, Chicago, IL 60604, (312) 922-1115, Fax: (312) 922-1157, www.euromonitor.com; *International Marketing Data and Statistics 2008* and *World Marketing Data and Statistics.*

International Monetary Fund (IMF), 700 Nineteenth Street, NW, Washington, DC 20431, (202) 623-7000, Fax: (202) 623-4661, www.imf.org; *Government Finance Statistics Yearbook (2008 Edition).*

Palgrave Macmillan Ltd., Houndmills, Basingstoke, Hampshire, RG21 6XS, England, (Telephone in U.S. (888) 330-8477), (Fax in U.S. (800) 672-2054), www.palgrave.com; *The Statesman's Yearbook 2008.*

Taylor and Francis Group, An Informa Business, 2 Park Square, Milton Park, Abingdon, Oxford OX14 4RN, United Kingdom, (Dial from U.S. (212) 216-7800), (Fax from U.S. (212) 564-7854), www.tandf.co.uk; *The Europa World Year Book.*

UNESCO Institute for Statistics, C.P. 6128 Succursale Centre-Ville, Montreal, Quebec, H3C 3J7 Canada, (Dial from U.S. (514) 343-6880), (Fax from U.S. (514) 343 6882), www.uis.unesco.org; *Statistical Tables.*

United Nations Statistics Division, New York, NY 10017, (800) 253-9646, Fax: (212) 963-4116, http://unstats.un.org; *Human Development Report 2006.*

The World Bank, 1818 H Street, NW, Washington, DC 20433, (202) 473-1000, Fax: (202) 477-6391, www.worldbank.org; *Grenada* and *World Development Indicators (WDI) 2008.*

GRENADA - ELECTRICITY

Palgrave Macmillan Ltd., Houndmills, Basingstoke, Hampshire, RG21 6XS, England, (Telephone in U.S. (888) 330-8477), (Fax in U.S. (800) 672-2054), www.palgrave.com; *The Statesman's Yearbook 2008.*

United Nations Statistics Division, New York, NY 10017, (800) 253-9646, Fax: (212) 963-4116, http://unstats.un.org; *Human Development Report 2006.*

GRENADA - EMPLOYMENT

Euromonitor International, Inc., 224 S. Michigan Avenue, Suite 1500, Chicago, IL 60604, (312) 922-1115, Fax: (312) 922-1157, www.euromonitor.com; *International Marketing Data and Statistics 2008.*

International Labour Office, I.L.O. Publications, 4 route des Morillons, CH-1211 Geneva 22, Switzerland, (Telephone in U.S. (202) 653-7652), (Fax in U.S. (202) 653-7687), www.ilo.org; *Yearbook of Labour Statistics 2006.*

The World Bank, 1818 H Street, NW, Washington, DC 20433, (202) 473-1000, Fax: (202) 477-6391, www.worldbank.org; *Grenada.*

GRENADA - ENVIRONMENTAL CONDITIONS

DSI Data Service Information, Xantener Strasse 51a, D-47495 Rheinberg, Germany, www.dsidata.com; *Campus Solution* and *DSI's Global Environmental Database.*

Economist Intelligence Unit, 111 West 57th Street, New York, NY 10019, (212) 554-0600, Fax: (212) 586-1181, www.eiu.com; *Organisation of Eastern Caribbean States.*

United Nations Statistics Division, New York, NY 10017, (800) 253-9646, Fax: (212) 963-4116, http://unstats.un.org; *World Statistics Pocketbook.*

GRENADA - EXCISE TAX

International Monetary Fund (IMF), 700 Nineteenth Street, NW, Washington, DC 20431, (202) 623-7000, Fax: (202) 623-4661, www.imf.org; *Government Finance Statistics Yearbook (2008 Edition)* and *International Financial Statistics Yearbook 2007.*

United Nations Statistics Division, New York, NY 10017, (800) 253-9646, Fax: (212) 963-4116, http://unstats.un.org; *Statistical Yearbook.*

GRENADA - EXPORTS

Central Intelligence Agency, Office of Public Affairs, Washington, DC 20505, (703) 482-0623, Fax: (703) 482-1739, www.cia.gov; *The World Factbook.*

Economist Intelligence Unit, 111 West 57th Street, New York, NY 10019, (212) 554-0600, Fax: (212) 586-1181, www.eiu.com; *Organisation of Eastern Caribbean States.*

Euromonitor International, Inc., 224 S. Michigan Avenue, Suite 1500, Chicago, IL 60604, (312) 922-1115, Fax: (312) 922-1157, www.euromonitor.com; *International Marketing Data and Statistics 2008* and *The World Economic Factbook 2008.*

International Monetary Fund (IMF), 700 Nineteenth Street, NW, Washington, DC 20431, (202) 623-7000, Fax: (202) 623-4661, www.imf.org; *Direction of Trade Statistics Yearbook 2007; Government Finance Statistics Yearbook (2008 Edition);* and *International Financial Statistics Yearbook 2007.*

Palgrave Macmillan Ltd., Houndmills, Basingstoke, Hampshire, RG21 6XS, England, (Telephone in U.S. (888) 330-8477), (Fax in U.S. (800) 672-2054), www.palgrave.com; *The Statesman's Yearbook 2008.*

Taylor and Francis Group, An Informa Business, 2 Park Square, Milton Park, Abingdon, Oxford OX14 4RN, United Kingdom, (Dial from U.S. (212) 216-7800), (Fax from U.S. (212) 564-7854), www.tandf.co.uk; *The Europa World Year Book.*

United Nations Conference on Trade and Development (UNCTAD), DC2-1120, United Nations, New York, NY 10017, (212) 963-0027, www.unctad.org; *Handbook of Statistics 2005.*

United Nations Food and Agricultural Organization (FAO), Viale delle Terme di Caracalla, 00100 Rome, Italy, (Dial from U.S. (202) 653-2400), (Fax from U.S. (202) 653 5760), www.fao.org; *The State of Food and Agriculture (SOFA) 2006.*

The World Bank, 1818 H Street, NW, Washington, DC 20433, (202) 473-1000, Fax: (202) 477-6391, www.worldbank.org; *World Development Indicators (WDI) 2008.*

GRENADA - FERTILITY, HUMAN

Central Intelligence Agency, Office of Public Affairs, Washington, DC 20505, (703) 482-0623, Fax: (703) 482-1739, www.cia.gov; *The World Factbook.*

United Nations Statistics Division, New York, NY 10017, (800) 253-9646, Fax: (212) 963-4116, http://unstats.un.org; *Demographic Yearbook* and *Human Development Report 2006.*

The World Bank, 1818 H Street, NW, Washington, DC 20433, (202) 473-1000, Fax: (202) 477-6391, www.worldbank.org; *The World Bank Atlas 2003-2004* and *World Development Indicators (WDI) 2008.*

World Health Organization (WHO), Avenue Appia 20, 1211 Geneve 27, Switzerland, (Telephone in U.S. (212) 331-9081), www.who.int; *World Health Report 2006.*

GRENADA - FERTILIZER INDUSTRY

United Nations Food and Agricultural Organization (FAO), Viale delle Terme di Caracalla, 00100 Rome, Italy, (Dial from U.S. (202) 653-2400), (Fax from U.S. (202) 653 5760), www.fao.org; *The State of Food and Agriculture (SOFA) 2006.*

GRENADA - FETAL MORTALITY

See GRENADA - MORTALITY

GRENADA - FINANCE

United Nations Statistics Division, New York, NY 10017, (800) 253-9646, Fax: (212) 963-4116, http://unstats.un.org; *National Accounts Statistics: Analysis of Main Aggregates* and *Statistical Yearbook.*

The World Bank, 1818 H Street, NW, Washington, DC 20433, (202) 473-1000, Fax: (202) 477-6391, www.worldbank.org; *Grenada.*

GRENADA - FINANCE, PUBLIC

Bernan Essential Government Publications, 4611-F Assembly Drive, Lanham MD, 20706-4391, (301) 459-2255, Fax: (800) 865-3450, www.bernan.com; *National Accounts Statistics.*

Economist Intelligence Unit, 111 West 57th Street, New York, NY 10019, (212) 554-0600, Fax: (212) 586-1181, www.eiu.com; *Organisation of Eastern Caribbean States.*

International Monetary Fund (IMF), 700 Nineteenth Street, NW, Washington, DC 20431, (202) 623-7000, Fax: (202) 623-4661, www.imf.org; *Government Finance Statistics Yearbook (2008 Edition); International Financial Statistics;* and *International Financial Statistics Online Service.*

Palgrave Macmillan Ltd., Houndmills, Basingstoke, Hampshire, RG21 6XS, England, (Telephone in U.S. (888) 330-8477), (Fax in U.S. (800) 672-2054), www.palgrave.com; *The Statesman's Yearbook 2008.*

Taylor and Francis Group, An Informa Business, 2 Park Square, Milton Park, Abingdon, Oxford OX14 4RN, United Kingdom, (Dial from U.S. (212) 216-7800), (Fax from U.S. (212) 564-7854), www.tandf.co.uk; *The Europa World Year Book.*

The World Bank, 1818 H Street, NW, Washington, DC 20433, (202) 473-1000, Fax: (202) 477-6391, www.worldbank.org; *Grenada.*

GRENADA - FISHERIES

Palgrave Macmillan Ltd., Houndmills, Basingstoke, Hampshire, RG21 6XS, England, (Telephone in U.S. (888) 330-8477), (Fax in U.S. (800) 672-2054), www.palgrave.com; *The Statesman's Yearbook 2008.*

Taylor and Francis Group, An Informa Business, 2 Park Square, Milton Park, Abingdon, Oxford OX14 4RN, United Kingdom, (Dial from U.S. (212) 216-7800), (Fax from U.S. (212) 564-7854), www.tandf.co.uk; *The Europa World Year Book.*

United Nations Conference on Trade and Development (UNCTAD), DC2-1120, United Nations, New York, NY 10017, (212) 963-0027, www.unctad.org; *UNCTAD Commodity Yearbook.*

United Nations Food and Agricultural Organization (FAO), Viale delle Terme di Caracalla, 00100 Rome, Italy, (Dial from U.S. (202) 653-2400), (Fax from U.S. (202) 653 5760), www.fao.org; *FAO Yearbook of Fishery Statistics;* Fishery Databases; FISHSTAT Database. Subjects covered include: Aquaculture production, capture production, fishery commodities; and *The State of Food and Agriculture (SOFA) 2006.*

United Nations Statistics Division, New York, NY 10017, (800) 253-9646, Fax: (212) 963-4116, http://unstats.un.org; *Statistical Yearbook.*

The World Bank, 1818 H Street, NW, Washington, DC 20433, (202) 473-1000, Fax: (202) 477-6391, www.worldbank.org; *Grenada.*

GRENADA - FOOD

United Nations Conference on Trade and Development (UNCTAD), DC2-1120, United Nations, New York, NY 10017, (212) 963-0027, www.unctad.org; *UNCTAD Commodity Yearbook.*

United Nations Food and Agricultural Organization (FAO), Viale delle Terme di Caracalla, 00100 Rome, Italy, (Dial from U.S. (202) 653-2400), (Fax from U.S. (202) 653 5760), www.fao.org; *FAO Production Yearbook 2002* and *The State of Food and Agriculture (SOFA) 2006.*

United Nations Statistics Division, New York, NY 10017, (800) 253-9646, Fax: (212) 963-4116, http://unstats.un.org; *Human Development Report 2006.*

GRENADA - FOREIGN EXCHANGE RATES

Central Intelligence Agency, Office of Public Affairs, Washington, DC 20505, (703) 482-0623, Fax: (703) 482-1739, www.cia.gov; *The World Factbook.*

Euromonitor International, Inc., 224 S. Michigan Avenue, Suite 1500, Chicago, IL 60604, (312) 922-1115, Fax: (312) 922-1157, www.euromonitor.com; *International Marketing Data and Statistics 2008* and *The World Economic Factbook 2008.*

International Monetary Fund (IMF), 700 Nineteenth Street, NW, Washington, DC 20431, (202) 623-7000, Fax: (202) 623-4661, www.imf.org; *International Financial Statistics Yearbook 2007.*

Organization of American States (OAS), 17th Street Constitution Avenue NW, Washington, DC 20006, (202) 458-3000, www.oas.org; *The OAS in Transition: 1994-2004.*

Taylor and Francis Group, An Informa Business, 2 Park Square, Milton Park, Abingdon, Oxford OX14 4RN, United Kingdom, (Dial from U.S. (212) 216-7800), (Fax from U.S. (212) 564-7854), www.tandf.co.uk; *The Europa World Year Book.*

United Nations Statistics Division, New York, NY 10017, (800) 253-9646, Fax: (212) 963-4116, http://unstats.un.org; *Statistical Yearbook* and *World Statistics Pocketbook.*

GRENADA - FORESTS AND FORESTRY

UNESCO Institute for Statistics, C.P. 6128 Succursale Centre-Ville, Montreal, Quebec, H3C 3J7 Canada, (Dial from U.S. (514) 343-6880), (Fax from U.S. (514) 343 6882), www.uis.unesco.org; *Statistical Tables.*

United Nations Conference on Trade and Development (UNCTAD), DC2-1120, United Nations, New York, NY 10017, (212) 963-0027, www.unctad.org; *UNCTAD Commodity Yearbook.*

United Nations Food and Agricultural Organization (FAO), Viale delle Terme di Caracalla, 00100 Rome, Italy, (Dial from U.S. (202) 653-2400), (Fax from U.S. (202) 653 5760), www.fao.org; *The State of Food and Agriculture (SOFA) 2006.*

United Nations Statistics Division, New York, NY 10017, (800) 253-9646, Fax: (212) 963-4116, http://unstats.un.org; *Statistical Yearbook.*

The World Bank, 1818 H Street, NW, Washington, DC 20433, (202) 473-1000, Fax: (202) 477-6391, www.worldbank.org; *Grenada.*

GRENADA - GEOGRAPHIC INFORMATION SYSTEMS

The World Bank, 1818 H Street, NW, Washington, DC 20433, (202) 473-1000, Fax: (202) 477-6391, www.worldbank.org; *Grenada.*

GRENADA - GOLD INDUSTRY

International Monetary Fund (IMF), 700 Nineteenth Street, NW, Washington, DC 20431, (202) 623-7000, Fax: (202) 623-4661, www.imf.org; *International Financial Statistics Yearbook 2007.*

United Nations Statistics Division, New York, NY 10017, (800) 253-9646, Fax: (212) 963-4116, http://unstats.un.org; *Statistical Yearbook.*

The World Bank, 1818 H Street, NW, Washington, DC 20433, (202) 473-1000, Fax: (202) 477-6391, www.worldbank.org; *World Development Indicators (WDI) 2008.*

GRENADA - GRANTS-IN-AID

International Monetary Fund (IMF), 700 Nineteenth Street, NW, Washington, DC 20431, (202) 623-7000, Fax: (202) 623-4661, www.imf.org; *Government Finance Statistics Yearbook (2008 Edition).*

GRENADA - GROSS DOMESTIC PRODUCT

Economist Intelligence Unit, 111 West 57th Street, New York, NY 10019, (212) 554-0600, Fax: (212) 586-1181, www.eiu.com; *Organisation of Eastern Caribbean States.*

Euromonitor International, Inc., 224 S. Michigan Avenue, Suite 1500, Chicago, IL 60604, (312) 922-1115, Fax: (312) 922-1157, www.euromonitor.com; *International Marketing Data and Statistics 2008* and *The World Economic Factbook 2008.*

Taylor and Francis Group, An Informa Business, 2 Park Square, Milton Park, Abingdon, Oxford OX14 4RN, United Kingdom, (Dial from U.S. (212) 216-7800), (Fax from U.S. (212) 564-7854), www.tandf.co.uk; *The Europa World Year Book.*

United Nations Statistics Division, New York, NY 10017, (800) 253-9646, Fax: (212) 963-4116, http://unstats.un.org; *Human Development Report 2006; National Accounts Statistics: Compendium of Income Distribution Statistics;* and *Statistical Yearbook.*

The World Bank, 1818 H Street, NW, Washington, DC 20433, (202) 473-1000, Fax: (202) 477-6391, www.worldbank.org; *World Development Indicators (WDI) 2008.*

GRENADA - GROSS NATIONAL PRODUCT

Palgrave Macmillan Ltd., Houndmills, Basingstoke, Hampshire, RG21 6XS, England, (Telephone in U.S. (888) 330-8477), (Fax in U.S. (800) 672-2054), www.palgrave.com; *The Statesman's Yearbook 2008.*

The World Bank, 1818 H Street, NW, Washington, DC 20433, (202) 473-1000, Fax: (202) 477-6391, www.worldbank.org; *The World Bank Atlas 2003-2004* and *World Development Indicators (WDI) 2008.*

GRENADA - HIDES AND SKINS INDUSTRY

United Nations Food and Agricultural Organization (FAO), Viale delle Terme di Caracalla, 00100 Rome, Italy, (Dial from U.S. (202) 653-2400), (Fax from U.S. (202) 653 5760), www.fao.org; *FAO Production Yearbook 2002.*

GRENADA - HOUSING

Euromonitor International, Inc., 224 S. Michigan Avenue, Suite 1500, Chicago, IL 60604, (312) 922-1115, Fax: (312) 922-1157, www.euromonitor.com; *World Marketing Data and Statistics.*

GRENADA - ILLITERATE PERSONS

Central Intelligence Agency, Office of Public Affairs, Washington, DC 20505, (703) 482-0623, Fax: (703) 482-1739, www.cia.gov; *The World Factbook.*

Euromonitor International, Inc., 224 S. Michigan Avenue, Suite 1500, Chicago, IL 60604, (312) 922-1115, Fax: (312) 922-1157, www.euromonitor.com; *The World Economic Factbook 2008.*

Palgrave Macmillan Ltd., Houndmills, Basingstoke, Hampshire, RG21 6XS, England, (Telephone in U.S. (888) 330-8477), (Fax in U.S. (800) 672-2054), www.palgrave.com; *The Statesman's Yearbook 2008.*

UNESCO Institute for Statistics, C.P. 6128 Succursale Centre-Ville, Montreal, Quebec, H3C 3J7 Canada, (Dial from U.S. (514) 343-6880), (Fax from U.S. (514) 343 6882), www.uis.unesco.org; *Statistical Tables.*

United Nations Statistics Division, New York, NY 10017, (800) 253-9646, Fax: (212) 963-4116, http://unstats.un.org; *Human Development Report 2006.*

GRENADA - IMPORTS

Central Intelligence Agency, Office of Public Affairs, Washington, DC 20505, (703) 482-0623, Fax: (703) 482-1739, www.cia.gov; *The World Factbook.*

Economist Intelligence Unit, 111 West 57th Street, New York, NY 10019, (212) 554-0600, Fax: (212) 586-1181, www.eiu.com; *Organisation of Eastern Caribbean States.*

Euromonitor International, Inc., 224 S. Michigan Avenue, Suite 1500, Chicago, IL 60604, (312) 922-1115, Fax: (312) 922-1157, www.euromonitor.com; *International Marketing Data and Statistics 2008* and *The World Economic Factbook 2008.*

International Monetary Fund (IMF), 700 Nineteenth Street, NW, Washington, DC 20431, (202) 623-7000, Fax: (202) 623-4661, www.imf.org; *Direction of Trade Statistics Yearbook 2007; Government Finance Statistics Yearbook (2008 Edition);* and *International Financial Statistics Yearbook 2007.*

Palgrave Macmillan Ltd., Houndmills, Basingstoke, Hampshire, RG21 6XS, England, (Telephone in U.S. (888) 330-8477), (Fax in U.S. (800) 672-2054), www.palgrave.com; *The Statesman's Yearbook 2008.*

Taylor and Francis Group, An Informa Business, 2 Park Square, Milton Park, Abingdon, Oxford OX14 4RN, United Kingdom, (Dial from U.S. (212) 216-7800), (Fax from U.S. (212) 564-7854), www.tandf.co.uk; *The Europa World Year Book.*

United Nations Conference on Trade and Development (UNCTAD), DC2-1120, United Nations, New York, NY 10017, (212) 963-0027, www.unctad.org; *Handbook of Statistics 2005.*

United Nations Food and Agricultural Organization (FAO), Viale delle Terme di Caracalla, 00100 Rome, Italy, (Dial from U.S. (202) 653-2400), (Fax from U.S. (202) 653 5760), www.fao.org; *The State of Food and Agriculture (SOFA) 2006.*

The World Bank, 1818 H Street, NW, Washington, DC 20433, (202) 473-1000, Fax: (202) 477-6391, www.worldbank.org; *World Development Indicators (WDI) 2008.*

GRENADA - INCOME TAXES

See GRENADA - TAXATION

GRENADA - INDUSTRIES

Central Intelligence Agency, Office of Public Affairs, Washington, DC 20505, (703) 482-0623, Fax: (703) 482-1739, www.cia.gov; *The World Factbook.*

Economist Intelligence Unit, 111 West 57th Street, New York, NY 10019, (212) 554-0600, Fax: (212) 586-1181, www.eiu.com; *Organisation of Eastern Caribbean States.*

Euromonitor International, Inc., 224 S. Michigan Avenue, Suite 1500, Chicago, IL 60604, (312) 922-1115, Fax: (312) 922-1157, www.euromonitor.com; *The World Economic Factbook 2008* and *World Marketing Data and Statistics.*

International Labour Office, I.L.O. Publications, 4 route des Morillons, CH-1211 Geneva 22, Switzerland, (Telephone in U.S. (202) 653-7652), (Fax in U.S. (202) 653-7687), www.ilo.org; *Yearbook of Labour Statistics 2006.*

Palgrave Macmillan Ltd., Houndmills, Basingstoke, Hampshire, RG21 6XS, England, (Telephone in U.S. (888) 330-8477), (Fax in U.S. (800) 672-2054), www.palgrave.com; *The Statesman's Yearbook 2008.*

Taylor and Francis Group, An Informa Business, 2 Park Square, Milton Park, Abingdon, Oxford OX14 4RN, United Kingdom, (Dial from U.S. (212) 216-7800), (Fax from U.S. (212) 564-7854), www.tandf.co.uk; *The Europa World Year Book.*

United Nations Industrial Development Organization (UNIDO), 1 United Nations Plaza, New York, NY 10017, (212) 963 6890, Fax: (212) 963-7904, http://unido.org; Industrial Statistics Database 2008 (INDSTAT) and *The International Yearbook of Industrial Statistics 2008.*

United Nations Statistics Division, New York, NY 10017, (800) 253-9646, Fax: (212) 963-4116, http://unstats.un.org; *Economic Survey of Latin America and the Caribbean 2004-2005.*

The World Bank, 1818 H Street, NW, Washington, DC 20433, (202) 473-1000, Fax: (202) 477-6391, www.worldbank.org; *Grenada* and *World Development Indicators (WDI) 2008.*

GRENADA - INFANT AND MATERNAL MORTALITY

See GRENADA - MORTALITY

GRENADA - INFLATION (FINANCE)

United Nations Statistics Division, New York, NY 10017, (800) 253-9646, Fax: (212) 963-4116, http://unstats.un.org; *Economic Survey of Latin America and the Caribbean 2004-2005.*

GRENADA - INTERNATIONAL LIQUIDITY

International Monetary Fund (IMF), 700 Nineteenth Street, NW, Washington, DC 20431, (202) 623-7000, Fax: (202) 623-4661, www.imf.org; *International Financial Statistics Yearbook 2007.*

GRENADA - INTERNATIONAL TRADE

Economist Intelligence Unit, 111 West 57th Street, New York, NY 10019, (212) 554-0600, Fax: (212) 586-1181, www.eiu.com; *Organisation of Eastern Caribbean States.*

Euromonitor International, Inc., 224 S. Michigan Avenue, Suite 1500, Chicago, IL 60604, (312) 922-1115, Fax: (312) 922-1157, www.euromonitor.com; *The World Economic Factbook 2008* and *World Marketing Data and Statistics.*

Palgrave Macmillan Ltd., Houndmills, Basingstoke, Hampshire, RG21 6XS, England, (Telephone in U.S. (888) 330-8477), (Fax in U.S. (800) 672-2054), www.palgrave.com; *The Statesman's Yearbook 2008.*

Taylor and Francis Group, An Informa Business, 2 Park Square, Milton Park, Abingdon, Oxford OX14 4RN, United Kingdom, (Dial from U.S. (212) 216-7800), (Fax from U.S. (212) 564-7854), www.tandf.co.uk; *The Europa World Year Book.*

United Nations Conference on Trade and Development (UNCTAD), DC2-1120, United Nations, New York, NY 10017, (212) 963-0027, www.unctad.org; *UNCTAD Commodity Yearbook.*

United Nations Food and Agricultural Organization (FAO), Viale delle Terme di Caracalla, 00100 Rome, Italy, (Dial from U.S. (202) 653-2400), (Fax from U.S. (202) 653 5760), www.fao.org; *FAO Trade Yearbook* and *The State of Food and Agriculture (SOFA) 2006.*

United Nations Statistics Division, New York, NY 10017, (800) 253-9646, Fax: (212) 963-4116, http://unstats.un.org; *Economic Survey of Latin America and the Caribbean 2004-2005.*

The World Bank, 1818 H Street, NW, Washington, DC 20433, (202) 473-1000, Fax: (202) 477-6391, www.worldbank.org; *Grenada* and *World Development Indicators (WDI) 2008.*

World Trade Organization (WTO), Centre William Rappard, Rue de Lausanne 154, CH-1211 Geneva 21, Switzerland, www.wto.org; *International Trade Statistics 2006.*

GRENADA - INTERNET USERS

International Telecommunication Union (ITU), Place des Nations, 1211 Geneva 20, Switzerland, www.itu.int; *World Telecommunication/ICT Indicators Database on CD-ROM; World Telecommunication/ICT Indicators Database Online;* and *Yearbook of Statistics - Telecommunication Services (Chronological Time Series 1997-2006).*

The World Bank, 1818 H Street, NW, Washington, DC 20433, (202) 473-1000, Fax: (202) 477-6391, www.worldbank.org; *Grenada.*

GRENADA - LABOR

Central Intelligence Agency, Office of Public Affairs, Washington, DC 20505, (703) 482-0623, Fax: (703) 482-1739, www.cia.gov; *The World Factbook.*

Euromonitor International, Inc., 224 S. Michigan Avenue, Suite 1500, Chicago, IL 60604, (312) 922-1115, Fax: (312) 922-1157, www.euromonitor.com; *International Marketing Data and Statistics 2008* and *World Marketing Data and Statistics.*

International Labour Office, I.L.O. Publications, 4 route des Morillons, CH-1211 Geneva 22, Switzerland, (Telephone in U.S. (202) 653-7652), (Fax in U.S. (202) 653-7687), www.ilo.org; *Yearbook of Labour Statistics 2006.*

Palgrave Macmillan Ltd., Houndmills, Basingstoke, Hampshire, RG21 6XS, England, (Telephone in U.S. (888) 330-8477), (Fax in U.S. (800) 672-2054), www.palgrave.com; *The Statesman's Yearbook 2008.*

Taylor and Francis Group, An Informa Business, 2 Park Square, Milton Park, Abingdon, Oxford OX14 4RN, United Kingdom, (Dial from U.S. (212) 216-7800), (Fax from U.S. (212) 564-7854), www.tandf.co.uk; *The Europa World Year Book.*

United Nations Food and Agricultural Organization (FAO), Viale delle Terme di Caracalla, 00100 Rome, Italy, (Dial from U.S. (202) 653-2400), (Fax from U.S. (202) 653 5760), www.fao.org; *The State of Food and Agriculture (SOFA) 2006.*

United Nations Statistics Division, New York, NY 10017, (800) 253-9646, Fax: (212) 963-4116, http://unstats.un.org; *Human Development Report 2006.*

The World Bank, 1818 H Street, NW, Washington, DC 20433, (202) 473-1000, Fax: (202) 477-6391, www.worldbank.org; *The World Bank Atlas 2003-2004* and *World Development Indicators (WDI) 2008.*

GRENADA - LAND USE

Central Intelligence Agency, Office of Public Affairs, Washington, DC 20505, (703) 482-0623, Fax: (703) 482-1739, www.cia.gov; *The World Factbook.*

Euromonitor International, Inc., 224 S. Michigan Avenue, Suite 1500, Chicago, IL 60604, (312) 922-1115, Fax: (312) 922-1157, www.euromonitor.com; *International Marketing Data and Statistics 2008.*

United Nations Food and Agricultural Organization (FAO), Viale delle Terme di Caracalla, 00100 Rome, Italy, (Dial from U.S. (202) 653-2400), (Fax from U.S. (202) 653 5760), www.fao.org; *FAO Production Yearbook 2002.*

GRENADA - LICENSES

International Monetary Fund (IMF), 700 Nineteenth Street, NW, Washington, DC 20431, (202) 623-7000, Fax: (202) 623-4661, www.imf.org; *Government Finance Statistics Yearbook (2008 Edition).*

GRENADA - LIFE EXPECTANCY

Central Intelligence Agency, Office of Public Affairs, Washington, DC 20505, (703) 482-0623, Fax: (703) 482-1739, www.cia.gov; *The World Factbook.*

Euromonitor International, Inc., 224 S. Michigan Avenue, Suite 1500, Chicago, IL 60604, (312) 922-1115, Fax: (312) 922-1157, www.euromonitor.com; *The World Economic Factbook 2008.*

United Nations Statistics Division, New York, NY 10017, (800) 253-9646, Fax: (212) 963-4116, http://unstats.un.org; *Human Development Report 2006* and *World Statistics Pocketbook.*

The World Bank, 1818 H Street, NW, Washington, DC 20433, (202) 473-1000, Fax: (202) 477-6391, www.worldbank.org; *The World Bank Atlas 2003-2004.*

GRENADA - LITERACY

Euromonitor International, Inc., 224 S. Michigan Avenue, Suite 1500, Chicago, IL 60604, (312) 922-1115, Fax: (312) 922-1157, www.euromonitor.com; *World Marketing Data and Statistics.*

GRENADA - LIVESTOCK

Palgrave Macmillan Ltd., Houndmills, Basingstoke, Hampshire, RG21 6XS, England, (Telephone in U.S. (888) 330-8477), (Fax in U.S. (800) 672-2054), www.palgrave.com; *The Statesman's Yearbook 2008.*

Taylor and Francis Group, An Informa Business, 2 Park Square, Milton Park, Abingdon, Oxford OX14 4RN, United Kingdom, (Dial from U.S. (212) 216-7800), (Fax from U.S. (212) 564-7854), www.tandf.co.uk; *The Europa World Year Book.*

United Nations Conference on Trade and Development (UNCTAD), DC2-1120, United Nations, New York, NY 10017, (212) 963-0027, www.unctad.org; *UNCTAD Commodity Yearbook.*

United Nations Food and Agricultural Organization (FAO), Viale delle Terme di Caracalla, 00100 Rome, Italy, (Dial from U.S. (202) 653-2400), (Fax from U.S. (202) 653 5760), www.fao.org; *FAO Production Yearbook 2002* and *The State of Food and Agriculture (SOFA) 2006.*

United Nations Statistics Division, New York, NY 10017, (800) 253-9646, Fax: (212) 963-4116, http://unstats.un.org; *Statistical Yearbook.*

GRENADA - MACE (SPICE)

International Monetary Fund (IMF), 700 Nineteenth Street, NW, Washington, DC 20431, (202) 623-7000, Fax: (202) 623-4661, www.imf.org; *International Financial Statistics Yearbook 2007.*

GRENADA - MANUFACTURES

The World Bank, 1818 H Street, NW, Washington, DC 20433, (202) 473-1000, Fax: (202) 477-6391, www.worldbank.org; *World Development Indicators (WDI) 2008.*

GRENADA - MARRIAGE

United Nations Statistics Division, New York, NY 10017, (800) 253-9646, Fax: (212) 963-4116, http://unstats.un.org; *Demographic Yearbook* and *Statistical Yearbook.*

GRENADA - MEAT PRODUCTION

See GRENADA - LIVESTOCK

GRENADA - MEDICAL CARE, COST OF

International Monetary Fund (IMF), 700 Nineteenth Street, NW, Washington, DC 20431, (202) 623-7000, Fax: (202) 623-4661, www.imf.org; *Government Finance Statistics Yearbook (2008 Edition).*

GRENADA - MINERAL INDUSTRIES

United Nations Conference on Trade and Development (UNCTAD), DC2-1120, United Nations, New York, NY 10017, (212) 963-0027, www.unctad.org; *UNCTAD Commodity Yearbook.*

GRENADA - MONEY EXCHANGE RATES

See GRENADA - FOREIGN EXCHANGE RATES

GRENADA - MONEY SUPPLY

Economist Intelligence Unit, 111 West 57th Street, New York, NY 10019, (212) 554-0600, Fax: (212) 586-1181, www.eiu.com; *Organisation of Eastern Caribbean States.*

International Monetary Fund (IMF), 700 Nineteenth Street, NW, Washington, DC 20431, (202) 623-7000, Fax: (202) 623-4661, www.imf.org; *International Financial Statistics Yearbook 2007.*

Taylor and Francis Group, An Informa Business, 2 Park Square, Milton Park, Abingdon, Oxford OX14 4RN, United Kingdom, (Dial from U.S. (212) 216-7800), (Fax from U.S. (212) 564-7854), www.tandf.co.uk; *The Europa World Year Book.*

The World Bank, 1818 H Street, NW, Washington, DC 20433, (202) 473-1000, Fax: (202) 477-6391, www.worldbank.org; *Grenada* and *World Development Indicators (WDI) 2008.*

GRENADA - MORTALITY

Central Intelligence Agency, Office of Public Affairs, Washington, DC 20505, (703) 482-0623, Fax: (703) 482-1739, www.cia.gov; *The World Factbook.*

Euromonitor International, Inc., 224 S. Michigan Avenue, Suite 1500, Chicago, IL 60604, (312) 922-1115, Fax: (312) 922-1157, www.euromonitor.com; *International Marketing Data and Statistics 2008* and *The World Economic Factbook 2008.*

Palgrave Macmillan Ltd., Houndmills, Basingstoke, Hampshire, RG21 6XS, England, (Telephone in U.S. (888) 330-8477), (Fax in U.S. (800) 672-2054), www.palgrave.com; *The Statesman's Yearbook 2008.*

Taylor and Francis Group, An Informa Business, 2 Park Square, Milton Park, Abingdon, Oxford OX14 4RN, United Kingdom, (Dial from U.S. (212) 216-7800), (Fax from U.S. (212) 564-7854), www.tandf.co.uk; *The Europa World Year Book.*

United Nations Statistics Division, New York, NY 10017, (800) 253-9646, Fax: (212) 963-4116, http://unstats.un.org; *Demographic Yearbook; Human Development Report 2006; Statistical Yearbook;* and *World Statistics Pocketbook.*

The World Bank, 1818 H Street, NW, Washington, DC 20433, (202) 473-1000, Fax: (202) 477-6391, www.worldbank.org; *The World Bank Atlas 2003-2004* and *World Development Indicators (WDI) 2008.*

World Health Organization (WHO), Avenue Appia 20, 1211 Geneve 27, Switzerland, (Telephone in U.S. (212) 331-9081), www.who.int; *The WHO Global Atlas of Infectious Diseases* and *World Health Report 2006.*

GRENADA - MOTION PICTURES

United Nations Statistics Division, New York, NY 10017, (800) 253-9646, Fax: (212) 963-4116, http://unstats.un.org; *Statistical Yearbook.*

GRENADA - MOTOR VEHICLES

Taylor and Francis Group, An Informa Business, 2 Park Square, Milton Park, Abingdon, Oxford OX14 4RN, United Kingdom, (Dial from U.S. (212) 216-7800), (Fax from U.S. (212) 564-7854), www.tandf.co.uk; *The Europa World Year Book.*

United Nations Statistics Division, New York, NY 10017, (800) 253-9646, Fax: (212) 963-4116, http://unstats.un.org; *Statistical Yearbook.*

GRENADA - MUSEUMS

UNESCO Institute for Statistics, C.P. 6128 Succursale Centre-Ville, Montreal, Quebec, H3C 3J7 Canada, (Dial from U.S. (514) 343-6880), (Fax from U.S. (514) 343 6882), www.uis.unesco.org; *Statistical Tables.*

GRENADA - NUTMEG INDUSTRY

International Monetary Fund (IMF), 700 Nineteenth Street, NW, Washington, DC 20431, (202) 623-7000, Fax: (202) 623-4661, www.imf.org; *International Financial Statistics Yearbook 2007.*

GRENADA - NUTRITION

United Nations Food and Agricultural Organization (FAO), Viale delle Terme di Caracalla, 00100 Rome, Italy, (Dial from U.S. (202) 653-2400), (Fax from U.S. (202) 653 5760), www.fao.org; *The State of Food and Agriculture (SOFA) 2006.*

GRENADA - PESTICIDES

United Nations Food and Agricultural Organization (FAO), Viale delle Terme di Caracalla, 00100 Rome, Italy, (Dial from U.S. (202) 653-2400), (Fax from U.S. (202) 653 5760), www.fao.org; *The State of Food and Agriculture (SOFA) 2006.*

GRENADA - PETROLEUM INDUSTRY AND TRADE

PennWell Corporation, 1421 South Sheridan Road, Tulsa, OK 74112, (918) 835-3161, www.pennwell.com; *International Petroleum Encyclopedia 2007.*

United Nations Conference on Trade and Development (UNCTAD), DC2-1120, United Nations, New York, NY 10017, (212) 963-0027, www.unctad.org; *UNCTAD Commodity Yearbook.*

United Nations Food and Agricultural Organization (FAO), Viale delle Terme di Caracalla, 00100 Rome, Italy, (Dial from U.S. (202) 653-2400), (Fax from U.S. (202) 653 5760), www.fao.org; *The State of Food and Agriculture (SOFA) 2006.*

GRENADA - POLITICAL SCIENCE

Central Intelligence Agency, Office of Public Affairs, Washington, DC 20505, (703) 482-0623, Fax: (703) 482-1739, www.cia.gov; *The World Factbook.*

International Monetary Fund (IMF), 700 Nineteenth Street, NW, Washington, DC 20431, (202) 623-7000, Fax: (202) 623-4661, www.imf.org; *Government Finance Statistics Yearbook (2008 Edition)* and *International Financial Statistics Yearbook 2007.*

Palgrave Macmillan Ltd., Houndmills, Basingstoke, Hampshire, RG21 6XS, England, (Telephone in U.S. (888) 330-8477), (Fax in U.S. (800) 672-2054), www.palgrave.com; *The Statesman's Yearbook 2008.*

Taylor and Francis Group, An Informa Business, 2 Park Square, Milton Park, Abingdon, Oxford OX14 4RN, United Kingdom, (Dial from U.S. (212) 216-7800), (Fax from U.S. (212) 564-7854), www.tandf.co.uk; *The Europa World Year Book.*

United Nations Statistics Division, New York, NY 10017, (800) 253-9646, Fax: (212) 963-4116, http://unstats.un.org; *National Accounts Statistics: Compendium of Income Distribution Statistics.*

The World Bank, 1818 H Street, NW, Washington, DC 20433, (202) 473-1000, Fax: (202) 477-6391, www.worldbank.org; *World Development Indicators (WDI) 2008.*

GRENADA - POPULATION

Caribbean Epidemiology Centre (CAREC), 16-18 Jamaica Boulevard, Federation Park, PO Box 164, Port of Spain, Republic of Trinidad and Tobago, (Dial from U.S. (868) 622-4261), (Fax from U.S. (868) 622-2792), www.carec.org; *Population Data.*

Central Intelligence Agency, Office of Public Affairs, Washington, DC 20505, (703) 482-0623, Fax: (703) 482-1739, www.cia.gov; *The World Factbook.*

Economist Intelligence Unit, 111 West 57th Street, New York, NY 10019, (212) 554-0600, Fax: (212) 586-1181, www.eiu.com; *Organisation of Eastern Caribbean States.*

Euromonitor International, Inc., 224 S. Michigan Avenue, Suite 1500, Chicago, IL 60604, (312) 922-1115, Fax: (312) 922-1157, www.euromonitor.com; *International Marketing Data and Statistics 2008* and *The World Economic Factbook 2008.*

Eurostat, Batiment Jean Monnet, Rue Alcide de Gasperi, L-2920 Luxembourg, http://epp.eurostat.ec.europa.eu; *Demographic Indicators - Population by Age-Classes.*

International Labour Office, I.L.O. Publications, 4 route des Morillons, CH-1211 Geneva 22, Switzerland, (Telephone in U.S. (202) 653-7652), (Fax in U.S. (202) 653-7687), www.ilo.org; *Yearbook of Labour Statistics 2006.*

Organization of American States (OAS), 17th Street Constitution Avenue NW, Washington, DC 20006, (202) 458-3000, www.oas.org; *The OAS in Transition: 1994-2004.*

Palgrave Macmillan Ltd., Houndmills, Basingstoke, Hampshire, RG21 6XS, England, (Telephone in U.S. (888) 330-8477), (Fax in U.S. (800) 672-2054), www.palgrave.com; *The Statesman's Yearbook 2008.*

Taylor and Francis Group, An Informa Business, 2 Park Square, Milton Park, Abingdon, Oxford OX14 4RN, United Kingdom, (Dial from U.S. (212) 216-7800), (Fax from U.S. (212) 564-7854), www.tandf.co.uk; *The Europa World Year Book.*

United Nations Food and Agricultural Organization (FAO), Viale delle Terme di Caracalla, 00100 Rome, Italy, (Dial from U.S. (202) 653-2400), (Fax from U.S. (202) 653 5760), www.fao.org; *FAO Production Yearbook 2002.*

United Nations Statistics Division, New York, NY 10017, (800) 253-9646, Fax: (212) 963-4116, http://unstats.un.org; *Demographic Yearbook; Human Development Report 2006; Statistical Yearbook;* and *World Statistics Pocketbook.*

The World Bank, 1818 H Street, NW, Washington, DC 20433, (202) 473-1000, Fax: (202) 477-6391, www.worldbank.org; *Grenada* and *The World Bank Atlas 2003-2004.*

World Health Organization (WHO), Avenue Appia 20, 1211 Geneve 27, Switzerland, (Telephone in U.S. (212) 331-9081), www.who.int; *World Health Report 2006.*

GRENADA - POPULATION DENSITY

Central Intelligence Agency, Office of Public Affairs, Washington, DC 20505, (703) 482-0623, Fax: (703) 482-1739, www.cia.gov; *The World Factbook.*

Euromonitor International, Inc., 224 S. Michigan Avenue, Suite 1500, Chicago, IL 60604, (312) 922-

1115, Fax: (312) 922-1157, www.euromonitor.com; *The World Economic Factbook 2008.*

Palgrave Macmillan Ltd., Houndmills, Basingstoke, Hampshire, RG21 6XS, England, (Telephone in U.S. (888) 330-8477), (Fax in U.S. (800) 672-2054), www.palgrave.com; *The Statesman's Yearbook 2008.*

Taylor and Francis Group, An Informa Business, 2 Park Square, Milton Park, Abingdon, Oxford OX14 4RN, United Kingdom, (Dial from U.S. (212) 216-7800), (Fax from U.S. (212) 564-7854), www.tandf.co.uk; *The Europa World Year Book.*

United Nations Food and Agricultural Organization (FAO), Viale delle Terme di Caracalla, 00100 Rome, Italy, (Dial from U.S. (202) 653-2400), (Fax from U.S. (202) 653 5760), www.fao.org; *The State of Food and Agriculture (SOFA) 2006.*

United Nations Statistics Division, New York, NY 10017, (800) 253-9646, Fax: (212) 963-4116, http://unstats.un.org; *Statistical Yearbook.*

The World Bank, 1818 H Street, NW, Washington, DC 20433, (202) 473-1000, Fax: (202) 477-6391, www.worldbank.org; *Grenada.*

GRENADA - POSTAL SERVICE

Palgrave Macmillan Ltd., Houndmills, Basingstoke, Hampshire, RG21 6XS, England, (Telephone in U.S. (888) 330-8477), (Fax in U.S. (800) 672-2054), www.palgrave.com; *The Statesman's Yearbook 2008.*

GRENADA - POWER RESOURCES

Euromonitor International, Inc., 224 S. Michigan Avenue, Suite 1500, Chicago, IL 60604, (312) 922-1115, Fax: (312) 922-1157, www.euromonitor.com; *International Marketing Data and Statistics 2008; The World Economic Factbook 2008;* and *World Marketing Data and Statistics.*

Palgrave Macmillan Ltd., Houndmills, Basingstoke, Hampshire, RG21 6XS, England, (Telephone in U.S. (888) 330-8477), (Fax in U.S. (800) 672-2054), www.palgrave.com; *The Statesman's Yearbook 2008.*

United Nations Food and Agricultural Organization (FAO), Viale delle Terme di Caracalla, 00100 Rome, Italy, (Dial from U.S. (202) 653-2400), (Fax from U.S. (202) 653 5760), www.fao.org; *The State of Food and Agriculture (SOFA) 2006.*

United Nations Statistics Division, New York, NY 10017, (800) 253-9646, Fax: (212) 963-4116, http://unstats.un.org; *Human Development Report 2006; Statistical Yearbook;* and *World Statistics Pocketbook.*

The World Bank, 1818 H Street, NW, Washington, DC 20433, (202) 473-1000, Fax: (202) 477-6391, www.worldbank.org; *The World Bank Atlas 2003-2004.*

GRENADA - PRICES

Euromonitor International, Inc., 224 S. Michigan Avenue, Suite 1500, Chicago, IL 60604, (312) 922-1115, Fax: (312) 922-1157, www.euromonitor.com; *World Marketing Data and Statistics.*

International Labour Office, I.L.O. Publications, 4 route des Morillons, CH-1211 Geneva 22, Switzerland, (Telephone in U.S. (202) 653-7652), (Fax in U.S. (202) 653-7687), www.ilo.org; *Yearbook of Labour Statistics 2006.*

Organization of American States (OAS), 17th Street Constitution Avenue NW, Washington, DC 20006, (202) 458-3000, www.oas.org; *The OAS in Transition: 1994-2004.*

United Nations Food and Agricultural Organization (FAO), Viale delle Terme di Caracalla, 00100 Rome, Italy, (Dial from U.S. (202) 653-2400), (Fax from U.S. (202) 653 5760), www.fao.org; *FAO Production Yearbook 2002* and *The State of Food and Agriculture (SOFA) 2006.*

United Nations Statistics Division, New York, NY 10017, (800) 253-9646, Fax: (212) 963-4116, http://unstats.un.org; *Economic Survey of Latin America and the Caribbean 2004-2005.*

The World Bank, 1818 H Street, NW, Washington, DC 20433, (202) 473-1000, Fax: (202) 477-6391, www.worldbank.org; *Grenada.*

GRENADA - PUBLIC HEALTH

Euromonitor International, Inc., 224 S. Michigan Avenue, Suite 1500, Chicago, IL 60604, (312) 922-1115, Fax: (312) 922-1157, www.euromonitor.com; *World Marketing Data and Statistics.*

Palgrave Macmillan Ltd., Houndmills, Basingstoke, Hampshire, RG21 6XS, England, (Telephone in U.S. (888) 330-8477), (Fax in U.S. (800) 672-2054), www.palgrave.com; *The Statesman's Yearbook 2008.*

United Nations Statistics Division, New York, NY 10017, (800) 253-9646, Fax: (212) 963-4116, http://unstats.un.org; *Human Development Report 2006* and *Statistical Yearbook.*

The World Bank, 1818 H Street, NW, Washington, DC 20433, (202) 473-1000, Fax: (202) 477-6391, www.worldbank.org; *Grenada.*

World Health Organization (WHO), Avenue Appia 20, 1211 Geneve 27, Switzerland, (Telephone in U.S. (212) 331-9081), www.who.int; The WHO Global Atlas of Infectious Diseases and *World Health Report 2006.*

GRENADA - PUBLISHERS AND PUBLISHING

Taylor and Francis Group, An Informa Business, 2 Park Square, Milton Park, Abingdon, Oxford OX14 4RN, United Kingdom, (Dial from U.S. (212) 216-7800), (Fax from U.S. (212) 564-7854), www.tandf.co.uk; *The Europa World Year Book.*

UNESCO Institute for Statistics, C.P. 6128 Succursale Centre-Ville, Montreal, Quebec, H3C 3J7 Canada, (Dial from U.S. (514) 343-6880), (Fax from U.S. (514) 343 6882), www.uis.unesco.org; *Statistical Tables.*

GRENADA - RADIO BROADCASTING

Palgrave Macmillan Ltd., Houndmills, Basingstoke, Hampshire, RG21 6XS, England, (Telephone in U.S. (888) 330-8477), (Fax in U.S. (800) 672-2054), www.palgrave.com; *The Statesman's Yearbook 2008.*

GRENADA - RELIGION

Central Intelligence Agency, Office of Public Affairs, Washington, DC 20505, (703) 482-0623, Fax: (703) 482-1739, www.cia.gov; *The World Factbook.*

Palgrave Macmillan Ltd., Houndmills, Basingstoke, Hampshire, RG21 6XS, England, (Telephone in U.S. (888) 330-8477), (Fax in U.S. (800) 672-2054), www.palgrave.com; *The Statesman's Yearbook 2008.*

GRENADA - RESERVES (ACCOUNTING)

Organization of American States (OAS), 17th Street Constitution Avenue NW, Washington, DC 20006, (202) 458-3000, www.oas.org; *The OAS in Transition: 1994-2004.*

United Nations Statistics Division, New York, NY 10017, (800) 253-9646, Fax: (212) 963-4116, http://unstats.un.org; *Statistical Yearbook.*

The World Bank, 1818 H Street, NW, Washington, DC 20433, (202) 473-1000, Fax: (202) 477-6391, www.worldbank.org; *World Development Indicators (WDI) 2008.*

GRENADA - RETAIL TRADE

Euromonitor International, Inc., 224 S. Michigan Avenue, Suite 1500, Chicago, IL 60604, (312) 922-1115, Fax: (312) 922-1157, www.euromonitor.com; *World Marketing Data and Statistics.*

GRENADA - ROADS

Central Intelligence Agency, Office of Public Affairs, Washington, DC 20505, (703) 482-0623, Fax: (703) 482-1739, www.cia.gov; *The World Factbook.*

Palgrave Macmillan Ltd., Houndmills, Basingstoke, Hampshire, RG21 6XS, England, (Telephone in U.S. (888) 330-8477), (Fax in U.S. (800) 672-2054), www.palgrave.com; *The Statesman's Yearbook 2008.*

GRENADA - SHEEP

See GRENADA - LIVESTOCK

GRENADA - SHIPPING

Palgrave Macmillan Ltd., Houndmills, Basingstoke, Hampshire, RG21 6XS, England, (Telephone in U.S. (888) 330-8477), (Fax in U.S. (800) 672-2054), www.palgrave.com; *The Statesman's Yearbook 2008.*

Taylor and Francis Group, An Informa Business, 2 Park Square, Milton Park, Abingdon, Oxford OX14 4RN, United Kingdom, (Dial from U.S. (212) 216-7800), (Fax from U.S. (212) 564-7854), www.tandf.co.uk; *The Europa World Year Book.*

United Nations Statistics Division, New York, NY 10017, (800) 253-9646, Fax: (212) 963-4116, http://unstats.un.org; *Statistical Yearbook.*

GRENADA - SOCIAL ECOLOGY

United Nations Statistics Division, New York, NY 10017, (800) 253-9646, Fax: (212) 963-4116, http://unstats.un.org; *World Statistics Pocketbook.*

GRENADA - SOCIAL SECURITY

International Monetary Fund (IMF), 700 Nineteenth Street, NW, Washington, DC 20431, (202) 623-7000, Fax: (202) 623-4661, www.imf.org; *Government Finance Statistics Yearbook (2008 Edition).*

United Nations Statistics Division, New York, NY 10017, (800) 253-9646, Fax: (212) 963-4116, http://unstats.un.org; *National Accounts Statistics: Compendium of Income Distribution Statistics.*

GRENADA - TAXATION

International Monetary Fund (IMF), 700 Nineteenth Street, NW, Washington, DC 20431, (202) 623-7000, Fax: (202) 623-4661, www.imf.org; *Government Finance Statistics Yearbook (2008 Edition).*

The World Bank, 1818 H Street, NW, Washington, DC 20433, (202) 473-1000, Fax: (202) 477-6391, www.worldbank.org; *World Development Indicators (WDI) 2008.*

GRENADA - TELEPHONE

International Telecommunication Union (ITU), Place des Nations, 1211 Geneva 20, Switzerland, www.itu.int; World Telecommunication Indicators Database.

Palgrave Macmillan Ltd., Houndmills, Basingstoke, Hampshire, RG21 6XS, England, (Telephone in U.S. (888) 330-8477), (Fax in U.S. (800) 672-2054), www.palgrave.com; *The Statesman's Yearbook 2008.*

Taylor and Francis Group, An Informa Business, 2 Park Square, Milton Park, Abingdon, Oxford OX14 4RN, United Kingdom, (Dial from U.S. (212) 216-7800), (Fax from U.S. (212) 564-7854), www.tandf.co.uk; *The Europa World Year Book.*

United Nations Statistics Division, New York, NY 10017, (800) 253-9646, Fax: (212) 963-4116, http://unstats.un.org; *Statistical Yearbook* and *World Statistics Pocketbook.*

GRENADA - TEXTILE INDUSTRY

Palgrave Macmillan Ltd., Houndmills, Basingstoke, Hampshire, RG21 6XS, England, (Telephone in U.S. (888) 330-8477), (Fax in U.S. (800) 672-2054), www.palgrave.com; *The Statesman's Yearbook 2008.*

United Nations Conference on Trade and Development (UNCTAD), DC2-1120, United Nations, New York, NY 10017, (212) 963-0027, www.unctad.org; *UNCTAD Commodity Yearbook.*

GRENADA - TOURISM

Euromonitor International, Inc., 224 S. Michigan Avenue, Suite 1500, Chicago, IL 60604, (312) 922-1115, Fax: (312) 922-1157, www.euromonitor.com; *The World Economic Factbook 2008* and *World Marketing Data and Statistics.*

Organization of American States (OAS), 17th Street Constitution Avenue NW, Washington, DC 20006, (202) 458-3000, www.oas.org; *The OAS in Transition: 1994-2004.*

Palgrave Macmillan Ltd., Houndmills, Basingstoke, Hampshire, RG21 6XS, England, (Telephone in U.S.

(888) 330-8477), (Fax in U.S. (800) 672-2054), www.palgrave.com; *The Statesman's Yearbook 2008.*

Taylor and Francis Group, An Informa Business, 2 Park Square, Milton Park, Abingdon, Oxford OX14 4RN, United Kingdom, (Dial from U.S. (212) 216-7800), (Fax from U.S. (212) 564-7854), www.tandf.co.uk; *The Europa World Year Book.*

United Nations Statistics Division, New York, NY 10017, (800) 253-9646, Fax: (212) 963-4116, http://unstats.un.org; *Statistical Yearbook.*

United Nations World Tourism Organization (UNWTO), Capitan Haya 42, 28020 Madrid, Spain, www.world-tourism.org; *Yearbook of Tourism Statistics.*

The World Bank, 1818 H Street, NW, Washington, DC 20433, (202) 473-1000, Fax: (202) 477-6391, www.worldbank.org; *Grenada.*

GRENADA - TRADE

See GRENADA - INTERNATIONAL TRADE

GRENADA - TRANSPORTATION

Central Intelligence Agency, Office of Public Affairs, Washington, DC 20505, (703) 482-0623, Fax: (703) 482-1739, www.cia.gov; *The World Factbook.*

Euromonitor International, Inc., 224 S. Michigan Avenue, Suite 1500, Chicago, IL 60604, (312) 922-1115, Fax: (312) 922-1157, www.euromonitor.com; *International Marketing Data and Statistics 2008* and *World Marketing Data and Statistics.*

Palgrave Macmillan Ltd., Houndmills, Basingstoke, Hampshire, RG21 6XS, England, (Telephone in U.S. (888) 330-8477), (Fax in U.S. (800) 672-2054), www.palgrave.com; *The Statesman's Yearbook 2008.*

Taylor and Francis Group, An Informa Business, 2 Park Square, Milton Park, Abingdon, Oxford OX14 4RN, United Kingdom, (Dial from U.S. (212) 216-7800), (Fax from U.S. (212) 564-7854), www.tandf.co.uk; *The Europa World Year Book.*

United Nations Statistics Division, New York, NY 10017, (800) 253-9646, Fax: (212) 963-4116, http://unstats.un.org; *Human Development Report 2006.*

The World Bank, 1818 H Street, NW, Washington, DC 20433, (202) 473-1000, Fax: (202) 477-6391, www.worldbank.org; *Grenada.*

GRENADA - UNEMPLOYMENT

Central Intelligence Agency, Office of Public Affairs, Washington, DC 20505, (703) 482-0623, Fax: (703) 482-1739, www.cia.gov; *The World Factbook.*

International Labour Office, I.L.O. Publications, 4 route des Morillons, CH-1211 Geneva 22, Switzerland, (Telephone in U.S. (202) 653-7652), (Fax in U.S. (202) 653-7687), www.ilo.org; *Yearbook of Labour Statistics 2006.*

Palgrave Macmillan Ltd., Houndmills, Basingstoke, Hampshire, RG21 6XS, England, (Telephone in U.S. (888) 330-8477), (Fax in U.S. (800) 672-2054), www.palgrave.com; *The Statesman's Yearbook 2008.*

GRENADA - VITAL STATISTICS

Palgrave Macmillan Ltd., Houndmills, Basingstoke, Hampshire, RG21 6XS, England, (Telephone in U.S. (888) 330-8477), (Fax in U.S. (800) 672-2054), www.palgrave.com; *The Statesman's Yearbook 2008.*

United Nations Statistics Division, New York, NY 10017, (800) 253-9646, Fax: (212) 963-4116, http://unstats.un.org; *Statistical Yearbook.*

World Health Organization (WHO), Avenue Appia 20, 1211 Geneve 27, Switzerland, (Telephone in U.S. (212) 331-9081), www.who.int; *World Health Report 2006.*

GRENADA - WAGES

International Labour Office, I.L.O. Publications, 4 route des Morillons, CH-1211 Geneva 22, Switzerland, (Telephone in U.S. (202) 653-7652), (Fax in U.S. (202) 653-7687), www.ilo.org; *Yearbook of Labour Statistics 2006.*

The World Bank, 1818 H Street, NW, Washington, DC 20433, (202) 473-1000, Fax: (202) 477-6391, www.worldbank.org; *Grenada.*

GRENADA - WELFARE STATE

International Monetary Fund (IMF), 700 Nineteenth Street, NW, Washington, DC 20431, (202) 623-7000, Fax: (202) 623-4661, www.imf.org; *Government Finance Statistics Yearbook (2008 Edition).*

GROCERY STORES

Economic Research Service (ERS), U.S. Department of Agriculture (USDA), 1800 M Street, NW, Washington, DC 20036-5831, (202) 694-5050, Fax: (202) 694-5689, www.ers.usda.gov; *Food Marketing and Price Spreads.*

Office of Trade and Industry Information (OTII), Manufacturing and Services, International Trade Administration, U.S. Department of Commerce, 1401 Constitution Ave, NW, Washington, DC 20230, (800) USA TRAD(E), http://trade.gov/index.asp; *TradeStats Express.*

U.S. Census Bureau, Center for Economic Studies, 4600 Silver Hill Road, Washington DC 20233, (301) 457-1235, www.ces.census.gov; *2002 Economic Census, Retail Trade* and *2002 Economic Census, Wholesale Trade.*

U.S. Census Bureau, Company Statistics Division, 4700 Silver Hill Road, Washington DC 20233-0001, (301) 763-3030, www.census.gov/csd/; *County Business Patterns 2004* and *Current Business Reports.*

GROCERY STORES - EARNINGS

Office of Trade and Industry Information (OTII), Manufacturing and Services, International Trade Administration, U.S. Department of Commerce, 1401 Constitution Ave, NW, Washington, DC 20230, (800) USA TRAD(E), http://trade.gov/index.asp; *TradeStats Express.*

Progressive Grocer, 770 Broadway, New York, NY 10003, (866) 890-8541, www.progressivegrocer.com; *Progressive Grocer 2006 Bakery Study* and *Progressive Grocer's 75th Annual Report of the Grocery Industry.*

U.S. Census Bureau, Center for Economic Studies, 4600 Silver Hill Road, Washington DC 20233, (301) 457-1235, www.ces.census.gov; *2002 Economic Census, Retail Trade.*

U.S. Census Bureau, Company Statistics Division, 4700 Silver Hill Road, Washington DC 20233-0001, (301) 763-3030, www.census.gov/csd/; *County Business Patterns 2004.*

GROCERY STORES - EMPLOYEES

U.S. Census Bureau, Center for Economic Studies, 4600 Silver Hill Road, Washington DC 20233, (301) 457-1235, www.ces.census.gov; *2002 Economic Census, Retail Trade.*

U.S. Census Bureau, Company Statistics Division, 4700 Silver Hill Road, Washington DC 20233-0001, (301) 763-3030, www.census.gov/csd/; *County Business Patterns 2004.*

GROCERY STORES - NONEMPLOYERS

U.S. Census Bureau, 4700 Silver Hill Road, Washington DC 20233-0001, (301) 763-3030, www.census.gov; *2002 Economic Census, Nonemployer Statistics.*

GROCERY STORES - PRODUCTIVITY

Progressive Grocer, 770 Broadway, New York, NY 10003, (866) 890-8541, www.progressivegrocer.com; *Progressive Grocer 2006 Bakery Study* and *Progressive Grocer's 75th Annual Report of the Grocery Industry.*

U.S. Bureau of Labor Statistics (BLS), Postal Square Building, 2 Massachusetts Avenue, NE, Washington, DC 20212-0001, (202) 691-5200, Fax: (202) 691-6325, www.bls.gov; *Industry Productivity and Costs.*

GROCERY STORES - SALES

Claritas, 5375 Mira Sorrento Place, Suite 400, San Diego, CA 92121, (800) 866-6520, Fax: (858) 550-5800, www.claritas.com; *Consumer Buying Power.*

Economic Research Service (ERS), U.S. Department of Agriculture (USDA), 1800 M Street, NW, Washington, DC 20036-5831, (202) 694-5050, Fax: (202) 694-5689, www.ers.usda.gov; *Food Marketing and Price Spreads.*

Progressive Grocer, 770 Broadway, New York, NY 10003, (866) 890-8541, www.progressivegrocer.com; *2006 Consumer Expenditures Study; Progressive Grocer 2006 Bakery Study; Progressive Grocer's 75th Annual Report of the Grocery Industry;* and *The VNU Retail Index.*

U.S. Census Bureau, Company Statistics Division, 4700 Silver Hill Road, Washington DC 20233-0001, (301) 763-3030, www.census.gov/csd/; *County Business Patterns 2004.*

GROCERY STORES - SERVICES - PRODUCTS OFFERED

Progressive Grocer, 770 Broadway, New York, NY 10003, (866) 890-8541, www.progressivegrocer.com; *Progressive Grocer 2006 Bakery Study* and *Progressive Grocer's 75th Annual Report of the Grocery Industry.*

GROSS DOMESTIC PRODUCT

Economist Intelligence Unit, 111 West 57th Street, New York, NY 10019, (212) 554-0600, Fax: (212) 586-1181, www.eiu.com; *United States of America Country Report.*

GROSS DOMESTIC PRODUCT - COMPONENTS - ANNUAL GROWTH RATES

Bureau of Economic Analysis (BEA), U.S. Department of Commerce (DOC), 1441 L Street NW, Washington, DC 20230, (202) 606-9900, www.bea.gov; *2007 Annual Revision of the National Income and Product Accounts (NIPA)* and *Survey of Current Business (SCB).*

GROSS DOMESTIC PRODUCT - FOREIGN COUNTRIES

Organisation for Economic Cooperation and Development (OECD), 2 rue Andre Pascal, F-75775 Paris Cedex 16, France, (Telephone in U.S. (202) 785-6323), (Fax in U.S. (202) 785-0350), www.oecd.org; *Comparison of Gross Domestic Product (GDP) for OECD Countries.*

GROSS DOMESTIC PRODUCT - IMPLICIT PRICE DEFLATORS

Organisation for Economic Cooperation and Development (OECD), 2 rue Andre Pascal, F-75775 Paris Cedex 16, France, (Telephone in U.S. (202) 785-6323), (Fax in U.S. (202) 785-0350), www.oecd.org; *Comparison of Gross Domestic Product (GDP) for OECD Countries.*

GROSS DOMESTIC PRODUCT - PER CAPITA

Organisation for Economic Cooperation and Development (OECD), 2 rue Andre Pascal, F-75775 Paris Cedex 16, France, (Telephone in U.S. (202) 785-6323), (Fax in U.S. (202) 785-0350), www.oecd.org; *Comparison of Gross Domestic Product (GDP) for OECD Countries.*

GROSS DOMESTIC PRODUCT - RELATION TO NATIONAL AND PERSONAL INCOME

Bureau of Economic Analysis (BEA), U.S. Department of Commerce (DOC), 1441 L Street NW, Washington, DC 20230, (202) 606-9900, www.bea.gov; *2007 Annual Revision of the National Income and Product Accounts (NIPA)* and *Survey of Current Business (SCB).*

GROSS DOMESTIC PRODUCT - STATE

Bureau of Economic Analysis (BEA), U.S. Department of Commerce (DOC), 1441 L Street NW, Washington, DC 20230, (202) 606-9900, www.bea.gov; *Survey of Current Business (SCB).*

GROSS NATIONAL PRODUCT

Bureau of Economic Analysis (BEA), U.S. Department of Commerce (DOC), 1441 L Street NW, Washington, DC 20230, (202) 606-9900, www.bea.gov; *2007 Annual Revision of the National Income and Product Accounts (NIPA)* and *Survey of Current Business (SCB).*

GROSS NATIONAL PRODUCT - FOREIGN COUNTRIES

The World Bank, 1818 H Street, NW, Washington, DC 20433, (202) 473-1000, Fax: (202) 477-6391, www.worldbank.org; *World Development Indicators (WDI) 2008.*

GROSS NATIONAL PRODUCT - NATIONAL DEFENSE OUTLAYS

The Office of Management and Budget (OMB), 725 17th Street, NW, Washington, DC 20503, (202) 395-3080, Fax: (202) 395-3888, www.whitehouse.gov/omb; *Historical Tables.*

GROSS PRIVATE DOMESTIC INVESTMENT

Bureau of Economic Analysis (BEA), U.S. Department of Commerce (DOC), 1441 L Street NW, Washington, DC 20230, (202) 606-9900, www.bea.gov; *2007 Annual Revision of the National Income and Product Accounts (NIPA)* and *Survey of Current Business (SCB).*

GROUND WATER - USED

U.S. Department of the Interior (DOI), U.S. Geological Survey (USGS), Water Resources Discipline (WRD), 12201 Sunrise Valley Drive, Reston, VA 20192, (888) 275-8747, http://water.usgs.gov; *Estimated Use of Water in the United States.*

GROUP HEALTH INSURANCE PLANS

Fingertip Formulary, LLC., 266 Harristown Road, Suite 202, Glen Rock, NJ 07452, (201) 652-3004, Fax: (201) 301-9177, www.fingertipformulary.com; *Fingertip Formulary Analytics* and *Fingertip Formulary Analytics Rx.*

HealthLeaders-InterStudy, One Vantage Way, B-300, Nashville, TN 37203, (615) 385-4131, Fax: (615) 385-4979, www.hmodata.com; *Blue Profiler; Competitive Edge; Employer Vantage; Health Plan Data Analysis ; HMO Financial Analyzer; Managed Market Surveyor-Rx;* and *Market Overviews.*

GROUP QUARTERS POPULATION

Office of Trade and Industry Information (OTII), Manufacturing and Services, International Trade Administration, U.S. Department of Commerce, 1401 Constitution Ave, NW, Washington, DC 20230, (800) USA TRAD(E), http://trade.gov/index.asp; *TradeStats Express.*

U.S. Census Bureau, Center for Economic Studies, 4600 Silver Hill Road, Washington DC 20233, (301) 457-1235, www.ces.census.gov; *2002 Economic Census, Retail Trade.*

U.S. Census Bureau, Housing and Household Economics Statistics Division, 4700 Silver Hill Road, Washington DC 20233-0001, (301) 763-3030, www.census.gov/hhes/www; *Census 2000 Summary File 1.*

GUADELOUPE - PRIMARY STATISTICS SOURCES

National Institute for Statistics and Economic Studies (Institut National de la Statistique et des Etudes Economiques (INSEE)), Tour "Gamma A", 195 Rue de Bercy, 75582, Paris Cedex 12, France, www.insee.fr; *Bilan demographique 2007; La population des departements d'outre-mer - Recensement de la population de 1999;* and *Tableaux Economiques Regionaux, Guadeloupe.*

GUADELOUPE - ABORTION

United Nations Statistics Division, New York, NY 10017, (800) 253-9646, Fax: (212) 963-4116, http://unstats.un.org; *Demographic Yearbook.*

GUADELOUPE - AGRICULTURAL MACHINERY

United Nations Statistics Division, New York, NY 10017, (800) 253-9646, Fax: (212) 963-4116, http://unstats.un.org; *Statistical Yearbook.*

GUADELOUPE - AGRICULTURE

Euromonitor International, Inc., 224 S. Michigan Avenue, Suite 1500, Chicago, IL 60604, (312) 922-1115, Fax: (312) 922-1157, www.euromonitor.com; *World Marketing Data and Statistics.*

Palgrave Macmillan Ltd., Houndmills, Basingstoke, Hampshire, RG21 6XS, England, (Telephone in U.S. (888) 330-8477), (Fax in U.S. (800) 672-2054), www.palgrave.com; *The Statesman's Yearbook 2008.*

Taylor and Francis Group, An Informa Business, 2 Park Square, Milton Park, Abingdon, Oxford OX14 4RN, United Kingdom, (Dial from U.S. (212) 216-7800), (Fax from U.S. (212) 564-7854), www.tandf.co.uk; *The Europa World Year Book.*

United Nations Conference on Trade and Development (UNCTAD), DC2-1120, United Nations, New York, NY 10017, (212) 963-0027, www.unctad.org; *UNCTAD Commodity Yearbook.*

United Nations Food and Agricultural Organization (FAO), Viale delle Terme di Caracalla, 00100 Rome, Italy, (Dial from U.S. (202) 653-2400), (Fax from U.S. (202) 653 5760), www.fao.org; AQUASTAT; *FAO Production Yearbook 2002; FAO Trade Yearbook;* and *The State of Food and Agriculture (SOFA) 2006.*

United Nations Statistics Division, New York, NY 10017, (800) 253-9646, Fax: (212) 963-4116, http://unstats.un.org; *Statistical Yearbook.*

GUADELOUPE - AIRLINES

Palgrave Macmillan Ltd., Houndmills, Basingstoke, Hampshire, RG21 6XS, England, (Telephone in U.S. (888) 330-8477), (Fax in U.S. (800) 672-2054), www.palgrave.com; *The Statesman's Yearbook 2008.*

Taylor and Francis Group, An Informa Business, 2 Park Square, Milton Park, Abingdon, Oxford OX14 4RN, United Kingdom, (Dial from U.S. (212) 216-7800), (Fax from U.S. (212) 564-7854), www.tandf.co.uk; *The Europa World Year Book.*

GUADELOUPE - AIRPORTS

Central Intelligence Agency, Office of Public Affairs, Washington, DC 20505, (703) 482-0623, Fax: (703) 482-1739, www.cia.gov; *The World Factbook.*

GUADELOUPE - ARMED FORCES

Central Intelligence Agency, Office of Public Affairs, Washington, DC 20505, (703) 482-0623, Fax: (703) 482-1739, www.cia.gov; *The World Factbook.*

Euromonitor International, Inc., 224 S. Michigan Avenue, Suite 1500, Chicago, IL 60604, (312) 922-1115, Fax: (312) 922-1157, www.euromonitor.com; *World Marketing Data and Statistics.*

GUADELOUPE - BANKS AND BANKING

Euromonitor International, Inc., 224 S. Michigan Avenue, Suite 1500, Chicago, IL 60604, (312) 922-1115, Fax: (312) 922-1157, www.euromonitor.com; *World Marketing Data and Statistics.*

Palgrave Macmillan Ltd., Houndmills, Basingstoke, Hampshire, RG21 6XS, England, (Telephone in U.S. (888) 330-8477), (Fax in U.S. (800) 672-2054), www.palgrave.com; *The Statesman's Yearbook 2008.*

GUADELOUPE - BROADCASTING

Central Intelligence Agency, Office of Public Affairs, Washington, DC 20505, (703) 482-0623, Fax: (703) 482-1739, www.cia.gov; *The World Factbook.*

Euromonitor International, Inc., 224 S. Michigan Avenue, Suite 1500, Chicago, IL 60604, (312) 922-1115, Fax: (312) 922-1157, www.euromonitor.com; *World Marketing Data and Statistics.*

Palgrave Macmillan Ltd., Houndmills, Basingstoke, Hampshire, RG21 6XS, England, (Telephone in U.S. (888) 330-8477), (Fax in U.S. (800) 672-2054), www.palgrave.com; *The Statesman's Yearbook 2008.*

GUADELOUPE - BUDGET

Central Intelligence Agency, Office of Public Affairs, Washington, DC 20505, (703) 482-0623, Fax: (703) 482-1739, www.cia.gov; *The World Factbook.*

GUADELOUPE - CATTLE

See GUADELOUPE - LIVESTOCK

GUADELOUPE - CHILDBIRTH - STATISTICS

Central Intelligence Agency, Office of Public Affairs, Washington, DC 20505, (703) 482-0623, Fax: (703) 482-1739, www.cia.gov; *The World Factbook.*

Euromonitor International, Inc., 224 S. Michigan Avenue, Suite 1500, Chicago, IL 60604, (312) 922-1115, Fax: (312) 922-1157, www.euromonitor.com; *International Marketing Data and Statistics 2008* and *The World Economic Factbook 2008.*

Taylor and Francis Group, An Informa Business, 2 Park Square, Milton Park, Abingdon, Oxford OX14 4RN, United Kingdom, (Dial from U.S. (212) 216-7800), (Fax from U.S. (212) 564-7854), www.tandf.co.uk; *The Europa World Year Book.*

United Nations Statistics Division, New York, NY 10017, (800) 253-9646, Fax: (212) 963-4116, http://unstats.un.org; *Demographic Yearbook* and *Statistical Yearbook.*

GUADELOUPE - CLIMATE

Palgrave Macmillan Ltd., Houndmills, Basingstoke, Hampshire, RG21 6XS, England, (Telephone in U.S. (888) 330-8477), (Fax in U.S. (800) 672-2054), www.palgrave.com; *The Statesman's Yearbook 2008.*

GUADELOUPE - COAL PRODUCTION

See GUADELOUPE - MINERAL INDUSTRIES

GUADELOUPE - COCOA PRODUCTION

See GUADELOUPE - CROPS

GUADELOUPE - COMMERCE

Palgrave Macmillan Ltd., Houndmills, Basingstoke, Hampshire, RG21 6XS, England, (Telephone in U.S. (888) 330-8477), (Fax in U.S. (800) 672-2054), www.palgrave.com; *The Statesman's Yearbook 2008.*

GUADELOUPE - COMMODITY EXCHANGES

Commodity Research Bureau, 330 South Wells Street, Suite 612, Chicago, IL 60606-7110, (800) 621-5271, Fax: (312) 939-4135, www.crbtrader.com; *2006 CRB Commodity Yearbook and CD.*

International Monetary Fund (IMF), 700 Nineteenth Street, NW, Washington, DC 20431, (202) 623-7000, Fax: (202) 623-4661, www.imf.org; *IMF Primary Commodity Prices.*

United Nations Food and Agricultural Organization (FAO), Viale delle Terme di Caracalla, 00100 Rome, Italy, (Dial from U.S. (202) 653-2400), (Fax from U.S. (202) 653 5760), www.fao.org; *The State of Food and Agriculture (SOFA) 2006.*

GUADELOUPE - CONSUMER PRICE INDEXES

Taylor and Francis Group, An Informa Business, 2 Park Square, Milton Park, Abingdon, Oxford OX14 4RN, United Kingdom, (Dial from U.S. (212) 216-7800), (Fax from U.S. (212) 564-7854), www.tandf.co.uk; *The Europa World Year Book.*

United Nations Statistics Division, New York, NY 10017, (800) 253-9646, Fax: (212) 963-4116, http://unstats.un.org; *Statistical Yearbook.*

GUADELOUPE - CORN INDUSTRY

See GUADELOUPE - CROPS

GUADELOUPE - CROPS

Palgrave Macmillan Ltd., Houndmills, Basingstoke, Hampshire, RG21 6XS, England, (Telephone in U.S. (888) 330-8477), (Fax in U.S. (800) 672-2054), www.palgrave.com; *The Statesman's Yearbook 2008.*

Taylor and Francis Group, An Informa Business, 2 Park Square, Milton Park, Abingdon, Oxford OX14 4RN, United Kingdom, (Dial from U.S. (212) 216-7800), (Fax from U.S. (212) 564-7854), www.tandf.co.uk; *The Europa World Year Book.*

United Nations Conference on Trade and Development (UNCTAD), DC2-1120, United Nations, New York, NY 10017, (212) 963-0027, www.unctad.org; *UNCTAD Commodity Yearbook.*

United Nations Food and Agricultural Organization (FAO), Viale delle Terme di Caracalla, 00100 Rome, Italy, (Dial from U.S. (202) 653-2400), (Fax from U.S. (202) 653 5760), www.fao.org; *FAO Production Yearbook 2002* and *The State of Food and Agriculture (SOFA) 2006.*

United Nations Statistics Division, New York, NY 10017, (800) 253-9646, Fax: (212) 963-4116, http://unstats.un.org; *Statistical Yearbook.*

GUADELOUPE - CUSTOMS ADMINISTRATION

Palgrave Macmillan Ltd., Houndmills, Basingstoke, Hampshire, RG21 6XS, England, (Telephone in U.S. (888) 330-8477), (Fax in U.S. (800) 672-2054), www.palgrave.com; *The Statesman's Yearbook 2008.*

GUADELOUPE - DAIRY PROCESSING

Palgrave Macmillan Ltd., Houndmills, Basingstoke, Hampshire, RG21 6XS, England, (Telephone in U.S. (888) 330-8477), (Fax in U.S. (800) 672-2054), www.palgrave.com; *The Statesman's Yearbook 2008.*

Taylor and Francis Group, An Informa Business, 2 Park Square, Milton Park, Abingdon, Oxford OX14 4RN, United Kingdom, (Dial from U.S. (212) 216-7800), (Fax from U.S. (212) 564-7854), www.tandf.co.uk; *The Europa World Year Book.*

United Nations Food and Agricultural Organization (FAO), Viale delle Terme di Caracalla, 00100 Rome, Italy, (Dial from U.S. (202) 653-2400), (Fax from U.S. (202) 653 5760), www.fao.org; *The State of Food and Agriculture (SOFA) 2006.*

GUADELOUPE - DEATH RATES

See GUADELOUPE - MORTALITY

GUADELOUPE - DEMOGRAPHY

Euromonitor International, Inc., 224 S. Michigan Avenue, Suite 1500, Chicago, IL 60604, (312) 922-1115, Fax: (312) 922-1157, www.euromonitor.com; *International Marketing Data and Statistics 2008; The World Economic Factbook 2008;* and *World Marketing Data and Statistics.*

GUADELOUPE - DISPOSABLE INCOME

United Nations Statistics Division, New York, NY 10017, (800) 253-9646, Fax: (212) 963-4116, http://unstats.un.org; *National Accounts Statistics: Compendium of Income Distribution Statistics* and *Statistical Yearbook.*

GUADELOUPE - DIVORCE

United Nations Statistics Division, New York, NY 10017, (800) 253-9646, Fax: (212) 963-4116, http://unstats.un.org; *Demographic Yearbook* and *Statistical Yearbook.*

GUADELOUPE - ECONOMIC ASSISTANCE

United Nations Statistics Division, New York, NY 10017, (800) 253-9646, Fax: (212) 963-4116, http://unstats.un.org; *Statistical Yearbook.*

GUADELOUPE - ECONOMIC CONDITIONS

Center for International Business Education Research (CIBER), Columbia Business School and School of International and Public Affairs, Uris Hall, Room 212, 3022 Broadway, New York, NY 10027-6902, Mr. Joshua Safier, (212) 854-4750, Fax: (212) 222-9821, www.columbia.edu/cu/ciber/; Datastream International.

Central Intelligence Agency, Office of Public Affairs, Washington, DC 20505, (703) 482-0623, Fax: (703) 482-1739, www.cia.gov; *The World Factbook.*

DSI Data Service Information, Xantener Strasse 51a, D-47495 Rheinberg, Germany, www.dsidata.com; *Campus Solution.*

Dun and Bradstreet (DB) Corporation, 103 JFK Parkway, Short Hills, NJ 07078, (973) 921-5500, www.dnb.com; *Country Report.*

Euromonitor International, Inc., 224 S. Michigan Avenue, Suite 1500, Chicago, IL 60604, (312) 922-1115, Fax: (312) 922-1157, www.euromonitor.com; *The World Economic Factbook 2008* and *World Marketing Data and Statistics.*

International Monetary Fund (IMF), 700 Nineteenth Street, NW, Washington, DC 20431, (202) 623-7000, Fax: (202) 623-4661, www.imf.org; *World Economic Outlook Reports.*

Palgrave Macmillan Ltd., Houndmills, Basingstoke, Hampshire, RG21 6XS, England, (Telephone in U.S. (888) 330-8477), (Fax in U.S. (800) 672-2054), www.palgrave.com; *The Statesman's Yearbook 2008.*

Taylor and Francis Group, An Informa Business, 2 Park Square, Milton Park, Abingdon, Oxford OX14 4RN, United Kingdom, (Dial from U.S. (212) 216-7800), (Fax from U.S. (212) 564-7854), www.tandf.co.uk; *The Europa World Year Book.*

United Nations Statistics Division, New York, NY 10017, (800) 253-9646, Fax: (212) 963-4116, http://unstats.un.org; *World Statistics Pocketbook.*

The World Bank, 1818 H Street, NW, Washington, DC 20433, (202) 473-1000, Fax: (202) 477-6391, www.worldbank.org; *Global Economic Monitor (GEM); Global Economic Prospects 2008;* and *The World Bank Atlas 2003-2004.*

GUADELOUPE - EDUCATION

Euromonitor International, Inc., 224 S. Michigan Avenue, Suite 1500, Chicago, IL 60604, (312) 922-1115, Fax: (312) 922-1157, www.euromonitor.com; *International Marketing Data and Statistics 2008* and *World Marketing Data and Statistics.*

Palgrave Macmillan Ltd., Houndmills, Basingstoke, Hampshire, RG21 6XS, England, (Telephone in U.S. (888) 330-8477), (Fax in U.S. (800) 672-2054), www.palgrave.com; *The Statesman's Yearbook 2008.*

Taylor and Francis Group, An Informa Business, 2 Park Square, Milton Park, Abingdon, Oxford OX14 4RN, United Kingdom, (Dial from U.S. (212) 216-7800), (Fax from U.S. (212) 564-7854), www.tandf.co.uk; *The Europa World Year Book.*

GUADELOUPE - ELECTRICITY

Palgrave Macmillan Ltd., Houndmills, Basingstoke, Hampshire, RG21 6XS, England, (Telephone in U.S. (888) 330-8477), (Fax in U.S. (800) 672-2054), www.palgrave.com; *The Statesman's Yearbook 2008.*

United Nations Statistics Division, New York, NY 10017, (800) 253-9646, Fax: (212) 963-4116, http://unstats.un.org; *Statistical Yearbook.*

GUADELOUPE - EMPLOYMENT

Euromonitor International, Inc., 224 S. Michigan Avenue, Suite 1500, Chicago, IL 60604, (312) 922-1115, Fax: (312) 922-1157, www.euromonitor.com; *International Marketing Data and Statistics 2008.*

International Labour Office, I.L.O. Publications, 4 route des Morillons, CH-1211 Geneva 22, Switzerland, (Telephone in U.S. (202) 653-7652), (Fax in U.S. (202) 653-7687), www.ilo.org; *Yearbook of Labour Statistics 2006.*

GUADELOUPE - ENVIRONMENTAL CONDITIONS

DSI Data Service Information, Xantener Strasse 51a, D-47495 Rheinberg, Germany, www.dsidata.com; *Campus Solution* and *DSI's Global Environmental Database.*

United Nations Statistics Division, New York, NY 10017, (800) 253-9646, Fax: (212) 963-4116, http://unstats.un.org; *World Statistics Pocketbook.*

GUADELOUPE - EXPORTS

Central Intelligence Agency, Office of Public Affairs, Washington, DC 20505, (703) 482-0623, Fax: (703) 482-1739, www.cia.gov; *The World Factbook.*

Euromonitor International, Inc., 224 S. Michigan Avenue, Suite 1500, Chicago, IL 60604, (312) 922-1115, Fax: (312) 922-1157, www.euromonitor.com; *International Marketing Data and Statistics 2008* and *The World Economic Factbook 2008.*

International Monetary Fund (IMF), 700 Nineteenth Street, NW, Washington, DC 20431, (202) 623-7000, Fax: (202) 623-4661, www.imf.org; *Direction of Trade Statistics Yearbook 2007.*

Palgrave Macmillan Ltd., Houndmills, Basingstoke, Hampshire, RG21 6XS, England, (Telephone in U.S. (888) 330-8477), (Fax in U.S. (800) 672-2054), www.palgrave.com; *The Statesman's Yearbook 2008.*

Taylor and Francis Group, An Informa Business, 2 Park Square, Milton Park, Abingdon, Oxford OX14 4RN, United Kingdom, (Dial from U.S. (212) 216-7800), (Fax from U.S. (212) 564-7854), www.tandf.co.uk; *The Europa World Year Book.*

United Nations Food and Agricultural Organization (FAO), Viale delle Terme di Caracalla, 00100 Rome, Italy, (Dial from U.S. (202) 653-2400), (Fax from U.S. (202) 653 5760), www.fao.org; *The State of Food and Agriculture (SOFA) 2006.*

GUADELOUPE - FERTILITY, HUMAN

Central Intelligence Agency, Office of Public Affairs, Washington, DC 20505, (703) 482-0623, Fax: (703) 482-1739, www.cia.gov; *The World Factbook.*

United Nations Statistics Division, New York, NY 10017, (800) 253-9646, Fax: (212) 963-4116, http://unstats.un.org; *Demographic Yearbook.*

The World Bank, 1818 H Street, NW, Washington, DC 20433, (202) 473-1000, Fax: (202) 477-6391, www.worldbank.org; *The World Bank Atlas 2003-2004.*

World Health Organization (WHO), Avenue Appia 20, 1211 Geneve 27, Switzerland, (Telephone in U.S. (212) 331-9081), www.who.int; *World Health Report 2006.*

GUADELOUPE - FERTILIZER INDUSTRY

United Nations Food and Agricultural Organization (FAO), Viale delle Terme di Caracalla, 00100 Rome, Italy, (Dial from U.S. (202) 653-2400), (Fax from U.S. (202) 653 5760), www.fao.org; *FAO Fertilizer Yearbook* and *The State of Food and Agriculture (SOFA) 2006.*

United Nations Statistics Division, New York, NY 10017, (800) 253-9646, Fax: (212) 963-4116, http://unstats.un.org; *Statistical Yearbook.*

GUADELOUPE - FETAL MORTALITY

See GUADELOUPE - MORTALITY

GUADELOUPE - FINANCE

United Nations Statistics Division, New York, NY 10017, (800) 253-9646, Fax: (212) 963-4116, http://unstats.un.org; *National Accounts Statistics: Compendium of Income Distribution Statistics* and *Statistical Yearbook.*

GUADELOUPE - FINANCE, PUBLIC

Bernan Essential Government Publications, 4611-F Assembly Drive, Lanham MD, 20706-4391, (301) 459-2255, Fax: (800) 865-3450, www.bernan.com; *National Accounts Statistics.*

International Monetary Fund (IMF), 700 Nineteenth Street, NW, Washington, DC 20431, (202) 623-7000, Fax: (202) 623-4661, www.imf.org; *International Financial Statistics* and *International Financial Statistics Online Service.*

Taylor and Francis Group, An Informa Business, 2 Park Square, Milton Park, Abingdon, Oxford OX14 4RN, United Kingdom, (Dial from U.S. (212) 216-7800), (Fax from U.S. (212) 564-7854), www.tandf.co.uk; *The Europa World Year Book.*

GUADELOUPE - FISHERIES

Palgrave Macmillan Ltd., Houndmills, Basingstoke, Hampshire, RG21 6XS, England, (Telephone in U.S. (888) 330-8477), (Fax in U.S. (800) 672-2054), www.palgrave.com; *The Statesman's Yearbook 2008.*

Taylor and Francis Group, An Informa Business, 2 Park Square, Milton Park, Abingdon, Oxford OX14 4RN, United Kingdom, (Dial from U.S. (212) 216-7800), (Fax from U.S. (212) 564-7854), www.tandf.co.uk; *The Europa World Year Book.*

United Nations Conference on Trade and Development (UNCTAD), DC2-1120, United Nations, New York, NY 10017, (212) 963-0027, www.unctad.org; *UNCTAD Commodity Yearbook.*

United Nations Food and Agricultural Organization (FAO), Viale delle Terme di Caracalla, 00100 Rome, Italy, (Dial from U.S. (202) 653-2400), (Fax from U.S. (202) 653 5760), www.fao.org; *FAO Yearbook of Fishery Statistics;* Fishery Databases; FISHSTAT Database. Subjects covered include: Aquaculture production, capture production, fishery commodities; and *The State of Food and Agriculture (SOFA) 2006.*

United Nations Statistics Division, New York, NY 10017, (800) 253-9646, Fax: (212) 963-4116, http://unstats.un.org; *Statistical Yearbook.*

GUADELOUPE - FLOUR INDUSTRY

United Nations Statistics Division, New York, NY 10017, (800) 253-9646, Fax: (212) 963-4116, http://unstats.un.org; *Statistical Yearbook.*

GUADELOUPE - FOOD

United Nations Conference on Trade and Development (UNCTAD), DC2-1120, United Nations, New York, NY 10017, (212) 963-0027, www.unctad.org; *UNCTAD Commodity Yearbook.*

United Nations Food and Agricultural Organization (FAO), Viale delle Terme di Caracalla, 00100 Rome, Italy, (Dial from U.S. (202) 653-2400), (Fax from U.S. (202) 653 5760), www.fao.org; *FAO Production Yearbook 2002* and *The State of Food and Agriculture (SOFA) 2006.*

GUADELOUPE - FOREIGN EXCHANGE RATES

Central Intelligence Agency, Office of Public Affairs, Washington, DC 20505, (703) 482-0623, Fax: (703) 482-1739, www.cia.gov; *The World Factbook.*

Euromonitor International, Inc., 224 S. Michigan Avenue, Suite 1500, Chicago, IL 60604, (312) 922-1115, Fax: (312) 922-1157, www.euromonitor.com; *International Marketing Data and Statistics 2008* and *The World Economic Factbook 2008.*

Taylor and Francis Group, An Informa Business, 2 Park Square, Milton Park, Abingdon, Oxford OX14 4RN, United Kingdom, (Dial from U.S. (212) 216-7800), (Fax from U.S. (212) 564-7854), www.tandf.co.uk; *The Europa World Year Book.*

United Nations Statistics Division, New York, NY 10017, (800) 253-9646, Fax: (212) 963-4116, http://unstats.un.org; *World Statistics Pocketbook.*

GUADELOUPE - FORESTS AND FORESTRY

Palgrave Macmillan Ltd., Houndmills, Basingstoke, Hampshire, RG21 6XS, England, (Telephone in U.S. (888) 330-8477), (Fax in U.S. (800) 672-2054), www.palgrave.com; *The Statesman's Yearbook 2008.*

Taylor and Francis Group, An Informa Business, 2 Park Square, Milton Park, Abingdon, Oxford OX14 4RN, United Kingdom, (Dial from U.S. (212) 216-7800), (Fax from U.S. (212) 564-7854), www.tandf.co.uk; *The Europa World Year Book.*

UNESCO Institute for Statistics, C.P. 6128 Succursale Centre-Ville, Montreal, Quebec, H3C 3J7 Canada, (Dial from U.S. (514) 343-6880), (Fax from U.S. (514) 343 6882), www.uis.unesco.org; *Statistical Tables.*

United Nations Conference on Trade and Development (UNCTAD), DC2-1120, United Nations, New York, NY 10017, (212) 963-0027, www.unctad.org; *UNCTAD Commodity Yearbook.*

United Nations Food and Agricultural Organization (FAO), Viale delle Terme di Caracalla, 00100 Rome, Italy, (Dial from U.S. (202) 653-2400), (Fax from U.S. (202) 653 5760), www.fao.org; *FAO Yearbook of Forest Products* and *The State of Food and Agriculture (SOFA) 2006.*

United Nations Statistics Division, New York, NY 10017, (800) 253-9646, Fax: (212) 963-4116, http://unstats.un.org; *Statistical Yearbook.*

GUADELOUPE - GROSS DOMESTIC PRODUCT

Euromonitor International, Inc., 224 S. Michigan Avenue, Suite 1500, Chicago, IL 60604, (312) 922-1115, Fax: (312) 922-1157, www.euromonitor.com; *International Marketing Data and Statistics 2008* and *The World Economic Factbook 2008.*

Taylor and Francis Group, An Informa Business, 2 Park Square, Milton Park, Abingdon, Oxford OX14 4RN, United Kingdom, (Dial from U.S. (212) 216-7800), (Fax from U.S. (212) 564-7854), www.tandf.co.uk; *The Europa World Year Book.*

United Nations Statistics Division, New York, NY 10017, (800) 253-9646, Fax: (212) 963-4116, http://unstats.un.org; *National Accounts Statistics: Compendium of Income Distribution Statistics* and *Statistical Yearbook.*

GUADELOUPE - GROSS NATIONAL PRODUCT

Taylor and Francis Group, An Informa Business, 2 Park Square, Milton Park, Abingdon, Oxford OX14 4RN, United Kingdom, (Dial from U.S. (212) 216-7800), (Fax from U.S. (212) 564-7854), www.tandf.co.uk; *The Europa World Year Book.*

The World Bank, 1818 H Street, NW, Washington, DC 20433, (202) 473-1000, Fax: (202) 477-6391, www.worldbank.org; *The World Bank Atlas 2003-2004.*

GUADELOUPE - HIDES AND SKINS INDUSTRY

United Nations Food and Agricultural Organization (FAO), Viale delle Terme di Caracalla, 00100 Rome, Italy, (Dial from U.S. (202) 653-2400), (Fax from U.S. (202) 653 5760), www.fao.org; *FAO Production Yearbook 2002.*

GUADELOUPE - HOURS OF LABOR

International Labour Office, I.L.O. Publications, 4 route des Morillons, CH-1211 Geneva 22, Switzerland, (Telephone in U.S. (202) 653-7652), (Fax in U.S. (202) 653-7687), www.ilo.org; *Yearbook of Labour Statistics 2006.*

GUADELOUPE - HOUSING

Euromonitor International, Inc., 224 S. Michigan Avenue, Suite 1500, Chicago, IL 60604, (312) 922-1115, Fax: (312) 922-1157, www.euromonitor.com; *World Marketing Data and Statistics.*

GUADELOUPE - ILLITERATE PERSONS

Euromonitor International, Inc., 224 S. Michigan Avenue, Suite 1500, Chicago, IL 60604, (312) 922-1115, Fax: (312) 922-1157, www.euromonitor.com; *The World Economic Factbook 2008.*

UNESCO Institute for Statistics, C.P. 6128 Succursale Centre-Ville, Montreal, Quebec, H3C 3J7 Canada, (Dial from U.S. (514) 343-6880), (Fax from U.S. (514) 343 6882), www.uis.unesco.org; *Statistical Tables.*

GUADELOUPE - IMPORTS

Central Intelligence Agency, Office of Public Affairs, Washington, DC 20505, (703) 482-0623, Fax: (703) 482-1739, www.cia.gov; *The World Factbook.*

Euromonitor International, Inc., 224 S. Michigan Avenue, Suite 1500, Chicago, IL 60604, (312) 922-1115, Fax: (312) 922-1157, www.euromonitor.com; *International Marketing Data and Statistics 2008* and *The World Economic Factbook 2008.*

International Monetary Fund (IMF), 700 Nineteenth Street, NW, Washington, DC 20431, (202) 623-7000, Fax: (202) 623-4661, www.imf.org; *Direction of Trade Statistics Yearbook 2007.*

Palgrave Macmillan Ltd., Houndmills, Basingstoke, Hampshire, RG21 6XS, England, (Telephone in U.S. (888) 330-8477), (Fax in U.S. (800) 672-2054), www.palgrave.com; *The Statesman's Yearbook 2008.*

Taylor and Francis Group, An Informa Business, 2 Park Square, Milton Park, Abingdon, Oxford OX14 4RN, United Kingdom, (Dial from U.S. (212) 216-7800), (Fax from U.S. (212) 564-7854), www.tandf.co.uk; *The Europa World Year Book.*

United Nations Food and Agricultural Organization (FAO), Viale delle Terme di Caracalla, 00100 Rome, Italy, (Dial from U.S. (202) 653-2400), (Fax from U.S. (202) 653 5760), www.fao.org; *The State of Food and Agriculture (SOFA) 2006.*

GUADELOUPE - INDUSTRIES

Central Intelligence Agency, Office of Public Affairs, Washington, DC 20505, (703) 482-0623, Fax: (703) 482-1739, www.cia.gov; *The World Factbook.*

Euromonitor International, Inc., 224 S. Michigan Avenue, Suite 1500, Chicago, IL 60604, (312) 922-1115, Fax: (312) 922-1157, www.euromonitor.com; *The World Economic Factbook 2008* and *World Marketing Data and Statistics.*

International Labour Office, I.L.O. Publications, 4 route des Morillons, CH-1211 Geneva 22, Switzerland, (Telephone in U.S. (202) 653-7652), (Fax in U.S. (202) 653-7687), www.ilo.org; *Yearbook of Labour Statistics 2006.*

Taylor and Francis Group, An Informa Business, 2 Park Square, Milton Park, Abingdon, Oxford OX14 4RN, United Kingdom, (Dial from U.S. (212) 216-7800), (Fax from U.S. (212) 564-7854), www.tandf.co.uk; *The Europa World Year Book.*

United Nations Industrial Development Organization (UNIDO), 1 United Nations Plaza, New York, NY 10017, (212) 963 6890, Fax: (212) 963-7904, http://unido.org; Industrial Statistics Database 2008 (INDSTAT) and *The International Yearbook of Industrial Statistics 2008.*

GUADELOUPE - INFANT AND MATERNAL MORTALITY

See GUADELOUPE - MORTALITY

GUADELOUPE - INTERNATIONAL TRADE

Euromonitor International, Inc., 224 S. Michigan Avenue, Suite 1500, Chicago, IL 60604, (312) 922-1115, Fax: (312) 922-1157, www.euromonitor.com; *The World Economic Factbook 2008* and *World Marketing Data and Statistics.*

Palgrave Macmillan Ltd., Houndmills, Basingstoke, Hampshire, RG21 6XS, England, (Telephone in U.S. (888) 330-8477), (Fax in U.S. (800) 672-2054), www.palgrave.com; *The Statesman's Yearbook 2008.*

Taylor and Francis Group, An Informa Business, 2 Park Square, Milton Park, Abingdon, Oxford OX14 4RN, United Kingdom, (Dial from U.S. (212) 216-7800), (Fax from U.S. (212) 564-7854), www.tandf.co.uk; *The Europa World Year Book.*

United Nations Conference on Trade and Development (UNCTAD), DC2-1120, United Nations, New York, NY 10017, (212) 963-0027, www.unctad.org; *UNCTAD Commodity Yearbook.*

United Nations Food and Agricultural Organization (FAO), Viale delle Terme di Caracalla, 00100 Rome, Italy, (Dial from U.S. (202) 653-2400), (Fax from

U.S. (202) 653 5760), www.fao.org; *FAO Trade Yearbook* and *The State of Food and Agriculture (SOFA) 2006.*

United Nations Statistics Division, New York, NY 10017, (800) 253-9646, Fax: (212) 963-4116, http://unstats.un.org; *International Trade Statistics Yearbook* and *Statistical Yearbook.*

World Trade Organization (WTO), Centre William Rappard, Rue de Lausanne 154, CH-1211 Geneva 21, Switzerland, www.wto.org; *International Trade Statistics 2006.*

GUADELOUPE - INTERNET USERS

International Telecommunication Union (ITU), Place des Nations, 1211 Geneva 20, Switzerland, www.itu.int; *World Telecommunication/ICT Indicators Database on CD-ROM; World Telecommunication/ICT Indicators Database Online;* and *Yearbook of Statistics - Telecommunication Services (Chronological Time Series 1997-2006).*

GUADELOUPE - LABOR

Central Intelligence Agency, Office of Public Affairs, Washington, DC 20505, (703) 482-0623, Fax: (703) 482-1739, www.cia.gov; *The World Factbook.*

Euromonitor International, Inc., 224 S. Michigan Avenue, Suite 1500, Chicago, IL 60604, (312) 922-1115, Fax: (312) 922-1157, www.euromonitor.com; *International Marketing Data and Statistics 2008* and *World Marketing Data and Statistics.*

International Labour Office, I.L.O. Publications, 4 route des Morillons, CH-1211 Geneva 22, Switzerland, (Telephone in U.S. (202) 653-7652), (Fax in U.S. (202) 653-7687), www.ilo.org; *Yearbook of Labour Statistics 2006.*

Palgrave Macmillan Ltd., Houndmills, Basingstoke, Hampshire, RG21 6XS, England, (Telephone in U.S. (888) 330-8477), (Fax in U.S. (800) 672-2054), www.palgrave.com; *The Statesman's Yearbook 2008.*

Taylor and Francis Group, An Informa Business, 2 Park Square, Milton Park, Abingdon, Oxford OX14 4RN, United Kingdom, (Dial from U.S. (212) 216-7800), (Fax from U.S. (212) 564-7854), www.tandf.co.uk; *The Europa World Year Book.*

United Nations Food and Agricultural Organization (FAO), Viale delle Terme di Caracalla, 00100 Rome, Italy, (Dial from U.S. (202) 653-2400), (Fax from U.S. (202) 653 5760), www.fao.org; *The State of Food and Agriculture (SOFA) 2006.*

The World Bank, 1818 H Street, NW, Washington, DC 20433, (202) 473-1000, Fax: (202) 477-6391, www.worldbank.org; *The World Bank Atlas 2003-2004.*

GUADELOUPE - LAND USE

Central Intelligence Agency, Office of Public Affairs, Washington, DC 20505, (703) 482-0623, Fax: (703) 482-1739, www.cia.gov; *The World Factbook.*

Euromonitor International, Inc., 224 S. Michigan Avenue, Suite 1500, Chicago, IL 60604, (312) 922-1115, Fax: (312) 922-1157, www.euromonitor.com; *International Marketing Data and Statistics 2008.*

United Nations Food and Agricultural Organization (FAO), Viale delle Terme di Caracalla, 00100 Rome, Italy, (Dial from U.S. (202) 653-2400), (Fax from U.S. (202) 653 5760), www.fao.org; *FAO Production Yearbook 2002.*

GUADELOUPE - LIFE EXPECTANCY

Central Intelligence Agency, Office of Public Affairs, Washington, DC 20505, (703) 482-0623, Fax: (703) 482-1739, www.cia.gov; *The World Factbook.*

Euromonitor International, Inc., 224 S. Michigan Avenue, Suite 1500, Chicago, IL 60604, (312) 922-1115, Fax: (312) 922-1157, www.euromonitor.com; *The World Economic Factbook 2008.*

United Nations Statistics Division, New York, NY 10017, (800) 253-9646, Fax: (212) 963-4116, http://unstats.un.org; *World Statistics Pocketbook.*

The World Bank, 1818 H Street, NW, Washington, DC 20433, (202) 473-1000, Fax: (202) 477-6391, www.worldbank.org; *The World Bank Atlas 2003-2004.*

GUADELOUPE - LITERACY

Euromonitor International, Inc., 224 S. Michigan Avenue, Suite 1500, Chicago, IL 60604, (312) 922-1115, Fax: (312) 922-1157, www.euromonitor.com; *World Marketing Data and Statistics.*

GUADELOUPE - LIVESTOCK

Palgrave Macmillan Ltd., Houndmills, Basingstoke, Hampshire, RG21 6XS, England, (Telephone in U.S. (888) 330-8477), (Fax in U.S. (800) 672-2054), www.palgrave.com; *The Statesman's Yearbook 2008.*

Taylor and Francis Group, An Informa Business, 2 Park Square, Milton Park, Abingdon, Oxford OX14 4RN, United Kingdom, (Dial from U.S. (212) 216-7800), (Fax from U.S. (212) 564-7854), www.tandf.co.uk; *The Europa World Year Book.*

United Nations Conference on Trade and Development (UNCTAD), DC2-1120, United Nations, New York, NY 10017, (212) 963-0027, www.unctad.org; *UNCTAD Commodity Yearbook.*

United Nations Food and Agricultural Organization (FAO), Viale delle Terme di Caracalla, 00100 Rome, Italy, (Dial from U.S. (202) 653-2400), (Fax from U.S. (202) 653 5760), www.fao.org; *FAO Production Yearbook 2002* and *The State of Food and Agriculture (SOFA) 2006.*

United Nations Statistics Division, New York, NY 10017, (800) 253-9646, Fax: (212) 963-4116, http://unstats.un.org; *Statistical Yearbook.*

GUADELOUPE - MARRIAGE

United Nations Statistics Division, New York, NY 10017, (800) 253-9646, Fax: (212) 963-4116, http://unstats.un.org; *Demographic Yearbook* and *Statistical Yearbook.*

GUADELOUPE - MEAT PRODUCTION

See GUADELOUPE - LIVESTOCK

GUADELOUPE - MINERAL INDUSTRIES

United Nations Conference on Trade and Development (UNCTAD), DC2-1120, United Nations, New York, NY 10017, (212) 963-0027, www.unctad.org; *UNCTAD Commodity Yearbook.*

United Nations Statistics Division, New York, NY 10017, (800) 253-9646, Fax: (212) 963-4116, http://unstats.un.org; *Statistical Yearbook.*

GUADELOUPE - MONEY SUPPLY

Taylor and Francis Group, An Informa Business, 2 Park Square, Milton Park, Abingdon, Oxford OX14 4RN, United Kingdom, (Dial from U.S. (212) 216-7800), (Fax from U.S. (212) 564-7854), www.tandf.co.uk; *The Europa World Year Book.*

GUADELOUPE - MONUMENTS AND HISTORIC SITES

UNESCO Institute for Statistics, C.P. 6128 Succursale Centre-Ville, Montreal, Quebec, H3C 3J7 Canada, (Dial from U.S. (514) 343-6880), (Fax from U.S. (514) 343 6882), www.uis.unesco.org; *Statistical Tables.*

GUADELOUPE - MORTALITY

Central Intelligence Agency, Office of Public Affairs, Washington, DC 20505, (703) 482-0623, Fax: (703) 482-1739, www.cia.gov; *The World Factbook.*

Euromonitor International, Inc., 224 S. Michigan Avenue, Suite 1500, Chicago, IL 60604, (312) 922-1115, Fax: (312) 922-1157, www.euromonitor.com; *International Marketing Data and Statistics 2008* and *The World Economic Factbook 2008.*

Palgrave Macmillan Ltd., Houndmills, Basingstoke, Hampshire, RG21 6XS, England, (Telephone in U.S. (888) 330-8477), (Fax in U.S. (800) 672-2054), www.palgrave.com; *The Statesman's Yearbook 2008.*

Taylor and Francis Group, An Informa Business, 2 Park Square, Milton Park, Abingdon, Oxford OX14 4RN, United Kingdom, (Dial from U.S. (212) 216-7800), (Fax from U.S. (212) 564-7854), www.tandf.co.uk; *The Europa World Year Book.*

United Nations Statistics Division, New York, NY 10017, (800) 253-9646, Fax: (212) 963-4116, http://unstats.un.org; *Demographic Yearbook; Statistical Yearbook;* and *World Statistics Pocketbook.*

The World Bank, 1818 H Street, NW, Washington, DC 20433, (202) 473-1000, Fax: (202) 477-6391, www.worldbank.org; *The World Bank Atlas 2003-2004.*

World Health Organization (WHO), Avenue Appia 20, 1211 Geneve 27, Switzerland, (Telephone in U.S. (212) 331-9081), www.who.int; The WHO Global Atlas of Infectious Diseases and *World Health Report 2006.*

GUADELOUPE - MOTOR VEHICLES

Taylor and Francis Group, An Informa Business, 2 Park Square, Milton Park, Abingdon, Oxford OX14 4RN, United Kingdom, (Dial from U.S. (212) 216-7800), (Fax from U.S. (212) 564-7854), www.tandf.co.uk; *The Europa World Year Book.*

United Nations Statistics Division, New York, NY 10017, (800) 253-9646, Fax: (212) 963-4116, http://unstats.un.org; *Statistical Yearbook.*

GUADELOUPE - MUSEUMS

UNESCO Institute for Statistics, C.P. 6128 Succursale Centre-Ville, Montreal, Quebec, H3C 3J7 Canada, (Dial from U.S. (514) 343-6880), (Fax from U.S. (514) 343 6882), www.uis.unesco.org; *Statistical Tables.*

GUADELOUPE - NUTRITION

United Nations Food and Agricultural Organization (FAO), Viale delle Terme di Caracalla, 00100 Rome, Italy, (Dial from U.S. (202) 653-2400), (Fax from U.S. (202) 653 5760), www.fao.org; *The State of Food and Agriculture (SOFA) 2006.*

GUADELOUPE - PAPER

See GUADELOUPE - FORESTS AND FORESTRY

GUADELOUPE - PERIODICALS

UNESCO Institute for Statistics, C.P. 6128 Succursale Centre-Ville, Montreal, Quebec, H3C 3J7 Canada, (Dial from U.S. (514) 343-6880), (Fax from U.S. (514) 343 6882), www.uis.unesco.org; *Statistical Tables.*

GUADELOUPE - PESTICIDES

United Nations Food and Agricultural Organization (FAO), Viale delle Terme di Caracalla, 00100 Rome, Italy, (Dial from U.S. (202) 653-2400), (Fax from U.S. (202) 653 5760), www.fao.org; *The State of Food and Agriculture (SOFA) 2006.*

GUADELOUPE - PETROLEUM INDUSTRY AND TRADE

PennWell Corporation, 1421 South Sheridan Road, Tulsa, OK 74112, (918) 835-3161, www.pennwell.com; *International Petroleum Encyclopedia 2007.*

United Nations Conference on Trade and Development (UNCTAD), DC2-1120, United Nations, New York, NY 10017, (212) 963-0027, www.unctad.org; *UNCTAD Commodity Yearbook.*

United Nations Food and Agricultural Organization (FAO), Viale delle Terme di Caracalla, 00100 Rome, Italy, (Dial from U.S. (202) 653-2400), (Fax from U.S. (202) 653 5760), www.fao.org; *The State of Food and Agriculture (SOFA) 2006.*

GUADELOUPE - POLITICAL SCIENCE

Central Intelligence Agency, Office of Public Affairs, Washington, DC 20505, (703) 482-0623, Fax: (703) 482-1739, www.cia.gov; *The World Factbook.*

Palgrave Macmillan Ltd., Houndmills, Basingstoke, Hampshire, RG21 6XS, England, (Telephone in U.S.

(888) 330-8477), (Fax in U.S. (800) 672-2054), www.palgrave.com; *The Statesman's Yearbook 2008.*

Taylor and Francis Group, An Informa Business, 2 Park Square, Milton Park, Abingdon, Oxford OX14 4RN, United Kingdom, (Dial from U.S. (212) 216-7800), (Fax from U.S. (212) 564-7854), www.tandf.co.uk; *The Europa World Year Book.*

United Nations Statistics Division, New York, NY 10017, (800) 253-9646, Fax: (212) 963-4116, http://unstats.un.org; *National Accounts Statistics: Compendium of Income Distribution Statistics.*

GUADELOUPE - POPULATION

Central Intelligence Agency, Office of Public Affairs, Washington, DC 20505, (703) 482-0623, Fax: (703) 482-1739, www.cia.gov; *The World Factbook.*

Euromonitor International, Inc., 224 S. Michigan Avenue, Suite 1500, Chicago, IL 60604, (312) 922-1115, Fax: (312) 922-1157, www.euromonitor.com; *International Marketing Data and Statistics 2008* and *The World Economic Factbook 2008.*

Eurostat, Batiment Jean Monnet, Rue Alcide de Gasperi, L-2920 Luxembourg, http://epp.eurostat.ec.europa.eu; *Demographic Indicators - Population by Age-Classes.*

International Labour Office, I.L.O. Publications, 4 route des Morillons, CH-1211 Geneva 22, Switzerland, (Telephone in U.S. (202) 653-7652), (Fax in U.S. (202) 653-7687), www.ilo.org; *Yearbook of Labour Statistics 2006.*

Palgrave Macmillan Ltd., Houndmills, Basingstoke, Hampshire, RG21 6XS, England, (Telephone in U.S. (888) 330-8477), (Fax in U.S. (800) 672-2054), www.palgrave.com; *The Statesman's Yearbook 2008.*

Taylor and Francis Group, An Informa Business, 2 Park Square, Milton Park, Abingdon, Oxford OX14 4RN, United Kingdom, (Dial from U.S. (212) 216-7800), (Fax from U.S. (212) 564-7854), www.tandf.co.uk; *The Europa World Year Book.*

United Nations Food and Agricultural Organization (FAO), Viale delle Terme di Caracalla, 00100 Rome, Italy, (Dial from U.S. (202) 653-2400), (Fax from U.S. (202) 653 5760), www.fao.org; *FAO Production Yearbook 2002.*

United Nations Statistics Division, New York, NY 10017, (800) 253-9646, Fax: (212) 963-4116, http://unstats.un.org; *Demographic Yearbook; Statistical Yearbook;* and *World Statistics Pocketbook.*

The World Bank, 1818 H Street, NW, Washington, DC 20433, (202) 473-1000, Fax: (202) 477-6391, www.worldbank.org; *The World Bank Atlas 2003-2004.*

World Health Organization (WHO), Avenue Appia 20, 1211 Geneve 27, Switzerland, (Telephone in U.S. (212) 331-9081), www.who.int; *World Health Report 2006.*

GUADELOUPE - POPULATION DENSITY

Central Intelligence Agency, Office of Public Affairs, Washington, DC 20505, (703) 482-0623, Fax: (703) 482-1739, www.cia.gov; *The World Factbook.*

Euromonitor International, Inc., 224 S. Michigan Avenue, Suite 1500, Chicago, IL 60604, (312) 922-1115, Fax: (312) 922-1157, www.euromonitor.com; *The World Economic Factbook 2008.*

Palgrave Macmillan Ltd., Houndmills, Basingstoke, Hampshire, RG21 6XS, England, (Telephone in U.S. (888) 330-8477), (Fax in U.S. (800) 672-2054), www.palgrave.com; *The Statesman's Yearbook 2008.*

Taylor and Francis Group, An Informa Business, 2 Park Square, Milton Park, Abingdon, Oxford OX14 4RN, United Kingdom, (Dial from U.S. (212) 216-7800), (Fax from U.S. (212) 564-7854), www.tandf.co.uk; *The Europa World Year Book.*

United Nations Food and Agricultural Organization (FAO), Viale delle Terme di Caracalla, 00100 Rome, Italy, (Dial from U.S. (202) 653-2400), (Fax from U.S. (202) 653 5760), www.fao.org; *The State of Food and Agriculture (SOFA) 2006.*

United Nations Statistics Division, New York, NY 10017, (800) 253-9646, Fax: (212) 963-4116, http://unstats.un.org; *Statistical Yearbook.*

GUADELOUPE - POSTAL SERVICE

Palgrave Macmillan Ltd., Houndmills, Basingstoke, Hampshire, RG21 6XS, England, (Telephone in U.S. (888) 330-8477), (Fax in U.S. (800) 672-2054), www.palgrave.com; *The Statesman's Yearbook 2008.*

GUADELOUPE - POWER RESOURCES

Euromonitor International, Inc., 224 S. Michigan Avenue, Suite 1500, Chicago, IL 60604, (312) 922-1115, Fax: (312) 922-1157, www.euromonitor.com; *International Marketing Data and Statistics 2008; The World Economic Factbook 2008;* and *World Marketing Data and Statistics.*

Palgrave Macmillan Ltd., Houndmills, Basingstoke, Hampshire, RG21 6XS, England, (Telephone in U.S. (888) 330-8477), (Fax in U.S. (800) 672-2054), www.palgrave.com; *The Statesman's Yearbook 2008.*

United Nations Food and Agricultural Organization (FAO), Viale delle Terme di Caracalla, 00100 Rome, Italy, (Dial from U.S. (202) 653-2400), (Fax from U.S. (202) 653 5760), www.fao.org; *The State of Food and Agriculture (SOFA) 2006.*

United Nations Statistics Division, New York, NY 10017, (800) 253-9646, Fax: (212) 963-4116, http://unstats.un.org; *Statistical Yearbook* and *World Statistics Pocketbook.*

The World Bank, 1818 H Street, NW, Washington, DC 20433, (202) 473-1000, Fax: (202) 477-6391, www.worldbank.org; *The World Bank Atlas 2003-2004.*

GUADELOUPE - PRICES

Euromonitor International, Inc., 224 S. Michigan Avenue, Suite 1500, Chicago, IL 60604, (312) 922-1115, Fax: (312) 922-1157, www.euromonitor.com; *World Marketing Data and Statistics.*

International Labour Office, I.L.O. Publications, 4 route des Morillons, CH-1211 Geneva 22, Switzerland, (Telephone in U.S. (202) 653-7652), (Fax in U.S. (202) 653-7687), www.ilo.org; *Yearbook of Labour Statistics 2006.*

United Nations Food and Agricultural Organization (FAO), Viale delle Terme di Caracalla, 00100 Rome, Italy, (Dial from U.S. (202) 653-2400), (Fax from U.S. (202) 653 5760), www.fao.org; *FAO Production Yearbook 2002* and *The State of Food and Agriculture (SOFA) 2006.*

GUADELOUPE - PUBLIC HEALTH

Euromonitor International, Inc., 224 S. Michigan Avenue, Suite 1500, Chicago, IL 60604, (312) 922-1115, Fax: (312) 922-1157, www.euromonitor.com; *World Marketing Data and Statistics.*

Palgrave Macmillan Ltd., Houndmills, Basingstoke, Hampshire, RG21 6XS, England, (Telephone in U.S. (888) 330-8477), (Fax in U.S. (800) 672-2054), www.palgrave.com; *The Statesman's Yearbook 2008.*

United Nations Statistics Division, New York, NY 10017, (800) 253-9646, Fax: (212) 963-4116, http://unstats.un.org; *Statistical Yearbook.*

World Health Organization (WHO), Avenue Appia 20, 1211 Geneve 27, Switzerland, (Telephone in U.S. (212) 331-9081), www.who.int; The WHO Global Atlas of Infectious Diseases and *World Health Report 2006.*

GUADELOUPE - RADIO BROADCASTING

Palgrave Macmillan Ltd., Houndmills, Basingstoke, Hampshire, RG21 6XS, England, (Telephone in U.S. (888) 330-8477), (Fax in U.S. (800) 672-2054), www.palgrave.com; *The Statesman's Yearbook 2008.*

GUADELOUPE - RELIGION

Central Intelligence Agency, Office of Public Affairs, Washington, DC 20505, (703) 482-0623, Fax: (703) 482-1739, www.cia.gov; *The World Factbook.*

Palgrave Macmillan Ltd., Houndmills, Basingstoke, Hampshire, RG21 6XS, England, (Telephone in U.S. (888) 330-8477), (Fax in U.S. (800) 672-2054), www.palgrave.com; *The Statesman's Yearbook 2008.*

GUADELOUPE - RENT CHARGES

International Labour Office, I.L.O. Publications, 4 route des Morillons, CH-1211 Geneva 22, Switzerland, (Telephone in U.S. (202) 653-7652), (Fax in U.S. (202) 653-7687), www.ilo.org; *Yearbook of Labour Statistics 2006.*

GUADELOUPE - RETAIL TRADE

Euromonitor International, Inc., 224 S. Michigan Avenue, Suite 1500, Chicago, IL 60604, (312) 922-1115, Fax: (312) 922-1157, www.euromonitor.com; *World Marketing Data and Statistics.*

GUADELOUPE - ROADS

Central Intelligence Agency, Office of Public Affairs, Washington, DC 20505, (703) 482-0623, Fax: (703) 482-1739, www.cia.gov; *The World Factbook.*

Palgrave Macmillan Ltd., Houndmills, Basingstoke, Hampshire, RG21 6XS, England, (Telephone in U.S. (888) 330-8477), (Fax in U.S. (800) 672-2054), www.palgrave.com; *The Statesman's Yearbook 2008.*

GUADELOUPE - SHEEP

See GUADELOUPE - LIVESTOCK

GUADELOUPE - SHIPPING

Palgrave Macmillan Ltd., Houndmills, Basingstoke, Hampshire, RG21 6XS, England, (Telephone in U.S. (888) 330-8477), (Fax in U.S. (800) 672-2054), www.palgrave.com; *The Statesman's Yearbook 2008.*

Taylor and Francis Group, An Informa Business, 2 Park Square, Milton Park, Abingdon, Oxford OX14 4RN, United Kingdom, (Dial from U.S. (212) 216-7800), (Fax from U.S. (212) 564-7854), www.tandf.co.uk; *The Europa World Year Book.*

United Nations Statistics Division, New York, NY 10017, (800) 253-9646, Fax: (212) 963-4116, http://unstats.un.org; *Statistical Yearbook.*

GUADELOUPE - SOCIAL ECOLOGY

United Nations Statistics Division, New York, NY 10017, (800) 253-9646, Fax: (212) 963-4116, http://unstats.un.org; *World Statistics Pocketbook.*

GUADELOUPE - SOCIAL SECURITY

United Nations Statistics Division, New York, NY 10017, (800) 253-9646, Fax: (212) 963-4116, http://unstats.un.org; *National Accounts Statistics: Compendium of Income Distribution Statistics.*

GUADELOUPE - SUGAR PRODUCTION

See GUADELOUPE - CROPS

GUADELOUPE - TELEPHONE

International Telecommunication Union (ITU), Place des Nations, 1211 Geneva 20, Switzerland, www.itu.int; World Telecommunication Indicators Database.

Palgrave Macmillan Ltd., Houndmills, Basingstoke, Hampshire, RG21 6XS, England, (Telephone in U.S. (888) 330-8477), (Fax in U.S. (800) 672-2054), www.palgrave.com; *The Statesman's Yearbook 2008.*

Taylor and Francis Group, An Informa Business, 2 Park Square, Milton Park, Abingdon, Oxford OX14 4RN, United Kingdom, (Dial from U.S. (212) 216-7800), (Fax from U.S. (212) 564-7854), www.tandf.co.uk; *The Europa World Year Book.*

United Nations Statistics Division, New York, NY 10017, (800) 253-9646, Fax: (212) 963-4116, http://unstats.un.org; *Statistical Yearbook* and *World Statistics Pocketbook.*

GUADELOUPE - TEXTILE INDUSTRY

United Nations Conference on Trade and Development (UNCTAD), DC2-1120, United Nations, New

York, NY 10017, (212) 963-0027, www.unctad.org; *UNCTAD Commodity Yearbook.*

GUADELOUPE - TOURISM

Euromonitor International, Inc., 224 S. Michigan Avenue, Suite 1500, Chicago, IL 60604, (312) 922-1115, Fax: (312) 922-1157, www.euromonitor.com; *The World Economic Factbook 2008* and *World Marketing Data and Statistics.*

Palgrave Macmillan Ltd., Houndmills, Basingstoke, Hampshire, RG21 6XS, England, (Telephone in U.S. (888) 330-8477), (Fax in U.S. (800) 672-2054), www.palgrave.com; *The Statesman's Yearbook 2008.*

Taylor and Francis Group, An Informa Business, 2 Park Square, Milton Park, Abingdon, Oxford OX14 4RN, United Kingdom, (Dial from U.S. (212) 216-7800), (Fax from U.S. (212) 564-7854), www.tandf.co.uk; *The Europa World Year Book.*

United Nations World Tourism Organization (UNWTO), Capitan Haya 42, 28020 Madrid, Spain, www.world-tourism.org; *Yearbook of Tourism Statistics.*

GUADELOUPE - TRADE

See GUADELOUPE - INTERNATIONAL TRADE

GUADELOUPE - TRANSPORTATION

Central Intelligence Agency, Office of Public Affairs, Washington, DC 20505, (703) 482-0623, Fax: (703) 482-1739, www.cia.gov; *The World Factbook.*

Euromonitor International, Inc., 224 S. Michigan Avenue, Suite 1500, Chicago, IL 60604, (312) 922-1115, Fax: (312) 922-1157, www.euromonitor.com; *International Marketing Data and Statistics 2008* and *World Marketing Data and Statistics.*

Palgrave Macmillan Ltd., Houndmills, Basingstoke, Hampshire, RG21 6XS, England, (Telephone in U.S. (888) 330-8477), (Fax in U.S. (800) 672-2054), www.palgrave.com; *The Statesman's Yearbook 2008.*

Taylor and Francis Group, An Informa Business, 2 Park Square, Milton Park, Abingdon, Oxford OX14 4RN, United Kingdom, (Dial from U.S. (212) 216-7800), (Fax from U.S. (212) 564-7854), www.tandf.co.uk; *The Europa World Year Book.*

GUADELOUPE - UNEMPLOYMENT

Central Intelligence Agency, Office of Public Affairs, Washington, DC 20505, (703) 482-0623, Fax: (703) 482-1739, www.cia.gov; *The World Factbook.*

International Labour Office, I.L.O. Publications, 4 route des Morillons, CH-1211 Geneva 22, Switzerland, (Telephone in U.S. (202) 653-7652), (Fax in U.S. (202) 653-7687), www.ilo.org; *Yearbook of Labour Statistics 2006.*

Palgrave Macmillan Ltd., Houndmills, Basingstoke, Hampshire, RG21 6XS, England, (Telephone in U.S. (888) 330-8477), (Fax in U.S. (800) 672-2054), www.palgrave.com; *The Statesman's Yearbook 2008.*

United Nations Statistics Division, New York, NY 10017, (800) 253-9646, Fax: (212) 963-4116, http://unstats.un.org; *Statistical Yearbook.*

GUADELOUPE - VITAL STATISTICS

Palgrave Macmillan Ltd., Houndmills, Basingstoke, Hampshire, RG21 6XS, England, (Telephone in U.S. (888) 330-8477), (Fax in U.S. (800) 672-2054), www.palgrave.com; *The Statesman's Yearbook 2008.*

United Nations Statistics Division, New York, NY 10017, (800) 253-9646, Fax: (212) 963-4116, http://unstats.un.org; *Statistical Yearbook.*

World Health Organization (WHO), Avenue Appia 20, 1211 Geneve 27, Switzerland, (Telephone in U.S. (212) 331-9081), www.who.int; *World Health Report 2006.*

GUADELOUPE - WAGES

International Labour Office, I.L.O. Publications, 4 route des Morillons, CH-1211 Geneva 22, Switzerland, (Telephone in U.S. (202) 653-7652), (Fax in U.S. (202) 653-7687), www.ilo.org; *Yearbook of Labour Statistics 2006.*

GUAM - NATIONAL STATISTICAL OFFICE

Department of Labor, Economic Research Center, PO Box 9970, Tamuning, Guam 96931, Mr. Gary Hiles, (Dial from U.S. (671) 475-7062), (Fax from U.S. (671) 475-7060), www.spc.int/prism/country/gu/stats; Data Center.

GUAM - PRIMARY STATISTICS SOURCES

Department of Labor, Economic Research Center, PO Box 9970, Tamuning, Guam 96931, Mr. Gary Hiles, (Dial from U.S. (671) 475-7062), (Fax from U.S. (671) 475-7060), www.spc.int/prism/country/gu/stats; *Guam Economic Review* and *2004 Guam Statistical Year Book.*

GUAM - AGRICULTURAL MACHINERY

United Nations Statistics Division, New York, NY 10017, (800) 253-9646, Fax: (212) 963-4116, http://unstats.un.org; *Statistical Yearbook.*

GUAM - AGRICULTURE

Economist Intelligence Unit, 111 West 57th Street, New York, NY 10019, (212) 554-0600, Fax: (212) 586-1181, www.eiu.com; *Guam Country Report.*

Euromonitor International, Inc., 224 S. Michigan Avenue, Suite 1500, Chicago, IL 60604, (312) 922-1115, Fax: (312) 922-1157, www.euromonitor.com; *World Marketing Data and Statistics.*

Palgrave Macmillan Ltd., Houndmills, Basingstoke, Hampshire, RG21 6XS, England, (Telephone in U.S. (888) 330-8477), (Fax in U.S. (800) 672-2054), www.palgrave.com; *The Statesman's Yearbook 2008.*

Taylor and Francis Group, An Informa Business, 2 Park Square, Milton Park, Abingdon, Oxford OX14 4RN, United Kingdom, (Dial from U.S. (212) 216-7800), (Fax from U.S. (212) 564-7854), www.tandf.co.uk; *The Europa World Year Book.*

United Nations Conference on Trade and Development (UNCTAD), DC2-1120, United Nations, New York, NY 10017, (212) 963-0027, www.unctad.org; *UNCTAD Commodity Yearbook.*

United Nations Food and Agricultural Organization (FAO), Viale delle Terme di Caracalla, 00100 Rome, Italy, (Dial from U.S. (202) 653-2400), (Fax from U.S. (202) 653 5760), www.fao.org; AQUASTAT; *FAO Production Yearbook 2002;* and *The State of Food and Agriculture (SOFA) 2006.*

United Nations Statistics Division, New York, NY 10017, (800) 253-9646, Fax: (212) 963-4116, http://unstats.un.org; *Asia-Pacific in Figures 2004* and *Statistical Yearbook.*

The World Bank, 1818 H Street, NW, Washington, DC 20433, (202) 473-1000, Fax: (202) 477-6391, www.worldbank.org; *Guam.*

GUAM - AIRLINES

Palgrave Macmillan Ltd., Houndmills, Basingstoke, Hampshire, RG21 6XS, England, (Telephone in U.S. (888) 330-8477), (Fax in U.S. (800) 672-2054), www.palgrave.com; *The Statesman's Yearbook 2008.*

Taylor and Francis Group, An Informa Business, 2 Park Square, Milton Park, Abingdon, Oxford OX14 4RN, United Kingdom, (Dial from U.S. (212) 216-7800), (Fax from U.S. (212) 564-7854), www.tandf.co.uk; *The Europa World Year Book.*

GUAM - AIRPORTS

Central Intelligence Agency, Office of Public Affairs, Washington, DC 20505, (703) 482-0623, Fax: (703) 482-1739, www.cia.gov; *The World Factbook.*

GUAM - ARMED FORCES

Central Intelligence Agency, Office of Public Affairs, Washington, DC 20505, (703) 482-0623, Fax: (703) 482-1739, www.cia.gov; *The World Factbook.*

Euromonitor International, Inc., 224 S. Michigan Avenue, Suite 1500, Chicago, IL 60604, (312) 922-1115, Fax: (312) 922-1157, www.euromonitor.com; *World Marketing Data and Statistics.*

GUAM - BANKS AND BANKING

Euromonitor International, Inc., 224 S. Michigan Avenue, Suite 1500, Chicago, IL 60604, (312) 922-1115, Fax: (312) 922-1157, www.euromonitor.com; *World Marketing Data and Statistics.*

Palgrave Macmillan Ltd., Houndmills, Basingstoke, Hampshire, RG21 6XS, England, (Telephone in U.S. (888) 330-8477), (Fax in U.S. (800) 672-2054), www.palgrave.com; *The Statesman's Yearbook 2008.*

GUAM - BROADCASTING

Central Intelligence Agency, Office of Public Affairs, Washington, DC 20505, (703) 482-0623, Fax: (703) 482-1739, www.cia.gov; *The World Factbook.*

Euromonitor International, Inc., 224 S. Michigan Avenue, Suite 1500, Chicago, IL 60604, (312) 922-1115, Fax: (312) 922-1157, www.euromonitor.com; *World Marketing Data and Statistics.*

Palgrave Macmillan Ltd., Houndmills, Basingstoke, Hampshire, RG21 6XS, England, (Telephone in U.S. (888) 330-8477), (Fax in U.S. (800) 672-2054), www.palgrave.com; *The Statesman's Yearbook 2008.*

UNESCO Institute for Statistics, C.P. 6128 Succursale Centre-Ville, Montreal, Quebec, H3C 3J7 Canada, (Dial from U.S. (514) 343-6880), (Fax from U.S. (514) 343 6882), www.uis.unesco.org; *Statistical Tables.*

GUAM - BUDGET

Central Intelligence Agency, Office of Public Affairs, Washington, DC 20505, (703) 482-0623, Fax: (703) 482-1739, www.cia.gov; *The World Factbook.*

GUAM - CATTLE

See GUAM - LIVESTOCK

GUAM - CHILDBIRTH - STATISTICS

Central Intelligence Agency, Office of Public Affairs, Washington, DC 20505, (703) 482-0623, Fax: (703) 482-1739, www.cia.gov; *The World Factbook.*

Euromonitor International, Inc., 224 S. Michigan Avenue, Suite 1500, Chicago, IL 60604, (312) 922-1115, Fax: (312) 922-1157, www.euromonitor.com; *International Marketing Data and Statistics 2008* and *The World Economic Factbook 2008.*

Palgrave Macmillan Ltd., Houndmills, Basingstoke, Hampshire, RG21 6XS, England, (Telephone in U.S. (888) 330-8477), (Fax in U.S. (800) 672-2054), www.palgrave.com; *The Statesman's Yearbook 2008.*

Taylor and Francis Group, An Informa Business, 2 Park Square, Milton Park, Abingdon, Oxford OX14 4RN, United Kingdom, (Dial from U.S. (212) 216-7800), (Fax from U.S. (212) 564-7854), www.tandf.co.uk; *The Europa World Year Book.*

United Nations Statistics Division, New York, NY 10017, (800) 253-9646, Fax: (212) 963-4116, http://unstats.un.org; *Asia-Pacific in Figures 2004; Demographic Yearbook;* and *Statistical Yearbook.*

GUAM - CLIMATE

Palgrave Macmillan Ltd., Houndmills, Basingstoke, Hampshire, RG21 6XS, England, (Telephone in U.S. (888) 330-8477), (Fax in U.S. (800) 672-2054), www.palgrave.com; *The Statesman's Yearbook 2008.*

GUAM - CLOTHING EXPORTS AND IMPORTS

See GUAM - TEXTILE INDUSTRY

GUAM - COMMERCE

Palgrave Macmillan Ltd., Houndmills, Basingstoke, Hampshire, RG21 6XS, England, (Telephone in U.S. (888) 330-8477), (Fax in U.S. (800) 672-2054), www.palgrave.com; *The Statesman's Yearbook 2008.*

GUAM - COMMODITY EXCHANGES

Commodity Research Bureau, 330 South Wells Street, Suite 612, Chicago, IL 60606-7110, (800) 621-5271, Fax: (312) 939-4135, www.crbtrader.com; *2006 CRB Commodity Yearbook and CD.*

International Monetary Fund (IMF), 700 Nineteenth Street, NW, Washington, DC 20431, (202) 623-7000, Fax: (202) 623-4661, www.imf.org; *IMF Primary Commodity Prices.*

United Nations Food and Agricultural Organization (FAO), Viale delle Terme di Caracalla, 00100 Rome, Italy, (Dial from U.S. (202) 653-2400), (Fax from U.S. (202) 653 5760), www.fao.org; *The State of Food and Agriculture (SOFA) 2006.*

GUAM - CONSTRUCTION INDUSTRY

Palgrave Macmillan Ltd., Houndmills, Basingstoke, Hampshire, RG21 6XS, England, (Telephone in U.S. (888) 330-8477), (Fax in U.S. (800) 672-2054), www.palgrave.com; *The Statesman's Yearbook 2008.*

GUAM - CONSUMER PRICE INDEXES

Taylor and Francis Group, An Informa Business, 2 Park Square, Milton Park, Abingdon, Oxford OX14 4RN, United Kingdom, (Dial from U.S. (212) 216-7800), (Fax from U.S. (212) 564-7854), www.tandf.co.uk; *The Europa World Year Book.*

United Nations Statistics Division, New York, NY 10017, (800) 253-9646, Fax: (212) 963-4116, http://unstats.un.org; *Statistical Yearbook.*

The World Bank, 1818 H Street, NW, Washington, DC 20433, (202) 473-1000, Fax: (202) 477-6391, www.worldbank.org; *Guam.*

GUAM - CONSUMPTION (ECONOMICS)

Secretariat of the Pacific Community (SPC), BP D5, 98848 Noumea Cedex, New Caledonia, www.spc.int/corp; *Selected Pacific Economies - a Statistical Summary (SPESS).*

GUAM - CORN INDUSTRY

See GUAM - CROPS

GUAM - COST AND STANDARD OF LIVING

Secretariat of the Pacific Community (SPC), BP D5, 98848 Noumea Cedex, New Caledonia, www.spc.int/corp; *Selected Pacific Economies - a Statistical Summary (SPESS).*

GUAM - CRIME

Yale University Press, PO Box 209040, New Haven, CT 06520-9040, (203) 432-0960, Fax: (203) 432-0948, http://yalepress.yale.edu/yupbooks; *Violence and Crime in Cross-National Perspective.*

GUAM - CROPS

Palgrave Macmillan Ltd., Houndmills, Basingstoke, Hampshire, RG21 6XS, England, (Telephone in U.S. (888) 330-8477), (Fax in U.S. (800) 672-2054), www.palgrave.com; *The Statesman's Yearbook 2008.*

Taylor and Francis Group, An Informa Business, 2 Park Square, Milton Park, Abingdon, Oxford OX14 4RN, United Kingdom, (Dial from U.S. (212) 216-7800), (Fax from U.S. (212) 564-7854), www.tandf.co.uk; *The Europa World Year Book.*

United Nations Conference on Trade and Development (UNCTAD), DC2-1120, United Nations, New York, NY 10017, (212) 963-0027, www.unctad.org; *UNCTAD Commodity Yearbook.*

United Nations Food and Agricultural Organization (FAO), Viale delle Terme di Caracalla, 00100 Rome, Italy, (Dial from U.S. (202) 653-2400), (Fax from U.S. (202) 653 5760), www.fao.org; *The State of Food and Agriculture (SOFA) 2006.*

GUAM - DAIRY PROCESSING

Palgrave Macmillan Ltd., Houndmills, Basingstoke, Hampshire, RG21 6XS, England, (Telephone in U.S. (888) 330-8477), (Fax in U.S. (800) 672-2054), www.palgrave.com; *The Statesman's Yearbook 2008.*

United Nations Food and Agricultural Organization (FAO), Viale delle Terme di Caracalla, 00100 Rome, Italy, (Dial from U.S. (202) 653-2400), (Fax from U.S. (202) 653 5760), www.fao.org; *The State of Food and Agriculture (SOFA) 2006.*

GUAM - DEATH RATES

See GUAM - MORTALITY

GUAM - DEBTS, EXTERNAL

The World Bank, 1818 H Street, NW, Washington, DC 20433, (202) 473-1000, Fax: (202) 477-6391, www.worldbank.org; *Global Development Finance 2007.*

Worldinformation.com, 2 Market Street, Saffron Walden, Essex CB10 1HZ, United Kingdom, www.worldinformation.com; The World of Information (www.worldinformation.com).

GUAM - DEMOGRAPHY

Euromonitor International, Inc., 224 S. Michigan Avenue, Suite 1500, Chicago, IL 60604, (312) 922-1115, Fax: (312) 922-1157, www.euromonitor.com; *International Marketing Data and Statistics 2008; The World Economic Factbook 2008;* and *World Marketing Data and Statistics.*

United Nations Statistics Division, New York, NY 10017, (800) 253-9646, Fax: (212) 963-4116, http://unstats.un.org; *Asia-Pacific in Figures 2004.*

The World Bank, 1818 H Street, NW, Washington, DC 20433, (202) 473-1000, Fax: (202) 477-6391, www.worldbank.org; *Guam.*

GUAM - DIVORCE

United Nations Statistics Division, New York, NY 10017, (800) 253-9646, Fax: (212) 963-4116, http://unstats.un.org; *Demographic Yearbook* and *Statistical Yearbook.*

GUAM - ECONOMIC CONDITIONS

Center for International Business Education Research (CIBER), Columbia Business School and School of International and Public Affairs, Uris Hall, Room 212, 3022 Broadway, New York, NY 10027-6902, Mr. Joshua Safier, (212) 854-4750, Fax: (212) 222-9821, www.columbia.edu/cu/ciber/; Datastream International.

Central Intelligence Agency, Office of Public Affairs, Washington, DC 20505, (703) 482-0623, Fax: (703) 482-1739, www.cia.gov; *The World Factbook.*

DSI Data Service Information, Xantener Strasse 51a, D-47495 Rheinberg, Germany, www.dsidata.com; *Campus Solution.*

Dun and Bradstreet (DB) Corporation, 103 JFK Parkway, Short Hills, NJ 07078, (973) 921-5500, www.dnb.com; *Country Report.*

Economist Intelligence Unit, 111 West 57th Street, New York, NY 10019, (212) 554-0600, Fax: (212) 586-1181, www.eiu.com; *Guam Country Report.*

Euromonitor International, Inc., 224 S. Michigan Avenue, Suite 1500, Chicago, IL 60604, (312) 922-1115, Fax: (312) 922-1157, www.euromonitor.com; *The World Economic Factbook 2008* and *World Marketing Data and Statistics.*

International Monetary Fund (IMF), 700 Nineteenth Street, NW, Washington, DC 20431, (202) 623-7000, Fax: (202) 623-4661, www.imf.org; *World Economic Outlook Reports.*

Palgrave Macmillan Ltd., Houndmills, Basingstoke, Hampshire, RG21 6XS, England, (Telephone in U.S. (888) 330-8477), (Fax in U.S. (800) 672-2054), www.palgrave.com; *The Statesman's Yearbook 2008.*

Secretariat of the Pacific Community (SPC), BP D5, 98848 Noumea Cedex, New Caledonia, www.spc.int/corp; PRISM (Pacific Regional Information System).

Taylor and Francis Group, An Informa Business, 2 Park Square, Milton Park, Abingdon, Oxford OX14 4RN, United Kingdom, (Dial from U.S. (212) 216-7800), (Fax from U.S. (212) 564-7854), www.tandf.co.uk; *The Europa World Year Book.*

United Nations Statistics Division, New York, NY 10017, (800) 253-9646, Fax: (212) 963-4116, http://unstats.un.org; *World Statistics Pocketbook.*

The World Bank, 1818 H Street, NW, Washington, DC 20433, (202) 473-1000, Fax: (202) 477-6391, www.worldbank.org; *Global Economic Monitor (GEM); Global Economic Prospects 2008; Guam;* and *The World Bank Atlas 2003-2004.*

GUAM - EDUCATION

Euromonitor International, Inc., 224 S. Michigan Avenue, Suite 1500, Chicago, IL 60604, (312) 922-1115, Fax: (312) 922-1157, www.euromonitor.com; *International Marketing Data and Statistics 2008* and *World Marketing Data and Statistics.*

Palgrave Macmillan Ltd., Houndmills, Basingstoke, Hampshire, RG21 6XS, England, (Telephone in U.S. (888) 330-8477), (Fax in U.S. (800) 672-2054), www.palgrave.com; *The Statesman's Yearbook 2008.*

Taylor and Francis Group, An Informa Business, 2 Park Square, Milton Park, Abingdon, Oxford OX14 4RN, United Kingdom, (Dial from U.S. (212) 216-7800), (Fax from U.S. (212) 564-7854), www.tandf.co.uk; *The Europa World Year Book.*

UNESCO Institute for Statistics, C.P. 6128 Succursale Centre-Ville, Montreal, Quebec, H3C 3J7 Canada, (Dial from U.S. (514) 343-6880), (Fax from U.S. (514) 343 6882), www.uis.unesco.org; *Statistical Tables.*

United Nations Statistics Division, New York, NY 10017, (800) 253-9646, Fax: (212) 963-4116, http://unstats.un.org; *Asia-Pacific in Figures 2004.*

The World Bank, 1818 H Street, NW, Washington, DC 20433, (202) 473-1000, Fax: (202) 477-6391, www.worldbank.org; *Guam.*

GUAM - ELECTRICITY

United Nations Statistics Division, New York, NY 10017, (800) 253-9646, Fax: (212) 963-4116, http://unstats.un.org; *Statistical Yearbook.*

GUAM - EMPLOYMENT

Euromonitor International, Inc., 224 S. Michigan Avenue, Suite 1500, Chicago, IL 60604, (312) 922-1115, Fax: (312) 922-1157, www.euromonitor.com; *International Marketing Data and Statistics 2008.*

International Labour Office, I.L.O. Publications, 4 route des Morillons, CH-1211 Geneva 22, Switzerland, (Telephone in U.S. (202) 653-7652), (Fax in U.S. (202) 653-7687), www.ilo.org; *Yearbook of Labour Statistics 2006.*

U.S. Department of Energy (DOE), Energy Information Administration (EIA), 1000 Independence Avenue, SW, Washington, DC 20585, (202) 586-8800, www.eia.doe.gov; *International Energy Annual 2004* and *International Energy Outlook 2006.*

United Nations Statistics Division, New York, NY 10017, (800) 253-9646, Fax: (212) 963-4116, http://unstats.un.org; *Asia-Pacific in Figures 2004.*

The World Bank, 1818 H Street, NW, Washington, DC 20433, (202) 473-1000, Fax: (202) 477-6391, www.worldbank.org; *Guam.*

GUAM - ENVIRONMENTAL CONDITIONS

DSI Data Service Information, Xantener Strasse 51a, D-47495 Rheinberg, Germany, www.dsidata.com; *Campus Solution* and *DSI's Global Environmental Database.*

Economist Intelligence Unit, 111 West 57th Street, New York, NY 10019, (212) 554-0600, Fax: (212) 586-1181, www.eiu.com; *Guam Country Report.*

United Nations Statistics Division, New York, NY 10017, (800) 253-9646, Fax: (212) 963-4116, http://unstats.un.org; *World Statistics Pocketbook.*

GUAM - EXPORTS

Central Intelligence Agency, Office of Public Affairs, Washington, DC 20505, (703) 482-0623, Fax: (703) 482-1739, www.cia.gov; *The World Factbook.*

Economist Intelligence Unit, 111 West 57th Street, New York, NY 10019, (212) 554-0600, Fax: (212) 586-1181, www.eiu.com; *Guam Country Report.*

Euromonitor International, Inc., 224 S. Michigan Avenue, Suite 1500, Chicago, IL 60604, (312) 922-1115, Fax: (312) 922-1157, www.euromonitor.com; *International Marketing Data and Statistics 2008* and *The World Economic Factbook 2008.*

International Monetary Fund (IMF), 700 Nineteenth Street, NW, Washington, DC 20431, (202) 623-7000, Fax: (202) 623-4661, www.imf.org; *Direction of Trade Statistics Yearbook 2007.*

Secretariat of the Pacific Community (SPC), BP D5, 98848 Noumea Cedex, New Caledonia, www.spc.int/corp; *Selected Pacific Economies - a Statistical Summary (SPESS).*

United Nations Food and Agricultural Organization (FAO), Viale delle Terme di Caracalla, 00100 Rome, Italy, (Dial from U.S. (202) 653-2400), (Fax from U.S. (202) 653 5760), www.fao.org; *The State of Food and Agriculture (SOFA) 2006.*

Worldinformation.com, 2 Market Street, Saffron Walden, Essex CB10 1HZ, United Kingdom, www.worldinformation.com; The World of Information (www.worldinformation.com).

GUAM - FERTILITY, HUMAN

Central Intelligence Agency, Office of Public Affairs, Washington, DC 20505, (703) 482-0623, Fax: (703) 482-1739, www.cia.gov; *The World Factbook.*

United Nations Statistics Division, New York, NY 10017, (800) 253-9646, Fax: (212) 963-4116, http://unstats.un.org; *Demographic Yearbook.*

The World Bank, 1818 H Street, NW, Washington, DC 20433, (202) 473-1000, Fax: (202) 477-6391, www.worldbank.org; *The World Bank Atlas 2003-2004.*

GUAM - FERTILIZER INDUSTRY

United Nations Food and Agricultural Organization (FAO), Viale delle Terme di Caracalla, 00100 Rome, Italy, (Dial from U.S. (202) 653-2400), (Fax from U.S. (202) 653 5760), www.fao.org; *The State of Food and Agriculture (SOFA) 2006.*

GUAM - FETAL MORTALITY

See GUAM - MORTALITY

GUAM - FINANCE

United Nations Statistics Division, New York, NY 10017, (800) 253-9646, Fax: (212) 963-4116, http://unstats.un.org; *Asia-Pacific in Figures 2004.*

The World Bank, 1818 H Street, NW, Washington, DC 20433, (202) 473-1000, Fax: (202) 477-6391, www.worldbank.org; *Guam.*

GUAM - FINANCE, PUBLIC

Bernan Essential Government Publications, 4611-F Assembly Drive, Lanham MD, 20706-4391, (301) 459-2255, Fax: (800) 865-3450, www.bernan.com; *National Accounts Statistics.*

Economist Intelligence Unit, 111 West 57th Street, New York, NY 10019, (212) 554-0600, Fax: (212) 586-1181, www.eiu.com; *Guam Country Report.*

International Monetary Fund (IMF), 700 Nineteenth Street, NW, Washington, DC 20431, (202) 623-7000, Fax: (202) 623-4661, www.imf.org; *International Financial Statistics* and *International Financial Statistics Online Service.*

Palgrave Macmillan Ltd., Houndmills, Basingstoke, Hampshire, RG21 6XS, England, (Telephone in U.S. (888) 330-8477), (Fax in U.S. (800) 672-2054), www.palgrave.com; *The Statesman's Yearbook 2008.*

Taylor and Francis Group, An Informa Business, 2 Park Square, Milton Park, Abingdon, Oxford OX14 4RN, United Kingdom, (Dial from U.S. (212) 216-7800), (Fax from U.S. (212) 564-7854), www.tandf.co.uk; *The Europa World Year Book.*

The World Bank, 1818 H Street, NW, Washington, DC 20433, (202) 473-1000, Fax: (202) 477-6391, www.worldbank.org; *Guam.*

GUAM - FISHERIES

Palgrave Macmillan Ltd., Houndmills, Basingstoke, Hampshire, RG21 6XS, England, (Telephone in U.S. (888) 330-8477), (Fax in U.S. (800) 672-2054), www.palgrave.com; *The Statesman's Yearbook 2008.*

Taylor and Francis Group, An Informa Business, 2 Park Square, Milton Park, Abingdon, Oxford OX14 4RN, United Kingdom, (Dial from U.S. (212) 216-7800), (Fax from U.S. (212) 564-7854), www.tandf.co.uk; *The Europa World Year Book.*

United Nations Conference on Trade and Development (UNCTAD), DC2-1120, United Nations, New York, NY 10017, (212) 963-0027, www.unctad.org; *UNCTAD Commodity Yearbook.*

United Nations Food and Agricultural Organization (FAO), Viale delle Terme di Caracalla, 00100 Rome, Italy, (Dial from U.S. (202) 653-2400), (Fax from U.S. (202) 653 5760), www.fao.org; *FAO Yearbook of Fishery Statistics;* Fishery Databases; FISHSTAT Database. Subjects covered include: Aquaculture production, capture production, fishery commodities; and *The State of Food and Agriculture (SOFA) 2006.*

The World Bank, 1818 H Street, NW, Washington, DC 20433, (202) 473-1000, Fax: (202) 477-6391, www.worldbank.org; *Guam.*

GUAM - FOOD

Secretariat of the Pacific Community (SPC), BP D5, 98848 Noumea Cedex, New Caledonia, www.spc.int/corp; *Selected Pacific Economies - a Statistical Summary (SPESS).*

United Nations Conference on Trade and Development (UNCTAD), DC2-1120, United Nations, New York, NY 10017, (212) 963-0027, www.unctad.org; *UNCTAD Commodity Yearbook.*

United Nations Food and Agricultural Organization (FAO), Viale delle Terme di Caracalla, 00100 Rome, Italy, (Dial from U.S. (202) 653-2400), (Fax from U.S. (202) 653 5760), www.fao.org; *FAO Production Yearbook 2002* and *The State of Food and Agriculture (SOFA) 2006.*

GUAM - FOREIGN EXCHANGE RATES

Central Intelligence Agency, Office of Public Affairs, Washington, DC 20505, (703) 482-0623, Fax: (703) 482-1739, www.cia.gov; *The World Factbook.*

Euromonitor International, Inc., 224 S. Michigan Avenue, Suite 1500, Chicago, IL 60604, (312) 922-1115, Fax: (312) 922-1157, www.euromonitor.com; *International Marketing Data and Statistics 2008* and *The World Economic Factbook 2008.*

Taylor and Francis Group, An Informa Business, 2 Park Square, Milton Park, Abingdon, Oxford OX14 4RN, United Kingdom, (Dial from U.S. (212) 216-7800), (Fax from U.S. (212) 564-7854), www.tandf.co.uk; *The Europa World Year Book.*

United Nations Statistics Division, New York, NY 10017, (800) 253-9646, Fax: (212) 963-4116, http://unstats.un.org; *World Statistics Pocketbook.*

Worldinformation.com, 2 Market Street, Saffron Walden, Essex CB10 1HZ, United Kingdom, www.worldinformation.com; The World of Information (www.worldinformation.com).

GUAM - FORESTS AND FORESTRY

UNESCO Institute for Statistics, C.P. 6128 Succursale Centre-Ville, Montreal, Quebec, H3C 3J7 Canada, (Dial from U.S. (514) 343-6880), (Fax from U.S. (514) 343 6882), www.uis.unesco.org; *Statistical Tables.*

United Nations Conference on Trade and Development (UNCTAD), DC2-1120, United Nations, New York, NY 10017, (212) 963-0027, www.unctad.org; *UNCTAD Commodity Yearbook.*

United Nations Food and Agricultural Organization (FAO), Viale delle Terme di Caracalla, 00100 Rome, Italy, (Dial from U.S. (202) 653-2400), (Fax from U.S. (202) 653 5760), www.fao.org; *The State of Food and Agriculture (SOFA) 2006.*

United Nations Statistics Division, New York, NY 10017, (800) 253-9646, Fax: (212) 963-4116, http://unstats.un.org; *Statistical Yearbook.*

The World Bank, 1818 H Street, NW, Washington, DC 20433, (202) 473-1000, Fax: (202) 477-6391, www.worldbank.org; *Guam.*

GUAM - GROSS DOMESTIC PRODUCT

Economist Intelligence Unit, 111 West 57th Street, New York, NY 10019, (212) 554-0600, Fax: (212) 586-1181, www.eiu.com; *Guam Country Report.*

Euromonitor International, Inc., 224 S. Michigan Avenue, Suite 1500, Chicago, IL 60604, (312) 922-1115, Fax: (312) 922-1157, www.euromonitor.com; *International Marketing Data and Statistics 2008* and *The World Economic Factbook 2008.*

GUAM - GROSS NATIONAL PRODUCT

The World Bank, 1818 H Street, NW, Washington, DC 20433, (202) 473-1000, Fax: (202) 477-6391, www.worldbank.org; *The World Bank Atlas 2003-2004.*

Worldinformation.com, 2 Market Street, Saffron Walden, Essex CB10 1HZ, United Kingdom, www.worldinformation.com; The World of Information (www.worldinformation.com).

GUAM - HIDES AND SKINS INDUSTRY

United Nations Food and Agricultural Organization (FAO), Viale delle Terme di Caracalla, 00100 Rome, Italy, (Dial from U.S. (202) 653-2400), (Fax from U.S. (202) 653 5760), www.fao.org; *FAO Production Yearbook 2002.*

GUAM - HOURS OF LABOR

International Labour Office, I.L.O. Publications, 4 route des Morillons, CH-1211 Geneva 22, Switzerland, (Telephone in U.S. (202) 653-7652), (Fax in U.S. (202) 653-7687), www.ilo.org; *Yearbook of Labour Statistics 2006.*

GUAM - HOUSING

Department of Labor, Economic Research Center, PO Box 9970, Tamuning, Guam 96931, Mr. Gary Hiles, (Dial from U.S. (671) 475-7062), (Fax from U.S. (671) 475-7060), www.spc.int/prism/country/gu/stats; *Guam: 2000 Census of Population and Housing.*

Euromonitor International, Inc., 224 S. Michigan Avenue, Suite 1500, Chicago, IL 60604, (312) 922-1115, Fax: (312) 922-1157, www.euromonitor.com; *World Marketing Data and Statistics.*

Secretariat of the Pacific Community (SPC), BP D5, 98848 Noumea Cedex, New Caledonia, www.spc.int/corp; *Selected Pacific Economies - a Statistical Summary (SPESS).*

GUAM - ILLITERATE PERSONS

Euromonitor International, Inc., 224 S. Michigan Avenue, Suite 1500, Chicago, IL 60604, (312) 922-1115, Fax: (312) 922-1157, www.euromonitor.com; *The World Economic Factbook 2008.*

United Nations Statistics Division, New York, NY 10017, (800) 253-9646, Fax: (212) 963-4116, http://unstats.un.org; *Asia-Pacific in Figures 2004.*

GUAM - IMPORTS

Central Intelligence Agency, Office of Public Affairs, Washington, DC 20505, (703) 482-0623, Fax: (703) 482-1739, www.cia.gov; *The World Factbook.*

Economist Intelligence Unit, 111 West 57th Street, New York, NY 10019, (212) 554-0600, Fax: (212) 586-1181, www.eiu.com; *Guam Country Report.*

Euromonitor International, Inc., 224 S. Michigan Avenue, Suite 1500, Chicago, IL 60604, (312) 922-1115, Fax: (312) 922-1157, www.euromonitor.com; *International Marketing Data and Statistics 2008* and *The World Economic Factbook 2008.*

International Monetary Fund (IMF), 700 Nineteenth Street, NW, Washington, DC 20431, (202) 623-

7000, Fax: (202) 623-4661, www.imf.org; *Direction of Trade Statistics Yearbook 2007.*

Secretariat of the Pacific Community (SPC), BP D5, 98848 Noumea Cedex, New Caledonia, www.spc.int/corp; *Selected Pacific Economies - a Statistical Summary (SPESS).*

United Nations Food and Agricultural Organization (FAO), Viale delle Terme di Caracalla, 00100 Rome, Italy, (Dial from U.S. (202) 653-2400), (Fax from U.S. (202) 653 5760), www.fao.org; *The State of Food and Agriculture (SOFA) 2006.*

Worldinformation.com, 2 Market Street, Saffron Walden, Essex CB10 1HZ, United Kingdom, www.worldinformation.com; The World of Information (www.worldinformation.com).

GUAM - INDUSTRIES

Central Intelligence Agency, Office of Public Affairs, Washington, DC 20505, (703) 482-0623, Fax: (703) 482-1739, www.cia.gov; *The World Factbook.*

Economist Intelligence Unit, 111 West 57th Street, New York, NY 10019, (212) 554-0600, Fax: (212) 586-1181, www.eiu.com; *Guam Country Report.*

Euromonitor International, Inc., 224 S. Michigan Avenue, Suite 1500, Chicago, IL 60604, (312) 922-1115, Fax: (312) 922-1157, www.euromonitor.com; *The World Economic Factbook 2008* and *World Marketing Data and Statistics.*

International Labour Office, I.L.O. Publications, 4 route des Morillons, CH-1211 Geneva 22, Switzerland, (Telephone in U.S. (202) 653-7652), (Fax in U.S. (202) 653-7687), www.ilo.org; *Yearbook of Labour Statistics 2006.*

Palgrave Macmillan Ltd., Houndmills, Basingstoke, Hampshire, RG21 6XS, England, (Telephone in U.S. (888) 330-8477), (Fax in U.S. (800) 672-2054), www.palgrave.com; *The Statesman's Yearbook 2008.*

United Nations Industrial Development Organization (UNIDO), 1 United Nations Plaza, New York, NY 10017, (212) 963 6890, Fax: (212) 963-7904, http://unido.org; Industrial Statistics Database 2008 (INDSTAT) and *The International Yearbook of Industrial Statistics 2008.*

United Nations Statistics Division, New York, NY 10017, (800) 253-9646, Fax: (212) 963-4116, http://unstats.un.org; *Asia-Pacific in Figures 2004.*

The World Bank, 1818 H Street, NW, Washington, DC 20433, (202) 473-1000, Fax: (202) 477-6391, www.worldbank.org; *Guam.*

GUAM - INFANT AND MATERNAL MORTALITY

See GUAM - MORTALITY

GUAM - INTERNATIONAL TRADE

Economist Intelligence Unit, 111 West 57th Street, New York, NY 10019, (212) 554-0600, Fax: (212) 586-1181, www.eiu.com; *Guam Country Report.*

Euromonitor International, Inc., 224 S. Michigan Avenue, Suite 1500, Chicago, IL 60604, (312) 922-1115, Fax: (312) 922-1157, www.euromonitor.com; *World Marketing Data and Statistics.*

Secretariat of the Pacific Community (SPC), BP D5, 98848 Noumea Cedex, New Caledonia, www.spc.int/corp; *Selected Pacific Economies - a Statistical Summary (SPESS).*

Taylor and Francis Group, An Informa Business, 2 Park Square, Milton Park, Abingdon, Oxford OX14 4RN, United Kingdom, (Dial from U.S. (212) 216-7800), (Fax from U.S. (212) 564-7854), www.tandf.co.uk; *The Europa World Year Book.*

United Nations Conference on Trade and Development (UNCTAD), DC2-1120, United Nations, New York, NY 10017, (212) 963-0027, www.unctad.org; *UNCTAD Commodity Yearbook.*

United Nations Food and Agricultural Organization (FAO), Viale delle Terme di Caracalla, 00100 Rome, Italy, (Dial from U.S. (202) 653-2400), (Fax from U.S. (202) 653 5760), www.fao.org; *FAO Trade Yearbook* and *The State of Food and Agriculture (SOFA) 2006.*

United Nations Statistics Division, New York, NY 10017, (800) 253-9646, Fax: (212) 963-4116, http://unstats.un.org; *Asia-Pacific in Figures 2004* and *Statistical Yearbook.*

The World Bank, 1818 H Street, NW, Washington, DC 20433, (202) 473-1000, Fax: (202) 477-6391, www.worldbank.org; *Guam.*

World Trade Organization (WTO), Centre William Rappard, Rue de Lausanne 154, CH-1211 Geneva 21, Switzerland, www.wto.org; *International Trade Statistics 2006.*

GUAM - INTERNET USERS

International Telecommunication Union (ITU), Place des Nations, 1211 Geneva 20, Switzerland, www.itu.int; *World Telecommunication/ICT Indicators Database on CD-ROM; World Telecommunication/ICT Indicators Database Online;* and *Yearbook of Statistics - Telecommunication Services (Chronological Time Series 1997-2006).*

The World Bank, 1818 H Street, NW, Washington, DC 20433, (202) 473-1000, Fax: (202) 477-6391, www.worldbank.org; *Guam.*

GUAM - LABOR

Central Intelligence Agency, Office of Public Affairs, Washington, DC 20505, (703) 482-0623, Fax: (703) 482-1739, www.cia.gov; *The World Factbook.*

Euromonitor International, Inc., 224 S. Michigan Avenue, Suite 1500, Chicago, IL 60604, (312) 922-1115, Fax: (312) 922-1157, www.euromonitor.com; *International Marketing Data and Statistics 2008* and *World Marketing Data and Statistics.*

International Labour Office, I.L.O. Publications, 4 route des Morillons, CH-1211 Geneva 22, Switzerland, (Telephone in U.S. (202) 653-7652), (Fax in U.S. (202) 653-7687), www.ilo.org; *Yearbook of Labour Statistics 2006.*

Palgrave Macmillan Ltd., Houndmills, Basingstoke, Hampshire, RG21 6XS, England, (Telephone in U.S. (888) 330-8477), (Fax in U.S. (800) 672-2054), www.palgrave.com; *The Statesman's Yearbook 2008.*

Taylor and Francis Group, An Informa Business, 2 Park Square, Milton Park, Abingdon, Oxford OX14 4RN, United Kingdom, (Dial from U.S. (212) 216-7800), (Fax from U.S. (212) 564-7854), www.tandf.co.uk; *The Europa World Year Book.*

United Nations Food and Agricultural Organization (FAO), Viale delle Terme di Caracalla, 00100 Rome, Italy, (Dial from U.S. (202) 653-2400), (Fax from U.S. (202) 653 5760), www.fao.org; *The State of Food and Agriculture (SOFA) 2006.*

The World Bank, 1818 H Street, NW, Washington, DC 20433, (202) 473-1000, Fax: (202) 477-6391, www.worldbank.org; *The World Bank Atlas 2003-2004.*

GUAM - LAND USE

Central Intelligence Agency, Office of Public Affairs, Washington, DC 20505, (703) 482-0623, Fax: (703) 482-1739, www.cia.gov; *The World Factbook.*

Euromonitor International, Inc., 224 S. Michigan Avenue, Suite 1500, Chicago, IL 60604, (312) 922-1115, Fax: (312) 922-1157, www.euromonitor.com; *International Marketing Data and Statistics 2008.*

United Nations Food and Agricultural Organization (FAO), Viale delle Terme di Caracalla, 00100 Rome, Italy, (Dial from U.S. (202) 653-2400), (Fax from U.S. (202) 653 5760), www.fao.org; *FAO Production Yearbook 2002.*

GUAM - LIFE EXPECTANCY

Central Intelligence Agency, Office of Public Affairs, Washington, DC 20505, (703) 482-0623, Fax: (703) 482-1739, www.cia.gov; *The World Factbook.*

Euromonitor International, Inc., 224 S. Michigan Avenue, Suite 1500, Chicago, IL 60604, (312) 922-1115, Fax: (312) 922-1157, www.euromonitor.com; *The World Economic Factbook 2008.*

United Nations Statistics Division, New York, NY 10017, (800) 253-9646, Fax: (212) 963-4116, http://unstats.un.org; *Asia-Pacific in Figures 2004* and *World Statistics Pocketbook.*

The World Bank, 1818 H Street, NW, Washington, DC 20433, (202) 473-1000, Fax: (202) 477-6391, www.worldbank.org; *The World Bank Atlas 2003-2004.*

GUAM - LITERACY

Euromonitor International, Inc., 224 S. Michigan Avenue, Suite 1500, Chicago, IL 60604, (312) 922-1115, Fax: (312) 922-1157, www.euromonitor.com; *World Marketing Data and Statistics.*

GUAM - LIVESTOCK

Palgrave Macmillan Ltd., Houndmills, Basingstoke, Hampshire, RG21 6XS, England, (Telephone in U.S. (888) 330-8477), (Fax in U.S. (800) 672-2054), www.palgrave.com; *The Statesman's Yearbook 2008.*

Taylor and Francis Group, An Informa Business, 2 Park Square, Milton Park, Abingdon, Oxford OX14 4RN, United Kingdom, (Dial from U.S. (212) 216-7800), (Fax from U.S. (212) 564-7854), www.tandf.co.uk; *The Europa World Year Book.*

United Nations Conference on Trade and Development (UNCTAD), DC2-1120, United Nations, New York, NY 10017, (212) 963-0027, www.unctad.org; *UNCTAD Commodity Yearbook.*

United Nations Food and Agricultural Organization (FAO), Viale delle Terme di Caracalla, 00100 Rome, Italy, (Dial from U.S. (202) 653-2400), (Fax from U.S. (202) 653 5760), www.fao.org; *FAO Production Yearbook 2002* and *The State of Food and Agriculture (SOFA) 2006.*

United Nations Statistics Division, New York, NY 10017, (800) 253-9646, Fax: (212) 963-4116, http://unstats.un.org; *Statistical Yearbook.*

GUAM - MARRIAGE

Taylor and Francis Group, An Informa Business, 2 Park Square, Milton Park, Abingdon, Oxford OX14 4RN, United Kingdom, (Dial from U.S. (212) 216-7800), (Fax from U.S. (212) 564-7854), www.tandf.co.uk; *The Europa World Year Book.*

United Nations Statistics Division, New York, NY 10017, (800) 253-9646, Fax: (212) 963-4116, http://unstats.un.org; *Demographic Yearbook* and *Statistical Yearbook.*

GUAM - MEAT PRODUCTION

See GUAM - LIVESTOCK

GUAM - MINERAL INDUSTRIES

United Nations Conference on Trade and Development (UNCTAD), DC2-1120, United Nations, New York, NY 10017, (212) 963-0027, www.unctad.org; *UNCTAD Commodity Yearbook.*

GUAM - MONEY SUPPLY

Economist Intelligence Unit, 111 West 57th Street, New York, NY 10019, (212) 554-0600, Fax: (212) 586-1181, www.eiu.com; *Guam Country Report.*

The World Bank, 1818 H Street, NW, Washington, DC 20433, (202) 473-1000, Fax: (202) 477-6391, www.worldbank.org; *Guam.*

GUAM - MORTALITY

Central Intelligence Agency, Office of Public Affairs, Washington, DC 20505, (703) 482-0623, Fax: (703) 482-1739, www.cia.gov; *The World Factbook.*

Euromonitor International, Inc., 224 S. Michigan Avenue, Suite 1500, Chicago, IL 60604, (312) 922-1115, Fax: (312) 922-1157, www.euromonitor.com; *International Marketing Data and Statistics 2008* and *The World Economic Factbook 2008.*

Palgrave Macmillan Ltd., Houndmills, Basingstoke, Hampshire, RG21 6XS, England, (Telephone in U.S. (888) 330-8477), (Fax in U.S. (800) 672-2054), www.palgrave.com; *The Statesman's Yearbook 2008.*

Taylor and Francis Group, An Informa Business, 2 Park Square, Milton Park, Abingdon, Oxford OX14

4RN, United Kingdom, (Dial from U.S. (212) 216-7800), (Fax from U.S. (212) 564-7854), www.tandf.co.uk; *The Europa World Year Book.*

United Nations Statistics Division, New York, NY 10017, (800) 253-9646, Fax: (212) 963-4116, http://unstats.un.org; *Asia-Pacific in Figures 2004; Demographic Yearbook; Statistical Yearbook;* and *World Statistics Pocketbook.*

The World Bank, 1818 H Street, NW, Washington, DC 20433, (202) 473-1000, Fax: (202) 477-6391, www.worldbank.org; *The World Bank Atlas 2003-2004.*

World Health Organization (WHO), Avenue Appia 20, 1211 Geneve 27, Switzerland, (Telephone in U.S. (212) 331-9081), www.who.int; The WHO Global Atlas of Infectious Diseases and *World Health Report 2006.*

GUAM - MOTION PICTURES

United Nations Statistics Division, New York, NY 10017, (800) 253-9646, Fax: (212) 963-4116, http://unstats.un.org; *Statistical Yearbook.*

GUAM - MOTOR VEHICLES

Taylor and Francis Group, An Informa Business, 2 Park Square, Milton Park, Abingdon, Oxford OX14 4RN, United Kingdom, (Dial from U.S. (212) 216-7800), (Fax from U.S. (212) 564-7854), www.tandf.co.uk; *The Europa World Year Book.*

United Nations Statistics Division, New York, NY 10017, (800) 253-9646, Fax: (212) 963-4116, http://unstats.un.org; *Statistical Yearbook.*

GUAM - NUTRITION

United Nations Food and Agricultural Organization (FAO), Viale delle Terme di Caracalla, 00100 Rome, Italy, (Dial from U.S. (202) 653-2400), (Fax from U.S. (202) 653 5760), www.fao.org; *The State of Food and Agriculture (SOFA) 2006.*

GUAM - PESTICIDES

United Nations Food and Agricultural Organization (FAO), Viale delle Terme di Caracalla, 00100 Rome, Italy, (Dial from U.S. (202) 653-2400), (Fax from U.S. (202) 653 5760), www.fao.org; *The State of Food and Agriculture (SOFA) 2006.*

GUAM - PETROLEUM INDUSTRY AND TRADE

PennWell Corporation, 1421 South Sheridan Road, Tulsa, OK 74112, (918) 835-3161, www.pennwell.com; *International Petroleum Encyclopedia 2007.*

U.S. Department of Energy (DOE), Energy Information Administration (EIA), 1000 Independence Avenue, SW, Washington, DC 20585, (202) 586-8800, www.eia.doe.gov; *International Energy Annual 2004* and *International Energy Outlook 2006.*

United Nations Conference on Trade and Development (UNCTAD), DC2-1120, United Nations, New York, NY 10017, (212) 963-0027, www.unctad.org; *UNCTAD Commodity Yearbook.*

United Nations Food and Agricultural Organization (FAO), Viale delle Terme di Caracalla, 00100 Rome, Italy, (Dial from U.S. (202) 653-2400), (Fax from U.S. (202) 653 5760), www.fao.org; *The State of Food and Agriculture (SOFA) 2006.*

United Nations Statistics Division, New York, NY 10017, (800) 253-9646, Fax: (212) 963-4116, http://unstats.un.org; *Statistical Yearbook.*

GUAM - POLITICAL SCIENCE

Central Intelligence Agency, Office of Public Affairs, Washington, DC 20505, (703) 482-0623, Fax: (703) 482-1739, www.cia.gov; *The World Factbook.*

Palgrave Macmillan Ltd., Houndmills, Basingstoke, Hampshire, RG21 6XS, England, (Telephone in U.S. (888) 330-8477), (Fax in U.S. (800) 672-2054), www.palgrave.com; *The Statesman's Yearbook 2008.*

Taylor and Francis Group, An Informa Business, 2 Park Square, Milton Park, Abingdon, Oxford OX14 4RN, United Kingdom, (Dial from U.S. (212) 216-7800), (Fax from U.S. (212) 564-7854), www.tandf.co.uk; *The Europa World Year Book.*

United Nations Statistics Division, New York, NY 10017, (800) 253-9646, Fax: (212) 963-4116, http://unstats.un.org; *Asia-Pacific in Figures 2004.*

GUAM - POPULATION

Central Intelligence Agency, Office of Public Affairs, Washington, DC 20505, (703) 482-0623, Fax: (703) 482-1739, www.cia.gov; *The World Factbook.*

Department of Labor, Economic Research Center, PO Box 9970, Tamuning, Guam 96931, Mr. Gary Hiles, (Dial from U.S. (671) 475-7062), (Fax from U.S. (671) 475-7060), www.spc.int/prism/country/gu/stats; *Guam: 2000 Census of Population and Housing.*

Economist Intelligence Unit, 111 West 57th Street, New York, NY 10019, (212) 554-0600, Fax: (212) 586-1181, www.eiu.com; *Guam Country Report.*

Euromonitor International, Inc., 224 S. Michigan Avenue, Suite 1500, Chicago, IL 60604, (312) 922-1115, Fax: (312) 922-1157, www.euromonitor.com; *International Marketing Data and Statistics 2008* and *The World Economic Factbook 2008.*

International Labour Office, I.L.O. Publications, 4 route des Morillons, CH-1211 Geneva 22, Switzerland, (Telephone in U.S. (202) 653-7652), (Fax in U.S. (202) 653-7687), www.ilo.org; *Yearbook of Labour Statistics 2006.*

Palgrave Macmillan Ltd., Houndmills, Basingstoke, Hampshire, RG21 6XS, England, (Telephone in U.S. (888) 330-8477), (Fax in U.S. (800) 672-2054), www.palgrave.com; *The Statesman's Yearbook 2008.*

Taylor and Francis Group, An Informa Business, 2 Park Square, Milton Park, Abingdon, Oxford OX14 4RN, United Kingdom, (Dial from U.S. (212) 216-7800), (Fax from U.S. (212) 564-7854), www.tandf.co.uk; *The Europa World Year Book.*

United Nations Food and Agricultural Organization (FAO), Viale delle Terme di Caracalla, 00100 Rome, Italy, (Dial from U.S. (202) 653-2400), (Fax from U.S. (202) 653 5760), www.fao.org; *FAO Production Yearbook 2002.*

United Nations Statistics Division, New York, NY 10017, (800) 253-9646, Fax: (212) 963-4116, http://unstats.un.org; *Asia-Pacific in Figures 2004; Demographic Yearbook; Statistical Yearbook;* and *World Statistics Pocketbook.*

The World Bank, 1818 H Street, NW, Washington, DC 20433, (202) 473-1000, Fax: (202) 477-6391, www.worldbank.org; *Guam.*

Worldinformation.com, 2 Market Street, Saffron Walden, Essex CB10 1HZ, United Kingdom, www.worldinformation.com; The World of Information (www.worldinformation.com).

GUAM - POPULATION DENSITY

Central Intelligence Agency, Office of Public Affairs, Washington, DC 20505, (703) 482-0623, Fax: (703) 482-1739, www.cia.gov; *The World Factbook.*

Euromonitor International, Inc., 224 S. Michigan Avenue, Suite 1500, Chicago, IL 60604, (312) 922-1115, Fax: (312) 922-1157, www.euromonitor.com; *The World Economic Factbook 2008.*

Palgrave Macmillan Ltd., Houndmills, Basingstoke, Hampshire, RG21 6XS, England, (Telephone in U.S. (888) 330-8477), (Fax in U.S. (800) 672-2054), www.palgrave.com; *The Statesman's Yearbook 2008.*

Taylor and Francis Group, An Informa Business, 2 Park Square, Milton Park, Abingdon, Oxford OX14 4RN, United Kingdom, (Dial from U.S. (212) 216-7800), (Fax from U.S. (212) 564-7854), www.tandf.co.uk; *The Europa World Year Book.*

United Nations Food and Agricultural Organization (FAO), Viale delle Terme di Caracalla, 00100 Rome, Italy, (Dial from U.S. (202) 653-2400), (Fax from U.S. (202) 653 5760), www.fao.org; *The State of Food and Agriculture (SOFA) 2006.*

United Nations Statistics Division, New York, NY 10017, (800) 253-9646, Fax: (212) 963-4116, http://unstats.un.org; *Statistical Yearbook.*

The World Bank, 1818 H Street, NW, Washington, DC 20433, (202) 473-1000, Fax: (202) 477-6391, www.worldbank.org; *Guam.*

GUAM - POWER RESOURCES

Euromonitor International, Inc., 224 S. Michigan Avenue, Suite 1500, Chicago, IL 60604, (312) 922-1115, Fax: (312) 922-1157, www.euromonitor.com; *International Marketing Data and Statistics 2008; The World Economic Factbook 2008;* and *World Marketing Data and Statistics.*

U.S. Department of Energy (DOE), Energy Information Administration (EIA), 1000 Independence Avenue, SW, Washington, DC 20585, (202) 586-8800, www.eia.doe.gov; *International Energy Annual 2004* and *International Energy Outlook 2006.*

United Nations Food and Agricultural Organization (FAO), Viale delle Terme di Caracalla, 00100 Rome, Italy, (Dial from U.S. (202) 653-2400), (Fax from U.S. (202) 653 5760), www.fao.org; *The State of Food and Agriculture (SOFA) 2006.*

United Nations Statistics Division, New York, NY 10017, (800) 253-9646, Fax: (212) 963-4116, http://unstats.un.org; *Asia-Pacific in Figures 2004; Statistical Yearbook;* and *World Statistics Pocketbook.*

The World Bank, 1818 H Street, NW, Washington, DC 20433, (202) 473-1000, Fax: (202) 477-6391, www.worldbank.org; *The World Bank Atlas 2003-2004.*

GUAM - PRICES

Euromonitor International, Inc., 224 S. Michigan Avenue, Suite 1500, Chicago, IL 60604, (312) 922-1115, Fax: (312) 922-1157, www.euromonitor.com; *World Marketing Data and Statistics.*

International Labour Office, I.L.O. Publications, 4 route des Morillons, CH-1211 Geneva 22, Switzerland, (Telephone in U.S. (202) 653-7652), (Fax in U.S. (202) 653-7687), www.ilo.org; *Yearbook of Labour Statistics 2006.*

Secretariat of the Pacific Community (SPC), BP D5, 98848 Noumea Cedex, New Caledonia, www.spc.int/corp; *Selected Pacific Economies - a Statistical Summary (SPESS).*

United Nations Food and Agricultural Organization (FAO), Viale delle Terme di Caracalla, 00100 Rome, Italy, (Dial from U.S. (202) 653-2400), (Fax from U.S. (202) 653 5760), www.fao.org; *FAO Production Yearbook 2002* and *The State of Food and Agriculture (SOFA) 2006.*

The World Bank, 1818 H Street, NW, Washington, DC 20433, (202) 473-1000, Fax: (202) 477-6391, www.worldbank.org; *Guam.*

GUAM - PROFESSIONS

United Nations Statistics Division, New York, NY 10017, (800) 253-9646, Fax: (212) 963-4116, http://unstats.un.org; *Statistical Yearbook.*

GUAM - PUBLIC HEALTH

Euromonitor International, Inc., 224 S. Michigan Avenue, Suite 1500, Chicago, IL 60604, (312) 922-1115, Fax: (312) 922-1157, www.euromonitor.com; *World Marketing Data and Statistics.*

Palgrave Macmillan Ltd., Houndmills, Basingstoke, Hampshire, RG21 6XS, England, (Telephone in U.S. (888) 330-8477), (Fax in U.S. (800) 672-2054), www.palgrave.com; *The Statesman's Yearbook 2008.*

Secretariat of the Pacific Community (SPC), BP D5, 98848 Noumea Cedex, New Caledonia, www.spc.int/corp; *Selected Pacific Economies - a Statistical Summary (SPESS).*

United Nations Statistics Division, New York, NY 10017, (800) 253-9646, Fax: (212) 963-4116, http://unstats.un.org; *Asia-Pacific in Figures 2004* and *Statistical Yearbook.*

The World Bank, 1818 H Street, NW, Washington, DC 20433, (202) 473-1000, Fax: (202) 477-6391, www.worldbank.org; *Guam.*

World Health Organization (WHO), Avenue Appia 20, 1211 Geneve 27, Switzerland, (Telephone in U.S. (212) 331-9081), www.who.int; The WHO Global Atlas of Infectious Diseases and *World Health Report 2006*.

GUAM - PUBLISHERS AND PUBLISHING

UNESCO Institute for Statistics, C.P. 6128 Succursale Centre-Ville, Montreal, Quebec, H3C 3J7 Canada, (Dial from U.S. (514) 343-6880), (Fax from U.S. (514) 343 6882), www.uis.unesco.org; *Statistical Tables*.

GUAM - RADIO BROADCASTING

Palgrave Macmillan Ltd., Houndmills, Basingstoke, Hampshire, RG21 6XS, England, (Telephone in U.S. (888) 330-8477), (Fax in U.S. (800) 672-2054), www.palgrave.com; *The Statesman's Yearbook 2008*.

GUAM - RELIGION

Central Intelligence Agency, Office of Public Affairs, Washington, DC 20505, (703) 482-0623, Fax: (703) 482-1739, www.cia.gov; *The World Factbook*.

Palgrave Macmillan Ltd., Houndmills, Basingstoke, Hampshire, RG21 6XS, England, (Telephone in U.S. (888) 330-8477), (Fax in U.S. (800) 672-2054), www.palgrave.com; *The Statesman's Yearbook 2008*.

GUAM - RENT CHARGES

International Labour Office, I.L.O. Publications, 4 route des Morillons, CH-1211 Geneva 22, Switzerland, (Telephone in U.S. (202) 653-7652), (Fax in U.S. (202) 653-7687), www.ilo.org; *Yearbook of Labour Statistics 2006*.

GUAM - RETAIL TRADE

Euromonitor International, Inc., 224 S. Michigan Avenue, Suite 1500, Chicago, IL 60604, (312) 922-1115, Fax: (312) 922-1157, www.euromonitor.com; *World Marketing Data and Statistics*.

GUAM - ROADS

Central Intelligence Agency, Office of Public Affairs, Washington, DC 20505, (703) 482-0623, Fax: (703) 482-1739, www.cia.gov; *The World Factbook*.

Palgrave Macmillan Ltd., Houndmills, Basingstoke, Hampshire, RG21 6XS, England, (Telephone in U.S. (888) 330-8477), (Fax in U.S. (800) 672-2054), www.palgrave.com; *The Statesman's Yearbook 2008*.

GUAM - SHIPPING

Taylor and Francis Group, An Informa Business, 2 Park Square, Milton Park, Abingdon, Oxford OX14 4RN, United Kingdom, (Dial from U.S. (212) 216-7800), (Fax from U.S. (212) 564-7854), www.tandf.co.uk; *The Europa World Year Book*.

United Nations Statistics Division, New York, NY 10017, (800) 253-9646, Fax: (212) 963-4116, http://unstats.un.org; *Statistical Yearbook*.

GUAM - SOCIAL ECOLOGY

United Nations Statistics Division, New York, NY 10017, (800) 253-9646, Fax: (212) 963-4116, http://unstats.un.org; *World Statistics Pocketbook*.

GUAM - SOCIAL SECURITY

Palgrave Macmillan Ltd., Houndmills, Basingstoke, Hampshire, RG21 6XS, England, (Telephone in U.S. (888) 330-8477), (Fax in U.S. (800) 672-2054), www.palgrave.com; *The Statesman's Yearbook 2008*.

GUAM - TELEPHONE

International Telecommunication Union (ITU), Place des Nations, 1211 Geneva 20, Switzerland, www.itu.int; World Telecommunication Indicators Database.

Palgrave Macmillan Ltd., Houndmills, Basingstoke, Hampshire, RG21 6XS, England, (Telephone in U.S. (888) 330-8477), (Fax in U.S. (800) 672-2054), www.palgrave.com; *The Statesman's Yearbook 2008*.

United Nations Statistics Division, New York, NY 10017, (800) 253-9646, Fax: (212) 963-4116, http://unstats.un.org; *Statistical Yearbook* and *World Statistics Pocketbook*.

GUAM - TEXTILE INDUSTRY

Palgrave Macmillan Ltd., Houndmills, Basingstoke, Hampshire, RG21 6XS, England, (Telephone in U.S. (888) 330-8477), (Fax in U.S. (800) 672-2054), www.palgrave.com; *The Statesman's Yearbook 2008*.

Secretariat of the Pacific Community (SPC), BP D5, 98848 Noumea Cedex, New Caledonia, www.spc.int/corp; *Selected Pacific Economies - a Statistical Summary (SPESS)*.

United Nations Conference on Trade and Development (UNCTAD), DC2-1120, United Nations, New York, NY 10017, (212) 963-0027, www.unctad.org; *UNCTAD Commodity Yearbook*.

GUAM - TOBACCO INDUSTRY

Foreign Agricultural Service (FAS), U.S. Department of Agriculture (USDA), 1400 Independence Avenue, SW, Washington, DC 20250, (202) 720-3935, www.fas.usda.gov; *Tobacco: World Markets and Trade*.

Secretariat of the Pacific Community (SPC), BP D5, 98848 Noumea Cedex, New Caledonia, www.spc.int/corp; *Selected Pacific Economies - a Statistical Summary (SPESS)*.

GUAM - TOURISM

Euromonitor International, Inc., 224 S. Michigan Avenue, Suite 1500, Chicago, IL 60604, (312) 922-1115, Fax: (312) 922-1157, www.euromonitor.com; *The World Economic Factbook 2008* and *World Marketing Data and Statistics*.

Palgrave Macmillan Ltd., Houndmills, Basingstoke, Hampshire, RG21 6XS, England, (Telephone in U.S. (888) 330-8477), (Fax in U.S. (800) 672-2054), www.palgrave.com; *The Statesman's Yearbook 2008*.

Taylor and Francis Group, An Informa Business, 2 Park Square, Milton Park, Abingdon, Oxford OX14 4RN, United Kingdom, (Dial from U.S. (212) 216-7800), (Fax from U.S. (212) 564-7854), www.tandf.co.uk; *The Europa World Year Book*.

United Nations World Tourism Organization (UNWTO), Capitan Haya 42, 28020 Madrid, Spain, www.world-tourism.org; *Yearbook of Tourism Statistics*.

The World Bank, 1818 H Street, NW, Washington, DC 20433, (202) 473-1000, Fax: (202) 477-6391, www.worldbank.org; *Guam*.

GUAM - TRADE

See GUAM - INTERNATIONAL TRADE

GUAM - TRANSPORTATION

Central Intelligence Agency, Office of Public Affairs, Washington, DC 20505, (703) 482-0623, Fax: (703) 482-1739, www.cia.gov; *The World Factbook*.

Euromonitor International, Inc., 224 S. Michigan Avenue, Suite 1500, Chicago, IL 60604, (312) 922-1115, Fax: (312) 922-1157, www.euromonitor.com; *International Marketing Data and Statistics 2008* and *World Marketing Data and Statistics*.

Palgrave Macmillan Ltd., Houndmills, Basingstoke, Hampshire, RG21 6XS, England, (Telephone in U.S. (888) 330-8477), (Fax in U.S. (800) 672-2054), www.palgrave.com; *The Statesman's Yearbook 2008*.

Secretariat of the Pacific Community (SPC), BP D5, 98848 Noumea Cedex, New Caledonia, www.spc.int/corp; *Selected Pacific Economies - a Statistical Summary (SPESS)*.

Taylor and Francis Group, An Informa Business, 2 Park Square, Milton Park, Abingdon, Oxford OX14 4RN, United Kingdom, (Dial from U.S. (212) 216-7800), (Fax from U.S. (212) 564-7854), www.tandf.co.uk; *The Europa World Year Book*.

The World Bank, 1818 H Street, NW, Washington, DC 20433, (202) 473-1000, Fax: (202) 477-6391, www.worldbank.org; *Guam*.

GUAM - UNEMPLOYMENT

Central Intelligence Agency, Office of Public Affairs, Washington, DC 20505, (703) 482-0623, Fax: (703) 482-1739, www.cia.gov; *The World Factbook*.

International Labour Office, I.L.O. Publications, 4 route des Morillons, CH-1211 Geneva 22, Switzerland, (Telephone in U.S. (202) 653-7652), (Fax in U.S. (202) 653-7687), www.ilo.org; *Yearbook of Labour Statistics 2006*.

Palgrave Macmillan Ltd., Houndmills, Basingstoke, Hampshire, RG21 6XS, England, (Telephone in U.S. (888) 330-8477), (Fax in U.S. (800) 672-2054), www.palgrave.com; *The Statesman's Yearbook 2008*.

United Nations Statistics Division, New York, NY 10017, (800) 253-9646, Fax: (212) 963-4116, http://unstats.un.org; *Statistical Yearbook*.

GUAM - VITAL STATISTICS

Palgrave Macmillan Ltd., Houndmills, Basingstoke, Hampshire, RG21 6XS, England, (Telephone in U.S. (888) 330-8477), (Fax in U.S. (800) 672-2054), www.palgrave.com; *The Statesman's Yearbook 2008*.

United Nations Statistics Division, New York, NY 10017, (800) 253-9646, Fax: (212) 963-4116, http://unstats.un.org; *Statistical Yearbook*.

GUAM - WAGES

International Labour Office, I.L.O. Publications, 4 route des Morillons, CH-1211 Geneva 22, Switzerland, (Telephone in U.S. (202) 653-7652), (Fax in U.S. (202) 653-7687), www.ilo.org; *Yearbook of Labour Statistics 2006*.

The World Bank, 1818 H Street, NW, Washington, DC 20433, (202) 473-1000, Fax: (202) 477-6391, www.worldbank.org; *Guam*.

GUAM - WELFARE STATE

Palgrave Macmillan Ltd., Houndmills, Basingstoke, Hampshire, RG21 6XS, England, (Telephone in U.S. (888) 330-8477), (Fax in U.S. (800) 672-2054), www.palgrave.com; *The Statesman's Yearbook 2008*.

GUAMAMIAN POPULATION

Population Reference Bureau, 1875 Connecticut Avenue, NW, Suite 520, Washington, DC, 20009-5728, (800) 877-9881, Fax: (202) 328-3937, www.prb.org; *The American People Series*.

U.S. Census Bureau, Population Division, 4700 Silver Hill Road, Washington DC 20233-0001, (301) 763-3030, www.census.gov/population/www/; *Census 2000 Profiles of General Demographic Characteristics*.

GUATEMALA - NATIONAL STATISTICAL OFFICE

Instituto Nacional de Estadistica (INE), 8va. Calle 9-55, zona 1 Guatemala, http://www.ine.gob.gt; National Data Center.

GUATEMALA - PRIMARY STATISTICS SOURCES

Instituto Nacional de Estadistica (INE), 8va. Calle 9-55, zona 1 Guatemala, http://www.ine.gob.gt; *Estadisticas Sociales* - (Social Statistics) and *Estados Financieros* (Financial Statements).

GUATEMALA - AGRICULTURAL MACHINERY

Economist Intelligence Unit, 111 West 57th Street, New York, NY 10019, (212) 554-0600, Fax: (212) 586-1181, www.eiu.com; *Business Latin America*.

United Nations Statistics Division, New York, NY 10017, (800) 253-9646, Fax: (212) 963-4116, http://unstats.un.org; *Statistical Yearbook*.

GUATEMALA - AGRICULTURE

Economist Intelligence Unit, 111 West 57th Street, New York, NY 10019, (212) 554-0600, Fax: (212)

586-1181, www.eiu.com; *Business Latin America* and *Guatemala Country Report.*

Euromonitor International, Inc., 224 S. Michigan Avenue, Suite 1500, Chicago, IL 60604, (312) 922-1115, Fax: (312) 922-1157, www.euromonitor.com; *International Marketing Data and Statistics 2008* and *World Marketing Data and Statistics.*

Inter-American Development Bank (IDB), 1300 New York Avenue, NW, Washington, DC 20577, (202) 623-1000, Fax: (202) 623-3096, www.iadb.org; *The Politics of Policies: Economic and Social Progress in Latin America - 2006 Report.*

M.E. Sharpe, 80 Business Park Drive, Armonk, NY 10504, (800) 541-6563, Fax: (914) 273-2106, www.mesharpe.com; *The Illustrated Book of World Rankings.*

Palgrave Macmillan Ltd., Houndmills, Basingstoke, Hampshire, RG21 6XS, England, (Telephone in U.S. (888) 330-8477), (Fax in U.S. (800) 672-2054), www.palgrave.com; *The Statesman's Yearbook 2008.*

Taylor and Francis Group, An Informa Business, 2 Park Square, Milton Park, Abingdon, Oxford OX14 4RN, United Kingdom, (Dial from U.S. (212) 216-7800), (Fax from U.S. (212) 564-7854), www.tandf.co.uk; *The Europa World Year Book.*

UCLA Latin American Institute, 10343 Bunche Hall, Box 951447, Los Angeles, CA 90095-1447, (310) 825-4571, Fax: (310) 206-6859, www.international.ucla.edu/lac; *Statistical Abstract of Latin America.*

United Nations Conference on Trade and Development (UNCTAD), DC2-1120, United Nations, New York, NY 10017, (212) 963-0027, www.unctad.org; *UNCTAD Commodity Yearbook.*

United Nations Food and Agricultural Organization (FAO), Viale delle Terme di Caracalla, 00100 Rome, Italy, (Dial from U.S. (202) 653-2400), (Fax from U.S. (202) 653 5760), www.fao.org; AQUASTAT; *FAO Production Yearbook 2002; FAO Trade Yearbook;* and *The State of Food and Agriculture (SOFA) 2006.*

United Nations Statistics Division, New York, NY 10017, (800) 253-9646, Fax: (212) 963-4116, http://unstats.un.org; *Statistical Yearbook* and *Statistical Yearbook for Latin America and the Caribbean 2004.*

The World Bank, 1818 H Street, NW, Washington, DC 20433, (202) 473-1000, Fax: (202) 477-6391, www.worldbank.org; *Guatemala* and *World Development Indicators (WDI) 2008.*

GUATEMALA - AIRLINES

Economist Intelligence Unit, 111 West 57th Street, New York, NY 10019, (212) 554-0600, Fax: (212) 586-1181, www.eiu.com; *Business Latin America.*

International Civil Aviation Organization (ICAO), External Relations and Public Information Office (EPO), 999 University Street, Montreal, Quebec H3C 5H7, Canada, (Dial from U.S. (514) 954-8219), (Fax from U.S. (514) 954-6077), www.icao.int; *Civil Aviation Statistics of the World.*

M.E. Sharpe, 80 Business Park Drive, Armonk, NY 10504, (800) 541-6563, Fax: (914) 273-2106, www.mesharpe.com; *The Illustrated Book of World Rankings.*

Palgrave Macmillan Ltd., Houndmills, Basingstoke, Hampshire, RG21 6XS, England, (Telephone in U.S. (888) 330-8477), (Fax in U.S. (800) 672-2054), www.palgrave.com; *The Statesman's Yearbook 2008.*

Taylor and Francis Group, An Informa Business, 2 Park Square, Milton Park, Abingdon, Oxford OX14 4RN, United Kingdom, (Dial from U.S. (212) 216-7800), (Fax from U.S. (212) 564-7854), www.tandf.co.uk; *The Europa World Year Book.*

United Nations Statistics Division, New York, NY 10017, (800) 253-9646, Fax: (212) 963-4116, http://unstats.un.org; *Statistical Yearbook.*

GUATEMALA - AIRPORTS

Central Intelligence Agency, Office of Public Affairs, Washington, DC 20505, (703) 482-0623, Fax: (703) 482-1739, www.cia.gov; *The World Factbook.*

GUATEMALA - ALUMINUM PRODUCTION

See GUATEMALA - MINERAL INDUSTRIES

GUATEMALA - AREA

Economist Intelligence Unit, 111 West 57th Street, New York, NY 10019, (212) 554-0600, Fax: (212) 586-1181, www.eiu.com; *Business Latin America.*

GUATEMALA - ARMED FORCES

Central Intelligence Agency, Office of Public Affairs, Washington, DC 20505, (703) 482-0623, Fax: (703) 482-1739, www.cia.gov; *The World Factbook.*

Economist Intelligence Unit, 111 West 57th Street, New York, NY 10019, (212) 554-0600, Fax: (212) 586-1181, www.eiu.com; *Business Latin America.*

Euromonitor International, Inc., 224 S. Michigan Avenue, Suite 1500, Chicago, IL 60604, (312) 922-1115, Fax: (312) 922-1157, www.euromonitor.com; *World Marketing Data and Statistics.*

International Institute for Strategic Studies (IISS), Arundel House, 13-15 Arundel Street, Temple Place, London WC2R 3DX, England, www.iiss.org; *The Military Balance 2007.*

International Monetary Fund (IMF), 700 Nineteenth Street, NW, Washington, DC 20431, (202) 623-7000, Fax: (202) 623-4661, www.imf.org; *Government Finance Statistics Yearbook (2008 Edition).*

Palgrave Macmillan Ltd., Houndmills, Basingstoke, Hampshire, RG21 6XS, England, (Telephone in U.S. (888) 330-8477), (Fax in U.S. (800) 672-2054), www.palgrave.com; *The Statesman's Yearbook 2008.*

U.S. Department of State (DOS), 2201 C Street NW, Washington, DC 20520, (202) 647-4000, www.state.gov; *World Military Expenditures and Arms Transfers (WMEAT).*

UCLA Latin American Institute, 10343 Bunche Hall, Box 951447, Los Angeles, CA 90095-1447, (310) 825-4571, Fax: (310) 206-6859, www.international.ucla.edu/lac; *Statistical Abstract of Latin America.*

United Nations Statistics Division, New York, NY 10017, (800) 253-9646, Fax: (212) 963-4116, http://unstats.un.org; *Human Development Report 2006.*

GUATEMALA - BALANCE OF PAYMENTS

Economist Intelligence Unit, 111 West 57th Street, New York, NY 10019, (212) 554-0600, Fax: (212) 586-1181, www.eiu.com; *Business Latin America.*

Inter-American Development Bank (IDB), 1300 New York Avenue, NW, Washington, DC 20577, (202) 623-1000, Fax: (202) 623-3096, www.iadb.org; *The Politics of Policies: Economic and Social Progress in Latin America - 2006 Report.*

International Monetary Fund (IMF), 700 Nineteenth Street, NW, Washington, DC 20431, (202) 623-7000, Fax: (202) 623-4661, www.imf.org; *Balance of Payments Statistics Newsletter; Balance of Payments Statistics Yearbook 2007;* and *International Financial Statistics Yearbook 2007.*

Organization of American States (OAS), 17th Street Constitution Avenue NW, Washington, DC 20006, (202) 458-3000, www.oas.org; *The OAS in Transition: 1994-2004.*

Taylor and Francis Group, An Informa Business, 2 Park Square, Milton Park, Abingdon, Oxford OX14 4RN, United Kingdom, (Dial from U.S. (212) 216-7800), (Fax from U.S. (212) 564-7854), www.tandf.co.uk; *The Europa World Year Book.*

UCLA Latin American Institute, 10343 Bunche Hall, Box 951447, Los Angeles, CA 90095-1447, (310) 825-4571, Fax: (310) 206-6859, www.international.ucla.edu/lac; *Statistical Abstract of Latin America.*

United Nations Conference on Trade and Development (UNCTAD), DC2-1120, United Nations, New York, NY 10017, (212) 963-0027, www.unctad.org; *Handbook of Statistics 2005.*

United Nations Statistics Division, New York, NY 10017, (800) 253-9646, Fax: (212) 963-4116, http://unstats.un.org; *Economic Survey of Latin America and the Caribbean 2004-2005* and *Statistical Yearbook for Latin America and the Caribbean 2004.*

The World Bank, 1818 H Street, NW, Washington, DC 20433, (202) 473-1000, Fax: (202) 477-6391, www.worldbank.org; *Guatemala; World Development Indicators (WDI) 2008;* and *World Development Report 2008.*

GUATEMALA - BANANAS

See GUATEMALA - CROPS

GUATEMALA - BANKS AND BANKING

Euromonitor International, Inc., 224 S. Michigan Avenue, Suite 1500, Chicago, IL 60604, (312) 922-1115, Fax: (312) 922-1157, www.euromonitor.com; *World Marketing Data and Statistics.*

Inter-American Development Bank (IDB), 1300 New York Avenue, NW, Washington, DC 20577, (202) 623-1000, Fax: (202) 623-3096, www.iadb.org; *The Politics of Policies: Economic and Social Progress in Latin America - 2006 Report.*

International Monetary Fund (IMF), 700 Nineteenth Street, NW, Washington, DC 20431, (202) 623-7000, Fax: (202) 623-4661, www.imf.org; *Government Finance Statistics Yearbook (2008 Edition)* and *International Financial Statistics Yearbook 2007.*

M.E. Sharpe, 80 Business Park Drive, Armonk, NY 10504, (800) 541-6563, Fax: (914) 273-2106, www.mesharpe.com; *The Illustrated Book of World Rankings.*

Palgrave Macmillan Ltd., Houndmills, Basingstoke, Hampshire, RG21 6XS, England, (Telephone in U.S. (888) 330-8477), (Fax in U.S. (800) 672-2054), www.palgrave.com; *The Statesman's Yearbook 2008.*

Taylor and Francis Group, An Informa Business, 2 Park Square, Milton Park, Abingdon, Oxford OX14 4RN, United Kingdom, (Dial from U.S. (212) 216-7800), (Fax from U.S. (212) 564-7854), www.tandf.co.uk; *The Europa World Year Book.*

GUATEMALA - BARLEY PRODUCTION

See GUATEMALA - CROPS

GUATEMALA - BEVERAGE INDUSTRY

M.E. Sharpe, 80 Business Park Drive, Armonk, NY 10504, (800) 541-6563, Fax: (914) 273-2106, www.mesharpe.com; *The Illustrated Book of World Rankings.*

United Nations Statistics Division, New York, NY 10017, (800) 253-9646, Fax: (212) 963-4116, http://unstats.un.org; *Statistical Yearbook.*

GUATEMALA - BIRTH CONTROL

UCLA Latin American Institute, 10343 Bunche Hall, Box 951447, Los Angeles, CA 90095-1447, (310) 825-4571, Fax: (310) 206-6859, www.international.ucla.edu/lac; *Statistical Abstract of Latin America.*

GUATEMALA - BONDS

Inter-American Development Bank (IDB), 1300 New York Avenue, NW, Washington, DC 20577, (202) 623-1000, Fax: (202) 623-3096, www.iadb.org; *The Politics of Policies: Economic and Social Progress in Latin America - 2006 Report.*

International Monetary Fund (IMF), 700 Nineteenth Street, NW, Washington, DC 20431, (202) 623-7000, Fax: (202) 623-4661, www.imf.org; *Government Finance Statistics Yearbook (2008 Edition).*

GUATEMALA - BROADCASTING

Central Intelligence Agency, Office of Public Affairs, Washington, DC 20505, (703) 482-0623, Fax: (703) 482-1739, www.cia.gov; *The World Factbook.*

Euromonitor International, Inc., 224 S. Michigan Avenue, Suite 1500, Chicago, IL 60604, (312) 922-1115, Fax: (312) 922-1157, www.euromonitor.com; *World Marketing Data and Statistics.*

M.E. Sharpe, 80 Business Park Drive, Armonk, NY 10504, (800) 541-6563, Fax: (914) 273-2106, www.mesharpe.com; *The Illustrated Book of World Rankings.*

Palgrave Macmillan Ltd., Houndmills, Basingstoke, Hampshire, RG21 6XS, England, (Telephone in U.S. (888) 330-8477), (Fax in U.S. (800) 672-2054), www.palgrave.com; *The Statesman's Yearbook 2008.*

WRTH Publications Limited, PO Box 290, Oxford OX2 7FT, UK, www.wrth.com; *World Radio TV Handbook 2007.*

GUATEMALA - BUDGET

Central Intelligence Agency, Office of Public Affairs, Washington, DC 20505, (703) 482-0623, Fax: (703) 482-1739, www.cia.gov; *The World Factbook.*

GUATEMALA - BUSINESS

Inter-American Development Bank (IDB), 1300 New York Avenue, NW, Washington, DC 20577, (202) 623-1000, Fax: (202) 623-3096, www.iadb.org; *The Politics of Policies: Economic and Social Progress in Latin America - 2006 Report.*

GUATEMALA - CAPITAL INVESTMENTS

Inter-American Development Bank (IDB), 1300 New York Avenue, NW, Washington, DC 20577, (202) 623-1000, Fax: (202) 623-3096, www.iadb.org; *The Politics of Policies: Economic and Social Progress in Latin America - 2006 Report.*

GUATEMALA - CAPITAL LEVY

Inter-American Development Bank (IDB), 1300 New York Avenue, NW, Washington, DC 20577, (202) 623-1000, Fax: (202) 623-3096, www.iadb.org; *The Politics of Policies: Economic and Social Progress in Latin America - 2006 Report.*

International Monetary Fund (IMF), 700 Nineteenth Street, NW, Washington, DC 20431, (202) 623-7000, Fax: (202) 623-4661, www.imf.org; *Government Finance Statistics Yearbook (2008 Edition).*

GUATEMALA - CATTLE

See GUATEMALA - LIVESTOCK

GUATEMALA - CHICKENS

See GUATEMALA - LIVESTOCK

GUATEMALA - CHILDBIRTH - STATISTICS

Central Intelligence Agency, Office of Public Affairs, Washington, DC 20505, (703) 482-0623, Fax: (703) 482-1739, www.cia.gov; *The World Factbook.*

Euromonitor International, Inc., 224 S. Michigan Avenue, Suite 1500, Chicago, IL 60604, (312) 922-1115, Fax: (312) 922-1157, www.euromonitor.com; *International Marketing Data and Statistics 2008* and *The World Economic Factbook 2008.*

M.E. Sharpe, 80 Business Park Drive, Armonk, NY 10504, (800) 541-6563, Fax: (914) 273-2106, www.mesharpe.com; *The Illustrated Book of World Rankings.*

Palgrave Macmillan Ltd., Houndmills, Basingstoke, Hampshire, RG21 6XS, England, (Telephone in U.S. (888) 330-8477), (Fax in U.S. (800) 672-2054), www.palgrave.com; *The Statesman's Yearbook 2008.*

Taylor and Francis Group, An Informa Business, 2 Park Square, Milton Park, Abingdon, Oxford OX14 4RN, United Kingdom, (Dial from U.S. (212) 216-7800), (Fax from U.S. (212) 564-7854), www.tandf.co.uk; *The Europa World Year Book.*

United Nations Statistics Division, New York, NY 10017, (800) 253-9646, Fax: (212) 963-4116, http://unstats.un.org; *Demographic Yearbook; Statistical Yearbook;* and *Statistical Yearbook for Latin America and the Caribbean 2004.*

The World Bank, 1818 H Street, NW, Washington, DC 20433, (202) 473-1000, Fax: (202) 477-6391, www.worldbank.org; *World Development Indicators (WDI) 2008.*

World Health Organization (WHO), Avenue Appia 20, 1211 Geneve 27, Switzerland, (Telephone in U.S. (212) 331-9081), www.who.int; *World Health Report 2006.*

GUATEMALA - CLIMATE

M.E. Sharpe, 80 Business Park Drive, Armonk, NY 10504, (800) 541-6563, Fax: (914) 273-2106, www.mesharpe.com; *The Illustrated Book of World Rankings.*

Palgrave Macmillan Ltd., Houndmills, Basingstoke, Hampshire, RG21 6XS, England, (Telephone in U.S. (888) 330-8477), (Fax in U.S. (800) 672-2054), www.palgrave.com; *The Statesman's Yearbook 2008.*

GUATEMALA - COAL PRODUCTION

See GUATEMALA - MINERAL INDUSTRIES

GUATEMALA - COCOA PRODUCTION

See GUATEMALA - CROPS

GUATEMALA - COFFEE

See GUATEMALA - CROPS

GUATEMALA - COMMERCE

Palgrave Macmillan Ltd., Houndmills, Basingstoke, Hampshire, RG21 6XS, England, (Telephone in U.S. (888) 330-8477), (Fax in U.S. (800) 672-2054), www.palgrave.com; *The Statesman's Yearbook 2008.*

GUATEMALA - COMMODITY EXCHANGES

Commodity Research Bureau, 330 South Wells Street, Suite 612, Chicago, IL 60606-7110, (800) 621-5271, Fax: (312) 939-4135, www.crbtrader.com; *2006 CRB Commodity Yearbook and CD.*

International Monetary Fund (IMF), 700 Nineteenth Street, NW, Washington, DC 20431, (202) 623-7000, Fax: (202) 623-4661, www.imf.org; *IMF Primary Commodity Prices.*

United Nations Food and Agricultural Organization (FAO), Viale delle Terme di Caracalla, 00100 Rome, Italy, (Dial from U.S. (202) 653-2400), (Fax from U.S. (202) 653 5760), www.fao.org; *The State of Food and Agriculture (SOFA) 2006.*

GUATEMALA - CONSTRUCTION INDUSTRY

Economist Intelligence Unit, 111 West 57th Street, New York, NY 10019, (212) 554-0600, Fax: (212) 586-1181, www.eiu.com; *Business Latin America.*

Inter-American Development Bank (IDB), 1300 New York Avenue, NW, Washington, DC 20577, (202) 623-1000, Fax: (202) 623-3096, www.iadb.org; *The Politics of Policies: Economic and Social Progress in Latin America - 2006 Report.*

M.E. Sharpe, 80 Business Park Drive, Armonk, NY 10504, (800) 541-6563, Fax: (914) 273-2106, www.mesharpe.com; *The Illustrated Book of World Rankings.*

Organization of American States (OAS), 17th Street Constitution Avenue NW, Washington, DC 20006, (202) 458-3000, www.oas.org; *The OAS in Transition: 1994-2004.*

UCLA Latin American Institute, 10343 Bunche Hall, Box 951447, Los Angeles, CA 90095-1447, (310) 825-4571, Fax: (310) 206-6859, www.international.ucla.edu/lac; *Statistical Abstract of Latin America.*

United Nations Statistics Division, New York, NY 10017, (800) 253-9646, Fax: (212) 963-4116, http://unstats.un.org; *Statistical Yearbook.*

GUATEMALA - CONSUMER COOPERATIVES

UCLA Latin American Institute, 10343 Bunche Hall, Box 951447, Los Angeles, CA 90095-1447, (310) 825-4571, Fax: (310) 206-6859, www.international.ucla.edu/lac; *Statistical Abstract of Latin America.*

GUATEMALA - CONSUMER PRICE INDEXES

Economist Intelligence Unit, 111 West 57th Street, New York, NY 10019, (212) 554-0600, Fax: (212) 586-1181, www.eiu.com; *Business Latin America.*

Euromonitor International, Inc., 224 S. Michigan Avenue, Suite 1500, Chicago, IL 60604, (312) 922-1115, Fax: (312) 922-1157, www.euromonitor.com; *World Marketing Data and Statistics.*

International Labour Office, I.L.O. Publications, 4 route des Morillons, CH-1211 Geneva 22, Switzerland, (Telephone in U.S. (202) 653-7652), (Fax in U.S. (202) 653-7687), www.ilo.org; *Yearbook of Labour Statistics 2006.*

International Monetary Fund (IMF), 700 Nineteenth Street, NW, Washington, DC 20431, (202) 623-7000, Fax: (202) 623-4661, www.imf.org; *International Financial Statistics Yearbook 2007.*

Organization of American States (OAS), 17th Street Constitution Avenue NW, Washington, DC 20006, (202) 458-3000, www.oas.org; *The OAS in Transition: 1994-2004.*

Taylor and Francis Group, An Informa Business, 2 Park Square, Milton Park, Abingdon, Oxford OX14 4RN, United Kingdom, (Dial from U.S. (212) 216-7800), (Fax from U.S. (212) 564-7854), www.tandf.co.uk; *The Europa World Year Book.*

UCLA Latin American Institute, 10343 Bunche Hall, Box 951447, Los Angeles, CA 90095-1447, (310) 825-4571, Fax: (310) 206-6859, www.international.ucla.edu/lac; *Statistical Abstract of Latin America.*

GUATEMALA - CONSUMPTION (ECONOMICS)

Economist Intelligence Unit, 111 West 57th Street, New York, NY 10019, (212) 554-0600, Fax: (212) 586-1181, www.eiu.com; *Business Latin America.*

Inter-American Development Bank (IDB), 1300 New York Avenue, NW, Washington, DC 20577, (202) 623-1000, Fax: (202) 623-3096, www.iadb.org; *The Politics of Policies: Economic and Social Progress in Latin America - 2006 Report.*

United Nations Statistics Division, New York, NY 10017, (800) 253-9646, Fax: (212) 963-4116, http://unstats.un.org; *Statistical Yearbook for Latin America and the Caribbean 2004.*

The World Bank, 1818 H Street, NW, Washington, DC 20433, (202) 473-1000, Fax: (202) 477-6391, www.worldbank.org; *World Development Report 2008.*

GUATEMALA - COPPER INDUSTRY AND TRADE

See GUATEMALA - MINERAL INDUSTRIES

GUATEMALA - CORN INDUSTRY

See GUATEMALA - CROPS

GUATEMALA - COST AND STANDARD OF LIVING

International Monetary Fund (IMF), 700 Nineteenth Street, NW, Washington, DC 20431, (202) 623-7000, Fax: (202) 623-4661, www.imf.org; *Government Finance Statistics Yearbook (2008 Edition).*

GUATEMALA - COTTON

See GUATEMALA - CROPS

GUATEMALA - CROPS

Economist Intelligence Unit, 111 West 57th Street, New York, NY 10019, (212) 554-0600, Fax: (212) 586-1181, www.eiu.com; *Business Latin America.*

International Monetary Fund (IMF), 700 Nineteenth Street, NW, Washington, DC 20431, (202) 623-7000, Fax: (202) 623-4661, www.imf.org; *International Financial Statistics Yearbook 2007.*

M.E. Sharpe, 80 Business Park Drive, Armonk, NY 10504, (800) 541-6563, Fax: (914) 273-2106, www.mesharpe.com; *The Illustrated Book of World Rankings.*

Organization of American States (OAS), 17th Street Constitution Avenue NW, Washington, DC 20006, (202) 458-3000, www.oas.org; *The OAS in Transition: 1994-2004.*

Palgrave Macmillan Ltd., Houndmills, Basingstoke, Hampshire, RG21 6XS, England, (Telephone in U.S. (888) 330-8477), (Fax in U.S. (800) 672-2054), www.palgrave.com; *The Statesman's Yearbook 2008.*

Taylor and Francis Group, An Informa Business, 2 Park Square, Milton Park, Abingdon, Oxford OX14 4RN, United Kingdom, (Dial from U.S. (212) 216-7800), (Fax from U.S. (212) 564-7854), www.tandf.co.uk; *The Europa World Year Book.*

United Nations Conference on Trade and Development (UNCTAD), DC2-1120, United Nations, New York, NY 10017, (212) 963-0027, www.unctad.org; *UNCTAD Commodity Yearbook.*

United Nations Food and Agricultural Organization (FAO), Viale delle Terme di Caracalla, 00100 Rome, Italy, (Dial from U.S. (202) 653-2400), (Fax from U.S. (202) 653 5760), www.fao.org; *FAO Production Yearbook 2002* and *The State of Food and Agriculture (SOFA) 2006.*

United Nations Statistics Division, New York, NY 10017, (800) 253-9646, Fax: (212) 963-4116, http://unstats.un.org; *Statistical Yearbook.*

GUATEMALA - CUSTOMS ADMINISTRATION

Inter-American Development Bank (IDB), 1300 New York Avenue, NW, Washington, DC 20577, (202) 623-1000, Fax: (202) 623-3096, www.iadb.org; *The Politics of Policies: Economic and Social Progress in Latin America - 2006 Report.*

International Monetary Fund (IMF), 700 Nineteenth Street, NW, Washington, DC 20431, (202) 623-7000, Fax: (202) 623-4661, www.imf.org; *Government Finance Statistics Yearbook (2008 Edition).*

Palgrave Macmillan Ltd., Houndmills, Basingstoke, Hampshire, RG21 6XS, England, (Telephone in U.S. (888) 330-8477), (Fax in U.S. (800) 672-2054), www.palgrave.com; *The Statesman's Yearbook 2008.*

GUATEMALA - DAIRY PROCESSING

M.E. Sharpe, 80 Business Park Drive, Armonk, NY 10504, (800) 541-6563, Fax: (914) 273-2106, www.mesharpe.com; *The Illustrated Book of World Rankings.*

Palgrave Macmillan Ltd., Houndmills, Basingstoke, Hampshire, RG21 6XS, England, (Telephone in U.S. (888) 330-8477), (Fax in U.S. (800) 672-2054), www.palgrave.com; *The Statesman's Yearbook 2008.*

Taylor and Francis Group, An Informa Business, 2 Park Square, Milton Park, Abingdon, Oxford OX14 4RN, United Kingdom, (Dial from U.S. (212) 216-7800), (Fax from U.S. (212) 564-7854), www.tandf.co.uk; *The Europa World Year Book.*

United Nations Food and Agricultural Organization (FAO), Viale delle Terme di Caracalla, 00100 Rome, Italy, (Dial from U.S. (202) 653-2400), (Fax from U.S. (202) 653 5760), www.fao.org; *FAO Production Yearbook 2002* and *The State of Food and Agriculture (SOFA) 2006.*

United Nations Statistics Division, New York, NY 10017, (800) 253-9646, Fax: (212) 963-4116, http://unstats.un.org; *Statistical Yearbook.*

GUATEMALA - DEATH RATES

See GUATEMALA - MORTALITY

GUATEMALA - DEBT

Economist Intelligence Unit, 111 West 57th Street, New York, NY 10019, (212) 554-0600, Fax: (212) 586-1181, www.eiu.com; *Business Latin America.*

The World Bank, 1818 H Street, NW, Washington, DC 20433, (202) 473-1000, Fax: (202) 477-6391, www.worldbank.org; *Global Development Finance 2007.*

GUATEMALA - DEBTS, EXTERNAL

Economist Intelligence Unit, 111 West 57th Street, New York, NY 10019, (212) 554-0600, Fax: (212) 586-1181, www.eiu.com; *Business Latin America.*

Inter-American Development Bank (IDB), 1300 New York Avenue, NW, Washington, DC 20577, (202) 623-1000, Fax: (202) 623-3096, www.iadb.org; *The Politics of Policies: Economic and Social Progress in Latin America - 2006 Report.*

International Monetary Fund (IMF), 700 Nineteenth Street, NW, Washington, DC 20431, (202) 623-7000, Fax: (202) 623-4661, www.imf.org; *Government Finance Statistics Yearbook (2008 Edition).*

Palgrave Macmillan Ltd., Houndmills, Basingstoke, Hampshire, RG21 6XS, England, (Telephone in U.S. (888) 330-8477), (Fax in U.S. (800) 672-2054), www.palgrave.com; *The Statesman's Yearbook 2008.*

United Nations Statistics Division, New York, NY 10017, (800) 253-9646, Fax: (212) 963-4116, http://unstats.un.org; *Economic Survey of Latin America and the Caribbean 2004-2005* and *Statistical Yearbook for Latin America and the Caribbean 2004.*

The World Bank, 1818 H Street, NW, Washington, DC 20433, (202) 473-1000, Fax: (202) 477-6391, www.worldbank.org; *Global Development Finance 2007; World Development Indicators (WDI) 2008;* and *World Development Report 2008.*

GUATEMALA - DEFENSE EXPENDITURES

See GUATEMALA - ARMED FORCES

GUATEMALA - DEMOGRAPHY

Euromonitor International, Inc., 224 S. Michigan Avenue, Suite 1500, Chicago, IL 60604, (312) 922-1115, Fax: (312) 922-1157, www.euromonitor.com; *International Marketing Data and Statistics 2008; The World Economic Factbook 2008;* and *World Marketing Data and Statistics.*

M.E. Sharpe, 80 Business Park Drive, Armonk, NY 10504, (800) 541-6563, Fax: (914) 273-2106, www.mesharpe.com; *The Illustrated Book of World Rankings.*

United Nations Statistics Division, New York, NY 10017, (800) 253-9646, Fax: (212) 963-4116, http://unstats.un.org; *Human Development Report 2006.*

The World Bank, 1818 H Street, NW, Washington, DC 20433, (202) 473-1000, Fax: (202) 477-6391, www.worldbank.org; *Guatemala.*

GUATEMALA - DIAMONDS

See GUATEMALA - MINERAL INDUSTRIES

GUATEMALA - DISPOSABLE INCOME

Inter-American Development Bank (IDB), 1300 New York Avenue, NW, Washington, DC 20577, (202) 623-1000, Fax: (202) 623-3096, www.iadb.org; *The Politics of Policies: Economic and Social Progress in Latin America - 2006 Report.*

M.E. Sharpe, 80 Business Park Drive, Armonk, NY 10504, (800) 541-6563, Fax: (914) 273-2106, www.mesharpe.com; *The Illustrated Book of World Rankings.*

United Nations Statistics Division, New York, NY 10017, (800) 253-9646, Fax: (212) 963-4116, http://unstats.un.org; *National Accounts Statistics: Compendium of Income Distribution Statistics* and *Statistical Yearbook.*

GUATEMALA - DIVORCE

M.E. Sharpe, 80 Business Park Drive, Armonk, NY 10504, (800) 541-6563, Fax: (914) 273-2106, www.mesharpe.com; *The Illustrated Book of World Rankings.*

United Nations Statistics Division, New York, NY 10017, (800) 253-9646, Fax: (212) 963-4116, http://unstats.un.org; *Statistical Yearbook.*

GUATEMALA - ECONOMIC ASSISTANCE

Inter-American Development Bank (IDB), 1300 New York Avenue, NW, Washington, DC 20577, (202) 623-1000, Fax: (202) 623-3096, www.iadb.org; *The Politics of Policies: Economic and Social Progress in Latin America - 2006 Report.*

United Nations Statistics Division, New York, NY 10017, (800) 253-9646, Fax: (212) 963-4116, http://unstats.un.org; *Statistical Yearbook.*

GUATEMALA - ECONOMIC CONDITIONS

Center for International Business Education Research (CIBER), Columbia Business School and School of International and Public Affairs, Uris Hall, Room 212, 3022 Broadway, New York, NY 10027-6902, Mr. Joshua Safier, (212) 854-4750, Fax: (212) 222-9821, www.columbia.edu/cu/ciber/; Datastream International.

Central Intelligence Agency, Office of Public Affairs, Washington, DC 20505, (703) 482-0623, Fax: (703) 482-1739, www.cia.gov; *The World Factbook.*

DSI Data Service Information, Xantener Strasse 51a, D-47495 Rheinberg, Germany, www.dsidata.com; *Campus Solution.*

Dun and Bradstreet (DB) Corporation, 103 JFK Parkway, Short Hills, NJ 07078, (973) 921-5500, www.dnb.com; *Country Report.*

Economist Intelligence Unit, 111 West 57th Street, New York, NY 10019, (212) 554-0600, Fax: (212) 586-1181, www.eiu.com; *Guatemala Country Report.*

Euromonitor International, Inc., 224 S. Michigan Avenue, Suite 1500, Chicago, IL 60604, (312) 922-1115, Fax: (312) 922-1157, www.euromonitor.com; *International Marketing Data and Statistics 2008; The World Economic Factbook 2008;* and *World Marketing Data and Statistics.*

Inter-American Development Bank (IDB), 1300 New York Avenue, NW, Washington, DC 20577, (202) 623-1000, Fax: (202) 623-3096, www.iadb.org; *The Politics of Policies: Economic and Social Progress in Latin America - 2006 Report.*

International Monetary Fund (IMF), 700 Nineteenth Street, NW, Washington, DC 20431, (202) 623-7000, Fax: (202) 623-4661, www.imf.org; *World Economic Outlook Reports.*

M.E. Sharpe, 80 Business Park Drive, Armonk, NY 10504, (800) 541-6563, Fax: (914) 273-2106, www.mesharpe.com; *The Illustrated Book of World Rankings.*

Organization of American States (OAS), 17th Street Constitution Avenue NW, Washington, DC 20006, (202) 458-3000, www.oas.org; *The OAS in Transition: 1994-2004.*

Palgrave Macmillan Ltd., Houndmills, Basingstoke, Hampshire, RG21 6XS, England, (Telephone in U.S. (888) 330-8477), (Fax in U.S. (800) 672-2054), www.palgrave.com; *The Statesman's Yearbook 2008.*

Taylor and Francis Group, An Informa Business, 2 Park Square, Milton Park, Abingdon, Oxford OX14 4RN, United Kingdom, (Dial from U.S. (212) 216-7800), (Fax from U.S. (212) 564-7854), www.tandf.co.uk; *The Europa World Year Book.*

UCLA Latin American Institute, 10343 Bunche Hall, Box 951447, Los Angeles, CA 90095-1447, (310) 825-4571, Fax: (310) 206-6859, www.international.ucla.edu/lac; *Statistical Abstract of Latin America.*

United Nations Statistics Division, New York, NY 10017, (800) 253-9646, Fax: (212) 963-4116, http://unstats.un.org; *Economic Survey of Latin America and the Caribbean 2004-2005* and *World Statistics Pocketbook.*

The World Bank, 1818 H Street, NW, Washington, DC 20433, (202) 473-1000, Fax: (202) 477-6391, www.worldbank.org; *Global Economic Monitor (GEM); Global Economic Prospects 2008; Guatemala; The World Bank Atlas 2003-2004;* and *World Development Report 2008.*

GUATEMALA - ECONOMICS - SOCIOLOGICAL ASPECTS

Inter-American Development Bank (IDB), 1300 New York Avenue, NW, Washington, DC 20577, (202) 623-1000, Fax: (202) 623-3096, www.iadb.org; *The Politics of Policies: Economic and Social Progress in Latin America - 2006 Report.*

UCLA Latin American Institute, 10343 Bunche Hall, Box 951447, Los Angeles, CA 90095-1447, (310) 825-4571, Fax: (310) 206-6859, www.international.ucla.edu/lac; *Statistical Abstract of Latin America.*

GUATEMALA - EDUCATION

Economist Intelligence Unit, 111 West 57th Street, New York, NY 10019, (212) 554-0600, Fax: (212) 586-1181, www.eiu.com; *Business Latin America.*

Euromonitor International, Inc., 224 S. Michigan Avenue, Suite 1500, Chicago, IL 60604, (312) 922-1115, Fax: (312) 922-1157, www.euromonitor.com; *International Marketing Data and Statistics 2008* and *World Marketing Data and Statistics.*

International Monetary Fund (IMF), 700 Nineteenth Street, NW, Washington, DC 20431, (202) 623-7000, Fax: (202) 623-4661, www.imf.org; *Government Finance Statistics Yearbook (2008 Edition).*

M.E. Sharpe, 80 Business Park Drive, Armonk, NY 10504, (800) 541-6563, Fax: (914) 273-2106, www.mesharpe.com; *The Illustrated Book of World Rankings.*

Palgrave Macmillan Ltd., Houndmills, Basingstoke, Hampshire, RG21 6XS, England, (Telephone in U.S. (888) 330-8477), (Fax in U.S. (800) 672-2054), www.palgrave.com; *The Statesman's Yearbook 2008.*

Taylor and Francis Group, An Informa Business, 2 Park Square, Milton Park, Abingdon, Oxford OX14 4RN, United Kingdom, (Dial from U.S. (212) 216-7800), (Fax from U.S. (212) 564-7854), www.tandf.co.uk; *The Europa World Year Book.*

UCLA Latin American Institute, 10343 Bunche Hall, Box 951447, Los Angeles, CA 90095-1447, (310) 825-4571, Fax: (310) 206-6859, www.international.ucla.edu/lac; *Statistical Abstract of Latin America.*

UNESCO Institute for Statistics, C.P. 6128 Succursale Centre-Ville, Montreal, Quebec, H3C 3J7 Canada, (Dial from U.S. (514) 343-6880), (Fax from U.S. (514) 343 6882), www.uis.unesco.org; *Statistical Tables.*

United Nations Statistics Division, New York, NY 10017, (800) 253-9646, Fax: (212) 963-4116, http://unstats.un.org; *Human Development Report 2006* and *Statistical Yearbook for Latin America and the Caribbean 2004.*

The World Bank, 1818 H Street, NW, Washington, DC 20433, (202) 473-1000, Fax: (202) 477-6391, www.worldbank.org; *Guatemala; World Development Indicators (WDI) 2008;* and *World Development Report 2008.*

GUATEMALA - ELECTRICITY

Economist Intelligence Unit, 111 West 57th Street, New York, NY 10019, (212) 554-0600, Fax: (212) 586-1181, www.eiu.com; *Business Latin America.*

Inter-American Development Bank (IDB), 1300 New York Avenue, NW, Washington, DC 20577, (202) 623-1000, Fax: (202) 623-3096, www.iadb.org; *The Politics of Policies: Economic and Social Progress in Latin America - 2006 Report.*

M.E. Sharpe, 80 Business Park Drive, Armonk, NY 10504, (800) 541-6563, Fax: (914) 273-2106, www.mesharpe.com; *The Illustrated Book of World Rankings.*

Organisation for Economic Cooperation and Development (OECD), 2 rue Andre Pascal, F-75775 Paris Cedex 16, France, (Telephone in U.S. (202) 785-6323), (Fax in U.S. (202) 785-0350), www.oecd.org; *World Energy Outlook 2007.*

Organization of American States (OAS), 17th Street Constitution Avenue NW, Washington, DC 20006, (202) 458-3000, www.oas.org; *The OAS in Transition: 1994-2004.*

Palgrave Macmillan Ltd., Houndmills, Basingstoke, Hampshire, RG21 6XS, England, (Telephone in U.S. (888) 330-8477), (Fax in U.S. (800) 672-2054), www.palgrave.com; *The Statesman's Yearbook 2008.*

U.S. Department of Energy (DOE), Energy Information Administration (EIA), 1000 Independence Avenue, SW, Washington, DC 20585, (202) 586-8800, www.eia.doe.gov; *International Energy Annual 2004* and *International Energy Outlook 2006.*

United Nations Statistics Division, New York, NY 10017, (800) 253-9646, Fax: (212) 963-4116, http://unstats.un.org; *Human Development Report 2006* and *Statistical Yearbook.*

GUATEMALA - EMIGRATION AND IMMIGRATION

UCLA Latin American Institute, 10343 Bunche Hall, Box 951447, Los Angeles, CA 90095-1447, (310) 825-4571, Fax: (310) 206-6859, www.international.ucla.edu/lac; *Statistical Abstract of Latin America.*

GUATEMALA - EMPLOYMENT

Euromonitor International, Inc., 224 S. Michigan Avenue, Suite 1500, Chicago, IL 60604, (312) 922-1115, Fax: (312) 922-1157, www.euromonitor.com; *International Marketing Data and Statistics 2008.*

International Labour Office, I.L.O. Publications, 4 route des Morillons, CH-1211 Geneva 22, Switzerland, (Telephone in U.S. (202) 653-7652), (Fax in U.S. (202) 653-7687), www.ilo.org; *Yearbook of Labour Statistics 2006.*

M.E. Sharpe, 80 Business Park Drive, Armonk, NY 10504, (800) 541-6563, Fax: (914) 273-2106, www.mesharpe.com; *The Illustrated Book of World Rankings.*

UCLA Latin American Institute, 10343 Bunche Hall, Box 951447, Los Angeles, CA 90095-1447, (310) 825-4571, Fax: (310) 206-6859, www.international.ucla.edu/lac; *Statistical Abstract of Latin America.*

United Nations Statistics Division, New York, NY 10017, (800) 253-9646, Fax: (212) 963-4116, http://unstats.un.org; *Statistical Yearbook* and *Statistical Yearbook for Latin America and the Caribbean 2004.*

The World Bank, 1818 H Street, NW, Washington, DC 20433, (202) 473-1000, Fax: (202) 477-6391, www.worldbank.org; *Guatemala.*

GUATEMALA - ENVIRONMENTAL CONDITIONS

DSI Data Service Information, Xantener Strasse 51a, D-47495 Rheinberg, Germany, www.dsidata.com; *Campus Solution* and *DSI's Global Environmental Database.*

Economist Intelligence Unit, 111 West 57th Street, New York, NY 10019, (212) 554-0600, Fax: (212) 586-1181, www.eiu.com; *Guatemala Country Report.*

United Nations Statistics Division, New York, NY 10017, (800) 253-9646, Fax: (212) 963-4116, http://unstats.un.org; *World Statistics Pocketbook.*

GUATEMALA - EXPENDITURES, PUBLIC

Inter-American Development Bank (IDB), 1300 New York Avenue, NW, Washington, DC 20577, (202) 623-1000, Fax: (202) 623-3096, www.iadb.org; *The Politics of Policies: Economic and Social Progress in Latin America - 2006 Report.*

Organization of American States (OAS), 17th Street Constitution Avenue NW, Washington, DC 20006, (202) 458-3000, www.oas.org; *The OAS in Transition: 1994-2004.*

United Nations Statistics Division, New York, NY 10017, (800) 253-9646, Fax: (212) 963-4116, http://unstats.un.org; *Statistical Yearbook for Latin America and the Caribbean 2004.*

GUATEMALA - EXPORTS

Central Intelligence Agency, Office of Public Affairs, Washington, DC 20505, (703) 482-0623, Fax: (703) 482-1739, www.cia.gov; *The World Factbook.*

Economist Intelligence Unit, 111 West 57th Street, New York, NY 10019, (212) 554-0600, Fax: (212) 586-1181, www.eiu.com; *Business Latin America* and *Guatemala Country Report.*

Euromonitor International, Inc., 224 S. Michigan Avenue, Suite 1500, Chicago, IL 60604, (312) 922-1115, Fax: (312) 922-1157, www.euromonitor.com; *International Marketing Data and Statistics 2008* and *The World Economic Factbook 2008.*

Inter-American Development Bank (IDB), 1300 New York Avenue, NW, Washington, DC 20577, (202) 623-1000, Fax: (202) 623-3096, www.iadb.org; *The Politics of Policies: Economic and Social Progress in Latin America - 2006 Report.*

International Monetary Fund (IMF), 700 Nineteenth Street, NW, Washington, DC 20431, (202) 623-7000, Fax: (202) 623-4661, www.imf.org; *Direction of Trade Statistics Yearbook 2007; Government Finance Statistics Yearbook (2008 Edition);* and *International Financial Statistics Yearbook 2007.*

Organization of American States (OAS), 17th Street Constitution Avenue NW, Washington, DC 20006, (202) 458-3000, www.oas.org; *The OAS in Transition: 1994-2004.*

Palgrave Macmillan Ltd., Houndmills, Basingstoke, Hampshire, RG21 6XS, England, (Telephone in U.S. (888) 330-8477), (Fax in U.S. (800) 672-2054), www.palgrave.com; *The Statesman's Yearbook 2008.*

Taylor and Francis Group, An Informa Business, 2 Park Square, Milton Park, Abingdon, Oxford OX14 4RN, United Kingdom, (Dial from U.S. (212) 216-7800), (Fax from U.S. (212) 564-7854), www.tandf.co.uk; *The Europa World Year Book.*

United Nations Conference on Trade and Development (UNCTAD), DC2-1120, United Nations, New York, NY 10017, (212) 963-0027, www.unctad.org; *Handbook of Statistics 2005.*

United Nations Food and Agricultural Organization (FAO), Viale delle Terme di Caracalla, 00100 Rome, Italy, (Dial from U.S. (202) 653-2400), (Fax from U.S. (202) 653 5760), www.fao.org; *The State of Food and Agriculture (SOFA) 2006.*

United Nations Statistics Division, New York, NY 10017, (800) 253-9646, Fax: (212) 963-4116, http://unstats.un.org; *Statistical Yearbook for Latin America and the Caribbean 2004.*

The World Bank, 1818 H Street, NW, Washington, DC 20433, (202) 473-1000, Fax: (202) 477-6391, www.worldbank.org; *World Development Indicators (WDI) 2008* and *World Development Report 2008.*

GUATEMALA - FEMALE WORKING POPULATION

See GUATEMALA - EMPLOYMENT

GUATEMALA - FERTILITY, HUMAN

Central Intelligence Agency, Office of Public Affairs, Washington, DC 20505, (703) 482-0623, Fax: (703) 482-1739, www.cia.gov; *The World Factbook.*

M.E. Sharpe, 80 Business Park Drive, Armonk, NY 10504, (800) 541-6563, Fax: (914) 273-2106, www.mesharpe.com; *The Illustrated Book of World Rankings.*

United Nations Statistics Division, New York, NY 10017, (800) 253-9646, Fax: (212) 963-4116, http://unstats.un.org; *Human Development Report 2006.*

The World Bank, 1818 H Street, NW, Washington, DC 20433, (202) 473-1000, Fax: (202) 477-6391, www.worldbank.org; *The World Bank Atlas 2003-2004; World Development Indicators (WDI) 2008;* and *World Development Report 2008.*

GUATEMALA - FERTILIZER INDUSTRY

Economist Intelligence Unit, 111 West 57th Street, New York, NY 10019, (212) 554-0600, Fax: (212) 586-1181, www.eiu.com; *Business Latin America.*

United Nations Food and Agricultural Organization (FAO), Viale delle Terme di Caracalla, 00100 Rome, Italy, (Dial from U.S. (202) 653-2400), (Fax from U.S. (202) 653 5760), www.fao.org; *The State of Food and Agriculture (SOFA) 2006.*

United Nations Statistics Division, New York, NY 10017, (800) 253-9646, Fax: (212) 963-4116, http://unstats.un.org; *Statistical Yearbook.*

GUATEMALA - FETAL MORTALITY

See GUATEMALA - MORTALITY

GUATEMALA - FINANCE

Inter-American Development Bank (IDB), 1300 New York Avenue, NW, Washington, DC 20577, (202)

623-1000, Fax: (202) 623-3096, www.iadb.org; *The Politics of Policies: Economic and Social Progress in Latin America - 2006 Report.*

International Monetary Fund (IMF), 700 Nineteenth Street, NW, Washington, DC 20431, (202) 623-7000, Fax: (202) 623-4661, www.imf.org; *International Financial Statistics Yearbook 2007.*

Organization of American States (OAS), 17th Street Constitution Avenue NW, Washington, DC 20006, (202) 458-3000, www.oas.org; *The OAS in Transition: 1994-2004.*

Taylor and Francis Group, An Informa Business, 2 Park Square, Milton Park, Abingdon, Oxford OX14 4RN, United Kingdom, (Dial from U.S. (212) 216-7800), (Fax from U.S. (212) 564-7854), www.tandf.co.uk; *The Europa World Year Book.*

United Nations Statistics Division, New York, NY 10017, (800) 253-9646, Fax: (212) 963-4116, http://unstats.un.org; *National Accounts Statistics: Analysis of Main Aggregates* and *Statistical Yearbook.*.

The World Bank, 1818 H Street, NW, Washington, DC 20433, (202) 473-1000, Fax: (202) 477-6391, www.worldbank.org; *Guatemala.*

GUATEMALA - FINANCE, PUBLIC

Bernan Essential Government Publications, 4611-F Assembly Drive, Lanham MD, 20706-4391, (301) 459-2255, Fax: (800) 865-3450, www.bernan.com; *National Accounts Statistics.*

Economist Intelligence Unit, 111 West 57th Street, New York, NY 10019, (212) 554-0600, Fax: (212) 586-1181, www.eiu.com; *Guatemala Country Report.*

Inter-American Development Bank (IDB), 1300 New York Avenue, NW, Washington, DC 20577, (202) 623-1000, Fax: (202) 623-3096, www.iadb.org; *The Politics of Policies: Economic and Social Progress in Latin America - 2006 Report.*

International Monetary Fund (IMF), 700 Nineteenth Street, NW, Washington, DC 20431, (202) 623-7000, Fax: (202) 623-4661, www.imf.org; *Government Finance Statistics Yearbook (2008 Edition); International Financial Statistics;* and *International Financial Statistics Online Service.*

M.E. Sharpe, 80 Business Park Drive, Armonk, NY 10504, (800) 541-6563, Fax: (914) 273-2106, www.mesharpe.com; *The Illustrated Book of World Rankings.*

Organization of American States (OAS), 17th Street Constitution Avenue NW, Washington, DC 20006, (202) 458-3000, www.oas.org; *The OAS in Transition: 1994-2004.*

Palgrave Macmillan Ltd., Houndmills, Basingstoke, Hampshire, RG21 6XS, England, (Telephone in U.S. (888) 330-8477), (Fax in U.S. (800) 672-2054), www.palgrave.com; *The Statesman's Yearbook 2008.*

Taylor and Francis Group, An Informa Business, 2 Park Square, Milton Park, Abingdon, Oxford OX14 4RN, United Kingdom, (Dial from U.S. (212) 216-7800), (Fax from U.S. (212) 564-7854), www.tandf.co.uk; *The Europa World Year Book.*

UCLA Latin American Institute, 10343 Bunche Hall, Box 951447, Los Angeles, CA 90095-1447, (310) 825-4571, Fax: (310) 206-6859, www.international.ucla.edu/lac; *Statistical Abstract of Latin America.*

The World Bank, 1818 H Street, NW, Washington, DC 20433, (202) 473-1000, Fax: (202) 477-6391, www.worldbank.org; *Guatemala.*

GUATEMALA - FISHERIES

Inter-American Development Bank (IDB), 1300 New York Avenue, NW, Washington, DC 20577, (202) 623-1000, Fax: (202) 623-3096, www.iadb.org; *The Politics of Policies: Economic and Social Progress in Latin America - 2006 Report.*

M.E. Sharpe, 80 Business Park Drive, Armonk, NY 10504, (800) 541-6563, Fax: (914) 273-2106, www.mesharpe.com; *The Illustrated Book of World Rankings.*

Taylor and Francis Group, An Informa Business, 2 Park Square, Milton Park, Abingdon, Oxford OX14 4RN, United Kingdom, (Dial from U.S. (212) 216-7800), (Fax from U.S. (212) 564-7854), www.tandf.co.uk; *The Europa World Year Book.*

UCLA Latin American Institute, 10343 Bunche Hall, Box 951447, Los Angeles, CA 90095-1447, (310) 825-4571, Fax: (310) 206-6859, www.international.ucla.edu/lac; *Statistical Abstract of Latin America.*

United Nations Conference on Trade and Development (UNCTAD), DC2-1120, United Nations, New York, NY 10017, (212) 963-0027, www.unctad.org; *UNCTAD Commodity Yearbook.*

United Nations Food and Agricultural Organization (FAO), Viale delle Terme di Caracalla, 00100 Rome, Italy, (Dial from U.S. (202) 653-2400), (Fax from U.S. (202) 653 5760), www.fao.org; *FAO Yearbook of Fishery Statistics;* Fishery Databases; FISHSTAT Database. Subjects covered include: Aquaculture production, capture production, fishery commodities; and *The State of Food and Agriculture (SOFA) 2006.*

United Nations Statistics Division, New York, NY 10017, (800) 253-9646, Fax: (212) 963-4116, http://unstats.un.org; *Statistical Yearbook.*

The World Bank, 1818 H Street, NW, Washington, DC 20433, (202) 473-1000, Fax: (202) 477-6391, www.worldbank.org; *Guatemala.*

GUATEMALA - FLOUR INDUSTRY

United Nations Statistics Division, New York, NY 10017, (800) 253-9646, Fax: (212) 963-4116, http://unstats.un.org; *Statistical Yearbook.*

GUATEMALA - FOOD

United Nations Conference on Trade and Development (UNCTAD), DC2-1120, United Nations, New York, NY 10017, (212) 963-0027, www.unctad.org; *UNCTAD Commodity Yearbook.*

United Nations Food and Agricultural Organization (FAO), Viale delle Terme di Caracalla, 00100 Rome, Italy, (Dial from U.S. (202) 653-2400), (Fax from U.S. (202) 653 5760), www.fao.org; *FAO Production Yearbook 2002* and *The State of Food and Agriculture (SOFA) 2006.*

United Nations Statistics Division, New York, NY 10017, (800) 253-9646, Fax: (212) 963-4116, http://unstats.un.org; *Human Development Report 2006.*

GUATEMALA - FOREIGN EXCHANGE RATES

Central Intelligence Agency, Office of Public Affairs, Washington, DC 20505, (703) 482-0623, Fax: (703) 482-1739, www.cia.gov; *The World Factbook.*

Euromonitor International, Inc., 224 S. Michigan Avenue, Suite 1500, Chicago, IL 60604, (312) 922-1115, Fax: (312) 922-1157, www.euromonitor.com; *International Marketing Data and Statistics 2008* and *The World Economic Factbook 2008.*

Inter-American Development Bank (IDB), 1300 New York Avenue, NW, Washington, DC 20577, (202) 623-1000, Fax: (202) 623-3096, www.iadb.org; *The Politics of Policies: Economic and Social Progress in Latin America - 2006 Report.*

International Civil Aviation Organization (ICAO), External Relations and Public Information Office (EPO), 999 University Street, Montreal, Quebec H3C 5H7, Canada, (Dial from U.S. (514) 954-8219), (Fax from U.S. (514) 954-6077), www.icao.int; *Civil Aviation Statistics of the World.*

International Monetary Fund (IMF), 700 Nineteenth Street, NW, Washington, DC 20431, (202) 623-7000, Fax: (202) 623-4661, www.imf.org; *International Financial Statistics Yearbook 2007.*

Organization of American States (OAS), 17th Street Constitution Avenue NW, Washington, DC 20006, (202) 458-3000, www.oas.org; *The OAS in Transition: 1994-2004.*

Taylor and Francis Group, An Informa Business, 2 Park Square, Milton Park, Abingdon, Oxford OX14 4RN, United Kingdom, (Dial from U.S. (212) 216-7800), (Fax from U.S. (212) 564-7854), www.tandf.co.uk; *The Europa World Year Book.*

UCLA Latin American Institute, 10343 Bunche Hall, Box 951447, Los Angeles, CA 90095-1447, (310) 825-4571, Fax: (310) 206-6859, www.international.ucla.edu/lac; *Statistical Abstract of Latin America.*

United Nations Statistics Division, New York, NY 10017, (800) 253-9646, Fax: (212) 963-4116, http://unstats.un.org; *Statistical Yearbook* and *World Statistics Pocketbook.*

GUATEMALA - FORESTS AND FORESTRY

American Forest Paper Association (AFPA), 1111 Nineteenth Street, NW, Suite 800, Washington, DC 20036, (800) 878-8878, www.afandpa.org; *2007 Annual Statistics of Paper, Paperboard, and Wood Pulp.*

Economist Intelligence Unit, 111 West 57th Street, New York, NY 10019, (212) 554-0600, Fax: (212) 586-1181, www.eiu.com; *Business Latin America.*

Inter-American Development Bank (IDB), 1300 New York Avenue, NW, Washington, DC 20577, (202) 623-1000, Fax: (202) 623-3096, www.iadb.org; *The Politics of Policies: Economic and Social Progress in Latin America - 2006 Report.*

M.E. Sharpe, 80 Business Park Drive, Armonk, NY 10504, (800) 541-6563, Fax: (914) 273-2106, www.mesharpe.com; *The Illustrated Book of World Rankings.*

Palgrave Macmillan Ltd., Houndmills, Basingstoke, Hampshire, RG21 6XS, England, (Telephone in U.S. (888) 330-8477), (Fax in U.S. (800) 672-2054), www.palgrave.com; *The Statesman's Yearbook 2008.*

Taylor and Francis Group, An Informa Business, 2 Park Square, Milton Park, Abingdon, Oxford OX14 4RN, United Kingdom, (Dial from U.S. (212) 216-7800), (Fax from U.S. (212) 564-7854), www.tandf.co.uk; *The Europa World Year Book.*

UCLA Latin American Institute, 10343 Bunche Hall, Box 951447, Los Angeles, CA 90095-1447, (310) 825-4571, Fax: (310) 206-6859, www.international.ucla.edu/lac; *Statistical Abstract of Latin America.*

UNESCO Institute for Statistics, C.P. 6128 Succursale Centre-Ville, Montreal, Quebec, H3C 3J7 Canada, (Dial from U.S. (514) 343-6880), (Fax from U.S. (514) 343 6882), www.uis.unesco.org; *Statistical Tables.*

United Nations Conference on Trade and Development (UNCTAD), DC2-1120, United Nations, New York, NY 10017, (212) 963-0027, www.unctad.org; *UNCTAD Commodity Yearbook.*

United Nations Food and Agricultural Organization (FAO), Viale delle Terme di Caracalla, 00100 Rome, Italy, (Dial from U.S. (202) 653-2400), (Fax from U.S. (202) 653 5760), www.fao.org; *FAO Yearbook of Forest Products* and *The State of Food and Agriculture (SOFA) 2006.*

United Nations Statistics Division, New York, NY 10017, (800) 253-9646, Fax: (212) 963-4116, http://unstats.un.org; *Statistical Yearbook.*

The World Bank, 1818 H Street, NW, Washington, DC 20433, (202) 473-1000, Fax: (202) 477-6391, www.worldbank.org; *Guatemala* and *World Development Report 2008.*

World Resources Institute (WRI), 10 G Street, NE, Suite 800 Washington, DC 20002, (202) 729-7600, www.wri.org; *Indigenous Peoples, Representation and Citizenship in Guatemalan Forestry.*

GUATEMALA - GAS PRODUCTION

See GUATEMALA - MINERAL INDUSTRIES

GUATEMALA - GEOGRAPHIC INFORMATION SYSTEMS

M.E. Sharpe, 80 Business Park Drive, Armonk, NY 10504, (800) 541-6563, Fax: (914) 273-2106, www.mesharpe.com; *The Illustrated Book of World Rankings.*

UCLA Latin American Institute, 10343 Bunche Hall, Box 951447, Los Angeles, CA 90095-1447, (310) 825-4571, Fax: (310) 206-6859, www.international.ucla.edu/lac; *Statistical Abstract of Latin America.*

GUATEMALA - GOLD INDUSTRY

Economist Intelligence Unit, 111 West 57th Street, New York, NY 10019, (212) 554-0600, Fax: (212) 586-1181, www.eiu.com; *Business Latin America.*

International Monetary Fund (IMF), 700 Nineteenth Street, NW, Washington, DC 20431, (202) 623-7000, Fax: (202) 623-4661, www.imf.org; *International Financial Statistics Yearbook 2007.*

United Nations Statistics Division, New York, NY 10017, (800) 253-9646, Fax: (212) 963-4116, http://unstats.un.org; *Statistical Yearbook.*

The World Bank, 1818 H Street, NW, Washington, DC 20433, (202) 473-1000, Fax: (202) 477-6391, www.worldbank.org; *World Development Indicators (WDI) 2008.*

GUATEMALA - GOLD PRODUCTION

See GUATEMALA - MINERAL INDUSTRIES

GUATEMALA - GRANTS-IN-AID

International Monetary Fund (IMF), 700 Nineteenth Street, NW, Washington, DC 20431, (202) 623-7000, Fax: (202) 623-4661, www.imf.org; *Government Finance Statistics Yearbook (2008 Edition).*

GUATEMALA - GROSS DOMESTIC PRODUCT

Economist Intelligence Unit, 111 West 57th Street, New York, NY 10019, (212) 554-0600, Fax: (212) 586-1181, www.eiu.com; *Business Latin America* and *Guatemala Country Report.*

Euromonitor International, Inc., 224 S. Michigan Avenue, Suite 1500, Chicago, IL 60604, (312) 922-1115, Fax: (312) 922-1157, www.euromonitor.com; *International Marketing Data and Statistics 2008* and *The World Economic Factbook 2008.*

Inter-American Development Bank (IDB), 1300 New York Avenue, NW, Washington, DC 20577, (202) 623-1000, Fax: (202) 623-3096, www.iadb.org; *The Politics of Policies: Economic and Social Progress in Latin America - 2006 Report.*

M.E. Sharpe, 80 Business Park Drive, Armonk, NY 10504, (800) 541-6563, Fax: (914) 273-2106, www.mesharpe.com; *The Illustrated Book of World Rankings.*

Organization of American States (OAS), 17th Street Constitution Avenue NW, Washington, DC 20006, (202) 458-3000, www.oas.org; *The OAS in Transition: 1994-2004.*

Taylor and Francis Group, An Informa Business, 2 Park Square, Milton Park, Abingdon, Oxford OX14 4RN, United Kingdom, (Dial from U.S. (212) 216-7800), (Fax from U.S. (212) 564-7854), www.tandf.co.uk; *The Europa World Year Book.*

United Nations Statistics Division, New York, NY 10017, (800) 253-9646, Fax: (212) 963-4116, http://unstats.un.org; *Human Development Report 2006; National Accounts Statistics: Compendium of Income Distribution Statistics; Statistical Yearbook;* and *Statistical Yearbook for Latin America and the Caribbean 2004.*

The World Bank, 1818 H Street, NW, Washington, DC 20433, (202) 473-1000, Fax: (202) 477-6391, www.worldbank.org; *World Development Indicators (WDI) 2008* and *World Development Report 2008.*

GUATEMALA - GROSS NATIONAL PRODUCT

Euromonitor International, Inc., 224 S. Michigan Avenue, Suite 1500, Chicago, IL 60604, (312) 922-1115, Fax: (312) 922-1157, www.euromonitor.com; *International Marketing Data and Statistics 2008.*

Inter-American Development Bank (IDB), 1300 New York Avenue, NW, Washington, DC 20577, (202) 623-1000, Fax: (202) 623-3096, www.iadb.org; *The Politics of Policies: Economic and Social Progress in Latin America - 2006 Report.*

M.E. Sharpe, 80 Business Park Drive, Armonk, NY 10504, (800) 541-6563, Fax: (914) 273-2106, www.mesharpe.com; *The Illustrated Book of World Rankings.*

Palgrave Macmillan Ltd., Houndmills, Basingstoke, Hampshire, RG21 6XS, England, (Telephone in U.S. (888) 330-8477), (Fax in U.S. (800) 672-2054), www.palgrave.com; *The Statesman's Yearbook 2008.*

U.S. Department of State (DOS), 2201 C Street NW, Washington, DC 20520, (202) 647-4000, www.state.gov; *World Military Expenditures and Arms Transfers (WMEAT).*

United Nations Statistics Division, New York, NY 10017, (800) 253-9646, Fax: (212) 963-4116, http://unstats.un.org; *Statistical Yearbook.*

The World Bank, 1818 H Street, NW, Washington, DC 20433, (202) 473-1000, Fax: (202) 477-6391, www.worldbank.org; *The World Bank Atlas 2003-2004; World Development Indicators (WDI) 2008;* and *World Development Report 2008.*

GUATEMALA - HIDES AND SKINS INDUSTRY

United Nations Food and Agricultural Organization (FAO), Viale delle Terme di Caracalla, 00100 Rome, Italy, (Dial from U.S. (202) 653-2400), (Fax from U.S. (202) 653 5760), www.fao.org; *FAO Production Yearbook 2002.*

GUATEMALA - HOUSING

Euromonitor International, Inc., 224 S. Michigan Avenue, Suite 1500, Chicago, IL 60604, (312) 922-1115, Fax: (312) 922-1157, www.euromonitor.com; *World Marketing Data and Statistics.*

M.E. Sharpe, 80 Business Park Drive, Armonk, NY 10504, (800) 541-6563, Fax: (914) 273-2106, www.mesharpe.com; *The Illustrated Book of World Rankings.*

UCLA Latin American Institute, 10343 Bunche Hall, Box 951447, Los Angeles, CA 90095-1447, (310) 825-4571, Fax: (310) 206-6859, www.international.ucla.edu/lac; *Statistical Abstract of Latin America.*

United Nations Statistics Division, New York, NY 10017, (800) 253-9646, Fax: (212) 963-4116, http://unstats.un.org; *Statistical Yearbook for Latin America and the Caribbean 2004.*

GUATEMALA - ILLITERATE PERSONS

Economist Intelligence Unit, 111 West 57th Street, New York, NY 10019, (212) 554-0600, Fax: (212) 586-1181, www.eiu.com; *Business Latin America.*

Euromonitor International, Inc., 224 S. Michigan Avenue, Suite 1500, Chicago, IL 60604, (312) 922-1115, Fax: (312) 922-1157, www.euromonitor.com; *The World Economic Factbook 2008.*

Palgrave Macmillan Ltd., Houndmills, Basingstoke, Hampshire, RG21 6XS, England, (Telephone in U.S. (888) 330-8477), (Fax in U.S. (800) 672-2054), www.palgrave.com; *The Statesman's Yearbook 2008.*

UNESCO Institute for Statistics, C.P. 6128 Succursale Centre-Ville, Montreal, Quebec, H3C 3J7 Canada, (Dial from U.S. (514) 343-6880), (Fax from U.S. (514) 343 6882), www.uis.unesco.org; *Statistical Tables.*

United Nations Statistics Division, New York, NY 10017, (800) 253-9646, Fax: (212) 963-4116, http://unstats.un.org; *Human Development Report 2006* and *Statistical Yearbook for Latin America and the Caribbean 2004.*

GUATEMALA - IMPORTS

Central Intelligence Agency, Office of Public Affairs, Washington, DC 20505, (703) 482-0623, Fax: (703) 482-1739, www.cia.gov; *The World Factbook.*

Economist Intelligence Unit, 111 West 57th Street, New York, NY 10019, (212) 554-0600, Fax: (212) 586-1181, www.eiu.com; *Business Latin America* and *Guatemala Country Report.*

Euromonitor International, Inc., 224 S. Michigan Avenue, Suite 1500, Chicago, IL 60604, (312) 922-1115, Fax: (312) 922-1157, www.euromonitor.com; *International Marketing Data and Statistics 2008* and *The World Economic Factbook 2008.*

Inter-American Development Bank (IDB), 1300 New York Avenue, NW, Washington, DC 20577, (202) 623-1000, Fax: (202) 623-3096, www.iadb.org; *The Politics of Policies: Economic and Social Progress in Latin America - 2006 Report.*

International Monetary Fund (IMF), 700 Nineteenth Street, NW, Washington, DC 20431, (202) 623-7000, Fax: (202) 623-4661, www.imf.org; *Direction of Trade Statistics Yearbook 2007; Government Finance Statistics Yearbook (2008 Edition);* and *International Financial Statistics Yearbook 2007.*

Organization of American States (OAS), 17th Street Constitution Avenue NW, Washington, DC 20006, (202) 458-3000, www.oas.org; *The OAS in Transition: 1994-2004.*

Palgrave Macmillan Ltd., Houndmills, Basingstoke, Hampshire, RG21 6XS, England, (Telephone in U.S. (888) 330-8477), (Fax in U.S. (800) 672-2054), www.palgrave.com; *The Statesman's Yearbook 2008.*

Taylor and Francis Group, An Informa Business, 2 Park Square, Milton Park, Abingdon, Oxford OX14 4RN, United Kingdom, (Dial from U.S. (212) 216-7800), (Fax from U.S. (212) 564-7854), www.tandf.co.uk; *The Europa World Year Book.*

United Nations Conference on Trade and Development (UNCTAD), DC2-1120, United Nations, New York, NY 10017, (212) 963-0027, www.unctad.org; *Handbook of Statistics 2005.*

United Nations Food and Agricultural Organization (FAO), Viale delle Terme di Caracalla, 00100 Rome, Italy, (Dial from U.S. (202) 653-2400), (Fax from U.S. (202) 653 5760), www.fao.org; *The State of Food and Agriculture (SOFA) 2006.*

United Nations Statistics Division, New York, NY 10017, (800) 253-9646, Fax: (212) 963-4116, http://unstats.un.org; *Statistical Yearbook for Latin America and the Caribbean 2004.*

The World Bank, 1818 H Street, NW, Washington, DC 20433, (202) 473-1000, Fax: (202) 477-6391, www.worldbank.org; *World Development Indicators (WDI) 2008* and *World Development Report 2008.*

GUATEMALA - INCOME DISTRIBUTION

UCLA Latin American Institute, 10343 Bunche Hall, Box 951447, Los Angeles, CA 90095-1447, (310) 825-4571, Fax: (310) 206-6859, www.international.ucla.edu/lac; *Statistical Abstract of Latin America.*

United Nations Statistics Division, New York, NY 10017, (800) 253-9646, Fax: (212) 963-4116, http://unstats.un.org; *Statistical Yearbook for Latin America and the Caribbean 2004.*

GUATEMALA - INCOME TAXES

See GUATEMALA - TAXATION

GUATEMALA - INDUSTRIAL PRODUCTIVITY

Euromonitor International, Inc., 224 S. Michigan Avenue, Suite 1500, Chicago, IL 60604, (312) 922-1115, Fax: (312) 922-1157, www.euromonitor.com; *International Marketing Data and Statistics 2008.*

M.E. Sharpe, 80 Business Park Drive, Armonk, NY 10504, (800) 541-6563, Fax: (914) 273-2106, www.mesharpe.com; *The Illustrated Book of World Rankings.*

GUATEMALA - INDUSTRIAL PROPERTY

United Nations Statistics Division, New York, NY 10017, (800) 253-9646, Fax: (212) 963-4116, http://unstats.un.org; *Statistical Yearbook.*

World Intellectual Property Organization (WIPO), PO Box 18, CH-1211 Geneva 20, Switzerland, www.wipo.int; *Industrial Property Statistics* and *Industrial Property Statistics Online Directory.*

GUATEMALA - INDUSTRIAL STATISTICS

United Nations Statistics Division, New York, NY 10017, (800) 253-9646, Fax: (212) 963-4116, http://unstats.un.org; *Economic Survey of Latin America and the Caribbean 2004-2005.*

GUATEMALA - INDUSTRIES

Central Intelligence Agency, Office of Public Affairs, Washington, DC 20505, (703) 482-0623, Fax: (703) 482-1739, www.cia.gov; *The World Factbook.*

Economist Intelligence Unit, 111 West 57th Street, New York, NY 10019, (212) 554-0600, Fax: (212) 586-1181, www.eiu.com; *Guatemala Country Report.*

Euromonitor International, Inc., 224 S. Michigan Avenue, Suite 1500, Chicago, IL 60604, (312) 922-1115, Fax: (312) 922-1157, www.euromonitor.com; *International Marketing Data and Statistics 2008; The World Economic Factbook 2008;* and *World Marketing Data and Statistics.*

International Labour Office, I.L.O. Publications, 4 route des Morillons, CH-1211 Geneva 22, Switzerland, (Telephone in U.S. (202) 653-7652), (Fax in U.S. (202) 653-7687), www.ilo.org; *Yearbook of Labour Statistics 2006.*

M.E. Sharpe, 80 Business Park Drive, Armonk, NY 10504, (800) 541-6563, Fax: (914) 273-2106, www.mesharpe.com; *The Illustrated Book of World Rankings.*

Palgrave Macmillan Ltd., Houndmills, Basingstoke, Hampshire, RG21 6XS, England, (Telephone in U.S. (888) 330-8477), (Fax in U.S. (800) 672-2054), www.palgrave.com; *The Statesman's Yearbook 2008.*

Taylor and Francis Group, An Informa Business, 2 Park Square, Milton Park, Abingdon, Oxford OX14 4RN, United Kingdom, (Dial from U.S. (212) 216-7800), (Fax from U.S. (212) 564-7854), www.tandf.co.uk; *The Europa World Year Book.*

UCLA Latin American Institute, 10343 Bunche Hall, Box 951447, Los Angeles, CA 90095-1447, (310) 825-4571, Fax: (310) 206-6859, www.international.ucla.edu/lac; *Statistical Abstract of Latin America.*

United Nations Industrial Development Organization (UNIDO), 1 United Nations Plaza, New York, NY 10017, (212) 963 6890, Fax: (212) 963-7904, http://unido.org; Industrial Statistics Database 2008 (INDSTAT) and *The International Yearbook of Industrial Statistics 2008.*

United Nations Statistics Division, New York, NY 10017, (800) 253-9646, Fax: (212) 963-4116, http://unstats.un.org; *2004 Industrial Commodity Statistics Yearbook* and *Statistical Yearbook.*

The World Bank, 1818 H Street, NW, Washington, DC 20433, (202) 473-1000, Fax: (202) 477-6391, www.worldbank.org; *Guatemala* and *World Development Indicators (WDI) 2008.*

GUATEMALA - INFANT AND MATERNAL MORTALITY

See GUATEMALA - MORTALITY

GUATEMALA - INFLATION (FINANCE)

United Nations Statistics Division, New York, NY 10017, (800) 253-9646, Fax: (212) 963-4116, http://unstats.un.org; *Economic Survey of Latin America and the Caribbean 2004-2005.*

GUATEMALA - INTEREST RATES

Inter-American Development Bank (IDB), 1300 New York Avenue, NW, Washington, DC 20577, (202) 623-1000, Fax: (202) 623-3096, www.iadb.org; *The Politics of Policies: Economic and Social Progress in Latin America - 2006 Report.*

GUATEMALA - INTERNAL REVENUE

Inter-American Development Bank (IDB), 1300 New York Avenue, NW, Washington, DC 20577, (202) 623-1000, Fax: (202) 623-3096, www.iadb.org; *The Politics of Policies: Economic and Social Progress in Latin America - 2006 Report.*

Organization of American States (OAS), 17th Street Constitution Avenue NW, Washington, DC 20006, (202) 458-3000, www.oas.org; *The OAS in Transition: 1994-2004.*

GUATEMALA - INTERNATIONAL FINANCE

Inter-American Development Bank (IDB), 1300 New York Avenue, NW, Washington, DC 20577, (202) 623-1000, Fax: (202) 623-3096, www.iadb.org; *The Politics of Policies: Economic and Social Progress in Latin America - 2006 Report.*

UCLA Latin American Institute, 10343 Bunche Hall, Box 951447, Los Angeles, CA 90095-1447, (310) 825-4571, Fax: (310) 206-6859, www.international.ucla.edu/lac; *Statistical Abstract of Latin America.*

United Nations Statistics Division, New York, NY 10017, (800) 253-9646, Fax: (212) 963-4116, http://unstats.un.org; *Statistical Yearbook for Latin America and the Caribbean 2004.*

GUATEMALA - INTERNATIONAL LIQUIDITY

Inter-American Development Bank (IDB), 1300 New York Avenue, NW, Washington, DC 20577, (202) 623-1000, Fax: (202) 623-3096, www.iadb.org; *The Politics of Policies: Economic and Social Progress in Latin America - 2006 Report.*

International Monetary Fund (IMF), 700 Nineteenth Street, NW, Washington, DC 20431, (202) 623-7000, Fax: (202) 623-4661, www.imf.org; *International Financial Statistics Yearbook 2007.*

GUATEMALA - INTERNATIONAL STATISTICS

Inter-American Development Bank (IDB), 1300 New York Avenue, NW, Washington, DC 20577, (202) 623-1000, Fax: (202) 623-3096, www.iadb.org; *The Politics of Policies: Economic and Social Progress in Latin America - 2006 Report.*

UCLA Latin American Institute, 10343 Bunche Hall, Box 951447, Los Angeles, CA 90095-1447, (310) 825-4571, Fax: (310) 206-6859, www.international.ucla.edu/lac; *Statistical Abstract of Latin America.*

GUATEMALA - INTERNATIONAL TRADE

Economist Intelligence Unit, 111 West 57th Street, New York, NY 10019, (212) 554-0600, Fax: (212) 586-1181, www.eiu.com; *Business Latin America* and *Guatemala Country Report.*

Euromonitor International, Inc., 224 S. Michigan Avenue, Suite 1500, Chicago, IL 60604, (312) 922-1115, Fax: (312) 922-1157, www.euromonitor.com; *International Marketing Data and Statistics 2008; The World Economic Factbook 2008;* and *World Marketing Data and Statistics.*

Inter-American Development Bank (IDB), 1300 New York Avenue, NW, Washington, DC 20577, (202) 623-1000, Fax: (202) 623-3096, www.iadb.org; *The Politics of Policies: Economic and Social Progress in Latin America - 2006 Report.*

International Monetary Fund (IMF), 700 Nineteenth Street, NW, Washington, DC 20431, (202) 623-7000, Fax: (202) 623-4661, www.imf.org; *International Financial Statistics Yearbook 2007.*

M.E. Sharpe, 80 Business Park Drive, Armonk, NY 10504, (800) 541-6563, Fax: (914) 273-2106, www.mesharpe.com; *The Illustrated Book of World Rankings.*

Palgrave Macmillan Ltd., Houndmills, Basingstoke, Hampshire, RG21 6XS, England, (Telephone in U.S. (888) 330-8477), (Fax in U.S. (800) 672-2054), www.palgrave.com; *The Statesman's Yearbook 2008.*

Taylor and Francis Group, An Informa Business, 2 Park Square, Milton Park, Abingdon, Oxford OX14 4RN, United Kingdom, (Dial from U.S. (212) 216-7800), (Fax from U.S. (212) 564-7854), www.tandf.co.uk; *The Europa World Year Book.*

UCLA Latin American Institute, 10343 Bunche Hall, Box 951447, Los Angeles, CA 90095-1447, (310) 825-4571, Fax: (310) 206-6859, www.international.ucla.edu/lac; *Statistical Abstract of Latin America.*

United Nations Conference on Trade and Development (UNCTAD), DC2-1120, United Nations, New York, NY 10017, (212) 963-0027, www.unctad.org; *UNCTAD Commodity Yearbook.*

United Nations Food and Agricultural Organization (FAO), Viale delle Terme di Caracalla, 00100 Rome, Italy, (Dial from U.S. (202) 653-2400), (Fax from U.S. (202) 653 5760), www.fao.org; *FAO Trade Yearbook* and *The State of Food and Agriculture (SOFA) 2006.*

United Nations Statistics Division, New York, NY 10017, (800) 253-9646, Fax: (212) 963-4116, http://unstats.un.org; *Economic Survey of Latin America and the Caribbean 2004-2005; International Trade Statistics Yearbook; Statistical Yearbook;* and *Statistical Yearbook for Latin America and the Caribbean 2004.*

The World Bank, 1818 H Street, NW, Washington, DC 20433, (202) 473-1000, Fax: (202) 477-6391, www.worldbank.org; *Guatemala; World Development Indicators (WDI) 2008;* and *World Development Report 2008.*

World Trade Organization (WTO), Centre William Rappard, Rue de Lausanne 154, CH-1211 Geneva 21, Switzerland, www.wto.org; *International Trade Statistics 2006.*

GUATEMALA - INTERNET USERS

International Telecommunication Union (ITU), Place des Nations, 1211 Geneva 20, Switzerland, www.itu.int; *World Telecommunication/ICT Indicators Database on CD-ROM; World Telecommunication/ICT Indicators Database Online;* and *Yearbook of Statistics - Telecommunication Services (Chronological Time Series 1997-2006).*

The World Bank, 1818 H Street, NW, Washington, DC 20433, (202) 473-1000, Fax: (202) 477-6391, www.worldbank.org; *Guatemala.*

GUATEMALA - INVESTMENTS

Inter-American Development Bank (IDB), 1300 New York Avenue, NW, Washington, DC 20577, (202) 623-1000, Fax: (202) 623-3096, www.iadb.org; *The Politics of Policies: Economic and Social Progress in Latin America - 2006 Report.*

International Monetary Fund (IMF), 700 Nineteenth Street, NW, Washington, DC 20431, (202) 623-7000, Fax: (202) 623-4661, www.imf.org; *International Financial Statistics Yearbook 2007.*

United Nations Statistics Division, New York, NY 10017, (800) 253-9646, Fax: (212) 963-4116, http://unstats.un.org; *Statistical Yearbook for Latin America and the Caribbean 2004.*

GUATEMALA - INVESTMENTS, FOREIGN

Economist Intelligence Unit, 111 West 57th Street, New York, NY 10019, (212) 554-0600, Fax: (212) 586-1181, www.eiu.com; *Business Latin America.*

GUATEMALA - IRON AND IRON ORE PRODUCTION

See GUATEMALA - MINERAL INDUSTRIES

GUATEMALA - IRRIGATION

Euromonitor International, Inc., 224 S. Michigan Avenue, Suite 1500, Chicago, IL 60604, (312) 922-1115, Fax: (312) 922-1157, www.euromonitor.com; *International Marketing Data and Statistics 2008.*

Inter-American Development Bank (IDB), 1300 New York Avenue, NW, Washington, DC 20577, (202) 623-1000, Fax: (202) 623-3096, www.iadb.org; *The Politics of Policies: Economic and Social Progress in Latin America - 2006 Report.*

GUATEMALA - LABOR

Central Intelligence Agency, Office of Public Affairs, Washington, DC 20505, (703) 482-0623, Fax: (703) 482-1739, www.cia.gov; *The World Factbook.*

Economist Intelligence Unit, 111 West 57th Street, New York, NY 10019, (212) 554-0600, Fax: (212) 586-1181, www.eiu.com; *Business Latin America.*

Euromonitor International, Inc., 224 S. Michigan Avenue, Suite 1500, Chicago, IL 60604, (312) 922-1115, Fax: (312) 922-1157, www.euromonitor.com; *International Marketing Data and Statistics 2008* and *World Marketing Data and Statistics.*

International Labour Office, I.L.O. Publications, 4 route des Morillons, CH-1211 Geneva 22, Switzerland, (Telephone in U.S. (202) 653-7652), (Fax in U.S. (202) 653-7687), www.ilo.org; *Yearbook of Labour Statistics 2006.*

M.E. Sharpe, 80 Business Park Drive, Armonk, NY 10504, (800) 541-6563, Fax: (914) 273-2106, www.mesharpe.com; *The Illustrated Book of World Rankings.*

Palgrave Macmillan Ltd., Houndmills, Basingstoke, Hampshire, RG21 6XS, England, (Telephone in U.S. (888) 330-8477), (Fax in U.S. (800) 672-2054), www.palgrave.com; *The Statesman's Yearbook 2008.*

United Nations Food and Agricultural Organization (FAO), Viale delle Terme di Caracalla, 00100 Rome, Italy, (Dial from U.S. (202) 653-2400), (Fax from U.S. (202) 653 5760), www.fao.org; *The State of Food and Agriculture (SOFA) 2006.*

United Nations Statistics Division, New York, NY 10017, (800) 253-9646, Fax: (212) 963-4116, http://unstats.un.org; *Human Development Report 2006.*

The World Bank, 1818 H Street, NW, Washington, DC 20433, (202) 473-1000, Fax: (202) 477-6391, www.worldbank.org; *The World Bank Atlas 2003-2004; World Development Indicators (WDI) 2008;* and *World Development Report 2008.*

GUATEMALA - LAND USE

Central Intelligence Agency, Office of Public Affairs, Washington, DC 20505, (703) 482-0623, Fax: (703) 482-1739, www.cia.gov; *The World Factbook.*

Euromonitor International, Inc., 224 S. Michigan Avenue, Suite 1500, Chicago, IL 60604, (312) 922-1115, Fax: (312) 922-1157, www.euromonitor.com; *International Marketing Data and Statistics 2008.*

Inter-American Development Bank (IDB), 1300 New York Avenue, NW, Washington, DC 20577, (202) 623-1000, Fax: (202) 623-3096, www.iadb.org; *The Politics of Policies: Economic and Social Progress in Latin America - 2006 Report.*

United Nations Food and Agricultural Organization (FAO), Viale delle Terme di Caracalla, 00100 Rome, Italy, (Dial from U.S. (202) 653-2400), (Fax from U.S. (202) 653 5760), www.fao.org; *FAO Production Yearbook 2002.*

The World Bank, 1818 H Street, NW, Washington, DC 20433, (202) 473-1000, Fax: (202) 477-6391, www.worldbank.org; *World Development Report 2008.*

GUATEMALA - LIBRARIES

M.E. Sharpe, 80 Business Park Drive, Armonk, NY 10504, (800) 541-6563, Fax: (914) 273-2106, www.mesharpe.com; *The Illustrated Book of World Rankings.*

UNESCO Institute for Statistics, C.P. 6128 Succursale Centre-Ville, Montreal, Quebec, H3C 3J7 Canada, (Dial from U.S. (514) 343-6880), (Fax from U.S. (514) 343 6882), www.uis.unesco.org; *Statistical Tables.*

GUATEMALA - LICENSES

International Monetary Fund (IMF), 700 Nineteenth Street, NW, Washington, DC 20431, (202) 623-7000, Fax: (202) 623-4661, www.imf.org; *Government Finance Statistics Yearbook (2008 Edition).*

GUATEMALA - LIFE EXPECTANCY

Central Intelligence Agency, Office of Public Affairs, Washington, DC 20505, (703) 482-0623, Fax: (703) 482-1739, www.cia.gov; *The World Factbook.*

Economist Intelligence Unit, 111 West 57th Street, New York, NY 10019, (212) 554-0600, Fax: (212) 586-1181, www.eiu.com; *Business Latin America.*

Euromonitor International, Inc., 224 S. Michigan Avenue, Suite 1500, Chicago, IL 60604, (312) 922-1115, Fax: (312) 922-1157, www.euromonitor.com; *The World Economic Factbook 2008.*

Palgrave Macmillan Ltd., Houndmills, Basingstoke, Hampshire, RG21 6XS, England, (Telephone in U.S. (888) 330-8477), (Fax in U.S. (800) 672-2054), www.palgrave.com; *The Statesman's Yearbook 2008.*

United Nations Statistics Division, New York, NY 10017, (800) 253-9646, Fax: (212) 963-4116, http://unstats.un.org; *Human Development Report 2006; Statistical Yearbook for Latin America and the Caribbean 2004;* and *World Statistics Pocketbook.*

The World Bank, 1818 H Street, NW, Washington, DC 20433, (202) 473-1000, Fax: (202) 477-6391, www.worldbank.org; *The World Bank Atlas 2003-2004* and *World Development Report 2008.*

GUATEMALA - LITERACY

Euromonitor International, Inc., 224 S. Michigan Avenue, Suite 1500, Chicago, IL 60604, (312) 922-1115, Fax: (312) 922-1157, www.euromonitor.com; *World Marketing Data and Statistics.*

GUATEMALA - LIVESTOCK

Euromonitor International, Inc., 224 S. Michigan Avenue, Suite 1500, Chicago, IL 60604, (312) 922-1115, Fax: (312) 922-1157, www.euromonitor.com; *International Marketing Data and Statistics 2008.*

M.E. Sharpe, 80 Business Park Drive, Armonk, NY 10504, (800) 541-6563, Fax: (914) 273-2106, www.mesharpe.com; *The Illustrated Book of World Rankings.*

Palgrave Macmillan Ltd., Houndmills, Basingstoke, Hampshire, RG21 6XS, England, (Telephone in U.S. (888) 330-8477), (Fax in U.S. (800) 672-2054), www.palgrave.com; *The Statesman's Yearbook 2008.*

Taylor and Francis Group, An Informa Business, 2 Park Square, Milton Park, Abingdon, Oxford OX14 4RN, United Kingdom, (Dial from U.S. (212) 216-7800), (Fax from U.S. (212) 564-7854), www.tandf.co.uk; *The Europa World Year Book.*

United Nations Conference on Trade and Development (UNCTAD), DC2-1120, United Nations, New York, NY 10017, (212) 963-0027, www.unctad.org; *UNCTAD Commodity Yearbook.*

United Nations Food and Agricultural Organization (FAO), Viale delle Terme di Caracalla, 00100 Rome, Italy, (Dial from U.S. (202) 653-2400), (Fax from U.S. (202) 653 5760), www.fao.org; *FAO Production Yearbook 2002* and *The State of Food and Agriculture (SOFA) 2006.*

United Nations Statistics Division, New York, NY 10017, (800) 253-9646, Fax: (212) 963-4116, http://unstats.un.org; *Statistical Yearbook.*

GUATEMALA - LOCAL TAXATION

Euromonitor International, Inc., 224 S. Michigan Avenue, Suite 1500, Chicago, IL 60604, (312) 922-1115, Fax: (312) 922-1157, www.euromonitor.com; *International Marketing Data and Statistics 2008.*

Inter-American Development Bank (IDB), 1300 New York Avenue, NW, Washington, DC 20577, (202) 623-1000, Fax: (202) 623-3096, www.iadb.org; *The Politics of Policies: Economic and Social Progress in Latin America - 2006 Report.*

GUATEMALA - MANUFACTURES

Economist Intelligence Unit, 111 West 57th Street, New York, NY 10019, (212) 554-0600, Fax: (212) 586-1181, www.eiu.com; *Business Latin America.*

Inter-American Development Bank (IDB), 1300 New York Avenue, NW, Washington, DC 20577, (202) 623-1000, Fax: (202) 623-3096, www.iadb.org; *The Politics of Policies: Economic and Social Progress in Latin America - 2006 Report.*

M.E. Sharpe, 80 Business Park Drive, Armonk, NY 10504, (800) 541-6563, Fax: (914) 273-2106, www.mesharpe.com; *The Illustrated Book of World Rankings.*

United Nations Statistics Division, New York, NY 10017, (800) 253-9646, Fax: (212) 963-4116, http://unstats.un.org; *Statistical Yearbook* and *Statistical Yearbook for Latin America and the Caribbean 2004.*

The World Bank, 1818 H Street, NW, Washington, DC 20433, (202) 473-1000, Fax: (202) 477-6391, www.worldbank.org; *World Development Indicators (WDI) 2008.*

GUATEMALA - MARRIAGE

M.E. Sharpe, 80 Business Park Drive, Armonk, NY 10504, (800) 541-6563, Fax: (914) 273-2106, www.mesharpe.com; *The Illustrated Book of World Rankings.*

Taylor and Francis Group, An Informa Business, 2 Park Square, Milton Park, Abingdon, Oxford OX14 4RN, United Kingdom, (Dial from U.S. (212) 216-7800), (Fax from U.S. (212) 564-7854), www.tandf.co.uk; *The Europa World Year Book.*

United Nations Statistics Division, New York, NY 10017, (800) 253-9646, Fax: (212) 963-4116, http://unstats.un.org; *Demographic Yearbook* and *Statistical Yearbook.*

GUATEMALA - MEAT INDUSTRY AND TRADE

International Monetary Fund (IMF), 700 Nineteenth Street, NW, Washington, DC 20431, (202) 623-7000, Fax: (202) 623-4661, www.imf.org; *International Financial Statistics Yearbook 2007.*

Organization of American States (OAS), 17th Street Constitution Avenue NW, Washington, DC 20006, (202) 458-3000, www.oas.org; *The OAS in Transition: 1994-2004.*

GUATEMALA - MEAT PRODUCTION

See GUATEMALA - LIVESTOCK

GUATEMALA - MEDICAL CARE, COST OF

International Monetary Fund (IMF), 700 Nineteenth Street, NW, Washington, DC 20431, (202) 623-7000, Fax: (202) 623-4661, www.imf.org; *Government Finance Statistics Yearbook (2008 Edition).*

United Nations Statistics Division, New York, NY 10017, (800) 253-9646, Fax: (212) 963-4116, http://unstats.un.org; *Statistical Yearbook for Latin America and the Caribbean 2004.*

GUATEMALA - MEDICAL PERSONNEL

UCLA Latin American Institute, 10343 Bunche Hall, Box 951447, Los Angeles, CA 90095-1447, (310) 825-4571, Fax: (310) 206-6859, www.international.ucla.edu/lac; *Statistical Abstract of Latin America.*

GUATEMALA - METAL PRODUCTS

United Nations Statistics Division, New York, NY 10017, (800) 253-9646, Fax: (212) 963-4116, http://unstats.un.org; *Statistical Yearbook.*

GUATEMALA - MILK PRODUCTION

See GUATEMALA - DAIRY PROCESSING

GUATEMALA - MINERAL INDUSTRIES

Economist Intelligence Unit, 111 West 57th Street, New York, NY 10019, (212) 554-0600, Fax: (212) 586-1181, www.eiu.com; *Business Latin America.*

Inter-American Development Bank (IDB), 1300 New York Avenue, NW, Washington, DC 20577, (202) 623-1000, Fax: (202) 623-3096, www.iadb.org; *The Politics of Policies: Economic and Social Progress in Latin America - 2006 Report.*

M.E. Sharpe, 80 Business Park Drive, Armonk, NY 10504, (800) 541-6563, Fax: (914) 273-2106, www.mesharpe.com; *The Illustrated Book of World Rankings.*

Organisation for Economic Cooperation and Development (OECD), 2 rue Andre Pascal, F-75775 Paris Cedex 16, France, (Telephone in U.S. (202) 785-6323), (Fax in U.S. (202) 785-0350), www.oecd.org; *World Energy Outlook 2007.*

Palgrave Macmillan Ltd., Houndmills, Basingstoke, Hampshire, RG21 6XS, England, (Telephone in U.S. (888) 330-8477), (Fax in U.S. (800) 672-2054), www.palgrave.com; *The Statesman's Yearbook 2008.*

Taylor and Francis Group, An Informa Business, 2 Park Square, Milton Park, Abingdon, Oxford OX14 4RN, United Kingdom, (Dial from U.S. (212) 216-7800), (Fax from U.S. (212) 564-7854), www.tandf.co.uk; *The Europa World Year Book.*

UCLA Latin American Institute, 10343 Bunche Hall, Box 951447, Los Angeles, CA 90095-1447, (310) 825-4571, Fax: (310) 206-6859, www.international.ucla.edu/lac; *Statistical Abstract of Latin America.*

United Nations Conference on Trade and Development (UNCTAD), DC2-1120, United Nations, New

York, NY 10017, (212) 963-0027, www.unctad.org; *UNCTAD Commodity Yearbook.*

United Nations Statistics Division, New York, NY 10017, (800) 253-9646, Fax: (212) 963-4116, http://unstats.un.org; *Statistical Yearbook* and *Statistical Yearbook for Latin America and the Caribbean 2004.*

GUATEMALA - MONEY EXCHANGE RATES

See GUATEMALA - FOREIGN EXCHANGE RATES

GUATEMALA - MONEY SUPPLY

Economist Intelligence Unit, 111 West 57th Street, New York, NY 10019, (212) 554-0600, Fax: (212) 586-1181, www.eiu.com; *Guatemala Country Report.*

Euromonitor International, Inc., 224 S. Michigan Avenue, Suite 1500, Chicago, IL 60604, (312) 922-1115, Fax: (312) 922-1157, www.euromonitor.com; *International Marketing Data and Statistics 2008.*

Inter-American Development Bank (IDB), 1300 New York Avenue, NW, Washington, DC 20577, (202) 623-1000, Fax: (202) 623-3096, www.iadb.org; *The Politics of Policies: Economic and Social Progress in Latin America - 2006 Report.*

International Monetary Fund (IMF), 700 Nineteenth Street, NW, Washington, DC 20431, (202) 623-7000, Fax: (202) 623-4661, www.imf.org; *International Financial Statistics Yearbook 2007.*

Taylor and Francis Group, An Informa Business, 2 Park Square, Milton Park, Abingdon, Oxford OX14 4RN, United Kingdom, (Dial from U.S. (212) 216-7800), (Fax from U.S. (212) 564-7854), www.tandf.co.uk; *The Europa World Year Book.*

UCLA Latin American Institute, 10343 Bunche Hall, Box 951447, Los Angeles, CA 90095-1447, (310) 825-4571, Fax: (310) 206-6859, www.international.ucla.edu/lac; *Statistical Abstract of Latin America.*

United Nations Statistics Division, New York, NY 10017, (800) 253-9646, Fax: (212) 963-4116, http://unstats.un.org; *Statistical Yearbook.*

The World Bank, 1818 H Street, NW, Washington, DC 20433, (202) 473-1000, Fax: (202) 477-6391, www.worldbank.org; *Guatemala* and *World Development Indicators (WDI) 2008.*

GUATEMALA - MORTALITY

Central Intelligence Agency, Office of Public Affairs, Washington, DC 20505, (703) 482-0623, Fax: (703) 482-1739, www.cia.gov; *The World Factbook.*

Economist Intelligence Unit, 111 West 57th Street, New York, NY 10019, (212) 554-0600, Fax: (212) 586-1181, www.eiu.com; *Business Latin America.*

Euromonitor International, Inc., 224 S. Michigan Avenue, Suite 1500, Chicago, IL 60604, (312) 922-1115, Fax: (312) 922-1157, www.euromonitor.com; *International Marketing Data and Statistics 2008* and *The World Economic Factbook 2008.*

Palgrave Macmillan Ltd., Houndmills, Basingstoke, Hampshire, RG21 6XS, England, (Telephone in U.S. (888) 330-8477), (Fax in U.S. (800) 672-2054), www.palgrave.com; *The Statesman's Yearbook 2008.*

Taylor and Francis Group, An Informa Business, 2 Park Square, Milton Park, Abingdon, Oxford OX14 4RN, United Kingdom, (Dial from U.S. (212) 216-7800), (Fax from U.S. (212) 564-7854), www.tandf.co.uk; *The Europa World Year Book.*

UNICEF, 3 United Nations Plaza, New York, NY 10017, (800) 253-9646, Fax: (212) 887-7465, www.unicef.org; *The State of the World's Children 2008.*

United Nations Statistics Division, New York, NY 10017, (800) 253-9646, Fax: (212) 963-4116, http://unstats.un.org; *Demographic Yearbook; Human Development Report 2006; Statistical Yearbook; Statistical Yearbook for Latin America and the Caribbean 2004;* and *World Statistics Pocketbook.*

The World Bank, 1818 H Street, NW, Washington, DC 20433, (202) 473-1000, Fax: (202) 477-6391, www.worldbank.org; *The World Bank Atlas 2003-2004; World Development Indicators (WDI) 2008;* and *World Development Report 2008.*

World Health Organization (WHO), Avenue Appia 20, 1211 Geneve 27, Switzerland, (Telephone in U.S. (212) 331-9081), www.who.int; *The WHO Global Atlas of Infectious Diseases* and *World Health Report 2006.*

GUATEMALA - MOTION PICTURES

Palgrave Macmillan Ltd., Houndmills, Basingstoke, Hampshire, RG21 6XS, England, (Telephone in U.S. (888) 330-8477), (Fax in U.S. (800) 672-2054), www.palgrave.com; *The Statesman's Yearbook 2008.*

United Nations Statistics Division, New York, NY 10017, (800) 253-9646, Fax: (212) 963-4116, http://unstats.un.org; *Statistical Yearbook.*

GUATEMALA - MOTOR VEHICLES

Economist Intelligence Unit, 111 West 57th Street, New York, NY 10019, (212) 554-0600, Fax: (212) 586-1181, www.eiu.com; *Business Latin America.*

Taylor and Francis Group, An Informa Business, 2 Park Square, Milton Park, Abingdon, Oxford OX14 4RN, United Kingdom, (Dial from U.S. (212) 216-7800), (Fax from U.S. (212) 564-7854), www.tandf.co.uk; *The Europa World Year Book.*

United Nations Statistics Division, New York, NY 10017, (800) 253-9646, Fax: (212) 963-4116, http://unstats.un.org; *Statistical Yearbook.*

GUATEMALA - MUSEUMS

M.E. Sharpe, 80 Business Park Drive, Armonk, NY 10504, (800) 541-6563, Fax: (914) 273-2106, www.mesharpe.com; *The Illustrated Book of World Rankings.*

UNESCO Institute for Statistics, C.P. 6128 Succursale Centre-Ville, Montreal, Quebec, H3C 3J7 Canada, (Dial from U.S. (514) 343-6880), (Fax from U.S. (514) 343 6882), www.uis.unesco.org; *Statistical Tables.*

GUATEMALA - NATURAL GAS PRODUCTION

See GUATEMALA - MINERAL INDUSTRIES

GUATEMALA - NUTRITION

United Nations Food and Agricultural Organization (FAO), Viale delle Terme di Caracalla, 00100 Rome, Italy, (Dial from U.S. (202) 653-2400), (Fax from U.S. (202) 653 5760), www.fao.org; *The State of Food and Agriculture (SOFA) 2006.*

United Nations Statistics Division, New York, NY 10017, (800) 253-9646, Fax: (212) 963-4116, http://unstats.un.org; *Statistical Yearbook for Latin America and the Caribbean 2004.*

GUATEMALA - OLDER PEOPLE

M.E. Sharpe, 80 Business Park Drive, Armonk, NY 10504, (800) 541-6563, Fax: (914) 273-2106, www.mesharpe.com; *The Illustrated Book of World Rankings.*

GUATEMALA - PAPER

See GUATEMALA - FORESTS AND FORESTRY

GUATEMALA - PEANUT PRODUCTION

See GUATEMALA - CROPS

GUATEMALA - PERIODICALS

UNESCO Institute for Statistics, C.P. 6128 Succursale Centre-Ville, Montreal, Quebec, H3C 3J7 Canada, (Dial from U.S. (514) 343-6880), (Fax from U.S. (514) 343 6882), www.uis.unesco.org; *Statistical Tables.*

GUATEMALA - PESTICIDES

United Nations Food and Agricultural Organization (FAO), Viale delle Terme di Caracalla, 00100 Rome, Italy, (Dial from U.S. (202) 653-2400), (Fax from U.S. (202) 653 5760), www.fao.org; *The State of Food and Agriculture (SOFA) 2006.*

GUATEMALA - PETROLEUM INDUSTRY AND TRADE

Economist Intelligence Unit, 111 West 57th Street, New York, NY 10019, (212) 554-0600, Fax: (212) 586-1181, www.eiu.com; *Business Latin America.*

Inter-American Development Bank (IDB), 1300 New York Avenue, NW, Washington, DC 20577, (202) 623-1000, Fax: (202) 623-3096, www.iadb.org; *The Politics of Policies: Economic and Social Progress in Latin America - 2006 Report.*

M.E. Sharpe, 80 Business Park Drive, Armonk, NY 10504, (800) 541-6563, Fax: (914) 273-2106, www.mesharpe.com; *The Illustrated Book of World Rankings.*

Organisation for Economic Cooperation and Development (OECD), 2 rue Andre Pascal, F-75775 Paris Cedex 16, France, (Telephone in U.S. (202) 785-6323), (Fax in U.S. (202) 785-0350), www.oecd.org; *World Energy Outlook 2007.*

PennWell Corporation, 1421 South Sheridan Road, Tulsa, OK 74112, (918) 835-3161, www.pennwell.com; *International Petroleum Encyclopedia 2007.*

U.S. Department of Energy (DOE), Energy Information Administration (EIA), 1000 Independence Avenue, SW, Washington, DC 20585, (202) 586-8800, www.eia.doe.gov; *International Energy Annual 2004* and *International Energy Outlook 2006.*

United Nations Conference on Trade and Development (UNCTAD), DC2-1120, United Nations, New York, NY 10017, (212) 963-0027, www.unctad.org; *UNCTAD Commodity Yearbook.*

United Nations Food and Agricultural Organization (FAO), Viale delle Terme di Caracalla, 00100 Rome, Italy, (Dial from U.S. (202) 653-2400), (Fax from U.S. (202) 653 5760), www.fao.org; *The State of Food and Agriculture (SOFA) 2006.*

United Nations Statistics Division, New York, NY 10017, (800) 253-9646, Fax: (212) 963-4116, http://unstats.un.org; *Statistical Yearbook.*

GUATEMALA - POLITICAL SCIENCE

Central Intelligence Agency, Office of Public Affairs, Washington, DC 20505, (703) 482-0623, Fax: (703) 482-1739, www.cia.gov; *The World Factbook.*

Inter-American Development Bank (IDB), 1300 New York Avenue, NW, Washington, DC 20577, (202) 623-1000, Fax: (202) 623-3096, www.iadb.org; *The Politics of Policies: Economic and Social Progress in Latin America - 2006 Report.*

International Monetary Fund (IMF), 700 Nineteenth Street, NW, Washington, DC 20431, (202) 623-7000, Fax: (202) 623-4661, www.imf.org; *Government Finance Statistics Yearbook (2008 Edition)* and *International Financial Statistics Yearbook 2007.*

Palgrave Macmillan Ltd., Houndmills, Basingstoke, Hampshire, RG21 6XS, England, (Telephone in U.S. (888) 330-8477), (Fax in U.S. (800) 672-2054), www.palgrave.com; *The Statesman's Yearbook 2008.*

Taylor and Francis Group, An Informa Business, 2 Park Square, Milton Park, Abingdon, Oxford OX14 4RN, United Kingdom, (Dial from U.S. (212) 216-7800), (Fax from U.S. (212) 564-7854), www.tandf.co.uk; *The Europa World Year Book.*

UCLA Latin American Institute, 10343 Bunche Hall, Box 951447, Los Angeles, CA 90095-1447, (310) 825-4571, Fax: (310) 206-6859, www.international.ucla.edu/lac; *Statistical Abstract of Latin America.*

United Nations Statistics Division, New York, NY 10017, (800) 253-9646, Fax: (212) 963-4116, http://unstats.un.org; *National Accounts Statistics: Compendium of Income Distribution Statistics* and *Statistical Yearbook.*

The World Bank, 1818 H Street, NW, Washington, DC 20433, (202) 473-1000, Fax: (202) 477-6391, www.worldbank.org; *World Development Indicators (WDI) 2008* and *World Development Report 2008.*

GUATEMALA - POPULATION

Central Intelligence Agency, Office of Public Affairs, Washington, DC 20505, (703) 482-0623, Fax: (703) 482-1739, www.cia.gov; *The World Factbook.*

Economist Intelligence Unit, 111 West 57th Street, New York, NY 10019, (212) 554-0600, Fax: (212) 586-1181, www.eiu.com; *Business Latin America* and *Guatemala Country Report.*

Euromonitor International, Inc., 224 S. Michigan Avenue, Suite 1500, Chicago, IL 60604, (312) 922-1115, Fax: (312) 922-1157, www.euromonitor.com; *International Marketing Data and Statistics 2008* and *The World Economic Factbook 2008.*

Inter-American Development Bank (IDB), 1300 New York Avenue, NW, Washington, DC 20577, (202) 623-1000, Fax: (202) 623-3096, www.iadb.org; *The Politics of Policies: Economic and Social Progress in Latin America - 2006 Report.*

International Labour Office, I.L.O. Publications, 4 route des Morillons, CH-1211 Geneva 22, Switzerland, (Telephone in U.S. (202) 653-7652), (Fax in U.S. (202) 653-7687), www.ilo.org; *Yearbook of Labour Statistics 2006.*

M.E. Sharpe, 80 Business Park Drive, Armonk, NY 10504, (800) 541-6563, Fax: (914) 273-2106, www.mesharpe.com; *The Illustrated Book of World Rankings.*

Organization of American States (OAS), 17th Street Constitution Avenue NW, Washington, DC 20006, (202) 458-3000, www.oas.org; *The OAS in Transition: 1994-2004.*

Palgrave Macmillan Ltd., Houndmills, Basingstoke, Hampshire, RG21 6XS, England, (Telephone in U.S. (888) 330-8477), (Fax in U.S. (800) 672-2054), www.palgrave.com; *The Statesman's Yearbook 2008.*

Taylor and Francis Group, An Informa Business, 2 Park Square, Milton Park, Abingdon, Oxford OX14 4RN, United Kingdom, (Dial from U.S. (212) 216-7800), (Fax from U.S. (212) 564-7854), www.tandf.co.uk; *The Europa World Year Book.*

U.S. Department of State (DOS), 2201 C Street NW, Washington, DC 20520, (202) 647-4000, www.state.gov; *World Military Expenditures and Arms Transfers (WMEAT).*

UCLA Latin American Institute, 10343 Bunche Hall, Box 951447, Los Angeles, CA 90095-1447, (310) 825-4571, Fax: (310) 206-6859, www.international.ucla.edu/lac; *Statistical Abstract of Latin America.*

UNESCO Institute for Statistics, C.P. 6128 Succursale Centre-Ville, Montreal, Quebec, H3C 3J7 Canada, (Dial from U.S. (514) 343-6880), (Fax from U.S. (514) 343 6882), www.uis.unesco.org; *Statistical Tables.*

United Nations Food and Agricultural Organization (FAO), Viale delle Terme di Caracalla, 00100 Rome, Italy, (Dial from U.S. (202) 653-2400), (Fax from U.S. (202) 653 5760), www.fao.org; *FAO Production Yearbook 2002.*

United Nations Statistics Division, New York, NY 10017, (800) 253-9646, Fax: (212) 963-4116, http://unstats.un.org; *Demographic Yearbook; Human Development Report 2006; Statistical Yearbook; Statistical Yearbook for Latin America and the Caribbean 2004;* and *World Statistics Pocketbook.*

The World Bank, 1818 H Street, NW, Washington, DC 20433, (202) 473-1000, Fax: (202) 477-6391, www.worldbank.org; *Guatemala; The World Bank Atlas 2003-2004;* and *World Development Report 2008.*

World Health Organization (WHO), Avenue Appia 20, 1211 Geneve 27, Switzerland, (Telephone in U.S. (212) 331-9081), www.who.int; *World Health Report 2006.*

World Resources Institute (WRI), 10 G Street, NE, Suite 800 Washington, DC 20002, (202) 729-7600, www.wri.org; *Indigenous Peoples, Representation and Citizenship in Guatemalan Forestry.*

GUATEMALA - POPULATION DENSITY

Central Intelligence Agency, Office of Public Affairs, Washington, DC 20505, (703) 482-0623, Fax: (703) 482-1739, www.cia.gov; *The World Factbook.*

Euromonitor International, Inc., 224 S. Michigan Avenue, Suite 1500, Chicago, IL 60604, (312) 922-1115, Fax: (312) 922-1157, www.euromonitor.com; *International Marketing Data and Statistics 2008* and *The World Economic Factbook 2008.*

Inter-American Development Bank (IDB), 1300 New York Avenue, NW, Washington, DC 20577, (202) 623-1000, Fax: (202) 623-3096, www.iadb.org; *The Politics of Policies: Economic and Social Progress in Latin America - 2006 Report.*

M.E. Sharpe, 80 Business Park Drive, Armonk, NY 10504, (800) 541-6563, Fax: (914) 273-2106, www.mesharpe.com; *The Illustrated Book of World Rankings.*

Palgrave Macmillan Ltd., Houndmills, Basingstoke, Hampshire, RG21 6XS, England, (Telephone in U.S. (888) 330-8477), (Fax in U.S. (800) 672-2054), www.palgrave.com; *The Statesman's Yearbook 2008.*

Taylor and Francis Group, An Informa Business, 2 Park Square, Milton Park, Abingdon, Oxford OX14 4RN, United Kingdom, (Dial from U.S. (212) 216-7800), (Fax from U.S. (212) 564-7854), www.tandf.co.uk; *The Europa World Year Book.*

UNESCO Institute for Statistics, C.P. 6128 Succursale Centre-Ville, Montreal, Quebec, H3C 3J7 Canada, (Dial from U.S. (514) 343-6880), (Fax from U.S. (514) 343 6882), www.uis.unesco.org; *Statistical Tables.*

United Nations Food and Agricultural Organization (FAO), Viale delle Terme di Caracalla, 00100 Rome, Italy, (Dial from U.S. (202) 653-2400), (Fax from U.S. (202) 653 5760), www.fao.org; *The State of Food and Agriculture (SOFA) 2006.*

United Nations Statistics Division, New York, NY 10017, (800) 253-9646, Fax: (212) 963-4116, http://unstats.un.org; *Statistical Yearbook.*

The World Bank, 1818 H Street, NW, Washington, DC 20433, (202) 473-1000, Fax: (202) 477-6391, www.worldbank.org; *Guatemala* and *World Development Report 2008.*

GUATEMALA - POSTAL SERVICE

M.E. Sharpe, 80 Business Park Drive, Armonk, NY 10504, (800) 541-6563, Fax: (914) 273-2106, www.mesharpe.com; *The Illustrated Book of World Rankings.*

United Nations Statistics Division, New York, NY 10017, (800) 253-9646, Fax: (212) 963-4116, http://unstats.un.org; *Statistical Yearbook.*

GUATEMALA - POWER RESOURCES

Economist Intelligence Unit, 111 West 57th Street, New York, NY 10019, (212) 554-0600, Fax: (212) 586-1181, www.eiu.com; *Business Latin America.*

Euromonitor International, Inc., 224 S. Michigan Avenue, Suite 1500, Chicago, IL 60604, (312) 922-1115, Fax: (312) 922-1157, www.euromonitor.com; *International Marketing Data and Statistics 2008; The World Economic Factbook 2008;* and *World Marketing Data and Statistics.*

M.E. Sharpe, 80 Business Park Drive, Armonk, NY 10504, (800) 541-6563, Fax: (914) 273-2106, www.mesharpe.com; *The Illustrated Book of World Rankings.*

Organisation for Economic Cooperation and Development (OECD), 2 rue Andre Pascal, F-75775 Paris Cedex 16, France, (Telephone in U.S. (202) 785-6323), (Fax in U.S. (202) 785-0350), www.oecd.org; *World Energy Outlook 2007.*

Palgrave Macmillan Ltd., Houndmills, Basingstoke, Hampshire, RG21 6XS, England, (Telephone in U.S. (888) 330-8477), (Fax in U.S. (800) 672-2054), www.palgrave.com; *The Statesman's Yearbook 2008.*

U.S. Department of Energy (DOE), Energy Information Administration (EIA), 1000 Independence Avenue, SW, Washington, DC 20585, (202) 586-8800, www.eia.doe.gov; *International Energy Annual 2004* and *International Energy Outlook 2006.*

UCLA Latin American Institute, 10343 Bunche Hall, Box 951447, Los Angeles, CA 90095-1447, (310) 825-4571, Fax: (310) 206-6859, www.international.ucla.edu/lac; *Statistical Abstract of Latin America.*

United Nations Food and Agricultural Organization (FAO), Viale delle Terme di Caracalla, 00100 Rome, Italy, (Dial from U.S. (202) 653-2400), (Fax from U.S. (202) 653 5760), www.fao.org; *The State of Food and Agriculture (SOFA) 2006.*

United Nations Statistics Division, New York, NY 10017, (800) 253-9646, Fax: (212) 963-4116, http://unstats.un.org; *Human Development Report 2006; Statistical Yearbook; Statistical Yearbook for Latin America and the Caribbean 2004;* and *World Statistics Pocketbook.*

The World Bank, 1818 H Street, NW, Washington, DC 20433, (202) 473-1000, Fax: (202) 477-6391, www.worldbank.org; *The World Bank Atlas 2003-2004* and *World Development Report 2008.*

GUATEMALA - PRICES

International Labour Office, I.L.O. Publications, 4 route des Morillons, CH-1211 Geneva 22, Switzerland, (Telephone in U.S. (202) 653-7652), (Fax in U.S. (202) 653-7687), www.ilo.org; *Yearbook of Labour Statistics 2006.*

International Monetary Fund (IMF), 700 Nineteenth Street, NW, Washington, DC 20431, (202) 623-7000, Fax: (202) 623-4661, www.imf.org; *International Financial Statistics Yearbook 2007.*

M.E. Sharpe, 80 Business Park Drive, Armonk, NY 10504, (800) 541-6563, Fax: (914) 273-2106, www.mesharpe.com; *The Illustrated Book of World Rankings.*

United Nations Food and Agricultural Organization (FAO), Viale delle Terme di Caracalla, 00100 Rome, Italy, (Dial from U.S. (202) 653-2400), (Fax from U.S. (202) 653 5760), www.fao.org; *FAO Production Yearbook 2002* and *The State of Food and Agriculture (SOFA) 2006.*

United Nations Statistics Division, New York, NY 10017, (800) 253-9646, Fax: (212) 963-4116, http://unstats.un.org; *Statistical Yearbook for Latin America and the Caribbean 2004.*

The World Bank, 1818 H Street, NW, Washington, DC 20433, (202) 473-1000, Fax: (202) 477-6391, www.worldbank.org; *Guatemala.*

GUATEMALA - PROFESSIONS

UCLA Latin American Institute, 10343 Bunche Hall, Box 951447, Los Angeles, CA 90095-1447, (310) 825-4571, Fax: (310) 206-6859, www.international.ucla.edu/lac; *Statistical Abstract of Latin America.*

United Nations Statistics Division, New York, NY 10017, (800) 253-9646, Fax: (212) 963-4116, http://unstats.un.org; *Statistical Yearbook.*

GUATEMALA - PUBLIC HEALTH

Economist Intelligence Unit, 111 West 57th Street, New York, NY 10019, (212) 554-0600, Fax: (212) 586-1181, www.eiu.com; *Business Latin America.*

Euromonitor International, Inc., 224 S. Michigan Avenue, Suite 1500, Chicago, IL 60604, (312) 922-1115, Fax: (312) 922-1157, www.euromonitor.com; *World Marketing Data and Statistics.*

M.E. Sharpe, 80 Business Park Drive, Armonk, NY 10504, (800) 541-6563, Fax: (914) 273-2106, www.mesharpe.com; *The Illustrated Book of World Rankings.*

Palgrave Macmillan Ltd., Houndmills, Basingstoke, Hampshire, RG21 6XS, England, (Telephone in U.S. (888) 330-8477), (Fax in U.S. (800) 672-2054), www.palgrave.com; *The Statesman's Yearbook 2008.*

UNICEF, 3 United Nations Plaza, New York, NY 10017, (800) 253-9646, Fax: (212) 887-7465, www.unicef.org; *The State of the World's Children 2008.*

United Nations Statistics Division, New York, NY 10017, (800) 253-9646, Fax: (212) 963-4116, http://unstats.un.org; *Human Development Report 2006; Statistical Yearbook;* and *Statistical Yearbook for Latin America and the Caribbean 2004.*

The World Bank, 1818 H Street, NW, Washington, DC 20433, (202) 473-1000, Fax: (202) 477-6391, www.worldbank.org; *Guatemala* and *World Development Report 2008.*

World Health Organization (WHO), Avenue Appia 20, 1211 Geneve 27, Switzerland, (Telephone in

U.S. (212) 331-9081), www.who.int; The WHO Global Atlas of Infectious Diseases and *World Health Report 2006.*

GUATEMALA - PUBLIC UTILITIES

UCLA Latin American Institute, 10343 Bunche Hall, Box 951447, Los Angeles, CA 90095-1447, (310) 825-4571, Fax: (310) 206-6859, www.international.ucla.edu/lac; *Statistical Abstract of Latin America.*

GUATEMALA - PUBLISHERS AND PUBLISHING

UNESCO Institute for Statistics, C.P. 6128 Succursale Centre-Ville, Montreal, Quebec, H3C 3J7 Canada, (Dial from U.S. (514) 343-6880), (Fax from U.S. (514) 343 6882), www.uis.unesco.org; *Statistical Tables.*

GUATEMALA - RADIO BROADCASTING

Palgrave Macmillan Ltd., Houndmills, Basingstoke, Hampshire, RG21 6XS, England, (Telephone in U.S. (888) 330-8477), (Fax in U.S. (800) 672-2054), www.palgrave.com; *The Statesman's Yearbook 2008.*

GUATEMALA - RAILROADS

Economist Intelligence Unit, 111 West 57th Street, New York, NY 10019, (212) 554-0600, Fax: (212) 586-1181, www.eiu.com; *Business Latin America.*

Jane's Information Group, 110 North Royal Street, Suite 200, Alexandria, VA 22314, (703) 683-3700, Fax: (800) 836-0297, www.janes.com; *Jane's World Railways.*

Palgrave Macmillan Ltd., Houndmills, Basingstoke, Hampshire, RG21 6XS, England, (Telephone in U.S. (888) 330-8477), (Fax in U.S. (800) 672-2054), www.palgrave.com; *The Statesman's Yearbook 2008.*

United Nations Statistics Division, New York, NY 10017, (800) 253-9646, Fax: (212) 963-4116, http://unstats.un.org; *Statistical Yearbook.*

GUATEMALA - RANCHING

UCLA Latin American Institute, 10343 Bunche Hall, Box 951447, Los Angeles, CA 90095-1447, (310) 825-4571, Fax: (310) 206-6859, www.international.ucla.edu/lac; *Statistical Abstract of Latin America.*

GUATEMALA - RELIGION

Central Intelligence Agency, Office of Public Affairs, Washington, DC 20505, (703) 482-0623, Fax: (703) 482-1739, www.cia.gov; *The World Factbook.*

M.E. Sharpe, 80 Business Park Drive, Armonk, NY 10504, (800) 541-6563, Fax: (914) 273-2106, www.mesharpe.com; *The Illustrated Book of World Rankings.*

Palgrave Macmillan Ltd., Houndmills, Basingstoke, Hampshire, RG21 6XS, England, (Telephone in U.S. (888) 330-8477), (Fax in U.S. (800) 672-2054), www.palgrave.com; *The Statesman's Yearbook 2008.*

UCLA Latin American Institute, 10343 Bunche Hall, Box 951447, Los Angeles, CA 90095-1447, (310) 825-4571, Fax: (310) 206-6859, www.international.ucla.edu/lac; *Statistical Abstract of Latin America.*

GUATEMALA - RENT CHARGES

International Labour Office, I.L.O. Publications, 4 route des Morillons, CH-1211 Geneva 22, Switzerland, (Telephone in U.S. (202) 653-7652), (Fax in U.S. (202) 653-7687), www.ilo.org; *Yearbook of Labour Statistics 2006.*

GUATEMALA - RESERVES (ACCOUNTING)

Economist Intelligence Unit, 111 West 57th Street, New York, NY 10019, (212) 554-0600, Fax: (212) 586-1181, www.eiu.com; *Business Latin America.*

Euromonitor International, Inc., 224 S. Michigan Avenue, Suite 1500, Chicago, IL 60604, (312) 922-1115, Fax: (312) 922-1157, www.euromonitor.com; *International Marketing Data and Statistics 2008.*

Inter-American Development Bank (IDB), 1300 New York Avenue, NW, Washington, DC 20577, (202) 623-1000, Fax: (202) 623-3096, www.iadb.org; *The Politics of Policies: Economic and Social Progress in Latin America - 2006 Report.*

Organization of American States (OAS), 17th Street Constitution Avenue NW, Washington, DC 20006, (202) 458-3000, www.oas.org; *The OAS in Transition: 1994-2004.*

United Nations Statistics Division, New York, NY 10017, (800) 253-9646, Fax: (212) 963-4116, http://unstats.un.org; *Statistical Yearbook.*

The World Bank, 1818 H Street, NW, Washington, DC 20433, (202) 473-1000, Fax: (202) 477-6391, www.worldbank.org; *World Development Indicators (WDI) 2008.*

GUATEMALA - RETAIL TRADE

Euromonitor International, Inc., 224 S. Michigan Avenue, Suite 1500, Chicago, IL 60604, (312) 922-1115, Fax: (312) 922-1157, www.euromonitor.com; *World Marketing Data and Statistics.*

Inter-American Development Bank (IDB), 1300 New York Avenue, NW, Washington, DC 20577, (202) 623-1000, Fax: (202) 623-3096, www.iadb.org; *The Politics of Policies: Economic and Social Progress in Latin America - 2006 Report.*

GUATEMALA - RICE PRODUCTION

See GUATEMALA - CROPS

GUATEMALA - ROADS

Central Intelligence Agency, Office of Public Affairs, Washington, DC 20505, (703) 482-0623, Fax: (703) 482-1739, www.cia.gov; *The World Factbook.*

Economist Intelligence Unit, 111 West 57th Street, New York, NY 10019, (212) 554-0600, Fax: (212) 586-1181, www.eiu.com; *Business Latin America.*

Palgrave Macmillan Ltd., Houndmills, Basingstoke, Hampshire, RG21 6XS, England, (Telephone in U.S. (888) 330-8477), (Fax in U.S. (800) 672-2054), www.palgrave.com; *The Statesman's Yearbook 2008.*

GUATEMALA - RUBBER INDUSTRY AND TRADE

International Rubber Study Group (IRSG), 1st Floor, Heron House, 109/115 Wembley Hill Road, Wembley, Middlesex HA9 8DA, United Kingdom, www.rubberstudy.com; *Rubber Statistical Bulletin; Summary of World Rubber Statistics 2005; World Rubber Statistics Handbook (Volume 6, 1975-2001);* and *World Rubber Statistics Historic Handbook.*

M.E. Sharpe, 80 Business Park Drive, Armonk, NY 10504, (800) 541-6563, Fax: (914) 273-2106, www.mesharpe.com; *The Illustrated Book of World Rankings.*

GUATEMALA - SALT PRODUCTION

See GUATEMALA - MINERAL INDUSTRIES

GUATEMALA - SESAME INDUSTRY

United Nations Food and Agricultural Organization (FAO), Viale delle Terme di Caracalla, 00100 Rome, Italy, (Dial from U.S. (202) 653-2400), (Fax from U.S. (202) 653 5760), www.fao.org; *FAO Production Yearbook 2002.*

GUATEMALA - SHEEP

See GUATEMALA - LIVESTOCK

GUATEMALA - SHELLFISH FISHERIES

International Monetary Fund (IMF), 700 Nineteenth Street, NW, Washington, DC 20431, (202) 623-7000, Fax: (202) 623-4661, www.imf.org; *Government Finance Statistics Yearbook (2008 Edition).*

GUATEMALA - SHIPPING

Palgrave Macmillan Ltd., Houndmills, Basingstoke, Hampshire, RG21 6XS, England, (Telephone in U.S. (888) 330-8477), (Fax in U.S. (800) 672-2054), www.palgrave.com; *The Statesman's Yearbook 2008.*

Taylor and Francis Group, An Informa Business, 2 Park Square, Milton Park, Abingdon, Oxford OX14 4RN, United Kingdom, (Dial from U.S. (212) 216-7800), (Fax from U.S. (212) 564-7854), www.tandf.co.uk; *The Europa World Year Book.*

U.S. Department of Transportation (DOT), Maritime Administration (MARAD), West Building, Southeast Federal Center, 1200 New Jersey Avenue, SE, Washington, DC 20590, (800) 99-MARAD, www.marad.dot.gov; *World Merchant Fleet 2005.*

United Nations Statistics Division, New York, NY 10017, (800) 253-9646, Fax: (212) 963-4116, http://unstats.un.org; *Statistical Yearbook.*

GUATEMALA - SILVER PRODUCTION

See GUATEMALA - MINERAL INDUSTRIES

GUATEMALA - SOCIAL ECOLOGY

M.E. Sharpe, 80 Business Park Drive, Armonk, NY 10504, (800) 541-6563, Fax: (914) 273-2106, www.mesharpe.com; *The Illustrated Book of World Rankings.*

UCLA Latin American Institute, 10343 Bunche Hall, Box 951447, Los Angeles, CA 90095-1447, (310) 825-4571, Fax: (310) 206-6859, www.international.ucla.edu/lac; *Statistical Abstract of Latin America.*

United Nations Statistics Division, New York, NY 10017, (800) 253-9646, Fax: (212) 963-4116, http://unstats.un.org; *World Statistics Pocketbook.*

GUATEMALA - SOCIAL SECURITY

Inter-American Development Bank (IDB), 1300 New York Avenue, NW, Washington, DC 20577, (202) 623-1000, Fax: (202) 623-3096, www.iadb.org; *The Politics of Policies: Economic and Social Progress in Latin America - 2006 Report.*

International Monetary Fund (IMF), 700 Nineteenth Street, NW, Washington, DC 20431, (202) 623-7000, Fax: (202) 623-4661, www.imf.org; *Government Finance Statistics Yearbook (2008 Edition).*

Palgrave Macmillan Ltd., Houndmills, Basingstoke, Hampshire, RG21 6XS, England, (Telephone in U.S. (888) 330-8477), (Fax in U.S. (800) 672-2054), www.palgrave.com; *The Statesman's Yearbook 2008.*

United Nations Statistics Division, New York, NY 10017, (800) 253-9646, Fax: (212) 963-4116, http://unstats.un.org; *National Accounts Statistics: Compendium of Income Distribution Statistics.*

GUATEMALA - SOYBEAN PRODUCTION

See GUATEMALA - CROPS

GUATEMALA - STEEL PRODUCTION

See GUATEMALA - MINERAL INDUSTRIES

GUATEMALA - SUGAR PRODUCTION

See GUATEMALA - CROPS

GUATEMALA - TAXATION

Inter-American Development Bank (IDB), 1300 New York Avenue, NW, Washington, DC 20577, (202) 623-1000, Fax: (202) 623-3096, www.iadb.org; *The Politics of Policies: Economic and Social Progress in Latin America - 2006 Report.*

International Monetary Fund (IMF), 700 Nineteenth Street, NW, Washington, DC 20431, (202) 623-7000, Fax: (202) 623-4661, www.imf.org; *Government Finance Statistics Yearbook (2008 Edition).*

Taylor and Francis Group, An Informa Business, 2 Park Square, Milton Park, Abingdon, Oxford OX14 4RN, United Kingdom, (Dial from U.S. (212) 216-7800), (Fax from U.S. (212) 564-7854), www.tandf.co.uk; *The Europa World Year Book.*

United Nations Statistics Division, New York, NY 10017, (800) 253-9646, Fax: (212) 963-4116, http://unstats.un.org; *Statistical Yearbook for Latin America and the Caribbean 2004.*

The World Bank, 1818 H Street, NW, Washington, DC 20433, (202) 473-1000, Fax: (202) 477-6391, www.worldbank.org; *World Development Indicators (WDI) 2008.*

GUATEMALA - TELEPHONE

Economist Intelligence Unit, 111 West 57th Street, New York, NY 10019, (212) 554-0600, Fax: (212) 586-1181, www.eiu.com; *Business Latin America.*

International Telecommunication Union (ITU), Place des Nations, 1211 Geneva 20, Switzerland, www.itu.int; World Telecommunication Indicators Database.

Palgrave Macmillan Ltd., Houndmills, Basingstoke, Hampshire, RG21 6XS, England, (Telephone in U.S. (888) 330-8477), (Fax in U.S. (800) 672-2054), www.palgrave.com; *The Statesman's Yearbook 2008.*

Taylor and Francis Group, An Informa Business, 2 Park Square, Milton Park, Abingdon, Oxford OX14 4RN, United Kingdom, (Dial from U.S. (212) 216-7800), (Fax from U.S. (212) 564-7854), www.tandf.co.uk; *The Europa World Year Book.*

United Nations Statistics Division, New York, NY 10017, (800) 253-9646, Fax: (212) 963-4116, http://unstats.un.org; *Statistical Yearbook* and *World Statistics Pocketbook.*

GUATEMALA - TEXTILE INDUSTRY

M.E. Sharpe, 80 Business Park Drive, Armonk, NY 10504, (800) 541-6563, Fax: (914) 273-2106, www.mesharpe.com; *The Illustrated Book of World Rankings.*

Palgrave Macmillan Ltd., Houndmills, Basingstoke, Hampshire, RG21 6XS, England, (Telephone in U.S. (888) 330-8477), (Fax in U.S. (800) 672-2054), www.palgrave.com; *The Statesman's Yearbook 2008.*

United Nations Conference on Trade and Development (UNCTAD), DC2-1120, United Nations, New York, NY 10017, (212) 963-0027, www.unctad.org; *UNCTAD Commodity Yearbook.*

United Nations Statistics Division, New York, NY 10017, (800) 253-9646, Fax: (212) 963-4116, http://unstats.un.org; *Statistical Yearbook.*

GUATEMALA - THEATER

UNESCO Institute for Statistics, C.P. 6128 Succursale Centre-Ville, Montreal, Quebec, H3C 3J7 Canada, (Dial from U.S. (514) 343-6880), (Fax from U.S. (514) 343 6882), www.uis.unesco.org; *Statistical Tables.*

GUATEMALA - TIN PRODUCTION

See GUATEMALA - MINERAL INDUSTRIES

GUATEMALA - TOBACCO INDUSTRY

Foreign Agricultural Service (FAS), U.S. Department of Agriculture (USDA), 1400 Independence Avenue, SW, Washington, DC 20250, (202) 720-3935, www.fas.usda.gov; *Tobacco: World Markets and Trade.*

M.E. Sharpe, 80 Business Park Drive, Armonk, NY 10504, (800) 541-6563, Fax: (914) 273-2106, www.mesharpe.com; *The Illustrated Book of World Rankings.*

United Nations Statistics Division, New York, NY 10017, (800) 253-9646, Fax: (212) 963-4116, http://unstats.un.org; *Statistical Yearbook.*

GUATEMALA - TOURISM

Economist Intelligence Unit, 111 West 57th Street, New York, NY 10019, (212) 554-0600, Fax: (212) 586-1181, www.eiu.com; *Business Latin America.*

Euromonitor International, Inc., 224 S. Michigan Avenue, Suite 1500, Chicago, IL 60604, (312) 922-1115, Fax: (312) 922-1157, www.euromonitor.com; *The World Economic Factbook 2008* and *World Marketing Data and Statistics.*

M.E. Sharpe, 80 Business Park Drive, Armonk, NY 10504, (800) 541-6563, Fax: (914) 273-2106, www.mesharpe.com; *The Illustrated Book of World Rankings.*

Organization of American States (OAS), 17th Street Constitution Avenue NW, Washington, DC 20006, (202) 458-3000, www.oas.org; *The OAS in Transition: 1994-2004.*

Taylor and Francis Group, An Informa Business, 2 Park Square, Milton Park, Abingdon, Oxford OX14 4RN, United Kingdom, (Dial from U.S. (212) 216-7800), (Fax from U.S. (212) 564-7854), www.tandf.co.uk; *The Europa World Year Book.*

UCLA Latin American Institute, 10343 Bunche Hall, Box 951447, Los Angeles, CA 90095-1447, (310) 825-4571, Fax: (310) 206-6859, www.international.ucla.edu/lac; *Statistical Abstract of Latin America.*

United Nations Statistics Division, New York, NY 10017, (800) 253-9646, Fax: (212) 963-4116, http://unstats.un.org; *Statistical Yearbook* and *Statistical Yearbook for Latin America and the Caribbean 2004.*

United Nations World Tourism Organization (UNWTO), Capitan Haya 42, 28020 Madrid, Spain, www.world-tourism.org; *Yearbook of Tourism Statistics.*

The World Bank, 1818 H Street, NW, Washington, DC 20433, (202) 473-1000, Fax: (202) 477-6391, www.worldbank.org; *Guatemala.*

GUATEMALA - TRADE

See GUATEMALA - INTERNATIONAL TRADE

GUATEMALA - TRANSPORTATION

Central Intelligence Agency, Office of Public Affairs, Washington, DC 20505, (703) 482-0623, Fax: (703) 482-1739, www.cia.gov; *The World Factbook.*

Economist Intelligence Unit, 111 West 57th Street, New York, NY 10019, (212) 554-0600, Fax: (212) 586-1181, www.eiu.com; *Business Latin America.*

Euromonitor International, Inc., 224 S. Michigan Avenue, Suite 1500, Chicago, IL 60604, (312) 922-1115, Fax: (312) 922-1157, www.euromonitor.com; *International Marketing Data and Statistics 2008* and *World Marketing Data and Statistics.*

Inter-American Development Bank (IDB), 1300 New York Avenue, NW, Washington, DC 20577, (202) 623-1000, Fax: (202) 623-3096, www.iadb.org; *The Politics of Policies: Economic and Social Progress in Latin America - 2006 Report.*

M.E. Sharpe, 80 Business Park Drive, Armonk, NY 10504, (800) 541-6563, Fax: (914) 273-2106, www.mesharpe.com; *The Illustrated Book of World Rankings.*

Palgrave Macmillan Ltd., Houndmills, Basingstoke, Hampshire, RG21 6XS, England, (Telephone in U.S. (888) 330-8477), (Fax in U.S. (800) 672-2054), www.palgrave.com; *The Statesman's Yearbook 2008.*

Taylor and Francis Group, An Informa Business, 2 Park Square, Milton Park, Abingdon, Oxford OX14 4RN, United Kingdom, (Dial from U.S. (212) 216-7800), (Fax from U.S. (212) 564-7854), www.tandf.co.uk; *The Europa World Year Book.*

UCLA Latin American Institute, 10343 Bunche Hall, Box 951447, Los Angeles, CA 90095-1447, (310) 825-4571, Fax: (310) 206-6859, www.international.ucla.edu/lac; *Statistical Abstract of Latin America.*

United Nations Statistics Division, New York, NY 10017, (800) 253-9646, Fax: (212) 963-4116, http://unstats.un.org; *Human Development Report 2006* and *Statistical Yearbook for Latin America and the Caribbean 2004.*

The World Bank, 1818 H Street, NW, Washington, DC 20433, (202) 473-1000, Fax: (202) 477-6391, www.worldbank.org; *Guatemala.*

GUATEMALA - UNEMPLOYMENT

Central Intelligence Agency, Office of Public Affairs, Washington, DC 20505, (703) 482-0623, Fax: (703) 482-1739, www.cia.gov; *The World Factbook.*

Economist Intelligence Unit, 111 West 57th Street, New York, NY 10019, (212) 554-0600, Fax: (212) 586-1181, www.eiu.com; *Business Latin America.*

Euromonitor International, Inc., 224 S. Michigan Avenue, Suite 1500, Chicago, IL 60604, (312) 922-1115, Fax: (312) 922-1157, www.euromonitor.com; *International Marketing Data and Statistics 2008.*

International Labour Office, I.L.O. Publications, 4 route des Morillons, CH-1211 Geneva 22, Switzerland, (Telephone in U.S. (202) 653-7652), (Fax in U.S. (202) 653-7687), www.ilo.org; *Yearbook of Labour Statistics 2006.*

UCLA Latin American Institute, 10343 Bunche Hall, Box 951447, Los Angeles, CA 90095-1447, (310) 825-4571, Fax: (310) 206-6859, www.international.ucla.edu/lac; *Statistical Abstract of Latin America.*

United Nations Statistics Division, New York, NY 10017, (800) 253-9646, Fax: (212) 963-4116, http://unstats.un.org; *Statistical Yearbook.*

GUATEMALA - VITAL STATISTICS

Euromonitor International, Inc., 224 S. Michigan Avenue, Suite 1500, Chicago, IL 60604, (312) 922-1115, Fax: (312) 922-1157, www.euromonitor.com; *International Marketing Data and Statistics 2008.*

Palgrave Macmillan Ltd., Houndmills, Basingstoke, Hampshire, RG21 6XS, England, (Telephone in U.S. (888) 330-8477), (Fax in U.S. (800) 672-2054), www.palgrave.com; *The Statesman's Yearbook 2008.*

United Nations Statistics Division, New York, NY 10017, (800) 253-9646, Fax: (212) 963-4116, http://unstats.un.org; *Statistical Yearbook.*

World Health Organization (WHO), Avenue Appia 20, 1211 Geneve 27, Switzerland, (Telephone in U.S. (212) 331-9081), www.who.int; *World Health Report 2006.*

GUATEMALA - WAGES

International Labour Office, I.L.O. Publications, 4 route des Morillons, CH-1211 Geneva 22, Switzerland, (Telephone in U.S. (202) 653-7652), (Fax in U.S. (202) 653-7687), www.ilo.org; *Yearbook of Labour Statistics 2006.*

UCLA Latin American Institute, 10343 Bunche Hall, Box 951447, Los Angeles, CA 90095-1447, (310) 825-4571, Fax: (310) 206-6859, www.international.ucla.edu/lac; *Statistical Abstract of Latin America.*

United Nations Statistics Division, New York, NY 10017, (800) 253-9646, Fax: (212) 963-4116, http://unstats.un.org; *Statistical Yearbook.*

The World Bank, 1818 H Street, NW, Washington, DC 20433, (202) 473-1000, Fax: (202) 477-6391, www.worldbank.org; *Guatemala.*

GUATEMALA - WEATHER

See GUATEMALA - CLIMATE

GUATEMALA - WELFARE STATE

Inter-American Development Bank (IDB), 1300 New York Avenue, NW, Washington, DC 20577, (202) 623-1000, Fax: (202) 623-3096, www.iadb.org; *The Politics of Policies: Economic and Social Progress in Latin America - 2006 Report.*

International Monetary Fund (IMF), 700 Nineteenth Street, NW, Washington, DC 20431, (202) 623-7000, Fax: (202) 623-4661, www.imf.org; *Government Finance Statistics Yearbook (2008 Edition).*

GUATEMALA - WHEAT PRODUCTION

See GUATEMALA - CROPS

GUATEMALA - WHOLESALE PRICE INDEXES

Inter-American Development Bank (IDB), 1300 New York Avenue, NW, Washington, DC 20577, (202) 623-1000, Fax: (202) 623-3096, www.iadb.org; *The Politics of Policies: Economic and Social Progress in Latin America - 2006 Report.*

International Monetary Fund (IMF), 700 Nineteenth Street, NW, Washington, DC 20431, (202) 623-7000, Fax: (202) 623-4661, www.imf.org; *International Financial Statistics Yearbook 2007.*

Organization of American States (OAS), 17th Street Constitution Avenue NW, Washington, DC 20006, (202) 458-3000, www.oas.org; *The OAS in Transition: 1994-2004.*

United Nations Statistics Division, New York, NY 10017, (800) 253-9646, Fax: (212) 963-4116, http://unstats.un.org; *Statistical Yearbook.*

GUATEMALA - WHOLESALE TRADE

Inter-American Development Bank (IDB), 1300 New York Avenue, NW, Washington, DC 20577, (202) 623-1000, Fax: (202) 623-3096, www.iadb.org; *The Politics of Policies: Economic and Social Progress in Latin America - 2006 Report.*

GUATEMALA - WINE PRODUCTION

See GUATEMALA - BEVERAGE INDUSTRY

GUATEMALA - WOOD AND WOOD PULP

See GUATEMALA - FORESTS AND FORESTRY

GUATEMALA - WOOL PRODUCTION

See GUATEMALA - TEXTILE INDUSTRY

GUATEMALA - ZINC AND ZINC ORE

See GUATEMALA - MINERAL INDUSTRIES

GUERNSEY - NATIONAL STATISTICAL OFFICE

Policy and Research Unit, Sir Charles Frossard House, La Charroterie, St Peter Port, GY1 1FH Channel Islands, Guernsey, www.gov.gg/esu; National Data Center.

GUERNSEY - PRIMARY STATISTICS SOURCES

Policy and Research Unit, Sir Charles Frossard House, La Charroterie, St Peter Port, GY1 1FH Channel Islands, Guernsey, www.gov.gg/esu; *2006 Facts and Figures* and *2006 Sustainable Guernsey.*

GUERNSEY - AGRICULTURE

Economist Intelligence Unit, 111 West 57th Street, New York, NY 10019, (212) 554-0600, Fax: (212) 586-1181, www.eiu.com; *Guernsey Country Report.*

United Nations Food and Agricultural Organization (FAO), Viale delle Terme di Caracalla, 00100 Rome, Italy, (Dial from U.S. (202) 653-2400), (Fax from U.S. (202) 653 5760), www.fao.org; AQUASTAT.

GUERNSEY - ECONOMIC CONDITIONS

Center for International Business Education Research (CIBER), Columbia Business School and School of International and Public Affairs, Uris Hall, Room 212, 3022 Broadway, New York, NY 10027-6902, Mr. Joshua Safier, (212) 854-4750, Fax: (212) 222-9821, www.columbia.edu/cu/ciber/; Datastream International.

DSI Data Service Information, Xantener Strasse 51a, D-47495 Rheinberg, Germany, www.dsidata.com; *Campus Solution.*

Dun and Bradstreet (DB) Corporation, 103 JFK Parkway, Short Hills, NJ 07078, (973) 921-5500, www.dnb.com; *Country Report.*

Economist Intelligence Unit, 111 West 57th Street, New York, NY 10019, (212) 554-0600, Fax: (212) 586-1181, www.eiu.com; *Guernsey Country Report.*

International Monetary Fund (IMF), 700 Nineteenth Street, NW, Washington, DC 20431, (202) 623-7000, Fax: (202) 623-4661, www.imf.org; *World Economic Outlook Reports.*

The World Bank, 1818 H Street, NW, Washington, DC 20433, (202) 473-1000, Fax: (202) 477-6391, www.worldbank.org; *Global Economic Monitor (GEM)* and *Global Economic Prospects 2008.*

GUERNSEY - ENVIRONMENTAL CONDITIONS

DSI Data Service Information, Xantener Strasse 51a, D-47495 Rheinberg, Germany, www.dsidata.com; *Campus Solution* and *DSI's Global Environmental Database.*

Economist Intelligence Unit, 111 West 57th Street, New York, NY 10019, (212) 554-0600, Fax: (212) 586-1181, www.eiu.com; *Guernsey Country Report.*

GUERNSEY - EXPORTS

Economist Intelligence Unit, 111 West 57th Street, New York, NY 10019, (212) 554-0600, Fax: (212) 586-1181, www.eiu.com; *Guernsey Country Report.*

GUERNSEY - FINANCE, PUBLIC

Banque de France, 48 rue Croix des Petits champs, 75001 Paris, France, www.banque-france.fr/home.htm; *Public Finance.*

Bernan Essential Government Publications, 4611-F Assembly Drive, Lanham MD, 20706-4391, (301) 459-2255, Fax: (800) 865-3450, www.bernan.com; *National Accounts Statistics.*

Economist Intelligence Unit, 111 West 57th Street, New York, NY 10019, (212) 554-0600, Fax: (212) 586-1181, www.eiu.com; *Guernsey Country Report.*

International Monetary Fund (IMF), 700 Nineteenth Street, NW, Washington, DC 20431, (202) 623-7000, Fax: (202) 623-4661, www.imf.org; *International Financial Statistics* and *International Financial Statistics Online Service.*

GUERNSEY - GROSS DOMESTIC PRODUCT

Economist Intelligence Unit, 111 West 57th Street, New York, NY 10019, (212) 554-0600, Fax: (212) 586-1181, www.eiu.com; *Guernsey Country Report.*

GUERNSEY - IMPORTS

Economist Intelligence Unit, 111 West 57th Street, New York, NY 10019, (212) 554-0600, Fax: (212) 586-1181, www.eiu.com; *Guernsey Country Report.*

GUERNSEY - INDUSTRIES

Economist Intelligence Unit, 111 West 57th Street, New York, NY 10019, (212) 554-0600, Fax: (212) 586-1181, www.eiu.com; *Guernsey Country Report.*

United Nations Industrial Development Organization (UNIDO), 1 United Nations Plaza, New York, NY 10017, (212) 963 6890, Fax: (212) 963-7904, http://unido.org; Industrial Statistics Database 2008 (INDSTAT) and *The International Yearbook of Industrial Statistics 2008.*

GUERNSEY - INTERNATIONAL TRADE

Banque de France, 48 rue Croix des Petits champs, 75001 Paris, France, www.banque-france.fr/home.htm; *Monthly Business Survey Overview.*

Economist Intelligence Unit, 111 West 57th Street, New York, NY 10019, (212) 554-0600, Fax: (212) 586-1181, www.eiu.com; *Guernsey Country Report.*

World Trade Organization (WTO), Centre William Rappard, Rue de Lausanne 154, CH-1211 Geneva 21, Switzerland, www.wto.org; *International Trade Statistics 2006.*

GUERNSEY - INTERNET USERS

International Telecommunication Union (ITU), Place des Nations, 1211 Geneva 20, Switzerland, www.itu.int; *World Telecommunication/ICT Indicators Database on CD-ROM; World Telecommunication/ICT Indicators Database Online;* and *Yearbook of Statistics - Telecommunication Services (Chronological Time Series 1997-2006).*

GUERNSEY - MONEY SUPPLY

Economist Intelligence Unit, 111 West 57th Street, New York, NY 10019, (212) 554-0600, Fax: (212) 586-1181, www.eiu.com; *Guernsey Country Report.*

GUERNSEY - POPULATION

Economist Intelligence Unit, 111 West 57th Street, New York, NY 10019, (212) 554-0600, Fax: (212) 586-1181, www.eiu.com; *Guernsey Country Report.*

GUINEA - NATIONAL STATISTICAL OFFICE

Direction Nationale de la Statistique, Ministere du Plan, BP 221 Conakry, Guinea, www.stat-guinee.org; National Data Center.

GUINEA - PRIMARY STATISTICS SOURCES

Direction Nationale de la Statistique, Ministere du Plan, BP 221 Conakry, Guinea, www.stat-guinee.org; *Bulletin de Statistique.*

GUINEA - AGRICULTURAL MACHINERY

United Nations Statistics Division, New York, NY 10017, (800) 253-9646, Fax: (212) 963-4116, http://unstats.un.org; *Statistical Yearbook.*

GUINEA - AGRICULTURE

Economist Intelligence Unit, 111 West 57th Street, New York, NY 10019, (212) 554-0600, Fax: (212) 586-1181, www.eiu.com; *Guinea Country Report.*

Euromonitor International, Inc., 224 S. Michigan Avenue, Suite 1500, Chicago, IL 60604, (312) 922-1115, Fax: (312) 922-1157, www.euromonitor.com; *International Marketing Data and Statistics 2008* and *World Marketing Data and Statistics.*

Inter-American Development Bank (IDB), 1300 New York Avenue, NW, Washington, DC 20577, (202) 623-1000, Fax: (202) 623-3096, www.iadb.org; *The Politics of Policies: Economic and Social Progress in Latin America - 2006 Report.*

M.E. Sharpe, 80 Business Park Drive, Armonk, NY 10504, (800) 541-6563, Fax: (914) 273-2106, www.mesharpe.com; *The Illustrated Book of World Rankings.*

Palgrave Macmillan Ltd., Houndmills, Basingstoke, Hampshire, RG21 6XS, England, (Telephone in U.S. (888) 330-8477), (Fax in U.S. (800) 672-2054), www.palgrave.com; *The Statesman's Yearbook 2008.*

Taylor and Francis Group, An Informa Business, 2 Park Square, Milton Park, Abingdon, Oxford OX14 4RN, United Kingdom, (Dial from U.S. (212) 216-7800), (Fax from U.S. (212) 564-7854), www.tandf.co.uk; *The Europa World Year Book.*

United Nations Conference on Trade and Development (UNCTAD), DC2-1120, United Nations, New York, NY 10017, (212) 963-0027, www.unctad.org; *UNCTAD Commodity Yearbook.*

United Nations Economic Commission for Africa (ECA), PO Box 3001, Addis Ababa, Ethiopia, (Telephone in U.S. (212) 963-4957), www.uneca.org; *African Statistical Yearbook 2006.*

United Nations Food and Agricultural Organization (FAO), Viale delle Terme di Caracalla, 00100 Rome, Italy, (Dial from U.S. (202) 653-2400), (Fax from U.S. (202) 653 5760), www.fao.org; AQUASTAT; *FAO Production Yearbook 2002; FAO Trade Yearbook;* and *The State of Food and Agriculture (SOFA) 2006.*

United Nations Statistics Division, New York, NY 10017, (800) 253-9646, Fax: (212) 963-4116, http://unstats.un.org; *Statistical Yearbook* and *Survey of Economic and Social Conditions in Africa 2005.*

The World Bank, 1818 H Street, NW, Washington, DC 20433, (202) 473-1000, Fax: (202) 477-6391, www.worldbank.org; *Africa Live Database (LDB); African Development Indicators (ADI) 2007;* and *Guinea.*

GUINEA - AIRLINES

M.E. Sharpe, 80 Business Park Drive, Armonk, NY 10504, (800) 541-6563, Fax: (914) 273-2106, www.mesharpe.com; *The Illustrated Book of World Rankings.*

Palgrave Macmillan Ltd., Houndmills, Basingstoke, Hampshire, RG21 6XS, England, (Telephone in U.S. (888) 330-8477), (Fax in U.S. (800) 672-2054), www.palgrave.com; *The Statesman's Yearbook 2008.*

Taylor and Francis Group, An Informa Business, 2 Park Square, Milton Park, Abingdon, Oxford OX14 4RN, United Kingdom, (Dial from U.S. (212) 216-7800), (Fax from U.S. (212) 564-7854), www.tandf.co.uk; *The Europa World Year Book.*

United Nations Economic Commission for Africa (ECA), PO Box 3001, Addis Ababa, Ethiopia,

(Telephone in U.S. (212) 963-4957), www.uneca.org; *African Statistical Yearbook 2006.*

United Nations Statistics Division, New York, NY 10017, (800) 253-9646, Fax: (212) 963-4116, http://unstats.un.org; *Statistical Yearbook.*

GUINEA - AIRPORTS

Central Intelligence Agency, Office of Public Affairs, Washington, DC 20505, (703) 482-0623, Fax: (703) 482-1739, www.cia.gov; *The World Factbook.*

GUINEA - ALUMINUM PRODUCTION

See GUINEA - MINERAL INDUSTRIES

GUINEA - ARMED FORCES

Central Intelligence Agency, Office of Public Affairs, Washington, DC 20505, (703) 482-0623, Fax: (703) 482-1739, www.cia.gov; *The World Factbook.*

Euromonitor International, Inc., 224 S. Michigan Avenue, Suite 1500, Chicago, IL 60604, (312) 922-1115, Fax: (312) 922-1157, www.euromonitor.com; *World Marketing Data and Statistics.*

International Institute for Strategic Studies (IISS), Arundel House, 13-15 Arundel Street, Temple Place, London WC2R 3DX, England, www.iiss.org; *The Military Balance 2007.*

Palgrave Macmillan Ltd., Houndmills, Basingstoke, Hampshire, RG21 6XS, England, (Telephone in U.S. (888) 330-8477), (Fax in U.S. (800) 672-2054), www.palgrave.com; *The Statesman's Yearbook 2008.*

U.S. Department of State (DOS), 2201 C Street NW, Washington, DC 20520, (202) 647-4000, www.state.gov; *World Military Expenditures and Arms Transfers (WMEAT).*

United Nations Statistics Division, New York, NY 10017, (800) 253-9646, Fax: (212) 963-4116, http://unstats.un.org; *Human Development Report 2006.*

GUINEA - BALANCE OF PAYMENTS

African Development Bank Group, Rue Joseph Anoma, 01 BP 1387 Abidjan 01, Cote d'Ivoire, www.afdb.org; *Statistics Pocketbook 2008.*

Inter-American Development Bank (IDB), 1300 New York Avenue, NW, Washington, DC 20577, (202) 623-1000, Fax: (202) 623-3096, www.iadb.org; *The Politics of Policies: Economic and Social Progress in Latin America - 2006 Report.*

Taylor and Francis Group, An Informa Business, 2 Park Square, Milton Park, Abingdon, Oxford OX14 4RN, United Kingdom, (Dial from U.S. (212) 216-7800), (Fax from U.S. (212) 564-7854), www.tandf.co.uk; *The Europa World Year Book.*

United Nations Conference on Trade and Development (UNCTAD), DC2-1120, United Nations, New York, NY 10017, (212) 963-0027, www.unctad.org; *Handbook of Statistics 2005.*

United Nations Economic Commission for Africa (ECA), PO Box 3001, Addis Ababa, Ethiopia, (Telephone in U.S. (212) 963-4957), www.uneca.org; *African Statistical Yearbook 2006.*

The World Bank, 1818 H Street, NW, Washington, DC 20433, (202) 473-1000, Fax: (202) 477-6391, www.worldbank.org; *Guinea* and *World Development Report 2008.*

GUINEA - BANKS AND BANKING

Euromonitor International, Inc., 224 S. Michigan Avenue, Suite 1500, Chicago, IL 60604, (312) 922-1115, Fax: (312) 922-1157, www.euromonitor.com; *World Marketing Data and Statistics.*

Inter-American Development Bank (IDB), 1300 New York Avenue, NW, Washington, DC 20577, (202) 623-1000, Fax: (202) 623-3096, www.iadb.org; *The Politics of Policies: Economic and Social Progress in Latin America - 2006 Report.*

M.E. Sharpe, 80 Business Park Drive, Armonk, NY 10504, (800) 541-6563, Fax: (914) 273-2106, www.mesharpe.com; *The Illustrated Book of World Rankings.*

Palgrave Macmillan Ltd., Houndmills, Basingstoke, Hampshire, RG21 6XS, England, (Telephone in U.S. (888) 330-8477), (Fax in U.S. (800) 672-2054), www.palgrave.com; *The Statesman's Yearbook 2008.*

United Nations Economic Commission for Africa (ECA), PO Box 3001, Addis Ababa, Ethiopia, (Telephone in U.S. (212) 963-4957), www.uneca.org; *African Statistical Yearbook 2006.*

GUINEA - BARLEY PRODUCTION

See GUINEA - CROPS

GUINEA - BEVERAGE INDUSTRY

M.E. Sharpe, 80 Business Park Drive, Armonk, NY 10504, (800) 541-6563, Fax: (914) 273-2106, www.mesharpe.com; *The Illustrated Book of World Rankings.*

GUINEA - BONDS

Inter-American Development Bank (IDB), 1300 New York Avenue, NW, Washington, DC 20577, (202) 623-1000, Fax: (202) 623-3096, www.iadb.org; *The Politics of Policies: Economic and Social Progress in Latin America - 2006 Report.*

GUINEA - BROADCASTING

Central Intelligence Agency, Office of Public Affairs, Washington, DC 20505, (703) 482-0623, Fax: (703) 482-1739, www.cia.gov; *The World Factbook.*

Euromonitor International, Inc., 224 S. Michigan Avenue, Suite 1500, Chicago, IL 60604, (312) 922-1115, Fax: (312) 922-1157, www.euromonitor.com; *World Marketing Data and Statistics.*

M.E. Sharpe, 80 Business Park Drive, Armonk, NY 10504, (800) 541-6563, Fax: (914) 273-2106, www.mesharpe.com; *The Illustrated Book of World Rankings.*

Palgrave Macmillan Ltd., Houndmills, Basingstoke, Hampshire, RG21 6XS, England, (Telephone in U.S. (888) 330-8477), (Fax in U.S. (800) 672-2054), www.palgrave.com; *The Statesman's Yearbook 2008.*

WRTH Publications Limited, PO Box 290, Oxford OX2 7FT, UK, www.wrth.com; *World Radio TV Handbook 2007.*

GUINEA - BUDGET

Central Intelligence Agency, Office of Public Affairs, Washington, DC 20505, (703) 482-0623, Fax: (703) 482-1739, www.cia.gov; *The World Factbook.*

GUINEA - BUSINESS

Economist Intelligence Unit, 111 West 57th Street, New York, NY 10019, (212) 554-0600, Fax: (212) 586-1181, www.eiu.com; *Business Africa.*

Inter-American Development Bank (IDB), 1300 New York Avenue, NW, Washington, DC 20577, (202) 623-1000, Fax: (202) 623-3096, www.iadb.org; *The Politics of Policies: Economic and Social Progress in Latin America - 2006 Report.*

GUINEA - CAPITAL INVESTMENTS

Inter-American Development Bank (IDB), 1300 New York Avenue, NW, Washington, DC 20577, (202) 623-1000, Fax: (202) 623-3096, www.iadb.org; *The Politics of Policies: Economic and Social Progress in Latin America - 2006 Report.*

GUINEA - CAPITAL LEVY

Inter-American Development Bank (IDB), 1300 New York Avenue, NW, Washington, DC 20577, (202) 623-1000, Fax: (202) 623-3096, www.iadb.org; *The Politics of Policies: Economic and Social Progress in Latin America - 2006 Report.*

GUINEA - CATTLE

See GUINEA - LIVESTOCK

GUINEA - CHICKENS

See GUINEA - LIVESTOCK

GUINEA - CHILDBIRTH - STATISTICS

Central Intelligence Agency, Office of Public Affairs, Washington, DC 20505, (703) 482-0623, Fax: (703) 482-1739, www.cia.gov; *The World Factbook.*

Euromonitor International, Inc., 224 S. Michigan Avenue, Suite 1500, Chicago, IL 60604, (312) 922-1115, Fax: (312) 922-1157, www.euromonitor.com; *International Marketing Data and Statistics 2008* and *The World Economic Factbook 2008.*

M.E. Sharpe, 80 Business Park Drive, Armonk, NY 10504, (800) 541-6563, Fax: (914) 273-2106, www.mesharpe.com; *The Illustrated Book of World Rankings.*

Taylor and Francis Group, An Informa Business, 2 Park Square, Milton Park, Abingdon, Oxford OX14 4RN, United Kingdom, (Dial from U.S. (212) 216-7800), (Fax from U.S. (212) 564-7854), www.tandf.co.uk; *The Europa World Year Book.*

United Nations Statistics Division, New York, NY 10017, (800) 253-9646, Fax: (212) 963-4116, http://unstats.un.org; *Demographic Yearbook; Statistical Yearbook;* and *Survey of Economic and Social Conditions in Africa 2005.*

GUINEA - CLIMATE

International Institute for Environment and Development (IIED), 3 Endsleigh Street, London, England, WC1H 0DD, United Kingdom, www.iied.org; *Environment Urbanization* and *Haramata - Bulletin of the Drylands.*

M.E. Sharpe, 80 Business Park Drive, Armonk, NY 10504, (800) 541-6563, Fax: (914) 273-2106, www.mesharpe.com; *The Illustrated Book of World Rankings.*

Palgrave Macmillan Ltd., Houndmills, Basingstoke, Hampshire, RG21 6XS, England, (Telephone in U.S. (888) 330-8477), (Fax in U.S. (800) 672-2054), www.palgrave.com; *The Statesman's Yearbook 2008.*

GUINEA - COAL PRODUCTION

See GUINEA - MINERAL INDUSTRIES

GUINEA - COFFEE

See GUINEA - CROPS

GUINEA - COMMERCE

Palgrave Macmillan Ltd., Houndmills, Basingstoke, Hampshire, RG21 6XS, England, (Telephone in U.S. (888) 330-8477), (Fax in U.S. (800) 672-2054), www.palgrave.com; *The Statesman's Yearbook 2008.*

GUINEA - COMMODITY EXCHANGES

Commodity Research Bureau, 330 South Wells Street, Suite 612, Chicago, IL 60606-7110, (800) 621-5271, Fax: (312) 939-4135, www.crbtrader.com; *2006 CRB Commodity Yearbook and CD.*

International Monetary Fund (IMF), 700 Nineteenth Street, NW, Washington, DC 20431, (202) 623-7000, Fax: (202) 623-4661, www.imf.org; *IMF Primary Commodity Prices.*

United Nations Food and Agricultural Organization (FAO), Viale delle Terme di Caracalla, 00100 Rome, Italy, (Dial from U.S. (202) 653-2400), (Fax from U.S. (202) 653 5760), www.fao.org; *The State of Food and Agriculture (SOFA) 2006.*

GUINEA - COMMUNICATION AND TRAFFIC

United Nations Statistics Division, New York, NY 10017, (800) 253-9646, Fax: (212) 963-4116, http://unstats.un.org; *Statistical Yearbook.*

GUINEA - CONSTRUCTION INDUSTRY

Inter-American Development Bank (IDB), 1300 New York Avenue, NW, Washington, DC 20577, (202) 623-1000, Fax: (202) 623-3096, www.iadb.org; *The Politics of Policies: Economic and Social Progress in Latin America - 2006 Report.*

M.E. Sharpe, 80 Business Park Drive, Armonk, NY 10504, (800) 541-6563, Fax: (914) 273-2106, www.mesharpe.com; *The Illustrated Book of World Rankings.*

United Nations Economic Commission for Africa (ECA), PO Box 3001, Addis Ababa, Ethiopia, (Telephone in U.S. (212) 963-4957), www.uneca.org; *African Statistical Yearbook 2006.*

GUINEA - CONSUMER PRICE INDEXES

Taylor and Francis Group, An Informa Business, 2 Park Square, Milton Park, Abingdon, Oxford OX14 4RN, United Kingdom, (Dial from U.S. (212) 216-7800), (Fax from U.S. (212) 564-7854), www.tandf.co.uk; *The Europa World Year Book.*

United Nations Statistics Division, New York, NY 10017, (800) 253-9646, Fax: (212) 963-4116, http://unstats.un.org; *Survey of Economic and Social Conditions in Africa 2005.*

GUINEA - CONSUMPTION (ECONOMICS)

African Development Bank Group, Rue Joseph Anoma, 01 BP 1387 Abidjan 01, Cote d'Ivoire, www.afdb.org; *Statistics Pocketbook 2008.*

Inter-American Development Bank (IDB), 1300 New York Avenue, NW, Washington, DC 20577, (202) 623-1000, Fax: (202) 623-3096, www.iadb.org; *The Politics of Policies: Economic and Social Progress in Latin America - 2006 Report.*

United Nations Statistics Division, New York, NY 10017, (800) 253-9646, Fax: (212) 963-4116, http://unstats.un.org; *Survey of Economic and Social Conditions in Africa 2005.*

The World Bank, 1818 H Street, NW, Washington, DC 20433, (202) 473-1000, Fax: (202) 477-6391, www.worldbank.org; *World Development Report 2008.*

GUINEA - COPPER INDUSTRY AND TRADE

See GUINEA - MINERAL INDUSTRIES

GUINEA - CORN INDUSTRY

See GUINEA - CROPS

GUINEA - COTTON

See GUINEA - CROPS

GUINEA - CROPS

M.E. Sharpe, 80 Business Park Drive, Armonk, NY 10504, (800) 541-6563, Fax: (914) 273-2106, www.mesharpe.com; *The Illustrated Book of World Rankings.*

Palgrave Macmillan Ltd., Houndmills, Basingstoke, Hampshire, RG21 6XS, England, (Telephone in U.S. (888) 330-8477), (Fax in U.S. (800) 672-2054), www.palgrave.com; *The Statesman's Yearbook 2008.*

Taylor and Francis Group, An Informa Business, 2 Park Square, Milton Park, Abingdon, Oxford OX14 4RN, United Kingdom, (Dial from U.S. (212) 216-7800), (Fax from U.S. (212) 564-7854), www.tandf.co.uk; *The Europa World Year Book.*

United Nations Conference on Trade and Development (UNCTAD), DC2-1120, United Nations, New York, NY 10017, (212) 963-0027, www.unctad.org; *UNCTAD Commodity Yearbook.*

United Nations Economic Commission for Africa (ECA), PO Box 3001, Addis Ababa, Ethiopia, (Telephone in U.S. (212) 963-4957), www.uneca.org; *African Statistical Yearbook 2006.*

United Nations Food and Agricultural Organization (FAO), Viale delle Terme di Caracalla, 00100 Rome, Italy, (Dial from U.S. (202) 653-2400), (Fax from U.S. (202) 653 5760), www.fao.org; *FAO Production Yearbook 2002* and *The State of Food and Agriculture (SOFA) 2006.*

United Nations Statistics Division, New York, NY 10017, (800) 253-9646, Fax: (212) 963-4116, http://unstats.un.org; *Statistical Yearbook.*

GUINEA - CUSTOMS ADMINISTRATION

Inter-American Development Bank (IDB), 1300 New York Avenue, NW, Washington, DC 20577, (202) 623-1000, Fax: (202) 623-3096, www.iadb.org; *The Politics of Policies: Economic and Social Progress in Latin America - 2006 Report.*

Palgrave Macmillan Ltd., Houndmills, Basingstoke, Hampshire, RG21 6XS, England, (Telephone in U.S. (888) 330-8477), (Fax in U.S. (800) 672-2054), www.palgrave.com; *The Statesman's Yearbook 2008.*

GUINEA - DAIRY PROCESSING

M.E. Sharpe, 80 Business Park Drive, Armonk, NY 10504, (800) 541-6563, Fax: (914) 273-2106, www.mesharpe.com; *The Illustrated Book of World Rankings.*

Palgrave Macmillan Ltd., Houndmills, Basingstoke, Hampshire, RG21 6XS, England, (Telephone in U.S. (888) 330-8477), (Fax in U.S. (800) 672-2054), www.palgrave.com; *The Statesman's Yearbook 2008.*

Taylor and Francis Group, An Informa Business, 2 Park Square, Milton Park, Abingdon, Oxford OX14 4RN, United Kingdom, (Dial from U.S. (212) 216-7800), (Fax from U.S. (212) 564-7854), www.tandf.co.uk; *The Europa World Year Book.*

United Nations Food and Agricultural Organization (FAO), Viale delle Terme di Caracalla, 00100 Rome, Italy, (Dial from U.S. (202) 653-2400), (Fax from U.S. (202) 653 5760), www.fao.org; *FAO Production Yearbook 2002* and *The State of Food and Agriculture (SOFA) 2006.*

United Nations Statistics Division, New York, NY 10017, (800) 253-9646, Fax: (212) 963-4116, http://unstats.un.org; *Statistical Yearbook.*

GUINEA - DEATH RATES

See GUINEA - MORTALITY

GUINEA - DEBTS, EXTERNAL

African Development Bank Group, Rue Joseph Anoma, 01 BP 1387 Abidjan 01, Cote d'Ivoire, www.afdb.org; *Statistics Pocketbook 2008.*

Inter-American Development Bank (IDB), 1300 New York Avenue, NW, Washington, DC 20577, (202) 623-1000, Fax: (202) 623-3096, www.iadb.org; *The Politics of Policies: Economic and Social Progress in Latin America - 2006 Report.*

Palgrave Macmillan Ltd., Houndmills, Basingstoke, Hampshire, RG21 6XS, England, (Telephone in U.S. (888) 330-8477), (Fax in U.S. (800) 672-2054), www.palgrave.com; *The Statesman's Yearbook 2008.*

United Nations Statistics Division, New York, NY 10017, (800) 253-9646, Fax: (212) 963-4116, http://unstats.un.org; *Survey of Economic and Social Conditions in Africa 2005.*

The World Bank, 1818 H Street, NW, Washington, DC 20433, (202) 473-1000, Fax: (202) 477-6391, www.worldbank.org; *Africa Live Database (LDB); African Development Indicators (ADI) 2007; Global Development Finance 2007;* and *World Development Report 2008.*

GUINEA - DEFENSE EXPENDITURES

See GUINEA - ARMED FORCES

GUINEA - DEMOGRAPHY

Euromonitor International, Inc., 224 S. Michigan Avenue, Suite 1500, Chicago, IL 60604, (312) 922-1115, Fax: (312) 922-1157, www.euromonitor.com; *International Marketing Data and Statistics 2008; The World Economic Factbook 2008;* and *World Marketing Data and Statistics.*

M.E. Sharpe, 80 Business Park Drive, Armonk, NY 10504, (800) 541-6563, Fax: (914) 273-2106, www.mesharpe.com; *The Illustrated Book of World Rankings.*

United Nations Statistics Division, New York, NY 10017, (800) 253-9646, Fax: (212) 963-4116, http://unstats.un.org; *Human Development Report 2006* and *Survey of Economic and Social Conditions in Africa 2005.*

The World Bank, 1818 H Street, NW, Washington, DC 20433, (202) 473-1000, Fax: (202) 477-6391, www.worldbank.org; *Guinea.*

GUINEA - DIAMONDS

See GUINEA - MINERAL INDUSTRIES

GUINEA - DISCOUNT

Inter-American Development Bank (IDB), 1300 New York Avenue, NW, Washington, DC 20577, (202) 623-1000, Fax: (202) 623-3096, www.iadb.org; *The Politics of Policies: Economic and Social Progress in Latin America - 2006 Report.*

GUINEA - DISPOSABLE INCOME

Inter-American Development Bank (IDB), 1300 New York Avenue, NW, Washington, DC 20577, (202) 623-1000, Fax: (202) 623-3096, www.iadb.org; *The Politics of Policies: Economic and Social Progress in Latin America - 2006 Report.*

M.E. Sharpe, 80 Business Park Drive, Armonk, NY 10504, (800) 541-6563, Fax: (914) 273-2106, www.mesharpe.com; *The Illustrated Book of World Rankings.*

United Nations Statistics Division, New York, NY 10017, (800) 253-9646, Fax: (212) 963-4116, http://unstats.un.org; *Statistical Yearbook.*

GUINEA - DIVORCE

M.E. Sharpe, 80 Business Park Drive, Armonk, NY 10504, (800) 541-6563, Fax: (914) 273-2106, www.mesharpe.com; *The Illustrated Book of World Rankings.*

United Nations Statistics Division, New York, NY 10017, (800) 253-9646, Fax: (212) 963-4116, http://unstats.un.org; *Demographic Yearbook.*

GUINEA - ECONOMIC ASSISTANCE

Inter-American Development Bank (IDB), 1300 New York Avenue, NW, Washington, DC 20577, (202) 623-1000, Fax: (202) 623-3096, www.iadb.org; *The Politics of Policies: Economic and Social Progress in Latin America - 2006 Report.*

United Nations Statistics Division, New York, NY 10017, (800) 253-9646, Fax: (212) 963-4116, http://unstats.un.org; *Statistical Yearbook.*

GUINEA - ECONOMIC CONDITIONS

African Development Bank Group, Rue Joseph Anoma, 01 BP 1387 Abidjan 01, Cote d'Ivoire, www.afdb.org; *The African Statistical Journal; Gender, Poverty and Environmental Indicators on African Countries 2007; Selected Statistics on African Countries 2007;* and *Statistics Pocketbook 2008.*

Center for International Business Education Research (CIBER), Columbia Business School and School of International and Public Affairs, Uris Hall, Room 212, 3022 Broadway, New York, NY 10027-6902, Mr. Joshua Safier, (212) 854-4750, Fax: (212) 222-9821, www.columbia.edu/cu/ciber/; Datastream International.

Central Intelligence Agency, Office of Public Affairs, Washington, DC 20505, (703) 482-0623, Fax: (703) 482-1739, www.cia.gov; *The World Factbook.*

DSI Data Service Information, Xantener Strasse 51a, D-47495 Rheinberg, Germany, www.dsidata.com; *Campus Solution.*

Dun and Bradstreet (DB) Corporation, 103 JFK Parkway, Short Hills, NJ 07078, (973) 921-5500, www.dnb.com; *Country Report.*

Economist Intelligence Unit, 111 West 57th Street, New York, NY 10019, (212) 554-0600, Fax: (212) 586-1181, www.eiu.com; *Business Africa* and *Guinea Country Report.*

Euromonitor International, Inc., 224 S. Michigan Avenue, Suite 1500, Chicago, IL 60604, (312) 922-1115, Fax: (312) 922-1157, www.euromonitor.com; *International Marketing Data and Statistics 2008; The World Economic Factbook 2008;* and *World Marketing Data and Statistics.*

Inter-American Development Bank (IDB), 1300 New York Avenue, NW, Washington, DC 20577, (202) 623-1000, Fax: (202) 623-3096, www.iadb.org; *The*

Politics of Policies: Economic and Social Progress in Latin America - 2006 Report.

International Monetary Fund (IMF), 700 Nineteenth Street, NW, Washington, DC 20431, (202) 623-7000, Fax: (202) 623-4661, www.imf.org; *World Economic Outlook Reports.*

M.E. Sharpe, 80 Business Park Drive, Armonk, NY 10504, (800) 541-6563, Fax: (914) 273-2106, www.mesharpe.com; *The Illustrated Book of World Rankings.*

Palgrave Macmillan Ltd., Houndmills, Basingstoke, Hampshire, RG21 6XS, England, (Telephone in U.S. (888) 330-8477), (Fax in U.S. (800) 672-2054), www.palgrave.com; *The Statesman's Yearbook 2008.*

Taylor and Francis Group, An Informa Business, 2 Park Square, Milton Park, Abingdon, Oxford OX14 4RN, United Kingdom, (Dial from U.S. (212) 216-7800), (Fax from U.S. (212) 564-7854), www.tandf.co.uk; *The Europa World Year Book.*

United Nations Statistics Division, New York, NY 10017, (800) 253-9646, Fax: (212) 963-4116, http://unstats.un.org; *Compendium of Intra-African and Related Foreign Trade Statistics 2003* and *World Statistics Pocketbook.*

The World Bank, 1818 H Street, NW, Washington, DC 20433, (202) 473-1000, Fax: (202) 477-6391, www.worldbank.org; *Africa Household Survey Databank; Africa Live Database (LDB); Africa Standardized Files and Indicators; African Development Indicators (ADI) 2007; Global Economic Monitor (GEM); Global Economic Prospects 2008; Guinea; The World Bank Atlas 2003-2004;* and *World Development Report 2008.*

GUINEA - ECONOMICS - SOCIOLOGICAL ASPECTS

Inter-American Development Bank (IDB), 1300 New York Avenue, NW, Washington, DC 20577, (202) 623-1000, Fax: (202) 623-3096, www.iadb.org; *The Politics of Policies: Economic and Social Progress in Latin America - 2006 Report.*

GUINEA - EDUCATION

African Development Bank Group, Rue Joseph Anoma, 01 BP 1387 Abidjan 01, Cote d'Ivoire, www.afdb.org; *Statistics Pocketbook 2008.*

Euromonitor International, Inc., 224 S. Michigan Avenue, Suite 1500, Chicago, IL 60604, (312) 922-1115, Fax: (312) 922-1157, www.euromonitor.com; *International Marketing Data and Statistics 2008* and *World Marketing Data and Statistics.*

M.E. Sharpe, 80 Business Park Drive, Armonk, NY 10504, (800) 541-6563, Fax: (914) 273-2106, www.mesharpe.com; *The Illustrated Book of World Rankings.*

Palgrave Macmillan Ltd., Houndmills, Basingstoke, Hampshire, RG21 6XS, England, (Telephone in U.S. (888) 330-8477), (Fax in U.S. (800) 672-2054), www.palgrave.com; *The Statesman's Yearbook 2008.*

Taylor and Francis Group, An Informa Business, 2 Park Square, Milton Park, Abingdon, Oxford OX14 4RN, United Kingdom, (Dial from U.S. (212) 216-7800), (Fax from U.S. (212) 564-7854), www.tandf.co.uk; *The Europa World Year Book.*

UNESCO Institute for Statistics, C.P. 6128 Succursale Centre-Ville, Montreal, Quebec, H3C 3J7 Canada, (Dial from U.S. (514) 343-6880), (Fax from U.S. (514) 343 6882), www.uis.unesco.org; *Statistical Tables.*

United Nations Economic Commission for Africa (ECA), PO Box 3001, Addis Ababa, Ethiopia, (Telephone in U.S. (212) 963-4957), www.uneca.org; *African Statistical Yearbook 2006.*

United Nations Statistics Division, New York, NY 10017, (800) 253-9646, Fax: (212) 963-4116, http://unstats.un.org; *Human Development Report 2006* and *Survey of Economic and Social Conditions in Africa 2005.*

The World Bank, 1818 H Street, NW, Washington, DC 20433, (202) 473-1000, Fax: (202) 477-6391, www.worldbank.org; *Guinea* and *World Development Report 2008.*

GUINEA - ELECTRICITY

Inter-American Development Bank (IDB), 1300 New York Avenue, NW, Washington, DC 20577, (202) 623-1000, Fax: (202) 623-3096, www.iadb.org; *The Politics of Policies: Economic and Social Progress in Latin America - 2006 Report.*

M.E. Sharpe, 80 Business Park Drive, Armonk, NY 10504, (800) 541-6563, Fax: (914) 273-2106, www.mesharpe.com; *The Illustrated Book of World Rankings.*

Palgrave Macmillan Ltd., Houndmills, Basingstoke, Hampshire, RG21 6XS, England, (Telephone in U.S. (888) 330-8477), (Fax in U.S. (800) 672-2054), www.palgrave.com; *The Statesman's Yearbook 2008.*

United Nations Economic Commission for Africa (ECA), PO Box 3001, Addis Ababa, Ethiopia, (Telephone in U.S. (212) 963-4957), www.uneca.org; *African Statistical Yearbook 2006.*

United Nations Statistics Division, New York, NY 10017, (800) 253-9646, Fax: (212) 963-4116, http://unstats.un.org; *Human Development Report 2006; Statistical Yearbook;* and *Survey of Economic and Social Conditions in Africa 2005.*

GUINEA - EMPLOYMENT

Euromonitor International, Inc., 224 S. Michigan Avenue, Suite 1500, Chicago, IL 60604, (312) 922-1115, Fax: (312) 922-1157, www.euromonitor.com; *International Marketing Data and Statistics 2008.*

M.E. Sharpe, 80 Business Park Drive, Armonk, NY 10504, (800) 541-6563, Fax: (914) 273-2106, www.mesharpe.com; *The Illustrated Book of World Rankings.*

United Nations Economic Commission for Africa (ECA), PO Box 3001, Addis Ababa, Ethiopia, (Telephone in U.S. (212) 963-4957), www.uneca.org; *African Statistical Yearbook 2006.*

United Nations Statistics Division, New York, NY 10017, (800) 253-9646, Fax: (212) 963-4116, http://unstats.un.org; *Survey of Economic and Social Conditions in Africa 2005.*

The World Bank, 1818 H Street, NW, Washington, DC 20433, (202) 473-1000, Fax: (202) 477-6391, www.worldbank.org; *Guinea.*

GUINEA - ENVIRONMENTAL CONDITIONS

DSI Data Service Information, Xantener Strasse 51a, D-47495 Rheinberg, Germany, www.dsidata.com; *Campus Solution* and *DSI's Global Environmental Database.*

Economist Intelligence Unit, 111 West 57th Street, New York, NY 10019, (212) 554-0600, Fax: (212) 586-1181, www.eiu.com; *Guinea Country Report.*

International Institute for Environment and Development (IIED), 3 Endsleigh Street, London, England, WC1H 0DD, United Kingdom, www.iied.org; *Environment Urbanization* and *Haramata - Bulletin of the Drylands.*

United Nations Statistics Division, New York, NY 10017, (800) 253-9646, Fax: (212) 963-4116, http://unstats.un.org; *World Statistics Pocketbook.*

GUINEA - EXPENDITURES, PUBLIC

Inter-American Development Bank (IDB), 1300 New York Avenue, NW, Washington, DC 20577, (202) 623-1000, Fax: (202) 623-3096, www.iadb.org; *The Politics of Policies: Economic and Social Progress in Latin America - 2006 Report.*

GUINEA - EXPORTS

African Development Bank Group, Rue Joseph Anoma, 01 BP 1387 Abidjan 01, Cote d'Ivoire, www.afdb.org; *Statistics Pocketbook 2008.*

Central Intelligence Agency, Office of Public Affairs, Washington, DC 20505, (703) 482-0623, Fax: (703) 482-1739, www.cia.gov; *The World Factbook.*

Economist Intelligence Unit, 111 West 57th Street, New York, NY 10019, (212) 554-0600, Fax: (212) 586-1181, www.eiu.com; *Guinea Country Report.*

Euromonitor International, Inc., 224 S. Michigan Avenue, Suite 1500, Chicago, IL 60604, (312) 922-1115, Fax: (312) 922-1157, www.euromonitor.com; *International Marketing Data and Statistics 2008* and *The World Economic Factbook 2008.*

Inter-American Development Bank (IDB), 1300 New York Avenue, NW, Washington, DC 20577, (202) 623-1000, Fax: (202) 623-3096, www.iadb.org; *The Politics of Policies: Economic and Social Progress in Latin America - 2006 Report.*

International Monetary Fund (IMF), 700 Nineteenth Street, NW, Washington, DC 20431, (202) 623-7000, Fax: (202) 623-4661, www.imf.org; *Direction of Trade Statistics Yearbook 2007.*

Palgrave Macmillan Ltd., Houndmills, Basingstoke, Hampshire, RG21 6XS, England, (Telephone in U.S. (888) 330-8477), (Fax in U.S. (800) 672-2054), www.palgrave.com; *The Statesman's Yearbook 2008.*

Taylor and Francis Group, An Informa Business, 2 Park Square, Milton Park, Abingdon, Oxford OX14 4RN, United Kingdom, (Dial from U.S. (212) 216-7800), (Fax from U.S. (212) 564-7854), www.tandf.co.uk; *The Europa World Year Book.*

United Nations Conference on Trade and Development (UNCTAD), DC2-1120, United Nations, New York, NY 10017, (212) 963-0027, www.unctad.org; *Handbook of Statistics 2005.*

United Nations Economic Commission for Africa (ECA), PO Box 3001, Addis Ababa, Ethiopia, (Telephone in U.S. (212) 963-4957), www.uneca.org; *African Statistical Yearbook 2006.*

United Nations Food and Agricultural Organization (FAO), Viale delle Terme di Caracalla, 00100 Rome, Italy, (Dial from U.S. (202) 653-2400), (Fax from U.S. (202) 653 5760), www.fao.org; *The State of Food and Agriculture (SOFA) 2006.*

United Nations Statistics Division, New York, NY 10017, (800) 253-9646, Fax: (212) 963-4116, http://unstats.un.org; *Compendium of Intra-African and Related Foreign Trade Statistics 2003* and *Survey of Economic and Social Conditions in Africa 2005.*

The World Bank, 1818 H Street, NW, Washington, DC 20433, (202) 473-1000, Fax: (202) 477-6391, www.worldbank.org; *World Development Report 2008.*

GUINEA - FEMALE WORKING POPULATION

See GUINEA - EMPLOYMENT

GUINEA - FERTILITY, HUMAN

Central Intelligence Agency, Office of Public Affairs, Washington, DC 20505, (703) 482-0623, Fax: (703) 482-1739, www.cia.gov; *The World Factbook.*

M.E. Sharpe, 80 Business Park Drive, Armonk, NY 10504, (800) 541-6563, Fax: (914) 273-2106, www.mesharpe.com; *The Illustrated Book of World Rankings.*

United Nations Statistics Division, New York, NY 10017, (800) 253-9646, Fax: (212) 963-4116, http://unstats.un.org; *Human Development Report 2006* and *Survey of Economic and Social Conditions in Africa 2005.*

The World Bank, 1818 H Street, NW, Washington, DC 20433, (202) 473-1000, Fax: (202) 477-6391, www.worldbank.org; *The World Bank Atlas 2003-2004* and *World Development Report 2008.*

GUINEA - FERTILIZER INDUSTRY

United Nations Food and Agricultural Organization (FAO), Viale delle Terme di Caracalla, 00100 Rome, Italy, (Dial from U.S. (202) 653-2400), (Fax from U.S. (202) 653 5760), www.fao.org; *FAO Fertilizer Yearbook* and *The State of Food and Agriculture (SOFA) 2006.*

United Nations Statistics Division, New York, NY 10017, (800) 253-9646, Fax: (212) 963-4116, http://unstats.un.org; *Statistical Yearbook.*

GUINEA - FETAL MORTALITY

See GUINEA - MORTALITY

GUINEA - FINANCE

Inter-American Development Bank (IDB), 1300 New York Avenue, NW, Washington, DC 20577, (202) 623-1000, Fax: (202) 623-3096, www.iadb.org; *The Politics of Policies: Economic and Social Progress in Latin America - 2006 Report.*

Taylor and Francis Group, An Informa Business, 2 Park Square, Milton Park, Abingdon, Oxford OX14 4RN, United Kingdom, (Dial from U.S. (212) 216-7800), (Fax from U.S. (212) 564-7854), www.tandf.co.uk; *The Europa World Year Book.*

United Nations Economic Commission for Africa (ECA), PO Box 3001, Addis Ababa, Ethiopia, (Telephone in U.S. (212) 963-4957), www.uneca.org; *African Statistical Yearbook 2006.*

United Nations Statistics Division, New York, NY 10017, (800) 253-9646, Fax: (212) 963-4116, http://unstats.un.org; *Statistical Yearbook.*

The World Bank, 1818 H Street, NW, Washington, DC 20433, (202) 473-1000, Fax: (202) 477-6391, www.worldbank.org; *Guinea.*

GUINEA - FINANCE, PUBLIC

African Development Bank Group, Rue Joseph Anoma, 01 BP 1387 Abidjan 01, Cote d'Ivoire, www.afdb.org; *Statistics Pocketbook 2008.*

Bernan Essential Government Publications, 4611-F Assembly Drive, Lanham MD, 20706-4391, (301) 459-2255, Fax: (800) 865-3450, www.bernan.com; *National Accounts Statistics.*

Economist Intelligence Unit, 111 West 57th Street, New York, NY 10019, (212) 554-0600, Fax: (212) 586-1181, www.eiu.com; *Guinea Country Report.*

Inter-American Development Bank (IDB), 1300 New York Avenue, NW, Washington, DC 20577, (202) 623-1000, Fax: (202) 623-3096, www.iadb.org; *The Politics of Policies: Economic and Social Progress in Latin America - 2006 Report.*

International Monetary Fund (IMF), 700 Nineteenth Street, NW, Washington, DC 20431, (202) 623-7000, Fax: (202) 623-4661, www.imf.org; *International Financial Statistics* and *International Financial Statistics Online Service.*

M.E. Sharpe, 80 Business Park Drive, Armonk, NY 10504, (800) 541-6563, Fax: (914) 273-2106, www.mesharpe.com; *The Illustrated Book of World Rankings.*

Palgrave Macmillan Ltd., Houndmills, Basingstoke, Hampshire, RG21 6XS, England, (Telephone in U.S. (888) 330-8477), (Fax in U.S. (800) 672-2054), www.palgrave.com; *The Statesman's Yearbook 2008.*

Taylor and Francis Group, An Informa Business, 2 Park Square, Milton Park, Abingdon, Oxford OX14 4RN, United Kingdom, (Dial from U.S. (212) 216-7800), (Fax from U.S. (212) 564-7854), www.tandf.co.uk; *The Europa World Year Book.*

United Nations Economic Commission for Africa (ECA), PO Box 3001, Addis Ababa, Ethiopia, (Telephone in U.S. (212) 963-4957), www.uneca.org; *African Statistical Yearbook 2006.*

The World Bank, 1818 H Street, NW, Washington, DC 20433, (202) 473-1000, Fax: (202) 477-6391, www.worldbank.org; *Guinea.*

GUINEA - FISHERIES

Inter-American Development Bank (IDB), 1300 New York Avenue, NW, Washington, DC 20577, (202) 623-1000, Fax: (202) 623-3096, www.iadb.org; *The Politics of Policies: Economic and Social Progress in Latin America - 2006 Report.*

M.E. Sharpe, 80 Business Park Drive, Armonk, NY 10504, (800) 541-6563, Fax: (914) 273-2106, www.mesharpe.com; *The Illustrated Book of World Rankings.*

Palgrave Macmillan Ltd., Houndmills, Basingstoke, Hampshire, RG21 6XS, England, (Telephone in U.S. (888) 330-8477), (Fax in U.S. (800) 672-2054), www.palgrave.com; *The Statesman's Yearbook 2008.*

Taylor and Francis Group, An Informa Business, 2 Park Square, Milton Park, Abingdon, Oxford OX14 4RN, United Kingdom, (Dial from U.S. (212) 216-7800), (Fax from U.S. (212) 564-7854), www.tandf.co.uk; *The Europa World Year Book.*

United Nations Conference on Trade and Development (UNCTAD), DC2-1120, United Nations, New York, NY 10017, (212) 963-0027, www.unctad.org; *UNCTAD Commodity Yearbook.*

United Nations Economic Commission for Africa (ECA), PO Box 3001, Addis Ababa, Ethiopia, (Telephone in U.S. (212) 963-4957), www.uneca.org; *African Statistical Yearbook 2006.*

United Nations Food and Agricultural Organization (FAO), Viale delle Terme di Caracalla, 00100 Rome, Italy, (Dial from U.S. (202) 653-2400), (Fax from U.S. (202) 653 5760), www.fao.org; *FAO Yearbook of Fishery Statistics;* Fishery Databases; FISHSTAT Database. Subjects covered include: Aquaculture production, capture production, fishery commodities; and *The State of Food and Agriculture (SOFA) 2006.*

United Nations Statistics Division, New York, NY 10017, (800) 253-9646, Fax: (212) 963-4116, http://unstats.un.org; *Statistical Yearbook* and *Survey of Economic and Social Conditions in Africa 2005.*

The World Bank, 1818 H Street, NW, Washington, DC 20433, (202) 473-1000, Fax: (202) 477-6391, www.worldbank.org; *Guinea.*

GUINEA - FOOD

African Development Bank Group, Rue Joseph Anoma, 01 BP 1387 Abidjan 01, Cote d'Ivoire, www.afdb.org; *Statistics Pocketbook 2008.*

United Nations Conference on Trade and Development (UNCTAD), DC2-1120, United Nations, New York, NY 10017, (212) 963-0027, www.unctad.org; *UNCTAD Commodity Yearbook.*

United Nations Food and Agricultural Organization (FAO), Viale delle Terme di Caracalla, 00100 Rome, Italy, (Dial from U.S. (202) 653-2400), (Fax from U.S. (202) 653 5760), www.fao.org; *FAO Production Yearbook 2002* and *The State of Food and Agriculture (SOFA) 2006.*

United Nations Statistics Division, New York, NY 10017, (800) 253-9646, Fax: (212) 963-4116, http://unstats.un.org; *Human Development Report 2006.*

GUINEA - FOREIGN EXCHANGE RATES

African Development Bank Group, Rue Joseph Anoma, 01 BP 1387 Abidjan 01, Cote d'Ivoire, www.afdb.org; *Statistics Pocketbook 2008.*

Central Intelligence Agency, Office of Public Affairs, Washington, DC 20505, (703) 482-0623, Fax: (703) 482-1739, www.cia.gov; *The World Factbook.*

Euromonitor International, Inc., 224 S. Michigan Avenue, Suite 1500, Chicago, IL 60604, (312) 922-1115, Fax: (312) 922-1157, www.euromonitor.com; *International Marketing Data and Statistics 2008* and *The World Economic Factbook 2008.*

Inter-American Development Bank (IDB), 1300 New York Avenue, NW, Washington, DC 20577, (202) 623-1000, Fax: (202) 623-3096, www.iadb.org; *The Politics of Policies: Economic and Social Progress in Latin America - 2006 Report.*

Taylor and Francis Group, An Informa Business, 2 Park Square, Milton Park, Abingdon, Oxford OX14 4RN, United Kingdom, (Dial from U.S. (212) 216-7800), (Fax from U.S. (212) 564-7854), www.tandf.co.uk; *The Europa World Year Book.*

United Nations Statistics Division, New York, NY 10017, (800) 253-9646, Fax: (212) 963-4116, http://unstats.un.org; *Compendium of Intra-African and Related Foreign Trade Statistics 2003; Statistical Yearbook;* and *World Statistics Pocketbook.*

GUINEA - FORESTS AND FORESTRY

Inter-American Development Bank (IDB), 1300 New York Avenue, NW, Washington, DC 20577, (202) 623-1000, Fax: (202) 623-3096, www.iadb.org; *The Politics of Policies: Economic and Social Progress in Latin America - 2006 Report.*

M.E. Sharpe, 80 Business Park Drive, Armonk, NY 10504, (800) 541-6563, Fax: (914) 273-2106, www.mesharpe.com; *The Illustrated Book of World Rankings.*

Palgrave Macmillan Ltd., Houndmills, Basingstoke, Hampshire, RG21 6XS, England, (Telephone in U.S. (888) 330-8477), (Fax in U.S. (800) 672-2054), www.palgrave.com; *The Statesman's Yearbook 2008.*

Taylor and Francis Group, An Informa Business, 2 Park Square, Milton Park, Abingdon, Oxford OX14 4RN, United Kingdom, (Dial from U.S. (212) 216-7800), (Fax from U.S. (212) 564-7854), www.tandf.co.uk; *The Europa World Year Book.*

UNESCO Institute for Statistics, C.P. 6128 Succursale Centre-Ville, Montreal, Quebec, H3C 3J7 Canada, (Dial from U.S. (514) 343-6880), (Fax from U.S. (514) 343 6882), www.uis.unesco.org; *Statistical Tables.*

United Nations Conference on Trade and Development (UNCTAD), DC2-1120, United Nations, New York, NY 10017, (212) 963-0027, www.unctad.org; *UNCTAD Commodity Yearbook.*

United Nations Economic Commission for Africa (ECA), PO Box 3001, Addis Ababa, Ethiopia, (Telephone in U.S. (212) 963-4957), www.uneca.org; *African Statistical Yearbook 2006.*

United Nations Food and Agricultural Organization (FAO), Viale delle Terme di Caracalla, 00100 Rome, Italy, (Dial from U.S. (202) 653-2400), (Fax from U.S. (202) 653 5760), www.fao.org; *FAO Yearbook of Forest Products* and *The State of Food and Agriculture (SOFA) 2006.*

United Nations Statistics Division, New York, NY 10017, (800) 253-9646, Fax: (212) 963-4116, http://unstats.un.org; *Statistical Yearbook.*

The World Bank, 1818 H Street, NW, Washington, DC 20433, (202) 473-1000, Fax: (202) 477-6391, www.worldbank.org; *Guinea* and *World Development Report 2008.*

GUINEA - GAS PRODUCTION

See GUINEA - MINERAL INDUSTRIES

GUINEA - GEOGRAPHIC INFORMATION SYSTEMS

M.E. Sharpe, 80 Business Park Drive, Armonk, NY 10504, (800) 541-6563, Fax: (914) 273-2106, www.mesharpe.com; *The Illustrated Book of World Rankings.*

GUINEA - GOLD PRODUCTION

See GUINEA - MINERAL INDUSTRIES

GUINEA - GROSS DOMESTIC PRODUCT

African Development Bank Group, Rue Joseph Anoma, 01 BP 1387 Abidjan 01, Cote d'Ivoire, www.afdb.org; *Statistics Pocketbook 2008.*

Economist Intelligence Unit, 111 West 57th Street, New York, NY 10019, (212) 554-0600, Fax: (212) 586-1181, www.eiu.com; *Guinea Country Report.*

Euromonitor International, Inc., 224 S. Michigan Avenue, Suite 1500, Chicago, IL 60604, (312) 922-1115, Fax: (312) 922-1157, www.euromonitor.com; *International Marketing Data and Statistics 2008* and *The World Economic Factbook 2008.*

Inter-American Development Bank (IDB), 1300 New York Avenue, NW, Washington, DC 20577, (202) 623-1000, Fax: (202) 623-3096, www.iadb.org; *The Politics of Policies: Economic and Social Progress in Latin America - 2006 Report.*

M.E. Sharpe, 80 Business Park Drive, Armonk, NY 10504, (800) 541-6563, Fax: (914) 273-2106, www.mesharpe.com; *The Illustrated Book of World Rankings.*

Taylor and Francis Group, An Informa Business, 2 Park Square, Milton Park, Abingdon, Oxford OX14 4RN, United Kingdom, (Dial from U.S. (212) 216-7800), (Fax from U.S. (212) 564-7854), www.tandf.co.uk; *The Europa World Year Book.*

United Nations Economic Commission for Africa (ECA), PO Box 3001, Addis Ababa, Ethiopia,

(Telephone in U.S. (212) 963-4957), www.uneca.org; *African Statistical Yearbook 2006.*

United Nations Statistics Division, New York, NY 10017, (800) 253-9646, Fax: (212) 963-4116, http://unstats.un.org; *Human Development Report 2006; Statistical Yearbook;* and *Survey of Economic and Social Conditions in Africa 2005.*

The World Bank, 1818 H Street, NW, Washington, DC 20433, (202) 473-1000, Fax: (202) 477-6391, www.worldbank.org; *World Development Report 2008.*

GUINEA - GROSS NATIONAL PRODUCT

Euromonitor International, Inc., 224 S. Michigan Avenue, Suite 1500, Chicago, IL 60604, (312) 922-1115, Fax: (312) 922-1157, www.euromonitor.com; *International Marketing Data and Statistics 2008.*

Inter-American Development Bank (IDB), 1300 New York Avenue, NW, Washington, DC 20577, (202) 623-1000, Fax: (202) 623-3096, www.iadb.org; *The Politics of Policies: Economic and Social Progress in Latin America - 2006 Report.*

M.E. Sharpe, 80 Business Park Drive, Armonk, NY 10504, (800) 541-6563, Fax: (914) 273-2106, www.mesharpe.com; *The Illustrated Book of World Rankings.*

Palgrave Macmillan Ltd., Houndmills, Basingstoke, Hampshire, RG21 6XS, England, (Telephone in U.S. (888) 330-8477), (Fax in U.S. (800) 672-2054), www.palgrave.com; *The Statesman's Yearbook 2008.*

U.S. Department of State (DOS), 2201 C Street NW, Washington, DC 20520, (202) 647-4000, www.state.gov; *World Military Expenditures and Arms Transfers (WMEAT).*

The World Bank, 1818 H Street, NW, Washington, DC 20433, (202) 473-1000, Fax: (202) 477-6391, www.worldbank.org; *The World Bank Atlas 2003-2004* and *World Development Report 2008.*

GUINEA - HIDES AND SKINS INDUSTRY

United Nations Food and Agricultural Organization (FAO), Viale delle Terme di Caracalla, 00100 Rome, Italy, (Dial from U.S. (202) 653-2400), (Fax from U.S. (202) 653 5760), www.fao.org; *FAO Production Yearbook 2002.*

GUINEA - HOUSING

Euromonitor International, Inc., 224 S. Michigan Avenue, Suite 1500, Chicago, IL 60604, (312) 922-1115, Fax: (312) 922-1157, www.euromonitor.com; *World Marketing Data and Statistics.*

M.E. Sharpe, 80 Business Park Drive, Armonk, NY 10504, (800) 541-6563, Fax: (914) 273-2106, www.mesharpe.com; *The Illustrated Book of World Rankings.*

GUINEA - ILLITERATE PERSONS

Euromonitor International, Inc., 224 S. Michigan Avenue, Suite 1500, Chicago, IL 60604, (312) 922-1115, Fax: (312) 922-1157, www.euromonitor.com; *The World Economic Factbook 2008.*

Palgrave Macmillan Ltd., Houndmills, Basingstoke, Hampshire, RG21 6XS, England, (Telephone in U.S. (888) 330-8477), (Fax in U.S. (800) 672-2054), www.palgrave.com; *The Statesman's Yearbook 2008.*

UNESCO Institute for Statistics, C.P. 6128 Succursale Centre-Ville, Montreal, Quebec, H3C 3J7 Canada, (Dial from U.S. (514) 343-6880), (Fax from U.S. (514) 343 6882), www.uis.unesco.org; *Statistical Tables.*

United Nations Statistics Division, New York, NY 10017, (800) 253-9646, Fax: (212) 963-4116, http://unstats.un.org; *Human Development Report 2006.*

GUINEA - IMPORTS

Central Intelligence Agency, Office of Public Affairs, Washington, DC 20505, (703) 482-0623, Fax: (703) 482-1739, www.cia.gov; *The World Factbook.*

Economist Intelligence Unit, 111 West 57th Street, New York, NY 10019, (212) 554-0600, Fax: (212) 586-1181, www.eiu.com; *Guinea Country Report.*

Euromonitor International, Inc., 224 S. Michigan Avenue, Suite 1500, Chicago, IL 60604, (312) 922-1115, Fax: (312) 922-1157, www.euromonitor.com; *International Marketing Data and Statistics 2008* and *The World Economic Factbook 2008.*

Inter-American Development Bank (IDB), 1300 New York Avenue, NW, Washington, DC 20577, (202) 623-1000, Fax: (202) 623-3096, www.iadb.org; *The Politics of Policies: Economic and Social Progress in Latin America - 2006 Report.*

International Monetary Fund (IMF), 700 Nineteenth Street, NW, Washington, DC 20431, (202) 623-7000, Fax: (202) 623-4661, www.imf.org; *Direction of Trade Statistics Yearbook 2007.*

Palgrave Macmillan Ltd., Houndmills, Basingstoke, Hampshire, RG21 6XS, England, (Telephone in U.S. (888) 330-8477), (Fax in U.S. (800) 672-2054), www.palgrave.com; *The Statesman's Yearbook 2008.*

Taylor and Francis Group, An Informa Business, 2 Park Square, Milton Park, Abingdon, Oxford OX14 4RN, United Kingdom, (Dial from U.S. (212) 216-7800), (Fax from U.S. (212) 564-7854), www.tandf.co.uk; *The Europa World Year Book.*

United Nations Conference on Trade and Development (UNCTAD), DC2-1120, United Nations, New York, NY 10017, (212) 963-0027, www.unctad.org; *Handbook of Statistics 2005.*

United Nations Economic Commission for Africa (ECA), PO Box 3001, Addis Ababa, Ethiopia, (Telephone in U.S. (212) 963-4957), www.uneca.org; *African Statistical Yearbook 2006.*

United Nations Food and Agricultural Organization (FAO), Viale delle Terme di Caracalla, 00100 Rome, Italy, (Dial from U.S. (202) 653-2400), (Fax from U.S. (202) 653 5760), www.fao.org; *The State of Food and Agriculture (SOFA) 2006.*

United Nations Statistics Division, New York, NY 10017, (800) 253-9646, Fax: (212) 963-4116, http://unstats.un.org; *Compendium of Intra-African and Related Foreign Trade Statistics 2003* and *Survey of Economic and Social Conditions in Africa 2005.*

The World Bank, 1818 H Street, NW, Washington, DC 20433, (202) 473-1000, Fax: (202) 477-6391, www.worldbank.org; *World Development Report 2008.*

GUINEA - INCOME TAXES

See GUINEA - TAXATION

GUINEA - INDUSTRIAL PRODUCTIVITY

Euromonitor International, Inc., 224 S. Michigan Avenue, Suite 1500, Chicago, IL 60604, (312) 922-1115, Fax: (312) 922-1157, www.euromonitor.com; *International Marketing Data and Statistics 2008.*

M.E. Sharpe, 80 Business Park Drive, Armonk, NY 10504, (800) 541-6563, Fax: (914) 273-2106, www.mesharpe.com; *The Illustrated Book of World Rankings.*

GUINEA - INDUSTRIES

Central Intelligence Agency, Office of Public Affairs, Washington, DC 20505, (703) 482-0623, Fax: (703) 482-1739, www.cia.gov; *The World Factbook.*

Economist Intelligence Unit, 111 West 57th Street, New York, NY 10019, (212) 554-0600, Fax: (212) 586-1181, www.eiu.com; *Guinea Country Report.*

Euromonitor International, Inc., 224 S. Michigan Avenue, Suite 1500, Chicago, IL 60604, (312) 922-1115, Fax: (312) 922-1157, www.euromonitor.com; *International Marketing Data and Statistics 2008; The World Economic Factbook 2008;* and *World Marketing Data and Statistics.*

M.E. Sharpe, 80 Business Park Drive, Armonk, NY 10504, (800) 541-6563, Fax: (914) 273-2106, www.mesharpe.com; *The Illustrated Book of World Rankings.*

Palgrave Macmillan Ltd., Houndmills, Basingstoke, Hampshire, RG21 6XS, England, (Telephone in U.S. (888) 330-8477), (Fax in U.S. (800) 672-2054), www.palgrave.com; *The Statesman's Yearbook 2008.*

Taylor and Francis Group, An Informa Business, 2 Park Square, Milton Park, Abingdon, Oxford OX14 4RN, United Kingdom, (Dial from U.S. (212) 216-7800), (Fax from U.S. (212) 564-7854), www.tandf.co.uk; *The Europa World Year Book.*

United Nations Economic Commission for Africa (ECA), PO Box 3001, Addis Ababa, Ethiopia, (Telephone in U.S. (212) 963-4957), www.uneca.org; *African Statistical Yearbook 2006.*

United Nations Industrial Development Organization (UNIDO), 1 United Nations Plaza, New York, NY 10017, (212) 963 6890, Fax: (212) 963-7904, http://unido.org; Industrial Statistics Database 2008 (INDSTAT) and *The International Yearbook of Industrial Statistics 2008.*

United Nations Statistics Division, New York, NY 10017, (800) 253-9646, Fax: (212) 963-4116, http://unstats.un.org; *Survey of Economic and Social Conditions in Africa 2005.*

The World Bank, 1818 H Street, NW, Washington, DC 20433, (202) 473-1000, Fax: (202) 477-6391, www.worldbank.org; *Guinea.*

GUINEA - INFANT AND MATERNAL MORTALITY

See GUINEA - MORTALITY

GUINEA - INTEREST RATES

Inter-American Development Bank (IDB), 1300 New York Avenue, NW, Washington, DC 20577, (202) 623-1000, Fax: (202) 623-3096, www.iadb.org; *The Politics of Policies: Economic and Social Progress in Latin America - 2006 Report.*

GUINEA - INTERNAL REVENUE

Inter-American Development Bank (IDB), 1300 New York Avenue, NW, Washington, DC 20577, (202) 623-1000, Fax: (202) 623-3096, www.iadb.org; *The Politics of Policies: Economic and Social Progress in Latin America - 2006 Report.*

GUINEA - INTERNATIONAL FINANCE

Inter-American Development Bank (IDB), 1300 New York Avenue, NW, Washington, DC 20577, (202) 623-1000, Fax: (202) 623-3096, www.iadb.org; *The Politics of Policies: Economic and Social Progress in Latin America - 2006 Report.*

GUINEA - INTERNATIONAL LIQUIDITY

Inter-American Development Bank (IDB), 1300 New York Avenue, NW, Washington, DC 20577, (202) 623-1000, Fax: (202) 623-3096, www.iadb.org; *The Politics of Policies: Economic and Social Progress in Latin America - 2006 Report.*

GUINEA - INTERNATIONAL STATISTICS

Inter-American Development Bank (IDB), 1300 New York Avenue, NW, Washington, DC 20577, (202) 623-1000, Fax: (202) 623-3096, www.iadb.org; *The Politics of Policies: Economic and Social Progress in Latin America - 2006 Report.*

GUINEA - INTERNATIONAL TRADE

African Development Bank Group, Rue Joseph Anoma, 01 BP 1387 Abidjan 01, Cote d'Ivoire, www.afdb.org; *Statistics Pocketbook 2008.*

Economist Intelligence Unit, 111 West 57th Street, New York, NY 10019, (212) 554-0600, Fax: (212) 586-1181, www.eiu.com; *Guinea Country Report.*

Euromonitor International, Inc., 224 S. Michigan Avenue, Suite 1500, Chicago, IL 60604, (312) 922-1115, Fax: (312) 922-1157, www.euromonitor.com; *International Marketing Data and Statistics 2008; The World Economic Factbook 2008;* and *World Marketing Data and Statistics.*

Inter-American Development Bank (IDB), 1300 New York Avenue, NW, Washington, DC 20577, (202) 623-1000, Fax: (202) 623-3096, www.iadb.org; *The Politics of Policies: Economic and Social Progress in Latin America - 2006 Report.*

M.E. Sharpe, 80 Business Park Drive, Armonk, NY 10504, (800) 541-6563, Fax: (914) 273-2106, www.mesharpe.com; *The Illustrated Book of World Rankings.*

Palgrave Macmillan Ltd., Houndmills, Basingstoke, Hampshire, RG21 6XS, England, (Telephone in U.S. (888) 330-8477), (Fax in U.S. (800) 672-2054), www.palgrave.com; *The Statesman's Yearbook 2008.*

Taylor and Francis Group, An Informa Business, 2 Park Square, Milton Park, Abingdon, Oxford OX14 4RN, United Kingdom, (Dial from U.S. (212) 216-7800), (Fax from U.S. (212) 564-7854), www.tandf.co.uk; *The Europa World Year Book.*

United Nations Conference on Trade and Development (UNCTAD), DC2-1120, United Nations, New York, NY 10017, (212) 963-0027, www.unctad.org; *UNCTAD Commodity Yearbook.*

United Nations Economic Commission for Africa (ECA), PO Box 3001, Addis Ababa, Ethiopia, (Telephone in U.S. (212) 963-4957), www.uneca.org; *African Statistical Yearbook 2006.*

United Nations Food and Agricultural Organization (FAO), Viale delle Terme di Caracalla, 00100 Rome, Italy, (Dial from U.S. (202) 653-2400), (Fax from U.S. (202) 653 5760), www.fao.org; *FAO Trade Yearbook* and *The State of Food and Agriculture (SOFA) 2006.*

United Nations Statistics Division, New York, NY 10017, (800) 253-9646, Fax: (212) 963-4116, http://unstats.un.org; Commodity Trade Statistics Database (COMTRADE); *Compendium of Intra-African and Related Foreign Trade Statistics 2003;* and *Statistical Yearbook.*

The World Bank, 1818 H Street, NW, Washington, DC 20433, (202) 473-1000, Fax: (202) 477-6391, www.worldbank.org; *Guinea* and *World Development Report 2008.*

World Trade Organization (WTO), Centre William Rappard, Rue de Lausanne 154, CH-1211 Geneva 21, Switzerland, www.wto.org; *International Trade Statistics 2006.*

GUINEA - INTERNET USERS

International Telecommunication Union (ITU), Place des Nations, 1211 Geneva 20, Switzerland, www.itu.int; *World Telecommunication/ICT Indicators Database on CD-ROM; World Telecommunication/ICT Indicators Database Online;* and *Yearbook of Statistics - Telecommunication Services (Chronological Time Series 1997-2006).*

The World Bank, 1818 H Street, NW, Washington, DC 20433, (202) 473-1000, Fax: (202) 477-6391, www.worldbank.org; *Guinea.*

GUINEA - INVESTMENTS

Inter-American Development Bank (IDB), 1300 New York Avenue, NW, Washington, DC 20577, (202) 623-1000, Fax: (202) 623-3096, www.iadb.org; *The Politics of Policies: Economic and Social Progress in Latin America - 2006 Report.*

GUINEA - IRON AND IRON ORE PRODUCTION

See GUINEA - MINERAL INDUSTRIES

GUINEA - IRRIGATION

Euromonitor International, Inc., 224 S. Michigan Avenue, Suite 1500, Chicago, IL 60604, (312) 922-1115, Fax: (312) 922-1157, www.euromonitor.com; *International Marketing Data and Statistics 2008.*

Inter-American Development Bank (IDB), 1300 New York Avenue, NW, Washington, DC 20577, (202) 623-1000, Fax: (202) 623-3096, www.iadb.org; *The Politics of Policies: Economic and Social Progress in Latin America - 2006 Report.*

GUINEA - LABOR

African Development Bank Group, Rue Joseph Anoma, 01 BP 1387 Abidjan 01, Cote d'Ivoire, www.afdb.org; *Statistics Pocketbook 2008.*

Central Intelligence Agency, Office of Public Affairs, Washington, DC 20505, (703) 482-0623, Fax: (703) 482-1739, www.cia.gov; *The World Factbook.*

Euromonitor International, Inc., 224 S. Michigan Avenue, Suite 1500, Chicago, IL 60604, (312) 922-1115, Fax: (312) 922-1157, www.euromonitor.com; *International Marketing Data and Statistics 2008* and *World Marketing Data and Statistics.*

M.E. Sharpe, 80 Business Park Drive, Armonk, NY 10504, (800) 541-6563, Fax: (914) 273-2106, www.mesharpe.com; *The Illustrated Book of World Rankings.*

Palgrave Macmillan Ltd., Houndmills, Basingstoke, Hampshire, RG21 6XS, England, (Telephone in U.S. (888) 330-8477), (Fax in U.S. (800) 672-2054), www.palgrave.com; *The Statesman's Yearbook 2008.*

Taylor and Francis Group, An Informa Business, 2 Park Square, Milton Park, Abingdon, Oxford OX14 4RN, United Kingdom, (Dial from U.S. (212) 216-7800), (Fax from U.S. (212) 564-7854), www.tandf.co.uk; *The Europa World Year Book.*

United Nations Food and Agricultural Organization (FAO), Viale delle Terme di Caracalla, 00100 Rome, Italy, (Dial from U.S. (202) 653-2400), (Fax from U.S. (202) 653 5760), www.fao.org; *The State of Food and Agriculture (SOFA) 2006.*

United Nations Statistics Division, New York, NY 10017, (800) 253-9646, Fax: (212) 963-4116, http://unstats.un.org; *Human Development Report 2006.*

The World Bank, 1818 H Street, NW, Washington, DC 20433, (202) 473-1000, Fax: (202) 477-6391, www.worldbank.org; *The World Bank Atlas 2003-2004* and *World Development Report 2008.*

GUINEA - LAND USE

Central Intelligence Agency, Office of Public Affairs, Washington, DC 20505, (703) 482-0623, Fax: (703) 482-1739, www.cia.gov; *The World Factbook.*

Euromonitor International, Inc., 224 S. Michigan Avenue, Suite 1500, Chicago, IL 60604, (312) 922-1115, Fax: (312) 922-1157, www.euromonitor.com; *International Marketing Data and Statistics 2008.*

Inter-American Development Bank (IDB), 1300 New York Avenue, NW, Washington, DC 20577, (202) 623-1000, Fax: (202) 623-3096, www.iadb.org; *The Politics of Policies: Economic and Social Progress in Latin America - 2006 Report.*

United Nations Food and Agricultural Organization (FAO), Viale delle Terme di Caracalla, 00100 Rome, Italy, (Dial from U.S. (202) 653-2400), (Fax from U.S. (202) 653 5760), www.fao.org; *FAO Production Yearbook 2002.*

The World Bank, 1818 H Street, NW, Washington, DC 20433, (202) 473-1000, Fax: (202) 477-6391, www.worldbank.org; *World Development Report 2008.*

GUINEA - LIBRARIES

M.E. Sharpe, 80 Business Park Drive, Armonk, NY 10504, (800) 541-6563, Fax: (914) 273-2106, www.mesharpe.com; *The Illustrated Book of World Rankings.*

GUINEA - LIFE EXPECTANCY

African Development Bank Group, Rue Joseph Anoma, 01 BP 1387 Abidjan 01, Cote d'Ivoire, www.afdb.org; *Statistics Pocketbook 2008.*

Central Intelligence Agency, Office of Public Affairs, Washington, DC 20505, (703) 482-0623, Fax: (703) 482-1739, www.cia.gov; *The World Factbook.*

Euromonitor International, Inc., 224 S. Michigan Avenue, Suite 1500, Chicago, IL 60604, (312) 922-1115, Fax: (312) 922-1157, www.euromonitor.com; *The World Economic Factbook 2008.*

United Nations Statistics Division, New York, NY 10017, (800) 253-9646, Fax: (212) 963-4116, http://unstats.un.org; *Human Development Report 2006* and *World Statistics Pocketbook.*

The World Bank, 1818 H Street, NW, Washington, DC 20433, (202) 473-1000, Fax: (202) 477-6391, www.worldbank.org; *The World Bank Atlas 2003-2004* and *World Development Report 2008.*

GUINEA - LITERACY

Euromonitor International, Inc., 224 S. Michigan Avenue, Suite 1500, Chicago, IL 60604, (312) 922-1115, Fax: (312) 922-1157, www.euromonitor.com; *World Marketing Data and Statistics.*

United Nations Statistics Division, New York, NY 10017, (800) 253-9646, Fax: (212) 963-4116, http://unstats.un.org; *Survey of Economic and Social Conditions in Africa 2005.*

GUINEA - LIVESTOCK

Euromonitor International, Inc., 224 S. Michigan Avenue, Suite 1500, Chicago, IL 60604, (312) 922-1115, Fax: (312) 922-1157, www.euromonitor.com; *International Marketing Data and Statistics 2008.*

M.E. Sharpe, 80 Business Park Drive, Armonk, NY 10504, (800) 541-6563, Fax: (914) 273-2106, www.mesharpe.com; *The Illustrated Book of World Rankings.*

Palgrave Macmillan Ltd., Houndmills, Basingstoke, Hampshire, RG21 6XS, England, (Telephone in U.S. (888) 330-8477), (Fax in U.S. (800) 672-2054), www.palgrave.com; *The Statesman's Yearbook 2008.*

Taylor and Francis Group, An Informa Business, 2 Park Square, Milton Park, Abingdon, Oxford OX14 4RN, United Kingdom, (Dial from U.S. (212) 216-7800), (Fax from U.S. (212) 564-7854), www.tandf.co.uk; *The Europa World Year Book.*

United Nations Conference on Trade and Development (UNCTAD), DC2-1120, United Nations, New York, NY 10017, (212) 963-0027, www.unctad.org; *UNCTAD Commodity Yearbook.*

United Nations Economic Commission for Africa (ECA), PO Box 3001, Addis Ababa, Ethiopia, (Telephone in U.S. (212) 963-4957), www.uneca.org; *African Statistical Yearbook 2006.*

United Nations Food and Agricultural Organization (FAO), Viale delle Terme di Caracalla, 00100 Rome, Italy, (Dial from U.S. (202) 653-2400), (Fax from U.S. (202) 653 5760), www.fao.org; *FAO Production Yearbook 2002* and *The State of Food and Agriculture (SOFA) 2006.*

United Nations Statistics Division, New York, NY 10017, (800) 253-9646, Fax: (212) 963-4116, http://unstats.un.org; *Statistical Yearbook* and *Survey of Economic and Social Conditions in Africa 2005.*

GUINEA - LOCAL TAXATION

Euromonitor International, Inc., 224 S. Michigan Avenue, Suite 1500, Chicago, IL 60604, (312) 922-1115, Fax: (312) 922-1157, www.euromonitor.com; *International Marketing Data and Statistics 2008.*

Inter-American Development Bank (IDB), 1300 New York Avenue, NW, Washington, DC 20577, (202) 623-1000, Fax: (202) 623-3096, www.iadb.org; *The Politics of Policies: Economic and Social Progress in Latin America - 2006 Report.*

GUINEA - MANUFACTURES

Inter-American Development Bank (IDB), 1300 New York Avenue, NW, Washington, DC 20577, (202) 623-1000, Fax: (202) 623-3096, www.iadb.org; *The Politics of Policies: Economic and Social Progress in Latin America - 2006 Report.*

M.E. Sharpe, 80 Business Park Drive, Armonk, NY 10504, (800) 541-6563, Fax: (914) 273-2106, www.mesharpe.com; *The Illustrated Book of World Rankings.*

United Nations Economic Commission for Africa (ECA), PO Box 3001, Addis Ababa, Ethiopia, (Telephone in U.S. (212) 963-4957), www.uneca.org; *African Statistical Yearbook 2006.*

United Nations Statistics Division, New York, NY 10017, (800) 253-9646, Fax: (212) 963-4116, http://unstats.un.org; *Survey of Economic and Social Conditions in Africa 2005.*

GUINEA - MARRIAGE

M.E. Sharpe, 80 Business Park Drive, Armonk, NY 10504, (800) 541-6563, Fax: (914) 273-2106, www.mesharpe.com; *The Illustrated Book of World Rankings.*

United Nations Statistics Division, New York, NY 10017, (800) 253-9646, Fax: (212) 963-4116, http://unstats.un.org; *Demographic Yearbook.*

GUINEA - MEAT PRODUCTION

See GUINEA - LIVESTOCK

GUINEA - MILK PRODUCTION

See GUINEA - DAIRY PROCESSING

GUINEA - MINERAL INDUSTRIES

Commodity Research Bureau, 330 South Wells Street, Suite 612, Chicago, IL 60606-7110, (800) 621-5271, Fax: (312) 939-4135, www.crbtrader.com; *2006 CRB Commodity Yearbook and CD.*

Inter-American Development Bank (IDB), 1300 New York Avenue, NW, Washington, DC 20577, (202) 623-1000, Fax: (202) 623-3096, www.iadb.org; *The Politics of Policies: Economic and Social Progress in Latin America - 2006 Report.*

M.E. Sharpe, 80 Business Park Drive, Armonk, NY 10504, (800) 541-6563, Fax: (914) 273-2106, www.mesharpe.com; *The Illustrated Book of World Rankings.*

Palgrave Macmillan Ltd., Houndmills, Basingstoke, Hampshire, RG21 6XS, England, (Telephone in U.S. (888) 330-8477), (Fax in U.S. (800) 672-2054), www.palgrave.com; *The Statesman's Yearbook 2008.*

Taylor and Francis Group, An Informa Business, 2 Park Square, Milton Park, Abingdon, Oxford OX14 4RN, United Kingdom, (Dial from U.S. (212) 216-7800), (Fax from U.S. (212) 564-7854), www.tandf.co.uk; *The Europa World Year Book.*

United Nations Conference on Trade and Development (UNCTAD), DC2-1120, United Nations, New York, NY 10017, (212) 963-0027, www.unctad.org; *UNCTAD Commodity Yearbook.*

United Nations Economic Commission for Africa (ECA), PO Box 3001, Addis Ababa, Ethiopia, (Telephone in U.S. (212) 963-4957), www.uneca.org; *African Statistical Yearbook 2006.*

United Nations Statistics Division, New York, NY 10017, (800) 253-9646, Fax: (212) 963-4116, http://unstats.un.org; *Statistical Yearbook.*

GUINEA - MONEY EXCHANGE RATES

See GUINEA - FOREIGN EXCHANGE RATES

GUINEA - MONEY SUPPLY

African Development Bank Group, Rue Joseph Anoma, 01 BP 1387 Abidjan 01, Cote d'Ivoire, www.afdb.org; *Statistics Pocketbook 2008.*

Economist Intelligence Unit, 111 West 57th Street, New York, NY 10019, (212) 554-0600, Fax: (212) 586-1181, www.eiu.com; *Guinea Country Report.*

Euromonitor International, Inc., 224 S. Michigan Avenue, Suite 1500, Chicago, IL 60604, (312) 922-1115, Fax: (312) 922-1157, www.euromonitor.com; *International Marketing Data and Statistics 2008.*

Inter-American Development Bank (IDB), 1300 New York Avenue, NW, Washington, DC 20577, (202) 623-1000, Fax: (202) 623-3096, www.iadb.org; *The Politics of Policies: Economic and Social Progress in Latin America - 2006 Report.*

The World Bank, 1818 H Street, NW, Washington, DC 20433, (202) 473-1000, Fax: (202) 477-6391, www.worldbank.org; *Guinea.*

GUINEA - MONUMENTS AND HISTORIC SITES

UNESCO Institute for Statistics, C.P. 6128 Succursale Centre-Ville, Montreal, Quebec, H3C 3J7 Canada, (Dial from U.S. (514) 343-6880), (Fax from U.S. (514) 343 6882), www.uis.unesco.org; *Statistical Tables.*

GUINEA - MORTALITY

Central Intelligence Agency, Office of Public Affairs, Washington, DC 20505, (703) 482-0623, Fax: (703) 482-1739, www.cia.gov; *The World Factbook.*

Euromonitor International, Inc., 224 S. Michigan Avenue, Suite 1500, Chicago, IL 60604, (312) 922-1115, Fax: (312) 922-1157, www.euromonitor.com; *International Marketing Data and Statistics 2008* and *The World Economic Factbook 2008.*

Taylor and Francis Group, An Informa Business, 2 Park Square, Milton Park, Abingdon, Oxford OX14 4RN, United Kingdom, (Dial from U.S. (212) 216-7800), (Fax from U.S. (212) 564-7854), www.tandf.co.uk; *The Europa World Year Book.*

UNICEF, 3 United Nations Plaza, New York, NY 10017, (800) 253-9646, Fax: (212) 887-7465, www.unicef.org; *The State of the World's Children 2008.*

United Nations Statistics Division, New York, NY 10017, (800) 253-9646, Fax: (212) 963-4116, http://unstats.un.org; *Demographic Yearbook; Human Development Report 2006; Statistical Yearbook; Survey of Economic and Social Conditions in Africa 2005;* and *World Statistics Pocketbook.*

The World Bank, 1818 H Street, NW, Washington, DC 20433, (202) 473-1000, Fax: (202) 477-6391, www.worldbank.org; *The World Bank Atlas 2003-2004* and *World Development Report 2008.*

World Health Organization (WHO), Avenue Appia 20, 1211 Geneve 27, Switzerland, (Telephone in U.S. (212) 331-9081), www.who.int; The WHO Global Atlas of Infectious Diseases.

GUINEA - MOTOR VEHICLES

Taylor and Francis Group, An Informa Business, 2 Park Square, Milton Park, Abingdon, Oxford OX14 4RN, United Kingdom, (Dial from U.S. (212) 216-7800), (Fax from U.S. (212) 564-7854), www.tandf.co.uk; *The Europa World Year Book.*

United Nations Statistics Division, New York, NY 10017, (800) 253-9646, Fax: (212) 963-4116, http://unstats.un.org; *Statistical Yearbook* and *Survey of Economic and Social Conditions in Africa 2005.*

GUINEA - MUSEUMS

M.E. Sharpe, 80 Business Park Drive, Armonk, NY 10504, (800) 541-6563, Fax: (914) 273-2106, www.mesharpe.com; *The Illustrated Book of World Rankings.*

UNESCO Institute for Statistics, C.P. 6128 Succursale Centre-Ville, Montreal, Quebec, H3C 3J7 Canada, (Dial from U.S. (514) 343-6880), (Fax from U.S. (514) 343 6882), www.uis.unesco.org; *Statistical Tables.*

GUINEA - NATURAL GAS PRODUCTION

See GUINEA - MINERAL INDUSTRIES

GUINEA - NUTRITION

African Development Bank Group, Rue Joseph Anoma, 01 BP 1387 Abidjan 01, Cote d'Ivoire, www.afdb.org; *Statistics Pocketbook 2008.*

United Nations Food and Agricultural Organization (FAO), Viale delle Terme di Caracalla, 00100 Rome, Italy, (Dial from U.S. (202) 653-2400), (Fax from U.S. (202) 653 5760), www.fao.org; *The State of Food and Agriculture (SOFA) 2006.*

GUINEA - OLDER PEOPLE

M.E. Sharpe, 80 Business Park Drive, Armonk, NY 10504, (800) 541-6563, Fax: (914) 273-2106, www.mesharpe.com; *The Illustrated Book of World Rankings.*

GUINEA - PALM OIL PRODUCTION

See GUINEA - CROPS

GUINEA - PEANUT PRODUCTION

See GUINEA - CROPS

GUINEA - PERIODICALS

UNESCO Institute for Statistics, C.P. 6128 Succursale Centre-Ville, Montreal, Quebec, H3C 3J7 Canada, (Dial from U.S. (514) 343-6880), (Fax from U.S. (514) 343 6882), www.uis.unesco.org; *Statistical Tables.*

GUINEA - PESTICIDES

United Nations Food and Agricultural Organization (FAO), Viale delle Terme di Caracalla, 00100 Rome, Italy, (Dial from U.S. (202) 653-2400), (Fax from U.S. (202) 653 5760), www.fao.org; *The State of Food and Agriculture (SOFA) 2006.*

GUINEA - PETROLEUM INDUSTRY AND TRADE

Inter-American Development Bank (IDB), 1300 New York Avenue, NW, Washington, DC 20577, (202) 623-1000, Fax: (202) 623-3096, www.iadb.org; *The Politics of Policies: Economic and Social Progress in Latin America - 2006 Report.*

M.E. Sharpe, 80 Business Park Drive, Armonk, NY 10504, (800) 541-6563, Fax: (914) 273-2106, www.mesharpe.com; *The Illustrated Book of World Rankings.*

PennWell Corporation, 1421 South Sheridan Road, Tulsa, OK 74112, (918) 835-3161, www.pennwell.com; *International Petroleum Encyclopedia 2007.*

United Nations Conference on Trade and Development (UNCTAD), DC2-1120, United Nations, New York, NY 10017, (212) 963-0027, www.unctad.org; *UNCTAD Commodity Yearbook.*

United Nations Food and Agricultural Organization (FAO), Viale delle Terme di Caracalla, 00100 Rome, Italy, (Dial from U.S. (202) 653-2400), (Fax from U.S. (202) 653 5760), www.fao.org; *The State of Food and Agriculture (SOFA) 2006.*

GUINEA - POLITICAL SCIENCE

Central Intelligence Agency, Office of Public Affairs, Washington, DC 20505, (703) 482-0623, Fax: (703) 482-1739, www.cia.gov; *The World Factbook.*

Inter-American Development Bank (IDB), 1300 New York Avenue, NW, Washington, DC 20577, (202) 623-1000, Fax: (202) 623-3096, www.iadb.org; *The Politics of Policies: Economic and Social Progress in Latin America - 2006 Report.*

Palgrave Macmillan Ltd., Houndmills, Basingstoke, Hampshire, RG21 6XS, England, (Telephone in U.S. (888) 330-8477), (Fax in U.S. (800) 672-2054), www.palgrave.com; *The Statesman's Yearbook 2008.*

Taylor and Francis Group, An Informa Business, 2 Park Square, Milton Park, Abingdon, Oxford OX14 4RN, United Kingdom, (Dial from U.S. (212) 216-7800), (Fax from U.S. (212) 564-7854), www.tandf.co.uk; *The Europa World Year Book.*

United Nations Statistics Division, New York, NY 10017, (800) 253-9646, Fax: (212) 963-4116, http://unstats.un.org; *Survey of Economic and Social Conditions in Africa 2005.*

The World Bank, 1818 H Street, NW, Washington, DC 20433, (202) 473-1000, Fax: (202) 477-6391, www.worldbank.org; *World Development Report 2008.*

GUINEA - POPULATION

African Development Bank Group, Rue Joseph Anoma, 01 BP 1387 Abidjan 01, Cote d'Ivoire, www.afdb.org; *The African Statistical Journal; Gender, Poverty and Environmental Indicators on African Countries 2007; Selected Statistics on African Countries 2007;* and *Statistics Pocketbook 2008.*

Central Intelligence Agency, Office of Public Affairs, Washington, DC 20505, (703) 482-0623, Fax: (703) 482-1739, www.cia.gov; *The World Factbook.*

Economist Intelligence Unit, 111 West 57th Street, New York, NY 10019, (212) 554-0600, Fax: (212) 586-1181, www.eiu.com; *Guinea Country Report.*

Euromonitor International, Inc., 224 S. Michigan Avenue, Suite 1500, Chicago, IL 60604, (312) 922-1115, Fax: (312) 922-1157, www.euromonitor.com; *International Marketing Data and Statistics 2008* and *The World Economic Factbook 2008.*

Eurostat, Batiment Jean Monnet, Rue Alcide de Gasperi, L-2920 Luxembourg, http://epp.eurostat.ec.europa.eu; *Demographic Indicators - Population by Age-Classes.*

Inter-American Development Bank (IDB), 1300 New York Avenue, NW, Washington, DC 20577, (202) 623-1000, Fax: (202) 623-3096, www.iadb.org; *The Politics of Policies: Economic and Social Progress in Latin America - 2006 Report.*

M.E. Sharpe, 80 Business Park Drive, Armonk, NY 10504, (800) 541-6563, Fax: (914) 273-2106, www.mesharpe.com; *The Illustrated Book of World Rankings.*

Palgrave Macmillan Ltd., Houndmills, Basingstoke, Hampshire, RG21 6XS, England, (Telephone in U.S. (888) 330-8477), (Fax in U.S. (800) 672-2054), www.palgrave.com; *The Statesman's Yearbook 2008.*

Taylor and Francis Group, An Informa Business, 2 Park Square, Milton Park, Abingdon, Oxford OX14 4RN, United Kingdom, (Dial from U.S. (212) 216-7800), (Fax from U.S. (212) 564-7854), www.tandf.co.uk; *The Europa World Year Book.*

U.S. Department of State (DOS), 2201 C Street NW, Washington, DC 20520, (202) 647-4000, www.state.gov; *World Military Expenditures and Arms Transfers (WMEAT).*

UNESCO Institute for Statistics, C.P. 6128 Succursale Centre-Ville, Montreal, Quebec, H3C 3J7 Canada, (Dial from U.S. (514) 343-6880), (Fax from U.S. (514) 343 6882), www.uis.unesco.org; *Statistical Tables.*

United Nations Food and Agricultural Organization (FAO), Viale delle Terme di Caracalla, 00100 Rome, Italy, (Dial from U.S. (202) 653-2400), (Fax from U.S. (202) 653 5760), www.fao.org; *FAO Production Yearbook 2002.*

United Nations Statistics Division, New York, NY 10017, (800) 253-9646, Fax: (212) 963-4116, http://unstats.un.org; *Demographic Yearbook; Human Development Report 2006; Statistical Yearbook; Survey of Economic and Social Conditions in Africa 2005;* and *World Statistics Pocketbook.*

The World Bank, 1818 H Street, NW, Washington, DC 20433, (202) 473-1000, Fax: (202) 477-6391, www.worldbank.org; *Guinea; The World Bank Atlas 2003-2004;* and *World Development Report 2008.*

World Health Organization (WHO), Avenue Appia 20, 1211 Geneve 27, Switzerland, (Telephone in U.S. (212) 331-9081), www.who.int; *World Health Report 2006.*

GUINEA - POPULATION DENSITY

African Development Bank Group, Rue Joseph Anoma, 01 BP 1387 Abidjan 01, Cote d'Ivoire, www.afdb.org; *Statistics Pocketbook 2008.*

Central Intelligence Agency, Office of Public Affairs, Washington, DC 20505, (703) 482-0623, Fax: (703) 482-1739, www.cia.gov; *The World Factbook.*

Euromonitor International, Inc., 224 S. Michigan Avenue, Suite 1500, Chicago, IL 60604, (312) 922-1115, Fax: (312) 922-1157, www.euromonitor.com; *International Marketing Data and Statistics 2008* and *The World Economic Factbook 2008.*

Inter-American Development Bank (IDB), 1300 New York Avenue, NW, Washington, DC 20577, (202) 623-1000, Fax: (202) 623-3096, www.iadb.org; *The Politics of Policies: Economic and Social Progress in Latin America - 2006 Report.*

M.E. Sharpe, 80 Business Park Drive, Armonk, NY 10504, (800) 541-6563, Fax: (914) 273-2106, www.mesharpe.com; *The Illustrated Book of World Rankings.*

Palgrave Macmillan Ltd., Houndmills, Basingstoke, Hampshire, RG21 6XS, England, (Telephone in U.S. (888) 330-8477), (Fax in U.S. (800) 672-2054), www.palgrave.com; *The Statesman's Yearbook 2008.*

Taylor and Francis Group, An Informa Business, 2 Park Square, Milton Park, Abingdon, Oxford OX14 4RN, United Kingdom, (Dial from U.S. (212) 216-7800), (Fax from U.S. (212) 564-7854), www.tandf.co.uk; *The Europa World Year Book.*

UNESCO Institute for Statistics, C.P. 6128 Succursale Centre-Ville, Montreal, Quebec, H3C 3J7 Canada, (Dial from U.S. (514) 343-6880), (Fax from U.S. (514) 343 6882), www.uis.unesco.org; *Statistical Tables.*

United Nations Food and Agricultural Organization (FAO), Viale delle Terme di Caracalla, 00100 Rome, Italy, (Dial from U.S. (202) 653-2400), (Fax from U.S. (202) 653 5760), www.fao.org; *The State of Food and Agriculture (SOFA) 2006.*

United Nations Statistics Division, New York, NY 10017, (800) 253-9646, Fax: (212) 963-4116, http://unstats.un.org; *Statistical Yearbook* and *Survey of Economic and Social Conditions in Africa 2005.*

The World Bank, 1818 H Street, NW, Washington, DC 20433, (202) 473-1000, Fax: (202) 477-6391, www.worldbank.org; *Guinea* and *World Development Report 2008.*

GUINEA - POSTAL SERVICE

M.E. Sharpe, 80 Business Park Drive, Armonk, NY 10504, (800) 541-6563, Fax: (914) 273-2106, www.mesharpe.com; *The Illustrated Book of World Rankings.*

United Nations Statistics Division, New York, NY 10017, (800) 253-9646, Fax: (212) 963-4116, http://unstats.un.org; *Statistical Yearbook.*

GUINEA - POWER RESOURCES

Euromonitor International, Inc., 224 S. Michigan Avenue, Suite 1500, Chicago, IL 60604, (312) 922-1115, Fax: (312) 922-1157, www.euromonitor.com; *International Marketing Data and Statistics 2008; The World Economic Factbook 2008;* and *World Marketing Data and Statistics.*

M.E. Sharpe, 80 Business Park Drive, Armonk, NY 10504, (800) 541-6563, Fax: (914) 273-2106, www.mesharpe.com; *The Illustrated Book of World Rankings.*

Palgrave Macmillan Ltd., Houndmills, Basingstoke, Hampshire, RG21 6XS, England, (Telephone in U.S. (888) 330-8477), (Fax in U.S. (800) 672-2054), www.palgrave.com; *The Statesman's Yearbook 2008.*

Platts, 2 Penn Plaza, 25th Floor, New York, NY 10121-2298, (212) 904-3070, www.platts.com; *Energy Economist.*

United Nations Economic Commission for Africa (ECA), PO Box 3001, Addis Ababa, Ethiopia, (Telephone in U.S. (212) 963-4957), www.uneca.org; *African Statistical Yearbook 2006.*

United Nations Food and Agricultural Organization (FAO), Viale delle Terme di Caracalla, 00100 Rome, Italy, (Dial from U.S. (202) 653-2400), (Fax from U.S. (202) 653 5760), www.fao.org; *The State of Food and Agriculture (SOFA) 2006.*

United Nations Statistics Division, New York, NY 10017, (800) 253-9646, Fax: (212) 963-4116, http://unstats.un.org; *Energy Statistics Yearbook 2003; Human Development Report 2006;* and *World Statistics Pocketbook.*

The World Bank, 1818 H Street, NW, Washington, DC 20433, (202) 473-1000, Fax: (202) 477-6391, www.worldbank.org; *The World Bank Atlas 2003-2004* and *World Development Report 2008.*

GUINEA - PRICES

Euromonitor International, Inc., 224 S. Michigan Avenue, Suite 1500, Chicago, IL 60604, (312) 922-1115, Fax: (312) 922-1157, www.euromonitor.com; *World Marketing Data and Statistics.*

M.E. Sharpe, 80 Business Park Drive, Armonk, NY 10504, (800) 541-6563, Fax: (914) 273-2106, www.mesharpe.com; *The Illustrated Book of World Rankings.*

United Nations Food and Agricultural Organization (FAO), Viale delle Terme di Caracalla, 00100 Rome, Italy, (Dial from U.S. (202) 653-2400), (Fax from U.S. (202) 653 5760), www.fao.org; *FAO Production Yearbook 2002* and *The State of Food and Agriculture (SOFA) 2006.*

The World Bank, 1818 H Street, NW, Washington, DC 20433, (202) 473-1000, Fax: (202) 477-6391, www.worldbank.org; *Guinea.*

GUINEA - PUBLIC HEALTH

African Development Bank Group, Rue Joseph Anoma, 01 BP 1387 Abidjan 01, Cote d'Ivoire, www.afdb.org; *Statistics Pocketbook 2008.*

Euromonitor International, Inc., 224 S. Michigan Avenue, Suite 1500, Chicago, IL 60604, (312) 922-1115, Fax: (312) 922-1157, www.euromonitor.com; *World Marketing Data and Statistics.*

M.E. Sharpe, 80 Business Park Drive, Armonk, NY 10504, (800) 541-6563, Fax: (914) 273-2106, www.mesharpe.com; *The Illustrated Book of World Rankings.*

Palgrave Macmillan Ltd., Houndmills, Basingstoke, Hampshire, RG21 6XS, England, (Telephone in U.S. (888) 330-8477), (Fax in U.S. (800) 672-2054), www.palgrave.com; *The Statesman's Yearbook 2008.*

UNICEF, 3 United Nations Plaza, New York, NY 10017, (800) 253-9646, Fax: (212) 887-7465, www.unicef.org; *The State of the World's Children 2008.*

United Nations Economic Commission for Africa (ECA), PO Box 3001, Addis Ababa, Ethiopia, (Telephone in U.S. (212) 963-4957), www.uneca.org; *African Statistical Yearbook 2006.*

United Nations Statistics Division, New York, NY 10017, (800) 253-9646, Fax: (212) 963-4116, http://unstats.un.org; *Human Development Report 2006* and *Statistical Yearbook.*

The World Bank, 1818 H Street, NW, Washington, DC 20433, (202) 473-1000, Fax: (202) 477-6391, www.worldbank.org; *Guinea* and *World Development Report 2008.*

World Health Organization (WHO), Avenue Appia 20, 1211 Geneve 27, Switzerland, (Telephone in U.S. (212) 331-9081), www.who.int; The WHO Global Atlas of Infectious Diseases.

GUINEA - RADIO BROADCASTING

Palgrave Macmillan Ltd., Houndmills, Basingstoke, Hampshire, RG21 6XS, England, (Telephone in U.S. (888) 330-8477), (Fax in U.S. (800) 672-2054), www.palgrave.com; *The Statesman's Yearbook 2008.*

GUINEA - RAILROADS

Jane's Information Group, 110 North Royal Street, Suite 200, Alexandria, VA 22314, (703) 683-3700, Fax: (800) 836-0297, www.janes.com; *Jane's World Railways.*

Palgrave Macmillan Ltd., Houndmills, Basingstoke, Hampshire, RG21 6XS, England, (Telephone in U.S. (888) 330-8477), (Fax in U.S. (800) 672-2054), www.palgrave.com; *The Statesman's Yearbook 2008.*

Taylor and Francis Group, An Informa Business, 2 Park Square, Milton Park, Abingdon, Oxford OX14 4RN, United Kingdom, (Dial from U.S. (212) 216-7800), (Fax from U.S. (212) 564-7854), www.tandf.co.uk; *The Europa World Year Book.*

United Nations Economic Commission for Africa (ECA), PO Box 3001, Addis Ababa, Ethiopia, (Telephone in U.S. (212) 963-4957), www.uneca.org; *African Statistical Yearbook 2006.*

GUINEA - RELIGION

Central Intelligence Agency, Office of Public Affairs, Washington, DC 20505, (703) 482-0623, Fax: (703) 482-1739, www.cia.gov; *The World Factbook.*

M.E. Sharpe, 80 Business Park Drive, Armonk, NY 10504, (800) 541-6563, Fax: (914) 273-2106, www.mesharpe.com; *The Illustrated Book of World Rankings.*

Palgrave Macmillan Ltd., Houndmills, Basingstoke, Hampshire, RG21 6XS, England, (Telephone in U.S. (888) 330-8477), (Fax in U.S. (800) 672-2054), www.palgrave.com; *The Statesman's Yearbook 2008.*

GUINEA - RESERVES (ACCOUNTING)

African Development Bank Group, Rue Joseph Anoma, 01 BP 1387 Abidjan 01, Cote d'Ivoire, www.afdb.org; *Statistics Pocketbook 2008.*

Euromonitor International, Inc., 224 S. Michigan Avenue, Suite 1500, Chicago, IL 60604, (312) 922-

1115, Fax: (312) 922-1157, www.euromonitor.com; *International Marketing Data and Statistics 2008.*

Inter-American Development Bank (IDB), 1300 New York Avenue, NW, Washington, DC 20577, (202) 623-1000, Fax: (202) 623-3096, www.iadb.org; *The Politics of Policies: Economic and Social Progress in Latin America - 2006 Report.*

GUINEA - RETAIL TRADE

Euromonitor International, Inc., 224 S. Michigan Avenue, Suite 1500, Chicago, IL 60604, (312) 922-1115, Fax: (312) 922-1157, www.euromonitor.com; *World Marketing Data and Statistics.*

Inter-American Development Bank (IDB), 1300 New York Avenue, NW, Washington, DC 20577, (202) 623-1000, Fax: (202) 623-3096, www.iadb.org; *The Politics of Policies: Economic and Social Progress in Latin America - 2006 Report.*

GUINEA - RICE PRODUCTION

See GUINEA - CROPS

GUINEA - ROADS

Central Intelligence Agency, Office of Public Affairs, Washington, DC 20505, (703) 482-0623, Fax: (703) 482-1739, www.cia.gov; *The World Factbook.*

Palgrave Macmillan Ltd., Houndmills, Basingstoke, Hampshire, RG21 6XS, England, (Telephone in U.S. (888) 330-8477), (Fax in U.S. (800) 672-2054), www.palgrave.com; *The Statesman's Yearbook 2008.*

United Nations Economic Commission for Africa (ECA), PO Box 3001, Addis Ababa, Ethiopia, (Telephone in U.S. (212) 963-4957), www.uneca.org; *African Statistical Yearbook 2006.*

United Nations Statistics Division, New York, NY 10017, (800) 253-9646, Fax: (212) 963-4116, http://unstats.un.org; *Survey of Economic and Social Conditions in Africa 2005.*

GUINEA - RUBBER INDUSTRY AND TRADE

International Rubber Study Group (IRSG), 1st Floor, Heron House, 109/115 Wembley Hill Road, Wembley, Middlesex HA9 8DA, United Kingdom, www.rubberstudy.com; *Rubber Statistical Bulletin; Summary of World Rubber Statistics 2005; World Rubber Statistics Handbook (Volume 6, 1975-2001);* and *World Rubber Statistics Historic Handbook.*

M.E. Sharpe, 80 Business Park Drive, Armonk, NY 10504, (800) 541-6563, Fax: (914) 273-2106, www.mesharpe.com; *The Illustrated Book of World Rankings.*

GUINEA - SHEEP

See GUINEA - LIVESTOCK

GUINEA - SHIPPING

Palgrave Macmillan Ltd., Houndmills, Basingstoke, Hampshire, RG21 6XS, England, (Telephone in U.S. (888) 330-8477), (Fax in U.S. (800) 672-2054), www.palgrave.com; *The Statesman's Yearbook 2008.*

Taylor and Francis Group, An Informa Business, 2 Park Square, Milton Park, Abingdon, Oxford OX14 4RN, United Kingdom, (Dial from U.S. (212) 216-7800), (Fax from U.S. (212) 564-7854), www.tandf.co.uk; *The Europa World Year Book.*

U.S. Department of Transportation (DOT), Maritime Administration (MARAD), West Building, Southeast Federal Center, 1200 New Jersey Avenue, SE, Washington, DC 20590, (800) 99-MARAD, www.marad.dot.gov; *World Merchant Fleet 2005.*

United Nations Economic Commission for Africa (ECA), PO Box 3001, Addis Ababa, Ethiopia, (Telephone in U.S. (212) 963-4957), www.uneca.org; *African Statistical Yearbook 2006.*

United Nations Statistics Division, New York, NY 10017, (800) 253-9646, Fax: (212) 963-4116, http://unstats.un.org; *Statistical Yearbook.*

GUINEA - SILVER PRODUCTION

See GUINEA - MINERAL INDUSTRIES

GUINEA - SOCIAL ECOLOGY

United Nations Statistics Division, New York, NY 10017, (800) 253-9646, Fax: (212) 963-4116, http://unstats.un.org; *World Statistics Pocketbook.*

GUINEA - SOCIAL SECURITY

Inter-American Development Bank (IDB), 1300 New York Avenue, NW, Washington, DC 20577, (202) 623-1000, Fax: (202) 623-3096, www.iadb.org; *The Politics of Policies: Economic and Social Progress in Latin America - 2006 Report.*

M.E. Sharpe, 80 Business Park Drive, Armonk, NY 10504, (800) 541-6563, Fax: (914) 273-2106, www.mesharpe.com; *The Illustrated Book of World Rankings.*

GUINEA - STEEL PRODUCTION

See GUINEA - MINERAL INDUSTRIES

GUINEA - SUGAR PRODUCTION

See GUINEA - CROPS

GUINEA - TAXATION

Inter-American Development Bank (IDB), 1300 New York Avenue, NW, Washington, DC 20577, (202) 623-1000, Fax: (202) 623-3096, www.iadb.org; *The Politics of Policies: Economic and Social Progress in Latin America - 2006 Report.*

Taylor and Francis Group, An Informa Business, 2 Park Square, Milton Park, Abingdon, Oxford OX14 4RN, United Kingdom, (Dial from U.S. (212) 216-7800), (Fax from U.S. (212) 564-7854), www.tandf.co.uk; *The Europa World Year Book.*

GUINEA - TELEPHONE

Central Intelligence Agency, Office of Public Affairs, Washington, DC 20505, (703) 482-0623, Fax: (703) 482-1739, www.cia.gov; *The World Factbook.*

International Telecommunication Union (ITU), Place des Nations, 1211 Geneva 20, Switzerland, www.itu.int; World Telecommunication Indicators Database.

Palgrave Macmillan Ltd., Houndmills, Basingstoke, Hampshire, RG21 6XS, England, (Telephone in U.S. (888) 330-8477), (Fax in U.S. (800) 672-2054), www.palgrave.com; *The Statesman's Yearbook 2008.*

Taylor and Francis Group, An Informa Business, 2 Park Square, Milton Park, Abingdon, Oxford OX14 4RN, United Kingdom, (Dial from U.S. (212) 216-7800), (Fax from U.S. (212) 564-7854), www.tandf.co.uk; *The Europa World Year Book.*

United Nations Statistics Division, New York, NY 10017, (800) 253-9646, Fax: (212) 963-4116, http://unstats.un.org; *Statistical Yearbook* and *World Statistics Pocketbook.*

GUINEA - TEXTILE INDUSTRY

Palgrave Macmillan Ltd., Houndmills, Basingstoke, Hampshire, RG21 6XS, England, (Telephone in U.S. (888) 330-8477), (Fax in U.S. (800) 672-2054), www.palgrave.com; *The Statesman's Yearbook 2008.*

United Nations Conference on Trade and Development (UNCTAD), DC2-1120, United Nations, New York, NY 10017, (212) 963-0027, www.unctad.org; *UNCTAD Commodity Yearbook.*

GUINEA - TOBACCO INDUSTRY

Foreign Agricultural Service (FAS), U.S. Department of Agriculture (USDA), 1400 Independence Avenue, SW, Washington, DC 20250, (202) 720-3935, www.fas.usda.gov; *Tobacco: World Markets and Trade.*

M.E. Sharpe, 80 Business Park Drive, Armonk, NY 10504, (800) 541-6563, Fax: (914) 273-2106, www.mesharpe.com; *The Illustrated Book of World Rankings.*

United Nations Statistics Division, New York, NY 10017, (800) 253-9646, Fax: (212) 963-4116, http://unstats.un.org; *Statistical Yearbook.*

GUINEA - TOURISM

Euromonitor International, Inc., 224 S. Michigan Avenue, Suite 1500, Chicago, IL 60604, (312) 922-1115, Fax: (312) 922-1157, www.euromonitor.com; *The World Economic Factbook 2008* and *World Marketing Data and Statistics.*

M.E. Sharpe, 80 Business Park Drive, Armonk, NY 10504, (800) 541-6563, Fax: (914) 273-2106, www.mesharpe.com; *The Illustrated Book of World Rankings.*

United Nations Economic Commission for Africa (ECA), PO Box 3001, Addis Ababa, Ethiopia, (Telephone in U.S. (212) 963-4957), www.uneca.org; *African Statistical Yearbook 2006.*

The World Bank, 1818 H Street, NW, Washington, DC 20433, (202) 473-1000, Fax: (202) 477-6391, www.worldbank.org; *Guinea.*

GUINEA - TRADE

See GUINEA - INTERNATIONAL TRADE

GUINEA - TRANSPORTATION

Central Intelligence Agency, Office of Public Affairs, Washington, DC 20505, (703) 482-0623, Fax: (703) 482-1739, www.cia.gov; *The World Factbook.*

Euromonitor International, Inc., 224 S. Michigan Avenue, Suite 1500, Chicago, IL 60604, (312) 922-1115, Fax: (312) 922-1157, www.euromonitor.com; *International Marketing Data and Statistics 2008* and *World Marketing Data and Statistics.*

Inter-American Development Bank (IDB), 1300 New York Avenue, NW, Washington, DC 20577, (202) 623-1000, Fax: (202) 623-3096, www.iadb.org; *The Politics of Policies: Economic and Social Progress in Latin America - 2006 Report.*

M.E. Sharpe, 80 Business Park Drive, Armonk, NY 10504, (800) 541-6563, Fax: (914) 273-2106, www.mesharpe.com; *The Illustrated Book of World Rankings.*

Palgrave Macmillan Ltd., Houndmills, Basingstoke, Hampshire, RG21 6XS, England, (Telephone in U.S. (888) 330-8477), (Fax in U.S. (800) 672-2054), www.palgrave.com; *The Statesman's Yearbook 2008.*

Taylor and Francis Group, An Informa Business, 2 Park Square, Milton Park, Abingdon, Oxford OX14 4RN, United Kingdom, (Dial from U.S. (212) 216-7800), (Fax from U.S. (212) 564-7854), www.tandf.co.uk; *The Europa World Year Book.*

United Nations Economic Commission for Africa (ECA), PO Box 3001, Addis Ababa, Ethiopia, (Telephone in U.S. (212) 963-4957), www.uneca.org; *African Statistical Yearbook 2006.*

United Nations Statistics Division, New York, NY 10017, (800) 253-9646, Fax: (212) 963-4116, http://unstats.un.org; *Human Development Report 2006.*

The World Bank, 1818 H Street, NW, Washington, DC 20433, (202) 473-1000, Fax: (202) 477-6391, www.worldbank.org; *Africa Live Database (LDB)* and *Guinea.*

GUINEA - UNEMPLOYMENT

Central Intelligence Agency, Office of Public Affairs, Washington, DC 20505, (703) 482-0623, Fax: (703) 482-1739, www.cia.gov; *The World Factbook.*

Euromonitor International, Inc., 224 S. Michigan Avenue, Suite 1500, Chicago, IL 60604, (312) 922-1115, Fax: (312) 922-1157, www.euromonitor.com; *International Marketing Data and Statistics 2008.*

GUINEA - VITAL STATISTICS

Euromonitor International, Inc., 224 S. Michigan Avenue, Suite 1500, Chicago, IL 60604, (312) 922-1115, Fax: (312) 922-1157, www.euromonitor.com; *International Marketing Data and Statistics 2008.*

United Nations Statistics Division, New York, NY 10017, (800) 253-9646, Fax: (212) 963-4116, http://unstats.un.org; *Statistical Yearbook.*

World Health Organization (WHO), Avenue Appia 20, 1211 Geneve 27, Switzerland, (Telephone in U.S. (212) 331-9081), www.who.int; *World Health Report 2006.*

GUINEA - WAGES

The World Bank, 1818 H Street, NW, Washington, DC 20433, (202) 473-1000, Fax: (202) 477-6391, www.worldbank.org; *Guinea.*

GUINEA - WEATHER

See GUINEA - CLIMATE

GUINEA - WELFARE STATE

Inter-American Development Bank (IDB), 1300 New York Avenue, NW, Washington, DC 20577, (202) 623-1000, Fax: (202) 623-3096, www.iadb.org; *The Politics of Policies: Economic and Social Progress in Latin America - 2006 Report.*

GUINEA - WHEAT PRODUCTION

See GUINEA - CROPS

GUINEA - WHOLESALE PRICE INDEXES

Inter-American Development Bank (IDB), 1300 New York Avenue, NW, Washington, DC 20577, (202) 623-1000, Fax: (202) 623-3096, www.iadb.org; *The Politics of Policies: Economic and Social Progress in Latin America - 2006 Report.*

GUINEA - WHOLESALE TRADE

Inter-American Development Bank (IDB), 1300 New York Avenue, NW, Washington, DC 20577, (202) 623-1000, Fax: (202) 623-3096, www.iadb.org; *The Politics of Policies: Economic and Social Progress in Latin America - 2006 Report.*

GUINEA - WINE PRODUCTION

See GUINEA - BEVERAGE INDUSTRY

GUINEA - WOOL PRODUCTION

See GUINEA - TEXTILE INDUSTRY

GUINEA - ZOOS

UNESCO Institute for Statistics, C.P. 6128 Succursale Centre-Ville, Montreal, Quebec, H3C 3J7 Canada, (Dial from U.S. (514) 343-6880), (Fax from U.S. (514) 343 6882), www.uis.unesco.org; *Statistical Tables.*

GUINEA-BISSAU - NATIONAL STATISTICAL OFFICE

Instituto Nacional de Estatistica e Censos (INEC), C.P. 06, Bissau, Guinea-Bissau, www.stat-guinebissau.com; National Data Center.

GUINEA-BISSAU - AGRICULTURAL MACHINERY

United Nations Statistics Division, New York, NY 10017, (800) 253-9646, Fax: (212) 963-4116, http://unstats.un.org; *Statistical Yearbook.*

GUINEA-BISSAU - AGRICULTURE

Economist Intelligence Unit, 111 West 57th Street, New York, NY 10019, (212) 554-0600, Fax: (212) 586-1181, www.eiu.com; *Guinea-Bissau Country Report.*

Euromonitor International, Inc., 224 S. Michigan Avenue, Suite 1500, Chicago, IL 60604, (312) 922-1115, Fax: (312) 922-1157, www.euromonitor.com; *World Marketing Data and Statistics.*

M.E. Sharpe, 80 Business Park Drive, Armonk, NY 10504, (800) 541-6563, Fax: (914) 273-2106, www.mesharpe.com; *The Illustrated Book of World Rankings.*

Palgrave Macmillan Ltd., Houndmills, Basingstoke, Hampshire, RG21 6XS, England, (Telephone in U.S. (888) 330-8477), (Fax in U.S. (800) 672-2054), www.palgrave.com; *The Statesman's Yearbook 2008.*

Taylor and Francis Group, An Informa Business, 2 Park Square, Milton Park, Abingdon, Oxford OX14 4RN, United Kingdom, (Dial from U.S. (212) 216-7800), (Fax from U.S. (212) 564-7854), www.tandf.co.uk; *The Europa World Year Book.*

United Nations Conference on Trade and Development (UNCTAD), DC2-1120, United Nations, New York, NY 10017, (212) 963-0027, www.unctad.org; *UNCTAD Commodity Yearbook.*

United Nations Economic Commission for Africa (ECA), PO Box 3001, Addis Ababa, Ethiopia, (Telephone in U.S. (212) 963-4957), www.uneca.org; *African Statistical Yearbook 2006.*

United Nations Food and Agricultural Organization (FAO), Viale delle Terme di Caracalla, 00100 Rome, Italy, (Dial from U.S. (202) 653-2400), (Fax from U.S. (202) 653 5760), www.fao.org; AQUASTAT; *FAO Production Yearbook 2002; FAO Trade Yearbook;* and *The State of Food and Agriculture (SOFA) 2006.*

United Nations Statistics Division, New York, NY 10017, (800) 253-9646, Fax: (212) 963-4116, http://unstats.un.org; *Statistical Yearbook* and *Survey of Economic and Social Conditions in Africa 2005.*

The World Bank, 1818 H Street, NW, Washington, DC 20433, (202) 473-1000, Fax: (202) 477-6391, www.worldbank.org; *Africa Live Database (LDB); African Development Indicators (ADI) 2007; Guinea-Bissau;* and *World Development Indicators (WDI) 2008.*

GUINEA-BISSAU - AIRLINES

M.E. Sharpe, 80 Business Park Drive, Armonk, NY 10504, (800) 541-6563, Fax: (914) 273-2106, www.mesharpe.com; *The Illustrated Book of World Rankings.*

Palgrave Macmillan Ltd., Houndmills, Basingstoke, Hampshire, RG21 6XS, England, (Telephone in U.S. (888) 330-8477), (Fax in U.S. (800) 672-2054), www.palgrave.com; *The Statesman's Yearbook 2008.*

Taylor and Francis Group, An Informa Business, 2 Park Square, Milton Park, Abingdon, Oxford OX14 4RN, United Kingdom, (Dial from U.S. (212) 216-7800), (Fax from U.S. (212) 564-7854), www.tandf.co.uk; *The Europa World Year Book.*

United Nations Economic Commission for Africa (ECA), PO Box 3001, Addis Ababa, Ethiopia, (Telephone in U.S. (212) 963-4957), www.uneca.org; *African Statistical Yearbook 2006.*

GUINEA-BISSAU - AIRPORTS

Central Intelligence Agency, Office of Public Affairs, Washington, DC 20505, (703) 482-0623, Fax: (703) 482-1739, www.cia.gov; *The World Factbook.*

GUINEA-BISSAU - ALUMINUM PRODUCTION

See GUINEA-BISSAU - MINERAL INDUSTRIES

GUINEA-BISSAU - ARMED FORCES

Central Intelligence Agency, Office of Public Affairs, Washington, DC 20505, (703) 482-0623, Fax: (703) 482-1739, www.cia.gov; *The World Factbook.*

Euromonitor International, Inc., 224 S. Michigan Avenue, Suite 1500, Chicago, IL 60604, (312) 922-1115, Fax: (312) 922-1157, www.euromonitor.com; *World Marketing Data and Statistics.*

International Institute for Strategic Studies (IISS), Arundel House, 13-15 Arundel Street, Temple Place, London WC2R 3DX, England, www.iiss.org; *The Military Balance 2007.*

Palgrave Macmillan Ltd., Houndmills, Basingstoke, Hampshire, RG21 6XS, England, (Telephone in U.S. (888) 330-8477), (Fax in U.S. (800) 672-2054), www.palgrave.com; *The Statesman's Yearbook 2008.*

U.S. Department of State (DOS), 2201 C Street NW, Washington, DC 20520, (202) 647-4000, www.state.gov; *World Military Expenditures and Arms Transfers (WMEAT).*

United Nations Statistics Division, New York, NY 10017, (800) 253-9646, Fax: (212) 963-4116, http://unstats.un.org; *Human Development Report 2006.*

GUINEA-BISSAU - BALANCE OF PAYMENTS

African Development Bank Group, Rue Joseph Anoma, 01 BP 1387 Abidjan 01, Cote d'Ivoire, www.afdb.org; *Statistics Pocketbook 2008.*

Taylor and Francis Group, An Informa Business, 2 Park Square, Milton Park, Abingdon, Oxford OX14 4RN, United Kingdom, (Dial from U.S. (212) 216-7800), (Fax from U.S. (212) 564-7854), www.tandf.co.uk; *The Europa World Year Book.*

United Nations Conference on Trade and Development (UNCTAD), DC2-1120, United Nations, New York, NY 10017, (212) 963-0027, www.unctad.org; *Handbook of Statistics 2005.*

United Nations Economic Commission for Africa (ECA), PO Box 3001, Addis Ababa, Ethiopia, (Telephone in U.S. (212) 963-4957), www.uneca.org; *African Statistical Yearbook 2006.*

The World Bank, 1818 H Street, NW, Washington, DC 20433, (202) 473-1000, Fax: (202) 477-6391, www.worldbank.org; *Guinea-Bissau* and *World Development Report 2008.*

GUINEA-BISSAU - BANKS AND BANKING

Euromonitor International, Inc., 224 S. Michigan Avenue, Suite 1500, Chicago, IL 60604, (312) 922-1115, Fax: (312) 922-1157, www.euromonitor.com; *World Marketing Data and Statistics.*

M.E. Sharpe, 80 Business Park Drive, Armonk, NY 10504, (800) 541-6563, Fax: (914) 273-2106, www.mesharpe.com; *The Illustrated Book of World Rankings.*

Palgrave Macmillan Ltd., Houndmills, Basingstoke, Hampshire, RG21 6XS, England, (Telephone in U.S. (888) 330-8477), (Fax in U.S. (800) 672-2054), www.palgrave.com; *The Statesman's Yearbook 2008.*

United Nations Economic Commission for Africa (ECA), PO Box 3001, Addis Ababa, Ethiopia, (Telephone in U.S. (212) 963-4957), www.uneca.org; *African Statistical Yearbook 2006.*

GUINEA-BISSAU - BARLEY PRODUCTION

See GUINEA-BISSAU - CROPS

GUINEA-BISSAU - BEVERAGE INDUSTRY

M.E. Sharpe, 80 Business Park Drive, Armonk, NY 10504, (800) 541-6563, Fax: (914) 273-2106, www.mesharpe.com; *The Illustrated Book of World Rankings.*

GUINEA-BISSAU - BROADCASTING

Central Intelligence Agency, Office of Public Affairs, Washington, DC 20505, (703) 482-0623, Fax: (703) 482-1739, www.cia.gov; *The World Factbook.*

Euromonitor International, Inc., 224 S. Michigan Avenue, Suite 1500, Chicago, IL 60604, (312) 922-1115, Fax: (312) 922-1157, www.euromonitor.com; *World Marketing Data and Statistics.*

M.E. Sharpe, 80 Business Park Drive, Armonk, NY 10504, (800) 541-6563, Fax: (914) 273-2106, www.mesharpe.com; *The Illustrated Book of World Rankings.*

Palgrave Macmillan Ltd., Houndmills, Basingstoke, Hampshire, RG21 6XS, England, (Telephone in U.S. (888) 330-8477), (Fax in U.S. (800) 672-2054), www.palgrave.com; *The Statesman's Yearbook 2008.*

WRTH Publications Limited, PO Box 290, Oxford OX2 7FT, UK, www.wrth.com; *World Radio TV Handbook 2007.*

GUINEA-BISSAU - BUDGET

Central Intelligence Agency, Office of Public Affairs, Washington, DC 20505, (703) 482-0623, Fax: (703) 482-1739, www.cia.gov; *The World Factbook.*

GUINEA-BISSAU - CATTLE

See GUINEA-BISSAU - LIVESTOCK

GUINEA-BISSAU - CHICKENS

See GUINEA-BISSAU - LIVESTOCK

GUINEA-BISSAU - CHILDBIRTH - STATISTICS

Central Intelligence Agency, Office of Public Affairs, Washington, DC 20505, (703) 482-0623, Fax: (703) 482-1739, www.cia.gov; *The World Factbook.*

Euromonitor International, Inc., 224 S. Michigan Avenue, Suite 1500, Chicago, IL 60604, (312) 922-1115, Fax: (312) 922-1157, www.euromonitor.com; *International Marketing Data and Statistics 2008* and *The World Economic Factbook 2008.*

M.E. Sharpe, 80 Business Park Drive, Armonk, NY 10504, (800) 541-6563, Fax: (914) 273-2106, www.mesharpe.com; *The Illustrated Book of World Rankings.*

Palgrave Macmillan Ltd., Houndmills, Basingstoke, Hampshire, RG21 6XS, England, (Telephone in U.S. (888) 330-8477), (Fax in U.S. (800) 672-2054), www.palgrave.com; *The Statesman's Yearbook 2008.*

Taylor and Francis Group, An Informa Business, 2 Park Square, Milton Park, Abingdon, Oxford OX14 4RN, United Kingdom, (Dial from U.S. (212) 216-7800), (Fax from U.S. (212) 564-7854), www.tandf.co.uk; *The Europa World Year Book.*

United Nations Statistics Division, New York, NY 10017, (800) 253-9646, Fax: (212) 963-4116, http://unstats.un.org; *Demographic Yearbook; Statistical Yearbook;* and *Survey of Economic and Social Conditions in Africa 2005.*

The World Bank, 1818 H Street, NW, Washington, DC 20433, (202) 473-1000, Fax: (202) 477-6391, www.worldbank.org; *World Development Indicators (WDI) 2008.*

GUINEA-BISSAU - CLIMATE

International Institute for Environment and Development (IIED), 3 Endsleigh Street, London, England, WC1H 0DD, United Kingdom, www.iied.org; *Environment Urbanization* and *Haramata - Bulletin of the Drylands.*

M.E. Sharpe, 80 Business Park Drive, Armonk, NY 10504, (800) 541-6563, Fax: (914) 273-2106, www.mesharpe.com; *The Illustrated Book of World Rankings.*

Palgrave Macmillan Ltd., Houndmills, Basingstoke, Hampshire, RG21 6XS, England, (Telephone in U.S. (888) 330-8477), (Fax in U.S. (800) 672-2054), www.palgrave.com; *The Statesman's Yearbook 2008.*

GUINEA-BISSAU - COAL PRODUCTION

See GUINEA-BISSAU - MINERAL INDUSTRIES

GUINEA-BISSAU - COFFEE

See GUINEA-BISSAU - CROPS

GUINEA-BISSAU - COMMERCE

Palgrave Macmillan Ltd., Houndmills, Basingstoke, Hampshire, RG21 6XS, England, (Telephone in U.S. (888) 330-8477), (Fax in U.S. (800) 672-2054), www.palgrave.com; *The Statesman's Yearbook 2008.*

GUINEA-BISSAU - COMMODITY EXCHANGES

Commodity Research Bureau, 330 South Wells Street, Suite 612, Chicago, IL 60606-7110, (800) 621-5271, Fax: (312) 939-4135, www.crbtrader.com; *2006 CRB Commodity Yearbook and CD.*

International Monetary Fund (IMF), 700 Nineteenth Street, NW, Washington, DC 20431, (202) 623-7000, Fax: (202) 623-4661, www.imf.org; *IMF Primary Commodity Prices.*

United Nations Food and Agricultural Organization (FAO), Viale delle Terme di Caracalla, 00100 Rome, Italy, (Dial from U.S. (202) 653-2400), (Fax from U.S. (202) 653 5760), www.fao.org; *The State of Food and Agriculture (SOFA) 2006.*

GUINEA-BISSAU - COMMUNICATION AND TRAFFIC

United Nations Statistics Division, New York, NY 10017, (800) 253-9646, Fax: (212) 963-4116, http://unstats.un.org; *Statistical Yearbook.*

GUINEA-BISSAU - CONSTRUCTION INDUSTRY

M.E. Sharpe, 80 Business Park Drive, Armonk, NY 10504, (800) 541-6563, Fax: (914) 273-2106, www.mesharpe.com; *The Illustrated Book of World Rankings.*

United Nations Economic Commission for Africa (ECA), PO Box 3001, Addis Ababa, Ethiopia, (Telephone in U.S. (212) 963-4957), www.uneca.org; *African Statistical Yearbook 2006.*

GUINEA-BISSAU - CONSUMER PRICE INDEXES

United Nations Statistics Division, New York, NY 10017, (800) 253-9646, Fax: (212) 963-4116, http://unstats.un.org; *Survey of Economic and Social Conditions in Africa 2005.*

GUINEA-BISSAU - CONSUMPTION (ECONOMICS)

African Development Bank Group, Rue Joseph Anoma, 01 BP 1387 Abidjan 01, Cote d'Ivoire, www.afdb.org; *Statistics Pocketbook 2008.*

United Nations Statistics Division, New York, NY 10017, (800) 253-9646, Fax: (212) 963-4116, http://unstats.un.org; *Survey of Economic and Social Conditions in Africa 2005.*

The World Bank, 1818 H Street, NW, Washington, DC 20433, (202) 473-1000, Fax: (202) 477-6391, www.worldbank.org; *World Development Report 2008.*

GUINEA-BISSAU - COPPER INDUSTRY AND TRADE

See GUINEA-BISSAU - MINERAL INDUSTRIES

GUINEA-BISSAU - CORN INDUSTRY

See GUINEA-BISSAU - CROPS

GUINEA-BISSAU - COTTON

See GUINEA-BISSAU - CROPS

GUINEA-BISSAU - CROPS

M.E. Sharpe, 80 Business Park Drive, Armonk, NY 10504, (800) 541-6563, Fax: (914) 273-2106, www.mesharpe.com; *The Illustrated Book of World Rankings.*

Palgrave Macmillan Ltd., Houndmills, Basingstoke, Hampshire, RG21 6XS, England, (Telephone in U.S. (888) 330-8477), (Fax in U.S. (800) 672-2054), www.palgrave.com; *The Statesman's Yearbook 2008.*

Taylor and Francis Group, An Informa Business, 2 Park Square, Milton Park, Abingdon, Oxford OX14 4RN, United Kingdom, (Dial from U.S. (212) 216-7800), (Fax from U.S. (212) 564-7854), www.tandf.co.uk; *The Europa World Year Book.*

United Nations Conference on Trade and Development (UNCTAD), DC2-1120, United Nations, New York, NY 10017, (212) 963-0027, www.unctad.org; *UNCTAD Commodity Yearbook.*

United Nations Economic Commission for Africa (ECA), PO Box 3001, Addis Ababa, Ethiopia, (Telephone in U.S. (212) 963-4957), www.uneca.org; *African Statistical Yearbook 2006.*

United Nations Food and Agricultural Organization (FAO), Viale delle Terme di Caracalla, 00100 Rome, Italy, (Dial from U.S. (202) 653-2400), (Fax from U.S. (202) 653 5760), www.fao.org; *FAO Production Yearbook 2002* and *The State of Food and Agriculture (SOFA) 2006.*

United Nations Statistics Division, New York, NY 10017, (800) 253-9646, Fax: (212) 963-4116, http://unstats.un.org; *Statistical Yearbook.*

GUINEA-BISSAU - DAIRY PROCESSING

M.E. Sharpe, 80 Business Park Drive, Armonk, NY 10504, (800) 541-6563, Fax: (914) 273-2106, www.mesharpe.com; *The Illustrated Book of World Rankings.*

Palgrave Macmillan Ltd., Houndmills, Basingstoke, Hampshire, RG21 6XS, England, (Telephone in U.S. (888) 330-8477), (Fax in U.S. (800) 672-2054), www.palgrave.com; *The Statesman's Yearbook 2008.*

Taylor and Francis Group, An Informa Business, 2 Park Square, Milton Park, Abingdon, Oxford OX14 4RN, United Kingdom, (Dial from U.S. (212) 216-7800), (Fax from U.S. (212) 564-7854), www.tandf.co.uk; *The Europa World Year Book.*

United Nations Food and Agricultural Organization (FAO), Viale delle Terme di Caracalla, 00100 Rome, Italy, (Dial from U.S. (202) 653-2400), (Fax from U.S. (202) 653 5760), www.fao.org; *FAO Production Yearbook 2002* and *The State of Food and Agriculture (SOFA) 2006.*

GUINEA-BISSAU - DEATH RATES

See GUINEA-BISSAU - MORTALITY

GUINEA-BISSAU - DEBTS, EXTERNAL

African Development Bank Group, Rue Joseph Anoma, 01 BP 1387 Abidjan 01, Cote d'Ivoire, www.afdb.org; *Statistics Pocketbook 2008.*

Palgrave Macmillan Ltd., Houndmills, Basingstoke, Hampshire, RG21 6XS, England, (Telephone in U.S. (888) 330-8477), (Fax in U.S. (800) 672-2054), www.palgrave.com; *The Statesman's Yearbook 2008.*

United Nations Statistics Division, New York, NY 10017, (800) 253-9646, Fax: (212) 963-4116, http://unstats.un.org; *Survey of Economic and Social Conditions in Africa 2005.*

The World Bank, 1818 H Street, NW, Washington, DC 20433, (202) 473-1000, Fax: (202) 477-6391, www.worldbank.org; *Africa Live Database (LDB); African Development Indicators (ADI) 2007; Global Development Finance 2007; World Development Indicators (WDI) 2008;* and *World Development Report 2008.*

GUINEA-BISSAU - DEFENSE EXPENDITURES

See GUINEA-BISSAU - ARMED FORCES

GUINEA-BISSAU - DEMOGRAPHY

Euromonitor International, Inc., 224 S. Michigan Avenue, Suite 1500, Chicago, IL 60604, (312) 922-1115, Fax: (312) 922-1157, www.euromonitor.com; *International Marketing Data and Statistics 2008; The World Economic Factbook 2008;* and *World Marketing Data and Statistics.*

M.E. Sharpe, 80 Business Park Drive, Armonk, NY 10504, (800) 541-6563, Fax: (914) 273-2106, www.mesharpe.com; *The Illustrated Book of World Rankings.*

United Nations Statistics Division, New York, NY 10017, (800) 253-9646, Fax: (212) 963-4116, http://unstats.un.org; *Human Development Report 2006* and *Survey of Economic and Social Conditions in Africa 2005.*

The World Bank, 1818 H Street, NW, Washington, DC 20433, (202) 473-1000, Fax: (202) 477-6391, www.worldbank.org; *Guinea-Bissau.*

GUINEA-BISSAU - DIAMONDS

See GUINEA-BISSAU - MINERAL INDUSTRIES

GUINEA-BISSAU - DISPOSABLE INCOME

M.E. Sharpe, 80 Business Park Drive, Armonk, NY 10504, (800) 541-6563, Fax: (914) 273-2106, www.mesharpe.com; *The Illustrated Book of World Rankings.*

United Nations Statistics Division, New York, NY 10017, (800) 253-9646, Fax: (212) 963-4116, http://unstats.un.org; *National Accounts Statistics: Compendium of Income Distribution Statistics* and *Statistical Yearbook.*

GUINEA-BISSAU - DIVORCE

M.E. Sharpe, 80 Business Park Drive, Armonk, NY 10504, (800) 541-6563, Fax: (914) 273-2106, www.mesharpe.com; *The Illustrated Book of World Rankings.*

United Nations Statistics Division, New York, NY 10017, (800) 253-9646, Fax: (212) 963-4116, http://unstats.un.org; *Demographic Yearbook* and *Statistical Yearbook.*

GUINEA-BISSAU - ECONOMIC ASSISTANCE

United Nations Statistics Division, New York, NY 10017, (800) 253-9646, Fax: (212) 963-4116, http://unstats.un.org; *Statistical Yearbook.*

GUINEA-BISSAU - ECONOMIC CONDITIONS

African Development Bank Group, Rue Joseph Anoma, 01 BP 1387 Abidjan 01, Cote d'Ivoire, www.afdb.org; *The African Statistical Journal; Gender, Poverty and Environmental Indicators on African Countries 2007; Selected Statistics on African Countries 2007;* and *Statistics Pocketbook 2008.*

Center for International Business Education Research (CIBER), Columbia Business School and School of International and Public Affairs, Uris Hall, Room 212, 3022 Broadway, New York, NY 10027-6902, Mr. Joshua Safier, (212) 854-4750, Fax: (212) 222-9821, www.columbia.edu/cu/ciber/; Datastream International.

Central Intelligence Agency, Office of Public Affairs, Washington, DC 20505, (703) 482-0623, Fax: (703) 482-1739, www.cia.gov; *The World Factbook.*

DSI Data Service Information, Xantener Strasse 51a, D-47495 Rheinberg, Germany, www.dsidata.com; *Campus Solution.*

Dun and Bradstreet (DB) Corporation, 103 JFK Parkway, Short Hills, NJ 07078, (973) 921-5500, www.dnb.com; *Country Report.*

Economist Intelligence Unit, 111 West 57th Street, New York, NY 10019, (212) 554-0600, Fax: (212) 586-1181, www.eiu.com; *Business Africa* and *Guinea-Bissau Country Report.*

Euromonitor International, Inc., 224 S. Michigan Avenue, Suite 1500, Chicago, IL 60604, (312) 922-1115, Fax: (312) 922-1157, www.euromonitor.com; *The World Economic Factbook 2008* and *World Marketing Data and Statistics.*

International Monetary Fund (IMF), 700 Nineteenth Street, NW, Washington, DC 20431, (202) 623-7000, Fax: (202) 623-4661, www.imf.org; *World Economic Outlook Reports.*

M.E. Sharpe, 80 Business Park Drive, Armonk, NY 10504, (800) 541-6563, Fax: (914) 273-2106, www.mesharpe.com; *The Illustrated Book of World Rankings.*

Palgrave Macmillan Ltd., Houndmills, Basingstoke, Hampshire, RG21 6XS, England, (Telephone in U.S. (888) 330-8477), (Fax in U.S. (800) 672-2054), www.palgrave.com; *The Statesman's Yearbook 2008.*

Taylor and Francis Group, An Informa Business, 2 Park Square, Milton Park, Abingdon, Oxford OX14 4RN, United Kingdom, (Dial from U.S. (212) 216-7800), (Fax from U.S. (212) 564-7854), www.tandf.co.uk; *The Europa World Year Book.*

United Nations Statistics Division, New York, NY 10017, (800) 253-9646, Fax: (212) 963-4116, http://unstats.un.org; *Compendium of Intra-African and Related Foreign Trade Statistics 2003* and *World Statistics Pocketbook.*

The World Bank, 1818 H Street, NW, Washington, DC 20433, (202) 473-1000, Fax: (202) 477-6391, www.worldbank.org; *Africa Household Survey Databank; Africa Live Database (LDB); Africa Standardized Files and Indicators; African Development Indicators (ADI) 2007; Global Economic Monitor (GEM); Global Economic Prospects 2008; Guinea-Bissau; The World Bank Atlas 2003-2004;* and *World Development Report 2008.*

GUINEA-BISSAU - EDUCATION

African Development Bank Group, Rue Joseph Anoma, 01 BP 1387 Abidjan 01, Cote d'Ivoire, www.afdb.org; *Statistics Pocketbook 2008.*

Euromonitor International, Inc., 224 S. Michigan Avenue, Suite 1500, Chicago, IL 60604, (312) 922-1115, Fax: (312) 922-1157, www.euromonitor.com; *International Marketing Data and Statistics 2008* and *World Marketing Data and Statistics.*

M.E. Sharpe, 80 Business Park Drive, Armonk, NY 10504, (800) 541-6563, Fax: (914) 273-2106, www.mesharpe.com; *The Illustrated Book of World Rankings.*

Palgrave Macmillan Ltd., Houndmills, Basingstoke, Hampshire, RG21 6XS, England, (Telephone in U.S. (888) 330-8477), (Fax in U.S. (800) 672-2054), www.palgrave.com; *The Statesman's Yearbook 2008.*

Taylor and Francis Group, An Informa Business, 2 Park Square, Milton Park, Abingdon, Oxford OX14 4RN, United Kingdom, (Dial from U.S. (212) 216-7800), (Fax from U.S. (212) 564-7854), www.tandf.co.uk; *The Europa World Year Book.*

UNESCO Institute for Statistics, C.P. 6128 Succursale Centre-Ville, Montreal, Quebec, H3C 3J7 Canada, (Dial from U.S. (514) 343-6880), (Fax from U.S. (514) 343 6882), www.uis.unesco.org; *Statistical Tables.*

United Nations Economic Commission for Africa (ECA), PO Box 3001, Addis Ababa, Ethiopia, (Telephone in U.S. (212) 963-4957), www.uneca.org; *African Statistical Yearbook 2006.*

United Nations Statistics Division, New York, NY 10017, (800) 253-9646, Fax: (212) 963-4116, http://unstats.un.org; *Human Development Report 2006* and *Survey of Economic and Social Conditions in Africa 2005.*

The World Bank, 1818 H Street, NW, Washington, DC 20433, (202) 473-1000, Fax: (202) 477-6391, www.worldbank.org; *Guinea-Bissau; World Development Indicators (WDI) 2008;* and *World Development Report 2008.*

GUINEA-BISSAU - ELECTRICITY

M.E. Sharpe, 80 Business Park Drive, Armonk, NY 10504, (800) 541-6563, Fax: (914) 273-2106, www.mesharpe.com; *The Illustrated Book of World Rankings.*

Palgrave Macmillan Ltd., Houndmills, Basingstoke, Hampshire, RG21 6XS, England, (Telephone in U.S. (888) 330-8477), (Fax in U.S. (800) 672-2054), www.palgrave.com; *The Statesman's Yearbook 2008.*

United Nations Economic Commission for Africa (ECA), PO Box 3001, Addis Ababa, Ethiopia, (Telephone in U.S. (212) 963-4957), www.uneca.org; *African Statistical Yearbook 2006.*

United Nations Statistics Division, New York, NY 10017, (800) 253-9646, Fax: (212) 963-4116, http://unstats.un.org; *Human Development Report 2006* and *Survey of Economic and Social Conditions in Africa 2005.*

GUINEA-BISSAU - EMPLOYMENT

Euromonitor International, Inc., 224 S. Michigan Avenue, Suite 1500, Chicago, IL 60604, (312) 922-1115, Fax: (312) 922-1157, www.euromonitor.com; *International Marketing Data and Statistics 2008.*

M.E. Sharpe, 80 Business Park Drive, Armonk, NY 10504, (800) 541-6563, Fax: (914) 273-2106, www.mesharpe.com; *The Illustrated Book of World Rankings.*

United Nations Economic Commission for Africa (ECA), PO Box 3001, Addis Ababa, Ethiopia, (Telephone in U.S. (212) 963-4957), www.uneca.org; *African Statistical Yearbook 2006.*

United Nations Statistics Division, New York, NY 10017, (800) 253-9646, Fax: (212) 963-4116, http://unstats.un.org; *Survey of Economic and Social Conditions in Africa 2005.*

The World Bank, 1818 H Street, NW, Washington, DC 20433, (202) 473-1000, Fax: (202) 477-6391, www.worldbank.org; *Guinea-Bissau.*

GUINEA-BISSAU - ENVIRONMENTAL CONDITIONS

DSI Data Service Information, Xantener Strasse 51a, D-47495 Rheinberg, Germany, www.dsidata.com; *Campus Solution* and *DSI's Global Environmental Database.*

Economist Intelligence Unit, 111 West 57th Street, New York, NY 10019, (212) 554-0600, Fax: (212) 586-1181, www.eiu.com; *Guinea-Bissau Country Report.*

International Institute for Environment and Development (IIED), 3 Endsleigh Street, London, England, WC1H 0DD, United Kingdom, www.iied.org; *Environment Urbanization* and *Haramata - Bulletin of the Drylands.*

United Nations Statistics Division, New York, NY 10017, (800) 253-9646, Fax: (212) 963-4116, http://unstats.un.org; *World Statistics Pocketbook.*

GUINEA-BISSAU - EXPORTS

African Development Bank Group, Rue Joseph Anoma, 01 BP 1387 Abidjan 01, Cote d'Ivoire, www.afdb.org; *Statistics Pocketbook 2008.*

Central Intelligence Agency, Office of Public Affairs, Washington, DC 20505, (703) 482-0623, Fax: (703) 482-1739, www.cia.gov; *The World Factbook.*

Economist Intelligence Unit, 111 West 57th Street, New York, NY 10019, (212) 554-0600, Fax: (212) 586-1181, www.eiu.com; *Guinea-Bissau Country Report.*

Euromonitor International, Inc., 224 S. Michigan Avenue, Suite 1500, Chicago, IL 60604, (312) 922-1115, Fax: (312) 922-1157, www.euromonitor.com; *International Marketing Data and Statistics 2008* and *The World Economic Factbook 2008.*

International Monetary Fund (IMF), 700 Nineteenth Street, NW, Washington, DC 20431, (202) 623-7000, Fax: (202) 623-4661, www.imf.org; *Direction of Trade Statistics Yearbook 2007.*

Palgrave Macmillan Ltd., Houndmills, Basingstoke, Hampshire, RG21 6XS, England, (Telephone in U.S. (888) 330-8477), (Fax in U.S. (800) 672-2054), www.palgrave.com; *The Statesman's Yearbook 2008.*

Taylor and Francis Group, An Informa Business, 2 Park Square, Milton Park, Abingdon, Oxford OX14 4RN, United Kingdom, (Dial from U.S. (212) 216-7800), (Fax from U.S. (212) 564-7854), www.tandf.co.uk; *The Europa World Year Book.*

United Nations Conference on Trade and Development (UNCTAD), DC2-1120, United Nations, New York, NY 10017, (212) 963-0027, www.unctad.org; *Handbook of Statistics 2005.*

United Nations Economic Commission for Africa (ECA), PO Box 3001, Addis Ababa, Ethiopia, (Telephone in U.S. (212) 963-4957), www.uneca.org; *African Statistical Yearbook 2006.*

United Nations Food and Agricultural Organization (FAO), Viale delle Terme di Caracalla, 00100 Rome, Italy, (Dial from U.S. (202) 653-2400), (Fax from U.S. (202) 653 5760), www.fao.org; *The State of Food and Agriculture (SOFA) 2006.*

United Nations Statistics Division, New York, NY 10017, (800) 253-9646, Fax: (212) 963-4116, http://unstats.un.org; *Compendium of Intra-African and Related Foreign Trade Statistics 2003* and *Survey of Economic and Social Conditions in Africa 2005.*

The World Bank, 1818 H Street, NW, Washington, DC 20433, (202) 473-1000, Fax: (202) 477-6391, www.worldbank.org; *World Development Indicators (WDI) 2008* and *World Development Report 2008.*

GUINEA-BISSAU - FERTILITY, HUMAN

Central Intelligence Agency, Office of Public Affairs, Washington, DC 20505, (703) 482-0623, Fax: (703) 482-1739, www.cia.gov; *The World Factbook.*

M.E. Sharpe, 80 Business Park Drive, Armonk, NY 10504, (800) 541-6563, Fax: (914) 273-2106, www.mesharpe.com; *The Illustrated Book of World Rankings.*

United Nations Statistics Division, New York, NY 10017, (800) 253-9646, Fax: (212) 963-4116, http://unstats.un.org; *Human Development Report 2006* and *Survey of Economic and Social Conditions in Africa 2005.*

The World Bank, 1818 H Street, NW, Washington, DC 20433, (202) 473-1000, Fax: (202) 477-6391,

www.worldbank.org; *The World Bank Atlas 2003-2004; World Development Indicators (WDI) 2008;* and *World Development Report 2008.*

GUINEA-BISSAU - FERTILIZER INDUSTRY

United Nations Food and Agricultural Organization (FAO), Viale delle Terme di Caracalla, 00100 Rome, Italy, (Dial from U.S. (202) 653-2400), (Fax from U.S. (202) 653 5760), www.fao.org; *The State of Food and Agriculture (SOFA) 2006.*

GUINEA-BISSAU - FETAL MORTALITY

See GUINEA-BISSAU - MORTALITY

GUINEA-BISSAU - FINANCE

United Nations Economic Commission for Africa (ECA), PO Box 3001, Addis Ababa, Ethiopia, (Telephone in U.S. (212) 963-4957), www.uneca.org; *African Statistical Yearbook 2006.*

The World Bank, 1818 H Street, NW, Washington, DC 20433, (202) 473-1000, Fax: (202) 477-6391, www.worldbank.org; *Guinea-Bissau.*

GUINEA-BISSAU - FINANCE, PUBLIC

African Development Bank Group, Rue Joseph Anoma, 01 BP 1387 Abidjan 01, Cote d'Ivoire, www.afdb.org; *Statistics Pocketbook 2008.*

Bernan Essential Government Publications, 4611-F Assembly Drive, Lanham MD, 20706-4391, (301) 459-2255, Fax: (800) 865-3450, www.bernan.com; *National Accounts Statistics.*

Economist Intelligence Unit, 111 West 57th Street, New York, NY 10019, (212) 554-0600, Fax: (212) 586-1181, www.eiu.com; *Guinea-Bissau Country Report.*

International Monetary Fund (IMF), 700 Nineteenth Street, NW, Washington, DC 20431, (202) 623-7000, Fax: (202) 623-4661, www.imf.org; *International Financial Statistics* and *International Financial Statistics Online Service.*

M.E. Sharpe, 80 Business Park Drive, Armonk, NY 10504, (800) 541-6563, Fax: (914) 273-2106, www.mesharpe.com; *The Illustrated Book of World Rankings.*

Palgrave Macmillan Ltd., Houndmills, Basingstoke, Hampshire, RG21 6XS, England, (Telephone in U.S. (888) 330-8477), (Fax in U.S. (800) 672-2054), www.palgrave.com; *The Statesman's Yearbook 2008.*

Taylor and Francis Group, An Informa Business, 2 Park Square, Milton Park, Abingdon, Oxford OX14 4RN, United Kingdom, (Dial from U.S. (212) 216-7800), (Fax from U.S. (212) 564-7854), www.tandf.co.uk; *The Europa World Year Book.*

United Nations Economic Commission for Africa (ECA), PO Box 3001, Addis Ababa, Ethiopia, (Telephone in U.S. (212) 963-4957), www.uneca.org; *African Statistical Yearbook 2006.*

The World Bank, 1818 H Street, NW, Washington, DC 20433, (202) 473-1000, Fax: (202) 477-6391, www.worldbank.org; *Guinea-Bissau.*

GUINEA-BISSAU - FISHERIES

M.E. Sharpe, 80 Business Park Drive, Armonk, NY 10504, (800) 541-6563, Fax: (914) 273-2106, www.mesharpe.com; *The Illustrated Book of World Rankings.*

Palgrave Macmillan Ltd., Houndmills, Basingstoke, Hampshire, RG21 6XS, England, (Telephone in U.S. (888) 330-8477), (Fax in U.S. (800) 672-2054), www.palgrave.com; *The Statesman's Yearbook 2008.*

Taylor and Francis Group, An Informa Business, 2 Park Square, Milton Park, Abingdon, Oxford OX14 4RN, United Kingdom, (Dial from U.S. (212) 216-7800), (Fax from U.S. (212) 564-7854), www.tandf.co.uk; *The Europa World Year Book.*

United Nations Conference on Trade and Development (UNCTAD), DC2-1120, United Nations, New York, NY 10017, (212) 963-0027, www.unctad.org; *UNCTAD Commodity Yearbook.*

United Nations Economic Commission for Africa (ECA), PO Box 3001, Addis Ababa, Ethiopia, (Telephone in U.S. (212) 963-4957), www.uneca.org; *African Statistical Yearbook 2006.*

United Nations Food and Agricultural Organization (FAO), Viale delle Terme di Caracalla, 00100 Rome, Italy, (Dial from U.S. (202) 653-2400), (Fax from U.S. (202) 653 5760), www.fao.org; *FAO Yearbook of Fishery Statistics;* Fishery Databases; FISHSTAT Database. Subjects covered include: Aquaculture production, capture production, fishery commodities; and *The State of Food and Agriculture (SOFA) 2006.*

United Nations Statistics Division, New York, NY 10017, (800) 253-9646, Fax: (212) 963-4116, http://unstats.un.org; *Statistical Yearbook* and *Survey of Economic and Social Conditions in Africa 2005.*

The World Bank, 1818 H Street, NW, Washington, DC 20433, (202) 473-1000, Fax: (202) 477-6391, www.worldbank.org; *Guinea-Bissau.*

GUINEA-BISSAU - FOOD

African Development Bank Group, Rue Joseph Anoma, 01 BP 1387 Abidjan 01, Cote d'Ivoire, www.afdb.org; *Statistics Pocketbook 2008.*

United Nations Conference on Trade and Development (UNCTAD), DC2-1120, United Nations, New York, NY 10017, (212) 963-0027, www.unctad.org; *UNCTAD Commodity Yearbook.*

United Nations Food and Agricultural Organization (FAO), Viale delle Terme di Caracalla, 00100 Rome, Italy, (Dial from U.S. (202) 653-2400), (Fax from U.S. (202) 653 5760), www.fao.org; *FAO Production Yearbook 2002* and *The State of Food and Agriculture (SOFA) 2006.*

United Nations Statistics Division, New York, NY 10017, (800) 253-9646, Fax: (212) 963-4116, http://unstats.un.org; *Human Development Report 2006.*

GUINEA-BISSAU - FOREIGN EXCHANGE RATES

African Development Bank Group, Rue Joseph Anoma, 01 BP 1387 Abidjan 01, Cote d'Ivoire, www.afdb.org; *Statistics Pocketbook 2008.*

Central Intelligence Agency, Office of Public Affairs, Washington, DC 20505, (703) 482-0623, Fax: (703) 482-1739, www.cia.gov; *The World Factbook.*

Euromonitor International, Inc., 224 S. Michigan Avenue, Suite 1500, Chicago, IL 60604, (312) 922-1115, Fax: (312) 922-1157, www.euromonitor.com; *International Marketing Data and Statistics 2008* and *The World Economic Factbook 2008.*

Taylor and Francis Group, An Informa Business, 2 Park Square, Milton Park, Abingdon, Oxford OX14 4RN, United Kingdom, (Dial from U.S. (212) 216-7800), (Fax from U.S. (212) 564-7854), www.tandf.co.uk; *The Europa World Year Book.*

United Nations Statistics Division, New York, NY 10017, (800) 253-9646, Fax: (212) 963-4116, http://unstats.un.org; *Compendium of Intra-African and Related Foreign Trade Statistics 2003; Statistical Yearbook;* and *World Statistics Pocketbook.*

GUINEA-BISSAU - FORESTS AND FORESTRY

M.E. Sharpe, 80 Business Park Drive, Armonk, NY 10504, (800) 541-6563, Fax: (914) 273-2106, www.mesharpe.com; *The Illustrated Book of World Rankings.*

Palgrave Macmillan Ltd., Houndmills, Basingstoke, Hampshire, RG21 6XS, England, (Telephone in U.S. (888) 330-8477), (Fax in U.S. (800) 672-2054), www.palgrave.com; *The Statesman's Yearbook 2008.*

Taylor and Francis Group, An Informa Business, 2 Park Square, Milton Park, Abingdon, Oxford OX14 4RN, United Kingdom, (Dial from U.S. (212) 216-7800), (Fax from U.S. (212) 564-7854), www.tandf.co.uk; *The Europa World Year Book.*

UNESCO Institute for Statistics, C.P. 6128 Succursale Centre-Ville, Montreal, Quebec, H3C 3J7 Canada, (Dial from U.S. (514) 343-6880), (Fax from U.S. (514) 343 6882), www.uis.unesco.org; *Statistical Tables.*

United Nations Conference on Trade and Development (UNCTAD), DC2-1120, United Nations, New York, NY 10017, (212) 963-0027, www.unctad.org; *UNCTAD Commodity Yearbook.*

United Nations Economic Commission for Africa (ECA), PO Box 3001, Addis Ababa, Ethiopia, (Telephone in U.S. (212) 963-4957), www.uneca.org; *African Statistical Yearbook 2006.*

United Nations Food and Agricultural Organization (FAO), Viale delle Terme di Caracalla, 00100 Rome, Italy, (Dial from U.S. (202) 653-2400), (Fax from U.S. (202) 653 5760), www.fao.org; *FAO Yearbook of Forest Products* and *The State of Food and Agriculture (SOFA) 2006.*

United Nations Statistics Division, New York, NY 10017, (800) 253-9646, Fax: (212) 963-4116, http://unstats.un.org; *Statistical Yearbook.*

The World Bank, 1818 H Street, NW, Washington, DC 20433, (202) 473-1000, Fax: (202) 477-6391, www.worldbank.org; *Guinea-Bissau* and *World Development Report 2008.*

GUINEA-BISSAU - GAS PRODUCTION

See GUINEA-BISSAU - MINERAL INDUSTRIES

GUINEA-BISSAU - GEOGRAPHIC INFORMATION SYSTEMS

M.E. Sharpe, 80 Business Park Drive, Armonk, NY 10504, (800) 541-6563, Fax: (914) 273-2106, www.mesharpe.com; *The Illustrated Book of World Rankings.*

GUINEA-BISSAU - GOLD INDUSTRY

The World Bank, 1818 H Street, NW, Washington, DC 20433, (202) 473-1000, Fax: (202) 477-6391, www.worldbank.org; *World Development Indicators (WDI) 2008.*

GUINEA-BISSAU - GOLD PRODUCTION

See GUINEA-BISSAU - MINERAL INDUSTRIES

GUINEA-BISSAU - GROSS DOMESTIC PRODUCT

African Development Bank Group, Rue Joseph Anoma, 01 BP 1387 Abidjan 01, Cote d'Ivoire, www.afdb.org; *Statistics Pocketbook 2008.*

Economist Intelligence Unit, 111 West 57th Street, New York, NY 10019, (212) 554-0600, Fax: (212) 586-1181, www.eiu.com; *Guinea-Bissau Country Report.*

Euromonitor International, Inc., 224 S. Michigan Avenue, Suite 1500, Chicago, IL 60604, (312) 922-1115, Fax: (312) 922-1157, www.euromonitor.com; *International Marketing Data and Statistics 2008* and *The World Economic Factbook 2008.*

M.E. Sharpe, 80 Business Park Drive, Armonk, NY 10504, (800) 541-6563, Fax: (914) 273-2106, www.mesharpe.com; *The Illustrated Book of World Rankings.*

United Nations Economic Commission for Africa (ECA), PO Box 3001, Addis Ababa, Ethiopia, (Telephone in U.S. (212) 963-4957), www.uneca.org; *African Statistical Yearbook 2006.*

United Nations Statistics Division, New York, NY 10017, (800) 253-9646, Fax: (212) 963-4116, http://unstats.un.org; *Human Development Report 2006; National Accounts Statistics: Compendium of Income Distribution Statistics; Statistical Yearbook;* and *Survey of Economic and Social Conditions in Africa 2005.*

The World Bank, 1818 H Street, NW, Washington, DC 20433, (202) 473-1000, Fax: (202) 477-6391, www.worldbank.org; *World Development Indicators (WDI) 2008* and *World Development Report 2008.*

GUINEA-BISSAU - GROSS NATIONAL PRODUCT

M.E. Sharpe, 80 Business Park Drive, Armonk, NY 10504, (800) 541-6563, Fax: (914) 273-2106, www.mesharpe.com; *The Illustrated Book of World Rankings.*

Palgrave Macmillan Ltd., Houndmills, Basingstoke, Hampshire, RG21 6XS, England, (Telephone in U.S. (888) 330-8477), (Fax in U.S. (800) 672-2054), www.palgrave.com; *The Statesman's Yearbook 2008.*

U.S. Department of State (DOS), 2201 C Street NW, Washington, DC 20520, (202) 647-4000, www.state.gov; *World Military Expenditures and Arms Transfers (WMEAT).*

The World Bank, 1818 H Street, NW, Washington, DC 20433, (202) 473-1000, Fax: (202) 477-6391, www.worldbank.org; *The World Bank Atlas 2003-2004; World Development Indicators (WDI) 2008;* and *World Development Report 2008.*

GUINEA-BISSAU - HIDES AND SKINS INDUSTRY

United Nations Food and Agricultural Organization (FAO), Viale delle Terme di Caracalla, 00100 Rome, Italy, (Dial from U.S. (202) 653-2400), (Fax from U.S. (202) 653 5760), www.fao.org; *FAO Production Yearbook 2002.*

GUINEA-BISSAU - HOUSING

Euromonitor International, Inc., 224 S. Michigan Avenue, Suite 1500, Chicago, IL 60604, (312) 922-1115, Fax: (312) 922-1157, www.euromonitor.com; *World Marketing Data and Statistics.*

M.E. Sharpe, 80 Business Park Drive, Armonk, NY 10504, (800) 541-6563, Fax: (914) 273-2106, www.mesharpe.com; *The Illustrated Book of World Rankings.*

GUINEA-BISSAU - ILLITERATE PERSONS

Euromonitor International, Inc., 224 S. Michigan Avenue, Suite 1500, Chicago, IL 60604, (312) 922-1115, Fax: (312) 922-1157, www.euromonitor.com; *The World Economic Factbook 2008.*

UNESCO Institute for Statistics, C.P. 6128 Succursale Centre-Ville, Montreal, Quebec, H3C 3J7 Canada, (Dial from U.S. (514) 343-6880), (Fax from U.S. (514) 343 6882), www.uis.unesco.org; *Statistical Tables.*

United Nations Statistics Division, New York, NY 10017, (800) 253-9646, Fax: (212) 963-4116, http://unstats.un.org; *Human Development Report 2006.*

GUINEA-BISSAU - IMPORTS

Central Intelligence Agency, Office of Public Affairs, Washington, DC 20505, (703) 482-0623, Fax: (703) 482-1739, www.cia.gov; *The World Factbook.*

Economist Intelligence Unit, 111 West 57th Street, New York, NY 10019, (212) 554-0600, Fax: (212) 586-1181, www.eiu.com; *Guinea-Bissau Country Report.*

Euromonitor International, Inc., 224 S. Michigan Avenue, Suite 1500, Chicago, IL 60604, (312) 922-1115, Fax: (312) 922-1157, www.euromonitor.com; *International Marketing Data and Statistics 2008* and *The World Economic Factbook 2008.*

International Monetary Fund (IMF), 700 Nineteenth Street, NW, Washington, DC 20431, (202) 623-7000, Fax: (202) 623-4661, www.imf.org; *Direction of Trade Statistics Yearbook 2007.*

Palgrave Macmillan Ltd., Houndmills, Basingstoke, Hampshire, RG21 6XS, England, (Telephone in U.S. (888) 330-8477), (Fax in U.S. (800) 672-2054), www.palgrave.com; *The Statesman's Yearbook 2008.*

Taylor and Francis Group, An Informa Business, 2 Park Square, Milton Park, Abingdon, Oxford OX14 4RN, United Kingdom, (Dial from U.S. (212) 216-7800), (Fax from U.S. (212) 564-7854), www.tandf.co.uk; *The Europa World Year Book.*

United Nations Conference on Trade and Development (UNCTAD), DC2-1120, United Nations, New York, NY 10017, (212) 963-0027, www.unctad.org; *Handbook of Statistics 2005.*

United Nations Economic Commission for Africa (ECA), PO Box 3001, Addis Ababa, Ethiopia, (Telephone in U.S. (212) 963-4957), www.uneca.org; *African Statistical Yearbook 2006.*

United Nations Food and Agricultural Organization (FAO), Viale delle Terme di Caracalla, 00100 Rome, Italy, (Dial from U.S. (202) 653-2400), (Fax from U.S. (202) 653 5760), www.fao.org; *The State of Food and Agriculture (SOFA) 2006.*

United Nations Statistics Division, New York, NY 10017, (800) 253-9646, Fax: (212) 963-4116, http://unstats.un.org; *Compendium of Intra-African and Related Foreign Trade Statistics 2003* and *Survey of Economic and Social Conditions in Africa 2005.*

The World Bank, 1818 H Street, NW, Washington, DC 20433, (202) 473-1000, Fax: (202) 477-6391, www.worldbank.org; *World Development Indicators (WDI) 2008* and *World Development Report 2008.*

GUINEA-BISSAU - INDUSTRIAL PRODUCTIVITY

M.E. Sharpe, 80 Business Park Drive, Armonk, NY 10504, (800) 541-6563, Fax: (914) 273-2106, www.mesharpe.com; *The Illustrated Book of World Rankings.*

GUINEA-BISSAU - INDUSTRIES

Central Intelligence Agency, Office of Public Affairs, Washington, DC 20505, (703) 482-0623, Fax: (703) 482-1739, www.cia.gov; *The World Factbook.*

Economist Intelligence Unit, 111 West 57th Street, New York, NY 10019, (212) 554-0600, Fax: (212) 586-1181, www.eiu.com; *Guinea-Bissau Country Report.*

Euromonitor International, Inc., 224 S. Michigan Avenue, Suite 1500, Chicago, IL 60604, (312) 922-1115, Fax: (312) 922-1157, www.euromonitor.com; *The World Economic Factbook 2008* and *World Marketing Data and Statistics.*

M.E. Sharpe, 80 Business Park Drive, Armonk, NY 10504, (800) 541-6563, Fax: (914) 273-2106, www.mesharpe.com; *The Illustrated Book of World Rankings.*

Palgrave Macmillan Ltd., Houndmills, Basingstoke, Hampshire, RG21 6XS, England, (Telephone in U.S. (888) 330-8477), (Fax in U.S. (800) 672-2054), www.palgrave.com; *The Statesman's Yearbook 2008.*

Taylor and Francis Group, An Informa Business, 2 Park Square, Milton Park, Abingdon, Oxford OX14 4RN, United Kingdom, (Dial from U.S. (212) 216-7800), (Fax from U.S. (212) 564-7854), www.tandf.co.uk; *The Europa World Year Book.*

United Nations Economic Commission for Africa (ECA), PO Box 3001, Addis Ababa, Ethiopia, (Telephone in U.S. (212) 963-4957), www.uneca.org; *African Statistical Yearbook 2006.*

United Nations Industrial Development Organization (UNIDO), 1 United Nations Plaza, New York, NY 10017, (212) 963 6890, Fax: (212) 963-7904, http://unido.org; Industrial Statistics Database 2008 (INDSTAT) and *The International Yearbook of Industrial Statistics 2008.*

United Nations Statistics Division, New York, NY 10017, (800) 253-9646, Fax: (212) 963-4116, http://unstats.un.org; *Survey of Economic and Social Conditions in Africa 2005.*

The World Bank, 1818 H Street, NW, Washington, DC 20433, (202) 473-1000, Fax: (202) 477-6391, www.worldbank.org; *Guinea-Bissau* and *World Development Indicators (WDI) 2008.*

GUINEA-BISSAU - INFANT AND MATERNAL MORTALITY

See GUINEA-BISSAU - MORTALITY

GUINEA-BISSAU - INTERNATIONAL TRADE

African Development Bank Group, Rue Joseph Anoma, 01 BP 1387 Abidjan 01, Cote d'Ivoire, www.afdb.org; *Statistics Pocketbook 2008.*

Economist Intelligence Unit, 111 West 57th Street, New York, NY 10019, (212) 554-0600, Fax: (212) 586-1181, www.eiu.com; *Guinea-Bissau Country Report.*

Euromonitor International, Inc., 224 S. Michigan Avenue, Suite 1500, Chicago, IL 60604, (312) 922-1115, Fax: (312) 922-1157, www.euromonitor.com; *The World Economic Factbook 2008* and *World Marketing Data and Statistics.*

M.E. Sharpe, 80 Business Park Drive, Armonk, NY 10504, (800) 541-6563, Fax: (914) 273-2106, www.mesharpe.com; *The Illustrated Book of World Rankings.*

Palgrave Macmillan Ltd., Houndmills, Basingstoke, Hampshire, RG21 6XS, England, (Telephone in U.S. (888) 330-8477), (Fax in U.S. (800) 672-2054), www.palgrave.com; *The Statesman's Yearbook 2008.*

Taylor and Francis Group, An Informa Business, 2 Park Square, Milton Park, Abingdon, Oxford OX14 4RN, United Kingdom, (Dial from U.S. (212) 216-7800), (Fax from U.S. (212) 564-7854), www.tandf.co.uk; *The Europa World Year Book.*

United Nations Conference on Trade and Development (UNCTAD), DC2-1120, United Nations, New York, NY 10017, (212) 963-0027, www.unctad.org; *UNCTAD Commodity Yearbook.*

United Nations Economic Commission for Africa (ECA), PO Box 3001, Addis Ababa, Ethiopia, (Telephone in U.S. (212) 963-4957), www.uneca.org; *African Statistical Yearbook 2006.*

United Nations Food and Agricultural Organization (FAO), Viale delle Terme di Caracalla, 00100 Rome, Italy, (Dial from U.S. (202) 653-2400), (Fax from U.S. (202) 653 5760), www.fao.org; *FAO Trade Yearbook* and *The State of Food and Agriculture (SOFA) 2006.*

United Nations Statistics Division, New York, NY 10017, (800) 253-9646, Fax: (212) 963-4116, http://unstats.un.org; *Compendium of Intra-African and Related Foreign Trade Statistics 2003; International Trade Statistics Yearbook;* and *Statistical Yearbook.*

The World Bank, 1818 H Street, NW, Washington, DC 20433, (202) 473-1000, Fax: (202) 477-6391, www.worldbank.org; *Guinea-Bissau; World Development Indicators (WDI) 2008;* and *World Development Report 2008.*

World Trade Organization (WTO), Centre William Rappard, Rue de Lausanne 154, CH-1211 Geneva 21, Switzerland, www.wto.org; *International Trade Statistics 2006.*

GUINEA-BISSAU - INTERNET USERS

International Telecommunication Union (ITU), Place des Nations, 1211 Geneva 20, Switzerland, www.itu.int; *World Telecommunication/ICT Indicators Database on CD-ROM; World Telecommunication/ICT Indicators Database Online;* and *Yearbook of Statistics - Telecommunication Services (Chronological Time Series 1997-2006).*

The World Bank, 1818 H Street, NW, Washington, DC 20433, (202) 473-1000, Fax: (202) 477-6391, www.worldbank.org; *Guinea-Bissau.*

GUINEA-BISSAU - IRON AND IRON ORE PRODUCTION

See GUINEA-BISSAU - MINERAL INDUSTRIES

GUINEA-BISSAU - LABOR

African Development Bank Group, Rue Joseph Anoma, 01 BP 1387 Abidjan 01, Cote d'Ivoire, www.afdb.org; *Statistics Pocketbook 2008.*

Central Intelligence Agency, Office of Public Affairs, Washington, DC 20505, (703) 482-0623, Fax: (703) 482-1739, www.cia.gov; *The World Factbook.*

Euromonitor International, Inc., 224 S. Michigan Avenue, Suite 1500, Chicago, IL 60604, (312) 922-1115, Fax: (312) 922-1157, www.euromonitor.com; *International Marketing Data and Statistics 2008* and *World Marketing Data and Statistics.*

M.E. Sharpe, 80 Business Park Drive, Armonk, NY 10504, (800) 541-6563, Fax: (914) 273-2106, www.mesharpe.com; *The Illustrated Book of World Rankings.*

Palgrave Macmillan Ltd., Houndmills, Basingstoke, Hampshire, RG21 6XS, England, (Telephone in U.S. (888) 330-8477), (Fax in U.S. (800) 672-2054), www.palgrave.com; *The Statesman's Yearbook 2008.*

United Nations Food and Agricultural Organization (FAO), Viale delle Terme di Caracalla, 00100 Rome, Italy, (Dial from U.S. (202) 653-2400), (Fax from U.S. (202) 653 5760), www.fao.org; *The State of Food and Agriculture (SOFA) 2006.*

United Nations Statistics Division, New York, NY 10017, (800) 253-9646, Fax: (212) 963-4116, http://unstats.un.org; *Human Development Report 2006.*

The World Bank, 1818 H Street, NW, Washington, DC 20433, (202) 473-1000, Fax: (202) 477-6391, www.worldbank.org; *The World Bank Atlas 2003-2004; World Development Indicators (WDI) 2008;* and *World Development Report 2008.*

GUINEA-BISSAU - LAND USE

Central Intelligence Agency, Office of Public Affairs, Washington, DC 20505, (703) 482-0623, Fax: (703) 482-1739, www.cia.gov; *The World Factbook.*

Euromonitor International, Inc., 224 S. Michigan Avenue, Suite 1500, Chicago, IL 60604, (312) 922-1115, Fax: (312) 922-1157, www.euromonitor.com; *International Marketing Data and Statistics 2008.*

United Nations Food and Agricultural Organization (FAO), Viale delle Terme di Caracalla, 00100 Rome, Italy, (Dial from U.S. (202) 653-2400), (Fax from U.S. (202) 653 5760), www.fao.org; *FAO Production Yearbook 2002.*

The World Bank, 1818 H Street, NW, Washington, DC 20433, (202) 473-1000, Fax: (202) 477-6391, www.worldbank.org; *World Development Report 2008.*

GUINEA-BISSAU - LIBRARIES

M.E. Sharpe, 80 Business Park Drive, Armonk, NY 10504, (800) 541-6563, Fax: (914) 273-2106, www.mesharpe.com; *The Illustrated Book of World Rankings.*

GUINEA-BISSAU - LIFE EXPECTANCY

African Development Bank Group, Rue Joseph Anoma, 01 BP 1387 Abidjan 01, Cote d'Ivoire, www.afdb.org; *Statistics Pocketbook 2008.*

Central Intelligence Agency, Office of Public Affairs, Washington, DC 20505, (703) 482-0623, Fax: (703) 482-1739, www.cia.gov; *The World Factbook.*

Euromonitor International, Inc., 224 S. Michigan Avenue, Suite 1500, Chicago, IL 60604, (312) 922-1115, Fax: (312) 922-1157, www.euromonitor.com; *The World Economic Factbook 2008.*

Palgrave Macmillan Ltd., Houndmills, Basingstoke, Hampshire, RG21 6XS, England, (Telephone in U.S. (888) 330-8477), (Fax in U.S. (800) 672-2054), www.palgrave.com; *The Statesman's Yearbook 2008.*

United Nations Statistics Division, New York, NY 10017, (800) 253-9646, Fax: (212) 963-4116, http://unstats.un.org; *Human Development Report 2006* and *World Statistics Pocketbook.*

The World Bank, 1818 H Street, NW, Washington, DC 20433, (202) 473-1000, Fax: (202) 477-6391, www.worldbank.org; *The World Bank Atlas 2003-2004* and *World Development Report 2008.*

GUINEA-BISSAU - LITERACY

Euromonitor International, Inc., 224 S. Michigan Avenue, Suite 1500, Chicago, IL 60604, (312) 922-1115, Fax: (312) 922-1157, www.euromonitor.com; *World Marketing Data and Statistics.*

United Nations Statistics Division, New York, NY 10017, (800) 253-9646, Fax: (212) 963-4116, http://unstats.un.org; *Survey of Economic and Social Conditions in Africa 2005.*

GUINEA-BISSAU - LIVESTOCK

M.E. Sharpe, 80 Business Park Drive, Armonk, NY 10504, (800) 541-6563, Fax: (914) 273-2106, www.mesharpe.com; *The Illustrated Book of World Rankings.*

Palgrave Macmillan Ltd., Houndmills, Basingstoke, Hampshire, RG21 6XS, England, (Telephone in U.S. (888) 330-8477), (Fax in U.S. (800) 672-2054), www.palgrave.com; *The Statesman's Yearbook 2008.*

Taylor and Francis Group, An Informa Business, 2 Park Square, Milton Park, Abingdon, Oxford OX14 4RN, United Kingdom, (Dial from U.S. (212) 216-7800), (Fax from U.S. (212) 564-7854), www.tandf.co.uk; *The Europa World Year Book.*

United Nations Conference on Trade and Development (UNCTAD), DC2-1120, United Nations, New York, NY 10017, (212) 963-0027, www.unctad.org; *UNCTAD Commodity Yearbook.*

United Nations Economic Commission for Africa (ECA), PO Box 3001, Addis Ababa, Ethiopia, (Telephone in U.S. (212) 963-4957), www.uneca.org; *African Statistical Yearbook 2006.*

United Nations Food and Agricultural Organization (FAO), Viale delle Terme di Caracalla, 00100 Rome, Italy, (Dial from U.S. (202) 653-2400), (Fax from U.S. (202) 653 5760), www.fao.org; *FAO Production Yearbook 2002* and *The State of Food and Agriculture (SOFA) 2006.*

United Nations Statistics Division, New York, NY 10017, (800) 253-9646, Fax: (212) 963-4116, http://unstats.un.org; *Statistical Yearbook* and *Survey of Economic and Social Conditions in Africa 2005.*

GUINEA-BISSAU - MANUFACTURES

M.E. Sharpe, 80 Business Park Drive, Armonk, NY 10504, (800) 541-6563, Fax: (914) 273-2106, www.mesharpe.com; *The Illustrated Book of World Rankings.*

United Nations Economic Commission for Africa (ECA), PO Box 3001, Addis Ababa, Ethiopia, (Telephone in U.S. (212) 963-4957), www.uneca.org; *African Statistical Yearbook 2006.*

United Nations Statistics Division, New York, NY 10017, (800) 253-9646, Fax: (212) 963-4116, http://unstats.un.org; *Survey of Economic and Social Conditions in Africa 2005.*

The World Bank, 1818 H Street, NW, Washington, DC 20433, (202) 473-1000, Fax: (202) 477-6391, www.worldbank.org; *World Development Indicators (WDI) 2008.*

GUINEA-BISSAU - MARRIAGE

M.E. Sharpe, 80 Business Park Drive, Armonk, NY 10504, (800) 541-6563, Fax: (914) 273-2106, www.mesharpe.com; *The Illustrated Book of World Rankings.*

United Nations Statistics Division, New York, NY 10017, (800) 253-9646, Fax: (212) 963-4116, http://unstats.un.org; *Demographic Yearbook* and *Statistical Yearbook.*

GUINEA-BISSAU - MEAT PRODUCTION

See GUINEA-BISSAU - LIVESTOCK

GUINEA-BISSAU - MILK PRODUCTION

See GUINEA-BISSAU - DAIRY PROCESSING

GUINEA-BISSAU - MINERAL INDUSTRIES

M.E. Sharpe, 80 Business Park Drive, Armonk, NY 10504, (800) 541-6563, Fax: (914) 273-2106, www.mesharpe.com; *The Illustrated Book of World Rankings.*

United Nations Conference on Trade and Development (UNCTAD), DC2-1120, United Nations, New York, NY 10017, (212) 963-0027, www.unctad.org; *UNCTAD Commodity Yearbook.*

United Nations Economic Commission for Africa (ECA), PO Box 3001, Addis Ababa, Ethiopia, (Telephone in U.S. (212) 963-4957), www.uneca.org; *African Statistical Yearbook 2006.*

GUINEA-BISSAU - MONEY EXCHANGE RATES

See GUINEA-BISSAU - FOREIGN EXCHANGE RATES

GUINEA-BISSAU - MONEY SUPPLY

African Development Bank Group, Rue Joseph Anoma, 01 BP 1387 Abidjan 01, Cote d'Ivoire, www.afdb.org; *Statistics Pocketbook 2008.*

Economist Intelligence Unit, 111 West 57th Street, New York, NY 10019, (212) 554-0600, Fax: (212) 586-1181, www.eiu.com; *Guinea-Bissau Country Report.*

The World Bank, 1818 H Street, NW, Washington, DC 20433, (202) 473-1000, Fax: (202) 477-6391, www.worldbank.org; *Guinea-Bissau* and *World Development Indicators (WDI) 2008.*

GUINEA-BISSAU - MORTALITY

Central Intelligence Agency, Office of Public Affairs, Washington, DC 20505, (703) 482-0623, Fax: (703) 482-1739, www.cia.gov; *The World Factbook.*

Euromonitor International, Inc., 224 S. Michigan Avenue, Suite 1500, Chicago, IL 60604, (312) 922-1115, Fax: (312) 922-1157, www.euromonitor.com; *International Marketing Data and Statistics 2008* and *The World Economic Factbook 2008.*

Palgrave Macmillan Ltd., Houndmills, Basingstoke, Hampshire, RG21 6XS, England, (Telephone in U.S. (888) 330-8477), (Fax in U.S. (800) 672-2054), www.palgrave.com; *The Statesman's Yearbook 2008.*

Taylor and Francis Group, An Informa Business, 2 Park Square, Milton Park, Abingdon, Oxford OX14 4RN, United Kingdom, (Dial from U.S. (212) 216-7800), (Fax from U.S. (212) 564-7854), www.tandf.co.uk; *The Europa World Year Book.*

UNICEF, 3 United Nations Plaza, New York, NY 10017, (800) 253-9646, Fax: (212) 887-7465, www.unicef.org; *The State of the World's Children 2008.*

United Nations Statistics Division, New York, NY 10017, (800) 253-9646, Fax: (212) 963-4116, http://unstats.un.org; *Demographic Yearbook; Human Development Report 2006; Statistical Yearbook; Survey of Economic and Social Conditions in Africa 2005;* and *World Statistics Pocketbook.*

The World Bank, 1818 H Street, NW, Washington, DC 20433, (202) 473-1000, Fax: (202) 477-6391, www.worldbank.org; *The World Bank Atlas 2003-2004; World Development Indicators (WDI) 2008;* and *World Development Report 2008.*

World Health Organization (WHO), Avenue Appia 20, 1211 Geneve 27, Switzerland, (Telephone in U.S. (212) 331-9081), www.who.int; The WHO Global Atlas of Infectious Diseases and *World Health Report 2006.*

GUINEA-BISSAU - MOTION PICTURES

Palgrave Macmillan Ltd., Houndmills, Basingstoke, Hampshire, RG21 6XS, England, (Telephone in U.S. (888) 330-8477), (Fax in U.S. (800) 672-2054), www.palgrave.com; *The Statesman's Yearbook 2008.*

United Nations Statistics Division, New York, NY 10017, (800) 253-9646, Fax: (212) 963-4116, http://unstats.un.org; *Statistical Yearbook.*

GUINEA-BISSAU - MOTOR VEHICLES

Taylor and Francis Group, An Informa Business, 2 Park Square, Milton Park, Abingdon, Oxford OX14 4RN, United Kingdom, (Dial from U.S. (212) 216-7800), (Fax from U.S. (212) 564-7854), www.tandf.co.uk; *The Europa World Year Book.*

United Nations Statistics Division, New York, NY 10017, (800) 253-9646, Fax: (212) 963-4116, http://unstats.un.org; *Survey of Economic and Social Conditions in Africa 2005.*

GUINEA-BISSAU - MUSEUMS

M.E. Sharpe, 80 Business Park Drive, Armonk, NY 10504, (800) 541-6563, Fax: (914) 273-2106, www.mesharpe.com; *The Illustrated Book of World Rankings.*

GUINEA-BISSAU - NATURAL GAS PRODUCTION

See GUINEA-BISSAU - MINERAL INDUSTRIES

GUINEA-BISSAU - NUTRITION

African Development Bank Group, Rue Joseph Anoma, 01 BP 1387 Abidjan 01, Cote d'Ivoire, www.afdb.org; *Statistics Pocketbook 2008.*

United Nations Food and Agricultural Organization (FAO), Viale delle Terme di Caracalla, 00100 Rome, Italy, (Dial from U.S. (202) 653-2400), (Fax from U.S. (202) 653 5760), www.fao.org; *The State of Food and Agriculture (SOFA) 2006.*

GUINEA-BISSAU - OLDER PEOPLE

M.E. Sharpe, 80 Business Park Drive, Armonk, NY 10504, (800) 541-6563, Fax: (914) 273-2106, www.mesharpe.com; *The Illustrated Book of World Rankings.*

GUINEA-BISSAU - PALM OIL PRODUCTION

See GUINEA-BISSAU - CROPS

GUINEA-BISSAU - PAPER

See GUINEA-BISSAU - FORESTS AND FORESTRY

GUINEA-BISSAU - PEANUT PRODUCTION

See GUINEA-BISSAU - CROPS

GUINEA-BISSAU - PESTICIDES

United Nations Food and Agricultural Organization (FAO), Viale delle Terme di Caracalla, 00100 Rome, Italy, (Dial from U.S. (202) 653-2400), (Fax from U.S. (202) 653 5760), www.fao.org; *The State of Food and Agriculture (SOFA) 2006.*

GUINEA-BISSAU - PETROLEUM INDUSTRY AND TRADE

M.E. Sharpe, 80 Business Park Drive, Armonk, NY 10504, (800) 541-6563, Fax: (914) 273-2106, www.mesharpe.com; *The Illustrated Book of World Rankings.*

PennWell Corporation, 1421 South Sheridan Road, Tulsa, OK 74112, (918) 835-3161, www.pennwell.com; *International Petroleum Encyclopedia 2007.*

United Nations Conference on Trade and Development (UNCTAD), DC2-1120, United Nations, New York, NY 10017, (212) 963-0027, www.unctad.org; *UNCTAD Commodity Yearbook.*

United Nations Food and Agricultural Organization (FAO), Viale delle Terme di Caracalla, 00100 Rome, Italy, (Dial from U.S. (202) 653-2400), (Fax from U.S. (202) 653 5760), www.fao.org; *The State of Food and Agriculture (SOFA) 2006.*

GUINEA-BISSAU - POLITICAL SCIENCE

Central Intelligence Agency, Office of Public Affairs, Washington, DC 20505, (703) 482-0623, Fax: (703) 482-1739, www.cia.gov; *The World Factbook.*

Palgrave Macmillan Ltd., Houndmills, Basingstoke, Hampshire, RG21 6XS, England, (Telephone in U.S. (888) 330-8477), (Fax in U.S. (800) 672-2054), www.palgrave.com; *The Statesman's Yearbook 2008.*

Taylor and Francis Group, An Informa Business, 2 Park Square, Milton Park, Abingdon, Oxford OX14 4RN, United Kingdom, (Dial from U.S. (212) 216-7800), (Fax from U.S. (212) 564-7854), www.tandf.co.uk; *The Europa World Year Book.*

United Nations Statistics Division, New York, NY 10017, (800) 253-9646, Fax: (212) 963-4116, http://unstats.un.org; *National Accounts Statistics: Compendium of Income Distribution Statistics* and *Survey of Economic and Social Conditions in Africa 2005.*

The World Bank, 1818 H Street, NW, Washington, DC 20433, (202) 473-1000, Fax: (202) 477-6391, www.worldbank.org; *World Development Indicators (WDI) 2008* and *World Development Report 2008.*

GUINEA-BISSAU - POPULATION

African Development Bank Group, Rue Joseph Anoma, 01 BP 1387 Abidjan 01, Cote d'Ivoire, www.afdb.org; *The African Statistical Journal; Gender, Poverty and Environmental Indicators on African Countries 2007; Selected Statistics on African Countries 2007;* and *Statistics Pocketbook 2008.*

Central Intelligence Agency, Office of Public Affairs, Washington, DC 20505, (703) 482-0623, Fax: (703) 482-1739, www.cia.gov; *The World Factbook.*

Economist Intelligence Unit, 111 West 57th Street, New York, NY 10019, (212) 554-0600, Fax: (212) 586-1181, www.eiu.com; *Guinea-Bissau Country Report.*

Euromonitor International, Inc., 224 S. Michigan Avenue, Suite 1500, Chicago, IL 60604, (312) 922-1115, Fax: (312) 922-1157, www.euromonitor.com; *International Marketing Data and Statistics 2008* and *The World Economic Factbook 2008.*

Eurostat, Batiment Jean Monnet, Rue Alcide de Gasperi, L-2920 Luxembourg, http://epp.eurostat.ec.europa.eu; *Demographic Indicators - Population by Age-Classes.*

M.E. Sharpe, 80 Business Park Drive, Armonk, NY 10504, (800) 541-6563, Fax: (914) 273-2106, www.mesharpe.com; *The Illustrated Book of World Rankings.*

Palgrave Macmillan Ltd., Houndmills, Basingstoke, Hampshire, RG21 6XS, England, (Telephone in U.S. (888) 330-8477), (Fax in U.S. (800) 672-2054), www.palgrave.com; *The Statesman's Yearbook 2008.*

Taylor and Francis Group, An Informa Business, 2 Park Square, Milton Park, Abingdon, Oxford OX14 4RN, United Kingdom, (Dial from U.S. (212) 216-7800), (Fax from U.S. (212) 564-7854), www.tandf.co.uk; *The Europa World Year Book.*

U.S. Department of State (DOS), 2201 C Street NW, Washington, DC 20520, (202) 647-4000, www.state.gov; *World Military Expenditures and Arms Transfers (WMEAT).*

United Nations Food and Agricultural Organization (FAO), Viale delle Terme di Caracalla, 00100 Rome, Italy, (Dial from U.S. (202) 653-2400), (Fax from U.S. (202) 653 5760), www.fao.org; *FAO Production Yearbook 2002.*

United Nations Statistics Division, New York, NY 10017, (800) 253-9646, Fax: (212) 963-4116, http://unstats.un.org; *Demographic Yearbook; Human Development Report 2006; Statistical Yearbook; Survey of Economic and Social Conditions in Africa 2005;* and *World Statistics Pocketbook.*

The World Bank, 1818 H Street, NW, Washington, DC 20433, (202) 473-1000, Fax: (202) 477-6391, www.worldbank.org; *Guinea-Bissau; The World Bank Atlas 2003-2004;* and *World Development Report 2008.*

World Health Organization (WHO), Avenue Appia 20, 1211 Geneve 27, Switzerland, (Telephone in U.S. (212) 331-9081), www.who.int; *World Health Report 2006.*

GUINEA-BISSAU - POPULATION DENSITY

African Development Bank Group, Rue Joseph Anoma, 01 BP 1387 Abidjan 01, Cote d'Ivoire, www.afdb.org; *Statistics Pocketbook 2008.*

Central Intelligence Agency, Office of Public Affairs, Washington, DC 20505, (703) 482-0623, Fax: (703) 482-1739, www.cia.gov; *The World Factbook.*

Euromonitor International, Inc., 224 S. Michigan Avenue, Suite 1500, Chicago, IL 60604, (312) 922-1115, Fax: (312) 922-1157, www.euromonitor.com; *The World Economic Factbook 2008.*

M.E. Sharpe, 80 Business Park Drive, Armonk, NY 10504, (800) 541-6563, Fax: (914) 273-2106, www.mesharpe.com; *The Illustrated Book of World Rankings.*

Palgrave Macmillan Ltd., Houndmills, Basingstoke, Hampshire, RG21 6XS, England, (Telephone in U.S. (888) 330-8477), (Fax in U.S. (800) 672-2054), www.palgrave.com; *The Statesman's Yearbook 2008.*

Taylor and Francis Group, An Informa Business, 2 Park Square, Milton Park, Abingdon, Oxford OX14 4RN, United Kingdom, (Dial from U.S. (212) 216-7800), (Fax from U.S. (212) 564-7854), www.tandf.co.uk; *The Europa World Year Book.*

United Nations Food and Agricultural Organization (FAO), Viale delle Terme di Caracalla, 00100 Rome, Italy, (Dial from U.S. (202) 653-2400), (Fax from U.S. (202) 653 5760), www.fao.org; *The State of Food and Agriculture (SOFA) 2006.*

United Nations Statistics Division, New York, NY 10017, (800) 253-9646, Fax: (212) 963-4116, http://unstats.un.org; *Statistical Yearbook* and *Survey of Economic and Social Conditions in Africa 2005.*

The World Bank, 1818 H Street, NW, Washington, DC 20433, (202) 473-1000, Fax: (202) 477-6391, www.worldbank.org; *Guinea-Bissau* and *World Development Report 2008.*

GUINEA-BISSAU - POSTAL SERVICE

M.E. Sharpe, 80 Business Park Drive, Armonk, NY 10504, (800) 541-6563, Fax: (914) 273-2106, www.mesharpe.com; *The Illustrated Book of World Rankings.*

GUINEA-BISSAU - POWER RESOURCES

Euromonitor International, Inc., 224 S. Michigan Avenue, Suite 1500, Chicago, IL 60604, (312) 922-1115, Fax: (312) 922-1157, www.euromonitor.com; *International Marketing Data and Statistics 2008; The World Economic Factbook 2008;* and *World Marketing Data and Statistics.*

M.E. Sharpe, 80 Business Park Drive, Armonk, NY 10504, (800) 541-6563, Fax: (914) 273-2106, www.mesharpe.com; *The Illustrated Book of World Rankings.*

Palgrave Macmillan Ltd., Houndmills, Basingstoke, Hampshire, RG21 6XS, England, (Telephone in U.S. (888) 330-8477), (Fax in U.S. (800) 672-2054), www.palgrave.com; *The Statesman's Yearbook 2008.*

Platts, 2 Penn Plaza, 25th Floor, New York, NY 10121-2298, (212) 904-3070, www.platts.com; *Energy Economist.*

United Nations Economic Commission for Africa (ECA), PO Box 3001, Addis Ababa, Ethiopia, (Telephone in U.S. (212) 963-4957), www.uneca.org; *African Statistical Yearbook 2006.*

United Nations Food and Agricultural Organization (FAO), Viale delle Terme di Caracalla, 00100 Rome, Italy, (Dial from U.S. (202) 653-2400), (Fax from U.S. (202) 653 5760), www.fao.org; *The State of Food and Agriculture (SOFA) 2006.*

United Nations Statistics Division, New York, NY 10017, (800) 253-9646, Fax: (212) 963-4116, http://unstats.un.org; *Energy Statistics Yearbook 2003; Human Development Report 2006; Statistical Yearbook;* and *World Statistics Pocketbook.*

The World Bank, 1818 H Street, NW, Washington, DC 20433, (202) 473-1000, Fax: (202) 477-6391, www.worldbank.org; *The World Bank Atlas 2003-2004* and *World Development Report 2008.*

GUINEA-BISSAU - PRICES

Euromonitor International, Inc., 224 S. Michigan Avenue, Suite 1500, Chicago, IL 60604, (312) 922-1115, Fax: (312) 922-1157, www.euromonitor.com; *World Marketing Data and Statistics.*

M.E. Sharpe, 80 Business Park Drive, Armonk, NY 10504, (800) 541-6563, Fax: (914) 273-2106, www.mesharpe.com; *The Illustrated Book of World Rankings.*

United Nations Food and Agricultural Organization (FAO), Viale delle Terme di Caracalla, 00100 Rome, Italy, (Dial from U.S. (202) 653-2400), (Fax from U.S. (202) 653 5760), www.fao.org; *FAO Production Yearbook 2002* and *The State of Food and Agriculture (SOFA) 2006.*

The World Bank, 1818 H Street, NW, Washington, DC 20433, (202) 473-1000, Fax: (202) 477-6391, www.worldbank.org; *Guinea-Bissau.*

GUINEA-BISSAU - PUBLIC HEALTH

African Development Bank Group, Rue Joseph Anoma, 01 BP 1387 Abidjan 01, Cote d'Ivoire, www.afdb.org; *Statistics Pocketbook 2008.*

Euromonitor International, Inc., 224 S. Michigan Avenue, Suite 1500, Chicago, IL 60604, (312) 922-1115, Fax: (312) 922-1157, www.euromonitor.com; *World Marketing Data and Statistics.*

M.E. Sharpe, 80 Business Park Drive, Armonk, NY 10504, (800) 541-6563, Fax: (914) 273-2106, www.mesharpe.com; *The Illustrated Book of World Rankings.*

Palgrave Macmillan Ltd., Houndmills, Basingstoke, Hampshire, RG21 6XS, England, (Telephone in U.S. (888) 330-8477), (Fax in U.S. (800) 672-2054), www.palgrave.com; *The Statesman's Yearbook 2008.*

UNICEF, 3 United Nations Plaza, New York, NY 10017, (800) 253-9646, Fax: (212) 887-7465, www.unicef.org; *The State of the World's Children 2008.*

United Nations Economic Commission for Africa (ECA), PO Box 3001, Addis Ababa, Ethiopia, (Telephone in U.S. (212) 963-4957), www.uneca.org; *African Statistical Yearbook 2006.*

United Nations Statistics Division, New York, NY 10017, (800) 253-9646, Fax: (212) 963-4116, http://unstats.un.org; *Human Development Report 2006* and *Statistical Yearbook.*

The World Bank, 1818 H Street, NW, Washington, DC 20433, (202) 473-1000, Fax: (202) 477-6391, www.worldbank.org; *Guinea-Bissau* and *World Development Report 2008.*

World Health Organization (WHO), Avenue Appia 20, 1211 Geneve 27, Switzerland, (Telephone in U.S. (212) 331-9081), www.who.int; The WHO Global Atlas of Infectious Diseases and *World Health Report 2006.*

GUINEA-BISSAU - RADIO BROADCASTING

Palgrave Macmillan Ltd., Houndmills, Basingstoke, Hampshire, RG21 6XS, England, (Telephone in U.S. (888) 330-8477), (Fax in U.S. (800) 672-2054), www.palgrave.com; *The Statesman's Yearbook 2008.*

GUINEA-BISSAU - RAILROADS

United Nations Economic Commission for Africa (ECA), PO Box 3001, Addis Ababa, Ethiopia, (Telephone in U.S. (212) 963-4957), www.uneca.org; *African Statistical Yearbook 2006.*

GUINEA-BISSAU - RELIGION

Central Intelligence Agency, Office of Public Affairs, Washington, DC 20505, (703) 482-0623, Fax: (703) 482-1739, www.cia.gov; *The World Factbook.*

M.E. Sharpe, 80 Business Park Drive, Armonk, NY 10504, (800) 541-6563, Fax: (914) 273-2106, www.mesharpe.com; *The Illustrated Book of World Rankings.*

Palgrave Macmillan Ltd., Houndmills, Basingstoke, Hampshire, RG21 6XS, England, (Telephone in U.S. (888) 330-8477), (Fax in U.S. (800) 672-2054), www.palgrave.com; *The Statesman's Yearbook 2008.*

GUINEA-BISSAU - RESERVES (ACCOUNTING)

African Development Bank Group, Rue Joseph Anoma, 01 BP 1387 Abidjan 01, Cote d'Ivoire, www.afdb.org; *Statistics Pocketbook 2008.*

The World Bank, 1818 H Street, NW, Washington, DC 20433, (202) 473-1000, Fax: (202) 477-6391, www.worldbank.org; *World Development Indicators (WDI) 2008.*

GUINEA-BISSAU - RETAIL TRADE

Euromonitor International, Inc., 224 S. Michigan Avenue, Suite 1500, Chicago, IL 60604, (312) 922-1115, Fax: (312) 922-1157, www.euromonitor.com; *World Marketing Data and Statistics.*

GUINEA-BISSAU - RICE PRODUCTION

See GUINEA-BISSAU - CROPS

GUINEA-BISSAU - ROADS

Central Intelligence Agency, Office of Public Affairs, Washington, DC 20505, (703) 482-0623, Fax: (703) 482-1739, www.cia.gov; *The World Factbook.*

Palgrave Macmillan Ltd., Houndmills, Basingstoke, Hampshire, RG21 6XS, England, (Telephone in U.S. (888) 330-8477), (Fax in U.S. (800) 672-2054), www.palgrave.com; *The Statesman's Yearbook 2008.*

United Nations Economic Commission for Africa (ECA), PO Box 3001, Addis Ababa, Ethiopia, (Telephone in U.S. (212) 963-4957), www.uneca.org; *African Statistical Yearbook 2006.*

United Nations Statistics Division, New York, NY 10017, (800) 253-9646, Fax: (212) 963-4116, http://unstats.un.org; *Survey of Economic and Social Conditions in Africa 2005.*

GUINEA-BISSAU - RUBBER INDUSTRY AND TRADE

International Rubber Study Group (IRSG), 1st Floor, Heron House, 109/115 Wembley Hill Road, Wembley, Middlesex HA9 8DA, United Kingdom, www.rubberstudy.com; *Rubber Statistical Bulletin; Summary of World Rubber Statistics 2005; World Rubber Statistics Handbook (Volume 6, 1975-2001);* and *World Rubber Statistics Historic Handbook.*

M.E. Sharpe, 80 Business Park Drive, Armonk, NY 10504, (800) 541-6563, Fax: (914) 273-2106, www.mesharpe.com; *The Illustrated Book of World Rankings.*

GUINEA-BISSAU - SHEEP

See GUINEA-BISSAU - LIVESTOCK

GUINEA-BISSAU - SHIPPING

Palgrave Macmillan Ltd., Houndmills, Basingstoke, Hampshire, RG21 6XS, England, (Telephone in U.S. (888) 330-8477), (Fax in U.S. (800) 672-2054), www.palgrave.com; *The Statesman's Yearbook 2008.*

Taylor and Francis Group, An Informa Business, 2 Park Square, Milton Park, Abingdon, Oxford OX14 4RN, United Kingdom, (Dial from U.S. (212) 216-7800), (Fax from U.S. (212) 564-7854), www.tandf.co.uk; *The Europa World Year Book.*

United Nations Economic Commission for Africa (ECA), PO Box 3001, Addis Ababa, Ethiopia, (Telephone in U.S. (212) 963-4957), www.uneca.org; *African Statistical Yearbook 2006.*

United Nations Statistics Division, New York, NY 10017, (800) 253-9646, Fax: (212) 963-4116, http://unstats.un.org; *Statistical Yearbook.*

GUINEA-BISSAU - SILVER PRODUCTION

See GUINEA-BISSAU - MINERAL INDUSTRIES

GUINEA-BISSAU - SOCIAL ECOLOGY

M.E. Sharpe, 80 Business Park Drive, Armonk, NY 10504, (800) 541-6563, Fax: (914) 273-2106, www.mesharpe.com; *The Illustrated Book of World Rankings.*

United Nations Statistics Division, New York, NY 10017, (800) 253-9646, Fax: (212) 963-4116, http://unstats.un.org; *World Statistics Pocketbook.*

GUINEA-BISSAU - SOCIAL SECURITY

United Nations Statistics Division, New York, NY 10017, (800) 253-9646, Fax: (212) 963-4116, http://unstats.un.org; *National Accounts Statistics: Compendium of Income Distribution Statistics.*

GUINEA-BISSAU - STEEL PRODUCTION

See GUINEA-BISSAU - MINERAL INDUSTRIES

GUINEA-BISSAU - SUGAR PRODUCTION

See GUINEA-BISSAU - CROPS

GUINEA-BISSAU - TAXATION

Taylor and Francis Group, An Informa Business, 2 Park Square, Milton Park, Abingdon, Oxford OX14 4RN, United Kingdom, (Dial from U.S. (212) 216-7800), (Fax from U.S. (212) 564-7854), www.tandf.co.uk; *The Europa World Year Book.*

The World Bank, 1818 H Street, NW, Washington, DC 20433, (202) 473-1000, Fax: (202) 477-6391, www.worldbank.org; *World Development Indicators (WDI) 2008.*

GUINEA-BISSAU - TELEPHONE

International Telecommunication Union (ITU), Place des Nations, 1211 Geneva 20, Switzerland, www.itu.int; World Telecommunication Indicators Database.

Palgrave Macmillan Ltd., Houndmills, Basingstoke, Hampshire, RG21 6XS, England, (Telephone in U.S. (888) 330-8477), (Fax in U.S. (800) 672-2054), www.palgrave.com; *The Statesman's Yearbook 2008.*

Taylor and Francis Group, An Informa Business, 2 Park Square, Milton Park, Abingdon, Oxford OX14 4RN, United Kingdom, (Dial from U.S. (212) 216-7800), (Fax from U.S. (212) 564-7854), www.tandf.co.uk; *The Europa World Year Book.*

United Nations Statistics Division, New York, NY 10017, (800) 253-9646, Fax: (212) 963-4116, http://unstats.un.org; *Statistical Yearbook* and *World Statistics Pocketbook.*

GUINEA-BISSAU - TEXTILE INDUSTRY

M.E. Sharpe, 80 Business Park Drive, Armonk, NY 10504, (800) 541-6563, Fax: (914) 273-2106, www.mesharpe.com; *The Illustrated Book of World Rankings.*

United Nations Conference on Trade and Development (UNCTAD), DC2-1120, United Nations, New York, NY 10017, (212) 963-0027, www.unctad.org; *UNCTAD Commodity Yearbook.*

GUINEA-BISSAU - TOBACCO INDUSTRY

Foreign Agricultural Service (FAS), U.S. Department of Agriculture (USDA), 1400 Independence Avenue, SW, Washington, DC 20250, (202) 720-3935, www.fas.usda.gov; *Tobacco: World Markets and Trade.*

M.E. Sharpe, 80 Business Park Drive, Armonk, NY 10504, (800) 541-6563, Fax: (914) 273-2106, www.mesharpe.com; *The Illustrated Book of World Rankings.*

GUINEA-BISSAU - TOURISM

Euromonitor International, Inc., 224 S. Michigan Avenue, Suite 1500, Chicago, IL 60604, (312) 922-1115, Fax: (312) 922-1157, www.euromonitor.com; *The World Economic Factbook 2008* and *World Marketing Data and Statistics.*

M.E. Sharpe, 80 Business Park Drive, Armonk, NY 10504, (800) 541-6563, Fax: (914) 273-2106, www.mesharpe.com; *The Illustrated Book of World Rankings.*

United Nations Economic Commission for Africa (ECA), PO Box 3001, Addis Ababa, Ethiopia, (Telephone in U.S. (212) 963-4957), www.uneca.org; *African Statistical Yearbook 2006.*

The World Bank, 1818 H Street, NW, Washington, DC 20433, (202) 473-1000, Fax: (202) 477-6391, www.worldbank.org; *Guinea-Bissau.*

GUINEA-BISSAU - TRADE

See GUINEA-BISSAU - INTERNATIONAL TRADE

GUINEA-BISSAU - TRANSPORTATION

Central Intelligence Agency, Office of Public Affairs, Washington, DC 20505, (703) 482-0623, Fax: (703) 482-1739, www.cia.gov; *The World Factbook.*

Euromonitor International, Inc., 224 S. Michigan Avenue, Suite 1500, Chicago, IL 60604, (312) 922-1115, Fax: (312) 922-1157, www.euromonitor.com; *International Marketing Data and Statistics 2008* and *World Marketing Data and Statistics.*

M.E. Sharpe, 80 Business Park Drive, Armonk, NY 10504, (800) 541-6563, Fax: (914) 273-2106, www.mesharpe.com; *The Illustrated Book of World Rankings.*

Palgrave Macmillan Ltd., Houndmills, Basingstoke, Hampshire, RG21 6XS, England, (Telephone in U.S. (888) 330-8477), (Fax in U.S. (800) 672-2054), www.palgrave.com; *The Statesman's Yearbook 2008.*

Taylor and Francis Group, An Informa Business, 2 Park Square, Milton Park, Abingdon, Oxford OX14 4RN, United Kingdom, (Dial from U.S. (212) 216-7800), (Fax from U.S. (212) 564-7854), www.tandf.co.uk; *The Europa World Year Book.*

United Nations Economic Commission for Africa (ECA), PO Box 3001, Addis Ababa, Ethiopia, (Telephone in U.S. (212) 963-4957), www.uneca.org; *African Statistical Yearbook 2006.*

United Nations Statistics Division, New York, NY 10017, (800) 253-9646, Fax: (212) 963-4116, http://unstats.un.org; *Human Development Report 2006.*

The World Bank, 1818 H Street, NW, Washington, DC 20433, (202) 473-1000, Fax: (202) 477-6391, www.worldbank.org; *Africa Live Database (LDB)* and *Guinea-Bissau.*

GUINEA-BISSAU - UNEMPLOYMENT

Central Intelligence Agency, Office of Public Affairs, Washington, DC 20505, (703) 482-0623, Fax: (703) 482-1739, www.cia.gov; *The World Factbook.*

GUINEA-BISSAU - VITAL STATISTICS

Palgrave Macmillan Ltd., Houndmills, Basingstoke, Hampshire, RG21 6XS, England, (Telephone in U.S. (888) 330-8477), (Fax in U.S. (800) 672-2054), www.palgrave.com; *The Statesman's Yearbook 2008.*

United Nations Statistics Division, New York, NY 10017, (800) 253-9646, Fax: (212) 963-4116, http://unstats.un.org; *Statistical Yearbook.*

World Health Organization (WHO), Avenue Appia 20, 1211 Geneve 27, Switzerland, (Telephone in U.S. (212) 331-9081), www.who.int; *World Health Report 2006.*

GUINEA-BISSAU - WAGES

The World Bank, 1818 H Street, NW, Washington, DC 20433, (202) 473-1000, Fax: (202) 477-6391, www.worldbank.org; *Guinea-Bissau.*

GUINEA-BISSAU - WEATHER

See GUINEA-BISSAU - CLIMATE

GUINEA-BISSAU - WHEAT PRODUCTION

See GUINEA-BISSAU - CROPS

GUINEA-BISSAU - WINE PRODUCTION

See GUINEA-BISSAU - BEVERAGE INDUSTRY

GUINEA-BISSAU - WOOL PRODUCTION

See GUINEA-BISSAU - TEXTILE INDUSTRY

GUNS

See FIREARMS

GUYANA - NATIONAL STATISTICAL OFFICE

Government Information Agency (GINA), Area B Homestretch Avenue, D'Urban Backlands, Georgetown, Guyana, www.gina.gov.gy; National Data Center.

GUYANA - PRIMARY STATISTICS SOURCES

Bank of Guyana, PO Box 1003, 1 Church Street Avenue of the Republic, Georgetown, Guyana, www.bankofguyana.org.gy; *Bank of Guyana Statistical Tables.*

Government Information Agency (GINA), Area B Homestretch Avenue, D'Urban Backlands, Georgetown, Guyana, www.gina.gov.gy; *Year In Review 2003.*

GUYANA - AGRICULTURAL MACHINERY

United Nations Statistics Division, New York, NY 10017, (800) 253-9646, Fax: (212) 963-4116, http://unstats.un.org; *Statistical Yearbook.*

GUYANA - AGRICULTURE

Economist Intelligence Unit, 111 West 57th Street, New York, NY 10019, (212) 554-0600, Fax: (212) 586-1181, www.eiu.com; *Guyana Country Report.*

Euromonitor International, Inc., 224 S. Michigan Avenue, Suite 1500, Chicago, IL 60604, (312) 922-1115, Fax: (312) 922-1157, www.euromonitor.com; *International Marketing Data and Statistics 2008* and *World Marketing Data and Statistics.*

Inter-American Development Bank (IDB), 1300 New York Avenue, NW, Washington, DC 20577, (202) 623-1000, Fax: (202) 623-3096, www.iadb.org; *The Politics of Policies: Economic and Social Progress in Latin America - 2006 Report.*

M.E. Sharpe, 80 Business Park Drive, Armonk, NY 10504, (800) 541-6563, Fax: (914) 273-2106, www.mesharpe.com; *The Illustrated Book of World Rankings.*

Palgrave Macmillan Ltd., Houndmills, Basingstoke, Hampshire, RG21 6XS, England, (Telephone in U.S. (888) 330-8477), (Fax in U.S. (800) 672-2054), www.palgrave.com; *The Statesman's Yearbook 2008.*

Taylor and Francis Group, An Informa Business, 2 Park Square, Milton Park, Abingdon, Oxford OX14 4RN, United Kingdom, (Dial from U.S. (212) 216-7800), (Fax from U.S. (212) 564-7854), www.tandf.co.uk; *The Europa World Year Book.*

United Nations Conference on Trade and Development (UNCTAD), DC2-1120, United Nations, New York, NY 10017, (212) 963-0027, www.unctad.org; *UNCTAD Commodity Yearbook.*

United Nations Food and Agricultural Organization (FAO), Viale delle Terme di Caracalla, 00100 Rome, Italy, (Dial from U.S. (202) 653-2400), (Fax from U.S. (202) 653 5760), www.fao.org; AQUASTAT; *FAO Production Yearbook 2002; FAO Trade Yearbook;* and *The State of Food and Agriculture (SOFA) 2006.*

United Nations Statistics Division, New York, NY 10017, (800) 253-9646, Fax: (212) 963-4116, http://unstats.un.org; *Statistical Yearbook* and *Statistical Yearbook for Latin America and the Caribbean 2004.*

The World Bank, 1818 H Street, NW, Washington, DC 20433, (202) 473-1000, Fax: (202) 477-6391, www.worldbank.org; *Guyana* and *World Development Indicators (WDI) 2008.*

GUYANA - AIRLINES

M.E. Sharpe, 80 Business Park Drive, Armonk, NY 10504, (800) 541-6563, Fax: (914) 273-2106, www.mesharpe.com; *The Illustrated Book of World Rankings.*

Palgrave Macmillan Ltd., Houndmills, Basingstoke, Hampshire, RG21 6XS, England, (Telephone in U.S. (888) 330-8477), (Fax in U.S. (800) 672-2054), www.palgrave.com; *The Statesman's Yearbook 2008.*

Taylor and Francis Group, An Informa Business, 2 Park Square, Milton Park, Abingdon, Oxford OX14 4RN, United Kingdom, (Dial from U.S. (212) 216-7800), (Fax from U.S. (212) 564-7854), www.tandf.co.uk; *The Europa World Year Book.*

GUYANA - AIRPORTS

Central Intelligence Agency, Office of Public Affairs, Washington, DC 20505, (703) 482-0623, Fax: (703) 482-1739, www.cia.gov; *The World Factbook.*

GUYANA - ALUMINUM PRODUCTION

See GUYANA - MINERAL INDUSTRIES

GUYANA - ARMED FORCES

Central Intelligence Agency, Office of Public Affairs, Washington, DC 20505, (703) 482-0623, Fax: (703) 482-1739, www.cia.gov; *The World Factbook.*

Euromonitor International, Inc., 224 S. Michigan Avenue, Suite 1500, Chicago, IL 60604, (312) 922-1115, Fax: (312) 922-1157, www.euromonitor.com; *World Marketing Data and Statistics.*

International Institute for Strategic Studies (IISS), Arundel House, 13-15 Arundel Street, Temple Place, London WC2R 3DX, England, www.iiss.org; *The Military Balance 2007.*

Palgrave Macmillan Ltd., Houndmills, Basingstoke, Hampshire, RG21 6XS, England, (Telephone in U.S. (888) 330-8477), (Fax in U.S. (800) 672-2054), www.palgrave.com; *The Statesman's Yearbook 2008.*

U.S. Department of State (DOS), 2201 C Street NW, Washington, DC 20520, (202) 647-4000, www.state.gov; *World Military Expenditures and Arms Transfers (WMEAT).*

United Nations Statistics Division, New York, NY 10017, (800) 253-9646, Fax: (212) 963-4116, http://unstats.un.org; *Human Development Report 2006.*

GUYANA - BALANCE OF PAYMENTS

Inter-American Development Bank (IDB), 1300 New York Avenue, NW, Washington, DC 20577, (202) 623-1000, Fax: (202) 623-3096, www.iadb.org; *The Politics of Policies: Economic and Social Progress in Latin America - 2006 Report.*

International Monetary Fund (IMF), 700 Nineteenth Street, NW, Washington, DC 20431, (202) 623-7000, Fax: (202) 623-4661, www.imf.org; *Balance of Payments Statistics Newsletter; Balance of Payments Statistics Yearbook 2007;* and *International Financial Statistics Yearbook 2007.*

Taylor and Francis Group, An Informa Business, 2 Park Square, Milton Park, Abingdon, Oxford OX14 4RN, United Kingdom, (Dial from U.S. (212) 216-7800), (Fax from U.S. (212) 564-7854), www.tandf.co.uk; *The Europa World Year Book.*

United Nations Conference on Trade and Development (UNCTAD), DC2-1120, United Nations, New York, NY 10017, (212) 963-0027, www.unctad.org; *Handbook of Statistics 2005.*

United Nations Statistics Division, New York, NY 10017, (800) 253-9646, Fax: (212) 963-4116, http://unstats.un.org; *Economic Survey of Latin America and the Caribbean 2004-2005* and *Statistical Yearbook for Latin America and the Caribbean 2004.*

The World Bank, 1818 H Street, NW, Washington, DC 20433, (202) 473-1000, Fax: (202) 477-6391, www.worldbank.org; *Guyana* and *World Development Indicators (WDI) 2008.*

GUYANA - BANKS AND BANKING

Euromonitor International, Inc., 224 S. Michigan Avenue, Suite 1500, Chicago, IL 60604, (312) 922-1115, Fax: (312) 922-1157, www.euromonitor.com; *World Marketing Data and Statistics.*

Inter-American Development Bank (IDB), 1300 New York Avenue, NW, Washington, DC 20577, (202) 623-1000, Fax: (202) 623-3096, www.iadb.org; *The Politics of Policies: Economic and Social Progress in Latin America - 2006 Report.*

International Monetary Fund (IMF), 700 Nineteenth Street, NW, Washington, DC 20431, (202) 623-7000, Fax: (202) 623-4661, www.imf.org; *Government Finance Statistics Yearbook (2008 Edition)* and *International Financial Statistics Yearbook 2007.*

M.E. Sharpe, 80 Business Park Drive, Armonk, NY 10504, (800) 541-6563, Fax: (914) 273-2106, www.mesharpe.com; *The Illustrated Book of World Rankings.*

Palgrave Macmillan Ltd., Houndmills, Basingstoke, Hampshire, RG21 6XS, England, (Telephone in U.S. (888) 330-8477), (Fax in U.S. (800) 672-2054), www.palgrave.com; *The Statesman's Yearbook 2008.*

Taylor and Francis Group, An Informa Business, 2 Park Square, Milton Park, Abingdon, Oxford OX14 4RN, United Kingdom, (Dial from U.S. (212) 216-7800), (Fax from U.S. (212) 564-7854), www.tandf.co.uk; *The Europa World Year Book.*

United Nations Statistics Division, New York, NY 10017, (800) 253-9646, Fax: (212) 963-4116, http://

unstats.un.org; *Statistical Yearbook for Latin America and the Caribbean 2004.*

GUYANA - BARLEY PRODUCTION

See GUYANA - CROPS

GUYANA - BEVERAGE INDUSTRY

M.E. Sharpe, 80 Business Park Drive, Armonk, NY 10504, (800) 541-6563, Fax: (914) 273-2106, www.mesharpe.com; *The Illustrated Book of World Rankings.*

United Nations Statistics Division, New York, NY 10017, (800) 253-9646, Fax: (212) 963-4116, http://unstats.un.org; *Statistical Yearbook.*

GUYANA - BONDS

Inter-American Development Bank (IDB), 1300 New York Avenue, NW, Washington, DC 20577, (202) 623-1000, Fax: (202) 623-3096, www.iadb.org; *The Politics of Policies: Economic and Social Progress in Latin America - 2006 Report.*

International Monetary Fund (IMF), 700 Nineteenth Street, NW, Washington, DC 20431, (202) 623-7000, Fax: (202) 623-4661, www.imf.org; *Government Finance Statistics Yearbook (2008 Edition).*

GUYANA - BROADCASTING

Central Intelligence Agency, Office of Public Affairs, Washington, DC 20505, (703) 482-0623, Fax: (703) 482-1739, www.cia.gov; *The World Factbook.*

Euromonitor International, Inc., 224 S. Michigan Avenue, Suite 1500, Chicago, IL 60604, (312) 922-1115, Fax: (312) 922-1157, www.euromonitor.com; *World Marketing Data and Statistics.*

M.E. Sharpe, 80 Business Park Drive, Armonk, NY 10504, (800) 541-6563, Fax: (914) 273-2106, www.mesharpe.com; *The Illustrated Book of World Rankings.*

Palgrave Macmillan Ltd., Houndmills, Basingstoke, Hampshire, RG21 6XS, England, (Telephone in U.S. (888) 330-8477), (Fax in U.S. (800) 672-2054), www.palgrave.com; *The Statesman's Yearbook 2008.*

WRTH Publications Limited, PO Box 290, Oxford OX2 7FT, UK, www.wrth.com; *World Radio TV Handbook 2007.*

GUYANA - BUDGET

Central Intelligence Agency, Office of Public Affairs, Washington, DC 20505, (703) 482-0623, Fax: (703) 482-1739, www.cia.gov; *The World Factbook.*

GUYANA - BUSINESS

Inter-American Development Bank (IDB), 1300 New York Avenue, NW, Washington, DC 20577, (202) 623-1000, Fax: (202) 623-3096, www.iadb.org; *The Politics of Policies: Economic and Social Progress in Latin America - 2006 Report.*

GUYANA - CAPITAL INVESTMENTS

Inter-American Development Bank (IDB), 1300 New York Avenue, NW, Washington, DC 20577, (202) 623-1000, Fax: (202) 623-3096, www.iadb.org; *The Politics of Policies: Economic and Social Progress in Latin America - 2006 Report.*

GUYANA - CAPITAL LEVY

Inter-American Development Bank (IDB), 1300 New York Avenue, NW, Washington, DC 20577, (202) 623-1000, Fax: (202) 623-3096, www.iadb.org; *The Politics of Policies: Economic and Social Progress in Latin America - 2006 Report.*

International Monetary Fund (IMF), 700 Nineteenth Street, NW, Washington, DC 20431, (202) 623-7000, Fax: (202) 623-4661, www.imf.org; *Government Finance Statistics Yearbook (2008 Edition).*

GUYANA - CATTLE

See GUYANA - LIVESTOCK

GUYANA - CHICKENS

See GUYANA - LIVESTOCK

GUYANA - CHILDBIRTH - STATISTICS

Central Intelligence Agency, Office of Public Affairs, Washington, DC 20505, (703) 482-0623, Fax: (703) 482-1739, www.cia.gov; *The World Factbook.*

Euromonitor International, Inc., 224 S. Michigan Avenue, Suite 1500, Chicago, IL 60604, (312) 922-1115, Fax: (312) 922-1157, www.euromonitor.com; *International Marketing Data and Statistics 2008* and *The World Economic Factbook 2008.*

M.E. Sharpe, 80 Business Park Drive, Armonk, NY 10504, (800) 541-6563, Fax: (914) 273-2106, www.mesharpe.com; *The Illustrated Book of World Rankings.*

Palgrave Macmillan Ltd., Houndmills, Basingstoke, Hampshire, RG21 6XS, England, (Telephone in U.S. (888) 330-8477), (Fax in U.S. (800) 672-2054), www.palgrave.com; *The Statesman's Yearbook 2008.*

Taylor and Francis Group, An Informa Business, 2 Park Square, Milton Park, Abingdon, Oxford OX14 4RN, United Kingdom, (Dial from U.S. (212) 216-7800), (Fax from U.S. (212) 564-7854), www.tandf.co.uk; *The Europa World Year Book.*

United Nations Statistics Division, New York, NY 10017, (800) 253-9646, Fax: (212) 963-4116, http://unstats.un.org; *Demographic Yearbook; Statistical Yearbook;* and *Statistical Yearbook for Latin America and the Caribbean 2004.*

The World Bank, 1818 H Street, NW, Washington, DC 20433, (202) 473-1000, Fax: (202) 477-6391, www.worldbank.org; *World Development Indicators (WDI) 2008.*

World Health Organization (WHO), Avenue Appia 20, 1211 Geneve 27, Switzerland, (Telephone in U.S. (212) 331-9081), www.who.int; *World Health Report 2006.*

GUYANA - CLIMATE

M.E. Sharpe, 80 Business Park Drive, Armonk, NY 10504, (800) 541-6563, Fax: (914) 273-2106, www.mesharpe.com; *The Illustrated Book of World Rankings.*

Palgrave Macmillan Ltd., Houndmills, Basingstoke, Hampshire, RG21 6XS, England, (Telephone in U.S. (888) 330-8477), (Fax in U.S. (800) 672-2054), www.palgrave.com; *The Statesman's Yearbook 2008.*

GUYANA - COAL PRODUCTION

See GUYANA - MINERAL INDUSTRIES

GUYANA - COFFEE

See GUYANA - CROPS

GUYANA - COMMERCE

Palgrave Macmillan Ltd., Houndmills, Basingstoke, Hampshire, RG21 6XS, England, (Telephone in U.S. (888) 330-8477), (Fax in U.S. (800) 672-2054), www.palgrave.com; *The Statesman's Yearbook 2008.*

GUYANA - COMMODITY EXCHANGES

Commodity Research Bureau, 330 South Wells Street, Suite 612, Chicago, IL 60606-7110, (800) 621-5271, Fax: (312) 939-4135, www.crbtrader.com; *2006 CRB Commodity Yearbook and CD.*

International Monetary Fund (IMF), 700 Nineteenth Street, NW, Washington, DC 20431, (202) 623-7000, Fax: (202) 623-4661, www.imf.org; *IMF Primary Commodity Prices.*

United Nations Food and Agricultural Organization (FAO), Viale delle Terme di Caracalla, 00100 Rome, Italy, (Dial from U.S. (202) 653-2400), (Fax from U.S. (202) 653 5760), www.fao.org; *The State of Food and Agriculture (SOFA) 2006.*

GUYANA - CONSTRUCTION INDUSTRY

Inter-American Development Bank (IDB), 1300 New York Avenue, NW, Washington, DC 20577, (202) 623-1000, Fax: (202) 623-3096, www.iadb.org; *The Politics of Policies: Economic and Social Progress in Latin America - 2006 Report.*

M.E. Sharpe, 80 Business Park Drive, Armonk, NY 10504, (800) 541-6563, Fax: (914) 273-2106, www.mesharpe.com; *The Illustrated Book of World Rankings.*

United Nations Statistics Division, New York, NY 10017, (800) 253-9646, Fax: (212) 963-4116, http://unstats.un.org; *Statistical Yearbook.*

GUYANA - CONSUMER PRICE INDEXES

Taylor and Francis Group, An Informa Business, 2 Park Square, Milton Park, Abingdon, Oxford OX14 4RN, United Kingdom, (Dial from U.S. (212) 216-7800), (Fax from U.S. (212) 564-7854), www.tandf.co.uk; *The Europa World Year Book.*

United Nations Statistics Division, New York, NY 10017, (800) 253-9646, Fax: (212) 963-4116, http://unstats.un.org; *Statistical Yearbook.*

The World Bank, 1818 H Street, NW, Washington, DC 20433, (202) 473-1000, Fax: (202) 477-6391, www.worldbank.org; *Guyana.*

GUYANA - CONSUMPTION (ECONOMICS)

Inter-American Development Bank (IDB), 1300 New York Avenue, NW, Washington, DC 20577, (202) 623-1000, Fax: (202) 623-3096, www.iadb.org; *The Politics of Policies: Economic and Social Progress in Latin America - 2006 Report.*

United Nations Statistics Division, New York, NY 10017, (800) 253-9646, Fax: (212) 963-4116, http://unstats.un.org; *Statistical Yearbook for Latin America and the Caribbean 2004.*

GUYANA - COPPER INDUSTRY AND TRADE

See GUYANA - MINERAL INDUSTRIES

GUYANA - CORN INDUSTRY

See GUYANA - CROPS

GUYANA - COTTON

See GUYANA - CROPS

GUYANA - CRIME

Yale University Press, PO Box 209040, New Haven, CT 06520-9040, (203) 432-0960, Fax: (203) 432-0948, http://yalepress.yale.edu/yupbooks; *Violence and Crime in Cross-National Perspective.*

GUYANA - CROPS

M.E. Sharpe, 80 Business Park Drive, Armonk, NY 10504, (800) 541-6563, Fax: (914) 273-2106, www.mesharpe.com; *The Illustrated Book of World Rankings.*

Palgrave Macmillan Ltd., Houndmills, Basingstoke, Hampshire, RG21 6XS, England, (Telephone in U.S. (888) 330-8477), (Fax in U.S. (800) 672-2054), www.palgrave.com; *The Statesman's Yearbook 2008.*

Taylor and Francis Group, An Informa Business, 2 Park Square, Milton Park, Abingdon, Oxford OX14 4RN, United Kingdom, (Dial from U.S. (212) 216-7800), (Fax from U.S. (212) 564-7854), www.tandf.co.uk; *The Europa World Year Book.*

United Nations Conference on Trade and Development (UNCTAD), DC2-1120, United Nations, New York, NY 10017, (212) 963-0027, www.unctad.org; *UNCTAD Commodity Yearbook.*

United Nations Food and Agricultural Organization (FAO), Viale delle Terme di Caracalla, 00100 Rome, Italy, (Dial from U.S. (202) 653-2400), (Fax from U.S. (202) 653 5760), www.fao.org; *FAO Production Yearbook 2002* and *The State of Food and Agriculture (SOFA) 2006.*

United Nations Statistics Division, New York, NY 10017, (800) 253-9646, Fax: (212) 963-4116, http://unstats.un.org; *Statistical Yearbook.*

GUYANA - CUSTOMS ADMINISTRATION

Inter-American Development Bank (IDB), 1300 New York Avenue, NW, Washington, DC 20577, (202) 623-1000, Fax: (202) 623-3096, www.iadb.org; *The*

Politics of Policies: Economic and Social Progress in Latin America - 2006 Report.

International Monetary Fund (IMF), 700 Nineteenth Street, NW, Washington, DC 20431, (202) 623-7000, Fax: (202) 623-4661, www.imf.org; *International Financial Statistics Yearbook 2007.*

Palgrave Macmillan Ltd., Houndmills, Basingstoke, Hampshire, RG21 6XS, England, (Telephone in U.S. (888) 330-8477), (Fax in U.S. (800) 672-2054), www.palgrave.com; *The Statesman's Yearbook 2008.*

GUYANA - DAIRY PROCESSING

M.E. Sharpe, 80 Business Park Drive, Armonk, NY 10504, (800) 541-6563, Fax: (914) 273-2106, www.mesharpe.com; *The Illustrated Book of World Rankings.*

Palgrave Macmillan Ltd., Houndmills, Basingstoke, Hampshire, RG21 6XS, England, (Telephone in U.S. (888) 330-8477), (Fax in U.S. (800) 672-2054), www.palgrave.com; *The Statesman's Yearbook 2008.*

Taylor and Francis Group, An Informa Business, 2 Park Square, Milton Park, Abingdon, Oxford OX14 4RN, United Kingdom, (Dial from U.S. (212) 216-7800), (Fax from U.S. (212) 564-7854), www.tandf.co.uk; *The Europa World Year Book.*

United Nations Food and Agricultural Organization (FAO), Viale delle Terme di Caracalla, 00100 Rome, Italy, (Dial from U.S. (202) 653-2400), (Fax from U.S. (202) 653 5760), www.fao.org; *The State of Food and Agriculture (SOFA) 2006.*

United Nations Statistics Division, New York, NY 10017, (800) 253-9646, Fax: (212) 963-4116, http://unstats.un.org; *Statistical Yearbook.*

GUYANA - DEATH RATES

See GUYANA - MORTALITY

GUYANA - DEBTS, EXTERNAL

Inter-American Development Bank (IDB), 1300 New York Avenue, NW, Washington, DC 20577, (202) 623-1000, Fax: (202) 623-3096, www.iadb.org; *The Politics of Policies: Economic and Social Progress in Latin America - 2006 Report.*

International Monetary Fund (IMF), 700 Nineteenth Street, NW, Washington, DC 20431, (202) 623-7000, Fax: (202) 623-4661, www.imf.org; *Government Finance Statistics Yearbook (2008 Edition).*

United Nations Statistics Division, New York, NY 10017, (800) 253-9646, Fax: (212) 963-4116, http://unstats.un.org; *Economic Survey of Latin America and the Caribbean 2004-2005.*

The World Bank, 1818 H Street, NW, Washington, DC 20433, (202) 473-1000, Fax: (202) 477-6391, www.worldbank.org; *Global Development Finance 2007* and *World Development Indicators (WDI) 2008.*

GUYANA - DEFENSE EXPENDITURES

See GUYANA - ARMED FORCES

GUYANA - DEMOGRAPHY

Euromonitor International, Inc., 224 S. Michigan Avenue, Suite 1500, Chicago, IL 60604, (312) 922-1115, Fax: (312) 922-1157, www.euromonitor.com; *International Marketing Data and Statistics 2008; The World Economic Factbook 2008;* and *World Marketing Data and Statistics.*

M.E. Sharpe, 80 Business Park Drive, Armonk, NY 10504, (800) 541-6563, Fax: (914) 273-2106, www.mesharpe.com; *The Illustrated Book of World Rankings.*

United Nations Statistics Division, New York, NY 10017, (800) 253-9646, Fax: (212) 963-4116, http://unstats.un.org; *Human Development Report 2006.*

The World Bank, 1818 H Street, NW, Washington, DC 20433, (202) 473-1000, Fax: (202) 477-6391, www.worldbank.org; *Guyana.*

GUYANA - DIAMONDS

See GUYANA - MINERAL INDUSTRIES

GUYANA - DISCOUNT

Inter-American Development Bank (IDB), 1300 New York Avenue, NW, Washington, DC 20577, (202) 623-1000, Fax: (202) 623-3096, www.iadb.org; *The Politics of Policies: Economic and Social Progress in Latin America - 2006 Report.*

GUYANA - DISPOSABLE INCOME

Inter-American Development Bank (IDB), 1300 New York Avenue, NW, Washington, DC 20577, (202) 623-1000, Fax: (202) 623-3096, www.iadb.org; *The Politics of Policies: Economic and Social Progress in Latin America - 2006 Report.*

M.E. Sharpe, 80 Business Park Drive, Armonk, NY 10504, (800) 541-6563, Fax: (914) 273-2106, www.mesharpe.com; *The Illustrated Book of World Rankings.*

United Nations Statistics Division, New York, NY 10017, (800) 253-9646, Fax: (212) 963-4116, http://unstats.un.org; *National Accounts Statistics: Compendium of Income Distribution Statistics; Statistical Yearbook;* and *Statistical Yearbook for Latin America and the Caribbean 2004.*

GUYANA - DIVORCE

M.E. Sharpe, 80 Business Park Drive, Armonk, NY 10504, (800) 541-6563, Fax: (914) 273-2106, www.mesharpe.com; *The Illustrated Book of World Rankings.*

United Nations Statistics Division, New York, NY 10017, (800) 253-9646, Fax: (212) 963-4116, http://unstats.un.org; *Demographic Yearbook* and *Statistical Yearbook.*

GUYANA - ECONOMIC ASSISTANCE

Inter-American Development Bank (IDB), 1300 New York Avenue, NW, Washington, DC 20577, (202) 623-1000, Fax: (202) 623-3096, www.iadb.org; *The Politics of Policies: Economic and Social Progress in Latin America - 2006 Report.*

United Nations Statistics Division, New York, NY 10017, (800) 253-9646, Fax: (212) 963-4116, http://unstats.un.org; *Statistical Yearbook.*

GUYANA - ECONOMIC CONDITIONS

Center for International Business Education Research (CIBER), Columbia Business School and School of International and Public Affairs, Uris Hall, Room 212, 3022 Broadway, New York, NY 10027-6902, Mr. Joshua Safier, (212) 854-4750, Fax: (212) 222-9821, www.columbia.edu/cu/ciber/; Datastream International.

Central Intelligence Agency, Office of Public Affairs, Washington, DC 20505, (703) 482-0623, Fax: (703) 482-1739, www.cia.gov; *The World Factbook.*

DSI Data Service Information, Xantener Strasse 51a, D-47495 Rheinberg, Germany, www.dsidata.com; *Campus Solution.*

Dun and Bradstreet (DB) Corporation, 103 JFK Parkway, Short Hills, NJ 07078, (973) 921-5500, www.dnb.com; *Country Report.*

Economist Intelligence Unit, 111 West 57th Street, New York, NY 10019, (212) 554-0600, Fax: (212) 586-1181, www.eiu.com; *Guyana Country Report.*

Euromonitor International, Inc., 224 S. Michigan Avenue, Suite 1500, Chicago, IL 60604, (312) 922-1115, Fax: (312) 922-1157, www.euromonitor.com; *International Marketing Data and Statistics 2008; The World Economic Factbook 2008;* and *World Marketing Data and Statistics.*

Inter-American Development Bank (IDB), 1300 New York Avenue, NW, Washington, DC 20577, (202) 623-1000, Fax: (202) 623-3096, www.iadb.org; *The Politics of Policies: Economic and Social Progress in Latin America - 2006 Report.*

International Monetary Fund (IMF), 700 Nineteenth Street, NW, Washington, DC 20431, (202) 623-7000, Fax: (202) 623-4661, www.imf.org; *World Economic Outlook Reports.*

M.E. Sharpe, 80 Business Park Drive, Armonk, NY 10504, (800) 541-6563, Fax: (914) 273-2106, www.mesharpe.com; *The Illustrated Book of World Rankings.*

Palgrave Macmillan Ltd., Houndmills, Basingstoke, Hampshire, RG21 6XS, England, (Telephone in U.S. (888) 330-8477), (Fax in U.S. (800) 672-2054), www.palgrave.com; *The Statesman's Yearbook 2008.*

Taylor and Francis Group, An Informa Business, 2 Park Square, Milton Park, Abingdon, Oxford OX14 4RN, United Kingdom, (Dial from U.S. (212) 216-7800), (Fax from U.S. (212) 564-7854), www.tandf.co.uk; *The Europa World Year Book.*

UCLA Latin American Institute, 10343 Bunche Hall, Box 951447, Los Angeles, CA 90095-1447, (310) 825-4571, Fax: (310) 206-6859, www.international.ucla.edu/lac; *Statistical Abstract of Latin America.*

United Nations Statistics Division, New York, NY 10017, (800) 253-9646, Fax: (212) 963-4116, http://unstats.un.org; *Economic Survey of Latin America and the Caribbean 2004-2005* and *World Statistics Pocketbook.*

The World Bank, 1818 H Street, NW, Washington, DC 20433, (202) 473-1000, Fax: (202) 477-6391, www.worldbank.org; *Global Economic Monitor (GEM); Global Economic Prospects 2008; Guyana;* and *The World Bank Atlas 2003-2004.*

GUYANA - ECONOMICS - SOCIOLOGICAL ASPECTS

Inter-American Development Bank (IDB), 1300 New York Avenue, NW, Washington, DC 20577, (202) 623-1000, Fax: (202) 623-3096, www.iadb.org; *The Politics of Policies: Economic and Social Progress in Latin America - 2006 Report.*

UCLA Latin American Institute, 10343 Bunche Hall, Box 951447, Los Angeles, CA 90095-1447, (310) 825-4571, Fax: (310) 206-6859, www.international.ucla.edu/lac; *Statistical Abstract of Latin America.*

GUYANA - EDUCATION

Euromonitor International, Inc., 224 S. Michigan Avenue, Suite 1500, Chicago, IL 60604, (312) 922-1115, Fax: (312) 922-1157, www.euromonitor.com; *International Marketing Data and Statistics 2008* and *World Marketing Data and Statistics.*

International Monetary Fund (IMF), 700 Nineteenth Street, NW, Washington, DC 20431, (202) 623-7000, Fax: (202) 623-4661, www.imf.org; *Government Finance Statistics Yearbook (2008 Edition).*

M.E. Sharpe, 80 Business Park Drive, Armonk, NY 10504, (800) 541-6563, Fax: (914) 273-2106, www.mesharpe.com; *The Illustrated Book of World Rankings.*

Palgrave Macmillan Ltd., Houndmills, Basingstoke, Hampshire, RG21 6XS, England, (Telephone in U.S. (888) 330-8477), (Fax in U.S. (800) 672-2054), www.palgrave.com; *The Statesman's Yearbook 2008.*

Taylor and Francis Group, An Informa Business, 2 Park Square, Milton Park, Abingdon, Oxford OX14 4RN, United Kingdom, (Dial from U.S. (212) 216-7800), (Fax from U.S. (212) 564-7854), www.tandf.co.uk; *The Europa World Year Book.*

UNESCO Institute for Statistics, C.P. 6128 Succursale Centre-Ville, Montreal, Quebec, H3C 3J7 Canada, (Dial from U.S. (514) 343-6880), (Fax from U.S. (514) 343 6882), www.uis.unesco.org; *Statistical Tables.*

United Nations Statistics Division, New York, NY 10017, (800) 253-9646, Fax: (212) 963-4116, http://unstats.un.org; *Human Development Report 2006* and *Statistical Yearbook for Latin America and the Caribbean 2004.*

The World Bank, 1818 H Street, NW, Washington, DC 20433, (202) 473-1000, Fax: (202) 477-6391, www.worldbank.org; *Guyana* and *World Development Indicators (WDI) 2008.*

GUYANA - ELECTRICITY

Inter-American Development Bank (IDB), 1300 New York Avenue, NW, Washington, DC 20577, (202)

623-1000, Fax: (202) 623-3096, www.iadb.org; *The Politics of Policies: Economic and Social Progress in Latin America - 2006 Report.*

M.E. Sharpe, 80 Business Park Drive, Armonk, NY 10504, (800) 541-6563, Fax: (914) 273-2106, www.mesharpe.com; *The Illustrated Book of World Rankings.*

Palgrave Macmillan Ltd., Houndmills, Basingstoke, Hampshire, RG21 6XS, England, (Telephone in U.S. (888) 330-8477), (Fax in U.S. (800) 672-2054), www.palgrave.com; *The Statesman's Yearbook 2008.*

United Nations Statistics Division, New York, NY 10017, (800) 253-9646, Fax: (212) 963-4116, http://unstats.un.org; *Human Development Report 2006* and *Statistical Yearbook.*

GUYANA - EMPLOYMENT

Euromonitor International, Inc., 224 S. Michigan Avenue, Suite 1500, Chicago, IL 60604, (312) 922-1115, Fax: (312) 922-1157, www.euromonitor.com; *International Marketing Data and Statistics 2008.*

International Labour Office, I.L.O. Publications, 4 route des Morillons, CH-1211 Geneva 22, Switzerland, (Telephone in U.S. (202) 653-7652), (Fax in U.S. (202) 653-7687), www.ilo.org; *Yearbook of Labour Statistics 2006.*

M.E. Sharpe, 80 Business Park Drive, Armonk, NY 10504, (800) 541-6563, Fax: (914) 273-2106, www.mesharpe.com; *The Illustrated Book of World Rankings.*

United Nations Statistics Division, New York, NY 10017, (800) 253-9646, Fax: (212) 963-4116, http://unstats.un.org; *Statistical Yearbook* and *Statistical Yearbook for Latin America and the Caribbean 2004.*

The World Bank, 1818 H Street, NW, Washington, DC 20433, (202) 473-1000, Fax: (202) 477-6391, www.worldbank.org; *Guyana.*

GUYANA - ENVIRONMENTAL CONDITIONS

DSI Data Service Information, Xantener Strasse 51a, D-47495 Rheinberg, Germany, www.dsidata.com; *Campus Solution* and *DSI's Global Environmental Database.*

Economist Intelligence Unit, 111 West 57th Street, New York, NY 10019, (212) 554-0600, Fax: (212) 586-1181, www.eiu.com; *Guyana Country Report.*

United Nations Statistics Division, New York, NY 10017, (800) 253-9646, Fax: (212) 963-4116, http://unstats.un.org; *World Statistics Pocketbook.*

GUYANA - EXPENDITURES, PUBLIC

Inter-American Development Bank (IDB), 1300 New York Avenue, NW, Washington, DC 20577, (202) 623-1000, Fax: (202) 623-3096, www.iadb.org; *The Politics of Policies: Economic and Social Progress in Latin America - 2006 Report.*

United Nations Statistics Division, New York, NY 10017, (800) 253-9646, Fax: (212) 963-4116, http://unstats.un.org; *Statistical Yearbook for Latin America and the Caribbean 2004.*

GUYANA - EXPORTS

Central Intelligence Agency, Office of Public Affairs, Washington, DC 20505, (703) 482-0623, Fax: (703) 482-1739, www.cia.gov; *The World Factbook.*

Economist Intelligence Unit, 111 West 57th Street, New York, NY 10019, (212) 554-0600, Fax: (212) 586-1181, www.eiu.com; *Guyana Country Report.*

Euromonitor International, Inc., 224 S. Michigan Avenue, Suite 1500, Chicago, IL 60604, (312) 922-1115, Fax: (312) 922-1157, www.euromonitor.com; *International Marketing Data and Statistics 2008* and *The World Economic Factbook 2008.*

Inter-American Development Bank (IDB), 1300 New York Avenue, NW, Washington, DC 20577, (202) 623-1000, Fax: (202) 623-3096, www.iadb.org; *The Politics of Policies: Economic and Social Progress in Latin America - 2006 Report.*

International Monetary Fund (IMF), 700 Nineteenth Street, NW, Washington, DC 20431, (202) 623-7000, Fax: (202) 623-4661, www.imf.org; *Direction of Trade Statistics Yearbook 2007; Government Finance Statistics Yearbook (2008 Edition);* and *International Financial Statistics Yearbook 2007.*

Palgrave Macmillan Ltd., Houndmills, Basingstoke, Hampshire, RG21 6XS, England, (Telephone in U.S. (888) 330-8477), (Fax in U.S. (800) 672-2054), www.palgrave.com; *The Statesman's Yearbook 2008.*

Taylor and Francis Group, An Informa Business, 2 Park Square, Milton Park, Abingdon, Oxford OX14 4RN, United Kingdom, (Dial from U.S. (212) 216-7800), (Fax from U.S. (212) 564-7854), www.tandf.co.uk; *The Europa World Year Book.*

United Nations Conference on Trade and Development (UNCTAD), DC2-1120, United Nations, New York, NY 10017, (212) 963-0027, www.unctad.org; *Handbook of Statistics 2005.*

United Nations Food and Agricultural Organization (FAO), Viale delle Terme di Caracalla, 00100 Rome, Italy, (Dial from U.S. (202) 653-2400), (Fax from U.S. (202) 653 5760), www.fao.org; *The State of Food and Agriculture (SOFA) 2006.*

United Nations Statistics Division, New York, NY 10017, (800) 253-9646, Fax: (212) 963-4116, http://unstats.un.org; *Statistical Yearbook for Latin America and the Caribbean 2004.*

The World Bank, 1818 H Street, NW, Washington, DC 20433, (202) 473-1000, Fax: (202) 477-6391, www.worldbank.org; *World Development Indicators (WDI) 2008.*

GUYANA - FEMALE WORKING POPULATION

See GUYANA - EMPLOYMENT

GUYANA - FERTILITY, HUMAN

Central Intelligence Agency, Office of Public Affairs, Washington, DC 20505, (703) 482-0623, Fax: (703) 482-1739, www.cia.gov; *The World Factbook.*

M.E. Sharpe, 80 Business Park Drive, Armonk, NY 10504, (800) 541-6563, Fax: (914) 273-2106, www.mesharpe.com; *The Illustrated Book of World Rankings.*

United Nations Statistics Division, New York, NY 10017, (800) 253-9646, Fax: (212) 963-4116, http://unstats.un.org; *Human Development Report 2006.*

The World Bank, 1818 H Street, NW, Washington, DC 20433, (202) 473-1000, Fax: (202) 477-6391, www.worldbank.org; *The World Bank Atlas 2003-2004* and *World Development Indicators (WDI) 2008.*

GUYANA - FERTILIZER INDUSTRY

United Nations Food and Agricultural Organization (FAO), Viale delle Terme di Caracalla, 00100 Rome, Italy, (Dial from U.S. (202) 653-2400), (Fax from U.S. (202) 653 5760), www.fao.org; *FAO Fertilizer Yearbook* and *The State of Food and Agriculture (SOFA) 2006.*

United Nations Statistics Division, New York, NY 10017, (800) 253-9646, Fax: (212) 963-4116, http://unstats.un.org; *Statistical Yearbook.*

GUYANA - FETAL MORTALITY

See GUYANA - MORTALITY

GUYANA - FILM

See GUYANA - MOTION PICTURES

GUYANA - FINANCE

Inter-American Development Bank (IDB), 1300 New York Avenue, NW, Washington, DC 20577, (202) 623-1000, Fax: (202) 623-3096, www.iadb.org; *The Politics of Policies: Economic and Social Progress in Latin America - 2006 Report.*

International Monetary Fund (IMF), 700 Nineteenth Street, NW, Washington, DC 20431, (202) 623-7000, Fax: (202) 623-4661, www.imf.org; *International Financial Statistics Yearbook 2007.*

United Nations Statistics Division, New York, NY 10017, (800) 253-9646, Fax: (212) 963-4116, http://unstats.un.org; *National Accounts Statistics: Compendium of Income Distribution Statistics* and *Statistical Yearbook.*

The World Bank, 1818 H Street, NW, Washington, DC 20433, (202) 473-1000, Fax: (202) 477-6391, www.worldbank.org; *Guyana.*

GUYANA - FINANCE, PUBLIC

Bernan Essential Government Publications, 4611-F Assembly Drive, Lanham MD, 20706-4391, (301) 459-2255, Fax: (800) 865-3450, www.bernan.com; *National Accounts Statistics.*

Economist Intelligence Unit, 111 West 57th Street, New York, NY 10019, (212) 554-0600, Fax: (212) 586-1181, www.eiu.com; *Guyana Country Report.*

Inter-American Development Bank (IDB), 1300 New York Avenue, NW, Washington, DC 20577, (202) 623-1000, Fax: (202) 623-3096, www.iadb.org; *The Politics of Policies: Economic and Social Progress in Latin America - 2006 Report.*

International Monetary Fund (IMF), 700 Nineteenth Street, NW, Washington, DC 20431, (202) 623-7000, Fax: (202) 623-4661, www.imf.org; *Government Finance Statistics Yearbook (2008 Edition); International Financial Statistics;* and *International Financial Statistics Online Service.*

M.E. Sharpe, 80 Business Park Drive, Armonk, NY 10504, (800) 541-6563, Fax: (914) 273-2106, www.mesharpe.com; *The Illustrated Book of World Rankings.*

Palgrave Macmillan Ltd., Houndmills, Basingstoke, Hampshire, RG21 6XS, England, (Telephone in U.S. (888) 330-8477), (Fax in U.S. (800) 672-2054), www.palgrave.com; *The Statesman's Yearbook 2008.*

Taylor and Francis Group, An Informa Business, 2 Park Square, Milton Park, Abingdon, Oxford OX14 4RN, United Kingdom, (Dial from U.S. (212) 216-7800), (Fax from U.S. (212) 564-7854), www.tandf.co.uk; *The Europa World Year Book.*

The World Bank, 1818 H Street, NW, Washington, DC 20433, (202) 473-1000, Fax: (202) 477-6391, www.worldbank.org; *Guyana.*

GUYANA - FISHERIES

Inter-American Development Bank (IDB), 1300 New York Avenue, NW, Washington, DC 20577, (202) 623-1000, Fax: (202) 623-3096, www.iadb.org; *The Politics of Policies: Economic and Social Progress in Latin America - 2006 Report.*

M.E. Sharpe, 80 Business Park Drive, Armonk, NY 10504, (800) 541-6563, Fax: (914) 273-2106, www.mesharpe.com; *The Illustrated Book of World Rankings.*

Palgrave Macmillan Ltd., Houndmills, Basingstoke, Hampshire, RG21 6XS, England, (Telephone in U.S. (888) 330-8477), (Fax in U.S. (800) 672-2054), www.palgrave.com; *The Statesman's Yearbook 2008.*

Taylor and Francis Group, An Informa Business, 2 Park Square, Milton Park, Abingdon, Oxford OX14 4RN, United Kingdom, (Dial from U.S. (212) 216-7800), (Fax from U.S. (212) 564-7854), www.tandf.co.uk; *The Europa World Year Book.*

United Nations Conference on Trade and Development (UNCTAD), DC2-1120, United Nations, New York, NY 10017, (212) 963-0027, www.unctad.org; *UNCTAD Commodity Yearbook.*

United Nations Food and Agricultural Organization (FAO), Viale delle Terme di Caracalla, 00100 Rome, Italy, (Dial from U.S. (202) 653-2400), (Fax from U.S. (202) 653 5760), www.fao.org; *FAO Yearbook of Fishery Statistics;* Fishery Databases; FISHSTAT Database. Subjects covered include: Aquaculture production, capture production, fishery commodities; and *The State of Food and Agriculture (SOFA) 2006.*

United Nations Statistics Division, New York, NY 10017, (800) 253-9646, Fax: (212) 963-4116, http://unstats.un.org; *Statistical Yearbook.*

The World Bank, 1818 H Street, NW, Washington, DC 20433, (202) 473-1000, Fax: (202) 477-6391, www.worldbank.org; *Guyana.*

GUYANA - FLOUR INDUSTRY

United Nations Statistics Division, New York, NY 10017, (800) 253-9646, Fax: (212) 963-4116, http://unstats.un.org; *Statistical Yearbook.*

GUYANA - FOOD

United Nations Conference on Trade and Development (UNCTAD), DC2-1120, United Nations, New York, NY 10017, (212) 963-0027, www.unctad.org; *UNCTAD Commodity Yearbook.*

United Nations Food and Agricultural Organization (FAO), Viale delle Terme di Caracalla, 00100 Rome, Italy, (Dial from U.S. (202) 653-2400), (Fax from U.S. (202) 653 5760), www.fao.org; *FAO Production Yearbook 2002* and *The State of Food and Agriculture (SOFA) 2006.*

GUYANA - FOREIGN EXCHANGE RATES

Central Intelligence Agency, Office of Public Affairs, Washington, DC 20505, (703) 482-0623, Fax: (703) 482-1739, www.cia.gov; *The World Factbook.*

Euromonitor International, Inc., 224 S. Michigan Avenue, Suite 1500, Chicago, IL 60604, (312) 922-1115, Fax: (312) 922-1157, www.euromonitor.com; *International Marketing Data and Statistics 2008* and *The World Economic Factbook 2008.*

Inter-American Development Bank (IDB), 1300 New York Avenue, NW, Washington, DC 20577, (202) 623-1000, Fax: (202) 623-3096, www.iadb.org; *The Politics of Policies: Economic and Social Progress in Latin America - 2006 Report.*

International Monetary Fund (IMF), 700 Nineteenth Street, NW, Washington, DC 20431, (202) 623-7000, Fax: (202) 623-4661, www.imf.org; *International Financial Statistics Yearbook 2007.*

Taylor and Francis Group, An Informa Business, 2 Park Square, Milton Park, Abingdon, Oxford OX14 4RN, United Kingdom, (Dial from U.S. (212) 216-7800), (Fax from U.S. (212) 564-7854), www.tandf.co.uk; *The Europa World Year Book.*

United Nations Statistics Division, New York, NY 10017, (800) 253-9646, Fax: (212) 963-4116, http://unstats.un.org; *Statistical Yearbook.*

GUYANA - FORESTS AND FORESTRY

Inter-American Development Bank (IDB), 1300 New York Avenue, NW, Washington, DC 20577, (202) 623-1000, Fax: (202) 623-3096, www.iadb.org; *The Politics of Policies: Economic and Social Progress in Latin America - 2006 Report.*

M.E. Sharpe, 80 Business Park Drive, Armonk, NY 10504, (800) 541-6563, Fax: (914) 273-2106, www.mesharpe.com; *The Illustrated Book of World Rankings.*

Palgrave Macmillan Ltd., Houndmills, Basingstoke, Hampshire, RG21 6XS, England, (Telephone in U.S. (888) 330-8477), (Fax in U.S. (800) 672-2054), www.palgrave.com; *The Statesman's Yearbook 2008.*

Taylor and Francis Group, An Informa Business, 2 Park Square, Milton Park, Abingdon, Oxford OX14 4RN, United Kingdom, (Dial from U.S. (212) 216-7800), (Fax from U.S. (212) 564-7854), www.tandf.co.uk; *The Europa World Year Book.*

UNESCO Institute for Statistics, C.P. 6128 Succursale Centre-Ville, Montreal, Quebec, H3C 3J7 Canada, (Dial from U.S. (514) 343-6880), (Fax from U.S. (514) 343 6882), www.uis.unesco.org; *Statistical Tables.*

United Nations Conference on Trade and Development (UNCTAD), DC2-1120, United Nations, New York, NY 10017, (212) 963-0027, www.unctad.org; *UNCTAD Commodity Yearbook.*

United Nations Food and Agricultural Organization (FAO), Viale delle Terme di Caracalla, 00100 Rome, Italy, (Dial from U.S. (202) 653-2400), (Fax from U.S. (202) 653 5760), www.fao.org; *FAO Yearbook of Forest Products* and *The State of Food and Agriculture (SOFA) 2006.*

United Nations Statistics Division, New York, NY 10017, (800) 253-9646, Fax: (212) 963-4116, http://unstats.un.org; *Statistical Yearbook.*

The World Bank, 1818 H Street, NW, Washington, DC 20433, (202) 473-1000, Fax: (202) 477-6391, www.worldbank.org; *Guyana.*

GUYANA - GAS PRODUCTION

See GUYANA - MINERAL INDUSTRIES

GUYANA - GEOGRAPHIC INFORMATION SYSTEMS

M.E. Sharpe, 80 Business Park Drive, Armonk, NY 10504, (800) 541-6563, Fax: (914) 273-2106, www.mesharpe.com; *The Illustrated Book of World Rankings.*

UCLA Latin American Institute, 10343 Bunche Hall, Box 951447, Los Angeles, CA 90095-1447, (310) 825-4571, Fax: (310) 206-6859, www.international.ucla.edu/lac; *Statistical Abstract of Latin America.*

The World Bank, 1818 H Street, NW, Washington, DC 20433, (202) 473-1000, Fax: (202) 477-6391, www.worldbank.org; *Guyana.*

GUYANA - GOLD INDUSTRY

International Monetary Fund (IMF), 700 Nineteenth Street, NW, Washington, DC 20431, (202) 623-7000, Fax: (202) 623-4661, www.imf.org; *International Financial Statistics Yearbook 2007.*

United Nations Statistics Division, New York, NY 10017, (800) 253-9646, Fax: (212) 963-4116, http://unstats.un.org; *Statistical Yearbook.*

The World Bank, 1818 H Street, NW, Washington, DC 20433, (202) 473-1000, Fax: (202) 477-6391, www.worldbank.org; *World Development Indicators (WDI) 2008.*

GUYANA - GOLD PRODUCTION

See GUYANA - MINERAL INDUSTRIES

GUYANA - GRANTS-IN-AID

International Monetary Fund (IMF), 700 Nineteenth Street, NW, Washington, DC 20431, (202) 623-7000, Fax: (202) 623-4661, www.imf.org; *Government Finance Statistics Yearbook (2008 Edition).*

GUYANA - GROSS DOMESTIC PRODUCT

Economist Intelligence Unit, 111 West 57th Street, New York, NY 10019, (212) 554-0600, Fax: (212) 586-1181, www.eiu.com; *Guyana Country Report.*

Euromonitor International, Inc., 224 S. Michigan Avenue, Suite 1500, Chicago, IL 60604, (312) 922-1115, Fax: (312) 922-1157, www.euromonitor.com; *International Marketing Data and Statistics 2008* and *The World Economic Factbook 2008.*

Inter-American Development Bank (IDB), 1300 New York Avenue, NW, Washington, DC 20577, (202) 623-1000, Fax: (202) 623-3096, www.iadb.org; *The Politics of Policies: Economic and Social Progress in Latin America - 2006 Report.*

M.E. Sharpe, 80 Business Park Drive, Armonk, NY 10504, (800) 541-6563, Fax: (914) 273-2106, www.mesharpe.com; *The Illustrated Book of World Rankings.*

Taylor and Francis Group, An Informa Business, 2 Park Square, Milton Park, Abingdon, Oxford OX14 4RN, United Kingdom, (Dial from U.S. (212) 216-7800), (Fax from U.S. (212) 564-7854), www.tandf.co.uk; *The Europa World Year Book.*

United Nations Statistics Division, New York, NY 10017, (800) 253-9646, Fax: (212) 963-4116, http://unstats.un.org; *Human Development Report 2006; National Accounts Statistics: Compendium of Income Distribution Statistics; Statistical Yearbook;* and *Statistical Yearbook for Latin America and the Caribbean 2004.*

The World Bank, 1818 H Street, NW, Washington, DC 20433, (202) 473-1000, Fax: (202) 477-6391, www.worldbank.org; *World Development Indicators (WDI) 2008.*

GUYANA - GROSS NATIONAL PRODUCT

Euromonitor International, Inc., 224 S. Michigan Avenue, Suite 1500, Chicago, IL 60604, (312) 922-1115, Fax: (312) 922-1157, www.euromonitor.com; *International Marketing Data and Statistics 2008.*

Inter-American Development Bank (IDB), 1300 New York Avenue, NW, Washington, DC 20577, (202) 623-1000, Fax: (202) 623-3096, www.iadb.org; *The Politics of Policies: Economic and Social Progress in Latin America - 2006 Report.*

M.E. Sharpe, 80 Business Park Drive, Armonk, NY 10504, (800) 541-6563, Fax: (914) 273-2106, www.mesharpe.com; *The Illustrated Book of World Rankings.*

Palgrave Macmillan Ltd., Houndmills, Basingstoke, Hampshire, RG21 6XS, England, (Telephone in U.S. (888) 330-8477), (Fax in U.S. (800) 672-2054), www.palgrave.com; *The Statesman's Yearbook 2008.*

U.S. Department of State (DOS), 2201 C Street NW, Washington, DC 20520, (202) 647-4000, www.state.gov; *World Military Expenditures and Arms Transfers (WMEAT).*

United Nations Statistics Division, New York, NY 10017, (800) 253-9646, Fax: (212) 963-4116, http://unstats.un.org; *Statistical Yearbook.*

The World Bank, 1818 H Street, NW, Washington, DC 20433, (202) 473-1000, Fax: (202) 477-6391, www.worldbank.org; *The World Bank Atlas 2003-2004* and *World Development Indicators (WDI) 2008.*

GUYANA - HIDES AND SKINS INDUSTRY

United Nations Food and Agricultural Organization (FAO), Viale delle Terme di Caracalla, 00100 Rome, Italy, (Dial from U.S. (202) 653-2400), (Fax from U.S. (202) 653 5760), www.fao.org; *FAO Production Yearbook 2002.*

GUYANA - HOUSING

Euromonitor International, Inc., 224 S. Michigan Avenue, Suite 1500, Chicago, IL 60604, (312) 922-1115, Fax: (312) 922-1157, www.euromonitor.com; *World Marketing Data and Statistics.*

M.E. Sharpe, 80 Business Park Drive, Armonk, NY 10504, (800) 541-6563, Fax: (914) 273-2106, www.mesharpe.com; *The Illustrated Book of World Rankings.*

United Nations Statistics Division, New York, NY 10017, (800) 253-9646, Fax: (212) 963-4116, http://unstats.un.org; *Statistical Yearbook for Latin America and the Caribbean 2004.*

GUYANA - ILLITERATE PERSONS

Euromonitor International, Inc., 224 S. Michigan Avenue, Suite 1500, Chicago, IL 60604, (312) 922-1115, Fax: (312) 922-1157, www.euromonitor.com; *The World Economic Factbook 2008.*

UNESCO Institute for Statistics, C.P. 6128 Succursale Centre-Ville, Montreal, Quebec, H3C 3J7 Canada, (Dial from U.S. (514) 343-6880), (Fax from U.S. (514) 343 6882), www.uis.unesco.org; *Statistical Tables.*

United Nations Statistics Division, New York, NY 10017, (800) 253-9646, Fax: (212) 963-4116, http://unstats.un.org; *Human Development Report 2006* and *Statistical Yearbook for Latin America and the Caribbean 2004.*

GUYANA - IMPORTS

Central Intelligence Agency, Office of Public Affairs, Washington, DC 20505, (703) 482-0623, Fax: (703) 482-1739, www.cia.gov; *The World Factbook.*

Economist Intelligence Unit, 111 West 57th Street, New York, NY 10019, (212) 554-0600, Fax: (212) 586-1181, www.eiu.com; *Guyana Country Report.*

Euromonitor International, Inc., 224 S. Michigan Avenue, Suite 1500, Chicago, IL 60604, (312) 922-1115, Fax: (312) 922-1157, www.euromonitor.com; *International Marketing Data and Statistics 2008* and *The World Economic Factbook 2008.*

Inter-American Development Bank (IDB), 1300 New York Avenue, NW, Washington, DC 20577, (202) 623-1000, Fax: (202) 623-3096, www.iadb.org; *The Politics of Policies: Economic and Social Progress in Latin America - 2006 Report.*

International Monetary Fund (IMF), 700 Nineteenth Street, NW, Washington, DC 20431, (202) 623-7000, Fax: (202) 623-4661, www.imf.org; *Direction of Trade Statistics Yearbook 2007; Government Finance Statistics Yearbook (2008 Edition);* and *International Financial Statistics Yearbook 2007.*

Palgrave Macmillan Ltd., Houndmills, Basingstoke, Hampshire, RG21 6XS, England, (Telephone in U.S. (888) 330-8477), (Fax in U.S. (800) 672-2054), www.palgrave.com; *The Statesman's Yearbook 2008.*

Taylor and Francis Group, An Informa Business, 2 Park Square, Milton Park, Abingdon, Oxford OX14 4RN, United Kingdom, (Dial from U.S. (212) 216-7800), (Fax from U.S. (212) 564-7854), www.tandf.co.uk; *The Europa World Year Book.*

United Nations Conference on Trade and Development (UNCTAD), DC2-1120, United Nations, New York, NY 10017, (212) 963-0027, www.unctad.org; *Handbook of Statistics 2005.*

United Nations Food and Agricultural Organization (FAO), Viale delle Terme di Caracalla, 00100 Rome, Italy, (Dial from U.S. (202) 653-2400), (Fax from U.S. (202) 653 5760), www.fao.org; *The State of Food and Agriculture (SOFA) 2006.*

United Nations Statistics Division, New York, NY 10017, (800) 253-9646, Fax: (212) 963-4116, http://unstats.un.org; *Statistical Yearbook for Latin America and the Caribbean 2004.*

The World Bank, 1818 H Street, NW, Washington, DC 20433, (202) 473-1000, Fax: (202) 477-6391, www.worldbank.org; *World Development Indicators (WDI) 2008.*

GUYANA - INCOME DISTRIBUTION

United Nations Statistics Division, New York, NY 10017, (800) 253-9646, Fax: (212) 963-4116, http://unstats.un.org; *Statistical Yearbook for Latin America and the Caribbean 2004.*

GUYANA - INCOME TAXES

See GUYANA - TAXATION

GUYANA - INDUSTRIAL PRODUCTIVITY

Euromonitor International, Inc., 224 S. Michigan Avenue, Suite 1500, Chicago, IL 60604, (312) 922-1115, Fax: (312) 922-1157, www.euromonitor.com; *International Marketing Data and Statistics 2008.*

M.E. Sharpe, 80 Business Park Drive, Armonk, NY 10504, (800) 541-6563, Fax: (914) 273-2106, www.mesharpe.com; *The Illustrated Book of World Rankings.*

GUYANA - INDUSTRIAL STATISTICS

United Nations Statistics Division, New York, NY 10017, (800) 253-9646, Fax: (212) 963-4116, http://unstats.un.org; *Economic Survey of Latin America and the Caribbean 2004-2005.*

GUYANA - INDUSTRIES

Central Intelligence Agency, Office of Public Affairs, Washington, DC 20505, (703) 482-0623, Fax: (703) 482-1739, www.cia.gov; *The World Factbook.*

Economist Intelligence Unit, 111 West 57th Street, New York, NY 10019, (212) 554-0600, Fax: (212) 586-1181, www.eiu.com; *Guyana Country Report.*

Euromonitor International, Inc., 224 S. Michigan Avenue, Suite 1500, Chicago, IL 60604, (312) 922-1115, Fax: (312) 922-1157, www.euromonitor.com; *International Marketing Data and Statistics 2008; The World Economic Factbook 2008;* and *World Marketing Data and Statistics.*

International Labour Office, I.L.O. Publications, 4 route des Morillons, CH-1211 Geneva 22, Switzerland, (Telephone in U.S. (202) 653-7652), (Fax in U.S. (202) 653-7687), www.ilo.org; *Yearbook of Labour Statistics 2006.*

M.E. Sharpe, 80 Business Park Drive, Armonk, NY 10504, (800) 541-6563, Fax: (914) 273-2106, www.mesharpe.com; *The Illustrated Book of World Rankings.*

Palgrave Macmillan Ltd., Houndmills, Basingstoke, Hampshire, RG21 6XS, England, (Telephone in U.S. (888) 330-8477), (Fax in U.S. (800) 672-2054), www.palgrave.com; *The Statesman's Yearbook 2008.*

Taylor and Francis Group, An Informa Business, 2 Park Square, Milton Park, Abingdon, Oxford OX14 4RN, United Kingdom, (Dial from U.S. (212) 216-7800), (Fax from U.S. (212) 564-7854), www.tandf.co.uk; *The Europa World Year Book.*

United Nations Industrial Development Organization (UNIDO), 1 United Nations Plaza, New York, NY 10017, (212) 963 6890, Fax: (212) 963-7904, http://unido.org; Industrial Statistics Database 2008 (INDSTAT) and *The International Yearbook of Industrial Statistics 2008.*

United Nations Statistics Division, New York, NY 10017, (800) 253-9646, Fax: (212) 963-4116, http://unstats.un.org; *2004 Industrial Commodity Statistics Yearbook.*

The World Bank, 1818 H Street, NW, Washington, DC 20433, (202) 473-1000, Fax: (202) 477-6391, www.worldbank.org; *Guyana* and *World Development Indicators (WDI) 2008.*

GUYANA - INFANT AND MATERNAL MORTALITY

See GUYANA - MORTALITY

GUYANA - INFLATION (FINANCE)

United Nations Statistics Division, New York, NY 10017, (800) 253-9646, Fax: (212) 963-4116, http://unstats.un.org; *Economic Survey of Latin America and the Caribbean 2004-2005.*

GUYANA - INTEREST RATES

Inter-American Development Bank (IDB), 1300 New York Avenue, NW, Washington, DC 20577, (202) 623-1000, Fax: (202) 623-3096, www.iadb.org; *The Politics of Policies: Economic and Social Progress in Latin America - 2006 Report.*

GUYANA - INTERNAL REVENUE

Inter-American Development Bank (IDB), 1300 New York Avenue, NW, Washington, DC 20577, (202) 623-1000, Fax: (202) 623-3096, www.iadb.org; *The Politics of Policies: Economic and Social Progress in Latin America - 2006 Report.*

GUYANA - INTERNATIONAL FINANCE

Inter-American Development Bank (IDB), 1300 New York Avenue, NW, Washington, DC 20577, (202) 623-1000, Fax: (202) 623-3096, www.iadb.org; *The Politics of Policies: Economic and Social Progress in Latin America - 2006 Report.*

United Nations Statistics Division, New York, NY 10017, (800) 253-9646, Fax: (212) 963-4116, http://unstats.un.org; *Statistical Yearbook for Latin America and the Caribbean 2004.*

GUYANA - INTERNATIONAL LIQUIDITY

Inter-American Development Bank (IDB), 1300 New York Avenue, NW, Washington, DC 20577, (202) 623-1000, Fax: (202) 623-3096, www.iadb.org; *The Politics of Policies: Economic and Social Progress in Latin America - 2006 Report.*

International Monetary Fund (IMF), 700 Nineteenth Street, NW, Washington, DC 20431, (202) 623-7000, Fax: (202) 623-4661, www.imf.org; *International Financial Statistics Yearbook 2007.*

GUYANA - INTERNATIONAL STATISTICS

Inter-American Development Bank (IDB), 1300 New York Avenue, NW, Washington, DC 20577, (202) 623-1000, Fax: (202) 623-3096, www.iadb.org; *The Politics of Policies: Economic and Social Progress in Latin America - 2006 Report.*

UCLA Latin American Institute, 10343 Bunche Hall, Box 951447, Los Angeles, CA 90095-1447, (310) 825-4571, Fax: (310) 206-6859, www.international.ucla.edu/lac; *Statistical Abstract of Latin America.*

GUYANA - INTERNATIONAL TRADE

Economist Intelligence Unit, 111 West 57th Street, New York, NY 10019, (212) 554-0600, Fax: (212) 586-1181, www.eiu.com; *Guyana Country Report.*

Euromonitor International, Inc., 224 S. Michigan Avenue, Suite 1500, Chicago, IL 60604, (312) 922-1115, Fax: (312) 922-1157, www.euromonitor.com; *International Marketing Data and Statistics 2008; The World Economic Factbook 2008;* and *World Marketing Data and Statistics.*

Inter-American Development Bank (IDB), 1300 New York Avenue, NW, Washington, DC 20577, (202) 623-1000, Fax: (202) 623-3096, www.iadb.org; *The Politics of Policies: Economic and Social Progress in Latin America - 2006 Report.*

International Monetary Fund (IMF), 700 Nineteenth Street, NW, Washington, DC 20431, (202) 623-7000, Fax: (202) 623-4661, www.imf.org; *International Financial Statistics Yearbook 2007.*

M.E. Sharpe, 80 Business Park Drive, Armonk, NY 10504, (800) 541-6563, Fax: (914) 273-2106, www.mesharpe.com; *The Illustrated Book of World Rankings.*

Palgrave Macmillan Ltd., Houndmills, Basingstoke, Hampshire, RG21 6XS, England, (Telephone in U.S. (888) 330-8477), (Fax in U.S. (800) 672-2054), www.palgrave.com; *The Statesman's Yearbook 2008.*

Taylor and Francis Group, An Informa Business, 2 Park Square, Milton Park, Abingdon, Oxford OX14 4RN, United Kingdom, (Dial from U.S. (212) 216-7800), (Fax from U.S. (212) 564-7854), www.tandf.co.uk; *The Europa World Year Book.*

United Nations Conference on Trade and Development (UNCTAD), DC2-1120, United Nations, New York, NY 10017, (212) 963-0027, www.unctad.org; *UNCTAD Commodity Yearbook.*

United Nations Food and Agricultural Organization (FAO), Viale delle Terme di Caracalla, 00100 Rome, Italy, (Dial from U.S. (202) 653-2400), (Fax from U.S. (202) 653 5760), www.fao.org; *FAO Trade Yearbook* and *The State of Food and Agriculture (SOFA) 2006.*

United Nations Statistics Division, New York, NY 10017, (800) 253-9646, Fax: (212) 963-4116, http://unstats.un.org; *Compendium of Intra-African and Related Foreign Trade Statistics 2003; International Trade Statistics Yearbook; Statistical Yearbook;* and *Statistical Yearbook for Latin America and the Caribbean 2004.*

The World Bank, 1818 H Street, NW, Washington, DC 20433, (202) 473-1000, Fax: (202) 477-6391, www.worldbank.org; *Guyana* and *World Development Indicators (WDI) 2008.*

World Trade Organization (WTO), Centre William Rappard, Rue de Lausanne 154, CH-1211 Geneva 21, Switzerland, www.wto.org; *International Trade Statistics 2006.*

GUYANA - INTERNET USERS

International Telecommunication Union (ITU), Place des Nations, 1211 Geneva 20, Switzerland, www.itu.int; *World Telecommunication/ICT Indicators Database on CD-ROM; World Telecommunication/ICT Indicators Database Online;* and *Yearbook of Statistics - Telecommunication Services (Chronological Time Series 1997-2006).*

The World Bank, 1818 H Street, NW, Washington, DC 20433, (202) 473-1000, Fax: (202) 477-6391, www.worldbank.org; *Guyana.*

GUYANA - INVESTMENTS

Inter-American Development Bank (IDB), 1300 New York Avenue, NW, Washington, DC 20577, (202) 623-1000, Fax: (202) 623-3096, www.iadb.org; *The Politics of Policies: Economic and Social Progress in Latin America - 2006 Report.*

United Nations Statistics Division, New York, NY 10017, (800) 253-9646, Fax: (212) 963-4116, http://unstats.un.org; *Statistical Yearbook for Latin America and the Caribbean 2004.*

GUYANA - IRON AND IRON ORE PRODUCTION

See GUYANA - MINERAL INDUSTRIES

GUYANA - IRRIGATION

Euromonitor International, Inc., 224 S. Michigan Avenue, Suite 1500, Chicago, IL 60604, (312) 922-1115, Fax: (312) 922-1157, www.euromonitor.com; *International Marketing Data and Statistics 2008.*

Inter-American Development Bank (IDB), 1300 New York Avenue, NW, Washington, DC 20577, (202) 623-1000, Fax: (202) 623-3096, www.iadb.org; *The Politics of Policies: Economic and Social Progress in Latin America - 2006 Report.*

GUYANA - LABOR

Central Intelligence Agency, Office of Public Affairs, Washington, DC 20505, (703) 482-0623, Fax: (703) 482-1739, www.cia.gov; *The World Factbook.*

Euromonitor International, Inc., 224 S. Michigan Avenue, Suite 1500, Chicago, IL 60604, (312) 922-1115, Fax: (312) 922-1157, www.euromonitor.com; *International Marketing Data and Statistics 2008* and *World Marketing Data and Statistics.*

International Labour Office, I.L.O. Publications, 4 route des Morillons, CH-1211 Geneva 22, Switzerland, (Telephone in U.S. (202) 653-7652), (Fax in U.S. (202) 653-7687), www.ilo.org; *Yearbook of Labour Statistics 2006.*

M.E. Sharpe, 80 Business Park Drive, Armonk, NY 10504, (800) 541-6563, Fax: (914) 273-2106, www.mesharpe.com; *The Illustrated Book of World Rankings.*

Palgrave Macmillan Ltd., Houndmills, Basingstoke, Hampshire, RG21 6XS, England, (Telephone in U.S. (888) 330-8477), (Fax in U.S. (800) 672-2054), www.palgrave.com; *The Statesman's Yearbook 2008.*

Taylor and Francis Group, An Informa Business, 2 Park Square, Milton Park, Abingdon, Oxford OX14 4RN, United Kingdom, (Dial from U.S. (212) 216-7800), (Fax from U.S. (212) 564-7854), www.tandf.co.uk; *The Europa World Year Book.*

United Nations Food and Agricultural Organization (FAO), Viale delle Terme di Caracalla, 00100 Rome, Italy, (Dial from U.S. (202) 653-2400), (Fax from U.S. (202) 653 5760), www.fao.org; *The State of Food and Agriculture (SOFA) 2006.*

United Nations Statistics Division, New York, NY 10017, (800) 253-9646, Fax: (212) 963-4116, http://unstats.un.org; *Human Development Report 2006.*

The World Bank, 1818 H Street, NW, Washington, DC 20433, (202) 473-1000, Fax: (202) 477-6391, www.worldbank.org; *The World Bank Atlas 2003-2004* and *World Development Indicators (WDI) 2008.*

GUYANA - LAND USE

Central Intelligence Agency, Office of Public Affairs, Washington, DC 20505, (703) 482-0623, Fax: (703) 482-1739, www.cia.gov; *The World Factbook.*

Euromonitor International, Inc., 224 S. Michigan Avenue, Suite 1500, Chicago, IL 60604, (312) 922-1115, Fax: (312) 922-1157, www.euromonitor.com; *International Marketing Data and Statistics 2008.*

Inter-American Development Bank (IDB), 1300 New York Avenue, NW, Washington, DC 20577, (202) 623-1000, Fax: (202) 623-3096, www.iadb.org; *The Politics of Policies: Economic and Social Progress in Latin America - 2006 Report.*

United Nations Food and Agricultural Organization (FAO), Viale delle Terme di Caracalla, 00100 Rome, Italy, (Dial from U.S. (202) 653-2400), (Fax from U.S. (202) 653 5760), www.fao.org; *FAO Production Yearbook 2002.*

GUYANA - LIBRARIES

M.E. Sharpe, 80 Business Park Drive, Armonk, NY 10504, (800) 541-6563, Fax: (914) 273-2106, www.mesharpe.com; *The Illustrated Book of World Rankings.*

GUYANA - LICENSES

International Monetary Fund (IMF), 700 Nineteenth Street, NW, Washington, DC 20431, (202) 623-7000, Fax: (202) 623-4661, www.imf.org; *Government Finance Statistics Yearbook (2008 Edition).*

GUYANA - LIFE EXPECTANCY

Central Intelligence Agency, Office of Public Affairs, Washington, DC 20505, (703) 482-0623, Fax: (703) 482-1739, www.cia.gov; *The World Factbook.*

Euromonitor International, Inc., 224 S. Michigan Avenue, Suite 1500, Chicago, IL 60604, (312) 922-1115, Fax: (312) 922-1157, www.euromonitor.com; *The World Economic Factbook 2008.*

Palgrave Macmillan Ltd., Houndmills, Basingstoke, Hampshire, RG21 6XS, England, (Telephone in U.S. (888) 330-8477), (Fax in U.S. (800) 672-2054), www.palgrave.com; *The Statesman's Yearbook 2008.*

United Nations Statistics Division, New York, NY 10017, (800) 253-9646, Fax: (212) 963-4116, http://unstats.un.org; *Human Development Report 2006* and *Statistical Yearbook for Latin America and the Caribbean 2004.*

The World Bank, 1818 H Street, NW, Washington, DC 20433, (202) 473-1000, Fax: (202) 477-6391, www.worldbank.org; *The World Bank Atlas 2003-2004.*

GUYANA - LITERACY

Euromonitor International, Inc., 224 S. Michigan Avenue, Suite 1500, Chicago, IL 60604, (312) 922-1115, Fax: (312) 922-1157, www.euromonitor.com; *World Marketing Data and Statistics.*

GUYANA - LIVESTOCK

Euromonitor International, Inc., 224 S. Michigan Avenue, Suite 1500, Chicago, IL 60604, (312) 922-1115, Fax: (312) 922-1157, www.euromonitor.com; *International Marketing Data and Statistics 2008.*

M.E. Sharpe, 80 Business Park Drive, Armonk, NY 10504, (800) 541-6563, Fax: (914) 273-2106, www.mesharpe.com; *The Illustrated Book of World Rankings.*

Palgrave Macmillan Ltd., Houndmills, Basingstoke, Hampshire, RG21 6XS, England, (Telephone in U.S. (888) 330-8477), (Fax in U.S. (800) 672-2054), www.palgrave.com; *The Statesman's Yearbook 2008.*

Taylor and Francis Group, An Informa Business, 2 Park Square, Milton Park, Abingdon, Oxford OX14 4RN, United Kingdom, (Dial from U.S. (212) 216-7800), (Fax from U.S. (212) 564-7854), www.tandf.co.uk; *The Europa World Year Book.*

United Nations Conference on Trade and Development (UNCTAD), DC2-1120, United Nations, New York, NY 10017, (212) 963-0027, www.unctad.org; *UNCTAD Commodity Yearbook.*

United Nations Food and Agricultural Organization (FAO), Viale delle Terme di Caracalla, 00100 Rome, Italy, (Dial from U.S. (202) 653-2400), (Fax from U.S. (202) 653 5760), www.fao.org; *FAO Production Yearbook 2002* and *The State of Food and Agriculture (SOFA) 2006.*

United Nations Statistics Division, New York, NY 10017, (800) 253-9646, Fax: (212) 963-4116, http://unstats.un.org; *Statistical Yearbook.*

GUYANA - LOCAL TAXATION

Euromonitor International, Inc., 224 S. Michigan Avenue, Suite 1500, Chicago, IL 60604, (312) 922-1115, Fax: (312) 922-1157, www.euromonitor.com; *International Marketing Data and Statistics 2008.*

Inter-American Development Bank (IDB), 1300 New York Avenue, NW, Washington, DC 20577, (202) 623-1000, Fax: (202) 623-3096, www.iadb.org; *The Politics of Policies: Economic and Social Progress in Latin America - 2006 Report.*

GUYANA - MANUFACTURES

Inter-American Development Bank (IDB), 1300 New York Avenue, NW, Washington, DC 20577, (202) 623-1000, Fax: (202) 623-3096, www.iadb.org; *The Politics of Policies: Economic and Social Progress in Latin America - 2006 Report.*

M.E. Sharpe, 80 Business Park Drive, Armonk, NY 10504, (800) 541-6563, Fax: (914) 273-2106, www.mesharpe.com; *The Illustrated Book of World Rankings.*

United Nations Statistics Division, New York, NY 10017, (800) 253-9646, Fax: (212) 963-4116, http://unstats.un.org; *Statistical Yearbook* and *Statistical Yearbook for Latin America and the Caribbean 2004.*

The World Bank, 1818 H Street, NW, Washington, DC 20433, (202) 473-1000, Fax: (202) 477-6391, www.worldbank.org; *World Development Indicators (WDI) 2008.*

GUYANA - MARRIAGE

M.E. Sharpe, 80 Business Park Drive, Armonk, NY 10504, (800) 541-6563, Fax: (914) 273-2106, www.mesharpe.com; *The Illustrated Book of World Rankings.*

United Nations Statistics Division, New York, NY 10017, (800) 253-9646, Fax: (212) 963-4116, http://unstats.un.org; *Demographic Yearbook* and *Statistical Yearbook.*

GUYANA - MEAT PRODUCTION

See GUYANA - LIVESTOCK

GUYANA - MEDICAL CARE, COST OF

United Nations Statistics Division, New York, NY 10017, (800) 253-9646, Fax: (212) 963-4116, http://unstats.un.org; *Statistical Yearbook for Latin America and the Caribbean 2004.*

GUYANA - MILK PRODUCTION

See GUYANA - DAIRY PROCESSING

GUYANA - MINERAL INDUSTRIES

Commodity Research Bureau, 330 South Wells Street, Suite 612, Chicago, IL 60606-7110, (800) 621-5271, Fax: (312) 939-4135, www.crbtrader.com; *2006 CRB Commodity Yearbook and CD.*

Inter-American Development Bank (IDB), 1300 New York Avenue, NW, Washington, DC 20577, (202) 623-1000, Fax: (202) 623-3096, www.iadb.org; *The Politics of Policies: Economic and Social Progress in Latin America - 2006 Report.*

International Monetary Fund (IMF), 700 Nineteenth Street, NW, Washington, DC 20431, (202) 623-7000, Fax: (202) 623-4661, www.imf.org; *International Financial Statistics Yearbook 2007.*

M.E. Sharpe, 80 Business Park Drive, Armonk, NY 10504, (800) 541-6563, Fax: (914) 273-2106, www.mesharpe.com; *The Illustrated Book of World Rankings.*

Palgrave Macmillan Ltd., Houndmills, Basingstoke, Hampshire, RG21 6XS, England, (Telephone in U.S. (888) 330-8477), (Fax in U.S. (800) 672-2054), www.palgrave.com; *The Statesman's Yearbook 2008.*

PennWell Corporation, 1421 South Sheridan Road, Tulsa, OK 74112, (918) 835-3161, www.pennwell.com; *Oil Gas Journal Latinoamericana.*

Taylor and Francis Group, An Informa Business, 2 Park Square, Milton Park, Abingdon, Oxford OX14 4RN, United Kingdom, (Dial from U.S. (212) 216-7800), (Fax from U.S. (212) 564-7854), www.tandf.co.uk; *The Europa World Year Book.*

United Nations Conference on Trade and Development (UNCTAD), DC2-1120, United Nations, New York, NY 10017, (212) 963-0027, www.unctad.org; *UNCTAD Commodity Yearbook.*

United Nations Statistics Division, New York, NY 10017, (800) 253-9646, Fax: (212) 963-4116, http://

unstats.un.org; *Statistical Yearbook* and *Statistical Yearbook for Latin America and the Caribbean 2004.*

GUYANA - MONEY EXCHANGE RATES

See GUYANA - FOREIGN EXCHANGE RATES

GUYANA - MONEY SUPPLY

Economist Intelligence Unit, 111 West 57th Street, New York, NY 10019, (212) 554-0600, Fax: (212) 586-1181, www.eiu.com; *Guyana Country Report.*

Euromonitor International, Inc., 224 S. Michigan Avenue, Suite 1500, Chicago, IL 60604, (312) 922-1115, Fax: (312) 922-1157, www.euromonitor.com; *International Marketing Data and Statistics 2008.*

Inter-American Development Bank (IDB), 1300 New York Avenue, NW, Washington, DC 20577, (202) 623-1000, Fax: (202) 623-3096, www.iadb.org; *The Politics of Policies: Economic and Social Progress in Latin America - 2006 Report.*

International Monetary Fund (IMF), 700 Nineteenth Street, NW, Washington, DC 20431, (202) 623-7000, Fax: (202) 623-4661, www.imf.org; *International Financial Statistics Yearbook 2007.*

Taylor and Francis Group, An Informa Business, 2 Park Square, Milton Park, Abingdon, Oxford OX14 4RN, United Kingdom, (Dial from U.S. (212) 216-7800), (Fax from U.S. (212) 564-7854), www.tandf.co.uk; *The Europa World Year Book.*

United Nations Statistics Division, New York, NY 10017, (800) 253-9646, Fax: (212) 963-4116, http://unstats.un.org; *Statistical Yearbook.*

The World Bank, 1818 H Street, NW, Washington, DC 20433, (202) 473-1000, Fax: (202) 477-6391, www.worldbank.org; *Guyana* and *World Development Indicators (WDI) 2008.*

GUYANA - MORTALITY

Central Intelligence Agency, Office of Public Affairs, Washington, DC 20505, (703) 482-0623, Fax: (703) 482-1739, www.cia.gov; *The World Factbook.*

Euromonitor International, Inc., 224 S. Michigan Avenue, Suite 1500, Chicago, IL 60604, (312) 922-1115, Fax: (312) 922-1157, www.euromonitor.com; *International Marketing Data and Statistics 2008* and *The World Economic Factbook 2008.*

Palgrave Macmillan Ltd., Houndmills, Basingstoke, Hampshire, RG21 6XS, England, (Telephone in U.S. (888) 330-8477), (Fax in U.S. (800) 672-2054), www.palgrave.com; *The Statesman's Yearbook 2008.*

Taylor and Francis Group, An Informa Business, 2 Park Square, Milton Park, Abingdon, Oxford OX14 4RN, United Kingdom, (Dial from U.S. (212) 216-7800), (Fax from U.S. (212) 564-7854), www.tandf.co.uk; *The Europa World Year Book.*

United Nations Statistics Division, New York, NY 10017, (800) 253-9646, Fax: (212) 963-4116, http://unstats.un.org; *Human Development Report 2006; Statistical Yearbook;* and *Statistical Yearbook for Latin America and the Caribbean 2004.*

The World Bank, 1818 H Street, NW, Washington, DC 20433, (202) 473-1000, Fax: (202) 477-6391, www.worldbank.org; *The World Bank Atlas 2003-2004* and *World Development Indicators (WDI) 2008.*

World Health Organization (WHO), Avenue Appia 20, 1211 Geneve 27, Switzerland, (Telephone in U.S. (212) 331-9081), www.who.int; The WHO Global Atlas of Infectious Diseases and *World Health Report 2006.*

GUYANA - MOTION PICTURES

Palgrave Macmillan Ltd., Houndmills, Basingstoke, Hampshire, RG21 6XS, England, (Telephone in U.S. (888) 330-8477), (Fax in U.S. (800) 672-2054), www.palgrave.com; *The Statesman's Yearbook 2008.*

UNESCO Institute for Statistics, C.P. 6128 Succursale Centre-Ville, Montreal, Quebec, H3C 3J7 Canada, (Dial from U.S. (514) 343-6880), (Fax from U.S. (514) 343 6882), www.uis.unesco.org; *Statistical Tables.*

United Nations Statistics Division, New York, NY 10017, (800) 253-9646, Fax: (212) 963-4116, http://unstats.un.org; *Statistical Yearbook.*

GUYANA - MOTOR VEHICLES

Taylor and Francis Group, An Informa Business, 2 Park Square, Milton Park, Abingdon, Oxford OX14 4RN, United Kingdom, (Dial from U.S. (212) 216-7800), (Fax from U.S. (212) 564-7854), www.tandf.co.uk; *The Europa World Year Book.*

United Nations Statistics Division, New York, NY 10017, (800) 253-9646, Fax: (212) 963-4116, http://unstats.un.org; *Statistical Yearbook.*

GUYANA - MUSEUMS

M.E. Sharpe, 80 Business Park Drive, Armonk, NY 10504, (800) 541-6563, Fax: (914) 273-2106, www.mesharpe.com; *The Illustrated Book of World Rankings.*

UNESCO Institute for Statistics, C.P. 6128 Succursale Centre-Ville, Montreal, Quebec, H3C 3J7 Canada, (Dial from U.S. (514) 343-6880), (Fax from U.S. (514) 343 6882), www.uis.unesco.org; *Statistical Tables.*

GUYANA - NATURAL GAS PRODUCTION

See GUYANA - MINERAL INDUSTRIES

GUYANA - NUTRITION

United Nations Food and Agricultural Organization (FAO), Viale delle Terme di Caracalla, 00100 Rome, Italy, (Dial from U.S. (202) 653-2400), (Fax from U.S. (202) 653 5760), www.fao.org; *The State of Food and Agriculture (SOFA) 2006.*

United Nations Statistics Division, New York, NY 10017, (800) 253-9646, Fax: (212) 963-4116, http://unstats.un.org; *Statistical Yearbook for Latin America and the Caribbean 2004.*

GUYANA - OLDER PEOPLE

M.E. Sharpe, 80 Business Park Drive, Armonk, NY 10504, (800) 541-6563, Fax: (914) 273-2106, www.mesharpe.com; *The Illustrated Book of World Rankings.*

GUYANA - PAPER

See GUYANA - FORESTS AND FORESTRY

GUYANA - PEANUT PRODUCTION

See GUYANA - CROPS

GUYANA - PERIODICALS

UNESCO Institute for Statistics, C.P. 6128 Succursale Centre-Ville, Montreal, Quebec, H3C 3J7 Canada, (Dial from U.S. (514) 343-6880), (Fax from U.S. (514) 343 6882), www.uis.unesco.org; *Statistical Tables.*

GUYANA - PESTICIDES

United Nations Food and Agricultural Organization (FAO), Viale delle Terme di Caracalla, 00100 Rome, Italy, (Dial from U.S. (202) 653-2400), (Fax from U.S. (202) 653 5760), www.fao.org; *The State of Food and Agriculture (SOFA) 2006.*

GUYANA - PETROLEUM INDUSTRY AND TRADE

Inter-American Development Bank (IDB), 1300 New York Avenue, NW, Washington, DC 20577, (202) 623-1000, Fax: (202) 623-3096, www.iadb.org; *The Politics of Policies: Economic and Social Progress in Latin America - 2006 Report.*

M.E. Sharpe, 80 Business Park Drive, Armonk, NY 10504, (800) 541-6563, Fax: (914) 273-2106, www.mesharpe.com; *The Illustrated Book of World Rankings.*

PennWell Corporation, 1421 South Sheridan Road, Tulsa, OK 74112, (918) 835-3161, www.pennwell.com; *International Petroleum Encyclopedia 2007* and *Oil Gas Journal Latinoamericana.*

United Nations Conference on Trade and Development (UNCTAD), DC2-1120, United Nations, New York, NY 10017, (212) 963-0027, www.unctad.org; *UNCTAD Commodity Yearbook.*

United Nations Food and Agricultural Organization (FAO), Viale delle Terme di Caracalla, 00100 Rome, Italy, (Dial from U.S. (202) 653-2400), (Fax from U.S. (202) 653 5760), www.fao.org; *The State of Food and Agriculture (SOFA) 2006.*

GUYANA - POLITICAL SCIENCE

Central Intelligence Agency, Office of Public Affairs, Washington, DC 20505, (703) 482-0623, Fax: (703) 482-1739, www.cia.gov; *The World Factbook.*

Inter-American Development Bank (IDB), 1300 New York Avenue, NW, Washington, DC 20577, (202) 623-1000, Fax: (202) 623-3096, www.iadb.org; *The Politics of Policies: Economic and Social Progress in Latin America - 2006 Report.*

International Monetary Fund (IMF), 700 Nineteenth Street, NW, Washington, DC 20431, (202) 623-7000, Fax: (202) 623-4661, www.imf.org; *Government Finance Statistics Yearbook (2008 Edition).*

Palgrave Macmillan Ltd., Houndmills, Basingstoke, Hampshire, RG21 6XS, England, (Telephone in U.S. (888) 330-8477), (Fax in U.S. (800) 672-2054), www.palgrave.com; *The Statesman's Yearbook 2008.*

Taylor and Francis Group, An Informa Business, 2 Park Square, Milton Park, Abingdon, Oxford OX14 4RN, United Kingdom, (Dial from U.S. (212) 216-7800), (Fax from U.S. (212) 564-7854), www.tandf.co.uk; *The Europa World Year Book.*

UCLA Latin American Institute, 10343 Bunche Hall, Box 951447, Los Angeles, CA 90095-1447, (310) 825-4571, Fax: (310) 206-6859, www.international.ucla.edu/lac; *Statistical Abstract of Latin America.*

United Nations Statistics Division, New York, NY 10017, (800) 253-9646, Fax: (212) 963-4116, http://unstats.un.org; *National Accounts Statistics: Compendium of Income Distribution Statistics* and *Statistical Yearbook.*

The World Bank, 1818 H Street, NW, Washington, DC 20433, (202) 473-1000, Fax: (202) 477-6391, www.worldbank.org; *World Development Indicators (WDI) 2008.*

GUYANA - POPULATION

Caribbean Epidemiology Centre (CAREC), 16-18 Jamaica Boulevard, Federation Park, PO Box 164, Port of Spain, Republic of Trinidad and Tobago, (Dial from U.S. (868) 622-4261), (Fax from U.S. (868) 622-2792), www.carec.org; *Population Data.*

Central Intelligence Agency, Office of Public Affairs, Washington, DC 20505, (703) 482-0623, Fax: (703) 482-1739, www.cia.gov; *The World Factbook.*

Economist Intelligence Unit, 111 West 57th Street, New York, NY 10019, (212) 554-0600, Fax: (212) 586-1181, www.eiu.com; *Guyana Country Report.*

Euromonitor International, Inc., 224 S. Michigan Avenue, Suite 1500, Chicago, IL 60604, (312) 922-1115, Fax: (312) 922-1157, www.euromonitor.com; *International Marketing Data and Statistics 2008* and *The World Economic Factbook 2008.*

Inter-American Development Bank (IDB), 1300 New York Avenue, NW, Washington, DC 20577, (202) 623-1000, Fax: (202) 623-3096, www.iadb.org; *The Politics of Policies: Economic and Social Progress in Latin America - 2006 Report.*

International Labour Office, I.L.O. Publications, 4 route des Morillons, CH-1211 Geneva 22, Switzerland, (Telephone in U.S. (202) 653-7652), (Fax in U.S. (202) 653-7687), www.ilo.org; *Yearbook of Labour Statistics 2006.*

M.E. Sharpe, 80 Business Park Drive, Armonk, NY 10504, (800) 541-6563, Fax: (914) 273-2106, www.mesharpe.com; *The Illustrated Book of World Rankings.*

Palgrave Macmillan Ltd., Houndmills, Basingstoke, Hampshire, RG21 6XS, England, (Telephone in U.S. (888) 330-8477), (Fax in U.S. (800) 672-2054), www.palgrave.com; *The Statesman's Yearbook 2008.*

Taylor and Francis Group, An Informa Business, 2 Park Square, Milton Park, Abingdon, Oxford OX14 4RN, United Kingdom, (Dial from U.S. (212) 216-7800), (Fax from U.S. (212) 564-7854), www.tandf.co.uk; *The Europa World Year Book.*

U.S. Department of State (DOS), 2201 C Street NW, Washington, DC 20520, (202) 647-4000, www.state.gov; *World Military Expenditures and Arms Transfers (WMEAT).*

UNESCO Institute for Statistics, C.P. 6128 Succursale Centre-Ville, Montreal, Quebec, H3C 3J7 Canada, (Dial from U.S. (514) 343-6880), (Fax from U.S. (514) 343 6882), www.uis.unesco.org; *Statistical Tables.*

United Nations Food and Agricultural Organization (FAO), Viale delle Terme di Caracalla, 00100 Rome, Italy, (Dial from U.S. (202) 653-2400), (Fax from U.S. (202) 653 5760), www.fao.org; *FAO Production Yearbook 2002.*

United Nations Statistics Division, New York, NY 10017, (800) 253-9646, Fax: (212) 963-4116, http://unstats.un.org; *Demographic Yearbook; Human Development Report 2006; Statistical Yearbook;* and *Statistical Yearbook for Latin America and the Caribbean 2004.*

The World Bank, 1818 H Street, NW, Washington, DC 20433, (202) 473-1000, Fax: (202) 477-6391, www.worldbank.org; *Guyana* and *The World Bank Atlas 2003-2004.*

World Health Organization (WHO), Avenue Appia 20, 1211 Geneve 27, Switzerland, (Telephone in U.S. (212) 331-9081), www.who.int; *World Health Report 2006.*

GUYANA - POPULATION DENSITY

Central Intelligence Agency, Office of Public Affairs, Washington, DC 20505, (703) 482-0623, Fax: (703) 482-1739, www.cia.gov; *The World Factbook.*

Euromonitor International, Inc., 224 S. Michigan Avenue, Suite 1500, Chicago, IL 60604, (312) 922-1115, Fax: (312) 922-1157, www.euromonitor.com; *International Marketing Data and Statistics 2008* and *The World Economic Factbook 2008.*

Inter-American Development Bank (IDB), 1300 New York Avenue, NW, Washington, DC 20577, (202) 623-1000, Fax: (202) 623-3096, www.iadb.org; *The Politics of Policies: Economic and Social Progress in Latin America - 2006 Report.*

M.E. Sharpe, 80 Business Park Drive, Armonk, NY 10504, (800) 541-6563, Fax: (914) 273-2106, www.mesharpe.com; *The Illustrated Book of World Rankings.*

Palgrave Macmillan Ltd., Houndmills, Basingstoke, Hampshire, RG21 6XS, England, (Telephone in U.S. (888) 330-8477), (Fax in U.S. (800) 672-2054), www.palgrave.com; *The Statesman's Yearbook 2008.*

Taylor and Francis Group, An Informa Business, 2 Park Square, Milton Park, Abingdon, Oxford OX14 4RN, United Kingdom, (Dial from U.S. (212) 216-7800), (Fax from U.S. (212) 564-7854), www.tandf.co.uk; *The Europa World Year Book.*

United Nations Food and Agricultural Organization (FAO), Viale delle Terme di Caracalla, 00100 Rome, Italy, (Dial from U.S. (202) 653-2400), (Fax from U.S. (202) 653 5760), www.fao.org; *The State of Food and Agriculture (SOFA) 2006.*

United Nations Statistics Division, New York, NY 10017, (800) 253-9646, Fax: (212) 963-4116, http://unstats.un.org; *Statistical Yearbook.*

The World Bank, 1818 H Street, NW, Washington, DC 20433, (202) 473-1000, Fax: (202) 477-6391, www.worldbank.org; *Guyana.*

GUYANA - POSTAL SERVICE

M.E. Sharpe, 80 Business Park Drive, Armonk, NY 10504, (800) 541-6563, Fax: (914) 273-2106, www.mesharpe.com; *The Illustrated Book of World Rankings.*

United Nations Statistics Division, New York, NY 10017, (800) 253-9646, Fax: (212) 963-4116, http://unstats.un.org; *Statistical Yearbook.*

GUYANA - POWER RESOURCES

Euromonitor International, Inc., 224 S. Michigan Avenue, Suite 1500, Chicago, IL 60604, (312) 922-1115, Fax: (312) 922-1157, www.euromonitor.com; *International Marketing Data and Statistics 2008; The World Economic Factbook 2008;* and *World Marketing Data and Statistics.*

M.E. Sharpe, 80 Business Park Drive, Armonk, NY 10504, (800) 541-6563, Fax: (914) 273-2106, www.mesharpe.com; *The Illustrated Book of World Rankings.*

Palgrave Macmillan Ltd., Houndmills, Basingstoke, Hampshire, RG21 6XS, England, (Telephone in U.S. (888) 330-8477), (Fax in U.S. (800) 672-2054), www.palgrave.com; *The Statesman's Yearbook 2008.*

Platts, 2 Penn Plaza, 25th Floor, New York, NY 10121-2298, (212) 904-3070, www.platts.com; *Energy Economist.*

United Nations Food and Agricultural Organization (FAO), Viale delle Terme di Caracalla, 00100 Rome, Italy, (Dial from U.S. (202) 653-2400), (Fax from U.S. (202) 653 5760), www.fao.org; *The State of Food and Agriculture (SOFA) 2006.*

United Nations Statistics Division, New York, NY 10017, (800) 253-9646, Fax: (212) 963-4116, http://unstats.un.org; *Energy Statistics Yearbook 2003; Human Development Report 2006; Statistical Yearbook; Statistical Yearbook for Latin America and the Caribbean 2004;* and *World Statistics Pocketbook.*

The World Bank, 1818 H Street, NW, Washington, DC 20433, (202) 473-1000, Fax: (202) 477-6391, www.worldbank.org; *The World Bank Atlas 2003-2004.*

GUYANA - PRICES

Euromonitor International, Inc., 224 S. Michigan Avenue, Suite 1500, Chicago, IL 60604, (312) 922-1115, Fax: (312) 922-1157, www.euromonitor.com; *World Marketing Data and Statistics.*

International Labour Office, I.L.O. Publications, 4 route des Morillons, CH-1211 Geneva 22, Switzerland, (Telephone in U.S. (202) 653-7652), (Fax in U.S. (202) 653-7687), www.ilo.org; *Yearbook of Labour Statistics 2006.*

International Monetary Fund (IMF), 700 Nineteenth Street, NW, Washington, DC 20431, (202) 623-7000, Fax: (202) 623-4661, www.imf.org; *International Financial Statistics Yearbook 2007.*

M.E. Sharpe, 80 Business Park Drive, Armonk, NY 10504, (800) 541-6563, Fax: (914) 273-2106, www.mesharpe.com; *The Illustrated Book of World Rankings.*

United Nations Food and Agricultural Organization (FAO), Viale delle Terme di Caracalla, 00100 Rome, Italy, (Dial from U.S. (202) 653-2400), (Fax from U.S. (202) 653 5760), www.fao.org; *FAO Production Yearbook 2002* and *The State of Food and Agriculture (SOFA) 2006.*

United Nations Statistics Division, New York, NY 10017, (800) 253-9646, Fax: (212) 963-4116, http://unstats.un.org; *Statistical Yearbook for Latin America and the Caribbean 2004.*

The World Bank, 1818 H Street, NW, Washington, DC 20433, (202) 473-1000, Fax: (202) 477-6391, www.worldbank.org; *Guyana.*

GUYANA - PROFESSIONS

United Nations Statistics Division, New York, NY 10017, (800) 253-9646, Fax: (212) 963-4116, http://unstats.un.org; *Statistical Yearbook.*

GUYANA - PUBLIC HEALTH

Euromonitor International, Inc., 224 S. Michigan Avenue, Suite 1500, Chicago, IL 60604, (312) 922-1115, Fax: (312) 922-1157, www.euromonitor.com; *World Marketing Data and Statistics.*

M.E. Sharpe, 80 Business Park Drive, Armonk, NY 10504, (800) 541-6563, Fax: (914) 273-2106, www.mesharpe.com; *The Illustrated Book of World Rankings.*

Palgrave Macmillan Ltd., Houndmills, Basingstoke, Hampshire, RG21 6XS, England, (Telephone in U.S. (888) 330-8477), (Fax in U.S. (800) 672-2054), www.palgrave.com; *The Statesman's Yearbook 2008.*

United Nations Statistics Division, New York, NY 10017, (800) 253-9646, Fax: (212) 963-4116, http://unstats.un.org; *Human Development Report 2006; Statistical Yearbook;* and *Statistical Yearbook for Latin America and the Caribbean 2004.*

The World Bank, 1818 H Street, NW, Washington, DC 20433, (202) 473-1000, Fax: (202) 477-6391, www.worldbank.org; *Guyana.*

World Health Organization (WHO), Avenue Appia 20, 1211 Geneve 27, Switzerland, (Telephone in U.S. (212) 331-9081), www.who.int; The WHO Global Atlas of Infectious Diseases and *World Health Report 2006.*

GUYANA - PUBLISHERS AND PUBLISHING

Taylor and Francis Group, An Informa Business, 2 Park Square, Milton Park, Abingdon, Oxford OX14 4RN, United Kingdom, (Dial from U.S. (212) 216-7800), (Fax from U.S. (212) 564-7854), www.tandf.co.uk; *The Europa World Year Book.*

UNESCO Institute for Statistics, C.P. 6128 Succursale Centre-Ville, Montreal, Quebec, H3C 3J7 Canada, (Dial from U.S. (514) 343-6880), (Fax from U.S. (514) 343 6882), www.uis.unesco.org; *Statistical Tables.*

GUYANA - RADIO BROADCASTING

Palgrave Macmillan Ltd., Houndmills, Basingstoke, Hampshire, RG21 6XS, England, (Telephone in U.S. (888) 330-8477), (Fax in U.S. (800) 672-2054), www.palgrave.com; *The Statesman's Yearbook 2008.*

GUYANA - RAILROADS

Palgrave Macmillan Ltd., Houndmills, Basingstoke, Hampshire, RG21 6XS, England, (Telephone in U.S. (888) 330-8477), (Fax in U.S. (800) 672-2054), www.palgrave.com; *The Statesman's Yearbook 2008.*

United Nations Statistics Division, New York, NY 10017, (800) 253-9646, Fax: (212) 963-4116, http://unstats.un.org; *Statistical Yearbook.*

GUYANA - RELIGION

Central Intelligence Agency, Office of Public Affairs, Washington, DC 20505, (703) 482-0623, Fax: (703) 482-1739, www.cia.gov; *The World Factbook.*

M.E. Sharpe, 80 Business Park Drive, Armonk, NY 10504, (800) 541-6563, Fax: (914) 273-2106, www.mesharpe.com; *The Illustrated Book of World Rankings.*

Palgrave Macmillan Ltd., Houndmills, Basingstoke, Hampshire, RG21 6XS, England, (Telephone in U.S. (888) 330-8477), (Fax in U.S. (800) 672-2054), www.palgrave.com; *The Statesman's Yearbook 2008.*

GUYANA - RENT CHARGES

International Labour Office, I.L.O. Publications, 4 route des Morillons, CH-1211 Geneva 22, Switzerland, (Telephone in U.S. (202) 653-7652), (Fax in U.S. (202) 653-7687), www.ilo.org; *Yearbook of Labour Statistics 2006.*

GUYANA - RESERVES (ACCOUNTING)

Euromonitor International, Inc., 224 S. Michigan Avenue, Suite 1500, Chicago, IL 60604, (312) 922-1115, Fax: (312) 922-1157, www.euromonitor.com; *International Marketing Data and Statistics 2008.*

Inter-American Development Bank (IDB), 1300 New York Avenue, NW, Washington, DC 20577, (202) 623-1000, Fax: (202) 623-3096, www.iadb.org; *The Politics of Policies: Economic and Social Progress in Latin America - 2006 Report.*

United Nations Statistics Division, New York, NY 10017, (800) 253-9646, Fax: (212) 963-4116, http://unstats.un.org; *Statistical Yearbook.*

The World Bank, 1818 H Street, NW, Washington, DC 20433, (202) 473-1000, Fax: (202) 477-6391, www.worldbank.org; *World Development Indicators (WDI) 2008.*

GUYANA - RETAIL TRADE

Euromonitor International, Inc., 224 S. Michigan Avenue, Suite 1500, Chicago, IL 60604, (312) 922-1115, Fax: (312) 922-1157, www.euromonitor.com; *World Marketing Data and Statistics.*

Inter-American Development Bank (IDB), 1300 New York Avenue, NW, Washington, DC 20577, (202) 623-1000, Fax: (202) 623-3096, www.iadb.org; *The Politics of Policies: Economic and Social Progress in Latin America - 2006 Report.*

GUYANA - RICE PRODUCTION

See GUYANA - CROPS

GUYANA - ROADS

Central Intelligence Agency, Office of Public Affairs, Washington, DC 20505, (703) 482-0623, Fax: (703) 482-1739, www.cia.gov; *The World Factbook.*

Palgrave Macmillan Ltd., Houndmills, Basingstoke, Hampshire, RG21 6XS, England, (Telephone in U.S. (888) 330-8477), (Fax in U.S. (800) 672-2054), www.palgrave.com; *The Statesman's Yearbook 2008.*

GUYANA - RUBBER INDUSTRY AND TRADE

International Rubber Study Group (IRSG), 1st Floor, Heron House, 109/115 Wembley Hill Road, Wembley, Middlesex HA9 8DA, United Kingdom, www.rubberstudy.com; *Rubber Statistical Bulletin; Summary of World Rubber Statistics 2005; World Rubber Statistics Handbook (Volume 6, 1975-2001);* and *World Rubber Statistics Historic Handbook.*

M.E. Sharpe, 80 Business Park Drive, Armonk, NY 10504, (800) 541-6563, Fax: (914) 273-2106, www.mesharpe.com; *The Illustrated Book of World Rankings.*

GUYANA - SHEEP

See GUYANA - LIVESTOCK

GUYANA - SHIPPING

Palgrave Macmillan Ltd., Houndmills, Basingstoke, Hampshire, RG21 6XS, England, (Telephone in U.S. (888) 330-8477), (Fax in U.S. (800) 672-2054), www.palgrave.com; *The Statesman's Yearbook 2008.*

Taylor and Francis Group, An Informa Business, 2 Park Square, Milton Park, Abingdon, Oxford OX14 4RN, United Kingdom, (Dial from U.S. (212) 216-7800), (Fax from U.S. (212) 564-7854), www.tandf.co.uk; *The Europa World Year Book.*

United Nations Statistics Division, New York, NY 10017, (800) 253-9646, Fax: (212) 963-4116, http://unstats.un.org; *Statistical Yearbook.*

GUYANA - SILVER PRODUCTION

See GUYANA - MINERAL INDUSTRIES

GUYANA - SOCIAL ECOLOGY

M.E. Sharpe, 80 Business Park Drive, Armonk, NY 10504, (800) 541-6563, Fax: (914) 273-2106, www.mesharpe.com; *The Illustrated Book of World Rankings.*

UCLA Latin American Institute, 10343 Bunche Hall, Box 951447, Los Angeles, CA 90095-1447, (310) 825-4571, Fax: (310) 206-6859, www.international.ucla.edu/lac; *Statistical Abstract of Latin America.*

GUYANA - SOCIAL SECURITY

Inter-American Development Bank (IDB), 1300 New York Avenue, NW, Washington, DC 20577, (202) 623-1000, Fax: (202) 623-3096, www.iadb.org; *The Politics of Policies: Economic and Social Progress in Latin America - 2006 Report.*

United Nations Statistics Division, New York, NY 10017, (800) 253-9646, Fax: (212) 963-4116, http://unstats.un.org; *Human Development Report 2006.*

GUYANA - STEEL PRODUCTION

See GUYANA - MINERAL INDUSTRIES

GUYANA - SUGAR PRODUCTION

See GUYANA - CROPS

GUYANA - TAXATION

Inter-American Development Bank (IDB), 1300 New York Avenue, NW, Washington, DC 20577, (202) 623-1000, Fax: (202) 623-3096, www.iadb.org; *The Politics of Policies: Economic and Social Progress in Latin America - 2006 Report.*

International Monetary Fund (IMF), 700 Nineteenth Street, NW, Washington, DC 20431, (202) 623-7000, Fax: (202) 623-4661, www.imf.org; *Government Finance Statistics Yearbook (2008 Edition).*

United Nations Statistics Division, New York, NY 10017, (800) 253-9646, Fax: (212) 963-4116, http://unstats.un.org; *Statistical Yearbook for Latin America and the Caribbean 2004.*

The World Bank, 1818 H Street, NW, Washington, DC 20433, (202) 473-1000, Fax: (202) 477-6391, www.worldbank.org; *World Development Indicators (WDI) 2008.*

GUYANA - TELEPHONE

International Telecommunication Union (ITU), Place des Nations, 1211 Geneva 20, Switzerland, www.itu.int; World Telecommunication Indicators Database.

Palgrave Macmillan Ltd., Houndmills, Basingstoke, Hampshire, RG21 6XS, England, (Telephone in U.S. (888) 330-8477), (Fax in U.S. (800) 672-2054), www.palgrave.com; *The Statesman's Yearbook 2008.*

Taylor and Francis Group, An Informa Business, 2 Park Square, Milton Park, Abingdon, Oxford OX14 4RN, United Kingdom, (Dial from U.S. (212) 216-7800), (Fax from U.S. (212) 564-7854), www.tandf.co.uk; *The Europa World Year Book.*

United Nations Statistics Division, New York, NY 10017, (800) 253-9646, Fax: (212) 963-4116, http://unstats.un.org; *Statistical Yearbook.*

GUYANA - TEXTILE INDUSTRY

M.E. Sharpe, 80 Business Park Drive, Armonk, NY 10504, (800) 541-6563, Fax: (914) 273-2106, www.mesharpe.com; *The Illustrated Book of World Rankings.*

United Nations Conference on Trade and Development (UNCTAD), DC2-1120, United Nations, New York, NY 10017, (212) 963-0027, www.unctad.org; *UNCTAD Commodity Yearbook.*

GUYANA - TOBACCO INDUSTRY

Foreign Agricultural Service (FAS), U.S. Department of Agriculture (USDA), 1400 Independence Avenue, SW, Washington, DC 20250, (202) 720-3935, www.fas.usda.gov; *Tobacco: World Markets and Trade.*

M.E. Sharpe, 80 Business Park Drive, Armonk, NY 10504, (800) 541-6563, Fax: (914) 273-2106, www.mesharpe.com; *The Illustrated Book of World Rankings.*

United Nations Statistics Division, New York, NY 10017, (800) 253-9646, Fax: (212) 963-4116, http://unstats.un.org; *Statistical Yearbook.*

GUYANA - TOURISM

Euromonitor International, Inc., 224 S. Michigan Avenue, Suite 1500, Chicago, IL 60604, (312) 922-1115, Fax: (312) 922-1157, www.euromonitor.com; *The World Economic Factbook 2008* and *World Marketing Data and Statistics.*

M.E. Sharpe, 80 Business Park Drive, Armonk, NY 10504, (800) 541-6563, Fax: (914) 273-2106, www.mesharpe.com; *The Illustrated Book of World Rankings.*

United Nations Statistics Division, New York, NY 10017, (800) 253-9646, Fax: (212) 963-4116, http://unstats.un.org; *Statistical Yearbook.*

The World Bank, 1818 H Street, NW, Washington, DC 20433, (202) 473-1000, Fax: (202) 477-6391, www.worldbank.org; *Guyana.*

GUYANA - TRADE

See GUYANA - INTERNATIONAL TRADE

GUYANA - TRANSPORTATION

Central Intelligence Agency, Office of Public Affairs, Washington, DC 20505, (703) 482-0623, Fax: (703) 482-1739, www.cia.gov; *The World Factbook.*

Euromonitor International, Inc., 224 S. Michigan Avenue, Suite 1500, Chicago, IL 60604, (312) 922-1115, Fax: (312) 922-1157, www.euromonitor.com; *International Marketing Data and Statistics 2008* and *World Marketing Data and Statistics.*

Inter-American Development Bank (IDB), 1300 New York Avenue, NW, Washington, DC 20577, (202) 623-1000, Fax: (202) 623-3096, www.iadb.org; *The Politics of Policies: Economic and Social Progress in Latin America - 2006 Report.*

M.E. Sharpe, 80 Business Park Drive, Armonk, NY 10504, (800) 541-6563, Fax: (914) 273-2106, www.mesharpe.com; *The Illustrated Book of World Rankings.*

Palgrave Macmillan Ltd., Houndmills, Basingstoke, Hampshire, RG21 6XS, England, (Telephone in U.S. (888) 330-8477), (Fax in U.S. (800) 672-2054), www.palgrave.com; *The Statesman's Yearbook 2008.*

Taylor and Francis Group, An Informa Business, 2 Park Square, Milton Park, Abingdon, Oxford OX14 4RN, United Kingdom, (Dial from U.S. (212) 216-7800), (Fax from U.S. (212) 564-7854), www.tandf.co.uk; *The Europa World Year Book.*

United Nations Statistics Division, New York, NY 10017, (800) 253-9646, Fax: (212) 963-4116, http://unstats.un.org; *Human Development Report 2006.*

The World Bank, 1818 H Street, NW, Washington, DC 20433, (202) 473-1000, Fax: (202) 477-6391, www.worldbank.org; *Guyana.*

GUYANA - UNEMPLOYMENT

Central Intelligence Agency, Office of Public Affairs, Washington, DC 20505, (703) 482-0623, Fax: (703) 482-1739, www.cia.gov; *The World Factbook.*

Euromonitor International, Inc., 224 S. Michigan Avenue, Suite 1500, Chicago, IL 60604, (312) 922-1115, Fax: (312) 922-1157, www.euromonitor.com; *International Marketing Data and Statistics 2008.*

International Labour Office, I.L.O. Publications, 4 route des Morillons, CH-1211 Geneva 22, Switzerland, (Telephone in U.S. (202) 653-7652), (Fax in U.S. (202) 653-7687), www.ilo.org; *Yearbook of Labour Statistics 2006.*

United Nations Statistics Division, New York, NY 10017, (800) 253-9646, Fax: (212) 963-4116, http://unstats.un.org; *Statistical Yearbook.*

GUYANA - VITAL STATISTICS

Euromonitor International, Inc., 224 S. Michigan Avenue, Suite 1500, Chicago, IL 60604, (312) 922-1115, Fax: (312) 922-1157, www.euromonitor.com; *International Marketing Data and Statistics 2008.*

Palgrave Macmillan Ltd., Houndmills, Basingstoke, Hampshire, RG21 6XS, England, (Telephone in U.S. (888) 330-8477), (Fax in U.S. (800) 672-2054), www.palgrave.com; *The Statesman's Yearbook 2008.*

United Nations Statistics Division, New York, NY 10017, (800) 253-9646, Fax: (212) 963-4116, http://unstats.un.org; *Statistical Yearbook.*

World Health Organization (WHO), Avenue Appia 20, 1211 Geneve 27, Switzerland, (Telephone in U.S. (212) 331-9081), www.who.int; *World Health Report 2006.*

GUYANA - WAGES

International Labour Office, I.L.O. Publications, 4 route des Morillons, CH-1211 Geneva 22, Switzerland, (Telephone in U.S. (202) 653-7652), (Fax in U.S. (202) 653-7687), www.ilo.org; *Yearbook of Labour Statistics 2006.*

United Nations Statistics Division, New York, NY 10017, (800) 253-9646, Fax: (212) 963-4116, http://unstats.un.org; *Statistical Yearbook.*

The World Bank, 1818 H Street, NW, Washington, DC 20433, (202) 473-1000, Fax: (202) 477-6391, www.worldbank.org; *Guyana.*

GUYANA - WELFARE STATE

Inter-American Development Bank (IDB), 1300 New York Avenue, NW, Washington, DC 20577, (202) 623-1000, Fax: (202) 623-3096, www.iadb.org; *The Politics of Policies: Economic and Social Progress in Latin America - 2006 Report.*

GUYANA - WHEAT PRODUCTION

See GUYANA - CROPS

GUYANA - WHOLESALE PRICE INDEXES

Inter-American Development Bank (IDB), 1300 New York Avenue, NW, Washington, DC 20577, (202) 623-1000, Fax: (202) 623-3096, www.iadb.org; *The Politics of Policies: Economic and Social Progress in Latin America - 2006 Report.*

GUYANA - WHOLESALE TRADE

Inter-American Development Bank (IDB), 1300 New York Avenue, NW, Washington, DC 20577, (202) 623-1000, Fax: (202) 623-3096, www.iadb.org; *The Politics of Policies: Economic and Social Progress in Latin America - 2006 Report.*

GUYANA - WINE PRODUCTION

See GUYANA - BEVERAGE INDUSTRY

GUYANA - WOOL PRODUCTION

See GUYANA - TEXTILE INDUSTRY

GYMNASTICS

National Collegiate Athletic Association (NCAA), 700 West Washington Street, PO Box 6222, Indianapolis, IN 46206-6222, (317) 917-6222, Fax: (317) 917-6888, www.ncaa.org; *1982-2003 Sports Sponsorship and Participation Rates Report.*

GYPSUM AND GYPSUM PRODUCTS

U.S. Bureau of Labor Statistics (BLS), Postal Square Building, 2 Massachusetts Avenue, NE, Washington, DC 20212-0001, (202) 691-5200, Fax: (202) 691-6325, www.bls.gov; *Producer Price Indexes (PPI).*

U.S. Department of the Interior (DOI), U.S. Geological Survey (USGS), Office of Minerals Information, 12201 Sunrise Valley Drive, Reston, VA 20192, Mr. Kenneth A. Beckman, (703) 648-4916, Fax: (703) 648-4995, http://minerals.usgs.gov/minerals; *Mineral Commodity Summaries* and *Minerals Yearbook.*
STATISTICS SOURCES, Thirty-second Edition - 2009STATISTICS SOURCES, Thirty-second Edition - 2009

HADDOCK

National Marine Fisheries Service (NMFS), National Oceanic and Atmospheric Administration (NOAA), Office of Constituent Services, 1315 East West Highway, 9th Floor, Silver Spring, MD 20910, (301) 713-2379, Fax: (301) 713-2385, www.nmfs.noaa.gov; *Fisheries of the United States - 2006.*

HAEMOPHILIUS INFLUENZA

Centers for Disease Control and Prevention (CDC), U.S. Department of Health and Human Services (HHS), 1600 Clifton Road, Atlanta, GA 30333, (800) 311-3435, www.cdc.gov; *Morbidity and Mortality Weekly Report (MMWR)* and *Summary of Notifiable Diseases, United States, 2006.*

HAITI - NATIONAL STATISTICAL OFFICE

Haitian Institute of Statistics and Information, Ministry of Finance, Haiti; National Data Center.

HAITI - PRIMARY STATISTICS SOURCES

Haitian Institute of Statistics and Information, Ministry of Finance, Haiti; *Bulletin Trimestriel de Statistique* (Quarterly Bulletin of Statistics).

HAITI - AGRICULTURAL MACHINERY

United Nations Statistics Division, New York, NY 10017, (800) 253-9646, Fax: (212) 963-4116, http://unstats.un.org; *Statistical Yearbook.*

HAITI - AGRICULTURE

Economist Intelligence Unit, 111 West 57th Street, New York, NY 10019, (212) 554-0600, Fax: (212) 586-1181, www.eiu.com; *Haiti Country Report.*

Euromonitor International, Inc., 224 S. Michigan Avenue, Suite 1500, Chicago, IL 60604, (312) 922-1115, Fax: (312) 922-1157, www.euromonitor.com; *World Marketing Data and Statistics.*

Inter-American Development Bank (IDB), 1300 New York Avenue, NW, Washington, DC 20577, (202) 623-1000, Fax: (202) 623-3096, www.iadb.org; *The Politics of Policies: Economic and Social Progress in Latin America - 2006 Report.*

M.E. Sharpe, 80 Business Park Drive, Armonk, NY 10504, (800) 541-6563, Fax: (914) 273-2106, www.mesharpe.com; *The Illustrated Book of World Rankings.*

Palgrave Macmillan Ltd., Houndmills, Basingstoke, Hampshire, RG21 6XS, England, (Telephone in U.S. (888) 330-8477), (Fax in U.S. (800) 672-2054), www.palgrave.com; *The Statesman's Yearbook 2008.*

Taylor and Francis Group, An Informa Business, 2 Park Square, Milton Park, Abingdon, Oxford OX14 4RN, United Kingdom, (Dial from U.S. (212) 216-7800), (Fax from U.S. (212) 564-7854), www.tandf.co.uk; *The Europa World Year Book.*

UCLA Latin American Institute, 10343 Bunche Hall, Box 951447, Los Angeles, CA 90095-1447, (310) 825-4571, Fax: (310) 206-6859, www.international.ucla.edu/lac; *Statistical Abstract of Latin America.*

United Nations Conference on Trade and Development (UNCTAD), DC2-1120, United Nations, New York, NY 10017, (212) 963-0027, www.unctad.org; *UNCTAD Commodity Yearbook.*

United Nations Food and Agricultural Organization (FAO), Viale delle Terme di Caracalla, 00100 Rome, Italy, (Dial from U.S. (202) 653-2400), (Fax from U.S. (202) 653 5760), www.fao.org; AQUASTAT; *FAO Production Yearbook 2002; FAO Trade Yearbook;* and *The State of Food and Agriculture (SOFA) 2006.*

United Nations Statistics Division, New York, NY 10017, (800) 253-9646, Fax: (212) 963-4116, http://unstats.un.org; *Statistical Yearbook* and *Statistical Yearbook for Latin America and the Caribbean 2004.*

The World Bank, 1818 H Street, NW, Washington, DC 20433, (202) 473-1000, Fax: (202) 477-6391, www.worldbank.org; *Haiti* and *World Development Indicators (WDI) 2008.*

HAITI - AIRLINES

M.E. Sharpe, 80 Business Park Drive, Armonk, NY 10504, (800) 541-6563, Fax: (914) 273-2106, www.mesharpe.com; *The Illustrated Book of World Rankings.*

Palgrave Macmillan Ltd., Houndmills, Basingstoke, Hampshire, RG21 6XS, England, (Telephone in U.S. (888) 330-8477), (Fax in U.S. (800) 672-2054), www.palgrave.com; *The Statesman's Yearbook 2008.*

Taylor and Francis Group, An Informa Business, 2 Park Square, Milton Park, Abingdon, Oxford OX14 4RN, United Kingdom, (Dial from U.S. (212) 216-7800), (Fax from U.S. (212) 564-7854), www.tandf.co.uk; *The Europa World Year Book.*

HAITI - AIRPORTS

Central Intelligence Agency, Office of Public Affairs, Washington, DC 20505, (703) 482-0623, Fax: (703) 482-1739, www.cia.gov; *The World Factbook.*

HAITI - ALUMINUM PRODUCTION

See HAITI - MINERAL INDUSTRIES

HAITI - ARMED FORCES

Central Intelligence Agency, Office of Public Affairs, Washington, DC 20505, (703) 482-0623, Fax: (703) 482-1739, www.cia.gov; *The World Factbook.*

Euromonitor International, Inc., 224 S. Michigan Avenue, Suite 1500, Chicago, IL 60604, (312) 922-1115, Fax: (312) 922-1157, www.euromonitor.com; *World Marketing Data and Statistics.*

International Institute for Strategic Studies (IISS), Arundel House, 13-15 Arundel Street, Temple Place, London WC2R 3DX, England, www.iiss.org; *The Military Balance 2007.*

Palgrave Macmillan Ltd., Houndmills, Basingstoke, Hampshire, RG21 6XS, England, (Telephone in U.S. (888) 330-8477), (Fax in U.S. (800) 672-2054), www.palgrave.com; *The Statesman's Yearbook 2008.*

U.S. Department of State (DOS), 2201 C Street NW, Washington, DC 20520, (202) 647-4000, www.state.gov; *World Military Expenditures and Arms Transfers (WMEAT).*

UCLA Latin American Institute, 10343 Bunche Hall, Box 951447, Los Angeles, CA 90095-1447, (310) 825-4571, Fax: (310) 206-6859, www.international.ucla.edu/lac; *Statistical Abstract of Latin America.*

United Nations Statistics Division, New York, NY 10017, (800) 253-9646, Fax: (212) 963-4116, http://unstats.un.org; *Human Development Report 2006.*

HAITI - BALANCE OF PAYMENTS

Inter-American Development Bank (IDB), 1300 New York Avenue, NW, Washington, DC 20577, (202) 623-1000, Fax: (202) 623-3096, www.iadb.org; *The Politics of Policies: Economic and Social Progress in Latin America - 2006 Report.*

International Monetary Fund (IMF), 700 Nineteenth Street, NW, Washington, DC 20431, (202) 623-7000, Fax: (202) 623-4661, www.imf.org; *Balance of Payments Statistics Newsletter; Balance of Payments Statistics Yearbook 2007;* and *International Financial Statistics Yearbook 2007.*

Organization of American States (OAS), 17th Street Constitution Avenue NW, Washington, DC 20006, (202) 458-3000, www.oas.org; *The OAS in Transition: 1994-2004.*

Taylor and Francis Group, An Informa Business, 2 Park Square, Milton Park, Abingdon, Oxford OX14 4RN, United Kingdom, (Dial from U.S. (212) 216-7800), (Fax from U.S. (212) 564-7854), www.tandf.co.uk; *The Europa World Year Book.*

UCLA Latin American Institute, 10343 Bunche Hall, Box 951447, Los Angeles, CA 90095-1447, (310) 825-4571, Fax: (310) 206-6859, www.international.ucla.edu/lac; *Statistical Abstract of Latin America.*

United Nations Conference on Trade and Development (UNCTAD), DC2-1120, United Nations, New York, NY 10017, (212) 963-0027, www.unctad.org; *Handbook of Statistics 2005.*

United Nations Statistics Division, New York, NY 10017, (800) 253-9646, Fax: (212) 963-4116, http://unstats.un.org; *Economic Survey of Latin America and the Caribbean 2004-2005* and *Statistical Yearbook for Latin America and the Caribbean 2004.*

The World Bank, 1818 H Street, NW, Washington, DC 20433, (202) 473-1000, Fax: (202) 477-6391, www.worldbank.org; *Haiti; World Development Indicators (WDI) 2008;* and *World Development Report 2008.*

HAITI - BANKS AND BANKING

Euromonitor International, Inc., 224 S. Michigan Avenue, Suite 1500, Chicago, IL 60604, (312) 922-1115, Fax: (312) 922-1157, www.euromonitor.com; *World Marketing Data and Statistics.*

Inter-American Development Bank (IDB), 1300 New York Avenue, NW, Washington, DC 20577, (202) 623-1000, Fax: (202) 623-3096, www.iadb.org; *The Politics of Policies: Economic and Social Progress in Latin America - 2006 Report.*

International Monetary Fund (IMF), 700 Nineteenth Street, NW, Washington, DC 20431, (202) 623-7000, Fax: (202) 623-4661, www.imf.org; *International Financial Statistics Yearbook 2007.*

M.E. Sharpe, 80 Business Park Drive, Armonk, NY 10504, (800) 541-6563, Fax: (914) 273-2106, www.mesharpe.com; *The Illustrated Book of World Rankings.*

Palgrave Macmillan Ltd., Houndmills, Basingstoke, Hampshire, RG21 6XS, England, (Telephone in U.S. (888) 330-8477), (Fax in U.S. (800) 672-2054), www.palgrave.com; *The Statesman's Yearbook 2008.*

Taylor and Francis Group, An Informa Business, 2 Park Square, Milton Park, Abingdon, Oxford OX14 4RN, United Kingdom, (Dial from U.S. (212) 216-7800), (Fax from U.S. (212) 564-7854), www.tandf.co.uk; *The Europa World Year Book.*

United Nations Statistics Division, New York, NY 10017, (800) 253-9646, Fax: (212) 963-4116, http://unstats.un.org; *Statistical Yearbook for Latin America and the Caribbean 2004.*

HAITI - BARLEY PRODUCTION

See HAITI - CROPS

HAITI - BEVERAGE INDUSTRY

M.E. Sharpe, 80 Business Park Drive, Armonk, NY 10504, (800) 541-6563, Fax: (914) 273-2106, www.mesharpe.com; *The Illustrated Book of World Rankings.*

HAITI - BIRTH CONTROL

UCLA Latin American Institute, 10343 Bunche Hall, Box 951447, Los Angeles, CA 90095-1447, (310) 825-4571, Fax: (310) 206-6859, www.international.ucla.edu/lac; *Statistical Abstract of Latin America.*

HAITI - BONDS

Inter-American Development Bank (IDB), 1300 New York Avenue, NW, Washington, DC 20577, (202) 623-1000, Fax: (202) 623-3096, www.iadb.org; *The Politics of Policies: Economic and Social Progress in Latin America - 2006 Report.*

HAITI - BROADCASTING

Central Intelligence Agency, Office of Public Affairs, Washington, DC 20505, (703) 482-0623, Fax: (703) 482-1739, www.cia.gov; *The World Factbook.*

Euromonitor International, Inc., 224 S. Michigan Avenue, Suite 1500, Chicago, IL 60604, (312) 922-1115, Fax: (312) 922-1157, www.euromonitor.com; *World Marketing Data and Statistics.*

M.E. Sharpe, 80 Business Park Drive, Armonk, NY 10504, (800) 541-6563, Fax: (914) 273-2106, www.mesharpe.com; *The Illustrated Book of World Rankings.*

Palgrave Macmillan Ltd., Houndmills, Basingstoke, Hampshire, RG21 6XS, England, (Telephone in U.S. (888) 330-8477), (Fax in U.S. (800) 672-2054), www.palgrave.com; *The Statesman's Yearbook 2008.*

WRTH Publications Limited, PO Box 290, Oxford OX2 7FT, UK, www.wrth.com; *World Radio TV Handbook 2007.*

HAITI - BUDGET

Central Intelligence Agency, Office of Public Affairs, Washington, DC 20505, (703) 482-0623, Fax: (703) 482-1739, www.cia.gov; *The World Factbook.*

HAITI - BUSINESS

Inter-American Development Bank (IDB), 1300 New York Avenue, NW, Washington, DC 20577, (202) 623-1000, Fax: (202) 623-3096, www.iadb.org; *The Politics of Policies: Economic and Social Progress in Latin America - 2006 Report.*

United Nations Statistics Division, New York, NY 10017, (800) 253-9646, Fax: (212) 963-4116, http://unstats.un.org; *Statistical Yearbook.*

HAITI - CAPITAL INVESTMENTS

Inter-American Development Bank (IDB), 1300 New York Avenue, NW, Washington, DC 20577, (202) 623-1000, Fax: (202) 623-3096, www.iadb.org; *The Politics of Policies: Economic and Social Progress in Latin America - 2006 Report.*

HAITI - CAPITAL LEVY

Inter-American Development Bank (IDB), 1300 New York Avenue, NW, Washington, DC 20577, (202) 623-1000, Fax: (202) 623-3096, www.iadb.org; *The Politics of Policies: Economic and Social Progress in Latin America - 2006 Report.*

International Monetary Fund (IMF), 700 Nineteenth Street, NW, Washington, DC 20431, (202) 623-7000, Fax: (202) 623-4661, www.imf.org; *Government Finance Statistics Yearbook (2008 Edition).*

HAITI - CATTLE

See HAITI - LIVESTOCK

HAITI - CHILDBIRTH - STATISTICS

Central Intelligence Agency, Office of Public Affairs, Washington, DC 20505, (703) 482-0623, Fax: (703) 482-1739, www.cia.gov; *The World Factbook.*

Euromonitor International, Inc., 224 S. Michigan Avenue, Suite 1500, Chicago, IL 60604, (312) 922-1115, Fax: (312) 922-1157, www.euromonitor.com; *International Marketing Data and Statistics 2008* and *The World Economic Factbook 2008.*

M.E. Sharpe, 80 Business Park Drive, Armonk, NY 10504, (800) 541-6563, Fax: (914) 273-2106, www.mesharpe.com; *The Illustrated Book of World Rankings.*

Palgrave Macmillan Ltd., Houndmills, Basingstoke, Hampshire, RG21 6XS, England, (Telephone in U.S. (888) 330-8477), (Fax in U.S. (800) 672-2054), www.palgrave.com; *The Statesman's Yearbook 2008.*

Taylor and Francis Group, An Informa Business, 2 Park Square, Milton Park, Abingdon, Oxford OX14 4RN, United Kingdom, (Dial from U.S. (212) 216-7800), (Fax from U.S. (212) 564-7854), www.tandf.co.uk; *The Europa World Year Book.*

United Nations Statistics Division, New York, NY 10017, (800) 253-9646, Fax: (212) 963-4116, http://unstats.un.org; *Demographic Yearbook; Statistical Yearbook;* and *Statistical Yearbook for Latin America and the Caribbean 2004.*

The World Bank, 1818 H Street, NW, Washington, DC 20433, (202) 473-1000, Fax: (202) 477-6391, www.worldbank.org; *World Development Indicators (WDI) 2008.*

HAITI - CLIMATE

M.E. Sharpe, 80 Business Park Drive, Armonk, NY 10504, (800) 541-6563, Fax: (914) 273-2106, www.mesharpe.com; *The Illustrated Book of World Rankings.*

Palgrave Macmillan Ltd., Houndmills, Basingstoke, Hampshire, RG21 6XS, England, (Telephone in U.S. (888) 330-8477), (Fax in U.S. (800) 672-2054), www.palgrave.com; *The Statesman's Yearbook 2008.*

HAITI - COAL PRODUCTION

See HAITI - MINERAL INDUSTRIES

HAITI - COCOA PRODUCTION

See HAITI - CROPS

HAITI - COFFEE

See HAITI - CROPS

HAITI - COMMERCE

Palgrave Macmillan Ltd., Houndmills, Basingstoke, Hampshire, RG21 6XS, England, (Telephone in U.S. (888) 330-8477), (Fax in U.S. (800) 672-2054), www.palgrave.com; *The Statesman's Yearbook 2008.*

HAITI - COMMODITY EXCHANGES

Commodity Research Bureau, 330 South Wells Street, Suite 612, Chicago, IL 60606-7110, (800) 621-5271, Fax: (312) 939-4135, www.crbtrader.com; *2006 CRB Commodity Yearbook and CD.*

International Monetary Fund (IMF), 700 Nineteenth Street, NW, Washington, DC 20431, (202) 623-7000, Fax: (202) 623-4661, www.imf.org; *IMF Primary Commodity Prices.*

United Nations Food and Agricultural Organization (FAO), Viale delle Terme di Caracalla, 00100 Rome, Italy, (Dial from U.S. (202) 653-2400), (Fax from U.S. (202) 653 5760), www.fao.org; *The State of Food and Agriculture (SOFA) 2006.*

HAITI - CONSTRUCTION INDUSTRY

Inter-American Development Bank (IDB), 1300 New York Avenue, NW, Washington, DC 20577, (202) 623-1000, Fax: (202) 623-3096, www.iadb.org; *The Politics of Policies: Economic and Social Progress in Latin America - 2006 Report.*

M.E. Sharpe, 80 Business Park Drive, Armonk, NY 10504, (800) 541-6563, Fax: (914) 273-2106, www.mesharpe.com; *The Illustrated Book of World Rankings.*

UCLA Latin American Institute, 10343 Bunche Hall, Box 951447, Los Angeles, CA 90095-1447, (310) 825-4571, Fax: (310) 206-6859, www.international.ucla.edu/lac; *Statistical Abstract of Latin America.*

United Nations Statistics Division, New York, NY 10017, (800) 253-9646, Fax: (212) 963-4116, http://unstats.un.org; *Statistical Yearbook.*

HAITI - CONSUMER COOPERATIVES

UCLA Latin American Institute, 10343 Bunche Hall, Box 951447, Los Angeles, CA 90095-1447, (310) 825-4571, Fax: (310) 206-6859, www.international.ucla.edu/lac; *Statistical Abstract of Latin America.*

HAITI - CONSUMER PRICE INDEXES

Taylor and Francis Group, An Informa Business, 2 Park Square, Milton Park, Abingdon, Oxford OX14 4RN, United Kingdom, (Dial from U.S. (212) 216-7800), (Fax from U.S. (212) 564-7854), www.tandf.co.uk; *The Europa World Year Book.*

United Nations Statistics Division, New York, NY 10017, (800) 253-9646, Fax: (212) 963-4116, http://unstats.un.org; *Statistical Yearbook.*

The World Bank, 1818 H Street, NW, Washington, DC 20433, (202) 473-1000, Fax: (202) 477-6391, www.worldbank.org; *Haiti.*

HAITI - CONSUMPTION (ECONOMICS)

Inter-American Development Bank (IDB), 1300 New York Avenue, NW, Washington, DC 20577, (202) 623-1000, Fax: (202) 623-3096, www.iadb.org; *The Politics of Policies: Economic and Social Progress in Latin America - 2006 Report.*

United Nations Statistics Division, New York, NY 10017, (800) 253-9646, Fax: (212) 963-4116, http://unstats.un.org; *Statistical Yearbook for Latin America and the Caribbean 2004.*

The World Bank, 1818 H Street, NW, Washington, DC 20433, (202) 473-1000, Fax: (202) 477-6391, www.worldbank.org; *World Development Report 2008.*

HAITI - COPPER INDUSTRY AND TRADE

See HAITI - MINERAL INDUSTRIES

HAITI - CORN INDUSTRY

See HAITI - CROPS

HAITI - COTTON

See HAITI - CROPS

HAITI - CROPS

International Monetary Fund (IMF), 700 Nineteenth Street, NW, Washington, DC 20431, (202) 623-7000, Fax: (202) 623-4661, www.imf.org; *International Financial Statistics Yearbook 2007.*

M.E. Sharpe, 80 Business Park Drive, Armonk, NY 10504, (800) 541-6563, Fax: (914) 273-2106, www.mesharpe.com; *The Illustrated Book of World Rankings.*

Organization of American States (OAS), 17th Street Constitution Avenue NW, Washington, DC 20006, (202) 458-3000, www.oas.org; *The OAS in Transition: 1994-2004.*

Palgrave Macmillan Ltd., Houndmills, Basingstoke, Hampshire, RG21 6XS, England, (Telephone in U.S. (888) 330-8477), (Fax in U.S. (800) 672-2054), www.palgrave.com; *The Statesman's Yearbook 2008.*

Taylor and Francis Group, An Informa Business, 2 Park Square, Milton Park, Abingdon, Oxford OX14 4RN, United Kingdom, (Dial from U.S. (212) 216-7800), (Fax from U.S. (212) 564-7854), www.tandf.co.uk; *The Europa World Year Book.*

United Nations Conference on Trade and Development (UNCTAD), DC2-1120, United Nations, New York, NY 10017, (212) 963-0027, www.unctad.org; *UNCTAD Commodity Yearbook.*

United Nations Food and Agricultural Organization (FAO), Viale delle Terme di Caracalla, 00100 Rome, Italy, (Dial from U.S. (202) 653-2400), (Fax from U.S. (202) 653 5760), www.fao.org; *FAO Production Yearbook 2002* and *The State of Food and Agriculture (SOFA) 2006.*

United Nations Statistics Division, New York, NY 10017, (800) 253-9646, Fax: (212) 963-4116, http://unstats.un.org; *Statistical Yearbook.*

HAITI - CUSTOMS ADMINISTRATION

Inter-American Development Bank (IDB), 1300 New York Avenue, NW, Washington, DC 20577, (202) 623-1000, Fax: (202) 623-3096, www.iadb.org; *The Politics of Policies: Economic and Social Progress in Latin America - 2006 Report.*

Palgrave Macmillan Ltd., Houndmills, Basingstoke, Hampshire, RG21 6XS, England, (Telephone in U.S. (888) 330-8477), (Fax in U.S. (800) 672-2054), www.palgrave.com; *The Statesman's Yearbook 2008.*

HAITI - DAIRY PROCESSING

M.E. Sharpe, 80 Business Park Drive, Armonk, NY 10504, (800) 541-6563, Fax: (914) 273-2106, www.mesharpe.com; *The Illustrated Book of World Rankings.*

Palgrave Macmillan Ltd., Houndmills, Basingstoke, Hampshire, RG21 6XS, England, (Telephone in U.S. (888) 330-8477), (Fax in U.S. (800) 672-2054), www.palgrave.com; *The Statesman's Yearbook 2008.*

Taylor and Francis Group, An Informa Business, 2 Park Square, Milton Park, Abingdon, Oxford OX14 4RN, United Kingdom, (Dial from U.S. (212) 216-7800), (Fax from U.S. (212) 564-7854), www.tandf.co.uk; *The Europa World Year Book.*

United Nations Food and Agricultural Organization (FAO), Viale delle Terme di Caracalla, 00100 Rome, Italy, (Dial from U.S. (202) 653-2400), (Fax from U.S. (202) 653 5760), www.fao.org; *FAO Production Yearbook 2002* and *The State of Food and Agriculture (SOFA) 2006.*

United Nations Statistics Division, New York, NY 10017, (800) 253-9646, Fax: (212) 963-4116, http://unstats.un.org; *Statistical Yearbook.*

HAITI - DEATH RATES

See HAITI - MORTALITY

HAITI - DEBTS, EXTERNAL

Inter-American Development Bank (IDB), 1300 New York Avenue, NW, Washington, DC 20577, (202) 623-1000, Fax: (202) 623-3096, www.iadb.org; *The Politics of Policies: Economic and Social Progress in Latin America - 2006 Report.*

United Nations Statistics Division, New York, NY 10017, (800) 253-9646, Fax: (212) 963-4116, http://unstats.un.org; *Economic Survey of Latin America and the Caribbean 2004-2005* and *Statistical Yearbook for Latin America and the Caribbean 2004.*

The World Bank, 1818 H Street, NW, Washington, DC 20433, (202) 473-1000, Fax: (202) 477-6391, www.worldbank.org; *Global Development Finance 2007; World Development Indicators (WDI) 2008;* and *World Development Report 2008.*

HAITI - DEFENSE EXPENDITURES

See HAITI - ARMED FORCES

HAITI - DEMOGRAPHY

Euromonitor International, Inc., 224 S. Michigan Avenue, Suite 1500, Chicago, IL 60604, (312) 922-1115, Fax: (312) 922-1157, www.euromonitor.com; *International Marketing Data and Statistics 2008; The World Economic Factbook 2008;* and *World Marketing Data and Statistics.*

M.E. Sharpe, 80 Business Park Drive, Armonk, NY 10504, (800) 541-6563, Fax: (914) 273-2106, www.mesharpe.com; *The Illustrated Book of World Rankings.*

United Nations Statistics Division, New York, NY 10017, (800) 253-9646, Fax: (212) 963-4116, http://unstats.un.org; *Human Development Report 2006.*

The World Bank, 1818 H Street, NW, Washington, DC 20433, (202) 473-1000, Fax: (202) 477-6391, www.worldbank.org; *Haiti.*

HAITI - DIAMONDS

See HAITI - MINERAL INDUSTRIES

HAITI - DISPOSABLE INCOME

Inter-American Development Bank (IDB), 1300 New York Avenue, NW, Washington, DC 20577, (202) 623-1000, Fax: (202) 623-3096, www.iadb.org; *The Politics of Policies: Economic and Social Progress in Latin America - 2006 Report.*

M.E. Sharpe, 80 Business Park Drive, Armonk, NY 10504, (800) 541-6563, Fax: (914) 273-2106, www.mesharpe.com; *The Illustrated Book of World Rankings.*

United Nations Statistics Division, New York, NY 10017, (800) 253-9646, Fax: (212) 963-4116, http://unstats.un.org; *National Accounts Statistics: Compendium of Income Distribution Statistics* and *Statistical Yearbook.*

HAITI - DIVORCE

M.E. Sharpe, 80 Business Park Drive, Armonk, NY 10504, (800) 541-6563, Fax: (914) 273-2106, www.mesharpe.com; *The Illustrated Book of World Rankings.*

United Nations Statistics Division, New York, NY 10017, (800) 253-9646, Fax: (212) 963-4116, http://unstats.un.org; *Demographic Yearbook.*

HAITI - ECONOMIC ASSISTANCE

Inter-American Development Bank (IDB), 1300 New York Avenue, NW, Washington, DC 20577, (202) 623-1000, Fax: (202) 623-3096, www.iadb.org; *The Politics of Policies: Economic and Social Progress in Latin America - 2006 Report.*

United Nations Statistics Division, New York, NY 10017, (800) 253-9646, Fax: (212) 963-4116, http://unstats.un.org; *Statistical Yearbook.*

HAITI - ECONOMIC CONDITIONS

Center for International Business Education Research (CIBER), Columbia Business School and School of International and Public Affairs, Uris Hall, Room 212, 3022 Broadway, New York, NY 10027-6902, Mr. Joshua Safier, (212) 854-4750, Fax: (212) 222-9821, www.columbia.edu/cu/ciber/; Datastream International.

Central Intelligence Agency, Office of Public Affairs, Washington, DC 20505, (703) 482-0623, Fax: (703) 482-1739, www.cia.gov; *The World Factbook.*

DSI Data Service Information, Xantener Strasse 51a, D-47495 Rheinberg, Germany, www.dsidata.com; *Campus Solution.*

Dun and Bradstreet (DB) Corporation, 103 JFK Parkway, Short Hills, NJ 07078, (973) 921-5500, www.dnb.com; *Country Report.*

Economist Intelligence Unit, 111 West 57th Street, New York, NY 10019, (212) 554-0600, Fax: (212) 586-1181, www.eiu.com; *Haiti Country Report.*

Euromonitor International, Inc., 224 S. Michigan Avenue, Suite 1500, Chicago, IL 60604, (312) 922-1115, Fax: (312) 922-1157, www.euromonitor.com; *The World Economic Factbook 2008* and *World Marketing Data and Statistics.*

Inter-American Development Bank (IDB), 1300 New York Avenue, NW, Washington, DC 20577, (202) 623-1000, Fax: (202) 623-3096, www.iadb.org; *The Politics of Policies: Economic and Social Progress in Latin America - 2006 Report.*

International Monetary Fund (IMF), 700 Nineteenth Street, NW, Washington, DC 20431, (202) 623-7000, Fax: (202) 623-4661, www.imf.org; *World Economic Outlook Reports.*

M.E. Sharpe, 80 Business Park Drive, Armonk, NY 10504, (800) 541-6563, Fax: (914) 273-2106, www.mesharpe.com; *The Illustrated Book of World Rankings.*

Organization of American States (OAS), 17th Street Constitution Avenue NW, Washington, DC 20006, (202) 458-3000, www.oas.org; *The OAS in Transition: 1994-2004.*

Palgrave Macmillan Ltd., Houndmills, Basingstoke, Hampshire, RG21 6XS, England, (Telephone in U.S. (888) 330-8477), (Fax in U.S. (800) 672-2054), www.palgrave.com; *The Statesman's Yearbook 2008.*

Taylor and Francis Group, An Informa Business, 2 Park Square, Milton Park, Abingdon, Oxford OX14 4RN, United Kingdom, (Dial from U.S. (212) 216-7800), (Fax from U.S. (212) 564-7854), www.tandf.co.uk; *The Europa World Year Book.*

UCLA Latin American Institute, 10343 Bunche Hall, Box 951447, Los Angeles, CA 90095-1447, (310) 825-4571, Fax: (310) 206-6859, www.international.ucla.edu/lac; *Statistical Abstract of Latin America.*

United Nations Statistics Division, New York, NY 10017, (800) 253-9646, Fax: (212) 963-4116, http://unstats.un.org; *Economic Survey of Latin America and the Caribbean 2004-2005* and *World Statistics Pocketbook.*

The World Bank, 1818 H Street, NW, Washington, DC 20433, (202) 473-1000, Fax: (202) 477-6391, www.worldbank.org; *Global Economic Monitor (GEM); Global Economic Prospects 2008; Haiti; The World Bank Atlas 2003-2004;* and *World Development Report 2008.*

HAITI - ECONOMICS - SOCIOLOGICAL ASPECTS

Inter-American Development Bank (IDB), 1300 New York Avenue, NW, Washington, DC 20577, (202) 623-1000, Fax: (202) 623-3096, www.iadb.org; *The Politics of Policies: Economic and Social Progress in Latin America - 2006 Report.*

UCLA Latin American Institute, 10343 Bunche Hall, Box 951447, Los Angeles, CA 90095-1447, (310) 825-4571, Fax: (310) 206-6859, www.international.ucla.edu/lac; *Statistical Abstract of Latin America.*

HAITI - EDUCATION

Euromonitor International, Inc., 224 S. Michigan Avenue, Suite 1500, Chicago, IL 60604, (312) 922-1115, Fax: (312) 922-1157, www.euromonitor.com; *International Marketing Data and Statistics 2008* and *World Marketing Data and Statistics.*

M.E. Sharpe, 80 Business Park Drive, Armonk, NY 10504, (800) 541-6563, Fax: (914) 273-2106, www.mesharpe.com; *The Illustrated Book of World Rankings.*

Palgrave Macmillan Ltd., Houndmills, Basingstoke, Hampshire, RG21 6XS, England, (Telephone in U.S.

(888) 330-8477), (Fax in U.S. (800) 672-2054), www.palgrave.com; *The Statesman's Yearbook 2008.*

Taylor and Francis Group, An Informa Business, 2 Park Square, Milton Park, Abingdon, Oxford OX14 4RN, United Kingdom, (Dial from U.S. (212) 216-7800), (Fax from U.S. (212) 564-7854), www.tandf.co.uk; *The Europa World Year Book.*

UCLA Latin American Institute, 10343 Bunche Hall, Box 951447, Los Angeles, CA 90095-1447, (310) 825-4571, Fax: (310) 206-6859, www.international.ucla.edu/lac; *Statistical Abstract of Latin America.*

UNESCO Institute for Statistics, C.P. 6128 Succursale Centre-Ville, Montreal, Quebec, H3C 3J7 Canada, (Dial from U.S. (514) 343-6880), (Fax from U.S. (514) 343 6882), www.uis.unesco.org; *Statistical Tables.*

United Nations Statistics Division, New York, NY 10017, (800) 253-9646, Fax: (212) 963-4116, http://unstats.un.org; *Human Development Report 2006* and *Statistical Yearbook for Latin America and the Caribbean 2004.*

The World Bank, 1818 H Street, NW, Washington, DC 20433, (202) 473-1000, Fax: (202) 477-6391, www.worldbank.org; *Haiti; World Development Indicators (WDI) 2008;* and *World Development Report 2008.*

HAITI - ELECTRICITY

Inter-American Development Bank (IDB), 1300 New York Avenue, NW, Washington, DC 20577, (202) 623-1000, Fax: (202) 623-3096, www.iadb.org; *The Politics of Policies: Economic and Social Progress in Latin America - 2006 Report.*

M.E. Sharpe, 80 Business Park Drive, Armonk, NY 10504, (800) 541-6563, Fax: (914) 273-2106, www.mesharpe.com; *The Illustrated Book of World Rankings.*

Palgrave Macmillan Ltd., Houndmills, Basingstoke, Hampshire, RG21 6XS, England, (Telephone in U.S. (888) 330-8477), (Fax in U.S. (800) 672-2054), www.palgrave.com; *The Statesman's Yearbook 2008.*

U.S. Department of Energy (DOE), Energy Information Administration (EIA), 1000 Independence Avenue, SW, Washington, DC 20585, (202) 586-8800, www.eia.doe.gov; *International Energy Annual 2004* and *International Energy Outlook 2006.*

United Nations Statistics Division, New York, NY 10017, (800) 253-9646, Fax: (212) 963-4116, http://unstats.un.org; *Human Development Report 2006* and *Statistical Yearbook.*

HAITI - EMIGRATION AND IMMIGRATION

UCLA Latin American Institute, 10343 Bunche Hall, Box 951447, Los Angeles, CA 90095-1447, (310) 825-4571, Fax: (310) 206-6859, www.international.ucla.edu/lac; *Statistical Abstract of Latin America.*

HAITI - EMPLOYMENT

Euromonitor International, Inc., 224 S. Michigan Avenue, Suite 1500, Chicago, IL 60604, (312) 922-1115, Fax: (312) 922-1157, www.euromonitor.com; *International Marketing Data and Statistics 2008.*

International Labour Office, I.L.O. Publications, 4 route des Morillons, CH-1211 Geneva 22, Switzerland, (Telephone in U.S. (202) 653-7652), (Fax in U.S. (202) 653-7687), www.ilo.org; *Yearbook of Labour Statistics 2006.*

M.E. Sharpe, 80 Business Park Drive, Armonk, NY 10504, (800) 541-6563, Fax: (914) 273-2106, www.mesharpe.com; *The Illustrated Book of World Rankings.*

UCLA Latin American Institute, 10343 Bunche Hall, Box 951447, Los Angeles, CA 90095-1447, (310) 825-4571, Fax: (310) 206-6859, www.international.ucla.edu/lac; *Statistical Abstract of Latin America.*

United Nations Statistics Division, New York, NY 10017, (800) 253-9646, Fax: (212) 963-4116, http://unstats.un.org; *Statistical Yearbook* and *Statistical Yearbook for Latin America and the Caribbean 2004.*

The World Bank, 1818 H Street, NW, Washington, DC 20433, (202) 473-1000, Fax: (202) 477-6391, www.worldbank.org; *Haiti.*

HAITI - ENERGY INDUSTRIES

Enerdata, 10 Rue Royale, 75008 Paris, France, www.enerdata.fr; *Global Energy Market Data.*

United Nations Statistics Division, New York, NY 10017, (800) 253-9646, Fax: (212) 963-4116, http://unstats.un.org; *Statistical Yearbook.*

HAITI - ENVIRONMENTAL CONDITIONS

DSI Data Service Information, Xantener Strasse 51a, D-47495 Rheinberg, Germany, www.dsidata.com; *Campus Solution* and *DSI's Global Environmental Database.*

Economist Intelligence Unit, 111 West 57th Street, New York, NY 10019, (212) 554-0600, Fax: (212) 586-1181, www.eiu.com; *Haiti Country Report.*

United Nations Statistics Division, New York, NY 10017, (800) 253-9646, Fax: (212) 963-4116, http://unstats.un.org; *World Statistics Pocketbook.*

HAITI - EXPENDITURES, PUBLIC

Inter-American Development Bank (IDB), 1300 New York Avenue, NW, Washington, DC 20577, (202) 623-1000, Fax: (202) 623-3096, www.iadb.org; *The Politics of Policies: Economic and Social Progress in Latin America - 2006 Report.*

Organization of American States (OAS), 17th Street Constitution Avenue NW, Washington, DC 20006, (202) 458-3000, www.oas.org; *The OAS in Transition: 1994-2004.*

United Nations Statistics Division, New York, NY 10017, (800) 253-9646, Fax: (212) 963-4116, http://unstats.un.org; *Statistical Yearbook for Latin America and the Caribbean 2004.*

HAITI - EXPORTS

Central Intelligence Agency, Office of Public Affairs, Washington, DC 20505, (703) 482-0623, Fax: (703) 482-1739, www.cia.gov; *The World Factbook.*

Economist Intelligence Unit, 111 West 57th Street, New York, NY 10019, (212) 554-0600, Fax: (212) 586-1181, www.eiu.com; *Haiti Country Report.*

Euromonitor International, Inc., 224 S. Michigan Avenue, Suite 1500, Chicago, IL 60604, (312) 922-1115, Fax: (312) 922-1157, www.euromonitor.com; *International Marketing Data and Statistics 2008* and *The World Economic Factbook 2008.*

Inter-American Development Bank (IDB), 1300 New York Avenue, NW, Washington, DC 20577, (202) 623-1000, Fax: (202) 623-3096, www.iadb.org; *The Politics of Policies: Economic and Social Progress in Latin America - 2006 Report.*

International Monetary Fund (IMF), 700 Nineteenth Street, NW, Washington, DC 20431, (202) 623-7000, Fax: (202) 623-4661, www.imf.org; *Direction of Trade Statistics Yearbook 2007; Government Finance Statistics Yearbook (2008 Edition);* and *International Financial Statistics Yearbook 2007.*

Organization of American States (OAS), 17th Street Constitution Avenue NW, Washington, DC 20006, (202) 458-3000, www.oas.org; *The OAS in Transition: 1994-2004.*

Palgrave Macmillan Ltd., Houndmills, Basingstoke, Hampshire, RG21 6XS, England, (Telephone in U.S. (888) 330-8477), (Fax in U.S. (800) 672-2054), www.palgrave.com; *The Statesman's Yearbook 2008.*

Taylor and Francis Group, An Informa Business, 2 Park Square, Milton Park, Abingdon, Oxford OX14 4RN, United Kingdom, (Dial from U.S. (212) 216-7800), (Fax from U.S. (212) 564-7854), www.tandf.co.uk; *The Europa World Year Book.*

United Nations Conference on Trade and Development (UNCTAD), DC2-1120, United Nations, New York, NY 10017, (212) 963-0027, www.unctad.org; *Handbook of Statistics 2005.*

United Nations Food and Agricultural Organization (FAO), Viale delle Terme di Caracalla, 00100 Rome, Italy, (Dial from U.S. (202) 653-2400), (Fax from U.S. (202) 653 5760), www.fao.org; *The State of Food and Agriculture (SOFA) 2006.*

United Nations Statistics Division, New York, NY 10017, (800) 253-9646, Fax: (212) 963-4116, http://unstats.un.org; *Statistical Yearbook for Latin America and the Caribbean 2004.*

The World Bank, 1818 H Street, NW, Washington, DC 20433, (202) 473-1000, Fax: (202) 477-6391, www.worldbank.org; *World Development Indicators (WDI) 2008* and *World Development Report 2008.*

HAITI - FERTILITY, HUMAN

Central Intelligence Agency, Office of Public Affairs, Washington, DC 20505, (703) 482-0623, Fax: (703) 482-1739, www.cia.gov; *The World Factbook.*

M.E. Sharpe, 80 Business Park Drive, Armonk, NY 10504, (800) 541-6563, Fax: (914) 273-2106, www.mesharpe.com; *The Illustrated Book of World Rankings.*

United Nations Statistics Division, New York, NY 10017, (800) 253-9646, Fax: (212) 963-4116, http://unstats.un.org; *Human Development Report 2006.*

The World Bank, 1818 H Street, NW, Washington, DC 20433, (202) 473-1000, Fax: (202) 477-6391, www.worldbank.org; *The World Bank Atlas 2003-2004; World Development Indicators (WDI) 2008;* and *World Development Report 2008.*

HAITI - FERTILIZER INDUSTRY

United Nations Food and Agricultural Organization (FAO), Viale delle Terme di Caracalla, 00100 Rome, Italy, (Dial from U.S. (202) 653-2400), (Fax from U.S. (202) 653 5760), www.fao.org; *FAO Fertilizer Yearbook* and *The State of Food and Agriculture (SOFA) 2006.*

United Nations Statistics Division, New York, NY 10017, (800) 253-9646, Fax: (212) 963-4116, http://unstats.un.org; *Statistical Yearbook.*

HAITI - FETAL MORTALITY

See HAITI - MORTALITY

HAITI - FINANCE

Inter-American Development Bank (IDB), 1300 New York Avenue, NW, Washington, DC 20577, (202) 623-1000, Fax: (202) 623-3096, www.iadb.org; *The Politics of Policies: Economic and Social Progress in Latin America - 2006 Report.*

Organization of American States (OAS), 17th Street Constitution Avenue NW, Washington, DC 20006, (202) 458-3000, www.oas.org; *The OAS in Transition: 1994-2004.*

Taylor and Francis Group, An Informa Business, 2 Park Square, Milton Park, Abingdon, Oxford OX14 4RN, United Kingdom, (Dial from U.S. (212) 216-7800), (Fax from U.S. (212) 564-7854), www.tandf.co.uk; *The Europa World Year Book.*

UCLA Latin American Institute, 10343 Bunche Hall, Box 951447, Los Angeles, CA 90095-1447, (310) 825-4571, Fax: (310) 206-6859, www.international.ucla.edu/lac; *Statistical Abstract of Latin America.*

United Nations Statistics Division, New York, NY 10017, (800) 253-9646, Fax: (212) 963-4116, http://unstats.un.org; *National Accounts Statistics: Compendium of Income Distribution Statistics* and *Statistical Yearbook.*

The World Bank, 1818 H Street, NW, Washington, DC 20433, (202) 473-1000, Fax: (202) 477-6391, www.worldbank.org; *Haiti.*

HAITI - FINANCE, PUBLIC

Bernan Essential Government Publications, 4611-F Assembly Drive, Lanham MD, 20706-4391, (301) 459-2255, Fax: (800) 865-3450, www.bernan.com; *National Accounts Statistics.*

Economist Intelligence Unit, 111 West 57th Street, New York, NY 10019, (212) 554-0600, Fax: (212) 586-1181, www.eiu.com; *Haiti Country Report.*

Inter-American Development Bank (IDB), 1300 New York Avenue, NW, Washington, DC 20577, (202) 623-1000, Fax: (202) 623-3096, www.iadb.org; *The Politics of Policies: Economic and Social Progress in Latin America - 2006 Report.*

International Monetary Fund (IMF), 700 Nineteenth Street, NW, Washington, DC 20431, (202) 623-7000, Fax: (202) 623-4661, www.imf.org; *International Financial Statistics* and *International Financial Statistics Online Service*.

M.E. Sharpe, 80 Business Park Drive, Armonk, NY 10504, (800) 541-6563, Fax: (914) 273-2106, www.mesharpe.com; *The Illustrated Book of World Rankings*.

Organization of American States (OAS), 17th Street Constitution Avenue NW, Washington, DC 20006, (202) 458-3000, www.oas.org; *The OAS in Transition: 1994-2004*.

Palgrave Macmillan Ltd., Houndmills, Basingstoke, Hampshire, RG21 6XS, England, (Telephone in U.S. (888) 330-8477), (Fax in U.S. (800) 672-2054), www.palgrave.com; *The Statesman's Yearbook 2008*.

Taylor and Francis Group, An Informa Business, 2 Park Square, Milton Park, Abingdon, Oxford OX14 4RN, United Kingdom, (Dial from U.S. (212) 216-7800), (Fax from U.S. (212) 564-7854), www.tandf.co.uk; *The Europa World Year Book*.

UCLA Latin American Institute, 10343 Bunche Hall, Box 951447, Los Angeles, CA 90095-1447, (310) 825-4571, Fax: (310) 206-6859, www.international.ucla.edu/lac; *Statistical Abstract of Latin America*.

The World Bank, 1818 H Street, NW, Washington, DC 20433, (202) 473-1000, Fax: (202) 477-6391, www.worldbank.org; *Haiti*.

HAITI - FISHERIES

Inter-American Development Bank (IDB), 1300 New York Avenue, NW, Washington, DC 20577, (202) 623-1000, Fax: (202) 623-3096, www.iadb.org; *The Politics of Policies: Economic and Social Progress in Latin America - 2006 Report*.

M.E. Sharpe, 80 Business Park Drive, Armonk, NY 10504, (800) 541-6563, Fax: (914) 273-2106, www.mesharpe.com; *The Illustrated Book of World Rankings*.

Palgrave Macmillan Ltd., Houndmills, Basingstoke, Hampshire, RG21 6XS, England, (Telephone in U.S. (888) 330-8477), (Fax in U.S. (800) 672-2054), www.palgrave.com; *The Statesman's Yearbook 2008*.

Taylor and Francis Group, An Informa Business, 2 Park Square, Milton Park, Abingdon, Oxford OX14 4RN, United Kingdom, (Dial from U.S. (212) 216-7800), (Fax from U.S. (212) 564-7854), www.tandf.co.uk; *The Europa World Year Book*.

UCLA Latin American Institute, 10343 Bunche Hall, Box 951447, Los Angeles, CA 90095-1447, (310) 825-4571, Fax: (310) 206-6859, www.international.ucla.edu/lac; *Statistical Abstract of Latin America*.

United Nations Conference on Trade and Development (UNCTAD), DC2-1120, United Nations, New York, NY 10017, (212) 963-0027, www.unctad.org; *UNCTAD Commodity Yearbook*.

United Nations Food and Agricultural Organization (FAO), Viale delle Terme di Caracalla, 00100 Rome, Italy, (Dial from U.S. (202) 653-2400), (Fax from U.S. (202) 653 5760), www.fao.org; *FAO Yearbook of Fishery Statistics;* Fishery Databases; FISHSTAT Database. Subjects covered include: Aquaculture production, capture production, fishery commodities; and *The State of Food and Agriculture (SOFA) 2006*.

United Nations Statistics Division, New York, NY 10017, (800) 253-9646, Fax: (212) 963-4116, http://unstats.un.org; *Statistical Yearbook*.

The World Bank, 1818 H Street, NW, Washington, DC 20433, (202) 473-1000, Fax: (202) 477-6391, www.worldbank.org; *Haiti*.

HAITI - FLOUR INDUSTRY

United Nations Statistics Division, New York, NY 10017, (800) 253-9646, Fax: (212) 963-4116, http://unstats.un.org; *Statistical Yearbook*.

HAITI - FOOD

United Nations Conference on Trade and Development (UNCTAD), DC2-1120, United Nations, New York, NY 10017, (212) 963-0027, www.unctad.org; *UNCTAD Commodity Yearbook*.

United Nations Food and Agricultural Organization (FAO), Viale delle Terme di Caracalla, 00100 Rome, Italy, (Dial from U.S. (202) 653-2400), (Fax from U.S. (202) 653 5760), www.fao.org; *FAO Production Yearbook 2002* and *The State of Food and Agriculture (SOFA) 2006*.

United Nations Statistics Division, New York, NY 10017, (800) 253-9646, Fax: (212) 963-4116, http://unstats.un.org; *Human Development Report 2006*.

HAITI - FOREIGN EXCHANGE RATES

Central Intelligence Agency, Office of Public Affairs, Washington, DC 20505, (703) 482-0623, Fax: (703) 482-1739, www.cia.gov; *The World Factbook*.

Euromonitor International, Inc., 224 S. Michigan Avenue, Suite 1500, Chicago, IL 60604, (312) 922-1115, Fax: (312) 922-1157, www.euromonitor.com; *International Marketing Data and Statistics 2008* and *The World Economic Factbook 2008*.

Inter-American Development Bank (IDB), 1300 New York Avenue, NW, Washington, DC 20577, (202) 623-1000, Fax: (202) 623-3096, www.iadb.org; *The Politics of Policies: Economic and Social Progress in Latin America - 2006 Report*.

International Monetary Fund (IMF), 700 Nineteenth Street, NW, Washington, DC 20431, (202) 623-7000, Fax: (202) 623-4661, www.imf.org; *International Financial Statistics Yearbook 2007*.

Organization of American States (OAS), 17th Street Constitution Avenue NW, Washington, DC 20006, (202) 458-3000, www.oas.org; *The OAS in Transition: 1994-2004*.

Taylor and Francis Group, An Informa Business, 2 Park Square, Milton Park, Abingdon, Oxford OX14 4RN, United Kingdom, (Dial from U.S. (212) 216-7800), (Fax from U.S. (212) 564-7854), www.tandf.co.uk; *The Europa World Year Book*.

UCLA Latin American Institute, 10343 Bunche Hall, Box 951447, Los Angeles, CA 90095-1447, (310) 825-4571, Fax: (310) 206-6859, www.international.ucla.edu/lac; *Statistical Abstract of Latin America*.

United Nations Statistics Division, New York, NY 10017, (800) 253-9646, Fax: (212) 963-4116, http://unstats.un.org; *Statistical Yearbook* and *World Statistics Pocketbook*.

HAITI - FORESTS AND FORESTRY

Inter-American Development Bank (IDB), 1300 New York Avenue, NW, Washington, DC 20577, (202) 623-1000, Fax: (202) 623-3096, www.iadb.org; *The Politics of Policies: Economic and Social Progress in Latin America - 2006 Report*.

M.E. Sharpe, 80 Business Park Drive, Armonk, NY 10504, (800) 541-6563, Fax: (914) 273-2106, www.mesharpe.com; *The Illustrated Book of World Rankings*.

Palgrave Macmillan Ltd., Houndmills, Basingstoke, Hampshire, RG21 6XS, England, (Telephone in U.S. (888) 330-8477), (Fax in U.S. (800) 672-2054), www.palgrave.com; *The Statesman's Yearbook 2008*.

Taylor and Francis Group, An Informa Business, 2 Park Square, Milton Park, Abingdon, Oxford OX14 4RN, United Kingdom, (Dial from U.S. (212) 216-7800), (Fax from U.S. (212) 564-7854), www.tandf.co.uk; *The Europa World Year Book*.

UCLA Latin American Institute, 10343 Bunche Hall, Box 951447, Los Angeles, CA 90095-1447, (310) 825-4571, Fax: (310) 206-6859, www.international.ucla.edu/lac; *Statistical Abstract of Latin America*.

UNESCO Institute for Statistics, C.P. 6128 Succursale Centre-Ville, Montreal, Quebec, H3C 3J7 Canada, (Dial from U.S. (514) 343-6880), (Fax from U.S. (514) 343 6882), www.uis.unesco.org; *Statistical Tables*.

United Nations Conference on Trade and Development (UNCTAD), DC2-1120, United Nations, New York, NY 10017, (212) 963-0027, www.unctad.org; *UNCTAD Commodity Yearbook*.

United Nations Food and Agricultural Organization (FAO), Viale delle Terme di Caracalla, 00100 Rome, Italy, (Dial from U.S. (202) 653-2400), (Fax from U.S. (202) 653 5760), www.fao.org; *FAO Yearbook of Forest Products* and *The State of Food and Agriculture (SOFA) 2006*.

United Nations Statistics Division, New York, NY 10017, (800) 253-9646, Fax: (212) 963-4116, http://unstats.un.org; *Statistical Yearbook*.

The World Bank, 1818 H Street, NW, Washington, DC 20433, (202) 473-1000, Fax: (202) 477-6391, www.worldbank.org; *Haiti* and *World Development Report 2008*.

HAITI - GAS PRODUCTION

See HAITI - MINERAL INDUSTRIES

HAITI - GEOGRAPHIC INFORMATION SYSTEMS

M.E. Sharpe, 80 Business Park Drive, Armonk, NY 10504, (800) 541-6563, Fax: (914) 273-2106, www.mesharpe.com; *The Illustrated Book of World Rankings*.

UCLA Latin American Institute, 10343 Bunche Hall, Box 951447, Los Angeles, CA 90095-1447, (310) 825-4571, Fax: (310) 206-6859, www.international.ucla.edu/lac; *Statistical Abstract of Latin America*.

The World Bank, 1818 H Street, NW, Washington, DC 20433, (202) 473-1000, Fax: (202) 477-6391, www.worldbank.org; *Haiti*.

HAITI - GOLD INDUSTRY

International Monetary Fund (IMF), 700 Nineteenth Street, NW, Washington, DC 20431, (202) 623-7000, Fax: (202) 623-4661, www.imf.org; *International Financial Statistics Yearbook 2007*.

United Nations Statistics Division, New York, NY 10017, (800) 253-9646, Fax: (212) 963-4116, http://unstats.un.org; *Statistical Yearbook*.

The World Bank, 1818 H Street, NW, Washington, DC 20433, (202) 473-1000, Fax: (202) 477-6391, www.worldbank.org; *World Development Indicators (WDI) 2008*.

HAITI - GOLD PRODUCTION

See HAITI - MINERAL INDUSTRIES

HAITI - GRANTS-IN-AID

International Monetary Fund (IMF), 700 Nineteenth Street, NW, Washington, DC 20431, (202) 623-7000, Fax: (202) 623-4661, www.imf.org; *Government Finance Statistics Yearbook (2008 Edition)*.

HAITI - GROSS DOMESTIC PRODUCT

Economist Intelligence Unit, 111 West 57th Street, New York, NY 10019, (212) 554-0600, Fax: (212) 586-1181, www.eiu.com; *Haiti Country Report*.

Euromonitor International, Inc., 224 S. Michigan Avenue, Suite 1500, Chicago, IL 60604, (312) 922-1115, Fax: (312) 922-1157, www.euromonitor.com; *International Marketing Data and Statistics 2008* and *The World Economic Factbook 2008*.

Inter-American Development Bank (IDB), 1300 New York Avenue, NW, Washington, DC 20577, (202) 623-1000, Fax: (202) 623-3096, www.iadb.org; *The Politics of Policies: Economic and Social Progress in Latin America - 2006 Report*.

M.E. Sharpe, 80 Business Park Drive, Armonk, NY 10504, (800) 541-6563, Fax: (914) 273-2106, www.mesharpe.com; *The Illustrated Book of World Rankings*.

Organization of American States (OAS), 17th Street Constitution Avenue NW, Washington, DC 20006, (202) 458-3000, www.oas.org; *The OAS in Transition: 1994-2004*.

Taylor and Francis Group, An Informa Business, 2 Park Square, Milton Park, Abingdon, Oxford OX14 4RN, United Kingdom, (Dial from U.S. (212) 216-7800), (Fax from U.S. (212) 564-7854), www.tandf.co.uk; *The Europa World Year Book*.

United Nations Statistics Division, New York, NY 10017, (800) 253-9646, Fax: (212) 963-4116, http://unstats.un.org; *Human Development Report 2006; National Accounts Statistics: Compendium of Income Distribution Statistics; Statistical Yearbook;* and *Statistical Yearbook for Latin America and the Caribbean 2004.*

The World Bank, 1818 H Street, NW, Washington, DC 20433, (202) 473-1000, Fax: (202) 477-6391, www.worldbank.org; *World Development Indicators (WDI) 2008* and *World Development Report 2008.*

HAITI - GROSS NATIONAL PRODUCT

Inter-American Development Bank (IDB), 1300 New York Avenue, NW, Washington, DC 20577, (202) 623-1000, Fax: (202) 623-3096, www.iadb.org; *The Politics of Policies: Economic and Social Progress in Latin America - 2006 Report.*

M.E. Sharpe, 80 Business Park Drive, Armonk, NY 10504, (800) 541-6563, Fax: (914) 273-2106, www.mesharpe.com; *The Illustrated Book of World Rankings.*

Palgrave Macmillan Ltd., Houndmills, Basingstoke, Hampshire, RG21 6XS, England, (Telephone in U.S. (888) 330-8477), (Fax in U.S. (800) 672-2054), www.palgrave.com; *The Statesman's Yearbook 2008.*

U.S. Department of State (DOS), 2201 C Street NW, Washington, DC 20520, (202) 647-4000, www.state.gov; *World Military Expenditures and Arms Transfers (WMEAT).*

United Nations Statistics Division, New York, NY 10017, (800) 253-9646, Fax: (212) 963-4116, http://unstats.un.org; *Statistical Yearbook.*

The World Bank, 1818 H Street, NW, Washington, DC 20433, (202) 473-1000, Fax: (202) 477-6391, www.worldbank.org; *The World Bank Atlas 2003-2004; World Development Indicators (WDI) 2008;* and *World Development Report 2008.*

HAITI - HIDES AND SKINS INDUSTRY

United Nations Food and Agricultural Organization (FAO), Viale delle Terme di Caracalla, 00100 Rome, Italy, (Dial from U.S. (202) 653-2400), (Fax from U.S. (202) 653 5760), www.fao.org; *FAO Production Yearbook 2002.*

HAITI - HOUSING

Euromonitor International, Inc., 224 S. Michigan Avenue, Suite 1500, Chicago, IL 60604, (312) 922-1115, Fax: (312) 922-1157, www.euromonitor.com; *World Marketing Data and Statistics.*

M.E. Sharpe, 80 Business Park Drive, Armonk, NY 10504, (800) 541-6563, Fax: (914) 273-2106, www.mesharpe.com; *The Illustrated Book of World Rankings.*

UCLA Latin American Institute, 10343 Bunche Hall, Box 951447, Los Angeles, CA 90095-1447, (310) 825-4571, Fax: (310) 206-6859, www.international.ucla.edu/lac; *Statistical Abstract of Latin America.*

United Nations Statistics Division, New York, NY 10017, (800) 253-9646, Fax: (212) 963-4116, http://unstats.un.org; *Statistical Yearbook for Latin America and the Caribbean 2004.*

HAITI - ILLITERATE PERSONS

Euromonitor International, Inc., 224 S. Michigan Avenue, Suite 1500, Chicago, IL 60604, (312) 922-1115, Fax: (312) 922-1157, www.euromonitor.com; *The World Economic Factbook 2008.*

UNESCO Institute for Statistics, C.P. 6128 Succursale Centre-Ville, Montreal, Quebec, H3C 3J7 Canada, (Dial from U.S. (514) 343-6880), (Fax from U.S. (514) 343 6882), www.uis.unesco.org; *Statistical Tables.*

United Nations Statistics Division, New York, NY 10017, (800) 253-9646, Fax: (212) 963-4116, http://unstats.un.org; *Human Development Report 2006* and *Statistical Yearbook for Latin America and the Caribbean 2004.*

HAITI - IMPORTS

Central Intelligence Agency, Office of Public Affairs, Washington, DC 20505, (703) 482-0623, Fax: (703) 482-1739, www.cia.gov; *The World Factbook.*

Economist Intelligence Unit, 111 West 57th Street, New York, NY 10019, (212) 554-0600, Fax: (212) 586-1181, www.eiu.com; *Haiti Country Report.*

Euromonitor International, Inc., 224 S. Michigan Avenue, Suite 1500, Chicago, IL 60604, (312) 922-1115, Fax: (312) 922-1157, www.euromonitor.com; *International Marketing Data and Statistics 2008* and *The World Economic Factbook 2008.*

Inter-American Development Bank (IDB), 1300 New York Avenue, NW, Washington, DC 20577, (202) 623-1000, Fax: (202) 623-3096, www.iadb.org; *The Politics of Policies: Economic and Social Progress in Latin America - 2006 Report.*

International Monetary Fund (IMF), 700 Nineteenth Street, NW, Washington, DC 20431, (202) 623-7000, Fax: (202) 623-4661, www.imf.org; *Direction of Trade Statistics Yearbook 2007; Government Finance Statistics Yearbook (2008 Edition);* and *International Financial Statistics Yearbook 2007.*

Organization of American States (OAS), 17th Street Constitution Avenue NW, Washington, DC 20006, (202) 458-3000, www.oas.org; *The OAS in Transition: 1994-2004.*

Palgrave Macmillan Ltd., Houndmills, Basingstoke, Hampshire, RG21 6XS, England, (Telephone in U.S. (888) 330-8477), (Fax in U.S. (800) 672-2054), www.palgrave.com; *The Statesman's Yearbook 2008.*

Taylor and Francis Group, An Informa Business, 2 Park Square, Milton Park, Abingdon, Oxford OX14 4RN, United Kingdom, (Dial from U.S. (212) 216-7800), (Fax from U.S. (212) 564-7854), www.tandf.co.uk; *The Europa World Year Book.*

United Nations Conference on Trade and Development (UNCTAD), DC2-1120, United Nations, New York, NY 10017, (212) 963-0027, www.unctad.org; *Handbook of Statistics 2005.*

United Nations Food and Agricultural Organization (FAO), Viale delle Terme di Caracalla, 00100 Rome, Italy, (Dial from U.S. (202) 653-2400), (Fax from U.S. (202) 653 5760), www.fao.org; *The State of Food and Agriculture (SOFA) 2006.*

United Nations Statistics Division, New York, NY 10017, (800) 253-9646, Fax: (212) 963-4116, http://unstats.un.org; *Statistical Yearbook for Latin America and the Caribbean 2004.*

The World Bank, 1818 H Street, NW, Washington, DC 20433, (202) 473-1000, Fax: (202) 477-6391, www.worldbank.org; *World Development Indicators (WDI) 2008* and *World Development Report 2008.*

HAITI - INCOME DISTRIBUTION

UCLA Latin American Institute, 10343 Bunche Hall, Box 951447, Los Angeles, CA 90095-1447, (310) 825-4571, Fax: (310) 206-6859, www.international.ucla.edu/lac; *Statistical Abstract of Latin America.*

United Nations Statistics Division, New York, NY 10017, (800) 253-9646, Fax: (212) 963-4116, http://unstats.un.org; *Statistical Yearbook for Latin America and the Caribbean 2004.*

HAITI - INCOME TAXES

See HAITI - TAXATION

HAITI - INDUSTRIAL PRODUCTIVITY

M.E. Sharpe, 80 Business Park Drive, Armonk, NY 10504, (800) 541-6563, Fax: (914) 273-2106, www.mesharpe.com; *The Illustrated Book of World Rankings.*

HAITI - INDUSTRIAL PROPERTY

United Nations Statistics Division, New York, NY 10017, (800) 253-9646, Fax: (212) 963-4116, http://unstats.un.org; *Statistical Yearbook.*

World Intellectual Property Organization (WIPO), PO Box 18, CH-1211 Geneva 20, Switzerland, www.wipo.int; *Industrial Property Statistics* and *Industrial Property Statistics Online Directory.*

HAITI - INDUSTRIES

Central Intelligence Agency, Office of Public Affairs, Washington, DC 20505, (703) 482-0623, Fax: (703) 482-1739, www.cia.gov; *The World Factbook.*

Economist Intelligence Unit, 111 West 57th Street, New York, NY 10019, (212) 554-0600, Fax: (212) 586-1181, www.eiu.com; *Haiti Country Report.*

Euromonitor International, Inc., 224 S. Michigan Avenue, Suite 1500, Chicago, IL 60604, (312) 922-1115, Fax: (312) 922-1157, www.euromonitor.com; *The World Economic Factbook 2008* and *World Marketing Data and Statistics.*

International Labour Office, I.L.O. Publications, 4 route des Morillons, CH-1211 Geneva 22, Switzerland, (Telephone in U.S. (202) 653-7652), (Fax in U.S. (202) 653-7687), www.ilo.org; *Yearbook of Labour Statistics 2006.*

M.E. Sharpe, 80 Business Park Drive, Armonk, NY 10504, (800) 541-6563, Fax: (914) 273-2106, www.mesharpe.com; *The Illustrated Book of World Rankings.*

Palgrave Macmillan Ltd., Houndmills, Basingstoke, Hampshire, RG21 6XS, England, (Telephone in U.S. (888) 330-8477), (Fax in U.S. (800) 672-2054), www.palgrave.com; *The Statesman's Yearbook 2008.*

Taylor and Francis Group, An Informa Business, 2 Park Square, Milton Park, Abingdon, Oxford OX14 4RN, United Kingdom, (Dial from U.S. (212) 216-7800), (Fax from U.S. (212) 564-7854), www.tandf.co.uk; *The Europa World Year Book.*

UCLA Latin American Institute, 10343 Bunche Hall, Box 951447, Los Angeles, CA 90095-1447, (310) 825-4571, Fax: (310) 206-6859, www.international.ucla.edu/lac; *Statistical Abstract of Latin America.*

United Nations Industrial Development Organization (UNIDO), 1 United Nations Plaza, New York, NY 10017, (212) 963 6890, Fax: (212) 963-7904, http://unido.org; Industrial Statistics Database 2008 (INDSTAT) and *The International Yearbook of Industrial Statistics 2008.*

United Nations Statistics Division, New York, NY 10017, (800) 253-9646, Fax: (212) 963-4116, http://unstats.un.org; *Economic Survey of Latin America and the Caribbean 2004-2005* and *2004 Industrial Commodity Statistics Yearbook.*

The World Bank, 1818 H Street, NW, Washington, DC 20433, (202) 473-1000, Fax: (202) 477-6391, www.worldbank.org; *Haiti* and *World Development Indicators (WDI) 2008.*

HAITI - INFANT AND MATERNAL MORTALITY

See HAITI - MORTALITY

HAITI - INFLATION (FINANCE)

United Nations Statistics Division, New York, NY 10017, (800) 253-9646, Fax: (212) 963-4116, http://unstats.un.org; *Economic Survey of Latin America and the Caribbean 2004-2005.*

HAITI - INTEREST RATES

Inter-American Development Bank (IDB), 1300 New York Avenue, NW, Washington, DC 20577, (202) 623-1000, Fax: (202) 623-3096, www.iadb.org; *The Politics of Policies: Economic and Social Progress in Latin America - 2006 Report.*

HAITI - INTERNAL REVENUE

Inter-American Development Bank (IDB), 1300 New York Avenue, NW, Washington, DC 20577, (202) 623-1000, Fax: (202) 623-3096, www.iadb.org; *The Politics of Policies: Economic and Social Progress in Latin America - 2006 Report.*

Organization of American States (OAS), 17th Street Constitution Avenue NW, Washington, DC 20006, (202) 458-3000, www.oas.org; *The OAS in Transition: 1994-2004.*

HAITI - INTERNATIONAL FINANCE

Inter-American Development Bank (IDB), 1300 New York Avenue, NW, Washington, DC 20577, (202) 623-1000, Fax: (202) 623-3096, www.iadb.org; *The Politics of Policies: Economic and Social Progress in Latin America - 2006 Report.*

UCLA Latin American Institute, 10343 Bunche Hall, Box 951447, Los Angeles, CA 90095-1447, (310) 825-4571, Fax: (310) 206-6859, www.international.ucla.edu/lac; *Statistical Abstract of Latin America.*

United Nations Statistics Division, New York, NY 10017, (800) 253-9646, Fax: (212) 963-4116, http://unstats.un.org; *Statistical Yearbook for Latin America and the Caribbean 2004.*

HAITI - INTERNATIONAL LIQUIDITY

Inter-American Development Bank (IDB), 1300 New York Avenue, NW, Washington, DC 20577, (202) 623-1000, Fax: (202) 623-3096, www.iadb.org; *The Politics of Policies: Economic and Social Progress in Latin America - 2006 Report.*

International Monetary Fund (IMF), 700 Nineteenth Street, NW, Washington, DC 20431, (202) 623-7000, Fax: (202) 623-4661, www.imf.org; *International Financial Statistics Yearbook 2007.*

HAITI - INTERNATIONAL STATISTICS

Inter-American Development Bank (IDB), 1300 New York Avenue, NW, Washington, DC 20577, (202) 623-1000, Fax: (202) 623-3096, www.iadb.org; *The Politics of Policies: Economic and Social Progress in Latin America - 2006 Report.*

UCLA Latin American Institute, 10343 Bunche Hall, Box 951447, Los Angeles, CA 90095-1447, (310) 825-4571, Fax: (310) 206-6859, www.international.ucla.edu/lac; *Statistical Abstract of Latin America.*

HAITI - INTERNATIONAL TRADE

Economist Intelligence Unit, 111 West 57th Street, New York, NY 10019, (212) 554-0600, Fax: (212) 586-1181, www.eiu.com; *Haiti Country Report.*

Euromonitor International, Inc., 224 S. Michigan Avenue, Suite 1500, Chicago, IL 60604, (312) 922-1115, Fax: (312) 922-1157, www.euromonitor.com; *The World Economic Factbook 2008* and *World Marketing Data and Statistics.*

Inter-American Development Bank (IDB), 1300 New York Avenue, NW, Washington, DC 20577, (202) 623-1000, Fax: (202) 623-3096, www.iadb.org; *The Politics of Policies: Economic and Social Progress in Latin America - 2006 Report.*

International Monetary Fund (IMF), 700 Nineteenth Street, NW, Washington, DC 20431, (202) 623-7000, Fax: (202) 623-4661, www.imf.org; *International Financial Statistics Yearbook 2007.*

M.E. Sharpe, 80 Business Park Drive, Armonk, NY 10504, (800) 541-6563, Fax: (914) 273-2106, www.mesharpe.com; *The Illustrated Book of World Rankings.*

Palgrave Macmillan Ltd., Houndmills, Basingstoke, Hampshire, RG21 6XS, England, (Telephone in U.S. (888) 330-8477), (Fax in U.S. (800) 672-2054), www.palgrave.com; *The Statesman's Yearbook 2008.*

Taylor and Francis Group, An Informa Business, 2 Park Square, Milton Park, Abingdon, Oxford OX14 4RN, United Kingdom, (Dial from U.S. (212) 216-7800), (Fax from U.S. (212) 564-7854), www.tandf.co.uk; *The Europa World Year Book.*

UCLA Latin American Institute, 10343 Bunche Hall, Box 951447, Los Angeles, CA 90095-1447, (310) 825-4571, Fax: (310) 206-6859, www.international.ucla.edu/lac; *Statistical Abstract of Latin America.*

United Nations Conference on Trade and Development (UNCTAD), DC2-1120, United Nations, New York, NY 10017, (212) 963-0027, www.unctad.org; *UNCTAD Commodity Yearbook.*

United Nations Food and Agricultural Organization (FAO), Viale delle Terme di Caracalla, 00100 Rome, Italy, (Dial from U.S. (202) 653-2400), (Fax from U.S. (202) 653 5760), www.fao.org; *FAO Trade Yearbook* and *The State of Food and Agriculture (SOFA) 2006.*

United Nations Statistics Division, New York, NY 10017, (800) 253-9646, Fax: (212) 963-4116, http://unstats.un.org; *Economic Survey of Latin America and the Caribbean 2004-2005; International Trade Statistics Yearbook; Statistical Yearbook;* and *Statistical Yearbook for Latin America and the Caribbean 2004.*

The World Bank, 1818 H Street, NW, Washington, DC 20433, (202) 473-1000, Fax: (202) 477-6391, www.worldbank.org; *Haiti; World Development Indicators (WDI) 2008;* and *World Development Report 2008.*

World Trade Organization (WTO), Centre William Rappard, Rue de Lausanne 154, CH-1211 Geneva 21, Switzerland, www.wto.org; *International Trade Statistics 2006.*

HAITI - INTERNET USERS

International Telecommunication Union (ITU), Place des Nations, 1211 Geneva 20, Switzerland, www.itu.int; *World Telecommunication/ICT Indicators Database on CD-ROM; World Telecommunication/ICT Indicators Database Online;* and *Yearbook of Statistics - Telecommunication Services (Chronological Time Series 1997-2006).*

The World Bank, 1818 H Street, NW, Washington, DC 20433, (202) 473-1000, Fax: (202) 477-6391, www.worldbank.org; *Haiti.*

HAITI - INVESTMENTS

Inter-American Development Bank (IDB), 1300 New York Avenue, NW, Washington, DC 20577, (202) 623-1000, Fax: (202) 623-3096, www.iadb.org; *The Politics of Policies: Economic and Social Progress in Latin America - 2006 Report.*

United Nations Statistics Division, New York, NY 10017, (800) 253-9646, Fax: (212) 963-4116, http://unstats.un.org; *Statistical Yearbook for Latin America and the Caribbean 2004.*

HAITI - IRON AND IRON ORE PRODUCTION

See HAITI - MINERAL INDUSTRIES

HAITI - IRRIGATION

Inter-American Development Bank (IDB), 1300 New York Avenue, NW, Washington, DC 20577, (202) 623-1000, Fax: (202) 623-3096, www.iadb.org; *The Politics of Policies: Economic and Social Progress in Latin America - 2006 Report.*

HAITI - LABOR

Central Intelligence Agency, Office of Public Affairs, Washington, DC 20505, (703) 482-0623, Fax: (703) 482-1739, www.cia.gov; *The World Factbook.*

Euromonitor International, Inc., 224 S. Michigan Avenue, Suite 1500, Chicago, IL 60604, (312) 922-1115, Fax: (312) 922-1157, www.euromonitor.com; *International Marketing Data and Statistics 2008* and *World Marketing Data and Statistics.*

International Labour Office, I.L.O. Publications, 4 route des Morillons, CH-1211 Geneva 22, Switzerland, (Telephone in U.S. (202) 653-7652), (Fax in U.S. (202) 653-7687), www.ilo.org; *Yearbook of Labour Statistics 2006.*

M.E. Sharpe, 80 Business Park Drive, Armonk, NY 10504, (800) 541-6563, Fax: (914) 273-2106, www.mesharpe.com; *The Illustrated Book of World Rankings.*

Palgrave Macmillan Ltd., Houndmills, Basingstoke, Hampshire, RG21 6XS, England, (Telephone in U.S. (888) 330-8477), (Fax in U.S. (800) 672-2054), www.palgrave.com; *The Statesman's Yearbook 2008.*

Taylor and Francis Group, An Informa Business, 2 Park Square, Milton Park, Abingdon, Oxford OX14 4RN, United Kingdom, (Dial from U.S. (212) 216-7800), (Fax from U.S. (212) 564-7854), www.tandf.co.uk; *The Europa World Year Book.*

United Nations Food and Agricultural Organization (FAO), Viale delle Terme di Caracalla, 00100 Rome, Italy, (Dial from U.S. (202) 653-2400), (Fax from U.S. (202) 653 5760), www.fao.org; *The State of Food and Agriculture (SOFA) 2006.*

United Nations Statistics Division, New York, NY 10017, (800) 253-9646, Fax: (212) 963-4116, http://unstats.un.org; *Human Development Report 2006.*

The World Bank, 1818 H Street, NW, Washington, DC 20433, (202) 473-1000, Fax: (202) 477-6391, www.worldbank.org; *The World Bank Atlas 2003-2004; World Development Indicators (WDI) 2008;* and *World Development Report 2008.*

HAITI - LAND USE

Central Intelligence Agency, Office of Public Affairs, Washington, DC 20505, (703) 482-0623, Fax: (703) 482-1739, www.cia.gov; *The World Factbook.*

Euromonitor International, Inc., 224 S. Michigan Avenue, Suite 1500, Chicago, IL 60604, (312) 922-1115, Fax: (312) 922-1157, www.euromonitor.com; *International Marketing Data and Statistics 2008.*

Inter-American Development Bank (IDB), 1300 New York Avenue, NW, Washington, DC 20577, (202) 623-1000, Fax: (202) 623-3096, www.iadb.org; *The Politics of Policies: Economic and Social Progress in Latin America - 2006 Report.*

United Nations Food and Agricultural Organization (FAO), Viale delle Terme di Caracalla, 00100 Rome, Italy, (Dial from U.S. (202) 653-2400), (Fax from U.S. (202) 653 5760), www.fao.org; *FAO Production Yearbook 2002.*

The World Bank, 1818 H Street, NW, Washington, DC 20433, (202) 473-1000, Fax: (202) 477-6391, www.worldbank.org; *World Development Report 2008.*

HAITI - LIBRARIES

M.E. Sharpe, 80 Business Park Drive, Armonk, NY 10504, (800) 541-6563, Fax: (914) 273-2106, www.mesharpe.com; *The Illustrated Book of World Rankings.*

UNESCO Institute for Statistics, C.P. 6128 Succursale Centre-Ville, Montreal, Quebec, H3C 3J7 Canada, (Dial from U.S. (514) 343-6880), (Fax from U.S. (514) 343 6882), www.uis.unesco.org; *Statistical Tables.*

HAITI - LICENSES

International Monetary Fund (IMF), 700 Nineteenth Street, NW, Washington, DC 20431, (202) 623-7000, Fax: (202) 623-4661, www.imf.org; *Government Finance Statistics Yearbook (2008 Edition).*

HAITI - LIFE EXPECTANCY

Central Intelligence Agency, Office of Public Affairs, Washington, DC 20505, (703) 482-0623, Fax: (703) 482-1739, www.cia.gov; *The World Factbook.*

Palgrave Macmillan Ltd., Houndmills, Basingstoke, Hampshire, RG21 6XS, England, (Telephone in U.S. (888) 330-8477), (Fax in U.S. (800) 672-2054), www.palgrave.com; *The Statesman's Yearbook 2008.*

United Nations Statistics Division, New York, NY 10017, (800) 253-9646, Fax: (212) 963-4116, http://unstats.un.org; *Human Development Report 2006; Statistical Yearbook for Latin America and the Caribbean 2004;* and *World Statistics Pocketbook.*

The World Bank, 1818 H Street, NW, Washington, DC 20433, (202) 473-1000, Fax: (202) 477-6391, www.worldbank.org; *The World Bank Atlas 2003-2004* and *World Development Report 2008.*

HAITI - LITERACY

Euromonitor International, Inc., 224 S. Michigan Avenue, Suite 1500, Chicago, IL 60604, (312) 922-1115, Fax: (312) 922-1157, www.euromonitor.com; *World Marketing Data and Statistics.*

HAITI - LIVESTOCK

M.E. Sharpe, 80 Business Park Drive, Armonk, NY 10504, (800) 541-6563, Fax: (914) 273-2106, www.mesharpe.com; *The Illustrated Book of World Rankings.*

Palgrave Macmillan Ltd., Houndmills, Basingstoke, Hampshire, RG21 6XS, England, (Telephone in U.S. (888) 330-8477), (Fax in U.S. (800) 672-2054), www.palgrave.com; *The Statesman's Yearbook 2008.*

Taylor and Francis Group, An Informa Business, 2 Park Square, Milton Park, Abingdon, Oxford OX14 4RN, United Kingdom, (Dial from U.S. (212) 216-7800), (Fax from U.S. (212) 564-7854), www.tandf.co.uk; *The Europa World Year Book.*

United Nations Conference on Trade and Development (UNCTAD), DC2-1120, United Nations, New York, NY 10017, (212) 963-0027, www.unctad.org; *UNCTAD Commodity Yearbook.*

United Nations Food and Agricultural Organization (FAO), Viale delle Terme di Caracalla, 00100 Rome, Italy, (Dial from U.S. (202) 653-2400), (Fax from U.S. (202) 653 5760), www.fao.org; *FAO Production Yearbook 2002* and *The State of Food and Agriculture (SOFA) 2006.*

United Nations Statistics Division, New York, NY 10017, (800) 253-9646, Fax: (212) 963-4116, http://unstats.un.org; *Statistical Yearbook.*

HAITI - LOCAL TAXATION

Inter-American Development Bank (IDB), 1300 New York Avenue, NW, Washington, DC 20577, (202) 623-1000, Fax: (202) 623-3096, www.iadb.org; *The Politics of Policies: Economic and Social Progress in Latin America - 2006 Report.*

HAITI - MANUFACTURES

Inter-American Development Bank (IDB), 1300 New York Avenue, NW, Washington, DC 20577, (202) 623-1000, Fax: (202) 623-3096, www.iadb.org; *The Politics of Policies: Economic and Social Progress in Latin America - 2006 Report.*

M.E. Sharpe, 80 Business Park Drive, Armonk, NY 10504, (800) 541-6563, Fax: (914) 273-2106, www.mesharpe.com; *The Illustrated Book of World Rankings.*

United Nations Statistics Division, New York, NY 10017, (800) 253-9646, Fax: (212) 963-4116, http://unstats.un.org; *Statistical Yearbook* and *Statistical Yearbook for Latin America and the Caribbean 2004.*

The World Bank, 1818 H Street, NW, Washington, DC 20433, (202) 473-1000, Fax: (202) 477-6391, www.worldbank.org; *World Development Indicators (WDI) 2008.*

HAITI - MARRIAGE

M.E. Sharpe, 80 Business Park Drive, Armonk, NY 10504, (800) 541-6563, Fax: (914) 273-2106, www.mesharpe.com; *The Illustrated Book of World Rankings.*

United Nations Statistics Division, New York, NY 10017, (800) 253-9646, Fax: (212) 963-4116, http://unstats.un.org; *Demographic Yearbook.*

HAITI - MEAT PRODUCTION

See HAITI - LIVESTOCK

HAITI - MEDICAL PERSONNEL

UCLA Latin American Institute, 10343 Bunche Hall, Box 951447, Los Angeles, CA 90095-1447, (310) 825-4571, Fax: (310) 206-6859, www.international.ucla.edu/lac; *Statistical Abstract of Latin America.*

HAITI - MILK PRODUCTION

See HAITI - DAIRY PROCESSING

HAITI - MINERAL INDUSTRIES

Inter-American Development Bank (IDB), 1300 New York Avenue, NW, Washington, DC 20577, (202) 623-1000, Fax: (202) 623-3096, www.iadb.org; *The Politics of Policies: Economic and Social Progress in Latin America - 2006 Report.*

International Monetary Fund (IMF), 700 Nineteenth Street, NW, Washington, DC 20431, (202) 623-7000, Fax: (202) 623-4661, www.imf.org; *International Financial Statistics Yearbook 2007.*

M.E. Sharpe, 80 Business Park Drive, Armonk, NY 10504, (800) 541-6563, Fax: (914) 273-2106, www.mesharpe.com; *The Illustrated Book of World Rankings.*

Organization of American States (OAS), 17th Street Constitution Avenue NW, Washington, DC 20006, (202) 458-3000, www.oas.org; *The OAS in Transition: 1994-2004.*

Palgrave Macmillan Ltd., Houndmills, Basingstoke, Hampshire, RG21 6XS, England, (Telephone in U.S. (888) 330-8477), (Fax in U.S. (800) 672-2054), www.palgrave.com; *The Statesman's Yearbook 2008.*

Taylor and Francis Group, An Informa Business, 2 Park Square, Milton Park, Abingdon, Oxford OX14 4RN, United Kingdom, (Dial from U.S. (212) 216-7800), (Fax from U.S. (212) 564-7854), www.tandf.co.uk; *The Europa World Year Book.*

UCLA Latin American Institute, 10343 Bunche Hall, Box 951447, Los Angeles, CA 90095-1447, (310) 825-4571, Fax: (310) 206-6859, www.international.ucla.edu/lac; *Statistical Abstract of Latin America.*

United Nations Conference on Trade and Development (UNCTAD), DC2-1120, United Nations, New York, NY 10017, (212) 963-0027, www.unctad.org; *UNCTAD Commodity Yearbook.*

United Nations Statistics Division, New York, NY 10017, (800) 253-9646, Fax: (212) 963-4116, http://unstats.un.org; *Statistical Yearbook* and *Statistical Yearbook for Latin America and the Caribbean 2004.*

HAITI - MONEY EXCHANGE RATES

See HAITI - FOREIGN EXCHANGE RATES

HAITI - MONEY SUPPLY

Economist Intelligence Unit, 111 West 57th Street, New York, NY 10019, (212) 554-0600, Fax: (212) 586-1181, www.eiu.com; *Haiti Country Report.*

Inter-American Development Bank (IDB), 1300 New York Avenue, NW, Washington, DC 20577, (202) 623-1000, Fax: (202) 623-3096, www.iadb.org; *The Politics of Policies: Economic and Social Progress in Latin America - 2006 Report.*

International Monetary Fund (IMF), 700 Nineteenth Street, NW, Washington, DC 20431, (202) 623-7000, Fax: (202) 623-4661, www.imf.org; *International Financial Statistics Yearbook 2007.*

Taylor and Francis Group, An Informa Business, 2 Park Square, Milton Park, Abingdon, Oxford OX14 4RN, United Kingdom, (Dial from U.S. (212) 216-7800), (Fax from U.S. (212) 564-7854), www.tandf.co.uk; *The Europa World Year Book.*

UCLA Latin American Institute, 10343 Bunche Hall, Box 951447, Los Angeles, CA 90095-1447, (310) 825-4571, Fax: (310) 206-6859, www.international.ucla.edu/lac; *Statistical Abstract of Latin America.*

United Nations Statistics Division, New York, NY 10017, (800) 253-9646, Fax: (212) 963-4116, http://unstats.un.org; *Statistical Yearbook.*

The World Bank, 1818 H Street, NW, Washington, DC 20433, (202) 473-1000, Fax: (202) 477-6391, www.worldbank.org; *Haiti* and *World Development Indicators (WDI) 2008.*

HAITI - MONUMENTS AND HISTORIC SITES

UNESCO Institute for Statistics, C.P. 6128 Succursale Centre-Ville, Montreal, Quebec, H3C 3J7 Canada, (Dial from U.S. (514) 343-6880), (Fax from U.S. (514) 343 6882), www.uis.unesco.org; *Statistical Tables.*

HAITI - MORTALITY

Central Intelligence Agency, Office of Public Affairs, Washington, DC 20505, (703) 482-0623, Fax: (703) 482-1739, www.cia.gov; *The World Factbook.*

Euromonitor International, Inc., 224 S. Michigan Avenue, Suite 1500, Chicago, IL 60604, (312) 922-1115, Fax: (312) 922-1157, www.euromonitor.com; *International Marketing Data and Statistics 2008.*

Palgrave Macmillan Ltd., Houndmills, Basingstoke, Hampshire, RG21 6XS, England, (Telephone in U.S. (888) 330-8477), (Fax in U.S. (800) 672-2054), www.palgrave.com; *The Statesman's Yearbook 2008.*

Taylor and Francis Group, An Informa Business, 2 Park Square, Milton Park, Abingdon, Oxford OX14 4RN, United Kingdom, (Dial from U.S. (212) 216-7800), (Fax from U.S. (212) 564-7854), www.tandf.co.uk; *The Europa World Year Book.*

UNICEF, 3 United Nations Plaza, New York, NY 10017, (800) 253-9646, Fax: (212) 887-7465, www.unicef.org; *The State of the World's Children 2008.*

United Nations Statistics Division, New York, NY 10017, (800) 253-9646, Fax: (212) 963-4116, http://unstats.un.org; *Demographic Yearbook; Human Development Report 2006; Statistical Yearbook; Statistical Yearbook for Latin America and the Caribbean 2004;* and *World Statistics Pocketbook.*

The World Bank, 1818 H Street, NW, Washington, DC 20433, (202) 473-1000, Fax: (202) 477-6391, www.worldbank.org; *The World Bank Atlas 2003-2004; World Development Indicators (WDI) 2008;* and *World Development Report 2008.*

World Health Organization (WHO), Avenue Appia 20, 1211 Geneve 27, Switzerland, (Telephone in U.S. (212) 331-9081), www.who.int; The WHO Global Atlas of Infectious Diseases and *World Health Report 2006.*

HAITI - MOTION PICTURES

Palgrave Macmillan Ltd., Houndmills, Basingstoke, Hampshire, RG21 6XS, England, (Telephone in U.S. (888) 330-8477), (Fax in U.S. (800) 672-2054), www.palgrave.com; *The Statesman's Yearbook 2008.*

HAITI - MOTOR VEHICLES

Taylor and Francis Group, An Informa Business, 2 Park Square, Milton Park, Abingdon, Oxford OX14 4RN, United Kingdom, (Dial from U.S. (212) 216-7800), (Fax from U.S. (212) 564-7854), www.tandf.co.uk; *The Europa World Year Book.*

United Nations Statistics Division, New York, NY 10017, (800) 253-9646, Fax: (212) 963-4116, http://unstats.un.org; *Statistical Yearbook.*

HAITI - MUSEUMS

M.E. Sharpe, 80 Business Park Drive, Armonk, NY 10504, (800) 541-6563, Fax: (914) 273-2106, www.mesharpe.com; *The Illustrated Book of World Rankings.*

UNESCO Institute for Statistics, C.P. 6128 Succursale Centre-Ville, Montreal, Quebec, H3C 3J7 Canada, (Dial from U.S. (514) 343-6880), (Fax from U.S. (514) 343 6882), www.uis.unesco.org; *Statistical Tables.*

HAITI - NATURAL GAS PRODUCTION

See HAITI - MINERAL INDUSTRIES

HAITI - NUTRITION

United Nations Food and Agricultural Organization (FAO), Viale delle Terme di Caracalla, 00100 Rome, Italy, (Dial from U.S. (202) 653-2400), (Fax from U.S. (202) 653 5760), www.fao.org; *The State of Food and Agriculture (SOFA) 2006.*

United Nations Statistics Division, New York, NY 10017, (800) 253-9646, Fax: (212) 963-4116, http://unstats.un.org; *Statistical Yearbook for Latin America and the Caribbean 2004.*

HAITI - OLDER PEOPLE

M.E. Sharpe, 80 Business Park Drive, Armonk, NY 10504, (800) 541-6563, Fax: (914) 273-2106, www.mesharpe.com; *The Illustrated Book of World Rankings.*

HAITI - PAPER

See HAITI - FORESTS AND FORESTRY

HAITI - PEANUT PRODUCTION

See HAITI - CROPS

HAITI - PESTICIDES

United Nations Food and Agricultural Organization (FAO), Viale delle Terme di Caracalla, 00100 Rome, Italy, (Dial from U.S. (202) 653-2400), (Fax from U.S. (202) 653 5760), www.fao.org; *The State of Food and Agriculture (SOFA) 2006.*

HAITI - PETROLEUM INDUSTRY AND TRADE

Inter-American Development Bank (IDB), 1300 New York Avenue, NW, Washington, DC 20577, (202) 623-1000, Fax: (202) 623-3096, www.iadb.org; *The Politics of Policies: Economic and Social Progress in Latin America - 2006 Report.*

M.E. Sharpe, 80 Business Park Drive, Armonk, NY 10504, (800) 541-6563, Fax: (914) 273-2106, www.mesharpe.com; *The Illustrated Book of World Rankings.*

Palgrave Macmillan Ltd., Houndmills, Basingstoke, Hampshire, RG21 6XS, England, (Telephone in U.S. (888) 330-8477), (Fax in U.S. (800) 672-2054), www.palgrave.com; *The Statesman's Yearbook 2008.*

PennWell Corporation, 1421 South Sheridan Road, Tulsa, OK 74112, (918) 835-3161, www.pennwell.com; *International Petroleum Encyclopedia 2007.*

U.S. Department of Energy (DOE), Energy Information Administration (EIA), 1000 Independence Avenue, SW, Washington, DC 20585, (202) 586-8800, www.eia.doe.gov; *International Energy Annual 2004* and *International Energy Outlook 2006.*

United Nations Conference on Trade and Development (UNCTAD), DC2-1120, United Nations, New York, NY 10017, (212) 963-0027, www.unctad.org; *UNCTAD Commodity Yearbook.*

United Nations Food and Agricultural Organization (FAO), Viale delle Terme di Caracalla, 00100 Rome, Italy, (Dial from U.S. (202) 653-2400), (Fax from U.S. (202) 653 5760), www.fao.org; *The State of Food and Agriculture (SOFA) 2006.*

HAITI - POLITICAL SCIENCE

Central Intelligence Agency, Office of Public Affairs, Washington, DC 20505, (703) 482-0623, Fax: (703) 482-1739, www.cia.gov; *The World Factbook.*

Inter-American Development Bank (IDB), 1300 New York Avenue, NW, Washington, DC 20577, (202) 623-1000, Fax: (202) 623-3096, www.iadb.org; *The Politics of Policies: Economic and Social Progress in Latin America - 2006 Report.*

International Monetary Fund (IMF), 700 Nineteenth Street, NW, Washington, DC 20431, (202) 623-7000, Fax: (202) 623-4661, www.imf.org; *Government Finance Statistics Yearbook (2008 Edition)* and *International Financial Statistics Yearbook 2007.*

Palgrave Macmillan Ltd., Houndmills, Basingstoke, Hampshire, RG21 6XS, England, (Telephone in U.S. (888) 330-8477), (Fax in U.S. (800) 672-2054), www.palgrave.com; *The Statesman's Yearbook 2008.*

Taylor and Francis Group, An Informa Business, 2 Park Square, Milton Park, Abingdon, Oxford OX14 4RN, United Kingdom, (Dial from U.S. (212) 216-7800), (Fax from U.S. (212) 564-7854), www.tandf.co.uk; *The Europa World Year Book.*

UCLA Latin American Institute, 10343 Bunche Hall, Box 951447, Los Angeles, CA 90095-1447, (310) 825-4571, Fax: (310) 206-6859, www.international.ucla.edu/lac; *Statistical Abstract of Latin America.*

United Nations Statistics Division, New York, NY 10017, (800) 253-9646, Fax: (212) 963-4116, http://unstats.un.org; *National Accounts Statistics: Compendium of Income Distribution Statistics* and *Statistical Yearbook.*

The World Bank, 1818 H Street, NW, Washington, DC 20433, (202) 473-1000, Fax: (202) 477-6391, www.worldbank.org; *World Development Indicators (WDI) 2008* and *World Development Report 2008.*

HAITI - POPULATION

Central Intelligence Agency, Office of Public Affairs, Washington, DC 20505, (703) 482-0623, Fax: (703) 482-1739, www.cia.gov; *The World Factbook.*

Economist Intelligence Unit, 111 West 57th Street, New York, NY 10019, (212) 554-0600, Fax: (212) 586-1181, www.eiu.com; *Haiti Country Report.*

Euromonitor International, Inc., 224 S. Michigan Avenue, Suite 1500, Chicago, IL 60604, (312) 922-1115, Fax: (312) 922-1157, www.euromonitor.com; *International Marketing Data and Statistics 2008* and *The World Economic Factbook 2008.*

Eurostat, Batiment Jean Monnet, Rue Alcide de Gasperi, L-2920 Luxembourg, http://epp.eurostat.ec.europa.eu; *Demographic Indicators - Population by Age-Classes.*

Inter-American Development Bank (IDB), 1300 New York Avenue, NW, Washington, DC 20577, (202) 623-1000, Fax: (202) 623-3096, www.iadb.org; *The Politics of Policies: Economic and Social Progress in Latin America - 2006 Report.*

International Labour Office, I.L.O. Publications, 4 route des Morillons, CH-1211 Geneva 22, Switzerland, (Telephone in U.S. (202) 653-7652), (Fax in U.S. (202) 653-7687), www.ilo.org; *Yearbook of Labour Statistics 2006.*

M.E. Sharpe, 80 Business Park Drive, Armonk, NY 10504, (800) 541-6563, Fax: (914) 273-2106, www.mesharpe.com; *The Illustrated Book of World Rankings.*

Organization of American States (OAS), 17th Street Constitution Avenue NW, Washington, DC 20006, (202) 458-3000, www.oas.org; *The OAS in Transition: 1994-2004.*

Palgrave Macmillan Ltd., Houndmills, Basingstoke, Hampshire, RG21 6XS, England, (Telephone in U.S. (888) 330-8477), (Fax in U.S. (800) 672-2054), www.palgrave.com; *The Statesman's Yearbook 2008.*

Taylor and Francis Group, An Informa Business, 2 Park Square, Milton Park, Abingdon, Oxford OX14 4RN, United Kingdom, (Dial from U.S. (212) 216-7800), (Fax from U.S. (212) 564-7854), www.tandf.co.uk; *The Europa World Year Book.*

U.S. Department of State (DOS), 2201 C Street NW, Washington, DC 20520, (202) 647-4000, www.state.gov; *World Military Expenditures and Arms Transfers (WMEAT).*

UCLA Latin American Institute, 10343 Bunche Hall, Box 951447, Los Angeles, CA 90095-1447, (310) 825-4571, Fax: (310) 206-6859, www.international.ucla.edu/lac; *Statistical Abstract of Latin America.*

UNESCO Institute for Statistics, C.P. 6128 Succursale Centre-Ville, Montreal, Quebec, H3C 3J7 Canada, (Dial from U.S. (514) 343-6880), (Fax from U.S. (514) 343 6882), www.uis.unesco.org; *Statistical Tables.*

United Nations Food and Agricultural Organization (FAO), Viale delle Terme di Caracalla, 00100 Rome, Italy, (Dial from U.S. (202) 653-2400), (Fax from U.S. (202) 653 5760), www.fao.org; *FAO Production Yearbook 2002.*

United Nations Statistics Division, New York, NY 10017, (800) 253-9646, Fax: (212) 963-4116, http://unstats.un.org; *Demographic Yearbook; Human Development Report 2006; Statistical Yearbook; Statistical Yearbook for Latin America and the Caribbean 2004;* and *World Statistics Pocketbook.*

The World Bank, 1818 H Street, NW, Washington, DC 20433, (202) 473-1000, Fax: (202) 477-6391, www.worldbank.org; *Haiti; The World Bank Atlas 2003-2004;* and *World Development Report 2008.*

World Health Organization (WHO), Avenue Appia 20, 1211 Geneve 27, Switzerland, (Telephone in U.S. (212) 331-9081), www.who.int; *World Health Report 2006.*

HAITI - POPULATION DENSITY

Central Intelligence Agency, Office of Public Affairs, Washington, DC 20505, (703) 482-0623, Fax: (703) 482-1739, www.cia.gov; *The World Factbook.*

Euromonitor International, Inc., 224 S. Michigan Avenue, Suite 1500, Chicago, IL 60604, (312) 922-1115, Fax: (312) 922-1157, www.euromonitor.com; *The World Economic Factbook 2008.*

Inter-American Development Bank (IDB), 1300 New York Avenue, NW, Washington, DC 20577, (202) 623-1000, Fax: (202) 623-3096, www.iadb.org; *The Politics of Policies: Economic and Social Progress in Latin America - 2006 Report.*

M.E. Sharpe, 80 Business Park Drive, Armonk, NY 10504, (800) 541-6563, Fax: (914) 273-2106, www.mesharpe.com; *The Illustrated Book of World Rankings.*

Palgrave Macmillan Ltd., Houndmills, Basingstoke, Hampshire, RG21 6XS, England, (Telephone in U.S. (888) 330-8477), (Fax in U.S. (800) 672-2054), www.palgrave.com; *The Statesman's Yearbook 2008.*

Taylor and Francis Group, An Informa Business, 2 Park Square, Milton Park, Abingdon, Oxford OX14 4RN, United Kingdom, (Dial from U.S. (212) 216-7800), (Fax from U.S. (212) 564-7854), www.tandf.co.uk; *The Europa World Year Book.*

UNESCO Institute for Statistics, C.P. 6128 Succursale Centre-Ville, Montreal, Quebec, H3C 3J7 Canada, (Dial from U.S. (514) 343-6880), (Fax from U.S. (514) 343 6882), www.uis.unesco.org; *Statistical Tables.*

United Nations Food and Agricultural Organization (FAO), Viale delle Terme di Caracalla, 00100 Rome, Italy, (Dial from U.S. (202) 653-2400), (Fax from U.S. (202) 653 5760), www.fao.org; *The State of Food and Agriculture (SOFA) 2006.*

United Nations Statistics Division, New York, NY 10017, (800) 253-9646, Fax: (212) 963-4116, http://unstats.un.org; *Statistical Yearbook.*

The World Bank, 1818 H Street, NW, Washington, DC 20433, (202) 473-1000, Fax: (202) 477-6391, www.worldbank.org; *Haiti* and *World Development Report 2008.*

HAITI - POSTAL SERVICE

M.E. Sharpe, 80 Business Park Drive, Armonk, NY 10504, (800) 541-6563, Fax: (914) 273-2106, www.mesharpe.com; *The Illustrated Book of World Rankings.*

United Nations Statistics Division, New York, NY 10017, (800) 253-9646, Fax: (212) 963-4116, http://unstats.un.org; *Statistical Yearbook.*

HAITI - POWER RESOURCES

Euromonitor International, Inc., 224 S. Michigan Avenue, Suite 1500, Chicago, IL 60604, (312) 922-1115, Fax: (312) 922-1157, www.euromonitor.com; *International Marketing Data and Statistics 2008; The World Economic Factbook 2008;* and *World Marketing Data and Statistics.*

M.E. Sharpe, 80 Business Park Drive, Armonk, NY 10504, (800) 541-6563, Fax: (914) 273-2106, www.mesharpe.com; *The Illustrated Book of World Rankings.*

Palgrave Macmillan Ltd., Houndmills, Basingstoke, Hampshire, RG21 6XS, England, (Telephone in U.S. (888) 330-8477), (Fax in U.S. (800) 672-2054), www.palgrave.com; *The Statesman's Yearbook 2008.*

Platts, 2 Penn Plaza, 25th Floor, New York, NY 10121-2298, (212) 904-3070, www.platts.com; *Energy Economist.*

U.S. Department of Energy (DOE), Energy Information Administration (EIA), 1000 Independence Avenue, SW, Washington, DC 20585, (202) 586-8800, www.eia.doe.gov; *International Energy Annual 2004* and *International Energy Outlook 2006.*

UCLA Latin American Institute, 10343 Bunche Hall, Box 951447, Los Angeles, CA 90095-1447, (310) 825-4571, Fax: (310) 206-6859, www.international.ucla.edu/lac; *Statistical Abstract of Latin America.*

United Nations Food and Agricultural Organization (FAO), Viale delle Terme di Caracalla, 00100 Rome, Italy, (Dial from U.S. (202) 653-2400), (Fax from U.S. (202) 653 5760), www.fao.org; *The State of Food and Agriculture (SOFA) 2006.*

United Nations Statistics Division, New York, NY 10017, (800) 253-9646, Fax: (212) 963-4116, http://unstats.un.org; *Energy Statistics Yearbook 2003;*

Human Development Report 2006; Statistical Yearbook; Statistical Yearbook for Latin America and the Caribbean 2004; and *World Statistics Pocketbook.*

The World Bank, 1818 H Street, NW, Washington, DC 20433, (202) 473-1000, Fax: (202) 477-6391, www.worldbank.org; *The World Bank Atlas 2003-2004* and *World Development Report 2008.*

HAITI - PRICES

Euromonitor International, Inc., 224 S. Michigan Avenue, Suite 1500, Chicago, IL 60604, (312) 922-1115, Fax: (312) 922-1157, www.euromonitor.com; *World Marketing Data and Statistics.*

International Labour Office, I.L.O. Publications, 4 route des Morillons, CH-1211 Geneva 22, Switzerland, (Telephone in U.S. (202) 653-7652), (Fax in U.S. (202) 653-7687), www.ilo.org; *Yearbook of Labour Statistics 2006.*

International Monetary Fund (IMF), 700 Nineteenth Street, NW, Washington, DC 20431, (202) 623-7000, Fax: (202) 623-4661, www.imf.org; *International Financial Statistics Yearbook 2007.*

M.E. Sharpe, 80 Business Park Drive, Armonk, NY 10504, (800) 541-6563, Fax: (914) 273-2106, www.mesharpe.com; *The Illustrated Book of World Rankings.*

Organization of American States (OAS), 17th Street Constitution Avenue NW, Washington, DC 20006, (202) 458-3000, www.oas.org; *The OAS in Transition: 1994-2004.*

UCLA Latin American Institute, 10343 Bunche Hall, Box 951447, Los Angeles, CA 90095-1447, (310) 825-4571, Fax: (310) 206-6859, www.international.ucla.edu/lac; *Statistical Abstract of Latin America.*

United Nations Food and Agricultural Organization (FAO), Viale delle Terme di Caracalla, 00100 Rome, Italy, (Dial from U.S. (202) 653-2400), (Fax from U.S. (202) 653 5760), www.fao.org; *FAO Production Yearbook 2002* and *The State of Food and Agriculture (SOFA) 2006.*

United Nations Statistics Division, New York, NY 10017, (800) 253-9646, Fax: (212) 963-4116, http://unstats.un.org; *Statistical Yearbook for Latin America and the Caribbean 2004.*

The World Bank, 1818 H Street, NW, Washington, DC 20433, (202) 473-1000, Fax: (202) 477-6391, www.worldbank.org; *Haiti.*

HAITI - PROFESSIONS

UCLA Latin American Institute, 10343 Bunche Hall, Box 951447, Los Angeles, CA 90095-1447, (310) 825-4571, Fax: (310) 206-6859, www.international.ucla.edu/lac; *Statistical Abstract of Latin America.*

UNESCO Institute for Statistics, C.P. 6128 Succursale Centre-Ville, Montreal, Quebec, H3C 3J7 Canada, (Dial from U.S. (514) 343-6880), (Fax from U.S. (514) 343 6882), www.uis.unesco.org; *Statistical Tables.*

HAITI - PUBLIC HEALTH

Euromonitor International, Inc., 224 S. Michigan Avenue, Suite 1500, Chicago, IL 60604, (312) 922-1115, Fax: (312) 922-1157, www.euromonitor.com; *World Marketing Data and Statistics.*

M.E. Sharpe, 80 Business Park Drive, Armonk, NY 10504, (800) 541-6563, Fax: (914) 273-2106, www.mesharpe.com; *The Illustrated Book of World Rankings.*

Palgrave Macmillan Ltd., Houndmills, Basingstoke, Hampshire, RG21 6XS, England, (Telephone in U.S. (888) 330-8477), (Fax in U.S. (800) 672-2054), www.palgrave.com; *The Statesman's Yearbook 2008.*

UCLA Latin American Institute, 10343 Bunche Hall, Box 951447, Los Angeles, CA 90095-1447, (310) 825-4571, Fax: (310) 206-6859, www.international.ucla.edu/lac; *Statistical Abstract of Latin America.*

UNICEF, 3 United Nations Plaza, New York, NY 10017, (800) 253-9646, Fax: (212) 887-7465, www.unicef.org; *The State of the World's Children 2008.*

United Nations Statistics Division, New York, NY 10017, (800) 253-9646, Fax: (212) 963-4116, http://unstats.un.org; *Human Development Report 2006; Statistical Yearbook;* and *Statistical Yearbook for Latin America and the Caribbean 2004.*

The World Bank, 1818 H Street, NW, Washington, DC 20433, (202) 473-1000, Fax: (202) 477-6391, www.worldbank.org; *Haiti* and *World Development Report 2008.*

World Health Organization (WHO), Avenue Appia 20, 1211 Geneve 27, Switzerland, (Telephone in U.S. (212) 331-9081), www.who.int; *The WHO Global Atlas of Infectious Diseases* and *World Health Report 2006.*

HAITI - PUBLIC UTILITIES

UCLA Latin American Institute, 10343 Bunche Hall, Box 951447, Los Angeles, CA 90095-1447, (310) 825-4571, Fax: (310) 206-6859, www.international.ucla.edu/lac; *Statistical Abstract of Latin America.*

HAITI - PUBLISHERS AND PUBLISHING

Taylor and Francis Group, An Informa Business, 2 Park Square, Milton Park, Abingdon, Oxford OX14 4RN, United Kingdom, (Dial from U.S. (212) 216-7800), (Fax from U.S. (212) 564-7854), www.tandf.co.uk; *The Europa World Year Book.*

HAITI - RADIO BROADCASTING

Palgrave Macmillan Ltd., Houndmills, Basingstoke, Hampshire, RG21 6XS, England, (Telephone in U.S. (888) 330-8477), (Fax in U.S. (800) 672-2054), www.palgrave.com; *The Statesman's Yearbook 2008.*

HAITI - RAILROADS

Palgrave Macmillan Ltd., Houndmills, Basingstoke, Hampshire, RG21 6XS, England, (Telephone in U.S. (888) 330-8477), (Fax in U.S. (800) 672-2054), www.palgrave.com; *The Statesman's Yearbook 2008.*

HAITI - RANCHING

UCLA Latin American Institute, 10343 Bunche Hall, Box 951447, Los Angeles, CA 90095-1447, (310) 825-4571, Fax: (310) 206-6859, www.international.ucla.edu/lac; *Statistical Abstract of Latin America.*

HAITI - RELIGION

Central Intelligence Agency, Office of Public Affairs, Washington, DC 20505, (703) 482-0623, Fax: (703) 482-1739, www.cia.gov; *The World Factbook.*

M.E. Sharpe, 80 Business Park Drive, Armonk, NY 10504, (800) 541-6563, Fax: (914) 273-2106, www.mesharpe.com; *The Illustrated Book of World Rankings.*

Palgrave Macmillan Ltd., Houndmills, Basingstoke, Hampshire, RG21 6XS, England, (Telephone in U.S. (888) 330-8477), (Fax in U.S. (800) 672-2054), www.palgrave.com; *The Statesman's Yearbook 2008.*

UCLA Latin American Institute, 10343 Bunche Hall, Box 951447, Los Angeles, CA 90095-1447, (310) 825-4571, Fax: (310) 206-6859, www.international.ucla.edu/lac; *Statistical Abstract of Latin America.*

HAITI - RENT CHARGES

International Labour Office, I.L.O. Publications, 4 route des Morillons, CH-1211 Geneva 22, Switzerland, (Telephone in U.S. (202) 653-7652), (Fax in U.S. (202) 653-7687), www.ilo.org; *Yearbook of Labour Statistics 2006.*

HAITI - RESERVES (ACCOUNTING)

Inter-American Development Bank (IDB), 1300 New York Avenue, NW, Washington, DC 20577, (202) 623-1000, Fax: (202) 623-3096, www.iadb.org; *The Politics of Policies: Economic and Social Progress in Latin America - 2006 Report.*

Organization of American States (OAS), 17th Street Constitution Avenue NW, Washington, DC 20006, (202) 458-3000, www.oas.org; *The OAS in Transition: 1994-2004.*

United Nations Statistics Division, New York, NY 10017, (800) 253-9646, Fax: (212) 963-4116, http://unstats.un.org; *Statistical Yearbook.*

The World Bank, 1818 H Street, NW, Washington, DC 20433, (202) 473-1000, Fax: (202) 477-6391, www.worldbank.org; *World Development Indicators (WDI) 2008.*

HAITI - RETAIL TRADE

Euromonitor International, Inc., 224 S. Michigan Avenue, Suite 1500, Chicago, IL 60604, (312) 922-1115, Fax: (312) 922-1157, www.euromonitor.com; *World Marketing Data and Statistics.*

Inter-American Development Bank (IDB), 1300 New York Avenue, NW, Washington, DC 20577, (202) 623-1000, Fax: (202) 623-3096, www.iadb.org; *The Politics of Policies: Economic and Social Progress in Latin America - 2006 Report.*

United Nations Statistics Division, New York, NY 10017, (800) 253-9646, Fax: (212) 963-4116, http://unstats.un.org; *Statistical Yearbook.*

HAITI - RICE PRODUCTION

See HAITI - CROPS

HAITI - ROADS

Central Intelligence Agency, Office of Public Affairs, Washington, DC 20505, (703) 482-0623, Fax: (703) 482-1739, www.cia.gov; *The World Factbook.*

Palgrave Macmillan Ltd., Houndmills, Basingstoke, Hampshire, RG21 6XS, England, (Telephone in U.S. (888) 330-8477), (Fax in U.S. (800) 672-2054), www.palgrave.com; *The Statesman's Yearbook 2008.*

HAITI - RUBBER INDUSTRY AND TRADE

International Rubber Study Group (IRSG), 1st Floor, Heron House, 109/115 Wembley Hill Road, Wembley, Middlesex HA9 8DA, United Kingdom, www.rubberstudy.com; *Rubber Statistical Bulletin; Summary of World Rubber Statistics 2005; World Rubber Statistics Handbook (Volume 6, 1975-2001);* and *World Rubber Statistics Historic Handbook.*

M.E. Sharpe, 80 Business Park Drive, Armonk, NY 10504, (800) 541-6563, Fax: (914) 273-2106, www.mesharpe.com; *The Illustrated Book of World Rankings.*

HAITI - SHEEP

See HAITI - LIVESTOCK

HAITI - SHIPPING

Palgrave Macmillan Ltd., Houndmills, Basingstoke, Hampshire, RG21 6XS, England, (Telephone in U.S. (888) 330-8477), (Fax in U.S. (800) 672-2054), www.palgrave.com; *The Statesman's Yearbook 2008.*

Taylor and Francis Group, An Informa Business, 2 Park Square, Milton Park, Abingdon, Oxford OX14 4RN, United Kingdom, (Dial from U.S. (212) 216-7800), (Fax from U.S. (212) 564-7854), www.tandf.co.uk; *The Europa World Year Book.*

United Nations Statistics Division, New York, NY 10017, (800) 253-9646, Fax: (212) 963-4116, http://unstats.un.org; *Statistical Yearbook.*

HAITI - SILVER PRODUCTION

See HAITI - MINERAL INDUSTRIES

HAITI - SOCIAL ECOLOGY

M.E. Sharpe, 80 Business Park Drive, Armonk, NY 10504, (800) 541-6563, Fax: (914) 273-2106, www.mesharpe.com; *The Illustrated Book of World Rankings.*

UCLA Latin American Institute, 10343 Bunche Hall, Box 951447, Los Angeles, CA 90095-1447, (310) 825-4571, Fax: (310) 206-6859, www.international.ucla.edu/lac; *Statistical Abstract of Latin America.*

United Nations Statistics Division, New York, NY 10017, (800) 253-9646, Fax: (212) 963-4116, http://unstats.un.org; *World Statistics Pocketbook.*

HAITI - SOCIAL SECURITY

Inter-American Development Bank (IDB), 1300 New York Avenue, NW, Washington, DC 20577, (202)

623-1000, Fax: (202) 623-3096, www.iadb.org; *The Politics of Policies: Economic and Social Progress in Latin America - 2006 Report.*

United Nations Statistics Division, New York, NY 10017, (800) 253-9646, Fax: (212) 963-4116, http://unstats.un.org; *National Accounts Statistics: Compendium of Income Distribution Statistics.*

HAITI - STEEL PRODUCTION

See HAITI - MINERAL INDUSTRIES

HAITI - SUGAR PRODUCTION

See HAITI - CROPS

HAITI - TAXATION

Inter-American Development Bank (IDB), 1300 New York Avenue, NW, Washington, DC 20577, (202) 623-1000, Fax: (202) 623-3096, www.iadb.org; *The Politics of Policies: Economic and Social Progress in Latin America - 2006 Report.*

International Monetary Fund (IMF), 700 Nineteenth Street, NW, Washington, DC 20431, (202) 623-7000, Fax: (202) 623-4661, www.imf.org; *Government Finance Statistics Yearbook (2008 Edition).*

Taylor and Francis Group, An Informa Business, 2 Park Square, Milton Park, Abingdon, Oxford OX14 4RN, United Kingdom, (Dial from U.S. (212) 216-7800), (Fax from U.S. (212) 564-7854), www.tandf.co.uk; *The Europa World Year Book.*

United Nations Statistics Division, New York, NY 10017, (800) 253-9646, Fax: (212) 963-4116, http://unstats.un.org; *Statistical Yearbook for Latin America and the Caribbean 2004.*

The World Bank, 1818 H Street, NW, Washington, DC 20433, (202) 473-1000, Fax: (202) 477-6391, www.worldbank.org; *World Development Indicators (WDI) 2008.*

HAITI - TELEPHONE

International Telecommunication Union (ITU), Place des Nations, 1211 Geneva 20, Switzerland, www.itu.int; World Telecommunication Indicators Database.

Palgrave Macmillan Ltd., Houndmills, Basingstoke, Hampshire, RG21 6XS, England, (Telephone in U.S. (888) 330-8477), (Fax in U.S. (800) 672-2054), www.palgrave.com; *The Statesman's Yearbook 2008.*

Taylor and Francis Group, An Informa Business, 2 Park Square, Milton Park, Abingdon, Oxford OX14 4RN, United Kingdom, (Dial from U.S. (212) 216-7800), (Fax from U.S. (212) 564-7854), www.tandf.co.uk; *The Europa World Year Book.*

United Nations Statistics Division, New York, NY 10017, (800) 253-9646, Fax: (212) 963-4116, http://unstats.un.org; *Statistical Yearbook* and *World Statistics Pocketbook.*

HAITI - TEXTILE INDUSTRY

Palgrave Macmillan Ltd., Houndmills, Basingstoke, Hampshire, RG21 6XS, England, (Telephone in U.S. (888) 330-8477), (Fax in U.S. (800) 672-2054), www.palgrave.com; *The Statesman's Yearbook 2008.*

United Nations Conference on Trade and Development (UNCTAD), DC2-1120, United Nations, New York, NY 10017, (212) 963-0027, www.unctad.org; *UNCTAD Commodity Yearbook.*

United Nations Statistics Division, New York, NY 10017, (800) 253-9646, Fax: (212) 963-4116, http://unstats.un.org; *Statistical Yearbook.*

HAITI - TOBACCO INDUSTRY

Foreign Agricultural Service (FAS), U.S. Department of Agriculture (USDA), 1400 Independence Avenue, SW, Washington, DC 20250, (202) 720-3935, www.fas.usda.gov; *Tobacco: World Markets and Trade.*

M.E. Sharpe, 80 Business Park Drive, Armonk, NY 10504, (800) 541-6563, Fax: (914) 273-2106, www.mesharpe.com; *The Illustrated Book of World Rankings.*

United Nations Statistics Division, New York, NY 10017, (800) 253-9646, Fax: (212) 963-4116, http://unstats.un.org; *Statistical Yearbook.*

HAITI - TOURISM

Euromonitor International, Inc., 224 S. Michigan Avenue, Suite 1500, Chicago, IL 60604, (312) 922-1115, Fax: (312) 922-1157, www.euromonitor.com; *The World Economic Factbook 2008* and *World Marketing Data and Statistics.*

M.E. Sharpe, 80 Business Park Drive, Armonk, NY 10504, (800) 541-6563, Fax: (914) 273-2106, www.mesharpe.com; *The Illustrated Book of World Rankings.*

Palgrave Macmillan Ltd., Houndmills, Basingstoke, Hampshire, RG21 6XS, England, (Telephone in U.S. (888) 330-8477), (Fax in U.S. (800) 672-2054), www.palgrave.com; *The Statesman's Yearbook 2008.*

Taylor and Francis Group, An Informa Business, 2 Park Square, Milton Park, Abingdon, Oxford OX14 4RN, United Kingdom, (Dial from U.S. (212) 216-7800), (Fax from U.S. (212) 564-7854), www.tandf.co.uk; *The Europa World Year Book.*

UCLA Latin American Institute, 10343 Bunche Hall, Box 951447, Los Angeles, CA 90095-1447, (310) 825-4571, Fax: (310) 206-6859, www.international.ucla.edu/lac; *Statistical Abstract of Latin America.*

United Nations Statistics Division, New York, NY 10017, (800) 253-9646, Fax: (212) 963-4116, http://unstats.un.org; *Statistical Yearbook* and *Statistical Yearbook for Latin America and the Caribbean 2004.*

United Nations World Tourism Organization (UNWTO), Capitan Haya 42, 28020 Madrid, Spain, www.world-tourism.org; *Yearbook of Tourism Statistics.*

The World Bank, 1818 H Street, NW, Washington, DC 20433, (202) 473-1000, Fax: (202) 477-6391, www.worldbank.org; *Haiti.*

HAITI - TRADE

See HAITI - INTERNATIONAL TRADE

HAITI - TRANSPORTATION

Central Intelligence Agency, Office of Public Affairs, Washington, DC 20505, (703) 482-0623, Fax: (703) 482-1739, www.cia.gov; *The World Factbook.*

Euromonitor International, Inc., 224 S. Michigan Avenue, Suite 1500, Chicago, IL 60604, (312) 922-1115, Fax: (312) 922-1157, www.euromonitor.com; *International Marketing Data and Statistics 2008* and *World Marketing Data and Statistics.*

Inter-American Development Bank (IDB), 1300 New York Avenue, NW, Washington, DC 20577, (202) 623-1000, Fax: (202) 623-3096, www.iadb.org; *The Politics of Policies: Economic and Social Progress in Latin America - 2006 Report.*

M.E. Sharpe, 80 Business Park Drive, Armonk, NY 10504, (800) 541-6563, Fax: (914) 273-2106, www.mesharpe.com; *The Illustrated Book of World Rankings.*

Palgrave Macmillan Ltd., Houndmills, Basingstoke, Hampshire, RG21 6XS, England, (Telephone in U.S. (888) 330-8477), (Fax in U.S. (800) 672-2054), www.palgrave.com; *The Statesman's Yearbook 2008.*

Taylor and Francis Group, An Informa Business, 2 Park Square, Milton Park, Abingdon, Oxford OX14 4RN, United Kingdom, (Dial from U.S. (212) 216-7800), (Fax from U.S. (212) 564-7854), www.tandf.co.uk; *The Europa World Year Book.*

UCLA Latin American Institute, 10343 Bunche Hall, Box 951447, Los Angeles, CA 90095-1447, (310) 825-4571, Fax: (310) 206-6859, www.international.ucla.edu/lac; *Statistical Abstract of Latin America.*

United Nations Statistics Division, New York, NY 10017, (800) 253-9646, Fax: (212) 963-4116, http://unstats.un.org; *Human Development Report 2006* and *Statistical Yearbook for Latin America and the Caribbean 2004.*

The World Bank, 1818 H Street, NW, Washington, DC 20433, (202) 473-1000, Fax: (202) 477-6391, www.worldbank.org; *Haiti.*

HAITI - TURKEYS

See HAITI - LIVESTOCK

HAITI - UNEMPLOYMENT

Central Intelligence Agency, Office of Public Affairs, Washington, DC 20505, (703) 482-0623, Fax: (703) 482-1739, www.cia.gov; *The World Factbook.*

International Labour Office, I.L.O. Publications, 4 route des Morillons, CH-1211 Geneva 22, Switzerland, (Telephone in U.S. (202) 653-7652), (Fax in U.S. (202) 653-7687), www.ilo.org; *Yearbook of Labour Statistics 2006.*

UCLA Latin American Institute, 10343 Bunche Hall, Box 951447, Los Angeles, CA 90095-1447, (310) 825-4571, Fax: (310) 206-6859, www.international.ucla.edu/lac; *Statistical Abstract of Latin America.*

HAITI - VITAL STATISTICS

Palgrave Macmillan Ltd., Houndmills, Basingstoke, Hampshire, RG21 6XS, England, (Telephone in U.S. (888) 330-8477), (Fax in U.S. (800) 672-2054), www.palgrave.com; *The Statesman's Yearbook 2008.*

United Nations Statistics Division, New York, NY 10017, (800) 253-9646, Fax: (212) 963-4116, http://unstats.un.org; *Statistical Yearbook.*

World Health Organization (WHO), Avenue Appia 20, 1211 Geneve 27, Switzerland, (Telephone in U.S. (212) 331-9081), www.who.int; *World Health Report 2006.*

HAITI - WAGES

International Labour Office, I.L.O. Publications, 4 route des Morillons, CH-1211 Geneva 22, Switzerland, (Telephone in U.S. (202) 653-7652), (Fax in U.S. (202) 653-7687), www.ilo.org; *Yearbook of Labour Statistics 2006.*

UCLA Latin American Institute, 10343 Bunche Hall, Box 951447, Los Angeles, CA 90095-1447, (310) 825-4571, Fax: (310) 206-6859, www.international.ucla.edu/lac; *Statistical Abstract of Latin America.*

The World Bank, 1818 H Street, NW, Washington, DC 20433, (202) 473-1000, Fax: (202) 477-6391, www.worldbank.org; *Haiti.*

HAITI - WELFARE STATE

Inter-American Development Bank (IDB), 1300 New York Avenue, NW, Washington, DC 20577, (202) 623-1000, Fax: (202) 623-3096, www.iadb.org; *The Politics of Policies: Economic and Social Progress in Latin America - 2006 Report.*

HAITI - WHEAT PRODUCTION

See HAITI - CROPS

HAITI - WHOLESALE PRICE INDEXES

Inter-American Development Bank (IDB), 1300 New York Avenue, NW, Washington, DC 20577, (202) 623-1000, Fax: (202) 623-3096, www.iadb.org; *The Politics of Policies: Economic and Social Progress in Latin America - 2006 Report.*

HAITI - WHOLESALE TRADE

Inter-American Development Bank (IDB), 1300 New York Avenue, NW, Washington, DC 20577, (202) 623-1000, Fax: (202) 623-3096, www.iadb.org; *The Politics of Policies: Economic and Social Progress in Latin America - 2006 Report.*

United Nations Statistics Division, New York, NY 10017, (800) 253-9646, Fax: (212) 963-4116, http://unstats.un.org; *Statistical Yearbook.*

HAITI - WINE AND WINE MAKING

M.E. Sharpe, 80 Business Park Drive, Armonk, NY 10504, (800) 541-6563, Fax: (914) 273-2106, www.mesharpe.com; *The Illustrated Book of World Rankings.*

HAITI - WOOL INDUSTRY

M.E. Sharpe, 80 Business Park Drive, Armonk, NY 10504, (800) 541-6563, Fax: (914) 273-2106, www.mesharpe.com; *The Illustrated Book of World Rankings.*

HAKE - PACIFIC WHITING - IMPORTS

National Marine Fisheries Service (NMFS), National Oceanic and Atmospheric Administration (NOAA), Office of Constituent Services, 1315 East West Highway, 9th Floor, Silver Spring, MD 20910, (301) 713-2379, Fax: (301) 713-2385, www.nmfs.noaa.gov; *Fisheries of the United States - 2006.*

HALIBUT

National Marine Fisheries Service (NMFS), National Oceanic and Atmospheric Administration (NOAA), Office of Constituent Services, 1315 East West Highway, 9th Floor, Silver Spring, MD 20910, (301) 713-2379, Fax: (301) 713-2385, www.nmfs.noaa.gov; *Fisheries of the United States - 2006.*

HALLUCINOGENIC DRUGS

Royal Canadian Mounted Police (RCMP), 1200 Vanier Parkway, Ottawa, ON K1A 0R2, Canada, (613) 993-7267, www.rcmp-grc.gc.ca; *Drug Situation in Canada - 2004.*

Substance Abuse and Mental Health Services Administration (SAMHSA), 1 Choke Cherry Road, Rockville, MD 20857, (240) 777-1311, www.oas.samhsa.gov; *National Survey on Drug Use Health (NSDUH).*

U.S. Department of Justice (DOJ), Bureau of Justice Statistics, 810 Seventh Street, NW, Washington, DC 20531, (202) 307-0765, www.ojp.usdoj.gov/bjs/; *Drugs Crime Facts.*

U.S. Department of Justice (DOJ), Drug Enforcement Administration (DEA), 2401 Jefferson Davis Highway, Alexandria, VA 22301, (202) 307-1000, www.usdoj.gov/dea; *State Factsheets.*

U.S. Department of Justice (DOJ), National Drug Intelligence Center, 319 Washington Street, 5th Floor, Johnstown, PA 15901-1622, (814) 532-4601, Fax: (814) 532-4690, www.usdoj.gov/ndic; *Drug Assessments* and *National Drug Threat Assessment 2007.*

United Nations Office on Drugs and Crime (UNODC), Vienna International Centre, PO Box 500, A-1400 Vienna, Austria, www.unodc.org; *World Drug Report 2006.*

HAM PRICE INDEXES

U.S. Bureau of Labor Statistics (BLS), Postal Square Building, 2 Massachusetts Avenue, NE, Washington, DC 20212-0001, (202) 691-5200, Fax: (202) 691-6325, www.bls.gov; *Consumer Price Index Detailed Report* and *Monthly Labor Review (MLR).*

HAM PRICES

U.S. Bureau of Labor Statistics (BLS), Postal Square Building, 2 Massachusetts Avenue, NE, Washington, DC 20212-0001, (202) 691-5200, Fax: (202) 691-6325, www.bls.gov; *Consumer Price Index Detailed Report* and *Monthly Labor Review (MLR).*

HANDGUNS

See FIREARMS

HANDICAPPED

See DISABILITY

HATE CRIMES

Justice Research and Statistics Association (JRSA), 777 N. Capitol Street, NE, Suite 801, Washington, DC 20002, (202) 842-9330, Fax: (202) 842-9329, www.jrsa.org; *Documenting the Extent and Nature of Drug and Violent Crime: Developing Jurisdiction-Specific Profiles of the Criminal Justice System; The Forum; Improving the Quality and Accuracy of Bias Crime Statistics Nationally: An Assessment of the First Ten Years of Bias Crime Data Collection; JRP Digest; Justice Research and Policy;* and *SAC Publication Digest.*

U.S. Department of Justice (DOJ), Bureau of Justice Statistics, 810 Seventh Street, NW, Washington, DC 20531, (202) 307-0765, www.ojp.usdoj.gov/bjs/; *Hate Crimes Reported by Victims and Police.*

HAWAII

See also - STATE DATA (FOR INDIVIDUAL STATES)

National Criminal Justice Reference Service (NCJRS), PO Box 6000, Rockville, MD 20849-6000, (800) 851-3420, Fax: (301) 519-5212, www.ncjrs.org; *Driving Under the Influence in the City and County of Honolulu.*

National Oceanographic Data Center (NOCD), National Oceanic and Atmospheric Administration (NOAA), SSMC3, 4th Floor, 1315 East-West Highway, Silver Spring, MD 20910-3282, (301) 713-3277, Fax: (301) 713-3302, www.nodc.noaa.gov; *Pacific Region Ocean Data and Information Portal.*

State of Hawaii Department of Business, Economic Development Tourism (DBEDT), Research and Economic Analysis Division (READ), PO Box 2359 Honolulu, HI 96804, (808) 586-2423, Fax: (808) 587-2790, www.hawaii.gov/dbedt/info/economic/census; *Construction and Hawaii's Economy; Hawaii's Emerging Technology Industry; Hawaii's Technology Sector: 2001 to 2005; Monthly Economic Indicators; Monthly Economic Indicators; New Measures of Tourism; 2002 State Input-Output Study;* and *Wage and Employment Structure: Comparing Recent Trends for Hawaii vs. the U.S.*

HAWAII - STATE DATA CENTERS

Department of Business, Economic Development Tourism, PO Box 2359, Honolulu, Hawaii 96804, (808) 586-2423, Fax: (808) 587-2790, www.hawaii.gov/dbedt; State Data Center.

Government Documents Collection, University of Hawaii Library, 2550 MaCarthy Mall, Honolulu, HI 96822, Ms. Gwen Sinclair, (808) 956-2549, Fax: (808) 956-5952, www.sinclair.hawaii.edu/govdocs; State Data Center.

State of Hawaii, Dept. of Business, Economic Development and Tourism, Research and Economic Analysis Division, PO Box 2359, Honolulu, HI 96804, (808) 586-2423, Fax: (808) 587-2790, http://hawaii.gov/dbedt; State Data Center.

HAWAII - PRIMARY STATISTICS SOURCES

State of Hawaii Department of Business, Economic Development Tourism (DBEDT), Research and Economic Analysis Division (READ), PO Box 2359 Honolulu, HI 96804, (808) 586-2423, Fax: (808) 587-2790, www.hawaii.gov/dbedt/info/economic/census; *Quarterly Statistical and Economic Report* and *2005 State of Hawaii Data Book: A Statistical Abstract.*

HAWAIIAN POPULATION

Bernan Essential Government Publications, 4611-F Assembly Drive, Lanham MD, 20706-4391, (301) 459-2255, Fax: (800) 865-3450, www.bernan.com; *Vital Statistics of the United States: Births, Life Expectancy, Deaths, and Selected Health Data.*

National Center for Health Statistics (NCHS), Centers for Disease Control and Prevention (CDC), U.S. Department of Health and Human Services (HHS), 3311 Toledo Road, Hyattsville, MD 20782, (866) 232-4636, www.cdc.gov/nchs; *National Vital Statistics Reports (NVSR); Vital Statistics of the United States (VSUS);* and unpublished data.

Population Reference Bureau, 1875 Connecticut Avenue, NW, Suite 520, Washington, DC, 20009-5728, (800) 877-9881, Fax: (202) 328-3937, www.prb.org; *The American People Series.*

U.S. Census Bureau, 4700 Silver Hill Road, Washington DC 20233-0001, (301) 763-3030, www.census.gov; American FactFinder (web app); *County and City Data Book 2007;* and *State and County QuickFacts.*

U.S. Census Bureau, Demographic Surveys Division, 4700 Silver Hill Road, Washington DC 20233-0001, (301) 763-3030, www.census.gov; *Census 2000: Demographic Profiles.*

U.S. Census Bureau, Population Division, 4700 Silver Hill Road, Washington DC 20233-0001, (301) 763-3030, www.census.gov/population/www/; *Census 2000 Profiles of General Demographic Characteristics* and *Current Population Reports.*

HAY

Economic Research Service (ERS), U.S. Department of Agriculture (USDA), 1800 M Street, NW, Washington, DC 20036-5831, (202) 694-5050, Fax: (202) 694-5689, www.ers.usda.gov; *Agricultural Outlook; Agricultural Statistics; Farm Balance Sheet;* and *Farm Income: Data Files.*

National Agricultural Statistics Service (NASS), U.S. Department of Agriculture (USDA), 1400 Independence Avenue, SW, Washington, DC 20250, (800) 727-9540, Fax: (202) 690-2090, www.nass.usda.gov; *Crop Production* and *Crop Values 2007 Summary.*

HAZARDOUS WASTES - SUPERFUND SITES

U.S. Environmental Protection Agency (EPA), Ariel Rios Building, 1200 Pennsylvania Avenue, NW, Washington, DC 20460, (202) 272-0167, www.epa.gov; Toxics Release Inventory (TRI) Database.

HAZARDOUS WASTES - TRANSPORTATION

U.S. Department of Transportation (DOT), Research and Innovative Technology Administration (RITA), Bureau of Transportation Statistics (BTS), 1200 New Jersey Avenue, SE, Washington, DC 20590, (800) 853-1351, www.bts.gov; *2007 Commodity Flow Survey (CFS)* and *TranStats.*

HAZARDOUS WASTES - WASTE MANAGEMENT

Environmental Business International, Inc., 4452 Park Boulevard, Suite 306, San Diego, CA 92116, (619) 295-7685, Fax: (619) 295-5743, www.ebiusa.com; *Environmental Business Journal (EBJ) 2006; Environmental Market Reports;* and *U.S. and Global Environmental Market Data.*

HAZELNUTS (FILBERTS)

National Agricultural Statistics Service (NASS), U.S. Department of Agriculture (USDA), 1400 Independence Avenue, SW, Washington, DC 20250, (800) 727-9540, Fax: (202) 690-2090, www.nass.usda.gov; *Noncitrus Fruits and Nuts: Final Estimates 1998-2003.*

HEAD START PROGRAM

Administration for Children and Families (ACF), Office of Planning, Research Evaluation (OPRE), U.S. Department of Health and Human Services (HHS), 370 L'Enfant Promenade, SW, Washington, DC 20201, (202) 401-9200, www.acf.hhs.gov/programs/opre; *Head Start Family and Child Experiences Survey (FACES), 1997-2010* and *Head Start Impact Study and Follow-up, 2000-2009.*

HEALTH AND HUMAN SERVICES, DEPARTMENT OF

National Science Foundation, Division of Science Resources Statistics (SRS), 4201 Wilson Boulevard, Arlington, VA 22230, (703) 292-8780, Fax: (703) 292-9092, www.nsf.gov; *Federal Funds for Research and Development: Fiscal Years 2004-2006.*

HEALTH AND MEDICAL ASSOCIATIONS

The Henry J. Kaiser Family Foundation, 2400 Sand Hill Road, Menlo Park, CA 94025, (650) 854-9400, Fax: (650) 854-4800, www.kff.org; *statehealthfacts.org.*

National Center for Health Statistics (NCHS), Centers for Disease Control and Prevention (CDC), U.S. Department of Health and Human Services

(HHS), 3311 Toledo Road, Hyattsville, MD 20782, (866) 232-4636, www.cdc.gov/nchs; *Faststats A to Z.*

National Committee for Quality Assurance (NCQA), 1100 13th Street, NW, Suite 1000 Washington, D.C. 20005, (202) 955-3500, www.ncqa.org; *Accreditation Statistics* and *2004 State of Health Care Quality Report.*

Thomson Gale, 27500 Drake Road, Farmington Hills, MI 48331, (248) 699-4253, www.galegroup.com; *Encyclopedia of Associations.*

HEALTH CARE AND SOCIAL ASSISTANCE INDUSTRY

Australian Institute of Health and Welfare (AIHW), GPO Box 570, Canberra ACT 2601, Australia, www.aihw.gov.au; *Expenditures on Health for Aboriginal and Torres Strait Islander Peoples 2004-05.*

The Brookings Institution, 1775 Massachusetts Avenue, NW, Washington, DC 20036, (202) 797-6000, Fax: (202) 797-6004, www.brook.edu; *Health Status and Access to Care Among Low-Income Washington, D.C. Residents.*

Fingertip Formulary, LLC., 266 Harristown Road, Suite 202, Glen Rock, NJ 07452, (201) 652-3004, Fax: (201) 301-9177, www.fingertipformulary.com; *Fingertip Formulary Analytics* and *Fingertip Formulary Analytics Rx.*

HealthLeaders-InterStudy, One Vantage Way, B-300, Nashville, TN 37203, (615) 385-4131, Fax: (615) 385-4979, www.hmodata.com; *Blue Profiler; Competitive Edge; HMO Financial Analyzer; Managed Market Surveyor-Rx; Medicare Outlook;* and *Strategic Assessment of Managed Markets (SAMM).*

The Henry J. Kaiser Family Foundation, 2400 Sand Hill Road, Menlo Park, CA 94025, (650) 854-9400, Fax: (650) 854-4800, www.kff.org; *Medicaid Benefits: Online Database; State Medicaid Fact Sheets;* and *statehealthfacts.org.*

HEALTH CARE AND SOCIAL ASSISTANCE INDUSTRY - EARNINGS, EMPLOYEES, AND ESTABLISHMENTS

U.S. Census Bureau, 4700 Silver Hill Road, Washington DC 20233-0001, (301) 763-3030, www.census.gov; *E-Stats - Measuring the Electronic Economy.*

U.S. Census Bureau, Center for Economic Studies, 4600 Silver Hill Road, Washington DC 20233, (301) 457-1235, www.ces.census.gov; Economic Census (web app).

U.S. Census Bureau, Company Statistics Division, 4700 Silver Hill Road, Washington DC 20233-0001, (301) 763-3030, www.census.gov/csd/; *County Business Patterns 2004* and *Statistics of U.S. Businesses (SUSB).*

U.S. Census Bureau, Service Sector Statistics Division, 4700 Silver Hill Road, Washington DC 20233-0001, (301) 763-3030, www.census.gov/svsd/www/economic.html; *2004 Service Annual Survey: Health Care and Social Assistance.*

HEALTH CLUBS

National Sporting Goods Association (NSGA), 1601 Feehanville Drive, Suite 300, Mount Prospect, IL 60056, (847) 296-6742, Fax: (847) 391-9827, www.nsga.org; *2006 Sports Participation.*

HEALTH INSURANCE

Fingertip Formulary, LLC., 266 Harristown Road, Suite 202, Glen Rock, NJ 07452, (201) 652-3004, Fax: (201) 301-9177, www.fingertipformulary.com; *Fingertip Formulary Analytics* and *Fingertip Formulary Analytics Rx.*

HealthLeaders-InterStudy, One Vantage Way, B-300, Nashville, TN 37203, (615) 385-4131, Fax: (615) 385-4979, www.hmodata.com; *Strategic Assessment of Managed Markets (SAMM).*

Robert Wood Johnson Foundation, PO Box 2316, College Road East and Route 1, Princeton, NJ 08543, (877) 843-7953, www.rwjf.org; *Medical Errors Involving Trainees: A Study of Closed Malpractice Claims From 5 Insurers; Report from Massachusetts: Employers Largely Support Health Care Reform, and Few Signs of Crowd-Out Appear;* and *What Factors Influence the Kind of Long-Term Services Patients with Private Insurance Choose Over Time.*

Thomson Healthcare, 200 First Stamford Place, 4th Floor, Stamford, CT 06902, (203) 539-8000, www.thomson.com; *Medstat Modeler.*

HEALTH INSURANCE - COVERAGE

Agency for Healthcare Research and Quality (AHRQ), Office of Communications and Knowledge Transfer, 540 Gaither Road, Suite 2000, Rockville, MD 20850, (301) 427-1364, www.ahrq.gov; The Healthcare Cost and Utilization Project (HCUP) and *Medical Expenditure Panel Survey (MEPS).*

The Brookings Institution, 1775 Massachusetts Avenue, NW, Washington, DC 20036, (202) 797-6000, Fax: (202) 797-6004, www.brook.edu; *Health Status and Access to Care Among Low-Income Washington, D.C. Residents.*

HealthLeaders-InterStudy, One Vantage Way, B-300, Nashville, TN 37203, (615) 385-4131, Fax: (615) 385-4979, www.hmodata.com; *Blue Profiler; Competitive Edge; Employer Vantage; Health Plan Data Analysis ; HMO Financial Analyzer; Managed Market Surveyor-Rx; Market Overviews; Medicare Outlook;* and *Pharmacy Benefit Evaluator.*

The Henry J. Kaiser Family Foundation, 2400 Sand Hill Road, Menlo Park, CA 94025, (650) 854-9400, Fax: (650) 854-4800, www.kff.org; *statehealthfacts.org.*

National Center for Health Statistics (NCHS), Centers for Disease Control and Prevention (CDC), U.S. Department of Health and Human Services (HHS), 3311 Toledo Road, Hyattsville, MD 20782, (866) 232-4636, www.cdc.gov/nchs; *Faststats A to Z.*

National Organization for Research at the University of Chicago (NORC), 1155 East 60th Street, Chicago, IL 60637, (773) 256-6000, www.norc.org; *Health Care: Americans Want More for Less.*

Robert Wood Johnson Foundation, PO Box 2316, College Road East and Route 1, Princeton, NJ 08543, (877) 843-7953, www.rwjf.org; *Leading the Way? Maine's Initial Experience in Expanding Coverage Through Dirigo Health Reforms.*

U.S. Bureau of Labor Statistics (BLS), Postal Square Building, 2 Massachusetts Avenue, NE, Washington, DC 20212-0001, (202) 691-5200, Fax: (202) 691-6325, www.bls.gov; unpublished data.

U.S. Census Bureau, 4700 Silver Hill Road, Washington DC 20233-0001, (301) 763-3030, www.census.gov; unpublished data.

U.S. Census Bureau, Center for Economic Studies, 4600 Silver Hill Road, Washington DC 20233, (301) 457-1235, www.ces.census.gov; *2002 Economic Census, Health Care and Social Assistance.*

U.S. Census Bureau, Housing and Household Economics Statistics Division, 4700 Silver Hill Road, Washington DC 20233-0001, (301) 763-3030, www.census.gov/hhes/www; *Health Insurance Coverage Status and Type of Coverage by Selected Characteristics for All People in Poverty Universe.*

U.S. Census Bureau, Population Division, 4700 Silver Hill Road, Washington DC 20233-0001, (301) 763-3030, www.census.gov/population/www/; *Current Population Reports.*

HEALTH INSURANCE - ENROLLMENT AND PAYMENTS

The Brookings Institution, 1775 Massachusetts Avenue, NW, Washington, DC 20036, (202) 797-6000, Fax: (202) 797-6004, www.brook.edu; *Health Status and Access to Care Among Low-Income Washington, D.C. Residents.*

Centers for Medicare and Medicaid Services (CMS), U.S. Department of Health and Human Services (HHS), 7500 Security Boulevard, Baltimore, MD 21244-1850, (410) 786-3000, http://cms.hhs.gov; The Medicare Current Beneficiary Survey (MCBS) (web app) and *Medicare Enrollment: National Trends 1966-2005.*

The Henry J. Kaiser Family Foundation, 2400 Sand Hill Road, Menlo Park, CA 94025, (650) 854-9400, Fax: (650) 854-4800, www.kff.org; *statehealthfacts.org.*

U.S. Census Bureau, Housing and Household Economics Statistics Division, 4700 Silver Hill Road, Washington DC 20233-0001, (301) 763-3030, www.census.gov/hhes/www; *Health Insurance Coverage Status and Type of Coverage by Selected Characteristics for All People in Poverty Universe.*

HEALTH INSURANCE - EXPENDITURES FOR

Centers for Medicare and Medicaid Services (CMS), U.S. Department of Health and Human Services (HHS), 7500 Security Boulevard, Baltimore, MD 21244-1850, (410) 786-3000, http://cms.hhs.gov; *Health Accounts.*

The Henry J. Kaiser Family Foundation, 2400 Sand Hill Road, Menlo Park, CA 94025, (650) 854-9400, Fax: (650) 854-4800, www.kff.org; *statehealthfacts.org.*

National Center for Health Statistics (NCHS), Centers for Disease Control and Prevention (CDC), U.S. Department of Health and Human Services (HHS), 3311 Toledo Road, Hyattsville, MD 20782, (866) 232-4636, www.cdc.gov/nchs; *Faststats A to Z.*

U.S. Bureau of Labor Statistics (BLS), Postal Square Building, 2 Massachusetts Avenue, NE, Washington, DC 20212-0001, (202) 691-5200, Fax: (202) 691-6325, www.bls.gov; *Consumer Expenditures in 2006.*

HEALTH INSURANCE - PREMIUMS AND EXPENSES

America's Health Insurance Plans (AHIP), 601 Pennsylvania Avenue, NW, South Building, Suite 500, Washington, DC 20004, (202) 778-3200, Fax: (202) 331-7487, www.ahip.org; *Cost Trends Chart Book.*

Centers for Medicare and Medicaid Services (CMS), U.S. Department of Health and Human Services (HHS), 7500 Security Boulevard, Baltimore, MD 21244-1850, (410) 786-3000, http://cms.hhs.gov; *Health Care Financing Review.*

The Henry J. Kaiser Family Foundation, 2400 Sand Hill Road, Menlo Park, CA 94025, (650) 854-9400, Fax: (650) 854-4800, www.kff.org; *statehealthfacts.org.*

National Center for Health Statistics (NCHS), Centers for Disease Control and Prevention (CDC), U.S. Department of Health and Human Services (HHS), 3311 Toledo Road, Hyattsville, MD 20782, (866) 232-4636, www.cdc.gov/nchs; *Faststats A to Z.*

Robert Wood Johnson Foundation, PO Box 2316, College Road East and Route 1, Princeton, NJ 08543, (877) 843-7953, www.rwjf.org; *Insurance Premiums Decline in States Capping Malpractice Payouts, Alabama University Study Finds* and *Leading the Way? Maine's Initial Experience in Expanding Coverage Through Dirigo Health Reforms.*

U.S. Bureau of Labor Statistics (BLS), Postal Square Building, 2 Massachusetts Avenue, NE, Washington, DC 20212-0001, (202) 691-5200, Fax: (202) 691-6325, www.bls.gov; unpublished data.

HEALTH INSURANCE - PREMIUMS AND POLICY RESERVES, LIFE INSURANCE COMPANIES

American Council of Life Insurers (ACLI), 101 Constitution Avenue, NW, Washington, DC 20001-2133, (202) 624-2000, www.acli.com; *Life Insurers Fact Book 2007.*

HEALTH MAINTENANCE ORGANIZATIONS

Agency for Healthcare Research and Quality (AHRQ), Office of Communications and Knowledge

Transfer, 540 Gaither Road, Suite 2000, Rockville, MD 20850, (301) 427-1364, www.ahrq.gov; The Healthcare Cost and Utilization Project (HCUP) and *Medical Expenditure Panel Survey (MEPS).*

HealthLeaders-InterStudy, One Vantage Way, B-300, Nashville, TN 37203, (615) 385-4131, Fax: (615) 385-4979, www.hmodata.com; *Competitive Edge; Health Plan Data Analysis ; HMO Financial Analyzer; Managed Market Surveyor-Rx; Market Overviews;* and *Pharmacy Benefit Evaluator.*

The Henry J. Kaiser Family Foundation, 2400 Sand Hill Road, Menlo Park, CA 94025, (650) 854-9400, Fax: (650) 854-4800, www.kff.org; *statehealthfacts.org.*

National Center for Health Statistics (NCHS), Centers for Disease Control and Prevention (CDC), U.S. Department of Health and Human Services (HHS), 3311 Toledo Road, Hyattsville, MD 20782, (866) 232-4636, www.cdc.gov/nchs; *Faststats A to Z.*

U.S. Bureau of Labor Statistics (BLS), Postal Square Building, 2 Massachusetts Avenue, NE, Washington, DC 20212-0001, (202) 691-5200, Fax: (202) 691-6325, www.bls.gov; unpublished data.

HEALTH SCIENCES - DEGREES CONFERRED

National Center for Education Statistics (NCES), 1990 K Street, NW, Washington, DC 20006, (202) 502-7300, http://nces.ed.gov; *Digest of Education Statistics 2007.*

HEALTH SERVICES

See also MEDICAL CARE

American Hospital Association (AHA), One North Franklin, Chicago, IL 60606-3421, (312) 422-3000, www.aha.org; *White Coats and Many Colors: Population Diversity and Its Implications for Health Care.*

American Medical Association, 515 North State Street, Chicago, IL 60610, (800) 621-8335, www.ama-assn.org; *AHA Hospital Statistics 2007* and *State Medical Licensure Requirements and Statistics 2008.*

Australian Institute of Health and Welfare (AIHW), GPO Box 570, Canberra ACT 2601, Australia, www.aihw.gov.au; *Australia's Health 2006; Rural, Regional and Remote Health: a Study on Mortality (2nd Edition); Rural, Regional and Remote Health: Indicators of Health Status and Determinants of Health;* and *Veterans' Use of Health Services.*

The Brookings Institution, 1775 Massachusetts Avenue, NW, Washington, DC 20036, (202) 797-6000, Fax: (202) 797-6004, www.brook.edu; *Health Status and Access to Care Among Low-Income Washington, D.C. Residents.*

Centers for Disease Control and Prevention (CDC), U.S. Department of Health and Human Services (HHS), 1600 Clifton Road, Atlanta, GA 30333, (800) 311-3435, www.cdc.gov; *2003 State Health Profiles.*

Decision Resources, Inc., 260 Charles Street, Waltham, MA 02453, (781) 296-2500, Fax: (781) 296-2550, www.decisionresources.com; Research Studies.

HealthLeaders-InterStudy, One Vantage Way, B-300, Nashville, TN 37203, (615) 385-4131, Fax: (615) 385-4979, www.hmodata.com; *Blue Profiler; Competitive Edge; HMO Financial Analyzer;* and *Managed Market Surveyor-Rx.*

The Henry J. Kaiser Family Foundation, 2400 Sand Hill Road, Menlo Park, CA 94025, (650) 854-9400, Fax: (650) 854-4800, www.kff.org; *Medicaid Benefits: Online Database; State Medicaid Fact Sheets;* and *statehealthfacts.org.*

International Organization for Migration (IOM), 17, Route des Morillons, CH-1211 Geneva 19, Switzerland, www.iom.int; *Migration Health Annual Report 2006.*

National Center for Children in Poverty (NCCP), 215 W. 125th Street, 3rd Floor, New York, NY 10027, (646) 284-9600, Fax: (646) 284-9623, www.nccp.org; *Promoting the Emotional Well-Being of Children and Families.*

National Center for Health Statistics (NCHS), Centers for Disease Control and Prevention (CDC), U.S. Department of Health and Human Services (HHS), 3311 Toledo Road, Hyattsville, MD 20782, (866) 232-4636, www.cdc.gov/nchs; *Faststats A to Z.*

National Organization for Research at the University of Chicago (NORC), 1155 East 60th Street, Chicago, IL 60637, (773) 256-6000, www.norc.org; *Health Care: Americans Want More for Less.*

Netherlands Institute for Health Services Research (NIVEL), PO Box 1568, 3500 BN Utrecht, The Netherlands, www.nivel.eu; *Health Care Utilisation by Ethnic Minorities in the Netherlands; Health Inequalities: Survey Data Compared to Doctor Defined Data; Health Policy Perception and Health Behaviours: A Multilevel Analysis and Implications for Public Health Psychology; Health Problems of Victims Before and After Disaster: A Longitudinal Study in General Practice;* and *Recently Enlisted Patients in General Practice Use More Health Care Resources.*

Robert Wood Johnson Foundation, PO Box 2316, College Road East and Route 1, Princeton, NJ 08543, (877) 843-7953, www.rwjf.org; *Accuracy of the Pain Numeric Rating Scale as a Screening Test in Primary Care; Promoting Smoking Cessation in the Healthcare Environment: 10 Years Later; Quality of Death and Dying is Significantly Higher for People Who Die at Home; Race Ethnicity, and the Education Gradient in Health; Reducing Racial and Ethnic Disparities and Improving Quality of Health Care;* and *Where People Die: A Multilevel Approach to Understanding Influences on Site of Death in America.*

Substance Abuse and Mental Health Services Administration (SAMHSA), 1 Choke Cherry Road, Rockville, MD 20857, (240) 777-1311, www.oas.samhsa.gov; *Health Services Utilization by Individuals with Substance Abuse and Mental Disorders* and *National Survey of Substance Abuse Treatment Services (N-SSATS).*

U.S. Department of Health and Human Services, 200 Independence Avenue, S.W., Washington, D.C. 20201, (202) 619-0257, www.hhs.gov; *Eliminating Health Disparities: Strengthening Data on Race, Ethnicity, and Primary Language in the United States.*

World Food Programme, Via C.G.Viola 68, Parco dei Medici, 00148 Rome, Italy, www.wfp.org; *World Hunger Series 2007: Hunger and Health.*

HEALTH SERVICES - CHARITABLE CONTRIBUTIONS

Independent Sector, 1200 Eighteenth Street, NW, Suite 200, Washington, DC 20036, (202) 467-6100, Fax: (202) 467-6101, www.independentsector.org; *Giving and Volunteering in the United States 2001.*

HEALTH SERVICES - COVERAGE

American Association of Retired Persons (AARP), 601 E Street, NW, Washington, DC 20049, (888) 687-2277, www.aarp.org; *State Profiles: Reforming the Health Care System 2005.*

The Brookings Institution, 1775 Massachusetts Avenue, NW, Washington, DC 20036, (202) 797-6000, Fax: (202) 797-6004, www.brook.edu; *Health Status and Access to Care Among Low-Income Washington, D.C. Residents.*

Centers for Medicare and Medicaid Services (CMS), U.S. Department of Health and Human Services (HHS), 7500 Security Boulevard, Baltimore, MD 21244-1850, (410) 786-3000, http://cms.hhs.gov; Data Compendium, 2007 (web app); The Medicare Current Beneficiary Survey (MCBS) (web app); and *Medicare Enrollment: National Trends 1966-2005.*

Health Resources and Services Administration (HRSA), National Center for Health Workforce Analysis (NCHWA), 5600 Fishers Lane, Rockville, MD 20857, (301) 443-2216, www.hrsa.gov; Area Resource File (ARF), 2003.

National Organization for Research at the University of Chicago (NORC), 1155 East 60th Street, Chicago, IL 60637, (773) 256-6000, www.norc.org; *Health Care: Americans Want More for Less.*

Social Security Administration (SSA), Office of Public Inquiries, Windsor Park Building, 6401 Security Boulevard, Baltimore, MD 21235, (800) 772-1213, www.ssa.gov; *Annual Statistical Supplement, 2007* and unpublished data.

U.S. Census Bureau, 4700 Silver Hill Road, Washington DC 20233-0001, (301) 763-3030, www.census.gov; unpublished data.

U.S. Census Bureau, Population Division, 4700 Silver Hill Road, Washington DC 20233-0001, (301) 763-3030, www.census.gov/population/www/; *Current Population Reports.*

HEALTH SERVICES - EMPLOYMENT BENEFITS

Agency for Healthcare Research and Quality (AHRQ), Office of Communications and Knowledge Transfer, 540 Gaither Road, Suite 2000, Rockville, MD 20850, (301) 427-1364, www.ahrq.gov; The Healthcare Cost and Utilization Project (HCUP) and *Medical Expenditure Panel Survey (MEPS).*

HealthLeaders-InterStudy, One Vantage Way, B-300, Nashville, TN 37203, (615) 385-4131, Fax: (615) 385-4979, www.hmodata.com; *Employer Vantage.*

U.S. Bureau of Labor Statistics (BLS), Postal Square Building, 2 Massachusetts Avenue, NE, Washington, DC 20212-0001, (202) 691-5200, Fax: (202) 691-6325, www.bls.gov; *Employee Benefits in Medium and Large Private Establishments* and unpublished data.

HEALTH SERVICES - EXPENDITURES, PUBLIC

Alan Guttmacher Institute, 125 Maiden Lane, 7th Floor, New York, NY 10038, (212) 248-1111, Fax: (212) 248-1951, www.agi-usa.org; *Public Funding for Contraceptive, Sterilization and Abortion Services, FY 1980-2001.*

American Association of Retired Persons (AARP), 601 E Street, NW, Washington, DC 20049, (888) 687-2277, www.aarp.org; *State Profiles: Reforming the Health Care System 2005.*

Australian Institute of Health and Welfare (AIHW), GPO Box 570, Canberra ACT 2601, Australia, www.aihw.gov.au; *Expenditures on Health for Aboriginal and Torres Strait Islander Peoples 2004-05* and *National Public Health Expenditure Report 2005-06.*

Centers for Medicare and Medicaid Services (CMS), U.S. Department of Health and Human Services (HHS), 7500 Security Boulevard, Baltimore, MD 21244-1850, (410) 786-3000, http://cms.hhs.gov; *Health Accounts.*

The Office of Management and Budget (OMB), 725 17th Street, NW, Washington, DC 20503, (202) 395-3080, Fax: (202) 395-3888, www.whitehouse.gov/omb; *Budget of the United States Government, Federal Year 2009.*

Robert Wood Johnson Foundation, PO Box 2316, College Road East and Route 1, Princeton, NJ 08543, (877) 843-7953, www.rwjf.org; *Leading the Way? Maine's Initial Experience in Expanding Coverage Through Dirigo Health Reforms.*

Social Security Administration (SSA), Office of Public Inquiries, Windsor Park Building, 6401 Security Boulevard, Baltimore, MD 21235, (800) 772-1213, www.ssa.gov; *Social Security Bulletin* and unpublished data.

U.S. Census Bureau, Governments Division, 4600 Silver Hill Road, Washington DC 20233, (800) 242-2184, www.census.gov/govs/www; *2002 Census of Governments, Government Finances.*

HEALTH SERVICES - EXPENDITURES, PUBLIC - CITY GOVERNMENTS

U.S. Census Bureau, 4700 Silver Hill Road, Washington DC 20233-0001, (301) 763-3030, www.census.gov; unpublished data.

HEALTH SERVICES - EXPENDITURES, PUBLIC - COUNTY GOVERNMENTS

Alan Guttmacher Institute, 125 Maiden Lane, 7th Floor, New York, NY 10038, (212) 248-1111, Fax: (212) 248-1951, www.agi-usa.org; *Public Funding for Contraceptive, Sterilization and Abortion Services, FY 1980-2001.*

U.S. Census Bureau, 4700 Silver Hill Road, Washington DC 20233-0001, (301) 763-3030, www.census.gov; unpublished data.

HEALTH SERVICES - EXPENDITURES, PUBLIC - FEDERAL GOVERNMENT

Alan Guttmacher Institute, 125 Maiden Lane, 7th Floor, New York, NY 10038, (212) 248-1111, Fax: (212) 248-1951, www.agi-usa.org; *Public Funding for Contraceptive, Sterilization and Abortion Services, FY 1980-2001.*

Centers for Medicare and Medicaid Services (CMS), U.S. Department of Health and Human Services (HHS), 7500 Security Boulevard, Baltimore, MD 21244-1850, (410) 786-3000, http://cms.hhs.gov; *Health Accounts.*

The Office of Management and Budget (OMB), 725 17th Street, NW, Washington, DC 20503, (202) 395-3080, Fax: (202) 395-3888, www.whitehouse.gov/omb; *Historical Tables.*

HEALTH SERVICES - EXPENDITURES, PUBLIC - FEDERAL GOVERNMENT - AID TO STATE AND LOCAL GOVERNMENTS

The Office of Management and Budget (OMB), 725 17th Street, NW, Washington, DC 20503, (202) 395-3080, Fax: (202) 395-3888, www.whitehouse.gov/omb; *Historical Tables.*

HEALTH SERVICES - EXPENDITURES, PUBLIC - STATE GOVERNMENTS

National Association of State Budget Officers (NASBO), Hall of the States Building - Suite 642, 444 North Capitol Street, NW, Washington, DC 20001-1511, (202) 624-5382, Fax: (202) 624-7745, www.nasbo.org; *Fiscal Survey of the States, Fall 2007* and *State Expenditure Report, Fiscal Year 2006.*

U.S. Census Bureau, Governments Division, 4600 Silver Hill Road, Washington DC 20233, (800) 242-2184, www.census.gov/govs/www; *2002 Census of Governments, Government Finances.*

HEALTH SERVICES - FEDERAL OUTLAYS FOR

Centers for Medicare and Medicaid Services (CMS), U.S. Department of Health and Human Services (HHS), 7500 Security Boulevard, Baltimore, MD 21244-1850, (410) 786-3000, http://cms.hhs.gov; *Health Accounts.*

The Office of Management and Budget (OMB), 725 17th Street, NW, Washington, DC 20503, (202) 395-3080, Fax: (202) 395-3888, www.whitehouse.gov/omb; *Historical Tables.*

HEALTH SERVICES - FOREIGN COUNTRIES

Lesotho Bureau of Statistics, Ministry of Finance and Development Planning, PO Box 455, Maseru 100, Lesotho, www.bos.gov.ls; *Health Statistics 2004.*

Netherlands Institute for Health Services Research (NIVEL), PO Box 1568, 3500 BN Utrecht, The Netherlands, www.nivel.eu; *Health Care Use by Diabetic Patients in the Netherlands: Patterns and Predicting Factors.*

Organisation for Economic Cooperation and Development (OECD), 2 rue Andre Pascal, F-75775 Paris Cedex 16, France, (Telephone in U.S. (202) 785-6323), (Fax in U.S. (202) 785-0350), www.oecd.org; *OECD Health Data 2007* and *OECD in Figures 2007.*

HEALTH SERVICES - GOVERNMENT EMPLOYMENT AND PAYROLLS

U.S. Census Bureau, Governments Division, 4600 Silver Hill Road, Washington DC 20233, (800) 242-2184, www.census.gov/govs/www; *2002 Census of Governments, Public Employment and Payroll.*

HEALTH SERVICES - HOSPITALS

American Hospital Association (AHA), One North Franklin, Chicago, IL 60606-3421, (312) 422-3000, www.aha.org; *Annual Survey of Hospitals; Hospital Statistics 2008;* and unpublished data.

National Center for Health Statistics (NCHS), Centers for Disease Control and Prevention (CDC), U.S. Department of Health and Human Services (HHS), 3311 Toledo Road, Hyattsville, MD 20782, (866) 232-4636, www.cdc.gov/nchs; *Health Care in America: Trends in Utilization (2004 Edition)* and *Health, United States, 2006, with Chartbook on Trends in the Health of Americans with Special Feature on Pain.*

U.S. Census Bureau, Company Statistics Division, 4700 Silver Hill Road, Washington DC 20233-0001, (301) 763-3030, www.census.gov/csd/; *County Business Patterns 2004* and *Current Business Reports.*

HEALTH SERVICES - INDUSTRY - CAPITAL EXPENDITURES

U.S. Census Bureau, Company Statistics Division, 4700 Silver Hill Road, Washington DC 20233-0001, (301) 763-3030, www.census.gov/csd/; *Annual Capital Expenditures Survey (ACES).*

HEALTH SERVICES - INDUSTRY - EARNINGS

U.S. Bureau of Labor Statistics (BLS), Postal Square Building, 2 Massachusetts Avenue, NE, Washington, DC 20212-0001, (202) 691-5200, Fax: (202) 691-6325, www.bls.gov; *Current Employment Statistics Survey (CES)* and *Employment and Earnings (EE).*

U.S. Census Bureau, 4700 Silver Hill Road, Washington DC 20233-0001, (301) 763-3030, www.census.gov; unpublished data.

U.S. Census Bureau, Center for Economic Studies, 4600 Silver Hill Road, Washington DC 20233, (301) 457-1235, www.ces.census.gov; *2002 Economic Census, Health Care and Social Assistance.*

U.S. Census Bureau, Company Statistics Division, 4700 Silver Hill Road, Washington DC 20233-0001, (301) 763-3030, www.census.gov/csd/; *County Business Patterns 2004.*

HEALTH SERVICES - INDUSTRY - EMPLOYEES

National Center for Health Statistics (NCHS), Centers for Disease Control and Prevention (CDC), U.S. Department of Health and Human Services (HHS), 3311 Toledo Road, Hyattsville, MD 20782, (866) 232-4636, www.cdc.gov/nchs; unpublished data.

U.S. Bureau of Labor Statistics (BLS), Postal Square Building, 2 Massachusetts Avenue, NE, Washington, DC 20212-0001, (202) 691-5200, Fax: (202) 691-6325, www.bls.gov; *Current Employment Statistics Survey (CES); Employment and Earnings (EE);* and *Industries at a Glance.*

U.S. Census Bureau, 4700 Silver Hill Road, Washington DC 20233-0001, (301) 763-3030, www.census.gov; unpublished data.

U.S. Census Bureau, Center for Economic Studies, 4600 Silver Hill Road, Washington DC 20233, (301) 457-1235, www.ces.census.gov; *2002 Economic Census, Health Care and Social Assistance.*

U.S. Census Bureau, Company Statistics Division, 4700 Silver Hill Road, Washington DC 20233-0001, (301) 763-3030, www.census.gov/csd/; *County Business Patterns 2004.*

HEALTH SERVICES - INDUSTRY - ESTABLISHMENTS

American Hospital Association (AHA), One North Franklin, Chicago, IL 60606-3421, (312) 422-3000, www.aha.org; *White Coats and Many Colors: Population Diversity and Its Implications for Health Care.*

HealthLeaders-InterStudy, One Vantage Way, B-300, Nashville, TN 37203, (615) 385-4131, Fax: (615) 385-4979, www.hmodata.com; *Blue Profiler; Competitive Edge; HMO Financial Analyzer;* and *Managed Market Surveyor-Rx.*

U.S. Census Bureau, 4700 Silver Hill Road, Washington DC 20233-0001, (301) 763-3030, www.census.gov; unpublished data.

U.S. Census Bureau, Center for Economic Studies, 4600 Silver Hill Road, Washington DC 20233, (301) 457-1235, www.ces.census.gov; *2002 Economic Census, Health Care and Social Assistance.*

U.S. Census Bureau, Company Statistics Division, 4700 Silver Hill Road, Washington DC 20233-0001, (301) 763-3030, www.census.gov/csd/; *County Business Patterns 2004.*

HEALTH SERVICES - INDUSTRY - FINANCES

U.S. Census Bureau, Company Statistics Division, 4700 Silver Hill Road, Washington DC 20233-0001, (301) 763-3030, www.census.gov/csd/; *Current Business Reports.*

HEALTH SERVICES - INDUSTRY - GROSS DOMESTIC PRODUCT

Bureau of Economic Analysis (BEA), U.S. Department of Commerce (DOC), 1441 L Street NW, Washington, DC 20230, (202) 606-9900, www.bea.gov; *Survey of Current Business (SCB).*

HEALTH SERVICES - INDUSTRY - MERGERS AND ACQUISITIONS

Thomson Financial, 195 Broadway, New York, NY 10007, (646) 822-2000, www.thomson.com; Thomson Research.

HEALTH SERVICES - INDUSTRY - MULTINATIONAL COMPANIES

Bureau of Economic Analysis (BEA), U.S. Department of Commerce (DOC), 1441 L Street NW, Washington, DC 20230, (202) 606-9900, www.bea.gov; *Survey of Current Business (SCB).*

HEALTH SERVICES - INDUSTRY - OCCUPATIONAL SAFETY

U.S. Bureau of Labor Statistics (BLS), Postal Square Building, 2 Massachusetts Avenue, NE, Washington, DC 20212-0001, (202) 691-5200, Fax: (202) 691-6325, www.bls.gov; *Injuries, Illnesses, and Fatalities (IIF).*

HEALTH SERVICES - INDUSTRY - SALES OR RECEIPTS

U.S. Census Bureau, 4700 Silver Hill Road, Washington DC 20233-0001, (301) 763-3030, www.census.gov; unpublished data.

U.S. Census Bureau, Center for Economic Studies, 4600 Silver Hill Road, Washington DC 20233, (301) 457-1235, www.ces.census.gov; *2002 Economic Census, Health Care and Social Assistance.*

U.S. Census Bureau, Company Statistics Division, 4700 Silver Hill Road, Washington DC 20233-0001, (301) 763-3030, www.census.gov/csd/; *Current Business Reports.*

U.S. Census Bureau, Service Sector Statistics Division, 4700 Silver Hill Road, Washington DC 20233-0001, (301) 763-3030, www.census.gov/svsd/www/economic.html; *2004 Service Annual Survey.*

HEALTH SERVICES - MEDICAID

The Brookings Institution, 1775 Massachusetts Avenue, NW, Washington, DC 20036, (202) 797-6000, Fax: (202) 797-6004, www.brook.edu; *Health Status and Access to Care Among Low-Income Washington, D.C. Residents.*

Centers for Medicare and Medicaid Services (CMS), U.S. Department of Health and Human Services (HHS), 7500 Security Boulevard, Baltimore, MD 21244-1850, (410) 786-3000, http://cms.hhs.gov; Data Compendium, 2007 (web app); *Health Ac-*

counts; The Medicare Current Beneficiary Survey (MCBS) (web app); and unpublished data.

The Office of Management and Budget (OMB), 725 17th Street, NW, Washington, DC 20503, (202) 395-3080, Fax: (202) 395-3888, www.whitehouse.gov/omb; *Historical Tables.*

Social Security Administration (SSA), Office of Public Inquiries, Windsor Park Building, 6401 Security Boulevard, Baltimore, MD 21235, (800) 772-1213, www.ssa.gov; *Social Security Bulletin* and unpublished data.

U.S. Census Bureau, Center for Economic Studies, 4600 Silver Hill Road, Washington DC 20233, (301) 457-1235, www.ces.census.gov; *2002 Economic Census, Health Care and Social Assistance.*

U.S. Census Bureau, Housing and Household Economics Statistics Division, 4700 Silver Hill Road, Washington DC 20233-0001, (301) 763-3030, www.census.gov/hhes/www; *Health Insurance Coverage Status and Type of Coverage by Selected Characteristics for All People in Poverty Universe.*

U.S. Census Bureau, Population Division, 4700 Silver Hill Road, Washington DC 20233-0001, (301) 763-3030, www.census.gov/population/www/; *Current Population Reports.*

U.S. Library of Congress (LOC), Congressional Research Service (CRS), The Library of Congress, 101 Independence Avenue, SE, Washington, DC 20540-7500, (202) 707-5700, www.loc.gov/crsinfo; *Cash and Non-cash Benefits for Persons With Limited Income: Eligibility Rules, Recipient and Expenditure Data.*

HEALTH SERVICES - MEDICARE

The Brookings Institution, 1775 Massachusetts Avenue, NW, Washington, DC 20036, (202) 797-6000, Fax: (202) 797-6004, www.brook.edu; *Health Status and Access to Care Among Low-Income Washington, D.C. Residents.*

Centers for Medicare and Medicaid Services (CMS), U.S. Department of Health and Human Services (HHS), 7500 Security Boulevard, Baltimore, MD 21244-1850, (410) 786-3000, http://cms.hhs.gov; Data Compendium, 2007 (web app); *Health Accounts;* and *Medicare Health Outcomes Survey (HOS)*.

HealthLeaders-InterStudy, One Vantage Way, B-300, Nashville, TN 37203, (615) 385-4131, Fax: (615) 385-4979, www.hmodata.com; *Medicare Outlook.*

The Office of Management and Budget (OMB), 725 17th Street, NW, Washington, DC 20503, (202) 395-3080, Fax: (202) 395-3888, www.whitehouse.gov/omb; *Budget of the United States Government, Federal Year 2009.*

Social Security Administration (SSA), Office of Public Inquiries, Windsor Park Building, 6401 Security Boulevard, Baltimore, MD 21235, (800) 772-1213, www.ssa.gov; *2006 Annual Report of the Board of Trustees of the Federal Old-Age and Survivors Insurance and Disability Insurance Trust Funds; Annual Statistical Supplement, 2007; Social Security Bulletin;* and unpublished data.

U.S. Census Bureau, Center for Economic Studies, 4600 Silver Hill Road, Washington DC 20233, (301) 457-1235, www.ces.census.gov; *2002 Economic Census, Health Care and Social Assistance.*

U.S. Census Bureau, Housing and Household Economics Statistics Division, 4700 Silver Hill Road, Washington DC 20233-0001, (301) 763-3030, www.census.gov/hhes/www; *Health Insurance Coverage Status and Type of Coverage by Selected Characteristics for All People in Poverty Universe.*

U.S. Census Bureau, Population Division, 4700 Silver Hill Road, Washington DC 20233-0001, (301) 763-3030, www.census.gov/population/www/; *Current Population Reports.*

HEALTH SERVICES - MENTAL HEALTH FACILITIES

National Center for Children in Poverty (NCCP), 215 W. 125th Street, 3rd Floor, New York, NY 10027, (646) 284-9600, Fax: (646) 284-9623, www.nccp.org; *Unclaimed Children Revisited.*

Substance Abuse and Mental Health Services Administration (SAMHSA), 1 Choke Cherry Road, Rockville, MD 20857, (240) 777-1311, www.oas.samhsa.gov; *Health Services Utilization by Individuals with Substance Abuse and Mental Disorders* and unpublished data.

HEALTH SERVICES - NURSING HOMES

Centers for Medicare and Medicaid Services (CMS), U.S. Department of Health and Human Services (HHS), 7500 Security Boulevard, Baltimore, MD 21244-1850, (410) 786-3000, http://cms.hhs.gov; *Health Accounts.*

National Center for Health Statistics (NCHS), Centers for Disease Control and Prevention (CDC), U.S. Department of Health and Human Services (HHS), 3311 Toledo Road, Hyattsville, MD 20782, (866) 232-4636, www.cdc.gov/nchs; *Health Care in America: Trends in Utilization (2004 Edition).*

HEALTH SERVICES - OCCUPATIONS

American Hospital Association (AHA), One North Franklin, Chicago, IL 60606-3421, (312) 422-3000, www.aha.org; *Annual Survey of Hospitals* and *Hospital Statistics 2008.*

American Medical Association, 515 North State Street, Chicago, IL 60610, (800) 621-8335, www.ama-assn.org; *Physician Characteristics and Distribution in the United States, 2008* and *Physician Compensation and Production Survey: 2007 Report Based on 2006 Data.*

National Center for Health Statistics (NCHS), Centers for Disease Control and Prevention (CDC), U.S. Department of Health and Human Services (HHS), 3311 Toledo Road, Hyattsville, MD 20782, (866) 232-4636, www.cdc.gov/nchs; unpublished data.

U.S. Bureau of Labor Statistics (BLS), Postal Square Building, 2 Massachusetts Avenue, NE, Washington, DC 20212-0001, (202) 691-5200, Fax: (202) 691-6325, www.bls.gov; *Employment and Earnings (EE)* and unpublished data.

United Nations Statistics Division, New York, NY 10017, (800) 253-9646, Fax: (212) 963-4116, http://unstats.un.org; *World Statistics Pocketbook.*

HEALTH SERVICES - PHILANTHROPY

Centers for Medicare and Medicaid Services (CMS), U.S. Department of Health and Human Services (HHS), 7500 Security Boulevard, Baltimore, MD 21244-1850, (410) 786-3000, http://cms.hhs.gov; *Health Care Financing Review.*

The Giving Institute, 4700 W. Lake Ave, Glenview, IL 60025, (800) 462-2372, Fax: (866) 607-0913, www.aafrc.org; *Giving USA 2006.*

HEALTH SERVICES - PRICE INDEXES

Bureau of Economic Analysis (BEA), U.S. Department of Commerce (DOC), 1441 L Street NW, Washington, DC 20230, (202) 606-9900, www.bea.gov; *2007 Annual Revision of the National Income and Product Accounts (NIPA)* and *Survey of Current Business (SCB).*

U.S. Bureau of Labor Statistics (BLS), Postal Square Building, 2 Massachusetts Avenue, NE, Washington, DC 20212-0001, (202) 691-5200, Fax: (202) 691-6325, www.bls.gov; *Consumer Price Index Detailed Report.*

U.S. Department of Labor (DOL), Bureau of Labor Statistics (BLS), Postal Square Building, 2 Massachusetts Avenue, NE, Washington, DC 20212-0001, (202) 691-5200, Fax: (202) 691-6325, www.bls.gov; *Consumer Price Indexes (CPI).*

HEALTH SERVICES - PRIVATE EXPENDITURES

American Hospital Association (AHA), One North Franklin, Chicago, IL 60606-3421, (312) 422-3000, www.aha.org; *White Coats and Many Colors: Population Diversity and Its Implications for Health Care.*

The Brookings Institution, 1775 Massachusetts Avenue, NW, Washington, DC 20036, (202) 797-6000, Fax: (202) 797-6004, www.brook.edu; *Health Status and Access to Care Among Low-Income Washington, D.C. Residents.*

Centers for Medicare and Medicaid Services (CMS), U.S. Department of Health and Human Services (HHS), 7500 Security Boulevard, Baltimore, MD 21244-1850, (410) 786-3000, http://cms.hhs.gov; *Health Accounts.*

Social Security Administration (SSA), Office of Public Inquiries, Windsor Park Building, 6401 Security Boulevard, Baltimore, MD 21235, (800) 772-1213, www.ssa.gov; *Annual Statistical Supplement, 2007.*

U.S. Bureau of Labor Statistics (BLS), Postal Square Building, 2 Massachusetts Avenue, NE, Washington, DC 20212-0001, (202) 691-5200, Fax: (202) 691-6325, www.bls.gov; *Consumer Expenditures in 2006.*

HEALTH SERVICES

See MEDICAL CARE

HEALTH SERVICES - VETERANS HEALTH CARE

Centers for Medicare and Medicaid Services (CMS), U.S. Department of Health and Human Services (HHS), 7500 Security Boulevard, Baltimore, MD 21244-1850, (410) 786-3000, http://cms.hhs.gov; *Health Accounts.*

U.S. Department of Veterans Affairs (VA), 810 Vermont Avenue, NW, Washington, DC 20420-0001, (202) 273-5400, www.va.gov; *Annual Accountability Report Statistical Appendix; Fact Sheets;* and unpublished data.

HEALTH SERVICES - VOLUNTEERS

Independent Sector, 1200 Eighteenth Street, NW, Suite 200, Washington, DC 20036, (202) 467-6100, Fax: (202) 467-6101, www.independentsector.org; *Giving and Volunteering in the United States 2001.*

HEARING IMPAIRED

National Center for Health Statistics (NCHS), Centers for Disease Control and Prevention (CDC), U.S. Department of Health and Human Services (HHS), 3311 Toledo Road, Hyattsville, MD 20782, (866) 232-4636, www.cdc.gov/nchs; unpublished data.

HEART

Robert Wood Johnson Foundation, PO Box 2316, College Road East and Route 1, Princeton, NJ 08543, (877) 843-7953, www.rwjf.org; *First-Year Achievements Signal Big Improvements in Heart Care for Minority Patients.*

HEART DISEASE

Bernan Essential Government Publications, 4611-F Assembly Drive, Lanham MD, 20706-4391, (301) 459-2255, Fax: (800) 865-3450, www.bernan.com; *Vital Statistics of the United States: Births, Life Expectancy, Deaths, and Selected Health Data.*

National Center for Chronic Disease Prevention and Health Promotion (NCCDPHP), Centers for Disease Control and Prevention (CDC), 4770 Buford Hwy, NE, MS K-40, Atlanta, GA 30341-3717, (404) 639-3311, www.cdc.gov/nccdphp; *The Atlas of Heart Disease and Stroke* and *Racial and Ethnic Approaches to Community Health (REACH 2010): Addressing Disparities in Health.*

National Center for Health Statistics (NCHS), Centers for Disease Control and Prevention (CDC), U.S. Department of Health and Human Services (HHS), 3311 Toledo Road, Hyattsville, MD 20782, (866) 232-4636, www.cdc.gov/nchs; *Faststats A to Z; Faststats A to Z; Health, United States, 2006, with Chartbook on Trends in the Health of Americans with Special Feature on Pain; National Vital Statistics Reports (NVSR); Vital Statistics of the United States (VSUS);* and unpublished data.

HEART DISEASE - DEATHS

Bernan Essential Government Publications, 4611-F Assembly Drive, Lanham MD, 20706-4391, (301) 459-2255, Fax: (800) 865-3450, www.bernan.com; *Vital Statistics of the United States: Births, Life Expectancy, Deaths, and Selected Health Data.*

National Center for Health Statistics (NCHS), Centers for Disease Control and Prevention (CDC), U.S. Department of Health and Human Services (HHS), 3311 Toledo Road, Hyattsville, MD 20782, (866) 232-4636, www.cdc.gov/nchs; *National Vital Statistics Reports (NVSR); Vital Statistics of the United States (VSUS);* and unpublished data.

HEART DISEASE - FOREIGN COUNTRIES

World Health Organization (WHO), Avenue Appia 20, 1211 Geneve 27, Switzerland, (Telephone in U.S. (212) 331-9081), www.who.int; *World Health Report 2006.*

HEAT

National Oceanographic Data Center (NOCD), National Oceanic and Atmospheric Administration (NOAA), SSMC3, 4th Floor, 1315 East-West Highway, Silver Spring, MD 20910-3282, (301) 713-3277, Fax: (301) 713-3302, www.nodc.noaa.gov; *Heat Content 2004* and *Warming of the World Ocean, 1955-2003.*

HEAT PUMPS

U.S. Census Bureau, Housing and Household Economics Statistics Division, 4700 Silver Hill Road, Washington DC 20233-0001, (301) 763-3030, www.census.gov/hhes/www; *2006 American Community Survey (ACS)* and *American Housing Survey (AHS).*

HEATING AND PLUMBING EQUIPMENT

U.S. Census Bureau, Housing and Household Economics Statistics Division, 4700 Silver Hill Road, Washington DC 20233-0001, (301) 763-3030, www.census.gov/hhes/www; *2006 American Community Survey (ACS)* and *American Housing Survey (AHS).*

U.S. Department of Energy (DOE), Energy Information Administration (EIA), 1000 Independence Avenue, SW, Washington, DC 20585, (202) 586-8800, www.eia.doe.gov; *Renewable Energy Annual 2004* and *Solar Thermal and Photovoltaic Collector Manufacturing Activities 2005.*

HEATING OIL PRICES

PennWell Corporation, 1421 South Sheridan Road, Tulsa, OK 74112, (918) 835-3161, www.pennwell.com; *Oil and Gas Financial Journal* and *Oil and Gas Journal.*

U.S. Department of Energy (DOE), Energy Information Administration (EIA), 1000 Independence Avenue, SW, Washington, DC 20585, (202) 586-8800, www.eia.doe.gov; *Annual Energy Review 2005; Monthly Energy Review (MER);* and *Petroleum Supply Annual 2004.*

HEIGHTS - AVERAGE - BY AGE AND SEX

National Center for Health Statistics (NCHS), Centers for Disease Control and Prevention (CDC), U.S. Department of Health and Human Services (HHS), 3311 Toledo Road, Hyattsville, MD 20782, (866) 232-4636, www.cdc.gov/nchs; unpublished data.

HELIUM

U.S. Department of the Interior (DOI), U.S. Geological Survey (USGS), Office of Minerals Information, 12201 Sunrise Valley Drive, Reston, VA 20192, Mr. Kenneth A. Beckman, (703) 648-4916, Fax: (703) 648-4995, http://minerals.usgs.gov/minerals; *Mineral Commodity Summaries.*

HEPATITIS

Centers for Disease Control and Prevention (CDC), U.S. Department of Health and Human Services (HHS), 1600 Clifton Road, Atlanta, GA 30333, (800) 311-3435, www.cdc.gov; *Morbidity and Mortality Weekly Report (MMWR)* and *Summary of Notifiable Diseases, United States, 2006.*

Health Protection Agency, 7th Floor, Holborn Gate, 330 High Holborn, London WC1V 7PP, United Kingdom, www.hpa.org.uk; *Hepatitis C in England.*

U.S. Department of Justice (DOJ), Bureau of Justice Statistics, 810 Seventh Street, NW, Washington, DC 20531, (202) 307-0765, www.ojp.usdoj.gov/bjs/; *Hepatitis Testing and Treatment in State Prisons.*

HERNIA AND INTESTINAL OBSTRUCTION - DEATHS

Bernan Essential Government Publications, 4611-F Assembly Drive, Lanham MD, 20706-4391, (301) 459-2255, Fax: (800) 865-3450, www.bernan.com; *Vital Statistics of the United States: Births, Life Expectancy, Deaths, and Selected Health Data.*

National Center for Health Statistics (NCHS), Centers for Disease Control and Prevention (CDC), U.S. Department of Health and Human Services (HHS), 3311 Toledo Road, Hyattsville, MD 20782, (866) 232-4636, www.cdc.gov/nchs; *National Vital Statistics Reports (NVSR); Vital Statistics of the United States (VSUS);* and unpublished data.

HEROIN

Federal Bureau of Investigation (FBI), J. Edgar Hoover Building, 935 Pennsylvania Avenue, NW, Washington, DC 20535-0001, (202) 324-3000, www.fbi.gov; *Crime in the United States (CIUS) 2007 (Preliminary).*

Justice Research and Statistics Association (JRSA), 777 N. Capitol Street, NE, Suite 801, Washington, DC 20002, (202) 842-9330, Fax: (202) 842-9329, www.jrsa.org; *Crime and Justice Atlas 2001.*

Royal Canadian Mounted Police (RCMP), 1200 Vanier Parkway, Ottawa, ON K1A 0R2, Canada, (613) 993-7267, www.rcmp-grc.gc.ca; *Drug Situation in Canada - 2004.*

Substance Abuse and Mental Health Services Administration (SAMHSA), 1 Choke Cherry Road, Rockville, MD 20857, (240) 777-1311, www.oas.samhsa.gov; *National Survey on Drug Use Health (NSDUH).*

U.S. Department of Justice (DOJ), Bureau of Justice Statistics, 810 Seventh Street, NW, Washington, DC 20531, (202) 307-0765, www.ojp.usdoj.gov/bjs/; *Drugs Crime Facts.*

U.S. Department of Justice (DOJ), Drug Enforcement Administration (DEA), 2401 Jefferson Davis Highway, Alexandria, VA 22301, (202) 307-1000, www.usdoj.gov/dea; *State Factsheets.*

U.S. Department of Justice (DOJ), National Drug Intelligence Center, 319 Washington Street, 5th Floor, Johnstown, PA 15901-1622, (814) 532-4601, Fax: (814) 532-4690, www.usdoj.gov/ndic; *Drug Assessments* and *National Drug Threat Assessment 2007.*

U.S. Department of Justice (DOJ), National Institute of Justice (NIJ), 810 Seventh Street, NW, Washington, DC 20531, (202) 307-2942, Fax: (202) 616-0275, www.ojp.usdoj.gov/nij/; *ADAM Preliminary 2000 Findings on Drug Use Drug Markets: Adult Male Arrestees; Drug Courts: The Second Decade;* and *I-ADAM in Eight Countries: Approaches and Challenges.*

United Nations Office on Drugs and Crime (UNODC), Vienna International Centre, PO Box 500, A-1400 Vienna, Austria, www.unodc.org; *World Drug Report 2006.*

HERRING - SEA

National Marine Fisheries Service (NMFS), National Oceanic and Atmospheric Administration (NOAA), Office of Constituent Services, 1315 East West Highway, 9th Floor, Silver Spring, MD 20910, (301) 713-2379, Fax: (301) 713-2385, www.nmfs.noaa.gov; *Fisheries of the United States - 2006.*

HIDES AND SKINS - INTERNATIONAL TRADE

Economic Research Service (ERS), U.S. Department of Agriculture (USDA), 1800 M Street, NW, Washington, DC 20036-5831, (202) 694-5050, Fax: (202) 694-5689, www.ers.usda.gov; *Agricultural Outlook; Agricultural Statistics; Foreign Agricultural Trade of the United States (FATUS);* and *U.S. Agricultural Trade Update: 2006.*

U.S. Census Bureau, Foreign Trade Division, 4700 Silver Hill Road, Washington DC 20233-0001, (301) 763-3030, www.census.gov/foreign-trade/www/; *U.S. International Trade in Goods and Services.*

HIGH SCHOOL STUDENTS

National Center for Education Statistics (NCES), 1990 K Street, NW, Washington, DC 20006, (202) 502-7300, http://nces.ed.gov; *Dual Enrollment of High School Students at Postsecondary Institutions: 2002-03.*

National Federation of State High School Associations, PO Box 690, Indianapolis, IN 46206, (317) 972-6900, Fax: (317) 822-5700, www.nfhs.org; *2008 National High School Sports Record Book.*

HIGHWAYS - ACCIDENTS

National Center for Statistics and Analysis (NCSA) of the National Highway Traffic Safety Administration, West Building, 1200 New Jersey Avenue, S.E., Washington, DC 20590, (202) 366-1503, Fax: (202) 366-7078, www.nhtsa.gov; *Fatality Analysis Reporting System (FARS); Large-Truck Crash Causation Study: An Initial Overview; Motor Vehicle Traffic Crashes as a Leading Cause of Death in the U.S., 2002 - A Demographic Perspective; Traffic Safety Fact Sheets, 2006 Data - Rural/Urban Comparison; Traffic Safety Facts Annual Report: 2005;* and *Trend and Pattern Analysis of Highway Crash Fatality by Month and Day.*

HIGHWAYS - BRIDGE INVENTORY

U.S. Department of Transportation (DOT), Federal Highway Administration (FHA), 1200 New Jersey Avenue, SE, Washington, DC 20590, (202) 366-0660, www.fhwa.dot.gov; unpublished data.

HIGHWAYS - CONSTRUCTION COSTS

U.S. Census Bureau, Center for Economic Studies, 4600 Silver Hill Road, Washington DC 20233, (301) 457-1235, www.ces.census.gov; *2002 Economic Census, Construction.*

HIGHWAYS - CONSTRUCTION COSTS - VALUE OF NEW CONSTRUCTION

U.S. Census Bureau, Manufacturing and Construction Division, 4600 Silver Hill Road, Washington DC 20233, (301) 763-4673, www.census.gov/mcd; *Current Construction Reports* and *Value of New Construction Put in Place.*

HIGHWAYS - DEBT - STATE AND LOCAL GOVERNMENTS

U.S. Department of Transportation (DOT), Federal Highway Administration (FHA), 1200 New Jersey Avenue, SE, Washington, DC 20590, (202) 366-0660, www.fhwa.dot.gov; *Highway Statistics 2006.*

HIGHWAYS - EMPLOYEES - GOVERNMENT

U.S. Census Bureau, Governments Division, 4600 Silver Hill Road, Washington DC 20233, (800) 242-2184, www.census.gov/govs/www; *2002 Census of Governments, Public Employment and Payroll.*

HIGHWAYS - EXPENDITURES - CITY GOVERNMENT

U.S. Census Bureau, Governments Division, 4600 Silver Hill Road, Washington DC 20233, (800) 242-2184, www.census.gov/govs/www; *2002 Census of Governments, Government Finances.*

HIGHWAYS - EXPENDITURES - COUNTY GOVERNMENT

U.S. Census Bureau, Governments Division, 4600 Silver Hill Road, Washington DC 20233, (800) 242-2184, www.census.gov/govs/www; *2002 Census of Governments, Government Finances.*

HIGHWAYS - EXPENDITURES - STATE AND LOCAL GOVERNMENT

U.S. Census Bureau, Governments Division, 4600 Silver Hill Road, Washington DC 20233, (800) 242-2184, www.census.gov/govs/www; *2002 Census of Governments, Government Finances* and *Federal Aid to States for Fiscal Year 2004.*

HIGHWAYS - EXPENDITURES - STATE GOVERNMENT

U.S. Census Bureau, Governments Division, 4600 Silver Hill Road, Washington DC 20233, (800) 242-2184, www.census.gov/govs/www; *2002 Census of Governments, Government Finances.*

HIGHWAYS - EXPENDITURES - UNITED STATES GOVERNMENT

U.S. Census Bureau, Governments Division, 4600 Silver Hill Road, Washington DC 20233, (800) 242-2184, www.census.gov/govs/www; *Federal Aid to States for Fiscal Year 2004.*

HIGHWAYS - EXPENDITURES - UNITED STATES GOVERNMENT - AID TO STATE AND LOCAL GOVERNMENTS

The Office of Management and Budget (OMB), 725 17th Street, NW, Washington, DC 20503, (202) 395-3080, Fax: (202) 395-3888, www.whitehouse.gov/omb; *Budget of the United States Government, Federal Year 2009* and *Historical Tables.*

HIGHWAYS - EXPENDITURES - UNITED STATES GOVERNMENT - HIGHWAY TRUST FUND

U.S. Census Bureau, Governments Division, 4600 Silver Hill Road, Washington DC 20233, (800) 242-2184, www.census.gov/govs/www; *Federal Aid to States for Fiscal Year 2004.*

HIGHWAYS - FEDERAL AID SYSTEMS

U.S. Department of Transportation (DOT), Federal Highway Administration (FHA), 1200 New Jersey Avenue, SE, Washington, DC 20590, (202) 366-0660, www.fhwa.dot.gov; *Highway Statistics 2006.*

HIGHWAYS - MILEAGE

National Center for Statistics and Analysis (NCSA) of the National Highway Traffic Safety Administration, West Building, 1200 New Jersey Avenue, S.E., Washington, DC 20590, (202) 366-1503, Fax: (202) 366-7078, www.nhtsa.gov; *Fatality Analysis Reporting System (FARS).*

U.S. Department of Transportation (DOT), Federal Highway Administration (FHA), 1200 New Jersey Avenue, SE, Washington, DC 20590, (202) 366-0660, www.fhwa.dot.gov; *Highway Statistics 2006.*

HIGHWAYS - MOTOR FUEL CONSUMPTION

U.S. Department of Transportation (DOT), Federal Highway Administration (FHA), 1200 New Jersey Avenue, SE, Washington, DC 20590, (202) 366-0660, www.fhwa.dot.gov; *Highway Statistics 2006.*

HIGHWAYS - MOTOR FUEL TAX

U.S. Department of Transportation (DOT), Federal Highway Administration (FHA), 1200 New Jersey Avenue, SE, Washington, DC 20590, (202) 366-0660, www.fhwa.dot.gov; *Highway Statistics 2006.*

HIGHWAYS - PAVEMENT CONDITION

U.S. Department of Transportation (DOT), Federal Highway Administration (FHA), 1200 New Jersey Avenue, SE, Washington, DC 20590, (202) 366-0660, www.fhwa.dot.gov; *Highway Statistics 2006.*

HIGHWAYS - TRAFFIC

National Center for Statistics and Analysis (NCSA) of the National Highway Traffic Safety Administration, West Building, 1200 New Jersey Avenue, S.E., Washington, DC 20590, (202) 366-1503, Fax: (202) 366-7078, www.nhtsa.gov; *Traffic Safety Fact Sheets, 2006 Data - Rural/Urban Comparison; Traffic Safety Facts Annual Report: 2005;* and *Trend and Pattern Analysis of Highway Crash Fatality by Month and Day.*

HIGHWAYS - TYPE AND CONTROL

U.S. Department of Transportation (DOT), Federal Highway Administration (FHA), 1200 New Jersey Avenue, SE, Washington, DC 20590, (202) 366-0660, www.fhwa.dot.gov; *Highway Statistics 2006.*

HIGHWAYS - TYPES OF ROADS TRAVELED

National Center for Statistics and Analysis (NCSA) of the National Highway Traffic Safety Administration, West Building, 1200 New Jersey Avenue, S.E., Washington, DC 20590, (202) 366-1503, Fax: (202) 366-7078, www.nhtsa.gov; *Fatality Analysis Reporting System (FARS).*

U.S. Department of Transportation (DOT), Federal Highway Administration (FHA), 1200 New Jersey Avenue, SE, Washington, DC 20590, (202) 366-0660, www.fhwa.dot.gov; *Highway Statistics 2006.*

HIKING

National Sporting Goods Association (NSGA), 1601 Feehanville Drive, Suite 300, Mount Prospect, IL 60056, (847) 296-6742, Fax: (847) 391-9827, www.nsga.org; *2006 Sports Participation.*

HINDU POPULATION

See RELIGION

HISPANIC ORIGIN POPULATION

The Annie E. Casey Foundation, 701 Saint Paul Street, Baltimore, MD 21202, (410) 547-6600, Fax: (410) 547-3610, www.aecf.org; *Faith Matters: Race/Ethnicity, Religion, and Substance Abuse.*

National Center for Health Statistics (NCHS), Centers for Disease Control and Prevention (CDC), U.S. Department of Health and Human Services (HHS), 3311 Toledo Road, Hyattsville, MD 20782, (866) 232-4636, www.cdc.gov/nchs; *Indicators of Social and Economic Well-Being by Race and Hispanic Origin.*

National Center for Statistics and Analysis (NCSA) of the National Highway Traffic Safety Administration, West Building, 1200 New Jersey Avenue, S.E., Washington, DC 20590, (202) 366-1503, Fax: (202) 366-7078, www.nhtsa.gov; *Race and Ethnicity in Fatal Motor Vehicle Traffic Crashes 1999-2004.*

Nielsen Media Research, Inc., 770 Broadway, New York, NY 10003, (646) 654-8300, www.nielsenmedia.com; *Nielsen Hispanic Television Index (NHTI).*

Population Reference Bureau, 1875 Connecticut Avenue, NW, Suite 520, Washington, DC, 20009-5728, (800) 877-9881, Fax: (202) 328-3937, www.prb.org; *The American People Series.*

Progressive Grocer, 770 Broadway, New York, NY 10003, (866) 890-8541, www.progressivegrocer.com; *Marketing to American Latinos, Part I* and *Marketing to American Latinos, Part II.*

U.S. Census Bureau, 4700 Silver Hill Road, Washington DC 20233-0001, (301) 763-3030, www.census.gov; American FactFinder (web app); *County and City Data Book 2007; County and City Data Book 2007;* and *State and County QuickFacts.*

U.S. Census Bureau, Population Division, 4700 Silver Hill Road, Washington DC 20233-0001, (301) 763-3030, www.census.gov/population/www/; *Census 2000 Profiles of General Demographic Characteristics; The Hispanic Population in the United States; National Population Projections;* and Population Estimates Program (web app).

U.S. Department of Justice (DOJ), National Institute of Justice (NIJ), 810 Seventh Street, NW, Washington, DC 20531, (202) 307-2942, Fax: (202) 616-0275, www.ojp.usdoj.gov/nij/; *Community Policing and "The New Immigrants": Latinos in Chicago.*

HISPANIC ORIGIN POPULATION - ADULT EDUCATION

National Center for Education Statistics (NCES), 1990 K Street, NW, Washington, DC 20006, (202) 502-7300, http://nces.ed.gov; *The National Household Education Surveys Program (NHES).*

HISPANIC ORIGIN POPULATION - AGE AND/OR SEX

U.S. Census Bureau, 4700 Silver Hill Road, Washington DC 20233-0001, (301) 763-3030, www.census.gov; unpublished data.

U.S. Census Bureau, Population Division, 4700 Silver Hill Road, Washington DC 20233-0001, (301) 763-3030, www.census.gov/population/www/; *The Hispanic Population in the United States; National Population Projections;* and Population Estimates Program (web app).

HISPANIC ORIGIN POPULATION - AIDS

Centers for Disease Control and Prevention (CDC), U.S. Department of Health and Human Services (HHS), 1600 Clifton Road, Atlanta, GA 30333, (800) 311-3435, www.cdc.gov; *HIV/AIDS Surveillance Report.*

HISPANIC ORIGIN POPULATION - BUSINESS OWNERS

U.S. Census Bureau, Company Statistics Division, 4700 Silver Hill Road, Washington DC 20233-0001, (301) 763-3030, www.census.gov/csd/; *2002 Survey of Business Owners (SBO).*

HISPANIC ORIGIN POPULATION - CANCER

National Cancer Institute (NCI), National Institutes of Health (NIH), Public Inquiries Office, 6116 Executive Boulevard, Room 3036A, Bethesda, MD 20892-8322, (800) 422-6237, www.cancer.gov; *2006-2007 Annual Report to the Nation; Assessing Progress, Advancing Change: 2005-2006 Annual President's Cancer Panel;* and *SEER Cancer Statistics Review, 1975-2005.*

HISPANIC ORIGIN POPULATION - CHILD CARE

National Center for Education Statistics (NCES), 1990 K Street, NW, Washington, DC 20006, (202) 502-7300, http://nces.ed.gov; *Digest of Education Statistics 2007.*

HISPANIC ORIGIN POPULATION - CHILDBIRTH - STATISTICS

Alan Guttmacher Institute, 125 Maiden Lane, 7th Floor, New York, NY 10038, (212) 248-1111, Fax: (212) 248-1951, www.agi-usa.org; *U.S. Teenage Pregnancy Statistics: Overall Trends, Trends by Race and Ethnicity and State-by-State Information* and *U.S. Teenage Pregnancy Statistics: Overall Trends, Trends by Race and Ethnicity and State-by-State Information.*

Bernan Essential Government Publications, 4611-F Assembly Drive, Lanham MD, 20706-4391, (301) 459-2255, Fax: (800) 865-3450, www.bernan.com; *Vital Statistics of the United States: Births, Life Expectancy, Deaths, and Selected Health Data.*

National Center for Health Statistics (NCHS), Centers for Disease Control and Prevention (CDC), U.S. Department of Health and Human Services (HHS), 3311 Toledo Road, Hyattsville, MD 20782, (866) 232-4636, www.cdc.gov/nchs; *National Vital Statistics Reports (NVSR); Vital Statistics of the United States (VSUS);* and unpublished data.

U.S. Census Bureau, Population Division, 4700 Silver Hill Road, Washington DC 20233-0001, (301) 763-3030, www.census.gov/population/www/; *The Hispanic Population in the United States.*

HISPANIC ORIGIN POPULATION - CHILDREN UNDER EIGHTEEN YEARS OLD

Federal Interagency Forum on Child and Family Statistics, 2070 Chain Bridge Road, Suite 450, Vienna, VA 22182-2536, (888) ASK-HRSA, www.childstats.gov; *America's Children: Key National Indicators of Well-Being 2006.*

U.S. Census Bureau, Population Division, 4700 Silver Hill Road, Washington DC 20233-0001, (301) 763-3030, www.census.gov/population/www/; *National Population Projections* and *Projected State Populations, by Sex, Race, and Hispanic Origin: 1995-2025.*

HISPANIC ORIGIN POPULATION - CHILDREN UNDER EIGHTEEN YEARS OLD - POVERTY

National Center for Children in Poverty (NCCP), 215 W. 125th Street, 3rd Floor, New York, NY 10027, (646) 284-9600, Fax: (646) 284-9623, www.nccp.org; *Basic Facts About Low-Income Children; Child Poverty in 21st Century America; Low-Income Children in the United States: National and State Trend Data, 1996-2006;* and *Predictors of Child Care Subsidy Use.*

Population Reference Bureau, 1875 Connecticut Avenue, NW, Suite 520, Washington, DC, 20009-5728, (800) 877-9881, Fax: (202) 328-3937, www.prb.org; *Child Poverty in Rural America* and *Strengthening Rural Families: America's Rural Children.*

U.S. Census Bureau, Housing and Household Economics Statistics Division, 4700 Silver Hill Road, Washington DC 20233-0001, (301) 763-3030, www.census.gov/hhes/www; *Historical Poverty Tables.*

HISPANIC ORIGIN POPULATION - COHABITATION EXPERIENCE

National Center for Health Statistics (NCHS), Centers for Disease Control and Prevention (CDC), U.S. Department of Health and Human Services (HHS), 3311 Toledo Road, Hyattsville, MD 20782, (866) 232-4636, www.cdc.gov/nchs; *National Survey of Family Growth (NSFG).*

HISPANIC ORIGIN POPULATION - COLLEGE ENROLLMENT

National Center for Education Statistics (NCES), 1990 K Street, NW, Washington, DC 20006, (202) 502-7300, http://nces.ed.gov; *Digest of Education Statistics 2007.*

HISPANIC ORIGIN POPULATION - COMPUTER USE

National Center for Education Statistics (NCES), 1990 K Street, NW, Washington, DC 20006, (202) 502-7300, http://nces.ed.gov; *Digest of Education Statistics 2007.*

National Telecommunications and Information Administration (NTIA), U.S. Department of Commerce (DOC), 1401 Constitution Avenue, NW, Washington, DC 20230, (202) 482-7002, www.ntia.doc.gov; *A Nation Online: Entering the Broadband Age.*

HISPANIC ORIGIN POPULATION - CONGRESS - MEMBERS OF

U.S. Government Printing Office (GPO), Office of Congressional Publishing Services (OCPS), 732 North Capitol Street NW, Washington, DC 20401, (202) 512-0224, www.gpo.gov/customerservices/cps.htm; *Congressional Directory.*

HISPANIC ORIGIN POPULATION - CONSUMER EXPENDITURES

Selig Center for Economic Growth, Terry College of Business, University of Georgia, Athens, GA 30602-6269, Mr. Jeffrey M. Humphreys, Director, (706) 425-2962, www.selig.uga.edu; *The Multicultural Economy: Minority Buying Power in 2006.*

HISPANIC ORIGIN POPULATION - CRIMINAL STATISTICS

RAND Corporation, 1776 Main Street, PO Box 2138, Santa Monica, CA 90407-2138, (310) 393-0411, www.rand.org; *Analysis of Racial Disparities in the New York Police Department's Stop, Question, and Frisk Practices.*

U.S. Department of Justice (DOJ), Bureau of Justice Statistics, 810 Seventh Street, NW, Washington, DC 20531, (202) 307-0765, www.ojp.usdoj.gov/bjs/; *Census of Jails; Crime and the Nation's Households, 2004; Hispanic Victims of Violent Crime, 1993-2000; Mental Health Problems of Prison and Jail Inmates; State Court Sentencing of Convicted Felons; Substance Dependence, Abuse, and Treatment of Jail Inmates, 2002; Violence by Gang Members, 1993-2003;* and *Violent Felons in Large Urban Counties.*

U.S. Department of Justice (DOJ), National Institute of Justice (NIJ), 810 Seventh Street, NW, Washington, DC 20531, (202) 307-2942, Fax: (202) 616-0275, www.ojp.usdoj.gov/nij/; *Community Policing and "The New Immigrants": Latinos in Chicago.*

HISPANIC ORIGIN POPULATION - CRIMINAL VICTIMIZATION

U.S. Department of Justice (DOJ), Bureau of Justice Statistics, 810 Seventh Street, NW, Washington, DC 20531, (202) 307-0765, www.ojp.usdoj.gov/bjs/; *Criminal Victimization, 2005; Hispanic Victims of Violent Crime, 1993-2000; Indicators of School Crime and Safety, 2005;* and *Weapon Use and Violent Crime, 1993-2001.*

HISPANIC ORIGIN POPULATION - DEATHS AND DEATH RATES

National Center for Statistics and Analysis (NCSA) of the National Highway Traffic Safety Administration, West Building, 1200 New Jersey Avenue, S.E., Washington, DC 20590, (202) 366-1503, Fax: (202) 366-7078, www.nhtsa.gov; *Motor Vehicle Traffic Crashes as a Leading Cause of Death in the U.S., 2002 - A Demographic Perspective* and *Race and Ethnicity in Fatal Motor Vehicle Traffic Crashes 1999-2004.*

RAND Corporation, 1776 Main Street, PO Box 2138, Santa Monica, CA 90407-2138, (310) 393-0411, www.rand.org; *Asthma Mortality in U.S. Hispanics of Mexican, Puerto Rican, and Cuban Heritage, 1990-1995.*

HISPANIC ORIGIN POPULATION - DISABILITY DAYS

National Center for Health Statistics (NCHS), Centers for Disease Control and Prevention (CDC), U.S. Department of Health and Human Services (HHS), 3311 Toledo Road, Hyattsville, MD 20782, (866) 232-4636, www.cdc.gov/nchs; unpublished data.

HISPANIC ORIGIN POPULATION - DISABLED PERSONS

U.S. Census Bureau, 4700 Silver Hill Road, Washington DC 20233-0001, (301) 763-3030, www.census.gov; unpublished data.

HISPANIC ORIGIN POPULATION - EDUCATIONAL ATTAINMENT

National Center for Education Statistics (NCES), 1990 K Street, NW, Washington, DC 20006, (202) 502-7300, http://nces.ed.gov; *Digest of Education Statistics 2007.*

National Science Foundation, Division of Science Resources Statistics (SRS), 4201 Wilson Boulevard, Arlington, VA 22230, (703) 292-8780, Fax: (703) 292-9092, www.nsf.gov; *Selected Data on Science and Engineering Doctorate Awards* and *Survey of Earned Doctorates 2006.*

Robert Wood Johnson Foundation, PO Box 2316, College Road East and Route 1, Princeton, NJ 08543, (877) 843-7953, www.rwjf.org; *Race Ethnicity, and the Education Gradient in Health.*

U.S. Census Bureau, Housing and Household Economics Statistics Division, 4700 Silver Hill Road, Washington DC 20233-0001, (301) 763-3030, www.census.gov/hhes/www; *2006 American Community Survey (ACS).*

U.S. Census Bureau, Population Division, 4700 Silver Hill Road, Washington DC 20233-0001, (301) 763-3030, www.census.gov/population/www/; *The Hispanic Population in the United States.*

HISPANIC ORIGIN POPULATION - ELECTED OFFICIALS

National Association of Latino Elected and Appointed Officials (NALEO) Educational Fund, 1122 West Washington Blvd., 3rd Floor, Los Angeles CA 90015, (213) 747-7606, Fax: (213) 747-7664, www.naleo.org; *2006 National Directory of Latino Elected Officials.*

U.S. Government Printing Office (GPO), Office of Congressional Publishing Services (OCPS), 732 North Capitol Street NW, Washington, DC 20401, (202) 512-0224, www.gpo.gov/customerservices/cps.htm; *Congressional Directory.*

HISPANIC ORIGIN POPULATION - ELECTIONS - VOTER REGISTRATION AND TURNOUT

Congressional Quarterly, Inc., 1255 22nd Street, NW, Washington, DC 20037, (202) 419-8500, www.cq.com; *Vital Statistics on American Politics 2007-2008.*

The Eagleton Institute of Politics, Rutgers, The State University of New Jersey, 191 Ryders Lane, New Brunswick, NJ 08901-8557, (732) 932-9384, Fax: (732) 932-6778, www.eagleton.rutgers.edu; *America's Newest Voters: Understanding Immigrant and Minority Voting Behavior.*

U.S. Census Bureau, 4700 Silver Hill Road, Washington DC 20233-0001, (301) 763-3030, www.census.gov; unpublished data.

U.S. Census Bureau, Population Division, 4700 Silver Hill Road, Washington DC 20233-0001, (301) 763-3030, www.census.gov/population/www/; *The Hispanic Population in the United States.*

HISPANIC ORIGIN POPULATION - FAMILIES - CHARACTERISTICS

Nielsen Media Research, Inc., 770 Broadway, New York, NY 10003, (646) 654-8300, www.nielsenmedia.com; *Nielsen Hispanic Television Index (NHTI).*

U.S. Census Bureau, Population Division, 4700 Silver Hill Road, Washington DC 20233-0001, (301) 763-3030, www.census.gov/population/www/; *The Hispanic Population in the United States.*

HISPANIC ORIGIN POPULATION - FARM OPERATORS AND WORKERS

National Agricultural Statistics Service (NASS), U.S. Department of Agriculture (USDA), 1400 Independence Avenue, SW, Washington, DC 20250, (800) 727-9540, Fax: (202) 690-2090, www.nass.usda.gov; *2007 Census of Agriculture.*

HISPANIC ORIGIN POPULATION - HEALTH INSURANCE COVERAGE

National Center for Health Statistics (NCHS), Centers for Disease Control and Prevention (CDC), U.S. Department of Health and Human Services (HHS), 3311 Toledo Road, Hyattsville, MD 20782, (866) 232-4636, www.cdc.gov/nchs; *Faststats A to Z.*

Robert Wood Johnson Foundation, PO Box 2316, College Road East and Route 1, Princeton, NJ 08543, (877) 843-7953, www.rwjf.org; *Medicare Race and Ethnicity Data: Prepared for the Study Panel on Sharpening Medicare's Tools to Reduce Racial and Ethnic Disparities.*

U.S. Census Bureau, Population Division, 4700 Silver Hill Road, Washington DC 20233-0001, (301) 763-3030, www.census.gov/population/www/; *The Hispanic Population in the United States.*

HISPANIC ORIGIN POPULATION - HIGH SCHOOL DROPOUTS

U.S. Census Bureau, Population Division, 4700 Silver Hill Road, Washington DC 20233-0001, (301) 763-3030, www.census.gov/population/www/; *The Hispanic Population in the United States.*

HISPANIC ORIGIN POPULATION - HOME-SCHOOLED

National Center for Education Statistics (NCES), 1990 K Street, NW, Washington, DC 20006, (202) 502-7300, http://nces.ed.gov; *Homeschooling in the United States: 2003.*

HISPANIC ORIGIN POPULATION - HOUSEHOLD OR FAMILY CHARACTERISTICS

U.S. Census Bureau, Population Division, 4700 Silver Hill Road, Washington DC 20233-0001, (301) 763-3030, www.census.gov/population/www/; *The Hispanic Population in the United States.*

HISPANIC ORIGIN POPULATION - HOUSING

U.S. Census Bureau, Housing and Household Economics Statistics Division, 4700 Silver Hill Road, Washington DC 20233-0001, (301) 763-3030, www.census.gov/hhes/www; *2006 American Community Survey (ACS)* and *Housing Characteristics: 2000.*

HISPANIC ORIGIN POPULATION - IMMUNIZATION OF CHILDREN

Centers for Disease Control and Prevention (CDC), U.S. Department of Health and Human Services (HHS), 1600 Clifton Road, Atlanta, GA 30333, (800) 311-3435, www.cdc.gov; *Immunization Coverage in the U.S.* and *Morbidity and Mortality Weekly Report (MMWR).*

National Center for Health Statistics (NCHS), Centers for Disease Control and Prevention (CDC), U.S. Department of Health and Human Services (HHS), 3311 Toledo Road, Hyattsville, MD 20782, (866) 232-4636, www.cdc.gov/nchs; *2005 National Immunization Survey (NIS).*

HISPANIC ORIGIN POPULATION - INCOME

Selig Center for Economic Growth, Terry College of Business, University of Georgia, Athens, GA 30602-6269, Mr. Jeffrey M. Humphreys, Director, (706) 425-2962, www.selig.uga.edu; *The Multicultural Economy: Minority Buying Power in 2006.*

U.S. Census Bureau, 4700 Silver Hill Road, Washington DC 20233-0001, (301) 763-3030, www.census.gov; unpublished data.

U.S. Census Bureau, Population Division, 4700 Silver Hill Road, Washington DC 20233-0001, (301) 763-3030, www.census.gov/population/www/; *The Hispanic Population in the United States.*

HISPANIC ORIGIN POPULATION - INCOME - FAMILY

U.S. Census Bureau, 4700 Silver Hill Road, Washington DC 20233-0001, (301) 763-3030, www.census.gov; unpublished data.

U.S. Census Bureau, Population Division, 4700 Silver Hill Road, Washington DC 20233-0001, (301) 763-3030, www.census.gov/population/www/; *The Hispanic Population in the United States.*

HISPANIC ORIGIN POPULATION - INCOME - HOUSEHOLD

U.S. Census Bureau, 4700 Silver Hill Road, Washington DC 20233-0001, (301) 763-3030, www.census.gov; unpublished data.

U.S. Census Bureau, Population Division, 4700 Silver Hill Road, Washington DC 20233-0001, (301) 763-3030, www.census.gov/population/www/; *The Hispanic Population in the United States.*

HISPANIC ORIGIN POPULATION - INTERNET ACCESS

National Telecommunications and Information Administration (NTIA), U.S. Department of Commerce (DOC), 1401 Constitution Avenue, NW, Washington, DC 20230, (202) 482-7002, www.ntia.doc.gov; *A Nation Online: Entering the Broadband Age.*

HISPANIC ORIGIN POPULATION - LABOR FORCE

Higher Education Research Institute (HERI), University of California, Los Angeles, 3005 Moore Hall/Box 951521, Los Angeles, CA 90095-1521, (310) 825-1925, Fax: (310) 206-2228, www.gseis.ucla.edu/heri/index.php; *Race and Ethnicity in the American Professoriate.*

HISPANIC ORIGIN POPULATION - LABOR FORCE - EARNINGS

U.S. Bureau of Labor Statistics (BLS), Postal Square Building, 2 Massachusetts Avenue, NE, Washington, DC 20212-0001, (202) 691-5200, Fax: (202) 691-6325, www.bls.gov; *Current Population Survey (CPS); Employment and Earnings (EE);* and unpublished data.

HISPANIC ORIGIN POPULATION - LABOR FORCE - EMPLOYED

U.S. Bureau of Labor Statistics (BLS), Postal Square Building, 2 Massachusetts Avenue, NE, Washington, DC 20212-0001, (202) 691-5200, Fax: (202) 691-6325, www.bls.gov; *Employment and Earnings (EE).*

U.S. Census Bureau, Population Division, 4700 Silver Hill Road, Washington DC 20233-0001, (301) 763-3030, www.census.gov/population/www/; *The Hispanic Population in the United States.*

HISPANIC ORIGIN POPULATION - LABOR FORCE - EMPLOYED - BY INDUSTRY

U.S. Bureau of Labor Statistics (BLS), Postal Square Building, 2 Massachusetts Avenue, NE, Washington, DC 20212-0001, (202) 691-5200, Fax: (202) 691-6325, www.bls.gov; *Employment and Earnings (EE)* and unpublished data.

HISPANIC ORIGIN POPULATION - LABOR FORCE - EMPLOYED - MINIMUM WAGE WORKERS

U.S. Bureau of Labor Statistics (BLS), Postal Square Building, 2 Massachusetts Avenue, NE, Washington, DC 20212-0001, (202) 691-5200, Fax: (202) 691-6325, www.bls.gov; *Employment and Earnings (EE)* and unpublished data.

HISPANIC ORIGIN POPULATION - LABOR FORCE - PERSONS WORKING AT HOME

U.S. Bureau of Labor Statistics (BLS), Postal Square Building, 2 Massachusetts Avenue, NE, Washington, DC 20212-0001, (202) 691-5200, Fax: (202) 691-6325, www.bls.gov; *Work at Home.*

HISPANIC ORIGIN POPULATION - LABOR FORCE - UNEMPLOYED

U.S. Bureau of Labor Statistics (BLS), Postal Square Building, 2 Massachusetts Avenue, NE, Washington, DC 20212-0001, (202) 691-5200, Fax: (202) 691-6325, www.bls.gov; *Employment and Earnings (EE)* and unpublished data.

HISPANIC ORIGIN POPULATION - LABOR FORCE - UNION MEMBERSHIP

U.S. Bureau of Labor Statistics (BLS), Postal Square Building, 2 Massachusetts Avenue, NE, Washington, DC 20212-0001, (202) 691-5200, Fax: (202) 691-6325, www.bls.gov; *Employment and Earnings (EE).*

HISPANIC ORIGIN POPULATION - LIVING ARRANGEMENTS

U.S. Census Bureau, 4700 Silver Hill Road, Washington DC 20233-0001, (301) 763-3030, www.census.gov; unpublished data.

U.S. Census Bureau, Housing and Household Economics Statistics Division, 4700 Silver Hill Road, Washington DC 20233-0001, (301) 763-3030, www.census.gov/hhes/www; *Families and Living Arrangements.*

U.S. Census Bureau, Population Division, 4700 Silver Hill Road, Washington DC 20233-0001, (301) 763-3030, www.census.gov/population/www/; *The Hispanic Population in the United States.*

HISPANIC ORIGIN POPULATION - MEDIA USERS

Mediamark Research, Inc., 75 Ninth Avenue, 5th Floor, New York, NY 10011, (212) 884-9200, Fax: (212) 884-9339, www.mediamark.com; MRI+.

Nielsen Media Research, Inc., 770 Broadway, New York, NY 10003, (646) 654-8300, www.nielsenmedia.com; *Nielsen Hispanic Television Index (NHTI).*

HISPANIC ORIGIN POPULATION - MEDICAL CARE

National Center for Chronic Disease Prevention and Health Promotion (NCCDPHP), Centers for Disease Control and Prevention (CDC), 4770 Buford Hwy, NE, MS K-40, Atlanta, GA 30341-3717, (404) 639-3311, www.cdc.gov/nccdphp; *Racial and Ethnic Approaches to Community Health (REACH 2010): Addressing Disparities in Health.*

National Center for Health Statistics (NCHS), Centers for Disease Control and Prevention (CDC), U.S. Department of Health and Human Services (HHS), 3311 Toledo Road, Hyattsville, MD 20782, (866) 232-4636, www.cdc.gov/nchs; *Faststats A to Z* and *Women's Health and Mortality Chartbook (2004 Edition).*

Robert Wood Johnson Foundation, PO Box 2316, College Road East and Route 1, Princeton, NJ 08543, (877) 843-7953, www.rwjf.org; *Medicare Race and Ethnicity Data: Prepared for the Study Panel on Sharpening Medicare's Tools to Reduce Racial and Ethnic Disparities; Race Ethnicity, and the Education Gradient in Health;* and *Reducing Racial and Ethnic Disparities and Improving Quality of Health Care.*

U.S. Department of Health and Human Services, 200 Independence Avenue, S.W., Washington, D.C. 20201, (202) 619-0257, www.hhs.gov; *Eliminating Health Disparities: Strengthening Data on Race, Ethnicity, and Primary Language in the United States.*

U.S. Department of Justice (DOJ), Bureau of Justice Statistics, 810 Seventh Street, NW, Washington, DC 20531, (202) 307-0765, www.ojp.usdoj.gov/bjs/; *Mental Health Problems of Prison and Jail Inmates.*

HISPANIC ORIGIN POPULATION - METROPOLITAN AREAS

U.S. Census Bureau, 4700 Silver Hill Road, Washington DC 20233-0001, (301) 763-3030, www.census.gov; unpublished data.

HISPANIC ORIGIN POPULATION - OLDER PEOPLE

U.S. Census Bureau, Population Division, 4700 Silver Hill Road, Washington DC 20233-0001, (301) 763-3030, www.census.gov/population/www/; *The Hispanic Population in the United States.*

HISPANIC ORIGIN POPULATION - PENSION PLAN COVERAGE

U.S. Census Bureau, Housing and Household Economics Statistics Division, 4700 Silver Hill Road, Washington DC 20233-0001, (301) 763-3030, www.census.gov/hhes/www; *Pension Plan Coverage of Workers by Selected Characteristics, Sex, Race and Hispanic Origin, and Poverty Status: 2003.*

HISPANIC ORIGIN POPULATION - POLICE CONTACT

RAND Corporation, 1776 Main Street, PO Box 2138, Santa Monica, CA 90407-2138, (310) 393-0411, www.rand.org; *Analysis of Racial Disparities in the New York Police Department's Stop, Question, and Frisk Practices.*

HISPANIC ORIGIN POPULATION - POVERTY

U.S. Census Bureau, 4700 Silver Hill Road, Washington DC 20233-0001, (301) 763-3030, www.census.gov; unpublished data.

U.S. Census Bureau, Housing and Household Economics Statistics Division, 4700 Silver Hill Road, Washington DC 20233-0001, (301) 763-3030, www.census.gov/hhes/www; *Historical Poverty Tables.*

U.S. Census Bureau, Population Division, 4700 Silver Hill Road, Washington DC 20233-0001, (301) 763-3030, www.census.gov/population/www/; *The Hispanic Population in the United States.*

HISPANIC ORIGIN POPULATION - PRISONERS

U.S. Department of Justice (DOJ), Bureau of Justice Statistics, 810 Seventh Street, NW, Washington, DC 20531, (202) 307-0765, www.ojp.usdoj.gov/bjs/; *Census of Jails; Drug Use and Dependence, State and Federal Prisoners, 2004; Mental Health Problems of Prison and Jail Inmates; National Corrections Reporting Program; Prison and Jail Inmates at Midyear 2005; Prisoners in 2004; Probation and Parole in the United States, 2004; Profile of Jail Inmates, 2002;* and *Veterans in Prison or Jail.*

HISPANIC ORIGIN POPULATION - RECREATIONAL ACTIVITIES

Nielsen Media Research, Inc., 770 Broadway, New York, NY 10003, (646) 654-8300, www.nielsenmedia.com; *Nielsen Hispanic Television Index (NHTI).*

HISPANIC ORIGIN POPULATION - SCHOOL ENROLLMENT

National Center for Education Statistics (NCES), 1990 K Street, NW, Washington, DC 20006, (202) 502-7300, http://nces.ed.gov; *Digest of Education Statistics 2007.*

U.S. Census Bureau, 4700 Silver Hill Road, Washington DC 20233-0001, (301) 763-3030, www.census.gov; unpublished data.

U.S. Census Bureau, Population Division, 4700 Silver Hill Road, Washington DC 20233-0001, (301) 763-3030, www.census.gov/population/www/; *The Hispanic Population in the United States.*

HISPANIC ORIGIN POPULATION - SCHOOL ENROLLMENT - PREPRIMARY SCHOOL

U.S. Census Bureau, 4700 Silver Hill Road, Washington DC 20233-0001, (301) 763-3030, www.census.gov; unpublished data.

U.S. Census Bureau, Population Division, 4700 Silver Hill Road, Washington DC 20233-0001, (301) 763-3030, www.census.gov/population/www/; *The Hispanic Population in the United States.*

HISPANIC ORIGIN POPULATION - STATES

Population Reference Bureau, 1875 Connecticut Avenue, NW, Suite 520, Washington, DC, 20009-5728, (800) 877-9881, Fax: (202) 328-3937, www.prb.org; *The American People Series.*

U.S. Census Bureau, 4700 Silver Hill Road, Washington DC 20233-0001, (301) 763-3030, www.census.gov; American FactFinder (web app) and *State and County QuickFacts.*

U.S. Census Bureau, Demographic Surveys Division, 4700 Silver Hill Road, Washington DC 20233-0001, (301) 763-3030, www.census.gov; *Census 2000: Demographic Profiles.*

U.S. Census Bureau, Population Division, 4700 Silver Hill Road, Washington DC 20233-0001, (301) 763-3030, www.census.gov/population/www/; *Census 2000 Profiles of General Demographic Characteristics; The Hispanic Population in the United States;* and *Projected State Populations, by Sex, Race, and Hispanic Origin: 1995-2025.*

HISPANIC ORIGIN POPULATION - SUBSTANCE ABUSE CLIENTS

Substance Abuse and Mental Health Services Administration (SAMHSA), 1 Choke Cherry Road, Rockville, MD 20857, (240) 777-1311, www.oas.samhsa.gov; *National Survey of Substance Abuse Treatment Services (N-SSATS).*

U.S. Department of Justice (DOJ), Bureau of Justice Statistics, 810 Seventh Street, NW, Washington, DC 20531, (202) 307-0765, www.ojp.usdoj.gov/bjs/; *Substance Dependence, Abuse, and Treatment of Jail Inmates, 2002.*

HISPANIC ORIGIN POPULATION - TEACHERS

National Center for Education Statistics (NCES), 1990 K Street, NW, Washington, DC 20006, (202) 502-7300, http://nces.ed.gov; *Digest of Education Statistics 2007.*

HISPANIC ORIGIN POPULATION - UNION MEMBERSHIP

U.S. Bureau of Labor Statistics (BLS), Postal Square Building, 2 Massachusetts Avenue, NE, Washington, DC 20212-0001, (202) 691-5200, Fax: (202) 691-6325, www.bls.gov; *Employment and Earnings (EE).*

HISPANIC ORIGIN POPULATION - VOLUNTEERS

Independent Sector, 1200 Eighteenth Street, NW, Suite 200, Washington, DC 20036, (202) 467-6100, Fax: (202) 467-6101, www.independentsector.org; *Giving and Volunteering in the United States 2001.*

HISPANIC ORIGIN POPULATION - VOTER REGISTRATION AND TURNOUT

The Eagleton Institute of Politics, Rutgers, The State University of New Jersey, 191 Ryders Lane, New Brunswick, NJ 08901-8557, (732) 932-9384, Fax: (732) 932-6778, www.eagleton.rutgers.edu; *America's Newest Voters: Understanding Immigrant and Minority Voting Behavior.*

U.S. Census Bureau, 4700 Silver Hill Road, Washington DC 20233-0001, (301) 763-3030, www.census.gov; unpublished data.

U.S. Census Bureau, Population Division, 4700 Silver Hill Road, Washington DC 20233-0001, (301) 763-3030, www.census.gov/population/www/; *The Hispanic Population in the United States.*

HIV INFECTION

See also AIDS (DISEASE)

Bernan Essential Government Publications, 4611-F Assembly Drive, Lanham MD, 20706-4391, (301) 459-2255, Fax: (800) 865-3450, www.bernan.com; *Vital Statistics of the United States: Births, Life Expectancy, Deaths, and Selected Health Data.*

European Centre for Disease Prevention and Control (ECDC), 171 83 Stockholm, Sweden, www.ecdc.europa.eu; *HIV Infection in Europe: 25 Years into the Pandemic.*

Health Protection Agency, 7th Floor, Holborn Gate, 330 High Holborn, London WC1V 7PP, United Kingdom, www.hpa.org.uk; *Testing Times - HIV and other Sexually Transmitted Infections in the United Kingdom: 2007.*

National Center for Chronic Disease Prevention and Health Promotion (NCCDPHP), Centers for Disease Control and Prevention (CDC), 4770 Buford Hwy, NE, MS K-40, Atlanta, GA 30341-3717, (404) 639-3311, www.cdc.gov/nccdphp; *Racial and Ethnic Approaches to Community Health (REACH 2010): Addressing Disparities in Health.*

National Center for Health Statistics (NCHS), Centers for Disease Control and Prevention (CDC), U.S. Department of Health and Human Services (HHS), 3311 Toledo Road, Hyattsville, MD 20782, (866) 232-4636, www.cdc.gov/nchs; *National Vital Statistics Reports (NVSR); Vital Statistics of the United States (VSUS);* and unpublished data.

Tonga Statistics Department, PO Box 149, Nuku'alofa, Tonga, www.spc.int/prism/country/to/stats/; *Surveillance Surveys of HIV, Other STIs and Risk Behaviours in 6 Pacific Island Countries 2004-2005.*

U.S. Department of Justice (DOJ), Bureau of Justice Statistics, 810 Seventh Street, NW, Washington, DC 20531, (202) 307-0765, www.ojp.usdoj.gov/bjs/; *HIV in Prisons, 2004.*

UNAIDS, 20, Avenue Appia, CH-1211 Geneva 27, Switzerland, www.unaids.org; *2007 AIDS Epidemic Update.*

HOBBY - AVOCATIONAL ASSOCIATIONS

Thomson Gale, 27500 Drake Road, Farmington Hills, MI 48331, (248) 699-4253, www.galegroup.com; *Encyclopedia of Associations.*

HOCKEY

National Collegiate Athletic Association (NCAA), 700 West Washington Street, PO Box 6222, Indianapolis, IN 46206-6222, (317) 917-6222, Fax: (317) 917-6888, www.ncaa.org; *1982-2003 Sports Sponsorship and Participation Rates Report.*

National Hockey League (NHL), 1251 Avenue of the Americas, New York, NY 10020-1104, (212) 789-2000, www.nhl.com; unpublished data.

National Hockey League Players Association (NHLPA), 20 Bay Street Suite 1700, Toronto, Ontario M5J 2N8, Canada, (Dial from U.S. (416) 408-4040), www.nhlpa.com; unpublished data.

Sports Reference LLC, 6757 Greene Street, Suite 315, Philadelphia PA 19119, (215) 301-9181, www.sports-reference.com; *Hockey-Reference.com.*

HOGS

Economic Research Service (ERS), U.S. Department of Agriculture (USDA), 1800 M Street, NW, Washington, DC 20036-5831, (202) 694-5050, Fax: (202) 694-5689, www.ers.usda.gov; *Agricultural Income and Finance Outlook; Agricultural Outlook; Agricultural Statistics; Farm Income: Data Files;* and *Livestock, Dairy, and Poultry Outlook.*

National Agricultural Statistics Service (NASS), U.S. Department of Agriculture (USDA), 1400 Independence Avenue, SW, Washington, DC 20250, (800) 727-9540, Fax: (202) 690-2090, www.nass.usda.gov; *2007 Census of Agriculture; Hogs and Pigs; Hogs and Pigs: Final Estimates 1998-2002; Livestock Slaughter;* and *Meat Animals Production, Disposition, and Income.*

HOLY

SEE (VATICAN CITY) - AGRICULTURE

United Nations Food and Agricultural Organization (FAO), Viale delle Terme di Caracalla, 00100 Rome, Italy, (Dial from U.S. (202) 653-2400), (Fax from U.S. (202) 653 5760), www.fao.org; AQUASTAT; *FAO Trade Yearbook;* and *The State of Food and Agriculture (SOFA) 2006.*

HOLY

SEE (VATICAN CITY) - AIRPORTS

Central Intelligence Agency, Office of Public Affairs, Washington, DC 20505, (703) 482-0623, Fax: (703) 482-1739, www.cia.gov; *The World Factbook.*

HOLY

SEE (VATICAN CITY) - ARMED FORCES

Central Intelligence Agency, Office of Public Affairs, Washington, DC 20505, (703) 482-0623, Fax: (703) 482-1739, www.cia.gov; *The World Factbook.*

HOLY

SEE (VATICAN CITY) - BROADCASTING

Central Intelligence Agency, Office of Public Affairs, Washington, DC 20505, (703) 482-0623, Fax: (703) 482-1739, www.cia.gov; *The World Factbook.*

HOLY

SEE (VATICAN CITY) - BUDGET

Central Intelligence Agency, Office of Public Affairs, Washington, DC 20505, (703) 482-0623, Fax: (703) 482-1739, www.cia.gov; *The World Factbook.*

HOLY

SEE (VATICAN CITY) - CHILDBIRTH - STATISTICS

Central Intelligence Agency, Office of Public Affairs, Washington, DC 20505, (703) 482-0623, Fax: (703) 482-1739, www.cia.gov; *The World Factbook.*

United Nations Statistics Division, New York, NY 10017, (800) 253-9646, Fax: (212) 963-4116, http://unstats.un.org; *Demographic Yearbook.*

HOLY

SEE (VATICAN CITY) - COMMODITY EXCHANGES

United Nations Food and Agricultural Organization (FAO), Viale delle Terme di Caracalla, 00100 Rome, Italy, (Dial from U.S. (202) 653-2400), (Fax from

U.S. (202) 653 5760), www.fao.org; *The State of Food and Agriculture (SOFA) 2006.*

HOLY

SEE (VATICAN CITY) - CORN INDUSTRY - See HOLY SEE (VATICAN CITY) - CROPS

HOLY

SEE (VATICAN CITY) - CROPS

United Nations Food and Agricultural Organization (FAO), Viale delle Terme di Caracalla, 00100 Rome, Italy, (Dial from U.S. (202) 653-2400), (Fax from U.S. (202) 653 5760), www.fao.org; *The State of Food and Agriculture (SOFA) 2006.*

HOLY

SEE (VATICAN CITY) - DAIRY PROCESSING

United Nations Food and Agricultural Organization (FAO), Viale delle Terme di Caracalla, 00100 Rome, Italy, (Dial from U.S. (202) 653-2400), (Fax from U.S. (202) 653 5760), www.fao.org; *The State of Food and Agriculture (SOFA) 2006.*

HOLY

SEE (VATICAN CITY) - ECONOMIC CONDITIONS

Central Intelligence Agency, Office of Public Affairs, Washington, DC 20505, (703) 482-0623, Fax: (703) 482-1739, www.cia.gov; *The World Factbook.*

HOLY

SEE (VATICAN CITY) - EXPORTS

Central Intelligence Agency, Office of Public Affairs, Washington, DC 20505, (703) 482-0623, Fax: (703) 482-1739, www.cia.gov; *The World Factbook.*

United Nations Food and Agricultural Organization (FAO), Viale delle Terme di Caracalla, 00100 Rome, Italy, (Dial from U.S. (202) 653-2400), (Fax from U.S. (202) 653 5760), www.fao.org; *The State of Food and Agriculture (SOFA) 2006.*

HOLY

SEE (VATICAN CITY) - FERTILITY, HUMAN

Central Intelligence Agency, Office of Public Affairs, Washington, DC 20505, (703) 482-0623, Fax: (703) 482-1739, www.cia.gov; *The World Factbook.*

HOLY

SEE (VATICAN CITY) - FERTILIZER INDUSTRY

United Nations Food and Agricultural Organization (FAO), Viale delle Terme di Caracalla, 00100 Rome, Italy, (Dial from U.S. (202) 653-2400), (Fax from U.S. (202) 653 5760), www.fao.org; *The State of Food and Agriculture (SOFA) 2006.*

HOLY

SEE (VATICAN CITY) - FETAL MORTALITY - See HOLY SEE (VATICAN CITY) - MORTALITY

HOLY

SEE (VATICAN CITY) - FISHERIES

United Nations Food and Agricultural Organization (FAO), Viale delle Terme di Caracalla, 00100 Rome, Italy, (Dial from U.S. (202) 653-2400), (Fax from U.S. (202) 653 5760), www.fao.org; *The State of Food and Agriculture (SOFA) 2006.*

HOLY

SEE (VATICAN CITY) - FOOD

United Nations Food and Agricultural Organization (FAO), Viale delle Terme di Caracalla, 00100 Rome, Italy, (Dial from U.S. (202) 653-2400), (Fax from U.S. (202) 653 5760), www.fao.org; *FAO Production Yearbook 2002* and *The State of Food and Agriculture (SOFA) 2006.*

HOLY

SEE (VATICAN CITY) - FOREIGN EXCHANGE RATES

Central Intelligence Agency, Office of Public Affairs, Washington, DC 20505, (703) 482-0623, Fax: (703) 482-1739, www.cia.gov; *The World Factbook.*

HOLY

SEE (VATICAN CITY) - FORESTS AND FORESTRY

United Nations Food and Agricultural Organization (FAO), Viale delle Terme di Caracalla, 00100 Rome, Italy, (Dial from U.S. (202) 653-2400), (Fax from U.S. (202) 653 5760), www.fao.org; *The State of Food and Agriculture (SOFA) 2006.*

HOLY

SEE (VATICAN CITY) - IMPORTS

Central Intelligence Agency, Office of Public Affairs, Washington, DC 20505, (703) 482-0623, Fax: (703) 482-1739, www.cia.gov; *The World Factbook.*

United Nations Food and Agricultural Organization (FAO), Viale delle Terme di Caracalla, 00100 Rome, Italy, (Dial from U.S. (202) 653-2400), (Fax from U.S. (202) 653 5760), www.fao.org; *The State of Food and Agriculture (SOFA) 2006.*

HOLY

SEE (VATICAN CITY) - INDUSTRIES

Central Intelligence Agency, Office of Public Affairs, Washington, DC 20505, (703) 482-0623, Fax: (703) 482-1739, www.cia.gov; *The World Factbook.*

HOLY

SEE (VATICAN CITY) - INFANT AND MATERNAL MORTALITY - See HOLY SEE (VATICAN CITY) - MORTALITY

HOLY

SEE (VATICAN CITY) - INTERNATIONAL TRADE

United Nations Food and Agricultural Organization (FAO), Viale delle Terme di Caracalla, 00100 Rome, Italy, (Dial from U.S. (202) 653-2400), (Fax from U.S. (202) 653 5760), www.fao.org; *FAO Trade Yearbook* and *The State of Food and Agriculture (SOFA) 2006.*

World Trade Organization (WTO), Centre William Rappard, Rue de Lausanne 154, CH-1211 Geneva 21, Switzerland, www.wto.org; *International Trade Statistics 2006.*

HOLY

SEE (VATICAN CITY) - LABOR

Central Intelligence Agency, Office of Public Affairs, Washington, DC 20505, (703) 482-0623, Fax: (703) 482-1739, www.cia.gov; *The World Factbook.*

United Nations Food and Agricultural Organization (FAO), Viale delle Terme di Caracalla, 00100 Rome, Italy, (Dial from U.S. (202) 653-2400), (Fax from U.S. (202) 653 5760), www.fao.org; *The State of Food and Agriculture (SOFA) 2006.*

HOLY

SEE (VATICAN CITY) - LAND USE

Central Intelligence Agency, Office of Public Affairs, Washington, DC 20505, (703) 482-0623, Fax: (703) 482-1739, www.cia.gov; *The World Factbook.*

United Nations Food and Agricultural Organization (FAO), Viale delle Terme di Caracalla, 00100 Rome, Italy, (Dial from U.S. (202) 653-2400), (Fax from U.S. (202) 653 5760), www.fao.org; *FAO Production Yearbook 2002.*

HOLY

SEE (VATICAN CITY) - LIBRARIES

UNESCO Institute for Statistics, C.P. 6128 Succursale Centre-Ville, Montreal, Quebec, H3C 3J7 Canada, (Dial from U.S. (514) 343-6880), (Fax from U.S. (514) 343 6882), www.uis.unesco.org; *Statistical Tables.*

HOLY

SEE (VATICAN CITY) - LIFE EXPECTANCY

Central Intelligence Agency, Office of Public Affairs, Washington, DC 20505, (703) 482-0623, Fax: (703) 482-1739, www.cia.gov; *The World Factbook.*

HOLY

SEE (VATICAN CITY) - LIVESTOCK

United Nations Food and Agricultural Organization (FAO), Viale delle Terme di Caracalla, 00100 Rome, Italy, (Dial from U.S. (202) 653-2400), (Fax from U.S. (202) 653 5760), www.fao.org; *The State of Food and Agriculture (SOFA) 2006.*

HOLY

SEE (VATICAN CITY) - MARRIAGE

United Nations Statistics Division, New York, NY 10017, (800) 253-9646, Fax: (212) 963-4116, http://unstats.un.org; *Demographic Yearbook.*

HOLY

SEE (VATICAN CITY) - MEAT PRODUCTION - See HOLY SEE (VATICAN CITY) - LIVESTOCK

HOLY

SEE (VATICAN CITY) - MORTALITY

Central Intelligence Agency, Office of Public Affairs, Washington, DC 20505, (703) 482-0623, Fax: (703) 482-1739, www.cia.gov; *The World Factbook.*

United Nations Statistics Division, New York, NY 10017, (800) 253-9646, Fax: (212) 963-4116, http://unstats.un.org; *Demographic Yearbook.*

HOLY

SEE (VATICAN CITY) - MUSEUMS

UNESCO Institute for Statistics, C.P. 6128 Succursale Centre-Ville, Montreal, Quebec, H3C 3J7 Canada, (Dial from U.S. (514) 343-6880), (Fax from U.S. (514) 343 6882), www.uis.unesco.org; *Statistical Tables.*

HOLY

SEE (VATICAN CITY) - NUTRITION

United Nations Food and Agricultural Organization (FAO), Viale delle Terme di Caracalla, 00100 Rome, Italy, (Dial from U.S. (202) 653-2400), (Fax from U.S. (202) 653 5760), www.fao.org; *The State of Food and Agriculture (SOFA) 2006.*

HOLY

SEE (VATICAN CITY) - PERIODICALS

UNESCO Institute for Statistics, C.P. 6128 Succursale Centre-Ville, Montreal, Quebec, H3C 3J7 Canada, (Dial from U.S. (514) 343-6880), (Fax from U.S. (514) 343 6882), www.uis.unesco.org; *Statistical Tables.*

HOLY

SEE (VATICAN CITY) - PESTICIDES

United Nations Food and Agricultural Organization (FAO), Viale delle Terme di Caracalla, 00100 Rome, Italy, (Dial from U.S. (202) 653-2400), (Fax from U.S. (202) 653 5760), www.fao.org; *The State of Food and Agriculture (SOFA) 2006.*

HOLY

SEE (VATICAN CITY) - PETROLEUM INDUSTRY AND TRADE

PennWell Corporation, 1421 South Sheridan Road, Tulsa, OK 74112, (918) 835-3161, www.pennwell.com; *International Petroleum Encyclopedia 2007.*

United Nations Food and Agricultural Organization (FAO), Viale delle Terme di Caracalla, 00100 Rome, Italy, (Dial from U.S. (202) 653-2400), (Fax from U.S. (202) 653 5760), www.fao.org; *The State of Food and Agriculture (SOFA) 2006.*

HOLY

SEE (VATICAN CITY) - POLITICAL SCIENCE

Central Intelligence Agency, Office of Public Affairs, Washington, DC 20505, (703) 482-0623, Fax: (703) 482-1739, www.cia.gov; *The World Factbook.*

HOLY

SEE (VATICAN CITY) - POPULATION

Central Intelligence Agency, Office of Public Affairs, Washington, DC 20505, (703) 482-0623, Fax: (703) 482-1739, www.cia.gov; *The World Factbook.*

United Nations Food and Agricultural Organization (FAO), Viale delle Terme di Caracalla, 00100 Rome, Italy, (Dial from U.S. (202) 653-2400), (Fax from U.S. (202) 653 5760), www.fao.org; *FAO Production Yearbook 2002.*

United Nations Statistics Division, New York, NY 10017, (800) 253-9646, Fax: (212) 963-4116, http://unstats.un.org; *Demographic Yearbook* and *Statistical Yearbook.*

World Health Organization (WHO), Avenue Appia 20, 1211 Geneve 27, Switzerland, (Telephone in U.S. (212) 331-9081), www.who.int; *World Health Report 2006.*

HOLY

SEE (VATICAN CITY) - POPULATION DENSITY

Central Intelligence Agency, Office of Public Affairs, Washington, DC 20505, (703) 482-0623, Fax: (703) 482-1739, www.cia.gov; *The World Factbook.*

United Nations Food and Agricultural Organization (FAO), Viale delle Terme di Caracalla, 00100 Rome, Italy, (Dial from U.S. (202) 653-2400), (Fax from U.S. (202) 653 5760), www.fao.org; *The State of Food and Agriculture (SOFA) 2006.*

United Nations Statistics Division, New York, NY 10017, (800) 253-9646, Fax: (212) 963-4116, http://unstats.un.org; *Statistical Yearbook.*

HOLY

SEE (VATICAN CITY) - POSTAL SERVICE

United Nations Statistics Division, New York, NY 10017, (800) 253-9646, Fax: (212) 963-4116, http://unstats.un.org; *Statistical Yearbook.*

HOLY

SEE (VATICAN CITY) - POWER RESOURCES

United Nations Food and Agricultural Organization (FAO), Viale delle Terme di Caracalla, 00100 Rome, Italy, (Dial from U.S. (202) 653-2400), (Fax from U.S. (202) 653 5760), www.fao.org; *The State of Food and Agriculture (SOFA) 2006.*

HOLY

SEE (VATICAN CITY) - PRICES

United Nations Food and Agricultural Organization (FAO), Viale delle Terme di Caracalla, 00100 Rome, Italy, (Dial from U.S. (202) 653-2400), (Fax from U.S. (202) 653 5760), www.fao.org; *FAO Production Yearbook 2002* and *The State of Food and Agriculture (SOFA) 2006.*

HOLY

SEE (VATICAN CITY) - PROFESSIONS

United Nations Statistics Division, New York, NY 10017, (800) 253-9646, Fax: (212) 963-4116, http://unstats.un.org; *Statistical Yearbook.*

HOLY

SEE (VATICAN CITY) - PUBLISHERS AND PUBLISHING

UNESCO Institute for Statistics, C.P. 6128 Succursale Centre-Ville, Montreal, Quebec, H3C 3J7 Canada, (Dial from U.S. (514) 343-6880), (Fax from U.S. (514) 343 6882), www.uis.unesco.org; *Statistical Tables.*

HOLY

SEE (VATICAN CITY) - RELIGION

Central Intelligence Agency, Office of Public Affairs, Washington, DC 20505, (703) 482-0623, Fax: (703) 482-1739, www.cia.gov; *The World Factbook.*

HOLY

SEE (VATICAN CITY) - ROADS

Central Intelligence Agency, Office of Public Affairs, Washington, DC 20505, (703) 482-0623, Fax: (703) 482-1739, www.cia.gov; *The World Factbook.*

HOLY

SEE (VATICAN CITY) - TRADE - See HOLY SEE (VATICAN CITY) - INTERNATIONAL TRADE

HOLY

SEE (VATICAN CITY) - TRANSPORTATION

Central Intelligence Agency, Office of Public Affairs, Washington, DC 20505, (703) 482-0623, Fax: (703) 482-1739, www.cia.gov; *The World Factbook.*

HOLY

SEE (VATICAN CITY) - UNEMPLOYMENT

Central Intelligence Agency, Office of Public Affairs, Washington, DC 20505, (703) 482-0623, Fax: (703) 482-1739, www.cia.gov; *The World Factbook.*

HOLY

SEE (VATICAN CITY) - VITAL STATISTICS

World Health Organization (WHO), Avenue Appia 20, 1211 Geneve 27, Switzerland, (Telephone in U.S. (212) 331-9081), www.who.int; *World Health Report 2006.*

HOME ECONOMICS - DEGREES CONFERRED

National Center for Education Statistics (NCES), 1990 K Street, NW, Washington, DC 20006, (202) 502-7300, http://nces.ed.gov; *Digest of Education Statistics 2007.*

U.S. Census Bureau, 4700 Silver Hill Road, Washington DC 20233-0001, (301) 763-3030, www.census.gov; unpublished data.

HOME EQUITY LOANS/LINES OF CREDIT

Board of Governors of the Federal Reserve System, Constitution Avenue, NW, Washington, DC 20551, (202) 452-3000, www.federalreserve.gov; *Federal Reserve Bulletin* and unpublished data.

Federal Deposit Insurance Corporation (FDIC), 550 Seventeenth Street, NW, Washington, DC 20429-0002, (877) 275-3342, www.fdic.gov; *2007 Annual Report; Quarterly Banking Profile (QBP);* and *State Banking Performance Summary.*

HOME FURNISHINGS

See FURNITURE AND HOME FURNISHING STORES

HOME HEALTH CARE SERVICES

National Center for Health Statistics (NCHS), Centers for Disease Control and Prevention (CDC), U.S. Department of Health and Human Services (HHS), 3311 Toledo Road, Hyattsville, MD 20782, (866) 232-4636, www.cdc.gov/nchs; *Faststats A to Z.*

Robert Wood Johnson Foundation, PO Box 2316, College Road East and Route 1, Princeton, NJ 08543, (877) 843-7953, www.rwjf.org; *Quality of Death and Dying is Significantly Higher for People Who Die at Home; What Factors Influence the Kind of Long-Term Services Patients with Private Insurance Choose Over Time;* and *Where People Die: A Multilevel Approach to Understanding Influences on Site of Death in America.*

U.S. Census Bureau, Center for Economic Studies, 4600 Silver Hill Road, Washington DC 20233, (301) 457-1235, www.ces.census.gov; *2002 Economic Census, Professional, Scientific and Technical Services.*

HOME HEALTH CARE SERVICES - EMPLOYEES

U.S. Census Bureau, 4700 Silver Hill Road, Washington DC 20233-0001, (301) 763-3030, www.census.gov; *2002 Economic Census, Nonemployer Statistics.*

U.S. Census Bureau, Service Sector Statistics Division, 4700 Silver Hill Road, Washington DC 20233-0001, (301) 763-3030, www.census.gov/svsd/www/economic.html; *2004 Service Annual Survey: Health Care and Social Assistance.*

HOME HEALTH CARE SERVICES - ESTABLISHMENTS

U.S. Census Bureau, 4700 Silver Hill Road, Washington DC 20233-0001, (301) 763-3030, www.census.gov; *2002 Economic Census, Nonemployer Statistics.*

U.S. Census Bureau, Service Sector Statistics Division, 4700 Silver Hill Road, Washington DC 20233-0001, (301) 763-3030, www.census.gov/svsd/www/economic.html; *2004 Service Annual Survey: Health Care and Social Assistance.*

HOME HEALTH CARE SERVICES - FINANCES

U.S. Census Bureau, 4700 Silver Hill Road, Washington DC 20233-0001, (301) 763-3030, www.census.gov; *2002 Economic Census, Nonemployer Statistics.*

U.S. Census Bureau, Service Sector Statistics Division, 4700 Silver Hill Road, Washington DC 20233-0001, (301) 763-3030, www.census.gov/svsd/www/economic.html; *2004 Service Annual Survey: Health Care and Social Assistance.*

HOME-BASED BUSINESSES

U.S. Bureau of Labor Statistics (BLS), Postal Square Building, 2 Massachusetts Avenue, NE, Washington, DC 20212-0001, (202) 691-5200, Fax: (202) 691-6325, www.bls.gov; unpublished data.

HOMELESSNESS

The Melville Charitable Trust, c/o The Philanthropic Initiative, Inc., 160 Federal Street, 8th Floor, Boston, MA 02110, (617) 338-2590, http://melvilletrust.org; unpublished data.

HOMES

See HOUSING AND HOUSING UNITS

HOMESCHOOLING

National Center for Education Statistics (NCES), 1990 K Street, NW, Washington, DC 20006, (202) 502-7300, http://nces.ed.gov; *1.1 Million Homeschooled Students in the United States in 2003* and *Homeschooling in the United States: 2003.*

HOMICIDES

Bernan Essential Government Publications, 4611-F Assembly Drive, Lanham MD, 20706-4391, (301) 459-2255, Fax: (800) 865-3450, www.bernan.com; *Vital Statistics of the United States: Births, Life Expectancy, Deaths, and Selected Health Data.*

Federal Bureau of Investigation (FBI), J. Edgar Hoover Building, 935 Pennsylvania Avenue, NW, Washington, DC 20535-0001, (202) 324-3000, www.fbi.gov; *Crime in the United States (CIUS) 2007 (Preliminary).*

Justice Research and Statistics Association (JRSA), 777 N. Capitol Street, NE, Suite 801, Washington, DC 20002, (202) 842-9330, Fax: (202) 842-9329, www.jrsa.org; *Crime and Justice Atlas 2001.*

National Center for Health Statistics (NCHS), Centers for Disease Control and Prevention (CDC), U.S. Department of Health and Human Services (HHS), 3311 Toledo Road, Hyattsville, MD 20782, (866) 232-4636, www.cdc.gov/nchs; *National Vital Statistics Reports (NVSR); Vital Statistics of the United States (VSUS);* and unpublished data.

U.S. Department of Justice (DOJ), Bureau of Justice Statistics, 810 Seventh Street, NW, Washington, DC 20531, (202) 307-0765, www.ojp.usdoj.gov/bjs/; *Homicide Trends in the United States: 2002 Update; Suicide and Homicide in State Prisons and Local Jails;* and *Weapon Use and Violent Crime, 1993-2001.*

U.S. Department of Justice (DOJ), National Institute of Justice (NIJ), 810 Seventh Street, NW, Washington, DC 20531, (202) 307-2942, Fax: (202) 616-0275, www.ojp.usdoj.gov/nij/; *Intimate Partner Homicide: An Overview; Reviewing Domestic Violence Deaths;* and *Risky Mix: Drinking, Drug Use, and Homicide.*

HOMOSEXUALITY

Hartford Institute for Religion Research, Hartford Seminary, 77 Sherman Street, Hartford, CT 06105-2260, (860) 509-9543, Fax: (860) 509-9551, http://hirr.hartsem.edu; *Homosexuality and Religion.*

HONDURAS - NATIONAL STATISTICAL OFFICE

Instituto Nacional de Estadistica (INE), Apartado Postal 9412, Boulevard Suyapa, Cl. Florencia Sur, Tegucigalpa, M.D.C. Honduras, www.ine-hn.org; National Data Center.

HONDURAS - PRIMARY STATISTICS SOURCES

Instituto Nacional de Estadistica (INE), Apartado Postal 9412, Boulevard Suyapa, Cl. Florencia Sur, Tegucigalpa, M.D.C. Honduras, www.ine-hn.org; *Anuario Estadistico Nacional 1995-2000.*

HONDURAS - AGRICULTURAL MACHINERY

Economist Intelligence Unit, 111 West 57th Street, New York, NY 10019, (212) 554-0600, Fax: (212) 586-1181, www.eiu.com; *Business Latin America.*

United Nations Statistics Division, New York, NY 10017, (800) 253-9646, Fax: (212) 963-4116, http://unstats.un.org; *Statistical Yearbook.*

HONDURAS - AGRICULTURE

Economist Intelligence Unit, 111 West 57th Street, New York, NY 10019, (212) 554-0600, Fax: (212) 586-1181, www.eiu.com; *Business Latin America* and *Honduras Country Report.*

Euromonitor International, Inc., 224 S. Michigan Avenue, Suite 1500, Chicago, IL 60604, (312) 922-1115, Fax: (312) 922-1157, www.euromonitor.com; *International Marketing Data and Statistics 2008* and *World Marketing Data and Statistics.*

Inter-American Development Bank (IDB), 1300 New York Avenue, NW, Washington, DC 20577, (202) 623-1000, Fax: (202) 623-3096, www.iadb.org; *The Politics of Policies: Economic and Social Progress in Latin America - 2006 Report.*

International Food Policy Research Institute (IFPRI), 2033 K Street, NW, Washington, D.C., 2006, (202) 862-5600, www.ifpri.org; *Rural Development Policies and Sustainable Land Use in the Hillside Areas of Honduras Survey, 2001-2002.*

M.E. Sharpe, 80 Business Park Drive, Armonk, NY 10504, (800) 541-6563, Fax: (914) 273-2106, www.mesharpe.com; *The Illustrated Book of World Rankings.*

Palgrave Macmillan Ltd., Houndmills, Basingstoke, Hampshire, RG21 6XS, England, (Telephone in U.S. (888) 330-8477), (Fax in U.S. (800) 672-2054), www.palgrave.com; *The Statesman's Yearbook 2008.*

Taylor and Francis Group, An Informa Business, 2 Park Square, Milton Park, Abingdon, Oxford OX14 4RN, United Kingdom, (Dial from U.S. (212) 216-7800), (Fax from U.S. (212) 564-7854), www.tandf.co.uk; *The Europa World Year Book.*

UCLA Latin American Institute, 10343 Bunche Hall, Box 951447, Los Angeles, CA 90095-1447, (310) 825-4571, Fax: (310) 206-6859, www.international.ucla.edu/lac; *Statistical Abstract of Latin America.*

United Nations Conference on Trade and Development (UNCTAD), DC2-1120, United Nations, New York, NY 10017, (212) 963-0027, www.unctad.org; *UNCTAD Commodity Yearbook.*

United Nations Food and Agricultural Organization (FAO), Viale delle Terme di Caracalla, 00100 Rome, Italy, (Dial from U.S. (202) 653-2400), (Fax from U.S. (202) 653 5760), www.fao.org; AQUASTAT; *FAO Production Yearbook 2002; FAO Trade Yearbook;* and *The State of Food and Agriculture (SOFA) 2006.*

United Nations Statistics Division, New York, NY 10017, (800) 253-9646, Fax: (212) 963-4116, http://unstats.un.org; *Statistical Yearbook* and *Statistical Yearbook for Latin America and the Caribbean 2004.*

The World Bank, 1818 H Street, NW, Washington, DC 20433, (202) 473-1000, Fax: (202) 477-6391, www.worldbank.org; *Honduras* and *World Development Indicators (WDI) 2008.*

HONDURAS - AIRLINES

Economist Intelligence Unit, 111 West 57th Street, New York, NY 10019, (212) 554-0600, Fax: (212) 586-1181, www.eiu.com; *Business Latin America.*

International Civil Aviation Organization (ICAO), External Relations and Public Information Office (EPO), 999 University Street, Montreal, Quebec H3C 5H7, Canada, (Dial from U.S. (514) 954-8219), (Fax from U.S. (514) 954-6077), www.icao.int; *Civil Aviation Statistics of the World.*

M.E. Sharpe, 80 Business Park Drive, Armonk, NY 10504, (800) 541-6563, Fax: (914) 273-2106, www.mesharpe.com; *The Illustrated Book of World Rankings.*

Palgrave Macmillan Ltd., Houndmills, Basingstoke, Hampshire, RG21 6XS, England, (Telephone in U.S. (888) 330-8477), (Fax in U.S. (800) 672-2054), www.palgrave.com; *The Statesman's Yearbook 2008.*

Taylor and Francis Group, An Informa Business, 2 Park Square, Milton Park, Abingdon, Oxford OX14 4RN, United Kingdom, (Dial from U.S. (212) 216-7800), (Fax from U.S. (212) 564-7854), www.tandf.co.uk; *The Europa World Year Book.*

United Nations Statistics Division, New York, NY 10017, (800) 253-9646, Fax: (212) 963-4116, http://unstats.un.org; *Statistical Yearbook.*

HONDURAS - AIRPORTS

Central Intelligence Agency, Office of Public Affairs, Washington, DC 20505, (703) 482-0623, Fax: (703) 482-1739, www.cia.gov; *The World Factbook.*

HONDURAS - ALUMINUM PRODUCTION

See HONDURAS - MINERAL INDUSTRIES

HONDURAS - AREA

Economist Intelligence Unit, 111 West 57th Street, New York, NY 10019, (212) 554-0600, Fax: (212) 586-1181, www.eiu.com; *Business Latin America.*

HONDURAS - ARMED FORCES

Central Intelligence Agency, Office of Public Affairs, Washington, DC 20505, (703) 482-0623, Fax: (703) 482-1739, www.cia.gov; *The World Factbook.*

Economist Intelligence Unit, 111 West 57th Street, New York, NY 10019, (212) 554-0600, Fax: (212) 586-1181, www.eiu.com; *Business Latin America.*

Euromonitor International, Inc., 224 S. Michigan Avenue, Suite 1500, Chicago, IL 60604, (312) 922-1115, Fax: (312) 922-1157, www.euromonitor.com; *World Marketing Data and Statistics.*

International Institute for Strategic Studies (IISS), Arundel House, 13-15 Arundel Street, Temple Place, London WC2R 3DX, England, www.iiss.org; *The Military Balance 2007.*

International Monetary Fund (IMF), 700 Nineteenth Street, NW, Washington, DC 20431, (202) 623-7000, Fax: (202) 623-4661, www.imf.org; *Government Finance Statistics Yearbook (2008 Edition).*

Palgrave Macmillan Ltd., Houndmills, Basingstoke, Hampshire, RG21 6XS, England, (Telephone in U.S. (888) 330-8477), (Fax in U.S. (800) 672-2054), www.palgrave.com; *The Statesman's Yearbook 2008.*

U.S. Department of State (DOS), 2201 C Street NW, Washington, DC 20520, (202) 647-4000, www.state.gov; *World Military Expenditures and Arms Transfers (WMEAT).*

UCLA Latin American Institute, 10343 Bunche Hall, Box 951447, Los Angeles, CA 90095-1447, (310) 825-4571, Fax: (310) 206-6859, www.international.ucla.edu/lac; *Statistical Abstract of Latin America.*

United Nations Statistics Division, New York, NY 10017, (800) 253-9646, Fax: (212) 963-4116, http://unstats.un.org; *Human Development Report 2006.*

HONDURAS - BALANCE OF PAYMENTS

Economist Intelligence Unit, 111 West 57th Street, New York, NY 10019, (212) 554-0600, Fax: (212) 586-1181, www.eiu.com; *Business Latin America.*

Inter-American Development Bank (IDB), 1300 New York Avenue, NW, Washington, DC 20577, (202) 623-1000, Fax: (202) 623-3096, www.iadb.org; *The Politics of Policies: Economic and Social Progress in Latin America - 2006 Report.*

International Monetary Fund (IMF), 700 Nineteenth Street, NW, Washington, DC 20431, (202) 623-7000, Fax: (202) 623-4661, www.imf.org; *Balance of Payments Statistics Newsletter; Balance of Payments Statistics Yearbook 2007;* and *International Financial Statistics Yearbook 2007.*

Organization of American States (OAS), 17th Street Constitution Avenue NW, Washington, DC 20006, (202) 458-3000, www.oas.org; *The OAS in Transition: 1994-2004.*

Taylor and Francis Group, An Informa Business, 2 Park Square, Milton Park, Abingdon, Oxford OX14 4RN, United Kingdom, (Dial from U.S. (212) 216-7800), (Fax from U.S. (212) 564-7854), www.tandf.co.uk; *The Europa World Year Book.*

UCLA Latin American Institute, 10343 Bunche Hall, Box 951447, Los Angeles, CA 90095-1447, (310) 825-4571, Fax: (310) 206-6859, www.international.ucla.edu/lac; *Statistical Abstract of Latin America.*

United Nations Conference on Trade and Development (UNCTAD), DC2-1120, United Nations, New York, NY 10017, (212) 963-0027, www.unctad.org; *Handbook of Statistics 2005.*

United Nations Statistics Division, New York, NY 10017, (800) 253-9646, Fax: (212) 963-4116, http://unstats.un.org; *Economic Survey of Latin America and the Caribbean 2004-2005* and *Statistical Yearbook for Latin America and the Caribbean 2004.*

The World Bank, 1818 H Street, NW, Washington, DC 20433, (202) 473-1000, Fax: (202) 477-6391, www.worldbank.org; *Honduras; World Development Indicators (WDI) 2008;* and *World Development Report 2008.*

HONDURAS - BANANAS

See HONDURAS - CROPS

HONDURAS - BANKS AND BANKING

Euromonitor International, Inc., 224 S. Michigan Avenue, Suite 1500, Chicago, IL 60604, (312) 922-1115, Fax: (312) 922-1157, www.euromonitor.com; *World Marketing Data and Statistics.*

Inter-American Development Bank (IDB), 1300 New York Avenue, NW, Washington, DC 20577, (202) 623-1000, Fax: (202) 623-3096, www.iadb.org; *The Politics of Policies: Economic and Social Progress in Latin America - 2006 Report.*

International Monetary Fund (IMF), 700 Nineteenth Street, NW, Washington, DC 20431, (202) 623-7000, Fax: (202) 623-4661, www.imf.org; *International Financial Statistics Yearbook 2007.*

M.E. Sharpe, 80 Business Park Drive, Armonk, NY 10504, (800) 541-6563, Fax: (914) 273-2106, www.mesharpe.com; *The Illustrated Book of World Rankings.*

Palgrave Macmillan Ltd., Houndmills, Basingstoke, Hampshire, RG21 6XS, England, (Telephone in U.S. (888) 330-8477), (Fax in U.S. (800) 672-2054), www.palgrave.com; *The Statesman's Yearbook 2008.*

Taylor and Francis Group, An Informa Business, 2 Park Square, Milton Park, Abingdon, Oxford OX14 4RN, United Kingdom, (Dial from U.S. (212) 216-7800), (Fax from U.S. (212) 564-7854), www.tandf.co.uk; *The Europa World Year Book.*

United Nations Statistics Division, New York, NY 10017, (800) 253-9646, Fax: (212) 963-4116, http://unstats.un.org; *Statistical Yearbook.*

HONDURAS - BARLEY PRODUCTION

See HONDURAS - CROPS

HONDURAS - BEVERAGE INDUSTRY

M.E. Sharpe, 80 Business Park Drive, Armonk, NY 10504, (800) 541-6563, Fax: (914) 273-2106, www.mesharpe.com; *The Illustrated Book of World Rankings.*

United Nations Statistics Division, New York, NY 10017, (800) 253-9646, Fax: (212) 963-4116, http://unstats.un.org; *Statistical Yearbook.*

HONDURAS - BIRTH CONTROL

UCLA Latin American Institute, 10343 Bunche Hall, Box 951447, Los Angeles, CA 90095-1447, (310) 825-4571, Fax: (310) 206-6859, www.international.ucla.edu/lac; *Statistical Abstract of Latin America.*

HONDURAS - BONDS

Inter-American Development Bank (IDB), 1300 New York Avenue, NW, Washington, DC 20577, (202) 623-1000, Fax: (202) 623-3096, www.iadb.org; *The Politics of Policies: Economic and Social Progress in Latin America - 2006 Report.*

International Monetary Fund (IMF), 700 Nineteenth Street, NW, Washington, DC 20431, (202) 623-7000, Fax: (202) 623-4661, www.imf.org; *Government Finance Statistics Yearbook (2008 Edition).*

HONDURAS - BROADCASTING

Central Intelligence Agency, Office of Public Affairs, Washington, DC 20505, (703) 482-0623, Fax: (703) 482-1739, www.cia.gov; *The World Factbook.*

Euromonitor International, Inc., 224 S. Michigan Avenue, Suite 1500, Chicago, IL 60604, (312) 922-1115, Fax: (312) 922-1157, www.euromonitor.com; *World Marketing Data and Statistics.*

M.E. Sharpe, 80 Business Park Drive, Armonk, NY 10504, (800) 541-6563, Fax: (914) 273-2106, www.mesharpe.com; *The Illustrated Book of World Rankings.*

Palgrave Macmillan Ltd., Houndmills, Basingstoke, Hampshire, RG21 6XS, England, (Telephone in U.S. (888) 330-8477), (Fax in U.S. (800) 672-2054), www.palgrave.com; *The Statesman's Yearbook 2008.*

WRTH Publications Limited, PO Box 290, Oxford OX2 7FT, UK, www.wrth.com; *World Radio TV Handbook 2007.*

HONDURAS - BUDGET

Central Intelligence Agency, Office of Public Affairs, Washington, DC 20505, (703) 482-0623, Fax: (703) 482-1739, www.cia.gov; *The World Factbook.*

HONDURAS - BUSINESS

Inter-American Development Bank (IDB), 1300 New York Avenue, NW, Washington, DC 20577, (202) 623-1000, Fax: (202) 623-3096, www.iadb.org; *The Politics of Policies: Economic and Social Progress in Latin America - 2006 Report.*

HONDURAS - CAPITAL INVESTMENTS

Inter-American Development Bank (IDB), 1300 New York Avenue, NW, Washington, DC 20577, (202) 623-1000, Fax: (202) 623-3096, www.iadb.org; *The Politics of Policies: Economic and Social Progress in Latin America - 2006 Report.*

HONDURAS - CAPITAL LEVY

Inter-American Development Bank (IDB), 1300 New York Avenue, NW, Washington, DC 20577, (202) 623-1000, Fax: (202) 623-3096, www.iadb.org; *The Politics of Policies: Economic and Social Progress in Latin America - 2006 Report.*

International Monetary Fund (IMF), 700 Nineteenth Street, NW, Washington, DC 20431, (202) 623-7000, Fax: (202) 623-4661, www.imf.org; *Government Finance Statistics Yearbook (2008 Edition).*

HONDURAS - CATTLE

See HONDURAS - LIVESTOCK

HONDURAS - CHICKENS

See HONDURAS - LIVESTOCK

HONDURAS - CHILDBIRTH - STATISTICS

Central Intelligence Agency, Office of Public Affairs, Washington, DC 20505, (703) 482-0623, Fax: (703) 482-1739, www.cia.gov; *The World Factbook.*

Euromonitor International, Inc., 224 S. Michigan Avenue, Suite 1500, Chicago, IL 60604, (312) 922-1115, Fax: (312) 922-1157, www.euromonitor.com; *International Marketing Data and Statistics 2008* and *The World Economic Factbook 2008.*

M.E. Sharpe, 80 Business Park Drive, Armonk, NY 10504, (800) 541-6563, Fax: (914) 273-2106, www.mesharpe.com; *The Illustrated Book of World Rankings.*

Palgrave Macmillan Ltd., Houndmills, Basingstoke, Hampshire, RG21 6XS, England, (Telephone in U.S. (888) 330-8477), (Fax in U.S. (800) 672-2054), www.palgrave.com; *The Statesman's Yearbook 2008.*

Taylor and Francis Group, An Informa Business, 2 Park Square, Milton Park, Abingdon, Oxford OX14 4RN, United Kingdom, (Dial from U.S. (212) 216-7800), (Fax from U.S. (212) 564-7854), www.tandf.co.uk; *The Europa World Year Book.*

United Nations Statistics Division, New York, NY 10017, (800) 253-9646, Fax: (212) 963-4116, http://unstats.un.org; *Demographic Yearbook; Statistical Yearbook;* and *Statistical Yearbook for Latin America and the Caribbean 2004.*

The World Bank, 1818 H Street, NW, Washington, DC 20433, (202) 473-1000, Fax: (202) 477-6391, www.worldbank.org; *World Development Indicators (WDI) 2008.*

World Health Organization (WHO), Avenue Appia 20, 1211 Geneve 27, Switzerland, (Telephone in U.S. (212) 331-9081), www.who.int; *World Health Report 2006.*

HONDURAS - CLIMATE

M.E. Sharpe, 80 Business Park Drive, Armonk, NY 10504, (800) 541-6563, Fax: (914) 273-2106, www.mesharpe.com; *The Illustrated Book of World Rankings.*

Palgrave Macmillan Ltd., Houndmills, Basingstoke, Hampshire, RG21 6XS, England, (Telephone in U.S. (888) 330-8477), (Fax in U.S. (800) 672-2054), www.palgrave.com; *The Statesman's Yearbook 2008.*

HONDURAS - COAL PRODUCTION

See HONDURAS - MINERAL INDUSTRIES

HONDURAS - COCOA PRODUCTION

See HONDURAS - CROPS

HONDURAS - COFFEE

See HONDURAS - CROPS

HONDURAS - COMMERCE

Palgrave Macmillan Ltd., Houndmills, Basingstoke, Hampshire, RG21 6XS, England, (Telephone in U.S. (888) 330-8477), (Fax in U.S. (800) 672-2054), www.palgrave.com; *The Statesman's Yearbook 2008.*

HONDURAS - COMMODITY EXCHANGES

Commodity Research Bureau, 330 South Wells Street, Suite 612, Chicago, IL 60606-7110, (800) 621-5271, Fax: (312) 939-4135, www.crbtrader.com; *2006 CRB Commodity Yearbook and CD.*

International Monetary Fund (IMF), 700 Nineteenth Street, NW, Washington, DC 20431, (202) 623-7000, Fax: (202) 623-4661, www.imf.org; *IMF Primary Commodity Prices.*

United Nations Food and Agricultural Organization (FAO), Viale delle Terme di Caracalla, 00100 Rome, Italy, (Dial from U.S. (202) 653-2400), (Fax from U.S. (202) 653 5760), www.fao.org; *The State of Food and Agriculture (SOFA) 2006.*

HONDURAS - CONSTRUCTION INDUSTRY

Economist Intelligence Unit, 111 West 57th Street, New York, NY 10019, (212) 554-0600, Fax: (212) 586-1181, www.eiu.com; *Business Latin America.*

Inter-American Development Bank (IDB), 1300 New York Avenue, NW, Washington, DC 20577, (202) 623-1000, Fax: (202) 623-3096, www.iadb.org; *The Politics of Policies: Economic and Social Progress in Latin America - 2006 Report.*

M.E. Sharpe, 80 Business Park Drive, Armonk, NY 10504, (800) 541-6563, Fax: (914) 273-2106, www.mesharpe.com; *The Illustrated Book of World Rankings.*

Palgrave Macmillan Ltd., Houndmills, Basingstoke, Hampshire, RG21 6XS, England, (Telephone in U.S. (888) 330-8477), (Fax in U.S. (800) 672-2054), www.palgrave.com; *The Statesman's Yearbook 2008.*

UCLA Latin American Institute, 10343 Bunche Hall, Box 951447, Los Angeles, CA 90095-1447, (310) 825-4571, Fax: (310) 206-6859, www.international.ucla.edu/lac; *Statistical Abstract of Latin America.*

United Nations Statistics Division, New York, NY 10017, (800) 253-9646, Fax: (212) 963-4116, http://unstats.un.org; *Statistical Yearbook.*

HONDURAS - CONSUMER COOPERATIVES

UCLA Latin American Institute, 10343 Bunche Hall, Box 951447, Los Angeles, CA 90095-1447, (310) 825-4571, Fax: (310) 206-6859, www.international.ucla.edu/lac; *Statistical Abstract of Latin America.*

HONDURAS - CONSUMER PRICE INDEXES

Taylor and Francis Group, An Informa Business, 2 Park Square, Milton Park, Abingdon, Oxford OX14 4RN, United Kingdom, (Dial from U.S. (212) 216-7800), (Fax from U.S. (212) 564-7854), www.tandf.co.uk; *The Europa World Year Book.*

United Nations Statistics Division, New York, NY 10017, (800) 253-9646, Fax: (212) 963-4116, http://unstats.un.org; *Statistical Yearbook.*

The World Bank, 1818 H Street, NW, Washington, DC 20433, (202) 473-1000, Fax: (202) 477-6391, www.worldbank.org; *Honduras.*

HONDURAS - CONSUMPTION (ECONOMICS)

Economist Intelligence Unit, 111 West 57th Street, New York, NY 10019, (212) 554-0600, Fax: (212) 586-1181, www.eiu.com; *Business Latin America.*

Inter-American Development Bank (IDB), 1300 New York Avenue, NW, Washington, DC 20577, (202) 623-1000, Fax: (202) 623-3096, www.iadb.org; *The Politics of Policies: Economic and Social Progress in Latin America - 2006 Report.*

United Nations Statistics Division, New York, NY 10017, (800) 253-9646, Fax: (212) 963-4116, http://unstats.un.org; *Statistical Yearbook for Latin America and the Caribbean 2004.*

The World Bank, 1818 H Street, NW, Washington, DC 20433, (202) 473-1000, Fax: (202) 477-6391, www.worldbank.org; *World Development Report 2008.*

HONDURAS - COPPER INDUSTRY AND TRADE

See HONDURAS - MINERAL INDUSTRIES

HONDURAS - CORN INDUSTRY

See HONDURAS - CROPS

HONDURAS - COST AND STANDARD OF LIVING

International Monetary Fund (IMF), 700 Nineteenth Street, NW, Washington, DC 20431, (202) 623-7000, Fax: (202) 623-4661, www.imf.org; *Government Finance Statistics Yearbook (2008 Edition).*

HONDURAS - COTTON

See HONDURAS - CROPS

HONDURAS - CROPS

Economist Intelligence Unit, 111 West 57th Street, New York, NY 10019, (212) 554-0600, Fax: (212) 586-1181, www.eiu.com; *Business Latin America.*

International Monetary Fund (IMF), 700 Nineteenth Street, NW, Washington, DC 20431, (202) 623-7000, Fax: (202) 623-4661, www.imf.org; *International Financial Statistics Yearbook 2007.*

M.E. Sharpe, 80 Business Park Drive, Armonk, NY 10504, (800) 541-6563, Fax: (914) 273-2106, www.mesharpe.com; *The Illustrated Book of World Rankings.*

Organization of American States (OAS), 17th Street Constitution Avenue NW, Washington, DC 20006, (202) 458-3000, www.oas.org; *The OAS in Transition: 1994-2004.*

Palgrave Macmillan Ltd., Houndmills, Basingstoke, Hampshire, RG21 6XS, England, (Telephone in U.S. (888) 330-8477), (Fax in U.S. (800) 672-2054), www.palgrave.com; *The Statesman's Yearbook 2008.*

Taylor and Francis Group, An Informa Business, 2 Park Square, Milton Park, Abingdon, Oxford OX14 4RN, United Kingdom, (Dial from U.S. (212) 216-7800), (Fax from U.S. (212) 564-7854), www.tandf.co.uk; *The Europa World Year Book.*

United Nations Conference on Trade and Development (UNCTAD), DC2-1120, United Nations, New York, NY 10017, (212) 963-0027, www.unctad.org; *UNCTAD Commodity Yearbook.*

United Nations Food and Agricultural Organization (FAO), Viale delle Terme di Caracalla, 00100 Rome, Italy, (Dial from U.S. (202) 653-2400), (Fax from U.S. (202) 653 5760), www.fao.org; *FAO Production Yearbook 2002* and *The State of Food and Agriculture (SOFA) 2006.*

United Nations Statistics Division, New York, NY 10017, (800) 253-9646, Fax: (212) 963-4116, http://unstats.un.org; *Statistical Yearbook.*

HONDURAS - CUSTOMS ADMINISTRATION

Inter-American Development Bank (IDB), 1300 New York Avenue, NW, Washington, DC 20577, (202) 623-1000, Fax: (202) 623-3096, www.iadb.org; *The Politics of Policies: Economic and Social Progress in Latin America - 2006 Report.*

International Monetary Fund (IMF), 700 Nineteenth Street, NW, Washington, DC 20431, (202) 623-7000, Fax: (202) 623-4661, www.imf.org; *Government Finance Statistics Yearbook (2008 Edition).*

Palgrave Macmillan Ltd., Houndmills, Basingstoke, Hampshire, RG21 6XS, England, (Telephone in U.S. (888) 330-8477), (Fax in U.S. (800) 672-2054), www.palgrave.com; *The Statesman's Yearbook 2008.*

HONDURAS - DAIRY PROCESSING

M.E. Sharpe, 80 Business Park Drive, Armonk, NY 10504, (800) 541-6563, Fax: (914) 273-2106, www.mesharpe.com; *The Illustrated Book of World Rankings.*

Palgrave Macmillan Ltd., Houndmills, Basingstoke, Hampshire, RG21 6XS, England, (Telephone in U.S. (888) 330-8477), (Fax in U.S. (800) 672-2054), www.palgrave.com; *The Statesman's Yearbook 2008.*

Taylor and Francis Group, An Informa Business, 2 Park Square, Milton Park, Abingdon, Oxford OX14 4RN, United Kingdom, (Dial from U.S. (212) 216-7800), (Fax from U.S. (212) 564-7854), www.tandf.co.uk; *The Europa World Year Book.*

United Nations Food and Agricultural Organization (FAO), Viale delle Terme di Caracalla, 00100 Rome, Italy, (Dial from U.S. (202) 653-2400), (Fax from U.S. (202) 653 5760), www.fao.org; *FAO Production Yearbook 2002* and *The State of Food and Agriculture (SOFA) 2006.*

United Nations Statistics Division, New York, NY 10017, (800) 253-9646, Fax: (212) 963-4116, http://unstats.un.org; *Statistical Yearbook.*

HONDURAS - DEATH RATES

See HONDURAS - MORTALITY

HONDURAS - DEBT

Economist Intelligence Unit, 111 West 57th Street, New York, NY 10019, (212) 554-0600, Fax: (212) 586-1181, www.eiu.com; *Business Latin America.*

The World Bank, 1818 H Street, NW, Washington, DC 20433, (202) 473-1000, Fax: (202) 477-6391, www.worldbank.org; *Global Development Finance 2007.*

HONDURAS - DEBTS, EXTERNAL

Economist Intelligence Unit, 111 West 57th Street, New York, NY 10019, (212) 554-0600, Fax: (212) 586-1181, www.eiu.com; *Business Latin America.*

Inter-American Development Bank (IDB), 1300 New York Avenue, NW, Washington, DC 20577, (202) 623-1000, Fax: (202) 623-3096, www.iadb.org; *The Politics of Policies: Economic and Social Progress in Latin America - 2006 Report.*

Palgrave Macmillan Ltd., Houndmills, Basingstoke, Hampshire, RG21 6XS, England, (Telephone in U.S. (888) 330-8477), (Fax in U.S. (800) 672-2054), www.palgrave.com; *The Statesman's Yearbook 2008.*

United Nations Statistics Division, New York, NY 10017, (800) 253-9646, Fax: (212) 963-4116, http://unstats.un.org; *Economic Survey of Latin America and the Caribbean 2004-2005* and *Statistical Yearbook for Latin America and the Caribbean 2004.*

The World Bank, 1818 H Street, NW, Washington, DC 20433, (202) 473-1000, Fax: (202) 477-6391, www.worldbank.org; *Global Development Finance 2007; World Development Indicators (WDI) 2008;* and *World Development Report 2008.*

HONDURAS - DEFENSE EXPENDITURES

See HONDURAS - ARMED FORCES

HONDURAS - DEMOGRAPHY

Euromonitor International, Inc., 224 S. Michigan Avenue, Suite 1500, Chicago, IL 60604, (312) 922-1115, Fax: (312) 922-1157, www.euromonitor.com; *International Marketing Data and Statistics 2008; The World Economic Factbook 2008;* and *World Marketing Data and Statistics.*

M.E. Sharpe, 80 Business Park Drive, Armonk, NY 10504, (800) 541-6563, Fax: (914) 273-2106, www.mesharpe.com; *The Illustrated Book of World Rankings.*

United Nations Statistics Division, New York, NY 10017, (800) 253-9646, Fax: (212) 963-4116, http://unstats.un.org; *Human Development Report 2006.*

The World Bank, 1818 H Street, NW, Washington, DC 20433, (202) 473-1000, Fax: (202) 477-6391, www.worldbank.org; *Honduras.*

HONDURAS - DIAMONDS

See HONDURAS - MINERAL INDUSTRIES

HONDURAS - DISPOSABLE INCOME

Inter-American Development Bank (IDB), 1300 New York Avenue, NW, Washington, DC 20577, (202) 623-1000, Fax: (202) 623-3096, www.iadb.org; *The Politics of Policies: Economic and Social Progress in Latin America - 2006 Report.*

International Monetary Fund (IMF), 700 Nineteenth Street, NW, Washington, DC 20431, (202) 623-7000, Fax: (202) 623-4661, www.imf.org; *International Financial Statistics Yearbook 2007.*

M.E. Sharpe, 80 Business Park Drive, Armonk, NY 10504, (800) 541-6563, Fax: (914) 273-2106, www.mesharpe.com; *The Illustrated Book of World Rankings.*

United Nations Statistics Division, New York, NY 10017, (800) 253-9646, Fax: (212) 963-4116, http://unstats.un.org; *National Accounts Statistics: Compendium of Income Distribution Statistics; Statistical Yearbook;* and *Statistical Yearbook for Latin America and the Caribbean 2004.*

HONDURAS - DIVORCE

M.E. Sharpe, 80 Business Park Drive, Armonk, NY 10504, (800) 541-6563, Fax: (914) 273-2106, www.mesharpe.com; *The Illustrated Book of World Rankings.*

United Nations Statistics Division, New York, NY 10017, (800) 253-9646, Fax: (212) 963-4116, http://unstats.un.org; *Demographic Yearbook* and *Statistical Yearbook.*

HONDURAS - ECONOMIC ASSISTANCE

Inter-American Development Bank (IDB), 1300 New York Avenue, NW, Washington, DC 20577, (202) 623-1000, Fax: (202) 623-3096, www.iadb.org; *The Politics of Policies: Economic and Social Progress in Latin America - 2006 Report.*

United Nations Statistics Division, New York, NY 10017, (800) 253-9646, Fax: (212) 963-4116, http://unstats.un.org; *Statistical Yearbook.*

HONDURAS - ECONOMIC CONDITIONS

Center for International Business Education Research (CIBER), Columbia Business School and School of International and Public Affairs, Uris Hall, Room 212, 3022 Broadway, New York, NY 10027-6902, Mr. Joshua Safier, (212) 854-4750, Fax: (212) 222-9821, www.columbia.edu/cu/ciber/; Datastream International.

Central Intelligence Agency, Office of Public Affairs, Washington, DC 20505, (703) 482-0623, Fax: (703) 482-1739, www.cia.gov; *The World Factbook.*

DSI Data Service Information, Xantener Strasse 51a, D-47495 Rheinberg, Germany, www.dsidata.com; *Campus Solution.*

Dun and Bradstreet (DB) Corporation, 103 JFK Parkway, Short Hills, NJ 07078, (973) 921-5500, www.dnb.com; *Country Report.*

Economist Intelligence Unit, 111 West 57th Street, New York, NY 10019, (212) 554-0600, Fax: (212) 586-1181, www.eiu.com; *Honduras Country Report.*

Euromonitor International, Inc., 224 S. Michigan Avenue, Suite 1500, Chicago, IL 60604, (312) 922-1115, Fax: (312) 922-1157, www.euromonitor.com; *International Marketing Data and Statistics 2008; The World Economic Factbook 2008;* and *World Marketing Data and Statistics.*

Inter-American Development Bank (IDB), 1300 New York Avenue, NW, Washington, DC 20577, (202) 623-1000, Fax: (202) 623-3096, www.iadb.org; *The Politics of Policies: Economic and Social Progress in Latin America - 2006 Report.*

International Monetary Fund (IMF), 700 Nineteenth Street, NW, Washington, DC 20431, (202) 623-7000, Fax: (202) 623-4661, www.imf.org; *World Economic Outlook Reports.*

M.E. Sharpe, 80 Business Park Drive, Armonk, NY 10504, (800) 541-6563, Fax: (914) 273-2106, www.mesharpe.com; *The Illustrated Book of World Rankings.*

Organization of American States (OAS), 17th Street Constitution Avenue NW, Washington, DC 20006, (202) 458-3000, www.oas.org; *The OAS in Transition: 1994-2004.*

Palgrave Macmillan Ltd., Houndmills, Basingstoke, Hampshire, RG21 6XS, England, (Telephone in U.S. (888) 330-8477), (Fax in U.S. (800) 672-2054), www.palgrave.com; *The Statesman's Yearbook 2008.*

Taylor and Francis Group, An Informa Business, 2 Park Square, Milton Park, Abingdon, Oxford OX14 4RN, United Kingdom, (Dial from U.S. (212) 216-7800), (Fax from U.S. (212) 564-7854), www.tandf.co.uk; *The Europa World Year Book.*

UCLA Latin American Institute, 10343 Bunche Hall, Box 951447, Los Angeles, CA 90095-1447, (310) 825-4571, Fax: (310) 206-6859, www.international.ucla.edu/lac; *Statistical Abstract of Latin America.*

United Nations Statistics Division, New York, NY 10017, (800) 253-9646, Fax: (212) 963-4116, http://unstats.un.org; *Economic Survey of Latin America and the Caribbean 2004-2005* and *World Statistics Pocketbook.*

The World Bank, 1818 H Street, NW, Washington, DC 20433, (202) 473-1000, Fax: (202) 477-6391, www.worldbank.org; *Global Economic Monitor (GEM); Global Economic Prospects 2008; Honduras; The World Bank Atlas 2003-2004;* and *World Development Report 2008.*

HONDURAS - ECONOMICS - SOCIOLOGICAL ASPECTS

Inter-American Development Bank (IDB), 1300 New York Avenue, NW, Washington, DC 20577, (202) 623-1000, Fax: (202) 623-3096, www.iadb.org; *The Politics of Policies: Economic and Social Progress in Latin America - 2006 Report.*

UCLA Latin American Institute, 10343 Bunche Hall, Box 951447, Los Angeles, CA 90095-1447, (310) 825-4571, Fax: (310) 206-6859, www.international.ucla.edu/lac; *Statistical Abstract of Latin America.*

HONDURAS - EDUCATION

Economist Intelligence Unit, 111 West 57th Street, New York, NY 10019, (212) 554-0600, Fax: (212) 586-1181, www.eiu.com; *Business Latin America.*

Euromonitor International, Inc., 224 S. Michigan Avenue, Suite 1500, Chicago, IL 60604, (312) 922-1115, Fax: (312) 922-1157, www.euromonitor.com; *International Marketing Data and Statistics 2008* and *World Marketing Data and Statistics.*

International Monetary Fund (IMF), 700 Nineteenth Street, NW, Washington, DC 20431, (202) 623-7000, Fax: (202) 623-4661, www.imf.org; *Government Finance Statistics Yearbook (2008 Edition).*

M.E. Sharpe, 80 Business Park Drive, Armonk, NY 10504, (800) 541-6563, Fax: (914) 273-2106, www.mesharpe.com; *The Illustrated Book of World Rankings.*

Palgrave Macmillan Ltd., Houndmills, Basingstoke, Hampshire, RG21 6XS, England, (Telephone in U.S. (888) 330-8477), (Fax in U.S. (800) 672-2054), www.palgrave.com; *The Statesman's Yearbook 2008.*

Taylor and Francis Group, An Informa Business, 2 Park Square, Milton Park, Abingdon, Oxford OX14 4RN, United Kingdom, (Dial from U.S. (212) 216-7800), (Fax from U.S. (212) 564-7854), www.tandf.co.uk; *The Europa World Year Book.*

UCLA Latin American Institute, 10343 Bunche Hall, Box 951447, Los Angeles, CA 90095-1447, (310) 825-4571, Fax: (310) 206-6859, www.international.ucla.edu/lac; *Statistical Abstract of Latin America.*

UNESCO Institute for Statistics, C.P. 6128 Succursale Centre-Ville, Montreal, Quebec, H3C 3J7 Canada, (Dial from U.S. (514) 343-6880), (Fax from U.S. (514) 343 6882), www.uis.unesco.org; *Statistical Tables.*

United Nations Statistics Division, New York, NY 10017, (800) 253-9646, Fax: (212) 963-4116, http://unstats.un.org; *Human Development Report 2006* and *Statistical Yearbook for Latin America and the Caribbean 2004.*

The World Bank, 1818 H Street, NW, Washington, DC 20433, (202) 473-1000, Fax: (202) 477-6391, www.worldbank.org; *Honduras; World Development Indicators (WDI) 2008;* and *World Development Report 2008.*

HONDURAS - ELECTRICITY

Economist Intelligence Unit, 111 West 57th Street, New York, NY 10019, (212) 554-0600, Fax: (212) 586-1181, www.eiu.com; *Business Latin America.*

Inter-American Development Bank (IDB), 1300 New York Avenue, NW, Washington, DC 20577, (202) 623-1000, Fax: (202) 623-3096, www.iadb.org; *The Politics of Policies: Economic and Social Progress in Latin America - 2006 Report.*

M.E. Sharpe, 80 Business Park Drive, Armonk, NY 10504, (800) 541-6563, Fax: (914) 273-2106, www.mesharpe.com; *The Illustrated Book of World Rankings.*

Organization of American States (OAS), 17th Street Constitution Avenue NW, Washington, DC 20006, (202) 458-3000, www.oas.org; *The OAS in Transition: 1994-2004.*

Palgrave Macmillan Ltd., Houndmills, Basingstoke, Hampshire, RG21 6XS, England, (Telephone in U.S. (888) 330-8477), (Fax in U.S. (800) 672-2054), www.palgrave.com; *The Statesman's Yearbook 2008.*

U.S. Department of Energy (DOE), Energy Information Administration (EIA), 1000 Independence Avenue, SW, Washington, DC 20585, (202) 586-8800, www.eia.doe.gov; *International Energy Annual 2004* and *International Energy Outlook 2006.*

United Nations Statistics Division, New York, NY 10017, (800) 253-9646, Fax: (212) 963-4116, http://unstats.un.org; *Human Development Report 2006* and *Statistical Yearbook.*

HONDURAS - EMIGRATION AND IMMIGRATION

UCLA Latin American Institute, 10343 Bunche Hall, Box 951447, Los Angeles, CA 90095-1447, (310) 825-4571, Fax: (310) 206-6859, www.international.ucla.edu/lac; *Statistical Abstract of Latin America.*

HONDURAS - EMPLOYMENT

Euromonitor International, Inc., 224 S. Michigan Avenue, Suite 1500, Chicago, IL 60604, (312) 922-1115, Fax: (312) 922-1157, www.euromonitor.com; *International Marketing Data and Statistics 2008.*

International Labour Office, I.L.O. Publications, 4 route des Morillons, CH-1211 Geneva 22, Switzerland, (Telephone in U.S. (202) 653-7652), (Fax in U.S. (202) 653-7687), www.ilo.org; *Yearbook of Labour Statistics 2006.*

M.E. Sharpe, 80 Business Park Drive, Armonk, NY 10504, (800) 541-6563, Fax: (914) 273-2106, www.mesharpe.com; *The Illustrated Book of World Rankings.*

UCLA Latin American Institute, 10343 Bunche Hall, Box 951447, Los Angeles, CA 90095-1447, (310) 825-4571, Fax: (310) 206-6859, www.international.ucla.edu/lac; *Statistical Abstract of Latin America.*

United Nations Statistics Division, New York, NY 10017, (800) 253-9646, Fax: (212) 963-4116, http://unstats.un.org; *Statistical Yearbook* and *Statistical Yearbook for Latin America and the Caribbean 2004.*

The World Bank, 1818 H Street, NW, Washington, DC 20433, (202) 473-1000, Fax: (202) 477-6391, www.worldbank.org; *Honduras.*

HONDURAS - ENERGY INDUSTRIES

Enerdata, 10 Rue Royale, 75008 Paris, France, www.enerdata.fr; *Global Energy Market Data.*

United Nations Statistics Division, New York, NY 10017, (800) 253-9646, Fax: (212) 963-4116, http://unstats.un.org; *Statistical Yearbook.*

HONDURAS - ENVIRONMENTAL CONDITIONS

DSI Data Service Information, Xantener Strasse 51a, D-47495 Rheinberg, Germany, www.dsidata.com; *Campus Solution* and *DSI's Global Environmental Database.*

Economist Intelligence Unit, 111 West 57th Street, New York, NY 10019, (212) 554-0600, Fax: (212) 586-1181, www.eiu.com; *Honduras Country Report.*

United Nations Statistics Division, New York, NY 10017, (800) 253-9646, Fax: (212) 963-4116, http://unstats.un.org; *World Statistics Pocketbook.*

HONDURAS - EXPENDITURES, PUBLIC

Inter-American Development Bank (IDB), 1300 New York Avenue, NW, Washington, DC 20577, (202) 623-1000, Fax: (202) 623-3096, www.iadb.org; *The Politics of Policies: Economic and Social Progress in Latin America - 2006 Report.*

Organization of American States (OAS), 17th Street Constitution Avenue NW, Washington, DC 20006, (202) 458-3000, www.oas.org; *The OAS in Transition: 1994-2004.*

United Nations Statistics Division, New York, NY 10017, (800) 253-9646, Fax: (212) 963-4116, http://unstats.un.org; *Statistical Yearbook for Latin America and the Caribbean 2004.*

HONDURAS - EXPORTS

Central Intelligence Agency, Office of Public Affairs, Washington, DC 20505, (703) 482-0623, Fax: (703) 482-1739, www.cia.gov; *The World Factbook.*

Economist Intelligence Unit, 111 West 57th Street, New York, NY 10019, (212) 554-0600, Fax: (212) 586-1181, www.eiu.com; *Business Latin America* and *Honduras Country Report.*

Euromonitor International, Inc., 224 S. Michigan Avenue, Suite 1500, Chicago, IL 60604, (312) 922-1115, Fax: (312) 922-1157, www.euromonitor.com; *International Marketing Data and Statistics 2008* and *The World Economic Factbook 2008.*

Inter-American Development Bank (IDB), 1300 New York Avenue, NW, Washington, DC 20577, (202) 623-1000, Fax: (202) 623-3096, www.iadb.org; *The Politics of Policies: Economic and Social Progress in Latin America - 2006 Report.*

International Monetary Fund (IMF), 700 Nineteenth Street, NW, Washington, DC 20431, (202) 623-7000, Fax: (202) 623-4661, www.imf.org; *Direction of Trade Statistics Yearbook 2007; Government Finance Statistics Yearbook (2008 Edition);* and *International Financial Statistics Yearbook 2007.*

Organization of American States (OAS), 17th Street Constitution Avenue NW, Washington, DC 20006, (202) 458-3000, www.oas.org; *The OAS in Transition: 1994-2004.*

Palgrave Macmillan Ltd., Houndmills, Basingstoke, Hampshire, RG21 6XS, England, (Telephone in U.S. (888) 330-8477), (Fax in U.S. (800) 672-2054), www.palgrave.com; *The Statesman's Yearbook 2008.*

Taylor and Francis Group, An Informa Business, 2 Park Square, Milton Park, Abingdon, Oxford OX14 4RN, United Kingdom, (Dial from U.S. (212) 216-7800), (Fax from U.S. (212) 564-7854), www.tandf.co.uk; *The Europa World Year Book.*

United Nations Conference on Trade and Development (UNCTAD), DC2-1120, United Nations, New York, NY 10017, (212) 963-0027, www.unctad.org; *Handbook of Statistics 2005.*

United Nations Food and Agricultural Organization (FAO), Viale delle Terme di Caracalla, 00100 Rome, Italy, (Dial from U.S. (202) 653-2400), (Fax from U.S. (202) 653 5760), www.fao.org; *The State of Food and Agriculture (SOFA) 2006.*

United Nations Statistics Division, New York, NY 10017, (800) 253-9646, Fax: (212) 963-4116, http://unstats.un.org; *Statistical Yearbook for Latin America and the Caribbean 2004.*

The World Bank, 1818 H Street, NW, Washington, DC 20433, (202) 473-1000, Fax: (202) 477-6391, www.worldbank.org; *World Development Indicators (WDI) 2008* and *World Development Report 2008.*

HONDURAS - FEMALE WORKING POPULATION

See HONDURAS - EMPLOYMENT

HONDURAS - FERTILITY, HUMAN

Central Intelligence Agency, Office of Public Affairs, Washington, DC 20505, (703) 482-0623, Fax: (703) 482-1739, www.cia.gov; *The World Factbook.*

M.E. Sharpe, 80 Business Park Drive, Armonk, NY 10504, (800) 541-6563, Fax: (914) 273-2106, www.mesharpe.com; *The Illustrated Book of World Rankings.*

United Nations Statistics Division, New York, NY 10017, (800) 253-9646, Fax: (212) 963-4116, http://unstats.un.org; *Human Development Report 2006.*

The World Bank, 1818 H Street, NW, Washington, DC 20433, (202) 473-1000, Fax: (202) 477-6391, www.worldbank.org; *The World Bank Atlas 2003-2004; World Development Indicators (WDI) 2008;* and *World Development Report 2008.*

HONDURAS - FERTILIZER INDUSTRY

Economist Intelligence Unit, 111 West 57th Street, New York, NY 10019, (212) 554-0600, Fax: (212) 586-1181, www.eiu.com; *Business Latin America.*

United Nations Food and Agricultural Organization (FAO), Viale delle Terme di Caracalla, 00100 Rome, Italy, (Dial from U.S. (202) 653-2400), (Fax from U.S. (202) 653 5760), www.fao.org; *The State of Food and Agriculture (SOFA) 2006.*

United Nations Statistics Division, New York, NY 10017, (800) 253-9646, Fax: (212) 963-4116, http://unstats.un.org; *Statistical Yearbook.*

HONDURAS - FETAL MORTALITY

See HONDURAS - MORTALITY

HONDURAS - FINANCE

Inter-American Development Bank (IDB), 1300 New York Avenue, NW, Washington, DC 20577, (202) 623-1000, Fax: (202) 623-3096, www.iadb.org; *The Politics of Policies: Economic and Social Progress in Latin America - 2006 Report.*

Organization of American States (OAS), 17th Street Constitution Avenue NW, Washington, DC 20006, (202) 458-3000, www.oas.org; *The OAS in Transition: 1994-2004.*

Taylor and Francis Group, An Informa Business, 2 Park Square, Milton Park, Abingdon, Oxford OX14 4RN, United Kingdom, (Dial from U.S. (212) 216-7800), (Fax from U.S. (212) 564-7854), www.tandf.co.uk; *The Europa World Year Book.*

UCLA Latin American Institute, 10343 Bunche Hall, Box 951447, Los Angeles, CA 90095-1447, (310) 825-4571, Fax: (310) 206-6859, www.international.ucla.edu/lac; *Statistical Abstract of Latin America.*

United Nations Statistics Division, New York, NY 10017, (800) 253-9646, Fax: (212) 963-4116, http://unstats.un.org; *National Accounts Statistics: Compendium of Income Distribution Statistics* and *Statistical Yearbook.*

The World Bank, 1818 H Street, NW, Washington, DC 20433, (202) 473-1000, Fax: (202) 477-6391, www.worldbank.org; *Honduras.*

HONDURAS - FINANCE, PUBLIC

Bernan Essential Government Publications, 4611-F Assembly Drive, Lanham MD, 20706-4391, (301) 459-2255, Fax: (800) 865-3450, www.bernan.com; *National Accounts Statistics.*

Economist Intelligence Unit, 111 West 57th Street, New York, NY 10019, (212) 554-0600, Fax: (212) 586-1181, www.eiu.com; *Honduras Country Report.*

Inter-American Development Bank (IDB), 1300 New York Avenue, NW, Washington, DC 20577, (202) 623-1000, Fax: (202) 623-3096, www.iadb.org; *The Politics of Policies: Economic and Social Progress in Latin America - 2006 Report.*

International Monetary Fund (IMF), 700 Nineteenth Street, NW, Washington, DC 20431, (202) 623-7000, Fax: (202) 623-4661, www.imf.org; *Government Finance Statistics Yearbook (2008 Edition); International Financial Statistics; International Financial Statistics Online Service;* and *International Financial Statistics Yearbook 2007.*

M.E. Sharpe, 80 Business Park Drive, Armonk, NY 10504, (800) 541-6563, Fax: (914) 273-2106, www.mesharpe.com; *The Illustrated Book of World Rankings.*

Organization of American States (OAS), 17th Street Constitution Avenue NW, Washington, DC 20006, (202) 458-3000, www.oas.org; *The OAS in Transition: 1994-2004.*

Palgrave Macmillan Ltd., Houndmills, Basingstoke, Hampshire, RG21 6XS, England, (Telephone in U.S. (888) 330-8477), (Fax in U.S. (800) 672-2054), www.palgrave.com; *The Statesman's Yearbook 2008.*

Taylor and Francis Group, An Informa Business, 2 Park Square, Milton Park, Abingdon, Oxford OX14 4RN, United Kingdom, (Dial from U.S. (212) 216-7800), (Fax from U.S. (212) 564-7854), www.tandf.co.uk; *The Europa World Year Book.*

UCLA Latin American Institute, 10343 Bunche Hall, Box 951447, Los Angeles, CA 90095-1447, (310) 825-4571, Fax: (310) 206-6859, www.international.ucla.edu/lac; *Statistical Abstract of Latin America.*

The World Bank, 1818 H Street, NW, Washington, DC 20433, (202) 473-1000, Fax: (202) 477-6391, www.worldbank.org; *Honduras.*

HONDURAS - FISHERIES

Inter-American Development Bank (IDB), 1300 New York Avenue, NW, Washington, DC 20577, (202) 623-1000, Fax: (202) 623-3096, www.iadb.org; *The Politics of Policies: Economic and Social Progress in Latin America - 2006 Report.*

M.E. Sharpe, 80 Business Park Drive, Armonk, NY 10504, (800) 541-6563, Fax: (914) 273-2106, www.mesharpe.com; *The Illustrated Book of World Rankings.*

Palgrave Macmillan Ltd., Houndmills, Basingstoke, Hampshire, RG21 6XS, England, (Telephone in U.S. (888) 330-8477), (Fax in U.S. (800) 672-2054), www.palgrave.com; *The Statesman's Yearbook 2008.*

Taylor and Francis Group, An Informa Business, 2 Park Square, Milton Park, Abingdon, Oxford OX14 4RN, United Kingdom, (Dial from U.S. (212) 216-7800), (Fax from U.S. (212) 564-7854), www.tandf.co.uk; *The Europa World Year Book.*

UCLA Latin American Institute, 10343 Bunche Hall, Box 951447, Los Angeles, CA 90095-1447, (310) 825-4571, Fax: (310) 206-6859, www.international.ucla.edu/lac; *Statistical Abstract of Latin America.*

United Nations Conference on Trade and Development (UNCTAD), DC2-1120, United Nations, New York, NY 10017, (212) 963-0027, www.unctad.org; *UNCTAD Commodity Yearbook.*

United Nations Food and Agricultural Organization (FAO), Viale delle Terme di Caracalla, 00100 Rome, Italy, (Dial from U.S. (202) 653-2400), (Fax from U.S. (202) 653 5760), www.fao.org; *FAO Yearbook of Fishery Statistics;* Fishery Databases; FISHSTAT Database. Subjects covered include: Aquaculture production, capture production, fishery commodities; and *The State of Food and Agriculture (SOFA) 2006.*

United Nations Statistics Division, New York, NY 10017, (800) 253-9646, Fax: (212) 963-4116, http://unstats.un.org; *Statistical Yearbook.*

The World Bank, 1818 H Street, NW, Washington, DC 20433, (202) 473-1000, Fax: (202) 477-6391, www.worldbank.org; *Honduras.*

HONDURAS - FLOUR INDUSTRY

United Nations Statistics Division, New York, NY 10017, (800) 253-9646, Fax: (212) 963-4116, http://unstats.un.org; *Statistical Yearbook.*

HONDURAS - FOOD

United Nations Conference on Trade and Development (UNCTAD), DC2-1120, United Nations, New York, NY 10017, (212) 963-0027, www.unctad.org; *UNCTAD Commodity Yearbook.*

United Nations Food and Agricultural Organization (FAO), Viale delle Terme di Caracalla, 00100 Rome, Italy, (Dial from U.S. (202) 653-2400), (Fax from U.S. (202) 653 5760), www.fao.org; *FAO Production Yearbook 2002* and *The State of Food and Agriculture (SOFA) 2006.*

United Nations Statistics Division, New York, NY 10017, (800) 253-9646, Fax: (212) 963-4116, http://unstats.un.org; *Human Development Report 2006.*

HONDURAS - FOREIGN EXCHANGE RATES

Central Intelligence Agency, Office of Public Affairs, Washington, DC 20505, (703) 482-0623, Fax: (703) 482-1739, www.cia.gov; *The World Factbook.*

Euromonitor International, Inc., 224 S. Michigan Avenue, Suite 1500, Chicago, IL 60604, (312) 922-1115, Fax: (312) 922-1157, www.euromonitor.com; *International Marketing Data and Statistics 2008* and *The World Economic Factbook 2008.*

Inter-American Development Bank (IDB), 1300 New York Avenue, NW, Washington, DC 20577, (202) 623-1000, Fax: (202) 623-3096, www.iadb.org; *The Politics of Policies: Economic and Social Progress in Latin America - 2006 Report.*

International Civil Aviation Organization (ICAO), External Relations and Public Information Office (EPO), 999 University Street, Montreal, Quebec H3C 5H7, Canada, (Dial from U.S. (514) 954-8219), (Fax from U.S. (514) 954-6077), www.icao.int; *Civil Aviation Statistics of the World.*

International Monetary Fund (IMF), 700 Nineteenth Street, NW, Washington, DC 20431, (202) 623-7000, Fax: (202) 623-4661, www.imf.org; *International Financial Statistics Yearbook 2007.*

Organization of American States (OAS), 17th Street Constitution Avenue NW, Washington, DC 20006, (202) 458-3000, www.oas.org; *The OAS in Transition: 1994-2004.*

Taylor and Francis Group, An Informa Business, 2 Park Square, Milton Park, Abingdon, Oxford OX14 4RN, United Kingdom, (Dial from U.S. (212) 216-7800), (Fax from U.S. (212) 564-7854), www.tandf.co.uk; *The Europa World Year Book.*

UCLA Latin American Institute, 10343 Bunche Hall, Box 951447, Los Angeles, CA 90095-1447, (310) 825-4571, Fax: (310) 206-6859, www.international.ucla.edu/lac; *Statistical Abstract of Latin America.*

United Nations Statistics Division, New York, NY 10017, (800) 253-9646, Fax: (212) 963-4116, http://unstats.un.org; *Statistical Yearbook* and *World Statistics Pocketbook.*

HONDURAS - FORESTS AND FORESTRY

Economist Intelligence Unit, 111 West 57th Street, New York, NY 10019, (212) 554-0600, Fax: (212) 586-1181, www.eiu.com; *Business Latin America.*

Inter-American Development Bank (IDB), 1300 New York Avenue, NW, Washington, DC 20577, (202) 623-1000, Fax: (202) 623-3096, www.iadb.org; *The Politics of Policies: Economic and Social Progress in Latin America - 2006 Report.*

International Monetary Fund (IMF), 700 Nineteenth Street, NW, Washington, DC 20431, (202) 623-7000, Fax: (202) 623-4661, www.imf.org; *International Financial Statistics Yearbook 2007.*

M.E. Sharpe, 80 Business Park Drive, Armonk, NY 10504, (800) 541-6563, Fax: (914) 273-2106, www.mesharpe.com; *The Illustrated Book of World Rankings.*

Palgrave Macmillan Ltd., Houndmills, Basingstoke, Hampshire, RG21 6XS, England, (Telephone in U.S. (888) 330-8477), (Fax in U.S. (800) 672-2054), www.palgrave.com; *The Statesman's Yearbook 2008.*

Taylor and Francis Group, An Informa Business, 2 Park Square, Milton Park, Abingdon, Oxford OX14 4RN, United Kingdom, (Dial from U.S. (212) 216-7800), (Fax from U.S. (212) 564-7854), www.tandf.co.uk; *The Europa World Year Book.*

UCLA Latin American Institute, 10343 Bunche Hall, Box 951447, Los Angeles, CA 90095-1447, (310) 825-4571, Fax: (310) 206-6859, www.international.ucla.edu/lac; *Statistical Abstract of Latin America.*

UNESCO Institute for Statistics, C.P. 6128 Succursale Centre-Ville, Montreal, Quebec, H3C 3J7

Canada, (Dial from U.S. (514) 343-6880), (Fax from U.S. (514) 343 6882), www.uis.unesco.org; *Statistical Tables.*

United Nations Conference on Trade and Development (UNCTAD), DC2-1120, United Nations, New York, NY 10017, (212) 963-0027, www.unctad.org; *UNCTAD Commodity Yearbook.*

United Nations Food and Agricultural Organization (FAO), Viale delle Terme di Caracalla, 00100 Rome, Italy, (Dial from U.S. (202) 653-2400), (Fax from U.S. (202) 653 5760), www.fao.org; *FAO Yearbook of Forest Products* and *The State of Food and Agriculture (SOFA) 2006.*

United Nations Statistics Division, New York, NY 10017, (800) 253-9646, Fax: (212) 963-4116, http://unstats.un.org; *Statistical Yearbook.*

The World Bank, 1818 H Street, NW, Washington, DC 20433, (202) 473-1000, Fax: (202) 477-6391, www.worldbank.org; *Honduras* and *World Development Report 2008.*

HONDURAS - GAS PRODUCTION

See HONDURAS - MINERAL INDUSTRIES

HONDURAS - GEOGRAPHIC INFORMATION SYSTEMS

M.E. Sharpe, 80 Business Park Drive, Armonk, NY 10504, (800) 541-6563, Fax: (914) 273-2106, www.mesharpe.com; *The Illustrated Book of World Rankings.*

UCLA Latin American Institute, 10343 Bunche Hall, Box 951447, Los Angeles, CA 90095-1447, (310) 825-4571, Fax: (310) 206-6859, www.international.ucla.edu/lac; *Statistical Abstract of Latin America.*

The World Bank, 1818 H Street, NW, Washington, DC 20433, (202) 473-1000, Fax: (202) 477-6391, www.worldbank.org; *Honduras.*

HONDURAS - GOLD INDUSTRY

Economist Intelligence Unit, 111 West 57th Street, New York, NY 10019, (212) 554-0600, Fax: (212) 586-1181, www.eiu.com; *Business Latin America.*

International Monetary Fund (IMF), 700 Nineteenth Street, NW, Washington, DC 20431, (202) 623-7000, Fax: (202) 623-4661, www.imf.org; *International Financial Statistics Yearbook 2007.*

United Nations Statistics Division, New York, NY 10017, (800) 253-9646, Fax: (212) 963-4116, http://unstats.un.org; *Statistical Yearbook.*

HONDURAS - GOLD PRODUCTION

See HONDURAS - MINERAL INDUSTRIES

HONDURAS - GRANTS-IN-AID

International Monetary Fund (IMF), 700 Nineteenth Street, NW, Washington, DC 20431, (202) 623-7000, Fax: (202) 623-4661, www.imf.org; *Government Finance Statistics Yearbook (2008 Edition).*

HONDURAS - GROSS DOMESTIC PRODUCT

Economist Intelligence Unit, 111 West 57th Street, New York, NY 10019, (212) 554-0600, Fax: (212) 586-1181, www.eiu.com; *Business Latin America* and *Honduras Country Report.*

Euromonitor International, Inc., 224 S. Michigan Avenue, Suite 1500, Chicago, IL 60604, (312) 922-1115, Fax: (312) 922-1157, www.euromonitor.com; *International Marketing Data and Statistics 2008* and *The World Economic Factbook 2008.*

Inter-American Development Bank (IDB), 1300 New York Avenue, NW, Washington, DC 20577, (202) 623-1000, Fax: (202) 623-3096, www.iadb.org; *The Politics of Policies: Economic and Social Progress in Latin America - 2006 Report.*

M.E. Sharpe, 80 Business Park Drive, Armonk, NY 10504, (800) 541-6563, Fax: (914) 273-2106, www.mesharpe.com; *The Illustrated Book of World Rankings.*

Organization of American States (OAS), 17th Street Constitution Avenue NW, Washington, DC 20006, (202) 458-3000, www.oas.org; *The OAS in Transition: 1994-2004.*

Taylor and Francis Group, An Informa Business, 2 Park Square, Milton Park, Abingdon, Oxford OX14 4RN, United Kingdom, (Dial from U.S. (212) 216-7800), (Fax from U.S. (212) 564-7854), www.tandf.co.uk; *The Europa World Year Book.*

United Nations Statistics Division, New York, NY 10017, (800) 253-9646, Fax: (212) 963-4116, http://unstats.un.org; *Human Development Report 2006; National Accounts Statistics: Compendium of Income Distribution Statistics; Statistical Yearbook;* and *Statistical Yearbook for Latin America and the Caribbean 2004.*

The World Bank, 1818 H Street, NW, Washington, DC 20433, (202) 473-1000, Fax: (202) 477-6391, www.worldbank.org; *World Development Indicators (WDI) 2008* and *World Development Report 2008.*

HONDURAS - GROSS NATIONAL PRODUCT

Euromonitor International, Inc., 224 S. Michigan Avenue, Suite 1500, Chicago, IL 60604, (312) 922-1115, Fax: (312) 922-1157, www.euromonitor.com; *International Marketing Data and Statistics 2008.*

Inter-American Development Bank (IDB), 1300 New York Avenue, NW, Washington, DC 20577, (202) 623-1000, Fax: (202) 623-3096, www.iadb.org; *The Politics of Policies: Economic and Social Progress in Latin America - 2006 Report.*

M.E. Sharpe, 80 Business Park Drive, Armonk, NY 10504, (800) 541-6563, Fax: (914) 273-2106, www.mesharpe.com; *The Illustrated Book of World Rankings.*

Palgrave Macmillan Ltd., Houndmills, Basingstoke, Hampshire, RG21 6XS, England, (Telephone in U.S. (888) 330-8477), (Fax in U.S. (800) 672-2054), www.palgrave.com; *The Statesman's Yearbook 2008.*

U.S. Department of State (DOS), 2201 C Street NW, Washington, DC 20520, (202) 647-4000, www.state.gov; *World Military Expenditures and Arms Transfers (WMEAT).*

United Nations Statistics Division, New York, NY 10017, (800) 253-9646, Fax: (212) 963-4116, http://unstats.un.org; *Statistical Yearbook.*

The World Bank, 1818 H Street, NW, Washington, DC 20433, (202) 473-1000, Fax: (202) 477-6391, www.worldbank.org; *The World Bank Atlas 2003-2004; World Development Indicators (WDI) 2008;* and *World Development Report 2008.*

HONDURAS - HIDES AND SKINS INDUSTRY

United Nations Food and Agricultural Organization (FAO), Viale delle Terme di Caracalla, 00100 Rome, Italy, (Dial from U.S. (202) 653-2400), (Fax from U.S. (202) 653 5760), www.fao.org; *FAO Production Yearbook 2002.*

HONDURAS - HOUSING

Euromonitor International, Inc., 224 S. Michigan Avenue, Suite 1500, Chicago, IL 60604, (312) 922-1115, Fax: (312) 922-1157, www.euromonitor.com; *World Marketing Data and Statistics.*

M.E. Sharpe, 80 Business Park Drive, Armonk, NY 10504, (800) 541-6563, Fax: (914) 273-2106, www.mesharpe.com; *The Illustrated Book of World Rankings.*

UCLA Latin American Institute, 10343 Bunche Hall, Box 951447, Los Angeles, CA 90095-1447, (310) 825-4571, Fax: (310) 206-6859, www.international.ucla.edu/lac; *Statistical Abstract of Latin America.*

United Nations Statistics Division, New York, NY 10017, (800) 253-9646, Fax: (212) 963-4116, http://unstats.un.org; *Statistical Yearbook for Latin America and the Caribbean 2004.*

HONDURAS - ILLITERATE PERSONS

Euromonitor International, Inc., 224 S. Michigan Avenue, Suite 1500, Chicago, IL 60604, (312) 922-1115, Fax: (312) 922-1157, www.euromonitor.com; *The World Economic Factbook 2008.*

Palgrave Macmillan Ltd., Houndmills, Basingstoke, Hampshire, RG21 6XS, England, (Telephone in U.S. (888) 330-8477), (Fax in U.S. (800) 672-2054), www.palgrave.com; *The Statesman's Yearbook 2008.*

UNESCO Institute for Statistics, C.P. 6128 Succursale Centre-Ville, Montreal, Quebec, H3C 3J7 Canada, (Dial from U.S. (514) 343-6880), (Fax from U.S. (514) 343 6882), www.uis.unesco.org; *Statistical Tables.*

United Nations Statistics Division, New York, NY 10017, (800) 253-9646, Fax: (212) 963-4116, http://unstats.un.org; *Human Development Report 2006* and *Statistical Yearbook for Latin America and the Caribbean 2004.*

HONDURAS - IMPORTS

Central Intelligence Agency, Office of Public Affairs, Washington, DC 20505, (703) 482-0623, Fax: (703) 482-1739, www.cia.gov; *The World Factbook.*

Economist Intelligence Unit, 111 West 57th Street, New York, NY 10019, (212) 554-0600, Fax: (212) 586-1181, www.eiu.com; *Business Latin America* and *Honduras Country Report.*

Euromonitor International, Inc., 224 S. Michigan Avenue, Suite 1500, Chicago, IL 60604, (312) 922-1115, Fax: (312) 922-1157, www.euromonitor.com; *International Marketing Data and Statistics 2008* and *The World Economic Factbook 2008.*

Inter-American Development Bank (IDB), 1300 New York Avenue, NW, Washington, DC 20577, (202) 623-1000, Fax: (202) 623-3096, www.iadb.org; *The Politics of Policies: Economic and Social Progress in Latin America - 2006 Report.*

International Monetary Fund (IMF), 700 Nineteenth Street, NW, Washington, DC 20431, (202) 623-7000, Fax: (202) 623-4661, www.imf.org; *Direction of Trade Statistics Yearbook 2007; Government Finance Statistics Yearbook (2008 Edition);* and *International Financial Statistics Yearbook 2007.*

Organization of American States (OAS), 17th Street Constitution Avenue NW, Washington, DC 20006, (202) 458-3000, www.oas.org; *The OAS in Transition: 1994-2004.*

Palgrave Macmillan Ltd., Houndmills, Basingstoke, Hampshire, RG21 6XS, England, (Telephone in U.S. (888) 330-8477), (Fax in U.S. (800) 672-2054), www.palgrave.com; *The Statesman's Yearbook 2008.*

Taylor and Francis Group, An Informa Business, 2 Park Square, Milton Park, Abingdon, Oxford OX14 4RN, United Kingdom, (Dial from U.S. (212) 216-7800), (Fax from U.S. (212) 564-7854), www.tandf.co.uk; *The Europa World Year Book.*

United Nations Conference on Trade and Development (UNCTAD), DC2-1120, United Nations, New York, NY 10017, (212) 963-0027, www.unctad.org; *Handbook of Statistics 2005.*

United Nations Food and Agricultural Organization (FAO), Viale delle Terme di Caracalla, 00100 Rome, Italy, (Dial from U.S. (202) 653-2400), (Fax from U.S. (202) 653 5760), www.fao.org; *The State of Food and Agriculture (SOFA) 2006.*

United Nations Statistics Division, New York, NY 10017, (800) 253-9646, Fax: (212) 963-4116, http://unstats.un.org; *Statistical Yearbook* and *Statistical Yearbook for Latin America and the Caribbean 2004.*

The World Bank, 1818 H Street, NW, Washington, DC 20433, (202) 473-1000, Fax: (202) 477-6391, www.worldbank.org; *World Development Indicators (WDI) 2008* and *World Development Report 2008.*

HONDURAS - INCOME DISTRIBUTION

UCLA Latin American Institute, 10343 Bunche Hall, Box 951447, Los Angeles, CA 90095-1447, (310) 825-4571, Fax: (310) 206-6859, www.international.ucla.edu/lac; *Statistical Abstract of Latin America.*

United Nations Statistics Division, New York, NY 10017, (800) 253-9646, Fax: (212) 963-4116, http://unstats.un.org; *Statistical Yearbook for Latin America and the Caribbean 2004.*

HONDURAS - INCOME TAXES

See HONDURAS - TAXATION

HONDURAS - INDUSTRIAL PRODUCTIVITY

Euromonitor International, Inc., 224 S. Michigan Avenue, Suite 1500, Chicago, IL 60604, (312) 922-1115, Fax: (312) 922-1157, www.euromonitor.com; *International Marketing Data and Statistics 2008.*

M.E. Sharpe, 80 Business Park Drive, Armonk, NY 10504, (800) 541-6563, Fax: (914) 273-2106, www.mesharpe.com; *The Illustrated Book of World Rankings.*

HONDURAS - INDUSTRIAL PROPERTY

United Nations Statistics Division, New York, NY 10017, (800) 253-9646, Fax: (212) 963-4116, http://unstats.un.org; *Statistical Yearbook.*

World Intellectual Property Organization (WIPO), PO Box 18, CH-1211 Geneva 20, Switzerland, www.wipo.int; *Industrial Property Statistics* and *Industrial Property Statistics Online Directory.*

HONDURAS - INDUSTRIAL STATISTICS

United Nations Statistics Division, New York, NY 10017, (800) 253-9646, Fax: (212) 963-4116, http://unstats.un.org; *Economic Survey of Latin America and the Caribbean 2004-2005.*

HONDURAS - INDUSTRIES

Central Intelligence Agency, Office of Public Affairs, Washington, DC 20505, (703) 482-0623, Fax: (703) 482-1739, www.cia.gov; *The World Factbook.*

Economist Intelligence Unit, 111 West 57th Street, New York, NY 10019, (212) 554-0600, Fax: (212) 586-1181, www.eiu.com; *Honduras Country Report.*

Euromonitor International, Inc., 224 S. Michigan Avenue, Suite 1500, Chicago, IL 60604, (312) 922-1115, Fax: (312) 922-1157, www.euromonitor.com; *International Marketing Data and Statistics 2008; The World Economic Factbook 2008;* and *World Marketing Data and Statistics.*

International Labour Office, I.L.O. Publications, 4 route des Morillons, CH-1211 Geneva 22, Switzerland, (Telephone in U.S. (202) 653-7652), (Fax in U.S. (202) 653-7687), www.ilo.org; *Yearbook of Labour Statistics 2006.*

M.E. Sharpe, 80 Business Park Drive, Armonk, NY 10504, (800) 541-6563, Fax: (914) 273-2106, www.mesharpe.com; *The Illustrated Book of World Rankings.*

Palgrave Macmillan Ltd., Houndmills, Basingstoke, Hampshire, RG21 6XS, England, (Telephone in U.S. (888) 330-8477), (Fax in U.S. (800) 672-2054), www.palgrave.com; *The Statesman's Yearbook 2008.*

Taylor and Francis Group, An Informa Business, 2 Park Square, Milton Park, Abingdon, Oxford OX14 4RN, United Kingdom, (Dial from U.S. (212) 216-7800), (Fax from U.S. (212) 564-7854), www.tandf.co.uk; *The Europa World Year Book.*

UCLA Latin American Institute, 10343 Bunche Hall, Box 951447, Los Angeles, CA 90095-1447, (310) 825-4571, Fax: (310) 206-6859, www.international.ucla.edu/lac; *Statistical Abstract of Latin America.*

United Nations Industrial Development Organization (UNIDO), 1 United Nations Plaza, New York, NY 10017, (212) 963 6890, Fax: (212) 963-7904, http://unido.org; Industrial Statistics Database 2008 (INDSTAT) and *The International Yearbook of Industrial Statistics 2008.*

United Nations Statistics Division, New York, NY 10017, (800) 253-9646, Fax: (212) 963-4116, http://unstats.un.org; *2004 Industrial Commodity Statistics Yearbook* and *Statistical Yearbook.*

The World Bank, 1818 H Street, NW, Washington, DC 20433, (202) 473-1000, Fax: (202) 477-6391, www.worldbank.org; *Honduras* and *World Development Indicators (WDI) 2008.*

HONDURAS - INFANT AND MATERNAL MORTALITY

See HONDURAS - MORTALITY

HONDURAS - INFLATION (FINANCE)

United Nations Statistics Division, New York, NY 10017, (800) 253-9646, Fax: (212) 963-4116, http://unstats.un.org; *Economic Survey of Latin America and the Caribbean 2004-2005.*

HONDURAS - INTEREST RATES

Inter-American Development Bank (IDB), 1300 New York Avenue, NW, Washington, DC 20577, (202) 623-1000, Fax: (202) 623-3096, www.iadb.org; *The Politics of Policies: Economic and Social Progress in Latin America - 2006 Report.*

Organization of American States (OAS), 17th Street Constitution Avenue NW, Washington, DC 20006, (202) 458-3000, www.oas.org; *The OAS in Transition: 1994-2004.*

HONDURAS - INTERNAL REVENUE

Inter-American Development Bank (IDB), 1300 New York Avenue, NW, Washington, DC 20577, (202) 623-1000, Fax: (202) 623-3096, www.iadb.org; *The Politics of Policies: Economic and Social Progress in Latin America - 2006 Report.*

Organization of American States (OAS), 17th Street Constitution Avenue NW, Washington, DC 20006, (202) 458-3000, www.oas.org; *The OAS in Transition: 1994-2004.*

HONDURAS - INTERNATIONAL FINANCE

Inter-American Development Bank (IDB), 1300 New York Avenue, NW, Washington, DC 20577, (202) 623-1000, Fax: (202) 623-3096, www.iadb.org; *The Politics of Policies: Economic and Social Progress in Latin America - 2006 Report.*

UCLA Latin American Institute, 10343 Bunche Hall, Box 951447, Los Angeles, CA 90095-1447, (310) 825-4571, Fax: (310) 206-6859, www.international.ucla.edu/lac; *Statistical Abstract of Latin America.*

United Nations Statistics Division, New York, NY 10017, (800) 253-9646, Fax: (212) 963-4116, http://unstats.un.org; *Statistical Yearbook for Latin America and the Caribbean 2004.*

HONDURAS - INTERNATIONAL LIQUIDITY

Inter-American Development Bank (IDB), 1300 New York Avenue, NW, Washington, DC 20577, (202) 623-1000, Fax: (202) 623-3096, www.iadb.org; *The Politics of Policies: Economic and Social Progress in Latin America - 2006 Report.*

International Monetary Fund (IMF), 700 Nineteenth Street, NW, Washington, DC 20431, (202) 623-7000, Fax: (202) 623-4661, www.imf.org; *International Financial Statistics Yearbook 2007.*

HONDURAS - INTERNATIONAL STATISTICS

Inter-American Development Bank (IDB), 1300 New York Avenue, NW, Washington, DC 20577, (202) 623-1000, Fax: (202) 623-3096, www.iadb.org; *The Politics of Policies: Economic and Social Progress in Latin America - 2006 Report.*

UCLA Latin American Institute, 10343 Bunche Hall, Box 951447, Los Angeles, CA 90095-1447, (310) 825-4571, Fax: (310) 206-6859, www.international.ucla.edu/lac; *Statistical Abstract of Latin America.*

HONDURAS - INTERNATIONAL TRADE

Economist Intelligence Unit, 111 West 57th Street, New York, NY 10019, (212) 554-0600, Fax: (212) 586-1181, www.eiu.com; *Business Latin America* and *Honduras Country Report.*

Euromonitor International, Inc., 224 S. Michigan Avenue, Suite 1500, Chicago, IL 60604, (312) 922-1115, Fax: (312) 922-1157, www.euromonitor.com; *International Marketing Data and Statistics 2008; The World Economic Factbook 2008;* and *World Marketing Data and Statistics.*

Inter-American Development Bank (IDB), 1300 New York Avenue, NW, Washington, DC 20577, (202) 623-1000, Fax: (202) 623-3096, www.iadb.org; *The Politics of Policies: Economic and Social Progress in Latin America - 2006 Report.*

International Monetary Fund (IMF), 700 Nineteenth Street, NW, Washington, DC 20431, (202) 623-7000, Fax: (202) 623-4661, www.imf.org; *International Financial Statistics Yearbook 2007.*

M.E. Sharpe, 80 Business Park Drive, Armonk, NY 10504, (800) 541-6563, Fax: (914) 273-2106, www.mesharpe.com; *The Illustrated Book of World Rankings.*

Palgrave Macmillan Ltd., Houndmills, Basingstoke, Hampshire, RG21 6XS, England, (Telephone in U.S. (888) 330-8477), (Fax in U.S. (800) 672-2054), www.palgrave.com; *The Statesman's Yearbook 2008.*

Taylor and Francis Group, An Informa Business, 2 Park Square, Milton Park, Abingdon, Oxford OX14 4RN, United Kingdom, (Dial from U.S. (212) 216-7800), (Fax from U.S. (212) 564-7854), www.tandf.co.uk; *The Europa World Year Book.*

UCLA Latin American Institute, 10343 Bunche Hall, Box 951447, Los Angeles, CA 90095-1447, (310) 825-4571, Fax: (310) 206-6859, www.international.ucla.edu/lac; *Statistical Abstract of Latin America.*

United Nations Conference on Trade and Development (UNCTAD), DC2-1120, United Nations, New York, NY 10017, (212) 963-0027, www.unctad.org; *UNCTAD Commodity Yearbook.*

United Nations Food and Agricultural Organization (FAO), Viale delle Terme di Caracalla, 00100 Rome, Italy, (Dial from U.S. (202) 653-2400), (Fax from U.S. (202) 653 5760), www.fao.org; *FAO Trade Yearbook* and *The State of Food and Agriculture (SOFA) 2006.*

United Nations Statistics Division, New York, NY 10017, (800) 253-9646, Fax: (212) 963-4116, http://unstats.un.org; *International Trade Statistics Yearbook; Statistical Yearbook;* and *Statistical Yearbook for Latin America and the Caribbean 2004.*

The World Bank, 1818 H Street, NW, Washington, DC 20433, (202) 473-1000, Fax: (202) 477-6391, www.worldbank.org; *Honduras; World Development Indicators (WDI) 2008;* and *World Development Report 2008.*

World Trade Organization (WTO), Centre William Rappard, Rue de Lausanne 154, CH-1211 Geneva 21, Switzerland, www.wto.org; *International Trade Statistics 2006.*

HONDURAS - INTERNET USERS

International Telecommunication Union (ITU), Place des Nations, 1211 Geneva 20, Switzerland, www.itu.int; *World Telecommunication/ICT Indicators Database on CD-ROM; World Telecommunication/ICT Indicators Database Online;* and *Yearbook of Statistics - Telecommunication Services (Chronological Time Series 1997-2006).*

The World Bank, 1818 H Street, NW, Washington, DC 20433, (202) 473-1000, Fax: (202) 477-6391, www.worldbank.org; *Honduras.*

HONDURAS - INVESTMENTS

Inter-American Development Bank (IDB), 1300 New York Avenue, NW, Washington, DC 20577, (202) 623-1000, Fax: (202) 623-3096, www.iadb.org; *The Politics of Policies: Economic and Social Progress in Latin America - 2006 Report.*

United Nations Statistics Division, New York, NY 10017, (800) 253-9646, Fax: (212) 963-4116, http://unstats.un.org; *Statistical Yearbook for Latin America and the Caribbean 2004.*

HONDURAS - INVESTMENTS, FOREIGN

Economist Intelligence Unit, 111 West 57th Street, New York, NY 10019, (212) 554-0600, Fax: (212) 586-1181, www.eiu.com; *Business Latin America.*

HONDURAS - IRON AND IRON ORE PRODUCTION

See HONDURAS - MINERAL INDUSTRIES

HONDURAS - IRRIGATION

Euromonitor International, Inc., 224 S. Michigan Avenue, Suite 1500, Chicago, IL 60604, (312) 922-

1115, Fax: (312) 922-1157, www.euromonitor.com; *International Marketing Data and Statistics 2008.*

Inter-American Development Bank (IDB), 1300 New York Avenue, NW, Washington, DC 20577, (202) 623-1000, Fax: (202) 623-3096, www.iadb.org; *The Politics of Policies: Economic and Social Progress in Latin America - 2006 Report.*

HONDURAS - LABOR

Central Intelligence Agency, Office of Public Affairs, Washington, DC 20505, (703) 482-0623, Fax: (703) 482-1739, www.cia.gov; *The World Factbook.*

Economist Intelligence Unit, 111 West 57th Street, New York, NY 10019, (212) 554-0600, Fax: (212) 586-1181, www.eiu.com; *Business Latin America.*

Euromonitor International, Inc., 224 S. Michigan Avenue, Suite 1500, Chicago, IL 60604, (312) 922-1115, Fax: (312) 922-1157, www.euromonitor.com; *International Marketing Data and Statistics 2008* and *World Marketing Data and Statistics.*

International Labour Office, I.L.O. Publications, 4 route des Morillons, CH-1211 Geneva 22, Switzerland, (Telephone in U.S. (202) 653-7652), (Fax in U.S. (202) 653-7687), www.ilo.org; *Yearbook of Labour Statistics 2006.*

M.E. Sharpe, 80 Business Park Drive, Armonk, NY 10504, (800) 541-6563, Fax: (914) 273-2106, www.mesharpe.com; *The Illustrated Book of World Rankings.*

Palgrave Macmillan Ltd., Houndmills, Basingstoke, Hampshire, RG21 6XS, England, (Telephone in U.S. (888) 330-8477), (Fax in U.S. (800) 672-2054), www.palgrave.com; *The Statesman's Yearbook 2008.*

United Nations Food and Agricultural Organization (FAO), Viale delle Terme di Caracalla, 00100 Rome, Italy, (Dial from U.S. (202) 653-2400), (Fax from U.S. (202) 653 5760), www.fao.org; *The State of Food and Agriculture (SOFA) 2006.*

United Nations Statistics Division, New York, NY 10017, (800) 253-9646, Fax: (212) 963-4116, http://unstats.un.org; *Human Development Report 2006.*

The World Bank, 1818 H Street, NW, Washington, DC 20433, (202) 473-1000, Fax: (202) 477-6391, www.worldbank.org; *The World Bank Atlas 2003-2004; World Development Indicators (WDI) 2008;* and *World Development Report 2008.*

HONDURAS - LAND USE

Central Intelligence Agency, Office of Public Affairs, Washington, DC 20505, (703) 482-0623, Fax: (703) 482-1739, www.cia.gov; *The World Factbook.*

Euromonitor International, Inc., 224 S. Michigan Avenue, Suite 1500, Chicago, IL 60604, (312) 922-1115, Fax: (312) 922-1157, www.euromonitor.com; *International Marketing Data and Statistics 2008.*

Inter-American Development Bank (IDB), 1300 New York Avenue, NW, Washington, DC 20577, (202) 623-1000, Fax: (202) 623-3096, www.iadb.org; *The Politics of Policies: Economic and Social Progress in Latin America - 2006 Report.*

International Food Policy Research Institute (IFPRI), 2033 K Street, NW, Washington, D.C., 2006, (202) 862-5600, www.ifpri.org; *Rural Development Policies and Sustainable Land Use in the Hillside Areas of Honduras Survey, 2001-2002.*

United Nations Food and Agricultural Organization (FAO), Viale delle Terme di Caracalla, 00100 Rome, Italy, (Dial from U.S. (202) 653-2400), (Fax from U.S. (202) 653 5760), www.fao.org; *FAO Production Yearbook 2002.*

The World Bank, 1818 H Street, NW, Washington, DC 20433, (202) 473-1000, Fax: (202) 477-6391, www.worldbank.org; *World Development Report 2008.*

HONDURAS - LIBRARIES

M.E. Sharpe, 80 Business Park Drive, Armonk, NY 10504, (800) 541-6563, Fax: (914) 273-2106, www.mesharpe.com; *The Illustrated Book of World Rankings.*

UNESCO Institute for Statistics, C.P. 6128 Succursale Centre-Ville, Montreal, Quebec, H3C 3J7 Canada, (Dial from U.S. (514) 343-6880), (Fax from U.S. (514) 343 6882), www.uis.unesco.org; *Statistical Tables.*

HONDURAS - LICENSES

International Monetary Fund (IMF), 700 Nineteenth Street, NW, Washington, DC 20431, (202) 623-7000, Fax: (202) 623-4661, www.imf.org; *Government Finance Statistics Yearbook (2008 Edition).*

HONDURAS - LIFE EXPECTANCY

Central Intelligence Agency, Office of Public Affairs, Washington, DC 20505, (703) 482-0623, Fax: (703) 482-1739, www.cia.gov; *The World Factbook.*

Economist Intelligence Unit, 111 West 57th Street, New York, NY 10019, (212) 554-0600, Fax: (212) 586-1181, www.eiu.com; *Business Latin America.*

Euromonitor International, Inc., 224 S. Michigan Avenue, Suite 1500, Chicago, IL 60604, (312) 922-1115, Fax: (312) 922-1157, www.euromonitor.com; *The World Economic Factbook 2008.*

Palgrave Macmillan Ltd., Houndmills, Basingstoke, Hampshire, RG21 6XS, England, (Telephone in U.S. (888) 330-8477), (Fax in U.S. (800) 672-2054), www.palgrave.com; *The Statesman's Yearbook 2008.*

United Nations Statistics Division, New York, NY 10017, (800) 253-9646, Fax: (212) 963-4116, http://unstats.un.org; *Human Development Report 2006; Statistical Yearbook for Latin America and the Caribbean 2004;* and *World Statistics Pocketbook.*

The World Bank, 1818 H Street, NW, Washington, DC 20433, (202) 473-1000, Fax: (202) 477-6391, www.worldbank.org; *The World Bank Atlas 2003-2004* and *World Development Report 2008.*

HONDURAS - LITERACY

Central Intelligence Agency, Office of Public Affairs, Washington, DC 20505, (703) 482-0623, Fax: (703) 482-1739, www.cia.gov; *The World Factbook.*

Economist Intelligence Unit, 111 West 57th Street, New York, NY 10019, (212) 554-0600, Fax: (212) 586-1181, www.eiu.com; *Business Latin America.*

Euromonitor International, Inc., 224 S. Michigan Avenue, Suite 1500, Chicago, IL 60604, (312) 922-1115, Fax: (312) 922-1157, www.euromonitor.com; *World Marketing Data and Statistics.*

HONDURAS - LIVESTOCK

Euromonitor International, Inc., 224 S. Michigan Avenue, Suite 1500, Chicago, IL 60604, (312) 922-1115, Fax: (312) 922-1157, www.euromonitor.com; *International Marketing Data and Statistics 2008.*

M.E. Sharpe, 80 Business Park Drive, Armonk, NY 10504, (800) 541-6563, Fax: (914) 273-2106, www.mesharpe.com; *The Illustrated Book of World Rankings.*

Organization of American States (OAS), 17th Street Constitution Avenue NW, Washington, DC 20006, (202) 458-3000, www.oas.org; *The OAS in Transition: 1994-2004.*

Palgrave Macmillan Ltd., Houndmills, Basingstoke, Hampshire, RG21 6XS, England, (Telephone in U.S. (888) 330-8477), (Fax in U.S. (800) 672-2054), www.palgrave.com; *The Statesman's Yearbook 2008.*

Taylor and Francis Group, An Informa Business, 2 Park Square, Milton Park, Abingdon, Oxford OX14 4RN, United Kingdom, (Dial from U.S. (212) 216-7800), (Fax from U.S. (212) 564-7854), www.tandf.co.uk; *The Europa World Year Book.*

United Nations Conference on Trade and Development (UNCTAD), DC2-1120, United Nations, New York, NY 10017, (212) 963-0027, www.unctad.org; *UNCTAD Commodity Yearbook.*

United Nations Food and Agricultural Organization (FAO), Viale delle Terme di Caracalla, 00100 Rome, Italy, (Dial from U.S. (202) 653-2400), (Fax from U.S. (202) 653 5760), www.fao.org; *FAO Production Yearbook 2002* and *The State of Food and Agriculture (SOFA) 2006.*

United Nations Statistics Division, New York, NY 10017, (800) 253-9646, Fax: (212) 963-4116, http://unstats.un.org; *Statistical Yearbook.*

HONDURAS - LOCAL TAXATION

Euromonitor International, Inc., 224 S. Michigan Avenue, Suite 1500, Chicago, IL 60604, (312) 922-1115, Fax: (312) 922-1157, www.euromonitor.com; *International Marketing Data and Statistics 2008.*

Inter-American Development Bank (IDB), 1300 New York Avenue, NW, Washington, DC 20577, (202) 623-1000, Fax: (202) 623-3096, www.iadb.org; *The Politics of Policies: Economic and Social Progress in Latin America - 2006 Report.*

HONDURAS - MANUFACTURES

Inter-American Development Bank (IDB), 1300 New York Avenue, NW, Washington, DC 20577, (202) 623-1000, Fax: (202) 623-3096, www.iadb.org; *The Politics of Policies: Economic and Social Progress in Latin America - 2006 Report.*

M.E. Sharpe, 80 Business Park Drive, Armonk, NY 10504, (800) 541-6563, Fax: (914) 273-2106, www.mesharpe.com; *The Illustrated Book of World Rankings.*

U.S. Department of State (DOS), 2201 C Street NW, Washington, DC 20520, (202) 647-4000, www.state.gov; *World Military Expenditures and Arms Transfers (WMEAT).*

United Nations Statistics Division, New York, NY 10017, (800) 253-9646, Fax: (212) 963-4116, http://unstats.un.org; *Statistical Yearbook* and *Statistical Yearbook for Latin America and the Caribbean 2004.*

The World Bank, 1818 H Street, NW, Washington, DC 20433, (202) 473-1000, Fax: (202) 477-6391, www.worldbank.org; *World Development Indicators (WDI) 2008.*

HONDURAS - MARRIAGE

M.E. Sharpe, 80 Business Park Drive, Armonk, NY 10504, (800) 541-6563, Fax: (914) 273-2106, www.mesharpe.com; *The Illustrated Book of World Rankings.*

United Nations Statistics Division, New York, NY 10017, (800) 253-9646, Fax: (212) 963-4116, http://unstats.un.org; *Demographic Yearbook* and *Statistical Yearbook.*

HONDURAS - MEAT INDUSTRY AND TRADE

International Monetary Fund (IMF), 700 Nineteenth Street, NW, Washington, DC 20431, (202) 623-7000, Fax: (202) 623-4661, www.imf.org; *International Financial Statistics Yearbook 2007.*

UCLA Latin American Institute, 10343 Bunche Hall, Box 951447, Los Angeles, CA 90095-1447, (310) 825-4571, Fax: (310) 206-6859, www.international.ucla.edu/lac; *Statistical Abstract of Latin America.*

HONDURAS - MEDICAL CARE, COST OF

International Monetary Fund (IMF), 700 Nineteenth Street, NW, Washington, DC 20431, (202) 623-7000, Fax: (202) 623-4661, www.imf.org; *Government Finance Statistics Yearbook (2008 Edition).*

United Nations Statistics Division, New York, NY 10017, (800) 253-9646, Fax: (212) 963-4116, http://unstats.un.org; *Statistical Yearbook for Latin America and the Caribbean 2004.*

HONDURAS - MILK PRODUCTION

See HONDURAS - DAIRY PROCESSING

HONDURAS - MINERAL INDUSTRIES

Economist Intelligence Unit, 111 West 57th Street, New York, NY 10019, (212) 554-0600, Fax: (212) 586-1181, www.eiu.com; *Business Latin America.*

Inter-American Development Bank (IDB), 1300 New York Avenue, NW, Washington, DC 20577, (202) 623-1000, Fax: (202) 623-3096, www.iadb.org; *The*

Politics of Policies: Economic and Social Progress in Latin America - 2006 Report.

M.E. Sharpe, 80 Business Park Drive, Armonk, NY 10504, (800) 541-6563, Fax: (914) 273-2106, www.mesharpe.com; *The Illustrated Book of World Rankings.*

Palgrave Macmillan Ltd., Houndmills, Basingstoke, Hampshire, RG21 6XS, England, (Telephone in U.S. (888) 330-8477), (Fax in U.S. (800) 672-2054), www.palgrave.com; *The Statesman's Yearbook 2008.*

PennWell Corporation, 1421 South Sheridan Road, Tulsa, OK 74112, (918) 835-3161, www.pennwell.com; *Oil Gas Journal Latinoamericana.*

Taylor and Francis Group, An Informa Business, 2 Park Square, Milton Park, Abingdon, Oxford OX14 4RN, United Kingdom, (Dial from U.S. (212) 216-7800), (Fax from U.S. (212) 564-7854), www.tandf.co.uk; *The Europa World Year Book.*

UCLA Latin American Institute, 10343 Bunche Hall, Box 951447, Los Angeles, CA 90095-1447, (310) 825-4571, Fax: (310) 206-6859, www.international.ucla.edu/lac; *Statistical Abstract of Latin America.*

United Nations Conference on Trade and Development (UNCTAD), DC2-1120, United Nations, New York, NY 10017, (212) 963-0027, www.unctad.org; *UNCTAD Commodity Yearbook.*

United Nations Statistics Division, New York, NY 10017, (800) 253-9646, Fax: (212) 963-4116, http://unstats.un.org; *Statistical Yearbook* and *Statistical Yearbook for Latin America and the Caribbean 2004.*

The World Bank, 1818 H Street, NW, Washington, DC 20433, (202) 473-1000, Fax: (202) 477-6391, www.worldbank.org; *World Development Indicators (WDI) 2008.*

HONDURAS - MONEY EXCHANGE RATES

See HONDURAS - FOREIGN EXCHANGE RATES

HONDURAS - MONEY SUPPLY

Economist Intelligence Unit, 111 West 57th Street, New York, NY 10019, (212) 554-0600, Fax: (212) 586-1181, www.eiu.com; *Honduras Country Report.*

Euromonitor International, Inc., 224 S. Michigan Avenue, Suite 1500, Chicago, IL 60604, (312) 922-1115, Fax: (312) 922-1157, www.euromonitor.com; *International Marketing Data and Statistics 2008.*

Inter-American Development Bank (IDB), 1300 New York Avenue, NW, Washington, DC 20577, (202) 623-1000, Fax: (202) 623-3096, www.iadb.org; *The Politics of Policies: Economic and Social Progress in Latin America - 2006 Report.*

International Monetary Fund (IMF), 700 Nineteenth Street, NW, Washington, DC 20431, (202) 623-7000, Fax: (202) 623-4661, www.imf.org; *International Financial Statistics Yearbook 2007.*

Taylor and Francis Group, An Informa Business, 2 Park Square, Milton Park, Abingdon, Oxford OX14 4RN, United Kingdom, (Dial from U.S. (212) 216-7800), (Fax from U.S. (212) 564-7854), www.tandf.co.uk; *The Europa World Year Book.*

UCLA Latin American Institute, 10343 Bunche Hall, Box 951447, Los Angeles, CA 90095-1447, (310) 825-4571, Fax: (310) 206-6859, www.international.ucla.edu/lac; *Statistical Abstract of Latin America.*

United Nations Statistics Division, New York, NY 10017, (800) 253-9646, Fax: (212) 963-4116, http://unstats.un.org; *Statistical Yearbook.*

The World Bank, 1818 H Street, NW, Washington, DC 20433, (202) 473-1000, Fax: (202) 477-6391, www.worldbank.org; *Honduras* and *World Development Indicators (WDI) 2008.*

HONDURAS - MONUMENTS AND HISTORIC SITES

UNESCO Institute for Statistics, C.P. 6128 Succursale Centre-Ville, Montreal, Quebec, H3C 3J7 Canada, (Dial from U.S. (514) 343-6880), (Fax from U.S. (514) 343 6882), www.uis.unesco.org; *Statistical Tables.*

HONDURAS - MORTALITY

Central Intelligence Agency, Office of Public Affairs, Washington, DC 20505, (703) 482-0623, Fax: (703) 482-1739, www.cia.gov; *The World Factbook.*

Economist Intelligence Unit, 111 West 57th Street, New York, NY 10019, (212) 554-0600, Fax: (212) 586-1181, www.eiu.com; *Business Latin America.*

Euromonitor International, Inc., 224 S. Michigan Avenue, Suite 1500, Chicago, IL 60604, (312) 922-1115, Fax: (312) 922-1157, www.euromonitor.com; *International Marketing Data and Statistics 2008* and *The World Economic Factbook 2008.*

Palgrave Macmillan Ltd., Houndmills, Basingstoke, Hampshire, RG21 6XS, England, (Telephone in U.S. (888) 330-8477), (Fax in U.S. (800) 672-2054), www.palgrave.com; *The Statesman's Yearbook 2008.*

Taylor and Francis Group, An Informa Business, 2 Park Square, Milton Park, Abingdon, Oxford OX14 4RN, United Kingdom, (Dial from U.S. (212) 216-7800), (Fax from U.S. (212) 564-7854), www.tandf.co.uk; *The Europa World Year Book.*

UNICEF, 3 United Nations Plaza, New York, NY 10017, (800) 253-9646, Fax: (212) 887-7465, www.unicef.org; *The State of the World's Children 2008.*

United Nations Statistics Division, New York, NY 10017, (800) 253-9646, Fax: (212) 963-4116, http://unstats.un.org; *Demographic Yearbook; Human Development Report 2006; Statistical Yearbook; Statistical Yearbook for Latin America and the Caribbean 2004;* and *World Statistics Pocketbook.*

The World Bank, 1818 H Street, NW, Washington, DC 20433, (202) 473-1000, Fax: (202) 477-6391, www.worldbank.org; *The World Bank Atlas 2003-2004; World Development Indicators (WDI) 2008;* and *World Development Report 2008.*

World Health Organization (WHO), Avenue Appia 20, 1211 Geneve 27, Switzerland, (Telephone in U.S. (212) 331-9081), www.who.int; The WHO Global Atlas of Infectious Diseases and *World Health Report 2006.*

HONDURAS - MOTION PICTURES

Palgrave Macmillan Ltd., Houndmills, Basingstoke, Hampshire, RG21 6XS, England, (Telephone in U.S. (888) 330-8477), (Fax in U.S. (800) 672-2054), www.palgrave.com; *The Statesman's Yearbook 2008.*

HONDURAS - MOTOR VEHICLES

Economist Intelligence Unit, 111 West 57th Street, New York, NY 10019, (212) 554-0600, Fax: (212) 586-1181, www.eiu.com; *Business Latin America.*

Taylor and Francis Group, An Informa Business, 2 Park Square, Milton Park, Abingdon, Oxford OX14 4RN, United Kingdom, (Dial from U.S. (212) 216-7800), (Fax from U.S. (212) 564-7854), www.tandf.co.uk; *The Europa World Year Book.*

United Nations Statistics Division, New York, NY 10017, (800) 253-9646, Fax: (212) 963-4116, http://unstats.un.org; *Statistical Yearbook.*

HONDURAS - MUSEUMS

M.E. Sharpe, 80 Business Park Drive, Armonk, NY 10504, (800) 541-6563, Fax: (914) 273-2106, www.mesharpe.com; *The Illustrated Book of World Rankings.*

UNESCO Institute for Statistics, C.P. 6128 Succursale Centre-Ville, Montreal, Quebec, H3C 3J7 Canada, (Dial from U.S. (514) 343-6880), (Fax from U.S. (514) 343 6882), www.uis.unesco.org; *Statistical Tables.*

HONDURAS - NATURAL GAS PRODUCTION

See HONDURAS - MINERAL INDUSTRIES

HONDURAS - NUTRITION

United Nations Food and Agricultural Organization (FAO), Viale delle Terme di Caracalla, 00100 Rome, Italy, (Dial from U.S. (202) 653-2400), (Fax from U.S. (202) 653 5760), www.fao.org; *The State of Food and Agriculture (SOFA) 2006.*

United Nations Statistics Division, New York, NY 10017, (800) 253-9646, Fax: (212) 963-4116, http://unstats.un.org; *Statistical Yearbook for Latin America and the Caribbean 2004.*

HONDURAS - OLDER PEOPLE

M.E. Sharpe, 80 Business Park Drive, Armonk, NY 10504, (800) 541-6563, Fax: (914) 273-2106, www.mesharpe.com; *The Illustrated Book of World Rankings.*

HONDURAS - PALM OIL PRODUCTION

See HONDURAS - CROPS

HONDURAS - PAPER

See HONDURAS - FORESTS AND FORESTRY

HONDURAS - PEANUT PRODUCTION

See HONDURAS - CROPS

HONDURAS - PESTICIDES

United Nations Food and Agricultural Organization (FAO), Viale delle Terme di Caracalla, 00100 Rome, Italy, (Dial from U.S. (202) 653-2400), (Fax from U.S. (202) 653 5760), www.fao.org; *The State of Food and Agriculture (SOFA) 2006.*

HONDURAS - PETROLEUM INDUSTRY AND TRADE

Economist Intelligence Unit, 111 West 57th Street, New York, NY 10019, (212) 554-0600, Fax: (212) 586-1181, www.eiu.com; *Business Latin America.*

Inter-American Development Bank (IDB), 1300 New York Avenue, NW, Washington, DC 20577, (202) 623-1000, Fax: (202) 623-3096, www.iadb.org; *The Politics of Policies: Economic and Social Progress in Latin America - 2006 Report.*

M.E. Sharpe, 80 Business Park Drive, Armonk, NY 10504, (800) 541-6563, Fax: (914) 273-2106, www.mesharpe.com; *The Illustrated Book of World Rankings.*

PennWell Corporation, 1421 South Sheridan Road, Tulsa, OK 74112, (918) 835-3161, www.pennwell.com; *International Petroleum Encyclopedia 2007.*

U.S. Department of Energy (DOE), Energy Information Administration (EIA), 1000 Independence Avenue, SW, Washington, DC 20585, (202) 586-8800, www.eia.doe.gov; *International Energy Annual 2004* and *International Energy Outlook 2006.*

United Nations Conference on Trade and Development (UNCTAD), DC2-1120, United Nations, New York, NY 10017, (212) 963-0027, www.unctad.org; *UNCTAD Commodity Yearbook.*

United Nations Food and Agricultural Organization (FAO), Viale delle Terme di Caracalla, 00100 Rome, Italy, (Dial from U.S. (202) 653-2400), (Fax from U.S. (202) 653 5760), www.fao.org; *The State of Food and Agriculture (SOFA) 2006.*

United Nations Statistics Division, New York, NY 10017, (800) 253-9646, Fax: (212) 963-4116, http://unstats.un.org; *Statistical Yearbook.*

HONDURAS - POLITICAL SCIENCE

Central Intelligence Agency, Office of Public Affairs, Washington, DC 20505, (703) 482-0623, Fax: (703) 482-1739, www.cia.gov; *The World Factbook.*

Inter-American Development Bank (IDB), 1300 New York Avenue, NW, Washington, DC 20577, (202) 623-1000, Fax: (202) 623-3096, www.iadb.org; *The Politics of Policies: Economic and Social Progress in Latin America - 2006 Report.*

International Monetary Fund (IMF), 700 Nineteenth Street, NW, Washington, DC 20431, (202) 623-7000, Fax: (202) 623-4661, www.imf.org; *Government Finance Statistics Yearbook (2008 Edition).*

Palgrave Macmillan Ltd., Houndmills, Basingstoke, Hampshire, RG21 6XS, England, (Telephone in U.S.

(888) 330-8477), (Fax in U.S. (800) 672-2054), www.palgrave.com; *The Statesman's Yearbook 2008.*

Taylor and Francis Group, An Informa Business, 2 Park Square, Milton Park, Abingdon, Oxford OX14 4RN, United Kingdom, (Dial from U.S. (212) 216-7800), (Fax from U.S. (212) 564-7854), www.tandf.co.uk; *The Europa World Year Book.*

UCLA Latin American Institute, 10343 Bunche Hall, Box 951447, Los Angeles, CA 90095-1447, (310) 825-4571, Fax: (310) 206-6859, www.international.ucla.edu/lac; *Statistical Abstract of Latin America.*

United Nations Statistics Division, New York, NY 10017, (800) 253-9646, Fax: (212) 963-4116, http://unstats.un.org; *National Accounts Statistics: Compendium of Income Distribution Statistics* and *Statistical Yearbook.*

The World Bank, 1818 H Street, NW, Washington, DC 20433, (202) 473-1000, Fax: (202) 477-6391, www.worldbank.org; *World Development Indicators (WDI) 2008* and *World Development Report 2008.*

HONDURAS - POPULATION

Central Intelligence Agency, Office of Public Affairs, Washington, DC 20505, (703) 482-0623, Fax: (703) 482-1739, www.cia.gov; *The World Factbook.*

Economist Intelligence Unit, 111 West 57th Street, New York, NY 10019, (212) 554-0600, Fax: (212) 586-1181, www.eiu.com; *Business Latin America* and *Honduras Country Report.*

Euromonitor International, Inc., 224 S. Michigan Avenue, Suite 1500, Chicago, IL 60604, (312) 922-1115, Fax: (312) 922-1157, www.euromonitor.com; *International Marketing Data and Statistics 2008* and *The World Economic Factbook 2008.*

Inter-American Development Bank (IDB), 1300 New York Avenue, NW, Washington, DC 20577, (202) 623-1000, Fax: (202) 623-3096, www.iadb.org; *The Politics of Policies: Economic and Social Progress in Latin America - 2006 Report.*

International Labour Office, I.L.O. Publications, 4 route des Morillons, CH-1211 Geneva 22, Switzerland, (Telephone in U.S. (202) 653-7652), (Fax in U.S. (202) 653-7687), www.ilo.org; *Yearbook of Labour Statistics 2006.*

M.E. Sharpe, 80 Business Park Drive, Armonk, NY 10504, (800) 541-6563, Fax: (914) 273-2106, www.mesharpe.com; *The Illustrated Book of World Rankings.*

Organization of American States (OAS), 17th Street Constitution Avenue NW, Washington, DC 20006, (202) 458-3000, www.oas.org; *The OAS in Transition: 1994-2004.*

Palgrave Macmillan Ltd., Houndmills, Basingstoke, Hampshire, RG21 6XS, England, (Telephone in U.S. (888) 330-8477), (Fax in U.S. (800) 672-2054), www.palgrave.com; *The Statesman's Yearbook 2008.*

Taylor and Francis Group, An Informa Business, 2 Park Square, Milton Park, Abingdon, Oxford OX14 4RN, United Kingdom, (Dial from U.S. (212) 216-7800), (Fax from U.S. (212) 564-7854), www.tandf.co.uk; *The Europa World Year Book.*

U.S. Department of State (DOS), 2201 C Street NW, Washington, DC 20520, (202) 647-4000, www.state.gov; *World Military Expenditures and Arms Transfers (WMEAT).*

UCLA Latin American Institute, 10343 Bunche Hall, Box 951447, Los Angeles, CA 90095-1447, (310) 825-4571, Fax: (310) 206-6859, www.international.ucla.edu/lac; *Statistical Abstract of Latin America.*

UNESCO Institute for Statistics, C.P. 6128 Succursale Centre-Ville, Montreal, Quebec, H3C 3J7 Canada, (Dial from U.S. (514) 343-6880), (Fax from U.S. (514) 343 6882), www.uis.unesco.org; *Statistical Tables.*

United Nations Food and Agricultural Organization (FAO), Viale delle Terme di Caracalla, 00100 Rome, Italy, (Dial from U.S. (202) 653-2400), (Fax from U.S. (202) 653 5760), www.fao.org; *FAO Production Yearbook 2002.*

United Nations Statistics Division, New York, NY 10017, (800) 253-9646, Fax: (212) 963-4116, http://unstats.un.org; *Demographic Yearbook; Human Development Report 2006; Statistical Yearbook; Statistical Yearbook for Latin America and the Caribbean 2004;* and *World Statistics Pocketbook.*

The World Bank, 1818 H Street, NW, Washington, DC 20433, (202) 473-1000, Fax: (202) 477-6391, www.worldbank.org; *Honduras; The World Bank Atlas 2003-2004;* and *World Development Report 2008.*

World Health Organization (WHO), Avenue Appia 20, 1211 Geneve 27, Switzerland, (Telephone in U.S. (212) 331-9081), www.who.int; *World Health Report 2006.*

HONDURAS - POPULATION DENSITY

Central Intelligence Agency, Office of Public Affairs, Washington, DC 20505, (703) 482-0623, Fax: (703) 482-1739, www.cia.gov; *The World Factbook.*

Euromonitor International, Inc., 224 S. Michigan Avenue, Suite 1500, Chicago, IL 60604, (312) 922-1115, Fax: (312) 922-1157, www.euromonitor.com; *International Marketing Data and Statistics 2008* and *The World Economic Factbook 2008.*

Inter-American Development Bank (IDB), 1300 New York Avenue, NW, Washington, DC 20577, (202) 623-1000, Fax: (202) 623-3096, www.iadb.org; *The Politics of Policies: Economic and Social Progress in Latin America - 2006 Report.*

M.E. Sharpe, 80 Business Park Drive, Armonk, NY 10504, (800) 541-6563, Fax: (914) 273-2106, www.mesharpe.com; *The Illustrated Book of World Rankings.*

Palgrave Macmillan Ltd., Houndmills, Basingstoke, Hampshire, RG21 6XS, England, (Telephone in U.S. (888) 330-8477), (Fax in U.S. (800) 672-2054), www.palgrave.com; *The Statesman's Yearbook 2008.*

Taylor and Francis Group, An Informa Business, 2 Park Square, Milton Park, Abingdon, Oxford OX14 4RN, United Kingdom, (Dial from U.S. (212) 216-7800), (Fax from U.S. (212) 564-7854), www.tandf.co.uk; *The Europa World Year Book.*

UNESCO Institute for Statistics, C.P. 6128 Succursale Centre-Ville, Montreal, Quebec, H3C 3J7 Canada, (Dial from U.S. (514) 343-6880), (Fax from U.S. (514) 343 6882), www.uis.unesco.org; *Statistical Tables.*

United Nations Food and Agricultural Organization (FAO), Viale delle Terme di Caracalla, 00100 Rome, Italy, (Dial from U.S. (202) 653-2400), (Fax from U.S. (202) 653 5760), www.fao.org; *The State of Food and Agriculture (SOFA) 2006.*

United Nations Statistics Division, New York, NY 10017, (800) 253-9646, Fax: (212) 963-4116, http://unstats.un.org; *Statistical Yearbook.*

The World Bank, 1818 H Street, NW, Washington, DC 20433, (202) 473-1000, Fax: (202) 477-6391, www.worldbank.org; *Honduras* and *World Development Report 2008.*

HONDURAS - POSTAL SERVICE

M.E. Sharpe, 80 Business Park Drive, Armonk, NY 10504, (800) 541-6563, Fax: (914) 273-2106, www.mesharpe.com; *The Illustrated Book of World Rankings.*

United Nations Statistics Division, New York, NY 10017, (800) 253-9646, Fax: (212) 963-4116, http://unstats.un.org; *Statistical Yearbook.*

HONDURAS - POWER RESOURCES

Economist Intelligence Unit, 111 West 57th Street, New York, NY 10019, (212) 554-0600, Fax: (212) 586-1181, www.eiu.com; *Business Latin America.*

Euromonitor International, Inc., 224 S. Michigan Avenue, Suite 1500, Chicago, IL 60604, (312) 922-1115, Fax: (312) 922-1157, www.euromonitor.com; *International Marketing Data and Statistics 2008; The World Economic Factbook 2008;* and *World Marketing Data and Statistics.*

M.E. Sharpe, 80 Business Park Drive, Armonk, NY 10504, (800) 541-6563, Fax: (914) 273-2106, www.mesharpe.com; *The Illustrated Book of World Rankings.*

Palgrave Macmillan Ltd., Houndmills, Basingstoke, Hampshire, RG21 6XS, England, (Telephone in U.S. (888) 330-8477), (Fax in U.S. (800) 672-2054), www.palgrave.com; *The Statesman's Yearbook 2008.*

Platts, 2 Penn Plaza, 25th Floor, New York, NY 10121-2298, (212) 904-3070, www.platts.com; *Energy Economist.*

U.S. Department of Energy (DOE), Energy Information Administration (EIA), 1000 Independence Avenue, SW, Washington, DC 20585, (202) 586-8800, www.eia.doe.gov; *International Energy Annual 2004* and *International Energy Outlook 2006.*

UCLA Latin American Institute, 10343 Bunche Hall, Box 951447, Los Angeles, CA 90095-1447, (310) 825-4571, Fax: (310) 206-6859, www.international.ucla.edu/lac; *Statistical Abstract of Latin America.*

United Nations Food and Agricultural Organization (FAO), Viale delle Terme di Caracalla, 00100 Rome, Italy, (Dial from U.S. (202) 653-2400), (Fax from U.S. (202) 653 5760), www.fao.org; *The State of Food and Agriculture (SOFA) 2006.*

United Nations Statistics Division, New York, NY 10017, (800) 253-9646, Fax: (212) 963-4116, http://unstats.un.org; *Energy Statistics Yearbook 2003; Human Development Report 2006; Statistical Yearbook; Statistical Yearbook for Latin America and the Caribbean 2004;* and *World Statistics Pocketbook.*

The World Bank, 1818 H Street, NW, Washington, DC 20433, (202) 473-1000, Fax: (202) 477-6391, www.worldbank.org; *The World Bank Atlas 2003-2004* and *World Development Report 2008.*

HONDURAS - PRICES

Economist Intelligence Unit, 111 West 57th Street, New York, NY 10019, (212) 554-0600, Fax: (212) 586-1181, www.eiu.com; *Business Latin America.*

Euromonitor International, Inc., 224 S. Michigan Avenue, Suite 1500, Chicago, IL 60604, (312) 922-1115, Fax: (312) 922-1157, www.euromonitor.com; *World Marketing Data and Statistics.*

International Labour Office, I.L.O. Publications, 4 route des Morillons, CH-1211 Geneva 22, Switzerland, (Telephone in U.S. (202) 653-7652), (Fax in U.S. (202) 653-7687), www.ilo.org; *Yearbook of Labour Statistics 2006.*

International Monetary Fund (IMF), 700 Nineteenth Street, NW, Washington, DC 20431, (202) 623-7000, Fax: (202) 623-4661, www.imf.org; *International Financial Statistics Yearbook 2007.*

M.E. Sharpe, 80 Business Park Drive, Armonk, NY 10504, (800) 541-6563, Fax: (914) 273-2106, www.mesharpe.com; *The Illustrated Book of World Rankings.*

Organization of American States (OAS), 17th Street Constitution Avenue NW, Washington, DC 20006, (202) 458-3000, www.oas.org; *The OAS in Transition: 1994-2004.*

UCLA Latin American Institute, 10343 Bunche Hall, Box 951447, Los Angeles, CA 90095-1447, (310) 825-4571, Fax: (310) 206-6859, www.international.ucla.edu/lac; *Statistical Abstract of Latin America.*

United Nations Food and Agricultural Organization (FAO), Viale delle Terme di Caracalla, 00100 Rome, Italy, (Dial from U.S. (202) 653-2400), (Fax from U.S. (202) 653 5760), www.fao.org; *FAO Production Yearbook 2002* and *The State of Food and Agriculture (SOFA) 2006.*

United Nations Statistics Division, New York, NY 10017, (800) 253-9646, Fax: (212) 963-4116, http://unstats.un.org; *Economic Survey of Latin America and the Caribbean 2004-2005* and *Statistical Yearbook for Latin America and the Caribbean 2004.*

The World Bank, 1818 H Street, NW, Washington, DC 20433, (202) 473-1000, Fax: (202) 477-6391, www.worldbank.org; *Honduras.*

HONDURAS - PROFESSIONS

UCLA Latin American Institute, 10343 Bunche Hall, Box 951447, Los Angeles, CA 90095-1447, (310) 825-4571, Fax: (310) 206-6859, www.international.ucla.edu/lac; *Statistical Abstract of Latin America.*

United Nations Statistics Division, New York, NY 10017, (800) 253-9646, Fax: (212) 963-4116, http://unstats.un.org; *Statistical Yearbook.*

HONDURAS - PUBLIC HEALTH

Economist Intelligence Unit, 111 West 57th Street, New York, NY 10019, (212) 554-0600, Fax: (212) 586-1181, www.eiu.com; *Business Latin America.*

Euromonitor International, Inc., 224 S. Michigan Avenue, Suite 1500, Chicago, IL 60604, (312) 922-1115, Fax: (312) 922-1157, www.euromonitor.com; *World Marketing Data and Statistics.*

M.E. Sharpe, 80 Business Park Drive, Armonk, NY 10504, (800) 541-6563, Fax: (914) 273-2106, www.mesharpe.com; *The Illustrated Book of World Rankings.*

Palgrave Macmillan Ltd., Houndmills, Basingstoke, Hampshire, RG21 6XS, England, (Telephone in U.S. (888) 330-8477), (Fax in U.S. (800) 672-2054), www.palgrave.com; *The Statesman's Yearbook 2008.*

UCLA Latin American Institute, 10343 Bunche Hall, Box 951447, Los Angeles, CA 90095-1447, (310) 825-4571, Fax: (310) 206-6859, www.international.ucla.edu/lac; *Statistical Abstract of Latin America.*

UNICEF, 3 United Nations Plaza, New York, NY 10017, (800) 253-9646, Fax: (212) 887-7465, www.unicef.org; *The State of the World's Children 2008.*

United Nations Statistics Division, New York, NY 10017, (800) 253-9646, Fax: (212) 963-4116, http://unstats.un.org; *Human Development Report 2006; Statistical Yearbook;* and *Statistical Yearbook for Latin America and the Caribbean 2004.*

The World Bank, 1818 H Street, NW, Washington, DC 20433, (202) 473-1000, Fax: (202) 477-6391, www.worldbank.org; *Honduras* and *World Development Report 2008.*

World Health Organization (WHO), Avenue Appia 20, 1211 Geneve 27, Switzerland, (Telephone in U.S. (212) 331-9081), www.who.int; The WHO Global Atlas of Infectious Diseases and *World Health Report 2006.*

HONDURAS - PUBLIC UTILITIES

UCLA Latin American Institute, 10343 Bunche Hall, Box 951447, Los Angeles, CA 90095-1447, (310) 825-4571, Fax: (310) 206-6859, www.international.ucla.edu/lac; *Statistical Abstract of Latin America.*

HONDURAS - RADIO BROADCASTING

Palgrave Macmillan Ltd., Houndmills, Basingstoke, Hampshire, RG21 6XS, England, (Telephone in U.S. (888) 330-8477), (Fax in U.S. (800) 672-2054), www.palgrave.com; *The Statesman's Yearbook 2008.*

HONDURAS - RAILROADS

Economist Intelligence Unit, 111 West 57th Street, New York, NY 10019, (212) 554-0600, Fax: (212) 586-1181, www.eiu.com; *Business Latin America.*

Jane's Information Group, 110 North Royal Street, Suite 200, Alexandria, VA 22314, (703) 683-3700, Fax: (800) 836-0297, www.janes.com; *Jane's World Railways.*

Palgrave Macmillan Ltd., Houndmills, Basingstoke, Hampshire, RG21 6XS, England, (Telephone in U.S. (888) 330-8477), (Fax in U.S. (800) 672-2054), www.palgrave.com; *The Statesman's Yearbook 2008.*

HONDURAS - RANCHING

UCLA Latin American Institute, 10343 Bunche Hall, Box 951447, Los Angeles, CA 90095-1447, (310) 825-4571, Fax: (310) 206-6859, www.international.ucla.edu/lac; *Statistical Abstract of Latin America.*

HONDURAS - RELIGION

Central Intelligence Agency, Office of Public Affairs, Washington, DC 20505, (703) 482-0623, Fax: (703) 482-1739, www.cia.gov; *The World Factbook.*

M.E. Sharpe, 80 Business Park Drive, Armonk, NY 10504, (800) 541-6563, Fax: (914) 273-2106, www.mesharpe.com; *The Illustrated Book of World Rankings.*

Palgrave Macmillan Ltd., Houndmills, Basingstoke, Hampshire, RG21 6XS, England, (Telephone in U.S. (888) 330-8477), (Fax in U.S. (800) 672-2054), www.palgrave.com; *The Statesman's Yearbook 2008.*

UCLA Latin American Institute, 10343 Bunche Hall, Box 951447, Los Angeles, CA 90095-1447, (310) 825-4571, Fax: (310) 206-6859, www.international.ucla.edu/lac; *Statistical Abstract of Latin America.*

HONDURAS - RENT CHARGES

International Labour Office, I.L.O. Publications, 4 route des Morillons, CH-1211 Geneva 22, Switzerland, (Telephone in U.S. (202) 653-7652), (Fax in U.S. (202) 653-7687), www.ilo.org; *Yearbook of Labour Statistics 2006.*

HONDURAS - RESERVES (ACCOUNTING)

Economist Intelligence Unit, 111 West 57th Street, New York, NY 10019, (212) 554-0600, Fax: (212) 586-1181, www.eiu.com; *Business Latin America.*

Euromonitor International, Inc., 224 S. Michigan Avenue, Suite 1500, Chicago, IL 60604, (312) 922-1115, Fax: (312) 922-1157, www.euromonitor.com; *International Marketing Data and Statistics 2008.*

Inter-American Development Bank (IDB), 1300 New York Avenue, NW, Washington, DC 20577, (202) 623-1000, Fax: (202) 623-3096, www.iadb.org; *The Politics of Policies: Economic and Social Progress in Latin America - 2006 Report.*

Organization of American States (OAS), 17th Street Constitution Avenue NW, Washington, DC 20006, (202) 458-3000, www.oas.org; *The OAS in Transition: 1994-2004.*

United Nations Statistics Division, New York, NY 10017, (800) 253-9646, Fax: (212) 963-4116, http://unstats.un.org; *Statistical Yearbook.*

The World Bank, 1818 H Street, NW, Washington, DC 20433, (202) 473-1000, Fax: (202) 477-6391, www.worldbank.org; *World Development Indicators (WDI) 2008.*

HONDURAS - RETAIL TRADE

Euromonitor International, Inc., 224 S. Michigan Avenue, Suite 1500, Chicago, IL 60604, (312) 922-1115, Fax: (312) 922-1157, www.euromonitor.com; *World Marketing Data and Statistics.*

Inter-American Development Bank (IDB), 1300 New York Avenue, NW, Washington, DC 20577, (202) 623-1000, Fax: (202) 623-3096, www.iadb.org; *The Politics of Policies: Economic and Social Progress in Latin America - 2006 Report.*

HONDURAS - RICE PRODUCTION

See HONDURAS - CROPS

HONDURAS - ROADS

Central Intelligence Agency, Office of Public Affairs, Washington, DC 20505, (703) 482-0623, Fax: (703) 482-1739, www.cia.gov; *The World Factbook.*

Economist Intelligence Unit, 111 West 57th Street, New York, NY 10019, (212) 554-0600, Fax: (212) 586-1181, www.eiu.com; *Business Latin America.*

Palgrave Macmillan Ltd., Houndmills, Basingstoke, Hampshire, RG21 6XS, England, (Telephone in U.S. (888) 330-8477), (Fax in U.S. (800) 672-2054), www.palgrave.com; *The Statesman's Yearbook 2008.*

HONDURAS - RUBBER INDUSTRY AND TRADE

International Rubber Study Group (IRSG), 1st Floor, Heron House, 109/115 Wembley Hill Road, Wembley, Middlesex HA9 8DA, United Kingdom, www.rubberstudy.com; *Rubber Statistical Bulletin; Summary of World Rubber Statistics 2005; World Rubber Statistics Handbook (Volume 6, 1975-2001);* and *World Rubber Statistics Historic Handbook.*

M.E. Sharpe, 80 Business Park Drive, Armonk, NY 10504, (800) 541-6563, Fax: (914) 273-2106, www.mesharpe.com; *The Illustrated Book of World Rankings.*

HONDURAS - SALT PRODUCTION

See HONDURAS - MINERAL INDUSTRIES

HONDURAS - SHEEP

See HONDURAS - LIVESTOCK

HONDURAS - SHIPPING

Palgrave Macmillan Ltd., Houndmills, Basingstoke, Hampshire, RG21 6XS, England, (Telephone in U.S. (888) 330-8477), (Fax in U.S. (800) 672-2054), www.palgrave.com; *The Statesman's Yearbook 2008.*

Taylor and Francis Group, An Informa Business, 2 Park Square, Milton Park, Abingdon, Oxford OX14 4RN, United Kingdom, (Dial from U.S. (212) 216-7800), (Fax from U.S. (212) 564-7854), www.tandf.co.uk; *The Europa World Year Book.*

U.S. Department of Transportation (DOT), Maritime Administration (MARAD), West Building, Southeast Federal Center, 1200 New Jersey Avenue, SE, Washington, DC 20590, (800) 99-MARAD, www.marad.dot.gov; *World Merchant Fleet 2005.*

United Nations Statistics Division, New York, NY 10017, (800) 253-9646, Fax: (212) 963-4116, http://unstats.un.org; *Statistical Yearbook.*

HONDURAS - SILVER PRODUCTION

See HONDURAS - MINERAL INDUSTRIES

HONDURAS - SOCIAL ECOLOGY

M.E. Sharpe, 80 Business Park Drive, Armonk, NY 10504, (800) 541-6563, Fax: (914) 273-2106, www.mesharpe.com; *The Illustrated Book of World Rankings.*

UCLA Latin American Institute, 10343 Bunche Hall, Box 951447, Los Angeles, CA 90095-1447, (310) 825-4571, Fax: (310) 206-6859, www.international.ucla.edu/lac; *Statistical Abstract of Latin America.*

United Nations Statistics Division, New York, NY 10017, (800) 253-9646, Fax: (212) 963-4116, http://unstats.un.org; *World Statistics Pocketbook.*

HONDURAS - SOCIAL SECURITY

Inter-American Development Bank (IDB), 1300 New York Avenue, NW, Washington, DC 20577, (202) 623-1000, Fax: (202) 623-3096, www.iadb.org; *The Politics of Policies: Economic and Social Progress in Latin America - 2006 Report.*

International Monetary Fund (IMF), 700 Nineteenth Street, NW, Washington, DC 20431, (202) 623-7000, Fax: (202) 623-4661, www.imf.org; *Government Finance Statistics Yearbook (2008 Edition).*

Palgrave Macmillan Ltd., Houndmills, Basingstoke, Hampshire, RG21 6XS, England, (Telephone in U.S. (888) 330-8477), (Fax in U.S. (800) 672-2054), www.palgrave.com; *The Statesman's Yearbook 2008.*

United Nations Statistics Division, New York, NY 10017, (800) 253-9646, Fax: (212) 963-4116, http://unstats.un.org; *National Accounts Statistics: Compendium of Income Distribution Statistics.*

HONDURAS - STEEL PRODUCTION

See HONDURAS - MINERAL INDUSTRIES

HONDURAS - SUGAR PRODUCTION

See HONDURAS - CROPS

HONDURAS - SUGAR TRADE

Inter-American Development Bank (IDB), 1300 New York Avenue, NW, Washington, DC 20577, (202) 623-1000, Fax: (202) 623-3096, www.iadb.org; *The Politics of Policies: Economic and Social Progress in Latin America - 2006 Report.*

International Monetary Fund (IMF), 700 Nineteenth Street, NW, Washington, DC 20431, (202) 623-

7000, Fax: (202) 623-4661, www.imf.org; *Government Finance Statistics Yearbook (2008 Edition).*

Taylor and Francis Group, An Informa Business, 2 Park Square, Milton Park, Abingdon, Oxford OX14 4RN, United Kingdom, (Dial from U.S. (212) 216-7800), (Fax from U.S. (212) 564-7854), www.tandf.co.uk; *The Europa World Year Book.*

United Nations Statistics Division, New York, NY 10017, (800) 253-9646, Fax: (212) 963-4116, http://unstats.un.org; *Statistical Yearbook for Latin America and the Caribbean 2004.*

The World Bank, 1818 H Street, NW, Washington, DC 20433, (202) 473-1000, Fax: (202) 477-6391, www.worldbank.org; *World Development Indicators (WDI) 2008.*

HONDURAS - TELEPHONE

Economist Intelligence Unit, 111 West 57th Street, New York, NY 10019, (212) 554-0600, Fax: (212) 586-1181, www.eiu.com; *Business Latin America.*

International Telecommunication Union (ITU), Place des Nations, 1211 Geneva 20, Switzerland, www.itu.int; World Telecommunication Indicators Database.

Palgrave Macmillan Ltd., Houndmills, Basingstoke, Hampshire, RG21 6XS, England, (Telephone in U.S. (888) 330-8477), (Fax in U.S. (800) 672-2054), www.palgrave.com; *The Statesman's Yearbook 2008.*

Taylor and Francis Group, An Informa Business, 2 Park Square, Milton Park, Abingdon, Oxford OX14 4RN, United Kingdom, (Dial from U.S. (212) 216-7800), (Fax from U.S. (212) 564-7854), www.tandf.co.uk; *The Europa World Year Book.*

United Nations Statistics Division, New York, NY 10017, (800) 253-9646, Fax: (212) 963-4116, http://unstats.un.org; *Statistical Yearbook* and *World Statistics Pocketbook.*

HONDURAS - TEXTILE INDUSTRY

M.E. Sharpe, 80 Business Park Drive, Armonk, NY 10504, (800) 541-6563, Fax: (914) 273-2106, www.mesharpe.com; *The Illustrated Book of World Rankings.*

United Nations Conference on Trade and Development (UNCTAD), DC2-1120, United Nations, New York, NY 10017, (212) 963-0027, www.unctad.org; *UNCTAD Commodity Yearbook.*

United Nations Statistics Division, New York, NY 10017, (800) 253-9646, Fax: (212) 963-4116, http://unstats.un.org; *Statistical Yearbook.*

HONDURAS - TOBACCO INDUSTRY

Foreign Agricultural Service (FAS), U.S. Department of Agriculture (USDA), 1400 Independence Avenue, SW, Washington, DC 20250, (202) 720-3935, www.fas.usda.gov; *Tobacco: World Markets and Trade.*

M.E. Sharpe, 80 Business Park Drive, Armonk, NY 10504, (800) 541-6563, Fax: (914) 273-2106, www.mesharpe.com; *The Illustrated Book of World Rankings.*

United Nations Statistics Division, New York, NY 10017, (800) 253-9646, Fax: (212) 963-4116, http://unstats.un.org; *Statistical Yearbook.*

HONDURAS - TOURISM

Economist Intelligence Unit, 111 West 57th Street, New York, NY 10019, (212) 554-0600, Fax: (212) 586-1181, www.eiu.com; *Business Latin America.*

Euromonitor International, Inc., 224 S. Michigan Avenue, Suite 1500, Chicago, IL 60604, (312) 922-1115, Fax: (312) 922-1157, www.euromonitor.com; *The World Economic Factbook 2008* and *World Marketing Data and Statistics.*

M.E. Sharpe, 80 Business Park Drive, Armonk, NY 10504, (800) 541-6563, Fax: (914) 273-2106, www.mesharpe.com; *The Illustrated Book of World Rankings.*

Organization of American States (OAS), 17th Street Constitution Avenue NW, Washington, DC 20006, (202) 458-3000, www.oas.org; *The OAS in Transition: 1994-2004.*

Palgrave Macmillan Ltd., Houndmills, Basingstoke, Hampshire, RG21 6XS, England, (Telephone in U.S. (888) 330-8477), (Fax in U.S. (800) 672-2054), www.palgrave.com; *The Statesman's Yearbook 2008.*

Taylor and Francis Group, An Informa Business, 2 Park Square, Milton Park, Abingdon, Oxford OX14 4RN, United Kingdom, (Dial from U.S. (212) 216-7800), (Fax from U.S. (212) 564-7854), www.tandf.co.uk; *The Europa World Year Book.*

UCLA Latin American Institute, 10343 Bunche Hall, Box 951447, Los Angeles, CA 90095-1447, (310) 825-4571, Fax: (310) 206-6859, www.international.ucla.edu/lac; *Statistical Abstract of Latin America.*

United Nations Statistics Division, New York, NY 10017, (800) 253-9646, Fax: (212) 963-4116, http://unstats.un.org; *Statistical Yearbook* and *Statistical Yearbook for Latin America and the Caribbean 2004.*

The World Bank, 1818 H Street, NW, Washington, DC 20433, (202) 473-1000, Fax: (202) 477-6391, www.worldbank.org; *Honduras.*

HONDURAS - TRADE

See HONDURAS - INTERNATIONAL TRADE

HONDURAS - TRANSPORTATION

Central Intelligence Agency, Office of Public Affairs, Washington, DC 20505, (703) 482-0623, Fax: (703) 482-1739, www.cia.gov; *The World Factbook.*

Economist Intelligence Unit, 111 West 57th Street, New York, NY 10019, (212) 554-0600, Fax: (212) 586-1181, www.eiu.com; *Business Latin America.*

Euromonitor International, Inc., 224 S. Michigan Avenue, Suite 1500, Chicago, IL 60604, (312) 922-1115, Fax: (312) 922-1157, www.euromonitor.com; *International Marketing Data and Statistics 2008* and *World Marketing Data and Statistics.*

Inter-American Development Bank (IDB), 1300 New York Avenue, NW, Washington, DC 20577, (202) 623-1000, Fax: (202) 623-3096, www.iadb.org; *The Politics of Policies: Economic and Social Progress in Latin America - 2006 Report.*

M.E. Sharpe, 80 Business Park Drive, Armonk, NY 10504, (800) 541-6563, Fax: (914) 273-2106, www.mesharpe.com; *The Illustrated Book of World Rankings.*

Palgrave Macmillan Ltd., Houndmills, Basingstoke, Hampshire, RG21 6XS, England, (Telephone in U.S. (888) 330-8477), (Fax in U.S. (800) 672-2054), www.palgrave.com; *The Statesman's Yearbook 2008.*

Taylor and Francis Group, An Informa Business, 2 Park Square, Milton Park, Abingdon, Oxford OX14 4RN, United Kingdom, (Dial from U.S. (212) 216-7800), (Fax from U.S. (212) 564-7854), www.tandf.co.uk; *The Europa World Year Book.*

UCLA Latin American Institute, 10343 Bunche Hall, Box 951447, Los Angeles, CA 90095-1447, (310) 825-4571, Fax: (310) 206-6859, www.international.ucla.edu/lac; *Statistical Abstract of Latin America.*

United Nations Statistics Division, New York, NY 10017, (800) 253-9646, Fax: (212) 963-4116, http://unstats.un.org; *Human Development Report 2006* and *Statistical Yearbook for Latin America and the Caribbean 2004.*

The World Bank, 1818 H Street, NW, Washington, DC 20433, (202) 473-1000, Fax: (202) 477-6391, www.worldbank.org; *Honduras.*

HONDURAS - UNEMPLOYMENT

Central Intelligence Agency, Office of Public Affairs, Washington, DC 20505, (703) 482-0623, Fax: (703) 482-1739, www.cia.gov; *The World Factbook.*

Economist Intelligence Unit, 111 West 57th Street, New York, NY 10019, (212) 554-0600, Fax: (212) 586-1181, www.eiu.com; *Business Latin America.*

Euromonitor International, Inc., 224 S. Michigan Avenue, Suite 1500, Chicago, IL 60604, (312) 922-1115, Fax: (312) 922-1157, www.euromonitor.com; *International Marketing Data and Statistics 2008.*

International Labour Office, I.L.O. Publications, 4 route des Morillons, CH-1211 Geneva 22, Switzerland, (Telephone in U.S. (202) 653-7652), (Fax in U.S. (202) 653-7687), www.ilo.org; *Yearbook of Labour Statistics 2006.*

UCLA Latin American Institute, 10343 Bunche Hall, Box 951447, Los Angeles, CA 90095-1447, (310) 825-4571, Fax: (310) 206-6859, www.international.ucla.edu/lac; *Statistical Abstract of Latin America.*

United Nations Statistics Division, New York, NY 10017, (800) 253-9646, Fax: (212) 963-4116, http://unstats.un.org; *Statistical Yearbook.*

HONDURAS - VITAL STATISTICS

Euromonitor International, Inc., 224 S. Michigan Avenue, Suite 1500, Chicago, IL 60604, (312) 922-1115, Fax: (312) 922-1157, www.euromonitor.com; *International Marketing Data and Statistics 2008.*

Palgrave Macmillan Ltd., Houndmills, Basingstoke, Hampshire, RG21 6XS, England, (Telephone in U.S. (888) 330-8477), (Fax in U.S. (800) 672-2054), www.palgrave.com; *The Statesman's Yearbook 2008.*

United Nations Statistics Division, New York, NY 10017, (800) 253-9646, Fax: (212) 963-4116, http://unstats.un.org; *Statistical Yearbook.*

World Health Organization (WHO), Avenue Appia 20, 1211 Geneve 27, Switzerland, (Telephone in U.S. (212) 331-9081), www.who.int; *World Health Report 2006.*

HONDURAS - WAGES

International Labour Office, I.L.O. Publications, 4 route des Morillons, CH-1211 Geneva 22, Switzerland, (Telephone in U.S. (202) 653-7652), (Fax in U.S. (202) 653-7687), www.ilo.org; *Yearbook of Labour Statistics 2006.*

UCLA Latin American Institute, 10343 Bunche Hall, Box 951447, Los Angeles, CA 90095-1447, (310) 825-4571, Fax: (310) 206-6859, www.international.ucla.edu/lac; *Statistical Abstract of Latin America.*

United Nations Statistics Division, New York, NY 10017, (800) 253-9646, Fax: (212) 963-4116, http://unstats.un.org; *Statistical Yearbook.*

The World Bank, 1818 H Street, NW, Washington, DC 20433, (202) 473-1000, Fax: (202) 477-6391, www.worldbank.org; *Honduras.*

HONDURAS - WEATHER

See HONDURAS - CLIMATE

HONDURAS - WELFARE STATE

Inter-American Development Bank (IDB), 1300 New York Avenue, NW, Washington, DC 20577, (202) 623-1000, Fax: (202) 623-3096, www.iadb.org; *The Politics of Policies: Economic and Social Progress in Latin America - 2006 Report.*

International Monetary Fund (IMF), 700 Nineteenth Street, NW, Washington, DC 20431, (202) 623-7000, Fax: (202) 623-4661, www.imf.org; *Government Finance Statistics Yearbook (2008 Edition).*

HONDURAS - WHEAT PRODUCTION

See HONDURAS - CROPS

HONDURAS - WHOLESALE PRICE INDEXES

Inter-American Development Bank (IDB), 1300 New York Avenue, NW, Washington, DC 20577, (202) 623-1000, Fax: (202) 623-3096, www.iadb.org; *The Politics of Policies: Economic and Social Progress in Latin America - 2006 Report.*

HONDURAS - WHOLESALE TRADE

Inter-American Development Bank (IDB), 1300 New York Avenue, NW, Washington, DC 20577, (202) 623-1000, Fax: (202) 623-3096, www.iadb.org; *The Politics of Policies: Economic and Social Progress in Latin America - 2006 Report.*

HONDURAS - WINE PRODUCTION

See HONDURAS - BEVERAGE INDUSTRY

HONDURAS - WOOD AND WOOD PULP

See HONDURAS - FORESTS AND FORESTRY

HONDURAS - WOOL PRODUCTION

See HONDURAS - TEXTILE INDUSTRY

HONDURAS - ZINC AND ZINC ORE

See HONDURAS - MINERAL INDUSTRIES

HONG KONG - NATIONAL STATISTICAL OFFICE

Census and Statistics Department (CSD), 21/F Wanchai Tower, 12 Harbour Road, Wan Chai, Hong Kong, China, www.censtatd.gov.hk; National Data Center.

HONG KONG - PRIMARY STATISTICS SOURCES

Census and Statistics Department (CSD), 21/F Wanchai Tower, 12 Harbour Road, Wan Chai, Hong Kong, China, www.censtatd.gov.hk; *Hong Kong Annual Digest of Statistics; Hong Kong in Figures;* and *Hong Kong Monthly Digest of Statistics.*

HONG KONG - AGRICULTURAL MACHINERY

United Nations Statistics Division, New York, NY 10017, (800) 253-9646, Fax: (212) 963-4116, http://unstats.un.org; *Statistical Yearbook.*

HONG KONG - AGRICULTURE

Asian Development Bank (ADB), PO Box 789, 0980 Manila, Philippines, www.adb.org; *Key Indicators of Developing Asian and Pacific Countries 2006.*

Economist Intelligence Unit, 111 West 57th Street, New York, NY 10019, (212) 554-0600, Fax: (212) 586-1181, www.eiu.com; *Business Asia* and *Hong Kong Country Report.*

Euromonitor International, Inc., 224 S. Michigan Avenue, Suite 1500, Chicago, IL 60604, (312) 922-1115, Fax: (312) 922-1157, www.euromonitor.com; *International Marketing Data and Statistics 2008* and *World Marketing Data and Statistics.*

M.E. Sharpe, 80 Business Park Drive, Armonk, NY 10504, (800) 541-6563, Fax: (914) 273-2106, www.mesharpe.com; *The Illustrated Book of World Rankings.*

Palgrave Macmillan Ltd., Houndmills, Basingstoke, Hampshire, RG21 6XS, England, (Telephone in U.S. (888) 330-8477), (Fax in U.S. (800) 672-2054), www.palgrave.com; *The Statesman's Yearbook 2008.*

Taylor and Francis Group, An Informa Business, 2 Park Square, Milton Park, Abingdon, Oxford OX14 4RN, United Kingdom, (Dial from U.S. (212) 216-7800), (Fax from U.S. (212) 564-7854), www.tandf.co.uk; *The Europa World Year Book.*

United Nations Conference on Trade and Development (UNCTAD), DC2-1120, United Nations, New York, NY 10017, (212) 963-0027, www.unctad.org; *UNCTAD Commodity Yearbook.*

United Nations Food and Agricultural Organization (FAO), Viale delle Terme di Caracalla, 00100 Rome, Italy, (Dial from U.S. (202) 653-2400), (Fax from U.S. (202) 653 5760), www.fao.org; AQUASTAT; *FAO Production Yearbook 2002;* and *The State of Food and Agriculture (SOFA) 2006.*

United Nations Statistics Division, New York, NY 10017, (800) 253-9646, Fax: (212) 963-4116, http://unstats.un.org; *Asia-Pacific in Figures 2004* and *Statistical Yearbook.*

The World Bank, 1818 H Street, NW, Washington, DC 20433, (202) 473-1000, Fax: (202) 477-6391, www.worldbank.org; *Hong Kong, China* and *World Development Indicators (WDI) 2008.*

HONG KONG - AIRLINES

Economist Intelligence Unit, 111 West 57th Street, New York, NY 10019, (212) 554-0600, Fax: (212) 586-1181, www.eiu.com; *Business Asia.*

International Civil Aviation Organization (ICAO), External Relations and Public Information Office (EPO), 999 University Street, Montreal, Quebec H3C 5H7, Canada, (Dial from U.S. (514) 954-8219), (Fax from U.S. (514) 954-6077), www.icao.int; *Civil Aviation Statistics of the World.*

M.E. Sharpe, 80 Business Park Drive, Armonk, NY 10504, (800) 541-6563, Fax: (914) 273-2106, www.mesharpe.com; *The Illustrated Book of World Rankings.*

Palgrave Macmillan Ltd., Houndmills, Basingstoke, Hampshire, RG21 6XS, England, (Telephone in U.S. (888) 330-8477), (Fax in U.S. (800) 672-2054), www.palgrave.com; *The Statesman's Yearbook 2008.*

Taylor and Francis Group, An Informa Business, 2 Park Square, Milton Park, Abingdon, Oxford OX14 4RN, United Kingdom, (Dial from U.S. (212) 216-7800), (Fax from U.S. (212) 564-7854), www.tandf.co.uk; *The Europa World Year Book.*

HONG KONG - AIRPORTS

Central Intelligence Agency, Office of Public Affairs, Washington, DC 20505, (703) 482-0623, Fax: (703) 482-1739, www.cia.gov; *The World Factbook.*

HONG KONG - ALUMINUM PRODUCTION

See HONG KONG - MINERAL INDUSTRIES

HONG KONG - ARMED FORCES

Central Intelligence Agency, Office of Public Affairs, Washington, DC 20505, (703) 482-0623, Fax: (703) 482-1739, www.cia.gov; *The World Factbook.*

Economist Intelligence Unit, 111 West 57th Street, New York, NY 10019, (212) 554-0600, Fax: (212) 586-1181, www.eiu.com; *Business Asia.*

Euromonitor International, Inc., 224 S. Michigan Avenue, Suite 1500, Chicago, IL 60604, (312) 922-1115, Fax: (312) 922-1157, www.euromonitor.com; *World Marketing Data and Statistics.*

Palgrave Macmillan Ltd., Houndmills, Basingstoke, Hampshire, RG21 6XS, England, (Telephone in U.S. (888) 330-8477), (Fax in U.S. (800) 672-2054), www.palgrave.com; *The Statesman's Yearbook 2008.*

United Nations Statistics Division, New York, NY 10017, (800) 253-9646, Fax: (212) 963-4116, http://unstats.un.org; *Human Development Report 2006.*

HONG KONG - BALANCE OF PAYMENTS

The World Bank, 1818 H Street, NW, Washington, DC 20433, (202) 473-1000, Fax: (202) 477-6391, www.worldbank.org; *Hong Kong, China; World Development Indicators (WDI) 2008;* and *World Development Report 2008.*

HONG KONG - BANKS AND BANKING

Asian Development Bank (ADB), PO Box 789, 0980 Manila, Philippines, www.adb.org; *Key Indicators of Developing Asian and Pacific Countries 2006.*

Economist Intelligence Unit, 111 West 57th Street, New York, NY 10019, (212) 554-0600, Fax: (212) 586-1181, www.eiu.com; *Business Asia.*

Euromonitor International, Inc., 224 S. Michigan Avenue, Suite 1500, Chicago, IL 60604, (312) 922-1115, Fax: (312) 922-1157, www.euromonitor.com; *World Marketing Data and Statistics.*

M.E. Sharpe, 80 Business Park Drive, Armonk, NY 10504, (800) 541-6563, Fax: (914) 273-2106, www.mesharpe.com; *The Illustrated Book of World Rankings.*

Palgrave Macmillan Ltd., Houndmills, Basingstoke, Hampshire, RG21 6XS, England, (Telephone in U.S. (888) 330-8477), (Fax in U.S. (800) 672-2054), www.palgrave.com; *The Statesman's Yearbook 2008.*

HONG KONG - BARLEY PRODUCTION

See HONG KONG - CROPS

HONG KONG - BEVERAGE INDUSTRY

M.E. Sharpe, 80 Business Park Drive, Armonk, NY 10504, (800) 541-6563, Fax: (914) 273-2106, www.mesharpe.com; *The Illustrated Book of World Rankings.*

United Nations Statistics Division, New York, NY 10017, (800) 253-9646, Fax: (212) 963-4116, http://unstats.un.org; *Statistical Yearbook.*

HONG KONG - BONDS

Asian Development Bank (ADB), PO Box 789, 0980 Manila, Philippines, www.adb.org; *Key Indicators of Developing Asian and Pacific Countries 2006.*

HONG KONG - BROADCASTING

Central Intelligence Agency, Office of Public Affairs, Washington, DC 20505, (703) 482-0623, Fax: (703) 482-1739, www.cia.gov; *The World Factbook.*

Economist Intelligence Unit, 111 West 57th Street, New York, NY 10019, (212) 554-0600, Fax: (212) 586-1181, www.eiu.com; *Business Asia.*

Euromonitor International, Inc., 224 S. Michigan Avenue, Suite 1500, Chicago, IL 60604, (312) 922-1115, Fax: (312) 922-1157, www.euromonitor.com; *World Marketing Data and Statistics.*

M.E. Sharpe, 80 Business Park Drive, Armonk, NY 10504, (800) 541-6563, Fax: (914) 273-2106, www.mesharpe.com; *The Illustrated Book of World Rankings.*

Palgrave Macmillan Ltd., Houndmills, Basingstoke, Hampshire, RG21 6XS, England, (Telephone in U.S. (888) 330-8477), (Fax in U.S. (800) 672-2054), www.palgrave.com; *The Statesman's Yearbook 2008.*

UNESCO Institute for Statistics, C.P. 6128 Succursale Centre-Ville, Montreal, Quebec, H3C 3J7 Canada, (Dial from U.S. (514) 343-6880), (Fax from U.S. (514) 343 6882), www.uis.unesco.org; *Statistical Tables.*

WRTH Publications Limited, PO Box 290, Oxford OX2 7FT, UK, www.wrth.com; *World Radio TV Handbook 2007.*

HONG KONG - BUDGET

Central Intelligence Agency, Office of Public Affairs, Washington, DC 20505, (703) 482-0623, Fax: (703) 482-1739, www.cia.gov; *The World Factbook.*

HONG KONG - BUSINESS

United Nations Statistics Division, New York, NY 10017, (800) 253-9646, Fax: (212) 963-4116, http://unstats.un.org; *Statistical Yearbook for Asia and the Pacific 2004.*

HONG KONG - CAPITAL INVESTMENTS

Asian Development Bank (ADB), PO Box 789, 0980 Manila, Philippines, www.adb.org; *Key Indicators of Developing Asian and Pacific Countries 2006.*

HONG KONG - CAPITAL LEVY

Asian Development Bank (ADB), PO Box 789, 0980 Manila, Philippines, www.adb.org; *Key Indicators of Developing Asian and Pacific Countries 2006.*

HONG KONG - CATTLE

See HONG KONG - LIVESTOCK

HONG KONG - CHICKENS

See HONG KONG - LIVESTOCK

HONG KONG - CHILDBIRTH - STATISTICS

Central Intelligence Agency, Office of Public Affairs, Washington, DC 20505, (703) 482-0623, Fax: (703) 482-1739, www.cia.gov; *The World Factbook.*

Economist Intelligence Unit, 111 West 57th Street, New York, NY 10019, (212) 554-0600, Fax: (212) 586-1181, www.eiu.com; *Business Asia.*

Euromonitor International, Inc., 224 S. Michigan Avenue, Suite 1500, Chicago, IL 60604, (312) 922-1115, Fax: (312) 922-1157, www.euromonitor.com; *International Marketing Data and Statistics 2008* and *The World Economic Factbook 2008.*

M.E. Sharpe, 80 Business Park Drive, Armonk, NY 10504, (800) 541-6563, Fax: (914) 273-2106, www.mesharpe.com; *The Illustrated Book of World Rankings.*

Palgrave Macmillan Ltd., Houndmills, Basingstoke, Hampshire, RG21 6XS, England, (Telephone in U.S. (888) 330-8477), (Fax in U.S. (800) 672-2054), www.palgrave.com; *The Statesman's Yearbook 2008.*

Taylor and Francis Group, An Informa Business, 2 Park Square, Milton Park, Abingdon, Oxford OX14 4RN, United Kingdom, (Dial from U.S. (212) 216-7800), (Fax from U.S. (212) 564-7854), www.tandf.co.uk; *The Europa World Year Book.*

United Nations Statistics Division, New York, NY 10017, (800) 253-9646, Fax: (212) 963-4116, http://unstats.un.org; *Asia-Pacific in Figures 2004; Demographic Yearbook;* and *Statistical Yearbook.*

The World Bank, 1818 H Street, NW, Washington, DC 20433, (202) 473-1000, Fax: (202) 477-6391, www.worldbank.org; *World Development Indicators (WDI) 2008.*

World Health Organization (WHO), Avenue Appia 20, 1211 Geneve 27, Switzerland, (Telephone in U.S. (212) 331-9081), www.who.int; *World Health Report 2006.*

HONG KONG - CLIMATE

Economist Intelligence Unit, 111 West 57th Street, New York, NY 10019, (212) 554-0600, Fax: (212) 586-1181, www.eiu.com; *Business Asia.*

M.E. Sharpe, 80 Business Park Drive, Armonk, NY 10504, (800) 541-6563, Fax: (914) 273-2106, www.mesharpe.com; *The Illustrated Book of World Rankings.*

Palgrave Macmillan Ltd., Houndmills, Basingstoke, Hampshire, RG21 6XS, England, (Telephone in U.S. (888) 330-8477), (Fax in U.S. (800) 672-2054), www.palgrave.com; *The Statesman's Yearbook 2008.*

HONG KONG - COAL PRODUCTION

See HONG KONG - MINERAL INDUSTRIES

HONG KONG - COFFEE

See HONG KONG - CROPS

HONG KONG - COMMERCE

Palgrave Macmillan Ltd., Houndmills, Basingstoke, Hampshire, RG21 6XS, England, (Telephone in U.S. (888) 330-8477), (Fax in U.S. (800) 672-2054), www.palgrave.com; *The Statesman's Yearbook 2008.*

HONG KONG - COMMODITY EXCHANGES

Commodity Research Bureau, 330 South Wells Street, Suite 612, Chicago, IL 60606-7110, (800) 621-5271, Fax: (312) 939-4135, www.crbtrader.com; *2006 CRB Commodity Yearbook and CD.*

International Monetary Fund (IMF), 700 Nineteenth Street, NW, Washington, DC 20431, (202) 623-7000, Fax: (202) 623-4661, www.imf.org; *IMF Primary Commodity Prices.*

United Nations Food and Agricultural Organization (FAO), Viale delle Terme di Caracalla, 00100 Rome, Italy, (Dial from U.S. (202) 653-2400), (Fax from U.S. (202) 653 5760), www.fao.org; *The State of Food and Agriculture (SOFA) 2006.*

HONG KONG - COMMUNICATION AND TRAFFIC

United Nations Statistics Division, New York, NY 10017, (800) 253-9646, Fax: (212) 963-4116, http://unstats.un.org; *Statistical Yearbook.*

HONG KONG - CONSTRUCTION INDUSTRY

M.E. Sharpe, 80 Business Park Drive, Armonk, NY 10504, (800) 541-6563, Fax: (914) 273-2106, www.mesharpe.com; *The Illustrated Book of World Rankings.*

Palgrave Macmillan Ltd., Houndmills, Basingstoke, Hampshire, RG21 6XS, England, (Telephone in U.S. (888) 330-8477), (Fax in U.S. (800) 672-2054), www.palgrave.com; *The Statesman's Yearbook 2008.*

United Nations Statistics Division, New York, NY 10017, (800) 253-9646, Fax: (212) 963-4116, http://unstats.un.org; *Statistical Yearbook.*

HONG KONG - CONSUMER PRICE INDEXES

Asian Development Bank (ADB), PO Box 789, 0980 Manila, Philippines, www.adb.org; *Key Indicators of Developing Asian and Pacific Countries 2006.*

Economist Intelligence Unit, 111 West 57th Street, New York, NY 10019, (212) 554-0600, Fax: (212) 586-1181, www.eiu.com; *Business Asia.*

Taylor and Francis Group, An Informa Business, 2 Park Square, Milton Park, Abingdon, Oxford OX14 4RN, United Kingdom, (Dial from U.S. (212) 216-7800), (Fax from U.S. (212) 564-7854), www.tandf.co.uk; *The Europa World Year Book.*

United Nations Statistics Division, New York, NY 10017, (800) 253-9646, Fax: (212) 963-4116, http://unstats.un.org; *Statistical Yearbook.*

The World Bank, 1818 H Street, NW, Washington, DC 20433, (202) 473-1000, Fax: (202) 477-6391, www.worldbank.org; *Hong Kong, China.*

HONG KONG - CONSUMPTION (ECONOMICS)

Economist Intelligence Unit, 111 West 57th Street, New York, NY 10019, (212) 554-0600, Fax: (212) 586-1181, www.eiu.com; *Business Asia.*

The World Bank, 1818 H Street, NW, Washington, DC 20433, (202) 473-1000, Fax: (202) 477-6391, www.worldbank.org; *World Development Report 2008.*

HONG KONG - COPPER INDUSTRY AND TRADE

See HONG KONG - MINERAL INDUSTRIES

HONG KONG - CORN INDUSTRY

See HONG KONG - CROPS

HONG KONG - COST AND STANDARD OF LIVING

United Nations Statistics Division, New York, NY 10017, (800) 253-9646, Fax: (212) 963-4116, http://unstats.un.org; *Statistical Yearbook for Asia and the Pacific 2004.*

HONG KONG - COTTON

See HONG KONG - CROPS

HONG KONG - CRIME

International Criminal Police Organization (INTERPOL), General Secretariat, 200 quai Charles de Gaulle, 69006 Lyon, France, www.interpol.int; *International Crime Statistics.*

U.S. Department of Justice (DOJ), Bureau of Justice Statistics, 810 Seventh Street, NW, Washington, DC 20531, (202) 307-0765, www.ojp.usdoj.gov/bjs/; *The World Factbook of Criminal Justice Systems.*

Yale University Press, PO Box 209040, New Haven, CT 06520-9040, (203) 432-0960, Fax: (203) 432-0948, http://yalepress.yale.edu/yupbooks; *Violence and Crime in Cross-National Perspective.*

HONG KONG - CROPS

Asian Development Bank (ADB), PO Box 789, 0980 Manila, Philippines, www.adb.org; *Key Indicators of Developing Asian and Pacific Countries 2006.*

M.E. Sharpe, 80 Business Park Drive, Armonk, NY 10504, (800) 541-6563, Fax: (914) 273-2106, www.mesharpe.com; *The Illustrated Book of World Rankings.*

Palgrave Macmillan Ltd., Houndmills, Basingstoke, Hampshire, RG21 6XS, England, (Telephone in U.S. (888) 330-8477), (Fax in U.S. (800) 672-2054), www.palgrave.com; *The Statesman's Yearbook 2008.*

Taylor and Francis Group, An Informa Business, 2 Park Square, Milton Park, Abingdon, Oxford OX14 4RN, United Kingdom, (Dial from U.S. (212) 216-7800), (Fax from U.S. (212) 564-7854), www.tandf.co.uk; *The Europa World Year Book.*

United Nations Conference on Trade and Development (UNCTAD), DC2-1120, United Nations, New York, NY 10017, (212) 963-0027, www.unctad.org; *UNCTAD Commodity Yearbook.*

United Nations Food and Agricultural Organization (FAO), Viale delle Terme di Caracalla, 00100 Rome, Italy, (Dial from U.S. (202) 653-2400), (Fax from U.S. (202) 653 5760), www.fao.org; *FAO Production Yearbook 2002* and *The State of Food and Agriculture (SOFA) 2006.*

United Nations Statistics Division, New York, NY 10017, (800) 253-9646, Fax: (212) 963-4116, http://unstats.un.org; *Statistical Yearbook.*

HONG KONG - CUSTOMS ADMINISTRATION

Palgrave Macmillan Ltd., Houndmills, Basingstoke, Hampshire, RG21 6XS, England, (Telephone in U.S. (888) 330-8477), (Fax in U.S. (800) 672-2054), www.palgrave.com; *The Statesman's Yearbook 2008.*

HONG KONG - DAIRY PROCESSING

Economist Intelligence Unit, 111 West 57th Street, New York, NY 10019, (212) 554-0600, Fax: (212) 586-1181, www.eiu.com; *Business Asia.*

M.E. Sharpe, 80 Business Park Drive, Armonk, NY 10504, (800) 541-6563, Fax: (914) 273-2106, www.mesharpe.com; *The Illustrated Book of World Rankings.*

Palgrave Macmillan Ltd., Houndmills, Basingstoke, Hampshire, RG21 6XS, England, (Telephone in U.S. (888) 330-8477), (Fax in U.S. (800) 672-2054), www.palgrave.com; *The Statesman's Yearbook 2008.*

United Nations Food and Agricultural Organization (FAO), Viale delle Terme di Caracalla, 00100 Rome, Italy, (Dial from U.S. (202) 653-2400), (Fax from U.S. (202) 653 5760), www.fao.org; *FAO Production Yearbook 2002* and *The State of Food and Agriculture (SOFA) 2006.*

United Nations Statistics Division, New York, NY 10017, (800) 253-9646, Fax: (212) 963-4116, http://unstats.un.org; *Statistical Yearbook.*

HONG KONG - DEATH RATES

See HONG KONG - MORTALITY

HONG KONG - DEBTS, EXTERNAL

Asian Development Bank (ADB), PO Box 789, 0980 Manila, Philippines, www.adb.org; *Key Indicators of Developing Asian and Pacific Countries 2006.*

Palgrave Macmillan Ltd., Houndmills, Basingstoke, Hampshire, RG21 6XS, England, (Telephone in U.S. (888) 330-8477), (Fax in U.S. (800) 672-2054), www.palgrave.com; *The Statesman's Yearbook 2008.*

The World Bank, 1818 H Street, NW, Washington, DC 20433, (202) 473-1000, Fax: (202) 477-6391, www.worldbank.org; *Global Development Finance 2007; World Development Indicators (WDI) 2008;* and *World Development Report 2008.*

Worldinformation.com, 2 Market Street, Saffron Walden, Essex CB10 1HZ, United Kingdom, www.worldinformation.com; The World of Information (www.worldinformation.com).

HONG KONG - DEMOGRAPHY

Economist Intelligence Unit, 111 West 57th Street, New York, NY 10019, (212) 554-0600, Fax: (212) 586-1181, www.eiu.com; *Business Asia.*

Euromonitor International, Inc., 224 S. Michigan Avenue, Suite 1500, Chicago, IL 60604, (312) 922-1115, Fax: (312) 922-1157, www.euromonitor.com; *International Marketing Data and Statistics 2008; The World Economic Factbook 2008;* and *World Marketing Data and Statistics.*

M.E. Sharpe, 80 Business Park Drive, Armonk, NY 10504, (800) 541-6563, Fax: (914) 273-2106, www.mesharpe.com; *The Illustrated Book of World Rankings.*

United Nations Statistics Division, New York, NY 10017, (800) 253-9646, Fax: (212) 963-4116, http://unstats.un.org; *Asia-Pacific in Figures 2004* and *Human Development Report 2006*.

The World Bank, 1818 H Street, NW, Washington, DC 20433, (202) 473-1000, Fax: (202) 477-6391, www.worldbank.org; *Hong Kong, China*.

HONG KONG - DIAMONDS

See HONG KONG - MINERAL INDUSTRIES

HONG KONG - DISPOSABLE INCOME

M.E. Sharpe, 80 Business Park Drive, Armonk, NY 10504, (800) 541-6563, Fax: (914) 273-2106, www.mesharpe.com; *The Illustrated Book of World Rankings*.

United Nations Statistics Division, New York, NY 10017, (800) 253-9646, Fax: (212) 963-4116, http://unstats.un.org; *National Accounts Statistics: Compendium of Income Distribution Statistics* and *Statistical Yearbook*.

HONG KONG - DIVORCE

M.E. Sharpe, 80 Business Park Drive, Armonk, NY 10504, (800) 541-6563, Fax: (914) 273-2106, www.mesharpe.com; *The Illustrated Book of World Rankings*.

United Nations Statistics Division, New York, NY 10017, (800) 253-9646, Fax: (212) 963-4116, http://unstats.un.org; *Demographic Yearbook* and *Statistical Yearbook*.

HONG KONG - ECONOMIC ASSISTANCE

Asian Development Bank (ADB), PO Box 789, 0980 Manila, Philippines, www.adb.org; *Key Indicators of Developing Asian and Pacific Countries 2006*.

United Nations Statistics Division, New York, NY 10017, (800) 253-9646, Fax: (212) 963-4116, http://unstats.un.org; *Statistical Yearbook*.

HONG KONG - ECONOMIC CONDITIONS

Asian Development Bank (ADB), PO Box 789, 0980 Manila, Philippines, www.adb.org; *Key Indicators of Developing Asian and Pacific Countries 2006*.

Census and Statistics Department (CSD), 21/F Wanchai Tower, 12 Harbour Road, Wan Chai, Hong Kong, China, www.censtatd.gov.hk; *A Graphic Guide on Hong Kong's Development (1967-2002); Hong Kong Economic Trends;* and *Hong Kong Social and Economic Trends*.

Center for International Business Education Research (CIBER), Columbia Business School and School of International and Public Affairs, Uris Hall, Room 212, 3022 Broadway, New York, NY 10027-6902, Mr. Joshua Safier, (212) 854-4750, Fax: (212) 222-9821, www.columbia.edu/cu/ciber/; Datastream International.

Central Intelligence Agency, Office of Public Affairs, Washington, DC 20505, (703) 482-0623, Fax: (703) 482-1739, www.cia.gov; *The World Factbook*.

DSI Data Service Information, Xantener Strasse 51a, D-47495 Rheinberg, Germany, www.dsidata.com; *Campus Solution*.

Dun and Bradstreet (DB) Corporation, 103 JFK Parkway, Short Hills, NJ 07078, (973) 921-5500, www.dnb.com; *Country Report*.

Economist Intelligence Unit, 111 West 57th Street, New York, NY 10019, (212) 554-0600, Fax: (212) 586-1181, www.eiu.com; *Business Asia* and *Hong Kong Country Report*.

Euromonitor International, Inc., 224 S. Michigan Avenue, Suite 1500, Chicago, IL 60604, (312) 922-1115, Fax: (312) 922-1157, www.euromonitor.com; *International Marketing Data and Statistics 2008; The World Economic Factbook 2008;* and *World Marketing Data and Statistics*.

International Monetary Fund (IMF), 700 Nineteenth Street, NW, Washington, DC 20431, (202) 623-7000, Fax: (202) 623-4661, www.imf.org; *World Economic Outlook Reports*.

M.E. Sharpe, 80 Business Park Drive, Armonk, NY 10504, (800) 541-6563, Fax: (914) 273-2106, www.mesharpe.com; *The Illustrated Book of World Rankings*.

Nomura Research Institute (NRI), 2 World Financial Center, Building B, 19th Fl., New York, NY 10281-1198, (212) 667-1670, www.nri.co.jp/english; *Asian Economic Outlook 2003-2004*.

Palgrave Macmillan Ltd., Houndmills, Basingstoke, Hampshire, RG21 6XS, England, (Telephone in U.S. (888) 330-8477), (Fax in U.S. (800) 672-2054), www.palgrave.com; *The Statesman's Yearbook 2008*.

Taylor and Francis Group, An Informa Business, 2 Park Square, Milton Park, Abingdon, Oxford OX14 4RN, United Kingdom, (Dial from U.S. (212) 216-7800), (Fax from U.S. (212) 564-7854), www.tandf.co.uk; *The Europa World Year Book*.

United Nations Statistics Division, New York, NY 10017, (800) 253-9646, Fax: (212) 963-4116, http://unstats.un.org; *World Statistics Pocketbook*.

The World Bank, 1818 H Street, NW, Washington, DC 20433, (202) 473-1000, Fax: (202) 477-6391, www.worldbank.org; *Global Economic Monitor (GEM); Global Economic Prospects 2008; Hong Kong, China; The World Bank Atlas 2003-2004;* and *World Development Report 2008*.

HONG KONG - EDUCATION

Economist Intelligence Unit, 111 West 57th Street, New York, NY 10019, (212) 554-0600, Fax: (212) 586-1181, www.eiu.com; *Business Asia*.

Euromonitor International, Inc., 224 S. Michigan Avenue, Suite 1500, Chicago, IL 60604, (312) 922-1115, Fax: (312) 922-1157, www.euromonitor.com; *International Marketing Data and Statistics 2008* and *World Marketing Data and Statistics*.

M.E. Sharpe, 80 Business Park Drive, Armonk, NY 10504, (800) 541-6563, Fax: (914) 273-2106, www.mesharpe.com; *The Illustrated Book of World Rankings*.

Palgrave Macmillan Ltd., Houndmills, Basingstoke, Hampshire, RG21 6XS, England, (Telephone in U.S. (888) 330-8477), (Fax in U.S. (800) 672-2054), www.palgrave.com; *The Statesman's Yearbook 2008*.

Taylor and Francis Group, An Informa Business, 2 Park Square, Milton Park, Abingdon, Oxford OX14 4RN, United Kingdom, (Dial from U.S. (212) 216-7800), (Fax from U.S. (212) 564-7854), www.tandf.co.uk; *The Europa World Year Book*.

UNESCO Institute for Statistics, C.P. 6128 Succursale Centre-Ville, Montreal, Quebec, H3C 3J7 Canada, (Dial from U.S. (514) 343-6880), (Fax from U.S. (514) 343 6882), www.uis.unesco.org; *Statistical Tables*.

United Nations Statistics Division, New York, NY 10017, (800) 253-9646, Fax: (212) 963-4116, http://unstats.un.org; *Asia-Pacific in Figures 2004* and *Human Development Report 2006*.

The World Bank, 1818 H Street, NW, Washington, DC 20433, (202) 473-1000, Fax: (202) 477-6391, www.worldbank.org; *Hong Kong, China; World Development Indicators (WDI) 2008;* and *World Development Report 2008*.

HONG KONG - ELECTRICITY

Asian Development Bank (ADB), PO Box 789, 0980 Manila, Philippines, www.adb.org; *Key Indicators of Developing Asian and Pacific Countries 2006*.

Central Intelligence Agency, Office of Public Affairs, Washington, DC 20505, (703) 482-0623, Fax: (703) 482-1739, www.cia.gov; *The World Factbook*.

Economist Intelligence Unit, 111 West 57th Street, New York, NY 10019, (212) 554-0600, Fax: (212) 586-1181, www.eiu.com; *Business Asia*.

M.E. Sharpe, 80 Business Park Drive, Armonk, NY 10504, (800) 541-6563, Fax: (914) 273-2106, www.mesharpe.com; *The Illustrated Book of World Rankings*.

Palgrave Macmillan Ltd., Houndmills, Basingstoke, Hampshire, RG21 6XS, England, (Telephone in U.S. (888) 330-8477), (Fax in U.S. (800) 672-2054), www.palgrave.com; *The Statesman's Yearbook 2008*.

Platts, 2 Penn Plaza, 25th Floor, New York, NY 10121-2298, (212) 904-3070, www.platts.com; *Asian Electricity Outlook 2006* and *Emissions Daily*.

U.S. Department of Energy (DOE), Energy Information Administration (EIA), 1000 Independence Avenue, SW, Washington, DC 20585, (202) 586-8800, www.eia.doe.gov; *International Energy Annual 2004* and *International Energy Outlook 2006*.

United Nations Statistics Division, New York, NY 10017, (800) 253-9646, Fax: (212) 963-4116, http://unstats.un.org; *Electric Power in Asia and the Pacific 2001 and 2002; Human Development Report 2006;* and *Statistical Yearbook*.

HONG KONG - EMPLOYMENT

Economist Intelligence Unit, 111 West 57th Street, New York, NY 10019, (212) 554-0600, Fax: (212) 586-1181, www.eiu.com; *Business Asia*.

Euromonitor International, Inc., 224 S. Michigan Avenue, Suite 1500, Chicago, IL 60604, (312) 922-1115, Fax: (312) 922-1157, www.euromonitor.com; *International Marketing Data and Statistics 2008*.

International Labour Office, I.L.O. Publications, 4 route des Morillons, CH-1211 Geneva 22, Switzerland, (Telephone in U.S. (202) 653-7652), (Fax in U.S. (202) 653-7687), www.ilo.org; *Yearbook of Labour Statistics 2006*.

M.E. Sharpe, 80 Business Park Drive, Armonk, NY 10504, (800) 541-6563, Fax: (914) 273-2106, www.mesharpe.com; *The Illustrated Book of World Rankings*.

United Nations Statistics Division, New York, NY 10017, (800) 253-9646, Fax: (212) 963-4116, http://unstats.un.org; *Asia-Pacific in Figures 2004* and *Statistical Yearbook*.

The World Bank, 1818 H Street, NW, Washington, DC 20433, (202) 473-1000, Fax: (202) 477-6391, www.worldbank.org; *Hong Kong, China*.

HONG KONG - ENERGY INDUSTRIES

Economist Intelligence Unit, 111 West 57th Street, New York, NY 10019, (212) 554-0600, Fax: (212) 586-1181, www.eiu.com; *Business Asia*.

Enerdata, 10 Rue Royale, 75008 Paris, France, www.enerdata.fr; *Global Energy Market Data*.

Platts, 2 Penn Plaza, 25th Floor, New York, NY 10121-2298, (212) 904-3070, www.platts.com; *Asian Electricity Outlook 2006* and *Emissions Daily*.

United Nations Statistics Division, New York, NY 10017, (800) 253-9646, Fax: (212) 963-4116, http://unstats.un.org; *Electric Power in Asia and the Pacific 2001 and 2002* and *Statistical Yearbook*.

HONG KONG - ENVIRONMENTAL CONDITIONS

DSI Data Service Information, Xantener Strasse 51a, D-47495 Rheinberg, Germany, www.dsidata.com; *Campus Solution* and *DSI's Global Environmental Database*.

Economist Intelligence Unit, 111 West 57th Street, New York, NY 10019, (212) 554-0600, Fax: (212) 586-1181, www.eiu.com; *Hong Kong Country Report*.

Platts, 2 Penn Plaza, 25th Floor, New York, NY 10121-2298, (212) 904-3070, www.platts.com; *Emissions Daily*.

United Nations Statistics Division, New York, NY 10017, (800) 253-9646, Fax: (212) 963-4116, http://unstats.un.org; *World Statistics Pocketbook*.

HONG KONG - EXPORTS

Asian Development Bank (ADB), PO Box 789, 0980 Manila, Philippines, www.adb.org; *Key Indicators of Developing Asian and Pacific Countries 2006*.

Central Intelligence Agency, Office of Public Affairs, Washington, DC 20505, (703) 482-0623, Fax: (703) 482-1739, www.cia.gov; *The World Factbook*.

Economist Intelligence Unit, 111 West 57th Street, New York, NY 10019, (212) 554-0600, Fax: (212) 586-1181, www.eiu.com; *Hong Kong Country Report.*

Euromonitor International, Inc., 224 S. Michigan Avenue, Suite 1500, Chicago, IL 60604, (312) 922-1115, Fax: (312) 922-1157, www.euromonitor.com; *International Marketing Data and Statistics 2008* and *The World Economic Factbook 2008.*

International Monetary Fund (IMF), 700 Nineteenth Street, NW, Washington, DC 20431, (202) 623-7000, Fax: (202) 623-4661, www.imf.org; *Direction of Trade Statistics Yearbook 2007.*

Palgrave Macmillan Ltd., Houndmills, Basingstoke, Hampshire, RG21 6XS, England, (Telephone in U.S. (888) 330-8477), (Fax in U.S. (800) 672-2054), www.palgrave.com; *The Statesman's Yearbook 2008.*

Taylor and Francis Group, An Informa Business, 2 Park Square, Milton Park, Abingdon, Oxford OX14 4RN, United Kingdom, (Dial from U.S. (212) 216-7800), (Fax from U.S. (212) 564-7854), www.tandf.co.uk; *The Europa World Year Book.*

United Nations Food and Agricultural Organization (FAO), Viale delle Terme di Caracalla, 00100 Rome, Italy, (Dial from U.S. (202) 653-2400), (Fax from U.S. (202) 653 5760), www.fao.org; *The State of Food and Agriculture (SOFA) 2006.*

United Nations Statistics Division, New York, NY 10017, (800) 253-9646, Fax: (212) 963-4116, http://unstats.un.org; *Foreign Trade Statistics of Asia and the Pacific 1996-2000.*

The World Bank, 1818 H Street, NW, Washington, DC 20433, (202) 473-1000, Fax: (202) 477-6391, www.worldbank.org; *World Development Indicators (WDI) 2008* and *World Development Report 2008.*

Worldinformation.com, 2 Market Street, Saffron Walden, Essex CB10 1HZ, United Kingdom, www.worldinformation.com; The World of Information (www.worldinformation.com).

HONG KONG - FEMALE WORKING POPULATION

See HONG KONG - EMPLOYMENT

HONG KONG - FERTILITY, HUMAN

Central Intelligence Agency, Office of Public Affairs, Washington, DC 20505, (703) 482-0623, Fax: (703) 482-1739, www.cia.gov; *The World Factbook.*

M.E. Sharpe, 80 Business Park Drive, Armonk, NY 10504, (800) 541-6563, Fax: (914) 273-2106, www.mesharpe.com; *The Illustrated Book of World Rankings.*

United Nations Statistics Division, New York, NY 10017, (800) 253-9646, Fax: (212) 963-4116, http://unstats.un.org; *Human Development Report 2006.*

The World Bank, 1818 H Street, NW, Washington, DC 20433, (202) 473-1000, Fax: (202) 477-6391, www.worldbank.org; *The World Bank Atlas 2003-2004; World Development Indicators (WDI) 2008;* and *World Development Report 2008.*

HONG KONG - FERTILIZER INDUSTRY

United Nations Food and Agricultural Organization (FAO), Viale delle Terme di Caracalla, 00100 Rome, Italy, (Dial from U.S. (202) 653-2400), (Fax from U.S. (202) 653 5760), www.fao.org; *FAO Fertilizer Yearbook* and *The State of Food and Agriculture (SOFA) 2006.*

HONG KONG - FETAL MORTALITY

See HONG KONG - MORTALITY

HONG KONG - FILM

See HONG KONG - MOTION PICTURES

HONG KONG - FINANCE

Taylor and Francis Group, An Informa Business, 2 Park Square, Milton Park, Abingdon, Oxford OX14 4RN, United Kingdom, (Dial from U.S. (212) 216-7800), (Fax from U.S. (212) 564-7854), www.tandf.co.uk; *The Europa World Year Book.*

United Nations Statistics Division, New York, NY 10017, (800) 253-9646, Fax: (212) 963-4116, http://unstats.un.org; *Asia-Pacific in Figures 2004; National Accounts Statistics: Compendium of Income Distribution Statistics; Statistical Yearbook;* and *Statistical Yearbook for Asia and the Pacific 2004.*

The World Bank, 1818 H Street, NW, Washington, DC 20433, (202) 473-1000, Fax: (202) 477-6391, www.worldbank.org; *Hong Kong, China.*

HONG KONG - FINANCE, PUBLIC

Asian Development Bank (ADB), PO Box 789, 0980 Manila, Philippines, www.adb.org; *Key Indicators of Developing Asian and Pacific Countries 2006.*

Bernan Essential Government Publications, 4611-F Assembly Drive, Lanham MD, 20706-4391, (301) 459-2255, Fax: (800) 865-3450, www.bernan.com; *National Accounts Statistics.*

Economist Intelligence Unit, 111 West 57th Street, New York, NY 10019, (212) 554-0600, Fax: (212) 586-1181, www.eiu.com; *Hong Kong Country Report.*

International Monetary Fund (IMF), 700 Nineteenth Street, NW, Washington, DC 20431, (202) 623-7000, Fax: (202) 623-4661, www.imf.org; *International Financial Statistics* and *International Financial Statistics Online Service.*

M.E. Sharpe, 80 Business Park Drive, Armonk, NY 10504, (800) 541-6563, Fax: (914) 273-2106, www.mesharpe.com; *The Illustrated Book of World Rankings.*

Palgrave Macmillan Ltd., Houndmills, Basingstoke, Hampshire, RG21 6XS, England, (Telephone in U.S. (888) 330-8477), (Fax in U.S. (800) 672-2054), www.palgrave.com; *The Statesman's Yearbook 2008.*

Taylor and Francis Group, An Informa Business, 2 Park Square, Milton Park, Abingdon, Oxford OX14 4RN, United Kingdom, (Dial from U.S. (212) 216-7800), (Fax from U.S. (212) 564-7854), www.tandf.co.uk; *The Europa World Year Book.*

United Nations Statistics Division, New York, NY 10017, (800) 253-9646, Fax: (212) 963-4116, http://unstats.un.org; *Statistical Yearbook for Asia and the Pacific 2004.*

The World Bank, 1818 H Street, NW, Washington, DC 20433, (202) 473-1000, Fax: (202) 477-6391, www.worldbank.org; *Hong Kong, China.*

HONG KONG - FISHERIES

Economist Intelligence Unit, 111 West 57th Street, New York, NY 10019, (212) 554-0600, Fax: (212) 586-1181, www.eiu.com; *Business Asia.*

M.E. Sharpe, 80 Business Park Drive, Armonk, NY 10504, (800) 541-6563, Fax: (914) 273-2106, www.mesharpe.com; *The Illustrated Book of World Rankings.*

Palgrave Macmillan Ltd., Houndmills, Basingstoke, Hampshire, RG21 6XS, England, (Telephone in U.S. (888) 330-8477), (Fax in U.S. (800) 672-2054), www.palgrave.com; *The Statesman's Yearbook 2008.*

Taylor and Francis Group, An Informa Business, 2 Park Square, Milton Park, Abingdon, Oxford OX14 4RN, United Kingdom, (Dial from U.S. (212) 216-7800), (Fax from U.S. (212) 564-7854), www.tandf.co.uk; *The Europa World Year Book.*

United Nations Conference on Trade and Development (UNCTAD), DC2-1120, United Nations, New York, NY 10017, (212) 963-0027, www.unctad.org; *UNCTAD Commodity Yearbook.*

United Nations Food and Agricultural Organization (FAO), Viale delle Terme di Caracalla, 00100 Rome, Italy, (Dial from U.S. (202) 653-2400), (Fax from U.S. (202) 653 5760), www.fao.org; *FAO Yearbook of Fishery Statistics;* Fishery Databases; FISHSTAT Database. Subjects covered include: Aquaculture production, capture production, fishery commodities; and *The State of Food and Agriculture (SOFA) 2006.*

United Nations Statistics Division, New York, NY 10017, (800) 253-9646, Fax: (212) 963-4116, http://unstats.un.org; *Statistical Yearbook.*

The World Bank, 1818 H Street, NW, Washington, DC 20433, (202) 473-1000, Fax: (202) 477-6391, www.worldbank.org; *Hong Kong, China.*

HONG KONG - FOOD

Euromonitor International, Inc., 224 S. Michigan Avenue, Suite 1500, Chicago, IL 60604, (312) 922-1115, Fax: (312) 922-1157, www.euromonitor.com; *Retail Trade International 2007.*

United Nations Conference on Trade and Development (UNCTAD), DC2-1120, United Nations, New York, NY 10017, (212) 963-0027, www.unctad.org; *UNCTAD Commodity Yearbook.*

United Nations Food and Agricultural Organization (FAO), Viale delle Terme di Caracalla, 00100 Rome, Italy, (Dial from U.S. (202) 653-2400), (Fax from U.S. (202) 653 5760), www.fao.org; *FAO Production Yearbook 2002* and *The State of Food and Agriculture (SOFA) 2006.*

United Nations Statistics Division, New York, NY 10017, (800) 253-9646, Fax: (212) 963-4116, http://unstats.un.org; *Human Development Report 2006* and *Statistical Yearbook for Asia and the Pacific 2004.*

HONG KONG - FOREIGN EXCHANGE RATES

Asian Development Bank (ADB), PO Box 789, 0980 Manila, Philippines, www.adb.org; *Key Indicators of Developing Asian and Pacific Countries 2006.*

Central Intelligence Agency, Office of Public Affairs, Washington, DC 20505, (703) 482-0623, Fax: (703) 482-1739, www.cia.gov; *The World Factbook.*

Economist Intelligence Unit, 111 West 57th Street, New York, NY 10019, (212) 554-0600, Fax: (212) 586-1181, www.eiu.com; *Business Asia.*

Euromonitor International, Inc., 224 S. Michigan Avenue, Suite 1500, Chicago, IL 60604, (312) 922-1115, Fax: (312) 922-1157, www.euromonitor.com; *International Marketing Data and Statistics 2008* and *The World Economic Factbook 2008.*

International Civil Aviation Organization (ICAO), External Relations and Public Information Office (EPO), 999 University Street, Montreal, Quebec H3C 5H7, Canada, (Dial from U.S. (514) 954-8219), (Fax from U.S. (514) 954-6077), www.icao.int; *Civil Aviation Statistics of the World.*

Taylor and Francis Group, An Informa Business, 2 Park Square, Milton Park, Abingdon, Oxford OX14 4RN, United Kingdom, (Dial from U.S. (212) 216-7800), (Fax from U.S. (212) 564-7854), www.tandf.co.uk; *The Europa World Year Book.*

United Nations Statistics Division, New York, NY 10017, (800) 253-9646, Fax: (212) 963-4116, http://unstats.un.org; *World Statistics Pocketbook.*

Worldinformation.com, 2 Market Street, Saffron Walden, Essex CB10 1HZ, United Kingdom, www.worldinformation.com; The World of Information (www.worldinformation.com).

HONG KONG - FORESTS AND FORESTRY

Economist Intelligence Unit, 111 West 57th Street, New York, NY 10019, (212) 554-0600, Fax: (212) 586-1181, www.eiu.com; *Business Asia.*

M.E. Sharpe, 80 Business Park Drive, Armonk, NY 10504, (800) 541-6563, Fax: (914) 273-2106, www.mesharpe.com; *The Illustrated Book of World Rankings.*

UNESCO Institute for Statistics, C.P. 6128 Succursale Centre-Ville, Montreal, Quebec, H3C 3J7 Canada, (Dial from U.S. (514) 343-6880), (Fax from U.S. (514) 343 6882), www.uis.unesco.org; *Statistical Tables.*

United Nations Conference on Trade and Development (UNCTAD), DC2-1120, United Nations, New York, NY 10017, (212) 963-0027, www.unctad.org; *UNCTAD Commodity Yearbook.*

United Nations Food and Agricultural Organization (FAO), Viale delle Terme di Caracalla, 00100 Rome, Italy, (Dial from U.S. (202) 653-2400), (Fax from U.S. (202) 653 5760), www.fao.org; *FAO Yearbook of Forest Products* and *The State of Food and Agriculture (SOFA) 2006*.

United Nations Statistics Division, New York, NY 10017, (800) 253-9646, Fax: (212) 963-4116, http://unstats.un.org; *Statistical Yearbook*.

The World Bank, 1818 H Street, NW, Washington, DC 20433, (202) 473-1000, Fax: (202) 477-6391, www.worldbank.org; *Hong Kong, China* and *World Development Report 2008*.

HONG KONG - GAS PRODUCTION

See HONG KONG - MINERAL INDUSTRIES

HONG KONG - GEOGRAPHIC INFORMATION SYSTEMS

M.E. Sharpe, 80 Business Park Drive, Armonk, NY 10504, (800) 541-6563, Fax: (914) 273-2106, www.mesharpe.com; *The Illustrated Book of World Rankings*.

HONG KONG - GOLD INDUSTRY

The World Bank, 1818 H Street, NW, Washington, DC 20433, (202) 473-1000, Fax: (202) 477-6391, www.worldbank.org; *World Development Indicators (WDI) 2008*.

HONG KONG - GOLD PRODUCTION

See HONG KONG - MINERAL INDUSTRIES

HONG KONG - GROSS DOMESTIC PRODUCT

Asian Development Bank (ADB), PO Box 789, 0980 Manila, Philippines, www.adb.org; *Key Indicators of Developing Asian and Pacific Countries 2006*.

Economist Intelligence Unit, 111 West 57th Street, New York, NY 10019, (212) 554-0600, Fax: (212) 586-1181, www.eiu.com; *Business Asia* and *Hong Kong Country Report*.

Euromonitor International, Inc., 224 S. Michigan Avenue, Suite 1500, Chicago, IL 60604, (312) 922-1115, Fax: (312) 922-1157, www.euromonitor.com; *International Marketing Data and Statistics 2008* and *The World Economic Factbook 2008*.

M.E. Sharpe, 80 Business Park Drive, Armonk, NY 10504, (800) 541-6563, Fax: (914) 273-2106, www.mesharpe.com; *The Illustrated Book of World Rankings*.

Taylor and Francis Group, An Informa Business, 2 Park Square, Milton Park, Abingdon, Oxford OX14 4RN, United Kingdom, (Dial from U.S. (212) 216-7800), (Fax from U.S. (212) 564-7854), www.tandf.co.uk; *The Europa World Year Book*.

United Nations Statistics Division, New York, NY 10017, (800) 253-9646, Fax: (212) 963-4116, http://unstats.un.org; *Human Development Report 2006; National Accounts Statistics: Compendium of Income Distribution Statistics;* and *Statistical Yearbook*.

The World Bank, 1818 H Street, NW, Washington, DC 20433, (202) 473-1000, Fax: (202) 477-6391, www.worldbank.org; *World Development Indicators (WDI) 2008* and *World Development Report 2008*.

HONG KONG - GROSS NATIONAL PRODUCT

Asian Development Bank (ADB), PO Box 789, 0980 Manila, Philippines, www.adb.org; *Key Indicators of Developing Asian and Pacific Countries 2006*.

Euromonitor International, Inc., 224 S. Michigan Avenue, Suite 1500, Chicago, IL 60604, (312) 922-1115, Fax: (312) 922-1157, www.euromonitor.com; *International Marketing Data and Statistics 2008*.

M.E. Sharpe, 80 Business Park Drive, Armonk, NY 10504, (800) 541-6563, Fax: (914) 273-2106, www.mesharpe.com; *The Illustrated Book of World Rankings*.

Palgrave Macmillan Ltd., Houndmills, Basingstoke, Hampshire, RG21 6XS, England, (Telephone in U.S. (888) 330-8477), (Fax in U.S. (800) 672-2054), www.palgrave.com; *The Statesman's Yearbook 2008*.

United Nations Statistics Division, New York, NY 10017, (800) 253-9646, Fax: (212) 963-4116, http://unstats.un.org; *Statistical Yearbook*.

The World Bank, 1818 H Street, NW, Washington, DC 20433, (202) 473-1000, Fax: (202) 477-6391, www.worldbank.org; *The World Bank Atlas 2003-2004; World Development Indicators (WDI) 2008;* and *World Development Report 2008*.

Worldinformation.com, 2 Market Street, Saffron Walden, Essex CB10 1HZ, United Kingdom, www.worldinformation.com; The World of Information (www.worldinformation.com).

HONG KONG - HANG SENG STOCK MARKET INDEX

Global Financial Data, Inc., 784 Fremont Villas, Los Angeles, CA 90042, (323) 924-1016, www.globalfindata.com; unpublished data.

HONG KONG - HIDES AND SKINS INDUSTRY

United Nations Food and Agricultural Organization (FAO), Viale delle Terme di Caracalla, 00100 Rome, Italy, (Dial from U.S. (202) 653-2400), (Fax from U.S. (202) 653 5760), www.fao.org; *FAO Production Yearbook 2002*.

HONG KONG - HOUSING

Economist Intelligence Unit, 111 West 57th Street, New York, NY 10019, (212) 554-0600, Fax: (212) 586-1181, www.eiu.com; *Business Asia*.

Euromonitor International, Inc., 224 S. Michigan Avenue, Suite 1500, Chicago, IL 60604, (312) 922-1115, Fax: (312) 922-1157, www.euromonitor.com; *World Marketing Data and Statistics*.

M.E. Sharpe, 80 Business Park Drive, Armonk, NY 10504, (800) 541-6563, Fax: (914) 273-2106, www.mesharpe.com; *The Illustrated Book of World Rankings*.

HONG KONG - ILLITERATE PERSONS

Economist Intelligence Unit, 111 West 57th Street, New York, NY 10019, (212) 554-0600, Fax: (212) 586-1181, www.eiu.com; *Business Asia*.

Euromonitor International, Inc., 224 S. Michigan Avenue, Suite 1500, Chicago, IL 60604, (312) 922-1115, Fax: (312) 922-1157, www.euromonitor.com; *The World Economic Factbook 2008*.

UNESCO Institute for Statistics, C.P. 6128 Succursale Centre-Ville, Montreal, Quebec, H3C 3J7 Canada, (Dial from U.S. (514) 343-6880), (Fax from U.S. (514) 343 6882), www.uis.unesco.org; *Statistical Tables*.

United Nations Statistics Division, New York, NY 10017, (800) 253-9646, Fax: (212) 963-4116, http://unstats.un.org; *Asia-Pacific in Figures 2004* and *Human Development Report 2006*.

HONG KONG - IMPORTS

Asian Development Bank (ADB), PO Box 789, 0980 Manila, Philippines, www.adb.org; *Key Indicators of Developing Asian and Pacific Countries 2006*.

Central Intelligence Agency, Office of Public Affairs, Washington, DC 20505, (703) 482-0623, Fax: (703) 482-1739, www.cia.gov; *The World Factbook*.

Economist Intelligence Unit, 111 West 57th Street, New York, NY 10019, (212) 554-0600, Fax: (212) 586-1181, www.eiu.com; *Hong Kong Country Report*.

Euromonitor International, Inc., 224 S. Michigan Avenue, Suite 1500, Chicago, IL 60604, (312) 922-1115, Fax: (312) 922-1157, www.euromonitor.com; *International Marketing Data and Statistics 2008* and *The World Economic Factbook 2008*.

International Monetary Fund (IMF), 700 Nineteenth Street, NW, Washington, DC 20431, (202) 623-7000, Fax: (202) 623-4661, www.imf.org; *Direction of Trade Statistics Yearbook 2007*.

Palgrave Macmillan Ltd., Houndmills, Basingstoke, Hampshire, RG21 6XS, England, (Telephone in U.S. (888) 330-8477), (Fax in U.S. (800) 672-2054), www.palgrave.com; *The Statesman's Yearbook 2008*.

Taylor and Francis Group, An Informa Business, 2 Park Square, Milton Park, Abingdon, Oxford OX14 4RN, United Kingdom, (Dial from U.S. (212) 216-7800), (Fax from U.S. (212) 564-7854), www.tandf.co.uk; *The Europa World Year Book*.

United Nations Food and Agricultural Organization (FAO), Viale delle Terme di Caracalla, 00100 Rome, Italy, (Dial from U.S. (202) 653-2400), (Fax from U.S. (202) 653 5760), www.fao.org; *The State of Food and Agriculture (SOFA) 2006*.

United Nations Statistics Division, New York, NY 10017, (800) 253-9646, Fax: (212) 963-4116, http://unstats.un.org; *Foreign Trade Statistics of Asia and the Pacific 1996-2000*.

The World Bank, 1818 H Street, NW, Washington, DC 20433, (202) 473-1000, Fax: (202) 477-6391, www.worldbank.org; *World Development Indicators (WDI) 2008* and *World Development Report 2008*.

Worldinformation.com, 2 Market Street, Saffron Walden, Essex CB10 1HZ, United Kingdom, www.worldinformation.com; The World of Information (www.worldinformation.com).

HONG KONG - INDUSTRIAL PRODUCTIVITY

Euromonitor International, Inc., 224 S. Michigan Avenue, Suite 1500, Chicago, IL 60604, (312) 922-1115, Fax: (312) 922-1157, www.euromonitor.com; *International Marketing Data and Statistics 2008*.

M.E. Sharpe, 80 Business Park Drive, Armonk, NY 10504, (800) 541-6563, Fax: (914) 273-2106, www.mesharpe.com; *The Illustrated Book of World Rankings*.

HONG KONG - INDUSTRIAL PROPERTY

United Nations Statistics Division, New York, NY 10017, (800) 253-9646, Fax: (212) 963-4116, http://unstats.un.org; *Statistical Yearbook*.

World Intellectual Property Organization (WIPO), PO Box 18, CH-1211 Geneva 20, Switzerland, www.wipo.int; *Industrial Property Statistics* and *Industrial Property Statistics Online Directory*.

HONG KONG - INDUSTRIES

Central Intelligence Agency, Office of Public Affairs, Washington, DC 20505, (703) 482-0623, Fax: (703) 482-1739, www.cia.gov; *The World Factbook*.

Economist Intelligence Unit, 111 West 57th Street, New York, NY 10019, (212) 554-0600, Fax: (212) 586-1181, www.eiu.com; *Hong Kong Country Report*.

Euromonitor International, Inc., 224 S. Michigan Avenue, Suite 1500, Chicago, IL 60604, (312) 922-1115, Fax: (312) 922-1157, www.euromonitor.com; *The World Economic Factbook 2008* and *World Marketing Data and Statistics*.

International Labour Office, I.L.O. Publications, 4 route des Morillons, CH-1211 Geneva 22, Switzerland, (Telephone in U.S. (202) 653-7652), (Fax in U.S. (202) 653-7687), www.ilo.org; *Yearbook of Labour Statistics 2006*.

M.E. Sharpe, 80 Business Park Drive, Armonk, NY 10504, (800) 541-6563, Fax: (914) 273-2106, www.mesharpe.com; *The Illustrated Book of World Rankings*.

Palgrave Macmillan Ltd., Houndmills, Basingstoke, Hampshire, RG21 6XS, England, (Telephone in U.S. (888) 330-8477), (Fax in U.S. (800) 672-2054), www.palgrave.com; *The Statesman's Yearbook 2008*.

Taylor and Francis Group, An Informa Business, 2 Park Square, Milton Park, Abingdon, Oxford OX14 4RN, United Kingdom, (Dial from U.S. (212) 216-7800), (Fax from U.S. (212) 564-7854), www.tandf.co.uk; *The Europa World Year Book*.

United Nations Industrial Development Organization (UNIDO), 1 United Nations Plaza, New York, NY 10017, (212) 963 6890, Fax: (212) 963-7904, http://unido.org; Industrial Statistics Database 2008 (INDSTAT) and *The International Yearbook of Industrial Statistics 2008.*

United Nations Statistics Division, New York, NY 10017, (800) 253-9646, Fax: (212) 963-4116, http://unstats.un.org; *Asia-Pacific in Figures 2004; 2004 Industrial Commodity Statistics Yearbook;* and *Statistical Yearbook for Asia and the Pacific 2004.*

The World Bank, 1818 H Street, NW, Washington, DC 20433, (202) 473-1000, Fax: (202) 477-6391, www.worldbank.org; *Hong Kong, China* and *World Development Indicators (WDI) 2008.*

HONG KONG - INFANT AND MATERNAL MORTALITY

See HONG KONG - MORTALITY

HONG KONG - INTERNATIONAL FINANCE

Asian Development Bank (ADB), PO Box 789, 0980 Manila, Philippines, www.adb.org; *Key Indicators of Developing Asian and Pacific Countries 2006.*

HONG KONG - INTERNATIONAL STATISTICS

Asian Development Bank (ADB), PO Box 789, 0980 Manila, Philippines, www.adb.org; *Key Indicators of Developing Asian and Pacific Countries 2006.*

HONG KONG - INTERNATIONAL TRADE

Asian Development Bank (ADB), PO Box 789, 0980 Manila, Philippines, www.adb.org; *Key Indicators of Developing Asian and Pacific Countries 2006.*

Economist Intelligence Unit, 111 West 57th Street, New York, NY 10019, (212) 554-0600, Fax: (212) 586-1181, www.eiu.com; *Business Asia* and *Hong Kong Country Report.*

Euromonitor International, Inc., 224 S. Michigan Avenue, Suite 1500, Chicago, IL 60604, (312) 922-1115, Fax: (312) 922-1157, www.euromonitor.com; *International Marketing Data and Statistics 2008; The World Economic Factbook 2008;* and *World Marketing Data and Statistics.*

M.E. Sharpe, 80 Business Park Drive, Armonk, NY 10504, (800) 541-6563, Fax: (914) 273-2106, www.mesharpe.com; *The Illustrated Book of World Rankings.*

Palgrave Macmillan Ltd., Houndmills, Basingstoke, Hampshire, RG21 6XS, England, (Telephone in U.S. (888) 330-8477), (Fax in U.S. (800) 672-2054), www.palgrave.com; *The Statesman's Yearbook 2008.*

Taylor and Francis Group, An Informa Business, 2 Park Square, Milton Park, Abingdon, Oxford OX14 4RN, United Kingdom, (Dial from U.S. (212) 216-7800), (Fax from U.S. (212) 564-7854), www.tandf.co.uk; *The Europa World Year Book.*

United Nations Conference on Trade and Development (UNCTAD), DC2-1120, United Nations, New York, NY 10017, (212) 963-0027, www.unctad.org; *UNCTAD Commodity Yearbook.*

United Nations Food and Agricultural Organization (FAO), Viale delle Terme di Caracalla, 00100 Rome, Italy, (Dial from U.S. (202) 653-2400), (Fax from U.S. (202) 653 5760), www.fao.org; *FAO Trade Yearbook* and *The State of Food and Agriculture (SOFA) 2006.*

United Nations Statistics Division, New York, NY 10017, (800) 253-9646, Fax: (212) 963-4116, http://unstats.un.org; *Asia-Pacific in Figures 2004; International Trade Statistics Yearbook; Statistical Yearbook;* and *Statistical Yearbook for Asia and the Pacific 2004.*

The World Bank, 1818 H Street, NW, Washington, DC 20433, (202) 473-1000, Fax: (202) 477-6391, www.worldbank.org; *Hong Kong, China; World Development Indicators (WDI) 2008;* and *World Development Report 2008.*

World Trade Organization (WTO), Centre William Rappard, Rue de Lausanne 154, CH-1211 Geneva 21, Switzerland, www.wto.org; *International Trade Statistics 2006.*

HONG KONG - INTERNET USERS

International Telecommunication Union (ITU), Place des Nations, 1211 Geneva 20, Switzerland, www.itu.int; *World Telecommunication/ICT Indicators Database on CD-ROM; World Telecommunication/ICT Indicators Database Online;* and *Yearbook of Statistics - Telecommunication Services (Chronological Time Series 1997-2006).*

The World Bank, 1818 H Street, NW, Washington, DC 20433, (202) 473-1000, Fax: (202) 477-6391, www.worldbank.org; *Hong Kong, China.*

HONG KONG - IRON AND IRON ORE PRODUCTION

See HONG KONG - MINERAL INDUSTRIES

HONG KONG - IRRIGATION

Euromonitor International, Inc., 224 S. Michigan Avenue, Suite 1500, Chicago, IL 60604, (312) 922-1115, Fax: (312) 922-1157, www.euromonitor.com; *International Marketing Data and Statistics 2008.*

HONG KONG - LABOR

Central Intelligence Agency, Office of Public Affairs, Washington, DC 20505, (703) 482-0623, Fax: (703) 482-1739, www.cia.gov; *The World Factbook.*

Economist Intelligence Unit, 111 West 57th Street, New York, NY 10019, (212) 554-0600, Fax: (212) 586-1181, www.eiu.com; *Business Asia.*

Euromonitor International, Inc., 224 S. Michigan Avenue, Suite 1500, Chicago, IL 60604, (312) 922-1115, Fax: (312) 922-1157, www.euromonitor.com; *International Marketing Data and Statistics 2008* and *World Marketing Data and Statistics.*

International Labour Office, I.L.O. Publications, 4 route des Morillons, CH-1211 Geneva 22, Switzerland, (Telephone in U.S. (202) 653-7652), (Fax in U.S. (202) 653-7687), www.ilo.org; *Yearbook of Labour Statistics 2006.*

M.E. Sharpe, 80 Business Park Drive, Armonk, NY 10504, (800) 541-6563, Fax: (914) 273-2106, www.mesharpe.com; *The Illustrated Book of World Rankings.*

Palgrave Macmillan Ltd., Houndmills, Basingstoke, Hampshire, RG21 6XS, England, (Telephone in U.S. (888) 330-8477), (Fax in U.S. (800) 672-2054), www.palgrave.com; *The Statesman's Yearbook 2008.*

Taylor and Francis Group, An Informa Business, 2 Park Square, Milton Park, Abingdon, Oxford OX14 4RN, United Kingdom, (Dial from U.S. (212) 216-7800), (Fax from U.S. (212) 564-7854), www.tandf.co.uk; *The Europa World Year Book.*

United Nations Food and Agricultural Organization (FAO), Viale delle Terme di Caracalla, 00100 Rome, Italy, (Dial from U.S. (202) 653-2400), (Fax from U.S. (202) 653 5760), www.fao.org; *The State of Food and Agriculture (SOFA) 2006.*

United Nations Statistics Division, New York, NY 10017, (800) 253-9646, Fax: (212) 963-4116, http://unstats.un.org; *Human Development Report 2006.*

The World Bank, 1818 H Street, NW, Washington, DC 20433, (202) 473-1000, Fax: (202) 477-6391, www.worldbank.org; *The World Bank Atlas 2003-2004; World Development Indicators (WDI) 2008;* and *World Development Report 2008.*

HONG KONG - LAND USE

Central Intelligence Agency, Office of Public Affairs, Washington, DC 20505, (703) 482-0623, Fax: (703) 482-1739, www.cia.gov; *The World Factbook.*

Euromonitor International, Inc., 224 S. Michigan Avenue, Suite 1500, Chicago, IL 60604, (312) 922-1115, Fax: (312) 922-1157, www.euromonitor.com; *International Marketing Data and Statistics 2008.*

United Nations Food and Agricultural Organization (FAO), Viale delle Terme di Caracalla, 00100 Rome, Italy, (Dial from U.S. (202) 653-2400), (Fax from U.S. (202) 653 5760), www.fao.org; *FAO Production Yearbook 2002.*

The World Bank, 1818 H Street, NW, Washington, DC 20433, (202) 473-1000, Fax: (202) 477-6391, www.worldbank.org; *World Development Report 2008.*

HONG KONG - LIBRARIES

M.E. Sharpe, 80 Business Park Drive, Armonk, NY 10504, (800) 541-6563, Fax: (914) 273-2106, www.mesharpe.com; *The Illustrated Book of World Rankings.*

UNESCO Institute for Statistics, C.P. 6128 Succursale Centre-Ville, Montreal, Quebec, H3C 3J7 Canada, (Dial from U.S. (514) 343-6880), (Fax from U.S. (514) 343 6882), www.uis.unesco.org; *Statistical Tables.*

HONG KONG - LIFE EXPECTANCY

Central Intelligence Agency, Office of Public Affairs, Washington, DC 20505, (703) 482-0623, Fax: (703) 482-1739, www.cia.gov; *The World Factbook.*

Economist Intelligence Unit, 111 West 57th Street, New York, NY 10019, (212) 554-0600, Fax: (212) 586-1181, www.eiu.com; *Business Asia.*

Euromonitor International, Inc., 224 S. Michigan Avenue, Suite 1500, Chicago, IL 60604, (312) 922-1115, Fax: (312) 922-1157, www.euromonitor.com; *The World Economic Factbook 2008.*

Palgrave Macmillan Ltd., Houndmills, Basingstoke, Hampshire, RG21 6XS, England, (Telephone in U.S. (888) 330-8477), (Fax in U.S. (800) 672-2054), www.palgrave.com; *The Statesman's Yearbook 2008.*

United Nations Statistics Division, New York, NY 10017, (800) 253-9646, Fax: (212) 963-4116, http://unstats.un.org; *Asia-Pacific in Figures 2004; Human Development Report 2006;* and *World Statistics Pocketbook.*

The World Bank, 1818 H Street, NW, Washington, DC 20433, (202) 473-1000, Fax: (202) 477-6391, www.worldbank.org; *The World Bank Atlas 2003-2004* and *World Development Report 2008.*

HONG KONG - LITERACY

Euromonitor International, Inc., 224 S. Michigan Avenue, Suite 1500, Chicago, IL 60604, (312) 922-1115, Fax: (312) 922-1157, www.euromonitor.com; *World Marketing Data and Statistics.*

HONG KONG - LIVESTOCK

Economist Intelligence Unit, 111 West 57th Street, New York, NY 10019, (212) 554-0600, Fax: (212) 586-1181, www.eiu.com; *Business Asia.*

M.E. Sharpe, 80 Business Park Drive, Armonk, NY 10504, (800) 541-6563, Fax: (914) 273-2106, www.mesharpe.com; *The Illustrated Book of World Rankings.*

Palgrave Macmillan Ltd., Houndmills, Basingstoke, Hampshire, RG21 6XS, England, (Telephone in U.S. (888) 330-8477), (Fax in U.S. (800) 672-2054), www.palgrave.com; *The Statesman's Yearbook 2008.*

Taylor and Francis Group, An Informa Business, 2 Park Square, Milton Park, Abingdon, Oxford OX14 4RN, United Kingdom, (Dial from U.S. (212) 216-7800), (Fax from U.S. (212) 564-7854), www.tandf.co.uk; *The Europa World Year Book.*

United Nations Conference on Trade and Development (UNCTAD), DC2-1120, United Nations, New York, NY 10017, (212) 963-0027, www.unctad.org; *UNCTAD Commodity Yearbook.*

United Nations Food and Agricultural Organization (FAO), Viale delle Terme di Caracalla, 00100 Rome, Italy, (Dial from U.S. (202) 653-2400), (Fax from U.S. (202) 653 5760), www.fao.org; *FAO Production Yearbook 2002* and *The State of Food and Agriculture (SOFA) 2006.*

United Nations Statistics Division, New York, NY 10017, (800) 253-9646, Fax: (212) 963-4116, http://unstats.un.org; *Statistical Yearbook.*

HONG KONG - LOCAL TAXATION

Euromonitor International, Inc., 224 S. Michigan Avenue, Suite 1500, Chicago, IL 60604, (312) 922-1115, Fax: (312) 922-1157, www.euromonitor.com; *International Marketing Data and Statistics 2008.*

HONG KONG - MANPOWER

United Nations Statistics Division, New York, NY 10017, (800) 253-9646, Fax: (212) 963-4116, http://unstats.un.org; *Statistical Yearbook for Asia and the Pacific 2004.*

HONG KONG - MANUFACTURES

Asian Development Bank (ADB), PO Box 789, 0980 Manila, Philippines, www.adb.org; *Key Indicators of Developing Asian and Pacific Countries 2006.*

M.E. Sharpe, 80 Business Park Drive, Armonk, NY 10504, (800) 541-6563, Fax: (914) 273-2106, www.mesharpe.com; *The Illustrated Book of World Rankings.*

United Nations Statistics Division, New York, NY 10017, (800) 253-9646, Fax: (212) 963-4116, http://unstats.un.org; *Statistical Yearbook.*

The World Bank, 1818 H Street, NW, Washington, DC 20433, (202) 473-1000, Fax: (202) 477-6391, www.worldbank.org; *World Development Indicators (WDI) 2008.*

HONG KONG - MARRIAGE

M.E. Sharpe, 80 Business Park Drive, Armonk, NY 10504, (800) 541-6563, Fax: (914) 273-2106, www.mesharpe.com; *The Illustrated Book of World Rankings.*

Taylor and Francis Group, An Informa Business, 2 Park Square, Milton Park, Abingdon, Oxford OX14 4RN, United Kingdom, (Dial from U.S. (212) 216-7800), (Fax from U.S. (212) 564-7854), www.tandf.co.uk; *The Europa World Year Book.*

United Nations Statistics Division, New York, NY 10017, (800) 253-9646, Fax: (212) 963-4116, http://unstats.un.org; *Demographic Yearbook* and *Statistical Yearbook.*

HONG KONG - MEAT PRODUCTION

See HONG KONG - LIVESTOCK

HONG KONG - MILK PRODUCTION

See HONG KONG - DAIRY PROCESSING

HONG KONG - MINERAL INDUSTRIES

Asian Development Bank (ADB), PO Box 789, 0980 Manila, Philippines, www.adb.org; *Key Indicators of Developing Asian and Pacific Countries 2006.*

Economist Intelligence Unit, 111 West 57th Street, New York, NY 10019, (212) 554-0600, Fax: (212) 586-1181, www.eiu.com; *Business Asia.*

Inter-American Development Bank (IDB), 1300 New York Avenue, NW, Washington, DC 20577, (202) 623-1000, Fax: (202) 623-3096, www.iadb.org; *The Politics of Policies: Economic and Social Progress in Latin America - 2006 Report.*

M.E. Sharpe, 80 Business Park Drive, Armonk, NY 10504, (800) 541-6563, Fax: (914) 273-2106, www.mesharpe.com; *The Illustrated Book of World Rankings.*

United Nations Conference on Trade and Development (UNCTAD), DC2-1120, United Nations, New York, NY 10017, (212) 963-0027, www.unctad.org; *UNCTAD Commodity Yearbook.*

United Nations Statistics Division, New York, NY 10017, (800) 253-9646, Fax: (212) 963-4116, http://unstats.un.org; *Statistical Yearbook* and *Statistical Yearbook for Asia and the Pacific 2004.*

The World Bank, 1818 H Street, NW, Washington, DC 20433, (202) 473-1000, Fax: (202) 477-6391, www.worldbank.org; *World Development Indicators (WDI) 2008.*

HONG KONG - MONEY EXCHANGE RATES

See HONG KONG - FOREIGN EXCHANGE RATES

HONG KONG - MONEY SUPPLY

Asian Development Bank (ADB), PO Box 789, 0980 Manila, Philippines, www.adb.org; *Key Indicators of Developing Asian and Pacific Countries 2006.*

Economist Intelligence Unit, 111 West 57th Street, New York, NY 10019, (212) 554-0600, Fax: (212) 586-1181, www.eiu.com; *Business Asia* and *Hong Kong Country Report.*

Euromonitor International, Inc., 224 S. Michigan Avenue, Suite 1500, Chicago, IL 60604, (312) 922-1115, Fax: (312) 922-1157, www.euromonitor.com; *International Marketing Data and Statistics 2008.*

Taylor and Francis Group, An Informa Business, 2 Park Square, Milton Park, Abingdon, Oxford OX14 4RN, United Kingdom, (Dial from U.S. (212) 216-7800), (Fax from U.S. (212) 564-7854), www.tandf.co.uk; *The Europa World Year Book.*

The World Bank, 1818 H Street, NW, Washington, DC 20433, (202) 473-1000, Fax: (202) 477-6391, www.worldbank.org; *Hong Kong, China* and *World Development Indicators (WDI) 2008.*

HONG KONG - MORTALITY

Central Intelligence Agency, Office of Public Affairs, Washington, DC 20505, (703) 482-0623, Fax: (703) 482-1739, www.cia.gov; *The World Factbook.*

Euromonitor International, Inc., 224 S. Michigan Avenue, Suite 1500, Chicago, IL 60604, (312) 922-1115, Fax: (312) 922-1157, www.euromonitor.com; *International Marketing Data and Statistics 2008* and *The World Economic Factbook 2008.*

Palgrave Macmillan Ltd., Houndmills, Basingstoke, Hampshire, RG21 6XS, England, (Telephone in U.S. (888) 330-8477), (Fax in U.S. (800) 672-2054), www.palgrave.com; *The Statesman's Yearbook 2008.*

Taylor and Francis Group, An Informa Business, 2 Park Square, Milton Park, Abingdon, Oxford OX14 4RN, United Kingdom, (Dial from U.S. (212) 216-7800), (Fax from U.S. (212) 564-7854), www.tandf.co.uk; *The Europa World Year Book.*

UNICEF, 3 United Nations Plaza, New York, NY 10017, (800) 253-9646, Fax: (212) 887-7465, www.unicef.org; *The State of the World's Children 2008.*

United Nations Statistics Division, New York, NY 10017, (800) 253-9646, Fax: (212) 963-4116, http://unstats.un.org; *Asia-Pacific in Figures 2004; Demographic Yearbook; Human Development Report 2006; Statistical Yearbook;* and *World Statistics Pocketbook.*

The World Bank, 1818 H Street, NW, Washington, DC 20433, (202) 473-1000, Fax: (202) 477-6391, www.worldbank.org; *The World Bank Atlas 2003-2004* and *World Development Report 2008.*

World Health Organization (WHO), Avenue Appia 20, 1211 Geneve 27, Switzerland, (Telephone in U.S. (212) 331-9081), www.who.int; The WHO Global Atlas of Infectious Diseases and *World Health Report 2006.*

HONG KONG - MOTION PICTURES

Palgrave Macmillan Ltd., Houndmills, Basingstoke, Hampshire, RG21 6XS, England, (Telephone in U.S. (888) 330-8477), (Fax in U.S. (800) 672-2054), www.palgrave.com; *The Statesman's Yearbook 2008.*

UNESCO Institute for Statistics, C.P. 6128 Succursale Centre-Ville, Montreal, Quebec, H3C 3J7 Canada, (Dial from U.S. (514) 343-6880), (Fax from U.S. (514) 343 6882), www.uis.unesco.org; *Statistical Tables.*

United Nations Statistics Division, New York, NY 10017, (800) 253-9646, Fax: (212) 963-4116, http://unstats.un.org; *Statistical Yearbook.*

HONG KONG - MOTOR VEHICLES

International Road Federation (IFR), Madison Place, 500 Montgomery Street, 5th Floor, Alexandria, VA 22314, (703) 535-1001, Fax: (703) 535-1007, www.irfnet.org; *World Road Statistics 2006.*

Taylor and Francis Group, An Informa Business, 2 Park Square, Milton Park, Abingdon, Oxford OX14 4RN, United Kingdom, (Dial from U.S. (212) 216-7800), (Fax from U.S. (212) 564-7854), www.tandf.co.uk; *The Europa World Year Book.*

United Nations Statistics Division, New York, NY 10017, (800) 253-9646, Fax: (212) 963-4116, http://unstats.un.org; *Statistical Yearbook.*

HONG KONG - MUSEUMS

M.E. Sharpe, 80 Business Park Drive, Armonk, NY 10504, (800) 541-6563, Fax: (914) 273-2106, www.mesharpe.com; *The Illustrated Book of World Rankings.*

UNESCO Institute for Statistics, C.P. 6128 Succursale Centre-Ville, Montreal, Quebec, H3C 3J7 Canada, (Dial from U.S. (514) 343-6880), (Fax from U.S. (514) 343 6882), www.uis.unesco.org; *Statistical Tables.*

HONG KONG - NATURAL GAS PRODUCTION

See HONG KONG - MINERAL INDUSTRIES

HONG KONG - NUTRITION

Asian Development Bank (ADB), PO Box 789, 0980 Manila, Philippines, www.adb.org; *Key Indicators of Developing Asian and Pacific Countries 2006.*

United Nations Food and Agricultural Organization (FAO), Viale delle Terme di Caracalla, 00100 Rome, Italy, (Dial from U.S. (202) 653-2400), (Fax from U.S. (202) 653 5760), www.fao.org; *The State of Food and Agriculture (SOFA) 2006.*

HONG KONG - OLDER PEOPLE

M.E. Sharpe, 80 Business Park Drive, Armonk, NY 10504, (800) 541-6563, Fax: (914) 273-2106, www.mesharpe.com; *The Illustrated Book of World Rankings.*

HONG KONG - PAPER

See HONG KONG - FORESTS AND FORESTRY

HONG KONG - PEANUT PRODUCTION

See HONG KONG - CROPS

HONG KONG - PERIODICALS

UNESCO Institute for Statistics, C.P. 6128 Succursale Centre-Ville, Montreal, Quebec, H3C 3J7 Canada, (Dial from U.S. (514) 343-6880), (Fax from U.S. (514) 343 6882), www.uis.unesco.org; *Statistical Tables.*

HONG KONG - PESTICIDES

United Nations Food and Agricultural Organization (FAO), Viale delle Terme di Caracalla, 00100 Rome, Italy, (Dial from U.S. (202) 653-2400), (Fax from U.S. (202) 653 5760), www.fao.org; *The State of Food and Agriculture (SOFA) 2006.*

HONG KONG - PETROLEUM INDUSTRY AND TRADE

Asian Development Bank (ADB), PO Box 789, 0980 Manila, Philippines, www.adb.org; *Key Indicators of Developing Asian and Pacific Countries 2006.*

Economist Intelligence Unit, 111 West 57th Street, New York, NY 10019, (212) 554-0600, Fax: (212) 586-1181, www.eiu.com; *Business Asia.*

M.E. Sharpe, 80 Business Park Drive, Armonk, NY 10504, (800) 541-6563, Fax: (914) 273-2106, www.mesharpe.com; *The Illustrated Book of World Rankings.*

PennWell Corporation, 1421 South Sheridan Road, Tulsa, OK 74112, (918) 835-3161, www.pennwell.com; *International Petroleum Encyclopedia 2007.*

U.S. Department of Energy (DOE), Energy Information Administration (EIA), 1000 Independence Avenue, SW, Washington, DC 20585, (202) 586-8800, www.eia.doe.gov; *International Energy Annual 2004* and *International Energy Outlook 2006.*

United Nations Conference on Trade and Development (UNCTAD), DC2-1120, United Nations, New

York, NY 10017, (212) 963-0027, www.unctad.org; *UNCTAD Commodity Yearbook.*

United Nations Food and Agricultural Organization (FAO), Viale delle Terme di Caracalla, 00100 Rome, Italy, (Dial from U.S. (202) 653-2400), (Fax from U.S. (202) 653 5760), www.fao.org; *The State of Food and Agriculture (SOFA) 2006.*

HONG KONG - POLITICAL SCIENCE

Asian Development Bank (ADB), PO Box 789, 0980 Manila, Philippines, www.adb.org; *Key Indicators of Developing Asian and Pacific Countries 2006.*

Central Intelligence Agency, Office of Public Affairs, Washington, DC 20505, (703) 482-0623, Fax: (703) 482-1739, www.cia.gov; *The World Factbook.*

Economist Intelligence Unit, 111 West 57th Street, New York, NY 10019, (212) 554-0600, Fax: (212) 586-1181, www.eiu.com; *Business Asia.*

Palgrave Macmillan Ltd., Houndmills, Basingstoke, Hampshire, RG21 6XS, England, (Telephone in U.S. (888) 330-8477), (Fax in U.S. (800) 672-2054), www.palgrave.com; *The Statesman's Yearbook 2008.*

Taylor and Francis Group, An Informa Business, 2 Park Square, Milton Park, Abingdon, Oxford OX14 4RN, United Kingdom, (Dial from U.S. (212) 216-7800), (Fax from U.S. (212) 564-7854), www.tandf.co.uk; *The Europa World Year Book.*

United Nations Statistics Division, New York, NY 10017, (800) 253-9646, Fax: (212) 963-4116, http://unstats.un.org; *Asia-Pacific in Figures 2004* and *National Accounts Statistics: Compendium of Income Distribution Statistics.*

The World Bank, 1818 H Street, NW, Washington, DC 20433, (202) 473-1000, Fax: (202) 477-6391, www.worldbank.org; *World Development Indicators (WDI) 2008* and *World Development Report 2008.*

HONG KONG - POPULATION

Asian Development Bank (ADB), PO Box 789, 0980 Manila, Philippines, www.adb.org; *Key Indicators of Developing Asian and Pacific Countries 2006.*

Census and Statistics Department (CSD), 21/F Wanchai Tower, 12 Harbour Road, Wan Chai, Hong Kong, China, www.censtatd.gov.hk; *Hong Kong Social and Economic Trends.*

Central Intelligence Agency, Office of Public Affairs, Washington, DC 20505, (703) 482-0623, Fax: (703) 482-1739, www.cia.gov; *The World Factbook.*

Economist Intelligence Unit, 111 West 57th Street, New York, NY 10019, (212) 554-0600, Fax: (212) 586-1181, www.eiu.com; *Business Asia* and *Hong Kong Country Report.*

Euromonitor International, Inc., 224 S. Michigan Avenue, Suite 1500, Chicago, IL 60604, (312) 922-1115, Fax: (312) 922-1157, www.euromonitor.com; *International Marketing Data and Statistics 2008* and *The World Economic Factbook 2008.*

International Labour Office, I.L.O. Publications, 4 route des Morillons, CH-1211 Geneva 22, Switzerland, (Telephone in U.S. (202) 653-7652), (Fax in U.S. (202) 653-7687), www.ilo.org; *Yearbook of Labour Statistics 2006.*

M.E. Sharpe, 80 Business Park Drive, Armonk, NY 10504, (800) 541-6563, Fax: (914) 273-2106, www.mesharpe.com; *The Illustrated Book of World Rankings.*

Palgrave Macmillan Ltd., Houndmills, Basingstoke, Hampshire, RG21 6XS, England, (Telephone in U.S. (888) 330-8477), (Fax in U.S. (800) 672-2054), www.palgrave.com; *The Statesman's Yearbook 2008.*

Taylor and Francis Group, An Informa Business, 2 Park Square, Milton Park, Abingdon, Oxford OX14 4RN, United Kingdom, (Dial from U.S. (212) 216-7800), (Fax from U.S. (212) 564-7854), www.tandf.co.uk; *The Europa World Year Book.*

UNESCO Institute for Statistics, C.P. 6128 Succursale Centre-Ville, Montreal, Quebec, H3C 3J7 Canada, (Dial from U.S. (514) 343-6880), (Fax from U.S. (514) 343 6882), www.uis.unesco.org; *Statistical Tables.*

United Nations Food and Agricultural Organization (FAO), Viale delle Terme di Caracalla, 00100 Rome, Italy, (Dial from U.S. (202) 653-2400), (Fax from U.S. (202) 653 5760), www.fao.org; *FAO Production Yearbook 2002.*

United Nations Statistics Division, New York, NY 10017, (800) 253-9646, Fax: (212) 963-4116, http://unstats.un.org; *Asia-Pacific in Figures 2004; Demographic Yearbook; Human Development Report 2006; Statistical Yearbook; Statistical Yearbook for Asia and the Pacific 2004;* and *World Statistics Pocketbook.*

The World Bank, 1818 H Street, NW, Washington, DC 20433, (202) 473-1000, Fax: (202) 477-6391, www.worldbank.org; *Hong Kong, China; The World Bank Atlas 2003-2004;* and *World Development Report 2008.*

World Health Organization (WHO), Avenue Appia 20, 1211 Geneve 27, Switzerland, (Telephone in U.S. (212) 331-9081), www.who.int; *World Health Report 2006.*

Worldinformation.com, 2 Market Street, Saffron Walden, Essex CB10 1HZ, United Kingdom, www.worldinformation.com; The World of Information (www.worldinformation.com).

HONG KONG - POPULATION DENSITY

Central Intelligence Agency, Office of Public Affairs, Washington, DC 20505, (703) 482-0623, Fax: (703) 482-1739, www.cia.gov; *The World Factbook.*

Economist Intelligence Unit, 111 West 57th Street, New York, NY 10019, (212) 554-0600, Fax: (212) 586-1181, www.eiu.com; *Business Asia.*

Euromonitor International, Inc., 224 S. Michigan Avenue, Suite 1500, Chicago, IL 60604, (312) 922-1115, Fax: (312) 922-1157, www.euromonitor.com; *International Marketing Data and Statistics 2008* and *The World Economic Factbook 2008.*

M.E. Sharpe, 80 Business Park Drive, Armonk, NY 10504, (800) 541-6563, Fax: (914) 273-2106, www.mesharpe.com; *The Illustrated Book of World Rankings.*

Palgrave Macmillan Ltd., Houndmills, Basingstoke, Hampshire, RG21 6XS, England, (Telephone in U.S. (888) 330-8477), (Fax in U.S. (800) 672-2054), www.palgrave.com; *The Statesman's Yearbook 2008.*

Taylor and Francis Group, An Informa Business, 2 Park Square, Milton Park, Abingdon, Oxford OX14 4RN, United Kingdom, (Dial from U.S. (212) 216-7800), (Fax from U.S. (212) 564-7854), www.tandf.co.uk; *The Europa World Year Book.*

UNESCO Institute for Statistics, C.P. 6128 Succursale Centre-Ville, Montreal, Quebec, H3C 3J7 Canada, (Dial from U.S. (514) 343-6880), (Fax from U.S. (514) 343 6882), www.uis.unesco.org; *Statistical Tables.*

United Nations Food and Agricultural Organization (FAO), Viale delle Terme di Caracalla, 00100 Rome, Italy, (Dial from U.S. (202) 653-2400), (Fax from U.S. (202) 653 5760), www.fao.org; *The State of Food and Agriculture (SOFA) 2006.*

United Nations Statistics Division, New York, NY 10017, (800) 253-9646, Fax: (212) 963-4116, http://unstats.un.org; *Statistical Yearbook.*

The World Bank, 1818 H Street, NW, Washington, DC 20433, (202) 473-1000, Fax: (202) 477-6391, www.worldbank.org; *Hong Kong, China* and *World Development Report 2008.*

HONG KONG - POSTAL SERVICE

Economist Intelligence Unit, 111 West 57th Street, New York, NY 10019, (212) 554-0600, Fax: (212) 586-1181, www.eiu.com; *Business Asia.*

M.E. Sharpe, 80 Business Park Drive, Armonk, NY 10504, (800) 541-6563, Fax: (914) 273-2106, www.mesharpe.com; *The Illustrated Book of World Rankings.*

Palgrave Macmillan Ltd., Houndmills, Basingstoke, Hampshire, RG21 6XS, England, (Telephone in U.S. (888) 330-8477), (Fax in U.S. (800) 672-2054), www.palgrave.com; *The Statesman's Yearbook 2008.*

United Nations Statistics Division, New York, NY 10017, (800) 253-9646, Fax: (212) 963-4116, http://unstats.un.org; *Statistical Yearbook.*

HONG KONG - POWER RESOURCES

Euromonitor International, Inc., 224 S. Michigan Avenue, Suite 1500, Chicago, IL 60604, (312) 922-1115, Fax: (312) 922-1157, www.euromonitor.com; *International Marketing Data and Statistics 2008* and *World Marketing Data and Statistics.*

M.E. Sharpe, 80 Business Park Drive, Armonk, NY 10504, (800) 541-6563, Fax: (914) 273-2106, www.mesharpe.com; *The Illustrated Book of World Rankings.*

Palgrave Macmillan Ltd., Houndmills, Basingstoke, Hampshire, RG21 6XS, England, (Telephone in U.S. (888) 330-8477), (Fax in U.S. (800) 672-2054), www.palgrave.com; *The Statesman's Yearbook 2008.*

Platts, 2 Penn Plaza, 25th Floor, New York, NY 10121-2298, (212) 904-3070, www.platts.com; *Asian Electricity Outlook 2006; Emissions Daily;* and *Energy Economist.*

U.S. Department of Energy (DOE), Energy Information Administration (EIA), 1000 Independence Avenue, SW, Washington, DC 20585, (202) 586-8800, www.eia.doe.gov; *International Energy Annual 2004* and *International Energy Outlook 2006.*

United Nations Food and Agricultural Organization (FAO), Viale delle Terme di Caracalla, 00100 Rome, Italy, (Dial from U.S. (202) 653-2400), (Fax from U.S. (202) 653 5760), www.fao.org; *The State of Food and Agriculture (SOFA) 2006.*

United Nations Statistics Division, New York, NY 10017, (800) 253-9646, Fax: (212) 963-4116, http://unstats.un.org; *Asia-Pacific in Figures 2004; Energy Statistics Yearbook 2003; Human Development Report 2006; Statistical Yearbook; Statistical Yearbook for Asia and the Pacific 2004;* and *World Statistics Pocketbook.*

The World Bank, 1818 H Street, NW, Washington, DC 20433, (202) 473-1000, Fax: (202) 477-6391, www.worldbank.org; *The World Bank Atlas 2003-2004* and *World Development Report 2008.*

HONG KONG - PRICES

Asian Development Bank (ADB), PO Box 789, 0980 Manila, Philippines, www.adb.org; *Key Indicators of Developing Asian and Pacific Countries 2006.*

Census and Statistics Department (CSD), 21/F Wanchai Tower, 12 Harbour Road, Wan Chai, Hong Kong, China, www.censtatd.gov.hk; *Hong Kong Social and Economic Trends.*

Euromonitor International, Inc., 224 S. Michigan Avenue, Suite 1500, Chicago, IL 60604, (312) 922-1115, Fax: (312) 922-1157, www.euromonitor.com; *World Marketing Data and Statistics.*

International Labour Office, I.L.O. Publications, 4 route des Morillons, CH-1211 Geneva 22, Switzerland, (Telephone in U.S. (202) 653-7652), (Fax in U.S. (202) 653-7687), www.ilo.org; *Yearbook of Labour Statistics 2006.*

M.E. Sharpe, 80 Business Park Drive, Armonk, NY 10504, (800) 541-6563, Fax: (914) 273-2106, www.mesharpe.com; *The Illustrated Book of World Rankings.*

United Nations Food and Agricultural Organization (FAO), Viale delle Terme di Caracalla, 00100 Rome, Italy, (Dial from U.S. (202) 653-2400), (Fax from U.S. (202) 653 5760), www.fao.org; *FAO Production Yearbook 2002* and *The State of Food and Agriculture (SOFA) 2006.*

The World Bank, 1818 H Street, NW, Washington, DC 20433, (202) 473-1000, Fax: (202) 477-6391, www.worldbank.org; *Hong Kong, China.*

HONG KONG - PROFESSIONS

UNESCO Institute for Statistics, C.P. 6128 Succursale Centre-Ville, Montreal, Quebec, H3C 3J7 Canada, (Dial from U.S. (514) 343-6880), (Fax from U.S. (514) 343 6882), www.uis.unesco.org; *Statistical Tables.*

United Nations Statistics Division, New York, NY 10017, (800) 253-9646, Fax: (212) 963-4116, http://unstats.un.org; *Statistical Yearbook.*

HONG KONG - PUBLIC HEALTH

Economist Intelligence Unit, 111 West 57th Street, New York, NY 10019, (212) 554-0600, Fax: (212) 586-1181, www.eiu.com; *Business Asia.*

Euromonitor International, Inc., 224 S. Michigan Avenue, Suite 1500, Chicago, IL 60604, (312) 922-1115, Fax: (312) 922-1157, www.euromonitor.com; *World Health Databook 2007/2008* and *World Marketing Data and Statistics.*

M.E. Sharpe, 80 Business Park Drive, Armonk, NY 10504, (800) 541-6563, Fax: (914) 273-2106, www.mesharpe.com; *The Illustrated Book of World Rankings.*

Palgrave Macmillan Ltd., Houndmills, Basingstoke, Hampshire, RG21 6XS, England, (Telephone in U.S. (888) 330-8477), (Fax in U.S. (800) 672-2054), www.palgrave.com; *The Statesman's Yearbook 2008.*

UNICEF, 3 United Nations Plaza, New York, NY 10017, (800) 253-9646, Fax: (212) 887-7465, www.unicef.org; *The State of the World's Children 2008.*

United Nations Statistics Division, New York, NY 10017, (800) 253-9646, Fax: (212) 963-4116, http://unstats.un.org; *Asia-Pacific in Figures 2004; Human Development Report 2006;* and *Statistical Yearbook.*

The World Bank, 1818 H Street, NW, Washington, DC 20433, (202) 473-1000, Fax: (202) 477-6391, www.worldbank.org; *Hong Kong, China* and *World Development Report 2008.*

World Health Organization (WHO), Avenue Appia 20, 1211 Geneve 27, Switzerland, (Telephone in U.S. (212) 331-9081), www.who.int; The WHO Global Atlas of Infectious Diseases and *World Health Report 2006.*

HONG KONG - PUBLIC UTILITIES

United Nations Statistics Division, New York, NY 10017, (800) 253-9646, Fax: (212) 963-4116, http://unstats.un.org; *Electric Power in Asia and the Pacific 2001 and 2002.*

HONG KONG - PUBLISHERS AND PUBLISHING

UNESCO Institute for Statistics, C.P. 6128 Succursale Centre-Ville, Montreal, Quebec, H3C 3J7 Canada, (Dial from U.S. (514) 343-6880), (Fax from U.S. (514) 343 6882), www.uis.unesco.org; *Statistical Tables.*

HONG KONG - RADIO BROADCASTING

Palgrave Macmillan Ltd., Houndmills, Basingstoke, Hampshire, RG21 6XS, England, (Telephone in U.S. (888) 330-8477), (Fax in U.S. (800) 672-2054), www.palgrave.com; *The Statesman's Yearbook 2008.*

United Nations Statistics Division, New York, NY 10017, (800) 253-9646, Fax: (212) 963-4116, http://unstats.un.org; *Statistical Yearbook.*

HONG KONG - RAILROADS

Jane's Information Group, 110 North Royal Street, Suite 200, Alexandria, VA 22314, (703) 683-3700, Fax: (800) 836-0297, www.janes.com; *Jane's World Railways.*

Palgrave Macmillan Ltd., Houndmills, Basingstoke, Hampshire, RG21 6XS, England, (Telephone in U.S. (888) 330-8477), (Fax in U.S. (800) 672-2054), www.palgrave.com; *The Statesman's Yearbook 2008.*

Taylor and Francis Group, An Informa Business, 2 Park Square, Milton Park, Abingdon, Oxford OX14 4RN, United Kingdom, (Dial from U.S. (212) 216-7800), (Fax from U.S. (212) 564-7854), www.tandf.co.uk; *The Europa World Year Book.*

United Nations Statistics Division, New York, NY 10017, (800) 253-9646, Fax: (212) 963-4116, http://unstats.un.org; *Statistical Yearbook.*

HONG KONG - RELIGION

Central Intelligence Agency, Office of Public Affairs, Washington, DC 20505, (703) 482-0623, Fax: (703) 482-1739, www.cia.gov; *The World Factbook.*

M.E. Sharpe, 80 Business Park Drive, Armonk, NY 10504, (800) 541-6563, Fax: (914) 273-2106, www.mesharpe.com; *The Illustrated Book of World Rankings.*

HONG KONG - RESERVES (ACCOUNTING)

Asian Development Bank (ADB), PO Box 789, 0980 Manila, Philippines, www.adb.org; *Key Indicators of Developing Asian and Pacific Countries 2006.*

Euromonitor International, Inc., 224 S. Michigan Avenue, Suite 1500, Chicago, IL 60604, (312) 922-1115, Fax: (312) 922-1157, www.euromonitor.com; *International Marketing Data and Statistics 2008.*

The World Bank, 1818 H Street, NW, Washington, DC 20433, (202) 473-1000, Fax: (202) 477-6391, www.worldbank.org; *World Development Indicators (WDI) 2008.*

HONG KONG - RETAIL TRADE

Economist Intelligence Unit, 111 West 57th Street, New York, NY 10019, (212) 554-0600, Fax: (212) 586-1181, www.eiu.com; *Business Asia.*

Euromonitor International, Inc., 224 S. Michigan Avenue, Suite 1500, Chicago, IL 60604, (312) 922-1115, Fax: (312) 922-1157, www.euromonitor.com; *Retail Trade International 2007* and *World Marketing Data and Statistics.*

HONG KONG - RICE PRODUCTION

See HONG KONG - CROPS

HONG KONG - ROADS

Central Intelligence Agency, Office of Public Affairs, Washington, DC 20505, (703) 482-0623, Fax: (703) 482-1739, www.cia.gov; *The World Factbook.*

Economist Intelligence Unit, 111 West 57th Street, New York, NY 10019, (212) 554-0600, Fax: (212) 586-1181, www.eiu.com; *Business Asia.*

International Road Federation (IFR), Madison Place, 500 Montgomery Street, 5th Floor, Alexandria, VA 22314, (703) 535-1001, Fax: (703) 535-1007, www.irfnet.org; *World Road Statistics 2006.*

Palgrave Macmillan Ltd., Houndmills, Basingstoke, Hampshire, RG21 6XS, England, (Telephone in U.S. (888) 330-8477), (Fax in U.S. (800) 672-2054), www.palgrave.com; *The Statesman's Yearbook 2008.*

HONG KONG - RUBBER INDUSTRY AND TRADE

International Rubber Study Group (IRSG), 1st Floor, Heron House, 109/115 Wembley Hill Road, Wembley, Middlesex HA9 8DA, United Kingdom, www.rubberstudy.com; *Rubber Statistical Bulletin; Summary of World Rubber Statistics 2005; World Rubber Statistics Handbook (Volume 6, 1975-2001);* and *World Rubber Statistics Historic Handbook.*

M.E. Sharpe, 80 Business Park Drive, Armonk, NY 10504, (800) 541-6563, Fax: (914) 273-2106, www.mesharpe.com; *The Illustrated Book of World Rankings.*

HONG KONG - SHEEP

See HONG KONG - LIVESTOCK

HONG KONG - SHIPPING

Lloyd's Register - Fairplay, 8410 N.W. 53rd Terrace, Suite 207, Miami FL 33166, (305) 718-9929, Fax: (305) 718-9663, www.lrfairplay.com; *Register of Ships 2007-2008; World Casualty Statistics 2007; World Fleet Statistics 2006; World Marine Propulsion Report 2006-2010; World Shipbuilding Statistics 2007;* and The World Shipping Encyclopaedia.

Palgrave Macmillan Ltd., Houndmills, Basingstoke, Hampshire, RG21 6XS, England, (Telephone in U.S. (888) 330-8477), (Fax in U.S. (800) 672-2054), www.palgrave.com; *The Statesman's Yearbook 2008.*

Taylor and Francis Group, An Informa Business, 2 Park Square, Milton Park, Abingdon, Oxford OX14 4RN, United Kingdom, (Dial from U.S. (212) 216-7800), (Fax from U.S. (212) 564-7854), www.tandf.co.uk; *The Europa World Year Book.*

United Nations Statistics Division, New York, NY 10017, (800) 253-9646, Fax: (212) 963-4116, http://unstats.un.org; *Statistical Yearbook.*

HONG KONG - SILVER PRODUCTION

See HONG KONG - MINERAL INDUSTRIES

HONG KONG - SOCIAL ECOLOGY

Asian Development Bank (ADB), PO Box 789, 0980 Manila, Philippines, www.adb.org; *Key Indicators of Developing Asian and Pacific Countries 2006.*

M.E. Sharpe, 80 Business Park Drive, Armonk, NY 10504, (800) 541-6563, Fax: (914) 273-2106, www.mesharpe.com; *The Illustrated Book of World Rankings.*

Palgrave Macmillan Ltd., Houndmills, Basingstoke, Hampshire, RG21 6XS, England, (Telephone in U.S. (888) 330-8477), (Fax in U.S. (800) 672-2054), www.palgrave.com; *The Statesman's Yearbook 2008.*

United Nations Statistics Division, New York, NY 10017, (800) 253-9646, Fax: (212) 963-4116, http://unstats.un.org; *World Statistics Pocketbook.*

HONG KONG - SOCIAL SECURITY

United Nations Statistics Division, New York, NY 10017, (800) 253-9646, Fax: (212) 963-4116, http://unstats.un.org; *National Accounts Statistics: Compendium of Income Distribution Statistics.*

HONG KONG - SOYBEAN PRODUCTION

See HONG KONG - CROPS

HONG KONG - STEEL PRODUCTION

See HONG KONG - MINERAL INDUSTRIES

HONG KONG - SUGAR PRODUCTION

See HONG KONG - CROPS

HONG KONG - TAXATION

International Road Federation (IFR), Madison Place, 500 Montgomery Street, 5th Floor, Alexandria, VA 22314, (703) 535-1001, Fax: (703) 535-1007, www.irfnet.org; *World Road Statistics 2006.*

Taylor and Francis Group, An Informa Business, 2 Park Square, Milton Park, Abingdon, Oxford OX14 4RN, United Kingdom, (Dial from U.S. (212) 216-7800), (Fax from U.S. (212) 564-7854), www.tandf.co.uk; *The Europa World Year Book.*

The World Bank, 1818 H Street, NW, Washington, DC 20433, (202) 473-1000, Fax: (202) 477-6391, www.worldbank.org; *World Development Indicators (WDI) 2008.*

HONG KONG - TEA TRADE

United Nations Statistics Division, New York, NY 10017, (800) 253-9646, Fax: (212) 963-4116, http://unstats.un.org; *Statistical Yearbook.*

HONG KONG - TELEPHONE

Economist Intelligence Unit, 111 West 57th Street, New York, NY 10019, (212) 554-0600, Fax: (212) 586-1181, www.eiu.com; *Business Asia.*

International Telecommunication Union (ITU), Place des Nations, 1211 Geneva 20, Switzerland, www.itu.int; World Telecommunication Indicators Database.

Palgrave Macmillan Ltd., Houndmills, Basingstoke, Hampshire, RG21 6XS, England, (Telephone in U.S. (888) 330-8477), (Fax in U.S. (800) 672-2054), www.palgrave.com; *The Statesman's Yearbook 2008.*

Taylor and Francis Group, An Informa Business, 2 Park Square, Milton Park, Abingdon, Oxford OX14 4RN, United Kingdom, (Dial from U.S. (212) 216-7800), (Fax from U.S. (212) 564-7854), www.tandf.co.uk; *The Europa World Year Book.*

United Nations Statistics Division, New York, NY 10017, (800) 253-9646, Fax: (212) 963-4116, http://unstats.un.org; *Statistical Yearbook* and *World Statistics Pocketbook.*

HONG KONG - TELEVISION - RECEIVERS AND RECEPTION

United Nations Statistics Division, New York, NY 10017, (800) 253-9646, Fax: (212) 963-4116, http://unstats.un.org; *Statistical Yearbook.*

HONG KONG - TEXTILE INDUSTRY

Economist Intelligence Unit, 111 West 57th Street, New York, NY 10019, (212) 554-0600, Fax: (212) 586-1181, www.eiu.com; *Business Asia.*

Euromonitor International, Inc., 224 S. Michigan Avenue, Suite 1500, Chicago, IL 60604, (312) 922-1115, Fax: (312) 922-1157, www.euromonitor.com; *Retail Trade International 2007.*

M.E. Sharpe, 80 Business Park Drive, Armonk, NY 10504, (800) 541-6563, Fax: (914) 273-2106, www.mesharpe.com; *The Illustrated Book of World Rankings.*

Palgrave Macmillan Ltd., Houndmills, Basingstoke, Hampshire, RG21 6XS, England, (Telephone in U.S. (888) 330-8477), (Fax in U.S. (800) 672-2054), www.palgrave.com; *The Statesman's Yearbook 2008.*

United Nations Conference on Trade and Development (UNCTAD), DC2-1120, United Nations, New York, NY 10017, (212) 963-0027, www.unctad.org; *UNCTAD Commodity Yearbook.*

United Nations Statistics Division, New York, NY 10017, (800) 253-9646, Fax: (212) 963-4116, http://unstats.un.org; *Statistical Yearbook.*

HONG KONG - THEATER

UNESCO Institute for Statistics, C.P. 6128 Succursale Centre-Ville, Montreal, Quebec, H3C 3J7 Canada, (Dial from U.S. (514) 343-6880), (Fax from U.S. (514) 343 6882), www.uis.unesco.org; *Statistical Tables.*

HONG KONG - TIN PRODUCTION

See HONG KONG - MINERAL INDUSTRIES

HONG KONG - TOBACCO INDUSTRY

Economist Intelligence Unit, 111 West 57th Street, New York, NY 10019, (212) 554-0600, Fax: (212) 586-1181, www.eiu.com; *Business Asia.*

Foreign Agricultural Service (FAS), U.S. Department of Agriculture (USDA), 1400 Independence Avenue, SW, Washington, DC 20250, (202) 720-3935, www.fas.usda.gov; *Tobacco: World Markets and Trade.*

M.E. Sharpe, 80 Business Park Drive, Armonk, NY 10504, (800) 541-6563, Fax: (914) 273-2106, www.mesharpe.com; *The Illustrated Book of World Rankings.*

United Nations Statistics Division, New York, NY 10017, (800) 253-9646, Fax: (212) 963-4116, http://unstats.un.org; *Statistical Yearbook.*

HONG KONG - TOURISM

Economist Intelligence Unit, 111 West 57th Street, New York, NY 10019, (212) 554-0600, Fax: (212) 586-1181, www.eiu.com; *Business Asia.*

Euromonitor International, Inc., 224 S. Michigan Avenue, Suite 1500, Chicago, IL 60604, (312) 922-1115, Fax: (312) 922-1157, www.euromonitor.com; *The World Economic Factbook 2008* and *World Marketing Data and Statistics.*

M.E. Sharpe, 80 Business Park Drive, Armonk, NY 10504, (800) 541-6563, Fax: (914) 273-2106, www.mesharpe.com; *The Illustrated Book of World Rankings.*

Palgrave Macmillan Ltd., Houndmills, Basingstoke, Hampshire, RG21 6XS, England, (Telephone in U.S. (888) 330-8477), (Fax in U.S. (800) 672-2054), www.palgrave.com; *The Statesman's Yearbook 2008.*

Taylor and Francis Group, An Informa Business, 2 Park Square, Milton Park, Abingdon, Oxford OX14 4RN, United Kingdom, (Dial from U.S. (212) 216-7800), (Fax from U.S. (212) 564-7854), www.tandf.co.uk; *The Europa World Year Book.*

United Nations Statistics Division, New York, NY 10017, (800) 253-9646, Fax: (212) 963-4116, http://unstats.un.org; *Statistical Yearbook.*

United Nations World Tourism Organization (UNWTO), Capitan Haya 42, 28020 Madrid, Spain, www.world-tourism.org; *Yearbook of Tourism Statistics.*

The World Bank, 1818 H Street, NW, Washington, DC 20433, (202) 473-1000, Fax: (202) 477-6391, www.worldbank.org; *Hong Kong, China.*

HONG KONG - TRADE

See HONG KONG - INTERNATIONAL TRADE

HONG KONG - TRANSPORTATION

Central Intelligence Agency, Office of Public Affairs, Washington, DC 20505, (703) 482-0623, Fax: (703) 482-1739, www.cia.gov; *The World Factbook.*

Economist Intelligence Unit, 111 West 57th Street, New York, NY 10019, (212) 554-0600, Fax: (212) 586-1181, www.eiu.com; *Business Asia.*

Euromonitor International, Inc., 224 S. Michigan Avenue, Suite 1500, Chicago, IL 60604, (312) 922-1115, Fax: (312) 922-1157, www.euromonitor.com; *International Marketing Data and Statistics 2008* and *World Marketing Data and Statistics.*

M.E. Sharpe, 80 Business Park Drive, Armonk, NY 10504, (800) 541-6563, Fax: (914) 273-2106, www.mesharpe.com; *The Illustrated Book of World Rankings.*

Palgrave Macmillan Ltd., Houndmills, Basingstoke, Hampshire, RG21 6XS, England, (Telephone in U.S. (888) 330-8477), (Fax in U.S. (800) 672-2054), www.palgrave.com; *The Statesman's Yearbook 2008.*

Taylor and Francis Group, An Informa Business, 2 Park Square, Milton Park, Abingdon, Oxford OX14 4RN, United Kingdom, (Dial from U.S. (212) 216-7800), (Fax from U.S. (212) 564-7854), www.tandf.co.uk; *The Europa World Year Book.*

United Nations Statistics Division, New York, NY 10017, (800) 253-9646, Fax: (212) 963-4116, http://unstats.un.org; *Human Development Report 2006* and *Statistical Yearbook for Asia and the Pacific 2004.*

The World Bank, 1818 H Street, NW, Washington, DC 20433, (202) 473-1000, Fax: (202) 477-6391, www.worldbank.org; *Hong Kong, China.*

HONG KONG - UNEMPLOYMENT

Central Intelligence Agency, Office of Public Affairs, Washington, DC 20505, (703) 482-0623, Fax: (703) 482-1739, www.cia.gov; *The World Factbook.*

Economist Intelligence Unit, 111 West 57th Street, New York, NY 10019, (212) 554-0600, Fax: (212) 586-1181, www.eiu.com; *Business Asia.*

Euromonitor International, Inc., 224 S. Michigan Avenue, Suite 1500, Chicago, IL 60604, (312) 922-1115, Fax: (312) 922-1157, www.euromonitor.com; *International Marketing Data and Statistics 2008.*

International Labour Office, I.L.O. Publications, 4 route des Morillons, CH-1211 Geneva 22, Switzerland, (Telephone in U.S. (202) 653-7652), (Fax in U.S. (202) 653-7687), www.ilo.org; *Yearbook of Labour Statistics 2006.*

Palgrave Macmillan Ltd., Houndmills, Basingstoke, Hampshire, RG21 6XS, England, (Telephone in U.S. (888) 330-8477), (Fax in U.S. (800) 672-2054), www.palgrave.com; *The Statesman's Yearbook 2008.*

United Nations Statistics Division, New York, NY 10017, (800) 253-9646, Fax: (212) 963-4116, http://unstats.un.org; *Statistical Yearbook.*

HONG KONG - VITAL STATISTICS

Census and Statistics Department (CSD), 21/F Wanchai Tower, 12 Harbour Road, Wan Chai, Hong Kong, China, www.censtatd.gov.hk; *Hong Kong in Figures.*

Euromonitor International, Inc., 224 S. Michigan Avenue, Suite 1500, Chicago, IL 60604, (312) 922-1115, Fax: (312) 922-1157, www.euromonitor.com; *International Marketing Data and Statistics 2008.*

Palgrave Macmillan Ltd., Houndmills, Basingstoke, Hampshire, RG21 6XS, England, (Telephone in U.S. (888) 330-8477), (Fax in U.S. (800) 672-2054), www.palgrave.com; *The Statesman's Yearbook 2008.*

United Nations Statistics Division, New York, NY 10017, (800) 253-9646, Fax: (212) 963-4116, http://unstats.un.org; *Statistical Yearbook.*

World Health Organization (WHO), Avenue Appia 20, 1211 Geneve 27, Switzerland, (Telephone in U.S. (212) 331-9081), www.who.int; *World Health Report 2006.*

HONG KONG - WAGES

Economist Intelligence Unit, 111 West 57th Street, New York, NY 10019, (212) 554-0600, Fax: (212) 586-1181, www.eiu.com; *Business Asia.*

International Labour Office, I.L.O. Publications, 4 route des Morillons, CH-1211 Geneva 22, Switzerland, (Telephone in U.S. (202) 653-7652), (Fax in U.S. (202) 653-7687), www.ilo.org; *Yearbook of Labour Statistics 2006.*

United Nations Statistics Division, New York, NY 10017, (800) 253-9646, Fax: (212) 963-4116, http://unstats.un.org; *Statistical Yearbook.*

The World Bank, 1818 H Street, NW, Washington, DC 20433, (202) 473-1000, Fax: (202) 477-6391, www.worldbank.org; *Hong Kong, China.*

HONG KONG - WEATHER

See HONG KONG - CLIMATE

HONG KONG - WELFARE STATE

Palgrave Macmillan Ltd., Houndmills, Basingstoke, Hampshire, RG21 6XS, England, (Telephone in U.S. (888) 330-8477), (Fax in U.S. (800) 672-2054), www.palgrave.com; *The Statesman's Yearbook 2008.*

HONG KONG - WHEAT PRODUCTION

See HONG KONG - CROPS

HONG KONG - WHOLESALE PRICE INDEXES

Asian Development Bank (ADB), PO Box 789, 0980 Manila, Philippines, www.adb.org; *Key Indicators of Developing Asian and Pacific Countries 2006.*

HONG KONG - WINE PRODUCTION

See HONG KONG - BEVERAGE INDUSTRY

HONG KONG - WOOD AND WOOD PULP

See HONG KONG - FORESTS AND FORESTRY

HONG KONG - WOOL PRODUCTION

See HONG KONG - TEXTILE INDUSTRY

HONG KONG - YARN PRODUCTION

See HONG KONG - TEXTILE INDUSTRY

HONG KONG - ZOOS

UNESCO Institute for Statistics, C.P. 6128 Succursale Centre-Ville, Montreal, Quebec, H3C 3J7 Canada, (Dial from U.S. (514) 343-6880), (Fax from U.S. (514) 343 6882), www.uis.unesco.org; *Statistical Tables.*

HORSES - RACING

Association of Racing Commissioners International (RCI), 2343 Alexandria Drive, Suite 200, Lexington, KY 40504, (859) 224-7070, Fax: (859) 224-7071, www.arci.com; unpublished data.

HORSES - RIDING

U.S. Department of the Interior (DOI), Fish Wildlife Service (FWS), 1849 C Street, NW, Washington, DC 20240, (800) 344-WILD, www.fws.gov; *2006 National Survey of Fishing, Hunting, and Wildlife-Associated Recreation (FHWAR).*

HORSES AND MULES

Economic Research Service (ERS), U.S. Department of Agriculture (USDA), 1800 M Street, NW,

Washington, DC 20036-5831, (202) 694-5050, Fax: (202) 694-5689, www.ers.usda.gov; *Farm Balance Sheet.*

HOSPICES

National Center for Health Statistics (NCHS), Centers for Disease Control and Prevention (CDC), U.S. Department of Health and Human Services (HHS), 3311 Toledo Road, Hyattsville, MD 20782, (866) 232-4636, www.cdc.gov/nchs; *Health, United States, 2006, with Chartbook on Trends in the Health of Americans with Special Feature on Pain* and unpublished data.

Robert Wood Johnson Foundation, PO Box 2316, College Road East and Route 1, Princeton, NJ 08543, (877) 843-7953, www.rwjf.org; *Quality of Death and Dying is Significantly Higher for People Who Die at Home; What Factors Influence the Kind of Long-Term Services Patients with Private Insurance Choose Over Time; What Length of Hospice Use Maximizes Reduction in Medical Expenditures Near Death in the U.S. Medicare Program?;* and *Where People Die: A Multilevel Approach to Understanding Influences on Site of Death in America.*

HOSPITALITY INDUSTRY

American Hospital Association (AHA), One North Franklin, Chicago, IL 60606-3421, (312) 422-3000, www.aha.org; *2008 AHA Environmental Assessment; Annual Survey of Hospitals;* and *White Coats and Many Colors: Population Diversity and Its Implications for Health Care.*

U.S. Bureau of Labor Statistics (BLS), Postal Square Building, 2 Massachusetts Avenue, NE, Washington, DC 20212-0001, (202) 691-5200, Fax: (202) 691-6325, www.bls.gov; *Industries at a Glance.*

HOSPITALITY INDUSTRY - CAPITAL

American Hospital Association (AHA), One North Franklin, Chicago, IL 60606-3421, (312) 422-3000, www.aha.org; *AHA White Paper: The State of Hospitals' Financial Health.*

U.S. Census Bureau, Company Statistics Division, 4700 Silver Hill Road, Washington DC 20233-0001, (301) 763-3030, www.census.gov/csd/; *Annual Capital Expenditures Survey (ACES).*

HOSPITALITY INDUSTRY - EARNINGS

American Hospital Association (AHA), One North Franklin, Chicago, IL 60606-3421, (312) 422-3000, www.aha.org; *AHA White Paper: The State of Hospitals' Financial Health* and *Beyond Health Care: The Economic Contribution of Hospitals.*

U.S. Census Bureau, 4700 Silver Hill Road, Washington DC 20233-0001, (301) 763-3030, www.census.gov; *2002 Economic Census, Nonemployer Statistics.*

U.S. Census Bureau, Center for Economic Studies, 4600 Silver Hill Road, Washington DC 20233, (301) 457-1235, www.ces.census.gov; *2002 Economic Census, Geographic Area Series.*

HOSPITALITY INDUSTRY - ELECTRONIC COMMERCE

U.S. Census Bureau, 4700 Silver Hill Road, Washington DC 20233-0001, (301) 763-3030, www.census.gov; *E-Stats - Measuring the Electronic Economy.*

HOSPITALITY INDUSTRY - EMPLOYEES

U.S. Census Bureau, 4700 Silver Hill Road, Washington DC 20233-0001, (301) 763-3030, www.census.gov; *2002 Economic Census, Nonemployer Statistics.*

U.S. Census Bureau, Center for Economic Studies, 4600 Silver Hill Road, Washington DC 20233, (301) 457-1235, www.ces.census.gov; *2002 Economic Census, Geographic Area Series.*

U.S. Census Bureau, Company Statistics Division, 4700 Silver Hill Road, Washington DC 20233-0001, (301) 763-3030, www.census.gov/csd/; *County Business Patterns 2004.*

HOSPITALITY INDUSTRY - ESTABLISHMENTS

American Hospital Association (AHA), One North Franklin, Chicago, IL 60606-3421, (312) 422-3000, www.aha.org; *2008 AHA Environmental Assessment; AHA White Paper: The State of Hospitals' Financial Health; Beyond Health Care: The Economic Contribution of Hospitals;* and *Impact of Physician-owned Limited-service Hospitals: A Summary of Four Case Studies.*

Small Business Administration (SBA), 409 3rd Street, SW, Washington, DC 20024-3212, (202) 205-6533, Fax: (202) 206-6928, www.sba.gov; *Small Business Economic Indicators.*

U.S. Census Bureau, 4700 Silver Hill Road, Washington DC 20233-0001, (301) 763-3030, www.census.gov; *2002 Economic Census, Nonemployer Statistics.*

U.S. Census Bureau, Center for Economic Studies, 4600 Silver Hill Road, Washington DC 20233, (301) 457-1235, www.ces.census.gov; *2002 Economic Census, Geographic Area Series.*

U.S. Census Bureau, Company Statistics Division, 4700 Silver Hill Road, Washington DC 20233-0001, (301) 763-3030, www.census.gov/csd/; *County Business Patterns 2004.*

HOSPITALITY INDUSTRY - FINANCES

American Hospital Association (AHA), One North Franklin, Chicago, IL 60606-3421, (312) 422-3000, www.aha.org; *AHA White Paper: The State of Hospitals' Financial Health* and *Beyond Health Care: The Economic Contribution of Hospitals.*

U.S. Department of the Treasury (DOT), Internal Revenue Service (IRS), Statistics of Income Division (SIS), PO Box 2608, Washington, DC, 20013-2608, (202) 874-0410, Fax: (202) 874-0964, www.irs.ustreas.gov; *Statistics of Income Bulletin* and various fact sheets.

HOSPITALITY INDUSTRY - NONEMPLOYERS

U.S. Census Bureau, 4700 Silver Hill Road, Washington DC 20233-0001, (301) 763-3030, www.census.gov; *2002 Economic Census, Nonemployer Statistics.*

HOSPITALITY INDUSTRY - SALES

American Hospital Association (AHA), One North Franklin, Chicago, IL 60606-3421, (312) 422-3000, www.aha.org; *AHA White Paper: The State of Hospitals' Financial Health.*

U.S. Department of the Treasury (DOT), Internal Revenue Service (IRS), Statistics of Income Division (SIS), PO Box 2608, Washington, DC, 20013-2608, (202) 874-0410, Fax: (202) 874-0964, www.irs.ustreas.gov; *Statistics of Income Bulletin* and various fact sheets.

HOSPITALS

American Medical Association, 515 North State Street, Chicago, IL 60610, (800) 621-8335, www.ama-assn.org; *AHA Hospital Statistics 2007.*

Decision Resources, Inc., 260 Charles Street, Waltham, MA 02453, (781) 296-2500, Fax: (781) 296-2550, www.decisionresources.com; Research Studies.

RAND Corporation, 1776 Main Street, PO Box 2138, Santa Monica, CA 90407-2138, (310) 393-0411, www.rand.org; *Hospital Competition, Managed Care, and Mortality After Hospitalization for Medical Conditions in California.*

Robert Wood Johnson Foundation, PO Box 2316, College Road East and Route 1, Princeton, NJ 08543, (877) 843-7953, www.rwjf.org; *Where People Die: A Multilevel Approach to Understanding Influences on Site of Death in America.*

HOSPITALS - AVERAGE DAILY ROOM CHARGE

American Hospital Association (AHA), One North Franklin, Chicago, IL 60606-3421, (312) 422-3000, www.aha.org; *Hospital Statistics 2008.*

HOSPITALS - BEDS

American Hospital Association (AHA), One North Franklin, Chicago, IL 60606-3421, (312) 422-3000, www.aha.org; *Hospital Statistics 2008.*

HOSPITALS - CHARGES AND PERSONAL EXPENDITURES FOR

American Hospital Association (AHA), One North Franklin, Chicago, IL 60606-3421, (312) 422-3000, www.aha.org; *AHA White Paper: The State of Hospitals' Financial Health.*

Centers for Medicare and Medicaid Services (CMS), U.S. Department of Health and Human Services (HHS), 7500 Security Boulevard, Baltimore, MD 21244-1850, (410) 786-3000, http://cms.hhs.gov; *Health Accounts* and The Medicare Current Beneficiary Survey (MCBS) (web app).

U.S. Bureau of Labor Statistics (BLS), Postal Square Building, 2 Massachusetts Avenue, NE, Washington, DC 20212-0001, (202) 691-5200, Fax: (202) 691-6325, www.bls.gov; *Consumer Price Index Detailed Report* and unpublished data.

HOSPITALS - CONSTRUCTION

American Hospital Association (AHA), One North Franklin, Chicago, IL 60606-3421, (312) 422-3000, www.aha.org; *2008 AHA Environmental Assessment.*

McGraw-Hill Construction, Dodge Analytics, 1221 Avenue of The Americas, Manhattan, NY 10020, (800) 393-6343, http://dodge.construction.com/analytics; *Construction Outlook 2008.*

U.S. Census Bureau, Manufacturing and Construction Division, 4600 Silver Hill Road, Washington DC 20233, (301) 763-4673, www.census.gov/mcd; *Current Construction Reports.*

HOSPITALS - COST TO HOSPITAL PER PATIENT

American Hospital Association (AHA), One North Franklin, Chicago, IL 60606-3421, (312) 422-3000, www.aha.org; *Hospital Statistics 2008.*

HOSPITALS - DIAGNOSTIC PROCEDURES

National Center for Health Statistics (NCHS), Centers for Disease Control and Prevention (CDC), U.S. Department of Health and Human Services (HHS), 3311 Toledo Road, Hyattsville, MD 20782, (866) 232-4636, www.cdc.gov/nchs; unpublished data.

Robert Wood Johnson Foundation, PO Box 2316, College Road East and Route 1, Princeton, NJ 08543, (877) 843-7953, www.rwjf.org; *Accuracy of the Pain Numeric Rating Scale as a Screening Test in Primary Care.*

HOSPITALS - DISCHARGES FROM

National Center for Health Statistics (NCHS), Centers for Disease Control and Prevention (CDC), U.S. Department of Health and Human Services (HHS), 3311 Toledo Road, Hyattsville, MD 20782, (866) 232-4636, www.cdc.gov/nchs; *Health, United States, 2006, with Chartbook on Trends in the Health of Americans with Special Feature on Pain* and unpublished data.

HOSPITALS - EARNINGS

American Hospital Association (AHA), One North Franklin, Chicago, IL 60606-3421, (312) 422-3000, www.aha.org; *AHA White Paper: The State of Hospitals' Financial Health* and *Annual Survey of Hospitals.*

U.S. Bureau of Labor Statistics (BLS), Postal Square Building, 2 Massachusetts Avenue, NE, Washington, DC 20212-0001, (202) 691-5200, Fax: (202) 691-6325, www.bls.gov; *Current Employment Statistics Survey (CES)* and *Employment and Earnings (EE).*

U.S. Census Bureau, Center for Economic Studies, 4600 Silver Hill Road, Washington DC 20233, (301)

457-1235, www.ces.census.gov; *2002 Economic Census, Health Care and Social Assistance* and *2002 Economic Census, Professional, Scientific and Technical Services.*

U.S. Census Bureau, Company Statistics Division, 4700 Silver Hill Road, Washington DC 20233-0001, (301) 763-3030, www.census.gov/csd/; *County Business Patterns 2004.*

HOSPITALS - EMPLOYEES

American Hospital Association (AHA), One North Franklin, Chicago, IL 60606-3421, (312) 422-3000, www.aha.org; *Hospital Statistics 2008.*

National Center for Health Statistics (NCHS), Centers for Disease Control and Prevention (CDC), U.S. Department of Health and Human Services (HHS), 3311 Toledo Road, Hyattsville, MD 20782, (866) 232-4636, www.cdc.gov/nchs; unpublished data.

U.S. Bureau of Labor Statistics (BLS), Postal Square Building, 2 Massachusetts Avenue, NE, Washington, DC 20212-0001, (202) 691-5200, Fax: (202) 691-6325, www.bls.gov; *Current Employment Statistics Survey (CES); Employment and Earnings (EE);* and *Monthly Labor Review (MLR).*

U.S. Census Bureau, Center for Economic Studies, 4600 Silver Hill Road, Washington DC 20233, (301) 457-1235, www.ces.census.gov; *2002 Economic Census, Health Care and Social Assistance* and *2002 Economic Census, Professional, Scientific and Technical Services.*

U.S. Census Bureau, Company Statistics Division, 4700 Silver Hill Road, Washington DC 20233-0001, (301) 763-3030, www.census.gov/csd/; *County Business Patterns 2004.*

U.S. Census Bureau, Governments Division, 4600 Silver Hill Road, Washington DC 20233, (800) 242-2184, www.census.gov/govs/www; *2002 Census of Governments, Public Employment and Payroll.*

HOSPITALS - ESTABLISHMENTS

American Hospital Association (AHA), One North Franklin, Chicago, IL 60606-3421, (312) 422-3000, www.aha.org; *2008 AHA Environmental Assessment; AHA White Paper: The State of Hospitals' Financial Health; Hospital Statistics 2008;* and *Impact of Physician-owned Limited-service Hospitals: A Summary of Four Case Studies.*

National Center for Health Statistics (NCHS), Centers for Disease Control and Prevention (CDC), U.S. Department of Health and Human Services (HHS), 3311 Toledo Road, Hyattsville, MD 20782, (866) 232-4636, www.cdc.gov/nchs; unpublished data.

U.S. Census Bureau, Center for Economic Studies, 4600 Silver Hill Road, Washington DC 20233, (301) 457-1235, www.ces.census.gov; *2002 Economic Census, Health Care and Social Assistance* and *2002 Economic Census, Professional, Scientific and Technical Services.*

U.S. Census Bureau, Company Statistics Division, 4700 Silver Hill Road, Washington DC 20233-0001, (301) 763-3030, www.census.gov/csd/; *County Business Patterns 2004.*

HOSPITALS - EXPENDITURES, PUBLIC

American Hospital Association (AHA), One North Franklin, Chicago, IL 60606-3421, (312) 422-3000, www.aha.org; *Annual Survey of Hospitals.*

Centers for Medicare and Medicaid Services (CMS), U.S. Department of Health and Human Services (HHS), 7500 Security Boulevard, Baltimore, MD 21244-1850, (410) 786-3000, http://cms.hhs.gov; *Health Accounts.*

HOSPITALS - EXPENDITURES, PUBLIC - CITY GOVERNMENTS

U.S. Census Bureau, Governments Division, 4600 Silver Hill Road, Washington DC 20233, (800) 242-2184, www.census.gov/govs/www; *2002 Census of Governments, Government Finances.*

HOSPITALS - EXPENDITURES, PUBLIC - COUNTY GOVERNMENTS

U.S. Census Bureau, Governments Division, 4600 Silver Hill Road, Washington DC 20233, (800) 242-2184, www.census.gov/govs/www; *2002 Census of Governments, Government Finances.*

HOSPITALS - EXPENDITURES, PUBLIC - STATE GOVERNMENTS

U.S. Census Bureau, Governments Division, 4600 Silver Hill Road, Washington DC 20233, (800) 242-2184, www.census.gov/govs/www; *2002 Census of Governments, Government Finances.*

HOSPITALS - FINANCES

American Hospital Association (AHA), One North Franklin, Chicago, IL 60606-3421, (312) 422-3000, www.aha.org; *AHA White Paper: The State of Hospitals' Financial Health; Annual Survey of Hospitals; Beyond Health Care: The Economic Contribution of Hospitals; Hospital Statistics 2008;* and *Impact of Physician-owned Limited-service Hospitals: A Summary of Four Case Studies.*

National Restaurant Association, 1200 17th Street, NW, Washington, DC 20036, (202) 331-5900, Fax: (202) 331-2429, www.restaurant.org; *2007 Restaurant Industry Forecast* and *Restaurant Industry Operations Report 2006/2007.*

U.S. Census Bureau, Center for Economic Studies, 4600 Silver Hill Road, Washington DC 20233, (301) 457-1235, www.ces.census.gov; *2002 Economic Census, Health Care and Social Assistance.*

U.S. Census Bureau, Company Statistics Division, 4700 Silver Hill Road, Washington DC 20233-0001, (301) 763-3030, www.census.gov/csd/; *Current Business Reports.*

U.S. Census Bureau, Service Sector Statistics Division, 4700 Silver Hill Road, Washington DC 20233-0001, (301) 763-3030, www.census.gov/svsd/www/economic.html; *2004 Service Annual Survey.*

HOSPITALS - GRANTS - FOUNDATIONS

The Foundation Center, 79 Fifth Avenue, New York, NY 10003-3076, (212) 620-4230, Fax: (212) 807-3677, www.fdncenter.org; *FC Stats - Grantmaker; FC Stats - Grants; Foundation Giving Trends (2008 Edition);* and *Top Funders: Top 100 U.S. Foundations by Asset Size.*

HOSPITALS - INSURANCE - MEDICARE PROGRAM

Centers for Medicare and Medicaid Services (CMS), U.S. Department of Health and Human Services (HHS), 7500 Security Boulevard, Baltimore, MD 21244-1850, (410) 786-3000, http://cms.hhs.gov; *CMS Facts Figures;* Data Compendium, 2007 (web app); *Health Care Financing Review;* and *Medicare Enrollment: National Trends 1966-2005.*

HOSPITALS - MENTAL HOSPITALS

American Hospital Association (AHA), One North Franklin, Chicago, IL 60606-3421, (312) 422-3000, www.aha.org; *Hospital Statistics 2008* and unpublished data.

Population Reference Bureau, 1875 Connecticut Avenue, NW, Suite 520, Washington, DC, 20009-5728, (800) 877-9881, Fax: (202) 328-3937, www.prb.org; *The American People Series.*

Substance Abuse and Mental Health Services Administration (SAMHSA), 1 Choke Cherry Road, Rockville, MD 20857, (240) 777-1311, www.oas.samhsa.gov; *Health Services Utilization by Individuals with Substance Abuse and Mental Disorders* and unpublished data.

U.S. Census Bureau, Population Division, 4700 Silver Hill Road, Washington DC 20233-0001, (301) 763-3030, www.census.gov/population/www/; *Census 2000 Profiles of General Demographic Characteristics.*

HOSPITALS - NATIONAL EXPENDITURES

American Hospital Association (AHA), One North Franklin, Chicago, IL 60606-3421, (312) 422-3000, www.aha.org; *AHA White Paper: The State of Hospitals' Financial Health.*

Centers for Medicare and Medicaid Services (CMS), U.S. Department of Health and Human Services (HHS), 7500 Security Boulevard, Baltimore, MD 21244-1850, (410) 786-3000, http://cms.hhs.gov; *Health Accounts.*

HOSPITALS - OUTPATIENT VISITS

American Hospital Association (AHA), One North Franklin, Chicago, IL 60606-3421, (312) 422-3000, www.aha.org; *Hospital Statistics 2008.*

HOSPITALS - PATIENTS

American Hospital Association (AHA), One North Franklin, Chicago, IL 60606-3421, (312) 422-3000, www.aha.org; *Hospital Statistics 2008.*

Australian Institute of Health and Welfare (AIHW), GPO Box 570, Canberra ACT 2601, Australia, www.aihw.gov.au; *Deaths and Hospitalisations Due to Drowning, Australia 1999-00 to 2003-04.*

Eurostat, Batiment Jean Monnet, Rue Alcide de Gasperi, L-2920 Luxembourg, http://epp.eurostat.ec.europa.eu; *In-Patient Average Length of Stay (ISHMT, in Days).*

Indian Health Service (IHS), U.S. Department of Health and Human Services, The Reyes Building, 801 Thompson Avenue, Suite 400, Rockville, MD 20852-1627, (301) 443-1180, www.ihs.gov; *Annual Federal Year 2001 IHS and Tribal Hospital Inpatient Statistics and Comparison with Federal Year 2000.*

National Center for Health Statistics (NCHS), Centers for Disease Control and Prevention (CDC), U.S. Department of Health and Human Services (HHS), 3311 Toledo Road, Hyattsville, MD 20782, (866) 232-4636, www.cdc.gov/nchs; unpublished data.

National Council on Compensation Insurance, Inc. (NCCI), 901 Peninsula Corporate Circle, Boca Raton, FL 33487, (800) NCCI-123, www.ncci.com; *NCCI Examines Emergency Room Treatment of Younger Workers vs. Older Workers - Fall 2007.*

Population Reference Bureau, 1875 Connecticut Avenue, NW, Suite 520, Washington, DC, 20009-5728, (800) 877-9881, Fax: (202) 328-3937, www.prb.org; *The American People Series.*

U.S. Census Bureau, Population Division, 4700 Silver Hill Road, Washington DC 20233-0001, (301) 763-3030, www.census.gov/population/www/; *Census 2000 Profiles of General Demographic Characteristics.*

HOSPITALS - RECEIPTS

American Hospital Association (AHA), One North Franklin, Chicago, IL 60606-3421, (312) 422-3000, www.aha.org; *2008 AHA Environmental Assessment; AHA White Paper: The State of Hospitals' Financial Health; Annual Survey of Hospitals; Beyond Health Care: The Economic Contribution of Hospitals;* and *Impact of Physician-owned Limited-service Hospitals: A Summary of Four Case Studies.*

U.S. Census Bureau, 4700 Silver Hill Road, Washington DC 20233-0001, (301) 763-3030, www.census.gov; unpublished data.

U.S. Census Bureau, Center for Economic Studies, 4600 Silver Hill Road, Washington DC 20233, (301) 457-1235, www.ces.census.gov; *2002 Economic Census, Health Care and Social Assistance* and *2002 Economic Census, Professional, Scientific and Technical Services.*

U.S. Census Bureau, Company Statistics Division, 4700 Silver Hill Road, Washington DC 20233-0001, (301) 763-3030, www.census.gov/csd/; *Current Business Reports.*

HOSPITALS - STATES

American Hospital Association (AHA), One North Franklin, Chicago, IL 60606-3421, (312) 422-3000, www.aha.org; *Hospital Statistics 2008* and unpublished data.

HOSPITALS - SURGERY

Arlington Medical Resources, Inc., 48 General Warren Boulevard, Malvern, PA 19355, (610) 722-5511, Fax: (610) 722-5514, www.amr-data.com; *The Imaging Market Guide.*

Health Protection Agency, 7th Floor, Holborn Gate, 330 High Holborn, London WC1V 7PP, United Kingdom, www.hpa.org.uk; *Third Report of the Mandatory Surveillance of Surgical Site Infection in Orthopaedic Surgery.*

National Center for Health Statistics (NCHS), Centers for Disease Control and Prevention (CDC), U.S. Department of Health and Human Services (HHS), 3311 Toledo Road, Hyattsville, MD 20782, (866) 232-4636, www.cdc.gov/nchs; unpublished data.

HOSPITALS - SURGERY - ORGAN TRANSPLANTS

American Association of Tissue Banks, 1320 Old Chain Bridge Road, Suite 450, McLean, VA 22101, (703) 827-9582, Fax: (703) 356-2198, www.aatb.org; unpublished data.

American Hospital Association (AHA), One North Franklin, Chicago, IL 60606-3421, (312) 422-3000, www.aha.org; *Annual Survey of Hospitals* and *Hospital Statistics 2008.*

Eye Bank Association of America (EBAA), 1015 18th Street, NW, Suite 1010, Washington, DC 20036, (202) 775-4999, Fax: (202) 429-6036, www.restoresight.org; unpublished data.

The Scientific Registry of Transplant Recipients (SRTR), University Renal Research and Education Association, 315 W. Huron, Suite 260, Ann Arbor, MI 48103, (800) 830-9664, Fax: (734) 665-2103, www.ustransplant.org; *2006 Annual Report.*

United Network for Organ Sharing (UNOS), PO Box 2484, Richmond, VA 23218, (804) 782-4800, Fax: (804) 782-4817, www.unos.org; Organ Procurement and Transplantation Network (OPTN).

HOSPITALS - USE - ADMISSIONS AND PATIENT DAYS

American Hospital Association (AHA), One North Franklin, Chicago, IL 60606-3421, (312) 422-3000, www.aha.org; *Hospital Statistics 2008* and unpublished data.

National Center for Health Statistics (NCHS), Centers for Disease Control and Prevention (CDC), U.S. Department of Health and Human Services (HHS), 3311 Toledo Road, Hyattsville, MD 20782, (866) 232-4636, www.cdc.gov/nchs; *Health, United States, 2006, with Chartbook on Trends in the Health of Americans with Special Feature on Pain* and unpublished data.

HOSPITALS - VETERANS - EXPENDITURES AND PATIENTS

Substance Abuse and Mental Health Services Administration (SAMHSA), 1 Choke Cherry Road, Rockville, MD 20857, (240) 777-1311, www.oas.samhsa.gov; unpublished data.

HOTELS AND OTHER LODGING PLACES - BUILDINGS AND FLOOR SPACE

U.S. Department of Energy (DOE), Energy Information Administration (EIA), 1000 Independence Avenue, SW, Washington, DC 20585, (202) 586-8800, www.eia.doe.gov; *Commercial Buildings Energy Consumption Survey (CBECS).*

HOTELS AND OTHER LODGING PLACES - EARNINGS

Tourism Intelligence International, An der Wolfskuhle 48, 33619 Bielefeld, Germany, www.tourism-intelligence.com; *Successful Hotel Resorts - Lessons from the Leaders.*

U.S. Bureau of Labor Statistics (BLS), Postal Square Building, 2 Massachusetts Avenue, NE, Washington, DC 20212-0001, (202) 691-5200, Fax: (202) 691-6325, www.bls.gov; *Current Employment Statistics Survey (CES)* and *Employment and Earnings (EE).*

U.S. Census Bureau, Center for Economic Studies, 4600 Silver Hill Road, Washington DC 20233, (301) 457-1235, www.ces.census.gov; *2002 Economic Census, Accommodation and Food Services.*

U.S. Census Bureau, Company Statistics Division, 4700 Silver Hill Road, Washington DC 20233-0001, (301) 763-3030, www.census.gov/csd/; *County Business Patterns 2004.*

U.S. Census Bureau, Service Sector Statistics Division, 4700 Silver Hill Road, Washington DC 20233-0001, (301) 763-3030, www.census.gov/svsd/www/economic.html; *2004 Service Annual Survey.*

HOTELS AND OTHER LODGING PLACES - EMPLOYEES

U.S. Census Bureau, Center for Economic Studies, 4600 Silver Hill Road, Washington DC 20233, (301) 457-1235, www.ces.census.gov; *2002 Economic Census, Professional, Scientific and Technical Services.*

U.S. Census Bureau, Company Statistics Division, 4700 Silver Hill Road, Washington DC 20233-0001, (301) 763-3030, www.census.gov/csd/; *County Business Patterns 2004.*

HOTELS AND OTHER LODGING PLACES - ESTABLISHMENTS

Tourism Intelligence International, An der Wolfskuhle 48, 33619 Bielefeld, Germany, www.tourism-intelligence.com; *Successful Hotel Resorts - Lessons from the Leaders.*

U.S. Census Bureau, Center for Economic Studies, 4600 Silver Hill Road, Washington DC 20233, (301) 457-1235, www.ces.census.gov; Economic Census (web app) and *2002 Economic Census, Professional, Scientific and Technical Services.*

U.S. Census Bureau, Company Statistics Division, 4700 Silver Hill Road, Washington DC 20233-0001, (301) 763-3030, www.census.gov/csd/; *County Business Patterns 2004.*

HOTELS AND OTHER LODGING PLACES - EXPENSES

U.S. Census Bureau, Company Statistics Division, 4700 Silver Hill Road, Washington DC 20233-0001, (301) 763-3030, www.census.gov/csd/; *Current Business Reports.*

HOTELS AND OTHER LODGING PLACES - GROSS DOMESTIC PRODUCT

Bureau of Economic Analysis (BEA), U.S. Department of Commerce (DOC), 1441 L Street NW, Washington, DC 20230, (202) 606-9900, www.bea.gov; *Survey of Current Business (SCB).*

HOTELS AND OTHER LODGING PLACES - INDUSTRIAL SAFETY

U.S. Bureau of Labor Statistics (BLS), Postal Square Building, 2 Massachusetts Avenue, NE, Washington, DC 20212-0001, (202) 691-5200, Fax: (202) 691-6325, www.bls.gov; *Injuries, Illnesses, and Fatalities (IIF).*

HOTELS AND OTHER LODGING PLACES - MERGERS AND ACQUISITIONS

Thomson Financial, 195 Broadway, New York, NY 10007, (646) 822-2000, www.thomson.com; Thomson Research.

HOTELS AND OTHER LODGING PLACES - MULTINATIONAL COMPANIES

Bureau of Economic Analysis (BEA), U.S. Department of Commerce (DOC), 1441 L Street NW, Washington, DC 20230, (202) 606-9900, www.bea.gov; *Survey of Current Business (SCB).*

HOTELS AND OTHER LODGING PLACES - NEW CONSTRUCTION

U.S. Census Bureau, Manufacturing and Construction Division, 4600 Silver Hill Road, Washington DC 20233, (301) 763-4673, www.census.gov/mcd; *Current Construction Reports* and *Value of New Construction Put in Place.*

HOTELS AND OTHER LODGING PLACES - OCCUPANCY RATE

American Hotel Lodging Association (AHLA), 1201 New York Avenue, NW, Suite 600, Washington, DC 20005-3931, (202) 289-3100, Fax: (202) 289-3199, www.ahla.com; *2006 Lodging Industry Profile.*

HOTELS AND OTHER LODGING PLACES - PRODUCTIVITY

U.S. Bureau of Labor Statistics (BLS), Postal Square Building, 2 Massachusetts Avenue, NE, Washington, DC 20212-0001, (202) 691-5200, Fax: (202) 691-6325, www.bls.gov; *Industry Productivity and Costs.*

HOTELS AND OTHER LODGING PLACES - RECEIPTS

National Restaurant Association, 1200 17th Street, NW, Washington, DC 20036, (202) 331-5900, Fax: (202) 331-2429, www.restaurant.org; *2007 Restaurant Industry Forecast* and *Restaurant Industry Operations Report 2006/2007.*

U.S. Census Bureau, Center for Economic Studies, 4600 Silver Hill Road, Washington DC 20233, (301) 457-1235, www.ces.census.gov; *2002 Economic Census, Accommodation and Food Services* and *2002 Economic Census, Professional, Scientific and Technical Services.*

U.S. Census Bureau, Company Statistics Division, 4700 Silver Hill Road, Washington DC 20233-0001, (301) 763-3030, www.census.gov/csd/; *Current Business Reports.*

HOTELS AND OTHER LODGING PLACES - TRAVEL SUMMARY

American Hotel Lodging Association (AHLA), 1201 New York Avenue, NW, Suite 600, Washington, DC 20005-3931, (202) 289-3100, Fax: (202) 289-3199, www.ahla.com; *2006 Lodging Industry Profile.*

HOUSE OF REPRESENTATIVES

Congressional Quarterly, Inc., 1255 22nd Street, NW, Washington, DC 20037, (202) 419-8500, www.cq.com; *America Votes 27: Election Returns by State, 2005-2006; Congressional Quarterly Weekly Report; CQ Congress Collection; Statistical History of the American Electorate;* and unpublished data.

U.S. Government Printing Office (GPO), Office of Congressional Publishing Services (OCPS), 732 North Capitol Street NW, Washington, DC 20401, (202) 512-0224, www.gpo.gov/customerservices/cps.htm; *Calendars of the U.S. House of Representatives and History of Legislation; Congressional Directory; Congressional Record;* and unpublished data.

HOUSEHOLD WORKERS

See DOMESTIC SERVICE

HOUSEHOLDS OR FAMILIES

See also HOUSING

The Annie E. Casey Foundation, 701 Saint Paul Street, Baltimore, MD 21202, (410) 547-6600, Fax: (410) 547-3610, www.aecf.org; *Change that Abides: A Retrospective Look at Five Community and Family Stengthening Projects and Their Enduring Results* and *Of, By, And For the Community: The Story of PUENTE Learning Center.*

DataPlace by KnowledgePlex, c/o Fannie Mae Foundation, 4000 Wisconsin Avenue, N.W., North Tower, Suite One, Washington, DC 20016-2804, www.dataplace.org; *Database. Subject coverage: Community, regional and national housing and demographic data.*

Office of Planning, District of Columbia, 801 North Capitol Street, NE, Suite 4000, Washington, DC 20002, (202) 442-7600, Fax: (202) 442-7637, www.planning.dc.gov; *District of Columbia Population and Housing Trends.*

Policy Research Bureau, 2a Tabernacle Street, London EC2A 4LU, United Kingdom, www.prb.org.

uk; *Parenting in Poor Environments: Stress, Support and Coping. A Summary of Key Messages for Policy and Practice from a Major National Study.*

U.S. Census Bureau, 4700 Silver Hill Road, Washington DC 20233-0001, (301) 763-3030, www.census.gov; American FactFinder (web app); *LandView 6; State and County QuickFacts;* and unpublished data.

U.S. Census Bureau, Housing and Household Economics Statistics Division, 4700 Silver Hill Road, Washington DC 20233-0001, (301) 763-3030, www.census.gov/hhes/www; Decennial Census of Population and Housing (web app) and *Housing Characteristics: 2000.*

U.S. Census Bureau, Population Division, 4700 Silver Hill Road, Washington DC 20233-0001, (301) 763-3030, www.census.gov/population/www/; *Current Population Reports.*

HOUSEHOLDS OR FAMILIES - AGE OF HOUSEHOLDER

U.S. Census Bureau, 4700 Silver Hill Road, Washington DC 20233-0001, (301) 763-3030, www.census.gov; unpublished data.

U.S. Census Bureau, Housing and Household Economics Statistics Division, 4700 Silver Hill Road, Washington DC 20233-0001, (301) 763-3030, www.census.gov/hhes/www; *Families and Living Arrangements.*

U.S. Census Bureau, Population Division, 4700 Silver Hill Road, Washington DC 20233-0001, (301) 763-3030, www.census.gov/population/www/; *Current Population Reports.*

HOUSEHOLDS OR FAMILIES - AMERICAN INDIAN, ESKIMO, AND ALEUT POPULATION

DataPlace by KnowledgePlex, c/o Fannie Mae Foundation, 4000 Wisconsin Avenue, N.W., North Tower, Suite One, Washington, DC 20016-2804, www.dataplace.org; *Database. Subject coverage: Community, regional and national housing and demographic data.*

U.S. Census Bureau, 4700 Silver Hill Road, Washington DC 20233-0001, (301) 763-3030, www.census.gov; unpublished data.

U.S. Census Bureau, Population Division, 4700 Silver Hill Road, Washington DC 20233-0001, (301) 763-3030, www.census.gov/population/www/; *Current Population Reports.*

HOUSEHOLDS OR FAMILIES - ASIAN AND PACIFIC ISLANDER POPULATION

DataPlace by KnowledgePlex, c/o Fannie Mae Foundation, 4000 Wisconsin Avenue, N.W., North Tower, Suite One, Washington, DC 20016-2804, www.dataplace.org; *Database. Subject coverage: Community, regional and national housing and demographic data.*

U.S. Census Bureau, 4700 Silver Hill Road, Washington DC 20233-0001, (301) 763-3030, www.census.gov; unpublished data.

U.S. Census Bureau, Population Division, 4700 Silver Hill Road, Washington DC 20233-0001, (301) 763-3030, www.census.gov/population/www/; *The Asian and Pacific Islander Population in the United States* and *Current Population Reports.*

HOUSEHOLDS OR FAMILIES - BALANCE SHEET

Board of Governors of the Federal Reserve System, Constitution Avenue, NW, Washington, DC 20551, (202) 452-3000, www.federalreserve.gov; *Flow of Funds Accounts of the United States.*

HOUSEHOLDS OR FAMILIES - BLACK POPULATION

U.S. Census Bureau, 4700 Silver Hill Road, Washington DC 20233-0001, (301) 763-3030, www.census.gov; unpublished data.

U.S. Census Bureau, Population Division, 4700 Silver Hill Road, Washington DC 20233-0001, (301) 763-3030, www.census.gov/population/www/; *The Black Population in the United States* and *Current Population Reports.*

HOUSEHOLDS OR FAMILIES - CHARACTERISTICS

DataPlace by KnowledgePlex, c/o Fannie Mae Foundation, 4000 Wisconsin Avenue, N.W., North Tower, Suite One, Washington, DC 20016-2804, www.dataplace.org; *Database. Subject coverage: Community, regional and national housing and demographic data* and *Database. Subject coverage: Community, regional and national housing and demographic data.*

Hartford Institute for Religion Research, Hartford Seminary, 77 Sherman Street, Hartford, CT 06105-2260, (860) 509-9543, Fax: (860) 509-9551, http://hirr.hartsem.edu; *Religion and the Family.*

National Center for Health Statistics (NCHS), Centers for Disease Control and Prevention (CDC), U.S. Department of Health and Human Services (HHS), 3311 Toledo Road, Hyattsville, MD 20782, (866) 232-4636, www.cdc.gov/nchs; *Indicators of Social and Economic Well-Being by Race and Hispanic Origin.*

U.S. Census Bureau, 4700 Silver Hill Road, Washington DC 20233-0001, (301) 763-3030, www.census.gov; unpublished data.

U.S. Census Bureau, Housing and Household Economics Statistics Division, 4700 Silver Hill Road, Washington DC 20233-0001, (301) 763-3030, www.census.gov/hhes/www; Decennial Census of Population and Housing (web app) and *Housing Vacancies and Homeownership (CPS/HVS)* .

U.S. Census Bureau, Population Division, 4700 Silver Hill Road, Washington DC 20233-0001, (301) 763-3030, www.census.gov/population/www/; *Current Population Reports.*

U.S. Department of Justice (DOJ), National Institute of Justice (NIJ), 810 Seventh Street, NW, Washington, DC 20531, (202) 307-2942, Fax: (202) 616-0275, www.ojp.usdoj.gov/nij/; *Does Parental Incarceration Increase a Child's Risk for Foster Care Placement?*

HOUSEHOLDS OR FAMILIES - CHILDREN UNDER 18 YEARS OLD

The Annie E. Casey Foundation, 701 Saint Paul Street, Baltimore, MD 21202, (410) 547-6600, Fax: (410) 547-3610, www.aecf.org; *Of, By, And For the Community: The Story of PUENTE Learning Center.*

Information and Documentation Centre, Institute de la statistique du Quebec, 200 Chemin Sainte-Foy, 3rd Floor, Quebec City, Quebec G1R 5T4, Canada, (Dial from U.S. (418) 691-2401), (Fax from U.S. (418) 643-4129), www.stat.gouv.qc.ca; *Disciplining Children in Quebec: Parenting Norms and Practices in 2004.*

National Center for Juvenile Justice (NCJJ), 3700 South Water Street, Suite 200, Pittsburgh, PA 15203, (412) 227-6950, Fax: (412) 227-6955, http://ncjj.servehttp.com/NCJJWebsite/main.htm; *Jury Trial in Termination of Parental Rights (2005 Update).*

Policy Research Bureau, 2a Tabernacle Street, London EC2A 4LU, United Kingdom, www.prb.org.uk; *Parenting in Poor Environments: Stress, Support and Coping. A Summary of Key Messages for Policy and Practice from a Major National Study.*

U.S. Census Bureau, 4700 Silver Hill Road, Washington DC 20233-0001, (301) 763-3030, www.census.gov; unpublished data.

U.S. Census Bureau, Housing and Household Economics Statistics Division, 4700 Silver Hill Road, Washington DC 20233-0001, (301) 763-3030, www.census.gov/hhes/www; Decennial Census of Population and Housing (web app) and *Families and Living Arrangements.*

U.S. Census Bureau, Population Division, 4700 Silver Hill Road, Washington DC 20233-0001, (301) 763-3030, www.census.gov/population/www/; *Current Population Reports.*

U.S. Department of Health and Human Services, Health Resources and Services Administration, Maternal and Child Health Bureau, Parklawn Building Room 18-05, 5600 Fishers Lane, Rockville, Maryland 20857, (301) 443-2170, http://mchb.hrsa.gov; *Data Summaries for Title V Expenditures and Individuals Served* and *Title V: A Snapshot of Maternal and Child Health.*

U.S. Department of Justice (DOJ), National Institute of Justice (NIJ), 810 Seventh Street, NW, Washington, DC 20531, (202) 307-2942, Fax: (202) 616-0275, www.ojp.usdoj.gov/nij/; *Does Parental Incarceration Increase a Child's Risk for Foster Care Placement?* and *Youth Victimization: Prevalence and Implications* .

HOUSEHOLDS OR FAMILIES - COMPUTER USE

Mediamark Research, Inc., 75 Ninth Avenue, 5th Floor, New York, NY 10011, (212) 884-9200, Fax: (212) 884-9339, www.mediamark.com; MRI+.

National Center for Education Statistics (NCES), 1990 K Street, NW, Washington, DC 20006, (202) 502-7300, http://nces.ed.gov; *Digest of Education Statistics 2007.*

National Telecommunications and Information Administration (NTIA), U.S. Department of Commerce (DOC), 1401 Constitution Avenue, NW, Washington, DC 20230, (202) 482-7002, www.ntia.doc.gov; *A Nation Online: Entering the Broadband Age.*

HOUSEHOLDS OR FAMILIES - CONSUMER EXPENDITURES

Department of Statistics (DOS), PO Box 2015, Amman 11181, Jordan, www.dos.gov.jo; *Household Income and Expenditure Survey.*

Mediamark Research, Inc., 75 Ninth Avenue, 5th Floor, New York, NY 10011, (212) 884-9200, Fax: (212) 884-9339, www.mediamark.com; *The American Kids Study.*

The NPD Group, Port Washington, 900 West Shore Road, Port Washington, NY 11050, (866) 444-1411, www.npd.com; *Market Research for the Appliances, Home Improvement, Home Textiles, and Housewares Industries.*

U.S. Bureau of Labor Statistics (BLS), Postal Square Building, 2 Massachusetts Avenue, NE, Washington, DC 20212-0001, (202) 691-5200, Fax: (202) 691-6325, www.bls.gov; *Consumer Expenditures in 2006.*

HOUSEHOLDS OR FAMILIES - CRIMINAL VICTIMIZATION

Australian Government Office for Women, Department of Families, Community Services and Indigenous Affairs, Box 7788, Canberra Mail Centre ACT 2610, Australia, http://ofw.facsia.gov.au; *Cost of Domestic Violence to the Australian Economy.*

U.S. Department of Justice (DOJ), Bureau of Justice Statistics, 810 Seventh Street, NW, Washington, DC 20531, (202) 307-0765, www.ojp.usdoj.gov/bjs/; *Crime and the Nation's Households, 2004; Criminal Victimization, 2005; Identity Theft, 2004;* and *Weapon Use and Violent Crime, 1993-2001.*

U.S. Department of Justice (DOJ), National Institute of Justice (NIJ), 810 Seventh Street, NW, Washington, DC 20531, (202) 307-2942, Fax: (202) 616-0275, www.ojp.usdoj.gov/nij/; *Youth Victimization: Prevalence and Implications* .

HOUSEHOLDS OR FAMILIES - DEBT

Board of Governors of the Federal Reserve System, Constitution Avenue, NW, Washington, DC 20551, (202) 452-3000, www.federalreserve.gov; *Federal Reserve Bulletin; Flow of Funds Accounts of the United States;* and unpublished data.

HOUSEHOLDS OR FAMILIES - EDUCATIONAL ATTAINMENT

The Annie E. Casey Foundation, 701 Saint Paul Street, Baltimore, MD 21202, (410) 547-6600, Fax:

(410) 547-3610, www.aecf.org; *Of, By, And For the Community: The Story of PUENTE Learning Center.*

U.S. Census Bureau, Housing and Household Economics Statistics Division, 4700 Silver Hill Road, Washington DC 20233-0001, (301) 763-3030, www.census.gov/hhes/www; *Families and Living Arrangements.*

U.S. Census Bureau, Population Division, 4700 Silver Hill Road, Washington DC 20233-0001, (301) 763-3030, www.census.gov/population/www/; *Current Population Reports.*

HOUSEHOLDS OR FAMILIES - FEMALE HOUSEHOLDER

U.S. Census Bureau, 4700 Silver Hill Road, Washington DC 20233-0001, (301) 763-3030, www.census.gov; unpublished data.

U.S. Census Bureau, Housing and Household Economics Statistics Division, 4700 Silver Hill Road, Washington DC 20233-0001, (301) 763-3030, www.census.gov/hhes/www; Decennial Census of Population and Housing (web app).

U.S. Census Bureau, Population Division, 4700 Silver Hill Road, Washington DC 20233-0001, (301) 763-3030, www.census.gov/population/www/; *Current Population Reports.*

U.S. Department of Justice (DOJ), National Institute of Justice (NIJ), 810 Seventh Street, NW, Washington, DC 20531, (202) 307-2942, Fax: (202) 616-0275, www.ojp.usdoj.gov/nij/; *Does Parental Incarceration Increase a Child's Risk for Foster Care Placement?*

HOUSEHOLDS OR FAMILIES - FLOW OF FUNDS

Board of Governors of the Federal Reserve System, Constitution Avenue, NW, Washington, DC 20551, (202) 452-3000, www.federalreserve.gov; *Flow of Funds Accounts of the United States.*

HOUSEHOLDS OR FAMILIES - HISPANIC ORIGIN POPULATION

DataPlace by KnowledgePlex, c/o Fannie Mae Foundation, 4000 Wisconsin Avenue, N.W., North Tower, Suite One, Washington, DC 20016-2804, www.dataplace.org; *Database. Subject coverage: Community, regional and national housing and demographic data.*

U.S. Census Bureau, 4700 Silver Hill Road, Washington DC 20233-0001, (301) 763-3030, www.census.gov; unpublished data.

U.S. Census Bureau, Population Division, 4700 Silver Hill Road, Washington DC 20233-0001, (301) 763-3030, www.census.gov/population/www/; *Current Population Reports* and *The Hispanic Population in the United States.*

HOUSEHOLDS OR FAMILIES - INCOME

Department of Statistics (DOS), PO Box 2015, Amman 11181, Jordan, www.dos.gov.jo; *Household Income and Expenditure Survey.*

National Center for Children in Poverty (NCCP), 215 W. 125th Street, 3rd Floor, New York, NY 10027, (646) 284-9600, Fax: (646) 284-9623, www.nccp.org; *Living at the Edge; Parent Employment and the Use of Child Care Subsidies; Predictors of Child Care Subsidy Use; Welfare Research Perspectives;* and *When Work Doesn't Pay: What Every Policymaker Should Know.*

National Center for Health Statistics (NCHS), Centers for Disease Control and Prevention (CDC), U.S. Department of Health and Human Services (HHS), 3311 Toledo Road, Hyattsville, MD 20782, (866) 232-4636, www.cdc.gov/nchs; *Indicators of Social and Economic Well-Being by Race and Hispanic Origin.*

U.S. Census Bureau, 4700 Silver Hill Road, Washington DC 20233-0001, (301) 763-3030, www.census.gov; unpublished data.

U.S. Census Bureau, Housing and Household Economics Statistics Division, 4700 Silver Hill Road, Washington DC 20233-0001, (301) 763-3030, www.census.gov/hhes/www; Decennial Census of Population and Housing (web app) and *Families and Living Arrangements.*

U.S. Census Bureau, Population Division, 4700 Silver Hill Road, Washington DC 20233-0001, (301) 763-3030, www.census.gov/population/www/; *Current Population Reports.*

HOUSEHOLDS OR FAMILIES - INTERNET ACCESS

Mediamark Research, Inc., 75 Ninth Avenue, 5th Floor, New York, NY 10011, (212) 884-9200, Fax: (212) 884-9339, www.mediamark.com; MRI+.

National Telecommunications and Information Administration (NTIA), U.S. Department of Commerce (DOC), 1401 Constitution Avenue, NW, Washington, DC 20230, (202) 482-7002, www.ntia.doc.gov; *A Nation Online: Entering the Broadband Age.*

Veronis Suhler Stevenson Partners LLC, 350 Park Avenue, New York, NY 10022, (212) 935-4990, Fax: (212) 381-8168, www.vss.com; Communications Industry Report.

HOUSEHOLDS OR FAMILIES - INTERRACIAL MARRIED COUPLES

U.S. Census Bureau, 4700 Silver Hill Road, Washington DC 20233-0001, (301) 763-3030, www.census.gov; unpublished data.

U.S. Census Bureau, Population Division, 4700 Silver Hill Road, Washington DC 20233-0001, (301) 763-3030, www.census.gov/population/www/; *Current Population Reports.*

HOUSEHOLDS OR FAMILIES - LIVING ARRANGEMENTS

State of Connecticut, Department of Economic and Community Development (DECD), 505 Hudson Street, Hartford, CT 06106-7107, (860) 270-8000, www.ct.gov/ecd/; *State of Connecticut Analysis of Impediments to Fair Housing Choice Update.*

U.S. Census Bureau, 4700 Silver Hill Road, Washington DC 20233-0001, (301) 763-3030, www.census.gov; unpublished data.

U.S. Census Bureau, Housing and Household Economics Statistics Division, 4700 Silver Hill Road, Washington DC 20233-0001, (301) 763-3030, www.census.gov/hhes/www; Decennial Census of Population and Housing (web app); *Families and Living Arrangements;* and *Housing Vacancies and Homeownership (CPS/HVS)* .

U.S. Census Bureau, Population Division, 4700 Silver Hill Road, Washington DC 20233-0001, (301) 763-3030, www.census.gov/population/www/; *Current Population Reports.*

HOUSEHOLDS OR FAMILIES - MARITAL STATUS

U.S. Census Bureau, 4700 Silver Hill Road, Washington DC 20233-0001, (301) 763-3030, www.census.gov; unpublished data.

U.S. Census Bureau, Housing and Household Economics Statistics Division, 4700 Silver Hill Road, Washington DC 20233-0001, (301) 763-3030, www.census.gov/hhes/www; *Families and Living Arrangements.*

U.S. Census Bureau, Population Division, 4700 Silver Hill Road, Washington DC 20233-0001, (301) 763-3030, www.census.gov/population/www/; *Current Population Reports.*

HOUSEHOLDS OR FAMILIES - MEDIA USERS

Mediamark Research, Inc., 75 Ninth Avenue, 5th Floor, New York, NY 10011, (212) 884-9200, Fax: (212) 884-9339, www.mediamark.com; MRI+.

HOUSEHOLDS OR FAMILIES - MOBILITY STATUS

U.S. Census Bureau, Population Division, 4700 Silver Hill Road, Washington DC 20233-0001, (301) 763-3030, www.census.gov/population/www/; *Current Population Reports.*

HOUSEHOLDS OR FAMILIES - NET WORTH

Board of Governors of the Federal Reserve System, Constitution Avenue, NW, Washington, DC 20551, (202) 452-3000, www.federalreserve.gov; *Federal Reserve Bulletin* and *Flow of Funds Accounts of the United States.*

HOUSEHOLDS OR FAMILIES - OLDER PEOPLE

U.S. Census Bureau, Housing and Household Economics Statistics Division, 4700 Silver Hill Road, Washington DC 20233-0001, (301) 763-3030, www.census.gov/hhes/www; *Families and Living Arrangements.*

U.S. Census Bureau, Population Division, 4700 Silver Hill Road, Washington DC 20233-0001, (301) 763-3030, www.census.gov/population/www/; *Current Population Reports.*

HOUSEHOLDS OR FAMILIES - PERSONS IN HOUSEHOLDS

U.S. Census Bureau, 4700 Silver Hill Road, Washington DC 20233-0001, (301) 763-3030, www.census.gov; unpublished data.

U.S. Census Bureau, Housing and Household Economics Statistics Division, 4700 Silver Hill Road, Washington DC 20233-0001, (301) 763-3030, www.census.gov/hhes/www; *Families and Living Arrangements.*

U.S. Census Bureau, Population Division, 4700 Silver Hill Road, Washington DC 20233-0001, (301) 763-3030, www.census.gov/population/www/; *Current Population Reports.*

HOUSEHOLDS OR FAMILIES - PERSONS LIVING ALONE

U.S. Census Bureau, 4700 Silver Hill Road, Washington DC 20233-0001, (301) 763-3030, www.census.gov; unpublished data.

U.S. Census Bureau, Housing and Household Economics Statistics Division, 4700 Silver Hill Road, Washington DC 20233-0001, (301) 763-3030, www.census.gov/hhes/www; Decennial Census of Population and Housing (web app) and *Families and Living Arrangements.*

U.S. Census Bureau, Population Division, 4700 Silver Hill Road, Washington DC 20233-0001, (301) 763-3030, www.census.gov/population/www/; *Current Population Reports.*

HOUSEHOLDS OR FAMILIES - POVERTY

The Annie E. Casey Foundation, 701 Saint Paul Street, Baltimore, MD 21202, (410) 547-6600, Fax: (410) 547-3610, www.aecf.org; *Beyond the Boundaries: Low-Income Residents, Faith-Based Organizations and Neighborhood Coalition Building; Children at Risk: State Trends 1990-2000; City and Rural KIDS COUNT Data Book; The High Cost of Being Poor: What It Takes for Low-Income Families to Get By and Get Ahead in Rural America; KIDS COUNT; National Tax Assistance for Working Families Campaign Report to the Annie E. Casey Foundation, 2004 Data; Rural KIDS COUNT Pocket Guide; Vermont Communities Count: Using Results to Strengthen Services for Families and Children;* and *Working Hard, Falling Short.*

National Center for Children in Poverty (NCCP), 215 W. 125th Street, 3rd Floor, New York, NY 10027, (646) 284-9600, Fax: (646) 284-9623, www.nccp.org; *2007 Annual Report; The Changing Demographics of Low-Income Families and Their Children; The Changing Face of Child Poverty in California; Child Poverty in States Hit by Hurricane Katrina; Early Childhood Poverty: A Statistical Profile; Geography of Low-Income Families and Children; Low-Income Families in the States: Results from the Family Resource Simulator; Parent Employment and the Use of Child Care Subsidies; Predictors of Child Care Subsidy Use; Promoting the Emotional Well-Being of Children and Families;* and *Welfare Research Perspectives.*

Policy Research Bureau, 2a Tabernacle Street, London EC2A 4LU, United Kingdom, www.prb.org.

uk; *Parenting in Poor Environments: Stress, Support and Coping. A Summary of Key Messages for Policy and Practice from a Major National Study.*

U.S. Census Bureau, Housing and Household Economics Statistics Division, 4700 Silver Hill Road, Washington DC 20233-0001, (301) 763-3030, www.census.gov/hhes/www; Decennial Census of Population and Housing (web app); *Families and Living Arrangements;* and *Historical Poverty Tables.*

U.S. Census Bureau, Population Division, 4700 Silver Hill Road, Washington DC 20233-0001, (301) 763-3030, www.census.gov/population/www/; *Current Population Reports.*

U.S. Department of Health and Human Services, Health Resources and Services Administration, Maternal and Child Health Bureau, Parklawn Building Room 18-05, 5600 Fishers Lane, Rockville, Maryland 20857, (301) 443-2170, http://mchb.hrsa.gov; *Data Summaries for Title V Expenditures and Individuals Served* and *Title V: A Snapshot of Maternal and Child Health.*

U.S. Department of Justice (DOJ), National Institute of Justice (NIJ), 810 Seventh Street, NW, Washington, DC 20531, (202) 307-2942, Fax: (202) 616-0275, www.ojp.usdoj.gov/nij/; *When Violence Hits Home: How Economics and Neighborhood Play a Role.*

HOUSEHOLDS OR FAMILIES - POVERTY - AMERICAN INDIAN, ESKIMO, ALEUT POPULATION

U.S. Census Bureau, Population Division, 4700 Silver Hill Road, Washington DC 20233-0001, (301) 763-3030, www.census.gov/population/www/; *2000 Census of Population and Housing: Characteristics of American Indians and Alaska Natives by Tribe and Language* and *Current Population Reports.*

HOUSEHOLDS OR FAMILIES - POVERTY - ASIAN AND PACIFIC ISLANDER POPULATION

U.S. Census Bureau, 4700 Silver Hill Road, Washington DC 20233-0001, (301) 763-3030, www.census.gov; unpublished data.

U.S. Census Bureau, Housing and Household Economics Statistics Division, 4700 Silver Hill Road, Washington DC 20233-0001, (301) 763-3030, www.census.gov/hhes/www; *Historical Poverty Tables.*

U.S. Census Bureau, Population Division, 4700 Silver Hill Road, Washington DC 20233-0001, (301) 763-3030, www.census.gov/population/www/; *Current Population Reports.*

HOUSEHOLDS OR FAMILIES - POVERTY - BLACK POPULATION

U.S. Census Bureau, 4700 Silver Hill Road, Washington DC 20233-0001, (301) 763-3030, www.census.gov; unpublished data.

U.S. Census Bureau, Housing and Household Economics Statistics Division, 4700 Silver Hill Road, Washington DC 20233-0001, (301) 763-3030, www.census.gov/hhes/www; *Historical Poverty Tables.*

U.S. Census Bureau, Population Division, 4700 Silver Hill Road, Washington DC 20233-0001, (301) 763-3030, www.census.gov/population/www/; *Current Population Reports.*

HOUSEHOLDS OR FAMILIES - POVERTY - HISPANIC ORIGIN POPULATION

U.S. Census Bureau, 4700 Silver Hill Road, Washington DC 20233-0001, (301) 763-3030, www.census.gov; unpublished data.

U.S. Census Bureau, Housing and Household Economics Statistics Division, 4700 Silver Hill Road, Washington DC 20233-0001, (301) 763-3030, www.census.gov/hhes/www; *Historical Poverty Tables.*

U.S. Census Bureau, Population Division, 4700 Silver Hill Road, Washington DC 20233-0001, (301) 763-3030, www.census.gov/population/www/; *Current Population Reports.*

HOUSEHOLDS OR FAMILIES - PUBLIC ASSISTANCE TO FAMILIES

Food and Nutrition Service (FNS), U.S. Department of Agriculture (USDA), 3101 Park Center Drive, Alexandria, VA 22302, (703) 305-2062, www.fns.usda.gov/fns; *WIC Participant and Program Characteristics 2006* and *WIC Program Coverage: How Many Eligible Individuals Participated in the Special Supplemental Nutrition Program for Women, Infants, and Children (WIC): 1994 to 2003?*

National Center for Children in Poverty (NCCP), 215 W. 125th Street, 3rd Floor, New York, NY 10027, (646) 284-9600, Fax: (646) 284-9623, www.nccp.org; *Parent Employment and the Use of Child Care Subsidies* and *Predictors of Child Care Subsidy Use.*

U.S. Census Bureau, Housing and Household Economics Statistics Division, 4700 Silver Hill Road, Washington DC 20233-0001, (301) 763-3030, www.census.gov/hhes/www; *Families and Living Arrangements* and *Pension Plan Coverage of Workers by Selected Characteristics, Sex, Race and Hispanic Origin, and Poverty Status: 2003.*

U.S. Census Bureau, Population Division, 4700 Silver Hill Road, Washington DC 20233-0001, (301) 763-3030, www.census.gov/population/www/; *Current Population Reports.*

U.S. Library of Congress (LOC), Congressional Research Service (CRS), The Library of Congress, 101 Independence Avenue, SE, Washington, DC 20540-7500, (202) 707-5700, www.loc.gov/crsinfo; *Cash and Non-cash Benefits for Persons With Limited Income: Eligibility Rules, Recipient and Expenditure Data.*

HOUSEHOLDS OR FAMILIES - RACE

U.S. Census Bureau, 4700 Silver Hill Road, Washington DC 20233-0001, (301) 763-3030, www.census.gov; unpublished data.

U.S. Census Bureau, Housing and Household Economics Statistics Division, 4700 Silver Hill Road, Washington DC 20233-0001, (301) 763-3030, www.census.gov/hhes/www; *Families and Living Arrangements.*

U.S. Census Bureau, Population Division, 4700 Silver Hill Road, Washington DC 20233-0001, (301) 763-3030, www.census.gov/population/www/; *Current Population Reports.*

HOUSEHOLDS OR FAMILIES - REGION OF HOUSEHOLDER

U.S. Census Bureau, 4700 Silver Hill Road, Washington DC 20233-0001, (301) 763-3030, www.census.gov; unpublished data.

U.S. Census Bureau, Housing and Household Economics Statistics Division, 4700 Silver Hill Road, Washington DC 20233-0001, (301) 763-3030, www.census.gov/hhes/www; Decennial Census of Population and Housing (web app).

U.S. Census Bureau, Population Division, 4700 Silver Hill Road, Washington DC 20233-0001, (301) 763-3030, www.census.gov/population/www/; *Current Population Reports.*

HOUSEHOLDS OR FAMILIES - SIZE

U.S. Census Bureau, Housing and Household Economics Statistics Division, 4700 Silver Hill Road, Washington DC 20233-0001, (301) 763-3030, www.census.gov/hhes/www; Decennial Census of Population and Housing (web app); *Families and Living Arrangements;* and *Families and Living Arrangements.*

U.S. Census Bureau, Population Division, 4700 Silver Hill Road, Washington DC 20233-0001, (301) 763-3030, www.census.gov/population/www/; *Current Population Reports.*

HOUSEHOLDS OR FAMILIES - STATES

DataPlace by KnowledgePlex, c/o Fannie Mae Foundation, 4000 Wisconsin Avenue, N.W., North Tower, Suite One, Washington, DC 20016-2804, www.dataplace.org; *Database. Subject coverage: Community, regional and national housing and demographic data.*

State of Connecticut, Department of Economic and Community Development (DECD), 505 Hudson Street, Hartford, CT 06106-7107, (860) 270-8000, www.ct.gov/ecd/; *State of Connecticut Analysis of Impediments to Fair Housing Choice Update* and *Tenant Demography Report and Survey Tables.*

U.S. Census Bureau, 4700 Silver Hill Road, Washington DC 20233-0001, (301) 763-3030, www.census.gov; unpublished data.

U.S. Census Bureau, Housing and Household Economics Statistics Division, 4700 Silver Hill Road, Washington DC 20233-0001, (301) 763-3030, www.census.gov/hhes/www; Decennial Census of Population and Housing (web app).

U.S. Census Bureau, Population Division, 4700 Silver Hill Road, Washington DC 20233-0001, (301) 763-3030, www.census.gov/population/www/; *Current Population Reports.*

U.S. Department of Health and Human Services, Health Resources and Services Administration, Maternal and Child Health Bureau, Parklawn Building Room 18-05, 5600 Fishers Lane, Rockville, Maryland 20857, (301) 443-2170, http://mchb.hrsa.gov; *Data Summaries for Title V Expenditures and Individuals Served* and *Title V: A Snapshot of Maternal and Child Health.*

HOUSEHOLDS OR FAMILIES - STOCK OWNERSHIP

Board of Governors of the Federal Reserve System, Constitution Avenue, NW, Washington, DC 20551, (202) 452-3000, www.federalreserve.gov; *Federal Reserve Bulletin* and unpublished data.

HOUSEHOLDS OR FAMILIES - TAXES PAID

U.S. Census Bureau, 4700 Silver Hill Road, Washington DC 20233-0001, (301) 763-3030, www.census.gov; *Survey of Income and Program Participation (SIPP).*

U.S. Census Bureau, Population Division, 4700 Silver Hill Road, Washington DC 20233-0001, (301) 763-3030, www.census.gov/population/www/; *Current Population Reports.*

HOUSEHOLDS OR FAMILIES - TELEPHONES

Federal Communications Commission (FCC), Wireline Competition Bureau (WCB), 445 12th Street, SW, Washington, DC 20554, (202) 418-1500, Fax: (202) 418-2825, www.fcc.gov/wcb; *Statistical Trends in Telephony 2007.*

HOUSEHOLDS OR FAMILIES - TYPES - MALE HOUSEHOLDER

U.S. Census Bureau, 4700 Silver Hill Road, Washington DC 20233-0001, (301) 763-3030, www.census.gov; unpublished data.

U.S. Census Bureau, Housing and Household Economics Statistics Division, 4700 Silver Hill Road, Washington DC 20233-0001, (301) 763-3030, www.census.gov/hhes/www; Decennial Census of Population and Housing (web app).

U.S. Census Bureau, Population Division, 4700 Silver Hill Road, Washington DC 20233-0001, (301) 763-3030, www.census.gov/population/www/; *Current Population Reports.*

HOUSEHOLDS OR FAMILIES - TYPES - MARRIED COUPLES WITH OR WITHOUT OWN HOUSEHOLD

U.S. Census Bureau, 4700 Silver Hill Road, Washington DC 20233-0001, (301) 763-3030, www.census.gov; unpublished data.

U.S. Census Bureau, Housing and Household Economics Statistics Division, 4700 Silver Hill Road, Washington DC 20233-0001, (301) 763-3030, www.census.gov/hhes/www; Decennial Census of Population and Housing (web app).

U.S. Census Bureau, Population Division, 4700 Silver Hill Road, Washington DC 20233-0001, (301) 763-3030, www.census.gov/population/www/; *Current Population Reports.*

HOUSEHOLDS OR FAMILIES - TYPES - NON-FAMILY

U.S. Census Bureau, 4700 Silver Hill Road, Washington DC 20233-0001, (301) 763-3030, www.census.gov; unpublished data.

U.S. Census Bureau, Housing and Household Economics Statistics Division, 4700 Silver Hill Road, Washington DC 20233-0001, (301) 763-3030, www.census.gov/hhes/www; Decennial Census of Population and Housing (web app).

U.S. Census Bureau, Population Division, 4700 Silver Hill Road, Washington DC 20233-0001, (301) 763-3030, www.census.gov/population/www/; *Current Population Reports.*

HOUSEHOLDS OR FAMILIES - TYPES - ONE-PERSON HOUSEHOLDS

U.S. Census Bureau, 4700 Silver Hill Road, Washington DC 20233-0001, (301) 763-3030, www.census.gov; unpublished data.

U.S. Census Bureau, Housing and Household Economics Statistics Division, 4700 Silver Hill Road, Washington DC 20233-0001, (301) 763-3030, www.census.gov/hhes/www; Decennial Census of Population and Housing (web app).

U.S. Census Bureau, Population Division, 4700 Silver Hill Road, Washington DC 20233-0001, (301) 763-3030, www.census.gov/population/www/; *Current Population Reports.*

HOUSEHOLDS OR FAMILIES - WEALTH

Board of Governors of the Federal Reserve System, Constitution Avenue, NW, Washington, DC 20551, (202) 452-3000, www.federalreserve.gov; *Federal Reserve Bulletin* and unpublished data.

HOUSEKEEPING SUPPLIES EXPENDITURES

U.S. Bureau of Labor Statistics (BLS), Postal Square Building, 2 Massachusetts Avenue, NE, Washington, DC 20212-0001, (202) 691-5200, Fax: (202) 691-6325, www.bls.gov; *Consumer Expenditures in 2006.*

HOUSING AND HOUSEHOLD OPERATIONS - PRICE INDEXES

Bureau of Economic Analysis (BEA), U.S. Department of Commerce (DOC), 1441 L Street NW, Washington, DC 20230, (202) 606-9900, www.bea.gov; *2007 Annual Revision of the National Income and Product Accounts (NIPA)* and *Survey of Current Business (SCB).*

U.S. Census Bureau, Housing and Household Economics Statistics Division, 4700 Silver Hill Road, Washington DC 20233-0001, (301) 763-3030, www.census.gov/hhes/www; *Housing Characteristics: 2000.*

HOUSING AND HOUSING UNITS

DataPlace by KnowledgePlex, c/o Fannie Mae Foundation, 4000 Wisconsin Avenue, N.W., North Tower, Suite One, Washington, DC 20016-2804, www.dataplace.org; *Database. Subject coverage: Community, regional and national housing and demographic data.*

HUD USER, PO Box 23268, Washington, DC 20026-3268, (800) 245-2691, Fax: (202) 708-9981, www.huduser.org; *The Sustainability of Homeownership: Factors Affecting the Duration of Homeownership and Rental Spells.*

The Melville Charitable Trust, c/o The Philanthropic Initiative, Inc., 160 Federal Street, 8th Floor, Boston, MA 02110, (617) 338-2590, http://melvilletrust.org; unpublished data.

NeighborhoodInfo DC, c/o The Urban Institute, 2100 M Street, NW, Washington, DC 20037, (202) 261-5760, Fax: (202) 872-9322, www.neighborhoodinfodc.org; *District of Columbia Housing Monitor.*

Office of Planning, District of Columbia, 801 North Capitol Street, NE, Suite 4000, Washington, DC 20002, (202) 442-7600, Fax: (202) 442-7637, www.planning.dc.gov; *District of Columbia Population and Housing Trends.*

State of Connecticut, Department of Economic and Community Development (DECD), 505 Hudson Street, Hartford, CT 06106-7107, (860) 270-8000, www.ct.gov/ecd/; *Housing a Region in Transition - An Analysis of Housing Needs in Southeastern Connecticut 2000-2005; State of Connecticut Analysis of Impediments to Fair Housing Choice Update;* and *Tenant Demography Report and Survey Tables.*

U.S. Census Bureau, 4700 Silver Hill Road, Washington DC 20233-0001, (301) 763-3030, www.census.gov; American FactFinder (web app); *LandView 6;* and *State and County QuickFacts.*

U.S. Census Bureau, Housing and Household Economics Statistics Division, 4700 Silver Hill Road, Washington DC 20233-0001, (301) 763-3030, www.census.gov/hhes/www; *Housing Characteristics: 2000* and *Housing Vacancies and Homeownership (CPS/HVS)* .

HOUSING AND HOUSING UNITS - AGE OF HOUSING STOCKS

U.S. Census Bureau, Demographic Surveys Division, 4700 Silver Hill Road, Washington DC 20233-0001, (301) 763-3030, www.census.gov; *Demographic Profiles: 100-percent and Sample Data.*

U.S. Census Bureau, Housing and Household Economics Statistics Division, 4700 Silver Hill Road, Washington DC 20233-0001, (301) 763-3030, www.census.gov/hhes/www; *2006 American Community Survey (ACS)* and *Housing Characteristics: 2000.*

HOUSING AND HOUSING UNITS - AMENITIES

U.S. Census Bureau, Housing and Household Economics Statistics Division, 4700 Silver Hill Road, Washington DC 20233-0001, (301) 763-3030, www.census.gov/hhes/www; *2006 American Community Survey (ACS)* and *American Housing Survey (AHS).*

HOUSING AND HOUSING UNITS - BUILDING PERMIT VALUE

U.S. Census Bureau, 4700 Silver Hill Road, Washington DC 20233-0001, (301) 763-3030, www.census.gov; unpublished data.

U.S. Census Bureau, Manufacturing and Construction Division, 4600 Silver Hill Road, Washington DC 20233, (301) 763-4673, www.census.gov/mcd; *Current Construction Reports.*

HOUSING AND HOUSING UNITS - CAPITAL

Bureau of Economic Analysis (BEA), U.S. Department of Commerce (DOC), 1441 L Street NW, Washington, DC 20230, (202) 606-9900, www.bea.gov; Fixed Assets Accounts Tables (web app); National Income and Product Accounts (NIPA) Tables (web app); and *Survey of Current Business (SCB).*

HOUSING AND HOUSING UNITS - CONDOMINIUMS

DataPlace by KnowledgePlex, c/o Fannie Mae Foundation, 4000 Wisconsin Avenue, N.W., North Tower, Suite One, Washington, DC 20016-2804, www.dataplace.org; *Database. Subject coverage: Community, regional and national housing and demographic data.*

National Association of Realtors (NAR), 430 North Michigan Avenue, Chicago, IL 60611-4087, (800) 874-6500, www.realtor.org; *Real Estate Outlook.*

U.S. Census Bureau, Housing and Household Economics Statistics Division, 4700 Silver Hill Road, Washington DC 20233-0001, (301) 763-3030, www.census.gov/hhes/www; *2006 American Community Survey (ACS).*

U.S. Census Bureau, Manufacturing and Construction Division, 4600 Silver Hill Road, Washington DC 20233, (301) 763-4673, www.census.gov/mcd; *Current Construction Reports* and *New Residential Construction.*

HOUSING AND HOUSING UNITS - CONSTRUCTION - APARTMENTS COMPLETED AND RENTED

DataPlace by KnowledgePlex, c/o Fannie Mae Foundation, 4000 Wisconsin Avenue, N.W., North Tower, Suite One, Washington, DC 20016-2804, www.dataplace.org; *Database. Subject coverage: Community, regional and national housing and demographic data.*

U.S. Census Bureau, 4700 Silver Hill Road, Washington DC 20233-0001, (301) 763-3030, www.census.gov; unpublished data.

U.S. Census Bureau, Housing and Household Economics Statistics Division, 4700 Silver Hill Road, Washington DC 20233-0001, (301) 763-3030, www.census.gov/hhes/www; *2006 American Community Survey (ACS).*

HOUSING AND HOUSING UNITS - CONSTRUCTION - NEW UNITS

DataPlace by KnowledgePlex, c/o Fannie Mae Foundation, 4000 Wisconsin Avenue, N.W., North Tower, Suite One, Washington, DC 20016-2804, www.dataplace.org; *Database. Subject coverage: Community, regional and national housing and demographic data.*

National Association of Home Builders (NAHB), 1201 15th Street, NW, Washington, DC 20005, (202) 266-8200, Fax: (202) 266-8400, www.nahb.com; HousingEconomics.com.

U.S. Census Bureau, Manufacturing and Construction Division, 4600 Silver Hill Road, Washington DC 20233, (301) 763-4673, www.census.gov/mcd; *Current Construction Reports.*

HOUSING AND HOUSING UNITS - CONSTRUCTION - VALUE

McGraw-Hill Construction, Dodge Analytics, 1221 Avenue of The Americas, Manhattan, NY 10020, (800) 393-6343, http://dodge.construction.com/analytics; *Construction Outlook 2008.*

U.S. Census Bureau, Manufacturing and Construction Division, 4600 Silver Hill Road, Washington DC 20233, (301) 763-4673, www.census.gov/mcd; *Current Construction Reports.*

HOUSING AND HOUSING UNITS - CONSUMER EXPENDITURES

U.S. Bureau of Labor Statistics (BLS), Postal Square Building, 2 Massachusetts Avenue, NE, Washington, DC 20212-0001, (202) 691-5200, Fax: (202) 691-6325, www.bls.gov; *Consumer Expenditures in 2006.*

HOUSING AND HOUSING UNITS - CONSUMER PRICE INDEXES

The Annie E. Casey Foundation, 701 Saint Paul Street, Baltimore, MD 21202, (410) 547-6600, Fax: (410) 547-3610, www.aecf.org; *City and Rural KIDS COUNT Data Book.*

U.S. Bureau of Labor Statistics (BLS), Postal Square Building, 2 Massachusetts Avenue, NE, Washington, DC 20212-0001, (202) 691-5200, Fax: (202) 691-6325, www.bls.gov; *Consumer Price Index Detailed Report* and *Monthly Labor Review (MLR).*

U.S. Department of Labor (DOL), Bureau of Labor Statistics (BLS), Postal Square Building, 2 Massachusetts Avenue, NE, Washington, DC 20212-0001, (202) 691-5200, Fax: (202) 691-6325, www.bls.gov; *Consumer Price Indexes (CPI).*

HOUSING AND HOUSING UNITS - COSTS

DataPlace by KnowledgePlex, c/o Fannie Mae Foundation, 4000 Wisconsin Avenue, N.W., North Tower, Suite One, Washington, DC 20016-2804, www.dataplace.org; *Database. Subject coverage: Community, regional and national housing and demographic data.*

U.S. Census Bureau, Housing and Household Economics Statistics Division, 4700 Silver Hill Road,

Washington DC 20233-0001, (301) 763-3030, www.census.gov/hhes/www; *2006 American Community Survey (ACS)* and *American Housing Survey (AHS).*

HOUSING AND HOUSING UNITS - ENERGY - CHARACTERISTICS

McGraw-Hill Construction, Dodge Analytics, 1221 Avenue of The Americas, Manhattan, NY 10020, (800) 393-6343, http://dodge.construction.com/analytics; *Green Building SmartMarket Report 2006.*

U.S. Census Bureau, Manufacturing and Construction Division, 4600 Silver Hill Road, Washington DC 20233, (301) 763-4673, www.census.gov/mcd; *Characteristics of New Housing* and *Current Construction Reports.*

HOUSING AND HOUSING UNITS - ENERGY - CONSUMPTION

U.S. Department of Energy (DOE), Energy Information Administration (EIA), 1000 Independence Avenue, SW, Washington, DC 20585, (202) 586-8800, www.eia.doe.gov; *Annual Energy Review 2005; Monthly Energy Review (MER); Residential Energy Consumption Survey (RECS);* and *State Energy Data Report.*

HOUSING AND HOUSING UNITS - ENERGY - EXPENDITURES

U.S. Department of Energy (DOE), Energy Information Administration (EIA), 1000 Independence Avenue, SW, Washington, DC 20585, (202) 586-8800, www.eia.doe.gov; *Residential Energy Consumption Survey (RECS)* and *State Energy Data 2003 Price and Expenditure Data.*

U.S. Library of Congress (LOC), Congressional Research Service (CRS), The Library of Congress, 101 Independence Avenue, SE, Washington, DC 20540-7500, (202) 707-5700, www.loc.gov/crsinfo; *The Low-Income Home Energy Assistance Program (LIHEAP): Program and Funding Issues.*

HOUSING AND HOUSING UNITS - FIRES AND PROPERTY LOSS

National Fire Protection Association (NFPA), One Batterymarch Park, Quincy, MA 02169-7471, (617) 770-3000, Fax: (617) 770-0700, www.nfpa.org; *Fire statistics.*

HOUSING AND HOUSING UNITS - GOVERNMENT EXPENDITURES

Australian Institute of Health and Welfare (AIHW), GPO Box 570, Canberra ACT 2601, Australia, www.aihw.gov.au; *Housing Assistance in Australia 2008* and *Housing Assistance in Australia 2008.*

U.S. Census Bureau, 4700 Silver Hill Road, Washington DC 20233-0001, (301) 763-3030, www.census.gov; unpublished data.

U.S. Census Bureau, Governments Division, 4600 Silver Hill Road, Washington DC 20233, (800) 242-2184, www.census.gov/govs/www; *2002 Census of Governments.*

U.S. Library of Congress (LOC), Congressional Research Service (CRS), The Library of Congress, 101 Independence Avenue, SE, Washington, DC 20540-7500, (202) 707-5700, www.loc.gov/crsinfo; *The Low-Income Home Energy Assistance Program (LIHEAP): Program and Funding Issues.*

HOUSING AND HOUSING UNITS - HEATING EQUIPMENT USED

U.S. Census Bureau, Housing and Household Economics Statistics Division, 4700 Silver Hill Road, Washington DC 20233-0001, (301) 763-3030, www.census.gov/hhes/www; *2006 American Community Survey (ACS).*

HOUSING AND HOUSING UNITS - HOUSING ASSISTANCE

Australian Institute of Health and Welfare (AIHW), GPO Box 570, Canberra ACT 2601, Australia, www.aihw.gov.au; *Housing Assistance in Australia 2008.*

Bureau of Economic Analysis (BEA), U.S. Department of Commerce (DOC), 1441 L Street NW, Washington, DC 20230, (202) 606-9900, www.bea.gov; *Survey of Current Business (SCB).*

HOUSING AND HOUSING UNITS - LOANS AND MORTGAGES

Australian Institute of Health and Welfare (AIHW), GPO Box 570, Canberra ACT 2601, Australia, www.aihw.gov.au; *Housing Assistance in Australia 2008.*

Board of Governors of the Federal Reserve System, Constitution Avenue, NW, Washington, DC 20551, (202) 452-3000, www.federalreserve.gov; *Federal Reserve Bulletin.*

DataPlace by KnowledgePlex, c/o Fannie Mae Foundation, 4000 Wisconsin Avenue, N.W., North Tower, Suite One, Washington, DC 20016-2804, www.dataplace.org; *Database. Subject coverage: Community, regional and national housing and demographic data.*

European Central Bank (ECB), Postfach 160319, D-60066 Frankfurt am Main, Germany, www.ecb.int; *Monetary Financial Institutions (MFI) Interest Rate Statistics (MIR).*

Federal Housing Finance Board (FHFB), 1625 Eye Street, NW, Washington, DC 20006-4001, (202) 408-2500, Fax: (202) 408-1435, www.fhfb.gov; *Monthly Interest Rate Survey (MIRS).*

HUD USER, PO Box 23268, Washington, DC 20026-3268, (800) 245-2691, Fax: (202) 708-9981, www.huduser.org; *Comprehensive Market Analysis Reports.*

Mortgage Bankers Association of America (MBA), 1919 Pennsylvania Avenue, NW, Washington, DC 20006-3404, (202) 557-2700, www.mbaa.org; *Commercial/Multifamily Quarterly Data Book; The Cost Study: Income and Cost for Origination and Servicing of One-to-Four-Unit Residential Loans; Mortgage Banking Compensation Survey;* and *National Delinquency Survey.*

U.S. Census Bureau, Manufacturing and Construction Division, 4600 Silver Hill Road, Washington DC 20233, (301) 763-4673, www.census.gov/mcd; *Characteristics of New Housing* and *Current Construction Reports.*

HOUSING AND HOUSING UNITS - LOANS AND MORTGAGES - FEDERAL HOUSING ADMINISTRATION (FHA)

U.S. Census Bureau, Manufacturing and Construction Division, 4600 Silver Hill Road, Washington DC 20233, (301) 763-4673, www.census.gov/mcd; *Characteristics of New Housing; Current Construction Reports;* and *New Residential Construction.*

HOUSING AND HOUSING UNITS - LOANS AND MORTGAGES - VETERANS ADMINISTRATION (VA)

U.S. Census Bureau, Manufacturing and Construction Division, 4600 Silver Hill Road, Washington DC 20233, (301) 763-4673, www.census.gov/mcd; *Characteristics of New Housing* and *Current Construction Reports.*

U.S. Department of Veterans Affairs (VA), 810 Vermont Avenue, NW, Washington, DC 20420-0001, (202) 273-5400, www.va.gov; *Annual Accountability Report Statistical Appendix.*

HOUSING AND HOUSING UNITS - MAINTENANCE AND REPAIR EXPENDITURES

U.S. Bureau of Labor Statistics (BLS), Postal Square Building, 2 Massachusetts Avenue, NE, Washington, DC 20212-0001, (202) 691-5200, Fax: (202) 691-6325, www.bls.gov; *Consumer Expenditures in 2006.*

U.S. Census Bureau, Manufacturing and Construction Division, 4600 Silver Hill Road, Washington DC 20233, (301) 763-4673, www.census.gov/mcd; *Current Construction Reports.*

HOUSING AND HOUSING UNITS - MOBILE HOMES

Bureau of Economic Analysis (BEA), U.S. Department of Commerce (DOC), 1441 L Street NW, Washington, DC 20230, (202) 606-9900, www.bea.gov; *Survey of Current Business (SCB).*

DataPlace by KnowledgePlex, c/o Fannie Mae Foundation, 4000 Wisconsin Avenue, N.W., North Tower, Suite One, Washington, DC 20016-2804, www.dataplace.org; *Database. Subject coverage: Community, regional and national housing and demographic data.*

U.S. Census Bureau, Housing and Household Economics Statistics Division, 4700 Silver Hill Road, Washington DC 20233-0001, (301) 763-3030, www.census.gov/hhes/www; *2006 American Community Survey (ACS)* and *Housing Characteristics: 2000.*

U.S. Census Bureau, Manufacturing and Construction Division, 4600 Silver Hill Road, Washington DC 20233, (301) 763-4673, www.census.gov/mcd; *Current Construction Reports.*

HOUSING AND HOUSING UNITS - NEW PRIVATELY-OWNED HOMES - CHARACTERISTICS

U.S. Census Bureau, Manufacturing and Construction Division, 4600 Silver Hill Road, Washington DC 20233, (301) 763-4673, www.census.gov/mcd; *Current Construction Reports.*

HOUSING AND HOUSING UNITS - OLDER PEOPLE

U.S. Census Bureau, Housing and Household Economics Statistics Division, 4700 Silver Hill Road, Washington DC 20233-0001, (301) 763-3030, www.census.gov/hhes/www; *Housing Characteristics: 2000* and *Housing Vacancies and Homeownership (CPS/HVS)* .

HOUSING AND HOUSING UNITS - PRICES

DataPlace by KnowledgePlex, c/o Fannie Mae Foundation, 4000 Wisconsin Avenue, N.W., North Tower, Suite One, Washington, DC 20016-2804, www.dataplace.org; *Database. Subject coverage: Community, regional and national housing and demographic data.*

DataQuick, 9620 Towne Centre Drive, San Diego, CA 92121, (858) 597-3100, www.dataquick.com; DQNews.com.

Inman News, 1100 Marina Village Parkway, Suite 102, Alameda, CA 94501, (800) 775-4662, Fax: (510) 658-9317, www.inman.com; *Real Estate News.*

National Association of Realtors (NAR), 430 North Michigan Avenue, Chicago, IL 60611-4087, (800) 874-6500, www.realtor.org; *Existing-Home Sales (EHS); Field Guide to Quick Real Estate Statistics; 2006 NAR Baby Boomers and Real Estate: Today and Tomorrow; 2007 NAR Member Profile; 2007 NAR Profile of Buyer's Home Feature Preferences; 2006 NAR Profile of Home Buyers and Sellers; 2006 NAR Profile of Real Estate Firms: An Industry Overview; Pending Home Sales Index;* Real Estate Intelligence Online (REIO); and *Real Estate Outlook.*

U.S. Census Bureau, Manufacturing and Construction Division, 4600 Silver Hill Road, Washington DC 20233, (301) 763-4673, www.census.gov/mcd; *Characteristics of New Housing; Current Construction Reports;* and *New Residential Construction.*

U.S. Library of Congress (LOC), Congressional Research Service (CRS), The Library of Congress, 101 Independence Avenue, SE, Washington, DC 20540-7500, (202) 707-5700, www.loc.gov/crsinfo; *Homeland Security Research and Development Funding, Organization, and Oversight.*

HOUSING AND HOUSING UNITS - PUBLIC HOUSING

DataPlace by KnowledgePlex, c/o Fannie Mae Foundation, 4000 Wisconsin Avenue, N.W., North Tower, Suite One, Washington, DC 20016-2804, www.dataplace.org; *Database. Subject coverage: Community, regional and national housing and demographic data.*

U.S. Census Bureau, Housing and Household Economics Statistics Division, 4700 Silver Hill Road, Washington DC 20233-0001, (301) 763-3030, www.census.gov/hhes/www; *Housing Characteristics: 2000* and *Pension Plan Coverage of Workers by Selected Characteristics, Sex, Race and Hispanic Origin, and Poverty Status: 2003.*

HOUSING AND HOUSING UNITS - PUBLIC HOUSING - FEDERAL AID TO STATE AND LOCAL GOVERNMENTS

The Office of Management and Budget (OMB), 725 17th Street, NW, Washington, DC 20503, (202) 395-3080, Fax: (202) 395-3888, www.whitehouse.gov/omb; *Budget of the United States Government, Federal Year 2009* and *Historical Tables.*

HOUSING AND HOUSING UNITS - PUBLIC HOUSING - GOVERNMENT EXPENDITURES

Social Security Administration (SSA), Office of Public Inquiries, Windsor Park Building, 6401 Security Boulevard, Baltimore, MD 21235, (800) 772-1213, www.ssa.gov; *Social Security Bulletin* and unpublished data.

U.S. Library of Congress (LOC), Congressional Research Service (CRS), The Library of Congress, 101 Independence Avenue, SE, Washington, DC 20540-7500, (202) 707-5700, www.loc.gov/crsinfo; *Cash and Non-cash Benefits for Persons With Limited Income: Eligibility Rules, Recipient and Expenditure Data.*

HOUSING AND HOUSING UNITS - RENTAL VALUE

U.S. Census Bureau, Housing and Household Economics Statistics Division, 4700 Silver Hill Road, Washington DC 20233-0001, (301) 763-3030, www.census.gov/hhes/www; *2006 American Community Survey (ACS)* and *Housing Vacancies and Homeownership (CPS/HVS)* .

HOUSING AND HOUSING UNITS - SALES

DataPlace by KnowledgePlex, c/o Fannie Mae Foundation, 4000 Wisconsin Avenue, N.W., North Tower, Suite One, Washington, DC 20016-2804, www.dataplace.org; *Database. Subject coverage: Community, regional and national housing and demographic data.*

DataQuick, 9620 Towne Centre Drive, San Diego, CA 92121, (858) 597-3100, www.dataquick.com; DQNews.com.

HUD USER, PO Box 23268, Washington, DC 20026-3268, (800) 245-2691, Fax: (202) 708-9981, www.huduser.org; *U.S. Housing Market Conditions.*

Inman News, 1100 Marina Village Parkway, Suite 102, Alameda, CA 94501, (800) 775-4662, Fax: (510) 658-9317, www.inman.com; *Real Estate News.*

National Association of Realtors (NAR), 430 North Michigan Avenue, Chicago, IL 60611-4087, (800) 874-6500, www.realtor.org; *Existing-Home Sales (EHS); Field Guide to Quick Real Estate Statistics; 2006 NAR Baby Boomers and Real Estate: Today and Tomorrow; 2007 NAR Member Profile; 2007 NAR Profile of Buyer's Home Feature Preferences; 2006 NAR Profile of Home Buyers and Sellers; 2006 NAR Profile of Real Estate Firms: An Industry Overview; Pending Home Sales Index;* Real Estate Intelligence Online (REIO); and *Real Estate Outlook.*

U.S. Census Bureau, Housing and Household Economics Statistics Division, 4700 Silver Hill Road, Washington DC 20233-0001, (301) 763-3030, www.census.gov/hhes/www; *Housing Vacancies and Homeownership (CPS/HVS)* .

U.S. Census Bureau, Manufacturing and Construction Division, 4600 Silver Hill Road, Washington DC 20233, (301) 763-4673, www.census.gov/mcd; *Characteristics of New Housing; Current Construction Reports;* and *New Residential Construction.*

U.S. Library of Congress (LOC), Congressional Research Service (CRS), The Library of Congress, 101 Independence Avenue, SE, Washington, DC 20540-7500, (202) 707-5700, www.loc.gov/crsinfo; *Homeland Security Research and Development Funding, Organization, and Oversight.*

HOUSING AND HOUSING UNITS - STATE DATA

DataPlace by KnowledgePlex, c/o Fannie Mae Foundation, 4000 Wisconsin Avenue, N.W., North Tower, Suite One, Washington, DC 20016-2804, www.dataplace.org; *Database. Subject coverage: Community, regional and national housing and demographic data.*

State of Connecticut, Department of Economic and Community Development (DECD), 505 Hudson Street, Hartford, CT 06106-7107, (860) 270-8000, www.ct.gov/ecd/; *Housing a Region in Transition - An Analysis of Housing Needs in Southeastern Connecticut 2000-2005; State of Connecticut Analysis of Impediments to Fair Housing Choice Update;* and *Tenant Demography Report and Survey Tables.*

U.S. Census Bureau, Governments Division, 4600 Silver Hill Road, Washington DC 20233, (800) 242-2184, www.census.gov/govs/www; *2002 Census of Governments.*

U.S. Census Bureau, Housing and Household Economics Statistics Division, 4700 Silver Hill Road, Washington DC 20233-0001, (301) 763-3030, www.census.gov/hhes/www; *Housing Characteristics: 2000.*

HOUSING AND HOUSING UNITS - STRUCTURAL TYPE

DataPlace by KnowledgePlex, c/o Fannie Mae Foundation, 4000 Wisconsin Avenue, N.W., North Tower, Suite One, Washington, DC 20016-2804, www.dataplace.org; *Database. Subject coverage: Community, regional and national housing and demographic data.*

U.S. Census Bureau, Housing and Household Economics Statistics Division, 4700 Silver Hill Road, Washington DC 20233-0001, (301) 763-3030, www.census.gov/hhes/www; *2006 American Community Survey (ACS).*

U.S. Census Bureau, Manufacturing and Construction Division, 4600 Silver Hill Road, Washington DC 20233, (301) 763-4673, www.census.gov/mcd; *Current Construction Reports.*

HOUSING AND HOUSING UNITS - TENURE

U.S. Census Bureau, Housing and Household Economics Statistics Division, 4700 Silver Hill Road, Washington DC 20233-0001, (301) 763-3030, www.census.gov/hhes/www; *2006 American Community Survey (ACS)* and *Housing Characteristics: 2000.*

U.S. Census Bureau, Population Division, 4700 Silver Hill Road, Washington DC 20233-0001, (301) 763-3030, www.census.gov/population/www/; *Current Population Reports.*

HOUSING AND HOUSING UNITS - VACANCIES

U.S. Census Bureau, Housing and Household Economics Statistics Division, 4700 Silver Hill Road, Washington DC 20233-0001, (301) 763-3030, www.census.gov/hhes/www; *Housing Characteristics: 2000* and *Housing Vacancies and Homeownership (CPS/HVS)* .

HOUSING AND HOUSING UNITS - VALUE

U.S. Census Bureau, Housing and Household Economics Statistics Division, 4700 Silver Hill Road, Washington DC 20233-0001, (301) 763-3030, www.census.gov/hhes/www; *2006 American Community Survey (ACS).*

HOUSING AND HOUSING UNITS - YEAR BUILT

U.S. Census Bureau, Housing and Household Economics Statistics Division, 4700 Silver Hill Road, Washington DC 20233-0001, (301) 763-3030, www.census.gov/hhes/www; *Housing Vacancies and Homeownership (CPS/HVS)* .

U.S. Department of Energy (DOE), Energy Information Administration (EIA), 1000 Independence Avenue, SW, Washington, DC 20585, (202) 586-8800, www.eia.doe.gov; *Residential Energy Consumption Survey (RECS).*

HOUSING AND URBAN DEVELOPMENT, DEPARTMENT OF - EMPLOYMENT

United States Office of Personnel Management (OMB), 1900 E Street, NW, Washington, DC 20415-1000, (202) 606-1800, www.opm.gov; *Employment and Trends of Federal Civilian Workforce Statistics.*

HOUSING AND URBAN DEVELOPMENT, DEPARTMENT OF - FEDERAL AID TO STATE AND LOCAL GOVERNMENTS

The Office of Management and Budget (OMB), 725 17th Street, NW, Washington, DC 20503, (202) 395-3080, Fax: (202) 395-3888, www.whitehouse.gov/omb; *Historical Tables.*

HUMAN IMMUNODEFICIENCY VIRUS (HIV) INFECTION

Bernan Essential Government Publications, 4611-F Assembly Drive, Lanham MD, 20706-4391, (301) 459-2255, Fax: (800) 865-3450, www.bernan.com; *Vital Statistics of the United States: Births, Life Expectancy, Deaths, and Selected Health Data.*

Caribbean Epidemiology Centre (CAREC), 16-18 Jamaica Boulevard, Federation Park, PO Box 164, Port of Spain, Republic of Trinidad and Tobago, (Dial from U.S. (868) 622-4261), (Fax from U.S. (868) 622-2792), www.carec.org; *20 Years of the HIV/AIDS Epidemic in the Caribbean* and AIDS Statistics.

European Centre for Disease Prevention and Control (ECDC), 171 83 Stockholm, Sweden, www.ecdc.europa.eu; *HIV Infection in Europe: 25 Years into the Pandemic.*

Health Protection Agency, 7th Floor, Holborn Gate, 330 High Holborn, London WC1V 7PP, United Kingdom, www.hpa.org.uk; *Testing Times - HIV and other Sexually Transmitted Infections in the United Kingdom: 2007.*

National Center for Health Statistics (NCHS), Centers for Disease Control and Prevention (CDC), U.S. Department of Health and Human Services (HHS), 3311 Toledo Road, Hyattsville, MD 20782, (866) 232-4636, www.cdc.gov/nchs; *National Vital Statistics Reports (NVSR); Vital Statistics of the United States (VSUS);* and unpublished data.

U.S. Department of Justice (DOJ), Bureau of Justice Statistics, 810 Seventh Street, NW, Washington, DC 20531, (202) 307-0765, www.ojp.usdoj.gov/bjs/; *HIV in Prisons, 2004.*

HUMAN RIGHTS

Congressional Quarterly, Inc., 1255 22nd Street, NW, Washington, DC 20037, (202) 419-8500, www.cq.com; *World at Risk: A Global Issues Sourcebook.*

Ford Foundation, 320 East 43rd Street, New York, NY 10017, (212) 573-5000, Fax: (212) 351-3677, www.fordfound.org; *Close to Home.*

HUMAN TRAFFICKING

Inter-American Commission of Women (CIM), Organization of American States (OAS), 17th Street and Constitution Avenue, NW, Washington, D.C. 20006, (202) 458-3000, www.oas.org/CIM/english/About.htm; *Trafficking in Women and Children: Research Findings and Follow-Up.*

International Organization for Migration (IOM), 17, Route des Morillons, CH-1211 Geneva 19, Switzerland, www.iom.int; *Migration, Human Smuggling and Trafficking from Nigeria to Europe* and *Trafficking in Human Beings and the 2006 World Cup in Germany.*

U.S. Department of Justice (DOJ), Bureau of Justice Statistics, 810 Seventh Street, NW, Washington, DC 20531, (202) 307-0765, www.ojp.usdoj.gov/bjs/; *Federal Prosecution of Human Trafficking, 2001-2005.*

U.S. Department of Justice (DOJ), Office of the Attorney General, 950 Pennsylvania Avenue, NW, Washington, DC 20530-0001, (202) 353-1555, www.usdoj.gov/ag; *Assessment of U.S. Government Activities to Combat Trafficking in Persons.*

HUNGARY - NATIONAL STATISTICAL OFFICE

Hungarian Central Statistical Office (HCSO) (Kozponti Statisztikai Hivatal (KSH)), PO Box 51, 1525 Budapest, Hungary, www.ksh.hu; National Data Center.

HUNGARY - PRIMARY STATISTICS SOURCES

Eurostat, Batiment Jean Monnet, Rue Alcide de Gasperi, L-2920 Luxembourg, http://epp.eurostat.ec.europa.eu; *Pocketbook on Candidate and Potential Candidate Countries.*

Hungarian Central Statistical Office (HCSO) (Kozponti Statisztikai Hivatal (KSH)), PO Box 51, 1525 Budapest, Hungary, www.ksh.hu; *Hungary in Figures, 2006* and *Hungary, 2006.*

HUNGARY - ABORTION

United Nations Statistics Division, New York, NY 10017, (800) 253-9646, Fax: (212) 963-4116, http://unstats.un.org; *Demographic Yearbook* and *Trends in Europe and North America: The Statistical Yearbook of the ECE 2005.*

HUNGARY - AGRICULTURAL MACHINERY

United Nations Statistics Division, New York, NY 10017, (800) 253-9646, Fax: (212) 963-4116, http://unstats.un.org; *Statistical Yearbook.*

HUNGARY - AGRICULTURE

Economist Intelligence Unit, 111 West 57th Street, New York, NY 10019, (212) 554-0600, Fax: (212) 586-1181, www.eiu.com; *Hungary Country Report.*

Euromonitor International, Inc., 224 S. Michigan Avenue, Suite 1500, Chicago, IL 60604, (312) 922-1115, Fax: (312) 922-1157, www.euromonitor.com; *World Marketing Data and Statistics.*

Eurostat, Batiment Jean Monnet, Rue Alcide de Gasperi, L-2920 Luxembourg, http://epp.eurostat.ec.europa.eu; *EU Agricultural Prices in 2007.*

M.E. Sharpe, 80 Business Park Drive, Armonk, NY 10504, (800) 541-6563, Fax: (914) 273-2106, www.mesharpe.com; *The Illustrated Book of World Rankings.*

Organisation for Economic Cooperation and Development (OECD), 2 rue Andre Pascal, F-75775 Paris Cedex 16, France, (Telephone in U.S. (202) 785-6323), (Fax in U.S. (202) 785-0350), www.oecd.org; *OECD Agricultural Outlook: 2007-2016* and *OECD Economic Survey - Hungary 2007.*

Palgrave Macmillan Ltd., Houndmills, Basingstoke, Hampshire, RG21 6XS, England, (Telephone in U.S. (888) 330-8477), (Fax in U.S. (800) 672-2054), www.palgrave.com; *The Statesman's Yearbook 2008.*

Taylor and Francis Group, An Informa Business, 2 Park Square, Milton Park, Abingdon, Oxford OX14 4RN, United Kingdom, (Dial from U.S. (212) 216-7800), (Fax from U.S. (212) 564-7854), www.tandf.co.uk; *The Europa World Year Book.*

United Nations Conference on Trade and Development (UNCTAD), DC2-1120, United Nations, New York, NY 10017, (212) 963-0027, www.unctad.org; *UNCTAD Commodity Yearbook.*

United Nations Food and Agricultural Organization (FAO), Viale delle Terme di Caracalla, 00100 Rome, Italy, (Dial from U.S. (202) 653-2400), (Fax from U.S. (202) 653 5760), www.fao.org; AQUASTAT; *FAO Production Yearbook 2002; FAO Trade Yearbook;* and *The State of Food and Agriculture (SOFA) 2006.*

United Nations Statistics Division, New York, NY 10017, (800) 253-9646, Fax: (212) 963-4116, http://unstats.un.org; *Statistical Yearbook.*

The World Bank, 1818 H Street, NW, Washington, DC 20433, (202) 473-1000, Fax: (202) 477-6391, www.worldbank.org; *Hungary* and *World Development Indicators (WDI) 2008.*

HUNGARY - AIRLINES

Eurostat, Batiment Jean Monnet, Rue Alcide de Gasperi, L-2920 Luxembourg, http://epp.eurostat.ec.europa.eu; *Regional Passenger and Freight Air Transport in Europe in 2006.*

International Civil Aviation Organization (ICAO), External Relations and Public Information Office (EPO), 999 University Street, Montreal, Quebec H3C 5H7, Canada, (Dial from U.S. (514) 954-8219), (Fax from U.S. (514) 954-6077), www.icao.int; *Civil Aviation Statistics of the World.*

M.E. Sharpe, 80 Business Park Drive, Armonk, NY 10504, (800) 541-6563, Fax: (914) 273-2106, www.mesharpe.com; *The Illustrated Book of World Rankings.*

Palgrave Macmillan Ltd., Houndmills, Basingstoke, Hampshire, RG21 6XS, England, (Telephone in U.S. (888) 330-8477), (Fax in U.S. (800) 672-2054), www.palgrave.com; *The Statesman's Yearbook 2008.*

Taylor and Francis Group, An Informa Business, 2 Park Square, Milton Park, Abingdon, Oxford OX14 4RN, United Kingdom, (Dial from U.S. (212) 216-7800), (Fax from U.S. (212) 564-7854), www.tandf.co.uk; *The Europa World Year Book.*

United Nations Statistics Division, New York, NY 10017, (800) 253-9646, Fax: (212) 963-4116, http://unstats.un.org; *Statistical Yearbook.*

HUNGARY - AIRPORTS

Central Intelligence Agency, Office of Public Affairs, Washington, DC 20505, (703) 482-0623, Fax: (703) 482-1739, www.cia.gov; *The World Factbook.*

HUNGARY - ALMOND PRODUCTION

See HUNGARY - CROPS

HUNGARY - ALUMINUM PRODUCTION

See HUNGARY - MINERAL INDUSTRIES

HUNGARY - ARMED FORCES

Central Intelligence Agency, Office of Public Affairs, Washington, DC 20505, (703) 482-0623, Fax: (703) 482-1739, www.cia.gov; *The World Factbook.*

Euromonitor International, Inc., 224 S. Michigan Avenue, Suite 1500, Chicago, IL 60604, (312) 922-1115, Fax: (312) 922-1157, www.euromonitor.com; *World Marketing Data and Statistics.*

International Institute for Strategic Studies (IISS), Arundel House, 13-15 Arundel Street, Temple Place, London WC2R 3DX, England, www.iiss.org; *The Military Balance 2007.*

Palgrave Macmillan Ltd., Houndmills, Basingstoke, Hampshire, RG21 6XS, England, (Telephone in U.S. (888) 330-8477), (Fax in U.S. (800) 672-2054), www.palgrave.com; *The Statesman's Yearbook 2008.*

U.S. Department of State (DOS), 2201 C Street NW, Washington, DC 20520, (202) 647-4000, www.state.gov; *World Military Expenditures and Arms Transfers (WMEAT).*

United Nations Statistics Division, New York, NY 10017, (800) 253-9646, Fax: (212) 963-4116, http://unstats.un.org; *Human Development Report 2006.*

HUNGARY - AUTOMOBILE INDUSTRY AND TRADE

United Nations Statistics Division, New York, NY 10017, (800) 253-9646, Fax: (212) 963-4116, http://unstats.un.org; *Statistical Yearbook.*

HUNGARY - BALANCE OF PAYMENTS

International Monetary Fund (IMF), 700 Nineteenth Street, NW, Washington, DC 20431, (202) 623-7000, Fax: (202) 623-4661, www.imf.org; *Balance of Payments Statistics Newsletter; Balance of Payments Statistics Yearbook 2007;* and *International Financial Statistics Yearbook 2007.*

Organisation for Economic Cooperation and Development (OECD), 2 rue Andre Pascal, F-75775 Paris Cedex 16, France, (Telephone in U.S. (202) 785-6323), (Fax in U.S. (202) 785-0350), www.oecd.org; *OECD Economic Survey - Hungary 2007.*

Taylor and Francis Group, An Informa Business, 2 Park Square, Milton Park, Abingdon, Oxford OX14 4RN, United Kingdom, (Dial from U.S. (212) 216-7800), (Fax from U.S. (212) 564-7854), www.tandf.co.uk; *The Europa World Year Book.*

United Nations Conference on Trade and Development (UNCTAD), DC2-1120, United Nations, New York, NY 10017, (212) 963-0027, www.unctad.org; *Handbook of Statistics 2005.*

The World Bank, 1818 H Street, NW, Washington, DC 20433, (202) 473-1000, Fax: (202) 477-6391, www.worldbank.org; *Hungary; World Development Indicators (WDI) 2008;* and *World Development Report 2008.*

HUNGARY - BANKS AND BANKING

Euromonitor International, Inc., 224 S. Michigan Avenue, Suite 1500, Chicago, IL 60604, (312) 922-1115, Fax: (312) 922-1157, www.euromonitor.com; *World Marketing Data and Statistics.*

European Union, Delegation of the European Commission to the United States, 2300 M Street, NW, Washington, DC 20037, (202) 862-9500, Fax: (202) 429-1766, www.eurunion.org; *The EU Economy, 2007 Review: Moving Europe's Productivity Frontier.*

International Monetary Fund (IMF), 700 Nineteenth Street, NW, Washington, DC 20431, (202) 623-7000, Fax: (202) 623-4661, www.imf.org; *International Financial Statistics Yearbook 2007.*

M.E. Sharpe, 80 Business Park Drive, Armonk, NY 10504, (800) 541-6563, Fax: (914) 273-2106, www.mesharpe.com; *The Illustrated Book of World Rankings.*

Organisation for Economic Cooperation and Development (OECD), 2 rue Andre Pascal, F-75775 Paris Cedex 16, France, (Telephone in U.S. (202) 785-6323), (Fax in U.S. (202) 785-0350), www.oecd.org; *OECD Economic Survey - Hungary 2007.*

Palgrave Macmillan Ltd., Houndmills, Basingstoke, Hampshire, RG21 6XS, England, (Telephone in U.S. (888) 330-8477), (Fax in U.S. (800) 672-2054), www.palgrave.com; *The Statesman's Yearbook 2008.*

Taylor and Francis Group, An Informa Business, 2 Park Square, Milton Park, Abingdon, Oxford OX14 4RN, United Kingdom, (Dial from U.S. (212) 216-7800), (Fax from U.S. (212) 564-7854), www.tandf.co.uk; *The Europa World Year Book.*

HUNGARY - BARLEY PRODUCTION

See HUNGARY - CROPS

HUNGARY - BEVERAGE INDUSTRY

M.E. Sharpe, 80 Business Park Drive, Armonk, NY 10504, (800) 541-6563, Fax: (914) 273-2106, www.mesharpe.com; *The Illustrated Book of World Rankings.*

United Nations Statistics Division, New York, NY 10017, (800) 253-9646, Fax: (212) 963-4116, http://unstats.un.org; *Statistical Yearbook.*

HUNGARY - BROADCASTING

Central Intelligence Agency, Office of Public Affairs, Washington, DC 20505, (703) 482-0623, Fax: (703) 482-1739, www.cia.gov; *The World Factbook.*

Euromonitor International, Inc., 224 S. Michigan Avenue, Suite 1500, Chicago, IL 60604, (312) 922-1115, Fax: (312) 922-1157, www.euromonitor.com; *World Marketing Data and Statistics.*

M.E. Sharpe, 80 Business Park Drive, Armonk, NY 10504, (800) 541-6563, Fax: (914) 273-2106, www.mesharpe.com; *The Illustrated Book of World Rankings.*

Palgrave Macmillan Ltd., Houndmills, Basingstoke, Hampshire, RG21 6XS, England, (Telephone in U.S. (888) 330-8477), (Fax in U.S. (800) 672-2054), www.palgrave.com; *The Statesman's Yearbook 2008.*

UNESCO Institute for Statistics, C.P. 6128 Succursale Centre-Ville, Montreal, Quebec, H3C 3J7 Canada, (Dial from U.S. (514) 343-6880), (Fax from U.S. (514) 343 6882), www.uis.unesco.org; *Statistical Tables.*

United Nations Statistics Division, New York, NY 10017, (800) 253-9646, Fax: (212) 963-4116, http://unstats.un.org; *Trends in Europe and North America: The Statistical Yearbook of the ECE 2005.*

WRTH Publications Limited, PO Box 290, Oxford OX2 7FT, UK, www.wrth.com; *World Radio TV Handbook 2007.*

HUNGARY - BUDGET

Central Intelligence Agency, Office of Public Affairs, Washington, DC 20505, (703) 482-0623, Fax: (703) 482-1739, www.cia.gov; *The World Factbook.*

Eurostat, Batiment Jean Monnet, Rue Alcide de Gasperi, L-2920 Luxembourg, http://epp.eurostat.ec.europa.eu; *Government Budgets.*

HUNGARY - BUSINESS

Economist Intelligence Unit, 111 West 57th Street, New York, NY 10019, (212) 554-0600, Fax: (212) 586-1181, www.eiu.com; *Business Eastern Europe.*

United Nations Statistics Division, New York, NY 10017, (800) 253-9646, Fax: (212) 963-4116, http://unstats.un.org; *Statistical Yearbook.*

HUNGARY - CATTLE

See HUNGARY - LIVESTOCK

HUNGARY - CHESTNUT PRODUCTION

See HUNGARY - CROPS

HUNGARY - CHILDBIRTH - STATISTICS

Central Intelligence Agency, Office of Public Affairs, Washington, DC 20505, (703) 482-0623, Fax: (703) 482-1739, www.cia.gov; *The World Factbook.*

M.E. Sharpe, 80 Business Park Drive, Armonk, NY 10504, (800) 541-6563, Fax: (914) 273-2106, www.mesharpe.com; *The Illustrated Book of World Rankings.*

Palgrave Macmillan Ltd., Houndmills, Basingstoke, Hampshire, RG21 6XS, England, (Telephone in U.S. (888) 330-8477), (Fax in U.S. (800) 672-2054), www.palgrave.com; *The Statesman's Yearbook 2008.*

Taylor and Francis Group, An Informa Business, 2 Park Square, Milton Park, Abingdon, Oxford OX14 4RN, United Kingdom, (Dial from U.S. (212) 216-7800), (Fax from U.S. (212) 564-7854), www.tandf.co.uk; *The Europa World Year Book.*

United Nations Statistics Division, New York, NY 10017, (800) 253-9646, Fax: (212) 963-4116, http://unstats.un.org; *Demographic Yearbook* and *Statistical Yearbook.*

The World Bank, 1818 H Street, NW, Washington, DC 20433, (202) 473-1000, Fax: (202) 477-6391, www.worldbank.org; *World Development Indicators (WDI) 2008.*

HUNGARY - CLIMATE

M.E. Sharpe, 80 Business Park Drive, Armonk, NY 10504, (800) 541-6563, Fax: (914) 273-2106, www.mesharpe.com; *The Illustrated Book of World Rankings.*

Palgrave Macmillan Ltd., Houndmills, Basingstoke, Hampshire, RG21 6XS, England, (Telephone in U.S. (888) 330-8477), (Fax in U.S. (800) 672-2054), www.palgrave.com; *The Statesman's Yearbook 2008.*

HUNGARY - COAL PRODUCTION

See HUNGARY - MINERAL INDUSTRIES

HUNGARY - COFFEE

See HUNGARY - CROPS

HUNGARY - COMMERCE

Palgrave Macmillan Ltd., Houndmills, Basingstoke, Hampshire, RG21 6XS, England, (Telephone in U.S. (888) 330-8477), (Fax in U.S. (800) 672-2054), www.palgrave.com; *The Statesman's Yearbook 2008.*

HUNGARY - COMMODITY EXCHANGES

Commodity Research Bureau, 330 South Wells Street, Suite 612, Chicago, IL 60606-7110, (800) 621-5271, Fax: (312) 939-4135, www.crbtrader.com; *2006 CRB Commodity Yearbook and CD.*

International Lead and Zinc Study Group (ILZSG), Rua Almirante Barroso 38, 5th Floor, Lisbon 1000 - 013, Portugal, www.ilzsg.org; Interactive Statistical Database.

International Monetary Fund (IMF), 700 Nineteenth Street, NW, Washington, DC 20431, (202) 623-7000, Fax: (202) 623-4661, www.imf.org; *IMF Primary Commodity Prices.*

United Nations Food and Agricultural Organization (FAO), Viale delle Terme di Caracalla, 00100 Rome, Italy, (Dial from U.S. (202) 653-2400), (Fax from U.S. (202) 653 5760), www.fao.org; *The State of Food and Agriculture (SOFA) 2006.*

HUNGARY - COMMUNICATION AND TRAFFIC

United Nations Statistics Division, New York, NY 10017, (800) 253-9646, Fax: (212) 963-4116, http://unstats.un.org; *Statistical Yearbook.*

HUNGARY - CONSTRUCTION INDUSTRY

M.E. Sharpe, 80 Business Park Drive, Armonk, NY 10504, (800) 541-6563, Fax: (914) 273-2106, www.mesharpe.com; *The Illustrated Book of World Rankings.*

Organisation for Economic Cooperation and Development (OECD), 2 rue Andre Pascal, F-75775 Paris Cedex 16, France, (Telephone in U.S. (202) 785-6323), (Fax in U.S. (202) 785-0350), www.oecd.org; *OECD Economic Survey - Hungary 2007.*

Palgrave Macmillan Ltd., Houndmills, Basingstoke, Hampshire, RG21 6XS, England, (Telephone in U.S. (888) 330-8477), (Fax in U.S. (800) 672-2054), www.palgrave.com; *The Statesman's Yearbook 2008.*

United Nations Statistics Division, New York, NY 10017, (800) 253-9646, Fax: (212) 963-4116, http://unstats.un.org; *Statistical Yearbook.*

HUNGARY - CONSUMER PRICE INDEXES

Taylor and Francis Group, An Informa Business, 2 Park Square, Milton Park, Abingdon, Oxford OX14 4RN, United Kingdom, (Dial from U.S. (212) 216-7800), (Fax from U.S. (212) 564-7854), www.tandf.co.uk; *The Europa World Year Book.*

United Nations Statistics Division, New York, NY 10017, (800) 253-9646, Fax: (212) 963-4116, http://unstats.un.org; *Statistical Yearbook* and *Trends in Europe and North America: The Statistical Yearbook of the ECE 2005.*

The World Bank, 1818 H Street, NW, Washington, DC 20433, (202) 473-1000, Fax: (202) 477-6391, www.worldbank.org; *Hungary.*

HUNGARY - CONSUMPTION (ECONOMICS)

International Lead and Zinc Study Group (ILZSG), Rua Almirante Barroso 38, 5th Floor, Lisbon 1000 - 013, Portugal, www.ilzsg.org; Interactive Statistical Database.

Organisation for Economic Cooperation and Development (OECD), 2 rue Andre Pascal, F-75775 Paris Cedex 16, France, (Telephone in U.S. (202) 785-6323), (Fax in U.S. (202) 785-0350), www.oecd.org; *Towards Sustainable Household Consumption?: Trends and Policies in OECD Countries.*

The World Bank, 1818 H Street, NW, Washington, DC 20433, (202) 473-1000, Fax: (202) 477-6391, www.worldbank.org; *World Development Report 2008.*

HUNGARY - COPPER INDUSTRY AND TRADE

See HUNGARY - MINERAL INDUSTRIES

HUNGARY - CORN INDUSTRY

See HUNGARY - CROPS

HUNGARY - COTTON

See HUNGARY - CROPS

HUNGARY - CRIME

Eurostat, Batiment Jean Monnet, Rue Alcide de Gasperi, L-2920 Luxembourg, http://epp.eurostat.ec.europa.eu; *Crime and Criminal Justice; General Government Expenditure and Revenue in the EU, 2006;* and *Study on Crime Victimisation.*

International Criminal Police Organization (INTERPOL), General Secretariat, 200 quai Charles de Gaulle, 69006 Lyon, France, www.interpol.int; *International Crime Statistics.*

U.S. Department of Justice (DOJ), Bureau of Justice Statistics, 810 Seventh Street, NW, Washington, DC 20531, (202) 307-0765, www.ojp.usdoj.gov/bjs/; *The World Factbook of Criminal Justice Systems.*

United Nations Statistics Division, New York, NY 10017, (800) 253-9646, Fax: (212) 963-4116, http://unstats.un.org; *Trends in Europe and North America: The Statistical Yearbook of the ECE 2005.*

Yale University Press, PO Box 209040, New Haven, CT 06520-9040, (203) 432-0960, Fax: (203) 432-0948, http://yalepress.yale.edu/yupbooks; *Violence and Crime in Cross-National Perspective.*

HUNGARY - CROPS

Euromonitor International, Inc., 224 S. Michigan Avenue, Suite 1500, Chicago, IL 60604, (312) 922-1115, Fax: (312) 922-1157, www.euromonitor.com; *European Marketing Data and Statistics 2008.*

M.E. Sharpe, 80 Business Park Drive, Armonk, NY 10504, (800) 541-6563, Fax: (914) 273-2106, www.mesharpe.com; *The Illustrated Book of World Rankings.*

Palgrave Macmillan Ltd., Houndmills, Basingstoke, Hampshire, RG21 6XS, England, (Telephone in U.S. (888) 330-8477), (Fax in U.S. (800) 672-2054), www.palgrave.com; *The Statesman's Yearbook 2008.*

Taylor and Francis Group, An Informa Business, 2 Park Square, Milton Park, Abingdon, Oxford OX14 4RN, United Kingdom, (Dial from U.S. (212) 216-7800), (Fax from U.S. (212) 564-7854), www.tandf.co.uk; *The Europa World Year Book.*

United Nations Conference on Trade and Development (UNCTAD), DC2-1120, United Nations, New York, NY 10017, (212) 963-0027, www.unctad.org; *UNCTAD Commodity Yearbook.*

United Nations Food and Agricultural Organization (FAO), Viale delle Terme di Caracalla, 00100 Rome, Italy, (Dial from U.S. (202) 653-2400), (Fax from U.S. (202) 653 5760), www.fao.org; *FAO Production Yearbook 2002* and *The State of Food and Agriculture (SOFA) 2006.*

United Nations Statistics Division, New York, NY 10017, (800) 253-9646, Fax: (212) 963-4116, http://unstats.un.org; *Statistical Yearbook.*

HUNGARY - CUSTOMS ADMINISTRATION

Palgrave Macmillan Ltd., Houndmills, Basingstoke, Hampshire, RG21 6XS, England, (Telephone in U.S. (888) 330-8477), (Fax in U.S. (800) 672-2054), www.palgrave.com; *The Statesman's Yearbook 2008.*

HUNGARY - DAIRY PROCESSING

M.E. Sharpe, 80 Business Park Drive, Armonk, NY 10504, (800) 541-6563, Fax: (914) 273-2106, www.mesharpe.com; *The Illustrated Book of World Rankings.*

Palgrave Macmillan Ltd., Houndmills, Basingstoke, Hampshire, RG21 6XS, England, (Telephone in U.S. (888) 330-8477), (Fax in U.S. (800) 672-2054), www.palgrave.com; *The Statesman's Yearbook 2008.*

Taylor and Francis Group, An Informa Business, 2 Park Square, Milton Park, Abingdon, Oxford OX14 4RN, United Kingdom, (Dial from U.S. (212) 216-7800), (Fax from U.S. (212) 564-7854), www.tandf.co.uk; *The Europa World Year Book.*

United Nations Food and Agricultural Organization (FAO), Viale delle Terme di Caracalla, 00100 Rome, Italy, (Dial from U.S. (202) 653-2400), (Fax from U.S. (202) 653 5760), www.fao.org; *FAO Production Yearbook 2002* and *The State of Food and Agriculture (SOFA) 2006.*

United Nations Statistics Division, New York, NY 10017, (800) 253-9646, Fax: (212) 963-4116, http://unstats.un.org; *Statistical Yearbook.*

HUNGARY - DEATH RATES

See HUNGARY - MORTALITY

HUNGARY - DEBTS, EXTERNAL

Palgrave Macmillan Ltd., Houndmills, Basingstoke, Hampshire, RG21 6XS, England, (Telephone in U.S. (888) 330-8477), (Fax in U.S. (800) 672-2054), www.palgrave.com; *The Statesman's Yearbook 2008.*

The World Bank, 1818 H Street, NW, Washington, DC 20433, (202) 473-1000, Fax: (202) 477-6391, www.worldbank.org; *Global Development Finance 2007; World Development Indicators (WDI) 2008;* and *World Development Report 2008.*

HUNGARY - DEFENSE EXPENDITURES

See HUNGARY - ARMED FORCES

HUNGARY - DEMOGRAPHY

Euromonitor International, Inc., 224 S. Michigan Avenue, Suite 1500, Chicago, IL 60604, (312) 922-1115, Fax: (312) 922-1157, www.euromonitor.com; *The World Economic Factbook 2008* and *World Marketing Data and Statistics.*

Eurostat, Batiment Jean Monnet, Rue Alcide de Gasperi, L-2920 Luxembourg, http://epp.eurostat.ec.europa.eu; *Demographic Outlook - National Reports on the Demographic Developments in 2006.*

M.E. Sharpe, 80 Business Park Drive, Armonk, NY 10504, (800) 541-6563, Fax: (914) 273-2106, www.mesharpe.com; *The Illustrated Book of World Rankings.*

United Nations Statistics Division, New York, NY 10017, (800) 253-9646, Fax: (212) 963-4116, http://unstats.un.org; *Human Development Report 2006.*

The World Bank, 1818 H Street, NW, Washington, DC 20433, (202) 473-1000, Fax: (202) 477-6391, www.worldbank.org; *Hungary.*

HUNGARY - DIAMONDS

See HUNGARY - MINERAL INDUSTRIES

HUNGARY - DISPOSABLE INCOME

M.E. Sharpe, 80 Business Park Drive, Armonk, NY 10504, (800) 541-6563, Fax: (914) 273-2106, www.mesharpe.com; *The Illustrated Book of World Rankings.*

United Nations Statistics Division, New York, NY 10017, (800) 253-9646, Fax: (212) 963-4116, http://unstats.un.org; *National Accounts Statistics: Compendium of Income Distribution Statistics* and *Statistical Yearbook.*

HUNGARY - DIVORCE

M.E. Sharpe, 80 Business Park Drive, Armonk, NY 10504, (800) 541-6563, Fax: (914) 273-2106, www.mesharpe.com; *The Illustrated Book of World Rankings.*

United Nations Statistics Division, New York, NY 10017, (800) 253-9646, Fax: (212) 963-4116, http://unstats.un.org; *Demographic Yearbook; Statistical Yearbook;* and *Trends in Europe and North America: The Statistical Yearbook of the ECE 2005.*

HUNGARY - ECONOMIC ASSISTANCE

United Nations Statistics Division, New York, NY 10017, (800) 253-9646, Fax: (212) 963-4116, http://unstats.un.org; *Statistical Yearbook.*

HUNGARY - ECONOMIC CONDITIONS

Banque de France, 48 rue Croix des Petits champs, 75001 Paris, France, www.banque-france.fr/home.htm; *Key Data for the Euro Area.*

Center for International Business Education Research (CIBER), Columbia Business School and School of International and Public Affairs, Uris Hall, Room 212, 3022 Broadway, New York, NY 10027-6902, Mr. Joshua Safier, (212) 854-4750, Fax: (212) 222-9821, www.columbia.edu/cu/ciber/; Datastream International.

Central Intelligence Agency, Office of Public Affairs, Washington, DC 20505, (703) 482-0623, Fax: (703) 482-1739, www.cia.gov; *The World Factbook.*

DSI Data Service Information, Xantener Strasse 51a, D-47495 Rheinberg, Germany, www.dsidata.com; *Campus Solution.*

Dun and Bradstreet (DB) Corporation, 103 JFK Parkway, Short Hills, NJ 07078, (973) 921-5500, www.dnb.com; *Country Report.*

Economist Intelligence Unit, 111 West 57th Street, New York, NY 10019, (212) 554-0600, Fax: (212) 586-1181, www.eiu.com; *Hungary Country Report.*

Euromonitor International, Inc., 224 S. Michigan Avenue, Suite 1500, Chicago, IL 60604, (312) 922-1115, Fax: (312) 922-1157, www.euromonitor.com; *European Marketing Data and Statistics 2008; The World Economic Factbook 2008;* and *World Marketing Data and Statistics.*

European Union, Delegation of the European Commission to the United States, 2300 M Street, NW, Washington, DC 20037, (202) 862-9500, Fax: (202) 429-1766, www.eurunion.org; *The EU Economy, 2007 Review: Moving Europe's Productivity Frontier.*

Eurostat, Batiment Jean Monnet, Rue Alcide de Gasperi, L-2920 Luxembourg, http://epp.eurostat.ec.europa.eu; *Consumers in Europe - Facts and Figures on Services of General Interest* and *EU Economic Data Pocketbook.*

Federal Statistical Office Germany, D-65180 Wiesbaden, Germany, www.destatis.de; *Hungary 2005.*

International Monetary Fund (IMF), 700 Nineteenth Street, NW, Washington, DC 20431, (202) 623-7000, Fax: (202) 623-4661, www.imf.org; *World Economic Outlook Reports.*

M.E. Sharpe, 80 Business Park Drive, Armonk, NY 10504, (800) 541-6563, Fax: (914) 273-2106, www.mesharpe.com; *The Illustrated Book of World Rankings.*

Organisation for Economic Cooperation and Development (OECD), 2 rue Andre Pascal, F-75775 Paris Cedex 16, France, (Telephone in U.S. (202) 785-6323), (Fax in U.S. (202) 785-0350), www.oecd.org; *ICT Sector Data and Metadata by Country; Labour Force Statistics: 1986-2005, 2007 Edition; OECD Composite Leading Indicators (CLIs), Updated September 2007; OECD Economic Survey - Hungary 2007;* and *OECD in Figures 2007.*

Palgrave Macmillan Ltd., Houndmills, Basingstoke, Hampshire, RG21 6XS, England, (Telephone in U.S. (888) 330-8477), (Fax in U.S. (800) 672-2054), www.palgrave.com; *The Statesman's Yearbook 2008.*

Taylor and Francis Group, An Informa Business, 2 Park Square, Milton Park, Abingdon, Oxford OX14 4RN, United Kingdom, (Dial from U.S. (212) 216-7800), (Fax from U.S. (212) 564-7854), www.tandf.co.uk; *The Europa World Year Book.*

United Nations Statistics Division, New York, NY 10017, (800) 253-9646, Fax: (212) 963-4116, http://unstats.un.org; *World Statistics Pocketbook.*

The World Bank, 1818 H Street, NW, Washington, DC 20433, (202) 473-1000, Fax: (202) 477-6391, www.worldbank.org; *Global Economic Monitor (GEM); Global Economic Prospects 2008; Hungary; The World Bank Atlas 2003-2004;* and *World Development Report 2008.*

HUNGARY - EDUCATION

Euromonitor International, Inc., 224 S. Michigan Avenue, Suite 1500, Chicago, IL 60604, (312) 922-1115, Fax: (312) 922-1157, www.euromonitor.com; *European Marketing Data and Statistics 2008* and *World Marketing Data and Statistics.*

European Union, Delegation of the European Commission to the United States, 2300 M Street, NW, Washington, DC 20037, (202) 862-9500, Fax: (202) 429-1766, www.eurunion.org; *Education across Europe 2003.*

Eurostat, Batiment Jean Monnet, Rue Alcide de Gasperi, L-2920 Luxembourg, http://epp.eurostat.ec.europa.eu; *Education, Science and Culture Statistics.*

M.E. Sharpe, 80 Business Park Drive, Armonk, NY 10504, (800) 541-6563, Fax: (914) 273-2106, www.mesharpe.com; *The Illustrated Book of World Rankings.*

Palgrave Macmillan Ltd., Houndmills, Basingstoke, Hampshire, RG21 6XS, England, (Telephone in U.S. (888) 330-8477), (Fax in U.S. (800) 672-2054), www.palgrave.com; *The Statesman's Yearbook 2008.*

Taylor and Francis Group, An Informa Business, 2 Park Square, Milton Park, Abingdon, Oxford OX14 4RN, United Kingdom, (Dial from U.S. (212) 216-7800), (Fax from U.S. (212) 564-7854), www.tandf.co.uk; *The Europa World Year Book.*

UNESCO Institute for Statistics, C.P. 6128 Succursale Centre-Ville, Montreal, Quebec, H3C 3J7 Canada, (Dial from U.S. (514) 343-6880), (Fax from U.S. (514) 343 6882), www.uis.unesco.org; *Statistical Tables.*

United Nations Statistics Division, New York, NY 10017, (800) 253-9646, Fax: (212) 963-4116, http://unstats.un.org; *Human Development Report 2006* and *Trends in Europe and North America: The Statistical Yearbook of the ECE 2005.*

The World Bank, 1818 H Street, NW, Washington, DC 20433, (202) 473-1000, Fax: (202) 477-6391, www.worldbank.org; *Hungary; World Development Indicators (WDI) 2008;* and *World Development Report 2008.*

HUNGARY - ELECTRICITY

Eurostat, Batiment Jean Monnet, Rue Alcide de Gasperi, L-2920 Luxembourg, http://epp.eurostat.ec.europa.eu; *Energy - Monthly Statistics* and *Panorama of Energy - 2007 Edition.*

M.E. Sharpe, 80 Business Park Drive, Armonk, NY 10504, (800) 541-6563, Fax: (914) 273-2106, www.mesharpe.com; *The Illustrated Book of World Rankings.*

Organisation for Economic Cooperation and Development (OECD), 2 rue Andre Pascal, F-75775 Paris Cedex 16, France, (Telephone in U.S. (202) 785-6323), (Fax in U.S. (202) 785-0350), www.oecd.org; *World Energy Outlook 2007.*

Palgrave Macmillan Ltd., Houndmills, Basingstoke, Hampshire, RG21 6XS, England, (Telephone in U.S. (888) 330-8477), (Fax in U.S. (800) 672-2054), www.palgrave.com; *The Statesman's Yearbook 2008.*

Platts, 2 Penn Plaza, 25th Floor, New York, NY 10121-2298, (212) 904-3070, www.platts.com; *EU Energy* and *European Electricity Review 2004.*

U.S. Department of Energy (DOE), Energy Information Administration (EIA), 1000 Independence Avenue, SW, Washington, DC 20585, (202) 586-8800, www.eia.doe.gov; *International Energy Annual 2004* and *International Energy Outlook 2006.*

United Nations Statistics Division, New York, NY 10017, (800) 253-9646, Fax: (212) 963-4116, http://unstats.un.org; *Human Development Report 2006* and *Trends in Europe and North America: The Statistical Yearbook of the ECE 2005.*

HUNGARY - EMPLOYMENT

Bernan Essential Government Publications, 4611-F Assembly Drive, Lanham MD, 20706-4391, (301) 459-2255, Fax: (800) 865-3450, www.bernan.com; *OECD Factbook 2006.*

Euromonitor International, Inc., 224 S. Michigan Avenue, Suite 1500, Chicago, IL 60604, (312) 922-

1115, Fax: (312) 922-1157, www.euromonitor.com; *European Marketing Data and Statistics 2008.*

International Labour Office, I.L.O. Publications, 4 route des Morillons, CH-1211 Geneva 22, Switzerland, (Telephone in U.S. (202) 653-7652), (Fax in U.S. (202) 653-7687), www.ilo.org; *Yearbook of Labour Statistics 2006.*

M.E. Sharpe, 80 Business Park Drive, Armonk, NY 10504, (800) 541-6563, Fax: (914) 273-2106, www.mesharpe.com; *The Illustrated Book of World Rankings.*

Organisation for Economic Cooperation and Development (OECD), 2 rue Andre Pascal, F-75775 Paris Cedex 16, France, (Telephone in U.S. (202) 785-6323), (Fax in U.S. (202) 785-0350), www.oecd.org; *ICT Sector Data and Metadata by Country; Labour Force Statistics: 1986-2005, 2007 Edition; OECD Composite Leading Indicators (CLIs), Updated September 2007; OECD Economic Survey - Hungary 2007;* and *OECD in Figures 2007.*

United Nations Statistics Division, New York, NY 10017, (800) 253-9646, Fax: (212) 963-4116, http://unstats.un.org; *Statistical Yearbook* and *Trends in Europe and North America: The Statistical Yearbook of the ECE 2005.*

The World Bank, 1818 H Street, NW, Washington, DC 20433, (202) 473-1000, Fax: (202) 477-6391, www.worldbank.org; *Hungary.*

HUNGARY - ENERGY INDUSTRIES

Enerdata, 10 Rue Royale, 75008 Paris, France, www.enerdata.fr; *Global Energy Market Data.*

Eurostat, Batiment Jean Monnet, Rue Alcide de Gasperi, L-2920 Luxembourg, http://epp.eurostat.ec.europa.eu; *Energy - Monthly Statistics* and *Panorama of Energy - 2007 Edition.*

International Energy Agency (IEA), 9, rue de la Federation, 75739 Paris Cedex 15, France, www.iea.org; *Key World Energy Statistics 2007.*

Organisation for Economic Cooperation and Development (OECD), 2 rue Andre Pascal, F-75775 Paris Cedex 16, France, (Telephone in U.S. (202) 785-6323), (Fax in U.S. (202) 785-0350), www.oecd.org; *Towards Sustainable Household Consumption?: Trends and Policies in OECD Countries.*

Platts, 2 Penn Plaza, 25th Floor, New York, NY 10121-2298, (212) 904-3070, www.platts.com; *Emissions Daily; EU Energy;* and *European Power Daily.*

United Nations Statistics Division, New York, NY 10017, (800) 253-9646, Fax: (212) 963-4116, http://unstats.un.org; *Statistical Yearbook.*

HUNGARY - ENVIRONMENTAL CONDITIONS

DSI Data Service Information, Xantener Strasse 51a, D-47495 Rheinberg, Germany, www.dsidata.com; *Campus Solution* and *DSI's Global Environmental Database.*

Economist Intelligence Unit, 111 West 57th Street, New York, NY 10019, (212) 554-0600, Fax: (212) 586-1181, www.eiu.com; *Hungary Country Report.*

Federal Statistical Office Germany, D-65180 Wiesbaden, Germany, www.destatis.de; *Hungary 2005.*

Platts, 2 Penn Plaza, 25th Floor, New York, NY 10121-2298, (212) 904-3070, www.platts.com; *Emissions Daily.*

United Nations Statistics Division, New York, NY 10017, (800) 253-9646, Fax: (212) 963-4116, http://unstats.un.org; *Trends in Europe and North America: The Statistical Yearbook of the ECE 2005* and *World Statistics Pocketbook.*

HUNGARY - EXPENDITURES, PUBLIC

Eurostat, Batiment Jean Monnet, Rue Alcide de Gasperi, L-2920 Luxembourg, http://epp.eurostat.ec.europa.eu; *European Social Statistics - Social Protection Expenditure and Receipts - Data 1997-2005.*

HUNGARY - EXPORTS

Central Intelligence Agency, Office of Public Affairs, Washington, DC 20505, (703) 482-0623, Fax: (703) 482-1739, www.cia.gov; *The World Factbook.*

Economist Intelligence Unit, 111 West 57th Street, New York, NY 10019, (212) 554-0600, Fax: (212) 586-1181, www.eiu.com; *Hungary Country Report.*

Euromonitor International, Inc., 224 S. Michigan Avenue, Suite 1500, Chicago, IL 60604, (312) 922-1115, Fax: (312) 922-1157, www.euromonitor.com; *The World Economic Factbook 2008.*

International Lead and Zinc Study Group (ILZSG), Rua Almirante Barroso 38, 5th Floor, Lisbon 1000 - 013, Portugal, www.ilzsg.org; Interactive Statistical Database.

International Monetary Fund (IMF), 700 Nineteenth Street, NW, Washington, DC 20431, (202) 623-7000, Fax: (202) 623-4661, www.imf.org; *Direction of Trade Statistics Yearbook 2007* and *International Financial Statistics Yearbook 2007.*

Organisation for Economic Cooperation and Development (OECD), 2 rue Andre Pascal, F-75775 Paris Cedex 16, France, (Telephone in U.S. (202) 785-6323), (Fax in U.S. (202) 785-0350), www.oecd.org; *OECD Economic Survey - Hungary 2007.*

Palgrave Macmillan Ltd., Houndmills, Basingstoke, Hampshire, RG21 6XS, England, (Telephone in U.S. (888) 330-8477), (Fax in U.S. (800) 672-2054), www.palgrave.com; *The Statesman's Yearbook 2008.*

Taylor and Francis Group, An Informa Business, 2 Park Square, Milton Park, Abingdon, Oxford OX14 4RN, United Kingdom, (Dial from U.S. (212) 216-7800), (Fax from U.S. (212) 564-7854), www.tandf.co.uk; *The Europa World Year Book.*

United Nations Conference on Trade and Development (UNCTAD), DC2-1120, United Nations, New York, NY 10017, (212) 963-0027, www.unctad.org; *Handbook of Statistics 2005.*

United Nations Food and Agricultural Organization (FAO), Viale delle Terme di Caracalla, 00100 Rome, Italy, (Dial from U.S. (202) 653-2400), (Fax from U.S. (202) 653 5760), www.fao.org; *The State of Food and Agriculture (SOFA) 2006.*

United Nations Statistics Division, New York, NY 10017, (800) 253-9646, Fax: (212) 963-4116, http://unstats.un.org; *Trends in Europe and North America: The Statistical Yearbook of the ECE 2005.*

The World Bank, 1818 H Street, NW, Washington, DC 20433, (202) 473-1000, Fax: (202) 477-6391, www.worldbank.org; *World Development Indicators (WDI) 2008* and *World Development Report 2008.*

HUNGARY - FERTILITY, HUMAN

Central Intelligence Agency, Office of Public Affairs, Washington, DC 20505, (703) 482-0623, Fax: (703) 482-1739, www.cia.gov; *The World Factbook.*

M.E. Sharpe, 80 Business Park Drive, Armonk, NY 10504, (800) 541-6563, Fax: (914) 273-2106, www.mesharpe.com; *The Illustrated Book of World Rankings.*

United Nations Statistics Division, New York, NY 10017, (800) 253-9646, Fax: (212) 963-4116, http://unstats.un.org; *Human Development Report 2006* and *Trends in Europe and North America: The Statistical Yearbook of the ECE 2005.*

The World Bank, 1818 H Street, NW, Washington, DC 20433, (202) 473-1000, Fax: (202) 477-6391, www.worldbank.org; *The World Bank Atlas 2003-2004; World Development Indicators (WDI) 2008;* and *World Development Report 2008.*

HUNGARY - FERTILIZER INDUSTRY

United Nations Food and Agricultural Organization (FAO), Viale delle Terme di Caracalla, 00100 Rome, Italy, (Dial from U.S. (202) 653-2400), (Fax from U.S. (202) 653 5760), www.fao.org; *The State of Food and Agriculture (SOFA) 2006.*

United Nations Statistics Division, New York, NY 10017, (800) 253-9646, Fax: (212) 963-4116, http://unstats.un.org; *Statistical Yearbook.*

HUNGARY - FETAL MORTALITY

See HUNGARY - MORTALITY

HUNGARY - FILM

See HUNGARY - MOTION PICTURES

HUNGARY - FINANCE

Taylor and Francis Group, An Informa Business, 2 Park Square, Milton Park, Abingdon, Oxford OX14 4RN, United Kingdom, (Dial from U.S. (212) 216-7800), (Fax from U.S. (212) 564-7854), www.tandf.co.uk; *The Europa World Year Book.*

United Nations Statistics Division, New York, NY 10017, (800) 253-9646, Fax: (212) 963-4116, http://unstats.un.org; *National Accounts Statistics: Compendium of Income Distribution Statistics* and *Statistical Yearbook.*

The World Bank, 1818 H Street, NW, Washington, DC 20433, (202) 473-1000, Fax: (202) 477-6391, www.worldbank.org; *Hungary.*

HUNGARY - FINANCE, PUBLIC

Banque de France, 48 rue Croix des Petits champs, 75001 Paris, France, www.banque-france.fr/home.htm; *Key Data for the Euro Area* and *Public Finance.*

Bernan Essential Government Publications, 4611-F Assembly Drive, Lanham MD, 20706-4391, (301) 459-2255, Fax: (800) 865-3450, www.bernan.com; *National Accounts Statistics.*

Economist Intelligence Unit, 111 West 57th Street, New York, NY 10019, (212) 554-0600, Fax: (212) 586-1181, www.eiu.com; *Hungary Country Report.*

International Monetary Fund (IMF), 700 Nineteenth Street, NW, Washington, DC 20431, (202) 623-7000, Fax: (202) 623-4661, www.imf.org; *International Financial Statistics* and *International Financial Statistics Online Service.*

M.E. Sharpe, 80 Business Park Drive, Armonk, NY 10504, (800) 541-6563, Fax: (914) 273-2106, www.mesharpe.com; *The Illustrated Book of World Rankings.*

Palgrave Macmillan Ltd., Houndmills, Basingstoke, Hampshire, RG21 6XS, England, (Telephone in U.S. (888) 330-8477), (Fax in U.S. (800) 672-2054), www.palgrave.com; *The Statesman's Yearbook 2008.*

Taylor and Francis Group, An Informa Business, 2 Park Square, Milton Park, Abingdon, Oxford OX14 4RN, United Kingdom, (Dial from U.S. (212) 216-7800), (Fax from U.S. (212) 564-7854), www.tandf.co.uk; *The Europa World Year Book.*

The World Bank, 1818 H Street, NW, Washington, DC 20433, (202) 473-1000, Fax: (202) 477-6391, www.worldbank.org; *Hungary.*

HUNGARY - FISHERIES

Euromonitor International, Inc., 224 S. Michigan Avenue, Suite 1500, Chicago, IL 60604, (312) 922-1115, Fax: (312) 922-1157, www.euromonitor.com; *European Marketing Data and Statistics 2008.*

M.E. Sharpe, 80 Business Park Drive, Armonk, NY 10504, (800) 541-6563, Fax: (914) 273-2106, www.mesharpe.com; *The Illustrated Book of World Rankings.*

Palgrave Macmillan Ltd., Houndmills, Basingstoke, Hampshire, RG21 6XS, England, (Telephone in U.S. (888) 330-8477), (Fax in U.S. (800) 672-2054), www.palgrave.com; *The Statesman's Yearbook 2008.*

Taylor and Francis Group, An Informa Business, 2 Park Square, Milton Park, Abingdon, Oxford OX14 4RN, United Kingdom, (Dial from U.S. (212) 216-7800), (Fax from U.S. (212) 564-7854), www.tandf.co.uk; *The Europa World Year Book.*

United Nations Conference on Trade and Development (UNCTAD), DC2-1120, United Nations, New York, NY 10017, (212) 963-0027, www.unctad.org; *UNCTAD Commodity Yearbook.*

United Nations Food and Agricultural Organization (FAO), Viale delle Terme di Caracalla, 00100 Rome, Italy, (Dial from U.S. (202) 653-2400), (Fax from

U.S. (202) 653 5760), www.fao.org; *FAO Yearbook of Fishery Statistics;* Fishery Databases; FISHSTAT Database. Subjects covered include: Aquaculture production, capture production, fishery commodities; and *The State of Food and Agriculture (SOFA) 2006.*

United Nations Statistics Division, New York, NY 10017, (800) 253-9646, Fax: (212) 963-4116, http://unstats.un.org; *Statistical Yearbook.*

The World Bank, 1818 H Street, NW, Washington, DC 20433, (202) 473-1000, Fax: (202) 477-6391, www.worldbank.org; *Hungary.*

HUNGARY - FLOUR INDUSTRY

United Nations Statistics Division, New York, NY 10017, (800) 253-9646, Fax: (212) 963-4116, http://unstats.un.org; *Statistical Yearbook.*

HUNGARY - FOOD

Euromonitor International, Inc., 224 S. Michigan Avenue, Suite 1500, Chicago, IL 60604, (312) 922-1115, Fax: (312) 922-1157, www.euromonitor.com; *Retail Trade International 2007.*

United Nations Conference on Trade and Development (UNCTAD), DC2-1120, United Nations, New York, NY 10017, (212) 963-0027, www.unctad.org; *UNCTAD Commodity Yearbook.*

United Nations Food and Agricultural Organization (FAO), Viale delle Terme di Caracalla, 00100 Rome, Italy, (Dial from U.S. (202) 653-2400), (Fax from U.S. (202) 653 5760), www.fao.org; *FAO Production Yearbook 2002* and *The State of Food and Agriculture (SOFA) 2006.*

United Nations Statistics Division, New York, NY 10017, (800) 253-9646, Fax: (212) 963-4116, http://unstats.un.org; *Human Development Report 2006.*

HUNGARY - FOREIGN EXCHANGE RATES

Central Intelligence Agency, Office of Public Affairs, Washington, DC 20505, (703) 482-0623, Fax: (703) 482-1739, www.cia.gov; *The World Factbook.*

Euromonitor International, Inc., 224 S. Michigan Avenue, Suite 1500, Chicago, IL 60604, (312) 922-1115, Fax: (312) 922-1157, www.euromonitor.com; *The World Economic Factbook 2008.*

International Civil Aviation Organization (ICAO), External Relations and Public Information Office (EPO), 999 University Street, Montreal, Quebec H3C 5H7, Canada, (Dial from U.S. (514) 954-8219), (Fax from U.S. (514) 954-6077), www.icao.int; *Civil Aviation Statistics of the World.*

International Monetary Fund (IMF), 700 Nineteenth Street, NW, Washington, DC 20431, (202) 623-7000, Fax: (202) 623-4661, www.imf.org; *International Financial Statistics Yearbook 2007.*

Taylor and Francis Group, An Informa Business, 2 Park Square, Milton Park, Abingdon, Oxford OX14 4RN, United Kingdom, (Dial from U.S. (212) 216-7800), (Fax from U.S. (212) 564-7854), www.tandf.co.uk; *The Europa World Year Book.*

United Nations Statistics Division, New York, NY 10017, (800) 253-9646, Fax: (212) 963-4116, http://unstats.un.org; *Statistical Yearbook; Trends in Europe and North America: The Statistical Yearbook of the ECE 2005;* and *World Statistics Pocketbook.*

HUNGARY - FORESTS AND FORESTRY

Euromonitor International, Inc., 224 S. Michigan Avenue, Suite 1500, Chicago, IL 60604, (312) 922-1115, Fax: (312) 922-1157, www.euromonitor.com; *European Marketing Data and Statistics 2008.*

M.E. Sharpe, 80 Business Park Drive, Armonk, NY 10504, (800) 541-6563, Fax: (914) 273-2106, www.mesharpe.com; *The Illustrated Book of World Rankings.*

Palgrave Macmillan Ltd., Houndmills, Basingstoke, Hampshire, RG21 6XS, England, (Telephone in U.S. (888) 330-8477), (Fax in U.S. (800) 672-2054), www.palgrave.com; *The Statesman's Yearbook 2008.*

Taylor and Francis Group, An Informa Business, 2 Park Square, Milton Park, Abingdon, Oxford OX14 4RN, United Kingdom, (Dial from U.S. (212) 216-7800), (Fax from U.S. (212) 564-7854), www.tandf.co.uk; *The Europa World Year Book.*

UNESCO Institute for Statistics, C.P. 6128 Succursale Centre-Ville, Montreal, Quebec, H3C 3J7 Canada, (Dial from U.S. (514) 343-6880), (Fax from U.S. (514) 343 6882), www.uis.unesco.org; *Statistical Tables.*

United Nations Conference on Trade and Development (UNCTAD), DC2-1120, United Nations, New York, NY 10017, (212) 963-0027, www.unctad.org; *UNCTAD Commodity Yearbook.*

United Nations Food and Agricultural Organization (FAO), Viale delle Terme di Caracalla, 00100 Rome, Italy, (Dial from U.S. (202) 653-2400), (Fax from U.S. (202) 653 5760), www.fao.org; *FAO Yearbook of Forest Products* and *The State of Food and Agriculture (SOFA) 2006.*

United Nations Statistics Division, New York, NY 10017, (800) 253-9646, Fax: (212) 963-4116, http://unstats.un.org; *Statistical Yearbook* and *Trends in Europe and North America: The Statistical Yearbook of the ECE 2005.*

The World Bank, 1818 H Street, NW, Washington, DC 20433, (202) 473-1000, Fax: (202) 477-6391, www.worldbank.org; *Hungary* and *World Development Report 2008.*

HUNGARY - GAS PRODUCTION

See HUNGARY - MINERAL INDUSTRIES

HUNGARY - GEOGRAPHIC INFORMATION SYSTEMS

M.E. Sharpe, 80 Business Park Drive, Armonk, NY 10504, (800) 541-6563, Fax: (914) 273-2106, www.mesharpe.com; *The Illustrated Book of World Rankings.*

The World Bank, 1818 H Street, NW, Washington, DC 20433, (202) 473-1000, Fax: (202) 477-6391, www.worldbank.org; *Hungary.*

HUNGARY - GOLD INDUSTRY

International Monetary Fund (IMF), 700 Nineteenth Street, NW, Washington, DC 20431, (202) 623-7000, Fax: (202) 623-4661, www.imf.org; *International Financial Statistics Yearbook 2007.*

The World Bank, 1818 H Street, NW, Washington, DC 20433, (202) 473-1000, Fax: (202) 477-6391, www.worldbank.org; *World Development Indicators (WDI) 2008.*

HUNGARY - GOLD PRODUCTION

See HUNGARY - MINERAL INDUSTRIES

HUNGARY - GREEN PEPPER AND CHILIE PRODUCTION

See HUNGARY - CROPS

HUNGARY - GROSS DOMESTIC PRODUCT

Economist Intelligence Unit, 111 West 57th Street, New York, NY 10019, (212) 554-0600, Fax: (212) 586-1181, www.eiu.com; *Hungary Country Report.*

Euromonitor International, Inc., 224 S. Michigan Avenue, Suite 1500, Chicago, IL 60604, (312) 922-1115, Fax: (312) 922-1157, www.euromonitor.com; *The World Economic Factbook 2008.*

M.E. Sharpe, 80 Business Park Drive, Armonk, NY 10504, (800) 541-6563, Fax: (914) 273-2106, www.mesharpe.com; *The Illustrated Book of World Rankings.*

Organisation for Economic Cooperation and Development (OECD), 2 rue Andre Pascal, F-75775 Paris Cedex 16, France, (Telephone in U.S. (202) 785-6323), (Fax in U.S. (202) 785-0350), www.oecd.org; *Comparison of Gross Domestic Product (GDP) for OECD Countries.*

Taylor and Francis Group, An Informa Business, 2 Park Square, Milton Park, Abingdon, Oxford OX14 4RN, United Kingdom, (Dial from U.S. (212) 216-7800), (Fax from U.S. (212) 564-7854), www.tandf.co.uk; *The Europa World Year Book.*

United Nations Statistics Division, New York, NY 10017, (800) 253-9646, Fax: (212) 963-4116, http://unstats.un.org; *Human Development Report 2006; National Accounts Statistics: Compendium of Income Distribution Statistics; Statistical Yearbook;* and *Trends in Europe and North America: The Statistical Yearbook of the ECE 2005.*

The World Bank, 1818 H Street, NW, Washington, DC 20433, (202) 473-1000, Fax: (202) 477-6391, www.worldbank.org; *World Development Indicators (WDI) 2008* and *World Development Report 2008.*

HUNGARY - GROSS NATIONAL PRODUCT

European Union, Delegation of the European Commission to the United States, 2300 M Street, NW, Washington, DC 20037, (202) 862-9500, Fax: (202) 429-1766, www.eurunion.org; *The EU Economy, 2007 Review: Moving Europe's Productivity Frontier.*

M.E. Sharpe, 80 Business Park Drive, Armonk, NY 10504, (800) 541-6563, Fax: (914) 273-2106, www.mesharpe.com; *The Illustrated Book of World Rankings.*

Organisation for Economic Cooperation and Development (OECD), 2 rue Andre Pascal, F-75775 Paris Cedex 16, France, (Telephone in U.S. (202) 785-6323), (Fax in U.S. (202) 785-0350), www.oecd.org; *OECD Composite Leading Indicators (CLIs), Updated September 2007.*

Palgrave Macmillan Ltd., Houndmills, Basingstoke, Hampshire, RG21 6XS, England, (Telephone in U.S. (888) 330-8477), (Fax in U.S. (800) 672-2054), www.palgrave.com; *The Statesman's Yearbook 2008.*

U.S. Department of State (DOS), 2201 C Street NW, Washington, DC 20520, (202) 647-4000, www.state.gov; *World Military Expenditures and Arms Transfers (WMEAT).*

United Nations Statistics Division, New York, NY 10017, (800) 253-9646, Fax: (212) 963-4116, http://unstats.un.org; *Statistical Yearbook.*

The World Bank, 1818 H Street, NW, Washington, DC 20433, (202) 473-1000, Fax: (202) 477-6391, www.worldbank.org; *The World Bank Atlas 2003-2004; World Development Indicators (WDI) 2008;* and *World Development Report 2008.*

HUNGARY - HAZELNUT PRODUCTION

See HUNGARY - CROPS

HUNGARY - HEMP FIBRE PRODUCTION

See HUNGARY - TEXTILE INDUSTRY

HUNGARY - HIDES AND SKINS INDUSTRY

United Nations Food and Agricultural Organization (FAO), Viale delle Terme di Caracalla, 00100 Rome, Italy, (Dial from U.S. (202) 653-2400), (Fax from U.S. (202) 653 5760), www.fao.org; *FAO Production Yearbook 2002.*

HUNGARY - HOPS PRODUCTION

See HUNGARY - CROPS

HUNGARY - HOUSING

Euromonitor International, Inc., 224 S. Michigan Avenue, Suite 1500, Chicago, IL 60604, (312) 922-1115, Fax: (312) 922-1157, www.euromonitor.com; *World Marketing Data and Statistics.*

M.E. Sharpe, 80 Business Park Drive, Armonk, NY 10504, (800) 541-6563, Fax: (914) 273-2106, www.mesharpe.com; *The Illustrated Book of World Rankings.*

United Nations Statistics Division, New York, NY 10017, (800) 253-9646, Fax: (212) 963-4116, http://unstats.un.org; *Trends in Europe and North America: The Statistical Yearbook of the ECE 2005.*

HUNGARY - ILLITERATE PERSONS

Central Intelligence Agency, Office of Public Affairs, Washington, DC 20505, (703) 482-0623, Fax: (703) 482-1739, www.cia.gov; *The World Factbook.*

Euromonitor International, Inc., 224 S. Michigan Avenue, Suite 1500, Chicago, IL 60604, (312) 922-1115, Fax: (312) 922-1157, www.euromonitor.com; *The World Economic Factbook 2008.*

UNESCO Institute for Statistics, C.P. 6128 Succursale Centre-Ville, Montreal, Quebec, H3C 3J7 Canada, (Dial from U.S. (514) 343-6880), (Fax from U.S. (514) 343 6882), www.uis.unesco.org; *Statistical Tables.*

United Nations Statistics Division, New York, NY 10017, (800) 253-9646, Fax: (212) 963-4116, http://unstats.un.org; *Human Development Report 2006.*

HUNGARY - IMPORTS

Central Intelligence Agency, Office of Public Affairs, Washington, DC 20505, (703) 482-0623, Fax: (703) 482-1739, www.cia.gov; *The World Factbook.*

Economist Intelligence Unit, 111 West 57th Street, New York, NY 10019, (212) 554-0600, Fax: (212) 586-1181, www.eiu.com; *Hungary Country Report.*

International Lead and Zinc Study Group (ILZSG), Rua Almirante Barroso 38, 5th Floor, Lisbon 1000 - 013, Portugal, www.ilzsg.org; Interactive Statistical Database.

International Monetary Fund (IMF), 700 Nineteenth Street, NW, Washington, DC 20431, (202) 623-7000, Fax: (202) 623-4661, www.imf.org; *Direction of Trade Statistics Yearbook 2007* and *International Financial Statistics Yearbook 2007.*

Organisation for Economic Cooperation and Development (OECD), 2 rue Andre Pascal, F-75775 Paris Cedex 16, France, (Telephone in U.S. (202) 785-6323), (Fax in U.S. (202) 785-0350), www.oecd.org; *OECD Economic Survey - Hungary 2007.*

Palgrave Macmillan Ltd., Houndmills, Basingstoke, Hampshire, RG21 6XS, England, (Telephone in U.S. (888) 330-8477), (Fax in U.S. (800) 672-2054), www.palgrave.com; *The Statesman's Yearbook 2008.*

Taylor and Francis Group, An Informa Business, 2 Park Square, Milton Park, Abingdon, Oxford OX14 4RN, United Kingdom, (Dial from U.S. (212) 216-7800), (Fax from U.S. (212) 564-7854), www.tandf.co.uk; *The Europa World Year Book.*

United Nations Conference on Trade and Development (UNCTAD), DC2-1120, United Nations, New York, NY 10017, (212) 963-0027, www.unctad.org; *Handbook of Statistics 2005.*

United Nations Food and Agricultural Organization (FAO), Viale delle Terme di Caracalla, 00100 Rome, Italy, (Dial from U.S. (202) 653-2400), (Fax from U.S. (202) 653 5760), www.fao.org; *The State of Food and Agriculture (SOFA) 2006.*

United Nations Statistics Division, New York, NY 10017, (800) 253-9646, Fax: (212) 963-4116, http://unstats.un.org; *Trends in Europe and North America: The Statistical Yearbook of the ECE 2005.*

The World Bank, 1818 H Street, NW, Washington, DC 20433, (202) 473-1000, Fax: (202) 477-6391, www.worldbank.org; *World Development Indicators (WDI) 2008* and *World Development Report 2008.*

HUNGARY - INDUSTRIAL METALS PRODUCTION

See HUNGARY - MINERAL INDUSTRIES

HUNGARY - INDUSTRIAL PRODUCTIVITY

International Lead and Zinc Study Group (ILZSG), Rua Almirante Barroso 38, 5th Floor, Lisbon 1000 - 013, Portugal, www.ilzsg.org; Interactive Statistical Database.

M.E. Sharpe, 80 Business Park Drive, Armonk, NY 10504, (800) 541-6563, Fax: (914) 273-2106, www.mesharpe.com; *The Illustrated Book of World Rankings.*

HUNGARY - INDUSTRIAL PROPERTY

United Nations Statistics Division, New York, NY 10017, (800) 253-9646, Fax: (212) 963-4116, http://unstats.un.org; *Statistical Yearbook.*

World Intellectual Property Organization (WIPO), PO Box 18, CH-1211 Geneva 20, Switzerland, www.wipo.int; *Industrial Property Statistics* and *Industrial Property Statistics Online Directory.*

HUNGARY - INDUSTRIES

Central Intelligence Agency, Office of Public Affairs, Washington, DC 20505, (703) 482-0623, Fax: (703) 482-1739, www.cia.gov; *The World Factbook.*

Economist Intelligence Unit, 111 West 57th Street, New York, NY 10019, (212) 554-0600, Fax: (212) 586-1181, www.eiu.com; *Hungary Country Report.*

Euromonitor International, Inc., 224 S. Michigan Avenue, Suite 1500, Chicago, IL 60604, (312) 922-1115, Fax: (312) 922-1157, www.euromonitor.com; *The World Economic Factbook 2008* and *World Marketing Data and Statistics.*

International Labour Office, I.L.O. Publications, 4 route des Morillons, CH-1211 Geneva 22, Switzerland, (Telephone in U.S. (202) 653-7652), (Fax in U.S. (202) 653-7687), www.ilo.org; *Yearbook of Labour Statistics 2006.*

M.E. Sharpe, 80 Business Park Drive, Armonk, NY 10504, (800) 541-6563, Fax: (914) 273-2106, www.mesharpe.com; *The Illustrated Book of World Rankings.*

Palgrave Macmillan Ltd., Houndmills, Basingstoke, Hampshire, RG21 6XS, England, (Telephone in U.S. (888) 330-8477), (Fax in U.S. (800) 672-2054), www.palgrave.com; *The Statesman's Yearbook 2008.*

Taylor and Francis Group, An Informa Business, 2 Park Square, Milton Park, Abingdon, Oxford OX14 4RN, United Kingdom, (Dial from U.S. (212) 216-7800), (Fax from U.S. (212) 564-7854), www.tandf.co.uk; *The Europa World Year Book.*

United Nations Industrial Development Organization (UNIDO), 1 United Nations Plaza, New York, NY 10017, (212) 963 6890, Fax: (212) 963-7904, http://unido.org; Industrial Statistics Database 2008 (INDSTAT) and *The International Yearbook of Industrial Statistics 2008.*

United Nations Statistics Division, New York, NY 10017, (800) 253-9646, Fax: (212) 963-4116, http://unstats.un.org; *2004 Industrial Commodity Statistics Yearbook; Statistical Yearbook;* and *Trends in Europe and North America: The Statistical Yearbook of the ECE 2005.*

The World Bank, 1818 H Street, NW, Washington, DC 20433, (202) 473-1000, Fax: (202) 477-6391, www.worldbank.org; *Hungary* and *World Development Indicators (WDI) 2008.*

HUNGARY - INFANT AND MATERNAL MORTALITY

See HUNGARY - MORTALITY

HUNGARY - INORGANIC ACIDS

United Nations Statistics Division, New York, NY 10017, (800) 253-9646, Fax: (212) 963-4116, http://unstats.un.org; *Statistical Yearbook.*

HUNGARY - INTERNATIONAL LIQUIDITY

International Monetary Fund (IMF), 700 Nineteenth Street, NW, Washington, DC 20431, (202) 623-7000, Fax: (202) 623-4661, www.imf.org; *International Financial Statistics Yearbook 2007.*

HUNGARY - INTERNATIONAL TRADE

Banque de France, 48 rue Croix des Petits champs, 75001 Paris, France, www.banque-france.fr/home.htm; *Monthly Business Survey Overview.*

Bernan Essential Government Publications, 4611-F Assembly Drive, Lanham MD, 20706-4391, (301) 459-2255, Fax: (800) 865-3450, www.bernan.com; *OECD Factbook 2006.*

Economist Intelligence Unit, 111 West 57th Street, New York, NY 10019, (212) 554-0600, Fax: (212) 586-1181, www.eiu.com; *Hungary Country Report.*

Euromonitor International, Inc., 224 S. Michigan Avenue, Suite 1500, Chicago, IL 60604, (312) 922-1115, Fax: (312) 922-1157, www.euromonitor.com; *European Marketing Data and Statistics 2008; The World Economic Factbook 2008;* and *World Marketing Data and Statistics.*

Eurostat, Batiment Jean Monnet, Rue Alcide de Gasperi, L-2920 Luxembourg, http://epp.eurostat.ec.europa.eu; Intra- and Extra-EU Trade.

M.E. Sharpe, 80 Business Park Drive, Armonk, NY 10504, (800) 541-6563, Fax: (914) 273-2106, www.mesharpe.com; *The Illustrated Book of World Rankings.*

Organisation for Economic Cooperation and Development (OECD), 2 rue Andre Pascal, F-75775 Paris Cedex 16, France, (Telephone in U.S. (202) 785-6323), (Fax in U.S. (202) 785-0350), www.oecd.org; *OECD Economic Survey - Hungary 2007* and *OECD in Figures 2007.*

Palgrave Macmillan Ltd., Houndmills, Basingstoke, Hampshire, RG21 6XS, England, (Telephone in U.S. (888) 330-8477), (Fax in U.S. (800) 672-2054), www.palgrave.com; *The Statesman's Yearbook 2008.*

Taylor and Francis Group, An Informa Business, 2 Park Square, Milton Park, Abingdon, Oxford OX14 4RN, United Kingdom, (Dial from U.S. (212) 216-7800), (Fax from U.S. (212) 564-7854), www.tandf.co.uk; *The Europa World Year Book.*

United Nations Conference on Trade and Development (UNCTAD), DC2-1120, United Nations, New York, NY 10017, (212) 963-0027, www.unctad.org; *UNCTAD Commodity Yearbook.*

United Nations Food and Agricultural Organization (FAO), Viale delle Terme di Caracalla, 00100 Rome, Italy, (Dial from U.S. (202) 653-2400), (Fax from U.S. (202) 653 5760), www.fao.org; *FAO Trade Yearbook* and *The State of Food and Agriculture (SOFA) 2006.*

United Nations Statistics Division, New York, NY 10017, (800) 253-9646, Fax: (212) 963-4116, http://unstats.un.org; *International Trade Statistics Yearbook* and *Statistical Yearbook.*

The World Bank, 1818 H Street, NW, Washington, DC 20433, (202) 473-1000, Fax: (202) 477-6391, www.worldbank.org; *Hungary; World Development Indicators (WDI) 2008;* and *World Development Report 2008.*

World Trade Organization (WTO), Centre William Rappard, Rue de Lausanne 154, CH-1211 Geneva 21, Switzerland, www.wto.org; *International Trade Statistics 2006.*

HUNGARY - INTERNET USERS

Eurostat, Batiment Jean Monnet, Rue Alcide de Gasperi, L-2920 Luxembourg, http://epp.eurostat.ec.europa.eu; *Internet Usage by Enterprises 2007.*

International Telecommunication Union (ITU), Place des Nations, 1211 Geneva 20, Switzerland, www.itu.int; *World Telecommunication/ICT Indicators Database on CD-ROM; World Telecommunication/ICT Indicators Database Online;* and *Yearbook of Statistics - Telecommunication Services (Chronological Time Series 1997-2006).*

The World Bank, 1818 H Street, NW, Washington, DC 20433, (202) 473-1000, Fax: (202) 477-6391, www.worldbank.org; *Hungary.*

HUNGARY - INVESTMENTS

International Monetary Fund (IMF), 700 Nineteenth Street, NW, Washington, DC 20431, (202) 623-7000, Fax: (202) 623-4661, www.imf.org; *International Financial Statistics Yearbook 2007.*

HUNGARY - IRON AND IRON ORE PRODUCTION

See HUNGARY - MINERAL INDUSTRIES

HUNGARY - LABOR

Central Intelligence Agency, Office of Public Affairs, Washington, DC 20505, (703) 482-0623, Fax: (703) 482-1739, www.cia.gov; *The World Factbook.*

Euromonitor International, Inc., 224 S. Michigan Avenue, Suite 1500, Chicago, IL 60604, (312) 922-

1115, Fax: (312) 922-1157, www.euromonitor.com; *World Marketing Data and Statistics.*

Federal Statistical Office Germany, D-65180 Wiesbaden, Germany, www.destatis.de; *Hungary 2005.*

International Labour Office, I.L.O. Publications, 4 route des Morillons, CH-1211 Geneva 22, Switzerland, (Telephone in U.S. (202) 653-7652), (Fax in U.S. (202) 653-7687), www.ilo.org; *Yearbook of Labour Statistics 2006.*

M.E. Sharpe, 80 Business Park Drive, Armonk, NY 10504, (800) 541-6563, Fax: (914) 273-2106, www.mesharpe.com; *The Illustrated Book of World Rankings.*

Organisation for Economic Cooperation and Development (OECD), 2 rue Andre Pascal, F-75775 Paris Cedex 16, France, (Telephone in U.S. (202) 785-6323), (Fax in U.S. (202) 785-0350), www.oecd.org; *OECD Economic Survey - Hungary 2007.*

Palgrave Macmillan Ltd., Houndmills, Basingstoke, Hampshire, RG21 6XS, England, (Telephone in U.S. (888) 330-8477), (Fax in U.S. (800) 672-2054), www.palgrave.com; *The Statesman's Yearbook 2008.*

United Nations Food and Agricultural Organization (FAO), Viale delle Terme di Caracalla, 00100 Rome, Italy, (Dial from U.S. (202) 653-2400), (Fax from U.S. (202) 653 5760), www.fao.org; *The State of Food and Agriculture (SOFA) 2006.*

United Nations Statistics Division, New York, NY 10017, (800) 253-9646, Fax: (212) 963-4116, http://unstats.un.org; *Human Development Report 2006.*

The World Bank, 1818 H Street, NW, Washington, DC 20433, (202) 473-1000, Fax: (202) 477-6391, www.worldbank.org; *The World Bank Atlas 2003-2004; World Development Indicators (WDI) 2008;* and *World Development Report 2008.*

HUNGARY - LAND USE

Central Intelligence Agency, Office of Public Affairs, Washington, DC 20505, (703) 482-0623, Fax: (703) 482-1739, www.cia.gov; *The World Factbook.*

Euromonitor International, Inc., 224 S. Michigan Avenue, Suite 1500, Chicago, IL 60604, (312) 922-1115, Fax: (312) 922-1157, www.euromonitor.com; *European Marketing Data and Statistics 2008.*

United Nations Food and Agricultural Organization (FAO), Viale delle Terme di Caracalla, 00100 Rome, Italy, (Dial from U.S. (202) 653-2400), (Fax from U.S. (202) 653 5760), www.fao.org; *FAO Production Yearbook 2002.*

The World Bank, 1818 H Street, NW, Washington, DC 20433, (202) 473-1000, Fax: (202) 477-6391, www.worldbank.org; *World Development Report 2008.*

HUNGARY - LIBRARIES

M.E. Sharpe, 80 Business Park Drive, Armonk, NY 10504, (800) 541-6563, Fax: (914) 273-2106, www.mesharpe.com; *The Illustrated Book of World Rankings.*

UNESCO Institute for Statistics, C.P. 6128 Succursale Centre-Ville, Montreal, Quebec, H3C 3J7 Canada, (Dial from U.S. (514) 343-6880), (Fax from U.S. (514) 343 6882), www.uis.unesco.org; *Statistical Tables.*

United Nations Statistics Division, New York, NY 10017, (800) 253-9646, Fax: (212) 963-4116, http://unstats.un.org; *Statistical Yearbook* and *Trends in Europe and North America: The Statistical Yearbook of the ECE 2005.*

HUNGARY - LIFE EXPECTANCY

Central Intelligence Agency, Office of Public Affairs, Washington, DC 20505, (703) 482-0623, Fax: (703) 482-1739, www.cia.gov; *The World Factbook.*

Euromonitor International, Inc., 224 S. Michigan Avenue, Suite 1500, Chicago, IL 60604, (312) 922-1115, Fax: (312) 922-1157, www.euromonitor.com; *The World Economic Factbook 2008.*

Palgrave Macmillan Ltd., Houndmills, Basingstoke, Hampshire, RG21 6XS, England, (Telephone in U.S. (888) 330-8477), (Fax in U.S. (800) 672-2054), www.palgrave.com; *The Statesman's Yearbook 2008.*

United Nations Statistics Division, New York, NY 10017, (800) 253-9646, Fax: (212) 963-4116, http://unstats.un.org; *Human Development Report 2006; Trends in Europe and North America: The Statistical Yearbook of the ECE 2005;* and *World Statistics Pocketbook.*

The World Bank, 1818 H Street, NW, Washington, DC 20433, (202) 473-1000, Fax: (202) 477-6391, www.worldbank.org; *The World Bank Atlas 2003-2004* and *World Development Report 2008.*

HUNGARY - LITERACY

Euromonitor International, Inc., 224 S. Michigan Avenue, Suite 1500, Chicago, IL 60604, (312) 922-1115, Fax: (312) 922-1157, www.euromonitor.com; *World Marketing Data and Statistics.*

HUNGARY - LIVESTOCK

Euromonitor International, Inc., 224 S. Michigan Avenue, Suite 1500, Chicago, IL 60604, (312) 922-1115, Fax: (312) 922-1157, www.euromonitor.com; *European Marketing Data and Statistics 2008.*

M.E. Sharpe, 80 Business Park Drive, Armonk, NY 10504, (800) 541-6563, Fax: (914) 273-2106, www.mesharpe.com; *The Illustrated Book of World Rankings.*

Palgrave Macmillan Ltd., Houndmills, Basingstoke, Hampshire, RG21 6XS, England, (Telephone in U.S. (888) 330-8477), (Fax in U.S. (800) 672-2054), www.palgrave.com; *The Statesman's Yearbook 2008.*

Taylor and Francis Group, An Informa Business, 2 Park Square, Milton Park, Abingdon, Oxford OX14 4RN, United Kingdom, (Dial from U.S. (212) 216-7800), (Fax from U.S. (212) 564-7854), www.tandf.co.uk; *The Europa World Year Book.*

United Nations Conference on Trade and Development (UNCTAD), DC2-1120, United Nations, New York, NY 10017, (212) 963-0027, www.unctad.org; *UNCTAD Commodity Yearbook.*

United Nations Food and Agricultural Organization (FAO), Viale delle Terme di Caracalla, 00100 Rome, Italy, (Dial from U.S. (202) 653-2400), (Fax from U.S. (202) 653 5760), www.fao.org; *FAO Production Yearbook 2002* and *The State of Food and Agriculture (SOFA) 2006.*

United Nations Statistics Division, New York, NY 10017, (800) 253-9646, Fax: (212) 963-4116, http://unstats.un.org; *Statistical Yearbook.*

HUNGARY - MANUFACTURES

M.E. Sharpe, 80 Business Park Drive, Armonk, NY 10504, (800) 541-6563, Fax: (914) 273-2106, www.mesharpe.com; *The Illustrated Book of World Rankings.*

Organisation for Economic Cooperation and Development (OECD), 2 rue Andre Pascal, F-75775 Paris Cedex 16, France, (Telephone in U.S. (202) 785-6323), (Fax in U.S. (202) 785-0350), www.oecd.org; *OECD Economic Survey - Hungary 2007.*

United Nations Statistics Division, New York, NY 10017, (800) 253-9646, Fax: (212) 963-4116, http://unstats.un.org; *Statistical Yearbook.*

The World Bank, 1818 H Street, NW, Washington, DC 20433, (202) 473-1000, Fax: (202) 477-6391, www.worldbank.org; *World Development Indicators (WDI) 2008.*

HUNGARY - MARRIAGE

M.E. Sharpe, 80 Business Park Drive, Armonk, NY 10504, (800) 541-6563, Fax: (914) 273-2106, www.mesharpe.com; *The Illustrated Book of World Rankings.*

Taylor and Francis Group, An Informa Business, 2 Park Square, Milton Park, Abingdon, Oxford OX14 4RN, United Kingdom, (Dial from U.S. (212) 216-7800), (Fax from U.S. (212) 564-7854), www.tandf.co.uk; *The Europa World Year Book.*

United Nations Statistics Division, New York, NY 10017, (800) 253-9646, Fax: (212) 963-4116, http://unstats.un.org; *Demographic Yearbook; Statistical Yearbook;* and *Trends in Europe and North America: The Statistical Yearbook of the ECE 2005.*

HUNGARY - MEAT PRODUCTION

See HUNGARY - LIVESTOCK

HUNGARY - MILK PRODUCTION

See HUNGARY - DAIRY PROCESSING

HUNGARY - MINERAL INDUSTRIES

Commodity Research Bureau, 330 South Wells Street, Suite 612, Chicago, IL 60606-7110, (800) 621-5271, Fax: (312) 939-4135, www.crbtrader.com; *2006 CRB Commodity Yearbook and CD.*

Eurostat, Batiment Jean Monnet, Rue Alcide de Gasperi, L-2920 Luxembourg, http://epp.eurostat.ec.europa.eu; *Energy - Monthly Statistics* and *Panorama of Energy - 2007 Edition.*

International Energy Agency (IEA), 9, rue de la Federation, 75739 Paris Cedex 15, France, www.iea.org; *Key World Energy Statistics 2007.*

International Lead and Zinc Study Group (ILZSG), Rua Almirante Barroso 38, 5th Floor, Lisbon 1000 - 013, Portugal, www.ilzsg.org; Interactive Statistical Database.

M.E. Sharpe, 80 Business Park Drive, Armonk, NY 10504, (800) 541-6563, Fax: (914) 273-2106, www.mesharpe.com; *The Illustrated Book of World Rankings.*

Organisation for Economic Cooperation and Development (OECD), 2 rue Andre Pascal, F-75775 Paris Cedex 16, France, (Telephone in U.S. (202) 785-6323), (Fax in U.S. (202) 785-0350), www.oecd.org; *OECD Economic Survey - Hungary 2007* and *World Energy Outlook 2007.*

Palgrave Macmillan Ltd., Houndmills, Basingstoke, Hampshire, RG21 6XS, England, (Telephone in U.S. (888) 330-8477), (Fax in U.S. (800) 672-2054), www.palgrave.com; *The Statesman's Yearbook 2008.*

Platts, 2 Penn Plaza, 25th Floor, New York, NY 10121-2298, (212) 904-3070, www.platts.com; *EU Energy.*

Taylor and Francis Group, An Informa Business, 2 Park Square, Milton Park, Abingdon, Oxford OX14 4RN, United Kingdom, (Dial from U.S. (212) 216-7800), (Fax from U.S. (212) 564-7854), www.tandf.co.uk; *The Europa World Year Book.*

United Nations Conference on Trade and Development (UNCTAD), DC2-1120, United Nations, New York, NY 10017, (212) 963-0027, www.unctad.org; *UNCTAD Commodity Yearbook.*

United Nations Statistics Division, New York, NY 10017, (800) 253-9646, Fax: (212) 963-4116, http://unstats.un.org; *Statistical Yearbook.*

HUNGARY - MONEY EXCHANGE RATES

See HUNGARY - FOREIGN EXCHANGE RATES

HUNGARY - MONEY SUPPLY

Economist Intelligence Unit, 111 West 57th Street, New York, NY 10019, (212) 554-0600, Fax: (212) 586-1181, www.eiu.com; *Hungary Country Report.*

International Monetary Fund (IMF), 700 Nineteenth Street, NW, Washington, DC 20431, (202) 623-7000, Fax: (202) 623-4661, www.imf.org; *International Financial Statistics Yearbook 2007.*

Organisation for Economic Cooperation and Development (OECD), 2 rue Andre Pascal, F-75775 Paris Cedex 16, France, (Telephone in U.S. (202) 785-6323), (Fax in U.S. (202) 785-0350), www.oecd.org; *OECD Economic Survey - Hungary 2007.*

Taylor and Francis Group, An Informa Business, 2 Park Square, Milton Park, Abingdon, Oxford OX14 4RN, United Kingdom, (Dial from U.S. (212) 216-7800), (Fax from U.S. (212) 564-7854), www.tandf.co.uk; *The Europa World Year Book.*

The World Bank, 1818 H Street, NW, Washington, DC 20433, (202) 473-1000, Fax: (202) 477-6391,

www.worldbank.org; *Hungary* and *World Development Indicators (WDI) 2008.*

HUNGARY - MONUMENTS AND HISTORIC SITES

UNESCO Institute for Statistics, C.P. 6128 Succursale Centre-Ville, Montreal, Quebec, H3C 3J7 Canada, (Dial from U.S. (514) 343-6880), (Fax from U.S. (514) 343 6882), www.uis.unesco.org; *Statistical Tables.*

HUNGARY - MORTALITY

Central Intelligence Agency, Office of Public Affairs, Washington, DC 20505, (703) 482-0623, Fax: (703) 482-1739, www.cia.gov; *The World Factbook.*

Euromonitor International, Inc., 224 S. Michigan Avenue, Suite 1500, Chicago, IL 60604, (312) 922-1115, Fax: (312) 922-1157, www.euromonitor.com; *The World Economic Factbook 2008.*

Palgrave Macmillan Ltd., Houndmills, Basingstoke, Hampshire, RG21 6XS, England, (Telephone in U.S. (888) 330-8477), (Fax in U.S. (800) 672-2054), www.palgrave.com; *The Statesman's Yearbook 2008.*

Taylor and Francis Group, An Informa Business, 2 Park Square, Milton Park, Abingdon, Oxford OX14 4RN, United Kingdom, (Dial from U.S. (212) 216-7800), (Fax from U.S. (212) 564-7854), www.tandf.co.uk; *The Europa World Year Book.*

UNICEF, 3 United Nations Plaza, New York, NY 10017, (800) 253-9646, Fax: (212) 887-7465, www.unicef.org; *The State of the World's Children 2008.*

United Nations Statistics Division, New York, NY 10017, (800) 253-9646, Fax: (212) 963-4116, http://unstats.un.org; *Demographic Yearbook; Human Development Report 2006; Statistical Yearbook; Trends in Europe and North America: The Statistical Yearbook of the ECE 2005;* and *World Statistics Pocketbook.*

The World Bank, 1818 H Street, NW, Washington, DC 20433, (202) 473-1000, Fax: (202) 477-6391, www.worldbank.org; *The World Bank Atlas 2003-2004; World Development Indicators (WDI) 2008;* and *World Development Report 2008.*

World Health Organization (WHO), Avenue Appia 20, 1211 Geneve 27, Switzerland, (Telephone in U.S. (212) 331-9081), www.who.int; *The WHO Global Atlas of Infectious Diseases* and *World Health Report 2006.*

HUNGARY - MOTION PICTURES

Palgrave Macmillan Ltd., Houndmills, Basingstoke, Hampshire, RG21 6XS, England, (Telephone in U.S. (888) 330-8477), (Fax in U.S. (800) 672-2054), www.palgrave.com; *The Statesman's Yearbook 2008.*

UNESCO Institute for Statistics, C.P. 6128 Succursale Centre-Ville, Montreal, Quebec, H3C 3J7 Canada, (Dial from U.S. (514) 343-6880), (Fax from U.S. (514) 343 6882), www.uis.unesco.org; *Statistical Tables.*

HUNGARY - MOTOR VEHICLES

International Road Federation (IFR), Madison Place, 500 Montgomery Street, 5th Floor, Alexandria, VA 22314, (703) 535-1001, Fax: (703) 535-1007, www.irfnet.org; *World Road Statistics 2006.*

Taylor and Francis Group, An Informa Business, 2 Park Square, Milton Park, Abingdon, Oxford OX14 4RN, United Kingdom, (Dial from U.S. (212) 216-7800), (Fax from U.S. (212) 564-7854), www.tandf.co.uk; *The Europa World Year Book.*

United Nations Statistics Division, New York, NY 10017, (800) 253-9646, Fax: (212) 963-4116, http://unstats.un.org; *Statistical Yearbook.*

HUNGARY - MUSEUMS

M.E. Sharpe, 80 Business Park Drive, Armonk, NY 10504, (800) 541-6563, Fax: (914) 273-2106, www.mesharpe.com; *The Illustrated Book of World Rankings.*

UNESCO Institute for Statistics, C.P. 6128 Succursale Centre-Ville, Montreal, Quebec, H3C 3J7 Canada, (Dial from U.S. (514) 343-6880), (Fax from U.S. (514) 343 6882), www.uis.unesco.org; *Statistical Tables.*

HUNGARY - NATIONAL INCOME

United Nations Statistics Division, New York, NY 10017, (800) 253-9646, Fax: (212) 963-4116, http://unstats.un.org; *Statistical Yearbook.*

HUNGARY - NATURAL GAS PRODUCTION

See HUNGARY - MINERAL INDUSTRIES

HUNGARY - NUTRITION

United Nations Food and Agricultural Organization (FAO), Viale delle Terme di Caracalla, 00100 Rome, Italy, (Dial from U.S. (202) 653-2400), (Fax from U.S. (202) 653 5760), www.fao.org; *The State of Food and Agriculture (SOFA) 2006.*

HUNGARY - OATS PRODUCTION

See HUNGARY - CROPS

HUNGARY - OLDER PEOPLE

M.E. Sharpe, 80 Business Park Drive, Armonk, NY 10504, (800) 541-6563, Fax: (914) 273-2106, www.mesharpe.com; *The Illustrated Book of World Rankings.*

HUNGARY - PAPER

See HUNGARY - FORESTS AND FORESTRY

HUNGARY - PEANUT PRODUCTION

See HUNGARY - CROPS

HUNGARY - PERIODICALS

UNESCO Institute for Statistics, C.P. 6128 Succursale Centre-Ville, Montreal, Quebec, H3C 3J7 Canada, (Dial from U.S. (514) 343-6880), (Fax from U.S. (514) 343 6882), www.uis.unesco.org; *Statistical Tables.*

HUNGARY - PESTICIDES

United Nations Food and Agricultural Organization (FAO), Viale delle Terme di Caracalla, 00100 Rome, Italy, (Dial from U.S. (202) 653-2400), (Fax from U.S. (202) 653 5760), www.fao.org; *The State of Food and Agriculture (SOFA) 2006.*

HUNGARY - PETROLEUM INDUSTRY AND TRADE

Euromonitor International, Inc., 224 S. Michigan Avenue, Suite 1500, Chicago, IL 60604, (312) 922-1115, Fax: (312) 922-1157, www.euromonitor.com; *European Marketing Data and Statistics 2008.*

International Energy Agency (IEA), 9, rue de la Federation, 75739 Paris Cedex 15, France, www.iea.org; *Key World Energy Statistics 2007.*

M.E. Sharpe, 80 Business Park Drive, Armonk, NY 10504, (800) 541-6563, Fax: (914) 273-2106, www.mesharpe.com; *The Illustrated Book of World Rankings.*

Organisation for Economic Cooperation and Development (OECD), 2 rue Andre Pascal, F-75775 Paris Cedex 16, France, (Telephone in U.S. (202) 785-6323), (Fax in U.S. (202) 785-0350), www.oecd.org; *World Energy Outlook 2007.*

Palgrave Macmillan Ltd., Houndmills, Basingstoke, Hampshire, RG21 6XS, England, (Telephone in U.S. (888) 330-8477), (Fax in U.S. (800) 672-2054), www.palgrave.com; *The Statesman's Yearbook 2008.*

PennWell Corporation, 1421 South Sheridan Road, Tulsa, OK 74112, (918) 835-3161, www.pennwell.com; *International Petroleum Encyclopedia 2007.*

U.S. Department of Energy (DOE), Energy Information Administration (EIA), 1000 Independence Avenue, SW, Washington, DC 20585, (202) 586-8800, www.eia.doe.gov; *International Energy Annual 2004* and *International Energy Outlook 2006.*

United Nations Conference on Trade and Development (UNCTAD), DC2-1120, United Nations, New York, NY 10017, (212) 963-0027, www.unctad.org; *UNCTAD Commodity Yearbook.*

United Nations Food and Agricultural Organization (FAO), Viale delle Terme di Caracalla, 00100 Rome, Italy, (Dial from U.S. (202) 653-2400), (Fax from U.S. (202) 653 5760), www.fao.org; *The State of Food and Agriculture (SOFA) 2006.*

United Nations Statistics Division, New York, NY 10017, (800) 253-9646, Fax: (212) 963-4116, http://unstats.un.org; *Statistical Yearbook* and *Trends in Europe and North America: The Statistical Yearbook of the ECE 2005.*

HUNGARY - PIPELINES

United Nations Statistics Division, New York, NY 10017, (800) 253-9646, Fax: (212) 963-4116, http://unstats.un.org; *Annual Bulletin of Transport Statistics for Europe and North America 2004.*

HUNGARY - PLASTICS INDUSTRY AND TRADE

United Nations Statistics Division, New York, NY 10017, (800) 253-9646, Fax: (212) 963-4116, http://unstats.un.org; *Statistical Yearbook.*

HUNGARY - POLITICAL SCIENCE

Central Intelligence Agency, Office of Public Affairs, Washington, DC 20505, (703) 482-0623, Fax: (703) 482-1739, www.cia.gov; *The World Factbook.*

International Monetary Fund (IMF), 700 Nineteenth Street, NW, Washington, DC 20431, (202) 623-7000, Fax: (202) 623-4661, www.imf.org; *International Financial Statistics Yearbook 2007.*

Palgrave Macmillan Ltd., Houndmills, Basingstoke, Hampshire, RG21 6XS, England, (Telephone in U.S. (888) 330-8477), (Fax in U.S. (800) 672-2054), www.palgrave.com; *The Statesman's Yearbook 2008.*

Taylor and Francis Group, An Informa Business, 2 Park Square, Milton Park, Abingdon, Oxford OX14 4RN, United Kingdom, (Dial from U.S. (212) 216-7800), (Fax from U.S. (212) 564-7854), www.tandf.co.uk; *The Europa World Year Book.*

United Nations Statistics Division, New York, NY 10017, (800) 253-9646, Fax: (212) 963-4116, http://unstats.un.org; *National Accounts Statistics: Compendium of Income Distribution Statistics* and *Statistical Yearbook.*

The World Bank, 1818 H Street, NW, Washington, DC 20433, (202) 473-1000, Fax: (202) 477-6391, www.worldbank.org; *World Development Indicators (WDI) 2008* and *World Development Report 2008.*

HUNGARY - POPULATION

Banque de France, 48 rue Croix des Petits champs, 75001 Paris, France, www.banque-france.fr/home.htm; *Key Data for the Euro Area.*

Central Intelligence Agency, Office of Public Affairs, Washington, DC 20505, (703) 482-0623, Fax: (703) 482-1739, www.cia.gov; *The World Factbook.*

Economist Intelligence Unit, 111 West 57th Street, New York, NY 10019, (212) 554-0600, Fax: (212) 586-1181, www.eiu.com; *Hungary Country Report.*

Euromonitor International, Inc., 224 S. Michigan Avenue, Suite 1500, Chicago, IL 60604, (312) 922-1115, Fax: (312) 922-1157, www.euromonitor.com; *European Marketing Data and Statistics 2008* and *The World Economic Factbook 2008.*

Eurostat, Batiment Jean Monnet, Rue Alcide de Gasperi, L-2920 Luxembourg, http://epp.eurostat.ec.europa.eu; *The Life of Women and Men in Europe - A Statistical Portrait.*

Federal Statistical Office Germany, D-65180 Wiesbaden, Germany, www.destatis.de; *Hungary 2005.*

International Labour Office, I.L.O. Publications, 4 route des Morillons, CH-1211 Geneva 22, Switzerland, (Telephone in U.S. (202) 653-7652), (Fax in U.S. (202) 653-7687), www.ilo.org; *Yearbook of Labour Statistics 2006.*

M.E. Sharpe, 80 Business Park Drive, Armonk, NY 10504, (800) 541-6563, Fax: (914) 273-2106, www.mesharpe.com; *The Illustrated Book of World Rankings.*

Organisation for Economic Cooperation and Development (OECD), 2 rue Andre Pascal, F-75775 Paris Cedex 16, France, (Telephone in U.S. (202) 785-6323), (Fax in U.S. (202) 785-0350), www.oecd.org; *Labour Force Statistics: 1986-2005, 2007 Edition.*

Palgrave Macmillan Ltd., Houndmills, Basingstoke, Hampshire, RG21 6XS, England, (Telephone in U.S. (888) 330-8477), (Fax in U.S. (800) 672-2054), www.palgrave.com; *The Statesman's Yearbook 2008.*

Taylor and Francis Group, An Informa Business, 2 Park Square, Milton Park, Abingdon, Oxford OX14 4RN, United Kingdom, (Dial from U.S. (212) 216-7800), (Fax from U.S. (212) 564-7854), www.tandf.co.uk; *The Europa World Year Book.*

U.S. Department of State (DOS), 2201 C Street NW, Washington, DC 20520, (202) 647-4000, www.state.gov; *World Military Expenditures and Arms Transfers (WMEAT).*

UNESCO Institute for Statistics, C.P. 6128 Succursale Centre-Ville, Montreal, Quebec, H3C 3J7 Canada, (Dial from U.S. (514) 343-6880), (Fax from U.S. (514) 343 6882), www.uis.unesco.org; *Statistical Tables.*

United Nations Food and Agricultural Organization (FAO), Viale delle Terme di Caracalla, 00100 Rome, Italy, (Dial from U.S. (202) 653-2400), (Fax from U.S. (202) 653 5760), www.fao.org; *FAO Production Yearbook 2002.*

United Nations Statistics Division, New York, NY 10017, (800) 253-9646, Fax: (212) 963-4116, http://unstats.un.org; *Demographic Yearbook; Human Development Report 2006; Statistical Yearbook; Trends in Europe and North America: The Statistical Yearbook of the ECE 2005;* and *World Statistics Pocketbook.*

The World Bank, 1818 H Street, NW, Washington, DC 20433, (202) 473-1000, Fax: (202) 477-6391, www.worldbank.org; *Hungary; The World Bank Atlas 2003-2004;* and *World Development Report 2008.*

World Health Organization (WHO), Avenue Appia 20, 1211 Geneve 27, Switzerland, (Telephone in U.S. (212) 331-9081), www.who.int; *World Health Report 2006.*

HUNGARY - POPULATION DENSITY

Central Intelligence Agency, Office of Public Affairs, Washington, DC 20505, (703) 482-0623, Fax: (703) 482-1739, www.cia.gov; *The World Factbook.*

Euromonitor International, Inc., 224 S. Michigan Avenue, Suite 1500, Chicago, IL 60604, (312) 922-1115, Fax: (312) 922-1157, www.euromonitor.com; *The World Economic Factbook 2008.*

M.E. Sharpe, 80 Business Park Drive, Armonk, NY 10504, (800) 541-6563, Fax: (914) 273-2106, www.mesharpe.com; *The Illustrated Book of World Rankings.*

Palgrave Macmillan Ltd., Houndmills, Basingstoke, Hampshire, RG21 6XS, England, (Telephone in U.S. (888) 330-8477), (Fax in U.S. (800) 672-2054), www.palgrave.com; *The Statesman's Yearbook 2008.*

Taylor and Francis Group, An Informa Business, 2 Park Square, Milton Park, Abingdon, Oxford OX14 4RN, United Kingdom, (Dial from U.S. (212) 216-7800), (Fax from U.S. (212) 564-7854), www.tandf.co.uk; *The Europa World Year Book.*

UNESCO Institute for Statistics, C.P. 6128 Succursale Centre-Ville, Montreal, Quebec, H3C 3J7 Canada, (Dial from U.S. (514) 343-6880), (Fax from U.S. (514) 343 6882), www.uis.unesco.org; *Statistical Tables.*

United Nations Food and Agricultural Organization (FAO), Viale delle Terme di Caracalla, 00100 Rome, Italy, (Dial from U.S. (202) 653-2400), (Fax from U.S. (202) 653 5760), www.fao.org; *The State of Food and Agriculture (SOFA) 2006.*

United Nations Statistics Division, New York, NY 10017, (800) 253-9646, Fax: (212) 963-4116, http://unstats.un.org; *Statistical Yearbook* and *Trends in Europe and North America: The Statistical Yearbook of the ECE 2005.*

The World Bank, 1818 H Street, NW, Washington, DC 20433, (202) 473-1000, Fax: (202) 477-6391, www.worldbank.org; *Hungary* and *World Development Report 2008.*

HUNGARY - POSTAL SERVICE

M.E. Sharpe, 80 Business Park Drive, Armonk, NY 10504, (800) 541-6563, Fax: (914) 273-2106, www.mesharpe.com; *The Illustrated Book of World Rankings.*

United Nations Statistics Division, New York, NY 10017, (800) 253-9646, Fax: (212) 963-4116, http://unstats.un.org; *Statistical Yearbook* and *Trends in Europe and North America: The Statistical Yearbook of the ECE 2005.*

HUNGARY - POWER RESOURCES

Euromonitor International, Inc., 224 S. Michigan Avenue, Suite 1500, Chicago, IL 60604, (312) 922-1115, Fax: (312) 922-1157, www.euromonitor.com; *European Marketing Data and Statistics 2008; The World Economic Factbook 2008;* and *World Marketing Data and Statistics.*

M.E. Sharpe, 80 Business Park Drive, Armonk, NY 10504, (800) 541-6563, Fax: (914) 273-2106, www.mesharpe.com; *The Illustrated Book of World Rankings.*

Organisation for Economic Cooperation and Development (OECD), 2 rue Andre Pascal, F-75775 Paris Cedex 16, France, (Telephone in U.S. (202) 785-6323), (Fax in U.S. (202) 785-0350), www.oecd.org; *World Energy Outlook 2007.*

Palgrave Macmillan Ltd., Houndmills, Basingstoke, Hampshire, RG21 6XS, England, (Telephone in U.S. (888) 330-8477), (Fax in U.S. (800) 672-2054), www.palgrave.com; *The Statesman's Yearbook 2008.*

Platts, 2 Penn Plaza, 25th Floor, New York, NY 10121-2298, (212) 904-3070, www.platts.com; *Energy Economist* and *European Power Daily.*

U.S. Department of Energy (DOE), Energy Information Administration (EIA), 1000 Independence Avenue, SW, Washington, DC 20585, (202) 586-8800, www.eia.doe.gov; *International Energy Annual 2004* and *International Energy Outlook 2006.*

United Nations Food and Agricultural Organization (FAO), Viale delle Terme di Caracalla, 00100 Rome, Italy, (Dial from U.S. (202) 653-2400), (Fax from U.S. (202) 653 5760), www.fao.org; *The State of Food and Agriculture (SOFA) 2006.*

United Nations Statistics Division, New York, NY 10017, (800) 253-9646, Fax: (212) 963-4116, http://unstats.un.org; *Energy Statistics Yearbook 2003; Human Development Report 2006; Statistical Yearbook; Trends in Europe and North America: The Statistical Yearbook of the ECE 2005;* and *World Statistics Pocketbook.*

The World Bank, 1818 H Street, NW, Washington, DC 20433, (202) 473-1000, Fax: (202) 477-6391, www.worldbank.org; *The World Bank Atlas 2003-2004* and *World Development Report 2008.*

HUNGARY - PRICES

Euromonitor International, Inc., 224 S. Michigan Avenue, Suite 1500, Chicago, IL 60604, (312) 922-1115, Fax: (312) 922-1157, www.euromonitor.com; *European Marketing Data and Statistics 2008* and *World Marketing Data and Statistics.*

International Labour Office, I.L.O. Publications, 4 route des Morillons, CH-1211 Geneva 22, Switzerland, (Telephone in U.S. (202) 653-7652), (Fax in U.S. (202) 653-7687), www.ilo.org; *Yearbook of Labour Statistics 2006.*

International Lead and Zinc Study Group (ILZSG), Rua Almirante Barroso 38, 5th Floor, Lisbon 1000 - 013, Portugal, www.ilzsg.org; Interactive Statistical Database.

International Monetary Fund (IMF), 700 Nineteenth Street, NW, Washington, DC 20431, (202) 623-7000, Fax: (202) 623-4661, www.imf.org; *International Financial Statistics Yearbook 2007.*

M.E. Sharpe, 80 Business Park Drive, Armonk, NY 10504, (800) 541-6563, Fax: (914) 273-2106, www.mesharpe.com; *The Illustrated Book of World Rankings.*

United Nations Food and Agricultural Organization (FAO), Viale delle Terme di Caracalla, 00100 Rome, Italy, (Dial from U.S. (202) 653-2400), (Fax from U.S. (202) 653 5760), www.fao.org; *FAO Production Yearbook 2002* and *The State of Food and Agriculture (SOFA) 2006.*

The World Bank, 1818 H Street, NW, Washington, DC 20433, (202) 473-1000, Fax: (202) 477-6391, www.worldbank.org; *Hungary.*

HUNGARY - PROFESSIONS

UNESCO Institute for Statistics, C.P. 6128 Succursale Centre-Ville, Montreal, Quebec, H3C 3J7 Canada, (Dial from U.S. (514) 343-6880), (Fax from U.S. (514) 343 6882), www.uis.unesco.org; *Statistical Tables.*

United Nations Statistics Division, New York, NY 10017, (800) 253-9646, Fax: (212) 963-4116, http://unstats.un.org; *Statistical Yearbook.*

HUNGARY - PUBLIC HEALTH

Euromonitor International, Inc., 224 S. Michigan Avenue, Suite 1500, Chicago, IL 60604, (312) 922-1115, Fax: (312) 922-1157, www.euromonitor.com; *World Health Databook 2007/2008* and *World Marketing Data and Statistics.*

Health and Consumer Protection Directorate-General, European Commission, B-1049 Brussels, Belgium, http://ec.europa.eu/dgs/health_consumer/index_en.htm; *Injuries in the European Union: Statistics Summary 2002-2004.*

M.E. Sharpe, 80 Business Park Drive, Armonk, NY 10504, (800) 541-6563, Fax: (914) 273-2106, www.mesharpe.com; *The Illustrated Book of World Rankings.*

Palgrave Macmillan Ltd., Houndmills, Basingstoke, Hampshire, RG21 6XS, England, (Telephone in U.S. (888) 330-8477), (Fax in U.S. (800) 672-2054), www.palgrave.com; *The Statesman's Yearbook 2008.*

Robert Koch Institute, Nordufer 20, D 13353 Berlin, Germany, www.rki.de; *EUVAC-NET Report: Pertussis-Surveillance 1998-2002.*

UNICEF, 3 United Nations Plaza, New York, NY 10017, (800) 253-9646, Fax: (212) 887-7465, www.unicef.org; *The State of the World's Children 2008.*

United Nations Statistics Division, New York, NY 10017, (800) 253-9646, Fax: (212) 963-4116, http://unstats.un.org; *Human Development Report 2006; Statistical Yearbook;* and *Trends in Europe and North America: The Statistical Yearbook of the ECE 2005.*

The World Bank, 1818 H Street, NW, Washington, DC 20433, (202) 473-1000, Fax: (202) 477-6391, www.worldbank.org; *Hungary* and *World Development Report 2008.*

World Health Organization (WHO), Avenue Appia 20, 1211 Geneve 27, Switzerland, (Telephone in U.S. (212) 331-9081), www.who.int; The WHO Global Atlas of Infectious Diseases and *World Health Report 2006.*

HUNGARY - PUBLISHERS AND PUBLISHING

Palgrave Macmillan Ltd., Houndmills, Basingstoke, Hampshire, RG21 6XS, England, (Telephone in U.S. (888) 330-8477), (Fax in U.S. (800) 672-2054), www.palgrave.com; *The Statesman's Yearbook 2008.*

Taylor and Francis Group, An Informa Business, 2 Park Square, Milton Park, Abingdon, Oxford OX14 4RN, United Kingdom, (Dial from U.S. (212) 216-7800), (Fax from U.S. (212) 564-7854), www.tandf.co.uk; *The Europa World Year Book.*

UNESCO Institute for Statistics, C.P. 6128 Succursale Centre-Ville, Montreal, Quebec, H3C 3J7

Canada, (Dial from U.S. (514) 343-6880), (Fax from U.S. (514) 343 6882), www.uis.unesco.org; *Statistical Tables.*

United Nations Statistics Division, New York, NY 10017, (800) 253-9646, Fax: (212) 963-4116, http://unstats.un.org; *Trends in Europe and North America: The Statistical Yearbook of the ECE 2005.*

HUNGARY - RADIO - RECEIVERS AND RECEPTION

Palgrave Macmillan Ltd., Houndmills, Basingstoke, Hampshire, RG21 6XS, England, (Telephone in U.S. (888) 330-8477), (Fax in U.S. (800) 672-2054), www.palgrave.com; *The Statesman's Yearbook 2008.*

United Nations Statistics Division, New York, NY 10017, (800) 253-9646, Fax: (212) 963-4116, http://unstats.un.org; *Statistical Yearbook.*

HUNGARY - RAILROADS

Euromonitor International, Inc., 224 S. Michigan Avenue, Suite 1500, Chicago, IL 60604, (312) 922-1115, Fax: (312) 922-1157, www.euromonitor.com; *European Marketing Data and Statistics 2008.*

Jane's Information Group, 110 North Royal Street, Suite 200, Alexandria, VA 22314, (703) 683-3700, Fax: (800) 836-0297, www.janes.com; *Jane's World Railways.*

Palgrave Macmillan Ltd., Houndmills, Basingstoke, Hampshire, RG21 6XS, England, (Telephone in U.S. (888) 330-8477), (Fax in U.S. (800) 672-2054), www.palgrave.com; *The Statesman's Yearbook 2008.*

Taylor and Francis Group, An Informa Business, 2 Park Square, Milton Park, Abingdon, Oxford OX14 4RN, United Kingdom, (Dial from U.S. (212) 216-7800), (Fax from U.S. (212) 564-7854), www.tandf.co.uk; *The Europa World Year Book.*

United Nations Statistics Division, New York, NY 10017, (800) 253-9646, Fax: (212) 963-4116, http://unstats.un.org; *Annual Bulletin of Transport Statistics for Europe and North America 2004; Statistical Yearbook;* and *Trends in Europe and North America: The Statistical Yearbook of the ECE 2005.*

HUNGARY - RELIGION

Central Intelligence Agency, Office of Public Affairs, Washington, DC 20505, (703) 482-0623, Fax: (703) 482-1739, www.cia.gov; *The World Factbook.*

M.E. Sharpe, 80 Business Park Drive, Armonk, NY 10504, (800) 541-6563, Fax: (914) 273-2106, www.mesharpe.com; *The Illustrated Book of World Rankings.*

Palgrave Macmillan Ltd., Houndmills, Basingstoke, Hampshire, RG21 6XS, England, (Telephone in U.S. (888) 330-8477), (Fax in U.S. (800) 672-2054), www.palgrave.com; *The Statesman's Yearbook 2008.*

HUNGARY - RENT CHARGES

International Labour Office, I.L.O. Publications, 4 route des Morillons, CH-1211 Geneva 22, Switzerland, (Telephone in U.S. (202) 653-7652), (Fax in U.S. (202) 653-7687), www.ilo.org; *Yearbook of Labour Statistics 2006.*

HUNGARY - RESERVES (ACCOUNTING)

The World Bank, 1818 H Street, NW, Washington, DC 20433, (202) 473-1000, Fax: (202) 477-6391, www.worldbank.org; *World Development Indicators (WDI) 2008.*

HUNGARY - RETAIL TRADE

Banque de France, 48 rue Croix des Petits champs, 75001 Paris, France, www.banque-france.fr/home.htm; *Monthly Business Survey Overview.*

Euromonitor International, Inc., 224 S. Michigan Avenue, Suite 1500, Chicago, IL 60604, (312) 922-1115, Fax: (312) 922-1157, www.euromonitor.com; *Retail Trade International 2007* and *World Marketing Data and Statistics.*

United Nations Statistics Division, New York, NY 10017, (800) 253-9646, Fax: (212) 963-4116, http://unstats.un.org; *Statistical Yearbook.*

HUNGARY - RICE PRODUCTION

See HUNGARY - CROPS

HUNGARY - ROADS

Central Intelligence Agency, Office of Public Affairs, Washington, DC 20505, (703) 482-0623, Fax: (703) 482-1739, www.cia.gov; *The World Factbook.*

International Road Federation (IFR), Madison Place, 500 Montgomery Street, 5th Floor, Alexandria, VA 22314, (703) 535-1001, Fax: (703) 535-1007, www.irfnet.org; *World Road Statistics 2006.*

Palgrave Macmillan Ltd., Houndmills, Basingstoke, Hampshire, RG21 6XS, England, (Telephone in U.S. (888) 330-8477), (Fax in U.S. (800) 672-2054), www.palgrave.com; *The Statesman's Yearbook 2008.*

United Nations Statistics Division, New York, NY 10017, (800) 253-9646, Fax: (212) 963-4116, http://unstats.un.org; *Annual Bulletin of Transport Statistics for Europe and North America 2004* and *Trends in Europe and North America: The Statistical Yearbook of the ECE 2005.*

HUNGARY - RUBBER INDUSTRY AND TRADE

International Rubber Study Group (IRSG), 1st Floor, Heron House, 109/115 Wembley Hill Road, Wembley, Middlesex HA9 8DA, United Kingdom, www.rubberstudy.com; *Rubber Statistical Bulletin; Summary of World Rubber Statistics 2005; World Rubber Statistics Handbook (Volume 6, 1975-2001);* and *World Rubber Statistics Historic Handbook.*

M.E. Sharpe, 80 Business Park Drive, Armonk, NY 10504, (800) 541-6563, Fax: (914) 273-2106, www.mesharpe.com; *The Illustrated Book of World Rankings.*

United Nations Statistics Division, New York, NY 10017, (800) 253-9646, Fax: (212) 963-4116, http://unstats.un.org; *Statistical Yearbook.*

HUNGARY - RYE PRODUCTION

See HUNGARY - CROPS

HUNGARY - SHEEP

See HUNGARY - LIVESTOCK

HUNGARY - SHIPPING

Palgrave Macmillan Ltd., Houndmills, Basingstoke, Hampshire, RG21 6XS, England, (Telephone in U.S. (888) 330-8477), (Fax in U.S. (800) 672-2054), www.palgrave.com; *The Statesman's Yearbook 2008.*

Taylor and Francis Group, An Informa Business, 2 Park Square, Milton Park, Abingdon, Oxford OX14 4RN, United Kingdom, (Dial from U.S. (212) 216-7800), (Fax from U.S. (212) 564-7854), www.tandf.co.uk; *The Europa World Year Book.*

U.S. Department of Transportation (DOT), Maritime Administration (MARAD), West Building, Southeast Federal Center, 1200 New Jersey Avenue, SE, Washington, DC 20590, (800) 99-MARAD, www.marad.dot.gov; *World Merchant Fleet 2005.*

United Nations Statistics Division, New York, NY 10017, (800) 253-9646, Fax: (212) 963-4116, http://unstats.un.org; *Annual Bulletin of Transport Statistics for Europe and North America 2004.*

HUNGARY - SILVER PRODUCTION

See HUNGARY - MINERAL INDUSTRIES

HUNGARY - SOCIAL ECOLOGY

M.E. Sharpe, 80 Business Park Drive, Armonk, NY 10504, (800) 541-6563, Fax: (914) 273-2106, www.mesharpe.com; *The Illustrated Book of World Rankings.*

United Nations Statistics Division, New York, NY 10017, (800) 253-9646, Fax: (212) 963-4116, http://unstats.un.org; *World Statistics Pocketbook.*

HUNGARY - SOCIAL SECURITY

Palgrave Macmillan Ltd., Houndmills, Basingstoke, Hampshire, RG21 6XS, England, (Telephone in U.S. (888) 330-8477), (Fax in U.S. (800) 672-2054), www.palgrave.com; *The Statesman's Yearbook 2008.*

United Nations Statistics Division, New York, NY 10017, (800) 253-9646, Fax: (212) 963-4116, http://unstats.un.org; *National Accounts Statistics: Compendium of Income Distribution Statistics.*

HUNGARY - SOYBEAN PRODUCTION

See HUNGARY - CROPS

HUNGARY - STEEL PRODUCTION

See HUNGARY - MINERAL INDUSTRIES

HUNGARY - SUGAR PRODUCTION

See HUNGARY - CROPS

HUNGARY - TAXATION

Eurostat, Batiment Jean Monnet, Rue Alcide de Gasperi, L-2920 Luxembourg, http://epp.eurostat.ec.europa.eu; *Taxation Trends in the European Union - Data for the EU Member States and Norway.*

International Road Federation (IFR), Madison Place, 500 Montgomery Street, 5th Floor, Alexandria, VA 22314, (703) 535-1001, Fax: (703) 535-1007, www.irfnet.org; *World Road Statistics 2006.*

Palgrave Macmillan Ltd., Houndmills, Basingstoke, Hampshire, RG21 6XS, England, (Telephone in U.S. (888) 330-8477), (Fax in U.S. (800) 672-2054), www.palgrave.com; *The Statesman's Yearbook 2008.*

Taylor and Francis Group, An Informa Business, 2 Park Square, Milton Park, Abingdon, Oxford OX14 4RN, United Kingdom, (Dial from U.S. (212) 216-7800), (Fax from U.S. (212) 564-7854), www.tandf.co.uk; *The Europa World Year Book.*

The World Bank, 1818 H Street, NW, Washington, DC 20433, (202) 473-1000, Fax: (202) 477-6391, www.worldbank.org; *World Development Indicators (WDI) 2008.*

HUNGARY - TELEPHONE

International Telecommunication Union (ITU), Place des Nations, 1211 Geneva 20, Switzerland, www.itu.int; World Telecommunication Indicators Database.

Palgrave Macmillan Ltd., Houndmills, Basingstoke, Hampshire, RG21 6XS, England, (Telephone in U.S. (888) 330-8477), (Fax in U.S. (800) 672-2054), www.palgrave.com; *The Statesman's Yearbook 2008.*

Taylor and Francis Group, An Informa Business, 2 Park Square, Milton Park, Abingdon, Oxford OX14 4RN, United Kingdom, (Dial from U.S. (212) 216-7800), (Fax from U.S. (212) 564-7854), www.tandf.co.uk; *The Europa World Year Book.*

United Nations Statistics Division, New York, NY 10017, (800) 253-9646, Fax: (212) 963-4116, http://unstats.un.org; *Statistical Yearbook; Trends in Europe and North America: The Statistical Yearbook of the ECE 2005;* and *World Statistics Pocketbook.*

HUNGARY - TEXTILE INDUSTRY

Euromonitor International, Inc., 224 S. Michigan Avenue, Suite 1500, Chicago, IL 60604, (312) 922-1115, Fax: (312) 922-1157, www.euromonitor.com; *Retail Trade International 2007.*

Palgrave Macmillan Ltd., Houndmills, Basingstoke, Hampshire, RG21 6XS, England, (Telephone in U.S. (888) 330-8477), (Fax in U.S. (800) 672-2054), www.palgrave.com; *The Statesman's Yearbook 2008.*

United Nations Conference on Trade and Development (UNCTAD), DC2-1120, United Nations, New York, NY 10017, (212) 963-0027, www.unctad.org; *UNCTAD Commodity Yearbook.*

United Nations Food and Agricultural Organization (FAO), Viale delle Terme di Caracalla, 00100 Rome, Italy, (Dial from U.S. (202) 653-2400), (Fax from U.S. (202) 653 5760), www.fao.org; *FAO Production Yearbook 2002.*

United Nations Statistics Division, New York, NY 10017, (800) 253-9646, Fax: (212) 963-4116, http://unstats.un.org; *Statistical Yearbook.*

HUNGARY - THEATER

UNESCO Institute for Statistics, C.P. 6128 Succursale Centre-Ville, Montreal, Quebec, H3C 3J7 Canada, (Dial from U.S. (514) 343-6880), (Fax from U.S. (514) 343 6882), www.uis.unesco.org; *Statistical Tables.*

HUNGARY - TIN PRODUCTION

See HUNGARY - MINERAL INDUSTRIES

HUNGARY - TIRE INDUSTRY

United Nations Statistics Division, New York, NY 10017, (800) 253-9646, Fax: (212) 963-4116, http://unstats.un.org; *Statistical Yearbook.*

HUNGARY - TOBACCO INDUSTRY

Foreign Agricultural Service (FAS), U.S. Department of Agriculture (USDA), 1400 Independence Avenue, SW, Washington, DC 20250, (202) 720-3935, www.fas.usda.gov; *Tobacco: World Markets and Trade.*

M.E. Sharpe, 80 Business Park Drive, Armonk, NY 10504, (800) 541-6563, Fax: (914) 273-2106, www.mesharpe.com; *The Illustrated Book of World Rankings.*

United Nations Statistics Division, New York, NY 10017, (800) 253-9646, Fax: (212) 963-4116, http://unstats.un.org; *Statistical Yearbook.*

HUNGARY - TOURISM

Euromonitor International, Inc., 224 S. Michigan Avenue, Suite 1500, Chicago, IL 60604, (312) 922-1115, Fax: (312) 922-1157, www.euromonitor.com; *European Marketing Data and Statistics 2008; The World Economic Factbook 2008;* and *World Marketing Data and Statistics.*

Eurostat, Batiment Jean Monnet, Rue Alcide de Gasperi, L-2920 Luxembourg, http://epp.eurostat.ec.europa.eu; *Tourism in Europe: First Results for 2007.*

M.E. Sharpe, 80 Business Park Drive, Armonk, NY 10504, (800) 541-6563, Fax: (914) 273-2106, www.mesharpe.com; *The Illustrated Book of World Rankings.*

Palgrave Macmillan Ltd., Houndmills, Basingstoke, Hampshire, RG21 6XS, England, (Telephone in U.S. (888) 330-8477), (Fax in U.S. (800) 672-2054), www.palgrave.com; *The Statesman's Yearbook 2008.*

Taylor and Francis Group, An Informa Business, 2 Park Square, Milton Park, Abingdon, Oxford OX14 4RN, United Kingdom, (Dial from U.S. (212) 216-7800), (Fax from U.S. (212) 564-7854), www.tandf.co.uk; *The Europa World Year Book.*

United Nations Statistics Division, New York, NY 10017, (800) 253-9646, Fax: (212) 963-4116, http://unstats.un.org; *Statistical Yearbook* and *Trends in Europe and North America: The Statistical Yearbook of the ECE 2005.*

United Nations World Tourism Organization (UNWTO), Capitan Haya 42, 28020 Madrid, Spain, www.world-tourism.org; *Tourism Market Trends 2004 - Europe* and *Yearbook of Tourism Statistics.*

The World Bank, 1818 H Street, NW, Washington, DC 20433, (202) 473-1000, Fax: (202) 477-6391, www.worldbank.org; *Hungary.*

HUNGARY - TRADE

See HUNGARY - INTERNATIONAL TRADE

HUNGARY - TRANSPORTATION

Central Intelligence Agency, Office of Public Affairs, Washington, DC 20505, (703) 482-0623, Fax: (703) 482-1739, www.cia.gov; *The World Factbook.*

Euromonitor International, Inc., 224 S. Michigan Avenue, Suite 1500, Chicago, IL 60604, (312) 922-1115, Fax: (312) 922-1157, www.euromonitor.com; *World Marketing Data and Statistics.*

Eurostat, Batiment Jean Monnet, Rue Alcide de Gasperi, L-2920 Luxembourg, http://epp.eurostat.ec.europa.eu; *Regional Passenger and Freight Air Transport in Europe in 2006* and *Regional Road and Rail Transport Networks.*

M.E. Sharpe, 80 Business Park Drive, Armonk, NY 10504, (800) 541-6563, Fax: (914) 273-2106, www.mesharpe.com; *The Illustrated Book of World Rankings.*

Palgrave Macmillan Ltd., Houndmills, Basingstoke, Hampshire, RG21 6XS, England, (Telephone in U.S. (888) 330-8477), (Fax in U.S. (800) 672-2054), www.palgrave.com; *The Statesman's Yearbook 2008.*

Taylor and Francis Group, An Informa Business, 2 Park Square, Milton Park, Abingdon, Oxford OX14 4RN, United Kingdom, (Dial from U.S. (212) 216-7800), (Fax from U.S. (212) 564-7854), www.tandf.co.uk; *The Europa World Year Book.*

United Nations Statistics Division, New York, NY 10017, (800) 253-9646, Fax: (212) 963-4116, http://unstats.un.org; *Human Development Report 2006* and *Trends in Europe and North America: The Statistical Yearbook of the ECE 2005.*

The World Bank, 1818 H Street, NW, Washington, DC 20433, (202) 473-1000, Fax: (202) 477-6391, www.worldbank.org; *Hungary.*

HUNGARY - TURKEYS

See HUNGARY - LIVESTOCK

HUNGARY - UNEMPLOYMENT

Central Intelligence Agency, Office of Public Affairs, Washington, DC 20505, (703) 482-0623, Fax: (703) 482-1739, www.cia.gov; *The World Factbook.*

Euromonitor International, Inc., 224 S. Michigan Avenue, Suite 1500, Chicago, IL 60604, (312) 922-1115, Fax: (312) 922-1157, www.euromonitor.com; *European Marketing Data and Statistics 2008.*

International Labour Office, I.L.O. Publications, 4 route des Morillons, CH-1211 Geneva 22, Switzerland, (Telephone in U.S. (202) 653-7652), (Fax in U.S. (202) 653-7687), www.ilo.org; *Yearbook of Labour Statistics 2006.*

Organisation for Economic Cooperation and Development (OECD), 2 rue Andre Pascal, F-75775 Paris Cedex 16, France, (Telephone in U.S. (202) 785-6323), (Fax in U.S. (202) 785-0350), www.oecd.org; *Labour Force Statistics: 1986-2005, 2007 Edition; OECD Composite Leading Indicators (CLIs), Updated September 2007;* and *OECD Economic Survey - Hungary 2007.*

Palgrave Macmillan Ltd., Houndmills, Basingstoke, Hampshire, RG21 6XS, England, (Telephone in U.S. (888) 330-8477), (Fax in U.S. (800) 672-2054), www.palgrave.com; *The Statesman's Yearbook 2008.*

United Nations Statistics Division, New York, NY 10017, (800) 253-9646, Fax: (212) 963-4116, http://unstats.un.org; *Trends in Europe and North America: The Statistical Yearbook of the ECE 2005.*

HUNGARY - VITAL STATISTICS

Palgrave Macmillan Ltd., Houndmills, Basingstoke, Hampshire, RG21 6XS, England, (Telephone in U.S. (888) 330-8477), (Fax in U.S. (800) 672-2054), www.palgrave.com; *The Statesman's Yearbook 2008.*

United Nations Statistics Division, New York, NY 10017, (800) 253-9646, Fax: (212) 963-4116, http://unstats.un.org; *Statistical Yearbook.*

World Health Organization (WHO), Avenue Appia 20, 1211 Geneve 27, Switzerland, (Telephone in U.S. (212) 331-9081), www.who.int; *World Health Report 2006.*

HUNGARY - WAGES

Euromonitor International, Inc., 224 S. Michigan Avenue, Suite 1500, Chicago, IL 60604, (312) 922-1115, Fax: (312) 922-1157, www.euromonitor.com; *European Marketing Data and Statistics 2008.*

International Labour Office, I.L.O. Publications, 4 route des Morillons, CH-1211 Geneva 22, Switzerland, (Telephone in U.S. (202) 653-7652), (Fax in U.S. (202) 653-7687), www.ilo.org; *Yearbook of Labour Statistics 2006.*

Organisation for Economic Cooperation and Development (OECD), 2 rue Andre Pascal, F-75775 Paris Cedex 16, France, (Telephone in U.S. (202) 785-6323), (Fax in U.S. (202) 785-0350), www.oecd.org; *ICT Sector Data and Metadata by Country.*

United Nations Statistics Division, New York, NY 10017, (800) 253-9646, Fax: (212) 963-4116, http://unstats.un.org; *Statistical Yearbook.*

The World Bank, 1818 H Street, NW, Washington, DC 20433, (202) 473-1000, Fax: (202) 477-6391, www.worldbank.org; *Hungary.*

HUNGARY - WALNUT PRODUCTION

See HUNGARY - CROPS

HUNGARY - WATERWAYS

United Nations Statistics Division, New York, NY 10017, (800) 253-9646, Fax: (212) 963-4116, http://unstats.un.org; *Annual Bulletin of Transport Statistics for Europe and North America 2004.*

HUNGARY - WEATHER

See HUNGARY - CLIMATE

HUNGARY - WHEAT PRODUCTION

See HUNGARY - CROPS

HUNGARY - WHOLESALE PRICE INDEXES

United Nations Statistics Division, New York, NY 10017, (800) 253-9646, Fax: (212) 963-4116, http://unstats.un.org; *Statistical Yearbook.*

HUNGARY - WHOLESALE TRADE

United Nations Statistics Division, New York, NY 10017, (800) 253-9646, Fax: (212) 963-4116, http://unstats.un.org; *Statistical Yearbook.*

HUNGARY - WINE PRODUCTION

See HUNGARY - BEVERAGE INDUSTRY

HUNGARY - WOOD AND WOOD PULP

See HUNGARY - FORESTS AND FORESTRY

HUNGARY - WOOL PRODUCTION

See HUNGARY - TEXTILE INDUSTRY

HUNGARY - YARN PRODUCTION

See HUNGARY - TEXTILE INDUSTRY

HUNGARY - ZINC AND ZINC ORE

See HUNGARY - MINERAL INDUSTRIES

HUNGER

Economic Research Service (ERS), U.S. Department of Agriculture (USDA), 1800 M Street, NW, Washington, DC 20036-5831, (202) 694-5050, Fax: (202) 694-5689, www.ers.usda.gov; *2007 Food Assistance and Nutrition Research Innovation and Development Grants in Economics (RIDGE) Conference; Food Assistance and Nutrition Research Program, Final Report: Fiscal 2007 Activities;* and *What Factors Account for State-to-State Differences in Food Security?*

Food and Nutrition Service (FNS), U.S. Department of Agriculture (USDA), 3101 Park Center Drive, Alexandria, VA 22302, (703) 305-2062, www.fns.usda.gov/fns; *Household Food Security in the United States, 2006.*

World Food Programme, Via C.G.Viola 68, Parco dei Medici, 00148 Rome, Italy, www.wfp.org; *Are We Reaching the Hungry?; Hunger Facts 2006; WFP in 2006; WFP in Africa: 2006 Facts, Figures and Partners; World Hunger Series 2006: Hunger and Learning;* and *World Hunger Series 2007: Hunger and Health.*

HUNTING AND FISHING

National Sporting Goods Association (NSGA), 1601 Feehanville Drive, Suite 300, Mount Prospect, IL

60056, (847) 296-6742, Fax: (847) 391-9827, www.nsga.org; *2006 Sports Participation* and *Ten-Year History of Selected Sports Participation, 1996-2006*.

U.S. Department of the Interior (DOI), Bureau of Land Management (BLM), 1849 C Street, Room 406-LS, Washington, DC 20240, (202) 452-5125, Fax: (202) 452-5124, www.blm.gov; *Public Land Statistics 2005*.

U.S. Department of the Interior (DOI), Fish Wildlife Service (FWS), 1849 C Street, NW, Washington, DC 20240, (800) 344-WILD, www.fws.gov; *2006 National Survey of Fishing, Hunting, and Wildlife-Associated Recreation (FHWAR)*.

HURRICANES

The Brookings Institution, 1775 Massachusetts Avenue, NW, Washington, DC 20036, (202) 797-6000, Fax: (202) 797-6004, www.brook.edu; *Katrina Index: Tracking Variables of Post-Katrina Recovery* and *Special Edition of the Katrina Index: A One-Year Review of Key Indicators of Recovery in Post-Storm New Orleans*.

Center for Research on the Epidemiology of Disasters (CRED), Universite Catholique de Louvain, Ecole de Sante Publique, 30.94 Clos Chapelle-aux-Champs, 1200 Brussels, Belgium, www.cred.be; *An Analytical Review of Selected Data Sets on Natural Disasters and Impacts;* Complex Emergency Database (CE-DAT): A Database on the Human Impact of Complex Emergencies; *EM-DAT: The International Disaster Database; Quality and Accuracy of Disaster Data: A Comparative Analysis of Three Global Data Sets;* and *Thirty Years of Natural Disasters 1974-2003: The Numbers*.

National Center for Children in Poverty (NCCP), 215 W. 125th Street, 3rd Floor, New York, NY 10027, (646) 284-9600, Fax: (646) 284-9623, www.nccp.org; *Child Poverty in 21st Century America* and *Child Poverty in States Hit by Hurricane Katrina*.

National Climatic Data Center (NCDC), National Oceanic and Atmospheric Administration (NOAA), Federal Building, 151 Patton Avenue, Asheville, NC 28801-5001, (828) 271-4800, Fax: (828) 271-4876, www.ncdc.noaa.gov; *Billion Dollar U.S. Weather Disasters, 1980-2007* and *Storm Data 2006*.

National Hurricane Center (NHC), Tropical Analysis and Forecast Branch (TAFB), 11691 SW 17th Street, Miami, FL 33165-2149, (305) 229-4400, www.nhc.noaa.gov/abouttafb.shtml; unpublished data.

National Oceanic and Atmospheric Administration (NOAA), 1401 Constitution Avenue, NW, Room 6217, Washington, DC 20230, (202) 482-6090, Fax: (202) 482-3154, www.noaa.gov; *Economic Statistics for NOAA*.

U.S. Census Bureau, Center for Economic Studies, 4600 Silver Hill Road, Washington DC 20233, (301) 457-1235, www.ces.census.gov; *The Impact of Hurricanes Katrina, Rita and Wilma on Business Establishments: A GIS Approach*.

U.S. Department of Labor (DOL), Bureau of Labor Statistics (BLS), Postal Square Building, 2 Massachusetts Avenue, NE, Washington, DC 20212-0001, (202) 691-5200, Fax: (202) 691-6325, www.bls.gov; *Hurricane Information: Katrina and Rita*.

United Nations Inter-Agency Secretariat of the International Strategy for Disaster Reduction (UN/ISDR), Palais des Nations, CH 1211 Geneva 10, Switzerland, www.unisdr.org; *Disaster Statistics 1991-2005*.

HYDROELECTRIC POWER

Environmental Business International, Inc., 4452 Park Boulevard, Suite 306, San Diego, CA 92116, (619) 295-7685, Fax: (619) 295-5743, www.ebiusa.com; *Environmental Business Journal (EBJ) 2006; Environmental Market Reports;* and *U.S. and Global Environmental Market Data*.

International Energy Agency (IEA), 9, rue de la Federation, 75739 Paris Cedex 15, France, www.iea.org; *Key World Energy Statistics 2007*.

National Hydropower Association (NHA), 1 Massachusetts Avenue, NW, Suite 850, Washington, DC 20001, (202) 682-1700, Fax: (202) 682-9478, www.hydro.org; unpublished data.

U.S. Department of Energy (DOE), Energy Information Administration (EIA), 1000 Independence Avenue, SW, Washington, DC 20585, (202) 586-8800, www.eia.doe.gov; *Renewable Energy Annual 2004*.

U.S. Department of Energy (DOE), Federal Energy Regulatory Commission (FERC), 888 First Street, NE, Washington, DC 20426, (866) 208-3372, www.ferc.gov; *Historical Hydroelectric Generation Compared to 16 Year Average for 1991-2006*.

HYDROELECTRIC POWER - CAPACITY

Edison Electric Institute (EEI), 701 Pennsylvania Avenue, NW, Washington, DC 20004-2696, (202) 508-5000, www.eei.org; *Historical Statistics of the Electric Utility Industry through 1992*.

U.S. Department of Energy (DOE), Energy Information Administration (EIA), 1000 Independence Avenue, SW, Washington, DC 20585, (202) 586-8800, www.eia.doe.gov; *Annual Energy Review 2005; Electric Power Annual;* and unpublished data.

U.S. Department of Energy (DOE), Federal Energy Regulatory Commission (FERC), 888 First Street, NE, Washington, DC 20426, (866) 208-3372, www.ferc.gov; *Historical Hydroelectric Generation Compared to 16 Year Average for 1991-2006* and unpublished data.

HYDROELECTRIC POWER - CONSUMPTION

Edison Electric Institute (EEI), 701 Pennsylvania Avenue, NW, Washington, DC 20004-2696, (202) 508-5000, www.eei.org; *Historical Statistics of the Electric Utility Industry through 1992*.

U.S. Department of Energy (DOE), Energy Information Administration (EIA), 1000 Independence Avenue, SW, Washington, DC 20585, (202) 586-8800, www.eia.doe.gov; *Annual Energy Review 2005; Electric Power Annual; Monthly Energy Review (MER);* and *State Energy Data Report*.

HYDROELECTRIC POWER - PRODUCTION

Edison Electric Institute (EEI), 701 Pennsylvania Avenue, NW, Washington, DC 20004-2696, (202) 508-5000, www.eei.org; *Historical Statistics of the Electric Utility Industry through 1992*.

International Energy Agency (IEA), 9, rue de la Federation, 75739 Paris Cedex 15, France, www.iea.org; *Key World Energy Statistics 2007*.

U.S. Department of Energy (DOE), Energy Information Administration (EIA), 1000 Independence Avenue, SW, Washington, DC 20585, (202) 586-8800, www.eia.doe.gov; *Annual Energy Review 2005; Electric Power Annual; Monthly Energy Review (MER);* and unpublished data.

HYPERTENSION

National Center for Health Statistics (NCHS), Centers for Disease Control and Prevention (CDC), U.S. Department of Health and Human Services (HHS), 3311 Toledo Road, Hyattsville, MD 20782, (866) 232-4636, www.cdc.gov/nchs; *Faststats A to Z* and unpublished data.

HYSTERECTOMY

National Center for Health Statistics (NCHS), Centers for Disease Control and Prevention (CDC), U.S. Department of Health and Human Services (HHS), 3311 Toledo Road, Hyattsville, MD 20782, (866) 232-4636, www.cdc.gov/nchs; *Faststats A to Z* and unpublished data.

RAND Corporation, 1776 Main Street, PO Box 2138, Santa Monica, CA 90407-2138, (310) 393-0411, www.rand.org; *Assessing Symptoms Before Hysterectomy: Is the Medical Record Accurate?*STATISTICS SOURCES, Thirty-second Edition - 2009STATISTICS SOURCES, Thirty-second Edition - 2009

ICE CREAM

Economic Research Service (ERS), U.S. Department of Agriculture (USDA), 1800 M Street, NW, Washington, DC 20036-5831, (202) 694-5050, Fax: (202) 694-5689, www.ers.usda.gov; *Agricultural Outlook* and *Food CPI, Prices, and Expenditures*.

National Agricultural Statistics Service (NASS), U.S. Department of Agriculture (USDA), 1400 Independence Avenue, SW, Washington, DC 20250, (800) 727-9540, Fax: (202) 690-2090, www.nass.usda.gov; *Dairy Products* and *Milk Cows and Milk Production*.

U.S. Bureau of Labor Statistics (BLS), Postal Square Building, 2 Massachusetts Avenue, NE, Washington, DC 20212-0001, (202) 691-5200, Fax: (202) 691-6325, www.bls.gov; *Consumer Price Index Detailed Report*.

ICE HOCKEY

Mediamark Research, Inc., 75 Ninth Avenue, 5th Floor, New York, NY 10011, (212) 884-9200, Fax: (212) 884-9339, www.mediamark.com; MRI+.

National Collegiate Athletic Association (NCAA), 700 West Washington Street, PO Box 6222, Indianapolis, IN 46206-6222, (317) 917-6222, Fax: (317) 917-6888, www.ncaa.org; *1982-2003 Sports Sponsorship and Participation Rates Report*.

National Sporting Goods Association (NSGA), 1601 Feehanville Drive, Suite 300, Mount Prospect, IL 60056, (847) 296-6742, Fax: (847) 391-9827, www.nsga.org; *2006 Sports Participation*.

ICE SKATING

National Sporting Goods Association (NSGA), 1601 Feehanville Drive, Suite 300, Mount Prospect, IL 60056, (847) 296-6742, Fax: (847) 391-9827, www.nsga.org; *2006 Sports Participation*.

ICELAND - NATIONAL STATISTICAL OFFICE

Statistics Iceland, Borgartuni 21a, 150 Reykjavik, Iceland, www.statice.is; National Data Center and *Statistical Series*.

ICELAND - PRIMARY STATISTICS SOURCES

Statistics Iceland, Borgartuni 21a, 150 Reykjavik, Iceland, www.statice.is; *Iceland in Figures 2007-2008; Icelandic Historical Statistics;* and *Statistical Yearbook of Iceland 2007*.

ICELAND - ABORTION

Nordic Council of Ministers, Store Strandstraede 18, DK-1255 Copenhagen K, Denmark, www.norden.org; *Nordic Statistical Yearbook 2004-2006*.

United Nations Statistics Division, New York, NY 10017, (800) 253-9646, Fax: (212) 963-4116, http://unstats.un.org; *Demographic Yearbook* and *Trends in Europe and North America: The Statistical Yearbook of the ECE 2005*.

ICELAND - AGRICULTURAL MACHINERY

United Nations Statistics Division, New York, NY 10017, (800) 253-9646, Fax: (212) 963-4116, http://unstats.un.org; *Statistical Yearbook*.

ICELAND - AGRICULTURE

Economist Intelligence Unit, 111 West 57th Street, New York, NY 10019, (212) 554-0600, Fax: (212) 586-1181, www.eiu.com; *Iceland Country Report*.

Euromonitor International, Inc., 224 S. Michigan Avenue, Suite 1500, Chicago, IL 60604, (312) 922-1115, Fax: (312) 922-1157, www.euromonitor.com; *World Marketing Data and Statistics*.

Eurostat, Batiment Jean Monnet, Rue Alcide de Gasperi, L-2920 Luxembourg, http://epp.eurostat.ec.europa.eu; *EU Agricultural Prices in 2007*.

M.E. Sharpe, 80 Business Park Drive, Armonk, NY 10504, (800) 541-6563, Fax: (914) 273-2106, www.mesharpe.com; *The Illustrated Book of World Rankings*.

Nordic Council of Ministers, Store Strandstraede 18, DK-1255 Copenhagen K, Denmark, www.norden.org; *Nordic Statistical Yearbook 2004-2006*.

Organisation for Economic Cooperation and Development (OECD), 2 rue Andre Pascal, F-75775 Paris Cedex 16, France, (Telephone in U.S. (202) 785-6323), (Fax in U.S. (202) 785-0350), www.oecd.org; *2005 OECD Agricultural Outlook Tables, 1970-2014; OECD Agricultural Outlook: 2007-2016; OECD Economic Survey - Iceland 2008;* and STructural ANalysis (STAN) database.

Palgrave Macmillan Ltd., Houndmills, Basingstoke, Hampshire, RG21 6XS, England, (Telephone in U.S. (888) 330-8477), (Fax in U.S. (800) 672-2054), www.palgrave.com; *The Statesman's Yearbook 2008*.

Taylor and Francis Group, An Informa Business, 2 Park Square, Milton Park, Abingdon, Oxford OX14 4RN, United Kingdom, (Dial from U.S. (212) 216-7800), (Fax from U.S. (212) 564-7854), www.tandf.co.uk; *The Europa World Year Book*.

U.S. Department of State (DOS), 2201 C Street NW, Washington, DC 20520, (202) 647-4000, www.state.gov; *World Military Expenditures and Arms Transfers (WMEAT)*.

United Nations Conference on Trade and Development (UNCTAD), DC2-1120, United Nations, New York, NY 10017, (212) 963-0027, www.unctad.org; *UNCTAD Commodity Yearbook*.

United Nations Food and Agricultural Organization (FAO), Viale delle Terme di Caracalla, 00100 Rome, Italy, (Dial from U.S. (202) 653-2400), (Fax from U.S. (202) 653 5760), www.fao.org; AQUASTAT; *FAO Production Yearbook 2002;* and *The State of Food and Agriculture (SOFA) 2006*.

United Nations Statistics Division, New York, NY 10017, (800) 253-9646, Fax: (212) 963-4116, http://unstats.un.org; *Statistical Yearbook*.

The World Bank, 1818 H Street, NW, Washington, DC 20433, (202) 473-1000, Fax: (202) 477-6391, www.worldbank.org; *Iceland* and *World Development Indicators (WDI) 2008*.

ICELAND - AIRLINES

International Civil Aviation Organization (ICAO), External Relations and Public Information Office (EPO), 999 University Street, Montreal, Quebec H3C 5H7, Canada, (Dial from U.S. (514) 954-8219), (Fax from U.S. (514) 954-6077), www.icao.int; *Civil Aviation Statistics of the World*.

M.E. Sharpe, 80 Business Park Drive, Armonk, NY 10504, (800) 541-6563, Fax: (914) 273-2106, www.mesharpe.com; *The Illustrated Book of World Rankings*.

Nordic Council of Ministers, Store Strandstraede 18, DK-1255 Copenhagen K, Denmark, www.norden.org; *Nordic Statistical Yearbook 2004-2006*.

Organisation for Economic Cooperation and Development (OECD), 2 rue Andre Pascal, F-75775 Paris Cedex 16, France, (Telephone in U.S. (202) 785-6323), (Fax in U.S. (202) 785-0350), www.oecd.org; *Household, Tourism, Travel: Trends, Environmental Impacts and Policy Responses*.

Palgrave Macmillan Ltd., Houndmills, Basingstoke, Hampshire, RG21 6XS, England, (Telephone in U.S. (888) 330-8477), (Fax in U.S. (800) 672-2054), www.palgrave.com; *The Statesman's Yearbook 2008*.

Taylor and Francis Group, An Informa Business, 2 Park Square, Milton Park, Abingdon, Oxford OX14 4RN, United Kingdom, (Dial from U.S. (212) 216-7800), (Fax from U.S. (212) 564-7854), www.tandf.co.uk; *The Europa World Year Book*.

United Nations Statistics Division, New York, NY 10017, (800) 253-9646, Fax: (212) 963-4116, http://unstats.un.org; *Statistical Yearbook*.

ICELAND - AIRPORTS

Central Intelligence Agency, Office of Public Affairs, Washington, DC 20505, (703) 482-0623, Fax: (703) 482-1739, www.cia.gov; *The World Factbook*.

ICELAND - ALUMINUM PRODUCTION

See ICELAND - MINERAL INDUSTRIES

ICELAND - ANIMAL FEEDING

Organisation for Economic Cooperation and Development (OECD), 2 rue Andre Pascal, F-75775 Paris Cedex 16, France, (Telephone in U.S. (202) 785-6323), (Fax in U.S. (202) 785-0350), www.oecd.org; *International Trade by Commodity Statistics (ITCS)*.

United Nations Statistics Division, New York, NY 10017, (800) 253-9646, Fax: (212) 963-4116, http://unstats.un.org; *Statistical Yearbook*.

ICELAND - ARMED FORCES

Central Intelligence Agency, Office of Public Affairs, Washington, DC 20505, (703) 482-0623, Fax: (703) 482-1739, www.cia.gov; *The World Factbook.*

Euromonitor International, Inc., 224 S. Michigan Avenue, Suite 1500, Chicago, IL 60604, (312) 922-1115, Fax: (312) 922-1157, www.euromonitor.com; *World Marketing Data and Statistics.*

International Institute for Strategic Studies (IISS), Arundel House, 13-15 Arundel Street, Temple Place, London WC2R 3DX, England, www.iiss.org; *The Military Balance 2007.*

Nordic Council of Ministers, Store Strandstraede 18, DK-1255 Copenhagen K, Denmark, www.norden.org; *Nordic Statistical Yearbook 2004-2006.*

Palgrave Macmillan Ltd., Houndmills, Basingstoke, Hampshire, RG21 6XS, England, (Telephone in U.S. (888) 330-8477), (Fax in U.S. (800) 672-2054), www.palgrave.com; *The Statesman's Yearbook 2008.*

U.S. Department of State (DOS), 2201 C Street NW, Washington, DC 20520, (202) 647-4000, www.state.gov; *World Military Expenditures and Arms Transfers (WMEAT).*

United Nations Statistics Division, New York, NY 10017, (800) 253-9646, Fax: (212) 963-4116, http://unstats.un.org; *Human Development Report 2006.*

ICELAND - AUTOMOBILE INDUSTRY AND TRADE

Organisation for Economic Cooperation and Development (OECD), 2 rue Andre Pascal, F-75775 Paris Cedex 16, France, (Telephone in U.S. (202) 785-6323), (Fax in U.S. (202) 785-0350), www.oecd.org; *International Trade by Commodity Statistics (ITCS).*

ICELAND - BALANCE OF PAYMENTS

International Monetary Fund (IMF), 700 Nineteenth Street, NW, Washington, DC 20431, (202) 623-7000, Fax: (202) 623-4661, www.imf.org; *Balance of Payments Statistics Newsletter* and *Balance of Payments Statistics Yearbook 2007.*

Nordic Council of Ministers, Store Strandstraede 18, DK-1255 Copenhagen K, Denmark, www.norden.org; *Nordic Statistical Yearbook 2004-2006.*

Organisation for Economic Cooperation and Development (OECD), 2 rue Andre Pascal, F-75775 Paris Cedex 16, France, (Telephone in U.S. (202) 785-6323), (Fax in U.S. (202) 785-0350), www.oecd.org; *Geographical Distribution of Financial Flows to Aid Recipients 2002-2006; OECD Economic Outlook 2008;* and *OECD Economic Survey - Iceland 2008.*

Taylor and Francis Group, An Informa Business, 2 Park Square, Milton Park, Abingdon, Oxford OX14 4RN, United Kingdom, (Dial from U.S. (212) 216-7800), (Fax from U.S. (212) 564-7854), www.tandf.co.uk; *The Europa World Year Book.*

United Nations Conference on Trade and Development (UNCTAD), DC2-1120, United Nations, New York, NY 10017, (212) 963-0027, www.unctad.org; *Handbook of Statistics 2005.*

The World Bank, 1818 H Street, NW, Washington, DC 20433, (202) 473-1000, Fax: (202) 477-6391, www.worldbank.org; *Iceland* and *World Development Indicators (WDI) 2008.*

ICELAND - BANKS AND BANKING

Euromonitor International, Inc., 224 S. Michigan Avenue, Suite 1500, Chicago, IL 60604, (312) 922-1115, Fax: (312) 922-1157, www.euromonitor.com; *World Marketing Data and Statistics.*

International Monetary Fund (IMF), 700 Nineteenth Street, NW, Washington, DC 20431, (202) 623-7000, Fax: (202) 623-4661, www.imf.org; *International Financial Statistics Yearbook 2007.*

M.E. Sharpe, 80 Business Park Drive, Armonk, NY 10504, (800) 541-6563, Fax: (914) 273-2106, www.mesharpe.com; *The Illustrated Book of World Rankings.*

Nordic Council of Ministers, Store Strandstraede 18, DK-1255 Copenhagen K, Denmark, www.norden.org; *Nordic Statistical Yearbook 2004-2006.*

Organisation for Economic Cooperation and Development (OECD), 2 rue Andre Pascal, F-75775 Paris Cedex 16, France, (Telephone in U.S. (202) 785-6323), (Fax in U.S. (202) 785-0350), www.oecd.org; *Financial Market Trends: OECD Periodical; OECD Economic Outlook 2008;* and *OECD Economic Survey - Iceland 2008.*

Palgrave Macmillan Ltd., Houndmills, Basingstoke, Hampshire, RG21 6XS, England, (Telephone in U.S. (888) 330-8477), (Fax in U.S. (800) 672-2054), www.palgrave.com; *The Statesman's Yearbook 2008.*

Taylor and Francis Group, An Informa Business, 2 Park Square, Milton Park, Abingdon, Oxford OX14 4RN, United Kingdom, (Dial from U.S. (212) 216-7800), (Fax from U.S. (212) 564-7854), www.tandf.co.uk; *The Europa World Year Book.*

United Nations Statistics Division, New York, NY 10017, (800) 253-9646, Fax: (212) 963-4116, http://unstats.un.org; *Statistical Yearbook.*

ICELAND - BARLEY PRODUCTION

See ICELAND - CROPS

ICELAND - BEVERAGE INDUSTRY

M.E. Sharpe, 80 Business Park Drive, Armonk, NY 10504, (800) 541-6563, Fax: (914) 273-2106, www.mesharpe.com; *The Illustrated Book of World Rankings.*

United Nations Statistics Division, New York, NY 10017, (800) 253-9646, Fax: (212) 963-4116, http://unstats.un.org; *Statistical Yearbook.*

ICELAND - BONDS

International Monetary Fund (IMF), 700 Nineteenth Street, NW, Washington, DC 20431, (202) 623-7000, Fax: (202) 623-4661, www.imf.org; *Government Finance Statistics Yearbook (2008 Edition).*

Organisation for Economic Cooperation and Development (OECD), 2 rue Andre Pascal, F-75775 Paris Cedex 16, France, (Telephone in U.S. (202) 785-6323), (Fax in U.S. (202) 785-0350), www.oecd.org; *Financial Market Trends: OECD Periodical.*

ICELAND - BROADCASTING

Central Intelligence Agency, Office of Public Affairs, Washington, DC 20505, (703) 482-0623, Fax: (703) 482-1739, www.cia.gov; *The World Factbook.*

Euromonitor International, Inc., 224 S. Michigan Avenue, Suite 1500, Chicago, IL 60604, (312) 922-1115, Fax: (312) 922-1157, www.euromonitor.com; *World Marketing Data and Statistics.*

M.E. Sharpe, 80 Business Park Drive, Armonk, NY 10504, (800) 541-6563, Fax: (914) 273-2106, www.mesharpe.com; *The Illustrated Book of World Rankings.*

Nordic Council of Ministers, Store Strandstraede 18, DK-1255 Copenhagen K, Denmark, www.norden.org; *Nordic Statistical Yearbook 2004-2006.*

Palgrave Macmillan Ltd., Houndmills, Basingstoke, Hampshire, RG21 6XS, England, (Telephone in U.S. (888) 330-8477), (Fax in U.S. (800) 672-2054), www.palgrave.com; *The Statesman's Yearbook 2008.*

UNESCO Institute for Statistics, C.P. 6128 Succursale Centre-Ville, Montreal, Quebec, H3C 3J7 Canada, (Dial from U.S. (514) 343-6880), (Fax from U.S. (514) 343 6882), www.uis.unesco.org; *Statistical Tables.*

United Nations Statistics Division, New York, NY 10017, (800) 253-9646, Fax: (212) 963-4116, http://unstats.un.org; *Trends in Europe and North America: The Statistical Yearbook of the ECE 2005.*

WRTH Publications Limited, PO Box 290, Oxford OX2 7FT, UK, www.wrth.com; *World Radio TV Handbook 2007.*

ICELAND - BUDGET

Central Intelligence Agency, Office of Public Affairs, Washington, DC 20505, (703) 482-0623, Fax: (703) 482-1739, www.cia.gov; *The World Factbook.*

Eurostat, Batiment Jean Monnet, Rue Alcide de Gasperi, L-2920 Luxembourg, http://epp.eurostat.ec.europa.eu; *Government Budgets.*

ICELAND - BUSINESS

Nordic Council of Ministers, Store Strandstraede 18, DK-1255 Copenhagen K, Denmark, www.norden.org; *Nordic Statistical Yearbook 2004-2006.*

United Nations Statistics Division, New York, NY 10017, (800) 253-9646, Fax: (212) 963-4116, http://unstats.un.org; *Statistical Yearbook.*

ICELAND - CAPITAL INVESTMENTS

Organisation for Economic Cooperation and Development (OECD), 2 rue Andre Pascal, F-75775 Paris Cedex 16, France, (Telephone in U.S. (202) 785-6323), (Fax in U.S. (202) 785-0350), www.oecd.org; *Financial Market Trends: OECD Periodical* and *OECD Economic Outlook 2008.*

ICELAND - CAPITAL LEVY

International Monetary Fund (IMF), 700 Nineteenth Street, NW, Washington, DC 20431, (202) 623-7000, Fax: (202) 623-4661, www.imf.org; *Government Finance Statistics Yearbook (2008 Edition).*

Organisation for Economic Cooperation and Development (OECD), 2 rue Andre Pascal, F-75775 Paris Cedex 16, France, (Telephone in U.S. (202) 785-6323), (Fax in U.S. (202) 785-0350), www.oecd.org; *Financial Market Trends: OECD Periodical* and *OECD Economic Outlook 2008.*

ICELAND - CATTLE

See ICELAND - LIVESTOCK

ICELAND - CHILDBIRTH - STATISTICS

Central Intelligence Agency, Office of Public Affairs, Washington, DC 20505, (703) 482-0623, Fax: (703) 482-1739, www.cia.gov; *The World Factbook.*

Euromonitor International, Inc., 224 S. Michigan Avenue, Suite 1500, Chicago, IL 60604, (312) 922-1115, Fax: (312) 922-1157, www.euromonitor.com; *The World Economic Factbook 2008.*

M.E. Sharpe, 80 Business Park Drive, Armonk, NY 10504, (800) 541-6563, Fax: (914) 273-2106, www.mesharpe.com; *The Illustrated Book of World Rankings.*

Nordic Council of Ministers, Store Strandstraede 18, DK-1255 Copenhagen K, Denmark, www.norden.org; *Nordic Statistical Yearbook 2004-2006.*

Palgrave Macmillan Ltd., Houndmills, Basingstoke, Hampshire, RG21 6XS, England, (Telephone in U.S. (888) 330-8477), (Fax in U.S. (800) 672-2054), www.palgrave.com; *The Statesman's Yearbook 2008.*

Taylor and Francis Group, An Informa Business, 2 Park Square, Milton Park, Abingdon, Oxford OX14 4RN, United Kingdom, (Dial from U.S. (212) 216-7800), (Fax from U.S. (212) 564-7854), www.tandf.co.uk; *The Europa World Year Book.*

United Nations Statistics Division, New York, NY 10017, (800) 253-9646, Fax: (212) 963-4116, http://unstats.un.org; *Demographic Yearbook* and *Statistical Yearbook.*

The World Bank, 1818 H Street, NW, Washington, DC 20433, (202) 473-1000, Fax: (202) 477-6391, www.worldbank.org; *World Development Indicators (WDI) 2008.*

World Health Organization (WHO), Avenue Appia 20, 1211 Geneve 27, Switzerland, (Telephone in U.S. (212) 331-9081), www.who.int; *World Health Report 2006.*

ICELAND - CLIMATE

M.E. Sharpe, 80 Business Park Drive, Armonk, NY 10504, (800) 541-6563, Fax: (914) 273-2106, www.mesharpe.com; *The Illustrated Book of World Rankings.*

Nordic Council of Ministers, Store Strandstraede 18, DK-1255 Copenhagen K, Denmark, www.norden.org; *Nordic Statistical Yearbook 2004-2006.*

Palgrave Macmillan Ltd., Houndmills, Basingstoke, Hampshire, RG21 6XS, England, (Telephone in U.S. (888) 330-8477), (Fax in U.S. (800) 672-2054), www.palgrave.com; *The Statesman's Yearbook 2008.*

ICELAND - CLOTHING EXPORTS AND IMPORTS

See ICELAND - TEXTILE INDUSTRY

ICELAND - COAL PRODUCTION

See ICELAND - MINERAL INDUSTRIES

ICELAND - COFFEE

See ICELAND - CROPS

ICELAND - COMMERCE

Palgrave Macmillan Ltd., Houndmills, Basingstoke, Hampshire, RG21 6XS, England, (Telephone in U.S. (888) 330-8477), (Fax in U.S. (800) 672-2054), www.palgrave.com; *The Statesman's Yearbook 2008.*

ICELAND - COMMODITY EXCHANGES

Commodity Research Bureau, 330 South Wells Street, Suite 612, Chicago, IL 60606-7110, (800) 621-5271, Fax: (312) 939-4135, www.crbtrader.com; *2006 CRB Commodity Yearbook and CD.*

International Monetary Fund (IMF), 700 Nineteenth Street, NW, Washington, DC 20431, (202) 623-7000, Fax: (202) 623-4661, www.imf.org; *IMF Primary Commodity Prices.*

United Nations Food and Agricultural Organization (FAO), Viale delle Terme di Caracalla, 00100 Rome, Italy, (Dial from U.S. (202) 653-2400), (Fax from U.S. (202) 653 5760), www.fao.org; *The State of Food and Agriculture (SOFA) 2006.*

ICELAND - COMMUNICATION AND TRAFFIC

Nordic Council of Ministers, Store Strandstraede 18, DK-1255 Copenhagen K, Denmark, www.norden.org; *Nordic Statistical Yearbook 2004-2006.*

United Nations Statistics Division, New York, NY 10017, (800) 253-9646, Fax: (212) 963-4116, http://unstats.un.org; *Statistical Yearbook.*

ICELAND - CONSTRUCTION INDUSTRY

M.E. Sharpe, 80 Business Park Drive, Armonk, NY 10504, (800) 541-6563, Fax: (914) 273-2106, www.mesharpe.com; *The Illustrated Book of World Rankings.*

Nordic Council of Ministers, Store Strandstraede 18, DK-1255 Copenhagen K, Denmark, www.norden.org; *Nordic Statistical Yearbook 2004-2006.*

Organisation for Economic Cooperation and Development (OECD), 2 rue Andre Pascal, F-75775 Paris Cedex 16, France, (Telephone in U.S. (202) 785-6323), (Fax in U.S. (202) 785-0350), www.oecd.org; *Iron and Steel Industry in 2004 (2006 Edition); OECD Economic Survey - Iceland 2008;* and STructural ANalysis (STAN) database.

United Nations Statistics Division, New York, NY 10017, (800) 253-9646, Fax: (212) 963-4116, http://unstats.un.org; *Statistical Yearbook.*

ICELAND - CONSUMER PRICE INDEXES

Nordic Council of Ministers, Store Strandstraede 18, DK-1255 Copenhagen K, Denmark, www.norden.org; *Nordic Statistical Yearbook 2004-2006.*

Organisation for Economic Cooperation and Development (OECD), 2 rue Andre Pascal, F-75775 Paris Cedex 16, France, (Telephone in U.S. (202) 785-6323), (Fax in U.S. (202) 785-0350), www.oecd.org; *OECD Economic Outlook 2008.*

Taylor and Francis Group, An Informa Business, 2 Park Square, Milton Park, Abingdon, Oxford OX14 4RN, United Kingdom, (Dial from U.S. (212) 216-7800), (Fax from U.S. (212) 564-7854), www.tandf.co.uk; *The Europa World Year Book.*

United Nations Statistics Division, New York, NY 10017, (800) 253-9646, Fax: (212) 963-4116, http://unstats.un.org; *Statistical Yearbook* and *Trends in Europe and North America: The Statistical Yearbook of the ECE 2005.*

The World Bank, 1818 H Street, NW, Washington, DC 20433, (202) 473-1000, Fax: (202) 477-6391, www.worldbank.org; *Iceland.*

ICELAND - CONSUMPTION (ECONOMICS)

Nordic Council of Ministers, Store Strandstraede 18, DK-1255 Copenhagen K, Denmark, www.norden.org; *Nordic Statistical Yearbook 2004-2006.*

Organisation for Economic Cooperation and Development (OECD), 2 rue Andre Pascal, F-75775 Paris Cedex 16, France, (Telephone in U.S. (202) 785-6323), (Fax in U.S. (202) 785-0350), www.oecd.org; *Environmental Impacts of Foreign Direct Investment in the Mining Sector in the Newly Independent States (NIS); Iron and Steel Industry in 2004 (2006 Edition); A New World Map in Textiles and Clothing: Adjusting to Change; 2005 OECD Agricultural Outlook Tables, 1970-2014;* and *Towards Sustainable Household Consumption?: Trends and Policies in OECD Countries.*

Technical Association of the Pulp and Paper Industry (TAPPI), 15 Technology Parkway South, Norcross, GA 30092, (770) 446-1400, Fax: (770) 446-6947, www.tappi.org; *TAPPI Annual Report.*

ICELAND - COPPER INDUSTRY AND TRADE

See ICELAND - MINERAL INDUSTRIES

ICELAND - CORN INDUSTRY

See ICELAND - CROPS

ICELAND - COST AND STANDARD OF LIVING

International Monetary Fund (IMF), 700 Nineteenth Street, NW, Washington, DC 20431, (202) 623-7000, Fax: (202) 623-4661, www.imf.org; *Government Finance Statistics Yearbook (2008 Edition).*

ICELAND - COTTON

See ICELAND - CROPS

ICELAND - CRIME

International Criminal Police Organization (INTERPOL), General Secretariat, 200 quai Charles de Gaulle, 69006 Lyon, France, www.interpol.int; *International Crime Statistics.*

Nordic Council of Ministers, Store Strandstraede 18, DK-1255 Copenhagen K, Denmark, www.norden.org; *Nordic Statistical Yearbook 2004-2006.*

United Nations Statistics Division, New York, NY 10017, (800) 253-9646, Fax: (212) 963-4116, http://unstats.un.org; *Trends in Europe and North America: The Statistical Yearbook of the ECE 2005.*

Yale University Press, PO Box 209040, New Haven, CT 06520-9040, (203) 432-0960, Fax: (203) 432-0948, http://yalepress.yale.edu/yupbooks; *Violence and Crime in Cross-National Perspective.*

ICELAND - CROPS

Euromonitor International, Inc., 224 S. Michigan Avenue, Suite 1500, Chicago, IL 60604, (312) 922-1115, Fax: (312) 922-1157, www.euromonitor.com; *European Marketing Data and Statistics 2008.*

M.E. Sharpe, 80 Business Park Drive, Armonk, NY 10504, (800) 541-6563, Fax: (914) 273-2106, www.mesharpe.com; *The Illustrated Book of World Rankings.*

Organisation for Economic Cooperation and Development (OECD), 2 rue Andre Pascal, F-75775 Paris Cedex 16, France, (Telephone in U.S. (202) 785-6323), (Fax in U.S. (202) 785-0350), www.oecd.org; *International Trade by Commodity Statistics (ITCS)* and *2005 OECD Agricultural Outlook Tables, 1970-2014.*

Palgrave Macmillan Ltd., Houndmills, Basingstoke, Hampshire, RG21 6XS, England, (Telephone in U.S. (888) 330-8477), (Fax in U.S. (800) 672-2054), www.palgrave.com; *The Statesman's Yearbook 2008.*

Taylor and Francis Group, An Informa Business, 2 Park Square, Milton Park, Abingdon, Oxford OX14 4RN, United Kingdom, (Dial from U.S. (212) 216-7800), (Fax from U.S. (212) 564-7854), www.tandf.co.uk; *The Europa World Year Book.*

United Nations Conference on Trade and Development (UNCTAD), DC2-1120, United Nations, New York, NY 10017, (212) 963-0027, www.unctad.org; *UNCTAD Commodity Yearbook.*

United Nations Food and Agricultural Organization (FAO), Viale delle Terme di Caracalla, 00100 Rome, Italy, (Dial from U.S. (202) 653-2400), (Fax from U.S. (202) 653 5760), www.fao.org; *FAO Production Yearbook 2002* and *The State of Food and Agriculture (SOFA) 2006.*

United Nations Statistics Division, New York, NY 10017, (800) 253-9646, Fax: (212) 963-4116, http://unstats.un.org; *Statistical Yearbook.*

ICELAND - CUSTOMS ADMINISTRATION

International Monetary Fund (IMF), 700 Nineteenth Street, NW, Washington, DC 20431, (202) 623-7000, Fax: (202) 623-4661, www.imf.org; *Government Finance Statistics Yearbook (2008 Edition).*

Organisation for Economic Cooperation and Development (OECD), 2 rue Andre Pascal, F-75775 Paris Cedex 16, France, (Telephone in U.S. (202) 785-6323), (Fax in U.S. (202) 785-0350), www.oecd.org; *Environmental Impacts of Foreign Direct Investment in the Mining Sector in the Newly Independent States (NIS).*

Palgrave Macmillan Ltd., Houndmills, Basingstoke, Hampshire, RG21 6XS, England, (Telephone in U.S. (888) 330-8477), (Fax in U.S. (800) 672-2054), www.palgrave.com; *The Statesman's Yearbook 2008.*

ICELAND - DAIRY PROCESSING

M.E. Sharpe, 80 Business Park Drive, Armonk, NY 10504, (800) 541-6563, Fax: (914) 273-2106, www.mesharpe.com; *The Illustrated Book of World Rankings.*

Nordic Council of Ministers, Store Strandstraede 18, DK-1255 Copenhagen K, Denmark, www.norden.org; *Nordic Statistical Yearbook 2004-2006.*

Organisation for Economic Cooperation and Development (OECD), 2 rue Andre Pascal, F-75775 Paris Cedex 16, France, (Telephone in U.S. (202) 785-6323), (Fax in U.S. (202) 785-0350), www.oecd.org; *2005 OECD Agricultural Outlook Tables, 1970-2014.*

Palgrave Macmillan Ltd., Houndmills, Basingstoke, Hampshire, RG21 6XS, England, (Telephone in U.S. (888) 330-8477), (Fax in U.S. (800) 672-2054), www.palgrave.com; *The Statesman's Yearbook 2008.*

Taylor and Francis Group, An Informa Business, 2 Park Square, Milton Park, Abingdon, Oxford OX14 4RN, United Kingdom, (Dial from U.S. (212) 216-7800), (Fax from U.S. (212) 564-7854), www.tandf.co.uk; *The Europa World Year Book.*

United Nations Food and Agricultural Organization (FAO), Viale delle Terme di Caracalla, 00100 Rome, Italy, (Dial from U.S. (202) 653-2400), (Fax from U.S. (202) 653 5760), www.fao.org; *The State of Food and Agriculture (SOFA) 2006.*

United Nations Statistics Division, New York, NY 10017, (800) 253-9646, Fax: (212) 963-4116, http://unstats.un.org; *Statistical Yearbook.*

ICELAND - DEATH RATES

See ICELAND - MORTALITY

ICELAND - DEBTS, EXTERNAL

International Monetary Fund (IMF), 700 Nineteenth Street, NW, Washington, DC 20431, (202) 623-7000, Fax: (202) 623-4661, www.imf.org; *Government Finance Statistics Yearbook (2008 Edition).*

Organisation for Economic Cooperation and Development (OECD), 2 rue Andre Pascal, F-75775 Paris Cedex 16, France, (Telephone in U.S. (202) 785-

6323), (Fax in U.S. (202) 785-0350), www.oecd.org; *Financial Market Trends: OECD Periodical; Geographical Distribution of Financial Flows to Aid Recipients 2002-2006;* and *OECD Economic Outlook 2008.*

Palgrave Macmillan Ltd., Houndmills, Basingstoke, Hampshire, RG21 6XS, England, (Telephone in U.S. (888) 330-8477), (Fax in U.S. (800) 672-2054), www.palgrave.com; *The Statesman's Yearbook 2008.*

The World Bank, 1818 H Street, NW, Washington, DC 20433, (202) 473-1000, Fax: (202) 477-6391, www.worldbank.org; *Global Development Finance 2007* and *World Development Indicators (WDI) 2008.*

ICELAND - DEFENSE EXPENDITURES

See ICELAND - ARMED FORCES

ICELAND - DEMOGRAPHY

Euromonitor International, Inc., 224 S. Michigan Avenue, Suite 1500, Chicago, IL 60604, (312) 922-1115, Fax: (312) 922-1157, www.euromonitor.com; *The World Economic Factbook 2008* and *World Marketing Data and Statistics.*

M.E. Sharpe, 80 Business Park Drive, Armonk, NY 10504, (800) 541-6563, Fax: (914) 273-2106, www.mesharpe.com; *The Illustrated Book of World Rankings.*

Nordic Council of Ministers, Store Strandstraede 18, DK-1255 Copenhagen K, Denmark, www.norden.org; *Nordic Statistical Yearbook 2004-2006.*

United Nations Statistics Division, New York, NY 10017, (800) 253-9646, Fax: (212) 963-4116, http://unstats.un.org; *Human Development Report 2006.*

The World Bank, 1818 H Street, NW, Washington, DC 20433, (202) 473-1000, Fax: (202) 477-6391, www.worldbank.org; *Iceland.*

ICELAND - DIAMONDS

See ICELAND - MINERAL INDUSTRIES

ICELAND - DISPOSABLE INCOME

M.E. Sharpe, 80 Business Park Drive, Armonk, NY 10504, (800) 541-6563, Fax: (914) 273-2106, www.mesharpe.com; *The Illustrated Book of World Rankings.*

Nordic Council of Ministers, Store Strandstraede 18, DK-1255 Copenhagen K, Denmark, www.norden.org; *Nordic Statistical Yearbook 2004-2006.*

Organisation for Economic Cooperation and Development (OECD), 2 rue Andre Pascal, F-75775 Paris Cedex 16, France, (Telephone in U.S. (202) 785-6323), (Fax in U.S. (202) 785-0350), www.oecd.org; *OECD Economic Outlook 2008.*

United Nations Statistics Division, New York, NY 10017, (800) 253-9646, Fax: (212) 963-4116, http://unstats.un.org; *National Accounts Statistics: Compendium of Income Distribution Statistics* and *Statistical Yearbook.*

ICELAND - DIVORCE

M.E. Sharpe, 80 Business Park Drive, Armonk, NY 10504, (800) 541-6563, Fax: (914) 273-2106, www.mesharpe.com; *The Illustrated Book of World Rankings.*

Nordic Council of Ministers, Store Strandstraede 18, DK-1255 Copenhagen K, Denmark, www.norden.org; *Nordic Statistical Yearbook 2004-2006.*

United Nations Statistics Division, New York, NY 10017, (800) 253-9646, Fax: (212) 963-4116, http://unstats.un.org; *Demographic Yearbook; Statistical Yearbook;* and *Trends in Europe and North America: The Statistical Yearbook of the ECE 2005.*

ICELAND - ECONOMIC ASSISTANCE

Organisation for Economic Cooperation and Development (OECD), 2 rue Andre Pascal, F-75775 Paris Cedex 16, France, (Telephone in U.S. (202) 785-6323), (Fax in U.S. (202) 785-0350), www.oecd.org; *Geographical Distribution of Financial Flows to Aid Recipients 2002-2006.*

ICELAND - ECONOMIC CONDITIONS

Center for International Business Education Research (CIBER), Columbia Business School and School of International and Public Affairs, Uris Hall, Room 212, 3022 Broadway, New York, NY 10027-6902, Mr. Joshua Safier, (212) 854-4750, Fax: (212) 222-9821, www.columbia.edu/cu/ciber/; Datastream International.

Central Intelligence Agency, Office of Public Affairs, Washington, DC 20505, (703) 482-0623, Fax: (703) 482-1739, www.cia.gov; *The World Factbook.*

DSI Data Service Information, Xantener Strasse 51a, D-47495 Rheinberg, Germany, www.dsidata.com; *Campus Solution.*

Dun and Bradstreet (DB) Corporation, 103 JFK Parkway, Short Hills, NJ 07078, (973) 921-5500, www.dnb.com; *Country Report.*

Economist Intelligence Unit, 111 West 57th Street, New York, NY 10019, (212) 554-0600, Fax: (212) 586-1181, www.eiu.com; *Iceland Country Report.*

Euromonitor International, Inc., 224 S. Michigan Avenue, Suite 1500, Chicago, IL 60604, (312) 922-1115, Fax: (312) 922-1157, www.euromonitor.com; *European Marketing Data and Statistics 2008; The World Economic Factbook 2008;* and *World Marketing Data and Statistics.*

Eurostat, Batiment Jean Monnet, Rue Alcide de Gasperi, L-2920 Luxembourg, http://epp.eurostat.ec.europa.eu; *Consumers in Europe - Facts and Figures on Services of General Interest.*

International Monetary Fund (IMF), 700 Nineteenth Street, NW, Washington, DC 20431, (202) 623-7000, Fax: (202) 623-4661, www.imf.org; *World Economic Outlook Reports.*

M.E. Sharpe, 80 Business Park Drive, Armonk, NY 10504, (800) 541-6563, Fax: (914) 273-2106, www.mesharpe.com; *The Illustrated Book of World Rankings.*

Organisation for Economic Cooperation and Development (OECD), 2 rue Andre Pascal, F-75775 Paris Cedex 16, France, (Telephone in U.S. (202) 785-6323), (Fax in U.S. (202) 785-0350), www.oecd.org; *Geographical Distribution of Financial Flows to Aid Recipients 2002-2006; ICT Sector Data and Metadata by Country; Labour Force Statistics: 1986-2005, 2007 Edition; OECD Composite Leading Indicators (CLIs), Updated September 2007; OECD Economic Outlook 2008; OECD Economic Survey - Iceland 2008; OECD Employment Outlook 2007; OECD in Figures 2007;* and *OECD Main Economic Indicators (MEI).*

Palgrave Macmillan Ltd., Houndmills, Basingstoke, Hampshire, RG21 6XS, England, (Telephone in U.S. (888) 330-8477), (Fax in U.S. (800) 672-2054), www.palgrave.com; *The Statesman's Yearbook 2008.*

Taylor and Francis Group, An Informa Business, 2 Park Square, Milton Park, Abingdon, Oxford OX14 4RN, United Kingdom, (Dial from U.S. (212) 216-7800), (Fax from U.S. (212) 564-7854), www.tandf.co.uk; *The Europa World Year Book.*

United Nations Statistics Division, New York, NY 10017, (800) 253-9646, Fax: (212) 963-4116, http://unstats.un.org; *World Statistics Pocketbook.*

The World Bank, 1818 H Street, NW, Washington, DC 20433, (202) 473-1000, Fax: (202) 477-6391, www.worldbank.org; *Global Economic Monitor (GEM); Global Economic Prospects 2008; Iceland;* and *The World Bank Atlas 2003-2004.*

ICELAND - ECONOMICS - SOCIOLOGICAL ASPECTS

Organisation for Economic Cooperation and Development (OECD), 2 rue Andre Pascal, F-75775 Paris Cedex 16, France, (Telephone in U.S. (202) 785-6323), (Fax in U.S. (202) 785-0350), www.oecd.org; *OECD Economic Outlook 2008.*

ICELAND - EDUCATION

Euromonitor International, Inc., 224 S. Michigan Avenue, Suite 1500, Chicago, IL 60604, (312) 922-1115, Fax: (312) 922-1157, www.euromonitor.com; *European Marketing Data and Statistics 2008* and *World Marketing Data and Statistics.*

European Union, Delegation of the European Commission to the United States, 2300 M Street, NW, Washington, DC 20037, (202) 862-9500, Fax: (202) 429-1766, www.eurunion.org; *Education across Europe 2003.*

International Monetary Fund (IMF), 700 Nineteenth Street, NW, Washington, DC 20431, (202) 623-7000, Fax: (202) 623-4661, www.imf.org; *Government Finance Statistics Yearbook (2008 Edition).*

M.E. Sharpe, 80 Business Park Drive, Armonk, NY 10504, (800) 541-6563, Fax: (914) 273-2106, www.mesharpe.com; *The Illustrated Book of World Rankings.*

Nordic Council of Ministers, Store Strandstraede 18, DK-1255 Copenhagen K, Denmark, www.norden.org; *Nordic Statistical Yearbook 2004-2006.*

Organisation for Economic Cooperation and Development (OECD), 2 rue Andre Pascal, F-75775 Paris Cedex 16, France, (Telephone in U.S. (202) 785-6323), (Fax in U.S. (202) 785-0350), www.oecd.org; *Education at a Glance* (2007 Edition).

Palgrave Macmillan Ltd., Houndmills, Basingstoke, Hampshire, RG21 6XS, England, (Telephone in U.S. (888) 330-8477), (Fax in U.S. (800) 672-2054), www.palgrave.com; *The Statesman's Yearbook 2008.*

Taylor and Francis Group, An Informa Business, 2 Park Square, Milton Park, Abingdon, Oxford OX14 4RN, United Kingdom, (Dial from U.S. (212) 216-7800), (Fax from U.S. (212) 564-7854), www.tandf.co.uk; *The Europa World Year Book.*

UNESCO Institute for Statistics, C.P. 6128 Succursale Centre-Ville, Montreal, Quebec, H3C 3J7 Canada, (Dial from U.S. (514) 343-6880), (Fax from U.S. (514) 343 6882), www.uis.unesco.org; *Statistical Tables.*

United Nations Statistics Division, New York, NY 10017, (800) 253-9646, Fax: (212) 963-4116, http://unstats.un.org; *Human Development Report 2006* and *Trends in Europe and North America: The Statistical Yearbook of the ECE 2005.*

The World Bank, 1818 H Street, NW, Washington, DC 20433, (202) 473-1000, Fax: (202) 477-6391, www.worldbank.org; *Iceland* and *World Development Indicators (WDI) 2008.*

ICELAND - ELECTRICITY

M.E. Sharpe, 80 Business Park Drive, Armonk, NY 10504, (800) 541-6563, Fax: (914) 273-2106, www.mesharpe.com; *The Illustrated Book of World Rankings.*

Nordic Council of Ministers, Store Strandstraede 18, DK-1255 Copenhagen K, Denmark, www.norden.org; *Nordic Statistical Yearbook 2004-2006.*

Organisation for Economic Cooperation and Development (OECD), 2 rue Andre Pascal, F-75775 Paris Cedex 16, France, (Telephone in U.S. (202) 785-6323), (Fax in U.S. (202) 785-0350), www.oecd.org; *Coal Information: 2007 Edition; Energy Statistics of OECD Countries* (2007 Edition); and STructural ANalysis (STAN) database.

Palgrave Macmillan Ltd., Houndmills, Basingstoke, Hampshire, RG21 6XS, England, (Telephone in U.S. (888) 330-8477), (Fax in U.S. (800) 672-2054), www.palgrave.com; *The Statesman's Yearbook 2008.*

U.S. Department of Energy (DOE), Energy Information Administration (EIA), 1000 Independence Avenue, SW, Washington, DC 20585, (202) 586-8800, www.eia.doe.gov; *International Energy Annual 2004* and *International Energy Outlook 2006.*

United Nations Statistics Division, New York, NY 10017, (800) 253-9646, Fax: (212) 963-4116, http://unstats.un.org; *Human Development Report 2006; Statistical Yearbook;* and *Trends in Europe and North America: The Statistical Yearbook of the ECE 2005.*

ICELAND - EMPLOYMENT

Bernan Essential Government Publications, 4611-F Assembly Drive, Lanham MD, 20706-4391, (301) 459-2255, Fax: (800) 865-3450, www.bernan.com; *OECD Factbook 2006.*

Euromonitor International, Inc., 224 S. Michigan Avenue, Suite 1500, Chicago, IL 60604, (312) 922-1115, Fax: (312) 922-1157, www.euromonitor.com; *European Marketing Data and Statistics 2008.*

International Labour Office, I.L.O. Publications, 4 route des Morillons, CH-1211 Geneva 22, Switzerland, (Telephone in U.S. (202) 653-7652), (Fax in U.S. (202) 653-7687), www.ilo.org; *Yearbook of Labour Statistics 2006.*

M.E. Sharpe, 80 Business Park Drive, Armonk, NY 10504, (800) 541-6563, Fax: (914) 273-2106, www.mesharpe.com; *The Illustrated Book of World Rankings.*

Nordic Council of Ministers, Store Strandstraede 18, DK-1255 Copenhagen K, Denmark, www.norden.org; *Nordic Statistical Yearbook 2004-2006.*

Organisation for Economic Cooperation and Development (OECD), 2 rue Andre Pascal, F-75775 Paris Cedex 16, France, (Telephone in U.S. (202) 785-6323), (Fax in U.S. (202) 785-0350), www.oecd.org; *Coal Information: 2007 Edition; ICT Sector Data and Metadata by Country; Iron and Steel Industry in 2004 (2006 Edition); Labour Force Statistics: 1986-2005, 2007 Edition; A New World Map in Textiles and Clothing: Adjusting to Change; OECD Composite Leading Indicators (CLIs), Updated September 2007; OECD Economic Outlook 2008; OECD Economic Survey - Iceland 2008; OECD Employment Outlook 2007;* and *OECD in Figures 2007.*

United Nations Statistics Division, New York, NY 10017, (800) 253-9646, Fax: (212) 963-4116, http://unstats.un.org; *Statistical Yearbook* and *Trends in Europe and North America: The Statistical Yearbook of the ECE 2005.*

The World Bank, 1818 H Street, NW, Washington, DC 20433, (202) 473-1000, Fax: (202) 477-6391, www.worldbank.org; *Iceland.*

ICELAND - ENVIRONMENTAL CONDITIONS

Center for Research on the Epidemiology of Disasters (CRED), Universite Catholique de Louvain, Ecole de Sante Publique, 30.94 Clos Chapelle-aux-Champs, 1200 Brussels, Belgium, www.cred.be; *Three Decades of Floods in Europe: A Preliminary Analysis of EMDAT Data.*

DSI Data Service Information, Xantener Strasse 51a, D-47495 Rheinberg, Germany, www.dsidata.com; *Campus Solution* and *DSI's Global Environmental Database.*

Economist Intelligence Unit, 111 West 57th Street, New York, NY 10019, (212) 554-0600, Fax: (212) 586-1181, www.eiu.com; *Iceland Country Report.*

Eurostat, Batiment Jean Monnet, Rue Alcide de Gasperi, L-2920 Luxembourg, http://epp.eurostat.ec.europa.eu; *Environmental Protection Expenditure in Europe.*

Organisation for Economic Cooperation and Development (OECD), 2 rue Andre Pascal, F-75775 Paris Cedex 16, France, (Telephone in U.S. (202) 785-6323), (Fax in U.S. (202) 785-0350), www.oecd.org; *Key Environmental Indicators 2004.*

Platts, 2 Penn Plaza, 25th Floor, New York, NY 10121-2298, (212) 904-3070, www.platts.com; *Emissions Daily.*

Statistics Iceland, Borgartuni 21a, 150 Reykjavik, Iceland, www.statice.is; *Environment and Pollutant Emissions.*

United Nations Statistics Division, New York, NY 10017, (800) 253-9646, Fax: (212) 963-4116, http://unstats.un.org; *Trends in Europe and North America: The Statistical Yearbook of the ECE 2005* and *World Statistics Pocketbook.*

ICELAND - EXPORTS

Central Intelligence Agency, Office of Public Affairs, Washington, DC 20505, (703) 482-0623, Fax: (703) 482-1739, www.cia.gov; *The World Factbook.*

Economist Intelligence Unit, 111 West 57th Street, New York, NY 10019, (212) 554-0600, Fax: (212) 586-1181, www.eiu.com; *Iceland Country Report.*

Euromonitor International, Inc., 224 S. Michigan Avenue, Suite 1500, Chicago, IL 60604, (312) 922-1115, Fax: (312) 922-1157, www.euromonitor.com; *The World Economic Factbook 2008.*

International Monetary Fund (IMF), 700 Nineteenth Street, NW, Washington, DC 20431, (202) 623-7000, Fax: (202) 623-4661, www.imf.org; *Direction of Trade Statistics Yearbook 2007; Government Finance Statistics Yearbook (2008 Edition);* and *International Financial Statistics Yearbook 2007.*

Nordic Council of Ministers, Store Strandstraede 18, DK-1255 Copenhagen K, Denmark, www.norden.org; *Nordic Statistical Yearbook 2004-2006.*

Organisation for Economic Cooperation and Development (OECD), 2 rue Andre Pascal, F-75775 Paris Cedex 16, France, (Telephone in U.S. (202) 785-6323), (Fax in U.S. (202) 785-0350), www.oecd.org; *Geographical Distribution of Financial Flows to Aid Recipients 2002-2006; International Trade by Commodity Statistics (ITCS); Iron and Steel Industry in 2004 (2006 Edition); 2005 OECD Agricultural Outlook Tables, 1970-2014; OECD Economic Outlook 2008; OECD Economic Survey - Iceland 2008; Review of Fisheries in OECD Countries: Country Statistics 2001 to 2003 - 2005 Edition;* and STructural ANalysis (STAN) database.

Palgrave Macmillan Ltd., Houndmills, Basingstoke, Hampshire, RG21 6XS, England, (Telephone in U.S. (888) 330-8477), (Fax in U.S. (800) 672-2054), www.palgrave.com; *The Statesman's Yearbook 2008.*

Taylor and Francis Group, An Informa Business, 2 Park Square, Milton Park, Abingdon, Oxford OX14 4RN, United Kingdom, (Dial from U.S. (212) 216-7800), (Fax from U.S. (212) 564-7854), www.tandf.co.uk; *The Europa World Year Book.*

Technical Association of the Pulp and Paper Industry (TAPPI), 15 Technology Parkway South, Norcross, GA 30092, (770) 446-1400, Fax: (770) 446-6947, www.tappi.org; *TAPPI Annual Report.*

United Nations Conference on Trade and Development (UNCTAD), DC2-1120, United Nations, New York, NY 10017, (212) 963-0027, www.unctad.org; *Handbook of Statistics 2005.*

United Nations Food and Agricultural Organization (FAO), Viale delle Terme di Caracalla, 00100 Rome, Italy, (Dial from U.S. (202) 653-2400), (Fax from U.S. (202) 653 5760), www.fao.org; *The State of Food and Agriculture (SOFA) 2006.*

United Nations Statistics Division, New York, NY 10017, (800) 253-9646, Fax: (212) 963-4116, http://unstats.un.org; *Trends in Europe and North America: The Statistical Yearbook of the ECE 2005.*

The World Bank, 1818 H Street, NW, Washington, DC 20433, (202) 473-1000, Fax: (202) 477-6391, www.worldbank.org; *World Development Indicators (WDI) 2008.*

ICELAND - FERTILITY, HUMAN

Central Intelligence Agency, Office of Public Affairs, Washington, DC 20505, (703) 482-0623, Fax: (703) 482-1739, www.cia.gov; *The World Factbook.*

M.E. Sharpe, 80 Business Park Drive, Armonk, NY 10504, (800) 541-6563, Fax: (914) 273-2106, www.mesharpe.com; *The Illustrated Book of World Rankings.*

Nordic Council of Ministers, Store Strandstraede 18, DK-1255 Copenhagen K, Denmark, www.norden.org; *Nordic Statistical Yearbook 2004-2006.*

United Nations Statistics Division, New York, NY 10017, (800) 253-9646, Fax: (212) 963-4116, http://unstats.un.org; *Human Development Report 2006* and *Trends in Europe and North America: The Statistical Yearbook of the ECE 2005.*

The World Bank, 1818 H Street, NW, Washington, DC 20433, (202) 473-1000, Fax: (202) 477-6391, www.worldbank.org; *The World Bank Atlas 2003-2004* and *World Development Indicators (WDI) 2008.*

ICELAND - FERTILIZER INDUSTRY

Organisation for Economic Cooperation and Development (OECD), 2 rue Andre Pascal, F-75775 Paris Cedex 16, France, (Telephone in U.S. (202) 785-6323), (Fax in U.S. (202) 785-0350), www.oecd.org; *International Trade by Commodity Statistics (ITCS)* and *2005 OECD Agricultural Outlook Tables, 1970-2014.*

United Nations Food and Agricultural Organization (FAO), Viale delle Terme di Caracalla, 00100 Rome, Italy, (Dial from U.S. (202) 653-2400), (Fax from U.S. (202) 653 5760), www.fao.org; *FAO Fertilizer Yearbook* and *The State of Food and Agriculture (SOFA) 2006.*

United Nations Statistics Division, New York, NY 10017, (800) 253-9646, Fax: (212) 963-4116, http://unstats.un.org; *Statistical Yearbook.*

ICELAND - FETAL MORTALITY

See ICELAND - MORTALITY

ICELAND - FINANCE

International Monetary Fund (IMF), 700 Nineteenth Street, NW, Washington, DC 20431, (202) 623-7000, Fax: (202) 623-4661, www.imf.org; *International Financial Statistics Yearbook 2007.*

Nordic Council of Ministers, Store Strandstraede 18, DK-1255 Copenhagen K, Denmark, www.norden.org; *Nordic Statistical Yearbook 2004-2006.*

Organisation for Economic Cooperation and Development (OECD), 2 rue Andre Pascal, F-75775 Paris Cedex 16, France, (Telephone in U.S. (202) 785-6323), (Fax in U.S. (202) 785-0350), www.oecd.org; *OECD Economic Outlook 2008.*

United Nations Statistics Division, New York, NY 10017, (800) 253-9646, Fax: (212) 963-4116, http://unstats.un.org; *National Accounts Statistics: Compendium of Income Distribution Statistics* and *Statistical Yearbook.*

The World Bank, 1818 H Street, NW, Washington, DC 20433, (202) 473-1000, Fax: (202) 477-6391, www.worldbank.org; *Iceland.*

ICELAND - FINANCE, PUBLIC

Banque de France, 48 rue Croix des Petits champs, 75001 Paris, France, www.banque-france.fr/home.htm; *Public Finance.*

Bernan Essential Government Publications, 4611-F Assembly Drive, Lanham MD, 20706-4391, (301) 459-2255, Fax: (800) 865-3450, www.bernan.com; *National Accounts Statistics.*

Economist Intelligence Unit, 111 West 57th Street, New York, NY 10019, (212) 554-0600, Fax: (212) 586-1181, www.eiu.com; *Iceland Country Report.*

International Monetary Fund (IMF), 700 Nineteenth Street, NW, Washington, DC 20431, (202) 623-7000, Fax: (202) 623-4661, www.imf.org; *International Financial Statistics; International Financial Statistics Online Service;* and *International Financial Statistics Yearbook 2007.*

M.E. Sharpe, 80 Business Park Drive, Armonk, NY 10504, (800) 541-6563, Fax: (914) 273-2106, www.mesharpe.com; *The Illustrated Book of World Rankings.*

Nordic Council of Ministers, Store Strandstraede 18, DK-1255 Copenhagen K, Denmark, www.norden.org; *Nordic Statistical Yearbook 2004-2006.*

Organisation for Economic Cooperation and Development (OECD), 2 rue Andre Pascal, F-75775 Paris Cedex 16, France, (Telephone in U.S. (202) 785-6323), (Fax in U.S. (202) 785-0350), www.oecd.org; *Financial Market Trends: OECD Periodical; Geographical Distribution of Financial Flows to Aid Recipients 2002-2006; OECD Economic Outlook 2008;* and *OECD Main Economic Indicators (MEI).*

Palgrave Macmillan Ltd., Houndmills, Basingstoke, Hampshire, RG21 6XS, England, (Telephone in U.S. (888) 330-8477), (Fax in U.S. (800) 672-2054), www.palgrave.com; *The Statesman's Yearbook 2008.*

Taylor and Francis Group, An Informa Business, 2 Park Square, Milton Park, Abingdon, Oxford OX14 4RN, United Kingdom, (Dial from U.S. (212) 216-7800), (Fax from U.S. (212) 564-7854), www.tandf.co.uk; *The Europa World Year Book.*

The World Bank, 1818 H Street, NW, Washington, DC 20433, (202) 473-1000, Fax: (202) 477-6391, www.worldbank.org; *Iceland.*

ICELAND - FISHERIES

Euromonitor International, Inc., 224 S. Michigan Avenue, Suite 1500, Chicago, IL 60604, (312) 922-1115, Fax: (312) 922-1157, www.euromonitor.com; *European Marketing Data and Statistics 2008.*

International Monetary Fund (IMF), 700 Nineteenth Street, NW, Washington, DC 20431, (202) 623-7000, Fax: (202) 623-4661, www.imf.org; *International Financial Statistics Yearbook 2007.*

M.E. Sharpe, 80 Business Park Drive, Armonk, NY 10504, (800) 541-6563, Fax: (914) 273-2106, www.mesharpe.com; *The Illustrated Book of World Rankings.*

Nordic Council of Ministers, Store Strandstraede 18, DK-1255 Copenhagen K, Denmark, www.norden.org; *Nordic Statistical Yearbook 2004-2006.*

Organisation for Economic Cooperation and Development (OECD), 2 rue Andre Pascal, F-75775 Paris Cedex 16, France, (Telephone in U.S. (202) 785-6323), (Fax in U.S. (202) 785-0350), www.oecd.org; *International Trade by Commodity Statistics (ITCS); OECD Main Economic Indicators (MEI); Review of Fisheries in OECD Countries: Country Statistics 2001 to 2003 - 2005 Edition;* and STructural ANalysis (STAN) database.

Palgrave Macmillan Ltd., Houndmills, Basingstoke, Hampshire, RG21 6XS, England, (Telephone in U.S. (888) 330-8477), (Fax in U.S. (800) 672-2054), www.palgrave.com; *The Statesman's Yearbook 2008.*

Taylor and Francis Group, An Informa Business, 2 Park Square, Milton Park, Abingdon, Oxford OX14 4RN, United Kingdom, (Dial from U.S. (212) 216-7800), (Fax from U.S. (212) 564-7854), www.tandf.co.uk; *The Europa World Year Book.*

United Nations Conference on Trade and Development (UNCTAD), DC2-1120, United Nations, New York, NY 10017, (212) 963-0027, www.unctad.org; *UNCTAD Commodity Yearbook.*

United Nations Food and Agricultural Organization (FAO), Viale delle Terme di Caracalla, 00100 Rome, Italy, (Dial from U.S. (202) 653-2400), (Fax from U.S. (202) 653 5760), www.fao.org; *FAO Yearbook of Fishery Statistics;* Fishery Databases; FISHSTAT Database. Subjects covered include: Aquaculture production, capture production, fishery commodities; and *The State of Food and Agriculture (SOFA) 2006.*

United Nations Statistics Division, New York, NY 10017, (800) 253-9646, Fax: (212) 963-4116, http://unstats.un.org; *Statistical Yearbook.*

The World Bank, 1818 H Street, NW, Washington, DC 20433, (202) 473-1000, Fax: (202) 477-6391, www.worldbank.org; *Iceland.*

ICELAND - FOOD

Euromonitor International, Inc., 224 S. Michigan Avenue, Suite 1500, Chicago, IL 60604, (312) 922-1115, Fax: (312) 922-1157, www.euromonitor.com; *Retail Trade International 2007.*

Organisation for Economic Cooperation and Development (OECD), 2 rue Andre Pascal, F-75775 Paris Cedex 16, France, (Telephone in U.S. (202) 785-6323), (Fax in U.S. (202) 785-0350), www.oecd.org; *International Trade by Commodity Statistics (ITCS).*

United Nations Conference on Trade and Development (UNCTAD), DC2-1120, United Nations, New York, NY 10017, (212) 963-0027, www.unctad.org; *UNCTAD Commodity Yearbook.*

United Nations Food and Agricultural Organization (FAO), Viale delle Terme di Caracalla, 00100 Rome, Italy, (Dial from U.S. (202) 653-2400), (Fax from U.S. (202) 653 5760), www.fao.org; *FAO Production Yearbook 2002* and *The State of Food and Agriculture (SOFA) 2006.*

United Nations Statistics Division, New York, NY 10017, (800) 253-9646, Fax: (212) 963-4116, http://unstats.un.org; *Human Development Report 2006.*

ICELAND - FOREIGN EXCHANGE RATES

Central Intelligence Agency, Office of Public Affairs, Washington, DC 20505, (703) 482-0623, Fax: (703) 482-1739, www.cia.gov; *The World Factbook.*

Euromonitor International, Inc., 224 S. Michigan Avenue, Suite 1500, Chicago, IL 60604, (312) 922-1115, Fax: (312) 922-1157, www.euromonitor.com; *The World Economic Factbook 2008.*

International Civil Aviation Organization (ICAO), External Relations and Public Information Office (EPO), 999 University Street, Montreal, Quebec H3C 5H7, Canada, (Dial from U.S. (514) 954-8219), (Fax from U.S. (514) 954-6077), www.icao.int; *Civil Aviation Statistics of the World.*

International Monetary Fund (IMF), 700 Nineteenth Street, NW, Washington, DC 20431, (202) 623-7000, Fax: (202) 623-4661, www.imf.org; *International Financial Statistics Yearbook 2007.*

Organisation for Economic Cooperation and Development (OECD), 2 rue Andre Pascal, F-75775 Paris Cedex 16, France, (Telephone in U.S. (202) 785-6323), (Fax in U.S. (202) 785-0350), www.oecd.org; *Financial Market Trends: OECD Periodical; Household, Tourism, Travel: Trends, Environmental Impacts and Policy Responses;* and *OECD Economic Outlook 2008.*

Taylor and Francis Group, An Informa Business, 2 Park Square, Milton Park, Abingdon, Oxford OX14 4RN, United Kingdom, (Dial from U.S. (212) 216-7800), (Fax from U.S. (212) 564-7854), www.tandf.co.uk; *The Europa World Year Book.*

United Nations Statistics Division, New York, NY 10017, (800) 253-9646, Fax: (212) 963-4116, http://unstats.un.org; *Statistical Yearbook; Trends in Europe and North America: The Statistical Yearbook of the ECE 2005;* and *World Statistics Pocketbook.*

ICELAND - FORESTS AND FORESTRY

Euromonitor International, Inc., 224 S. Michigan Avenue, Suite 1500, Chicago, IL 60604, (312) 922-1115, Fax: (312) 922-1157, www.euromonitor.com; *European Marketing Data and Statistics 2008.*

M.E. Sharpe, 80 Business Park Drive, Armonk, NY 10504, (800) 541-6563, Fax: (914) 273-2106, www.mesharpe.com; *The Illustrated Book of World Rankings.*

Nordic Council of Ministers, Store Strandstraede 18, DK-1255 Copenhagen K, Denmark, www.norden.org; *Nordic Statistical Yearbook 2004-2006.*

Organisation for Economic Cooperation and Development (OECD), 2 rue Andre Pascal, F-75775 Paris Cedex 16, France, (Telephone in U.S. (202) 785-6323), (Fax in U.S. (202) 785-0350), www.oecd.org; *International Trade by Commodity Statistics (ITCS)* and STructural ANalysis (STAN) database.

Technical Association of the Pulp and Paper Industry (TAPPI), 15 Technology Parkway South, Norcross, GA 30092, (770) 446-1400, Fax: (770) 446-6947, www.tappi.org; *TAPPI Annual Report.*

UNESCO Institute for Statistics, C.P. 6128 Succursale Centre-Ville, Montreal, Quebec, H3C 3J7 Canada, (Dial from U.S. (514) 343-6880), (Fax from U.S. (514) 343 6882), www.uis.unesco.org; *Statistical Tables.*

United Nations Conference on Trade and Development (UNCTAD), DC2-1120, United Nations, New York, NY 10017, (212) 963-0027, www.unctad.org; *UNCTAD Commodity Yearbook.*

United Nations Food and Agricultural Organization (FAO), Viale delle Terme di Caracalla, 00100 Rome, Italy, (Dial from U.S. (202) 653-2400), (Fax from U.S. (202) 653 5760), www.fao.org; *FAO Yearbook of Forest Products* and *The State of Food and Agriculture (SOFA) 2006.*

United Nations Statistics Division, New York, NY 10017, (800) 253-9646, Fax: (212) 963-4116, http://unstats.un.org; *Statistical Yearbook* and *Trends in Europe and North America: The Statistical Yearbook of the ECE 2005.*

The World Bank, 1818 H Street, NW, Washington, DC 20433, (202) 473-1000, Fax: (202) 477-6391, www.worldbank.org; *Iceland.*

ICELAND - FRUIT PRODUCTION

See ICELAND - CROPS

ICELAND - GAS PRODUCTION

See ICELAND - MINERAL INDUSTRIES

ICELAND - GEOGRAPHIC INFORMATION SYSTEMS

M.E. Sharpe, 80 Business Park Drive, Armonk, NY 10504, (800) 541-6563, Fax: (914) 273-2106, www.mesharpe.com; *The Illustrated Book of World Rankings.*

The World Bank, 1818 H Street, NW, Washington, DC 20433, (202) 473-1000, Fax: (202) 477-6391, www.worldbank.org; *Iceland.*

ICELAND - GOLD INDUSTRY

International Monetary Fund (IMF), 700 Nineteenth Street, NW, Washington, DC 20431, (202) 623-7000, Fax: (202) 623-4661, www.imf.org; *International Financial Statistics Yearbook 2007.*

United Nations Statistics Division, New York, NY 10017, (800) 253-9646, Fax: (212) 963-4116, http://unstats.un.org; *Statistical Yearbook.*

The World Bank, 1818 H Street, NW, Washington, DC 20433, (202) 473-1000, Fax: (202) 477-6391, www.worldbank.org; *World Development Indicators (WDI) 2008.*

ICELAND - GOLD PRODUCTION

See ICELAND - MINERAL INDUSTRIES

ICELAND - GRANTS-IN-AID

International Monetary Fund (IMF), 700 Nineteenth Street, NW, Washington, DC 20431, (202) 623-7000, Fax: (202) 623-4661, www.imf.org; *Government Finance Statistics Yearbook (2008 Edition).*

Organisation for Economic Cooperation and Development (OECD), 2 rue Andre Pascal, F-75775 Paris Cedex 16, France, (Telephone in U.S. (202) 785-6323), (Fax in U.S. (202) 785-0350), www.oecd.org; *Geographical Distribution of Financial Flows to Aid Recipients 2002-2006.*

ICELAND - GROSS DOMESTIC PRODUCT

Economist Intelligence Unit, 111 West 57th Street, New York, NY 10019, (212) 554-0600, Fax: (212) 586-1181, www.eiu.com; *Iceland Country Report.*

Euromonitor International, Inc., 224 S. Michigan Avenue, Suite 1500, Chicago, IL 60604, (312) 922-1115, Fax: (312) 922-1157, www.euromonitor.com; *The World Economic Factbook 2008.*

M.E. Sharpe, 80 Business Park Drive, Armonk, NY 10504, (800) 541-6563, Fax: (914) 273-2106, www.mesharpe.com; *The Illustrated Book of World Rankings.*

Nordic Council of Ministers, Store Strandstraede 18, DK-1255 Copenhagen K, Denmark, www.norden.org; *Nordic Statistical Yearbook 2004-2006.*

Organisation for Economic Cooperation and Development (OECD), 2 rue Andre Pascal, F-75775 Paris Cedex 16, France, (Telephone in U.S. (202) 785-6323), (Fax in U.S. (202) 785-0350), www.oecd.org; *Comparison of Gross Domestic Product (GDP) for OECD Countries; Geographical Distribution of Financial Flows to Aid Recipients 2002-2006;* and *OECD Economic Outlook 2008.*

Taylor and Francis Group, An Informa Business, 2 Park Square, Milton Park, Abingdon, Oxford OX14 4RN, United Kingdom, (Dial from U.S. (212) 216-7800), (Fax from U.S. (212) 564-7854), www.tandf.co.uk; *The Europa World Year Book.*

United Nations Statistics Division, New York, NY 10017, (800) 253-9646, Fax: (212) 963-4116, http://unstats.un.org; *Human Development Report 2006; National Accounts Statistics: Compendium of Income Distribution Statistics; Statistical Yearbook;* and *Trends in Europe and North America: The Statistical Yearbook of the ECE 2005.*

The World Bank, 1818 H Street, NW, Washington, DC 20433, (202) 473-1000, Fax: (202) 477-6391, www.worldbank.org; *World Development Indicators (WDI) 2008.*

ICELAND - GROSS NATIONAL PRODUCT

M.E. Sharpe, 80 Business Park Drive, Armonk, NY 10504, (800) 541-6563, Fax: (914) 273-2106, www.mesharpe.com; *The Illustrated Book of World Rankings.*

Organisation for Economic Cooperation and Development (OECD), 2 rue Andre Pascal, F-75775 Paris Cedex 16, France, (Telephone in U.S. (202) 785-6323), (Fax in U.S. (202) 785-0350), www.oecd.org; *Geographical Distribution of Financial Flows to Aid Recipients 2002-2006; OECD Composite Leading Indicators (CLIs), Updated September 2007;* and *OECD Economic Outlook 2008.*

Palgrave Macmillan Ltd., Houndmills, Basingstoke, Hampshire, RG21 6XS, England, (Telephone in U.S. (888) 330-8477), (Fax in U.S. (800) 672-2054), www.palgrave.com; *The Statesman's Yearbook 2008.*

U.S. Department of State (DOS), 2201 C Street NW, Washington, DC 20520, (202) 647-4000, www.state.gov; *World Military Expenditures and Arms Transfers (WMEAT).*

United Nations Statistics Division, New York, NY 10017, (800) 253-9646, Fax: (212) 963-4116, http://unstats.un.org; *Statistical Yearbook.*

The World Bank, 1818 H Street, NW, Washington, DC 20433, (202) 473-1000, Fax: (202) 477-6391, www.worldbank.org; *The World Bank Atlas 2003-2004* and *World Development Indicators (WDI) 2008.*

ICELAND - HIDES AND SKINS INDUSTRY

Organisation for Economic Cooperation and Development (OECD), 2 rue Andre Pascal, F-75775 Paris Cedex 16, France, (Telephone in U.S. (202) 785-6323), (Fax in U.S. (202) 785-0350), www.oecd.org; *International Trade by Commodity Statistics (ITCS).*

United Nations Food and Agricultural Organization (FAO), Viale delle Terme di Caracalla, 00100 Rome, Italy, (Dial from U.S. (202) 653-2400), (Fax from U.S. (202) 653 5760), www.fao.org; *FAO Production Yearbook 2002.*

ICELAND - HOUSING

Euromonitor International, Inc., 224 S. Michigan Avenue, Suite 1500, Chicago, IL 60604, (312) 922-1115, Fax: (312) 922-1157, www.euromonitor.com; *World Marketing Data and Statistics.*

M.E. Sharpe, 80 Business Park Drive, Armonk, NY 10504, (800) 541-6563, Fax: (914) 273-2106, www.mesharpe.com; *The Illustrated Book of World Rankings.*

Nordic Council of Ministers, Store Strandstraede 18, DK-1255 Copenhagen K, Denmark, www.norden.org; *Nordic Statistical Yearbook 2004-2006.*

United Nations Statistics Division, New York, NY 10017, (800) 253-9646, Fax: (212) 963-4116, http://unstats.un.org; *Trends in Europe and North America: The Statistical Yearbook of the ECE 2005.*

ICELAND - HOUSING - FINANCE

Organisation for Economic Cooperation and Development (OECD), 2 rue Andre Pascal, F-75775 Paris Cedex 16, France, (Telephone in U.S. (202) 785-6323), (Fax in U.S. (202) 785-0350), www.oecd.org; *OECD Main Economic Indicators (MEI).*

ICELAND - HOUSING CONSTRUCTION

See ICELAND - CONSTRUCTION INDUSTRY

ICELAND - ILLITERATE PERSONS

Euromonitor International, Inc., 224 S. Michigan Avenue, Suite 1500, Chicago, IL 60604, (312) 922-1115, Fax: (312) 922-1157, www.euromonitor.com; *The World Economic Factbook 2008.*

United Nations Statistics Division, New York, NY 10017, (800) 253-9646, Fax: (212) 963-4116, http://unstats.un.org; *Human Development Report 2006.*

ICELAND - IMPORTS

Central Intelligence Agency, Office of Public Affairs, Washington, DC 20505, (703) 482-0623, Fax: (703) 482-1739, www.cia.gov; *The World Factbook.*

Economist Intelligence Unit, 111 West 57th Street, New York, NY 10019, (212) 554-0600, Fax: (212) 586-1181, www.eiu.com; *Iceland Country Report.*

Euromonitor International, Inc., 224 S. Michigan Avenue, Suite 1500, Chicago, IL 60604, (312) 922-1115, Fax: (312) 922-1157, www.euromonitor.com; *The World Economic Factbook 2008.*

International Monetary Fund (IMF), 700 Nineteenth Street, NW, Washington, DC 20431, (202) 623-7000, Fax: (202) 623-4661, www.imf.org; *Direction of Trade Statistics Yearbook 2007; Government Finance Statistics Yearbook (2008 Edition);* and *International Financial Statistics Yearbook 2007.*

Nordic Council of Ministers, Store Strandstraede 18, DK-1255 Copenhagen K, Denmark, www.norden.org; *Nordic Statistical Yearbook 2004-2006.*

Organisation for Economic Cooperation and Development (OECD), 2 rue Andre Pascal, F-75775 Paris Cedex 16, France, (Telephone in U.S. (202) 785-6323), (Fax in U.S. (202) 785-0350), www.oecd.org; *Iron and Steel Industry in 2004 (2006 Edition); 2005 OECD Agricultural Outlook Tables, 1970-2014; OECD Economic Outlook 2008; OECD Economic Survey - Iceland 2008; Review of Fisheries in OECD Countries: Country Statistics 2001 to 2003 - 2005 Edition;* and STructural ANalysis (STAN) database.

Palgrave Macmillan Ltd., Houndmills, Basingstoke, Hampshire, RG21 6XS, England, (Telephone in U.S. (888) 330-8477), (Fax in U.S. (800) 672-2054), www.palgrave.com; *The Statesman's Yearbook 2008.*

Taylor and Francis Group, An Informa Business, 2 Park Square, Milton Park, Abingdon, Oxford OX14 4RN, United Kingdom, (Dial from U.S. (212) 216-7800), (Fax from U.S. (212) 564-7854), www.tandf.co.uk; *The Europa World Year Book.*

Technical Association of the Pulp and Paper Industry (TAPPI), 15 Technology Parkway South, Norcross, GA 30092, (770) 446-1400, Fax: (770) 446-6947, www.tappi.org; *TAPPI Annual Report.*

United Nations Conference on Trade and Development (UNCTAD), DC2-1120, United Nations, New York, NY 10017, (212) 963-0027, www.unctad.org; *Handbook of Statistics 2005.*

United Nations Food and Agricultural Organization (FAO), Viale delle Terme di Caracalla, 00100 Rome, Italy, (Dial from U.S. (202) 653-2400), (Fax from U.S. (202) 653 5760), www.fao.org; *The State of Food and Agriculture (SOFA) 2006.*

United Nations Statistics Division, New York, NY 10017, (800) 253-9646, Fax: (212) 963-4116, http://unstats.un.org; *Trends in Europe and North America: The Statistical Yearbook of the ECE 2005.*

The World Bank, 1818 H Street, NW, Washington, DC 20433, (202) 473-1000, Fax: (202) 477-6391, www.worldbank.org; *World Development Indicators (WDI) 2008.*

ICELAND - INCOME TAXES

See ICELAND - TAXATION

ICELAND - INDUSTRIAL METALS PRODUCTION

See ICELAND - MINERAL INDUSTRIES

ICELAND - INDUSTRIAL PRODUCTIVITY

M.E. Sharpe, 80 Business Park Drive, Armonk, NY 10504, (800) 541-6563, Fax: (914) 273-2106, www.mesharpe.com; *The Illustrated Book of World Rankings.*

Organisation for Economic Cooperation and Development (OECD), 2 rue Andre Pascal, F-75775 Paris Cedex 16, France, (Telephone in U.S. (202) 785-6323), (Fax in U.S. (202) 785-0350), www.oecd.org; *Environmental Impacts of Foreign Direct Investment in the Mining Sector in the Newly Independent States (NIS); Iron and Steel Industry in 2004 (2006 Edition); A New World Map in Textiles and Clothing: Adjusting to Change; 2005 OECD Agricultural Outlook Tables, 1970-2014; OECD Economic Outlook 2008;* and STructural ANalysis (STAN) database.

Technical Association of the Pulp and Paper Industry (TAPPI), 15 Technology Parkway South, Norcross, GA 30092, (770) 446-1400, Fax: (770) 446-6947, www.tappi.org; *TAPPI Annual Report.*

ICELAND - INDUSTRIAL PROPERTY

Nordic Council of Ministers, Store Strandstraede 18, DK-1255 Copenhagen K, Denmark, www.norden.org; *Nordic Statistical Yearbook 2004-2006.*

United Nations Statistics Division, New York, NY 10017, (800) 253-9646, Fax: (212) 963-4116, http://unstats.un.org; *Statistical Yearbook.*

World Intellectual Property Organization (WIPO), PO Box 18, CH-1211 Geneva 20, Switzerland, www.wipo.int; *Industrial Property Statistics* and *Industrial Property Statistics Online Directory.*

ICELAND - INDUSTRIES

Central Intelligence Agency, Office of Public Affairs, Washington, DC 20505, (703) 482-0623, Fax: (703) 482-1739, www.cia.gov; *The World Factbook.*

Economist Intelligence Unit, 111 West 57th Street, New York, NY 10019, (212) 554-0600, Fax: (212) 586-1181, www.eiu.com; *Iceland Country Report.*

Euromonitor International, Inc., 224 S. Michigan Avenue, Suite 1500, Chicago, IL 60604, (312) 922-1115, Fax: (312) 922-1157, www.euromonitor.com; *The World Economic Factbook 2008* and *World Marketing Data and Statistics.*

International Labour Office, I.L.O. Publications, 4 route des Morillons, CH-1211 Geneva 22, Switzerland, (Telephone in U.S. (202) 653-7652), (Fax in U.S. (202) 653-7687), www.ilo.org; *Yearbook of Labour Statistics 2006.*

M.E. Sharpe, 80 Business Park Drive, Armonk, NY 10504, (800) 541-6563, Fax: (914) 273-2106, www.mesharpe.com; *The Illustrated Book of World Rankings.*

Nordic Council of Ministers, Store Strandstraede 18, DK-1255 Copenhagen K, Denmark, www.norden.org; *Nordic Statistical Yearbook 2004-2006.*

Organisation for Economic Cooperation and Development (OECD), 2 rue Andre Pascal, F-75775 Paris Cedex 16, France, (Telephone in U.S. (202) 785-6323), (Fax in U.S. (202) 785-0350), www.oecd.org; *Key Environmental Indicators 2004; OECD Economic Outlook 2008;* and STructural ANalysis (STAN) database.

Palgrave Macmillan Ltd., Houndmills, Basingstoke, Hampshire, RG21 6XS, England, (Telephone in U.S. (888) 330-8477), (Fax in U.S. (800) 672-2054), www.palgrave.com; *The Statesman's Yearbook 2008.*

Taylor and Francis Group, An Informa Business, 2 Park Square, Milton Park, Abingdon, Oxford OX14 4RN, United Kingdom, (Dial from U.S. (212) 216-7800), (Fax from U.S. (212) 564-7854), www.tandf.co.uk; *The Europa World Year Book.*

United Nations Industrial Development Organization (UNIDO), 1 United Nations Plaza, New York, NY 10017, (212) 963 6890, Fax: (212) 963-7904, http://unido.org; Industrial Statistics Database 2008 (INDSTAT) and *The International Yearbook of Industrial Statistics 2008.*

United Nations Statistics Division, New York, NY 10017, (800) 253-9646, Fax: (212) 963-4116, http://unstats.un.org; *2004 Industrial Commodity Statistics Yearbook* and *Trends in Europe and North America: The Statistical Yearbook of the ECE 2005.*

The World Bank, 1818 H Street, NW, Washington, DC 20433, (202) 473-1000, Fax: (202) 477-6391, www.worldbank.org; *Iceland* and *World Development Indicators (WDI) 2008.*

ICELAND - INFANT AND MATERNAL MORTALITY

See ICELAND - MORTALITY

ICELAND - INFORMATION TECHNOLOGY

Statistics Iceland, Borgartuni 21a, 150 Reykjavik, Iceland, www.statice.is; *Icelandic Information Society in a European Context 2006.*

ICELAND - INTEREST RATES

Organisation for Economic Cooperation and Development (OECD), 2 rue Andre Pascal, F-75775 Paris Cedex 16, France, (Telephone in U.S. (202) 785-6323), (Fax in U.S. (202) 785-0350), www.oecd.org; *Financial Market Trends: OECD Periodical* and *OECD Economic Outlook 2008.*

ICELAND - INTERNATIONAL FINANCE

Organisation for Economic Cooperation and Development (OECD), 2 rue Andre Pascal, F-75775 Paris Cedex 16, France, (Telephone in U.S. (202) 785-6323), (Fax in U.S. (202) 785-0350), www.oecd.org; *Financial Market Trends: OECD Periodical* and *OECD Economic Outlook 2008.*

The World Bank, 1818 H Street, NW, Washington, DC 20433, (202) 473-1000, Fax: (202) 477-6391, www.worldbank.org; *Iceland.*

ICELAND - INTERNATIONAL LIQUIDITY

International Monetary Fund (IMF), 700 Nineteenth Street, NW, Washington, DC 20431, (202) 623-7000, Fax: (202) 623-4661, www.imf.org; *International Financial Statistics Yearbook 2007.*

Organisation for Economic Cooperation and Development (OECD), 2 rue Andre Pascal, F-75775 Paris Cedex 16, France, (Telephone in U.S. (202) 785-6323), (Fax in U.S. (202) 785-0350), www.oecd.org; *Financial Market Trends: OECD Periodical* and *OECD Economic Outlook 2008.*

ICELAND - INTERNATIONAL STATISTICS

Organisation for Economic Cooperation and Development (OECD), 2 rue Andre Pascal, F-75775 Paris Cedex 16, France, (Telephone in U.S. (202) 785-6323), (Fax in U.S. (202) 785-0350), www.oecd.org; *Financial Market Trends: OECD Periodical* and *Household, Tourism, Travel: Trends, Environmental Impacts and Policy Responses.*

ICELAND - INTERNATIONAL TRADE

Banque de France, 48 rue Croix des Petits champs, 75001 Paris, France, www.banque-france.fr/home.htm; *Monthly Business Survey Overview.*

Bernan Essential Government Publications, 4611-F Assembly Drive, Lanham MD, 20706-4391, (301) 459-2255, Fax: (800) 865-3450, www.bernan.com; *OECD Factbook 2006.*

Economist Intelligence Unit, 111 West 57th Street, New York, NY 10019, (212) 554-0600, Fax: (212) 586-1181, www.eiu.com; *Iceland Country Report.*

Euromonitor International, Inc., 224 S. Michigan Avenue, Suite 1500, Chicago, IL 60604, (312) 922-1115, Fax: (312) 922-1157, www.euromonitor.com; *European Marketing Data and Statistics 2008; The World Economic Factbook 2008;* and *World Marketing Data and Statistics.*

International Monetary Fund (IMF), 700 Nineteenth Street, NW, Washington, DC 20431, (202) 623-7000, Fax: (202) 623-4661, www.imf.org; *International Financial Statistics Yearbook 2007.*

M.E. Sharpe, 80 Business Park Drive, Armonk, NY 10504, (800) 541-6563, Fax: (914) 273-2106, www.mesharpe.com; *The Illustrated Book of World Rankings.*

Nordic Council of Ministers, Store Strandstraede 18, DK-1255 Copenhagen K, Denmark, www.norden.org; *Nordic Statistical Yearbook 2004-2006.*

Organisation for Economic Cooperation and Development (OECD), 2 rue Andre Pascal, F-75775 Paris Cedex 16, France, (Telephone in U.S. (202) 785-6323), (Fax in U.S. (202) 785-0350), www.oecd.org; *International Trade by Commodity Statistics (ITCS); 2005 OECD Agricultural Outlook Tables, 1970-2014; OECD Economic Outlook 2008; OECD Economic Survey - Iceland 2008; OECD in Figures 2007; OECD Main Economic Indicators (MEI);* and *Statistics on Ship Production, Exports and Orders in 2004.*

Palgrave Macmillan Ltd., Houndmills, Basingstoke, Hampshire, RG21 6XS, England, (Telephone in U.S. (888) 330-8477), (Fax in U.S. (800) 672-2054), www.palgrave.com; *The Statesman's Yearbook 2008.*

Taylor and Francis Group, An Informa Business, 2 Park Square, Milton Park, Abingdon, Oxford OX14 4RN, United Kingdom, (Dial from U.S. (212) 216-7800), (Fax from U.S. (212) 564-7854), www.tandf.co.uk; *The Europa World Year Book.*

United Nations Conference on Trade and Development (UNCTAD), DC2-1120, United Nations, New York, NY 10017, (212) 963-0027, www.unctad.org; *UNCTAD Commodity Yearbook.*

United Nations Food and Agricultural Organization (FAO), Viale delle Terme di Caracalla, 00100 Rome, Italy, (Dial from U.S. (202) 653-2400), (Fax from U.S. (202) 653 5760), www.fao.org; *FAO Trade Yearbook* and *The State of Food and Agriculture (SOFA) 2006.*

United Nations Statistics Division, New York, NY 10017, (800) 253-9646, Fax: (212) 963-4116, http://unstats.un.org; *International Trade Statistics Yearbook* and *Statistical Yearbook.*

The World Bank, 1818 H Street, NW, Washington, DC 20433, (202) 473-1000, Fax: (202) 477-6391, www.worldbank.org; *Iceland* and *World Development Indicators (WDI) 2008.*

World Trade Organization (WTO), Centre William Rappard, Rue de Lausanne 154, CH-1211 Geneva 21, Switzerland, www.wto.org; *International Trade Statistics 2006.*

ICELAND - INTERNET USERS

International Telecommunication Union (ITU), Place des Nations, 1211 Geneva 20, Switzerland, www.itu.int; *World Telecommunication/ICT Indicators Database on CD-ROM; World Telecommunication/ICT Indicators Database Online;* and *Yearbook of Statistics - Telecommunication Services (Chronological Time Series 1997-2006).*

The World Bank, 1818 H Street, NW, Washington, DC 20433, (202) 473-1000, Fax: (202) 477-6391, www.worldbank.org; *Iceland.*

ICELAND - INVESTMENTS

Organisation for Economic Cooperation and Development (OECD), 2 rue Andre Pascal, F-75775 Paris Cedex 16, France, (Telephone in U.S. (202) 785-6323), (Fax in U.S. (202) 785-0350), www.oecd.org; *Financial Market Trends: OECD Periodical; Iron and Steel Industry in 2004 (2006 Edition); A New World Map in Textiles and Clothing: Adjusting to Change; OECD Economic Outlook 2008;* and STructural ANalysis (STAN) database.

ICELAND - IRON AND IRON ORE PRODUCTION

See ICELAND - MINERAL INDUSTRIES

ICELAND - LABOR

Central Intelligence Agency, Office of Public Affairs, Washington, DC 20505, (703) 482-0623, Fax: (703) 482-1739, www.cia.gov; *The World Factbook.*

Euromonitor International, Inc., 224 S. Michigan Avenue, Suite 1500, Chicago, IL 60604, (312) 922-1115, Fax: (312) 922-1157, www.euromonitor.com; *World Marketing Data and Statistics.*

International Labour Office, I.L.O. Publications, 4 route des Morillons, CH-1211 Geneva 22, Switzerland, (Telephone in U.S. (202) 653-7652), (Fax in U.S. (202) 653-7687), www.ilo.org; *Yearbook of Labour Statistics 2006.*

M.E. Sharpe, 80 Business Park Drive, Armonk, NY 10504, (800) 541-6563, Fax: (914) 273-2106, www.mesharpe.com; *The Illustrated Book of World Rankings.*

Nordic Council of Ministers, Store Strandstraede 18, DK-1255 Copenhagen K, Denmark, www.norden.org; *Nordic Statistical Yearbook 2004-2006.*

Organisation for Economic Cooperation and Development (OECD), 2 rue Andre Pascal, F-75775 Paris Cedex 16, France, (Telephone in U.S. (202) 785-6323), (Fax in U.S. (202) 785-0350), www.oecd.org; *Iron and Steel Industry in 2004 (2006 Edition); A New World Map in Textiles and Clothing: Adjusting to Change; OECD Economic Outlook 2008; OECD Economic Survey - Iceland 2008; OECD Employment Outlook 2007;* and *Statistics on Ship Production, Exports and Orders in 2004.*

Palgrave Macmillan Ltd., Houndmills, Basingstoke, Hampshire, RG21 6XS, England, (Telephone in U.S. (888) 330-8477), (Fax in U.S. (800) 672-2054), www.palgrave.com; *The Statesman's Yearbook 2008.*

Statistics Iceland, Borgartuni 21a, 150 Reykjavik, Iceland, www.statice.is; *Associations of Media People, Graphic Designers and Artists 1980-2005.*

United Nations Food and Agricultural Organization (FAO), Viale delle Terme di Caracalla, 00100 Rome, Italy, (Dial from U.S. (202) 653-2460), (Fax from U.S. (202) 653 5760), www.fao.org; *The State of Food and Agriculture (SOFA) 2006.*

United Nations Statistics Division, New York, NY 10017, (800) 253-9646, Fax: (212) 963-4116, http://unstats.un.org; *Human Development Report 2006.*

The World Bank, 1818 H Street, NW, Washington, DC 20433, (202) 473-1000, Fax: (202) 477-6391, www.worldbank.org; *The World Bank Atlas 2003-2004* and *World Development Indicators (WDI) 2008.*

ICELAND - LAND USE

Central Intelligence Agency, Office of Public Affairs, Washington, DC 20505, (703) 482-0623, Fax: (703) 482-1739, www.cia.gov; *The World Factbook.*

Euromonitor International, Inc., 224 S. Michigan Avenue, Suite 1500, Chicago, IL 60604, (312) 922-1115, Fax: (312) 922-1157, www.euromonitor.com; *European Marketing Data and Statistics 2008.*

United Nations Food and Agricultural Organization (FAO), Viale delle Terme di Caracalla, 00100 Rome, Italy, (Dial from U.S. (202) 653-2400), (Fax from U.S. (202) 653 5760), www.fao.org; *FAO Production Yearbook 2002.*

ICELAND - LIBRARIES

M.E. Sharpe, 80 Business Park Drive, Armonk, NY 10504, (800) 541-6563, Fax: (914) 273-2106, www.mesharpe.com; *The Illustrated Book of World Rankings.*

Nordic Council of Ministers, Store Strandstraede 18, DK-1255 Copenhagen K, Denmark, www.norden.org; *Nordic Statistical Yearbook 2004-2006.*

UNESCO Institute for Statistics, C.P. 6128 Succursale Centre-Ville, Montreal, Quebec, H3C 3J7 Canada, (Dial from U.S. (514) 343-6880), (Fax from U.S. (514) 343 6882), www.uis.unesco.org; *Statistical Tables.*

United Nations Statistics Division, New York, NY 10017, (800) 253-9646, Fax: (212) 963-4116, http://unstats.un.org; *Trends in Europe and North America: The Statistical Yearbook of the ECE 2005.*

ICELAND - LICENSES

International Monetary Fund (IMF), 700 Nineteenth Street, NW, Washington, DC 20431, (202) 623-

7000, Fax: (202) 623-4661, www.imf.org; *Government Finance Statistics Yearbook (2008 Edition).*

ICELAND - LIFE EXPECTANCY

Central Intelligence Agency, Office of Public Affairs, Washington, DC 20505, (703) 482-0623, Fax: (703) 482-1739, www.cia.gov; *The World Factbook.*

Euromonitor International, Inc., 224 S. Michigan Avenue, Suite 1500, Chicago, IL 60604, (312) 922-1115, Fax: (312) 922-1157, www.euromonitor.com; *The World Economic Factbook 2008.*

Organisation for Economic Cooperation and Development (OECD), 2 rue Andre Pascal, F-75775 Paris Cedex 16, France, (Telephone in U.S. (202) 785-6323), (Fax in U.S. (202) 785-0350), www.oecd.org; *OECD Economic Outlook 2008.*

Palgrave Macmillan Ltd., Houndmills, Basingstoke, Hampshire, RG21 6XS, England, (Telephone in U.S. (888) 330-8477), (Fax in U.S. (800) 672-2054), www.palgrave.com; *The Statesman's Yearbook 2008.*

United Nations Statistics Division, New York, NY 10017, (800) 253-9646, Fax: (212) 963-4116, http://unstats.un.org; *Human Development Report 2006; Trends in Europe and North America: The Statistical Yearbook of the ECE 2005;* and *World Statistics Pocketbook.*

The World Bank, 1818 H Street, NW, Washington, DC 20433, (202) 473-1000, Fax: (202) 477-6391, www.worldbank.org; *The World Bank Atlas 2003-2004.*

ICELAND - LITERACY

Euromonitor International, Inc., 224 S. Michigan Avenue, Suite 1500, Chicago, IL 60604, (312) 922-1115, Fax: (312) 922-1157, www.euromonitor.com; *World Marketing Data and Statistics.*

ICELAND - LIVESTOCK

Euromonitor International, Inc., 224 S. Michigan Avenue, Suite 1500, Chicago, IL 60604, (312) 922-1115, Fax: (312) 922-1157, www.euromonitor.com; *European Marketing Data and Statistics 2008.*

M.E. Sharpe, 80 Business Park Drive, Armonk, NY 10504, (800) 541-6563, Fax: (914) 273-2106, www.mesharpe.com; *The Illustrated Book of World Rankings.*

Nordic Council of Ministers, Store Strandstraede 18, DK-1255 Copenhagen K, Denmark, www.norden.org; *Nordic Statistical Yearbook 2004-2006.*

Organisation for Economic Cooperation and Development (OECD), 2 rue Andre Pascal, F-75775 Paris Cedex 16, France, (Telephone in U.S. (202) 785-6323), (Fax in U.S. (202) 785-0350), www.oecd.org; *2005 OECD Agricultural Outlook Tables, 1970-2014.*

Palgrave Macmillan Ltd., Houndmills, Basingstoke, Hampshire, RG21 6XS, England, (Telephone in U.S. (888) 330-8477), (Fax in U.S. (800) 672-2054), www.palgrave.com; *The Statesman's Yearbook 2008.*

Taylor and Francis Group, An Informa Business, 2 Park Square, Milton Park, Abingdon, Oxford OX14 4RN, United Kingdom, (Dial from U.S. (212) 216-7800), (Fax from U.S. (212) 564-7854), www.tandf.co.uk; *The Europa World Year Book.*

United Nations Conference on Trade and Development (UNCTAD), DC2-1120, United Nations, New York, NY 10017, (212) 963-0027, www.unctad.org; *UNCTAD Commodity Yearbook.*

United Nations Food and Agricultural Organization (FAO), Viale delle Terme di Caracalla, 00100 Rome, Italy, (Dial from U.S. (202) 653-2400), (Fax from U.S. (202) 653 5760), www.fao.org; *FAO Production Yearbook 2002* and *The State of Food and Agriculture (SOFA) 2006.*

United Nations Statistics Division, New York, NY 10017, (800) 253-9646, Fax: (212) 963-4116, http://unstats.un.org; *Statistical Yearbook.*

ICELAND - MANUFACTURES

M.E. Sharpe, 80 Business Park Drive, Armonk, NY 10504, (800) 541-6563, Fax: (914) 273-2106, www.mesharpe.com; *The Illustrated Book of World Rankings.*

Nordic Council of Ministers, Store Strandstraede 18, DK-1255 Copenhagen K, Denmark, www.norden.org; *Nordic Statistical Yearbook 2004-2006.*

Organisation for Economic Cooperation and Development (OECD), 2 rue Andre Pascal, F-75775 Paris Cedex 16, France, (Telephone in U.S. (202) 785-6323), (Fax in U.S. (202) 785-0350), www.oecd.org; *International Trade by Commodity Statistics (ITCS); OECD Economic Survey - Iceland 2008;* and STructural ANalysis (STAN) database.

The World Bank, 1818 H Street, NW, Washington, DC 20433, (202) 473-1000, Fax: (202) 477-6391, www.worldbank.org; *World Development Indicators (WDI) 2008.*

ICELAND - MARRIAGE

M.E. Sharpe, 80 Business Park Drive, Armonk, NY 10504, (800) 541-6563, Fax: (914) 273-2106, www.mesharpe.com; *The Illustrated Book of World Rankings.*

Nordic Council of Ministers, Store Strandstraede 18, DK-1255 Copenhagen K, Denmark, www.norden.org; *Nordic Statistical Yearbook 2004-2006.*

Taylor and Francis Group, An Informa Business, 2 Park Square, Milton Park, Abingdon, Oxford OX14 4RN, United Kingdom, (Dial from U.S. (212) 216-7800), (Fax from U.S. (212) 564-7854), www.tandf.co.uk; *The Europa World Year Book.*

United Nations Statistics Division, New York, NY 10017, (800) 253-9646, Fax: (212) 963-4116, http://unstats.un.org; *Demographic Yearbook; Statistical Yearbook;* and *Trends in Europe and North America: The Statistical Yearbook of the ECE 2005.*

ICELAND - MEAT PRODUCTION

See ICELAND - LIVESTOCK

ICELAND - MEDICAL CARE, COST OF

International Monetary Fund (IMF), 700 Nineteenth Street, NW, Washington, DC 20431, (202) 623-7000, Fax: (202) 623-4661, www.imf.org; *Government Finance Statistics Yearbook (2008 Edition).*

ICELAND - MILK PRODUCTION

See ICELAND - DAIRY PROCESSING

ICELAND - MINERAL INDUSTRIES

International Energy Agency (IEA), 9, rue de la Federation, 75739 Paris Cedex 15, France, www.iea.org; *Key World Energy Statistics 2007.*

International Monetary Fund (IMF), 700 Nineteenth Street, NW, Washington, DC 20431, (202) 623-7000, Fax: (202) 623-4661, www.imf.org; *International Financial Statistics Yearbook 2007.*

M.E. Sharpe, 80 Business Park Drive, Armonk, NY 10504, (800) 541-6563, Fax: (914) 273-2106, www.mesharpe.com; *The Illustrated Book of World Rankings.*

Nordic Council of Ministers, Store Strandstraede 18, DK-1255 Copenhagen K, Denmark, www.norden.org; *Nordic Statistical Yearbook 2004-2006.*

Organisation for Economic Cooperation and Development (OECD), 2 rue Andre Pascal, F-75775 Paris Cedex 16, France, (Telephone in U.S. (202) 785-6323), (Fax in U.S. (202) 785-0350), www.oecd.org; *Coal Information: 2007 Edition; Energy Statistics of OECD Countries* (2007 Edition); *Environmental Impacts of Foreign Direct Investment in the Mining Sector in the Newly Independent States (NIS); International Trade by Commodity Statistics (ITCS); Iron and Steel Industry in 2004 (2006 Edition); OECD Economic Survey - Iceland 2008;* and STructural ANalysis (STAN) database.

United Nations Conference on Trade and Development (UNCTAD), DC2-1120, United Nations, New York, NY 10017, (212) 963-0027, www.unctad.org; *UNCTAD Commodity Yearbook.*

United Nations Statistics Division, New York, NY 10017, (800) 253-9646, Fax: (212) 963-4116, http://unstats.un.org; *Statistical Yearbook.*

The World Bank, 1818 H Street, NW, Washington, DC 20433, (202) 473-1000, Fax: (202) 477-6391, www.worldbank.org; *Iceland.*

ICELAND - MONEY

European Central Bank (ECB), Postfach 160319, D-60066 Frankfurt am Main, Germany, www.ecb.int; *Monetary Developments in the Euro Area; Monthly Bulletin;* and *Statistics Pocket Book.*

Organisation for Economic Cooperation and Development (OECD), 2 rue Andre Pascal, F-75775 Paris Cedex 16, France, (Telephone in U.S. (202) 785-6323), (Fax in U.S. (202) 785-0350), www.oecd.org; *OECD Economic Survey - Iceland 2008.*

ICELAND - MONEY EXCHANGE RATES

See ICELAND - FOREIGN EXCHANGE RATES

ICELAND - MONEY SUPPLY

Economist Intelligence Unit, 111 West 57th Street, New York, NY 10019, (212) 554-0600, Fax: (212) 586-1181, www.eiu.com; *Iceland Country Report.*

International Monetary Fund (IMF), 700 Nineteenth Street, NW, Washington, DC 20431, (202) 623-7000, Fax: (202) 623-4661, www.imf.org; *International Financial Statistics Yearbook 2007.*

Nordic Council of Ministers, Store Strandstraede 18, DK-1255 Copenhagen K, Denmark, www.norden.org; *Nordic Statistical Yearbook 2004-2006.*

Organisation for Economic Cooperation and Development (OECD), 2 rue Andre Pascal, F-75775 Paris Cedex 16, France, (Telephone in U.S. (202) 785-6323), (Fax in U.S. (202) 785-0350), www.oecd.org; *OECD Economic Outlook 2008.*

Taylor and Francis Group, An Informa Business, 2 Park Square, Milton Park, Abingdon, Oxford OX14 4RN, United Kingdom, (Dial from U.S. (212) 216-7800), (Fax from U.S. (212) 564-7854), www.tandf.co.uk; *The Europa World Year Book.*

United Nations Statistics Division, New York, NY 10017, (800) 253-9646, Fax: (212) 963-4116, http://unstats.un.org; *Statistical Yearbook.*

The World Bank, 1818 H Street, NW, Washington, DC 20433, (202) 473-1000, Fax: (202) 477-6391, www.worldbank.org; *Iceland* and *World Development Indicators (WDI) 2008.*

ICELAND - MORTALITY

Central Intelligence Agency, Office of Public Affairs, Washington, DC 20505, (703) 482-0623, Fax: (703) 482-1739, www.cia.gov; *The World Factbook.*

Euromonitor International, Inc., 224 S. Michigan Avenue, Suite 1500, Chicago, IL 60604, (312) 922-1115, Fax: (312) 922-1157, www.euromonitor.com; *The World Economic Factbook 2008.*

Nordic Council of Ministers, Store Strandstraede 18, DK-1255 Copenhagen K, Denmark, www.norden.org; *Nordic Statistical Yearbook 2004-2006.*

Palgrave Macmillan Ltd., Houndmills, Basingstoke, Hampshire, RG21 6XS, England, (Telephone in U.S. (888) 330-8477), (Fax in U.S. (800) 672-2054), www.palgrave.com; *The Statesman's Yearbook 2008.*

Taylor and Francis Group, An Informa Business, 2 Park Square, Milton Park, Abingdon, Oxford OX14 4RN, United Kingdom, (Dial from U.S. (212) 216-7800), (Fax from U.S. (212) 564-7854), www.tandf.co.uk; *The Europa World Year Book.*

United Nations Statistics Division, New York, NY 10017, (800) 253-9646, Fax: (212) 963-4116, http://unstats.un.org; *Demographic Yearbook; Human Development Report 2006; Statistical Yearbook; Trends in Europe and North America: The Statistical Yearbook of the ECE 2005;* and *World Statistics Pocketbook.*

The World Bank, 1818 H Street, NW, Washington, DC 20433, (202) 473-1000, Fax: (202) 477-6391, www.worldbank.org; *The World Bank Atlas 2003-2004* and *World Development Indicators (WDI) 2008.*

World Health Organization (WHO), Avenue Appia 20, 1211 Geneve 27, Switzerland, (Telephone in

U.S. (212) 331-9081), www.who.int; The WHO Global Atlas of Infectious Diseases and *World Health Report 2006.*

ICELAND - MOTION PICTURES

Palgrave Macmillan Ltd., Houndmills, Basingstoke, Hampshire, RG21 6XS, England, (Telephone in U.S. (888) 330-8477), (Fax in U.S. (800) 672-2054), www.palgrave.com; *The Statesman's Yearbook 2008.*

United Nations Statistics Division, New York, NY 10017, (800) 253-9646, Fax: (212) 963-4116, http://unstats.un.org; *Statistical Yearbook.*

ICELAND - MOTOR VEHICLES

International Road Federation (IFR), Madison Place, 500 Montgomery Street, 5th Floor, Alexandria, VA 22314, (703) 535-1001, Fax: (703) 535-1007, www.irfnet.org; *World Road Statistics 2006.*

Nordic Council of Ministers, Store Strandstraede 18, DK-1255 Copenhagen K, Denmark, www.norden.org; *Nordic Statistical Yearbook 2004-2006.*

Taylor and Francis Group, An Informa Business, 2 Park Square, Milton Park, Abingdon, Oxford OX14 4RN, United Kingdom, (Dial from U.S. (212) 216-7800), (Fax from U.S. (212) 564-7854), www.tandf.co.uk; *The Europa World Year Book.*

United Nations Statistics Division, New York, NY 10017, (800) 253-9646, Fax: (212) 963-4116, http://unstats.un.org; *Statistical Yearbook.*

ICELAND - MUSEUMS

M.E. Sharpe, 80 Business Park Drive, Armonk, NY 10504, (800) 541-6563, Fax: (914) 273-2106, www.mesharpe.com; *The Illustrated Book of World Rankings.*

Nordic Council of Ministers, Store Strandstraede 18, DK-1255 Copenhagen K, Denmark, www.norden.org; *Nordic Statistical Yearbook 2004-2006.*

UNESCO Institute for Statistics, C.P. 6128 Succursale Centre-Ville, Montreal, Quebec, H3C 3J7 Canada, (Dial from U.S. (514) 343-6880), (Fax from U.S. (514) 343 6882), www.uis.unesco.org; *Statistical Tables.*

ICELAND - NATURAL GAS PRODUCTION

See ICELAND - MINERAL INDUSTRIES

ICELAND - NICKEL AND NICKEL ORE

See ICELAND - MINERAL INDUSTRIES

ICELAND - NUTRITION

United Nations Food and Agricultural Organization (FAO), Viale delle Terme di Caracalla, 00100 Rome, Italy, (Dial from U.S. (202) 653-2400), (Fax from U.S. (202) 653 5760), www.fao.org; *The State of Food and Agriculture (SOFA) 2006.*

ICELAND - OILSEED PLANTS

Organisation for Economic Cooperation and Development (OECD), 2 rue Andre Pascal, F-75775 Paris Cedex 16, France, (Telephone in U.S. (202) 785-6323), (Fax in U.S. (202) 785-0350), www.oecd.org; *International Trade by Commodity Statistics (ITCS).*

ICELAND - OLDER PEOPLE

M.E. Sharpe, 80 Business Park Drive, Armonk, NY 10504, (800) 541-6563, Fax: (914) 273-2106, www.mesharpe.com; *The Illustrated Book of World Rankings.*

ICELAND - PAPER

See ICELAND - FORESTS AND FORESTRY

ICELAND - PEANUT PRODUCTION

See ICELAND - CROPS

ICELAND - PERIODICALS

UNESCO Institute for Statistics, C.P. 6128 Succursale Centre-Ville, Montreal, Quebec, H3C 3J7 Canada, (Dial from U.S. (514) 343-6880), (Fax from U.S. (514) 343 6882), www.uis.unesco.org; *Statistical Tables.*

ICELAND - PESTICIDES

United Nations Food and Agricultural Organization (FAO), Viale delle Terme di Caracalla, 00100 Rome, Italy, (Dial from U.S. (202) 653-2400), (Fax from U.S. (202) 653 5760), www.fao.org; *The State of Food and Agriculture (SOFA) 2006.*

ICELAND - PETROLEUM INDUSTRY AND TRADE

Euromonitor International, Inc., 224 S. Michigan Avenue, Suite 1500, Chicago, IL 60604, (312) 922-1115, Fax: (312) 922-1157, www.euromonitor.com; *European Marketing Data and Statistics 2008.*

International Energy Agency (IEA), 9, rue de la Federation, 75739 Paris Cedex 15, France, www.iea.org; *Key World Energy Statistics 2007.*

M.E. Sharpe, 80 Business Park Drive, Armonk, NY 10504, (800) 541-6563, Fax: (914) 273-2106, www.mesharpe.com; *The Illustrated Book of World Rankings.*

Organisation for Economic Cooperation and Development (OECD), 2 rue Andre Pascal, F-75775 Paris Cedex 16, France, (Telephone in U.S. (202) 785-6323), (Fax in U.S. (202) 785-0350), www.oecd.org; *Energy Statistics of OECD Countries* (2007 Edition); *International Trade by Commodity Statistics (ITCS);* and *Oil Information 2006 Edition.*

PennWell Corporation, 1421 South Sheridan Road, Tulsa, OK 74112, (918) 835-3161, www.pennwell.com; *International Petroleum Encyclopedia 2007.*

U.S. Department of Energy (DOE), Energy Information Administration (EIA), 1000 Independence Avenue, SW, Washington, DC 20585, (202) 586-8800, www.eia.doe.gov; *International Energy Annual 2004* and *International Energy Outlook 2006.*

United Nations Conference on Trade and Development (UNCTAD), DC2-1120, United Nations, New York, NY 10017, (212) 963-0027, www.unctad.org; *UNCTAD Commodity Yearbook.*

United Nations Food and Agricultural Organization (FAO), Viale delle Terme di Caracalla, 00100 Rome, Italy, (Dial from U.S. (202) 653-2400), (Fax from U.S. (202) 653 5760), www.fao.org; *The State of Food and Agriculture (SOFA) 2006.*

United Nations Statistics Division, New York, NY 10017, (800) 253-9646, Fax: (212) 963-4116, http://unstats.un.org; *Trends in Europe and North America: The Statistical Yearbook of the ECE 2005.*

ICELAND - PLASTICS INDUSTRY AND TRADE

Organisation for Economic Cooperation and Development (OECD), 2 rue Andre Pascal, F-75775 Paris Cedex 16, France, (Telephone in U.S. (202) 785-6323), (Fax in U.S. (202) 785-0350), www.oecd.org; *International Trade by Commodity Statistics (ITCS).*

ICELAND - POLITICAL SCIENCE

Central Intelligence Agency, Office of Public Affairs, Washington, DC 20505, (703) 482-0623, Fax: (703) 482-1739, www.cia.gov; *The World Factbook.*

International Monetary Fund (IMF), 700 Nineteenth Street, NW, Washington, DC 20431, (202) 623-7000, Fax: (202) 623-4661, www.imf.org; *Government Finance Statistics Yearbook (2008 Edition)* and *International Financial Statistics Yearbook 2007.*

Nordic Council of Ministers, Store Strandstraede 18, DK-1255 Copenhagen K, Denmark, www.norden.org; *Nordic Statistical Yearbook 2004-2006.*

Organisation for Economic Cooperation and Development (OECD), 2 rue Andre Pascal, F-75775 Paris Cedex 16, France, (Telephone in U.S. (202) 785-6323), (Fax in U.S. (202) 785-0350), www.oecd.org; *OECD Economic Outlook 2008.*

Palgrave Macmillan Ltd., Houndmills, Basingstoke, Hampshire, RG21 6XS, England, (Telephone in U.S. (888) 330-8477), (Fax in U.S. (800) 672-2054), www.palgrave.com; *The Statesman's Yearbook 2008.*

Taylor and Francis Group, An Informa Business, 2 Park Square, Milton Park, Abingdon, Oxford OX14 4RN, United Kingdom, (Dial from U.S. (212) 216-7800), (Fax from U.S. (212) 564-7854), www.tandf.co.uk; *The Europa World Year Book.*

United Nations Statistics Division, New York, NY 10017, (800) 253-9646, Fax: (212) 963-4116, http://unstats.un.org; *National Accounts Statistics: Compendium of Income Distribution Statistics.*

The World Bank, 1818 H Street, NW, Washington, DC 20433, (202) 473-1000, Fax: (202) 477-6391, www.worldbank.org; *World Development Indicators (WDI) 2008.*

ICELAND - POPULATION

Central Intelligence Agency, Office of Public Affairs, Washington, DC 20505, (703) 482-0623, Fax: (703) 482-1739, www.cia.gov; *The World Factbook.*

Economist Intelligence Unit, 111 West 57th Street, New York, NY 10019, (212) 554-0600, Fax: (212) 586-1181, www.eiu.com; *Iceland Country Report.*

Euromonitor International, Inc., 224 S. Michigan Avenue, Suite 1500, Chicago, IL 60604, (312) 922-1115, Fax: (312) 922-1157, www.euromonitor.com; *European Marketing Data and Statistics 2008* and *The World Economic Factbook 2008.*

International Labour Office, I.L.O. Publications, 4 route des Morillons, CH-1211 Geneva 22, Switzerland, (Telephone in U.S. (202) 653-7652), (Fax in U.S. (202) 653-7687), www.ilo.org; *Yearbook of Labour Statistics 2006.*

M.E. Sharpe, 80 Business Park Drive, Armonk, NY 10504, (800) 541-6563, Fax: (914) 273-2106, www.mesharpe.com; *The Illustrated Book of World Rankings.*

Nordic Council of Ministers, Store Strandstraede 18, DK-1255 Copenhagen K, Denmark, www.norden.org; *Nordic Statistical Yearbook 2004-2006.*

Organisation for Economic Cooperation and Development (OECD), 2 rue Andre Pascal, F-75775 Paris Cedex 16, France, (Telephone in U.S. (202) 785-6323), (Fax in U.S. (202) 785-0350), www.oecd.org; *Labour Force Statistics: 1986-2005, 2007 Edition.*

Palgrave Macmillan Ltd., Houndmills, Basingstoke, Hampshire, RG21 6XS, England, (Telephone in U.S. (888) 330-8477), (Fax in U.S. (800) 672-2054), www.palgrave.com; *The Statesman's Yearbook 2008.*

Statistics Iceland, Borgartuni 21a, 150 Reykjavik, Iceland, www.statice.is; *Associations of Media People, Graphic Designers and Artists 1980-2005.*

Taylor and Francis Group, An Informa Business, 2 Park Square, Milton Park, Abingdon, Oxford OX14 4RN, United Kingdom, (Dial from U.S. (212) 216-7800), (Fax from U.S. (212) 564-7854), www.tandf.co.uk; *The Europa World Year Book.*

U.S. Department of State (DOS), 2201 C Street NW, Washington, DC 20520, (202) 647-4000, www.state.gov; *World Military Expenditures and Arms Transfers (WMEAT).*

UNESCO Institute for Statistics, C.P. 6128 Succursale Centre-Ville, Montreal, Quebec, H3C 3J7 Canada, (Dial from U.S. (514) 343-6880), (Fax from U.S. (514) 343 6882), www.uis.unesco.org; *Statistical Tables.*

United Nations Food and Agricultural Organization (FAO), Viale delle Terme di Caracalla, 00100 Rome, Italy, (Dial from U.S. (202) 653-2400), (Fax from U.S. (202) 653 5760), www.fao.org; *FAO Production Yearbook 2002.*

United Nations Statistics Division, New York, NY 10017, (800) 253-9646, Fax: (212) 963-4116, http://unstats.un.org; *Demographic Yearbook; Human Development Report 2006; Statistical Yearbook; Trends in Europe and North America: The Statistical Yearbook of the ECE 2005;* and *World Statistics Pocketbook.*

The World Bank, 1818 H Street, NW, Washington, DC 20433, (202) 473-1000, Fax: (202) 477-6391, www.worldbank.org; *Iceland* and *The World Bank Atlas 2003-2004.*

World Health Organization (WHO), Avenue Appia 20, 1211 Geneve 27, Switzerland, (Telephone in U.S. (212) 331-9081), www.who.int; *World Health Report 2006.*

ICELAND - POPULATION DENSITY

Central Intelligence Agency, Office of Public Affairs, Washington, DC 20505, (703) 482-0623, Fax: (703) 482-1739, www.cia.gov; *The World Factbook.*

Euromonitor International, Inc., 224 S. Michigan Avenue, Suite 1500, Chicago, IL 60604, (312) 922-1115, Fax: (312) 922-1157, www.euromonitor.com; *The World Economic Factbook 2008.*

M.E. Sharpe, 80 Business Park Drive, Armonk, NY 10504, (800) 541-6563, Fax: (914) 273-2106, www.mesharpe.com; *The Illustrated Book of World Rankings.*

Nordic Council of Ministers, Store Strandstraede 18, DK-1255 Copenhagen K, Denmark, www.norden.org; *Nordic Statistical Yearbook 2004-2006.*

Palgrave Macmillan Ltd., Houndmills, Basingstoke, Hampshire, RG21 6XS, England, (Telephone in U.S. (888) 330-8477), (Fax in U.S. (800) 672-2054), www.palgrave.com; *The Statesman's Yearbook 2008.*

Taylor and Francis Group, An Informa Business, 2 Park Square, Milton Park, Abingdon, Oxford OX14 4RN, United Kingdom, (Dial from U.S. (212) 216-7800), (Fax from U.S. (212) 564-7854), www.tandf.co.uk; *The Europa World Year Book.*

UNESCO Institute for Statistics, C.P. 6128 Succursale Centre-Ville, Montreal, Quebec, H3C 3J7 Canada, (Dial from U.S. (514) 343-6880), (Fax from U.S. (514) 343 6882), www.uis.unesco.org; *Statistical Tables.*

United Nations Food and Agricultural Organization (FAO), Viale delle Terme di Caracalla, 00100 Rome, Italy, (Dial from U.S. (202) 653-2400), (Fax from U.S. (202) 653 5760), www.fao.org; *The State of Food and Agriculture (SOFA) 2006.*

United Nations Statistics Division, New York, NY 10017, (800) 253-9646, Fax: (212) 963-4116, http://unstats.un.org; *Statistical Yearbook* and *Trends in Europe and North America: The Statistical Yearbook of the ECE 2005.*

The World Bank, 1818 H Street, NW, Washington, DC 20433, (202) 473-1000, Fax: (202) 477-6391, www.worldbank.org; *Iceland.*

ICELAND - POSTAL SERVICE

M.E. Sharpe, 80 Business Park Drive, Armonk, NY 10504, (800) 541-6563, Fax: (914) 273-2106, www.mesharpe.com; *The Illustrated Book of World Rankings.*

Nordic Council of Ministers, Store Strandstraede 18, DK-1255 Copenhagen K, Denmark, www.norden.org; *Nordic Statistical Yearbook 2004-2006.*

Palgrave Macmillan Ltd., Houndmills, Basingstoke, Hampshire, RG21 6XS, England, (Telephone in U.S. (888) 330-8477), (Fax in U.S. (800) 672-2054), www.palgrave.com; *The Statesman's Yearbook 2008.*

United Nations Statistics Division, New York, NY 10017, (800) 253-9646, Fax: (212) 963-4116, http://unstats.un.org; *Statistical Yearbook* and *Trends in Europe and North America: The Statistical Yearbook of the ECE 2005.*

ICELAND - POWER RESOURCES

Euromonitor International, Inc., 224 S. Michigan Avenue, Suite 1500, Chicago, IL 60604, (312) 922-1115, Fax: (312) 922-1157, www.euromonitor.com; *European Marketing Data and Statistics 2008; The World Economic Factbook 2008;* and *World Marketing Data and Statistics.*

M.E. Sharpe, 80 Business Park Drive, Armonk, NY 10504, (800) 541-6563, Fax: (914) 273-2106, www.mesharpe.com; *The Illustrated Book of World Rankings.*

Nordic Council of Ministers, Store Strandstraede 18, DK-1255 Copenhagen K, Denmark, www.norden.org; *Nordic Statistical Yearbook 2004-2006.*

Organisation for Economic Cooperation and Development (OECD), 2 rue Andre Pascal, F-75775 Paris Cedex 16, France, (Telephone in U.S. (202) 785-6323), (Fax in U.S. (202) 785-0350), www.oecd.org; *Coal Information: 2007 Edition; Energy Statistics of OECD Countries* (2007 Edition); *Key Environmental Indicators 2004;* and *Oil Information 2006 Edition.*

Palgrave Macmillan Ltd., Houndmills, Basingstoke, Hampshire, RG21 6XS, England, (Telephone in U.S. (888) 330-8477), (Fax in U.S. (800) 672-2054), www.palgrave.com; *The Statesman's Yearbook 2008.*

Platts, 2 Penn Plaza, 25th Floor, New York, NY 10121-2298, (212) 904-3070, www.platts.com; *Energy Economist.*

U.S. Department of Energy (DOE), Energy Information Administration (EIA), 1000 Independence Avenue, SW, Washington, DC 20585, (202) 586-8800, www.eia.doe.gov; *International Energy Annual 2004* and *International Energy Outlook 2006.*

United Nations Food and Agricultural Organization (FAO), Viale delle Terme di Caracalla, 00100 Rome, Italy, (Dial from U.S. (202) 653-2400), (Fax from U.S. (202) 653 5760), www.fao.org; *The State of Food and Agriculture (SOFA) 2006.*

United Nations Statistics Division, New York, NY 10017, (800) 253-9646, Fax: (212) 963-4116, http://unstats.un.org; *Energy Statistics Yearbook 2003; Human Development Report 2006; Statistical Yearbook; Trends in Europe and North America: The Statistical Yearbook of the ECE 2005;* and *World Statistics Pocketbook.*

The World Bank, 1818 H Street, NW, Washington, DC 20433, (202) 473-1000, Fax: (202) 477-6391, www.worldbank.org; *The World Bank Atlas 2003-2004.*

ICELAND - PRICES

Euromonitor International, Inc., 224 S. Michigan Avenue, Suite 1500, Chicago, IL 60604, (312) 922-1115, Fax: (312) 922-1157, www.euromonitor.com; *European Marketing Data and Statistics 2008* and *World Marketing Data and Statistics.*

International Labour Office, I.L.O. Publications, 4 route des Morillons, CH-1211 Geneva 22, Switzerland, (Telephone in U.S. (202) 653-7652), (Fax in U.S. (202) 653-7687), www.ilo.org; *Yearbook of Labour Statistics 2006.*

International Monetary Fund (IMF), 700 Nineteenth Street, NW, Washington, DC 20431, (202) 623-7000, Fax: (202) 623-4661, www.imf.org; *International Financial Statistics Yearbook 2007.*

M.E. Sharpe, 80 Business Park Drive, Armonk, NY 10504, (800) 541-6563, Fax: (914) 273-2106, www.mesharpe.com; *The Illustrated Book of World Rankings.*

Nordic Council of Ministers, Store Strandstraede 18, DK-1255 Copenhagen K, Denmark, www.norden.org; *Nordic Statistical Yearbook 2004-2006.*

Organisation for Economic Cooperation and Development (OECD), 2 rue Andre Pascal, F-75775 Paris Cedex 16, France, (Telephone in U.S. (202) 785-6323), (Fax in U.S. (202) 785-0350), www.oecd.org; *Iron and Steel Industry in 2004 (2006 Edition); OECD Economic Outlook 2008;* and *OECD Main Economic Indicators (MEI).*

Technical Association of the Pulp and Paper Industry (TAPPI), 15 Technology Parkway South, Norcross, GA 30092, (770) 446-1400, Fax: (770) 446-6947, www.tappi.org; *TAPPI Annual Report.*

United Nations Food and Agricultural Organization (FAO), Viale delle Terme di Caracalla, 00100 Rome, Italy, (Dial from U.S. (202) 653-2400), (Fax from U.S. (202) 653 5760), www.fao.org; *FAO Production Yearbook 2002* and *The State of Food and Agriculture (SOFA) 2006.*

The World Bank, 1818 H Street, NW, Washington, DC 20433, (202) 473-1000, Fax: (202) 477-6391, www.worldbank.org; *Iceland.*

ICELAND - PROFESSIONS

UNESCO Institute for Statistics, C.P. 6128 Succursale Centre-Ville, Montreal, Quebec, H3C 3J7 Canada, (Dial from U.S. (514) 343-6880), (Fax from U.S. (514) 343 6882), www.uis.unesco.org; *Statistical Tables.*

United Nations Statistics Division, New York, NY 10017, (800) 253-9646, Fax: (212) 963-4116, http://unstats.un.org; *Statistical Yearbook.*

ICELAND - PUBLIC HEALTH

Directorate of Health, Austurstrond 5, IS - 170 Seltjarnarnes, Iceland, www.landlaeknir.is; *Annus Medicus: Directorate of Health.*

Euromonitor International, Inc., 224 S. Michigan Avenue, Suite 1500, Chicago, IL 60604, (312) 922-1115, Fax: (312) 922-1157, www.euromonitor.com; *World Marketing Data and Statistics.*

M.E. Sharpe, 80 Business Park Drive, Armonk, NY 10504, (800) 541-6563, Fax: (914) 273-2106, www.mesharpe.com; *The Illustrated Book of World Rankings.*

Nordic Council of Ministers, Store Strandstraede 18, DK-1255 Copenhagen K, Denmark, www.norden.org; *Nordic Statistical Yearbook 2004-2006.*

Organisation for Economic Cooperation and Development (OECD), 2 rue Andre Pascal, F-75775 Paris Cedex 16, France, (Telephone in U.S. (202) 785-6323), (Fax in U.S. (202) 785-0350), www.oecd.org; *Health at a Glance 2007 - OECD Indicators.*

Palgrave Macmillan Ltd., Houndmills, Basingstoke, Hampshire, RG21 6XS, England, (Telephone in U.S. (888) 330-8477), (Fax in U.S. (800) 672-2054), www.palgrave.com; *The Statesman's Yearbook 2008.*

United Nations Statistics Division, New York, NY 10017, (800) 253-9646, Fax: (212) 963-4116, http://unstats.un.org; *Human Development Report 2006; Statistical Yearbook;* and *Trends in Europe and North America: The Statistical Yearbook of the ECE 2005.*

The World Bank, 1818 H Street, NW, Washington, DC 20433, (202) 473-1000, Fax: (202) 477-6391, www.worldbank.org; *Iceland.*

World Health Organization (WHO), Avenue Appia 20, 1211 Geneve 27, Switzerland, (Telephone in U.S. (212) 331-9081), www.who.int; The WHO Global Atlas of Infectious Diseases and *World Health Report 2006.*

ICELAND - PUBLISHERS AND PUBLISHING

Nordic Council of Ministers, Store Strandstraede 18, DK-1255 Copenhagen K, Denmark, www.norden.org; *Nordic Statistical Yearbook 2004-2006.*

Taylor and Francis Group, An Informa Business, 2 Park Square, Milton Park, Abingdon, Oxford OX14 4RN, United Kingdom, (Dial from U.S. (212) 216-7800), (Fax from U.S. (212) 564-7854), www.tandf.co.uk; *The Europa World Year Book.*

UNESCO Institute for Statistics, C.P. 6128 Succursale Centre-Ville, Montreal, Quebec, H3C 3J7 Canada, (Dial from U.S. (514) 343-6880), (Fax from U.S. (514) 343 6882), www.uis.unesco.org; *Statistical Tables.*

United Nations Statistics Division, New York, NY 10017, (800) 253-9646, Fax: (212) 963-4116, http://unstats.un.org; *Trends in Europe and North America: The Statistical Yearbook of the ECE 2005.*

ICELAND - RADIO BROADCASTING

Palgrave Macmillan Ltd., Houndmills, Basingstoke, Hampshire, RG21 6XS, England, (Telephone in U.S. (888) 330-8477), (Fax in U.S. (800) 672-2054), www.palgrave.com; *The Statesman's Yearbook 2008.*

ICELAND - RAILROADS

Euromonitor International, Inc., 224 S. Michigan Avenue, Suite 1500, Chicago, IL 60604, (312) 922-1115, Fax: (312) 922-1157, www.euromonitor.com; *European Marketing Data and Statistics 2008.*

Nordic Council of Ministers, Store Strandstraede 18, DK-1255 Copenhagen K, Denmark, www.norden.org; *Nordic Statistical Yearbook 2004-2006.*

United Nations Statistics Division, New York, NY 10017, (800) 253-9646, Fax: (212) 963-4116, http://unstats.un.org; *Trends in Europe and North America: The Statistical Yearbook of the ECE 2005.*

ICELAND - RELIGION

Central Intelligence Agency, Office of Public Affairs, Washington, DC 20505, (703) 482-0623, Fax: (703) 482-1739, www.cia.gov; *The World Factbook.*

M.E. Sharpe, 80 Business Park Drive, Armonk, NY 10504, (800) 541-6563, Fax: (914) 273-2106, www.mesharpe.com; *The Illustrated Book of World Rankings.*

Palgrave Macmillan Ltd., Houndmills, Basingstoke, Hampshire, RG21 6XS, England, (Telephone in U.S. (888) 330-8477), (Fax in U.S. (800) 672-2054), www.palgrave.com; *The Statesman's Yearbook 2008.*

ICELAND - RENT CHARGES

International Labour Office, I.L.O. Publications, 4 route des Morillons, CH-1211 Geneva 22, Switzerland, (Telephone in U.S. (202) 653-7652), (Fax in U.S. (202) 653-7687), www.ilo.org; *Yearbook of Labour Statistics 2006.*

ICELAND - RESERVES (ACCOUNTING)

Organisation for Economic Cooperation and Development (OECD), 2 rue Andre Pascal, F-75775 Paris Cedex 16, France, (Telephone in U.S. (202) 785-6323), (Fax in U.S. (202) 785-0350), www.oecd.org; *Financial Market Trends: OECD Periodical* and *OECD Economic Outlook 2008.*

United Nations Statistics Division, New York, NY 10017, (800) 253-9646, Fax: (212) 963-4116, http://unstats.un.org; *Statistical Yearbook.*

The World Bank, 1818 H Street, NW, Washington, DC 20433, (202) 473-1000, Fax: (202) 477-6391, www.worldbank.org; *World Development Indicators (WDI) 2008.*

ICELAND - RETAIL TRADE

Banque de France, 48 rue Croix des Petits champs, 75001 Paris, France, www.banque-france.fr/home.htm; *Monthly Business Survey Overview.*

Euromonitor International, Inc., 224 S. Michigan Avenue, Suite 1500, Chicago, IL 60604, (312) 922-1115, Fax: (312) 922-1157, www.euromonitor.com; *Retail Trade International 2007* and *World Marketing Data and Statistics.*

ICELAND - RICE PRODUCTION

See ICELAND - CROPS

ICELAND - ROADS

Central Intelligence Agency, Office of Public Affairs, Washington, DC 20505, (703) 482-0623, Fax: (703) 482-1739, www.cia.gov; *The World Factbook.*

International Road Federation (IFR), Madison Place, 500 Montgomery Street, 5th Floor, Alexandria, VA 22314, (703) 535-1001, Fax: (703) 535-1007, www.irfnet.org; *World Road Statistics 2006.*

Nordic Council of Ministers, Store Strandstraede 18, DK-1255 Copenhagen K, Denmark, www.norden.org; *Nordic Statistical Yearbook 2004-2006.*

Palgrave Macmillan Ltd., Houndmills, Basingstoke, Hampshire, RG21 6XS, England, (Telephone in U.S. (888) 330-8477), (Fax in U.S. (800) 672-2054), www.palgrave.com; *The Statesman's Yearbook 2008.*

United Nations Statistics Division, New York, NY 10017, (800) 253-9646, Fax: (212) 963-4116, http://unstats.un.org; *Annual Bulletin of Transport Statistics for Europe and North America 2004* and *Trends in Europe and North America: The Statistical Yearbook of the ECE 2005.*

ICELAND - RUBBER INDUSTRY AND TRADE

International Rubber Study Group (IRSG), 1st Floor, Heron House, 109/115 Wembley Hill Road, Wembley, Middlesex HA9 8DA, United Kingdom, www.rubberstudy.com; *Rubber Statistical Bulletin; Summary of World Rubber Statistics 2005; World Rubber Statistics Handbook (Volume 6, 1975-2001);* and *World Rubber Statistics Historic Handbook.*

M.E. Sharpe, 80 Business Park Drive, Armonk, NY 10504, (800) 541-6563, Fax: (914) 273-2106, www.mesharpe.com; *The Illustrated Book of World Rankings.*

Organisation for Economic Cooperation and Development (OECD), 2 rue Andre Pascal, F-75775 Paris Cedex 16, France, (Telephone in U.S. (202) 785-6323), (Fax in U.S. (202) 785-0350), www.oecd.org; *International Trade by Commodity Statistics (ITCS).*

ICELAND - SHEEP

See ICELAND - LIVESTOCK

ICELAND - SHIPPING

Lloyd's Register - Fairplay, 8410 N.W. 53rd Terrace, Suite 207, Miami FL 33166, (305) 718-9929, Fax: (305) 718-9663, www.lrfairplay.com; *Register of Ships 2007-2008; World Casualty Statistics 2007; World Fleet Statistics 2006; World Marine Propulsion Report 2006-2010; World Shipbuilding Statistics 2007;* and The World Shipping Encyclopaedia.

Nordic Council of Ministers, Store Strandstraede 18, DK-1255 Copenhagen K, Denmark, www.norden.org; *Nordic Statistical Yearbook 2004-2006.*

Organisation for Economic Cooperation and Development (OECD), 2 rue Andre Pascal, F-75775 Paris Cedex 16, France, (Telephone in U.S. (202) 785-6323), (Fax in U.S. (202) 785-0350), www.oecd.org; *Statistics on Ship Production, Exports and Orders in 2004.*

Palgrave Macmillan Ltd., Houndmills, Basingstoke, Hampshire, RG21 6XS, England, (Telephone in U.S. (888) 330-8477), (Fax in U.S. (800) 672-2054), www.palgrave.com; *The Statesman's Yearbook 2008.*

Taylor and Francis Group, An Informa Business, 2 Park Square, Milton Park, Abingdon, Oxford OX14 4RN, United Kingdom, (Dial from U.S. (212) 216-7800), (Fax from U.S. (212) 564-7854), www.tandf.co.uk; *The Europa World Year Book.*

U.S. Department of Transportation (DOT), Maritime Administration (MARAD), West Building, Southeast Federal Center, 1200 New Jersey Avenue, SE, Washington, DC 20590, (800) 99-MARAD, www.marad.dot.gov; *World Merchant Fleet 2005.*

United Nations Statistics Division, New York, NY 10017, (800) 253-9646, Fax: (212) 963-4116, http://unstats.un.org; *Statistical Yearbook.*

ICELAND - SILVER PRODUCTION

See ICELAND - MINERAL INDUSTRIES

ICELAND - SOCIAL ECOLOGY

M.E. Sharpe, 80 Business Park Drive, Armonk, NY 10504, (800) 541-6563, Fax: (914) 273-2106, www.mesharpe.com; *The Illustrated Book of World Rankings.*

United Nations Statistics Division, New York, NY 10017, (800) 253-9646, Fax: (212) 963-4116, http://unstats.un.org; *World Statistics Pocketbook.*

ICELAND - SOCIAL SECURITY

International Monetary Fund (IMF), 700 Nineteenth Street, NW, Washington, DC 20431, (202) 623-7000, Fax: (202) 623-4661, www.imf.org; *Government Finance Statistics Yearbook (2008 Edition).*

Nordic Council of Ministers, Store Strandstraede 18, DK-1255 Copenhagen K, Denmark, www.norden.org; *Nordic Statistical Yearbook 2004-2006.*

Palgrave Macmillan Ltd., Houndmills, Basingstoke, Hampshire, RG21 6XS, England, (Telephone in U.S. (888) 330-8477), (Fax in U.S. (800) 672-2054), www.palgrave.com; *The Statesman's Yearbook 2008.*

United Nations Statistics Division, New York, NY 10017, (800) 253-9646, Fax: (212) 963-4116, http://unstats.un.org; *Human Development Report 2006.*

ICELAND - STEEL PRODUCTION

See ICELAND - MINERAL INDUSTRIES

ICELAND - SUGAR PRODUCTION

See ICELAND - CROPS

ICELAND - TAXATION

International Monetary Fund (IMF), 700 Nineteenth Street, NW, Washington, DC 20431, (202) 623-7000, Fax: (202) 623-4661, www.imf.org; *Government Finance Statistics Yearbook (2008 Edition).*

International Road Federation (IFR), Madison Place, 500 Montgomery Street, 5th Floor, Alexandria, VA 22314, (703) 535-1001, Fax: (703) 535-1007, www.irfnet.org; *World Road Statistics 2006.*

Nordic Council of Ministers, Store Strandstraede 18, DK-1255 Copenhagen K, Denmark, www.norden.org; *Nordic Statistical Yearbook 2004-2006.*

Palgrave Macmillan Ltd., Houndmills, Basingstoke, Hampshire, RG21 6XS, England, (Telephone in U.S. (888) 330-8477), (Fax in U.S. (800) 672-2054), www.palgrave.com; *The Statesman's Yearbook 2008.*

Taylor and Francis Group, An Informa Business, 2 Park Square, Milton Park, Abingdon, Oxford OX14 4RN, United Kingdom, (Dial from U.S. (212) 216-7800), (Fax from U.S. (212) 564-7854), www.tandf.co.uk; *The Europa World Year Book.*

The World Bank, 1818 H Street, NW, Washington, DC 20433, (202) 473-1000, Fax: (202) 477-6391, www.worldbank.org; *World Development Indicators (WDI) 2008.*

ICELAND - TELEPHONE

International Telecommunication Union (ITU), Place des Nations, 1211 Geneva 20, Switzerland, www.itu.int; World Telecommunication Indicators Database.

Nordic Council of Ministers, Store Strandstraede 18, DK-1255 Copenhagen K, Denmark, www.norden.org; *Nordic Statistical Yearbook 2004-2006.*

Palgrave Macmillan Ltd., Houndmills, Basingstoke, Hampshire, RG21 6XS, England, (Telephone in U.S. (888) 330-8477), (Fax in U.S. (800) 672-2054), www.palgrave.com; *The Statesman's Yearbook 2008.*

Taylor and Francis Group, An Informa Business, 2 Park Square, Milton Park, Abingdon, Oxford OX14 4RN, United Kingdom, (Dial from U.S. (212) 216-7800), (Fax from U.S. (212) 564-7854), www.tandf.co.uk; *The Europa World Year Book.*

United Nations Statistics Division, New York, NY 10017, (800) 253-9646, Fax: (212) 963-4116, http://unstats.un.org; *Statistical Yearbook; Trends in Europe and North America: The Statistical Yearbook of the ECE 2005;* and *World Statistics Pocketbook.*

ICELAND - TEXTILE INDUSTRY

Euromonitor International, Inc., 224 S. Michigan Avenue, Suite 1500, Chicago, IL 60604, (312) 922-1115, Fax: (312) 922-1157, www.euromonitor.com; *Retail Trade International 2007.*

M.E. Sharpe, 80 Business Park Drive, Armonk, NY 10504, (800) 541-6563, Fax: (914) 273-2106, www.mesharpe.com; *The Illustrated Book of World Rankings.*

Organisation for Economic Cooperation and Development (OECD), 2 rue Andre Pascal, F-75775 Paris Cedex 16, France, (Telephone in U.S. (202) 785-6323), (Fax in U.S. (202) 785-0350), www.oecd.org; *International Trade by Commodity Statistics (ITCS); A New World Map in Textiles and Clothing: Adjusting to Change; 2005 OECD Agricultural Outlook Tables, 1970-2014;* and STructural ANalysis (STAN) database.

United Nations Conference on Trade and Development (UNCTAD), DC2-1120, United Nations, New York, NY 10017, (212) 963-0027, www.unctad.org; *UNCTAD Commodity Yearbook.*

United Nations Statistics Division, New York, NY 10017, (800) 253-9646, Fax: (212) 963-4116, http://unstats.un.org; *Statistical Yearbook.*

ICELAND - TIN INDUSTRY

Organisation for Economic Cooperation and Development (OECD), 2 rue Andre Pascal, F-75775 Paris Cedex 16, France, (Telephone in U.S. (202) 785-6323), (Fax in U.S. (202) 785-0350), www.oecd.org; *Environmental Impacts of Foreign Direct Investment in the Mining Sector in the Newly Independent States (NIS).*

ICELAND - TOBACCO INDUSTRY

Euromonitor International, Inc., 224 S. Michigan Avenue, Suite 1500, Chicago, IL 60604, (312) 922-1115, Fax: (312) 922-1157, www.euromonitor.com; *European Marketing Data and Statistics 2008.*

Foreign Agricultural Service (FAS), U.S. Department of Agriculture (USDA), 1400 Independence Avenue, SW, Washington, DC 20250, (202) 720-3935, www.fas.usda.gov; *Tobacco: World Markets and Trade.*

M.E. Sharpe, 80 Business Park Drive, Armonk, NY 10504, (800) 541-6563, Fax: (914) 273-2106, www.mesharpe.com; *The Illustrated Book of World Rankings.*

Organisation for Economic Cooperation and Development (OECD), 2 rue Andre Pascal, F-75775 Paris Cedex 16, France, (Telephone in U.S. (202) 785-6323), (Fax in U.S. (202) 785-0350), www.oecd.org; *International Trade by Commodity Statistics (ITCS)* and STructural ANalysis (STAN) database.

United Nations Statistics Division, New York, NY 10017, (800) 253-9646, Fax: (212) 963-4116, http://unstats.un.org; *Statistical Yearbook.*

ICELAND - TOURISM

Euromonitor International, Inc., 224 S. Michigan Avenue, Suite 1500, Chicago, IL 60604, (312) 922-1115, Fax: (312) 922-1157, www.euromonitor.com; *European Marketing Data and Statistics 2008; The World Economic Factbook 2008;* and *World Marketing Data and Statistics.*

Eurostat, Batiment Jean Monnet, Rue Alcide de Gasperi, L-2920 Luxembourg, http://epp.eurostat.ec.europa.eu; *Tourism in Europe: First Results for 2007.*

M.E. Sharpe, 80 Business Park Drive, Armonk, NY 10504, (800) 541-6563, Fax: (914) 273-2106, www.mesharpe.com; *The Illustrated Book of World Rankings.*

Organisation for Economic Cooperation and Development (OECD), 2 rue Andre Pascal, F-75775 Paris Cedex 16, France, (Telephone in U.S. (202) 785-6323), (Fax in U.S. (202) 785-0350), www.oecd.org; *Household, Tourism, Travel: Trends, Environmental Impacts and Policy Responses.*

Palgrave Macmillan Ltd., Houndmills, Basingstoke, Hampshire, RG21 6XS, England, (Telephone in U.S. (888) 330-8477), (Fax in U.S. (800) 672-2054), www.palgrave.com; *The Statesman's Yearbook 2008.*

Taylor and Francis Group, An Informa Business, 2 Park Square, Milton Park, Abingdon, Oxford OX14 4RN, United Kingdom, (Dial from U.S. (212) 216-7800), (Fax from U.S. (212) 564-7854), www.tandf.co.uk; *The Europa World Year Book.*

United Nations Statistics Division, New York, NY 10017, (800) 253-9646, Fax: (212) 963-4116, http://unstats.un.org; *Statistical Yearbook* and *Trends in Europe and North America: The Statistical Yearbook of the ECE 2005.*

United Nations World Tourism Organization (UNWTO), Capitan Haya 42, 28020 Madrid, Spain, www.world-tourism.org; *Tourism Market Trends 2004 - Europe* and *Yearbook of Tourism Statistics.*

The World Bank, 1818 H Street, NW, Washington, DC 20433, (202) 473-1000, Fax: (202) 477-6391, www.worldbank.org; *Iceland.*

ICELAND - TRADE

See ICELAND - INTERNATIONAL TRADE

ICELAND - TRANSPORTATION

Central Intelligence Agency, Office of Public Affairs, Washington, DC 20505, (703) 482-0623, Fax: (703) 482-1739, www.cia.gov; *The World Factbook.*

Euromonitor International, Inc., 224 S. Michigan Avenue, Suite 1500, Chicago, IL 60604, (312) 922-1115, Fax: (312) 922-1157, www.euromonitor.com; *World Marketing Data and Statistics.*

M.E. Sharpe, 80 Business Park Drive, Armonk, NY 10504, (800) 541-6563, Fax: (914) 273-2106, www.mesharpe.com; *The Illustrated Book of World Rankings.*

Nordic Council of Ministers, Store Strandstraede 18, DK-1255 Copenhagen K, Denmark, www.norden.org; *Nordic Statistical Yearbook 2004-2006.*

Palgrave Macmillan Ltd., Houndmills, Basingstoke, Hampshire, RG21 6XS, England, (Telephone in U.S. (888) 330-8477), (Fax in U.S. (800) 672-2054), www.palgrave.com; *The Statesman's Yearbook 2008.*

Taylor and Francis Group, An Informa Business, 2 Park Square, Milton Park, Abingdon, Oxford OX14 4RN, United Kingdom, (Dial from U.S. (212) 216-7800), (Fax from U.S. (212) 564-7854), www.tandf.co.uk; *The Europa World Year Book.*

United Nations Statistics Division, New York, NY 10017, (800) 253-9646, Fax: (212) 963-4116, http://unstats.un.org; *Human Development Report 2006* and *Trends in Europe and North America: The Statistical Yearbook of the ECE 2005.*

The World Bank, 1818 H Street, NW, Washington, DC 20433, (202) 473-1000, Fax: (202) 477-6391, www.worldbank.org; *Iceland.*

ICELAND - UNEMPLOYMENT

Central Intelligence Agency, Office of Public Affairs, Washington, DC 20505, (703) 482-0623, Fax: (703) 482-1739, www.cia.gov; *The World Factbook.*

Euromonitor International, Inc., 224 S. Michigan Avenue, Suite 1500, Chicago, IL 60604, (312) 922-1115, Fax: (312) 922-1157, www.euromonitor.com; *European Marketing Data and Statistics 2008.*

International Labour Office, I.L.O. Publications, 4 route des Morillons, CH-1211 Geneva 22, Switzerland, (Telephone in U.S. (202) 653-7652), (Fax in U.S. (202) 653-7687), www.ilo.org; *Yearbook of Labour Statistics 2006.*

Nordic Council of Ministers, Store Strandstraede 18, DK-1255 Copenhagen K, Denmark, www.norden.org; *Nordic Statistical Yearbook 2004-2006.*

Organisation for Economic Cooperation and Development (OECD), 2 rue Andre Pascal, F-75775 Paris Cedex 16, France, (Telephone in U.S. (202) 785-6323), (Fax in U.S. (202) 785-0350), www.oecd.org; *Labour Force Statistics: 1986-2005, 2007 Edition; OECD Composite Leading Indicators (CLIs), Updated September 2007; OECD Economic Outlook 2008; OECD Economic Survey - Iceland 2008;* and *OECD Employment Outlook 2007.*

Palgrave Macmillan Ltd., Houndmills, Basingstoke, Hampshire, RG21 6XS, England, (Telephone in U.S. (888) 330-8477), (Fax in U.S. (800) 672-2054), www.palgrave.com; *The Statesman's Yearbook 2008.*

United Nations Statistics Division, New York, NY 10017, (800) 253-9646, Fax: (212) 963-4116, http://unstats.un.org; *Statistical Yearbook* and *Trends in Europe and North America: The Statistical Yearbook of the ECE 2005.*

The World Bank, 1818 H Street, NW, Washington, DC 20433, (202) 473-1000, Fax: (202) 477-6391, www.worldbank.org; *Iceland.*

ICELAND - VITAL STATISTICS

Nordic Council of Ministers, Store Strandstraede 18, DK-1255 Copenhagen K, Denmark, www.norden.org; *Nordic Statistical Yearbook 2004-2006.*

Palgrave Macmillan Ltd., Houndmills, Basingstoke, Hampshire, RG21 6XS, England, (Telephone in U.S. (888) 330-8477), (Fax in U.S. (800) 672-2054), www.palgrave.com; *The Statesman's Yearbook 2008.*

Statistics Iceland, Borgartuni 21a, 150 Reykjavik, Iceland, www.statice.is; *Icelandic Information Society in a European Context 2006.*

United Nations Statistics Division, New York, NY 10017, (800) 253-9646, Fax: (212) 963-4116, http://unstats.un.org; *Statistical Yearbook.*

World Health Organization (WHO), Avenue Appia 20, 1211 Geneve 27, Switzerland, (Telephone in U.S. (212) 331-9081), www.who.int; *World Health Report 2006.*

ICELAND - WAGES

Euromonitor International, Inc., 224 S. Michigan Avenue, Suite 1500, Chicago, IL 60604, (312) 922-1115, Fax: (312) 922-1157, www.euromonitor.com; *European Marketing Data and Statistics 2008.*

International Labour Office, I.L.O. Publications, 4 route des Morillons, CH-1211 Geneva 22, Switzerland, (Telephone in U.S. (202) 653-7652), (Fax in U.S. (202) 653-7687), www.ilo.org; *Yearbook of Labour Statistics 2006.*

Nordic Council of Ministers, Store Strandstraede 18, DK-1255 Copenhagen K, Denmark, www.norden.org; *Nordic Statistical Yearbook 2004-2006.*

Organisation for Economic Cooperation and Development (OECD), 2 rue Andre Pascal, F-75775 Paris Cedex 16, France, (Telephone in U.S. (202) 785-6323), (Fax in U.S. (202) 785-0350), www.oecd.org; *ICT Sector Data and Metadata by Country; OECD Economic Outlook 2008;* and STructural ANalysis (STAN) database.

The World Bank, 1818 H Street, NW, Washington, DC 20433, (202) 473-1000, Fax: (202) 477-6391, www.worldbank.org; *Iceland.*

ICELAND - WEATHER

See ICELAND - CLIMATE

ICELAND - WELFARE STATE

International Monetary Fund (IMF), 700 Nineteenth Street, NW, Washington, DC 20431, (202) 623-7000, Fax: (202) 623-4661, www.imf.org; *Government Finance Statistics Yearbook (2008 Edition).*

Nordic Council of Ministers, Store Strandstraede 18, DK-1255 Copenhagen K, Denmark, www.norden.org; *Nordic Statistical Yearbook 2004-2006.*

Palgrave Macmillan Ltd., Houndmills, Basingstoke, Hampshire, RG21 6XS, England, (Telephone in U.S. (888) 330-8477), (Fax in U.S. (800) 672-2054), www.palgrave.com; *The Statesman's Yearbook 2008.*

ICELAND - WHALES

See ICELAND - FISHERIES

ICELAND - WHEAT PRODUCTION

See ICELAND - CROPS

ICELAND - WHOLESALE PRICE INDEXES

Nordic Council of Ministers, Store Strandstraede 18, DK-1255 Copenhagen K, Denmark, www.norden.org; *Nordic Statistical Yearbook 2004-2006.*

ICELAND - WINE PRODUCTION

See ICELAND - BEVERAGE INDUSTRY

ICELAND - WOOD AND WOOD PULP

See ICELAND - FORESTS AND FORESTRY

ICELAND - WOOD PRODUCTS

Organisation for Economic Cooperation and Development (OECD), 2 rue Andre Pascal, F-75775 Paris Cedex 16, France, (Telephone in U.S. (202) 785-6323), (Fax in U.S. (202) 785-0350), www.oecd.org; *International Trade by Commodity Statistics (ITCS)* and STructural ANalysis (STAN) database.

ICELAND - WOOL PRODUCTION

See ICELAND - TEXTILE INDUSTRY

ICELAND - YARN PRODUCTION

See ICELAND - TEXTILE INDUSTRY

ICELAND - ZINC AND ZINC ORE

See ICELAND - MINERAL INDUSTRIES

IDAHO

See also - STATE DATA (FOR INDIVIDUAL STATES)

The Urban Institute, 2100 M Street, N.W., Washington, DC 20037, (202) 833-7200, www.urban.org; *Prisoner Reentry in Idaho.*

IDAHO - STATE DATA CENTERS

College of Business, Idaho State University, Campus Box 80201, Pocatello, ID 83209, (208) 282-3585, http://cob.isu.edu; State Data Center.

Idaho Commerce Labor, 317 West Main Street, Boise, ID 83735, (208) 334-2470, Fax: (208) 334-2631, www.idoc.state.id.us; State Data Center.

Idaho Commission for Libraries, 325 West State Street, Boise, ID 83702, (208) 334-2150, Fax: (208) 334-4016, www.lili.org; State Data Center.

IDAHO - PRIMARY STATISTICS SOURCES

Idaho Commerce Labor, 317 West Main Street, Boise, ID 83735, (208) 334-2470, Fax: (208) 334-2631, www.idoc.state.id.us; *Community Profiles; County Profiles;* and *Profile of Rural Idaho.*

INSIDE Idaho (Interactive Numeric Spatial Information Data Engine), University of Idaho Library, PO Box 442350, Moscow, ID 83844-2350, Gail Eckwright, Project Director, (208) 885-2507, http://inside.uidaho.edu; *Idaho Statistical Abstract.*

IDENTITY THEFT

Federal Trade Commission (FTC), 600 Pennsylvania Avenue, NW, Washington, DC 20580, (202) 326-2222, www.ftc.gov; *2003 Identity Theft Survey Report; Identity Theft Victim Complaint Data 2006;* and *National and State Trends in Fraud and Identity Theft, January-December 2004.*

U.S. Department of Justice (DOJ), Bureau of Justice Statistics, 810 Seventh Street, NW, Washington, DC 20531, (202) 307-0765, www.ojp.usdoj.gov/bjs/; *Identity Theft, 2004.*

U.S. Government Accountablity Office (GAO), 441 G Street, NW, Washington, DC 20548, (202) 512-3000, www.gao.gov; *Identity Theft: Greater Awareness and Use of Existing Data Are Needed.*

ILLEGAL IMMIGRATION

See IMMIGRANTS

ILLINOIS

See also - STATE DATA (FOR INDIVIDUAL STATES)

The Urban Institute, 2100 M Street, N.W., Washington, DC 20037, (202) 833-7200, www.urban.org; *A Portrait of Prisoner Reentry in Illinois.*

ILLINOIS - STATE DATA CENTERS

Chicago Area Geographic Information Study (CAGIS), m/c 092, 1007 West Harrison Street, Room 2102, University of Illinois at Chicago, Chicago, IL 60607-7138, (312) 996-5274, www.cagis.uic.edu; State Data Center.

Chicago Metropolitan Agency for Planning (CMAP), 233 South Wacker Drive, Suite 800, Sears Tower, Chicago, Illinois 60606, (312) 454-0400, Fax: (312) 454-0411, www.chicagoareaplanning.org; State Data Center.

Illinois Department of Commerce and Economic Opportunity (DCEO), 620 East Adams Street, Springfield, IL 62701, (217) 782-7500, www.commerce.state.il.us; State Data Center.

Regional Development Institute (RDI), Northern Illinois University, 148 North Third Street, DeKalb, Illinois 60115-2854, Robert Gleeson, Director (815) 753-0912, Fax: (815) 753-2305, www.nibidc.com; State Data Center.

ILLINOIS - PRIMARY STATISTICS SOURCES

Institute of Government and Public Affairs at the University of Illinois (IGPA), 1007 W. Nevada Street, Urbana, IL 61801 MC-037, Mr. Robert F. Rich, Director (217) 333-3340, Fax: (217) 244-4817, www.igpa.uillinois.edu; *Illinois Statistical Abstract 2004.*

ILLNESS

See also MORTALITY and Particular Illnesses

European Centre for Disease Prevention and Control (ECDC), 171 83 Stockholm, Sweden, www.ecdc.europa.eu; *Avian Influenza A/H5N1 in Bathing and Potable (Drinking) Water and Risks to Human Health; The Community Summary Report on Trends and Sources of Zoonoses, Zoonotic Agents, Antimicrobial resistance and Foodborne outbreaks in the European Union in 2006; The ECDC Avian Influenza Portofolio; HIV Infection in Europe: 25 Years into the Pandemic;* and *Influenza News.*

Health Protection Agency, 7th Floor, Holborn Gate, 330 High Holborn, London WC1V 7PP, United Kingdom, www.hpa.org.uk; *Antimicrobial Resistance in England, Wales, and Northern Ireland; Communicable Disease in London 2002-05; Foreign Travel Associated Illness, England, Wales, and Northern Ireland: 2007 Report; Fungal Diseases in the UK; Hepatitis C in England; Indications of Public Health in the English Regions: Sexual Health (November 2006); Migrant Health: Infectious Diseases in Non-UK Born Populations in England, Wales and Northern Ireland (A Baseline Report - 2006); National Confidential Study of Deaths Following Meticillin Resistant Staphylococcus aureus (MRSA) Infection; Shooting Up: Infections Among Injecting Drug Users in the United Kingdom 2006 (An Update: 2007); Surveillance of Healthcare Associated Infections Report 2007; Testing Times - HIV and other Sexually Transmitted Infections in the United Kingdom: 2007; Third Report of the Mandatory Surveillance of Surgical Site Infection in Orthopaedic Surgery;* and *Tuberculosis in the UK: Annual Report on Tuberculosis Surveillance and Control in the UK 2007.*

National Center for Chronic Disease Prevention and Health Promotion (NCCDPHP), Centers for Disease Control and Prevention (CDC), 4770 Buford Hwy, NE, MS K-40, Atlanta, GA 30341-3717, (404) 639-3311, www.cdc.gov/nccdphp; *Chronic Diseases: The Leading Causes of Death.*

National Center for Health Statistics (NCHS), Centers for Disease Control and Prevention (CDC), U.S. Department of Health and Human Services (HHS), 3311 Toledo Road, Hyattsville, MD 20782, (866) 232-4636, www.cdc.gov/nchs; *Faststats A to Z* and unpublished data.

Robert Koch Institute, Nordufer 20, D 13353 Berlin, Germany, www.rki.de; *Health in Germany 2006.*

ILLNESS - BED DISABILITY - DAYS

National Center for Health Statistics (NCHS), Centers for Disease Control and Prevention (CDC), U.S. Department of Health and Human Services (HHS), 3311 Toledo Road, Hyattsville, MD 20782, (866) 232-4636, www.cdc.gov/nchs; unpublished data.

ILLNESS - DAYS LOST FROM WORK, SCHOOL

National Center for Health Statistics (NCHS), Centers for Disease Control and Prevention (CDC), U.S. Department of Health and Human Services (HHS), 3311 Toledo Road, Hyattsville, MD 20782, (866) 232-4636, www.cdc.gov/nchs; unpublished data.

ILLNESS - EMPLOYEE PROTECTION AGAINST INCOME LOSS

Social Security Administration (SSA), Office of Public Inquiries, Windsor Park Building, 6401 Security Boulevard, Baltimore, MD 21235, (800) 772-1213, www.ssa.gov; *Social Security Bulletin* and unpublished data.

ILLNESS - PRIVATE EXPENDITURES FOR INCOME MAINTENANCE

Social Security Administration (SSA), Office of Public Inquiries, Windsor Park Building, 6401 Security Boulevard, Baltimore, MD 21235, (800) 772-1213, www.ssa.gov; *Annual Statistical Supplement, 2007; Social Security Bulletin;* and unpublished data.

ILLNESS - RESTRICTED ACTIVITY

National Center for Health Statistics (NCHS), Centers for Disease Control and Prevention (CDC), U.S. Department of Health and Human Services (HHS), 3311 Toledo Road, Hyattsville, MD 20782, (866) 232-4636, www.cdc.gov/nchs; unpublished data.

IMMIGRANTS

The Annie E. Casey Foundation, 701 Saint Paul Street, Baltimore, MD 21202, (410) 547-6600, Fax: (410) 547-3610, www.aecf.org; *Undercounted, Underserved: Immigrant and Refugee Families in the Child Welfare System.*

The Brookings Institution, 1775 Massachusetts Avenue, NW, Washington, DC 20036, (202) 797-6000, Fax: (202) 797-6004, www.brook.edu; *From 'There' to 'Here': Refugee Resettlement in Metropolitan America.*

International Organization for Migration (IOM), 17, Route des Morillons, CH-1211 Geneva 19, Switzerland, www.iom.int; *International Migration; IOM Worldwide; Migration and Development: New Strategic Outlooks and Practical Ways Forward - The Cases of Angola and Zambia; Migration from Latin America to Europe: Trends and Policy Challenges; Migration, Development and Natural Disasters: Insights from the Indian Ocean Tsunami; World Migration 2003: Managing Migration - Challenges and Responses for People on the Move; World Migration 2005: Costs and Benefits of International Migration;* and *World Migration Report 2000.*

Migration Information Source, Migration Policy Institute (MPI), 1400 16th Street NW, Suite 300, Washington, DC 20036-2257, (202) 266-1940, Fax: (202) 266-1900, www.migrationinformation.org; *Analyzing Asylum Applications; Country Resources; Global Data Center; Maps of the Foreign Born in the United States; US Census Data on the Foreign Born; US Historical Trends;* and *Who's Where in the United States?*

National Center for Children in Poverty (NCCP), 215 W. 125th Street, 3rd Floor, New York, NY 10027, (646) 284-9600, Fax: (646) 284-9623, www.nccp.org; *Children in Low-Income Immigrant Families* and *Children of Immigrants: A Statistical Profile.*

U.S. Citizenship and Immigration Services (USCIS), Washington District Office, 2675 Prosperity Avenue, Fairfax, VA 22031, (800) 375-5283, http://uscis.gov; *2005 Yearbook of Immigration Statistics.*

U.S. Department of Homeland Security (DHS), Office of Immigration Statistics, Washington, DC 20528, (202) 282-8000, www.dhs.gov; *Characteristics of Diversity Legal Permanent Residents: 2004; Characteristics of Employment-Based Legal Permanent Residents: 2004; Estimates of the Legal Permanent Resident Population and Population Eligible to Naturalize in 2004; Estimates of the Unauthorized Immigrant Population Residing in the United States: 1990 to 2000; Estimates of the Unauthorized Immigrant Population Residing in the United States: January 2005; Fiscal Year End Statistical Reports; Immigration Enforcement Actions: 2005; IRCA Legalization Effects: Lawful Permanent Residence and Naturalization through 2001; Legal Permanent Residents: 2005; Mapping Immigration: Legal Permanent Residents (LPRs);*

Mapping Trends in Naturalizations: 1980 to 2003; Mapping Trends in U.S. Legal Immigration: 1980 to 2003; Monthly Statistical Report; Naturalizations in the United States: 2005; Profiles on Legal Permanent Residents; Profiles on Naturalized Citizens; Refugee Applicants and Admissions to the United States: 2004; and *Refugees and Asylees: 2005.*

U.S. Department of Justice (DOJ), Bureau of Justice Statistics, 810 Seventh Street, NW, Washington, DC 20531, (202) 307-0765, www.ojp.usdoj.gov/bjs/; *Assessing Measurement Techniques for Identifying Race, Ethnicity, and Gender: Observation-Based Data Collection in Airports and at Immigration Checkpoints* and *Immigration Offenders in the Federal Criminal Justice System, 2000.*

U.S. Department of Justice (DOJ), National Institute of Justice (NIJ), 810 Seventh Street, NW, Washington, DC 20531, (202) 307-2942, Fax: (202) 616-0275, www.ojp.usdoj.gov/nij/; *Community Policing and "The New Immigrants": Latinos in Chicago.*

U.S. Library of Congress (LOC), Congressional Research Service (CRS), The Library of Congress, 101 Independence Avenue, SE, Washington, DC 20540-7500, (202) 707-5700, www.loc.gov/crsinfo; *Border Security: The Role of the U.S. Border Patrol* and *Immigration Fraud: Policies, Investigations, and Issues.*

IMMIGRANTS - BY AREA OF RESIDENCE

The Brookings Institution, 1775 Massachusetts Avenue, NW, Washington, DC 20036, (202) 797-6000, Fax: (202) 797-6004, www.brook.edu; *From 'There' to 'Here': Refugee Resettlement in Metropolitan America.*

U.S. Citizenship and Immigration Services (USCIS), Washington District Office, 2675 Prosperity Avenue, Fairfax, VA 22031, (800) 375-5283, http://uscis.gov; *2005 Yearbook of Immigration Statistics.*

U.S. Department of Homeland Security (DHS), Office of Immigration Statistics, Washington, DC 20528, (202) 282-8000, www.dhs.gov; *Mapping Immigration: Legal Permanent Residents (LPRs); Mapping Trends in Naturalizations: 1980 to 2003; Mapping Trends in U.S. Legal Immigration: 1980 to 2003; Profiles on Legal Permanent Residents;* and *Profiles on Naturalized Citizens.*

IMMIGRANTS - BY CLASS OF ADMISSION

U.S. Citizenship and Immigration Services (USCIS), Washington District Office, 2675 Prosperity Avenue, Fairfax, VA 22031, (800) 375-5283, http://uscis.gov; *2005 Yearbook of Immigration Statistics.*

IMMIGRANTS - BY COUNTRY OF BIRTH

U.S. Citizenship and Immigration Services (USCIS), Washington District Office, 2675 Prosperity Avenue, Fairfax, VA 22031, (800) 375-5283, http://uscis.gov; *2005 Yearbook of Immigration Statistics.*

U.S. Department of Homeland Security (DHS), Office of Immigration Statistics, Washington, DC 20528, (202) 282-8000, www.dhs.gov; *Mapping Immigration: Legal Permanent Residents (LPRs); Mapping Trends in Naturalizations: 1980 to 2003; Mapping Trends in U.S. Legal Immigration: 1980 to 2003; Naturalizations in the United States: 2005; Profiles on Legal Permanent Residents; Profiles on Naturalized Citizens; Refugee Applicants and Admissions to the United States: 2004;* and *Refugees and Asylees: 2005.*

IMMIGRANTS - HEALTH CARE

Health Protection Agency, 7th Floor, Holborn Gate, 330 High Holborn, London WC1V 7PP, United Kingdom, www.hpa.org.uk; *Migrant Health: Infectious Diseases in Non-UK Born Populations in England, Wales and Northern Ireland (A Baseline Report - 2006).*

International Organization for Migration (IOM), 17, Route des Morillons, CH-1211 Geneva 19, Switzerland, www.iom.int; *Migration Health Annual Report 2006.*

IMMIGRANTS - REFUGEES

The Annie E. Casey Foundation, 701 Saint Paul Street, Baltimore, MD 21202, (410) 547-6600, Fax: (410) 547-3610, www.aecf.org; *Undercounted, Underserved: Immigrant and Refugee Families in the Child Welfare System.*

The Brookings Institution, 1775 Massachusetts Avenue, NW, Washington, DC 20036, (202) 797-6000, Fax: (202) 797-6004, www.brook.edu; *From 'There' to 'Here': Refugee Resettlement in Metropolitan America.*

U.S. Citizenship and Immigration Services (USCIS), Washington District Office, 2675 Prosperity Avenue, Fairfax, VA 22031, (800) 375-5283, http://uscis.gov; *2005 Yearbook of Immigration Statistics.*

U.S. Department of Homeland Security (DHS), Office of Immigration Statistics, Washington, DC 20528, (202) 282-8000, www.dhs.gov; *Profiles on Legal Permanent Residents; Profiles on Naturalized Citizens; Refugee Applicants and Admissions to the United States: 2004;* and *Refugees and Asylees: 2005.*

United Nations High Commissioner for Refugees (UNHCR), Case Postale 2500, CH-1211 Geneve 2 Depot, Switzerland, www.unhcr.org; *Measuring Protection by Numbers; The State of the World's Refugees 2006; Unaccompanied and Separated Children Seeking Asylum, 2001-2003;* and *UNHCR Statistical Yearbook 2006.*

IMMUNIZATION OF CHILDREN

Centers for Disease Control and Prevention (CDC), U.S. Department of Health and Human Services (HHS), 1600 Clifton Road, Atlanta, GA 30333, (800) 311-3435, www.cdc.gov; *Immunization Coverage in the U.S.* and *Morbidity and Mortality Weekly Report (MMWR).*

European Centre for Disease Prevention and Control (ECDC), 171 83 Stockholm, Sweden, www.ecdc.europa.eu; *Infant and Children Seasonal Immunisation Against Influenza on a Routine Basis During Inter-pandemic Period; Sudden Deaths and Influenza Vaccinations in Israel - ECDC Interim Risk Assessment;* and *Vaccines and Immunisation - VI news.*

National Center for Health Statistics (NCHS), Centers for Disease Control and Prevention (CDC), U.S. Department of Health and Human Services (HHS), 3311 Toledo Road, Hyattsville, MD 20782, (866) 232-4636, www.cdc.gov/nchs; *Faststats A to Z* and *2005 National Immunization Survey (NIS).*

IMPORTS

See INTERNATIONAL TRADE

INCOME - ADULT EDUCATION

National Center for Education Statistics (NCES), 1990 K Street, NW, Washington, DC 20006, (202) 502-7300, http://nces.ed.gov; *The National Household Education Surveys Program (NHES).*

INCOME - AGGREGATE INCOME

U.S. Census Bureau, 4700 Silver Hill Road, Washington DC 20233-0001, (301) 763-3030, www.census.gov; *Survey of Income and Program Participation (SIPP).*

U.S. Census Bureau, Population Division, 4700 Silver Hill Road, Washington DC 20233-0001, (301) 763-3030, www.census.gov/population/www/; *Current Population Reports.*

INCOME - AMERICAN INDIAN, ESKIMO, ALEUT POPULATION

U.S. Census Bureau, Population Division, 4700 Silver Hill Road, Washington DC 20233-0001, (301) 763-3030, www.census.gov/population/www/; *The Asian and Pacific Islander Population in the United States; 2000 Census of Population and Housing: Characteristics of American Indians and Alaska Natives by Tribe and Language;* and *Current Population Reports.*

INCOME - ASIAN AND PACIFIC ISLANDER POPULATION

U.S. Census Bureau, Population Division, 4700 Silver Hill Road, Washington DC 20233-0001, (301) 763-3030, www.census.gov/population/www/; *The Asian and Pacific Islander Population in the United States* and *Current Population Reports.*

INCOME - BLACK POPULATION

U.S. Census Bureau, Population Division, 4700 Silver Hill Road, Washington DC 20233-0001, (301) 763-3030, www.census.gov/population/www/; *Current Population Reports.*

INCOME - CORPORATE

U.S. Department of the Treasury (DOT), Internal Revenue Service (IRS), Statistics of Income Division (SIS), PO Box 2608, Washington, DC, 20013-2608, (202) 874-0410, Fax: (202) 874-0964, www.irs.ustreas.gov; *Statistics of Income Bulletin, Corporation Income Tax Returns.*

INCOME - DISPOSABLE PERSONAL

Bureau of Economic Analysis (BEA), U.S. Department of Commerce (DOC), 1441 L Street NW, Washington, DC 20230, (202) 606-9900, www.bea.gov; *2007 Annual Revision of the National Income and Product Accounts (NIPA)* and *Survey of Current Business (SCB).*

INCOME - DISTRIBUTION

Bureau of Economic Analysis (BEA), U.S. Department of Commerce (DOC), 1441 L Street NW, Washington, DC 20230, (202) 606-9900, www.bea.gov; *2007 Annual Revision of the National Income and Product Accounts (NIPA)* and *Survey of Current Business (SCB).*

U.S. Census Bureau, 4700 Silver Hill Road, Washington DC 20233-0001, (301) 763-3030, www.census.gov; *Survey of Income and Program Participation (SIPP).*

U.S. Census Bureau, Population Division, 4700 Silver Hill Road, Washington DC 20233-0001, (301) 763-3030, www.census.gov/population/www/; *Current Population Reports.*

U.S. Department of Commerce (DOC), Economics and Statistics Administration (ESA), 1401 Constitution Avenue, NW, Washington, DC 20230, (800) 782-8872, www.esa.doc.gov; *A Chance to Advance: A Look at Income Variability in the U.S.*

INCOME - ENERGY CONSUMPTION

U.S. Department of Energy (DOE), Energy Information Administration (EIA), 1000 Independence Avenue, SW, Washington, DC 20585, (202) 586-8800, www.eia.doe.gov; *Residential Energy Consumption Survey (RECS).*

INCOME - FAMILIES

National Center for Children in Poverty (NCCP), 215 W. 125th Street, 3rd Floor, New York, NY 10027, (646) 284-9600, Fax: (646) 284-9623, www.nccp.org; *Living at the Edge; Parent Employment and the Use of Child Care Subsidies;* and *When Work Doesn't Pay: What Every Policymaker Should Know.*

Office of Planning, District of Columbia, 801 North Capitol Street, NE, Suite 4000, Washington, DC 20002, (202) 442-7600, Fax: (202) 442-7637, www.planning.dc.gov; *Income and Poverty in the District of Columbia: 1990-2004.*

U.S. Bureau of Labor Statistics (BLS), Postal Square Building, 2 Massachusetts Avenue, NE, Washington, DC 20212-0001, (202) 691-5200, Fax: (202) 691-6325, www.bls.gov; *Current Population Survey (CPS).*

U.S. Census Bureau, 4700 Silver Hill Road, Washington DC 20233-0001, (301) 763-3030, www.census.gov; American FactFinder (web app); *County and City Data Book 2007; State and County QuickFacts; Survey of Income and Program Participation (SIPP);* and unpublished data.

U.S. Census Bureau, Housing and Household Economics Statistics Division, 4700 Silver Hill Road, Washington DC 20233-0001, (301) 763-3030, www.census.gov/hhes/www; Decennial Census of Population and Housing (web app).

U.S. Census Bureau, Population Division, 4700 Silver Hill Road, Washington DC 20233-0001, (301) 763-3030, www.census.gov/population/www/; *Current Population Reports.*

U.S. Department of Commerce (DOC), Economics and Statistics Administration (ESA), 1401 Constitution Avenue, NW, Washington, DC 20230, (800) 782-8872, www.esa.doc.gov; *A Chance to Advance: A Look at Income Variability in the U.S.*

INCOME - FAMILIES - COMPUTER USE

National Telecommunications and Information Administration (NTIA), U.S. Department of Commerce (DOC), 1401 Constitution Avenue, NW, Washington, DC 20230, (202) 482-7002, www.ntia.doc.gov; *A Nation Online: Entering the Broadband Age.*

INCOME - FAMILIES - LABOR FORCE PARTICIPATION

U.S. Census Bureau, Population Division, 4700 Silver Hill Road, Washington DC 20233-0001, (301) 763-3030, www.census.gov/population/www/; *Current Population Reports.*

INCOME - FAMILIES - OUTLYING AREAS

Oficina del Censo, Programa de Planificacion Economica y Social, Junta de Planificacion, PO Box 41119, Santurce, Puerto Rico 00940, (Dial from U.S. (787) 723-6200), (Fax from U.S. (787) 268-0506), www.censo.gobierno.pr; unpublished data.

INCOME - FAMILIES - TYPE OF FAMILY

U.S. Census Bureau, 4700 Silver Hill Road, Washington DC 20233-0001, (301) 763-3030, www.census.gov; *Survey of Income and Program Participation (SIPP).*

U.S. Census Bureau, Population Division, 4700 Silver Hill Road, Washington DC 20233-0001, (301) 763-3030, www.census.gov/population/www/; *Current Population Reports.*

INCOME - FARM

Bureau of Economic Analysis (BEA), U.S. Department of Commerce (DOC), 1441 L Street NW, Washington, DC 20230, (202) 606-9900, www.bea.gov; *2007 Annual Revision of the National Income and Product Accounts (NIPA)* and *Survey of Current Business (SCB).*

Economic Research Service (ERS), U.S. Department of Agriculture (USDA), 1800 M Street, NW, Washington, DC 20036-5831, (202) 694-5050, Fax: (202) 694-5689, www.ers.usda.gov; *Agricultural Income and Finance Outlook; 2008 Farm Income Forecast;* and *Farm Income: Data Files.*

National Agricultural Statistics Service (NASS), U.S. Department of Agriculture (USDA), 1400 Independence Avenue, SW, Washington, DC 20250, (800) 727-9540, Fax: (202) 690-2090, www.nass.usda.gov; *Farm Labor.*

INCOME - HISPANIC ORIGIN POPULATION

U.S. Census Bureau, 4700 Silver Hill Road, Washington DC 20233-0001, (301) 763-3030, www.census.gov; *Survey of Income and Program Participation (SIPP)* and unpublished data.

U.S. Census Bureau, Population Division, 4700 Silver Hill Road, Washington DC 20233-0001, (301) 763-3030, www.census.gov/population/www/; *Current Population Reports.*

INCOME - HOUSEHOLD

Office of Planning, District of Columbia, 801 North Capitol Street, NE, Suite 4000, Washington, DC 20002, (202) 442-7600, Fax: (202) 442-7637, www.planning.dc.gov; *Income and Poverty in the District of Columbia: 1990-2004.*

U.S. Census Bureau, 4700 Silver Hill Road, Washington DC 20233-0001, (301) 763-3030, www.census.gov; American FactFinder (web app); *County and City Data Book 2007;* and *State and County QuickFacts.*

U.S. Department of Commerce (DOC), Economics and Statistics Administration (ESA), 1401 Constitution Avenue, NW, Washington, DC 20230, (800) 782-8872, www.esa.doc.gov; *A Chance to Advance: A Look at Income Variability in the U.S.*

INCOME - HOUSEHOLD - AGE

U.S. Census Bureau, 4700 Silver Hill Road, Washington DC 20233-0001, (301) 763-3030, www.census.gov; *Survey of Income and Program Participation (SIPP).*

U.S. Census Bureau, Population Division, 4700 Silver Hill Road, Washington DC 20233-0001, (301) 763-3030, www.census.gov/population/www/; *Current Population Reports.*

INCOME - HOUSEHOLD - BLACK POPULATION

U.S. Census Bureau, 4700 Silver Hill Road, Washington DC 20233-0001, (301) 763-3030, www.census.gov; *Survey of Income and Program Participation (SIPP).*

U.S. Census Bureau, Population Division, 4700 Silver Hill Road, Washington DC 20233-0001, (301) 763-3030, www.census.gov/population/www/; *Current Population Reports.*

INCOME - HOUSEHOLD - EDUCATIONAL ATTAINMENT

U.S. Census Bureau, Population Division, 4700 Silver Hill Road, Washington DC 20233-0001, (301) 763-3030, www.census.gov/population/www/; *Current Population Reports.*

INCOME - HOUSEHOLD - HISPANIC ORIGIN POPULATION

U.S. Census Bureau, Population Division, 4700 Silver Hill Road, Washington DC 20233-0001, (301) 763-3030, www.census.gov/population/www/; *Current Population Reports.*

INCOME - HOUSEHOLD - OLDER PEOPLE

U.S. Census Bureau, Population Division, 4700 Silver Hill Road, Washington DC 20233-0001, (301) 763-3030, www.census.gov/population/www/; *Current Population Reports.*

INCOME - HOUSEHOLD - RECREATION ACTIVITIES

National Sporting Goods Association (NSGA), 1601 Feehanville Drive, Suite 300, Mount Prospect, IL 60056, (847) 296-6742, Fax: (847) 391-9827, www.nsga.org; *2006 Sports Participation* and *Ten-Year History of Selected Sports Participation, 1996-2006.*

INCOME - HOUSEHOLD - TENURE

U.S. Census Bureau, Population Division, 4700 Silver Hill Road, Washington DC 20233-0001, (301) 763-3030, www.census.gov/population/www/; *Current Population Reports.*

INCOME - LOSS FROM SHORT-TERM SICKNESS

Social Security Administration (SSA), Office of Public Inquiries, Windsor Park Building, 6401 Security Boulevard, Baltimore, MD 21235, (800) 772-1213, www.ssa.gov; *Social Security Bulletin* and unpublished data.

INCOME - NATIONAL INCOME

Bureau of Economic Analysis (BEA), U.S. Department of Commerce (DOC), 1441 L Street NW, Washington, DC 20230, (202) 606-9900, www.bea.gov; *2007 Annual Revision of the National Income and Product Accounts (NIPA)* and *Survey of Current Business (SCB).*

U.S. Department of Commerce (DOC), Economics and Statistics Administration (ESA), 1401 Constitution Avenue, NW, Washington, DC 20230, (800) 782-8872, www.esa.doc.gov; *A Chance to Advance: A Look at Income Variability in the U.S.*

United Nations Statistics Division, New York, NY 10017, (800) 253-9646, Fax: (212) 963-4116, http://unstats.un.org; United Nations Common Database (UNCDB).

INCOME - NATIONAL INCOME - BY TYPE OF INCOME

Bureau of Economic Analysis (BEA), U.S. Department of Commerce (DOC), 1441 L Street NW, Washington, DC 20230, (202) 606-9900, www.bea.gov; *2007 Annual Revision of the National Income and Product Accounts (NIPA)* and *Survey of Current Business (SCB).*

INCOME - NATIONAL INCOME - ORIGINATING IN FARMING

Bureau of Economic Analysis (BEA), U.S. Department of Commerce (DOC), 1441 L Street NW, Washington, DC 20230, (202) 606-9900, www.bea.gov; *2007 Annual Revision of the National Income and Product Accounts (NIPA)* and *Survey of Current Business (SCB).*

Economic Research Service (ERS), U.S. Department of Agriculture (USDA), 1800 M Street, NW, Washington, DC 20036-5831, (202) 694-5050, Fax: (202) 694-5689, www.ers.usda.gov; *2008 Farm Income Forecast.*

INCOME - PER CAPITA

Bureau of Economic Analysis (BEA), U.S. Department of Commerce (DOC), 1441 L Street NW, Washington, DC 20230, (202) 606-9900, www.bea.gov; *2007 Annual Revision of the National Income and Product Accounts (NIPA)* and *Survey of Current Business (SCB).*

U.S. Census Bureau, Population Division, 4700 Silver Hill Road, Washington DC 20233-0001, (301) 763-3030, www.census.gov/population/www/; *Current Population Reports.*

INCOME - PERSONAL

Bureau of Economic Analysis (BEA), U.S. Department of Commerce (DOC), 1441 L Street NW, Washington, DC 20230, (202) 606-9900, www.bea.gov; *2007 Annual Revision of the National Income and Product Accounts (NIPA); Survey of Current Business (SCB);* and unpublished data.

Office of Planning, District of Columbia, 801 North Capitol Street, NE, Suite 4000, Washington, DC 20002, (202) 442-7600, Fax: (202) 442-7637, www.planning.dc.gov; *Income and Poverty in the District of Columbia: 1990-2004.*

State of Hawaii Department of Business, Economic Development Tourism (DBEDT), Research and Economic Analysis Division (READ), PO Box 2359 Honolulu, HI 96804, (808) 586-2423, Fax: (808) 587-2790, www.hawaii.gov/dbedt/info/economic/census; *Wage and Employment Structure: Comparing Recent Trends for Hawaii vs. the U.S.*

U.S. Department of Labor (DOL), Bureau of Labor Statistics (BLS), Postal Square Building, 2 Massachusetts Avenue, NE, Washington, DC 20212-0001, (202) 691-5200, Fax: (202) 691-6325, www.bls.gov; *Wages by Area and Occupation.*

INCOME - PERSONS

American Medical Association, 515 North State Street, Chicago, IL 60610, (800) 621-8335, www.ama-assn.org; *Physician Compensation and Production Survey: 2007 Report Based on 2006 Data.*

Forbes, Inc., 60 Fifth Avenue, New York, NY 10011, (212) 366-8900, www.forbes.com; *The 400 Richest Americans* and *The World's Billionaires.*

State of Hawaii Department of Business, Economic Development Tourism (DBEDT), Research and Economic Analysis Division (READ), PO Box 2359 Honolulu, HI 96804, (808) 586-2423, Fax: (808)

587-2790, www.hawaii.gov/dbedt/info/economic/census; *Wage and Employment Structure: Comparing Recent Trends for Hawaii vs. the U.S.*

U.S. Census Bureau, 4700 Silver Hill Road, Washington DC 20233-0001, (301) 763-3030, www.census.gov; American FactFinder (web app) and *County and City Data Book 2007*.

U.S. Census Bureau, Population Division, 4700 Silver Hill Road, Washington DC 20233-0001, (301) 763-3030, www.census.gov/population/www/; *Current Population Reports*.

U.S. Department of Commerce (DOC), Economics and Statistics Administration (ESA), 1401 Constitution Avenue, NW, Washington, DC 20230, (800) 782-8872, www.esa.doc.gov; *A Chance to Advance: A Look at Income Variability in the U.S.*

U.S. Department of Labor (DOL), Bureau of Labor Statistics (BLS), Postal Square Building, 2 Massachusetts Avenue, NE, Washington, DC 20212-0001, (202) 691-5200, Fax: (202) 691-6325, www.bls.gov; *Current Employment Statistics (CES)* and *Employment and Wages, Annual Averages 2005*.

U.S. Library of Congress (LOC), Congressional Research Service (CRS), The Library of Congress, 101 Independence Avenue, SE, Washington, DC 20540-7500, (202) 707-5700, www.loc.gov/crsinfo; *Federal Employees: Pay and Pension Increases Since 1969*.

INCOME - PERSONS - BELOW POVERTY LEVEL

The Annie E. Casey Foundation, 701 Saint Paul Street, Baltimore, MD 21202, (410) 547-6600, Fax: (410) 547-3610, www.aecf.org; *The High Cost of Being Poor: What It Takes for Low-Income Families to Get By and Get Ahead in Rural America* and *Working Hard, Falling Short*.

National Center for Children in Poverty (NCCP), 215 W. 125th Street, 3rd Floor, New York, NY 10027, (646) 284-9600, Fax: (646) 284-9623, www.nccp.org; *Living at the Edge* and *When Work Doesn't Pay: What Every Policymaker Should Know*.

Population Reference Bureau, 1875 Connecticut Avenue, NW, Suite 520, Washington, DC, 20009-5728, (800) 877-9881, Fax: (202) 328-3937, www.prb.org; *The American People Series*.

U.S. Census Bureau, 4700 Silver Hill Road, Washington DC 20233-0001, (301) 763-3030, www.census.gov; American FactFinder (web app) and *County and City Data Book 2007*.

U.S. Census Bureau, Demographic Surveys Division, 4700 Silver Hill Road, Washington DC 20233-0001, (301) 763-3030, www.census.gov; *Demographic Profiles: 100-percent and Sample Data*.

U.S. Census Bureau, Population Division, 4700 Silver Hill Road, Washington DC 20233-0001, (301) 763-3030, www.census.gov/population/www/; *Census 2000 Profiles of General Demographic Characteristics* and *Current Population Reports*.

INCOME - POVERTY

The Annie E. Casey Foundation, 701 Saint Paul Street, Baltimore, MD 21202, (410) 547-6600, Fax: (410) 547-3610, www.aecf.org; *The High Cost of Being Poor: What It Takes for Low-Income Families to Get By and Get Ahead in Rural America* and *Working Hard, Falling Short*.

National Center for Children in Poverty (NCCP), 215 W. 125th Street, 3rd Floor, New York, NY 10027, (646) 284-9600, Fax: (646) 284-9623, www.nccp.org; *2007 Annual Report; The Changing Demographics of Low-Income Families and Their Children; The Changing Face of Child Poverty in California; Early Childhood Poverty: A Statistical Profile; Geography of Low-Income Families and Children; Living at the Edge; Low-Income Families in the States: Results from the Family Resource Simulator; Parent Employment and the Use of Child Care Subsidies;* and *When Work Doesn't Pay: What Every Policymaker Should Know*.

Office of Planning, District of Columbia, 801 North Capitol Street, NE, Suite 4000, Washington, DC 20002, (202) 442-7600, Fax: (202) 442-7637, www.planning.dc.gov; *Income and Poverty in the District of Columbia: 1990-2004*.

U.S. Census Bureau, Population Division, 4700 Silver Hill Road, Washington DC 20233-0001, (301) 763-3030, www.census.gov/population/www/; *Current Population Reports*.

U.S. Department of Justice (DOJ), National Institute of Justice (NIJ), 810 Seventh Street, NW, Washington, DC 20531, (202) 307-2942, Fax: (202) 616-0275, www.ojp.usdoj.gov/nij/; *When Violence Hits Home: How Economics and Neighborhood Play a Role*.

INCOME - SAVINGS

Board of Governors of the Federal Reserve System, Constitution Avenue, NW, Washington, DC 20551, (202) 452-3000, www.federalreserve.gov; *Flow of Funds Accounts of the United States*.

Bureau of Economic Analysis (BEA), U.S. Department of Commerce (DOC), 1441 L Street NW, Washington, DC 20230, (202) 606-9900, www.bea.gov; *2007 Annual Revision of the National Income and Product Accounts (NIPA)* and *Survey of Current Business (SCB)*.

INCOME - SPORTS PARTICIPATION - GOODS

National Sporting Goods Association (NSGA), 1601 Feehanville Drive, Suite 300, Mount Prospect, IL 60056, (847) 296-6742, Fax: (847) 391-9827, www.nsga.org; *2006 Sports Participation* and *Ten-Year History of Selected Sports Participation, 1996-2006*.

INCOME TAX

See also TAX RECEIPTS

Economic and Policy Analysis Research Center (EPARC), University of Missouri-Columbia, 10 Professional Building, Columbia, MO 65211, (573) 882-4805, Fax: (573) 882-5563, http://econ.missouri.edu/eparc; *Missouri Historical Tax Summary 1965-2007* and *Tax Expenditure Report 2007*.

INCOME TAX - AVERAGE TAX BY INCOME LEVEL

U.S. Department of the Treasury (DOT), Internal Revenue Service (IRS), Statistics of Income Division (SIS), PO Box 2608, Washington, DC, 20013-2608, (202) 874-0410, Fax: (202) 874-0964, www.irs.ustreas.gov; *IRS Data Book 2004-2005* and *Statistics of Income Bulletin, Individual Income Tax Returns*.

INCOME TAX - CORPORATION

Economic and Policy Analysis Research Center (EPARC), University of Missouri-Columbia, 10 Professional Building, Columbia, MO 65211, (573) 882-4805, Fax: (573) 882-5563, http://econ.missouri.edu/eparc; *Missouri Historical Tax Summary 1965-2007* and *Tax Expenditure Report 2007*.

U.S. Census Bureau, Governments Division, 4600 Silver Hill Road, Washington DC 20233, (800) 242-2184, www.census.gov/govs/www; *2002 Census of Governments, Government Finances* and *Federal, State, and Local Governments: State Government Tax Collections (STC)*.

U.S. Department of the Treasury (DOT), Internal Revenue Service (IRS), Statistics of Income Division (SIS), PO Box 2608, Washington, DC, 20013-2608, (202) 874-0410, Fax: (202) 874-0964, www.irs.ustreas.gov; *IRS Data Book 2004-2005* and *Statistics of Income Bulletin, Corporation Income Tax Returns*.

INCOME TAX - FOREIGN COUNTRIES

Organisation for Economic Cooperation and Development (OECD), 2 rue Andre Pascal, F-75775 Paris Cedex 16, France, (Telephone in U.S. (202) 785-6323), (Fax in U.S. (202) 785-0350), www.oecd.org; *Taxing Wages 2006/2007: 2007 Edition*.

INCOME TAX - STATE COLLECTIONS

Economic and Policy Analysis Research Center (EPARC), University of Missouri-Columbia, 10 Professional Building, Columbia, MO 65211, (573) 882-4805, Fax: (573) 882-5563, http://econ.missouri.edu/eparc; *Missouri Historical Tax Summary 1965-2007* and *Tax Expenditure Report 2007*.

U.S. Census Bureau, Governments Division, 4600 Silver Hill Road, Washington DC 20233, (800) 242-2184, www.census.gov/govs/www; *2002 Census of Governments, Government Finances*.

INDIA - NATIONAL STATISTICAL OFFICE

Central Statistical Organization, Ministry of Statistics and Programme Implementation, Computer Centre, East Block-10, R.K. Puram, New Delhi 110066, India, www.mospi.nic.in; National Data Center.

INDIA - PRIMARY STATISTICS SOURCES

Census of India, Office of the Registrar General, 2A, Mansingh Road, New Delhi-110 011, India, www.censusindia.net; *2001 Census Data*.

Central Statistical Organization, Ministry of Statistics and Programme Implementation, Computer Centre, East Block-10, R.K. Puram, New Delhi 110066, India, www.mospi.nic.in; *India In Figures 2007; Monthly Abstract of Statistics; Statistical Abstract India 2007;* and *Statistical Pocketbook of India 2006/2007*.

Directorate General of Commercial Intelligence and Statistics (DGCIS), Ministry of Commerce and Industry, 1, Council House Street, Calcutta-700 001, India, www.dgciskol.nic.in; *Indian Trade Journal*.

INDIA - ABORTION

United Nations Statistics Division, New York, NY 10017, (800) 253-9646, Fax: (212) 963-4116, http://unstats.un.org; *Demographic Yearbook*.

INDIA - AGRICULTURAL MACHINERY

United Nations Statistics Division, New York, NY 10017, (800) 253-9646, Fax: (212) 963-4116, http://unstats.un.org; *Statistical Yearbook*.

INDIA - AGRICULTURE

Economist Intelligence Unit, 111 West 57th Street, New York, NY 10019, (212) 554-0600, Fax: (212) 586-1181, www.eiu.com; *India Country Report*.

Euromonitor International, Inc., 224 S. Michigan Avenue, Suite 1500, Chicago, IL 60604, (312) 922-1115, Fax: (312) 922-1157, www.euromonitor.com; *International Marketing Data and Statistics 2008* and *World Marketing Data and Statistics*.

Federal Statistical Office Germany, D-65180 Wiesbaden, Germany, www.destatis.de; *India 2006*.

Palgrave Macmillan Ltd., Houndmills, Basingstoke, Hampshire, RG21 6XS, England, (Telephone in U.S. (888) 330-8477), (Fax in U.S. (800) 672-2054), www.palgrave.com; *The Statesman's Yearbook 2008*.

Taylor and Francis Group, An Informa Business, 2 Park Square, Milton Park, Abingdon, Oxford OX14 4RN, United Kingdom, (Dial from U.S. (212) 216-7800), (Fax from U.S. (212) 564-7854), www.tandf.co.uk; *The Europa World Year Book*.

United Nations Conference on Trade and Development (UNCTAD), DC2-1120, United Nations, New York, NY 10017, (212) 963-0027, www.unctad.org; *UNCTAD Commodity Yearbook*.

United Nations Food and Agricultural Organization (FAO), Viale delle Terme di Caracalla, 00100 Rome, Italy, (Dial from U.S. (202) 653-2400), (Fax from U.S. (202) 653 5760), www.fao.org; AQUASTAT; *FAO Production Yearbook 2002; FAO Trade Yearbook;* and *The State of Food and Agriculture (SOFA) 2006*.

United Nations Statistics Division, New York, NY 10017, (800) 253-9646, Fax: (212) 963-4116, http://

unstats.un.org; *Asia-Pacific in Figures 2004; Statistical Yearbook;* and *Statistical Yearbook for Asia and the Pacific 2004.*

The World Bank, 1818 H Street, NW, Washington, DC 20433, (202) 473-1000, Fax: (202) 477-6391, www.worldbank.org; *India* and *World Development Indicators (WDI) 2008.*

INDIA - AIRLINES

Economist Intelligence Unit, 111 West 57th Street, New York, NY 10019, (212) 554-0600, Fax: (212) 586-1181, www.eiu.com; *Business Asia.*

International Civil Aviation Organization (ICAO), External Relations and Public Information Office (EPO), 999 University Street, Montreal, Quebec H3C 5H7, Canada, (Dial from U.S. (514) 954-8219), (Fax from U.S. (514) 954-6077), www.icao.int; *Civil Aviation Statistics of the World.*

Palgrave Macmillan Ltd., Houndmills, Basingstoke, Hampshire, RG21 6XS, England, (Telephone in U.S. (888) 330-8477), (Fax in U.S. (800) 672-2054), www.palgrave.com; *The Statesman's Yearbook 2008.*

Taylor and Francis Group, An Informa Business, 2 Park Square, Milton Park, Abingdon, Oxford OX14 4RN, United Kingdom, (Dial from U.S. (212) 216-7800), (Fax from U.S. (212) 564-7854), www.tandf.co.uk; *The Europa World Year Book.*

United Nations Statistics Division, New York, NY 10017, (800) 253-9646, Fax: (212) 963-4116, http://unstats.un.org; *Statistical Yearbook.*

INDIA - AIRPORTS

Central Intelligence Agency, Office of Public Affairs, Washington, DC 20505, (703) 482-0623, Fax: (703) 482-1739, www.cia.gov; *The World Factbook.*

INDIA - ALUMINUM PRODUCTION

See INDIA - MINERAL INDUSTRIES

INDIA - ARMED FORCES

Central Intelligence Agency, Office of Public Affairs, Washington, DC 20505, (703) 482-0623, Fax: (703) 482-1739, www.cia.gov; *The World Factbook.*

Economist Intelligence Unit, 111 West 57th Street, New York, NY 10019, (212) 554-0600, Fax: (212) 586-1181, www.eiu.com; *Business Asia.*

Euromonitor International, Inc., 224 S. Michigan Avenue, Suite 1500, Chicago, IL 60604, (312) 922-1115, Fax: (312) 922-1157, www.euromonitor.com; *World Marketing Data and Statistics.*

International Institute for Strategic Studies (IISS), Arundel House, 13-15 Arundel Street, Temple Place, London WC2R 3DX, England, www.iiss.org; *The Military Balance 2007.*

International Monetary Fund (IMF), 700 Nineteenth Street, NW, Washington, DC 20431, (202) 623-7000, Fax: (202) 623-4661, www.imf.org; *Government Finance Statistics Yearbook (2008 Edition).*

Palgrave Macmillan Ltd., Houndmills, Basingstoke, Hampshire, RG21 6XS, England, (Telephone in U.S. (888) 330-8477), (Fax in U.S. (800) 672-2054), www.palgrave.com; *The Statesman's Yearbook 2008.*

U.S. Department of State (DOS), 2201 C Street NW, Washington, DC 20520, (202) 647-4000, www.state.gov; *World Military Expenditures and Arms Transfers (WMEAT).*

United Nations Statistics Division, New York, NY 10017, (800) 253-9646, Fax: (212) 963-4116, http://unstats.un.org; *Human Development Report 2006.*

INDIA - AUTOMOBILE INDUSTRY AND TRADE

United Nations Statistics Division, New York, NY 10017, (800) 253-9646, Fax: (212) 963-4116, http://unstats.un.org; *Statistical Yearbook.*

INDIA - BALANCE OF PAYMENTS

Federal Statistical Office Germany, D-65180 Wiesbaden, Germany, www.destatis.de; *India 2006.*

International Monetary Fund (IMF), 700 Nineteenth Street, NW, Washington, DC 20431, (202) 623-7000, Fax: (202) 623-4661, www.imf.org; *Balance of Payments Statistics Newsletter; Balance of Payments Statistics Yearbook 2007;* and *International Financial Statistics Yearbook 2007.*

Taylor and Francis Group, An Informa Business, 2 Park Square, Milton Park, Abingdon, Oxford OX14 4RN, United Kingdom, (Dial from U.S. (212) 216-7800), (Fax from U.S. (212) 564-7854), www.tandf.co.uk; *The Europa World Year Book.*

United Nations Conference on Trade and Development (UNCTAD), DC2-1120, United Nations, New York, NY 10017, (212) 963-0027, www.unctad.org; *Handbook of Statistics 2005.*

The World Bank, 1818 H Street, NW, Washington, DC 20433, (202) 473-1000, Fax: (202) 477-6391, www.worldbank.org; *India* and *World Development Report 2008.*

INDIA - BANKS AND BANKING

Euromonitor International, Inc., 224 S. Michigan Avenue, Suite 1500, Chicago, IL 60604, (312) 922-1115, Fax: (312) 922-1157, www.euromonitor.com; *World Marketing Data and Statistics.*

International Monetary Fund (IMF), 700 Nineteenth Street, NW, Washington, DC 20431, (202) 623-7000, Fax: (202) 623-4661, www.imf.org; *International Financial Statistics Yearbook 2007.*

Palgrave Macmillan Ltd., Houndmills, Basingstoke, Hampshire, RG21 6XS, England, (Telephone in U.S. (888) 330-8477), (Fax in U.S. (800) 672-2054), www.palgrave.com; *The Statesman's Yearbook 2008.*

Taylor and Francis Group, An Informa Business, 2 Park Square, Milton Park, Abingdon, Oxford OX14 4RN, United Kingdom, (Dial from U.S. (212) 216-7800), (Fax from U.S. (212) 564-7854), www.tandf.co.uk; *The Europa World Year Book.*

United Nations Statistics Division, New York, NY 10017, (800) 253-9646, Fax: (212) 963-4116, http://unstats.un.org; *Statistical Yearbook.*

INDIA - BARLEY PRODUCTION

See INDIA - CROPS

INDIA - BEVERAGE INDUSTRY

United Nations Statistics Division, New York, NY 10017, (800) 253-9646, Fax: (212) 963-4116, http://unstats.un.org; *Statistical Yearbook.*

INDIA - BONDS

International Monetary Fund (IMF), 700 Nineteenth Street, NW, Washington, DC 20431, (202) 623-7000, Fax: (202) 623-4661, www.imf.org; *Government Finance Statistics Yearbook (2008 Edition).*

United Nations Statistics Division, New York, NY 10017, (800) 253-9646, Fax: (212) 963-4116, http://unstats.un.org; *Statistical Yearbook.*

INDIA - BROADCASTING

Central Intelligence Agency, Office of Public Affairs, Washington, DC 20505, (703) 482-0623, Fax: (703) 482-1739, www.cia.gov; *The World Factbook.*

Economist Intelligence Unit, 111 West 57th Street, New York, NY 10019, (212) 554-0600, Fax: (212) 586-1181, www.eiu.com; *Business Asia.*

Euromonitor International, Inc., 224 S. Michigan Avenue, Suite 1500, Chicago, IL 60604, (312) 922-1115, Fax: (312) 922-1157, www.euromonitor.com; *World Marketing Data and Statistics.*

Palgrave Macmillan Ltd., Houndmills, Basingstoke, Hampshire, RG21 6XS, England, (Telephone in U.S. (888) 330-8477), (Fax in U.S. (800) 672-2054), www.palgrave.com; *The Statesman's Yearbook 2008.*

UNESCO Institute for Statistics, C.P. 6128 Succursale Centre-Ville, Montreal, Quebec, H3C 3J7 Canada, (Dial from U.S. (514) 343-6880), (Fax from U.S. (514) 343 6882), www.uis.unesco.org; *Statistical Tables.*

WRTH Publications Limited, PO Box 290, Oxford OX2 7FT, UK, www.wrth.com; *World Radio TV Handbook 2007.*

INDIA - BUDGET

Central Intelligence Agency, Office of Public Affairs, Washington, DC 20505, (703) 482-0623, Fax: (703) 482-1739, www.cia.gov; *The World Factbook.*

INDIA - BUSINESS

Directorate General of Commercial Intelligence and Statistics (DGCIS), Ministry of Commerce and Industry, 1, Council House Street, Calcutta-700 001, India, www.dgciskol.nic.in; *Inter-State Movements/ Flows of Goods by Rail, River and Air.*

United Nations Statistics Division, New York, NY 10017, (800) 253-9646, Fax: (212) 963-4116, http://unstats.un.org; *Statistical Yearbook for Asia and the Pacific 2004.*

INDIA - CADMIUM PRODUCTION

See INDIA - MINERAL INDUSTRIES

INDIA - CAPITAL LEVY

International Monetary Fund (IMF), 700 Nineteenth Street, NW, Washington, DC 20431, (202) 623-7000, Fax: (202) 623-4661, www.imf.org; *Government Finance Statistics Yearbook (2008 Edition).*

INDIA - CATTLE

See INDIA - LIVESTOCK

INDIA - CHICK PEA PRODUCTION

See INDIA - CROPS

INDIA - CHICKENS

See INDIA - LIVESTOCK

INDIA - CHILDBIRTH - STATISTICS

Central Intelligence Agency, Office of Public Affairs, Washington, DC 20505, (703) 482-0623, Fax: (703) 482-1739, www.cia.gov; *The World Factbook.*

Economist Intelligence Unit, 111 West 57th Street, New York, NY 10019, (212) 554-0600, Fax: (212) 586-1181, www.eiu.com; *Business Asia.*

Euromonitor International, Inc., 224 S. Michigan Avenue, Suite 1500, Chicago, IL 60604, (312) 922-1115, Fax: (312) 922-1157, www.euromonitor.com; *International Marketing Data and Statistics 2008* and *The World Economic Factbook 2008.*

Palgrave Macmillan Ltd., Houndmills, Basingstoke, Hampshire, RG21 6XS, England, (Telephone in U.S. (888) 330-8477), (Fax in U.S. (800) 672-2054), www.palgrave.com; *The Statesman's Yearbook 2008.*

Taylor and Francis Group, An Informa Business, 2 Park Square, Milton Park, Abingdon, Oxford OX14 4RN, United Kingdom, (Dial from U.S. (212) 216-7800), (Fax from U.S. (212) 564-7854), www.tandf.co.uk; *The Europa World Year Book.*

United Nations Statistics Division, New York, NY 10017, (800) 253-9646, Fax: (212) 963-4116, http://unstats.un.org; *Asia-Pacific in Figures 2004; Demographic Yearbook;* and *Statistical Yearbook.*

The World Bank, 1818 H Street, NW, Washington, DC 20433, (202) 473-1000, Fax: (202) 477-6391, www.worldbank.org; *World Development Report 2008.*

World Health Organization (WHO), Avenue Appia 20, 1211 Geneve 27, Switzerland, (Telephone in U.S. (212) 331-9081), www.who.int; *World Health Report 2006.*

INDIA - CLIMATE

International Institute for Environment and Development (IIED), 3 Endsleigh Street, London, England, WC1H 0DD, United Kingdom, www.iied.org; *Environment Urbanization.*

Palgrave Macmillan Ltd., Houndmills, Basingstoke, Hampshire, RG21 6XS, England, (Telephone in U.S.

(888) 330-8477), (Fax in U.S. (800) 672-2054), www.palgrave.com; *The Statesman's Yearbook 2008.*

INDIA - COAL PRODUCTION

See INDIA - MINERAL INDUSTRIES

INDIA - COBALT PRODUCTION

See INDIA - MINERAL INDUSTRIES

INDIA - COFFEE

See INDIA - CROPS

INDIA - COMMERCE

Palgrave Macmillan Ltd., Houndmills, Basingstoke, Hampshire, RG21 6XS, England, (Telephone in U.S. (888) 330-8477), (Fax in U.S. (800) 672-2054), www.palgrave.com; *The Statesman's Yearbook 2008.*

INDIA - COMMODITY EXCHANGES

Commodity Research Bureau, 330 South Wells Street, Suite 612, Chicago, IL 60606-7110, (800) 621-5271, Fax: (312) 939-4135, www.crbtrader.com; *2006 CRB Commodity Yearbook and CD.*

International Lead and Zinc Study Group (ILZSG), Rua Almirante Barroso 38, 5th Floor, Lisbon 1000 - 013, Portugal, www.ilzsg.org; Interactive Statistical Database.

International Monetary Fund (IMF), 700 Nineteenth Street, NW, Washington, DC 20431, (202) 623-7000, Fax: (202) 623-4661, www.imf.org; *IMF Primary Commodity Prices.*

United Nations Food and Agricultural Organization (FAO), Viale delle Terme di Caracalla, 00100 Rome, Italy, (Dial from U.S. (202) 653-2400), (Fax from U.S. (202) 653 5760), www.fao.org; *The State of Food and Agriculture (SOFA) 2006.*

United Nations Statistics Division, New York, NY 10017, (800) 253-9646, Fax: (212) 963-4116, http://unstats.un.org; *Statistical Yearbook.*

World Bureau of Metal Statistics (WBMS), 27a High Street, Ware, Hertfordshire, SG12 9BA, United Kingdom, www.world-bureau.com; *Annual Stainless Steel Statistics; World Flow Charts; World Metal Statistics; World Nickel Statistics;* and *World Tin Statistics.*

INDIA - COMMUNICATION AND TRAFFIC

United Nations Statistics Division, New York, NY 10017, (800) 253-9646, Fax: (212) 963-4116, http://unstats.un.org; *Statistical Yearbook.*

INDIA - CONSTRUCTION INDUSTRY

Palgrave Macmillan Ltd., Houndmills, Basingstoke, Hampshire, RG21 6XS, England, (Telephone in U.S. (888) 330-8477), (Fax in U.S. (800) 672-2054), www.palgrave.com; *The Statesman's Yearbook 2008.*

United Nations Statistics Division, New York, NY 10017, (800) 253-9646, Fax: (212) 963-4116, http://unstats.un.org; *Statistical Yearbook.*

INDIA - CONSUMER PRICE INDEXES

Federal Statistical Office Germany, D-65180 Wiesbaden, Germany, www.destatis.de; *India 2006.*

International Labour Office, I.L.O. Publications, 4 route des Morillons, CH-1211 Geneva 22, Switzerland, (Telephone in U.S. (202) 653-7652), (Fax in U.S. (202) 653-7687), www.ilo.org; *Yearbook of Labour Statistics 2006.*

Taylor and Francis Group, An Informa Business, 2 Park Square, Milton Park, Abingdon, Oxford OX14 4RN, United Kingdom, (Dial from U.S. (212) 216-7800), (Fax from U.S. (212) 564-7854), www.tandf.co.uk; *The Europa World Year Book.*

United Nations Statistics Division, New York, NY 10017, (800) 253-9646, Fax: (212) 963-4116, http://unstats.un.org; *Statistical Yearbook.*

INDIA - CONSUMPTION (ECONOMICS)

International Lead and Zinc Study Group (ILZSG), Rua Almirante Barroso 38, 5th Floor, Lisbon 1000 - 013, Portugal, www.ilzsg.org; Interactive Statistical Database.

The World Bank, 1818 H Street, NW, Washington, DC 20433, (202) 473-1000, Fax: (202) 477-6391, www.worldbank.org; *World Development Report 2008.*

INDIA - COPPER INDUSTRY AND TRADE

See INDIA - MINERAL INDUSTRIES

INDIA - CORN INDUSTRY

See INDIA - CROPS

INDIA - COST AND STANDARD OF LIVING

International Monetary Fund (IMF), 700 Nineteenth Street, NW, Washington, DC 20431, (202) 623-7000, Fax: (202) 623-4661, www.imf.org; *Government Finance Statistics Yearbook (2008 Edition).*

United Nations Statistics Division, New York, NY 10017, (800) 253-9646, Fax: (212) 963-4116, http://unstats.un.org; *Statistical Yearbook for Asia and the Pacific 2004.*

INDIA - COTTON

See INDIA - CROPS

INDIA - CRIME

International Criminal Police Organization (INTERPOL), General Secretariat, 200 quai Charles de Gaulle, 69006 Lyon, France, www.interpol.int; *International Crime Statistics.*

U.S. Department of Justice (DOJ), Bureau of Justice Statistics, 810 Seventh Street, NW, Washington, DC 20531, (202) 307-0765, www.ojp.usdoj.gov/bjs/; *The World Factbook of Criminal Justice Systems.*

Yale University Press, PO Box 209040, New Haven, CT 06520-9040, (203) 432-0960, Fax: (203) 432-0948, http://yalepress.yale.edu/yupbooks; *Violence and Crime in Cross-National Perspective.*

INDIA - CROPS

International Labour Office, I.L.O. Publications, 4 route des Morillons, CH-1211 Geneva 22, Switzerland, (Telephone in U.S. (202) 653-7652), (Fax in U.S. (202) 653-7687), www.ilo.org; *Yearbook of Labour Statistics 2006.*

International Monetary Fund (IMF), 700 Nineteenth Street, NW, Washington, DC 20431, (202) 623-7000, Fax: (202) 623-4661, www.imf.org; *International Financial Statistics Yearbook 2007.*

Palgrave Macmillan Ltd., Houndmills, Basingstoke, Hampshire, RG21 6XS, England, (Telephone in U.S. (888) 330-8477), (Fax in U.S. (800) 672-2054), www.palgrave.com; *The Statesman's Yearbook 2008.*

Taylor and Francis Group, An Informa Business, 2 Park Square, Milton Park, Abingdon, Oxford OX14 4RN, United Kingdom, (Dial from U.S. (212) 216-7800), (Fax from U.S. (212) 564-7854), www.tandf.co.uk; *The Europa World Year Book.*

United Nations Conference on Trade and Development (UNCTAD), DC2-1120, United Nations, New York, NY 10017, (212) 963-0027, www.unctad.org; *UNCTAD Commodity Yearbook.*

United Nations Food and Agricultural Organization (FAO), Viale delle Terme di Caracalla, 00100 Rome, Italy, (Dial from U.S. (202) 653-2400), (Fax from U.S. (202) 653 5760), www.fao.org; *FAO Production Yearbook 2002* and *The State of Food and Agriculture (SOFA) 2006.*

United Nations Statistics Division, New York, NY 10017, (800) 253-9646, Fax: (212) 963-4116, http://unstats.un.org; *Statistical Yearbook.*

INDIA - CUSTOMS ADMINISTRATION

International Monetary Fund (IMF), 700 Nineteenth Street, NW, Washington, DC 20431, (202) 623-7000, Fax: (202) 623-4661, www.imf.org; *Government Finance Statistics Yearbook (2008 Edition).*

Palgrave Macmillan Ltd., Houndmills, Basingstoke, Hampshire, RG21 6XS, England, (Telephone in U.S. (888) 330-8477), (Fax in U.S. (800) 672-2054), www.palgrave.com; *The Statesman's Yearbook 2008.*

INDIA - DAIRY PROCESSING

Palgrave Macmillan Ltd., Houndmills, Basingstoke, Hampshire, RG21 6XS, England, (Telephone in U.S. (888) 330-8477), (Fax in U.S. (800) 672-2054), www.palgrave.com; *The Statesman's Yearbook 2008.*

Taylor and Francis Group, An Informa Business, 2 Park Square, Milton Park, Abingdon, Oxford OX14 4RN, United Kingdom, (Dial from U.S. (212) 216-7800), (Fax from U.S. (212) 564-7854), www.tandf.co.uk; *The Europa World Year Book.*

United Nations Food and Agricultural Organization (FAO), Viale delle Terme di Caracalla, 00100 Rome, Italy, (Dial from U.S. (202) 653-2400), (Fax from U.S. (202) 653 5760), www.fao.org; *FAO Production Yearbook 2002* and *The State of Food and Agriculture (SOFA) 2006.*

United Nations Statistics Division, New York, NY 10017, (800) 253-9646, Fax: (212) 963-4116, http://unstats.un.org; *Statistical Yearbook.*

INDIA - DEATH RATES

See INDIA - MORTALITY

INDIA - DEBTS, EXTERNAL

International Monetary Fund (IMF), 700 Nineteenth Street, NW, Washington, DC 20431, (202) 623-7000, Fax: (202) 623-4661, www.imf.org; *Government Finance Statistics Yearbook (2008 Edition).*

Palgrave Macmillan Ltd., Houndmills, Basingstoke, Hampshire, RG21 6XS, England, (Telephone in U.S. (888) 330-8477), (Fax in U.S. (800) 672-2054), www.palgrave.com; *The Statesman's Yearbook 2008.*

The World Bank, 1818 H Street, NW, Washington, DC 20433, (202) 473-1000, Fax: (202) 477-6391, www.worldbank.org; *Global Development Finance 2007* and *World Development Report 2008.*

Worldinformation.com, 2 Market Street, Saffron Walden, Essex CB10 1HZ, United Kingdom, www.worldinformation.com; The World of Information (www.worldinformation.com).

INDIA - DEFENSE EXPENDITURES

See INDIA - ARMED FORCES

INDIA - DEMOGRAPHY

Economist Intelligence Unit, 111 West 57th Street, New York, NY 10019, (212) 554-0600, Fax: (212) 586-1181, www.eiu.com; *Business Asia.*

Euromonitor International, Inc., 224 S. Michigan Avenue, Suite 1500, Chicago, IL 60604, (312) 922-1115, Fax: (312) 922-1157, www.euromonitor.com; *International Marketing Data and Statistics 2008; The World Economic Factbook 2008;* and *World Marketing Data and Statistics.*

Federal Statistical Office Germany, D-65180 Wiesbaden, Germany, www.destatis.de; *India 2006.*

United Nations Statistics Division, New York, NY 10017, (800) 253-9646, Fax: (212) 963-4116, http://unstats.un.org; *Asia-Pacific in Figures 2004* and *Human Development Report 2006.*

The World Bank, 1818 H Street, NW, Washington, DC 20433, (202) 473-1000, Fax: (202) 477-6391, www.worldbank.org; *India.*

INDIA - DIAMONDS

See INDIA - MINERAL INDUSTRIES

INDIA - DISPOSABLE INCOME

United Nations Statistics Division, New York, NY 10017, (800) 253-9646, Fax: (212) 963-4116, http://unstats.un.org; *National Accounts Statistics: Compendium of Income Distribution Statistics* and *Statistical Yearbook.*

INDIA - DIVORCE

United Nations Statistics Division, New York, NY 10017, (800) 253-9646, Fax: (212) 963-4116, http://unstats.un.org; *Demographic Yearbook.*

INDIA - ECONOMIC ASSISTANCE

United Nations Statistics Division, New York, NY 10017, (800) 253-9646, Fax: (212) 963-4116, http://unstats.un.org; *Statistical Yearbook.*

INDIA - ECONOMIC CONDITIONS

Center for International Business Education Research (CIBER), Columbia Business School and School of International and Public Affairs, Uris Hall, Room 212, 3022 Broadway, New York, NY 10027-6902, Mr. Joshua Safier, (212) 854-4750, Fax: (212) 222-9821, www.columbia.edu/cu/ciber/; Datastream International.

Central Intelligence Agency, Office of Public Affairs, Washington, DC 20505, (703) 482-0623, Fax: (703) 482-1739, www.cia.gov; *The World Factbook.*

Directorate General of Commercial Intelligence and Statistics (DGCIS), Ministry of Commerce and Industry, 1, Council House Street, Calcutta-700 001, India, www.dgciskol.nic.in; *Foreign Trade Statistics of India by Principal Commodities Countries; Inter-State Movements/Flows of Goods by Rail, River and Air;* and *Statistics of Foreign Trade in India by Countries.*

DSI Data Service Information, Xantener Strasse 51a, D-47495 Rheinberg, Germany, www.dsidata.com; *Campus Solution.*

Dun and Bradstreet (DB) Corporation, 103 JFK Parkway, Short Hills, NJ 07078, (973) 921-5500, www.dnb.com; *Country Report.*

Economist Intelligence Unit, 111 West 57th Street, New York, NY 10019, (212) 554-0600, Fax: (212) 586-1181, www.eiu.com; *India Country Report.*

Euromonitor International, Inc., 224 S. Michigan Avenue, Suite 1500, Chicago, IL 60604, (312) 922-1115, Fax: (312) 922-1157, www.euromonitor.com; *International Marketing Data and Statistics 2008; The World Economic Factbook 2008;* and *World Marketing Data and Statistics.*

Federal Statistical Office Germany, D-65180 Wiesbaden, Germany, www.destatis.de; *India 2006.*

International Monetary Fund (IMF), 700 Nineteenth Street, NW, Washington, DC 20431, (202) 623-7000, Fax: (202) 623-4661, www.imf.org; *World Economic Outlook Reports.*

Nomura Research Institute (NRI), 2 World Financial Center, Building B, 19th Fl., New York, NY 10281-1198, (212) 667-1670, www.nri.co.jp/english; *Asian Economic Outlook 2003-2004.*

Palgrave Macmillan Ltd., Houndmills, Basingstoke, Hampshire, RG21 6XS, England, (Telephone in U.S. (888) 330-8477), (Fax in U.S. (800) 672-2054), www.palgrave.com; *The Statesman's Yearbook 2008.*

Taylor and Francis Group, An Informa Business, 2 Park Square, Milton Park, Abingdon, Oxford OX14 4RN, United Kingdom, (Dial from U.S. (212) 216-7800), (Fax from U.S. (212) 564-7854), www.tandf.co.uk; *The Europa World Year Book.*

United Nations Statistics Division, New York, NY 10017, (800) 253-9646, Fax: (212) 963-4116, http://unstats.un.org; *World Statistics Pocketbook.*

The World Bank, 1818 H Street, NW, Washington, DC 20433, (202) 473-1000, Fax: (202) 477-6391, www.worldbank.org; *Global Economic Monitor (GEM); Global Economic Prospects 2008; India; The World Bank Atlas 2003-2004;* and *World Development Report 2008.*

INDIA - EDUCATION

Economist Intelligence Unit, 111 West 57th Street, New York, NY 10019, (212) 554-0600, Fax: (212) 586-1181, www.eiu.com; *Business Asia.*

Euromonitor International, Inc., 224 S. Michigan Avenue, Suite 1500, Chicago, IL 60604, (312) 922-1115, Fax: (312) 922-1157, www.euromonitor.com; *International Marketing Data and Statistics 2008* and *World Marketing Data and Statistics.*

Federal Statistical Office Germany, D-65180 Wiesbaden, Germany, www.destatis.de; *India 2006.*

International Monetary Fund (IMF), 700 Nineteenth Street, NW, Washington, DC 20431, (202) 623-7000, Fax: (202) 623-4661, www.imf.org; *Government Finance Statistics Yearbook (2008 Edition).*

Palgrave Macmillan Ltd., Houndmills, Basingstoke, Hampshire, RG21 6XS, England, (Telephone in U.S. (888) 330-8477), (Fax in U.S. (800) 672-2054), www.palgrave.com; *The Statesman's Yearbook 2008.*

Taylor and Francis Group, An Informa Business, 2 Park Square, Milton Park, Abingdon, Oxford OX14 4RN, United Kingdom, (Dial from U.S. (212) 216-7800), (Fax from U.S. (212) 564-7854), www.tandf.co.uk; *The Europa World Year Book.*

UNESCO Institute for Statistics, C.P. 6128 Succursale Centre-Ville, Montreal, Quebec, H3C 3J7 Canada, (Dial from U.S. (514) 343-6880), (Fax from U.S. (514) 343 6882), www.uis.unesco.org; *Statistical Tables.*

United Nations Statistics Division, New York, NY 10017, (800) 253-9646, Fax: (212) 963-4116, http://unstats.un.org; *Asia-Pacific in Figures 2004* and *Human Development Report 2006.*

The World Bank, 1818 H Street, NW, Washington, DC 20433, (202) 473-1000, Fax: (202) 477-6391, www.worldbank.org; *India* and *World Development Report 2008.*

INDIA - ELECTRICITY

Organisation for Economic Cooperation and Development (OECD), 2 rue Andre Pascal, F-75775 Paris Cedex 16, France, (Telephone in U.S. (202) 785-6323), (Fax in U.S. (202) 785-0350), www.oecd.org; *Coal Information: 2007 Edition* and *World Energy Outlook 2007.*

Palgrave Macmillan Ltd., Houndmills, Basingstoke, Hampshire, RG21 6XS, England, (Telephone in U.S. (888) 330-8477), (Fax in U.S. (800) 672-2054), www.palgrave.com; *The Statesman's Yearbook 2008.*

Platts, 2 Penn Plaza, 25th Floor, New York, NY 10121-2298, (212) 904-3070, www.platts.com; *Asian Electricity Outlook 2006* and *Emissions Daily.*

U.S. Department of Energy (DOE), Energy Information Administration (EIA), 1000 Independence Avenue, SW, Washington, DC 20585, (202) 586-8800, www.eia.doe.gov; *International Energy Annual 2004* and *International Energy Outlook 2006.*

United Nations Statistics Division, New York, NY 10017, (800) 253-9646, Fax: (212) 963-4116, http://unstats.un.org; *Electric Power in Asia and the Pacific 2001 and 2002; Human Development Report 2006;* and *Statistical Yearbook.*

INDIA - EMPLOYMENT

Euromonitor International, Inc., 224 S. Michigan Avenue, Suite 1500, Chicago, IL 60604, (312) 922-1115, Fax: (312) 922-1157, www.euromonitor.com; *International Marketing Data and Statistics 2008.*

Federal Statistical Office Germany, D-65180 Wiesbaden, Germany, www.destatis.de; *India 2006.*

International Labour Office, I.L.O. Publications, 4 route des Morillons, CH-1211 Geneva 22, Switzerland, (Telephone in U.S. (202) 653-7652), (Fax in U.S. (202) 653-7687), www.ilo.org; *Yearbook of Labour Statistics 2006.*

United Nations Statistics Division, New York, NY 10017, (800) 253-9646, Fax: (212) 963-4116, http://unstats.un.org; *Asia-Pacific in Figures 2004* and *Statistical Yearbook.*

The World Bank, 1818 H Street, NW, Washington, DC 20433, (202) 473-1000, Fax: (202) 477-6391, www.worldbank.org; *India.*

INDIA - ENERGY INDUSTRIES

Enerdata, 10 Rue Royale, 75008 Paris, France, www.enerdata.fr; *Global Energy Market Data.*

Federal Statistical Office Germany, D-65180 Wiesbaden, Germany, www.destatis.de; *India 2006.*

Platts, 2 Penn Plaza, 25th Floor, New York, NY 10121-2298, (212) 904-3070, www.platts.com; *Asian Electricity Outlook 2006* and *Emissions Daily.*

United Nations Statistics Division, New York, NY 10017, (800) 253-9646, Fax: (212) 963-4116, http://unstats.un.org; *Electric Power in Asia and the Pacific 2001 and 2002* and *Statistical Yearbook.*

INDIA - ENVIRONMENTAL CONDITIONS

DSI Data Service Information, Xantener Strasse 51a, D-47495 Rheinberg, Germany, www.dsidata.com; *Campus Solution* and *DSI's Global Environmental Database.*

Economist Intelligence Unit, 111 West 57th Street, New York, NY 10019, (212) 554-0600, Fax: (212) 586-1181, www.eiu.com; *India Country Report.*

International Institute for Environment and Development (IIED), 3 Endsleigh Street, London, England, WC1H 0DD, United Kingdom, www.iied.org; *Environment Urbanization* and *Up in Smoke? Asia and the Pacific.*

Platts, 2 Penn Plaza, 25th Floor, New York, NY 10121-2298, (212) 904-3070, www.platts.com; *Emissions Daily.*

United Nations Statistics Division, New York, NY 10017, (800) 253-9646, Fax: (212) 963-4116, http://unstats.un.org; *World Statistics Pocketbook.*

INDIA - EXPORTS

Central Intelligence Agency, Office of Public Affairs, Washington, DC 20505, (703) 482-0623, Fax: (703) 482-1739, www.cia.gov; *The World Factbook.*

Economist Intelligence Unit, 111 West 57th Street, New York, NY 10019, (212) 554-0600, Fax: (212) 586-1181, www.eiu.com; *India Country Report.*

Euromonitor International, Inc., 224 S. Michigan Avenue, Suite 1500, Chicago, IL 60604, (312) 922-1115, Fax: (312) 922-1157, www.euromonitor.com; *International Marketing Data and Statistics 2008* and *The World Economic Factbook 2008.*

International Lead and Zinc Study Group (ILZSG), Rua Almirante Barroso 38, 5th Floor, Lisbon 1000-013, Portugal, www.ilzsg.org; Interactive Statistical Database.

International Monetary Fund (IMF), 700 Nineteenth Street, NW, Washington, DC 20431, (202) 623-7000, Fax: (202) 623-4661, www.imf.org; *Direction of Trade Statistics Yearbook 2007; Government Finance Statistics Yearbook (2008 Edition);* and *International Financial Statistics Yearbook 2007.*

Palgrave Macmillan Ltd., Houndmills, Basingstoke, Hampshire, RG21 6XS, England, (Telephone in U.S. (888) 330-8477), (Fax in U.S. (800) 672-2054), www.palgrave.com; *The Statesman's Yearbook 2008.*

Taylor and Francis Group, An Informa Business, 2 Park Square, Milton Park, Abingdon, Oxford OX14 4RN, United Kingdom, (Dial from U.S. (212) 216-7800), (Fax from U.S. (212) 564-7854), www.tandf.co.uk; *The Europa World Year Book.*

United Nations Conference on Trade and Development (UNCTAD), DC2-1120, United Nations, New York, NY 10017, (212) 963-0027, www.unctad.org; *Handbook of Statistics 2005.*

United Nations Food and Agricultural Organization (FAO), Viale delle Terme di Caracalla, 00100 Rome, Italy, (Dial from U.S. (202) 653-2400), (Fax from U.S. (202) 653 5760), www.fao.org; *The State of Food and Agriculture (SOFA) 2006.*

United Nations Statistics Division, New York, NY 10017, (800) 253-9646, Fax: (212) 963-4116, http://unstats.un.org; *Foreign Trade Statistics of Asia and the Pacific 1996-2000.*

The World Bank, 1818 H Street, NW, Washington, DC 20433, (202) 473-1000, Fax: (202) 477-6391, www.worldbank.org; *World Development Report 2008.*

Worldinformation.com, 2 Market Street, Saffron Walden, Essex CB10 1HZ, United Kingdom, www.worldinformation.com; The World of Information (www.worldinformation.com).

INDIA - FERTILITY, HUMAN

Central Intelligence Agency, Office of Public Affairs, Washington, DC 20505, (703) 482-0623, Fax: (703) 482-1739, www.cia.gov; *The World Factbook.*

United Nations Statistics Division, New York, NY 10017, (800) 253-9646, Fax: (212) 963-4116, http://unstats.un.org; *Human Development Report 2006.*

The World Bank, 1818 H Street, NW, Washington, DC 20433, (202) 473-1000, Fax: (202) 477-6391, www.worldbank.org; *The World Bank Atlas 2003-2004* and *World Development Report 2008.*

INDIA - FERTILIZER INDUSTRY

United Nations Food and Agricultural Organization (FAO), Viale delle Terme di Caracalla, 00100 Rome, Italy, (Dial from U.S. (202) 653-2400), (Fax from U.S. (202) 653 5760), www.fao.org; *FAO Fertilizer Yearbook* and *The State of Food and Agriculture (SOFA) 2006.*

United Nations Statistics Division, New York, NY 10017, (800) 253-9646, Fax: (212) 963-4116, http://unstats.un.org; *Statistical Yearbook.*

INDIA - FETAL MORTALITY

See INDIA - MORTALITY

INDIA - FILM

See INDIA - MOTION PICTURES

INDIA - FINANCE

Federal Statistical Office Germany, D-65180 Wiesbaden, Germany, www.destatis.de; *India 2006.*

International Monetary Fund (IMF), 700 Nineteenth Street, NW, Washington, DC 20431, (202) 623-7000, Fax: (202) 623-4661, www.imf.org; *International Financial Statistics Yearbook 2007.*

Taylor and Francis Group, An Informa Business, 2 Park Square, Milton Park, Abingdon, Oxford OX14 4RN, United Kingdom, (Dial from U.S. (212) 216-7800), (Fax from U.S. (212) 564-7854), www.tandf.co.uk; *The Europa World Year Book.*

United Nations Statistics Division, New York, NY 10017, (800) 253-9646, Fax: (212) 963-4116, http://unstats.un.org; *Asia-Pacific in Figures 2004; National Accounts Statistics: Compendium of Income Distribution Statistics; Statistical Yearbook;* and *Statistical Yearbook for Asia and the Pacific 2004.*

The World Bank, 1818 H Street, NW, Washington, DC 20433, (202) 473-1000, Fax: (202) 477-6391, www.worldbank.org; *India.*

INDIA - FINANCE, PUBLIC

Bernan Essential Government Publications, 4611-F Assembly Drive, Lanham MD, 20706-4391, (301) 459-2255, Fax: (800) 865-3450, www.bernan.com; *National Accounts Statistics.*

Economist Intelligence Unit, 111 West 57th Street, New York, NY 10019, (212) 554-0600, Fax: (212) 586-1181, www.eiu.com; *India Country Report.*

Federal Statistical Office Germany, D-65180 Wiesbaden, Germany, www.destatis.de; *India 2006.*

International Monetary Fund (IMF), 700 Nineteenth Street, NW, Washington, DC 20431, (202) 623-7000, Fax: (202) 623-4661, www.imf.org; *Government Finance Statistics Yearbook (2008 Edition); International Financial Statistics; International Financial Statistics Online Service;* and *International Financial Statistics Yearbook 2007.*

Palgrave Macmillan Ltd., Houndmills, Basingstoke, Hampshire, RG21 6XS, England, (Telephone in U.S. (888) 330-8477), (Fax in U.S. (800) 672-2054), www.palgrave.com; *The Statesman's Yearbook 2008.*

Taylor and Francis Group, An Informa Business, 2 Park Square, Milton Park, Abingdon, Oxford OX14 4RN, United Kingdom, (Dial from U.S. (212) 216-7800), (Fax from U.S. (212) 564-7854), www.tandf.co.uk; *The Europa World Year Book.*

United Nations Statistics Division, New York, NY 10017, (800) 253-9646, Fax: (212) 963-4116, http://unstats.un.org; *Statistical Yearbook for Asia and the Pacific 2004.*

The World Bank, 1818 H Street, NW, Washington, DC 20433, (202) 473-1000, Fax: (202) 477-6391, www.worldbank.org; *India.*

INDIA - FISHERIES

Federal Statistical Office Germany, D-65180 Wiesbaden, Germany, www.destatis.de; *India 2006.*

Palgrave Macmillan Ltd., Houndmills, Basingstoke, Hampshire, RG21 6XS, England, (Telephone in U.S. (888) 330-8477), (Fax in U.S. (800) 672-2054), www.palgrave.com; *The Statesman's Yearbook 2008.*

Taylor and Francis Group, An Informa Business, 2 Park Square, Milton Park, Abingdon, Oxford OX14 4RN, United Kingdom, (Dial from U.S. (212) 216-7800), (Fax from U.S. (212) 564-7854), www.tandf.co.uk; *The Europa World Year Book.*

United Nations Conference on Trade and Development (UNCTAD), DC2-1120, United Nations, New York, NY 10017, (212) 963-0027, www.unctad.org; *UNCTAD Commodity Yearbook.*

United Nations Food and Agricultural Organization (FAO), Viale delle Terme di Caracalla, 00100 Rome, Italy, (Dial from U.S. (202) 653-2400), (Fax from U.S. (202) 653 5760), www.fao.org; *FAO Yearbook of Fishery Statistics;* Fishery Databases; FISHSTAT Database. Subjects covered include: Aquaculture production, capture production, fishery commodities; and *The State of Food and Agriculture (SOFA) 2006.*

United Nations Statistics Division, New York, NY 10017, (800) 253-9646, Fax: (212) 963-4116, http://unstats.un.org; *Statistical Yearbook.*

The World Bank, 1818 H Street, NW, Washington, DC 20433, (202) 473-1000, Fax: (202) 477-6391, www.worldbank.org; *India.*

INDIA - FLOUR INDUSTRY

United Nations Statistics Division, New York, NY 10017, (800) 253-9646, Fax: (212) 963-4116, http://unstats.un.org; *Statistical Yearbook.*

INDIA - FOOD

Euromonitor International, Inc., 224 S. Michigan Avenue, Suite 1500, Chicago, IL 60604, (312) 922-1115, Fax: (312) 922-1157, www.euromonitor.com; *Retail Trade International 2007.*

United Nations Conference on Trade and Development (UNCTAD), DC2-1120, United Nations, New York, NY 10017, (212) 963-0027, www.unctad.org; *UNCTAD Commodity Yearbook.*

United Nations Food and Agricultural Organization (FAO), Viale delle Terme di Caracalla, 00100 Rome, Italy, (Dial from U.S. (202) 653-2400), (Fax from U.S. (202) 653 5760), www.fao.org; *FAO Production Yearbook 2002* and *The State of Food and Agriculture (SOFA) 2006.*

United Nations Statistics Division, New York, NY 10017, (800) 253-9646, Fax: (212) 963-4116, http://unstats.un.org; *Human Development Report 2006* and *Statistical Yearbook for Asia and the Pacific 2004.*

INDIA - FOREIGN EXCHANGE RATES

Central Intelligence Agency, Office of Public Affairs, Washington, DC 20505, (703) 482-0623, Fax: (703) 482-1739, www.cia.gov; *The World Factbook.*

Economist Intelligence Unit, 111 West 57th Street, New York, NY 10019, (212) 554-0600, Fax: (212) 586-1181, www.eiu.com; *Business Asia.*

Euromonitor International, Inc., 224 S. Michigan Avenue, Suite 1500, Chicago, IL 60604, (312) 922-1115, Fax: (312) 922-1157, www.euromonitor.com; *International Marketing Data and Statistics 2008* and *The World Economic Factbook 2008.*

International Civil Aviation Organization (ICAO), External Relations and Public Information Office (EPO), 999 University Street, Montreal, Quebec H3C 5H7, Canada, (Dial from U.S. (514) 954-8219), (Fax from U.S. (514) 954-6077), www.icao.int; *Civil Aviation Statistics of the World.*

International Monetary Fund (IMF), 700 Nineteenth Street, NW, Washington, DC 20431, (202) 623-7000, Fax: (202) 623-4661, www.imf.org; *International Financial Statistics Yearbook 2007.*

Taylor and Francis Group, An Informa Business, 2 Park Square, Milton Park, Abingdon, Oxford OX14 4RN, United Kingdom, (Dial from U.S. (212) 216-7800), (Fax from U.S. (212) 564-7854), www.tandf.co.uk; *The Europa World Year Book.*

United Nations Statistics Division, New York, NY 10017, (800) 253-9646, Fax: (212) 963-4116, http://unstats.un.org; *Statistical Yearbook* and *World Statistics Pocketbook.*

Worldinformation.com, 2 Market Street, Saffron Walden, Essex CB10 1HZ, United Kingdom, www.worldinformation.com; The World of Information (www.worldinformation.com).

INDIA - FORESTS AND FORESTRY

American Forest Paper Association (AFPA), 1111 Nineteenth Street, NW, Suite 800, Washington, DC 20036, (800) 878-8878, www.afandpa.org; *2007 Annual Statistics of Paper, Paperboard, and Wood Pulp.*

Economist Intelligence Unit, 111 West 57th Street, New York, NY 10019, (212) 554-0600, Fax: (212) 586-1181, www.eiu.com; *Business Asia.*

Federal Statistical Office Germany, D-65180 Wiesbaden, Germany, www.destatis.de; *India 2006.*

Palgrave Macmillan Ltd., Houndmills, Basingstoke, Hampshire, RG21 6XS, England, (Telephone in U.S. (888) 330-8477), (Fax in U.S. (800) 672-2054), www.palgrave.com; *The Statesman's Yearbook 2008.*

Taylor and Francis Group, An Informa Business, 2 Park Square, Milton Park, Abingdon, Oxford OX14 4RN, United Kingdom, (Dial from U.S. (212) 216-7800), (Fax from U.S. (212) 564-7854), www.tandf.co.uk; *The Europa World Year Book.*

UNESCO Institute for Statistics, C.P. 6128 Succursale Centre-Ville, Montreal, Quebec, H3C 3J7 Canada, (Dial from U.S. (514) 343-6880), (Fax from U.S. (514) 343 6882), www.uis.unesco.org; *Statistical Tables.*

United Nations Conference on Trade and Development (UNCTAD), DC2-1120, United Nations, New York, NY 10017, (212) 963-0027, www.unctad.org; *UNCTAD Commodity Yearbook.*

United Nations Food and Agricultural Organization (FAO), Viale delle Terme di Caracalla, 00100 Rome, Italy, (Dial from U.S. (202) 653-2400), (Fax from U.S. (202) 653 5760), www.fao.org; *FAO Yearbook of Forest Products* and *The State of Food and Agriculture (SOFA) 2006.*

United Nations Statistics Division, New York, NY 10017, (800) 253-9646, Fax: (212) 963-4116, http://unstats.un.org; *Statistical Yearbook.*

The World Bank, 1818 H Street, NW, Washington, DC 20433, (202) 473-1000, Fax: (202) 477-6391, www.worldbank.org; *India* and *World Development Report 2008.*

INDIA - GAS PRODUCTION

See INDIA - MINERAL INDUSTRIES

INDIA - GOLD INDUSTRY

International Monetary Fund (IMF), 700 Nineteenth Street, NW, Washington, DC 20431, (202) 623-7000, Fax: (202) 623-4661, www.imf.org; *International Financial Statistics Yearbook 2007.*

United Nations Statistics Division, New York, NY 10017, (800) 253-9646, Fax: (212) 963-4116, http://unstats.un.org; *Statistical Yearbook.*

The World Bank, 1818 H Street, NW, Washington, DC 20433, (202) 473-1000, Fax: (202) 477-6391, www.worldbank.org; *World Development Report 2008.*

INDIA - GOLD PRODUCTION

See INDIA - MINERAL INDUSTRIES

INDIA - GRANTS-IN-AID

International Monetary Fund (IMF), 700 Nineteenth Street, NW, Washington, DC 20431, (202) 623-7000, Fax: (202) 623-4661, www.imf.org; *Government Finance Statistics Yearbook (2008 Edition).*

INDIA - GROSS DOMESTIC PRODUCT

Economist Intelligence Unit, 111 West 57th Street, New York, NY 10019, (212) 554-0600, Fax: (212) 586-1181, www.eiu.com; *Business Asia* and *India Country Report.*

Euromonitor International, Inc., 224 S. Michigan Avenue, Suite 1500, Chicago, IL 60604, (312) 922-1115, Fax: (312) 922-1157, www.euromonitor.com; *International Marketing Data and Statistics 2008* and *The World Economic Factbook 2008.*

Taylor and Francis Group, An Informa Business, 2 Park Square, Milton Park, Abingdon, Oxford OX14 4RN, United Kingdom, (Dial from U.S. (212) 216-7800), (Fax from U.S. (212) 564-7854), www.tandf.co.uk; *The Europa World Year Book.*

United Nations Statistics Division, New York, NY 10017, (800) 253-9646, Fax: (212) 963-4116, http://unstats.un.org; *Human Development Report 2006; National Accounts Statistics: Compendium of Income Distribution Statistics;* and *Statistical Yearbook.*

The World Bank, 1818 H Street, NW, Washington, DC 20433, (202) 473-1000, Fax: (202) 477-6391, www.worldbank.org; *World Development Report 2008.*

INDIA - GROSS NATIONAL PRODUCT

Euromonitor International, Inc., 224 S. Michigan Avenue, Suite 1500, Chicago, IL 60604, (312) 922-1115, Fax: (312) 922-1157, www.euromonitor.com; *International Marketing Data and Statistics 2008.*

Palgrave Macmillan Ltd., Houndmills, Basingstoke, Hampshire, RG21 6XS, England, (Telephone in U.S. (888) 330-8477), (Fax in U.S. (800) 672-2054), www.palgrave.com; *The Statesman's Yearbook 2008.*

Taylor and Francis Group, An Informa Business, 2 Park Square, Milton Park, Abingdon, Oxford OX14 4RN, United Kingdom, (Dial from U.S. (212) 216-7800), (Fax from U.S. (212) 564-7854), www.tandf.co.uk; *The Europa World Year Book.*

U.S. Department of State (DOS), 2201 C Street NW, Washington, DC 20520, (202) 647-4000, www.state.gov; *World Military Expenditures and Arms Transfers (WMEAT).*

United Nations Statistics Division, New York, NY 10017, (800) 253-9646, Fax: (212) 963-4116, http://unstats.un.org; *Statistical Yearbook.*

The World Bank, 1818 H Street, NW, Washington, DC 20433, (202) 473-1000, Fax: (202) 477-6391, www.worldbank.org; *The World Bank Atlas 2003-2004* and *World Development Report 2008.*

Worldinformation.com, 2 Market Street, Saffron Walden, Essex CB10 1HZ, United Kingdom, www.worldinformation.com; The World of Information (www.worldinformation.com).

INDIA - HEMP FIBRE PRODUCTION

See INDIA - TEXTILE INDUSTRY

INDIA - HIDES AND SKINS INDUSTRY

United Nations Food and Agricultural Organization (FAO), Viale delle Terme di Caracalla, 00100 Rome, Italy, (Dial from U.S. (202) 653-2400), (Fax from U.S. (202) 653 5760), www.fao.org; *FAO Production Yearbook 2002.*

INDIA - HOUSING

Euromonitor International, Inc., 224 S. Michigan Avenue, Suite 1500, Chicago, IL 60604, (312) 922-1115, Fax: (312) 922-1157, www.euromonitor.com; *World Marketing Data and Statistics.*

INDIA - ILLITERATE PERSONS

Euromonitor International, Inc., 224 S. Michigan Avenue, Suite 1500, Chicago, IL 60604, (312) 922-1115, Fax: (312) 922-1157, www.euromonitor.com; *The World Economic Factbook 2008.*

Palgrave Macmillan Ltd., Houndmills, Basingstoke, Hampshire, RG21 6XS, England, (Telephone in U.S. (888) 330-8477), (Fax in U.S. (800) 672-2054), www.palgrave.com; *The Statesman's Yearbook 2008.*

UNESCO Institute for Statistics, C.P. 6128 Succursale Centre-Ville, Montreal, Quebec, H3C 3J7 Canada, (Dial from U.S. (514) 343-6880), (Fax from U.S. (514) 343 6882), www.uis.unesco.org; *Statistical Tables.*

United Nations Statistics Division, New York, NY 10017, (800) 253-9646, Fax: (212) 963-4116, http://unstats.un.org; *Asia-Pacific in Figures 2004* and *Human Development Report 2006.*

INDIA - IMPORTS

Central Intelligence Agency, Office of Public Affairs, Washington, DC 20505, (703) 482-0623, Fax: (703) 482-1739, www.cia.gov; *The World Factbook.*

Economist Intelligence Unit, 111 West 57th Street, New York, NY 10019, (212) 554-0600, Fax: (212) 586-1181, www.eiu.com; *India Country Report.*

Euromonitor International, Inc., 224 S. Michigan Avenue, Suite 1500, Chicago, IL 60604, (312) 922-1115, Fax: (312) 922-1157, www.euromonitor.com; *International Marketing Data and Statistics 2008* and *The World Economic Factbook 2008.*

International Lead and Zinc Study Group (ILZSG), Rua Almirante Barroso 38, 5th Floor, Lisbon 1000 - 013, Portugal, www.ilzsg.org; Interactive Statistical Database.

International Monetary Fund (IMF), 700 Nineteenth Street, NW, Washington, DC 20431, (202) 623-7000, Fax: (202) 623-4661, www.imf.org; *Direction of Trade Statistics Yearbook 2007; Government Finance Statistics Yearbook (2008 Edition);* and *International Financial Statistics Yearbook 2007.*

Palgrave Macmillan Ltd., Houndmills, Basingstoke, Hampshire, RG21 6XS, England, (Telephone in U.S. (888) 330-8477), (Fax in U.S. (800) 672-2054), www.palgrave.com; *The Statesman's Yearbook 2008.*

Taylor and Francis Group, An Informa Business, 2 Park Square, Milton Park, Abingdon, Oxford OX14 4RN, United Kingdom, (Dial from U.S. (212) 216-7800), (Fax from U.S. (212) 564-7854), www.tandf.co.uk; *The Europa World Year Book.*

United Nations Conference on Trade and Development (UNCTAD), DC2-1120, United Nations, New York, NY 10017, (212) 963-0027, www.unctad.org; *Handbook of Statistics 2005.*

United Nations Food and Agricultural Organization (FAO), Viale delle Terme di Caracalla, 00100 Rome, Italy, (Dial from U.S. (202) 653-2400), (Fax from U.S. (202) 653 5760), www.fao.org; *The State of Food and Agriculture (SOFA) 2006.*

United Nations Statistics Division, New York, NY 10017, (800) 253-9646, Fax: (212) 963-4116, http://unstats.un.org; *Foreign Trade Statistics of Asia and the Pacific 1996-2000.*

The World Bank, 1818 H Street, NW, Washington, DC 20433, (202) 473-1000, Fax: (202) 477-6391, www.worldbank.org; *World Development Report 2008.*

Worldinformation.com, 2 Market Street, Saffron Walden, Essex CB10 1HZ, United Kingdom, www.worldinformation.com; The World of Information (www.worldinformation.com).

INDIA - INCOME TAXES

See INDIA - TAXATION

INDIA - INDUSTRIAL METALS PRODUCTION

See INDIA - MINERAL INDUSTRIES

INDIA - INDUSTRIAL PRODUCTIVITY

Euromonitor International, Inc., 224 S. Michigan Avenue, Suite 1500, Chicago, IL 60604, (312) 922-1115, Fax: (312) 922-1157, www.euromonitor.com; *International Marketing Data and Statistics 2008.*

International Lead and Zinc Study Group (ILZSG), Rua Almirante Barroso 38, 5th Floor, Lisbon 1000 - 013, Portugal, www.ilzsg.org; Interactive Statistical Database.

INDIA - INDUSTRIAL PROPERTY

United Nations Statistics Division, New York, NY 10017, (800) 253-9646, Fax: (212) 963-4116, http://unstats.un.org; *Statistical Yearbook.*

World Intellectual Property Organization (WIPO), PO Box 18, CH-1211 Geneva 20, Switzerland, www.wipo.int; *Industrial Property Statistics* and *Industrial Property Statistics Online Directory.*

INDIA - INDUSTRIES

Central Intelligence Agency, Office of Public Affairs, Washington, DC 20505, (703) 482-0623, Fax: (703) 482-1739, www.cia.gov; *The World Factbook.*

Economist Intelligence Unit, 111 West 57th Street, New York, NY 10019, (212) 554-0600, Fax: (212) 586-1181, www.eiu.com; *India Country Report.*

Euromonitor International, Inc., 224 S. Michigan Avenue, Suite 1500, Chicago, IL 60604, (312) 922-1115, Fax: (312) 922-1157, www.euromonitor.com; *The World Economic Factbook 2008* and *World Marketing Data and Statistics.*

Federal Statistical Office Germany, D-65180 Wiesbaden, Germany, www.destatis.de; *India 2006.*

International Labour Office, I.L.O. Publications, 4 route des Morillons, CH-1211 Geneva 22, Switzerland, (Telephone in U.S. (202) 653-7652), (Fax in U.S. (202) 653-7687), www.ilo.org; *Yearbook of Labour Statistics 2006.*

Palgrave Macmillan Ltd., Houndmills, Basingstoke, Hampshire, RG21 6XS, England, (Telephone in U.S. (888) 330-8477), (Fax in U.S. (800) 672-2054), www.palgrave.com; *The Statesman's Yearbook 2008.*

Taylor and Francis Group, An Informa Business, 2 Park Square, Milton Park, Abingdon, Oxford OX14 4RN, United Kingdom, (Dial from U.S. (212) 216-7800), (Fax from U.S. (212) 564-7854), www.tandf.co.uk; *The Europa World Year Book.*

United Nations Industrial Development Organization (UNIDO), 1 United Nations Plaza, New York, NY 10017, (212) 963 6890, Fax: (212) 963-7904, http://unido.org; Industrial Statistics Database 2008 (INDSTAT) and *The International Yearbook of Industrial Statistics 2008.*

United Nations Statistics Division, New York, NY 10017, (800) 253-9646, Fax: (212) 963-4116, http://unstats.un.org; *Asia-Pacific in Figures 2004; 2004 Industrial Commodity Statistics Yearbook;* and *Statistical Yearbook for Asia and the Pacific 2004.*

The World Bank, 1818 H Street, NW, Washington, DC 20433, (202) 473-1000, Fax: (202) 477-6391, www.worldbank.org; *India* and *World Development Report 2008.*

INDIA - INFANT AND MATERNAL MORTALITY

See INDIA - MORTALITY

INDIA - INORGANIC ACIDS

United Nations Statistics Division, New York, NY 10017, (800) 253-9646, Fax: (212) 963-4116, http://unstats.un.org; *Statistical Yearbook.*

INDIA - INTEREST RATES

United Nations Statistics Division, New York, NY 10017, (800) 253-9646, Fax: (212) 963-4116, http://unstats.un.org; *Statistical Yearbook.*

INDIA - INTERNATIONAL LIQUIDITY

International Monetary Fund (IMF), 700 Nineteenth Street, NW, Washington, DC 20431, (202) 623-7000, Fax: (202) 623-4661, www.imf.org; *International Financial Statistics Yearbook 2007.*

INDIA - INTERNATIONAL TRADE

Directorate General of Commercial Intelligence and Statistics (DGCIS), Ministry of Commerce and Industry, 1, Council House Street, Calcutta-700 001, India, www.dgciskol.nic.in; *Foreign Trade Statistics of India by Principal Commodities Countries; Indian Trade Journal;* and *Statistics of Foreign Trade in India by Countries.*

Economist Intelligence Unit, 111 West 57th Street, New York, NY 10019, (212) 554-0600, Fax: (212) 586-1181, www.eiu.com; *Business Asia* and *India Country Report.*

Euromonitor International, Inc., 224 S. Michigan Avenue, Suite 1500, Chicago, IL 60604, (312) 922-1115, Fax: (312) 922-1157, www.euromonitor.com; *International Marketing Data and Statistics 2008; The World Economic Factbook 2008;* and *World Marketing Data and Statistics.*

Federal Statistical Office Germany, D-65180 Wiesbaden, Germany, www.destatis.de; *India 2006.*

International Monetary Fund (IMF), 700 Nineteenth Street, NW, Washington, DC 20431, (202) 623-7000, Fax: (202) 623-4661, www.imf.org; *International Financial Statistics Yearbook 2007.*

Palgrave Macmillan Ltd., Houndmills, Basingstoke, Hampshire, RG21 6XS, England, (Telephone in U.S. (888) 330-8477), (Fax in U.S. (800) 672-2054), www.palgrave.com; *The Statesman's Yearbook 2008.*

Taylor and Francis Group, An Informa Business, 2 Park Square, Milton Park, Abingdon, Oxford OX14 4RN, United Kingdom, (Dial from U.S. (212) 216-7800), (Fax from U.S. (212) 564-7854), www.tandf.co.uk; *The Europa World Year Book.*

United Nations Conference on Trade and Development (UNCTAD), DC2-1120, United Nations, New York, NY 10017, (212) 963-0027, www.unctad.org; *UNCTAD Commodity Yearbook.*

United Nations Food and Agricultural Organization (FAO), Viale delle Terme di Caracalla, 00100 Rome, Italy, (Dial from U.S. (202) 653-2400), (Fax from U.S. (202) 653 5760), www.fao.org; *FAO Trade Yearbook* and *The State of Food and Agriculture (SOFA) 2006.*

United Nations Statistics Division, New York, NY 10017, (800) 253-9646, Fax: (212) 963-4116, http://unstats.un.org; *Asia-Pacific in Figures 2004; International Trade Statistics Yearbook; Statistical Yearbook;* and *Statistical Yearbook for Asia and the Pacific 2004.*

The World Bank, 1818 H Street, NW, Washington, DC 20433, (202) 473-1000, Fax: (202) 477-6391, www.worldbank.org; *India* and *World Development Report 2008.*

World Bureau of Metal Statistics (WBMS), 27a High Street, Ware, Hertfordshire, SG12 9BA, United Kingdom, www.world-bureau.com; *World Flow Charts* and *World Metal Statistics.*

World Trade Organization (WTO), Centre William Rappard, Rue de Lausanne 154, CH-1211 Geneva 21, Switzerland, www.wto.org; *International Trade Statistics 2006.*

INDIA - INTERNET USERS

Federal Statistical Office Germany, D-65180 Wiesbaden, Germany, www.destatis.de; *India 2006.*

International Telecommunication Union (ITU), Place des Nations, 1211 Geneva 20, Switzerland, www.itu.int; *World Telecommunication/ICT Indicators Database on CD-ROM; World Telecommunication/ICT Indicators Database Online;* and *Yearbook of Statistics - Telecommunication Services (Chronological Time Series 1997-2006).*

The World Bank, 1818 H Street, NW, Washington, DC 20433, (202) 473-1000, Fax: (202) 477-6391, www.worldbank.org; *India.*

INDIA - INVESTMENTS

International Monetary Fund (IMF), 700 Nineteenth Street, NW, Washington, DC 20431, (202) 623-7000, Fax: (202) 623-4661, www.imf.org; *International Financial Statistics Yearbook 2007.*

INDIA - IRON AND IRON ORE PRODUCTION

See INDIA - MINERAL INDUSTRIES

INDIA - IRRIGATION

Euromonitor International, Inc., 224 S. Michigan Avenue, Suite 1500, Chicago, IL 60604, (312) 922-1115, Fax: (312) 922-1157, www.euromonitor.com; *International Marketing Data and Statistics 2008.*

INDIA - JUTE PRODUCTION

See INDIA - CROPS

INDIA - LABOR

Central Intelligence Agency, Office of Public Affairs, Washington, DC 20505, (703) 482-0623, Fax: (703) 482-1739, www.cia.gov; *The World Factbook.*

Economist Intelligence Unit, 111 West 57th Street, New York, NY 10019, (212) 554-0600, Fax: (212) 586-1181, www.eiu.com; *Business Asia.*

Euromonitor International, Inc., 224 S. Michigan Avenue, Suite 1500, Chicago, IL 60604, (312) 922-1115, Fax: (312) 922-1157, www.euromonitor.com; *International Marketing Data and Statistics 2008* and *World Marketing Data and Statistics.*

International Labour Office, I.L.O. Publications, 4 route des Morillons, CH-1211 Geneva 22, Switzerland, (Telephone in U.S. (202) 653-7652), (Fax in U.S. (202) 653-7687), www.ilo.org; *Yearbook of Labour Statistics 2006.*

Palgrave Macmillan Ltd., Houndmills, Basingstoke, Hampshire, RG21 6XS, England, (Telephone in U.S. (888) 330-8477), (Fax in U.S. (800) 672-2054), www.palgrave.com; *The Statesman's Yearbook 2008.*

United Nations Food and Agricultural Organization (FAO), Viale delle Terme di Caracalla, 00100 Rome, Italy, (Dial from U.S. (202) 653-2400), (Fax from U.S. (202) 653 5760), www.fao.org; *The State of Food and Agriculture (SOFA) 2006.*

United Nations Statistics Division, New York, NY 10017, (800) 253-9646, Fax: (212) 963-4116, http://unstats.un.org; *Human Development Report 2006.*

The World Bank, 1818 H Street, NW, Washington, DC 20433, (202) 473-1000, Fax: (202) 477-6391, www.worldbank.org; *The World Bank Atlas 2003-2004* and *World Development Report 2008.*

INDIA - LAND USE

Central Intelligence Agency, Office of Public Affairs, Washington, DC 20505, (703) 482-0623, Fax: (703) 482-1739, www.cia.gov; *The World Factbook.*

Euromonitor International, Inc., 224 S. Michigan Avenue, Suite 1500, Chicago, IL 60604, (312) 922-1115, Fax: (312) 922-1157, www.euromonitor.com; *International Marketing Data and Statistics 2008.*

United Nations Food and Agricultural Organization (FAO), Viale delle Terme di Caracalla, 00100 Rome, Italy, (Dial from U.S. (202) 653-2400), (Fax from U.S. (202) 653 5760), www.fao.org; *FAO Production Yearbook 2002.*

The World Bank, 1818 H Street, NW, Washington, DC 20433, (202) 473-1000, Fax: (202) 477-6391, www.worldbank.org; *World Development Report 2008.*

INDIA - LIBRARIES

UNESCO Institute for Statistics, C.P. 6128 Succursale Centre-Ville, Montreal, Quebec, H3C 3J7 Canada, (Dial from U.S. (514) 343-6880), (Fax from U.S. (514) 343 6882), www.uis.unesco.org; *Statistical Tables.*

INDIA - LIFE EXPECTANCY

Central Intelligence Agency, Office of Public Affairs, Washington, DC 20505, (703) 482-0623, Fax: (703) 482-1739, www.cia.gov; *The World Factbook.*

Economist Intelligence Unit, 111 West 57th Street, New York, NY 10019, (212) 554-0600, Fax: (212) 586-1181, www.eiu.com; *Business Asia.*

Euromonitor International, Inc., 224 S. Michigan Avenue, Suite 1500, Chicago, IL 60604, (312) 922-1115, Fax: (312) 922-1157, www.euromonitor.com; *The World Economic Factbook 2008.*

Palgrave Macmillan Ltd., Houndmills, Basingstoke, Hampshire, RG21 6XS, England, (Telephone in U.S. (888) 330-8477), (Fax in U.S. (800) 672-2054), www.palgrave.com; *The Statesman's Yearbook 2008.*

United Nations Statistics Division, New York, NY 10017, (800) 253-9646, Fax: (212) 963-4116, http://unstats.un.org; *Asia-Pacific in Figures 2004; Human Development Report 2006;* and *World Statistics Pocketbook.*

The World Bank, 1818 H Street, NW, Washington, DC 20433, (202) 473-1000, Fax: (202) 477-6391, www.worldbank.org; *The World Bank Atlas 2003-2004* and *World Development Report 2008.*

INDIA - LITERACY

Euromonitor International, Inc., 224 S. Michigan Avenue, Suite 1500, Chicago, IL 60604, (312) 922-1115, Fax: (312) 922-1157, www.euromonitor.com; *World Marketing Data and Statistics.*

INDIA - LIVESTOCK

Palgrave Macmillan Ltd., Houndmills, Basingstoke, Hampshire, RG21 6XS, England, (Telephone in U.S. (888) 330-8477), (Fax in U.S. (800) 672-2054), www.palgrave.com; *The Statesman's Yearbook 2008.*

Taylor and Francis Group, An Informa Business, 2 Park Square, Milton Park, Abingdon, Oxford OX14 4RN, United Kingdom, (Dial from U.S. (212) 216-7800), (Fax from U.S. (212) 564-7854), www.tandf.co.uk; *The Europa World Year Book.*

United Nations Conference on Trade and Development (UNCTAD), DC2-1120, United Nations, New York, NY 10017, (212) 963-0027, www.unctad.org; *UNCTAD Commodity Yearbook.*

United Nations Food and Agricultural Organization (FAO), Viale delle Terme di Caracalla, 00100 Rome, Italy, (Dial from U.S. (202) 653-2400), (Fax from U.S. (202) 653 5760), www.fao.org; *FAO Production Yearbook 2002* and *The State of Food and Agriculture (SOFA) 2006.*

United Nations Statistics Division, New York, NY 10017, (800) 253-9646, Fax: (212) 963-4116, http://unstats.un.org; *Statistical Yearbook.*

INDIA - LOCAL TAXATION

Euromonitor International, Inc., 224 S. Michigan Avenue, Suite 1500, Chicago, IL 60604, (312) 922-1115, Fax: (312) 922-1157, www.euromonitor.com; *International Marketing Data and Statistics 2008.*

INDIA - MAGNESIUM PRODUCTION AND CONSUMPTION

See INDIA - MINERAL INDUSTRIES

INDIA - MANPOWER

United Nations Statistics Division, New York, NY 10017, (800) 253-9646, Fax: (212) 963-4116, http://unstats.un.org; *Statistical Yearbook for Asia and the Pacific 2004.*

INDIA - MANUFACTURES

United Nations Statistics Division, New York, NY 10017, (800) 253-9646, Fax: (212) 963-4116, http://unstats.un.org; *Statistical Yearbook.*

The World Bank, 1818 H Street, NW, Washington, DC 20433, (202) 473-1000, Fax: (202) 477-6391, www.worldbank.org; *World Development Report 2008.*

INDIA - MARRIAGE

United Nations Statistics Division, New York, NY 10017, (800) 253-9646, Fax: (212) 963-4116, http://unstats.un.org; *Demographic Yearbook.*

INDIA - MEAT PRODUCTION

See INDIA - LIVESTOCK

INDIA - MEDICAL CARE, COST OF

International Monetary Fund (IMF), 700 Nineteenth Street, NW, Washington, DC 20431, (202) 623-7000, Fax: (202) 623-4661, www.imf.org; *Government Finance Statistics Yearbook (2008 Edition).*

INDIA - MILK PRODUCTION

See INDIA - DAIRY PROCESSING

INDIA - MINERAL INDUSTRIES

Commodity Research Bureau, 330 South Wells Street, Suite 612, Chicago, IL 60606-7110, (800) 621-5271, Fax: (312) 939-4135, www.crbtrader.com; *2006 CRB Commodity Yearbook and CD.*

Federal Statistical Office Germany, D-65180 Wiesbaden, Germany, www.destatis.de; *India 2006.*

International Lead and Zinc Study Group (ILZSG), Rua Almirante Barroso 38, 5th Floor, Lisbon 1000 - 013, Portugal, www.ilzsg.org; Interactive Statistical Database.

M.E. Sharpe, 80 Business Park Drive, Armonk, NY 10504, (800) 541-6563, Fax: (914) 273-2106, www.mesharpe.com; *The Illustrated Book of World Rankings.*

Organisation for Economic Cooperation and Development (OECD), 2 rue Andre Pascal, F-75775 Paris Cedex 16, France, (Telephone in U.S. (202) 785-6323), (Fax in U.S. (202) 785-0350), www.oecd.org; *Coal Information: 2007 Edition* and *World Energy Outlook 2007.*

Palgrave Macmillan Ltd., Houndmills, Basingstoke, Hampshire, RG21 6XS, England, (Telephone in U.S. (888) 330-8477), (Fax in U.S. (800) 672-2054), www.palgrave.com; *The Statesman's Yearbook 2008.*

Taylor and Francis Group, An Informa Business, 2 Park Square, Milton Park, Abingdon, Oxford OX14 4RN, United Kingdom, (Dial from U.S. (212) 216-7800), (Fax from U.S. (212) 564-7854), www.tandf.co.uk; *The Europa World Year Book.*

United Nations Conference on Trade and Development (UNCTAD), DC2-1120, United Nations, New York, NY 10017, (212) 963-0027, www.unctad.org; *UNCTAD Commodity Yearbook.*

United Nations Statistics Division, New York, NY 10017, (800) 253-9646, Fax: (212) 963-4116, http://unstats.un.org; *Statistical Yearbook.*

World Bureau of Metal Statistics (WBMS), 27a High Street, Ware, Hertfordshire, SG12 9BA, United Kingdom, www.world-bureau.com; *Annual Stainless Steel Statistics; World Flow Charts; World Metal Statistics; World Nickel Statistics;* and *World Tin Statistics.*

INDIA - MOLASSES PRODUCTION

See INDIA - CROPS

INDIA - MONEY EXCHANGE RATES

See INDIA - FOREIGN EXCHANGE RATES

INDIA - MONEY SUPPLY

Economist Intelligence Unit, 111 West 57th Street, New York, NY 10019, (212) 554-0600, Fax: (212) 586-1181, www.eiu.com; *India Country Report.*

Euromonitor International, Inc., 224 S. Michigan Avenue, Suite 1500, Chicago, IL 60604, (312) 922-1115, Fax: (312) 922-1157, www.euromonitor.com; *International Marketing Data and Statistics 2008.*

Federal Statistical Office Germany, D-65180 Wiesbaden, Germany, www.destatis.de; *India 2006.*

International Monetary Fund (IMF), 700 Nineteenth Street, NW, Washington, DC 20431, (202) 623-7000, Fax: (202) 623-4661, www.imf.org; *International Financial Statistics Yearbook 2007.*

Taylor and Francis Group, An Informa Business, 2 Park Square, Milton Park, Abingdon, Oxford OX14 4RN, United Kingdom, (Dial from U.S. (212) 216-7800), (Fax from U.S. (212) 564-7854), www.tandf.co.uk; *The Europa World Year Book.*

United Nations Statistics Division, New York, NY 10017, (800) 253-9646, Fax: (212) 963-4116, http://unstats.un.org; *Statistical Yearbook.*

The World Bank, 1818 H Street, NW, Washington, DC 20433, (202) 473-1000, Fax: (202) 477-6391, www.worldbank.org; *India* and *World Development Report 2008.*

INDIA - MORTALITY

Central Intelligence Agency, Office of Public Affairs, Washington, DC 20505, (703) 482-0623, Fax: (703) 482-1739, www.cia.gov; *The World Factbook.*

Euromonitor International, Inc., 224 S. Michigan Avenue, Suite 1500, Chicago, IL 60604, (312) 922-1115, Fax: (312) 922-1157, www.euromonitor.com; *International Marketing Data and Statistics 2008* and *The World Economic Factbook 2008.*

Palgrave Macmillan Ltd., Houndmills, Basingstoke, Hampshire, RG21 6XS, England, (Telephone in U.S. (888) 330-8477), (Fax in U.S. (800) 672-2054), www.palgrave.com; *The Statesman's Yearbook 2008.*

Taylor and Francis Group, An Informa Business, 2 Park Square, Milton Park, Abingdon, Oxford OX14 4RN, United Kingdom, (Dial from U.S. (212) 216-7800), (Fax from U.S. (212) 564-7854), www.tandf.co.uk; *The Europa World Year Book.*

UNICEF, 3 United Nations Plaza, New York, NY 10017, (800) 253-9646, Fax: (212) 887-7465, www.unicef.org; *The State of the World's Children 2008.*

United Nations Statistics Division, New York, NY 10017, (800) 253-9646, Fax: (212) 963-4116, http://unstats.un.org; *Asia-Pacific in Figures 2004; Demographic Yearbook; Human Development Report 2006; Statistical Yearbook;* and *World Statistics Pocketbook.*

The World Bank, 1818 H Street, NW, Washington, DC 20433, (202) 473-1000, Fax: (202) 477-6391, www.worldbank.org; *The World Bank Atlas 2003-2004* and *World Development Report 2008.*

World Health Organization (WHO), Avenue Appia 20, 1211 Geneve 27, Switzerland, (Telephone in U.S. (212) 331-9081), www.who.int; The WHO Global Atlas of Infectious Diseases and *World Health Report 2006.*

INDIA - MOTION PICTURES

Palgrave Macmillan Ltd., Houndmills, Basingstoke, Hampshire, RG21 6XS, England, (Telephone in U.S. (888) 330-8477), (Fax in U.S. (800) 672-2054), www.palgrave.com; *The Statesman's Yearbook 2008.*

UNESCO Institute for Statistics, C.P. 6128 Succursale Centre-Ville, Montreal, Quebec, H3C 3J7 Canada, (Dial from U.S. (514) 343-6880), (Fax from U.S. (514) 343 6882), www.uis.unesco.org; *Statistical Tables.*

United Nations Statistics Division, New York, NY 10017, (800) 253-9646, Fax: (212) 963-4116, http://unstats.un.org; *Statistical Yearbook.*

INDIA - MOTOR VEHICLES

International Road Federation (IFR), Madison Place, 500 Montgomery Street, 5th Floor, Alexandria, VA 22314, (703) 535-1001, Fax: (703) 535-1007, www.irfnet.org; *World Road Statistics 2006.*

Taylor and Francis Group, An Informa Business, 2 Park Square, Milton Park, Abingdon, Oxford OX14 4RN, United Kingdom, (Dial from U.S. (212) 216-7800), (Fax from U.S. (212) 564-7854), www.tandf.co.uk; *The Europa World Year Book.*

United Nations Statistics Division, New York, NY 10017, (800) 253-9646, Fax: (212) 963-4116, http://unstats.un.org; *Statistical Yearbook.*

INDIA - NATURAL GAS PRODUCTION

See INDIA - MINERAL INDUSTRIES

INDIA - NICKEL AND NICKEL ORE

See INDIA - MINERAL INDUSTRIES

INDIA - NUTRITION

United Nations Food and Agricultural Organization (FAO), Viale delle Terme di Caracalla, 00100 Rome, Italy, (Dial from U.S. (202) 653-2400), (Fax from U.S. (202) 653 5760), www.fao.org; *The State of Food and Agriculture (SOFA) 2006.*

INDIA - ONION PRODUCTION

See INDIA - CROPS

INDIA - PAPER

See INDIA - FORESTS AND FORESTRY

INDIA - PEANUT PRODUCTION

See INDIA - CROPS

INDIA - PEPPER PRODUCTION

See INDIA - CROPS

INDIA - PERIODICALS

UNESCO Institute for Statistics, C.P. 6128 Succursale Centre-Ville, Montreal, Quebec, H3C 3J7 Canada, (Dial from U.S. (514) 343-6880), (Fax from U.S. (514) 343 6882), www.uis.unesco.org; *Statistical Tables.*

INDIA - PESTICIDES

United Nations Food and Agricultural Organization (FAO), Viale delle Terme di Caracalla, 00100 Rome, Italy, (Dial from U.S. (202) 653-2400), (Fax from U.S. (202) 653 5760), www.fao.org; *The State of Food and Agriculture (SOFA) 2006.*

INDIA - PETROLEUM INDUSTRY AND TRADE

Organisation for Economic Cooperation and Development (OECD), 2 rue Andre Pascal, F-75775 Paris Cedex 16, France, (Telephone in U.S. (202) 785-6323), (Fax in U.S. (202) 785-0350), www.oecd.org; *World Energy Outlook 2007.*

Palgrave Macmillan Ltd., Houndmills, Basingstoke, Hampshire, RG21 6XS, England, (Telephone in U.S. (888) 330-8477), (Fax in U.S. (800) 672-2054), www.palgrave.com; *The Statesman's Yearbook 2008.*

PennWell Corporation, 1421 South Sheridan Road, Tulsa, OK 74112, (918) 835-3161, www.pennwell.com; *International Petroleum Encyclopedia 2007.*

U.S. Department of Energy (DOE), Energy Information Administration (EIA), 1000 Independence Avenue, SW, Washington, DC 20585, (202) 586-8800, www.eia.doe.gov; *International Energy Annual 2004* and *International Energy Outlook 2006.*

United Nations Conference on Trade and Development (UNCTAD), DC2-1120, United Nations, New York, NY 10017, (212) 963-0027, www.unctad.org; *UNCTAD Commodity Yearbook.*

United Nations Food and Agricultural Organization (FAO), Viale delle Terme di Caracalla, 00100 Rome, Italy, (Dial from U.S. (202) 653-2400), (Fax from U.S. (202) 653 5760), www.fao.org; *The State of Food and Agriculture (SOFA) 2006.*

United Nations Statistics Division, New York, NY 10017, (800) 253-9646, Fax: (212) 963-4116, http://unstats.un.org; *Statistical Yearbook.*

INDIA - PHOSPHATES PRODUCTION

See INDIA - MINERAL INDUSTRIES

INDIA - PLASTICS INDUSTRY AND TRADE

United Nations Statistics Division, New York, NY 10017, (800) 253-9646, Fax: (212) 963-4116, http://unstats.un.org; *Statistical Yearbook.*

INDIA - POLITICAL SCIENCE

Central Intelligence Agency, Office of Public Affairs, Washington, DC 20505, (703) 482-0623, Fax: (703) 482-1739, www.cia.gov; *The World Factbook.*

International Monetary Fund (IMF), 700 Nineteenth Street, NW, Washington, DC 20431, (202) 623-7000, Fax: (202) 623-4661, www.imf.org; *Government Finance Statistics Yearbook (2008 Edition)* and *International Financial Statistics Yearbook 2007.*

Palgrave Macmillan Ltd., Houndmills, Basingstoke, Hampshire, RG21 6XS, England, (Telephone in U.S. (888) 330-8477), (Fax in U.S. (800) 672-2054), www.palgrave.com; *The Statesman's Yearbook 2008.*

Taylor and Francis Group, An Informa Business, 2 Park Square, Milton Park, Abingdon, Oxford OX14 4RN, United Kingdom, (Dial from U.S. (212) 216-7800), (Fax from U.S. (212) 564-7854), www.tandf.co.uk; *The Europa World Year Book.*

United Nations Statistics Division, New York, NY 10017, (800) 253-9646, Fax: (212) 963-4116, http://unstats.un.org; *Asia-Pacific in Figures 2004; National Accounts Statistics: Compendium of Income Distribution Statistics;* and *Statistical Yearbook.*

The World Bank, 1818 H Street, NW, Washington, DC 20433, (202) 473-1000, Fax: (202) 477-6391, www.worldbank.org; *World Development Report 2008.*

INDIA - POPULATION

Central Intelligence Agency, Office of Public Affairs, Washington, DC 20505, (703) 482-0623, Fax: (703) 482-1739, www.cia.gov; *The World Factbook.*

Economist Intelligence Unit, 111 West 57th Street, New York, NY 10019, (212) 554-0600, Fax: (212) 586-1181, www.eiu.com; *Business Asia* and *India Country Report.*

Euromonitor International, Inc., 224 S. Michigan Avenue, Suite 1500, Chicago, IL 60604, (312) 922-1115, Fax: (312) 922-1157, www.euromonitor.com; *International Marketing Data and Statistics 2008* and *The World Economic Factbook 2008.*

Federal Statistical Office Germany, D-65180 Wiesbaden, Germany, www.destatis.de; *India 2006.*

International Labour Office, I.L.O. Publications, 4 route des Morillons, CH-1211 Geneva 22, Switzerland, (Telephone in U.S. (202) 653-7652), (Fax in U.S. (202) 653-7687), www.ilo.org; *Yearbook of Labour Statistics 2006.*

Palgrave Macmillan Ltd., Houndmills, Basingstoke, Hampshire, RG21 6XS, England, (Telephone in U.S. (888) 330-8477), (Fax in U.S. (800) 672-2054), www.palgrave.com; *The Statesman's Yearbook 2008.*

Taylor and Francis Group, An Informa Business, 2 Park Square, Milton Park, Abingdon, Oxford OX14 4RN, United Kingdom, (Dial from U.S. (212) 216-7800), (Fax from U.S. (212) 564-7854), www.tandf.co.uk; *The Europa World Year Book.*

U.S. Department of State (DOS), 2201 C Street NW, Washington, DC 20520, (202) 647-4000, www.state.gov; *World Military Expenditures and Arms Transfers (WMEAT).*

UNESCO Institute for Statistics, C.P. 6128 Succursale Centre-Ville, Montreal, Quebec, H3C 3J7 Canada, (Dial from U.S. (514) 343-6880), (Fax from U.S. (514) 343 6882), www.uis.unesco.org; *Statistical Tables.*

United Nations Food and Agricultural Organization (FAO), Viale delle Terme di Caracalla, 00100 Rome, Italy, (Dial from U.S. (202) 653-2400), (Fax from U.S. (202) 653 5760), www.fao.org; *FAO Production Yearbook 2002.*

United Nations Statistics Division, New York, NY 10017, (800) 253-9646, Fax: (212) 963-4116, http://unstats.un.org; *Asia-Pacific in Figures 2004; Demographic Yearbook; Human Development Report 2006; Statistical Yearbook; Statistical Yearbook for Asia and the Pacific 2004;* and *World Statistics Pocketbook.*

The World Bank, 1818 H Street, NW, Washington, DC 20433, (202) 473-1000, Fax: (202) 477-6391, www.worldbank.org; *India; The World Bank Atlas 2003-2004;* and *World Development Report 2008.*

World Health Organization (WHO), Avenue Appia 20, 1211 Geneve 27, Switzerland, (Telephone in U.S. (212) 331-9081), www.who.int; *World Health Report 2006.*

Worldinformation.com, 2 Market Street, Saffron Walden, Essex CB10 1HZ, United Kingdom, www.worldinformation.com; The World of Information (www.worldinformation.com).

INDIA - POPULATION DENSITY

Central Intelligence Agency, Office of Public Affairs, Washington, DC 20505, (703) 482-0623, Fax: (703) 482-1739, www.cia.gov; *The World Factbook.*

Euromonitor International, Inc., 224 S. Michigan Avenue, Suite 1500, Chicago, IL 60604, (312) 922-1115, Fax: (312) 922-1157, www.euromonitor.com; *International Marketing Data and Statistics 2008* and *The World Economic Factbook 2008.*

Federal Statistical Office Germany, D-65180 Wiesbaden, Germany, www.destatis.de; *India 2006.*

Palgrave Macmillan Ltd., Houndmills, Basingstoke, Hampshire, RG21 6XS, England, (Telephone in U.S. (888) 330-8477), (Fax in U.S. (800) 672-2054), www.palgrave.com; *The Statesman's Yearbook 2008.*

Taylor and Francis Group, An Informa Business, 2 Park Square, Milton Park, Abingdon, Oxford OX14 4RN, United Kingdom, (Dial from U.S. (212) 216-7800), (Fax from U.S. (212) 564-7854), www.tandf.co.uk; *The Europa World Year Book.*

UNESCO Institute for Statistics, C.P. 6128 Succursale Centre-Ville, Montreal, Quebec, H3C 3J7 Canada, (Dial from U.S. (514) 343-6880), (Fax from U.S. (514) 343 6882), www.uis.unesco.org; *Statistical Tables.*

United Nations Food and Agricultural Organization (FAO), Viale delle Terme di Caracalla, 00100 Rome, Italy, (Dial from U.S. (202) 653-2400), (Fax from U.S. (202) 653 5760), www.fao.org; *The State of Food and Agriculture (SOFA) 2006.*

United Nations Statistics Division, New York, NY 10017, (800) 253-9646, Fax: (212) 963-4116, http://unstats.un.org; *Statistical Yearbook.*

The World Bank, 1818 H Street, NW, Washington, DC 20433, (202) 473-1000, Fax: (202) 477-6391, www.worldbank.org; *India* and *World Development Report 2008.*

INDIA - POSTAL SERVICE

Palgrave Macmillan Ltd., Houndmills, Basingstoke, Hampshire, RG21 6XS, England, (Telephone in U.S. (888) 330-8477), (Fax in U.S. (800) 672-2054), www.palgrave.com; *The Statesman's Yearbook 2008.*

United Nations Statistics Division, New York, NY 10017, (800) 253-9646, Fax: (212) 963-4116, http://unstats.un.org; *Statistical Yearbook.*

INDIA - POWER RESOURCES

Euromonitor International, Inc., 224 S. Michigan Avenue, Suite 1500, Chicago, IL 60604, (312) 922-1115, Fax: (312) 922-1157, www.euromonitor.com; *International Marketing Data and Statistics 2008; The World Economic Factbook 2008;* and *World Marketing Data and Statistics.*

Organisation for Economic Cooperation and Development (OECD), 2 rue Andre Pascal, F-75775 Paris Cedex 16, France, (Telephone in U.S. (202) 785-6323), (Fax in U.S. (202) 785-0350), www.oecd.org; *Coal Information: 2007 Edition* and *World Energy Outlook 2007.*

Palgrave Macmillan Ltd., Houndmills, Basingstoke, Hampshire, RG21 6XS, England, (Telephone in U.S. (888) 330-8477), (Fax in U.S. (800) 672-2054), www.palgrave.com; *The Statesman's Yearbook 2008.*

Platts, 2 Penn Plaza, 25th Floor, New York, NY 10121-2298, (212) 904-3070, www.platts.com; *Asian Electricity Outlook 2006; Emissions Daily;* and *Energy Economist.*

U.S. Department of Energy (DOE), Energy Information Administration (EIA), 1000 Independence Avenue, SW, Washington, DC 20585, (202) 586-8800, www.eia.doe.gov; *International Energy Annual 2004* and *International Energy Outlook 2006.*

United Nations Food and Agricultural Organization (FAO), Viale delle Terme di Caracalla, 00100 Rome, Italy, (Dial from U.S. (202) 653-2400), (Fax from U.S. (202) 653 5760), www.fao.org; *The State of Food and Agriculture (SOFA) 2006.*

United Nations Statistics Division, New York, NY 10017, (800) 253-9646, Fax: (212) 963-4116, http://unstats.un.org; *Asia-Pacific in Figures 2004; Energy Statistics Yearbook 2003; Human Development Report 2006; Statistical Yearbook; Statistical Yearbook for Asia and the Pacific 2004;* and *World Statistics Pocketbook.*

The World Bank, 1818 H Street, NW, Washington, DC 20433, (202) 473-1000, Fax: (202) 477-6391, www.worldbank.org; *The World Bank Atlas 2003-2004* and *World Development Report 2008.*

INDIA - PRICES

Euromonitor International, Inc., 224 S. Michigan Avenue, Suite 1500, Chicago, IL 60604, (312) 922-1115, Fax: (312) 922-1157, www.euromonitor.com; *World Marketing Data and Statistics.*

Federal Statistical Office Germany, D-65180 Wiesbaden, Germany, www.destatis.de; *India 2006.*

International Labour Office, I.L.O. Publications, 4 route des Morillons, CH-1211 Geneva 22, Switzerland, (Telephone in U.S. (202) 653-7652), (Fax in U.S. (202) 653-7687), www.ilo.org; *Yearbook of Labour Statistics 2006.*

International Lead and Zinc Study Group (ILZSG), Rua Almirante Barroso 38, 5th Floor, Lisbon 1000 - 013, Portugal, www.ilzsg.org; Interactive Statistical Database.

International Monetary Fund (IMF), 700 Nineteenth Street, NW, Washington, DC 20431, (202) 623-7000, Fax: (202) 623-4661, www.imf.org; *International Financial Statistics Yearbook 2007.*

United Nations Food and Agricultural Organization (FAO), Viale delle Terme di Caracalla, 00100 Rome, Italy, (Dial from U.S. (202) 653-2400), (Fax from U.S. (202) 653 5760), www.fao.org; *FAO Production Yearbook 2002* and *The State of Food and Agriculture (SOFA) 2006.*

The World Bank, 1818 H Street, NW, Washington, DC 20433, (202) 473-1000, Fax: (202) 477-6391, www.worldbank.org; *India.*

World Bureau of Metal Statistics (WBMS), 27a High Street, Ware, Hertfordshire, SG12 9BA, United Kingdom, www.world-bureau.com; *World Flow Charts* and *World Metal Statistics.*

INDIA - PROFESSIONS

United Nations Statistics Division, New York, NY 10017, (800) 253-9646, Fax: (212) 963-4116, http://unstats.un.org; *Statistical Yearbook.*

INDIA - PUBLIC HEALTH

Economist Intelligence Unit, 111 West 57th Street, New York, NY 10019, (212) 554-0600, Fax: (212) 586-1181, www.eiu.com; *Business Asia.*

Euromonitor International, Inc., 224 S. Michigan Avenue, Suite 1500, Chicago, IL 60604, (312) 922-1115, Fax: (312) 922-1157, www.euromonitor.com; *World Health Databook 2007/2008* and *World Marketing Data and Statistics.*

Federal Statistical Office Germany, D-65180 Wiesbaden, Germany, www.destatis.de; *India 2006.*

Palgrave Macmillan Ltd., Houndmills, Basingstoke, Hampshire, RG21 6XS, England, (Telephone in U.S. (888) 330-8477), (Fax in U.S. (800) 672-2054), www.palgrave.com; *The Statesman's Yearbook 2008.*

UNICEF, 3 United Nations Plaza, New York, NY 10017, (800) 253-9646, Fax: (212) 887-7465, www.unicef.org; *The State of the World's Children 2008.*

United Nations Statistics Division, New York, NY 10017, (800) 253-9646, Fax: (212) 963-4116, http://unstats.un.org; *Asia-Pacific in Figures 2004; Human Development Report 2006;* and *Statistical Yearbook.*

The World Bank, 1818 H Street, NW, Washington, DC 20433, (202) 473-1000, Fax: (202) 477-6391, www.worldbank.org; *India* and *World Development Report 2008.*

World Health Organization (WHO), Avenue Appia 20, 1211 Geneve 27, Switzerland, (Telephone in U.S. (212) 331-9081), www.who.int; The WHO Global Atlas of Infectious Diseases and *World Health Report 2006.*

INDIA - PUBLIC UTILITIES

United Nations Statistics Division, New York, NY 10017, (800) 253-9646, Fax: (212) 963-4116, http://unstats.un.org; *Electric Power in Asia and the Pacific 2001 and 2002.*

INDIA - PUBLISHERS AND PUBLISHING

Palgrave Macmillan Ltd., Houndmills, Basingstoke, Hampshire, RG21 6XS, England, (Telephone in U.S. (888) 330-8477), (Fax in U.S. (800) 672-2054), www.palgrave.com; *The Statesman's Yearbook 2008.*

UNESCO Institute for Statistics, C.P. 6128 Succursale Centre-Ville, Montreal, Quebec, H3C 3J7 Canada, (Dial from U.S. (514) 343-6880), (Fax from U.S. (514) 343 6882), www.uis.unesco.org; *Statistical Tables.*

INDIA - RADIO - RECEIVERS AND RECEPTION

Palgrave Macmillan Ltd., Houndmills, Basingstoke, Hampshire, RG21 6XS, England, (Telephone in U.S. (888) 330-8477), (Fax in U.S. (800) 672-2054), www.palgrave.com; *The Statesman's Yearbook 2008.*

United Nations Statistics Division, New York, NY 10017, (800) 253-9646, Fax: (212) 963-4116, http://unstats.un.org; *Statistical Yearbook.*

INDIA - RAILROADS

Jane's Information Group, 110 North Royal Street, Suite 200, Alexandria, VA 22314, (703) 683-3700, Fax: (800) 836-0297, www.janes.com; *Jane's World Railways.*

Palgrave Macmillan Ltd., Houndmills, Basingstoke, Hampshire, RG21 6XS, England, (Telephone in U.S. (888) 330-8477), (Fax in U.S. (800) 672-2054), www.palgrave.com; *The Statesman's Yearbook 2008.*

Taylor and Francis Group, An Informa Business, 2 Park Square, Milton Park, Abingdon, Oxford OX14 4RN, United Kingdom, (Dial from U.S. (212) 216-7800), (Fax from U.S. (212) 564-7854), www.tandf.co.uk; *The Europa World Year Book.*

United Nations Statistics Division, New York, NY 10017, (800) 253-9646, Fax: (212) 963-4116, http://unstats.un.org; *Statistical Yearbook.*

INDIA - RELIGION

Central Intelligence Agency, Office of Public Affairs, Washington, DC 20505, (703) 482-0623, Fax: (703) 482-1739, www.cia.gov; *The World Factbook.*

Palgrave Macmillan Ltd., Houndmills, Basingstoke, Hampshire, RG21 6XS, England, (Telephone in U.S. (888) 330-8477), (Fax in U.S. (800) 672-2054), www.palgrave.com; *The Statesman's Yearbook 2008.*

INDIA - RENT CHARGES

International Labour Office, I.L.O. Publications, 4 route des Morillons, CH-1211 Geneva 22, Switzerland, (Telephone in U.S. (202) 653-7652), (Fax in U.S. (202) 653-7687), www.ilo.org; *Yearbook of Labour Statistics 2006.*

INDIA - RESERVES (ACCOUNTING)

Euromonitor International, Inc., 224 S. Michigan Avenue, Suite 1500, Chicago, IL 60604, (312) 922-1115, Fax: (312) 922-1157, www.euromonitor.com; *International Marketing Data and Statistics 2008.*

United Nations Statistics Division, New York, NY 10017, (800) 253-9646, Fax: (212) 963-4116, http://unstats.un.org; *Statistical Yearbook.*

The World Bank, 1818 H Street, NW, Washington, DC 20433, (202) 473-1000, Fax: (202) 477-6391, www.worldbank.org; *World Development Report 2008.*

INDIA - RETAIL TRADE

Euromonitor International, Inc., 224 S. Michigan Avenue, Suite 1500, Chicago, IL 60604, (312) 922-1115, Fax: (312) 922-1157, www.euromonitor.com; *Retail Trade International 2007* and *World Marketing Data and Statistics.*

INDIA - RICE PRODUCTION

See INDIA - CROPS

INDIA - ROADS

Central Intelligence Agency, Office of Public Affairs, Washington, DC 20505, (703) 482-0623, Fax: (703) 482-1739, www.cia.gov; *The World Factbook.*

International Road Federation (IFR), Madison Place, 500 Montgomery Street, 5th Floor, Alexandria, VA 22314, (703) 535-1001, Fax: (703) 535-1007, www.irfnet.org; *World Road Statistics 2006.*

Palgrave Macmillan Ltd., Houndmills, Basingstoke, Hampshire, RG21 6XS, England, (Telephone in U.S. (888) 330-8477), (Fax in U.S. (800) 672-2054), www.palgrave.com; *The Statesman's Yearbook 2008.*

INDIA - RUBBER INDUSTRY AND TRADE

International Rubber Study Group (IRSG), 1st Floor, Heron House, 109/115 Wembley Hill Road, Wembley, Middlesex HA9 8DA, United Kingdom, www.rubberstudy.com; *Rubber Statistical Bulletin; Summary of World Rubber Statistics 2005; World Rubber Statistics Handbook (Volume 6, 1975-2001);* and *World Rubber Statistics Historic Handbook.*

United Nations Statistics Division, New York, NY 10017, (800) 253-9646, Fax: (212) 963-4116, http://unstats.un.org; *Statistical Yearbook.*

INDIA - SALT PRODUCTION

See INDIA - MINERAL INDUSTRIES

INDIA - SHEEP

See INDIA - LIVESTOCK

INDIA - SHIPPING

Lloyd's Register - Fairplay, 8410 N.W. 53rd Terrace, Suite 207, Miami FL 33166, (305) 718-9929, Fax: (305) 718-9663, www.lrfairplay.com; *Register of Ships 2007-2008; World Casualty Statistics 2007; World Fleet Statistics 2006; World Marine Propulsion Report 2006-2010; World Shipbuilding Statistics 2007;* and The World Shipping Encyclopaedia.

Palgrave Macmillan Ltd., Houndmills, Basingstoke, Hampshire, RG21 6XS, England, (Telephone in U.S. (888) 330-8477), (Fax in U.S. (800) 672-2054), www.palgrave.com; *The Statesman's Yearbook 2008.*

Taylor and Francis Group, An Informa Business, 2 Park Square, Milton Park, Abingdon, Oxford OX14 4RN, United Kingdom, (Dial from U.S. (212) 216-7800), (Fax from U.S. (212) 564-7854), www.tandf.co.uk; *The Europa World Year Book.*

U.S. Department of Transportation (DOT), Maritime Administration (MARAD), West Building, Southeast Federal Center, 1200 New Jersey Avenue, SE, Washington, DC 20590, (800) 99-MARAD, www.marad.dot.gov; *World Merchant Fleet 2005.*

United Nations Statistics Division, New York, NY 10017, (800) 253-9646, Fax: (212) 963-4116, http://unstats.un.org; *Statistical Yearbook.*

INDIA - SILVER PRODUCTION

See INDIA - MINERAL INDUSTRIES

INDIA - SOCIAL ECOLOGY

United Nations Statistics Division, New York, NY 10017, (800) 253-9646, Fax: (212) 963-4116, http://unstats.un.org; *World Statistics Pocketbook.*

INDIA - SOCIAL SECURITY

International Monetary Fund (IMF), 700 Nineteenth Street, NW, Washington, DC 20431, (202) 623-7000, Fax: (202) 623-4661, www.imf.org; *Government Finance Statistics Yearbook (2008 Edition).*

United Nations Statistics Division, New York, NY 10017, (800) 253-9646, Fax: (212) 963-4116, http://unstats.un.org; *National Accounts Statistics: Compendium of Income Distribution Statistics.*

INDIA - SOYBEAN PRODUCTION

See INDIA - CROPS

INDIA - STEEL PRODUCTION

See INDIA - MINERAL INDUSTRIES

INDIA - SUGAR PRODUCTION

See INDIA - CROPS

INDIA - SULPHUR PRODUCTION

See INDIA - MINERAL INDUSTRIES

INDIA - TAXATION

International Monetary Fund (IMF), 700 Nineteenth Street, NW, Washington, DC 20431, (202) 623-7000, Fax: (202) 623-4661, www.imf.org; *Government Finance Statistics Yearbook (2008 Edition).*

International Road Federation (IFR), Madison Place, 500 Montgomery Street, 5th Floor, Alexandria, VA 22314, (703) 535-1001, Fax: (703) 535-1007, www.irfnet.org; *World Road Statistics 2006.*

Palgrave Macmillan Ltd., Houndmills, Basingstoke, Hampshire, RG21 6XS, England, (Telephone in U.S. (888) 330-8477), (Fax in U.S. (800) 672-2054), www.palgrave.com; *The Statesman's Yearbook 2008.*

Taylor and Francis Group, An Informa Business, 2 Park Square, Milton Park, Abingdon, Oxford OX14 4RN, United Kingdom, (Dial from U.S. (212) 216-7800), (Fax from U.S. (212) 564-7854), www.tandf.co.uk; *The Europa World Year Book.*

The World Bank, 1818 H Street, NW, Washington, DC 20433, (202) 473-1000, Fax: (202) 477-6391, www.worldbank.org; *World Development Report 2008.*

INDIA - TEA PRODUCTION

See INDIA - CROPS

INDIA - TELEPHONE

Economist Intelligence Unit, 111 West 57th Street, New York, NY 10019, (212) 554-0600, Fax: (212) 586-1181, www.eiu.com; *Business Asia.*

International Telecommunication Union (ITU), Place des Nations, 1211 Geneva 20, Switzerland, www.itu.int; World Telecommunication Indicators Database.

Palgrave Macmillan Ltd., Houndmills, Basingstoke, Hampshire, RG21 6XS, England, (Telephone in U.S. (888) 330-8477), (Fax in U.S. (800) 672-2054), www.palgrave.com; *The Statesman's Yearbook 2008.*

Taylor and Francis Group, An Informa Business, 2 Park Square, Milton Park, Abingdon, Oxford OX14 4RN, United Kingdom, (Dial from U.S. (212) 216-7800), (Fax from U.S. (212) 564-7854), www.tandf.co.uk; *The Europa World Year Book.*

United Nations Statistics Division, New York, NY 10017, (800) 253-9646, Fax: (212) 963-4116, http://unstats.un.org; *Statistical Yearbook* and *World Statistics Pocketbook.*

INDIA - TEXTILE INDUSTRY

Euromonitor International, Inc., 224 S. Michigan Avenue, Suite 1500, Chicago, IL 60604, (312) 922-1115, Fax: (312) 922-1157, www.euromonitor.com; *Retail Trade International 2007.*

Palgrave Macmillan Ltd., Houndmills, Basingstoke, Hampshire, RG21 6XS, England, (Telephone in U.S. (888) 330-8477), (Fax in U.S. (800) 672-2054), www.palgrave.com; *The Statesman's Yearbook 2008.*

United Nations Conference on Trade and Development (UNCTAD), DC2-1120, United Nations, New York, NY 10017, (212) 963-0027, www.unctad.org; *UNCTAD Commodity Yearbook.*

United Nations Food and Agricultural Organization (FAO), Viale delle Terme di Caracalla, 00100 Rome, Italy, (Dial from U.S. (202) 653-2400), (Fax from U.S. (202) 653 5760), www.fao.org; *FAO Production Yearbook 2002.*

United Nations Statistics Division, New York, NY 10017, (800) 253-9646, Fax: (212) 963-4116, http://unstats.un.org; *Statistical Yearbook.*

INDIA - TIN PRODUCTION

See INDIA - MINERAL INDUSTRIES

INDIA - TIRE INDUSTRY

United Nations Statistics Division, New York, NY 10017, (800) 253-9646, Fax: (212) 963-4116, http://unstats.un.org; *Statistical Yearbook.*

INDIA - TOBACCO INDUSTRY

Foreign Agricultural Service (FAS), U.S. Department of Agriculture (USDA), 1400 Independence Avenue, SW, Washington, DC 20250, (202) 720-3935, www.fas.usda.gov; *Tobacco: World Markets and Trade.*

United Nations Statistics Division, New York, NY 10017, (800) 253-9646, Fax: (212) 963-4116, http://unstats.un.org; *Statistical Yearbook.*

INDIA - TOURISM

Euromonitor International, Inc., 224 S. Michigan Avenue, Suite 1500, Chicago, IL 60604, (312) 922-1115, Fax: (312) 922-1157, www.euromonitor.com; *The World Economic Factbook 2008* and *World Marketing Data and Statistics.*

Federal Statistical Office Germany, D-65180 Wiesbaden, Germany, www.destatis.de; *India 2006.*

Palgrave Macmillan Ltd., Houndmills, Basingstoke, Hampshire, RG21 6XS, England, (Telephone in U.S. (888) 330-8477), (Fax in U.S. (800) 672-2054), www.palgrave.com; *The Statesman's Yearbook 2008.*

Taylor and Francis Group, An Informa Business, 2 Park Square, Milton Park, Abingdon, Oxford OX14 4RN, United Kingdom, (Dial from U.S. (212) 216-7800), (Fax from U.S. (212) 564-7854), www.tandf.co.uk; *The Europa World Year Book.*

United Nations Statistics Division, New York, NY 10017, (800) 253-9646, Fax: (212) 963-4116, http://unstats.un.org; *Statistical Yearbook.*

United Nations World Tourism Organization (UNWTO), Capitan Haya 42, 28020 Madrid, Spain, www.world-tourism.org; *Yearbook of Tourism Statistics.*

The World Bank, 1818 H Street, NW, Washington, DC 20433, (202) 473-1000, Fax: (202) 477-6391, www.worldbank.org; *India.*

INDIA - TRADE

See INDIA - INTERNATIONAL TRADE

INDIA - TRANSPORTATION

Central Intelligence Agency, Office of Public Affairs, Washington, DC 20505, (703) 482-0623, Fax: (703) 482-1739, www.cia.gov; *The World Factbook.*

Directorate General of Commercial Intelligence and Statistics (DGCIS), Ministry of Commerce and Industry, 1, Council House Street, Calcutta-700 001, India, www.dgciskol.nic.in; *Inter-State Movements/ Flows of Goods by Rail, River and Air.*

Economist Intelligence Unit, 111 West 57th Street, New York, NY 10019, (212) 554-0600, Fax: (212) 586-1181, www.eiu.com; *Business Asia.*

Euromonitor International, Inc., 224 S. Michigan Avenue, Suite 1500, Chicago, IL 60604, (312) 922-1115, Fax: (312) 922-1157, www.euromonitor.com; *International Marketing Data and Statistics 2008* and *World Marketing Data and Statistics.*

Federal Statistical Office Germany, D-65180 Wiesbaden, Germany, www.destatis.de; *India 2006.*

Palgrave Macmillan Ltd., Houndmills, Basingstoke, Hampshire, RG21 6XS, England, (Telephone in U.S. (888) 330-8477), (Fax in U.S. (800) 672-2054), www.palgrave.com; *The Statesman's Yearbook 2008.*

Taylor and Francis Group, An Informa Business, 2 Park Square, Milton Park, Abingdon, Oxford OX14 4RN, United Kingdom, (Dial from U.S. (212) 216-7800), (Fax from U.S. (212) 564-7854), www.tandf.co.uk; *The Europa World Year Book.*

United Nations Statistics Division, New York, NY 10017, (800) 253-9646, Fax: (212) 963-4116, http://unstats.un.org; *Human Development Report 2006* and *Statistical Yearbook for Asia and the Pacific 2004.*

The World Bank, 1818 H Street, NW, Washington, DC 20433, (202) 473-1000, Fax: (202) 477-6391, www.worldbank.org; *India.*

INDIA - UNEMPLOYMENT

Central Intelligence Agency, Office of Public Affairs, Washington, DC 20505, (703) 482-0623, Fax: (703) 482-1739, www.cia.gov; *The World Factbook.*

Euromonitor International, Inc., 224 S. Michigan Avenue, Suite 1500, Chicago, IL 60604, (312) 922-1115, Fax: (312) 922-1157, www.euromonitor.com; *International Marketing Data and Statistics 2008.*

Federal Statistical Office Germany, D-65180 Wiesbaden, Germany, www.destatis.de; *India 2006.*

International Labour Office, I.L.O. Publications, 4 route des Morillons, CH-1211 Geneva 22, Switzerland, (Telephone in U.S. (202) 653-7652), (Fax in U.S. (202) 653-7687), www.ilo.org; *Yearbook of Labour Statistics 2006.*

Palgrave Macmillan Ltd., Houndmills, Basingstoke, Hampshire, RG21 6XS, England, (Telephone in U.S. (888) 330-8477), (Fax in U.S. (800) 672-2054), www.palgrave.com; *The Statesman's Yearbook 2008.*

United Nations Statistics Division, New York, NY 10017, (800) 253-9646, Fax: (212) 963-4116, http://unstats.un.org; *Statistical Yearbook.*

INDIA - URANIUM PRODUCTION AND CONSUMPTION

See INDIA - MINERAL INDUSTRIES

INDIA - VITAL STATISTICS

Euromonitor International, Inc., 224 S. Michigan Avenue, Suite 1500, Chicago, IL 60604, (312) 922-1115, Fax: (312) 922-1157, www.euromonitor.com; *International Marketing Data and Statistics 2008.*

Palgrave Macmillan Ltd., Houndmills, Basingstoke, Hampshire, RG21 6XS, England, (Telephone in U.S. (888) 330-8477), (Fax in U.S. (800) 672-2054), www.palgrave.com; *The Statesman's Yearbook 2008.*

United Nations Statistics Division, New York, NY 10017, (800) 253-9646, Fax: (212) 963-4116, http://unstats.un.org; *Statistical Yearbook.*

World Health Organization (WHO), Avenue Appia 20, 1211 Geneve 27, Switzerland, (Telephone in U.S. (212) 331-9081), www.who.int; *World Health Report 2006.*

INDIA - WAGES

Federal Statistical Office Germany, D-65180 Wiesbaden, Germany, www.destatis.de; *India 2006.*

International Labour Office, I.L.O. Publications, 4 route des Morillons, CH-1211 Geneva 22, Switzerland, (Telephone in U.S. (202) 653-7652), (Fax in U.S. (202) 653-7687), www.ilo.org; *Yearbook of Labour Statistics 2006.*

United Nations Statistics Division, New York, NY 10017, (800) 253-9646, Fax: (212) 963-4116, http://unstats.un.org; *Statistical Yearbook.*

The World Bank, 1818 H Street, NW, Washington, DC 20433, (202) 473-1000, Fax: (202) 477-6391, www.worldbank.org; *India.*

INDIA - WALNUT PRODUCTION

See INDIA - CROPS

INDIA - WELFARE STATE

International Monetary Fund (IMF), 700 Nineteenth Street, NW, Washington, DC 20431, (202) 623-7000, Fax: (202) 623-4661, www.imf.org; *Government Finance Statistics Yearbook (2008 Edition).*

Palgrave Macmillan Ltd., Houndmills, Basingstoke, Hampshire, RG21 6XS, England, (Telephone in U.S. (888) 330-8477), (Fax in U.S. (800) 672-2054), www.palgrave.com; *The Statesman's Yearbook 2008.*

INDIA - WHEAT PRODUCTION

See INDIA - CROPS

INDIA - WHOLESALE PRICE INDEXES

International Monetary Fund (IMF), 700 Nineteenth Street, NW, Washington, DC 20431, (202) 623-7000, Fax: (202) 623-4661, www.imf.org; *International Financial Statistics Yearbook 2007.*

United Nations Statistics Division, New York, NY 10017, (800) 253-9646, Fax: (212) 963-4116, http://unstats.un.org; *Statistical Yearbook.*

INDIA - WOOD AND WOOD PULP

See INDIA - FORESTS AND FORESTRY

INDIA - WOOL PRODUCTION

See INDIA - TEXTILE INDUSTRY

INDIA - YARN PRODUCTION

See INDIA - TEXTILE INDUSTRY

INDIA - ZINC AND ZINC ORE

See INDIA - MINERAL INDUSTRIES

INDIAN-ASIAN POPULATION

Casey Family Programs, 1300 Dexter Avenue North, Floor 3, Seattle, WA 98109-3542, (206) 282-7300, Fax: (206) 282-3555, www.casey.org; *The Indian Child Welfare Act: An Examination of State Compliance in Arizona; Native American Children and Youth Well-Being Indicators: A Strengths Perspective;* and *Native American Kids 2002: Indian Children's Well-Being Indicators Data Book for 13 States.*

U.S. Census Bureau, 4700 Silver Hill Road, Washington DC 20233-0001, (301) 763-3030, www.census.gov; unpublished data.

U.S. Census Bureau, Housing and Household Economics Statistics Division, 4700 Silver Hill Road, Washington DC 20233-0001, (301) 763-3030, www.census.gov/hhes/www; Decennial Census of Population and Housing (web app).

U.S. Census Bureau, Population Division, 4700 Silver Hill Road, Washington DC 20233-0001, (301) 763-3030, www.census.gov/population/www/; *Current Population Reports.*

INDIANA

See also - STATE DATA (FOR INDIVIDUAL STATES)

INDIANA - STATE DATA CENTERS

Indiana Business Research Center (IBRC) Bloomington, Kelley School of Business, William J. Godfrey Graduate and Executive Education Center, Suite 3110, 1275 East Tenth Street, Bloomington, IN 47405, (812) 855-5507, Fax: (812) 855-7763, www.ibrc.indiana.edu; State Data Center.

Indiana Business Research Center (IBRC) Indianapolis, Kelley School of Business, IUPUI Campus, 777 Indiana Avenue, Suite 210, Indianapolis, IN 46202, (317) 274-2979, Fax: (317) 278-8400, www.ibrc.indiana.edu; State Data Center.

Indiana Economic Development Corporation (IEDC), 1 North Capitol, Suite 700, Indianapolis, IN 46204, (317) 232-8800, Fax: (317) 232-4146, www.indianacommerce.com; State Data Center.

Indiana State Data Center, Indiana State Library, 140 North Senate Avenue, Indianapolis, IN 46204-2296, (317) 232-3675, www.statelib.lib.in.us/WWW/isl/whoweare/datacenter.html; State Data Center.

INDIANA - PRIMARY STATISTICS SOURCES

Indiana Business Research Center (IBRC) Indianapolis, Kelley School of Business, IUPUI Campus,

777 Indiana Avenue, Suite 210, Indianapolis, IN 46202, (317) 274-2979, Fax: (317) 278-8400, www.ibrc.indiana.edu; *Stats Indiana.*

INDIANS OF NORTH AMERICA

Indian Health Service (IHS), U.S. Department of Health and Human Services, The Reyes Building, 801 Thompson Avenue, Suite 400, Rockville, MD 20852-1627, (301) 443-1180, www.ihs.gov; *Indian Health Focus - Women.*

National Indian Child Welfare Association (NICWA), 5100 SW Macadam Avenue, Suite 300, Portland, Oregon 97239, (503) 222-4044, www.nicwa.org; unpublished data.

INDIANS OF NORTH AMERICA - CHILDREN UNDER EIGHTEEN YEARS OLD

Casey Family Programs, 1300 Dexter Avenue North, Floor 3, Seattle, WA 98109-3542, (206) 282-7300, Fax: (206) 282-3555, www.casey.org; *The Indian Child Welfare Act: An Examination of State Compliance in Arizona; Native American Children and Youth Well-Being Indicators: A Strengths Perspective;* and *Native American Kids 2002: Indian Children's Well-Being Indicators Data Book for 13 States.*

Indian Health Service (IHS), U.S. Department of Health and Human Services, The Reyes Building, 801 Thompson Avenue, Suite 400, Rockville, MD 20852-1627, (301) 443-1180, www.ihs.gov; *Indian Health Focus - Youth.*

INDIANS OF NORTH AMERICA - CRIMINAL STATISTICS

U.S. Department of Justice (DOJ), Bureau of Justice Statistics, 810 Seventh Street, NW, Washington, DC 20531, (202) 307-0765, www.ojp.usdoj.gov/bjs/; *American Indians and Crime: A BJS Statistical Profile, 1992-2002.*

INDIANS OF NORTH AMERICA - CRIMINAL VICTIMIZATION

Robert Wood Johnson Foundation, PO Box 2316, College Road East and Route 1, Princeton, NJ 08543, (877) 843-7953, www.rwjf.org; *Race Ethnicity, and the Education Gradient in Health.*

U.S. Department of Justice (DOJ), Bureau of Justice Statistics, 810 Seventh Street, NW, Washington, DC 20531, (202) 307-0765, www.ojp.usdoj.gov/bjs/; *American Indians and Crime: A BJS Statistical Profile, 1992-2002.*

INDIANS OF NORTH AMERICA - HEALTH CARE VISITS TO PROFESSIONALS

British Columbia Vital Statistics Agency, PO Box 9657 STN PROV GOVT, Victoria BC V8W 9P3, Canada, (Dial from U.S. (250) 952-2681), (Fax from U.S. (250) 952-2527), www.vs.gov.bc.ca; *Regional Analysis of Health Statistics for Status Indians in British Columbia, 1992-2002.*

Indian Health Service (IHS), U.S. Department of Health and Human Services, The Reyes Building, 801 Thompson Avenue, Suite 400, Rockville, MD 20852-1627, (301) 443-1180, www.ihs.gov; *Annual Federal Year 2001 IHS and Tribal Hospital Inpatient Statistics and Comparison with Federal Year 2000; Indian Health Focus - Women; Regional Differences in Indian Health 2000-2001;* and *Trends in Indian Health 2000-2001.*

Robert Wood Johnson Foundation, PO Box 2316, College Road East and Route 1, Princeton, NJ 08543, (877) 843-7953, www.rwjf.org; *Race Ethnicity, and the Education Gradient in Health* and *Reducing Racial and Ethnic Disparities and Improving Quality of Health Care.*

INDIANS OF NORTH AMERICA - HEALTH INSURANCE COVERAGE

British Columbia Vital Statistics Agency, PO Box 9657 STN PROV GOVT, Victoria BC V8W 9P3, Canada, (Dial from U.S. (250) 952-2681), (Fax from U.S. (250) 952-2527), www.vs.gov.bc.ca; *Regional Analysis of Health Statistics for Status Indians in British Columbia, 1992-2002.*

INDIANS OF NORTH AMERICA - HOSPITAL UTILIZATION

British Columbia Vital Statistics Agency, PO Box 9657 STN PROV GOVT, Victoria BC V8W 9P3, Canada, (Dial from U.S. (250) 952-2681), (Fax from U.S. (250) 952-2527), www.vs.gov.bc.ca; *Regional Analysis of Health Statistics for Status Indians in British Columbia, 1992-2002.*

Indian Health Service (IHS), U.S. Department of Health and Human Services, The Reyes Building, 801 Thompson Avenue, Suite 400, Rockville, MD 20852-1627, (301) 443-1180, www.ihs.gov; *Annual Federal Year 2001 IHS and Tribal Hospital Inpatient Statistics and Comparison with Federal Year 2000.*

INDIANS OF NORTH AMERICA - MEDICAL CARE

British Columbia Vital Statistics Agency, PO Box 9657 STN PROV GOVT, Victoria BC V8W 9P3, Canada, (Dial from U.S. (250) 952-2681), (Fax from U.S. (250) 952-2527), www.vs.gov.bc.ca; *Regional Analysis of Health Statistics for Status Indians in British Columbia, 1992-2002.*

Indian Health Service (IHS), U.S. Department of Health and Human Services, The Reyes Building, 801 Thompson Avenue, Suite 400, Rockville, MD 20852-1627, (301) 443-1180, www.ihs.gov; *Annual Federal Year 2001 IHS and Tribal Hospital Inpatient Statistics and Comparison with Federal Year 2000; Indian Health Focus - Injuries; Regional Differences in Indian Health 2000-2001;* and *Trends in Indian Health 2000-2001.*

Robert Wood Johnson Foundation, PO Box 2316, College Road East and Route 1, Princeton, NJ 08543, (877) 843-7953, www.rwjf.org; *Race Ethnicity, and the Education Gradient in Health* and *Reducing Racial and Ethnic Disparities and Improving Quality of Health Care.*

INDIANS OF NORTH AMERICA - OLDER PEOPLE

Indian Health Service (IHS), U.S. Department of Health and Human Services, The Reyes Building, 801 Thompson Avenue, Suite 400, Rockville, MD 20852-1627, (301) 443-1180, www.ihs.gov; *Indian Health Focus - Elders.*

INDIANS OF NORTH AMERICA - SCHOOLS AND EDUCATION - ATTAINMENT

Robert Wood Johnson Foundation, PO Box 2316, College Road East and Route 1, Princeton, NJ 08543, (877) 843-7953, www.rwjf.org; *Race Ethnicity, and the Education Gradient in Health.*

INDIUM

U.S. Department of the Interior (DOI), U.S. Geological Survey (USGS), Office of Minerals Information, 12201 Sunrise Valley Drive, Reston, VA 20192, Mr. Kenneth A. Beckman, (703) 648-4916, Fax: (703) 648-4995, http://minerals.usgs.gov/minerals; *Mineral Commodity Summaries.*

INDIVIDUAL RETIREMENT ACCOUNTS (IRA'S)

Investment Company Institute (ICI), 1401 H Street, NW, Suite 1200, Washington, DC 20005-2040, (202) 326-5800, www.ici.org; *Equity Ownership in America, 2005; IRA Ownership in 2004;* and *Profile of Mutual Fund Shareholders.*

INDONESIA - NATIONAL STATISTICAL OFFICE

Statistics Indonesia (Badan Pusat Statistik (BPS)), Jl. Dr. Sutomo 6-8, Jakarta 10710, Indonesia, www.bps.go.id; National Data Center.

INDONESIA - PRIMARY STATISTICS SOURCES

Statistics Indonesia (Badan Pusat Statistik (BPS)), Jl. Dr. Sutomo 6-8, Jakarta 10710, Indonesia, www.bps.go.id; *Statistical Yearbook of Indonesia 2007.*

INDONESIA - AGRICULTURAL MACHINERY

United Nations Statistics Division, New York, NY 10017, (800) 253-9646, Fax: (212) 963-4116, http://unstats.un.org; *Statistical Yearbook.*

INDONESIA - AGRICULTURE

Asian Development Bank (ADB), PO Box 789, 0980 Manila, Philippines, www.adb.org; *Key Indicators of Developing Asian and Pacific Countries 2006.*

Economist Intelligence Unit, 111 West 57th Street, New York, NY 10019, (212) 554-0600, Fax: (212) 586-1181, www.eiu.com; *Indonesia Country Report.*

Euromonitor International, Inc., 224 S. Michigan Avenue, Suite 1500, Chicago, IL 60604, (312) 922-1115, Fax: (312) 922-1157, www.euromonitor.com; *International Marketing Data and Statistics 2008* and *World Marketing Data and Statistics.*

M.E. Sharpe, 80 Business Park Drive, Armonk, NY 10504, (800) 541-6563, Fax: (914) 273-2106, www.mesharpe.com; *The Illustrated Book of World Rankings.*

Palgrave Macmillan Ltd., Houndmills, Basingstoke, Hampshire, RG21 6XS, England, (Telephone in U.S. (888) 330-8477), (Fax in U.S. (800) 672-2054), www.palgrave.com; *The Statesman's Yearbook 2008.*

Taylor and Francis Group, An Informa Business, 2 Park Square, Milton Park, Abingdon, Oxford OX14 4RN, United Kingdom, (Dial from U.S. (212) 216-7800), (Fax from U.S. (212) 564-7854), www.tandf.co.uk; *The Europa World Year Book.*

United Nations Conference on Trade and Development (UNCTAD), DC2-1120, United Nations, New York, NY 10017, (212) 963-0027, www.unctad.org; *UNCTAD Commodity Yearbook.*

United Nations Food and Agricultural Organization (FAO), Viale delle Terme di Caracalla, 00100 Rome, Italy, (Dial from U.S. (202) 653-2400), (Fax from U.S. (202) 653 5760), www.fao.org; AQUASTAT; *FAO Production Yearbook 2002;* and *The State of Food and Agriculture (SOFA) 2006.*

United Nations Statistics Division, New York, NY 10017, (800) 253-9646, Fax: (212) 963-4116, http://unstats.un.org; *Asia-Pacific in Figures 2004; Statistical Yearbook;* and *Statistical Yearbook for Asia and the Pacific 2004.*

The World Bank, 1818 H Street, NW, Washington, DC 20433, (202) 473-1000, Fax: (202) 477-6391, www.worldbank.org; *India; Indonesia;* and *World Development Report 2008.*

INDONESIA - AIRLINES

Economist Intelligence Unit, 111 West 57th Street, New York, NY 10019, (212) 554-0600, Fax: (212) 586-1181, www.eiu.com; *Business Asia.*

M.E. Sharpe, 80 Business Park Drive, Armonk, NY 10504, (800) 541-6563, Fax: (914) 273-2106, www.mesharpe.com; *The Illustrated Book of World Rankings.*

Palgrave Macmillan Ltd., Houndmills, Basingstoke, Hampshire, RG21 6XS, England, (Telephone in U.S.

(888) 330-8477), (Fax in U.S. (800) 672-2054), www.palgrave.com; *The Statesman's Yearbook 2008.*

Taylor and Francis Group, An Informa Business, 2 Park Square, Milton Park, Abingdon, Oxford OX14 4RN, United Kingdom, (Dial from U.S. (212) 216-7800), (Fax from U.S. (212) 564-7854), www.tandf.co.uk; *The Europa World Year Book.*

United Nations Statistics Division, New York, NY 10017, (800) 253-9646, Fax: (212) 963-4116, http://unstats.un.org; *Statistical Yearbook.*

INDONESIA - AIRPORTS

Central Intelligence Agency, Office of Public Affairs, Washington, DC 20505, (703) 482-0623, Fax: (703) 482-1739, www.cia.gov; *The World Factbook.*

INDONESIA - ALUMINUM PRODUCTION

See INDONESIA - MINERAL INDUSTRIES

INDONESIA - ARMED FORCES

Central Intelligence Agency, Office of Public Affairs, Washington, DC 20505, (703) 482-0623, Fax: (703) 482-1739, www.cia.gov; *The World Factbook.*

Economist Intelligence Unit, 111 West 57th Street, New York, NY 10019, (212) 554-0600, Fax: (212) 586-1181, www.eiu.com; *Business Asia.*

Euromonitor International, Inc., 224 S. Michigan Avenue, Suite 1500, Chicago, IL 60604, (312) 922-1115, Fax: (312) 922-1157, www.euromonitor.com; *World Marketing Data and Statistics.*

International Institute for Strategic Studies (IISS), Arundel House, 13-15 Arundel Street, Temple Place, London WC2R 3DX, England, www.iiss.org; *The Military Balance 2007.*

Palgrave Macmillan Ltd., Houndmills, Basingstoke, Hampshire, RG21 6XS, England, (Telephone in U.S. (888) 330-8477), (Fax in U.S. (800) 672-2054), www.palgrave.com; *The Statesman's Yearbook 2008.*

U.S. Department of State (DOS), 2201 C Street NW, Washington, DC 20520, (202) 647-4000, www.state.gov; *World Military Expenditures and Arms Transfers (WMEAT).*

United Nations Statistics Division, New York, NY 10017, (800) 253-9646, Fax: (212) 963-4116, http://unstats.un.org; *Human Development Report 2006.*

INDONESIA - AUTOMOBILE INDUSTRY AND TRADE

United Nations Statistics Division, New York, NY 10017, (800) 253-9646, Fax: (212) 963-4116, http://unstats.un.org; *Statistical Yearbook.*

INDONESIA - BALANCE OF PAYMENTS

International Monetary Fund (IMF), 700 Nineteenth Street, NW, Washington, DC 20431, (202) 623-7000, Fax: (202) 623-4661, www.imf.org; *Balance of Payments Statistics Newsletter; Balance of Payments Statistics Yearbook 2007;* and *International Financial Statistics Yearbook 2007.*

Taylor and Francis Group, An Informa Business, 2 Park Square, Milton Park, Abingdon, Oxford OX14 4RN, United Kingdom, (Dial from U.S. (212) 216-7800), (Fax from U.S. (212) 564-7854), www.tandf.co.uk; *The Europa World Year Book.*

United Nations Conference on Trade and Development (UNCTAD), DC2-1120, United Nations, New York, NY 10017, (212) 963-0027, www.unctad.org; *Handbook of Statistics 2005.*

The World Bank, 1818 H Street, NW, Washington, DC 20433, (202) 473-1000, Fax: (202) 477-6391, www.worldbank.org; *India; Indonesia;* and *World Development Report 2008.*

INDONESIA - BANKS AND BANKING

Asian Development Bank (ADB), PO Box 789, 0980 Manila, Philippines, www.adb.org; *Key Indicators of Developing Asian and Pacific Countries 2006.*

Euromonitor International, Inc., 224 S. Michigan Avenue, Suite 1500, Chicago, IL 60604, (312) 922-1115, Fax: (312) 922-1157, www.euromonitor.com; *World Marketing Data and Statistics.*

International Monetary Fund (IMF), 700 Nineteenth Street, NW, Washington, DC 20431, (202) 623-7000, Fax: (202) 623-4661, www.imf.org; *International Financial Statistics Yearbook 2007.*

M.E. Sharpe, 80 Business Park Drive, Armonk, NY 10504, (800) 541-6563, Fax: (914) 273-2106, www.mesharpe.com; *The Illustrated Book of World Rankings.*

Palgrave Macmillan Ltd., Houndmills, Basingstoke, Hampshire, RG21 6XS, England, (Telephone in U.S. (888) 330-8477), (Fax in U.S. (800) 672-2054), www.palgrave.com; *The Statesman's Yearbook 2008.*

Taylor and Francis Group, An Informa Business, 2 Park Square, Milton Park, Abingdon, Oxford OX14 4RN, United Kingdom, (Dial from U.S. (212) 216-7800), (Fax from U.S. (212) 564-7854), www.tandf.co.uk; *The Europa World Year Book.*

INDONESIA - BARLEY PRODUCTION

See INDONESIA - CROPS

INDONESIA - BEVERAGE INDUSTRY

M.E. Sharpe, 80 Business Park Drive, Armonk, NY 10504, (800) 541-6563, Fax: (914) 273-2106, www.mesharpe.com; *The Illustrated Book of World Rankings.*

United Nations Statistics Division, New York, NY 10017, (800) 253-9646, Fax: (212) 963-4116, http://unstats.un.org; *Statistical Yearbook.*

INDONESIA - BONDS

Asian Development Bank (ADB), PO Box 789, 0980 Manila, Philippines, www.adb.org; *Key Indicators of Developing Asian and Pacific Countries 2006.*

INDONESIA - BROADCASTING

Central Intelligence Agency, Office of Public Affairs, Washington, DC 20505, (703) 482-0623, Fax: (703) 482-1739, www.cia.gov; *The World Factbook.*

Economist Intelligence Unit, 111 West 57th Street, New York, NY 10019, (212) 554-0600, Fax: (212) 586-1181, www.eiu.com; *Business Asia.*

Euromonitor International, Inc., 224 S. Michigan Avenue, Suite 1500, Chicago, IL 60604, (312) 922-1115, Fax: (312) 922-1157, www.euromonitor.com; *World Marketing Data and Statistics.*

M.E. Sharpe, 80 Business Park Drive, Armonk, NY 10504, (800) 541-6563, Fax: (914) 273-2106, www.mesharpe.com; *The Illustrated Book of World Rankings.*

Palgrave Macmillan Ltd., Houndmills, Basingstoke, Hampshire, RG21 6XS, England, (Telephone in U.S. (888) 330-8477), (Fax in U.S. (800) 672-2054), www.palgrave.com; *The Statesman's Yearbook 2008.*

UNESCO Institute for Statistics, C.P. 6128 Succursale Centre-Ville, Montreal, Quebec, H3C 3J7 Canada, (Dial from U.S. (514) 343-6880), (Fax from U.S. (514) 343 6882), www.uis.unesco.org; *Statistical Tables.*

WRTH Publications Limited, PO Box 290, Oxford OX2 7FT, UK, www.wrth.com; *World Radio TV Handbook 2007.*

INDONESIA - BUDGET

Central Intelligence Agency, Office of Public Affairs, Washington, DC 20505, (703) 482-0623, Fax: (703) 482-1739, www.cia.gov; *The World Factbook.*

INDONESIA - BUSINESS

United Nations Statistics Division, New York, NY 10017, (800) 253-9646, Fax: (212) 963-4116, http://unstats.un.org; *Statistical Yearbook for Asia and the Pacific 2004.*

INDONESIA - CAPITAL INVESTMENTS

Asian Development Bank (ADB), PO Box 789, 0980 Manila, Philippines, www.adb.org; *Key Indicators of Developing Asian and Pacific Countries 2006.*

INDONESIA - CAPITAL LEVY

Asian Development Bank (ADB), PO Box 789, 0980 Manila, Philippines, www.adb.org; *Key Indicators of Developing Asian and Pacific Countries 2006.*

International Monetary Fund (IMF), 700 Nineteenth Street, NW, Washington, DC 20431, (202) 623-7000, Fax: (202) 623-4661, www.imf.org; *Government Finance Statistics Yearbook (2008 Edition).*

INDONESIA - CATTLE

See INDONESIA - LIVESTOCK

INDONESIA - CHICKENS

See INDONESIA - LIVESTOCK

INDONESIA - CHILDBIRTH - STATISTICS

Central Intelligence Agency, Office of Public Affairs, Washington, DC 20505, (703) 482-0623, Fax: (703) 482-1739, www.cia.gov; *The World Factbook.*

Economist Intelligence Unit, 111 West 57th Street, New York, NY 10019, (212) 554-0600, Fax: (212) 586-1181, www.eiu.com; *Business Asia.*

Euromonitor International, Inc., 224 S. Michigan Avenue, Suite 1500, Chicago, IL 60604, (312) 922-1115, Fax: (312) 922-1157, www.euromonitor.com; *International Marketing Data and Statistics 2008* and *The World Economic Factbook 2008.*

M.E. Sharpe, 80 Business Park Drive, Armonk, NY 10504, (800) 541-6563, Fax: (914) 273-2106, www.mesharpe.com; *The Illustrated Book of World Rankings.*

Palgrave Macmillan Ltd., Houndmills, Basingstoke, Hampshire, RG21 6XS, England, (Telephone in U.S. (888) 330-8477), (Fax in U.S. (800) 672-2054), www.palgrave.com; *The Statesman's Yearbook 2008.*

Statistics Indonesia (Badan Pusat Statistik (BPS)), Jl. Dr. Sutomo 6-8, Jakarta 10710, Indonesia, www.bps.go.id; *Statistical Profile of Women, Mothers and Children in Indonesia.*

Taylor and Francis Group, An Informa Business, 2 Park Square, Milton Park, Abingdon, Oxford OX14 4RN, United Kingdom, (Dial from U.S. (212) 216-7800), (Fax from U.S. (212) 564-7854), www.tandf.co.uk; *The Europa World Year Book.*

United Nations Statistics Division, New York, NY 10017, (800) 253-9646, Fax: (212) 963-4116, http://unstats.un.org; *Asia-Pacific in Figures 2004; Demographic Yearbook;* and *Statistical Yearbook.*

The World Bank, 1818 H Street, NW, Washington, DC 20433, (202) 473-1000, Fax: (202) 477-6391, www.worldbank.org; *World Development Report 2008.*

INDONESIA - CLIMATE

International Institute for Environment and Development (IIED), 3 Endsleigh Street, London, England, WC1H 0DD, United Kingdom, www.iied.org; *Environment Urbanization.*

M.E. Sharpe, 80 Business Park Drive, Armonk, NY 10504, (800) 541-6563, Fax: (914) 273-2106, www.mesharpe.com; *The Illustrated Book of World Rankings.*

Palgrave Macmillan Ltd., Houndmills, Basingstoke, Hampshire, RG21 6XS, England, (Telephone in U.S. (888) 330-8477), (Fax in U.S. (800) 672-2054), www.palgrave.com; *The Statesman's Yearbook 2008.*

Statistics Indonesia (Badan Pusat Statistik (BPS)), Jl. Dr. Sutomo 6-8, Jakarta 10710, Indonesia, www.bps.go.id; *Environmental Statistical of Indonesia 2005.*

INDONESIA - COAL PRODUCTION

See INDONESIA - MINERAL INDUSTRIES

INDONESIA - COCOA PRODUCTION

See INDONESIA - CROPS

INDONESIA - COFFEE

See INDONESIA - CROPS

INDONESIA - COMMERCE

Palgrave Macmillan Ltd., Houndmills, Basingstoke, Hampshire, RG21 6XS, England, (Telephone in U.S. (888) 330-8477), (Fax in U.S. (800) 672-2054), www.palgrave.com; *The Statesman's Yearbook 2008.*

INDONESIA - COMMODITY EXCHANGES

Commodity Research Bureau, 330 South Wells Street, Suite 612, Chicago, IL 60606-7110, (800) 621-5271, Fax: (312) 939-4135, www.crbtrader.com; *2006 CRB Commodity Yearbook and CD.*

International Monetary Fund (IMF), 700 Nineteenth Street, NW, Washington, DC 20431, (202) 623-7000, Fax: (202) 623-4661, www.imf.org; *IMF Primary Commodity Prices.*

United Nations Food and Agricultural Organization (FAO), Viale delle Terme di Caracalla, 00100 Rome, Italy, (Dial from U.S. (202) 653-2400), (Fax from U.S. (202) 653 5760), www.fao.org; *The State of Food and Agriculture (SOFA) 2006.*

INDONESIA - COMMUNICATION AND TRAFFIC

United Nations Statistics Division, New York, NY 10017, (800) 253-9646, Fax: (212) 963-4116, http://unstats.un.org; *Statistical Yearbook.*

INDONESIA - CONSTRUCTION INDUSTRY

M.E. Sharpe, 80 Business Park Drive, Armonk, NY 10504, (800) 541-6563, Fax: (914) 273-2106, www.mesharpe.com; *The Illustrated Book of World Rankings.*

Palgrave Macmillan Ltd., Houndmills, Basingstoke, Hampshire, RG21 6XS, England, (Telephone in U.S. (888) 330-8477), (Fax in U.S. (800) 672-2054), www.palgrave.com; *The Statesman's Yearbook 2008.*

United Nations Statistics Division, New York, NY 10017, (800) 253-9646, Fax: (212) 963-4116, http://unstats.un.org; *Statistical Yearbook.*

INDONESIA - CONSUMER PRICE INDEXES

Asian Development Bank (ADB), PO Box 789, 0980 Manila, Philippines, www.adb.org; *Key Indicators of Developing Asian and Pacific Countries 2006.*

Taylor and Francis Group, An Informa Business, 2 Park Square, Milton Park, Abingdon, Oxford OX14 4RN, United Kingdom, (Dial from U.S. (212) 216-7800), (Fax from U.S. (212) 564-7854), www.tandf.co.uk; *The Europa World Year Book.*

United Nations Statistics Division, New York, NY 10017, (800) 253-9646, Fax: (212) 963-4116, http://unstats.un.org; *Statistical Yearbook.*

The World Bank, 1818 H Street, NW, Washington, DC 20433, (202) 473-1000, Fax: (202) 477-6391, www.worldbank.org; *Indonesia.*

INDONESIA - CONSUMPTION (ECONOMICS)

The World Bank, 1818 H Street, NW, Washington, DC 20433, (202) 473-1000, Fax: (202) 477-6391, www.worldbank.org; *World Development Report 2008.*

INDONESIA - COPPER INDUSTRY AND TRADE

See INDONESIA - MINERAL INDUSTRIES

INDONESIA - CORN INDUSTRY

See INDONESIA - CROPS

INDONESIA - COTTON

See INDONESIA - CROPS

INDONESIA - CRIME

International Criminal Police Organization (INTERPOL), General Secretariat, 200 quai Charles de Gaulle, 69006 Lyon, France, www.interpol.int; *International Crime Statistics.*

Yale University Press, PO Box 209040, New Haven, CT 06520-9040, (203) 432-0960, Fax: (203) 432-0948, http://yalepress.yale.edu/yupbooks; *Violence and Crime in Cross-National Perspective.*

INDONESIA - CROPS

Asian Development Bank (ADB), PO Box 789, 0980 Manila, Philippines, www.adb.org; *Key Indicators of Developing Asian and Pacific Countries 2006.*

M.E. Sharpe, 80 Business Park Drive, Armonk, NY 10504, (800) 541-6563, Fax: (914) 273-2106, www.mesharpe.com; *The Illustrated Book of World Rankings.*

Palgrave Macmillan Ltd., Houndmills, Basingstoke, Hampshire, RG21 6XS, England, (Telephone in U.S. (888) 330-8477), (Fax in U.S. (800) 672-2054), www.palgrave.com; *The Statesman's Yearbook 2008.*

Taylor and Francis Group, An Informa Business, 2 Park Square, Milton Park, Abingdon, Oxford OX14 4RN, United Kingdom, (Dial from U.S. (212) 216-7800), (Fax from U.S. (212) 564-7854), www.tandf.co.uk; *The Europa World Year Book.*

United Nations Conference on Trade and Development (UNCTAD), DC2-1120, United Nations, New York, NY 10017, (212) 963-0027, www.unctad.org; *UNCTAD Commodity Yearbook.*

United Nations Food and Agricultural Organization (FAO), Viale delle Terme di Caracalla, 00100 Rome, Italy, (Dial from U.S. (202) 653-2400), (Fax from U.S. (202) 653 5760), www.fao.org; *FAO Production Yearbook 2002* and *The State of Food and Agriculture (SOFA) 2006.*

United Nations Statistics Division, New York, NY 10017, (800) 253-9646, Fax: (212) 963-4116, http://unstats.un.org; *Statistical Yearbook.*

INDONESIA - CUSTOMS ADMINISTRATION

International Monetary Fund (IMF), 700 Nineteenth Street, NW, Washington, DC 20431, (202) 623-7000, Fax: (202) 623-4661, www.imf.org; *Government Finance Statistics Yearbook (2008 Edition).*

Palgrave Macmillan Ltd., Houndmills, Basingstoke, Hampshire, RG21 6XS, England, (Telephone in U.S. (888) 330-8477), (Fax in U.S. (800) 672-2054), www.palgrave.com; *The Statesman's Yearbook 2008.*

INDONESIA - DAIRY PROCESSING

M.E. Sharpe, 80 Business Park Drive, Armonk, NY 10504, (800) 541-6563, Fax: (914) 273-2106, www.mesharpe.com; *The Illustrated Book of World Rankings.*

Palgrave Macmillan Ltd., Houndmills, Basingstoke, Hampshire, RG21 6XS, England, (Telephone in U.S. (888) 330-8477), (Fax in U.S. (800) 672-2054), www.palgrave.com; *The Statesman's Yearbook 2008.*

Taylor and Francis Group, An Informa Business, 2 Park Square, Milton Park, Abingdon, Oxford OX14 4RN, United Kingdom, (Dial from U.S. (212) 216-7800), (Fax from U.S. (212) 564-7854), www.tandf.co.uk; *The Europa World Year Book.*

United Nations Food and Agricultural Organization (FAO), Viale delle Terme di Caracalla, 00100 Rome, Italy, (Dial from U.S. (202) 653-2400), (Fax from U.S. (202) 653 5760), www.fao.org; *FAO Production Yearbook 2002* and *The State of Food and Agriculture (SOFA) 2006.*

United Nations Statistics Division, New York, NY 10017, (800) 253-9646, Fax: (212) 963-4116, http://unstats.un.org; *Statistical Yearbook.*

INDONESIA - DEATH RATES

See INDONESIA - MORTALITY

INDONESIA - DEBTS, EXTERNAL

Asian Development Bank (ADB), PO Box 789, 0980 Manila, Philippines, www.adb.org; *Key Indicators of Developing Asian and Pacific Countries 2006.*

International Monetary Fund (IMF), 700 Nineteenth Street, NW, Washington, DC 20431, (202) 623-7000, Fax: (202) 623-4661, www.imf.org; *Government Finance Statistics Yearbook (2008 Edition).*

The World Bank, 1818 H Street, NW, Washington, DC 20433, (202) 473-1000, Fax: (202) 477-6391, www.worldbank.org; *Global Development Finance 2007* and *World Development Report 2008.*

Worldinformation.com, 2 Market Street, Saffron Walden, Essex CB10 1HZ, United Kingdom, www.worldinformation.com; The World of Information (www.worldinformation.com).

INDONESIA - DEFENSE EXPENDITURES

See INDONESIA - ARMED FORCES

INDONESIA - DEMOGRAPHY

Economist Intelligence Unit, 111 West 57th Street, New York, NY 10019, (212) 554-0600, Fax: (212) 586-1181, www.eiu.com; *Business Asia.*

Euromonitor International, Inc., 224 S. Michigan Avenue, Suite 1500, Chicago, IL 60604, (312) 922-1115, Fax: (312) 922-1157, www.euromonitor.com; *International Marketing Data and Statistics 2008; The World Economic Factbook 2008;* and *World Marketing Data and Statistics.*

M.E. Sharpe, 80 Business Park Drive, Armonk, NY 10504, (800) 541-6563, Fax: (914) 273-2106, www.mesharpe.com; *The Illustrated Book of World Rankings.*

Statistics Indonesia (Badan Pusat Statistik (BPS)), Jl. Dr. Sutomo 6-8, Jakarta 10710, Indonesia, www.bps.go.id; *Statistical Profile of Women, Mothers and Children in Indonesia.*

United Nations Statistics Division, New York, NY 10017, (800) 253-9646, Fax: (212) 963-4116, http://unstats.un.org; *Asia-Pacific in Figures 2004* and *Human Development Report 2006.*

The World Bank, 1818 H Street, NW, Washington, DC 20433, (202) 473-1000, Fax: (202) 477-6391, www.worldbank.org; *India* and *Indonesia.*

INDONESIA - DIAMONDS

See INDONESIA - MINERAL INDUSTRIES

INDONESIA - DISPOSABLE INCOME

M.E. Sharpe, 80 Business Park Drive, Armonk, NY 10504, (800) 541-6563, Fax: (914) 273-2106, www.mesharpe.com; *The Illustrated Book of World Rankings.*

United Nations Statistics Division, New York, NY 10017, (800) 253-9646, Fax: (212) 963-4116, http://unstats.un.org; *National Accounts Statistics: Compendium of Income Distribution Statistics* and *Statistical Yearbook.*

INDONESIA - DIVORCE

M.E. Sharpe, 80 Business Park Drive, Armonk, NY 10504, (800) 541-6563, Fax: (914) 273-2106, www.mesharpe.com; *The Illustrated Book of World Rankings.*

United Nations Statistics Division, New York, NY 10017, (800) 253-9646, Fax: (212) 963-4116, http://unstats.un.org; *Demographic Yearbook.*

INDONESIA - ECONOMIC ASSISTANCE

Asian Development Bank (ADB), PO Box 789, 0980 Manila, Philippines, www.adb.org; *Key Indicators of Developing Asian and Pacific Countries 2006.*

United Nations Statistics Division, New York, NY 10017, (800) 253-9646, Fax: (212) 963-4116, http://unstats.un.org; *Statistical Yearbook.*

INDONESIA - ECONOMIC CONDITIONS

Asian Development Bank (ADB), PO Box 789, 0980 Manila, Philippines, www.adb.org; *Key Indicators of Developing Asian and Pacific Countries 2006.*

Center for International Business Education Research (CIBER), Columbia Business School and School of International and Public Affairs, Uris Hall, Room 212, 3022 Broadway, New York, NY 10027-

6902, Mr. Joshua Safier, (212) 854-4750, Fax: (212) 222-9821, www.columbia.edu/cu/ciber/; Datastream International.

Central Intelligence Agency, Office of Public Affairs, Washington, DC 20505, (703) 482-0623, Fax: (703) 482-1739, www.cia.gov; *The World Factbook.*

DSI Data Service Information, Xantener Strasse 51a, D-47495 Rheinberg, Germany, www.dsidata.com; *Campus Solution.*

Dun and Bradstreet (DB) Corporation, 103 JFK Parkway, Short Hills, NJ 07078, (973) 921-5500, www.dnb.com; *Country Report.*

Economist Intelligence Unit, 111 West 57th Street, New York, NY 10019, (212) 554-0600, Fax: (212) 586-1181, www.eiu.com; *Indonesia Country Report.*

Euromonitor International, Inc., 224 S. Michigan Avenue, Suite 1500, Chicago, IL 60604, (312) 922-1115, Fax: (312) 922-1157, www.euromonitor.com; *International Marketing Data and Statistics 2008; The World Economic Factbook 2008;* and *World Marketing Data and Statistics.*

International Monetary Fund (IMF), 700 Nineteenth Street, NW, Washington, DC 20431, (202) 623-7000, Fax: (202) 623-4661, www.imf.org; *World Economic Outlook Reports.*

International Organization for Migration (IOM), 17, Route des Morillons, CH-1211 Geneva 19, Switzerland, www.iom.int; *Migration, Development and Natural Disasters: Insights from the Indian Ocean Tsunami.*

M.E. Sharpe, 80 Business Park Drive, Armonk, NY 10504, (800) 541-6563, Fax: (914) 273-2106, www.mesharpe.com; *The Illustrated Book of World Rankings.*

Nomura Research Institute (NRI), 2 World Financial Center, Building B, 19th Fl., New York, NY 10281-1198, (212) 667-1670, www.nri.co.jp/english; *Asian Economic Outlook 2003-2004.*

Palgrave Macmillan Ltd., Houndmills, Basingstoke, Hampshire, RG21 6XS, England, (Telephone in U.S. (888) 330-8477), (Fax in U.S. (800) 672-2054), www.palgrave.com; *The Statesman's Yearbook 2008.*

Statistics Indonesia (Badan Pusat Statistik (BPS)), Jl. Dr. Sutomo 6-8, Jakarta 10710, Indonesia, www.bps.go.id; *Financial Statistics of State Enterprises and Local Corporate.*

Taylor and Francis Group, An Informa Business, 2 Park Square, Milton Park, Abingdon, Oxford OX14 4RN, United Kingdom, (Dial from U.S. (212) 216-7800), (Fax from U.S. (212) 564-7854), www.tandf.co.uk; *The Europa World Year Book.*

United Nations Statistics Division, New York, NY 10017, (800) 253-9646, Fax: (212) 963-4116, http://unstats.un.org; *World Statistics Pocketbook.*

The World Bank, 1818 H Street, NW, Washington, DC 20433, (202) 473-1000, Fax: (202) 477-6391, www.worldbank.org; *Global Economic Monitor (GEM); Global Economic Prospects 2008; India; Indonesia; The World Bank Atlas 2003-2004;* and *World Development Report 2008.*

INDONESIA - EDUCATION

Economist Intelligence Unit, 111 West 57th Street, New York, NY 10019, (212) 554-0600, Fax: (212) 586-1181, www.eiu.com; *Business Asia.*

Euromonitor International, Inc., 224 S. Michigan Avenue, Suite 1500, Chicago, IL 60604, (312) 922-1115, Fax: (312) 922-1157, www.euromonitor.com; *International Marketing Data and Statistics 2008* and *World Marketing Data and Statistics.*

M.E. Sharpe, 80 Business Park Drive, Armonk, NY 10504, (800) 541-6563, Fax: (914) 273-2106, www.mesharpe.com; *The Illustrated Book of World Rankings.*

Palgrave Macmillan Ltd., Houndmills, Basingstoke, Hampshire, RG21 6XS, England, (Telephone in U.S. (888) 330-8477), (Fax in U.S. (800) 672-2054), www.palgrave.com; *The Statesman's Yearbook 2008.*

Taylor and Francis Group, An Informa Business, 2 Park Square, Milton Park, Abingdon, Oxford OX14 4RN, United Kingdom, (Dial from U.S. (212) 216-7800), (Fax from U.S. (212) 564-7854), www.tandf.co.uk; *The Europa World Year Book.*

UNESCO Institute for Statistics, C.P. 6128 Succursale Centre-Ville, Montreal, Quebec, H3C 3J7 Canada, (Dial from U.S. (514) 343-6880), (Fax from U.S. (514) 343 6882), www.uis.unesco.org; *Statistical Tables.*

United Nations Statistics Division, New York, NY 10017, (800) 253-9646, Fax: (212) 963-4116, http://unstats.un.org; *Asia-Pacific in Figures 2004* and *Human Development Report 2006.*

The World Bank, 1818 H Street, NW, Washington, DC 20433, (202) 473-1000, Fax: (202) 477-6391, www.worldbank.org; *India; Indonesia;* and *World Development Report 2008.*

INDONESIA - ELECTRICITY

Asian Development Bank (ADB), PO Box 789, 0980 Manila, Philippines, www.adb.org; *Key Indicators of Developing Asian and Pacific Countries 2006.*

M.E. Sharpe, 80 Business Park Drive, Armonk, NY 10504, (800) 541-6563, Fax: (914) 273-2106, www.mesharpe.com; *The Illustrated Book of World Rankings.*

Organisation for Economic Cooperation and Development (OECD), 2 rue Andre Pascal, F-75775 Paris Cedex 16, France, (Telephone in U.S. (202) 785-6323), (Fax in U.S. (202) 785-0350), www.oecd.org; *World Energy Outlook 2007.*

Palgrave Macmillan Ltd., Houndmills, Basingstoke, Hampshire, RG21 6XS, England, (Telephone in U.S. (888) 330-8477), (Fax in U.S. (800) 672-2054), www.palgrave.com; *The Statesman's Yearbook 2008.*

Platts, 2 Penn Plaza, 25th Floor, New York, NY 10121-2298, (212) 904-3070, www.platts.com; *Asian Electricity Outlook 2006* and *Emissions Daily.*

U.S. Department of Energy (DOE), Energy Information Administration (EIA), 1000 Independence Avenue, SW, Washington, DC 20585, (202) 586-8800, www.eia.doe.gov; *International Energy Annual 2004* and *International Energy Outlook 2006.*

United Nations Statistics Division, New York, NY 10017, (800) 253-9646, Fax: (212) 963-4116, http://unstats.un.org; *Electric Power in Asia and the Pacific 2001 and 2002; Human Development Report 2006;* and *Statistical Yearbook.*

INDONESIA - EMIGRATION AND IMMIGRATION

International Organization for Migration (IOM), 17, Route des Morillons, CH-1211 Geneva 19, Switzerland, www.iom.int; *Migration, Development and Natural Disasters: Insights from the Indian Ocean Tsunami.*

INDONESIA - EMPLOYMENT

Euromonitor International, Inc., 224 S. Michigan Avenue, Suite 1500, Chicago, IL 60604, (312) 922-1115, Fax: (312) 922-1157, www.euromonitor.com; *International Marketing Data and Statistics 2008.*

International Labour Office, I.L.O. Publications, 4 route des Morillons, CH-1211 Geneva 22, Switzerland, (Telephone in U.S. (202) 653-7652), (Fax in U.S. (202) 653-7687), www.ilo.org; *Yearbook of Labour Statistics 2006.*

M.E. Sharpe, 80 Business Park Drive, Armonk, NY 10504, (800) 541-6563, Fax: (914) 273-2106, www.mesharpe.com; *The Illustrated Book of World Rankings.*

United Nations Statistics Division, New York, NY 10017, (800) 253-9646, Fax: (212) 963-4116, http://unstats.un.org; *Asia-Pacific in Figures 2004* and *Statistical Yearbook.*

The World Bank, 1818 H Street, NW, Washington, DC 20433, (202) 473-1000, Fax: (202) 477-6391, www.worldbank.org; *India* and *Indonesia.*

INDONESIA - ENERGY INDUSTRIES

Enerdata, 10 Rue Royale, 75008 Paris, France, www.enerdata.fr; *Global Energy Market Data.*

Platts, 2 Penn Plaza, 25th Floor, New York, NY 10121-2298, (212) 904-3070, www.platts.com; *Asian Electricity Outlook 2006* and *Emissions Daily.*

United Nations Statistics Division, New York, NY 10017, (800) 253-9646, Fax: (212) 963-4116, http://unstats.un.org; *Electric Power in Asia and the Pacific 2001 and 2002* and *Statistical Yearbook.*

The World Bank, 1818 H Street, NW, Washington, DC 20433, (202) 473-1000, Fax: (202) 477-6391, www.worldbank.org; *Indonesia.*

INDONESIA - ENVIRONMENTAL CONDITIONS

DSI Data Service Information, Xantener Strasse 51a, D-47495 Rheinberg, Germany, www.dsidata.com; *Campus Solution* and *DSI's Global Environmental Database.*

Economist Intelligence Unit, 111 West 57th Street, New York, NY 10019, (212) 554-0600, Fax: (212) 586-1181, www.eiu.com; *Indonesia Country Report.*

International Institute for Environment and Development (IIED), 3 Endsleigh Street, London, England, WC1H 0DD, United Kingdom, www.iied.org; *Environment Urbanization.*

Platts, 2 Penn Plaza, 25th Floor, New York, NY 10121-2298, (212) 904-3070, www.platts.com; *Emissions Daily.*

Statistics Indonesia (Badan Pusat Statistik (BPS)), Jl. Dr. Sutomo 6-8, Jakarta 10710, Indonesia, www.bps.go.id; *Environmental Statistical of Indonesia 2005.*

United Nations Statistics Division, New York, NY 10017, (800) 253-9646, Fax: (212) 963-4116, http://unstats.un.org; *World Statistics Pocketbook.*

INDONESIA - EXPORTS

Asian Development Bank (ADB), PO Box 789, 0980 Manila, Philippines, www.adb.org; *Key Indicators of Developing Asian and Pacific Countries 2006.*

Central Intelligence Agency, Office of Public Affairs, Washington, DC 20505, (703) 482-0623, Fax: (703) 482-1739, www.cia.gov; *The World Factbook.*

Economist Intelligence Unit, 111 West 57th Street, New York, NY 10019, (212) 554-0600, Fax: (212) 586-1181, www.eiu.com; *Indonesia Country Report.*

Euromonitor International, Inc., 224 S. Michigan Avenue, Suite 1500, Chicago, IL 60604, (312) 922-1115, Fax: (312) 922-1157, www.euromonitor.com; *International Marketing Data and Statistics 2008* and *The World Economic Factbook 2008.*

International Monetary Fund (IMF), 700 Nineteenth Street, NW, Washington, DC 20431, (202) 623-7000, Fax: (202) 623-4661, www.imf.org; *Direction of Trade Statistics Yearbook 2007; Government Finance Statistics Yearbook (2008 Edition);* and *International Financial Statistics Yearbook 2007.*

Organization of Petroleum Exporting Countries (OPEC), Obere Donaustrasse 93, A-1020, Vienna, Austria, www.opec.org; *Annual Statistical Bulletin 2006.*

Palgrave Macmillan Ltd., Houndmills, Basingstoke, Hampshire, RG21 6XS, England, (Telephone in U.S. (888) 330-8477), (Fax in U.S. (800) 672-2054), www.palgrave.com; *The Statesman's Yearbook 2008.*

Taylor and Francis Group, An Informa Business, 2 Park Square, Milton Park, Abingdon, Oxford OX14 4RN, United Kingdom, (Dial from U.S. (212) 216-7800), (Fax from U.S. (212) 564-7854), www.tandf.co.uk; *The Europa World Year Book.*

United Nations Conference on Trade and Development (UNCTAD), DC2-1120, United Nations, New York, NY 10017, (212) 963-0027, www.unctad.org; *Handbook of Statistics 2005.*

United Nations Food and Agricultural Organization (FAO), Viale delle Terme di Caracalla, 00100 Rome, Italy, (Dial from U.S. (202) 653-2400), (Fax from U.S. (202) 653 5760), www.fao.org; *The State of Food and Agriculture (SOFA) 2006.*

United Nations Statistics Division, New York, NY 10017, (800) 253-9646, Fax: (212) 963-4116, http://unstats.un.org; *Foreign Trade Statistics of Asia and the Pacific 1996-2000.*

The World Bank, 1818 H Street, NW, Washington, DC 20433, (202) 473-1000, Fax: (202) 477-6391, www.worldbank.org; *World Development Report 2008.*

Worldinformation.com, 2 Market Street, Saffron Walden, Essex CB10 1HZ, United Kingdom, www.worldinformation.com; The World of Information (www.worldinformation.com).

INDONESIA - FERTILITY, HUMAN

Central Intelligence Agency, Office of Public Affairs, Washington, DC 20505, (703) 482-0623, Fax: (703) 482-1739, www.cia.gov; *The World Factbook.*

M.E. Sharpe, 80 Business Park Drive, Armonk, NY 10504, (800) 541-6563, Fax: (914) 273-2106, www.mesharpe.com; *The Illustrated Book of World Rankings.*

United Nations Statistics Division, New York, NY 10017, (800) 253-9646, Fax: (212) 963-4116, http://unstats.un.org; *Human Development Report 2006.*

The World Bank, 1818 H Street, NW, Washington, DC 20433, (202) 473-1000, Fax: (202) 477-6391, www.worldbank.org; *The World Bank Atlas 2003-2004* and *World Development Report 2008.*

INDONESIA - FERTILIZER INDUSTRY

United Nations Food and Agricultural Organization (FAO), Viale delle Terme di Caracalla, 00100 Rome, Italy, (Dial from U.S. (202) 653-2400), (Fax from U.S. (202) 653 5760), www.fao.org; *FAO Fertilizer Yearbook* and *The State of Food and Agriculture (SOFA) 2006.*

United Nations Statistics Division, New York, NY 10017, (800) 253-9646, Fax: (212) 963-4116, http://unstats.un.org; *Statistical Yearbook.*

INDONESIA - FETAL MORTALITY

See INDONESIA - MORTALITY

INDONESIA - FILM

See INDONESIA - MOTION PICTURES

INDONESIA - FINANCE

Statistics Indonesia (Badan Pusat Statistik (BPS)), Jl. Dr. Sutomo 6-8, Jakarta 10710, Indonesia, www.bps.go.id; *Financial Statistics of State Enterprises and Local Corporate.*

Taylor and Francis Group, An Informa Business, 2 Park Square, Milton Park, Abingdon, Oxford OX14 4RN, United Kingdom, (Dial from U.S. (212) 216-7800), (Fax from U.S. (212) 564-7854), www.tandf.co.uk; *The Europa World Year Book.*

United Nations Statistics Division, New York, NY 10017, (800) 253-9646, Fax: (212) 963-4116, http://unstats.un.org; *Asia-Pacific in Figures 2004; National Accounts Statistics: Compendium of Income Distribution Statistics; Statistical Yearbook;* and *Statistical Yearbook for Asia and the Pacific 2004.*

The World Bank, 1818 H Street, NW, Washington, DC 20433, (202) 473-1000, Fax: (202) 477-6391, www.worldbank.org; *India* and *Indonesia.*

INDONESIA - FINANCE, PUBLIC

Asian Development Bank (ADB), PO Box 789, 0980 Manila, Philippines, www.adb.org; *Key Indicators of Developing Asian and Pacific Countries 2006.*

Bernan Essential Government Publications, 4611-F Assembly Drive, Lanham MD, 20706-4391, (301) 459-2255, Fax: (800) 865-3450, www.bernan.com; *National Accounts Statistics.*

Economist Intelligence Unit, 111 West 57th Street, New York, NY 10019, (212) 554-0600, Fax: (212) 586-1181, www.eiu.com; *Indonesia Country Report.*

International Monetary Fund (IMF), 700 Nineteenth Street, NW, Washington, DC 20431, (202) 623-7000, Fax: (202) 623-4661, www.imf.org; *International Financial Statistics; International Financial Statistics Online Service;* and *International Financial Statistics Yearbook 2007.*

M.E. Sharpe, 80 Business Park Drive, Armonk, NY 10504, (800) 541-6563, Fax: (914) 273-2106, www.mesharpe.com; *The Illustrated Book of World Rankings.*

Palgrave Macmillan Ltd., Houndmills, Basingstoke, Hampshire, RG21 6XS, England, (Telephone in U.S. (888) 330-8477), (Fax in U.S. (800) 672-2054), www.palgrave.com; *The Statesman's Yearbook 2008.*

Statistics Indonesia (Badan Pusat Statistik (BPS)), Jl. Dr. Sutomo 6-8, Jakarta 10710, Indonesia, www.bps.go.id; *Financial Statistics of State Enterprises and Local Corporate.*

Taylor and Francis Group, An Informa Business, 2 Park Square, Milton Park, Abingdon, Oxford OX14 4RN, United Kingdom, (Dial from U.S. (212) 216-7800), (Fax from U.S. (212) 564-7854), www.tandf.co.uk; *The Europa World Year Book.*

United Nations Statistics Division, New York, NY 10017, (800) 253-9646, Fax: (212) 963-4116, http://unstats.un.org; *Statistical Yearbook for Asia and the Pacific 2004.*

The World Bank, 1818 H Street, NW, Washington, DC 20433, (202) 473-1000, Fax: (202) 477-6391, www.worldbank.org; *India* and *Indonesia.*

INDONESIA - FISHERIES

M.E. Sharpe, 80 Business Park Drive, Armonk, NY 10504, (800) 541-6563, Fax: (914) 273-2106, www.mesharpe.com; *The Illustrated Book of World Rankings.*

Palgrave Macmillan Ltd., Houndmills, Basingstoke, Hampshire, RG21 6XS, England, (Telephone in U.S. (888) 330-8477), (Fax in U.S. (800) 672-2054), www.palgrave.com; *The Statesman's Yearbook 2008.*

Taylor and Francis Group, An Informa Business, 2 Park Square, Milton Park, Abingdon, Oxford OX14 4RN, United Kingdom, (Dial from U.S. (212) 216-7800), (Fax from U.S. (212) 564-7854), www.tandf.co.uk; *The Europa World Year Book.*

United Nations Conference on Trade and Development (UNCTAD), DC2-1120, United Nations, New York, NY 10017, (212) 963-0027, www.unctad.org; *UNCTAD Commodity Yearbook.*

United Nations Food and Agricultural Organization (FAO), Viale delle Terme di Caracalla, 00100 Rome, Italy, (Dial from U.S. (202) 653-2400), (Fax from U.S. (202) 653 5760), www.fao.org; *FAO Yearbook of Fishery Statistics;* Fishery Databases; FISHSTAT Database. Subjects covered include: Aquaculture production, capture production, fishery commodities; and *The State of Food and Agriculture (SOFA) 2006.*

United Nations Statistics Division, New York, NY 10017, (800) 253-9646, Fax: (212) 963-4116, http://unstats.un.org; *Statistical Yearbook.*

The World Bank, 1818 H Street, NW, Washington, DC 20433, (202) 473-1000, Fax: (202) 477-6391, www.worldbank.org; *India* and *Indonesia.*

INDONESIA - FLOUR INDUSTRY

United Nations Statistics Division, New York, NY 10017, (800) 253-9646, Fax: (212) 963-4116, http://unstats.un.org; *Statistical Yearbook.*

INDONESIA - FOOD

Euromonitor International, Inc., 224 S. Michigan Avenue, Suite 1500, Chicago, IL 60604, (312) 922-1115, Fax: (312) 922-1157, www.euromonitor.com; *Retail Trade International 2007.*

United Nations Conference on Trade and Development (UNCTAD), DC2-1120, United Nations, New York, NY 10017, (212) 963-0027, www.unctad.org; *UNCTAD Commodity Yearbook.*

United Nations Food and Agricultural Organization (FAO), Viale delle Terme di Caracalla, 00100 Rome, Italy, (Dial from U.S. (202) 653-2400), (Fax from U.S. (202) 653 5760), www.fao.org; *FAO Production Yearbook 2002* and *The State of Food and Agriculture (SOFA) 2006.*

United Nations Statistics Division, New York, NY 10017, (800) 253-9646, Fax: (212) 963-4116, http://unstats.un.org; *Human Development Report 2006* and *Statistical Yearbook for Asia and the Pacific 2004.*

INDONESIA - FOREIGN EXCHANGE RATES

Asian Development Bank (ADB), PO Box 789, 0980 Manila, Philippines, www.adb.org; *Key Indicators of Developing Asian and Pacific Countries 2006.*

Central Intelligence Agency, Office of Public Affairs, Washington, DC 20505, (703) 482-0623, Fax: (703) 482-1739, www.cia.gov; *The World Factbook.*

Economist Intelligence Unit, 111 West 57th Street, New York, NY 10019, (212) 554-0600, Fax: (212) 586-1181, www.eiu.com; *Business Asia.*

Euromonitor International, Inc., 224 S. Michigan Avenue, Suite 1500, Chicago, IL 60604, (312) 922-1115, Fax: (312) 922-1157, www.euromonitor.com; *International Marketing Data and Statistics 2008* and *The World Economic Factbook 2008.*

International Monetary Fund (IMF), 700 Nineteenth Street, NW, Washington, DC 20431, (202) 623-7000, Fax: (202) 623-4661, www.imf.org; *International Financial Statistics Yearbook 2007.*

Organization of Petroleum Exporting Countries (OPEC), Obere Donaustrasse 93, A-1020, Vienna, Austria, www.opec.org; *Annual Statistical Bulletin 2006.*

Taylor and Francis Group, An Informa Business, 2 Park Square, Milton Park, Abingdon, Oxford OX14 4RN, United Kingdom, (Dial from U.S. (212) 216-7800), (Fax from U.S. (212) 564-7854), www.tandf.co.uk; *The Europa World Year Book.*

United Nations Statistics Division, New York, NY 10017, (800) 253-9646, Fax: (212) 963-4116, http://unstats.un.org; *Statistical Yearbook* and *World Statistics Pocketbook.*

Worldinformation.com, 2 Market Street, Saffron Walden, Essex CB10 1HZ, United Kingdom, www.worldinformation.com; The World of Information (www.worldinformation.com).

INDONESIA - FORESTS AND FORESTRY

American Forest Paper Association (AFPA), 1111 Nineteenth Street, NW, Suite 800, Washington, DC 20036, (800) 878-8878, www.afandpa.org; *2007 Annual Statistics of Paper, Paperboard, and Wood Pulp.*

Economist Intelligence Unit, 111 West 57th Street, New York, NY 10019, (212) 554-0600, Fax: (212) 586-1181, www.eiu.com; *Business Asia.*

International Monetary Fund (IMF), 700 Nineteenth Street, NW, Washington, DC 20431, (202) 623-7000, Fax: (202) 623-4661, www.imf.org; *International Financial Statistics Yearbook 2007.*

M.E. Sharpe, 80 Business Park Drive, Armonk, NY 10504, (800) 541-6563, Fax: (914) 273-2106, www.mesharpe.com; *The Illustrated Book of World Rankings.*

Palgrave Macmillan Ltd., Houndmills, Basingstoke, Hampshire, RG21 6XS, England, (Telephone in U.S. (888) 330-8477), (Fax in U.S. (800) 672-2054), www.palgrave.com; *The Statesman's Yearbook 2008.*

Statistics Indonesia (Badan Pusat Statistik (BPS)), Jl. Dr. Sutomo 6-8, Jakarta 10710, Indonesia, www.bps.go.id; *Natural Forest Concession Enterprises.*

Taylor and Francis Group, An Informa Business, 2 Park Square, Milton Park, Abingdon, Oxford OX14 4RN, United Kingdom, (Dial from U.S. (212) 216-7800), (Fax from U.S. (212) 564-7854), www.tandf.co.uk; *The Europa World Year Book.*

UNESCO Institute for Statistics, C.P. 6128 Succursale Centre-Ville, Montreal, Quebec, H3C 3J7 Canada, (Dial from U.S. (514) 343-6880), (Fax from U.S. (514) 343 6882), www.uis.unesco.org; *Statistical Tables.*

United Nations Conference on Trade and Development (UNCTAD), DC2-1120, United Nations, New York, NY 10017, (212) 963-0027, www.unctad.org; *UNCTAD Commodity Yearbook.*

United Nations Food and Agricultural Organization (FAO), Viale delle Terme di Caracalla, 00100 Rome, Italy, (Dial from U.S. (202) 653-2400), (Fax from U.S. (202) 653 5760), www.fao.org; *FAO Yearbook of Forest Products* and *The State of Food and Agriculture (SOFA) 2006.*

United Nations Statistics Division, New York, NY 10017, (800) 253-9646, Fax: (212) 963-4116, http://unstats.un.org; *Statistical Yearbook.*

The World Bank, 1818 H Street, NW, Washington, DC 20433, (202) 473-1000, Fax: (202) 477-6391, www.worldbank.org; *India; Indonesia;* and *World Development Report 2008.*

INDONESIA - GAS PRODUCTION

See INDONESIA - MINERAL INDUSTRIES

INDONESIA - GEOGRAPHIC INFORMATION SYSTEMS

M.E. Sharpe, 80 Business Park Drive, Armonk, NY 10504, (800) 541-6563, Fax: (914) 273-2106, www.mesharpe.com; *The Illustrated Book of World Rankings.*

The World Bank, 1818 H Street, NW, Washington, DC 20433, (202) 473-1000, Fax: (202) 477-6391, www.worldbank.org; *Indonesia.*

INDONESIA - GOLD INDUSTRY

International Monetary Fund (IMF), 700 Nineteenth Street, NW, Washington, DC 20431, (202) 623-7000, Fax: (202) 623-4661, www.imf.org; *International Financial Statistics Yearbook 2007.*

United Nations Statistics Division, New York, NY 10017, (800) 253-9646, Fax: (212) 963-4116, http://unstats.un.org; *Statistical Yearbook.*

The World Bank, 1818 H Street, NW, Washington, DC 20433, (202) 473-1000, Fax: (202) 477-6391, www.worldbank.org; *World Development Report 2008.*

INDONESIA - GOLD PRODUCTION

See INDONESIA - MINERAL INDUSTRIES

INDONESIA - GRANTS-IN-AID

International Monetary Fund (IMF), 700 Nineteenth Street, NW, Washington, DC 20431, (202) 623-7000, Fax: (202) 623-4661, www.imf.org; *Government Finance Statistics Yearbook (2008 Edition).*

INDONESIA - GROSS DOMESTIC PRODUCT

Asian Development Bank (ADB), PO Box 789, 0980 Manila, Philippines, www.adb.org; *Key Indicators of Developing Asian and Pacific Countries 2006.*

Economist Intelligence Unit, 111 West 57th Street, New York, NY 10019, (212) 554-0600, Fax: (212) 586-1181, www.eiu.com; *Business Asia* and *Indonesia Country Report.*

Euromonitor International, Inc., 224 S. Michigan Avenue, Suite 1500, Chicago, IL 60604, (312) 922-1115, Fax: (312) 922-1157, www.euromonitor.com; *International Marketing Data and Statistics 2008* and *The World Economic Factbook 2008.*

M.E. Sharpe, 80 Business Park Drive, Armonk, NY 10504, (800) 541-6563, Fax: (914) 273-2106, www.mesharpe.com; *The Illustrated Book of World Rankings.*

Taylor and Francis Group, An Informa Business, 2 Park Square, Milton Park, Abingdon, Oxford OX14 4RN, United Kingdom, (Dial from U.S. (212) 216-7800), (Fax from U.S. (212) 564-7854), www.tandf.co.uk; *The Europa World Year Book.*

United Nations Statistics Division, New York, NY 10017, (800) 253-9646, Fax: (212) 963-4116, http://unstats.un.org; *Human Development Report 2006; National Accounts Statistics: Compendium of Income Distribution Statistics;* and *Statistical Yearbook.*

The World Bank, 1818 H Street, NW, Washington, DC 20433, (202) 473-1000, Fax: (202) 477-6391, www.worldbank.org; *World Development Report 2008.*

INDONESIA - GROSS NATIONAL PRODUCT

Asian Development Bank (ADB), PO Box 789, 0980 Manila, Philippines, www.adb.org; *Key Indicators of Developing Asian and Pacific Countries 2006.*

Euromonitor International, Inc., 224 S. Michigan Avenue, Suite 1500, Chicago, IL 60604, (312) 922-1115, Fax: (312) 922-1157, www.euromonitor.com; *International Marketing Data and Statistics 2008.*

M.E. Sharpe, 80 Business Park Drive, Armonk, NY 10504, (800) 541-6563, Fax: (914) 273-2106, www.mesharpe.com; *The Illustrated Book of World Rankings.*

Organization of Petroleum Exporting Countries (OPEC), Obere Donaustrasse 93, A-1020, Vienna, Austria, www.opec.org; *Annual Statistical Bulletin 2006.*

Palgrave Macmillan Ltd., Houndmills, Basingstoke, Hampshire, RG21 6XS, England, (Telephone in U.S. (888) 330-8477), (Fax in U.S. (800) 672-2054), www.palgrave.com; *The Statesman's Yearbook 2008.*

Taylor and Francis Group, An Informa Business, 2 Park Square, Milton Park, Abingdon, Oxford OX14 4RN, United Kingdom, (Dial from U.S. (212) 216-7800), (Fax from U.S. (212) 564-7854), www.tandf.co.uk; *The Europa World Year Book.*

U.S. Department of State (DOS), 2201 C Street NW, Washington, DC 20520, (202) 647-4000, www.state.gov; *World Military Expenditures and Arms Transfers (WMEAT).*

United Nations Statistics Division, New York, NY 10017, (800) 253-9646, Fax: (212) 963-4116, http://unstats.un.org; *Statistical Yearbook.*

The World Bank, 1818 H Street, NW, Washington, DC 20433, (202) 473-1000, Fax: (202) 477-6391, www.worldbank.org; *The World Bank Atlas 2003-2004* and *World Development Report 2008.*

Worldinformation.com, 2 Market Street, Saffron Walden, Essex CB10 1HZ, United Kingdom, www.worldinformation.com; The World of Information (www.worldinformation.com).

INDONESIA - HIDES AND SKINS INDUSTRY

United Nations Food and Agricultural Organization (FAO), Viale delle Terme di Caracalla, 00100 Rome, Italy, (Dial from U.S. (202) 653-2400), (Fax from U.S. (202) 653 5760), www.fao.org; *FAO Production Yearbook 2002.*

INDONESIA - HOUSING

Euromonitor International, Inc., 224 S. Michigan Avenue, Suite 1500, Chicago, IL 60604, (312) 922-1115, Fax: (312) 922-1157, www.euromonitor.com; *World Marketing Data and Statistics.*

M.E. Sharpe, 80 Business Park Drive, Armonk, NY 10504, (800) 541-6563, Fax: (914) 273-2106, www.mesharpe.com; *The Illustrated Book of World Rankings.*

INDONESIA - ILLITERATE PERSONS

Euromonitor International, Inc., 224 S. Michigan Avenue, Suite 1500, Chicago, IL 60604, (312) 922-1115, Fax: (312) 922-1157, www.euromonitor.com; *The World Economic Factbook 2008.*

Palgrave Macmillan Ltd., Houndmills, Basingstoke, Hampshire, RG21 6XS, England, (Telephone in U.S. (888) 330-8477), (Fax in U.S. (800) 672-2054), www.palgrave.com; *The Statesman's Yearbook 2008.*

UNESCO Institute for Statistics, C.P. 6128 Succursale Centre-Ville, Montreal, Quebec, H3C 3J7 Canada, (Dial from U.S. (514) 343-6880), (Fax from U.S. (514) 343 6882), www.uis.unesco.org; *Statistical Tables.*

United Nations Statistics Division, New York, NY 10017, (800) 253-9646, Fax: (212) 963-4116, http://unstats.un.org; *Asia-Pacific in Figures 2004* and *Human Development Report 2006.*

INDONESIA - IMPORTS

Asian Development Bank (ADB), PO Box 789, 0980 Manila, Philippines, www.adb.org; *Key Indicators of Developing Asian and Pacific Countries 2006.*

Central Intelligence Agency, Office of Public Affairs, Washington, DC 20505, (703) 482-0623, Fax: (703) 482-1739, www.cia.gov; *The World Factbook.*

Economist Intelligence Unit, 111 West 57th Street, New York, NY 10019, (212) 554-0600, Fax: (212) 586-1181, www.eiu.com; *Indonesia Country Report.*

Euromonitor International, Inc., 224 S. Michigan Avenue, Suite 1500, Chicago, IL 60604, (312) 922-1115, Fax: (312) 922-1157, www.euromonitor.com; *International Marketing Data and Statistics 2008* and *The World Economic Factbook 2008.*

International Monetary Fund (IMF), 700 Nineteenth Street, NW, Washington, DC 20431, (202) 623-7000, Fax: (202) 623-4661, www.imf.org; *Direction of Trade Statistics Yearbook 2007; Government Finance Statistics Yearbook (2008 Edition);* and *International Financial Statistics Yearbook 2007.*

Palgrave Macmillan Ltd., Houndmills, Basingstoke, Hampshire, RG21 6XS, England, (Telephone in U.S. (888) 330-8477), (Fax in U.S. (800) 672-2054), www.palgrave.com; *The Statesman's Yearbook 2008.*

Taylor and Francis Group, An Informa Business, 2 Park Square, Milton Park, Abingdon, Oxford OX14 4RN, United Kingdom, (Dial from U.S. (212) 216-7800), (Fax from U.S. (212) 564-7854), www.tandf.co.uk; *The Europa World Year Book.*

United Nations Conference on Trade and Development (UNCTAD), DC2-1120, United Nations, New York, NY 10017, (212) 963-0027, www.unctad.org; *Handbook of Statistics 2005.*

United Nations Food and Agricultural Organization (FAO), Viale delle Terme di Caracalla, 00100 Rome, Italy, (Dial from U.S. (202) 653-2400), (Fax from U.S. (202) 653 5760), www.fao.org; *The State of Food and Agriculture (SOFA) 2006.*

United Nations Statistics Division, New York, NY 10017, (800) 253-9646, Fax: (212) 963-4116, http://unstats.un.org; *Foreign Trade Statistics of Asia and the Pacific 1996-2000.*

The World Bank, 1818 H Street, NW, Washington, DC 20433, (202) 473-1000, Fax: (202) 477-6391, www.worldbank.org; *World Development Report 2008.*

Worldinformation.com, 2 Market Street, Saffron Walden, Essex CB10 1HZ, United Kingdom, www.worldinformation.com; The World of Information (www.worldinformation.com).

INDONESIA - INCOME TAXES

See INDONESIA - TAXATION

INDONESIA - INDUSTRIAL PRODUCTIVITY

Euromonitor International, Inc., 224 S. Michigan Avenue, Suite 1500, Chicago, IL 60604, (312) 922-1115, Fax: (312) 922-1157, www.euromonitor.com; *International Marketing Data and Statistics 2008.*

M.E. Sharpe, 80 Business Park Drive, Armonk, NY 10504, (800) 541-6563, Fax: (914) 273-2106, www.mesharpe.com; *The Illustrated Book of World Rankings.*

INDONESIA - INDUSTRIAL PROPERTY

United Nations Statistics Division, New York, NY 10017, (800) 253-9646, Fax: (212) 963-4116, http://unstats.un.org; *Statistical Yearbook.*

World Intellectual Property Organization (WIPO), PO Box 18, CH-1211 Geneva 20, Switzerland, www.wipo.int; *Industrial Property Statistics* and *Industrial Property Statistics Online Directory.*

INDONESIA - INDUSTRIES

Central Intelligence Agency, Office of Public Affairs, Washington, DC 20505, (703) 482-0623, Fax: (703) 482-1739, www.cia.gov; *The World Factbook.*

Economist Intelligence Unit, 111 West 57th Street, New York, NY 10019, (212) 554-0600, Fax: (212) 586-1181, www.eiu.com; *Indonesia Country Report.*

Euromonitor International, Inc., 224 S. Michigan Avenue, Suite 1500, Chicago, IL 60604, (312) 922-1115, Fax: (312) 922-1157, www.euromonitor.com; *International Marketing Data and Statistics 2008; The World Economic Factbook 2008;* and *World Marketing Data and Statistics.*

International Labour Office, I.L.O. Publications, 4 route des Morillons, CH-1211 Geneva 22, Switzerland, (Telephone in U.S. (202) 653-7652), (Fax in U.S. (202) 653-7687), www.ilo.org; *Yearbook of Labour Statistics 2006.*

M.E. Sharpe, 80 Business Park Drive, Armonk, NY 10504, (800) 541-6563, Fax: (914) 273-2106, www.mesharpe.com; *The Illustrated Book of World Rankings.*

Palgrave Macmillan Ltd., Houndmills, Basingstoke, Hampshire, RG21 6XS, England, (Telephone in U.S. (888) 330-8477), (Fax in U.S. (800) 672-2054), www.palgrave.com; *The Statesman's Yearbook 2008.*

Statistics Indonesia (Badan Pusat Statistik (BPS)), Jl. Dr. Sutomo 6-8, Jakarta 10710, Indonesia, www.bps.go.id; *Financial Statistics of State Enterprises and Local Corporate.*

Taylor and Francis Group, An Informa Business, 2 Park Square, Milton Park, Abingdon, Oxford OX14 4RN, United Kingdom, (Dial from U.S. (212) 216-7800), (Fax from U.S. (212) 564-7854), www.tandf.co.uk; *The Europa World Year Book.*

United Nations Industrial Development Organization (UNIDO), 1 United Nations Plaza, New York, NY 10017, (212) 963 6890, Fax: (212) 963-7904, http://unido.org; Industrial Statistics Database 2008 (INDSTAT) and *The International Yearbook of Industrial Statistics 2008.*

United Nations Statistics Division, New York, NY 10017, (800) 253-9646, Fax: (212) 963-4116, http://unstats.un.org; *Asia-Pacific in Figures 2004; 2004 Industrial Commodity Statistics Yearbook;* and *Statistical Yearbook for Asia and the Pacific 2004.*

The World Bank, 1818 H Street, NW, Washington, DC 20433, (202) 473-1000, Fax: (202) 477-6391, www.worldbank.org; *India; Indonesia;* and *World Development Report 2008.*

INDONESIA - INFANT AND MATERNAL MORTALITY

See INDONESIA - MORTALITY

INDONESIA - INORGANIC ACIDS

United Nations Statistics Division, New York, NY 10017, (800) 253-9646, Fax: (212) 963-4116, http://unstats.un.org; *Statistical Yearbook.*

INDONESIA - INTERNATIONAL FINANCE

Asian Development Bank (ADB), PO Box 789, 0980 Manila, Philippines, www.adb.org; *Key Indicators of Developing Asian and Pacific Countries 2006.*

The World Bank, 1818 H Street, NW, Washington, DC 20433, (202) 473-1000, Fax: (202) 477-6391, www.worldbank.org; *Indonesia.*

INDONESIA - INTERNATIONAL LIQUIDITY

International Monetary Fund (IMF), 700 Nineteenth Street, NW, Washington, DC 20431, (202) 623-7000, Fax: (202) 623-4661, www.imf.org; *International Financial Statistics Yearbook 2007.*

INDONESIA - INTERNATIONAL STATISTICS

Asian Development Bank (ADB), PO Box 789, 0980 Manila, Philippines, www.adb.org; *Key Indicators of Developing Asian and Pacific Countries 2006.*

INDONESIA - INTERNATIONAL TRADE

Asian Development Bank (ADB), PO Box 789, 0980 Manila, Philippines, www.adb.org; *Key Indicators of Developing Asian and Pacific Countries 2006.*

Economist Intelligence Unit, 111 West 57th Street, New York, NY 10019, (212) 554-0600, Fax: (212) 586-1181, www.eiu.com; *Business Asia* and *Indonesia Country Report.*

Euromonitor International, Inc., 224 S. Michigan Avenue, Suite 1500, Chicago, IL 60604, (312) 922-1115, Fax: (312) 922-1157, www.euromonitor.com; *International Marketing Data and Statistics 2008; The World Economic Factbook 2008;* and *World Marketing Data and Statistics.*

M.E. Sharpe, 80 Business Park Drive, Armonk, NY 10504, (800) 541-6563, Fax: (914) 273-2106, www.mesharpe.com; *The Illustrated Book of World Rankings.*

Palgrave Macmillan Ltd., Houndmills, Basingstoke, Hampshire, RG21 6XS, England, (Telephone in U.S. (888) 330-8477), (Fax in U.S. (800) 672-2054), www.palgrave.com; *The Statesman's Yearbook 2008.*

Taylor and Francis Group, An Informa Business, 2 Park Square, Milton Park, Abingdon, Oxford OX14 4RN, United Kingdom, (Dial from U.S. (212) 216-7800), (Fax from U.S. (212) 564-7854), www.tandf.co.uk; *The Europa World Year Book.*

United Nations Conference on Trade and Development (UNCTAD), DC2-1120, United Nations, New York, NY 10017, (212) 963-0027, www.unctad.org; *UNCTAD Commodity Yearbook.*

United Nations Food and Agricultural Organization (FAO), Viale delle Terme di Caracalla, 00100 Rome, Italy, (Dial from U.S. (202) 653-2400), (Fax from U.S. (202) 653 5760), www.fao.org; *FAO Trade Yearbook* and *The State of Food and Agriculture (SOFA) 2006.*

United Nations Statistics Division, New York, NY 10017, (800) 253-9646, Fax: (212) 963-4116, http://unstats.un.org; *Asia-Pacific in Figures 2004; International Trade Statistics Yearbook; Statistical Yearbook;* and *Statistical Yearbook for Asia and the Pacific 2004.*

The World Bank, 1818 H Street, NW, Washington, DC 20433, (202) 473-1000, Fax: (202) 477-6391, www.worldbank.org; *India; Indonesia;* and *World Development Report 2008.*

World Trade Organization (WTO), Centre William Rappard, Rue de Lausanne 154, CH-1211 Geneva 21, Switzerland, www.wto.org; *International Trade Statistics 2006.*

INDONESIA - INTERNET USERS

International Telecommunication Union (ITU), Place des Nations, 1211 Geneva 20, Switzerland, www.itu.int; *World Telecommunication/ICT Indicators Database on CD-ROM; World Telecommunication/ICT Indicators Database Online;* and *Yearbook of Statistics - Telecommunication Services (Chronological Time Series 1997-2006).*

The World Bank, 1818 H Street, NW, Washington, DC 20433, (202) 473-1000, Fax: (202) 477-6391, www.worldbank.org; *Indonesia.*

INDONESIA - INVESTMENTS

International Monetary Fund (IMF), 700 Nineteenth Street, NW, Washington, DC 20431, (202) 623-7000, Fax: (202) 623-4661, www.imf.org; *International Financial Statistics Yearbook 2007.*

INDONESIA - IRON AND IRON ORE PRODUCTION

See INDONESIA - MINERAL INDUSTRIES

INDONESIA - IRRIGATION

Euromonitor International, Inc., 224 S. Michigan Avenue, Suite 1500, Chicago, IL 60604, (312) 922-1115, Fax: (312) 922-1157, www.euromonitor.com; *International Marketing Data and Statistics 2008.*

INDONESIA - JUTE PRODUCTION

See INDONESIA - CROPS

INDONESIA - LABOR

Central Intelligence Agency, Office of Public Affairs, Washington, DC 20505, (703) 482-0623, Fax: (703) 482-1739, www.cia.gov; *The World Factbook.*

Economist Intelligence Unit, 111 West 57th Street, New York, NY 10019, (212) 554-0600, Fax: (212) 586-1181, www.eiu.com; *Business Asia.*

Euromonitor International, Inc., 224 S. Michigan Avenue, Suite 1500, Chicago, IL 60604, (312) 922-1115, Fax: (312) 922-1157, www.euromonitor.com; *International Marketing Data and Statistics 2008* and *World Marketing Data and Statistics.*

International Labour Office, I.L.O. Publications, 4 route des Morillons, CH-1211 Geneva 22, Switzerland, (Telephone in U.S. (202) 653-7652), (Fax in U.S. (202) 653-7687), www.ilo.org; *Yearbook of Labour Statistics 2006.*

M.E. Sharpe, 80 Business Park Drive, Armonk, NY 10504, (800) 541-6563, Fax: (914) 273-2106, www.mesharpe.com; *The Illustrated Book of World Rankings.*

Palgrave Macmillan Ltd., Houndmills, Basingstoke, Hampshire, RG21 6XS, England, (Telephone in U.S. (888) 330-8477), (Fax in U.S. (800) 672-2054), www.palgrave.com; *The Statesman's Yearbook 2008.*

United Nations Food and Agricultural Organization (FAO), Viale delle Terme di Caracalla, 00100 Rome, Italy, (Dial from U.S. (202) 653-2400), (Fax from U.S. (202) 653 5760), www.fao.org; *The State of Food and Agriculture (SOFA) 2006.*

United Nations Statistics Division, New York, NY 10017, (800) 253-9646, Fax: (212) 963-4116, http://unstats.un.org; *Human Development Report 2006.*

The World Bank, 1818 H Street, NW, Washington, DC 20433, (202) 473-1000, Fax: (202) 477-6391, www.worldbank.org; *The World Bank Atlas 2003-2004* and *World Development Report 2008.*

INDONESIA - LAND USE

Central Intelligence Agency, Office of Public Affairs, Washington, DC 20505, (703) 482-0623, Fax: (703) 482-1739, www.cia.gov; *The World Factbook.*

Euromonitor International, Inc., 224 S. Michigan Avenue, Suite 1500, Chicago, IL 60604, (312) 922-1115, Fax: (312) 922-1157, www.euromonitor.com; *International Marketing Data and Statistics 2008.*

Statistics Indonesia (Badan Pusat Statistik (BPS)), Jl. Dr. Sutomo 6-8, Jakarta 10710, Indonesia, www.bps.go.id; *Natural Forest Concession Enterprises.*

United Nations Food and Agricultural Organization (FAO), Viale delle Terme di Caracalla, 00100 Rome, Italy, (Dial from U.S. (202) 653-2400), (Fax from U.S. (202) 653 5760), www.fao.org; *FAO Production Yearbook 2002.*

The World Bank, 1818 H Street, NW, Washington, DC 20433, (202) 473-1000, Fax: (202) 477-6391, www.worldbank.org; *World Development Report 2008.*

INDONESIA - LIBRARIES

M.E. Sharpe, 80 Business Park Drive, Armonk, NY 10504, (800) 541-6563, Fax: (914) 273-2106, www.mesharpe.com; *The Illustrated Book of World Rankings.*

UNESCO Institute for Statistics, C.P. 6128 Succursale Centre-Ville, Montreal, Quebec, H3C 3J7 Canada, (Dial from U.S. (514) 343-6880), (Fax from U.S. (514) 343 6882), www.uis.unesco.org; *Statistical Tables.*

INDONESIA - LIFE EXPECTANCY

Central Intelligence Agency, Office of Public Affairs, Washington, DC 20505, (703) 482-0623, Fax: (703) 482-1739, www.cia.gov; *The World Factbook.*

Economist Intelligence Unit, 111 West 57th Street, New York, NY 10019, (212) 554-0600, Fax: (212) 586-1181, www.eiu.com; *Business Asia.*

Euromonitor International, Inc., 224 S. Michigan Avenue, Suite 1500, Chicago, IL 60604, (312) 922-

1115, Fax: (312) 922-1157, www.euromonitor.com; *The World Economic Factbook 2008.*

Palgrave Macmillan Ltd., Houndmills, Basingstoke, Hampshire, RG21 6XS, England, (Telephone in U.S. (888) 330-8477), (Fax in U.S. (800) 672-2054), www.palgrave.com; *The Statesman's Yearbook 2008.*

United Nations Statistics Division, New York, NY 10017, (800) 253-9646, Fax: (212) 963-4116, http://unstats.un.org; *Asia-Pacific in Figures 2004; Human Development Report 2006;* and *World Statistics Pocketbook.*

The World Bank, 1818 H Street, NW, Washington, DC 20433, (202) 473-1000, Fax: (202) 477-6391, www.worldbank.org; *The World Bank Atlas 2003-2004* and *World Development Report 2008.*

INDONESIA - LITERACY

Euromonitor International, Inc., 224 S. Michigan Avenue, Suite 1500, Chicago, IL 60604, (312) 922-1115, Fax: (312) 922-1157, www.euromonitor.com; *World Marketing Data and Statistics.*

INDONESIA - LIVESTOCK

M.E. Sharpe, 80 Business Park Drive, Armonk, NY 10504, (800) 541-6563, Fax: (914) 273-2106, www.mesharpe.com; *The Illustrated Book of World Rankings.*

Palgrave Macmillan Ltd., Houndmills, Basingstoke, Hampshire, RG21 6XS, England, (Telephone in U.S. (888) 330-8477), (Fax in U.S. (800) 672-2054), www.palgrave.com; *The Statesman's Yearbook 2008.*

Taylor and Francis Group, An Informa Business, 2 Park Square, Milton Park, Abingdon, Oxford OX14 4RN, United Kingdom, (Dial from U.S. (212) 216-7800), (Fax from U.S. (212) 564-7854), www.tandf.co.uk; *The Europa World Year Book.*

United Nations Conference on Trade and Development (UNCTAD), DC2-1120, United Nations, New York, NY 10017, (212) 963-0027, www.unctad.org; *UNCTAD Commodity Yearbook.*

United Nations Food and Agricultural Organization (FAO), Viale delle Terme di Caracalla, 00100 Rome, Italy, (Dial from U.S. (202) 653-2400), (Fax from U.S. (202) 653 5760), www.fao.org; *FAO Production Yearbook 2002* and *The State of Food and Agriculture (SOFA) 2006.*

United Nations Statistics Division, New York, NY 10017, (800) 253-9646, Fax: (212) 963-4116, http://unstats.un.org; *Statistical Yearbook.*

INDONESIA - LOCAL TAXATION

Euromonitor International, Inc., 224 S. Michigan Avenue, Suite 1500, Chicago, IL 60604, (312) 922-1115, Fax: (312) 922-1157, www.euromonitor.com; *International Marketing Data and Statistics 2008.*

INDONESIA - MANPOWER

United Nations Statistics Division, New York, NY 10017, (800) 253-9646, Fax: (212) 963-4116, http://unstats.un.org; *Statistical Yearbook for Asia and the Pacific 2004.*

INDONESIA - MANUFACTURES

Asian Development Bank (ADB), PO Box 789, 0980 Manila, Philippines, www.adb.org; *Key Indicators of Developing Asian and Pacific Countries 2006.*

M.E. Sharpe, 80 Business Park Drive, Armonk, NY 10504, (800) 541-6563, Fax: (914) 273-2106, www.mesharpe.com; *The Illustrated Book of World Rankings.*

United Nations Statistics Division, New York, NY 10017, (800) 253-9646, Fax: (212) 963-4116, http://unstats.un.org; *Statistical Yearbook.*

The World Bank, 1818 H Street, NW, Washington, DC 20433, (202) 473-1000, Fax: (202) 477-6391, www.worldbank.org; *World Development Report 2008.*

INDONESIA - MARRIAGE

M.E. Sharpe, 80 Business Park Drive, Armonk, NY 10504, (800) 541-6563, Fax: (914) 273-2106, www.mesharpe.com; *The Illustrated Book of World Rankings.*

Taylor and Francis Group, An Informa Business, 2 Park Square, Milton Park, Abingdon, Oxford OX14 4RN, United Kingdom, (Dial from U.S. (212) 216-7800), (Fax from U.S. (212) 564-7854), www.tandf.co.uk; *The Europa World Year Book.*

United Nations Statistics Division, New York, NY 10017, (800) 253-9646, Fax: (212) 963-4116, http://unstats.un.org; *Demographic Yearbook* and *Statistical Yearbook.*

INDONESIA - MEAT PRODUCTION

See INDONESIA - LIVESTOCK

INDONESIA - METAL PRODUCTS

United Nations Statistics Division, New York, NY 10017, (800) 253-9646, Fax: (212) 963-4116, http://unstats.un.org; *Statistical Yearbook.*

INDONESIA - MILK PRODUCTION

See INDONESIA - DAIRY PROCESSING

INDONESIA - MINERAL INDUSTRIES

Asian Development Bank (ADB), PO Box 789, 0980 Manila, Philippines, www.adb.org; *Key Indicators of Developing Asian and Pacific Countries 2006.*

Commodity Research Bureau, 330 South Wells Street, Suite 612, Chicago, IL 60606-7110, (800) 621-5271, Fax: (312) 939-4135, www.crbtrader.com; *2006 CRB Commodity Yearbook and CD.*

Euromonitor International, Inc., 224 S. Michigan Avenue, Suite 1500, Chicago, IL 60604, (312) 922-1115, Fax: (312) 922-1157, www.euromonitor.com; *International Marketing Data and Statistics 2008.*

M.E. Sharpe, 80 Business Park Drive, Armonk, NY 10504, (800) 541-6563, Fax: (914) 273-2106, www.mesharpe.com; *The Illustrated Book of World Rankings.*

Organisation for Economic Cooperation and Development (OECD), 2 rue Andre Pascal, F-75775 Paris Cedex 16, France, (Telephone in U.S. (202) 785-6323), (Fax in U.S. (202) 785-0350), www.oecd.org; *World Energy Outlook 2007.*

Organization of Petroleum Exporting Countries (OPEC), Obere Donaustrasse 93, A-1020, Vienna, Austria, www.opec.org; *Annual Statistical Bulletin 2006.*

Palgrave Macmillan Ltd., Houndmills, Basingstoke, Hampshire, RG21 6XS, England, (Telephone in U.S. (888) 330-8477), (Fax in U.S. (800) 672-2054), www.palgrave.com; *The Statesman's Yearbook 2008.*

Taylor and Francis Group, An Informa Business, 2 Park Square, Milton Park, Abingdon, Oxford OX14 4RN, United Kingdom, (Dial from U.S. (212) 216-7800), (Fax from U.S. (212) 564-7854), www.tandf.co.uk; *The Europa World Year Book.*

United Nations Conference on Trade and Development (UNCTAD), DC2-1120, United Nations, New York, NY 10017, (212) 963-0027, www.unctad.org; *UNCTAD Commodity Yearbook.*

United Nations Statistics Division, New York, NY 10017, (800) 253-9646, Fax: (212) 963-4116, http://unstats.un.org; *Statistical Yearbook.*

The World Bank, 1818 H Street, NW, Washington, DC 20433, (202) 473-1000, Fax: (202) 477-6391, www.worldbank.org; *Indonesia.*

INDONESIA - MONEY EXCHANGE RATES

See INDONESIA - FOREIGN EXCHANGE RATES

INDONESIA - MONEY SUPPLY

Asian Development Bank (ADB), PO Box 789, 0980 Manila, Philippines, www.adb.org; *Key Indicators of Developing Asian and Pacific Countries 2006.*

Economist Intelligence Unit, 111 West 57th Street, New York, NY 10019, (212) 554-0600, Fax: (212) 586-1181, www.eiu.com; *Indonesia Country Report.*

Euromonitor International, Inc., 224 S. Michigan Avenue, Suite 1500, Chicago, IL 60604, (312) 922-1115, Fax: (312) 922-1157, www.euromonitor.com; *International Marketing Data and Statistics 2008.*

International Monetary Fund (IMF), 700 Nineteenth Street, NW, Washington, DC 20431, (202) 623-7000, Fax: (202) 623-4661, www.imf.org; *International Financial Statistics Yearbook 2007.*

Taylor and Francis Group, An Informa Business, 2 Park Square, Milton Park, Abingdon, Oxford OX14 4RN, United Kingdom, (Dial from U.S. (212) 216-7800), (Fax from U.S. (212) 564-7854), www.tandf.co.uk; *The Europa World Year Book.*

United Nations Statistics Division, New York, NY 10017, (800) 253-9646, Fax: (212) 963-4116, http://unstats.un.org; *Statistical Yearbook.*

The World Bank, 1818 H Street, NW, Washington, DC 20433, (202) 473-1000, Fax: (202) 477-6391, www.worldbank.org; *India; Indonesia;* and *World Development Report 2008.*

INDONESIA - MONUMENTS AND HISTORIC SITES

UNESCO Institute for Statistics, C.P. 6128 Succursale Centre-Ville, Montreal, Quebec, H3C 3J7 Canada, (Dial from U.S. (514) 343-6880), (Fax from U.S. (514) 343 6882), www.uis.unesco.org; *Statistical Tables.*

INDONESIA - MORTALITY

Central Intelligence Agency, Office of Public Affairs, Washington, DC 20505, (703) 482-0623, Fax: (703) 482-1739, www.cia.gov; *The World Factbook.*

Euromonitor International, Inc., 224 S. Michigan Avenue, Suite 1500, Chicago, IL 60604, (312) 922-1115, Fax: (312) 922-1157, www.euromonitor.com; *International Marketing Data and Statistics 2008* and *The World Economic Factbook 2008.*

Palgrave Macmillan Ltd., Houndmills, Basingstoke, Hampshire, RG21 6XS, England, (Telephone in U.S. (888) 330-8477), (Fax in U.S. (800) 672-2054), www.palgrave.com; *The Statesman's Yearbook 2008.*

Taylor and Francis Group, An Informa Business, 2 Park Square, Milton Park, Abingdon, Oxford OX14 4RN, United Kingdom, (Dial from U.S. (212) 216-7800), (Fax from U.S. (212) 564-7854), www.tandf.co.uk; *The Europa World Year Book.*

UNICEF, 3 United Nations Plaza, New York, NY 10017, (800) 253-9646, Fax: (212) 887-7465, www.unicef.org; *The State of the World's Children 2008.*

United Nations Statistics Division, New York, NY 10017, (800) 253-9646, Fax: (212) 963-4116, http://unstats.un.org; *Asia-Pacific in Figures 2004; Demographic Yearbook; Human Development Report 2006; Statistical Yearbook;* and *World Statistics Pocketbook.*

The World Bank, 1818 H Street, NW, Washington, DC 20433, (202) 473-1000, Fax: (202) 477-6391, www.worldbank.org; *The World Bank Atlas 2003-2004* and *World Development Report 2008.*

World Health Organization (WHO), Avenue Appia 20, 1211 Geneve 27, Switzerland, (Telephone in U.S. (212) 331-9081), www.who.int; The WHO Global Atlas of Infectious Diseases and *World Health Report 2006.*

INDONESIA - MOTION PICTURES

Palgrave Macmillan Ltd., Houndmills, Basingstoke, Hampshire, RG21 6XS, England, (Telephone in U.S. (888) 330-8477), (Fax in U.S. (800) 672-2054), www.palgrave.com; *The Statesman's Yearbook 2008.*

UNESCO Institute for Statistics, C.P. 6128 Succursale Centre-Ville, Montreal, Quebec, H3C 3J7 Canada, (Dial from U.S. (514) 343-6880), (Fax from U.S. (514) 343 6882), www.uis.unesco.org; *Statistical Tables.*

United Nations Statistics Division, New York, NY 10017, (800) 253-9646, Fax: (212) 963-4116, http://unstats.un.org; *Statistical Yearbook.*

INDONESIA - MOTOR VEHICLES

International Road Federation (IFR), Madison Place, 500 Montgomery Street, 5th Floor, Alexandria, VA

22314, (703) 535-1001, Fax: (703) 535-1007, www.irfnet.org; *World Road Statistics 2006.*

Taylor and Francis Group, An Informa Business, 2 Park Square, Milton Park, Abingdon, Oxford OX14 4RN, United Kingdom, (Dial from U.S. (212) 216-7800), (Fax from U.S. (212) 564-7854), www.tandf.co.uk; *The Europa World Year Book.*

United Nations Statistics Division, New York, NY 10017, (800) 253-9646, Fax: (212) 963-4116, http://unstats.un.org; *Statistical Yearbook.*

INDONESIA - MUSEUMS

M.E. Sharpe, 80 Business Park Drive, Armonk, NY 10504, (800) 541-6563, Fax: (914) 273-2106, www.mesharpe.com; *The Illustrated Book of World Rankings.*

UNESCO Institute for Statistics, C.P. 6128 Succursale Centre-Ville, Montreal, Quebec, H3C 3J7 Canada, (Dial from U.S. (514) 343-6880), (Fax from U.S. (514) 343 6882), www.uis.unesco.org; *Statistical Tables.*

INDONESIA - NATURAL GAS PRODUCTION

See INDONESIA - MINERAL INDUSTRIES

INDONESIA - NICKEL AND NICKEL ORE

See INDONESIA - MINERAL INDUSTRIES

INDONESIA - NUTRITION

Asian Development Bank (ADB), PO Box 789, 0980 Manila, Philippines, www.adb.org; *Key Indicators of Developing Asian and Pacific Countries 2006.*

United Nations Food and Agricultural Organization (FAO), Viale delle Terme di Caracalla, 00100 Rome, Italy, (Dial from U.S. (202) 653-2400), (Fax from U.S. (202) 653 5760), www.fao.org; *The State of Food and Agriculture (SOFA) 2006.*

INDONESIA - OLDER PEOPLE

M.E. Sharpe, 80 Business Park Drive, Armonk, NY 10504, (800) 541-6563, Fax: (914) 273-2106, www.mesharpe.com; *The Illustrated Book of World Rankings.*

INDONESIA - PALM OIL PRODUCTION

See INDONESIA - CROPS

INDONESIA - PAPER

See INDONESIA - FORESTS AND FORESTRY

INDONESIA - PEANUT PRODUCTION

See INDONESIA - CROPS

INDONESIA - PEPPER PRODUCTION

See INDONESIA - CROPS

INDONESIA - PESTICIDES

United Nations Food and Agricultural Organization (FAO), Viale delle Terme di Caracalla, 00100 Rome, Italy, (Dial from U.S. (202) 653-2400), (Fax from U.S. (202) 653 5760), www.fao.org; *The State of Food and Agriculture (SOFA) 2006.*

INDONESIA - PETROLEUM INDUSTRY AND TRADE

Asian Development Bank (ADB), PO Box 789, 0980 Manila, Philippines, www.adb.org; *Key Indicators of Developing Asian and Pacific Countries 2006.*

International Monetary Fund (IMF), 700 Nineteenth Street, NW, Washington, DC 20431, (202) 623-7000, Fax: (202) 623-4661, www.imf.org; *International Financial Statistics Yearbook 2007.*

M.E. Sharpe, 80 Business Park Drive, Armonk, NY 10504, (800) 541-6563, Fax: (914) 273-2106, www.mesharpe.com; *The Illustrated Book of World Rankings.*

Organisation for Economic Cooperation and Development (OECD), 2 rue Andre Pascal, F-75775 Paris Cedex 16, France, (Telephone in U.S. (202) 785-6323), (Fax in U.S. (202) 785-0350), www.oecd.org; *World Energy Outlook 2007.*

Organization of Petroleum Exporting Countries (OPEC), Obere Donaustrasse 93, A-1020, Vienna, Austria, www.opec.org; *Annual Statistical Bulletin 2006.*

Palgrave Macmillan Ltd., Houndmills, Basingstoke, Hampshire, RG21 6XS, England, (Telephone in U.S. (888) 330-8477), (Fax in U.S. (800) 672-2054), www.palgrave.com; *The Statesman's Yearbook 2008.*

PennWell Corporation, 1421 South Sheridan Road, Tulsa, OK 74112, (918) 835-3161, www.pennwell.com; *International Petroleum Encyclopedia 2007.*

U.S. Department of Energy (DOE), Energy Information Administration (EIA), 1000 Independence Avenue, SW, Washington, DC 20585, (202) 586-8800, www.eia.doe.gov; *International Energy Annual 2004* and *International Energy Outlook 2006.*

United Nations Conference on Trade and Development (UNCTAD), DC2-1120, United Nations, New York, NY 10017, (212) 963-0027, www.unctad.org; *UNCTAD Commodity Yearbook.*

United Nations Food and Agricultural Organization (FAO), Viale delle Terme di Caracalla, 00100 Rome, Italy, (Dial from U.S. (202) 653-2400), (Fax from U.S. (202) 653 5760), www.fao.org; *The State of Food and Agriculture (SOFA) 2006.*

United Nations Statistics Division, New York, NY 10017, (800) 253-9646, Fax: (212) 963-4116, http://unstats.un.org; *Statistical Yearbook.*

INDONESIA - PHOSPHATES PRODUCTION

See INDONESIA - MINERAL INDUSTRIES

INDONESIA - PIPELINES

Organization of Petroleum Exporting Countries (OPEC), Obere Donaustrasse 93, A-1020, Vienna, Austria, www.opec.org; *Annual Statistical Bulletin 2006.*

INDONESIA - POLITICAL SCIENCE

Asian Development Bank (ADB), PO Box 789, 0980 Manila, Philippines, www.adb.org; *Key Indicators of Developing Asian and Pacific Countries 2006.*

Central Intelligence Agency, Office of Public Affairs, Washington, DC 20505, (703) 482-0623, Fax: (703) 482-1739, www.cia.gov; *The World Factbook.*

International Monetary Fund (IMF), 700 Nineteenth Street, NW, Washington, DC 20431, (202) 623-7000, Fax: (202) 623-4661, www.imf.org; *Government Finance Statistics Yearbook (2008 Edition)* and *International Financial Statistics Yearbook 2007.*

Palgrave Macmillan Ltd., Houndmills, Basingstoke, Hampshire, RG21 6XS, England, (Telephone in U.S. (888) 330-8477), (Fax in U.S. (800) 672-2054), www.palgrave.com; *The Statesman's Yearbook 2008.*

Taylor and Francis Group, An Informa Business, 2 Park Square, Milton Park, Abingdon, Oxford OX14 4RN, United Kingdom, (Dial from U.S. (212) 216-7800), (Fax from U.S. (212) 564-7854), www.tandf.co.uk; *The Europa World Year Book.*

United Nations Statistics Division, New York, NY 10017, (800) 253-9646, Fax: (212) 963-4116, http://unstats.un.org; *Asia-Pacific in Figures 2004; National Accounts Statistics: Compendium of Income Distribution Statistics;* and *Statistical Yearbook.*

The World Bank, 1818 H Street, NW, Washington, DC 20433, (202) 473-1000, Fax: (202) 477-6391, www.worldbank.org; *World Development Report 2008.*

INDONESIA - POPULATION

Asian Development Bank (ADB), PO Box 789, 0980 Manila, Philippines, www.adb.org; *Key Indicators of Developing Asian and Pacific Countries 2006.*

Central Intelligence Agency, Office of Public Affairs, Washington, DC 20505, (703) 482-0623, Fax: (703) 482-1739, www.cia.gov; *The World Factbook.*

Economist Intelligence Unit, 111 West 57th Street, New York, NY 10019, (212) 554-0600, Fax: (212) 586-1181, www.eiu.com; *Indonesia Country Report.*

Euromonitor International, Inc., 224 S. Michigan Avenue, Suite 1500, Chicago, IL 60604, (312) 922-1115, Fax: (312) 922-1157, www.euromonitor.com; *International Marketing Data and Statistics 2008* and *The World Economic Factbook 2008.*

International Labour Office, I.L.O. Publications, 4 route des Morillons, CH-1211 Geneva 22, Switzerland, (Telephone in U.S. (202) 653-7652), (Fax in U.S. (202) 653-7687), www.ilo.org; *Yearbook of Labour Statistics 2006.*

International Organization for Migration (IOM), 17, Route des Morillons, CH-1211 Geneva 19, Switzerland, www.iom.int; *Migration, Development and Natural Disasters: Insights from the Indian Ocean Tsunami.*

M.E. Sharpe, 80 Business Park Drive, Armonk, NY 10504, (800) 541-6563, Fax: (914) 273-2106, www.mesharpe.com; *The Illustrated Book of World Rankings.*

Palgrave Macmillan Ltd., Houndmills, Basingstoke, Hampshire, RG21 6XS, England, (Telephone in U.S. (888) 330-8477), (Fax in U.S. (800) 672-2054), www.palgrave.com; *The Statesman's Yearbook 2008.*

Statistics Indonesia (Badan Pusat Statistik (BPS)), Jl. Dr. Sutomo 6-8, Jakarta 10710, Indonesia, www.bps.go.id; *Statistical Profile of Women, Mothers and Children in Indonesia.*

Taylor and Francis Group, An Informa Business, 2 Park Square, Milton Park, Abingdon, Oxford OX14 4RN, United Kingdom, (Dial from U.S. (212) 216-7800), (Fax from U.S. (212) 564-7854), www.tandf.co.uk; *The Europa World Year Book.*

U.S. Department of State (DOS), 2201 C Street NW, Washington, DC 20520, (202) 647-4000, www.state.gov; *World Military Expenditures and Arms Transfers (WMEAT).*

UNESCO Institute for Statistics, C.P. 6128 Succursale Centre-Ville, Montreal, Quebec, H3C 3J7 Canada, (Dial from U.S. (514) 343-6880), (Fax from U.S. (514) 343 6882), www.uis.unesco.org; *Statistical Tables.*

United Nations Food and Agricultural Organization (FAO), Viale delle Terme di Caracalla, 00100 Rome, Italy, (Dial from U.S. (202) 653-2400), (Fax from U.S. (202) 653 5760), www.fao.org; *FAO Production Yearbook 2002.*

United Nations Statistics Division, New York, NY 10017, (800) 253-9646, Fax: (212) 963-4116, http://unstats.un.org; *Asia-Pacific in Figures 2004; Demographic Yearbook; Human Development Report 2006; Statistical Yearbook; Statistical Yearbook for Asia and the Pacific 2004;* and *World Statistics Pocketbook.*

The World Bank, 1818 H Street, NW, Washington, DC 20433, (202) 473-1000, Fax: (202) 477-6391, www.worldbank.org; *India; Indonesia; The World Bank Atlas 2003-2004;* and *World Development Report 2008.*

World Health Organization (WHO), Avenue Appia 20, 1211 Geneve 27, Switzerland, (Telephone in U.S. (212) 331-9081), www.who.int; *World Health Report 2006.*

Worldinformation.com, 2 Market Street, Saffron Walden, Essex CB10 1HZ, United Kingdom, www.worldinformation.com; The World of Information (www.worldinformation.com).

INDONESIA - POPULATION DENSITY

Central Intelligence Agency, Office of Public Affairs, Washington, DC 20505, (703) 482-0623, Fax: (703) 482-1739, www.cia.gov; *The World Factbook.*

Euromonitor International, Inc., 224 S. Michigan Avenue, Suite 1500, Chicago, IL 60604, (312) 922-1115, Fax: (312) 922-1157, www.euromonitor.com; *International Marketing Data and Statistics 2008* and *The World Economic Factbook 2008.*

M.E. Sharpe, 80 Business Park Drive, Armonk, NY 10504, (800) 541-6563, Fax: (914) 273-2106, www.mesharpe.com; *The Illustrated Book of World Rankings.*

Palgrave Macmillan Ltd., Houndmills, Basingstoke, Hampshire, RG21 6XS, England, (Telephone in U.S. (888) 330-8477), (Fax in U.S. (800) 672-2054), www.palgrave.com; *The Statesman's Yearbook 2008.*

Taylor and Francis Group, An Informa Business, 2 Park Square, Milton Park, Abingdon, Oxford OX14 4RN, United Kingdom, (Dial from U.S. (212) 216-7800), (Fax from U.S. (212) 564-7854), www.tandf.co.uk; *The Europa World Year Book.*

UNESCO Institute for Statistics, C.P. 6128 Succursale Centre-Ville, Montreal, Quebec, H3C 3J7 Canada, (Dial from U.S. (514) 343-6880), (Fax from U.S. (514) 343 6882), www.uis.unesco.org; *Statistical Tables.*

United Nations Food and Agricultural Organization (FAO), Viale delle Terme di Caracalla, 00100 Rome, Italy, (Dial from U.S. (202) 653-2400), (Fax from U.S. (202) 653 5760), www.fao.org; *The State of Food and Agriculture (SOFA) 2006.*

United Nations Statistics Division, New York, NY 10017, (800) 253-9646, Fax: (212) 963-4116, http://unstats.un.org; *Statistical Yearbook.*

The World Bank, 1818 H Street, NW, Washington, DC 20433, (202) 473-1000, Fax: (202) 477-6391, www.worldbank.org; *India; Indonesia;* and *World Development Report 2008.*

INDONESIA - POSTAL SERVICE

M.E. Sharpe, 80 Business Park Drive, Armonk, NY 10504, (800) 541-6563, Fax: (914) 273-2106, www.mesharpe.com; *The Illustrated Book of World Rankings.*

United Nations Statistics Division, New York, NY 10017, (800) 253-9646, Fax: (212) 963-4116, http://unstats.un.org; *Statistical Yearbook.*

INDONESIA - POWER RESOURCES

Euromonitor International, Inc., 224 S. Michigan Avenue, Suite 1500, Chicago, IL 60604, (312) 922-1115, Fax: (312) 922-1157, www.euromonitor.com; *International Marketing Data and Statistics 2008; The World Economic Factbook 2008;* and *World Marketing Data and Statistics.*

M.E. Sharpe, 80 Business Park Drive, Armonk, NY 10504, (800) 541-6563, Fax: (914) 273-2106, www.mesharpe.com; *The Illustrated Book of World Rankings.*

Organisation for Economic Cooperation and Development (OECD), 2 rue Andre Pascal, F-75775 Paris Cedex 16, France, (Telephone in U.S. (202) 785-6323), (Fax in U.S. (202) 785-0350), www.oecd.org; *World Energy Outlook 2007.*

Palgrave Macmillan Ltd., Houndmills, Basingstoke, Hampshire, RG21 6XS, England, (Telephone in U.S. (888) 330-8477), (Fax in U.S. (800) 672-2054), www.palgrave.com; *The Statesman's Yearbook 2008.*

Platts, 2 Penn Plaza, 25th Floor, New York, NY 10121-2298, (212) 904-3070, www.platts.com; *Asian Electricity Outlook 2006; Emissions Daily;* and *Energy Economist.*

U.S. Department of Energy (DOE), Energy Information Administration (EIA), 1000 Independence Avenue, SW, Washington, DC 20585, (202) 586-8800, www.eia.doe.gov; *International Energy Annual 2004* and *International Energy Outlook 2006.*

United Nations Food and Agricultural Organization (FAO), Viale delle Terme di Caracalla, 00100 Rome, Italy, (Dial from U.S. (202) 653-2400), (Fax from U.S. (202) 653 5760), www.fao.org; *The State of Food and Agriculture (SOFA) 2006.*

United Nations Statistics Division, New York, NY 10017, (800) 253-9646, Fax: (212) 963-4116, http://unstats.un.org; *Asia-Pacific in Figures 2004; Energy Statistics Yearbook 2003; Human Development Report 2006; Statistical Yearbook; Statistical Yearbook for Asia and the Pacific 2004; World Energy Assessment 2004 Update: Overview;* and *World Statistics Pocketbook.*

The World Bank, 1818 H Street, NW, Washington, DC 20433, (202) 473-1000, Fax: (202) 477-6391, www.worldbank.org; *The World Bank Atlas 2003-2004* and *World Development Report 2008.*

INDONESIA - PRICES

Asian Development Bank (ADB), PO Box 789, 0980 Manila, Philippines, www.adb.org; *Key Indicators of Developing Asian and Pacific Countries 2006.*

Euromonitor International, Inc., 224 S. Michigan Avenue, Suite 1500, Chicago, IL 60604, (312) 922-1115, Fax: (312) 922-1157, www.euromonitor.com; *World Marketing Data and Statistics.*

International Labour Office, I.L.O. Publications, 4 route des Morillons, CH-1211 Geneva 22, Switzerland, (Telephone in U.S. (202) 653-7652), (Fax in U.S. (202) 653-7687), www.ilo.org; *Yearbook of Labour Statistics 2006.*

International Monetary Fund (IMF), 700 Nineteenth Street, NW, Washington, DC 20431, (202) 623-7000, Fax: (202) 623-4661, www.imf.org; *International Financial Statistics Yearbook 2007.*

M.E. Sharpe, 80 Business Park Drive, Armonk, NY 10504, (800) 541-6563, Fax: (914) 273-2106, www.mesharpe.com; *The Illustrated Book of World Rankings.*

United Nations Food and Agricultural Organization (FAO), Viale delle Terme di Caracalla, 00100 Rome, Italy, (Dial from U.S. (202) 653-2400), (Fax from U.S. (202) 653 5760), www.fao.org; *FAO Production Yearbook 2002* and *The State of Food and Agriculture (SOFA) 2006.*

The World Bank, 1818 H Street, NW, Washington, DC 20433, (202) 473-1000, Fax: (202) 477-6391, www.worldbank.org; *India* and *Indonesia.*

INDONESIA - PROFESSIONS

United Nations Statistics Division, New York, NY 10017, (800) 253-9646, Fax: (212) 963-4116, http://unstats.un.org; *Statistical Yearbook.*

INDONESIA - PUBLIC HEALTH

Economist Intelligence Unit, 111 West 57th Street, New York, NY 10019, (212) 554-0600, Fax: (212) 586-1181, www.eiu.com; *Business Asia.*

Euromonitor International, Inc., 224 S. Michigan Avenue, Suite 1500, Chicago, IL 60604, (312) 922-1115, Fax: (312) 922-1157, www.euromonitor.com; *World Health Databook 2007/2008* and *World Marketing Data and Statistics.*

M.E. Sharpe, 80 Business Park Drive, Armonk, NY 10504, (800) 541-6563, Fax: (914) 273-2106, www.mesharpe.com; *The Illustrated Book of World Rankings.*

Palgrave Macmillan Ltd., Houndmills, Basingstoke, Hampshire, RG21 6XS, England, (Telephone in U.S. (888) 330-8477), (Fax in U.S. (800) 672-2054), www.palgrave.com; *The Statesman's Yearbook 2008.*

UNICEF, 3 United Nations Plaza, New York, NY 10017, (800) 253-9646, Fax: (212) 887-7465, www.unicef.org; *The State of the World's Children 2008.*

United Nations Statistics Division, New York, NY 10017, (800) 253-9646, Fax: (212) 963-4116, http://unstats.un.org; *Asia-Pacific in Figures 2004; Human Development Report 2006;* and *Statistical Yearbook.*

The World Bank, 1818 H Street, NW, Washington, DC 20433, (202) 473-1000, Fax: (202) 477-6391, www.worldbank.org; *India; Indonesia;* and *World Development Report 2008.*

World Health Organization (WHO), Avenue Appia 20, 1211 Geneve 27, Switzerland, (Telephone in U.S. (212) 331-9081), www.who.int; The WHO Global Atlas of Infectious Diseases and *World Health Report 2006.*

INDONESIA - PUBLIC UTILITIES

United Nations Statistics Division, New York, NY 10017, (800) 253-9646, Fax: (212) 963-4116, http://unstats.un.org; *Electric Power in Asia and the Pacific 2001 and 2002.*

INDONESIA - PUBLISHERS AND PUBLISHING

Palgrave Macmillan Ltd., Houndmills, Basingstoke, Hampshire, RG21 6XS, England, (Telephone in U.S. (888) 330-8477), (Fax in U.S. (800) 672-2054), www.palgrave.com; *The Statesman's Yearbook 2008.*

Taylor and Francis Group, An Informa Business, 2 Park Square, Milton Park, Abingdon, Oxford OX14 4RN, United Kingdom, (Dial from U.S. (212) 216-7800), (Fax from U.S. (212) 564-7854), www.tandf.co.uk; *The Europa World Year Book.*

UNESCO Institute for Statistics, C.P. 6128 Succursale Centre-Ville, Montreal, Quebec, H3C 3J7 Canada, (Dial from U.S. (514) 343-6880), (Fax from U.S. (514) 343 6882), www.uis.unesco.org; *Statistical Tables.*

INDONESIA - RADIO - RECEIVERS AND RECEPTION

Palgrave Macmillan Ltd., Houndmills, Basingstoke, Hampshire, RG21 6XS, England, (Telephone in U.S. (888) 330-8477), (Fax in U.S. (800) 672-2054), www.palgrave.com; *The Statesman's Yearbook 2008.*

United Nations Statistics Division, New York, NY 10017, (800) 253-9646, Fax: (212) 963-4116, http://unstats.un.org; *Statistical Yearbook.*

INDONESIA - RAILROADS

Jane's Information Group, 110 North Royal Street, Suite 200, Alexandria, VA 22314, (703) 683-3700, Fax: (800) 836-0297, www.janes.com; *Jane's World Railways.*

Palgrave Macmillan Ltd., Houndmills, Basingstoke, Hampshire, RG21 6XS, England, (Telephone in U.S. (888) 330-8477), (Fax in U.S. (800) 672-2054), www.palgrave.com; *The Statesman's Yearbook 2008.*

Taylor and Francis Group, An Informa Business, 2 Park Square, Milton Park, Abingdon, Oxford OX14 4RN, United Kingdom, (Dial from U.S. (212) 216-7800), (Fax from U.S. (212) 564-7854), www.tandf.co.uk; *The Europa World Year Book.*

United Nations Statistics Division, New York, NY 10017, (800) 253-9646, Fax: (212) 963-4116, http://unstats.un.org; *Statistical Yearbook.*

INDONESIA - RELIGION

Central Intelligence Agency, Office of Public Affairs, Washington, DC 20505, (703) 482-0623, Fax: (703) 482-1739, www.cia.gov; *The World Factbook.*

M.E. Sharpe, 80 Business Park Drive, Armonk, NY 10504, (800) 541-6563, Fax: (914) 273-2106, www.mesharpe.com; *The Illustrated Book of World Rankings.*

Palgrave Macmillan Ltd., Houndmills, Basingstoke, Hampshire, RG21 6XS, England, (Telephone in U.S. (888) 330-8477), (Fax in U.S. (800) 672-2054), www.palgrave.com; *The Statesman's Yearbook 2008.*

INDONESIA - RENT CHARGES

International Labour Office, I.L.O. Publications, 4 route des Morillons, CH-1211 Geneva 22, Switzerland, (Telephone in U.S. (202) 653-7652), (Fax in U.S. (202) 653-7687), www.ilo.org; *Yearbook of Labour Statistics 2006.*

INDONESIA - RESERVES (ACCOUNTING)

Asian Development Bank (ADB), PO Box 789, 0980 Manila, Philippines, www.adb.org; *Key Indicators of Developing Asian and Pacific Countries 2006.*

Euromonitor International, Inc., 224 S. Michigan Avenue, Suite 1500, Chicago, IL 60604, (312) 922-1115, Fax: (312) 922-1157, www.euromonitor.com; *International Marketing Data and Statistics 2008.*

United Nations Statistics Division, New York, NY 10017, (800) 253-9646, Fax: (212) 963-4116, http://unstats.un.org; *Statistical Yearbook.*

The World Bank, 1818 H Street, NW, Washington, DC 20433, (202) 473-1000, Fax: (202) 477-6391, www.worldbank.org; *World Development Report 2008.*

INDONESIA - RETAIL TRADE

Euromonitor International, Inc., 224 S. Michigan Avenue, Suite 1500, Chicago, IL 60604, (312) 922-1115, Fax: (312) 922-1157, www.euromonitor.com; *Retail Trade International 2007* and *World Marketing Data and Statistics.*

INDONESIA - RICE PRODUCTION

See INDONESIA - CROPS

INDONESIA - ROADS

Central Intelligence Agency, Office of Public Affairs, Washington, DC 20505, (703) 482-0623, Fax: (703) 482-1739, www.cia.gov; *The World Factbook.*

Economist Intelligence Unit, 111 West 57th Street, New York, NY 10019, (212) 554-0600, Fax: (212) 586-1181, www.eiu.com; *Business Asia.*

International Road Federation (IFR), Madison Place, 500 Montgomery Street, 5th Floor, Alexandria, VA 22314, (703) 535-1001, Fax: (703) 535-1007, www.irfnet.org; *World Road Statistics 2006.*

Palgrave Macmillan Ltd., Houndmills, Basingstoke, Hampshire, RG21 6XS, England, (Telephone in U.S. (888) 330-8477), (Fax in U.S. (800) 672-2054), www.palgrave.com; *The Statesman's Yearbook 2008.*

INDONESIA - RUBBER INDUSTRY AND TRADE

International Monetary Fund (IMF), 700 Nineteenth Street, NW, Washington, DC 20431, (202) 623-7000, Fax: (202) 623-4661, www.imf.org; *International Financial Statistics Yearbook 2007.*

International Rubber Study Group (IRSG), 1st Floor, Heron House, 109/115 Wembley Hill Road, Wembley, Middlesex HA9 8DA, United Kingdom, www.rubberstudy.com; *Rubber Statistical Bulletin; Summary of World Rubber Statistics 2005; World Rubber Statistics Handbook (Volume 6, 1975-2001);* and *World Rubber Statistics Historic Handbook.*

M.E. Sharpe, 80 Business Park Drive, Armonk, NY 10504, (800) 541-6563, Fax: (914) 273-2106, www.mesharpe.com; *The Illustrated Book of World Rankings.*

United Nations Statistics Division, New York, NY 10017, (800) 253-9646, Fax: (212) 963-4116, http://unstats.un.org; *Statistical Yearbook.*

INDONESIA - SALT PRODUCTION

See INDONESIA - MINERAL INDUSTRIES

INDONESIA - SHEEP

See INDONESIA - LIVESTOCK

INDONESIA - SHIPPING

Lloyd's Register - Fairplay, 8410 N.W. 53rd Terrace, Suite 207, Miami FL 33166, (305) 718-9929, Fax: (305) 718-9663, www.lrfairplay.com; *Register of Ships 2007-2008; World Casualty Statistics 2007; World Fleet Statistics 2006; World Marine Propulsion Report 2006-2010; World Shipbuilding Statistics 2007;* and The World Shipping Encyclopaedia.

Organization of Petroleum Exporting Countries (OPEC), Obere Donaustrasse 93, A-1020, Vienna, Austria, www.opec.org; *Annual Statistical Bulletin 2006.*

Palgrave Macmillan Ltd., Houndmills, Basingstoke, Hampshire, RG21 6XS, England, (Telephone in U.S. (888) 330-8477), (Fax in U.S. (800) 672-2054), www.palgrave.com; *The Statesman's Yearbook 2008.*

Taylor and Francis Group, An Informa Business, 2 Park Square, Milton Park, Abingdon, Oxford OX14 4RN, United Kingdom, (Dial from U.S. (212) 216-7800), (Fax from U.S. (212) 564-7854), www.tandf.co.uk; *The Europa World Year Book.*

U.S. Department of Transportation (DOT), Maritime Administration (MARAD), West Building, Southeast Federal Center, 1200 New Jersey Avenue, SE, Washington, DC 20590, (800) 99-MARAD, www.marad.dot.gov; *World Merchant Fleet 2005.*

United Nations Statistics Division, New York, NY 10017, (800) 253-9646, Fax: (212) 963-4116, http://unstats.un.org; *Statistical Yearbook.*

INDONESIA - SILVER PRODUCTION

See INDONESIA - MINERAL INDUSTRIES

INDONESIA - SOCIAL ECOLOGY

Asian Development Bank (ADB), PO Box 789, 0980 Manila, Philippines, www.adb.org; *Key Indicators of Developing Asian and Pacific Countries 2006.*

M.E. Sharpe, 80 Business Park Drive, Armonk, NY 10504, (800) 541-6563, Fax: (914) 273-2106, www.mesharpe.com; *The Illustrated Book of World Rankings.*

United Nations Statistics Division, New York, NY 10017, (800) 253-9646, Fax: (212) 963-4116, http://unstats.un.org; *World Statistics Pocketbook.*

INDONESIA - SOCIAL SECURITY

Palgrave Macmillan Ltd., Houndmills, Basingstoke, Hampshire, RG21 6XS, England, (Telephone in U.S. (888) 330-8477), (Fax in U.S. (800) 672-2054), www.palgrave.com; *The Statesman's Yearbook 2008.*

United Nations Statistics Division, New York, NY 10017, (800) 253-9646, Fax: (212) 963-4116, http://unstats.un.org; *National Accounts Statistics: Compendium of Income Distribution Statistics.*

INDONESIA - SOYBEAN PRODUCTION

See INDONESIA - CROPS

INDONESIA - STEEL PRODUCTION

See INDONESIA - MINERAL INDUSTRIES

INDONESIA - SUGAR PRODUCTION

See INDONESIA - CROPS

INDONESIA - TAXATION

International Monetary Fund (IMF), 700 Nineteenth Street, NW, Washington, DC 20431, (202) 623-7000, Fax: (202) 623-4661, www.imf.org; *Government Finance Statistics Yearbook (2008 Edition).*

International Road Federation (IFR), Madison Place, 500 Montgomery Street, 5th Floor, Alexandria, VA 22314, (703) 535-1001, Fax: (703) 535-1007, www.irfnet.org; *World Road Statistics 2006.*

Taylor and Francis Group, An Informa Business, 2 Park Square, Milton Park, Abingdon, Oxford OX14 4RN, United Kingdom, (Dial from U.S. (212) 216-7800), (Fax from U.S. (212) 564-7854), www.tandf.co.uk; *The Europa World Year Book.*

The World Bank, 1818 H Street, NW, Washington, DC 20433, (202) 473-1000, Fax: (202) 477-6391, www.worldbank.org; *World Development Report 2008.*

INDONESIA - TEA PRODUCTION

See INDONESIA - CROPS

INDONESIA - TELEPHONE

International Telecommunication Union (ITU), Place des Nations, 1211 Geneva 20, Switzerland, www.itu.int; World Telecommunication Indicators Database.

Palgrave Macmillan Ltd., Houndmills, Basingstoke, Hampshire, RG21 6XS, England, (Telephone in U.S. (888) 330-8477), (Fax in U.S. (800) 672-2054), www.palgrave.com; *The Statesman's Yearbook 2008.*

Taylor and Francis Group, An Informa Business, 2 Park Square, Milton Park, Abingdon, Oxford OX14 4RN, United Kingdom, (Dial from U.S. (212) 216-7800), (Fax from U.S. (212) 564-7854), www.tandf.co.uk; *The Europa World Year Book.*

United Nations Statistics Division, New York, NY 10017, (800) 253-9646, Fax: (212) 963-4116, http://unstats.un.org; *Statistical Yearbook* and *World Statistics Pocketbook.*

INDONESIA - TELEVISION - RECEIVERS AND RECEPTION

United Nations Statistics Division, New York, NY 10017, (800) 253-9646, Fax: (212) 963-4116, http://unstats.un.org; *Statistical Yearbook.*

INDONESIA - TEXTILE INDUSTRY

Euromonitor International, Inc., 224 S. Michigan Avenue, Suite 1500, Chicago, IL 60604, (312) 922-1115, Fax: (312) 922-1157, www.euromonitor.com; *Retail Trade International 2007.*

M.E. Sharpe, 80 Business Park Drive, Armonk, NY 10504, (800) 541-6563, Fax: (914) 273-2106, www.mesharpe.com; *The Illustrated Book of World Rankings.*

Palgrave Macmillan Ltd., Houndmills, Basingstoke, Hampshire, RG21 6XS, England, (Telephone in U.S. (888) 330-8477), (Fax in U.S. (800) 672-2054), www.palgrave.com; *The Statesman's Yearbook 2008.*

United Nations Conference on Trade and Development (UNCTAD), DC2-1120, United Nations, New York, NY 10017, (212) 963-0027, www.unctad.org; *UNCTAD Commodity Yearbook.*

United Nations Statistics Division, New York, NY 10017, (800) 253-9646, Fax: (212) 963-4116, http://unstats.un.org; *Statistical Yearbook.*

INDONESIA - THEATER

UNESCO Institute for Statistics, C.P. 6128 Succursale Centre-Ville, Montreal, Quebec, H3C 3J7 Canada, (Dial from U.S. (514) 343-6880), (Fax from U.S. (514) 343 6882), www.uis.unesco.org; *Statistical Tables.*

INDONESIA - TIN PRODUCTION

See INDONESIA - MINERAL INDUSTRIES

INDONESIA - TIRE INDUSTRY

United Nations Statistics Division, New York, NY 10017, (800) 253-9646, Fax: (212) 963-4116, http://unstats.un.org; *Statistical Yearbook.*

INDONESIA - TOBACCO INDUSTRY

Foreign Agricultural Service (FAS), U.S. Department of Agriculture (USDA), 1400 Independence Avenue, SW, Washington, DC 20250, (202) 720-3935, www.fas.usda.gov; *Tobacco: World Markets and Trade.*

M.E. Sharpe, 80 Business Park Drive, Armonk, NY 10504, (800) 541-6563, Fax: (914) 273-2106, www.mesharpe.com; *The Illustrated Book of World Rankings.*

United Nations Statistics Division, New York, NY 10017, (800) 253-9646, Fax: (212) 963-4116, http://unstats.un.org; *Statistical Yearbook.*

INDONESIA - TOURISM

Euromonitor International, Inc., 224 S. Michigan Avenue, Suite 1500, Chicago, IL 60604, (312) 922-1115, Fax: (312) 922-1157, www.euromonitor.com; *The World Economic Factbook 2008* and *World Marketing Data and Statistics.*

M.E. Sharpe, 80 Business Park Drive, Armonk, NY 10504, (800) 541-6563, Fax: (914) 273-2106, www.mesharpe.com; *The Illustrated Book of World Rankings.*

Palgrave Macmillan Ltd., Houndmills, Basingstoke, Hampshire, RG21 6XS, England, (Telephone in U.S. (888) 330-8477), (Fax in U.S. (800) 672-2054), www.palgrave.com; *The Statesman's Yearbook 2008.*

Taylor and Francis Group, An Informa Business, 2 Park Square, Milton Park, Abingdon, Oxford OX14 4RN, United Kingdom, (Dial from U.S. (212) 216-7800), (Fax from U.S. (212) 564-7854), www.tandf.co.uk; *The Europa World Year Book.*

United Nations Statistics Division, New York, NY 10017, (800) 253-9646, Fax: (212) 963-4116, http://unstats.un.org; *Statistical Yearbook.*

United Nations World Tourism Organization (UNWTO), Capitan Haya 42, 28020 Madrid, Spain, www.world-tourism.org; *Yearbook of Tourism Statistics.*

The World Bank, 1818 H Street, NW, Washington, DC 20433, (202) 473-1000, Fax: (202) 477-6391, www.worldbank.org; *India* and *Indonesia*.

INDONESIA - TRADE

See INDONESIA - INTERNATIONAL TRADE

INDONESIA - TRANSPORTATION

Central Intelligence Agency, Office of Public Affairs, Washington, DC 20505, (703) 482-0623, Fax: (703) 482-1739, www.cia.gov; *The World Factbook*.

Euromonitor International, Inc., 224 S. Michigan Avenue, Suite 1500, Chicago, IL 60604, (312) 922-1115, Fax: (312) 922-1157, www.euromonitor.com; *International Marketing Data and Statistics 2008* and *World Marketing Data and Statistics*.

M.E. Sharpe, 80 Business Park Drive, Armonk, NY 10504, (800) 541-6563, Fax: (914) 273-2106, www.mesharpe.com; *The Illustrated Book of World Rankings*.

Palgrave Macmillan Ltd., Houndmills, Basingstoke, Hampshire, RG21 6XS, England, (Telephone in U.S. (888) 330-8477), (Fax in U.S. (800) 672-2054), www.palgrave.com; *The Statesman's Yearbook 2008*.

Taylor and Francis Group, An Informa Business, 2 Park Square, Milton Park, Abingdon, Oxford OX14 4RN, United Kingdom, (Dial from U.S. (212) 216-7800), (Fax from U.S. (212) 564-7854), www.tandf.co.uk; *The Europa World Year Book*.

United Nations Statistics Division, New York, NY 10017, (800) 253-9646, Fax: (212) 963-4116, http://unstats.un.org; *Human Development Report 2006* and *Statistical Yearbook for Asia and the Pacific 2004*.

The World Bank, 1818 H Street, NW, Washington, DC 20433, (202) 473-1000, Fax: (202) 477-6391, www.worldbank.org; *India* and *Indonesia*.

INDONESIA - UNEMPLOYMENT

Central Intelligence Agency, Office of Public Affairs, Washington, DC 20505, (703) 482-0623, Fax: (703) 482-1739, www.cia.gov; *The World Factbook*.

Euromonitor International, Inc., 224 S. Michigan Avenue, Suite 1500, Chicago, IL 60604, (312) 922-1115, Fax: (312) 922-1157, www.euromonitor.com; *International Marketing Data and Statistics 2008*.

International Labour Office, I.L.O. Publications, 4 route des Morillons, CH-1211 Geneva 22, Switzerland, (Telephone in U.S. (202) 653-7652), (Fax in U.S. (202) 653-7687), www.ilo.org; *Yearbook of Labour Statistics 2006*.

Palgrave Macmillan Ltd., Houndmills, Basingstoke, Hampshire, RG21 6XS, England, (Telephone in U.S. (888) 330-8477), (Fax in U.S. (800) 672-2054), www.palgrave.com; *The Statesman's Yearbook 2008*.

United Nations Statistics Division, New York, NY 10017, (800) 253-9646, Fax: (212) 963-4116, http://unstats.un.org; *Statistical Yearbook*.

The World Bank, 1818 H Street, NW, Washington, DC 20433, (202) 473-1000, Fax: (202) 477-6391, www.worldbank.org; *Indonesia*.

INDONESIA - VITAL STATISTICS

Euromonitor International, Inc., 224 S. Michigan Avenue, Suite 1500, Chicago, IL 60604, (312) 922-1115, Fax: (312) 922-1157, www.euromonitor.com; *International Marketing Data and Statistics 2008*.

International Organization for Migration (IOM), 17, Route des Morillons, CH-1211 Geneva 19, Switzerland, www.iom.int; *Migration, Development and Natural Disasters: Insights from the Indian Ocean Tsunami*.

Palgrave Macmillan Ltd., Houndmills, Basingstoke, Hampshire, RG21 6XS, England, (Telephone in U.S. (888) 330-8477), (Fax in U.S. (800) 672-2054), www.palgrave.com; *The Statesman's Yearbook 2008*.

Statistics Indonesia (Badan Pusat Statistik (BPS)), Jl. Dr. Sutomo 6-8, Jakarta 10710, Indonesia, www.bps.go.id; *Statistical Profile of Women, Mothers and Children in Indonesia*.

United Nations Statistics Division, New York, NY 10017, (800) 253-9646, Fax: (212) 963-4116, http://unstats.un.org; *Statistical Yearbook*.

World Health Organization (WHO), Avenue Appia 20, 1211 Geneve 27, Switzerland, (Telephone in U.S. (212) 331-9081), www.who.int; *World Health Report 2006*.

INDONESIA - WAGES

International Labour Office, I.L.O. Publications, 4 route des Morillons, CH-1211 Geneva 22, Switzerland, (Telephone in U.S. (202) 653-7652), (Fax in U.S. (202) 653-7687), www.ilo.org; *Yearbook of Labour Statistics 2006*.

United Nations Statistics Division, New York, NY 10017, (800) 253-9646, Fax: (212) 963-4116, http://unstats.un.org; *Statistical Yearbook for Asia and the Pacific 2004*.

The World Bank, 1818 H Street, NW, Washington, DC 20433, (202) 473-1000, Fax: (202) 477-6391, www.worldbank.org; *India* and *Indonesia*.

INDONESIA - WEATHER

See INDONESIA - CLIMATE

INDONESIA - WHEAT PRODUCTION

See INDONESIA - CROPS

INDONESIA - WHOLESALE PRICE INDEXES

Asian Development Bank (ADB), PO Box 789, 0980 Manila, Philippines, www.adb.org; *Key Indicators of Developing Asian and Pacific Countries 2006*.

INDONESIA - WINE PRODUCTION

See INDONESIA - BEVERAGE INDUSTRY

INDONESIA - WOOD AND WOOD PULP

See INDONESIA - FORESTS AND FORESTRY

INDONESIA - WOOL PRODUCTION

See INDONESIA - TEXTILE INDUSTRY

INDONESIA - YARN PRODUCTION

See INDONESIA - TEXTILE INDUSTRY

INDONESIA - ZOOS

UNESCO Institute for Statistics, C.P. 6128 Succursale Centre-Ville, Montreal, Quebec, H3C 3J7 Canada, (Dial from U.S. (514) 343-6880), (Fax from U.S. (514) 343 6882), www.uis.unesco.org; *Statistical Tables*.

INDUSTRIAL AND COMMERCIAL ENTERPRISES - FAILURES

U.S. Census Bureau, Company Statistics Division, 4700 Silver Hill Road, Washington DC 20233-0001, (301) 763-3030, www.census.gov/csd/; *County Business Patterns 2004*.

INDUSTRIAL MACHINERY AND EQUIPMENT - CAPITAL

Bureau of Economic Analysis (BEA), U.S. Department of Commerce (DOC), 1441 L Street NW, Washington, DC 20230, (202) 606-9900, www.bea.gov; National Income and Product Accounts (NIPA) Tables (web app) and *Survey of Current Business (SCB)*.

INDUSTRIAL MACHINERY AND EQUIPMENT - EARNINGS

U.S. Bureau of Labor Statistics (BLS), Postal Square Building, 2 Massachusetts Avenue, NE, Washington, DC 20212-0001, (202) 691-5200, Fax: (202) 691-6325, www.bls.gov; *Current Employment Statistics Survey (CES)* and *Employment and Earnings (EE)*.

U.S. Census Bureau, 4700 Silver Hill Road, Washington DC 20233-0001, (301) 763-3030, www.census.gov; *2002 Economic Census, Nonemployer Statistics*.

U.S. Census Bureau, Center for Economic Studies, 4600 Silver Hill Road, Washington DC 20233, (301) 457-1235, www.ces.census.gov; *2002 Economic Census, Geographic Area Series*.

U.S. Census Bureau, Company Statistics Division, 4700 Silver Hill Road, Washington DC 20233-0001, (301) 763-3030, www.census.gov/csd/; *County Business Patterns 2004*.

U.S. Census Bureau, Manufacturing and Construction Division, 4600 Silver Hill Road, Washington DC 20233, (301) 763-4673, www.census.gov/mcd; *Annual Survey of Manufactures (ASM)* and *Census of Manufactures*.

U.S. Department of Commerce (DOC), Economics and Statistics Administration (ESA), 1401 Constitution Avenue, NW, Washington, DC 20230, (800) 782-8872, www.esa.doc.gov; *The Digital Economy 2003*.

INDUSTRIAL MACHINERY AND EQUIPMENT - EMPLOYEES

U.S. Bureau of Labor Statistics (BLS), Postal Square Building, 2 Massachusetts Avenue, NE, Washington, DC 20212-0001, (202) 691-5200, Fax: (202) 691-6325, www.bls.gov; *Current Employment Statistics Survey (CES)* and *Employment and Earnings (EE)*.

U.S. Census Bureau, Company Statistics Division, 4700 Silver Hill Road, Washington DC 20233-0001, (301) 763-3030, www.census.gov/csd/; *County Business Patterns 2004*.

U.S. Census Bureau, Manufacturing and Construction Division, 4600 Silver Hill Road, Washington DC 20233, (301) 763-4673, www.census.gov/mcd; *Annual Survey of Manufactures (ASM)* and *Census of Manufactures*.

U.S. Department of Commerce (DOC), Economics and Statistics Administration (ESA), 1401 Constitution Avenue, NW, Washington, DC 20230, (800) 782-8872, www.esa.doc.gov; *The Digital Economy 2003*.

INDUSTRIAL MACHINERY AND EQUIPMENT - ENERGY CONSUMPTION

U.S. Department of Energy (DOE), Energy Information Administration (EIA), 1000 Independence Avenue, SW, Washington, DC 20585, (202) 586-8800, www.eia.doe.gov; *Manufacturing Energy Consumption Survey (MECS) 2002*.

INDUSTRIAL MACHINERY AND EQUIPMENT - ESTABLISHMENTS

U.S. Census Bureau, Company Statistics Division, 4700 Silver Hill Road, Washington DC 20233-0001, (301) 763-3030, www.census.gov/csd/; *County Business Patterns 2004*.

U.S. Census Bureau, Manufacturing and Construction Division, 4600 Silver Hill Road, Washington DC 20233, (301) 763-4673, www.census.gov/mcd; *Annual Survey of Manufactures (ASM)* and *Census of Manufactures*.

INDUSTRIAL MACHINERY AND EQUIPMENT - FOREIGN COUNTRIES

Organisation for Economic Cooperation and Development (OECD), 2 rue Andre Pascal, F-75775 Paris Cedex 16, France, (Telephone in U.S. (202) 785-6323), (Fax in U.S. (202) 785-0350), www.oecd.org; *ICT Sector Data and Metadata by Country*.

INDUSTRIAL MACHINERY AND EQUIPMENT - GROSS DOMESTIC PRODUCT

Bureau of Economic Analysis (BEA), U.S. Department of Commerce (DOC), 1441 L Street NW, Washington, DC 20230, (202) 606-9900, www.bea.gov; *Survey of Current Business (SCB)*.

INDUSTRIAL MACHINERY AND EQUIPMENT - INDUSTRIAL SAFETY

U.S. Bureau of Labor Statistics (BLS), Postal Square Building, 2 Massachusetts Avenue, NE,

Washington, DC 20212-0001, (202) 691-5200, Fax: (202) 691-6325, www.bls.gov; *Injuries, Illnesses, and Fatalities (IIF).*

INDUSTRIAL MACHINERY AND EQUIPMENT - INVENTORIES

U.S. Census Bureau, Manufacturing and Construction Division, 4600 Silver Hill Road, Washington DC 20233, (301) 763-4673, www.census.gov/mcd; *Current Industrial Reports* and *Manufacturers Shipments, Inventories and Orders.*

INDUSTRIAL MACHINERY AND EQUIPMENT - MERGERS AND ACQUISITIONS

Thomson Financial, 195 Broadway, New York, NY 10007, (646) 822-2000, www.thomson.com; Thomson Research.

INDUSTRIAL MACHINERY AND EQUIPMENT - MULTINATIONAL COMPANIES

Bureau of Economic Analysis (BEA), U.S. Department of Commerce (DOC), 1441 L Street NW, Washington, DC 20230, (202) 606-9900, www.bea.gov; *Survey of Current Business (SCB).*

INDUSTRIAL MACHINERY AND EQUIPMENT - PATENTS

U.S. Patent and Trademark Office (USPTO), PO Box 1450, Alexandria, VA 22313-1450, (571) 272-1000, www.uspto.gov; *Patenting Trends Calendar Year 2003.*

INDUSTRIAL MACHINERY AND EQUIPMENT - PRODUCTIVITY

U.S. Bureau of Labor Statistics (BLS), Postal Square Building, 2 Massachusetts Avenue, NE, Washington, DC 20212-0001, (202) 691-5200, Fax: (202) 691-6325, www.bls.gov; *Industry Productivity and Costs.*

INDUSTRIAL MACHINERY AND EQUIPMENT - RESEARCH AND DEVELOPMENT

National Science Foundation, Division of Science Resources Statistics (SRS), 4201 Wilson Boulevard, Arlington, VA 22230, (703) 292-8780, Fax: (703) 292-9092, www.nsf.gov; *Research and Development in Industry: 2003.*

INDUSTRIAL MACHINERY AND EQUIPMENT - SHIPMENTS

U.S. Census Bureau, Manufacturing and Construction Division, 4600 Silver Hill Road, Washington DC 20233, (301) 763-4673, www.census.gov/mcd; *Annual Survey of Manufactures (ASM); Census of Manufactures; Current Industrial Reports;* and *Manufacturers Shipments, Inventories and Orders.*

INDUSTRIAL MACHINERY AND EQUIPMENT - TOXIC CHEMICAL RELEASES

U.S. Environmental Protection Agency (EPA), Ariel Rios Building, 1200 Pennsylvania Avenue, NW, Washington, DC 20460, (202) 272-0167, www.epa.gov; Toxics Release Inventory (TRI) Database.

INDUSTRIAL MINERALS

U.S. Department of the Interior (DOI), U.S. Geological Survey (USGS), Office of Minerals Information, 12201 Sunrise Valley Drive, Reston, VA 20192, Mr. Kenneth A. Beckman, (703) 648-4916, Fax: (703) 648-4995, http://minerals.usgs.gov/minerals; *Mineral Commodity Summaries; Minerals Yearbook;* and *Nonmetallic Mineral Products Industry Indexes.*

INDUSTRIAL PRODUCTION INDEXES

Board of Governors of the Federal Reserve System, Constitution Avenue, NW, Washington, DC 20551, (202) 452-3000, www.federalreserve.gov; *Federal Reserve Bulletin* and *Industrial Production and Capacity Utilization.*

U.S. Department of Commerce (DOC), Economics and Statistics Administration (ESA), 1401 Constitution Avenue, NW, Washington, DC 20230, (800) 782-8872, www.esa.doc.gov; *Impact of Increased Natural Gas Prices on U.S. Economy and Industries: Report to Congress.*

INDUSTRIAL PRODUCTION INDEXES - FOREIGN COUNTRIES

Organisation for Economic Cooperation and Development (OECD), 2 rue Andre Pascal, F-75775 Paris Cedex 16, France, (Telephone in U.S. (202) 785-6323), (Fax in U.S. (202) 785-0350), www.oecd.org; *OECD Composite Leading Indicators (CLIs), Updated September 2007* and *OECD Main Economic Indicators (MEI).*

INDUSTRIAL PROPERTY

State of Hawaii Department of Business, Economic Development Tourism (DBEDT), Research and Economic Analysis Division (READ), PO Box 2359 Honolulu, HI 96804, (808) 586-2423, Fax: (808) 587-2790, www.hawaii.gov/dbedt/info/economic/census; *2005 State of Hawaii Data Book: A Statistical Abstract.*

World Intellectual Property Organization (WIPO), PO Box 18, CH-1211 Geneva 20, Switzerland, www.wipo.int; *Industrial Property Statistics.*

INDUSTRIAL SAFETY

National Agricultural Statistics Service (NASS), U.S. Department of Agriculture (USDA), 1400 Independence Avenue, SW, Washington, DC 20250, (800) 727-9540, Fax: (202) 690-2090, www.nass.usda.gov; *Adult Agricultural Related Injuries 2004.*

U.S. Department of Labor (DOL), Mine Safety and Health Administration (MSHA), 1100 Wilson Boulevard, 21st Floor, Arlington, VA 22209-3939, (202) 693-9400, Fax: (202) 693-9401, www.msha.gov; *Mine Injury and Worktime Quarterly Statistics; Mine Safety and Health at a Glance;* and *Statistics Single Source Page.*

INDUSTRY

See CORPORATIONS

Economist Intelligence Unit, 111 West 57th Street, New York, NY 10019, (212) 554-0600, Fax: (212) 586-1181, www.eiu.com; *United States of America Country Report.*

INFANT DEATHS

See also FETAL DEATHS

Bernan Essential Government Publications, 4611-F Assembly Drive, Lanham MD, 20706-4391, (301) 459-2255, Fax: (800) 865-3450, www.bernan.com; *Vital Statistics of the United States: Births, Life Expectancy, Deaths, and Selected Health Data.*

Child Welfare League of America (CWLA), 440 First Street, NW, Third Floor, Washington, DC 20001-2085, (202) 638-2952, Fax: (202) 638-4004, www.cwla.org; *Mortality Trends Among U.S. Children and Youth.*

National Center for Health Statistics (NCHS), Centers for Disease Control and Prevention (CDC), U.S. Department of Health and Human Services (HHS), 3311 Toledo Road, Hyattsville, MD 20782, (866) 232-4636, www.cdc.gov/nchs; *National Vital Statistics Reports (NVSR); Vital Statistics of the United States (VSUS);* and unpublished data.

INFANT DEATHS - CAUSE

Bernan Essential Government Publications, 4611-F Assembly Drive, Lanham MD, 20706-4391, (301) 459-2255, Fax: (800) 865-3450, www.bernan.com; *Vital Statistics of the United States: Births, Life Expectancy, Deaths, and Selected Health Data.*

National Center for Health Statistics (NCHS), Centers for Disease Control and Prevention (CDC), U.S. Department of Health and Human Services (HHS), 3311 Toledo Road, Hyattsville, MD 20782, (866) 232-4636, www.cdc.gov/nchs; *National Vital Statistics Reports (NVSR); Vital Statistics of the United States (VSUS);* and unpublished data.

INFANT DEATHS - METROPOLITAN AREAS

National Center for Health Statistics (NCHS), Centers for Disease Control and Prevention (CDC), U.S. Department of Health and Human Services (HHS), 3311 Toledo Road, Hyattsville, MD 20782, (866) 232-4636, www.cdc.gov/nchs; *Vital Statistics of the United States (VSUS)* and unpublished data.

INFERTILITY

National Center for Health Statistics (NCHS), Centers for Disease Control and Prevention (CDC), U.S. Department of Health and Human Services (HHS), 3311 Toledo Road, Hyattsville, MD 20782, (866) 232-4636, www.cdc.gov/nchs; *Faststats A to Z* and *National Survey of Family Growth (NSFG).*

INFLUENZA

European Centre for Disease Prevention and Control (ECDC), 171 83 Stockholm, Sweden, www.ecdc.europa.eu; *Avian Influenza A/H5N1 in Bathing and Potable (Drinking) Water and Risks to Human Health; The ECDC Avian Influenza Portofolio; HIV Infection in Europe: 25 Years into the Pandemic; Infant and Children Seasonal Immunisation Against Influenza on a Routine Basis During Inter-pandemic Period; Influenza News; Sudden Deaths and Influenza Vaccinations in Israel - ECDC Interim Risk Assessment;* and *Technical Report of the Scientific Panel on Influenza in Reply to Eight Questions Concerning Avian Flu.*

National Center for Health Statistics (NCHS), Centers for Disease Control and Prevention (CDC), U.S. Department of Health and Human Services (HHS), 3311 Toledo Road, Hyattsville, MD 20782, (866) 232-4636, www.cdc.gov/nchs; *Faststats A to Z; National Vital Statistics Reports (NVSR); Vital Statistics of the United States (VSUS);* and unpublished data.

INFORMATION INDUSTRY

International Telecommunication Union (ITU), Place des Nations, 1211 Geneva 20, Switzerland, www.itu.int; *African Telecommunication/ICT Indicators 2008: At a Crossroads; World Telecommunication/ICT Indicators Database on CD-ROM; World Telecommunication/ICT Indicators Database Online;* and *Yearbook of Statistics - Telecommunication Services (Chronological Time Series 1997-2006).*

LISU, Holywell Park, Loughborough University, Leicestershire, LE11 3TU, United Kingdom, www.lboro.ac.uk/departments/dis/lisu; *Availability of Accessible Publications; 2004 Library and Information Statistics Tables; Statistics in Practice - Measuring and Managing;* and *A Survey of NHS Libraries: Statistics From the NHS Regional Librarians Group.*

Lithuanian Department of Statistics (Statistics Lithuania), Gedimino av. 29, LT-01500 Vilnius, Lithuania, www.stat.gov.lt/en; *Transport and Communications 2006.*

U.S. Bureau of Labor Statistics (BLS), Postal Square Building, 2 Massachusetts Avenue, NE, Washington, DC 20212-0001, (202) 691-5200, Fax: (202) 691-6325, www.bls.gov; *Industries at a Glance.*

U.S. Census Bureau, Center for Economic Studies, 4600 Silver Hill Road, Washington DC 20233, (301) 457-1235, www.ces.census.gov; Economic Census (web app).

U.S. Census Bureau, Service Sector Statistics Division, 4700 Silver Hill Road, Washington DC 20233-0001, (301) 763-3030, www.census.gov/svsd/www/economic.html; *2004 Service Annual Survey: Information Sector Services.*

Veronis Suhler Stevenson Partners LLC, 350 Park Avenue, New York, NY 10022, (212) 935-4990, Fax: (212) 381-8168, www.vss.com; *Investment Considerations for the Communications Industry.*

INFORMATION INDUSTRY - EMPLOYEES

U.S. Census Bureau, 4700 Silver Hill Road, Washington DC 20233-0001, (301) 763-3030, www.census.gov; *2002 Economic Census, Nonemployer Statistics.*

U.S. Census Bureau, Center for Economic Studies, 4600 Silver Hill Road, Washington DC 20233, (301) 457-1235, www.ces.census.gov; *2002 Economic Census, Information.*

U.S. Census Bureau, Company Statistics Division, 4700 Silver Hill Road, Washington DC 20233-0001, (301) 763-3030, www.census.gov/csd/; *Statistics of U.S. Businesses (SUSB).*

INFORMATION INDUSTRY - ESTABLISHMENTS

U.S. Census Bureau, 4700 Silver Hill Road, Washington DC 20233-0001, (301) 763-3030, www.census.gov; *2002 Economic Census, Nonemployer Statistics.*

U.S. Census Bureau, Center for Economic Studies, 4600 Silver Hill Road, Washington DC 20233, (301) 457-1235, www.ces.census.gov; *2002 Economic Census, Information.*

U.S. Census Bureau, Company Statistics Division, 4700 Silver Hill Road, Washington DC 20233-0001, (301) 763-3030, www.census.gov/csd/; *Statistics of U.S. Businesses (SUSB).*

INFORMATION INDUSTRY - PAYROLL

U.S. Census Bureau, Center for Economic Studies, 4600 Silver Hill Road, Washington DC 20233, (301) 457-1235, www.ces.census.gov; *2002 Economic Census, Information.*

U.S. Census Bureau, Company Statistics Division, 4700 Silver Hill Road, Washington DC 20233-0001, (301) 763-3030, www.census.gov/csd/; *Statistics of U.S. Businesses (SUSB).*

INFORMATION INDUSTRY - SHIPMENTS - REVENUE

U.S. Census Bureau, Center for Economic Studies, 4600 Silver Hill Road, Washington DC 20233, (301) 457-1235, www.ces.census.gov; *2002 Economic Census, Information.*

INFORMATION TECHNOLOGY

Eurostat, Batiment Jean Monnet, Rue Alcide de Gasperi, L-2920 Luxembourg, http://epp.eurostat.ec.europa.eu; *Patent Applications to the EPO in the ICT Sector 1993 to 2003.*

Market Data Retrieval (MDR), 6 Armstrong Road, Shelton, CT 06484, (800) 333-8802, www.schooldata.com; *The College Technology Review 2006* and *Educator Buying Trends: A National Survey - 2007.*

National Science Foundation, Division of Science Resources Statistics (SRS), 4201 Wilson Boulevard, Arlington, VA 22230, (703) 292-8780, Fax: (703) 292-9092, www.nsf.gov; *Social and Economic Implications of Information Technologies: A Bibliographic Database Pilot Project (Archived 2006).*

National Technical Information Service (NTIS), U.S. Department of Commerce (DOC), 5285 Port Royal Road, Springfield, VA 22161, (703) 605-6000, www.ntis.gov; unpublished data.

The NPD Group, Port Washington, 900 West Shore Road, Port Washington, NY 11050, (866) 444-1411, www.npd.com; *Market Research for the Consumer Technology Industry* and *Wireless.*

Organisation for Economic Cooperation and Development (OECD), 2 rue Andre Pascal, F-75775 Paris Cedex 16, France, (Telephone in U.S. (202) 785-6323), (Fax in U.S. (202) 785-0350), www.oecd.org; *OECD Information Technology Outlook 2006.*

Statistics Iceland, Borgartuni 21a, 150 Reykjavik, Iceland, www.statice.is; *Icelandic Information Society in a European Context 2006.*

U.S. Census Bureau, Company Statistics Division, 4700 Silver Hill Road, Washington DC 20233-0001, (301) 763-3030, www.census.gov/csd/; *Information and Communication Technology (ICT) Survey.*

U.S. Census Bureau, Service Sector Statistics Division, 4700 Silver Hill Road, Washington DC 20233-0001, (301) 763-3030, www.census.gov/svsd/www/economic.html; *2004 Service Annual Survey: Information Sector Services.*

U.S. Library of Congress (LOC), Congressional Research Service (CRS), The Library of Congress, 101 Independence Avenue, SE, Washington, DC 20540-7500, (202) 707-5700, www.loc.gov/crsinfo; *The Economic Impact of Cyber-Attacks.*

INFRASTRUCTURE EXPENDITURES

See GOVERNMENT

INHALANTS - PERSONS USING

Substance Abuse and Mental Health Services Administration (SAMHSA), 1 Choke Cherry Road, Rockville, MD 20857, (240) 777-1311, www.oas.samhsa.gov; *National Survey on Drug Use Health (NSDUH).*

INJURIES

See also ACCIDENTS

Bernan Essential Government Publications, 4611-F Assembly Drive, Lanham MD, 20706-4391, (301) 459-2255, Fax: (800) 865-3450, www.bernan.com; *Vital Statistics of the United States: Births, Life Expectancy, Deaths, and Selected Health Data.*

Health and Consumer Protection Directorate-General, European Commission, B-1049 Brussels, Belgium, http://ec.europa.eu/dgs/health_consumer/index_en.htm; *Injuries in the European Union: Statistics Summary 2002-2004.*

Indian Health Service (IHS), U.S. Department of Health and Human Services, The Reyes Building, 801 Thompson Avenue, Suite 400, Rockville, MD 20852-1627, (301) 443-1180, www.ihs.gov; *Indian Health Focus - Injuries.*

National Agricultural Statistics Service (NASS), U.S. Department of Agriculture (USDA), 1400 Independence Avenue, SW, Washington, DC 20250, (800) 727-9540, Fax: (202) 690-2090, www.nass.usda.gov; *Adult Agricultural Related Injuries 2004.*

National Center for Health Statistics (NCHS), Centers for Disease Control and Prevention (CDC), U.S. Department of Health and Human Services (HHS), 3311 Toledo Road, Hyattsville, MD 20782, (866) 232-4636, www.cdc.gov/nchs; *Faststats A to Z; Health, United States, 2006, with Chartbook on Trends in the Health of Americans with Special Feature on Pain; National Vital Statistics Reports (NVSR);* and unpublished data.

National Center for Statistics and Analysis (NCSA) of the National Highway Traffic Safety Administration, West Building, 1200 New Jersey Avenue, S.E., Washington, DC 20590, (202) 366-1503, Fax: (202) 366-7078, www.nhtsa.gov; *Alcohol Involvement in Fatal Motor Vehicle Traffic Crashes, 2003; Analysis of Crashes Involving 15-Passenger Vans; Analysis of Speeding-Related Fatal Motor Vehicle Traffic Crashes; An Assessment of the Crash-Reducing Effectiveness of Passenger Vehicle Daytime Running Lamps (DRLs); Child Passenger Fatalities and Injuries, Based on Restraint Use, Vehicle Type, Seat Position, and Number of Vehicles in the Crash; Fatal Motor Vehicle Crashes on Indian Reservations 1975-2002; Impaired Motorcycle Operators Involved in Fatal Crashes; Individual State Data from the State Alcohol Related Fatality Report; Most Fatalities in Young (15- to 20-Year-Old) Driver Crashes Are Young Drivers and Their Young Passengers; Motor Vehicle Traffic Crashes as a Leading Cause of Death in the U.S., 2002 - A Demographic Perspective; Motorcycle Helmet Effectiveness Revisited; New England Low Fatality Rates versus Low Safety Belt Use; Pedestrian Roadway Fatalities; Race and Ethnicity in Fatal Motor Vehicle Traffic Crashes 1999-2004; The Relationship between Occupant Compartment Deformation and Occupant Injury; Rollover Crash Mechanisms and Injury Outcomes for Restrained Occupants; Safety Belt Use in 2003: Demographic Characteristics; Safety Belt Use in 2003: Use Rates in the States and Territories; State Alcohol-Related Fatality Rates 2003; States With Primary Enforcement Laws Have Lower Fatality Rates; Traffic Safety Fact Sheets, 2006 Data - Bicyclists and Other Cyclists; Traffic Safety Fact Sheets, 2006 Data - Children; Traffic Safety Fact Sheets, 2006 Data - Large Trucks; Traffic Safety Fact Sheets, 2006 Data - Motorcycles; Traffic Safety Fact Sheets, 2006 Data - Older Population; Traffic Safety Fact Sheets, 2006 Data - Pedestrians; Traffic Safety Fact Sheets, 2006 Data - School Transportation-Related Crashes; Traffic Safety Fact Sheets, 2006 Data - Speeding; Traffic Safety Facts Annual Report: 2005;* and *Trend and Pattern Analysis of Highway Crash Fatality by Month and Day.*

National Safety Council (NSC), 1121 Spring Lake Drive, Itasca, IL 60143-3201, (630) 285-1121, www.nsc.org; *Injury Facts.*

U.S. Bureau of Labor Statistics (BLS), Postal Square Building, 2 Massachusetts Avenue, NE, Washington, DC 20212-0001, (202) 691-5200, Fax: (202) 691-6325, www.bls.gov; *Fatal Occupational Injuries to Members of the Resident Military, 1992-2003* and *Injuries, Illnesses, and Fatalities (IIF).*

U.S. Department of Labor (DOL), Bureau of Labor Statistics (BLS), Postal Square Building, 2 Massachusetts Avenue, NE, Washington, DC 20212-0001, (202) 691-5200, Fax: (202) 691-6325, www.bls.gov; *Injuries, Illnesses, and Fatalities (IIF).*

U.S. Department of Labor (DOL), Mine Safety and Health Administration (MSHA), 1100 Wilson Boulevard, 21st Floor, Arlington, VA 22209-3939, (202) 693-9400, Fax: (202) 693-9401, www.msha.gov; unpublished data.

U.S. Department of Transportation (DOT), Federal Railroad Administration (FRA), 1200 New Jersey Avenue, SE, Washington, DC 20590, (202) 366-4000, www.fra.dot.gov; FRA Office of Safety Analysis Web Site.

U.S. Department of Transportation (DOT), Research and Innovative Technology Administration (RITA), Bureau of Transportation Statistics (BTS), 1200 New Jersey Avenue, SE, Washington, DC 20590, (800) 853-1351, www.bts.gov; *TranStats.*

INMATES

See also CORRECTIONAL INSTITUTIONS

Justice Research and Statistics Association (JRSA), 777 N. Capitol Street, NE, Suite 801, Washington, DC 20002, (202) 842-9330, Fax: (202) 842-9329, www.jrsa.org; *The Forum; JRP Digest; Justice Research and Policy;* and *SAC Publication Digest.*

Lesotho Bureau of Statistics, Ministry of Finance and Development Planning, PO Box 455, Maseru 100, Lesotho, www.bos.gov.ls; *Crime Statistics 2005* and *Prison Statistics.*

National Center for Juvenile Justice (NCJJ), 3700 South Water Street, Suite 200, Pittsburgh, PA 15203, (412) 227-6950, Fax: (412) 227-6955, http://ncjj.servehttp.com/NCJJWebsite/main.htm; *Juveniles in Corrections (2004).*

U.S. Department of Justice (DOJ), Bureau of Justice Statistics, 810 Seventh Street, NW, Washington, DC 20531, (202) 307-0765, www.ojp.usdoj.gov/bjs/; *Census of State and Federal Correctional Facilities; Correctional Populations in the United States; Drug Use and Dependence, State and Federal Prisoners, 2004; Drug Use, Testing, and Treatment in Jails; Education and Correctional Populations; Prevalence of Imprisonment in the U.S. Population, 1974-2001; Prison and Jail Inmates at Midyear 2005; Prisoners in 2004; Profile of Jail Inmates, 2002; Reentry Trends in the United States;* and *Substance Dependence, Abuse, and Treatment of Jail Inmates, 2002.*

INORGANIC MATERIALS

U.S. Census Bureau, Manufacturing and Construction Division, 4600 Silver Hill Road, Washington DC 20233, (301) 763-4673, www.census.gov/mcd; *Current Industrial Reports* and *Current Industrial Reports, Manufacturing Profiles.*

INSTALLMENT LOANS

See also LOANS and MORTGAGES

Board of Governors of the Federal Reserve System, Constitution Avenue, NW, Washington, DC 20551, (202) 452-3000, www.federalreserve.gov; *Federal Reserve Bulletin* and unpublished data.

INSTITUTIONAL CARE FACILITIES

See also HOSPITALS and NURSING PERSONNEL

American Hospital Association (AHA), One North Franklin, Chicago, IL 60606-3421, (312) 422-3000, www.aha.org; *Annual Survey of Hospitals; Hospital Statistics 2008;* and unpublished data.

Centers for Medicare and Medicaid Services (CMS), U.S. Department of Health and Human Services (HHS), 7500 Security Boulevard, Baltimore, MD 21244-1850, (410) 786-3000, http://cms.hhs.gov; Data Compendium, 2007 (web app) and unpublished data.

National Center for Health Statistics (NCHS), Centers for Disease Control and Prevention (CDC), U.S. Department of Health and Human Services (HHS), 3311 Toledo Road, Hyattsville, MD 20782, (866) 232-4636, www.cdc.gov/nchs; unpublished data.

INSTITUTIONAL POPULATION - MENTALLY ILL RETARDED

Substance Abuse and Mental Health Services Administration (SAMHSA), 1 Choke Cherry Road, Rockville, MD 20857, (240) 777-1311, www.oas.samhsa.gov; unpublished data.

INSTITUTIONAL POPULATION - PRISONERS

Australian Institute of Criminology, 74 Leichhardt Street, Griffith ACT 2603 Australia, www.aic.gov.au/; *Deaths in Custody in Australia: National Deaths in Custody Program Annual Report 2004.*

Lesotho Bureau of Statistics, Ministry of Finance and Development Planning, PO Box 455, Maseru 100, Lesotho, www.bos.gov.ls; *Prison Statistics.*

U.S. Department of Justice (DOJ), Bureau of Justice Statistics, 810 Seventh Street, NW, Washington, DC 20531, (202) 307-0765, www.ojp.usdoj.gov/bjs/; *Census of Jails; Challenging the Conditions of Prisons and Jails: A Report on Section 1983 Litigation; Hepatitis Testing and Treatment in State Prisons; HIV in Prisons, 2004; Medical Problems of Jail Inmates; Mental Health Problems of Prison and Jail Inmates; Mental Health Treatment in State Prisons, 2000; National Corrections Reporting Program; Prison and Jail Inmates at Midyear 2005; Prisoners in 2004; Profile of Jail Inmates, 2002; Profile of Nonviolent Offenders Exiting State Prisons; Sexual Violence Reported by Correctional Authorities, 2005; Suicide and Homicide in State Prisons and Local Jails;* and *Veterans in Prison or Jail.*

U.S. Department of Justice (DOJ), National Institute of Justice (NIJ), 810 Seventh Street, NW, Washington, DC 20531, (202) 307-2942, Fax: (202) 616-0275, www.ojp.usdoj.gov/nij/; *Correctional Boot Camps: Lessons From a Decade of Research* and *Does Parental Incarceration Increase a Child's Risk for Foster Care Placement?*

INSTITUTIONS OF HIGHER EDUCATION

See EDUCATION - HIGHER EDUCATION INSTITUTIONS

INSTRUMENTS AND RELATED PRODUCTS

Arlington Medical Resources, Inc., 48 General Warren Boulevard, Malvern, PA 19355, (610) 722-5511, Fax: (610) 722-5514, www.amr-data.com; *The Imaging Market Guide.*

INSTRUMENTS AND RELATED PRODUCTS - MANUFACTURING - CAPITAL

Bureau of Economic Analysis (BEA), U.S. Department of Commerce (DOC), 1441 L Street NW, Washington, DC 20230, (202) 606-9900, www.bea.gov; *Survey of Current Business (SCB).*

INSTRUMENTS AND RELATED PRODUCTS - MANUFACTURING - EARNINGS

U.S. Bureau of Labor Statistics (BLS), Postal Square Building, 2 Massachusetts Avenue, NE, Washington, DC 20212-0001, (202) 691-5200, Fax: (202) 691-6325, www.bls.gov; *Current Employment Statistics Survey (CES)* and *Employment and Earnings (EE).*

U.S. Census Bureau, Company Statistics Division, 4700 Silver Hill Road, Washington DC 20233-0001, (301) 763-3030, www.census.gov/csd/; *County Business Patterns 2004.*

U.S. Census Bureau, Manufacturing and Construction Division, 4600 Silver Hill Road, Washington DC 20233, (301) 763-4673, www.census.gov/mcd; *Annual Survey of Manufactures (ASM)* and *Census of Manufactures.*

INSTRUMENTS AND RELATED PRODUCTS - MANUFACTURING - EMPLOYEES

U.S. Bureau of Labor Statistics (BLS), Postal Square Building, 2 Massachusetts Avenue, NE, Washington, DC 20212-0001, (202) 691-5200, Fax: (202) 691-6325, www.bls.gov; *Current Employment Statistics Survey (CES)* and *Employment and Earnings (EE).*

U.S. Census Bureau, Company Statistics Division, 4700 Silver Hill Road, Washington DC 20233-0001, (301) 763-3030, www.census.gov/csd/; *County Business Patterns 2004.*

U.S. Census Bureau, Manufacturing and Construction Division, 4600 Silver Hill Road, Washington DC 20233, (301) 763-4673, www.census.gov/mcd; *Annual Survey of Manufactures (ASM)* and *Census of Manufactures.*

INSTRUMENTS AND RELATED PRODUCTS - MANUFACTURING - ENERGY CONSUMPTION

U.S. Department of Energy (DOE), Energy Information Administration (EIA), 1000 Independence Avenue, SW, Washington, DC 20585, (202) 586-8800, www.eia.doe.gov; *Manufacturing Energy Consumption Survey (MECS) 2002.*

INSTRUMENTS AND RELATED PRODUCTS - MANUFACTURING - ESTABLISHMENTS

U.S. Census Bureau, Company Statistics Division, 4700 Silver Hill Road, Washington DC 20233-0001, (301) 763-3030, www.census.gov/csd/; *County Business Patterns 2004.*

INSTRUMENTS AND RELATED PRODUCTS - MANUFACTURING - GROSS DOMESTIC PRODUCT

Bureau of Economic Analysis (BEA), U.S. Department of Commerce (DOC), 1441 L Street NW, Washington, DC 20230, (202) 606-9900, www.bea.gov; *2007 Annual Revision of the National Income and Product Accounts (NIPA)* and *Survey of Current Business (SCB).*

INSTRUMENTS AND RELATED PRODUCTS - MANUFACTURING - INTERNATIONAL TRADE

U.S. Census Bureau, Foreign Trade Division, 4700 Silver Hill Road, Washington DC 20233-0001, (301) 763-3030, www.census.gov/foreign-trade/www/; *U.S. International Trade in Goods and Services.*

INSTRUMENTS AND RELATED PRODUCTS - MANUFACTURING - INVENTORIES

U.S. Census Bureau, Manufacturing and Construction Division, 4600 Silver Hill Road, Washington DC 20233, (301) 763-4673, www.census.gov/mcd; *Current Industrial Reports* and *Manufacturers Shipments, Inventories and Orders.*

INSTRUMENTS AND RELATED PRODUCTS - MANUFACTURING - MERGERS AND ACQUISITIONS

Thomson Financial, 195 Broadway, New York, NY 10007, (646) 822-2000, www.thomson.com; Thomson Research.

INSTRUMENTS AND RELATED PRODUCTS - MANUFACTURING - OCCUPATIONAL SAFETY

U.S. Bureau of Labor Statistics (BLS), Postal Square Building, 2 Massachusetts Avenue, NE, Washington, DC 20212-0001, (202) 691-5200, Fax: (202) 691-6325, www.bls.gov; *Injuries, Illnesses, and Fatalities (IIF).*

INSTRUMENTS AND RELATED PRODUCTS - MANUFACTURING - PATENTS

U.S. Patent and Trademark Office (USPTO), PO Box 1450, Alexandria, VA 22313-1450, (571) 272-1000, www.uspto.gov; *Patenting Trends Calendar Year 2003.*

INSTRUMENTS AND RELATED PRODUCTS - MANUFACTURING - PRODUCTIVITY

Board of Governors of the Federal Reserve System, Constitution Avenue, NW, Washington, DC 20551, (202) 452-3000, www.federalreserve.gov; *Federal Reserve Bulletin* and *Industrial Production and Capacity Utilization.*

U.S. Bureau of Labor Statistics (BLS), Postal Square Building, 2 Massachusetts Avenue, NE, Washington, DC 20212-0001, (202) 691-5200, Fax: (202) 691-6325, www.bls.gov; *Current Employment Statistics Survey (CES)* and *Employment and Earnings (EE).*

INSTRUMENTS AND RELATED PRODUCTS - MANUFACTURING - PROFITS

Executive Office of the President, Council of Economic Advisors, The White House, 1600 Pennsylvania Avenue NW, Washington, DC 20500, (202) 456-1414, www.whitehouse.gov/cea; *2007 Economic Report of the President.*

U.S. Census Bureau, Manufacturing and Construction Division, 4600 Silver Hill Road, Washington DC 20233, (301) 763-4673, www.census.gov/mcd; *Quarterly Financial Report for Manufacturing, Mining and Trade Corporations.*

INSTRUMENTS AND RELATED PRODUCTS - MANUFACTURING - RESEARCH AND DEVELOPMENT

National Science Foundation, Division of Science Resources Statistics (SRS), 4201 Wilson Boulevard, Arlington, VA 22230, (703) 292-8780, Fax: (703) 292-9092, www.nsf.gov; *Research and Development in Industry: 2003.*

INSTRUMENTS AND RELATED PRODUCTS - MANUFACTURING - SHIPMENTS

U.S. Census Bureau, Manufacturing and Construction Division, 4600 Silver Hill Road, Washington DC 20233, (301) 763-4673, www.census.gov/mcd; *Annual Survey of Manufactures (ASM); Census of Manufactures; Current Industrial Reports;* and *Manufacturers Shipments, Inventories and Orders.*

INSTRUMENTS AND RELATED PRODUCTS - MANUFACTURING - TOXIC CHEMICAL RELEASES

U.S. Environmental Protection Agency (EPA), Ariel Rios Building, 1200 Pennsylvania Avenue, NW, Washington, DC 20460, (202) 272-0167, www.epa.gov; Toxics Release Inventory (TRI) Database.

INSURANCE

See also Individual Forms of Insurance

National Bureau of Statistics of China (NBS), No. 57, Yuetan Nanjie, Sanlihe, Xicheng District, Beijing 100826, China, www.stats.gov.cn/english; *Banking and Insurance.*

National Council on Compensation Insurance, Inc. (NCCI), 901 Peninsula Corporate Circle, Boca Raton, FL 33487, (800) NCCI-123, www.ncci.com; *An*

Emerging Issue for Workers Compensation - Aging Baby Boomers and a Growing Long-Term Care Industry.

NeighborhoodInfo DC, c/o The Urban Institute, 2100 M Street, NW, Washington, DC 20037, (202) 261-5760, Fax: (202) 872-9322, www.neighborhoodinfodc.org; *Insurance and Uninsurance in the District of Columbia: Starting with the Numbers.*

Standard and Poor's Corporation, 55 Water Street, New York, NY 10041, (212) 438-1000, www.standardandpoors.com; *Marine Mutual Report 2006.*

INSURANCE - MEDICAL CARE

America's Health Insurance Plans (AHIP), 601 Pennsylvania Avenue, NW, South Building, Suite 500, Washington, DC 20004, (202) 778-3200, Fax: (202) 331-7487, www.ahip.org; *Cost Trends Chart Book.*

Centers for Medicare and Medicaid Services (CMS), U.S. Department of Health and Human Services (HHS), 7500 Security Boulevard, Baltimore, MD 21244-1850, (410) 786-3000, http://cms.hhs.gov; *Health Care Financing Review.*

HealthLeaders-InterStudy, One Vantage Way, B-300, Nashville, TN 37203, (615) 385-4131, Fax: (615) 385-4979, www.hmodata.com; *Pharmacy Benefit Evaluator.*

NeighborhoodInfo DC, c/o The Urban Institute, 2100 M Street, NW, Washington, DC 20037, (202) 261-5760, Fax: (202) 872-9322, www.neighborhoodinfodc.org; *Insurance and Uninsurance in the District of Columbia: Starting with the Numbers.*

Robert Wood Johnson Foundation, PO Box 2316, College Road East and Route 1, Princeton, NJ 08543, (877) 843-7953, www.rwjf.org; *Insurance Premiums Decline in States Capping Malpractice Payouts, Alabama University Study Finds; Medical Errors Involving Trainees: A Study of Closed Malpractice Claims From 5 Insurers;* and *Medicare Race and Ethnicity Data: Prepared for the Study Panel on Sharpening Medicare's Tools to Reduce Racial and Ethnic Disparities.*

U.S. Bureau of Labor Statistics (BLS), Postal Square Building, 2 Massachusetts Avenue, NE, Washington, DC 20212-0001, (202) 691-5200, Fax: (202) 691-6325, www.bls.gov; *Consumer Price Index Detailed Report.*

INSURANCE AGENTS, BROKERS AND SERVICE - ADVERTISING EXPENDITURES

Magazine Publishers of America (MPA), 810 Seventh Avenue, 24th Floor, New York, NY 10019, (212) 872-3700, www.magazine.org; *The Media Research Index.*

INSURANCE AGENTS, BROKERS AND SERVICE - EARNINGS

U.S. Bureau of Labor Statistics (BLS), Postal Square Building, 2 Massachusetts Avenue, NE, Washington, DC 20212-0001, (202) 691-5200, Fax: (202) 691-6325, www.bls.gov; *Current Employment Statistics Survey (CES)* and *Employment and Earnings (EE).*

U.S. Census Bureau, Center for Economic Studies, 4600 Silver Hill Road, Washington DC 20233, (301) 457-1235, www.ces.census.gov; *2002 Economic Census, Professional, Scientific and Technical Services.*

U.S. Census Bureau, Company Statistics Division, 4700 Silver Hill Road, Washington DC 20233-0001, (301) 763-3030, www.census.gov/csd/; *County Business Patterns 2004.*

INSURANCE AGENTS, BROKERS AND SERVICE - EMPLOYEES

Bureau of Economic Analysis (BEA), U.S. Department of Commerce (DOC), 1441 L Street NW, Washington, DC 20230, (202) 606-9900, www.bea.gov; *2007 Annual Revision of the National Income and Product Accounts (NIPA)* and *Survey of Current Business (SCB).*

U.S. Bureau of Labor Statistics (BLS), Postal Square Building, 2 Massachusetts Avenue, NE, Washington, DC 20212-0001, (202) 691-5200, Fax: (202) 691-6325, www.bls.gov; *Current Employment Statistics Survey (CES)* and *Employment and Earnings (EE).*

U.S. Census Bureau, Center for Economic Studies, 4600 Silver Hill Road, Washington DC 20233, (301) 457-1235, www.ces.census.gov; *2002 Economic Census, Professional, Scientific and Technical Services.*

U.S. Census Bureau, Company Statistics Division, 4700 Silver Hill Road, Washington DC 20233-0001, (301) 763-3030, www.census.gov/csd/; *County Business Patterns 2004.*

INSURANCE AGENTS, BROKERS AND SERVICE - ESTABLISHMENTS

Federal Deposit Insurance Corporation (FDIC), 550 Seventeenth Street, NW, Washington, DC 20429-0002, (877) 275-3342, www.fdic.gov; *Quarterly Banking Profile (QBP)* and *State Banking Performance Summary.*

U.S. Census Bureau, Center for Economic Studies, 4600 Silver Hill Road, Washington DC 20233, (301) 457-1235, www.ces.census.gov; *2002 Economic Census, Professional, Scientific and Technical Services.*

U.S. Census Bureau, Company Statistics Division, 4700 Silver Hill Road, Washington DC 20233-0001, (301) 763-3030, www.census.gov/csd/; *County Business Patterns 2004.*

INSURANCE AGENTS, BROKERS AND SERVICE - FINANCES

America's Health Insurance Plans (AHIP), 601 Pennsylvania Avenue, NW, South Building, Suite 500, Washington, DC 20004, (202) 778-3200, Fax: (202) 331-7487, www.ahip.org; *Cost Trends Chart Book.*

Board of Governors of the Federal Reserve System, Constitution Avenue, NW, Washington, DC 20551, (202) 452-3000, www.federalreserve.gov; *Flow of Funds Accounts of the United States.*

Centers for Medicare and Medicaid Services (CMS), U.S. Department of Health and Human Services (HHS), 7500 Security Boulevard, Baltimore, MD 21244-1850, (410) 786-3000, http://cms.hhs.gov; *Health Care Financing Review.*

Insurance Information Institute (III), 110 William Street, New York, NY 10038, (212) 346-5500, www.iii.org; *Insurance Fact Book 2007.*

U.S. Census Bureau, Center for Economic Studies, 4600 Silver Hill Road, Washington DC 20233, (301) 457-1235, www.ces.census.gov; *2002 Economic Census, Finance and Insurance.*

INSURANCE AGENTS, BROKERS AND SERVICE - FOREIGN INVESTMENT IN THE UNITED STATES

Bureau of Economic Analysis (BEA), U.S. Department of Commerce (DOC), 1441 L Street NW, Washington, DC 20230, (202) 606-9900, www.bea.gov; *Survey of Current Business (SCB).*

INSURANCE AGENTS, BROKERS AND SERVICE - GROSS DOMESTIC PRODUCT

Bureau of Economic Analysis (BEA), U.S. Department of Commerce (DOC), 1441 L Street NW, Washington, DC 20230, (202) 606-9900, www.bea.gov; *Survey of Current Business (SCB).*

INSURANCE AGENTS, BROKERS AND SERVICE - INDUSTRIAL SAFETY

U.S. Bureau of Labor Statistics (BLS), Postal Square Building, 2 Massachusetts Avenue, NE, Washington, DC 20212-0001, (202) 691-5200, Fax: (202) 691-6325, www.bls.gov; *Injuries, Illnesses, and Fatalities (IIF).*

INSURANCE AGENTS, BROKERS AND SERVICE - MERGERS AND ACQUISITIONS

Thomson Financial, 195 Broadway, New York, NY 10007, (646) 822-2000, www.thomson.com; Thomson Research.

INSURANCE CARRIERS - EARNINGS

U.S. Bureau of Labor Statistics (BLS), Postal Square Building, 2 Massachusetts Avenue, NE, Washington, DC 20212-0001, (202) 691-5200, Fax: (202) 691-6325, www.bls.gov; *Current Employment Statistics Survey (CES)* and *Employment and Earnings (EE).*

U.S. Census Bureau, Center for Economic Studies, 4600 Silver Hill Road, Washington DC 20233, (301) 457-1235, www.ces.census.gov; *2002 Economic Census, Professional, Scientific and Technical Services.*

U.S. Census Bureau, Company Statistics Division, 4700 Silver Hill Road, Washington DC 20233-0001, (301) 763-3030, www.census.gov/csd/; *County Business Patterns 2004.*

INSURANCE CARRIERS - EMPLOYEES

Bureau of Economic Analysis (BEA), U.S. Department of Commerce (DOC), 1441 L Street NW, Washington, DC 20230, (202) 606-9900, www.bea.gov; *2007 Annual Revision of the National Income and Product Accounts (NIPA)* and *Survey of Current Business (SCB).*

U.S. Bureau of Labor Statistics (BLS), Postal Square Building, 2 Massachusetts Avenue, NE, Washington, DC 20212-0001, (202) 691-5200, Fax: (202) 691-6325, www.bls.gov; *Current Employment Statistics Survey (CES)* and *Employment and Earnings (EE).*

U.S. Census Bureau, Center for Economic Studies, 4600 Silver Hill Road, Washington DC 20233, (301) 457-1235, www.ces.census.gov; *2002 Economic Census, Professional, Scientific and Technical Services.*

U.S. Census Bureau, Company Statistics Division, 4700 Silver Hill Road, Washington DC 20233-0001, (301) 763-3030, www.census.gov/csd/; *County Business Patterns 2004.*

INSURANCE CARRIERS - ESTABLISHMENTS

U.S. Census Bureau, Center for Economic Studies, 4600 Silver Hill Road, Washington DC 20233, (301) 457-1235, www.ces.census.gov; *2002 Economic Census, Professional, Scientific and Technical Services.*

U.S. Census Bureau, Company Statistics Division, 4700 Silver Hill Road, Washington DC 20233-0001, (301) 763-3030, www.census.gov/csd/; *County Business Patterns 2004.*

INSURANCE CARRIERS - FINANCES

Board of Governors of the Federal Reserve System, Constitution Avenue, NW, Washington, DC 20551, (202) 452-3000, www.federalreserve.gov; *Flow of Funds Accounts of the United States.*

Insurance Information Institute (III), 110 William Street, New York, NY 10038, (212) 346-5500, www.iii.org; *Insurance Fact Book 2007.*

U.S. Census Bureau, Center for Economic Studies, 4600 Silver Hill Road, Washington DC 20233, (301) 457-1235, www.ces.census.gov; *2002 Economic Census, Finance and Insurance.*

INSURANCE CARRIERS - GROSS DOMESTIC PRODUCT

Bureau of Economic Analysis (BEA), U.S. Department of Commerce (DOC), 1441 L Street NW, Washington, DC 20230, (202) 606-9900, www.bea.gov; *Survey of Current Business (SCB).*

INSURANCE CARRIERS - INDUSTRIAL SAFETY

U.S. Bureau of Labor Statistics (BLS), Postal Square Building, 2 Massachusetts Avenue, NE,

Washington, DC 20212-0001, (202) 691-5200, Fax: (202) 691-6325, www.bls.gov; *Injuries, Illnesses, and Fatalities (IIF).*

INSURANCE CARRIERS - PROFITS

Board of Governors of the Federal Reserve System, Constitution Avenue, NW, Washington, DC 20551, (202) 452-3000, www.federalreserve.gov; *Flow of Funds Accounts of the United States.*

Insurance Information Institute (III), 110 William Street, New York, NY 10038, (212) 346-5500, www.iii.org; *Insurance Fact Book 2007.*

U.S. Census Bureau, Center for Economic Studies, 4600 Silver Hill Road, Washington DC 20233, (301) 457-1235, www.ces.census.gov; *2002 Economic Census, Finance and Insurance.*

INSURANCE, GOVERNMENT

See SOCIAL INSURANCE

INTER-AMERICAN DEVELOPMENT BANK

Bureau of Economic Analysis (BEA), U.S. Department of Commerce (DOC), 1441 L Street NW, Washington, DC 20230, (202) 606-9900, www.bea.gov; unpublished data.

INTERACTIVE DIGITAL MEDIA

Veronis Suhler Stevenson Partners LLC, 350 Park Avenue, New York, NY 10022, (212) 935-4990, Fax: (212) 381-8168, www.vss.com; Communications Industry Report.

INTERCITY TRAFFIC

Eno Transportation Foundation, 1634 I Street, NW, Suite 500, Washington, DC 20006, (202) 879-4700, Fax: (202) 879-4719, www.enotrans.com; *Transportation in America.*

National Center for Statistics and Analysis (NCSA) of the National Highway Traffic Safety Administration, West Building, 1200 New Jersey Avenue, S.E., Washington, DC 20590, (202) 366-1503, Fax: (202) 366-7078, www.nhtsa.gov; *Traffic Safety Facts Annual Report: 2005.*

National Transportation Safety Board (NTSB), 490 L'Enfant Plaza, SW, Washington, DC 20594, (202) 314-6000, www.ntsb.gov; *Transportation Safety Databases.*

U.S. Department of Transportation (DOT), Research and Innovative Technology Administration (RITA), Bureau of Transportation Statistics (BTS), 1200 New Jersey Avenue, SE, Washington, DC 20590, (800) 853-1351, www.bts.gov; *Motor Carrier Financial and Operating Information Program* and *TranStats.*

INTEREST - PAYMENTS - FEDERAL GOVERNMENT

The Office of Management and Budget (OMB), 725 17th Street, NW, Washington, DC 20503, (202) 395-3080, Fax: (202) 395-3888, www.whitehouse.gov/omb; *Historical Tables.*

INTEREST - RECEIPTS BY SOURCE - INDIVIDUAL INCOME TAX RETURNS

U.S. Department of the Treasury (DOT), Internal Revenue Service (IRS), Statistics of Income Division (SIS), PO Box 2608, Washington, DC, 20013-2608, (202) 874-0410, Fax: (202) 874-0964, www.irs.ustreas.gov; *Statistics of Income Bulletin* and *Statistics of Income Bulletin, Individual Income Tax Returns.*

INTEREST - RECEIPTS BY SOURCE - NATIONAL AND PERSONAL INCOME COMPONENT

Bureau of Economic Analysis (BEA), U.S. Department of Commerce (DOC), 1441 L Street NW, Washington, DC 20230, (202) 606-9900, www.bea.gov; *2007 Annual Revision of the National Income and Product Accounts (NIPA)* and *Survey of Current Business (SCB).*

INTEREST RATES

Board of Governors of the Federal Reserve System, Constitution Avenue, NW, Washington, DC 20551, (202) 452-3000, www.federalreserve.gov; *Federal Reserve Bulletin* and *Statistical Digest.*

European Central Bank (ECB), Postfach 160319, D-60066 Frankfurt am Main, Germany, www.ecb.int; *Monetary Financial Institutions (MFI) Interest Rate Statistics (MIR).*

MSCI Barra, 88 Pine Street, 2nd Floor, New York, NY 10005, (212) 785-9630, http://www.mscibarra.com; Investment Portfolio Analysis Products.

INTEREST RATES - MORTGAGES

Board of Governors of the Federal Reserve System, Constitution Avenue, NW, Washington, DC 20551, (202) 452-3000, www.federalreserve.gov; *Federal Reserve Bulletin* and *Statistical Digest.*

Federal Housing Finance Board (FHFB), 1625 Eye Street, NW, Washington, DC 20006-4001, (202) 408-2500, Fax: (202) 408-1435, www.fhfb.gov; *Monthly Interest Rate Survey (MIRS).*

INTERNAL WATERWAYS - TRAFFIC

Waterborne Commerce Statistics Center (WCSC), Navigation Data Center (NDC), U.S. Army Corps of Engineers, PO Box 61280, New Orleans, LA 70161-1280, (504) 862-1426, www.iwr.usace.army.mil/ndc/wcsc/wcsc.htm; *2006 Waterborne Commerce of the United States (WCUS).*

INTERNATIONAL AFFAIRS

Congressional Quarterly, Inc., 1255 22nd Street, NW, Washington, DC 20037, (202) 419-8500, www.cq.com; *Political Handbook of the World 2008.*

The Economist, 25 St. James's Street, London SW1A 1HG, United Kingdom, www.economist.com; *The World in 2007.*

International Finance Corporation (IFC), 2121 Pennsylvania Avenue, NW, Washington, DC 20433 USA, (202) 473-1000, Fax: (202) 974-4384, www.ifc.org; *Annual Report 2007.*

NewsBank, 4501 Tamiami Trail North, Suite 316, Naples, FL 34103, (800) 762-8182, Fax: (239) 263-3004, www.newsbank.com; *Access Statistics.*

Thomson Financial, 195 Broadway, New York, NY 10007, (646) 822-2000, www.thomson.com; *International Financing Review (IFR)* and *Thomson Financial News.*

Tourism Intelligence International, An der Wolfskuhle 48, 33619 Bielefeld, Germany, www.tourism-intelligence.com; *Impact of Terrorism on World Tourism.*

U.S. Department of Homeland Security (DHS), National Counterterrorism Center (NCTC), Washington, DC 20528, (202) 282-8000, www.nctc.gov; *A Chronology of Significant International Terrorism for 2004; NCTC Fact Sheet and Observations Related to 2005 Terrorist Incidents;* and *NCTC Report on Incidents of Terrorism 2006.*

U.S. Department of State (DOS), 2201 C Street NW, Washington, DC 20520, (202) 647-4000, www.state.gov; *Patterns of Global Terrorism.*

U.S. Department of State (DOS) Office of the Coordinator for Counterterrorism, Office of Public Affairs, Room 2509, 2201 C Street NW, Washington, DC 20520, (202) 647-4000, www.state.gov/s/ct; *Country Reports on Terrorism 2007.*

United Nations Environment Programme (UNEP), PO Box 30552, Nairobi, Kenya, www.unep.org; *Atlas of International Freshwater Agreements.*

INTERNATIONAL AFFAIRS - BALANCE OF TRADE

Eurostat, Batiment Jean Monnet, Rue Alcide de Gasperi, L-2920 Luxembourg, http://epp.eurostat.ec.europa.eu; Intra- and Extra-EU Trade.

International Trade Administration (ITA), U.S. Department of Commerce (DOC), 1401 Constitution Avenue, NW, Washington, DC 20230, (800) USA-TRAD(E), Fax: (202) 482-4473, www.ita.doc.gov; unpublished data.

INTERNATIONAL AFFAIRS - COMMERCE

DSI Data Service Information, Xantener Strasse 51a, D-47495 Rheinberg, Germany, www.dsidata.com; *International Statistical Yearbook 2007.*

International Monetary Fund (IMF), 700 Nineteenth Street, NW, Washington, DC 20431, (202) 623-7000, Fax: (202) 623-4661, www.imf.org; *International Financial Statistics Yearbook 2007.*

International Trade Administration (ITA), U.S. Department of Commerce (DOC), 1401 Constitution Avenue, NW, Washington, DC 20230, (800) USA-TRAD(E), Fax: (202) 482-4473, www.ita.doc.gov; unpublished data.

U.S. Census Bureau, Foreign Trade Division, 4700 Silver Hill Road, Washington DC 20233-0001, (301) 763-3030, www.census.gov/foreign-trade/www/; *U.S. International Trade in Goods and Services* and *U.S. Trade with Puerto Rico and U.S. Possessions.*

The World Bank, 1818 H Street, NW, Washington, DC 20433, (202) 473-1000, Fax: (202) 477-6391, www.worldbank.org; *Global Economic Monitor (GEM)* and *Global Economic Prospects 2008.*

INTERNATIONAL AFFAIRS - FEDERAL OUTLAYS

The Office of Management and Budget (OMB), 725 17th Street, NW, Washington, DC 20503, (202) 395-3080, Fax: (202) 395-3888, www.whitehouse.gov/omb; *Budget of the United States Government, Federal Year 2009* and *Historical Tables.*

INTERNATIONAL AFFAIRS - FOREIGN EXCHANGE RATES

DSI Data Service Information, Xantener Strasse 51a, D-47495 Rheinberg, Germany, www.dsidata.com; *International Statistical Yearbook 2007.*

Federal Financial Institutions Examination Council (FFIEC), 3501 Fairfax Drive, Room D8073A, Arlington, VA 22226, (202) 872-7500, www.ffiec.gov; *Country Exposure Lending Survey.*

International Trade Administration (ITA), U.S. Department of Commerce (DOC), 1401 Constitution Avenue, NW, Washington, DC 20230, (800) USA-TRAD(E), Fax: (202) 482-4473, www.ita.doc.gov; unpublished data.

The World Bank, 1818 H Street, NW, Washington, DC 20433, (202) 473-1000, Fax: (202) 477-6391, www.worldbank.org; *Global Economic Monitor (GEM)* and *Global Economic Prospects 2008.*

INTERNATIONAL AFFAIRS - FOREIGN INVESTMENT IN THE UNITED STATES

Bureau of Economic Analysis (BEA), U.S. Department of Commerce (DOC), 1441 L Street NW, Washington, DC 20230, (202) 606-9900, www.bea.gov; *Survey of Current Business (SCB).*

Department of Employment and Economic Development, Minnesota Trade Office, 1st National Bank Building, Suite E200, 332 Minnesota Street, St. Paul, MN 55101-1351, (651) 297-4222, Fax: (651) 296-3555, http://www.exportminnesota.com/mtomap.htm; *Foreign Direct Investment in Minnesota.*

INTERNATIONAL AFFAIRS - INTERNATIONAL TRANSACTIONS - UNITED STATES

Bureau of Economic Analysis (BEA), U.S. Department of Commerce (DOC), 1441 L Street NW, Washington, DC 20230, (202) 606-9900, www.bea.gov; *Survey of Current Business (SCB).*

INTERNATIONAL AFFAIRS - RECEIPTS AND PAYMENTS FOR TRANSPORTATION

Bureau of Economic Analysis (BEA), U.S. Department of Commerce (DOC), 1441 L Street NW, Washington, DC 20230, (202) 606-9900, www.bea.gov; *Survey of Current Business (SCB)* and unpublished data.

INTERNATIONAL AFFAIRS - UNITED STATES GOVERNMENT AID

Bureau of Economic Analysis (BEA), U.S. Department of Commerce (DOC), 1441 L Street NW, Washington, DC 20230, (202) 606-9900, www.bea.gov; unpublished data.

U.S. Agency for International Development (USAID), Information Center, Ronald Reagan Building, Washington, D.C. 20523, (202) 712-0000, Fax: (202) 216-3524, www.usaid.gov; *U.S. Overseas Loans and Grants and Assistance from International Organizations* and unpublished data.

INTERNATIONAL AFFAIRS - UNITED STATES INVESTMENTS

Bureau of Economic Analysis (BEA), U.S. Department of Commerce (DOC), 1441 L Street NW, Washington, DC 20230, (202) 606-9900, www.bea.gov; *Survey of Current Business (SCB).*

INTERNATIONAL BANK FOR RECONSTRUCTION AND DEVELOPMENT

Bureau of Economic Analysis (BEA), U.S. Department of Commerce (DOC), 1441 L Street NW, Washington, DC 20230, (202) 606-9900, www.bea.gov; unpublished data.

INTERNATIONAL DEVELOPMENT ASSOCIATION

Bureau of Economic Analysis (BEA), U.S. Department of Commerce (DOC), 1441 L Street NW, Washington, DC 20230, (202) 606-9900, www.bea.gov; unpublished data.

INTERNATIONAL EDUCATION

Council of Graduate Schools, One Dupont Circle NW, Suite 230, Washington, DC 20036, (202) 223-3791, www.cgsnet.org; *Findings from the 2007 CGS International Graduate Admissions Survey: Phase I - Applications; Findings from the 2007 CGS International Graduate Admissions Survey: Phase II - Final Applications and Initial Offers of Acceptance; Findings from the 2007 CGS International Graduate Amissions Survey: Phase III - Admissions and Enrollment;* and *Graduate Enrollment and Degrees Report.*

Institute of International Education (IIE), 809 United Nations Plaza, New York, NY 10017-3580, (212) 883-8200, Fax: (212) 984-5452, www.iie.org; *International Student Enrollment Survey: Survey Report Fall 2007* and *Open Doors 1948-2004: CD-ROM.*

INTERNATIONAL FINANCE CORPORATION

Bureau of Economic Analysis (BEA), U.S. Department of Commerce (DOC), 1441 L Street NW, Washington, DC 20230, (202) 606-9900, www.bea.gov; unpublished data.

INTERNATIONAL INVESTMENT POSITION - UNITED STATES

Bureau of Economic Analysis (BEA), U.S. Department of Commerce (DOC), 1441 L Street NW, Washington, DC 20230, (202) 606-9900, www.bea.gov; *Survey of Current Business (SCB)* and unpublished data.

INTERNATIONAL MAIL - UNITED STATES POSTAL

U.S. Postal Service (USPS), 475 L'Enfant Plaza West, SW, Washington, DC 20260, (202) 268-2500, Fax: (202) 268-4860, www.usps.gov; *Quarterly Statistics Report (QSR)* and unpublished data.

INTERNATIONAL TRADE

See also FOREIGN COUNTRIES and Individual Commodities

Bernan Essential Government Publications, 4611-F Assembly Drive, Lanham MD, 20706-4391, (301) 459-2255, Fax: (800) 865-3450, www.bernan.com; *United States Foreign Trade Highlights: Trends in the Global Market, 2007.*

Department of Statistics (DOS), PO Box 2015, Amman 11181, Jordan, www.dos.gov.jo; *External Trade Statistics 2006.*

Directorate General of Commercial Intelligence and Statistics (DGCIS), Ministry of Commerce and Industry, 1, Council House Street, Calcutta-700 001, India, www.dgciskol.nic.in; *Foreign Trade Statistics of India by Principal Commodities Countries* and *Statistics of Foreign Trade in India by Countries.*

DSI Data Service Information, Xantener Strasse 51a, D-47495 Rheinberg, Germany, www.dsidata.com; *International Statistical Yearbook 2007.*

Dun and Bradstreet (DB) Corporation, 103 JFK Parkway, Short Hills, NJ 07078, (973) 921-5500, www.dnb.com; *Country Report.*

The Economist, 25 St. James's Street, London SW1A 1HG, United Kingdom, www.economist.com; *The World in 2007.*

Economist Intelligence Unit, 111 West 57th Street, New York, NY 10019, (212) 554-0600, Fax: (212) 586-1181, www.eiu.com; *United States of America Country Report.*

Eurostat, Batiment Jean Monnet, Rue Alcide de Gasperi, L-2920 Luxembourg, http://epp.eurostat.ec.europa.eu; Intra- and Extra-EU Trade.

International Monetary Fund (IMF), 700 Nineteenth Street, NW, Washington, DC 20431, (202) 623-7000, Fax: (202) 623-4661, www.imf.org; *GFSR Market Update; Global Financial Stability Report (April 2008 Edition); International Financial Statistics Yearbook 2007;* and *World Economic Outlook Database (April 2008 Edition).*

International Trade Administration (ITA), U.S. Department of Commerce (DOC), 1401 Constitution Avenue, NW, Washington, DC 20230, (800) USA-TRAD(E), Fax: (202) 482-4473, www.ita.doc.gov; *CAFTA-DR: A State Export Overview, 2000-2004; Exports, Jobs, and Foreign Investment;* and *NAFTA - 10 Years Later.*

Lithuanian Department of Statistics (Statistics Lithuania), Gedimino av. 29, LT-01500 Vilnius, Lithuania, www.stat.gov.lt/en; *Foreign Trade 2006.*

MSCI Barra, 88 Pine Street, 2nd Floor, New York, NY 10005, (212) 785-9630, http://www.mscibarra.com; Investment Portfolio Analysis Products.

Organization of American States (OAS), 17th Street Constitution Avenue NW, Washington, DC 20006, (202) 458-3000, www.oas.org; Foreign Trade Information System (SICE).

STAT-USA, HCHB Room 4885, U.S. Department of Commerce, Washington, DC 20230, (202) 482-1986, Fax: (202) 482-2164, www.stat-usa.gov; USA Trade Online.

Thomson Financial, 195 Broadway, New York, NY 10007, (646) 822-2000, www.thomson.com; *International Financing Review (IFR)* and *Thomson Financial News.*

Thomson Scientific, 3501 Market Street, Philadelphia, PA 19104-3302, (800) 336-4474, www.thomson.com; *Dialog TradStat.*

U.S. Census Bureau, Center for Economic Studies, 4600 Silver Hill Road, Washington DC 20233, (301) 457-1235, www.ces.census.gov; *Downsizing, Layoffs and Plant Closure: The Impacts of Import Price Pressure and Technological Growth on U.S. Textile Producers* and *Import Price Pressure on Firm Productivity and Employment: The Case of U.S. Textiles.*

U.S. Census Bureau, Foreign Trade Division, 4700 Silver Hill Road, Washington DC 20233-0001, (301) 763-3030, www.census.gov/foreign-trade/www/; *U.S. International Trade in Goods and Services.*

U.S. Customs and Border Protection (CBP), U.S. Department of Homeland Security (DHS), 1300 Pennsylvania Avenue, NW Washington, DC 20004-3002, (202) 354-1000, www.cbp.gov; *FY04 Year-End Import Trade Trends Report.*

U.S. Department of Labor (DOL), Bureau of International Labor Affairs (ILAB), Frances Perkins Building, Room C-4325, 200 Constitution Avenue, NW, Washington, DC 20210, (202) 693-4770, Fax: (202) 693-4780, www.dol.gov/ilab; *United States Employment Impact Review.*

U.S. Library of Congress (LOC), Congressional Research Service (CRS), The Library of Congress, 101 Independence Avenue, SE, Washington, DC 20540-7500, (202) 707-5700, www.loc.gov/crsinfo; *Ports in Louisiana: New Orleans, South Louisiana, and Baton Rouge; U.S.-World Merchandise Trade Data: 1948-2006;* and *What's the Difference? Comparing U.S. and Chinese Trade Data.*

United Nations Conference on Trade and Development (UNCTAD), DC2-1120, United Nations, New York, NY 10017, (212) 963-0027, www.unctad.org; UNCTAD-TRAINS (TRade Analysis and INformation System).

United Nations Statistics Division, New York, NY 10017, (800) 253-9646, Fax: (212) 963-4116, http://unstats.un.org; United Nations Common Database (UNCDB).

The World Bank, 1818 H Street, NW, Washington, DC 20433, (202) 473-1000, Fax: (202) 477-6391, www.worldbank.org; *Global Economic Monitor (GEM)* and *Global Economic Prospects 2008.*

World Trade Organization (WTO), Centre William Rappard, Rue de Lausanne 154, CH-1211 Geneva 21, Switzerland, www.wto.org; *Statistics Database.*

INTERNATIONAL TRADE - AEROSPACE PRODUCTS

Aerospace Industries Association (AIA), 1000 Wilson Boulevard, Suite 1700, Arlington, VA 22209-3928, (703) 358-1000, www.aia-aerospace.org; *Aerospace Facts and Figures 2007; Aerospace Statistics;* and *AIA's Year-End Review and Forecast.*

Federal Aviation Administration (FAA), 800 Independence Avenue, SW, Washington, DC 20591, (866) 835-5322, www.faa.gov; *FAA Aerospace Forecasts - Fiscal Years 2007-2020.*

U.S. Census Bureau, Foreign Trade Division, 4700 Silver Hill Road, Washington DC 20233-0001, (301) 763-3030, www.census.gov/foreign-trade/www/; *U.S. International Trade in Goods and Services.*

U.S. Census Bureau, Manufacturing and Construction Division, 4600 Silver Hill Road, Washington DC 20233, (301) 763-4673, www.census.gov/mcd; *Aerospace Industry.*

INTERNATIONAL TRADE - AGRICULTURAL PRODUCTS

Economic Research Service (ERS), U.S. Department of Agriculture (USDA), 1800 M Street, NW, Washington, DC 20036-5831, (202) 694-5050, Fax: (202) 694-5689, www.ers.usda.gov; *Agricultural Outlook; Agricultural Statistics;* and *Foreign Agricultural Trade of the United States (FATUS).*

National Agricultural Statistics Service (NASS), U.S. Department of Agriculture (USDA), 1400 Independence Avenue, SW, Washington, DC 20250, (800) 727-9540, Fax: (202) 690-2090, www.nass.usda.gov; *2006 Agricultural Statistics.*

INTERNATIONAL TRADE - AIRCRAFT AND AIRCRAFT PARTS

Aerospace Industries Association (AIA), 1000 Wilson Boulevard, Suite 1700, Arlington, VA 22209-3928, (703) 358-1000, www.aia-aerospace.org; *Aerospace Facts and Figures 2007; Aerospace Statistics;* and *AIA's Year-End Review and Forecast.*

Federal Aviation Administration (FAA), 800 Independence Avenue, SW, Washington, DC 20591, (866) 835-5322, www.faa.gov; *FAA Aerospace Forecasts - Fiscal Years 2007-2020.*

U.S. Census Bureau, Foreign Trade Division, 4700 Silver Hill Road, Washington DC 20233-0001, (301) 763-3030, www.census.gov/foreign-trade/www/; *U.S. International Trade in Goods and Services.*

U.S. Census Bureau, Manufacturing and Construction Division, 4600 Silver Hill Road, Washington DC 20233, (301) 763-4673, www.census.gov/mcd; *Aerospace Industry.*

INTERNATIONAL TRADE - AUTOMOBILES

Alliance of Automobile Manufacturers (AAM), 1401 Eye Street, NW, Suite 900, Washington, DC 20005, (202) 326-5500, Fax: (202) 326-5598, www.autoalliance.org; various fact sheets.

Bureau of Economic Analysis (BEA), U.S. Department of Commerce (DOC), 1441 L Street NW, Washington, DC 20230, (202) 606-9900, www.bea.gov; *2007 Annual Revision of the National Income and Product Accounts (NIPA)* and *Survey of Current Business (SCB).*

U.S. Census Bureau, Foreign Trade Division, 4700 Silver Hill Road, Washington DC 20233-0001, (301) 763-3030, www.census.gov/foreign-trade/www/; *U.S. International Trade in Goods and Services.*

Ward's Communications, 3000 Town Center, Suite 2750, Southfield, MI 48075, (248) 799-2645, Fax: (248) 357-0810, http://wardsauto.com; *Ward's Automotive Reports.*

INTERNATIONAL TRADE - BALANCE OF TRADE

DSI Data Service Information, Xantener Strasse 51a, D-47495 Rheinberg, Germany, www.dsidata.com; *International Statistical Yearbook 2007.*

MSCI Barra, 88 Pine Street, 2nd Floor, New York, NY 10005, (212) 785-9630, http://www.mscibarra.com; Investment Portfolio Analysis Products.

U.S. Census Bureau, Foreign Trade Division, 4700 Silver Hill Road, Washington DC 20233-0001, (301) 763-3030, www.census.gov/foreign-trade/www/; *U.S. International Trade in Goods and Services.*

The World Bank, 1818 H Street, NW, Washington, DC 20433, (202) 473-1000, Fax: (202) 477-6391, www.worldbank.org; *Global Economic Monitor (GEM)* and *Global Economic Prospects 2008.*

INTERNATIONAL TRADE - COAL

U.S. Department of Energy (DOE), Energy Information Administration (EIA), 1000 Independence Avenue, SW, Washington, DC 20585, (202) 586-8800, www.eia.doe.gov; *Annual Coal Report 2005; Annual Energy Review 2005;* and unpublished data.

INTERNATIONAL TRADE - COMPANIES EXPORTING

U.S. Census Bureau, Foreign Trade Division, 4700 Silver Hill Road, Washington DC 20233-0001, (301) 763-3030, www.census.gov/foreign-trade/www/; *U.S. International Trade in Goods and Services.*

INTERNATIONAL TRADE - COUNTRIES

DSI Data Service Information, Xantener Strasse 51a, D-47495 Rheinberg, Germany, www.dsidata.com; *International Statistical Yearbook 2007.*

U.S. Census Bureau, Foreign Trade Division, 4700 Silver Hill Road, Washington DC 20233-0001, (301) 763-3030, www.census.gov/foreign-trade/www/; *U.S. International Trade in Goods and Services.*

United Nations Conference on Trade and Development (UNCTAD), DC2-1120, United Nations, New York, NY 10017, (212) 963-0027, www.unctad.org; *Development and Globalization: Facts and Figures.*

The World Bank, 1818 H Street, NW, Washington, DC 20433, (202) 473-1000, Fax: (202) 477-6391, www.worldbank.org; *Global Economic Monitor (GEM)* and *Global Economic Prospects 2008.*

INTERNATIONAL TRADE - CRUDE OIL

American Petroleum Institute (API), 1220 L Street, NW, Washington, DC 20005-4070, (202) 682-8000, http://api-ec.api.org; *Crude Oil and Product Import Chart; Monthly Statistical Report;* and *Weekly Statistical Bulletin.*

Lundberg Survey, Incorporated (LSI), 911 Via Alondra, Camarillo, CA 93012, (805) 383-2400, Fax: (805) 383-2424, www.lundbergsurvey.com; *Energy Detente; Lundberg Letter; National Retail Gasoline and Diesel Price Survey;* and *National Share of Market Report.*

PennWell Corporation, 1421 South Sheridan Road, Tulsa, OK 74112, (918) 835-3161, www.pennwell.com; *Oil and Gas Financial Journal; Oil and Gas Journal;* and *Oil Gas Journal Latinoamericana.*

U.S. Department of Energy (DOE), Energy Information Administration (EIA), 1000 Independence Avenue, SW, Washington, DC 20585, (202) 586-8800, www.eia.doe.gov; *Annual Energy Review 2005; Monthly Energy Review (MER);* and *Petroleum Supply Annual 2004.*

U.S. Department of the Interior (DOI), Minerals Management Service (MMS), 1849 C Street, NW, Washington, DC 20240, (202) 208-3985, www.mms.gov; *Federal Offshore Statistics.*

INTERNATIONAL TRADE - CUSTOMS AND DISTRICTS

U.S. Census Bureau, Foreign Trade Division, 4700 Silver Hill Road, Washington DC 20233-0001, (301) 763-3030, www.census.gov/foreign-trade/www/; *U.S. International Trade in Goods and Services.*

INTERNATIONAL TRADE - FISH PRODUCTS

National Marine Fisheries Service (NMFS), National Oceanic and Atmospheric Administration (NOAA), Office of Constituent Services, 1315 East West Highway, 9th Floor, Silver Spring, MD 20910, (301) 713-2379, Fax: (301) 713-2385, www.nmfs.noaa.gov; *Fisheries of the United States - 2006.*

INTERNATIONAL TRADE - INDEXES - UNIT VALUE

International Monetary Fund (IMF), 700 Nineteenth Street, NW, Washington, DC 20431, (202) 623-7000, Fax: (202) 623-4661, www.imf.org; *International Financial Statistics Yearbook 2007.*

INTERNATIONAL TRADE - INFORMATION AND COMMUNICATION TECHNOLOGY SECTOR

The NPD Group, Port Washington, 900 West Shore Road, Port Washington, NY 11050, (866) 444-1411, www.npd.com; *Market Research for the Consumer Technology Industry.*

Organisation for Economic Cooperation and Development (OECD), 2 rue Andre Pascal, F-75775 Paris Cedex 16, France, (Telephone in U.S. (202) 785-6323), (Fax in U.S. (202) 785-0350), www.oecd.org; *ICT Sector Data and Metadata by Country.*

INTERNATIONAL TRADE - INTERNATIONAL TRANSACTIONS - UNITED STATES

Bureau of Economic Analysis (BEA), U.S. Department of Commerce (DOC), 1441 L Street NW, Washington, DC 20230, (202) 606-9900, www.bea.gov; *Survey of Current Business (SCB).*

U.S. Census Bureau, Foreign Trade Division, 4700 Silver Hill Road, Washington DC 20233-0001, (301) 763-3030, www.census.gov/foreign-trade/www/; *U.S. International Trade in Goods and Services.*

U.S. Department of Labor (DOL), Bureau of International Labor Affairs (ILAB), Frances Perkins Building, Room C-4325, 200 Constitution Avenue, NW, Washington, DC 20210, (202) 693-4770, Fax: (202) 693-4780, www.dol.gov/ilab; *United States Employment Impact Review.*

INTERNATIONAL TRADE - MANUFACTURES - UNITED STATES COMPARED TO WORLD

International Trade Administration (ITA), U.S. Department of Commerce (DOC), 1401 Constitution Avenue, NW, Washington, DC 20230, (800) USA-TRAD(E), Fax: (202) 482-4473, www.ita.doc.gov; unpublished data.

U.S. Census Bureau, Center for Economic Studies, 4600 Silver Hill Road, Washington DC 20233, (301) 457-1235, www.ces.census.gov; *Downsizing, Layoffs and Plant Closure: The Impacts of Import Price Pressure and Technological Growth on U.S. Textile Producers* and *Import Price Pressure on Firm Productivity and Employment: The Case of U.S. Textiles.*

INTERNATIONAL TRADE - MINERAL IMPORTS

U.S. Census Bureau, Foreign Trade Division, 4700 Silver Hill Road, Washington DC 20233-0001, (301) 763-3030, www.census.gov/foreign-trade/www/; *U.S. International Trade in Goods and Services.*

U.S. Department of the Interior (DOI), U.S. Geological Survey (USGS), Office of Minerals Information, 12201 Sunrise Valley Drive, Reston, VA 20192, Mr. Kenneth A. Beckman, (703) 648-4916, Fax: (703) 648-4995, http://minerals.usgs.gov/minerals; *Mineral Commodity Summaries* and *Minerals Yearbook.*

INTERNATIONAL TRADE - PETROLEUM INDUSTRY

American Petroleum Institute (API), 1220 L Street, NW, Washington, DC 20005-4070, (202) 682-8000, http://api-ec.api.org; *Monthly Statistical Report* and *Weekly Statistical Bulletin.*

Organization of Petroleum Exporting Countries (OPEC), Obere Donaustrasse 93, A-1020, Vienna, Austria, www.opec.org; *Annual Statistical Bulletin 2006* and *World Oil Outlook 2007.*

PennWell Corporation, 1421 South Sheridan Road, Tulsa, OK 74112, (918) 835-3161, www.pennwell.com; *Oil and Gas Financial Journal* and *Oil and Gas Journal.*

INTERNATIONAL TRADE - TIMBER PRODUCTS

USDA Forest Service, 1400 Independence Ave, SW, Washington, DC 20250-0003, (202) 205-8333, www.fs.fed.us; *Timber Products Supply and Demand.*

INTERNATIONAL TRADE - UNITED STATES AFFILIATES OF FOREIGN COMPANIES

Bureau of Economic Analysis (BEA), U.S. Department of Commerce (DOC), 1441 L Street NW, Washington, DC 20230, (202) 606-9900, www.bea.gov; *Foreign Direct Investment in the United States (FDIUS); Survey of Current Business (SCB);* and *U.S. Direct Investment Abroad (USDIA).*

INTERNATIONAL TRADE - WORLD SUMMARY - EXTERNAL TRADE

DSI Data Service Information, Xantener Strasse 51a, D-47495 Rheinberg, Germany, www.dsidata.com; *International Statistical Yearbook 2007.*

Thomson Scientific, 3501 Market Street, Philadelphia, PA 19104-3302, (800) 336-4474, www.thomson.com; *Dialog TradStat.*

United Nations Conference on Trade and Development (UNCTAD), DC2-1120, United Nations, New York, NY 10017, (212) 963-0027, www.unctad.org; *Development and Globalization: Facts and Figures.*

United Nations Statistics Division, New York, NY 10017, (800) 253-9646, Fax: (212) 963-4116, http://unstats.un.org; *Monthly Bulletin of Statistics.*

The World Bank, 1818 H Street, NW, Washington, DC 20433, (202) 473-1000, Fax: (202) 477-6391, www.worldbank.org; *Global Economic Monitor (GEM)* and *Global Economic Prospects 2008.*

INTERNET USE

Eurostat, Batiment Jean Monnet, Rue Alcide de Gasperi, L-2920 Luxembourg, http://epp.eurostat.ec.europa.eu; *Internet Usage by Enterprises 2007* and *Internet Usage in 2007 - Households and Individuals.*

Information Institute, Florida State University, Room 010 Louis Shores Building, 142 Collegiate Loop, PO Box 3062100, Tallahassee, FL 32306-2100, (850) 645-5683, www.ii.fsu.edu; *Public Libraries and the Internet 2007.*

International Telecommunication Union (ITU), Place des Nations, 1211 Geneva 20, Switzerland, www.itu.int; *Asia-Pacific Telecommunication Indicators.*

International Telecommunication Union (ITU), Place des Nations, 1211 Geneva 20, Switzerland, www.itu.int; *World Telecommunication/ICT Indicators Database on CD-ROM; World Telecommunication/ICT Indicators Database Online;* and *Yearbook of Statistics - Telecommunication Services (Chronological Time Series 1997-2006).*

Mediamark Research, Inc., 75 Ninth Avenue, 5th Floor, New York, NY 10011, (212) 884-9200, Fax: (212) 884-9339, www.mediamark.com; MRI+.

National Center for Education Statistics (NCES), 1990 K Street, NW, Washington, DC 20006, (202) 502-7300, http://nces.ed.gov; *Advanced Telecommunications in U.S. Private Schools; Internet Access in U.S. Public Schools and Classrooms: 1994-2005;* and *Teacher Use of Computers and the Internet in Public Schools.*

National Telecommunications and Information Administration (NTIA), U.S. Department of Commerce (DOC), 1401 Constitution Avenue, NW, Washington, DC 20230, (202) 482-7002, www.ntia.doc.gov; *A Nation Online: Entering the Broadband Age.*

U.S. Department of Commerce (DOC), Economics and Statistics Administration (ESA), 1401 Constitution Avenue, NW, Washington, DC 20230, (800) 782-8872, www.esa.doc.gov; *Falling Through the Net: Toward Digital Inclusion; Main Street in the Digital Age: How Small and Medium-sized Businesses Are Using the Tools of the New Economy;* and *A Nation Online.*

U.S. National Commission on Libraries and Information Science (NCLIS), 1800 M Street, NW, Suite 350 North Tower, Washington, DC 20036-5841, (202) 606-9200, Fax: (202) 606-9203, www.nclis.gov; *Public Libraries and the Internet 2000: Summary Findings and Data Table.*

Veronis Suhler Stevenson Partners LLC, 350 Park Avenue, New York, NY 10022, (212) 935-4990, Fax: (212) 381-8168, www.vss.com; Communications Industry Report.

The World Bank, 1818 H Street, NW, Washington, DC 20433, (202) 473-1000, Fax: (202) 477-6391, www.worldbank.org; *United States.*

INTERRACIAL MARRIED COUPLES

U.S. Census Bureau, Population Division, 4700 Silver Hill Road, Washington DC 20233-0001, (301) 763-3030, www.census.gov/population/www/; *Current Population Reports.*

INTRACITY TRANSPORTATION PRICE INDEXES

U.S. Bureau of Labor Statistics (BLS), Postal Square Building, 2 Massachusetts Avenue, NE, Washington, DC 20212-0001, (202) 691-5200, Fax: (202) 691-6325, www.bls.gov; *Consumer Price Index Detailed Report* and *Monthly Labor Review (MLR).*

INVENTORIES

Office of Trade and Industry Information (OTII), Manufacturing and Services, International Trade Administration, U.S. Department of Commerce, 1401 Constitution Ave, NW, Washington, DC 20230, (800) USA TRAD(E), http://trade.gov/index.asp; *TradeStats Express.*

U.S. Census Bureau, Center for Economic Studies, 4600 Silver Hill Road, Washington DC 20233, (301) 457-1235, www.ces.census.gov; *2002 Economic Census, Retail Trade* and *2002 Economic Census, Wholesale Trade.*

U.S. Census Bureau, Company Statistics Division, 4700 Silver Hill Road, Washington DC 20233-0001, (301) 763-3030, www.census.gov/csd/; *Current Business Reports.*

U.S. Census Bureau, Manufacturing and Construction Division, 4600 Silver Hill Road, Washington DC 20233, (301) 763-4673, www.census.gov/mcd; *Current Industrial Reports* and *Manufacturers Shipments, Inventories and Orders.*

U.S. Census Bureau, Service Sector Statistics Division, 4700 Silver Hill Road, Washington DC 20233-0001, (301) 763-3030, www.census.gov/svsd/www/economic.html; *Annual Benchmark Report for Wholesale Trade.*

INVENTORIES - BUSINESS (GDP)

Bureau of Economic Analysis (BEA), U.S. Department of Commerce (DOC), 1441 L Street NW, Washington, DC 20230, (202) 606-9900, www.bea.gov; *2007 Annual Revision of the National Income and Product Accounts (NIPA)* and *Survey of Current Business (SCB).*

INVESTMENTS

Bond Market Association, 360 Madison Avenue, New York, NY 10017-7111, (646) 637-9200, Fax: (646) 637-9126, www.bondmarket.com; *The African-American Book Buyers Study.*

MSCI Barra, 88 Pine Street, 2nd Floor, New York, NY 10005, (212) 785-9630, http://www.mscibarra.com; Investment Portfolio Analysis Products.

Standard and Poor's Corporation, 55 Water Street, New York, NY 10041, (212) 438-1000, www.standardandpoors.com; *Compustat Global; Compustat North America; KENNYBASE: Comprehensive Online Fixed Income Database;* and *Marine Mutual Report 2006.*

INVESTMENTS - FOREIGN - IN UNITED STATES

Bureau of Economic Analysis (BEA), U.S. Department of Commerce (DOC), 1441 L Street NW, Washington, DC 20230, (202) 606-9900, www.bea.gov; *Foreign Direct Investment in the United States (FDIUS); Survey of Current Business (SCB); U.S. Direct Investment Abroad (USDIA);* and unpublished data.

MSCI Barra, 88 Pine Street, 2nd Floor, New York, NY 10005, (212) 785-9630, http://www.mscibarra.com; Investment Portfolio Analysis Products.

United Nations Conference on Trade and Development (UNCTAD), DC2-1120, United Nations, New York, NY 10017, (212) 963-0027, www.unctad.org; Foreign Direct Investment (FDI) and *World Investment Report, 2006.*

INVESTMENTS - PRIVATE DOMESTIC - GROSS

Bureau of Economic Analysis (BEA), U.S. Department of Commerce (DOC), 1441 L Street NW, Washington, DC 20230, (202) 606-9900, www.bea.gov; *2007 Annual Revision of the National Income and Product Accounts (NIPA)* and *Survey of Current Business (SCB).*

MSCI Barra, 88 Pine Street, 2nd Floor, New York, NY 10005, (212) 785-9630, http://www.mscibarra.com; Investment Portfolio Analysis Products.

INVESTMENTS - UNITED STATES GOVERNMENT OBLIGATIONS

Federal Deposit Insurance Corporation (FDIC), 550 Seventeenth Street, NW, Washington, DC 20429-0002, (877) 275-3342, www.fdic.gov; *2007 Annual Report; Quarterly Banking Profile (QBP);* and Statistics on Depository Institutions (SDI) (web app).

INVESTMENTS - UNITED STATES INTERNATIONAL

Bureau of Economic Analysis (BEA), U.S. Department of Commerce (DOC), 1441 L Street NW, Washington, DC 20230, (202) 606-9900, www.bea.gov; *Survey of Current Business (SCB).*

INVESTMENTS - VENTURE CAPITAL

Thomson Financial, 195 Broadway, New York, NY 10007, (646) 822-2000, www.thomson.com; *Venture Capital Journal.*

IOWA

See also - STATE DATA (FOR INDIVIDUAL STATES)

IOWA - STATE DATA CENTERS

Center for Social and Behavioral Research (CSBR), University of Northern Iowa, 221 Sabin Hall, Cedar Falls, IA 50614-0402, Dr. Mary Losch (319) 273-2105, Fax: (319) 273-3104, www.uni.edu/csbr; State Data Center.

Department of Sociology, University of Iowa, W140 Seashore Hall, Iowa City, IA 52242-1401, Mr. Ben Earnhart, (319) 335-2887, Fax: (319) 335-2509, www.uiowa.edu/[]soc/icpsr_frm.htm; State Data Center.

Office of Social and Economic Trend Analysis (SETA), Iowa State University, 303 East Hall, Ames, IA 50010-1070, (515) 294-9903, Fax: (515) 294-0592, www.seta.iastate.edu; State Data Center.

State Library of Iowa, Ola Babcock Miller Building, 1112 East Grand, Des Moines, IA 50319-0233, Ms. Beth Henning, (515) 281-4350, Fax: (515) 242-6543, www.iowadatacenter.org; State Data Center.

IOWA - PRIMARY STATISTICS SOURCES

Public Interest Institute, Iowa Wesleyan College, 600 North Jackson Street, Mt. Pleasant, IA 52641-1328, (319) 385-3462, www.limitedgovernment.org; *Iowa Economic Scorecard.*

IRAN - NATIONAL STATISTICAL OFFICE

Statistical Centre of Iran (SCI), Dr. Fatemi Avenue, PO Box 14155-6133, Tehran 1414663111, Iran, www.sci.org.ir/portal/faces/public/sci_en/; National Data Center.

IRAN - PRIMARY STATISTICS SOURCES

Statistical Centre of Iran (SCI), Dr. Fatemi Avenue, PO Box 14155-6133, Tehran 1414663111, Iran, www.sci.org.ir/portal/faces/public/sci_en/; *Iran Statistical Digest* and *Iran Statistical Yearbook 1385 (2006-2007).*

IRAN - AGRICULTURAL MACHINERY

United Nations Statistics Division, New York, NY 10017, (800) 253-9646, Fax: (212) 963-4116, http://unstats.un.org; *Statistical Yearbook.*

IRAN - AGRICULTURE

Economist Intelligence Unit, 111 West 57th Street, New York, NY 10019, (212) 554-0600, Fax: (212) 586-1181, www.eiu.com; *Iran Country Report.*

Euromonitor International, Inc., 224 S. Michigan Avenue, Suite 1500, Chicago, IL 60604, (312) 922-1115, Fax: (312) 922-1157, www.euromonitor.com; *International Marketing Data and Statistics 2008* and *World Marketing Data and Statistics.*

M.E. Sharpe, 80 Business Park Drive, Armonk, NY 10504, (800) 541-6563, Fax: (914) 273-2106, www.mesharpe.com; *The Illustrated Book of World Rankings.*

Palgrave Macmillan Ltd., Houndmills, Basingstoke, Hampshire, RG21 6XS, England, (Telephone in U.S. (888) 330-8477), (Fax in U.S. (800) 672-2054), www.palgrave.com; *The Statesman's Yearbook 2008.*

Taylor and Francis Group, An Informa Business, 2 Park Square, Milton Park, Abingdon, Oxford OX14 4RN, United Kingdom, (Dial from U.S. (212) 216-7800), (Fax from U.S. (212) 564-7854), www.tandf.co.uk; *The Europa World Year Book.*

United Nations Conference on Trade and Development (UNCTAD), DC2-1120, United Nations, New York, NY 10017, (212) 963-0027, www.unctad.org; *UNCTAD Commodity Yearbook.*

United Nations Food and Agricultural Organization (FAO), Viale delle Terme di Caracalla, 00100 Rome, Italy, (Dial from U.S. (202) 653-2400), (Fax from U.S. (202) 653 5760), www.fao.org; AQUASTAT; *FAO Production Yearbook 2002;* and *The State of Food and Agriculture (SOFA) 2006.*

United Nations Statistics Division, New York, NY 10017, (800) 253-9646, Fax: (212) 963-4116, http://unstats.un.org; *Asia-Pacific in Figures 2004; Statistical Yearbook;* and *Statistical Yearbook for Asia and the Pacific 2004.*

The World Bank, 1818 H Street, NW, Washington, DC 20433, (202) 473-1000, Fax: (202) 477-6391, www.worldbank.org; *Iran, Islamic Republic of.*

IRAN - AIRLINES

International Civil Aviation Organization (ICAO), External Relations and Public Information Office (EPO), 999 University Street, Montreal, Quebec H3C 5H7, Canada, (Dial from U.S. (514) 954-8219), (Fax from U.S. (514) 954-6077), www.icao.int; *Civil Aviation Statistics of the World.*

M.E. Sharpe, 80 Business Park Drive, Armonk, NY 10504, (800) 541-6563, Fax: (914) 273-2106, www.mesharpe.com; *The Illustrated Book of World Rankings.*

Palgrave Macmillan Ltd., Houndmills, Basingstoke, Hampshire, RG21 6XS, England, (Telephone in U.S. (888) 330-8477), (Fax in U.S. (800) 672-2054), www.palgrave.com; *The Statesman's Yearbook 2008.*

Taylor and Francis Group, An Informa Business, 2 Park Square, Milton Park, Abingdon, Oxford OX14 4RN, United Kingdom, (Dial from U.S. (212) 216-7800), (Fax from U.S. (212) 564-7854), www.tandf.co.uk; *The Europa World Year Book.*

United Nations Statistics Division, New York, NY 10017, (800) 253-9646, Fax: (212) 963-4116, http://unstats.un.org; *Statistical Yearbook.*

IRAN - AIRPORTS

Central Intelligence Agency, Office of Public Affairs, Washington, DC 20505, (703) 482-0623, Fax: (703) 482-1739, www.cia.gov; *The World Factbook.*

IRAN - ALMOND PRODUCTION

See IRAN - CROPS

IRAN - ALUMINUM PRODUCTION

See IRAN - MINERAL INDUSTRIES

IRAN - ARMED FORCES

Central Intelligence Agency, Office of Public Affairs, Washington, DC 20505, (703) 482-0623, Fax: (703) 482-1739, www.cia.gov; *The World Factbook.*

Euromonitor International, Inc., 224 S. Michigan Avenue, Suite 1500, Chicago, IL 60604, (312) 922-1115, Fax: (312) 922-1157, www.euromonitor.com; *World Marketing Data and Statistics.*

International Institute for Strategic Studies (IISS), Arundel House, 13-15 Arundel Street, Temple Place, London WC2R 3DX, England, www.iiss.org; *The Military Balance 2007.*

International Monetary Fund (IMF), 700 Nineteenth Street, NW, Washington, DC 20431, (202) 623-7000, Fax: (202) 623-4661, www.imf.org; *Government Finance Statistics Yearbook (2008 Edition).*

Palgrave Macmillan Ltd., Houndmills, Basingstoke, Hampshire, RG21 6XS, England, (Telephone in U.S. (888) 330-8477), (Fax in U.S. (800) 672-2054), www.palgrave.com; *The Statesman's Yearbook 2008.*

U.S. Department of State (DOS), 2201 C Street NW, Washington, DC 20520, (202) 647-4000, www.state.gov; *World Military Expenditures and Arms Transfers (WMEAT).*

United Nations Statistics Division, New York, NY 10017, (800) 253-9646, Fax: (212) 963-4116, http://unstats.un.org; *Human Development Report 2006.*

IRAN - AUTOMOBILE INDUSTRY AND TRADE

United Nations Statistics Division, New York, NY 10017, (800) 253-9646, Fax: (212) 963-4116, http://unstats.un.org; *Statistical Yearbook.*

IRAN - BALANCE OF PAYMENTS

International Monetary Fund (IMF), 700 Nineteenth Street, NW, Washington, DC 20431, (202) 623-7000, Fax: (202) 623-4661, www.imf.org; *Balance of Payments Statistics Newsletter* and *Balance of Payments Statistics Yearbook 2007.*

Statistical Centre of Iran (SCI), Dr. Fatemi Avenue, PO Box 14155-6133, Tehran 1414663111, Iran, www.sci.org.ir/portal/faces/public/sci_en/; *National Accounts of Iran 2003-2004.*

Taylor and Francis Group, An Informa Business, 2 Park Square, Milton Park, Abingdon, Oxford OX14 4RN, United Kingdom, (Dial from U.S. (212) 216-7800), (Fax from U.S. (212) 564-7854), www.tandf.co.uk; *The Europa World Year Book.*

United Nations Conference on Trade and Development (UNCTAD), DC2-1120, United Nations, New York, NY 10017, (212) 963-0027, www.unctad.org; *Handbook of Statistics 2005.*

The World Bank, 1818 H Street, NW, Washington, DC 20433, (202) 473-1000, Fax: (202) 477-6391, www.worldbank.org; *Iran, Islamic Republic of* and *World Development Report 2008.*

IRAN - BANKS AND BANKING

Euromonitor International, Inc., 224 S. Michigan Avenue, Suite 1500, Chicago, IL 60604, (312) 922-1115, Fax: (312) 922-1157, www.euromonitor.com; *World Marketing Data and Statistics.*

International Monetary Fund (IMF), 700 Nineteenth Street, NW, Washington, DC 20431, (202) 623-7000, Fax: (202) 623-4661, www.imf.org; *International Financial Statistics Yearbook 2007.*

M.E. Sharpe, 80 Business Park Drive, Armonk, NY 10504, (800) 541-6563, Fax: (914) 273-2106, www.mesharpe.com; *The Illustrated Book of World Rankings.*

Palgrave Macmillan Ltd., Houndmills, Basingstoke, Hampshire, RG21 6XS, England, (Telephone in U.S. (888) 330-8477), (Fax in U.S. (800) 672-2054), www.palgrave.com; *The Statesman's Yearbook 2008.*

Statistical Centre of Iran (SCI), Dr. Fatemi Avenue, PO Box 14155-6133, Tehran 1414663111, Iran, www.sci.org.ir/portal/faces/public/sci_en/; *National Accounts of Iran 2003-2004.*

Taylor and Francis Group, An Informa Business, 2 Park Square, Milton Park, Abingdon, Oxford OX14 4RN, United Kingdom, (Dial from U.S. (212) 216-7800), (Fax from U.S. (212) 564-7854), www.tandf.co.uk; *The Europa World Year Book.*

United Nations Statistics Division, New York, NY 10017, (800) 253-9646, Fax: (212) 963-4116, http://unstats.un.org; *Statistical Yearbook.*

IRAN - BARLEY PRODUCTION

See IRAN - CROPS

IRAN - BEVERAGE INDUSTRY

M.E. Sharpe, 80 Business Park Drive, Armonk, NY 10504, (800) 541-6563, Fax: (914) 273-2106, www.mesharpe.com; *The Illustrated Book of World Rankings.*

United Nations Statistics Division, New York, NY 10017, (800) 253-9646, Fax: (212) 963-4116, http://unstats.un.org; *Statistical Yearbook.*

IRAN - BONDS

International Monetary Fund (IMF), 700 Nineteenth Street, NW, Washington, DC 20431, (202) 623-7000, Fax: (202) 623-4661, www.imf.org; *Government Finance Statistics Yearbook (2008 Edition).*

IRAN - BROADCASTING

Central Intelligence Agency, Office of Public Affairs, Washington, DC 20505, (703) 482-0623, Fax: (703) 482-1739, www.cia.gov; *The World Factbook.*

Euromonitor International, Inc., 224 S. Michigan Avenue, Suite 1500, Chicago, IL 60604, (312) 922-1115, Fax: (312) 922-1157, www.euromonitor.com; *World Marketing Data and Statistics.*

M.E. Sharpe, 80 Business Park Drive, Armonk, NY 10504, (800) 541-6563, Fax: (914) 273-2106, www.mesharpe.com; *The Illustrated Book of World Rankings.*

Palgrave Macmillan Ltd., Houndmills, Basingstoke, Hampshire, RG21 6XS, England, (Telephone in U.S. (888) 330-8477), (Fax in U.S. (800) 672-2054), www.palgrave.com; *The Statesman's Yearbook 2008.*

WRTH Publications Limited, PO Box 290, Oxford OX2 7FT, UK, www.wrth.com; *World Radio TV Handbook 2007.*

IRAN - BUDGET

Central Intelligence Agency, Office of Public Affairs, Washington, DC 20505, (703) 482-0623, Fax: (703) 482-1739, www.cia.gov; *The World Factbook.*

IRAN - BUSINESS

United Nations Statistics Division, New York, NY 10017, (800) 253-9646, Fax: (212) 963-4116, http://unstats.un.org; *Statistical Yearbook* and *Statistical Yearbook for Asia and the Pacific 2004.*

IRAN - CAPITAL LEVY

International Monetary Fund (IMF), 700 Nineteenth Street, NW, Washington, DC 20431, (202) 623-7000, Fax: (202) 623-4661, www.imf.org; *Government Finance Statistics Yearbook (2008 Edition).*

IRAN - CATTLE

See IRAN - LIVESTOCK

IRAN - CHICK PEA PRODUCTION

See IRAN - CROPS

IRAN - CHICKENS

See IRAN - LIVESTOCK

IRAN - CHILDBIRTH - STATISTICS

Central Intelligence Agency, Office of Public Affairs, Washington, DC 20505, (703) 482-0623, Fax: (703) 482-1739, www.cia.gov; *The World Factbook.*

Euromonitor International, Inc., 224 S. Michigan Avenue, Suite 1500, Chicago, IL 60604, (312) 922-1115, Fax: (312) 922-1157, www.euromonitor.com; *International Marketing Data and Statistics 2008* and *The World Economic Factbook 2008.*

M.E. Sharpe, 80 Business Park Drive, Armonk, NY 10504, (800) 541-6563, Fax: (914) 273-2106, www.mesharpe.com; *The Illustrated Book of World Rankings.*

Statistical Centre of Iran (SCI), Dr. Fatemi Avenue, PO Box 14155-6133, Tehran 1414663111, Iran, www.sci.org.ir/portal/faces/public/sci_en/; *A Study on the Effects of Women's Activity on Fertility in Iran.*

Taylor and Francis Group, An Informa Business, 2 Park Square, Milton Park, Abingdon, Oxford OX14 4RN, United Kingdom, (Dial from U.S. (212) 216-7800), (Fax from U.S. (212) 564-7854), www.tandf.co.uk; *The Europa World Year Book.*

United Nations Statistics Division, New York, NY 10017, (800) 253-9646, Fax: (212) 963-4116, http://unstats.un.org; *Asia-Pacific in Figures 2004; Demographic Yearbook;* and *Statistical Yearbook.*

World Health Organization (WHO), Avenue Appia 20, 1211 Geneve 27, Switzerland, (Telephone in U.S. (212) 331-9081), www.who.int; *World Health Report 2006.*

IRAN - CLIMATE

M.E. Sharpe, 80 Business Park Drive, Armonk, NY 10504, (800) 541-6563, Fax: (914) 273-2106, www.mesharpe.com; *The Illustrated Book of World Rankings.*

Palgrave Macmillan Ltd., Houndmills, Basingstoke, Hampshire, RG21 6XS, England, (Telephone in U.S. (888) 330-8477), (Fax in U.S. (800) 672-2054), www.palgrave.com; *The Statesman's Yearbook 2008.*

IRAN - COAL PRODUCTION

See IRAN - MINERAL INDUSTRIES

IRAN - COFFEE

See IRAN - CROPS

IRAN - COMMERCE

Palgrave Macmillan Ltd., Houndmills, Basingstoke, Hampshire, RG21 6XS, England, (Telephone in U.S. (888) 330-8477), (Fax in U.S. (800) 672-2054), www.palgrave.com; *The Statesman's Yearbook 2008.*

IRAN - COMMODITY EXCHANGES

Commodity Research Bureau, 330 South Wells Street, Suite 612, Chicago, IL 60606-7110, (800) 621-5271, Fax: (312) 939-4135, www.crbtrader.com; *2006 CRB Commodity Yearbook and CD.*

International Lead and Zinc Study Group (ILZSG), Rua Almirante Barroso 38, 5th Floor, Lisbon 1000 - 013, Portugal, www.ilzsg.org; Interactive Statistical Database.

International Monetary Fund (IMF), 700 Nineteenth Street, NW, Washington, DC 20431, (202) 623-7000, Fax: (202) 623-4661, www.imf.org; *IMF Primary Commodity Prices.*

United Nations Food and Agricultural Organization (FAO), Viale delle Terme di Caracalla, 00100 Rome, Italy, (Dial from U.S. (202) 653-2400), (Fax from U.S. (202) 653 5760), www.fao.org; *The State of Food and Agriculture (SOFA) 2006.*

IRAN - CONSTRUCTION INDUSTRY

M.E. Sharpe, 80 Business Park Drive, Armonk, NY 10504, (800) 541-6563, Fax: (914) 273-2106, www.mesharpe.com; *The Illustrated Book of World Rankings.*

United Nations Statistics Division, New York, NY 10017, (800) 253-9646, Fax: (212) 963-4116, http://unstats.un.org; *Statistical Yearbook.*

IRAN - CONSUMER PRICE INDEXES

Taylor and Francis Group, An Informa Business, 2 Park Square, Milton Park, Abingdon, Oxford OX14 4RN, United Kingdom, (Dial from U.S. (212) 216-7800), (Fax from U.S. (212) 564-7854), www.tandf.co.uk; *The Europa World Year Book.*

United Nations Statistics Division, New York, NY 10017, (800) 253-9646, Fax: (212) 963-4116, http://unstats.un.org; *Statistical Yearbook.*

IRAN - CONSUMPTION (ECONOMICS)

International Lead and Zinc Study Group (ILZSG), Rua Almirante Barroso 38, 5th Floor, Lisbon 1000 - 013, Portugal, www.ilzsg.org; Interactive Statistical Database.

The World Bank, 1818 H Street, NW, Washington, DC 20433, (202) 473-1000, Fax: (202) 477-6391, www.worldbank.org; *World Development Report 2008.*

IRAN - COPPER INDUSTRY AND TRADE

See IRAN - MINERAL INDUSTRIES

IRAN - CORN INDUSTRY

See IRAN - CROPS

IRAN - COST AND STANDARD OF LIVING

International Monetary Fund (IMF), 700 Nineteenth Street, NW, Washington, DC 20431, (202) 623-7000, Fax: (202) 623-4661, www.imf.org; *Government Finance Statistics Yearbook (2008 Edition).*

United Nations Statistics Division, New York, NY 10017, (800) 253-9646, Fax: (212) 963-4116, http://unstats.un.org; *Statistical Yearbook for Asia and the Pacific 2004.*

IRAN - COTTON

See IRAN - CROPS

IRAN - CRIME

Yale University Press, PO Box 209040, New Haven, CT 06520-9040, (203) 432-0960, Fax: (203) 432-0948, http://yalepress.yale.edu/yupbooks; *Violence and Crime in Cross-National Perspective.*

IRAN - CROPS

M.E. Sharpe, 80 Business Park Drive, Armonk, NY 10504, (800) 541-6563, Fax: (914) 273-2106, www.mesharpe.com; *The Illustrated Book of World Rankings.*

Palgrave Macmillan Ltd., Houndmills, Basingstoke, Hampshire, RG21 6XS, England, (Telephone in U.S. (888) 330-8477), (Fax in U.S. (800) 672-2054), www.palgrave.com; *The Statesman's Yearbook 2008.*

Taylor and Francis Group, An Informa Business, 2 Park Square, Milton Park, Abingdon, Oxford OX14 4RN, United Kingdom, (Dial from U.S. (212) 216-7800), (Fax from U.S. (212) 564-7854), www.tandf.co.uk; *The Europa World Year Book.*

United Nations Conference on Trade and Development (UNCTAD), DC2-1120, United Nations, New York, NY 10017, (212) 963-0027, www.unctad.org; *UNCTAD Commodity Yearbook.*

United Nations Food and Agricultural Organization (FAO), Viale delle Terme di Caracalla, 00100 Rome, Italy, (Dial from U.S. (202) 653-2400), (Fax from U.S. (202) 653 5760), www.fao.org; *FAO Production Yearbook 2002* and *The State of Food and Agriculture (SOFA) 2006.*

United Nations Statistics Division, New York, NY 10017, (800) 253-9646, Fax: (212) 963-4116, http://unstats.un.org; *Statistical Yearbook.*

IRAN - CUSTOMS ADMINISTRATION

International Monetary Fund (IMF), 700 Nineteenth Street, NW, Washington, DC 20431, (202) 623-7000, Fax: (202) 623-4661, www.imf.org; *Government Finance Statistics Yearbook (2008 Edition).*

Palgrave Macmillan Ltd., Houndmills, Basingstoke, Hampshire, RG21 6XS, England, (Telephone in U.S. (888) 330-8477), (Fax in U.S. (800) 672-2054), www.palgrave.com; *The Statesman's Yearbook 2008.*

IRAN - DAIRY PROCESSING

M.E. Sharpe, 80 Business Park Drive, Armonk, NY 10504, (800) 541-6563, Fax: (914) 273-2106, www.mesharpe.com; *The Illustrated Book of World Rankings.*

Palgrave Macmillan Ltd., Houndmills, Basingstoke, Hampshire, RG21 6XS, England, (Telephone in U.S. (888) 330-8477), (Fax in U.S. (800) 672-2054), www.palgrave.com; *The Statesman's Yearbook 2008.*

Taylor and Francis Group, An Informa Business, 2 Park Square, Milton Park, Abingdon, Oxford OX14 4RN, United Kingdom, (Dial from U.S. (212) 216-7800), (Fax from U.S. (212) 564-7854), www.tandf.co.uk; *The Europa World Year Book.*

United Nations Food and Agricultural Organization (FAO), Viale delle Terme di Caracalla, 00100 Rome, Italy, (Dial from U.S. (202) 653-2400), (Fax from U.S. (202) 653 5760), www.fao.org; *FAO Production Yearbook 2002* and *The State of Food and Agriculture (SOFA) 2006.*

United Nations Statistics Division, New York, NY 10017, (800) 253-9646, Fax: (212) 963-4116, http://unstats.un.org; *Statistical Yearbook.*

IRAN - DEATH RATES

See IRAN - MORTALITY

IRAN - DEBTS, EXTERNAL

Palgrave Macmillan Ltd., Houndmills, Basingstoke, Hampshire, RG21 6XS, England, (Telephone in U.S. (888) 330-8477), (Fax in U.S. (800) 672-2054), www.palgrave.com; *The Statesman's Yearbook 2008.*

Statistical Centre of Iran (SCI), Dr. Fatemi Avenue, PO Box 14155-6133, Tehran 1414663111, Iran, www.sci.org.ir/portal/faces/public/sci_en/; *National Accounts of Iran 2003-2004.*

The World Bank, 1818 H Street, NW, Washington, DC 20433, (202) 473-1000, Fax: (202) 477-6391, www.worldbank.org; *Global Development Finance 2007* and *World Development Report 2008.*

IRAN - DEFENSE EXPENDITURES

See IRAN - ARMED FORCES

IRAN - DEMOGRAPHY

Euromonitor International, Inc., 224 S. Michigan Avenue, Suite 1500, Chicago, IL 60604, (312) 922-1115, Fax: (312) 922-1157, www.euromonitor.com; *International Marketing Data and Statistics 2008; The World Economic Factbook 2008;* and *World Marketing Data and Statistics.*

M.E. Sharpe, 80 Business Park Drive, Armonk, NY 10504, (800) 541-6563, Fax: (914) 273-2106, www.mesharpe.com; *The Illustrated Book of World Rankings.*

United Nations Statistics Division, New York, NY 10017, (800) 253-9646, Fax: (212) 963-4116, http://unstats.un.org; *Asia-Pacific in Figures 2004* and *Human Development Report 2006.*

The World Bank, 1818 H Street, NW, Washington, DC 20433, (202) 473-1000, Fax: (202) 477-6391, www.worldbank.org; *Iran, Islamic Republic of.*

IRAN - DIAMONDS

See IRAN - MINERAL INDUSTRIES

IRAN - DISPOSABLE INCOME

M.E. Sharpe, 80 Business Park Drive, Armonk, NY 10504, (800) 541-6563, Fax: (914) 273-2106, www.mesharpe.com; *The Illustrated Book of World Rankings.*

United Nations Statistics Division, New York, NY 10017, (800) 253-9646, Fax: (212) 963-4116, http://unstats.un.org; *National Accounts Statistics: Compendium of Income Distribution Statistics* and *Statistical Yearbook.*

IRAN - DIVORCE

M.E. Sharpe, 80 Business Park Drive, Armonk, NY 10504, (800) 541-6563, Fax: (914) 273-2106, www.mesharpe.com; *The Illustrated Book of World Rankings.*

United Nations Statistics Division, New York, NY 10017, (800) 253-9646, Fax: (212) 963-4116, http://unstats.un.org; *Demographic Yearbook* and *Statistical Yearbook.*

IRAN - ECONOMIC ASSISTANCE

United Nations Statistics Division, New York, NY 10017, (800) 253-9646, Fax: (212) 963-4116, http://unstats.un.org; *Statistical Yearbook.*

IRAN - ECONOMIC CONDITIONS

Center for International Business Education Research (CIBER), Columbia Business School and School of International and Public Affairs, Uris Hall, Room 212, 3022 Broadway, New York, NY 10027-6902, Mr. Joshua Safier, (212) 854-4750, Fax: (212) 222-9821, www.columbia.edu/cu/ciber/; Datastream International.

Central Intelligence Agency, Office of Public Affairs, Washington, DC 20505, (703) 482-0623, Fax: (703) 482-1739, www.cia.gov; *The World Factbook.*

DSI Data Service Information, Xantener Strasse 51a, D-47495 Rheinberg, Germany, www.dsidata.com; *Campus Solution.*

Dun and Bradstreet (DB) Corporation, 103 JFK Parkway, Short Hills, NJ 07078, (973) 921-5500, www.dnb.com; *Country Report.*

Economist Intelligence Unit, 111 West 57th Street, New York, NY 10019, (212) 554-0600, Fax: (212) 586-1181, www.eiu.com; *Iran Country Report.*

Euromonitor International, Inc., 224 S. Michigan Avenue, Suite 1500, Chicago, IL 60604, (312) 922-1115, Fax: (312) 922-1157, www.euromonitor.com; *International Marketing Data and Statistics 2008; The World Economic Factbook 2008;* and *World Marketing Data and Statistics.*

Federal Statistical Office Germany, D-65180 Wiesbaden, Germany, www.destatis.de; *Iran 2006*.

International Monetary Fund (IMF), 700 Nineteenth Street, NW, Washington, DC 20431, (202) 623-7000, Fax: (202) 623-4661, www.imf.org; *World Economic Outlook Reports*.

M.E. Sharpe, 80 Business Park Drive, Armonk, NY 10504, (800) 541-6563, Fax: (914) 273-2106, www.mesharpe.com; *The Illustrated Book of World Rankings*.

Palgrave Macmillan Ltd., Houndmills, Basingstoke, Hampshire, RG21 6XS, England, (Telephone in U.S. (888) 330-8477), (Fax in U.S. (800) 672-2054), www.palgrave.com; *The Statesman's Yearbook 2008*.

Statistical Centre of Iran (SCI), Dr. Fatemi Avenue, PO Box 14155-6133, Tehran 1414663111, Iran, www.sci.org.ir/portal/faces/public/sci_en/; *National Accounts of Iran 2003-2004* and *Women Heads of Households (Socio-Economic Characteristics)*.

Taylor and Francis Group, An Informa Business, 2 Park Square, Milton Park, Abingdon, Oxford OX14 4RN, United Kingdom, (Dial from U.S. (212) 216-7800), (Fax from U.S. (212) 564-7854), www.tandf.co.uk; *The Europa World Year Book*.

United Nations Statistics Division, New York, NY 10017, (800) 253-9646, Fax: (212) 963-4116, http://unstats.un.org; *World Statistics Pocketbook*.

The World Bank, 1818 H Street, NW, Washington, DC 20433, (202) 473-1000, Fax: (202) 477-6391, www.worldbank.org; *Global Economic Monitor (GEM); Global Economic Prospects 2008; Iran, Islamic Republic of; The World Bank Atlas 2003-2004;* and *World Development Report 2008*.

IRAN - EDUCATION

Euromonitor International, Inc., 224 S. Michigan Avenue, Suite 1500, Chicago, IL 60604, (312) 922-1115, Fax: (312) 922-1157, www.euromonitor.com; *International Marketing Data and Statistics 2008* and *World Marketing Data and Statistics*.

International Monetary Fund (IMF), 700 Nineteenth Street, NW, Washington, DC 20431, (202) 623-7000, Fax: (202) 623-4661, www.imf.org; *Government Finance Statistics Yearbook (2008 Edition)*.

M.E. Sharpe, 80 Business Park Drive, Armonk, NY 10504, (800) 541-6563, Fax: (914) 273-2106, www.mesharpe.com; *The Illustrated Book of World Rankings*.

Palgrave Macmillan Ltd., Houndmills, Basingstoke, Hampshire, RG21 6XS, England, (Telephone in U.S. (888) 330-8477), (Fax in U.S. (800) 672-2054), www.palgrave.com; *The Statesman's Yearbook 2008*.

Taylor and Francis Group, An Informa Business, 2 Park Square, Milton Park, Abingdon, Oxford OX14 4RN, United Kingdom, (Dial from U.S. (212) 216-7800), (Fax from U.S. (212) 564-7854), www.tandf.co.uk; *The Europa World Year Book*.

UNESCO Institute for Statistics, C.P. 6128 Succursale Centre-Ville, Montreal, Quebec, H3C 3J7 Canada, (Dial from U.S. (514) 343-6880), (Fax from U.S. (514) 343 6882), www.uis.unesco.org; *Statistical Tables*.

United Nations Statistics Division, New York, NY 10017, (800) 253-9646, Fax: (212) 963-4116, http://unstats.un.org; *Asia-Pacific in Figures 2004* and *Human Development Report 2006*.

The World Bank, 1818 H Street, NW, Washington, DC 20433, (202) 473-1000, Fax: (202) 477-6391, www.worldbank.org; *Iran, Islamic Republic of* and *World Development Report 2008*.

IRAN - ELECTRICITY

M.E. Sharpe, 80 Business Park Drive, Armonk, NY 10504, (800) 541-6563, Fax: (914) 273-2106, www.mesharpe.com; *The Illustrated Book of World Rankings*.

Organisation for Economic Cooperation and Development (OECD), 2 rue Andre Pascal, F-75775 Paris Cedex 16, France, (Telephone in U.S. (202) 785-6323), (Fax in U.S. (202) 785-0350), www.oecd.org; *World Energy Outlook 2007*.

Palgrave Macmillan Ltd., Houndmills, Basingstoke, Hampshire, RG21 6XS, England, (Telephone in U.S. (888) 330-8477), (Fax in U.S. (800) 672-2054), www.palgrave.com; *The Statesman's Yearbook 2008*.

U.S. Department of Energy (DOE), Energy Information Administration (EIA), 1000 Independence Avenue, SW, Washington, DC 20585, (202) 586-8800, www.eia.doe.gov; *International Energy Annual 2004* and *International Energy Outlook 2006*.

United Nations Statistics Division, New York, NY 10017, (800) 253-9646, Fax: (212) 963-4116, http://unstats.un.org; *Electric Power in Asia and the Pacific 2001 and 2002; Human Development Report 2006;* and *Statistical Yearbook*.

IRAN - EMPLOYMENT

Euromonitor International, Inc., 224 S. Michigan Avenue, Suite 1500, Chicago, IL 60604, (312) 922-1115, Fax: (312) 922-1157, www.euromonitor.com; *International Marketing Data and Statistics 2008*.

International Labour Office, I.L.O. Publications, 4 route des Morillons, CH-1211 Geneva 22, Switzerland, (Telephone in U.S. (202) 653-7652), (Fax in U.S. (202) 653-7687), www.ilo.org; *Yearbook of Labour Statistics 2006*.

M.E. Sharpe, 80 Business Park Drive, Armonk, NY 10504, (800) 541-6563, Fax: (914) 273-2106, www.mesharpe.com; *The Illustrated Book of World Rankings*.

Statistical Centre of Iran (SCI), Dr. Fatemi Avenue, PO Box 14155-6133, Tehran 1414663111, Iran, www.sci.org.ir/portal/faces/public/sci_en/; *A Study on the Effects of Women's Activity on Fertility in Iran*.

United Nations Statistics Division, New York, NY 10017, (800) 253-9646, Fax: (212) 963-4116, http://unstats.un.org; *Asia-Pacific in Figures 2004* and *Statistical Yearbook*.

The World Bank, 1818 H Street, NW, Washington, DC 20433, (202) 473-1000, Fax: (202) 477-6391, www.worldbank.org; *Iran, Islamic Republic of*.

IRAN - ENERGY INDUSTRIES

Enerdata, 10 Rue Royale, 75008 Paris, France, www.enerdata.fr; *Global Energy Market Data*.

United Nations Statistics Division, New York, NY 10017, (800) 253-9646, Fax: (212) 963-4116, http://unstats.un.org; *Electric Power in Asia and the Pacific 2001 and 2002*.

IRAN - ENVIRONMENTAL CONDITIONS

DSI Data Service Information, Xantener Strasse 51a, D-47495 Rheinberg, Germany, www.dsidata.com; *Campus Solution* and *DSI's Global Environmental Database*.

Economist Intelligence Unit, 111 West 57th Street, New York, NY 10019, (212) 554-0600, Fax: (212) 586-1181, www.eiu.com; *Iran Country Report*.

Federal Statistical Office Germany, D-65180 Wiesbaden, Germany, www.destatis.de; *Iran 2006*.

United Nations Statistics Division, New York, NY 10017, (800) 253-9646, Fax: (212) 963-4116, http://unstats.un.org; *World Statistics Pocketbook*.

IRAN - EXPORTS

Central Intelligence Agency, Office of Public Affairs, Washington, DC 20505, (703) 482-0623, Fax: (703) 482-1739, www.cia.gov; *The World Factbook*.

Economist Intelligence Unit, 111 West 57th Street, New York, NY 10019, (212) 554-0600, Fax: (212) 586-1181, www.eiu.com; *Iran Country Report*.

Euromonitor International, Inc., 224 S. Michigan Avenue, Suite 1500, Chicago, IL 60604, (312) 922-1115, Fax: (312) 922-1157, www.euromonitor.com; *International Marketing Data and Statistics 2008* and *The World Economic Factbook 2008*.

International Lead and Zinc Study Group (ILZSG), Rua Almirante Barroso 38, 5th Floor, Lisbon 1000-013, Portugal, www.ilzsg.org; Interactive Statistical Database.

International Monetary Fund (IMF), 700 Nineteenth Street, NW, Washington, DC 20431, (202) 623-7000, Fax: (202) 623-4661, www.imf.org; *Direction of Trade Statistics Yearbook 2007* and *International Financial Statistics Yearbook 2007*.

Organization of Petroleum Exporting Countries (OPEC), Obere Donaustrasse 93, A-1020, Vienna, Austria, www.opec.org; *Annual Statistical Bulletin 2006*.

Palgrave Macmillan Ltd., Houndmills, Basingstoke, Hampshire, RG21 6XS, England, (Telephone in U.S. (888) 330-8477), (Fax in U.S. (800) 672-2054), www.palgrave.com; *The Statesman's Yearbook 2008*.

Statistical Centre of Iran (SCI), Dr. Fatemi Avenue, PO Box 14155-6133, Tehran 1414663111, Iran, www.sci.org.ir/portal/faces/public/sci_en/; *National Accounts of Iran 2003-2004*.

Taylor and Francis Group, An Informa Business, 2 Park Square, Milton Park, Abingdon, Oxford OX14 4RN, United Kingdom, (Dial from U.S. (212) 216-7800), (Fax from U.S. (212) 564-7854), www.tandf.co.uk; *The Europa World Year Book*.

United Nations Conference on Trade and Development (UNCTAD), DC2-1120, United Nations, New York, NY 10017, (212) 963-0027, www.unctad.org; *Handbook of Statistics 2005*.

United Nations Food and Agricultural Organization (FAO), Viale delle Terme di Caracalla, 00100 Rome, Italy, (Dial from U.S. (202) 653-2400), (Fax from U.S. (202) 653 5760), www.fao.org; *The State of Food and Agriculture (SOFA) 2006*.

The World Bank, 1818 H Street, NW, Washington, DC 20433, (202) 473-1000, Fax: (202) 477-6391, www.worldbank.org; *World Development Report 2008*.

IRAN - FEMALE WORKING POPULATION

See IRAN - EMPLOYMENT

IRAN - FERTILITY, HUMAN

Central Intelligence Agency, Office of Public Affairs, Washington, DC 20505, (703) 482-0623, Fax: (703) 482-1739, www.cia.gov; *The World Factbook*.

M.E. Sharpe, 80 Business Park Drive, Armonk, NY 10504, (800) 541-6563, Fax: (914) 273-2106, www.mesharpe.com; *The Illustrated Book of World Rankings*.

Statistical Centre of Iran (SCI), Dr. Fatemi Avenue, PO Box 14155-6133, Tehran 1414663111, Iran, www.sci.org.ir/portal/faces/public/sci_en/; *Knowledge and Attitude of Students on Reproductive Health and Gender Issues in Selected Districts of the I.R. of Iran* and *A Study on the Effects of Women's Activity on Fertility in Iran*.

United Nations Statistics Division, New York, NY 10017, (800) 253-9646, Fax: (212) 963-4116, http://unstats.un.org; *Human Development Report 2006*.

The World Bank, 1818 H Street, NW, Washington, DC 20433, (202) 473-1000, Fax: (202) 477-6391, www.worldbank.org; *The World Bank Atlas 2003-2004* and *World Development Report 2008*.

IRAN - FERTILIZER INDUSTRY

United Nations Food and Agricultural Organization (FAO), Viale delle Terme di Caracalla, 00100 Rome, Italy, (Dial from U.S. (202) 653-2400), (Fax from U.S. (202) 653 5760), www.fao.org; *FAO Fertilizer Yearbook* and *The State of Food and Agriculture (SOFA) 2006*.

United Nations Statistics Division, New York, NY 10017, (800) 253-9646, Fax: (212) 963-4116, http://unstats.un.org; *Statistical Yearbook*.

IRAN - FETAL MORTALITY

See IRAN - MORTALITY

IRAN - FILM

See IRAN - MOTION PICTURES

IRAN - FINANCE

International Monetary Fund (IMF), 700 Nineteenth Street, NW, Washington, DC 20431, (202) 623-

7000, Fax: (202) 623-4661, www.imf.org; *International Financial Statistics Yearbook 2007.*

Taylor and Francis Group, An Informa Business, 2 Park Square, Milton Park, Abingdon, Oxford OX14 4RN, United Kingdom, (Dial from U.S. (212) 216-7800), (Fax from U.S. (212) 564-7854), www.tandf.co.uk; *The Europa World Year Book.*

United Nations Statistics Division, New York, NY 10017, (800) 253-9646, Fax: (212) 963-4116, http://unstats.un.org; *Asia-Pacific in Figures 2004; National Accounts Statistics: Compendium of Income Distribution Statistics; Statistical Yearbook;* and *Statistical Yearbook for Asia and the Pacific 2004.*

The World Bank, 1818 H Street, NW, Washington, DC 20433, (202) 473-1000, Fax: (202) 477-6391, www.worldbank.org; *Iran, Islamic Republic of.*

IRAN - FINANCE, PUBLIC

Bernan Essential Government Publications, 4611-F Assembly Drive, Lanham MD, 20706-4391, (301) 459-2255, Fax: (800) 865-3450, www.bernan.com; *National Accounts Statistics.*

Economist Intelligence Unit, 111 West 57th Street, New York, NY 10019, (212) 554-0600, Fax: (212) 586-1181, www.eiu.com; *Iran Country Report.*

International Monetary Fund (IMF), 700 Nineteenth Street, NW, Washington, DC 20431, (202) 623-7000, Fax: (202) 623-4661, www.imf.org; *Government Finance Statistics Yearbook (2008 Edition); International Financial Statistics; International Financial Statistics Online Service;* and *International Financial Statistics Yearbook 2007.*

M.E. Sharpe, 80 Business Park Drive, Armonk, NY 10504, (800) 541-6563, Fax: (914) 273-2106, www.mesharpe.com; *The Illustrated Book of World Rankings.*

Palgrave Macmillan Ltd., Houndmills, Basingstoke, Hampshire, RG21 6XS, England, (Telephone in U.S. (888) 330-8477), (Fax in U.S. (800) 672-2054), www.palgrave.com; *The Statesman's Yearbook 2008.*

Statistical Centre of Iran (SCI), Dr. Fatemi Avenue, PO Box 14155-6133, Tehran 1414663111, Iran, www.sci.org.ir/portal/faces/public/sci_en/; *National Accounts of Iran 2003-2004.*

Taylor and Francis Group, An Informa Business, 2 Park Square, Milton Park, Abingdon, Oxford OX14 4RN, United Kingdom, (Dial from U.S. (212) 216-7800), (Fax from U.S. (212) 564-7854), www.tandf.co.uk; *The Europa World Year Book.*

United Nations Statistics Division, New York, NY 10017, (800) 253-9646, Fax: (212) 963-4116, http://unstats.un.org; *Statistical Yearbook for Asia and the Pacific 2004.*

The World Bank, 1818 H Street, NW, Washington, DC 20433, (202) 473-1000, Fax: (202) 477-6391, www.worldbank.org; *Iran, Islamic Republic of.*

IRAN - FISHERIES

M.E. Sharpe, 80 Business Park Drive, Armonk, NY 10504, (800) 541-6563, Fax: (914) 273-2106, www.mesharpe.com; *The Illustrated Book of World Rankings.*

Palgrave Macmillan Ltd., Houndmills, Basingstoke, Hampshire, RG21 6XS, England, (Telephone in U.S. (888) 330-8477), (Fax in U.S. (800) 672-2054), www.palgrave.com; *The Statesman's Yearbook 2008.*

Taylor and Francis Group, An Informa Business, 2 Park Square, Milton Park, Abingdon, Oxford OX14 4RN, United Kingdom, (Dial from U.S. (212) 216-7800), (Fax from U.S. (212) 564-7854), www.tandf.co.uk; *The Europa World Year Book.*

United Nations Conference on Trade and Development (UNCTAD), DC2-1120, United Nations, New York, NY 10017, (212) 963-0027, www.unctad.org; *UNCTAD Commodity Yearbook.*

United Nations Food and Agricultural Organization (FAO), Viale delle Terme di Caracalla, 00100 Rome, Italy, (Dial from U.S. (202) 653-2400), (Fax from U.S. (202) 653 5760), www.fao.org; *FAO Yearbook of Fishery Statistics;* Fishery Databases; FISHSTAT Database. Subjects covered include: Aquaculture production, capture production, fishery commodities; and *The State of Food and Agriculture (SOFA) 2006.*

United Nations Statistics Division, New York, NY 10017, (800) 253-9646, Fax: (212) 963-4116, http://unstats.un.org; *Statistical Yearbook.*

The World Bank, 1818 H Street, NW, Washington, DC 20433, (202) 473-1000, Fax: (202) 477-6391, www.worldbank.org; *Iran, Islamic Republic of.*

IRAN - FLOUR INDUSTRY

United Nations Statistics Division, New York, NY 10017, (800) 253-9646, Fax: (212) 963-4116, http://unstats.un.org; *Statistical Yearbook.*

IRAN - FOOD

United Nations Conference on Trade and Development (UNCTAD), DC2-1120, United Nations, New York, NY 10017, (212) 963-0027, www.unctad.org; *UNCTAD Commodity Yearbook.*

United Nations Food and Agricultural Organization (FAO), Viale delle Terme di Caracalla, 00100 Rome, Italy, (Dial from U.S. (202) 653-2400), (Fax from U.S. (202) 653 5760), www.fao.org; *FAO Production Yearbook 2002* and *The State of Food and Agriculture (SOFA) 2006.*

United Nations Statistics Division, New York, NY 10017, (800) 253-9646, Fax: (212) 963-4116, http://unstats.un.org; *Human Development Report 2006* and *Statistical Yearbook for Asia and the Pacific 2004.*

IRAN - FOREIGN EXCHANGE RATES

Central Intelligence Agency, Office of Public Affairs, Washington, DC 20505, (703) 482-0623, Fax: (703) 482-1739, www.cia.gov; *The World Factbook.*

Euromonitor International, Inc., 224 S. Michigan Avenue, Suite 1500, Chicago, IL 60604, (312) 922-1115, Fax: (312) 922-1157, www.euromonitor.com; *International Marketing Data and Statistics 2008* and *The World Economic Factbook 2008.*

International Civil Aviation Organization (ICAO), External Relations and Public Information Office (EPO), 999 University Street, Montreal, Quebec H3C 5H7, Canada, (Dial from U.S. (514) 954-8219), (Fax from U.S. (514) 954-6077), www.icao.int; *Civil Aviation Statistics of the World.*

International Monetary Fund (IMF), 700 Nineteenth Street, NW, Washington, DC 20431, (202) 623-7000, Fax: (202) 623-4661, www.imf.org; *International Financial Statistics Yearbook 2007.*

Organization of Petroleum Exporting Countries (OPEC), Obere Donaustrasse 93, A-1020, Vienna, Austria, www.opec.org; *Annual Statistical Bulletin 2006.*

Taylor and Francis Group, An Informa Business, 2 Park Square, Milton Park, Abingdon, Oxford OX14 4RN, United Kingdom, (Dial from U.S. (212) 216-7800), (Fax from U.S. (212) 564-7854), www.tandf.co.uk; *The Europa World Year Book.*

United Nations Statistics Division, New York, NY 10017, (800) 253-9646, Fax: (212) 963-4116, http://unstats.un.org; *Statistical Yearbook* and *World Statistics Pocketbook.*

IRAN - FORESTS AND FORESTRY

International Monetary Fund (IMF), 700 Nineteenth Street, NW, Washington, DC 20431, (202) 623-7000, Fax: (202) 623-4661, www.imf.org; *International Financial Statistics Yearbook 2007.*

M.E. Sharpe, 80 Business Park Drive, Armonk, NY 10504, (800) 541-6563, Fax: (914) 273-2106, www.mesharpe.com; *The Illustrated Book of World Rankings.*

Taylor and Francis Group, An Informa Business, 2 Park Square, Milton Park, Abingdon, Oxford OX14 4RN, United Kingdom, (Dial from U.S. (212) 216-7800), (Fax from U.S. (212) 564-7854), www.tandf.co.uk; *The Europa World Year Book.*

UNESCO Institute for Statistics, C.P. 6128 Succursale Centre-Ville, Montreal, Quebec, H3C 3J7 Canada, (Dial from U.S. (514) 343-6880), (Fax from U.S. (514) 343 6882), www.uis.unesco.org; *Statistical Tables.*

United Nations Conference on Trade and Development (UNCTAD), DC2-1120, United Nations, New York, NY 10017, (212) 963-0027, www.unctad.org; *UNCTAD Commodity Yearbook.*

United Nations Food and Agricultural Organization (FAO), Viale delle Terme di Caracalla, 00100 Rome, Italy, (Dial from U.S. (202) 653-2400), (Fax from U.S. (202) 653 5760), www.fao.org; *FAO Yearbook of Forest Products* and *The State of Food and Agriculture (SOFA) 2006.*

United Nations Statistics Division, New York, NY 10017, (800) 253-9646, Fax: (212) 963-4116, http://unstats.un.org; *Statistical Yearbook.*

The World Bank, 1818 H Street, NW, Washington, DC 20433, (202) 473-1000, Fax: (202) 477-6391, www.worldbank.org; *Iran, Islamic Republic of* and *World Development Report 2008.*

IRAN - GAS PRODUCTION

See IRAN - MINERAL INDUSTRIES

IRAN - GEOGRAPHIC INFORMATION SYSTEMS

M.E. Sharpe, 80 Business Park Drive, Armonk, NY 10504, (800) 541-6563, Fax: (914) 273-2106, www.mesharpe.com; *The Illustrated Book of World Rankings.*

IRAN - GOLD INDUSTRY

International Monetary Fund (IMF), 700 Nineteenth Street, NW, Washington, DC 20431, (202) 623-7000, Fax: (202) 623-4661, www.imf.org; *International Financial Statistics Yearbook 2007.*

United Nations Statistics Division, New York, NY 10017, (800) 253-9646, Fax: (212) 963-4116, http://unstats.un.org; *Statistical Yearbook.*

IRAN - GOLD PRODUCTION

See IRAN - MINERAL INDUSTRIES

IRAN - GRANTS-IN-AID

International Monetary Fund (IMF), 700 Nineteenth Street, NW, Washington, DC 20431, (202) 623-7000, Fax: (202) 623-4661, www.imf.org; *Government Finance Statistics Yearbook (2008 Edition).*

IRAN - GROSS DOMESTIC PRODUCT

Economist Intelligence Unit, 111 West 57th Street, New York, NY 10019, (212) 554-0600, Fax: (212) 586-1181, www.eiu.com; *Iran Country Report.*

Euromonitor International, Inc., 224 S. Michigan Avenue, Suite 1500, Chicago, IL 60604, (312) 922-1115, Fax: (312) 922-1157, www.euromonitor.com; *International Marketing Data and Statistics 2008* and *The World Economic Factbook 2008.*

M.E. Sharpe, 80 Business Park Drive, Armonk, NY 10504, (800) 541-6563, Fax: (914) 273-2106, www.mesharpe.com; *The Illustrated Book of World Rankings.*

Taylor and Francis Group, An Informa Business, 2 Park Square, Milton Park, Abingdon, Oxford OX14 4RN, United Kingdom, (Dial from U.S. (212) 216-7800), (Fax from U.S. (212) 564-7854), www.tandf.co.uk; *The Europa World Year Book.*

United Nations Statistics Division, New York, NY 10017, (800) 253-9646, Fax: (212) 963-4116, http://unstats.un.org; *Human Development Report 2006; National Accounts Statistics: Compendium of Income Distribution Statistics;* and *Statistical Yearbook.*

The World Bank, 1818 H Street, NW, Washington, DC 20433, (202) 473-1000, Fax: (202) 477-6391, www.worldbank.org; *World Development Report 2008.*

IRAN - GROSS NATIONAL PRODUCT

Euromonitor International, Inc., 224 S. Michigan Avenue, Suite 1500, Chicago, IL 60604, (312) 922-

1115, Fax: (312) 922-1157, www.euromonitor.com; *International Marketing Data and Statistics 2008.*

M.E. Sharpe, 80 Business Park Drive, Armonk, NY 10504, (800) 541-6563, Fax: (914) 273-2106, www.mesharpe.com; *The Illustrated Book of World Rankings.*

Organization of Petroleum Exporting Countries (OPEC), Obere Donaustrasse 93, A-1020, Vienna, Austria, www.opec.org; *Annual Statistical Bulletin 2006.*

Palgrave Macmillan Ltd., Houndmills, Basingstoke, Hampshire, RG21 6XS, England, (Telephone in U.S. (888) 330-8477), (Fax in U.S. (800) 672-2054), www.palgrave.com; *The Statesman's Yearbook 2008.*

Taylor and Francis Group, An Informa Business, 2 Park Square, Milton Park, Abingdon, Oxford OX14 4RN, United Kingdom, (Dial from U.S. (212) 216-7800), (Fax from U.S. (212) 564-7854), www.tandf.co.uk; *The Europa World Year Book.*

U.S. Department of State (DOS), 2201 C Street NW, Washington, DC 20520, (202) 647-4000, www.state.gov; *World Military Expenditures and Arms Transfers (WMEAT).*

United Nations Statistics Division, New York, NY 10017, (800) 253-9646, Fax: (212) 963-4116, http://unstats.un.org; *Statistical Yearbook.*

The World Bank, 1818 H Street, NW, Washington, DC 20433, (202) 473-1000, Fax: (202) 477-6391, www.worldbank.org; *The World Bank Atlas 2003-2004* and *World Development Report 2008.*

IRAN - HAZELNUT PRODUCTION

See IRAN - CROPS

IRAN - HIDES AND SKINS INDUSTRY

United Nations Food and Agricultural Organization (FAO), Viale delle Terme di Caracalla, 00100 Rome, Italy, (Dial from U.S. (202) 653-2400), (Fax from U.S. (202) 653 5760), www.fao.org; *FAO Production Yearbook 2002.*

IRAN - HOUSING

Euromonitor International, Inc., 224 S. Michigan Avenue, Suite 1500, Chicago, IL 60604, (312) 922-1115, Fax: (312) 922-1157, www.euromonitor.com; *World Marketing Data and Statistics.*

M.E. Sharpe, 80 Business Park Drive, Armonk, NY 10504, (800) 541-6563, Fax: (914) 273-2106, www.mesharpe.com; *The Illustrated Book of World Rankings.*

IRAN - ILLITERATE PERSONS

Euromonitor International, Inc., 224 S. Michigan Avenue, Suite 1500, Chicago, IL 60604, (312) 922-1115, Fax: (312) 922-1157, www.euromonitor.com; *The World Economic Factbook 2008.*

Palgrave Macmillan Ltd., Houndmills, Basingstoke, Hampshire, RG21 6XS, England, (Telephone in U.S. (888) 330-8477), (Fax in U.S. (800) 672-2054), www.palgrave.com; *The Statesman's Yearbook 2008.*

UNESCO Institute for Statistics, C.P. 6128 Succursale Centre-Ville, Montreal, Quebec, H3C 3J7 Canada, (Dial from U.S. (514) 343-6880), (Fax from U.S. (514) 343 6882), www.uis.unesco.org; *Statistical Tables.*

United Nations Statistics Division, New York, NY 10017, (800) 253-9646, Fax: (212) 963-4116, http://unstats.un.org; *Asia-Pacific in Figures 2004* and *Human Development Report 2006.*

IRAN - IMPORTS

Central Intelligence Agency, Office of Public Affairs, Washington, DC 20505, (703) 482-0623, Fax: (703) 482-1739, www.cia.gov; *The World Factbook.*

Economist Intelligence Unit, 111 West 57th Street, New York, NY 10019, (212) 554-0600, Fax: (212) 586-1181, www.eiu.com; *Iran Country Report.*

Euromonitor International, Inc., 224 S. Michigan Avenue, Suite 1500, Chicago, IL 60604, (312) 922-1115, Fax: (312) 922-1157, www.euromonitor.com; *International Marketing Data and Statistics 2008* and *The World Economic Factbook 2008.*

International Lead and Zinc Study Group (ILZSG), Rua Almirante Barroso 38, 5th Floor, Lisbon 1000 - 013, Portugal, www.ilzsg.org; Interactive Statistical Database.

International Monetary Fund (IMF), 700 Nineteenth Street, NW, Washington, DC 20431, (202) 623-7000, Fax: (202) 623-4661, www.imf.org; *Direction of Trade Statistics Yearbook 2007; Government Finance Statistics Yearbook (2008 Edition);* and *International Financial Statistics Yearbook 2007.*

Palgrave Macmillan Ltd., Houndmills, Basingstoke, Hampshire, RG21 6XS, England, (Telephone in U.S. (888) 330-8477), (Fax in U.S. (800) 672-2054), www.palgrave.com; *The Statesman's Yearbook 2008.*

Statistical Centre of Iran (SCI), Dr. Fatemi Avenue, PO Box 14155-6133, Tehran 1414663111, Iran, www.sci.org.ir/portal/faces/public/sci_en/; *National Accounts of Iran 2003-2004.*

Taylor and Francis Group, An Informa Business, 2 Park Square, Milton Park, Abingdon, Oxford OX14 4RN, United Kingdom, (Dial from U.S. (212) 216-7800), (Fax from U.S. (212) 564-7854), www.tandf.co.uk; *The Europa World Year Book.*

United Nations Conference on Trade and Development (UNCTAD), DC2-1120, United Nations, New York, NY 10017, (212) 963-0027, www.unctad.org; *Handbook of Statistics 2005.*

United Nations Food and Agricultural Organization (FAO), Viale delle Terme di Caracalla, 00100 Rome, Italy, (Dial from U.S. (202) 653-2400), (Fax from U.S. (202) 653 5760), www.fao.org; *The State of Food and Agriculture (SOFA) 2006.*

The World Bank, 1818 H Street, NW, Washington, DC 20433, (202) 473-1000, Fax: (202) 477-6391, www.worldbank.org; *World Development Report 2008.*

IRAN - INCOME TAXES

See IRAN - TAXATION

IRAN - INDUSTRIAL METALS PRODUCTION

See IRAN - MINERAL INDUSTRIES

IRAN - INDUSTRIAL PRODUCTIVITY

Euromonitor International, Inc., 224 S. Michigan Avenue, Suite 1500, Chicago, IL 60604, (312) 922-1115, Fax: (312) 922-1157, www.euromonitor.com; *International Marketing Data and Statistics 2008.*

International Lead and Zinc Study Group (ILZSG), Rua Almirante Barroso 38, 5th Floor, Lisbon 1000 - 013, Portugal, www.ilzsg.org; Interactive Statistical Database.

M.E. Sharpe, 80 Business Park Drive, Armonk, NY 10504, (800) 541-6563, Fax: (914) 273-2106, www.mesharpe.com; *The Illustrated Book of World Rankings.*

IRAN - INDUSTRIAL PROPERTY

United Nations Statistics Division, New York, NY 10017, (800) 253-9646, Fax: (212) 963-4116, http://unstats.un.org; *Statistical Yearbook.*

World Intellectual Property Organization (WIPO), PO Box 18, CH-1211 Geneva 20, Switzerland, www.wipo.int; *Industrial Property Statistics* and *Industrial Property Statistics Online Directory.*

IRAN - INDUSTRIES

Central Intelligence Agency, Office of Public Affairs, Washington, DC 20505, (703) 482-0623, Fax: (703) 482-1739, www.cia.gov; *The World Factbook.*

Economist Intelligence Unit, 111 West 57th Street, New York, NY 10019, (212) 554-0600, Fax: (212) 586-1181, www.eiu.com; *Iran Country Report.*

Euromonitor International, Inc., 224 S. Michigan Avenue, Suite 1500, Chicago, IL 60604, (312) 922-1115, Fax: (312) 922-1157, www.euromonitor.com; *The World Economic Factbook 2008* and *World Marketing Data and Statistics.*

International Labour Office, I.L.O. Publications, 4 route des Morillons, CH-1211 Geneva 22, Switzerland, (Telephone in U.S. (202) 653-7652), (Fax in U.S. (202) 653-7687), www.ilo.org; *Yearbook of Labour Statistics 2006.*

M.E. Sharpe, 80 Business Park Drive, Armonk, NY 10504, (800) 541-6563, Fax: (914) 273-2106, www.mesharpe.com; *The Illustrated Book of World Rankings.*

Palgrave Macmillan Ltd., Houndmills, Basingstoke, Hampshire, RG21 6XS, England, (Telephone in U.S. (888) 330-8477), (Fax in U.S. (800) 672-2054), www.palgrave.com; *The Statesman's Yearbook 2008.*

Taylor and Francis Group, An Informa Business, 2 Park Square, Milton Park, Abingdon, Oxford OX14 4RN, United Kingdom, (Dial from U.S. (212) 216-7800), (Fax from U.S. (212) 564-7854), www.tandf.co.uk; *The Europa World Year Book.*

United Nations Industrial Development Organization (UNIDO), 1 United Nations Plaza, New York, NY 10017, (212) 963 6890, Fax: (212) 963-7904, http://unido.org; Industrial Statistics Database 2008 (INDSTAT) and *The International Yearbook of Industrial Statistics 2008.*

United Nations Statistics Division, New York, NY 10017, (800) 253-9646, Fax: (212) 963-4116, http://unstats.un.org; *Asia-Pacific in Figures 2004; 2004 Industrial Commodity Statistics Yearbook; Statistical Yearbook;* and *Statistical Yearbook for Asia and the Pacific 2004.*

The World Bank, 1818 H Street, NW, Washington, DC 20433, (202) 473-1000, Fax: (202) 477-6391, www.worldbank.org; *Iran, Islamic Republic of.*

IRAN - INFANT AND MATERNAL MORTALITY

See IRAN - MORTALITY

IRAN - INORGANIC ACIDS

United Nations Statistics Division, New York, NY 10017, (800) 253-9646, Fax: (212) 963-4116, http://unstats.un.org; *Statistical Yearbook.*

IRAN - INTERNATIONAL LIQUIDITY

International Monetary Fund (IMF), 700 Nineteenth Street, NW, Washington, DC 20431, (202) 623-7000, Fax: (202) 623-4661, www.imf.org; *International Financial Statistics Yearbook 2007.*

IRAN - INTERNATIONAL TRADE

Economist Intelligence Unit, 111 West 57th Street, New York, NY 10019, (212) 554-0600, Fax: (212) 586-1181, www.eiu.com; *Iran Country Report.*

Euromonitor International, Inc., 224 S. Michigan Avenue, Suite 1500, Chicago, IL 60604, (312) 922-1115, Fax: (312) 922-1157, www.euromonitor.com; *International Marketing Data and Statistics 2008; The World Economic Factbook 2008;* and *World Marketing Data and Statistics.*

International Monetary Fund (IMF), 700 Nineteenth Street, NW, Washington, DC 20431, (202) 623-7000, Fax: (202) 623-4661, www.imf.org; *International Financial Statistics Yearbook 2007.*

M.E. Sharpe, 80 Business Park Drive, Armonk, NY 10504, (800) 541-6563, Fax: (914) 273-2106, www.mesharpe.com; *The Illustrated Book of World Rankings.*

Palgrave Macmillan Ltd., Houndmills, Basingstoke, Hampshire, RG21 6XS, England, (Telephone in U.S. (888) 330-8477), (Fax in U.S. (800) 672-2054), www.palgrave.com; *The Statesman's Yearbook 2008.*

Statistical Centre of Iran (SCI), Dr. Fatemi Avenue, PO Box 14155-6133, Tehran 1414663111, Iran, www.sci.org.ir/portal/faces/public/sci_en/; *National Accounts of Iran 2003-2004.*

Taylor and Francis Group, An Informa Business, 2 Park Square, Milton Park, Abingdon, Oxford OX14

4RN, United Kingdom, (Dial from U.S. (212) 216-7800), (Fax from U.S. (212) 564-7854), www.tandf.co.uk; *The Europa World Year Book.*

United Nations Conference on Trade and Development (UNCTAD), DC2-1120, United Nations, New York, NY 10017, (212) 963-0027, www.unctad.org; *UNCTAD Commodity Yearbook.*

United Nations Food and Agricultural Organization (FAO), Viale delle Terme di Caracalla, 00100 Rome, Italy, (Dial from U.S. (202) 653-2400), (Fax from U.S. (202) 653 5760), www.fao.org; *FAO Trade Yearbook* and *The State of Food and Agriculture (SOFA) 2006.*

United Nations Statistics Division, New York, NY 10017, (800) 253-9646, Fax: (212) 963-4116, http://unstats.un.org; *Asia-Pacific in Figures 2004; International Trade Statistics Yearbook; Statistical Yearbook;* and *Statistical Yearbook for Asia and the Pacific 2004.*

The World Bank, 1818 H Street, NW, Washington, DC 20433, (202) 473-1000, Fax: (202) 477-6391, www.worldbank.org; *Iran, Islamic Republic of* and *World Development Report 2008.*

World Trade Organization (WTO), Centre William Rappard, Rue de Lausanne 154, CH-1211 Geneva 21, Switzerland, www.wto.org; *International Trade Statistics 2006.*

IRAN - INTERNET USERS

International Telecommunication Union (ITU), Place des Nations, 1211 Geneva 20, Switzerland, www.itu.int; *World Telecommunication/ICT Indicators Database on CD-ROM; World Telecommunication/ICT Indicators Database Online;* and *Yearbook of Statistics - Telecommunication Services (Chronological Time Series 1997-2006).*

The World Bank, 1818 H Street, NW, Washington, DC 20433, (202) 473-1000, Fax: (202) 477-6391, www.worldbank.org; *Iran, Islamic Republic of.*

IRAN - IRON AND IRON ORE PRODUCTION

See IRAN - MINERAL INDUSTRIES

IRAN - IRRIGATION

Euromonitor International, Inc., 224 S. Michigan Avenue, Suite 1500, Chicago, IL 60604, (312) 922-1115, Fax: (312) 922-1157, www.euromonitor.com; *International Marketing Data and Statistics 2008.*

IRAN - JUTE PRODUCTION

See IRAN - CROPS

IRAN - LABOR

Central Intelligence Agency, Office of Public Affairs, Washington, DC 20505, (703) 482-0623, Fax: (703) 482-1739, www.cia.gov; *The World Factbook.*

Euromonitor International, Inc., 224 S. Michigan Avenue, Suite 1500, Chicago, IL 60604, (312) 922-1115, Fax: (312) 922-1157, www.euromonitor.com; *International Marketing Data and Statistics 2008* and *World Marketing Data and Statistics.*

Federal Statistical Office Germany, D-65180 Wiesbaden, Germany, www.destatis.de; *Iran 2006.*

International Labour Office, I.L.O. Publications, 4 route des Morillons, CH-1211 Geneva 22, Switzerland, (Telephone in U.S. (202) 653-7652), (Fax in U.S. (202) 653-7687), www.ilo.org; *Yearbook of Labour Statistics 2006.*

M.E. Sharpe, 80 Business Park Drive, Armonk, NY 10504, (800) 541-6563, Fax: (914) 273-2106, www.mesharpe.com; *The Illustrated Book of World Rankings.*

Palgrave Macmillan Ltd., Houndmills, Basingstoke, Hampshire, RG21 6XS, England, (Telephone in U.S. (888) 330-8477), (Fax in U.S. (800) 672-2054), www.palgrave.com; *The Statesman's Yearbook 2008.*

Taylor and Francis Group, An Informa Business, 2 Park Square, Milton Park, Abingdon, Oxford OX14 4RN, United Kingdom, (Dial from U.S. (212) 216-7800), (Fax from U.S. (212) 564-7854), www.tandf.co.uk; *The Europa World Year Book.*

United Nations Food and Agricultural Organization (FAO), Viale delle Terme di Caracalla, 00100 Rome, Italy, (Dial from U.S. (202) 653-2400), (Fax from U.S. (202) 653 5760), www.fao.org; *The State of Food and Agriculture (SOFA) 2006.*

United Nations Statistics Division, New York, NY 10017, (800) 253-9646, Fax: (212) 963-4116, http://unstats.un.org; *Human Development Report 2006.*

The World Bank, 1818 H Street, NW, Washington, DC 20433, (202) 473-1000, Fax: (202) 477-6391, www.worldbank.org; *The World Bank Atlas 2003-2004* and *World Development Report 2008.*

IRAN - LAND USE

Central Intelligence Agency, Office of Public Affairs, Washington, DC 20505, (703) 482-0623, Fax: (703) 482-1739, www.cia.gov; *The World Factbook.*

Euromonitor International, Inc., 224 S. Michigan Avenue, Suite 1500, Chicago, IL 60604, (312) 922-1115, Fax: (312) 922-1157, www.euromonitor.com; *International Marketing Data and Statistics 2008.*

United Nations Food and Agricultural Organization (FAO), Viale delle Terme di Caracalla, 00100 Rome, Italy, (Dial from U.S. (202) 653-2400), (Fax from U.S. (202) 653 5760), www.fao.org; *FAO Production Yearbook 2002.*

The World Bank, 1818 H Street, NW, Washington, DC 20433, (202) 473-1000, Fax: (202) 477-6391, www.worldbank.org; *World Development Report 2008.*

IRAN - LIBRARIES

M.E. Sharpe, 80 Business Park Drive, Armonk, NY 10504, (800) 541-6563, Fax: (914) 273-2106, www.mesharpe.com; *The Illustrated Book of World Rankings.*

IRAN - LIFE EXPECTANCY

Central Intelligence Agency, Office of Public Affairs, Washington, DC 20505, (703) 482-0623, Fax: (703) 482-1739, www.cia.gov; *The World Factbook.*

Euromonitor International, Inc., 224 S. Michigan Avenue, Suite 1500, Chicago, IL 60604, (312) 922-1115, Fax: (312) 922-1157, www.euromonitor.com; *The World Economic Factbook 2008.*

United Nations Statistics Division, New York, NY 10017, (800) 253-9646, Fax: (212) 963-4116, http://unstats.un.org; *Asia-Pacific in Figures 2004; Human Development Report 2006;* and *World Statistics Pocketbook.*

The World Bank, 1818 H Street, NW, Washington, DC 20433, (202) 473-1000, Fax: (202) 477-6391, www.worldbank.org; *The World Bank Atlas 2003-2004* and *World Development Report 2008.*

IRAN - LITERACY

Euromonitor International, Inc., 224 S. Michigan Avenue, Suite 1500, Chicago, IL 60604, (312) 922-1115, Fax: (312) 922-1157, www.euromonitor.com; *World Marketing Data and Statistics.*

Statistical Centre of Iran (SCI), Dr. Fatemi Avenue, PO Box 14155-6133, Tehran 1414663111, Iran, www.sci.org.ir/portal/faces/public/sci_en/; *Knowledge and Attitude of Students on Reproductive Health and Gender Issues in Selected Districts of the I.R. of Iran.*

IRAN - LIVESTOCK

M.E. Sharpe, 80 Business Park Drive, Armonk, NY 10504, (800) 541-6563, Fax: (914) 273-2106, www.mesharpe.com; *The Illustrated Book of World Rankings.*

Palgrave Macmillan Ltd., Houndmills, Basingstoke, Hampshire, RG21 6XS, England, (Telephone in U.S. (888) 330-8477), (Fax in U.S. (800) 672-2054), www.palgrave.com; *The Statesman's Yearbook 2008.*

Taylor and Francis Group, An Informa Business, 2 Park Square, Milton Park, Abingdon, Oxford OX14 4RN, United Kingdom, (Dial from U.S. (212) 216-7800), (Fax from U.S. (212) 564-7854), www.tandf.co.uk; *The Europa World Year Book.*

United Nations Conference on Trade and Development (UNCTAD), DC2-1120, United Nations, New York, NY 10017, (212) 963-0027, www.unctad.org; *UNCTAD Commodity Yearbook.*

United Nations Food and Agricultural Organization (FAO), Viale delle Terme di Caracalla, 00100 Rome, Italy, (Dial from U.S. (202) 653-2400), (Fax from U.S. (202) 653 5760), www.fao.org; *FAO Production Yearbook 2002* and *The State of Food and Agriculture (SOFA) 2006.*

United Nations Statistics Division, New York, NY 10017, (800) 253-9646, Fax: (212) 963-4116, http://unstats.un.org; *Statistical Yearbook.*

IRAN - LOCAL TAXATION

Euromonitor International, Inc., 224 S. Michigan Avenue, Suite 1500, Chicago, IL 60604, (312) 922-1115, Fax: (312) 922-1157, www.euromonitor.com; *International Marketing Data and Statistics 2008.*

IRAN - MANPOWER

United Nations Statistics Division, New York, NY 10017, (800) 253-9646, Fax: (212) 963-4116, http://unstats.un.org; *Statistical Yearbook for Asia and the Pacific 2004.*

IRAN - MANUFACTURES

M.E. Sharpe, 80 Business Park Drive, Armonk, NY 10504, (800) 541-6563, Fax: (914) 273-2106, www.mesharpe.com; *The Illustrated Book of World Rankings.*

United Nations Statistics Division, New York, NY 10017, (800) 253-9646, Fax: (212) 963-4116, http://unstats.un.org; *Statistical Yearbook.*

IRAN - MARRIAGE

M.E. Sharpe, 80 Business Park Drive, Armonk, NY 10504, (800) 541-6563, Fax: (914) 273-2106, www.mesharpe.com; *The Illustrated Book of World Rankings.*

United Nations Statistics Division, New York, NY 10017, (800) 253-9646, Fax: (212) 963-4116, http://unstats.un.org; *Demographic Yearbook* and *Statistical Yearbook.*

IRAN - MEAT PRODUCTION

See IRAN - LIVESTOCK

IRAN - MEDICAL CARE, COST OF

International Monetary Fund (IMF), 700 Nineteenth Street, NW, Washington, DC 20431, (202) 623-7000, Fax: (202) 623-4661, www.imf.org; *Government Finance Statistics Yearbook (2008 Edition).*

IRAN - MERCHANT SHIPS

See IRAN - SHIPPING

IRAN - MILK PRODUCTION

See IRAN - DAIRY PROCESSING

IRAN - MINERAL INDUSTRIES

Commodity Research Bureau, 330 South Wells Street, Suite 612, Chicago, IL 60606-7110, (800) 621-5271, Fax: (312) 939-4135, www.crbtrader.com; *2006 CRB Commodity Yearbook and CD.*

International Lead and Zinc Study Group (ILZSG), Rua Almirante Barroso 38, 5th Floor, Lisbon 1000-013, Portugal, www.ilzsg.org; Interactive Statistical Database.

M.E. Sharpe, 80 Business Park Drive, Armonk, NY 10504, (800) 541-6563, Fax: (914) 273-2106, www.mesharpe.com; *The Illustrated Book of World Rankings.*

Organisation for Economic Cooperation and Development (OECD), 2 rue Andre Pascal, F-75775 Paris Cedex 16, France, (Telephone in U.S. (202) 785-

6323), (Fax in U.S. (202) 785-0350), www.oecd.org; *World Energy Outlook 2007.*

Organization of Petroleum Exporting Countries (OPEC), Obere Donaustrasse 93, A-1020, Vienna, Austria, www.opec.org; *Annual Statistical Bulletin 2006.*

Palgrave Macmillan Ltd., Houndmills, Basingstoke, Hampshire, RG21 6XS, England, (Telephone in U.S. (888) 330-8477), (Fax in U.S. (800) 672-2054), www.palgrave.com; *The Statesman's Yearbook 2008.*

Taylor and Francis Group, An Informa Business, 2 Park Square, Milton Park, Abingdon, Oxford OX14 4RN, United Kingdom, (Dial from U.S. (212) 216-7800), (Fax from U.S. (212) 564-7854), www.tandf.co.uk; *The Europa World Year Book.*

United Nations Conference on Trade and Development (UNCTAD), DC2-1120, United Nations, New York, NY 10017, (212) 963-0027, www.unctad.org; *UNCTAD Commodity Yearbook.*

United Nations Statistics Division, New York, NY 10017, (800) 253-9646, Fax: (212) 963-4116, http://unstats.un.org; *Statistical Yearbook.*

IRAN - MONEY EXCHANGE RATES

See IRAN - FOREIGN EXCHANGE RATES

IRAN - MONEY SUPPLY

Economist Intelligence Unit, 111 West 57th Street, New York, NY 10019, (212) 554-0600, Fax: (212) 586-1181, www.eiu.com; *Iran Country Report.*

Euromonitor International, Inc., 224 S. Michigan Avenue, Suite 1500, Chicago, IL 60604, (312) 922-1115, Fax: (312) 922-1157, www.euromonitor.com; *International Marketing Data and Statistics 2008.*

International Monetary Fund (IMF), 700 Nineteenth Street, NW, Washington, DC 20431, (202) 623-7000, Fax: (202) 623-4661, www.imf.org; *International Financial Statistics Yearbook 2007.*

Taylor and Francis Group, An Informa Business, 2 Park Square, Milton Park, Abingdon, Oxford OX14 4RN, United Kingdom, (Dial from U.S. (212) 216-7800), (Fax from U.S. (212) 564-7854), www.tandf.co.uk; *The Europa World Year Book.*

United Nations Statistics Division, New York, NY 10017, (800) 253-9646, Fax: (212) 963-4116, http://unstats.un.org; *Statistical Yearbook.*

The World Bank, 1818 H Street, NW, Washington, DC 20433, (202) 473-1000, Fax: (202) 477-6391, www.worldbank.org; *Iran, Islamic Republic of.*

IRAN - MORTALITY

Central Intelligence Agency, Office of Public Affairs, Washington, DC 20505, (703) 482-0623, Fax: (703) 482-1739, www.cia.gov; *The World Factbook.*

Euromonitor International, Inc., 224 S. Michigan Avenue, Suite 1500, Chicago, IL 60604, (312) 922-1115, Fax: (312) 922-1157, www.euromonitor.com; *International Marketing Data and Statistics 2008* and *The World Economic Factbook 2008.*

Taylor and Francis Group, An Informa Business, 2 Park Square, Milton Park, Abingdon, Oxford OX14 4RN, United Kingdom, (Dial from U.S. (212) 216-7800), (Fax from U.S. (212) 564-7854), www.tandf.co.uk; *The Europa World Year Book.*

UNICEF, 3 United Nations Plaza, New York, NY 10017, (800) 253-9646, Fax: (212) 887-7465, www.unicef.org; *The State of the World's Children 2008.*

United Nations Statistics Division, New York, NY 10017, (800) 253-9646, Fax: (212) 963-4116, http://unstats.un.org; *Asia-Pacific in Figures 2004; Demographic Yearbook; Human Development Report 2006; Statistical Yearbook;* and *World Statistics Pocketbook.*

The World Bank, 1818 H Street, NW, Washington, DC 20433, (202) 473-1000, Fax: (202) 477-6391, www.worldbank.org; *The World Bank Atlas 2003-2004* and *World Development Report 2008.*

World Health Organization (WHO), Avenue Appia 20, 1211 Geneve 27, Switzerland, (Telephone in U.S. (212) 331-9081), www.who.int; The WHO Global Atlas of Infectious Diseases and *World Health Report 2006.*

IRAN - MOTION PICTURES

Palgrave Macmillan Ltd., Houndmills, Basingstoke, Hampshire, RG21 6XS, England, (Telephone in U.S. (888) 330-8477), (Fax in U.S. (800) 672-2054), www.palgrave.com; *The Statesman's Yearbook 2008.*

UNESCO Institute for Statistics, C.P. 6128 Succursale Centre-Ville, Montreal, Quebec, H3C 3J7 Canada, (Dial from U.S. (514) 343-6880), (Fax from U.S. (514) 343 6882), www.uis.unesco.org; *Statistical Tables.*

United Nations Statistics Division, New York, NY 10017, (800) 253-9646, Fax: (212) 963-4116, http://unstats.un.org; *Statistical Yearbook.*

IRAN - MOTOR VEHICLES

International Road Federation (IFR), Madison Place, 500 Montgomery Street, 5th Floor, Alexandria, VA 22314, (703) 535-1001, Fax: (703) 535-1007, www.irfnet.org; *World Road Statistics 2006.*

Taylor and Francis Group, An Informa Business, 2 Park Square, Milton Park, Abingdon, Oxford OX14 4RN, United Kingdom, (Dial from U.S. (212) 216-7800), (Fax from U.S. (212) 564-7854), www.tandf.co.uk; *The Europa World Year Book.*

United Nations Statistics Division, New York, NY 10017, (800) 253-9646, Fax: (212) 963-4116, http://unstats.un.org; *Statistical Yearbook.*

IRAN - MUSEUMS

M.E. Sharpe, 80 Business Park Drive, Armonk, NY 10504, (800) 541-6563, Fax: (914) 273-2106, www.mesharpe.com; *The Illustrated Book of World Rankings.*

UNESCO Institute for Statistics, C.P. 6128 Succursale Centre-Ville, Montreal, Quebec, H3C 3J7 Canada, (Dial from U.S. (514) 343-6880), (Fax from U.S. (514) 343 6882), www.uis.unesco.org; *Statistical Tables.*

IRAN - NATURAL GAS PRODUCTION

See IRAN - MINERAL INDUSTRIES

IRAN - NUTRITION

United Nations Food and Agricultural Organization (FAO), Viale delle Terme di Caracalla, 00100 Rome, Italy, (Dial from U.S. (202) 653-2400), (Fax from U.S. (202) 653 5760), www.fao.org; *The State of Food and Agriculture (SOFA) 2006.*

IRAN - OLDER PEOPLE

M.E. Sharpe, 80 Business Park Drive, Armonk, NY 10504, (800) 541-6563, Fax: (914) 273-2106, www.mesharpe.com; *The Illustrated Book of World Rankings.*

IRAN - PAPER

See IRAN - FORESTS AND FORESTRY

IRAN - PEANUT PRODUCTION

See IRAN - CROPS

IRAN - PESTICIDES

United Nations Food and Agricultural Organization (FAO), Viale delle Terme di Caracalla, 00100 Rome, Italy, (Dial from U.S. (202) 653-2400), (Fax from U.S. (202) 653 5760), www.fao.org; *The State of Food and Agriculture (SOFA) 2006.*

IRAN - PETROLEUM INDUSTRY AND TRADE

M.E. Sharpe, 80 Business Park Drive, Armonk, NY 10504, (800) 541-6563, Fax: (914) 273-2106, www.mesharpe.com; *The Illustrated Book of World Rankings.*

Organisation for Economic Cooperation and Development (OECD), 2 rue Andre Pascal, F-75775 Paris Cedex 16, France, (Telephone in U.S. (202) 785-6323), (Fax in U.S. (202) 785-0350), www.oecd.org; *World Energy Outlook 2007.*

Organization of Petroleum Exporting Countries (OPEC), Obere Donaustrasse 93, A-1020, Vienna, Austria, www.opec.org; *Annual Statistical Bulletin 2006.*

Palgrave Macmillan Ltd., Houndmills, Basingstoke, Hampshire, RG21 6XS, England, (Telephone in U.S. (888) 330-8477), (Fax in U.S. (800) 672-2054), www.palgrave.com; *The Statesman's Yearbook 2008.*

PennWell Corporation, 1421 South Sheridan Road, Tulsa, OK 74112, (918) 835-3161, www.pennwell.com; *International Petroleum Encyclopedia 2007.*

U.S. Department of Energy (DOE), Energy Information Administration (EIA), 1000 Independence Avenue, SW, Washington, DC 20585, (202) 586-8800, www.eia.doe.gov; *International Energy Annual 2004* and *International Energy Outlook 2006.*

United Nations Conference on Trade and Development (UNCTAD), DC2-1120, United Nations, New York, NY 10017, (212) 963-0027, www.unctad.org; *UNCTAD Commodity Yearbook.*

United Nations Food and Agricultural Organization (FAO), Viale delle Terme di Caracalla, 00100 Rome, Italy, (Dial from U.S. (202) 653-2400), (Fax from U.S. (202) 653 5760), www.fao.org; *The State of Food and Agriculture (SOFA) 2006.*

United Nations Statistics Division, New York, NY 10017, (800) 253-9646, Fax: (212) 963-4116, http://unstats.un.org; *Statistical Yearbook.*

IRAN - PIPELINES

Organization of Petroleum Exporting Countries (OPEC), Obere Donaustrasse 93, A-1020, Vienna, Austria, www.opec.org; *Annual Statistical Bulletin 2006.*

IRAN - PISTACHIO PRODUCTION

See IRAN - CROPS

IRAN - PLASTICS INDUSTRY AND TRADE

United Nations Statistics Division, New York, NY 10017, (800) 253-9646, Fax: (212) 963-4116, http://unstats.un.org; *Statistical Yearbook.*

IRAN - POLITICAL SCIENCE

Central Intelligence Agency, Office of Public Affairs, Washington, DC 20505, (703) 482-0623, Fax: (703) 482-1739, www.cia.gov; *The World Factbook.*

International Monetary Fund (IMF), 700 Nineteenth Street, NW, Washington, DC 20431, (202) 623-7000, Fax: (202) 623-4661, www.imf.org; *Government Finance Statistics Yearbook (2008 Edition)* and *International Financial Statistics Yearbook 2007.*

Palgrave Macmillan Ltd., Houndmills, Basingstoke, Hampshire, RG21 6XS, England, (Telephone in U.S. (888) 330-8477), (Fax in U.S. (800) 672-2054), www.palgrave.com; *The Statesman's Yearbook 2008.*

Taylor and Francis Group, An Informa Business, 2 Park Square, Milton Park, Abingdon, Oxford OX14 4RN, United Kingdom, (Dial from U.S. (212) 216-7800), (Fax from U.S. (212) 564-7854), www.tandf.co.uk; *The Europa World Year Book.*

United Nations Statistics Division, New York, NY 10017, (800) 253-9646, Fax: (212) 963-4116, http://unstats.un.org; *Asia-Pacific in Figures 2004; National Accounts Statistics: Compendium of Income Distribution Statistics;* and *Statistical Yearbook.*

The World Bank, 1818 H Street, NW, Washington, DC 20433, (202) 473-1000, Fax: (202) 477-6391, www.worldbank.org; *World Development Report 2008.*

IRAN - POPULATION

Central Intelligence Agency, Office of Public Affairs, Washington, DC 20505, (703) 482-0623, Fax: (703) 482-1739, www.cia.gov; *The World Factbook.*

Economist Intelligence Unit, 111 West 57th Street, New York, NY 10019, (212) 554-0600, Fax: (212) 586-1181, www.eiu.com; *Iran Country Report.*

Euromonitor International, Inc., 224 S. Michigan Avenue, Suite 1500, Chicago, IL 60604, (312) 922-1115, Fax: (312) 922-1157, www.euromonitor.com; *International Marketing Data and Statistics 2008* and *The World Economic Factbook 2008.*

Federal Statistical Office Germany, D-65180 Wiesbaden, Germany, www.destatis.de; *Iran 2006.*

International Labour Office, I.L.O. Publications, 4 route des Morillons, CH-1211 Geneva 22, Switzerland, (Telephone in U.S. (202) 653-7652), (Fax in U.S. (202) 653-7687), www.ilo.org; *Yearbook of Labour Statistics 2006.*

M.E. Sharpe, 80 Business Park Drive, Armonk, NY 10504, (800) 541-6563, Fax: (914) 273-2106, www.mesharpe.com; *The Illustrated Book of World Rankings.*

Palgrave Macmillan Ltd., Houndmills, Basingstoke, Hampshire, RG21 6XS, England, (Telephone in U.S. (888) 330-8477), (Fax in U.S. (800) 672-2054), www.palgrave.com; *The Statesman's Yearbook 2008.*

Statistical Centre of Iran (SCI), Dr. Fatemi Avenue, PO Box 14155-6133, Tehran 1414663111, Iran, www.sci.org.ir/portal/faces/public/sci_en/; *A Study on the Effects of Women's Activity on Fertility in Iran* and *Women Heads of Households (Socio-Economic Characteristics).*

Taylor and Francis Group, An Informa Business, 2 Park Square, Milton Park, Abingdon, Oxford OX14 4RN, United Kingdom, (Dial from U.S. (212) 216-7800), (Fax from U.S. (212) 564-7854), www.tandf.co.uk; *The Europa World Year Book.*

U.S. Department of State (DOS), 2201 C Street NW, Washington, DC 20520, (202) 647-4000, www.state.gov; *World Military Expenditures and Arms Transfers (WMEAT).*

UNESCO Institute for Statistics, C.P. 6128 Succursale Centre-Ville, Montreal, Quebec, H3C 3J7 Canada, (Dial from U.S. (514) 343-6880), (Fax from U.S. (514) 343 6882), www.uis.unesco.org; *Statistical Tables.*

United Nations Food and Agricultural Organization (FAO), Viale delle Terme di Caracalla, 00100 Rome, Italy, (Dial from U.S. (202) 653-2400), (Fax from U.S. (202) 653 5760), www.fao.org; *FAO Production Yearbook 2002.*

United Nations Statistics Division, New York, NY 10017, (800) 253-9646, Fax: (212) 963-4116, http://unstats.un.org; *Asia-Pacific in Figures 2004; Demographic Yearbook; Human Development Report 2006; Statistical Yearbook; Statistical Yearbook for Asia and the Pacific 2004;* and *World Statistics Pocketbook.*

The World Bank, 1818 H Street, NW, Washington, DC 20433, (202) 473-1000, Fax: (202) 477-6391, www.worldbank.org; *Iran, Islamic Republic of; The World Bank Atlas 2003-2004;* and *World Development Report 2008.*

World Health Organization (WHO), Avenue Appia 20, 1211 Geneve 27, Switzerland, (Telephone in U.S. (212) 331-9081), www.who.int; *World Health Report 2006.*

IRAN - POPULATION DENSITY

Central Intelligence Agency, Office of Public Affairs, Washington, DC 20505, (703) 482-0623, Fax: (703) 482-1739, www.cia.gov; *The World Factbook.*

Euromonitor International, Inc., 224 S. Michigan Avenue, Suite 1500, Chicago, IL 60604, (312) 922-1115, Fax: (312) 922-1157, www.euromonitor.com; *International Marketing Data and Statistics 2008* and *The World Economic Factbook 2008.*

M.E. Sharpe, 80 Business Park Drive, Armonk, NY 10504, (800) 541-6563, Fax: (914) 273-2106, www.mesharpe.com; *The Illustrated Book of World Rankings.*

Palgrave Macmillan Ltd., Houndmills, Basingstoke, Hampshire, RG21 6XS, England, (Telephone in U.S. (888) 330-8477), (Fax in U.S. (800) 672-2054), www.palgrave.com; *The Statesman's Yearbook 2008.*

Taylor and Francis Group, An Informa Business, 2 Park Square, Milton Park, Abingdon, Oxford OX14 4RN, United Kingdom, (Dial from U.S. (212) 216-7800), (Fax from U.S. (212) 564-7854), www.tandf.co.uk; *The Europa World Year Book.*

UNESCO Institute for Statistics, C.P. 6128 Succursale Centre-Ville, Montreal, Quebec, H3C 3J7 Canada, (Dial from U.S. (514) 343-6880), (Fax from U.S. (514) 343 6882), www.uis.unesco.org; *Statistical Tables.*

United Nations Food and Agricultural Organization (FAO), Viale delle Terme di Caracalla, 00100 Rome, Italy, (Dial from U.S. (202) 653-2400), (Fax from U.S. (202) 653 5760), www.fao.org; *The State of Food and Agriculture (SOFA) 2006.*

United Nations Statistics Division, New York, NY 10017, (800) 253-9646, Fax: (212) 963-4116, http://unstats.un.org; *Statistical Yearbook.*

The World Bank, 1818 H Street, NW, Washington, DC 20433, (202) 473-1000, Fax: (202) 477-6391, www.worldbank.org; *Iran, Islamic Republic of* and *World Development Report 2008.*

IRAN - POSTAL SERVICE

M.E. Sharpe, 80 Business Park Drive, Armonk, NY 10504, (800) 541-6563, Fax: (914) 273-2106, www.mesharpe.com; *The Illustrated Book of World Rankings.*

United Nations Statistics Division, New York, NY 10017, (800) 253-9646, Fax: (212) 963-4116, http://unstats.un.org; *Statistical Yearbook.*

IRAN - POWER RESOURCES

Euromonitor International, Inc., 224 S. Michigan Avenue, Suite 1500, Chicago, IL 60604, (312) 922-1115, Fax: (312) 922-1157, www.euromonitor.com; *International Marketing Data and Statistics 2008; The World Economic Factbook 2008;* and *World Marketing Data and Statistics.*

M.E. Sharpe, 80 Business Park Drive, Armonk, NY 10504, (800) 541-6563, Fax: (914) 273-2106, www.mesharpe.com; *The Illustrated Book of World Rankings.*

Organisation for Economic Cooperation and Development (OECD), 2 rue Andre Pascal, F-75775 Paris Cedex 16, France, (Telephone in U.S. (202) 785-6323), (Fax in U.S. (202) 785-0350), www.oecd.org; *World Energy Outlook 2007.*

Palgrave Macmillan Ltd., Houndmills, Basingstoke, Hampshire, RG21 6XS, England, (Telephone in U.S. (888) 330-8477), (Fax in U.S. (800) 672-2054), www.palgrave.com; *The Statesman's Yearbook 2008.*

Platts, 2 Penn Plaza, 25th Floor, New York, NY 10121-2298, (212) 904-3070, www.platts.com; *Energy Economist.*

U.S. Department of Energy (DOE), Energy Information Administration (EIA), 1000 Independence Avenue, SW, Washington, DC 20585, (202) 586-8800, www.eia.doe.gov; *International Energy Annual 2004* and *International Energy Outlook 2006.*

United Nations Food and Agricultural Organization (FAO), Viale delle Terme di Caracalla, 00100 Rome, Italy, (Dial from U.S. (202) 653-2400), (Fax from U.S. (202) 653 5760), www.fao.org; *The State of Food and Agriculture (SOFA) 2006.*

United Nations Statistics Division, New York, NY 10017, (800) 253-9646, Fax: (212) 963-4116, http://unstats.un.org; *Asia-Pacific in Figures 2004; Energy Statistics Yearbook 2003; Human Development Report 2006; Statistical Yearbook; Statistical Yearbook for Asia and the Pacific 2004;* and *World Statistics Pocketbook.*

The World Bank, 1818 H Street, NW, Washington, DC 20433, (202) 473-1000, Fax: (202) 477-6391, www.worldbank.org; *The World Bank Atlas 2003-2004* and *World Development Report 2008.*

IRAN - PRICES

Euromonitor International, Inc., 224 S. Michigan Avenue, Suite 1500, Chicago, IL 60604, (312) 922-1115, Fax: (312) 922-1157, www.euromonitor.com; *World Marketing Data and Statistics.*

International Labour Office, I.L.O. Publications, 4 route des Morillons, CH-1211 Geneva 22, Switzerland, (Telephone in U.S. (202) 653-7652), (Fax in U.S. (202) 653-7687), www.ilo.org; *Yearbook of Labour Statistics 2006.*

International Lead and Zinc Study Group (ILZSG), Rua Almirante Barroso 38, 5th Floor, Lisbon 1000 - 013, Portugal, www.ilzsg.org; Interactive Statistical Database.

International Monetary Fund (IMF), 700 Nineteenth Street, NW, Washington, DC 20431, (202) 623-7000, Fax: (202) 623-4661, www.imf.org; *International Financial Statistics Yearbook 2007.*

M.E. Sharpe, 80 Business Park Drive, Armonk, NY 10504, (800) 541-6563, Fax: (914) 273-2106, www.mesharpe.com; *The Illustrated Book of World Rankings.*

United Nations Food and Agricultural Organization (FAO), Viale delle Terme di Caracalla, 00100 Rome, Italy, (Dial from U.S. (202) 653-2400), (Fax from U.S. (202) 653 5760), www.fao.org; *FAO Production Yearbook 2002* and *The State of Food and Agriculture (SOFA) 2006.*

The World Bank, 1818 H Street, NW, Washington, DC 20433, (202) 473-1000, Fax: (202) 477-6391, www.worldbank.org; *Iran, Islamic Republic of.*

IRAN - PROFESSIONS

UNESCO Institute for Statistics, C.P. 6128 Succursale Centre-Ville, Montreal, Quebec, H3C 3J7 Canada, (Dial from U.S. (514) 343-6880), (Fax from U.S. (514) 343 6882), www.uis.unesco.org; *Statistical Tables.*

United Nations Statistics Division, New York, NY 10017, (800) 253-9646, Fax: (212) 963-4116, http://unstats.un.org; *Statistical Yearbook.*

IRAN - PUBLIC HEALTH

Euromonitor International, Inc., 224 S. Michigan Avenue, Suite 1500, Chicago, IL 60604, (312) 922-1115, Fax: (312) 922-1157, www.euromonitor.com; *World Marketing Data and Statistics.*

M.E. Sharpe, 80 Business Park Drive, Armonk, NY 10504, (800) 541-6563, Fax: (914) 273-2106, www.mesharpe.com; *The Illustrated Book of World Rankings.*

Palgrave Macmillan Ltd., Houndmills, Basingstoke, Hampshire, RG21 6XS, England, (Telephone in U.S. (888) 330-8477), (Fax in U.S. (800) 672-2054), www.palgrave.com; *The Statesman's Yearbook 2008.*

Statistical Centre of Iran (SCI), Dr. Fatemi Avenue, PO Box 14155-6133, Tehran 1414663111, Iran, www.sci.org.ir/portal/faces/public/sci_en/; *Knowledge and Attitude of Students on Reproductive Health and Gender Issues in Selected Districts of the I.R. of Iran.*

UNICEF, 3 United Nations Plaza, New York, NY 10017, (800) 253-9646, Fax: (212) 887-7465, www.unicef.org; *The State of the World's Children 2008.*

United Nations Statistics Division, New York, NY 10017, (800) 253-9646, Fax: (212) 963-4116, http://unstats.un.org; *Asia-Pacific in Figures 2004; Human Development Report 2006;* and *Statistical Yearbook.*

The World Bank, 1818 H Street, NW, Washington, DC 20433, (202) 473-1000, Fax: (202) 477-6391, www.worldbank.org; *Iran, Islamic Republic of* and *World Development Report 2008.*

World Health Organization (WHO), Avenue Appia 20, 1211 Geneve 27, Switzerland, (Telephone in U.S. (212) 331-9081), www.who.int; The WHO Global Atlas of Infectious Diseases and *World Health Report 2006.*

IRAN - PUBLIC UTILITIES

United Nations Statistics Division, New York, NY 10017, (800) 253-9646, Fax: (212) 963-4116, http://unstats.un.org; *Electric Power in Asia and the Pacific 2001 and 2002.*

IRAN - PUBLISHERS AND PUBLISHING

Taylor and Francis Group, An Informa Business, 2 Park Square, Milton Park, Abingdon, Oxford OX14

4RN, United Kingdom, (Dial from U.S. (212) 216-7800), (Fax from U.S. (212) 564-7854), www.tandf.co.uk; *The Europa World Year Book.*

UNESCO Institute for Statistics, C.P. 6128 Succursale Centre-Ville, Montreal, Quebec, H3C 3J7 Canada, (Dial from U.S. (514) 343-6880), (Fax from U.S. (514) 343 6882), www.uis.unesco.org; *Statistical Tables.*

IRAN - RADIO - RECEIVERS AND RECEPTION

Palgrave Macmillan Ltd., Houndmills, Basingstoke, Hampshire, RG21 6XS, England, (Telephone in U.S. (888) 330-8477), (Fax in U.S. (800) 672-2054), www.palgrave.com; *The Statesman's Yearbook 2008.*

United Nations Statistics Division, New York, NY 10017, (800) 253-9646, Fax: (212) 963-4116, http://unstats.un.org; *Statistical Yearbook.*

IRAN - RAILROADS

Jane's Information Group, 110 North Royal Street, Suite 200, Alexandria, VA 22314, (703) 683-3700, Fax: (800) 836-0297, www.janes.com; *Jane's World Railways.*

Palgrave Macmillan Ltd., Houndmills, Basingstoke, Hampshire, RG21 6XS, England, (Telephone in U.S. (888) 330-8477), (Fax in U.S. (800) 672-2054), www.palgrave.com; *The Statesman's Yearbook 2008.*

Taylor and Francis Group, An Informa Business, 2 Park Square, Milton Park, Abingdon, Oxford OX14 4RN, United Kingdom, (Dial from U.S. (212) 216-7800), (Fax from U.S. (212) 564-7854), www.tandf.co.uk; *The Europa World Year Book.*

United Nations Statistics Division, New York, NY 10017, (800) 253-9646, Fax: (212) 963-4116, http://unstats.un.org; *Statistical Yearbook.*

IRAN - RELIGION

Central Intelligence Agency, Office of Public Affairs, Washington, DC 20505, (703) 482-0623, Fax: (703) 482-1739, www.cia.gov; *The World Factbook.*

M.E. Sharpe, 80 Business Park Drive, Armonk, NY 10504, (800) 541-6563, Fax: (914) 273-2106, www.mesharpe.com; *The Illustrated Book of World Rankings.*

Palgrave Macmillan Ltd., Houndmills, Basingstoke, Hampshire, RG21 6XS, England, (Telephone in U.S. (888) 330-8477), (Fax in U.S. (800) 672-2054), www.palgrave.com; *The Statesman's Yearbook 2008.*

IRAN - RENT CHARGES

International Labour Office, I.L.O. Publications, 4 route des Morillons, CH-1211 Geneva 22, Switzerland, (Telephone in U.S. (202) 653-7652), (Fax in U.S. (202) 653-7687), www.ilo.org; *Yearbook of Labour Statistics 2006.*

IRAN - RESERVES (ACCOUNTING)

Euromonitor International, Inc., 224 S. Michigan Avenue, Suite 1500, Chicago, IL 60604, (312) 922-1115, Fax: (312) 922-1157, www.euromonitor.com; *International Marketing Data and Statistics 2008.*

Statistical Centre of Iran (SCI), Dr. Fatemi Avenue, PO Box 14155-6133, Tehran 1414663111, Iran, www.sci.org.ir/portal/faces/public/sci_en/; *National Accounts of Iran 2003-2004.*

United Nations Statistics Division, New York, NY 10017, (800) 253-9646, Fax: (212) 963-4116, http://unstats.un.org; *Statistical Yearbook.*

IRAN - RETAIL TRADE

Euromonitor International, Inc., 224 S. Michigan Avenue, Suite 1500, Chicago, IL 60604, (312) 922-1115, Fax: (312) 922-1157, www.euromonitor.com; *World Marketing Data and Statistics.*

United Nations Statistics Division, New York, NY 10017, (800) 253-9646, Fax: (212) 963-4116, http://unstats.un.org; *Statistical Yearbook.*

IRAN - RICE PRODUCTION

See IRAN - CROPS

IRAN - ROADS

Central Intelligence Agency, Office of Public Affairs, Washington, DC 20505, (703) 482-0623, Fax: (703) 482-1739, www.cia.gov; *The World Factbook.*

International Road Federation (IFR), Madison Place, 500 Montgomery Street, 5th Floor, Alexandria, VA 22314, (703) 535-1001, Fax: (703) 535-1007, www.irfnet.org; *World Road Statistics 2006.*

Palgrave Macmillan Ltd., Houndmills, Basingstoke, Hampshire, RG21 6XS, England, (Telephone in U.S. (888) 330-8477), (Fax in U.S. (800) 672-2054), www.palgrave.com; *The Statesman's Yearbook 2008.*

IRAN - RUBBER INDUSTRY AND TRADE

International Rubber Study Group (IRSG), 1st Floor, Heron House, 109/115 Wembley Hill Road, Wembley, Middlesex HA9 8DA, United Kingdom, www.rubberstudy.com; *Rubber Statistical Bulletin; Summary of World Rubber Statistics 2005; World Rubber Statistics Handbook (Volume 6, 1975-2001);* and *World Rubber Statistics Historic Handbook.*

M.E. Sharpe, 80 Business Park Drive, Armonk, NY 10504, (800) 541-6563, Fax: (914) 273-2106, www.mesharpe.com; *The Illustrated Book of World Rankings.*

IRAN - SAFFLOWER SEED PRODUCTION

See IRAN - CROPS

IRAN - SALT PRODUCTION

See IRAN - MINERAL INDUSTRIES

IRAN - SHEEP

See IRAN - LIVESTOCK

IRAN - SHIPPING

Lloyd's Register - Fairplay, 8410 N.W. 53rd Terrace, Suite 207, Miami FL 33166, (305) 718-9929, Fax: (305) 718-9663, www.lrfairplay.com; *Register of Ships 2007-2008; World Casualty Statistics 2007; World Fleet Statistics 2006; World Marine Propulsion Report 2006-2010; World Shipbuilding Statistics 2007;* and The World Shipping Encyclopaedia.

Organization of Petroleum Exporting Countries (OPEC), Obere Donaustrasse 93, A-1020, Vienna, Austria, www.opec.org; *Annual Statistical Bulletin 2006.*

Palgrave Macmillan Ltd., Houndmills, Basingstoke, Hampshire, RG21 6XS, England, (Telephone in U.S. (888) 330-8477), (Fax in U.S. (800) 672-2054), www.palgrave.com; *The Statesman's Yearbook 2008.*

Taylor and Francis Group, An Informa Business, 2 Park Square, Milton Park, Abingdon, Oxford OX14 4RN, United Kingdom, (Dial from U.S. (212) 216-7800), (Fax from U.S. (212) 564-7854), www.tandf.co.uk; *The Europa World Year Book.*

U.S. Department of Transportation (DOT), Maritime Administration (MARAD), West Building, Southeast Federal Center, 1200 New Jersey Avenue, SE, Washington, DC 20590, (800) 99-MARAD, www.marad.dot.gov; *World Merchant Fleet 2005.*

United Nations Statistics Division, New York, NY 10017, (800) 253-9646, Fax: (212) 963-4116, http://unstats.un.org; *Statistical Yearbook.*

IRAN - SILVER PRODUCTION

See IRAN - MINERAL INDUSTRIES

IRAN - SOCIAL ECOLOGY

M.E. Sharpe, 80 Business Park Drive, Armonk, NY 10504, (800) 541-6563, Fax: (914) 273-2106, www.mesharpe.com; *The Illustrated Book of World Rankings.*

United Nations Statistics Division, New York, NY 10017, (800) 253-9646, Fax: (212) 963-4116, http://unstats.un.org; *World Statistics Pocketbook.*

IRAN - SOCIAL SECURITY

International Monetary Fund (IMF), 700 Nineteenth Street, NW, Washington, DC 20431, (202) 623-7000, Fax: (202) 623-4661, www.imf.org; *Government Finance Statistics Yearbook (2008 Edition).*

United Nations Statistics Division, New York, NY 10017, (800) 253-9646, Fax: (212) 963-4116, http://unstats.un.org; *National Accounts Statistics: Compendium of Income Distribution Statistics.*

IRAN - SOYBEAN PRODUCTION

See IRAN - CROPS

IRAN - STEEL PRODUCTION

See IRAN - MINERAL INDUSTRIES

IRAN - SUGAR PRODUCTION

See IRAN - CROPS

IRAN - TAXATION

International Monetary Fund (IMF), 700 Nineteenth Street, NW, Washington, DC 20431, (202) 623-7000, Fax: (202) 623-4661, www.imf.org; *Government Finance Statistics Yearbook (2008 Edition).*

International Road Federation (IFR), Madison Place, 500 Montgomery Street, 5th Floor, Alexandria, VA 22314, (703) 535-1001, Fax: (703) 535-1007, www.irfnet.org; *World Road Statistics 2006.*

Taylor and Francis Group, An Informa Business, 2 Park Square, Milton Park, Abingdon, Oxford OX14 4RN, United Kingdom, (Dial from U.S. (212) 216-7800), (Fax from U.S. (212) 564-7854), www.tandf.co.uk; *The Europa World Year Book.*

IRAN - TEA PRODUCTION

See IRAN - CROPS

IRAN - TELEPHONE

International Telecommunication Union (ITU), Place des Nations, 1211 Geneva 20, Switzerland, www.itu.int; World Telecommunication Indicators Database.

Palgrave Macmillan Ltd., Houndmills, Basingstoke, Hampshire, RG21 6XS, England, (Telephone in U.S. (888) 330-8477), (Fax in U.S. (800) 672-2054), www.palgrave.com; *The Statesman's Yearbook 2008.*

Taylor and Francis Group, An Informa Business, 2 Park Square, Milton Park, Abingdon, Oxford OX14 4RN, United Kingdom, (Dial from U.S. (212) 216-7800), (Fax from U.S. (212) 564-7854), www.tandf.co.uk; *The Europa World Year Book.*

United Nations Statistics Division, New York, NY 10017, (800) 253-9646, Fax: (212) 963-4116, http://unstats.un.org; *Statistical Yearbook* and *World Statistics Pocketbook.*

IRAN - TELEVISION - RECEIVERS AND RECEPTION

United Nations Statistics Division, New York, NY 10017, (800) 253-9646, Fax: (212) 963-4116, http://unstats.un.org; *Statistical Yearbook.*

IRAN - TEXTILE INDUSTRY

M.E. Sharpe, 80 Business Park Drive, Armonk, NY 10504, (800) 541-6563, Fax: (914) 273-2106, www.mesharpe.com; *The Illustrated Book of World Rankings.*

United Nations Conference on Trade and Development (UNCTAD), DC2-1120, United Nations, New York, NY 10017, (212) 963-0027, www.unctad.org; *UNCTAD Commodity Yearbook.*

United Nations Statistics Division, New York, NY 10017, (800) 253-9646, Fax: (212) 963-4116, http://unstats.un.org; *Statistical Yearbook.*

IRAN - THEATER

UNESCO Institute for Statistics, C.P. 6128 Succursale Centre-Ville, Montreal, Quebec, H3C 3J7 Canada, (Dial from U.S. (514) 343-6880), (Fax from U.S. (514) 343 6882), www.uis.unesco.org; *Statistical Tables.*

IRAN - TIN PRODUCTION

See IRAN - MINERAL INDUSTRIES

IRAN - TIRE INDUSTRY

United Nations Statistics Division, New York, NY 10017, (800) 253-9646, Fax: (212) 963-4116, http://unstats.un.org; *Statistical Yearbook.*

IRAN - TOBACCO INDUSTRY

Foreign Agricultural Service (FAS), U.S. Department of Agriculture (USDA), 1400 Independence Avenue, SW, Washington, DC 20250, (202) 720-3935, www.fas.usda.gov; *Tobacco: World Markets and Trade.*

M.E. Sharpe, 80 Business Park Drive, Armonk, NY 10504, (800) 541-6563, Fax: (914) 273-2106, www.mesharpe.com; *The Illustrated Book of World Rankings.*

United Nations Statistics Division, New York, NY 10017, (800) 253-9646, Fax: (212) 963-4116, http://unstats.un.org; *Statistical Yearbook.*

IRAN - TOURISM

Euromonitor International, Inc., 224 S. Michigan Avenue, Suite 1500, Chicago, IL 60604, (312) 922-1115, Fax: (312) 922-1157, www.euromonitor.com; *The World Economic Factbook 2008* and *World Marketing Data and Statistics.*

M.E. Sharpe, 80 Business Park Drive, Armonk, NY 10504, (800) 541-6563, Fax: (914) 273-2106, www.mesharpe.com; *The Illustrated Book of World Rankings.*

Palgrave Macmillan Ltd., Houndmills, Basingstoke, Hampshire, RG21 6XS, England, (Telephone in U.S. (888) 330-8477), (Fax in U.S. (800) 672-2054), www.palgrave.com; *The Statesman's Yearbook 2008.*

Taylor and Francis Group, An Informa Business, 2 Park Square, Milton Park, Abingdon, Oxford OX14 4RN, United Kingdom, (Dial from U.S. (212) 216-7800), (Fax from U.S. (212) 564-7854), www.tandf.co.uk; *The Europa World Year Book.*

United Nations Statistics Division, New York, NY 10017, (800) 253-9646, Fax: (212) 963-4116, http://unstats.un.org; *Statistical Yearbook.*

United Nations World Tourism Organization (UNWTO), Capitan Haya 42, 28020 Madrid, Spain, www.world-tourism.org; *Yearbook of Tourism Statistics.*

The World Bank, 1818 H Street, NW, Washington, DC 20433, (202) 473-1000, Fax: (202) 477-6391, www.worldbank.org; *Iran, Islamic Republic of.*

IRAN - TRADE

See IRAN - INTERNATIONAL TRADE

IRAN - TRANSPORTATION

Central Intelligence Agency, Office of Public Affairs, Washington, DC 20505, (703) 482-0623, Fax: (703) 482-1739, www.cia.gov; *The World Factbook.*

Euromonitor International, Inc., 224 S. Michigan Avenue, Suite 1500, Chicago, IL 60604, (312) 922-1115, Fax: (312) 922-1157, www.euromonitor.com; *International Marketing Data and Statistics 2008* and *World Marketing Data and Statistics.*

M.E. Sharpe, 80 Business Park Drive, Armonk, NY 10504, (800) 541-6563, Fax: (914) 273-2106, www.mesharpe.com; *The Illustrated Book of World Rankings.*

Palgrave Macmillan Ltd., Houndmills, Basingstoke, Hampshire, RG21 6XS, England, (Telephone in U.S. (888) 330-8477), (Fax in U.S. (800) 672-2054), www.palgrave.com; *The Statesman's Yearbook 2008.*

Taylor and Francis Group, An Informa Business, 2 Park Square, Milton Park, Abingdon, Oxford OX14 4RN, United Kingdom, (Dial from U.S. (212) 216-7800), (Fax from U.S. (212) 564-7854), www.tandf.co.uk; *The Europa World Year Book.*

United Nations Statistics Division, New York, NY 10017, (800) 253-9646, Fax: (212) 963-4116, http://unstats.un.org; *Human Development Report 2006* and *Statistical Yearbook for Asia and the Pacific 2004.*

The World Bank, 1818 H Street, NW, Washington, DC 20433, (202) 473-1000, Fax: (202) 477-6391, www.worldbank.org; *Iran, Islamic Republic of.*

IRAN - UNEMPLOYMENT

Central Intelligence Agency, Office of Public Affairs, Washington, DC 20505, (703) 482-0623, Fax: (703) 482-1739, www.cia.gov; *The World Factbook.*

Euromonitor International, Inc., 224 S. Michigan Avenue, Suite 1500, Chicago, IL 60604, (312) 922-1115, Fax: (312) 922-1157, www.euromonitor.com; *International Marketing Data and Statistics 2008.*

International Labour Office, I.L.O. Publications, 4 route des Morillons, CH-1211 Geneva 22, Switzerland, (Telephone in U.S. (202) 653-7652), (Fax in U.S. (202) 653-7687), www.ilo.org; *Yearbook of Labour Statistics 2006.*

IRAN - VITAL STATISTICS

Euromonitor International, Inc., 224 S. Michigan Avenue, Suite 1500, Chicago, IL 60604, (312) 922-1115, Fax: (312) 922-1157, www.euromonitor.com; *International Marketing Data and Statistics 2008.*

Statistical Centre of Iran (SCI), Dr. Fatemi Avenue, PO Box 14155-6133, Tehran 1414663111, Iran, www.sci.org.ir/portal/faces/public/sci_en/; *Iran Statistical Digest; Knowledge and Attitude of Students on Reproductive Health and Gender Issues in Selected Districts of the I.R. of Iran; A Study on the Effects of Women's Activity on Fertility in Iran;* and *Women Heads of Households (Socio-Economic Characteristics).*

United Nations Statistics Division, New York, NY 10017, (800) 253-9646, Fax: (212) 963-4116, http://unstats.un.org; *Statistical Yearbook.*

World Health Organization (WHO), Avenue Appia 20, 1211 Geneve 27, Switzerland, (Telephone in U.S. (212) 331-9081), www.who.int; *World Health Report 2006.*

IRAN - WAGES

International Labour Office, I.L.O. Publications, 4 route des Morillons, CH-1211 Geneva 22, Switzerland, (Telephone in U.S. (202) 653-7652), (Fax in U.S. (202) 653-7687), www.ilo.org; *Yearbook of Labour Statistics 2006.*

The World Bank, 1818 H Street, NW, Washington, DC 20433, (202) 473-1000, Fax: (202) 477-6391, www.worldbank.org; *Iran, Islamic Republic of.*

IRAN - WALNUT PRODUCTION

See IRAN - CROPS

IRAN - WEATHER

See IRAN - CLIMATE

IRAN - WELFARE STATE

International Monetary Fund (IMF), 700 Nineteenth Street, NW, Washington, DC 20431, (202) 623-7000, Fax: (202) 623-4661, www.imf.org; *Government Finance Statistics Yearbook (2008 Edition).*

IRAN - WHEAT PRODUCTION

See IRAN - CROPS

IRAN - WHOLESALE PRICE INDEXES

International Monetary Fund (IMF), 700 Nineteenth Street, NW, Washington, DC 20431, (202) 623-7000, Fax: (202) 623-4661, www.imf.org; *International Financial Statistics Yearbook 2007.*

United Nations Statistics Division, New York, NY 10017, (800) 253-9646, Fax: (212) 963-4116, http://unstats.un.org; *Statistical Yearbook.*

IRAN - WHOLESALE TRADE

United Nations Statistics Division, New York, NY 10017, (800) 253-9646, Fax: (212) 963-4116, http://unstats.un.org; *Statistical Yearbook.*

IRAN - WINE PRODUCTION

See IRAN - BEVERAGE INDUSTRY

IRAN - WOOD AND WOOD PULP

See IRAN - FORESTS AND FORESTRY

IRAN - WOOL PRODUCTION

See IRAN - TEXTILE INDUSTRY

IRAN - YARN PRODUCTION

See IRAN - TEXTILE INDUSTRY

IRAN - ZINC AND ZINC ORE

See IRAN - MINERAL INDUSTRIES

IRAQ - NATIONAL STATISTICAL OFFICE

Minister of Planning and Cooperative Development, Central Bureau of Statistics, PO Box 8001, Baghdad, Iraq; National Data Center.

IRAQ - PRIMARY STATISTICS SOURCES

Minister of Planning and Cooperative Development, Central Bureau of Statistics, PO Box 8001, Baghdad, Iraq; *Annual Abstract of Statistics.*

IRAQ - AGRICULTURAL MACHINERY

United Nations Statistics Division, New York, NY 10017, (800) 253-9646, Fax: (212) 963-4116, http://unstats.un.org; *Statistical Yearbook.*

IRAQ - AGRICULTURE

Economist Intelligence Unit, 111 West 57th Street, New York, NY 10019, (212) 554-0600, Fax: (212) 586-1181, www.eiu.com; *Iraq Country Report.*

Euromonitor International, Inc., 224 S. Michigan Avenue, Suite 1500, Chicago, IL 60604, (312) 922-1115, Fax: (312) 922-1157, www.euromonitor.com; *International Marketing Data and Statistics 2008* and *World Marketing Data and Statistics.*

M.E. Sharpe, 80 Business Park Drive, Armonk, NY 10504, (800) 541-6563, Fax: (914) 273-2106, www.mesharpe.com; *The Illustrated Book of World Rankings.*

Palgrave Macmillan Ltd., Houndmills, Basingstoke, Hampshire, RG21 6XS, England, (Telephone in U.S. (888) 330-8477), (Fax in U.S. (800) 672-2054), www.palgrave.com; *The Statesman's Yearbook 2008.*

Taylor and Francis Group, An Informa Business, 2 Park Square, Milton Park, Abingdon, Oxford OX14 4RN, United Kingdom, (Dial from U.S. (212) 216-7800), (Fax from U.S. (212) 564-7854), www.tandf.co.uk; *The Europa World Year Book.*

United Nations Conference on Trade and Development (UNCTAD), DC2-1120, United Nations, New York, NY 10017, (212) 963-0027, www.unctad.org; *UNCTAD Commodity Yearbook.*

United Nations Economic and Social Commission for Western Asia (ESCWA), PO Box 11-8575, Riad el-Solh Square, Beirut, Lebanon, www.escwa.un.org; *Annual Report 2006* and *Statistical Abstract of the ESCWA Region 2007.*

United Nations Food and Agricultural Organization (FAO), Viale delle Terme di Caracalla, 00100 Rome, Italy, (Dial from U.S. (202) 653-2400), (Fax from U.S. (202) 653 5760), www.fao.org; AQUASTAT; *FAO Production Yearbook 2002; FAO Trade Yearbook;* and *The State of Food and Agriculture (SOFA) 2006.*

United Nations Statistics Division, New York, NY 10017, (800) 253-9646, Fax: (212) 963-4116, http://unstats.un.org; *Statistical Yearbook.*

The World Bank, 1818 H Street, NW, Washington, DC 20433, (202) 473-1000, Fax: (202) 477-6391, www.worldbank.org; *Iraq.*

IRAQ - AIRLINES

M.E. Sharpe, 80 Business Park Drive, Armonk, NY 10504, (800) 541-6563, Fax: (914) 273-2106, www.mesharpe.com; *The Illustrated Book of World Rankings.*

Palgrave Macmillan Ltd., Houndmills, Basingstoke, Hampshire, RG21 6XS, England, (Telephone in U.S. (888) 330-8477), (Fax in U.S. (800) 672-2054), www.palgrave.com; *The Statesman's Yearbook 2008.*

Taylor and Francis Group, An Informa Business, 2 Park Square, Milton Park, Abingdon, Oxford OX14 4RN, United Kingdom, (Dial from U.S. (212) 216-7800), (Fax from U.S. (212) 564-7854), www.tandf.co.uk; *The Europa World Year Book.*

United Nations Statistics Division, New York, NY 10017, (800) 253-9646, Fax: (212) 963-4116, http://unstats.un.org; *Statistical Yearbook.*

IRAQ - AIRPORTS

Central Intelligence Agency, Office of Public Affairs, Washington, DC 20505, (703) 482-0623, Fax: (703) 482-1739, www.cia.gov; *The World Factbook.*

IRAQ - ALMOND PRODUCTION

See IRAQ - CROPS

IRAQ - ALUMINUM PRODUCTION

See IRAQ - MINERAL INDUSTRIES

IRAQ - ARMED FORCES

Central Intelligence Agency, Office of Public Affairs, Washington, DC 20505, (703) 482-0623, Fax: (703) 482-1739, www.cia.gov; *The World Factbook.*

Euromonitor International, Inc., 224 S. Michigan Avenue, Suite 1500, Chicago, IL 60604, (312) 922-1115, Fax: (312) 922-1157, www.euromonitor.com; *World Marketing Data and Statistics.*

International Institute for Strategic Studies (IISS), Arundel House, 13-15 Arundel Street, Temple Place, London WC2R 3DX, England, www.iiss.org; *The Military Balance 2007.*

Palgrave Macmillan Ltd., Houndmills, Basingstoke, Hampshire, RG21 6XS, England, (Telephone in U.S. (888) 330-8477), (Fax in U.S. (800) 672-2054), www.palgrave.com; *The Statesman's Yearbook 2008.*

U.S. Department of State (DOS), 2201 C Street NW, Washington, DC 20520, (202) 647-4000, www.state.gov; *World Military Expenditures and Arms Transfers (WMEAT).*

United Nations Statistics Division, New York, NY 10017, (800) 253-9646, Fax: (212) 963-4116, http://unstats.un.org; *Human Development Report 2006.*

IRAQ - BALANCE OF PAYMENTS

International Monetary Fund (IMF), 700 Nineteenth Street, NW, Washington, DC 20431, (202) 623-7000, Fax: (202) 623-4661, www.imf.org; *Balance of Payments Statistics Newsletter* and *Balance of Payments Statistics Yearbook 2007.*

United Nations Conference on Trade and Development (UNCTAD), DC2-1120, United Nations, New York, NY 10017, (212) 963-0027, www.unctad.org; *Handbook of Statistics 2005.*

United Nations Economic and Social Commission for Western Asia (ESCWA), PO Box 11-8575, Riad el-Solh Square, Beirut, Lebanon, www.escwa.un.org; *Annual Report 2006* and *Statistical Abstract of the ESCWA Region 2007.*

The World Bank, 1818 H Street, NW, Washington, DC 20433, (202) 473-1000, Fax: (202) 477-6391, www.worldbank.org; *Iraq.*

IRAQ - BANKS AND BANKING

Euromonitor International, Inc., 224 S. Michigan Avenue, Suite 1500, Chicago, IL 60604, (312) 922-1115, Fax: (312) 922-1157, www.euromonitor.com; *World Marketing Data and Statistics.*

International Monetary Fund (IMF), 700 Nineteenth Street, NW, Washington, DC 20431, (202) 623-7000, Fax: (202) 623-4661, www.imf.org; *International Financial Statistics Yearbook 2007.*

M.E. Sharpe, 80 Business Park Drive, Armonk, NY 10504, (800) 541-6563, Fax: (914) 273-2106, www.mesharpe.com; *The Illustrated Book of World Rankings.*

Palgrave Macmillan Ltd., Houndmills, Basingstoke, Hampshire, RG21 6XS, England, (Telephone in U.S. (888) 330-8477), (Fax in U.S. (800) 672-2054), www.palgrave.com; *The Statesman's Yearbook 2008.*

Taylor and Francis Group, An Informa Business, 2 Park Square, Milton Park, Abingdon, Oxford OX14 4RN, United Kingdom, (Dial from U.S. (212) 216-7800), (Fax from U.S. (212) 564-7854), www.tandf.co.uk; *The Europa World Year Book.*

United Nations Economic and Social Commission for Western Asia (ESCWA), PO Box 11-8575, Riad el-Solh Square, Beirut, Lebanon, www.escwa.un.org; *Annual Report 2006* and *Statistical Abstract of the ESCWA Region 2007.*

IRAQ - BARLEY PRODUCTION

See IRAQ - CROPS

IRAQ - BEVERAGE INDUSTRY

M.E. Sharpe, 80 Business Park Drive, Armonk, NY 10504, (800) 541-6563, Fax: (914) 273-2106, www.mesharpe.com; *The Illustrated Book of World Rankings.*

United Nations Statistics Division, New York, NY 10017, (800) 253-9646, Fax: (212) 963-4116, http://unstats.un.org; *Statistical Yearbook.*

IRAQ - BROADCASTING

Central Intelligence Agency, Office of Public Affairs, Washington, DC 20505, (703) 482-0623, Fax: (703) 482-1739, www.cia.gov; *The World Factbook.*

Euromonitor International, Inc., 224 S. Michigan Avenue, Suite 1500, Chicago, IL 60604, (312) 922-1115, Fax: (312) 922-1157, www.euromonitor.com; *World Marketing Data and Statistics.*

M.E. Sharpe, 80 Business Park Drive, Armonk, NY 10504, (800) 541-6563, Fax: (914) 273-2106, www.mesharpe.com; *The Illustrated Book of World Rankings.*

Palgrave Macmillan Ltd., Houndmills, Basingstoke, Hampshire, RG21 6XS, England, (Telephone in U.S. (888) 330-8477), (Fax in U.S. (800) 672-2054), www.palgrave.com; *The Statesman's Yearbook 2008.*

UNESCO Institute for Statistics, C.P. 6128 Succursale Centre-Ville, Montreal, Quebec, H3C 3J7 Canada, (Dial from U.S. (514) 343-6880), (Fax from U.S. (514) 343 6882), www.uis.unesco.org; *Statistical Tables.*

WRTH Publications Limited, PO Box 290, Oxford OX2 7FT, UK, www.wrth.com; *World Radio TV Handbook 2007.*

IRAQ - BUDGET

Central Intelligence Agency, Office of Public Affairs, Washington, DC 20505, (703) 482-0623, Fax: (703) 482-1739, www.cia.gov; *The World Factbook.*

IRAQ - CATTLE

See IRAQ - LIVESTOCK

IRAQ - CHICK PEA PRODUCTION

See IRAQ - CROPS

IRAQ - CHICKENS

See IRAQ - LIVESTOCK

IRAQ - CHILDBIRTH - STATISTICS

Central Intelligence Agency, Office of Public Affairs, Washington, DC 20505, (703) 482-0623, Fax: (703) 482-1739, www.cia.gov; *The World Factbook.*

Euromonitor International, Inc., 224 S. Michigan Avenue, Suite 1500, Chicago, IL 60604, (312) 922-1115, Fax: (312) 922-1157, www.euromonitor.com; *International Marketing Data and Statistics 2008* and *The World Economic Factbook 2008.*

M.E. Sharpe, 80 Business Park Drive, Armonk, NY 10504, (800) 541-6563, Fax: (914) 273-2106, www.mesharpe.com; *The Illustrated Book of World Rankings.*

Taylor and Francis Group, An Informa Business, 2 Park Square, Milton Park, Abingdon, Oxford OX14 4RN, United Kingdom, (Dial from U.S. (212) 216-7800), (Fax from U.S. (212) 564-7854), www.tandf.co.uk; *The Europa World Year Book.*

United Nations Statistics Division, New York, NY 10017, (800) 253-9646, Fax: (212) 963-4116, http://unstats.un.org; *Demographic Yearbook* and *Statistical Yearbook.*

World Health Organization (WHO), Avenue Appia 20, 1211 Geneve 27, Switzerland, (Telephone in U.S. (212) 331-9081), www.who.int; *World Health Report 2006.*

IRAQ - CLIMATE

M.E. Sharpe, 80 Business Park Drive, Armonk, NY 10504, (800) 541-6563, Fax: (914) 273-2106, www.mesharpe.com; *The Illustrated Book of World Rankings.*

Palgrave Macmillan Ltd., Houndmills, Basingstoke, Hampshire, RG21 6XS, England, (Telephone in U.S. (888) 330-8477), (Fax in U.S. (800) 672-2054), www.palgrave.com; *The Statesman's Yearbook 2008.*

IRAQ - COAL PRODUCTION

See IRAQ - MINERAL INDUSTRIES

IRAQ - COFFEE

See IRAQ - CROPS

IRAQ - COMMERCE

Palgrave Macmillan Ltd., Houndmills, Basingstoke, Hampshire, RG21 6XS, England, (Telephone in U.S. (888) 330-8477), (Fax in U.S. (800) 672-2054), www.palgrave.com; *The Statesman's Yearbook 2008.*

IRAQ - COMMODITY EXCHANGES

Commodity Research Bureau, 330 South Wells Street, Suite 612, Chicago, IL 60606-7110, (800) 621-5271, Fax: (312) 939-4135, www.crbtrader.com; *2006 CRB Commodity Yearbook and CD.*

International Monetary Fund (IMF), 700 Nineteenth Street, NW, Washington, DC 20431, (202) 623-7000, Fax: (202) 623-4661, www.imf.org; *IMF Primary Commodity Prices.*

United Nations Food and Agricultural Organization (FAO), Viale delle Terme di Caracalla, 00100 Rome, Italy, (Dial from U.S. (202) 653-2400), (Fax from U.S. (202) 653 5760), www.fao.org; *The State of Food and Agriculture (SOFA) 2006.*

IRAQ - COMMUNICATION AND TRAFFIC

United Nations Statistics Division, New York, NY 10017, (800) 253-9646, Fax: (212) 963-4116, http://unstats.un.org; *Statistical Yearbook.*

IRAQ - CONSTRUCTION INDUSTRY

M.E. Sharpe, 80 Business Park Drive, Armonk, NY 10504, (800) 541-6563, Fax: (914) 273-2106, www.mesharpe.com; *The Illustrated Book of World Rankings.*

United Nations Statistics Division, New York, NY 10017, (800) 253-9646, Fax: (212) 963-4116, http://unstats.un.org; *Statistical Yearbook.*

IRAQ - CONSUMER PRICE INDEXES

Taylor and Francis Group, An Informa Business, 2 Park Square, Milton Park, Abingdon, Oxford OX14 4RN, United Kingdom, (Dial from U.S. (212) 216-7800), (Fax from U.S. (212) 564-7854), www.tandf.co.uk; *The Europa World Year Book.*

United Nations Statistics Division, New York, NY 10017, (800) 253-9646, Fax: (212) 963-4116, http://unstats.un.org; *Statistical Yearbook.*

IRAQ - COPPER INDUSTRY AND TRADE

See IRAQ - MINERAL INDUSTRIES

IRAQ - CORN INDUSTRY

See IRAQ - CROPS

IRAQ - COTTON

See IRAQ - CROPS

IRAQ - CRIME

International Criminal Police Organization (INTERPOL), General Secretariat, 200 quai Charles de Gaulle, 69006 Lyon, France, www.interpol.int; *International Crime Statistics.*

Yale University Press, PO Box 209040, New Haven, CT 06520-9040, (203) 432-0960, Fax: (203) 432-0948, http://yalepress.yale.edu/yupbooks; *Violence and Crime in Cross-National Perspective.*

IRAQ - CROPS

M.E. Sharpe, 80 Business Park Drive, Armonk, NY 10504, (800) 541-6563, Fax: (914) 273-2106, www.mesharpe.com; *The Illustrated Book of World Rankings.*

Palgrave Macmillan Ltd., Houndmills, Basingstoke, Hampshire, RG21 6XS, England, (Telephone in U.S. (888) 330-8477), (Fax in U.S. (800) 672-2054), www.palgrave.com; *The Statesman's Yearbook 2008.*

Taylor and Francis Group, An Informa Business, 2 Park Square, Milton Park, Abingdon, Oxford OX14 4RN, United Kingdom, (Dial from U.S. (212) 216-7800), (Fax from U.S. (212) 564-7854), www.tandf.co.uk; *The Europa World Year Book.*

United Nations Conference on Trade and Development (UNCTAD), DC2-1120, United Nations, New York, NY 10017, (212) 963-0027, www.unctad.org; *UNCTAD Commodity Yearbook.*

United Nations Food and Agricultural Organization (FAO), Viale delle Terme di Caracalla, 00100 Rome, Italy, (Dial from U.S. (202) 653-2400), (Fax from U.S. (202) 653 5760), www.fao.org; *FAO Production Yearbook 2002* and *The State of Food and Agriculture (SOFA) 2006.*

United Nations Statistics Division, New York, NY 10017, (800) 253-9646, Fax: (212) 963-4116, http://unstats.un.org; *Statistical Yearbook.*

IRAQ - CUSTOMS ADMINISTRATION

Palgrave Macmillan Ltd., Houndmills, Basingstoke, Hampshire, RG21 6XS, England, (Telephone in U.S. (888) 330-8477), (Fax in U.S. (800) 672-2054), www.palgrave.com; *The Statesman's Yearbook 2008.*

IRAQ - DAIRY PROCESSING

M.E. Sharpe, 80 Business Park Drive, Armonk, NY 10504, (800) 541-6563, Fax: (914) 273-2106, www.mesharpe.com; *The Illustrated Book of World Rankings.*

Palgrave Macmillan Ltd., Houndmills, Basingstoke, Hampshire, RG21 6XS, England, (Telephone in U.S. (888) 330-8477), (Fax in U.S. (800) 672-2054), www.palgrave.com; *The Statesman's Yearbook 2008.*

Taylor and Francis Group, An Informa Business, 2 Park Square, Milton Park, Abingdon, Oxford OX14 4RN, United Kingdom, (Dial from U.S. (212) 216-7800), (Fax from U.S. (212) 564-7854), www.tandf.co.uk; *The Europa World Year Book.*

United Nations Food and Agricultural Organization (FAO), Viale delle Terme di Caracalla, 00100 Rome, Italy, (Dial from U.S. (202) 653-2400), (Fax from U.S. (202) 653 5760), www.fao.org; *FAO Production Yearbook 2002* and *The State of Food and Agriculture (SOFA) 2006.*

United Nations Statistics Division, New York, NY 10017, (800) 253-9646, Fax: (212) 963-4116, http://unstats.un.org; *Statistical Yearbook.*

IRAQ - DEATH RATES

See IRAQ - MORTALITY

IRAQ - DEFENSE EXPENDITURES

See IRAQ - ARMED FORCES

IRAQ - DEMOGRAPHY

Euromonitor International, Inc., 224 S. Michigan Avenue, Suite 1500, Chicago, IL 60604, (312) 922-1115, Fax: (312) 922-1157, www.euromonitor.com; *International Marketing Data and Statistics 2008; The World Economic Factbook 2008;* and *World Marketing Data and Statistics.*

M.E. Sharpe, 80 Business Park Drive, Armonk, NY 10504, (800) 541-6563, Fax: (914) 273-2106, www.mesharpe.com; *The Illustrated Book of World Rankings.*

United Nations Statistics Division, New York, NY 10017, (800) 253-9646, Fax: (212) 963-4116, http://unstats.un.org; *Human Development Report 2006.*

The World Bank, 1818 H Street, NW, Washington, DC 20433, (202) 473-1000, Fax: (202) 477-6391, www.worldbank.org; *Iraq.*

IRAQ - DIAMONDS

See IRAQ - MINERAL INDUSTRIES

IRAQ - DISPOSABLE INCOME

M.E. Sharpe, 80 Business Park Drive, Armonk, NY 10504, (800) 541-6563, Fax: (914) 273-2106, www.mesharpe.com; *The Illustrated Book of World Rankings.*

United Nations Statistics Division, New York, NY 10017, (800) 253-9646, Fax: (212) 963-4116, http://unstats.un.org; *National Accounts Statistics: Compendium of Income Distribution Statistics* and *Statistical Yearbook.*

IRAQ - DIVORCE

M.E. Sharpe, 80 Business Park Drive, Armonk, NY 10504, (800) 541-6563, Fax: (914) 273-2106, www.mesharpe.com; *The Illustrated Book of World Rankings.*

United Nations Statistics Division, New York, NY 10017, (800) 253-9646, Fax: (212) 963-4116, http://unstats.un.org; *Statistical Yearbook.*

IRAQ - ECONOMIC ASSISTANCE

United Nations Statistics Division, New York, NY 10017, (800) 253-9646, Fax: (212) 963-4116, http://unstats.un.org; *Statistical Yearbook.*

IRAQ - ECONOMIC CONDITIONS

Center for International Business Education Research (CIBER), Columbia Business School and School of International and Public Affairs, Uris Hall, Room 212, 3022 Broadway, New York, NY 10027-6902, Mr. Joshua Safier, (212) 854-4750, Fax: (212) 222-9821, www.columbia.edu/cu/ciber/; Datastream International.

Central Intelligence Agency, Office of Public Affairs, Washington, DC 20505, (703) 482-0623, Fax: (703) 482-1739, www.cia.gov; *The World Factbook.*

DSI Data Service Information, Xantener Strasse 51a, D-47495 Rheinberg, Germany, www.dsidata.com; *Campus Solution.*

Dun and Bradstreet (DB) Corporation, 103 JFK Parkway, Short Hills, NJ 07078, (973) 921-5500, www.dnb.com; *Country Report.*

Economist Intelligence Unit, 111 West 57th Street, New York, NY 10019, (212) 554-0600, Fax: (212) 586-1181, www.eiu.com; *Iraq Country Report.*

Euromonitor International, Inc., 224 S. Michigan Avenue, Suite 1500, Chicago, IL 60604, (312) 922-1115, Fax: (312) 922-1157, www.euromonitor.com; *International Marketing Data and Statistics 2008; The World Economic Factbook 2008;* and *World Marketing Data and Statistics.*

International Monetary Fund (IMF), 700 Nineteenth Street, NW, Washington, DC 20431, (202) 623-7000, Fax: (202) 623-4661, www.imf.org; *World Economic Outlook Reports.*

M.E. Sharpe, 80 Business Park Drive, Armonk, NY 10504, (800) 541-6563, Fax: (914) 273-2106, www.mesharpe.com; *The Illustrated Book of World Rankings.*

Palgrave Macmillan Ltd., Houndmills, Basingstoke, Hampshire, RG21 6XS, England, (Telephone in U.S. (888) 330-8477), (Fax in U.S. (800) 672-2054), www.palgrave.com; *The Statesman's Yearbook 2008.*

Taylor and Francis Group, An Informa Business, 2 Park Square, Milton Park, Abingdon, Oxford OX14 4RN, United Kingdom, (Dial from U.S. (212) 216-7800), (Fax from U.S. (212) 564-7854), www.tandf.co.uk; *The Europa World Year Book.*

United Nations Economic and Social Commission for Western Asia (ESCWA), PO Box 11-8575, Riad el-Solh Square, Beirut, Lebanon, www.escwa.un.org; *Annual Report 2006; Bulletin on Population and Vital Statistics in the ESCWA Region;* and *Survey of Economic and Social Developments in the ESCWA Region 2006-2007.*

United Nations Statistics Division, New York, NY 10017, (800) 253-9646, Fax: (212) 963-4116, http://unstats.un.org; *World Statistics Pocketbook.*

The World Bank, 1818 H Street, NW, Washington, DC 20433, (202) 473-1000, Fax: (202) 477-6391, www.worldbank.org; *Global Economic Monitor (GEM); Global Economic Prospects 2008; Iraq;* and *The World Bank Atlas 2003-2004.*

IRAQ - EDUCATION

Euromonitor International, Inc., 224 S. Michigan Avenue, Suite 1500, Chicago, IL 60604, (312) 922-1115, Fax: (312) 922-1157, www.euromonitor.com; *International Marketing Data and Statistics 2008* and *World Marketing Data and Statistics.*

M.E. Sharpe, 80 Business Park Drive, Armonk, NY 10504, (800) 541-6563, Fax: (914) 273-2106, www.mesharpe.com; *The Illustrated Book of World Rankings.*

Palgrave Macmillan Ltd., Houndmills, Basingstoke, Hampshire, RG21 6XS, England, (Telephone in U.S. (888) 330-8477), (Fax in U.S. (800) 672-2054), www.palgrave.com; *The Statesman's Yearbook 2008.*

Taylor and Francis Group, An Informa Business, 2 Park Square, Milton Park, Abingdon, Oxford OX14 4RN, United Kingdom, (Dial from U.S. (212) 216-7800), (Fax from U.S. (212) 564-7854), www.tandf.co.uk; *The Europa World Year Book.*

UNESCO Institute for Statistics, C.P. 6128 Succursale Centre-Ville, Montreal, Quebec, H3C 3J7 Canada, (Dial from U.S. (514) 343-6880), (Fax from U.S. (514) 343 6882), www.uis.unesco.org; *Statistical Tables.*

United Nations Economic and Social Commission for Western Asia (ESCWA), PO Box 11-8575, Riad el-Solh Square, Beirut, Lebanon, www.escwa.un.org; *Annual Report 2006* and *Statistical Abstract of the ESCWA Region 2007.*

United Nations Statistics Division, New York, NY 10017, (800) 253-9646, Fax: (212) 963-4116, http://unstats.un.org; *Human Development Report 2006.*

The World Bank, 1818 H Street, NW, Washington, DC 20433, (202) 473-1000, Fax: (202) 477-6391, www.worldbank.org; *Iraq.*

IRAQ - EGGPLANT PRODUCTION

See IRAQ - CROPS

IRAQ - ELECTRICITY

M.E. Sharpe, 80 Business Park Drive, Armonk, NY 10504, (800) 541-6563, Fax: (914) 273-2106, www.mesharpe.com; *The Illustrated Book of World Rankings.*

Organisation for Economic Cooperation and Development (OECD), 2 rue Andre Pascal, F-75775 Paris Cedex 16, France, (Telephone in U.S. (202) 785-6323), (Fax in U.S. (202) 785-0350), www.oecd.org; *World Energy Outlook 2007.*

Palgrave Macmillan Ltd., Houndmills, Basingstoke, Hampshire, RG21 6XS, England, (Telephone in U.S.

(888) 330-8477), (Fax in U.S. (800) 672-2054), www.palgrave.com; *The Statesman's Yearbook 2008.*

U.S. Department of Energy (DOE), Energy Information Administration (EIA), 1000 Independence Avenue, SW, Washington, DC 20585, (202) 586-8800, www.eia.doe.gov; *International Energy Annual 2004* and *International Energy Outlook 2006.*

United Nations Statistics Division, New York, NY 10017, (800) 253-9646, Fax: (212) 963-4116, http://unstats.un.org; *Human Development Report 2006* and *Statistical Yearbook.*

IRAQ - EMPLOYMENT

Euromonitor International, Inc., 224 S. Michigan Avenue, Suite 1500, Chicago, IL 60604, (312) 922-1115, Fax: (312) 922-1157, www.euromonitor.com; *International Marketing Data and Statistics 2008.*

International Labour Office, I.L.O. Publications, 4 route des Morillons, CH-1211 Geneva 22, Switzerland, (Telephone in U.S. (202) 653-7652), (Fax in U.S. (202) 653-7687), www.ilo.org; *Yearbook of Labour Statistics 2006.*

M.E. Sharpe, 80 Business Park Drive, Armonk, NY 10504, (800) 541-6563, Fax: (914) 273-2106, www.mesharpe.com; *The Illustrated Book of World Rankings.*

United Nations Economic and Social Commission for Western Asia (ESCWA), PO Box 11-8575, Riad el-Solh Square, Beirut, Lebanon, www.escwa.un.org; *Annual Report 2006* and *Statistical Abstract of the ESCWA Region 2007.*

United Nations Statistics Division, New York, NY 10017, (800) 253-9646, Fax: (212) 963-4116, http://unstats.un.org; *Bulletin of Industrial Statistics for the Arab Countries* and *Statistical Yearbook.*

The World Bank, 1818 H Street, NW, Washington, DC 20433, (202) 473-1000, Fax: (202) 477-6391, www.worldbank.org; *Iraq.*

IRAQ - ENERGY INDUSTRIES

Enerdata, 10 Rue Royale, 75008 Paris, France, www.enerdata.fr; *Global Energy Market Data.*

United Nations Statistics Division, New York, NY 10017, (800) 253-9646, Fax: (212) 963-4116, http://unstats.un.org; *Statistical Yearbook.*

IRAQ - ENVIRONMENTAL CONDITIONS

DSI Data Service Information, Xantener Strasse 51a, D-47495 Rheinberg, Germany, www.dsidata.com; *Campus Solution* and *DSI's Global Environmental Database.*

Economist Intelligence Unit, 111 West 57th Street, New York, NY 10019, (212) 554-0600, Fax: (212) 586-1181, www.eiu.com; *Iraq Country Report.*

United Nations Statistics Division, New York, NY 10017, (800) 253-9646, Fax: (212) 963-4116, http://unstats.un.org; *World Statistics Pocketbook.*

IRAQ - EXPORTS

Central Intelligence Agency, Office of Public Affairs, Washington, DC 20505, (703) 482-0623, Fax: (703) 482-1739, www.cia.gov; *The World Factbook.*

Economist Intelligence Unit, 111 West 57th Street, New York, NY 10019, (212) 554-0600, Fax: (212) 586-1181, www.eiu.com; *Iraq Country Report.*

Euromonitor International, Inc., 224 S. Michigan Avenue, Suite 1500, Chicago, IL 60604, (312) 922-1115, Fax: (312) 922-1157, www.euromonitor.com; *International Marketing Data and Statistics 2008.*

International Monetary Fund (IMF), 700 Nineteenth Street, NW, Washington, DC 20431, (202) 623-7000, Fax: (202) 623-4661, www.imf.org; *Direction of Trade Statistics Yearbook 2007* and *International Financial Statistics Yearbook 2007.*

Organization of Petroleum Exporting Countries (OPEC), Obere Donaustrasse 93, A-1020, Vienna, Austria, www.opec.org; *Annual Statistical Bulletin 2006.*

Palgrave Macmillan Ltd., Houndmills, Basingstoke, Hampshire, RG21 6XS, England, (Telephone in U.S. (888) 330-8477), (Fax in U.S. (800) 672-2054), www.palgrave.com; *The Statesman's Yearbook 2008.*

Taylor and Francis Group, An Informa Business, 2 Park Square, Milton Park, Abingdon, Oxford OX14 4RN, United Kingdom, (Dial from U.S. (212) 216-7800), (Fax from U.S. (212) 564-7854), www.tandf.co.uk; *The Europa World Year Book.*

United Nations Conference on Trade and Development (UNCTAD), DC2-1120, United Nations, New York, NY 10017, (212) 963-0027, www.unctad.org; *Handbook of Statistics 2005.*

United Nations Economic and Social Commission for Western Asia (ESCWA), PO Box 11-8575, Riad el-Solh Square, Beirut, Lebanon, www.escwa.un.org; *Annual Report 2006* and *Statistical Abstract of the ESCWA Region 2007.*

United Nations Food and Agricultural Organization (FAO), Viale delle Terme di Caracalla, 00100 Rome, Italy, (Dial from U.S. (202) 653-2400), (Fax from U.S. (202) 653 5760), www.fao.org; *The State of Food and Agriculture (SOFA) 2006.*

United Nations Statistics Division, New York, NY 10017, (800) 253-9646, Fax: (212) 963-4116, http://unstats.un.org; *Bulletin of Industrial Statistics for the Arab Countries.*

IRAQ - FERTILITY, HUMAN

Central Intelligence Agency, Office of Public Affairs, Washington, DC 20505, (703) 482-0623, Fax: (703) 482-1739, www.cia.gov; *The World Factbook.*

M.E. Sharpe, 80 Business Park Drive, Armonk, NY 10504, (800) 541-6563, Fax: (914) 273-2106, www.mesharpe.com; *The Illustrated Book of World Rankings.*

United Nations Statistics Division, New York, NY 10017, (800) 253-9646, Fax: (212) 963-4116, http://unstats.un.org; *Human Development Report 2006.*

The World Bank, 1818 H Street, NW, Washington, DC 20433, (202) 473-1000, Fax: (202) 477-6391, www.worldbank.org; *The World Bank Atlas 2003-2004.*

IRAQ - FERTILIZER INDUSTRY

United Nations Food and Agricultural Organization (FAO), Viale delle Terme di Caracalla, 00100 Rome, Italy, (Dial from U.S. (202) 653-2400), (Fax from U.S. (202) 653 5760), www.fao.org; *FAO Fertilizer Yearbook* and *The State of Food and Agriculture (SOFA) 2006.*

United Nations Statistics Division, New York, NY 10017, (800) 253-9646, Fax: (212) 963-4116, http://unstats.un.org; *Statistical Yearbook.*

IRAQ - FETAL MORTALITY

See IRAQ - MORTALITY

IRAQ - FINANCE

International Monetary Fund (IMF), 700 Nineteenth Street, NW, Washington, DC 20431, (202) 623-7000, Fax: (202) 623-4661, www.imf.org; *International Financial Statistics Yearbook 2007.*

Taylor and Francis Group, An Informa Business, 2 Park Square, Milton Park, Abingdon, Oxford OX14 4RN, United Kingdom, (Dial from U.S. (212) 216-7800), (Fax from U.S. (212) 564-7854), www.tandf.co.uk; *The Europa World Year Book.*

United Nations Economic and Social Commission for Western Asia (ESCWA), PO Box 11-8575, Riad el-Solh Square, Beirut, Lebanon, www.escwa.un.org; *Annual Report 2006* and *Statistical Abstract of the ESCWA Region 2007.*

United Nations Statistics Division, New York, NY 10017, (800) 253-9646, Fax: (212) 963-4116, http://unstats.un.org; *National Accounts Statistics: Compendium of Income Distribution Statistics.*

The World Bank, 1818 H Street, NW, Washington, DC 20433, (202) 473-1000, Fax: (202) 477-6391, www.worldbank.org; *Iraq.*

IRAQ - FINANCE, PUBLIC

Bernan Essential Government Publications, 4611-F Assembly Drive, Lanham MD, 20706-4391, (301) 459-2255, Fax: (800) 865-3450, www.bernan.com; *National Accounts Statistics.*

Economist Intelligence Unit, 111 West 57th Street, New York, NY 10019, (212) 554-0600, Fax: (212) 586-1181, www.eiu.com; *Iraq Country Report.*

International Monetary Fund (IMF), 700 Nineteenth Street, NW, Washington, DC 20431, (202) 623-7000, Fax: (202) 623-4661, www.imf.org; *International Financial Statistics; International Financial Statistics Online Service;* and *International Financial Statistics Yearbook 2007.*

M.E. Sharpe, 80 Business Park Drive, Armonk, NY 10504, (800) 541-6563, Fax: (914) 273-2106, www.mesharpe.com; *The Illustrated Book of World Rankings.*

Palgrave Macmillan Ltd., Houndmills, Basingstoke, Hampshire, RG21 6XS, England, (Telephone in U.S. (888) 330-8477), (Fax in U.S. (800) 672-2054), www.palgrave.com; *The Statesman's Yearbook 2008.*

Taylor and Francis Group, An Informa Business, 2 Park Square, Milton Park, Abingdon, Oxford OX14 4RN, United Kingdom, (Dial from U.S. (212) 216-7800), (Fax from U.S. (212) 564-7854), www.tandf.co.uk; *The Europa World Year Book.*

United Nations Economic and Social Commission for Western Asia (ESCWA), PO Box 11-8575, Riad el-Solh Square, Beirut, Lebanon, www.escwa.un.org; *Annual Report 2006* and *Statistical Abstract of the ESCWA Region 2007.*

The World Bank, 1818 H Street, NW, Washington, DC 20433, (202) 473-1000, Fax: (202) 477-6391, www.worldbank.org; *Iraq.*

IRAQ - FISHERIES

M.E. Sharpe, 80 Business Park Drive, Armonk, NY 10504, (800) 541-6563, Fax: (914) 273-2106, www.mesharpe.com; *The Illustrated Book of World Rankings.*

Palgrave Macmillan Ltd., Houndmills, Basingstoke, Hampshire, RG21 6XS, England, (Telephone in U.S. (888) 330-8477), (Fax in U.S. (800) 672-2054), www.palgrave.com; *The Statesman's Yearbook 2008.*

Taylor and Francis Group, An Informa Business, 2 Park Square, Milton Park, Abingdon, Oxford OX14 4RN, United Kingdom, (Dial from U.S. (212) 216-7800), (Fax from U.S. (212) 564-7854), www.tandf.co.uk; *The Europa World Year Book.*

United Nations Conference on Trade and Development (UNCTAD), DC2-1120, United Nations, New York, NY 10017, (212) 963-0027, www.unctad.org; *UNCTAD Commodity Yearbook.*

United Nations Economic and Social Commission for Western Asia (ESCWA), PO Box 11-8575, Riad el-Solh Square, Beirut, Lebanon, www.escwa.un.org; *Annual Report 2006* and *Statistical Abstract of the ESCWA Region 2007.*

United Nations Food and Agricultural Organization (FAO), Viale delle Terme di Caracalla, 00100 Rome, Italy, (Dial from U.S. (202) 653-2400), (Fax from U.S. (202) 653 5760), www.fao.org; *FAO Yearbook of Fishery Statistics;* Fishery Databases; FISHSTAT Database. Subjects covered include: Aquaculture production, capture production, fishery commodities; and *The State of Food and Agriculture (SOFA) 2006.*

United Nations Statistics Division, New York, NY 10017, (800) 253-9646, Fax: (212) 963-4116, http://unstats.un.org; *Statistical Yearbook.*

The World Bank, 1818 H Street, NW, Washington, DC 20433, (202) 473-1000, Fax: (202) 477-6391, www.worldbank.org; *Iraq.*

IRAQ - FLOUR INDUSTRY

United Nations Statistics Division, New York, NY 10017, (800) 253-9646, Fax: (212) 963-4116, http://unstats.un.org; *Statistical Yearbook.*

IRAQ - FOOD

United Nations Conference on Trade and Development (UNCTAD), DC2-1120, United Nations, New

York, NY 10017, (212) 963-0027, www.unctad.org; *UNCTAD Commodity Yearbook.*

United Nations Food and Agricultural Organization (FAO), Viale delle Terme di Caracalla, 00100 Rome, Italy, (Dial from U.S. (202) 653-2400), (Fax from U.S. (202) 653 5760), www.fao.org; *FAO Production Yearbook 2002* and *The State of Food and Agriculture (SOFA) 2006.*

United Nations Statistics Division, New York, NY 10017, (800) 253-9646, Fax: (212) 963-4116, http://unstats.un.org; *Human Development Report 2006.*

IRAQ - FOREIGN EXCHANGE RATES

Central Intelligence Agency, Office of Public Affairs, Washington, DC 20505, (703) 482-0623, Fax: (703) 482-1739, www.cia.gov; *The World Factbook.*

Euromonitor International, Inc., 224 S. Michigan Avenue, Suite 1500, Chicago, IL 60604, (312) 922-1115, Fax: (312) 922-1157, www.euromonitor.com; *International Marketing Data and Statistics 2008* and *The World Economic Factbook 2008.*

International Monetary Fund (IMF), 700 Nineteenth Street, NW, Washington, DC 20431, (202) 623-7000, Fax: (202) 623-4661, www.imf.org; *International Financial Statistics Yearbook 2007.*

Organization of Petroleum Exporting Countries (OPEC), Obere Donaustrasse 93, A-1020, Vienna, Austria, www.opec.org; *Annual Statistical Bulletin 2006.*

Taylor and Francis Group, An Informa Business, 2 Park Square, Milton Park, Abingdon, Oxford OX14 4RN, United Kingdom, (Dial from U.S. (212) 216-7800), (Fax from U.S. (212) 564-7854), www.tandf.co.uk; *The Europa World Year Book.*

United Nations Statistics Division, New York, NY 10017, (800) 253-9646, Fax: (212) 963-4116, http://unstats.un.org; *Bulletin of Industrial Statistics for the Arab Countries; Statistical Yearbook;* and *World Statistics Pocketbook.*

IRAQ - FORESTS AND FORESTRY

M.E. Sharpe, 80 Business Park Drive, Armonk, NY 10504, (800) 541-6563, Fax: (914) 273-2106, www.mesharpe.com; *The Illustrated Book of World Rankings.*

Taylor and Francis Group, An Informa Business, 2 Park Square, Milton Park, Abingdon, Oxford OX14 4RN, United Kingdom, (Dial from U.S. (212) 216-7800), (Fax from U.S. (212) 564-7854), www.tandf.co.uk; *The Europa World Year Book.*

UNESCO Institute for Statistics, C.P. 6128 Succursale Centre-Ville, Montreal, Quebec, H3C 3J7 Canada, (Dial from U.S. (514) 343-6880), (Fax from U.S. (514) 343 6882), www.uis.unesco.org; *Statistical Tables.*

United Nations Conference on Trade and Development (UNCTAD), DC2-1120, United Nations, New York, NY 10017, (212) 963-0027, www.unctad.org; *UNCTAD Commodity Yearbook.*

United Nations Food and Agricultural Organization (FAO), Viale delle Terme di Caracalla, 00100 Rome, Italy, (Dial from U.S. (202) 653-2400), (Fax from U.S. (202) 653 5760), www.fao.org; *FAO Yearbook of Forest Products* and *The State of Food and Agriculture (SOFA) 2006.*

United Nations Statistics Division, New York, NY 10017, (800) 253-9646, Fax: (212) 963-4116, http://unstats.un.org; *Statistical Yearbook.*

The World Bank, 1818 H Street, NW, Washington, DC 20433, (202) 473-1000, Fax: (202) 477-6391, www.worldbank.org; *Iraq.*

IRAQ - GAS PRODUCTION

See IRAQ - MINERAL INDUSTRIES

IRAQ - GEOGRAPHIC INFORMATION SYSTEMS

M.E. Sharpe, 80 Business Park Drive, Armonk, NY 10504, (800) 541-6563, Fax: (914) 273-2106, www.mesharpe.com; *The Illustrated Book of World Rankings.*

IRAQ - GOLD INDUSTRY

International Monetary Fund (IMF), 700 Nineteenth Street, NW, Washington, DC 20431, (202) 623-7000, Fax: (202) 623-4661, www.imf.org; *International Financial Statistics Yearbook 2007.*

United Nations Statistics Division, New York, NY 10017, (800) 253-9646, Fax: (212) 963-4116, http://unstats.un.org; *Statistical Yearbook.*

IRAQ - GOLD PRODUCTION

See IRAQ - MINERAL INDUSTRIES

IRAQ - GREEN PEPPER AND CHILIE PRODUCTION

See IRAQ - CROPS

IRAQ - GROSS DOMESTIC PRODUCT

Economist Intelligence Unit, 111 West 57th Street, New York, NY 10019, (212) 554-0600, Fax: (212) 586-1181, www.eiu.com; *Iraq Country Report.*

Euromonitor International, Inc., 224 S. Michigan Avenue, Suite 1500, Chicago, IL 60604, (312) 922-1115, Fax: (312) 922-1157, www.euromonitor.com; *International Marketing Data and Statistics 2008* and *The World Economic Factbook 2008.*

M.E. Sharpe, 80 Business Park Drive, Armonk, NY 10504, (800) 541-6563, Fax: (914) 273-2106, www.mesharpe.com; *The Illustrated Book of World Rankings.*

Taylor and Francis Group, An Informa Business, 2 Park Square, Milton Park, Abingdon, Oxford OX14 4RN, United Kingdom, (Dial from U.S. (212) 216-7800), (Fax from U.S. (212) 564-7854), www.tandf.co.uk; *The Europa World Year Book.*

United Nations Economic and Social Commission for Western Asia (ESCWA), PO Box 11-8575, Riad el-Solh Square, Beirut, Lebanon, www.escwa.un.org; *Annual Report 2006* and *Statistical Abstract of the ESCWA Region 2007.*

United Nations Statistics Division, New York, NY 10017, (800) 253-9646, Fax: (212) 963-4116, http://unstats.un.org; *Bulletin of Industrial Statistics for the Arab Countries; Human Development Report 2006; National Accounts Statistics: Compendium of Income Distribution Statistics;* and *Statistical Yearbook.*

IRAQ - GROSS NATIONAL PRODUCT

Euromonitor International, Inc., 224 S. Michigan Avenue, Suite 1500, Chicago, IL 60604, (312) 922-1115, Fax: (312) 922-1157, www.euromonitor.com; *International Marketing Data and Statistics 2008.*

M.E. Sharpe, 80 Business Park Drive, Armonk, NY 10504, (800) 541-6563, Fax: (914) 273-2106, www.mesharpe.com; *The Illustrated Book of World Rankings.*

Organization of Petroleum Exporting Countries (OPEC), Obere Donaustrasse 93, A-1020, Vienna, Austria, www.opec.org; *Annual Statistical Bulletin 2006.*

Palgrave Macmillan Ltd., Houndmills, Basingstoke, Hampshire, RG21 6XS, England, (Telephone in U.S. (888) 330-8477), (Fax in U.S. (800) 672-2054), www.palgrave.com; *The Statesman's Yearbook 2008.*

Taylor and Francis Group, An Informa Business, 2 Park Square, Milton Park, Abingdon, Oxford OX14 4RN, United Kingdom, (Dial from U.S. (212) 216-7800), (Fax from U.S. (212) 564-7854), www.tandf.co.uk; *The Europa World Year Book.*

U.S. Department of State (DOS), 2201 C Street NW, Washington, DC 20520, (202) 647-4000, www.state.gov; *World Military Expenditures and Arms Transfers (WMEAT).*

United Nations Statistics Division, New York, NY 10017, (800) 253-9646, Fax: (212) 963-4116, http://unstats.un.org; *Statistical Yearbook.*

The World Bank, 1818 H Street, NW, Washington, DC 20433, (202) 473-1000, Fax: (202) 477-6391, www.worldbank.org; *The World Bank Atlas 2003-2004.*

IRAQ - HIDES AND SKINS INDUSTRY

United Nations Food and Agricultural Organization (FAO), Viale delle Terme di Caracalla, 00100 Rome, Italy, (Dial from U.S. (202) 653-2400), (Fax from U.S. (202) 653 5760), www.fao.org; *FAO Production Yearbook 2002.*

IRAQ - HOUSING

Euromonitor International, Inc., 224 S. Michigan Avenue, Suite 1500, Chicago, IL 60604, (312) 922-1115, Fax: (312) 922-1157, www.euromonitor.com; *World Marketing Data and Statistics.*

M.E. Sharpe, 80 Business Park Drive, Armonk, NY 10504, (800) 541-6563, Fax: (914) 273-2106, www.mesharpe.com; *The Illustrated Book of World Rankings.*

IRAQ - ILLITERATE PERSONS

Euromonitor International, Inc., 224 S. Michigan Avenue, Suite 1500, Chicago, IL 60604, (312) 922-1115, Fax: (312) 922-1157, www.euromonitor.com; *The World Economic Factbook 2008.*

UNESCO Institute for Statistics, C.P. 6128 Succursale Centre-Ville, Montreal, Quebec, H3C 3J7 Canada, (Dial from U.S. (514) 343-6880), (Fax from U.S. (514) 343 6882), www.uis.unesco.org; *Statistical Tables.*

United Nations Statistics Division, New York, NY 10017, (800) 253-9646, Fax: (212) 963-4116, http://unstats.un.org; *Human Development Report 2006.*

IRAQ - IMPORTS

Central Intelligence Agency, Office of Public Affairs, Washington, DC 20505, (703) 482-0623, Fax: (703) 482-1739, www.cia.gov; *The World Factbook.*

Economist Intelligence Unit, 111 West 57th Street, New York, NY 10019, (212) 554-0600, Fax: (212) 586-1181, www.eiu.com; *Iraq Country Report.*

Euromonitor International, Inc., 224 S. Michigan Avenue, Suite 1500, Chicago, IL 60604, (312) 922-1115, Fax: (312) 922-1157, www.euromonitor.com; *International Marketing Data and Statistics 2008* and *The World Economic Factbook 2008.*

International Monetary Fund (IMF), 700 Nineteenth Street, NW, Washington, DC 20431, (202) 623-7000, Fax: (202) 623-4661, www.imf.org; *Direction of Trade Statistics Yearbook 2007* and *International Financial Statistics Yearbook 2007.*

Palgrave Macmillan Ltd., Houndmills, Basingstoke, Hampshire, RG21 6XS, England, (Telephone in U.S. (888) 330-8477), (Fax in U.S. (800) 672-2054), www.palgrave.com; *The Statesman's Yearbook 2008.*

Taylor and Francis Group, An Informa Business, 2 Park Square, Milton Park, Abingdon, Oxford OX14 4RN, United Kingdom, (Dial from U.S. (212) 216-7800), (Fax from U.S. (212) 564-7854), www.tandf.co.uk; *The Europa World Year Book.*

United Nations Conference on Trade and Development (UNCTAD), DC2-1120, United Nations, New York, NY 10017, (212) 963-0027, www.unctad.org; *Handbook of Statistics 2005.*

United Nations Economic and Social Commission for Western Asia (ESCWA), PO Box 11-8575, Riad el-Solh Square, Beirut, Lebanon, www.escwa.un.org; *Annual Report 2006* and *Statistical Abstract of the ESCWA Region 2007.*

United Nations Food and Agricultural Organization (FAO), Viale delle Terme di Caracalla, 00100 Rome, Italy, (Dial from U.S. (202) 653-2400), (Fax from U.S. (202) 653 5760), www.fao.org; *The State of Food and Agriculture (SOFA) 2006.*

United Nations Statistics Division, New York, NY 10017, (800) 253-9646, Fax: (212) 963-4116, http://unstats.un.org; *Bulletin of Industrial Statistics for the Arab Countries.*

IRAQ - INDUSTRIAL PRODUCTIVITY

Euromonitor International, Inc., 224 S. Michigan Avenue, Suite 1500, Chicago, IL 60604, (312) 922-1115, Fax: (312) 922-1157, www.euromonitor.com; *International Marketing Data and Statistics 2008.*

M.E. Sharpe, 80 Business Park Drive, Armonk, NY 10504, (800) 541-6563, Fax: (914) 273-2106, www.mesharpe.com; *The Illustrated Book of World Rankings.*

IRAQ - INDUSTRIAL PROPERTY

United Nations Statistics Division, New York, NY 10017, (800) 253-9646, Fax: (212) 963-4116, http://unstats.un.org; *Statistical Yearbook.*

IRAQ - INDUSTRIES

Central Intelligence Agency, Office of Public Affairs, Washington, DC 20505, (703) 482-0623, Fax: (703) 482-1739, www.cia.gov; *The World Factbook.*

Economist Intelligence Unit, 111 West 57th Street, New York, NY 10019, (212) 554-0600, Fax: (212) 586-1181, www.eiu.com; *Iraq Country Report.*

Euromonitor International, Inc., 224 S. Michigan Avenue, Suite 1500, Chicago, IL 60604, (312) 922-1115, Fax: (312) 922-1157, www.euromonitor.com; *The World Economic Factbook 2008* and *World Marketing Data and Statistics.*

International Labour Office, I.L.O. Publications, 4 route des Morillons, CH-1211 Geneva 22, Switzerland, (Telephone in U.S. (202) 653-7652), (Fax in U.S. (202) 653-7687), www.ilo.org; *Yearbook of Labour Statistics 2006.*

M.E. Sharpe, 80 Business Park Drive, Armonk, NY 10504, (800) 541-6563, Fax: (914) 273-2106, www.mesharpe.com; *The Illustrated Book of World Rankings.*

Palgrave Macmillan Ltd., Houndmills, Basingstoke, Hampshire, RG21 6XS, England, (Telephone in U.S. (888) 330-8477), (Fax in U.S. (800) 672-2054), www.palgrave.com; *The Statesman's Yearbook 2008.*

Taylor and Francis Group, An Informa Business, 2 Park Square, Milton Park, Abingdon, Oxford OX14 4RN, United Kingdom, (Dial from U.S. (212) 216-7800), (Fax from U.S. (212) 564-7854), www.tandf.co.uk; *The Europa World Year Book.*

United Nations Industrial Development Organization (UNIDO), 1 United Nations Plaza, New York, NY 10017, (212) 963 6890, Fax: (212) 963-7904, http://unido.org; Industrial Statistics Database 2008 (INDSTAT) and *The International Yearbook of Industrial Statistics 2008.*

United Nations Statistics Division, New York, NY 10017, (800) 253-9646, Fax: (212) 963-4116, http://unstats.un.org; *Bulletin of Industrial Statistics for the Arab Countries; 2004 Industrial Commodity Statistics Yearbook;* and *Statistical Yearbook.*

The World Bank, 1818 H Street, NW, Washington, DC 20433, (202) 473-1000, Fax: (202) 477-6391, www.worldbank.org; *Iraq.*

IRAQ - INFANT AND MATERNAL MORTALITY

See IRAQ - MORTALITY

IRAQ - INORGANIC ACIDS

United Nations Statistics Division, New York, NY 10017, (800) 253-9646, Fax: (212) 963-4116, http://unstats.un.org; *Statistical Yearbook.*

IRAQ - INTERNATIONAL LIQUIDITY

International Monetary Fund (IMF), 700 Nineteenth Street, NW, Washington, DC 20431, (202) 623-7000, Fax: (202) 623-4661, www.imf.org; *International Financial Statistics Yearbook 2007.*

IRAQ - INTERNATIONAL TRADE

Economist Intelligence Unit, 111 West 57th Street, New York, NY 10019, (212) 554-0600, Fax: (212) 586-1181, www.eiu.com; *Iraq Country Report.*

Euromonitor International, Inc., 224 S. Michigan Avenue, Suite 1500, Chicago, IL 60604, (312) 922-1115, Fax: (312) 922-1157, www.euromonitor.com; *International Marketing Data and Statistics 2008; The World Economic Factbook 2008;* and *World Marketing Data and Statistics.*

International Monetary Fund (IMF), 700 Nineteenth Street, NW, Washington, DC 20431, (202) 623-7000, Fax: (202) 623-4661, www.imf.org; *International Financial Statistics Yearbook 2007.*

M.E. Sharpe, 80 Business Park Drive, Armonk, NY 10504, (800) 541-6563, Fax: (914) 273-2106, www.mesharpe.com; *The Illustrated Book of World Rankings.*

Palgrave Macmillan Ltd., Houndmills, Basingstoke, Hampshire, RG21 6XS, England, (Telephone in U.S. (888) 330-8477), (Fax in U.S. (800) 672-2054), www.palgrave.com; *The Statesman's Yearbook 2008.*

Taylor and Francis Group, An Informa Business, 2 Park Square, Milton Park, Abingdon, Oxford OX14 4RN, United Kingdom, (Dial from U.S. (212) 216-7800), (Fax from U.S. (212) 564-7854), www.tandf.co.uk; *The Europa World Year Book.*

United Nations Conference on Trade and Development (UNCTAD), DC2-1120, United Nations, New York, NY 10017, (212) 963-0027, www.unctad.org; *UNCTAD Commodity Yearbook.*

United Nations Economic and Social Commission for Western Asia (ESCWA), PO Box 11-8575, Riad el-Solh Square, Beirut, Lebanon, www.escwa.un.org; *Annual Report 2006* and *Statistical Abstract of the ESCWA Region 2007.*

United Nations Food and Agricultural Organization (FAO), Viale delle Terme di Caracalla, 00100 Rome, Italy, (Dial from U.S. (202) 653-2400), (Fax from U.S. (202) 653 5760), www.fao.org; *FAO Trade Yearbook* and *The State of Food and Agriculture (SOFA) 2006.*

United Nations Statistics Division, New York, NY 10017, (800) 253-9646, Fax: (212) 963-4116, http://unstats.un.org; *Bulletin of Industrial Statistics for the Arab Countries; International Trade Statistics Yearbook;* and *Statistical Yearbook.*

The World Bank, 1818 H Street, NW, Washington, DC 20433, (202) 473-1000, Fax: (202) 477-6391, www.worldbank.org; *Iraq.*

World Trade Organization (WTO), Centre William Rappard, Rue de Lausanne 154, CH-1211 Geneva 21, Switzerland, www.wto.org; *International Trade Statistics 2006.*

IRAQ - INTERNET USERS

International Telecommunication Union (ITU), Place des Nations, 1211 Geneva 20, Switzerland, www.itu.int; *World Telecommunication/ICT Indicators Database on CD-ROM; World Telecommunication/ICT Indicators Database Online;* and *Yearbook of Statistics - Telecommunication Services (Chronological Time Series 1997-2006).*

The World Bank, 1818 H Street, NW, Washington, DC 20433, (202) 473-1000, Fax: (202) 477-6391, www.worldbank.org; *Iraq.*

IRAQ - IRON AND IRON ORE PRODUCTION

See IRAQ - MINERAL INDUSTRIES

IRAQ - IRRIGATION

Euromonitor International, Inc., 224 S. Michigan Avenue, Suite 1500, Chicago, IL 60604, (312) 922-1115, Fax: (312) 922-1157, www.euromonitor.com; *International Marketing Data and Statistics 2008.*

IRAQ - LABOR

Central Intelligence Agency, Office of Public Affairs, Washington, DC 20505, (703) 482-0623, Fax: (703) 482-1739, www.cia.gov; *The World Factbook.*

Euromonitor International, Inc., 224 S. Michigan Avenue, Suite 1500, Chicago, IL 60604, (312) 922-1115, Fax: (312) 922-1157, www.euromonitor.com; *International Marketing Data and Statistics 2008* and *World Marketing Data and Statistics.*

International Labour Office, I.L.O. Publications, 4 route des Morillons, CH-1211 Geneva 22, Switzerland, (Telephone in U.S. (202) 653-7652), (Fax in U.S. (202) 653-7687), www.ilo.org; *Yearbook of Labour Statistics 2006.*

M.E. Sharpe, 80 Business Park Drive, Armonk, NY 10504, (800) 541-6563, Fax: (914) 273-2106, www.mesharpe.com; *The Illustrated Book of World Rankings.*

Palgrave Macmillan Ltd., Houndmills, Basingstoke, Hampshire, RG21 6XS, England, (Telephone in U.S. (888) 330-8477), (Fax in U.S. (800) 672-2054), www.palgrave.com; *The Statesman's Yearbook 2008.*

Taylor and Francis Group, An Informa Business, 2 Park Square, Milton Park, Abingdon, Oxford OX14 4RN, United Kingdom, (Dial from U.S. (212) 216-7800), (Fax from U.S. (212) 564-7854), www.tandf.co.uk; *The Europa World Year Book.*

United Nations Economic and Social Commission for Western Asia (ESCWA), PO Box 11-8575, Riad el-Solh Square, Beirut, Lebanon, www.escwa.un.org; *Annual Report 2006* and *Statistical Abstract of the ESCWA Region 2007.*

United Nations Food and Agricultural Organization (FAO), Viale delle Terme di Caracalla, 00100 Rome, Italy, (Dial from U.S. (202) 653-2400), (Fax from U.S. (202) 653 5760), www.fao.org; *The State of Food and Agriculture (SOFA) 2006.*

United Nations Statistics Division, New York, NY 10017, (800) 253-9646, Fax: (212) 963-4116, http://unstats.un.org; *Human Development Report 2006.*

The World Bank, 1818 H Street, NW, Washington, DC 20433, (202) 473-1000, Fax: (202) 477-6391, www.worldbank.org; *The World Bank Atlas 2003-2004.*

IRAQ - LAND USE

Central Intelligence Agency, Office of Public Affairs, Washington, DC 20505, (703) 482-0623, Fax: (703) 482-1739, www.cia.gov; *The World Factbook.*

Euromonitor International, Inc., 224 S. Michigan Avenue, Suite 1500, Chicago, IL 60604, (312) 922-1115, Fax: (312) 922-1157, www.euromonitor.com; *International Marketing Data and Statistics 2008.*

United Nations Food and Agricultural Organization (FAO), Viale delle Terme di Caracalla, 00100 Rome, Italy, (Dial from U.S. (202) 653-2400), (Fax from U.S. (202) 653 5760), www.fao.org; *FAO Production Yearbook 2002.*

IRAQ - LIBRARIES

M.E. Sharpe, 80 Business Park Drive, Armonk, NY 10504, (800) 541-6563, Fax: (914) 273-2106, www.mesharpe.com; *The Illustrated Book of World Rankings.*

UNESCO Institute for Statistics, C.P. 6128 Succursale Centre-Ville, Montreal, Quebec, H3C 3J7 Canada, (Dial from U.S. (514) 343-6880), (Fax from U.S. (514) 343 6882), www.uis.unesco.org; *Statistical Tables.*

IRAQ - LIFE EXPECTANCY

Central Intelligence Agency, Office of Public Affairs, Washington, DC 20505, (703) 482-0623, Fax: (703) 482-1739, www.cia.gov; *The World Factbook.*

Euromonitor International, Inc., 224 S. Michigan Avenue, Suite 1500, Chicago, IL 60604, (312) 922-1115, Fax: (312) 922-1157, www.euromonitor.com; *The World Economic Factbook 2008.*

Palgrave Macmillan Ltd., Houndmills, Basingstoke, Hampshire, RG21 6XS, England, (Telephone in U.S. (888) 330-8477), (Fax in U.S. (800) 672-2054), www.palgrave.com; *The Statesman's Yearbook 2008.*

United Nations Statistics Division, New York, NY 10017, (800) 253-9646, Fax: (212) 963-4116, http://unstats.un.org; *Human Development Report 2006* and *World Statistics Pocketbook.*

The World Bank, 1818 H Street, NW, Washington, DC 20433, (202) 473-1000, Fax: (202) 477-6391, www.worldbank.org; *The World Bank Atlas 2003-2004.*

IRAQ - LITERACY

Euromonitor International, Inc., 224 S. Michigan Avenue, Suite 1500, Chicago, IL 60604, (312) 922-

1115, Fax: (312) 922-1157, www.euromonitor.com; *World Marketing Data and Statistics.*

IRAQ - LIVESTOCK

Euromonitor International, Inc., 224 S. Michigan Avenue, Suite 1500, Chicago, IL 60604, (312) 922-1115, Fax: (312) 922-1157, www.euromonitor.com; *International Marketing Data and Statistics 2008.*

M.E. Sharpe, 80 Business Park Drive, Armonk, NY 10504, (800) 541-6563, Fax: (914) 273-2106, www.mesharpe.com; *The Illustrated Book of World Rankings.*

Palgrave Macmillan Ltd., Houndmills, Basingstoke, Hampshire, RG21 6XS, England, (Telephone in U.S. (888) 330-8477), (Fax in U.S. (800) 672-2054), www.palgrave.com; *The Statesman's Yearbook 2008.*

Taylor and Francis Group, An Informa Business, 2 Park Square, Milton Park, Abingdon, Oxford OX14 4RN, United Kingdom, (Dial from U.S. (212) 216-7800), (Fax from U.S. (212) 564-7854), www.tandf.co.uk; *The Europa World Year Book.*

United Nations Conference on Trade and Development (UNCTAD), DC2-1120, United Nations, New York, NY 10017, (212) 963-0027, www.unctad.org; *UNCTAD Commodity Yearbook.*

United Nations Food and Agricultural Organization (FAO), Viale delle Terme di Caracalla, 00100 Rome, Italy, (Dial from U.S. (202) 653-2400), (Fax from U.S. (202) 653 5760), www.fao.org; *FAO Production Yearbook 2002* and *The State of Food and Agriculture (SOFA) 2006.*

United Nations Statistics Division, New York, NY 10017, (800) 253-9646, Fax: (212) 963-4116, http://unstats.un.org; *Statistical Yearbook.*

IRAQ - LOCAL TAXATION

Euromonitor International, Inc., 224 S. Michigan Avenue, Suite 1500, Chicago, IL 60604, (312) 922-1115, Fax: (312) 922-1157, www.euromonitor.com; *International Marketing Data and Statistics 2008.*

IRAQ - MANUFACTURES

M.E. Sharpe, 80 Business Park Drive, Armonk, NY 10504, (800) 541-6563, Fax: (914) 273-2106, www.mesharpe.com; *The Illustrated Book of World Rankings.*

United Nations Statistics Division, New York, NY 10017, (800) 253-9646, Fax: (212) 963-4116, http://unstats.un.org; *Bulletin of Industrial Statistics for the Arab Countries* and *Statistical Yearbook.*

IRAQ - MARRIAGE

M.E. Sharpe, 80 Business Park Drive, Armonk, NY 10504, (800) 541-6563, Fax: (914) 273-2106, www.mesharpe.com; *The Illustrated Book of World Rankings.*

United Nations Statistics Division, New York, NY 10017, (800) 253-9646, Fax: (212) 963-4116, http://unstats.un.org; *Demographic Yearbook* and *Statistical Yearbook.*

IRAQ - MEAT PRODUCTION

See IRAQ - LIVESTOCK

IRAQ - MILK PRODUCTION

See IRAQ - DAIRY PROCESSING

IRAQ - MINERAL INDUSTRIES

Euromonitor International, Inc., 224 S. Michigan Avenue, Suite 1500, Chicago, IL 60604, (312) 922-1115, Fax: (312) 922-1157, www.euromonitor.com; *International Marketing Data and Statistics 2008.*

International Lead and Zinc Study Group (ILZSG), Rua Almirante Barroso 38, 5th Floor, Lisbon 1000 - 013, Portugal, www.ilzsg.org; Interactive Statistical Database.

M.E. Sharpe, 80 Business Park Drive, Armonk, NY 10504, (800) 541-6563, Fax: (914) 273-2106, www.mesharpe.com; *The Illustrated Book of World Rankings.*

Organisation for Economic Cooperation and Development (OECD), 2 rue Andre Pascal, F-75775 Paris Cedex 16, France, (Telephone in U.S. (202) 785-6323), (Fax in U.S. (202) 785-0350), www.oecd.org; *World Energy Outlook 2007.*

Organization of Petroleum Exporting Countries (OPEC), Obere Donaustrasse 93, A-1020, Vienna, Austria, www.opec.org; *Annual Statistical Bulletin 2006.*

Taylor and Francis Group, An Informa Business, 2 Park Square, Milton Park, Abingdon, Oxford OX14 4RN, United Kingdom, (Dial from U.S. (212) 216-7800), (Fax from U.S. (212) 564-7854), www.tandf.co.uk; *The Europa World Year Book.*

United Nations Conference on Trade and Development (UNCTAD), DC2-1120, United Nations, New York, NY 10017, (212) 963-0027, www.unctad.org; *UNCTAD Commodity Yearbook.*

United Nations Economic and Social Commission for Western Asia (ESCWA), PO Box 11-8575, Riad el-Solh Square, Beirut, Lebanon, www.escwa.un.org; *Annual Report 2006* and *Statistical Abstract of the ESCWA Region 2007.*

United Nations Statistics Division, New York, NY 10017, (800) 253-9646, Fax: (212) 963-4116, http://unstats.un.org; *Bulletin of Industrial Statistics for the Arab Countries* and *Statistical Yearbook.*

IRAQ - MONEY EXCHANGE RATES

See IRAQ - FOREIGN EXCHANGE RATES

IRAQ - MONEY SUPPLY

Economist Intelligence Unit, 111 West 57th Street, New York, NY 10019, (212) 554-0600, Fax: (212) 586-1181, www.eiu.com; *Iraq Country Report.*

Euromonitor International, Inc., 224 S. Michigan Avenue, Suite 1500, Chicago, IL 60604, (312) 922-1115, Fax: (312) 922-1157, www.euromonitor.com; *International Marketing Data and Statistics 2008.*

International Monetary Fund (IMF), 700 Nineteenth Street, NW, Washington, DC 20431, (202) 623-7000, Fax: (202) 623-4661, www.imf.org; *International Financial Statistics Yearbook 2007.*

United Nations Economic and Social Commission for Western Asia (ESCWA), PO Box 11-8575, Riad el-Solh Square, Beirut, Lebanon, www.escwa.un.org; *Annual Report 2006* and *Statistical Abstract of the ESCWA Region 2007.*

United Nations Statistics Division, New York, NY 10017, (800) 253-9646, Fax: (212) 963-4116, http://unstats.un.org; *Statistical Yearbook.*

The World Bank, 1818 H Street, NW, Washington, DC 20433, (202) 473-1000, Fax: (202) 477-6391, www.worldbank.org; *Iraq.*

IRAQ - MORTALITY

Central Intelligence Agency, Office of Public Affairs, Washington, DC 20505, (703) 482-0623, Fax: (703) 482-1739, www.cia.gov; *The World Factbook.*

Euromonitor International, Inc., 224 S. Michigan Avenue, Suite 1500, Chicago, IL 60604, (312) 922-1115, Fax: (312) 922-1157, www.euromonitor.com; *International Marketing Data and Statistics 2008* and *The World Economic Factbook 2008.*

Taylor and Francis Group, An Informa Business, 2 Park Square, Milton Park, Abingdon, Oxford OX14 4RN, United Kingdom, (Dial from U.S. (212) 216-7800), (Fax from U.S. (212) 564-7854), www.tandf.co.uk; *The Europa World Year Book.*

U.S. Library of Congress (LOC), Congressional Research Service (CRS), The Library of Congress, 101 Independence Avenue, SE, Washington, DC 20540-7500, (202) 707-5700, www.loc.gov/crsinfo; *Iraqi Civilian Deaths Estimates* and *Iraqi Police and Security Forces Deaths Estimates.*

UNICEF, 3 United Nations Plaza, New York, NY 10017, (800) 253-9646, Fax: (212) 887-7465, www.unicef.org; *The State of the World's Children 2008.*

United Nations Statistics Division, New York, NY 10017, (800) 253-9646, Fax: (212) 963-4116, http://unstats.un.org; *Demographic Yearbook; Human Development Report 2006; Statistical Yearbook;* and *World Statistics Pocketbook.*

The World Bank, 1818 H Street, NW, Washington, DC 20433, (202) 473-1000, Fax: (202) 477-6391, www.worldbank.org; *The World Bank Atlas 2003-2004.*

World Health Organization (WHO), Avenue Appia 20, 1211 Geneve 27, Switzerland, (Telephone in U.S. (212) 331-9081), www.who.int; The WHO Global Atlas of Infectious Diseases and *World Health Report 2006.*

IRAQ - MOTOR VEHICLES

International Road Federation (IFR), Madison Place, 500 Montgomery Street, 5th Floor, Alexandria, VA 22314, (703) 535-1001, Fax: (703) 535-1007, www.irfnet.org; *World Road Statistics 2006.*

Taylor and Francis Group, An Informa Business, 2 Park Square, Milton Park, Abingdon, Oxford OX14 4RN, United Kingdom, (Dial from U.S. (212) 216-7800), (Fax from U.S. (212) 564-7854), www.tandf.co.uk; *The Europa World Year Book.*

United Nations Statistics Division, New York, NY 10017, (800) 253-9646, Fax: (212) 963-4116, http://unstats.un.org; *Statistical Yearbook.*

IRAQ - MUSEUMS

M.E. Sharpe, 80 Business Park Drive, Armonk, NY 10504, (800) 541-6563, Fax: (914) 273-2106, www.mesharpe.com; *The Illustrated Book of World Rankings.*

UNESCO Institute for Statistics, C.P. 6128 Succursale Centre-Ville, Montreal, Quebec, H3C 3J7 Canada, (Dial from U.S. (514) 343-6880), (Fax from U.S. (514) 343 6882), www.uis.unesco.org; *Statistical Tables.*

IRAQ - NATURAL GAS PRODUCTION

See IRAQ - MINERAL INDUSTRIES

IRAQ - NUTRITION

United Nations Food and Agricultural Organization (FAO), Viale delle Terme di Caracalla, 00100 Rome, Italy, (Dial from U.S. (202) 653-2400), (Fax from U.S. (202) 653 5760), www.fao.org; *The State of Food and Agriculture (SOFA) 2006.*

IRAQ - OLDER PEOPLE

M.E. Sharpe, 80 Business Park Drive, Armonk, NY 10504, (800) 541-6563, Fax: (914) 273-2106, www.mesharpe.com; *The Illustrated Book of World Rankings.*

IRAQ - PAPER

See IRAQ - FORESTS AND FORESTRY

IRAQ - PEANUT PRODUCTION

See IRAQ - CROPS

IRAQ - PESTICIDES

United Nations Food and Agricultural Organization (FAO), Viale delle Terme di Caracalla, 00100 Rome, Italy, (Dial from U.S. (202) 653-2400), (Fax from U.S. (202) 653 5760), www.fao.org; *The State of Food and Agriculture (SOFA) 2006.*

IRAQ - PETROLEUM INDUSTRY AND TRADE

M.E. Sharpe, 80 Business Park Drive, Armonk, NY 10504, (800) 541-6563, Fax: (914) 273-2106, www.mesharpe.com; *The Illustrated Book of World Rankings.*

Organisation for Economic Cooperation and Development (OECD), 2 rue Andre Pascal, F-75775 Paris Cedex 16, France, (Telephone in U.S. (202) 785-6323), (Fax in U.S. (202) 785-0350), www.oecd.org; *World Energy Outlook 2007.*

Organization of Petroleum Exporting Countries (OPEC), Obere Donaustrasse 93, A-1020, Vienna, Austria, www.opec.org; *Annual Statistical Bulletin 2006.*

Palgrave Macmillan Ltd., Houndmills, Basingstoke, Hampshire, RG21 6XS, England, (Telephone in U.S. (888) 330-8477), (Fax in U.S. (800) 672-2054), www.palgrave.com; *The Statesman's Yearbook 2008.*

PennWell Corporation, 1421 South Sheridan Road, Tulsa, OK 74112, (918) 835-3161, www.pennwell.com; *International Petroleum Encyclopedia 2007.*

U.S. Department of Energy (DOE), Energy Information Administration (EIA), 1000 Independence Avenue, SW, Washington, DC 20585, (202) 586-8800, www.eia.doe.gov; *International Energy Annual 2004* and *International Energy Outlook 2006.*

United Nations Conference on Trade and Development (UNCTAD), DC2-1120, United Nations, New York, NY 10017, (212) 963-0027, www.unctad.org; *UNCTAD Commodity Yearbook.*

United Nations Food and Agricultural Organization (FAO), Viale delle Terme di Caracalla, 00100 Rome, Italy, (Dial from U.S. (202) 653-2400), (Fax from U.S. (202) 653 5760), www.fao.org; *The State of Food and Agriculture (SOFA) 2006.*

United Nations Statistics Division, New York, NY 10017, (800) 253-9646, Fax: (212) 963-4116, http://unstats.un.org; *Statistical Yearbook.*

IRAQ - PIPELINES

Organization of Petroleum Exporting Countries (OPEC), Obere Donaustrasse 93, A-1020, Vienna, Austria, www.opec.org; *Annual Statistical Bulletin 2006.*

IRAQ - POLITICAL SCIENCE

Central Intelligence Agency, Office of Public Affairs, Washington, DC 20505, (703) 482-0623, Fax: (703) 482-1739, www.cia.gov; *The World Factbook.*

International Monetary Fund (IMF), 700 Nineteenth Street, NW, Washington, DC 20431, (202) 623-7000, Fax: (202) 623-4661, www.imf.org; *International Financial Statistics Yearbook 2007.*

Palgrave Macmillan Ltd., Houndmills, Basingstoke, Hampshire, RG21 6XS, England, (Telephone in U.S. (888) 330-8477), (Fax in U.S. (800) 672-2054), www.palgrave.com; *The Statesman's Yearbook 2008.*

Taylor and Francis Group, An Informa Business, 2 Park Square, Milton Park, Abingdon, Oxford OX14 4RN, United Kingdom, (Dial from U.S. (212) 216-7800), (Fax from U.S. (212) 564-7854), www.tandf.co.uk; *The Europa World Year Book.*

United Nations Statistics Division, New York, NY 10017, (800) 253-9646, Fax: (212) 963-4116, http://unstats.un.org; *National Accounts Statistics: Compendium of Income Distribution Statistics* and *Statistical Yearbook.*

IRAQ - POPULATION

Central Intelligence Agency, Office of Public Affairs, Washington, DC 20505, (703) 482-0623, Fax: (703) 482-1739, www.cia.gov; *The World Factbook.*

Economist Intelligence Unit, 111 West 57th Street, New York, NY 10019, (212) 554-0600, Fax: (212) 586-1181, www.eiu.com; *Iraq Country Report.*

Euromonitor International, Inc., 224 S. Michigan Avenue, Suite 1500, Chicago, IL 60604, (312) 922-1115, Fax: (312) 922-1157, www.euromonitor.com; *International Marketing Data and Statistics 2008* and *The World Economic Factbook 2008.*

International Labour Office, I.L.O. Publications, 4 route des Morillons, CH-1211 Geneva 22, Switzerland, (Telephone in U.S. (202) 653-7652), (Fax in U.S. (202) 653-7687), www.ilo.org; *Yearbook of Labour Statistics 2006.*

International Organization for Migration (IOM), 17, Route des Morillons, CH-1211 Geneva 19, Switzerland, www.iom.int; *IOM Emergency Needs Assesments: Post-February 2006 Displacement in Iraq* and *IOM Monitoring and Needs Assessments: Assessment of Iraqi Return.*

M.E. Sharpe, 80 Business Park Drive, Armonk, NY 10504, (800) 541-6563, Fax: (914) 273-2106, www.mesharpe.com; *The Illustrated Book of World Rankings.*

Palgrave Macmillan Ltd., Houndmills, Basingstoke, Hampshire, RG21 6XS, England, (Telephone in U.S. (888) 330-8477), (Fax in U.S. (800) 672-2054), www.palgrave.com; *The Statesman's Yearbook 2008.*

Taylor and Francis Group, An Informa Business, 2 Park Square, Milton Park, Abingdon, Oxford OX14 4RN, United Kingdom, (Dial from U.S. (212) 216-7800), (Fax from U.S. (212) 564-7854), www.tandf.co.uk; *The Europa World Year Book.*

U.S. Department of State (DOS), 2201 C Street NW, Washington, DC 20520, (202) 647-4000, www.state.gov; *World Military Expenditures and Arms Transfers (WMEAT).*

UNESCO Institute for Statistics, C.P. 6128 Succursale Centre-Ville, Montreal, Quebec, H3C 3J7 Canada, (Dial from U.S. (514) 343-6880), (Fax from U.S. (514) 343 6882), www.uis.unesco.org; *Statistical Tables.*

United Nations Economic and Social Commission for Western Asia (ESCWA), PO Box 11-8575, Riad el-Solh Square, Beirut, Lebanon, www.escwa.un.org; *Annual Report 2006* and *Statistical Abstract of the ESCWA Region 2007.*

United Nations Food and Agricultural Organization (FAO), Viale delle Terme di Caracalla, 00100 Rome, Italy, (Dial from U.S. (202) 653-2400), (Fax from U.S. (202) 653 5760), www.fao.org; *FAO Production Yearbook 2002.*

United Nations Statistics Division, New York, NY 10017, (800) 253-9646, Fax: (212) 963-4116, http://unstats.un.org; *Demographic Yearbook; Human Development Report 2006; Statistical Yearbook;* and *World Statistics Pocketbook.*

The World Bank, 1818 H Street, NW, Washington, DC 20433, (202) 473-1000, Fax: (202) 477-6391, www.worldbank.org; *Iraq* and *The World Bank Atlas 2003-2004.*

World Health Organization (WHO), Avenue Appia 20, 1211 Geneve 27, Switzerland, (Telephone in U.S. (212) 331-9081), www.who.int; *World Health Report 2006.*

IRAQ - POPULATION DENSITY

Central Intelligence Agency, Office of Public Affairs, Washington, DC 20505, (703) 482-0623, Fax: (703) 482-1739, www.cia.gov; *The World Factbook.*

Euromonitor International, Inc., 224 S. Michigan Avenue, Suite 1500, Chicago, IL 60604, (312) 922-1115, Fax: (312) 922-1157, www.euromonitor.com; *International Marketing Data and Statistics 2008* and *The World Economic Factbook 2008.*

M.E. Sharpe, 80 Business Park Drive, Armonk, NY 10504, (800) 541-6563, Fax: (914) 273-2106, www.mesharpe.com; *The Illustrated Book of World Rankings.*

Palgrave Macmillan Ltd., Houndmills, Basingstoke, Hampshire, RG21 6XS, England, (Telephone in U.S. (888) 330-8477), (Fax in U.S. (800) 672-2054), www.palgrave.com; *The Statesman's Yearbook 2008.*

Taylor and Francis Group, An Informa Business, 2 Park Square, Milton Park, Abingdon, Oxford OX14 4RN, United Kingdom, (Dial from U.S. (212) 216-7800), (Fax from U.S. (212) 564-7854), www.tandf.co.uk; *The Europa World Year Book.*

UNESCO Institute for Statistics, C.P. 6128 Succursale Centre-Ville, Montreal, Quebec, H3C 3J7 Canada, (Dial from U.S. (514) 343-6880), (Fax from U.S. (514) 343 6882), www.uis.unesco.org; *Statistical Tables.*

United Nations Food and Agricultural Organization (FAO), Viale delle Terme di Caracalla, 00100 Rome, Italy, (Dial from U.S. (202) 653-2400), (Fax from U.S. (202) 653 5760), www.fao.org; *The State of Food and Agriculture (SOFA) 2006.*

United Nations Statistics Division, New York, NY 10017, (800) 253-9646, Fax: (212) 963-4116, http://unstats.un.org; *Statistical Yearbook.*

The World Bank, 1818 H Street, NW, Washington, DC 20433, (202) 473-1000, Fax: (202) 477-6391, www.worldbank.org; *Iraq.*

IRAQ - POSTAL SERVICE

M.E. Sharpe, 80 Business Park Drive, Armonk, NY 10504, (800) 541-6563, Fax: (914) 273-2106, www.mesharpe.com; *The Illustrated Book of World Rankings.*

United Nations Statistics Division, New York, NY 10017, (800) 253-9646, Fax: (212) 963-4116, http://unstats.un.org; *Statistical Yearbook.*

IRAQ - POWER RESOURCES

Euromonitor International, Inc., 224 S. Michigan Avenue, Suite 1500, Chicago, IL 60604, (312) 922-1115, Fax: (312) 922-1157, www.euromonitor.com; *International Marketing Data and Statistics 2008; The World Economic Factbook 2008;* and *World Marketing Data and Statistics.*

M.E. Sharpe, 80 Business Park Drive, Armonk, NY 10504, (800) 541-6563, Fax: (914) 273-2106, www.mesharpe.com; *The Illustrated Book of World Rankings.*

Organisation for Economic Cooperation and Development (OECD), 2 rue Andre Pascal, F-75775 Paris Cedex 16, France, (Telephone in U.S. (202) 785-6323), (Fax in U.S. (202) 785-0350), www.oecd.org; *World Energy Outlook 2007.*

Palgrave Macmillan Ltd., Houndmills, Basingstoke, Hampshire, RG21 6XS, England, (Telephone in U.S. (888) 330-8477), (Fax in U.S. (800) 672-2054), www.palgrave.com; *The Statesman's Yearbook 2008.*

Platts, 2 Penn Plaza, 25th Floor, New York, NY 10121-2298, (212) 904-3070, www.platts.com; *Energy Economist.*

U.S. Department of Energy (DOE), Energy Information Administration (EIA), 1000 Independence Avenue, SW, Washington, DC 20585, (202) 586-8800, www.eia.doe.gov; *International Energy Annual 2004* and *International Energy Outlook 2006.*

United Nations Economic and Social Commission for Western Asia (ESCWA), PO Box 11-8575, Riad el-Solh Square, Beirut, Lebanon, www.escwa.un.org; *Annual Report 2006* and *Statistical Abstract of the ESCWA Region 2007.*

United Nations Food and Agricultural Organization (FAO), Viale delle Terme di Caracalla, 00100 Rome, Italy, (Dial from U.S. (202) 653-2400), (Fax from U.S. (202) 653 5760), www.fao.org; *The State of Food and Agriculture (SOFA) 2006.*

United Nations Statistics Division, New York, NY 10017, (800) 253-9646, Fax: (212) 963-4116, http://unstats.un.org; *Energy Statistics Yearbook 2003; Human Development Report 2006; Statistical Yearbook;* and *World Statistics Pocketbook.*

The World Bank, 1818 H Street, NW, Washington, DC 20433, (202) 473-1000, Fax: (202) 477-6391, www.worldbank.org; *The World Bank Atlas 2003-2004.*

IRAQ - PRICES

Euromonitor International, Inc., 224 S. Michigan Avenue, Suite 1500, Chicago, IL 60604, (312) 922-1115, Fax: (312) 922-1157, www.euromonitor.com; *World Marketing Data and Statistics.*

International Labour Office, I.L.O. Publications, 4 route des Morillons, CH-1211 Geneva 22, Switzerland, (Telephone in U.S. (202) 653-7652), (Fax in U.S. (202) 653-7687), www.ilo.org; *Yearbook of Labour Statistics 2006.*

International Monetary Fund (IMF), 700 Nineteenth Street, NW, Washington, DC 20431, (202) 623-7000, Fax: (202) 623-4661, www.imf.org; *International Financial Statistics Yearbook 2007.*

M.E. Sharpe, 80 Business Park Drive, Armonk, NY 10504, (800) 541-6563, Fax: (914) 273-2106, www.mesharpe.com; *The Illustrated Book of World Rankings.*

United Nations Food and Agricultural Organization (FAO), Viale delle Terme di Caracalla, 00100 Rome, Italy, (Dial from U.S. (202) 653-2400), (Fax from U.S. (202) 653 5760), www.fao.org; *FAO Production Yearbook 2002* and *The State of Food and Agriculture (SOFA) 2006.*

The World Bank, 1818 H Street, NW, Washington, DC 20433, (202) 473-1000, Fax: (202) 477-6391, www.worldbank.org; *Iraq.*

IRAQ - PROFESSIONS

UNESCO Institute for Statistics, C.P. 6128 Succursale Centre-Ville, Montreal, Quebec, H3C 3J7 Canada, (Dial from U.S. (514) 343-6880), (Fax from U.S. (514) 343 6882), www.uis.unesco.org; *Statistical Tables.*

United Nations Statistics Division, New York, NY 10017, (800) 253-9646, Fax: (212) 963-4116, http://unstats.un.org; *Statistical Yearbook.*

IRAQ - PUBLIC HEALTH

Euromonitor International, Inc., 224 S. Michigan Avenue, Suite 1500, Chicago, IL 60604, (312) 922-1115, Fax: (312) 922-1157, www.euromonitor.com; *World Marketing Data and Statistics.*

M.E. Sharpe, 80 Business Park Drive, Armonk, NY 10504, (800) 541-6563, Fax: (914) 273-2106, www.mesharpe.com; *The Illustrated Book of World Rankings.*

Palgrave Macmillan Ltd., Houndmills, Basingstoke, Hampshire, RG21 6XS, England, (Telephone in U.S. (888) 330-8477), (Fax in U.S. (800) 672-2054), www.palgrave.com; *The Statesman's Yearbook 2008.*

UNICEF, 3 United Nations Plaza, New York, NY 10017, (800) 253-9646, Fax: (212) 887-7465, www.unicef.org; *The State of the World's Children 2008.*

United Nations Economic and Social Commission for Western Asia (ESCWA), PO Box 11-8575, Riad el-Solh Square, Beirut, Lebanon, www.escwa.un.org; *Annual Report 2006* and *Statistical Abstract of the ESCWA Region 2007.*

United Nations Statistics Division, New York, NY 10017, (800) 253-9646, Fax: (212) 963-4116, http://unstats.un.org; *Human Development Report 2006* and *Statistical Yearbook.*

The World Bank, 1818 H Street, NW, Washington, DC 20433, (202) 473-1000, Fax: (202) 477-6391, www.worldbank.org; *Iraq.*

World Health Organization (WHO), Avenue Appia 20, 1211 Geneve 27, Switzerland, (Telephone in U.S. (212) 331-9081), www.who.int; The WHO Global Atlas of Infectious Diseases and *World Health Report 2006.*

IRAQ - PUBLISHERS AND PUBLISHING

UNESCO Institute for Statistics, C.P. 6128 Succursale Centre-Ville, Montreal, Quebec, H3C 3J7 Canada, (Dial from U.S. (514) 343-6880), (Fax from U.S. (514) 343 6882), www.uis.unesco.org; *Statistical Tables.*

IRAQ - RADIO BROADCASTING

Palgrave Macmillan Ltd., Houndmills, Basingstoke, Hampshire, RG21 6XS, England, (Telephone in U.S. (888) 330-8477), (Fax in U.S. (800) 672-2054), www.palgrave.com; *The Statesman's Yearbook 2008.*

IRAQ - RAILROADS

Jane's Information Group, 110 North Royal Street, Suite 200, Alexandria, VA 22314, (703) 683-3700, Fax: (800) 836-0297, www.janes.com; *Jane's World Railways.*

Palgrave Macmillan Ltd., Houndmills, Basingstoke, Hampshire, RG21 6XS, England, (Telephone in U.S. (888) 330-8477), (Fax in U.S. (800) 672-2054), www.palgrave.com; *The Statesman's Yearbook 2008.*

Taylor and Francis Group, An Informa Business, 2 Park Square, Milton Park, Abingdon, Oxford OX14 4RN, United Kingdom, (Dial from U.S. (212) 216-7800), (Fax from U.S. (212) 564-7854), www.tandf.co.uk; *The Europa World Year Book.*

United Nations Statistics Division, New York, NY 10017, (800) 253-9646, Fax: (212) 963-4116, http://unstats.un.org; *Statistical Yearbook.*

IRAQ - RELIGION

Central Intelligence Agency, Office of Public Affairs, Washington, DC 20505, (703) 482-0623, Fax: (703) 482-1739, www.cia.gov; *The World Factbook.*

M.E. Sharpe, 80 Business Park Drive, Armonk, NY 10504, (800) 541-6563, Fax: (914) 273-2106, www.mesharpe.com; *The Illustrated Book of World Rankings.*

Palgrave Macmillan Ltd., Houndmills, Basingstoke, Hampshire, RG21 6XS, England, (Telephone in U.S. (888) 330-8477), (Fax in U.S. (800) 672-2054), www.palgrave.com; *The Statesman's Yearbook 2008.*

IRAQ - RENT CHARGES

International Labour Office, I.L.O. Publications, 4 route des Morillons, CH-1211 Geneva 22, Switzerland, (Telephone in U.S. (202) 653-7652), (Fax in U.S. (202) 653-7687), www.ilo.org; *Yearbook of Labour Statistics 2006.*

IRAQ - RESERVES (ACCOUNTING)

Euromonitor International, Inc., 224 S. Michigan Avenue, Suite 1500, Chicago, IL 60604, (312) 922-1115, Fax: (312) 922-1157, www.euromonitor.com; *International Marketing Data and Statistics 2008.*

United Nations Statistics Division, New York, NY 10017, (800) 253-9646, Fax: (212) 963-4116, http://unstats.un.org; *Statistical Yearbook.*

IRAQ - RETAIL TRADE

Euromonitor International, Inc., 224 S. Michigan Avenue, Suite 1500, Chicago, IL 60604, (312) 922-1115, Fax: (312) 922-1157, www.euromonitor.com; *World Marketing Data and Statistics.*

United Nations Statistics Division, New York, NY 10017, (800) 253-9646, Fax: (212) 963-4116, http://unstats.un.org; *Statistical Yearbook.*

IRAQ - RICE PRODUCTION

See IRAQ - CROPS

IRAQ - ROADS

Central Intelligence Agency, Office of Public Affairs, Washington, DC 20505, (703) 482-0623, Fax: (703) 482-1739, www.cia.gov; *The World Factbook.*

International Road Federation (IFR), Madison Place, 500 Montgomery Street, 5th Floor, Alexandria, VA 22314, (703) 535-1001, Fax: (703) 535-1007, www.irfnet.org; *World Road Statistics 2006.*

Palgrave Macmillan Ltd., Houndmills, Basingstoke, Hampshire, RG21 6XS, England, (Telephone in U.S. (888) 330-8477), (Fax in U.S. (800) 672-2054), www.palgrave.com; *The Statesman's Yearbook 2008.*

IRAQ - RUBBER INDUSTRY AND TRADE

International Rubber Study Group (IRSG), 1st Floor, Heron House, 109/115 Wembley Hill Road, Wembley, Middlesex HA9 8DA, United Kingdom, www.rubberstudy.com; *Rubber Statistical Bulletin; Summary of World Rubber Statistics 2005; World Rubber Statistics Handbook (Volume 6, 1975-2001);* and *World Rubber Statistics Historic Handbook.*

M.E. Sharpe, 80 Business Park Drive, Armonk, NY 10504, (800) 541-6563, Fax: (914) 273-2106, www.mesharpe.com; *The Illustrated Book of World Rankings.*

IRAQ - SALT PRODUCTION

See IRAQ - MINERAL INDUSTRIES

IRAQ - SHEEP

See IRAQ - LIVESTOCK

IRAQ - SHIPPING

Organization of Petroleum Exporting Countries (OPEC), Obere Donaustrasse 93, A-1020, Vienna, Austria, www.opec.org; *Annual Statistical Bulletin 2006.*

Palgrave Macmillan Ltd., Houndmills, Basingstoke, Hampshire, RG21 6XS, England, (Telephone in U.S. (888) 330-8477), (Fax in U.S. (800) 672-2054), www.palgrave.com; *The Statesman's Yearbook 2008.*

U.S. Department of Transportation (DOT), Maritime Administration (MARAD), West Building, Southeast Federal Center, 1200 New Jersey Avenue, SE, Washington, DC 20590, (800) 99-MARAD, www.marad.dot.gov; *World Merchant Fleet 2005.*

United Nations Statistics Division, New York, NY 10017, (800) 253-9646, Fax: (212) 963-4116, http://unstats.un.org; *Statistical Yearbook.*

IRAQ - SILVER PRODUCTION

See IRAQ - MINERAL INDUSTRIES

IRAQ - SOCIAL ECOLOGY

M.E. Sharpe, 80 Business Park Drive, Armonk, NY 10504, (800) 541-6563, Fax: (914) 273-2106, www.mesharpe.com; *The Illustrated Book of World Rankings.*

United Nations Statistics Division, New York, NY 10017, (800) 253-9646, Fax: (212) 963-4116, http://unstats.un.org; *World Statistics Pocketbook.*

IRAQ - SOCIAL SECURITY

United Nations Statistics Division, New York, NY 10017, (800) 253-9646, Fax: (212) 963-4116, http://unstats.un.org; *National Accounts Statistics: Compendium of Income Distribution Statistics.*

IRAQ - SOYBEAN PRODUCTION

See IRAQ - CROPS

IRAQ - STEEL PRODUCTION

See IRAQ - MINERAL INDUSTRIES

IRAQ - SUGAR PRODUCTION

See IRAQ - CROPS

IRAQ - TAXATION

International Road Federation (IFR), Madison Place, 500 Montgomery Street, 5th Floor, Alexandria, VA 22314, (703) 535-1001, Fax: (703) 535-1007, www.irfnet.org; *World Road Statistics 2006.*

IRAQ - TEA TRADE

United Nations Statistics Division, New York, NY 10017, (800) 253-9646, Fax: (212) 963-4116, http://unstats.un.org; *Statistical Yearbook.*

IRAQ - TELEPHONE

International Telecommunication Union (ITU), Place des Nations, 1211 Geneva 20, Switzerland, www.itu.int; World Telecommunication Indicators Database.

Palgrave Macmillan Ltd., Houndmills, Basingstoke, Hampshire, RG21 6XS, England, (Telephone in U.S. (888) 330-8477), (Fax in U.S. (800) 672-2054), www.palgrave.com; *The Statesman's Yearbook 2008.*

Taylor and Francis Group, An Informa Business, 2 Park Square, Milton Park, Abingdon, Oxford OX14 4RN, United Kingdom, (Dial from U.S. (212) 216-7800), (Fax from U.S. (212) 564-7854), www.tandf.co.uk; *The Europa World Year Book.*

United Nations Statistics Division, New York, NY 10017, (800) 253-9646, Fax: (212) 963-4116, http://unstats.un.org; *Statistical Yearbook* and *World Statistics Pocketbook.*

IRAQ - TELEVISION - RECEIVERS AND RECEPTION

United Nations Statistics Division, New York, NY 10017, (800) 253-9646, Fax: (212) 963-4116, http://unstats.un.org; *Statistical Yearbook.*

IRAQ - TEXTILE INDUSTRY

M.E. Sharpe, 80 Business Park Drive, Armonk, NY 10504, (800) 541-6563, Fax: (914) 273-2106, www.mesharpe.com; *The Illustrated Book of World Rankings.*

United Nations Conference on Trade and Development (UNCTAD), DC2-1120, United Nations, New York, NY 10017, (212) 963-0027, www.unctad.org; *UNCTAD Commodity Yearbook.*

United Nations Statistics Division, New York, NY 10017, (800) 253-9646, Fax: (212) 963-4116, http://unstats.un.org; *Statistical Yearbook.*

IRAQ - THEATER

UNESCO Institute for Statistics, C.P. 6128 Succursale Centre-Ville, Montreal, Quebec, H3C 3J7 Canada, (Dial from U.S. (514) 343-6880), (Fax from U.S. (514) 343 6882), www.uis.unesco.org; *Statistical Tables.*

IRAQ - TOBACCO INDUSTRY

Foreign Agricultural Service (FAS), U.S. Department of Agriculture (USDA), 1400 Independence Avenue, SW, Washington, DC 20250, (202) 720-3935, www.fas.usda.gov; *Tobacco: World Markets and Trade.*

M.E. Sharpe, 80 Business Park Drive, Armonk, NY 10504, (800) 541-6563, Fax: (914) 273-2106, www.mesharpe.com; *The Illustrated Book of World Rankings.*

United Nations Statistics Division, New York, NY 10017, (800) 253-9646, Fax: (212) 963-4116, http://unstats.un.org; *Statistical Yearbook.*

IRAQ - TOURISM

Euromonitor International, Inc., 224 S. Michigan Avenue, Suite 1500, Chicago, IL 60604, (312) 922-1115, Fax: (312) 922-1157, www.euromonitor.com; *The World Economic Factbook 2008* and *World Marketing Data and Statistics.*

M.E. Sharpe, 80 Business Park Drive, Armonk, NY 10504, (800) 541-6563, Fax: (914) 273-2106, www.mesharpe.com; *The Illustrated Book of World Rankings.*

Palgrave Macmillan Ltd., Houndmills, Basingstoke, Hampshire, RG21 6XS, England, (Telephone in U.S. (888) 330-8477), (Fax in U.S. (800) 672-2054), www.palgrave.com; *The Statesman's Yearbook 2008.*

Taylor and Francis Group, An Informa Business, 2 Park Square, Milton Park, Abingdon, Oxford OX14 4RN, United Kingdom, (Dial from U.S. (212) 216-7800), (Fax from U.S. (212) 564-7854), www.tandf.co.uk; *The Europa World Year Book.*

United Nations Economic and Social Commission for Western Asia (ESCWA), PO Box 11-8575, Riad el-Solh Square, Beirut, Lebanon, www.escwa.un.org; *Annual Report 2006* and *Statistical Abstract of the ESCWA Region 2007.*

United Nations Statistics Division, New York, NY 10017, (800) 253-9646, Fax: (212) 963-4116, http://unstats.un.org; *Statistical Yearbook.*

United Nations World Tourism Organization (UNWTO), Capitan Haya 42, 28020 Madrid, Spain, www.world-tourism.org; *Yearbook of Tourism Statistics.*

The World Bank, 1818 H Street, NW, Washington, DC 20433, (202) 473-1000, Fax: (202) 477-6391, www.worldbank.org; *Iraq.*

IRAQ - TRADE

See IRAQ - INTERNATIONAL TRADE

IRAQ - TRANSPORTATION

Central Intelligence Agency, Office of Public Affairs, Washington, DC 20505, (703) 482-0623, Fax: (703) 482-1739, www.cia.gov; *The World Factbook.*

Euromonitor International, Inc., 224 S. Michigan Avenue, Suite 1500, Chicago, IL 60604, (312) 922-1115, Fax: (312) 922-1157, www.euromonitor.com; *World Marketing Data and Statistics.*

M.E. Sharpe, 80 Business Park Drive, Armonk, NY 10504, (800) 541-6563, Fax: (914) 273-2106, www.mesharpe.com; *The Illustrated Book of World Rankings.*

Palgrave Macmillan Ltd., Houndmills, Basingstoke, Hampshire, RG21 6XS, England, (Telephone in U.S. (888) 330-8477), (Fax in U.S. (800) 672-2054), www.palgrave.com; *The Statesman's Yearbook 2008.*

Taylor and Francis Group, An Informa Business, 2 Park Square, Milton Park, Abingdon, Oxford OX14 4RN, United Kingdom, (Dial from U.S. (212) 216-7800), (Fax from U.S. (212) 564-7854), www.tandf.co.uk; *The Europa World Year Book.*

United Nations Economic and Social Commission for Western Asia (ESCWA), PO Box 11-8575, Riad el-Solh Square, Beirut, Lebanon, www.escwa.un.org; *Annual Report 2006* and *Statistical Abstract of the ESCWA Region 2007.*

United Nations Statistics Division, New York, NY 10017, (800) 253-9646, Fax: (212) 963-4116, http://unstats.un.org; *Human Development Report 2006.*

The World Bank, 1818 H Street, NW, Washington, DC 20433, (202) 473-1000, Fax: (202) 477-6391, www.worldbank.org; *Iraq.*

IRAQ - UNEMPLOYMENT

Central Intelligence Agency, Office of Public Affairs, Washington, DC 20505, (703) 482-0623, Fax: (703) 482-1739, www.cia.gov; *The World Factbook.*

Euromonitor International, Inc., 224 S. Michigan Avenue, Suite 1500, Chicago, IL 60604, (312) 922-1115, Fax: (312) 922-1157, www.euromonitor.com; *International Marketing Data and Statistics 2008.*

International Labour Office, I.L.O. Publications, 4 route des Morillons, CH-1211 Geneva 22, Switzerland, (Telephone in U.S. (202) 653-7652), (Fax in U.S. (202) 653-7687), www.ilo.org; *Yearbook of Labour Statistics 2006.*

United Nations Statistics Division, New York, NY 10017, (800) 253-9646, Fax: (212) 963-4116, http://unstats.un.org; *Statistical Yearbook.*

IRAQ - VITAL STATISTICS

Euromonitor International, Inc., 224 S. Michigan Avenue, Suite 1500, Chicago, IL 60604, (312) 922-1115, Fax: (312) 922-1157, www.euromonitor.com; *International Marketing Data and Statistics 2008.*

United Nations Economic and Social Commission for Western Asia (ESCWA), PO Box 11-8575, Riad el-Solh Square, Beirut, Lebanon, www.escwa.un.org; *Annual Report 2006; Bulletin on Population and Vital Statistics in the ESCWA Region;* and *Survey of Economic and Social Developments in the ESCWA Region 2006-2007.*

United Nations Statistics Division, New York, NY 10017, (800) 253-9646, Fax: (212) 963-4116, http://unstats.un.org; *Statistical Yearbook.*

World Health Organization (WHO), Avenue Appia 20, 1211 Geneve 27, Switzerland, (Telephone in U.S. (212) 331-9081), www.who.int; *World Health Report 2006.*

IRAQ - WAGES

International Labour Office, I.L.O. Publications, 4 route des Morillons, CH-1211 Geneva 22, Switzerland, (Telephone in U.S. (202) 653-7652), (Fax in U.S. (202) 653-7687), www.ilo.org; *Yearbook of Labour Statistics 2006.*

The World Bank, 1818 H Street, NW, Washington, DC 20433, (202) 473-1000, Fax: (202) 477-6391, www.worldbank.org; *Iraq.*

IRAQ - WALNUT PRODUCTION

See IRAQ - CROPS

IRAQ - WEATHER

See IRAN - CLIMATE

IRAQ - WHEAT PRODUCTION

See IRAQ - CROPS

IRAQ - WHOLESALE PRICE INDEXES

International Monetary Fund (IMF), 700 Nineteenth Street, NW, Washington, DC 20431, (202) 623-7000, Fax: (202) 623-4661, www.imf.org; *International Financial Statistics Yearbook 2007.*

United Nations Statistics Division, New York, NY 10017, (800) 253-9646, Fax: (212) 963-4116, http://unstats.un.org; *Statistical Yearbook.*

IRAQ - WHOLESALE TRADE

United Nations Statistics Division, New York, NY 10017, (800) 253-9646, Fax: (212) 963-4116, http://unstats.un.org; *Statistical Yearbook.*

IRAQ - WINE PRODUCTION

See IRAQ - BEVERAGE INDUSTRY

IRAQ - WOOD AND WOOD PULP

See IRAQ - FORESTS AND FORESTRY

IRAQ - WOOL PRODUCTION

See IRAQ - TEXTILE INDUSTRY

IRAQ - YARN PRODUCTION

See IRAQ - TEXTILE INDUSTRY

IRELAND - NATIONAL STATISTICAL OFFICE

Central Statistics Office (CSO) Ireland, Skehard Road, Cork, Ireland, www.cso.ie; National Data Center.

IRELAND - PRIMARY STATISTICS SOURCES

Central Statistics Office (CSO) Ireland, Skehard Road, Cork, Ireland, www.cso.ie; *Ireland North and South: A Statistical Profile 2003* and *Statistical Bulletin.*

Eurostat, Batiment Jean Monnet, Rue Alcide de Gasperi, L-2920 Luxembourg, http://epp.eurostat.ec.europa.eu; *Pocketbook on Candidate and Potential Candidate Countries.*

IRELAND - DATABASES

Central Statistics Office (CSO) Ireland, Skehard Road, Cork, Ireland, www.cso.ie; Database. Subject coverage: People and society, labour market and earnings, business sectors, economy, and environment.

IRELAND - ABORTION

European Union, Delegation of the European Commission to the United States, 2300 M Street, NW, Washington, DC 20037, (202) 862-9500, Fax: (202) 429-1766, www.eurunion.org; *First Demographic Estimates for 2006.*

United Nations Statistics Division, New York, NY 10017, (800) 253-9646, Fax: (212) 963-4116, http://unstats.un.org; *Trends in Europe and North America: The Statistical Yearbook of the ECE 2005.*

IRELAND - AGRICULTURAL MACHINERY

European Union, Delegation of the European Commission to the United States, 2300 M Street, NW, Washington, DC 20037, (202) 862-9500, Fax: (202) 429-1766, www.eurunion.org; *Statistical Overview of Transport in the European Union (Data 1970-2001).*

United Nations Statistics Division, New York, NY 10017, (800) 253-9646, Fax: (212) 963-4116, http://unstats.un.org; *Statistical Yearbook.*

IRELAND - AGRICULTURE

Economist Intelligence Unit, 111 West 57th Street, New York, NY 10019, (212) 554-0600, Fax: (212) 586-1181, www.eiu.com; *Ireland Country Report.*

Euromonitor International, Inc., 224 S. Michigan Avenue, Suite 1500, Chicago, IL 60604, (312) 922-1115, Fax: (312) 922-1157, www.euromonitor.com; *World Marketing Data and Statistics.*

European Union, Delegation of the European Commission to the United States, 2300 M Street, NW, Washington, DC 20037, (202) 862-9500, Fax: (202)

429-1766, www.eurunion.org; *Agricultural Statistics: Data 1995-2005; European Union Labour Force Survey; Eurostatistics: Data for Short-Term Economic Analysis (2007 edition);* and *Regions - Statistical Yearbook 2006.*

Eurostat, Batiment Jean Monnet, Rue Alcide de Gasperi, L-2920 Luxembourg, http://epp.eurostat.ec.europa.eu; *Eurostat Yearbook 2006-2007.*

M.E. Sharpe, 80 Business Park Drive, Armonk, NY 10504, (800) 541-6563, Fax: (914) 273-2106, www.mesharpe.com; *The Illustrated Book of World Rankings.*

Organisation for Economic Cooperation and Development (OECD), 2 rue Andre Pascal, F-75775 Paris Cedex 16, France, (Telephone in U.S. (202) 785-6323), (Fax in U.S. (202) 785-0350), www.oecd.org; *Indicators of Industrial Activity; 2005 OECD Agricultural Outlook Tables, 1970-2014; OECD Agricultural Outlook: 2007-2016;* and *OECD Economic Survey - Ireland 2008.*

Palgrave Macmillan Ltd., Houndmills, Basingstoke, Hampshire, RG21 6XS, England, (Telephone in U.S. (888) 330-8477), (Fax in U.S. (800) 672-2054), www.palgrave.com; *The Statesman's Yearbook 2008.*

Taylor and Francis Group, An Informa Business, 2 Park Square, Milton Park, Abingdon, Oxford OX14 4RN, United Kingdom, (Dial from U.S. (212) 216-7800), (Fax from U.S. (212) 564-7854), www.tandf.co.uk; *The Europa World Year Book.*

Teagasc, Oak Park, Carlow, Ireland, www.teagasc.ie; *Beef and Sheep Production Research; Irish Journal of Agricultural and Food Research;* and *National Farm Survey 2005.*

United Nations Conference on Trade and Development (UNCTAD), DC2-1120, United Nations, New York, NY 10017, (212) 963-0027, www.unctad.org; *UNCTAD Commodity Yearbook.*

United Nations Food and Agricultural Organization (FAO), Viale delle Terme di Caracalla, 00100 Rome, Italy, (Dial from U.S. (202) 653-2400), (Fax from U.S. (202) 653 5760), www.fao.org; AQUASTAT; *FAO Production Yearbook 2002;* and *The State of Food and Agriculture (SOFA) 2006.*

United Nations Statistics Division, New York, NY 10017, (800) 253-9646, Fax: (212) 963-4116, http://unstats.un.org; *Statistical Yearbook.*

The World Bank, 1818 H Street, NW, Washington, DC 20433, (202) 473-1000, Fax: (202) 477-6391, www.worldbank.org; *Ireland* and *World Development Indicators (WDI) 2008.*

IRELAND - AIRLINES

European Union, Delegation of the European Commission to the United States, 2300 M Street, NW, Washington, DC 20037, (202) 862-9500, Fax: (202) 429-1766, www.eurunion.org; *Regions - Statistical Yearbook 2006.*

Eurostat, Batiment Jean Monnet, Rue Alcide de Gasperi, L-2920 Luxembourg, http://epp.eurostat.ec.europa.eu; *Eurostat Yearbook 2006-2007* and *Regional Passenger and Freight Air Transport in Europe in 2006.*

International Civil Aviation Organization (ICAO), External Relations and Public Information Office (EPO), 999 University Street, Montreal, Quebec H3C 5H7, Canada, (Dial from U.S. (514) 954-8219), (Fax from U.S. (514) 954-6077), www.icao.int; *Civil Aviation Statistics of the World.*

M.E. Sharpe, 80 Business Park Drive, Armonk, NY 10504, (800) 541-6563, Fax: (914) 273-2106, www.mesharpe.com; *The Illustrated Book of World Rankings.*

Organisation for Economic Cooperation and Development (OECD), 2 rue Andre Pascal, F-75775 Paris Cedex 16, France, (Telephone in U.S. (202) 785-6323), (Fax in U.S. (202) 785-0350), www.oecd.org; *Household, Tourism, Travel: Trends, Environmental Impacts and Policy Responses.*

Palgrave Macmillan Ltd., Houndmills, Basingstoke, Hampshire, RG21 6XS, England, (Telephone in U.S. (888) 330-8477), (Fax in U.S. (800) 672-2054), www.palgrave.com; *The Statesman's Yearbook 2008.*

Taylor and Francis Group, An Informa Business, 2 Park Square, Milton Park, Abingdon, Oxford OX14 4RN, United Kingdom, (Dial from U.S. (212) 216-7800), (Fax from U.S. (212) 564-7854), www.tandf.co.uk; *The Europa World Year Book.*

United Nations Statistics Division, New York, NY 10017, (800) 253-9646, Fax: (212) 963-4116, http://unstats.un.org; *Statistical Yearbook.*

IRELAND - AIRPORTS

Central Intelligence Agency, Office of Public Affairs, Washington, DC 20505, (703) 482-0623, Fax: (703) 482-1739, www.cia.gov; *The World Factbook.*

IRELAND - ALMOND PRODUCTION

See IRELAND - CROPS

IRELAND - ALUMINUM PRODUCTION

See IRELAND - MINERAL INDUSTRIES

IRELAND - ANIMAL FEEDING

Organisation for Economic Cooperation and Development (OECD), 2 rue Andre Pascal, F-75775 Paris Cedex 16, France, (Telephone in U.S. (202) 785-6323), (Fax in U.S. (202) 785-0350), www.oecd.org; *International Trade by Commodity Statistics (ITCS).*

IRELAND - APPLE PRODUCTION

See IRELAND - CROPS

IRELAND - ARMED FORCES

Central Intelligence Agency, Office of Public Affairs, Washington, DC 20505, (703) 482-0623, Fax: (703) 482-1739, www.cia.gov; *The World Factbook.*

Euromonitor International, Inc., 224 S. Michigan Avenue, Suite 1500, Chicago, IL 60604, (312) 922-1115, Fax: (312) 922-1157, www.euromonitor.com; *World Marketing Data and Statistics.*

European Union, Delegation of the European Commission to the United States, 2300 M Street, NW, Washington, DC 20037, (202) 862-9500, Fax: (202) 429-1766, www.eurunion.org; *RD Expenditure in Europe (2006 edition).*

International Institute for Strategic Studies (IISS), Arundel House, 13-15 Arundel Street, Temple Place, London WC2R 3DX, England, www.iiss.org; *The Military Balance 2007.*

International Road Federation (IFR), Madison Place, 500 Montgomery Street, 5th Floor, Alexandria, VA 22314, (703) 535-1001, Fax: (703) 535-1007, www.irfnet.org; *World Road Statistics 2006.*

Palgrave Macmillan Ltd., Houndmills, Basingstoke, Hampshire, RG21 6XS, England, (Telephone in U.S. (888) 330-8477), (Fax in U.S. (800) 672-2054), www.palgrave.com; *The Statesman's Yearbook 2008.*

U.S. Department of State (DOS), 2201 C Street NW, Washington, DC 20520, (202) 647-4000, www.state.gov; *World Military Expenditures and Arms Transfers (WMEAT).*

United Nations Statistics Division, New York, NY 10017, (800) 253-9646, Fax: (212) 963-4116, http://unstats.un.org; *Human Development Report 2006.*

IRELAND - AUTOMOBILE INDUSTRY AND TRADE

European Union, Delegation of the European Commission to the United States, 2300 M Street, NW, Washington, DC 20037, (202) 862-9500, Fax: (202) 429-1766, www.eurunion.org; *Eurostatistics: Data for Short-Term Economic Analysis (2007 edition).*

Eurostat, Batiment Jean Monnet, Rue Alcide de Gasperi, L-2920 Luxembourg, http://epp.eurostat.ec.europa.eu; *Eurostat Yearbook 2006-2007.*

Organisation for Economic Cooperation and Development (OECD), 2 rue Andre Pascal, F-75775 Paris Cedex 16, France, (Telephone in U.S. (202) 785-6323), (Fax in U.S. (202) 785-0350), www.oecd.org; *Indicators of Industrial Activity* and *International Trade by Commodity Statistics (ITCS).*

United Nations Statistics Division, New York, NY 10017, (800) 253-9646, Fax: (212) 963-4116, http://unstats.un.org; *Statistical Yearbook.*

IRELAND - BALANCE OF PAYMENTS

European Union, Delegation of the European Commission to the United States, 2300 M Street, NW, Washington, DC 20037, (202) 862-9500, Fax: (202) 429-1766, www.eurunion.org; *Eurostatistics: Data for Short-Term Economic Analysis (2007 edition).*

Eurostat, Batiment Jean Monnet, Rue Alcide de Gasperi, L-2920 Luxembourg, http://epp.eurostat.ec.europa.eu; *Eurostat Yearbook 2006-2007.*

International Monetary Fund (IMF), 700 Nineteenth Street, NW, Washington, DC 20431, (202) 623-7000, Fax: (202) 623-4661, www.imf.org; *Balance of Payments Statistics Newsletter* and *Balance of Payments Statistics Yearbook 2007.*

Organisation for Economic Cooperation and Development (OECD), 2 rue Andre Pascal, F-75775 Paris Cedex 16, France, (Telephone in U.S. (202) 785-6323), (Fax in U.S. (202) 785-0350), www.oecd.org; *Geographical Distribution of Financial Flows to Aid Recipients 2002-2006; OECD Economic Outlook 2008;* and *OECD Economic Survey - Ireland 2008.*

Platts, 2 Penn Plaza, 25th Floor, New York, NY 10121-2298, (212) 904-3070, www.platts.com; *Energy Economist.*

Taylor and Francis Group, An Informa Business, 2 Park Square, Milton Park, Abingdon, Oxford OX14 4RN, United Kingdom, (Dial from U.S. (212) 216-7800), (Fax from U.S. (212) 564-7854), www.tandf.co.uk; *The Europa World Year Book.*

United Nations Conference on Trade and Development (UNCTAD), DC2-1120, United Nations, New York, NY 10017, (212) 963-0027, www.unctad.org; *Handbook of Statistics 2005.*

United Nations Statistics Division, New York, NY 10017, (800) 253-9646, Fax: (212) 963-4116, http://unstats.un.org; *Energy Statistics Yearbook 2003.*

The World Bank, 1818 H Street, NW, Washington, DC 20433, (202) 473-1000, Fax: (202) 477-6391, www.worldbank.org; *Ireland; World Development Indicators (WDI) 2008;* and *World Development Report 2008.*

IRELAND - BANANAS

See IRELAND - CROPS

IRELAND - BANKS AND BANKING

Euromonitor International, Inc., 224 S. Michigan Avenue, Suite 1500, Chicago, IL 60604, (312) 922-1115, Fax: (312) 922-1157, www.euromonitor.com; *World Marketing Data and Statistics.*

European Union, Delegation of the European Commission to the United States, 2300 M Street, NW, Washington, DC 20037, (202) 862-9500, Fax: (202) 429-1766, www.eurunion.org; *The EU Economy, 2007 Review: Moving Europe's Productivity Frontier* and *Eurostatistics: Data for Short-Term Economic Analysis (2007 edition).*

Eurostat, Batiment Jean Monnet, Rue Alcide de Gasperi, L-2920 Luxembourg, http://epp.eurostat.ec.europa.eu; *Eurostat Yearbook 2006-2007.*

International Monetary Fund (IMF), 700 Nineteenth Street, NW, Washington, DC 20431, (202) 623-7000, Fax: (202) 623-4661, www.imf.org; *International Financial Statistics Yearbook 2007.*

M.E. Sharpe, 80 Business Park Drive, Armonk, NY 10504, (800) 541-6563, Fax: (914) 273-2106, www.mesharpe.com; *The Illustrated Book of World Rankings.*

Organisation for Economic Cooperation and Development (OECD), 2 rue Andre Pascal, F-75775 Paris Cedex 16, France, (Telephone in U.S. (202) 785-6323), (Fax in U.S. (202) 785-0350), www.oecd.org; *Financial Market Trends: OECD Periodical; OECD Economic Outlook 2008;* and *OECD Economic Survey - Ireland 2008.*

Palgrave Macmillan Ltd., Houndmills, Basingstoke, Hampshire, RG21 6XS, England, (Telephone in U.S. (888) 330-8477), (Fax in U.S. (800) 672-2054), www.palgrave.com; *The Statesman's Yearbook 2008.*

Taylor and Francis Group, An Informa Business, 2 Park Square, Milton Park, Abingdon, Oxford OX14 4RN, United Kingdom, (Dial from U.S. (212) 216-7800), (Fax from U.S. (212) 564-7854), www.tandf.co.uk; *The Europa World Year Book.*

IRELAND - BARLEY PRODUCTION

See IRELAND - CROPS

IRELAND - BEVERAGE INDUSTRY

Eurostat, Batiment Jean Monnet, Rue Alcide de Gasperi, L-2920 Luxembourg, http://epp.eurostat.ec.europa.eu; *Eurostat Yearbook 2006-2007.*

M.E. Sharpe, 80 Business Park Drive, Armonk, NY 10504, (800) 541-6563, Fax: (914) 273-2106, www.mesharpe.com; *The Illustrated Book of World Rankings.*

Organisation for Economic Cooperation and Development (OECD), 2 rue Andre Pascal, F-75775 Paris Cedex 16, France, (Telephone in U.S. (202) 785-6323), (Fax in U.S. (202) 785-0350), www.oecd.org; *Indicators of Industrial Activity.*

United Nations Statistics Division, New York, NY 10017, (800) 253-9646, Fax: (212) 963-4116, http://unstats.un.org; *Statistical Yearbook.*

IRELAND - BONDS

Eurostat, Batiment Jean Monnet, Rue Alcide de Gasperi, L-2920 Luxembourg, http://epp.eurostat.ec.europa.eu; *Eurostat Yearbook 2006-2007.*

Organisation for Economic Cooperation and Development (OECD), 2 rue Andre Pascal, F-75775 Paris Cedex 16, France, (Telephone in U.S. (202) 785-6323), (Fax in U.S. (202) 785-0350), www.oecd.org; *Financial Market Trends: OECD Periodical.*

United Nations Statistics Division, New York, NY 10017, (800) 253-9646, Fax: (212) 963-4116, http://unstats.un.org; *Statistical Yearbook.*

IRELAND - BROADCASTING

Central Intelligence Agency, Office of Public Affairs, Washington, DC 20505, (703) 482-0623, Fax: (703) 482-1739, www.cia.gov; *The World Factbook.*

Euromonitor International, Inc., 224 S. Michigan Avenue, Suite 1500, Chicago, IL 60604, (312) 922-1115, Fax: (312) 922-1157, www.euromonitor.com; *World Marketing Data and Statistics.*

Eurostat, Batiment Jean Monnet, Rue Alcide de Gasperi, L-2920 Luxembourg, http://epp.eurostat.ec.europa.eu; *Eurostat Yearbook 2006-2007.*

M.E. Sharpe, 80 Business Park Drive, Armonk, NY 10504, (800) 541-6563, Fax: (914) 273-2106, www.mesharpe.com; *The Illustrated Book of World Rankings.*

Palgrave Macmillan Ltd., Houndmills, Basingstoke, Hampshire, RG21 6XS, England, (Telephone in U.S. (888) 330-8477), (Fax in U.S. (800) 672-2054), www.palgrave.com; *The Statesman's Yearbook 2008.*

UNESCO Institute for Statistics, C.P. 6128 Succursale Centre-Ville, Montreal, Quebec, H3C 3J7 Canada, (Dial from U.S. (514) 343-6880), (Fax from U.S. (514) 343 6882), www.uis.unesco.org; *Statistical Tables.*

United Nations Statistics Division, New York, NY 10017, (800) 253-9646, Fax: (212) 963-4116, http://unstats.un.org; *Trends in Europe and North America: The Statistical Yearbook of the ECE 2005.*

WRTH Publications Limited, PO Box 290, Oxford OX2 7FT, UK, www.wrth.com; *World Radio TV Handbook 2007.*

IRELAND - BUDGET

Central Intelligence Agency, Office of Public Affairs, Washington, DC 20505, (703) 482-0623, Fax: (703) 482-1739, www.cia.gov; *The World Factbook.*

Eurostat, Batiment Jean Monnet, Rue Alcide de Gasperi, L-2920 Luxembourg, http://epp.eurostat.ec.europa.eu; *Government Budgets.*

IRELAND - BUSINESS

Eurostat, Batiment Jean Monnet, Rue Alcide de Gasperi, L-2920 Luxembourg, http://epp.eurostat.ec.europa.eu; *Eurostat Yearbook 2006-2007.*

Organisation for Economic Cooperation and Development (OECD), 2 rue Andre Pascal, F-75775 Paris Cedex 16, France, (Telephone in U.S. (202) 785-6323), (Fax in U.S. (202) 785-0350), www.oecd.org; *OECD Main Economic Indicators (MEI).*

IRELAND - CADMIUM PRODUCTION

See IRELAND - MINERAL INDUSTRIES

IRELAND - CAPITAL INVESTMENTS

Organisation for Economic Cooperation and Development (OECD), 2 rue Andre Pascal, F-75775 Paris Cedex 16, France, (Telephone in U.S. (202) 785-6323), (Fax in U.S. (202) 785-0350), www.oecd.org; *Financial Market Trends: OECD Periodical* and *OECD Economic Outlook 2008.*

IRELAND - CAPITAL LEVY

International Monetary Fund (IMF), 700 Nineteenth Street, NW, Washington, DC 20431, (202) 623-7000, Fax: (202) 623-4661, www.imf.org; *Government Finance Statistics Yearbook (2008 Edition).*

Organisation for Economic Cooperation and Development (OECD), 2 rue Andre Pascal, F-75775 Paris Cedex 16, France, (Telephone in U.S. (202) 785-6323), (Fax in U.S. (202) 785-0350), www.oecd.org; *Financial Market Trends: OECD Periodical* and *OECD Economic Outlook 2008.*

IRELAND - CATTLE

See IRELAND - LIVESTOCK

IRELAND - CHESTNUT PRODUCTION

See IRELAND - CROPS

IRELAND - CHICKENS

See IRELAND - LIVESTOCK

IRELAND - CHILDBIRTH - STATISTICS

Central Intelligence Agency, Office of Public Affairs, Washington, DC 20505, (703) 482-0623, Fax: (703) 482-1739, www.cia.gov; *The World Factbook.*

Euromonitor International, Inc., 224 S. Michigan Avenue, Suite 1500, Chicago, IL 60604, (312) 922-1115, Fax: (312) 922-1157, www.euromonitor.com; *The World Economic Factbook 2008.*

European Union, Delegation of the European Commission to the United States, 2300 M Street, NW, Washington, DC 20037, (202) 862-9500, Fax: (202) 429-1766, www.eurunion.org; *First Demographic Estimates for 2006.*

Eurostat, Batiment Jean Monnet, Rue Alcide de Gasperi, L-2920 Luxembourg, http://epp.eurostat.ec.europa.eu; *Eurostat Yearbook 2006-2007.*

M.E. Sharpe, 80 Business Park Drive, Armonk, NY 10504, (800) 541-6563, Fax: (914) 273-2106, www.mesharpe.com; *The Illustrated Book of World Rankings.*

Palgrave Macmillan Ltd., Houndmills, Basingstoke, Hampshire, RG21 6XS, England, (Telephone in U.S. (888) 330-8477), (Fax in U.S. (800) 672-2054), www.palgrave.com; *The Statesman's Yearbook 2008.*

Taylor and Francis Group, An Informa Business, 2 Park Square, Milton Park, Abingdon, Oxford OX14 4RN, United Kingdom, (Dial from U.S. (212) 216-7800), (Fax from U.S. (212) 564-7854), www.tandf.co.uk; *The Europa World Year Book.*

United Nations Statistics Division, New York, NY 10017, (800) 253-9646, Fax: (212) 963-4116, http://unstats.un.org; *Demographic Yearbook* and *Statistical Yearbook.*

The World Bank, 1818 H Street, NW, Washington, DC 20433, (202) 473-1000, Fax: (202) 477-6391, www.worldbank.org; *World Development Indicators (WDI) 2008.*

World Health Organization (WHO), Avenue Appia 20, 1211 Geneve 27, Switzerland, (Telephone in U.S. (212) 331-9081), www.who.int; *World Health Report 2006.*

IRELAND - CLIMATE

M.E. Sharpe, 80 Business Park Drive, Armonk, NY 10504, (800) 541-6563, Fax: (914) 273-2106, www.mesharpe.com; *The Illustrated Book of World Rankings.*

Palgrave Macmillan Ltd., Houndmills, Basingstoke, Hampshire, RG21 6XS, England, (Telephone in U.S. (888) 330-8477), (Fax in U.S. (800) 672-2054), www.palgrave.com; *The Statesman's Yearbook 2008.*

IRELAND - CLOTHING EXPORTS AND IMPORTS

See IRELAND - TEXTILE INDUSTRY

IRELAND - COAL PRODUCTION

See IRELAND - MINERAL INDUSTRIES

IRELAND - COBALT PRODUCTION

See IRELAND - MINERAL INDUSTRIES

IRELAND - COCOA PRODUCTION

See IRELAND - CROPS

IRELAND - COFFEE

See IRELAND - CROPS

IRELAND - COMMERCE

Palgrave Macmillan Ltd., Houndmills, Basingstoke, Hampshire, RG21 6XS, England, (Telephone in U.S. (888) 330-8477), (Fax in U.S. (800) 672-2054), www.palgrave.com; *The Statesman's Yearbook 2008.*

IRELAND - COMMODITY EXCHANGES

Commodity Research Bureau, 330 South Wells Street, Suite 612, Chicago, IL 60606-7110, (800) 621-5271, Fax: (312) 939-4135, www.crbtrader.com; *2006 CRB Commodity Yearbook and CD.*

International Lead and Zinc Study Group (ILZSG), Rua Almirante Barroso 38, 5th Floor, Lisbon 1000 - 013, Portugal, www.ilzsg.org; Interactive Statistical Database.

International Monetary Fund (IMF), 700 Nineteenth Street, NW, Washington, DC 20431, (202) 623-7000, Fax: (202) 623-4661, www.imf.org; *IMF Primary Commodity Prices.*

United Nations Food and Agricultural Organization (FAO), Viale delle Terme di Caracalla, 00100 Rome, Italy, (Dial from U.S. (202) 653-2400), (Fax from U.S. (202) 653 5760), www.fao.org; *The State of Food and Agriculture (SOFA) 2006.*

United Nations Statistics Division, New York, NY 10017, (800) 253-9646, Fax: (212) 963-4116, http://unstats.un.org; *Statistical Yearbook.*

IRELAND - COMMUNICATION AND TRAFFIC

European Union, Delegation of the European Commission to the United States, 2300 M Street, NW, Washington, DC 20037, (202) 862-9500, Fax: (202) 429-1766, www.eurunion.org; *Statistical Overview of Transport in the European Union (Data 1970-2001).*

United Nations Statistics Division, New York, NY 10017, (800) 253-9646, Fax: (212) 963-4116, http://unstats.un.org; *Statistical Yearbook.*

IRELAND - CONSTRUCTION INDUSTRY

European Union, Delegation of the European Commission to the United States, 2300 M Street, NW,

Washington, DC 20037, (202) 862-9500, Fax: (202) 429-1766, www.eurunion.org; *European Union Labour Force Survey.*

Eurostat, Batiment Jean Monnet, Rue Alcide de Gasperi, L-2920 Luxembourg, http://epp.eurostat.ec.europa.eu; *Eurostat Yearbook 2006-2007.*

M.E. Sharpe, 80 Business Park Drive, Armonk, NY 10504, (800) 541-6563, Fax: (914) 273-2106, www.mesharpe.com; *The Illustrated Book of World Rankings.*

Organisation for Economic Cooperation and Development (OECD), 2 rue Andre Pascal, F-75775 Paris Cedex 16, France, (Telephone in U.S. (202) 785-6323), (Fax in U.S. (202) 785-0350), www.oecd.org; *Iron and Steel Industry in 2004 (2006 Edition); OECD Economic Survey - Ireland 2008; OECD Main Economic Indicators (MEI);* and STructural ANalysis (STAN) database.

Palgrave Macmillan Ltd., Houndmills, Basingstoke, Hampshire, RG21 6XS, England, (Telephone in U.S. (888) 330-8477), (Fax in U.S. (800) 672-2054), www.palgrave.com; *The Statesman's Yearbook 2008.*

United Nations Statistics Division, New York, NY 10017, (800) 253-9646, Fax: (212) 963-4116, http://unstats.un.org; *Statistical Yearbook.*

IRELAND - CONSUMER PRICE INDEXES

Eurostat, Batiment Jean Monnet, Rue Alcide de Gasperi, L-2920 Luxembourg, http://epp.eurostat.ec.europa.eu; *Eurostat Yearbook 2006-2007.*

International Labour Office, I.L.O. Publications, 4 route des Morillons, CH-1211 Geneva 22, Switzerland, (Telephone in U.S. (202) 653-7652), (Fax in U.S. (202) 653-7687), www.ilo.org; *Yearbook of Labour Statistics 2006.*

Organisation for Economic Cooperation and Development (OECD), 2 rue Andre Pascal, F-75775 Paris Cedex 16, France, (Telephone in U.S. (202) 785-6323), (Fax in U.S. (202) 785-0350), www.oecd.org; *OECD Economic Outlook 2008.*

Taylor and Francis Group, An Informa Business, 2 Park Square, Milton Park, Abingdon, Oxford OX14 4RN, United Kingdom, (Dial from U.S. (212) 216-7800), (Fax from U.S. (212) 564-7854), www.tandf.co.uk; *The Europa World Year Book.*

United Nations Statistics Division, New York, NY 10017, (800) 253-9646, Fax: (212) 963-4116, http://unstats.un.org; *Statistical Yearbook* and *Trends in Europe and North America: The Statistical Yearbook of the ECE 2005.*

The World Bank, 1818 H Street, NW, Washington, DC 20433, (202) 473-1000, Fax: (202) 477-6391, www.worldbank.org; *Ireland.*

IRELAND - CONSUMPTION (ECONOMICS)

Eurostat, Batiment Jean Monnet, Rue Alcide de Gasperi, L-2920 Luxembourg, http://epp.eurostat.ec.europa.eu; *Eurostat Yearbook 2006-2007.*

International Lead and Zinc Study Group (ILZSG), Rua Almirante Barroso 38, 5th Floor, Lisbon 1000 - 013, Portugal, www.ilzsg.org; Interactive Statistical Database.

Organisation for Economic Cooperation and Development (OECD), 2 rue Andre Pascal, F-75775 Paris Cedex 16, France, (Telephone in U.S. (202) 785-6323), (Fax in U.S. (202) 785-0350), www.oecd.org; *Environmental Impacts of Foreign Direct Investment in the Mining Sector in the Newly Independent States (NIS); Iron and Steel Industry in 2004 (2006 Edition); A New World Map in Textiles and Clothing: Adjusting to Change; 2005 OECD Agricultural Outlook Tables, 1970-2014; Revenue Statistics 1965-2006 - 2007 Edition;* and *Towards Sustainable Household Consumption?: Trends and Policies in OECD Countries.*

Technical Association of the Pulp and Paper Industry (TAPPI), 15 Technology Parkway South, Norcross, GA 30092, (770) 446-1400, Fax: (770) 446-6947, www.tappi.org; *TAPPI Annual Report.*

The World Bank, 1818 H Street, NW, Washington, DC 20433, (202) 473-1000, Fax: (202) 477-6391, www.worldbank.org; *World Development Report 2008.*

IRELAND - COPPER INDUSTRY AND TRADE

See IRELAND - MINERAL INDUSTRIES

IRELAND - CORN INDUSTRY

See IRELAND - CROPS

IRELAND - COST AND STANDARD OF LIVING

Eurostat, Batiment Jean Monnet, Rue Alcide de Gasperi, L-2920 Luxembourg, http://epp.eurostat.ec.europa.eu; *Eurostat Yearbook 2006-2007.*

IRELAND - COTTON

See IRELAND - CROPS

IRELAND - CRIME

Central Statistics Office (CSO) Ireland, Skehard Road, Cork, Ireland, www.cso.ie; *Women and Men in Ireland, 2007.*

Eurostat, Batiment Jean Monnet, Rue Alcide de Gasperi, L-2920 Luxembourg, http://epp.eurostat.ec.europa.eu; *Crime and Criminal Justice; General Government Expenditure and Revenue in the EU, 2006;* and *Study on Crime Victimisation.*

International Criminal Police Organization (INTERPOL), General Secretariat, 200 quai Charles de Gaulle, 69006 Lyon, France, www.interpol.int; *International Crime Statistics.*

U.S. Department of Justice (DOJ), Bureau of Justice Statistics, 810 Seventh Street, NW, Washington, DC 20531, (202) 307-0765, www.ojp.usdoj.gov/bjs/; *The World Factbook of Criminal Justice Systems.*

United Nations Statistics Division, New York, NY 10017, (800) 253-9646, Fax: (212) 963-4116, http://unstats.un.org; *Trends in Europe and North America: The Statistical Yearbook of the ECE 2005.*

Yale University Press, PO Box 209040, New Haven, CT 06520-9040, (203) 432-0960, Fax: (203) 432-0948, http://yalepress.yale.edu/yupbooks; *Violence and Crime in Cross-National Perspective.*

IRELAND - CROPS

Euromonitor International, Inc., 224 S. Michigan Avenue, Suite 1500, Chicago, IL 60604, (312) 922-1115, Fax: (312) 922-1157, www.euromonitor.com; *European Marketing Data and Statistics 2008.*

European Union, Delegation of the European Commission to the United States, 2300 M Street, NW, Washington, DC 20037, (202) 862-9500, Fax: (202) 429-1766, www.eurunion.org; *Agricultural Statistics: Data 1995-2005; Agriculture in the European Union: Statistical and Economic Information 2006; Eurostatistics: Data for Short-Term Economic Analysis (2007 edition);* and *Regions - Statistical Yearbook 2006.*

Eurostat, Batiment Jean Monnet, Rue Alcide de Gasperi, L-2920 Luxembourg, http://epp.eurostat.ec.europa.eu; *Eurostat Yearbook 2006-2007.*

M.E. Sharpe, 80 Business Park Drive, Armonk, NY 10504, (800) 541-6563, Fax: (914) 273-2106, www.mesharpe.com; *The Illustrated Book of World Rankings.*

Organisation for Economic Cooperation and Development (OECD), 2 rue Andre Pascal, F-75775 Paris Cedex 16, France, (Telephone in U.S. (202) 785-6323), (Fax in U.S. (202) 785-0350), www.oecd.org; *International Trade by Commodity Statistics (ITCS)* and *2005 OECD Agricultural Outlook Tables, 1970-2014.*

Palgrave Macmillan Ltd., Houndmills, Basingstoke, Hampshire, RG21 6XS, England, (Telephone in U.S. (888) 330-8477), (Fax in U.S. (800) 672-2054), www.palgrave.com; *The Statesman's Yearbook 2008.*

Taylor and Francis Group, An Informa Business, 2 Park Square, Milton Park, Abingdon, Oxford OX14 4RN, United Kingdom, (Dial from U.S. (212) 216-7800), (Fax from U.S. (212) 564-7854), www.tandf.co.uk; *The Europa World Year Book.*

United Nations Conference on Trade and Development (UNCTAD), DC2-1120, United Nations, New York, NY 10017, (212) 963-0027, www.unctad.org; *UNCTAD Commodity Yearbook.*

United Nations Food and Agricultural Organization (FAO), Viale delle Terme di Caracalla, 00100 Rome, Italy, (Dial from U.S. (202) 653-2400), (Fax from U.S. (202) 653 5760), www.fao.org; *FAO Production Yearbook 2002* and *The State of Food and Agriculture (SOFA) 2006.*

United Nations Statistics Division, New York, NY 10017, (800) 253-9646, Fax: (212) 963-4116, http://unstats.un.org; *Statistical Yearbook.*

IRELAND - CUSTOMS ADMINISTRATION

Eurostat, Batiment Jean Monnet, Rue Alcide de Gasperi, L-2920 Luxembourg, http://epp.eurostat.ec.europa.eu; *Eurostat Yearbook 2006-2007.*

International Monetary Fund (IMF), 700 Nineteenth Street, NW, Washington, DC 20431, (202) 623-7000, Fax: (202) 623-4661, www.imf.org; *Government Finance Statistics Yearbook (2008 Edition).*

Organisation for Economic Cooperation and Development (OECD), 2 rue Andre Pascal, F-75775 Paris Cedex 16, France, (Telephone in U.S. (202) 785-6323), (Fax in U.S. (202) 785-0350), www.oecd.org; *Environmental Impacts of Foreign Direct Investment in the Mining Sector in the Newly Independent States (NIS).*

Palgrave Macmillan Ltd., Houndmills, Basingstoke, Hampshire, RG21 6XS, England, (Telephone in U.S. (888) 330-8477), (Fax in U.S. (800) 672-2054), www.palgrave.com; *The Statesman's Yearbook 2008.*

IRELAND - DAIRY PROCESSING

European Union, Delegation of the European Commission to the United States, 2300 M Street, NW, Washington, DC 20037, (202) 862-9500, Fax: (202) 429-1766, www.eurunion.org; *Eurostatistics: Data for Short-Term Economic Analysis (2007 edition).*

Eurostat, Batiment Jean Monnet, Rue Alcide de Gasperi, L-2920 Luxembourg, http://epp.eurostat.ec.europa.eu; *Eurostat Yearbook 2006-2007.*

M.E. Sharpe, 80 Business Park Drive, Armonk, NY 10504, (800) 541-6563, Fax: (914) 273-2106, www.mesharpe.com; *The Illustrated Book of World Rankings.*

Organisation for Economic Cooperation and Development (OECD), 2 rue Andre Pascal, F-75775 Paris Cedex 16, France, (Telephone in U.S. (202) 785-6323), (Fax in U.S. (202) 785-0350), www.oecd.org; *2005 OECD Agricultural Outlook Tables, 1970-2014.*

Palgrave Macmillan Ltd., Houndmills, Basingstoke, Hampshire, RG21 6XS, England, (Telephone in U.S. (888) 330-8477), (Fax in U.S. (800) 672-2054), www.palgrave.com; *The Statesman's Yearbook 2008.*

Taylor and Francis Group, An Informa Business, 2 Park Square, Milton Park, Abingdon, Oxford OX14 4RN, United Kingdom, (Dial from U.S. (212) 216-7800), (Fax from U.S. (212) 564-7854), www.tandf.co.uk; *The Europa World Year Book.*

United Nations Food and Agricultural Organization (FAO), Viale delle Terme di Caracalla, 00100 Rome, Italy, (Dial from U.S. (202) 653-2400), (Fax from U.S. (202) 653 5760), www.fao.org; *FAO Production Yearbook 2002* and *The State of Food and Agriculture (SOFA) 2006.*

United Nations Statistics Division, New York, NY 10017, (800) 253-9646, Fax: (212) 963-4116, http://unstats.un.org; *Statistical Yearbook.*

IRELAND - DEATH RATES

See IRELAND - MORTALITY

IRELAND - DEBTS, EXTERNAL

International Monetary Fund (IMF), 700 Nineteenth Street, NW, Washington, DC 20431, (202) 623-

7000, Fax: (202) 623-4661, www.imf.org; *Government Finance Statistics Yearbook (2008 Edition).*

Organisation for Economic Cooperation and Development (OECD), 2 rue Andre Pascal, F-75775 Paris Cedex 16, France, (Telephone in U.S. (202) 785-6323), (Fax in U.S. (202) 785-0350), www.oecd.org; *Financial Market Trends: OECD Periodical; Geographical Distribution of Financial Flows to Aid Recipients 2002-2006;* and *OECD Economic Outlook 2008.*

Palgrave Macmillan Ltd., Houndmills, Basingstoke, Hampshire, RG21 6XS, England, (Telephone in U.S. (888) 330-8477), (Fax in U.S. (800) 672-2054), www.palgrave.com; *The Statesman's Yearbook 2008.*

The World Bank, 1818 H Street, NW, Washington, DC 20433, (202) 473-1000, Fax: (202) 477-6391, www.worldbank.org; *Global Development Finance 2007; World Development Indicators (WDI) 2008;* and *World Development Report 2008.*

IRELAND - DEFENSE EXPENDITURES

See IRELAND - ARMED FORCES

IRELAND - DEMOGRAPHY

Central Statistics Office (CSO) Ireland, Skehard Road, Cork, Ireland, www.cso.ie; *Measuring Ireland's Progress, 2006* and *Women and Men in Ireland, 2007.*

Euromonitor International, Inc., 224 S. Michigan Avenue, Suite 1500, Chicago, IL 60604, (312) 922-1115, Fax: (312) 922-1157, www.euromonitor.com; *The World Economic Factbook 2008* and *World Marketing Data and Statistics.*

European Union, Delegation of the European Commission to the United States, 2300 M Street, NW, Washington, DC 20037, (202) 862-9500, Fax: (202) 429-1766, www.eurunion.org; *First Demographic Estimates for 2006* and *Regions - Statistical Yearbook 2006.*

Eurostat, Batiment Jean Monnet, Rue Alcide de Gasperi, L-2920 Luxembourg, http://epp.eurostat.ec.europa.eu; *Demographic Outlook - National Reports on the Demographic Developments in 2006* and *Eurostat Yearbook 2006-2007.*

M.E. Sharpe, 80 Business Park Drive, Armonk, NY 10504, (800) 541-6563, Fax: (914) 273-2106, www.mesharpe.com; *The Illustrated Book of World Rankings.*

United Nations Statistics Division, New York, NY 10017, (800) 253-9646, Fax: (212) 963-4116, http://unstats.un.org; *Human Development Report 2006.*

The World Bank, 1818 H Street, NW, Washington, DC 20433, (202) 473-1000, Fax: (202) 477-6391, www.worldbank.org; *Ireland.*

IRELAND - DIAMONDS

See IRELAND - MINERAL INDUSTRIES

IRELAND - DISPOSABLE INCOME

M.E. Sharpe, 80 Business Park Drive, Armonk, NY 10504, (800) 541-6563, Fax: (914) 273-2106, www.mesharpe.com; *The Illustrated Book of World Rankings.*

Organisation for Economic Cooperation and Development (OECD), 2 rue Andre Pascal, F-75775 Paris Cedex 16, France, (Telephone in U.S. (202) 785-6323), (Fax in U.S. (202) 785-0350), www.oecd.org; *OECD Economic Outlook 2008.*

United Nations Statistics Division, New York, NY 10017, (800) 253-9646, Fax: (212) 963-4116, http://unstats.un.org; *National Accounts Statistics: Compendium of Income Distribution Statistics* and *Statistical Yearbook.*

IRELAND - DIVORCE

European Union, Delegation of the European Commission to the United States, 2300 M Street, NW, Washington, DC 20037, (202) 862-9500, Fax: (202) 429-1766, www.eurunion.org; *First Demographic Estimates for 2006.*

M.E. Sharpe, 80 Business Park Drive, Armonk, NY 10504, (800) 541-6563, Fax: (914) 273-2106, www.mesharpe.com; *The Illustrated Book of World Rankings.*

United Nations Statistics Division, New York, NY 10017, (800) 253-9646, Fax: (212) 963-4116, http://unstats.un.org; *Demographic Yearbook* and *Trends in Europe and North America: The Statistical Yearbook of the ECE 2005.*

IRELAND - ECONOMIC ASSISTANCE

European Union, Delegation of the European Commission to the United States, 2300 M Street, NW, Washington, DC 20037, (202) 862-9500, Fax: (202) 429-1766, www.eurunion.org; *RD Expenditure in Europe (2006 edition).*

Eurostat, Batiment Jean Monnet, Rue Alcide de Gasperi, L-2920 Luxembourg, http://epp.eurostat.ec.europa.eu; *Eurostat Yearbook 2006-2007.*

Organisation for Economic Cooperation and Development (OECD), 2 rue Andre Pascal, F-75775 Paris Cedex 16, France, (Telephone in U.S. (202) 785-6323), (Fax in U.S. (202) 785-0350), www.oecd.org; *Geographical Distribution of Financial Flows to Aid Recipients 2002-2006.*

IRELAND - ECONOMIC CONDITIONS

Banque de France, 48 rue Croix des Petits champs, 75001 Paris, France, www.banque-france.fr/home.htm; *Key Data for the Euro Area.*

Center for International Business Education Research (CIBER), Columbia Business School and School of International and Public Affairs, Uris Hall, Room 212, 3022 Broadway, New York, NY 10027-6902, Mr. Joshua Safier, (212) 854-4750, Fax: (212) 222-9821, www.columbia.edu/cu/ciber/; Datastream International.

Central Intelligence Agency, Office of Public Affairs, Washington, DC 20505, (703) 482-0623, Fax: (703) 482-1739, www.cia.gov; *The World Factbook.*

Central Statistics Office (CSO) Ireland, Skehard Road, Cork, Ireland, www.cso.ie; *Measuring Ireland's Progress, 2006.*

DSI Data Service Information, Xantener Strasse 51a, D-47495 Rheinberg, Germany, www.dsidata.com; *Campus Solution.*

Dun and Bradstreet (DB) Corporation, 103 JFK Parkway, Short Hills, NJ 07078, (973) 921-5500, www.dnb.com; *Country Report.*

Economist Intelligence Unit, 111 West 57th Street, New York, NY 10019, (212) 554-0600, Fax: (212) 586-1181, www.eiu.com; *Ireland Country Report.*

Euromonitor International, Inc., 224 S. Michigan Avenue, Suite 1500, Chicago, IL 60604, (312) 922-1115, Fax: (312) 922-1157, www.euromonitor.com; *European Marketing Data and Statistics 2008; The World Economic Factbook 2008;* and *World Marketing Data and Statistics.*

European Union, Delegation of the European Commission to the United States, 2300 M Street, NW, Washington, DC 20037, (202) 862-9500, Fax: (202) 429-1766, www.eurunion.org; *The EU Economy, 2007 Review: Moving Europe's Productivity Frontier* and *European Union Labour Force Survey.*

Eurostat, Batiment Jean Monnet, Rue Alcide de Gasperi, L-2920 Luxembourg, http://epp.eurostat.ec.europa.eu; *Consumers in Europe - Facts and Figures on Services of General Interest; EU Economic Data Pocketbook;* and *Eurostat Yearbook 2006-2007.*

International Monetary Fund (IMF), 700 Nineteenth Street, NW, Washington, DC 20431, (202) 623-7000, Fax: (202) 623-4661, www.imf.org; *World Economic Outlook Reports.*

M.E. Sharpe, 80 Business Park Drive, Armonk, NY 10504, (800) 541-6563, Fax: (914) 273-2106, www.mesharpe.com; *The Illustrated Book of World Rankings.*

Organisation for Economic Cooperation and Development (OECD), 2 rue Andre Pascal, F-75775 Paris Cedex 16, France, (Telephone in U.S. (202) 785-6323), (Fax in U.S. (202) 785-0350), www.oecd.org; *Geographical Distribution of Financial Flows to Aid Recipients 2002-2006; ICT Sector Data and Metadata by Country; Labour Force Statistics: 1986-2005, 2007 Edition; OECD Composite Leading Indicators (CLIs), Updated September 2007; OECD Economic Outlook 2008; OECD Economic Survey - Ireland 2008; OECD Employment Outlook 2007; OECD in Figures 2007;* and *OECD Main Economic Indicators (MEI).*

Palgrave Macmillan Ltd., Houndmills, Basingstoke, Hampshire, RG21 6XS, England, (Telephone in U.S. (888) 330-8477), (Fax in U.S. (800) 672-2054), www.palgrave.com; *The Statesman's Yearbook 2008.*

Platts, 2 Penn Plaza, 25th Floor, New York, NY 10121-2298, (212) 904-3070, www.platts.com; *Energy Economist.*

Taylor and Francis Group, An Informa Business, 2 Park Square, Milton Park, Abingdon, Oxford OX14 4RN, United Kingdom, (Dial from U.S. (212) 216-7800), (Fax from U.S. (212) 564-7854), www.tandf.co.uk; *The Europa World Year Book.*

United Nations Statistics Division, New York, NY 10017, (800) 253-9646, Fax: (212) 963-4116, http://unstats.un.org; *Energy Statistics Yearbook 2003* and *World Statistics Pocketbook.*

The World Bank, 1818 H Street, NW, Washington, DC 20433, (202) 473-1000, Fax: (202) 477-6391, www.worldbank.org; *Global Economic Monitor (GEM); Global Economic Prospects 2008; Ireland; The World Bank Atlas 2003-2004;* and *World Development Report 2008.*

IRELAND - ECONOMICS - SOCIOLOGICAL ASPECTS

Eurostat, Batiment Jean Monnet, Rue Alcide de Gasperi, L-2920 Luxembourg, http://epp.eurostat.ec.europa.eu; *Eurostat Yearbook 2006-2007.*

Organisation for Economic Cooperation and Development (OECD), 2 rue Andre Pascal, F-75775 Paris Cedex 16, France, (Telephone in U.S. (202) 785-6323), (Fax in U.S. (202) 785-0350), www.oecd.org; *OECD Economic Outlook 2008.*

IRELAND - EDUCATION

Central Statistics Office (CSO) Ireland, Skehard Road, Cork, Ireland, www.cso.ie; *Measuring Ireland's Progress, 2006* and *Women and Men in Ireland, 2007.*

Euromonitor International, Inc., 224 S. Michigan Avenue, Suite 1500, Chicago, IL 60604, (312) 922-1115, Fax: (312) 922-1157, www.euromonitor.com; *European Marketing Data and Statistics 2008* and *World Marketing Data and Statistics.*

European Union, Delegation of the European Commission to the United States, 2300 M Street, NW, Washington, DC 20037, (202) 862-9500, Fax: (202) 429-1766, www.eurunion.org; *Education across Europe 2003* and *Regions - Statistical Yearbook 2006.*

Eurostat, Batiment Jean Monnet, Rue Alcide de Gasperi, L-2920 Luxembourg, http://epp.eurostat.ec.europa.eu; *Education, Science and Culture Statistics* and *Eurostat Yearbook 2006-2007.*

M.E. Sharpe, 80 Business Park Drive, Armonk, NY 10504, (800) 541-6563, Fax: (914) 273-2106, www.mesharpe.com; *The Illustrated Book of World Rankings.*

Organisation for Economic Cooperation and Development (OECD), 2 rue Andre Pascal, F-75775 Paris Cedex 16, France, (Telephone in U.S. (202) 785-6323), (Fax in U.S. (202) 785-0350), www.oecd.org; *Education at a Glance* (2007 Edition).

Palgrave Macmillan Ltd., Houndmills, Basingstoke, Hampshire, RG21 6XS, England, (Telephone in U.S. (888) 330-8477), (Fax in U.S. (800) 672-2054), www.palgrave.com; *The Statesman's Yearbook 2008.*

Taylor and Francis Group, An Informa Business, 2 Park Square, Milton Park, Abingdon, Oxford OX14 4RN, United Kingdom, (Dial from U.S. (212) 216-

7800), (Fax from U.S. (212) 564-7854), www.tandf.co.uk; *The Europa World Year Book.*

UNESCO Institute for Statistics, C.P. 6128 Succursale Centre-Ville, Montreal, Quebec, H3C 3J7 Canada, (Dial from U.S. (514) 343-6880), (Fax from U.S. (514) 343 6882), www.uis.unesco.org; *Statistical Tables.*

United Nations Statistics Division, New York, NY 10017, (800) 253-9646, Fax: (212) 963-4116, http://unstats.un.org; *Human Development Report 2006* and *Trends in Europe and North America: The Statistical Yearbook of the ECE 2005.*

The World Bank, 1818 H Street, NW, Washington, DC 20433, (202) 473-1000, Fax: (202) 477-6391, www.worldbank.org; *Ireland; World Development Indicators (WDI) 2008;* and *World Development Report 2008.*

IRELAND - ELECTRICITY

European Union, Delegation of the European Commission to the United States, 2300 M Street, NW, Washington, DC 20037, (202) 862-9500, Fax: (202) 429-1766, www.eurunion.org; *European Union Energy Transport in Figures 2006; Eurostatistics: Data for Short-Term Economic Analysis (2007 edition);* and *Regions - Statistical Yearbook 2006.*

Eurostat, Batiment Jean Monnet, Rue Alcide de Gasperi, L-2920 Luxembourg, http://epp.eurostat.ec.europa.eu; *Energy - Monthly Statistics; Eurostat Yearbook 2006-2007;* and *Panorama of Energy - 2007 Edition.*

M.E. Sharpe, 80 Business Park Drive, Armonk, NY 10504, (800) 541-6563, Fax: (914) 273-2106, www.mesharpe.com; *The Illustrated Book of World Rankings.*

Organisation for Economic Cooperation and Development (OECD), 2 rue Andre Pascal, F-75775 Paris Cedex 16, France, (Telephone in U.S. (202) 785-6323), (Fax in U.S. (202) 785-0350), www.oecd.org; *Coal Information: 2007 Edition; Energy Statistics of OECD Countries* (2007 Edition); *Indicators of Industrial Activity;* and STructural ANalysis (STAN) database.

Palgrave Macmillan Ltd., Houndmills, Basingstoke, Hampshire, RG21 6XS, England, (Telephone in U.S. (888) 330-8477), (Fax in U.S. (800) 672-2054), www.palgrave.com; *The Statesman's Yearbook 2008.*

Platts, 2 Penn Plaza, 25th Floor, New York, NY 10121-2298, (212) 904-3070, www.platts.com; *Energy Economist; EU Energy;* and *European Electricity Review 2004.*

U.S. Department of Energy (DOE), Energy Information Administration (EIA), 1000 Independence Avenue, SW, Washington, DC 20585, (202) 586-8800, www.eia.doe.gov; *International Energy Annual 2004* and *International Energy Outlook 2006.*

United Nations Statistics Division, New York, NY 10017, (800) 253-9646, Fax: (212) 963-4116, http://unstats.un.org; *Energy Statistics Yearbook 2003; Human Development Report 2006; Statistical Yearbook;* and *Trends in Europe and North America: The Statistical Yearbook of the ECE 2005.*

IRELAND - EMPLOYMENT

Bernan Essential Government Publications, 4611-F Assembly Drive, Lanham MD, 20706-4391, (301) 459-2255, Fax: (800) 865-3450, www.bernan.com; *OECD Factbook 2006.*

Central Statistics Office (CSO) Ireland, Skehard Road, Cork, Ireland, www.cso.ie; *Measuring Ireland's Progress, 2006* and *Women and Men in Ireland, 2007.*

Euromonitor International, Inc., 224 S. Michigan Avenue, Suite 1500, Chicago, IL 60604, (312) 922-1115, Fax: (312) 922-1157, www.euromonitor.com; *European Marketing Data and Statistics 2008.*

European Union, Delegation of the European Commission to the United States, 2300 M Street, NW, Washington, DC 20037, (202) 862-9500, Fax: (202) 429-1766, www.eurunion.org; *Agriculture in the European Union: Statistical and Economic Information 2006; European Union Labour Force Survey; Eurostatistics: Data for Short-Term Economic Analysis (2007 edition);* and *Iron and Steel.*

Eurostat, Batiment Jean Monnet, Rue Alcide de Gasperi, L-2920 Luxembourg, http://epp.eurostat.ec.europa.eu; *Eurostat Yearbook 2006-2007.*

International Labour Office, I.L.O. Publications, 4 route des Morillons, CH-1211 Geneva 22, Switzerland, (Telephone in U.S. (202) 653-7652), (Fax in U.S. (202) 653-7687), www.ilo.org; *Yearbook of Labour Statistics 2006.*

M.E. Sharpe, 80 Business Park Drive, Armonk, NY 10504, (800) 541-6563, Fax: (914) 273-2106, www.mesharpe.com; *The Illustrated Book of World Rankings.*

Organisation for Economic Cooperation and Development (OECD), 2 rue Andre Pascal, F-75775 Paris Cedex 16, France, (Telephone in U.S. (202) 785-6323), (Fax in U.S. (202) 785-0350), www.oecd.org; *ICT Sector Data and Metadata by Country; Iron and Steel Industry in 2004 (2006 Edition); Labour Force Statistics: 1986-2005, 2007 Edition; A New World Map in Textiles and Clothing: Adjusting to Change; OECD Composite Leading Indicators (CLIs), Updated September 2007; OECD Economic Outlook 2008; OECD Economic Survey - Ireland 2008; OECD Employment Outlook 2007;* and *OECD in Figures 2007.*

United Nations Statistics Division, New York, NY 10017, (800) 253-9646, Fax: (212) 963-4116, http://unstats.un.org; *Statistical Yearbook* and *Trends in Europe and North America: The Statistical Yearbook of the ECE 2005.*

The World Bank, 1818 H Street, NW, Washington, DC 20433, (202) 473-1000, Fax: (202) 477-6391, www.worldbank.org; *Ireland.*

IRELAND - ENERGY INDUSTRIES

Enerdata, 10 Rue Royale, 75008 Paris, France, www.enerdata.fr; *Global Energy Market Data.*

Eurostat, Batiment Jean Monnet, Rue Alcide de Gasperi, L-2920 Luxembourg, http://epp.eurostat.ec.europa.eu; *Energy - Monthly Statistics; Eurostat Yearbook 2006-2007;* and *Panorama of Energy - 2007 Edition.*

International Energy Agency (IEA), 9, rue de la Federation, 75739 Paris Cedex 15, France, www.iea.org; *Key World Energy Statistics 2007.*

Organisation for Economic Cooperation and Development (OECD), 2 rue Andre Pascal, F-75775 Paris Cedex 16, France, (Telephone in U.S. (202) 785-6323), (Fax in U.S. (202) 785-0350), www.oecd.org; *Towards Sustainable Household Consumption?: Trends and Policies in OECD Countries.*

Platts, 2 Penn Plaza, 25th Floor, New York, NY 10121-2298, (212) 904-3070, www.platts.com; *EU Energy* and *European Power Daily.*

United Nations Statistics Division, New York, NY 10017, (800) 253-9646, Fax: (212) 963-4116, http://unstats.un.org; *Statistical Yearbook.*

The World Bank, 1818 H Street, NW, Washington, DC 20433, (202) 473-1000, Fax: (202) 477-6391, www.worldbank.org; *Ireland.*

IRELAND - ENVIRONMENTAL CONDITIONS

Central Statistics Office (CSO) Ireland, Skehard Road, Cork, Ireland, www.cso.ie; *Measuring Ireland's Progress, 2006.*

DSI Data Service Information, Xantener Strasse 51a, D-47495 Rheinberg, Germany, www.dsidata.com; *Campus Solution* and *DSI's Global Environmental Database.*

Economist Intelligence Unit, 111 West 57th Street, New York, NY 10019, (212) 554-0600, Fax: (212) 586-1181, www.eiu.com; *Ireland Country Report.*

United Nations Statistics Division, New York, NY 10017, (800) 253-9646, Fax: (212) 963-4116, http://unstats.un.org; *Trends in Europe and North America: The Statistical Yearbook of the ECE 2005* and *World Statistics Pocketbook.*

IRELAND - EXPENDITURES, PUBLIC

Eurostat, Batiment Jean Monnet, Rue Alcide de Gasperi, L-2920 Luxembourg, http://epp.eurostat.ec.europa.eu; *European Social Statistics - Social Protection Expenditure and Receipts - Data 1997-2005* and *Eurostat Yearbook 2006-2007.*

Organisation for Economic Cooperation and Development (OECD), 2 rue Andre Pascal, F-75775 Paris Cedex 16, France, (Telephone in U.S. (202) 785-6323), (Fax in U.S. (202) 785-0350), www.oecd.org; *Revenue Statistics 1965-2006 - 2007 Edition.*

IRELAND - EXPORTS

Central Intelligence Agency, Office of Public Affairs, Washington, DC 20505, (703) 482-0623, Fax: (703) 482-1739, www.cia.gov; *The World Factbook.*

Economist Intelligence Unit, 111 West 57th Street, New York, NY 10019, (212) 554-0600, Fax: (212) 586-1181, www.eiu.com; *Ireland Country Report.*

Euromonitor International, Inc., 224 S. Michigan Avenue, Suite 1500, Chicago, IL 60604, (312) 922-1115, Fax: (312) 922-1157, www.euromonitor.com; *The World Economic Factbook 2008.*

European Union, Delegation of the European Commission to the United States, 2300 M Street, NW, Washington, DC 20037, (202) 862-9500, Fax: (202) 429-1766, www.eurunion.org; *European Union Energy Transport in Figures 2006; Eurostatistics: Data for Short-Term Economic Analysis (2007 edition); External and Intra-European Union Trade: Data 1958-2002; External and Intra-European Union Trade: Data 1999-2004;* and *Fishery Statistics - 1990-2006.*

Eurostat, Batiment Jean Monnet, Rue Alcide de Gasperi, L-2920 Luxembourg, http://epp.eurostat.ec.europa.eu; *Eurostat Yearbook 2006-2007.*

International Lead and Zinc Study Group (ILZSG), Rua Almirante Barroso 38, 5th Floor, Lisbon 1000 - 013, Portugal, www.ilzsg.org; Interactive Statistical Database.

International Monetary Fund (IMF), 700 Nineteenth Street, NW, Washington, DC 20431, (202) 623-7000, Fax: (202) 623-4661, www.imf.org; *Direction of Trade Statistics Yearbook 2007; Government Finance Statistics Yearbook (2008 Edition);* and *International Financial Statistics Yearbook 2007.*

Organisation for Economic Cooperation and Development (OECD), 2 rue Andre Pascal, F-75775 Paris Cedex 16, France, (Telephone in U.S. (202) 785-6323), (Fax in U.S. (202) 785-0350), www.oecd.org; *Geographical Distribution of Financial Flows to Aid Recipients 2002-2006; International Trade by Commodity Statistics (ITCS); Iron and Steel Industry in 2004 (2006 Edition); 2005 OECD Agricultural Outlook Tables, 1970-2014; OECD Economic Outlook 2008; OECD Economic Survey - Ireland 2008; Review of Fisheries in OECD Countries: Country Statistics 2001 to 2003 - 2005 Edition;* and STructural ANalysis (STAN) database.

Palgrave Macmillan Ltd., Houndmills, Basingstoke, Hampshire, RG21 6XS, England, (Telephone in U.S. (888) 330-8477), (Fax in U.S. (800) 672-2054), www.palgrave.com; *The Statesman's Yearbook 2008.*

Platts, 2 Penn Plaza, 25th Floor, New York, NY 10121-2298, (212) 904-3070, www.platts.com; *Energy Economist.*

Taylor and Francis Group, An Informa Business, 2 Park Square, Milton Park, Abingdon, Oxford OX14 4RN, United Kingdom, (Dial from U.S. (212) 216-7800), (Fax from U.S. (212) 564-7854), www.tandf.co.uk; *The Europa World Year Book.*

Technical Association of the Pulp and Paper Industry (TAPPI), 15 Technology Parkway South, Norcross, GA 30092, (770) 446-1400, Fax: (770) 446-6947, www.tappi.org; *TAPPI Annual Report.*

United Nations Conference on Trade and Development (UNCTAD), DC2-1120, United Nations, New York, NY 10017, (212) 963-0027, www.unctad.org; *Handbook of Statistics 2005.*

United Nations Food and Agricultural Organization (FAO), Viale delle Terme di Caracalla, 00100 Rome,

Italy, (Dial from U.S. (202) 653-2400), (Fax from U.S. (202) 653 5760), www.fao.org; *The State of Food and Agriculture (SOFA) 2006.*

United Nations Statistics Division, New York, NY 10017, (800) 253-9646, Fax: (212) 963-4116, http://unstats.un.org; *Energy Statistics Yearbook 2003* and *Trends in Europe and North America: The Statistical Yearbook of the ECE 2005.*

The World Bank, 1818 H Street, NW, Washington, DC 20433, (202) 473-1000, Fax: (202) 477-6391, www.worldbank.org; *World Development Indicators (WDI) 2008* and *World Development Report 2008.*

IRELAND - FERTILITY, HUMAN

Central Intelligence Agency, Office of Public Affairs, Washington, DC 20505, (703) 482-0623, Fax: (703) 482-1739, www.cia.gov; *The World Factbook.*

European Union, Delegation of the European Commission to the United States, 2300 M Street, NW, Washington, DC 20037, (202) 862-9500, Fax: (202) 429-1766, www.eurunion.org; *First Demographic Estimates for 2006.*

M.E. Sharpe, 80 Business Park Drive, Armonk, NY 10504, (800) 541-6563, Fax: (914) 273-2106, www.mesharpe.com; *The Illustrated Book of World Rankings.*

United Nations Statistics Division, New York, NY 10017, (800) 253-9646, Fax: (212) 963-4116, http://unstats.un.org; *Human Development Report 2006* and *Trends in Europe and North America: The Statistical Yearbook of the ECE 2005.*

The World Bank, 1818 H Street, NW, Washington, DC 20433, (202) 473-1000, Fax: (202) 477-6391, www.worldbank.org; *The World Bank Atlas 2003-2004; World Development Indicators (WDI) 2008;* and *World Development Report 2008.*

IRELAND - FERTILIZER INDUSTRY

Eurostat, Batiment Jean Monnet, Rue Alcide de Gasperi, L-2920 Luxembourg, http://epp.eurostat.ec.europa.eu; *Eurostat Yearbook 2006-2007.*

Organisation for Economic Cooperation and Development (OECD), 2 rue Andre Pascal, F-75775 Paris Cedex 16, France, (Telephone in U.S. (202) 785-6323), (Fax in U.S. (202) 785-0350), www.oecd.org; *International Trade by Commodity Statistics (ITCS)* and *2005 OECD Agricultural Outlook Tables, 1970-2014.*

United Nations Food and Agricultural Organization (FAO), Viale delle Terme di Caracalla, 00100 Rome, Italy, (Dial from U.S. (202) 653-2400), (Fax from U.S. (202) 653 5760), www.fao.org; *FAO Fertilizer Yearbook* and *The State of Food and Agriculture (SOFA) 2006.*

United Nations Statistics Division, New York, NY 10017, (800) 253-9646, Fax: (212) 963-4116, http://unstats.un.org; *Statistical Yearbook.*

IRELAND - FETAL MORTALITY

See IRELAND - MORTALITY

IRELAND - FILM

See IRELAND - MOTION PICTURES

IRELAND - FINANCE

European Union, Delegation of the European Commission to the United States, 2300 M Street, NW, Washington, DC 20037, (202) 862-9500, Fax: (202) 429-1766, www.eurunion.org; *Eurostatistics: Data for Short-Term Economic Analysis (2007 edition).*

Eurostat, Batiment Jean Monnet, Rue Alcide de Gasperi, L-2920 Luxembourg, http://epp.eurostat.ec.europa.eu; *Eurostat Yearbook 2006-2007.*

International Monetary Fund (IMF), 700 Nineteenth Street, NW, Washington, DC 20431, (202) 623-7000, Fax: (202) 623-4661, www.imf.org; *International Financial Statistics Yearbook 2007.*

Organisation for Economic Cooperation and Development (OECD), 2 rue Andre Pascal, F-75775 Paris Cedex 16, France, (Telephone in U.S. (202) 785-6323), (Fax in U.S. (202) 785-0350), www.oecd.org; *OECD Economic Outlook 2008.*

Taylor and Francis Group, An Informa Business, 2 Park Square, Milton Park, Abingdon, Oxford OX14 4RN, United Kingdom, (Dial from U.S. (212) 216-7800), (Fax from U.S. (212) 564-7854), www.tandf.co.uk; *The Europa World Year Book.*

United Nations Statistics Division, New York, NY 10017, (800) 253-9646, Fax: (212) 963-4116, http://unstats.un.org; *National Accounts Statistics: Compendium of Income Distribution Statistics* and *Statistical Yearbook.*

The World Bank, 1818 H Street, NW, Washington, DC 20433, (202) 473-1000, Fax: (202) 477-6391, www.worldbank.org; *Ireland.*

IRELAND - FINANCE, PUBLIC

Banque de France, 48 rue Croix des Petits champs, 75001 Paris, France, www.banque-france.fr/home.htm; *Key Data for the Euro Area* and *Public Finance.*

Bernan Essential Government Publications, 4611-F Assembly Drive, Lanham MD, 20706-4391, (301) 459-2255, Fax: (800) 865-3450, www.bernan.com; *National Accounts Statistics.*

Economist Intelligence Unit, 111 West 57th Street, New York, NY 10019, (212) 554-0600, Fax: (212) 586-1181, www.eiu.com; *Ireland Country Report.*

European Union, Delegation of the European Commission to the United States, 2300 M Street, NW, Washington, DC 20037, (202) 862-9500, Fax: (202) 429-1766, www.eurunion.org; *Eurostatistics: Data for Short-Term Economic Analysis (2007 edition)* and *Fishery Statistics - 1990-2006.*

Eurostat, Batiment Jean Monnet, Rue Alcide de Gasperi, L-2920 Luxembourg, http://epp.eurostat.ec.europa.eu; *Eurostat Yearbook 2006-2007.*

International Monetary Fund (IMF), 700 Nineteenth Street, NW, Washington, DC 20431, (202) 623-7000, Fax: (202) 623-4661, www.imf.org; *International Financial Statistics; International Financial Statistics Online Service;* and *International Financial Statistics Yearbook 2007.*

M.E. Sharpe, 80 Business Park Drive, Armonk, NY 10504, (800) 541-6563, Fax: (914) 273-2106, www.mesharpe.com; *The Illustrated Book of World Rankings.*

Organisation for Economic Cooperation and Development (OECD), 2 rue Andre Pascal, F-75775 Paris Cedex 16, France, (Telephone in U.S. (202) 785-6323), (Fax in U.S. (202) 785-0350), www.oecd.org; *Financial Market Trends: OECD Periodical; Geographical Distribution of Financial Flows to Aid Recipients 2002-2006; International Trade by Commodity Statistics (ITCS); OECD Economic Outlook 2008; OECD Main Economic Indicators (MEI); Revenue Statistics 1965-2006 - 2007 Edition;* and *Review of Fisheries in OECD Countries: Country Statistics 2001 to 2003 - 2005 Edition.*

Palgrave Macmillan Ltd., Houndmills, Basingstoke, Hampshire, RG21 6XS, England, (Telephone in U.S. (888) 330-8477), (Fax in U.S. (800) 672-2054), www.palgrave.com; *The Statesman's Yearbook 2008.*

Taylor and Francis Group, An Informa Business, 2 Park Square, Milton Park, Abingdon, Oxford OX14 4RN, United Kingdom, (Dial from U.S. (212) 216-7800), (Fax from U.S. (212) 564-7854), www.tandf.co.uk; *The Europa World Year Book.*

The World Bank, 1818 H Street, NW, Washington, DC 20433, (202) 473-1000, Fax: (202) 477-6391, www.worldbank.org; *Ireland.*

IRELAND - FISHERIES

Euromonitor International, Inc., 224 S. Michigan Avenue, Suite 1500, Chicago, IL 60604, (312) 922-1115, Fax: (312) 922-1157, www.euromonitor.com; *European Marketing Data and Statistics 2008.*

European Union, Delegation of the European Commission to the United States, 2300 M Street, NW, Washington, DC 20037, (202) 862-9500, Fax: (202) 429-1766, www.eurunion.org; *Agricultural Statistics: Data 1995-2005* and *Fishery Statistics - 1990-2006.*

M.E. Sharpe, 80 Business Park Drive, Armonk, NY 10504, (800) 541-6563, Fax: (914) 273-2106, www.mesharpe.com; *The Illustrated Book of World Rankings.*

Organisation for Economic Cooperation and Development (OECD), 2 rue Andre Pascal, F-75775 Paris Cedex 16, France, (Telephone in U.S. (202) 785-6323), (Fax in U.S. (202) 785-0350), www.oecd.org; *Review of Fisheries in OECD Countries: Country Statistics 2001 to 2003 - 2005 Edition* and STructural ANalysis (STAN) database.

Palgrave Macmillan Ltd., Houndmills, Basingstoke, Hampshire, RG21 6XS, England, (Telephone in U.S. (888) 330-8477), (Fax in U.S. (800) 672-2054), www.palgrave.com; *The Statesman's Yearbook 2008.*

Taylor and Francis Group, An Informa Business, 2 Park Square, Milton Park, Abingdon, Oxford OX14 4RN, United Kingdom, (Dial from U.S. (212) 216-7800), (Fax from U.S. (212) 564-7854), www.tandf.co.uk; *The Europa World Year Book.*

United Nations Conference on Trade and Development (UNCTAD), DC2-1120, United Nations, New York, NY 10017, (212) 963-0027, www.unctad.org; *UNCTAD Commodity Yearbook.*

United Nations Food and Agricultural Organization (FAO), Viale delle Terme di Caracalla, 00100 Rome, Italy, (Dial from U.S. (202) 653-2400), (Fax from U.S. (202) 653 5760), www.fao.org; *FAO Yearbook of Fishery Statistics;* Fishery Databases; FISHSTAT Database. Subjects covered include: Aquaculture production, capture production, fishery commodities; and *The State of Food and Agriculture (SOFA) 2006.*

United Nations Statistics Division, New York, NY 10017, (800) 253-9646, Fax: (212) 963-4116, http://unstats.un.org; *Statistical Yearbook.*

The World Bank, 1818 H Street, NW, Washington, DC 20433, (202) 473-1000, Fax: (202) 477-6391, www.worldbank.org; *Ireland.*

IRELAND - FLOUR INDUSTRY

Eurostat, Batiment Jean Monnet, Rue Alcide de Gasperi, L-2920 Luxembourg, http://epp.eurostat.ec.europa.eu; *Eurostat Yearbook 2006-2007.*

United Nations Statistics Division, New York, NY 10017, (800) 253-9646, Fax: (212) 963-4116, http://unstats.un.org; *Statistical Yearbook.*

IRELAND - FOOD

Eurostat, Batiment Jean Monnet, Rue Alcide de Gasperi, L-2920 Luxembourg, http://epp.eurostat.ec.europa.eu; *Eurostat Yearbook 2006-2007.*

Organisation for Economic Cooperation and Development (OECD), 2 rue Andre Pascal, F-75775 Paris Cedex 16, France, (Telephone in U.S. (202) 785-6323), (Fax in U.S. (202) 785-0350), www.oecd.org; *International Trade by Commodity Statistics (ITCS)* and *Towards Sustainable Household Consumption?: Trends and Policies in OECD Countries.*

United Nations Conference on Trade and Development (UNCTAD), DC2-1120, United Nations, New York, NY 10017, (212) 963-0027, www.unctad.org; *UNCTAD Commodity Yearbook.*

United Nations Food and Agricultural Organization (FAO), Viale delle Terme di Caracalla, 00100 Rome, Italy, (Dial from U.S. (202) 653-2400), (Fax from U.S. (202) 653 5760), www.fao.org; *FAO Production Yearbook 2002* and *The State of Food and Agriculture (SOFA) 2006.*

United Nations Statistics Division, New York, NY 10017, (800) 253-9646, Fax: (212) 963-4116, http://unstats.un.org; *Human Development Report 2006.*

IRELAND - FOOTWEAR

Organisation for Economic Cooperation and Development (OECD), 2 rue Andre Pascal, F-75775 Paris Cedex 16, France, (Telephone in U.S. (202) 785-6323), (Fax in U.S. (202) 785-0350), www.oecd.org; *Indicators of Industrial Activity.*

IRELAND - FOREIGN EXCHANGE RATES

Central Intelligence Agency, Office of Public Affairs, Washington, DC 20505, (703) 482-0623, Fax: (703) 482-1739, www.cia.gov; *The World Factbook*.

Euromonitor International, Inc., 224 S. Michigan Avenue, Suite 1500, Chicago, IL 60604, (312) 922-1115, Fax: (312) 922-1157, www.euromonitor.com; *The World Economic Factbook 2008*.

European Union, Delegation of the European Commission to the United States, 2300 M Street, NW, Washington, DC 20037, (202) 862-9500, Fax: (202) 429-1766, www.eurunion.org; *Eurostatistics: Data for Short-Term Economic Analysis (2007 edition)*.

Eurostat, Batiment Jean Monnet, Rue Alcide de Gasperi, L-2920 Luxembourg, http://epp.eurostat.ec.europa.eu; *Eurostat Yearbook 2006-2007*.

International Civil Aviation Organization (ICAO), External Relations and Public Information Office (EPO), 999 University Street, Montreal, Quebec H3C 5H7, Canada, (Dial from U.S. (514) 954-8219), (Fax from U.S. (514) 954-6077), www.icao.int; *Civil Aviation Statistics of the World*.

International Monetary Fund (IMF), 700 Nineteenth Street, NW, Washington, DC 20431, (202) 623-7000, Fax: (202) 623-4661, www.imf.org; *International Financial Statistics Yearbook 2007*.

Organisation for Economic Cooperation and Development (OECD), 2 rue Andre Pascal, F-75775 Paris Cedex 16, France, (Telephone in U.S. (202) 785-6323), (Fax in U.S. (202) 785-0350), www.oecd.org; *Financial Market Trends: OECD Periodical; Household, Tourism, Travel: Trends, Environmental Impacts and Policy Responses; OECD Economic Outlook 2008;* and *Revenue Statistics 1965-2006 - 2007 Edition*.

Taylor and Francis Group, An Informa Business, 2 Park Square, Milton Park, Abingdon, Oxford OX14 4RN, United Kingdom, (Dial from U.S. (212) 216-7800), (Fax from U.S. (212) 564-7854), www.tandf.co.uk; *The Europa World Year Book*.

United Nations Statistics Division, New York, NY 10017, (800) 253-9646, Fax: (212) 963-4116, http://unstats.un.org; *Statistical Yearbook; Trends in Europe and North America: The Statistical Yearbook of the ECE 2005;* and *World Statistics Pocketbook*.

IRELAND - FORESTS AND FORESTRY

American Forest Paper Association (AFPA), 1111 Nineteenth Street, NW, Suite 800, Washington, DC 20036, (800) 878-8878, www.afandpa.org; *2007 Annual Statistics of Paper, Paperboard, and Wood Pulp*.

Euromonitor International, Inc., 224 S. Michigan Avenue, Suite 1500, Chicago, IL 60604, (312) 922-1115, Fax: (312) 922-1157, www.euromonitor.com; *European Marketing Data and Statistics 2008*.

European Union, Delegation of the European Commission to the United States, 2300 M Street, NW, Washington, DC 20037, (202) 862-9500, Fax: (202) 429-1766, www.eurunion.org; *Agricultural Statistics: Data 1995-2005*.

Eurostat, Batiment Jean Monnet, Rue Alcide de Gasperi, L-2920 Luxembourg, http://epp.eurostat.ec.europa.eu; *Eurostat Yearbook 2006-2007*.

M.E. Sharpe, 80 Business Park Drive, Armonk, NY 10504, (800) 541-6563, Fax: (914) 273-2106, www.mesharpe.com; *The Illustrated Book of World Rankings*.

Organisation for Economic Cooperation and Development (OECD), 2 rue Andre Pascal, F-75775 Paris Cedex 16, France, (Telephone in U.S. (202) 785-6323), (Fax in U.S. (202) 785-0350), www.oecd.org; *Indicators of Industrial Activity; International Trade by Commodity Statistics (ITCS);* and STructural ANalysis (STAN) database.

Palgrave Macmillan Ltd., Houndmills, Basingstoke, Hampshire, RG21 6XS, England, (Telephone in U.S. (888) 330-8477), (Fax in U.S. (800) 672-2054), www.palgrave.com; *The Statesman's Yearbook 2008*.

Taylor and Francis Group, An Informa Business, 2 Park Square, Milton Park, Abingdon, Oxford OX14 4RN, United Kingdom, (Dial from U.S. (212) 216-7800), (Fax from U.S. (212) 564-7854), www.tandf.co.uk; *The Europa World Year Book*.

Technical Association of the Pulp and Paper Industry (TAPPI), 15 Technology Parkway South, Norcross, GA 30092, (770) 446-1400, Fax: (770) 446-6947, www.tappi.org; *TAPPI Annual Report*.

UNESCO Institute for Statistics, C.P. 6128 Succursale Centre-Ville, Montreal, Quebec, H3C 3J7 Canada, (Dial from U.S. (514) 343-6880), (Fax from U.S. (514) 343 6882), www.uis.unesco.org; *Statistical Tables*.

United Nations Conference on Trade and Development (UNCTAD), DC2-1120, United Nations, New York, NY 10017, (212) 963-0027, www.unctad.org; *UNCTAD Commodity Yearbook*.

United Nations Food and Agricultural Organization (FAO), Viale delle Terme di Caracalla, 00100 Rome, Italy, (Dial from U.S. (202) 653-2400), (Fax from U.S. (202) 653 5760), www.fao.org; *FAO Yearbook of Forest Products* and *The State of Food and Agriculture (SOFA) 2006*.

United Nations Statistics Division, New York, NY 10017, (800) 253-9646, Fax: (212) 963-4116, http://unstats.un.org; *Statistical Yearbook* and *Trends in Europe and North America: The Statistical Yearbook of the ECE 2005*.

The World Bank, 1818 H Street, NW, Washington, DC 20433, (202) 473-1000, Fax: (202) 477-6391, www.worldbank.org; *Ireland* and *World Development Report 2008*.

IRELAND - FRUIT PRODUCTION

See IRELAND - CROPS

IRELAND - GAS PRODUCTION

See IRELAND - MINERAL INDUSTRIES

IRELAND - GEOGRAPHIC INFORMATION SYSTEMS

Eurostat, Batiment Jean Monnet, Rue Alcide de Gasperi, L-2920 Luxembourg, http://epp.eurostat.ec.europa.eu; *Eurostat Yearbook 2006-2007*.

M.E. Sharpe, 80 Business Park Drive, Armonk, NY 10504, (800) 541-6563, Fax: (914) 273-2106, www.mesharpe.com; *The Illustrated Book of World Rankings*.

The World Bank, 1818 H Street, NW, Washington, DC 20433, (202) 473-1000, Fax: (202) 477-6391, www.worldbank.org; *Ireland*.

IRELAND - GLASS TRADE

Organisation for Economic Cooperation and Development (OECD), 2 rue Andre Pascal, F-75775 Paris Cedex 16, France, (Telephone in U.S. (202) 785-6323), (Fax in U.S. (202) 785-0350), www.oecd.org; *Indicators of Industrial Activity*.

IRELAND - GOLD INDUSTRY

International Monetary Fund (IMF), 700 Nineteenth Street, NW, Washington, DC 20431, (202) 623-7000, Fax: (202) 623-4661, www.imf.org; *International Financial Statistics Yearbook 2007*.

Organisation for Economic Cooperation and Development (OECD), 2 rue Andre Pascal, F-75775 Paris Cedex 16, France, (Telephone in U.S. (202) 785-6323), (Fax in U.S. (202) 785-0350), www.oecd.org; *Indicators of Industrial Activity*.

United Nations Statistics Division, New York, NY 10017, (800) 253-9646, Fax: (212) 963-4116, http://unstats.un.org; *Statistical Yearbook*.

The World Bank, 1818 H Street, NW, Washington, DC 20433, (202) 473-1000, Fax: (202) 477-6391, www.worldbank.org; *World Development Indicators (WDI) 2008*.

IRELAND - GOLD PRODUCTION

See IRELAND - MINERAL INDUSTRIES

IRELAND - GRANTS-IN-AID

International Monetary Fund (IMF), 700 Nineteenth Street, NW, Washington, DC 20431, (202) 623-7000, Fax: (202) 623-4661, www.imf.org; *Government Finance Statistics Yearbook (2008 Edition)*.

Organisation for Economic Cooperation and Development (OECD), 2 rue Andre Pascal, F-75775 Paris Cedex 16, France, (Telephone in U.S. (202) 785-6323), (Fax in U.S. (202) 785-0350), www.oecd.org; *Geographical Distribution of Financial Flows to Aid Recipients 2002-2006*.

IRELAND - GREEN PEPPER AND CHILIE PRODUCTION

See IRELAND - CROPS

IRELAND - GROSS DOMESTIC PRODUCT

Economist Intelligence Unit, 111 West 57th Street, New York, NY 10019, (212) 554-0600, Fax: (212) 586-1181, www.eiu.com; *Ireland Country Report*.

European Union, Delegation of the European Commission to the United States, 2300 M Street, NW, Washington, DC 20037, (202) 862-9500, Fax: (202) 429-1766, www.eurunion.org; *Eurostatistics: Data for Short-Term Economic Analysis (2007 edition); Iron and Steel;* and *RD Expenditure in Europe (2006 edition)*.

Eurostat, Batiment Jean Monnet, Rue Alcide de Gasperi, L-2920 Luxembourg, http://epp.eurostat.ec.europa.eu; *Eurostat Yearbook 2006-2007*.

M.E. Sharpe, 80 Business Park Drive, Armonk, NY 10504, (800) 541-6563, Fax: (914) 273-2106, www.mesharpe.com; *The Illustrated Book of World Rankings*.

Organisation for Economic Cooperation and Development (OECD), 2 rue Andre Pascal, F-75775 Paris Cedex 16, France, (Telephone in U.S. (202) 785-6323), (Fax in U.S. (202) 785-0350), www.oecd.org; *Comparison of Gross Domestic Product (GDP) for OECD Countries; Geographical Distribution of Financial Flows to Aid Recipients 2002-2006; OECD Economic Outlook 2008;* and *Revenue Statistics 1965-2006 - 2007 Edition*.

Palgrave Macmillan Ltd., Houndmills, Basingstoke, Hampshire, RG21 6XS, England, (Telephone in U.S. (888) 330-8477), (Fax in U.S. (800) 672-2054), www.palgrave.com; *The Statesman's Yearbook 2008*.

Taylor and Francis Group, An Informa Business, 2 Park Square, Milton Park, Abingdon, Oxford OX14 4RN, United Kingdom, (Dial from U.S. (212) 216-7800), (Fax from U.S. (212) 564-7854), www.tandf.co.uk; *The Europa World Year Book*.

United Nations Statistics Division, New York, NY 10017, (800) 253-9646, Fax: (212) 963-4116, http://unstats.un.org; *Human Development Report 2006; National Accounts Statistics: Compendium of Income Distribution Statistics; Statistical Yearbook;* and *Trends in Europe and North America: The Statistical Yearbook of the ECE 2005*.

The World Bank, 1818 H Street, NW, Washington, DC 20433, (202) 473-1000, Fax: (202) 477-6391, www.worldbank.org; *World Development Indicators (WDI) 2008* and *World Development Report 2008*.

IRELAND - GROSS NATIONAL PRODUCT

European Union, Delegation of the European Commission to the United States, 2300 M Street, NW, Washington, DC 20037, (202) 862-9500, Fax: (202) 429-1766, www.eurunion.org; *The EU Economy, 2007 Review: Moving Europe's Productivity Frontier*.

Eurostat, Batiment Jean Monnet, Rue Alcide de Gasperi, L-2920 Luxembourg, http://epp.eurostat.ec.europa.eu; *Eurostat Yearbook 2006-2007*.

M.E. Sharpe, 80 Business Park Drive, Armonk, NY 10504, (800) 541-6563, Fax: (914) 273-2106, www.mesharpe.com; *The Illustrated Book of World Rankings*.

Organisation for Economic Cooperation and Development (OECD), 2 rue Andre Pascal, F-75775 Paris Cedex 16, France, (Telephone in U.S. (202) 785-6323), (Fax in U.S. (202) 785-0350), www.oecd.org; *Geographical Distribution of Financial Flows to Aid Recipients 2002-2006; OECD Composite Leading Indicators (CLIs), Updated September 2007;* and *OECD Economic Outlook 2008*.

Palgrave Macmillan Ltd., Houndmills, Basingstoke, Hampshire, RG21 6XS, England, (Telephone in U.S. (888) 330-8477), (Fax in U.S. (800) 672-2054), www.palgrave.com; *The Statesman's Yearbook 2008.*

Taylor and Francis Group, An Informa Business, 2 Park Square, Milton Park, Abingdon, Oxford OX14 4RN, United Kingdom, (Dial from U.S. (212) 216-7800), (Fax from U.S. (212) 564-7854), www.tandf.co.uk; *The Europa World Year Book.*

U.S. Department of State (DOS), 2201 C Street NW, Washington, DC 20520, (202) 647-4000, www.state.gov; *World Military Expenditures and Arms Transfers (WMEAT).*

United Nations Statistics Division, New York, NY 10017, (800) 253-9646, Fax: (212) 963-4116, http://unstats.un.org; *Statistical Yearbook.*

The World Bank, 1818 H Street, NW, Washington, DC 20433, (202) 473-1000, Fax: (202) 477-6391, www.worldbank.org; *The World Bank Atlas 2003-2004; World Development Indicators (WDI) 2008;* and *World Development Report 2008.*

IRELAND - HAY PRODUCTION

See IRELAND - CROPS

IRELAND - HAZELNUT PRODUCTION

See IRELAND - CROPS

IRELAND - HEALTH

See IRELAND - PUBLIC HEALTH

IRELAND - HEMP FIBRE PRODUCTION

See IRELAND - TEXTILE INDUSTRY

IRELAND - HIDES AND SKINS INDUSTRY

Organisation for Economic Cooperation and Development (OECD), 2 rue Andre Pascal, F-75775 Paris Cedex 16, France, (Telephone in U.S. (202) 785-6323), (Fax in U.S. (202) 785-0350), www.oecd.org; *Indicators of Industrial Activity* and *International Trade by Commodity Statistics (ITCS).*

United Nations Food and Agricultural Organization (FAO), Viale delle Terme di Caracalla, 00100 Rome, Italy, (Dial from U.S. (202) 653-2400), (Fax from U.S. (202) 653 5760), www.fao.org; *FAO Production Yearbook 2002.*

IRELAND - HOPS PRODUCTION

See IRELAND - CROPS

IRELAND - HOUSING

Euromonitor International, Inc., 224 S. Michigan Avenue, Suite 1500, Chicago, IL 60604, (312) 922-1115, Fax: (312) 922-1157, www.euromonitor.com; *World Marketing Data and Statistics.*

European Union, Delegation of the European Commission to the United States, 2300 M Street, NW, Washington, DC 20037, (202) 862-9500, Fax: (202) 429-1766, www.eurunion.org; *European Union Labour Force Survey* and *Regions - Statistical Yearbook 2006.*

Eurostat, Batiment Jean Monnet, Rue Alcide de Gasperi, L-2920 Luxembourg, http://epp.eurostat.ec.europa.eu; *Eurostat Yearbook 2006-2007.*

M.E. Sharpe, 80 Business Park Drive, Armonk, NY 10504, (800) 541-6563, Fax: (914) 273-2106, www.mesharpe.com; *The Illustrated Book of World Rankings.*

United Nations Statistics Division, New York, NY 10017, (800) 253-9646, Fax: (212) 963-4116, http://unstats.un.org; *Trends in Europe and North America: The Statistical Yearbook of the ECE 2005.*

IRELAND - HOUSING - FINANCE

Organisation for Economic Cooperation and Development (OECD), 2 rue Andre Pascal, F-75775 Paris Cedex 16, France, (Telephone in U.S. (202) 785-6323), (Fax in U.S. (202) 785-0350), www.oecd.org; *OECD Main Economic Indicators (MEI).*

IRELAND - HOUSING CONSTRUCTION

See IRELAND - CONSTRUCTION INDUSTRY

IRELAND - ILLITERATE PERSONS

Central Intelligence Agency, Office of Public Affairs, Washington, DC 20505, (703) 482-0623, Fax: (703) 482-1739, www.cia.gov; *The World Factbook.*

Euromonitor International, Inc., 224 S. Michigan Avenue, Suite 1500, Chicago, IL 60604, (312) 922-1115, Fax: (312) 922-1157, www.euromonitor.com; *The World Economic Factbook 2008.*

Palgrave Macmillan Ltd., Houndmills, Basingstoke, Hampshire, RG21 6XS, England, (Telephone in U.S. (888) 330-8477), (Fax in U.S. (800) 672-2054), www.palgrave.com; *The Statesman's Yearbook 2008.*

United Nations Statistics Division, New York, NY 10017, (800) 253-9646, Fax: (212) 963-4116, http://unstats.un.org; *Human Development Report 2006.*

IRELAND - IMPORTS

Central Intelligence Agency, Office of Public Affairs, Washington, DC 20505, (703) 482-0623, Fax: (703) 482-1739, www.cia.gov; *The World Factbook.*

Economist Intelligence Unit, 111 West 57th Street, New York, NY 10019, (212) 554-0600, Fax: (212) 586-1181, www.eiu.com; *Ireland Country Report.*

Euromonitor International, Inc., 224 S. Michigan Avenue, Suite 1500, Chicago, IL 60604, (312) 922-1115, Fax: (312) 922-1157, www.euromonitor.com; *The World Economic Factbook 2008.*

European Union, Delegation of the European Commission to the United States, 2300 M Street, NW, Washington, DC 20037, (202) 862-9500, Fax: (202) 429-1766, www.eurunion.org; *European Union Energy Transport in Figures 2006; Eurostatistics: Data for Short-Term Economic Analysis (2007 edition); External and Intra-European Union Trade: Data 1958-2002; External and Intra-European Union Trade: Data 1999-2004;* and *Fishery Statistics - 1990-2006.*

Eurostat, Batiment Jean Monnet, Rue Alcide de Gasperi, L-2920 Luxembourg, http://epp.eurostat.ec.europa.eu; *Eurostat Yearbook 2006-2007.*

International Lead and Zinc Study Group (ILZSG), Rua Almirante Barroso 38, 5th Floor, Lisbon 1000 - 013, Portugal, www.ilzsg.org; Interactive Statistical Database.

International Monetary Fund (IMF), 700 Nineteenth Street, NW, Washington, DC 20431, (202) 623-7000, Fax: (202) 623-4661, www.imf.org; *Direction of Trade Statistics Yearbook 2007; Government Finance Statistics Yearbook (2008 Edition);* and *International Financial Statistics Yearbook 2007.*

Organisation for Economic Cooperation and Development (OECD), 2 rue Andre Pascal, F-75775 Paris Cedex 16, France, (Telephone in U.S. (202) 785-6323), (Fax in U.S. (202) 785-0350), www.oecd.org; *Iron and Steel Industry in 2004 (2006 Edition); 2005 OECD Agricultural Outlook Tables, 1970-2014; OECD Economic Outlook 2008; OECD Economic Survey - Ireland 2008; Review of Fisheries in OECD Countries: Country Statistics 2001 to 2003 - 2005 Edition;* and STructural ANalysis (STAN) database.

Palgrave Macmillan Ltd., Houndmills, Basingstoke, Hampshire, RG21 6XS, England, (Telephone in U.S. (888) 330-8477), (Fax in U.S. (800) 672-2054), www.palgrave.com; *The Statesman's Yearbook 2008.*

Platts, 2 Penn Plaza, 25th Floor, New York, NY 10121-2298, (212) 904-3070, www.platts.com; *Energy Economist.*

Taylor and Francis Group, An Informa Business, 2 Park Square, Milton Park, Abingdon, Oxford OX14 4RN, United Kingdom, (Dial from U.S. (212) 216-7800), (Fax from U.S. (212) 564-7854), www.tandf.co.uk; *The Europa World Year Book.*

Technical Association of the Pulp and Paper Industry (TAPPI), 15 Technology Parkway South, Norcross, GA 30092, (770) 446-1400, Fax: (770) 446-6947, www.tappi.org; *TAPPI Annual Report.*

United Nations Conference on Trade and Development (UNCTAD), DC2-1120, United Nations, New York, NY 10017, (212) 963-0027, www.unctad.org; *Handbook of Statistics 2005.*

United Nations Food and Agricultural Organization (FAO), Viale delle Terme di Caracalla, 00100 Rome, Italy, (Dial from U.S. (202) 653-2400), (Fax from U.S. (202) 653 5760), www.fao.org; *The State of Food and Agriculture (SOFA) 2006.*

United Nations Statistics Division, New York, NY 10017, (800) 253-9646, Fax: (212) 963-4116, http://unstats.un.org; *Energy Statistics Yearbook 2003* and *Trends in Europe and North America: The Statistical Yearbook of the ECE 2005.*

The World Bank, 1818 H Street, NW, Washington, DC 20433, (202) 473-1000, Fax: (202) 477-6391, www.worldbank.org; *World Development Indicators (WDI) 2008* and *World Development Report 2008.*

IRELAND - INCOME TAXES

See IRELAND - TAXATION

IRELAND - INDUSTRIAL METALS PRODUCTION

See IRELAND - MINERAL INDUSTRIES

IRELAND - INDUSTRIAL PRODUCTIVITY

European Union, Delegation of the European Commission to the United States, 2300 M Street, NW, Washington, DC 20037, (202) 862-9500, Fax: (202) 429-1766, www.eurunion.org; *Eurostatistics: Data for Short-Term Economic Analysis (2007 edition); Fishery Statistics - 1990-2006;* and *RD Expenditure in Europe (2006 edition).*

Eurostat, Batiment Jean Monnet, Rue Alcide de Gasperi, L-2920 Luxembourg, http://epp.eurostat.ec.europa.eu; *Eurostat Yearbook 2006-2007.*

International Lead and Zinc Study Group (ILZSG), Rua Almirante Barroso 38, 5th Floor, Lisbon 1000 - 013, Portugal, www.ilzsg.org; Interactive Statistical Database.

M.E. Sharpe, 80 Business Park Drive, Armonk, NY 10504, (800) 541-6563, Fax: (914) 273-2106, www.mesharpe.com; *The Illustrated Book of World Rankings.*

Organisation for Economic Cooperation and Development (OECD), 2 rue Andre Pascal, F-75775 Paris Cedex 16, France, (Telephone in U.S. (202) 785-6323), (Fax in U.S. (202) 785-0350), www.oecd.org; *Environmental Impacts of Foreign Direct Investment in the Mining Sector in the Newly Independent States (NIS); Indicators of Industrial Activity; Iron and Steel Industry in 2004 (2006 Edition); A New World Map in Textiles and Clothing: Adjusting to Change; 2005 OECD Agricultural Outlook Tables, 1970-2014; OECD Economic Outlook 2008;* and STructural ANalysis (STAN) database.

Technical Association of the Pulp and Paper Industry (TAPPI), 15 Technology Parkway South, Norcross, GA 30092, (770) 446-1400, Fax: (770) 446-6947, www.tappi.org; *TAPPI Annual Report.*

IRELAND - INDUSTRIAL PROPERTY

United Nations Statistics Division, New York, NY 10017, (800) 253-9646, Fax: (212) 963-4116, http://unstats.un.org; *Statistical Yearbook.*

World Intellectual Property Organization (WIPO), PO Box 18, CH-1211 Geneva 20, Switzerland, www.wipo.int; *Industrial Property Statistics* and *Industrial Property Statistics Online Directory.*

IRELAND - INDUSTRIES

Central Intelligence Agency, Office of Public Affairs, Washington, DC 20505, (703) 482-0623, Fax: (703) 482-1739, www.cia.gov; *The World Factbook.*

Economist Intelligence Unit, 111 West 57th Street, New York, NY 10019, (212) 554-0600, Fax: (212) 586-1181, www.eiu.com; *Ireland Country Report.*

Euromonitor International, Inc., 224 S. Michigan Avenue, Suite 1500, Chicago, IL 60604, (312) 922-1115, Fax: (312) 922-1157, www.euromonitor.com; *The World Economic Factbook 2008* and *World Marketing Data and Statistics.*

European Union, Delegation of the European Commission to the United States, 2300 M Street, NW, Washington, DC 20037, (202) 862-9500, Fax: (202) 429-1766, www.eurunion.org; *European Union Labour Force Survey* and *Eurostatistics: Data for Short-Term Economic Analysis (2007 edition).*

Eurostat, Batiment Jean Monnet, Rue Alcide de Gasperi, L-2920 Luxembourg, http://epp.eurostat.ec.europa.eu; *Eurostat Yearbook 2006-2007.*

International Labour Office, I.L.O. Publications, 4 route des Morillons, CH-1211 Geneva 22, Switzerland, (Telephone in U.S. (202) 653-7652), (Fax in U.S. (202) 653-7687), www.ilo.org; *Yearbook of Labour Statistics 2006.*

M.E. Sharpe, 80 Business Park Drive, Armonk, NY 10504, (800) 541-6563, Fax: (914) 273-2106, www.mesharpe.com; *The Illustrated Book of World Rankings.*

Organisation for Economic Cooperation and Development (OECD), 2 rue Andre Pascal, F-75775 Paris Cedex 16, France, (Telephone in U.S. (202) 785-6323), (Fax in U.S. (202) 785-0350), www.oecd.org; *Key Environmental Indicators 2004; OECD Economic Outlook 2008;* and STructural ANalysis (STAN) database.

Palgrave Macmillan Ltd., Houndmills, Basingstoke, Hampshire, RG21 6XS, England, (Telephone in U.S. (888) 330-8477), (Fax in U.S. (800) 672-2054), www.palgrave.com; *The Statesman's Yearbook 2008.*

Taylor and Francis Group, An Informa Business, 2 Park Square, Milton Park, Abingdon, Oxford OX14 4RN, United Kingdom, (Dial from U.S. (212) 216-7800), (Fax from U.S. (212) 564-7854), www.tandf.co.uk; *The Europa World Year Book.*

United Nations Industrial Development Organization (UNIDO), 1 United Nations Plaza, New York, NY 10017, (212) 963 6890, Fax: (212) 963-7904, http://unido.org; Industrial Statistics Database 2008 (INDSTAT) and *The International Yearbook of Industrial Statistics 2008.*

United Nations Statistics Division, New York, NY 10017, (800) 253-9646, Fax: (212) 963-4116, http://unstats.un.org; *2004 Industrial Commodity Statistics Yearbook; Statistical Yearbook;* and *Trends in Europe and North America: The Statistical Yearbook of the ECE 2005.*

The World Bank, 1818 H Street, NW, Washington, DC 20433, (202) 473-1000, Fax: (202) 477-6391, www.worldbank.org; *Ireland* and *World Development Indicators (WDI) 2008.*

IRELAND - INFANT AND MATERNAL MORTALITY

See IRELAND - MORTALITY

IRELAND - INORGANIC ACIDS

Eurostat, Batiment Jean Monnet, Rue Alcide de Gasperi, L-2920 Luxembourg, http://epp.eurostat.ec.europa.eu; *Eurostat Yearbook 2006-2007.*

Organisation for Economic Cooperation and Development (OECD), 2 rue Andre Pascal, F-75775 Paris Cedex 16, France, (Telephone in U.S. (202) 785-6323), (Fax in U.S. (202) 785-0350), www.oecd.org; *Indicators of Industrial Activity.*

IRELAND - INTEREST RATES

Eurostat, Batiment Jean Monnet, Rue Alcide de Gasperi, L-2920 Luxembourg, http://epp.eurostat.ec.europa.eu; *Eurostat Yearbook 2006-2007.*

Organisation for Economic Cooperation and Development (OECD), 2 rue Andre Pascal, F-75775 Paris Cedex 16, France, (Telephone in U.S. (202) 785-6323), (Fax in U.S. (202) 785-0350), www.oecd.org; *Financial Market Trends: OECD Periodical; OECD Economic Outlook 2008;* and *OECD Main Economic Indicators (MEI).*

IRELAND - INTERNAL REVENUE

Organisation for Economic Cooperation and Development (OECD), 2 rue Andre Pascal, F-75775 Paris Cedex 16, France, (Telephone in U.S. (202) 785-6323), (Fax in U.S. (202) 785-0350), www.oecd.org; *2005 OECD Agricultural Outlook Tables, 1970-2014.*

IRELAND - INTERNATIONAL FINANCE

Eurostat, Batiment Jean Monnet, Rue Alcide de Gasperi, L-2920 Luxembourg, http://epp.eurostat.ec.europa.eu; *Eurostat Yearbook 2006-2007.*

Organisation for Economic Cooperation and Development (OECD), 2 rue Andre Pascal, F-75775 Paris Cedex 16, France, (Telephone in U.S. (202) 785-6323), (Fax in U.S. (202) 785-0350), www.oecd.org; *Financial Market Trends: OECD Periodical* and *OECD Economic Outlook 2008.*

The World Bank, 1818 H Street, NW, Washington, DC 20433, (202) 473-1000, Fax: (202) 477-6391, www.worldbank.org; *Ireland.*

IRELAND - INTERNATIONAL LIQUIDITY

Organisation for Economic Cooperation and Development (OECD), 2 rue Andre Pascal, F-75775 Paris Cedex 16, France, (Telephone in U.S. (202) 785-6323), (Fax in U.S. (202) 785-0350), www.oecd.org; *Financial Market Trends: OECD Periodical* and *OECD Economic Outlook 2008.*

IRELAND - INTERNATIONAL STATISTICS

Organisation for Economic Cooperation and Development (OECD), 2 rue Andre Pascal, F-75775 Paris Cedex 16, France, (Telephone in U.S. (202) 785-6323), (Fax in U.S. (202) 785-0350), www.oecd.org; *Financial Market Trends: OECD Periodical* and *Household, Tourism, Travel: Trends, Environmental Impacts and Policy Responses.*

IRELAND - INTERNATIONAL TRADE

Banque de France, 48 rue Croix des Petits champs, 75001 Paris, France, www.banque-france.fr/home.htm; *Monthly Business Survey Overview.*

Bernan Essential Government Publications, 4611-F Assembly Drive, Lanham MD, 20706-4391, (301) 459-2255, Fax: (800) 865-3450, www.bernan.com; *OECD Factbook 2006.*

Central Statistics Office (CSO) Ireland, Skehard Road, Cork, Ireland, www.cso.ie; *Trade Statistics of Ireland.*

Economist Intelligence Unit, 111 West 57th Street, New York, NY 10019, (212) 554-0600, Fax: (212) 586-1181, www.eiu.com; *Ireland Country Report.*

Euromonitor International, Inc., 224 S. Michigan Avenue, Suite 1500, Chicago, IL 60604, (312) 922-1115, Fax: (312) 922-1157, www.euromonitor.com; *European Marketing Data and Statistics 2008; The World Economic Factbook 2008;* and *World Marketing Data and Statistics.*

European Union, Delegation of the European Commission to the United States, 2300 M Street, NW, Washington, DC 20037, (202) 862-9500, Fax: (202) 429-1766, www.eurunion.org; *Eurostatistics: Data for Short-Term Economic Analysis (2007 edition); External and Intra-European Union Trade: Data 1958-2002; External and Intra-European Union Trade: Data 1999-2004;* and *Iron and Steel.*

Eurostat, Batiment Jean Monnet, Rue Alcide de Gasperi, L-2920 Luxembourg, http://epp.eurostat.ec.europa.eu; *Eurostat Yearbook 2006-2007* and Intra- and Extra-EU Trade.

International Monetary Fund (IMF), 700 Nineteenth Street, NW, Washington, DC 20431, (202) 623-7000, Fax: (202) 623-4661, www.imf.org; *International Financial Statistics Yearbook 2007.*

M.E. Sharpe, 80 Business Park Drive, Armonk, NY 10504, (800) 541-6563, Fax: (914) 273-2106, www.mesharpe.com; *The Illustrated Book of World Rankings.*

Organisation for Economic Cooperation and Development (OECD), 2 rue Andre Pascal, F-75775 Paris Cedex 16, France, (Telephone in U.S. (202) 785-6323), (Fax in U.S. (202) 785-0350), www.oecd.org; *International Trade by Commodity Statistics (ITCS); 2005 OECD Agricultural Outlook Tables, 1970-2014; OECD Economic Outlook 2008; OECD Economic Survey - Ireland 2008; OECD in Figures 2007; OECD Main Economic Indicators (MEI);* and *Statistics on Ship Production, Exports and Orders in 2004.*

Palgrave Macmillan Ltd., Houndmills, Basingstoke, Hampshire, RG21 6XS, England, (Telephone in U.S. (888) 330-8477), (Fax in U.S. (800) 672-2054), www.palgrave.com; *The Statesman's Yearbook 2008.*

Platts, 2 Penn Plaza, 25th Floor, New York, NY 10121-2298, (212) 904-3070, www.platts.com; *Energy Economist.*

Taylor and Francis Group, An Informa Business, 2 Park Square, Milton Park, Abingdon, Oxford OX14 4RN, United Kingdom, (Dial from U.S. (212) 216-7800), (Fax from U.S. (212) 564-7854), www.tandf.co.uk; *The Europa World Year Book.*

United Nations Conference on Trade and Development (UNCTAD), DC2-1120, United Nations, New York, NY 10017, (212) 963-0027, www.unctad.org; *UNCTAD Commodity Yearbook.*

United Nations Food and Agricultural Organization (FAO), Viale delle Terme di Caracalla, 00100 Rome, Italy, (Dial from U.S. (202) 653-2400), (Fax from U.S. (202) 653 5760), www.fao.org; *FAO Trade Yearbook* and *The State of Food and Agriculture (SOFA) 2006.*

United Nations Statistics Division, New York, NY 10017, (800) 253-9646, Fax: (212) 963-4116, http://unstats.un.org; *Energy Statistics Yearbook 2003; International Trade Statistics Yearbook;* and *Statistical Yearbook.*

The World Bank, 1818 H Street, NW, Washington, DC 20433, (202) 473-1000, Fax: (202) 477-6391, www.worldbank.org; *Ireland; World Development Indicators (WDI) 2008;* and *World Development Report 2008.*

World Trade Organization (WTO), Centre William Rappard, Rue de Lausanne 154, CH-1211 Geneva 21, Switzerland, www.wto.org; *International Trade Statistics 2006.*

IRELAND - INTERNET USERS

Eurostat, Batiment Jean Monnet, Rue Alcide de Gasperi, L-2920 Luxembourg, http://epp.eurostat.ec.europa.eu; *Internet Usage by Enterprises 2007.*

International Telecommunication Union (ITU), Place des Nations, 1211 Geneva 20, Switzerland, www.itu.int; *World Telecommunication/ICT Indicators Database on CD-ROM; World Telecommunication/ICT Indicators Database Online;* and *Yearbook of Statistics - Telecommunication Services (Chronological Time Series 1997-2006).*

The World Bank, 1818 H Street, NW, Washington, DC 20433, (202) 473-1000, Fax: (202) 477-6391, www.worldbank.org; *Ireland.*

IRELAND - INVESTMENTS

Organisation for Economic Cooperation and Development (OECD), 2 rue Andre Pascal, F-75775 Paris Cedex 16, France, (Telephone in U.S. (202) 785-6323), (Fax in U.S. (202) 785-0350), www.oecd.org; *Financial Market Trends: OECD Periodical; A New World Map in Textiles and Clothing: Adjusting to Change; OECD Economic Outlook 2008;* and STructural ANalysis (STAN) database.

IRELAND - IRON AND IRON ORE PRODUCTION

See IRELAND - MINERAL INDUSTRIES

IRELAND - JUTE PRODUCTION

See IRELAND - CROPS

IRELAND - LABOR

Central Intelligence Agency, Office of Public Affairs, Washington, DC 20505, (703) 482-0623, Fax: (703) 482-1739, www.cia.gov; *The World Factbook.*

Euromonitor International, Inc., 224 S. Michigan Avenue, Suite 1500, Chicago, IL 60604, (312) 922-1115, Fax: (312) 922-1157, www.euromonitor.com; *World Marketing Data and Statistics.*

European Union, Delegation of the European Commission to the United States, 2300 M Street, NW, Washington, DC 20037, (202) 862-9500, Fax: (202) 429-1766, www.eurunion.org; *European Union Labour Force Survey* and *Regions - Statistical Yearbook 2006*.

Eurostat, Batiment Jean Monnet, Rue Alcide de Gasperi, L-2920 Luxembourg, http://epp.eurostat.ec.europa.eu; *Eurostat Yearbook 2006-2007*.

International Labour Office, I.L.O. Publications, 4 route des Morillons, CH-1211 Geneva 22, Switzerland, (Telephone in U.S. (202) 653-7652), (Fax in U.S. (202) 653-7687), www.ilo.org; *Yearbook of Labour Statistics 2006*.

M.E. Sharpe, 80 Business Park Drive, Armonk, NY 10504, (800) 541-6563, Fax: (914) 273-2106, www.mesharpe.com; *The Illustrated Book of World Rankings*.

Organisation for Economic Cooperation and Development (OECD), 2 rue Andre Pascal, F-75775 Paris Cedex 16, France, (Telephone in U.S. (202) 785-6323), (Fax in U.S. (202) 785-0350), www.oecd.org; *Iron and Steel Industry in 2004 (2006 Edition); A New World Map in Textiles and Clothing: Adjusting to Change; OECD Economic Outlook 2008; OECD Economic Survey - Ireland 2008; OECD Employment Outlook 2007; OECD Main Economic Indicators (MEI);* and *Statistics on Ship Production, Exports and Orders in 2004*.

Palgrave Macmillan Ltd., Houndmills, Basingstoke, Hampshire, RG21 6XS, England, (Telephone in U.S. (888) 330-8477), (Fax in U.S. (800) 672-2054), www.palgrave.com; *The Statesman's Yearbook 2008*.

United Nations Food and Agricultural Organization (FAO), Viale delle Terme di Caracalla, 00100 Rome, Italy, (Dial from U.S. (202) 653-2400), (Fax from U.S. (202) 653 5760), www.fao.org; *The State of Food and Agriculture (SOFA) 2006*.

United Nations Statistics Division, New York, NY 10017, (800) 253-9646, Fax: (212) 963-4116, http://unstats.un.org; *Human Development Report 2006*.

The World Bank, 1818 H Street, NW, Washington, DC 20433, (202) 473-1000, Fax: (202) 477-6391, www.worldbank.org; *The World Bank Atlas 2003-2004; World Development Indicators (WDI) 2008;* and *World Development Report 2008*.

IRELAND - LAND USE

Central Intelligence Agency, Office of Public Affairs, Washington, DC 20505, (703) 482-0623, Fax: (703) 482-1739, www.cia.gov; *The World Factbook*.

Euromonitor International, Inc., 224 S. Michigan Avenue, Suite 1500, Chicago, IL 60604, (312) 922-1115, Fax: (312) 922-1157, www.euromonitor.com; *European Marketing Data and Statistics 2008*.

European Union, Delegation of the European Commission to the United States, 2300 M Street, NW, Washington, DC 20037, (202) 862-9500, Fax: (202) 429-1766, www.eurunion.org; *Agricultural Statistics: Data 1995-2005; Agriculture in the European Union: Statistical and Economic Information 2006;* and *Regions - Statistical Yearbook 2006*.

Eurostat, Batiment Jean Monnet, Rue Alcide de Gasperi, L-2920 Luxembourg, http://epp.eurostat.ec.europa.eu; *Eurostat Yearbook 2006-2007*.

United Nations Food and Agricultural Organization (FAO), Viale delle Terme di Caracalla, 00100 Rome, Italy, (Dial from U.S. (202) 653-2400), (Fax from U.S. (202) 653 5760), www.fao.org; *FAO Production Yearbook 2002*.

The World Bank, 1818 H Street, NW, Washington, DC 20433, (202) 473-1000, Fax: (202) 477-6391, www.worldbank.org; *World Development Report 2008*.

IRELAND - LEATHER INDUSTRY AND TRADE

Eurostat, Batiment Jean Monnet, Rue Alcide de Gasperi, L-2920 Luxembourg, http://epp.eurostat.ec.europa.eu; *Eurostat Yearbook 2006-2007*.

Organisation for Economic Cooperation and Development (OECD), 2 rue Andre Pascal, F-75775 Paris Cedex 16, France, (Telephone in U.S. (202) 785-6323), (Fax in U.S. (202) 785-0350), www.oecd.org; *Indicators of Industrial Activity*.

IRELAND - LIBRARIES

M.E. Sharpe, 80 Business Park Drive, Armonk, NY 10504, (800) 541-6563, Fax: (914) 273-2106, www.mesharpe.com; *The Illustrated Book of World Rankings*.

UNESCO Institute for Statistics, C.P. 6128 Succursale Centre-Ville, Montreal, Quebec, H3C 3J7 Canada, (Dial from U.S. (514) 343-6880), (Fax from U.S. (514) 343 6882), www.uis.unesco.org; *Statistical Tables*.

United Nations Statistics Division, New York, NY 10017, (800) 253-9646, Fax: (212) 963-4116, http://unstats.un.org; *Trends in Europe and North America: The Statistical Yearbook of the ECE 2005*.

IRELAND - LIFE EXPECTANCY

Central Intelligence Agency, Office of Public Affairs, Washington, DC 20505, (703) 482-0623, Fax: (703) 482-1739, www.cia.gov; *The World Factbook*.

Euromonitor International, Inc., 224 S. Michigan Avenue, Suite 1500, Chicago, IL 60604, (312) 922-1115, Fax: (312) 922-1157, www.euromonitor.com; *The World Economic Factbook 2008*.

Organisation for Economic Cooperation and Development (OECD), 2 rue Andre Pascal, F-75775 Paris Cedex 16, France, (Telephone in U.S. (202) 785-6323), (Fax in U.S. (202) 785-0350), www.oecd.org; *OECD Economic Outlook 2008*.

United Nations Statistics Division, New York, NY 10017, (800) 253-9646, Fax: (212) 963-4116, http://unstats.un.org; *Human Development Report 2006; Trends in Europe and North America: The Statistical Yearbook of the ECE 2005;* and *World Statistics Pocketbook*.

The World Bank, 1818 H Street, NW, Washington, DC 20433, (202) 473-1000, Fax: (202) 477-6391, www.worldbank.org; *The World Bank Atlas 2003-2004* and *World Development Report 2008*.

IRELAND - LITERACY

Euromonitor International, Inc., 224 S. Michigan Avenue, Suite 1500, Chicago, IL 60604, (312) 922-1115, Fax: (312) 922-1157, www.euromonitor.com; *World Marketing Data and Statistics*.

IRELAND - LIVESTOCK

Euromonitor International, Inc., 224 S. Michigan Avenue, Suite 1500, Chicago, IL 60604, (312) 922-1115, Fax: (312) 922-1157, www.euromonitor.com; *European Marketing Data and Statistics 2008*.

European Union, Delegation of the European Commission to the United States, 2300 M Street, NW, Washington, DC 20037, (202) 862-9500, Fax: (202) 429-1766, www.eurunion.org; *Agricultural Statistics: Data 1995-2005* and *Regions - Statistical Yearbook 2006*.

Eurostat, Batiment Jean Monnet, Rue Alcide de Gasperi, L-2920 Luxembourg, http://epp.eurostat.ec.europa.eu; *Eurostat Yearbook 2006-2007*.

M.E. Sharpe, 80 Business Park Drive, Armonk, NY 10504, (800) 541-6563, Fax: (914) 273-2106, www.mesharpe.com; *The Illustrated Book of World Rankings*.

Organisation for Economic Cooperation and Development (OECD), 2 rue Andre Pascal, F-75775 Paris Cedex 16, France, (Telephone in U.S. (202) 785-6323), (Fax in U.S. (202) 785-0350), www.oecd.org; *2005 OECD Agricultural Outlook Tables, 1970-2014*.

Palgrave Macmillan Ltd., Houndmills, Basingstoke, Hampshire, RG21 6XS, England, (Telephone in U.S. (888) 330-8477), (Fax in U.S. (800) 672-2054), www.palgrave.com; *The Statesman's Yearbook 2008*.

Taylor and Francis Group, An Informa Business, 2 Park Square, Milton Park, Abingdon, Oxford OX14 4RN, United Kingdom, (Dial from U.S. (212) 216-7800), (Fax from U.S. (212) 564-7854), www.tandf.co.uk; *The Europa World Year Book*.

Teagasc, Oak Park, Carlow, Ireland, www.teagasc.ie; *Beef and Sheep Production Research*.

United Nations Conference on Trade and Development (UNCTAD), DC2-1120, United Nations, New York, NY 10017, (212) 963-0027, www.unctad.org; *UNCTAD Commodity Yearbook*.

United Nations Food and Agricultural Organization (FAO), Viale delle Terme di Caracalla, 00100 Rome, Italy, (Dial from U.S. (202) 653-2400), (Fax from U.S. (202) 653 5760), www.fao.org; *FAO Production Yearbook 2002* and *The State of Food and Agriculture (SOFA) 2006*.

United Nations Statistics Division, New York, NY 10017, (800) 253-9646, Fax: (212) 963-4116, http://unstats.un.org; *Statistical Yearbook*.

IRELAND - MACHINERY

Organisation for Economic Cooperation and Development (OECD), 2 rue Andre Pascal, F-75775 Paris Cedex 16, France, (Telephone in U.S. (202) 785-6323), (Fax in U.S. (202) 785-0350), www.oecd.org; *Indicators of Industrial Activity*.

IRELAND - MAGNESIUM PRODUCTION AND CONSUMPTION

See IRELAND - MINERAL INDUSTRIES

IRELAND - MANUFACTURES

European Union, Delegation of the European Commission to the United States, 2300 M Street, NW, Washington, DC 20037, (202) 862-9500, Fax: (202) 429-1766, www.eurunion.org; *European Union Labour Force Survey; Eurostatistics: Data for Short-Term Economic Analysis (2007 edition);* and *The Textile Industry in the EU*.

Eurostat, Batiment Jean Monnet, Rue Alcide de Gasperi, L-2920 Luxembourg, http://epp.eurostat.ec.europa.eu; *Eurostat Yearbook 2006-2007*.

M.E. Sharpe, 80 Business Park Drive, Armonk, NY 10504, (800) 541-6563, Fax: (914) 273-2106, www.mesharpe.com; *The Illustrated Book of World Rankings*.

Organisation for Economic Cooperation and Development (OECD), 2 rue Andre Pascal, F-75775 Paris Cedex 16, France, (Telephone in U.S. (202) 785-6323), (Fax in U.S. (202) 785-0350), www.oecd.org; *Indicators of Industrial Activity; International Trade by Commodity Statistics (ITCS); OECD Economic Survey - Ireland 2008;* and STructural ANalysis (STAN) database.

United Nations Statistics Division, New York, NY 10017, (800) 253-9646, Fax: (212) 963-4116, http://unstats.un.org; *Statistical Yearbook*.

The World Bank, 1818 H Street, NW, Washington, DC 20433, (202) 473-1000, Fax: (202) 477-6391, www.worldbank.org; *World Development Indicators (WDI) 2008*.

IRELAND - MARRIAGE

Eurostat, Batiment Jean Monnet, Rue Alcide de Gasperi, L-2920 Luxembourg, http://epp.eurostat.ec.europa.eu; *Eurostat Yearbook 2006-2007*.

M.E. Sharpe, 80 Business Park Drive, Armonk, NY 10504, (800) 541-6563, Fax: (914) 273-2106, www.mesharpe.com; *The Illustrated Book of World Rankings*.

Taylor and Francis Group, An Informa Business, 2 Park Square, Milton Park, Abingdon, Oxford OX14 4RN, United Kingdom, (Dial from U.S. (212) 216-7800), (Fax from U.S. (212) 564-7854), www.tandf.co.uk; *The Europa World Year Book*.

United Nations Statistics Division, New York, NY 10017, (800) 253-9646, Fax: (212) 963-4116, http://unstats.un.org; *Demographic Yearbook; Statistical Yearbook;* and *Trends in Europe and North America: The Statistical Yearbook of the ECE 2005*.

IRELAND - MEAT PRODUCTION

See IRELAND - LIVESTOCK

IRELAND - MERCURY INDUSTRY AND TRADE

Eurostat, Batiment Jean Monnet, Rue Alcide de Gasperi, L-2920 Luxembourg, http://epp.eurostat.ec.europa.eu; *Eurostat Yearbook 2006-2007.*

Organisation for Economic Cooperation and Development (OECD), 2 rue Andre Pascal, F-75775 Paris Cedex 16, France, (Telephone in U.S. (202) 785-6323), (Fax in U.S. (202) 785-0350), www.oecd.org; *Indicators of Industrial Activity.*

United Nations Statistics Division, New York, NY 10017, (800) 253-9646, Fax: (212) 963-4116, http://unstats.un.org; *Statistical Yearbook.*

IRELAND - METAL PRODUCTS

Eurostat, Batiment Jean Monnet, Rue Alcide de Gasperi, L-2920 Luxembourg, http://epp.eurostat.ec.europa.eu; *Eurostat Yearbook 2006-2007.*

IRELAND - MINERAL INDUSTRIES

European Union, Delegation of the European Commission to the United States, 2300 M Street, NW, Washington, DC 20037, (202) 862-9500, Fax: (202) 429-1766, www.eurunion.org; *European Union Energy Transport in Figures 2006; European Union Labour Force Survey; Eurostatistics: Data for Short-Term Economic Analysis (2007 edition); Iron and Steel;* and *Regions - Statistical Yearbook 2006.*

Eurostat, Batiment Jean Monnet, Rue Alcide de Gasperi, L-2920 Luxembourg, http://epp.eurostat.ec.europa.eu; *Energy - Monthly Statistics; Eurostat Yearbook 2006-2007;* and *Panorama of Energy - 2007 Edition.*

International Energy Agency (IEA), 9, rue de la Federation, 75739 Paris Cedex 15, France, www.iea.org; *Key World Energy Statistics 2007.*

International Lead and Zinc Study Group (ILZSG), Rua Almirante Barroso 38, 5th Floor, Lisbon 1000 - 013, Portugal, www.ilzsg.org; Interactive Statistical Database.

M.E. Sharpe, 80 Business Park Drive, Armonk, NY 10504, (800) 541-6563, Fax: (914) 273-2106, www.mesharpe.com; *The Illustrated Book of World Rankings.*

Organisation for Economic Cooperation and Development (OECD), 2 rue Andre Pascal, F-75775 Paris Cedex 16, France, (Telephone in U.S. (202) 785-6323), (Fax in U.S. (202) 785-0350), www.oecd.org; *Coal Information: 2007 Edition; Energy Statistics of OECD Countries (2007 Edition); Environmental Impacts of Foreign Direct Investment in the Mining Sector in the Newly Independent States (NIS); Indicators of Industrial Activity; International Trade by Commodity Statistics (ITCS); Iron and Steel Industry in 2004 (2006 Edition); OECD Economic Outlook 2008; OECD Economic Survey - Ireland 2008; OECD Main Economic Indicators (MEI);* and STructural ANalysis (STAN) database.

Palgrave Macmillan Ltd., Houndmills, Basingstoke, Hampshire, RG21 6XS, England, (Telephone in U.S. (888) 330-8477), (Fax in U.S. (800) 672-2054), www.palgrave.com; *The Statesman's Yearbook 2008.*

Platts, 2 Penn Plaza, 25th Floor, New York, NY 10121-2298, (212) 904-3070, www.platts.com; *Energy Economist* and *EU Energy.*

Taylor and Francis Group, An Informa Business, 2 Park Square, Milton Park, Abingdon, Oxford OX14 4RN, United Kingdom, (Dial from U.S. (212) 216-7800), (Fax from U.S. (212) 564-7854), www.tandf.co.uk; *The Europa World Year Book.*

United Nations Conference on Trade and Development (UNCTAD), DC2-1120, United Nations, New York, NY 10017, (212) 963-0027, www.unctad.org; *UNCTAD Commodity Yearbook.*

United Nations Statistics Division, New York, NY 10017, (800) 253-9646, Fax: (212) 963-4116, http://unstats.un.org; *Energy Statistics Yearbook 2003* and *Statistical Yearbook.*

The World Bank, 1818 H Street, NW, Washington, DC 20433, (202) 473-1000, Fax: (202) 477-6391, www.worldbank.org; *Ireland.*

IRELAND - MONEY

European Central Bank (ECB), Postfach 160319, D-60066 Frankfurt am Main, Germany, www.ecb.int; *Monetary Developments in the Euro Area; Monthly Bulletin;* and *Statistics Pocket Book.*

Organisation for Economic Cooperation and Development (OECD), 2 rue Andre Pascal, F-75775 Paris Cedex 16, France, (Telephone in U.S. (202) 785-6323), (Fax in U.S. (202) 785-0350), www.oecd.org; *OECD Economic Survey - Ireland 2008.*

IRELAND - MONEY EXCHANGE RATES

See IRELAND - FOREIGN EXCHANGE RATES

IRELAND - MONEY SUPPLY

Economist Intelligence Unit, 111 West 57th Street, New York, NY 10019, (212) 554-0600, Fax: (212) 586-1181, www.eiu.com; *Ireland Country Report.*

European Union, Delegation of the European Commission to the United States, 2300 M Street, NW, Washington, DC 20037, (202) 862-9500, Fax: (202) 429-1766, www.eurunion.org; *Eurostatistics: Data for Short-Term Economic Analysis (2007 edition).*

Eurostat, Batiment Jean Monnet, Rue Alcide de Gasperi, L-2920 Luxembourg, http://epp.eurostat.ec.europa.eu; *Eurostat Yearbook 2006-2007.*

International Monetary Fund (IMF), 700 Nineteenth Street, NW, Washington, DC 20431, (202) 623-7000, Fax: (202) 623-4661, www.imf.org; *International Financial Statistics Yearbook 2007.*

Organisation for Economic Cooperation and Development (OECD), 2 rue Andre Pascal, F-75775 Paris Cedex 16, France, (Telephone in U.S. (202) 785-6323), (Fax in U.S. (202) 785-0350), www.oecd.org; *OECD Economic Outlook 2008.*

United Nations Statistics Division, New York, NY 10017, (800) 253-9646, Fax: (212) 963-4116, http://unstats.un.org; *Statistical Yearbook.*

The World Bank, 1818 H Street, NW, Washington, DC 20433, (202) 473-1000, Fax: (202) 477-6391, www.worldbank.org; *Ireland* and *World Development Indicators (WDI) 2008.*

IRELAND - MORTALITY

Central Intelligence Agency, Office of Public Affairs, Washington, DC 20505, (703) 482-0623, Fax: (703) 482-1739, www.cia.gov; *The World Factbook.*

Euromonitor International, Inc., 224 S. Michigan Avenue, Suite 1500, Chicago, IL 60604, (312) 922-1115, Fax: (312) 922-1157, www.euromonitor.com; *The World Economic Factbook 2008.*

European Union, Delegation of the European Commission to the United States, 2300 M Street, NW, Washington, DC 20037, (202) 862-9500, Fax: (202) 429-1766, www.eurunion.org; *First Demographic Estimates for 2006.*

Eurostat, Batiment Jean Monnet, Rue Alcide de Gasperi, L-2920 Luxembourg, http://epp.eurostat.ec.europa.eu; *Eurostat Yearbook 2006-2007.*

Palgrave Macmillan Ltd., Houndmills, Basingstoke, Hampshire, RG21 6XS, England, (Telephone in U.S. (888) 330-8477), (Fax in U.S. (800) 672-2054), www.palgrave.com; *The Statesman's Yearbook 2008.*

Taylor and Francis Group, An Informa Business, 2 Park Square, Milton Park, Abingdon, Oxford OX14 4RN, United Kingdom, (Dial from U.S. (212) 216-7800), (Fax from U.S. (212) 564-7854), www.tandf.co.uk; *The Europa World Year Book.*

UNICEF, 3 United Nations Plaza, New York, NY 10017, (800) 253-9646, Fax: (212) 887-7465, www.unicef.org; *The State of the World's Children 2008.*

United Nations Statistics Division, New York, NY 10017, (800) 253-9646, Fax: (212) 963-4116, http://unstats.un.org; *Demographic Yearbook; Human Development Report 2006; Statistical Yearbook; Trends in Europe and North America: The Statistical Yearbook of the ECE 2005;* and *World Statistics Pocketbook.*

The World Bank, 1818 H Street, NW, Washington, DC 20433, (202) 473-1000, Fax: (202) 477-6391, www.worldbank.org; *The World Bank Atlas 2003-2004; World Development Indicators (WDI) 2008;* and *World Development Report 2008.*

World Health Organization (WHO), Avenue Appia 20, 1211 Geneve 27, Switzerland, (Telephone in U.S. (212) 331-9081), www.who.int; The WHO Global Atlas of Infectious Diseases and *World Health Report 2006.*

IRELAND - MOTION PICTURES

Palgrave Macmillan Ltd., Houndmills, Basingstoke, Hampshire, RG21 6XS, England, (Telephone in U.S. (888) 330-8477), (Fax in U.S. (800) 672-2054), www.palgrave.com; *The Statesman's Yearbook 2008.*

UNESCO Institute for Statistics, C.P. 6128 Succursale Centre-Ville, Montreal, Quebec, H3C 3J7 Canada, (Dial from U.S. (514) 343-6880), (Fax from U.S. (514) 343 6882), www.uis.unesco.org; *Statistical Tables.*

United Nations Statistics Division, New York, NY 10017, (800) 253-9646, Fax: (212) 963-4116, http://unstats.un.org; *Statistical Yearbook.*

IRELAND - MOTOR VEHICLES

European Union, Delegation of the European Commission to the United States, 2300 M Street, NW, Washington, DC 20037, (202) 862-9500, Fax: (202) 429-1766, www.eurunion.org; *Statistical Overview of Transport in the European Union (Data 1970-2001).*

Eurostat, Batiment Jean Monnet, Rue Alcide de Gasperi, L-2920 Luxembourg, http://epp.eurostat.ec.europa.eu; *Eurostat Yearbook 2006-2007.*

International Road Federation (IFR), Madison Place, 500 Montgomery Street, 5th Floor, Alexandria, VA 22314, (703) 535-1001, Fax: (703) 535-1007, www.irfnet.org; *World Road Statistics 2006.*

Taylor and Francis Group, An Informa Business, 2 Park Square, Milton Park, Abingdon, Oxford OX14 4RN, United Kingdom, (Dial from U.S. (212) 216-7800), (Fax from U.S. (212) 564-7854), www.tandf.co.uk; *The Europa World Year Book.*

United Nations Statistics Division, New York, NY 10017, (800) 253-9646, Fax: (212) 963-4116, http://unstats.un.org; *Statistical Yearbook.*

IRELAND - MUSEUMS

M.E. Sharpe, 80 Business Park Drive, Armonk, NY 10504, (800) 541-6563, Fax: (914) 273-2106, www.mesharpe.com; *The Illustrated Book of World Rankings.*

UNESCO Institute for Statistics, C.P. 6128 Succursale Centre-Ville, Montreal, Quebec, H3C 3J7 Canada, (Dial from U.S. (514) 343-6880), (Fax from U.S. (514) 343 6882), www.uis.unesco.org; *Statistical Tables.*

IRELAND - NATURAL GAS PRODUCTION

See IRELAND - MINERAL INDUSTRIES

IRELAND - NICKEL AND NICKEL ORE

See IRELAND - MINERAL INDUSTRIES

IRELAND - NUTRITION

United Nations Food and Agricultural Organization (FAO), Viale delle Terme di Caracalla, 00100 Rome, Italy, (Dial from U.S. (202) 653-2400), (Fax from U.S. (202) 653 5760), www.fao.org; *The State of Food and Agriculture (SOFA) 2006.*

IRELAND - OATS PRODUCTION

See IRELAND - CROPS

IRELAND - OILSEED PLANTS

Eurostat, Batiment Jean Monnet, Rue Alcide de Gasperi, L-2920 Luxembourg, http://epp.eurostat.ec.europa.eu; *Eurostat Yearbook 2006-2007.*

Organisation for Economic Cooperation and Development (OECD), 2 rue Andre Pascal, F-75775 Paris Cedex 16, France, (Telephone in U.S. (202) 785-

6323), (Fax in U.S. (202) 785-0350), www.oecd.org; *International Trade by Commodity Statistics (ITCS)*.

IRELAND - OLDER PEOPLE

M.E. Sharpe, 80 Business Park Drive, Armonk, NY 10504, (800) 541-6563, Fax: (914) 273-2106, www.mesharpe.com; *The Illustrated Book of World Rankings*.

IRELAND - ONION PRODUCTION

See IRELAND - CROPS

IRELAND - PALM OIL PRODUCTION

See IRELAND - CROPS

IRELAND - PAPER

See IRELAND - FORESTS AND FORESTRY

IRELAND - PEANUT PRODUCTION

See IRELAND - CROPS

IRELAND - PERIODICALS

UNESCO Institute for Statistics, C.P. 6128 Succursale Centre-Ville, Montreal, Quebec, H3C 3J7 Canada, (Dial from U.S. (514) 343-6880), (Fax from U.S. (514) 343 6882), www.uis.unesco.org; *Statistical Tables*.

IRELAND - PESTICIDES

United Nations Food and Agricultural Organization (FAO), Viale delle Terme di Caracalla, 00100 Rome, Italy, (Dial from U.S. (202) 653-2400), (Fax from U.S. (202) 653 5760), www.fao.org; *The State of Food and Agriculture (SOFA) 2006*.

IRELAND - PETROLEUM INDUSTRY AND TRADE

Euromonitor International, Inc., 224 S. Michigan Avenue, Suite 1500, Chicago, IL 60604, (312) 922-1115, Fax: (312) 922-1157, www.euromonitor.com; *European Marketing Data and Statistics 2008*.

Eurostat, Batiment Jean Monnet, Rue Alcide de Gasperi, L-2920 Luxembourg, http://epp.eurostat.ec.europa.eu; *Eurostat Yearbook 2006-2007*.

International Energy Agency (IEA), 9, rue de la Federation, 75739 Paris Cedex 15, France, www.iea.org; *Key World Energy Statistics 2007*.

M.E. Sharpe, 80 Business Park Drive, Armonk, NY 10504, (800) 541-6563, Fax: (914) 273-2106, www.mesharpe.com; *The Illustrated Book of World Rankings*.

Organisation for Economic Cooperation and Development (OECD), 2 rue Andre Pascal, F-75775 Paris Cedex 16, France, (Telephone in U.S. (202) 785-6323), (Fax in U.S. (202) 785-0350), www.oecd.org; *Energy Statistics of OECD Countries* (2007 Edition); *Indicators of Industrial Activity; International Trade by Commodity Statistics (ITCS)*; and *Oil Information 2006 Edition*.

Palgrave Macmillan Ltd., Houndmills, Basingstoke, Hampshire, RG21 6XS, England, (Telephone in U.S. (888) 330-8477), (Fax in U.S. (800) 672-2054), www.palgrave.com; *The Statesman's Yearbook 2008*.

PennWell Corporation, 1421 South Sheridan Road, Tulsa, OK 74112, (918) 835-3161, www.pennwell.com; *International Petroleum Encyclopedia 2007*.

Platts, 2 Penn Plaza, 25th Floor, New York, NY 10121-2298, (212) 904-3070, www.platts.com; *Energy Economist*.

U.S. Department of Energy (DOE), Energy Information Administration (EIA), 1000 Independence Avenue, SW, Washington, DC 20585, (202) 586-8800, www.eia.doe.gov; *International Energy Annual 2004* and *International Energy Outlook 2006*.

United Nations Conference on Trade and Development (UNCTAD), DC2-1120, United Nations, New York, NY 10017, (212) 963-0027, www.unctad.org; *UNCTAD Commodity Yearbook*.

United Nations Statistics Division, New York, NY 10017, (800) 253-9646, Fax: (212) 963-4116, http://unstats.un.org; *Energy Statistics Yearbook 2003* and *Trends in Europe and North America: The Statistical Yearbook of the ECE 2005*.

IRELAND - PHOSPHATES PRODUCTION

See IRELAND - MINERAL INDUSTRIES

IRELAND - PIPELINES

European Union, Delegation of the European Commission to the United States, 2300 M Street, NW, Washington, DC 20037, (202) 862-9500, Fax: (202) 429-1766, www.eurunion.org; *Statistical Overview of Transport in the European Union (Data 1970-2001)*.

IRELAND - PLASTICS INDUSTRY AND TRADE

Eurostat, Batiment Jean Monnet, Rue Alcide de Gasperi, L-2920 Luxembourg, http://epp.eurostat.ec.europa.eu; *Eurostat Yearbook 2006-2007*.

Organisation for Economic Cooperation and Development (OECD), 2 rue Andre Pascal, F-75775 Paris Cedex 16, France, (Telephone in U.S. (202) 785-6323), (Fax in U.S. (202) 785-0350), www.oecd.org; *International Trade by Commodity Statistics (ITCS)*.

IRELAND - PLATINUM PRODUCTION

See IRELAND - MINERAL INDUSTRIES

IRELAND - POLITICAL SCIENCE

Central Intelligence Agency, Office of Public Affairs, Washington, DC 20505, (703) 482-0623, Fax: (703) 482-1739, www.cia.gov; *The World Factbook*.

European Union, Delegation of the European Commission to the United States, 2300 M Street, NW, Washington, DC 20037, (202) 862-9500, Fax: (202) 429-1766, www.eurunion.org; *RD Expenditure in Europe (2006 edition)*.

Eurostat, Batiment Jean Monnet, Rue Alcide de Gasperi, L-2920 Luxembourg, http://epp.eurostat.ec.europa.eu; *Eurostat Yearbook 2006-2007*.

International Monetary Fund (IMF), 700 Nineteenth Street, NW, Washington, DC 20431, (202) 623-7000, Fax: (202) 623-4661, www.imf.org; *Government Finance Statistics Yearbook (2008 Edition)* and *International Financial Statistics Yearbook 2007*.

Organisation for Economic Cooperation and Development (OECD), 2 rue Andre Pascal, F-75775 Paris Cedex 16, France, (Telephone in U.S. (202) 785-6323), (Fax in U.S. (202) 785-0350), www.oecd.org; *OECD Economic Outlook 2008* and *Revenue Statistics 1965-2006 - 2007 Edition*.

Palgrave Macmillan Ltd., Houndmills, Basingstoke, Hampshire, RG21 6XS, England, (Telephone in U.S. (888) 330-8477), (Fax in U.S. (800) 672-2054), www.palgrave.com; *The Statesman's Yearbook 2008*.

Taylor and Francis Group, An Informa Business, 2 Park Square, Milton Park, Abingdon, Oxford OX14 4RN, United Kingdom, (Dial from U.S. (212) 216-7800), (Fax from U.S. (212) 564-7854), www.tandf.co.uk; *The Europa World Year Book*.

United Nations Statistics Division, New York, NY 10017, (800) 253-9646, Fax: (212) 963-4116, http://unstats.un.org; *National Accounts Statistics: Compendium of Income Distribution Statistics* and *Statistical Yearbook*.

The World Bank, 1818 H Street, NW, Washington, DC 20433, (202) 473-1000, Fax: (202) 477-6391, www.worldbank.org; *World Development Indicators (WDI) 2008* and *World Development Report 2008*.

IRELAND - POPULATION

Banque de France, 48 rue Croix des Petits champs, 75001 Paris, France, www.banque-france.fr/home.htm; *Key Data for the Euro Area*.

Central Intelligence Agency, Office of Public Affairs, Washington, DC 20505, (703) 482-0623, Fax: (703) 482-1739, www.cia.gov; *The World Factbook*.

Central Statistics Office (CSO) Ireland, Skehard Road, Cork, Ireland, www.cso.ie; *Measuring Ireland's Progress, 2006; Statistical Yearbook of Ireland 2007;* and *Women and Men in Ireland, 2007*.

Economist Intelligence Unit, 111 West 57th Street, New York, NY 10019, (212) 554-0600, Fax: (212) 586-1181, www.eiu.com; *Ireland Country Report*.

Euromonitor International, Inc., 224 S. Michigan Avenue, Suite 1500, Chicago, IL 60604, (312) 922-1115, Fax: (312) 922-1157, www.euromonitor.com; *European Marketing Data and Statistics 2008* and *The World Economic Factbook 2008*.

European Union, Delegation of the European Commission to the United States, 2300 M Street, NW, Washington, DC 20037, (202) 862-9500, Fax: (202) 429-1766, www.eurunion.org; *European Union Labour Force Survey; First Demographic Estimates for 2006;* and *Regions - Statistical Yearbook 2006*.

Eurostat, Batiment Jean Monnet, Rue Alcide de Gasperi, L-2920 Luxembourg, http://epp.eurostat.ec.europa.eu; *Eurostat Yearbook 2006-2007* and *The Life of Women and Men in Europe - A Statistical Portrait*.

International Labour Office, I.L.O. Publications, 4 route des Morillons, CH-1211 Geneva 22, Switzerland, (Telephone in U.S. (202) 653-7652), (Fax in U.S. (202) 653-7687), www.ilo.org; *Yearbook of Labour Statistics 2006*.

M.E. Sharpe, 80 Business Park Drive, Armonk, NY 10504, (800) 541-6563, Fax: (914) 273-2106, www.mesharpe.com; *The Illustrated Book of World Rankings*.

Organisation for Economic Cooperation and Development (OECD), 2 rue Andre Pascal, F-75775 Paris Cedex 16, France, (Telephone in U.S. (202) 785-6323), (Fax in U.S. (202) 785-0350), www.oecd.org; *Labour Force Statistics: 1986-2005, 2007 Edition*.

Palgrave Macmillan Ltd., Houndmills, Basingstoke, Hampshire, RG21 6XS, England, (Telephone in U.S. (888) 330-8477), (Fax in U.S. (800) 672-2054), www.palgrave.com; *The Statesman's Yearbook 2008*.

Taylor and Francis Group, An Informa Business, 2 Park Square, Milton Park, Abingdon, Oxford OX14 4RN, United Kingdom, (Dial from U.S. (212) 216-7800), (Fax from U.S. (212) 564-7854), www.tandf.co.uk; *The Europa World Year Book*.

U.S. Department of State (DOS), 2201 C Street NW, Washington, DC 20520, (202) 647-4000, www.state.gov; *World Military Expenditures and Arms Transfers (WMEAT)*.

UNESCO Institute for Statistics, C.P. 6128 Succursale Centre-Ville, Montreal, Quebec, H3C 3J7 Canada, (Dial from U.S. (514) 343-6880), (Fax from U.S. (514) 343 6882), www.uis.unesco.org; *Statistical Tables*.

United Nations Food and Agricultural Organization (FAO), Viale delle Terme di Caracalla, 00100 Rome, Italy, (Dial from U.S. (202) 653-2400), (Fax from U.S. (202) 653 5760), www.fao.org; *FAO Production Yearbook 2002*.

United Nations Statistics Division, New York, NY 10017, (800) 253-9646, Fax: (212) 963-4116, http://unstats.un.org; *Demographic Yearbook; Human Development Report 2006; Statistical Yearbook; Trends in Europe and North America: The Statistical Yearbook of the ECE 2005;* and *World Statistics Pocketbook*.

The World Bank, 1818 H Street, NW, Washington, DC 20433, (202) 473-1000, Fax: (202) 477-6391, www.worldbank.org; *Ireland; The World Bank Atlas 2003-2004;* and *World Development Report 2008*.

World Health Organization (WHO), Avenue Appia 20, 1211 Geneve 27, Switzerland, (Telephone in U.S. (212) 331-9081), www.who.int; *World Health Report 2006*.

IRELAND - POPULATION DENSITY

Central Intelligence Agency, Office of Public Affairs, Washington, DC 20505, (703) 482-0623, Fax: (703) 482-1739, www.cia.gov; *The World Factbook*.

Euromonitor International, Inc., 224 S. Michigan Avenue, Suite 1500, Chicago, IL 60604, (312) 922-1115, Fax: (312) 922-1157, www.euromonitor.com; *The World Economic Factbook 2008.*

European Union, Delegation of the European Commission to the United States, 2300 M Street, NW, Washington, DC 20037, (202) 862-9500, Fax: (202) 429-1766, www.eurunion.org; *First Demographic Estimates for 2006.*

Eurostat, Batiment Jean Monnet, Rue Alcide de Gasperi, L-2920 Luxembourg, http://epp.eurostat.ec.europa.eu; *Eurostat Yearbook 2006-2007.*

M.E. Sharpe, 80 Business Park Drive, Armonk, NY 10504, (800) 541-6563, Fax: (914) 273-2106, www.mesharpe.com; *The Illustrated Book of World Rankings.*

Palgrave Macmillan Ltd., Houndmills, Basingstoke, Hampshire, RG21 6XS, England, (Telephone in U.S. (888) 330-8477), (Fax in U.S. (800) 672-2054), www.palgrave.com; *The Statesman's Yearbook 2008.*

Taylor and Francis Group, An Informa Business, 2 Park Square, Milton Park, Abingdon, Oxford OX14 4RN, United Kingdom, (Dial from U.S. (212) 216-7800), (Fax from U.S. (212) 564-7854), www.tandf.co.uk; *The Europa World Year Book.*

UNESCO Institute for Statistics, C.P. 6128 Succursale Centre-Ville, Montreal, Quebec, H3C 3J7 Canada, (Dial from U.S. (514) 343-6880), (Fax from U.S. (514) 343 6882), www.uis.unesco.org; *Statistical Tables.*

United Nations Food and Agricultural Organization (FAO), Viale delle Terme di Caracalla, 00100 Rome, Italy, (Dial from U.S. (202) 653-2400), (Fax from U.S. (202) 653 5760), www.fao.org; *The State of Food and Agriculture (SOFA) 2006.*

United Nations Statistics Division, New York, NY 10017, (800) 253-9646, Fax: (212) 963-4116, http://unstats.un.org; *Statistical Yearbook* and *Trends in Europe and North America: The Statistical Yearbook of the ECE 2005.*

The World Bank, 1818 H Street, NW, Washington, DC 20433, (202) 473-1000, Fax: (202) 477-6391, www.worldbank.org; *Ireland* and *World Development Report 2008.*

IRELAND - POSTAL SERVICE

European Union, Delegation of the European Commission to the United States, 2300 M Street, NW, Washington, DC 20037, (202) 862-9500, Fax: (202) 429-1766, www.eurunion.org; *Statistical Overview of Transport in the European Union (Data 1970-2001).*

M.E. Sharpe, 80 Business Park Drive, Armonk, NY 10504, (800) 541-6563, Fax: (914) 273-2106, www.mesharpe.com; *The Illustrated Book of World Rankings.*

Palgrave Macmillan Ltd., Houndmills, Basingstoke, Hampshire, RG21 6XS, England, (Telephone in U.S. (888) 330-8477), (Fax in U.S. (800) 672-2054), www.palgrave.com; *The Statesman's Yearbook 2008.*

United Nations Statistics Division, New York, NY 10017, (800) 253-9646, Fax: (212) 963-4116, http://unstats.un.org; *Statistical Yearbook* and *Trends in Europe and North America: The Statistical Yearbook of the ECE 2005.*

IRELAND - POWER RESOURCES

Euromonitor International, Inc., 224 S. Michigan Avenue, Suite 1500, Chicago, IL 60604, (312) 922-1115, Fax: (312) 922-1157, www.euromonitor.com; *European Marketing Data and Statistics 2008; The World Economic Factbook 2008;* and *World Marketing Data and Statistics.*

European Union, Delegation of the European Commission to the United States, 2300 M Street, NW, Washington, DC 20037, (202) 862-9500, Fax: (202) 429-1766, www.eurunion.org; *European Union Energy Transport in Figures 2006; European Union Labour Force Survey;* and *Regions - Statistical Yearbook 2006.*

Eurostat, Batiment Jean Monnet, Rue Alcide de Gasperi, L-2920 Luxembourg, http://epp.eurostat.ec.europa.eu; *Eurostat Yearbook 2006-2007.*

M.E. Sharpe, 80 Business Park Drive, Armonk, NY 10504, (800) 541-6563, Fax: (914) 273-2106, www.mesharpe.com; *The Illustrated Book of World Rankings.*

Organisation for Economic Cooperation and Development (OECD), 2 rue Andre Pascal, F-75775 Paris Cedex 16, France, (Telephone in U.S. (202) 785-6323), (Fax in U.S. (202) 785-0350), www.oecd.org; *Coal Information: 2007 Edition; Energy Statistics of OECD Countries* (2007 Edition); *Key Environmental Indicators 2004;* and *Oil Information 2006 Edition.*

Palgrave Macmillan Ltd., Houndmills, Basingstoke, Hampshire, RG21 6XS, England, (Telephone in U.S. (888) 330-8477), (Fax in U.S. (800) 672-2054), www.palgrave.com; *The Statesman's Yearbook 2008.*

Platts, 2 Penn Plaza, 25th Floor, New York, NY 10121-2298, (212) 904-3070, www.platts.com; *Energy Economist* and *European Power Daily.*

U.S. Department of Energy (DOE), Energy Information Administration (EIA), 1000 Independence Avenue, SW, Washington, DC 20585, (202) 586-8800, www.eia.doe.gov; *International Energy Annual 2004* and *International Energy Outlook 2006.*

United Nations Food and Agricultural Organization (FAO), Viale delle Terme di Caracalla, 00100 Rome, Italy, (Dial from U.S. (202) 653-2400), (Fax from U.S. (202) 653 5760), www.fao.org; *The State of Food and Agriculture (SOFA) 2006.*

United Nations Statistics Division, New York, NY 10017, (800) 253-9646, Fax: (212) 963-4116, http://unstats.un.org; *Energy Statistics Yearbook 2003; Human Development Report 2006; Statistical Yearbook; Trends in Europe and North America: The Statistical Yearbook of the ECE 2005;* and *World Statistics Pocketbook.*

The World Bank, 1818 H Street, NW, Washington, DC 20433, (202) 473-1000, Fax: (202) 477-6391, www.worldbank.org; *The World Bank Atlas 2003-2004* and *World Development Report 2008.*

IRELAND - PRICES

Central Statistics Office (CSO) Ireland, Skehard Road, Cork, Ireland, www.cso.ie; *Consumer Price Index.*

Euromonitor International, Inc., 224 S. Michigan Avenue, Suite 1500, Chicago, IL 60604, (312) 922-1115, Fax: (312) 922-1157, www.euromonitor.com; *European Marketing Data and Statistics 2008* and *World Marketing Data and Statistics.*

European Union, Delegation of the European Commission to the United States, 2300 M Street, NW, Washington, DC 20037, (202) 862-9500, Fax: (202) 429-1766, www.eurunion.org; *Eurostatistics: Data for Short-Term Economic Analysis (2007 edition).*

Eurostat, Batiment Jean Monnet, Rue Alcide de Gasperi, L-2920 Luxembourg, http://epp.eurostat.ec.europa.eu; *Eurostat Yearbook 2006-2007.*

International Labour Office, I.L.O. Publications, 4 route des Morillons, CH-1211 Geneva 22, Switzerland, (Telephone in U.S. (202) 653-7652), (Fax in U.S. (202) 653-7687), www.ilo.org; *Yearbook of Labour Statistics 2006.*

International Lead and Zinc Study Group (ILZSG), Rua Almirante Barroso 38, 5th Floor, Lisbon 1000 - 013, Portugal, www.ilzsg.org; Interactive Statistical Database.

International Monetary Fund (IMF), 700 Nineteenth Street, NW, Washington, DC 20431, (202) 623-7000, Fax: (202) 623-4661, www.imf.org; *International Financial Statistics Yearbook 2007.*

M.E. Sharpe, 80 Business Park Drive, Armonk, NY 10504, (800) 541-6563, Fax: (914) 273-2106, www.mesharpe.com; *The Illustrated Book of World Rankings.*

Organisation for Economic Cooperation and Development (OECD), 2 rue Andre Pascal, F-75775 Paris Cedex 16, France, (Telephone in U.S. (202) 785-6323), (Fax in U.S. (202) 785-0350), www.oecd.org; *Indicators of Industrial Activity; Iron and Steel Industry in 2004 (2006 Edition); OECD Economic Outlook 2008;* and *OECD Main Economic Indicators (MEI).*

Technical Association of the Pulp and Paper Industry (TAPPI), 15 Technology Parkway South, Norcross, GA 30092, (770) 446-1400, Fax: (770) 446-6947, www.tappi.org; *TAPPI Annual Report.*

United Nations Food and Agricultural Organization (FAO), Viale delle Terme di Caracalla, 00100 Rome, Italy, (Dial from U.S. (202) 653-2400), (Fax from U.S. (202) 653 5760), www.fao.org; *FAO Production Yearbook 2002* and *The State of Food and Agriculture (SOFA) 2006.*

The World Bank, 1818 H Street, NW, Washington, DC 20433, (202) 473-1000, Fax: (202) 477-6391, www.worldbank.org; *Ireland.*

IRELAND - PROFESSIONS

Eurostat, Batiment Jean Monnet, Rue Alcide de Gasperi, L-2920 Luxembourg, http://epp.eurostat.ec.europa.eu; *Eurostat Yearbook 2006-2007.*

UNESCO Institute for Statistics, C.P. 6128 Succursale Centre-Ville, Montreal, Quebec, H3C 3J7 Canada, (Dial from U.S. (514) 343-6880), (Fax from U.S. (514) 343 6882), www.uis.unesco.org; *Statistical Tables.*

United Nations Statistics Division, New York, NY 10017, (800) 253-9646, Fax: (212) 963-4116, http://unstats.un.org; *Statistical Yearbook.*

IRELAND - PUBLIC HEALTH

Central Statistics Office (CSO) Ireland, Skehard Road, Cork, Ireland, www.cso.ie; *Measuring Ireland's Progress, 2006* and *Women and Men in Ireland, 2007.*

Euromonitor International, Inc., 224 S. Michigan Avenue, Suite 1500, Chicago, IL 60604, (312) 922-1115, Fax: (312) 922-1157, www.euromonitor.com; *World Health Databook 2007/2008* and *World Marketing Data and Statistics.*

European Centre for Disease Prevention and Control (ECDC), 171 83 Stockholm, Sweden, www.ecdc.europa.eu; *Eurosurveillance.*

European Union, Delegation of the European Commission to the United States, 2300 M Street, NW, Washington, DC 20037, (202) 862-9500, Fax: (202) 429-1766, www.eurunion.org; *Regions - Statistical Yearbook 2006.*

Eurostat, Batiment Jean Monnet, Rue Alcide de Gasperi, L-2920 Luxembourg, http://epp.eurostat.ec.europa.eu; *Eurostat Yearbook 2006-2007.*

Health and Consumer Protection Directorate-General, European Commission, B-1049 Brussels, Belgium, http://ec.europa.eu/dgs/health_consumer/index_en.htm; *Injuries in the European Union: Statistics Summary 2002-2004.*

Health Protection Agency, 7th Floor, Holborn Gate, 330 High Holborn, London WC1V 7PP, United Kingdom, www.hpa.org.uk; *Antimicrobial Resistance in England, Wales, and Northern Ireland* and *Foreign Travel Associated Illness, England, Wales, and Northern Ireland: 2007 Report.*

Health Protection Surveillance Centre (HPSC), 25-27 Middle Gardiner Street, Dublin 1, Ireland, www.ndsc.ie/hpsc; *Acute Gastroenteritis in Ireland, North and South: A Telephone Survey* and *Report on the Epidemiology of Tuberculosis in Ireland 2005.*

M.E. Sharpe, 80 Business Park Drive, Armonk, NY 10504, (800) 541-6563, Fax: (914) 273-2106, www.mesharpe.com; *The Illustrated Book of World Rankings.*

National Cancer Institute (NCI), National Institutes of Health (NIH), Public Inquiries Office, 6116 Executive Boulevard, Room 3036A, Bethesda, MD 20892-8322, (800) 422-6237, www.cancer.gov; *Cancer Research Across Borders: Second Report 2001-2002.*

Organisation for Economic Cooperation and Development (OECD), 2 rue Andre Pascal, F-75775 Paris

Cedex 16, France, (Telephone in U.S. (202) 785-6323), (Fax in U.S. (202) 785-0350), www.oecd.org; *Health at a Glance 2007 - OECD Indicators.*

Palgrave Macmillan Ltd., Houndmills, Basingstoke, Hampshire, RG21 6XS, England, (Telephone in U.S. (888) 330-8477), (Fax in U.S. (800) 672-2054), www.palgrave.com; *The Statesman's Yearbook 2008.*

Robert Koch Institute, Nordufer 20, D 13353 Berlin, Germany, www.rki.de; *EUVAC-NET Report: Pertussis-Surveillance 1998-2002.*

UNICEF, 3 United Nations Plaza, New York, NY 10017, (800) 253-9646, Fax: (212) 887-7465, www.unicef.org; *The State of the World's Children 2008.*

United Nations Statistics Division, New York, NY 10017, (800) 253-9646, Fax: (212) 963-4116, http://unstats.un.org; *Human Development Report 2006; Statistical Yearbook;* and *Trends in Europe and North America: The Statistical Yearbook of the ECE 2005.*

The World Bank, 1818 H Street, NW, Washington, DC 20433, (202) 473-1000, Fax: (202) 477-6391, www.worldbank.org; *Ireland* and *World Development Report 2008.*

World Health Organization (WHO), Avenue Appia 20, 1211 Geneve 27, Switzerland, (Telephone in U.S. (212) 331-9081), www.who.int; The WHO Global Atlas of Infectious Diseases and *World Health Report 2006.*

IRELAND - PUBLIC UTILITIES

Eurostat, Batiment Jean Monnet, Rue Alcide de Gasperi, L-2920 Luxembourg, http://epp.eurostat.ec.europa.eu; *Eurostat Yearbook 2006-2007.*

IRELAND - PUBLISHERS AND PUBLISHING

Organisation for Economic Cooperation and Development (OECD), 2 rue Andre Pascal, F-75775 Paris Cedex 16, France, (Telephone in U.S. (202) 785-6323), (Fax in U.S. (202) 785-0350), www.oecd.org; *Indicators of Industrial Activity.*

Taylor and Francis Group, An Informa Business, 2 Park Square, Milton Park, Abingdon, Oxford OX14 4RN, United Kingdom, (Dial from U.S. (212) 216-7800), (Fax from U.S. (212) 564-7854), www.tandf.co.uk; *The Europa World Year Book.*

UNESCO Institute for Statistics, C.P. 6128 Succursale Centre-Ville, Montreal, Quebec, H3C 3J7 Canada, (Dial from U.S. (514) 343-6880), (Fax from U.S. (514) 343 6882), www.uis.unesco.org; *Statistical Tables.*

United Nations Statistics Division, New York, NY 10017, (800) 253-9646, Fax: (212) 963-4116, http://unstats.un.org; *Trends in Europe and North America: The Statistical Yearbook of the ECE 2005.*

IRELAND - RADIO - RECEIVERS AND RECEPTION

Palgrave Macmillan Ltd., Houndmills, Basingstoke, Hampshire, RG21 6XS, England, (Telephone in U.S. (888) 330-8477), (Fax in U.S. (800) 672-2054), www.palgrave.com; *The Statesman's Yearbook 2008.*

United Nations Statistics Division, New York, NY 10017, (800) 253-9646, Fax: (212) 963-4116, http://unstats.un.org; *Statistical Yearbook.*

IRELAND - RAILROADS

Euromonitor International, Inc., 224 S. Michigan Avenue, Suite 1500, Chicago, IL 60604, (312) 922-1115, Fax: (312) 922-1157, www.euromonitor.com; *European Marketing Data and Statistics 2008.*

European Union, Delegation of the European Commission to the United States, 2300 M Street, NW, Washington, DC 20037, (202) 862-9500, Fax: (202) 429-1766, www.eurunion.org; *Regions - Statistical Yearbook 2006* and *Statistical Overview of Transport in the European Union (Data 1970-2001).*

Eurostat, Batiment Jean Monnet, Rue Alcide de Gasperi, L-2920 Luxembourg, http://epp.eurostat.ec.europa.eu; *Eurostat Yearbook 2006-2007.*

Jane's Information Group, 110 North Royal Street, Suite 200, Alexandria, VA 22314, (703) 683-3700, Fax: (800) 836-0297, www.janes.com; *Jane's World Railways.*

Palgrave Macmillan Ltd., Houndmills, Basingstoke, Hampshire, RG21 6XS, England, (Telephone in U.S. (888) 330-8477), (Fax in U.S. (800) 672-2054), www.palgrave.com; *The Statesman's Yearbook 2008.*

Taylor and Francis Group, An Informa Business, 2 Park Square, Milton Park, Abingdon, Oxford OX14 4RN, United Kingdom, (Dial from U.S. (212) 216-7800), (Fax from U.S. (212) 564-7854), www.tandf.co.uk; *The Europa World Year Book.*

United Nations Statistics Division, New York, NY 10017, (800) 253-9646, Fax: (212) 963-4116, http://unstats.un.org; *Annual Bulletin of Transport Statistics for Europe and North America 2004; Statistical Yearbook;* and *Trends in Europe and North America: The Statistical Yearbook of the ECE 2005.*

IRELAND - RANCHING

Eurostat, Batiment Jean Monnet, Rue Alcide de Gasperi, L-2920 Luxembourg, http://epp.eurostat.ec.europa.eu; *Eurostat Yearbook 2006-2007.*

IRELAND - RELIGION

Central Intelligence Agency, Office of Public Affairs, Washington, DC 20505, (703) 482-0623, Fax: (703) 482-1739, www.cia.gov; *The World Factbook.*

M.E. Sharpe, 80 Business Park Drive, Armonk, NY 10504, (800) 541-6563, Fax: (914) 273-2106, www.mesharpe.com; *The Illustrated Book of World Rankings.*

Palgrave Macmillan Ltd., Houndmills, Basingstoke, Hampshire, RG21 6XS, England, (Telephone in U.S. (888) 330-8477), (Fax in U.S. (800) 672-2054), www.palgrave.com; *The Statesman's Yearbook 2008.*

IRELAND - RENT CHARGES

International Labour Office, I.L.O. Publications, 4 route des Morillons, CH-1211 Geneva 22, Switzerland, (Telephone in U.S. (202) 653-7652), (Fax in U.S. (202) 653-7687), www.ilo.org; *Yearbook of Labour Statistics 2006.*

IRELAND - RESERVES (ACCOUNTING)

Eurostat, Batiment Jean Monnet, Rue Alcide de Gasperi, L-2920 Luxembourg, http://epp.eurostat.ec.europa.eu; *Eurostat Yearbook 2006-2007.*

Organisation for Economic Cooperation and Development (OECD), 2 rue Andre Pascal, F-75775 Paris Cedex 16, France, (Telephone in U.S. (202) 785-6323), (Fax in U.S. (202) 785-0350), www.oecd.org; *Financial Market Trends: OECD Periodical* and *OECD Economic Outlook 2008.*

United Nations Statistics Division, New York, NY 10017, (800) 253-9646, Fax: (212) 963-4116, http://unstats.un.org; *Statistical Yearbook.*

The World Bank, 1818 H Street, NW, Washington, DC 20433, (202) 473-1000, Fax: (202) 477-6391, www.worldbank.org; *World Development Indicators (WDI) 2008.*

IRELAND - RETAIL TRADE

Banque de France, 48 rue Croix des Petits champs, 75001 Paris, France, www.banque-france.fr/home.htm; *Monthly Business Survey Overview.*

Euromonitor International, Inc., 224 S. Michigan Avenue, Suite 1500, Chicago, IL 60604, (312) 922-1115, Fax: (312) 922-1157, www.euromonitor.com; *World Marketing Data and Statistics.*

European Union, Delegation of the European Commission to the United States, 2300 M Street, NW, Washington, DC 20037, (202) 862-9500, Fax: (202) 429-1766, www.eurunion.org; *Eurostatistics: Data for Short-Term Economic Analysis (2007 edition).*

Eurostat, Batiment Jean Monnet, Rue Alcide de Gasperi, L-2920 Luxembourg, http://epp.eurostat.ec.europa.eu; *Eurostat Yearbook 2006-2007.*

United Nations Statistics Division, New York, NY 10017, (800) 253-9646, Fax: (212) 963-4116, http://unstats.un.org; *Statistical Yearbook.*

IRELAND - RICE PRODUCTION

See IRELAND - CROPS

IRELAND - ROADS

Central Intelligence Agency, Office of Public Affairs, Washington, DC 20505, (703) 482-0623, Fax: (703) 482-1739, www.cia.gov; *The World Factbook.*

Eurostat, Batiment Jean Monnet, Rue Alcide de Gasperi, L-2920 Luxembourg, http://epp.eurostat.ec.europa.eu; *Eurostat Yearbook 2006-2007.*

International Road Federation (IFR), Madison Place, 500 Montgomery Street, 5th Floor, Alexandria, VA 22314, (703) 535-1001, Fax: (703) 535-1007, www.irfnet.org; *World Road Statistics 2006.*

Palgrave Macmillan Ltd., Houndmills, Basingstoke, Hampshire, RG21 6XS, England, (Telephone in U.S. (888) 330-8477), (Fax in U.S. (800) 672-2054), www.palgrave.com; *The Statesman's Yearbook 2008.*

United Nations Statistics Division, New York, NY 10017, (800) 253-9646, Fax: (212) 963-4116, http://unstats.un.org; *Annual Bulletin of Transport Statistics for Europe and North America 2004* and *Trends in Europe and North America: The Statistical Yearbook of the ECE 2005.*

IRELAND - RUBBER INDUSTRY AND TRADE

Eurostat, Batiment Jean Monnet, Rue Alcide de Gasperi, L-2920 Luxembourg, http://epp.eurostat.ec.europa.eu; *Eurostat Yearbook 2006-2007.*

International Rubber Study Group (IRSG), 1st Floor, Heron House, 109/115 Wembley Hill Road, Wembley, Middlesex HA9 8DA, United Kingdom, www.rubberstudy.com; *Rubber Statistical Bulletin; Summary of World Rubber Statistics 2005; World Rubber Statistics Handbook (Volume 6, 1975-2001);* and *World Rubber Statistics Historic Handbook.*

M.E. Sharpe, 80 Business Park Drive, Armonk, NY 10504, (800) 541-6563, Fax: (914) 273-2106, www.mesharpe.com; *The Illustrated Book of World Rankings.*

Organisation for Economic Cooperation and Development (OECD), 2 rue Andre Pascal, F-75775 Paris Cedex 16, France, (Telephone in U.S. (202) 785-6323), (Fax in U.S. (202) 785-0350), www.oecd.org; *International Trade by Commodity Statistics (ITCS).*

IRELAND - RYE PRODUCTION

See IRELAND - CROPS

IRELAND - SAFFLOWER SEED PRODUCTION

See IRELAND - CROPS

IRELAND - SALT PRODUCTION

See IRELAND - MINERAL INDUSTRIES

IRELAND - SAVINGS ACCOUNT DEPOSITS

See IRELAND - BANKS AND BANKING

IRELAND - SHEEP

See IRELAND - LIVESTOCK

IRELAND - SHIPBUILDING

Organisation for Economic Cooperation and Development (OECD), 2 rue Andre Pascal, F-75775 Paris Cedex 16, France, (Telephone in U.S. (202) 785-6323), (Fax in U.S. (202) 785-0350), www.oecd.org; *Indicators of Industrial Activity.*

IRELAND - SHIPPING

European Union, Delegation of the European Commission to the United States, 2300 M Street, NW, Washington, DC 20037, (202) 862-9500, Fax: (202) 429-1766, www.eurunion.org; *Fishery Statistics - 1990-2006; Regions - Statistical Yearbook 2006;* and *Statistical Overview of Transport in the European Union (Data 1970-2001).*

Eurostat, Batiment Jean Monnet, Rue Alcide de Gasperi, L-2920 Luxembourg, http://epp.eurostat.ec.europa.eu; *Eurostat Yearbook 2006-2007.*

Organisation for Economic Cooperation and Development (OECD), 2 rue Andre Pascal, F-75775 Paris Cedex 16, France, (Telephone in U.S. (202) 785-6323), (Fax in U.S. (202) 785-0350), www.oecd.org; *Statistics on Ship Production, Exports and Orders in 2004.*

Palgrave Macmillan Ltd., Houndmills, Basingstoke, Hampshire, RG21 6XS, England, (Telephone in U.S. (888) 330-8477), (Fax in U.S. (800) 672-2054), www.palgrave.com; *The Statesman's Yearbook 2008.*

Taylor and Francis Group, An Informa Business, 2 Park Square, Milton Park, Abingdon, Oxford OX14 4RN, United Kingdom, (Dial from U.S. (212) 216-7800), (Fax from U.S. (212) 564-7854), www.tandf.co.uk; *The Europa World Year Book.*

U.S. Department of Transportation (DOT), Maritime Administration (MARAD), West Building, Southeast Federal Center, 1200 New Jersey Avenue, SE, Washington, DC 20590, (800) 99-MARAD, www.marad.dot.gov; *World Merchant Fleet 2005.*

United Nations Statistics Division, New York, NY 10017, (800) 253-9646, Fax: (212) 963-4116, http://unstats.un.org; *Statistical Yearbook.*

IRELAND - SILVER PRODUCTION

See IRELAND - MINERAL INDUSTRIES

IRELAND - SOCIAL CLASSES

European Union, Delegation of the European Commission to the United States, 2300 M Street, NW, Washington, DC 20037, (202) 862-9500, Fax: (202) 429-1766, www.eurunion.org; *European Union Labour Force Survey.*

Eurostat, Batiment Jean Monnet, Rue Alcide de Gasperi, L-2920 Luxembourg, http://epp.eurostat.ec.europa.eu; *Eurostat Yearbook 2006-2007.*

IRELAND - SOCIAL ECOLOGY

Eurostat, Batiment Jean Monnet, Rue Alcide de Gasperi, L-2920 Luxembourg, http://epp.eurostat.ec.europa.eu; *Eurostat Yearbook 2006-2007.*

M.E. Sharpe, 80 Business Park Drive, Armonk, NY 10504, (800) 541-6563, Fax: (914) 273-2106, www.mesharpe.com; *The Illustrated Book of World Rankings.*

United Nations Statistics Division, New York, NY 10017, (800) 253-9646, Fax: (212) 963-4116, http://unstats.un.org; *World Statistics Pocketbook.*

IRELAND - SOCIAL SECURITY

Eurostat, Batiment Jean Monnet, Rue Alcide de Gasperi, L-2920 Luxembourg, http://epp.eurostat.ec.europa.eu; *Eurostat Yearbook 2006-2007.*

Organisation for Economic Cooperation and Development (OECD), 2 rue Andre Pascal, F-75775 Paris Cedex 16, France, (Telephone in U.S. (202) 785-6323), (Fax in U.S. (202) 785-0350), www.oecd.org; *Revenue Statistics 1965-2006 - 2007 Edition.*

Palgrave Macmillan Ltd., Houndmills, Basingstoke, Hampshire, RG21 6XS, England, (Telephone in U.S. (888) 330-8477), (Fax in U.S. (800) 672-2054), www.palgrave.com; *The Statesman's Yearbook 2008.*

United Nations Statistics Division, New York, NY 10017, (800) 253-9646, Fax: (212) 963-4116, http://unstats.un.org; *National Accounts Statistics: Compendium of Income Distribution Statistics.*

IRELAND - SOYBEAN PRODUCTION

See IRELAND - CROPS

IRELAND - STEEL PRODUCTION

See IRELAND - MINERAL INDUSTRIES

IRELAND - STRAW PRODUCTION

See IRELAND - CROPS

IRELAND - SUGAR PRODUCTION

See IRELAND - CROPS

IRELAND - SULPHUR PRODUCTION

See IRELAND - MINERAL INDUSTRIES

IRELAND - SUNFLOWER PRODUCTION

See IRELAND - CROPS

IRELAND - TAXATION

Eurostat, Batiment Jean Monnet, Rue Alcide de Gasperi, L-2920 Luxembourg, http://epp.eurostat.ec.europa.eu; *Eurostat Yearbook 2006-2007* and *Taxation Trends in the European Union - Data for the EU Member States and Norway.*

International Monetary Fund (IMF), 700 Nineteenth Street, NW, Washington, DC 20431, (202) 623-7000, Fax: (202) 623-4661, www.imf.org; *Government Finance Statistics Yearbook (2008 Edition).*

International Road Federation (IFR), Madison Place, 500 Montgomery Street, 5th Floor, Alexandria, VA 22314, (703) 535-1001, Fax: (703) 535-1007, www.irfnet.org; *World Road Statistics 2006.*

Organisation for Economic Cooperation and Development (OECD), 2 rue Andre Pascal, F-75775 Paris Cedex 16, France, (Telephone in U.S. (202) 785-6323), (Fax in U.S. (202) 785-0350), www.oecd.org; *Revenue Statistics 1965-2006 - 2007 Edition.*

Palgrave Macmillan Ltd., Houndmills, Basingstoke, Hampshire, RG21 6XS, England, (Telephone in U.S. (888) 330-8477), (Fax in U.S. (800) 672-2054), www.palgrave.com; *The Statesman's Yearbook 2008.*

Taylor and Francis Group, An Informa Business, 2 Park Square, Milton Park, Abingdon, Oxford OX14 4RN, United Kingdom, (Dial from U.S. (212) 216-7800), (Fax from U.S. (212) 564-7854), www.tandf.co.uk; *The Europa World Year Book.*

The World Bank, 1818 H Street, NW, Washington, DC 20433, (202) 473-1000, Fax: (202) 477-6391, www.worldbank.org; *World Development Indicators (WDI) 2008.*

IRELAND - TEA PRODUCTION

See IRELAND - CROPS

IRELAND - TELEPHONE

European Union, Delegation of the European Commission to the United States, 2300 M Street, NW, Washington, DC 20037, (202) 862-9500, Fax: (202) 429-1766, www.eurunion.org; *Statistical Overview of Transport in the European Union (Data 1970-2001).*

Eurostat, Batiment Jean Monnet, Rue Alcide de Gasperi, L-2920 Luxembourg, http://epp.eurostat.ec.europa.eu; *Eurostat Yearbook 2006-2007.*

International Telecommunication Union (ITU), Place des Nations, 1211 Geneva 20, Switzerland, www.itu.int; World Telecommunication Indicators Database.

Palgrave Macmillan Ltd., Houndmills, Basingstoke, Hampshire, RG21 6XS, England, (Telephone in U.S. (888) 330-8477), (Fax in U.S. (800) 672-2054), www.palgrave.com; *The Statesman's Yearbook 2008.*

Taylor and Francis Group, An Informa Business, 2 Park Square, Milton Park, Abingdon, Oxford OX14 4RN, United Kingdom, (Dial from U.S. (212) 216-7800), (Fax from U.S. (212) 564-7854), www.tandf.co.uk; *The Europa World Year Book.*

United Nations Statistics Division, New York, NY 10017, (800) 253-9646, Fax: (212) 963-4116, http://unstats.un.org; *Statistical Yearbook; Trends in Europe and North America: The Statistical Yearbook of the ECE 2005;* and *World Statistics Pocketbook.*

IRELAND - TELEVISION - RECEIVERS AND RECEPTION

Eurostat, Batiment Jean Monnet, Rue Alcide de Gasperi, L-2920 Luxembourg, http://epp.eurostat.ec.europa.eu; *Eurostat Yearbook 2006-2007.*

United Nations Statistics Division, New York, NY 10017, (800) 253-9646, Fax: (212) 963-4116, http://unstats.un.org; *Statistical Yearbook.*

IRELAND - TEXTILE INDUSTRY

European Union, Delegation of the European Commission to the United States, 2300 M Street, NW, Washington, DC 20037, (202) 862-9500, Fax: (202) 429-1766, www.eurunion.org; *Eurostatistics: Data for Short-Term Economic Analysis (2007 edition)* and *The Textile Industry in the EU.*

Eurostat, Batiment Jean Monnet, Rue Alcide de Gasperi, L-2920 Luxembourg, http://epp.eurostat.ec.europa.eu; *Eurostat Yearbook 2006-2007.*

M.E. Sharpe, 80 Business Park Drive, Armonk, NY 10504, (800) 541-6563, Fax: (914) 273-2106, www.mesharpe.com; *The Illustrated Book of World Rankings.*

Organisation for Economic Cooperation and Development (OECD), 2 rue Andre Pascal, F-75775 Paris Cedex 16, France, (Telephone in U.S. (202) 785-6323), (Fax in U.S. (202) 785-0350), www.oecd.org; *Indicators of Industrial Activity; International Trade by Commodity Statistics (ITCS); A New World Map in Textiles and Clothing: Adjusting to Change; 2005 OECD Agricultural Outlook Tables, 1970-2014;* and STructural ANalysis (STAN) database.

Palgrave Macmillan Ltd., Houndmills, Basingstoke, Hampshire, RG21 6XS, England, (Telephone in U.S. (888) 330-8477), (Fax in U.S. (800) 672-2054), www.palgrave.com; *The Statesman's Yearbook 2008.*

United Nations Conference on Trade and Development (UNCTAD), DC2-1120, United Nations, New York, NY 10017, (212) 963-0027, www.unctad.org; *UNCTAD Commodity Yearbook.*

United Nations Statistics Division, New York, NY 10017, (800) 253-9646, Fax: (212) 963-4116, http://unstats.un.org; *Statistical Yearbook.*

IRELAND - THEATER

UNESCO Institute for Statistics, C.P. 6128 Succursale Centre-Ville, Montreal, Quebec, H3C 3J7 Canada, (Dial from U.S. (514) 343-6880), (Fax from U.S. (514) 343 6882), www.uis.unesco.org; *Statistical Tables.*

IRELAND - TIMBER

See IRELAND - FORESTS AND FORESTRY

IRELAND - TIN PRODUCTION

See IRELAND - MINERAL INDUSTRIES

IRELAND - TOBACCO INDUSTRY

Euromonitor International, Inc., 224 S. Michigan Avenue, Suite 1500, Chicago, IL 60604, (312) 922-1115, Fax: (312) 922-1157, www.euromonitor.com; *European Marketing Data and Statistics 2008.*

Eurostat, Batiment Jean Monnet, Rue Alcide de Gasperi, L-2920 Luxembourg, http://epp.eurostat.ec.europa.eu; *Eurostat Yearbook 2006-2007.*

Foreign Agricultural Service (FAS), U.S. Department of Agriculture (USDA), 1400 Independence Avenue, SW, Washington, DC 20250, (202) 720-3935, www.fas.usda.gov; *Tobacco: World Markets and Trade.*

M.E. Sharpe, 80 Business Park Drive, Armonk, NY 10504, (800) 541-6563, Fax: (914) 273-2106, www.mesharpe.com; *The Illustrated Book of World Rankings.*

Organisation for Economic Cooperation and Development (OECD), 2 rue Andre Pascal, F-75775 Paris Cedex 16, France, (Telephone in U.S. (202) 785-6323), (Fax in U.S. (202) 785-0350), www.oecd.org; *Indicators of Industrial Activity; International Trade by Commodity Statistics (ITCS);* and STructural ANalysis (STAN) database.

United Nations Statistics Division, New York, NY 10017, (800) 253-9646, Fax: (212) 963-4116, http://unstats.un.org; *Statistical Yearbook.*

IRELAND - TOURISM

Euromonitor International, Inc., 224 S. Michigan Avenue, Suite 1500, Chicago, IL 60604, (312) 922-

1115, Fax: (312) 922-1157, www.euromonitor.com; *European Marketing Data and Statistics 2008; The World Economic Factbook 2008;* and *World Marketing Data and Statistics.*

European Union, Delegation of the European Commission to the United States, 2300 M Street, NW, Washington, DC 20037, (202) 862-9500, Fax: (202) 429-1766, www.eurunion.org; *Statistical Overview of Transport in the European Union (Data 1970-2001).*

Eurostat, Batiment Jean Monnet, Rue Alcide de Gasperi, L-2920 Luxembourg, http://epp.eurostat.ec.europa.eu; *Tourism in Europe: First Results for 2007.*

M.E. Sharpe, 80 Business Park Drive, Armonk, NY 10504, (800) 541-6563, Fax: (914) 273-2106, www.mesharpe.com; *The Illustrated Book of World Rankings.*

Organisation for Economic Cooperation and Development (OECD), 2 rue Andre Pascal, F-75775 Paris Cedex 16, France, (Telephone in U.S. (202) 785-6323), (Fax in U.S. (202) 785-0350), www.oecd.org; *Household, Tourism, Travel: Trends, Environmental Impacts and Policy Responses.*

Palgrave Macmillan Ltd., Houndmills, Basingstoke, Hampshire, RG21 6XS, England, (Telephone in U.S. (888) 330-8477), (Fax in U.S. (800) 672-2054), www.palgrave.com; *The Statesman's Yearbook 2008.*

Taylor and Francis Group, An Informa Business, 2 Park Square, Milton Park, Abingdon, Oxford OX14 4RN, United Kingdom, (Dial from U.S. (212) 216-7800), (Fax from U.S. (212) 564-7854), www.tandf.co.uk; *The Europa World Year Book.*

United Nations Statistics Division, New York, NY 10017, (800) 253-9646, Fax: (212) 963-4116, http://unstats.un.org; *Statistical Yearbook* and *Trends in Europe and North America: The Statistical Yearbook of the ECE 2005.*

United Nations World Tourism Organization (UNWTO), Capitan Haya 42, 28020 Madrid, Spain, www.world-tourism.org; *Tourism Market Trends 2004 - Europe* and *Yearbook of Tourism Statistics.*

The World Bank, 1818 H Street, NW, Washington, DC 20433, (202) 473-1000, Fax: (202) 477-6391, www.worldbank.org; *Ireland.*

IRELAND - TRADE

See IRELAND - INTERNATIONAL TRADE

IRELAND - TRANSPORTATION

Central Statistics Office (CSO) Ireland, Skehard Road, Cork, Ireland, www.cso.ie; *Women and Men in Ireland, 2007.*

Euromonitor International, Inc., 224 S. Michigan Avenue, Suite 1500, Chicago, IL 60604, (312) 922-1115, Fax: (312) 922-1157, www.euromonitor.com; *World Marketing Data and Statistics.*

European Union, Delegation of the European Commission to the United States, 2300 M Street, NW, Washington, DC 20037, (202) 862-9500, Fax: (202) 429-1766, www.eurunion.org; *Regions - Statistical Yearbook 2006* and *Statistical Overview of Transport in the European Union (Data 1970-2001).*

Eurostat, Batiment Jean Monnet, Rue Alcide de Gasperi, L-2920 Luxembourg, http://epp.eurostat.ec.europa.eu; *Eurostat Yearbook 2006-2007; Regional Passenger and Freight Air Transport in Europe in 2006;* and *Regional Road and Rail Transport Networks.*

M.E. Sharpe, 80 Business Park Drive, Armonk, NY 10504, (800) 541-6563, Fax: (914) 273-2106, www.mesharpe.com; *The Illustrated Book of World Rankings.*

Palgrave Macmillan Ltd., Houndmills, Basingstoke, Hampshire, RG21 6XS, England, (Telephone in U.S. (888) 330-8477), (Fax in U.S. (800) 672-2054), www.palgrave.com; *The Statesman's Yearbook 2008.*

Platts, 2 Penn Plaza, 25th Floor, New York, NY 10121-2298, (212) 904-3070, www.platts.com; *Energy Economist.*

Taylor and Francis Group, An Informa Business, 2 Park Square, Milton Park, Abingdon, Oxford OX14 4RN, United Kingdom, (Dial from U.S. (212) 216-7800), (Fax from U.S. (212) 564-7854), www.tandf.co.uk; *The Europa World Year Book.*

United Nations Statistics Division, New York, NY 10017, (800) 253-9646, Fax: (212) 963-4116, http://unstats.un.org; *Energy Statistics Yearbook 2003; Human Development Report 2006;* and *Trends in Europe and North America: The Statistical Yearbook of the ECE 2005.*

The World Bank, 1818 H Street, NW, Washington, DC 20433, (202) 473-1000, Fax: (202) 477-6391, www.worldbank.org; *Ireland.*

IRELAND - TURKEYS

See IRELAND - LIVESTOCK

IRELAND - UNEMPLOYMENT

Central Statistics Office (CSO) Ireland, Skehard Road, Cork, Ireland, www.cso.ie; *Measuring Ireland's Progress, 2006.*

Euromonitor International, Inc., 224 S. Michigan Avenue, Suite 1500, Chicago, IL 60604, (312) 922-1115, Fax: (312) 922-1157, www.euromonitor.com; *European Marketing Data and Statistics 2008.*

European Union, Delegation of the European Commission to the United States, 2300 M Street, NW, Washington, DC 20037, (202) 862-9500, Fax: (202) 429-1766, www.eurunion.org; *European Union Labour Force Survey; Eurostatistics: Data for Short-Term Economic Analysis (2007 edition);* and *Regions - Statistical Yearbook 2006.*

Eurostat, Batiment Jean Monnet, Rue Alcide de Gasperi, L-2920 Luxembourg, http://epp.eurostat.ec.europa.eu; *Eurostat Yearbook 2006-2007.*

International Labour Office, I.L.O. Publications, 4 route des Morillons, CH-1211 Geneva 22, Switzerland, (Telephone in U.S. (202) 653-7652), (Fax in U.S. (202) 653-7687), www.ilo.org; *Yearbook of Labour Statistics 2006.*

Organisation for Economic Cooperation and Development (OECD), 2 rue Andre Pascal, F-75775 Paris Cedex 16, France, (Telephone in U.S. (202) 785-6323), (Fax in U.S. (202) 785-0350), www.oecd.org; *Labour Force Statistics: 1986-2005, 2007 Edition; OECD Composite Leading Indicators (CLIs), Updated September 2007; OECD Economic Outlook 2008; OECD Economic Survey - Ireland 2008;* and *OECD Employment Outlook 2007.*

Palgrave Macmillan Ltd., Houndmills, Basingstoke, Hampshire, RG21 6XS, England, (Telephone in U.S. (888) 330-8477), (Fax in U.S. (800) 672-2054), www.palgrave.com; *The Statesman's Yearbook 2008.*

United Nations Statistics Division, New York, NY 10017, (800) 253-9646, Fax: (212) 963-4116, http://unstats.un.org; *Statistical Yearbook* and *Trends in Europe and North America: The Statistical Yearbook of the ECE 2005.*

The World Bank, 1818 H Street, NW, Washington, DC 20433, (202) 473-1000, Fax: (202) 477-6391, www.worldbank.org; *Ireland.*

IRELAND - URANIUM PRODUCTION AND CONSUMPTION

See IRELAND - MINERAL INDUSTRIES

IRELAND - VITAL STATISTICS

Central Statistics Office (CSO) Ireland, Skehard Road, Cork, Ireland, www.cso.ie; *Measuring Ireland's Progress, 2006* and *Women and Men in Ireland, 2007.*

Palgrave Macmillan Ltd., Houndmills, Basingstoke, Hampshire, RG21 6XS, England, (Telephone in U.S. (888) 330-8477), (Fax in U.S. (800) 672-2054), www.palgrave.com; *The Statesman's Yearbook 2008.*

IRELAND - WAGES

European Union, Delegation of the European Commission to the United States, 2300 M Street, NW, Washington, DC 20037, (202) 862-9500, Fax: (202) 429-1766, www.eurunion.org; *Eurostatistics: Data for Short-Term Economic Analysis (2007 edition).*

Organisation for Economic Cooperation and Development (OECD), 2 rue Andre Pascal, F-75775 Paris Cedex 16, France, (Telephone in U.S. (202) 785-6323), (Fax in U.S. (202) 785-0350), www.oecd.org; *ICT Sector Data and Metadata by Country.*

The World Bank, 1818 H Street, NW, Washington, DC 20433, (202) 473-1000, Fax: (202) 477-6391, www.worldbank.org; *Ireland.*

IRELAND - WALNUT PRODUCTION

See IRELAND - CROPS

IRELAND - WELFARE STATE

Eurostat, Batiment Jean Monnet, Rue Alcide de Gasperi, L-2920 Luxembourg, http://epp.eurostat.ec.europa.eu; *Eurostat Yearbook 2006-2007.*

Palgrave Macmillan Ltd., Houndmills, Basingstoke, Hampshire, RG21 6XS, England, (Telephone in U.S. (888) 330-8477), (Fax in U.S. (800) 672-2054), www.palgrave.com; *The Statesman's Yearbook 2008.*

IRELAND - WHEAT PRODUCTION

See IRELAND - CROPS

IRELAND - WOOD AND WOOD PULP

See IRELAND - FORESTS AND FORESTRY

IRELAND - WOOD PRODUCTS

Eurostat, Batiment Jean Monnet, Rue Alcide de Gasperi, L-2920 Luxembourg, http://epp.eurostat.ec.europa.eu; *Eurostat Yearbook 2006-2007.*

Organisation for Economic Cooperation and Development (OECD), 2 rue Andre Pascal, F-75775 Paris Cedex 16, France, (Telephone in U.S. (202) 785-6323), (Fax in U.S. (202) 785-0350), www.oecd.org; *International Trade by Commodity Statistics (ITCS)* and STructural ANalysis (STAN) database.

IRELAND - WOOL PRODUCTION

See IRELAND - TEXTILE INDUSTRY

IRELAND - YARN PRODUCTION

See IRELAND - TEXTILE INDUSTRY

IRELAND - ZINC AND ZINC ORE

See IRELAND - MINERAL INDUSTRIES

IRON - INTERNATIONAL TRADE

U.S. Census Bureau, Foreign Trade Division, 4700 Silver Hill Road, Washington DC 20233-0001, (301) 763-3030, www.census.gov/foreign-trade/www/; *U.S. International Trade in Goods and Services.*

U.S. Department of the Interior (DOI), U.S. Geological Survey (USGS), Office of Minerals Information, 12201 Sunrise Valley Drive, Reston, VA 20192, Mr. Kenneth A. Beckman, (703) 648-4916, Fax: (703) 648-4995, http://minerals.usgs.gov/minerals; *Mineral Commodity Summaries* and *Minerals Yearbook.*

IRON - MINING INDUSTRY

U.S. Bureau of Labor Statistics (BLS), Postal Square Building, 2 Massachusetts Avenue, NE, Washington, DC 20212-0001, (202) 691-5200, Fax: (202) 691-6325, www.bls.gov; *Current Employment Statistics Survey (CES)* and *Employment and Earnings (EE).*

U.S. Census Bureau, Center for Economic Studies, 4600 Silver Hill Road, Washington DC 20233, (301) 457-1235, www.ces.census.gov; *2002 Economic Census, Mining.*

U.S. Census Bureau, Manufacturing and Construction Division, 4600 Silver Hill Road, Washington DC 20233, (301) 763-4673, www.census.gov/mcd; *Census of Mineral Industries.*

IRON - MINING INDUSTRY - PRODUCTIVITY

U.S. Bureau of Labor Statistics (BLS), Postal Square Building, 2 Massachusetts Avenue, NE,

Washington, DC 20212-0001, (202) 691-5200, Fax: (202) 691-6325, www.bls.gov; *Industry Productivity and Costs.*

IRON - PRICES

U.S. Department of the Interior (DOI), U.S. Geological Survey (USGS), Office of Minerals Information, 12201 Sunrise Valley Drive, Reston, VA 20192, Mr. Kenneth A. Beckman, (703) 648-4916, Fax: (703) 648-4995, http://minerals.usgs.gov/minerals; *Mineral Commodity Summaries.*

IRON - PRODUCTION

U.S. Department of the Interior (DOI), U.S. Geological Survey (USGS), Office of Minerals Information, 12201 Sunrise Valley Drive, Reston, VA 20192, Mr. Kenneth A. Beckman, (703) 648-4916, Fax: (703) 648-4995, http://minerals.usgs.gov/minerals; *Mineral Commodity Summaries* and *Minerals Yearbook.*

IRON - WORLD PRODUCTION

U.S. Department of the Interior (DOI), U.S. Geological Survey (USGS), Office of Minerals Information, 12201 Sunrise Valley Drive, Reston, VA 20192, Mr. Kenneth A. Beckman, (703) 648-4916, Fax: (703) 648-4995, http://minerals.usgs.gov/minerals; *Mineral Commodity Summaries* and *Minerals Yearbook.*

United Nations Statistics Division, New York, NY 10017, (800) 253-9646, Fax: (212) 963-4116, http://unstats.un.org; *Monthly Bulletin of Statistics.*

IRON AND STEEL - MANUFACTURING

See also METAL TRADE

IRON AND STEEL - MANUFACTURING - CAPITAL

American Iron and Steel Institute, 1140 Connecticut Avenue, NW, Suite 705, Washington, DC 20036, (202) 452-7100, www.steel.org; *2005 Annual Statistical Report.*

U.S. Census Bureau, Foreign Trade Division, 4700 Silver Hill Road, Washington DC 20233-0001, (301) 763-3030, www.census.gov/foreign-trade/www/; *U.S. International Trade in Goods and Services.*

IRON AND STEEL - MANUFACTURING - EARNINGS

U.S. Bureau of Labor Statistics (BLS), Postal Square Building, 2 Massachusetts Avenue, NE, Washington, DC 20212-0001, (202) 691-5200, Fax: (202) 691-6325, www.bls.gov; *Current Employment Statistics Survey (CES)* and *Employment and Earnings (EE).*

IRON AND STEEL - MANUFACTURING - EMPLOYEES

U.S. Bureau of Labor Statistics (BLS), Postal Square Building, 2 Massachusetts Avenue, NE, Washington, DC 20212-0001, (202) 691-5200, Fax: (202) 691-6325, www.bls.gov; *Current Employment Statistics Survey (CES)* and *Employment and Earnings (EE).*

U.S. Census Bureau, Foreign Trade Division, 4700 Silver Hill Road, Washington DC 20233-0001, (301) 763-3030, www.census.gov/foreign-trade/www/; *U.S. International Trade in Goods and Services.*

IRON AND STEEL - MANUFACTURING - INTERNATIONAL TRADE

U.S. Census Bureau, Foreign Trade Division, 4700 Silver Hill Road, Washington DC 20233-0001, (301) 763-3030, www.census.gov/foreign-trade/www/; *U.S. International Trade in Goods and Services.*

IRON AND STEEL - MANUFACTURING - OCCUPATIONAL SAFETY

U.S. Bureau of Labor Statistics (BLS), Postal Square Building, 2 Massachusetts Avenue, NE, Washington, DC 20212-0001, (202) 691-5200, Fax: (202) 691-6325, www.bls.gov; *Injuries, Illnesses, and Fatalities (IIF).*

IRON AND STEEL - MANUFACTURING - PRODUCTIVITY

Board of Governors of the Federal Reserve System, Constitution Avenue, NW, Washington, DC 20551, (202) 452-3000, www.federalreserve.gov; *Federal Reserve Bulletin* and *Industrial Production and Capacity Utilization.*

U.S. Bureau of Labor Statistics (BLS), Postal Square Building, 2 Massachusetts Avenue, NE, Washington, DC 20212-0001, (202) 691-5200, Fax: (202) 691-6325, www.bls.gov; *Industry Productivity and Costs.*

IRON AND STEEL - MANUFACTURING - PROFITS

Executive Office of the President, Council of Economic Advisors, The White House, 1600 Pennsylvania Avenue NW, Washington, DC 20500, (202) 456-1414, www.whitehouse.gov/cea; *2007 Economic Report of the President.*

U.S. Census Bureau, Manufacturing and Construction Division, 4600 Silver Hill Road, Washington DC 20233, (301) 763-4673, www.census.gov/mcd; *Quarterly Financial Report for Manufacturing, Mining and Trade Corporations.*

IRON AND STEEL - MANUFACTURING - SHIPMENTS

American Iron and Steel Institute, 1140 Connecticut Avenue, NW, Suite 705, Washington, DC 20036, (202) 452-7100, www.steel.org; *2005 Annual Statistical Report.*

U.S. Census Bureau, Foreign Trade Division, 4700 Silver Hill Road, Washington DC 20233-0001, (301) 763-3030, www.census.gov/foreign-trade/www/; *U.S. International Trade in Goods and Services.*

IRON AND STEEL PRODUCTS

American Iron and Steel Institute, 1140 Connecticut Avenue, NW, Suite 705, Washington, DC 20036, (202) 452-7100, www.steel.org; *2005 Annual Statistical Report.*

U.S. Census Bureau, Foreign Trade Division, 4700 Silver Hill Road, Washington DC 20233-0001, (301) 763-3030, www.census.gov/foreign-trade/www/; *U.S. International Trade in Goods and Services.*

U.S. Department of the Interior (DOI), U.S. Geological Survey (USGS), Office of Minerals Information, 12201 Sunrise Valley Drive, Reston, VA 20192, Mr. Kenneth A. Beckman, (703) 648-4916, Fax: (703) 648-4995, http://minerals.usgs.gov/minerals; *Mineral Commodity Summaries* and *Minerals Yearbook.*

IRON AND STEEL PRODUCTS - PRODUCTION AND VALUE

American Iron and Steel Institute, 1140 Connecticut Avenue, NW, Suite 705, Washington, DC 20036, (202) 452-7100, www.steel.org; *2005 Annual Statistical Report.*

U.S. Department of the Interior (DOI), U.S. Geological Survey (USGS), Office of Minerals Information, 12201 Sunrise Valley Drive, Reston, VA 20192, Mr. Kenneth A. Beckman, (703) 648-4916, Fax: (703) 648-4995, http://minerals.usgs.gov/minerals; *Mineral Commodity Summaries* and *Minerals Yearbook.*

IRON AND STEEL SCRAP

U.S. Department of the Interior (DOI), U.S. Geological Survey (USGS), Office of Minerals Information, 12201 Sunrise Valley Drive, Reston, VA 20192, Mr. Kenneth A. Beckman, (703) 648-4916, Fax: (703) 648-4995, http://minerals.usgs.gov/minerals; *Mineral Commodity Summaries.*

IRON AND STEEL SLAG

U.S. Department of the Interior (DOI), U.S. Geological Survey (USGS), Office of Minerals Information, 12201 Sunrise Valley Drive, Reston, VA 20192, Mr. Kenneth A. Beckman, (703) 648-4916, Fax: (703) 648-4995, http://minerals.usgs.gov/minerals; *Mineral Commodity Summaries.*

IRRIGATION

National Agricultural Statistics Service (NASS), U.S. Department of Agriculture (USDA), 1400 Independence Avenue, SW, Washington, DC 20250, (800) 727-9540, Fax: (202) 690-2090, www.nass.usda.gov; *2007 Census of Agriculture.*

U.S. Department of the Interior (DOI), U.S. Geological Survey (USGS), Water Resources Discipline (WRD), 12201 Sunrise Valley Drive, Reston, VA 20192, (888) 275-8747, http://water.usgs.gov; *Estimated Use of Water in the United States.*

ISLAMIC POPULATION

See RELIGION

ISRAEL - NATIONAL STATISTICAL OFFICE

Central Bureau of Statistics (CBS) Israel, PO Box 34525, Jerusalem 91342, Israel, www.cbs.gov.il/engindex.htm; National Data Center.

ISRAEL - PRIMARY STATISTICS SOURCES

Central Bureau of Statistics (CBS) Israel, PO Box 34525, Jerusalem 91342, Israel, www.cbs.gov.il/engindex.htm; *Monthly Bulletin of Statistics* and *Statistical Abstract of Israel 2007.*

ISRAEL - ABORTION

United Nations Statistics Division, New York, NY 10017, (800) 253-9646, Fax: (212) 963-4116, http://unstats.un.org; *Trends in Europe and North America: The Statistical Yearbook of the ECE 2005.*

ISRAEL - AGRICULTURAL MACHINERY

United Nations Statistics Division, New York, NY 10017, (800) 253-9646, Fax: (212) 963-4116, http://unstats.un.org; *Statistical Yearbook.*

ISRAEL - AGRICULTURE

Economist Intelligence Unit, 111 West 57th Street, New York, NY 10019, (212) 554-0600, Fax: (212) 586-1181, www.eiu.com; *Israel Country Report.*

Euromonitor International, Inc., 224 S. Michigan Avenue, Suite 1500, Chicago, IL 60604, (312) 922-1115, Fax: (312) 922-1157, www.euromonitor.com; *International Marketing Data and Statistics 2008* and *World Marketing Data and Statistics.*

M.E. Sharpe, 80 Business Park Drive, Armonk, NY 10504, (800) 541-6563, Fax: (914) 273-2106, www.mesharpe.com; *The Illustrated Book of World Rankings.*

Palgrave Macmillan Ltd., Houndmills, Basingstoke, Hampshire, RG21 6XS, England, (Telephone in U.S. (888) 330-8477), (Fax in U.S. (800) 672-2054), www.palgrave.com; *The Statesman's Yearbook 2008.*

Taylor and Francis Group, An Informa Business, 2 Park Square, Milton Park, Abingdon, Oxford OX14 4RN, United Kingdom, (Dial from U.S. (212) 216-7800), (Fax from U.S. (212) 564-7854), www.tandf.co.uk; *The Europa World Year Book.*

United Nations Conference on Trade and Development (UNCTAD), DC2-1120, United Nations, New York, NY 10017, (212) 963-0027, www.unctad.org; *UNCTAD Commodity Yearbook.*

United Nations Food and Agricultural Organization (FAO), Viale delle Terme di Caracalla, 00100 Rome, Italy, (Dial from U.S. (202) 653-2400), (Fax from U.S. (202) 653 5760), www.fao.org; AQUASTAT; *FAO Production Yearbook 2002; FAO Trade Yearbook;* and *The State of Food and Agriculture (SOFA) 2006.*

United Nations Statistics Division, New York, NY 10017, (800) 253-9646, Fax: (212) 963-4116, http://unstats.un.org; *Statistical Yearbook.*

The World Bank, 1818 H Street, NW, Washington, DC 20433, (202) 473-1000, Fax: (202) 477-6391, www.worldbank.org; *Israel* and *World Development Indicators (WDI) 2008.*

ISRAEL - AIRLINES

International Civil Aviation Organization (ICAO), External Relations and Public Information Office (EPO), 999 University Street, Montreal, Quebec H3C 5H7, Canada, (Dial from U.S. (514) 954-8219), (Fax from U.S. (514) 954-6077), www.icao.int; *Civil Aviation Statistics of the World.*

M.E. Sharpe, 80 Business Park Drive, Armonk, NY 10504, (800) 541-6563, Fax: (914) 273-2106, www.mesharpe.com; *The Illustrated Book of World Rankings.*

Palgrave Macmillan Ltd., Houndmills, Basingstoke, Hampshire, RG21 6XS, England, (Telephone in U.S. (888) 330-8477), (Fax in U.S. (800) 672-2054), www.palgrave.com; *The Statesman's Yearbook 2008.*

Taylor and Francis Group, An Informa Business, 2 Park Square, Milton Park, Abingdon, Oxford OX14 4RN, United Kingdom, (Dial from U.S. (212) 216-7800), (Fax from U.S. (212) 564-7854), www.tandf.co.uk; *The Europa World Year Book.*

United Nations Statistics Division, New York, NY 10017, (800) 253-9646, Fax: (212) 963-4116, http://unstats.un.org; *Statistical Yearbook.*

ISRAEL - AIRPORTS

Central Intelligence Agency, Office of Public Affairs, Washington, DC 20505, (703) 482-0623, Fax: (703) 482-1739, www.cia.gov; *The World Factbook.*

ISRAEL - ALMOND PRODUCTION

See ISRAEL - CROPS

ISRAEL - ALUMINUM PRODUCTION

See ISRAEL - MINERAL INDUSTRIES

ISRAEL - ARMED FORCES

Central Intelligence Agency, Office of Public Affairs, Washington, DC 20505, (703) 482-0623, Fax: (703) 482-1739, www.cia.gov; *The World Factbook.*

Euromonitor International, Inc., 224 S. Michigan Avenue, Suite 1500, Chicago, IL 60604, (312) 922-1115, Fax: (312) 922-1157, www.euromonitor.com; *World Marketing Data and Statistics.*

International Institute for Strategic Studies (IISS), Arundel House, 13-15 Arundel Street, Temple Place, London WC2R 3DX, England, www.iiss.org; *The Military Balance 2007.*

International Monetary Fund (IMF), 700 Nineteenth Street, NW, Washington, DC 20431, (202) 623-7000, Fax: (202) 623-4661, www.imf.org; *Government Finance Statistics Yearbook (2008 Edition).*

Palgrave Macmillan Ltd., Houndmills, Basingstoke, Hampshire, RG21 6XS, England, (Telephone in U.S. (888) 330-8477), (Fax in U.S. (800) 672-2054), www.palgrave.com; *The Statesman's Yearbook 2008.*

U.S. Department of State (DOS), 2201 C Street NW, Washington, DC 20520, (202) 647-4000, www.state.gov; *World Military Expenditures and Arms Transfers (WMEAT).*

United Nations Statistics Division, New York, NY 10017, (800) 253-9646, Fax: (212) 963-4116, http://unstats.un.org; *Human Development Report 2006.*

ISRAEL - ARTICHOKE PRODUCTION

See ISRAEL - CROPS

ISRAEL - AUTOMOBILE INDUSTRY AND TRADE

United Nations Statistics Division, New York, NY 10017, (800) 253-9646, Fax: (212) 963-4116, http://unstats.un.org; *Statistical Yearbook.*

ISRAEL - BALANCE OF PAYMENTS

International Monetary Fund (IMF), 700 Nineteenth Street, NW, Washington, DC 20431, (202) 623-7000, Fax: (202) 623-4661, www.imf.org; *Balance of Payments Statistics Newsletter; Balance of Payments Statistics Yearbook 2007;* and *International Financial Statistics Yearbook 2007.*

Taylor and Francis Group, An Informa Business, 2 Park Square, Milton Park, Abingdon, Oxford OX14 4RN, United Kingdom, (Dial from U.S. (212) 216-7800), (Fax from U.S. (212) 564-7854), www.tandf.co.uk; *The Europa World Year Book.*

United Nations Conference on Trade and Development (UNCTAD), DC2-1120, United Nations, New York, NY 10017, (212) 963-0027, www.unctad.org; *Handbook of Statistics 2005.*

The World Bank, 1818 H Street, NW, Washington, DC 20433, (202) 473-1000, Fax: (202) 477-6391, www.worldbank.org; *Israel; World Development Indicators (WDI) 2008;* and *World Development Report 2008.*

ISRAEL - BANKS AND BANKING

Euromonitor International, Inc., 224 S. Michigan Avenue, Suite 1500, Chicago, IL 60604, (312) 922-1115, Fax: (312) 922-1157, www.euromonitor.com; *World Marketing Data and Statistics.*

International Monetary Fund (IMF), 700 Nineteenth Street, NW, Washington, DC 20431, (202) 623-7000, Fax: (202) 623-4661, www.imf.org; *Government Finance Statistics Yearbook (2008 Edition)* and *International Financial Statistics Yearbook 2007.*

M.E. Sharpe, 80 Business Park Drive, Armonk, NY 10504, (800) 541-6563, Fax: (914) 273-2106, www.mesharpe.com; *The Illustrated Book of World Rankings.*

Palgrave Macmillan Ltd., Houndmills, Basingstoke, Hampshire, RG21 6XS, England, (Telephone in U.S. (888) 330-8477), (Fax in U.S. (800) 672-2054), www.palgrave.com; *The Statesman's Yearbook 2008.*

Taylor and Francis Group, An Informa Business, 2 Park Square, Milton Park, Abingdon, Oxford OX14 4RN, United Kingdom, (Dial from U.S. (212) 216-7800), (Fax from U.S. (212) 564-7854), www.tandf.co.uk; *The Europa World Year Book.*

ISRAEL - BARLEY PRODUCTION

See ISRAEL - CROPS

ISRAEL - BEVERAGE INDUSTRY

M.E. Sharpe, 80 Business Park Drive, Armonk, NY 10504, (800) 541-6563, Fax: (914) 273-2106, www.mesharpe.com; *The Illustrated Book of World Rankings.*

United Nations Statistics Division, New York, NY 10017, (800) 253-9646, Fax: (212) 963-4116, http://unstats.un.org; *Statistical Yearbook.*

ISRAEL - BONDS

International Monetary Fund (IMF), 700 Nineteenth Street, NW, Washington, DC 20431, (202) 623-7000, Fax: (202) 623-4661, www.imf.org; *Government Finance Statistics Yearbook (2008 Edition).*

ISRAEL - BROADCASTING

Central Intelligence Agency, Office of Public Affairs, Washington, DC 20505, (703) 482-0623, Fax: (703) 482-1739, www.cia.gov; *The World Factbook.*

Euromonitor International, Inc., 224 S. Michigan Avenue, Suite 1500, Chicago, IL 60604, (312) 922-1115, Fax: (312) 922-1157, www.euromonitor.com; *World Marketing Data and Statistics.*

M.E. Sharpe, 80 Business Park Drive, Armonk, NY 10504, (800) 541-6563, Fax: (914) 273-2106, www.mesharpe.com; *The Illustrated Book of World Rankings.*

Palgrave Macmillan Ltd., Houndmills, Basingstoke, Hampshire, RG21 6XS, England, (Telephone in U.S. (888) 330-8477), (Fax in U.S. (800) 672-2054), www.palgrave.com; *The Statesman's Yearbook 2008.*

United Nations Statistics Division, New York, NY 10017, (800) 253-9646, Fax: (212) 963-4116, http://unstats.un.org; *Trends in Europe and North America: The Statistical Yearbook of the ECE 2005.*

WRTH Publications Limited, PO Box 290, Oxford OX2 7FT, UK, www.wrth.com; *World Radio TV Handbook 2007.*

ISRAEL - BUDGET

Central Intelligence Agency, Office of Public Affairs, Washington, DC 20505, (703) 482-0623, Fax: (703) 482-1739, www.cia.gov; *The World Factbook.*

ISRAEL - CAPITAL LEVY

International Monetary Fund (IMF), 700 Nineteenth Street, NW, Washington, DC 20431, (202) 623-7000, Fax: (202) 623-4661, www.imf.org; *Government Finance Statistics Yearbook (2008 Edition).*

ISRAEL - CATTLE

See ISRAEL - LIVESTOCK

ISRAEL - CHICK PEA PRODUCTION

See ISRAEL - CROPS

ISRAEL - CHICKENS

See ISRAEL - LIVESTOCK

ISRAEL - CHILDBIRTH - STATISTICS

Central Intelligence Agency, Office of Public Affairs, Washington, DC 20505, (703) 482-0623, Fax: (703) 482-1739, www.cia.gov; *The World Factbook.*

Euromonitor International, Inc., 224 S. Michigan Avenue, Suite 1500, Chicago, IL 60604, (312) 922-1115, Fax: (312) 922-1157, www.euromonitor.com; *International Marketing Data and Statistics 2008* and *The World Economic Factbook 2008.*

M.E. Sharpe, 80 Business Park Drive, Armonk, NY 10504, (800) 541-6563, Fax: (914) 273-2106, www.mesharpe.com; *The Illustrated Book of World Rankings.*

Palgrave Macmillan Ltd., Houndmills, Basingstoke, Hampshire, RG21 6XS, England, (Telephone in U.S. (888) 330-8477), (Fax in U.S. (800) 672-2054), www.palgrave.com; *The Statesman's Yearbook 2008.*

Taylor and Francis Group, An Informa Business, 2 Park Square, Milton Park, Abingdon, Oxford OX14 4RN, United Kingdom, (Dial from U.S. (212) 216-7800), (Fax from U.S. (212) 564-7854), www.tandf.co.uk; *The Europa World Year Book.*

United Nations Statistics Division, New York, NY 10017, (800) 253-9646, Fax: (212) 963-4116, http://unstats.un.org; *Demographic Yearbook* and *Statistical Yearbook.*

The World Bank, 1818 H Street, NW, Washington, DC 20433, (202) 473-1000, Fax: (202) 477-6391, www.worldbank.org; *World Development Indicators (WDI) 2008.*

World Health Organization (WHO), Avenue Appia 20, 1211 Geneve 27, Switzerland, (Telephone in U.S. (212) 331-9081), www.who.int; *World Health Report 2006.*

ISRAEL - CITRUS EXPORTS

See ISRAEL - CROPS

ISRAEL - CLIMATE

M.E. Sharpe, 80 Business Park Drive, Armonk, NY 10504, (800) 541-6563, Fax: (914) 273-2106, www.mesharpe.com; *The Illustrated Book of World Rankings.*

Palgrave Macmillan Ltd., Houndmills, Basingstoke, Hampshire, RG21 6XS, England, (Telephone in U.S. (888) 330-8477), (Fax in U.S. (800) 672-2054), www.palgrave.com; *The Statesman's Yearbook 2008.*

ISRAEL - COAL PRODUCTION

See ISRAEL - MINERAL INDUSTRIES

ISRAEL - COFFEE

See ISRAEL - CROPS

ISRAEL - COMMERCE

Palgrave Macmillan Ltd., Houndmills, Basingstoke, Hampshire, RG21 6XS, England, (Telephone in U.S.

(888) 330-8477), (Fax in U.S. (800) 672-2054), www.palgrave.com; *The Statesman's Yearbook 2008.*

ISRAEL - COMMODITY EXCHANGES

Commodity Research Bureau, 330 South Wells Street, Suite 612, Chicago, IL 60606-7110, (800) 621-5271, Fax: (312) 939-4135, www.crbtrader.com; *2006 CRB Commodity Yearbook and CD.*

International Monetary Fund (IMF), 700 Nineteenth Street, NW, Washington, DC 20431, (202) 623-7000, Fax: (202) 623-4661, www.imf.org; *IMF Primary Commodity Prices.*

United Nations Food and Agricultural Organization (FAO), Viale delle Terme di Caracalla, 00100 Rome, Italy, (Dial from U.S. (202) 653-2400), (Fax from U.S. (202) 653 5760), www.fao.org; *The State of Food and Agriculture (SOFA) 2006.*

United Nations Statistics Division, New York, NY 10017, (800) 253-9646, Fax: (212) 963-4116, http://unstats.un.org; *Statistical Yearbook.*

ISRAEL - COMMUNICATION AND TRAFFIC

United Nations Statistics Division, New York, NY 10017, (800) 253-9646, Fax: (212) 963-4116, http://unstats.un.org; *Statistical Yearbook.*

ISRAEL - CONSTRUCTION INDUSTRY

M.E. Sharpe, 80 Business Park Drive, Armonk, NY 10504, (800) 541-6563, Fax: (914) 273-2106, www.mesharpe.com; *The Illustrated Book of World Rankings.*

United Nations Statistics Division, New York, NY 10017, (800) 253-9646, Fax: (212) 963-4116, http://unstats.un.org; *Statistical Yearbook.*

ISRAEL - CONSUMER PRICE INDEXES

International Labour Office, I.L.O. Publications, 4 route des Morillons, CH-1211 Geneva 22, Switzerland, (Telephone in U.S. (202) 653-7652), (Fax in U.S. (202) 653-7687), www.ilo.org; *Yearbook of Labour Statistics 2006.*

Taylor and Francis Group, An Informa Business, 2 Park Square, Milton Park, Abingdon, Oxford OX14 4RN, United Kingdom, (Dial from U.S. (212) 216-7800), (Fax from U.S. (212) 564-7854), www.tandf.co.uk; *The Europa World Year Book.*

United Nations Statistics Division, New York, NY 10017, (800) 253-9646, Fax: (212) 963-4116, http://unstats.un.org; *Statistical Yearbook* and *Trends in Europe and North America: The Statistical Yearbook of the ECE 2005.*

The World Bank, 1818 H Street, NW, Washington, DC 20433, (202) 473-1000, Fax: (202) 477-6391, www.worldbank.org; *Israel.*

ISRAEL - CONSUMPTION (ECONOMICS)

International Monetary Fund (IMF), 700 Nineteenth Street, NW, Washington, DC 20431, (202) 623-7000, Fax: (202) 623-4661, www.imf.org; *International Financial Statistics Yearbook 2007.*

The World Bank, 1818 H Street, NW, Washington, DC 20433, (202) 473-1000, Fax: (202) 477-6391, www.worldbank.org; *World Development Report 2008.*

ISRAEL - COPPER INDUSTRY AND TRADE

See ISRAEL - MINERAL INDUSTRIES

ISRAEL - CORN INDUSTRY

See ISRAEL - CROPS

ISRAEL - COST AND STANDARD OF LIVING

International Monetary Fund (IMF), 700 Nineteenth Street, NW, Washington, DC 20431, (202) 623-7000, Fax: (202) 623-4661, www.imf.org; *Government Finance Statistics Yearbook (2008 Edition).*

M.E. Sharpe, 80 Business Park Drive, Armonk, NY 10504, (800) 541-6563, Fax: (914) 273-2106, www.mesharpe.com; *The Illustrated Book of World Rankings.*

ISRAEL - COTTON

See ISRAEL - CROPS

ISRAEL - CRIME

International Criminal Police Organization (INTERPOL), General Secretariat, 200 quai Charles de Gaulle, 69006 Lyon, France, www.interpol.int; *International Crime Statistics.*

U.S. Department of Justice (DOJ), Bureau of Justice Statistics, 810 Seventh Street, NW, Washington, DC 20531, (202) 307-0765, www.ojp.usdoj.gov/bjs/; *The World Factbook of Criminal Justice Systems.*

United Nations Statistics Division, New York, NY 10017, (800) 253-9646, Fax: (212) 963-4116, http://unstats.un.org; *Trends in Europe and North America: The Statistical Yearbook of the ECE 2005.*

Yale University Press, PO Box 209040, New Haven, CT 06520-9040, (203) 432-0960, Fax: (203) 432-0948, http://yalepress.yale.edu/yupbooks; *Violence and Crime in Cross-National Perspective.*

ISRAEL - CROPS

International Monetary Fund (IMF), 700 Nineteenth Street, NW, Washington, DC 20431, (202) 623-7000, Fax: (202) 623-4661, www.imf.org; *International Financial Statistics Yearbook 2007.*

M.E. Sharpe, 80 Business Park Drive, Armonk, NY 10504, (800) 541-6563, Fax: (914) 273-2106, www.mesharpe.com; *The Illustrated Book of World Rankings.*

Palgrave Macmillan Ltd., Houndmills, Basingstoke, Hampshire, RG21 6XS, England, (Telephone in U.S. (888) 330-8477), (Fax in U.S. (800) 672-2054), www.palgrave.com; *The Statesman's Yearbook 2008.*

Taylor and Francis Group, An Informa Business, 2 Park Square, Milton Park, Abingdon, Oxford OX14 4RN, United Kingdom, (Dial from U.S. (212) 216-7800), (Fax from U.S. (212) 564-7854), www.tandf.co.uk; *The Europa World Year Book.*

United Nations Conference on Trade and Development (UNCTAD), DC2-1120, United Nations, New York, NY 10017, (212) 963-0027, www.unctad.org; *UNCTAD Commodity Yearbook.*

United Nations Food and Agricultural Organization (FAO), Viale delle Terme di Caracalla, 00100 Rome, Italy, (Dial from U.S. (202) 653-2400), (Fax from U.S. (202) 653 5760), www.fao.org; *FAO Production Yearbook 2002* and *The State of Food and Agriculture (SOFA) 2006.*

United Nations Statistics Division, New York, NY 10017, (800) 253-9646, Fax: (212) 963-4116, http://unstats.un.org; *Statistical Yearbook.*

ISRAEL - CUSTOMS ADMINISTRATION

International Monetary Fund (IMF), 700 Nineteenth Street, NW, Washington, DC 20431, (202) 623-7000, Fax: (202) 623-4661, www.imf.org; *Government Finance Statistics Yearbook (2008 Edition).*

Palgrave Macmillan Ltd., Houndmills, Basingstoke, Hampshire, RG21 6XS, England, (Telephone in U.S. (888) 330-8477), (Fax in U.S. (800) 672-2054), www.palgrave.com; *The Statesman's Yearbook 2008.*

ISRAEL - DAIRY PROCESSING

M.E. Sharpe, 80 Business Park Drive, Armonk, NY 10504, (800) 541-6563, Fax: (914) 273-2106, www.mesharpe.com; *The Illustrated Book of World Rankings.*

Palgrave Macmillan Ltd., Houndmills, Basingstoke, Hampshire, RG21 6XS, England, (Telephone in U.S. (888) 330-8477), (Fax in U.S. (800) 672-2054), www.palgrave.com; *The Statesman's Yearbook 2008.*

Taylor and Francis Group, An Informa Business, 2 Park Square, Milton Park, Abingdon, Oxford OX14 4RN, United Kingdom, (Dial from U.S. (212) 216-7800), (Fax from U.S. (212) 564-7854), www.tandf.co.uk; *The Europa World Year Book.*

United Nations Food and Agricultural Organization (FAO), Viale delle Terme di Caracalla, 00100 Rome, Italy, (Dial from U.S. (202) 653-2400), (Fax from U.S. (202) 653 5760), www.fao.org; *FAO Production Yearbook 2002* and *The State of Food and Agriculture (SOFA) 2006.*

United Nations Statistics Division, New York, NY 10017, (800) 253-9646, Fax: (212) 963-4116, http://unstats.un.org; *Statistical Yearbook.*

ISRAEL - DEATH RATES

See ISRAEL - MORTALITY

ISRAEL - DEBTS, EXTERNAL

International Monetary Fund (IMF), 700 Nineteenth Street, NW, Washington, DC 20431, (202) 623-7000, Fax: (202) 623-4661, www.imf.org; *Government Finance Statistics Yearbook (2008 Edition).*

Palgrave Macmillan Ltd., Houndmills, Basingstoke, Hampshire, RG21 6XS, England, (Telephone in U.S. (888) 330-8477), (Fax in U.S. (800) 672-2054), www.palgrave.com; *The Statesman's Yearbook 2008.*

The World Bank, 1818 H Street, NW, Washington, DC 20433, (202) 473-1000, Fax: (202) 477-6391, www.worldbank.org; *Global Development Finance 2007; World Development Indicators (WDI) 2008;* and *World Development Report 2008.*

ISRAEL - DEFENSE EXPENDITURES

See ISRAEL - ARMED FORCES

ISRAEL - DEMOGRAPHY

Euromonitor International, Inc., 224 S. Michigan Avenue, Suite 1500, Chicago, IL 60604, (312) 922-1115, Fax: (312) 922-1157, www.euromonitor.com; *International Marketing Data and Statistics 2008; The World Economic Factbook 2008;* and *World Marketing Data and Statistics.*

M.E. Sharpe, 80 Business Park Drive, Armonk, NY 10504, (800) 541-6563, Fax: (914) 273-2106, www.mesharpe.com; *The Illustrated Book of World Rankings.*

United Nations Statistics Division, New York, NY 10017, (800) 253-9646, Fax: (212) 963-4116, http://unstats.un.org; *Human Development Report 2006.*

The World Bank, 1818 H Street, NW, Washington, DC 20433, (202) 473-1000, Fax: (202) 477-6391, www.worldbank.org; *Israel.*

ISRAEL - DIAMONDS

See ISRAEL - MINERAL INDUSTRIES

ISRAEL - DISPOSABLE INCOME

M.E. Sharpe, 80 Business Park Drive, Armonk, NY 10504, (800) 541-6563, Fax: (914) 273-2106, www.mesharpe.com; *The Illustrated Book of World Rankings.*

United Nations Statistics Division, New York, NY 10017, (800) 253-9646, Fax: (212) 963-4116, http://unstats.un.org; *National Accounts Statistics: Compendium of Income Distribution Statistics* and *Statistical Yearbook.*

ISRAEL - DIVORCE

M.E. Sharpe, 80 Business Park Drive, Armonk, NY 10504, (800) 541-6563, Fax: (914) 273-2106, www.mesharpe.com; *The Illustrated Book of World Rankings.*

United Nations Statistics Division, New York, NY 10017, (800) 253-9646, Fax: (212) 963-4116, http://unstats.un.org; *Demographic Yearbook; Statistical Yearbook;* and *Trends in Europe and North America: The Statistical Yearbook of the ECE 2005.*

ISRAEL - ECONOMIC ASSISTANCE

United Nations Statistics Division, New York, NY 10017, (800) 253-9646, Fax: (212) 963-4116, http://unstats.un.org; *Statistical Yearbook.*

ISRAEL - ECONOMIC CONDITIONS

Center for International Business Education Research (CIBER), Columbia Business School and School of International and Public Affairs, Uris Hall, Room 212, 3022 Broadway, New York, NY 10027-6902, Mr. Joshua Safier, (212) 854-4750, Fax: (212) 222-9821, www.columbia.edu/cu/ciber/; Datastream International.

Central Intelligence Agency, Office of Public Affairs, Washington, DC 20505, (703) 482-0623, Fax: (703) 482-1739, www.cia.gov; *The World Factbook.*

DSI Data Service Information, Xantener Strasse 51a, D-47495 Rheinberg, Germany, www.dsidata.com; *Campus Solution.*

Dun and Bradstreet (DB) Corporation, 103 JFK Parkway, Short Hills, NJ 07078, (973) 921-5500, www.dnb.com; *Country Report.*

Economist Intelligence Unit, 111 West 57th Street, New York, NY 10019, (212) 554-0600, Fax: (212) 586-1181, www.eiu.com; *Israel Country Report.*

Euromonitor International, Inc., 224 S. Michigan Avenue, Suite 1500, Chicago, IL 60604, (312) 922-1115, Fax: (312) 922-1157, www.euromonitor.com; *International Marketing Data and Statistics 2008; The World Economic Factbook 2008;* and *World Marketing Data and Statistics.*

International Monetary Fund (IMF), 700 Nineteenth Street, NW, Washington, DC 20431, (202) 623-7000, Fax: (202) 623-4661, www.imf.org; *World Economic Outlook Reports.*

M.E. Sharpe, 80 Business Park Drive, Armonk, NY 10504, (800) 541-6563, Fax: (914) 273-2106, www.mesharpe.com; *The Illustrated Book of World Rankings.*

Palgrave Macmillan Ltd., Houndmills, Basingstoke, Hampshire, RG21 6XS, England, (Telephone in U.S. (888) 330-8477), (Fax in U.S. (800) 672-2054), www.palgrave.com; *The Statesman's Yearbook 2008.*

Taylor and Francis Group, An Informa Business, 2 Park Square, Milton Park, Abingdon, Oxford OX14 4RN, United Kingdom, (Dial from U.S. (212) 216-7800), (Fax from U.S. (212) 564-7854), www.tandf.co.uk; *The Europa World Year Book.*

United Nations Economic and Social Commission for Western Asia (ESCWA), PO Box 11-8575, Riad el-Solh Square, Beirut, Lebanon, www.escwa.un.org; *Annual Report 2006; Bulletin on Population and Vital Statistics in the ESCWA Region;* and *Survey of Economic and Social Developments in the ESCWA Region 2006-2007.*

United Nations Statistics Division, New York, NY 10017, (800) 253-9646, Fax: (212) 963-4116, http://unstats.un.org; *World Statistics Pocketbook.*

The World Bank, 1818 H Street, NW, Washington, DC 20433, (202) 473-1000, Fax: (202) 477-6391, www.worldbank.org; *Global Economic Monitor (GEM); Global Economic Prospects 2008; Israel; The World Bank Atlas 2003-2004;* and *World Development Report 2008.*

ISRAEL - EDUCATION

Euromonitor International, Inc., 224 S. Michigan Avenue, Suite 1500, Chicago, IL 60604, (312) 922-1115, Fax: (312) 922-1157, www.euromonitor.com; *International Marketing Data and Statistics 2008* and *World Marketing Data and Statistics.*

International Monetary Fund (IMF), 700 Nineteenth Street, NW, Washington, DC 20431, (202) 623-7000, Fax: (202) 623-4661, www.imf.org; *Government Finance Statistics Yearbook (2008 Edition).*

M.E. Sharpe, 80 Business Park Drive, Armonk, NY 10504, (800) 541-6563, Fax: (914) 273-2106, www.mesharpe.com; *The Illustrated Book of World Rankings.*

Palgrave Macmillan Ltd., Houndmills, Basingstoke, Hampshire, RG21 6XS, England, (Telephone in U.S. (888) 330-8477), (Fax in U.S. (800) 672-2054), www.palgrave.com; *The Statesman's Yearbook 2008.*

Taylor and Francis Group, An Informa Business, 2 Park Square, Milton Park, Abingdon, Oxford OX14 4RN, United Kingdom, (Dial from U.S. (212) 216-7800), (Fax from U.S. (212) 564-7854), www.tandf.co.uk; *The Europa World Year Book.*

UNESCO Institute for Statistics, C.P. 6128 Succursale Centre-Ville, Montreal, Quebec, H3C 3J7 Canada, (Dial from U.S. (514) 343-6880), (Fax from U.S. (514) 343 6882), www.uis.unesco.org; *Statistical Tables.*

United Nations Statistics Division, New York, NY 10017, (800) 253-9646, Fax: (212) 963-4116, http://unstats.un.org; *Human Development Report 2006* and *Trends in Europe and North America: The Statistical Yearbook of the ECE 2005.*

The World Bank, 1818 H Street, NW, Washington, DC 20433, (202) 473-1000, Fax: (202) 477-6391, www.worldbank.org; *Israel; World Development Indicators (WDI) 2008;* and *World Development Report 2008.*

ISRAEL - EGGPLANT PRODUCTION

See ISRAEL - CROPS

ISRAEL - ELECTRICITY

M.E. Sharpe, 80 Business Park Drive, Armonk, NY 10504, (800) 541-6563, Fax: (914) 273-2106, www.mesharpe.com; *The Illustrated Book of World Rankings.*

Organisation for Economic Cooperation and Development (OECD), 2 rue Andre Pascal, F-75775 Paris Cedex 16, France, (Telephone in U.S. (202) 785-6323), (Fax in U.S. (202) 785-0350), www.oecd.org; *World Energy Outlook 2007.*

Palgrave Macmillan Ltd., Houndmills, Basingstoke, Hampshire, RG21 6XS, England, (Telephone in U.S. (888) 330-8477), (Fax in U.S. (800) 672-2054), www.palgrave.com; *The Statesman's Yearbook 2008.*

U.S. Department of Energy (DOE), Energy Information Administration (EIA), 1000 Independence Avenue, SW, Washington, DC 20585, (202) 586-8800, www.eia.doe.gov; *International Energy Annual 2004* and *International Energy Outlook 2006.*

United Nations Statistics Division, New York, NY 10017, (800) 253-9646, Fax: (212) 963-4116, http://unstats.un.org; *Human Development Report 2006; Statistical Yearbook;* and *Trends in Europe and North America: The Statistical Yearbook of the ECE 2005.*

ISRAEL - EMPLOYMENT

Euromonitor International, Inc., 224 S. Michigan Avenue, Suite 1500, Chicago, IL 60604, (312) 922-1115, Fax: (312) 922-1157, www.euromonitor.com; *International Marketing Data and Statistics 2008.*

International Labour Office, I.L.O. Publications, 4 route des Morillons, CH-1211 Geneva 22, Switzerland, (Telephone in U.S. (202) 653-7652), (Fax in U.S. (202) 653-7687), www.ilo.org; *Yearbook of Labour Statistics 2006.*

M.E. Sharpe, 80 Business Park Drive, Armonk, NY 10504, (800) 541-6563, Fax: (914) 273-2106, www.mesharpe.com; *The Illustrated Book of World Rankings.*

United Nations Statistics Division, New York, NY 10017, (800) 253-9646, Fax: (212) 963-4116, http://unstats.un.org; *Statistical Yearbook* and *Trends in Europe and North America: The Statistical Yearbook of the ECE 2005.*

The World Bank, 1818 H Street, NW, Washington, DC 20433, (202) 473-1000, Fax: (202) 477-6391, www.worldbank.org; *Israel.*

ISRAEL - ENVIRONMENTAL CONDITIONS

DSI Data Service Information, Xantener Strasse 51a, D-47495 Rheinberg, Germany, www.dsidata.com; *Campus Solution* and *DSI's Global Environmental Database.*

Economist Intelligence Unit, 111 West 57th Street, New York, NY 10019, (212) 554-0600, Fax: (212) 586-1181, www.eiu.com; *Israel Country Report.*

United Nations Statistics Division, New York, NY 10017, (800) 253-9646, Fax: (212) 963-4116, http://unstats.un.org; *Trends in Europe and North America: The Statistical Yearbook of the ECE 2005* and *World Statistics Pocketbook.*

ISRAEL - EXPORTS

Central Intelligence Agency, Office of Public Affairs, Washington, DC 20505, (703) 482-0623, Fax: (703) 482-1739, www.cia.gov; *The World Factbook.*

Economist Intelligence Unit, 111 West 57th Street, New York, NY 10019, (212) 554-0600, Fax: (212) 586-1181, www.eiu.com; *Israel Country Report.*

Euromonitor International, Inc., 224 S. Michigan Avenue, Suite 1500, Chicago, IL 60604, (312) 922-1115, Fax: (312) 922-1157, www.euromonitor.com; *International Marketing Data and Statistics 2008* and *The World Economic Factbook 2008.*

International Monetary Fund (IMF), 700 Nineteenth Street, NW, Washington, DC 20431, (202) 623-7000, Fax: (202) 623-4661, www.imf.org; *Direction of Trade Statistics Yearbook 2007* and *International Financial Statistics Yearbook 2007.*

Palgrave Macmillan Ltd., Houndmills, Basingstoke, Hampshire, RG21 6XS, England, (Telephone in U.S. (888) 330-8477), (Fax in U.S. (800) 672-2054), www.palgrave.com; *The Statesman's Yearbook 2008.*

Taylor and Francis Group, An Informa Business, 2 Park Square, Milton Park, Abingdon, Oxford OX14 4RN, United Kingdom, (Dial from U.S. (212) 216-7800), (Fax from U.S. (212) 564-7854), www.tandf.co.uk; *The Europa World Year Book.*

United Nations Conference on Trade and Development (UNCTAD), DC2-1120, United Nations, New York, NY 10017, (212) 963-0027, www.unctad.org; *Handbook of Statistics 2005.*

United Nations Food and Agricultural Organization (FAO), Viale delle Terme di Caracalla, 00100 Rome, Italy, (Dial from U.S. (202) 653-2400), (Fax from U.S. (202) 653 5760), www.fao.org; *The State of Food and Agriculture (SOFA) 2006.*

United Nations Statistics Division, New York, NY 10017, (800) 253-9646, Fax: (212) 963-4116, http://unstats.un.org; *Trends in Europe and North America: The Statistical Yearbook of the ECE 2005.*

The World Bank, 1818 H Street, NW, Washington, DC 20433, (202) 473-1000, Fax: (202) 477-6391, www.worldbank.org; *World Development Indicators (WDI) 2008* and *World Development Report 2008.*

ISRAEL - FEMALE WORKING POPULATION

See ISRAEL - EMPLOYMENT

ISRAEL - FERTILITY, HUMAN

Central Intelligence Agency, Office of Public Affairs, Washington, DC 20505, (703) 482-0623, Fax: (703) 482-1739, www.cia.gov; *The World Factbook.*

M.E. Sharpe, 80 Business Park Drive, Armonk, NY 10504, (800) 541-6563, Fax: (914) 273-2106, www.mesharpe.com; *The Illustrated Book of World Rankings.*

United Nations Statistics Division, New York, NY 10017, (800) 253-9646, Fax: (212) 963-4116, http://unstats.un.org; *Human Development Report 2006* and *Trends in Europe and North America: The Statistical Yearbook of the ECE 2005.*

The World Bank, 1818 H Street, NW, Washington, DC 20433, (202) 473-1000, Fax: (202) 477-6391, www.worldbank.org; *The World Bank Atlas 2003-2004; World Development Indicators (WDI) 2008;* and *World Development Report 2008.*

ISRAEL - FERTILIZER INDUSTRY

United Nations Food and Agricultural Organization (FAO), Viale delle Terme di Caracalla, 00100 Rome, Italy, (Dial from U.S. (202) 653-2400), (Fax from U.S. (202) 653 5760), www.fao.org; *FAO Fertilizer Yearbook* and *The State of Food and Agriculture (SOFA) 2006.*

United Nations Statistics Division, New York, NY 10017, (800) 253-9646, Fax: (212) 963-4116, http://unstats.un.org; *Statistical Yearbook.*

ISRAEL - FETAL MORTALITY

See ISRAEL - MORTALITY

ISRAEL - FILM

See ISRAEL - MOTION PICTURES

ISRAEL - FINANCE

International Monetary Fund (IMF), 700 Nineteenth Street, NW, Washington, DC 20431, (202) 623-7000, Fax: (202) 623-4661, www.imf.org; *International Financial Statistics Yearbook 2007.*

Taylor and Francis Group, An Informa Business, 2 Park Square, Milton Park, Abingdon, Oxford OX14 4RN, United Kingdom, (Dial from U.S. (212) 216-7800), (Fax from U.S. (212) 564-7854), www.tandf.co.uk; *The Europa World Year Book.*

United Nations Statistics Division, New York, NY 10017, (800) 253-9646, Fax: (212) 963-4116, http://unstats.un.org; *National Accounts Statistics: Compendium of Income Distribution Statistics* and *Statistical Yearbook.*

The World Bank, 1818 H Street, NW, Washington, DC 20433, (202) 473-1000, Fax: (202) 477-6391, www.worldbank.org; *Israel.*

ISRAEL - FINANCE, PUBLIC

Bernan Essential Government Publications, 4611-F Assembly Drive, Lanham MD, 20706-4391, (301) 459-2255, Fax: (800) 865-3450, www.bernan.com; *National Accounts Statistics.*

Economist Intelligence Unit, 111 West 57th Street, New York, NY 10019, (212) 554-0600, Fax: (212) 586-1181, www.eiu.com; *Israel Country Report.*

International Monetary Fund (IMF), 700 Nineteenth Street, NW, Washington, DC 20431, (202) 623-7000, Fax: (202) 623-4661, www.imf.org; *Government Finance Statistics Yearbook (2008 Edition); International Financial Statistics; International Financial Statistics Online Service;* and *International Financial Statistics Yearbook 2007.*

M.E. Sharpe, 80 Business Park Drive, Armonk, NY 10504, (800) 541-6563, Fax: (914) 273-2106, www.mesharpe.com; *The Illustrated Book of World Rankings.*

Palgrave Macmillan Ltd., Houndmills, Basingstoke, Hampshire, RG21 6XS, England, (Telephone in U.S. (888) 330-8477), (Fax in U.S. (800) 672-2054), www.palgrave.com; *The Statesman's Yearbook 2008.*

Taylor and Francis Group, An Informa Business, 2 Park Square, Milton Park, Abingdon, Oxford OX14 4RN, United Kingdom, (Dial from U.S. (212) 216-7800), (Fax from U.S. (212) 564-7854), www.tandf.co.uk; *The Europa World Year Book.*

The World Bank, 1818 H Street, NW, Washington, DC 20433, (202) 473-1000, Fax: (202) 477-6391, www.worldbank.org; *Israel.*

ISRAEL - FISHERIES

M.E. Sharpe, 80 Business Park Drive, Armonk, NY 10504, (800) 541-6563, Fax: (914) 273-2106, www.mesharpe.com; *The Illustrated Book of World Rankings.*

Taylor and Francis Group, An Informa Business, 2 Park Square, Milton Park, Abingdon, Oxford OX14 4RN, United Kingdom, (Dial from U.S. (212) 216-7800), (Fax from U.S. (212) 564-7854), www.tandf.co.uk; *The Europa World Year Book.*

United Nations Conference on Trade and Development (UNCTAD), DC2-1120, United Nations, New York, NY 10017, (212) 963-0027, www.unctad.org; *UNCTAD Commodity Yearbook.*

United Nations Food and Agricultural Organization (FAO), Viale delle Terme di Caracalla, 00100 Rome, Italy, (Dial from U.S. (202) 653-2400), (Fax from U.S. (202) 653 5760), www.fao.org; *FAO Yearbook of Fishery Statistics;* Fishery Databases; FISHSTAT Database. Subjects covered include: Aquaculture production, capture production, fishery commodities; and *The State of Food and Agriculture (SOFA) 2006.*

United Nations Statistics Division, New York, NY 10017, (800) 253-9646, Fax: (212) 963-4116, http://unstats.un.org; *Statistical Yearbook.*

The World Bank, 1818 H Street, NW, Washington, DC 20433, (202) 473-1000, Fax: (202) 477-6391, www.worldbank.org; *Israel.*

ISRAEL - FLOUR INDUSTRY

United Nations Statistics Division, New York, NY 10017, (800) 253-9646, Fax: (212) 963-4116, http://unstats.un.org; *Statistical Yearbook.*

ISRAEL - FOOD

Euromonitor International, Inc., 224 S. Michigan Avenue, Suite 1500, Chicago, IL 60604, (312) 922-1115, Fax: (312) 922-1157, www.euromonitor.com; *Retail Trade International 2007.*

United Nations Conference on Trade and Development (UNCTAD), DC2-1120, United Nations, New York, NY 10017, (212) 963-0027, www.unctad.org; *UNCTAD Commodity Yearbook.*

United Nations Food and Agricultural Organization (FAO), Viale delle Terme di Caracalla, 00100 Rome, Italy, (Dial from U.S. (202) 653-2400), (Fax from U.S. (202) 653 5760), www.fao.org; *FAO Production Yearbook 2002* and *The State of Food and Agriculture (SOFA) 2006.*

United Nations Statistics Division, New York, NY 10017, (800) 253-9646, Fax: (212) 963-4116, http://unstats.un.org; *Human Development Report 2006.*

ISRAEL - FOREIGN EXCHANGE RATES

Central Intelligence Agency, Office of Public Affairs, Washington, DC 20505, (703) 482-0623, Fax: (703) 482-1739, www.cia.gov; *The World Factbook.*

Euromonitor International, Inc., 224 S. Michigan Avenue, Suite 1500, Chicago, IL 60604, (312) 922-1115, Fax: (312) 922-1157, www.euromonitor.com; *International Marketing Data and Statistics 2008* and *The World Economic Factbook 2008.*

International Civil Aviation Organization (ICAO), External Relations and Public Information Office (EPO), 999 University Street, Montreal, Quebec H3C 5H7, Canada, (Dial from U.S. (514) 954-8219), (Fax from U.S. (514) 954-6077), www.icao.int; *Civil Aviation Statistics of the World.*

International Monetary Fund (IMF), 700 Nineteenth Street, NW, Washington, DC 20431, (202) 623-7000, Fax: (202) 623-4661, www.imf.org; *International Financial Statistics Yearbook 2007.*

Taylor and Francis Group, An Informa Business, 2 Park Square, Milton Park, Abingdon, Oxford OX14 4RN, United Kingdom, (Dial from U.S. (212) 216-7800), (Fax from U.S. (212) 564-7854), www.tandf.co.uk; *The Europa World Year Book.*

United Nations Statistics Division, New York, NY 10017, (800) 253-9646, Fax: (212) 963-4116, http://unstats.un.org; *Statistical Yearbook; Trends in Europe and North America: The Statistical Yearbook of the ECE 2005;* and *World Statistics Pocketbook.*

ISRAEL - FORESTS AND FORESTRY

American Forest Paper Association (AFPA), 1111 Nineteenth Street, NW, Suite 800, Washington, DC 20036, (800) 878-8878, www.afandpa.org; *2007 Annual Statistics of Paper, Paperboard, and Wood Pulp.*

M.E. Sharpe, 80 Business Park Drive, Armonk, NY 10504, (800) 541-6563, Fax: (914) 273-2106, www.mesharpe.com; *The Illustrated Book of World Rankings.*

Taylor and Francis Group, An Informa Business, 2 Park Square, Milton Park, Abingdon, Oxford OX14 4RN, United Kingdom, (Dial from U.S. (212) 216-7800), (Fax from U.S. (212) 564-7854), www.tandf.co.uk; *The Europa World Year Book.*

UNESCO Institute for Statistics, C.P. 6128 Succursale Centre-Ville, Montreal, Quebec, H3C 3J7 Canada, (Dial from U.S. (514) 343-6880), (Fax from U.S. (514) 343 6882), www.uis.unesco.org; *Statistical Tables.*

United Nations Conference on Trade and Development (UNCTAD), DC2-1120, United Nations, New York, NY 10017, (212) 963-0027, www.unctad.org; *UNCTAD Commodity Yearbook.*

United Nations Food and Agricultural Organization (FAO), Viale delle Terme di Caracalla, 00100 Rome, Italy, (Dial from U.S. (202) 653-2400), (Fax from U.S. (202) 653 5760), www.fao.org; *FAO Yearbook of Forest Products* and *The State of Food and Agriculture (SOFA) 2006.*

United Nations Statistics Division, New York, NY 10017, (800) 253-9646, Fax: (212) 963-4116, http://unstats.un.org; *Statistical Yearbook* and *Trends in Europe and North America: The Statistical Yearbook of the ECE 2005.*

The World Bank, 1818 H Street, NW, Washington, DC 20433, (202) 473-1000, Fax: (202) 477-6391, www.worldbank.org; *Israel* and *World Development Report 2008.*

ISRAEL - GAS PRODUCTION

See ISRAEL - MINERAL INDUSTRIES

ISRAEL - GEOGRAPHIC INFORMATION SYSTEMS

M.E. Sharpe, 80 Business Park Drive, Armonk, NY 10504, (800) 541-6563, Fax: (914) 273-2106, www.mesharpe.com; *The Illustrated Book of World Rankings.*

The World Bank, 1818 H Street, NW, Washington, DC 20433, (202) 473-1000, Fax: (202) 477-6391, www.worldbank.org; *Israel.*

ISRAEL - GOLD INDUSTRY

International Monetary Fund (IMF), 700 Nineteenth Street, NW, Washington, DC 20431, (202) 623-7000, Fax: (202) 623-4661, www.imf.org; *International Financial Statistics Yearbook 2007.*

United Nations Statistics Division, New York, NY 10017, (800) 253-9646, Fax: (212) 963-4116, http://unstats.un.org; *Statistical Yearbook.*

The World Bank, 1818 H Street, NW, Washington, DC 20433, (202) 473-1000, Fax: (202) 477-6391, www.worldbank.org; *World Development Indicators (WDI) 2008.*

ISRAEL - GOLD PRODUCTION

See ISRAEL - MINERAL INDUSTRIES

ISRAEL - GRANTS-IN-AID

International Monetary Fund (IMF), 700 Nineteenth Street, NW, Washington, DC 20431, (202) 623-7000, Fax: (202) 623-4661, www.imf.org; *Government Finance Statistics Yearbook (2008 Edition).*

ISRAEL - GREEN PEPPER AND CHILIE PRODUCTION

See ISRAEL - CROPS

ISRAEL - GROSS DOMESTIC PRODUCT

Economist Intelligence Unit, 111 West 57th Street, New York, NY 10019, (212) 554-0600, Fax: (212) 586-1181, www.eiu.com; *Israel Country Report.*

Euromonitor International, Inc., 224 S. Michigan Avenue, Suite 1500, Chicago, IL 60604, (312) 922-1115, Fax: (312) 922-1157, www.euromonitor.com; *International Marketing Data and Statistics 2008* and *The World Economic Factbook 2008.*

International Monetary Fund (IMF), 700 Nineteenth Street, NW, Washington, DC 20431, (202) 623-7000, Fax: (202) 623-4661, www.imf.org; *International Financial Statistics Yearbook 2007.*

M.E. Sharpe, 80 Business Park Drive, Armonk, NY 10504, (800) 541-6563, Fax: (914) 273-2106, www.mesharpe.com; *The Illustrated Book of World Rankings.*

Taylor and Francis Group, An Informa Business, 2 Park Square, Milton Park, Abingdon, Oxford OX14 4RN, United Kingdom, (Dial from U.S. (212) 216-

7800), (Fax from U.S. (212) 564-7854), www.tandf.co.uk; *The Europa World Year Book.*

United Nations Statistics Division, New York, NY 10017, (800) 253-9646, Fax: (212) 963-4116, http://unstats.un.org; *Human Development Report 2006; National Accounts Statistics: Compendium of Income Distribution Statistics; Statistical Yearbook;* and *Trends in Europe and North America: The Statistical Yearbook of the ECE 2005.*

The World Bank, 1818 H Street, NW, Washington, DC 20433, (202) 473-1000, Fax: (202) 477-6391, www.worldbank.org; *World Development Indicators (WDI) 2008* and *World Development Report 2008.*

ISRAEL - GROSS NATIONAL PRODUCT

Euromonitor International, Inc., 224 S. Michigan Avenue, Suite 1500, Chicago, IL 60604, (312) 922-1115, Fax: (312) 922-1157, www.euromonitor.com; *International Marketing Data and Statistics 2008.*

M.E. Sharpe, 80 Business Park Drive, Armonk, NY 10504, (800) 541-6563, Fax: (914) 273-2106, www.mesharpe.com; *The Illustrated Book of World Rankings.*

Palgrave Macmillan Ltd., Houndmills, Basingstoke, Hampshire, RG21 6XS, England, (Telephone in U.S. (888) 330-8477), (Fax in U.S. (800) 672-2054), www.palgrave.com; *The Statesman's Yearbook 2008.*

Taylor and Francis Group, An Informa Business, 2 Park Square, Milton Park, Abingdon, Oxford OX14 4RN, United Kingdom, (Dial from U.S. (212) 216-7800), (Fax from U.S. (212) 564-7854), www.tandf.co.uk; *The Europa World Year Book.*

U.S. Department of State (DOS), 2201 C Street NW, Washington, DC 20520, (202) 647-4000, www.state.gov; *World Military Expenditures and Arms Transfers (WMEAT).*

United Nations Statistics Division, New York, NY 10017, (800) 253-9646, Fax: (212) 963-4116, http://unstats.un.org; *Statistical Yearbook.*

The World Bank, 1818 H Street, NW, Washington, DC 20433, (202) 473-1000, Fax: (202) 477-6391, www.worldbank.org; *The World Bank Atlas 2003-2004; World Development Indicators (WDI) 2008;* and *World Development Report 2008.*

ISRAEL - HIDES AND SKINS INDUSTRY

United Nations Food and Agricultural Organization (FAO), Viale delle Terme di Caracalla, 00100 Rome, Italy, (Dial from U.S. (202) 653-2400), (Fax from U.S. (202) 653 5760), www.fao.org; *FAO Production Yearbook 2002.*

ISRAEL - HOUSING

Euromonitor International, Inc., 224 S. Michigan Avenue, Suite 1500, Chicago, IL 60604, (312) 922-1115, Fax: (312) 922-1157, www.euromonitor.com; *World Marketing Data and Statistics.*

United Nations Statistics Division, New York, NY 10017, (800) 253-9646, Fax: (212) 963-4116, http://unstats.un.org; *Trends in Europe and North America: The Statistical Yearbook of the ECE 2005.*

ISRAEL - ILLITERATE PERSONS

Central Intelligence Agency, Office of Public Affairs, Washington, DC 20505, (703) 482-0623, Fax: (703) 482-1739, www.cia.gov; *The World Factbook.*

Euromonitor International, Inc., 224 S. Michigan Avenue, Suite 1500, Chicago, IL 60604, (312) 922-1115, Fax: (312) 922-1157, www.euromonitor.com; *The World Economic Factbook 2008.*

UNESCO Institute for Statistics, C.P. 6128 Succursale Centre-Ville, Montreal, Quebec, H3C 3J7 Canada, (Dial from U.S. (514) 343-6880), (Fax from U.S. (514) 343 6882), www.uis.unesco.org; *Statistical Tables.*

United Nations Statistics Division, New York, NY 10017, (800) 253-9646, Fax: (212) 963-4116, http://unstats.un.org; *Human Development Report 2006.*

ISRAEL - IMPORTS

Central Intelligence Agency, Office of Public Affairs, Washington, DC 20505, (703) 482-0623, Fax: (703) 482-1739, www.cia.gov; *The World Factbook.*

Economist Intelligence Unit, 111 West 57th Street, New York, NY 10019, (212) 554-0600, Fax: (212) 586-1181, www.eiu.com; *Israel Country Report.*

Euromonitor International, Inc., 224 S. Michigan Avenue, Suite 1500, Chicago, IL 60604, (312) 922-1115, Fax: (312) 922-1157, www.euromonitor.com; *International Marketing Data and Statistics 2008* and *The World Economic Factbook 2008.*

International Monetary Fund (IMF), 700 Nineteenth Street, NW, Washington, DC 20431, (202) 623-7000, Fax: (202) 623-4661, www.imf.org; *Direction of Trade Statistics Yearbook 2007; Government Finance Statistics Yearbook (2008 Edition);* and *International Financial Statistics Yearbook 2007.*

Palgrave Macmillan Ltd., Houndmills, Basingstoke, Hampshire, RG21 6XS, England, (Telephone in U.S. (888) 330-8477), (Fax in U.S. (800) 672-2054), www.palgrave.com; *The Statesman's Yearbook 2008.*

Taylor and Francis Group, An Informa Business, 2 Park Square, Milton Park, Abingdon, Oxford OX14 4RN, United Kingdom, (Dial from U.S. (212) 216-7800), (Fax from U.S. (212) 564-7854), www.tandf.co.uk; *The Europa World Year Book.*

United Nations Conference on Trade and Development (UNCTAD), DC2-1120, United Nations, New York, NY 10017, (212) 963-0027, www.unctad.org; *Handbook of Statistics 2005.*

United Nations Food and Agricultural Organization (FAO), Viale delle Terme di Caracalla, 00100 Rome, Italy, (Dial from U.S. (202) 653-2400), (Fax from U.S. (202) 653 5760), www.fao.org; *The State of Food and Agriculture (SOFA) 2006.*

United Nations Statistics Division, New York, NY 10017, (800) 253-9646, Fax: (212) 963-4116, http://unstats.un.org; *Trends in Europe and North America: The Statistical Yearbook of the ECE 2005.*

The World Bank, 1818 H Street, NW, Washington, DC 20433, (202) 473-1000, Fax: (202) 477-6391, www.worldbank.org; *World Development Indicators (WDI) 2008* and *World Development Report 2008.*

ISRAEL - INCOME TAXES

See ISRAEL - TAXATION

ISRAEL - INDUSTRIAL METALS PRODUCTION

See ISRAEL - MINERAL INDUSTRIES

ISRAEL - INDUSTRIAL PRODUCTIVITY

Euromonitor International, Inc., 224 S. Michigan Avenue, Suite 1500, Chicago, IL 60604, (312) 922-1115, Fax: (312) 922-1157, www.euromonitor.com; *International Marketing Data and Statistics 2008.*

M.E. Sharpe, 80 Business Park Drive, Armonk, NY 10504, (800) 541-6563, Fax: (914) 273-2106, www.mesharpe.com; *The Illustrated Book of World Rankings.*

ISRAEL - INDUSTRIAL PROPERTY

United Nations Statistics Division, New York, NY 10017, (800) 253-9646, Fax: (212) 963-4116, http://unstats.un.org; *Statistical Yearbook.*

World Intellectual Property Organization (WIPO), PO Box 18, CH-1211 Geneva 20, Switzerland, www.wipo.int; *Industrial Property Statistics* and *Industrial Property Statistics Online Directory.*

ISRAEL - INDUSTRIES

Central Intelligence Agency, Office of Public Affairs, Washington, DC 20505, (703) 482-0623, Fax: (703) 482-1739, www.cia.gov; *The World Factbook.*

Economist Intelligence Unit, 111 West 57th Street, New York, NY 10019, (212) 554-0600, Fax: (212) 586-1181, www.eiu.com; *Israel Country Report.*

Euromonitor International, Inc., 224 S. Michigan Avenue, Suite 1500, Chicago, IL 60604, (312) 922-1115, Fax: (312) 922-1157, www.euromonitor.com; *International Marketing Data and Statistics 2008; The World Economic Factbook 2008;* and *World Marketing Data and Statistics.*

International Labour Office, I.L.O. Publications, 4 route des Morillons, CH-1211 Geneva 22, Switzerland, (Telephone in U.S. (202) 653-7652), (Fax in U.S. (202) 653-7687), www.ilo.org; *Yearbook of Labour Statistics 2006.*

M.E. Sharpe, 80 Business Park Drive, Armonk, NY 10504, (800) 541-6563, Fax: (914) 273-2106, www.mesharpe.com; *The Illustrated Book of World Rankings.*

Palgrave Macmillan Ltd., Houndmills, Basingstoke, Hampshire, RG21 6XS, England, (Telephone in U.S. (888) 330-8477), (Fax in U.S. (800) 672-2054), www.palgrave.com; *The Statesman's Yearbook 2008.*

Taylor and Francis Group, An Informa Business, 2 Park Square, Milton Park, Abingdon, Oxford OX14 4RN, United Kingdom, (Dial from U.S. (212) 216-7800), (Fax from U.S. (212) 564-7854), www.tandf.co.uk; *The Europa World Year Book.*

United Nations Industrial Development Organization (UNIDO), 1 United Nations Plaza, New York, NY 10017, (212) 963 6890, Fax: (212) 963-7904, http://unido.org; Industrial Statistics Database 2008 (INDSTAT) and *The International Yearbook of Industrial Statistics 2008.*

United Nations Statistics Division, New York, NY 10017, (800) 253-9646, Fax: (212) 963-4116, http://unstats.un.org; *2004 Industrial Commodity Statistics Yearbook; Statistical Yearbook;* and *Trends in Europe and North America: The Statistical Yearbook of the ECE 2005.*

The World Bank, 1818 H Street, NW, Washington, DC 20433, (202) 473-1000, Fax: (202) 477-6391, www.worldbank.org; *Israel* and *World Development Indicators (WDI) 2008.*

ISRAEL - INFANT AND MATERNAL MORTALITY

See ISRAEL - MORTALITY

ISRAEL - INORGANIC ACIDS

United Nations Statistics Division, New York, NY 10017, (800) 253-9646, Fax: (212) 963-4116, http://unstats.un.org; *Statistical Yearbook.*

ISRAEL - INTERNATIONAL LIQUIDITY

International Monetary Fund (IMF), 700 Nineteenth Street, NW, Washington, DC 20431, (202) 623-7000, Fax: (202) 623-4661, www.imf.org; *International Financial Statistics Yearbook 2007.*

ISRAEL - INTERNATIONAL TRADE

Economist Intelligence Unit, 111 West 57th Street, New York, NY 10019, (212) 554-0600, Fax: (212) 586-1181, www.eiu.com; *Israel Country Report.*

Euromonitor International, Inc., 224 S. Michigan Avenue, Suite 1500, Chicago, IL 60604, (312) 922-1115, Fax: (312) 922-1157, www.euromonitor.com; *International Marketing Data and Statistics 2008; The World Economic Factbook 2008;* and *World Marketing Data and Statistics.*

International Monetary Fund (IMF), 700 Nineteenth Street, NW, Washington, DC 20431, (202) 623-7000, Fax: (202) 623-4661, www.imf.org; *International Financial Statistics Yearbook 2007.*

M.E. Sharpe, 80 Business Park Drive, Armonk, NY 10504, (800) 541-6563, Fax: (914) 273-2106, www.mesharpe.com; *The Illustrated Book of World Rankings.*

Palgrave Macmillan Ltd., Houndmills, Basingstoke, Hampshire, RG21 6XS, England, (Telephone in U.S. (888) 330-8477), (Fax in U.S. (800) 672-2054), www.palgrave.com; *The Statesman's Yearbook 2008.*

Taylor and Francis Group, An Informa Business, 2 Park Square, Milton Park, Abingdon, Oxford OX14 4RN, United Kingdom, (Dial from U.S. (212) 216-7800), (Fax from U.S. (212) 564-7854), www.tandf.co.uk; *The Europa World Year Book.*

United Nations Conference on Trade and Development (UNCTAD), DC2-1120, United Nations, New York, NY 10017, (212) 963-0027, www.unctad.org; *UNCTAD Commodity Yearbook.*

United Nations Food and Agricultural Organization (FAO), Viale delle Terme di Caracalla, 00100 Rome, Italy, (Dial from U.S. (202) 653-2400), (Fax from U.S. (202) 653 5760), www.fao.org; *FAO Trade Yearbook* and *The State of Food and Agriculture (SOFA) 2006.*

United Nations Statistics Division, New York, NY 10017, (800) 253-9646, Fax: (212) 963-4116, http://unstats.un.org; *International Trade Statistics Yearbook* and *Statistical Yearbook.*

The World Bank, 1818 H Street, NW, Washington, DC 20433, (202) 473-1000, Fax: (202) 477-6391, www.worldbank.org; *Israel; World Development Indicators (WDI) 2008;* and *World Development Report 2008.*

World Trade Organization (WTO), Centre William Rappard, Rue de Lausanne 154, CH-1211 Geneva 21, Switzerland, www.wto.org; *International Trade Statistics 2006.*

ISRAEL - INTERNET USERS

International Telecommunication Union (ITU), Place des Nations, 1211 Geneva 20, Switzerland, www.itu.int; *World Telecommunication/ICT Indicators Database on CD-ROM; World Telecommunication/ICT Indicators Database Online;* and *Yearbook of Statistics - Telecommunication Services (Chronological Time Series 1997-2006).*

The World Bank, 1818 H Street, NW, Washington, DC 20433, (202) 473-1000, Fax: (202) 477-6391, www.worldbank.org; *Israel.*

ISRAEL - INVESTMENTS

International Monetary Fund (IMF), 700 Nineteenth Street, NW, Washington, DC 20431, (202) 623-7000, Fax: (202) 623-4661, www.imf.org; *International Financial Statistics Yearbook 2007.*

ISRAEL - IRON AND IRON ORE PRODUCTION

See ISRAEL - MINERAL INDUSTRIES

ISRAEL - IRRIGATION

Euromonitor International, Inc., 224 S. Michigan Avenue, Suite 1500, Chicago, IL 60604, (312) 922-1115, Fax: (312) 922-1157, www.euromonitor.com; *International Marketing Data and Statistics 2008.*

ISRAEL - LABOR

Central Intelligence Agency, Office of Public Affairs, Washington, DC 20505, (703) 482-0623, Fax: (703) 482-1739, www.cia.gov; *The World Factbook.*

Euromonitor International, Inc., 224 S. Michigan Avenue, Suite 1500, Chicago, IL 60604, (312) 922-1115, Fax: (312) 922-1157, www.euromonitor.com; *International Marketing Data and Statistics 2008* and *World Marketing Data and Statistics.*

International Labour Office, I.L.O. Publications, 4 route des Morillons, CH-1211 Geneva 22, Switzerland, (Telephone in U.S. (202) 653-7652), (Fax in U.S. (202) 653-7687), www.ilo.org; *Yearbook of Labour Statistics 2006.*

M.E. Sharpe, 80 Business Park Drive, Armonk, NY 10504, (800) 541-6563, Fax: (914) 273-2106, www.mesharpe.com; *The Illustrated Book of World Rankings.*

Palgrave Macmillan Ltd., Houndmills, Basingstoke, Hampshire, RG21 6XS, England, (Telephone in U.S. (888) 330-8477), (Fax in U.S. (800) 672-2054), www.palgrave.com; *The Statesman's Yearbook 2008.*

Taylor and Francis Group, An Informa Business, 2 Park Square, Milton Park, Abingdon, Oxford OX14 4RN, United Kingdom, (Dial from U.S. (212) 216-7800), (Fax from U.S. (212) 564-7854), www.tandf.co.uk; *The Europa World Year Book.*

United Nations Food and Agricultural Organization (FAO), Viale delle Terme di Caracalla, 00100 Rome, Italy, (Dial from U.S. (202) 653-2400), (Fax from U.S. (202) 653 5760), www.fao.org; *The State of Food and Agriculture (SOFA) 2006.*

United Nations Statistics Division, New York, NY 10017, (800) 253-9646, Fax: (212) 963-4116, http://unstats.un.org; *Human Development Report 2006.*

The World Bank, 1818 H Street, NW, Washington, DC 20433, (202) 473-1000, Fax: (202) 477-6391, www.worldbank.org; *The World Bank Atlas 2003-2004; World Development Indicators (WDI) 2008;* and *World Development Report 2008.*

ISRAEL - LAND USE

Central Intelligence Agency, Office of Public Affairs, Washington, DC 20505, (703) 482-0623, Fax: (703) 482-1739, www.cia.gov; *The World Factbook.*

Euromonitor International, Inc., 224 S. Michigan Avenue, Suite 1500, Chicago, IL 60604, (312) 922-1115, Fax: (312) 922-1157, www.euromonitor.com; *International Marketing Data and Statistics 2008.*

United Nations Food and Agricultural Organization (FAO), Viale delle Terme di Caracalla, 00100 Rome, Italy, (Dial from U.S. (202) 653-2400), (Fax from U.S. (202) 653 5760), www.fao.org; *FAO Production Yearbook 2002.*

The World Bank, 1818 H Street, NW, Washington, DC 20433, (202) 473-1000, Fax: (202) 477-6391, www.worldbank.org; *World Development Report 2008.*

ISRAEL - LIBRARIES

M.E. Sharpe, 80 Business Park Drive, Armonk, NY 10504, (800) 541-6563, Fax: (914) 273-2106, www.mesharpe.com; *The Illustrated Book of World Rankings.*

UNESCO Institute for Statistics, C.P. 6128 Succursale Centre-Ville, Montreal, Quebec, H3C 3J7 Canada, (Dial from U.S. (514) 343-6880), (Fax from U.S. (514) 343 6882), www.uis.unesco.org; *Statistical Tables.*

United Nations Statistics Division, New York, NY 10017, (800) 253-9646, Fax: (212) 963-4116, http://unstats.un.org; *Trends in Europe and North America: The Statistical Yearbook of the ECE 2005.*

ISRAEL - LIFE EXPECTANCY

Central Intelligence Agency, Office of Public Affairs, Washington, DC 20505, (703) 482-0623, Fax: (703) 482-1739, www.cia.gov; *The World Factbook.*

Euromonitor International, Inc., 224 S. Michigan Avenue, Suite 1500, Chicago, IL 60604, (312) 922-1115, Fax: (312) 922-1157, www.euromonitor.com; *The World Economic Factbook 2008.*

Palgrave Macmillan Ltd., Houndmills, Basingstoke, Hampshire, RG21 6XS, England, (Telephone in U.S. (888) 330-8477), (Fax in U.S. (800) 672-2054), www.palgrave.com; *The Statesman's Yearbook 2008.*

United Nations Statistics Division, New York, NY 10017, (800) 253-9646, Fax: (212) 963-4116, http://unstats.un.org; *Human Development Report 2006; Trends in Europe and North America: The Statistical Yearbook of the ECE 2005;* and *World Statistics Pocketbook.*

The World Bank, 1818 H Street, NW, Washington, DC 20433, (202) 473-1000, Fax: (202) 477-6391, www.worldbank.org; *The World Bank Atlas 2003-2004* and *World Development Report 2008.*

ISRAEL - LITERACY

Euromonitor International, Inc., 224 S. Michigan Avenue, Suite 1500, Chicago, IL 60604, (312) 922-1115, Fax: (312) 922-1157, www.euromonitor.com; *World Marketing Data and Statistics.*

ISRAEL - LIVESTOCK

Euromonitor International, Inc., 224 S. Michigan Avenue, Suite 1500, Chicago, IL 60604, (312) 922-1115, Fax: (312) 922-1157, www.euromonitor.com; *International Marketing Data and Statistics 2008.*

M.E. Sharpe, 80 Business Park Drive, Armonk, NY 10504, (800) 541-6563, Fax: (914) 273-2106, www.mesharpe.com; *The Illustrated Book of World Rankings.*

Palgrave Macmillan Ltd., Houndmills, Basingstoke, Hampshire, RG21 6XS, England, (Telephone in U.S. (888) 330-8477), (Fax in U.S. (800) 672-2054), www.palgrave.com; *The Statesman's Yearbook 2008.*

Taylor and Francis Group, An Informa Business, 2 Park Square, Milton Park, Abingdon, Oxford OX14 4RN, United Kingdom, (Dial from U.S. (212) 216-7800), (Fax from U.S. (212) 564-7854), www.tandf.co.uk; *The Europa World Year Book.*

United Nations Conference on Trade and Development (UNCTAD), DC2-1120, United Nations, New York, NY 10017, (212) 963-0027, www.unctad.org; *UNCTAD Commodity Yearbook.*

United Nations Food and Agricultural Organization (FAO), Viale delle Terme di Caracalla, 00100 Rome, Italy, (Dial from U.S. (202) 653-2400), (Fax from U.S. (202) 653 5760), www.fao.org; *FAO Production Yearbook 2002* and *The State of Food and Agriculture (SOFA) 2006.*

United Nations Statistics Division, New York, NY 10017, (800) 253-9646, Fax: (212) 963-4116, http://unstats.un.org; *Statistical Yearbook.*

ISRAEL - LOCAL TAXATION

Euromonitor International, Inc., 224 S. Michigan Avenue, Suite 1500, Chicago, IL 60604, (312) 922-1115, Fax: (312) 922-1157, www.euromonitor.com; *International Marketing Data and Statistics 2008.*

ISRAEL - MANUFACTURES

M.E. Sharpe, 80 Business Park Drive, Armonk, NY 10504, (800) 541-6563, Fax: (914) 273-2106, www.mesharpe.com; *The Illustrated Book of World Rankings.*

United Nations Statistics Division, New York, NY 10017, (800) 253-9646, Fax: (212) 963-4116, http://unstats.un.org; *Statistical Yearbook.*

The World Bank, 1818 H Street, NW, Washington, DC 20433, (202) 473-1000, Fax: (202) 477-6391, www.worldbank.org; *World Development Indicators (WDI) 2008.*

ISRAEL - MARRIAGE

M.E. Sharpe, 80 Business Park Drive, Armonk, NY 10504, (800) 541-6563, Fax: (914) 273-2106, www.mesharpe.com; *The Illustrated Book of World Rankings.*

Taylor and Francis Group, An Informa Business, 2 Park Square, Milton Park, Abingdon, Oxford OX14 4RN, United Kingdom, (Dial from U.S. (212) 216-7800), (Fax from U.S. (212) 564-7854), www.tandf.co.uk; *The Europa World Year Book.*

United Nations Statistics Division, New York, NY 10017, (800) 253-9646, Fax: (212) 963-4116, http://unstats.un.org; *Demographic Yearbook; Statistical Yearbook;* and *Trends in Europe and North America: The Statistical Yearbook of the ECE 2005.*

ISRAEL - MEAT PRODUCTION

See ISRAEL - LIVESTOCK

ISRAEL - MEDICAL CARE, COST OF

International Monetary Fund (IMF), 700 Nineteenth Street, NW, Washington, DC 20431, (202) 623-7000, Fax: (202) 623-4661, www.imf.org; *Government Finance Statistics Yearbook (2008 Edition).*

ISRAEL - MILK PRODUCTION

See ISRAEL - DAIRY PROCESSING

ISRAEL - MINERAL INDUSTRIES

International Monetary Fund (IMF), 700 Nineteenth Street, NW, Washington, DC 20431, (202) 623-7000, Fax: (202) 623-4661, www.imf.org; *International Financial Statistics Yearbook 2007.*

M.E. Sharpe, 80 Business Park Drive, Armonk, NY 10504, (800) 541-6563, Fax: (914) 273-2106, www.mesharpe.com; *The Illustrated Book of World Rankings.*

Organisation for Economic Cooperation and Development (OECD), 2 rue Andre Pascal, F-75775 Paris Cedex 16, France, (Telephone in U.S. (202) 785-6323), (Fax in U.S. (202) 785-0350), www.oecd.org; *World Energy Outlook 2007.*

Palgrave Macmillan Ltd., Houndmills, Basingstoke, Hampshire, RG21 6XS, England, (Telephone in U.S. (888) 330-8477), (Fax in U.S. (800) 672-2054), www.palgrave.com; *The Statesman's Yearbook 2008.*

Taylor and Francis Group, An Informa Business, 2 Park Square, Milton Park, Abingdon, Oxford OX14 4RN, United Kingdom, (Dial from U.S. (212) 216-7800), (Fax from U.S. (212) 564-7854), www.tandf.co.uk; *The Europa World Year Book.*

United Nations Conference on Trade and Development (UNCTAD), DC2-1120, United Nations, New York, NY 10017, (212) 963-0027, www.unctad.org; *UNCTAD Commodity Yearbook.*

United Nations Statistics Division, New York, NY 10017, (800) 253-9646, Fax: (212) 963-4116, http://unstats.un.org; *Statistical Yearbook.*

The World Bank, 1818 H Street, NW, Washington, DC 20433, (202) 473-1000, Fax: (202) 477-6391, www.worldbank.org; *Israel.*

ISRAEL - MONEY EXCHANGE RATES

See ISRAEL - FOREIGN EXCHANGE RATES

ISRAEL - MONEY SUPPLY

Economist Intelligence Unit, 111 West 57th Street, New York, NY 10019, (212) 554-0600, Fax: (212) 586-1181, www.eiu.com; *Israel Country Report.*

Euromonitor International, Inc., 224 S. Michigan Avenue, Suite 1500, Chicago, IL 60604, (312) 922-1115, Fax: (312) 922-1157, www.euromonitor.com; *International Marketing Data and Statistics 2008.*

International Monetary Fund (IMF), 700 Nineteenth Street, NW, Washington, DC 20431, (202) 623-7000, Fax: (202) 623-4661, www.imf.org; *International Financial Statistics Yearbook 2007.*

Taylor and Francis Group, An Informa Business, 2 Park Square, Milton Park, Abingdon, Oxford OX14 4RN, United Kingdom, (Dial from U.S. (212) 216-7800), (Fax from U.S. (212) 564-7854), www.tandf.co.uk; *The Europa World Year Book.*

United Nations Statistics Division, New York, NY 10017, (800) 253-9646, Fax: (212) 963-4116, http://unstats.un.org; *Statistical Yearbook.*

The World Bank, 1818 H Street, NW, Washington, DC 20433, (202) 473-1000, Fax: (202) 477-6391, www.worldbank.org; *Israel.*

ISRAEL - MORTALITY

Central Intelligence Agency, Office of Public Affairs, Washington, DC 20505, (703) 482-0623, Fax: (703) 482-1739, www.cia.gov; *The World Factbook.*

Euromonitor International, Inc., 224 S. Michigan Avenue, Suite 1500, Chicago, IL 60604, (312) 922-1115, Fax: (312) 922-1157, www.euromonitor.com; *International Marketing Data and Statistics 2008* and *The World Economic Factbook 2008.*

European Centre for Disease Prevention and Control (ECDC), 171 83 Stockholm, Sweden, www.ecdc.europa.eu; *Sudden Deaths and Influenza Vaccinations in Israel - ECDC Interim Risk Assessment.*

Palgrave Macmillan Ltd., Houndmills, Basingstoke, Hampshire, RG21 6XS, England, (Telephone in U.S. (888) 330-8477), (Fax in U.S. (800) 672-2054), www.palgrave.com; *The Statesman's Yearbook 2008.*

Taylor and Francis Group, An Informa Business, 2 Park Square, Milton Park, Abingdon, Oxford OX14 4RN, United Kingdom, (Dial from U.S. (212) 216-7800), (Fax from U.S. (212) 564-7854), www.tandf.co.uk; *The Europa World Year Book.*

UNICEF, 3 United Nations Plaza, New York, NY 10017, (800) 253-9646, Fax: (212) 887-7465, www.unicef.org; *The State of the World's Children 2008.*

United Nations Statistics Division, New York, NY 10017, (800) 253-9646, Fax: (212) 963-4116, http://unstats.un.org; *Demographic Yearbook; Human Development Report 2006; Statistical Yearbook; Trends in Europe and North America: The Statistical Yearbook of the ECE 2005;* and *World Statistics Pocketbook.*

The World Bank, 1818 H Street, NW, Washington, DC 20433, (202) 473-1000, Fax: (202) 477-6391, www.worldbank.org; *The World Bank Atlas 2003-2004; World Development Indicators (WDI) 2008;* and *World Development Report 2008.*

World Health Organization (WHO), Avenue Appia 20, 1211 Geneve 27, Switzerland, (Telephone in U.S. (212) 331-9081), www.who.int; The WHO Global Atlas of Infectious Diseases and *World Health Report 2006.*

ISRAEL - MOTION PICTURES

Palgrave Macmillan Ltd., Houndmills, Basingstoke, Hampshire, RG21 6XS, England, (Telephone in U.S. (888) 330-8477), (Fax in U.S. (800) 672-2054), www.palgrave.com; *The Statesman's Yearbook 2008.*

UNESCO Institute for Statistics, C.P. 6128 Succursale Centre-Ville, Montreal, Quebec, H3C 3J7 Canada, (Dial from U.S. (514) 343-6880), (Fax from U.S. (514) 343 6882), www.uis.unesco.org; *Statistical Tables.*

United Nations Statistics Division, New York, NY 10017, (800) 253-9646, Fax: (212) 963-4116, http://unstats.un.org; *Statistical Yearbook.*

ISRAEL - MOTOR VEHICLES

Taylor and Francis Group, An Informa Business, 2 Park Square, Milton Park, Abingdon, Oxford OX14 4RN, United Kingdom, (Dial from U.S. (212) 216-7800), (Fax from U.S. (212) 564-7854), www.tandf.co.uk; *The Europa World Year Book.*

United Nations Statistics Division, New York, NY 10017, (800) 253-9646, Fax: (212) 963-4116, http://unstats.un.org; *Statistical Yearbook.*

ISRAEL - MUSEUMS

M.E. Sharpe, 80 Business Park Drive, Armonk, NY 10504, (800) 541-6563, Fax: (914) 273-2106, www.mesharpe.com; *The Illustrated Book of World Rankings.*

UNESCO Institute for Statistics, C.P. 6128 Succursale Centre-Ville, Montreal, Quebec, H3C 3J7 Canada, (Dial from U.S. (514) 343-6880), (Fax from U.S. (514) 343 6882), www.uis.unesco.org; *Statistical Tables.*

ISRAEL - NATURAL GAS PRODUCTION

See ISRAEL - MINERAL INDUSTRIES

ISRAEL - NUTRITION

United Nations Food and Agricultural Organization (FAO), Viale delle Terme di Caracalla, 00100 Rome, Italy, (Dial from U.S. (202) 653-2400), (Fax from U.S. (202) 653 5760), www.fao.org; *The State of Food and Agriculture (SOFA) 2006.*

ISRAEL - OLDER PEOPLE

M.E. Sharpe, 80 Business Park Drive, Armonk, NY 10504, (800) 541-6563, Fax: (914) 273-2106, www.mesharpe.com; *The Illustrated Book of World Rankings.*

ISRAEL - ORANGES PRODUCTION

See ISRAEL - CROPS

ISRAEL - PAPER

See ISRAEL - FORESTS AND FORESTRY

ISRAEL - PEANUT PRODUCTION

See ISRAEL - CROPS

ISRAEL - PERIODICALS

UNESCO Institute for Statistics, C.P. 6128 Succursale Centre-Ville, Montreal, Quebec, H3C 3J7 Canada, (Dial from U.S. (514) 343-6880), (Fax from U.S. (514) 343 6882), www.uis.unesco.org; *Statistical Tables.*

ISRAEL - PESTICIDES

United Nations Food and Agricultural Organization (FAO), Viale delle Terme di Caracalla, 00100 Rome, Italy, (Dial from U.S. (202) 653-2400), (Fax from U.S. (202) 653 5760), www.fao.org; *The State of Food and Agriculture (SOFA) 2006.*

ISRAEL - PETROLEUM INDUSTRY AND TRADE

M.E. Sharpe, 80 Business Park Drive, Armonk, NY 10504, (800) 541-6563, Fax: (914) 273-2106, www.mesharpe.com; *The Illustrated Book of World Rankings.*

Organisation for Economic Cooperation and Development (OECD), 2 rue Andre Pascal, F-75775 Paris Cedex 16, France, (Telephone in U.S. (202) 785-6323), (Fax in U.S. (202) 785-0350), www.oecd.org; *World Energy Outlook 2007.*

Palgrave Macmillan Ltd., Houndmills, Basingstoke, Hampshire, RG21 6XS, England, (Telephone in U.S. (888) 330-8477), (Fax in U.S. (800) 672-2054), www.palgrave.com; *The Statesman's Yearbook 2008.*

PennWell Corporation, 1421 South Sheridan Road, Tulsa, OK 74112, (918) 835-3161, www.pennwell.com; *International Petroleum Encyclopedia 2007.*

U.S. Department of Energy (DOE), Energy Information Administration (EIA), 1000 Independence Avenue, SW, Washington, DC 20585, (202) 586-8800, www.eia.doe.gov; *International Energy Annual 2004* and *International Energy Outlook 2006.*

United Nations Conference on Trade and Development (UNCTAD), DC2-1120, United Nations, New York, NY 10017, (212) 963-0027, www.unctad.org; *UNCTAD Commodity Yearbook.*

United Nations Food and Agricultural Organization (FAO), Viale delle Terme di Caracalla, 00100 Rome, Italy, (Dial from U.S. (202) 653-2400), (Fax from U.S. (202) 653 5760), www.fao.org; *The State of Food and Agriculture (SOFA) 2006.*

United Nations Statistics Division, New York, NY 10017, (800) 253-9646, Fax: (212) 963-4116, http://unstats.un.org; *Statistical Yearbook* and *Trends in Europe and North America: The Statistical Yearbook of the ECE 2005.*

ISRAEL - PHOSPHATES PRODUCTION

See ISRAEL - MINERAL INDUSTRIES

ISRAEL - PLASTICS INDUSTRY AND TRADE

United Nations Statistics Division, New York, NY 10017, (800) 253-9646, Fax: (212) 963-4116, http://unstats.un.org; *Statistical Yearbook.*

ISRAEL - POLITICAL SCIENCE

Central Intelligence Agency, Office of Public Affairs, Washington, DC 20505, (703) 482-0623, Fax: (703) 482-1739, www.cia.gov; *The World Factbook.*

International Monetary Fund (IMF), 700 Nineteenth Street, NW, Washington, DC 20431, (202) 623-7000, Fax: (202) 623-4661, www.imf.org; *Government Finance Statistics Yearbook (2008 Edition)* and *International Financial Statistics Yearbook 2007.*

Palgrave Macmillan Ltd., Houndmills, Basingstoke, Hampshire, RG21 6XS, England, (Telephone in U.S. (888) 330-8477), (Fax in U.S. (800) 672-2054), www.palgrave.com; *The Statesman's Yearbook 2008.*

Taylor and Francis Group, An Informa Business, 2 Park Square, Milton Park, Abingdon, Oxford OX14 4RN, United Kingdom, (Dial from U.S. (212) 216-7800), (Fax from U.S. (212) 564-7854), www.tandf.co.uk; *The Europa World Year Book.*

United Nations Statistics Division, New York, NY 10017, (800) 253-9646, Fax: (212) 963-4116, http://unstats.un.org; *National Accounts Statistics: Compendium of Income Distribution Statistics* and *Statistical Yearbook.*

The World Bank, 1818 H Street, NW, Washington, DC 20433, (202) 473-1000, Fax: (202) 477-6391, www.worldbank.org; *World Development Indicators (WDI) 2008* and *World Development Report 2008.*

ISRAEL - POPULATION

Central Intelligence Agency, Office of Public Affairs, Washington, DC 20505, (703) 482-0623, Fax: (703) 482-1739, www.cia.gov; *The World Factbook.*

Economist Intelligence Unit, 111 West 57th Street, New York, NY 10019, (212) 554-0600, Fax: (212) 586-1181, www.eiu.com; *Israel Country Report.*

Euromonitor International, Inc., 224 S. Michigan Avenue, Suite 1500, Chicago, IL 60604, (312) 922-1115, Fax: (312) 922-1157, www.euromonitor.com; *International Marketing Data and Statistics 2008* and *The World Economic Factbook 2008.*

International Labour Office, I.L.O. Publications, 4 route des Morillons, CH-1211 Geneva 22, Switzerland, (Telephone in U.S. (202) 653-7652), (Fax in U.S. (202) 653-7687), www.ilo.org; *Yearbook of Labour Statistics 2006.*

M.E. Sharpe, 80 Business Park Drive, Armonk, NY 10504, (800) 541-6563, Fax: (914) 273-2106, www.mesharpe.com; *The Illustrated Book of World Rankings.*

Palgrave Macmillan Ltd., Houndmills, Basingstoke, Hampshire, RG21 6XS, England, (Telephone in U.S. (888) 330-8477), (Fax in U.S. (800) 672-2054), www.palgrave.com; *The Statesman's Yearbook 2008.*

Taylor and Francis Group, An Informa Business, 2 Park Square, Milton Park, Abingdon, Oxford OX14 4RN, United Kingdom, (Dial from U.S. (212) 216-7800), (Fax from U.S. (212) 564-7854), www.tandf.co.uk; *The Europa World Year Book.*

U.S. Department of State (DOS), 2201 C Street NW, Washington, DC 20520, (202) 647-4000, www.state.gov; *World Military Expenditures and Arms Transfers (WMEAT).*

UNESCO Institute for Statistics, C.P. 6128 Succursale Centre-Ville, Montreal, Quebec, H3C 3J7 Canada, (Dial from U.S. (514) 343-6880), (Fax from U.S. (514) 343 6882), www.uis.unesco.org; *Statistical Tables.*

United Nations Food and Agricultural Organization (FAO), Viale delle Terme di Caracalla, 00100 Rome, Italy, (Dial from U.S. (202) 653-2400), (Fax from U.S. (202) 653 5760), www.fao.org; *FAO Production Yearbook 2002.*

United Nations Statistics Division, New York, NY 10017, (800) 253-9646, Fax: (212) 963-4116, http://unstats.un.org; *Demographic Yearbook; Human Development Report 2006; Statistical Yearbook; Trends in Europe and North America: The Statistical Yearbook of the ECE 2005;* and *World Statistics Pocketbook.*

The World Bank, 1818 H Street, NW, Washington, DC 20433, (202) 473-1000, Fax: (202) 477-6391, www.worldbank.org; *Israel; The World Bank Atlas 2003-2004;* and *World Development Report 2008.*

World Health Organization (WHO), Avenue Appia 20, 1211 Geneve 27, Switzerland, (Telephone in U.S. (212) 331-9081), www.who.int; *World Health Report 2006.*

ISRAEL - POPULATION DENSITY

Central Intelligence Agency, Office of Public Affairs, Washington, DC 20505, (703) 482-0623, Fax: (703) 482-1739, www.cia.gov; *The World Factbook.*

Euromonitor International, Inc., 224 S. Michigan Avenue, Suite 1500, Chicago, IL 60604, (312) 922-1115, Fax: (312) 922-1157, www.euromonitor.com; *International Marketing Data and Statistics 2008* and *The World Economic Factbook 2008.*

M.E. Sharpe, 80 Business Park Drive, Armonk, NY 10504, (800) 541-6563, Fax: (914) 273-2106, www.mesharpe.com; *The Illustrated Book of World Rankings.*

Palgrave Macmillan Ltd., Houndmills, Basingstoke, Hampshire, RG21 6XS, England, (Telephone in U.S. (888) 330-8477), (Fax in U.S. (800) 672-2054), www.palgrave.com; *The Statesman's Yearbook 2008.*

Taylor and Francis Group, An Informa Business, 2 Park Square, Milton Park, Abingdon, Oxford OX14 4RN, United Kingdom, (Dial from U.S. (212) 216-7800), (Fax from U.S. (212) 564-7854), www.tandf.co.uk; *The Europa World Year Book.*

UNESCO Institute for Statistics, C.P. 6128 Succursale Centre-Ville, Montreal, Quebec, H3C 3J7 Canada, (Dial from U.S. (514) 343-6880), (Fax from U.S. (514) 343 6882), www.uis.unesco.org; *Statistical Tables.*

United Nations Food and Agricultural Organization (FAO), Viale delle Terme di Caracalla, 00100 Rome, Italy, (Dial from U.S. (202) 653-2400), (Fax from U.S. (202) 653 5760), www.fao.org; *The State of Food and Agriculture (SOFA) 2006.*

United Nations Statistics Division, New York, NY 10017, (800) 253-9646, Fax: (212) 963-4116, http://unstats.un.org; *Statistical Yearbook* and *Trends in Europe and North America: The Statistical Yearbook of the ECE 2005.*

The World Bank, 1818 H Street, NW, Washington, DC 20433, (202) 473-1000, Fax: (202) 477-6391, www.worldbank.org; *Israel* and *World Development Report 2008.*

ISRAEL - POSTAL SERVICE

M.E. Sharpe, 80 Business Park Drive, Armonk, NY 10504, (800) 541-6563, Fax: (914) 273-2106, www.mesharpe.com; *The Illustrated Book of World Rankings.*

Palgrave Macmillan Ltd., Houndmills, Basingstoke, Hampshire, RG21 6XS, England, (Telephone in U.S. (888) 330-8477), (Fax in U.S. (800) 672-2054), www.palgrave.com; *The Statesman's Yearbook 2008.*

United Nations Statistics Division, New York, NY 10017, (800) 253-9646, Fax: (212) 963-4116, http://unstats.un.org; *Statistical Yearbook* and *Trends in Europe and North America: The Statistical Yearbook of the ECE 2005.*

ISRAEL - POWER RESOURCES

Euromonitor International, Inc., 224 S. Michigan Avenue, Suite 1500, Chicago, IL 60604, (312) 922-1115, Fax: (312) 922-1157, www.euromonitor.com; *International Marketing Data and Statistics 2008; The World Economic Factbook 2008;* and *World Marketing Data and Statistics.*

M.E. Sharpe, 80 Business Park Drive, Armonk, NY 10504, (800) 541-6563, Fax: (914) 273-2106, www.mesharpe.com; *The Illustrated Book of World Rankings.*

Organisation for Economic Cooperation and Development (OECD), 2 rue Andre Pascal, F-75775 Paris Cedex 16, France, (Telephone in U.S. (202) 785-6323), (Fax in U.S. (202) 785-0350), www.oecd.org; *World Energy Outlook 2007.*

Palgrave Macmillan Ltd., Houndmills, Basingstoke, Hampshire, RG21 6XS, England, (Telephone in U.S. (888) 330-8477), (Fax in U.S. (800) 672-2054), www.palgrave.com; *The Statesman's Yearbook 2008.*

Platts, 2 Penn Plaza, 25th Floor, New York, NY 10121-2298, (212) 904-3070, www.platts.com; *Energy Economist.*

U.S. Department of Energy (DOE), Energy Information Administration (EIA), 1000 Independence Avenue, SW, Washington, DC 20585, (202) 586-8800, www.eia.doe.gov; *International Energy Annual 2004* and *International Energy Outlook 2006.*

United Nations Food and Agricultural Organization (FAO), Viale delle Terme di Caracalla, 00100 Rome, Italy, (Dial from U.S. (202) 653-2400), (Fax from U.S. (202) 653 5760), www.fao.org; *The State of Food and Agriculture (SOFA) 2006.*

United Nations Statistics Division, New York, NY 10017, (800) 253-9646, Fax: (212) 963-4116, http://unstats.un.org; *Energy Statistics Yearbook 2003; Human Development Report 2006; Statistical Yearbook; Trends in Europe and North America: The Statistical Yearbook of the ECE 2005;* and *World Statistics Pocketbook.*

The World Bank, 1818 H Street, NW, Washington, DC 20433, (202) 473-1000, Fax: (202) 477-6391, www.worldbank.org; *The World Bank Atlas 2003-2004* and *World Development Report 2008.*

ISRAEL - PRICES

Euromonitor International, Inc., 224 S. Michigan Avenue, Suite 1500, Chicago, IL 60604, (312) 922-1115, Fax: (312) 922-1157, www.euromonitor.com; *World Marketing Data and Statistics.*

International Labour Office, I.L.O. Publications, 4 route des Morillons, CH-1211 Geneva 22, Switzerland, (Telephone in U.S. (202) 653-7652), (Fax in U.S. (202) 653-7687), www.ilo.org; *Yearbook of Labour Statistics 2006.*

International Monetary Fund (IMF), 700 Nineteenth Street, NW, Washington, DC 20431, (202) 623-7000, Fax: (202) 623-4661, www.imf.org; *International Financial Statistics Yearbook 2007.*

M.E. Sharpe, 80 Business Park Drive, Armonk, NY 10504, (800) 541-6563, Fax: (914) 273-2106, www.mesharpe.com; *The Illustrated Book of World Rankings.*

United Nations Food and Agricultural Organization (FAO), Viale delle Terme di Caracalla, 00100 Rome, Italy, (Dial from U.S. (202) 653-2400), (Fax from U.S. (202) 653 5760), www.fao.org; *FAO Production Yearbook 2002* and *The State of Food and Agriculture (SOFA) 2006.*

The World Bank, 1818 H Street, NW, Washington, DC 20433, (202) 473-1000, Fax: (202) 477-6391, www.worldbank.org; *Israel.*

ISRAEL - PROFESSIONS

UNESCO Institute for Statistics, C.P. 6128 Succursale Centre-Ville, Montreal, Quebec, H3C 3J7 Canada, (Dial from U.S. (514) 343-6880), (Fax from U.S. (514) 343 6882), www.uis.unesco.org; *Statistical Tables.*

United Nations Statistics Division, New York, NY 10017, (800) 253-9646, Fax: (212) 963-4116, http://unstats.un.org; *Statistical Yearbook.*

ISRAEL - PUBLIC HEALTH

Euromonitor International, Inc., 224 S. Michigan Avenue, Suite 1500, Chicago, IL 60604, (312) 922-1115, Fax: (312) 922-1157, www.euromonitor.com; *World Health Databook 2007/2008* and *World Marketing Data and Statistics.*

European Centre for Disease Prevention and Control (ECDC), 171 83 Stockholm, Sweden, www.ecdc.europa.eu; *Sudden Deaths and Influenza Vaccinations in Israel - ECDC Interim Risk Assessment.*

M.E. Sharpe, 80 Business Park Drive, Armonk, NY 10504, (800) 541-6563, Fax: (914) 273-2106, www.mesharpe.com; *The Illustrated Book of World Rankings.*

Palgrave Macmillan Ltd., Houndmills, Basingstoke, Hampshire, RG21 6XS, England, (Telephone in U.S. (888) 330-8477), (Fax in U.S. (800) 672-2054), www.palgrave.com; *The Statesman's Yearbook 2008.*

UNICEF, 3 United Nations Plaza, New York, NY 10017, (800) 253-9646, Fax: (212) 887-7465, www.unicef.org; *The State of the World's Children 2008.*

United Nations Statistics Division, New York, NY 10017, (800) 253-9646, Fax: (212) 963-4116, http://unstats.un.org; *Human Development Report 2006; Statistical Yearbook;* and *Trends in Europe and North America: The Statistical Yearbook of the ECE 2005.*

The World Bank, 1818 H Street, NW, Washington, DC 20433, (202) 473-1000, Fax: (202) 477-6391, www.worldbank.org; *Israel* and *World Development Report 2008.*

World Health Organization (WHO), Avenue Appia 20, 1211 Geneve 27, Switzerland, (Telephone in U.S. (212) 331-9081), www.who.int; The WHO Global Atlas of Infectious Diseases.

ISRAEL - PUBLISHERS AND PUBLISHING

Taylor and Francis Group, An Informa Business, 2 Park Square, Milton Park, Abingdon, Oxford OX14 4RN, United Kingdom, (Dial from U.S. (212) 216-7800), (Fax from U.S. (212) 564-7854), www.tandf.co.uk; *The Europa World Year Book.*

UNESCO Institute for Statistics, C.P. 6128 Succursale Centre-Ville, Montreal, Quebec, H3C 3J7 Canada, (Dial from U.S. (514) 343-6880), (Fax from U.S. (514) 343 6882), www.uis.unesco.org; *Statistical Tables.*

United Nations Statistics Division, New York, NY 10017, (800) 253-9646, Fax: (212) 963-4116, http://unstats.un.org; *Trends in Europe and North America: The Statistical Yearbook of the ECE 2005.*

ISRAEL - RADIO - RECEIVERS AND RECEPTION

Palgrave Macmillan Ltd., Houndmills, Basingstoke, Hampshire, RG21 6XS, England, (Telephone in U.S. (888) 330-8477), (Fax in U.S. (800) 672-2054), www.palgrave.com; *The Statesman's Yearbook 2008.*

United Nations Statistics Division, New York, NY 10017, (800) 253-9646, Fax: (212) 963-4116, http://unstats.un.org; *Statistical Yearbook.*

ISRAEL - RAILROADS

Jane's Information Group, 110 North Royal Street, Suite 200, Alexandria, VA 22314, (703) 683-3700, Fax: (800) 836-0297, www.janes.com; *Jane's World Railways.*

Palgrave Macmillan Ltd., Houndmills, Basingstoke, Hampshire, RG21 6XS, England, (Telephone in U.S. (888) 330-8477), (Fax in U.S. (800) 672-2054), www.palgrave.com; *The Statesman's Yearbook 2008.*

Taylor and Francis Group, An Informa Business, 2 Park Square, Milton Park, Abingdon, Oxford OX14 4RN, United Kingdom, (Dial from U.S. (212) 216-7800), (Fax from U.S. (212) 564-7854), www.tandf.co.uk; *The Europa World Year Book.*

United Nations Statistics Division, New York, NY 10017, (800) 253-9646, Fax: (212) 963-4116, http://unstats.un.org; *Trends in Europe and North America: The Statistical Yearbook of the ECE 2005.*

ISRAEL - RELIGION

Central Intelligence Agency, Office of Public Affairs, Washington, DC 20505, (703) 482-0623, Fax: (703) 482-1739, www.cia.gov; *The World Factbook.*

M.E. Sharpe, 80 Business Park Drive, Armonk, NY 10504, (800) 541-6563, Fax: (914) 273-2106, www.mesharpe.com; *The Illustrated Book of World Rankings.*

Palgrave Macmillan Ltd., Houndmills, Basingstoke, Hampshire, RG21 6XS, England, (Telephone in U.S. (888) 330-8477), (Fax in U.S. (800) 672-2054), www.palgrave.com; *The Statesman's Yearbook 2008.*

ISRAEL - RENT CHARGES

International Labour Office, I.L.O. Publications, 4 route des Morillons, CH-1211 Geneva 22, Switzerland, (Telephone in U.S. (202) 653-7652), (Fax in U.S. (202) 653-7687), www.ilo.org; *Yearbook of Labour Statistics 2006.*

ISRAEL - RESERVES (ACCOUNTING)

Euromonitor International, Inc., 224 S. Michigan Avenue, Suite 1500, Chicago, IL 60604, (312) 922-1115, Fax: (312) 922-1157, www.euromonitor.com; *International Marketing Data and Statistics 2008.*

United Nations Statistics Division, New York, NY 10017, (800) 253-9646, Fax: (212) 963-4116, http://unstats.un.org; *Statistical Yearbook.*

The World Bank, 1818 H Street, NW, Washington, DC 20433, (202) 473-1000, Fax: (202) 477-6391; www.worldbank.org; *World Development Indicators (WDI) 2008.*

ISRAEL - RETAIL TRADE

Euromonitor International, Inc., 224 S. Michigan Avenue, Suite 1500, Chicago, IL 60604, (312) 922-1115, Fax: (312) 922-1157, www.euromonitor.com; *Retail Trade International 2007* and *World Marketing Data and Statistics.*

United Nations Statistics Division, New York, NY 10017, (800) 253-9646, Fax: (212) 963-4116, http://unstats.un.org; *Statistical Yearbook.*

ISRAEL - RICE PRODUCTION

See ISRAEL - CROPS

ISRAEL - ROADS

Central Intelligence Agency, Office of Public Affairs, Washington, DC 20505, (703) 482-0623, Fax: (703) 482-1739, www.cia.gov; *The World Factbook.*

Palgrave Macmillan Ltd., Houndmills, Basingstoke, Hampshire, RG21 6XS, England, (Telephone in U.S. (888) 330-8477), (Fax in U.S. (800) 672-2054), www.palgrave.com; *The Statesman's Yearbook 2008.*

United Nations Statistics Division, New York, NY 10017, (800) 253-9646, Fax: (212) 963-4116, http://unstats.un.org; *Trends in Europe and North America: The Statistical Yearbook of the ECE 2005.*

ISRAEL - RUBBER INDUSTRY AND TRADE

International Rubber Study Group (IRSG), 1st Floor, Heron House, 109/115 Wembley Hill Road, Wembley, Middlesex HA9 8DA, United Kingdom, www.rubberstudy.com; *Rubber Statistical Bulletin; Summary of World Rubber Statistics 2005; World Rubber Statistics Handbook (Volume 6, 1975-2001);* and *World Rubber Statistics Historic Handbook.*

M.E. Sharpe, 80 Business Park Drive, Armonk, NY 10504, (800) 541-6563, Fax: (914) 273-2106, www.mesharpe.com; *The Illustrated Book of World Rankings.*

ISRAEL - SAFFLOWER SEED PRODUCTION

See ISRAEL - CROPS

ISRAEL - SALT PRODUCTION

See ISRAEL - MINERAL INDUSTRIES

ISRAEL - SHEEP

See ISRAEL - LIVESTOCK

ISRAEL - SHIPPING

Lloyd's Register - Fairplay, 8410 N.W. 53rd Terrace, Suite 207, Miami FL 33166, (305) 718-9929, Fax: (305) 718-9663, www.lrfairplay.com; *Register of Ships 2007-2008; World Casualty Statistics 2007; World Fleet Statistics 2006; World Marine Propulsion Report 2006-2010; World Shipbuilding Statistics 2007;* and The World Shipping Encyclopaedia.

Palgrave Macmillan Ltd., Houndmills, Basingstoke, Hampshire, RG21 6XS, England, (Telephone in U.S. (888) 330-8477), (Fax in U.S. (800) 672-2054), www.palgrave.com; *The Statesman's Yearbook 2008.*

Taylor and Francis Group, An Informa Business, 2 Park Square, Milton Park, Abingdon, Oxford OX14 4RN, United Kingdom, (Dial from U.S. (212) 216-7800), (Fax from U.S. (212) 564-7854), www.tandf.co.uk; *The Europa World Year Book.*

U.S. Department of Transportation (DOT), Maritime Administration (MARAD), West Building, Southeast Federal Center, 1200 New Jersey Avenue, SE, Washington, DC 20590, (800) 99-MARAD, www.marad.dot.gov; *World Merchant Fleet 2005.*

United Nations Statistics Division, New York, NY 10017, (800) 253-9646, Fax: (212) 963-4116, http://unstats.un.org; *Statistical Yearbook.*

ISRAEL - SILVER PRODUCTION

See ISRAEL - MINERAL INDUSTRIES

ISRAEL - SOCIAL ECOLOGY

M.E. Sharpe, 80 Business Park Drive, Armonk, NY 10504, (800) 541-6563, Fax: (914) 273-2106, www.mesharpe.com; *The Illustrated Book of World Rankings.*

United Nations Statistics Division, New York, NY 10017, (800) 253-9646, Fax: (212) 963-4116, http://unstats.un.org; *World Statistics Pocketbook.*

ISRAEL - SOCIAL SECURITY

International Monetary Fund (IMF), 700 Nineteenth Street, NW, Washington, DC 20431, (202) 623-7000, Fax: (202) 623-4661, www.imf.org; *Government Finance Statistics Yearbook (2008 Edition).*

United Nations Statistics Division, New York, NY 10017, (800) 253-9646, Fax: (212) 963-4116, http://unstats.un.org; *National Accounts Statistics: Compendium of Income Distribution Statistics.*

ISRAEL - STEEL PRODUCTION

See ISRAEL - MINERAL INDUSTRIES

ISRAEL - SUGAR PRODUCTION

See ISRAEL - CROPS

ISRAEL - SULPHUR PRODUCTION

See ISRAEL - MINERAL INDUSTRIES

ISRAEL - TAXATION

International Monetary Fund (IMF), 700 Nineteenth Street, NW, Washington, DC 20431, (202) 623-7000, Fax: (202) 623-4661, www.imf.org; *Government Finance Statistics Yearbook (2008 Edition).*

Taylor and Francis Group, An Informa Business, 2 Park Square, Milton Park, Abingdon, Oxford OX14 4RN, United Kingdom, (Dial from U.S. (212) 216-7800), (Fax from U.S. (212) 564-7854), www.tandf.co.uk; *The Europa World Year Book.*

The World Bank, 1818 H Street, NW, Washington, DC 20433, (202) 473-1000, Fax: (202) 477-6391, www.worldbank.org; *World Development Indicators (WDI) 2008.*

ISRAEL - TELEPHONE

International Telecommunication Union (ITU), Place des Nations, 1211 Geneva 20, Switzerland, www.itu.int; World Telecommunication Indicators Database.

Taylor and Francis Group, An Informa Business, 2 Park Square, Milton Park, Abingdon, Oxford OX14 4RN, United Kingdom, (Dial from U.S. (212) 216-7800), (Fax from U.S. (212) 564-7854), www.tandf.co.uk; *The Europa World Year Book.*

United Nations Statistics Division, New York, NY 10017, (800) 253-9646, Fax: (212) 963-4116, http://unstats.un.org; *Statistical Yearbook; Trends in Europe and North America: The Statistical Yearbook of the ECE 2005;* and *World Statistics Pocketbook.*

ISRAEL - TELEVISION - RECEIVERS AND RECEPTION

United Nations Statistics Division, New York, NY 10017, (800) 253-9646, Fax: (212) 963-4116, http://unstats.un.org; *Statistical Yearbook.*

ISRAEL - TEXTILE INDUSTRY

Euromonitor International, Inc., 224 S. Michigan Avenue, Suite 1500, Chicago, IL 60604, (312) 922-1115, Fax: (312) 922-1157, www.euromonitor.com; *Retail Trade International 2007.*

M.E. Sharpe, 80 Business Park Drive, Armonk, NY 10504, (800) 541-6563, Fax: (914) 273-2106, www.mesharpe.com; *The Illustrated Book of World Rankings.*

United Nations Conference on Trade and Development (UNCTAD), DC2-1120, United Nations, New York, NY 10017, (212) 963-0027, www.unctad.org; *UNCTAD Commodity Yearbook.*

United Nations Statistics Division, New York, NY 10017, (800) 253-9646, Fax: (212) 963-4116, http://unstats.un.org; *Statistical Yearbook.*

ISRAEL - TIN PRODUCTION

See ISRAEL - MINERAL INDUSTRIES

ISRAEL - TIRE INDUSTRY

United Nations Statistics Division, New York, NY 10017, (800) 253-9646, Fax: (212) 963-4116, http://unstats.un.org; *Statistical Yearbook.*

ISRAEL - TOBACCO INDUSTRY

Foreign Agricultural Service (FAS), U.S. Department of Agriculture (USDA), 1400 Independence Avenue,

SW, Washington, DC 20250, (202) 720-3935, www.fas.usda.gov; *Tobacco: World Markets and Trade.*

M.E. Sharpe, 80 Business Park Drive, Armonk, NY 10504, (800) 541-6563, Fax: (914) 273-2106, www.mesharpe.com; *The Illustrated Book of World Rankings.*

United Nations Statistics Division, New York, NY 10017, (800) 253-9646, Fax: (212) 963-4116, http://unstats.un.org; *Statistical Yearbook.*

ISRAEL - TOURISM

Euromonitor International, Inc., 224 S. Michigan Avenue, Suite 1500, Chicago, IL 60604, (312) 922-1115, Fax: (312) 922-1157, www.euromonitor.com; *The World Economic Factbook 2008* and *World Marketing Data and Statistics.*

M.E. Sharpe, 80 Business Park Drive, Armonk, NY 10504, (800) 541-6563, Fax: (914) 273-2106, www.mesharpe.com; *The Illustrated Book of World Rankings.*

Taylor and Francis Group, An Informa Business, 2 Park Square, Milton Park, Abingdon, Oxford OX14 4RN, United Kingdom, (Dial from U.S. (212) 216-7800), (Fax from U.S. (212) 564-7854), www.tandf.co.uk; *The Europa World Year Book.*

United Nations Statistics Division, New York, NY 10017, (800) 253-9646, Fax: (212) 963-4116, http://unstats.un.org; *Statistical Yearbook* and *Trends in Europe and North America: The Statistical Yearbook of the ECE 2005.*

United Nations World Tourism Organization (UNWTO), Capitan Haya 42, 28020 Madrid, Spain, www.world-tourism.org; *Yearbook of Tourism Statistics.*

The World Bank, 1818 H Street, NW, Washington, DC 20433, (202) 473-1000, Fax: (202) 477-6391, www.worldbank.org; *Israel.*

ISRAEL - TRANSPORTATION

Central Intelligence Agency, Office of Public Affairs, Washington, DC 20505, (703) 482-0623, Fax: (703) 482-1739, www.cia.gov; *The World Factbook.*

Euromonitor International, Inc., 224 S. Michigan Avenue, Suite 1500, Chicago, IL 60604, (312) 922-1115, Fax: (312) 922-1157, www.euromonitor.com; *World Marketing Data and Statistics.*

M.E. Sharpe, 80 Business Park Drive, Armonk, NY 10504, (800) 541-6563, Fax: (914) 273-2106, www.mesharpe.com; *The Illustrated Book of World Rankings.*

Taylor and Francis Group, An Informa Business, 2 Park Square, Milton Park, Abingdon, Oxford OX14 4RN, United Kingdom, (Dial from U.S. (212) 216-7800), (Fax from U.S. (212) 564-7854), www.tandf.co.uk; *The Europa World Year Book.*

United Nations Statistics Division, New York, NY 10017, (800) 253-9646, Fax: (212) 963-4116, http://unstats.un.org; *Human Development Report 2006* and *Trends in Europe and North America: The Statistical Yearbook of the ECE 2005.*

The World Bank, 1818 H Street, NW, Washington, DC 20433, (202) 473-1000, Fax: (202) 477-6391, www.worldbank.org; *Israel.*

ISRAEL - UNEMPLOYMENT

Central Intelligence Agency, Office of Public Affairs, Washington, DC 20505, (703) 482-0623, Fax: (703) 482-1739, www.cia.gov; *The World Factbook.*

Euromonitor International, Inc., 224 S. Michigan Avenue, Suite 1500, Chicago, IL 60604, (312) 922-1115, Fax: (312) 922-1157, www.euromonitor.com; *International Marketing Data and Statistics 2008.*

International Labour Office, I.L.O. Publications, 4 route des Morillons, CH-1211 Geneva 22, Switzerland, (Telephone in U.S. (202) 653-7652), (Fax in U.S. (202) 653-7687), www.ilo.org; *Yearbook of Labour Statistics 2006.*

United Nations Statistics Division, New York, NY 10017, (800) 253-9646, Fax: (212) 963-4116, http://unstats.un.org; *Statistical Yearbook* and *Trends in Europe and North America: The Statistical Yearbook of the ECE 2005.*

The World Bank, 1818 H Street, NW, Washington, DC 20433, (202) 473-1000, Fax: (202) 477-6391, www.worldbank.org; *Israel.*

ISRAEL - VITAL STATISTICS

Euromonitor International, Inc., 224 S. Michigan Avenue, Suite 1500, Chicago, IL 60604, (312) 922-1115, Fax: (312) 922-1157, www.euromonitor.com; *International Marketing Data and Statistics 2008.*

United Nations Economic and Social Commission for Western Asia (ESCWA), PO Box 11-8575, Riad el-Solh Square, Beirut, Lebanon, www.escwa.un.org; *Annual Report 2006; Bulletin on Population and Vital Statistics in the ESCWA Region;* and *Survey of Economic and Social Developments in the ESCWA Region 2006-2007.*

United Nations Statistics Division, New York, NY 10017, (800) 253-9646, Fax: (212) 963-4116, http://unstats.un.org; *Statistical Yearbook.*

World Health Organization (WHO), Avenue Appia 20, 1211 Geneve 27, Switzerland, (Telephone in U.S. (212) 331-9081), www.who.int; *World Health Report 2006.*

ISRAEL - WAGES

International Labour Office, I.L.O. Publications, 4 route des Morillons, CH-1211 Geneva 22, Switzerland, (Telephone in U.S. (202) 653-7652), (Fax in U.S. (202) 653-7687), www.ilo.org; *Yearbook of Labour Statistics 2006.*

United Nations Statistics Division, New York, NY 10017, (800) 253-9646, Fax: (212) 963-4116, http://unstats.un.org; *Statistical Yearbook.*

The World Bank, 1818 H Street, NW, Washington, DC 20433, (202) 473-1000, Fax: (202) 477-6391, www.worldbank.org; *Israel.*

ISRAEL - WEATHER

See ISRAEL - CLIMATE

ISRAEL - WELFARE STATE

International Monetary Fund (IMF), 700 Nineteenth Street, NW, Washington, DC 20431, (202) 623-7000, Fax: (202) 623-4661, www.imf.org; *Government Finance Statistics Yearbook (2008 Edition).*

ISRAEL - WHEAT PRODUCTION

See ISRAEL - CROPS

ISRAEL - WHOLESALE PRICE INDEXES

International Monetary Fund (IMF), 700 Nineteenth Street, NW, Washington, DC 20431, (202) 623-7000, Fax: (202) 623-4661, www.imf.org; *International Financial Statistics Yearbook 2007.*

United Nations Statistics Division, New York, NY 10017, (800) 253-9646, Fax: (212) 963-4116, http://unstats.un.org; *Statistical Yearbook.*

ISRAEL - WHOLESALE TRADE

United Nations Statistics Division, New York, NY 10017, (800) 253-9646, Fax: (212) 963-4116, http://unstats.un.org; *Statistical Yearbook.*

ISRAEL - WINE PRODUCTION

See ISRAEL - BEVERAGE INDUSTRY

ISRAEL - WOOD AND WOOD PULP

See ISRAEL - FORESTS AND FORESTRY

ISRAEL - WOOL PRODUCTION

See ISRAEL - TEXTILE INDUSTRY

ISRAEL - YARN PRODUCTION

See ISRAEL - TEXTILE INDUSTRY

ISRAEL - ZOOS

UNESCO Institute for Statistics, C.P. 6128 Succursale Centre-Ville, Montreal, Quebec, H3C 3J7 Canada, (Dial from U.S. (514) 343-6880), (Fax from U.S. (514) 343 6882), www.uis.unesco.org; *Statistical Tables.*

ITALY - NATIONAL STATISTICAL OFFICE

Istat - National Institute of Statistics (Instituto Nazionale di Statistica), Via Cesare Balbo 16, 00184 Rome, Italy, www.istat.it/english; National Data Center.

ITALY - PRIMARY STATISTICS SOURCES

Eurostat, Batiment Jean Monnet, Rue Alcide de Gasperi, L-2920 Luxembourg, http://epp.eurostat.ec.europa.eu; *Euro-Mediterranean Statistics 2007* and *Pocketbook on Candidate and Potential Candidate Countries.*

Istat - National Institute of Statistics (Instituto Nazionale di Statistica), Via Cesare Balbo 16, 00184 Rome, Italy, www.istat.it/english; *Italian Statistical Yearbook.*

ITALY - DATABASES

Istat - National Institute of Statistics (Instituto Nazionale di Statistica), Via Cesare Balbo 16, 00184 Rome, Italy, www.istat.it/english; Coeweb: Foreign Trade Statistics; Conlstat: Short-Term Indicators; and Prezzi al Consumo (Consumer price indexes).

ITALY - ABORTION

European Union, Delegation of the European Commission to the United States, 2300 M Street, NW, Washington, DC 20037, (202) 862-9500, Fax: (202) 429-1766, www.eurunion.org; *First Demographic Estimates for 2006.*

United Nations Statistics Division, New York, NY 10017, (800) 253-9646, Fax: (212) 963-4116, http://unstats.un.org; *Trends in Europe and North America: The Statistical Yearbook of the ECE 2005.*

ITALY - AGRICULTURAL MACHINERY

European Union, Delegation of the European Commission to the United States, 2300 M Street, NW, Washington, DC 20037, (202) 862-9500, Fax: (202) 429-1766, www.eurunion.org; *Statistical Overview of Transport in the European Union (Data 1970-2001).*

United Nations Statistics Division, New York, NY 10017, (800) 253-9646, Fax: (212) 963-4116, http://unstats.un.org; *Statistical Yearbook.*

ITALY - AGRICULTURE

Economist Intelligence Unit, 111 West 57th Street, New York, NY 10019, (212) 554-0600, Fax: (212) 586-1181, www.eiu.com; *Italy Country Report.*

Euromonitor International, Inc., 224 S. Michigan Avenue, Suite 1500, Chicago, IL 60604, (312) 922-1115, Fax: (312) 922-1157, www.euromonitor.com; *World Marketing Data and Statistics.*

European Union, Delegation of the European Commission to the United States, 2300 M Street, NW, Washington, DC 20037, (202) 862-9500, Fax: (202) 429-1766, www.eurunion.org; *Agricultural Statistics: Data 1995-2005; European Union Labour Force Survey; Eurostatistics: Data for Short-Term Economic Analysis (2007 edition);* and *Regions - Statistical Yearbook 2006.*

Eurostat, Batiment Jean Monnet, Rue Alcide de Gasperi, L-2920 Luxembourg, http://epp.eurostat.ec.europa.eu; *EU Agricultural Prices in 2007* and *Eurostat Yearbook 2006-2007.*

M.E. Sharpe, 80 Business Park Drive, Armonk, NY 10504, (800) 541-6563, Fax: (914) 273-2106, www.mesharpe.com; *The Illustrated Book of World Rankings.*

Organisation for Economic Cooperation and Development (OECD), 2 rue Andre Pascal, F-75775 Paris Cedex 16, France, (Telephone in U.S. (202) 785-6323), (Fax in U.S. (202) 785-0350), www.oecd.org; *Indicators of Industrial Activity; 2005 OECD Agricultural Outlook Tables, 1970-2014; OECD Agricultural Outlook: 2007-2016; OECD Economic Survey - Italy 2007;* and STructural ANalysis (STAN) database.

Palgrave Macmillan Ltd., Houndmills, Basingstoke, Hampshire, RG21 6XS, England, (Telephone in U.S. (888) 330-8477), (Fax in U.S. (800) 672-2054), www.palgrave.com; *The Statesman's Yearbook 2008.*

Taylor and Francis Group, An Informa Business, 2 Park Square, Milton Park, Abingdon, Oxford OX14 4RN, United Kingdom, (Dial from U.S. (212) 216-7800), (Fax from U.S. (212) 564-7854), www.tandf.co.uk; *The Europa World Year Book.*

United Nations Conference on Trade and Development (UNCTAD), DC2-1120, United Nations, New York, NY 10017, (212) 963-0027, www.unctad.org; *UNCTAD Commodity Yearbook.*

United Nations Food and Agricultural Organization (FAO), Viale delle Terme di Caracalla, 00100 Rome, Italy, (Dial from U.S. (202) 653-2400), (Fax from U.S. (202) 653 5760), www.fao.org; AQUASTAT; *FAO Production Yearbook 2002; FAO Trade Yearbook;* and *The State of Food and Agriculture (SOFA) 2006.*

United Nations Statistics Division, New York, NY 10017, (800) 253-9646, Fax: (212) 963-4116, http://unstats.un.org; *Statistical Yearbook.*

The World Bank, 1818 H Street, NW, Washington, DC 20433, (202) 473-1000, Fax: (202) 477-6391, www.worldbank.org; *Italy* and *World Development Indicators (WDI) 2008.*

ITALY - AIRLINES

European Union, Delegation of the European Commission to the United States, 2300 M Street, NW, Washington, DC 20037, (202) 862-9500, Fax: (202) 429-1766, www.eurunion.org; *Regions - Statistical Yearbook 2006* and *Statistical Overview of Transport in the European Union (Data 1970-2001).*

Eurostat, Batiment Jean Monnet, Rue Alcide de Gasperi, L-2920 Luxembourg, http://epp.eurostat.ec.europa.eu; *Eurostat Yearbook 2006-2007* and *Regional Passenger and Freight Air Transport in Europe in 2006.*

International Civil Aviation Organization (ICAO), External Relations and Public Information Office (EPO), 999 University Street, Montreal, Quebec H3C 5H7, Canada, (Dial from U.S. (514) 954-8219), (Fax from U.S. (514) 954-6077), www.icao.int; *Civil Aviation Statistics of the World.*

M.E. Sharpe, 80 Business Park Drive, Armonk, NY 10504, (800) 541-6563, Fax: (914) 273-2106, www.mesharpe.com; *The Illustrated Book of World Rankings.*

Organisation for Economic Cooperation and Development (OECD), 2 rue Andre Pascal, F-75775 Paris Cedex 16, France, (Telephone in U.S. (202) 785-6323), (Fax in U.S. (202) 785-0350), www.oecd.org; *Household, Tourism, Travel: Trends, Environmental Impacts and Policy Responses.*

Palgrave Macmillan Ltd., Houndmills, Basingstoke, Hampshire, RG21 6XS, England, (Telephone in U.S. (888) 330-8477), (Fax in U.S. (800) 672-2054), www.palgrave.com; *The Statesman's Yearbook 2008.*

Taylor and Francis Group, An Informa Business, 2 Park Square, Milton Park, Abingdon, Oxford OX14 4RN, United Kingdom, (Dial from U.S. (212) 216-7800), (Fax from U.S. (212) 564-7854), www.tandf.co.uk; *The Europa World Year Book.*

United Nations Statistics Division, New York, NY 10017, (800) 253-9646, Fax: (212) 963-4116, http://unstats.un.org; *Statistical Yearbook.*

ITALY - AIRPORTS

Central Intelligence Agency, Office of Public Affairs, Washington, DC 20505, (703) 482-0623, Fax: (703) 482-1739, www.cia.gov; *The World Factbook.*

ITALY - ALMOND PRODUCTION

See ITALY - CROPS

ITALY - ALUMINUM PRODUCTION

See ITALY - MINERAL INDUSTRIES

ITALY - ANIMAL FEEDING

Organisation for Economic Cooperation and Development (OECD), 2 rue Andre Pascal, F-75775 Paris Cedex 16, France, (Telephone in U.S. (202) 785-6323), (Fax in U.S. (202) 785-0350), www.oecd.org; *International Trade by Commodity Statistics (ITCS).*

ITALY - APPLE PRODUCTION

See ITALY - CROPS

ITALY - ARMED FORCES

Central Intelligence Agency, Office of Public Affairs, Washington, DC 20505, (703) 482-0623, Fax: (703) 482-1739, www.cia.gov; *The World Factbook.*

Euromonitor International, Inc., 224 S. Michigan Avenue, Suite 1500, Chicago, IL 60604, (312) 922-1115, Fax: (312) 922-1157, www.euromonitor.com; *World Marketing Data and Statistics.*

European Union, Delegation of the European Commission to the United States, 2300 M Street, NW, Washington, DC 20037, (202) 862-9500, Fax: (202) 429-1766, www.eurunion.org; *RD Expenditure in Europe (2006 edition).*

International Institute for Strategic Studies (IISS), Arundel House, 13-15 Arundel Street, Temple Place, London WC2R 3DX, England, www.iiss.org; *The Military Balance 2007.*

International Monetary Fund (IMF), 700 Nineteenth Street, NW, Washington, DC 20431, (202) 623-7000, Fax: (202) 623-4661, www.imf.org; *Government Finance Statistics Yearbook (2008 Edition).*

Palgrave Macmillan Ltd., Houndmills, Basingstoke, Hampshire, RG21 6XS, England, (Telephone in U.S. (888) 330-8477), (Fax in U.S. (800) 672-2054), www.palgrave.com; *The Statesman's Yearbook 2008.*

U.S. Department of State (DOS), 2201 C Street NW, Washington, DC 20520, (202) 647-4000, www.state.gov; *World Military Expenditures and Arms Transfers (WMEAT).*

United Nations Statistics Division, New York, NY 10017, (800) 253-9646, Fax: (212) 963-4116, http://unstats.un.org; *Human Development Report 2006.*

ITALY - ARTICHOKE PRODUCTION

See ITALY - CROPS

ITALY - AUTOMOBILE INDUSTRY AND TRADE

European Union, Delegation of the European Commission to the United States, 2300 M Street, NW, Washington, DC 20037, (202) 862-9500, Fax: (202) 429-1766, www.eurunion.org; *Eurostatistics: Data for Short-Term Economic Analysis (2007 edition).*

Eurostat, Batiment Jean Monnet, Rue Alcide de Gasperi, L-2920 Luxembourg, http://epp.eurostat.ec.europa.eu; *Eurostat Yearbook 2006-2007.*

Organisation for Economic Cooperation and Development (OECD), 2 rue Andre Pascal, F-75775 Paris Cedex 16, France, (Telephone in U.S. (202) 785-6323), (Fax in U.S. (202) 785-0350), www.oecd.org; *Indicators of Industrial Activity* and *International Trade by Commodity Statistics (ITCS).*

United Nations Statistics Division, New York, NY 10017, (800) 253-9646, Fax: (212) 963-4116, http://unstats.un.org; *Statistical Yearbook.*

ITALY - BALANCE OF PAYMENTS

European Union, Delegation of the European Commission to the United States, 2300 M Street, NW, Washington, DC 20037, (202) 862-9500, Fax: (202) 429-1766, www.eurunion.org; *Eurostatistics: Data for Short-Term Economic Analysis (2007 edition).*

Eurostat, Batiment Jean Monnet, Rue Alcide de Gasperi, L-2920 Luxembourg, http://epp.eurostat.ec.europa.eu; *Eurostat Yearbook 2006-2007.*

International Monetary Fund (IMF), 700 Nineteenth Street, NW, Washington, DC 20431, (202) 623-7000, Fax: (202) 623-4661, www.imf.org; *Balance of Payments Statistics Newsletter; Balance of Payments Statistics Yearbook 2007;* and *International Financial Statistics Yearbook 2007.*

Organisation for Economic Cooperation and Development (OECD), 2 rue Andre Pascal, F-75775 Paris Cedex 16, France, (Telephone in U.S. (202) 785-6323), (Fax in U.S. (202) 785-0350), www.oecd.org; *Geographical Distribution of Financial Flows to Aid Recipients 2002-2006; OECD Economic Outlook 2008; OECD Economic Survey - Italy 2007;* and *OECD Main Economic Indicators (MEI).*

Platts, 2 Penn Plaza, 25th Floor, New York, NY 10121-2298, (212) 904-3070, www.platts.com; *Energy Economist.*

Taylor and Francis Group, An Informa Business, 2 Park Square, Milton Park, Abingdon, Oxford OX14 4RN, United Kingdom, (Dial from U.S. (212) 216-7800), (Fax from U.S. (212) 564-7854), www.tandf.co.uk; *The Europa World Year Book.*

United Nations Conference on Trade and Development (UNCTAD), DC2-1120, United Nations, New York, NY 10017, (212) 963-0027, www.unctad.org; *Handbook of Statistics 2005.*

United Nations Statistics Division, New York, NY 10017, (800) 253-9646, Fax: (212) 963-4116, http://unstats.un.org; *Energy Statistics Yearbook 2003.*

The World Bank, 1818 H Street, NW, Washington, DC 20433, (202) 473-1000, Fax: (202) 477-6391, www.worldbank.org; *Italy; World Development Indicators (WDI) 2008;* and *World Development Report 2008.*

ITALY - BANANAS

See ITALY - CROPS

ITALY - BANKS AND BANKING

Euromonitor International, Inc., 224 S. Michigan Avenue, Suite 1500, Chicago, IL 60604, (312) 922-1115, Fax: (312) 922-1157, www.euromonitor.com; *World Marketing Data and Statistics.*

European Union, Delegation of the European Commission to the United States, 2300 M Street, NW, Washington, DC 20037, (202) 862-9500, Fax: (202) 429-1766, www.eurunion.org; *The EU Economy, 2007 Review: Moving Europe's Productivity Frontier* and *Eurostatistics: Data for Short-Term Economic Analysis (2007 edition).*

Eurostat, Batiment Jean Monnet, Rue Alcide de Gasperi, L-2920 Luxembourg, http://epp.eurostat.ec.europa.eu; *Eurostat Yearbook 2006-2007.*

International Monetary Fund (IMF), 700 Nineteenth Street, NW, Washington, DC 20431, (202) 623-7000, Fax: (202) 623-4661, www.imf.org; *International Financial Statistics Yearbook 2007.*

M.E. Sharpe, 80 Business Park Drive, Armonk, NY 10504, (800) 541-6563, Fax: (914) 273-2106, www.mesharpe.com; *The Illustrated Book of World Rankings.*

Organisation for Economic Cooperation and Development (OECD), 2 rue Andre Pascal, F-75775 Paris Cedex 16, France, (Telephone in U.S. (202) 785-6323), (Fax in U.S. (202) 785-0350), www.oecd.org; *Financial Market Trends: OECD Periodical; OECD Economic Outlook 2008;* and *OECD Economic Survey - Italy 2007.*

Palgrave Macmillan Ltd., Houndmills, Basingstoke, Hampshire, RG21 6XS, England, (Telephone in U.S. (888) 330-8477), (Fax in U.S. (800) 672-2054), www.palgrave.com; *The Statesman's Yearbook 2008.*

Taylor and Francis Group, An Informa Business, 2 Park Square, Milton Park, Abingdon, Oxford OX14 4RN, United Kingdom, (Dial from U.S. (212) 216-7800), (Fax from U.S. (212) 564-7854), www.tandf.co.uk; *The Europa World Year Book.*

United Nations Statistics Division, New York, NY 10017, (800) 253-9646, Fax: (212) 963-4116, http://unstats.un.org; *Statistical Yearbook.*

ITALY - BARLEY PRODUCTION

See ITALY - CROPS

ITALY - BEVERAGE INDUSTRY

Eurostat, Batiment Jean Monnet, Rue Alcide de Gasperi, L-2920 Luxembourg, http://epp.eurostat.ec.europa.eu; *Eurostat Yearbook 2006-2007.*

M.E. Sharpe, 80 Business Park Drive, Armonk, NY 10504, (800) 541-6563, Fax: (914) 273-2106, www.mesharpe.com; *The Illustrated Book of World Rankings.*

Organisation for Economic Cooperation and Development (OECD), 2 rue Andre Pascal, F-75775 Paris Cedex 16, France, (Telephone in U.S. (202) 785-6323), (Fax in U.S. (202) 785-0350), www.oecd.org; *Indicators of Industrial Activity.*

United Nations Statistics Division, New York, NY 10017, (800) 253-9646, Fax: (212) 963-4116, http://unstats.un.org; *Statistical Yearbook.*

ITALY - BONDS

Eurostat, Batiment Jean Monnet, Rue Alcide de Gasperi, L-2920 Luxembourg, http://epp.eurostat.ec.europa.eu; *Eurostat Yearbook 2006-2007.*

International Monetary Fund (IMF), 700 Nineteenth Street, NW, Washington, DC 20431, (202) 623-7000, Fax: (202) 623-4661, www.imf.org; *Government Finance Statistics Yearbook (2008 Edition).*

Organisation for Economic Cooperation and Development (OECD), 2 rue Andre Pascal, F-75775 Paris Cedex 16, France, (Telephone in U.S. (202) 785-6323), (Fax in U.S. (202) 785-0350), www.oecd.org; *Financial Market Trends: OECD Periodical.*

United Nations Statistics Division, New York, NY 10017, (800) 253-9646, Fax: (212) 963-4116, http://unstats.un.org; *Statistical Yearbook.*

ITALY - BROADCASTING

Central Intelligence Agency, Office of Public Affairs, Washington, DC 20505, (703) 482-0623, Fax: (703) 482-1739, www.cia.gov; *The World Factbook.*

Euromonitor International, Inc., 224 S. Michigan Avenue, Suite 1500, Chicago, IL 60604, (312) 922-1115, Fax: (312) 922-1157, www.euromonitor.com; *World Marketing Data and Statistics.*

Eurostat, Batiment Jean Monnet, Rue Alcide de Gasperi, L-2920 Luxembourg, http://epp.eurostat.ec.europa.eu; *Eurostat Yearbook 2006-2007.*

M.E. Sharpe, 80 Business Park Drive, Armonk, NY 10504, (800) 541-6563, Fax: (914) 273-2106, www.mesharpe.com; *The Illustrated Book of World Rankings.*

Palgrave Macmillan Ltd., Houndmills, Basingstoke, Hampshire, RG21 6XS, England, (Telephone in U.S. (888) 330-8477), (Fax in U.S. (800) 672-2054), www.palgrave.com; *The Statesman's Yearbook 2008.*

UNESCO Institute for Statistics, C.P. 6128 Succursale Centre-Ville, Montreal, Quebec, H3C 3J7 Canada, (Dial from U.S. (514) 343-6880), (Fax from U.S. (514) 343 6882), www.uis.unesco.org; *Statistical Tables.*

United Nations Statistics Division, New York, NY 10017, (800) 253-9646, Fax: (212) 963-4116, http://unstats.un.org; *Trends in Europe and North America: The Statistical Yearbook of the ECE 2005.*

WRTH Publications Limited, PO Box 290, Oxford OX2 7FT, UK, www.wrth.com; *World Radio TV Handbook 2007.*

ITALY - BUDGET

Central Intelligence Agency, Office of Public Affairs, Washington, DC 20505, (703) 482-0623, Fax: (703) 482-1739, www.cia.gov; *The World Factbook.*

ITALY - BUSINESS

Eurostat, Batiment Jean Monnet, Rue Alcide de Gasperi, L-2920 Luxembourg, http://epp.eurostat.ec.europa.eu; *Eurostat Yearbook 2006-2007.*

Organisation for Economic Cooperation and Development (OECD), 2 rue Andre Pascal, F-75775 Paris Cedex 16, France, (Telephone in U.S. (202) 785-6323), (Fax in U.S. (202) 785-0350), www.oecd.org; *OECD Main Economic Indicators (MEI).*

ITALY - CADMIUM PRODUCTION

See ITALY - MINERAL INDUSTRIES

ITALY - CAPITAL INVESTMENTS

Organisation for Economic Cooperation and Development (OECD), 2 rue Andre Pascal, F-75775 Paris Cedex 16, France, (Telephone in U.S. (202) 785-6323), (Fax in U.S. (202) 785-0350), www.oecd.org; *Financial Market Trends: OECD Periodical* and *OECD Economic Outlook 2008.*

ITALY - CAPITAL LEVY

International Monetary Fund (IMF), 700 Nineteenth Street, NW, Washington, DC 20431, (202) 623-7000, Fax: (202) 623-4661, www.imf.org; *Government Finance Statistics Yearbook (2008 Edition).*

Organisation for Economic Cooperation and Development (OECD), 2 rue Andre Pascal, F-75775 Paris Cedex 16, France, (Telephone in U.S. (202) 785-6323), (Fax in U.S. (202) 785-0350), www.oecd.org; *Financial Market Trends: OECD Periodical* and *OECD Economic Outlook 2008.*

ITALY - CATTLE

See ITALY - LIVESTOCK

ITALY - CHESTNUT PRODUCTION

See ITALY - CROPS

ITALY - CHICK PEA PRODUCTION

See ITALY - CROPS

ITALY - CHICKENS

See ITALY - LIVESTOCK

ITALY - CHILDBIRTH - STATISTICS

Central Intelligence Agency, Office of Public Affairs, Washington, DC 20505, (703) 482-0623, Fax: (703) 482-1739, www.cia.gov; *The World Factbook.*

Euromonitor International, Inc., 224 S. Michigan Avenue, Suite 1500, Chicago, IL 60604, (312) 922-1115, Fax: (312) 922-1157, www.euromonitor.com; *The World Economic Factbook 2008.*

European Union, Delegation of the European Commission to the United States, 2300 M Street, NW, Washington, DC 20037, (202) 862-9500, Fax: (202) 429-1766, www.eurunion.org; *First Demographic Estimates for 2006.*

Eurostat, Batiment Jean Monnet, Rue Alcide de Gasperi, L-2920 Luxembourg, http://epp.eurostat.ec.europa.eu; *Eurostat Yearbook 2006-2007.*

M.E. Sharpe, 80 Business Park Drive, Armonk, NY 10504, (800) 541-6563, Fax: (914) 273-2106, www.mesharpe.com; *The Illustrated Book of World Rankings.*

Palgrave Macmillan Ltd., Houndmills, Basingstoke, Hampshire, RG21 6XS, England, (Telephone in U.S. (888) 330-8477), (Fax in U.S. (800) 672-2054), www.palgrave.com; *The Statesman's Yearbook 2008.*

Taylor and Francis Group, An Informa Business, 2 Park Square, Milton Park, Abingdon, Oxford OX14 4RN, United Kingdom, (Dial from U.S. (212) 216-7800), (Fax from U.S. (212) 564-7854), www.tandf.co.uk; *The Europa World Year Book.*

United Nations Statistics Division, New York, NY 10017, (800) 253-9646, Fax: (212) 963-4116, http://unstats.un.org; *Demographic Yearbook* and *Statistical Yearbook.*

The World Bank, 1818 H Street, NW, Washington, DC 20433, (202) 473-1000, Fax: (202) 477-6391, www.worldbank.org; *World Development Indicators (WDI) 2008.*

World Health Organization (WHO), Avenue Appia 20, 1211 Geneve 27, Switzerland, (Telephone in U.S. (212) 331-9081), www.who.int; *World Health Report 2006.*

ITALY - CLIMATE

M.E. Sharpe, 80 Business Park Drive, Armonk, NY 10504, (800) 541-6563, Fax: (914) 273-2106, www.mesharpe.com; *The Illustrated Book of World Rankings.*

Palgrave Macmillan Ltd., Houndmills, Basingstoke, Hampshire, RG21 6XS, England, (Telephone in U.S. (888) 330-8477), (Fax in U.S. (800) 672-2054), www.palgrave.com; *The Statesman's Yearbook 2008.*

ITALY - CLOTHING EXPORTS AND IMPORTS

See ITALY - TEXTILE INDUSTRY

ITALY - COAL PRODUCTION

See ITALY - MINERAL INDUSTRIES

ITALY - COBALT PRODUCTION

See ITALY - MINERAL INDUSTRIES

ITALY - COCOA PRODUCTION

See ITALY - CROPS

ITALY - COFFEE

See ITALY - CROPS

ITALY - COMMERCE

Palgrave Macmillan Ltd., Houndmills, Basingstoke, Hampshire, RG21 6XS, England, (Telephone in U.S. (888) 330-8477), (Fax in U.S. (800) 672-2054), www.palgrave.com; *The Statesman's Yearbook 2008.*

ITALY - COMMODITY EXCHANGES

Commodity Research Bureau, 330 South Wells Street, Suite 612, Chicago, IL 60606-7110, (800) 621-5271, Fax: (312) 939-4135, www.crbtrader.com; *2006 CRB Commodity Yearbook and CD.*

International Lead and Zinc Study Group (ILZSG), Rua Almirante Barroso 38, 5th Floor, Lisbon 1000 - 013, Portugal, www.ilzsg.org; Interactive Statistical Database.

International Monetary Fund (IMF), 700 Nineteenth Street, NW, Washington, DC 20431, (202) 623-7000, Fax: (202) 623-4661, www.imf.org; *IMF Primary Commodity Prices.*

United Nations Food and Agricultural Organization (FAO), Viale delle Terme di Caracalla, 00100 Rome, Italy, (Dial from U.S. (202) 653-2400), (Fax from U.S. (202) 653 5760), www.fao.org; *The State of Food and Agriculture (SOFA) 2006.*

United Nations Statistics Division, New York, NY 10017, (800) 253-9646, Fax: (212) 963-4116, http://unstats.un.org; *Statistical Yearbook.*

World Bureau of Metal Statistics (WBMS), 27a High Street, Ware, Hertfordshire, SG12 9BA, United Kingdom, www.world-bureau.com; *Annual Stainless Steel Statistics; World Flow Charts; World Metal Statistics; World Nickel Statistics;* and *World Tin Statistics.*

ITALY - COMMUNICATION AND TRAFFIC

European Union, Delegation of the European Commission to the United States, 2300 M Street, NW, Washington, DC 20037, (202) 862-9500, Fax: (202) 429-1766, www.eurunion.org; *Statistical Overview of Transport in the European Union (Data 1970-2001).*

United Nations Statistics Division, New York, NY 10017, (800) 253-9646, Fax: (212) 963-4116, http://unstats.un.org; *Statistical Yearbook.*

ITALY - CONSTRUCTION INDUSTRY

European Union, Delegation of the European Commission to the United States, 2300 M Street, NW,

Washington, DC 20037, (202) 862-9500, Fax: (202) 429-1766, www.eurunion.org; *European Union Labour Force Survey.*

Eurostat, Batiment Jean Monnet, Rue Alcide de Gasperi, L-2920 Luxembourg, http://epp.eurostat.ec.europa.eu; *Eurostat Yearbook 2006-2007.*

M.E. Sharpe, 80 Business Park Drive, Armonk, NY 10504, (800) 541-6563, Fax: (914) 273-2106, www.mesharpe.com; *The Illustrated Book of World Rankings.*

Organisation for Economic Cooperation and Development (OECD), 2 rue Andre Pascal, F-75775 Paris Cedex 16, France, (Telephone in U.S. (202) 785-6323), (Fax in U.S. (202) 785-0350), www.oecd.org; *Iron and Steel Industry in 2004 (2006 Edition); OECD Economic Survey - Italy 2007; OECD Main Economic Indicators (MEI);* and STructural ANalysis (STAN) database.

Palgrave Macmillan Ltd., Houndmills, Basingstoke, Hampshire, RG21 6XS, England, (Telephone in U.S. (888) 330-8477), (Fax in U.S. (800) 672-2054), www.palgrave.com; *The Statesman's Yearbook 2008.*

United Nations Statistics Division, New York, NY 10017, (800) 253-9646, Fax: (212) 963-4116, http://unstats.un.org; *Statistical Yearbook.*

ITALY - CONSUMER PRICE INDEXES

European Union, Delegation of the European Commission to the United States, 2300 M Street, NW, Washington, DC 20037, (202) 862-9500, Fax: (202) 429-1766, www.eurunion.org; *Eurostatistics: Data for Short-Term Economic Analysis (2007 edition).*

Eurostat, Batiment Jean Monnet, Rue Alcide de Gasperi, L-2920 Luxembourg, http://epp.eurostat.ec.europa.eu; *Eurostat Yearbook 2006-2007.*

Organisation for Economic Cooperation and Development (OECD), 2 rue Andre Pascal, F-75775 Paris Cedex 16, France, (Telephone in U.S. (202) 785-6323), (Fax in U.S. (202) 785-0350), www.oecd.org; *OECD Economic Outlook 2008.*

Taylor and Francis Group, An Informa Business, 2 Park Square, Milton Park, Abingdon, Oxford OX14 4RN, United Kingdom, (Dial from U.S. (212) 216-7800), (Fax from U.S. (212) 564-7854), www.tandf.co.uk; *The Europa World Year Book.*

United Nations Statistics Division, New York, NY 10017, (800) 253-9646, Fax: (212) 963-4116, http://unstats.un.org; *Statistical Yearbook* and *Trends in Europe and North America: The Statistical Yearbook of the ECE 2005.*

The World Bank, 1818 H Street, NW, Washington, DC 20433, (202) 473-1000, Fax: (202) 477-6391, www.worldbank.org; *Italy.*

ITALY - CONSUMPTION (ECONOMICS)

Eurostat, Batiment Jean Monnet, Rue Alcide de Gasperi, L-2920 Luxembourg, http://epp.eurostat.ec.europa.eu; *Eurostat Yearbook 2006-2007.*

International Iron and Steel Institute (IISI), Rue Colonel Bourg 120, B-1140 Brussels, Belgium, www.worldsteel.org; *Steel Statistical Yearbook 2006.*

International Lead and Zinc Study Group (ILZSG), Rua Almirante Barroso 38, 5th Floor, Lisbon 1000 - 013, Portugal, www.ilzsg.org; Interactive Statistical Database.

International Monetary Fund (IMF), 700 Nineteenth Street, NW, Washington, DC 20431, (202) 623-7000, Fax: (202) 623-4661, www.imf.org; *International Financial Statistics Yearbook 2007.*

Organisation for Economic Cooperation and Development (OECD), 2 rue Andre Pascal, F-75775 Paris Cedex 16, France, (Telephone in U.S. (202) 785-6323), (Fax in U.S. (202) 785-0350), www.oecd.org; *Environmental Impacts of Foreign Direct Investment in the Mining Sector in the Newly Independent States (NIS); Iron and Steel Industry in 2004 (2006 Edition); A New World Map in Textiles and Clothing: Adjusting to Change; 2005 OECD Agricultural Outlook Tables, 1970-2014;* and *Towards Sustainable Household Consumption?: Trends and Policies in OECD Countries.*

Technical Association of the Pulp and Paper Industry (TAPPI), 15 Technology Parkway South, Norcross, GA 30092, (770) 446-1400, Fax: (770) 446-6947, www.tappi.org; *TAPPI Annual Report.*

The World Bank, 1818 H Street, NW, Washington, DC 20433, (202) 473-1000, Fax: (202) 477-6391, www.worldbank.org; *World Development Report 2008.*

ITALY - COPPER INDUSTRY AND TRADE

See ITALY - MINERAL INDUSTRIES

ITALY - CORN INDUSTRY

See ITALY - CROPS

ITALY - COST AND STANDARD OF LIVING

Eurostat, Batiment Jean Monnet, Rue Alcide de Gasperi, L-2920 Luxembourg, http://epp.eurostat.ec.europa.eu; *Eurostat Yearbook 2006-2007.*

International Monetary Fund (IMF), 700 Nineteenth Street, NW, Washington, DC 20431, (202) 623-7000, Fax: (202) 623-4661, www.imf.org; *Government Finance Statistics Yearbook (2008 Edition).*

ITALY - COTTON

See ITALY - CROPS

ITALY - CRIME

Eurostat, Batiment Jean Monnet, Rue Alcide de Gasperi, L-2920 Luxembourg, http://epp.eurostat.ec.europa.eu; *Crime and Criminal Justice; General Government Expenditure and Revenue in the EU, 2006;* and *Study on Crime Victimisation.*

U.S. Department of Justice (DOJ), Bureau of Justice Statistics, 810 Seventh Street, NW, Washington, DC 20531, (202) 307-0765, www.ojp.usdoj.gov/bjs/; *The World Factbook of Criminal Justice Systems.*

United Nations Statistics Division, New York, NY 10017, (800) 253-9646, Fax: (212) 963-4116, http://unstats.un.org; *Trends in Europe and North America: The Statistical Yearbook of the ECE 2005.*

Yale University Press, PO Box 209040, New Haven, CT 06520-9040, (203) 432-0960, Fax: (203) 432-0948, http://yalepress.yale.edu/yupbooks; *Violence and Crime in Cross-National Perspective.*

ITALY - CROPS

Euromonitor International, Inc., 224 S. Michigan Avenue, Suite 1500, Chicago, IL 60604, (312) 922-1115, Fax: (312) 922-1157, www.euromonitor.com; *European Marketing Data and Statistics 2008.*

European Union, Delegation of the European Commission to the United States, 2300 M Street, NW, Washington, DC 20037, (202) 862-9500, Fax: (202) 429-1766, www.eurunion.org; *Agricultural Statistics: Data 1995-2005; Agriculture in the European Union: Statistical and Economic Information 2006; Eurostatistics: Data for Short-Term Economic Analysis (2007 edition);* and *Regions - Statistical Yearbook 2006.*

Eurostat, Batiment Jean Monnet, Rue Alcide de Gasperi, L-2920 Luxembourg, http://epp.eurostat.ec.europa.eu; *Eurostat Yearbook 2006-2007.*

M.E. Sharpe, 80 Business Park Drive, Armonk, NY 10504, (800) 541-6563, Fax: (914) 273-2106, www.mesharpe.com; *The Illustrated Book of World Rankings.*

Organisation for Economic Cooperation and Development (OECD), 2 rue Andre Pascal, F-75775 Paris Cedex 16, France, (Telephone in U.S. (202) 785-6323), (Fax in U.S. (202) 785-0350), www.oecd.org; *International Trade by Commodity Statistics (ITCS)* and *2005 OECD Agricultural Outlook Tables, 1970-2014.*

Palgrave Macmillan Ltd., Houndmills, Basingstoke, Hampshire, RG21 6XS, England, (Telephone in U.S. (888) 330-8477), (Fax in U.S. (800) 672-2054), www.palgrave.com; *The Statesman's Yearbook 2008.*

Taylor and Francis Group, An Informa Business, 2 Park Square, Milton Park, Abingdon, Oxford OX14 4RN, United Kingdom, (Dial from U.S. (212) 216-7800), (Fax from U.S. (212) 564-7854), www.tandf.co.uk; *The Europa World Year Book.*

United Nations Conference on Trade and Development (UNCTAD), DC2-1120, United Nations, New York, NY 10017, (212) 963-0027, www.unctad.org; *UNCTAD Commodity Yearbook.*

United Nations Food and Agricultural Organization (FAO), Viale delle Terme di Caracalla, 00100 Rome, Italy, (Dial from U.S. (202) 653-2400), (Fax from U.S. (202) 653 5760), www.fao.org; *FAO Production Yearbook 2002* and *The State of Food and Agriculture (SOFA) 2006.*

United Nations Statistics Division, New York, NY 10017, (800) 253-9646, Fax: (212) 963-4116, http://unstats.un.org; *Statistical Yearbook.*

ITALY - CUSTOMS ADMINISTRATION

Eurostat, Batiment Jean Monnet, Rue Alcide de Gasperi, L-2920 Luxembourg, http://epp.eurostat.ec.europa.eu; *Eurostat Yearbook 2006-2007.*

International Monetary Fund (IMF), 700 Nineteenth Street, NW, Washington, DC 20431, (202) 623-7000, Fax: (202) 623-4661, www.imf.org; *Government Finance Statistics Yearbook (2008 Edition).*

Organisation for Economic Cooperation and Development (OECD), 2 rue Andre Pascal, F-75775 Paris Cedex 16, France, (Telephone in U.S. (202) 785-6323), (Fax in U.S. (202) 785-0350), www.oecd.org; *Environmental Impacts of Foreign Direct Investment in the Mining Sector in the Newly Independent States (NIS).*

ITALY - DAIRY PROCESSING

European Union, Delegation of the European Commission to the United States, 2300 M Street, NW, Washington, DC 20037, (202) 862-9500, Fax: (202) 429-1766, www.eurunion.org; *Eurostatistics: Data for Short-Term Economic Analysis (2007 edition).*

Eurostat, Batiment Jean Monnet, Rue Alcide de Gasperi, L-2920 Luxembourg, http://epp.eurostat.ec.europa.eu; *Eurostat Yearbook 2006-2007.*

M.E. Sharpe, 80 Business Park Drive, Armonk, NY 10504, (800) 541-6563, Fax: (914) 273-2106, www.mesharpe.com; *The Illustrated Book of World Rankings.*

Organisation for Economic Cooperation and Development (OECD), 2 rue Andre Pascal, F-75775 Paris Cedex 16, France, (Telephone in U.S. (202) 785-6323), (Fax in U.S. (202) 785-0350), www.oecd.org; *2005 OECD Agricultural Outlook Tables, 1970-2014.*

Palgrave Macmillan Ltd., Houndmills, Basingstoke, Hampshire, RG21 6XS, England, (Telephone in U.S. (888) 330-8477), (Fax in U.S. (800) 672-2054), www.palgrave.com; *The Statesman's Yearbook 2008.*

Taylor and Francis Group, An Informa Business, 2 Park Square, Milton Park, Abingdon, Oxford OX14 4RN, United Kingdom, (Dial from U.S. (212) 216-7800), (Fax from U.S. (212) 564-7854), www.tandf.co.uk; *The Europa World Year Book.*

United Nations Food and Agricultural Organization (FAO), Viale delle Terme di Caracalla, 00100 Rome, Italy, (Dial from U.S. (202) 653-2400), (Fax from U.S. (202) 653 5760), www.fao.org; *FAO Production Yearbook 2002* and *The State of Food and Agriculture (SOFA) 2006.*

United Nations Statistics Division, New York, NY 10017, (800) 253-9646, Fax: (212) 963-4116, http://unstats.un.org; *Statistical Yearbook.*

ITALY - DEATH RATES

See ITALY - MORTALITY

ITALY - DEBTS, EXTERNAL

Organisation for Economic Cooperation and Development (OECD), 2 rue Andre Pascal, F-75775 Paris Cedex 16, France, (Telephone in U.S. (202) 785-6323), (Fax in U.S. (202) 785-0350), www.oecd.org; *Financial Market Trends: OECD Periodical; Geographical Distribution of Financial Flows to Aid Recipients 2002-2006;* and *OECD Economic Outlook 2008.*

Palgrave Macmillan Ltd., Houndmills, Basingstoke, Hampshire, RG21 6XS, England, (Telephone in U.S. (888) 330-8477), (Fax in U.S. (800) 672-2054), www.palgrave.com; *The Statesman's Yearbook 2008.*

The World Bank, 1818 H Street, NW, Washington, DC 20433, (202) 473-1000, Fax: (202) 477-6391, www.worldbank.org; *Global Development Finance 2007; World Development Indicators (WDI) 2008;* and *World Development Report 2008.*

ITALY - DEFENSE EXPENDITURES

See ITALY - ARMED FORCES

ITALY - DEMOGRAPHY

Euromonitor International, Inc., 224 S. Michigan Avenue, Suite 1500, Chicago, IL 60604, (312) 922-1115, Fax: (312) 922-1157, www.euromonitor.com; *The World Economic Factbook 2008* and *World Marketing Data and Statistics.*

European Union, Delegation of the European Commission to the United States, 2300 M Street, NW, Washington, DC 20037, (202) 862-9500, Fax: (202) 429-1766, www.eurunion.org; *First Demographic Estimates for 2006* and *Regions - Statistical Yearbook 2006.*

Eurostat, Batiment Jean Monnet, Rue Alcide de Gasperi, L-2920 Luxembourg, http://epp.eurostat.ec.europa.eu; *Demographic Outlook - National Reports on the Demographic Developments in 2006* and *Eurostat Yearbook 2006-2007.*

M.E. Sharpe, 80 Business Park Drive, Armonk, NY 10504, (800) 541-6563, Fax: (914) 273-2106, www.mesharpe.com; *The Illustrated Book of World Rankings.*

United Nations Statistics Division, New York, NY 10017, (800) 253-9646, Fax: (212) 963-4116, http://unstats.un.org; *Human Development Report 2006.*

The World Bank, 1818 H Street, NW, Washington, DC 20433, (202) 473-1000, Fax: (202) 477-6391, www.worldbank.org; *Italy.*

ITALY - DIAMONDS

See ITALY - MINERAL INDUSTRIES

ITALY - DISPOSABLE INCOME

M.E. Sharpe, 80 Business Park Drive, Armonk, NY 10504, (800) 541-6563, Fax: (914) 273-2106, www.mesharpe.com; *The Illustrated Book of World Rankings.*

Organisation for Economic Cooperation and Development (OECD), 2 rue Andre Pascal, F-75775 Paris Cedex 16, France, (Telephone in U.S. (202) 785-6323), (Fax in U.S. (202) 785-0350), www.oecd.org; *OECD Economic Outlook 2008.*

United Nations Statistics Division, New York, NY 10017, (800) 253-9646, Fax: (212) 963-4116, http://unstats.un.org; *National Accounts Statistics: Compendium of Income Distribution Statistics* and *Statistical Yearbook.*

ITALY - DIVORCE

European Union, Delegation of the European Commission to the United States, 2300 M Street, NW, Washington, DC 20037, (202) 862-9500, Fax: (202) 429-1766, www.eurunion.org; *First Demographic Estimates for 2006.*

M.E. Sharpe, 80 Business Park Drive, Armonk, NY 10504, (800) 541-6563, Fax: (914) 273-2106, www.mesharpe.com; *The Illustrated Book of World Rankings.*

United Nations Statistics Division, New York, NY 10017, (800) 253-9646, Fax: (212) 963-4116, http://unstats.un.org; *Demographic Yearbook; Statistical Yearbook;* and *Trends in Europe and North America: The Statistical Yearbook of the ECE 2005.*

ITALY - ECONOMIC ASSISTANCE

European Union, Delegation of the European Commission to the United States, 2300 M Street, NW, Washington, DC 20037, (202) 862-9500, Fax: (202) 429-1766, www.eurunion.org; *RD Expenditure in Europe (2006 edition).*

Eurostat, Batiment Jean Monnet, Rue Alcide de Gasperi, L-2920 Luxembourg, http://epp.eurostat.ec.europa.eu; *Eurostat Yearbook 2006-2007.*

Organisation for Economic Cooperation and Development (OECD), 2 rue Andre Pascal, F-75775 Paris Cedex 16, France, (Telephone in U.S. (202) 785-6323), (Fax in U.S. (202) 785-0350), www.oecd.org; *Geographical Distribution of Financial Flows to Aid Recipients 2002-2006.*

United Nations Statistics Division, New York, NY 10017, (800) 253-9646, Fax: (212) 963-4116, http://unstats.un.org; *Statistical Yearbook.*

ITALY - ECONOMIC CONDITIONS

Center for International Business Education Research (CIBER), Columbia Business School and School of International and Public Affairs, Uris Hall, Room 212, 3022 Broadway, New York, NY 10027-6902, Mr. Joshua Safier, (212) 854-4750, Fax: (212) 222-9821, www.columbia.edu/cu/ciber/; Datastream International.

Central Intelligence Agency, Office of Public Affairs, Washington, DC 20505, (703) 482-0623, Fax: (703) 482-1739, www.cia.gov; *The World Factbook.*

DSI Data Service Information, Xantener Strasse 51a, D-47495 Rheinberg, Germany, www.dsidata.com; *Campus Solution.*

Dun and Bradstreet (DB) Corporation, 103 JFK Parkway, Short Hills, NJ 07078, (973) 921-5500, www.dnb.com; *Country Report.*

Economist Intelligence Unit, 111 West 57th Street, New York, NY 10019, (212) 554-0600, Fax: (212) 586-1181, www.eiu.com; *Italy Country Report.*

Euromonitor International, Inc., 224 S. Michigan Avenue, Suite 1500, Chicago, IL 60604, (312) 922-1115, Fax: (312) 922-1157, www.euromonitor.com; *European Marketing Data and Statistics 2008; The World Economic Factbook 2008;* and *World Marketing Data and Statistics.*

European Union, Delegation of the European Commission to the United States, 2300 M Street, NW, Washington, DC 20037, (202) 862-9500, Fax: (202) 429-1766, www.eurunion.org; *The EU Economy, 2007 Review: Moving Europe's Productivity Frontier* and *European Union Labour Force Survey.*

Eurostat, Batiment Jean Monnet, Rue Alcide de Gasperi, L-2920 Luxembourg, http://epp.eurostat.ec.europa.eu; *Consumers in Europe - Facts and Figures on Services of General Interest; EU Economic Data Pocketbook;* and *Eurostat Yearbook 2006-2007.*

Federal Statistical Office Germany, D-65180 Wiesbaden, Germany, www.destatis.de; *Italy 2006.*

International Monetary Fund (IMF), 700 Nineteenth Street, NW, Washington, DC 20431, (202) 623-7000, Fax: (202) 623-4661, www.imf.org; *International Financial Statistics Yearbook 2007* and *World Economic Outlook Reports.*

M.E. Sharpe, 80 Business Park Drive, Armonk, NY 10504, (800) 541-6563, Fax: (914) 273-2106, www.mesharpe.com; *The Illustrated Book of World Rankings.*

Organisation for Economic Cooperation and Development (OECD), 2 rue Andre Pascal, F-75775 Paris Cedex 16, France, (Telephone in U.S. (202) 785-6323), (Fax in U.S. (202) 785-0350), www.oecd.org; *Geographical Distribution of Financial Flows to Aid Recipients 2002-2006; ICT Sector Data and Metadata by Country; Labour Force Statistics: 1986-2005, 2007 Edition; OECD Composite Leading Indicators (CLIs), Updated September 2007; OECD Economic Outlook 2008; OECD Economic Survey - Italy 2007; OECD Employment Outlook 2007;* and *OECD in Figures 2007.*

Palgrave Macmillan Ltd., Houndmills, Basingstoke, Hampshire, RG21 6XS, England, (Telephone in U.S. (888) 330-8477), (Fax in U.S. (800) 672-2054), www.palgrave.com; *The Statesman's Yearbook 2008.*

Platts, 2 Penn Plaza, 25th Floor, New York, NY 10121-2298, (212) 904-3070, www.platts.com; *Energy Economist.*

Taylor and Francis Group, An Informa Business, 2 Park Square, Milton Park, Abingdon, Oxford OX14 4RN, United Kingdom, (Dial from U.S. (212) 216-7800), (Fax from U.S. (212) 564-7854), www.tandf.co.uk; *The Europa World Year Book.*

United Nations Statistics Division, New York, NY 10017, (800) 253-9646, Fax: (212) 963-4116, http://unstats.un.org; *Energy Statistics Yearbook 2003* and *World Statistics Pocketbook.*

The World Bank, 1818 H Street, NW, Washington, DC 20433, (202) 473-1000, Fax: (202) 477-6391, www.worldbank.org; *Global Economic Monitor (GEM); Global Economic Prospects 2008; Italy; The World Bank Atlas 2003-2004;* and *World Development Report 2008.*

ITALY - ECONOMICS - SOCIOLOGICAL ASPECTS

Eurostat, Batiment Jean Monnet, Rue Alcide de Gasperi, L-2920 Luxembourg, http://epp.eurostat.ec.europa.eu; *Eurostat Yearbook 2006-2007.*

Organisation for Economic Cooperation and Development (OECD), 2 rue Andre Pascal, F-75775 Paris Cedex 16, France, (Telephone in U.S. (202) 785-6323), (Fax in U.S. (202) 785-0350), www.oecd.org; *OECD Economic Outlook 2008.*

ITALY - EDUCATION

Euromonitor International, Inc., 224 S. Michigan Avenue, Suite 1500, Chicago, IL 60604, (312) 922-1115, Fax: (312) 922-1157, www.euromonitor.com; *European Marketing Data and Statistics 2008* and *World Marketing Data and Statistics.*

European Union, Delegation of the European Commission to the United States, 2300 M Street, NW, Washington, DC 20037, (202) 862-9500, Fax: (202) 429-1766, www.eurunion.org; *Education across Europe 2003* and *Regions - Statistical Yearbook 2006.*

Eurostat, Batiment Jean Monnet, Rue Alcide de Gasperi, L-2920 Luxembourg, http://epp.eurostat.ec.europa.eu; *Education, Science and Culture Statistics* and *Eurostat Yearbook 2006-2007.*

International Monetary Fund (IMF), 700 Nineteenth Street, NW, Washington, DC 20431, (202) 623-7000, Fax: (202) 623-4661, www.imf.org; *Government Finance Statistics Yearbook (2008 Edition).*

M.E. Sharpe, 80 Business Park Drive, Armonk, NY 10504, (800) 541-6563, Fax: (914) 273-2106, www.mesharpe.com; *The Illustrated Book of World Rankings.*

Organisation for Economic Cooperation and Development (OECD), 2 rue Andre Pascal, F-75775 Paris Cedex 16, France, (Telephone in U.S. (202) 785-6323), (Fax in U.S. (202) 785-0350), www.oecd.org; *Education at a Glance* (2007 Edition).

Palgrave Macmillan Ltd., Houndmills, Basingstoke, Hampshire, RG21 6XS, England, (Telephone in U.S. (888) 330-8477), (Fax in U.S. (800) 672-2054), www.palgrave.com; *The Statesman's Yearbook 2008.*

Taylor and Francis Group, An Informa Business, 2 Park Square, Milton Park, Abingdon, Oxford OX14 4RN, United Kingdom, (Dial from U.S. (212) 216-7800), (Fax from U.S. (212) 564-7854), www.tandf.co.uk; *The Europa World Year Book.*

UNESCO Institute for Statistics, C.P. 6128 Succursale Centre-Ville, Montreal, Quebec, H3C 3J7 Canada, (Dial from U.S. (514) 343-6880), (Fax from U.S. (514) 343 6882), www.uis.unesco.org; *Statistical Tables.*

United Nations Statistics Division, New York, NY 10017, (800) 253-9646, Fax: (212) 963-4116, http://unstats.un.org; *Human Development Report 2006* and *Trends in Europe and North America: The Statistical Yearbook of the ECE 2005.*

The World Bank, 1818 H Street, NW, Washington, DC 20433, (202) 473-1000, Fax: (202) 477-6391, www.worldbank.org; *Italy; World Development Indicators (WDI) 2008;* and *World Development Report 2008.*

ITALY - EGGPLANT PRODUCTION

See ITALY - CROPS

ITALY - ELECTRICITY

Central Intelligence Agency, Office of Public Affairs, Washington, DC 20505, (703) 482-0623, Fax: (703) 482-1739, www.cia.gov; *The World Factbook.*

European Union, Delegation of the European Commission to the United States, 2300 M Street, NW, Washington, DC 20037, (202) 862-9500, Fax: (202) 429-1766, www.eurunion.org; *European Union Energy Transport in Figures 2006; Eurostatistics: Data for Short-Term Economic Analysis (2007 edition);* and *Regions - Statistical Yearbook 2006.*

Eurostat, Batiment Jean Monnet, Rue Alcide de Gasperi, L-2920 Luxembourg, http://epp.eurostat.ec.europa.eu; *Energy - Monthly Statistics; Eurostat Yearbook 2006-2007;* and *Panorama of Energy - 2007 Edition.*

M.E. Sharpe, 80 Business Park Drive, Armonk, NY 10504, (800) 541-6563, Fax: (914) 273-2106, www.mesharpe.com; *The Illustrated Book of World Rankings.*

Organisation for Economic Cooperation and Development (OECD), 2 rue Andre Pascal, F-75775 Paris Cedex 16, France, (Telephone in U.S. (202) 785-6323), (Fax in U.S. (202) 785-0350), www.oecd.org; *Coal Information: 2007 Edition; Energy Statistics of OECD Countries* (2007 Edition); *Indicators of Industrial Activity;* STructural ANalysis (STAN) database; and *World Energy Outlook 2007.*

Palgrave Macmillan Ltd., Houndmills, Basingstoke, Hampshire, RG21 6XS, England, (Telephone in U.S. (888) 330-8477), (Fax in U.S. (800) 672-2054), www.palgrave.com; *The Statesman's Yearbook 2008.*

Platts, 2 Penn Plaza, 25th Floor, New York, NY 10121-2298, (212) 904-3070, www.platts.com; *Energy Economist; EU Energy;* and *European Electricity Review 2004.*

U.S. Department of Energy (DOE), Energy Information Administration (EIA), 1000 Independence Avenue, SW, Washington, DC 20585, (202) 586-8800, www.eia.doe.gov; *International Energy Annual 2004* and *International Energy Outlook 2006.*

United Nations Statistics Division, New York, NY 10017, (800) 253-9646, Fax: (212) 963-4116, http://unstats.un.org; *Energy Statistics Yearbook 2003; Human Development Report 2006;* and *Trends in Europe and North America: The Statistical Yearbook of the ECE 2005.*

ITALY - EMPLOYMENT

Bernan Essential Government Publications, 4611-F Assembly Drive, Lanham MD, 20706-4391, (301) 459-2255, Fax: (800) 865-3450, www.bernan.com; *OECD Factbook 2006.*

Euromonitor International, Inc., 224 S. Michigan Avenue, Suite 1500, Chicago, IL 60604, (312) 922-1115, Fax: (312) 922-1157, www.euromonitor.com; *European Marketing Data and Statistics 2008.*

European Union, Delegation of the European Commission to the United States, 2300 M Street, NW, Washington, DC 20037, (202) 862-9500, Fax: (202) 429-1766, www.eurunion.org; *Agriculture in the European Union: Statistical and Economic Information 2006; European Union Labour Force Survey; Eurostatistics: Data for Short-Term Economic Analysis (2007 edition);* and *Iron and Steel.*

Eurostat, Batiment Jean Monnet, Rue Alcide de Gasperi, L-2920 Luxembourg, http://epp.eurostat.ec.europa.eu; *Eurostat Yearbook 2006-2007.*

International Labour Office, I.L.O. Publications, 4 route des Morillons, CH-1211 Geneva 22, Switzerland, (Telephone in U.S. (202) 653-7652), (Fax in U.S. (202) 653-7687), www.ilo.org; *Yearbook of Labour Statistics 2006.*

M.E. Sharpe, 80 Business Park Drive, Armonk, NY 10504, (800) 541-6563, Fax: (914) 273-2106, www.mesharpe.com; *The Illustrated Book of World Rankings.*

Organisation for Economic Cooperation and Development (OECD), 2 rue Andre Pascal, F-75775 Paris Cedex 16, France, (Telephone in U.S. (202) 785-6323), (Fax in U.S. (202) 785-0350), www.oecd.org; *ICT Sector Data and Metadata by Country; Iron and Steel Industry in 2004 (2006 Edition); Labour Force Statistics: 1986-2005, 2007 Edition; A New World Map in Textiles and Clothing: Adjusting to Change; OECD Composite Leading Indicators (CLIs), Updated September 2007; OECD Economic Outlook 2008; OECD Economic Survey - Italy 2007; OECD Employment Outlook 2007;* and *OECD in Figures 2007.*

United Nations Statistics Division, New York, NY 10017, (800) 253-9646, Fax: (212) 963-4116, http://unstats.un.org; *Statistical Yearbook* and *Trends in Europe and North America: The Statistical Yearbook of the ECE 2005.*

The World Bank, 1818 H Street, NW, Washington, DC 20433, (202) 473-1000, Fax: (202) 477-6391, www.worldbank.org; *Italy.*

ITALY - ENERGY INDUSTRIES

Enerdata, 10 Rue Royale, 75008 Paris, France, www.enerdata.fr; *Global Energy Market Data.*

Eurostat, Batiment Jean Monnet, Rue Alcide de Gasperi, L-2920 Luxembourg, http://epp.eurostat.ec.europa.eu; *Energy - Monthly Statistics; Eurostat Yearbook 2006-2007;* and *Panorama of Energy - 2007 Edition.*

International Energy Agency (IEA), 9, rue de la Federation, 75739 Paris Cedex 15, France, www.iea.org; *Key World Energy Statistics 2007.*

Organisation for Economic Cooperation and Development (OECD), 2 rue Andre Pascal, F-75775 Paris Cedex 16, France, (Telephone in U.S. (202) 785-6323), (Fax in U.S. (202) 785-0350), www.oecd.org; *Towards Sustainable Household Consumption?: Trends and Policies in OECD Countries.*

Platts, 2 Penn Plaza, 25th Floor, New York, NY 10121-2298, (212) 904-3070, www.platts.com; *EU Energy* and *European Power Daily.*

United Nations Statistics Division, New York, NY 10017, (800) 253-9646, Fax: (212) 963-4116, http://unstats.un.org; *Statistical Yearbook.*

The World Bank, 1818 H Street, NW, Washington, DC 20433, (202) 473-1000, Fax: (202) 477-6391, www.worldbank.org; *Italy.*

ITALY - ENVIRONMENTAL CONDITIONS

Center for Research on the Epidemiology of Disasters (CRED), Universite Catholique de Louvain, Ecole de Sante Publique, 30.94 Clos Chapelle-aux-Champs, 1200 Brussels, Belgium, www.cred.be; *Three Decades of Floods in Europe: A Preliminary Analysis of EMDAT Data.*

DSI Data Service Information, Xantener Strasse 51a, D-47495 Rheinberg, Germany, www.dsidata.com; *Campus Solution* and *DSI's Global Environmental Database.*

Economist Intelligence Unit, 111 West 57th Street, New York, NY 10019, (212) 554-0600, Fax: (212) 586-1181, www.eiu.com; *Italy Country Report.*

Eurostat, Batiment Jean Monnet, Rue Alcide de Gasperi, L-2920 Luxembourg, http://epp.eurostat.ec.europa.eu; *Environmental Protection Expenditure in Europe.*

Federal Statistical Office Germany, D-65180 Wiesbaden, Germany, www.destatis.de; *Italy 2006.*

Organisation for Economic Cooperation and Development (OECD), 2 rue Andre Pascal, F-75775 Paris Cedex 16, France, (Telephone in U.S. (202) 785-6323), (Fax in U.S. (202) 785-0350), www.oecd.org; *Key Environmental Indicators 2004.*

Platts, 2 Penn Plaza, 25th Floor, New York, NY 10121-2298, (212) 904-3070, www.platts.com; *Emissions Daily.*

United Nations Statistics Division, New York, NY 10017, (800) 253-9646, Fax: (212) 963-4116, http://unstats.un.org; *Trends in Europe and North America: The Statistical Yearbook of the ECE 2005* and *World Statistics Pocketbook.*

ITALY - EXPENDITURES, PUBLIC

Eurostat, Batiment Jean Monnet, Rue Alcide de Gasperi, L-2920 Luxembourg, http://epp.eurostat.ec.europa.eu; *European Social Statistics - Social Protection Expenditure and Receipts - Data 1997-2005* and *Eurostat Yearbook 2006-2007.*

Organisation for Economic Cooperation and Development (OECD), 2 rue Andre Pascal, F-75775 Paris Cedex 16, France, (Telephone in U.S. (202) 785-6323), (Fax in U.S. (202) 785-0350), www.oecd.org; *Revenue Statistics 1965-2006 - 2007 Edition.*

ITALY - EXPORTS

Central Intelligence Agency, Office of Public Affairs, Washington, DC 20505, (703) 482-0623, Fax: (703) 482-1739, www.cia.gov; *The World Factbook.*

Economist Intelligence Unit, 111 West 57th Street, New York, NY 10019, (212) 554-0600, Fax: (212) 586-1181, www.eiu.com; *Italy Country Report.*

Euromonitor International, Inc., 224 S. Michigan Avenue, Suite 1500, Chicago, IL 60604, (312) 922-1115, Fax: (312) 922-1157, www.euromonitor.com; *The World Economic Factbook 2008.*

European Union, Delegation of the European Commission to the United States, 2300 M Street, NW, Washington, DC 20037, (202) 862-9500, Fax: (202) 429-1766, www.eurunion.org; *European Union Energy Transport in Figures 2006; Eurostatistics: Data for Short-Term Economic Analysis (2007 edition); External and Intra-European Union Trade: Data 1958-2002; External and Intra-European Union Trade: Data 1999-2004;* and *Fishery Statistics - 1990-2006.*

Eurostat, Batiment Jean Monnet, Rue Alcide de Gasperi, L-2920 Luxembourg, http://epp.eurostat.ec.europa.eu; *Eurostat Yearbook 2006-2007.*

International Iron and Steel Institute (IISI), Rue Colonel Bourg 120, B-1140 Brussels, Belgium, www.worldsteel.org; *Steel Statistical Yearbook 2006.*

International Lead and Zinc Study Group (ILZSG), Rua Almirante Barroso 38, 5th Floor, Lisbon 1000 - 013, Portugal, www.ilzsg.org; Interactive Statistical Database.

International Monetary Fund (IMF), 700 Nineteenth Street, NW, Washington, DC 20431, (202) 623-7000, Fax: (202) 623-4661, www.imf.org; *Direction of Trade Statistics Yearbook 2007; Government Finance Statistics Yearbook (2008 Edition);* and *International Financial Statistics Yearbook 2007.*

Organisation for Economic Cooperation and Development (OECD), 2 rue Andre Pascal, F-75775 Paris Cedex 16, France, (Telephone in U.S. (202) 785-6323), (Fax in U.S. (202) 785-0350), www.oecd.org; *Geographical Distribution of Financial Flows to Aid Recipients 2002-2006; Indicators of Industrial Activity; International Trade by Commodity Statistics (ITCS); Iron and Steel Industry in 2004 (2006 Edition); 2005 OECD Agricultural Outlook Tables, 1970-2014; OECD Economic Outlook 2008; OECD Economic Survey - Italy 2007;* and *Review of Fisheries in OECD Countries: Country Statistics 2001 to 2003 - 2005 Edition.*

Palgrave Macmillan Ltd., Houndmills, Basingstoke, Hampshire, RG21 6XS, England, (Telephone in U.S. (888) 330-8477), (Fax in U.S. (800) 672-2054), www.palgrave.com; *The Statesman's Yearbook 2008.*

Platts, 2 Penn Plaza, 25th Floor, New York, NY 10121-2298, (212) 904-3070, www.platts.com; *Energy Economist.*

Taylor and Francis Group, An Informa Business, 2 Park Square, Milton Park, Abingdon, Oxford OX14 4RN, United Kingdom, (Dial from U.S. (212) 216-7800), (Fax from U.S. (212) 564-7854), www.tandf.co.uk; *The Europa World Year Book.*

Technical Association of the Pulp and Paper Industry (TAPPI), 15 Technology Parkway South, Norcross, GA 30092, (770) 446-1400, Fax: (770) 446-6947, www.tappi.org; *TAPPI Annual Report.*

United Nations Conference on Trade and Development (UNCTAD), DC2-1120, United Nations, New York, NY 10017, (212) 963-0027, www.unctad.org; *Handbook of Statistics 2005.*

United Nations Food and Agricultural Organization (FAO), Viale delle Terme di Caracalla, 00100 Rome, Italy, (Dial from U.S. (202) 653-2400), (Fax from U.S. (202) 653 5760), www.fao.org; *The State of Food and Agriculture (SOFA) 2006.*

United Nations Statistics Division, New York, NY 10017, (800) 253-9646, Fax: (212) 963-4116, http://unstats.un.org; *Energy Statistics Yearbook 2003* and *Trends in Europe and North America: The Statistical Yearbook of the ECE 2005.*

The World Bank, 1818 H Street, NW, Washington, DC 20433, (202) 473-1000, Fax: (202) 477-6391, www.worldbank.org; *World Development Indicators (WDI) 2008* and *World Development Report 2008.*

ITALY - FEMALE WORKING POPULATION

See ITALY - EMPLOYMENT

ITALY - FERTILITY, HUMAN

Central Intelligence Agency, Office of Public Affairs, Washington, DC 20505, (703) 482-0623, Fax: (703) 482-1739, www.cia.gov; *The World Factbook.*

European Union, Delegation of the European Commission to the United States, 2300 M Street, NW, Washington, DC 20037, (202) 862-9500, Fax: (202) 429-1766, www.eurunion.org; *First Demographic Estimates for 2006.*

M.E. Sharpe, 80 Business Park Drive, Armonk, NY 10504, (800) 541-6563, Fax: (914) 273-2106, www.mesharpe.com; *The Illustrated Book of World Rankings.*

United Nations Statistics Division, New York, NY 10017, (800) 253-9646, Fax: (212) 963-4116, http://unstats.un.org; *Human Development Report 2006* and *Trends in Europe and North America: The Statistical Yearbook of the ECE 2005.*

The World Bank, 1818 H Street, NW, Washington, DC 20433, (202) 473-1000, Fax: (202) 477-6391, www.worldbank.org; *The World Bank Atlas 2003-2004; World Development Indicators (WDI) 2008;* and *World Development Report 2008.*

ITALY - FERTILIZER INDUSTRY

Eurostat, Batiment Jean Monnet, Rue Alcide de Gasperi, L-2920 Luxembourg, http://epp.eurostat.ec.europa.eu; *Eurostat Yearbook 2006-2007.*

Organisation for Economic Cooperation and Development (OECD), 2 rue Andre Pascal, F-75775 Paris Cedex 16, France, (Telephone in U.S. (202) 785-6323), (Fax in U.S. (202) 785-0350), www.oecd.org; *International Trade by Commodity Statistics (ITCS)* and *2005 OECD Agricultural Outlook Tables, 1970-2014.*

United Nations Food and Agricultural Organization (FAO), Viale delle Terme di Caracalla, 00100 Rome, Italy, (Dial from U.S. (202) 653-2400), (Fax from U.S. (202) 653 5760), www.fao.org; *FAO Fertilizer Yearbook* and *The State of Food and Agriculture (SOFA) 2006.*

United Nations Statistics Division, New York, NY 10017, (800) 253-9646, Fax: (212) 963-4116, http://unstats.un.org; *Statistical Yearbook.*

ITALY - FETAL MORTALITY

See ITALY - MORTALITY

ITALY - FILM

See ITALY - MOTION PICTURES

ITALY - FINANCE

European Union, Delegation of the European Commission to the United States, 2300 M Street, NW, Washington, DC 20037, (202) 862-9500, Fax: (202) 429-1766, www.eurunion.org; *Eurostatistics: Data for Short-Term Economic Analysis (2007 edition).*

Eurostat, Batiment Jean Monnet, Rue Alcide de Gasperi, L-2920 Luxembourg, http://epp.eurostat.ec.europa.eu; *Eurostat Yearbook 2006-2007.*

International Monetary Fund (IMF), 700 Nineteenth Street, NW, Washington, DC 20431, (202) 623-7000, Fax: (202) 623-4661, www.imf.org; *International Financial Statistics Yearbook 2007.*

Organisation for Economic Cooperation and Development (OECD), 2 rue Andre Pascal, F-75775 Paris Cedex 16, France, (Telephone in U.S. (202) 785-6323), (Fax in U.S. (202) 785-0350), www.oecd.org; *OECD Economic Outlook 2008.*

Taylor and Francis Group, An Informa Business, 2 Park Square, Milton Park, Abingdon, Oxford OX14 4RN, United Kingdom, (Dial from U.S. (212) 216-7800), (Fax from U.S. (212) 564-7854), www.tandf.co.uk; *The Europa World Year Book.*

United Nations Statistics Division, New York, NY 10017, (800) 253-9646, Fax: (212) 963-4116, http://unstats.un.org; *National Accounts Statistics: Compendium of Income Distribution Statistics* and *Statistical Yearbook.*

The World Bank, 1818 H Street, NW, Washington, DC 20433, (202) 473-1000, Fax: (202) 477-6391, www.worldbank.org; *Italy.*

ITALY - FINANCE, PUBLIC

Bernan Essential Government Publications, 4611-F Assembly Drive, Lanham MD, 20706-4391, (301) 459-2255, Fax: (800) 865-3450, www.bernan.com; *National Accounts Statistics.*

Economist Intelligence Unit, 111 West 57th Street, New York, NY 10019, (212) 554-0600, Fax: (212) 586-1181, www.eiu.com; *Italy Country Report.*

European Union, Delegation of the European Commission to the United States, 2300 M Street, NW, Washington, DC 20037, (202) 862-9500, Fax: (202) 429-1766, www.eurunion.org; *Eurostatistics: Data for Short-Term Economic Analysis (2007 edition).*

Eurostat, Batiment Jean Monnet, Rue Alcide de Gasperi, L-2920 Luxembourg, http://epp.eurostat.ec.europa.eu; *Eurostat Yearbook 2006-2007.*

International Monetary Fund (IMF), 700 Nineteenth Street, NW, Washington, DC 20431, (202) 623-7000, Fax: (202) 623-4661, www.imf.org; *Government Finance Statistics Yearbook (2008 Edition); International Financial Statistics; International Financial Statistics Online Service;* and *International Financial Statistics Yearbook 2007.*

M.E. Sharpe, 80 Business Park Drive, Armonk, NY 10504, (800) 541-6563, Fax: (914) 273-2106, www.mesharpe.com; *The Illustrated Book of World Rankings.*

Organisation for Economic Cooperation and Development (OECD), 2 rue Andre Pascal, F-75775 Paris Cedex 16, France, (Telephone in U.S. (202) 785-6323), (Fax in U.S. (202) 785-0350), www.oecd.org; *Financial Market Trends: OECD Periodical; Geographical Distribution of Financial Flows to Aid Recipients 2002-2006; OECD Economic Outlook 2008;* and *Revenue Statistics 1965-2006 - 2007 Edition.*

Palgrave Macmillan Ltd., Houndmills, Basingstoke, Hampshire, RG21 6XS, England, (Telephone in U.S. (888) 330-8477), (Fax in U.S. (800) 672-2054), www.palgrave.com; *The Statesman's Yearbook 2008.*

Taylor and Francis Group, An Informa Business, 2 Park Square, Milton Park, Abingdon, Oxford OX14 4RN, United Kingdom, (Dial from U.S. (212) 216-7800), (Fax from U.S. (212) 564-7854), www.tandf.co.uk; *The Europa World Year Book.*

The World Bank, 1818 H Street, NW, Washington, DC 20433, (202) 473-1000, Fax: (202) 477-6391, www.worldbank.org; *Italy.*

ITALY - FISHERIES

Euromonitor International, Inc., 224 S. Michigan Avenue, Suite 1500, Chicago, IL 60604, (312) 922-1115, Fax: (312) 922-1157, www.euromonitor.com; *European Marketing Data and Statistics 2008.*

European Union, Delegation of the European Commission to the United States, 2300 M Street, NW, Washington, DC 20037, (202) 862-9500, Fax: (202) 429-1766, www.eurunion.org; *Agricultural Statistics: Data 1995-2005* and *Fishery Statistics - 1990-2006.*

Eurostat, Batiment Jean Monnet, Rue Alcide de Gasperi, L-2920 Luxembourg, http://epp.eurostat.ec.europa.eu; *Eurostat Yearbook 2006-2007.*

M.E. Sharpe, 80 Business Park Drive, Armonk, NY 10504, (800) 541-6563, Fax: (914) 273-2106, www.mesharpe.com; *The Illustrated Book of World Rankings.*

Organisation for Economic Cooperation and Development (OECD), 2 rue Andre Pascal, F-75775 Paris Cedex 16, France, (Telephone in U.S. (202) 785-6323), (Fax in U.S. (202) 785-0350), www.oecd.org; *Indicators of Industrial Activity; International Trade by Commodity Statistics (ITCS);* and *Review of Fisheries in OECD Countries: Country Statistics 2001 to 2003 - 2005 Edition.*

Palgrave Macmillan Ltd., Houndmills, Basingstoke, Hampshire, RG21 6XS, England, (Telephone in U.S. (888) 330-8477), (Fax in U.S. (800) 672-2054), www.palgrave.com; *The Statesman's Yearbook 2008.*

Taylor and Francis Group, An Informa Business, 2 Park Square, Milton Park, Abingdon, Oxford OX14 4RN, United Kingdom, (Dial from U.S. (212) 216-7800), (Fax from U.S. (212) 564-7854), www.tandf.co.uk; *The Europa World Year Book.*

United Nations Conference on Trade and Development (UNCTAD), DC2-1120, United Nations, New York, NY 10017, (212) 963-0027, www.unctad.org; *UNCTAD Commodity Yearbook.*

United Nations Food and Agricultural Organization (FAO), Viale delle Terme di Caracalla, 00100 Rome, Italy, (Dial from U.S. (202) 653-2400), (Fax from U.S. (202) 653 5760), www.fao.org; *FAO Yearbook of Fishery Statistics;* Fishery Databases; FISHSTAT Database. Subjects covered include: Aquaculture production, capture production, fishery commodities; and *The State of Food and Agriculture (SOFA) 2006.*

United Nations Statistics Division, New York, NY 10017, (800) 253-9646, Fax: (212) 963-4116, http://unstats.un.org; *Statistical Yearbook.*

The World Bank, 1818 H Street, NW, Washington, DC 20433, (202) 473-1000, Fax: (202) 477-6391, www.worldbank.org; *Italy.*

ITALY - FOOD

Euromonitor International, Inc., 224 S. Michigan Avenue, Suite 1500, Chicago, IL 60604, (312) 922-1115, Fax: (312) 922-1157, www.euromonitor.com; *Retail Trade International 2007.*

Eurostat, Batiment Jean Monnet, Rue Alcide de Gasperi, L-2920 Luxembourg, http://epp.eurostat.ec.europa.eu; *Eurostat Yearbook 2006-2007.*

Organisation for Economic Cooperation and Development (OECD), 2 rue Andre Pascal, F-75775 Paris Cedex 16, France, (Telephone in U.S. (202) 785-6323), (Fax in U.S. (202) 785-0350), www.oecd.org; *International Trade by Commodity Statistics (ITCS)* and *Towards Sustainable Household Consumption?: Trends and Policies in OECD Countries.*

United Nations Conference on Trade and Development (UNCTAD), DC2-1120, United Nations, New York, NY 10017, (212) 963-0027, www.unctad.org; *UNCTAD Commodity Yearbook.*

United Nations Food and Agricultural Organization (FAO), Viale delle Terme di Caracalla, 00100 Rome, Italy, (Dial from U.S. (202) 653-2400), (Fax from U.S. (202) 653 5760), www.fao.org; *FAO Production Yearbook 2002* and *The State of Food and Agriculture (SOFA) 2006.*

United Nations Statistics Division, New York, NY 10017, (800) 253-9646, Fax: (212) 963-4116, http://unstats.un.org; *Human Development Report 2006.*

ITALY - FOOTWEAR

Organisation for Economic Cooperation and Development (OECD), 2 rue Andre Pascal, F-75775 Paris Cedex 16, France, (Telephone in U.S. (202) 785-6323), (Fax in U.S. (202) 785-0350), www.oecd.org; *Indicators of Industrial Activity.*

ITALY - FOREIGN EXCHANGE RATES

Central Intelligence Agency, Office of Public Affairs, Washington, DC 20505, (703) 482-0623, Fax: (703) 482-1739, www.cia.gov; *The World Factbook.*

Euromonitor International, Inc., 224 S. Michigan Avenue, Suite 1500, Chicago, IL 60604, (312) 922-1115, Fax: (312) 922-1157, www.euromonitor.com; *The World Economic Factbook 2008.*

European Union, Delegation of the European Commission to the United States, 2300 M Street, NW, Washington, DC 20037, (202) 862-9500, Fax: (202) 429-1766, www.eurunion.org; *Eurostatistics: Data for Short-Term Economic Analysis (2007 edition).*

Eurostat, Batiment Jean Monnet, Rue Alcide de Gasperi, L-2920 Luxembourg, http://epp.eurostat.ec.europa.eu; *Eurostat Yearbook 2006-2007.*

International Civil Aviation Organization (ICAO), External Relations and Public Information Office (EPO), 999 University Street, Montreal, Quebec H3C 5H7, Canada, (Dial from U.S. (514) 954-8219), (Fax from U.S. (514) 954-6077), www.icao.int; *Civil Aviation Statistics of the World.*

International Monetary Fund (IMF), 700 Nineteenth Street, NW, Washington, DC 20431, (202) 623-7000, Fax: (202) 623-4661, www.imf.org; *International Financial Statistics Yearbook 2007.*

Organisation for Economic Cooperation and Development (OECD), 2 rue Andre Pascal, F-75775 Paris Cedex 16, France, (Telephone in U.S. (202) 785-6323), (Fax in U.S. (202) 785-0350), www.oecd.org; *Financial Market Trends: OECD Periodical; Household, Tourism, Travel: Trends, Environmental Impacts and Policy Responses; OECD Economic Outlook 2008;* and *Revenue Statistics 1965-2006 - 2007 Edition.*

Taylor and Francis Group, An Informa Business, 2 Park Square, Milton Park, Abingdon, Oxford OX14 4RN, United Kingdom, (Dial from U.S. (212) 216-7800), (Fax from U.S. (212) 564-7854), www.tandf.co.uk; *The Europa World Year Book.*

United Nations Statistics Division, New York, NY 10017, (800) 253-9646, Fax: (212) 963-4116, http://unstats.un.org; *Statistical Yearbook; Trends in Europe and North America: The Statistical Yearbook of the ECE 2005;* and *World Statistics Pocketbook.*

ITALY - FORESTS AND FORESTRY

Euromonitor International, Inc., 224 S. Michigan Avenue, Suite 1500, Chicago, IL 60604, (312) 922-1115, Fax: (312) 922-1157, www.euromonitor.com; *European Marketing Data and Statistics 2008.*

European Union, Delegation of the European Commission to the United States, 2300 M Street, NW, Washington, DC 20037, (202) 862-9500, Fax: (202) 429-1766, www.eurunion.org; *Agricultural Statistics: Data 1995-2005.*

Eurostat, Batiment Jean Monnet, Rue Alcide de Gasperi, L-2920 Luxembourg, http://epp.eurostat.ec.europa.eu; *Eurostat Yearbook 2006-2007.*

M.E. Sharpe, 80 Business Park Drive, Armonk, NY 10504, (800) 541-6563, Fax: (914) 273-2106, www.mesharpe.com; *The Illustrated Book of World Rankings.*

Organisation for Economic Cooperation and Development (OECD), 2 rue Andre Pascal, F-75775 Paris Cedex 16, France, (Telephone in U.S. (202) 785-6323), (Fax in U.S. (202) 785-0350), www.oecd.org; *Indicators of Industrial Activity; International Trade by Commodity Statistics (ITCS);* and STructural ANalysis (STAN) database.

Taylor and Francis Group, An Informa Business, 2 Park Square, Milton Park, Abingdon, Oxford OX14 4RN, United Kingdom, (Dial from U.S. (212) 216-7800), (Fax from U.S. (212) 564-7854), www.tandf.co.uk; *The Europa World Year Book.*

Technical Association of the Pulp and Paper Industry (TAPPI), 15 Technology Parkway South, Norcross, GA 30092, (770) 446-1400, Fax: (770) 446-6947, www.tappi.org; *TAPPI Annual Report.*

UNESCO Institute for Statistics, C.P. 6128 Succursale Centre-Ville, Montreal, Quebec, H3C 3J7 Canada, (Dial from U.S. (514) 343-6880), (Fax from U.S. (514) 343 6882), www.uis.unesco.org; *Statistical Tables.*

United Nations Conference on Trade and Development (UNCTAD), DC2-1120, United Nations, New York, NY 10017, (212) 963-0027, www.unctad.org; *UNCTAD Commodity Yearbook.*

United Nations Food and Agricultural Organization (FAO), Viale delle Terme di Caracalla, 00100 Rome, Italy, (Dial from U.S. (202) 653-2400), (Fax from U.S. (202) 653 5760), www.fao.org; *FAO Yearbook of Forest Products* and *The State of Food and Agriculture (SOFA) 2006.*

United Nations Statistics Division, New York, NY 10017, (800) 253-9646, Fax: (212) 963-4116, http://unstats.un.org; *Statistical Yearbook* and *Trends in Europe and North America: The Statistical Yearbook of the ECE 2005.*

The World Bank, 1818 H Street, NW, Washington, DC 20433, (202) 473-1000, Fax: (202) 477-6391, www.worldbank.org; *Italy* and *World Development Report 2008.*

ITALY - FRUIT PRODUCTION

See ITALY - CROPS

ITALY - GAS PRODUCTION

See ITALY - MINERAL INDUSTRIES

ITALY - GEOGRAPHIC INFORMATION SYSTEMS

Eurostat, Batiment Jean Monnet, Rue Alcide de Gasperi, L-2920 Luxembourg, http://epp.eurostat.ec.europa.eu; *Eurostat Yearbook 2006-2007.*

M.E. Sharpe, 80 Business Park Drive, Armonk, NY 10504, (800) 541-6563, Fax: (914) 273-2106, www.mesharpe.com; *The Illustrated Book of World Rankings.*

The World Bank, 1818 H Street, NW, Washington, DC 20433, (202) 473-1000, Fax: (202) 477-6391, www.worldbank.org; *Italy.*

ITALY - GLASS TRADE

Organisation for Economic Cooperation and Development (OECD), 2 rue Andre Pascal, F-75775 Paris Cedex 16, France, (Telephone in U.S. (202) 785-6323), (Fax in U.S. (202) 785-0350), www.oecd.org; *Indicators of Industrial Activity.*

ITALY - GOLD INDUSTRY

International Monetary Fund (IMF), 700 Nineteenth Street, NW, Washington, DC 20431, (202) 623-7000, Fax: (202) 623-4661, www.imf.org; *International Financial Statistics Yearbook 2007.*

United Nations Statistics Division, New York, NY 10017, (800) 253-9646, Fax: (212) 963-4116, http://unstats.un.org; *Statistical Yearbook.*

The World Bank, 1818 H Street, NW, Washington, DC 20433, (202) 473-1000, Fax: (202) 477-6391, www.worldbank.org; *World Development Indicators (WDI) 2008.*

ITALY - GOLD PRODUCTION

See ITALY - MINERAL INDUSTRIES

ITALY - GRANTS-IN-AID

International Monetary Fund (IMF), 700 Nineteenth Street, NW, Washington, DC 20431, (202) 623-7000, Fax: (202) 623-4661, www.imf.org; *Government Finance Statistics Yearbook (2008 Edition).*

Organisation for Economic Cooperation and Development (OECD), 2 rue Andre Pascal, F-75775 Paris Cedex 16, France, (Telephone in U.S. (202) 785-6323), (Fax in U.S. (202) 785-0350), www.oecd.org; *Geographical Distribution of Financial Flows to Aid Recipients 2002-2006.*

ITALY - GREEN PEPPER AND CHILIE PRODUCTION

See ITALY - CROPS

ITALY - GROSS DOMESTIC PRODUCT

Economist Intelligence Unit, 111 West 57th Street, New York, NY 10019, (212) 554-0600, Fax: (212) 586-1181, www.eiu.com; *Italy Country Report.*

Euromonitor International, Inc., 224 S. Michigan Avenue, Suite 1500, Chicago, IL 60604, (312) 922-1115, Fax: (312) 922-1157, www.euromonitor.com; *The World Economic Factbook 2008.*

European Union, Delegation of the European Commission to the United States, 2300 M Street, NW, Washington, DC 20037, (202) 862-9500, Fax: (202) 429-1766, www.eurunion.org; *Eurostatistics: Data for Short-Term Economic Analysis (2007 edition); Iron and Steel;* and *RD Expenditure in Europe (2006 edition).*

Eurostat, Batiment Jean Monnet, Rue Alcide de Gasperi, L-2920 Luxembourg, http://epp.eurostat.ec.europa.eu; *Eurostat Yearbook 2006-2007.*

International Monetary Fund (IMF), 700 Nineteenth Street, NW, Washington, DC 20431, (202) 623-7000, Fax: (202) 623-4661, www.imf.org; *International Financial Statistics Yearbook 2007.*

M.E. Sharpe, 80 Business Park Drive, Armonk, NY 10504, (800) 541-6563, Fax: (914) 273-2106, www.mesharpe.com; *The Illustrated Book of World Rankings.*

Organisation for Economic Cooperation and Development (OECD), 2 rue Andre Pascal, F-75775 Paris Cedex 16, France, (Telephone in U.S. (202) 785-6323), (Fax in U.S. (202) 785-0350), www.oecd.org; *Comparison of Gross Domestic Product (GDP) for OECD Countries; Geographical Distribution of Financial Flows to Aid Recipients 2002-2006; OECD Economic Outlook 2008;* and *Revenue Statistics 1965-2006 - 2007 Edition.*

Taylor and Francis Group, An Informa Business, 2 Park Square, Milton Park, Abingdon, Oxford OX14 4RN, United Kingdom, (Dial from U.S. (212) 216-7800), (Fax from U.S. (212) 564-7854), www.tandf.co.uk; *The Europa World Year Book.*

United Nations Statistics Division, New York, NY 10017, (800) 253-9646, Fax: (212) 963-4116, http://unstats.un.org; *Human Development Report 2006; National Accounts Statistics: Compendium of Income Distribution Statistics; Statistical Yearbook;* and *Trends in Europe and North America: The Statistical Yearbook of the ECE 2005.*

The World Bank, 1818 H Street, NW, Washington, DC 20433, (202) 473-1000, Fax: (202) 477-6391, www.worldbank.org; *World Development Indicators (WDI) 2008* and *World Development Report 2008.*

ITALY - GROSS NATIONAL PRODUCT

European Union, Delegation of the European Commission to the United States, 2300 M Street, NW, Washington, DC 20037, (202) 862-9500, Fax: (202) 429-1766, www.eurunion.org; *The EU Economy, 2007 Review: Moving Europe's Productivity Frontier.*

Eurostat, Batiment Jean Monnet, Rue Alcide de Gasperi, L-2920 Luxembourg, http://epp.eurostat.ec.europa.eu; *Eurostat Yearbook 2006-2007.*

M.E. Sharpe, 80 Business Park Drive, Armonk, NY 10504, (800) 541-6563, Fax: (914) 273-2106, www.mesharpe.com; *The Illustrated Book of World Rankings.*

Organisation for Economic Cooperation and Development (OECD), 2 rue Andre Pascal, F-75775 Paris Cedex 16, France, (Telephone in U.S. (202) 785-6323), (Fax in U.S. (202) 785-0350), www.oecd.org; *Geographical Distribution of Financial Flows to Aid Recipients 2002-2006; OECD Composite Leading Indicators (CLIs), Updated September 2007; OECD Economic Outlook 2008;* and *OECD Main Economic Indicators (MEI).*

Palgrave Macmillan Ltd., Houndmills, Basingstoke, Hampshire, RG21 6XS, England, (Telephone in U.S. (888) 330-8477), (Fax in U.S. (800) 672-2054), www.palgrave.com; *The Statesman's Yearbook 2008.*

Taylor and Francis Group, An Informa Business, 2 Park Square, Milton Park, Abingdon, Oxford OX14 4RN, United Kingdom, (Dial from U.S. (212) 216-

7800), (Fax from U.S. (212) 564-7854), www.tandf.co.uk; *The Europa World Year Book.*

U.S. Department of State (DOS), 2201 C Street NW, Washington, DC 20520, (202) 647-4000, www.state.gov; *World Military Expenditures and Arms Transfers (WMEAT).*

United Nations Statistics Division, New York, NY 10017, (800) 253-9646, Fax: (212) 963-4116, http://unstats.un.org; *Statistical Yearbook.*

The World Bank, 1818 H Street, NW, Washington, DC 20433, (202) 473-1000, Fax: (202) 477-6391, www.worldbank.org; *The World Bank Atlas 2003-2004; World Development Indicators (WDI) 2008;* and *World Development Report 2008.*

ITALY - HAY PRODUCTION

See ITALY - CROPS

ITALY - HAZELNUT PRODUCTION

See ITALY - CROPS

ITALY - HEALTH

See ITALY - PUBLIC HEALTH

ITALY - HEMP FIBRE PRODUCTION

See ITALY - TEXTILE INDUSTRY

ITALY - HIDES AND SKINS INDUSTRY

Organisation for Economic Cooperation and Development (OECD), 2 rue Andre Pascal, F-75775 Paris Cedex 16, France, (Telephone in U.S. (202) 785-6323), (Fax in U.S. (202) 785-0350), www.oecd.org; *Indicators of Industrial Activity* and *International Trade by Commodity Statistics (ITCS).*

United Nations Food and Agricultural Organization (FAO), Viale delle Terme di Caracalla, 00100 Rome, Italy, (Dial from U.S. (202) 653-2400), (Fax from U.S. (202) 653 5760), www.fao.org; *FAO Production Yearbook 2002.*

ITALY - HOPS PRODUCTION

See ITALY - CROPS

ITALY - HOUSING

Euromonitor International, Inc., 224 S. Michigan Avenue, Suite 1500, Chicago, IL 60604, (312) 922-1115, Fax: (312) 922-1157, www.euromonitor.com; *World Marketing Data and Statistics.*

European Union, Delegation of the European Commission to the United States, 2300 M Street, NW, Washington, DC 20037, (202) 862-9500, Fax: (202) 429-1766, www.eurunion.org; *European Union Labour Force Survey* and *Regions - Statistical Yearbook 2006.*

Eurostat, Batiment Jean Monnet, Rue Alcide de Gasperi, L-2920 Luxembourg, http://epp.eurostat.ec.europa.eu; *Eurostat Yearbook 2006-2007.*

M.E. Sharpe, 80 Business Park Drive, Armonk, NY 10504, (800) 541-6563, Fax: (914) 273-2106, www.mesharpe.com; *The Illustrated Book of World Rankings.*

United Nations Statistics Division, New York, NY 10017, (800) 253-9646, Fax: (212) 963-4116, http://unstats.un.org; *Trends in Europe and North America: The Statistical Yearbook of the ECE 2005.*

ITALY - HOUSING - FINANCE

Organisation for Economic Cooperation and Development (OECD), 2 rue Andre Pascal, F-75775 Paris Cedex 16, France, (Telephone in U.S. (202) 785-6323), (Fax in U.S. (202) 785-0350), www.oecd.org; *OECD Main Economic Indicators (MEI).*

The World Bank, 1818 H Street, NW, Washington, DC 20433, (202) 473-1000, Fax: (202) 477-6391, www.worldbank.org; *Italy.*

ITALY - HOUSING CONSTRUCTION

See ITALY - CONSTRUCTION INDUSTRY

ITALY - ILLITERATE PERSONS

Euromonitor International, Inc., 224 S. Michigan Avenue, Suite 1500, Chicago, IL 60604, (312) 922-1115, Fax: (312) 922-1157, www.euromonitor.com; *The World Economic Factbook 2008.*

UNESCO Institute for Statistics, C.P. 6128 Succursale Centre-Ville, Montreal, Quebec, H3C 3J7 Canada, (Dial from U.S. (514) 343-6880), (Fax from U.S. (514) 343 6882), www.uis.unesco.org; *Statistical Tables.*

United Nations Statistics Division, New York, NY 10017, (800) 253-9646, Fax: (212) 963-4116, http://unstats.un.org; *Human Development Report 2006.*

ITALY - IMPORTS

Central Intelligence Agency, Office of Public Affairs, Washington, DC 20505, (703) 482-0623, Fax: (703) 482-1739, www.cia.gov; *The World Factbook.*

Economist Intelligence Unit, 111 West 57th Street, New York, NY 10019, (212) 554-0600, Fax: (212) 586-1181, www.eiu.com; *Italy Country Report.*

Euromonitor International, Inc., 224 S. Michigan Avenue, Suite 1500, Chicago, IL 60604, (312) 922-1115, Fax: (312) 922-1157, www.euromonitor.com; *The World Economic Factbook 2008.*

European Union, Delegation of the European Commission to the United States, 2300 M Street, NW, Washington, DC 20037, (202) 862-9500, Fax: (202) 429-1766, www.eurunion.org; *European Union Energy Transport in Figures 2006; Eurostatistics: Data for Short-Term Economic Analysis (2007 edition); External and Intra-European Union Trade: Data 1958-2002; External and Intra-European Union Trade: Data 1999-2004;* and *Fishery Statistics - 1990-2006.*

Eurostat, Batiment Jean Monnet, Rue Alcide de Gasperi, L-2920 Luxembourg, http://epp.eurostat.ec.europa.eu; *Eurostat Yearbook 2006-2007.*

International Iron and Steel Institute (IISI), Rue Colonel Bourg 120, B-1140 Brussels, Belgium, www.worldsteel.org; *Steel Statistical Yearbook 2006.*

International Lead and Zinc Study Group (ILZSG), Rua Almirante Barroso 38, 5th Floor, Lisbon 1000 - 013, Portugal, www.ilzsg.org; Interactive Statistical Database.

International Monetary Fund (IMF), 700 Nineteenth Street, NW, Washington, DC 20431, (202) 623-7000, Fax: (202) 623-4661, www.imf.org; *Direction of Trade Statistics Yearbook 2007; Government Finance Statistics Yearbook (2008 Edition);* and *International Financial Statistics Yearbook 2007.*

Organisation for Economic Cooperation and Development (OECD), 2 rue Andre Pascal, F-75775 Paris Cedex 16, France, (Telephone in U.S. (202) 785-6323), (Fax in U.S. (202) 785-0350), www.oecd.org; *Iron and Steel Industry in 2004 (2006 Edition); 2005 OECD Agricultural Outlook Tables, 1970-2014; OECD Economic Outlook 2008; Review of Fisheries in OECD Countries: Country Statistics 2001 to 2003 - 2005 Edition;* and STructural ANalysis (STAN) database.

Palgrave Macmillan Ltd., Houndmills, Basingstoke, Hampshire, RG21 6XS, England, (Telephone in U.S. (888) 330-8477), (Fax in U.S. (800) 672-2054), www.palgrave.com; *The Statesman's Yearbook 2008.*

Platts, 2 Penn Plaza, 25th Floor, New York, NY 10121-2298, (212) 904-3070, www.platts.com; *Energy Economist.*

Taylor and Francis Group, An Informa Business, 2 Park Square, Milton Park, Abingdon, Oxford OX14 4RN, United Kingdom, (Dial from U.S. (212) 216-7800), (Fax from U.S. (212) 564-7854), www.tandf.co.uk; *The Europa World Year Book.*

Technical Association of the Pulp and Paper Industry (TAPPI), 15 Technology Parkway South, Norcross, GA 30092, (770) 446-1400, Fax: (770) 446-6947, www.tappi.org; *TAPPI Annual Report.*

United Nations Conference on Trade and Development (UNCTAD), DC2-1120, United Nations, New York, NY 10017, (212) 963-0027, www.unctad.org; *Handbook of Statistics 2005.*

United Nations Food and Agricultural Organization (FAO), Viale delle Terme di Caracalla, 00100 Rome, Italy, (Dial from U.S. (202) 653-2400), (Fax from U.S. (202) 653 5760), www.fao.org; *The State of Food and Agriculture (SOFA) 2006.*

United Nations Statistics Division, New York, NY 10017, (800) 253-9646, Fax: (212) 963-4116, http://unstats.un.org; *Energy Statistics Yearbook 2003* and *Trends in Europe and North America: The Statistical Yearbook of the ECE 2005.*

The World Bank, 1818 H Street, NW, Washington, DC 20433, (202) 473-1000, Fax: (202) 477-6391, www.worldbank.org; *World Development Indicators (WDI) 2008* and *World Development Report 2008.*

ITALY - INCOME TAXES

See ITALY - TAXATION

ITALY - INDUSTRIAL METALS PRODUCTION

See ITALY - MINERAL INDUSTRIES

ITALY - INDUSTRIAL PRODUCTIVITY

European Union, Delegation of the European Commission to the United States, 2300 M Street, NW, Washington, DC 20037, (202) 862-9500, Fax: (202) 429-1766, www.eurunion.org; *Eurostatistics: Data for Short-Term Economic Analysis (2007 edition); Fishery Statistics - 1990-2006;* and *RD Expenditure in Europe (2006 edition).*

Eurostat, Batiment Jean Monnet, Rue Alcide de Gasperi, L-2920 Luxembourg, http://epp.eurostat.ec.europa.eu; *Eurostat Yearbook 2006-2007.*

International Iron and Steel Institute (IISI), Rue Colonel Bourg 120, B-1140 Brussels, Belgium, www.worldsteel.org; *Steel Statistical Yearbook 2006.*

International Lead and Zinc Study Group (ILZSG), Rua Almirante Barroso 38, 5th Floor, Lisbon 1000 - 013, Portugal, www.ilzsg.org; Interactive Statistical Database.

M.E. Sharpe, 80 Business Park Drive, Armonk, NY 10504, (800) 541-6563, Fax: (914) 273-2106, www.mesharpe.com; *The Illustrated Book of World Rankings.*

Organisation for Economic Cooperation and Development (OECD), 2 rue Andre Pascal, F-75775 Paris Cedex 16, France, (Telephone in U.S. (202) 785-6323), (Fax in U.S. (202) 785-0350), www.oecd.org; *Environmental Impacts of Foreign Direct Investment in the Mining Sector in the Newly Independent States (NIS); Indicators of Industrial Activity; Iron and Steel Industry in 2004 (2006 Edition); A New World Map in Textiles and Clothing: Adjusting to Change; 2005 OECD Agricultural Outlook Tables, 1970-2014; OECD Economic Outlook 2008;* and STructural ANalysis (STAN) database.

Technical Association of the Pulp and Paper Industry (TAPPI), 15 Technology Parkway South, Norcross, GA 30092, (770) 446-1400, Fax: (770) 446-6947, www.tappi.org; *TAPPI Annual Report.*

ITALY - INDUSTRIAL PROPERTY

United Nations Statistics Division, New York, NY 10017, (800) 253-9646, Fax: (212) 963-4116, http://unstats.un.org; *Statistical Yearbook.*

World Intellectual Property Organization (WIPO), PO Box 18, CH-1211 Geneva 20, Switzerland, www.wipo.int; *Industrial Property Statistics* and *Industrial Property Statistics Online Directory.*

ITALY - INDUSTRIES

Central Intelligence Agency, Office of Public Affairs, Washington, DC 20505, (703) 482-0623, Fax: (703) 482-1739, www.cia.gov; *The World Factbook.*

Economist Intelligence Unit, 111 West 57th Street, New York, NY 10019, (212) 554-0600, Fax: (212) 586-1181, www.eiu.com; *Italy Country Report.*

Euromonitor International, Inc., 224 S. Michigan Avenue, Suite 1500, Chicago, IL 60604, (312) 922-1115, Fax: (312) 922-1157, www.euromonitor.com;

The World Economic Factbook 2008 and *World Marketing Data and Statistics.*

European Union, Delegation of the European Commission to the United States, 2300 M Street, NW, Washington, DC 20037, (202) 862-9500, Fax: (202) 429-1766, www.eurunion.org; *European Union Labour Force Survey* and *Eurostatistics: Data for Short-Term Economic Analysis (2007 edition).*

Eurostat, Batiment Jean Monnet, Rue Alcide de Gasperi, L-2920 Luxembourg, http://epp.eurostat.ec.europa.eu; *Eurostat Yearbook 2006-2007.*

International Labour Office, I.L.O. Publications, 4 route des Morillons, CH-1211 Geneva 22, Switzerland, (Telephone in U.S. (202) 653-7652), (Fax in U.S. (202) 653-7687), www.ilo.org; *Yearbook of Labour Statistics 2006.*

M.E. Sharpe, 80 Business Park Drive, Armonk, NY 10504, (800) 541-6563, Fax: (914) 273-2106, www.mesharpe.com; *The Illustrated Book of World Rankings.*

Organisation for Economic Cooperation and Development (OECD), 2 rue Andre Pascal, F-75775 Paris Cedex 16, France, (Telephone in U.S. (202) 785-6323), (Fax in U.S. (202) 785-0350), www.oecd.org; *Indicators of Industrial Activity; Key Environmental Indicators 2004; OECD Economic Outlook 2008; OECD Main Economic Indicators (MEI);* and STructural ANalysis (STAN) database.

Palgrave Macmillan Ltd., Houndmills, Basingstoke, Hampshire, RG21 6XS, England, (Telephone in U.S. (888) 330-8477), (Fax in U.S. (800) 672-2054), www.palgrave.com; *The Statesman's Yearbook 2008.*

Taylor and Francis Group, An Informa Business, 2 Park Square, Milton Park, Abingdon, Oxford OX14 4RN, United Kingdom, (Dial from U.S. (212) 216-7800), (Fax from U.S. (212) 564-7854), www.tandf.co.uk; *The Europa World Year Book.*

United Nations Industrial Development Organization (UNIDO), 1 United Nations Plaza, New York, NY 10017, (212) 963 6890, Fax: (212) 963-7904, http://unido.org; Industrial Statistics Database 2008 (INDSTAT) and *The International Yearbook of Industrial Statistics 2008.*

United Nations Statistics Division, New York, NY 10017, (800) 253-9646, Fax: (212) 963-4116, http://unstats.un.org; *Human Development Report 2006; 2004 Industrial Commodity Statistics Yearbook; Statistical Yearbook;* and *Trends in Europe and North America: The Statistical Yearbook of the ECE 2005.*

The World Bank, 1818 H Street, NW, Washington, DC 20433, (202) 473-1000, Fax: (202) 477-6391, www.worldbank.org; *Italy* and *World Development Indicators (WDI) 2008.*

ITALY - INFANT AND MATERNAL MORTALITY

See ITALY - MORTALITY

ITALY - INORGANIC ACIDS

Eurostat, Batiment Jean Monnet, Rue Alcide de Gasperi, L-2920 Luxembourg, http://epp.eurostat.ec.europa.eu; *Eurostat Yearbook 2006-2007.*

Organisation for Economic Cooperation and Development (OECD), 2 rue Andre Pascal, F-75775 Paris Cedex 16, France, (Telephone in U.S. (202) 785-6323), (Fax in U.S. (202) 785-0350), www.oecd.org; *Indicators of Industrial Activity.*

United Nations Statistics Division, New York, NY 10017, (800) 253-9646, Fax: (212) 963-4116, http://unstats.un.org; *Statistical Yearbook.*

ITALY - INTEREST RATES

Eurostat, Batiment Jean Monnet, Rue Alcide de Gasperi, L-2920 Luxembourg, http://epp.eurostat.ec.europa.eu; *Eurostat Yearbook 2006-2007.*

Organisation for Economic Cooperation and Development (OECD), 2 rue Andre Pascal, F-75775 Paris Cedex 16, France, (Telephone in U.S. (202) 785-6323), (Fax in U.S. (202) 785-0350), www.oecd.org; *Financial Market Trends: OECD Periodical; OECD Economic Outlook 2008;* and *OECD Main Economic Indicators (MEI).*

ITALY - INTERNAL REVENUE

Organisation for Economic Cooperation and Development (OECD), 2 rue Andre Pascal, F-75775 Paris Cedex 16, France, (Telephone in U.S. (202) 785-6323), (Fax in U.S. (202) 785-0350), www.oecd.org; *Revenue Statistics 1965-2006 - 2007 Edition.*

ITALY - INTERNATIONAL FINANCE

Eurostat, Batiment Jean Monnet, Rue Alcide de Gasperi, L-2920 Luxembourg, http://epp.eurostat.ec.europa.eu; *Eurostat Yearbook 2006-2007.*

International Finance Corporation (IFC), 2121 Pennsylvania Avenue, NW, Washington, DC 20433 USA, (202) 473-1000, Fax: (202) 974-4384, www.ifc.org; *Annual Report 2007.*

Organisation for Economic Cooperation and Development (OECD), 2 rue Andre Pascal, F-75775 Paris Cedex 16, France, (Telephone in U.S. (202) 785-6323), (Fax in U.S. (202) 785-0350), www.oecd.org; *Financial Market Trends: OECD Periodical; 2005 OECD Agricultural Outlook Tables, 1970-2014; OECD Economic Outlook 2008;* and *OECD Main Economic Indicators (MEI).*

The World Bank, 1818 H Street, NW, Washington, DC 20433, (202) 473-1000, Fax: (202) 477-6391, www.worldbank.org; *Italy.*

ITALY - INTERNATIONAL LIQUIDITY

International Monetary Fund (IMF), 700 Nineteenth Street, NW, Washington, DC 20431, (202) 623-7000, Fax: (202) 623-4661, www.imf.org; *International Financial Statistics Yearbook 2007.*

Organisation for Economic Cooperation and Development (OECD), 2 rue Andre Pascal, F-75775 Paris Cedex 16, France, (Telephone in U.S. (202) 785-6323), (Fax in U.S. (202) 785-0350), www.oecd.org; *Financial Market Trends: OECD Periodical* and *OECD Economic Outlook 2008.*

ITALY - INTERNATIONAL STATISTICS

Organisation for Economic Cooperation and Development (OECD), 2 rue Andre Pascal, F-75775 Paris Cedex 16, France, (Telephone in U.S. (202) 785-6323), (Fax in U.S. (202) 785-0350), www.oecd.org; *Financial Market Trends: OECD Periodical* and *Household, Tourism, Travel: Trends, Environmental Impacts and Policy Responses.*

ITALY - INTERNATIONAL TRADE

Bernan Essential Government Publications, 4611-F Assembly Drive, Lanham MD, 20706-4391, (301) 459-2255, Fax: (800) 865-3450, www.bernan.com; *OECD Factbook 2006.*

Economist Intelligence Unit, 111 West 57th Street, New York, NY 10019, (212) 554-0600, Fax: (212) 586-1181, www.eiu.com; *Italy Country Report.*

Euromonitor International, Inc., 224 S. Michigan Avenue, Suite 1500, Chicago, IL 60604, (312) 922-1115, Fax: (312) 922-1157, www.euromonitor.com; *European Marketing Data and Statistics 2008; The World Economic Factbook 2008;* and *World Marketing Data and Statistics.*

European Union, Delegation of the European Commission to the United States, 2300 M Street, NW, Washington, DC 20037, (202) 862-9500, Fax: (202) 429-1766, www.eurunion.org; *Eurostatistics: Data for Short-Term Economic Analysis (2007 edition); External and Intra-European Union Trade: Data 1958-2002; External and Intra-European Union Trade: Data 1999-2004;* and *Iron and Steel.*

Eurostat, Batiment Jean Monnet, Rue Alcide de Gasperi, L-2920 Luxembourg, http://epp.eurostat.ec.europa.eu; *Eurostat Yearbook 2006-2007* and Intra- and Extra-EU Trade.

International Iron and Steel Institute (IISI), Rue Colonel Bourg 120, B-1140 Brussels, Belgium, www.worldsteel.org; *Steel Statistical Yearbook 2006.*

International Monetary Fund (IMF), 700 Nineteenth Street, NW, Washington, DC 20431, (202) 623-7000, Fax: (202) 623-4661, www.imf.org; *International Financial Statistics Yearbook 2007.*

M.E. Sharpe, 80 Business Park Drive, Armonk, NY 10504, (800) 541-6563, Fax: (914) 273-2106, www.mesharpe.com; *The Illustrated Book of World Rankings.*

Organisation for Economic Cooperation and Development (OECD), 2 rue Andre Pascal, F-75775 Paris Cedex 16, France, (Telephone in U.S. (202) 785-6323), (Fax in U.S. (202) 785-0350), www.oecd.org; *International Trade by Commodity Statistics (ITCS); 2005 OECD Agricultural Outlook Tables, 1970-2014; OECD Economic Outlook 2008; OECD Economic Survey - Italy 2007; OECD in Figures 2007; OECD Main Economic Indicators (MEI);* and *Statistics on Ship Production, Exports and Orders in 2004.*

Palgrave Macmillan Ltd., Houndmills, Basingstoke, Hampshire, RG21 6XS, England, (Telephone in U.S. (888) 330-8477), (Fax in U.S. (800) 672-2054), www.palgrave.com; *The Statesman's Yearbook 2008.*

Platts, 2 Penn Plaza, 25th Floor, New York, NY 10121-2298, (212) 904-3070, www.platts.com; *Energy Economist.*

Taylor and Francis Group, An Informa Business, 2 Park Square, Milton Park, Abingdon, Oxford OX14 4RN, United Kingdom, (Dial from U.S. (212) 216-7800), (Fax from U.S. (212) 564-7854), www.tandf.co.uk; *The Europa World Year Book.*

United Nations Conference on Trade and Development (UNCTAD), DC2-1120, United Nations, New York, NY 10017, (212) 963-0027, www.unctad.org; *UNCTAD Commodity Yearbook.*

United Nations Food and Agricultural Organization (FAO), Viale delle Terme di Caracalla, 00100 Rome, Italy, (Dial from U.S. (202) 653-2400), (Fax from U.S. (202) 653 5760), www.fao.org; *FAO Trade Yearbook* and *The State of Food and Agriculture (SOFA) 2006.*

United Nations Statistics Division, New York, NY 10017, (800) 253-9646, Fax: (212) 963-4116, http://unstats.un.org; Commodity Trade Statistics Database (COMTRADE); *Energy Statistics Yearbook 2003; International Trade Statistics Yearbook;* and *Statistical Yearbook.*

The World Bank, 1818 H Street, NW, Washington, DC 20433, (202) 473-1000, Fax: (202) 477-6391, www.worldbank.org; *Italy* and *World Development Report 2008.*

World Bureau of Metal Statistics (WBMS), 27a High Street, Ware, Hertfordshire, SG12 9BA, United Kingdom, www.world-bureau.com; *World Flow Charts* and *World Metal Statistics.*

World Trade Organization (WTO), Centre William Rappard, Rue de Lausanne 154, CH-1211 Geneva 21, Switzerland, www.wto.org; *International Trade Statistics 2006.*

ITALY - INTERNET USERS

Eurostat, Batiment Jean Monnet, Rue Alcide de Gasperi, L-2920 Luxembourg, http://epp.eurostat.ec.europa.eu; *Internet Usage by Enterprises 2007.*

International Telecommunication Union (ITU), Place des Nations, 1211 Geneva 20, Switzerland, www.itu.int; *World Telecommunication/ICT Indicators Database on CD-ROM; World Telecommunication/ICT Indicators Database Online;* and *Yearbook of Statistics - Telecommunication Services (Chronological Time Series 1997-2006).*

The World Bank, 1818 H Street, NW, Washington, DC 20433, (202) 473-1000, Fax: (202) 477-6391, www.worldbank.org; *Italy.*

ITALY - INVESTMENTS

International Monetary Fund (IMF), 700 Nineteenth Street, NW, Washington, DC 20431, (202) 623-7000, Fax: (202) 623-4661, www.imf.org; *International Financial Statistics Yearbook 2007.*

Organisation for Economic Cooperation and Development (OECD), 2 rue Andre Pascal, F-75775 Paris Cedex 16, France, (Telephone in U.S. (202) 785-6323), (Fax in U.S. (202) 785-0350), www.oecd.org; *Financial Market Trends: OECD Periodical; Iron and Steel Industry in 2004 (2006 Edition); A New World Map in Textiles and Clothing: Adjusting to Change;*

OECD Economic Outlook 2008; and STructural ANalysis (STAN) database.

ITALY - IRON AND IRON ORE PRODUCTION

See ITALY - MINERAL INDUSTRIES

ITALY - JUTE PRODUCTION

See ITALY - CROPS

ITALY - LABOR

Central Intelligence Agency, Office of Public Affairs, Washington, DC 20505, (703) 482-0623, Fax: (703) 482-1739, www.cia.gov; *The World Factbook.*

Euromonitor International, Inc., 224 S. Michigan Avenue, Suite 1500, Chicago, IL 60604, (312) 922-1115, Fax: (312) 922-1157, www.euromonitor.com; *World Marketing Data and Statistics.*

European Union, Delegation of the European Commission to the United States, 2300 M Street, NW, Washington, DC 20037, (202) 862-9500, Fax: (202) 429-1766, www.eurunion.org; *European Union Labour Force Survey* and *Regions - Statistical Yearbook 2006.*

Eurostat, Batiment Jean Monnet, Rue Alcide de Gasperi, L-2920 Luxembourg, http://epp.eurostat.ec.europa.eu; *Eurostat Yearbook 2006-2007.*

Federal Statistical Office Germany, D-65180 Wiesbaden, Germany, www.destatis.de; *Italy 2006.*

International Labour Office, I.L.O. Publications, 4 route des Morillons, CH-1211 Geneva 22, Switzerland, (Telephone in U.S. (202) 653-7652), (Fax in U.S. (202) 653-7687), www.ilo.org; *Yearbook of Labour Statistics 2006.*

M.E. Sharpe, 80 Business Park Drive, Armonk, NY 10504, (800) 541-6563, Fax: (914) 273-2106, www.mesharpe.com; *The Illustrated Book of World Rankings.*

Organisation for Economic Cooperation and Development (OECD), 2 rue Andre Pascal, F-75775 Paris Cedex 16, France, (Telephone in U.S. (202) 785-6323), (Fax in U.S. (202) 785-0350), www.oecd.org; *Iron and Steel Industry in 2004 (2006 Edition); A New World Map in Textiles and Clothing: Adjusting to Change; OECD Economic Outlook 2008; OECD Economic Survey - Italy 2007; OECD Employment Outlook 2007; OECD Main Economic Indicators (MEI);* and *Statistics on Ship Production, Exports and Orders in 2004.*

Palgrave Macmillan Ltd., Houndmills, Basingstoke, Hampshire, RG21 6XS, England, (Telephone in U.S. (888) 330-8477), (Fax in U.S. (800) 672-2054), www.palgrave.com; *The Statesman's Yearbook 2008.*

Taylor and Francis Group, An Informa Business, 2 Park Square, Milton Park, Abingdon, Oxford OX14 4RN, United Kingdom, (Dial from U.S. (212) 216-7800), (Fax from U.S. (212) 564-7854), www.tandf.co.uk; *The Europa World Year Book.*

United Nations Food and Agricultural Organization (FAO), Viale delle Terme di Caracalla, 00100 Rome, Italy, (Dial from U.S. (202) 653-2400), (Fax from U.S. (202) 653 5760), www.fao.org; *The State of Food and Agriculture (SOFA) 2006.*

The World Bank, 1818 H Street, NW, Washington, DC 20433, (202) 473-1000, Fax: (202) 477-6391, www.worldbank.org; *The World Bank Atlas 2003-2004; World Development Indicators (WDI) 2008;* and *World Development Report 2008.*

ITALY - LAND USE

Central Intelligence Agency, Office of Public Affairs, Washington, DC 20505, (703) 482-0623, Fax: (703) 482-1739, www.cia.gov; *The World Factbook.*

Euromonitor International, Inc., 224 S. Michigan Avenue, Suite 1500, Chicago, IL 60604, (312) 922-1115, Fax: (312) 922-1157, www.euromonitor.com; *European Marketing Data and Statistics 2008.*

European Union, Delegation of the European Commission to the United States, 2300 M Street, NW, Washington, DC 20037, (202) 862-9500, Fax: (202) 429-1766, www.eurunion.org; *Agricultural Statistics: Data 1995-2005; Agriculture in the European Union: Statistical and Economic Information 2006;* and *Regions - Statistical Yearbook 2006.*

Eurostat, Batiment Jean Monnet, Rue Alcide de Gasperi, L-2920 Luxembourg, http://epp.eurostat.ec.europa.eu; *Eurostat Yearbook 2006-2007.*

United Nations Food and Agricultural Organization (FAO), Viale delle Terme di Caracalla, 00100 Rome, Italy, (Dial from U.S. (202) 653-2400), (Fax from U.S. (202) 653 5760), www.fao.org; *FAO Production Yearbook 2002.*

The World Bank, 1818 H Street, NW, Washington, DC 20433, (202) 473-1000, Fax: (202) 477-6391, www.worldbank.org; *World Development Report 2008.*

ITALY - LEATHER INDUSTRY AND TRADE

Eurostat, Batiment Jean Monnet, Rue Alcide de Gasperi, L-2920 Luxembourg, http://epp.eurostat.ec.europa.eu; *Eurostat Yearbook 2006-2007.*

Organisation for Economic Cooperation and Development (OECD), 2 rue Andre Pascal, F-75775 Paris Cedex 16, France, (Telephone in U.S. (202) 785-6323), (Fax in U.S. (202) 785-0350), www.oecd.org; *Indicators of Industrial Activity.*

ITALY - LIBRARIES

M.E. Sharpe, 80 Business Park Drive, Armonk, NY 10504, (800) 541-6563, Fax: (914) 273-2106, www.mesharpe.com; *The Illustrated Book of World Rankings.*

UNESCO Institute for Statistics, C.P. 6128 Succursale Centre-Ville, Montreal, Quebec, H3C 3J7 Canada, (Dial from U.S. (514) 343-6880), (Fax from U.S. (514) 343 6882), www.uis.unesco.org; *Statistical Tables.*

United Nations Statistics Division, New York, NY 10017, (800) 253-9646, Fax: (212) 963-4116, http://unstats.un.org; *Trends in Europe and North America: The Statistical Yearbook of the ECE 2005.*

ITALY - LIFE EXPECTANCY

Central Intelligence Agency, Office of Public Affairs, Washington, DC 20505, (703) 482-0623, Fax: (703) 482-1739, www.cia.gov; *The World Factbook.*

Euromonitor International, Inc., 224 S. Michigan Avenue, Suite 1500, Chicago, IL 60604, (312) 922-1115, Fax: (312) 922-1157, www.euromonitor.com; *The World Economic Factbook 2008.*

Organisation for Economic Cooperation and Development (OECD), 2 rue Andre Pascal, F-75775 Paris Cedex 16, France, (Telephone in U.S. (202) 785-6323), (Fax in U.S. (202) 785-0350), www.oecd.org; *OECD Economic Outlook 2008.*

Palgrave Macmillan Ltd., Houndmills, Basingstoke, Hampshire, RG21 6XS, England, (Telephone in U.S. (888) 330-8477), (Fax in U.S. (800) 672-2054), www.palgrave.com; *The Statesman's Yearbook 2008.*

United Nations Statistics Division, New York, NY 10017, (800) 253-9646, Fax: (212) 963-4116, http://unstats.un.org; *Human Development Report 2006; Trends in Europe and North America: The Statistical Yearbook of the ECE 2005;* and *World Statistics Pocketbook.*

The World Bank, 1818 H Street, NW, Washington, DC 20433, (202) 473-1000, Fax: (202) 477-6391, www.worldbank.org; *The World Bank Atlas 2003-2004* and *World Development Report 2008.*

ITALY - LITERACY

Euromonitor International, Inc., 224 S. Michigan Avenue, Suite 1500, Chicago, IL 60604, (312) 922-1115, Fax: (312) 922-1157, www.euromonitor.com; *World Marketing Data and Statistics.*

ITALY - LIVESTOCK

Euromonitor International, Inc., 224 S. Michigan Avenue, Suite 1500, Chicago, IL 60604, (312) 922-1115, Fax: (312) 922-1157, www.euromonitor.com; *European Marketing Data and Statistics 2008.*

European Union, Delegation of the European Commission to the United States, 2300 M Street, NW, Washington, DC 20037, (202) 862-9500, Fax: (202) 429-1766, www.eurunion.org; *Agricultural Statistics: Data 1995-2005; Eurostatistics: Data for Short-Term Economic Analysis (2007 edition);* and *Regions - Statistical Yearbook 2006.*

Eurostat, Batiment Jean Monnet, Rue Alcide de Gasperi, L-2920 Luxembourg, http://epp.eurostat.ec.europa.eu; *Eurostat Yearbook 2006-2007.*

M.E. Sharpe, 80 Business Park Drive, Armonk, NY 10504, (800) 541-6563, Fax: (914) 273-2106, www.mesharpe.com; *The Illustrated Book of World Rankings.*

Organisation for Economic Cooperation and Development (OECD), 2 rue Andre Pascal, F-75775 Paris Cedex 16, France, (Telephone in U.S. (202) 785-6323), (Fax in U.S. (202) 785-0350), www.oecd.org; *2005 OECD Agricultural Outlook Tables, 1970-2014.*

Palgrave Macmillan Ltd., Houndmills, Basingstoke, Hampshire, RG21 6XS, England, (Telephone in U.S. (888) 330-8477), (Fax in U.S. (800) 672-2054), www.palgrave.com; *The Statesman's Yearbook 2008.*

Taylor and Francis Group, An Informa Business, 2 Park Square, Milton Park, Abingdon, Oxford OX14 4RN, United Kingdom, (Dial from U.S. (212) 216-7800), (Fax from U.S. (212) 564-7854), www.tandf.co.uk; *The Europa World Year Book.*

United Nations Food and Agricultural Organization (FAO), Viale delle Terme di Caracalla, 00100 Rome, Italy, (Dial from U.S. (202) 653-2400), (Fax from U.S. (202) 653 5760), www.fao.org; *FAO Production Yearbook 2002* and *The State of Food and Agriculture (SOFA) 2006.*

United Nations Statistics Division, New York, NY 10017, (800) 253-9646, Fax: (212) 963-4116, http://unstats.un.org; *Statistical Yearbook.*

ITALY - MACHINERY

Organisation for Economic Cooperation and Development (OECD), 2 rue Andre Pascal, F-75775 Paris Cedex 16, France, (Telephone in U.S. (202) 785-6323), (Fax in U.S. (202) 785-0350), www.oecd.org; *Indicators of Industrial Activity.*

ITALY - MAGNESIUM PRODUCTION AND CONSUMPTION

See ITALY - MINERAL INDUSTRIES

ITALY - MANUFACTURES

European Union, Delegation of the European Commission to the United States, 2300 M Street, NW, Washington, DC 20037, (202) 862-9500, Fax: (202) 429-1766, www.eurunion.org; *European Union Labour Force Survey; Eurostatistics: Data for Short-Term Economic Analysis (2007 edition);* and *The Textile Industry in the EU.*

Eurostat, Batiment Jean Monnet, Rue Alcide de Gasperi, L-2920 Luxembourg, http://epp.eurostat.ec.europa.eu; *Eurostat Yearbook 2006-2007.*

M.E. Sharpe, 80 Business Park Drive, Armonk, NY 10504, (800) 541-6563, Fax: (914) 273-2106, www.mesharpe.com; *The Illustrated Book of World Rankings.*

Organisation for Economic Cooperation and Development (OECD), 2 rue Andre Pascal, F-75775 Paris Cedex 16, France, (Telephone in U.S. (202) 785-6323), (Fax in U.S. (202) 785-0350), www.oecd.org; *Indicators of Industrial Activity; International Trade by Commodity Statistics (ITCS); OECD Economic Survey - Italy 2007;* and STructural ANalysis (STAN) database.

United Nations Statistics Division, New York, NY 10017, (800) 253-9646, Fax: (212) 963-4116, http://unstats.un.org; *Statistical Yearbook.*

The World Bank, 1818 H Street, NW, Washington, DC 20433, (202) 473-1000, Fax: (202) 477-6391, www.worldbank.org; *World Development Indicators (WDI) 2008.*

ITALY - MARRIAGE

Eurostat, Batiment Jean Monnet, Rue Alcide de Gasperi, L-2920 Luxembourg, http://epp.eurostat.ec.europa.eu; *Eurostat Yearbook 2006-2007.*

M.E. Sharpe, 80 Business Park Drive, Armonk, NY 10504, (800) 541-6563, Fax: (914) 273-2106, www.mesharpe.com; *The Illustrated Book of World Rankings.*

Taylor and Francis Group, An Informa Business, 2 Park Square, Milton Park, Abingdon, Oxford OX14 4RN, United Kingdom, (Dial from U.S. (212) 216-7800), (Fax from U.S. (212) 564-7854), www.tandf.co.uk; *The Europa World Year Book.*

United Nations Statistics Division, New York, NY 10017, (800) 253-9646, Fax: (212) 963-4116, http://unstats.un.org; *Demographic Yearbook; Statistical Yearbook;* and *Trends in Europe and North America: The Statistical Yearbook of the ECE 2005.*

ITALY - MEAT PRODUCTION

See ITALY - LIVESTOCK

ITALY - MEDICAL CARE, COST OF

International Monetary Fund (IMF), 700 Nineteenth Street, NW, Washington, DC 20431, (202) 623-7000, Fax: (202) 623-4661, www.imf.org; *Government Finance Statistics Yearbook (2008 Edition).*

ITALY - MERCURY PRODUCTION

See ITALY - MINERAL INDUSTRIES

ITALY - METAL PRODUCTS

Eurostat, Batiment Jean Monnet, Rue Alcide de Gasperi, L-2920 Luxembourg, http://epp.eurostat.ec.europa.eu; *Eurostat Yearbook 2006-2007.*

ITALY - MILK PRODUCTION

See ITALY - DAIRY PROCESSING

ITALY - MINERAL INDUSTRIES

Commodity Research Bureau, 330 South Wells Street, Suite 612, Chicago, IL 60606-7110, (800) 621-5271, Fax: (312) 939-4135, www.crbtrader.com; *2006 CRB Commodity Yearbook and CD.*

European Union, Delegation of the European Commission to the United States, 2300 M Street, NW, Washington, DC 20037, (202) 862-9500, Fax: (202) 429-1766, www.eurunion.org; *European Union Energy Transport in Figures 2006; European Union Labour Force Survey; Eurostatistics: Data for Short-Term Economic Analysis (2007 edition); Iron and Steel;* and *Regions - Statistical Yearbook 2006.*

Eurostat, Batiment Jean Monnet, Rue Alcide de Gasperi, L-2920 Luxembourg, http://epp.eurostat.ec.europa.eu; *Energy - Monthly Statistics; Eurostat Yearbook 2006-2007;* and *Panorama of Energy - 2007 Edition.*

International Energy Agency (IEA), 9, rue de la Federation, 75739 Paris Cedex 15, France, www.iea.org; *Key World Energy Statistics 2007.*

International Iron and Steel Institute (IISI), Rue Colonel Bourg 120, B-1140 Brussels, Belgium, www.worldsteel.org; *Steel Statistical Yearbook 2006.*

International Lead and Zinc Study Group (ILZSG), Rua Almirante Barroso 38, 5th Floor, Lisbon 1000 - 013, Portugal, www.ilzsg.org; Interactive Statistical Database.

M.E. Sharpe, 80 Business Park Drive, Armonk, NY 10504, (800) 541-6563, Fax: (914) 273-2106, www.mesharpe.com; *The Illustrated Book of World Rankings.*

Organisation for Economic Cooperation and Development (OECD), 2 rue Andre Pascal, F-75775 Paris Cedex 16, France, (Telephone in U.S. (202) 785-6323), (Fax in U.S. (202) 785-0350), www.oecd.org; *Coal Information: 2007 Edition; Energy Statistics of OECD Countries* (2007 Edition); *Environmental Impacts of Foreign Direct Investment in the Mining Sector in the Newly Independent States (NIS); Indicators of Industrial Activity; International Trade by Commodity Statistics (ITCS); Iron and Steel Industry in 2004 (2006 Edition); OECD Economic Survey - Italy 2007;* STructural ANalysis (STAN) database; and *World Energy Outlook 2007.*

Palgrave Macmillan Ltd., Houndmills, Basingstoke, Hampshire, RG21 6XS, England, (Telephone in U.S. (888) 330-8477), (Fax in U.S. (800) 672-2054), www.palgrave.com; *The Statesman's Yearbook 2008.*

Platts, 2 Penn Plaza, 25th Floor, New York, NY 10121-2298, (212) 904-3070, www.platts.com; *EU Energy.*

Taylor and Francis Group, An Informa Business, 2 Park Square, Milton Park, Abingdon, Oxford OX14 4RN, United Kingdom, (Dial from U.S. (212) 216-7800), (Fax from U.S. (212) 564-7854), www.tandf.co.uk; *The Europa World Year Book.*

United Nations Conference on Trade and Development (UNCTAD), DC2-1120, United Nations, New York, NY 10017, (212) 963-0027, www.unctad.org; *UNCTAD Commodity Yearbook.*

United Nations Statistics Division, New York, NY 10017, (800) 253-9646, Fax: (212) 963-4116, http://unstats.un.org; *Statistical Yearbook.*

The World Bank, 1818 H Street, NW, Washington, DC 20433, (202) 473-1000, Fax: (202) 477-6391, www.worldbank.org; *Italy.*

World Bureau of Metal Statistics (WBMS), 27a High Street, Ware, Hertfordshire, SG12 9BA, United Kingdom, www.world-bureau.com; *Annual Stainless Steel Statistics; World Flow Charts; World Metal Statistics; World Nickel Statistics;* and *World Tin Statistics.*

ITALY - MOLASSES PRODUCTION

See ITALY - CROPS

ITALY - MONEY

European Central Bank (ECB), Postfach 160319, D-60066 Frankfurt am Main, Germany, www.ecb.int; *Monetary Developments in the Euro Area; Monthly Bulletin;* and *Statistics Pocket Book.*

Organisation for Economic Cooperation and Development (OECD), 2 rue Andre Pascal, F-75775 Paris Cedex 16, France, (Telephone in U.S. (202) 785-6323), (Fax in U.S. (202) 785-0350), www.oecd.org; *OECD Economic Survey - Italy 2007.*

ITALY - MONEY EXCHANGE RATES

See ITALY - FOREIGN EXCHANGE RATES

ITALY - MONEY SUPPLY

Economist Intelligence Unit, 111 West 57th Street, New York, NY 10019, (212) 554-0600, Fax: (212) 586-1181, www.eiu.com; *Italy Country Report.*

European Union, Delegation of the European Commission to the United States, 2300 M Street, NW, Washington, DC 20037, (202) 862-9500, Fax: (202) 429-1766, www.eurunion.org; *Eurostatistics: Data for Short-Term Economic Analysis (2007 edition).*

Eurostat, Batiment Jean Monnet, Rue Alcide de Gasperi, L-2920 Luxembourg, http://epp.eurostat.ec.europa.eu; *Eurostat Yearbook 2006-2007.*

International Monetary Fund (IMF), 700 Nineteenth Street, NW, Washington, DC 20431, (202) 623-7000, Fax: (202) 623-4661, www.imf.org; *International Financial Statistics Yearbook 2007.*

Organisation for Economic Cooperation and Development (OECD), 2 rue Andre Pascal, F-75775 Paris Cedex 16, France, (Telephone in U.S. (202) 785-6323), (Fax in U.S. (202) 785-0350), www.oecd.org; *OECD Economic Outlook 2008.*

Taylor and Francis Group, An Informa Business, 2 Park Square, Milton Park, Abingdon, Oxford OX14 4RN, United Kingdom, (Dial from U.S. (212) 216-7800), (Fax from U.S. (212) 564-7854), www.tandf.co.uk; *The Europa World Year Book.*

United Nations Statistics Division, New York, NY 10017, (800) 253-9646, Fax: (212) 963-4116, http://unstats.un.org; *Statistical Yearbook.*

The World Bank, 1818 H Street, NW, Washington, DC 20433, (202) 473-1000, Fax: (202) 477-6391, www.worldbank.org; *Italy* and *World Development Indicators (WDI) 2008.*

ITALY - MONUMENTS AND HISTORIC SITES

UNESCO Institute for Statistics, C.P. 6128 Succursale Centre-Ville, Montreal, Quebec, H3C 3J7 Canada, (Dial from U.S. (514) 343-6880), (Fax from U.S. (514) 343 6882), www.uis.unesco.org; *Statistical Tables.*

ITALY - MORTALITY

Central Intelligence Agency, Office of Public Affairs, Washington, DC 20505, (703) 482-0623, Fax: (703) 482-1739, www.cia.gov; *The World Factbook.*

Euromonitor International, Inc., 224 S. Michigan Avenue, Suite 1500, Chicago, IL 60604, (312) 922-1115, Fax: (312) 922-1157, www.euromonitor.com; *The World Economic Factbook 2008.*

European Union, Delegation of the European Commission to the United States, 2300 M Street, NW, Washington, DC 20037, (202) 862-9500, Fax: (202) 429-1766, www.eurunion.org; *First Demographic Estimates for 2006.*

Eurostat, Batiment Jean Monnet, Rue Alcide de Gasperi, L-2920 Luxembourg, http://epp.eurostat.ec.europa.eu; *Eurostat Yearbook 2006-2007.*

Palgrave Macmillan Ltd., Houndmills, Basingstoke, Hampshire, RG21 6XS, England, (Telephone in U.S. (888) 330-8477), (Fax in U.S. (800) 672-2054), www.palgrave.com; *The Statesman's Yearbook 2008.*

Taylor and Francis Group, An Informa Business, 2 Park Square, Milton Park, Abingdon, Oxford OX14 4RN, United Kingdom, (Dial from U.S. (212) 216-7800), (Fax from U.S. (212) 564-7854), www.tandf.co.uk; *The Europa World Year Book.*

UNICEF, 3 United Nations Plaza, New York, NY 10017, (800) 253-9646, Fax: (212) 887-7465, www.unicef.org; *The State of the World's Children 2008.*

United Nations Statistics Division, New York, NY 10017, (800) 253-9646, Fax: (212) 963-4116, http://unstats.un.org; *Demographic Yearbook; Human Development Report 2006; Statistical Yearbook; Trends in Europe and North America: The Statistical Yearbook of the ECE 2005;* and *World Statistics Pocketbook.*

The World Bank, 1818 H Street, NW, Washington, DC 20433, (202) 473-1000, Fax: (202) 477-6391, www.worldbank.org; *The World Bank Atlas 2003-2004; World Development Indicators (WDI) 2008;* and *World Development Report 2008.*

World Health Organization (WHO), Avenue Appia 20, 1211 Geneve 27, Switzerland, (Telephone in U.S. (212) 331-9081), www.who.int; The WHO Global Atlas of Infectious Diseases and *World Health Report 2006.*

ITALY - MOTION PICTURES

Palgrave Macmillan Ltd., Houndmills, Basingstoke, Hampshire, RG21 6XS, England, (Telephone in U.S. (888) 330-8477), (Fax in U.S. (800) 672-2054), www.palgrave.com; *The Statesman's Yearbook 2008.*

UNESCO Institute for Statistics, C.P. 6128 Succursale Centre-Ville, Montreal, Quebec, H3C 3J7 Canada, (Dial from U.S. (514) 343-6880), (Fax from U.S. (514) 343 6882), www.uis.unesco.org; *Statistical Tables.*

United Nations Statistics Division, New York, NY 10017, (800) 253-9646, Fax: (212) 963-4116, http://unstats.un.org; *Statistical Yearbook.*

ITALY - MOTOR VEHICLES

European Union, Delegation of the European Commission to the United States, 2300 M Street, NW, Washington, DC 20037, (202) 862-9500, Fax: (202) 429-1766, www.eurunion.org; *Statistical Overview of Transport in the European Union (Data 1970-2001).*

Eurostat, Batiment Jean Monnet, Rue Alcide de Gasperi, L-2920 Luxembourg, http://epp.eurostat.ec.europa.eu; *Eurostat Yearbook 2006-2007.*

International Road Federation (IFR), Madison Place, 500 Montgomery Street, 5th Floor, Alexandria, VA 22314, (703) 535-1001, Fax: (703) 535-1007, www.irfnet.org; *World Road Statistics 2006.*

Taylor and Francis Group, An Informa Business, 2 Park Square, Milton Park, Abingdon, Oxford OX14 4RN, United Kingdom, (Dial from U.S. (212) 216-7800), (Fax from U.S. (212) 564-7854), www.tandf.co.uk; *The Europa World Year Book.*

United Nations Statistics Division, New York, NY 10017, (800) 253-9646, Fax: (212) 963-4116, http://unstats.un.org; *Statistical Yearbook.*

ITALY - MUSEUMS

M.E. Sharpe, 80 Business Park Drive, Armonk, NY 10504, (800) 541-6563, Fax: (914) 273-2106, www.mesharpe.com; *The Illustrated Book of World Rankings.*

UNESCO Institute for Statistics, C.P. 6128 Succursale Centre-Ville, Montreal, Quebec, H3C 3J7 Canada, (Dial from U.S. (514) 343-6880), (Fax from U.S. (514) 343 6882), www.uis.unesco.org; *Statistical Tables.*

ITALY - NATURAL GAS PRODUCTION

See ITALY - MINERAL INDUSTRIES

ITALY - NICKEL AND NICKEL ORE

See ITALY - MINERAL INDUSTRIES

ITALY - NUTRITION

United Nations Food and Agricultural Organization (FAO), Viale delle Terme di Caracalla, 00100 Rome, Italy, (Dial from U.S. (202) 653-2400), (Fax from U.S. (202) 653 5760), www.fao.org; *The State of Food and Agriculture (SOFA) 2006.*

ITALY - OATS PRODUCTION

See ITALY - CROPS

ITALY - OIL PRODUCING CROPS

See ITALY - CROPS

ITALY - OLDER PEOPLE

M.E. Sharpe, 80 Business Park Drive, Armonk, NY 10504, (800) 541-6563, Fax: (914) 273-2106, www.mesharpe.com; *The Illustrated Book of World Rankings.*

ITALY - ONION PRODUCTION

See ITALY - CROPS

ITALY - ORANGES PRODUCTION

See ITALY - CROPS

ITALY - PALM OIL PRODUCTION

See ITALY - CROPS

ITALY - PAPER

See ITALY - FORESTS AND FORESTRY

ITALY - PEANUT PRODUCTION

See ITALY - CROPS

ITALY - PEPPER PRODUCTION

See ITALY - CROPS

ITALY - PERIODICALS

UNESCO Institute for Statistics, C.P. 6128 Succursale Centre-Ville, Montreal, Quebec, H3C 3J7 Canada, (Dial from U.S. (514) 343-6880), (Fax from U.S. (514) 343 6882), www.uis.unesco.org; *Statistical Tables.*

ITALY - PESTICIDES

United Nations Food and Agricultural Organization (FAO), Viale delle Terme di Caracalla, 00100 Rome, Italy, (Dial from U.S. (202) 653-2400), (Fax from U.S. (202) 653 5760), www.fao.org; *The State of Food and Agriculture (SOFA) 2006.*

ITALY - PETROLEUM INDUSTRY AND TRADE

Euromonitor International, Inc., 224 S. Michigan Avenue, Suite 1500, Chicago, IL 60604, (312) 922-1115, Fax: (312) 922-1157, www.euromonitor.com; *European Marketing Data and Statistics 2008.*

Eurostat, Batiment Jean Monnet, Rue Alcide de Gasperi, L-2920 Luxembourg, http://epp.eurostat.ec.europa.eu; *Eurostat Yearbook 2006-2007.*

International Energy Agency (IEA), 9, rue de la Federation, 75739 Paris Cedex 15, France, www.iea.org; *Key World Energy Statistics 2007.*

M.E. Sharpe, 80 Business Park Drive, Armonk, NY 10504, (800) 541-6563, Fax: (914) 273-2106, www.mesharpe.com; *The Illustrated Book of World Rankings.*

Organisation for Economic Cooperation and Development (OECD), 2 rue Andre Pascal, F-75775 Paris Cedex 16, France, (Telephone in U.S. (202) 785-6323), (Fax in U.S. (202) 785-0350), www.oecd.org; *Energy Statistics of OECD Countries* (2007 Edition); *International Trade by Commodity Statistics (ITCS); Oil Information 2006 Edition;* and *World Energy Outlook 2007.*

Palgrave Macmillan Ltd., Houndmills, Basingstoke, Hampshire, RG21 6XS, England, (Telephone in U.S. (888) 330-8477), (Fax in U.S. (800) 672-2054), www.palgrave.com; *The Statesman's Yearbook 2008.*

PennWell Corporation, 1421 South Sheridan Road, Tulsa, OK 74112, (918) 835-3161, www.pennwell.com; *International Petroleum Encyclopedia 2007.*

Platts, 2 Penn Plaza, 25th Floor, New York, NY 10121-2298, (212) 904-3070, www.platts.com; *Energy Economist.*

U.S. Department of Energy (DOE), Energy Information Administration (EIA), 1000 Independence Avenue, SW, Washington, DC 20585, (202) 586-8800, www.eia.doe.gov; *International Energy Annual 2004* and *International Energy Outlook 2006.*

United Nations Conference on Trade and Development (UNCTAD), DC2-1120, United Nations, New York, NY 10017, (212) 963-0027, www.unctad.org; *UNCTAD Commodity Yearbook.*

United Nations Statistics Division, New York, NY 10017, (800) 253-9646, Fax: (212) 963-4116, http://unstats.un.org; *Energy Statistics Yearbook 2003; Statistical Yearbook;* and *Trends in Europe and North America: The Statistical Yearbook of the ECE 2005.*

ITALY - PHOSPHATES PRODUCTION

See ITALY - MINERAL INDUSTRIES

ITALY - PIPELINES

European Union, Delegation of the European Commission to the United States, 2300 M Street, NW, Washington, DC 20037, (202) 862-9500, Fax: (202) 429-1766, www.eurunion.org; *Statistical Overview of Transport in the European Union (Data 1970-2001).*

United Nations Statistics Division, New York, NY 10017, (800) 253-9646, Fax: (212) 963-4116, http://unstats.un.org; *Annual Bulletin of Transport Statistics for Europe and North America 2004.*

ITALY - PISTACHIO PRODUCTION

See ITALY - CROPS

ITALY - PLASTICS INDUSTRY AND TRADE

Eurostat, Batiment Jean Monnet, Rue Alcide de Gasperi, L-2920 Luxembourg, http://epp.eurostat.ec.europa.eu; *Eurostat Yearbook 2006-2007.*

Organisation for Economic Cooperation and Development (OECD), 2 rue Andre Pascal, F-75775 Paris Cedex 16, France, (Telephone in U.S. (202) 785-6323), (Fax in U.S. (202) 785-0350), www.oecd.org; *International Trade by Commodity Statistics (ITCS).*

United Nations Statistics Division, New York, NY 10017, (800) 253-9646, Fax: (212) 963-4116, http://unstats.un.org; *Statistical Yearbook.*

ITALY - PLATINUM PRODUCTION

See ITALY - MINERAL INDUSTRIES

ITALY - POLITICAL SCIENCE

Central Intelligence Agency, Office of Public Affairs, Washington, DC 20505, (703) 482-0623, Fax: (703) 482-1739, www.cia.gov; *The World Factbook.*

European Union, Delegation of the European Commission to the United States, 2300 M Street, NW, Washington, DC 20037, (202) 862-9500, Fax: (202) 429-1766, www.eurunion.org; *RD Expenditure in Europe (2006 edition).*

Eurostat, Batiment Jean Monnet, Rue Alcide de Gasperi, L-2920 Luxembourg, http://epp.eurostat.ec.europa.eu; *Eurostat Yearbook 2006-2007.*

International Monetary Fund (IMF), 700 Nineteenth Street, NW, Washington, DC 20431, (202) 623-7000, Fax: (202) 623-4661, www.imf.org; *Government Finance Statistics Yearbook (2008 Edition)* and *International Financial Statistics Yearbook 2007.*

Organisation for Economic Cooperation and Development (OECD), 2 rue Andre Pascal, F-75775 Paris Cedex 16, France, (Telephone in U.S. (202) 785-6323), (Fax in U.S. (202) 785-0350), www.oecd.org; *OECD Economic Outlook 2008* and *Revenue Statistics 1965-2006 - 2007 Edition.*

Palgrave Macmillan Ltd., Houndmills, Basingstoke, Hampshire, RG21 6XS, England, (Telephone in U.S. (888) 330-8477), (Fax in U.S. (800) 672-2054), www.palgrave.com; *The Statesman's Yearbook 2008.*

Taylor and Francis Group, An Informa Business, 2 Park Square, Milton Park, Abingdon, Oxford OX14 4RN, United Kingdom, (Dial from U.S. (212) 216-7800), (Fax from U.S. (212) 564-7854), www.tandf.co.uk; *The Europa World Year Book.*

United Nations Statistics Division, New York, NY 10017, (800) 253-9646, Fax: (212) 963-4116, http://unstats.un.org; *National Accounts Statistics: Compendium of Income Distribution Statistics.*

The World Bank, 1818 H Street, NW, Washington, DC 20433, (202) 473-1000, Fax: (202) 477-6391, www.worldbank.org; *World Development Indicators (WDI) 2008* and *World Development Report 2008.*

ITALY - POPULATION

Central Intelligence Agency, Office of Public Affairs, Washington, DC 20505, (703) 482-0623, Fax: (703) 482-1739, www.cia.gov; *The World Factbook.*

Economist Intelligence Unit, 111 West 57th Street, New York, NY 10019, (212) 554-0600, Fax: (212) 586-1181, www.eiu.com; *Italy Country Report.*

Euromonitor International, Inc., 224 S. Michigan Avenue, Suite 1500, Chicago, IL 60604, (312) 922-1115, Fax: (312) 922-1157, www.euromonitor.com; *European Marketing Data and Statistics 2008* and *The World Economic Factbook 2008.*

European Union, Delegation of the European Commission to the United States, 2300 M Street, NW, Washington, DC 20037, (202) 862-9500, Fax: (202) 429-1766, www.eurunion.org; *European Union Labour Force Survey; First Demographic Estimates for 2006;* and *Regions - Statistical Yearbook 2006.*

Eurostat, Batiment Jean Monnet, Rue Alcide de Gasperi, L-2920 Luxembourg, http://epp.eurostat.ec.europa.eu; *Eurostat Yearbook 2006-2007* and *The Life of Women and Men in Europe - A Statistical Portrait.*

Federal Statistical Office Germany, D-65180 Wiesbaden, Germany, www.destatis.de; *Italy 2006.*

International Labour Office, I.L.O. Publications, 4 route des Morillons, CH-1211 Geneva 22, Switzerland, (Telephone in U.S. (202) 653-7652), (Fax in U.S. (202) 653-7687), www.ilo.org; *Yearbook of Labour Statistics 2006.*

M.E. Sharpe, 80 Business Park Drive, Armonk, NY 10504, (800) 541-6563, Fax: (914) 273-2106, www.mesharpe.com; *The Illustrated Book of World Rankings.*

Organisation for Economic Cooperation and Development (OECD), 2 rue Andre Pascal, F-75775 Paris Cedex 16, France, (Telephone in U.S. (202) 785-6323), (Fax in U.S. (202) 785-0350), www.oecd.org; *Labour Force Statistics: 1986-2005, 2007 Edition.*

Palgrave Macmillan Ltd., Houndmills, Basingstoke, Hampshire, RG21 6XS, England, (Telephone in U.S. (888) 330-8477), (Fax in U.S. (800) 672-2054), www.palgrave.com; *The Statesman's Yearbook 2008.*

Taylor and Francis Group, An Informa Business, 2 Park Square, Milton Park, Abingdon, Oxford OX14 4RN, United Kingdom, (Dial from U.S. (212) 216-7800), (Fax from U.S. (212) 564-7854), www.tandf.co.uk; *The Europa World Year Book.*

U.S. Department of State (DOS), 2201 C Street NW, Washington, DC 20520, (202) 647-4000, www.state.gov; *World Military Expenditures and Arms Transfers (WMEAT).*

UNESCO Institute for Statistics, C.P. 6128 Succursale Centre-Ville, Montreal, Quebec, H3C 3J7 Canada, (Dial from U.S. (514) 343-6880), (Fax from U.S. (514) 343 6882), www.uis.unesco.org; *Statistical Tables.*

United Nations Food and Agricultural Organization (FAO), Viale delle Terme di Caracalla, 00100 Rome, Italy, (Dial from U.S. (202) 653-2400), (Fax from U.S. (202) 653 5760), www.fao.org; *FAO Production Yearbook 2002.*

United Nations Statistics Division, New York, NY 10017, (800) 253-9646, Fax: (212) 963-4116, http://unstats.un.org; *Demographic Yearbook; Human Development Report 2006; Statistical Yearbook; Trends in Europe and North America: The Statistical Yearbook of the ECE 2005;* and *World Statistics Pocketbook.*

The World Bank, 1818 H Street, NW, Washington, DC 20433, (202) 473-1000, Fax: (202) 477-6391, www.worldbank.org; *Italy; The World Bank Atlas 2003-2004;* and *World Development Report 2008.*

World Health Organization (WHO), Avenue Appia 20, 1211 Geneve 27, Switzerland, (Telephone in U.S. (212) 331-9081), www.who.int; *World Health Report 2006.*

ITALY - POPULATION DENSITY

Central Intelligence Agency, Office of Public Affairs, Washington, DC 20505, (703) 482-0623, Fax: (703) 482-1739, www.cia.gov; *The World Factbook.*

Euromonitor International, Inc., 224 S. Michigan Avenue, Suite 1500, Chicago, IL 60604, (312) 922-1115, Fax: (312) 922-1157, www.euromonitor.com; *The World Economic Factbook 2008.*

European Union, Delegation of the European Commission to the United States, 2300 M Street, NW, Washington, DC 20037, (202) 862-9500, Fax: (202) 429-1766, www.eurunion.org; *First Demographic Estimates for 2006.*

Eurostat, Batiment Jean Monnet, Rue Alcide de Gasperi, L-2920 Luxembourg, http://epp.eurostat.ec.europa.eu; *Eurostat Yearbook 2006-2007.*

M.E. Sharpe, 80 Business Park Drive, Armonk, NY 10504, (800) 541-6563, Fax: (914) 273-2106, www.mesharpe.com; *The Illustrated Book of World Rankings.*

Palgrave Macmillan Ltd., Houndmills, Basingstoke, Hampshire, RG21 6XS, England, (Telephone in U.S. (888) 330-8477), (Fax in U.S. (800) 672-2054), www.palgrave.com; *The Statesman's Yearbook 2008.*

Taylor and Francis Group, An Informa Business, 2 Park Square, Milton Park, Abingdon, Oxford OX14 4RN, United Kingdom, (Dial from U.S. (212) 216-7800), (Fax from U.S. (212) 564-7854), www.tandf.co.uk; *The Europa World Year Book.*

UNESCO Institute for Statistics, C.P. 6128 Succursale Centre-Ville, Montreal, Quebec, H3C 3J7 Canada, (Dial from U.S. (514) 343-6880), (Fax from U.S. (514) 343 6882), www.uis.unesco.org; *Statistical Tables.*

United Nations Food and Agricultural Organization (FAO), Viale delle Terme di Caracalla, 00100 Rome, Italy, (Dial from U.S. (202) 653-2400), (Fax from U.S. (202) 653 5760), www.fao.org; *The State of Food and Agriculture (SOFA) 2006.*

United Nations Statistics Division, New York, NY 10017, (800) 253-9646, Fax: (212) 963-4116, http://unstats.un.org; *Statistical Yearbook* and *Trends in Europe and North America: The Statistical Yearbook of the ECE 2005.*

The World Bank, 1818 H Street, NW, Washington, DC 20433, (202) 473-1000, Fax: (202) 477-6391, www.worldbank.org; *Italy* and *World Development Report 2008.*

ITALY - POSTAL SERVICE

European Union, Delegation of the European Commission to the United States, 2300 M Street, NW, Washington, DC 20037, (202) 862-9500, Fax: (202) 429-1766, www.eurunion.org; *Statistical Overview of Transport in the European Union (Data 1970-2001).*

M.E. Sharpe, 80 Business Park Drive, Armonk, NY 10504, (800) 541-6563, Fax: (914) 273-2106, www.mesharpe.com; *The Illustrated Book of World Rankings.*

Palgrave Macmillan Ltd., Houndmills, Basingstoke, Hampshire, RG21 6XS, England, (Telephone in U.S. (888) 330-8477), (Fax in U.S. (800) 672-2054), www.palgrave.com; *The Statesman's Yearbook 2008.*

United Nations Statistics Division, New York, NY 10017, (800) 253-9646, Fax: (212) 963-4116, http://unstats.un.org; *Statistical Yearbook* and *Trends in Europe and North America: The Statistical Yearbook of the ECE 2005.*

ITALY - POWER RESOURCES

Euromonitor International, Inc., 224 S. Michigan Avenue, Suite 1500, Chicago, IL 60604, (312) 922-1115, Fax: (312) 922-1157, www.euromonitor.com; *European Marketing Data and Statistics 2008; The World Economic Factbook 2008;* and *World Marketing Data and Statistics.*

European Union, Delegation of the European Commission to the United States, 2300 M Street, NW, Washington, DC 20037, (202) 862-9500, Fax: (202) 429-1766, www.eurunion.org; *European Union Energy Transport in Figures 2006; European Union Labour Force Survey; Regions - Statistical Yearbook 2006;* and *Statistical Overview of Transport in the European Union (Data 1970-2001).*

Eurostat, Batiment Jean Monnet, Rue Alcide de Gasperi, L-2920 Luxembourg, http://epp.eurostat.ec.europa.eu; *Eurostat Yearbook 2006-2007.*

M.E. Sharpe, 80 Business Park Drive, Armonk, NY 10504, (800) 541-6563, Fax: (914) 273-2106, www.mesharpe.com; *The Illustrated Book of World Rankings.*

Organisation for Economic Cooperation and Development (OECD), 2 rue Andre Pascal, F-75775 Paris Cedex 16, France, (Telephone in U.S. (202) 785-6323), (Fax in U.S. (202) 785-0350), www.oecd.org; *Coal Information: 2007 Edition; Energy Statistics of OECD Countries* (2007 Edition); *Key Environmental Indicators 2004; Oil Information 2006 Edition;* and *World Energy Outlook 2007.*

Palgrave Macmillan Ltd., Houndmills, Basingstoke, Hampshire, RG21 6XS, England, (Telephone in U.S. (888) 330-8477), (Fax in U.S. (800) 672-2054), www.palgrave.com; *The Statesman's Yearbook 2008.*

Platts, 2 Penn Plaza, 25th Floor, New York, NY 10121-2298, (212) 904-3070, www.platts.com; *Energy Economist* and *European Power Daily.*

U.S. Department of Energy (DOE), Energy Information Administration (EIA), 1000 Independence Avenue, SW, Washington, DC 20585, (202) 586-8800, www.eia.doe.gov; *International Energy Annual 2004* and *International Energy Outlook 2006.*

United Nations Statistics Division, New York, NY 10017, (800) 253-9646, Fax: (212) 963-4116, http://unstats.un.org; *Energy Statistics Yearbook 2003; Human Development Report 2006; Statistical Yearbook; Trends in Europe and North America: The Statistical Yearbook of the ECE 2005;* and *World Statistics Pocketbook.*

The World Bank, 1818 H Street, NW, Washington, DC 20433, (202) 473-1000, Fax: (202) 477-6391, www.worldbank.org; *The World Bank Atlas 2003-2004* and *World Development Report 2008.*

ITALY - PRICES

Euromonitor International, Inc., 224 S. Michigan Avenue, Suite 1500, Chicago, IL 60604, (312) 922-1115, Fax: (312) 922-1157, www.euromonitor.com; *European Marketing Data and Statistics 2008* and *World Marketing Data and Statistics.*

European Union, Delegation of the European Commission to the United States, 2300 M Street, NW, Washington, DC 20037, (202) 862-9500, Fax: (202) 429-1766, www.eurunion.org; *Eurostatistics: Data for Short-Term Economic Analysis (2007 edition).*

Eurostat, Batiment Jean Monnet, Rue Alcide de Gasperi, L-2920 Luxembourg, http://epp.eurostat.ec.europa.eu; *Eurostat Yearbook 2006-2007.*

International Labour Office, I.L.O. Publications, 4 route des Morillons, CH-1211 Geneva 22, Switzerland, (Telephone in U.S. (202) 653-7652), (Fax in U.S. (202) 653-7687), www.ilo.org; *Yearbook of Labour Statistics 2006.*

International Lead and Zinc Study Group (ILZSG), Rua Almirante Barroso 38, 5th Floor, Lisbon 1000 - 013, Portugal, www.ilzsg.org; Interactive Statistical Database.

International Monetary Fund (IMF), 700 Nineteenth Street, NW, Washington, DC 20431, (202) 623-7000, Fax: (202) 623-4661, www.imf.org; *International Financial Statistics Yearbook 2007.*

M.E. Sharpe, 80 Business Park Drive, Armonk, NY 10504, (800) 541-6563, Fax: (914) 273-2106, www.mesharpe.com; *The Illustrated Book of World Rankings.*

Organisation for Economic Cooperation and Development (OECD), 2 rue Andre Pascal, F-75775 Paris Cedex 16, France, (Telephone in U.S. (202) 785-6323), (Fax in U.S. (202) 785-0350), www.oecd.org; *Indicators of Industrial Activity; Iron and Steel Industry in 2004 (2006 Edition); OECD Economic Outlook 2008;* and *OECD Main Economic Indicators (MEI).*

Technical Association of the Pulp and Paper Industry (TAPPI), 15 Technology Parkway South, Norcross, GA 30092, (770) 446-1400, Fax: (770) 446-6947, www.tappi.org; *TAPPI Annual Report.*

United Nations Food and Agricultural Organization (FAO), Viale delle Terme di Caracalla, 00100 Rome, Italy, (Dial from U.S. (202) 653-2400), (Fax from U.S. (202) 653 5760), www.fao.org; *The State of Food and Agriculture (SOFA) 2006.*

The World Bank, 1818 H Street, NW, Washington, DC 20433, (202) 473-1000, Fax: (202) 477-6391, www.worldbank.org; *Italy.*

World Bureau of Metal Statistics (WBMS), 27a High Street, Ware, Hertfordshire, SG12 9BA, United Kingdom, www.world-bureau.com; *World Flow Charts* and *World Metal Statistics.*

ITALY - PROFESSIONS

Eurostat, Batiment Jean Monnet, Rue Alcide de Gasperi, L-2920 Luxembourg, http://epp.eurostat.ec.europa.eu; *Eurostat Yearbook 2006-2007.*

UNESCO Institute for Statistics, C.P. 6128 Succursale Centre-Ville, Montreal, Quebec, H3C 3J7 Canada, (Dial from U.S. (514) 343-6880), (Fax from U.S. (514) 343 6882), www.uis.unesco.org; *Statistical Tables.*

United Nations Statistics Division, New York, NY 10017, (800) 253-9646, Fax: (212) 963-4116, http://unstats.un.org; *Statistical Yearbook.*

ITALY - PROPERTY TAX

Eurostat, Batiment Jean Monnet, Rue Alcide de Gasperi, L-2920 Luxembourg, http://epp.eurostat.ec.europa.eu; *Eurostat Yearbook 2006-2007.*

Organisation for Economic Cooperation and Development (OECD), 2 rue Andre Pascal, F-75775 Paris Cedex 16, France, (Telephone in U.S. (202) 785-6323), (Fax in U.S. (202) 785-0350), www.oecd.org; *Revenue Statistics 1965-2006 - 2007 Edition.*

ITALY - PUBLIC HEALTH

Euromonitor International, Inc., 224 S. Michigan Avenue, Suite 1500, Chicago, IL 60604, (312) 922-1115, Fax: (312) 922-1157, www.euromonitor.com; *World Health Databook 2007/2008* and *World Marketing Data and Statistics.*

European Centre for Disease Prevention and Control (ECDC), 171 83 Stockholm, Sweden, www.ecdc.europa.eu; *Eurosurveillance.*

European Union, Delegation of the European Commission to the United States, 2300 M Street, NW, Washington, DC 20037, (202) 862-9500, Fax: (202) 429-1766, www.eurunion.org; *Regions - Statistical Yearbook 2006.*

Eurostat, Batiment Jean Monnet, Rue Alcide de Gasperi, L-2920 Luxembourg, http://epp.eurostat.ec.europa.eu; *Eurostat Yearbook 2006-2007.*

Health and Consumer Protection Directorate-General, European Commission, B-1049 Brussels, Belgium, http://ec.europa.eu/dgs/health_consumer/index_en.htm; *Injuries in the European Union: Statistics Summary 2002-2004.*

M.E. Sharpe, 80 Business Park Drive, Armonk, NY 10504, (800) 541-6563, Fax: (914) 273-2106, www.mesharpe.com; *The Illustrated Book of World Rankings.*

Organisation for Economic Cooperation and Development (OECD), 2 rue Andre Pascal, F-75775 Paris Cedex 16, France, (Telephone in U.S. (202) 785-6323), (Fax in U.S. (202) 785-0350), www.oecd.org; *Health at a Glance 2007 - OECD Indicators.*

Palgrave Macmillan Ltd., Houndmills, Basingstoke, Hampshire, RG21 6XS, England, (Telephone in U.S. (888) 330-8477), (Fax in U.S. (800) 672-2054), www.palgrave.com; *The Statesman's Yearbook 2008.*

Robert Koch Institute, Nordufer 20, D 13353 Berlin, Germany, www.rki.de; *EUVAC-NET Report: Pertussis-Surveillance 1998-2002.*

UNICEF, 3 United Nations Plaza, New York, NY 10017, (800) 253-9646, Fax: (212) 887-7465, www.unicef.org; *The State of the World's Children 2008.*

United Nations Statistics Division, New York, NY 10017, (800) 253-9646, Fax: (212) 963-4116, http://unstats.un.org; *Human Development Report 2006; Statistical Yearbook;* and *Trends in Europe and North America: The Statistical Yearbook of the ECE 2005.*

The World Bank, 1818 H Street, NW, Washington, DC 20433, (202) 473-1000, Fax: (202) 477-6391, www.worldbank.org; *Italy* and *World Development Report 2008.*

World Health Organization (WHO), Avenue Appia 20, 1211 Geneve 27, Switzerland, (Telephone in U.S. (212) 331-9081), www.who.int; The WHO Global Atlas of Infectious Diseases and *World Health Report 2006.*

ITALY - PUBLIC UTILITIES

Eurostat, Batiment Jean Monnet, Rue Alcide de Gasperi, L-2920 Luxembourg, http://epp.eurostat.ec.europa.eu; *Eurostat Yearbook 2006-2007.*

ITALY - PUBLISHERS AND PUBLISHING

Organisation for Economic Cooperation and Development (OECD), 2 rue Andre Pascal, F-75775 Paris Cedex 16, France, (Telephone in U.S. (202) 785-6323), (Fax in U.S. (202) 785-0350), www.oecd.org; *Indicators of Industrial Activity.*

Taylor and Francis Group, An Informa Business, 2 Park Square, Milton Park, Abingdon, Oxford OX14 4RN, United Kingdom, (Dial from U.S. (212) 216-7800), (Fax from U.S. (212) 564-7854), www.tandf.co.uk; *The Europa World Year Book.*

UNESCO Institute for Statistics, C.P. 6128 Succursale Centre-Ville, Montreal, Quebec, H3C 3J7 Canada, (Dial from U.S. (514) 343-6880), (Fax from U.S. (514) 343 6882), www.uis.unesco.org; *Statistical Tables.*

United Nations Statistics Division, New York, NY 10017, (800) 253-9646, Fax: (212) 963-4116, http://unstats.un.org; *Trends in Europe and North America: The Statistical Yearbook of the ECE 2005.*

ITALY - RADIO - RECEIVERS AND RECEPTION

Palgrave Macmillan Ltd., Houndmills, Basingstoke, Hampshire, RG21 6XS, England, (Telephone in U.S. (888) 330-8477), (Fax in U.S. (800) 672-2054), www.palgrave.com; *The Statesman's Yearbook 2008.*

United Nations Statistics Division, New York, NY 10017, (800) 253-9646, Fax: (212) 963-4116, http://unstats.un.org; *Statistical Yearbook.*

ITALY - RAILROADS

Euromonitor International, Inc., 224 S. Michigan Avenue, Suite 1500, Chicago, IL 60604, (312) 922-1115, Fax: (312) 922-1157, www.euromonitor.com; *European Marketing Data and Statistics 2008.*

European Union, Delegation of the European Commission to the United States, 2300 M Street, NW, Washington, DC 20037, (202) 862-9500, Fax: (202) 429-1766, www.eurunion.org; *Regions - Statistical Yearbook 2006* and *Statistical Overview of Transport in the European Union (Data 1970-2001).*

Eurostat, Batiment Jean Monnet, Rue Alcide de Gasperi, L-2920 Luxembourg, http://epp.eurostat.ec.europa.eu; *Eurostat Yearbook 2006-2007.*

Jane's Information Group, 110 North Royal Street, Suite 200, Alexandria, VA 22314, (703) 683-3700, Fax: (800) 836-0297, www.janes.com; *Jane's World Railways.*

Palgrave Macmillan Ltd., Houndmills, Basingstoke, Hampshire, RG21 6XS, England, (Telephone in U.S. (888) 330-8477), (Fax in U.S. (800) 672-2054), www.palgrave.com; *The Statesman's Yearbook 2008.*

Taylor and Francis Group, An Informa Business, 2 Park Square, Milton Park, Abingdon, Oxford OX14 4RN, United Kingdom, (Dial from U.S. (212) 216-7800), (Fax from U.S. (212) 564-7854), www.tandf.co.uk; *The Europa World Year Book.*

United Nations Statistics Division, New York, NY 10017, (800) 253-9646, Fax: (212) 963-4116, http://unstats.un.org; *Annual Bulletin of Transport Statistics for Europe and North America 2004; Statistical Yearbook;* and *Trends in Europe and North America: The Statistical Yearbook of the ECE 2005.*

ITALY - RANCHING

Eurostat, Batiment Jean Monnet, Rue Alcide de Gasperi, L-2920 Luxembourg, http://epp.eurostat.ec.europa.eu; *Eurostat Yearbook 2006-2007.*

ITALY - RELIGION

Central Intelligence Agency, Office of Public Affairs, Washington, DC 20505, (703) 482-0623, Fax: (703) 482-1739, www.cia.gov; *The World Factbook.*

M.E. Sharpe, 80 Business Park Drive, Armonk, NY 10504, (800) 541-6563, Fax: (914) 273-2106, www.mesharpe.com; *The Illustrated Book of World Rankings.*

Palgrave Macmillan Ltd., Houndmills, Basingstoke, Hampshire, RG21 6XS, England, (Telephone in U.S. (888) 330-8477), (Fax in U.S. (800) 672-2054), www.palgrave.com; *The Statesman's Yearbook 2008.*

ITALY - RENT CHARGES

International Labour Office, I.L.O. Publications, 4 route des Morillons, CH-1211 Geneva 22, Switzerland, (Telephone in U.S. (202) 653-7652), (Fax in U.S. (202) 653-7687), www.ilo.org; *Yearbook of Labour Statistics 2006.*

ITALY - RESERVES (ACCOUNTING)

Eurostat, Batiment Jean Monnet, Rue Alcide de Gasperi, L-2920 Luxembourg, http://epp.eurostat.ec.europa.eu; *Eurostat Yearbook 2006-2007.*

Organisation for Economic Cooperation and Development (OECD), 2 rue Andre Pascal, F-75775 Paris Cedex 16, France, (Telephone in U.S. (202) 785-6323), (Fax in U.S. (202) 785-0350), www.oecd.org; *Financial Market Trends: OECD Periodical* and *OECD Economic Outlook 2008.*

United Nations Statistics Division, New York, NY 10017, (800) 253-9646, Fax: (212) 963-4116, http://unstats.un.org; *Statistical Yearbook.*

The World Bank, 1818 H Street, NW, Washington, DC 20433, (202) 473-1000, Fax: (202) 477-6391, www.worldbank.org; *World Development Indicators (WDI) 2008.*

ITALY - RETAIL TRADE

Euromonitor International, Inc., 224 S. Michigan Avenue, Suite 1500, Chicago, IL 60604, (312) 922-1115, Fax: (312) 922-1157, www.euromonitor.com; *Retail Trade International 2007* and *World Marketing Data and Statistics.*

European Union, Delegation of the European Commission to the United States, 2300 M Street, NW, Washington, DC 20037, (202) 862-9500, Fax: (202) 429-1766, www.eurunion.org; *Eurostatistics: Data for Short-Term Economic Analysis (2007 edition).*

Eurostat, Batiment Jean Monnet, Rue Alcide de Gasperi, L-2920 Luxembourg, http://epp.eurostat.ec.europa.eu; *Eurostat Yearbook 2006-2007.*

United Nations Statistics Division, New York, NY 10017, (800) 253-9646, Fax: (212) 963-4116, http://unstats.un.org; *Statistical Yearbook.*

ITALY - RICE PRODUCTION

See ITALY - CROPS

ITALY - ROADS

Central Intelligence Agency, Office of Public Affairs, Washington, DC 20505, (703) 482-0623, Fax: (703) 482-1739, www.cia.gov; *The World Factbook.*

European Union, Delegation of the European Commission to the United States, 2300 M Street, NW, Washington, DC 20037, (202) 862-9500, Fax: (202) 429-1766, www.eurunion.org; *Statistical Overview of Transport in the European Union (Data 1970-2001).*

Eurostat, Batiment Jean Monnet, Rue Alcide de Gasperi, L-2920 Luxembourg, http://epp.eurostat.ec.europa.eu; *Eurostat Yearbook 2006-2007.*

International Road Federation (IFR), Madison Place, 500 Montgomery Street, 5th Floor, Alexandria, VA 22314, (703) 535-1001, Fax: (703) 535-1007, www.irfnet.org; *World Road Statistics 2006.*

Palgrave Macmillan Ltd., Houndmills, Basingstoke, Hampshire, RG21 6XS, England, (Telephone in U.S. (888) 330-8477), (Fax in U.S. (800) 672-2054), www.palgrave.com; *The Statesman's Yearbook 2008.*

United Nations Statistics Division, New York, NY 10017, (800) 253-9646, Fax: (212) 963-4116, http://unstats.un.org; *Annual Bulletin of Transport Statistics for Europe and North America 2004* and *Trends in Europe and North America: The Statistical Yearbook of the ECE 2005.*

ITALY - RUBBER INDUSTRY AND TRADE

Eurostat, Batiment Jean Monnet, Rue Alcide de Gasperi, L-2920 Luxembourg, http://epp.eurostat.ec.europa.eu; *Eurostat Yearbook 2006-2007.*

International Rubber Study Group (IRSG), 1st Floor, Heron House, 109/115 Wembley Hill Road, Wembley, Middlesex HA9 8DA, United Kingdom, www.rubberstudy.com; *Rubber Statistical Bulletin; Summary of World Rubber Statistics 2005; World Rubber Statistics Handbook (Volume 6, 1975-2001);* and *World Rubber Statistics Historic Handbook.*

M.E. Sharpe, 80 Business Park Drive, Armonk, NY 10504, (800) 541-6563, Fax: (914) 273-2106, www.mesharpe.com; *The Illustrated Book of World Rankings.*

Organisation for Economic Cooperation and Development (OECD), 2 rue Andre Pascal, F-75775 Paris Cedex 16, France, (Telephone in U.S. (202) 785-6323), (Fax in U.S. (202) 785-0350), www.oecd.org; *International Trade by Commodity Statistics (ITCS).*

United Nations Statistics Division, New York, NY 10017, (800) 253-9646, Fax: (212) 963-4116, http://unstats.un.org; *Statistical Yearbook.*

ITALY - RYE PRODUCTION

See ITALY - CROPS

ITALY - SAFFLOWER SEED PRODUCTION

See ITALY - CROPS

ITALY - SALT PRODUCTION

See ITALY - MINERAL INDUSTRIES

ITALY - SAVINGS ACCOUNT DEPOSITS

See ITALY - BANKS AND BANKING

ITALY - SHEEP

See ITALY - LIVESTOCK

ITALY - SHIPBUILDING

Organisation for Economic Cooperation and Development (OECD), 2 rue Andre Pascal, F-75775 Paris Cedex 16, France, (Telephone in U.S. (202) 785-6323), (Fax in U.S. (202) 785-0350), www.oecd.org; *Indicators of Industrial Activity.*

ITALY - SHIPPING

European Union, Delegation of the European Commission to the United States, 2300 M Street, NW, Washington, DC 20037, (202) 862-9500, Fax: (202) 429-1766, www.eurunion.org; *Fishery Statistics - 1990-2006; Regions - Statistical Yearbook 2006;* and *Statistical Overview of Transport in the European Union (Data 1970-2001).*

Eurostat, Batiment Jean Monnet, Rue Alcide de Gasperi, L-2920 Luxembourg, http://epp.eurostat.ec.europa.eu; *Eurostat Yearbook 2006-2007.*

Lloyd's Register - Fairplay, 8410 N.W. 53rd Terrace, Suite 207, Miami FL 33166, (305) 718-9929, Fax: (305) 718-9663, www.lrfairplay.com; *Register of Ships 2007-2008; World Casualty Statistics 2007; World Fleet Statistics 2006; World Marine Propulsion Report 2006-2010; World Shipbuilding Statistics 2007;* and The World Shipping Encyclopaedia.

Organisation for Economic Cooperation and Development (OECD), 2 rue Andre Pascal, F-75775 Paris Cedex 16, France, (Telephone in U.S. (202) 785-6323), (Fax in U.S. (202) 785-0350), www.oecd.org; *Statistics on Ship Production, Exports and Orders in 2004.*

Palgrave Macmillan Ltd., Houndmills, Basingstoke, Hampshire, RG21 6XS, England, (Telephone in U.S. (888) 330-8477), (Fax in U.S. (800) 672-2054), www.palgrave.com; *The Statesman's Yearbook 2008.*

Taylor and Francis Group, An Informa Business, 2 Park Square, Milton Park, Abingdon, Oxford OX14 4RN, United Kingdom, (Dial from U.S. (212) 216-7800), (Fax from U.S. (212) 564-7854), www.tandf.co.uk; *The Europa World Year Book.*

U.S. Department of Transportation (DOT), Maritime Administration (MARAD), West Building, Southeast Federal Center, 1200 New Jersey Avenue, SE, Washington, DC 20590, (800) 99-MARAD, www.marad.dot.gov; *World Merchant Fleet 2005.*

United Nations Statistics Division, New York, NY 10017, (800) 253-9646, Fax: (212) 963-4116, http://unstats.un.org; *Annual Bulletin of Transport Statistics for Europe and North America 2004* and *Statistical Yearbook.*

ITALY - SILVER PRODUCTION

See ITALY - MINERAL INDUSTRIES

ITALY - SOCIAL CLASSES

European Union, Delegation of the European Commission to the United States, 2300 M Street, NW, Washington, DC 20037, (202) 862-9500, Fax: (202) 429-1766, www.eurunion.org; *European Union Labour Force Survey.*

ITALY - SOCIAL ECOLOGY

Eurostat, Batiment Jean Monnet, Rue Alcide de Gasperi, L-2920 Luxembourg, http://epp.eurostat.ec.europa.eu; *Eurostat Yearbook 2006-2007.*

M.E. Sharpe, 80 Business Park Drive, Armonk, NY 10504, (800) 541-6563, Fax: (914) 273-2106, www.mesharpe.com; *The Illustrated Book of World Rankings.*

United Nations Statistics Division, New York, NY 10017, (800) 253-9646, Fax: (212) 963-4116, http://unstats.un.org; *World Statistics Pocketbook.*

ITALY - SOCIAL SECURITY

Eurostat, Batiment Jean Monnet, Rue Alcide de Gasperi, L-2920 Luxembourg, http://epp.eurostat.ec.europa.eu; *Eurostat Yearbook 2006-2007.*

International Monetary Fund (IMF), 700 Nineteenth Street, NW, Washington, DC 20431, (202) 623-7000, Fax: (202) 623-4661, www.imf.org; *Government Finance Statistics Yearbook (2008 Edition).*

Organisation for Economic Cooperation and Development (OECD), 2 rue Andre Pascal, F-75775 Paris Cedex 16, France, (Telephone in U.S. (202) 785-6323), (Fax in U.S. (202) 785-0350), www.oecd.org; *Revenue Statistics 1965-2006 - 2007 Edition.*

Palgrave Macmillan Ltd., Houndmills, Basingstoke, Hampshire, RG21 6XS, England, (Telephone in U.S. (888) 330-8477), (Fax in U.S. (800) 672-2054), www.palgrave.com; *The Statesman's Yearbook 2008.*

United Nations Statistics Division, New York, NY 10017, (800) 253-9646, Fax: (212) 963-4116, http://unstats.un.org; *National Accounts Statistics: Compendium of Income Distribution Statistics.*

ITALY - SOYBEAN PRODUCTION

See ITALY - CROPS

ITALY - STEEL PRODUCTION

See ITALY - MINERAL INDUSTRIES

ITALY - STRAW PRODUCTION

See ITALY - CROPS

ITALY - SUGAR PRODUCTION

See ITALY - CROPS

ITALY - SULPHUR PRODUCTION

See ITALY - MINERAL INDUSTRIES

ITALY - SUNFLOWER PRODUCTION

See ITALY - CROPS

ITALY - TAXATION

Eurostat, Batiment Jean Monnet, Rue Alcide de Gasperi, L-2920 Luxembourg, http://epp.eurostat.ec.europa.eu; *Eurostat Yearbook 2006-2007* and *Taxation Trends in the European Union - Data for the EU Member States and Norway.*

International Monetary Fund (IMF), 700 Nineteenth Street, NW, Washington, DC 20431, (202) 623-7000, Fax: (202) 623-4661, www.imf.org; *Government Finance Statistics Yearbook (2008 Edition).*

International Road Federation (IFR), Madison Place, 500 Montgomery Street, 5th Floor, Alexandria, VA 22314, (703) 535-1001, Fax: (703) 535-1007, www.irfnet.org; *World Road Statistics 2006.*

Organisation for Economic Cooperation and Development (OECD), 2 rue Andre Pascal, F-75775 Paris Cedex 16, France, (Telephone in U.S. (202) 785-6323), (Fax in U.S. (202) 785-0350), www.oecd.org; *Revenue Statistics 1965-2006 - 2007 Edition.*

Palgrave Macmillan Ltd., Houndmills, Basingstoke, Hampshire, RG21 6XS, England, (Telephone in U.S. (888) 330-8477), (Fax in U.S. (800) 672-2054), www.palgrave.com; *The Statesman's Yearbook 2008.*

Taylor and Francis Group, An Informa Business, 2 Park Square, Milton Park, Abingdon, Oxford OX14 4RN, United Kingdom, (Dial from U.S. (212) 216-7800), (Fax from U.S. (212) 564-7854), www.tandf.co.uk; *The Europa World Year Book.*

The World Bank, 1818 H Street, NW, Washington, DC 20433, (202) 473-1000, Fax: (202) 477-6391, www.worldbank.org; *World Development Indicators (WDI) 2008.*

ITALY - TEA PRODUCTION

See ITALY - CROPS

ITALY - TELEPHONE

European Union, Delegation of the European Commission to the United States, 2300 M Street, NW, Washington, DC 20037, (202) 862-9500, Fax: (202) 429-1766, www.eurunion.org; *Statistical Overview of Transport in the European Union (Data 1970-2001).*

Eurostat, Batiment Jean Monnet, Rue Alcide de Gasperi, L-2920 Luxembourg, http://epp.eurostat.ec.europa.eu; *Eurostat Yearbook 2006-2007.*

International Telecommunication Union (ITU), Place des Nations, 1211 Geneva 20, Switzerland, www.itu.int; World Telecommunication Indicators Database.

Palgrave Macmillan Ltd., Houndmills, Basingstoke, Hampshire, RG21 6XS, England, (Telephone in U.S. (888) 330-8477), (Fax in U.S. (800) 672-2054), www.palgrave.com; *The Statesman's Yearbook 2008.*

Taylor and Francis Group, An Informa Business, 2 Park Square, Milton Park, Abingdon, Oxford OX14 4RN, United Kingdom, (Dial from U.S. (212) 216-7800), (Fax from U.S. (212) 564-7854), www.tandf.co.uk; *The Europa World Year Book.*

United Nations Statistics Division, New York, NY 10017, (800) 253-9646, Fax: (212) 963-4116, http://unstats.un.org; *Statistical Yearbook; Trends in Europe and North America: The Statistical Yearbook of the ECE 2005;* and *World Statistics Pocketbook.*

ITALY - TELEVISION - RECEIVERS AND RECEPTION

Eurostat, Batiment Jean Monnet, Rue Alcide de Gasperi, L-2920 Luxembourg, http://epp.eurostat.ec.europa.eu; *Eurostat Yearbook 2006-2007.*

United Nations Statistics Division, New York, NY 10017, (800) 253-9646, Fax: (212) 963-4116, http://unstats.un.org; *Statistical Yearbook.*

ITALY - TEXTILE INDUSTRY

Euromonitor International, Inc., 224 S. Michigan Avenue, Suite 1500, Chicago, IL 60604, (312) 922-1115, Fax: (312) 922-1157, www.euromonitor.com; *Retail Trade International 2007.*

European Union, Delegation of the European Commission to the United States, 2300 M Street, NW, Washington, DC 20037, (202) 862-9500, Fax: (202) 429-1766, www.eurunion.org; *Eurostatistics: Data for Short-Term Economic Analysis (2007 edition)* and *The Textile Industry in the EU.*

Eurostat, Batiment Jean Monnet, Rue Alcide de Gasperi, L-2920 Luxembourg, http://epp.eurostat.ec.europa.eu; *Eurostat Yearbook 2006-2007.*

M.E. Sharpe, 80 Business Park Drive, Armonk, NY 10504, (800) 541-6563, Fax: (914) 273-2106, www.mesharpe.com; *The Illustrated Book of World Rankings.*

Organisation for Economic Cooperation and Development (OECD), 2 rue Andre Pascal, F-75775 Paris Cedex 16, France, (Telephone in U.S. (202) 785-6323), (Fax in U.S. (202) 785-0350), www.oecd.org; *Indicators of Industrial Activity; International Trade by Commodity Statistics (ITCS); A New World Map in Textiles and Clothing: Adjusting to Change; 2005 OECD Agricultural Outlook Tables, 1970-2014;* and STructural ANalysis (STAN) database.

Palgrave Macmillan Ltd., Houndmills, Basingstoke, Hampshire, RG21 6XS, England, (Telephone in U.S.

(888) 330-8477), (Fax in U.S. (800) 672-2054), www.palgrave.com; *The Statesman's Yearbook 2008.*

United Nations Conference on Trade and Development (UNCTAD), DC2-1120, United Nations, New York, NY 10017, (212) 963-0027, www.unctad.org; *UNCTAD Commodity Yearbook.*

United Nations Food and Agricultural Organization (FAO), Viale delle Terme di Caracalla, 00100 Rome, Italy, (Dial from U.S. (202) 653-2400), (Fax from U.S. (202) 653 5760), www.fao.org; *FAO Production Yearbook 2002.*

United Nations Statistics Division, New York, NY 10017, (800) 253-9646, Fax: (212) 963-4116, http://unstats.un.org; *Statistical Yearbook.*

ITALY - THEATER

UNESCO Institute for Statistics, C.P. 6128 Succursale Centre-Ville, Montreal, Quebec, H3C 3J7 Canada, (Dial from U.S. (514) 343-6880), (Fax from U.S. (514) 343 6882), www.uis.unesco.org; *Statistical Tables.*

ITALY - TIMBER

See ITALY - FORESTS AND FORESTRY

ITALY - TIN PRODUCTION

See ITALY - MINERAL INDUSTRIES

ITALY - TIRE INDUSTRY

International Rubber Study Group (IRSG), 1st Floor, Heron House, 109/115 Wembley Hill Road, Wembley, Middlesex HA9 8DA, United Kingdom, www.rubberstudy.com; *World Rubber Statistics Handbook (Volume 6, 1975-2001).*

United Nations Statistics Division, New York, NY 10017, (800) 253-9646, Fax: (212) 963-4116, http://unstats.un.org; *Statistical Yearbook.*

ITALY - TOBACCO INDUSTRY

Euromonitor International, Inc., 224 S. Michigan Avenue, Suite 1500, Chicago, IL 60604, (312) 922-1115, Fax: (312) 922-1157, www.euromonitor.com; *European Marketing Data and Statistics 2008.*

Eurostat, Batiment Jean Monnet, Rue Alcide de Gasperi, L-2920 Luxembourg, http://epp.eurostat.ec.europa.eu; *Eurostat Yearbook 2006-2007.*

Foreign Agricultural Service (FAS), U.S. Department of Agriculture (USDA), 1400 Independence Avenue, SW, Washington, DC 20250, (202) 720-3935, www.fas.usda.gov; *Tobacco: World Markets and Trade.*

M.E. Sharpe, 80 Business Park Drive, Armonk, NY 10504, (800) 541-6563, Fax: (914) 273-2106, www.mesharpe.com; *The Illustrated Book of World Rankings.*

Organisation for Economic Cooperation and Development (OECD), 2 rue Andre Pascal, F-75775 Paris Cedex 16, France, (Telephone in U.S. (202) 785-6323), (Fax in U.S. (202) 785-0350), www.oecd.org; *Indicators of Industrial Activity; International Trade by Commodity Statistics (ITCS);* and STructural ANalysis (STAN) database.

United Nations Statistics Division, New York, NY 10017, (800) 253-9646, Fax: (212) 963-4116, http://unstats.un.org; *Statistical Yearbook.*

ITALY - TOURISM

Euromonitor International, Inc., 224 S. Michigan Avenue, Suite 1500, Chicago, IL 60604, (312) 922-1115, Fax: (312) 922-1157, www.euromonitor.com; *European Marketing Data and Statistics 2008; The World Economic Factbook 2008;* and *World Marketing Data and Statistics.*

European Union, Delegation of the European Commission to the United States, 2300 M Street, NW, Washington, DC 20037, (202) 862-9500, Fax: (202) 429-1766, www.eurunion.org; *Statistical Overview of Transport in the European Union (Data 1970-2001).*

Eurostat, Batiment Jean Monnet, Rue Alcide de Gasperi, L-2920 Luxembourg, http://epp.eurostat.ec.europa.eu; *Tourism in Europe: First Results for 2007.*

M.E. Sharpe, 80 Business Park Drive, Armonk, NY 10504, (800) 541-6563, Fax: (914) 273-2106, www.mesharpe.com; *The Illustrated Book of World Rankings.*

Organisation for Economic Cooperation and Development (OECD), 2 rue Andre Pascal, F-75775 Paris Cedex 16, France, (Telephone in U.S. (202) 785-6323), (Fax in U.S. (202) 785-0350), www.oecd.org; *Household, Tourism, Travel: Trends, Environmental Impacts and Policy Responses.*

Palgrave Macmillan Ltd., Houndmills, Basingstoke, Hampshire, RG21 6XS, England, (Telephone in U.S. (888) 330-8477), (Fax in U.S. (800) 672-2054), www.palgrave.com; *The Statesman's Yearbook 2008.*

Taylor and Francis Group, An Informa Business, 2 Park Square, Milton Park, Abingdon, Oxford OX14 4RN, United Kingdom, (Dial from U.S. (212) 216-7800), (Fax from U.S. (212) 564-7854), www.tandf.co.uk; *The Europa World Year Book.*

United Nations Statistics Division, New York, NY 10017, (800) 253-9646, Fax: (212) 963-4116, http://unstats.un.org; *Statistical Yearbook* and *Trends in Europe and North America: The Statistical Yearbook of the ECE 2005.*

United Nations World Tourism Organization (UNWTO), Capitan Haya 42, 28020 Madrid, Spain, www.world-tourism.org; *The Italian Ecotourism Market; Tourism Market Trends 2004 - Europe;* and *Yearbook of Tourism Statistics.*

The World Bank, 1818 H Street, NW, Washington, DC 20433, (202) 473-1000, Fax: (202) 477-6391, www.worldbank.org; *Italy.*

ITALY - TRADE

See ITALY - INTERNATIONAL TRADE

ITALY - TRANSPORTATION

Central Intelligence Agency, Office of Public Affairs, Washington, DC 20505, (703) 482-0623, Fax: (703) 482-1739, www.cia.gov; *The World Factbook.*

Euromonitor International, Inc., 224 S. Michigan Avenue, Suite 1500, Chicago, IL 60604, (312) 922-1115, Fax: (312) 922-1157, www.euromonitor.com; *World Marketing Data and Statistics.*

European Union, Delegation of the European Commission to the United States, 2300 M Street, NW, Washington, DC 20037, (202) 862-9500, Fax: (202) 429-1766, www.eurunion.org; *Regions - Statistical Yearbook 2006* and *Statistical Overview of Transport in the European Union (Data 1970-2001).*

Eurostat, Batiment Jean Monnet, Rue Alcide de Gasperi, L-2920 Luxembourg, http://epp.eurostat.ec.europa.eu; *Eurostat Yearbook 2006-2007; Regional Passenger and Freight Air Transport in Europe in 2006;* and *Regional Road and Rail Transport Networks.*

M.E. Sharpe, 80 Business Park Drive, Armonk, NY 10504, (800) 541-6563, Fax: (914) 273-2106, www.mesharpe.com; *The Illustrated Book of World Rankings.*

Palgrave Macmillan Ltd., Houndmills, Basingstoke, Hampshire, RG21 6XS, England, (Telephone in U.S. (888) 330-8477), (Fax in U.S. (800) 672-2054), www.palgrave.com; *The Statesman's Yearbook 2008.*

Platts, 2 Penn Plaza, 25th Floor, New York, NY 10121-2298, (212) 904-3070, www.platts.com; *Energy Economist.*

Taylor and Francis Group, An Informa Business, 2 Park Square, Milton Park, Abingdon, Oxford OX14 4RN, United Kingdom, (Dial from U.S. (212) 216-7800), (Fax from U.S. (212) 564-7854), www.tandf.co.uk; *The Europa World Year Book.*

United Nations Statistics Division, New York, NY 10017, (800) 253-9646, Fax: (212) 963-4116, http://unstats.un.org; *Energy Statistics Yearbook 2003; Human Development Report 2006;* and *Trends in Europe and North America: The Statistical Yearbook of the ECE 2005.*

The World Bank, 1818 H Street, NW, Washington, DC 20433, (202) 473-1000, Fax: (202) 477-6391, www.worldbank.org; *Italy.*

ITALY - TURKEYS

See ITALY - LIVESTOCK

ITALY - UNEMPLOYMENT

Central Intelligence Agency, Office of Public Affairs, Washington, DC 20505, (703) 482-0623, Fax: (703) 482-1739, www.cia.gov; *The World Factbook.*

Euromonitor International, Inc., 224 S. Michigan Avenue, Suite 1500, Chicago, IL 60604, (312) 922-1115, Fax: (312) 922-1157, www.euromonitor.com; *European Marketing Data and Statistics 2008.*

European Union, Delegation of the European Commission to the United States, 2300 M Street, NW, Washington, DC 20037, (202) 862-9500, Fax: (202) 429-1766, www.eurunion.org; *European Union Labour Force Survey; Eurostatistics: Data for Short-Term Economic Analysis (2007 edition);* and *Regions - Statistical Yearbook 2006.*

Eurostat, Batiment Jean Monnet, Rue Alcide de Gasperi, L-2920 Luxembourg, http://epp.eurostat.ec.europa.eu; *Eurostat Yearbook 2006-2007.*

International Labour Office, I.L.O. Publications, 4 route des Morillons, CH-1211 Geneva 22, Switzerland, (Telephone in U.S. (202) 653-7652), (Fax in U.S. (202) 653-7687), www.ilo.org; *Yearbook of Labour Statistics 2006.*

Organisation for Economic Cooperation and Development (OECD), 2 rue Andre Pascal, F-75775 Paris Cedex 16, France, (Telephone in U.S. (202) 785-6323), (Fax in U.S. (202) 785-0350), www.oecd.org; *Labour Force Statistics: 1986-2005, 2007 Edition; OECD Composite Leading Indicators (CLIs), Updated September 2007; OECD Economic Outlook 2008; OECD Economic Survey - Italy 2007;* and *OECD Employment Outlook 2007.*

Palgrave Macmillan Ltd., Houndmills, Basingstoke, Hampshire, RG21 6XS, England, (Telephone in U.S. (888) 330-8477), (Fax in U.S. (800) 672-2054), www.palgrave.com; *The Statesman's Yearbook 2008.*

United Nations Statistics Division, New York, NY 10017, (800) 253-9646, Fax: (212) 963-4116, http://unstats.un.org; *Statistical Yearbook* and *Trends in Europe and North America: The Statistical Yearbook of the ECE 2005.*

The World Bank, 1818 H Street, NW, Washington, DC 20433, (202) 473-1000, Fax: (202) 477-6391, www.worldbank.org; *Italy.*

ITALY - URANIUM PRODUCTION AND CONSUMPTION

See ITALY - MINERAL INDUSTRIES

ITALY - VITAL STATISTICS

Eurostat, Batiment Jean Monnet, Rue Alcide de Gasperi, L-2920 Luxembourg, http://epp.eurostat.ec.europa.eu; *Eurostat Yearbook 2006-2007.*

Palgrave Macmillan Ltd., Houndmills, Basingstoke, Hampshire, RG21 6XS, England, (Telephone in U.S. (888) 330-8477), (Fax in U.S. (800) 672-2054), www.palgrave.com; *The Statesman's Yearbook 2008.*

United Nations Statistics Division, New York, NY 10017, (800) 253-9646, Fax: (212) 963-4116, http://unstats.un.org; *Statistical Yearbook.*

World Health Organization (WHO), Avenue Appia 20, 1211 Geneve 27, Switzerland, (Telephone in U.S. (212) 331-9081), www.who.int; *World Health Report 2006.*

ITALY - WAGES

Euromonitor International, Inc., 224 S. Michigan Avenue, Suite 1500, Chicago, IL 60604, (312) 922-1115, Fax: (312) 922-1157, www.euromonitor.com; *European Marketing Data and Statistics 2008.*

European Union, Delegation of the European Commission to the United States, 2300 M Street, NW, Washington, DC 20037, (202) 862-9500, Fax: (202) 429-1766, www.eurunion.org; *Agriculture in the European Union: Statistical and Economic Information 2006* and *Eurostatistics: Data for Short-Term Economic Analysis (2007 edition).*

Eurostat, Batiment Jean Monnet, Rue Alcide de Gasperi, L-2920 Luxembourg, http://epp.eurostat.ec.europa.eu; *Eurostat Yearbook 2006-2007.*

International Labour Office, I.L.O. Publications, 4 route des Morillons, CH-1211 Geneva 22, Switzerland, (Telephone in U.S. (202) 653-7652), (Fax in U.S. (202) 653-7687), www.ilo.org; *Yearbook of Labour Statistics 2006.*

Organisation for Economic Cooperation and Development (OECD), 2 rue Andre Pascal, F-75775 Paris Cedex 16, France, (Telephone in U.S. (202) 785-6323), (Fax in U.S. (202) 785-0350), www.oecd.org; *ICT Sector Data and Metadata by Country; OECD Economic Outlook 2008; OECD Main Economic Indicators (MEI);* and STructural ANalysis (STAN) database.

United Nations Statistics Division, New York, NY 10017, (800) 253-9646, Fax: (212) 963-4116, http://unstats.un.org; *Statistical Yearbook.*

The World Bank, 1818 H Street, NW, Washington, DC 20433, (202) 473-1000, Fax: (202) 477-6391, www.worldbank.org; *Italy.*

ITALY - WALNUT PRODUCTION

See ITALY - CROPS

ITALY - WEATHER

See ITALY - CLIMATE

ITALY - WELFARE STATE

Eurostat, Batiment Jean Monnet, Rue Alcide de Gasperi, L-2920 Luxembourg, http://epp.eurostat.ec.europa.eu; *Eurostat Yearbook 2006-2007.*

International Monetary Fund (IMF), 700 Nineteenth Street, NW, Washington, DC 20431, (202) 623-7000, Fax: (202) 623-4661, www.imf.org; *Government Finance Statistics Yearbook (2008 Edition).*

ITALY - WHEAT PRODUCTION

See ITALY - CROPS

ITALY - WHOLESALE PRICE INDEXES

Eurostat, Batiment Jean Monnet, Rue Alcide de Gasperi, L-2920 Luxembourg, http://epp.eurostat.ec.europa.eu; *Eurostat Yearbook 2006-2007.*

International Monetary Fund (IMF), 700 Nineteenth Street, NW, Washington, DC 20431, (202) 623-7000, Fax: (202) 623-4661, www.imf.org; *International Financial Statistics Yearbook 2007.*

United Nations Statistics Division, New York, NY 10017, (800) 253-9646, Fax: (212) 963-4116, http://unstats.un.org; *Statistical Yearbook.*

ITALY - WHOLESALE TRADE

Eurostat, Batiment Jean Monnet, Rue Alcide de Gasperi, L-2920 Luxembourg, http://epp.eurostat.ec.europa.eu; *Eurostat Yearbook 2006-2007.*

United Nations Statistics Division, New York, NY 10017, (800) 253-9646, Fax: (212) 963-4116, http://unstats.un.org; *Statistical Yearbook.*

ITALY - WINE PRODUCTION

See ITALY - BEVERAGE INDUSTRY

ITALY - WOOD AND WOOD PULP

See ITALY - FORESTS AND FORESTRY

ITALY - WOOD PRODUCTS

Eurostat, Batiment Jean Monnet, Rue Alcide de Gasperi, L-2920 Luxembourg, http://epp.eurostat.ec.europa.eu; *Eurostat Yearbook 2006-2007.*

Organisation for Economic Cooperation and Development (OECD), 2 rue Andre Pascal, F-75775 Paris Cedex 16, France, (Telephone in U.S. (202) 785-6323), (Fax in U.S. (202) 785-0350), www.oecd.org; *International Trade by Commodity Statistics (ITCS); OECD Economic Survey - Italy 2007;* and STructural ANalysis (STAN) database.

ITALY - WOOL PRODUCTION

See ITALY - TEXTILE INDUSTRY

ITALY - YARN PRODUCTION

See ITALY - TEXTILE INDUSTRY

ITALY - ZINC AND ZINC ORE

See ITALY - MINERAL INDUSTRIES

ITALY - ZOOS

UNESCO Institute for Statistics, C.P. 6128 Succursale Centre-Ville, Montreal, Quebec, H3C 3J7 Canada, (Dial from U.S. (514) 343-6880), (Fax from U.S. (514) 343 6882), www.uis.unesco.org; *Statistical Tables.*

ITEMIZED DEDUCTIONS (TAXES)

Independent Sector, 1200 Eighteenth Street, NW, Suite 200, Washington, DC 20036, (202) 467-6100, Fax: (202) 467-6101, www.independentsector.org; *Giving and Volunteering in the United States 2001.*

U.S. Department of the Treasury (DOT), Internal Revenue Service (IRS), Statistics of Income Division (SIS), PO Box 2608, Washington, DC, 20013-2608, (202) 874-0410, Fax: (202) 874-0964, www.irs.ustreas.gov; *Statistics of Income Bulletin* and *Statistics of Income Bulletin, Individual Income Tax Returns.*STATISTICS SOURCES, Thirty-second Edition - 2009STATISTICS SOURCES, Thirty-second Edition - 2009

JAILS

Lesotho Bureau of Statistics, Ministry of Finance and Development Planning, PO Box 455, Maseru 100, Lesotho, www.bos.gov.ls; *Crime Statistics 2005* and *Prison Statistics*.

U.S. Department of Justice (DOJ), Bureau of Justice Statistics, 810 Seventh Street, NW, Washington, DC 20531, (202) 307-0765, www.ojp.usdoj.gov/bjs/; *Census of Jails; Challenging the Conditions of Prisons and Jails: A Report on Section 1983 Litigation; Correctional Populations in the United States; Jails in Indian Country, 2003; Prison and Jail Inmates at Midyear 2005; Prisoners in 2004; Profile of Jail Inmates, 2002; Suicide and Homicide in State Prisons and Local Jails;* and *Veterans in Prison or Jail.*

JAMAICA - NATIONAL STATISTICAL OFFICE

Statistical Institute of Jamaica (STATIN), 7 Cecelio Avenue, Kingston 10, Jamaica, (Dial from U.S. (876) 926-5311), (Fax from U.S. (876) 926-1138), www.statinja.com; National Data Center.

JAMAICA - PRIMARY STATISTICS SOURCES

Statistical Institute of Jamaica (STATIN), 7 Cecelio Avenue, Kingston 10, Jamaica, (Dial from U.S. (876) 926-5311), (Fax from U.S. (876) 926-1138), www.statinja.com; *Pocketbook of Statistics 2003* and *Statistical Yearbook of Jamaica.*

JAMAICA - AGRICULTURAL MACHINERY

Economist Intelligence Unit, 111 West 57th Street, New York, NY 10019, (212) 554-0600, Fax: (212) 586-1181, www.eiu.com; *Business Latin America.*

United Nations Statistics Division, New York, NY 10017, (800) 253-9646, Fax: (212) 963-4116, http://unstats.un.org; *Statistical Yearbook.*

JAMAICA - AGRICULTURE

Economist Intelligence Unit, 111 West 57th Street, New York, NY 10019, (212) 554-0600, Fax: (212) 586-1181, www.eiu.com; *Business Latin America* and *Jamaica Country Report.*

Euromonitor International, Inc., 224 S. Michigan Avenue, Suite 1500, Chicago, IL 60604, (312) 922-1115, Fax: (312) 922-1157, www.euromonitor.com; *World Marketing Data and Statistics.*

Inter-American Development Bank (IDB), 1300 New York Avenue, NW, Washington, DC 20577, (202) 623-1000, Fax: (202) 623-3096, www.iadb.org; *The Politics of Policies: Economic and Social Progress in Latin America - 2006 Report.*

M.E. Sharpe, 80 Business Park Drive, Armonk, NY 10504, (800) 541-6563, Fax: (914) 273-2106, www.mesharpe.com; *The Illustrated Book of World Rankings.*

Palgrave Macmillan Ltd., Houndmills, Basingstoke, Hampshire, RG21 6XS, England, (Telephone in U.S. (888) 330-8477), (Fax in U.S. (800) 672-2054), www.palgrave.com; *The Statesman's Yearbook 2008.*

Statistical Institute of Jamaica (STATIN), 7 Cecelio Avenue, Kingston 10, Jamaica, (Dial from U.S. (876) 926-5311), (Fax from U.S. (876) 926-1138), www.statinja.com; *Production Statistics 2007.*

Taylor and Francis Group, An Informa Business, 2 Park Square, Milton Park, Abingdon, Oxford OX14 4RN, United Kingdom, (Dial from U.S. (212) 216-7800), (Fax from U.S. (212) 564-7854), www.tandf.co.uk; *The Europa World Year Book.*

United Nations Conference on Trade and Development (UNCTAD), DC2-1120, United Nations, New York, NY 10017, (212) 963-0027, www.unctad.org; *UNCTAD Commodity Yearbook.*

United Nations Food and Agricultural Organization (FAO), Viale delle Terme di Caracalla, 00100 Rome, Italy, (Dial from U.S. (202) 653-2400), (Fax from U.S. (202) 653 5760), www.fao.org; AQUASTAT; *FAO Trade Yearbook;* and *The State of Food and Agriculture (SOFA) 2006.*

United Nations Statistics Division, New York, NY 10017, (800) 253-9646, Fax: (212) 963-4116, http://unstats.un.org; *Statistical Yearbook for Latin America and the Caribbean 2004.*

The World Bank, 1818 H Street, NW, Washington, DC 20433, (202) 473-1000, Fax: (202) 477-6391, www.worldbank.org; *Jamaica.*

JAMAICA - AIRLINES

Economist Intelligence Unit, 111 West 57th Street, New York, NY 10019, (212) 554-0600, Fax: (212) 586-1181, www.eiu.com; *Business Latin America.*

International Civil Aviation Organization (ICAO), External Relations and Public Information Office (EPO), 999 University Street, Montreal, Quebec H3C 5H7, Canada, (Dial from U.S. (514) 954-8219), (Fax from U.S. (514) 954-6077), www.icao.int; *Civil Aviation Statistics of the World.*

M.E. Sharpe, 80 Business Park Drive, Armonk, NY 10504, (800) 541-6563, Fax: (914) 273-2106, www.mesharpe.com; *The Illustrated Book of World Rankings.*

Palgrave Macmillan Ltd., Houndmills, Basingstoke, Hampshire, RG21 6XS, England, (Telephone in U.S. (888) 330-8477), (Fax in U.S. (800) 672-2054), www.palgrave.com; *The Statesman's Yearbook 2008.*

Taylor and Francis Group, An Informa Business, 2 Park Square, Milton Park, Abingdon, Oxford OX14 4RN, United Kingdom, (Dial from U.S. (212) 216-7800), (Fax from U.S. (212) 564-7854), www.tandf.co.uk; *The Europa World Year Book.*

United Nations Statistics Division, New York, NY 10017, (800) 253-9646, Fax: (212) 963-4116, http://unstats.un.org; *Statistical Yearbook.*

JAMAICA - ALUMINUM MINES AND MINING

International Monetary Fund (IMF), 700 Nineteenth Street, NW, Washington, DC 20431, (202) 623-7000, Fax: (202) 623-4661, www.imf.org; *International Financial Statistics Yearbook 2007.*

Organization of American States (OAS), 17th Street Constitution Avenue NW, Washington, DC 20006, (202) 458-3000, www.oas.org; *The OAS in Transition: 1994-2004.*

JAMAICA - ALUMINUM PRODUCTION

See JAMAICA - MINERAL INDUSTRIES

JAMAICA - AREA

Economist Intelligence Unit, 111 West 57th Street, New York, NY 10019, (212) 554-0600, Fax: (212) 586-1181, www.eiu.com; *Business Latin America.*

JAMAICA - ARMED FORCES

Central Intelligence Agency, Office of Public Affairs, Washington, DC 20505, (703) 482-0623, Fax: (703) 482-1739, www.cia.gov; *The World Factbook.*

Economist Intelligence Unit, 111 West 57th Street, New York, NY 10019, (212) 554-0600, Fax: (212) 586-1181, www.eiu.com; *Business Latin America.*

Euromonitor International, Inc., 224 S. Michigan Avenue, Suite 1500, Chicago, IL 60604, (312) 922-1115, Fax: (312) 922-1157, www.euromonitor.com; *World Marketing Data and Statistics.*

International Institute for Strategic Studies (IISS), Arundel House, 13-15 Arundel Street, Temple Place, London WC2R 3DX, England, www.iiss.org; *The Military Balance 2007.*

International Monetary Fund (IMF), 700 Nineteenth Street, NW, Washington, DC 20431, (202) 623-7000, Fax: (202) 623-4661, www.imf.org; *Government Finance Statistics Yearbook (2008 Edition).*

Palgrave Macmillan Ltd., Houndmills, Basingstoke, Hampshire, RG21 6XS, England, (Telephone in U.S. (888) 330-8477), (Fax in U.S. (800) 672-2054), www.palgrave.com; *The Statesman's Yearbook 2008.*

U.S. Department of State (DOS), 2201 C Street NW, Washington, DC 20520, (202) 647-4000, www.state.gov; *World Military Expenditures and Arms Transfers (WMEAT).*

United Nations Statistics Division, New York, NY 10017, (800) 253-9646, Fax: (212) 963-4116, http://unstats.un.org; *Human Development Report 2006.*

JAMAICA - BALANCE OF PAYMENTS

Economist Intelligence Unit, 111 West 57th Street, New York, NY 10019, (212) 554-0600, Fax: (212) 586-1181, www.eiu.com; *Business Latin America.*

Inter-American Development Bank (IDB), 1300 New York Avenue, NW, Washington, DC 20577, (202) 623-1000, Fax: (202) 623-3096, www.iadb.org; *The Politics of Policies: Economic and Social Progress in Latin America - 2006 Report.*

International Monetary Fund (IMF), 700 Nineteenth Street, NW, Washington, DC 20431, (202) 623-7000, Fax: (202) 623-4661, www.imf.org; *Balance of Payments Statistics Newsletter* and *Balance of Payments Statistics Yearbook 2007.*

Taylor and Francis Group, An Informa Business, 2 Park Square, Milton Park, Abingdon, Oxford OX14 4RN, United Kingdom, (Dial from U.S. (212) 216-7800), (Fax from U.S. (212) 564-7854), www.tandf.co.uk; *The Europa World Year Book.*

United Nations Conference on Trade and Development (UNCTAD), DC2-1120, United Nations, New York, NY 10017, (212) 963-0027, www.unctad.org; *Handbook of Statistics 2005.*

The World Bank, 1818 H Street, NW, Washington, DC 20433, (202) 473-1000, Fax: (202) 477-6391, www.worldbank.org; *Jamaica* and *World Development Report 2008.*

JAMAICA - BANKS AND BANKING

Euromonitor International, Inc., 224 S. Michigan Avenue, Suite 1500, Chicago, IL 60604, (312) 922-1115, Fax: (312) 922-1157, www.euromonitor.com; *World Marketing Data and Statistics.*

Inter-American Development Bank (IDB), 1300 New York Avenue, NW, Washington, DC 20577, (202) 623-1000, Fax: (202) 623-3096, www.iadb.org; *The Politics of Policies: Economic and Social Progress in Latin America - 2006 Report.*

International Monetary Fund (IMF), 700 Nineteenth Street, NW, Washington, DC 20431, (202) 623-7000, Fax: (202) 623-4661, www.imf.org; *International Financial Statistics Yearbook 2007.*

M.E. Sharpe, 80 Business Park Drive, Armonk, NY 10504, (800) 541-6563, Fax: (914) 273-2106, www.mesharpe.com; *The Illustrated Book of World Rankings.*

Organization of American States (OAS), 17th Street Constitution Avenue NW, Washington, DC 20006, (202) 458-3000, www.oas.org; *The OAS in Transition: 1994-2004.*

Palgrave Macmillan Ltd., Houndmills, Basingstoke, Hampshire, RG21 6XS, England, (Telephone in U.S. (888) 330-8477), (Fax in U.S. (800) 672-2054), www.palgrave.com; *The Statesman's Yearbook 2008.*

Taylor and Francis Group, An Informa Business, 2 Park Square, Milton Park, Abingdon, Oxford OX14 4RN, United Kingdom, (Dial from U.S. (212) 216-7800), (Fax from U.S. (212) 564-7854), www.tandf.co.uk; *The Europa World Year Book.*

United Nations Statistics Division, New York, NY 10017, (800) 253-9646, Fax: (212) 963-4116, http://unstats.un.org; *Statistical Yearbook* and *Statistical Yearbook for Latin America and the Caribbean 2004.*

JAMAICA - BARLEY PRODUCTION

See JAMAICA - CROPS

JAMAICA - BEVERAGE INDUSTRY

M.E. Sharpe, 80 Business Park Drive, Armonk, NY 10504, (800) 541-6563, Fax: (914) 273-2106, www.mesharpe.com; *The Illustrated Book of World Rankings.*

United Nations Statistics Division, New York, NY 10017, (800) 253-9646, Fax: (212) 963-4116, http://unstats.un.org; *Statistical Yearbook.*

JAMAICA - BONDS

Inter-American Development Bank (IDB), 1300 New York Avenue, NW, Washington, DC 20577, (202) 623-1000, Fax: (202) 623-3096, www.iadb.org; *The Politics of Policies: Economic and Social Progress in Latin America - 2006 Report.*

Organization of American States (OAS), 17th Street Constitution Avenue NW, Washington, DC 20006, (202) 458-3000, www.oas.org; *The OAS in Transition: 1994-2004.*

United Nations Statistics Division, New York, NY 10017, (800) 253-9646, Fax: (212) 963-4116, http://unstats.un.org; *Statistical Yearbook.*

JAMAICA - BROADCASTING

Central Intelligence Agency, Office of Public Affairs, Washington, DC 20505, (703) 482-0623, Fax: (703) 482-1739, www.cia.gov; *The World Factbook.*

Euromonitor International, Inc., 224 S. Michigan Avenue, Suite 1500, Chicago, IL 60604, (312) 922-1115, Fax: (312) 922-1157, www.euromonitor.com; *World Marketing Data and Statistics.*

M.E. Sharpe, 80 Business Park Drive, Armonk, NY 10504, (800) 541-6563, Fax: (914) 273-2106, www.mesharpe.com; *The Illustrated Book of World Rankings.*

Palgrave Macmillan Ltd., Houndmills, Basingstoke, Hampshire, RG21 6XS, England, (Telephone in U.S. (888) 330-8477), (Fax in U.S. (800) 672-2054), www.palgrave.com; *The Statesman's Yearbook 2008.*

WRTH Publications Limited, PO Box 290, Oxford OX2 7FT, UK, www.wrth.com; *World Radio TV Handbook 2007.*

JAMAICA - BUDGET

Central Intelligence Agency, Office of Public Affairs, Washington, DC 20505, (703) 482-0623, Fax: (703) 482-1739, www.cia.gov; *The World Factbook.*

JAMAICA - BUSINESS

Inter-American Development Bank (IDB), 1300 New York Avenue, NW, Washington, DC 20577, (202) 623-1000, Fax: (202) 623-3096, www.iadb.org; *The Politics of Policies: Economic and Social Progress in Latin America - 2006 Report.*

Statistical Institute of Jamaica (STATIN), 7 Cecelio Avenue, Kingston 10, Jamaica, (Dial from U.S. (876) 926-5311), (Fax from U.S. (876) 926-1138), www.statinja.com; *Production Statistics 2007.*

JAMAICA - CAPITAL INVESTMENTS

Inter-American Development Bank (IDB), 1300 New York Avenue, NW, Washington, DC 20577, (202) 623-1000, Fax: (202) 623-3096, www.iadb.org; *The Politics of Policies: Economic and Social Progress in Latin America - 2006 Report.*

JAMAICA - CAPITAL LEVY

Inter-American Development Bank (IDB), 1300 New York Avenue, NW, Washington, DC 20577, (202) 623-1000, Fax: (202) 623-3096, www.iadb.org; *The Politics of Policies: Economic and Social Progress in Latin America - 2006 Report.*

International Monetary Fund (IMF), 700 Nineteenth Street, NW, Washington, DC 20431, (202) 623-7000, Fax: (202) 623-4661, www.imf.org; *Government Finance Statistics Yearbook (2008 Edition).*

JAMAICA - CATTLE

See JAMAICA - LIVESTOCK

JAMAICA - CHICKENS

See JAMAICA - LIVESTOCK

JAMAICA - CHILDBIRTH - STATISTICS

Central Intelligence Agency, Office of Public Affairs, Washington, DC 20505, (703) 482-0623, Fax: (703) 482-1739, www.cia.gov; *The World Factbook.*

Euromonitor International, Inc., 224 S. Michigan Avenue, Suite 1500, Chicago, IL 60604, (312) 922-1115, Fax: (312) 922-1157, www.euromonitor.com; *International Marketing Data and Statistics 2008* and *The World Economic Factbook 2008.*

M.E. Sharpe, 80 Business Park Drive, Armonk, NY 10504, (800) 541-6563, Fax: (914) 273-2106, www.mesharpe.com; *The Illustrated Book of World Rankings.*

Palgrave Macmillan Ltd., Houndmills, Basingstoke, Hampshire, RG21 6XS, England, (Telephone in U.S. (888) 330-8477), (Fax in U.S. (800) 672-2054), www.palgrave.com; *The Statesman's Yearbook 2008.*

Taylor and Francis Group, An Informa Business, 2 Park Square, Milton Park, Abingdon, Oxford OX14 4RN, United Kingdom, (Dial from U.S. (212) 216-7800), (Fax from U.S. (212) 564-7854), www.tandf.co.uk; *The Europa World Year Book.*

United Nations Statistics Division, New York, NY 10017, (800) 253-9646, Fax: (212) 963-4116, http://unstats.un.org; *Demographic Yearbook; Statistical Yearbook;* and *Statistical Yearbook for Latin America and the Caribbean 2004.*

World Health Organization (WHO), Avenue Appia 20, 1211 Geneve 27, Switzerland, (Telephone in U.S. (212) 331-9081), www.who.int; *World Health Report 2006.*

JAMAICA - CLIMATE

M.E. Sharpe, 80 Business Park Drive, Armonk, NY 10504, (800) 541-6563, Fax: (914) 273-2106, www.mesharpe.com; *The Illustrated Book of World Rankings.*

Palgrave Macmillan Ltd., Houndmills, Basingstoke, Hampshire, RG21 6XS, England, (Telephone in U.S. (888) 330-8477), (Fax in U.S. (800) 672-2054), www.palgrave.com; *The Statesman's Yearbook 2008.*

JAMAICA - COAL PRODUCTION

See JAMAICA - MINERAL INDUSTRIES

JAMAICA - COCOA PRODUCTION

See JAMAICA - CROPS

JAMAICA - COFFEE

See JAMAICA - CROPS

JAMAICA - COMMERCE

Palgrave Macmillan Ltd., Houndmills, Basingstoke, Hampshire, RG21 6XS, England, (Telephone in U.S. (888) 330-8477), (Fax in U.S. (800) 672-2054), www.palgrave.com; *The Statesman's Yearbook 2008.*

JAMAICA - COMMODITY EXCHANGES

Commodity Research Bureau, 330 South Wells Street, Suite 612, Chicago, IL 60606-7110, (800) 621-5271, Fax: (312) 939-4135, www.crbtrader.com; *2006 CRB Commodity Yearbook and CD.*

International Monetary Fund (IMF), 700 Nineteenth Street, NW, Washington, DC 20431, (202) 623-7000, Fax: (202) 623-4661, www.imf.org; *IMF Primary Commodity Prices.*

United Nations Food and Agricultural Organization (FAO), Viale delle Terme di Caracalla, 00100 Rome, Italy, (Dial from U.S. (202) 653-2400), (Fax from U.S. (202) 653 5760), www.fao.org; *The State of Food and Agriculture (SOFA) 2006.*

JAMAICA - CONSTRUCTION INDUSTRY

Economist Intelligence Unit, 111 West 57th Street, New York, NY 10019, (212) 554-0600, Fax: (212) 586-1181, www.eiu.com; *Business Latin America.*

Inter-American Development Bank (IDB), 1300 New York Avenue, NW, Washington, DC 20577, (202) 623-1000, Fax: (202) 623-3096, www.iadb.org; *The Politics of Policies: Economic and Social Progress in Latin America - 2006 Report.*

M.E. Sharpe, 80 Business Park Drive, Armonk, NY 10504, (800) 541-6563, Fax: (914) 273-2106, www.mesharpe.com; *The Illustrated Book of World Rankings.*

Palgrave Macmillan Ltd., Houndmills, Basingstoke, Hampshire, RG21 6XS, England, (Telephone in U.S. (888) 330-8477), (Fax in U.S. (800) 672-2054), www.palgrave.com; *The Statesman's Yearbook 2008.*

United Nations Statistics Division, New York, NY 10017, (800) 253-9646, Fax: (212) 963-4116, http://unstats.un.org; *Statistical Yearbook.*

JAMAICA - CONSUMER PRICE INDEXES

International Labour Office, I.L.O. Publications, 4 route des Morillons, CH-1211 Geneva 22, Switzerland, (Telephone in U.S. (202) 653-7652), (Fax in U.S. (202) 653-7687), www.ilo.org; *Yearbook of Labour Statistics 2006.*

Taylor and Francis Group, An Informa Business, 2 Park Square, Milton Park, Abingdon, Oxford OX14 4RN, United Kingdom, (Dial from U.S. (212) 216-7800), (Fax from U.S. (212) 564-7854), www.tandf.co.uk; *The Europa World Year Book.*

United Nations Statistics Division, New York, NY 10017, (800) 253-9646, Fax: (212) 963-4116, http://unstats.un.org; *Statistical Yearbook.*

The World Bank, 1818 H Street, NW, Washington, DC 20433, (202) 473-1000, Fax: (202) 477-6391, www.worldbank.org; *Jamaica.*

JAMAICA - CONSUMPTION (ECONOMICS)

Economist Intelligence Unit, 111 West 57th Street, New York, NY 10019, (212) 554-0600, Fax: (212) 586-1181, www.eiu.com; *Business Latin America.*

Inter-American Development Bank (IDB), 1300 New York Avenue, NW, Washington, DC 20577, (202) 623-1000, Fax: (202) 623-3096, www.iadb.org; *The Politics of Policies: Economic and Social Progress in Latin America - 2006 Report.*

United Nations Statistics Division, New York, NY 10017, (800) 253-9646, Fax: (212) 963-4116, http://unstats.un.org; *Statistical Yearbook for Latin America and the Caribbean 2004.*

The World Bank, 1818 H Street, NW, Washington, DC 20433, (202) 473-1000, Fax: (202) 477-6391, www.worldbank.org; *World Development Report 2008.*

JAMAICA - CORN INDUSTRY

See JAMAICA - CROPS

JAMAICA - COST AND STANDARD OF LIVING

International Monetary Fund (IMF), 700 Nineteenth Street, NW, Washington, DC 20431, (202) 623-7000, Fax: (202) 623-4661, www.imf.org; *Government Finance Statistics Yearbook (2008 Edition).*

JAMAICA - COTTON

See JAMAICA - CROPS

JAMAICA - CRIME

Yale University Press, PO Box 209040, New Haven, CT 06520-9040, (203) 432-0960, Fax: (203) 432-0948, http://yalepress.yale.edu/yupbooks; *Violence and Crime in Cross-National Perspective.*

JAMAICA - CROPS

Economist Intelligence Unit, 111 West 57th Street, New York, NY 10019, (212) 554-0600, Fax: (212) 586-1181, www.eiu.com; *Business Latin America.*

International Monetary Fund (IMF), 700 Nineteenth Street, NW, Washington, DC 20431, (202) 623-7000, Fax: (202) 623-4661, www.imf.org; *International Financial Statistics Yearbook 2007.*

M.E. Sharpe, 80 Business Park Drive, Armonk, NY 10504, (800) 541-6563, Fax: (914) 273-2106, www.mesharpe.com; *The Illustrated Book of World Rankings.*

Organization of American States (OAS), 17th Street Constitution Avenue NW, Washington, DC 20006, (202) 458-3000, www.oas.org; *The OAS in Transition: 1994-2004.*

Palgrave Macmillan Ltd., Houndmills, Basingstoke, Hampshire, RG21 6XS, England, (Telephone in U.S. (888) 330-8477), (Fax in U.S. (800) 672-2054), www.palgrave.com; *The Statesman's Yearbook 2008.*

Taylor and Francis Group, An Informa Business, 2 Park Square, Milton Park, Abingdon, Oxford OX14 4RN, United Kingdom, (Dial from U.S. (212) 216-7800), (Fax from U.S. (212) 564-7854), www.tandf.co.uk; *The Europa World Year Book.*

United Nations Conference on Trade and Development (UNCTAD), DC2-1120, United Nations, New York, NY 10017, (212) 963-0027, www.unctad.org; *UNCTAD Commodity Yearbook.*

United Nations Food and Agricultural Organization (FAO), Viale delle Terme di Caracalla, 00100 Rome, Italy, (Dial from U.S. (202) 653-2400), (Fax from U.S. (202) 653 5760), www.fao.org; *FAO Production Yearbook 2002* and *The State of Food and Agriculture (SOFA) 2006.*

United Nations Statistics Division, New York, NY 10017, (800) 253-9646, Fax: (212) 963-4116, http://unstats.un.org; *Statistical Yearbook.*

JAMAICA - CUSTOMS ADMINISTRATION

Inter-American Development Bank (IDB), 1300 New York Avenue, NW, Washington, DC 20577, (202) 623-1000, Fax: (202) 623-3096, www.iadb.org; *The Politics of Policies: Economic and Social Progress in Latin America - 2006 Report.*

International Monetary Fund (IMF), 700 Nineteenth Street, NW, Washington, DC 20431, (202) 623-7000, Fax: (202) 623-4661, www.imf.org; *Government Finance Statistics Yearbook (2008 Edition).*

Palgrave Macmillan Ltd., Houndmills, Basingstoke, Hampshire, RG21 6XS, England, (Telephone in U.S. (888) 330-8477), (Fax in U.S. (800) 672-2054), www.palgrave.com; *The Statesman's Yearbook 2008.*

JAMAICA - DAIRY PROCESSING

M.E. Sharpe, 80 Business Park Drive, Armonk, NY 10504, (800) 541-6563, Fax: (914) 273-2106, www.mesharpe.com; *The Illustrated Book of World Rankings.*

Palgrave Macmillan Ltd., Houndmills, Basingstoke, Hampshire, RG21 6XS, England, (Telephone in U.S. (888) 330-8477), (Fax in U.S. (800) 672-2054), www.palgrave.com; *The Statesman's Yearbook 2008.*

Taylor and Francis Group, An Informa Business, 2 Park Square, Milton Park, Abingdon, Oxford OX14 4RN, United Kingdom, (Dial from U.S. (212) 216-7800), (Fax from U.S. (212) 564-7854), www.tandf.co.uk; *The Europa World Year Book.*

United Nations Food and Agricultural Organization (FAO), Viale delle Terme di Caracalla, 00100 Rome, Italy, (Dial from U.S. (202) 653-2400), (Fax from U.S. (202) 653 5760), www.fao.org; *FAO Production Yearbook 2002* and *The State of Food and Agriculture (SOFA) 2006.*

United Nations Statistics Division, New York, NY 10017, (800) 253-9646, Fax: (212) 963-4116, http://unstats.un.org; *Statistical Yearbook.*

JAMAICA - DEATH RATES

See JAMAICA - MORTALITY

JAMAICA - DEBT

Economist Intelligence Unit, 111 West 57th Street, New York, NY 10019, (212) 554-0600, Fax: (212) 586-1181, www.eiu.com; *Business Latin America.*

The World Bank, 1818 H Street, NW, Washington, DC 20433, (202) 473-1000, Fax: (202) 477-6391, www.worldbank.org; *Global Development Finance 2007.*

JAMAICA - DEBTS, EXTERNAL

Economist Intelligence Unit, 111 West 57th Street, New York, NY 10019, (212) 554-0600, Fax: (212) 586-1181, www.eiu.com; *Business Latin America.*

Inter-American Development Bank (IDB), 1300 New York Avenue, NW, Washington, DC 20577, (202) 623-1000, Fax: (202) 623-3096, www.iadb.org; *The Politics of Policies: Economic and Social Progress in Latin America - 2006 Report.*

Palgrave Macmillan Ltd., Houndmills, Basingstoke, Hampshire, RG21 6XS, England, (Telephone in U.S. (888) 330-8477), (Fax in U.S. (800) 672-2054), www.palgrave.com; *The Statesman's Yearbook 2008.*

United Nations Statistics Division, New York, NY 10017, (800) 253-9646, Fax: (212) 963-4116, http://unstats.un.org; *Economic Survey of Latin America and the Caribbean 2004-2005* and *Statistical Yearbook for Latin America and the Caribbean 2004.*

The World Bank, 1818 H Street, NW, Washington, DC 20433, (202) 473-1000, Fax: (202) 477-6391, www.worldbank.org; *Global Development Finance 2007* and *World Development Report 2008.*

JAMAICA - DEFENSE EXPENDITURES

See JAMAICA - ARMED FORCES

JAMAICA - DEFENSE INDUSTRIES

Economist Intelligence Unit, 111 West 57th Street, New York, NY 10019, (212) 554-0600, Fax: (212) 586-1181, www.eiu.com; *Business Latin America.*

The World Bank, 1818 H Street, NW, Washington, DC 20433, (202) 473-1000, Fax: (202) 477-6391, www.worldbank.org; *Jamaica.*

JAMAICA - DEMOGRAPHY

Euromonitor International, Inc., 224 S. Michigan Avenue, Suite 1500, Chicago, IL 60604, (312) 922-1115, Fax: (312) 922-1157, www.euromonitor.com; *International Marketing Data and Statistics 2008; The World Economic Factbook 2008;* and *World Marketing Data and Statistics.*

M.E. Sharpe, 80 Business Park Drive, Armonk, NY 10504, (800) 541-6563, Fax: (914) 273-2106, www.mesharpe.com; *The Illustrated Book of World Rankings.*

Statistical Institute of Jamaica (STATIN), 7 Cecelio Avenue, Kingston 10, Jamaica, (Dial from U.S. (876) 926-5311), (Fax from U.S. (876) 926-1138), www.statinja.com; *Demographic Statistics 2007.*

United Nations Statistics Division, New York, NY 10017, (800) 253-9646, Fax: (212) 963-4116, http://unstats.un.org; *Human Development Report 2006.*

The World Bank, 1818 H Street, NW, Washington, DC 20433, (202) 473-1000, Fax: (202) 477-6391, www.worldbank.org; *Jamaica.*

JAMAICA - DIAMONDS

See JAMAICA - MINERAL INDUSTRIES

JAMAICA - DISPOSABLE INCOME

Inter-American Development Bank (IDB), 1300 New York Avenue, NW, Washington, DC 20577, (202) 623-1000, Fax: (202) 623-3096, www.iadb.org; *The Politics of Policies: Economic and Social Progress in Latin America - 2006 Report.*

M.E. Sharpe, 80 Business Park Drive, Armonk, NY 10504, (800) 541-6563, Fax: (914) 273-2106, www.mesharpe.com; *The Illustrated Book of World Rankings.*

United Nations Statistics Division, New York, NY 10017, (800) 253-9646, Fax: (212) 963-4116, http://unstats.un.org; *National Accounts Statistics: Compendium of Income Distribution Statistics; Statistical Yearbook;* and *Statistical Yearbook for Latin America and the Caribbean 2004.*

JAMAICA - DIVORCE

M.E. Sharpe, 80 Business Park Drive, Armonk, NY 10504, (800) 541-6563, Fax: (914) 273-2106, www.mesharpe.com; *The Illustrated Book of World Rankings.*

United Nations Statistics Division, New York, NY 10017, (800) 253-9646, Fax: (212) 963-4116, http://unstats.un.org; *Demographic Yearbook* and *Statistical Yearbook.*

JAMAICA - ECONOMIC ASSISTANCE

Inter-American Development Bank (IDB), 1300 New York Avenue, NW, Washington, DC 20577, (202) 623-1000, Fax: (202) 623-3096, www.iadb.org; *The Politics of Policies: Economic and Social Progress in Latin America - 2006 Report.*

United Nations Statistics Division, New York, NY 10017, (800) 253-9646, Fax: (212) 963-4116, http://unstats.un.org; *Statistical Yearbook.*

JAMAICA - ECONOMIC CONDITIONS

Center for International Business Education Research (CIBER), Columbia Business School and School of International and Public Affairs, Uris Hall,

Room 212, 3022 Broadway, New York, NY 10027-6902, Mr. Joshua Safier, (212) 854-4750, Fax: (212) 222-9821, www.columbia.edu/cu/ciber/; Datastream International.

Central Intelligence Agency, Office of Public Affairs, Washington, DC 20505, (703) 482-0623, Fax: (703) 482-1739, www.cia.gov; *The World Factbook.*

DSI Data Service Information, Xantener Strasse 51a, D-47495 Rheinberg, Germany, www.dsidata.com; *Campus Solution.*

Dun and Bradstreet (DB) Corporation, 103 JFK Parkway, Short Hills, NJ 07078, (973) 921-5500, www.dnb.com; *Country Report.*

Economist Intelligence Unit, 111 West 57th Street, New York, NY 10019, (212) 554-0600, Fax: (212) 586-1181, www.eiu.com; *Jamaica Country Report.*

Euromonitor International, Inc., 224 S. Michigan Avenue, Suite 1500, Chicago, IL 60604, (312) 922-1115, Fax: (312) 922-1157, www.euromonitor.com; *International Marketing Data and Statistics 2008; The World Economic Factbook 2008;* and *World Marketing Data and Statistics.*

Inter-American Development Bank (IDB), 1300 New York Avenue, NW, Washington, DC 20577, (202) 623-1000, Fax: (202) 623-3096, www.iadb.org; *The Politics of Policies: Economic and Social Progress in Latin America - 2006 Report.*

International Monetary Fund (IMF), 700 Nineteenth Street, NW, Washington, DC 20431, (202) 623-7000, Fax: (202) 623-4661, www.imf.org; *World Economic Outlook Reports.*

M.E. Sharpe, 80 Business Park Drive, Armonk, NY 10504, (800) 541-6563, Fax: (914) 273-2106, www.mesharpe.com; *The Illustrated Book of World Rankings.*

Organization of American States (OAS), 17th Street Constitution Avenue NW, Washington, DC 20006, (202) 458-3000, www.oas.org; *The OAS in Transition: 1994-2004.*

Palgrave Macmillan Ltd., Houndmills, Basingstoke, Hampshire, RG21 6XS, England, (Telephone in U.S. (888) 330-8477), (Fax in U.S. (800) 672-2054), www.palgrave.com; *The Statesman's Yearbook 2008.*

Statistical Institute of Jamaica (STATIN), 7 Cecelio Avenue, Kingston 10, Jamaica, (Dial from U.S. (876) 926-5311), (Fax from U.S. (876) 926-1138), www.statinja.com; *Production Statistics 2007.*

Taylor and Francis Group, An Informa Business, 2 Park Square, Milton Park, Abingdon, Oxford OX14 4RN, United Kingdom, (Dial from U.S. (212) 216-7800), (Fax from U.S. (212) 564-7854), www.tandf.co.uk; *The Europa World Year Book.*

United Nations Statistics Division, New York, NY 10017, (800) 253-9646, Fax: (212) 963-4116, http://unstats.un.org; *Economic Survey of Latin America and the Caribbean 2004-2005* and *World Statistics Pocketbook.*

The World Bank, 1818 H Street, NW, Washington, DC 20433, (202) 473-1000, Fax: (202) 477-6391, www.worldbank.org; *Global Economic Monitor (GEM); Global Economic Prospects 2008; Jamaica; The World Bank Atlas 2003-2004;* and *World Development Report 2008.*

JAMAICA - ECONOMICS - SOCIOLOGICAL ASPECTS

Inter-American Development Bank (IDB), 1300 New York Avenue, NW, Washington, DC 20577, (202) 623-1000, Fax: (202) 623-3096, www.iadb.org; *The Politics of Policies: Economic and Social Progress in Latin America - 2006 Report.*

JAMAICA - EDUCATION

Economist Intelligence Unit, 111 West 57th Street, New York, NY 10019, (212) 554-0600, Fax: (212) 586-1181, www.eiu.com; *Business Latin America.*

Euromonitor International, Inc., 224 S. Michigan Avenue, Suite 1500, Chicago, IL 60604, (312) 922-1115, Fax: (312) 922-1157, www.euromonitor.com; *International Marketing Data and Statistics 2008* and *World Marketing Data and Statistics.*

International Monetary Fund (IMF), 700 Nineteenth Street, NW, Washington, DC 20431, (202) 623-7000, Fax: (202) 623-4661, www.imf.org; *Government Finance Statistics Yearbook (2008 Edition).*

M.E. Sharpe, 80 Business Park Drive, Armonk, NY 10504, (800) 541-6563, Fax: (914) 273-2106, www.mesharpe.com; *The Illustrated Book of World Rankings.*

Palgrave Macmillan Ltd., Houndmills, Basingstoke, Hampshire, RG21 6XS, England, (Telephone in U.S. (888) 330-8477), (Fax in U.S. (800) 672-2054), www.palgrave.com; *The Statesman's Yearbook 2008.*

Taylor and Francis Group, An Informa Business, 2 Park Square, Milton Park, Abingdon, Oxford OX14 4RN, United Kingdom, (Dial from U.S. (212) 216-7800), (Fax from U.S. (212) 564-7854), www.tandf.co.uk; *The Europa World Year Book.*

UNESCO Institute for Statistics, C.P. 6128 Succursale Centre-Ville, Montreal, Quebec, H3C 3J7 Canada, (Dial from U.S. (514) 343-6880), (Fax from U.S. (514) 343 6882), www.uis.unesco.org; *Statistical Tables.*

United Nations Statistics Division, New York, NY 10017, (800) 253-9646, Fax: (212) 963-4116, http://unstats.un.org; *Human Development Report 2006* and *Statistical Yearbook for Latin America and the Caribbean 2004.*

The World Bank, 1818 H Street, NW, Washington, DC 20433, (202) 473-1000, Fax: (202) 477-6391, www.worldbank.org; *Jamaica* and *World Development Report 2008.*

JAMAICA - ELECTRICITY

Economist Intelligence Unit, 111 West 57th Street, New York, NY 10019, (212) 554-0600, Fax: (212) 586-1181, www.eiu.com; *Business Latin America.*

Inter-American Development Bank (IDB), 1300 New York Avenue, NW, Washington, DC 20577, (202) 623-1000, Fax: (202) 623-3096, www.iadb.org; *The Politics of Policies: Economic and Social Progress in Latin America - 2006 Report.*

M.E. Sharpe, 80 Business Park Drive, Armonk, NY 10504, (800) 541-6563, Fax: (914) 273-2106, www.mesharpe.com; *The Illustrated Book of World Rankings.*

Organization of American States (OAS), 17th Street Constitution Avenue NW, Washington, DC 20006, (202) 458-3000, www.oas.org; *The OAS in Transition: 1994-2004.*

Palgrave Macmillan Ltd., Houndmills, Basingstoke, Hampshire, RG21 6XS, England, (Telephone in U.S. (888) 330-8477), (Fax in U.S. (800) 672-2054), www.palgrave.com; *The Statesman's Yearbook 2008.*

U.S. Department of Energy (DOE), Energy Information Administration (EIA), 1000 Independence Avenue, SW, Washington, DC 20585, (202) 586-8800, www.eia.doe.gov; *International Energy Annual 2004* and *International Energy Outlook 2006.*

United Nations Statistics Division, New York, NY 10017, (800) 253-9646, Fax: (212) 963-4116, http://unstats.un.org; *Human Development Report 2006* and *Statistical Yearbook.*

JAMAICA - EMPLOYMENT

Euromonitor International, Inc., 224 S. Michigan Avenue, Suite 1500, Chicago, IL 60604, (312) 922-1115, Fax: (312) 922-1157, www.euromonitor.com; *International Marketing Data and Statistics 2008.*

International Labour Office, I.L.O. Publications, 4 route des Morillons, CH-1211 Geneva 22, Switzerland, (Telephone in U.S. (202) 653-7652), (Fax in U.S. (202) 653-7687), www.ilo.org; *Yearbook of Labour Statistics 2006.*

M.E. Sharpe, 80 Business Park Drive, Armonk, NY 10504, (800) 541-6563, Fax: (914) 273-2106, www.mesharpe.com; *The Illustrated Book of World Rankings.*

Statistical Institute of Jamaica (STATIN), 7 Cecelio Avenue, Kingston 10, Jamaica, (Dial from U.S. (876) 926-5311), (Fax from U.S. (876) 926-1138), www.statinja.com; *Labour Force 2007.*

United Nations Statistics Division, New York, NY 10017, (800) 253-9646, Fax: (212) 963-4116, http://unstats.un.org; *Statistical Yearbook for Latin America and the Caribbean 2004.*

The World Bank, 1818 H Street, NW, Washington, DC 20433, (202) 473-1000, Fax: (202) 477-6391, www.worldbank.org; *Jamaica.*

JAMAICA - ENERGY INDUSTRIES

Enerdata, 10 Rue Royale, 75008 Paris, France, www.enerdata.fr; *Global Energy Market Data.*

United Nations Statistics Division, New York, NY 10017, (800) 253-9646, Fax: (212) 963-4116, http://unstats.un.org; *Statistical Yearbook.*

The World Bank, 1818 H Street, NW, Washington, DC 20433, (202) 473-1000, Fax: (202) 477-6391, www.worldbank.org; *Jamaica.*

JAMAICA - ENVIRONMENTAL CONDITIONS

DSI Data Service Information, Xantener Strasse 51a, D-47495 Rheinberg, Germany, www.dsidata.com; *Campus Solution* and *DSI's Global Environmental Database.*

Economist Intelligence Unit, 111 West 57th Street, New York, NY 10019, (212) 554-0600, Fax: (212) 586-1181, www.eiu.com; *Jamaica Country Report.*

Statistical Institute of Jamaica (STATIN), 7 Cecelio Avenue, Kingston 10, Jamaica, (Dial from U.S. (876) 926-5311), (Fax from U.S. (876) 926-1138), www.statinja.com; *Environmental Statistics 2001.*

United Nations Statistics Division, New York, NY 10017, (800) 253-9646, Fax: (212) 963-4116, http://unstats.un.org; *Bulletin of Industrial Statistics for the Arab Countries.*

JAMAICA - EXPENDITURES, PUBLIC

Inter-American Development Bank (IDB), 1300 New York Avenue, NW, Washington, DC 20577, (202) 623-1000, Fax: (202) 623-3096, www.iadb.org; *The Politics of Policies: Economic and Social Progress in Latin America - 2006 Report.*

Organization of American States (OAS), 17th Street Constitution Avenue NW, Washington, DC 20006, (202) 458-3000, www.oas.org; *The OAS in Transition: 1994-2004.*

United Nations Statistics Division, New York, NY 10017, (800) 253-9646, Fax: (212) 963-4116, http://unstats.un.org; *Statistical Yearbook for Latin America and the Caribbean 2004.*

JAMAICA - EXPORTS

Central Intelligence Agency, Office of Public Affairs, Washington, DC 20505, (703) 482-0623, Fax: (703) 482-1739, www.cia.gov; *The World Factbook.*

Economist Intelligence Unit, 111 West 57th Street, New York, NY 10019, (212) 554-0600, Fax: (212) 586-1181, www.eiu.com; *Business Latin America* and *Jamaica Country Report.*

Euromonitor International, Inc., 224 S. Michigan Avenue, Suite 1500, Chicago, IL 60604, (312) 922-1115, Fax: (312) 922-1157, www.euromonitor.com; *International Marketing Data and Statistics 2008* and *The World Economic Factbook 2008.*

Inter-American Development Bank (IDB), 1300 New York Avenue, NW, Washington, DC 20577, (202) 623-1000, Fax: (202) 623-3096, www.iadb.org; *The Politics of Policies: Economic and Social Progress in Latin America - 2006 Report.*

International Monetary Fund (IMF), 700 Nineteenth Street, NW, Washington, DC 20431, (202) 623-7000, Fax: (202) 623-4661, www.imf.org; *Direction of Trade Statistics Yearbook 2007; Government Finance Statistics Yearbook (2008 Edition);* and *International Financial Statistics Yearbook 2007.*

Organization of American States (OAS), 17th Street Constitution Avenue NW, Washington, DC 20006, (202) 458-3000, www.oas.org; *The OAS in Transition: 1994-2004.*

Palgrave Macmillan Ltd., Houndmills, Basingstoke, Hampshire, RG21 6XS, England, (Telephone in U.S.

(888) 330-8477), (Fax in U.S. (800) 672-2054), www.palgrave.com; *The Statesman's Yearbook 2008.*

Taylor and Francis Group, An Informa Business, 2 Park Square, Milton Park, Abingdon, Oxford OX14 4RN, United Kingdom, (Dial from U.S. (212) 216-7800), (Fax from U.S. (212) 564-7854), www.tandf.co.uk; *The Europa World Year Book.*

United Nations Conference on Trade and Development (UNCTAD), DC2-1120, United Nations, New York, NY 10017, (212) 963-0027, www.unctad.org; *Handbook of Statistics 2005.*

United Nations Food and Agricultural Organization (FAO), Viale delle Terme di Caracalla, 00100 Rome, Italy, (Dial from U.S. (202) 653-2400), (Fax from U.S. (202) 653 5760), www.fao.org; *The State of Food and Agriculture (SOFA) 2006.*

United Nations Statistics Division, New York, NY 10017, (800) 253-9646, Fax: (212) 963-4116, http://unstats.un.org; *Statistical Yearbook for Latin America and the Caribbean 2004.*

The World Bank, 1818 H Street, NW, Washington, DC 20433, (202) 473-1000, Fax: (202) 477-6391, www.worldbank.org; *World Development Report 2008.*

JAMAICA - FEMALE WORKING POPULATION

See JAMAICA - EMPLOYMENT

JAMAICA - FERTILITY, HUMAN

Central Intelligence Agency, Office of Public Affairs, Washington, DC 20505, (703) 482-0623, Fax: (703) 482-1739, www.cia.gov; *The World Factbook.*

M.E. Sharpe, 80 Business Park Drive, Armonk, NY 10504, (800) 541-6563, Fax: (914) 273-2106, www.mesharpe.com; *The Illustrated Book of World Rankings.*

United Nations Statistics Division, New York, NY 10017, (800) 253-9646, Fax: (212) 963-4116, http://unstats.un.org; *Human Development Report 2006.*

The World Bank, 1818 H Street, NW, Washington, DC 20433, (202) 473-1000, Fax: (202) 477-6391, www.worldbank.org; *The World Bank Atlas 2003-2004* and *World Development Report 2008.*

JAMAICA - FERTILIZER INDUSTRY

Economist Intelligence Unit, 111 West 57th Street, New York, NY 10019, (212) 554-0600, Fax: (212) 586-1181, www.eiu.com; *Business Latin America.*

United Nations Food and Agricultural Organization (FAO), Viale delle Terme di Caracalla, 00100 Rome, Italy, (Dial from U.S. (202) 653-2400), (Fax from U.S. (202) 653 5760), www.fao.org; *FAO Fertilizer Yearbook* and *The State of Food and Agriculture (SOFA) 2006.*

United Nations Statistics Division, New York, NY 10017, (800) 253-9646, Fax: (212) 963-4116, http://unstats.un.org; *Statistical Yearbook.*

JAMAICA - FETAL MORTALITY

See JAMAICA - MORTALITY

JAMAICA - FINANCE

Inter-American Development Bank (IDB), 1300 New York Avenue, NW, Washington, DC 20577, (202) 623-1000, Fax: (202) 623-3096, www.iadb.org; *The Politics of Policies: Economic and Social Progress in Latin America - 2006 Report.*

International Monetary Fund (IMF), 700 Nineteenth Street, NW, Washington, DC 20431, (202) 623-7000, Fax: (202) 623-4661, www.imf.org; *International Financial Statistics Yearbook 2007.*

Organization of American States (OAS), 17th Street Constitution Avenue NW, Washington, DC 20006, (202) 458-3000, www.oas.org; *The OAS in Transition: 1994-2004.*

Taylor and Francis Group, An Informa Business, 2 Park Square, Milton Park, Abingdon, Oxford OX14 4RN, United Kingdom, (Dial from U.S. (212) 216-7800), (Fax from U.S. (212) 564-7854), www.tandf.co.uk; *The Europa World Year Book.*

United Nations Statistics Division, New York, NY 10017, (800) 253-9646, Fax: (212) 963-4116, http://unstats.un.org; *National Accounts Statistics: Compendium of Income Distribution Statistics* and *Statistical Yearbook.*

The World Bank, 1818 H Street, NW, Washington, DC 20433, (202) 473-1000, Fax: (202) 477-6391, www.worldbank.org; *Jamaica.*

JAMAICA - FINANCE, PUBLIC

Bernan Essential Government Publications, 4611-F Assembly Drive, Lanham MD, 20706-4391, (301) 459-2255, Fax: (800) 865-3450, www.bernan.com; *National Accounts Statistics.*

Economist Intelligence Unit, 111 West 57th Street, New York, NY 10019, (212) 554-0600, Fax: (212) 586-1181, www.eiu.com; *Jamaica Country Report.*

Inter-American Development Bank (IDB), 1300 New York Avenue, NW, Washington, DC 20577, (202) 623-1000, Fax: (202) 623-3096, www.iadb.org; *The Politics of Policies: Economic and Social Progress in Latin America - 2006 Report.*

International Monetary Fund (IMF), 700 Nineteenth Street, NW, Washington, DC 20431, (202) 623-7000, Fax: (202) 623-4661, www.imf.org; *International Financial Statistics; International Financial Statistics Online Service;* and *International Financial Statistics Yearbook 2007.*

M.E. Sharpe, 80 Business Park Drive, Armonk, NY 10504, (800) 541-6563, Fax: (914) 273-2106, www.mesharpe.com; *The Illustrated Book of World Rankings.*

Organization of American States (OAS), 17th Street Constitution Avenue NW, Washington, DC 20006, (202) 458-3000, www.oas.org; *The OAS in Transition: 1994-2004.*

Palgrave Macmillan Ltd., Houndmills, Basingstoke, Hampshire, RG21 6XS, England, (Telephone in U.S. (888) 330-8477), (Fax in U.S. (800) 672-2054), www.palgrave.com; *The Statesman's Yearbook 2008.*

Taylor and Francis Group, An Informa Business, 2 Park Square, Milton Park, Abingdon, Oxford OX14 4RN, United Kingdom, (Dial from U.S. (212) 216-7800), (Fax from U.S. (212) 564-7854), www.tandf.co.uk; *The Europa World Year Book.*

The World Bank, 1818 H Street, NW, Washington, DC 20433, (202) 473-1000, Fax: (202) 477-6391, www.worldbank.org; *Jamaica.*

JAMAICA - FISHERIES

Inter-American Development Bank (IDB), 1300 New York Avenue, NW, Washington, DC 20577, (202) 623-1000, Fax: (202) 623-3096, www.iadb.org; *The Politics of Policies: Economic and Social Progress in Latin America - 2006 Report.*

M.E. Sharpe, 80 Business Park Drive, Armonk, NY 10504, (800) 541-6563, Fax: (914) 273-2106, www.mesharpe.com; *The Illustrated Book of World Rankings.*

Taylor and Francis Group, An Informa Business, 2 Park Square, Milton Park, Abingdon, Oxford OX14 4RN, United Kingdom, (Dial from U.S. (212) 216-7800), (Fax from U.S. (212) 564-7854), www.tandf.co.uk; *The Europa World Year Book.*

United Nations Conference on Trade and Development (UNCTAD), DC2-1120, United Nations, New York, NY 10017, (212) 963-0027, www.unctad.org; *UNCTAD Commodity Yearbook.*

United Nations Food and Agricultural Organization (FAO), Viale delle Terme di Caracalla, 00100 Rome, Italy, (Dial from U.S. (202) 653-2400), (Fax from U.S. (202) 653 5760), www.fao.org; *FAO Yearbook of Fishery Statistics;* Fishery Databases; FISHSTAT Database. Subjects covered include: Aquaculture production, capture production, fishery commodities; and *The State of Food and Agriculture (SOFA) 2006.*

United Nations Statistics Division, New York, NY 10017, (800) 253-9646, Fax: (212) 963-4116, http://unstats.un.org; *Statistical Yearbook.*

The World Bank, 1818 H Street, NW, Washington, DC 20433, (202) 473-1000, Fax: (202) 477-6391, www.worldbank.org; *Jamaica.*

JAMAICA - FLOUR INDUSTRY

United Nations Statistics Division, New York, NY 10017, (800) 253-9646, Fax: (212) 963-4116, http://unstats.un.org; *Statistical Yearbook.*

JAMAICA - FOOD

United Nations Conference on Trade and Development (UNCTAD), DC2-1120, United Nations, New York, NY 10017, (212) 963-0027, www.unctad.org; *UNCTAD Commodity Yearbook.*

United Nations Food and Agricultural Organization (FAO), Viale delle Terme di Caracalla, 00100 Rome, Italy, (Dial from U.S. (202) 653-2400), (Fax from U.S. (202) 653 5760), www.fao.org; *FAO Production Yearbook 2002* and *The State of Food and Agriculture (SOFA) 2006.*

United Nations Statistics Division, New York, NY 10017, (800) 253-9646, Fax: (212) 963-4116, http://unstats.un.org; *Human Development Report 2006.*

JAMAICA - FOREIGN EXCHANGE RATES

Central Intelligence Agency, Office of Public Affairs, Washington, DC 20505, (703) 482-0623, Fax: (703) 482-1739, www.cia.gov; *The World Factbook.*

Euromonitor International, Inc., 224 S. Michigan Avenue, Suite 1500, Chicago, IL 60604, (312) 922-1115, Fax: (312) 922-1157, www.euromonitor.com; *International Marketing Data and Statistics 2008* and *The World Economic Factbook 2008.*

Inter-American Development Bank (IDB), 1300 New York Avenue, NW, Washington, DC 20577, (202) 623-1000, Fax: (202) 623-3096, www.iadb.org; *The Politics of Policies: Economic and Social Progress in Latin America - 2006 Report.*

International Civil Aviation Organization (ICAO), External Relations and Public Information Office (EPO), 999 University Street, Montreal, Quebec H3C 5H7, Canada, (Dial from U.S. (514) 954-8219), (Fax from U.S. (514) 954-6077), www.icao.int; *Civil Aviation Statistics of the World.*

International Monetary Fund (IMF), 700 Nineteenth Street, NW, Washington, DC 20431, (202) 623-7000, Fax: (202) 623-4661, www.imf.org; *International Financial Statistics Yearbook 2007.*

Organization of American States (OAS), 17th Street Constitution Avenue NW, Washington, DC 20006, (202) 458-3000, www.oas.org; *The OAS in Transition: 1994-2004.*

Taylor and Francis Group, An Informa Business, 2 Park Square, Milton Park, Abingdon, Oxford OX14 4RN, United Kingdom, (Dial from U.S. (212) 216-7800), (Fax from U.S. (212) 564-7854), www.tandf.co.uk; *The Europa World Year Book.*

United Nations Statistics Division, New York, NY 10017, (800) 253-9646, Fax: (212) 963-4116, http://unstats.un.org; *Statistical Yearbook* and *World Statistics Pocketbook.*

JAMAICA - FORESTS AND FORESTRY

Economist Intelligence Unit, 111 West 57th Street, New York, NY 10019, (212) 554-0600, Fax: (212) 586-1181, www.eiu.com; *Business Latin America.*

Inter-American Development Bank (IDB), 1300 New York Avenue, NW, Washington, DC 20577, (202) 623-1000, Fax: (202) 623-3096, www.iadb.org; *The Politics of Policies: Economic and Social Progress in Latin America - 2006 Report.*

M.E. Sharpe, 80 Business Park Drive, Armonk, NY 10504, (800) 541-6563, Fax: (914) 273-2106, www.mesharpe.com; *The Illustrated Book of World Rankings.*

Taylor and Francis Group, An Informa Business, 2 Park Square, Milton Park, Abingdon, Oxford OX14

4RN, United Kingdom, (Dial from U.S. (212) 216-7800), (Fax from U.S. (212) 564-7854), www.tandf.co.uk; *The Europa World Year Book.*

UNESCO Institute for Statistics, C.P. 6128 Succursale Centre-Ville, Montreal, Quebec, H3C 3J7 Canada, (Dial from U.S. (514) 343-6880), (Fax from U.S. (514) 343 6882), www.uis.unesco.org; *Statistical Tables.*

United Nations Conference on Trade and Development (UNCTAD), DC2-1120, United Nations, New York, NY 10017, (212) 963-0027, www.unctad.org; *UNCTAD Commodity Yearbook.*

United Nations Food and Agricultural Organization (FAO), Viale delle Terme di Caracalla, 00100 Rome, Italy, (Dial from U.S. (202) 653-2400), (Fax from U.S. (202) 653 5760), www.fao.org; *FAO Yearbook of Forest Products* and *The State of Food and Agriculture (SOFA) 2006.*

United Nations Statistics Division, New York, NY 10017, (800) 253-9646, Fax: (212) 963-4116, http://unstats.un.org; *Statistical Yearbook.*

The World Bank, 1818 H Street, NW, Washington, DC 20433, (202) 473-1000, Fax: (202) 477-6391, www.worldbank.org; *Jamaica* and *World Development Report 2008.*

JAMAICA - GAS PRODUCTION

See JAMAICA - MINERAL INDUSTRIES

JAMAICA - GEOGRAPHIC INFORMATION SYSTEMS

M.E. Sharpe, 80 Business Park Drive, Armonk, NY 10504, (800) 541-6563, Fax: (914) 273-2106, www.mesharpe.com; *The Illustrated Book of World Rankings.*

The World Bank, 1818 H Street, NW, Washington, DC 20433, (202) 473-1000, Fax: (202) 477-6391, www.worldbank.org; *Jamaica.*

JAMAICA - GOLD INDUSTRY

Economist Intelligence Unit, 111 West 57th Street, New York, NY 10019, (212) 554-0600, Fax: (212) 586-1181, www.eiu.com; *Business Latin America.*

International Monetary Fund (IMF), 700 Nineteenth Street, NW, Washington, DC 20431, (202) 623-7000, Fax: (202) 623-4661, www.imf.org; *International Financial Statistics Yearbook 2007.*

United Nations Statistics Division, New York, NY 10017, (800) 253-9646, Fax: (212) 963-4116, http://unstats.un.org; *Statistical Yearbook.*

JAMAICA - GOLD PRODUCTION

See JAMAICA - MINERAL INDUSTRIES

JAMAICA - GRANTS-IN-AID

International Monetary Fund (IMF), 700 Nineteenth Street, NW, Washington, DC 20431, (202) 623-7000, Fax: (202) 623-4661, www.imf.org; *Government Finance Statistics Yearbook (2008 Edition).*

JAMAICA - GROSS DOMESTIC PRODUCT

Economist Intelligence Unit, 111 West 57th Street, New York, NY 10019, (212) 554-0600, Fax: (212) 586-1181, www.eiu.com; *Business Latin America* and *Jamaica Country Report.*

Euromonitor International, Inc., 224 S. Michigan Avenue, Suite 1500, Chicago, IL 60604, (312) 922-1115, Fax: (312) 922-1157, www.euromonitor.com; *International Marketing Data and Statistics 2008* and *The World Economic Factbook 2008.*

Inter-American Development Bank (IDB), 1300 New York Avenue, NW, Washington, DC 20577, (202) 623-1000, Fax: (202) 623-3096, www.iadb.org; *The Politics of Policies: Economic and Social Progress in Latin America - 2006 Report.*

M.E. Sharpe, 80 Business Park Drive, Armonk, NY 10504, (800) 541-6563, Fax: (914) 273-2106, www.mesharpe.com; *The Illustrated Book of World Rankings.*

Organization of American States (OAS), 17th Street Constitution Avenue NW, Washington, DC 20006, (202) 458-3000, www.oas.org; *The OAS in Transition: 1994-2004.*

Taylor and Francis Group, An Informa Business, 2 Park Square, Milton Park, Abingdon, Oxford OX14 4RN, United Kingdom, (Dial from U.S. (212) 216-7800), (Fax from U.S. (212) 564-7854), www.tandf.co.uk; *The Europa World Year Book.*

United Nations Statistics Division, New York, NY 10017, (800) 253-9646, Fax: (212) 963-4116, http://unstats.un.org; *Human Development Report 2006; National Accounts Statistics: Compendium of Income Distribution Statistics; Statistical Yearbook;* and *Statistical Yearbook for Latin America and the Caribbean 2004.*

The World Bank, 1818 H Street, NW, Washington, DC 20433, (202) 473-1000, Fax: (202) 477-6391, www.worldbank.org; *World Development Report 2008.*

JAMAICA - GROSS NATIONAL PRODUCT

Euromonitor International, Inc., 224 S. Michigan Avenue, Suite 1500, Chicago, IL 60604, (312) 922-1115, Fax: (312) 922-1157, www.euromonitor.com; *International Marketing Data and Statistics 2008.*

Inter-American Development Bank (IDB), 1300 New York Avenue, NW, Washington, DC 20577, (202) 623-1000, Fax: (202) 623-3096, www.iadb.org; *The Politics of Policies: Economic and Social Progress in Latin America - 2006 Report.*

M.E. Sharpe, 80 Business Park Drive, Armonk, NY 10504, (800) 541-6563, Fax: (914) 273-2106, www.mesharpe.com; *The Illustrated Book of World Rankings.*

Palgrave Macmillan Ltd., Houndmills, Basingstoke, Hampshire, RG21 6XS, England, (Telephone in U.S. (888) 330-8477), (Fax in U.S. (800) 672-2054), www.palgrave.com; *The Statesman's Yearbook 2008.*

U.S. Department of State (DOS), 2201 C Street NW, Washington, DC 20520, (202) 647-4000, www.state.gov; *World Military Expenditures and Arms Transfers (WMEAT).*

United Nations Statistics Division, New York, NY 10017, (800) 253-9646, Fax: (212) 963-4116, http://unstats.un.org; *Statistical Yearbook.*

The World Bank, 1818 H Street, NW, Washington, DC 20433, (202) 473-1000, Fax: (202) 477-6391, www.worldbank.org; *The World Bank Atlas 2003-2004* and *World Development Report 2008.*

JAMAICA - HIDES AND SKINS INDUSTRY

United Nations Food and Agricultural Organization (FAO), Viale delle Terme di Caracalla, 00100 Rome, Italy, (Dial from U.S. (202) 653-2400), (Fax from U.S. (202) 653 5760), www.fao.org; *FAO Production Yearbook 2002.*

JAMAICA - HOUSING

Euromonitor International, Inc., 224 S. Michigan Avenue, Suite 1500, Chicago, IL 60604, (312) 922-1115, Fax: (312) 922-1157, www.euromonitor.com; *World Marketing Data and Statistics.*

M.E. Sharpe, 80 Business Park Drive, Armonk, NY 10504, (800) 541-6563, Fax: (914) 273-2106, www.mesharpe.com; *The Illustrated Book of World Rankings.*

United Nations Statistics Division, New York, NY 10017, (800) 253-9646, Fax: (212) 963-4116, http://unstats.un.org; *Statistical Yearbook for Latin America and the Caribbean 2004.*

JAMAICA - ILLITERATE PERSONS

Euromonitor International, Inc., 224 S. Michigan Avenue, Suite 1500, Chicago, IL 60604, (312) 922-1115, Fax: (312) 922-1157, www.euromonitor.com; *The World Economic Factbook 2008.*

UNESCO Institute for Statistics, C.P. 6128 Succursale Centre-Ville, Montreal, Quebec, H3C 3J7 Canada, (Dial from U.S. (514) 343-6880), (Fax from U.S. (514) 343 6882), www.uis.unesco.org; *Statistical Tables.*

United Nations Statistics Division, New York, NY 10017, (800) 253-9646, Fax: (212) 963-4116, http://unstats.un.org; *Human Development Report 2006* and *Statistical Yearbook for Latin America and the Caribbean 2004.*

JAMAICA - IMPORTS

Central Intelligence Agency, Office of Public Affairs, Washington, DC 20505, (703) 482-0623, Fax: (703) 482-1739, www.cia.gov; *The World Factbook.*

Economist Intelligence Unit, 111 West 57th Street, New York, NY 10019, (212) 554-0600, Fax: (212) 586-1181, www.eiu.com; *Business Latin America* and *Jamaica Country Report.*

Euromonitor International, Inc., 224 S. Michigan Avenue, Suite 1500, Chicago, IL 60604, (312) 922-1115, Fax: (312) 922-1157, www.euromonitor.com; *International Marketing Data and Statistics 2008* and *The World Economic Factbook 2008.*

Inter-American Development Bank (IDB), 1300 New York Avenue, NW, Washington, DC 20577, (202) 623-1000, Fax: (202) 623-3096, www.iadb.org; *The Politics of Policies: Economic and Social Progress in Latin America - 2006 Report.*

International Monetary Fund (IMF), 700 Nineteenth Street, NW, Washington, DC 20431, (202) 623-7000, Fax: (202) 623-4661, www.imf.org; *Direction of Trade Statistics Yearbook 2007; Government Finance Statistics Yearbook (2008 Edition);* and *International Financial Statistics Yearbook 2007.*

Organization of American States (OAS), 17th Street Constitution Avenue NW, Washington, DC 20006, (202) 458-3000, www.oas.org; *The OAS in Transition: 1994-2004.*

Palgrave Macmillan Ltd., Houndmills, Basingstoke, Hampshire, RG21 6XS, England, (Telephone in U.S. (888) 330-8477), (Fax in U.S. (800) 672-2054), www.palgrave.com; *The Statesman's Yearbook 2008.*

Taylor and Francis Group, An Informa Business, 2 Park Square, Milton Park, Abingdon, Oxford OX14 4RN, United Kingdom, (Dial from U.S. (212) 216-7800), (Fax from U.S. (212) 564-7854), www.tandf.co.uk; *The Europa World Year Book.*

United Nations Conference on Trade and Development (UNCTAD), DC2-1120, United Nations, New York, NY 10017, (212) 963-0027, www.unctad.org; *Handbook of Statistics 2005.*

United Nations Food and Agricultural Organization (FAO), Viale delle Terme di Caracalla, 00100 Rome, Italy, (Dial from U.S. (202) 653-2400), (Fax from U.S. (202) 653 5760), www.fao.org; *The State of Food and Agriculture (SOFA) 2006.*

United Nations Statistics Division, New York, NY 10017, (800) 253-9646, Fax: (212) 963-4116, http://unstats.un.org; *Statistical Yearbook for Latin America and the Caribbean 2004.*

The World Bank, 1818 H Street, NW, Washington, DC 20433, (202) 473-1000, Fax: (202) 477-6391, www.worldbank.org; *World Development Report 2008.*

JAMAICA - INCOME DISTRIBUTION

United Nations Statistics Division, New York, NY 10017, (800) 253-9646, Fax: (212) 963-4116, http://unstats.un.org; *Statistical Yearbook for Latin America and the Caribbean 2004.*

JAMAICA - INCOME TAXES

See JAMAICA - TAXATION

JAMAICA - INDUSTRIAL PRODUCTIVITY

Euromonitor International, Inc., 224 S. Michigan Avenue, Suite 1500, Chicago, IL 60604, (312) 922-1115, Fax: (312) 922-1157, www.euromonitor.com; *International Marketing Data and Statistics 2008.*

M.E. Sharpe, 80 Business Park Drive, Armonk, NY 10504, (800) 541-6563, Fax: (914) 273-2106, www.mesharpe.com; *The Illustrated Book of World Rankings.*

JAMAICA - INDUSTRIAL PROPERTY

United Nations Statistics Division, New York, NY 10017, (800) 253-9646, Fax: (212) 963-4116, http://unstats.un.org; *Statistical Yearbook.*

JAMAICA - INDUSTRIES

Central Intelligence Agency, Office of Public Affairs, Washington, DC 20505, (703) 482-0623, Fax: (703) 482-1739, www.cia.gov; *The World Factbook.*

Economist Intelligence Unit, 111 West 57th Street, New York, NY 10019, (212) 554-0600, Fax: (212) 586-1181, www.eiu.com; *Jamaica Country Report.*

Euromonitor International, Inc., 224 S. Michigan Avenue, Suite 1500, Chicago, IL 60604, (312) 922-1115, Fax: (312) 922-1157, www.euromonitor.com; *International Marketing Data and Statistics 2008; The World Economic Factbook 2008;* and *World Marketing Data and Statistics.*

International Labour Office, I.L.O. Publications, 4 route des Morillons, CH-1211 Geneva 22, Switzerland, (Telephone in U.S. (202) 653-7652), (Fax in U.S. (202) 653-7687), www.ilo.org; *Yearbook of Labour Statistics 2006.*

M.E. Sharpe, 80 Business Park Drive, Armonk, NY 10504, (800) 541-6563, Fax: (914) 273-2106, www.mesharpe.com; *The Illustrated Book of World Rankings.*

Palgrave Macmillan Ltd., Houndmills, Basingstoke, Hampshire, RG21 6XS, England, (Telephone in U.S. (888) 330-8477), (Fax in U.S. (800) 672-2054), www.palgrave.com; *The Statesman's Yearbook 2008.*

Taylor and Francis Group, An Informa Business, 2 Park Square, Milton Park, Abingdon, Oxford OX14 4RN, United Kingdom, (Dial from U.S. (212) 216-7800), (Fax from U.S. (212) 564-7854), www.tandf.co.uk; *The Europa World Year Book.*

United Nations Industrial Development Organization (UNIDO), 1 United Nations Plaza, New York, NY 10017, (212) 963 6890, Fax: (212) 963-7904, http://unido.org; Industrial Statistics Database 2008 (INDSTAT) and *The International Yearbook of Industrial Statistics 2008.*

United Nations Statistics Division, New York, NY 10017, (800) 253-9646, Fax: (212) 963-4116, http://unstats.un.org; *Economic Survey of Latin America and the Caribbean 2004-2005; 2004 Industrial Commodity Statistics Yearbook;* and *Statistical Yearbook.*

The World Bank, 1818 H Street, NW, Washington, DC 20433, (202) 473-1000, Fax: (202) 477-6391, www.worldbank.org; *Jamaica.*

JAMAICA - INFANT AND MATERNAL MORTALITY

See JAMAICA - MORTALITY

JAMAICA - INFLATION (FINANCE)

United Nations Statistics Division, New York, NY 10017, (800) 253-9646, Fax: (212) 963-4116, http://unstats.un.org; *Economic Survey of Latin America and the Caribbean 2004-2005.*

JAMAICA - INTEREST RATES

Inter-American Development Bank (IDB), 1300 New York Avenue, NW, Washington, DC 20577, (202) 623-1000, Fax: (202) 623-3096, www.iadb.org; *The Politics of Policies: Economic and Social Progress in Latin America - 2006 Report.*

Organization of American States (OAS), 17th Street Constitution Avenue NW, Washington, DC 20006, (202) 458-3000, www.oas.org; *The OAS in Transition: 1994-2004.*

United Nations Statistics Division, New York, NY 10017, (800) 253-9646, Fax: (212) 963-4116, http://unstats.un.org; *Statistical Yearbook.*

JAMAICA - INTERNAL REVENUE

Inter-American Development Bank (IDB), 1300 New York Avenue, NW, Washington, DC 20577, (202) 623-1000, Fax: (202) 623-3096, www.iadb.org; *The Politics of Policies: Economic and Social Progress in Latin America - 2006 Report.*

Organization of American States (OAS), 17th Street Constitution Avenue NW, Washington, DC 20006, (202) 458-3000, www.oas.org; *The OAS in Transition: 1994-2004.*

JAMAICA - INTERNATIONAL FINANCE

Inter-American Development Bank (IDB), 1300 New York Avenue, NW, Washington, DC 20577, (202) 623-1000, Fax: (202) 623-3096, www.iadb.org; *The Politics of Policies: Economic and Social Progress in Latin America - 2006 Report.*

United Nations Statistics Division, New York, NY 10017, (800) 253-9646, Fax: (212) 963-4116, http://unstats.un.org; *Statistical Yearbook for Latin America and the Caribbean 2004.*

The World Bank, 1818 H Street, NW, Washington, DC 20433, (202) 473-1000, Fax: (202) 477-6391, www.worldbank.org; *Jamaica.*

JAMAICA - INTERNATIONAL LIQUIDITY

Inter-American Development Bank (IDB), 1300 New York Avenue, NW, Washington, DC 20577, (202) 623-1000, Fax: (202) 623-3096, www.iadb.org; *The Politics of Policies: Economic and Social Progress in Latin America - 2006 Report.*

International Monetary Fund (IMF), 700 Nineteenth Street, NW, Washington, DC 20431, (202) 623-7000, Fax: (202) 623-4661, www.imf.org; *International Financial Statistics Yearbook 2007.*

JAMAICA - INTERNATIONAL STATISTICS

Inter-American Development Bank (IDB), 1300 New York Avenue, NW, Washington, DC 20577, (202) 623-1000, Fax: (202) 623-3096, www.iadb.org; *The Politics of Policies: Economic and Social Progress in Latin America - 2006 Report.*

JAMAICA - INTERNATIONAL TRADE

Economist Intelligence Unit, 111 West 57th Street, New York, NY 10019, (212) 554-0600, Fax: (212) 586-1181, www.eiu.com; *Business Latin America* and *Jamaica Country Report.*

Euromonitor International, Inc., 224 S. Michigan Avenue, Suite 1500, Chicago, IL 60604, (312) 922-1115, Fax: (312) 922-1157, www.euromonitor.com; *International Marketing Data and Statistics 2008; The World Economic Factbook 2008;* and *World Marketing Data and Statistics.*

Inter-American Development Bank (IDB), 1300 New York Avenue, NW, Washington, DC 20577, (202) 623-1000, Fax: (202) 623-3096, www.iadb.org; *The Politics of Policies: Economic and Social Progress in Latin America - 2006 Report.*

International Monetary Fund (IMF), 700 Nineteenth Street, NW, Washington, DC 20431, (202) 623-7000, Fax: (202) 623-4661, www.imf.org; *International Financial Statistics Yearbook 2007.*

M.E. Sharpe, 80 Business Park Drive, Armonk, NY 10504, (800) 541-6563, Fax: (914) 273-2106, www.mesharpe.com; *The Illustrated Book of World Rankings.*

Palgrave Macmillan Ltd., Houndmills, Basingstoke, Hampshire, RG21 6XS, England, (Telephone in U.S. (888) 330-8477), (Fax in U.S. (800) 672-2054), www.palgrave.com; *The Statesman's Yearbook 2008.*

Taylor and Francis Group, An Informa Business, 2 Park Square, Milton Park, Abingdon, Oxford OX14 4RN, United Kingdom, (Dial from U.S. (212) 216-7800), (Fax from U.S. (212) 564-7854), www.tandf.co.uk; *The Europa World Year Book.*

United Nations Conference on Trade and Development (UNCTAD), DC2-1120, United Nations, New York, NY 10017, (212) 963-0027, www.unctad.org; *UNCTAD Commodity Yearbook.*

United Nations Food and Agricultural Organization (FAO), Viale delle Terme di Caracalla, 00100 Rome, Italy, (Dial from U.S. (202) 653-2400), (Fax from U.S. (202) 653 5760), www.fao.org; *FAO Trade Yearbook* and *The State of Food and Agriculture (SOFA) 2006.*

United Nations Statistics Division, New York, NY 10017, (800) 253-9646, Fax: (212) 963-4116, http://unstats.un.org; *Economic Survey of Latin America and the Caribbean 2004-2005; International Trade Statistics Yearbook; Statistical Yearbook;* and *Statistical Yearbook for Latin America and the Caribbean 2004.*

The World Bank, 1818 H Street, NW, Washington, DC 20433, (202) 473-1000, Fax: (202) 477-6391, www.worldbank.org; *Jamaica* and *World Development Report 2008.*

World Trade Organization (WTO), Centre William Rappard, Rue de Lausanne 154, CH-1211 Geneva 21, Switzerland, www.wto.org; *International Trade Statistics 2006.*

JAMAICA - INTERNET USERS

International Telecommunication Union (ITU), Place des Nations, 1211 Geneva 20, Switzerland, www.itu.int; *World Telecommunication/ICT Indicators Database on CD-ROM; World Telecommunication/ICT Indicators Database Online;* and *Yearbook of Statistics - Telecommunication Services (Chronological Time Series 1997-2006).*

The World Bank, 1818 H Street, NW, Washington, DC 20433, (202) 473-1000, Fax: (202) 477-6391, www.worldbank.org; *Jamaica.*

JAMAICA - INVESTMENTS

Inter-American Development Bank (IDB), 1300 New York Avenue, NW, Washington, DC 20577, (202) 623-1000, Fax: (202) 623-3096, www.iadb.org; *The Politics of Policies: Economic and Social Progress in Latin America - 2006 Report.*

United Nations Statistics Division, New York, NY 10017, (800) 253-9646, Fax: (212) 963-4116, http://unstats.un.org; *Statistical Yearbook for Latin America and the Caribbean 2004.*

JAMAICA - INVESTMENTS, FOREIGN

Economist Intelligence Unit, 111 West 57th Street, New York, NY 10019, (212) 554-0600, Fax: (212) 586-1181, www.eiu.com; *Business Latin America.*

JAMAICA - IRON AND IRON ORE PRODUCTION

See JAMAICA - MINERAL INDUSTRIES

JAMAICA - IRRIGATION

Euromonitor International, Inc., 224 S. Michigan Avenue, Suite 1500, Chicago, IL 60604, (312) 922-1115, Fax: (312) 922-1157, www.euromonitor.com; *International Marketing Data and Statistics 2008.*

Inter-American Development Bank (IDB), 1300 New York Avenue, NW, Washington, DC 20577, (202) 623-1000, Fax: (202) 623-3096, www.iadb.org; *The Politics of Policies: Economic and Social Progress in Latin America - 2006 Report.*

JAMAICA - LABOR

Central Intelligence Agency, Office of Public Affairs, Washington, DC 20505, (703) 482-0623, Fax: (703) 482-1739, www.cia.gov; *The World Factbook.*

Economist Intelligence Unit, 111 West 57th Street, New York, NY 10019, (212) 554-0600, Fax: (212) 586-1181, www.eiu.com; *Business Latin America.*

Euromonitor International, Inc., 224 S. Michigan Avenue, Suite 1500, Chicago, IL 60604, (312) 922-1115, Fax: (312) 922-1157, www.euromonitor.com; *International Marketing Data and Statistics 2008* and *World Marketing Data and Statistics.*

International Labour Office, I.L.O. Publications, 4 route des Morillons, CH-1211 Geneva 22, Switzerland, (Telephone in U.S. (202) 653-7652), (Fax in U.S. (202) 653-7687), www.ilo.org; *Yearbook of Labour Statistics 2006.*

M.E. Sharpe, 80 Business Park Drive, Armonk, NY 10504, (800) 541-6563, Fax: (914) 273-2106, www.mesharpe.com; *The Illustrated Book of World Rankings.*

Palgrave Macmillan Ltd., Houndmills, Basingstoke, Hampshire, RG21 6XS, England, (Telephone in U.S. (888) 330-8477), (Fax in U.S. (800) 672-2054), www.palgrave.com; *The Statesman's Yearbook 2008.*

Statistical Institute of Jamaica (STATIN), 7 Cecelio Avenue, Kingston 10, Jamaica, (Dial from U.S. (876) 926-5311), (Fax from U.S. (876) 926-1138), www.statinja.com; *Labour Force 2007.*

Taylor and Francis Group, An Informa Business, 2 Park Square, Milton Park, Abingdon, Oxford OX14 4RN, United Kingdom, (Dial from U.S. (212) 216-7800), (Fax from U.S. (212) 564-7854), www.tandf.co.uk; *The Europa World Year Book.*

United Nations Food and Agricultural Organization (FAO), Viale delle Terme di Caracalla, 00100 Rome, Italy, (Dial from U.S. (202) 653-2400), (Fax from U.S. (202) 653 5760), www.fao.org; *The State of Food and Agriculture (SOFA) 2006.*

United Nations Statistics Division, New York, NY 10017, (800) 253-9646, Fax: (212) 963-4116, http://unstats.un.org; *Human Development Report 2006.*

The World Bank, 1818 H Street, NW, Washington, DC 20433, (202) 473-1000, Fax: (202) 477-6391, www.worldbank.org; *The World Bank Atlas 2003-2004* and *World Development Report 2008.*

JAMAICA - LAND USE

Central Intelligence Agency, Office of Public Affairs, Washington, DC 20505, (703) 482-0623, Fax: (703) 482-1739, www.cia.gov; *The World Factbook.*

Euromonitor International, Inc., 224 S. Michigan Avenue, Suite 1500, Chicago, IL 60604, (312) 922-1115, Fax: (312) 922-1157, www.euromonitor.com; *International Marketing Data and Statistics 2008.*

Inter-American Development Bank (IDB), 1300 New York Avenue, NW, Washington, DC 20577, (202) 623-1000, Fax: (202) 623-3096, www.iadb.org; *The Politics of Policies: Economic and Social Progress in Latin America - 2006 Report.*

United Nations Food and Agricultural Organization (FAO), Viale delle Terme di Caracalla, 00100 Rome, Italy, (Dial from U.S. (202) 653-2400), (Fax from U.S. (202) 653 5760), www.fao.org; *FAO Production Yearbook 2002.*

The World Bank, 1818 H Street, NW, Washington, DC 20433, (202) 473-1000, Fax: (202) 477-6391, www.worldbank.org; *World Development Report 2008.*

JAMAICA - LIBRARIES

M.E. Sharpe, 80 Business Park Drive, Armonk, NY 10504, (800) 541-6563, Fax: (914) 273-2106, www.mesharpe.com; *The Illustrated Book of World Rankings.*

UNESCO Institute for Statistics, C.P. 6128 Succursale Centre-Ville, Montreal, Quebec, H3C 3J7 Canada, (Dial from U.S. (514) 343-6880), (Fax from U.S. (514) 343 6882), www.uis.unesco.org; *Statistical Tables.*

JAMAICA - LICENSES

International Monetary Fund (IMF), 700 Nineteenth Street, NW, Washington, DC 20431, (202) 623-7000, Fax: (202) 623-4661, www.imf.org; *Government Finance Statistics Yearbook (2008 Edition).*

JAMAICA - LIFE EXPECTANCY

Central Intelligence Agency, Office of Public Affairs, Washington, DC 20505, (703) 482-0623, Fax: (703) 482-1739, www.cia.gov; *The World Factbook.*

Economist Intelligence Unit, 111 West 57th Street, New York, NY 10019, (212) 554-0600, Fax: (212) 586-1181, www.eiu.com; *Business Latin America.*

Euromonitor International, Inc., 224 S. Michigan Avenue, Suite 1500, Chicago, IL 60604, (312) 922-1115, Fax: (312) 922-1157, www.euromonitor.com; *The World Economic Factbook 2008.*

United Nations Statistics Division, New York, NY 10017, (800) 253-9646, Fax: (212) 963-4116, http://unstats.un.org; *Human Development Report 2006; Statistical Yearbook for Latin America and the Caribbean 2004;* and *World Statistics Pocketbook.*

The World Bank, 1818 H Street, NW, Washington, DC 20433, (202) 473-1000, Fax: (202) 477-6391, www.worldbank.org; *The World Bank Atlas 2003-2004* and *World Development Report 2008.*

JAMAICA - LITERACY

Economist Intelligence Unit, 111 West 57th Street, New York, NY 10019, (212) 554-0600, Fax: (212) 586-1181, www.eiu.com; *Business Latin America.*

Euromonitor International, Inc,, 224 S. Michigan Avenue, Suite 1500, Chicago, IL 60604, (312) 922-1115, Fax: (312) 922-1157, www.euromonitor.com; *World Marketing Data and Statistics.*

JAMAICA - LIVESTOCK

Euromonitor International, Inc., 224 S. Michigan Avenue, Suite 1500, Chicago, IL 60604, (312) 922-1115, Fax: (312) 922-1157, www.euromonitor.com; *International Marketing Data and Statistics 2008.*

M.E. Sharpe, 80 Business Park Drive, Armonk, NY 10504, (800) 541-6563, Fax: (914) 273-2106, www.mesharpe.com; *The Illustrated Book of World Rankings.*

Palgrave Macmillan Ltd., Houndmills, Basingstoke, Hampshire, RG21 6XS, England, (Telephone in U.S. (888) 330-8477), (Fax in U.S. (800) 672-2054), www.palgrave.com; *The Statesman's Yearbook 2008.*

Taylor and Francis Group, An Informa Business, 2 Park Square, Milton Park, Abingdon, Oxford OX14 4RN, United Kingdom, (Dial from U.S. (212) 216-7800), (Fax from U.S. (212) 564-7854), www.tandf.co.uk; *The Europa World Year Book.*

United Nations Conference on Trade and Development (UNCTAD), DC2-1120, United Nations, New York, NY 10017, (212) 963-0027, www.unctad.org; *UNCTAD Commodity Yearbook.*

United Nations Food and Agricultural Organization (FAO), Viale delle Terme di Caracalla, 00100 Rome, Italy, (Dial from U.S. (202) 653-2400), (Fax from U.S. (202) 653 5760), www.fao.org; *FAO Production Yearbook 2002* and *The State of Food and Agriculture (SOFA) 2006.*

United Nations Statistics Division, New York, NY 10017, (800) 253-9646, Fax: (212) 963-4116, http://unstats.un.org; *Statistical Yearbook.*

JAMAICA - LOCAL TAXATION

Euromonitor International, Inc., 224 S. Michigan Avenue, Suite 1500, Chicago, IL 60604, (312) 922-1115, Fax: (312) 922-1157, www.euromonitor.com; *International Marketing Data and Statistics 2008.*

Inter-American Development Bank (IDB), 1300 New York Avenue, NW, Washington, DC 20577, (202) 623-1000, Fax: (202) 623-3096, www.iadb.org; *The Politics of Policies: Economic and Social Progress in Latin America - 2006 Report.*

JAMAICA - MANUFACTURES

Economist Intelligence Unit, 111 West 57th Street, New York, NY 10019, (212) 554-0600, Fax: (212) 586-1181, www.eiu.com; *Business Latin America.*

Inter-American Development Bank (IDB), 1300 New York Avenue, NW, Washington, DC 20577, (202) 623-1000, Fax: (202) 623-3096, www.iadb.org; *The Politics of Policies: Economic and Social Progress in Latin America - 2006 Report.*

M.E. Sharpe, 80 Business Park Drive, Armonk, NY 10504, (800) 541-6563, Fax: (914) 273-2106, www.mesharpe.com; *The Illustrated Book of World Rankings.*

Statistical Institute of Jamaica (STATIN), 7 Cecelio Avenue, Kingston 10, Jamaica, (Dial from U.S. (876) 926-5311), (Fax from U.S. (876) 926-1138), www.statinja.com; *Production Statistics 2007.*

United Nations Statistics Division, New York, NY 10017, (800) 253-9646, Fax: (212) 963-4116, http://unstats.un.org; *Statistical Yearbook* and *Statistical Yearbook for Latin America and the Caribbean 2004.*

JAMAICA - MARRIAGE

M.E. Sharpe, 80 Business Park Drive, Armonk, NY 10504, (800) 541-6563, Fax: (914) 273-2106, www.mesharpe.com; *The Illustrated Book of World Rankings.*

Taylor and Francis Group, An Informa Business, 2 Park Square, Milton Park, Abingdon, Oxford OX14 4RN, United Kingdom, (Dial from U.S. (212) 216-7800), (Fax from U.S. (212) 564-7854), www.tandf.co.uk; *The Europa World Year Book.*

United Nations Statistics Division, New York, NY 10017, (800) 253-9646, Fax: (212) 963-4116, http://unstats.un.org; *Demographic Yearbook* and *Statistical Yearbook.*

JAMAICA - MEAT PRODUCTION

See JAMAICA - LIVESTOCK

JAMAICA - MEDICAL CARE, COST OF

International Monetary Fund (IMF), 700 Nineteenth Street, NW, Washington, DC 20431, (202) 623-7000, Fax: (202) 623-4661, www.imf.org; *Government Finance Statistics Yearbook (2008 Edition).*

United Nations Statistics Division, New York, NY 10017, (800) 253-9646, Fax: (212) 963-4116, http://unstats.un.org; *Statistical Yearbook for Latin America and the Caribbean 2004.*

JAMAICA - MILK PRODUCTION

See JAMAICA - DAIRY PROCESSING

JAMAICA - MINERAL INDUSTRIES

Commodity Research Bureau, 330 South Wells Street, Suite 612, Chicago, IL 60606-7110, (800) 621-5271, Fax: (312) 939-4135, www.crbtrader.com; *2006 CRB Commodity Yearbook and CD.*

Economist Intelligence Unit, 111 West 57th Street, New York, NY 10019, (212) 554-0600, Fax: (212) 586-1181, www.eiu.com; *Business Latin America.*

Inter-American Development Bank (IDB), 1300 New York Avenue, NW, Washington, DC 20577, (202) 623-1000, Fax: (202) 623-3096, www.iadb.org; *The Politics of Policies: Economic and Social Progress in Latin America - 2006 Report.*

M.E. Sharpe, 80 Business Park Drive, Armonk, NY 10504, (800) 541-6563, Fax: (914) 273-2106, www.mesharpe.com; *The Illustrated Book of World Rankings.*

Palgrave Macmillan Ltd., Houndmills, Basingstoke, Hampshire, RG21 6XS, England, (Telephone in U.S. (888) 330-8477), (Fax in U.S. (800) 672-2054), www.palgrave.com; *The Statesman's Yearbook 2008.*

Taylor and Francis Group, An Informa Business, 2 Park Square, Milton Park, Abingdon, Oxford OX14 4RN, United Kingdom, (Dial from U.S. (212) 216-7800), (Fax from U.S. (212) 564-7854), www.tandf.co.uk; *The Europa World Year Book.*

United Nations Conference on Trade and Development (UNCTAD), DC2-1120, United Nations, New York, NY 10017, (212) 963-0027, www.unctad.org; *UNCTAD Commodity Yearbook.*

United Nations Statistics Division, New York, NY 10017, (800) 253-9646, Fax: (212) 963-4116, http://unstats.un.org; *Statistical Yearbook* and *Statistical Yearbook for Latin America and the Caribbean 2004.*

The World Bank, 1818 H Street, NW, Washington, DC 20433, (202) 473-1000, Fax: (202) 477-6391, www.worldbank.org; *Jamaica.*

JAMAICA - MONEY EXCHANGE RATES

See JAMAICA - FOREIGN EXCHANGE RATES

JAMAICA - MONEY SUPPLY

Economist Intelligence Unit, 111 West 57th Street, New York, NY 10019, (212) 554-0600, Fax: (212) 586-1181, www.eiu.com; *Jamaica Country Report.*

Euromonitor International, Inc., 224 S. Michigan Avenue, Suite 1500, Chicago, IL 60604, (312) 922-

1115, Fax: (312) 922-1157, www.euromonitor.com; *International Marketing Data and Statistics 2008.*

Inter-American Development Bank (IDB), 1300 New York Avenue, NW, Washington, DC 20577, (202) 623-1000, Fax: (202) 623-3096, www.iadb.org; *The Politics of Policies: Economic and Social Progress in Latin America - 2006 Report.*

International Monetary Fund (IMF), 700 Nineteenth Street, NW, Washington, DC 20431, (202) 623-7000, Fax: (202) 623-4661, www.imf.org; *International Financial Statistics Yearbook 2007.*

Taylor and Francis Group, An Informa Business, 2 Park Square, Milton Park, Abingdon, Oxford OX14 4RN, United Kingdom, (Dial from U.S. (212) 216-7800), (Fax from U.S. (212) 564-7854), www.tandf.co.uk; *The Europa World Year Book.*

United Nations Statistics Division, New York, NY 10017, (800) 253-9646, Fax: (212) 963-4116, http://unstats.un.org; *Statistical Yearbook.*

The World Bank, 1818 H Street, NW, Washington, DC 20433, (202) 473-1000, Fax: (202) 477-6391, www.worldbank.org; *Jamaica.*

JAMAICA - MORTALITY

Central Intelligence Agency, Office of Public Affairs, Washington, DC 20505, (703) 482-0623, Fax: (703) 482-1739, www.cia.gov; *The World Factbook.*

Economist Intelligence Unit, 111 West 57th Street, New York, NY 10019, (212) 554-0600, Fax: (212) 586-1181, www.eiu.com; *Business Latin America.*

Euromonitor International, Inc., 224 S. Michigan Avenue, Suite 1500, Chicago, IL 60604, (312) 922-1115, Fax: (312) 922-1157, www.euromonitor.com; *International Marketing Data and Statistics 2008* and *The World Economic Factbook 2008.*

Palgrave Macmillan Ltd., Houndmills, Basingstoke, Hampshire, RG21 6XS, England, (Telephone in U.S. (888) 330-8477), (Fax in U.S. (800) 672-2054), www.palgrave.com; *The Statesman's Yearbook 2008.*

Taylor and Francis Group, An Informa Business, 2 Park Square, Milton Park, Abingdon, Oxford OX14 4RN, United Kingdom, (Dial from U.S. (212) 216-7800), (Fax from U.S. (212) 564-7854), www.tandf.co.uk; *The Europa World Year Book.*

UNICEF, 3 United Nations Plaza, New York, NY 10017, (800) 253-9646, Fax: (212) 887-7465, www.unicef.org; *The State of the World's Children 2008.*

United Nations Statistics Division, New York, NY 10017, (800) 253-9646, Fax: (212) 963-4116, http://unstats.un.org; *Demographic Yearbook; Human Development Report 2006; Statistical Yearbook;* and *World Statistics Pocketbook.*

The World Bank, 1818 H Street, NW, Washington, DC 20433, (202) 473-1000, Fax: (202) 477-6391, www.worldbank.org; *The World Bank Atlas 2003-2004* and *World Development Report 2008.*

World Health Organization (WHO), Avenue Appia 20, 1211 Geneve 27, Switzerland, (Telephone in U.S. (212) 331-9081), www.who.int; The WHO Global Atlas of Infectious Diseases and *World Health Report 2006.*

JAMAICA - MOTION PICTURES

Palgrave Macmillan Ltd., Houndmills, Basingstoke, Hampshire, RG21 6XS, England, (Telephone in U.S. (888) 330-8477), (Fax in U.S. (800) 672-2054), www.palgrave.com; *The Statesman's Yearbook 2008.*

United Nations Statistics Division, New York, NY 10017, (800) 253-9646, Fax: (212) 963-4116, http://unstats.un.org; *Statistical Yearbook.*

JAMAICA - MOTOR VEHICLES

Economist Intelligence Unit, 111 West 57th Street, New York, NY 10019, (212) 554-0600, Fax: (212) 586-1181, www.eiu.com; *Business Latin America.*

Taylor and Francis Group, An Informa Business, 2 Park Square, Milton Park, Abingdon, Oxford OX14 4RN, United Kingdom, (Dial from U.S. (212) 216-7800), (Fax from U.S. (212) 564-7854), www.tandf.co.uk; *The Europa World Year Book.*

United Nations Statistics Division, New York, NY 10017, (800) 253-9646, Fax: (212) 963-4116, http://unstats.un.org; *Statistical Yearbook.*

JAMAICA - MUSEUMS

M.E. Sharpe, 80 Business Park Drive, Armonk, NY 10504, (800) 541-6563, Fax: (914) 273-2106, www.mesharpe.com; *The Illustrated Book of World Rankings.*

UNESCO Institute for Statistics, C.P. 6128 Succursale Centre-Ville, Montreal, Quebec, H3C 3J7 Canada, (Dial from U.S. (514) 343-6880), (Fax from U.S. (514) 343 6882), www.uis.unesco.org; *Statistical Tables.*

JAMAICA - NATURAL GAS PRODUCTION

See JAMAICA - MINERAL INDUSTRIES

JAMAICA - NUTRITION

United Nations Food and Agricultural Organization (FAO), Viale delle Terme di Caracalla, 00100 Rome, Italy, (Dial from U.S. (202) 653-2400), (Fax from U.S. (202) 653 5760), www.fao.org; *The State of Food and Agriculture (SOFA) 2006.*

United Nations Statistics Division, New York, NY 10017, (800) 253-9646, Fax: (212) 963-4116, http://unstats.un.org; *Statistical Yearbook for Latin America and the Caribbean 2004.*

JAMAICA - OLDER PEOPLE

M.E. Sharpe, 80 Business Park Drive, Armonk, NY 10504, (800) 541-6563, Fax: (914) 273-2106, www.mesharpe.com; *The Illustrated Book of World Rankings.*

JAMAICA - PAPER

See JAMAICA - FORESTS AND FORESTRY

JAMAICA - PEANUT PRODUCTION

See JAMAICA - CROPS

JAMAICA - PESTICIDES

United Nations Food and Agricultural Organization (FAO), Viale delle Terme di Caracalla, 00100 Rome, Italy, (Dial from U.S. (202) 653-2400), (Fax from U.S. (202) 653 5760), www.fao.org; *The State of Food and Agriculture (SOFA) 2006.*

JAMAICA - PETROLEUM INDUSTRY AND TRADE

Economist Intelligence Unit, 111 West 57th Street, New York, NY 10019, (212) 554-0600, Fax: (212) 586-1181, www.eiu.com; *Business Latin America.*

Inter-American Development Bank (IDB), 1300 New York Avenue, NW, Washington, DC 20577, (202) 623-1000, Fax: (202) 623-3096, www.iadb.org; *The Politics of Policies: Economic and Social Progress in Latin America - 2006 Report.*

M.E. Sharpe, 80 Business Park Drive, Armonk, NY 10504, (800) 541-6563, Fax: (914) 273-2106, www.mesharpe.com; *The Illustrated Book of World Rankings.*

PennWell Corporation, 1421 South Sheridan Road, Tulsa, OK 74112, (918) 835-3161, www.pennwell.com; *International Petroleum Encyclopedia 2007.*

U.S. Department of Energy (DOE), Energy Information Administration (EIA), 1000 Independence Avenue, SW, Washington, DC 20585, (202) 586-8800, www.eia.doe.gov; *International Energy Annual 2004* and *International Energy Outlook 2006.*

United Nations Conference on Trade and Development (UNCTAD), DC2-1120, United Nations, New York, NY 10017, (212) 963-0027, www.unctad.org; *UNCTAD Commodity Yearbook.*

United Nations Food and Agricultural Organization (FAO), Viale delle Terme di Caracalla, 00100 Rome, Italy, (Dial from U.S. (202) 653-2400), (Fax from U.S. (202) 653 5760), www.fao.org; *The State of Food and Agriculture (SOFA) 2006.*

United Nations Statistics Division, New York, NY 10017, (800) 253-9646, Fax: (212) 963-4116, http://unstats.un.org; *Statistical Yearbook.*

JAMAICA - POLITICAL SCIENCE

Central Intelligence Agency, Office of Public Affairs, Washington, DC 20505, (703) 482-0623, Fax: (703) 482-1739, www.cia.gov; *The World Factbook.*

Inter-American Development Bank (IDB), 1300 New York Avenue, NW, Washington, DC 20577, (202) 623-1000, Fax: (202) 623-3096, www.iadb.org; *The Politics of Policies: Economic and Social Progress in Latin America - 2006 Report.*

International Monetary Fund (IMF), 700 Nineteenth Street, NW, Washington, DC 20431, (202) 623-7000, Fax: (202) 623-4661, www.imf.org; *Government Finance Statistics Yearbook (2008 Edition)* and *International Financial Statistics Yearbook 2007.*

Palgrave Macmillan Ltd., Houndmills, Basingstoke, Hampshire, RG21 6XS, England, (Telephone in U.S. (888) 330-8477), (Fax in U.S. (800) 672-2054), www.palgrave.com; *The Statesman's Yearbook 2008.*

Taylor and Francis Group, An Informa Business, 2 Park Square, Milton Park, Abingdon, Oxford OX14 4RN, United Kingdom, (Dial from U.S. (212) 216-7800), (Fax from U.S. (212) 564-7854), www.tandf.co.uk; *The Europa World Year Book.*

United Nations Statistics Division, New York, NY 10017, (800) 253-9646, Fax: (212) 963-4116, http://unstats.un.org; *National Accounts Statistics: Compendium of Income Distribution Statistics* and *Statistical Yearbook.*

The World Bank, 1818 H Street, NW, Washington, DC 20433, (202) 473-1000, Fax: (202) 477-6391, www.worldbank.org; *World Development Report 2008.*

JAMAICA - POPULATION

Caribbean Epidemiology Centre (CAREC), 16-18 Jamaica Boulevard, Federation Park, PO Box 164, Port of Spain, Republic of Trinidad and Tobago, (Dial from U.S. (868) 622-4261), (Fax from U.S. (868) 622-2792), www.carec.org; *Population Data.*

Central Intelligence Agency, Office of Public Affairs, Washington, DC 20505, (703) 482-0623, Fax: (703) 482-1739, www.cia.gov; *The World Factbook.*

Economist Intelligence Unit, 111 West 57th Street, New York, NY 10019, (212) 554-0600, Fax: (212) 586-1181, www.eiu.com; *Business Latin America* and *Jamaica Country Report.*

Euromonitor International, Inc., 224 S. Michigan Avenue, Suite 1500, Chicago, IL 60604, (312) 922-1115, Fax: (312) 922-1157, www.euromonitor.com; *International Marketing Data and Statistics 2008* and *The World Economic Factbook 2008.*

Eurostat, Batiment Jean Monnet, Rue Alcide de Gasperi, L-2920 Luxembourg, http://epp.eurostat.ec.europa.eu; *Demographic Indicators - Population by Age-Classes.*

Inter-American Development Bank (IDB), 1300 New York Avenue, NW, Washington, DC 20577, (202) 623-1000, Fax: (202) 623-3096, www.iadb.org; *The Politics of Policies: Economic and Social Progress in Latin America - 2006 Report.*

International Labour Office, I.L.O. Publications, 4 route des Morillons, CH-1211 Geneva 22, Switzerland, (Telephone in U.S. (202) 653-7652), (Fax in U.S. (202) 653-7687), www.ilo.org; *Yearbook of Labour Statistics 2006.*

M.E. Sharpe, 80 Business Park Drive, Armonk, NY 10504, (800) 541-6563, Fax: (914) 273-2106, www.mesharpe.com; *The Illustrated Book of World Rankings.*

Organization of American States (OAS), 17th Street Constitution Avenue NW, Washington, DC 20006, (202) 458-3000, www.oas.org; *The OAS in Transition: 1994-2004.*

Palgrave Macmillan Ltd., Houndmills, Basingstoke, Hampshire, RG21 6XS, England, (Telephone in U.S. (888) 330-8477), (Fax in U.S. (800) 672-2054), www.palgrave.com; *The Statesman's Yearbook 2008.*

Statistical Institute of Jamaica (STATIN), 7 Cecelio Avenue, Kingston 10, Jamaica, (Dial from U.S. (876) 926-5311), (Fax from U.S. (876) 926-1138), www.statinja.com; *Demographic Statistics 2007.*

Taylor and Francis Group, An Informa Business, 2 Park Square, Milton Park, Abingdon, Oxford OX14 4RN, United Kingdom, (Dial from U.S. (212) 216-7800), (Fax from U.S. (212) 564-7854), www.tandf.co.uk; *The Europa World Year Book.*

U.S. Department of State (DOS), 2201 C Street NW, Washington, DC 20520, (202) 647-4000, www.state.gov; *World Military Expenditures and Arms Transfers (WMEAT).*

UNESCO Institute for Statistics, C.P. 6128 Succursale Centre-Ville, Montreal, Quebec, H3C 3J7 Canada, (Dial from U.S. (514) 343-6880), (Fax from U.S. (514) 343 6882), www.uis.unesco.org; *Statistical Tables.*

United Nations Food and Agricultural Organization (FAO), Viale delle Terme di Caracalla, 00100 Rome, Italy, (Dial from U.S. (202) 653-2400), (Fax from U.S. (202) 653 5760), www.fao.org; *FAO Production Yearbook 2002.*

United Nations Statistics Division, New York, NY 10017, (800) 253-9646, Fax: (212) 963-4116, http://unstats.un.org; *Demographic Yearbook; Human Development Report 2006; Statistical Yearbook; Statistical Yearbook for Latin America and the Caribbean 2004;* and *World Statistics Pocketbook.*

The World Bank, 1818 H Street, NW, Washington, DC 20433, (202) 473-1000, Fax: (202) 477-6391, www.worldbank.org; *Jamaica; The World Bank Atlas 2003-2004;* and *World Development Report 2008.*

World Health Organization (WHO), Avenue Appia 20, 1211 Geneve 27, Switzerland, (Telephone in U.S. (212) 331-9081), www.who.int; *World Health Report 2006.*

JAMAICA - POPULATION DENSITY

Central Intelligence Agency, Office of Public Affairs, Washington, DC 20505, (703) 482-0623, Fax: (703) 482-1739, www.cia.gov; *The World Factbook.*

Euromonitor International, Inc., 224 S. Michigan Avenue, Suite 1500, Chicago, IL 60604, (312) 922-1115, Fax: (312) 922-1157, www.euromonitor.com; *International Marketing Data and Statistics 2008* and *The World Economic Factbook 2008.*

Inter-American Development Bank (IDB), 1300 New York Avenue, NW, Washington, DC 20577, (202) 623-1000, Fax: (202) 623-3096, www.iadb.org; *The Politics of Policies: Economic and Social Progress in Latin America - 2006 Report.*

M.E. Sharpe, 80 Business Park Drive, Armonk, NY 10504, (800) 541-6563, Fax: (914) 273-2106, www.mesharpe.com; *The Illustrated Book of World Rankings.*

Palgrave Macmillan Ltd., Houndmills, Basingstoke, Hampshire, RG21 6XS, England, (Telephone in U.S. (888) 330-8477), (Fax in U.S. (800) 672-2054), www.palgrave.com; *The Statesman's Yearbook 2008.*

Taylor and Francis Group, An Informa Business, 2 Park Square, Milton Park, Abingdon, Oxford OX14 4RN, United Kingdom, (Dial from U.S. (212) 216-7800), (Fax from U.S. (212) 564-7854), www.tandf.co.uk; *The Europa World Year Book.*

UNESCO Institute for Statistics, C.P. 6128 Succursale Centre-Ville, Montreal, Quebec, H3C 3J7 Canada, (Dial from U.S. (514) 343-6880), (Fax from U.S. (514) 343 6882), www.uis.unesco.org; *Statistical Tables.*

United Nations Food and Agricultural Organization (FAO), Viale delle Terme di Caracalla, 00100 Rome, Italy, (Dial from U.S. (202) 653-2400), (Fax from U.S. (202) 653 5760), www.fao.org; *The State of Food and Agriculture (SOFA) 2006.*

United Nations Statistics Division, New York, NY 10017, (800) 253-9646, Fax: (212) 963-4116, http://unstats.un.org; *Statistical Yearbook.*

The World Bank, 1818 H Street, NW, Washington, DC 20433, (202) 473-1000, Fax: (202) 477-6391, www.worldbank.org; *Jamaica* and *World Development Report 2008.*

JAMAICA - POSTAL SERVICE

M.E. Sharpe, 80 Business Park Drive, Armonk, NY 10504, (800) 541-6563, Fax: (914) 273-2106, www.mesharpe.com; *The Illustrated Book of World Rankings.*

Palgrave Macmillan Ltd., Houndmills, Basingstoke, Hampshire, RG21 6XS, England, (Telephone in U.S. (888) 330-8477), (Fax in U.S. (800) 672-2054), www.palgrave.com; *The Statesman's Yearbook 2008.*

United Nations Statistics Division, New York, NY 10017, (800) 253-9646, Fax: (212) 963-4116, http://unstats.un.org; *Statistical Yearbook.*

JAMAICA - POWER RESOURCES

Economist Intelligence Unit, 111 West 57th Street, New York, NY 10019, (212) 554-0600, Fax: (212) 586-1181, www.eiu.com; *Business Latin America.*

Euromonitor International, Inc., 224 S. Michigan Avenue, Suite 1500, Chicago, IL 60604, (312) 922-1115, Fax: (312) 922-1157, www.euromonitor.com; *International Marketing Data and Statistics 2008; The World Economic Factbook 2008;* and *World Marketing Data and Statistics.*

M.E. Sharpe, 80 Business Park Drive, Armonk, NY 10504, (800) 541-6563, Fax: (914) 273-2106, www.mesharpe.com; *The Illustrated Book of World Rankings.*

Palgrave Macmillan Ltd., Houndmills, Basingstoke, Hampshire, RG21 6XS, England, (Telephone in U.S. (888) 330-8477), (Fax in U.S. (800) 672-2054), www.palgrave.com; *The Statesman's Yearbook 2008.*

Platts, 2 Penn Plaza, 25th Floor, New York, NY 10121-2298, (212) 904-3070, www.platts.com; *Energy Economist.*

U.S. Department of Energy (DOE), Energy Information Administration (EIA), 1000 Independence Avenue, SW, Washington, DC 20585, (202) 586-8800, www.eia.doe.gov; *International Energy Annual 2004* and *International Energy Outlook 2006.*

United Nations Food and Agricultural Organization (FAO), Viale delle Terme di Caracalla, 00100 Rome, Italy, (Dial from U.S. (202) 653-2400), (Fax from U.S. (202) 653 5760), www.fao.org; *The State of Food and Agriculture (SOFA) 2006.*

United Nations Statistics Division, New York, NY 10017, (800) 253-9646, Fax: (212) 963-4116, http://unstats.un.org; *Energy Statistics Yearbook 2003; Human Development Report 2006; Statistical Yearbook; Statistical Yearbook for Latin America and the Caribbean 2004;* and *World Statistics Pocketbook.*

The World Bank, 1818 H Street, NW, Washington, DC 20433, (202) 473-1000, Fax: (202) 477-6391, www.worldbank.org; *The World Bank Atlas 2003-2004* and *World Development Report 2008.*

JAMAICA - PRICES

Economist Intelligence Unit, 111 West 57th Street, New York, NY 10019, (212) 554-0600, Fax: (212) 586-1181, www.eiu.com; *Business Latin America.*

Euromonitor International, Inc., 224 S. Michigan Avenue, Suite 1500, Chicago, IL 60604, (312) 922-1115, Fax: (312) 922-1157, www.euromonitor.com; *World Marketing Data and Statistics.*

International Labour Office, I.L.O. Publications, 4 route des Morillons, CH-1211 Geneva 22, Switzerland, (Telephone in U.S. (202) 653-7652), (Fax in U.S. (202) 653-7687), www.ilo.org; *Yearbook of Labour Statistics 2006.*

International Monetary Fund (IMF), 700 Nineteenth Street, NW, Washington, DC 20431, (202) 623-7000, Fax: (202) 623-4661, www.imf.org; *International Financial Statistics Yearbook 2007.*

M.E. Sharpe, 80 Business Park Drive, Armonk, NY 10504, (800) 541-6563, Fax: (914) 273-2106, www.mesharpe.com; *The Illustrated Book of World Rankings.*

Organization of American States (OAS), 17th Street Constitution Avenue NW, Washington, DC 20006, (202) 458-3000, www.oas.org; *The OAS in Transition: 1994-2004.*

United Nations Food and Agricultural Organization (FAO), Viale delle Terme di Caracalla, 00100 Rome, Italy, (Dial from U.S. (202) 653-2400), (Fax from U.S. (202) 653 5760), www.fao.org; *FAO Production Yearbook 2002* and *The State of Food and Agriculture (SOFA) 2006.*

United Nations Statistics Division, New York, NY 10017, (800) 253-9646, Fax: (212) 963-4116, http://unstats.un.org; *Economic Survey of Latin America and the Caribbean 2004-2005* and *Statistical Yearbook for Latin America and the Caribbean 2004.*

The World Bank, 1818 H Street, NW, Washington, DC 20433, (202) 473-1000, Fax: (202) 477-6391, www.worldbank.org; *Jamaica.*

JAMAICA - PROFESSIONS

United Nations Statistics Division, New York, NY 10017, (800) 253-9646, Fax: (212) 963-4116, http://unstats.un.org; *Statistical Yearbook.*

JAMAICA - PUBLIC HEALTH

Economist Intelligence Unit, 111 West 57th Street, New York, NY 10019, (212) 554-0600, Fax: (212) 586-1181, www.eiu.com; *Business Latin America.*

Euromonitor International, Inc., 224 S. Michigan Avenue, Suite 1500, Chicago, IL 60604, (312) 922-1115, Fax: (312) 922-1157, www.euromonitor.com; *World Marketing Data and Statistics.*

M.E. Sharpe, 80 Business Park Drive, Armonk, NY 10504, (800) 541-6563, Fax: (914) 273-2106, www.mesharpe.com; *The Illustrated Book of World Rankings.*

Palgrave Macmillan Ltd., Houndmills, Basingstoke, Hampshire, RG21 6XS, England, (Telephone in U.S. (888) 330-8477), (Fax in U.S. (800) 672-2054), www.palgrave.com; *The Statesman's Yearbook 2008.*

UNICEF, 3 United Nations Plaza, New York, NY 10017, (800) 253-9646, Fax: (212) 887-7465, www.unicef.org; *The State of the World's Children 2008.*

United Nations Statistics Division, New York, NY 10017, (800) 253-9646, Fax: (212) 963-4116, http://unstats.un.org; *Human Development Report 2006; Statistical Yearbook;* and *Statistical Yearbook for Latin America and the Caribbean 2004.*

The World Bank, 1818 H Street, NW, Washington, DC 20433, (202) 473-1000, Fax: (202) 477-6391, www.worldbank.org; *Jamaica* and *World Development Report 2008.*

World Health Organization (WHO), Avenue Appia 20, 1211 Geneve 27, Switzerland, (Telephone in U.S. (212) 331-9081), www.who.int; The WHO Global Atlas of Infectious Diseases and *World Health Report 2006.*

JAMAICA - PUBLISHERS AND PUBLISHING

UNESCO Institute for Statistics, C.P. 6128 Succursale Centre-Ville, Montreal, Quebec, H3C 3J7 Canada, (Dial from U.S. (514) 343-6880), (Fax from U.S. (514) 343 6882), www.uis.unesco.org; *Statistical Tables.*

JAMAICA - RADIO BROADCASTING

Palgrave Macmillan Ltd., Houndmills, Basingstoke, Hampshire, RG21 6XS, England, (Telephone in U.S. (888) 330-8477), (Fax in U.S. (800) 672-2054), www.palgrave.com; *The Statesman's Yearbook 2008.*

United Nations Statistics Division, New York, NY 10017, (800) 253-9646, Fax: (212) 963-4116, http://unstats.un.org; *Statistical Yearbook.*

JAMAICA - RAILROADS

Economist Intelligence Unit, 111 West 57th Street, New York, NY 10019, (212) 554-0600, Fax: (212) 586-1181, www.eiu.com; *Business Latin America.*

Jane's Information Group, 110 North Royal Street, Suite 200, Alexandria, VA 22314, (703) 683-3700, Fax: (800) 836-0297, www.janes.com; *Jane's World Railways.*

Taylor and Francis Group, An Informa Business, 2 Park Square, Milton Park, Abingdon, Oxford OX14 4RN, United Kingdom, (Dial from U.S. (212) 216-7800), (Fax from U.S. (212) 564-7854), www.tandf.co.uk; *The Europa World Year Book.*

United Nations Statistics Division, New York, NY 10017, (800) 253-9646, Fax: (212) 963-4116, http://unstats.un.org; *Statistical Yearbook.*

JAMAICA - RELIGION

Central Intelligence Agency, Office of Public Affairs, Washington, DC 20505, (703) 482-0623, Fax: (703) 482-1739, www.cia.gov; *The World Factbook.*

M.E. Sharpe, 80 Business Park Drive, Armonk, NY 10504, (800) 541-6563, Fax: (914) 273-2106, www.mesharpe.com; *The Illustrated Book of World Rankings.*

Palgrave Macmillan Ltd., Houndmills, Basingstoke, Hampshire, RG21 6XS, England, (Telephone in U.S. (888) 330-8477), (Fax in U.S. (800) 672-2054), www.palgrave.com; *The Statesman's Yearbook 2008.*

JAMAICA - RENT CHARGES

International Labour Office, I.L.O. Publications, 4 route des Morillons, CH-1211 Geneva 22, Switzerland, (Telephone in U.S. (202) 653-7652), (Fax in U.S. (202) 653-7687), www.ilo.org; *Yearbook of Labour Statistics 2006.*

JAMAICA - RESERVES (ACCOUNTING)

Economist Intelligence Unit, 111 West 57th Street, New York, NY 10019, (212) 554-0600, Fax: (212) 586-1181, www.eiu.com; *Business Latin America.*

Euromonitor International, Inc., 224 S. Michigan Avenue, Suite 1500, Chicago, IL 60604, (312) 922-1115, Fax: (312) 922-1157, www.euromonitor.com; *International Marketing Data and Statistics 2008.*

Inter-American Development Bank (IDB), 1300 New York Avenue, NW, Washington, DC 20577, (202) 623-1000, Fax: (202) 623-3096, www.iadb.org; *The Politics of Policies: Economic and Social Progress in Latin America - 2006 Report.*

Organization of American States (OAS), 17th Street Constitution Avenue NW, Washington, DC 20006, (202) 458-3000, www.oas.org; *The OAS in Transition: 1994-2004.*

United Nations Statistics Division, New York, NY 10017, (800) 253-9646, Fax: (212) 963-4116, http://unstats.un.org; *Statistical Yearbook.*

JAMAICA - RETAIL TRADE

Euromonitor International, Inc., 224 S. Michigan Avenue, Suite 1500, Chicago, IL 60604, (312) 922-1115, Fax: (312) 922-1157, www.euromonitor.com; *World Marketing Data and Statistics.*

Inter-American Development Bank (IDB), 1300 New York Avenue, NW, Washington, DC 20577, (202) 623-1000, Fax: (202) 623-3096, www.iadb.org; *The Politics of Policies: Economic and Social Progress in Latin America - 2006 Report.*

JAMAICA - RICE PRODUCTION

See JAMAICA - CROPS

JAMAICA - ROADS

Central Intelligence Agency, Office of Public Affairs, Washington, DC 20505, (703) 482-0623, Fax: (703) 482-1739, www.cia.gov; *The World Factbook.*

Economist Intelligence Unit, 111 West 57th Street, New York, NY 10019, (212) 554-0600, Fax: (212) 586-1181, www.eiu.com; *Business Latin America.*

Palgrave Macmillan Ltd., Houndmills, Basingstoke, Hampshire, RG21 6XS, England, (Telephone in U.S. (888) 330-8477), (Fax in U.S. (800) 672-2054), www.palgrave.com; *The Statesman's Yearbook 2008.*

JAMAICA - RUBBER INDUSTRY AND TRADE

International Rubber Study Group (IRSG), 1st Floor, Heron House, 109/115 Wembley Hill Road, Wembley, Middlesex HA9 8DA, United Kingdom, www.rubberstudy.com; *Rubber Statistical Bulletin; Summary of World Rubber Statistics 2005; World Rubber Statistics Handbook (Volume 6, 1975-2001);* and *World Rubber Statistics Historic Handbook.*

M.E. Sharpe, 80 Business Park Drive, Armonk, NY 10504, (800) 541-6563, Fax: (914) 273-2106, www.mesharpe.com; *The Illustrated Book of World Rankings.*

JAMAICA - SHEEP

See JAMAICA - LIVESTOCK

JAMAICA - SHIPPING

Palgrave Macmillan Ltd., Houndmills, Basingstoke, Hampshire, RG21 6XS, England, (Telephone in U.S. (888) 330-8477), (Fax in U.S. (800) 672-2054), www.palgrave.com; *The Statesman's Yearbook 2008.*

Taylor and Francis Group, An Informa Business, 2 Park Square, Milton Park, Abingdon, Oxford OX14 4RN, United Kingdom, (Dial from U.S. (212) 216-7800), (Fax from U.S. (212) 564-7854), www.tandf.co.uk; *The Europa World Year Book.*

U.S. Department of Transportation (DOT), Maritime Administration (MARAD), West Building, Southeast Federal Center, 1200 New Jersey Avenue, SE, Washington, DC 20590, (800) 99-MARAD, www.marad.dot.gov; *World Merchant Fleet 2005.*

United Nations Statistics Division, New York, NY 10017, (800) 253-9646, Fax: (212) 963-4116, http://unstats.un.org; *Statistical Yearbook.*

JAMAICA - SILVER PRODUCTION

See JAMAICA - MINERAL INDUSTRIES

JAMAICA - SOCIAL ECOLOGY

M.E. Sharpe, 80 Business Park Drive, Armonk, NY 10504, (800) 541-6563, Fax: (914) 273-2106, www.mesharpe.com; *The Illustrated Book of World Rankings.*

United Nations Statistics Division, New York, NY 10017, (800) 253-9646, Fax: (212) 963-4116, http://unstats.un.org; *Bulletin of Industrial Statistics for the Arab Countries.*

JAMAICA - SOCIAL SECURITY

Inter-American Development Bank (IDB), 1300 New York Avenue, NW, Washington, DC 20577, (202) 623-1000, Fax: (202) 623-3096, www.iadb.org; *The Politics of Policies: Economic and Social Progress in Latin America - 2006 Report.*

International Monetary Fund (IMF), 700 Nineteenth Street, NW, Washington, DC 20431, (202) 623-7000, Fax: (202) 623-4661, www.imf.org; *Government Finance Statistics Yearbook (2008 Edition).*

United Nations Statistics Division, New York, NY 10017, (800) 253-9646, Fax: (212) 963-4116, http://unstats.un.org; *National Accounts Statistics: Compendium of Income Distribution Statistics.*

JAMAICA - SOYBEAN PRODUCTION

See JAMAICA - CROPS

JAMAICA - STEEL PRODUCTION

See JAMAICA - MINERAL INDUSTRIES

JAMAICA - SUGAR PRODUCTION

See JAMAICA - CROPS

JAMAICA - SULPHUR PRODUCTION

See JAMAICA - MINERAL INDUSTRIES

JAMAICA - TAXATION

Inter-American Development Bank (IDB), 1300 New York Avenue, NW, Washington, DC 20577, (202) 623-1000, Fax: (202) 623-3096, www.iadb.org; *The Politics of Policies: Economic and Social Progress in Latin America - 2006 Report.*

International Monetary Fund (IMF), 700 Nineteenth Street, NW, Washington, DC 20431, (202) 623-7000, Fax: (202) 623-4661, www.imf.org; *Government Finance Statistics Yearbook (2008 Edition).*

Taylor and Francis Group, An Informa Business, 2 Park Square, Milton Park, Abingdon, Oxford OX14 4RN, United Kingdom, (Dial from U.S. (212) 216-7800), (Fax from U.S. (212) 564-7854), www.tandf.co.uk; *The Europa World Year Book.*

United Nations Statistics Division, New York, NY 10017, (800) 253-9646, Fax: (212) 963-4116, http://unstats.un.org; *Statistical Yearbook for Latin America and the Caribbean 2004.*

JAMAICA - TELEPHONE

Economist Intelligence Unit, 111 West 57th Street, New York, NY 10019, (212) 554-0600, Fax: (212) 586-1181, www.eiu.com; *Business Latin America.*

International Telecommunication Union (ITU), Place des Nations, 1211 Geneva 20, Switzerland, www.itu.int; World Telecommunication Indicators Database.

Palgrave Macmillan Ltd., Houndmills, Basingstoke, Hampshire, RG21 6XS, England, (Telephone in U.S. (888) 330-8477), (Fax in U.S. (800) 672-2054), www.palgrave.com; *The Statesman's Yearbook 2008.*

Taylor and Francis Group, An Informa Business, 2 Park Square, Milton Park, Abingdon, Oxford OX14 4RN, United Kingdom, (Dial from U.S. (212) 216-7800), (Fax from U.S. (212) 564-7854), www.tandf.co.uk; *The Europa World Year Book.*

United Nations Statistics Division, New York, NY 10017, (800) 253-9646, Fax: (212) 963-4116, http://unstats.un.org; *Statistical Yearbook* and *World Statistics Pocketbook.*

JAMAICA - TELEVISION - RECEIVERS AND RECEPTION

United Nations Statistics Division, New York, NY 10017, (800) 253-9646, Fax: (212) 963-4116, http://unstats.un.org; *Statistical Yearbook.*

JAMAICA - TEXTILE INDUSTRY

United Nations Conference on Trade and Development (UNCTAD), DC2-1120, United Nations, New York, NY 10017, (212) 963-0027, www.unctad.org; *UNCTAD Commodity Yearbook.*

United Nations Statistics Division, New York, NY 10017, (800) 253-9646, Fax: (212) 963-4116, http://unstats.un.org; *Statistical Yearbook.*

JAMAICA - THEATER

UNESCO Institute for Statistics, C.P. 6128 Succursale Centre-Ville, Montreal, Quebec, H3C 3J7 Canada, (Dial from U.S. (514) 343-6880), (Fax from U.S. (514) 343 6882), www.uis.unesco.org; *Statistical Tables.*

JAMAICA - TIRE INDUSTRY

United Nations Statistics Division, New York, NY 10017, (800) 253-9646, Fax: (212) 963-4116, http://unstats.un.org; *Statistical Yearbook.*

JAMAICA - TOBACCO INDUSTRY

Foreign Agricultural Service (FAS), U.S. Department of Agriculture (USDA), 1400 Independence Avenue, SW, Washington, DC 20250, (202) 720-3935, www.fas.usda.gov; *Tobacco: World Markets and Trade.*

M.E. Sharpe, 80 Business Park Drive, Armonk, NY 10504, (800) 541-6563, Fax: (914) 273-2106, www.mesharpe.com; *The Illustrated Book of World Rankings.*

United Nations Statistics Division, New York, NY 10017, (800) 253-9646, Fax: (212) 963-4116, http://unstats.un.org; *Statistical Yearbook.*

JAMAICA - TOURISM

Economist Intelligence Unit, 111 West 57th Street, New York, NY 10019, (212) 554-0600, Fax: (212) 586-1181, www.eiu.com; *Business Latin America.*

Euromonitor International, Inc., 224 S. Michigan Avenue, Suite 1500, Chicago, IL 60604, (312) 922-1115, Fax: (312) 922-1157, www.euromonitor.com; *The World Economic Factbook 2008* and *World Marketing Data and Statistics.*

M.E. Sharpe, 80 Business Park Drive, Armonk, NY 10504, (800) 541-6563, Fax: (914) 273-2106, www.mesharpe.com; *The Illustrated Book of World Rankings.*

Organization of American States (OAS), 17th Street Constitution Avenue NW, Washington, DC 20006, (202) 458-3000, www.oas.org; *The OAS in Transition: 1994-2004.*

Palgrave Macmillan Ltd., Houndmills, Basingstoke, Hampshire, RG21 6XS, England, (Telephone in U.S. (888) 330-8477), (Fax in U.S. (800) 672-2054), www.palgrave.com; *The Statesman's Yearbook 2008.*

Taylor and Francis Group, An Informa Business, 2 Park Square, Milton Park, Abingdon, Oxford OX14 4RN, United Kingdom, (Dial from U.S. (212) 216-7800), (Fax from U.S. (212) 564-7854), www.tandf.co.uk; *The Europa World Year Book.*

United Nations Statistics Division, New York, NY 10017, (800) 253-9646, Fax: (212) 963-4116, http://unstats.un.org; *Statistical Yearbook* and *Statistical Yearbook for Latin America and the Caribbean 2004.*

United Nations World Tourism Organization (UNWTO), Capitan Haya 42, 28020 Madrid, Spain, www.world-tourism.org; *Yearbook of Tourism Statistics.*

The World Bank, 1818 H Street, NW, Washington, DC 20433, (202) 473-1000, Fax: (202) 477-6391, www.worldbank.org; *Jamaica.*

JAMAICA - TRADE

See JAMAICA - INTERNATIONAL TRADE

JAMAICA - TRANSPORTATION

Central Intelligence Agency, Office of Public Affairs, Washington, DC 20505, (703) 482-0623, Fax: (703) 482-1739, www.cia.gov; *The World Factbook.*

Economist Intelligence Unit, 111 West 57th Street, New York, NY 10019, (212) 554-0600, Fax: (212) 586-1181, www.eiu.com; *Business Latin America.*

Euromonitor International, Inc., 224 S. Michigan Avenue, Suite 1500, Chicago, IL 60604, (312) 922-1115, Fax: (312) 922-1157, www.euromonitor.com; *World Marketing Data and Statistics.*

Inter-American Development Bank (IDB), 1300 New York Avenue, NW, Washington, DC 20577, (202) 623-1000, Fax: (202) 623-3096, www.iadb.org; *The Politics of Policies: Economic and Social Progress in Latin America - 2006 Report.*

M.E. Sharpe, 80 Business Park Drive, Armonk, NY 10504, (800) 541-6563, Fax: (914) 273-2106, www.mesharpe.com; *The Illustrated Book of World Rankings.*

Palgrave Macmillan Ltd., Houndmills, Basingstoke, Hampshire, RG21 6XS, England, (Telephone in U.S. (888) 330-8477), (Fax in U.S. (800) 672-2054), www.palgrave.com; *The Statesman's Yearbook 2008.*

Taylor and Francis Group, An Informa Business, 2 Park Square, Milton Park, Abingdon, Oxford OX14 4RN, United Kingdom, (Dial from U.S. (212) 216-7800), (Fax from U.S. (212) 564-7854), www.tandf.co.uk; *The Europa World Year Book.*

United Nations Statistics Division, New York, NY 10017, (800) 253-9646, Fax: (212) 963-4116, http://unstats.un.org; *Human Development Report 2006* and *Statistical Yearbook for Latin America and the Caribbean 2004.*

The World Bank, 1818 H Street, NW, Washington, DC 20433, (202) 473-1000, Fax: (202) 477-6391, www.worldbank.org; *Jamaica.*

JAMAICA - TREASURY BILLS

Organization of American States (OAS), 17th Street Constitution Avenue NW, Washington, DC 20006, (202) 458-3000, www.oas.org; *The OAS in Transition: 1994-2004.*

JAMAICA - UNEMPLOYMENT

Central Intelligence Agency, Office of Public Affairs, Washington, DC 20505, (703) 482-0623, Fax: (703) 482-1739, www.cia.gov; *The World Factbook.*

Economist Intelligence Unit, 111 West 57th Street, New York, NY 10019, (212) 554-0600, Fax: (212) 586-1181, www.eiu.com; *Business Latin America.*

Euromonitor International, Inc., 224 S. Michigan Avenue, Suite 1500, Chicago, IL 60604, (312) 922-1115, Fax: (312) 922-1157, www.euromonitor.com; *International Marketing Data and Statistics 2008.*

International Labour Office, I.L.O. Publications, 4 route des Morillons, CH-1211 Geneva 22, Switzerland, (Telephone in U.S. (202) 653-7652), (Fax in U.S. (202) 653-7687), www.ilo.org; *Yearbook of Labour Statistics 2006.*

Organization of American States (OAS), 17th Street Constitution Avenue NW, Washington, DC 20006, (202) 458-3000, www.oas.org; *The OAS in Transition: 1994-2004.*

Palgrave Macmillan Ltd., Houndmills, Basingstoke, Hampshire, RG21 6XS, England, (Telephone in U.S. (888) 330-8477), (Fax in U.S. (800) 672-2054), www.palgrave.com; *The Statesman's Yearbook 2008.*

United Nations Statistics Division, New York, NY 10017, (800) 253-9646, Fax: (212) 963-4116, http://unstats.un.org; *Statistical Yearbook.*

The World Bank, 1818 H Street, NW, Washington, DC 20433, (202) 473-1000, Fax: (202) 477-6391, www.worldbank.org; *Jamaica.*

JAMAICA - VITAL STATISTICS

Euromonitor International, Inc., 224 S. Michigan Avenue, Suite 1500, Chicago, IL 60604, (312) 922-1115, Fax: (312) 922-1157, www.euromonitor.com; *International Marketing Data and Statistics 2008.*

Palgrave Macmillan Ltd., Houndmills, Basingstoke, Hampshire, RG21 6XS, England, (Telephone in U.S. (888) 330-8477), (Fax in U.S. (800) 672-2054), www.palgrave.com; *The Statesman's Yearbook 2008.*

Statistical Institute of Jamaica (STATIN), 7 Cecelio Avenue, Kingston 10, Jamaica, (Dial from U.S. (876) 926-5311), (Fax from U.S. (876) 926-1138), www.statinja.com; *Demographic Statistics 2007.*

United Nations Statistics Division, New York, NY 10017, (800) 253-9646, Fax: (212) 963-4116, http://unstats.un.org; *Statistical Yearbook.*

World Health Organization (WHO), Avenue Appia 20, 1211 Geneve 27, Switzerland, (Telephone in U.S. (212) 331-9081), www.who.int; *World Health Report 2006.*

JAMAICA - WAGES

International Labour Office, I.L.O. Publications, 4 route des Morillons, CH-1211 Geneva 22, Switzerland, (Telephone in U.S. (202) 653-7652), (Fax in U.S. (202) 653-7687), www.ilo.org; *Yearbook of Labour Statistics 2006.*

Organization of American States (OAS), 17th Street Constitution Avenue NW, Washington, DC 20006, (202) 458-3000, www.oas.org; *The OAS in Transition: 1994-2004.*

The World Bank, 1818 H Street, NW, Washington, DC 20433, (202) 473-1000, Fax: (202) 477-6391, www.worldbank.org; *Jamaica.*

JAMAICA - WEATHER

See JAMAICA - CLIMATE

JAMAICA - WELFARE STATE

Inter-American Development Bank (IDB), 1300 New York Avenue, NW, Washington, DC 20577, (202) 623-1000, Fax: (202) 623-3096, www.iadb.org; *The Politics of Policies: Economic and Social Progress in Latin America - 2006 Report.*

International Monetary Fund (IMF), 700 Nineteenth Street, NW, Washington, DC 20431, (202) 623-7000, Fax: (202) 623-4661, www.imf.org; *Government Finance Statistics Yearbook (2008 Edition).*

JAMAICA - WHEAT PRODUCTION

See JAMAICA - CROPS

JAMAICA - WHOLESALE PRICE INDEXES

Inter-American Development Bank (IDB), 1300 New York Avenue, NW, Washington, DC 20577, (202) 623-1000, Fax: (202) 623-3096, www.iadb.org; *The Politics of Policies: Economic and Social Progress in Latin America - 2006 Report.*

JAMAICA - WHOLESALE TRADE

Inter-American Development Bank (IDB), 1300 New York Avenue, NW, Washington, DC 20577, (202) 623-1000, Fax: (202) 623-3096, www.iadb.org; *The Politics of Policies: Economic and Social Progress in Latin America - 2006 Report.*

JAMAICA - WINE PRODUCTION

See JAMAICA - BEVERAGE INDUSTRY

JAMAICA - WOOL PRODUCTION

See JAMAICA - TEXTILE INDUSTRY

JAPAN - NATIONAL STATISTICAL OFFICE

Statistics Bureau, the Director-General for Policy Planning (Statistical Standards), 19-1 Wakamatsucho, Shinjuku-ku, Tokyo 162-8668, Japan, www.stat.go.jp/english; National Data Center.

JAPAN - PRIMARY STATISTICS SOURCES

Ministry of Economy, Trade and Industry (METI), 1-3-1 Kasumigaseki, Chiyoda-ku, Tokyo 100, www.meti.go.jp/english; *Revised Report on Indices of Industrial Production (February 2007).*

Nomura Research Institute (NRI), 2 World Financial Center, Building B, 19th Fl., New York, NY 10281-1198, (212) 667-1670, www.nri.co.jp/english; unpublished data.

Statistics Bureau, the Director-General for Policy Planning (Statistical Standards), 19-1 Wakamatsucho, Shinjuku-ku, Tokyo 162-8668, Japan, www.stat.go.jp/english; *Historical Statistics of Japan; Japan Monthly Statistics; Japan Statistical Yearbook 2008;* and *Statistical Handbook of Japan 2007 (SHJ).*

JAPAN - DATABASES

Nikkei Inc., 1-9-5 Ohtemachi Chiyoda-ku, Tokyo 100-8066, Japan, www.nni.nikkei.co.jp; Markets Japan (database: subject coverage: Japan's financial markets with the latest market data and news).

JAPAN - ABORTION

United Nations Statistics Division, New York, NY 10017, (800) 253-9646, Fax: (212) 963-4116, http://unstats.un.org; *Demographic Yearbook.*

JAPAN - AGRICULTURAL MACHINERY

United Nations Statistics Division, New York, NY 10017, (800) 253-9646, Fax: (212) 963-4116, http://unstats.un.org; *Statistical Yearbook.*

JAPAN - AGRICULTURE

Economist Intelligence Unit, 111 West 57th Street, New York, NY 10019, (212) 554-0600, Fax: (212) 586-1181, www.eiu.com; *Japan Country Report.*

Euromonitor International, Inc., 224 S. Michigan Avenue, Suite 1500, Chicago, IL 60604, (312) 922-1115, Fax: (312) 922-1157, www.euromonitor.com; *International Marketing Data and Statistics 2008* and *World Marketing Data and Statistics.*

M.E. Sharpe, 80 Business Park Drive, Armonk, NY 10504, (800) 541-6563, Fax: (914) 273-2106, www.mesharpe.com; *The Illustrated Book of World Rankings.*

Organisation for Economic Cooperation and Development (OECD), 2 rue Andre Pascal, F-75775 Paris Cedex 16, France, (Telephone in U.S. (202) 785-6323), (Fax in U.S. (202) 785-0350), www.oecd.org; *Indicators of Industrial Activity; 2005 OECD Agricultural Outlook Tables, 1970-2014; OECD Agricultural Outlook: 2007-2016;* and *OECD Economic Survey - Japan 2008.*

Palgrave Macmillan Ltd., Houndmills, Basingstoke, Hampshire, RG21 6XS, England, (Telephone in U.S. (888) 330-8477), (Fax in U.S. (800) 672-2054), www.palgrave.com; *The Statesman's Yearbook 2008.*

Statistics Bureau, the Director-General for Policy Planning (Statistical Standards), 19-1 Wakamatsu-cho, Shinjuku-ku, Tokyo 162-8668, Japan, www.stat.go.jp/english; *Japan Statistical Yearbook 2008.*

Taylor and Francis Group, An Informa Business, 2 Park Square, Milton Park, Abingdon, Oxford OX14 4RN, United Kingdom, (Dial from U.S. (212) 216-7800), (Fax from U.S. (212) 564-7854), www.tandf.co.uk; *The Europa World Year Book.*

United Nations Conference on Trade and Development (UNCTAD), DC2-1120, United Nations, New York, NY 10017, (212) 963-0027, www.unctad.org; *UNCTAD Commodity Yearbook.*

United Nations Food and Agricultural Organization (FAO), Viale delle Terme di Caracalla, 00100 Rome, Italy, (Dial from U.S. (202) 653-2400), (Fax from U.S. (202) 653 5760), www.fao.org; AQUASTAT; *FAO Production Yearbook 2002;* and *The State of Food and Agriculture (SOFA) 2006.*

United Nations Statistics Division, New York, NY 10017, (800) 253-9646, Fax: (212) 963-4116, http://unstats.un.org; *Asia-Pacific in Figures 2004; Statistical Yearbook;* and *Statistical Yearbook for Asia and the Pacific 2004.*

The World Bank, 1818 H Street, NW, Washington, DC 20433, (202) 473-1000, Fax: (202) 477-6391, www.worldbank.org; *Japan.*

JAPAN - AIRLINES

Economist Intelligence Unit, 111 West 57th Street, New York, NY 10019, (212) 554-0600, Fax: (212) 586-1181, www.eiu.com; *Business Asia.*

International Civil Aviation Organization (ICAO), External Relations and Public Information Office (EPO), 999 University Street, Montreal, Quebec H3C 5H7, Canada, (Dial from U.S. (514) 954-8219), (Fax from U.S. (514) 954-6077), www.icao.int; *Civil Aviation Statistics of the World.*

M.E. Sharpe, 80 Business Park Drive, Armonk, NY 10504, (800) 541-6563, Fax: (914) 273-2106, www.mesharpe.com; *The Illustrated Book of World Rankings.*

Organisation for Economic Cooperation and Development (OECD), 2 rue Andre Pascal, F-75775 Paris Cedex 16, France, (Telephone in U.S. (202) 785-6323), (Fax in U.S. (202) 785-0350), www.oecd.org; *Household, Tourism, Travel: Trends, Environmental Impacts and Policy Responses.*

Palgrave Macmillan Ltd., Houndmills, Basingstoke, Hampshire, RG21 6XS, England, (Telephone in U.S. (888) 330-8477), (Fax in U.S. (800) 672-2054), www.palgrave.com; *The Statesman's Yearbook 2008.*

Taylor and Francis Group, An Informa Business, 2 Park Square, Milton Park, Abingdon, Oxford OX14 4RN, United Kingdom, (Dial from U.S. (212) 216-7800), (Fax from U.S. (212) 564-7854), www.tandf.co.uk; *The Europa World Year Book.*

United Nations Statistics Division, New York, NY 10017, (800) 253-9646, Fax: (212) 963-4116, http://unstats.un.org; *Statistical Yearbook.*

JAPAN - ALMOND PRODUCTION

See JAPAN - CROPS

JAPAN - ALUMINUM PRODUCTION

See JAPAN - MINERAL INDUSTRIES

JAPAN - ANIMAL FEEDING

Organisation for Economic Cooperation and Development (OECD), 2 rue Andre Pascal, F-75775 Paris Cedex 16, France, (Telephone in U.S. (202) 785-6323), (Fax in U.S. (202) 785-0350), www.oecd.org; *International Trade by Commodity Statistics (ITCS).*

United Nations Statistics Division, New York, NY 10017, (800) 253-9646, Fax: (212) 963-4116, http://unstats.un.org; *Statistical Yearbook.*

JAPAN - APPLE PRODUCTION

See JAPAN - CROPS

JAPAN - ARMED FORCES

Central Intelligence Agency, Office of Public Affairs, Washington, DC 20505, (703) 482-0623, Fax: (703) 482-1739, www.cia.gov; *The World Factbook.*

Economist Intelligence Unit, 111 West 57th Street, New York, NY 10019, (212) 554-0600, Fax: (212) 586-1181, www.eiu.com; *Business Asia.*

Euromonitor International, Inc., 224 S. Michigan Avenue, Suite 1500, Chicago, IL 60604, (312) 922-1115, Fax: (312) 922-1157, www.euromonitor.com; *World Marketing Data and Statistics.*

International Institute for Strategic Studies (IISS), Arundel House, 13-15 Arundel Street, Temple Place, London WC2R 3DX, England, www.iiss.org; *The Military Balance 2007.*

Palgrave Macmillan Ltd., Houndmills, Basingstoke, Hampshire, RG21 6XS, England, (Telephone in U.S. (888) 330-8477), (Fax in U.S. (800) 672-2054), www.palgrave.com; *The Statesman's Yearbook 2008.*

U.S. Department of State (DOS), 2201 C Street NW, Washington, DC 20520, (202) 647-4000, www.state.gov; *World Military Expenditures and Arms Transfers (WMEAT).*

United Nations Statistics Division, New York, NY 10017, (800) 253-9646, Fax: (212) 963-4116, http://unstats.un.org; *Human Development Report 2006.*

JAPAN - AUTOMOBILE INDUSTRY AND TRADE

Organisation for Economic Cooperation and Development (OECD), 2 rue Andre Pascal, F-75775 Paris Cedex 16, France, (Telephone in U.S. (202) 785-6323), (Fax in U.S. (202) 785-0350), www.oecd.org; *Indicators of Industrial Activity* and *International Trade by Commodity Statistics (ITCS).*

United Nations Statistics Division, New York, NY 10017, (800) 253-9646, Fax: (212) 963-4116, http://unstats.un.org; *Statistical Yearbook.*

JAPAN - BALANCE OF PAYMENTS

International Monetary Fund (IMF), 700 Nineteenth Street, NW, Washington, DC 20431, (202) 623-7000, Fax: (202) 623-4661, www.imf.org; *Balance of Payments Statistics Newsletter; Balance of Payments Statistics Yearbook 2007;* and *International Financial Statistics Yearbook 2007.*

Japan Center for Economic Research (JCER), Nikkei Kayabacho Building, Nihombashi Kayabacho, 2-6-1, Chuo-ku, Tokyo 103-0025, Japan, www.jcer.or.jp/eng; *Japan Financial Report.*

Organisation for Economic Cooperation and Development (OECD), 2 rue Andre Pascal, F-75775 Paris Cedex 16, France, (Telephone in U.S. (202) 785-6323), (Fax in U.S. (202) 785-0350), www.oecd.org; *Geographical Distribution of Financial Flows to Aid Recipients 2002-2006; OECD Economic Outlook 2008; OECD Economic Survey - Japan 2008;* and *OECD Main Economic Indicators (MEI).*

Taylor and Francis Group, An Informa Business, 2 Park Square, Milton Park, Abingdon, Oxford OX14 4RN, United Kingdom, (Dial from U.S. (212) 216-7800), (Fax from U.S. (212) 564-7854), www.tandf.co.uk; *The Europa World Year Book.*

United Nations Conference on Trade and Development (UNCTAD), DC2-1120, United Nations, New York, NY 10017, (212) 963-0027, www.unctad.org; *Handbook of Statistics 2005.*

The World Bank, 1818 H Street, NW, Washington, DC 20433, (202) 473-1000, Fax: (202) 477-6391, www.worldbank.org; *Japan* and *World Development Report 2008.*

JAPAN - BANKS AND BANKING

Euromonitor International, Inc., 224 S. Michigan Avenue, Suite 1500, Chicago, IL 60604, (312) 922-1115, Fax: (312) 922-1157, www.euromonitor.com; *World Marketing Data and Statistics.*

International Monetary Fund (IMF), 700 Nineteenth Street, NW, Washington, DC 20431, (202) 623-7000, Fax: (202) 623-4661, www.imf.org; *Government Finance Statistics Yearbook (2008 Edition)* and *International Financial Statistics Yearbook 2007.*

Japan Center for Economic Research (JCER), Nikkei Kayabacho Building, Nihombashi Kayabacho, 2-6-1, Chuo-ku, Tokyo 103-0025, Japan, www.jcer.or.jp/eng; *Japan Financial Report.*

M.E. Sharpe, 80 Business Park Drive, Armonk, NY 10504, (800) 541-6563, Fax: (914) 273-2106, www.mesharpe.com; *The Illustrated Book of World Rankings.*

Organisation for Economic Cooperation and Development (OECD), 2 rue Andre Pascal, F-75775 Paris Cedex 16, France, (Telephone in U.S. (202) 785-6323), (Fax in U.S. (202) 785-0350), www.oecd.org; *Financial Market Trends: OECD Periodical; OECD Economic Outlook 2008;* and *OECD Economic Survey - Japan 2008.*

Palgrave Macmillan Ltd., Houndmills, Basingstoke, Hampshire, RG21 6XS, England, (Telephone in U.S. (888) 330-8477), (Fax in U.S. (800) 672-2054), www.palgrave.com; *The Statesman's Yearbook 2008.*

Taylor and Francis Group, An Informa Business, 2 Park Square, Milton Park, Abingdon, Oxford OX14 4RN, United Kingdom, (Dial from U.S. (212) 216-7800), (Fax from U.S. (212) 564-7854), www.tandf.co.uk; *The Europa World Year Book.*

United Nations Statistics Division, New York, NY 10017, (800) 253-9646, Fax: (212) 963-4116, http://unstats.un.org; *Statistical Yearbook.*

JAPAN - BARLEY PRODUCTION

See JAPAN - CROPS

JAPAN - BEVERAGE INDUSTRY

M.E. Sharpe, 80 Business Park Drive, Armonk, NY 10504, (800) 541-6563, Fax: (914) 273-2106, www.mesharpe.com; *The Illustrated Book of World Rankings.*

Organisation for Economic Cooperation and Development (OECD), 2 rue Andre Pascal, F-75775 Paris Cedex 16, France, (Telephone in U.S. (202) 785-6323), (Fax in U.S. (202) 785-0350), www.oecd.org; *Indicators of Industrial Activity.*

United Nations Statistics Division, New York, NY 10017, (800) 253-9646, Fax: (212) 963-4116, http://unstats.un.org; *Statistical Yearbook.*

JAPAN - BONDS

Organisation for Economic Cooperation and Development (OECD), 2 rue Andre Pascal, F-75775 Paris Cedex 16, France, (Telephone in U.S. (202) 785-6323), (Fax in U.S. (202) 785-0350), www.oecd.org; *Financial Market Trends: OECD Periodical.*

United Nations Statistics Division, New York, NY 10017, (800) 253-9646, Fax: (212) 963-4116, http://unstats.un.org; *Statistical Yearbook.*

JAPAN - BROADCASTING

Central Intelligence Agency, Office of Public Affairs, Washington, DC 20505, (703) 482-0623, Fax: (703) 482-1739, www.cia.gov; *The World Factbook.*

Economist Intelligence Unit, 111 West 57th Street, New York, NY 10019, (212) 554-0600, Fax: (212) 586-1181, www.eiu.com; *Business Asia.*

Euromonitor International, Inc., 224 S. Michigan Avenue, Suite 1500, Chicago, IL 60604, (312) 922-1115, Fax: (312) 922-1157, www.euromonitor.com; *World Marketing Data and Statistics.*

M.E. Sharpe, 80 Business Park Drive, Armonk, NY 10504, (800) 541-6563, Fax: (914) 273-2106, www.mesharpe.com; *The Illustrated Book of World Rankings.*

Palgrave Macmillan Ltd., Houndmills, Basingstoke, Hampshire, RG21 6XS, England, (Telephone in U.S. (888) 330-8477), (Fax in U.S. (800) 672-2054), www.palgrave.com; *The Statesman's Yearbook 2008.*

UNESCO Institute for Statistics, C.P. 6128 Succursale Centre-Ville, Montreal, Quebec, H3C 3J7 Canada, (Dial from U.S. (514) 343-6880), (Fax from U.S. (514) 343 6882), www.uis.unesco.org; *Statistical Tables.*

WRTH Publications Limited, PO Box 290, Oxford OX2 7FT, UK, www.wrth.com; *World Radio TV Handbook 2007.*

JAPAN - BUSINESS

Central Intelligence Agency, Office of Public Affairs, Washington, DC 20505, (703) 482-0623, Fax: (703) 482-1739, www.cia.gov; *The World Factbook.*

Japan Center for Economic Research (JCER), Nikkei Kayabacho Building, Nihombashi Kayabacho, 2-6-1, Chuo-ku, Tokyo 103-0025, Japan, www.jcer.or.jp/eng; *Industry Research Report 2003* and *Japan Financial Report.*

Organisation for Economic Cooperation and Development (OECD), 2 rue Andre Pascal, F-75775 Paris Cedex 16, France, (Telephone in U.S. (202) 785-6323), (Fax in U.S. (202) 785-0350), www.oecd.org; *OECD Main Economic Indicators (MEI).*

United Nations Statistics Division, New York, NY 10017, (800) 253-9646, Fax: (212) 963-4116, http://unstats.un.org; *Statistical Yearbook* and *Statistical Yearbook for Asia and the Pacific 2004.*

JAPAN - CADMIUM PRODUCTION

See JAPAN - MINERAL INDUSTRIES

JAPAN - CAPITAL INVESTMENTS

Organisation for Economic Cooperation and Development (OECD), 2 rue Andre Pascal, F-75775 Paris Cedex 16, France, (Telephone in U.S. (202) 785-6323), (Fax in U.S. (202) 785-0350), www.oecd.org; *Financial Market Trends: OECD Periodical* and *OECD Economic Outlook 2008.*

JAPAN - CAPITAL LEVY

International Monetary Fund (IMF), 700 Nineteenth Street, NW, Washington, DC 20431, (202) 623-7000, Fax: (202) 623-4661, www.imf.org; *Government Finance Statistics Yearbook (2008 Edition).*

Organisation for Economic Cooperation and Development (OECD), 2 rue Andre Pascal, F-75775 Paris Cedex 16, France, (Telephone in U.S. (202) 785-6323), (Fax in U.S. (202) 785-0350), www.oecd.org; *Financial Market Trends: OECD Periodical* and *OECD Economic Outlook 2008.*

JAPAN - CATTLE

See JAPAN - LIVESTOCK

JAPAN - CHESTNUT PRODUCTION

See JAPAN - CROPS

JAPAN - CHICKENS

See JAPAN - LIVESTOCK

JAPAN - CHILDBIRTH - STATISTICS

Central Intelligence Agency, Office of Public Affairs, Washington, DC 20505, (703) 482-0623, Fax: (703) 482-1739, www.cia.gov; *The World Factbook.*

Economist Intelligence Unit, 111 West 57th Street, New York, NY 10019, (212) 554-0600, Fax: (212) 586-1181, www.eiu.com; *Business Asia.*

Euromonitor International, Inc., 224 S. Michigan Avenue, Suite 1500, Chicago, IL 60604, (312) 922-1115, Fax: (312) 922-1157, www.euromonitor.com; *The World Economic Factbook 2008.*

M.E. Sharpe, 80 Business Park Drive, Armonk, NY 10504, (800) 541-6563, Fax: (914) 273-2106, www.mesharpe.com; *The Illustrated Book of World Rankings.*

Palgrave Macmillan Ltd., Houndmills, Basingstoke, Hampshire, RG21 6XS, England, (Telephone in U.S. (888) 330-8477), (Fax in U.S. (800) 672-2054), www.palgrave.com; *The Statesman's Yearbook 2008.*

Statistics Bureau, the Director-General for Policy Planning (Statistical Standards), 19-1 Wakamatsucho, Shinjuku-ku, Tokyo 162-8668, Japan, www.stat.go.jp/english; *Japan Statistical Yearbook 2008.*

Taylor and Francis Group, An Informa Business, 2 Park Square, Milton Park, Abingdon, Oxford OX14 4RN, United Kingdom, (Dial from U.S. (212) 216-7800), (Fax from U.S. (212) 564-7854), www.tandf.co.uk; *The Europa World Year Book.*

United Nations Statistics Division, New York, NY 10017, (800) 253-9646, Fax: (212) 963-4116, http://unstats.un.org; *Asia-Pacific in Figures 2004; Demographic Yearbook;* and *Statistical Yearbook.*

World Health Organization (WHO), Avenue Appia 20, 1211 Geneve 27, Switzerland, (Telephone in U.S. (212) 331-9081), www.who.int; *World Health Report 2006.*

JAPAN - CLIMATE

International Institute for Environment and Development (IIED), 3 Endsleigh Street, London, England, WC1H 0DD, United Kingdom, www.iied.org; *Environment Urbanization.*

M.E. Sharpe, 80 Business Park Drive, Armonk, NY 10504, (800) 541-6563, Fax: (914) 273-2106, www.mesharpe.com; *The Illustrated Book of World Rankings.*

Palgrave Macmillan Ltd., Houndmills, Basingstoke, Hampshire, RG21 6XS, England, (Telephone in U.S. (888) 330-8477), (Fax in U.S. (800) 672-2054), www.palgrave.com; *The Statesman's Yearbook 2008.*

Statistics Bureau, the Director-General for Policy Planning (Statistical Standards), 19-1 Wakamatsucho, Shinjuku-ku, Tokyo 162-8668, Japan, www.stat.go.jp/english; *Japan Statistical Yearbook 2008.*

JAPAN - CLOTHING EXPORTS AND IMPORTS

See JAPAN - TEXTILE INDUSTRY

JAPAN - COAL PRODUCTION

See JAPAN - MINERAL INDUSTRIES

JAPAN - COBALT PRODUCTION

See JAPAN - MINERAL INDUSTRIES

JAPAN - COCOA PRODUCTION

See JAPAN - CROPS

JAPAN - COFFEE

See JAPAN - CROPS

JAPAN - COMMERCE

Japan Center for Economic Research (JCER), Nikkei Kayabacho Building, Nihombashi Kayabacho, 2-6-1, Chuo-ku, Tokyo 103-0025, Japan, www.jcer.or.jp/eng; *Japan Financial Report.*

Palgrave Macmillan Ltd., Houndmills, Basingstoke, Hampshire, RG21 6XS, England, (Telephone in U.S. (888) 330-8477), (Fax in U.S. (800) 672-2054), www.palgrave.com; *The Statesman's Yearbook 2008.*

JAPAN - COMMODITY EXCHANGES

Commodity Research Bureau, 330 South Wells Street, Suite 612, Chicago, IL 60606-7110, (800) 621-5271, Fax: (312) 939-4135, www.crbtrader.com; *2006 CRB Commodity Yearbook and CD.*

International Lead and Zinc Study Group (ILZSG), Rua Almirante Barroso 38, 5th Floor, Lisbon 1000 - 013, Portugal, www.ilzsg.org; Interactive Statistical Database.

International Monetary Fund (IMF), 700 Nineteenth Street, NW, Washington, DC 20431, (202) 623-7000, Fax: (202) 623-4661, www.imf.org; *IMF Primary Commodity Prices.*

United Nations Food and Agricultural Organization (FAO), Viale delle Terme di Caracalla, 00100 Rome, Italy, (Dial from U.S. (202) 653-2400), (Fax from U.S. (202) 653 5760), www.fao.org; *The State of Food and Agriculture (SOFA) 2006.*

United Nations Statistics Division, New York, NY 10017, (800) 253-9646, Fax: (212) 963-4116, http://unstats.un.org; *Statistical Yearbook.*

World Bureau of Metal Statistics (WBMS), 27a High Street, Ware, Hertfordshire, SG12 9BA, United Kingdom, www.world-bureau.com; *Annual Stainless Steel Statistics; World Flow Charts; World Metal Statistics; World Nickel Statistics;* and *World Tin Statistics.*

JAPAN - COMMUNICATION AND TRAFFIC

United Nations Statistics Division, New York, NY 10017, (800) 253-9646, Fax: (212) 963-4116, http://unstats.un.org; *Statistical Yearbook.*

JAPAN - CONSTRUCTION INDUSTRY

M.E. Sharpe, 80 Business Park Drive, Armonk, NY 10504, (800) 541-6563, Fax: (914) 273-2106, www.mesharpe.com; *The Illustrated Book of World Rankings.*

Organisation for Economic Cooperation and Development (OECD), 2 rue Andre Pascal, F-75775 Paris Cedex 16, France, (Telephone in U.S. (202) 785-6323), (Fax in U.S. (202) 785-0350), www.oecd.org; *Iron and Steel Industry in 2004 (2006 Edition); OECD Economic Survey - Japan 2008; OECD Main Economic Indicators (MEI);* and STructural ANalysis (STAN) database.

Palgrave Macmillan Ltd., Houndmills, Basingstoke, Hampshire, RG21 6XS, England, (Telephone in U.S. (888) 330-8477), (Fax in U.S. (800) 672-2054), www.palgrave.com; *The Statesman's Yearbook 2008.*

United Nations Statistics Division, New York, NY 10017, (800) 253-9646, Fax: (212) 963-4116, http://unstats.un.org; *Statistical Yearbook.*

JAPAN - CONSUMER PRICE INDEXES

Organisation for Economic Cooperation and Development (OECD), 2 rue Andre Pascal, F-75775 Paris Cedex 16, France, (Telephone in U.S. (202) 785-6323), (Fax in U.S. (202) 785-0350), www.oecd.org; *OECD Economic Outlook 2008.*

Taylor and Francis Group, An Informa Business, 2 Park Square, Milton Park, Abingdon, Oxford OX14 4RN, United Kingdom, (Dial from U.S. (212) 216-7800), (Fax from U.S. (212) 564-7854), www.tandf.co.uk; *The Europa World Year Book.*

United Nations Statistics Division, New York, NY 10017, (800) 253-9646, Fax: (212) 963-4116, http://unstats.un.org; *Statistical Yearbook.*

The World Bank, 1818 H Street, NW, Washington, DC 20433, (202) 473-1000, Fax: (202) 477-6391, www.worldbank.org; *Japan.*

JAPAN - CONSUMPTION (ECONOMICS)

International Lead and Zinc Study Group (ILZSG), Rua Almirante Barroso 38, 5th Floor, Lisbon 1000 - 013, Portugal, www.ilzsg.org; Interactive Statistical Database and *Monthly Bulletin of the International Lead and Zinc Study Group.*

International Monetary Fund (IMF), 700 Nineteenth Street, NW, Washington, DC 20431, (202) 623-7000, Fax: (202) 623-4661, www.imf.org; *International Financial Statistics Yearbook 2007.*

Organisation for Economic Cooperation and Development (OECD), 2 rue Andre Pascal, F-75775 Paris Cedex 16, France, (Telephone in U.S. (202) 785-6323), (Fax in U.S. (202) 785-0350), www.oecd.org; *Environmental Impacts of Foreign Direct Investment in the Mining Sector in the Newly Independent States (NIS); Iron and Steel Industry in 2004 (2006 Edition); A New World Map in Textiles and Clothing: Adjusting to Change; 2005 OECD Agricultural Outlook Tables, 1970-2014; Revenue Statistics 1965-2006 - 2007 Edition;* and *Towards Sustainable Household Consumption?: Trends and Policies in OECD Countries.*

Statistics Bureau, the Director-General for Policy Planning (Statistical Standards), 19-1 Wakamatsu-cho, Shinjuku-ku, Tokyo 162-8668, Japan, www.stat.go.jp/english; *Japan Statistical Yearbook 2008.*

Technical Association of the Pulp and Paper Industry (TAPPI), 15 Technology Parkway South, Norcross, GA 30092, (770) 446-1400, Fax: (770) 446-6947, www.tappi.org; *TAPPI Annual Report.*

The World Bank, 1818 H Street, NW, Washington, DC 20433, (202) 473-1000, Fax: (202) 477-6391, www.worldbank.org; *World Development Report 2008.*

JAPAN - COPPER INDUSTRY AND TRADE

See JAPAN - MINERAL INDUSTRIES

JAPAN - CORN INDUSTRY

See JAPAN - CROPS

JAPAN - COTTON

See JAPAN - CROPS

JAPAN - CRIME

International Criminal Police Organization (INTERPOL), General Secretariat, 200 quai Charles de Gaulle, 69006 Lyon, France, www.interpol.int; *International Crime Statistics.*

Statistics Bureau, the Director-General for Policy Planning (Statistical Standards), 19-1 Wakamatsu-cho, Shinjuku-ku, Tokyo 162-8668, Japan, www.stat.go.jp/english; *Japan Statistical Yearbook 2008.*

U.S. Department of Justice (DOJ), Bureau of Justice Statistics, 810 Seventh Street, NW, Washington, DC 20531, (202) 307-0765, www.ojp.usdoj.gov/bjs/; *The World Factbook of Criminal Justice Systems.*

Yale University Press, PO Box 209040, New Haven, CT 06520-9040, (203) 432-0960, Fax: (203) 432-0948, http://yalepress.yale.edu/yupbooks; *Violence and Crime in Cross-National Perspective.*

JAPAN - CROPS

M.E. Sharpe, 80 Business Park Drive, Armonk, NY 10504, (800) 541-6563, Fax: (914) 273-2106, www.mesharpe.com; *The Illustrated Book of World Rankings.*

Organisation for Economic Cooperation and Development (OECD), 2 rue Andre Pascal, F-75775 Paris Cedex 16, France, (Telephone in U.S. (202) 785-6323), (Fax in U.S. (202) 785-0350), www.oecd.org; *Indicators of Industrial Activity; International Trade by Commodity Statistics (ITCS);* and *2005 OECD Agricultural Outlook Tables, 1970-2014.*

Palgrave Macmillan Ltd., Houndmills, Basingstoke, Hampshire, RG21 6XS, England, (Telephone in U.S. (888) 330-8477), (Fax in U.S. (800) 672-2054), www.palgrave.com; *The Statesman's Yearbook 2008.*

Statistics Bureau, the Director-General for Policy Planning (Statistical Standards), 19-1 Wakamatsu-cho, Shinjuku-ku, Tokyo 162-8668, Japan, www.stat.go.jp/english; *Japan Statistical Yearbook 2008.*

Taylor and Francis Group, An Informa Business, 2 Park Square, Milton Park, Abingdon, Oxford OX14 4RN, United Kingdom, (Dial from U.S. (212) 216-7800), (Fax from U.S. (212) 564-7854), www.tandf.co.uk; *The Europa World Year Book.*

United Nations Conference on Trade and Development (UNCTAD), DC2-1120, United Nations, New York, NY 10017, (212) 963-0027, www.unctad.org; *UNCTAD Commodity Yearbook.*

United Nations Food and Agricultural Organization (FAO), Viale delle Terme di Caracalla, 00100 Rome, Italy, (Dial from U.S. (202) 653-2400), (Fax from U.S. (202) 653 5760), www.fao.org; *FAO Production Yearbook 2002* and *The State of Food and Agriculture (SOFA) 2006.*

United Nations Statistics Division, New York, NY 10017, (800) 253-9646, Fax: (212) 963-4116, http://unstats.un.org; *Statistical Yearbook.*

JAPAN - CUSTOMS ADMINISTRATION

International Monetary Fund (IMF), 700 Nineteenth Street, NW, Washington, DC 20431, (202) 623-7000, Fax: (202) 623-4661, www.imf.org; *Government Finance Statistics Yearbook (2008 Edition).*

Organisation for Economic Cooperation and Development (OECD), 2 rue Andre Pascal, F-75775 Paris Cedex 16, France, (Telephone in U.S. (202) 785-6323), (Fax in U.S. (202) 785-0350), www.oecd.org; *Environmental Impacts of Foreign Direct Investment in the Mining Sector in the Newly Independent States (NIS)* and *2005 OECD Agricultural Outlook Tables, 1970-2014.*

Palgrave Macmillan Ltd., Houndmills, Basingstoke, Hampshire, RG21 6XS, England, (Telephone in U.S. (888) 330-8477), (Fax in U.S. (800) 672-2054), www.palgrave.com; *The Statesman's Yearbook 2008.*

JAPAN - DAIRY PROCESSING

M.E. Sharpe, 80 Business Park Drive, Armonk, NY 10504, (800) 541-6563, Fax: (914) 273-2106, www.mesharpe.com; *The Illustrated Book of World Rankings.*

Organisation for Economic Cooperation and Development (OECD), 2 rue Andre Pascal, F-75775 Paris Cedex 16, France, (Telephone in U.S. (202) 785-6323), (Fax in U.S. (202) 785-0350), www.oecd.org; *2005 OECD Agricultural Outlook Tables, 1970-2014.*

Palgrave Macmillan Ltd., Houndmills, Basingstoke, Hampshire, RG21 6XS, England, (Telephone in U.S. (888) 330-8477), (Fax in U.S. (800) 672-2054), www.palgrave.com; *The Statesman's Yearbook 2008.*

Taylor and Francis Group, An Informa Business, 2 Park Square, Milton Park, Abingdon, Oxford OX14 4RN, United Kingdom, (Dial from U.S. (212) 216-7800), (Fax from U.S. (212) 564-7854), www.tandf.co.uk; *The Europa World Year Book.*

United Nations Food and Agricultural Organization (FAO), Viale delle Terme di Caracalla, 00100 Rome, Italy, (Dial from U.S. (202) 653-2400), (Fax from U.S. (202) 653 5760), www.fao.org; *FAO Production Yearbook 2002* and *The State of Food and Agriculture (SOFA) 2006.*

United Nations Statistics Division, New York, NY 10017, (800) 253-9646, Fax: (212) 963-4116, http://unstats.un.org; *Statistical Yearbook.*

JAPAN - DEBTS, EXTERNAL

International Monetary Fund (IMF), 700 Nineteenth Street, NW, Washington, DC 20431, (202) 623-7000, Fax: (202) 623-4661, www.imf.org; *Government Finance Statistics Yearbook (2008 Edition).*

Organisation for Economic Cooperation and Development (OECD), 2 rue Andre Pascal, F-75775 Paris Cedex 16, France, (Telephone in U.S. (202) 785-6323), (Fax in U.S. (202) 785-0350), www.oecd.org; *Financial Market Trends: OECD Periodical; Geographical Distribution of Financial Flows to Aid Recipients 2002-2006;* and *OECD Economic Outlook 2008.*

Palgrave Macmillan Ltd., Houndmills, Basingstoke, Hampshire, RG21 6XS, England, (Telephone in U.S. (888) 330-8477), (Fax in U.S. (800) 672-2054), www.palgrave.com; *The Statesman's Yearbook 2008.*

The World Bank, 1818 H Street, NW, Washington, DC 20433, (202) 473-1000, Fax: (202) 477-6391, www.worldbank.org; *Global Development Finance 2007* and *World Development Report 2008.*

Worldinformation.com, 2 Market Street, Saffron Walden, Essex CB10 1HZ, United Kingdom, www.worldinformation.com; The World of Information (www.worldinformation.com).

JAPAN - DEFENSE EXPENDITURES

See JAPAN - ARMED FORCES

JAPAN - DEMOGRAPHY

Economist Intelligence Unit, 111 West 57th Street, New York, NY 10019, (212) 554-0600, Fax: (212) 586-1181, www.eiu.com; *Business Asia.*

Euromonitor International, Inc., 224 S. Michigan Avenue, Suite 1500, Chicago, IL 60604, (312) 922-1115, Fax: (312) 922-1157, www.euromonitor.com; *The World Economic Factbook 2008* and *World Marketing Data and Statistics.*

M.E. Sharpe, 80 Business Park Drive, Armonk, NY 10504, (800) 541-6563, Fax: (914) 273-2106, www.mesharpe.com; *The Illustrated Book of World Rankings.*

United Nations Statistics Division, New York, NY 10017, (800) 253-9646, Fax: (212) 963-4116, http://unstats.un.org; *Asia-Pacific in Figures 2004* and *Human Development Report 2006.*

The World Bank, 1818 H Street, NW, Washington, DC 20433, (202) 473-1000, Fax: (202) 477-6391, www.worldbank.org; *Japan.*

JAPAN - DIAMONDS

See JAPAN - MINERAL INDUSTRIES

JAPAN - DISPOSABLE INCOME

M.E. Sharpe, 80 Business Park Drive, Armonk, NY 10504, (800) 541-6563, Fax: (914) 273-2106, www.mesharpe.com; *The Illustrated Book of World Rankings.*

Organisation for Economic Cooperation and Development (OECD), 2 rue Andre Pascal, F-75775 Paris Cedex 16, France, (Telephone in U.S. (202) 785-6323), (Fax in U.S. (202) 785-0350), www.oecd.org; *OECD Economic Outlook 2008.*

United Nations Statistics Division, New York, NY 10017, (800) 253-9646, Fax: (212) 963-4116, http://unstats.un.org; *National Accounts Statistics: Compendium of Income Distribution Statistics* and *Statistical Yearbook.*

JAPAN - DIVORCE

M.E. Sharpe, 80 Business Park Drive, Armonk, NY 10504, (800) 541-6563, Fax: (914) 273-2106, www.mesharpe.com; *The Illustrated Book of World Rankings.*

Statistics Bureau, the Director-General for Policy Planning (Statistical Standards), 19-1 Wakamatsu-cho, Shinjuku-ku, Tokyo 162-8668, Japan, www.stat.go.jp/english; *Japan Statistical Yearbook 2008.*

United Nations Statistics Division, New York, NY 10017, (800) 253-9646, Fax: (212) 963-4116, http://unstats.un.org; *Demographic Yearbook* and *Statistical Yearbook.*

JAPAN - ECONOMIC ASSISTANCE

Organisation for Economic Cooperation and Development (OECD), 2 rue Andre Pascal, F-75775 Paris Cedex 16, France, (Telephone in U.S. (202) 785-6323), (Fax in U.S. (202) 785-0350), www.oecd.org; *Geographical Distribution of Financial Flows to Aid Recipients 2002-2006.*

United Nations Statistics Division, New York, NY 10017, (800) 253-9646, Fax: (212) 963-4116, http://unstats.un.org; *Statistical Yearbook.*

JAPAN - ECONOMIC CONDITIONS

Center for International Business Education Research (CIBER), Columbia Business School and School of International and Public Affairs, Uris Hall, Room 212, 3022 Broadway, New York, NY 10027-6902, Mr. Joshua Safier, (212) 854-4750, Fax: (212) 222-9821, www.columbia.edu/cu/ciber/; Datastream International.

Central Intelligence Agency, Office of Public Affairs, Washington, DC 20505, (703) 482-0623, Fax: (703) 482-1739, www.cia.gov; *The World Factbook.*

DSI Data Service Information, Xantener Strasse 51a, D-47495 Rheinberg, Germany, www.dsidata.com; *Campus Solution.*

Dun and Bradstreet (DB) Corporation, 103 JFK Parkway, Short Hills, NJ 07078, (973) 921-5500, www.dnb.com; *Country Report.*

Economist Intelligence Unit, 111 West 57th Street, New York, NY 10019, (212) 554-0600, Fax: (212) 586-1181, www.eiu.com; *Japan Country Report.*

Euromonitor International, Inc., 224 S. Michigan Avenue, Suite 1500, Chicago, IL 60604, (312) 922-1115, Fax: (312) 922-1157, www.euromonitor.com; *International Marketing Data and Statistics 2008; The World Economic Factbook 2008;* and *World Marketing Data and Statistics.*

Federal Statistical Office Germany, D-65180 Wiesbaden, Germany, www.destatis.de; *Japan 2008.*

International Monetary Fund (IMF), 700 Nineteenth Street, NW, Washington, DC 20431, (202) 623-7000, Fax: (202) 623-4661, www.imf.org; *World Economic Outlook Reports.*

Japan Center for Economic Research (JCER), Nikkei Kayabacho Building, Nihombashi Kayabacho, 2-6-1, Chuo-ku, Tokyo 103-0025, Japan, www.jcer.or.jp/eng; *Asia Research Report; Industry Research Report 2003;* and *Japan Financial Report.*

M.E. Sharpe, 80 Business Park Drive, Armonk, NY 10504, (800) 541-6563, Fax: (914) 273-2106, www.mesharpe.com; *The Illustrated Book of World Rankings.*

Nomura Research Institute (NRI), 2 World Financial Center, Building B, 19th Fl., New York, NY 10281-1198, (212) 667-1670, www.nri.co.jp/english; *Asian Economic Outlook 2003-2004.*

Organisation for Economic Cooperation and Development (OECD), 2 rue Andre Pascal, F-75775 Paris Cedex 16, France, (Telephone in U.S. (202) 785-6323), (Fax in U.S. (202) 785-0350), www.oecd.org; *Geographical Distribution of Financial Flows to Aid Recipients 2002-2006; ICT Sector Data and Metadata by Country; Labour Force Statistics: 1986-2005, 2007 Edition; OECD Composite Leading Indicators (CLIs), Updated September 2007; OECD Economic Outlook 2008; OECD Economic Survey - Japan 2008; OECD Employment Outlook 2007; OECD in Figures 2007;* and *OECD Main Economic Indicators (MEI).*

Palgrave Macmillan Ltd., Houndmills, Basingstoke, Hampshire, RG21 6XS, England, (Telephone in U.S. (888) 330-8477), (Fax in U.S. (800) 672-2054), www.palgrave.com; *The Statesman's Yearbook 2008.*

Statistics Bureau, the Director-General for Policy Planning (Statistical Standards), 19-1 Wakamatsucho, Shinjuku-ku, Tokyo 162-8668, Japan, www.stat.go.jp/english; *Japan Statistical Yearbook 2008.*

Taylor and Francis Group, An Informa Business, 2 Park Square, Milton Park, Abingdon, Oxford OX14 4RN, United Kingdom, (Dial from U.S. (212) 216-7800), (Fax from U.S. (212) 564-7854), www.tandf.co.uk; *The Europa World Year Book.*

United Nations Statistics Division, New York, NY 10017, (800) 253-9646, Fax: (212) 963-4116, http://unstats.un.org; *World Statistics Pocketbook.*

The World Bank, 1818 H Street, NW, Washington, DC 20433, (202) 473-1000, Fax: (202) 477-6391, www.worldbank.org; *Global Economic Monitor (GEM); Global Economic Prospects 2008; Japan; The World Bank Atlas 2003-2004;* and *World Development Report 2008.*

JAPAN - ECONOMICS - SOCIOLOGICAL ASPECTS

Organisation for Economic Cooperation and Development (OECD), 2 rue Andre Pascal, F-75775 Paris Cedex 16, France, (Telephone in U.S. (202) 785-6323), (Fax in U.S. (202) 785-0350), www.oecd.org; *OECD Economic Outlook 2008.*

JAPAN - EDUCATION

Economist Intelligence Unit, 111 West 57th Street, New York, NY 10019, (212) 554-0600, Fax: (212) 586-1181, www.eiu.com; *Business Asia.*

Euromonitor International, Inc., 224 S. Michigan Avenue, Suite 1500, Chicago, IL 60604, (312) 922-1115, Fax: (312) 922-1157, www.euromonitor.com; *World Marketing Data and Statistics.*

M.E. Sharpe, 80 Business Park Drive, Armonk, NY 10504, (800) 541-6563, Fax: (914) 273-2106, www.mesharpe.com; *The Illustrated Book of World Rankings.*

Organisation for Economic Cooperation and Development (OECD), 2 rue Andre Pascal, F-75775 Paris Cedex 16, France, (Telephone in U.S. (202) 785-6323), (Fax in U.S. (202) 785-0350), www.oecd.org; *Education at a Glance* (2007 Edition).

Palgrave Macmillan Ltd., Houndmills, Basingstoke, Hampshire, RG21 6XS, England, (Telephone in U.S. (888) 330-8477), (Fax in U.S. (800) 672-2054), www.palgrave.com; *The Statesman's Yearbook 2008.*

Statistics Bureau, the Director-General for Policy Planning (Statistical Standards), 19-1 Wakamatsucho, Shinjuku-ku, Tokyo 162-8668, Japan, www.stat.go.jp/english; *Japan Statistical Yearbook 2008.*

Taylor and Francis Group, An Informa Business, 2 Park Square, Milton Park, Abingdon, Oxford OX14 4RN, United Kingdom, (Dial from U.S. (212) 216-7800), (Fax from U.S. (212) 564-7854), www.tandf.co.uk; *The Europa World Year Book.*

UNESCO Institute for Statistics, C.P. 6128 Succursale Centre-Ville, Montreal, Quebec, H3C 3J7 Canada, (Dial from U.S. (514) 343-6880), (Fax from U.S. (514) 343 6882), www.uis.unesco.org; *Statistical Tables.*

United Nations Statistics Division, New York, NY 10017, (800) 253-9646, Fax: (212) 963-4116, http://unstats.un.org; *Asia-Pacific in Figures 2004; Human Development Report 2006;* and *Statistical Yearbook for Asia and the Pacific 2004.*

The World Bank, 1818 H Street, NW, Washington, DC 20433, (202) 473-1000, Fax: (202) 477-6391, www.worldbank.org; *Japan* and *World Development Report 2008.*

JAPAN - EGGPLANT PRODUCTION

See JAPAN - CROPS

JAPAN - ELECTRICITY

M.E. Sharpe, 80 Business Park Drive, Armonk, NY 10504, (800) 541-6563, Fax: (914) 273-2106, www.mesharpe.com; *The Illustrated Book of World Rankings.*

Organisation for Economic Cooperation and Development (OECD), 2 rue Andre Pascal, F-75775 Paris Cedex 16, France, (Telephone in U.S. (202) 785-6323), (Fax in U.S. (202) 785-0350), www.oecd.org; *Energy Statistics of OECD Countries* (2007 Edition); *Indicators of Industrial Activity;* STructural ANalysis (STAN) database; and *World Energy Outlook 2007.*

Palgrave Macmillan Ltd., Houndmills, Basingstoke, Hampshire, RG21 6XS, England, (Telephone in U.S. (888) 330-8477), (Fax in U.S. (800) 672-2054), www.palgrave.com; *The Statesman's Yearbook 2008.*

Platts, 2 Penn Plaza, 25th Floor, New York, NY 10121-2298, (212) 904-3070, www.platts.com; *Asian Electricity Outlook 2006* and *Emissions Daily.*

U.S. Department of Energy (DOE), Energy Information Administration (EIA), 1000 Independence Avenue, SW, Washington, DC 20585, (202) 586-8800, www.eia.doe.gov; *International Energy Annual 2004* and *International Energy Outlook 2006.*

United Nations Statistics Division, New York, NY 10017, (800) 253-9646, Fax: (212) 963-4116, http://unstats.un.org; *Electric Power in Asia and the Pacific 2001 and 2002; Human Development Report 2006;* and *Statistical Yearbook.*

JAPAN - EMPLOYMENT

Bernan Essential Government Publications, 4611-F Assembly Drive, Lanham MD, 20706-4391, (301) 459-2255, Fax: (800) 865-3450, www.bernan.com; *OECD Factbook 2006.*

Euromonitor International, Inc., 224 S. Michigan Avenue, Suite 1500, Chicago, IL 60604, (312) 922-1115, Fax: (312) 922-1157, www.euromonitor.com; *International Marketing Data and Statistics 2008.*

International Labour Office, I.L.O. Publications, 4 route des Morillons, CH-1211 Geneva 22, Switzerland, (Telephone in U.S. (202) 653-7652), (Fax in U.S. (202) 653-7687), www.ilo.org; *Yearbook of Labour Statistics 2006.*

M.E. Sharpe, 80 Business Park Drive, Armonk, NY 10504, (800) 541-6563, Fax: (914) 273-2106, www.mesharpe.com; *The Illustrated Book of World Rankings.*

Organisation for Economic Cooperation and Development (OECD), 2 rue Andre Pascal, F-75775 Paris Cedex 16, France, (Telephone in U.S. (202) 785-6323), (Fax in U.S. (202) 785-0350), www.oecd.org; *ICT Sector Data and Metadata by Country; Iron and Steel Industry in 2004 (2006 Edition); Labour Force Statistics: 1986-2005, 2007 Edition; A New World Map in Textiles and Clothing: Adjusting to Change; OECD Composite Leading Indicators (CLIs), Updated September 2007; OECD Economic Survey - Japan 2008; OECD Employment Outlook 2007;* and *OECD in Figures 2007.*

Statistics Bureau, the Director-General for Policy Planning (Statistical Standards), 19-1 Wakamatsucho, Shinjuku-ku, Tokyo 162-8668, Japan, www.stat.go.jp/english; *Japan Statistical Yearbook 2008.*

United Nations Statistics Division, New York, NY 10017, (800) 253-9646, Fax: (212) 963-4116, http://unstats.un.org; *Asia-Pacific in Figures 2004* and *Statistical Yearbook.*

The World Bank, 1818 H Street, NW, Washington, DC 20433, (202) 473-1000, Fax: (202) 477-6391, www.worldbank.org; *Japan.*

JAPAN - ENERGY INDUSTRIES

Enerdata, 10 Rue Royale, 75008 Paris, France, www.enerdata.fr; *Global Energy Market Data.*

International Energy Agency (IEA), 9, rue de la Federation, 75739 Paris Cedex 15, France, www.iea.org; *Key World Energy Statistics 2007.*

Organisation for Economic Cooperation and Development (OECD), 2 rue Andre Pascal, F-75775 Paris Cedex 16, France, (Telephone in U.S. (202) 785-6323), (Fax in U.S. (202) 785-0350), www.oecd.org; *Towards Sustainable Household Consumption?: Trends and Policies in OECD Countries.*

Platts, 2 Penn Plaza, 25th Floor, New York, NY 10121-2298, (212) 904-3070, www.platts.com; *Asian Electricity Outlook 2006* and *Emissions Daily.*

United Nations Statistics Division, New York, NY 10017, (800) 253-9646, Fax: (212) 963-4116, http://unstats.un.org; *Electric Power in Asia and the Pacific 2001 and 2002* and *Statistical Yearbook.*

The World Bank, 1818 H Street, NW, Washington, DC 20433, (202) 473-1000, Fax: (202) 477-6391, www.worldbank.org; *Japan.*

JAPAN - ENVIRONMENTAL CONDITIONS

DSI Data Service Information, Xantener Strasse 51a, D-47495 Rheinberg, Germany, www.dsidata.com; *Campus Solution* and *DSI's Global Environmental Database.*

Economist Intelligence Unit, 111 West 57th Street, New York, NY 10019, (212) 554-0600, Fax: (212) 586-1181, www.eiu.com; *Japan Country Report.*

Federal Statistical Office Germany, D-65180 Wiesbaden, Germany, www.destatis.de; *Japan 2008.*

International Institute for Environment and Development (IIED), 3 Endsleigh Street, London, England, WC1H 0DD, United Kingdom, www.iied.org; *Environment Urbanization* and *Up in Smoke? Asia and the Pacific.*

Organisation for Economic Cooperation and Development (OECD), 2 rue Andre Pascal, F-75775 Paris Cedex 16, France, (Telephone in U.S. (202) 785-6323), (Fax in U.S. (202) 785-0350), www.oecd.org; *Key Environmental Indicators 2004.*

Platts, 2 Penn Plaza, 25th Floor, New York, NY 10121-2298, (212) 904-3070, www.platts.com; *Emissions Daily.*

United Nations Statistics Division, New York, NY 10017, (800) 253-9646, Fax: (212) 963-4116, http://unstats.un.org; *World Statistics Pocketbook.*

JAPAN - EXPENDITURES, PUBLIC

Japan Center for Economic Research (JCER), Nikkei Kayabacho Building, Nihombashi Kayabacho,

2-6-1, Chuo-ku, Tokyo 103-0025, Japan, www.jcer.or.jp/eng; *Japan Financial Report*.

Organisation for Economic Cooperation and Development (OECD), 2 rue Andre Pascal, F-75775 Paris Cedex 16, France, (Telephone in U.S. (202) 785-6323), (Fax in U.S. (202) 785-0350), www.oecd.org; *Revenue Statistics 1965-2006 - 2007 Edition*.

Statistics Bureau, the Director-General for Policy Planning (Statistical Standards), 19-1 Wakamatsu-cho, Shinjuku-ku, Tokyo 162-8668, Japan, www.stat.go.jp/english; *Japan Statistical Yearbook 2008*.

JAPAN - EXPORTS

Central Intelligence Agency, Office of Public Affairs, Washington, DC 20505, (703) 482-0623, Fax: (703) 482-1739, www.cia.gov; *The World Factbook*.

Economist Intelligence Unit, 111 West 57th Street, New York, NY 10019, (212) 554-0600, Fax: (212) 586-1181, www.eiu.com; *Japan Country Report*.

Euromonitor International, Inc., 224 S. Michigan Avenue, Suite 1500, Chicago, IL 60604, (312) 922-1115, Fax: (312) 922-1157, www.euromonitor.com; *International Marketing Data and Statistics 2008* and *The World Economic Factbook 2008*.

International Lead and Zinc Study Group (ILZSG), Rua Almirante Barroso 38, 5th Floor, Lisbon 1000 - 013, Portugal, www.ilzsg.org; Interactive Statistical Database.

International Monetary Fund (IMF), 700 Nineteenth Street, NW, Washington, DC 20431, (202) 623-7000, Fax: (202) 623-4661, www.imf.org; *Direction of Trade Statistics Yearbook 2007* and *International Financial Statistics Yearbook 2007*.

Japan Center for Economic Research (JCER), Nikkei Kayabacho Building, Nihombashi Kayabacho, 2-6-1, Chuo-ku, Tokyo 103-0025, Japan, www.jcer.or.jp/eng; *Japan Financial Report*.

Organisation for Economic Cooperation and Development (OECD), 2 rue Andre Pascal, F-75775 Paris Cedex 16, France, (Telephone in U.S. (202) 785-6323), (Fax in U.S. (202) 785-0350), www.oecd.org; *Geographical Distribution of Financial Flows to Aid Recipients 2002-2006; International Trade by Commodity Statistics (ITCS); Iron and Steel Industry in 2004 (2006 Edition); 2005 OECD Agricultural Outlook Tables, 1970-2014; OECD Economic Outlook 2008; OECD Economic Survey - Japan 2008; Review of Fisheries in OECD Countries: Country Statistics 2001 to 2003 - 2005 Edition;* and STructural ANalysis (STAN) database.

Palgrave Macmillan Ltd., Houndmills, Basingstoke, Hampshire, RG21 6XS, England, (Telephone in U.S. (888) 330-8477), (Fax in U.S. (800) 672-2054), www.palgrave.com; *The Statesman's Yearbook 2008*.

Statistics Bureau, the Director-General for Policy Planning (Statistical Standards), 19-1 Wakamatsu-cho, Shinjuku-ku, Tokyo 162-8668, Japan, www.stat.go.jp/english; *Japan Statistical Yearbook 2008*.

Taylor and Francis Group, An Informa Business, 2 Park Square, Milton Park, Abingdon, Oxford OX14 4RN, United Kingdom, (Dial from U.S. (212) 216-7800), (Fax from U.S. (212) 564-7854), www.tandf.co.uk; *The Europa World Year Book*.

Technical Association of the Pulp and Paper Industry (TAPPI), 15 Technology Parkway South, Norcross, GA 30092, (770) 446-1400, Fax: (770) 446-6947, www.tappi.org; *TAPPI Annual Report*.

United Nations Conference on Trade and Development (UNCTAD), DC2-1120, United Nations, New York, NY 10017, (212) 963-0027, www.unctad.org; *Handbook of Statistics 2005*.

United Nations Food and Agricultural Organization (FAO), Viale delle Terme di Caracalla, 00100 Rome, Italy, (Dial from U.S. (202) 653-2400), (Fax from U.S. (202) 653 5760), www.fao.org; *The State of Food and Agriculture (SOFA) 2006*.

United Nations Statistics Division, New York, NY 10017, (800) 253-9646, Fax: (212) 963-4116, http://unstats.un.org; *Foreign Trade Statistics of Asia and the Pacific 1996-2000*.

The World Bank, 1818 H Street, NW, Washington, DC 20433, (202) 473-1000, Fax: (202) 477-6391, www.worldbank.org; *World Development Report 2008*.

Worldinformation.com, 2 Market Street, Saffron Walden, Essex CB10 1HZ, United Kingdom, www.worldinformation.com; The World of Information (www.worldinformation.com).

JAPAN - FEMALE WORKING POPULATION

See JAPAN - EMPLOYMENT

JAPAN - FERTILITY, HUMAN

Central Intelligence Agency, Office of Public Affairs, Washington, DC 20505, (703) 482-0623, Fax: (703) 482-1739, www.cia.gov; *The World Factbook*.

M.E. Sharpe, 80 Business Park Drive, Armonk, NY 10504, (800) 541-6563, Fax: (914) 273-2106, www.mesharpe.com; *The Illustrated Book of World Rankings*.

United Nations Statistics Division, New York, NY 10017, (800) 253-9646, Fax: (212) 963-4116, http://unstats.un.org; *Human Development Report 2006*.

The World Bank, 1818 H Street, NW, Washington, DC 20433, (202) 473-1000, Fax: (202) 477-6391, www.worldbank.org; *The World Bank Atlas 2003-2004* and *World Development Report 2008*.

JAPAN - FERTILIZER INDUSTRY

Organisation for Economic Cooperation and Development (OECD), 2 rue Andre Pascal, F-75775 Paris Cedex 16, France, (Telephone in U.S. (202) 785-6323), (Fax in U.S. (202) 785-0350), www.oecd.org; *International Trade by Commodity Statistics (ITCS)* and *2005 OECD Agricultural Outlook Tables, 1970-2014*.

United Nations Food and Agricultural Organization (FAO), Viale delle Terme di Caracalla, 00100 Rome, Italy, (Dial from U.S. (202) 653-2400), (Fax from U.S. (202) 653 5760), www.fao.org; *FAO Fertilizer Yearbook* and *The State of Food and Agriculture (SOFA) 2006*.

United Nations Statistics Division, New York, NY 10017, (800) 253-9646, Fax: (212) 963-4116, http://unstats.un.org; *Statistical Yearbook*.

JAPAN - FETAL MORTALITY

See JAPAN - MORTALITY

JAPAN - FILM

See JAPAN - MOTION PICTURES

JAPAN - FINANCE

International Monetary Fund (IMF), 700 Nineteenth Street, NW, Washington, DC 20431, (202) 623-7000, Fax: (202) 623-4661, www.imf.org; *International Financial Statistics Yearbook 2007*.

Japan Center for Economic Research (JCER), Nikkei Kayabacho Building, Nihombashi Kayabacho, 2-6-1, Chuo-ku, Tokyo 103-0025, Japan, www.jcer.or.jp/eng; *Japan Financial Report*.

Organisation for Economic Cooperation and Development (OECD), 2 rue Andre Pascal, F-75775 Paris Cedex 16, France, (Telephone in U.S. (202) 785-6323), (Fax in U.S. (202) 785-0350), www.oecd.org; *OECD Economic Outlook 2008*.

Taylor and Francis Group, An Informa Business, 2 Park Square, Milton Park, Abingdon, Oxford OX14 4RN, United Kingdom, (Dial from U.S. (212) 216-7800), (Fax from U.S. (212) 564-7854), www.tandf.co.uk; *The Europa World Year Book*.

United Nations Statistics Division, New York, NY 10017, (800) 253-9646, Fax: (212) 963-4116, http://unstats.un.org; *Asia-Pacific in Figures 2004; National Accounts Statistics: Compendium of Income Distribution Statistics; Statistical Yearbook;* and *Statistical Yearbook for Asia and the Pacific 2004*.

The World Bank, 1818 H Street, NW, Washington, DC 20433, (202) 473-1000, Fax: (202) 477-6391, www.worldbank.org; *Japan*.

JAPAN - FINANCE, PUBLIC

Bernan Essential Government Publications, 4611-F Assembly Drive, Lanham MD, 20706-4391, (301) 459-2255, Fax: (800) 865-3450, www.bernan.com; *National Accounts Statistics*.

Economist Intelligence Unit, 111 West 57th Street, New York, NY 10019, (212) 554-0600, Fax: (212) 586-1181, www.eiu.com; *Japan Country Report*.

International Monetary Fund (IMF), 700 Nineteenth Street, NW, Washington, DC 20431, (202) 623-7000, Fax: (202) 623-4661, www.imf.org; *International Financial Statistics; International Financial Statistics Online Service;* and *International Financial Statistics Yearbook 2007*.

Japan Center for Economic Research (JCER), Nikkei Kayabacho Building, Nihombashi Kayabacho, 2-6-1, Chuo-ku, Tokyo 103-0025, Japan, www.jcer.or.jp/eng; *Japan Financial Report*.

M.E. Sharpe, 80 Business Park Drive, Armonk, NY 10504, (800) 541-6563, Fax: (914) 273-2106, www.mesharpe.com; *The Illustrated Book of World Rankings*.

Organisation for Economic Cooperation and Development (OECD), 2 rue Andre Pascal, F-75775 Paris Cedex 16, France, (Telephone in U.S. (202) 785-6323), (Fax in U.S. (202) 785-0350), www.oecd.org; *Financial Market Trends: OECD Periodical; Geographical Distribution of Financial Flows to Aid Recipients 2002-2006; OECD Economic Outlook 2008; OECD Main Economic Indicators (MEI);* and *Revenue Statistics 1965-2006 - 2007 Edition*.

Palgrave Macmillan Ltd., Houndmills, Basingstoke, Hampshire, RG21 6XS, England, (Telephone in U.S. (888) 330-8477), (Fax in U.S. (800) 672-2054), www.palgrave.com; *The Statesman's Yearbook 2008*.

Statistics Bureau, the Director-General for Policy Planning (Statistical Standards), 19-1 Wakamatsu-cho, Shinjuku-ku, Tokyo 162-8668, Japan, www.stat.go.jp/english; *Japan Statistical Yearbook 2008*.

Taylor and Francis Group, An Informa Business, 2 Park Square, Milton Park, Abingdon, Oxford OX14 4RN, United Kingdom, (Dial from U.S. (212) 216-7800), (Fax from U.S. (212) 564-7854), www.tandf.co.uk; *The Europa World Year Book*.

United Nations Statistics Division, New York, NY 10017, (800) 253-9646, Fax: (212) 963-4116, http://unstats.un.org; *Statistical Yearbook for Asia and the Pacific 2004*.

The World Bank, 1818 H Street, NW, Washington, DC 20433, (202) 473-1000, Fax: (202) 477-6391, www.worldbank.org; *Japan*.

JAPAN - FISHERIES

M.E. Sharpe, 80 Business Park Drive, Armonk, NY 10504, (800) 541-6563, Fax: (914) 273-2106, www.mesharpe.com; *The Illustrated Book of World Rankings*.

Organisation for Economic Cooperation and Development (OECD), 2 rue Andre Pascal, F-75775 Paris Cedex 16, France, (Telephone in U.S. (202) 785-6323), (Fax in U.S. (202) 785-0350), www.oecd.org; *International Trade by Commodity Statistics (ITCS)* and *Review of Fisheries in OECD Countries: Country Statistics 2001 to 2003 - 2005 Edition*.

Palgrave Macmillan Ltd., Houndmills, Basingstoke, Hampshire, RG21 6XS, England, (Telephone in U.S. (888) 330-8477), (Fax in U.S. (800) 672-2054), www.palgrave.com; *The Statesman's Yearbook 2008*.

Taylor and Francis Group, An Informa Business, 2 Park Square, Milton Park, Abingdon, Oxford OX14 4RN, United Kingdom, (Dial from U.S. (212) 216-7800), (Fax from U.S. (212) 564-7854), www.tandf.co.uk; *The Europa World Year Book*.

United Nations Conference on Trade and Development (UNCTAD), DC2-1120, United Nations, New York, NY 10017, (212) 963-0027, www.unctad.org; *UNCTAD Commodity Yearbook*.

United Nations Food and Agricultural Organization (FAO), Viale delle Terme di Caracalla, 00100 Rome, Italy, (Dial from U.S. (202) 653-2400), (Fax from

U.S. (202) 653 5760), www.fao.org; *The State of Food and Agriculture (SOFA) 2006.*

United Nations Statistics Division, New York, NY 10017, (800) 253-9646, Fax: (212) 963-4116, http://unstats.un.org; *Statistical Yearbook.*

The World Bank, 1818 H Street, NW, Washington, DC 20433, (202) 473-1000, Fax: (202) 477-6391, www.worldbank.org; *Japan.*

JAPAN - FLOUR INDUSTRY

United Nations Statistics Division, New York, NY 10017, (800) 253-9646, Fax: (212) 963-4116, http://unstats.un.org; *Statistical Yearbook.*

JAPAN - FOOD

Euromonitor International, Inc., 224 S. Michigan Avenue, Suite 1500, Chicago, IL 60604, (312) 922-1115, Fax: (312) 922-1157, www.euromonitor.com; *Retail Trade International 2007.*

Organisation for Economic Cooperation and Development (OECD), 2 rue Andre Pascal, F-75775 Paris Cedex 16, France, (Telephone in U.S. (202) 785-6323), (Fax in U.S. (202) 785-0350), www.oecd.org; *International Trade by Commodity Statistics (ITCS)* and *Towards Sustainable Household Consumption?: Trends and Policies in OECD Countries.*

United Nations Conference on Trade and Development (UNCTAD), DC2-1120, United Nations, New York, NY 10017, (212) 963-0027, www.unctad.org; *UNCTAD Commodity Yearbook.*

United Nations Food and Agricultural Organization (FAO), Viale delle Terme di Caracalla, 00100 Rome, Italy, (Dial from U.S. (202) 653-2400), (Fax from U.S. (202) 653 5760), www.fao.org; *FAO Production Yearbook 2002* and *The State of Food and Agriculture (SOFA) 2006.*

United Nations Statistics Division, New York, NY 10017, (800) 253-9646, Fax: (212) 963-4116, http://unstats.un.org; *Human Development Report 2006* and *Statistical Yearbook for Asia and the Pacific 2004.*

JAPAN - FOOTWEAR

Organisation for Economic Cooperation and Development (OECD), 2 rue Andre Pascal, F-75775 Paris Cedex 16, France, (Telephone in U.S. (202) 785-6323), (Fax in U.S. (202) 785-0350), www.oecd.org; *Indicators of Industrial Activity.*

JAPAN - FOREIGN EXCHANGE RATES

Central Intelligence Agency, Office of Public Affairs, Washington, DC 20505, (703) 482-0623, Fax: (703) 482-1739, www.cia.gov; *The World Factbook.*

Economist Intelligence Unit, 111 West 57th Street, New York, NY 10019, (212) 554-0600, Fax: (212) 586-1181, www.eiu.com; *Business Asia.*

Euromonitor International, Inc., 224 S. Michigan Avenue, Suite 1500, Chicago, IL 60604, (312) 922-1115, Fax: (312) 922-1157, www.euromonitor.com; *International Marketing Data and Statistics 2008* and *The World Economic Factbook 2008.*

International Civil Aviation Organization (ICAO), External Relations and Public Information Office (EPO), 999 University Street, Montreal, Quebec H3C 5H7, Canada, (Dial from U.S. (514) 954-8219), (Fax from U.S. (514) 954-6077), www.icao.int; *Civil Aviation Statistics of the World.*

International Monetary Fund (IMF), 700 Nineteenth Street, NW, Washington, DC 20431, (202) 623-7000, Fax: (202) 623-4661, www.imf.org; *International Financial Statistics Yearbook 2007.*

Organisation for Economic Cooperation and Development (OECD), 2 rue Andre Pascal, F-75775 Paris Cedex 16, France, (Telephone in U.S. (202) 785-6323), (Fax in U.S. (202) 785-0350), www.oecd.org; *Financial Market Trends: OECD Periodical; Household, Tourism, Travel: Trends, Environmental Impacts and Policy Responses; OECD Economic Outlook 2008;* and *Revenue Statistics 1965-2006 - 2007 Edition.*

Taylor and Francis Group, An Informa Business, 2 Park Square, Milton Park, Abingdon, Oxford OX14 4RN, United Kingdom, (Dial from U.S. (212) 216-7800), (Fax from U.S. (212) 564-7854), www.tandf.co.uk; *The Europa World Year Book.*

United Nations Statistics Division, New York, NY 10017, (800) 253-9646, Fax: (212) 963-4116, http://unstats.un.org; *Statistical Yearbook* and *World Statistics Pocketbook.*

Worldinformation.com, 2 Market Street, Saffron Walden, Essex CB10 1HZ, United Kingdom, www.worldinformation.com; The World of Information (www.worldinformation.com).

JAPAN - FORESTS AND FORESTRY

American Forest Paper Association (AFPA), 1111 Nineteenth Street, NW, Suite 800, Washington, DC 20036, (800) 878-8878, www.afandpa.org; *2007 Annual Statistics of Paper, Paperboard, and Wood Pulp.*

Economist Intelligence Unit, 111 West 57th Street, New York, NY 10019, (212) 554-0600, Fax: (212) 586-1181, www.eiu.com; *Business Asia.*

M.E. Sharpe, 80 Business Park Drive, Armonk, NY 10504, (800) 541-6563, Fax: (914) 273-2106, www.mesharpe.com; *The Illustrated Book of World Rankings.*

Organisation for Economic Cooperation and Development (OECD), 2 rue Andre Pascal, F-75775 Paris Cedex 16, France, (Telephone in U.S. (202) 785-6323), (Fax in U.S. (202) 785-0350), www.oecd.org; *Indicators of Industrial Activity; International Trade by Commodity Statistics (ITCS);* and STructural ANalysis (STAN) database.

Palgrave Macmillan Ltd., Houndmills, Basingstoke, Hampshire, RG21 6XS, England, (Telephone in U.S. (888) 330-8477), (Fax in U.S. (800) 672-2054), www.palgrave.com; *The Statesman's Yearbook 2008.*

Taylor and Francis Group, An Informa Business, 2 Park Square, Milton Park, Abingdon, Oxford OX14 4RN, United Kingdom, (Dial from U.S. (212) 216-7800), (Fax from U.S. (212) 564-7854), www.tandf.co.uk; *The Europa World Year Book.*

Technical Association of the Pulp and Paper Industry (TAPPI), 15 Technology Parkway South, Norcross, GA 30092, (770) 446-1400, Fax: (770) 446-6947, www.tappi.org; *TAPPI Annual Report.*

UNESCO Institute for Statistics, C.P. 6128 Succursale Centre-Ville, Montreal, Quebec, H3C 3J7 Canada, (Dial from U.S. (514) 343-6880), (Fax from U.S. (514) 343 6882), www.uis.unesco.org; *Statistical Tables.*

United Nations Conference on Trade and Development (UNCTAD), DC2-1120, United Nations, New York, NY 10017, (212) 963-0027, www.unctad.org; *UNCTAD Commodity Yearbook.*

United Nations Food and Agricultural Organization (FAO), Viale delle Terme di Caracalla, 00100 Rome, Italy, (Dial from U.S. (202) 653-2400), (Fax from U.S. (202) 653 5760), www.fao.org; *FAO Yearbook of Forest Products* and *The State of Food and Agriculture (SOFA) 2006.*

United Nations Statistics Division, New York, NY 10017, (800) 253-9646, Fax: (212) 963-4116, http://unstats.un.org; *Statistical Yearbook.*

The World Bank, 1818 H Street, NW, Washington, DC 20433, (202) 473-1000, Fax: (202) 477-6391, www.worldbank.org; *Japan* and *World Development Report 2008.*

JAPAN - FRUIT TRADE

Organisation for Economic Cooperation and Development (OECD), 2 rue Andre Pascal, F-75775 Paris Cedex 16, France, (Telephone in U.S. (202) 785-6323), (Fax in U.S. (202) 785-0350), www.oecd.org; *International Trade by Commodity Statistics (ITCS)* and *2005 OECD Agricultural Outlook Tables, 1970-2014.*

JAPAN - GAS PRODUCTION

See JAPAN - MINERAL INDUSTRIES

JAPAN - GEOGRAPHIC INFORMATION SYSTEMS

M.E. Sharpe, 80 Business Park Drive, Armonk, NY 10504, (800) 541-6563, Fax: (914) 273-2106, www.mesharpe.com; *The Illustrated Book of World Rankings.*

The World Bank, 1818 H Street, NW, Washington, DC 20433, (202) 473-1000, Fax: (202) 477-6391, www.worldbank.org; *Japan.*

JAPAN - GLASS TRADE

Organisation for Economic Cooperation and Development (OECD), 2 rue Andre Pascal, F-75775 Paris Cedex 16, France, (Telephone in U.S. (202) 785-6323), (Fax in U.S. (202) 785-0350), www.oecd.org; *Indicators of Industrial Activity.*

JAPAN - GOLD INDUSTRY

International Monetary Fund (IMF), 700 Nineteenth Street, NW, Washington, DC 20431, (202) 623-7000, Fax: (202) 623-4661, www.imf.org; *International Financial Statistics Yearbook 2007.*

United Nations Statistics Division, New York, NY 10017, (800) 253-9646, Fax: (212) 963-4116, http://unstats.un.org; *Statistical Yearbook.*

JAPAN - GOLD PRODUCTION

See JAPAN - MINERAL INDUSTRIES

JAPAN - GRANTS-IN-AID

International Monetary Fund (IMF), 700 Nineteenth Street, NW, Washington, DC 20431, (202) 623-7000, Fax: (202) 623-4661, www.imf.org; *Government Finance Statistics Yearbook (2008 Edition).*

Organisation for Economic Cooperation and Development (OECD), 2 rue Andre Pascal, F-75775 Paris Cedex 16, France, (Telephone in U.S. (202) 785-6323), (Fax in U.S. (202) 785-0350), www.oecd.org; *Geographical Distribution of Financial Flows to Aid Recipients 2002-2006.*

JAPAN - GREEN PEPPER AND CHILIE PRODUCTION

See JAPAN - CROPS

JAPAN - GROSS DOMESTIC PRODUCT

Economist Intelligence Unit, 111 West 57th Street, New York, NY 10019, (212) 554-0600, Fax: (212) 586-1181, www.eiu.com; *Business Asia* and *Japan Country Report.*

Euromonitor International, Inc., 224 S. Michigan Avenue, Suite 1500, Chicago, IL 60604, (312) 922-1115, Fax: (312) 922-1157, www.euromonitor.com; *International Marketing Data and Statistics 2008* and *The World Economic Factbook 2008.*

International Monetary Fund (IMF), 700 Nineteenth Street, NW, Washington, DC 20431, (202) 623-7000, Fax: (202) 623-4661, www.imf.org; *International Financial Statistics Yearbook 2007.*

M.E. Sharpe, 80 Business Park Drive, Armonk, NY 10504, (800) 541-6563, Fax: (914) 273-2106, www.mesharpe.com; *The Illustrated Book of World Rankings.*

Organisation for Economic Cooperation and Development (OECD), 2 rue Andre Pascal, F-75775 Paris Cedex 16, France, (Telephone in U.S. (202) 785-6323), (Fax in U.S. (202) 785-0350), www.oecd.org; *Comparison of Gross Domestic Product (GDP) for OECD Countries; Geographical Distribution of Financial Flows to Aid Recipients 2002-2006; OECD Economic Outlook 2008;* and *Revenue Statistics 1965-2006 - 2007 Edition.*

Palgrave Macmillan Ltd., Houndmills, Basingstoke, Hampshire, RG21 6XS, England, (Telephone in U.S. (888) 330-8477), (Fax in U.S. (800) 672-2054), www.palgrave.com; *The Statesman's Yearbook 2008.*

Taylor and Francis Group, An Informa Business, 2 Park Square, Milton Park, Abingdon, Oxford OX14 4RN, United Kingdom, (Dial from U.S. (212) 216-7800), (Fax from U.S. (212) 564-7854), www.tandf.co.uk; *The Europa World Year Book.*

United Nations Statistics Division, New York, NY 10017, (800) 253-9646, Fax: (212) 963-4116, http://unstats.un.org; *Human Development Report 2006; National Accounts Statistics: Compendium of Income Distribution Statistics;* and *Statistical Yearbook.*

The World Bank, 1818 H Street, NW, Washington, DC 20433, (202) 473-1000, Fax: (202) 477-6391, www.worldbank.org; *World Development Report 2008.*

JAPAN - GROSS NATIONAL PRODUCT

Euromonitor International, Inc., 224 S. Michigan Avenue, Suite 1500, Chicago, IL 60604, (312) 922-1115, Fax: (312) 922-1157, www.euromonitor.com; *International Marketing Data and Statistics 2008.*

M.E. Sharpe, 80 Business Park Drive, Armonk, NY 10504, (800) 541-6563, Fax: (914) 273-2106, www.mesharpe.com; *The Illustrated Book of World Rankings.*

Organisation for Economic Cooperation and Development (OECD), 2 rue Andre Pascal, F-75775 Paris Cedex 16, France, (Telephone in U.S. (202) 785-6323), (Fax in U.S. (202) 785-0350), www.oecd.org; *Geographical Distribution of Financial Flows to Aid Recipients 2002-2006; OECD Composite Leading Indicators (CLIs), Updated September 2007; OECD Economic Outlook 2008;* and *OECD Main Economic Indicators (MEI).*

Taylor and Francis Group, An Informa Business, 2 Park Square, Milton Park, Abingdon, Oxford OX14 4RN, United Kingdom, (Dial from U.S. (212) 216-7800), (Fax from U.S. (212) 564-7854), www.tandf.co.uk; *The Europa World Year Book.*

U.S. Department of State (DOS), 2201 C Street NW, Washington, DC 20520, (202) 647-4000, www.state.gov; *World Military Expenditures and Arms Transfers (WMEAT).*

United Nations Statistics Division, New York, NY 10017, (800) 253-9646, Fax: (212) 963-4116, http://unstats.un.org; *Statistical Yearbook.*

The World Bank, 1818 H Street, NW, Washington, DC 20433, (202) 473-1000, Fax: (202) 477-6391, www.worldbank.org; *The World Bank Atlas 2003-2004* and *World Development Report 2008.*

Worldinformation.com, 2 Market Street, Saffron Walden, Essex CB10 1HZ, United Kingdom, www.worldinformation.com; The World of Information (www.worldinformation.com).

JAPAN - HAY PRODUCTION

See JAPAN - CROPS

JAPAN - HAZELNUT PRODUCTION

See JAPAN - CROPS

JAPAN - HEALTH

See JAPAN - PUBLIC HEALTH

JAPAN - HEMP FIBRE PRODUCTION

See JAPAN - TEXTILE INDUSTRY

JAPAN - HIDES AND SKINS INDUSTRY

Organisation for Economic Cooperation and Development (OECD), 2 rue Andre Pascal, F-75775 Paris Cedex 16, France, (Telephone in U.S. (202) 785-6323), (Fax in U.S. (202) 785-0350), www.oecd.org; *Indicators of Industrial Activity* and *International Trade by Commodity Statistics (ITCS).*

United Nations Food and Agricultural Organization (FAO), Viale delle Terme di Caracalla, 00100 Rome, Italy, (Dial from U.S. (202) 653-2400), (Fax from U.S. (202) 653 5760), www.fao.org; *FAO Production Yearbook 2002.*

JAPAN - HOPS PRODUCTION

See JAPAN - CROPS

JAPAN - HOUSING

Euromonitor International, Inc., 224 S. Michigan Avenue, Suite 1500, Chicago, IL 60604, (312) 922-1115, Fax: (312) 922-1157, www.euromonitor.com; *World Marketing Data and Statistics.*

M.E. Sharpe, 80 Business Park Drive, Armonk, NY 10504, (800) 541-6563, Fax: (914) 273-2106, www.mesharpe.com; *The Illustrated Book of World Rankings.*

Statistics Bureau, the Director-General for Policy Planning (Statistical Standards), 19-1 Wakamatsucho, Shinjuku-ku, Tokyo 162-8668, Japan, www.stat.go.jp/english; *Japan Statistical Yearbook 2008.*

United Nations Statistics Division, New York, NY 10017, (800) 253-9646, Fax: (212) 963-4116, http://unstats.un.org; *Statistical Yearbook.*

JAPAN - HOUSING - FINANCE

Organisation for Economic Cooperation and Development (OECD), 2 rue Andre Pascal, F-75775 Paris Cedex 16, France, (Telephone in U.S. (202) 785-6323), (Fax in U.S. (202) 785-0350), www.oecd.org; *OECD Main Economic Indicators (MEI).*

The World Bank, 1818 H Street, NW, Washington, DC 20433, (202) 473-1000, Fax: (202) 477-6391, www.worldbank.org; *Japan.*

JAPAN - HOUSING CONSTRUCTION

See JAPAN - CONSTRUCTION INDUSTRY

JAPAN - ILLITERATE PERSONS

Euromonitor International, Inc., 224 S. Michigan Avenue, Suite 1500, Chicago, IL 60604, (312) 922-1115, Fax: (312) 922-1157, www.euromonitor.com; *The World Economic Factbook 2008.*

UNESCO Institute for Statistics, C.P. 6128 Succursale Centre-Ville, Montreal, Quebec, H3C 3J7 Canada, (Dial from U.S. (514) 343-6880), (Fax from U.S. (514) 343 6882), www.uis.unesco.org; *Statistical Tables.*

United Nations Statistics Division, New York, NY 10017, (800) 253-9646, Fax: (212) 963-4116, http://unstats.un.org; *Asia-Pacific in Figures 2004* and *Human Development Report 2006.*

JAPAN - IMPORTS

Central Intelligence Agency, Office of Public Affairs, Washington, DC 20505, (703) 482-0623, Fax: (703) 482-1739, www.cia.gov; *The World Factbook.*

Economist Intelligence Unit, 111 West 57th Street, New York, NY 10019, (212) 554-0600, Fax: (212) 586-1181, www.eiu.com; *Japan Country Report.*

Euromonitor International, Inc., 224 S. Michigan Avenue, Suite 1500, Chicago, IL 60604, (312) 922-1115, Fax: (312) 922-1157, www.euromonitor.com; *International Marketing Data and Statistics 2008* and *The World Economic Factbook 2008.*

International Lead and Zinc Study Group (ILZSG), Rua Almirante Barroso 38, 5th Floor, Lisbon 1000 - 013, Portugal, www.ilzsg.org; Interactive Statistical Database.

International Monetary Fund (IMF), 700 Nineteenth Street, NW, Washington, DC 20431, (202) 623-7000, Fax: (202) 623-4661, www.imf.org; *Direction of Trade Statistics Yearbook 2007* and *International Financial Statistics Yearbook 2007.*

Japan Center for Economic Research (JCER), Nikkei Kayabacho Building, Nihombashi Kayabacho, 2-6-1, Chuo-ku, Tokyo 103-0025, Japan, www.jcer.or.jp/eng; *Japan Financial Report.*

Organisation for Economic Cooperation and Development (OECD), 2 rue Andre Pascal, F-75775 Paris Cedex 16, France, (Telephone in U.S. (202) 785-6323), (Fax in U.S. (202) 785-0350), www.oecd.org; *Iron and Steel Industry in 2004 (2006 Edition); 2005 OECD Agricultural Outlook Tables, 1970-2014; OECD Economic Outlook 2008; OECD Economic Survey - Japan 2008; Review of Fisheries in OECD Countries: Country Statistics 2001 to 2003 - 2005 Edition;* and STructural ANalysis (STAN) database.

Palgrave Macmillan Ltd., Houndmills, Basingstoke, Hampshire, RG21 6XS, England, (Telephone in U.S. (888) 330-8477), (Fax in U.S. (800) 672-2054), www.palgrave.com; *The Statesman's Yearbook 2008.*

Taylor and Francis Group, An Informa Business, 2 Park Square, Milton Park, Abingdon, Oxford OX14 4RN, United Kingdom, (Dial from U.S. (212) 216-7800), (Fax from U.S. (212) 564-7854), www.tandf.co.uk; *The Europa World Year Book.*

Technical Association of the Pulp and Paper Industry (TAPPI), 15 Technology Parkway South, Norcross, GA 30092, (770) 446-1400, Fax: (770) 446-6947, www.tappi.org; *TAPPI Annual Report.*

United Nations Conference on Trade and Development (UNCTAD), DC2-1120, United Nations, New York, NY 10017, (212) 963-0027, www.unctad.org; *Handbook of Statistics 2005.*

United Nations Food and Agricultural Organization (FAO), Viale delle Terme di Caracalla, 00100 Rome, Italy, (Dial from U.S. (202) 653-2400), (Fax from U.S. (202) 653 5760), www.fao.org; *The State of Food and Agriculture (SOFA) 2006.*

United Nations Statistics Division, New York, NY 10017, (800) 253-9646, Fax: (212) 963-4116, http://unstats.un.org; *Foreign Trade Statistics of Asia and the Pacific 1996-2000.*

The World Bank, 1818 H Street, NW, Washington, DC 20433, (202) 473-1000, Fax: (202) 477-6391, www.worldbank.org; *World Development Report 2008.*

Worldinformation.com, 2 Market Street, Saffron Walden, Essex CB10 1HZ, United Kingdom, www.worldinformation.com; The World of Information (www.worldinformation.com).

JAPAN - INCOME TAXES

See JAPAN - TAXATION

JAPAN - INDUSTRIAL METALS PRODUCTION

See JAPAN - MINERAL INDUSTRIES

JAPAN - INDUSTRIAL PRODUCTIVITY

Euromonitor International, Inc., 224 S. Michigan Avenue, Suite 1500, Chicago, IL 60604, (312) 922-1115, Fax: (312) 922-1157, www.euromonitor.com; *International Marketing Data and Statistics 2008.*

International Lead and Zinc Study Group (ILZSG), Rua Almirante Barroso 38, 5th Floor, Lisbon 1000 - 013, Portugal, www.ilzsg.org; Interactive Statistical Database.

M.E. Sharpe, 80 Business Park Drive, Armonk, NY 10504, (800) 541-6563, Fax: (914) 273-2106, www.mesharpe.com; *The Illustrated Book of World Rankings.*

Organisation for Economic Cooperation and Development (OECD), 2 rue Andre Pascal, F-75775 Paris Cedex 16, France, (Telephone in U.S. (202) 785-6323), (Fax in U.S. (202) 785-0350), www.oecd.org; *Environmental Impacts of Foreign Direct Investment in the Mining Sector in the Newly Independent States (NIS); Indicators of Industrial Activity; Iron and Steel Industry in 2004 (2006 Edition); A New World Map in Textiles and Clothing: Adjusting to Change; 2005 OECD Agricultural Outlook Tables, 1970-2014; OECD Economic Outlook 2008;* and STructural ANalysis (STAN) database.

Statistics Bureau, the Director-General for Policy Planning (Statistical Standards), 19-1 Wakamatsucho, Shinjuku-ku, Tokyo 162-8668, Japan, www.stat.go.jp/english; *Japan Statistical Yearbook 2008.*

Technical Association of the Pulp and Paper Industry (TAPPI), 15 Technology Parkway South, Norcross, GA 30092, (770) 446-1400, Fax: (770) 446-6947, www.tappi.org; *TAPPI Annual Report.*

JAPAN - INDUSTRIAL PROPERTY

United Nations Statistics Division, New York, NY 10017, (800) 253-9646, Fax: (212) 963-4116, http://unstats.un.org; *Statistical Yearbook.*

World Intellectual Property Organization (WIPO), PO Box 18, CH-1211 Geneva 20, Switzerland, www.wipo.int; *Industrial Property Statistics* and *Industrial Property Statistics Online Directory.*

JAPAN - INDUSTRIES

Central Intelligence Agency, Office of Public Affairs, Washington, DC 20505, (703) 482-0623, Fax: (703) 482-1739, www.cia.gov; *The World Factbook.*

Economist Intelligence Unit, 111 West 57th Street, New York, NY 10019, (212) 554-0600, Fax: (212) 586-1181, www.eiu.com; *Japan Country Report.*

Euromonitor International, Inc., 224 S. Michigan Avenue, Suite 1500, Chicago, IL 60604, (312) 922-1115, Fax: (312) 922-1157; www.euromonitor.com; *International Marketing Data and Statistics 2008; The World Economic Factbook 2008;* and *World Marketing Data and Statistics.*

International Labour Office, I.L.O. Publications, 4 route des Morillons, CH-1211 Geneva 22, Switzerland, (Telephone in U.S. (202) 653-7652), (Fax in U.S. (202) 653-7687), www.ilo.org; *Yearbook of Labour Statistics 2006.*

Japan Center for Economic Research (JCER), Nikkei Kayabacho Building, Nihombashi Kayabacho, 2-6-1, Chuo-ku, Tokyo 103-0025, Japan, www.jcer.or.jp/eng; *Industry Research Report 2003.*

M.E. Sharpe, 80 Business Park Drive, Armonk, NY 10504, (800) 541-6563, Fax: (914) 273-2106, www.mesharpe.com; *The Illustrated Book of World Rankings.*

Organisation for Economic Cooperation and Development (OECD), 2 rue Andre Pascal, F-75775 Paris Cedex 16, France, (Telephone in U.S. (202) 785-6323), (Fax in U.S. (202) 785-0350), www.oecd.org; *Key Environmental Indicators 2004; OECD Economic Outlook 2008; OECD Main Economic Indicators (MEI);* and STructural ANalysis (STAN) database.

Palgrave Macmillan Ltd., Houndmills, Basingstoke, Hampshire, RG21 6XS, England, (Telephone in U.S. (888) 330-8477), (Fax in U.S. (800) 672-2054), www.palgrave.com; *The Statesman's Yearbook 2008.*

Statistics Bureau, the Director-General for Policy Planning (Statistical Standards), 19-1 Wakamatsucho, Shinjuku-ku, Tokyo 162-8668, Japan, www.stat.go.jp/english; *Japan Statistical Yearbook 2008.*

Taylor and Francis Group, An Informa Business, 2 Park Square, Milton Park, Abingdon, Oxford OX14 4RN, United Kingdom, (Dial from U.S. (212) 216-7800), (Fax from U.S. (212) 564-7854), www.tandf.co.uk; *The Europa World Year Book.*

United Nations Industrial Development Organization (UNIDO), 1 United Nations Plaza, New York, NY 10017, (212) 963 6890, Fax: (212) 963-7904, http://unido.org; Industrial Statistics Database 2008 (INDSTAT) and *The International Yearbook of Industrial Statistics 2008.*

United Nations Statistics Division, New York, NY 10017, (800) 253-9646, Fax: (212) 963-4116, http://unstats.un.org; *Asia-Pacific in Figures 2004; 2004 Industrial Commodity Statistics Yearbook; Statistical Yearbook;* and *Statistical Yearbook for Asia and the Pacific 2004.*

The World Bank, 1818 H Street, NW, Washington, DC 20433, (202) 473-1000, Fax: (202) 477-6391, www.worldbank.org; *Japan.*

JAPAN - INFANT AND MATERNAL MORTALITY

See JAPAN - MORTALITY

JAPAN - INORGANIC ACIDS

United Nations Statistics Division, New York, NY 10017, (800) 253-9646, Fax: (212) 963-4116, http://unstats.un.org; *Statistical Yearbook.*

JAPAN - INTEREST RATES

Organisation for Economic Cooperation and Development (OECD), 2 rue Andre Pascal, F-75775 Paris Cedex 16, France, (Telephone in U.S. (202) 785-6323), (Fax in U.S. (202) 785-0350), www.oecd.org; *Financial Market Trends: OECD Periodical; OECD Economic Outlook 2008;* and *OECD Main Economic Indicators (MEI).*

United Nations Statistics Division, New York, NY 10017, (800) 253-9646, Fax: (212) 963-4116, http://unstats.un.org; *Statistical Yearbook.*

JAPAN - INTERNAL REVENUE

Organisation for Economic Cooperation and Development (OECD), 2 rue Andre Pascal, F-75775 Paris Cedex 16, France, (Telephone in U.S. (202) 785-6323), (Fax in U.S. (202) 785-0350), www.oecd.org; *Revenue Statistics 1965-2006 - 2007 Edition.*

JAPAN - INTERNATIONAL FINANCE

International Finance Corporation (IFC), 2121 Pennsylvania Avenue, NW, Washington, DC 20433 USA, (202) 473-1000, Fax: (202) 974-4384, www.ifc.org; *Annual Report 2007.*

Organisation for Economic Cooperation and Development (OECD), 2 rue Andre Pascal, F-75775 Paris Cedex 16, France, (Telephone in U.S. (202) 785-6323), (Fax in U.S. (202) 785-0350), www.oecd.org; *Financial Market Trends: OECD Periodical* and *OECD Economic Outlook 2008.*

The World Bank, 1818 H Street, NW, Washington, DC 20433, (202) 473-1000, Fax: (202) 477-6391, www.worldbank.org; *Japan.*

JAPAN - INTERNATIONAL LIQUIDITY

International Monetary Fund (IMF), 700 Nineteenth Street, NW, Washington, DC 20431, (202) 623-7000, Fax: (202) 623-4661, www.imf.org; *International Financial Statistics Yearbook 2007.*

Organisation for Economic Cooperation and Development (OECD), 2 rue Andre Pascal, F-75775 Paris Cedex 16, France, (Telephone in U.S. (202) 785-6323), (Fax in U.S. (202) 785-0350), www.oecd.org; *Financial Market Trends: OECD Periodical* and *OECD Economic Outlook 2008.*

JAPAN - INTERNATIONAL STATISTICS

Organisation for Economic Cooperation and Development (OECD), 2 rue Andre Pascal, F-75775 Paris Cedex 16, France, (Telephone in U.S. (202) 785-6323), (Fax in U.S. (202) 785-0350), www.oecd.org; *Financial Market Trends: OECD Periodical* and *Household, Tourism, Travel: Trends, Environmental Impacts and Policy Responses.*

JAPAN - INTERNATIONAL TRADE

Bernan Essential Government Publications, 4611-F Assembly Drive, Lanham MD, 20706-4391, (301) 459-2255, Fax: (800) 865-3450, www.bernan.com; *OECD Factbook 2006.*

Economist Intelligence Unit, 111 West 57th Street, New York, NY 10019, (212) 554-0600, Fax: (212) 586-1181, www.eiu.com; *Business Asia* and *Japan Country Report.*

Euromonitor International, Inc., 224 S. Michigan Avenue, Suite 1500, Chicago, IL 60604, (312) 922-1115, Fax: (312) 922-1157, www.euromonitor.com; *International Marketing Data and Statistics 2008; The World Economic Factbook 2008;* and *World Marketing Data and Statistics.*

International Monetary Fund (IMF), 700 Nineteenth Street, NW, Washington, DC 20431, (202) 623-7000, Fax: (202) 623-4661, www.imf.org; *International Financial Statistics Yearbook 2007.*

Japan Center for Economic Research (JCER), Nikkei Kayabacho Building, Nihombashi Kayabacho, 2-6-1, Chuo-ku, Tokyo 103-0025, Japan, www.jcer.or.jp/eng; *Japan Financial Report.*

M.E. Sharpe, 80 Business Park Drive, Armonk, NY 10504, (800) 541-6563, Fax: (914) 273-2106, www.mesharpe.com; *The Illustrated Book of World Rankings.*

Organisation for Economic Cooperation and Development (OECD), 2 rue Andre Pascal, F-75775 Paris Cedex 16, France, (Telephone in U.S. (202) 785-6323), (Fax in U.S. (202) 785-0350), www.oecd.org; *International Trade by Commodity Statistics (ITCS); 2005 OECD Agricultural Outlook Tables, 1970-2014; OECD Economic Outlook 2008; OECD Economic Survey - Japan 2008; OECD in Figures 2007; OECD Main Economic Indicators (MEI);* and *Statistics on Ship Production, Exports and Orders in 2004.*

Palgrave Macmillan Ltd., Houndmills, Basingstoke, Hampshire, RG21 6XS, England, (Telephone in U.S. (888) 330-8477), (Fax in U.S. (800) 672-2054), www.palgrave.com; *The Statesman's Yearbook 2008.*

Taylor and Francis Group, An Informa Business, 2 Park Square, Milton Park, Abingdon, Oxford OX14 4RN, United Kingdom, (Dial from U.S. (212) 216-7800), (Fax from U.S. (212) 564-7854), www.tandf.co.uk; *The Europa World Year Book.*

United Nations Conference on Trade and Development (UNCTAD), DC2-1120, United Nations, New York, NY 10017, (212) 963-0027, www.unctad.org; *UNCTAD Commodity Yearbook.*

United Nations Food and Agricultural Organization (FAO), Viale delle Terme di Caracalla, 00100 Rome, Italy, (Dial from U.S. (202) 653-2400), (Fax from U.S. (202) 653 5760), www.fao.org; *FAO Trade Yearbook* and *The State of Food and Agriculture (SOFA) 2006.*

United Nations Statistics Division, New York, NY 10017, (800) 253-9646, Fax: (212) 963-4116, http://unstats.un.org; *Asia-Pacific in Figures 2004; International Trade Statistics Yearbook; Statistical Yearbook;* and *Statistical Yearbook for Asia and the Pacific 2004.*

The World Bank, 1818 H Street, NW, Washington, DC 20433, (202) 473-1000, Fax: (202) 477-6391, www.worldbank.org; *Japan* and *World Development Report 2008.*

World Bureau of Metal Statistics (WBMS), 27a High Street, Ware, Hertfordshire, SG12 9BA, United Kingdom, www.world-bureau.com; *World Flow Charts* and *World Metal Statistics.*

World Trade Organization (WTO), Centre William Rappard, Rue de Lausanne 154, CH-1211 Geneva 21, Switzerland, www.wto.org; *International Trade Statistics 2006.*

JAPAN - INTERNET USERS

International Telecommunication Union (ITU), Place des Nations, 1211 Geneva 20, Switzerland, www.itu.int; *World Telecommunication/ICT Indicators Database on CD-ROM; World Telecommunication/ICT Indicators Database Online;* and *Yearbook of Statistics - Telecommunication Services (Chronological Time Series 1997-2006).*

The World Bank, 1818 H Street, NW, Washington, DC 20433, (202) 473-1000, Fax: (202) 477-6391, www.worldbank.org; *Japan.*

JAPAN - INVESTMENTS

International Monetary Fund (IMF), 700 Nineteenth Street, NW, Washington, DC 20431, (202) 623-7000, Fax: (202) 623-4661, www.imf.org; *International Financial Statistics Yearbook 2007.*

Organisation for Economic Cooperation and Development (OECD), 2 rue Andre Pascal, F-75775 Paris Cedex 16, France, (Telephone in U.S. (202) 785-6323), (Fax in U.S. (202) 785-0350), www.oecd.org; *Financial Market Trends: OECD Periodical; Iron and Steel Industry in 2004 (2006 Edition); A New World Map in Textiles and Clothing: Adjusting to Change; OECD Economic Outlook 2008;* and STructural ANalysis (STAN) database.

JAPAN - IRON AND IRON ORE PRODUCTION

See JAPAN - MINERAL INDUSTRIES

JAPAN - IRRIGATION

Euromonitor International, Inc., 224 S. Michigan Avenue, Suite 1500, Chicago, IL 60604, (312) 922-1115, Fax: (312) 922-1157, www.euromonitor.com; *International Marketing Data and Statistics 2008.*

JAPAN - JUTE PRODUCTION

See JAPAN - CROPS

JAPAN - LABOR

Central Intelligence Agency, Office of Public Affairs, Washington, DC 20505, (703) 482-0623, Fax: (703) 482-1739, www.cia.gov; *The World Factbook.*

Economist Intelligence Unit, 111 West 57th Street, New York, NY 10019, (212) 554-0600, Fax: (212) 586-1181, www.eiu.com; *Business Asia.*

Euromonitor International, Inc., 224 S. Michigan Avenue, Suite 1500, Chicago, IL 60604, (312) 922-1115, Fax: (312) 922-1157, www.euromonitor.com; *International Marketing Data and Statistics 2008* and *World Marketing Data and Statistics.*

Federal Statistical Office Germany, D-65180 Wiesbaden, Germany, www.destatis.de; *Japan 2008.*

International Labour Office, I.L.O. Publications, 4 route des Morillons, CH-1211 Geneva 22, Switzerland, (Telephone in U.S. (202) 653-7652), (Fax in U.S. (202) 653-7687), www.ilo.org; *Yearbook of Labour Statistics 2006.*

M.E. Sharpe, 80 Business Park Drive, Armonk, NY 10504, (800) 541-6563, Fax: (914) 273-2106, www.mesharpe.com; *The Illustrated Book of World Rankings.*

Organisation for Economic Cooperation and Development (OECD), 2 rue Andre Pascal, F-75775 Paris Cedex 16, France, (Telephone in U.S. (202) 785-6323), (Fax in U.S. (202) 785-0350), www.oecd.org; *Iron and Steel Industry in 2004 (2006 Edition); A New World Map in Textiles and Clothing: Adjusting to Change; OECD Economic Outlook 2008; OECD Economic Survey - Japan 2008; OECD Employment Outlook 2007; OECD Main Economic Indicators (MEI);* and *Statistics on Ship Production, Exports and Orders in 2004.*

Palgrave Macmillan Ltd., Houndmills, Basingstoke, Hampshire, RG21 6XS, England, (Telephone in U.S. (888) 330-8477), (Fax in U.S. (800) 672-2054), www.palgrave.com; *The Statesman's Yearbook 2008.*

Statistics Bureau, the Director-General for Policy Planning (Statistical Standards), 19-1 Wakamatsucho, Shinjuku-ku, Tokyo 162-8668, Japan, www.stat.go.jp/english; *Japan Statistical Yearbook 2008.*

Taylor and Francis Group, An Informa Business, 2 Park Square, Milton Park, Abingdon, Oxford OX14 4RN, United Kingdom, (Dial from U.S. (212) 216-7800), (Fax from U.S. (212) 564-7854), www.tandf.co.uk; *The Europa World Year Book.*

United Nations Food and Agricultural Organization (FAO), Viale delle Terme di Caracalla, 00100 Rome, Italy, (Dial from U.S. (202) 653-2400), (Fax from U.S. (202) 653 5760), www.fao.org; *The State of Food and Agriculture (SOFA) 2006.*

United Nations Statistics Division, New York, NY 10017, (800) 253-9646, Fax: (212) 963-4116, http://unstats.un.org; *Human Development Report 2006.*

The World Bank, 1818 H Street, NW, Washington, DC 20433, (202) 473-1000, Fax: (202) 477-6391, www.worldbank.org; *The World Bank Atlas 2003-2004* and *World Development Report 2008.*

JAPAN - LAND USE

Central Intelligence Agency, Office of Public Affairs, Washington, DC 20505, (703) 482-0623, Fax: (703) 482-1739, www.cia.gov; *The World Factbook.*

Euromonitor International, Inc., 224 S. Michigan Avenue, Suite 1500, Chicago, IL 60604, (312) 922-1115, Fax: (312) 922-1157, www.euromonitor.com; *International Marketing Data and Statistics 2008.*

United Nations Food and Agricultural Organization (FAO), Viale delle Terme di Caracalla, 00100 Rome, Italy, (Dial from U.S. (202) 653-2400), (Fax from U.S. (202) 653 5760), www.fao.org; *FAO Production Yearbook 2002.*

The World Bank, 1818 H Street, NW, Washington, DC 20433, (202) 473-1000, Fax: (202) 477-6391, www.worldbank.org; *World Development Report 2008.*

JAPAN - LEATHER INDUSTRY AND TRADE

Organisation for Economic Cooperation and Development (OECD), 2 rue Andre Pascal, F-75775 Paris Cedex 16, France, (Telephone in U.S. (202) 785-6323), (Fax in U.S. (202) 785-0350), www.oecd.org; *Indicators of Industrial Activity.*

JAPAN - LIBRARIES

M.E. Sharpe, 80 Business Park Drive, Armonk, NY 10504, (800) 541-6563, Fax: (914) 273-2106, www.mesharpe.com; *The Illustrated Book of World Rankings.*

UNESCO Institute for Statistics, C.P. 6128 Succursale Centre-Ville, Montreal, Quebec, H3C 3J7 Canada, (Dial from U.S. (514) 343-6880), (Fax from U.S. (514) 343 6882), www.uis.unesco.org; *Statistical Tables.*

JAPAN - LIFE EXPECTANCY

Central Intelligence Agency, Office of Public Affairs, Washington, DC 20505, (703) 482-0623, Fax: (703) 482-1739, www.cia.gov; *The World Factbook.*

Economist Intelligence Unit, 111 West 57th Street, New York, NY 10019, (212) 554-0600, Fax: (212) 586-1181, www.eiu.com; *Business Asia.*

Euromonitor International, Inc., 224 S. Michigan Avenue, Suite 1500, Chicago, IL 60604, (312) 922-1115, Fax: (312) 922-1157, www.euromonitor.com; *The World Economic Factbook 2008.*

Organisation for Economic Cooperation and Development (OECD), 2 rue Andre Pascal, F-75775 Paris Cedex 16, France, (Telephone in U.S. (202) 785-6323), (Fax in U.S. (202) 785-0350), www.oecd.org; *OECD Economic Outlook 2008.*

Palgrave Macmillan Ltd., Houndmills, Basingstoke, Hampshire, RG21 6XS, England, (Telephone in U.S. (888) 330-8477), (Fax in U.S. (800) 672-2054), www.palgrave.com; *The Statesman's Yearbook 2008.*

Statistics Bureau, the Director-General for Policy Planning (Statistical Standards), 19-1 Wakamatsucho, Shinjuku-ku, Tokyo 162-8668, Japan, www.stat.go.jp/english; *Japan Statistical Yearbook 2008.*

United Nations Statistics Division, New York, NY 10017, (800) 253-9646, Fax: (212) 963-4116, http://unstats.un.org; *Asia-Pacific in Figures 2004; Human Development Report 2006;* and *World Statistics Pocketbook.*

The World Bank, 1818 H Street, NW, Washington, DC 20433, (202) 473-1000, Fax: (202) 477-6391, www.worldbank.org; *The World Bank Atlas 2003-2004* and *World Development Report 2008.*

JAPAN - LITERACY

Euromonitor International, Inc., 224 S. Michigan Avenue, Suite 1500, Chicago, IL 60604, (312) 922-1115, Fax: (312) 922-1157, www.euromonitor.com; *World Marketing Data and Statistics.*

JAPAN - LIVESTOCK

Euromonitor International, Inc., 224 S. Michigan Avenue, Suite 1500, Chicago, IL 60604, (312) 922-1115, Fax: (312) 922-1157, www.euromonitor.com; *International Marketing Data and Statistics 2008.*

M.E. Sharpe, 80 Business Park Drive, Armonk, NY 10504, (800) 541-6563, Fax: (914) 273-2106, www.mesharpe.com; *The Illustrated Book of World Rankings.*

Organisation for Economic Cooperation and Development (OECD), 2 rue Andre Pascal, F-75775 Paris Cedex 16, France, (Telephone in U.S. (202) 785-6323), (Fax in U.S. (202) 785-0350), www.oecd.org; *Indicators of Industrial Activity* and *2005 OECD Agricultural Outlook Tables, 1970-2014.*

Palgrave Macmillan Ltd., Houndmills, Basingstoke, Hampshire, RG21 6XS, England, (Telephone in U.S. (888) 330-8477), (Fax in U.S. (800) 672-2054), www.palgrave.com; *The Statesman's Yearbook 2008.*

Taylor and Francis Group, An Informa Business, 2 Park Square, Milton Park, Abingdon, Oxford OX14 4RN, United Kingdom, (Dial from U.S. (212) 216-7800), (Fax from U.S. (212) 564-7854), www.tandf.co.uk; *The Europa World Year Book.*

United Nations Conference on Trade and Development (UNCTAD), DC2-1120, United Nations, New York, NY 10017, (212) 963-0027, www.unctad.org; *UNCTAD Commodity Yearbook.*

United Nations Food and Agricultural Organization (FAO), Viale delle Terme di Caracalla, 00100 Rome, Italy, (Dial from U.S. (202) 653-2400), (Fax from U.S. (202) 653 5760), www.fao.org; *FAO Production Yearbook 2002* and *The State of Food and Agriculture (SOFA) 2006.*

United Nations Statistics Division, New York, NY 10017, (800) 253-9646, Fax: (212) 963-4116, http://unstats.un.org; *Statistical Yearbook.*

JAPAN - LOCAL TAXATION

Euromonitor International, Inc., 224 S. Michigan Avenue, Suite 1500, Chicago, IL 60604, (312) 922-1115, Fax: (312) 922-1157, www.euromonitor.com; *International Marketing Data and Statistics 2008.*

JAPAN - MACHINERY

Organisation for Economic Cooperation and Development (OECD), 2 rue Andre Pascal, F-75775 Paris Cedex 16, France, (Telephone in U.S. (202) 785-6323), (Fax in U.S. (202) 785-0350), www.oecd.org; *Indicators of Industrial Activity.*

JAPAN - MAGNESIUM PRODUCTION AND CONSUMPTION

See JAPAN - MINERAL INDUSTRIES

JAPAN - MANPOWER

United Nations Statistics Division, New York, NY 10017, (800) 253-9646, Fax: (212) 963-4116, http://unstats.un.org; *Statistical Yearbook for Asia and the Pacific 2004.*

JAPAN - MANUFACTURES

M.E. Sharpe, 80 Business Park Drive, Armonk, NY 10504, (800) 541-6563, Fax: (914) 273-2106, www.mesharpe.com; *The Illustrated Book of World Rankings.*

Organisation for Economic Cooperation and Development (OECD), 2 rue Andre Pascal, F-75775 Paris Cedex 16, France, (Telephone in U.S. (202) 785-6323), (Fax in U.S. (202) 785-0350), www.oecd.org; *Indicators of Industrial Activity; International Trade by Commodity Statistics (ITCS); OECD Economic Survey - Japan 2008;* and STructural ANalysis (STAN) database.

Statistics Bureau, the Director-General for Policy Planning (Statistical Standards), 19-1 Wakamatsucho, Shinjuku-ku, Tokyo 162-8668, Japan, www.stat.go.jp/english; *Japan Statistical Yearbook 2008.*

United Nations Statistics Division, New York, NY 10017, (800) 253-9646, Fax: (212) 963-4116, http://unstats.un.org; *Statistical Yearbook.*

JAPAN - MARRIAGE

M.E. Sharpe, 80 Business Park Drive, Armonk, NY 10504, (800) 541-6563, Fax: (914) 273-2106, www.mesharpe.com; *The Illustrated Book of World Rankings.*

Statistics Bureau, the Director-General for Policy Planning (Statistical Standards), 19-1 Wakamatsucho, Shinjuku-ku, Tokyo 162-8668, Japan, www.stat.go.jp/english; *Japan Statistical Yearbook 2008.*

Taylor and Francis Group, An Informa Business, 2 Park Square, Milton Park, Abingdon, Oxford OX14 4RN, United Kingdom, (Dial from U.S. (212) 216-7800), (Fax from U.S. (212) 564-7854), www.tandf.co.uk; *The Europa World Year Book.*

United Nations Statistics Division, New York, NY 10017, (800) 253-9646, Fax: (212) 963-4116, http://unstats.un.org; *Demographic Yearbook* and *Statistical Yearbook.*

JAPAN - MEAT PRODUCTION

See JAPAN - LIVESTOCK

JAPAN - MERCURY PRODUCTION

See JAPAN - MINERAL INDUSTRIES

JAPAN - MILK PRODUCTION

See JAPAN - DAIRY PROCESSING

JAPAN - MINERAL INDUSTRIES

Commodity Research Bureau, 330 South Wells Street, Suite 612, Chicago, IL 60606-7110, (800) 621-5271, Fax: (312) 939-4135, www.crbtrader.com; *2006 CRB Commodity Yearbook and CD.*

International Energy Agency (IEA), 9, rue de la Federation, 75739 Paris Cedex 15, France, www.iea.org; *Key World Energy Statistics 2007.*

International Lead and Zinc Study Group (ILZSG), Rua Almirante Barroso 38, 5th Floor, Lisbon 1000 - 013, Portugal, www.ilzsg.org; Interactive Statistical Database.

M.E. Sharpe, 80 Business Park Drive, Armonk, NY 10504, (800) 541-6563, Fax: (914) 273-2106, www.mesharpe.com; *The Illustrated Book of World Rankings.*

Organisation for Economic Cooperation and Development (OECD), 2 rue Andre Pascal, F-75775 Paris Cedex 16, France, (Telephone in U.S. (202) 785-6323), (Fax in U.S. (202) 785-0350), www.oecd.org; *Coal Information: 2007 Edition; Energy Statistics of OECD Countries* (2007 Edition); *Environmental Impacts of Foreign Direct Investment in the Mining Sector in the Newly Independent States (NIS); Indicators of Industrial Activity; International Trade by Commodity Statistics (ITCS); Iron and Steel Industry in 2004 (2006 Edition); OECD Economic Survey - Japan 2008;* STructural ANalysis (STAN) database; and *World Energy Outlook 2007.*

Palgrave Macmillan Ltd., Houndmills, Basingstoke, Hampshire, RG21 6XS, England, (Telephone in U.S. (888) 330-8477), (Fax in U.S. (800) 672-2054), www.palgrave.com; *The Statesman's Yearbook 2008.*

Taylor and Francis Group, An Informa Business, 2 Park Square, Milton Park, Abingdon, Oxford OX14 4RN, United Kingdom, (Dial from U.S. (212) 216-7800), (Fax from U.S. (212) 564-7854), www.tandf.co.uk; *The Europa World Year Book.*

United Nations Conference on Trade and Development (UNCTAD), DC2-1120, United Nations, New York, NY 10017, (212) 963-0027, www.unctad.org; *UNCTAD Commodity Yearbook.*

United Nations Statistics Division, New York, NY 10017, (800) 253-9646, Fax: (212) 963-4116, http://unstats.un.org; *Statistical Yearbook.*

The World Bank, 1818 H Street, NW, Washington, DC 20433, (202) 473-1000, Fax: (202) 477-6391, www.worldbank.org; *Japan.*

World Bureau of Metal Statistics (WBMS), 27a High Street, Ware, Hertfordshire, SG12 9BA, United Kingdom, www.world-bureau.com; *Annual Stainless Steel Statistics; World Flow Charts; World Metal Statistics; World Nickel Statistics;* and *World Tin Statistics.*

JAPAN - MONEY

European Central Bank (ECB), Postfach 160319, D-60066 Frankfurt am Main, Germany, www.ecb.int; *Monetary Developments in the Euro Area; Monthly Bulletin;* and *Statistics Pocket Book.*

Japan Center for Economic Research (JCER), Nikkei Kayabacho Building, Nihombashi Kayabacho, 2-6-1, Chuo-ku, Tokyo 103-0025, Japan, www.jcer.or.jp/eng; *Japan Financial Report.*

Organisation for Economic Cooperation and Development (OECD), 2 rue Andre Pascal, F-75775 Paris Cedex 16, France, (Telephone in U.S. (202) 785-6323), (Fax in U.S. (202) 785-0350), www.oecd.org; *OECD Economic Survey - Japan 2008.*

JAPAN - MONEY EXCHANGE RATES

See JAPAN - FOREIGN EXCHANGE RATES

JAPAN - MONEY SUPPLY

Economist Intelligence Unit, 111 West 57th Street, New York, NY 10019, (212) 554-0600, Fax: (212) 586-1181, www.eiu.com; *Japan Country Report.*

Euromonitor International, Inc., 224 S. Michigan Avenue, Suite 1500, Chicago, IL 60604, (312) 922-1115, Fax: (312) 922-1157, www.euromonitor.com; *International Marketing Data and Statistics 2008.*

International Monetary Fund (IMF), 700 Nineteenth Street, NW, Washington, DC 20431, (202) 623-7000, Fax: (202) 623-4661, www.imf.org; *International Financial Statistics Yearbook 2007.*

Organisation for Economic Cooperation and Development (OECD), 2 rue Andre Pascal, F-75775 Paris Cedex 16, France, (Telephone in U.S. (202) 785-6323), (Fax in U.S. (202) 785-0350), www.oecd.org; *OECD Economic Outlook 2008.*

Taylor and Francis Group, An Informa Business, 2 Park Square, Milton Park, Abingdon, Oxford OX14 4RN, United Kingdom, (Dial from U.S. (212) 216-7800), (Fax from U.S. (212) 564-7854), www.tandf.co.uk; *The Europa World Year Book.*

United Nations Statistics Division, New York, NY 10017, (800) 253-9646, Fax: (212) 963-4116, http://unstats.un.org; *Statistical Yearbook.*

The World Bank, 1818 H Street, NW, Washington, DC 20433, (202) 473-1000, Fax: (202) 477-6391, www.worldbank.org; *Japan.*

JAPAN - MORTALITY

Central Intelligence Agency, Office of Public Affairs, Washington, DC 20505, (703) 482-0623, Fax: (703) 482-1739, www.cia.gov; *The World Factbook.*

Euromonitor International, Inc., 224 S. Michigan Avenue, Suite 1500, Chicago, IL 60604, (312) 922-1115, Fax: (312) 922-1157, www.euromonitor.com; *The World Economic Factbook 2008.*

Palgrave Macmillan Ltd., Houndmills, Basingstoke, Hampshire, RG21 6XS, England, (Telephone in U.S. (888) 330-8477), (Fax in U.S. (800) 672-2054), www.palgrave.com; *The Statesman's Yearbook 2008.*

Statistics Bureau, the Director-General for Policy Planning (Statistical Standards), 19-1 Wakamatsucho, Shinjuku-ku, Tokyo 162-8668, Japan, www.stat.go.jp/english; *Japan Statistical Yearbook 2008.*

Taylor and Francis Group, An Informa Business, 2 Park Square, Milton Park, Abingdon, Oxford OX14 4RN, United Kingdom, (Dial from U.S. (212) 216-7800), (Fax from U.S. (212) 564-7854), www.tandf.co.uk; *The Europa World Year Book.*

UNICEF, 3 United Nations Plaza, New York, NY 10017, (800) 253-9646, Fax: (212) 887-7465, www.unicef.org; *The State of the World's Children 2008.*

United Nations Statistics Division, New York, NY 10017, (800) 253-9646, Fax: (212) 963-4116, http://unstats.un.org; *Asia-Pacific in Figures 2004; Demographic Yearbook; Human Development Report 2006; Statistical Yearbook;* and *World Statistics Pocketbook.*

The World Bank, 1818 H Street, NW, Washington, DC 20433, (202) 473-1000, Fax: (202) 477-6391, www.worldbank.org; *The World Bank Atlas 2003-2004* and *World Development Report 2008.*

World Health Organization (WHO), Avenue Appia 20, 1211 Geneve 27, Switzerland, (Telephone in U.S. (212) 331-9081), www.who.int; The WHO Global Atlas of Infectious Diseases and *World Health Report 2006.*

JAPAN - MOTION PICTURES

Palgrave Macmillan Ltd., Houndmills, Basingstoke, Hampshire, RG21 6XS, England, (Telephone in U.S. (888) 330-8477), (Fax in U.S. (800) 672-2054), www.palgrave.com; *The Statesman's Yearbook 2008.*

UNESCO Institute for Statistics, C.P. 6128 Succursale Centre-Ville, Montreal, Quebec, H3C 3J7 Canada, (Dial from U.S. (514) 343-6880), (Fax from U.S. (514) 343 6882), www.uis.unesco.org; *Statistical Tables.*

United Nations Statistics Division, New York, NY 10017, (800) 253-9646, Fax: (212) 963-4116, http://unstats.un.org; *Statistical Yearbook.*

JAPAN - MOTOR VEHICLES

International Road Federation (IFR), Madison Place, 500 Montgomery Street, 5th Floor, Alexandria, VA 22314, (703) 535-1001, Fax: (703) 535-1007, www.irfnet.org; *World Road Statistics 2006.*

Taylor and Francis Group, An Informa Business, 2 Park Square, Milton Park, Abingdon, Oxford OX14 4RN, United Kingdom, (Dial from U.S. (212) 216-7800), (Fax from U.S. (212) 564-7854), www.tandf.co.uk; *The Europa World Year Book.*

United Nations Statistics Division, New York, NY 10017, (800) 253-9646, Fax: (212) 963-4116, http://unstats.un.org; *Statistical Yearbook.*

JAPAN - MUSEUMS

M.E. Sharpe, 80 Business Park Drive, Armonk, NY 10504, (800) 541-6563, Fax: (914) 273-2106, www.mesharpe.com; *The Illustrated Book of World Rankings.*

Statistics Bureau, the Director-General for Policy Planning (Statistical Standards), 19-1 Wakamatsucho, Shinjuku-ku, Tokyo 162-8668, Japan, www.stat.go.jp/english; *Japan Statistical Yearbook 2008.*

UNESCO Institute for Statistics, C.P. 6128 Succursale Centre-Ville, Montreal, Quebec, H3C 3J7 Canada, (Dial from U.S. (514) 343-6880), (Fax from U.S. (514) 343 6882), www.uis.unesco.org; *Statistical Tables.*

JAPAN - NATURAL GAS PRODUCTION

See JAPAN - MINERAL INDUSTRIES

JAPAN - NICKEL AND NICKEL ORE

See JAPAN - MINERAL INDUSTRIES

JAPAN - NUTRITION

United Nations Food and Agricultural Organization (FAO), Viale delle Terme di Caracalla, 00100 Rome, Italy, (Dial from U.S. (202) 653-2400), (Fax from U.S. (202) 653 5760), www.fao.org; *The State of Food and Agriculture (SOFA) 2006.*

JAPAN - OATS PRODUCTION

See JAPAN - CROPS

JAPAN - OILSEED PLANTS

Organisation for Economic Cooperation and Development (OECD), 2 rue Andre Pascal, F-75775 Paris Cedex 16, France, (Telephone in U.S. (202) 785-6323), (Fax in U.S. (202) 785-0350), www.oecd.org; *International Trade by Commodity Statistics (ITCS).*

JAPAN - OLDER PEOPLE

M.E. Sharpe, 80 Business Park Drive, Armonk, NY 10504, (800) 541-6563, Fax: (914) 273-2106, www.mesharpe.com; *The Illustrated Book of World Rankings.*

JAPAN - ONION PRODUCTION

See JAPAN - CROPS

JAPAN - ORANGES PRODUCTION

See JAPAN - CROPS

JAPAN - PALM OIL PRODUCTION

See JAPAN - CROPS

JAPAN - PAPER

See JAPAN - FORESTS AND FORESTRY

JAPAN - PEANUT PRODUCTION

See JAPAN - CROPS

JAPAN - PEPPER PRODUCTION

See JAPAN - CROPS

JAPAN - PERIODICALS

UNESCO Institute for Statistics, C.P. 6128 Succursale Centre-Ville, Montreal, Quebec, H3C 3J7 Canada, (Dial from U.S. (514) 343-6880), (Fax from U.S. (514) 343 6882), www.uis.unesco.org; *Statistical Tables.*

JAPAN - PESTICIDES

United Nations Food and Agricultural Organization (FAO), Viale delle Terme di Caracalla, 00100 Rome, Italy, (Dial from U.S. (202) 653-2400), (Fax from U.S. (202) 653 5760), www.fao.org; *The State of Food and Agriculture (SOFA) 2006.*

JAPAN - PETROLEUM INDUSTRY AND TRADE

International Energy Agency (IEA), 9, rue de la Federation, 75739 Paris Cedex 15, France, www.iea.org; *Key World Energy Statistics 2007.*

M.E. Sharpe, 80 Business Park Drive, Armonk, NY 10504, (800) 541-6563, Fax: (914) 273-2106, www.mesharpe.com; *The Illustrated Book of World Rankings.*

Organisation for Economic Cooperation and Development (OECD), 2 rue Andre Pascal, F-75775 Paris Cedex 16, France, (Telephone in U.S. (202) 785-6323), (Fax in U.S. (202) 785-0350), www.oecd.org; *Energy Statistics of OECD Countries* (2007 Edition); *Indicators of Industrial Activity; International Trade by Commodity Statistics (ITCS); Oil Information 2006 Edition;* and *World Energy Outlook 2007.*

Palgrave Macmillan Ltd., Houndmills, Basingstoke, Hampshire, RG21 6XS, England, (Telephone in U.S. (888) 330-8477), (Fax in U.S. (800) 672-2054), www.palgrave.com; *The Statesman's Yearbook 2008.*

PennWell Corporation, 1421 South Sheridan Road, Tulsa, OK 74112, (918) 835-3161, www.pennwell.com; *International Petroleum Encyclopedia 2007.*

U.S. Department of Energy (DOE), Energy Information Administration (EIA), 1000 Independence Avenue, SW, Washington, DC 20585, (202) 586-8800, www.eia.doe.gov; *International Energy Annual 2004* and *International Energy Outlook 2006.*

United Nations Conference on Trade and Development (UNCTAD), DC2-1120, United Nations, New York, NY 10017, (212) 963-0027, www.unctad.org; *UNCTAD Commodity Yearbook.*

United Nations Food and Agricultural Organization (FAO), Viale delle Terme di Caracalla, 00100 Rome, Italy, (Dial from U.S. (202) 653-2400), (Fax from U.S. (202) 653 5760), www.fao.org; *The State of Food and Agriculture (SOFA) 2006.*

United Nations Statistics Division, New York, NY 10017, (800) 253-9646, Fax: (212) 963-4116, http://unstats.un.org; *Statistical Yearbook.*

JAPAN - PHOSPHATES PRODUCTION

See JAPAN - MINERAL INDUSTRIES

JAPAN - PLASTICS INDUSTRY AND TRADE

Organisation for Economic Cooperation and Development (OECD), 2 rue Andre Pascal, F-75775 Paris Cedex 16, France, (Telephone in U.S. (202) 785-6323), (Fax in U.S. (202) 785-0350), www.oecd.org; *International Trade by Commodity Statistics (ITCS).*

United Nations Statistics Division, New York, NY 10017, (800) 253-9646, Fax: (212) 963-4116, http://unstats.un.org; *Statistical Yearbook.*

JAPAN - PLATINUM PRODUCTION

See JAPAN - MINERAL INDUSTRIES

JAPAN - POLITICAL SCIENCE

Central Intelligence Agency, Office of Public Affairs, Washington, DC 20505, (703) 482-0623, Fax: (703) 482-1739, www.cia.gov; *The World Factbook.*

International Monetary Fund (IMF), 700 Nineteenth Street, NW, Washington, DC 20431, (202) 623-7000, Fax: (202) 623-4661, www.imf.org; *Government Finance Statistics Yearbook (2008 Edition)* and *International Financial Statistics Yearbook 2007.*

Organisation for Economic Cooperation and Development (OECD), 2 rue Andre Pascal, F-75775 Paris Cedex 16, France, (Telephone in U.S. (202) 785-6323), (Fax in U.S. (202) 785-0350), www.oecd.org; *OECD Economic Outlook 2008* and *Revenue Statistics 1965-2006 - 2007 Edition.*

Palgrave Macmillan Ltd., Houndmills, Basingstoke, Hampshire, RG21 6XS, England, (Telephone in U.S. (888) 330-8477), (Fax in U.S. (800) 672-2054), www.palgrave.com; *The Statesman's Yearbook 2008.*

Taylor and Francis Group, An Informa Business, 2 Park Square, Milton Park, Abingdon, Oxford OX14 4RN, United Kingdom, (Dial from U.S. (212) 216-7800), (Fax from U.S. (212) 564-7854), www.tandf.co.uk; *The Europa World Year Book.*

United Nations Statistics Division, New York, NY 10017, (800) 253-9646, Fax: (212) 963-4116, http://unstats.un.org; *Asia-Pacific in Figures 2004; National Accounts Statistics: Compendium of Income Distribution Statistics;* and *Statistical Yearbook.*

The World Bank, 1818 H Street, NW, Washington, DC 20433, (202) 473-1000, Fax: (202) 477-6391, www.worldbank.org; *World Development Report 2008.*

JAPAN - POPULATION

Central Intelligence Agency, Office of Public Affairs, Washington, DC 20505, (703) 482-0623, Fax: (703) 482-1739, www.cia.gov; *The World Factbook.*

Economist Intelligence Unit, 111 West 57th Street, New York, NY 10019, (212) 554-0600, Fax: (212) 586-1181, www.eiu.com; *Business Asia* and *Japan Country Report.*

Euromonitor International, Inc., 224 S. Michigan Avenue, Suite 1500, Chicago, IL 60604, (312) 922-1115, Fax: (312) 922-1157, www.euromonitor.com; *International Marketing Data and Statistics 2008* and *The World Economic Factbook 2008.*

Federal Statistical Office Germany, D-65180 Wiesbaden, Germany, www.destatis.de; *Japan 2008.*

International Labour Office, I.L.O. Publications, 4 route des Morillons, CH-1211 Geneva 22, Switzerland, (Telephone in U.S. (202) 653-7652), (Fax in U.S. (202) 653-7687), www.ilo.org; *Yearbook of Labour Statistics 2006.*

M.E. Sharpe, 80 Business Park Drive, Armonk, NY 10504, (800) 541-6563, Fax: (914) 273-2106, www.mesharpe.com; *The Illustrated Book of World Rankings.*

Organisation for Economic Cooperation and Development (OECD), 2 rue Andre Pascal, F-75775 Paris Cedex 16, France, (Telephone in U.S. (202) 785-6323), (Fax in U.S. (202) 785-0350), www.oecd.org; *Labour Force Statistics: 1986-2005, 2007 Edition.*

Palgrave Macmillan Ltd., Houndmills, Basingstoke, Hampshire, RG21 6XS, England, (Telephone in U.S. (888) 330-8477), (Fax in U.S. (800) 672-2054), www.palgrave.com; *The Statesman's Yearbook 2008.*

Statistics Bureau, the Director-General for Policy Planning (Statistical Standards), 19-1 Wakamatsucho, Shinjuku-ku, Tokyo 162-8668, Japan, www.stat.go.jp/english; *Japan Statistical Yearbook 2008.*

Taylor and Francis Group, An Informa Business, 2 Park Square, Milton Park, Abingdon, Oxford OX14 4RN, United Kingdom, (Dial from U.S. (212) 216-7800), (Fax from U.S. (212) 564-7854), www.tandf.co.uk; *The Europa World Year Book.*

Tourism Intelligence International, An der Wolfskuhle 48, 33619 Bielefeld, Germany, www.tourism-intelligence.com; *How the Japanese Will Travel 2007.*

U.S. Department of State (DOS), 2201 C Street NW, Washington, DC 20520, (202) 647-4000, www.state.gov; *World Military Expenditures and Arms Transfers (WMEAT).*

UNESCO Institute for Statistics, C.P. 6128 Succursale Centre-Ville, Montreal, Quebec, H3C 3J7 Canada, (Dial from U.S. (514) 343-6880), (Fax from U.S. (514) 343 6882), www.uis.unesco.org; *Statistical Tables.*

United Nations Food and Agricultural Organization (FAO), Viale delle Terme di Caracalla, 00100 Rome, Italy, (Dial from U.S. (202) 653-2400), (Fax from U.S. (202) 653 5760), www.fao.org; *FAO Production Yearbook 2002.*

United Nations Statistics Division, New York, NY 10017, (800) 253-9646, Fax: (212) 963-4116, http://unstats.un.org; *Asia-Pacific in Figures 2004; Demographic Yearbook; Human Development Report 2006; Statistical Yearbook; Statistical Yearbook for Asia and the Pacific 2004;* and *World Statistics Pocketbook.*

The World Bank, 1818 H Street, NW, Washington, DC 20433, (202) 473-1000, Fax: (202) 477-6391, www.worldbank.org; *Japan; The World Bank Atlas 2003-2004;* and *World Development Report 2008.*

World Health Organization (WHO), Avenue Appia 20, 1211 Geneve 27, Switzerland, (Telephone in U.S. (212) 331-9081), www.who.int; *World Health Report 2006.*

Worldinformation.com, 2 Market Street, Saffron Walden, Essex CB10 1HZ, United Kingdom, www.worldinformation.com; The World of Information (www.worldinformation.com).

JAPAN - POPULATION DENSITY

Central Intelligence Agency, Office of Public Affairs, Washington, DC 20505, (703) 482-0623, Fax: (703) 482-1739, www.cia.gov; *The World Factbook.*

Euromonitor International, Inc., 224 S. Michigan Avenue, Suite 1500, Chicago, IL 60604, (312) 922-1115, Fax: (312) 922-1157, www.euromonitor.com; *International Marketing Data and Statistics 2008* and *The World Economic Factbook 2008.*

M.E. Sharpe, 80 Business Park Drive, Armonk, NY 10504, (800) 541-6563, Fax: (914) 273-2106, www.mesharpe.com; *The Illustrated Book of World Rankings.*

Palgrave Macmillan Ltd., Houndmills, Basingstoke, Hampshire, RG21 6XS, England, (Telephone in U.S. (888) 330-8477), (Fax in U.S. (800) 672-2054), www.palgrave.com; *The Statesman's Yearbook 2008.*

Statistics Bureau, the Director-General for Policy Planning (Statistical Standards), 19-1 Wakamatsucho, Shinjuku-ku, Tokyo 162-8668, Japan, www.stat.go.jp/english; *Japan Statistical Yearbook 2008.*

Taylor and Francis Group, An Informa Business, 2 Park Square, Milton Park, Abingdon, Oxford OX14 4RN, United Kingdom, (Dial from U.S. (212) 216-7800), (Fax from U.S. (212) 564-7854), www.tandf.co.uk; *The Europa World Year Book.*

UNESCO Institute for Statistics, C.P. 6128 Succursale Centre-Ville, Montreal, Quebec, H3C 3J7 Canada, (Dial from U.S. (514) 343-6880), (Fax from U.S. (514) 343 6882), www.uis.unesco.org; *Statistical Tables.*

United Nations Food and Agricultural Organization (FAO), Viale delle Terme di Caracalla, 00100 Rome, Italy, (Dial from U.S. (202) 653-2400), (Fax from U.S. (202) 653 5760), www.fao.org; *The State of Food and Agriculture (SOFA) 2006.*

United Nations Statistics Division, New York, NY 10017, (800) 253-9646, Fax: (212) 963-4116, http://unstats.un.org; *Statistical Yearbook.*

The World Bank, 1818 H Street, NW, Washington, DC 20433, (202) 473-1000, Fax: (202) 477-6391, www.worldbank.org; *Japan* and *World Development Report 2008.*

JAPAN - POSTAL SERVICE

M.E. Sharpe, 80 Business Park Drive, Armonk, NY 10504, (800) 541-6563, Fax: (914) 273-2106, www.mesharpe.com; *The Illustrated Book of World Rankings.*

United Nations Statistics Division, New York, NY 10017, (800) 253-9646, Fax: (212) 963-4116, http://unstats.un.org; *Statistical Yearbook.*

JAPAN - POWER RESOURCES

Euromonitor International, Inc., 224 S. Michigan Avenue, Suite 1500, Chicago, IL 60604, (312) 922-1115, Fax: (312) 922-1157, www.euromonitor.com; *The World Economic Factbook 2008* and *World Marketing Data and Statistics*.

M.E. Sharpe, 80 Business Park Drive, Armonk, NY 10504, (800) 541-6563, Fax: (914) 273-2106, www.mesharpe.com; *The Illustrated Book of World Rankings*.

Organisation for Economic Cooperation and Development (OECD), 2 rue Andre Pascal, F-75775 Paris Cedex 16, France, (Telephone in U.S. (202) 785-6323), (Fax in U.S. (202) 785-0350), www.oecd.org; *Coal Information: 2007 Edition; Energy Statistics of OECD Countries* (2007 Edition); *Key Environmental Indicators 2004; Oil Information 2006 Edition;* and *World Energy Outlook 2007*.

Palgrave Macmillan Ltd., Houndmills, Basingstoke, Hampshire, RG21 6XS, England, (Telephone in U.S. (888) 330-8477), (Fax in U.S. (800) 672-2054), www.palgrave.com; *The Statesman's Yearbook 2008*.

Platts, 2 Penn Plaza, 25th Floor, New York, NY 10121-2298, (212) 904-3070, www.platts.com; *Asian Electricity Outlook 2006; Emissions Daily;* and *Energy Economist*.

U.S. Department of Energy (DOE), Energy Information Administration (EIA), 1000 Independence Avenue, SW, Washington, DC 20585, (202) 586-8800, www.eia.doe.gov; *International Energy Annual 2004* and *International Energy Outlook 2006*.

United Nations Food and Agricultural Organization (FAO), Viale delle Terme di Caracalla, 00100 Rome, Italy, (Dial from U.S. (202) 653-2400), (Fax from U.S. (202) 653 5760), www.fao.org; *The State of Food and Agriculture (SOFA) 2006*.

United Nations Statistics Division, New York, NY 10017, (800) 253-9646, Fax: (212) 963-4116, http://unstats.un.org; *Asia-Pacific in Figures 2004; Energy Statistics Yearbook 2003; Human Development Report 2006; Statistical Yearbook;* and *World Statistics Pocketbook*.

The World Bank, 1818 H Street, NW, Washington, DC 20433, (202) 473-1000, Fax: (202) 477-6391, www.worldbank.org; *The World Bank Atlas 2003-2004* and *World Development Report 2008*.

JAPAN - PRICES

Euromonitor International, Inc., 224 S. Michigan Avenue, Suite 1500, Chicago, IL 60604, (312) 922-1115, Fax: (312) 922-1157, www.euromonitor.com; *World Marketing Data and Statistics*.

International Labour Office, I.L.O. Publications, 4 route des Morillons, CH-1211 Geneva 22, Switzerland, (Telephone in U.S. (202) 653-7652), (Fax in U.S. (202) 653-7687), www.ilo.org; *Yearbook of Labour Statistics 2006*.

International Lead and Zinc Study Group (ILZSG), Rua Almirante Barroso 38, 5th Floor, Lisbon 1000 - 013, Portugal, www.ilzsg.org; Interactive Statistical Database.

International Monetary Fund (IMF), 700 Nineteenth Street, NW, Washington, DC 20431, (202) 623-7000, Fax: (202) 623-4661, www.imf.org; *International Financial Statistics Yearbook 2007*.

M.E. Sharpe, 80 Business Park Drive, Armonk, NY 10504, (800) 541-6563, Fax: (914) 273-2106, www.mesharpe.com; *The Illustrated Book of World Rankings*.

Organisation for Economic Cooperation and Development (OECD), 2 rue Andre Pascal, F-75775 Paris Cedex 16, France, (Telephone in U.S. (202) 785-6323), (Fax in U.S. (202) 785-0350), www.oecd.org; *Indicators of Industrial Activity; Iron and Steel Industry in 2004 (2006 Edition); OECD Economic Outlook 2008;* and *OECD Main Economic Indicators (MEI)*.

Technical Association of the Pulp and Paper Industry (TAPPI), 15 Technology Parkway South, Norcross, GA 30092, (770) 446-1400, Fax: (770) 446-6947, www.tappi.org; *TAPPI Annual Report*.

United Nations Food and Agricultural Organization (FAO), Viale delle Terme di Caracalla, 00100 Rome, Italy, (Dial from U.S. (202) 653-2400), (Fax from U.S. (202) 653 5760), www.fao.org; *FAO Production Yearbook 2002* and *The State of Food and Agriculture (SOFA) 2006*.

The World Bank, 1818 H Street, NW, Washington, DC 20433, (202) 473-1000, Fax: (202) 477-6391, www.worldbank.org; *Japan*.

World Bureau of Metal Statistics (WBMS), 27a High Street, Ware, Hertfordshire, SG12 9BA, United Kingdom, www.world-bureau.com; *World Flow Charts* and *World Metal Statistics*.

JAPAN - PROFESSIONS

UNESCO Institute for Statistics, C.P. 6128 Succursale Centre-Ville, Montreal, Quebec, H3C 3J7 Canada, (Dial from U.S. (514) 343-6880), (Fax from U.S. (514) 343 6882), www.uis.unesco.org; *Statistical Tables*.

United Nations Statistics Division, New York, NY 10017, (800) 253-9646, Fax: (212) 963-4116, http://unstats.un.org; *Statistical Yearbook*.

JAPAN - PUBLIC HEALTH

Economist Intelligence Unit, 111 West 57th Street, New York, NY 10019, (212) 554-0600, Fax: (212) 586-1181, www.eiu.com; *Business Asia*.

Euromonitor International, Inc., 224 S. Michigan Avenue, Suite 1500, Chicago, IL 60604, (312) 922-1115, Fax: (312) 922-1157, www.euromonitor.com; *World Health Databook 2007/2008* and *World Marketing Data and Statistics*.

M.E. Sharpe, 80 Business Park Drive, Armonk, NY 10504, (800) 541-6563, Fax: (914) 273-2106, www.mesharpe.com; *The Illustrated Book of World Rankings*.

Organisation for Economic Cooperation and Development (OECD), 2 rue Andre Pascal, F-75775 Paris Cedex 16, France, (Telephone in U.S. (202) 785-6323), (Fax in U.S. (202) 785-0350), www.oecd.org; *Health at a Glance 2007 - OECD Indicators*.

Palgrave Macmillan Ltd., Houndmills, Basingstoke, Hampshire, RG21 6XS, England, (Telephone in U.S. (888) 330-8477), (Fax in U.S. (800) 672-2054), www.palgrave.com; *The Statesman's Yearbook 2008*.

Statistics Bureau, the Director-General for Policy Planning (Statistical Standards), 19-1 Wakamatsucho, Shinjuku-ku, Tokyo 162-8668, Japan, www.stat.go.jp/english; *Japan Statistical Yearbook 2008*.

UNICEF, 3 United Nations Plaza, New York, NY 10017, (800) 253-9646, Fax: (212) 887-7465, www.unicef.org; *The State of the World's Children 2008*.

United Nations Statistics Division, New York, NY 10017, (800) 253-9646, Fax: (212) 963-4116, http://unstats.un.org; *Asia-Pacific in Figures 2004; Human Development Report 2006;* and *Statistical Yearbook*.

The World Bank, 1818 H Street, NW, Washington, DC 20433, (202) 473-1000, Fax: (202) 477-6391, www.worldbank.org; *Japan* and *World Development Report 2008*.

World Health Organization (WHO), Avenue Appia 20, 1211 Geneve 27, Switzerland, (Telephone in U.S. (212) 331-9081), www.who.int; The WHO Global Atlas of Infectious Diseases and *World Health Report 2006*.

JAPAN - PUBLIC UTILITIES

United Nations Statistics Division, New York, NY 10017, (800) 253-9646, Fax: (212) 963-4116, http://unstats.un.org; *Electric Power in Asia and the Pacific 2001 and 2002*.

JAPAN - PUBLISHERS AND PUBLISHING

Organisation for Economic Cooperation and Development (OECD), 2 rue Andre Pascal, F-75775 Paris Cedex 16, France, (Telephone in U.S. (202) 785-6323), (Fax in U.S. (202) 785-0350), www.oecd.org; *Indicators of Industrial Activity*.

UNESCO Institute for Statistics, C.P. 6128 Succursale Centre-Ville, Montreal, Quebec, H3C 3J7 Canada, (Dial from U.S. (514) 343-6880), (Fax from U.S. (514) 343 6882), www.uis.unesco.org; *Statistical Tables*.

JAPAN - RADIO BROADCASTING

Palgrave Macmillan Ltd., Houndmills, Basingstoke, Hampshire, RG21 6XS, England, (Telephone in U.S. (888) 330-8477), (Fax in U.S. (800) 672-2054), www.palgrave.com; *The Statesman's Yearbook 2008*.

United Nations Statistics Division, New York, NY 10017, (800) 253-9646, Fax: (212) 963-4116, http://unstats.un.org; *Statistical Yearbook*.

JAPAN - RAILROADS

Jane's Information Group, 110 North Royal Street, Suite 200, Alexandria, VA 22314, (703) 683-3700, Fax: (800) 836-0297, www.janes.com; *Jane's World Railways*.

Palgrave Macmillan Ltd., Houndmills, Basingstoke, Hampshire, RG21 6XS, England, (Telephone in U.S. (888) 330-8477), (Fax in U.S. (800) 672-2054), www.palgrave.com; *The Statesman's Yearbook 2008*.

Taylor and Francis Group, An Informa Business, 2 Park Square, Milton Park, Abingdon, Oxford OX14 4RN, United Kingdom, (Dial from U.S. (212) 216-7800), (Fax from U.S. (212) 564-7854), www.tandf.co.uk; *The Europa World Year Book*.

United Nations Statistics Division, New York, NY 10017, (800) 253-9646, Fax: (212) 963-4116, http://unstats.un.org; *Statistical Yearbook*.

JAPAN - RELIGION

Central Intelligence Agency, Office of Public Affairs, Washington, DC 20505, (703) 482-0623, Fax: (703) 482-1739, www.cia.gov; *The World Factbook*.

M.E. Sharpe, 80 Business Park Drive, Armonk, NY 10504, (800) 541-6563, Fax: (914) 273-2106, www.mesharpe.com; *The Illustrated Book of World Rankings*.

Palgrave Macmillan Ltd., Houndmills, Basingstoke, Hampshire, RG21 6XS, England, (Telephone in U.S. (888) 330-8477), (Fax in U.S. (800) 672-2054), www.palgrave.com; *The Statesman's Yearbook 2008*.

JAPAN - RENT CHARGES

International Labour Office, I.L.O. Publications, 4 route des Morillons, CH-1211 Geneva 22, Switzerland, (Telephone in U.S. (202) 653-7652), (Fax in U.S. (202) 653-7687), www.ilo.org; *Yearbook of Labour Statistics 2006*.

JAPAN - RESERVES (ACCOUNTING)

Euromonitor International, Inc., 224 S. Michigan Avenue, Suite 1500, Chicago, IL 60604, (312) 922-1115, Fax: (312) 922-1157, www.euromonitor.com; *International Marketing Data and Statistics 2008*.

Organisation for Economic Cooperation and Development (OECD), 2 rue Andre Pascal, F-75775 Paris Cedex 16, France, (Telephone in U.S. (202) 785-6323), (Fax in U.S. (202) 785-0350), www.oecd.org; *Financial Market Trends: OECD Periodical* and *OECD Economic Outlook 2008*.

United Nations Statistics Division, New York, NY 10017, (800) 253-9646, Fax: (212) 963-4116, http://unstats.un.org; *Statistical Yearbook*.

JAPAN - RETAIL TRADE

Euromonitor International, Inc., 224 S. Michigan Avenue, Suite 1500, Chicago, IL 60604, (312) 922-1115, Fax: (312) 922-1157, www.euromonitor.com; *Retail Trade International 2007* and *World Marketing Data and Statistics*.

United Nations Statistics Division, New York, NY 10017, (800) 253-9646, Fax: (212) 963-4116, http://unstats.un.org; *Statistical Yearbook*.

JAPAN - RICE PRODUCTION

See JAPAN - CROPS

JAPAN - ROADS

Central Intelligence Agency, Office of Public Affairs, Washington, DC 20505, (703) 482-0623, Fax: (703) 482-1739, www.cia.gov; *The World Factbook*.

Economist Intelligence Unit, 111 West 57th Street, New York, NY 10019, (212) 554-0600, Fax: (212) 586-1181, www.eiu.com; *Business Asia.*

International Road Federation (IFR), Madison Place, 500 Montgomery Street, 5th Floor, Alexandria, VA 22314, (703) 535-1001, Fax: (703) 535-1007, www.irfnet.org; *World Road Statistics 2006.*

Palgrave Macmillan Ltd., Houndmills, Basingstoke, Hampshire, RG21 6XS, England, (Telephone in U.S. (888) 330-8477), (Fax in U.S. (800) 672-2054), www.palgrave.com; *The Statesman's Yearbook 2008.*

JAPAN - RUBBER INDUSTRY AND TRADE

International Rubber Study Group (IRSG), 1st Floor, Heron House, 109/115 Wembley Hill Road, Wembley, Middlesex HA9 8DA, United Kingdom, www.rubberstudy.com; *Rubber Statistical Bulletin; Summary of World Rubber Statistics 2005; World Rubber Statistics Handbook (Volume 6, 1975-2001);* and *World Rubber Statistics Historic Handbook.*

M.E. Sharpe, 80 Business Park Drive, Armonk, NY 10504, (800) 541-6563, Fax: (914) 273-2106, www.mesharpe.com; *The Illustrated Book of World Rankings.*

Organisation for Economic Cooperation and Development (OECD), 2 rue Andre Pascal, F-75775 Paris Cedex 16, France, (Telephone in U.S. (202) 785-6323), (Fax in U.S. (202) 785-0350), www.oecd.org; *International Trade by Commodity Statistics (ITCS).*

United Nations Statistics Division, New York, NY 10017, (800) 253-9646, Fax: (212) 963-4116, http://unstats.un.org; *Statistical Yearbook.*

JAPAN - RYE PRODUCTION

See JAPAN - CROPS

JAPAN - SAFFLOWER SEED PRODUCTION

See JAPAN - CROPS

JAPAN - SALT PRODUCTION

See JAPAN - MINERAL INDUSTRIES

JAPAN - SHEEP

See JAPAN - LIVESTOCK

JAPAN - SHIPBUILDING

Organisation for Economic Cooperation and Development (OECD), 2 rue Andre Pascal, F-75775 Paris Cedex 16, France, (Telephone in U.S. (202) 785-6323), (Fax in U.S. (202) 785-0350), www.oecd.org; *Indicators of Industrial Activity.*

JAPAN - SHIPPING

Lloyd's Register - Fairplay, 8410 N.W. 53rd Terrace, Suite 207, Miami FL 33166, (305) 718-9929, Fax: (305) 718-9663, www.lrfairplay.com; *Register of Ships 2007-2008; World Casualty Statistics 2007; World Fleet Statistics 2006; World Marine Propulsion Report 2006-2010; World Shipbuilding Statistics 2007;* and The World Shipping Encyclopaedia.

Organisation for Economic Cooperation and Development (OECD), 2 rue Andre Pascal, F-75775 Paris Cedex 16, France, (Telephone in U.S. (202) 785-6323), (Fax in U.S. (202) 785-0350), www.oecd.org; *Statistics on Ship Production, Exports and Orders in 2004.*

Palgrave Macmillan Ltd., Houndmills, Basingstoke, Hampshire, RG21 6XS, England, (Telephone in U.S. (888) 330-8477), (Fax in U.S. (800) 672-2054), www.palgrave.com; *The Statesman's Yearbook 2008.*

Taylor and Francis Group, An Informa Business, 2 Park Square, Milton Park, Abingdon, Oxford OX14 4RN, United Kingdom, (Dial from U.S. (212) 216-7800), (Fax from U.S. (212) 564-7854), www.tandf.co.uk; *The Europa World Year Book.*

U.S. Department of Transportation (DOT), Maritime Administration (MARAD), West Building, Southeast Federal Center, 1200 New Jersey Avenue, SE, Washington, DC 20590, (800) 99-MARAD, www.marad.dot.gov; *World Merchant Fleet 2005.*

United Nations Statistics Division, New York, NY 10017, (800) 253-9646, Fax: (212) 963-4116, http://unstats.un.org; *Statistical Yearbook.*

JAPAN - SILVER PRODUCTION

See JAPAN - MINERAL INDUSTRIES

JAPAN - SOCIAL ECOLOGY

M.E. Sharpe, 80 Business Park Drive, Armonk, NY 10504, (800) 541-6563, Fax: (914) 273-2106, www.mesharpe.com; *The Illustrated Book of World Rankings.*

United Nations Statistics Division, New York, NY 10017, (800) 253-9646, Fax: (212) 963-4116, http://unstats.un.org; *World Statistics Pocketbook.*

JAPAN - SOCIAL SECURITY

Organisation for Economic Cooperation and Development (OECD), 2 rue Andre Pascal, F-75775 Paris Cedex 16, France, (Telephone in U.S. (202) 785-6323), (Fax in U.S. (202) 785-0350), www.oecd.org; *Revenue Statistics 1965-2006 - 2007 Edition.*

Palgrave Macmillan Ltd., Houndmills, Basingstoke, Hampshire, RG21 6XS, England, (Telephone in U.S. (888) 330-8477), (Fax in U.S. (800) 672-2054), www.palgrave.com; *The Statesman's Yearbook 2008.*

United Nations Statistics Division, New York, NY 10017, (800) 253-9646, Fax: (212) 963-4116, http://unstats.un.org; *National Accounts Statistics: Compendium of Income Distribution Statistics.*

JAPAN - SOYBEAN PRODUCTION

See JAPAN - CROPS

JAPAN - STEEL PRODUCTION

See JAPAN - MINERAL INDUSTRIES

JAPAN - STRAW PRODUCTION

See JAPAN - CROPS

JAPAN - SUGAR PRODUCTION

See JAPAN - CROPS

JAPAN - SULPHUR PRODUCTION

See JAPAN - MINERAL INDUSTRIES

JAPAN - SUNFLOWER PRODUCTION

See JAPAN - CROPS

JAPAN - TAXATION

International Monetary Fund (IMF), 700 Nineteenth Street, NW, Washington, DC 20431, (202) 623-7000, Fax: (202) 623-4661, www.imf.org; *Government Finance Statistics Yearbook (2008 Edition).*

International Road Federation (IFR), Madison Place, 500 Montgomery Street, 5th Floor, Alexandria, VA 22314, (703) 535-1001, Fax: (703) 535-1007, www.irfnet.org; *World Road Statistics 2006.*

Organisation for Economic Cooperation and Development (OECD), 2 rue Andre Pascal, F-75775 Paris Cedex 16, France, (Telephone in U.S. (202) 785-6323), (Fax in U.S. (202) 785-0350), www.oecd.org; *Revenue Statistics 1965-2006 - 2007 Edition.*

Taylor and Francis Group, An Informa Business, 2 Park Square, Milton Park, Abingdon, Oxford OX14 4RN, United Kingdom, (Dial from U.S. (212) 216-7800), (Fax from U.S. (212) 564-7854), www.tandf.co.uk; *The Europa World Year Book.*

JAPAN - TEA PRODUCTION

See JAPAN - CROPS

JAPAN - TELEPHONE

Economist Intelligence Unit, 111 West 57th Street, New York, NY 10019, (212) 554-0600, Fax: (212) 586-1181, www.eiu.com; *Business Asia.*

International Telecommunication Union (ITU), Place des Nations, 1211 Geneva 20, Switzerland, www.itu.int; World Telecommunication Indicators Database.

Palgrave Macmillan Ltd., Houndmills, Basingstoke, Hampshire, RG21 6XS, England, (Telephone in U.S. (888) 330-8477), (Fax in U.S. (800) 672-2054), www.palgrave.com; *The Statesman's Yearbook 2008.*

United Nations Statistics Division, New York, NY 10017, (800) 253-9646, Fax: (212) 963-4116, http://unstats.un.org; *Statistical Yearbook* and *World Statistics Pocketbook.*

JAPAN - TELEVISION - RECEIVERS AND RECEPTION

United Nations Statistics Division, New York, NY 10017, (800) 253-9646, Fax: (212) 963-4116, http://unstats.un.org; *Statistical Yearbook.*

JAPAN - TEXTILE INDUSTRY

Euromonitor International, Inc., 224 S. Michigan Avenue, Suite 1500, Chicago, IL 60604, (312) 922-1115, Fax: (312) 922-1157, www.euromonitor.com; *Retail Trade International 2007.*

M.E. Sharpe, 80 Business Park Drive, Armonk, NY 10504, (800) 541-6563, Fax: (914) 273-2106, www.mesharpe.com; *The Illustrated Book of World Rankings.*

Organisation for Economic Cooperation and Development (OECD), 2 rue Andre Pascal, F-75775 Paris Cedex 16, France, (Telephone in U.S. (202) 785-6323), (Fax in U.S. (202) 785-0350), www.oecd.org; *Indicators of Industrial Activity; International Trade by Commodity Statistics (ITCS); A New World Map in Textiles and Clothing: Adjusting to Change; 2005 OECD Agricultural Outlook Tables, 1970-2014;* and STructural ANalysis (STAN) database.

Palgrave Macmillan Ltd., Houndmills, Basingstoke, Hampshire, RG21 6XS, England, (Telephone in U.S. (888) 330-8477), (Fax in U.S. (800) 672-2054), www.palgrave.com; *The Statesman's Yearbook 2008.*

United Nations Conference on Trade and Development (UNCTAD), DC2-1120, United Nations, New York, NY 10017, (212) 963-0027, www.unctad.org; *UNCTAD Commodity Yearbook.*

United Nations Food and Agricultural Organization (FAO), Viale delle Terme di Caracalla, 00100 Rome, Italy, (Dial from U.S. (202) 653-2400), (Fax from U.S. (202) 653 5760), www.fao.org; *FAO Production Yearbook 2002.*

United Nations Statistics Division, New York, NY 10017, (800) 253-9646, Fax: (212) 963-4116, http://unstats.un.org; *Statistical Yearbook.*

JAPAN - THEATER

UNESCO Institute for Statistics, C.P. 6128 Succursale Centre-Ville, Montreal, Quebec, H3C 3J7 Canada, (Dial from U.S. (514) 343-6880), (Fax from U.S. (514) 343 6882), www.uis.unesco.org; *Statistical Tables.*

JAPAN - TIMBER

See JAPAN - FORESTS AND FORESTRY

JAPAN - TIN PRODUCTION

See JAPAN - MINERAL INDUSTRIES

JAPAN - TIRE INDUSTRY

United Nations Statistics Division, New York, NY 10017, (800) 253-9646, Fax: (212) 963-4116, http://unstats.un.org; *Statistical Yearbook.*

JAPAN - TOBACCO INDUSTRY

Foreign Agricultural Service (FAS), U.S. Department of Agriculture (USDA), 1400 Independence Avenue, SW, Washington, DC 20250, (202) 720-3935, www.fas.usda.gov; *Tobacco: World Markets and Trade.*

M.E. Sharpe, 80 Business Park Drive, Armonk, NY 10504, (800) 541-6563, Fax: (914) 273-2106, www.mesharpe.com; *The Illustrated Book of World Rankings.*

Organisation for Economic Cooperation and Development (OECD), 2 rue Andre Pascal, F-75775 Paris Cedex 16, France, (Telephone in U.S. (202) 785-6323), (Fax in U.S. (202) 785-0350), www.oecd.org; *Indicators of Industrial Activity; International Trade by Commodity Statistics (ITCS);* and STructural ANalysis (STAN) database.

United Nations Statistics Division, New York, NY 10017, (800) 253-9646, Fax: (212) 963-4116, http://unstats.un.org; *Statistical Yearbook.*

JAPAN - TOURISM

Euromonitor International, Inc., 224 S. Michigan Avenue, Suite 1500, Chicago, IL 60604, (312) 922-1115, Fax: (312) 922-1157, www.euromonitor.com; *The World Economic Factbook 2008* and *World Marketing Data and Statistics.*

M.E. Sharpe, 80 Business Park Drive, Armonk, NY 10504, (800) 541-6563, Fax: (914) 273-2106, www.mesharpe.com; *The Illustrated Book of World Rankings.*

Organisation for Economic Cooperation and Development (OECD), 2 rue Andre Pascal, F-75775 Paris Cedex 16, France, (Telephone in U.S. (202) 785-6323), (Fax in U.S. (202) 785-0350), www.oecd.org; *Household, Tourism, Travel: Trends, Environmental Impacts and Policy Responses.*

Palgrave Macmillan Ltd., Houndmills, Basingstoke, Hampshire, RG21 6XS, England, (Telephone in U.S. (888) 330-8477), (Fax in U.S. (800) 672-2054), www.palgrave.com; *The Statesman's Yearbook 2008.*

Taylor and Francis Group, An Informa Business, 2 Park Square, Milton Park, Abingdon, Oxford OX14 4RN, United Kingdom, (Dial from U.S. (212) 216-7800), (Fax from U.S. (212) 564-7854), www.tandf.co.uk; *The Europa World Year Book.*

United Nations Statistics Division, New York, NY 10017, (800) 253-9646, Fax: (212) 963-4116, http://unstats.un.org; *Statistical Yearbook.*

United Nations World Tourism Organization (UNWTO), Capitan Haya 42, 28020 Madrid, Spain, www.world-tourism.org; *Yearbook of Tourism Statistics.*

The World Bank, 1818 H Street, NW, Washington, DC 20433, (202) 473-1000, Fax: (202) 477-6391, www.worldbank.org; *Japan.*

JAPAN - TRADE

See JAPAN - INTERNATIONAL TRADE

JAPAN - TRANSPORTATION

Central Intelligence Agency, Office of Public Affairs, Washington, DC 20505, (703) 482-0623, Fax: (703) 482-1739, www.cia.gov; *The World Factbook.*

Economist Intelligence Unit, 111 West 57th Street, New York, NY 10019, (212) 554-0600, Fax: (212) 586-1181, www.eiu.com; *Business Asia.*

Euromonitor International, Inc., 224 S. Michigan Avenue, Suite 1500, Chicago, IL 60604, (312) 922-1115, Fax: (312) 922-1157, www.euromonitor.com; *World Marketing Data and Statistics.*

M.E. Sharpe, 80 Business Park Drive, Armonk, NY 10504, (800) 541-6563, Fax: (914) 273-2106, www.mesharpe.com; *The Illustrated Book of World Rankings.*

Palgrave Macmillan Ltd., Houndmills, Basingstoke, Hampshire, RG21 6XS, England, (Telephone in U.S. (888) 330-8477), (Fax in U.S. (800) 672-2054), www.palgrave.com; *The Statesman's Yearbook 2008.*

Taylor and Francis Group, An Informa Business, 2 Park Square, Milton Park, Abingdon, Oxford OX14 4RN, United Kingdom, (Dial from U.S. (212) 216-7800), (Fax from U.S. (212) 564-7854), www.tandf.co.uk; *The Europa World Year Book.*

United Nations Statistics Division, New York, NY 10017, (800) 253-9646, Fax: (212) 963-4116, http://unstats.un.org; *Human Development Report 2006* and *Statistical Yearbook for Asia and the Pacific 2004.*

The World Bank, 1818 H Street, NW, Washington, DC 20433, (202) 473-1000, Fax: (202) 477-6391, www.worldbank.org; *Japan.*

JAPAN - TURKEYS

See JAPAN - LIVESTOCK

JAPAN - UNEMPLOYMENT

Central Intelligence Agency, Office of Public Affairs, Washington, DC 20505, (703) 482-0623, Fax: (703) 482-1739, www.cia.gov; *The World Factbook.*

Euromonitor International, Inc., 224 S. Michigan Avenue, Suite 1500, Chicago, IL 60604, (312) 922-1115, Fax: (312) 922-1157, www.euromonitor.com; *International Marketing Data and Statistics 2008.*

International Labour Office, I.L.O. Publications, 4 route des Morillons, CH-1211 Geneva 22, Switzerland, (Telephone in U.S. (202) 653-7652), (Fax in U.S. (202) 653-7687), www.ilo.org; *Yearbook of Labour Statistics 2006.*

Organisation for Economic Cooperation and Development (OECD), 2 rue Andre Pascal, F-75775 Paris Cedex 16, France, (Telephone in U.S. (202) 785-6323), (Fax in U.S. (202) 785-0350), www.oecd.org; *Labour Force Statistics: 1986-2005, 2007 Edition; OECD Composite Leading Indicators (CLIs), Updated September 2007; OECD Economic Outlook 2008; OECD Economic Survey - Japan 2008;* and *OECD Employment Outlook 2007.*

Palgrave Macmillan Ltd., Houndmills, Basingstoke, Hampshire, RG21 6XS, England, (Telephone in U.S. (888) 330-8477), (Fax in U.S. (800) 672-2054), www.palgrave.com; *The Statesman's Yearbook 2008.*

Statistics Bureau, the Director-General for Policy Planning (Statistical Standards), 19-1 Wakamatsu-cho, Shinjuku-ku, Tokyo 162-8668, Japan, www.stat.go.jp/english; *Japan Statistical Yearbook 2008.*

United Nations Statistics Division, New York, NY 10017, (800) 253-9646, Fax: (212) 963-4116, http://unstats.un.org; *Statistical Yearbook.*

The World Bank, 1818 H Street, NW, Washington, DC 20433, (202) 473-1000, Fax: (202) 477-6391, www.worldbank.org; *Japan.*

JAPAN - URANIUM PRODUCTION AND CONSUMPTION

See JAPAN - MINERAL INDUSTRIES

JAPAN - VITAL STATISTICS

Euromonitor International, Inc., 224 S. Michigan Avenue, Suite 1500, Chicago, IL 60604, (312) 922-1115, Fax: (312) 922-1157, www.euromonitor.com; *International Marketing Data and Statistics 2008.*

Palgrave Macmillan Ltd., Houndmills, Basingstoke, Hampshire, RG21 6XS, England, (Telephone in U.S. (888) 330-8477), (Fax in U.S. (800) 672-2054), www.palgrave.com; *The Statesman's Yearbook 2008.*

JAPAN - WELFARE STATE

Palgrave Macmillan Ltd., Houndmills, Basingstoke, Hampshire, RG21 6XS, England, (Telephone in U.S. (888) 330-8477), (Fax in U.S. (800) 672-2054), www.palgrave.com; *The Statesman's Yearbook 2008.*

JAPAN - WHOLESALE TRADE

United Nations Statistics Division, New York, NY 10017, (800) 253-9646, Fax: (212) 963-4116, http://unstats.un.org; *Statistical Yearbook.*

JAPAN - WINE PRODUCTION

See JAPAN - BEVERAGE INDUSTRY

JAPAN - WOOD AND WOOD PULP

See JAPAN - FORESTS AND FORESTRY

JAPAN - WOOD PRODUCTS

Organisation for Economic Cooperation and Development (OECD), 2 rue Andre Pascal, F-75775 Paris Cedex 16, France, (Telephone in U.S. (202) 785-6323), (Fax in U.S. (202) 785-0350), www.oecd.org; *International Trade by Commodity Statistics (ITCS)* and STructural ANalysis (STAN) database.

JAPAN - WOOL PRODUCTION

See JAPAN - TEXTILE INDUSTRY

JAPAN - YARN PRODUCTION

See JAPAN - TEXTILE INDUSTRY

JAPAN - ZINC AND ZINC ORE

See JAPAN - MINERAL INDUSTRIES

JAPAN - ZOOS

UNESCO Institute for Statistics, C.P. 6128 Succursale Centre-Ville, Montreal, Quebec, H3C 3J7 Canada, (Dial from U.S. (514) 343-6880), (Fax from U.S. (514) 343 6882), www.uis.unesco.org; *Statistical Tables.*

JAPANESE POPULATION

U.S. Census Bureau, Demographic Surveys Division, 4700 Silver Hill Road, Washington DC 20233-0001, (301) 763-3030, www.census.gov; *Census 2000: Demographic Profiles.*

JAZZ

National Endowment for the Arts (NEA), 1100 Pennsylvania Avenue, NW, Washington, DC 20506-0001, (202) 682-5400, www.arts.gov; *2002 Survey of Public Participation in the Arts.*

Recording Industry Association of America (RIAA), 10th Floor, 1025 F Street, NW, Washington, DC 20004, (202) 775-0101, www.riaa.com; *The 2007 Annual Consumer Profile Chart.*

JERSEY - AGRICULTURE

Economist Intelligence Unit, 111 West 57th Street, New York, NY 10019, (212) 554-0600, Fax: (212) 586-1181, www.eiu.com; *Jersey.*

United Nations Food and Agricultural Organization (FAO), Viale delle Terme di Caracalla, 00100 Rome, Italy, (Dial from U.S. (202) 653-2400), (Fax from U.S. (202) 653 5760), www.fao.org; AQUASTAT.

JERSEY - ECONOMIC CONDITIONS

Center for International Business Education Research (CIBER), Columbia Business School and School of International and Public Affairs, Uris Hall, Room 212, 3022 Broadway, New York, NY 10027-6902, Mr. Joshua Safier, (212) 854-4750, Fax: (212) 222-9821, www.columbia.edu/cu/ciber/; Datastream International.

DSI Data Service Information, Xantener Strasse 51a, D-47495 Rheinberg, Germany, www.dsidata.com; *Campus Solution.*

Dun and Bradstreet (DB) Corporation, 103 JFK Parkway, Short Hills, NJ 07078, (973) 921-5500, www.dnb.com; *Country Report.*

Economist Intelligence Unit, 111 West 57th Street, New York, NY 10019, (212) 554-0600, Fax: (212) 586-1181, www.eiu.com; *Jersey.*

International Monetary Fund (IMF), 700 Nineteenth Street, NW, Washington, DC 20431, (202) 623-7000, Fax: (202) 623-4661, www.imf.org; *World Economic Outlook Reports.*

The World Bank, 1818 H Street, NW, Washington, DC 20433, (202) 473-1000, Fax: (202) 477-6391, www.worldbank.org; *Global Economic Monitor (GEM)* and *Global Economic Prospects 2008.*

JERSEY - ENVIRONMENTAL CONDITIONS

DSI Data Service Information, Xantener Strasse 51a, D-47495 Rheinberg, Germany, www.dsidata.com; *Campus Solution* and *DSI's Global Environmental Database.*

Economist Intelligence Unit, 111 West 57th Street, New York, NY 10019, (212) 554-0600, Fax: (212) 586-1181, www.eiu.com; *Jersey.*

JERSEY - EXPORTS

Economist Intelligence Unit, 111 West 57th Street, New York, NY 10019, (212) 554-0600, Fax: (212) 586-1181, www.eiu.com; *Jersey.*

JERSEY - FINANCE, PUBLIC

Banque de France, 48 rue Croix des Petits champs, 75001 Paris, France, www.banque-france.fr/home.htm; *Public Finance.*

Bernan Essential Government Publications, 4611-F Assembly Drive, Lanham MD, 20706-4391, (301) 459-2255, Fax: (800) 865-3450, www.bernan.com; *National Accounts Statistics.*

Economist Intelligence Unit, 111 West 57th Street, New York, NY 10019, (212) 554-0600, Fax: (212) 586-1181, www.eiu.com; *Jersey.*

International Monetary Fund (IMF), 700 Nineteenth Street, NW, Washington, DC 20431, (202) 623-7000, Fax: (202) 623-4661, www.imf.org; *International Financial Statistics* and *International Financial Statistics Online Service.*

JERSEY - GROSS DOMESTIC PRODUCT

Economist Intelligence Unit, 111 West 57th Street, New York, NY 10019, (212) 554-0600, Fax: (212) 586-1181, www.eiu.com; *Jersey.*

JERSEY - IMPORTS

Economist Intelligence Unit, 111 West 57th Street, New York, NY 10019, (212) 554-0600, Fax: (212) 586-1181, www.eiu.com; *Jersey.*

JERSEY - INDUSTRIES

Economist Intelligence Unit, 111 West 57th Street, New York, NY 10019, (212) 554-0600, Fax: (212) 586-1181, www.eiu.com; *Jersey.*

United Nations Industrial Development Organization (UNIDO), 1 United Nations Plaza, New York, NY 10017, (212) 963 6890, Fax: (212) 963-7904, http://unido.org; Industrial Statistics Database 2008 (INDSTAT) and *The International Yearbook of Industrial Statistics 2008.*

JERSEY - INTERNATIONAL TRADE

Economist Intelligence Unit, 111 West 57th Street, New York, NY 10019, (212) 554-0600, Fax: (212) 586-1181, www.eiu.com; *Jersey.*

World Trade Organization (WTO), Centre William Rappard, Rue de Lausanne 154, CH-1211 Geneva 21, Switzerland, www.wto.org; *International Trade Statistics 2006.*

JERSEY - INTERNET USERS

International Telecommunication Union (ITU), Place des Nations, 1211 Geneva 20, Switzerland, www.itu.int; *World Telecommunication/ICT Indicators Database on CD-ROM; World Telecommunication/ICT Indicators Database Online;* and *Yearbook of Statistics - Telecommunication Services (Chronological Time Series 1997-2006).*

JERSEY - MONEY SUPPLY

Economist Intelligence Unit, 111 West 57th Street, New York, NY 10019, (212) 554-0600, Fax: (212) 586-1181, www.eiu.com; *Jersey.*

JERSEY - POPULATION

Economist Intelligence Unit, 111 West 57th Street, New York, NY 10019, (212) 554-0600, Fax: (212) 586-1181, www.eiu.com; *Jersey.*

JEWELRY SALES

Office of Trade and Industry Information (OTII), Manufacturing and Services, International Trade Administration, U.S. Department of Commerce, 1401 Constitution Ave, NW, Washington, DC 20230, (800) USA TRAD(E), http://trade.gov/index.asp; *TradeStats Express.*

U.S. Census Bureau, Center for Economic Studies, 4600 Silver Hill Road, Washington DC 20233, (301) 457-1235, www.ces.census.gov; *2002 Economic Census, Retail Trade* and *2002 Economic Census, Wholesale Trade.*

U.S. Census Bureau, Company Statistics Division, 4700 Silver Hill Road, Washington DC 20233-0001, (301) 763-3030, www.census.gov/csd/; *County Business Patterns 2004* and *Current Business Reports.*

JEWELRY, SILVERWARE, AND PLATED WARE - MANUFACTURING

U.S. Bureau of Labor Statistics (BLS), Postal Square Building, 2 Massachusetts Avenue, NE, Washington, DC 20212-0001, (202) 691-5200, Fax: (202) 691-6325, www.bls.gov; *Current Employment Statistics Survey (CES)* and *Employment and Earnings (EE).*

U.S. Census Bureau, Manufacturing and Construction Division, 4600 Silver Hill Road, Washington DC 20233, (301) 763-4673, www.census.gov/mcd; *Annual Survey of Manufactures (ASM)* and *Census of Manufactures.*

JEWISH POPULATION

See RELIGION

JOB CORPS

U.S. Library of Congress (LOC), Congressional Research Service (CRS), The Library of Congress, 101 Independence Avenue, SE, Washington, DC 20540-7500, (202) 707-5700, www.loc.gov/crsinfo; *Cash and Non-cash Benefits for Persons With Limited Income: Eligibility Rules, Recipient and Expenditure Data.*

JOGGING

National Sporting Goods Association (NSGA), 1601 Feehanville Drive, Suite 300, Mount Prospect, IL 60056, (847) 296-6742, Fax: (847) 391-9827, www.nsga.org; *2006 Sports Participation* and *Ten-Year History of Selected Sports Participation, 1996-2006.*

JORDAN - NATIONAL STATISTICAL OFFICE

Department of Statistics (DOS), PO Box 2015, Amman 11181, Jordan, www.dos.gov.jo; National Data Center.

JORDAN - PRIMARY STATISTICS SOURCES

Department of Statistics (DOS), PO Box 2015, Amman 11181, Jordan, www.dos.gov.jo; *Statistical Yearbook 2006.*

JORDAN - AGRICULTURAL MACHINERY

United Nations Statistics Division, New York, NY 10017, (800) 253-9646, Fax: (212) 963-4116, http://unstats.un.org; *Statistical Yearbook.*

JORDAN - AGRICULTURE

Department of Statistics (DOS), PO Box 2015, Amman 11181, Jordan, www.dos.gov.jo; *Agricultural Statistics 2006.*

Economist Intelligence Unit, 111 West 57th Street, New York, NY 10019, (212) 554-0600, Fax: (212) 586-1181, www.eiu.com; *Jordan Country Report.*

Euromonitor International, Inc., 224 S. Michigan Avenue, Suite 1500, Chicago, IL 60604, (312) 922-1115, Fax: (312) 922-1157, www.euromonitor.com; *World Marketing Data and Statistics.*

M.E. Sharpe, 80 Business Park Drive, Armonk, NY 10504, (800) 541-6563, Fax: (914) 273-2106, www.mesharpe.com; *The Illustrated Book of World Rankings.*

Palgrave Macmillan Ltd., Houndmills, Basingstoke, Hampshire, RG21 6XS, England, (Telephone in U.S. (888) 330-8477), (Fax in U.S. (800) 672-2054), www.palgrave.com; *The Statesman's Yearbook 2008.*

Taylor and Francis Group, An Informa Business, 2 Park Square, Milton Park, Abingdon, Oxford OX14 4RN, United Kingdom, (Dial from U.S. (212) 216-7800), (Fax from U.S. (212) 564-7854), www.tandf.co.uk; *The Europa World Year Book.*

United Nations Conference on Trade and Development (UNCTAD), DC2-1120, United Nations, New York, NY 10017, (212) 963-0027, www.unctad.org; *UNCTAD Commodity Yearbook.*

United Nations Economic and Social Commission for Western Asia (ESCWA), PO Box 11-8575, Riad el-Solh Square, Beirut, Lebanon, www.escwa.un.org; *Annual Report 2006* and *Statistical Abstract of the ESCWA Region 2007.*

United Nations Food and Agricultural Organization (FAO), Viale delle Terme di Caracalla, 00100 Rome, Italy, (Dial from U.S. (202) 653-2400), (Fax from U.S. (202) 653 5760), www.fao.org; AQUASTAT; *FAO Production Yearbook 2002; FAO Trade Yearbook;* and *The State of Food and Agriculture (SOFA) 2006.*

United Nations Statistics Division, New York, NY 10017, (800) 253-9646, Fax: (212) 963-4116, http://unstats.un.org; *Statistical Yearbook.*

The World Bank, 1818 H Street, NW, Washington, DC 20433, (202) 473-1000, Fax: (202) 477-6391, www.worldbank.org; *Jordan.*

JORDAN - AIRLINES

International Civil Aviation Organization (ICAO), External Relations and Public Information Office (EPO), 999 University Street, Montreal, Quebec H3C 5H7, Canada, (Dial from U.S. (514) 954-8219), (Fax from U.S. (514) 954-6077), www.icao.int; *Civil Aviation Statistics of the World.*

M.E. Sharpe, 80 Business Park Drive, Armonk, NY 10504, (800) 541-6563, Fax: (914) 273-2106, www.mesharpe.com; *The Illustrated Book of World Rankings.*

Palgrave Macmillan Ltd., Houndmills, Basingstoke, Hampshire, RG21 6XS, England, (Telephone in U.S. (888) 330-8477), (Fax in U.S. (800) 672-2054), www.palgrave.com; *The Statesman's Yearbook 2008.*

Taylor and Francis Group, An Informa Business, 2 Park Square, Milton Park, Abingdon, Oxford OX14 4RN, United Kingdom, (Dial from U.S. (212) 216-7800), (Fax from U.S. (212) 564-7854), www.tandf.co.uk; *The Europa World Year Book.*

United Nations Statistics Division, New York, NY 10017, (800) 253-9646, Fax: (212) 963-4116, http://unstats.un.org; *Statistical Yearbook.*

JORDAN - ALUMINUM PRODUCTION

See JORDAN - MINERAL INDUSTRIES

JORDAN - ARMED FORCES

Central Intelligence Agency, Office of Public Affairs, Washington, DC 20505, (703) 482-0623, Fax: (703) 482-1739, www.cia.gov; *The World Factbook.*

Euromonitor International, Inc., 224 S. Michigan Avenue, Suite 1500, Chicago, IL 60604, (312) 922-1115, Fax: (312) 922-1157, www.euromonitor.com; *World Marketing Data and Statistics.*

International Institute for Strategic Studies (IISS), Arundel House, 13-15 Arundel Street, Temple Place, London WC2R 3DX, England, www.iiss.org; *The Military Balance 2007.*

International Monetary Fund (IMF), 700 Nineteenth Street, NW, Washington, DC 20431, (202) 623-7000, Fax: (202) 623-4661, www.imf.org; *Government Finance Statistics Yearbook (2008 Edition).*

Palgrave Macmillan Ltd., Houndmills, Basingstoke, Hampshire, RG21 6XS, England, (Telephone in U.S. (888) 330-8477), (Fax in U.S. (800) 672-2054), www.palgrave.com; *The Statesman's Yearbook 2008.*

U.S. Department of State (DOS), 2201 C Street NW, Washington, DC 20520, (202) 647-4000, www.state.gov; *World Military Expenditures and Arms Transfers (WMEAT).*

United Nations Statistics Division, New York, NY 10017, (800) 253-9646, Fax: (212) 963-4116, http://unstats.un.org; *Human Development Report 2006.*

JORDAN - BALANCE OF PAYMENTS

International Monetary Fund (IMF), 700 Nineteenth Street, NW, Washington, DC 20431, (202) 623-7000, Fax: (202) 623-4661, www.imf.org; *Balance of Payments Statistics Newsletter; Balance of Payments Statistics Yearbook 2007;* and *International Financial Statistics Yearbook 2007.*

Taylor and Francis Group, An Informa Business, 2 Park Square, Milton Park, Abingdon, Oxford OX14 4RN, United Kingdom, (Dial from U.S. (212) 216-7800), (Fax from U.S. (212) 564-7854), www.tandf.co.uk; *The Europa World Year Book.*

United Nations Conference on Trade and Development (UNCTAD), DC2-1120, United Nations, New York, NY 10017, (212) 963-0027, www.unctad.org; *Handbook of Statistics 2005.*

United Nations Economic and Social Commission for Western Asia (ESCWA), PO Box 11-8575, Riad el-Solh Square, Beirut, Lebanon, www.escwa.un.org; *Annual Report 2006* and *Statistical Abstract of the ESCWA Region 2007.*

The World Bank, 1818 H Street, NW, Washington, DC 20433, (202) 473-1000, Fax: (202) 477-6391, www.worldbank.org; *Jordan* and *World Development Report 2008.*

JORDAN - BANKS AND BANKING

Euromonitor International, Inc., 224 S. Michigan Avenue, Suite 1500, Chicago, IL 60604, (312) 922-1115, Fax: (312) 922-1157, www.euromonitor.com; *World Marketing Data and Statistics.*

International Monetary Fund (IMF), 700 Nineteenth Street, NW, Washington, DC 20431, (202) 623-7000, Fax: (202) 623-4661, www.imf.org; *Government Finance Statistics Yearbook (2008 Edition)* and *International Financial Statistics Yearbook 2007.*

M.E. Sharpe, 80 Business Park Drive, Armonk, NY 10504, (800) 541-6563, Fax: (914) 273-2106, www.mesharpe.com; *The Illustrated Book of World Rankings.*

Palgrave Macmillan Ltd., Houndmills, Basingstoke, Hampshire, RG21 6XS, England, (Telephone in U.S. (888) 330-8477), (Fax in U.S. (800) 672-2054), www.palgrave.com; *The Statesman's Yearbook 2008.*

Taylor and Francis Group, An Informa Business, 2 Park Square, Milton Park, Abingdon, Oxford OX14 4RN, United Kingdom, (Dial from U.S. (212) 216-7800), (Fax from U.S. (212) 564-7854), www.tandf.co.uk; *The Europa World Year Book.*

United Nations Economic and Social Commission for Western Asia (ESCWA), PO Box 11-8575, Riad el-Solh Square, Beirut, Lebanon, www.escwa.un.org; *Annual Report 2006* and *Statistical Abstract of the ESCWA Region 2007.*

United Nations Statistics Division, New York, NY 10017, (800) 253-9646, Fax: (212) 963-4116, http://unstats.un.org; *Statistical Yearbook.*

JORDAN - BARLEY PRODUCTION

See JORDAN - CROPS

JORDAN - BEVERAGE INDUSTRY

M.E. Sharpe, 80 Business Park Drive, Armonk, NY 10504, (800) 541-6563, Fax: (914) 273-2106, www.mesharpe.com; *The Illustrated Book of World Rankings.*

United Nations Statistics Division, New York, NY 10017, (800) 253-9646, Fax: (212) 963-4116, http://unstats.un.org; *Statistical Yearbook.*

JORDAN - BONDS

International Monetary Fund (IMF), 700 Nineteenth Street, NW, Washington, DC 20431, (202) 623-7000, Fax: (202) 623-4661, www.imf.org; *Government Finance Statistics Yearbook (2008 Edition).*

JORDAN - BROADCASTING

Central Intelligence Agency, Office of Public Affairs, Washington, DC 20505, (703) 482-0623, Fax: (703) 482-1739, www.cia.gov; *The World Factbook.*

Euromonitor International, Inc., 224 S. Michigan Avenue, Suite 1500, Chicago, IL 60604, (312) 922-1115, Fax: (312) 922-1157, www.euromonitor.com; *World Marketing Data and Statistics.*

M.E. Sharpe, 80 Business Park Drive, Armonk, NY 10504, (800) 541-6563, Fax: (914) 273-2106, www.mesharpe.com; *The Illustrated Book of World Rankings.*

Palgrave Macmillan Ltd., Houndmills, Basingstoke, Hampshire, RG21 6XS, England, (Telephone in U.S. (888) 330-8477), (Fax in U.S. (800) 672-2054), www.palgrave.com; *The Statesman's Yearbook 2008.*

WRTH Publications Limited, PO Box 290, Oxford OX2 7FT, UK, www.wrth.com; *World Radio TV Handbook 2007.*

JORDAN - BUDGET

Central Intelligence Agency, Office of Public Affairs, Washington, DC 20505, (703) 482-0623, Fax: (703) 482-1739, www.cia.gov; *The World Factbook.*

JORDAN - CAPITAL LEVY

International Monetary Fund (IMF), 700 Nineteenth Street, NW, Washington, DC 20431, (202) 623-7000, Fax: (202) 623-4661, www.imf.org; *Government Finance Statistics Yearbook (2008 Edition).*

JORDAN - CATTLE

See JORDAN - LIVESTOCK

JORDAN - CHICK PEA PRODUCTION

See JORDAN - CROPS

JORDAN - CHICKENS

See JORDAN - LIVESTOCK

JORDAN - CHILDBIRTH - STATISTICS

Central Intelligence Agency, Office of Public Affairs, Washington, DC 20505, (703) 482-0623, Fax: (703) 482-1739, www.cia.gov; *The World Factbook.*

Euromonitor International, Inc., 224 S. Michigan Avenue, Suite 1500, Chicago, IL 60604, (312) 922-1115, Fax: (312) 922-1157, www.euromonitor.com; *International Marketing Data and Statistics 2008* and *The World Economic Factbook 2008.*

M.E. Sharpe, 80 Business Park Drive, Armonk, NY 10504, (800) 541-6563, Fax: (914) 273-2106, www.mesharpe.com; *The Illustrated Book of World Rankings.*

Palgrave Macmillan Ltd., Houndmills, Basingstoke, Hampshire, RG21 6XS, England, (Telephone in U.S. (888) 330-8477), (Fax in U.S. (800) 672-2054), www.palgrave.com; *The Statesman's Yearbook 2008.*

Taylor and Francis Group, An Informa Business, 2 Park Square, Milton Park, Abingdon, Oxford OX14 4RN, United Kingdom, (Dial from U.S. (212) 216-7800), (Fax from U.S. (212) 564-7854), www.tandf.co.uk; *The Europa World Year Book.*

United Nations Statistics Division, New York, NY 10017, (800) 253-9646, Fax: (212) 963-4116, http://unstats.un.org; *Demographic Yearbook* and *Statistical Yearbook.*

World Health Organization (WHO), Avenue Appia 20, 1211 Geneve 27, Switzerland, (Telephone in U.S. (212) 331-9081), www.who.int; *World Health Report 2006.*

JORDAN - CLIMATE

M.E. Sharpe, 80 Business Park Drive, Armonk, NY 10504, (800) 541-6563, Fax: (914) 273-2106, www.mesharpe.com; *The Illustrated Book of World Rankings.*

Palgrave Macmillan Ltd., Houndmills, Basingstoke, Hampshire, RG21 6XS, England, (Telephone in U.S. (888) 330-8477), (Fax in U.S. (800) 672-2054), www.palgrave.com; *The Statesman's Yearbook 2008.*

JORDAN - COAL PRODUCTION

See JORDAN - MINERAL INDUSTRIES

JORDAN - COFFEE

See JORDAN - CROPS

JORDAN - COMMERCE

Palgrave Macmillan Ltd., Houndmills, Basingstoke, Hampshire, RG21 6XS, England, (Telephone in U.S. (888) 330-8477), (Fax in U.S. (800) 672-2054), www.palgrave.com; *The Statesman's Yearbook 2008.*

JORDAN - COMMODITY EXCHANGES

Commodity Research Bureau, 330 South Wells Street, Suite 612, Chicago, IL 60606-7110, (800) 621-5271, Fax: (312) 939-4135, www.crbtrader.com; *2006 CRB Commodity Yearbook and CD.*

International Monetary Fund (IMF), 700 Nineteenth Street, NW, Washington, DC 20431, (202) 623-7000, Fax: (202) 623-4661, www.imf.org; *IMF Primary Commodity Prices.*

United Nations Food and Agricultural Organization (FAO), Viale delle Terme di Caracalla, 00100 Rome, Italy, (Dial from U.S. (202) 653-2400), (Fax from U.S. (202) 653 5760), www.fao.org; *The State of Food and Agriculture (SOFA) 2006.*

JORDAN - CONSTRUCTION INDUSTRY

M.E. Sharpe, 80 Business Park Drive, Armonk, NY 10504, (800) 541-6563, Fax: (914) 273-2106, www.mesharpe.com; *The Illustrated Book of World Rankings.*

Palgrave Macmillan Ltd., Houndmills, Basingstoke, Hampshire, RG21 6XS, England, (Telephone in U.S. (888) 330-8477), (Fax in U.S. (800) 672-2054), www.palgrave.com; *The Statesman's Yearbook 2008.*

United Nations Statistics Division, New York, NY 10017, (800) 253-9646, Fax: (212) 963-4116, http://unstats.un.org; *Statistical Yearbook.*

JORDAN - CONSUMER PRICE INDEXES

Euromonitor International, Inc., 224 S. Michigan Avenue, Suite 1500, Chicago, IL 60604, (312) 922-1115, Fax: (312) 922-1157, www.euromonitor.com; *World Marketing Data and Statistics.*

Taylor and Francis Group, An Informa Business, 2 Park Square, Milton Park, Abingdon, Oxford OX14 4RN, United Kingdom, (Dial from U.S. (212) 216-7800), (Fax from U.S. (212) 564-7854), www.tandf.co.uk; *The Europa World Year Book.*

United Nations Statistics Division, New York, NY 10017, (800) 253-9646, Fax: (212) 963-4116, http://unstats.un.org; *Statistical Yearbook.*

JORDAN - CONSUMPTION (ECONOMICS)

The World Bank, 1818 H Street, NW, Washington, DC 20433, (202) 473-1000, Fax: (202) 477-6391, www.worldbank.org; *World Development Report 2008.*

JORDAN - COPPER INDUSTRY AND TRADE

See JORDAN - MINERAL INDUSTRIES

JORDAN - CORN INDUSTRY

See JORDAN - CROPS

JORDAN - COST AND STANDARD OF LIVING

International Monetary Fund (IMF), 700 Nineteenth Street, NW, Washington, DC 20431, (202) 623-7000, Fax: (202) 623-4661, www.imf.org; *Government Finance Statistics Yearbook (2008 Edition).*

JORDAN - COTTON

See JORDAN - CROPS

JORDAN - CRIME

International Criminal Police Organization (INTERPOL), General Secretariat, 200 quai Charles de Gaulle, 69006 Lyon, France, www.interpol.int; *International Crime Statistics.*

Yale University Press, PO Box 209040, New Haven, CT 06520-9040, (203) 432-0960, Fax: (203) 432-0948, http://yalepress.yale.edu/yupbooks; *Violence and Crime in Cross-National Perspective.*

JORDAN - CROPS

M.E. Sharpe, 80 Business Park Drive, Armonk, NY 10504, (800) 541-6563, Fax: (914) 273-2106, www.mesharpe.com; *The Illustrated Book of World Rankings.*

Palgrave Macmillan Ltd., Houndmills, Basingstoke, Hampshire, RG21 6XS, England, (Telephone in U.S. (888) 330-8477), (Fax in U.S. (800) 672-2054), www.palgrave.com; *The Statesman's Yearbook 2008.*

Taylor and Francis Group, An Informa Business, 2 Park Square, Milton Park, Abingdon, Oxford OX14 4RN, United Kingdom, (Dial from U.S. (212) 216-7800), (Fax from U.S. (212) 564-7854), www.tandf.co.uk; *The Europa World Year Book.*

United Nations Conference on Trade and Development (UNCTAD), DC2-1120, United Nations, New York, NY 10017, (212) 963-0027, www.unctad.org; *UNCTAD Commodity Yearbook.*

United Nations Food and Agricultural Organization (FAO), Viale delle Terme di Caracalla, 00100 Rome, Italy, (Dial from U.S. (202) 653-2400), (Fax from U.S. (202) 653 5760), www.fao.org; *FAO Production Yearbook 2002* and *The State of Food and Agriculture (SOFA) 2006.*

United Nations Statistics Division, New York, NY 10017, (800) 253-9646, Fax: (212) 963-4116, http://unstats.un.org; *Statistical Yearbook.*

JORDAN - CUSTOMS ADMINISTRATION

International Monetary Fund (IMF), 700 Nineteenth Street, NW, Washington, DC 20431, (202) 623-7000, Fax: (202) 623-4661, www.imf.org; *Government Finance Statistics Yearbook (2008 Edition).*

Palgrave Macmillan Ltd., Houndmills, Basingstoke, Hampshire, RG21 6XS, England, (Telephone in U.S. (888) 330-8477), (Fax in U.S. (800) 672-2054), www.palgrave.com; *The Statesman's Yearbook 2008.*

JORDAN - DAIRY PROCESSING

M.E. Sharpe, 80 Business Park Drive, Armonk, NY 10504, (800) 541-6563, Fax: (914) 273-2106, www.mesharpe.com; *The Illustrated Book of World Rankings.*

Palgrave Macmillan Ltd., Houndmills, Basingstoke, Hampshire, RG21 6XS, England, (Telephone in U.S. (888) 330-8477), (Fax in U.S. (800) 672-2054), www.palgrave.com; *The Statesman's Yearbook 2008.*

United Nations Economic and Social Commission for Western Asia (ESCWA), PO Box 11-8575, Riad el-Solh Square, Beirut, Lebanon, www.escwa.un.org; *Annual Report 2006* and *Statistical Abstract of the ESCWA Region 2007.*

United Nations Food and Agricultural Organization (FAO), Viale delle Terme di Caracalla, 00100 Rome, Italy, (Dial from U.S. (202) 653-2400), (Fax from U.S. (202) 653 5760), www.fao.org; *FAO Production Yearbook 2002* and *The State of Food and Agriculture (SOFA) 2006.*

United Nations Statistics Division, New York, NY 10017, (800) 253-9646, Fax: (212) 963-4116, http://unstats.un.org; *Statistical Yearbook.*

JORDAN - DEATH RATES

See JORDAN - MORTALITY

JORDAN - DEBTS, EXTERNAL

International Monetary Fund (IMF), 700 Nineteenth Street, NW, Washington, DC 20431, (202) 623-7000, Fax: (202) 623-4661, www.imf.org; *Government Finance Statistics Yearbook (2008 Edition).*

Palgrave Macmillan Ltd., Houndmills, Basingstoke, Hampshire, RG21 6XS, England, (Telephone in U.S. (888) 330-8477), (Fax in U.S. (800) 672-2054), www.palgrave.com; *The Statesman's Yearbook 2008.*

The World Bank, 1818 H Street, NW, Washington, DC 20433, (202) 473-1000, Fax: (202) 477-6391, www.worldbank.org; *Global Development Finance 2007* and *World Development Report 2008.*

JORDAN - DEFENSE EXPENDITURES

See JORDAN - ARMED FORCES

JORDAN - DEMOGRAPHY

Euromonitor International, Inc., 224 S. Michigan Avenue, Suite 1500, Chicago, IL 60604, (312) 922-1115, Fax: (312) 922-1157, www.euromonitor.com; *International Marketing Data and Statistics 2008; The World Economic Factbook 2008;* and *World Marketing Data and Statistics.*

M.E. Sharpe, 80 Business Park Drive, Armonk, NY 10504, (800) 541-6563, Fax: (914) 273-2106, www.mesharpe.com; *The Illustrated Book of World Rankings.*

United Nations Statistics Division, New York, NY 10017, (800) 253-9646, Fax: (212) 963-4116, http://unstats.un.org; *Human Development Report 2006.*

The World Bank, 1818 H Street, NW, Washington, DC 20433, (202) 473-1000, Fax: (202) 477-6391, www.worldbank.org; *Jordan.*

JORDAN - DIAMONDS

See JORDAN - MINERAL INDUSTRIES

JORDAN - DISPOSABLE INCOME

M.E. Sharpe, 80 Business Park Drive, Armonk, NY 10504, (800) 541-6563, Fax: (914) 273-2106, www.mesharpe.com; *The Illustrated Book of World Rankings.*

United Nations Statistics Division, New York, NY 10017, (800) 253-9646, Fax: (212) 963-4116, http://unstats.un.org; *National Accounts Statistics: Compendium of Income Distribution Statistics* and *Statistical Yearbook.*

JORDAN - DIVORCE

M.E. Sharpe, 80 Business Park Drive, Armonk, NY 10504, (800) 541-6563, Fax: (914) 273-2106, www.mesharpe.com; *The Illustrated Book of World Rankings.*

United Nations Statistics Division, New York, NY 10017, (800) 253-9646, Fax: (212) 963-4116, http://unstats.un.org; *Demographic Yearbook* and *Statistical Yearbook.*

JORDAN - ECONOMIC ASSISTANCE

United Nations Statistics Division, New York, NY 10017, (800) 253-9646, Fax: (212) 963-4116, http://unstats.un.org; *Statistical Yearbook.*

JORDAN - ECONOMIC CONDITIONS

Center for International Business Education Research (CIBER), Columbia Business School and School of International and Public Affairs, Uris Hall, Room 212, 3022 Broadway, New York, NY 10027-6902, Mr. Joshua Safier, (212) 854-4750, Fax: (212) 222-9821, www.columbia.edu/cu/ciber/; Datastream International.

Central Intelligence Agency, Office of Public Affairs, Washington, DC 20505, (703) 482-0623, Fax: (703) 482-1739, www.cia.gov; *The World Factbook.*

Department of Statistics (DOS), PO Box 2015, Amman 11181, Jordan, www.dos.gov.jo; Economic Surveys and *Household Income and Expenditure Survey.*

DSI Data Service Information, Xantener Strasse 51a, D-47495 Rheinberg, Germany, www.dsidata.com; *Campus Solution.*

Dun and Bradstreet (DB) Corporation, 103 JFK Parkway, Short Hills, NJ 07078, (973) 921-5500, www.dnb.com; *Country Report.*

Economist Intelligence Unit, 111 West 57th Street, New York, NY 10019, (212) 554-0600, Fax: (212) 586-1181, www.eiu.com; *Jordan Country Report.*

Euromonitor International, Inc., 224 S. Michigan Avenue, Suite 1500, Chicago, IL 60604, (312) 922-1115, Fax: (312) 922-1157, www.euromonitor.com; *International Marketing Data and Statistics 2008; The World Economic Factbook 2008;* and *World Marketing Data and Statistics.*

International Monetary Fund (IMF), 700 Nineteenth Street, NW, Washington, DC 20431, (202) 623-7000, Fax: (202) 623-4661, www.imf.org; *World Economic Outlook Reports.*

M.E. Sharpe, 80 Business Park Drive, Armonk, NY 10504, (800) 541-6563, Fax: (914) 273-2106, www.mesharpe.com; *The Illustrated Book of World Rankings.*

Palgrave Macmillan Ltd., Houndmills, Basingstoke, Hampshire, RG21 6XS, England, (Telephone in U.S. (888) 330-8477), (Fax in U.S. (800) 672-2054), www.palgrave.com; *The Statesman's Yearbook 2008.*

Taylor and Francis Group, An Informa Business, 2 Park Square, Milton Park, Abingdon, Oxford OX14 4RN, United Kingdom, (Dial from U.S. (212) 216-7800), (Fax from U.S. (212) 564-7854), www.tandf.co.uk; *The Europa World Year Book.*

United Nations Economic and Social Commission for Western Asia (ESCWA), PO Box 11-8575, Riad el-Solh Square, Beirut, Lebanon, www.escwa.un.org; *Annual Report 2006; Bulletin on Population and Vital Statistics in the ESCWA Region;* and *Survey of Economic and Social Developments in the ESCWA Region 2006-2007.*

United Nations Statistics Division, New York, NY 10017, (800) 253-9646, Fax: (212) 963-4116, http://unstats.un.org; *World Statistics Pocketbook.*

The World Bank, 1818 H Street, NW, Washington, DC 20433, (202) 473-1000, Fax: (202) 477-6391, www.worldbank.org; *Global Economic Monitor (GEM); Global Economic Prospects 2008; Jordan; The World Bank Atlas 2003-2004;* and *World Development Report 2008.*

JORDAN - EDUCATION

Euromonitor International, Inc., 224 S. Michigan Avenue, Suite 1500, Chicago, IL 60604, (312) 922-1115, Fax: (312) 922-1157, www.euromonitor.com; *International Marketing Data and Statistics 2008* and *World Marketing Data and Statistics.*

M.E. Sharpe, 80 Business Park Drive, Armonk, NY 10504, (800) 541-6563, Fax: (914) 273-2106, www.mesharpe.com; *The Illustrated Book of World Rankings.*

Palgrave Macmillan Ltd., Houndmills, Basingstoke, Hampshire, RG21 6XS, England, (Telephone in U.S. (888) 330-8477), (Fax in U.S. (800) 672-2054), www.palgrave.com; *The Statesman's Yearbook 2008.*

Taylor and Francis Group, An Informa Business, 2 Park Square, Milton Park, Abingdon, Oxford OX14 4RN, United Kingdom, (Dial from U.S. (212) 216-7800), (Fax from U.S. (212) 564-7854), www.tandf.co.uk; *The Europa World Year Book.*

UNESCO Institute for Statistics, C.P. 6128 Succursale Centre-Ville, Montreal, Quebec, H3C 3J7 Canada, (Dial from U.S. (514) 343-6880), (Fax from U.S. (514) 343 6882), www.uis.unesco.org; *Statistical Tables.*

United Nations Economic and Social Commission for Western Asia (ESCWA), PO Box 11-8575, Riad el-Solh Square, Beirut, Lebanon, www.escwa.un.org; *Annual Report 2006* and *Statistical Abstract of the ESCWA Region 2007.*

United Nations Statistics Division, New York, NY 10017, (800) 253-9646, Fax: (212) 963-4116, http://unstats.un.org; *Human Development Report 2006.*

The World Bank, 1818 H Street, NW, Washington, DC 20433, (202) 473-1000, Fax: (202) 477-6391, www.worldbank.org; *Jordan* and *World Development Report 2008.*

JORDAN - EGGPLANT PRODUCTION

See JORDAN - CROPS

JORDAN - ELECTRICITY

M.E. Sharpe, 80 Business Park Drive, Armonk, NY 10504, (800) 541-6563, Fax: (914) 273-2106, www.mesharpe.com; *The Illustrated Book of World Rankings.*

Organisation for Economic Cooperation and Development (OECD), 2 rue Andre Pascal, F-75775 Paris Cedex 16, France, (Telephone in U.S. (202) 785-6323), (Fax in U.S. (202) 785-0350), www.oecd.org; *World Energy Outlook 2007.*

Palgrave Macmillan Ltd., Houndmills, Basingstoke, Hampshire, RG21 6XS, England, (Telephone in U.S. (888) 330-8477), (Fax in U.S. (800) 672-2054), www.palgrave.com; *The Statesman's Yearbook 2008.*

U.S. Department of Energy (DOE), Energy Information Administration (EIA), 1000 Independence Avenue, SW, Washington, DC 20585, (202) 586-8800, www.eia.doe.gov; *International Energy Annual 2004* and *International Energy Outlook 2006.*

United Nations Statistics Division, New York, NY 10017, (800) 253-9646, Fax: (212) 963-4116, http://unstats.un.org; *Human Development Report 2006* and *Statistical Yearbook.*

JORDAN - EMPLOYMENT

Department of Statistics (DOS), PO Box 2015, Amman 11181, Jordan, www.dos.gov.jo; *Employment Survey 2005.*

Euromonitor International, Inc., 224 S. Michigan Avenue, Suite 1500, Chicago, IL 60604, (312) 922-1115, Fax: (312) 922-1157, www.euromonitor.com; *International Marketing Data and Statistics 2008.*

International Labour Office, I.L.O. Publications, 4 route des Morillons, CH-1211 Geneva 22, Switzerland, (Telephone in U.S. (202) 653-7652), (Fax in U.S. (202) 653-7687), www.ilo.org; *Yearbook of Labour Statistics 2006.*

M.E. Sharpe, 80 Business Park Drive, Armonk, NY 10504, (800) 541-6563, Fax: (914) 273-2106, www.mesharpe.com; *The Illustrated Book of World Rankings.*

United Nations Economic and Social Commission for Western Asia (ESCWA), PO Box 11-8575, Riad el-Solh Square, Beirut, Lebanon, www.escwa.un.org; *Annual Report 2006* and *Statistical Abstract of the ESCWA Region 2007.*

United Nations Statistics Division, New York, NY 10017, (800) 253-9646, Fax: (212) 963-4116, http://unstats.un.org; *Bulletin of Industrial Statistics for the Arab Countries* and *Statistical Yearbook.*

The World Bank, 1818 H Street, NW, Washington, DC 20433, (202) 473-1000, Fax: (202) 477-6391, www.worldbank.org; *Jordan.*

JORDAN - ENERGY INDUSTRIES

Enerdata, 10 Rue Royale, 75008 Paris, France, www.enerdata.fr; *Global Energy Market Data.*

United Nations Statistics Division, New York, NY 10017, (800) 253-9646, Fax: (212) 963-4116, http://unstats.un.org; *Statistical Yearbook.*

JORDAN - ENVIRONMENTAL CONDITIONS

Department of Statistics (DOS), PO Box 2015, Amman 11181, Jordan, www.dos.gov.jo; *Annual Environmental Statistic 2006.*

DSI Data Service Information, Xantener Strasse 51a, D-47495 Rheinberg, Germany, www.dsidata.com; *Campus Solution* and *DSI's Global Environmental Database.*

Economist Intelligence Unit, 111 West 57th Street, New York, NY 10019, (212) 554-0600, Fax: (212) 586-1181, www.eiu.com; *Jordan Country Report.*

United Nations Statistics Division, New York, NY 10017, (800) 253-9646, Fax: (212) 963-4116, http://unstats.un.org; *World Statistics Pocketbook.*

JORDAN - EXPORTS

Central Intelligence Agency, Office of Public Affairs, Washington, DC 20505, (703) 482-0623, Fax: (703) 482-1739, www.cia.gov; *The World Factbook.*

Economist Intelligence Unit, 111 West 57th Street, New York, NY 10019, (212) 554-0600, Fax: (212) 586-1181, www.eiu.com; *Jordan Country Report.*

Euromonitor International, Inc., 224 S. Michigan Avenue, Suite 1500, Chicago, IL 60604, (312) 922-1115, Fax: (312) 922-1157, www.euromonitor.com; *International Marketing Data and Statistics 2008* and *The World Economic Factbook 2008.*

International Monetary Fund (IMF), 700 Nineteenth Street, NW, Washington, DC 20431, (202) 623-7000, Fax: (202) 623-4661, www.imf.org; *Direction of Trade Statistics Yearbook 2007; Government Finance Statistics Yearbook (2008 Edition);* and *International Financial Statistics Yearbook 2007.*

Palgrave Macmillan Ltd., Houndmills, Basingstoke, Hampshire, RG21 6XS, England, (Telephone in U.S. (888) 330-8477), (Fax in U.S. (800) 672-2054), www.palgrave.com; *The Statesman's Yearbook 2008.*

Taylor and Francis Group, An Informa Business, 2 Park Square, Milton Park, Abingdon, Oxford OX14 4RN, United Kingdom, (Dial from U.S. (212) 216-7800), (Fax from U.S. (212) 564-7854), www.tandf.co.uk; *The Europa World Year Book.*

United Nations Conference on Trade and Development (UNCTAD), DC2-1120, United Nations, New York, NY 10017, (212) 963-0027, www.unctad.org; *Handbook of Statistics 2005.*

United Nations Economic and Social Commission for Western Asia (ESCWA), PO Box 11-8575, Riad el-Solh Square, Beirut, Lebanon, www.escwa.un.org; *Annual Report 2006* and *Statistical Abstract of the ESCWA Region 2007.*

United Nations Food and Agricultural Organization (FAO), Viale delle Terme di Caracalla, 00100 Rome, Italy, (Dial from U.S. (202) 653-2400), (Fax from U.S. (202) 653 5760), www.fao.org; *The State of Food and Agriculture (SOFA) 2006.*

United Nations Statistics Division, New York, NY 10017, (800) 253-9646, Fax: (212) 963-4116, http://unstats.un.org; *Bulletin of Industrial Statistics for the Arab Countries.*

The World Bank, 1818 H Street, NW, Washington, DC 20433, (202) 473-1000, Fax: (202) 477-6391, www.worldbank.org; *World Development Report 2008.*

JORDAN - FEMALE WORKING POPULATION

See JORDAN - EMPLOYMENT

JORDAN - FERTILITY, HUMAN

Central Intelligence Agency, Office of Public Affairs, Washington, DC 20505, (703) 482-0623, Fax: (703) 482-1739, www.cia.gov; *The World Factbook.*

M.E. Sharpe, 80 Business Park Drive, Armonk, NY 10504, (800) 541-6563, Fax: (914) 273-2106, www.mesharpe.com; *The Illustrated Book of World Rankings.*

United Nations Statistics Division, New York, NY 10017, (800) 253-9646, Fax: (212) 963-4116, http://unstats.un.org; *Human Development Report 2006.*

The World Bank, 1818 H Street, NW, Washington, DC 20433, (202) 473-1000, Fax: (202) 477-6391, www.worldbank.org; *The World Bank Atlas 2003-2004* and *World Development Report 2008.*

JORDAN - FERTILIZER INDUSTRY

United Nations Food and Agricultural Organization (FAO), Viale delle Terme di Caracalla, 00100 Rome, Italy, (Dial from U.S. (202) 653-2400), (Fax from U.S. (202) 653 5760), www.fao.org; *FAO Fertilizer Yearbook* and *The State of Food and Agriculture (SOFA) 2006.*

United Nations Statistics Division, New York, NY 10017, (800) 253-9646, Fax: (212) 963-4116, http://unstats.un.org; *Statistical Yearbook.*

JORDAN - FETAL MORTALITY

See JORDAN - MORTALITY

JORDAN - FINANCE

International Monetary Fund (IMF), 700 Nineteenth Street, NW, Washington, DC 20431, (202) 623-7000, Fax: (202) 623-4661, www.imf.org; *International Financial Statistics Yearbook 2007.*

Taylor and Francis Group, An Informa Business, 2 Park Square, Milton Park, Abingdon, Oxford OX14 4RN, United Kingdom, (Dial from U.S. (212) 216-7800), (Fax from U.S. (212) 564-7854), www.tandf.co.uk; *The Europa World Year Book.*

United Nations Economic and Social Commission for Western Asia (ESCWA), PO Box 11-8575, Riad el-Solh Square, Beirut, Lebanon, www.escwa.un.org; *Annual Report 2006* and *Statistical Abstract of the ESCWA Region 2007.*

United Nations Statistics Division, New York, NY 10017, (800) 253-9646, Fax: (212) 963-4116, http://unstats.un.org; *National Accounts Statistics: Compendium of Income Distribution Statistics* and *Statistical Yearbook.*

The World Bank, 1818 H Street, NW, Washington, DC 20433, (202) 473-1000, Fax: (202) 477-6391, www.worldbank.org; *Jordan.*

JORDAN - FINANCE, PUBLIC

Bernan Essential Government Publications, 4611-F Assembly Drive, Lanham MD, 20706-4391, (301) 459-2255, Fax: (800) 865-3450, www.bernan.com; *National Accounts Statistics.*

Economist Intelligence Unit, 111 West 57th Street, New York, NY 10019, (212) 554-0600, Fax: (212) 586-1181, www.eiu.com; *Jordan Country Report.*

International Monetary Fund (IMF), 700 Nineteenth Street, NW, Washington, DC 20431, (202) 623-7000, Fax: (202) 623-4661, www.imf.org; *Government Finance Statistics Yearbook (2008 Edition); International Financial Statistics; International Financial Statistics Online Service;* and *International Financial Statistics Yearbook 2007.*

M.E. Sharpe, 80 Business Park Drive, Armonk, NY 10504, (800) 541-6563, Fax: (914) 273-2106, www.mesharpe.com; *The Illustrated Book of World Rankings.*

Palgrave Macmillan Ltd., Houndmills, Basingstoke, Hampshire, RG21 6XS, England, (Telephone in U.S. (888) 330-8477), (Fax in U.S. (800) 672-2054), www.palgrave.com; *The Statesman's Yearbook 2008.*

Taylor and Francis Group, An Informa Business, 2 Park Square, Milton Park, Abingdon, Oxford OX14 4RN, United Kingdom, (Dial from U.S. (212) 216-7800), (Fax from U.S. (212) 564-7854), www.tandf.co.uk; *The Europa World Year Book.*

United Nations Economic and Social Commission for Western Asia (ESCWA), PO Box 11-8575, Riad el-Solh Square, Beirut, Lebanon, www.escwa.un.org; *Annual Report 2006* and *Statistical Abstract of the ESCWA Region 2007.*

The World Bank, 1818 H Street, NW, Washington, DC 20433, (202) 473-1000, Fax: (202) 477-6391, www.worldbank.org; *Jordan.*

JORDAN - FISHERIES

M.E. Sharpe, 80 Business Park Drive, Armonk, NY 10504, (800) 541-6563, Fax: (914) 273-2106, www.mesharpe.com; *The Illustrated Book of World Rankings.*

United Nations Conference on Trade and Development (UNCTAD), DC2-1120, United Nations, New York, NY 10017, (212) 963-0027, www.unctad.org; *UNCTAD Commodity Yearbook.*

United Nations Economic and Social Commission for Western Asia (ESCWA), PO Box 11-8575, Riad el-Solh Square, Beirut, Lebanon, www.escwa.un.org; *Annual Report 2006* and *Statistical Abstract of the ESCWA Region 2007.*

United Nations Food and Agricultural Organization (FAO), Viale delle Terme di Caracalla, 00100 Rome,

Italy, (Dial from U.S. (202) 653-2400), (Fax from U.S. (202) 653 5760), www.fao.org; *FAO Yearbook of Fishery Statistics;* Fishery Databases; FISHSTAT Database. Subjects covered include: Aquaculture production, capture production, fishery commodities; and *The State of Food and Agriculture (SOFA) 2006.*

The World Bank, 1818 H Street, NW, Washington, DC 20433, (202) 473-1000, Fax: (202) 477-6391, www.worldbank.org; *Jordan.*

JORDAN - FLOUR INDUSTRY

United Nations Statistics Division, New York, NY 10017, (800) 253-9646, Fax: (212) 963-4116, http://unstats.un.org; *Statistical Yearbook.*

JORDAN - FOOD

United Nations Conference on Trade and Development (UNCTAD), DC2-1120, United Nations, New York, NY 10017, (212) 963-0027, www.unctad.org; *UNCTAD Commodity Yearbook.*

United Nations Food and Agricultural Organization (FAO), Viale delle Terme di Caracalla, 00100 Rome, Italy, (Dial from U.S. (202) 653-2400), (Fax from U.S. (202) 653 5760), www.fao.org; *FAO Production Yearbook 2002* and *The State of Food and Agriculture (SOFA) 2006.*

United Nations Statistics Division, New York, NY 10017, (800) 253-9646, Fax: (212) 963-4116, http://unstats.un.org; *Human Development Report 2006.*

JORDAN - FOREIGN EXCHANGE RATES

Central Intelligence Agency, Office of Public Affairs, Washington, DC 20505, (703) 482-0623, Fax: (703) 482-1739, www.cia.gov; *The World Factbook.*

Euromonitor International, Inc., 224 S. Michigan Avenue, Suite 1500, Chicago, IL 60604, (312) 922-1115, Fax: (312) 922-1157, www.euromonitor.com; *International Marketing Data and Statistics 2008* and *The World Economic Factbook 2008.*

International Civil Aviation Organization (ICAO), External Relations and Public Information Office (EPO), 999 University Street, Montreal, Quebec H3C 5H7, Canada, (Dial from U.S. (514) 954-8219), (Fax from U.S. (514) 954-6077), www.icao.int; *Civil Aviation Statistics of the World.*

International Monetary Fund (IMF), 700 Nineteenth Street, NW, Washington, DC 20431, (202) 623-7000, Fax: (202) 623-4661, www.imf.org; *International Financial Statistics Yearbook 2007.*

Taylor and Francis Group, An Informa Business, 2 Park Square, Milton Park, Abingdon, Oxford OX14 4RN, United Kingdom, (Dial from U.S. (212) 216-7800), (Fax from U.S. (212) 564-7854), www.tandf.co.uk; *The Europa World Year Book.*

United Nations Statistics Division, New York, NY 10017, (800) 253-9646, Fax: (212) 963-4116, http://unstats.un.org; *Bulletin of Industrial Statistics for the Arab Countries; Statistical Yearbook;* and *World Statistics Pocketbook.*

JORDAN - FORESTS AND FORESTRY

M.E. Sharpe, 80 Business Park Drive, Armonk, NY 10504, (800) 541-6563, Fax: (914) 273-2106, www.mesharpe.com; *The Illustrated Book of World Rankings.*

Palgrave Macmillan Ltd., Houndmills, Basingstoke, Hampshire, RG21 6XS, England, (Telephone in U.S. (888) 330-8477), (Fax in U.S. (800) 672-2054), www.palgrave.com; *The Statesman's Yearbook 2008.*

Taylor and Francis Group, An Informa Business, 2 Park Square, Milton Park, Abingdon, Oxford OX14 4RN, United Kingdom, (Dial from U.S. (212) 216-7800), (Fax from U.S. (212) 564-7854), www.tandf.co.uk; *The Europa World Year Book.*

UNESCO Institute for Statistics, C.P. 6128 Succursale Centre-Ville, Montreal, Quebec, H3C 3J7 Canada, (Dial from U.S. (514) 343-6880), (Fax from U.S. (514) 343 6882), www.uis.unesco.org; *Statistical Tables.*

United Nations Conference on Trade and Development (UNCTAD), DC2-1120, United Nations, New York, NY 10017, (212) 963-0027, www.unctad.org; *UNCTAD Commodity Yearbook.*

United Nations Food and Agricultural Organization (FAO), Viale delle Terme di Caracalla, 00100 Rome, Italy, (Dial from U.S. (202) 653-2400), (Fax from U.S. (202) 653 5760), www.fao.org; *FAO Yearbook of Forest Products* and *The State of Food and Agriculture (SOFA) 2006.*

United Nations Statistics Division, New York, NY 10017, (800) 253-9646, Fax: (212) 963-4116, http://unstats.un.org; *Statistical Yearbook.*

The World Bank, 1818 H Street, NW, Washington, DC 20433, (202) 473-1000, Fax: (202) 477-6391, www.worldbank.org; *Jordan* and *World Development Report 2008.*

JORDAN - GAS PRODUCTION

See JORDAN - MINERAL INDUSTRIES

JORDAN - GEOGRAPHIC INFORMATION SYSTEMS

M.E. Sharpe, 80 Business Park Drive, Armonk, NY 10504, (800) 541-6563, Fax: (914) 273-2106, www.mesharpe.com; *The Illustrated Book of World Rankings.*

JORDAN - GOLD INDUSTRY

International Monetary Fund (IMF), 700 Nineteenth Street, NW, Washington, DC 20431, (202) 623-7000, Fax: (202) 623-4661, www.imf.org; *International Financial Statistics Yearbook 2007.*

United Nations Statistics Division, New York, NY 10017, (800) 253-9646, Fax: (212) 963-4116, http://unstats.un.org; *Statistical Yearbook.*

JORDAN - GOLD PRODUCTION

See JORDAN - MINERAL INDUSTRIES

JORDAN - GRANTS-IN-AID

International Monetary Fund (IMF), 700 Nineteenth Street, NW, Washington, DC 20431, (202) 623-7000, Fax: (202) 623-4661, www.imf.org; *Government Finance Statistics Yearbook (2008 Edition).*

JORDAN - GREEN PEPPER AND CHILIE PRODUCTION

See JORDAN - CROPS

JORDAN - GROSS DOMESTIC PRODUCT

Economist Intelligence Unit, 111 West 57th Street, New York, NY 10019, (212) 554-0600, Fax: (212) 586-1181, www.eiu.com; *Jordan Country Report.*

Euromonitor International, Inc., 224 S. Michigan Avenue, Suite 1500, Chicago, IL 60604, (312) 922-1115, Fax: (312) 922-1157, www.euromonitor.com; *International Marketing Data and Statistics 2008* and *The World Economic Factbook 2008.*

M.E. Sharpe, 80 Business Park Drive, Armonk, NY 10504, (800) 541-6563, Fax: (914) 273-2106, www.mesharpe.com; *The Illustrated Book of World Rankings.*

Taylor and Francis Group, An Informa Business, 2 Park Square, Milton Park, Abingdon, Oxford OX14 4RN, United Kingdom, (Dial from U.S. (212) 216-7800), (Fax from U.S. (212) 564-7854), www.tandf.co.uk; *The Europa World Year Book.*

United Nations Economic and Social Commission for Western Asia (ESCWA), PO Box 11-8575, Riad el-Solh Square, Beirut, Lebanon, www.escwa.un.org; *Annual Report 2006* and *Statistical Abstract of the ESCWA Region 2007.*

United Nations Statistics Division, New York, NY 10017, (800) 253-9646, Fax: (212) 963-4116, http://unstats.un.org; *Bulletin of Industrial Statistics for the Arab Countries; Human Development Report 2006; National Accounts Statistics: Compendium of Income Distribution Statistics;* and *Statistical Yearbook.*

The World Bank, 1818 H Street, NW, Washington, DC 20433, (202) 473-1000, Fax: (202) 477-6391, www.worldbank.org; *World Development Report 2008.*

JORDAN - GROSS NATIONAL PRODUCT

Euromonitor International, Inc., 224 S. Michigan Avenue, Suite 1500, Chicago, IL 60604, (312) 922-1115, Fax: (312) 922-1157, www.euromonitor.com; *International Marketing Data and Statistics 2008.*

M.E. Sharpe, 80 Business Park Drive, Armonk, NY 10504, (800) 541-6563, Fax: (914) 273-2106, www.mesharpe.com; *The Illustrated Book of World Rankings.*

Palgrave Macmillan Ltd., Houndmills, Basingstoke, Hampshire, RG21 6XS, England, (Telephone in U.S. (888) 330-8477), (Fax in U.S. (800) 672-2054), www.palgrave.com; *The Statesman's Yearbook 2008.*

U.S. Department of State (DOS), 2201 C Street NW, Washington, DC 20520, (202) 647-4000, www.state.gov; *World Military Expenditures and Arms Transfers (WMEAT).*

The World Bank, 1818 H Street, NW, Washington, DC 20433, (202) 473-1000, Fax: (202) 477-6391, www.worldbank.org; *The World Bank Atlas 2003-2004* and *World Development Report 2008.*

JORDAN - HIDES AND SKINS INDUSTRY

United Nations Food and Agricultural Organization (FAO), Viale delle Terme di Caracalla, 00100 Rome, Italy, (Dial from U.S. (202) 653-2400), (Fax from U.S. (202) 653 5760), www.fao.org; *FAO Production Yearbook 2002.*

JORDAN - HOUSING

Euromonitor International, Inc., 224 S. Michigan Avenue, Suite 1500, Chicago, IL 60604, (312) 922-1115, Fax: (312) 922-1157, www.euromonitor.com; *World Marketing Data and Statistics.*

M.E. Sharpe, 80 Business Park Drive, Armonk, NY 10504, (800) 541-6563, Fax: (914) 273-2106, www.mesharpe.com; *The Illustrated Book of World Rankings.*

JORDAN - ILLITERATE PERSONS

Euromonitor International, Inc., 224 S. Michigan Avenue, Suite 1500, Chicago, IL 60604, (312) 922-1115, Fax: (312) 922-1157, www.euromonitor.com; *The World Economic Factbook 2008.*

UNESCO Institute for Statistics, C.P. 6128 Succursale Centre-Ville, Montreal, Quebec, H3C 3J7 Canada, (Dial from U.S. (514) 343-6880), (Fax from U.S. (514) 343 6882), www.uis.unesco.org; *Statistical Tables.*

United Nations Statistics Division, New York, NY 10017, (800) 253-9646, Fax: (212) 963-4116, http://unstats.un.org; *Human Development Report 2006.*

JORDAN - IMPORTS

Central Intelligence Agency, Office of Public Affairs, Washington, DC 20505, (703) 482-0623, Fax: (703) 482-1739, www.cia.gov; *The World Factbook.*

Economist Intelligence Unit, 111 West 57th Street, New York, NY 10019, (212) 554-0600, Fax: (212) 586-1181, www.eiu.com; *Jordan Country Report.*

Euromonitor International, Inc., 224 S. Michigan Avenue, Suite 1500, Chicago, IL 60604, (312) 922-1115, Fax: (312) 922-1157, www.euromonitor.com; *International Marketing Data and Statistics 2008* and *The World Economic Factbook 2008.*

International Monetary Fund (IMF), 700 Nineteenth Street, NW, Washington, DC 20431, (202) 623-7000, Fax: (202) 623-4661, www.imf.org; *Direction of Trade Statistics Yearbook 2007; Government Finance Statistics Yearbook (2008 Edition);* and *International Financial Statistics Yearbook 2007.*

Palgrave Macmillan Ltd., Houndmills, Basingstoke, Hampshire, RG21 6XS, England, (Telephone in U.S. (888) 330-8477), (Fax in U.S. (800) 672-2054), www.palgrave.com; *The Statesman's Yearbook 2008.*

Taylor and Francis Group, An Informa Business, 2 Park Square, Milton Park, Abingdon, Oxford OX14 4RN, United Kingdom, (Dial from U.S. (212) 216-7800), (Fax from U.S. (212) 564-7854), www.tandf.co.uk; *The Europa World Year Book.*

United Nations Conference on Trade and Development (UNCTAD), DC2-1120, United Nations, New York, NY 10017, (212) 963-0027, www.unctad.org; *Handbook of Statistics 2005.*

United Nations Economic and Social Commission for Western Asia (ESCWA), PO Box 11-8575, Riad el-Solh Square, Beirut, Lebanon, www.escwa.un.org; *Annual Report 2006* and *Statistical Abstract of the ESCWA Region 2007.*

United Nations Food and Agricultural Organization (FAO), Viale delle Terme di Caracalla, 00100 Rome, Italy, (Dial from U.S. (202) 653-2400), (Fax from U.S. (202) 653 5760), www.fao.org; *The State of Food and Agriculture (SOFA) 2006.*

United Nations Statistics Division, New York, NY 10017, (800) 253-9646, Fax: (212) 963-4116, http://unstats.un.org; *Bulletin of Industrial Statistics for the Arab Countries.*

The World Bank, 1818 H Street, NW, Washington, DC 20433, (202) 473-1000, Fax: (202) 477-6391, www.worldbank.org; *World Development Report 2008.*

JORDAN - INCOME TAXES

See JORDAN - TAXATION

JORDAN - INDUSTRIAL PRODUCTIVITY

Euromonitor International, Inc., 224 S. Michigan Avenue, Suite 1500, Chicago, IL 60604, (312) 922-1115, Fax: (312) 922-1157, www.euromonitor.com; *International Marketing Data and Statistics 2008.*

M.E. Sharpe, 80 Business Park Drive, Armonk, NY 10504, (800) 541-6563, Fax: (914) 273-2106, www.mesharpe.com; *The Illustrated Book of World Rankings.*

JORDAN - INDUSTRIAL PROPERTY

United Nations Statistics Division, New York, NY 10017, (800) 253-9646, Fax: (212) 963-4116, http://unstats.un.org; *Statistical Yearbook.*

JORDAN - INDUSTRIES

Central Intelligence Agency, Office of Public Affairs, Washington, DC 20505, (703) 482-0623, Fax: (703) 482-1739, www.cia.gov; *The World Factbook.*

Economist Intelligence Unit, 111 West 57th Street, New York, NY 10019, (212) 554-0600, Fax: (212) 586-1181, www.eiu.com; *Jordan Country Report.*

Euromonitor International, Inc., 224 S. Michigan Avenue, Suite 1500, Chicago, IL 60604, (312) 922-1115, Fax: (312) 922-1157, www.euromonitor.com; *International Marketing Data and Statistics 2008; The World Economic Factbook 2008;* and *World Marketing Data and Statistics.*

International Labour Office, I.L.O. Publications, 4 route des Morillons, CH-1211 Geneva 22, Switzerland, (Telephone in U.S. (202) 653-7652), (Fax in U.S. (202) 653-7687), www.ilo.org; *Yearbook of Labour Statistics 2006.*

M.E. Sharpe, 80 Business Park Drive, Armonk, NY 10504, (800) 541-6563, Fax: (914) 273-2106, www.mesharpe.com; *The Illustrated Book of World Rankings.*

Palgrave Macmillan Ltd., Houndmills, Basingstoke, Hampshire, RG21 6XS, England, (Telephone in U.S. (888) 330-8477), (Fax in U.S. (800) 672-2054), www.palgrave.com; *The Statesman's Yearbook 2008.*

Taylor and Francis Group, An Informa Business, 2 Park Square, Milton Park, Abingdon, Oxford OX14 4RN, United Kingdom, (Dial from U.S. (212) 216-7800), (Fax from U.S. (212) 564-7854), www.tandf.co.uk; *The Europa World Year Book.*

United Nations Industrial Development Organization (UNIDO), 1 United Nations Plaza, New York, NY 10017, (212) 963 6890, Fax: (212) 963-7904, http://unido.org; Industrial Statistics Database 2008 (INDSTAT) and *The International Yearbook of Industrial Statistics 2008.*

United Nations Statistics Division, New York, NY 10017, (800) 253-9646, Fax: (212) 963-4116, http://unstats.un.org; *Bulletin of Industrial Statistics for the Arab Countries* and *2004 Industrial Commodity Statistics Yearbook.*

The World Bank, 1818 H Street, NW, Washington, DC 20433, (202) 473-1000, Fax: (202) 477-6391, www.worldbank.org; *Jordan.*

JORDAN - INFANT AND MATERNAL MORTALITY

See JORDAN - MORTALITY

JORDAN - INTERNATIONAL LIQUIDITY

International Monetary Fund (IMF), 700 Nineteenth Street, NW, Washington, DC 20431, (202) 623-7000, Fax: (202) 623-4661, www.imf.org; *International Financial Statistics Yearbook 2007.*

JORDAN - INTERNATIONAL TRADE

Department of Statistics (DOS), PO Box 2015, Amman 11181, Jordan, www.dos.gov.jo; *External Trade Statistics 2006.*

Economist Intelligence Unit, 111 West 57th Street, New York, NY 10019, (212) 554-0600, Fax: (212) 586-1181, www.eiu.com; *Jordan Country Report.*

Euromonitor International, Inc., 224 S. Michigan Avenue, Suite 1500, Chicago, IL 60604, (312) 922-1115, Fax: (312) 922-1157, www.euromonitor.com; *International Marketing Data and Statistics 2008; The World Economic Factbook 2008;* and *World Marketing Data and Statistics.*

International Monetary Fund (IMF), 700 Nineteenth Street, NW, Washington, DC 20431, (202) 623-7000, Fax: (202) 623-4661, www.imf.org; *International Financial Statistics Yearbook 2007.*

M.E. Sharpe, 80 Business Park Drive, Armonk, NY 10504, (800) 541-6563, Fax: (914) 273-2106, www.mesharpe.com; *The Illustrated Book of World Rankings.*

Palgrave Macmillan Ltd., Houndmills, Basingstoke, Hampshire, RG21 6XS, England, (Telephone in U.S. (888) 330-8477), (Fax in U.S. (800) 672-2054), www.palgrave.com; *The Statesman's Yearbook 2008.*

Taylor and Francis Group, An Informa Business, 2 Park Square, Milton Park, Abingdon, Oxford OX14 4RN, United Kingdom, (Dial from U.S. (212) 216-7800), (Fax from U.S. (212) 564-7854), www.tandf.co.uk; *The Europa World Year Book.*

United Nations Conference on Trade and Development (UNCTAD), DC2-1120, United Nations, New York, NY 10017, (212) 963-0027, www.unctad.org; *UNCTAD Commodity Yearbook.*

United Nations Economic and Social Commission for Western Asia (ESCWA), PO Box 11-8575, Riad el-Solh Square, Beirut, Lebanon, www.escwa.un.org; *Annual Report 2006* and *Statistical Abstract of the ESCWA Region 2007.*

United Nations Food and Agricultural Organization (FAO), Viale delle Terme di Caracalla, 00100 Rome, Italy, (Dial from U.S. (202) 653-2400), (Fax from U.S. (202) 653 5760), www.fao.org; *FAO Trade Yearbook* and *The State of Food and Agriculture (SOFA) 2006.*

United Nations Statistics Division, New York, NY 10017, (800) 253-9646, Fax: (212) 963-4116, http://unstats.un.org; *Bulletin of Industrial Statistics for the Arab Countries; International Trade Statistics Yearbook;* and *Statistical Yearbook.*

The World Bank, 1818 H Street, NW, Washington, DC 20433, (202) 473-1000, Fax: (202) 477-6391, www.worldbank.org; *Jordan* and *World Development Report 2008.*

World Trade Organization (WTO), Centre William Rappard, Rue de Lausanne 154, CH-1211 Geneva 21, Switzerland, www.wto.org; *International Trade Statistics 2006.*

JORDAN - INTERNET USERS

International Telecommunication Union (ITU), Place des Nations, 1211 Geneva 20, Switzerland, www.itu.int; *World Telecommunication/ICT Indicators Database on CD-ROM; World Telecommunication/ICT Indicators Database Online;* and *Yearbook of Statistics - Telecommunication Services (Chronological Time Series 1997-2006).*

The World Bank, 1818 H Street, NW, Washington, DC 20433, (202) 473-1000, Fax: (202) 477-6391, www.worldbank.org; *Jordan.*

JORDAN - INVESTMENTS

International Monetary Fund (IMF), 700 Nineteenth Street, NW, Washington, DC 20431, (202) 623-7000, Fax: (202) 623-4661, www.imf.org; *International Financial Statistics Yearbook 2007.*

JORDAN - IRON AND IRON ORE PRODUCTION

See JORDAN - MINERAL INDUSTRIES

JORDAN - IRRIGATION

Euromonitor International, Inc., 224 S. Michigan Avenue, Suite 1500, Chicago, IL 60604, (312) 922-1115, Fax: (312) 922-1157, www.euromonitor.com; *International Marketing Data and Statistics 2008.*

JORDAN - LABOR

Central Intelligence Agency, Office of Public Affairs, Washington, DC 20505, (703) 482-0623, Fax: (703) 482-1739, www.cia.gov; *The World Factbook.*

Euromonitor International, Inc., 224 S. Michigan Avenue, Suite 1500, Chicago, IL 60604, (312) 922-1115, Fax: (312) 922-1157, www.euromonitor.com; *International Marketing Data and Statistics 2008* and *World Marketing Data and Statistics.*

International Labour Office, I.L.O. Publications, 4 route des Morillons, CH-1211 Geneva 22, Switzerland, (Telephone in U.S. (202) 653-7652), (Fax in U.S. (202) 653-7687), www.ilo.org; *Yearbook of Labour Statistics 2006.*

M.E. Sharpe, 80 Business Park Drive, Armonk, NY 10504, (800) 541-6563, Fax: (914) 273-2106, www.mesharpe.com; *The Illustrated Book of World Rankings.*

Palgrave Macmillan Ltd., Houndmills, Basingstoke, Hampshire, RG21 6XS, England, (Telephone in U.S. (888) 330-8477), (Fax in U.S. (800) 672-2054), www.palgrave.com; *The Statesman's Yearbook 2008.*

Taylor and Francis Group, An Informa Business, 2 Park Square, Milton Park, Abingdon, Oxford OX14 4RN, United Kingdom, (Dial from U.S. (212) 216-7800), (Fax from U.S. (212) 564-7854), www.tandf.co.uk; *The Europa World Year Book.*

United Nations Economic and Social Commission for Western Asia (ESCWA), PO Box 11-8575, Riad el-Solh Square, Beirut, Lebanon, www.escwa.un.org; *Annual Report 2006* and *Statistical Abstract of the ESCWA Region 2007.*

United Nations Food and Agricultural Organization (FAO), Viale delle Terme di Caracalla, 00100 Rome, Italy, (Dial from U.S. (202) 653-2400), (Fax from U.S. (202) 653 5760), www.fao.org; *The State of Food and Agriculture (SOFA) 2006.*

United Nations Statistics Division, New York, NY 10017, (800) 253-9646, Fax: (212) 963-4116, http://unstats.un.org; *Human Development Report 2006.*

The World Bank, 1818 H Street, NW, Washington, DC 20433, (202) 473-1000, Fax: (202) 477-6391, www.worldbank.org; *The World Bank Atlas 2003-2004* and *World Development Report 2008.*

JORDAN - LAND USE

Central Intelligence Agency, Office of Public Affairs, Washington, DC 20505, (703) 482-0623, Fax: (703) 482-1739, www.cia.gov; *The World Factbook.*

Euromonitor International, Inc., 224 S. Michigan Avenue, Suite 1500, Chicago, IL 60604, (312) 922-1115, Fax: (312) 922-1157, www.euromonitor.com; *International Marketing Data and Statistics 2008.*

United Nations Food and Agricultural Organization (FAO), Viale delle Terme di Caracalla, 00100 Rome,

Italy, (Dial from U.S. (202) 653-2400), (Fax from U.S. (202) 653 5760), www.fao.org; *FAO Production Yearbook 2002.*

The World Bank, 1818 H Street, NW, Washington, DC 20433, (202) 473-1000, Fax: (202) 477-6391, www.worldbank.org; *World Development Report 2008.*

JORDAN - LIBRARIES

M.E. Sharpe, 80 Business Park Drive, Armonk, NY 10504, (800) 541-6563, Fax: (914) 273-2106, www.mesharpe.com; *The Illustrated Book of World Rankings.*

UNESCO Institute for Statistics, C.P. 6128 Succursale Centre-Ville, Montreal, Quebec, H3C 3J7 Canada, (Dial from U.S. (514) 343-6880), (Fax from U.S. (514) 343 6882), www.uis.unesco.org; *Statistical Tables.*

JORDAN - LICENSES

International Monetary Fund (IMF), 700 Nineteenth Street, NW, Washington, DC 20431, (202) 623-7000, Fax: (202) 623-4661, www.imf.org; *Government Finance Statistics Yearbook (2008 Edition).*

JORDAN - LIFE EXPECTANCY

Central Intelligence Agency, Office of Public Affairs, Washington, DC 20505, (703) 482-0623, Fax: (703) 482-1739, www.cia.gov; *The World Factbook.*

Euromonitor International, Inc., 224 S. Michigan Avenue, Suite 1500, Chicago, IL 60604, (312) 922-1115, Fax: (312) 922-1157, www.euromonitor.com; *The World Economic Factbook 2008.*

Palgrave Macmillan Ltd., Houndmills, Basingstoke, Hampshire, RG21 6XS, England, (Telephone in U.S. (888) 330-8477), (Fax in U.S. (800) 672-2054), www.palgrave.com; *The Statesman's Yearbook 2008.*

United Nations Statistics Division, New York, NY 10017, (800) 253-9646, Fax: (212) 963-4116, http://unstats.un.org; *Human Development Report 2006* and *World Statistics Pocketbook.*

The World Bank, 1818 H Street, NW, Washington, DC 20433, (202) 473-1000, Fax: (202) 477-6391, www.worldbank.org; *The World Bank Atlas 2003-2004* and *World Development Report 2008.*

JORDAN - LITERACY

Euromonitor International, Inc., 224 S. Michigan Avenue, Suite 1500, Chicago, IL 60604, (312) 922-1115, Fax: (312) 922-1157, www.euromonitor.com; *World Marketing Data and Statistics.*

JORDAN - LIVESTOCK

Euromonitor International, Inc., 224 S. Michigan Avenue, Suite 1500, Chicago, IL 60604, (312) 922-1115, Fax: (312) 922-1157, www.euromonitor.com; *International Marketing Data and Statistics 2008.*

M.E. Sharpe, 80 Business Park Drive, Armonk, NY 10504, (800) 541-6563, Fax: (914) 273-2106, www.mesharpe.com; *The Illustrated Book of World Rankings.*

Palgrave Macmillan Ltd., Houndmills, Basingstoke, Hampshire, RG21 6XS, England, (Telephone in U.S. (888) 330-8477), (Fax in U.S. (800) 672-2054), www.palgrave.com; *The Statesman's Yearbook 2008.*

Taylor and Francis Group, An Informa Business, 2 Park Square, Milton Park, Abingdon, Oxford OX14 4RN, United Kingdom, (Dial from U.S. (212) 216-7800), (Fax from U.S. (212) 564-7854), www.tandf.co.uk; *The Europa World Year Book.*

United Nations Conference on Trade and Development (UNCTAD), DC2-1120, United Nations, New York, NY 10017, (212) 963-0027, www.unctad.org; *UNCTAD Commodity Yearbook.*

United Nations Food and Agricultural Organization (FAO), Viale delle Terme di Caracalla, 00100 Rome, Italy, (Dial from U.S. (202) 653-2400), (Fax from U.S. (202) 653 5760), www.fao.org; *FAO Production Yearbook 2002* and *The State of Food and Agriculture (SOFA) 2006.*

United Nations Statistics Division, New York, NY 10017, (800) 253-9646, Fax: (212) 963-4116, http://unstats.un.org; *Statistical Yearbook.*

JORDAN - LOCAL TAXATION

Euromonitor International, Inc., 224 S. Michigan Avenue, Suite 1500, Chicago, IL 60604, (312) 922-1115, Fax: (312) 922-1157, www.euromonitor.com; *International Marketing Data and Statistics 2008.*

JORDAN - MANUFACTURES

M.E. Sharpe, 80 Business Park Drive, Armonk, NY 10504, (800) 541-6563, Fax: (914) 273-2106, www.mesharpe.com; *The Illustrated Book of World Rankings.*

United Nations Statistics Division, New York, NY 10017, (800) 253-9646, Fax: (212) 963-4116, http://unstats.un.org; *Bulletin of Industrial Statistics for the Arab Countries* and *Statistical Yearbook.*

JORDAN - MARRIAGE

M.E. Sharpe, 80 Business Park Drive, Armonk, NY 10504, (800) 541-6563, Fax: (914) 273-2106, www.mesharpe.com; *The Illustrated Book of World Rankings.*

Taylor and Francis Group, An Informa Business, 2 Park Square, Milton Park, Abingdon, Oxford OX14 4RN, United Kingdom, (Dial from U.S. (212) 216-7800), (Fax from U.S. (212) 564-7854), www.tandf.co.uk; *The Europa World Year Book.*

United Nations Statistics Division, New York, NY 10017, (800) 253-9646, Fax: (212) 963-4116, http://unstats.un.org; *Demographic Yearbook* and *Statistical Yearbook.*

JORDAN - MEAT PRODUCTION

See JORDAN - LIVESTOCK

JORDAN - MEDICAL CARE, COST OF

International Monetary Fund (IMF), 700 Nineteenth Street, NW, Washington, DC 20431, (202) 623-7000, Fax: (202) 623-4661, www.imf.org; *Government Finance Statistics Yearbook (2008 Edition).*

JORDAN - MILK PRODUCTION

See JORDAN - DAIRY PROCESSING

JORDAN - MINERAL INDUSTRIES

M.E. Sharpe, 80 Business Park Drive, Armonk, NY 10504, (800) 541-6563, Fax: (914) 273-2106, www.mesharpe.com; *The Illustrated Book of World Rankings.*

Organisation for Economic Cooperation and Development (OECD), 2 rue Andre Pascal, F-75775 Paris Cedex 16, France, (Telephone in U.S. (202) 785-6323), (Fax in U.S. (202) 785-0350), www.oecd.org; *World Energy Outlook 2007.*

Palgrave Macmillan Ltd., Houndmills, Basingstoke, Hampshire, RG21 6XS, England, (Telephone in U.S. (888) 330-8477), (Fax in U.S. (800) 672-2054), www.palgrave.com; *The Statesman's Yearbook 2008.*

Taylor and Francis Group, An Informa Business, 2 Park Square, Milton Park, Abingdon, Oxford OX14 4RN, United Kingdom, (Dial from U.S. (212) 216-7800), (Fax from U.S. (212) 564-7854), www.tandf.co.uk; *The Europa World Year Book.*

United Nations Conference on Trade and Development (UNCTAD), DC2-1120, United Nations, New York, NY 10017, (212) 963-0027, www.unctad.org; *UNCTAD Commodity Yearbook.*

United Nations Economic and Social Commission for Western Asia (ESCWA), PO Box 11-8575, Riad el-Solh Square, Beirut, Lebanon, www.escwa.un.org; *Annual Report 2006* and *Statistical Abstract of the ESCWA Region 2007.*

United Nations Statistics Division, New York, NY 10017, (800) 253-9646, Fax: (212) 963-4116, http://unstats.un.org; *Bulletin of Industrial Statistics for the Arab Countries* and *Statistical Yearbook.*

JORDAN - MONEY EXCHANGE RATES

See JORDAN - FOREIGN EXCHANGE RATES

JORDAN - MONEY SUPPLY

Economist Intelligence Unit, 111 West 57th Street, New York, NY 10019, (212) 554-0600, Fax: (212) 586-1181, www.eiu.com; *Jordan Country Report.*

Euromonitor International, Inc., 224 S. Michigan Avenue, Suite 1500, Chicago, IL 60604, (312) 922-1115, Fax: (312) 922-1157, www.euromonitor.com; *International Marketing Data and Statistics 2008.*

International Monetary Fund (IMF), 700 Nineteenth Street, NW, Washington, DC 20431, (202) 623-7000, Fax: (202) 623-4661, www.imf.org; *International Financial Statistics Yearbook 2007.*

Taylor and Francis Group, An Informa Business, 2 Park Square, Milton Park, Abingdon, Oxford OX14 4RN, United Kingdom, (Dial from U.S. (212) 216-7800), (Fax from U.S. (212) 564-7854), www.tandf.co.uk; *The Europa World Year Book.*

United Nations Economic and Social Commission for Western Asia (ESCWA), PO Box 11-8575, Riad el-Solh Square, Beirut, Lebanon, www.escwa.un.org; *Annual Report 2006* and *Statistical Abstract of the ESCWA Region 2007.*

United Nations Statistics Division, New York, NY 10017, (800) 253-9646, Fax: (212) 963-4116, http://unstats.un.org; *Statistical Yearbook.*

The World Bank, 1818 H Street, NW, Washington, DC 20433, (202) 473-1000, Fax: (202) 477-6391, www.worldbank.org; *Jordan.*

JORDAN - MONUMENTS AND HISTORIC SITES

UNESCO Institute for Statistics, C.P. 6128 Succursale Centre-Ville, Montreal, Quebec, H3C 3J7 Canada, (Dial from U.S. (514) 343-6880), (Fax from U.S. (514) 343 6882), www.uis.unesco.org; *Statistical Tables.*

JORDAN - MORTALITY

Central Intelligence Agency, Office of Public Affairs, Washington, DC 20505, (703) 482-0623, Fax: (703) 482-1739, www.cia.gov; *The World Factbook.*

Euromonitor International, Inc., 224 S. Michigan Avenue, Suite 1500, Chicago, IL 60604, (312) 922-1115, Fax: (312) 922-1157, www.euromonitor.com; *International Marketing Data and Statistics 2008* and *The World Economic Factbook 2008.*

Palgrave Macmillan Ltd., Houndmills, Basingstoke, Hampshire, RG21 6XS, England, (Telephone in U.S. (888) 330-8477), (Fax in U.S. (800) 672-2054), www.palgrave.com; *The Statesman's Yearbook 2008.*

Taylor and Francis Group, An Informa Business, 2 Park Square, Milton Park, Abingdon, Oxford OX14 4RN, United Kingdom, (Dial from U.S. (212) 216-7800), (Fax from U.S. (212) 564-7854), www.tandf.co.uk; *The Europa World Year Book.*

UNICEF, 3 United Nations Plaza, New York, NY 10017, (800) 253-9646, Fax: (212) 887-7465, www.unicef.org; *The State of the World's Children 2008.*

United Nations Statistics Division, New York, NY 10017, (800) 253-9646, Fax: (212) 963-4116, http://unstats.un.org; *Demographic Yearbook; Human Development Report 2006; Statistical Yearbook;* and *World Statistics Pocketbook.*

The World Bank, 1818 H Street, NW, Washington, DC 20433, (202) 473-1000, Fax: (202) 477-6391, www.worldbank.org; *The World Bank Atlas 2003-2004* and *World Development Report 2008.*

World Health Organization (WHO), Avenue Appia 20, 1211 Geneve 27, Switzerland, (Telephone in U.S. (212) 331-9081), www.who.int; The WHO Global Atlas of Infectious Diseases and *World Health Report 2006.*

JORDAN - MOTION PICTURES

United Nations Statistics Division, New York, NY 10017, (800) 253-9646, Fax: (212) 963-4116, http://unstats.un.org; *Statistical Yearbook.*

JORDAN - MOTOR VEHICLES

International Road Federation (IFR), Madison Place, 500 Montgomery Street, 5th Floor, Alexandria, VA 22314, (703) 535-1001, Fax: (703) 535-1007, www.irfnet.org; *World Road Statistics 2006.*

Taylor and Francis Group, An Informa Business, 2 Park Square, Milton Park, Abingdon, Oxford OX14 4RN, United Kingdom, (Dial from U.S. (212) 216-7800), (Fax from U.S. (212) 564-7854), www.tandf.co.uk; *The Europa World Year Book.*

United Nations Statistics Division, New York, NY 10017, (800) 253-9646, Fax: (212) 963-4116, http://unstats.un.org; *Statistical Yearbook.*

JORDAN - MUSEUMS

M.E. Sharpe, 80 Business Park Drive, Armonk, NY 10504, (800) 541-6563, Fax: (914) 273-2106, www.mesharpe.com; *The Illustrated Book of World Rankings.*

UNESCO Institute for Statistics, C.P. 6128 Succursale Centre-Ville, Montreal, Quebec, H3C 3J7 Canada, (Dial from U.S. (514) 343-6880), (Fax from U.S. (514) 343 6882), www.uis.unesco.org; *Statistical Tables.*

JORDAN - NATURAL GAS PRODUCTION

See JORDAN - MINERAL INDUSTRIES

JORDAN - NUTRITION

United Nations Food and Agricultural Organization (FAO), Viale delle Terme di Caracalla, 00100 Rome, Italy, (Dial from U.S. (202) 653-2400), (Fax from U.S. (202) 653 5760), www.fao.org; *The State of Food and Agriculture (SOFA) 2006.*

JORDAN - OLDER PEOPLE

M.E. Sharpe, 80 Business Park Drive, Armonk, NY 10504, (800) 541-6563, Fax: (914) 273-2106, www.mesharpe.com; *The Illustrated Book of World Rankings.*

JORDAN - PAPER

See JORDAN - FORESTS AND FORESTRY

JORDAN - PEANUT PRODUCTION

See JORDAN - CROPS

JORDAN - PERIODICALS

UNESCO Institute for Statistics, C.P. 6128 Succursale Centre-Ville, Montreal, Quebec, H3C 3J7 Canada, (Dial from U.S. (514) 343-6880), (Fax from U.S. (514) 343 6882), www.uis.unesco.org; *Statistical Tables.*

JORDAN - PESTICIDES

United Nations Food and Agricultural Organization (FAO), Viale delle Terme di Caracalla, 00100 Rome, Italy, (Dial from U.S. (202) 653-2400), (Fax from U.S. (202) 653 5760), www.fao.org; *The State of Food and Agriculture (SOFA) 2006.*

JORDAN - PETROLEUM INDUSTRY AND TRADE

M.E. Sharpe, 80 Business Park Drive, Armonk, NY 10504, (800) 541-6563, Fax: (914) 273-2106, www.mesharpe.com; *The Illustrated Book of World Rankings.*

Organisation for Economic Cooperation and Development (OECD), 2 rue Andre Pascal, F-75775 Paris Cedex 16, France, (Telephone in U.S. (202) 785-6323), (Fax in U.S. (202) 785-0350), www.oecd.org; *World Energy Outlook 2007.*

PennWell Corporation, 1421 South Sheridan Road, Tulsa, OK 74112, (918) 835-3161, www.pennwell.com; *International Petroleum Encyclopedia 2007.*

U.S. Department of Energy (DOE), Energy Information Administration (EIA), 1000 Independence Avenue, SW, Washington, DC 20585, (202) 586-8800, www.eia.doe.gov; *International Energy Annual 2004* and *International Energy Outlook 2006.*

United Nations Conference on Trade and Development (UNCTAD), DC2-1120, United Nations, New York, NY 10017, (212) 963-0027, www.unctad.org; *UNCTAD Commodity Yearbook.*

United Nations Food and Agricultural Organization (FAO), Viale delle Terme di Caracalla, 00100 Rome, Italy, (Dial from U.S. (202) 653-2400), (Fax from U.S. (202) 653 5760), www.fao.org; *The State of Food and Agriculture (SOFA) 2006.*

United Nations Statistics Division, New York, NY 10017, (800) 253-9646, Fax: (212) 963-4116, http://unstats.un.org; *Statistical Yearbook.*

JORDAN - PHOSPHATES

International Monetary Fund (IMF), 700 Nineteenth Street, NW, Washington, DC 20431, (202) 623-7000, Fax: (202) 623-4661, www.imf.org; *International Financial Statistics Yearbook 2007.*

JORDAN - PHOSPHATES PRODUCTION

See JORDAN - MINERAL INDUSTRIES

JORDAN - POLITICAL SCIENCE

Central Intelligence Agency, Office of Public Affairs, Washington, DC 20505, (703) 482-0623, Fax: (703) 482-1739, www.cia.gov; *The World Factbook.*

International Monetary Fund (IMF), 700 Nineteenth Street, NW, Washington, DC 20431, (202) 623-7000, Fax: (202) 623-4661, www.imf.org; *Government Finance Statistics Yearbook (2008 Edition)* and *International Financial Statistics Yearbook 2007.*

Palgrave Macmillan Ltd., Houndmills, Basingstoke, Hampshire, RG21 6XS, England, (Telephone in U.S. (888) 330-8477), (Fax in U.S. (800) 672-2054), www.palgrave.com; *The Statesman's Yearbook 2008.*

Taylor and Francis Group, An Informa Business, 2 Park Square, Milton Park, Abingdon, Oxford OX14 4RN, United Kingdom, (Dial from U.S. (212) 216-7800), (Fax from U.S. (212) 564-7854), www.tandf.co.uk; *The Europa World Year Book.*

United Nations Statistics Division, New York, NY 10017, (800) 253-9646, Fax: (212) 963-4116, http://unstats.un.org; *National Accounts Statistics: Compendium of Income Distribution Statistics* and *Statistical Yearbook.*

The World Bank, 1818 H Street, NW, Washington, DC 20433, (202) 473-1000, Fax: (202) 477-6391, www.worldbank.org; *World Development Report 2008.*

JORDAN - POPULATION

Central Intelligence Agency, Office of Public Affairs, Washington, DC 20505, (703) 482-0623, Fax: (703) 482-1739, www.cia.gov; *The World Factbook.*

Economist Intelligence Unit, 111 West 57th Street, New York, NY 10019, (212) 554-0600, Fax: (212) 586-1181, www.eiu.com; *Jordan Country Report.*

Euromonitor International, Inc., 224 S. Michigan Avenue, Suite 1500, Chicago, IL 60604, (312) 922-1115, Fax: (312) 922-1157, www.euromonitor.com; *International Marketing Data and Statistics 2008* and *The World Economic Factbook 2008.*

International Labour Office, I.L.O. Publications, 4 route des Morillons, CH-1211 Geneva 22, Switzerland, (Telephone in U.S. (202) 653-7652), (Fax in U.S. (202) 653-7687), www.ilo.org; *Yearbook of Labour Statistics 2006.*

M.E. Sharpe, 80 Business Park Drive, Armonk, NY 10504, (800) 541-6563, Fax: (914) 273-2106, www.mesharpe.com; *The Illustrated Book of World Rankings.*

Palgrave Macmillan Ltd., Houndmills, Basingstoke, Hampshire, RG21 6XS, England, (Telephone in U.S. (888) 330-8477), (Fax in U.S. (800) 672-2054), www.palgrave.com; *The Statesman's Yearbook 2008.*

Taylor and Francis Group, An Informa Business, 2 Park Square, Milton Park, Abingdon, Oxford OX14 4RN, United Kingdom, (Dial from U.S. (212) 216-7800), (Fax from U.S. (212) 564-7854), www.tandf.co.uk; *The Europa World Year Book.*

U.S. Department of State (DOS), 2201 C Street NW, Washington, DC 20520, (202) 647-4000, www.state.gov; *World Military Expenditures and Arms Transfers (WMEAT).*

UNESCO Institute for Statistics, C.P. 6128 Succursale Centre-Ville, Montreal, Quebec, H3C 3J7 Canada, (Dial from U.S. (514) 343-6880), (Fax from U.S. (514) 343 6882), www.uis.unesco.org; *Statistical Tables.*

United Nations Economic and Social Commission for Western Asia (ESCWA), PO Box 11-8575, Riad el-Solh Square, Beirut, Lebanon, www.escwa.un.org; *Annual Report 2006* and *Statistical Abstract of the ESCWA Region 2007.*

United Nations Food and Agricultural Organization (FAO), Viale delle Terme di Caracalla, 00100 Rome, Italy, (Dial from U.S. (202) 653-2400), (Fax from U.S. (202) 653 5760), www.fao.org; *FAO Production Yearbook 2002.*

United Nations Statistics Division, New York, NY 10017, (800) 253-9646, Fax: (212) 963-4116, http://unstats.un.org; *Demographic Yearbook; Human Development Report 2006; Statistical Yearbook;* and *World Statistics Pocketbook.*

The World Bank, 1818 H Street, NW, Washington, DC 20433, (202) 473-1000, Fax: (202) 477-6391, www.worldbank.org; *Jordan; The World Bank Atlas 2003-2004;* and *World Development Report 2008.*

World Health Organization (WHO), Avenue Appia 20, 1211 Geneve 27, Switzerland, (Telephone in U.S. (212) 331-9081), www.who.int; *World Health Report 2006.*

JORDAN - POPULATION DENSITY

Central Intelligence Agency, Office of Public Affairs, Washington, DC 20505, (703) 482-0623, Fax: (703) 482-1739, www.cia.gov; *The World Factbook.*

Euromonitor International, Inc., 224 S. Michigan Avenue, Suite 1500, Chicago, IL 60604, (312) 922-1115, Fax: (312) 922-1157, www.euromonitor.com; *International Marketing Data and Statistics 2008* and *The World Economic Factbook 2008.*

M.E. Sharpe, 80 Business Park Drive, Armonk, NY 10504, (800) 541-6563, Fax: (914) 273-2106, www.mesharpe.com; *The Illustrated Book of World Rankings.*

Palgrave Macmillan Ltd., Houndmills, Basingstoke, Hampshire, RG21 6XS, England, (Telephone in U.S. (888) 330-8477), (Fax in U.S. (800) 672-2054), www.palgrave.com; *The Statesman's Yearbook 2008.*

Taylor and Francis Group, An Informa Business, 2 Park Square, Milton Park, Abingdon, Oxford OX14 4RN, United Kingdom, (Dial from U.S. (212) 216-7800), (Fax from U.S. (212) 564-7854), www.tandf.co.uk; *The Europa World Year Book.*

UNESCO Institute for Statistics, C.P. 6128 Succursale Centre-Ville, Montreal, Quebec, H3C 3J7 Canada, (Dial from U.S. (514) 343-6880), (Fax from U.S. (514) 343 6882), www.uis.unesco.org; *Statistical Tables.*

United Nations Food and Agricultural Organization (FAO), Viale delle Terme di Caracalla, 00100 Rome, Italy, (Dial from U.S. (202) 653-2400), (Fax from U.S. (202) 653 5760), www.fao.org; *The State of Food and Agriculture (SOFA) 2006.*

United Nations Statistics Division, New York, NY 10017, (800) 253-9646, Fax: (212) 963-4116, http://unstats.un.org; *Statistical Yearbook.*

The World Bank, 1818 H Street, NW, Washington, DC 20433, (202) 473-1000, Fax: (202) 477-6391, www.worldbank.org; *Jordan* and *World Development Report 2008.*

JORDAN - POSTAL SERVICE

M.E. Sharpe, 80 Business Park Drive, Armonk, NY 10504, (800) 541-6563, Fax: (914) 273-2106, www.mesharpe.com; *The Illustrated Book of World Rankings.*

Palgrave Macmillan Ltd., Houndmills, Basingstoke, Hampshire, RG21 6XS, England, (Telephone in U.S.

(888) 330-8477), (Fax in U.S. (800) 672-2054), www.palgrave.com; *The Statesman's Yearbook 2008.*

United Nations Statistics Division, New York, NY 10017, (800) 253-9646, Fax: (212) 963-4116, http://unstats.un.org; *Statistical Yearbook.*

JORDAN - POWER RESOURCES

Euromonitor International, Inc., 224 S. Michigan Avenue, Suite 1500, Chicago, IL 60604, (312) 922-1115, Fax: (312) 922-1157, www.euromonitor.com; *International Marketing Data and Statistics 2008; The World Economic Factbook 2008;* and *World Marketing Data and Statistics.*

M.E. Sharpe, 80 Business Park Drive, Armonk, NY 10504, (800) 541-6563, Fax: (914) 273-2106, www.mesharpe.com; *The Illustrated Book of World Rankings.*

Organisation for Economic Cooperation and Development (OECD), 2 rue Andre Pascal, F-75775 Paris Cedex 16, France, (Telephone in U.S. (202) 785-6323), (Fax in U.S. (202) 785-0350), www.oecd.org; *World Energy Outlook 2007.*

Palgrave Macmillan Ltd., Houndmills, Basingstoke, Hampshire, RG21 6XS, England, (Telephone in U.S. (888) 330-8477), (Fax in U.S. (800) 672-2054), www.palgrave.com; *The Statesman's Yearbook 2008.*

Platts, 2 Penn Plaza, 25th Floor, New York, NY 10121-2298, (212) 904-3070, www.platts.com; *Energy Economist.*

U.S. Department of Energy (DOE), Energy Information Administration (EIA), 1000 Independence Avenue, SW, Washington, DC 20585, (202) 586-8800, www.eia.doe.gov; *International Energy Annual 2004* and *International Energy Outlook 2006.*

United Nations Economic and Social Commission for Western Asia (ESCWA), PO Box 11-8575, Riad el-Solh Square, Beirut, Lebanon, www.escwa.un.org; *Annual Report 2006* and *Statistical Abstract of the ESCWA Region 2007.*

United Nations Food and Agricultural Organization (FAO), Viale delle Terme di Caracalla, 00100 Rome, Italy, (Dial from U.S. (202) 653-2400), (Fax from U.S. (202) 653 5760), www.fao.org; *The State of Food and Agriculture (SOFA) 2006.*

United Nations Statistics Division, New York, NY 10017, (800) 253-9646, Fax: (212) 963-4116, http://unstats.un.org; *Energy Statistics Yearbook 2003; Human Development Report 2006; Statistical Yearbook;* and *World Statistics Pocketbook.*

The World Bank, 1818 H Street, NW, Washington, DC 20433, (202) 473-1000, Fax: (202) 477-6391, www.worldbank.org; *The World Bank Atlas 2003-2004* and *World Development Report 2008.*

JORDAN - PRICES

International Labour Office, I.L.O. Publications, 4 route des Morillons, CH-1211 Geneva 22, Switzerland, (Telephone in U.S. (202) 653-7652), (Fax in U.S. (202) 653-7687), www.ilo.org; *Yearbook of Labour Statistics 2006.*

International Monetary Fund (IMF), 700 Nineteenth Street, NW, Washington, DC 20431, (202) 623-7000, Fax: (202) 623-4661, www.imf.org; *International Financial Statistics Yearbook 2007.*

M.E. Sharpe, 80 Business Park Drive, Armonk, NY 10504, (800) 541-6563, Fax: (914) 273-2106, www.mesharpe.com; *The Illustrated Book of World Rankings.*

United Nations Food and Agricultural Organization (FAO), Viale delle Terme di Caracalla, 00100 Rome, Italy, (Dial from U.S. (202) 653-2400), (Fax from U.S. (202) 653 5760), www.fao.org; *FAO Production Yearbook 2002* and *The State of Food and Agriculture (SOFA) 2006.*

The World Bank, 1818 H Street, NW, Washington, DC 20433, (202) 473-1000, Fax: (202) 477-6391, www.worldbank.org; *Jordan.*

JORDAN - PROFESSIONS

United Nations Statistics Division, New York, NY 10017, (800) 253-9646, Fax: (212) 963-4116, http://unstats.un.org; *Statistical Yearbook.*

JORDAN - PUBLIC HEALTH

Euromonitor International, Inc., 224 S. Michigan Avenue, Suite 1500, Chicago, IL 60604, (312) 922-1115, Fax: (312) 922-1157, www.euromonitor.com; *World Health Databook 2007/2008* and *World Marketing Data and Statistics.*

M.E. Sharpe, 80 Business Park Drive, Armonk, NY 10504, (800) 541-6563, Fax: (914) 273-2106, www.mesharpe.com; *The Illustrated Book of World Rankings.*

Palgrave Macmillan Ltd., Houndmills, Basingstoke, Hampshire, RG21 6XS, England, (Telephone in U.S. (888) 330-8477), (Fax in U.S. (800) 672-2054), www.palgrave.com; *The Statesman's Yearbook 2008.*

UNICEF, 3 United Nations Plaza, New York, NY 10017, (800) 253-9646, Fax: (212) 887-7465, www.unicef.org; *The State of the World's Children 2008.*

United Nations Economic and Social Commission for Western Asia (ESCWA), PO Box 11-8575, Riad el-Solh Square, Beirut, Lebanon, www.escwa.un.org; *Annual Report 2006* and *Statistical Abstract of the ESCWA Region 2007.*

United Nations Statistics Division, New York, NY 10017, (800) 253-9646, Fax: (212) 963-4116, http://unstats.un.org; *Human Development Report 2006* and *Statistical Yearbook.*

The World Bank, 1818 H Street, NW, Washington, DC 20433, (202) 473-1000, Fax: (202) 477-6391, www.worldbank.org; *Jordan* and *World Development Report 2008.*

World Health Organization (WHO), Avenue Appia 20, 1211 Geneve 27, Switzerland, (Telephone in U.S. (212) 331-9081), www.who.int; The WHO Global Atlas of Infectious Diseases and *World Health Report 2006.*

JORDAN - PUBLISHERS AND PUBLISHING

UNESCO Institute for Statistics, C.P. 6128 Succursale Centre-Ville, Montreal, Quebec, H3C 3J7 Canada, (Dial from U.S. (514) 343-6880), (Fax from U.S. (514) 343 6882), www.uis.unesco.org; *Statistical Tables.*

JORDAN - RADIO BROADCASTING

Palgrave Macmillan Ltd., Houndmills, Basingstoke, Hampshire, RG21 6XS, England, (Telephone in U.S. (888) 330-8477), (Fax in U.S. (800) 672-2054), www.palgrave.com; *The Statesman's Yearbook 2008.*

JORDAN - RAILROADS

Jane's Information Group, 110 North Royal Street, Suite 200, Alexandria, VA 22314, (703) 683-3700, Fax: (800) 836-0297, www.janes.com; *Jane's World Railways.*

Palgrave Macmillan Ltd., Houndmills, Basingstoke, Hampshire, RG21 6XS, England, (Telephone in U.S. (888) 330-8477), (Fax in U.S. (800) 672-2054), www.palgrave.com; *The Statesman's Yearbook 2008.*

Taylor and Francis Group, An Informa Business, 2 Park Square, Milton Park, Abingdon, Oxford OX14 4RN, United Kingdom, (Dial from U.S. (212) 216-7800), (Fax from U.S. (212) 564-7854), www.tandf.co.uk; *The Europa World Year Book.*

JORDAN - RELIGION

Central Intelligence Agency, Office of Public Affairs, Washington, DC 20505, (703) 482-0623, Fax: (703) 482-1739, www.cia.gov; *The World Factbook.*

M.E. Sharpe, 80 Business Park Drive, Armonk, NY 10504, (800) 541-6563, Fax: (914) 273-2106, www.mesharpe.com; *The Illustrated Book of World Rankings.*

Palgrave Macmillan Ltd., Houndmills, Basingstoke, Hampshire, RG21 6XS, England, (Telephone in U.S. (888) 330-8477), (Fax in U.S. (800) 672-2054), www.palgrave.com; *The Statesman's Yearbook 2008.*

JORDAN - RENT CHARGES

International Labour Office, I.L.O. Publications, 4 route des Morillons, CH-1211 Geneva 22, Switzerland, (Telephone in U.S. (202) 653-7652), (Fax in U.S. (202) 653-7687), www.ilo.org; *Yearbook of Labour Statistics 2006.*

JORDAN - RESERVES (ACCOUNTING)

United Nations Statistics Division, New York, NY 10017, (800) 253-9646, Fax: (212) 963-4116, http://unstats.un.org; *Statistical Yearbook.*

JORDAN - RETAIL TRADE

Euromonitor International, Inc., 224 S. Michigan Avenue, Suite 1500, Chicago, IL 60604, (312) 922-1115, Fax: (312) 922-1157, www.euromonitor.com; *World Marketing Data and Statistics.*

JORDAN - RICE PRODUCTION

See JORDAN - CROPS

JORDAN - ROADS

Central Intelligence Agency, Office of Public Affairs, Washington, DC 20505, (703) 482-0623, Fax: (703) 482-1739, www.cia.gov; *The World Factbook.*

International Road Federation (IFR), Madison Place, 500 Montgomery Street, 5th Floor, Alexandria, VA 22314, (703) 535-1001, Fax: (703) 535-1007, www.irfnet.org; *World Road Statistics 2006.*

Palgrave Macmillan Ltd., Houndmills, Basingstoke, Hampshire, RG21 6XS, England, (Telephone in U.S. (888) 330-8477), (Fax in U.S. (800) 672-2054), www.palgrave.com; *The Statesman's Yearbook 2008.*

JORDAN - RUBBER INDUSTRY AND TRADE

International Rubber Study Group (IRSG), 1st Floor, Heron House, 109/115 Wembley Hill Road, Wembley, Middlesex HA9 8DA, United Kingdom, www.rubberstudy.com; *Rubber Statistical Bulletin; Summary of World Rubber Statistics 2005; World Rubber Statistics Handbook (Volume 6, 1975-2001);* and *World Rubber Statistics Historic Handbook.*

M.E. Sharpe, 80 Business Park Drive, Armonk, NY 10504, (800) 541-6563, Fax: (914) 273-2106, www.mesharpe.com; *The Illustrated Book of World Rankings.*

JORDAN - SALT PRODUCTION

See JORDAN - MINERAL INDUSTRIES

JORDAN - SHEEP

See JORDAN - LIVESTOCK

JORDAN - SHIPPING

Palgrave Macmillan Ltd., Houndmills, Basingstoke, Hampshire, RG21 6XS, England, (Telephone in U.S. (888) 330-8477), (Fax in U.S. (800) 672-2054), www.palgrave.com; *The Statesman's Yearbook 2008.*

Taylor and Francis Group, An Informa Business, 2 Park Square, Milton Park, Abingdon, Oxford OX14 4RN, United Kingdom, (Dial from U.S. (212) 216-7800), (Fax from U.S. (212) 564-7854), www.tandf.co.uk; *The Europa World Year Book.*

United Nations Statistics Division, New York, NY 10017, (800) 253-9646, Fax: (212) 963-4116, http://unstats.un.org; *Statistical Yearbook.*

JORDAN - SILVER PRODUCTION

See JORDAN - MINERAL INDUSTRIES

JORDAN - SOCIAL ECOLOGY

M.E. Sharpe, 80 Business Park Drive, Armonk, NY 10504, (800) 541-6563, Fax: (914) 273-2106, www.mesharpe.com; *The Illustrated Book of World Rankings.*

United Nations Statistics Division, New York, NY 10017, (800) 253-9646, Fax: (212) 963-4116, http://unstats.un.org; *World Statistics Pocketbook.*

JORDAN - SOCIAL SECURITY

International Monetary Fund (IMF), 700 Nineteenth Street, NW, Washington, DC 20431, (202) 623-

7000, Fax: (202) 623-4661, www.imf.org; *Government Finance Statistics Yearbook (2008 Edition).*

United Nations Statistics Division, New York, NY 10017, (800) 253-9646, Fax: (212) 963-4116, http://unstats.un.org; *National Accounts Statistics: Compendium of Income Distribution Statistics.*

JORDAN - STEEL PRODUCTION

See JORDAN - MINERAL INDUSTRIES

JORDAN - SUGAR PRODUCTION

See JORDAN - CROPS

JORDAN - TAXATION

International Monetary Fund (IMF), 700 Nineteenth Street, NW, Washington, DC 20431, (202) 623-7000, Fax: (202) 623-4661, www.imf.org; *Government Finance Statistics Yearbook (2008 Edition).*

International Road Federation (IFR), Madison Place, 500 Montgomery Street, 5th Floor, Alexandria, VA 22314, (703) 535-1001, Fax: (703) 535-1007, www.irfnet.org; *World Road Statistics 2006.*

Taylor and Francis Group, An Informa Business, 2 Park Square, Milton Park, Abingdon, Oxford OX14 4RN, United Kingdom, (Dial from U.S. (212) 216-7800), (Fax from U.S. (212) 564-7854), www.tandf.co.uk; *The Europa World Year Book.*

JORDAN - TEA PRODUCTION

See JORDAN - CROPS

JORDAN - TELEPHONE

International Telecommunication Union (ITU), Place des Nations, 1211 Geneva 20, Switzerland, www.itu.int; World Telecommunication Indicators Database.

Palgrave Macmillan Ltd., Houndmills, Basingstoke, Hampshire, RG21 6XS, England, (Telephone in U.S. (888) 330-8477), (Fax in U.S. (800) 672-2054), www.palgrave.com; *The Statesman's Yearbook 2008.*

Taylor and Francis Group, An Informa Business, 2 Park Square, Milton Park, Abingdon, Oxford OX14 4RN, United Kingdom, (Dial from U.S. (212) 216-7800), (Fax from U.S. (212) 564-7854), www.tandf.co.uk; *The Europa World Year Book.*

United Nations Statistics Division, New York, NY 10017, (800) 253-9646, Fax: (212) 963-4116, http://unstats.un.org; *Statistical Yearbook* and *World Statistics Pocketbook.*

JORDAN - TEXTILE INDUSTRY

M.E. Sharpe, 80 Business Park Drive, Armonk, NY 10504, (800) 541-6563, Fax: (914) 273-2106, www.mesharpe.com; *The Illustrated Book of World Rankings.*

JORDAN - THEATER

UNESCO Institute for Statistics, C.P. 6128 Succursale Centre-Ville, Montreal, Quebec, H3C 3J7 Canada, (Dial from U.S. (514) 343-6880), (Fax from U.S. (514) 343 6882), www.uis.unesco.org; *Statistical Tables.*

JORDAN - TOBACCO INDUSTRY

Foreign Agricultural Service (FAS), U.S. Department of Agriculture (USDA), 1400 Independence Avenue, SW, Washington, DC 20250, (202) 720-3935, www.fas.usda.gov; *Tobacco: World Markets and Trade.*

M.E. Sharpe, 80 Business Park Drive, Armonk, NY 10504, (800) 541-6563, Fax: (914) 273-2106, www.mesharpe.com; *The Illustrated Book of World Rankings.*

United Nations Statistics Division, New York, NY 10017, (800) 253-9646, Fax: (212) 963-4116, http://unstats.un.org; *Statistical Yearbook.*

JORDAN - TOURISM

Euromonitor International, Inc., 224 S. Michigan Avenue, Suite 1500, Chicago, IL 60604, (312) 922-1115, Fax: (312) 922-1157, www.euromonitor.com; *The World Economic Factbook 2008* and *World Marketing Data and Statistics.*

M.E. Sharpe, 80 Business Park Drive, Armonk, NY 10504, (800) 541-6563, Fax: (914) 273-2106, www.mesharpe.com; *The Illustrated Book of World Rankings.*

Palgrave Macmillan Ltd., Houndmills, Basingstoke, Hampshire, RG21 6XS, England, (Telephone in U.S. (888) 330-8477), (Fax in U.S. (800) 672-2054), www.palgrave.com; *The Statesman's Yearbook 2008.*

Taylor and Francis Group, An Informa Business, 2 Park Square, Milton Park, Abingdon, Oxford OX14 4RN, United Kingdom, (Dial from U.S. (212) 216-7800), (Fax from U.S. (212) 564-7854), www.tandf.co.uk; *The Europa World Year Book.*

United Nations Economic and Social Commission for Western Asia (ESCWA), PO Box 11-8575, Riad el-Solh Square, Beirut, Lebanon, www.escwa.un.org; *Annual Report 2006* and *Statistical Abstract of the ESCWA Region 2007.*

United Nations Statistics Division, New York, NY 10017, (800) 253-9646, Fax: (212) 963-4116, http://unstats.un.org; *Statistical Yearbook.*

United Nations World Tourism Organization (UNWTO), Capitan Haya 42, 28020 Madrid, Spain, www.world-tourism.org; *Yearbook of Tourism Statistics.*

The World Bank, 1818 H Street, NW, Washington, DC 20433, (202) 473-1000, Fax: (202) 477-6391, www.worldbank.org; *Jordan.*

JORDAN - TRADE

See JORDAN - INTERNATIONAL TRADE

JORDAN - TRANSPORTATION

Central Intelligence Agency, Office of Public Affairs, Washington, DC 20505, (703) 482-0623, Fax: (703) 482-1739, www.cia.gov; *The World Factbook.*

Euromonitor International, Inc., 224 S. Michigan Avenue, Suite 1500, Chicago, IL 60604, (312) 922-1115, Fax: (312) 922-1157, www.euromonitor.com; *International Marketing Data and Statistics 2008* and *World Marketing Data and Statistics.*

M.E. Sharpe, 80 Business Park Drive, Armonk, NY 10504, (800) 541-6563, Fax: (914) 273-2106, www.mesharpe.com; *The Illustrated Book of World Rankings.*

Palgrave Macmillan Ltd., Houndmills, Basingstoke, Hampshire, RG21 6XS, England, (Telephone in U.S. (888) 330-8477), (Fax in U.S. (800) 672-2054), www.palgrave.com; *The Statesman's Yearbook 2008.*

Taylor and Francis Group, An Informa Business, 2 Park Square, Milton Park, Abingdon, Oxford OX14 4RN, United Kingdom, (Dial from U.S. (212) 216-7800), (Fax from U.S. (212) 564-7854), www.tandf.co.uk; *The Europa World Year Book.*

United Nations Economic and Social Commission for Western Asia (ESCWA), PO Box 11-8575, Riad el-Solh Square, Beirut, Lebanon, www.escwa.un.org; *Annual Report 2006* and *Statistical Abstract of the ESCWA Region 2007.*

United Nations Statistics Division, New York, NY 10017, (800) 253-9646, Fax: (212) 963-4116, http://unstats.un.org; *Human Development Report 2006.*

The World Bank, 1818 H Street, NW, Washington, DC 20433, (202) 473-1000, Fax: (202) 477-6391, www.worldbank.org; *Jordan.*

JORDAN - TURKEYS

See JORDAN - LIVESTOCK

JORDAN - UNEMPLOYMENT

Central Intelligence Agency, Office of Public Affairs, Washington, DC 20505, (703) 482-0623, Fax: (703) 482-1739, www.cia.gov; *The World Factbook.*

Department of Statistics (DOS), PO Box 2015, Amman 11181, Jordan, www.dos.gov.jo; *Employment Survey 2005.*

Euromonitor International, Inc., 224 S. Michigan Avenue, Suite 1500, Chicago, IL 60604, (312) 922-1115, Fax: (312) 922-1157, www.euromonitor.com; *International Marketing Data and Statistics 2008.*

International Labour Office, I.L.O. Publications, 4 route des Morillons, CH-1211 Geneva 22, Switzerland, (Telephone in U.S. (202) 653-7652), (Fax in U.S. (202) 653-7687), www.ilo.org; *Yearbook of Labour Statistics 2006.*

Palgrave Macmillan Ltd., Houndmills, Basingstoke, Hampshire, RG21 6XS, England, (Telephone in U.S. (888) 330-8477), (Fax in U.S. (800) 672-2054), www.palgrave.com; *The Statesman's Yearbook 2008.*

JORDAN - VITAL STATISTICS

Euromonitor International, Inc., 224 S. Michigan Avenue, Suite 1500, Chicago, IL 60604, (312) 922-1115, Fax: (312) 922-1157, www.euromonitor.com; *International Marketing Data and Statistics 2008.*

Palgrave Macmillan Ltd., Houndmills, Basingstoke, Hampshire, RG21 6XS, England, (Telephone in U.S. (888) 330-8477), (Fax in U.S. (800) 672-2054), www.palgrave.com; *The Statesman's Yearbook 2008.*

United Nations Economic and Social Commission for Western Asia (ESCWA), PO Box 11-8575, Riad el-Solh Square, Beirut, Lebanon, www.escwa.un.org; *Annual Report 2006; Bulletin on Population and Vital Statistics in the ESCWA Region;* and *Survey of Economic and Social Developments in the ESCWA Region 2006-2007.*

United Nations Statistics Division, New York, NY 10017, (800) 253-9646, Fax: (212) 963-4116, http://unstats.un.org; *Statistical Yearbook.*

World Health Organization (WHO), Avenue Appia 20, 1211 Geneve 27, Switzerland, (Telephone in U.S. (212) 331-9081), www.who.int; *World Health Report 2006.*

JORDAN - WAGES

International Labour Office, I.L.O. Publications, 4 route des Morillons, CH-1211 Geneva 22, Switzerland, (Telephone in U.S. (202) 653-7652), (Fax in U.S. (202) 653-7687), www.ilo.org; *Yearbook of Labour Statistics 2006.*

United Nations Statistics Division, New York, NY 10017, (800) 253-9646, Fax: (212) 963-4116, http://unstats.un.org; *Statistical Yearbook.*

The World Bank, 1818 H Street, NW, Washington, DC 20433, (202) 473-1000, Fax: (202) 477-6391, www.worldbank.org; *Jordan.*

JORDAN - WALNUT PRODUCTION

See JORDAN - CROPS

JORDAN - WEATHER

See JORDAN - CLIMATE

JORDAN - WELFARE STATE

International Monetary Fund (IMF), 700 Nineteenth Street, NW, Washington, DC 20431, (202) 623-7000, Fax: (202) 623-4661, www.imf.org; *Government Finance Statistics Yearbook (2008 Edition).*

JORDAN - WHEAT PRODUCTION

See JORDAN - CROPS

JORDAN - WHOLESALE PRICE INDEXES

United Nations Statistics Division, New York, NY 10017, (800) 253-9646, Fax: (212) 963-4116, http://unstats.un.org; *Statistical Yearbook.*

JORDAN - WINE PRODUCTION

See JORDAN - BEVERAGE INDUSTRY

JORDAN - WOOL PRODUCTION

See JORDAN - TEXTILE INDUSTRY

JUDICIAL SERVICE, FEDERAL - EMPLOYEES AND PAYROLLS

United States Office of Personnel Management (OMB), 1900 E Street, NW, Washington, DC 20415-1000, (202) 606-1800, www.opm.gov; *Employment and Trends of Federal Civilian Workforce Statistics* and unpublished data.

JUDICIAL SERVICE, FEDERAL - FEDERAL OUTLAYS

The Office of Management and Budget (OMB), 725 17th Street, NW, Washington, DC 20503, (202) 395-3080, Fax: (202) 395-3888, www.whitehouse.gov/omb; *Budget of the United States Government, Federal Year 2009* and *Historical Tables.*

JUICES

Economic Research Service (ERS), U.S. Department of Agriculture (USDA), 1800 M Street, NW, Washington, DC 20036-5831, (202) 694-5050, Fax: (202) 694-5689, www.ers.usda.gov; *Agricultural Outlook* and *Food CPI, Prices, and Expenditures.*

JUSTICE

Justice Research and Statistics Association (JRSA), 777 N. Capitol Street, NE, Suite 801, Washington, DC 20002, (202) 842-9330, Fax: (202) 842-9329, www.jrsa.org; *Crime and Justice Atlas 2001; Directory of Justice Issues in the States; Documenting the Extent and Nature of Drug and Violent Crime: Developing Jurisdiction-Specific Profiles of the Criminal Justice System; The Forum;* InfoBase of State Activities and Research (ISAR); *JRP Digest; Justice Research and Policy;* and *SAC Publication Digest.*

National Center for Juvenile Justice (NCJJ), 3700 South Water Street, Suite 200, Pittsburgh, PA 15203, (412) 227-6950, Fax: (412) 227-6955, http://ncjj.servehttp.com/NCJJWebsite/main.htm; *How Does the Juvenile Justice System Measure Up? Applying Performance Measures in Five Jurisdictions (2006).*

U.S. Department of Justice (DOJ), Bureau of Justice Statistics, 810 Seventh Street, NW, Washington, DC 20531, (202) 307-0765, www.ojp.usdoj.gov/bjs/; *Bureau of Justice Statistics, 2002: At a Glance; Census of Tribal Justice Agencies in Indian Country, 2002; Cross-National Studies in Crime and Justice; Federal Criminal Justice Trends, 2003; Federal Justice Statistics Resource Center; Justice Assistance Grant (JAG) Program, 2005;* and *The Sourcebook of Criminal Justice Statistics, 2003.*

JUVENILES - ARRESTS

Center for Substance Abuse Research (CESAR), 4321 Hartwick Road, Suite 501, College Park, MD 20740, (301) 405-9770, Fax: (301) 403-8342, www.cesar.umd.edu; *Juvenile Offender Population Urinalysis Screening Program (OPUS) Detention Study, February-June 2005.*

Federal Bureau of Investigation (FBI), J. Edgar Hoover Building, 935 Pennsylvania Avenue, NW, Washington, DC 20535-0001, (202) 324-3000, www.fbi.gov; *Crime in the United States (CIUS) 2007 (Preliminary).*

Justice Research and Statistics Association (JRSA), 777 N. Capitol Street, NE, Suite 801, Washington, DC 20002, (202) 842-9330, Fax: (202) 842-9329, www.jrsa.org; *Crime and Justice Atlas 2001.*

National Center for Juvenile Justice (NCJJ), 3700 South Water Street, Suite 200, Pittsburgh, PA 15203, (412) 227-6950, Fax: (412) 227-6955, http://ncjj.servehttp.com/NCJJWebsite/main.htm; *Detention and Delinquency Cases 1990-1999 (2003); Good News: Measuring Juvenile Court Outcomes at Case Closing, 2003 (2003); How Does the Juvenile Justice System Measure Up? Applying Performance Measures in Five Jurisdictions (2006); Juvenile Arrests 2003 (2005); Juvenile Court Statistics 2000 (2004); Juvenile Offenders and Victims: 2006 National Report; Juveniles in Corrections (2004);* and *Person Offenses in Juvenile Court, 1990-1999 (2003).*

Royal Canadian Mounted Police (RCMP), 1200 Vanier Parkway, Ottawa, ON K1A 0R2, Canada, (613) 993-7267, www.rcmp-grc.gc.ca; *The Direct and Indirect Impacts of Organized Crime on Youth, as Offenders and Victims.*

U.S. Department of Justice (DOJ), Bureau of Justice Statistics, 810 Seventh Street, NW, Washington, DC 20531, (202) 307-0765, www.ojp.usdoj.gov/bjs/; *Juvenile Victimization and Offending, 1993-2003.*

U.S. Department of Justice (DOJ), National Institute of Justice (NIJ), 810 Seventh Street, NW, Washington, DC 20531, (202) 307-2942, Fax: (202) 616-0275, www.ojp.usdoj.gov/nij/; *Co-Offending and Patterns of Juvenile Crime.*

The Urban Institute, 2100 M Street, N.W., Washington, DC 20037, (202) 833-7200, www.urban.org; *Juvenile Crime in Washington, D.C.; The Rise and Fall of American Youth Violence: 1980 to 2000;* and *Youth Crime Drop.*

JUVENILES - COURT CASES

Justice Research and Statistics Association (JRSA), 777 N. Capitol Street, NE, Suite 801, Washington, DC 20002, (202) 842-9330, Fax: (202) 842-9329, www.jrsa.org; *Documenting the Extent and Nature of Drug and Violent Crime: Developing Jurisdiction-Specific Profiles of the Criminal Justice System; The Forum; JRP Digest; Justice Research and Policy;* and *SAC Publication Digest.*

National Center for Juvenile Justice (NCJJ), 3700 South Water Street, Suite 200, Pittsburgh, PA 15203, (412) 227-6950, Fax: (412) 227-6955, http://ncjj.servehttp.com/NCJJWebsite/main.htm; *Detention and Delinquency Cases 1990-1999 (2003); Good News: Measuring Juvenile Court Outcomes at Case Closing, 2003 (2003); How Does the Juvenile Justice System Measure Up? Applying Performance Measures in Five Jurisdictions (2006); Jury Trial in Abuse, Neglect, Dependency Cases; Jury Trial in Termination of Parental Rights (2005 Update); Juvenile Arrests 2003 (2005); Juvenile Court Statistics 2000 (2004); Juvenile Offenders and Victims: 2006 National Report; Juveniles in Corrections (2004);* and *Person Offenses in Juvenile Court, 1990-1999 (2003).*

National Criminal Justice Reference Service (NCJRS), PO Box 6000, Rockville, MD 20849-6000, (800) 851-3420, Fax: (301) 519-5212, www.ncjrs.org; *Delaware Juvenile Recidivism 1994-2005 Juvenile Level III, IV and V Recidivism Study* and *Presence of Learning Disabled Youth in Our Juvenile Institutions: Excusable or Gross Negligence?*

Office of Juvenile Justice and Delinquency Prevention (OJJDP), 810 Seventh Street, NW, Washington, DC 20531, (202) 307-5911, www.ojjdp.ncjrs.org; *Statistical Briefing Book (SBB).*

U.S. Department of Justice (DOJ), National Institute of Justice (NIJ), 810 Seventh Street, NW, Washington, DC 20531, (202) 307-2942, Fax: (202) 616-0275, www.ojp.usdoj.gov/nij/; *Co-Offending and Patterns of Juvenile Crime.*

The Urban Institute, 2100 M Street, N.W., Washington, DC 20037, (202) 833-7200, www.urban.org; *Juvenile Crime in Washington, D.C.; The Rise and Fall of American Youth Violence: 1980 to 2000;* and *Youth Crime Drop.*STATISTICS SOURCES, Thirty-second Edition - 2009STATISTICS SOURCES, Thirty-second Edition - 2009

KANSAS

See also - STATE DATA (FOR INDIVIDUAL STATES)

Institute for Policy and Social Research (IPSR), University of Kansas, 1541 Lilac Lane, 607 Blake Hall, Lawrence, KS 66044-3177, (785) 864-3701, Fax: (785) 864-3683, www.ipsr.ku.edu; *Indicators of the Kansas Economy: Assessment and Prototypes Project Final Report* and *Trends in the Kansas Economy: 1985-2006.*

KANSAS - STATE DATA CENTERS

Center for Economic Development and Business Research (CEDBR), Wichita State University, 1845 Fairmount, 2nd Floor, Devlin Hall, Wichita, KS 67260-0121, (316) 978-3225, Fax: (316) 978-3950, http://webs.wichita.edu/?u=cedbr; State Data Center.

Institute for Policy and Social Research (IPRS), University of Kansas, 1541 Lilac Lane, 607 Blake Hall, Lawrence, KS 66044-3177, (785) 864-3701, Fax: (785) 864-3683, www.ipsr.ku.edu/ksdata; State Data Center.

Kansas Division of the Budget, 900 SW Jackson, Suite 504, Topeka, KS 66612, (785) 296-2436, Fax: (785) 296-0231, http://da.state.ks.us/budget; State Data Center.

Kansas Population Center, 255 Waters Hall, Kansas State University, Manhattan, KS 66506, Mr. Laszlo J. Kulcsar, Director (785) 532-4959, Fax: (785) 532-6978, www.k-state.edu/sasw/kpc; State Data Center.

Kansas State Library, 300 SW Tenth Ave, Room 343-N, Topeka, KS 66612, Mr. Marc Galbraith, (785) 296-3296, www.skyways.org/KSL/ref/census; State Data Center.

KANSAS - PRIMARY STATISTICS SOURCES

Institute for Policy and Social Research (IPSR), University of Kansas, 1541 Lilac Lane, 607 Blake Hall, Lawrence, KS 66044-3177, (785) 864-3701, Fax: (785) 864-3683, www.ipsr.ku.edu; *Kansas Statistical Abstract 2005.*

KAZAKHSTAN - NATIONAL STATISTICAL OFFICE

National Statistical Agency of the Republic of Kazakhstan, Prospekt Abaya 125, 480008 Almaty, Kazakhstan, www.stat.kz; National Data Center.

KAZAKHSTAN - ABORTION

United Nations Statistics Division, New York, NY 10017, (800) 253-9646, Fax: (212) 963-4116, http://unstats.un.org; *Trends in Europe and North America: The Statistical Yearbook of the ECE 2005.*

KAZAKHSTAN - AGRICULTURE

Academic International Press, PO Box 1111, Gulf Breeze, FL 32562-1111, Fax: (850) 934-0953, www.ai-press.com; *Russia and Eurasia Facts and Figures Annual.*

Economist Intelligence Unit, 111 West 57th Street, New York, NY 10019, (212) 554-0600, Fax: (212) 586-1181, www.eiu.com; *Kazakhstan Country Report.*

Euromonitor International, Inc., 224 S. Michigan Avenue, Suite 1500, Chicago, IL 60604, (312) 922-1115, Fax: (312) 922-1157, www.euromonitor.com; *World Marketing Data and Statistics.*

Palgrave Macmillan Ltd., Houndmills, Basingstoke, Hampshire, RG21 6XS, England, (Telephone in U.S. (888) 330-8477), (Fax in U.S. (800) 672-2054), www.palgrave.com; *The Statesman's Yearbook 2008.*

Taylor and Francis Group, An Informa Business, 2 Park Square, Milton Park, Abingdon, Oxford OX14 4RN, United Kingdom, (Dial from U.S. (212) 216-7800), (Fax from U.S. (212) 564-7854), www.tandf.co.uk; *The Europa World Year Book.*

United Nations Food and Agricultural Organization (FAO), Viale delle Terme di Caracalla, 00100 Rome, Italy, (Dial from U.S. (202) 653-2400), (Fax from U.S. (202) 653 5760), www.fao.org; AQUASTAT; *FAO Production Yearbook 2002; FAO Trade Yearbook;* and *The State of Food and Agriculture (SOFA) 2006.*

United Nations Statistics Division, New York, NY 10017, (800) 253-9646, Fax: (212) 963-4116, http://unstats.un.org; *2004 Industrial Commodity Statistics Yearbook* and *Statistical Yearbook.*

The World Bank, 1818 H Street, NW, Washington, DC 20433, (202) 473-1000, Fax: (202) 477-6391, www.worldbank.org; *Kazakhstan; Statistical Handbook: States of the Former USSR;* and *World Development Indicators (WDI) 2008.*

KAZAKHSTAN - AIRLINES

International Civil Aviation Organization (ICAO), External Relations and Public Information Office (EPO), 999 University Street, Montreal, Quebec H3C 5H7, Canada, (Dial from U.S. (514) 954-8219), (Fax from U.S. (514) 954-6077), www.icao.int; *Civil Aviation Statistics of the World.*

Palgrave Macmillan Ltd., Houndmills, Basingstoke, Hampshire, RG21 6XS, England, (Telephone in U.S. (888) 330-8477), (Fax in U.S. (800) 672-2054), www.palgrave.com; *The Statesman's Yearbook 2008.*

United Nations Statistics Division, New York, NY 10017, (800) 253-9646, Fax: (212) 963-4116, http://unstats.un.org; *Statistical Yearbook.*

KAZAKHSTAN - ARMED FORCES

Academic International Press, PO Box 1111, Gulf Breeze, FL 32562-1111, Fax: (850) 934-0953, www.ai-press.com; *Russia and Eurasia Facts and Figures Annual.*

Central Intelligence Agency, Office of Public Affairs, Washington, DC 20505, (703) 482-0623, Fax: (703) 482-1739, www.cia.gov; *The World Factbook.*

Euromonitor International, Inc., 224 S. Michigan Avenue, Suite 1500, Chicago, IL 60604, (312) 922-1115, Fax: (312) 922-1157, www.euromonitor.com; *World Marketing Data and Statistics.*

International Institute for Strategic Studies (IISS), Arundel House, 13-15 Arundel Street, Temple Place, London WC2R 3DX, England, www.iiss.org; *The Military Balance 2007.*

Palgrave Macmillan Ltd., Houndmills, Basingstoke, Hampshire, RG21 6XS, England, (Telephone in U.S. (888) 330-8477), (Fax in U.S. (800) 672-2054), www.palgrave.com; *The Statesman's Yearbook 2008.*

United Nations Statistics Division, New York, NY 10017, (800) 253-9646, Fax: (212) 963-4116, http://unstats.un.org; *Human Development Report 2006.*

KAZAKHSTAN - AUTOMOBILE INDUSTRY AND TRADE

United Nations Statistics Division, New York, NY 10017, (800) 253-9646, Fax: (212) 963-4116, http://unstats.un.org; *Statistical Yearbook.*

KAZAKHSTAN - BALANCE OF PAYMENTS

Taylor and Francis Group, An Informa Business, 2 Park Square, Milton Park, Abingdon, Oxford OX14 4RN, United Kingdom, (Dial from U.S. (212) 216-7800), (Fax from U.S. (212) 564-7854), www.tandf.co.uk; *The Europa World Year Book.*

United Nations Conference on Trade and Development (UNCTAD), DC2-1120, United Nations, New York, NY 10017, (212) 963-0027, www.unctad.org; *Handbook of Statistics 2005.*

The World Bank, 1818 H Street, NW, Washington, DC 20433, (202) 473-1000, Fax: (202) 477-6391, www.worldbank.org; *Kazakhstan; World Development Indicators (WDI) 2008;* and *World Development Report 2008.*

KAZAKHSTAN - BANKS AND BANKING

Euromonitor International, Inc., 224 S. Michigan Avenue, Suite 1500, Chicago, IL 60604, (312) 922-1115, Fax: (312) 922-1157, www.euromonitor.com; *World Marketing Data and Statistics.*

KAZAKHSTAN - BEVERAGE INDUSTRY

United Nations Statistics Division, New York, NY 10017, (800) 253-9646, Fax: (212) 963-4116, http://unstats.un.org; *Statistical Yearbook.*

KAZAKHSTAN - BROADCASTING

Central Intelligence Agency, Office of Public Affairs, Washington, DC 20505, (703) 482-0623, Fax: (703) 482-1739, www.cia.gov; *The World Factbook.*

Euromonitor International, Inc., 224 S. Michigan Avenue, Suite 1500, Chicago, IL 60604, (312) 922-1115, Fax: (312) 922-1157, www.euromonitor.com; *World Marketing Data and Statistics.*

Palgrave Macmillan Ltd., Houndmills, Basingstoke, Hampshire, RG21 6XS, England, (Telephone in U.S. (888) 330-8477), (Fax in U.S. (800) 672-2054), www.palgrave.com; *The Statesman's Yearbook 2008.*

UNESCO Institute for Statistics, C.P. 6128 Succursale Centre-Ville, Montreal, Quebec, H3C 3J7 Canada, (Dial from U.S. (514) 343-6880), (Fax from U.S. (514) 343 6882), www.uis.unesco.org; *Statistical Tables.*

United Nations Statistics Division, New York, NY 10017, (800) 253-9646, Fax: (212) 963-4116, http://unstats.un.org; *Trends in Europe and North America: The Statistical Yearbook of the ECE 2005.*

KAZAKHSTAN - BUDGET

Central Intelligence Agency, Office of Public Affairs, Washington, DC 20505, (703) 482-0623, Fax: (703) 482-1739, www.cia.gov; *The World Factbook.*

KAZAKHSTAN - BUSINESS

United Nations Statistics Division, New York, NY 10017, (800) 253-9646, Fax: (212) 963-4116, http://unstats.un.org; *Statistical Yearbook.*

KAZAKHSTAN - CAPITAL INVESTMENTS

The World Bank, 1818 H Street, NW, Washington, DC 20433, (202) 473-1000, Fax: (202) 477-6391, www.worldbank.org; *Statistical Handbook: States of the Former USSR.*

KAZAKHSTAN - CATTLE

See KAZAKHSTAN - LIVESTOCK

KAZAKHSTAN - CHILDBIRTH - STATISTICS

Central Intelligence Agency, Office of Public Affairs, Washington, DC 20505, (703) 482-0623, Fax: (703) 482-1739, www.cia.gov; *The World Factbook.*

Euromonitor International, Inc., 224 S. Michigan Avenue, Suite 1500, Chicago, IL 60604, (312) 922-1115, Fax: (312) 922-1157, www.euromonitor.com; *International Marketing Data and Statistics 2008* and *The World Economic Factbook 2008.*

Palgrave Macmillan Ltd., Houndmills, Basingstoke, Hampshire, RG21 6XS, England, (Telephone in U.S. (888) 330-8477), (Fax in U.S. (800) 672-2054), www.palgrave.com; *The Statesman's Yearbook 2008.*

Taylor and Francis Group, An Informa Business, 2 Park Square, Milton Park, Abingdon, Oxford OX14 4RN, United Kingdom, (Dial from U.S. (212) 216-7800), (Fax from U.S. (212) 564-7854), www.tandf.co.uk; *The Europa World Year Book.*

United Nations Statistics Division, New York, NY 10017, (800) 253-9646, Fax: (212) 963-4116, http://unstats.un.org; *Statistical Yearbook.*

World Health Organization (WHO), Avenue Appia 20, 1211 Geneve 27, Switzerland, (Telephone in U.S. (212) 331-9081), www.who.int; *World Health Report 2006.*

KAZAKHSTAN - COAL PRODUCTION

See KAZAKHSTAN - MINERAL INDUSTRIES

KAZAKHSTAN - COMMERCE

Palgrave Macmillan Ltd., Houndmills, Basingstoke, Hampshire, RG21 6XS, England, (Telephone in U.S. (888) 330-8477), (Fax in U.S. (800) 672-2054), www.palgrave.com; *The Statesman's Yearbook 2008.*

KAZAKHSTAN - CONSTRUCTION INDUSTRY

Academic International Press, PO Box 1111, Gulf Breeze, FL 32562-1111, Fax: (850) 934-0953, www.ai-press.com; *Russia and Eurasia Facts and Figures Annual.*

Palgrave Macmillan Ltd., Houndmills, Basingstoke, Hampshire, RG21 6XS, England, (Telephone in U.S. (888) 330-8477), (Fax in U.S. (800) 672-2054), www.palgrave.com; *The Statesman's Yearbook 2008.*

United Nations Statistics Division, New York, NY 10017, (800) 253-9646, Fax: (212) 963-4116, http://unstats.un.org; *Statistical Yearbook.*

KAZAKHSTAN - CONSUMER PRICE INDEXES

United Nations Statistics Division, New York, NY 10017, (800) 253-9646, Fax: (212) 963-4116, http://unstats.un.org; *Statistical Yearbook* and *Trends in Europe and North America: The Statistical Yearbook of the ECE 2005.*

The World Bank, 1818 H Street, NW, Washington, DC 20433, (202) 473-1000, Fax: (202) 477-6391, www.worldbank.org; *Kazakhstan.*

KAZAKHSTAN - CONSUMPTION (ECONOMICS)

The World Bank, 1818 H Street, NW, Washington, DC 20433, (202) 473-1000, Fax: (202) 477-6391, www.worldbank.org; *Statistical Handbook: States of the Former USSR* and *World Development Report 2008.*

KAZAKHSTAN - COTTON

See KAZAKHSTAN - CROPS

KAZAKHSTAN - CRIME

Academic International Press, PO Box 1111, Gulf Breeze, FL 32562-1111, Fax: (850) 934-0953, www.ai-press.com; *Russia and Eurasia Facts and Figures Annual.*

United Nations Statistics Division, New York, NY 10017, (800) 253-9646, Fax: (212) 963-4116, http://unstats.un.org; *Trends in Europe and North America: The Statistical Yearbook of the ECE 2005.*

KAZAKHSTAN - CROPS

Palgrave Macmillan Ltd., Houndmills, Basingstoke, Hampshire, RG21 6XS, England, (Telephone in U.S. (888) 330-8477), (Fax in U.S. (800) 672-2054), www.palgrave.com; *The Statesman's Yearbook 2008.*

Taylor and Francis Group, An Informa Business, 2 Park Square, Milton Park, Abingdon, Oxford OX14 4RN, United Kingdom, (Dial from U.S. (212) 216-7800), (Fax from U.S. (212) 564-7854), www.tandf.co.uk; *The Europa World Year Book.*

United Nations Food and Agricultural Organization (FAO), Viale delle Terme di Caracalla, 00100 Rome, Italy, (Dial from U.S. (202) 653-2400), (Fax from U.S. (202) 653 5760), www.fao.org; *FAO Production Yearbook 2002* and *The State of Food and Agriculture (SOFA) 2006.*

United Nations Statistics Division, New York, NY 10017, (800) 253-9646, Fax: (212) 963-4116, http://unstats.un.org; *2004 Industrial Commodity Statistics Yearbook* and *Statistical Yearbook.*

The World Bank, 1818 H Street, NW, Washington, DC 20433, (202) 473-1000, Fax: (202) 477-6391, www.worldbank.org; *Statistical Handbook: States of the Former USSR.*

KAZAKHSTAN - DAIRY PROCESSING

Palgrave Macmillan Ltd., Houndmills, Basingstoke, Hampshire, RG21 6XS, England, (Telephone in U.S. (888) 330-8477), (Fax in U.S. (800) 672-2054), www.palgrave.com; *The Statesman's Yearbook 2008.*

Taylor and Francis Group, An Informa Business, 2 Park Square, Milton Park, Abingdon, Oxford OX14 4RN, United Kingdom, (Dial from U.S. (212) 216-7800), (Fax from U.S. (212) 564-7854), www.tandf.co.uk; *The Europa World Year Book.*

United Nations Food and Agricultural Organization (FAO), Viale delle Terme di Caracalla, 00100 Rome, Italy, (Dial from U.S. (202) 653-2400), (Fax from U.S. (202) 653 5760), www.fao.org; *FAO Production Yearbook 2002* and *The State of Food and Agriculture (SOFA) 2006.*

United Nations Statistics Division, New York, NY 10017, (800) 253-9646, Fax: (212) 963-4116, http://unstats.un.org; *2004 Industrial Commodity Statistics Yearbook* and *Statistical Yearbook.*

KAZAKHSTAN - DEATH RATES

See KAZAKHSTAN - MORTALITY

KAZAKHSTAN - DEBTS, EXTERNAL

The World Bank, 1818 H Street, NW, Washington, DC 20433, (202) 473-1000, Fax: (202) 477-6391, www.worldbank.org; *Global Development Finance 2007; World Development Indicators (WDI) 2008;* and *World Development Report 2008.*

Worldinformation.com, 2 Market Street, Saffron Walden, Essex CB10 1HZ, United Kingdom, www.worldinformation.com; The World of Information (www.worldinformation.com).

KAZAKHSTAN - DEMOGRAPHY

Euromonitor International, Inc., 224 S. Michigan Avenue, Suite 1500, Chicago, IL 60604, (312) 922-1115, Fax: (312) 922-1157, www.euromonitor.com; *International Marketing Data and Statistics 2008; The World Economic Factbook 2008;* and *World Marketing Data and Statistics.*

United Nations Statistics Division, New York, NY 10017, (800) 253-9646, Fax: (212) 963-4116, http://unstats.un.org; *Demographic Yearbook* and *Human Development Report 2006.*

The World Bank, 1818 H Street, NW, Washington, DC 20433, (202) 473-1000, Fax: (202) 477-6391, www.worldbank.org; *Kazakhstan* and *Statistical Handbook: States of the Former USSR.*

KAZAKHSTAN - DISPOSABLE INCOME

United Nations Statistics Division, New York, NY 10017, (800) 253-9646, Fax: (212) 963-4116, http://unstats.un.org; *National Accounts Statistics: Compendium of Income Distribution Statistics* and *Statistical Yearbook.*

KAZAKHSTAN - DIVORCE

United Nations Statistics Division, New York, NY 10017, (800) 253-9646, Fax: (212) 963-4116, http://unstats.un.org; *Demographic Yearbook; Statistical Yearbook;* and *Trends in Europe and North America: The Statistical Yearbook of the ECE 2005.*

KAZAKHSTAN - ECONOMIC CONDITIONS

Academic International Press, PO Box 1111, Gulf Breeze, FL 32562-1111, Fax: (850) 934-0953, www.ai-press.com; *Russia and Eurasia Facts and Figures Annual.*

Center for International Business Education Research (CIBER), Columbia Business School and School of International and Public Affairs, Uris Hall, Room 212, 3022 Broadway, New York, NY 10027-6902, Mr. Joshua Safier, (212) 854-4750, Fax: (212) 222-9821, www.columbia.edu/cu/ciber/; Datastream International.

Central Intelligence Agency, Office of Public Affairs, Washington, DC 20505, (703) 482-0623, Fax: (703) 482-1739, www.cia.gov; *The World Factbook.*

DSI Data Service Information, Xantener Strasse 51a, D-47495 Rheinberg, Germany, www.dsidata.com; *Campus Solution.*

Dun and Bradstreet (DB) Corporation, 103 JFK Parkway, Short Hills, NJ 07078, (973) 921-5500, www.dnb.com; *Country Report.*

Economist Intelligence Unit, 111 West 57th Street, New York, NY 10019, (212) 554-0600, Fax: (212) 586-1181, www.eiu.com; *Kazakhstan Country Report.*

Euromonitor International, Inc., 224 S. Michigan Avenue, Suite 1500, Chicago, IL 60604, (312) 922-1115, Fax: (312) 922-1157, www.euromonitor.com; *The World Economic Factbook 2008* and *World Marketing Data and Statistics.*

International Monetary Fund (IMF), 700 Nineteenth Street, NW, Washington, DC 20431, (202) 623-

7000, Fax: (202) 623-4661, www.imf.org; *World Economic Outlook Reports.*

Nomura Research Institute (NRI), 2 World Financial Center, Building B, 19th Fl., New York, NY 10281-1198, (212) 667-1670, www.nri.co.jp/english; *Asian Economic Outlook 2003-2004.*

Palgrave Macmillan Ltd., Houndmills, Basingstoke, Hampshire, RG21 6XS, England, (Telephone in U.S. (888) 330-8477), (Fax in U.S. (800) 672-2054), www.palgrave.com; *The Statesman's Yearbook 2008.*

United Nations Statistics Division, New York, NY 10017, (800) 253-9646, Fax: (212) 963-4116, http://unstats.un.org; *World Statistics Pocketbook.*

The World Bank, 1818 H Street, NW, Washington, DC 20433, (202) 473-1000, Fax: (202) 477-6391, www.worldbank.org; *Global Economic Monitor (GEM); Global Economic Prospects 2008; Kazakhstan; The World Bank Atlas 2003-2004;* and *World Development Report 2008.*

KAZAKHSTAN - EDUCATION

Academic International Press, PO Box 1111, Gulf Breeze, FL 32562-1111, Fax: (850) 934-0953, www.ai-press.com; *Russia and Eurasia Facts and Figures Annual.*

Euromonitor International, Inc., 224 S. Michigan Avenue, Suite 1500, Chicago, IL 60604, (312) 922-1115, Fax: (312) 922-1157, www.euromonitor.com; *International Marketing Data and Statistics 2008* and *World Marketing Data and Statistics.*

Palgrave Macmillan Ltd., Houndmills, Basingstoke, Hampshire, RG21 6XS, England, (Telephone in U.S. (888) 330-8477), (Fax in U.S. (800) 672-2054), www.palgrave.com; *The Statesman's Yearbook 2008.*

Taylor and Francis Group, An Informa Business, 2 Park Square, Milton Park, Abingdon, Oxford OX14 4RN, United Kingdom, (Dial from U.S. (212) 216-7800), (Fax from U.S. (212) 564-7854), www.tandf.co.uk; *The Europa World Year Book.*

UNESCO Institute for Statistics, C.P. 6128 Succursale Centre-Ville, Montreal, Quebec, H3C 3J7 Canada, (Dial from U.S. (514) 343-6880), (Fax from U.S. (514) 343 6882), www.uis.unesco.org; *Statistical Tables.*

United Nations Statistics Division, New York, NY 10017, (800) 253-9646, Fax: (212) 963-4116, http://unstats.un.org; *Human Development Report 2006* and *Trends in Europe and North America: The Statistical Yearbook of the ECE 2005.*

The World Bank, 1818 H Street, NW, Washington, DC 20433, (202) 473-1000, Fax: (202) 477-6391, www.worldbank.org; *Kazakhstan* and *World Development Report 2008.*

KAZAKHSTAN - ELECTRICITY

Central Intelligence Agency, Office of Public Affairs, Washington, DC 20505, (703) 482-0623, Fax: (703) 482-1739, www.cia.gov; *The World Factbook.*

Palgrave Macmillan Ltd., Houndmills, Basingstoke, Hampshire, RG21 6XS, England, (Telephone in U.S. (888) 330-8477), (Fax in U.S. (800) 672-2054), www.palgrave.com; *The Statesman's Yearbook 2008.*

Platts, 2 Penn Plaza, 25th Floor, New York, NY 10121-2298, (212) 904-3070, www.platts.com; *Energy Economist.*

U.S. Department of Energy (DOE), Energy Information Administration (EIA), 1000 Independence Avenue, SW, Washington, DC 20585, (202) 586-8800, www.eia.doe.gov; *International Energy Annual 2004* and *International Energy Outlook 2006.*

United Nations Statistics Division, New York, NY 10017, (800) 253-9646, Fax: (212) 963-4116, http://unstats.un.org; *Energy Statistics Yearbook 2003; Human Development Report 2006; Statistical Yearbook;* and *Trends in Europe and North America: The Statistical Yearbook of the ECE 2005.*

The World Bank, 1818 H Street, NW, Washington, DC 20433, (202) 473-1000, Fax: (202) 477-6391, www.worldbank.org; *Statistical Handbook: States of the Former USSR.*

KAZAKHSTAN - EMPLOYMENT

Euromonitor International, Inc., 224 S. Michigan Avenue, Suite 1500, Chicago, IL 60604, (312) 922-1115, Fax: (312) 922-1157, www.euromonitor.com; *International Marketing Data and Statistics 2008.*

United Nations Statistics Division, New York, NY 10017, (800) 253-9646, Fax: (212) 963-4116, http://unstats.un.org; *Statistical Yearbook* and *Trends in Europe and North America: The Statistical Yearbook of the ECE 2005.*

The World Bank, 1818 H Street, NW, Washington, DC 20433, (202) 473-1000, Fax: (202) 477-6391, www.worldbank.org; *Kazakhstan* and *Statistical Handbook: States of the Former USSR.*

KAZAKHSTAN - ENVIRONMENTAL CONDITIONS

DSI Data Service Information, Xantener Strasse 51a, D-47495 Rheinberg, Germany, www.dsidata.com; *Campus Solution* and *DSI's Global Environmental Database.*

Economist Intelligence Unit, 111 West 57th Street, New York, NY 10019, (212) 554-0600, Fax: (212) 586-1181, www.eiu.com; *Kazakhstan Country Report.*

United Nations Statistics Division, New York, NY 10017, (800) 253-9646, Fax: (212) 963-4116, http://unstats.un.org; *Statistical Yearbook; Trends in Europe and North America: The Statistical Yearbook of the ECE 2005;* and *World Statistics Pocketbook.*

KAZAKHSTAN - EXPORTS

Academic International Press, PO Box 1111, Gulf Breeze, FL 32562-1111, Fax: (850) 934-0953, www.ai-press.com; *Russia and Eurasia Facts and Figures Annual.*

Central Intelligence Agency, Office of Public Affairs, Washington, DC 20505, (703) 482-0623, Fax: (703) 482-1739, www.cia.gov; *The World Factbook.*

Economist Intelligence Unit, 111 West 57th Street, New York, NY 10019, (212) 554-0600, Fax: (212) 586-1181, www.eiu.com; *Kazakhstan Country Report.*

Euromonitor International, Inc., 224 S. Michigan Avenue, Suite 1500, Chicago, IL 60604, (312) 922-1115, Fax: (312) 922-1157, www.euromonitor.com; *International Marketing Data and Statistics 2008* and *The World Economic Factbook 2008.*

International Monetary Fund (IMF), 700 Nineteenth Street, NW, Washington, DC 20431, (202) 623-7000, Fax: (202) 623-4661, www.imf.org; *Direction of Trade Statistics Yearbook 2007.*

Palgrave Macmillan Ltd., Houndmills, Basingstoke, Hampshire, RG21 6XS, England, (Telephone in U.S. (888) 330-8477), (Fax in U.S. (800) 672-2054), www.palgrave.com; *The Statesman's Yearbook 2008.*

Taylor and Francis Group, An Informa Business, 2 Park Square, Milton Park, Abingdon, Oxford OX14 4RN, United Kingdom, (Dial from U.S. (212) 216-7800), (Fax from U.S. (212) 564-7854), www.tandf.co.uk; *The Europa World Year Book.*

United Nations Conference on Trade and Development (UNCTAD), DC2-1120, United Nations, New York, NY 10017, (212) 963-0027, www.unctad.org; *Handbook of Statistics 2005.*

United Nations Statistics Division, New York, NY 10017, (800) 253-9646, Fax: (212) 963-4116, http://unstats.un.org; *International Trade Statistics Yearbook* and *Trends in Europe and North America: The Statistical Yearbook of the ECE 2005.*

The World Bank, 1818 H Street, NW, Washington, DC 20433, (202) 473-1000, Fax: (202) 477-6391, www.worldbank.org; *Statistical Handbook: States of the Former USSR; World Development Indicators (WDI) 2008;* and *World Development Report 2008.*

Worldinformation.com, 2 Market Street, Saffron Walden, Essex CB10 1HZ, United Kingdom, www.worldinformation.com; The World of Information (www.worldinformation.com).

KAZAKHSTAN - FERTILITY, HUMAN

Central Intelligence Agency, Office of Public Affairs, Washington, DC 20505, (703) 482-0623, Fax: (703) 482-1739, www.cia.gov; *The World Factbook.*

United Nations Statistics Division, New York, NY 10017, (800) 253-9646, Fax: (212) 963-4116, http://unstats.un.org; *Human Development Report 2006* and *Trends in Europe and North America: The Statistical Yearbook of the ECE 2005.*

The World Bank, 1818 H Street, NW, Washington, DC 20433, (202) 473-1000, Fax: (202) 477-6391, www.worldbank.org; *Statistical Handbook: States of the Former USSR; The World Bank Atlas 2003-2004; World Development Indicators (WDI) 2008;* and *World Development Report 2008.*

World Health Organization (WHO), Avenue Appia 20, 1211 Geneve 27, Switzerland, (Telephone in U.S. (212) 331-9081), www.who.int; *World Health Report 2006.*

KAZAKHSTAN - FERTILIZER INDUSTRY

United Nations Food and Agricultural Organization (FAO), Viale delle Terme di Caracalla, 00100 Rome, Italy, (Dial from U.S. (202) 653-2400), (Fax from U.S. (202) 653 5760), www.fao.org; *FAO Fertilizer Yearbook.*

United Nations Statistics Division, New York, NY 10017, (800) 253-9646, Fax: (212) 963-4116, http://unstats.un.org; *2004 Industrial Commodity Statistics Yearbook* and *Statistical Yearbook.*

KAZAKHSTAN - FINANCE

United Nations Statistics Division, New York, NY 10017, (800) 253-9646, Fax: (212) 963-4116, http://unstats.un.org; *National Accounts Statistics: Compendium of Income Distribution Statistics* and *Statistical Yearbook.*

The World Bank, 1818 H Street, NW, Washington, DC 20433, (202) 473-1000, Fax: (202) 477-6391, www.worldbank.org; *Kazakhstan* and *Statistical Handbook: States of the Former USSR.*

KAZAKHSTAN - FINANCE, PUBLIC

Bernan Essential Government Publications, 4611-F Assembly Drive, Lanham MD, 20706-4391, (301) 459-2255, Fax: (800) 865-3450, www.bernan.com; *National Accounts Statistics.*

Economist Intelligence Unit, 111 West 57th Street, New York, NY 10019, (212) 554-0600, Fax: (212) 586-1181, www.eiu.com; *Kazakhstan Country Report.*

International Monetary Fund (IMF), 700 Nineteenth Street, NW, Washington, DC 20431, (202) 623-7000, Fax: (202) 623-4661, www.imf.org; *International Financial Statistics* and *International Financial Statistics Online Service.*

Taylor and Francis Group, An Informa Business, 2 Park Square, Milton Park, Abingdon, Oxford OX14 4RN, United Kingdom, (Dial from U.S. (212) 216-7800), (Fax from U.S. (212) 564-7854), www.tandf.co.uk; *The Europa World Year Book.*

The World Bank, 1818 H Street, NW, Washington, DC 20433, (202) 473-1000, Fax: (202) 477-6391, www.worldbank.org; *Kazakhstan* and *Statistical Handbook: States of the Former USSR.*

KAZAKHSTAN - FISHERIES

United Nations Food and Agricultural Organization (FAO), Viale delle Terme di Caracalla, 00100 Rome, Italy, (Dial from U.S. (202) 653-2400), (Fax from U.S. (202) 653 5760), www.fao.org; *FAO Yearbook of Fishery Statistics;* Fishery Databases; FISHSTAT Database. Subjects covered include: Aquaculture production, capture production, fishery commodities; and *The State of Food and Agriculture (SOFA) 2006.*

United Nations Statistics Division, New York, NY 10017, (800) 253-9646, Fax: (212) 963-4116, http://unstats.un.org; *2004 Industrial Commodity Statistics Yearbook* and *Statistical Yearbook.*

The World Bank, 1818 H Street, NW, Washington, DC 20433, (202) 473-1000, Fax: (202) 477-6391, www.worldbank.org; *Kazakhstan.*

KAZAKHSTAN - FOOD

United Nations Food and Agricultural Organization (FAO), Viale delle Terme di Caracalla, 00100 Rome, Italy, (Dial from U.S. (202) 653-2400), (Fax from U.S. (202) 653 5760), www.fao.org; *FAO Production Yearbook 2002* and *The State of Food and Agriculture (SOFA) 2006.*

United Nations Statistics Division, New York, NY 10017, (800) 253-9646, Fax: (212) 963-4116, http://unstats.un.org; *Human Development Report 2006* and *2004 Industrial Commodity Statistics Yearbook.*

KAZAKHSTAN - FOREIGN EXCHANGE RATES

Central Intelligence Agency, Office of Public Affairs, Washington, DC 20505, (703) 482-0623, Fax: (703) 482-1739, www.cia.gov; *The World Factbook.*

Euromonitor International, Inc., 224 S. Michigan Avenue, Suite 1500, Chicago, IL 60604, (312) 922-1115, Fax: (312) 922-1157, www.euromonitor.com; *International Marketing Data and Statistics 2008* and *The World Economic Factbook 2008.*

Taylor and Francis Group, An Informa Business, 2 Park Square, Milton Park, Abingdon, Oxford OX14 4RN, United Kingdom, (Dial from U.S. (212) 216-7800), (Fax from U.S. (212) 564-7854), www.tandf.co.uk; *The Europa World Year Book.*

United Nations Statistics Division, New York, NY 10017, (800) 253-9646, Fax: (212) 963-4116, http://unstats.un.org; *Statistical Yearbook; Trends in Europe and North America: The Statistical Yearbook of the ECE 2005;* and *World Statistics Pocketbook.*

Worldinformation.com, 2 Market Street, Saffron Walden, Essex CB10 1HZ, United Kingdom, www.worldinformation.com; The World of Information (www.worldinformation.com).

KAZAKHSTAN - FORESTS AND FORESTRY

Academic International Press, PO Box 1111, Gulf Breeze, FL 32562-1111, Fax: (850) 934-0953, www.ai-press.com; *Russia and Eurasia Facts and Figures Annual.*

Palgrave Macmillan Ltd., Houndmills, Basingstoke, Hampshire, RG21 6XS, England, (Telephone in U.S. (888) 330-8477), (Fax in U.S. (800) 672-2054), www.palgrave.com; *The Statesman's Yearbook 2008.*

UNESCO Institute for Statistics, C.P. 6128 Succursale Centre-Ville, Montreal, Quebec, H3C 3J7 Canada, (Dial from U.S. (514) 343-6880), (Fax from U.S. (514) 343 6882), www.uis.unesco.org; *Statistical Tables.*

United Nations Food and Agricultural Organization (FAO), Viale delle Terme di Caracalla, 00100 Rome, Italy, (Dial from U.S. (202) 653-2400), (Fax from U.S. (202) 653 5760), www.fao.org; *FAO Yearbook of Forest Products* and *The State of Food and Agriculture (SOFA) 2006.*

United Nations Statistics Division, New York, NY 10017, (800) 253-9646, Fax: (212) 963-4116, http://unstats.un.org; *2004 Industrial Commodity Statistics Yearbook; Statistical Yearbook;* and *Trends in Europe and North America: The Statistical Yearbook of the ECE 2005.*

The World Bank, 1818 H Street, NW, Washington, DC 20433, (202) 473-1000, Fax: (202) 477-6391, www.worldbank.org; *Kazakhstan* and *World Development Report 2008.*

KAZAKHSTAN - GROSS DOMESTIC PRODUCT

Academic International Press, PO Box 1111, Gulf Breeze, FL 32562-1111, Fax: (850) 934-0953, www.ai-press.com; *Russia and Eurasia Facts and Figures Annual.*

Economist Intelligence Unit, 111 West 57th Street, New York, NY 10019, (212) 554-0600, Fax: (212) 586-1181, www.eiu.com; *Kazakhstan Country Report.*

Euromonitor International, Inc., 224 S. Michigan Avenue, Suite 1500, Chicago, IL 60604, (312) 922-1115, Fax: (312) 922-1157, www.euromonitor.com; *International Marketing Data and Statistics 2008* and *The World Economic Factbook 2008.*

United Nations Statistics Division, New York, NY 10017, (800) 253-9646, Fax: (212) 963-4116, http://unstats.un.org; *Human Development Report 2006; National Accounts Statistics: Compendium of Income Distribution Statistics; Statistical Yearbook;* and *Trends in Europe and North America: The Statistical Yearbook of the ECE 2005.*

The World Bank, 1818 H Street, NW, Washington, DC 20433, (202) 473-1000, Fax: (202) 477-6391, www.worldbank.org; *Statistical Handbook: States of the Former USSR; World Development Indicators (WDI) 2008;* and *World Development Report 2008.*

KAZAKHSTAN - GROSS NATIONAL PRODUCT

Palgrave Macmillan Ltd., Houndmills, Basingstoke, Hampshire, RG21 6XS, England, (Telephone in U.S. (888) 330-8477), (Fax in U.S. (800) 672-2054), www.palgrave.com; *The Statesman's Yearbook 2008.*

United Nations Statistics Division, New York, NY 10017, (800) 253-9646, Fax: (212) 963-4116, http://unstats.un.org; *Statistical Yearbook.*

The World Bank, 1818 H Street, NW, Washington, DC 20433, (202) 473-1000, Fax: (202) 477-6391, www.worldbank.org; *The World Bank Atlas 2003-2004; World Development Indicators (WDI) 2008;* and *World Development Report 2008.*

Worldinformation.com, 2 Market Street, Saffron Walden, Essex CB10 1HZ, United Kingdom, www.worldinformation.com; The World of Information (www.worldinformation.com).

KAZAKHSTAN - HOUSING

Euromonitor International, Inc., 224 S. Michigan Avenue, Suite 1500, Chicago, IL 60604, (312) 922-1115, Fax: (312) 922-1157, www.euromonitor.com; *World Marketing Data and Statistics.*

United Nations Statistics Division, New York, NY 10017, (800) 253-9646, Fax: (212) 963-4116, http://unstats.un.org; *Trends in Europe and North America: The Statistical Yearbook of the ECE 2005.*

KAZAKHSTAN - ILLITERATE PERSONS

Euromonitor International, Inc., 224 S. Michigan Avenue, Suite 1500, Chicago, IL 60604, (312) 922-1115, Fax: (312) 922-1157, www.euromonitor.com; *The World Economic Factbook 2008.*

UNESCO Institute for Statistics, C.P. 6128 Succursale Centre-Ville, Montreal, Quebec, H3C 3J7 Canada, (Dial from U.S. (514) 343-6880), (Fax from U.S. (514) 343 6882), www.uis.unesco.org; *Statistical Tables.*

United Nations Statistics Division, New York, NY 10017, (800) 253-9646, Fax: (212) 963-4116, http://unstats.un.org; *Human Development Report 2006.*

KAZAKHSTAN - IMPORTS

Academic International Press, PO Box 1111, Gulf Breeze, FL 32562-1111, Fax: (850) 934-0953, www.ai-press.com; *Russia and Eurasia Facts and Figures Annual.*

Central Intelligence Agency, Office of Public Affairs, Washington, DC 20505, (703) 482-0623, Fax: (703) 482-1739, www.cia.gov; *The World Factbook.*

Economist Intelligence Unit, 111 West 57th Street, New York, NY 10019, (212) 554-0600, Fax: (212) 586-1181, www.eiu.com; *Kazakhstan Country Report.*

Euromonitor International, Inc., 224 S. Michigan Avenue, Suite 1500, Chicago, IL 60604, (312) 922-1115, Fax: (312) 922-1157, www.euromonitor.com; *International Marketing Data and Statistics 2008* and *The World Economic Factbook 2008.*

International Monetary Fund (IMF), 700 Nineteenth Street, NW, Washington, DC 20431, (202) 623-7000, Fax: (202) 623-4661, www.imf.org; *Direction of Trade Statistics Yearbook 2007.*

Palgrave Macmillan Ltd., Houndmills, Basingstoke, Hampshire, RG21 6XS, England, (Telephone in U.S. (888) 330-8477), (Fax in U.S. (800) 672-2054), www.palgrave.com; *The Statesman's Yearbook 2008.*

Taylor and Francis Group, An Informa Business, 2 Park Square, Milton Park, Abingdon, Oxford OX14 4RN, United Kingdom, (Dial from U.S. (212) 216-7800), (Fax from U.S. (212) 564-7854), www.tandf.co.uk; *The Europa World Year Book.*

United Nations Conference on Trade and Development (UNCTAD), DC2-1120, United Nations, New York, NY 10017, (212) 963-0027, www.unctad.org; *Handbook of Statistics 2005.*

United Nations Statistics Division, New York, NY 10017, (800) 253-9646, Fax: (212) 963-4116, http://unstats.un.org; *International Trade Statistics Yearbook* and *Trends in Europe and North America: The Statistical Yearbook of the ECE 2005.*

The World Bank, 1818 H Street, NW, Washington, DC 20433, (202) 473-1000, Fax: (202) 477-6391, www.worldbank.org; *Statistical Handbook: States of the Former USSR; World Development Indicators (WDI) 2008;* and *World Development Report 2008.*

Worldinformation.com, 2 Market Street, Saffron Walden, Essex CB10 1HZ, United Kingdom, www.worldinformation.com; The World of Information (www.worldinformation.com).

KAZAKHSTAN - INDUSTRIAL PRODUCTIVITY

The World Bank, 1818 H Street, NW, Washington, DC 20433, (202) 473-1000, Fax: (202) 477-6391, www.worldbank.org; *Statistical Handbook: States of the Former USSR.*

KAZAKHSTAN - INDUSTRIAL PROPERTY

United Nations Statistics Division, New York, NY 10017, (800) 253-9646, Fax: (212) 963-4116, http://unstats.un.org; *Statistical Yearbook.*

KAZAKHSTAN - INDUSTRIES

Academic International Press, PO Box 1111, Gulf Breeze, FL 32562-1111, Fax: (850) 934-0953, www.ai-press.com; *Russia and Eurasia Facts and Figures Annual.*

Central Intelligence Agency, Office of Public Affairs, Washington, DC 20505, (703) 482-0623, Fax: (703) 482-1739, www.cia.gov; *The World Factbook.*

Economist Intelligence Unit, 111 West 57th Street, New York, NY 10019, (212) 554-0600, Fax: (212) 586-1181, www.eiu.com; *Kazakhstan Country Report.*

Euromonitor International, Inc., 224 S. Michigan Avenue, Suite 1500, Chicago, IL 60604, (312) 922-1115, Fax: (312) 922-1157, www.euromonitor.com; *The World Economic Factbook 2008* and *World Marketing Data and Statistics.*

Palgrave Macmillan Ltd., Houndmills, Basingstoke, Hampshire, RG21 6XS, England, (Telephone in U.S. (888) 330-8477), (Fax in U.S. (800) 672-2054), www.palgrave.com; *The Statesman's Yearbook 2008.*

Taylor and Francis Group, An Informa Business, 2 Park Square, Milton Park, Abingdon, Oxford OX14 4RN, United Kingdom, (Dial from U.S. (212) 216-7800), (Fax from U.S. (212) 564-7854), www.tandf.co.uk; *The Europa World Year Book.*

United Nations Industrial Development Organization (UNIDO), 1 United Nations Plaza, New York, NY 10017, (212) 963 6890, Fax: (212) 963-7904, http://unido.org; Industrial Statistics Database 2008 (INDSTAT) and *The International Yearbook of Industrial Statistics 2008.*

United Nations Statistics Division, New York, NY 10017, (800) 253-9646, Fax: (212) 963-4116, http://unstats.un.org; *2004 Industrial Commodity Statistics Yearbook; Statistical Yearbook;* and *Trends in Europe and North America: The Statistical Yearbook of the ECE 2005.*

The World Bank, 1818 H Street, NW, Washington, DC 20433, (202) 473-1000, Fax: (202) 477-6391, www.worldbank.org; *Kazakhstan; Statistical Hand-*

book: States of the Former USSR; and *World Development Indicators (WDI) 2008.*

KAZAKHSTAN - INFANT AND MATERNAL MORTALITY

See KAZAKHSTAN - MORTALITY

KAZAKHSTAN - INTERNATIONAL TRADE

Academic International Press, PO Box 1111, Gulf Breeze, FL 32562-1111, Fax: (850) 934-0953, www.ai-press.com; *Russia and Eurasia Facts and Figures Annual.*

Economist Intelligence Unit, 111 West 57th Street, New York, NY 10019, (212) 554-0600, Fax: (212) 586-1181, www.eiu.com; *Kazakhstan Country Report.*

Euromonitor International, Inc., 224 S. Michigan Avenue, Suite 1500, Chicago, IL 60604, (312) 922-1115, Fax: (312) 922-1157, www.euromonitor.com; *The World Economic Factbook 2008* and *World Marketing Data and Statistics.*

International Monetary Fund (IMF), 700 Nineteenth Street, NW, Washington, DC 20431, (202) 623-7000, Fax: (202) 623-4661, www.imf.org; *Direction of Trade Statistics Yearbook 2007.*

Palgrave Macmillan Ltd., Houndmills, Basingstoke, Hampshire, RG21 6XS, England, (Telephone in U.S. (888) 330-8477), (Fax in U.S. (800) 672-2054), www.palgrave.com; *The Statesman's Yearbook 2008.*

United Nations Food and Agricultural Organization (FAO), Viale delle Terme di Caracalla, 00100 Rome, Italy, (Dial from U.S. (202) 653-2400), (Fax from U.S. (202) 653 5760), www.fao.org; *FAO Trade Yearbook.*

United Nations Statistics Division, New York, NY 10017, (800) 253-9646, Fax: (212) 963-4116, http://unstats.un.org; *International Trade Statistics Yearbook* and *Statistical Yearbook.*

The World Bank, 1818 H Street, NW, Washington, DC 20433, (202) 473-1000, Fax: (202) 477-6391, www.worldbank.org; *Kazakhstan; Statistical Handbook: States of the Former USSR; World Development Indicators (WDI) 2008;* and *World Development Report 2008.*

World Trade Organization (WTO), Centre William Rappard, Rue de Lausanne 154, CH-1211 Geneva 21, Switzerland, www.wto.org; *International Trade Statistics 2006.*

KAZAKHSTAN - INTERNET USERS

International Telecommunication Union (ITU), Place des Nations, 1211 Geneva 20, Switzerland, www.itu.int; *World Telecommunication/ICT Indicators Database on CD-ROM; World Telecommunication/ICT Indicators Database Online;* and *Yearbook of Statistics - Telecommunication Services (Chronological Time Series 1997-2006).*

The World Bank, 1818 H Street, NW, Washington, DC 20433, (202) 473-1000, Fax: (202) 477-6391, www.worldbank.org; *Kazakhstan.*

KAZAKHSTAN - LABOR

Academic International Press, PO Box 1111, Gulf Breeze, FL 32562-1111, Fax: (850) 934-0953, www.ai-press.com; *Russia and Eurasia Facts and Figures Annual.*

Central Intelligence Agency, Office of Public Affairs, Washington, DC 20505, (703) 482-0623, Fax: (703) 482-1739, www.cia.gov; *The World Factbook.*

Euromonitor International, Inc., 224 S. Michigan Avenue, Suite 1500, Chicago, IL 60604, (312) 922-1115, Fax: (312) 922-1157, www.euromonitor.com; *International Marketing Data and Statistics 2008* and *World Marketing Data and Statistics.*

Palgrave Macmillan Ltd., Houndmills, Basingstoke, Hampshire, RG21 6XS, England, (Telephone in U.S. (888) 330-8477), (Fax in U.S. (800) 672-2054), www.palgrave.com; *The Statesman's Yearbook 2008.*

United Nations Statistics Division, New York, NY 10017, (800) 253-9646, Fax: (212) 963-4116, http://unstats.un.org; *Human Development Report 2006* and *Statistical Yearbook.*

The World Bank, 1818 H Street, NW, Washington, DC 20433, (202) 473-1000, Fax: (202) 477-6391, www.worldbank.org; *Statistical Handbook: States of the Former USSR; The World Bank Atlas 2003-2004; World Development Indicators (WDI) 2008;* and *World Development Report 2008.*

KAZAKHSTAN - LAND USE

Central Intelligence Agency, Office of Public Affairs, Washington, DC 20505, (703) 482-0623, Fax: (703) 482-1739, www.cia.gov; *The World Factbook.*

Euromonitor International, Inc., 224 S. Michigan Avenue, Suite 1500, Chicago, IL 60604, (312) 922-1115, Fax: (312) 922-1157, www.euromonitor.com; *International Marketing Data and Statistics 2008.*

United Nations Food and Agricultural Organization (FAO), Viale delle Terme di Caracalla, 00100 Rome, Italy, (Dial from U.S. (202) 653-2400), (Fax from U.S. (202) 653 5760), www.fao.org; *FAO Production Yearbook 2002.*

The World Bank, 1818 H Street, NW, Washington, DC 20433, (202) 473-1000, Fax: (202) 477-6391, www.worldbank.org; *World Development Report 2008.*

KAZAKHSTAN - LIBRARIES

UNESCO Institute for Statistics, C.P. 6128 Succursale Centre-Ville, Montreal, Quebec, H3C 3J7 Canada, (Dial from U.S. (514) 343-6880), (Fax from U.S. (514) 343 6882), www.uis.unesco.org; *Statistical Tables.*

United Nations Statistics Division, New York, NY 10017, (800) 253-9646, Fax: (212) 963-4116, http://unstats.un.org; *Trends in Europe and North America: The Statistical Yearbook of the ECE 2005.*

KAZAKHSTAN - LIFE EXPECTANCY

Central Intelligence Agency, Office of Public Affairs, Washington, DC 20505, (703) 482-0623, Fax: (703) 482-1739, www.cia.gov; *The World Factbook.*

Euromonitor International, Inc., 224 S. Michigan Avenue, Suite 1500, Chicago, IL 60604, (312) 922-1115, Fax: (312) 922-1157, www.euromonitor.com; *The World Economic Factbook 2008.*

United Nations Statistics Division, New York, NY 10017, (800) 253-9646, Fax: (212) 963-4116, http://unstats.un.org; *Demographic Yearbook; Human Development Report 2006; Trends in Europe and North America: The Statistical Yearbook of the ECE 2005;* and *World Statistics Pocketbook.*

The World Bank, 1818 H Street, NW, Washington, DC 20433, (202) 473-1000, Fax: (202) 477-6391, www.worldbank.org; *The World Bank Atlas 2003-2004; World Development Indicators (WDI) 2008;* and *World Development Report 2008.*

World Health Organization (WHO), Avenue Appia 20, 1211 Geneve 27, Switzerland, (Telephone in U.S. (212) 331-9081), www.who.int; *World Health Report 2006.*

KAZAKHSTAN - LIVESTOCK

Academic International Press, PO Box 1111, Gulf Breeze, FL 32562-1111, Fax: (850) 934-0953, www.ai-press.com; *Russia and Eurasia Facts and Figures Annual.*

Palgrave Macmillan Ltd., Houndmills, Basingstoke, Hampshire, RG21 6XS, England, (Telephone in U.S. (888) 330-8477), (Fax in U.S. (800) 672-2054), www.palgrave.com; *The Statesman's Yearbook 2008.*

Taylor and Francis Group, An Informa Business, 2 Park Square, Milton Park, Abingdon, Oxford OX14 4RN, United Kingdom, (Dial from U.S. (212) 216-7800), (Fax from U.S. (212) 564-7854), www.tandf.co.uk; *The Europa World Year Book.*

United Nations Food and Agricultural Organization (FAO), Viale delle Terme di Caracalla, 00100 Rome, Italy, (Dial from U.S. (202) 653-2400), (Fax from U.S. (202) 653 5760), www.fao.org; *FAO Production Yearbook 2002* and *The State of Food and Agriculture (SOFA) 2006.*

United Nations Statistics Division, New York, NY 10017, (800) 253-9646, Fax: (212) 963-4116, http://unstats.un.org; *2004 Industrial Commodity Statistics Yearbook* and *Statistical Yearbook.*

KAZAKHSTAN - MACHINERY

United Nations Statistics Division, New York, NY 10017, (800) 253-9646, Fax: (212) 963-4116, http://unstats.un.org; *2004 Industrial Commodity Statistics Yearbook.*

KAZAKHSTAN - MANUFACTURES

United Nations Statistics Division, New York, NY 10017, (800) 253-9646, Fax: (212) 963-4116, http://unstats.un.org; *2004 Industrial Commodity Statistics Yearbook* and *Statistical Yearbook.*

The World Bank, 1818 H Street, NW, Washington, DC 20433, (202) 473-1000, Fax: (202) 477-6391, www.worldbank.org; *World Development Indicators (WDI) 2008.*

KAZAKHSTAN - MARRIAGE

United Nations Statistics Division, New York, NY 10017, (800) 253-9646, Fax: (212) 963-4116, http://unstats.un.org; *Demographic Yearbook; Statistical Yearbook;* and *Trends in Europe and North America: The Statistical Yearbook of the ECE 2005.*

KAZAKHSTAN - MEAT PRODUCTION

See KAZAKHSTAN - LIVESTOCK

KAZAKHSTAN - MINERAL INDUSTRIES

Academic International Press, PO Box 1111, Gulf Breeze, FL 32562-1111, Fax: (850) 934-0953, www.ai-press.com; *Russia and Eurasia Facts and Figures Annual.*

Palgrave Macmillan Ltd., Houndmills, Basingstoke, Hampshire, RG21 6XS, England, (Telephone in U.S. (888) 330-8477), (Fax in U.S. (800) 672-2054), www.palgrave.com; *The Statesman's Yearbook 2008.*

Platts, 2 Penn Plaza, 25th Floor, New York, NY 10121-2298, (212) 904-3070, www.platts.com; *Energy Economist.*

Taylor and Francis Group, An Informa Business, 2 Park Square, Milton Park, Abingdon, Oxford OX14 4RN, United Kingdom, (Dial from U.S. (212) 216-7800), (Fax from U.S. (212) 564-7854), www.tandf.co.uk; *The Europa World Year Book.*

United Nations Statistics Division, New York, NY 10017, (800) 253-9646, Fax: (212) 963-4116, http://unstats.un.org; *Energy Statistics Yearbook 2003* and *Statistical Yearbook.*

The World Bank, 1818 H Street, NW, Washington, DC 20433, (202) 473-1000, Fax: (202) 477-6391, www.worldbank.org; *Kazakhstan.*

KAZAKHSTAN - MONEY SUPPLY

Economist Intelligence Unit, 111 West 57th Street, New York, NY 10019, (212) 554-0600, Fax: (212) 586-1181, www.eiu.com; *Kazakhstan Country Report.*

The World Bank, 1818 H Street, NW, Washington, DC 20433, (202) 473-1000, Fax: (202) 477-6391, www.worldbank.org; *Kazakhstan.*

KAZAKHSTAN - MONUMENTS AND HISTORIC SITES

UNESCO Institute for Statistics, C.P. 6128 Succursale Centre-Ville, Montreal, Quebec, H3C 3J7 Canada, (Dial from U.S. (514) 343-6880), (Fax from U.S. (514) 343 6882), www.uis.unesco.org; *Statistical Tables.*

KAZAKHSTAN - MORTALITY

Central Intelligence Agency, Office of Public Affairs, Washington, DC 20505, (703) 482-0623, Fax: (703) 482-1739, www.cia.gov; *The World Factbook.*

Euromonitor International, Inc., 224 S. Michigan Avenue, Suite 1500, Chicago, IL 60604, (312) 922-1115, Fax: (312) 922-1157, www.euromonitor.com; *International Marketing Data and Statistics 2008* and *The World Economic Factbook 2008.*

Palgrave Macmillan Ltd., Houndmills, Basingstoke, Hampshire, RG21 6XS, England, (Telephone in U.S. (888) 330-8477), (Fax in U.S. (800) 672-2054), www.palgrave.com; *The Statesman's Yearbook 2008.*

Taylor and Francis Group, An Informa Business, 2 Park Square, Milton Park, Abingdon, Oxford OX14 4RN, United Kingdom, (Dial from U.S. (212) 216-7800), (Fax from U.S. (212) 564-7854), www.tandf.co.uk; *The Europa World Year Book.*

UNICEF, 3 United Nations Plaza, New York, NY 10017, (800) 253-9646, Fax: (212) 887-7465, www.unicef.org; *The State of the World's Children 2008.*

United Nations Statistics Division, New York, NY 10017, (800) 253-9646, Fax: (212) 963-4116, http://unstats.un.org; *Demographic Yearbook; Human Development Report 2006; Statistical Yearbook; Trends in Europe and North America: The Statistical Yearbook of the ECE 2005;* and *World Statistics Pocketbook.*

The World Bank, 1818 H Street, NW, Washington, DC 20433, (202) 473-1000, Fax: (202) 477-6391, www.worldbank.org; *The World Bank Atlas 2003-2004; World Development Indicators (WDI) 2008;* and *World Development Report 2008.*

World Health Organization (WHO), Avenue Appia 20, 1211 Geneve 27, Switzerland, (Telephone in U.S. (212) 331-9081), www.who.int; The WHO Global Atlas of Infectious Diseases and *World Health Report 2006.*

KAZAKHSTAN - MOTION PICTURES

UNESCO Institute for Statistics, C.P. 6128 Succursale Centre-Ville, Montreal, Quebec, H3C 3J7 Canada, (Dial from U.S. (514) 343-6880), (Fax from U.S. (514) 343 6882), www.uis.unesco.org; *Statistical Tables.*

United Nations Statistics Division, New York, NY 10017, (800) 253-9646, Fax: (212) 963-4116, http://unstats.un.org; *Statistical Yearbook.*

KAZAKHSTAN - MUSEUMS

UNESCO Institute for Statistics, C.P. 6128 Succursale Centre-Ville, Montreal, Quebec, H3C 3J7 Canada, (Dial from U.S. (514) 343-6880), (Fax from U.S. (514) 343 6882), www.uis.unesco.org; *Statistical Tables.*

KAZAKHSTAN - PERIODICALS

UNESCO Institute for Statistics, C.P. 6128 Succursale Centre-Ville, Montreal, Quebec, H3C 3J7 Canada, (Dial from U.S. (514) 343-6880), (Fax from U.S. (514) 343 6882), www.uis.unesco.org; *Statistical Tables.*

KAZAKHSTAN - PETROLEUM INDUSTRY AND TRADE

Palgrave Macmillan Ltd., Houndmills, Basingstoke, Hampshire, RG21 6XS, England, (Telephone in U.S. (888) 330-8477), (Fax in U.S. (800) 672-2054), www.palgrave.com; *The Statesman's Yearbook 2008.*

PennWell Corporation, 1421 South Sheridan Road, Tulsa, OK 74112, (918) 835-3161, www.pennwell.com; *International Petroleum Encyclopedia 2007.*

Platts, 2 Penn Plaza, 25th Floor, New York, NY 10121-2298, (212) 904-3070, www.platts.com; *Energy Economist.*

U.S. Department of Energy (DOE), Energy Information Administration (EIA), 1000 Independence Avenue, SW, Washington, DC 20585, (202) 586-8800, www.eia.doe.gov; *International Energy Annual 2004* and *International Energy Outlook 2006.*

United Nations Food and Agricultural Organization (FAO), Viale delle Terme di Caracalla, 00100 Rome, Italy, (Dial from U.S. (202) 653-2400), (Fax from U.S. (202) 653 5760), www.fao.org; *The State of Food and Agriculture (SOFA) 2006.*

United Nations Statistics Division, New York, NY 10017, (800) 253-9646, Fax: (212) 963-4116, http://unstats.un.org; *Energy Statistics Yearbook 2003; 2004 Industrial Commodity Statistics Yearbook; Statistical Yearbook;* and *Trends in Europe and North America: The Statistical Yearbook of the ECE 2005.*

KAZAKHSTAN - POLITICAL SCIENCE

Academic International Press, PO Box 1111, Gulf Breeze, FL 32562-1111, Fax: (850) 934-0953, www.ai-press.com; *Russia and Eurasia Facts and Figures Annual.*

Central Intelligence Agency, Office of Public Affairs, Washington, DC 20505, (703) 482-0623, Fax: (703) 482-1739, www.cia.gov; *The World Factbook.*

Palgrave Macmillan Ltd., Houndmills, Basingstoke, Hampshire, RG21 6XS, England, (Telephone in U.S. (888) 330-8477), (Fax in U.S. (800) 672-2054), www.palgrave.com; *The Statesman's Yearbook 2008.*

Taylor and Francis Group, An Informa Business, 2 Park Square, Milton Park, Abingdon, Oxford OX14 4RN, United Kingdom, (Dial from U.S. (212) 216-7800), (Fax from U.S. (212) 564-7854), www.tandf.co.uk; *The Europa World Year Book.*

United Nations Statistics Division, New York, NY 10017, (800) 253-9646, Fax: (212) 963-4116, http://unstats.un.org; *National Accounts Statistics: Compendium of Income Distribution Statistics* and *Statistical Yearbook.*

The World Bank, 1818 H Street, NW, Washington, DC 20433, (202) 473-1000, Fax: (202) 477-6391, www.worldbank.org; *Statistical Handbook: States of the Former USSR* and *World Development Report 2008.*

KAZAKHSTAN - POPULATION

Academic International Press, PO Box 1111, Gulf Breeze, FL 32562-1111, Fax: (850) 934-0953, www.ai-press.com; *Russia and Eurasia Facts and Figures Annual.*

Central Intelligence Agency, Office of Public Affairs, Washington, DC 20505, (703) 482-0623, Fax: (703) 482-1739, www.cia.gov; *The World Factbook.*

Economist Intelligence Unit, 111 West 57th Street, New York, NY 10019, (212) 554-0600, Fax: (212) 586-1181, www.eiu.com; *Kazakhstan Country Report.*

Euromonitor International, Inc., 224 S. Michigan Avenue, Suite 1500, Chicago, IL 60604, (312) 922-1115, Fax: (312) 922-1157, www.euromonitor.com; *International Marketing Data and Statistics 2008* and *The World Economic Factbook 2008.*

Palgrave Macmillan Ltd., Houndmills, Basingstoke, Hampshire, RG21 6XS, England, (Telephone in U.S. (888) 330-8477), (Fax in U.S. (800) 672-2054), www.palgrave.com; *The Statesman's Yearbook 2008.*

UNESCO Institute for Statistics, C.P. 6128 Succursale Centre-Ville, Montreal, Quebec, H3C 3J7 Canada, (Dial from U.S. (514) 343-6880), (Fax from U.S. (514) 343 6882), www.uis.unesco.org; *Statistical Tables.*

United Nations Food and Agricultural Organization (FAO), Viale delle Terme di Caracalla, 00100 Rome, Italy, (Dial from U.S. (202) 653-2400), (Fax from U.S. (202) 653 5760), www.fao.org; *FAO Production Yearbook 2002.*

United Nations Statistics Division, New York, NY 10017, (800) 253-9646, Fax: (212) 963-4116, http://unstats.un.org; *Demographic Yearbook; Human Development Report 2006; Statistical Yearbook; Trends in Europe and North America: The Statistical Yearbook of the ECE 2005;* and *World Statistics Pocketbook.*

The World Bank, 1818 H Street, NW, Washington, DC 20433, (202) 473-1000, Fax: (202) 477-6391, www.worldbank.org; *Kazakhstan; Statistical Handbook: States of the Former USSR; The World Bank Atlas 2003-2004; World Development Indicators (WDI) 2008;* and *World Development Report 2008.*

World Health Organization (WHO), Avenue Appia 20, 1211 Geneve 27, Switzerland, (Telephone in U.S. (212) 331-9081), www.who.int; *World Health Report 2006.*

Worldinformation.com, 2 Market Street, Saffron Walden, Essex CB10 1HZ, United Kingdom, www.worldinformation.com; The World of Information (www.worldinformation.com).

KAZAKHSTAN - POPULATION DENSITY

Central Intelligence Agency, Office of Public Affairs, Washington, DC 20505, (703) 482-0623, Fax: (703) 482-1739, www.cia.gov; *The World Factbook.*

Euromonitor International, Inc., 224 S. Michigan Avenue, Suite 1500, Chicago, IL 60604, (312) 922-1115, Fax: (312) 922-1157, www.euromonitor.com; *The World Economic Factbook 2008.*

Palgrave Macmillan Ltd., Houndmills, Basingstoke, Hampshire, RG21 6XS, England, (Telephone in U.S. (888) 330-8477), (Fax in U.S. (800) 672-2054), www.palgrave.com; *The Statesman's Yearbook 2008.*

Taylor and Francis Group, An Informa Business, 2 Park Square, Milton Park, Abingdon, Oxford OX14 4RN, United Kingdom, (Dial from U.S. (212) 216-7800), (Fax from U.S. (212) 564-7854), www.tandf.co.uk; *The Europa World Year Book.*

UNESCO Institute for Statistics, C.P. 6128 Succursale Centre-Ville, Montreal, Quebec, H3C 3J7 Canada, (Dial from U.S. (514) 343-6880), (Fax from U.S. (514) 343 6882), www.uis.unesco.org; *Statistical Tables.*

United Nations Statistics Division, New York, NY 10017, (800) 253-9646, Fax: (212) 963-4116, http://unstats.un.org; *Statistical Yearbook* and *Trends in Europe and North America: The Statistical Yearbook of the ECE 2005.*

The World Bank, 1818 H Street, NW, Washington, DC 20433, (202) 473-1000, Fax: (202) 477-6391, www.worldbank.org; *Kazakhstan* and *World Development Report 2008.*

KAZAKHSTAN - POSTAL SERVICE

United Nations Statistics Division, New York, NY 10017, (800) 253-9646, Fax: (212) 963-4116, http://unstats.un.org; *Statistical Yearbook* and *Trends in Europe and North America: The Statistical Yearbook of the ECE 2005.*

KAZAKHSTAN - POULTRY

See KAZAKHSTAN - LIVESTOCK

KAZAKHSTAN - POWER RESOURCES

Academic International Press, PO Box 1111, Gulf Breeze, FL 32562-1111, Fax: (850) 934-0953, www.ai-press.com; *Russia and Eurasia Facts and Figures Annual.*

Euromonitor International, Inc., 224 S. Michigan Avenue, Suite 1500, Chicago, IL 60604, (312) 922-1115, Fax: (312) 922-1157, www.euromonitor.com; *International Marketing Data and Statistics 2008; The World Economic Factbook 2008;* and *World Marketing Data and Statistics.*

Palgrave Macmillan Ltd., Houndmills, Basingstoke, Hampshire, RG21 6XS, England, (Telephone in U.S. (888) 330-8477), (Fax in U.S. (800) 672-2054), www.palgrave.com; *The Statesman's Yearbook 2008.*

Platts, 2 Penn Plaza, 25th Floor, New York, NY 10121-2298, (212) 904-3070, www.platts.com; *Energy Economist.*

U.S. Department of Energy (DOE), Energy Information Administration (EIA), 1000 Independence Avenue, SW, Washington, DC 20585, (202) 586-8800, www.eia.doe.gov; *International Energy Annual 2004* and *International Energy Outlook 2006.*

United Nations Statistics Division, New York, NY 10017, (800) 253-9646, Fax: (212) 963-4116, http://unstats.un.org; *Energy Statistics Yearbook 2003; Human Development Report 2006; Statistical Yearbook; Trends in Europe and North America: The Statistical Yearbook of the ECE 2005;* and *World Statistics Pocketbook.*

The World Bank, 1818 H Street, NW, Washington, DC 20433, (202) 473-1000, Fax: (202) 477-6391, www.worldbank.org; *Statistical Handbook: States of the Former USSR; The World Bank Atlas 2003-2004;* and *World Development Report 2008.*

KAZAKHSTAN - PRICES

Euromonitor International, Inc., 224 S. Michigan Avenue, Suite 1500, Chicago, IL 60604, (312) 922-

1115, Fax: (312) 922-1157, www.euromonitor.com; *World Marketing Data and Statistics.*

United Nations Food and Agricultural Organization (FAO), Viale delle Terme di Caracalla, 00100 Rome, Italy, (Dial from U.S. (202) 653-2400), (Fax from U.S. (202) 653 5760), www.fao.org; *FAO Production Yearbook 2002.*

The World Bank, 1818 H Street, NW, Washington, DC 20433, (202) 473-1000, Fax: (202) 477-6391, www.worldbank.org; *Kazakhstan* and *Statistical Handbook: States of the Former USSR.*

KAZAKHSTAN - PROFESSIONS

United Nations Statistics Division, New York, NY 10017, (800) 253-9646, Fax: (212) 963-4116, http://unstats.un.org; *Statistical Yearbook.*

KAZAKHSTAN - PUBLIC HEALTH

Academic International Press, PO Box 1111, Gulf Breeze, FL 32562-1111, Fax: (850) 934-0953, www.ai-press.com; *Russia and Eurasia Facts and Figures Annual.*

Euromonitor International, Inc., 224 S. Michigan Avenue, Suite 1500, Chicago, IL 60604, (312) 922-1115, Fax: (312) 922-1157, www.euromonitor.com; *World Health Databook 2007/2008* and *World Marketing Data and Statistics.*

UNICEF, 3 United Nations Plaza, New York, NY 10017, (800) 253-9646, Fax: (212) 887-7465, www.unicef.org; *The State of the World's Children 2008.*

United Nations Statistics Division, New York, NY 10017, (800) 253-9646, Fax: (212) 963-4116, http://unstats.un.org; *Human Development Report 2006; Statistical Yearbook;* and *Trends in Europe and North America: The Statistical Yearbook of the ECE 2005.*

The World Bank, 1818 H Street, NW, Washington, DC 20433, (202) 473-1000, Fax: (202) 477-6391, www.worldbank.org; *Kazakhstan* and *World Development Report 2008.*

World Health Organization (WHO), Avenue Appia 20, 1211 Geneve 27, Switzerland, (Telephone in U.S. (212) 331-9081), www.who.int; The WHO Global Atlas of Infectious Diseases and *World Health Report 2006.*

KAZAKHSTAN - PUBLISHERS AND PUBLISHING

UNESCO Institute for Statistics, C.P. 6128 Succursale Centre-Ville, Montreal, Quebec, H3C 3J7 Canada, (Dial from U.S. (514) 343-6880), (Fax from U.S. (514) 343 6882), www.uis.unesco.org; *Statistical Tables.*

United Nations Statistics Division, New York, NY 10017, (800) 253-9646, Fax: (212) 963-4116, http://unstats.un.org; *Trends in Europe and North America: The Statistical Yearbook of the ECE 2005.*

KAZAKHSTAN - RADIO BROADCASTING

Palgrave Macmillan Ltd., Houndmills, Basingstoke, Hampshire, RG21 6XS, England, (Telephone in U.S. (888) 330-8477), (Fax in U.S. (800) 672-2054), www.palgrave.com; *The Statesman's Yearbook 2008.*

United Nations Statistics Division, New York, NY 10017, (800) 253-9646, Fax: (212) 963-4116, http://unstats.un.org; *Statistical Yearbook.*

KAZAKHSTAN - RAILROADS

Palgrave Macmillan Ltd., Houndmills, Basingstoke, Hampshire, RG21 6XS, England, (Telephone in U.S. (888) 330-8477), (Fax in U.S. (800) 672-2054), www.palgrave.com; *The Statesman's Yearbook 2008.*

United Nations Statistics Division, New York, NY 10017, (800) 253-9646, Fax: (212) 963-4116, http://unstats.un.org; *Statistical Yearbook* and *Trends in Europe and North America: The Statistical Yearbook of the ECE 2005.*

KAZAKHSTAN - RELIGION

Academic International Press, PO Box 1111, Gulf Breeze, FL 32562-1111, Fax: (850) 934-0953, www.ai-press.com; *Russia and Eurasia Facts and Figures Annual.*

Central Intelligence Agency, Office of Public Affairs, Washington, DC 20505, (703) 482-0623, Fax: (703) 482-1739, www.cia.gov; *The World Factbook.*

Palgrave Macmillan Ltd., Houndmills, Basingstoke, Hampshire, RG21 6XS, England, (Telephone in U.S. (888) 330-8477), (Fax in U.S. (800) 672-2054), www.palgrave.com; *The Statesman's Yearbook 2008.*

KAZAKHSTAN - RETAIL TRADE

Euromonitor International, Inc., 224 S. Michigan Avenue, Suite 1500, Chicago, IL 60604, (312) 922-1115, Fax: (312) 922-1157, www.euromonitor.com; *World Marketing Data and Statistics.*

United Nations Statistics Division, New York, NY 10017, (800) 253-9646, Fax: (212) 963-4116, http://unstats.un.org; *Statistical Yearbook.*

KAZAKHSTAN - ROADS

Central Intelligence Agency, Office of Public Affairs, Washington, DC 20505, (703) 482-0623, Fax: (703) 482-1739, www.cia.gov; *The World Factbook.*

Palgrave Macmillan Ltd., Houndmills, Basingstoke, Hampshire, RG21 6XS, England, (Telephone in U.S. (888) 330-8477), (Fax in U.S. (800) 672-2054), www.palgrave.com; *The Statesman's Yearbook 2008.*

United Nations Statistics Division, New York, NY 10017, (800) 253-9646, Fax: (212) 963-4116, http://unstats.un.org; *Trends in Europe and North America: The Statistical Yearbook of the ECE 2005.*

KAZAKHSTAN - RUBBER INDUSTRY AND TRADE

International Rubber Study Group (IRSG), 1st Floor, Heron House, 109/115 Wembley Hill Road, Wembley, Middlesex HA9 8DA, United Kingdom, www.rubberstudy.com; *Rubber Statistical Bulletin; Summary of World Rubber Statistics 2005; World Rubber Statistics Handbook (Volume 6, 1975-2001);* and *World Rubber Statistics Historic Handbook.*

United Nations Statistics Division, New York, NY 10017, (800) 253-9646, Fax: (212) 963-4116, http://unstats.un.org; *Statistical Yearbook.*

KAZAKHSTAN - SHEEP

See KAZAKHSTAN - LIVESTOCK

KAZAKHSTAN - SHIPPING

United Nations Statistics Division, New York, NY 10017, (800) 253-9646, Fax: (212) 963-4116, http://unstats.un.org; *Statistical Yearbook.*

KAZAKHSTAN - SOCIAL ECOLOGY

United Nations Statistics Division, New York, NY 10017, (800) 253-9646, Fax: (212) 963-4116, http://unstats.un.org; *World Statistics Pocketbook.*

KAZAKHSTAN - SOCIAL SECURITY

United Nations Statistics Division, New York, NY 10017, (800) 253-9646, Fax: (212) 963-4116, http://unstats.un.org; *National Accounts Statistics: Compendium of Income Distribution Statistics.*

KAZAKHSTAN - STEEL PRODUCTION

See KAZAKHSTAN - MINERAL INDUSTRIES

KAZAKHSTAN - TAXATION

Taylor and Francis Group, An Informa Business, 2 Park Square, Milton Park, Abingdon, Oxford OX14 4RN, United Kingdom, (Dial from U.S. (212) 216-7800), (Fax from U.S. (212) 564-7854), www.tandf.co.uk; *The Europa World Year Book.*

KAZAKHSTAN - TELEPHONE

Central Intelligence Agency, Office of Public Affairs, Washington, DC 20505, (703) 482-0623, Fax: (703) 482-1739, www.cia.gov; *The World Factbook.*

United Nations Statistics Division, New York, NY 10017, (800) 253-9646, Fax: (212) 963-4116, http://unstats.un.org; *Statistical Yearbook; Trends in Europe and North America: The Statistical Yearbook of the ECE 2005;* and *World Statistics Pocketbook.*

KAZAKHSTAN - TEXTILE INDUSTRY

United Nations Statistics Division, New York, NY 10017, (800) 253-9646, Fax: (212) 963-4116, http://unstats.un.org; *2004 Industrial Commodity Statistics Yearbook* and *Statistical Yearbook.*

KAZAKHSTAN - THEATER

UNESCO Institute for Statistics, C.P. 6128 Succursale Centre-Ville, Montreal, Quebec, H3C 3J7 Canada, (Dial from U.S. (514) 343-6880), (Fax from U.S. (514) 343 6882), www.uis.unesco.org; *Statistical Tables.*

KAZAKHSTAN - TIRE INDUSTRY

United Nations Statistics Division, New York, NY 10017, (800) 253-9646, Fax: (212) 963-4116, http://unstats.un.org; *Statistical Yearbook.*

KAZAKHSTAN - TOBACCO INDUSTRY

Foreign Agricultural Service (FAS), U.S. Department of Agriculture (USDA), 1400 Independence Avenue, SW, Washington, DC 20250, (202) 720-3935, www.fas.usda.gov; *Tobacco: World Markets and Trade.*

United Nations Statistics Division, New York, NY 10017, (800) 253-9646, Fax: (212) 963-4116, http://unstats.un.org; *Statistical Yearbook.*

KAZAKHSTAN - TOURISM

Euromonitor International, Inc., 224 S. Michigan Avenue, Suite 1500, Chicago, IL 60604, (312) 922-1115, Fax: (312) 922-1157, www.euromonitor.com; *The World Economic Factbook 2008.*

United Nations Statistics Division, New York, NY 10017, (800) 253-9646, Fax: (212) 963-4116, http://unstats.un.org; *Statistical Yearbook* and *Trends in Europe and North America: The Statistical Yearbook of the ECE 2005.*

The World Bank, 1818 H Street, NW, Washington, DC 20433, (202) 473-1000, Fax: (202) 477-6391, www.worldbank.org; *Kazakhstan.*

KAZAKHSTAN - TRANSPORTATION

Academic International Press, PO Box 1111, Gulf Breeze, FL 32562-1111, Fax: (850) 934-0953, www.ai-press.com; *Russia and Eurasia Facts and Figures Annual.*

Central Intelligence Agency, Office of Public Affairs, Washington, DC 20505, (703) 482-0623, Fax: (703) 482-1739, www.cia.gov; *The World Factbook.*

Euromonitor International, Inc., 224 S. Michigan Avenue, Suite 1500, Chicago, IL 60604, (312) 922-1115, Fax: (312) 922-1157, www.euromonitor.com; *International Marketing Data and Statistics 2008* and *World Marketing Data and Statistics.*

Palgrave Macmillan Ltd., Houndmills, Basingstoke, Hampshire, RG21 6XS, England, (Telephone in U.S. (888) 330-8477), (Fax in U.S. (800) 672-2054), www.palgrave.com; *The Statesman's Yearbook 2008.*

United Nations Statistics Division, New York, NY 10017, (800) 253-9646, Fax: (212) 963-4116, http://unstats.un.org; *Human Development Report 2006* and *Trends in Europe and North America: The Statistical Yearbook of the ECE 2005.*

The World Bank, 1818 H Street, NW, Washington, DC 20433, (202) 473-1000, Fax: (202) 477-6391, www.worldbank.org; *Kazakhstan.*

KAZAKHSTAN - UNEMPLOYMENT

Central Intelligence Agency, Office of Public Affairs, Washington, DC 20505, (703) 482-0623, Fax: (703) 482-1739, www.cia.gov; *The World Factbook.*

Palgrave Macmillan Ltd., Houndmills, Basingstoke, Hampshire, RG21 6XS, England, (Telephone in U.S. (888) 330-8477), (Fax in U.S. (800) 672-2054), www.palgrave.com; *The Statesman's Yearbook 2008.*

United Nations Statistics Division, New York, NY 10017, (800) 253-9646, Fax: (212) 963-4116, http://

unstats.un.org; *Statistical Yearbook* and *Trends in Europe and North America: The Statistical Yearbook of the ECE 2005.*

The World Bank, 1818 H Street, NW, Washington, DC 20433, (202) 473-1000, Fax: (202) 477-6391, www.worldbank.org; *Kazakhstan.*

KAZAKHSTAN - VITAL STATISTICS

Palgrave Macmillan Ltd., Houndmills, Basingstoke, Hampshire, RG21 6XS, England, (Telephone in U.S. (888) 330-8477), (Fax in U.S. (800) 672-2054), www.palgrave.com; *The Statesman's Yearbook 2008.*

United Nations Statistics Division, New York, NY 10017, (800) 253-9646, Fax: (212) 963-4116, http://unstats.un.org; *Statistical Yearbook.*

World Health Organization (WHO), Avenue Appia 20, 1211 Geneve 27, Switzerland, (Telephone in U.S. (212) 331-9081), www.who.int; *World Health Report 2006.*

KAZAKHSTAN - WAGES

United Nations Statistics Division, New York, NY 10017, (800) 253-9646, Fax: (212) 963-4116, http://unstats.un.org; *Statistical Yearbook.*

The World Bank, 1818 H Street, NW, Washington, DC 20433, (202) 473-1000, Fax: (202) 477-6391, www.worldbank.org; *Kazakhstan* and *Statistical Handbook: States of the Former USSR.*

KAZAKHSTAN - WELFARE STATE

Palgrave Macmillan Ltd., Houndmills, Basingstoke, Hampshire, RG21 6XS, England, (Telephone in U.S. (888) 330-8477), (Fax in U.S. (800) 672-2054), www.palgrave.com; *The Statesman's Yearbook 2008.*

KAZAKHSTAN - WHOLESALE PRICE INDEXES

United Nations Statistics Division, New York, NY 10017, (800) 253-9646, Fax: (212) 963-4116, http://unstats.un.org; *Statistical Yearbook.*

KAZAKHSTAN - WHOLESALE TRADE

United Nations Statistics Division, New York, NY 10017, (800) 253-9646, Fax: (212) 963-4116, http://unstats.un.org; *Statistical Yearbook.*

KAZAKHSTAN - WOOL PRODUCTION

See KAZAKHSTAN - TEXTILE INDUSTRY

KENTUCKY

See also - STATE DATA (FOR INDIVIDUAL STATES)

KENTUCKY - STATE DATA CENTERS

Governor's Office for Policy and Management (GOPM), 702 Capitol Avenue, Room 284, Capitol Annex, Frankfort, KY 40601, (502) 564-7300, Fax: (502) 564-6684, www.osbd.ky.gov/contactus/gopm.htm; State Data Center.

Kentucky State Data Center, School of Urban and Public Affairs, University of Louisville, 426 W. Bloom Street, Louisville, KY 40208, (502) 852-7990, Fax: (502) 852-7386, http://ksdc.louisville.edu; State Data Center.

State Library Services Division, Department for Libraries and Archives, 300 Coffee Tree Road, Frankfort, KY 40601, Ms. Leigh Troutman, (502) 564-8300, http://kdla.ky.gov/home.htm; State Data Center.

KENTUCKY - PRIMARY STATISTICS SOURCES

Kentucky Cabinet for Economic Development, Old Capitol Annex, 300 West Broadway, Frankfort, KY 40601, (800) 626-2930, Fax: (502) 564-3256, www.thinkkentucky.com; Kentucky Deskbook of Economic Statistics (web app).

KENYA - NATIONAL STATISTICAL OFFICE

Central Bureau of Statistics (CBS), Ministry of Economic Planning and Development, PO Box 30266, 00200 GPO Nairobi, Kenya, www.cbs.go.ke; National Data Center.

Government of Kenya, Ministry of Finance, Treasury Building, Harambee Avenue, PO Box 30007, Nairobi, Kenya, www.treasury.go.ke; National Data Center.

KENYA - PRIMARY STATISTICS SOURCES

Central Bureau of Statistics (CBS), Ministry of Economic Planning and Development, PO Box 30266, 00200 GPO Nairobi, Kenya, www.cbs.go.ke; *Statistical Abstract 2004.*

KENYA - AGRICULTURAL MACHINERY

United Nations Statistics Division, New York, NY 10017, (800) 253-9646, Fax: (212) 963-4116, http://unstats.un.org; *Statistical Yearbook.*

KENYA - AGRICULTURE

Central Bureau of Statistics (CBS), Ministry of Economic Planning and Development, PO Box 30266, 00200 GPO Nairobi, Kenya, www.cbs.go.ke; *Statistical Abstract 2004.*

Economist Intelligence Unit, 111 West 57th Street, New York, NY 10019, (212) 554-0600, Fax: (212) 586-1181, www.eiu.com; *Kenya Country Report.*

Euromonitor International, Inc., 224 S. Michigan Avenue, Suite 1500, Chicago, IL 60604, (312) 922-1115, Fax: (312) 922-1157, www.euromonitor.com; *International Marketing Data and Statistics 2008* and *World Marketing Data and Statistics.*

International Food Policy Research Institute (IFPRI), 2033 K Street, NW, Washington, D.C., 2006, (202) 862-5600, www.ifpri.org; *Kenya: The Influence of Social Capital on Sustainable Agriculture in Marginal Areas, 2003.*

M.E. Sharpe, 80 Business Park Drive, Armonk, NY 10504, (800) 541-6563, Fax: (914) 273-2106, www.mesharpe.com; *The Illustrated Book of World Rankings.*

Palgrave Macmillan Ltd., Houndmills, Basingstoke, Hampshire, RG21 6XS, England, (Telephone in U.S. (888) 330-8477), (Fax in U.S. (800) 672-2054), www.palgrave.com; *The Statesman's Yearbook 2008.*

Taylor and Francis Group, An Informa Business, 2 Park Square, Milton Park, Abingdon, Oxford OX14 4RN, United Kingdom, (Dial from U.S. (212) 216-7800), (Fax from U.S. (212) 564-7854), www.tandf.co.uk; *The Europa World Year Book.*

United Nations Conference on Trade and Development (UNCTAD), DC2-1120, United Nations, New York, NY 10017, (212) 963-0027, www.unctad.org; *UNCTAD Commodity Yearbook.*

United Nations Economic Commission for Africa (ECA), PO Box 3001, Addis Ababa, Ethiopia, (Telephone in U.S. (212) 963-4957), www.uneca.org; *African Statistical Yearbook 2006.*

United Nations Food and Agricultural Organization (FAO), Viale delle Terme di Caracalla, 00100 Rome, Italy, (Dial from U.S. (202) 653-2400), (Fax from U.S. (202) 653 5760), www.fao.org; AQUASTAT; *FAO Production Yearbook 2002; FAO Trade Yearbook;* and *The State of Food and Agriculture (SOFA) 2006.*

United Nations Statistics Division, New York, NY 10017, (800) 253-9646, Fax: (212) 963-4116, http://unstats.un.org; *Statistical Yearbook* and *Survey of Economic and Social Conditions in Africa 2005.*

The World Bank, 1818 H Street, NW, Washington, DC 20433, (202) 473-1000, Fax: (202) 477-6391, www.worldbank.org; *Africa Live Database (LDB); African Development Indicators (ADI) 2007; Kenya;* and *World Development Indicators (WDI) 2008.*

KENYA - AIRLINES

M.E. Sharpe, 80 Business Park Drive, Armonk, NY 10504, (800) 541-6563, Fax: (914) 273-2106, www.mesharpe.com; *The Illustrated Book of World Rankings.*

Palgrave Macmillan Ltd., Houndmills, Basingstoke, Hampshire, RG21 6XS, England, (Telephone in U.S. (888) 330-8477), (Fax in U.S. (800) 672-2054), www.palgrave.com; *The Statesman's Yearbook 2008.*

Taylor and Francis Group, An Informa Business, 2 Park Square, Milton Park, Abingdon, Oxford OX14 4RN, United Kingdom, (Dial from U.S. (212) 216-7800), (Fax from U.S. (212) 564-7854), www.tandf.co.uk; *The Europa World Year Book.*

United Nations Economic Commission for Africa (ECA), PO Box 3001, Addis Ababa, Ethiopia, (Telephone in U.S. (212) 963-4957), www.uneca.org; *African Statistical Yearbook 2006.*

United Nations Statistics Division, New York, NY 10017, (800) 253-9646, Fax: (212) 963-4116, http://unstats.un.org; *Statistical Yearbook.*

KENYA - ALUMINUM PRODUCTION

See KENYA - MINERAL INDUSTRIES

KENYA - ARMED FORCES

Central Intelligence Agency, Office of Public Affairs, Washington, DC 20505, (703) 482-0623, Fax: (703) 482-1739, www.cia.gov; *The World Factbook.*

Euromonitor International, Inc., 224 S. Michigan Avenue, Suite 1500, Chicago, IL 60604, (312) 922-1115, Fax: (312) 922-1157, www.euromonitor.com; *World Marketing Data and Statistics.*

International Institute for Strategic Studies (IISS), Arundel House, 13-15 Arundel Street, Temple Place, London WC2R 3DX, England, www.iiss.org; *The Military Balance 2007.*

International Monetary Fund (IMF), 700 Nineteenth Street, NW, Washington, DC 20431, (202) 623-7000, Fax: (202) 623-4661, www.imf.org; *Government Finance Statistics Yearbook (2008 Edition).*

Palgrave Macmillan Ltd., Houndmills, Basingstoke, Hampshire, RG21 6XS, England, (Telephone in U.S. (888) 330-8477), (Fax in U.S. (800) 672-2054), www.palgrave.com; *The Statesman's Yearbook 2008.*

United Nations Statistics Division, New York, NY 10017, (800) 253-9646, Fax: (212) 963-4116, http://unstats.un.org; *Human Development Report 2006.*

KENYA - BALANCE OF PAYMENTS

African Development Bank Group, Rue Joseph Anoma, 01 BP 1387 Abidjan 01, Cote d'Ivoire, www.afdb.org; *Statistics Pocketbook 2008.*

International Monetary Fund (IMF), 700 Nineteenth Street, NW, Washington, DC 20431, (202) 623-7000, Fax: (202) 623-4661, www.imf.org; *Balance of Payments Statistics Newsletter* and *Balance of Payments Statistics Yearbook 2007.*

Taylor and Francis Group, An Informa Business, 2 Park Square, Milton Park, Abingdon, Oxford OX14 4RN, United Kingdom, (Dial from U.S. (212) 216-7800), (Fax from U.S. (212) 564-7854), www.tandf.co.uk; *The Europa World Year Book.*

United Nations Conference on Trade and Development (UNCTAD), DC2-1120, United Nations, New York, NY 10017, (212) 963-0027, www.unctad.org; *Handbook of Statistics 2005.*

United Nations Economic Commission for Africa (ECA), PO Box 3001, Addis Ababa, Ethiopia, (Telephone in U.S. (212) 963-4957), www.uneca.org; *African Statistical Yearbook 2006.*

The World Bank, 1818 H Street, NW, Washington, DC 20433, (202) 473-1000, Fax: (202) 477-6391,

www.worldbank.org; *Kenya; World Development Indicators (WDI) 2008;* and *World Development Report 2008.*

KENYA - BANKS AND BANKING

Euromonitor International, Inc., 224 S. Michigan Avenue, Suite 1500, Chicago, IL 60604, (312) 922-1115, Fax: (312) 922-1157, www.euromonitor.com; *World Marketing Data and Statistics.*

International Monetary Fund (IMF), 700 Nineteenth Street, NW, Washington, DC 20431, (202) 623-7000, Fax: (202) 623-4661, www.imf.org; *Government Finance Statistics Yearbook (2008 Edition)* and *International Financial Statistics Yearbook 2007.*

M.E. Sharpe, 80 Business Park Drive, Armonk, NY 10504, (800) 541-6563, Fax: (914) 273-2106, www.mesharpe.com; *The Illustrated Book of World Rankings.*

Palgrave Macmillan Ltd., Houndmills, Basingstoke, Hampshire, RG21 6XS, England, (Telephone in U.S. (888) 330-8477), (Fax in U.S. (800) 672-2054), www.palgrave.com; *The Statesman's Yearbook 2008.*

United Nations Economic Commission for Africa (ECA), PO Box 3001, Addis Ababa, Ethiopia, (Telephone in U.S. (212) 963-4957), www.uneca.org; *African Statistical Yearbook 2006.*

KENYA - BARLEY PRODUCTION

See KENYA - CROPS

KENYA - BEVERAGE INDUSTRY

M.E. Sharpe, 80 Business Park Drive, Armonk, NY 10504, (800) 541-6563, Fax: (914) 273-2106, www.mesharpe.com; *The Illustrated Book of World Rankings.*

United Nations Statistics Division, New York, NY 10017, (800) 253-9646, Fax: (212) 963-4116, http://unstats.un.org; *Statistical Yearbook.*

KENYA - BONDS

International Monetary Fund (IMF), 700 Nineteenth Street, NW, Washington, DC 20431, (202) 623-7000, Fax: (202) 623-4661, www.imf.org; *Government Finance Statistics Yearbook (2008 Edition).*

KENYA - BROADCASTING

Central Intelligence Agency, Office of Public Affairs, Washington, DC 20505, (703) 482-0623, Fax: (703) 482-1739, www.cia.gov; *The World Factbook.*

Euromonitor International, Inc., 224 S. Michigan Avenue, Suite 1500, Chicago, IL 60604, (312) 922-1115, Fax: (312) 922-1157, www.euromonitor.com; *World Marketing Data and Statistics.*

M.E. Sharpe, 80 Business Park Drive, Armonk, NY 10504, (800) 541-6563, Fax: (914) 273-2106, www.mesharpe.com; *The Illustrated Book of World Rankings.*

Palgrave Macmillan Ltd., Houndmills, Basingstoke, Hampshire, RG21 6XS, England, (Telephone in U.S. (888) 330-8477), (Fax in U.S. (800) 672-2054), www.palgrave.com; *The Statesman's Yearbook 2008.*

WRTH Publications Limited, PO Box 290, Oxford OX2 7FT, UK, www.wrth.com; *World Radio TV Handbook 2007.*

KENYA - BUDGET

Central Intelligence Agency, Office of Public Affairs, Washington, DC 20505, (703) 482-0623, Fax: (703) 482-1739, www.cia.gov; *The World Factbook.*

KENYA - BUSINESS

Economist Intelligence Unit, 111 West 57th Street, New York, NY 10019, (212) 554-0600, Fax: (212) 586-1181, www.eiu.com; *Business Africa.*

United Nations Statistics Division, New York, NY 10017, (800) 253-9646, Fax: (212) 963-4116, http://unstats.un.org; *Statistical Yearbook.*

KENYA - CAPITAL LEVY

International Monetary Fund (IMF), 700 Nineteenth Street, NW, Washington, DC 20431, (202) 623-7000, Fax: (202) 623-4661, www.imf.org; *Government Finance Statistics Yearbook (2008 Edition).*

KENYA - CATTLE

See KENYA - LIVESTOCK

KENYA - CHICKENS

See KENYA - LIVESTOCK

KENYA - CHILDBIRTH - STATISTICS

Central Intelligence Agency, Office of Public Affairs, Washington, DC 20505, (703) 482-0623, Fax: (703) 482-1739, www.cia.gov; *The World Factbook.*

Euromonitor International, Inc., 224 S. Michigan Avenue, Suite 1500, Chicago, IL 60604, (312) 922-1115, Fax: (312) 922-1157, www.euromonitor.com; *International Marketing Data and Statistics 2008* and *The World Economic Factbook 2008.*

M.E. Sharpe, 80 Business Park Drive, Armonk, NY 10504, (800) 541-6563, Fax: (914) 273-2106, www.mesharpe.com; *The Illustrated Book of World Rankings.*

Taylor and Francis Group, An Informa Business, 2 Park Square, Milton Park, Abingdon, Oxford OX14 4RN, United Kingdom, (Dial from U.S. (212) 216-7800), (Fax from U.S. (212) 564-7854), www.tandf.co.uk; *The Europa World Year Book.*

United Nations Statistics Division, New York, NY 10017, (800) 253-9646, Fax: (212) 963-4116, http://unstats.un.org; *Demographic Yearbook; Statistical Yearbook;* and *Survey of Economic and Social Conditions in Africa 2005.*

The World Bank, 1818 H Street, NW, Washington, DC 20433, (202) 473-1000, Fax: (202) 477-6391, www.worldbank.org; *World Development Indicators (WDI) 2008.*

KENYA - CLIMATE

Central Bureau of Statistics (CBS), Ministry of Economic Planning and Development, PO Box 30266, 00200 GPO Nairobi, Kenya, www.cbs.go.ke; *Statistical Abstract 2004.*

International Institute for Environment and Development (IIED), 3 Endsleigh Street, London, England, WC1H 0DD, United Kingdom, www.iied.org; *Environment Urbanization* and *Haramata - Bulletin of the Drylands.*

M.E. Sharpe, 80 Business Park Drive, Armonk, NY 10504, (800) 541-6563, Fax: (914) 273-2106, www.mesharpe.com; *The Illustrated Book of World Rankings.*

Palgrave Macmillan Ltd., Houndmills, Basingstoke, Hampshire, RG21 6XS, England, (Telephone in U.S. (888) 330-8477), (Fax in U.S. (800) 672-2054), www.palgrave.com; *The Statesman's Yearbook 2008.*

World Resources Institute (WRI), 10 G Street, NE, Suite 800 Washington, DC 20002, (202) 729-7600, www.wri.org; *Nature's Benefits in Kenya: An Atlas of Ecosystems and Human Well-Being.*

KENYA - COAL PRODUCTION

See KENYA - MINERAL INDUSTRIES

KENYA - COFFEE

See KENYA - CROPS

KENYA - COMMERCE

Palgrave Macmillan Ltd., Houndmills, Basingstoke, Hampshire, RG21 6XS, England, (Telephone in U.S. (888) 330-8477), (Fax in U.S. (800) 672-2054), www.palgrave.com; *The Statesman's Yearbook 2008.*

KENYA - COMMODITY EXCHANGES

Commodity Research Bureau, 330 South Wells Street, Suite 612, Chicago, IL 60606-7110, (800) 621-5271, Fax: (312) 939-4135, www.crbtrader.com; *2006 CRB Commodity Yearbook and CD.*

International Monetary Fund (IMF), 700 Nineteenth Street, NW, Washington, DC 20431, (202) 623-7000, Fax: (202) 623-4661, www.imf.org; *IMF Primary Commodity Prices.*

United Nations Food and Agricultural Organization (FAO), Viale delle Terme di Caracalla, 00100 Rome, Italy, (Dial from U.S. (202) 653-2400), (Fax from U.S. (202) 653 5760), www.fao.org; *The State of Food and Agriculture (SOFA) 2006.*

KENYA - COMMUNICATION AND TRAFFIC

United Nations Statistics Division, New York, NY 10017, (800) 253-9646, Fax: (212) 963-4116, http://unstats.un.org; *Statistical Yearbook.*

KENYA - CONSTRUCTION INDUSTRY

M.E. Sharpe, 80 Business Park Drive, Armonk, NY 10504, (800) 541-6563, Fax: (914) 273-2106, www.mesharpe.com; *The Illustrated Book of World Rankings.*

United Nations Economic Commission for Africa (ECA), PO Box 3001, Addis Ababa, Ethiopia, (Telephone in U.S. (212) 963-4957), www.uneca.org; *African Statistical Yearbook 2006.*

United Nations Statistics Division, New York, NY 10017, (800) 253-9646, Fax: (212) 963-4116, http://unstats.un.org; *Statistical Yearbook.*

KENYA - CONSUMER PRICE INDEXES

Taylor and Francis Group, An Informa Business, 2 Park Square, Milton Park, Abingdon, Oxford OX14 4RN, United Kingdom, (Dial from U.S. (212) 216-7800), (Fax from U.S. (212) 564-7854), www.tandf.co.uk; *The Europa World Year Book.*

United Nations Economic Commission for Africa (ECA), PO Box 3001, Addis Ababa, Ethiopia, (Telephone in U.S. (212) 963-4957), www.uneca.org; *African Statistical Yearbook 2006.*

United Nations Statistics Division, New York, NY 10017, (800) 253-9646, Fax: (212) 963-4116, http://unstats.un.org; *Statistical Yearbook* and *Survey of Economic and Social Conditions in Africa 2005.*

The World Bank, 1818 H Street, NW, Washington, DC 20433, (202) 473-1000, Fax: (202) 477-6391, www.worldbank.org; *Kenya.*

KENYA - CONSUMPTION (ECONOMICS)

African Development Bank Group, Rue Joseph Anoma, 01 BP 1387 Abidjan 01, Cote d'Ivoire, www.afdb.org; *Statistics Pocketbook 2008.*

United Nations Statistics Division, New York, NY 10017, (800) 253-9646, Fax: (212) 963-4116, http://unstats.un.org; *Survey of Economic and Social Conditions in Africa 2005.*

The World Bank, 1818 H Street, NW, Washington, DC 20433, (202) 473-1000, Fax: (202) 477-6391, www.worldbank.org; *World Development Report 2008.*

KENYA - COPPER INDUSTRY AND TRADE

See KENYA - MINERAL INDUSTRIES

KENYA - CORN INDUSTRY

See KENYA - CROPS

KENYA - COST AND STANDARD OF LIVING

International Monetary Fund (IMF), 700 Nineteenth Street, NW, Washington, DC 20431, (202) 623-7000, Fax: (202) 623-4661, www.imf.org; *Government Finance Statistics Yearbook (2008 Edition).*

KENYA - COTTON

See KENYA - CROPS

KENYA - CRIME

U.S. Department of Justice (DOJ), Bureau of Justice Statistics, 810 Seventh Street, NW, Washington, DC 20531, (202) 307-0765, www.ojp.usdoj.gov/bjs/; *The World Factbook of Criminal Justice Systems.*

Yale University Press, PO Box 209040, New Haven, CT 06520-9040, (203) 432-0960, Fax: (203) 432-0948, http://yalepress.yale.edu/yupbooks; *Violence and Crime in Cross-National Perspective.*

KENYA - CROPS

International Monetary Fund (IMF), 700 Nineteenth Street, NW, Washington, DC 20431, (202) 623-7000, Fax: (202) 623-4661, www.imf.org; *International Financial Statistics Yearbook 2007.*

M.E. Sharpe, 80 Business Park Drive, Armonk, NY 10504, (800) 541-6563, Fax: (914) 273-2106, www.mesharpe.com; *The Illustrated Book of World Rankings.*

Palgrave Macmillan Ltd., Houndmills, Basingstoke, Hampshire, RG21 6XS, England, (Telephone in U.S. (888) 330-8477), (Fax in U.S. (800) 672-2054), www.palgrave.com; *The Statesman's Yearbook 2008.*

Taylor and Francis Group, An Informa Business, 2 Park Square, Milton Park, Abingdon, Oxford OX14 4RN, United Kingdom, (Dial from U.S. (212) 216-7800), (Fax from U.S. (212) 564-7854), www.tandf.co.uk; *The Europa World Year Book.*

United Nations Conference on Trade and Development (UNCTAD), DC2-1120, United Nations, New York, NY 10017, (212) 963-0027, www.unctad.org; *UNCTAD Commodity Yearbook.*

United Nations Economic Commission for Africa (ECA), PO Box 3001, Addis Ababa, Ethiopia, (Telephone in U.S. (212) 963-4957), www.uneca.org; *African Statistical Yearbook 2006.*

United Nations Food and Agricultural Organization (FAO), Viale delle Terme di Caracalla, 00100 Rome, Italy, (Dial from U.S. (202) 653-2400), (Fax from U.S. (202) 653 5760), www.fao.org; *FAO Production Yearbook 2002* and *The State of Food and Agriculture (SOFA) 2006.*

United Nations Statistics Division, New York, NY 10017, (800) 253-9646, Fax: (212) 963-4116, http://unstats.un.org; *Statistical Yearbook.*

KENYA - CUSTOMS ADMINISTRATION

International Monetary Fund (IMF), 700 Nineteenth Street, NW, Washington, DC 20431, (202) 623-7000, Fax: (202) 623-4661, www.imf.org; *Government Finance Statistics Yearbook (2008 Edition).*

Palgrave Macmillan Ltd., Houndmills, Basingstoke, Hampshire, RG21 6XS, England, (Telephone in U.S. (888) 330-8477), (Fax in U.S. (800) 672-2054), www.palgrave.com; *The Statesman's Yearbook 2008.*

KENYA - DAIRY PROCESSING

M.E. Sharpe, 80 Business Park Drive, Armonk, NY 10504, (800) 541-6563, Fax: (914) 273-2106, www.mesharpe.com; *The Illustrated Book of World Rankings.*

Palgrave Macmillan Ltd., Houndmills, Basingstoke, Hampshire, RG21 6XS, England, (Telephone in U.S. (888) 330-8477), (Fax in U.S. (800) 672-2054), www.palgrave.com; *The Statesman's Yearbook 2008.*

Taylor and Francis Group, An Informa Business, 2 Park Square, Milton Park, Abingdon, Oxford OX14 4RN, United Kingdom, (Dial from U.S. (212) 216-7800), (Fax from U.S. (212) 564-7854), www.tandf.co.uk; *The Europa World Year Book.*

United Nations Food and Agricultural Organization (FAO), Viale delle Terme di Caracalla, 00100 Rome, Italy, (Dial from U.S. (202) 653-2400), (Fax from U.S. (202) 653 5760), www.fao.org; *FAO Production Yearbook 2002* and *The State of Food and Agriculture (SOFA) 2006.*

United Nations Statistics Division, New York, NY 10017, (800) 253-9646, Fax: (212) 963-4116, http://unstats.un.org; *Statistical Yearbook.*

KENYA - DEATH RATES

See KENYA - MORTALITY

KENYA - DEBTS, EXTERNAL

African Development Bank Group, Rue Joseph Anoma, 01 BP 1387 Abidjan 01, Cote d'Ivoire, www.afdb.org; *Statistics Pocketbook 2008.*

International Monetary Fund (IMF), 700 Nineteenth Street, NW, Washington, DC 20431, (202) 623-7000, Fax: (202) 623-4661, www.imf.org; *Government Finance Statistics Yearbook (2008 Edition).*

Palgrave Macmillan Ltd., Houndmills, Basingstoke, Hampshire, RG21 6XS, England, (Telephone in U.S. (888) 330-8477), (Fax in U.S. (800) 672-2054), www.palgrave.com; *The Statesman's Yearbook 2008.*

United Nations Statistics Division, New York, NY 10017, (800) 253-9646, Fax: (212) 963-4116, http://unstats.un.org; *Survey of Economic and Social Conditions in Africa 2005.*

The World Bank, 1818 H Street, NW, Washington, DC 20433, (202) 473-1000, Fax: (202) 477-6391, www.worldbank.org; *Africa Live Database (LDB); African Development Indicators (ADI) 2007; Global Development Finance 2007;* and *World Development Report 2008.*

KENYA - DEFENSE EXPENDITURES

See KENYA - ARMED FORCES

KENYA - DEMOGRAPHY

Euromonitor International, Inc., 224 S. Michigan Avenue, Suite 1500, Chicago, IL 60604, (312) 922-1115, Fax: (312) 922-1157, www.euromonitor.com; *International Marketing Data and Statistics 2008; The World Economic Factbook 2008;* and *World Marketing Data and Statistics.*

M.E. Sharpe, 80 Business Park Drive, Armonk, NY 10504, (800) 541-6563, Fax: (914) 273-2106, www.mesharpe.com; *The Illustrated Book of World Rankings.*

United Nations Statistics Division, New York, NY 10017, (800) 253-9646, Fax: (212) 963-4116, http://unstats.un.org; *Human Development Report 2006* and *Survey of Economic and Social Conditions in Africa 2005.*

The World Bank, 1818 H Street, NW, Washington, DC 20433, (202) 473-1000, Fax: (202) 477-6391, www.worldbank.org; *Kenya.*

KENYA - DIAMONDS

See KENYA - MINERAL INDUSTRIES

KENYA - DISPOSABLE INCOME

M.E. Sharpe, 80 Business Park Drive, Armonk, NY 10504, (800) 541-6563, Fax: (914) 273-2106, www.mesharpe.com; *The Illustrated Book of World Rankings.*

United Nations Statistics Division, New York, NY 10017, (800) 253-9646, Fax: (212) 963-4116, http://unstats.un.org; *National Accounts Statistics: Compendium of Income Distribution Statistics* and *Statistical Yearbook.*

KENYA - DIVORCE

M.E. Sharpe, 80 Business Park Drive, Armonk, NY 10504, (800) 541-6563, Fax: (914) 273-2106, www.mesharpe.com; *The Illustrated Book of World Rankings.*

United Nations Statistics Division, New York, NY 10017, (800) 253-9646, Fax: (212) 963-4116, http://unstats.un.org; *Demographic Yearbook.*

KENYA - ECONOMIC ASSISTANCE

United Nations Statistics Division, New York, NY 10017, (800) 253-9646, Fax: (212) 963-4116, http://unstats.un.org; *Statistical Yearbook.*

KENYA - ECONOMIC CONDITIONS

African Development Bank Group, Rue Joseph Anoma, 01 BP 1387 Abidjan 01, Cote d'Ivoire, www.afdb.org; *The African Statistical Journal; Gender, Poverty and Environmental Indicators on African Countries 2007; Selected Statistics on African Countries 2007;* and *Statistics Pocketbook 2008.*

Center for International Business Education Research (CIBER), Columbia Business School and School of International and Public Affairs, Uris Hall, Room 212, 3022 Broadway, New York, NY 10027-6902, Mr. Joshua Safier, (212) 854-4750, Fax: (212) 222-9821, www.columbia.edu/cu/ciber/; Datastream International.

DSI Data Service Information, Xantener Strasse 51a, D-47495 Rheinberg, Germany, www.dsidata.com; *Campus Solution.*

Dun and Bradstreet (DB) Corporation, 103 JFK Parkway, Short Hills, NJ 07078, (973) 921-5500, www.dnb.com; *Country Report.*

Economist Intelligence Unit, 111 West 57th Street, New York, NY 10019, (212) 554-0600, Fax: (212) 586-1181, www.eiu.com; *Business Africa* and *Kenya Country Report.*

Euromonitor International, Inc., 224 S. Michigan Avenue, Suite 1500, Chicago, IL 60604, (312) 922-1115, Fax: (312) 922-1157, www.euromonitor.com; *International Marketing Data and Statistics 2008; The World Economic Factbook 2008;* and *World Marketing Data and Statistics.*

International Food Policy Research Institute (IFPRI), 2033 K Street, NW, Washington, D.C., 2006, (202) 862-5600, www.ifpri.org; *Kenya: The Influence of Social Capital on Sustainable Agriculture in Marginal Areas, 2003.*

International Monetary Fund (IMF), 700 Nineteenth Street, NW, Washington, DC 20431, (202) 623-7000, Fax: (202) 623-4661, www.imf.org; *World Economic Outlook Reports.*

M.E. Sharpe, 80 Business Park Drive, Armonk, NY 10504, (800) 541-6563, Fax: (914) 273-2106, www.mesharpe.com; *The Illustrated Book of World Rankings.*

Palgrave Macmillan Ltd., Houndmills, Basingstoke, Hampshire, RG21 6XS, England, (Telephone in U.S. (888) 330-8477), (Fax in U.S. (800) 672-2054), www.palgrave.com; *The Statesman's Yearbook 2008.*

Taylor and Francis Group, An Informa Business, 2 Park Square, Milton Park, Abingdon, Oxford OX14 4RN, United Kingdom, (Dial from U.S. (212) 216-7800), (Fax from U.S. (212) 564-7854), www.tandf.co.uk; *The Europa World Year Book.*

United Nations Statistics Division, New York, NY 10017, (800) 253-9646, Fax: (212) 963-4116, http://unstats.un.org; *Compendium of Intra-African and Related Foreign Trade Statistics 2003* and *World Statistics Pocketbook.*

The World Bank, 1818 H Street, NW, Washington, DC 20433, (202) 473-1000, Fax: (202) 477-6391, www.worldbank.org; *Africa Household Survey Databank; Africa Live Database (LDB); Africa Standardized Files and Indicators; African Development Indicators (ADI) 2007; Global Economic Monitor (GEM); Global Economic Prospects 2008; Kenya; The World Bank Atlas 2003-2004;* and *World Development Report 2008.*

KENYA - EDUCATION

African Development Bank Group, Rue Joseph Anoma, 01 BP 1387 Abidjan 01, Cote d'Ivoire, www.afdb.org; *Statistics Pocketbook 2008.*

Central Bureau of Statistics (CBS), Ministry of Economic Planning and Development, PO Box 30266, 00200 GPO Nairobi, Kenya, www.cbs.go.ke; *Statistical Abstract 2004.*

Euromonitor International, Inc., 224 S. Michigan Avenue, Suite 1500, Chicago, IL 60604, (312) 922-1115, Fax: (312) 922-1157, www.euromonitor.com; *International Marketing Data and Statistics 2008* and *World Marketing Data and Statistics.*

International Monetary Fund (IMF), 700 Nineteenth Street, NW, Washington, DC 20431, (202) 623-7000, Fax: (202) 623-4661, www.imf.org; *Government Finance Statistics Yearbook (2008 Edition).*

M.E. Sharpe, 80 Business Park Drive, Armonk, NY 10504, (800) 541-6563, Fax: (914) 273-2106, www.mesharpe.com; *The Illustrated Book of World Rankings.*

Palgrave Macmillan Ltd., Houndmills, Basingstoke, Hampshire, RG21 6XS, England, (Telephone in U.S.

(888) 330-8477), (Fax in U.S. (800) 672-2054), www.palgrave.com; *The Statesman's Yearbook 2008.*

Taylor and Francis Group, An Informa Business, 2 Park Square, Milton Park, Abingdon, Oxford OX14 4RN, United Kingdom, (Dial from U.S. (212) 216-7800), (Fax from U.S. (212) 564-7854), www.tandf.co.uk; *The Europa World Year Book.*

UNESCO Institute for Statistics, C.P. 6128 Succursale Centre-Ville, Montreal, Quebec, H3C 3J7 Canada, (Dial from U.S. (514) 343-6880), (Fax from U.S. (514) 343 6882), www.uis.unesco.org; *Statistical Tables.*

United Nations Economic Commission for Africa (ECA), PO Box 3001, Addis Ababa, Ethiopia, (Telephone in U.S. (212) 963-4957), www.uneca.org; *African Statistical Yearbook 2006.*

United Nations Statistics Division, New York, NY 10017, (800) 253-9646, Fax: (212) 963-4116, http://unstats.un.org; *Human Development Report 2006* and *Survey of Economic and Social Conditions in Africa 2005.*

The World Bank, 1818 H Street, NW, Washington, DC 20433, (202) 473-1000, Fax: (202) 477-6391, www.worldbank.org; *Kenya; World Development Indicators (WDI) 2008;* and *World Development Report 2008.*

KENYA - ELECTRICITY

M.E. Sharpe, 80 Business Park Drive, Armonk, NY 10504, (800) 541-6563, Fax: (914) 273-2106, www.mesharpe.com; *The Illustrated Book of World Rankings.*

Palgrave Macmillan Ltd., Houndmills, Basingstoke, Hampshire, RG21 6XS, England, (Telephone in U.S. (888) 330-8477), (Fax in U.S. (800) 672-2054), www.palgrave.com; *The Statesman's Yearbook 2008.*

U.S. Department of Energy (DOE), Energy Information Administration (EIA), 1000 Independence Avenue, SW, Washington, DC 20585, (202) 586-8800, www.eia.doe.gov; *International Energy Annual 2004* and *International Energy Outlook 2006.*

United Nations Economic Commission for Africa (ECA), PO Box 3001, Addis Ababa, Ethiopia, (Telephone in U.S. (212) 963-4957), www.uneca.org; *African Statistical Yearbook 2006.*

United Nations Statistics Division, New York, NY 10017, (800) 253-9646, Fax: (212) 963-4116, http://unstats.un.org; *Human Development Report 2006; Statistical Yearbook;* and *Survey of Economic and Social Conditions in Africa 2005.*

KENYA - EMPLOYMENT

Euromonitor International, Inc., 224 S. Michigan Avenue, Suite 1500, Chicago, IL 60604, (312) 922-1115, Fax: (312) 922-1157, www.euromonitor.com; *International Marketing Data and Statistics 2008.*

International Labour Office, I.L.O. Publications, 4 route des Morillons, CH-1211 Geneva 22, Switzerland, (Telephone in U.S. (202) 653-7652), (Fax in U.S. (202) 653-7687), www.ilo.org; *Yearbook of Labour Statistics 2006.*

M.E. Sharpe, 80 Business Park Drive, Armonk, NY 10504, (800) 541-6563, Fax: (914) 273-2106, www.mesharpe.com; *The Illustrated Book of World Rankings.*

United Nations Economic Commission for Africa (ECA), PO Box 3001, Addis Ababa, Ethiopia, (Telephone in U.S. (212) 963-4957), www.uneca.org; *African Statistical Yearbook 2006.*

United Nations Statistics Division, New York, NY 10017, (800) 253-9646, Fax: (212) 963-4116, http://unstats.un.org; *Statistical Yearbook* and *Survey of Economic and Social Conditions in Africa 2005.*

The World Bank, 1818 H Street, NW, Washington, DC 20433, (202) 473-1000, Fax: (202) 477-6391, www.worldbank.org; *Kenya.*

KENYA - ENVIRONMENTAL CONDITIONS

DSI Data Service Information, Xantener Strasse 51a, D-47495 Rheinberg, Germany, www.dsidata.com; *Campus Solution* and *DSI's Global Environmental Database.*

Economist Intelligence Unit, 111 West 57th Street, New York, NY 10019, (212) 554-0600, Fax: (212) 586-1181, www.eiu.com; *Kenya Country Report.*

International Institute for Environment and Development (IIED), 3 Endsleigh Street, London, England, WC1H 0DD, United Kingdom, www.iied.org; *Environment Urbanization* and *Haramata - Bulletin of the Drylands.*

United Nations Statistics Division, New York, NY 10017, (800) 253-9646, Fax: (212) 963-4116, http://unstats.un.org; *World Statistics Pocketbook.*

KENYA - EXPORTS

African Development Bank Group, Rue Joseph Anoma, 01 BP 1387 Abidjan 01, Cote d'Ivoire, www.afdb.org; *Statistics Pocketbook 2008.*

Central Intelligence Agency, Office of Public Affairs, Washington, DC 20505, (703) 482-0623, Fax: (703) 482-1739, www.cia.gov; *The World Factbook.*

Economist Intelligence Unit, 111 West 57th Street, New York, NY 10019, (212) 554-0600, Fax: (212) 586-1181, www.eiu.com; *Kenya Country Report.*

Euromonitor International, Inc., 224 S. Michigan Avenue, Suite 1500, Chicago, IL 60604, (312) 922-1115, Fax: (312) 922-1157, www.euromonitor.com; *International Marketing Data and Statistics 2008* and *The World Economic Factbook 2008.*

International Monetary Fund (IMF), 700 Nineteenth Street, NW, Washington, DC 20431, (202) 623-7000, Fax: (202) 623-4661, www.imf.org; *Direction of Trade Statistics Yearbook 2007; Government Finance Statistics Yearbook (2008 Edition);* and *International Financial Statistics Yearbook 2007.*

Palgrave Macmillan Ltd., Houndmills, Basingstoke, Hampshire, RG21 6XS, England, (Telephone in U.S. (888) 330-8477), (Fax in U.S. (800) 672-2054), www.palgrave.com; *The Statesman's Yearbook 2008.*

Taylor and Francis Group, An Informa Business, 2 Park Square, Milton Park, Abingdon, Oxford OX14 4RN, United Kingdom, (Dial from U.S. (212) 216-7800), (Fax from U.S. (212) 564-7854), www.tandf.co.uk; *The Europa World Year Book.*

United Nations Conference on Trade and Development (UNCTAD), DC2-1120, United Nations, New York, NY 10017, (212) 963-0027, www.unctad.org; *Handbook of Statistics 2005.*

United Nations Economic Commission for Africa (ECA), PO Box 3001, Addis Ababa, Ethiopia, (Telephone in U.S. (212) 963-4957), www.uneca.org; *African Statistical Yearbook 2006.*

United Nations Food and Agricultural Organization (FAO), Viale delle Terme di Caracalla, 00100 Rome, Italy, (Dial from U.S. (202) 653-2400), (Fax from U.S. (202) 653 5760), www.fao.org; *The State of Food and Agriculture (SOFA) 2006.*

United Nations Statistics Division, New York, NY 10017, (800) 253-9646, Fax: (212) 963-4116, http://unstats.un.org; *Compendium of Intra-African and Related Foreign Trade Statistics 2003* and *Survey of Economic and Social Conditions in Africa 2005.*

The World Bank, 1818 H Street, NW, Washington, DC 20433, (202) 473-1000, Fax: (202) 477-6391, www.worldbank.org; *World Development Indicators (WDI) 2008* and *World Development Report 2008.*

KENYA - FEMALE WORKING POPULATION

See KENYA - EMPLOYMENT

KENYA - FERTILITY, HUMAN

Central Intelligence Agency, Office of Public Affairs, Washington, DC 20505, (703) 482-0623, Fax: (703) 482-1739, www.cia.gov; *The World Factbook.*

M.E. Sharpe, 80 Business Park Drive, Armonk, NY 10504, (800) 541-6563, Fax: (914) 273-2106, www.mesharpe.com; *The Illustrated Book of World Rankings.*

United Nations Statistics Division, New York, NY 10017, (800) 253-9646, Fax: (212) 963-4116, http://unstats.un.org; *Human Development Report 2006* and *Survey of Economic and Social Conditions in Africa 2005.*

The World Bank, 1818 H Street, NW, Washington, DC 20433, (202) 473-1000, Fax: (202) 477-6391, www.worldbank.org; *The World Bank Atlas 2003-2004; World Development Indicators (WDI) 2008;* and *World Development Report 2008.*

KENYA - FERTILIZER INDUSTRY

United Nations Food and Agricultural Organization (FAO), Viale delle Terme di Caracalla, 00100 Rome, Italy, (Dial from U.S. (202) 653-2400), (Fax from U.S. (202) 653 5760), www.fao.org; *FAO Fertilizer Yearbook* and *The State of Food and Agriculture (SOFA) 2006.*

United Nations Statistics Division, New York, NY 10017, (800) 253-9646, Fax: (212) 963-4116, http://unstats.un.org; *Statistical Yearbook.*

KENYA - FETAL MORTALITY

See KENYA - MORTALITY

KENYA - FINANCE

Central Bureau of Statistics (CBS), Ministry of Economic Planning and Development, PO Box 30266, 00200 GPO Nairobi, Kenya, www.cbs.go.ke; *Statistical Abstract 2004.*

International Monetary Fund (IMF), 700 Nineteenth Street, NW, Washington, DC 20431, (202) 623-7000, Fax: (202) 623-4661, www.imf.org; *International Financial Statistics Yearbook 2007.*

Taylor and Francis Group, An Informa Business, 2 Park Square, Milton Park, Abingdon, Oxford OX14 4RN, United Kingdom, (Dial from U.S. (212) 216-7800), (Fax from U.S. (212) 564-7854), www.tandf.co.uk; *The Europa World Year Book.*

United Nations Economic Commission for Africa (ECA), PO Box 3001, Addis Ababa, Ethiopia, (Telephone in U.S. (212) 963-4957), www.uneca.org; *African Statistical Yearbook 2006.*

United Nations Statistics Division, New York, NY 10017, (800) 253-9646, Fax: (212) 963-4116, http://unstats.un.org; *National Accounts Statistics: Compendium of Income Distribution Statistics* and *Statistical Yearbook.*

The World Bank, 1818 H Street, NW, Washington, DC 20433, (202) 473-1000, Fax: (202) 477-6391, www.worldbank.org; *Kenya.*

KENYA - FINANCE, PUBLIC

African Development Bank Group, Rue Joseph Anoma, 01 BP 1387 Abidjan 01, Cote d'Ivoire, www.afdb.org; *Statistics Pocketbook 2008.*

Bernan Essential Government Publications, 4611-F Assembly Drive, Lanham MD, 20706-4391, (301) 459-2255, Fax: (800) 865-3450, www.bernan.com; *National Accounts Statistics.*

Central Bureau of Statistics (CBS), Ministry of Economic Planning and Development, PO Box 30266, 00200 GPO Nairobi, Kenya, www.cbs.go.ke; *Statistical Abstract 2004.*

Economist Intelligence Unit, 111 West 57th Street, New York, NY 10019, (212) 554-0600, Fax: (212) 586-1181, www.eiu.com; *Kenya Country Report.*

International Monetary Fund (IMF), 700 Nineteenth Street, NW, Washington, DC 20431, (202) 623-7000, Fax: (202) 623-4661, www.imf.org; *International Financial Statistics; International Financial Statistics Online Service;* and *International Financial Statistics Yearbook 2007.*

M.E. Sharpe, 80 Business Park Drive, Armonk, NY 10504, (800) 541-6563, Fax: (914) 273-2106, www.mesharpe.com; *The Illustrated Book of World Rankings.*

Palgrave Macmillan Ltd., Houndmills, Basingstoke, Hampshire, RG21 6XS, England, (Telephone in U.S. (888) 330-8477), (Fax in U.S. (800) 672-2054), www.palgrave.com; *The Statesman's Yearbook 2008.*

Taylor and Francis Group, An Informa Business, 2 Park Square, Milton Park, Abingdon, Oxford OX14

4RN, United Kingdom, (Dial from U.S. (212) 216-7800), (Fax from U.S. (212) 564-7854), www.tandf.co.uk; *The Europa World Year Book.*

United Nations Economic Commission for Africa (ECA), PO Box 3001, Addis Ababa, Ethiopia, (Telephone in U.S. (212) 963-4957), www.uneca.org; *African Statistical Yearbook 2006.*

The World Bank, 1818 H Street, NW, Washington, DC 20433, (202) 473-1000, Fax: (202) 477-6391, www.worldbank.org; *Kenya.*

KENYA - FISHERIES

Central Bureau of Statistics (CBS), Ministry of Economic Planning and Development, PO Box 30266, 00200 GPO Nairobi, Kenya, www.cbs.go.ke; *Statistical Abstract 2004.*

M.E. Sharpe, 80 Business Park Drive, Armonk, NY 10504, (800) 541-6563, Fax: (914) 273-2106, www.mesharpe.com; *The Illustrated Book of World Rankings.*

Palgrave Macmillan Ltd., Houndmills, Basingstoke, Hampshire, RG21 6XS, England, (Telephone in U.S. (888) 330-8477), (Fax in U.S. (800) 672-2054), www.palgrave.com; *The Statesman's Yearbook 2008.*

Taylor and Francis Group, An Informa Business, 2 Park Square, Milton Park, Abingdon, Oxford OX14 4RN, United Kingdom, (Dial from U.S. (212) 216-7800), (Fax from U.S. (212) 564-7854), www.tandf.co.uk; *The Europa World Year Book.*

United Nations Conference on Trade and Development (UNCTAD), DC2-1120, United Nations, New York, NY 10017, (212) 963-0027, www.unctad.org; *UNCTAD Commodity Yearbook.*

United Nations Economic Commission for Africa (ECA), PO Box 3001, Addis Ababa, Ethiopia, (Telephone in U.S. (212) 963-4957), www.uneca.org; *African Statistical Yearbook 2006.*

United Nations Food and Agricultural Organization (FAO), Viale delle Terme di Caracalla, 00100 Rome, Italy, (Dial from U.S. (202) 653-2400), (Fax from U.S. (202) 653 5760), www.fao.org; *The State of Food and Agriculture (SOFA) 2006.*

United Nations Statistics Division, New York, NY 10017, (800) 253-9646, Fax: (212) 963-4116, http://unstats.un.org; *Statistical Yearbook* and *Survey of Economic and Social Conditions in Africa 2005.*

The World Bank, 1818 H Street, NW, Washington, DC 20433, (202) 473-1000, Fax: (202) 477-6391, www.worldbank.org; *Kenya.*

KENYA - FLOUR INDUSTRY

United Nations Statistics Division, New York, NY 10017, (800) 253-9646, Fax: (212) 963-4116, http://unstats.un.org; *Statistical Yearbook.*

KENYA - FOOD

African Development Bank Group, Rue Joseph Anoma, 01 BP 1387 Abidjan 01, Cote d'Ivoire, www.afdb.org; *Statistics Pocketbook 2008.*

United Nations Conference on Trade and Development (UNCTAD), DC2-1120, United Nations, New York, NY 10017, (212) 963-0027, www.unctad.org; *UNCTAD Commodity Yearbook.*

United Nations Food and Agricultural Organization (FAO), Viale delle Terme di Caracalla, 00100 Rome, Italy, (Dial from U.S. (202) 653-2400), (Fax from U.S. (202) 653 5760), www.fao.org; *FAO Production Yearbook 2002* and *The State of Food and Agriculture (SOFA) 2006.*

United Nations Statistics Division, New York, NY 10017, (800) 253-9646, Fax: (212) 963-4116, http://unstats.un.org; *Human Development Report 2006.*

KENYA - FOREIGN EXCHANGE RATES

African Development Bank Group, Rue Joseph Anoma, 01 BP 1387 Abidjan 01, Cote d'Ivoire, www.afdb.org; *Statistics Pocketbook 2008.*

Central Intelligence Agency, Office of Public Affairs, Washington, DC 20505, (703) 482-0623, Fax: (703) 482-1739, www.cia.gov; *The World Factbook.*

Euromonitor International, Inc., 224 S. Michigan Avenue, Suite 1500, Chicago, IL 60604, (312) 922-1115, Fax: (312) 922-1157, www.euromonitor.com; *International Marketing Data and Statistics 2008* and *The World Economic Factbook 2008.*

International Monetary Fund (IMF), 700 Nineteenth Street, NW, Washington, DC 20431, (202) 623-7000, Fax: (202) 623-4661, www.imf.org; *International Financial Statistics Yearbook 2007.*

Taylor and Francis Group, An Informa Business, 2 Park Square, Milton Park, Abingdon, Oxford OX14 4RN, United Kingdom, (Dial from U.S. (212) 216-7800), (Fax from U.S. (212) 564-7854), www.tandf.co.uk; *The Europa World Year Book.*

United Nations Statistics Division, New York, NY 10017, (800) 253-9646, Fax: (212) 963-4116, http://unstats.un.org; *Compendium of Intra-African and Related Foreign Trade Statistics 2003; Statistical Yearbook;* and *World Statistics Pocketbook.*

KENYA - FORESTS AND FORESTRY

Central Bureau of Statistics (CBS), Ministry of Economic Planning and Development, PO Box 30266, 00200 GPO Nairobi, Kenya, www.cbs.go.ke; *Statistical Abstract 2004.*

M.E. Sharpe, 80 Business Park Drive, Armonk, NY 10504, (800) 541-6563, Fax: (914) 273-2106, www.mesharpe.com; *The Illustrated Book of World Rankings.*

Palgrave Macmillan Ltd., Houndmills, Basingstoke, Hampshire, RG21 6XS, England, (Telephone in U.S. (888) 330-8477), (Fax in U.S. (800) 672-2054), www.palgrave.com; *The Statesman's Yearbook 2008.*

Taylor and Francis Group, An Informa Business, 2 Park Square, Milton Park, Abingdon, Oxford OX14 4RN, United Kingdom, (Dial from U.S. (212) 216-7800), (Fax from U.S. (212) 564-7854), www.tandf.co.uk; *The Europa World Year Book.*

UNESCO Institute for Statistics, C.P. 6128 Succursale Centre-Ville, Montreal, Quebec, H3C 3J7 Canada, (Dial from U.S. (514) 343-6880), (Fax from U.S. (514) 343 6882), www.uis.unesco.org; *Statistical Tables.*

United Nations Conference on Trade and Development (UNCTAD), DC2-1120, United Nations, New York, NY 10017, (212) 963-0027, www.unctad.org; *UNCTAD Commodity Yearbook.*

United Nations Economic Commission for Africa (ECA), PO Box 3001, Addis Ababa, Ethiopia, (Telephone in U.S. (212) 963-4957), www.uneca.org; *African Statistical Yearbook 2006.*

United Nations Food and Agricultural Organization (FAO), Viale delle Terme di Caracalla, 00100 Rome, Italy, (Dial from U.S. (202) 653-2400), (Fax from U.S. (202) 653 5760), www.fao.org; *FAO Yearbook of Forest Products* and *The State of Food and Agriculture (SOFA) 2006.*

United Nations Statistics Division, New York, NY 10017, (800) 253-9646, Fax: (212) 963-4116, http://unstats.un.org; *Statistical Yearbook.*

The World Bank, 1818 H Street, NW, Washington, DC 20433, (202) 473-1000, Fax: (202) 477-6391, www.worldbank.org; *Kenya* and *World Development Report 2008.*

KENYA - GAS PRODUCTION

See KENYA - MINERAL INDUSTRIES

KENYA - GEOGRAPHIC INFORMATION SYSTEMS

M.E. Sharpe, 80 Business Park Drive, Armonk, NY 10504, (800) 541-6563, Fax: (914) 273-2106, www.mesharpe.com; *The Illustrated Book of World Rankings.*

The World Bank, 1818 H Street, NW, Washington, DC 20433, (202) 473-1000, Fax: (202) 477-6391, www.worldbank.org; *Kenya.*

KENYA - GOLD INDUSTRY

International Monetary Fund (IMF), 700 Nineteenth Street, NW, Washington, DC 20431, (202) 623-7000, Fax: (202) 623-4661, www.imf.org; *International Financial Statistics Yearbook 2007.*

United Nations Statistics Division, New York, NY 10017, (800) 253-9646, Fax: (212) 963-4116, http://unstats.un.org; *Statistical Yearbook.*

The World Bank, 1818 H Street, NW, Washington, DC 20433, (202) 473-1000, Fax: (202) 477-6391, www.worldbank.org; *World Development Indicators (WDI) 2008.*

KENYA - GOLD PRODUCTION

See KENYA - MINERAL INDUSTRIES

KENYA - GRANTS-IN-AID

International Monetary Fund (IMF), 700 Nineteenth Street, NW, Washington, DC 20431, (202) 623-7000, Fax: (202) 623-4661, www.imf.org; *Government Finance Statistics Yearbook (2008 Edition).*

KENYA - GROSS DOMESTIC PRODUCT

African Development Bank Group, Rue Joseph Anoma, 01 BP 1387 Abidjan 01, Cote d'Ivoire, www.afdb.org; *Statistics Pocketbook 2008.*

Economist Intelligence Unit, 111 West 57th Street, New York, NY 10019, (212) 554-0600, Fax: (212) 586-1181, www.eiu.com; *Kenya Country Report.*

Euromonitor International, Inc., 224 S. Michigan Avenue, Suite 1500, Chicago, IL 60604, (312) 922-1115, Fax: (312) 922-1157, www.euromonitor.com; *International Marketing Data and Statistics 2008* and *The World Economic Factbook 2008.*

M.E. Sharpe, 80 Business Park Drive, Armonk, NY 10504, (800) 541-6563, Fax: (914) 273-2106, www.mesharpe.com; *The Illustrated Book of World Rankings.*

Taylor and Francis Group, An Informa Business, 2 Park Square, Milton Park, Abingdon, Oxford OX14 4RN, United Kingdom, (Dial from U.S. (212) 216-7800), (Fax from U.S. (212) 564-7854), www.tandf.co.uk; *The Europa World Year Book.*

United Nations Economic Commission for Africa (ECA), PO Box 3001, Addis Ababa, Ethiopia, (Telephone in U.S. (212) 963-4957), www.uneca.org; *African Statistical Yearbook 2006.*

United Nations Statistics Division, New York, NY 10017, (800) 253-9646, Fax: (212) 963-4116, http://unstats.un.org; *Human Development Report 2006; National Accounts Statistics: Compendium of Income Distribution Statistics; Statistical Yearbook;* and *Survey of Economic and Social Conditions in Africa 2005.*

The World Bank, 1818 H Street, NW, Washington, DC 20433, (202) 473-1000, Fax: (202) 477-6391, www.worldbank.org; *World Development Indicators (WDI) 2008* and *World Development Report 2008.*

KENYA - GROSS NATIONAL PRODUCT

Euromonitor International, Inc., 224 S. Michigan Avenue, Suite 1500, Chicago, IL 60604, (312) 922-1115, Fax: (312) 922-1157, www.euromonitor.com; *International Marketing Data and Statistics 2008.*

M.E. Sharpe, 80 Business Park Drive, Armonk, NY 10504, (800) 541-6563, Fax: (914) 273-2106, www.mesharpe.com; *The Illustrated Book of World Rankings.*

Palgrave Macmillan Ltd., Houndmills, Basingstoke, Hampshire, RG21 6XS, England, (Telephone in U.S. (888) 330-8477), (Fax in U.S. (800) 672-2054), www.palgrave.com; *The Statesman's Yearbook 2008.*

Taylor and Francis Group, An Informa Business, 2 Park Square, Milton Park, Abingdon, Oxford OX14 4RN, United Kingdom, (Dial from U.S. (212) 216-7800), (Fax from U.S. (212) 564-7854), www.tandf.co.uk; *The Europa World Year Book.*

United Nations Statistics Division, New York, NY 10017, (800) 253-9646, Fax: (212) 963-4116, http://unstats.un.org; *Statistical Yearbook.*

The World Bank, 1818 H Street, NW, Washington, DC 20433, (202) 473-1000, Fax: (202) 477-6391,

www.worldbank.org; *The World Bank Atlas 2003-2004; World Development Indicators (WDI) 2008;* and *World Development Report 2008.*

KENYA - HIDES AND SKINS INDUSTRY

United Nations Food and Agricultural Organization (FAO), Viale delle Terme di Caracalla, 00100 Rome, Italy, (Dial from U.S. (202) 653-2400), (Fax from U.S. (202) 653 5760), www.fao.org; *FAO Production Yearbook 2002.*

KENYA - HOUSING

Euromonitor International, Inc., 224 S. Michigan Avenue, Suite 1500, Chicago, IL 60604, (312) 922-1115, Fax: (312) 922-1157, www.euromonitor.com; *World Marketing Data and Statistics.*

M.E. Sharpe, 80 Business Park Drive, Armonk, NY 10504, (800) 541-6563, Fax: (914) 273-2106, www.mesharpe.com; *The Illustrated Book of World Rankings.*

KENYA - ILLITERATE PERSONS

Euromonitor International, Inc., 224 S. Michigan Avenue, Suite 1500, Chicago, IL 60604, (312) 922-1115, Fax: (312) 922-1157, www.euromonitor.com; *The World Economic Factbook 2008.*

UNESCO Institute for Statistics, C.P. 6128 Succursale Centre-Ville, Montreal, Quebec, H3C 3J7 Canada, (Dial from U.S. (514) 343-6880), (Fax from U.S. (514) 343 6882), www.uis.unesco.org; *Statistical Tables.*

United Nations Statistics Division, New York, NY 10017, (800) 253-9646, Fax: (212) 963-4116, http://unstats.un.org; *Human Development Report 2006.*

KENYA - IMPORTS

Central Intelligence Agency, Office of Public Affairs, Washington, DC 20505, (703) 482-0623, Fax: (703) 482-1739, www.cia.gov; *The World Factbook.*

Economist Intelligence Unit, 111 West 57th Street, New York, NY 10019, (212) 554-0600, Fax: (212) 586-1181, www.eiu.com; *Kenya Country Report.*

Euromonitor International, Inc., 224 S. Michigan Avenue, Suite 1500, Chicago, IL 60604, (312) 922-1115, Fax: (312) 922-1157, www.euromonitor.com; *International Marketing Data and Statistics 2008* and *The World Economic Factbook 2008.*

International Monetary Fund (IMF), 700 Nineteenth Street, NW, Washington, DC 20431, (202) 623-7000, Fax: (202) 623-4661, www.imf.org; *Direction of Trade Statistics Yearbook 2007; Government Finance Statistics Yearbook (2008 Edition);* and *International Financial Statistics Yearbook 2007.*

Palgrave Macmillan Ltd., Houndmills, Basingstoke, Hampshire, RG21 6XS, England, (Telephone in U.S. (888) 330-8477), (Fax in U.S. (800) 672-2054), www.palgrave.com; *The Statesman's Yearbook 2008.*

Taylor and Francis Group, An Informa Business, 2 Park Square, Milton Park, Abingdon, Oxford OX14 4RN, United Kingdom, (Dial from U.S. (212) 216-7800), (Fax from U.S. (212) 564-7854), www.tandf.co.uk; *The Europa World Year Book.*

United Nations Conference on Trade and Development (UNCTAD), DC2-1120, United Nations, New York, NY 10017, (212) 963-0027, www.unctad.org; *Handbook of Statistics 2005.*

United Nations Economic Commission for Africa (ECA), PO Box 3001, Addis Ababa, Ethiopia, (Telephone in U.S. (212) 963-4957), www.uneca.org; *African Statistical Yearbook 2006.*

United Nations Food and Agricultural Organization (FAO), Viale delle Terme di Caracalla, 00100 Rome, Italy, (Dial from U.S. (202) 653-2400), (Fax from U.S. (202) 653 5760), www.fao.org; *The State of Food and Agriculture (SOFA) 2006.*

United Nations Statistics Division, New York, NY 10017, (800) 253-9646, Fax: (212) 963-4116, http://unstats.un.org; *Compendium of Intra-African and Related Foreign Trade Statistics 2003.*

The World Bank, 1818 H Street, NW, Washington, DC 20433, (202) 473-1000, Fax: (202) 477-6391, www.worldbank.org; *World Development Indicators (WDI) 2008* and *World Development Report 2008.*

KENYA - INCOME TAXES

See KENYA - TAXATION

KENYA - INDUSTRIAL PRODUCTIVITY

Euromonitor International, Inc., 224 S. Michigan Avenue, Suite 1500, Chicago, IL 60604, (312) 922-1115, Fax: (312) 922-1157, www.euromonitor.com; *International Marketing Data and Statistics 2008.*

M.E. Sharpe, 80 Business Park Drive, Armonk, NY 10504, (800) 541-6563, Fax: (914) 273-2106, www.mesharpe.com; *The Illustrated Book of World Rankings.*

KENYA - INDUSTRIAL PROPERTY

United Nations Statistics Division, New York, NY 10017, (800) 253-9646, Fax: (212) 963-4116, http://unstats.un.org; *Statistical Yearbook.*

World Intellectual Property Organization (WIPO), PO Box 18, CH-1211 Geneva 20, Switzerland, www.wipo.int; *Industrial Property Statistics* and *Industrial Property Statistics Online Directory.*

KENYA - INDUSTRIES

Central Bureau of Statistics (CBS), Ministry of Economic Planning and Development, PO Box 30266, 00200 GPO Nairobi, Kenya, www.cbs.go.ke; *Statistical Abstract 2004.*

Central Intelligence Agency, Office of Public Affairs, Washington, DC 20505, (703) 482-0623, Fax: (703) 482-1739, www.cia.gov; *The World Factbook.*

Economist Intelligence Unit, 111 West 57th Street, New York, NY 10019, (212) 554-0600, Fax: (212) 586-1181, www.eiu.com; *Kenya Country Report.*

Euromonitor International, Inc., 224 S. Michigan Avenue, Suite 1500, Chicago, IL 60604, (312) 922-1115, Fax: (312) 922-1157, www.euromonitor.com; *International Marketing Data and Statistics 2008; The World Economic Factbook 2008;* and *World Marketing Data and Statistics.*

International Labour Office, I.L.O. Publications, 4 route des Morillons, CH-1211 Geneva 22, Switzerland, (Telephone in U.S. (202) 653-7652), (Fax in U.S. (202) 653-7687), www.ilo.org; *Yearbook of Labour Statistics 2006.*

M.E. Sharpe, 80 Business Park Drive, Armonk, NY 10504, (800) 541-6563, Fax: (914) 273-2106, www.mesharpe.com; *The Illustrated Book of World Rankings.*

Palgrave Macmillan Ltd., Houndmills, Basingstoke, Hampshire, RG21 6XS, England, (Telephone in U.S. (888) 330-8477), (Fax in U.S. (800) 672-2054), www.palgrave.com; *The Statesman's Yearbook 2008.*

Taylor and Francis Group, An Informa Business, 2 Park Square, Milton Park, Abingdon, Oxford OX14 4RN, United Kingdom, (Dial from U.S. (212) 216-7800), (Fax from U.S. (212) 564-7854), www.tandf.co.uk; *The Europa World Year Book.*

United Nations Economic Commission for Africa (ECA), PO Box 3001, Addis Ababa, Ethiopia, (Telephone in U.S. (212) 963-4957), www.uneca.org; *African Statistical Yearbook 2006.*

United Nations Industrial Development Organization (UNIDO), 1 United Nations Plaza, New York, NY 10017, (212) 963 6890, Fax: (212) 963-7904, http://unido.org; Industrial Statistics Database 2008 (INDSTAT) and *The International Yearbook of Industrial Statistics 2008.*

United Nations Statistics Division, New York, NY 10017, (800) 253-9646, Fax: (212) 963-4116, http://unstats.un.org; *2004 Industrial Commodity Statistics Yearbook; Statistical Yearbook;* and *Survey of Economic and Social Conditions in Africa 2005.*

The World Bank, 1818 H Street, NW, Washington, DC 20433, (202) 473-1000, Fax: (202) 477-6391, www.worldbank.org; *Kenya; Statistical Handbook: States of the Former USSR;* and *World Development Indicators (WDI) 2008.*

KENYA - INFANT AND MATERNAL MORTALITY

See KENYA - MORTALITY

KENYA - INTERNATIONAL LIQUIDITY

International Monetary Fund (IMF), 700 Nineteenth Street, NW, Washington, DC 20431, (202) 623-7000, Fax: (202) 623-4661, www.imf.org; *International Financial Statistics Yearbook 2007.*

KENYA - INTERNATIONAL TRADE

African Development Bank Group, Rue Joseph Anoma, 01 BP 1387 Abidjan 01, Cote d'Ivoire, www.afdb.org; *Statistics Pocketbook 2008.*

Economist Intelligence Unit, 111 West 57th Street, New York, NY 10019, (212) 554-0600, Fax: (212) 586-1181, www.eiu.com; *Kenya Country Report.*

Euromonitor International, Inc., 224 S. Michigan Avenue, Suite 1500, Chicago, IL 60604, (312) 922-1115, Fax: (312) 922-1157, www.euromonitor.com; *International Marketing Data and Statistics 2008; The World Economic Factbook 2008;* and *World Marketing Data and Statistics.*

International Monetary Fund (IMF), 700 Nineteenth Street, NW, Washington, DC 20431, (202) 623-7000, Fax: (202) 623-4661, www.imf.org; *International Financial Statistics Yearbook 2007.*

M.E. Sharpe, 80 Business Park Drive, Armonk, NY 10504, (800) 541-6563, Fax: (914) 273-2106, www.mesharpe.com; *The Illustrated Book of World Rankings.*

Palgrave Macmillan Ltd., Houndmills, Basingstoke, Hampshire, RG21 6XS, England, (Telephone in U.S. (888) 330-8477), (Fax in U.S. (800) 672-2054), www.palgrave.com; *The Statesman's Yearbook 2008.*

Taylor and Francis Group, An Informa Business, 2 Park Square, Milton Park, Abingdon, Oxford OX14 4RN, United Kingdom, (Dial from U.S. (212) 216-7800), (Fax from U.S. (212) 564-7854), www.tandf.co.uk; *The Europa World Year Book.*

United Nations Conference on Trade and Development (UNCTAD), DC2-1120, United Nations, New York, NY 10017, (212) 963-0027, www.unctad.org; *UNCTAD Commodity Yearbook.*

United Nations Economic Commission for Africa (ECA), PO Box 3001, Addis Ababa, Ethiopia, (Telephone in U.S. (212) 963-4957), www.uneca.org; *African Statistical Yearbook 2006.*

United Nations Food and Agricultural Organization (FAO), Viale delle Terme di Caracalla, 00100 Rome, Italy, (Dial from U.S. (202) 653-2400), (Fax from U.S. (202) 653 5760), www.fao.org; *FAO Trade Yearbook* and *The State of Food and Agriculture (SOFA) 2006.*

United Nations Statistics Division, New York, NY 10017, (800) 253-9646, Fax: (212) 963-4116, http://unstats.un.org; *Compendium of Intra-African and Related Foreign Trade Statistics 2003; International Trade Statistics Yearbook;* and *Statistical Yearbook.*

The World Bank, 1818 H Street, NW, Washington, DC 20433, (202) 473-1000, Fax: (202) 477-6391, www.worldbank.org; *Kenya; World Development Indicators (WDI) 2008;* and *World Development Report 2008.*

World Trade Organization (WTO), Centre William Rappard, Rue de Lausanne 154, CH-1211 Geneva 21, Switzerland, www.wto.org; *International Trade Statistics 2006.*

KENYA - INTERNET USERS

International Telecommunication Union (ITU), Place des Nations, 1211 Geneva 20, Switzerland, www.itu.int; *World Telecommunication/ICT Indicators Database on CD-ROM; World Telecommunication/ICT Indicators Database Online;* and *Yearbook of Statistics - Telecommunication Services (Chronological Time Series 1997-2006).*

The World Bank, 1818 H Street, NW, Washington, DC 20433, (202) 473-1000, Fax: (202) 477-6391, www.worldbank.org; *Kenya.*

KENYA - IRON AND IRON ORE PRODUCTION

See KENYA - MINERAL INDUSTRIES

KENYA - IRRIGATION

Euromonitor International, Inc., 224 S. Michigan Avenue, Suite 1500, Chicago, IL 60604, (312) 922-1115, Fax: (312) 922-1157, www.euromonitor.com; *International Marketing Data and Statistics 2008.*

KENYA - LABOR

African Development Bank Group, Rue Joseph Anoma, 01 BP 1387 Abidjan 01, Cote d'Ivoire, www.afdb.org; *Statistics Pocketbook 2008.*

Central Bureau of Statistics (CBS), Ministry of Economic Planning and Development, PO Box 30266, 00200 GPO Nairobi, Kenya, www.cbs.go.ke; *Statistical Abstract 2004.*

Central Intelligence Agency, Office of Public Affairs, Washington, DC 20505, (703) 482-0623, Fax: (703) 482-1739, www.cia.gov; *The World Factbook.*

Euromonitor International, Inc., 224 S. Michigan Avenue, Suite 1500, Chicago, IL 60604, (312) 922-1115, Fax: (312) 922-1157, www.euromonitor.com; *International Marketing Data and Statistics 2008* and *World Marketing Data and Statistics.*

International Labour Office, I.L.O. Publications, 4 route des Morillons, CH-1211 Geneva 22, Switzerland, (Telephone in U.S. (202) 653-7652), (Fax in U.S. (202) 653-7687), www.ilo.org; *Yearbook of Labour Statistics 2006.*

M.E. Sharpe, 80 Business Park Drive, Armonk, NY 10504, (800) 541-6563, Fax: (914) 273-2106, www.mesharpe.com; *The Illustrated Book of World Rankings.*

Palgrave Macmillan Ltd., Houndmills, Basingstoke, Hampshire, RG21 6XS, England, (Telephone in U.S. (888) 330-8477), (Fax in U.S. (800) 672-2054), www.palgrave.com; *The Statesman's Yearbook 2008.*

Taylor and Francis Group, An Informa Business, 2 Park Square, Milton Park, Abingdon, Oxford OX14 4RN, United Kingdom, (Dial from U.S. (212) 216-7800), (Fax from U.S. (212) 564-7854), www.tandf.co.uk; *The Europa World Year Book.*

United Nations Food and Agricultural Organization (FAO), Viale delle Terme di Caracalla, 00100 Rome, Italy, (Dial from U.S. (202) 653-2400), (Fax from U.S. (202) 653 5760), www.fao.org; *The State of Food and Agriculture (SOFA) 2006.*

United Nations Statistics Division, New York, NY 10017, (800) 253-9646, Fax: (212) 963-4116, http://unstats.un.org; *Human Development Report 2006.*

The World Bank, 1818 H Street, NW, Washington, DC 20433, (202) 473-1000, Fax: (202) 477-6391, www.worldbank.org; *The World Bank Atlas 2003-2004; World Development Indicators (WDI) 2008;* and *World Development Report 2008.*

KENYA - LAND USE

Central Intelligence Agency, Office of Public Affairs, Washington, DC 20505, (703) 482-0623, Fax: (703) 482-1739, www.cia.gov; *The World Factbook.*

Euromonitor International, Inc., 224 S. Michigan Avenue, Suite 1500, Chicago, IL 60604, (312) 922-1115, Fax: (312) 922-1157, www.euromonitor.com; *International Marketing Data and Statistics 2008.*

United Nations Food and Agricultural Organization (FAO), Viale delle Terme di Caracalla, 00100 Rome, Italy, (Dial from U.S. (202) 653-2400), (Fax from U.S. (202) 653 5760), www.fao.org; *FAO Production Yearbook 2002.*

The World Bank, 1818 H Street, NW, Washington, DC 20433, (202) 473-1000, Fax: (202) 477-6391, www.worldbank.org; *World Development Report 2008.*

KENYA - LIBRARIES

M.E. Sharpe, 80 Business Park Drive, Armonk, NY 10504, (800) 541-6563, Fax: (914) 273-2106, www.mesharpe.com; *The Illustrated Book of World Rankings.*

UNESCO Institute for Statistics, C.P. 6128 Succursale Centre-Ville, Montreal, Quebec, H3C 3J7 Canada, (Dial from U.S. (514) 343-6880), (Fax from U.S. (514) 343 6882), www.uis.unesco.org; *Statistical Tables.*

KENYA - LICENSES

International Monetary Fund (IMF), 700 Nineteenth Street, NW, Washington, DC 20431, (202) 623-7000, Fax: (202) 623-4661, www.imf.org; *Government Finance Statistics Yearbook (2008 Edition).*

KENYA - LIFE EXPECTANCY

African Development Bank Group, Rue Joseph Anoma, 01 BP 1387 Abidjan 01, Cote d'Ivoire, www.afdb.org; *Statistics Pocketbook 2008.*

Central Intelligence Agency, Office of Public Affairs, Washington, DC 20505, (703) 482-0623, Fax: (703) 482-1739, www.cia.gov; *The World Factbook.*

Euromonitor International, Inc., 224 S. Michigan Avenue, Suite 1500, Chicago, IL 60604, (312) 922-1115, Fax: (312) 922-1157, www.euromonitor.com; *The World Economic Factbook 2008.*

Palgrave Macmillan Ltd., Houndmills, Basingstoke, Hampshire, RG21 6XS, England, (Telephone in U.S. (888) 330-8477), (Fax in U.S. (800) 672-2054), www.palgrave.com; *The Statesman's Yearbook 2008.*

United Nations Statistics Division, New York, NY 10017, (800) 253-9646, Fax: (212) 963-4116, http://unstats.un.org; *Human Development Report 2006* and *World Statistics Pocketbook.*

The World Bank, 1818 H Street, NW, Washington, DC 20433, (202) 473-1000, Fax: (202) 477-6391, www.worldbank.org; *The World Bank Atlas 2003-2004* and *World Development Report 2008.*

KENYA - LITERACY

Euromonitor International, Inc., 224 S. Michigan Avenue, Suite 1500, Chicago, IL 60604, (312) 922-1115, Fax: (312) 922-1157, www.euromonitor.com; *World Marketing Data and Statistics.*

United Nations Statistics Division, New York, NY 10017, (800) 253-9646, Fax: (212) 963-4116, http://unstats.un.org; *Survey of Economic and Social Conditions in Africa 2005.*

KENYA - LIVESTOCK

Euromonitor International, Inc., 224 S. Michigan Avenue, Suite 1500, Chicago, IL 60604, (312) 922-1115, Fax: (312) 922-1157, www.euromonitor.com; *International Marketing Data and Statistics 2008.*

M.E. Sharpe, 80 Business Park Drive, Armonk, NY 10504, (800) 541-6563, Fax: (914) 273-2106, www.mesharpe.com; *The Illustrated Book of World Rankings.*

Palgrave Macmillan Ltd., Houndmills, Basingstoke, Hampshire, RG21 6XS, England, (Telephone in U.S. (888) 330-8477), (Fax in U.S. (800) 672-2054), www.palgrave.com; *The Statesman's Yearbook 2008.*

Taylor and Francis Group, An Informa Business, 2 Park Square, Milton Park, Abingdon, Oxford OX14 4RN, United Kingdom, (Dial from U.S. (212) 216-7800), (Fax from U.S. (212) 564-7854), www.tandf.co.uk; *The Europa World Year Book.*

United Nations Conference on Trade and Development (UNCTAD), DC2-1120, United Nations, New York, NY 10017, (212) 963-0027, www.unctad.org; *UNCTAD Commodity Yearbook.*

United Nations Food and Agricultural Organization (FAO), Viale delle Terme di Caracalla, 00100 Rome, Italy, (Dial from U.S. (202) 653-2400), (Fax from U.S. (202) 653 5760), www.fao.org; *FAO Production Yearbook 2002* and *The State of Food and Agriculture (SOFA) 2006.*

United Nations Statistics Division, New York, NY 10017, (800) 253-9646, Fax: (212) 963-4116, http://unstats.un.org; *Statistical Yearbook* and *Survey of Economic and Social Conditions in Africa 2005.*

KENYA - LOCAL TAXATION

Euromonitor International, Inc., 224 S. Michigan Avenue, Suite 1500, Chicago, IL 60604, (312) 922-1115, Fax: (312) 922-1157, www.euromonitor.com; *International Marketing Data and Statistics 2008.*

KENYA - MANUFACTURES

M.E. Sharpe, 80 Business Park Drive, Armonk, NY 10504, (800) 541-6563, Fax: (914) 273-2106, www.mesharpe.com; *The Illustrated Book of World Rankings.*

United Nations Economic Commission for Africa (ECA), PO Box 3001, Addis Ababa, Ethiopia, (Telephone in U.S. (212) 963-4957), www.uneca.org; *African Statistical Yearbook 2006.*

United Nations Statistics Division, New York, NY 10017, (800) 253-9646, Fax: (212) 963-4116, http://unstats.un.org; *Statistical Yearbook* and *Survey of Economic and Social Conditions in Africa 2005.*

The World Bank, 1818 H Street, NW, Washington, DC 20433, (202) 473-1000, Fax: (202) 477-6391, www.worldbank.org; *World Development Indicators (WDI) 2008.*

KENYA - MARRIAGE

M.E. Sharpe, 80 Business Park Drive, Armonk, NY 10504, (800) 541-6563, Fax: (914) 273-2106, www.mesharpe.com; *The Illustrated Book of World Rankings.*

United Nations Statistics Division, New York, NY 10017, (800) 253-9646, Fax: (212) 963-4116, http://unstats.un.org; *Demographic Yearbook.*

KENYA - MEAT PRODUCTION

See KENYA - LIVESTOCK

KENYA - MEDICAL CARE, COST OF

International Monetary Fund (IMF), 700 Nineteenth Street, NW, Washington, DC 20431, (202) 623-7000, Fax: (202) 623-4661, www.imf.org; *Government Finance Statistics Yearbook (2008 Edition).*

KENYA - MILK PRODUCTION

See KENYA - DAIRY PROCESSING

KENYA - MINERAL INDUSTRIES

M.E. Sharpe, 80 Business Park Drive, Armonk, NY 10504, (800) 541-6563, Fax: (914) 273-2106, www.mesharpe.com; *The Illustrated Book of World Rankings.*

Palgrave Macmillan Ltd., Houndmills, Basingstoke, Hampshire, RG21 6XS, England, (Telephone in U.S. (888) 330-8477), (Fax in U.S. (800) 672-2054), www.palgrave.com; *The Statesman's Yearbook 2008.*

Taylor and Francis Group, An Informa Business, 2 Park Square, Milton Park, Abingdon, Oxford OX14 4RN, United Kingdom, (Dial from U.S. (212) 216-7800), (Fax from U.S. (212) 564-7854), www.tandf.co.uk; *The Europa World Year Book.*

United Nations Conference on Trade and Development (UNCTAD), DC2-1120, United Nations, New York, NY 10017, (212) 963-0027, www.unctad.org; *UNCTAD Commodity Yearbook.*

United Nations Economic Commission for Africa (ECA), PO Box 3001, Addis Ababa, Ethiopia, (Telephone in U.S. (212) 963-4957), www.uneca.org; *African Statistical Yearbook 2006.*

United Nations Statistics Division, New York, NY 10017, (800) 253-9646, Fax: (212) 963-4116, http://unstats.un.org; *Statistical Yearbook.*

The World Bank, 1818 H Street, NW, Washington, DC 20433, (202) 473-1000, Fax: (202) 477-6391, www.worldbank.org; *Kenya.*

KENYA - MONEY EXCHANGE RATES

See KENYA - FOREIGN EXCHANGE RATES

KENYA - MONEY SUPPLY

African Development Bank Group, Rue Joseph Anoma, 01 BP 1387 Abidjan 01, Cote d'Ivoire, www.afdb.org; *Statistics Pocketbook 2008.*

Economist Intelligence Unit, 111 West 57th Street, New York, NY 10019, (212) 554-0600, Fax: (212) 586-1181, www.eiu.com; *Kenya Country Report.*

Euromonitor International, Inc., 224 S. Michigan Avenue, Suite 1500, Chicago, IL 60604, (312) 922-1115, Fax: (312) 922-1157, www.euromonitor.com; *International Marketing Data and Statistics 2008.*

International Monetary Fund (IMF), 700 Nineteenth Street, NW, Washington, DC 20431, (202) 623-7000, Fax: (202) 623-4661, www.imf.org; *International Financial Statistics Yearbook 2007.*

Taylor and Francis Group, An Informa Business, 2 Park Square, Milton Park, Abingdon, Oxford OX14 4RN, United Kingdom, (Dial from U.S. (212) 216-7800), (Fax from U.S. (212) 564-7854), www.tandf.co.uk; *The Europa World Year Book.*

United Nations Statistics Division, New York, NY 10017, (800) 253-9646, Fax: (212) 963-4116, http://unstats.un.org; *Statistical Yearbook.*

The World Bank, 1818 H Street, NW, Washington, DC 20433, (202) 473-1000, Fax: (202) 477-6391, www.worldbank.org; *Kenya* and *World Development Indicators (WDI) 2008.*

KENYA - MONUMENTS AND HISTORIC SITES

UNESCO Institute for Statistics, C.P. 6128 Succursale Centre-Ville, Montreal, Quebec, H3C 3J7 Canada, (Dial from U.S. (514) 343-6880), (Fax from U.S. (514) 343 6882), www.uis.unesco.org; *Statistical Tables.*

KENYA - MORTALITY

Central Intelligence Agency, Office of Public Affairs, Washington, DC 20505, (703) 482-0623, Fax: (703) 482-1739, www.cia.gov; *The World Factbook.*

Euromonitor International, Inc., 224 S. Michigan Avenue, Suite 1500, Chicago, IL 60604, (312) 922-1115, Fax: (312) 922-1157, www.euromonitor.com; *International Marketing Data and Statistics 2008* and *The World Economic Factbook 2008.*

Taylor and Francis Group, An Informa Business, 2 Park Square, Milton Park, Abingdon, Oxford OX14 4RN, United Kingdom, (Dial from U.S. (212) 216-7800), (Fax from U.S. (212) 564-7854), www.tandf.co.uk; *The Europa World Year Book.*

UNICEF, 3 United Nations Plaza, New York, NY 10017, (800) 253-9646, Fax: (212) 887-7465, www.unicef.org; *The State of the World's Children 2008.*

United Nations Statistics Division, New York, NY 10017, (800) 253-9646, Fax: (212) 963-4116, http://unstats.un.org; *Demographic Yearbook; Human Development Report 2006; Statistical Yearbook; Survey of Economic and Social Conditions in Africa 2005;* and *World Statistics Pocketbook.*

The World Bank, 1818 H Street, NW, Washington, DC 20433, (202) 473-1000, Fax: (202) 477-6391, www.worldbank.org; *The World Bank Atlas 2003-2004; World Development Indicators (WDI) 2008;* and *World Development Report 2008.*

World Health Organization (WHO), Avenue Appia 20, 1211 Geneve 27, Switzerland, (Telephone in U.S. (212) 331-9081), www.who.int; The WHO Global Atlas of Infectious Diseases.

KENYA - MOTION PICTURES

United Nations Statistics Division, New York, NY 10017, (800) 253-9646, Fax: (212) 963-4116, http://unstats.un.org; *Statistical Yearbook.*

KENYA - MOTOR VEHICLES

International Road Federation (IFR), Madison Place, 500 Montgomery Street, 5th Floor, Alexandria, VA 22314, (703) 535-1001, Fax: (703) 535-1007, www.irfnet.org; *World Road Statistics 2006.*

Taylor and Francis Group, An Informa Business, 2 Park Square, Milton Park, Abingdon, Oxford OX14 4RN, United Kingdom, (Dial from U.S. (212) 216-7800), (Fax from U.S. (212) 564-7854), www.tandf.co.uk; *The Europa World Year Book.*

United Nations Statistics Division, New York, NY 10017, (800) 253-9646, Fax: (212) 963-4116, http://unstats.un.org; *Statistical Yearbook* and *Survey of Economic and Social Conditions in Africa 2005.*

KENYA - MUSEUMS

M.E. Sharpe, 80 Business Park Drive, Armonk, NY 10504, (800) 541-6563, Fax: (914) 273-2106, www.mesharpe.com; *The Illustrated Book of World Rankings.*

UNESCO Institute for Statistics, C.P. 6128 Succursale Centre-Ville, Montreal, Quebec, H3C 3J7 Canada, (Dial from U.S. (514) 343-6880), (Fax from U.S. (514) 343 6882), www.uis.unesco.org; *Statistical Tables.*

KENYA - NATURAL GAS PRODUCTION

See KENYA - MINERAL INDUSTRIES

KENYA - NUTRITION

African Development Bank Group, Rue Joseph Anoma, 01 BP 1387 Abidjan 01, Cote d'Ivoire, www.afdb.org; *Statistics Pocketbook 2008.*

United Nations Food and Agricultural Organization (FAO), Viale delle Terme di Caracalla, 00100 Rome, Italy, (Dial from U.S. (202) 653-2400), (Fax from U.S. (202) 653 5760), www.fao.org; *The State of Food and Agriculture (SOFA) 2006.*

KENYA - OATS PRODUCTION

See KENYA - CROPS

KENYA - OLDER PEOPLE

M.E. Sharpe, 80 Business Park Drive, Armonk, NY 10504, (800) 541-6563, Fax: (914) 273-2106, www.mesharpe.com; *The Illustrated Book of World Rankings.*

KENYA - PAPER

See KENYA - FORESTS AND FORESTRY

KENYA - PEANUT PRODUCTION

See KENYA - CROPS

KENYA - PESTICIDES

United Nations Food and Agricultural Organization (FAO), Viale delle Terme di Caracalla, 00100 Rome, Italy, (Dial from U.S. (202) 653-2400), (Fax from U.S. (202) 653 5760), www.fao.org; *The State of Food and Agriculture (SOFA) 2006.*

KENYA - PETROLEUM INDUSTRY AND TRADE

International Monetary Fund (IMF), 700 Nineteenth Street, NW, Washington, DC 20431, (202) 623-7000, Fax: (202) 623-4661, www.imf.org; *International Financial Statistics Yearbook 2007.*

M.E. Sharpe, 80 Business Park Drive, Armonk, NY 10504, (800) 541-6563, Fax: (914) 273-2106, www.mesharpe.com; *The Illustrated Book of World Rankings.*

Palgrave Macmillan Ltd., Houndmills, Basingstoke, Hampshire, RG21 6XS, England, (Telephone in U.S. (888) 330-8477), (Fax in U.S. (800) 672-2054), www.palgrave.com; *The Statesman's Yearbook 2008.*

PennWell Corporation, 1421 South Sheridan Road, Tulsa, OK 74112, (918) 835-3161, www.pennwell.com; *International Petroleum Encyclopedia 2007.*

U.S. Department of Energy (DOE), Energy Information Administration (EIA), 1000 Independence Avenue, SW, Washington, DC 20585, (202) 586-8800, www.eia.doe.gov; *International Energy Annual 2004* and *International Energy Outlook 2006.*

United Nations Conference on Trade and Development (UNCTAD), DC2-1120, United Nations, New York, NY 10017, (212) 963-0027, www.unctad.org; *UNCTAD Commodity Yearbook.*

United Nations Food and Agricultural Organization (FAO), Viale delle Terme di Caracalla, 00100 Rome, Italy, (Dial from U.S. (202) 653-2400), (Fax from U.S. (202) 653 5760), www.fao.org; *The State of Food and Agriculture (SOFA) 2006.*

United Nations Statistics Division, New York, NY 10017, (800) 253-9646, Fax: (212) 963-4116, http://unstats.un.org; *Statistical Yearbook.*

KENYA - POLITICAL SCIENCE

Central Intelligence Agency, Office of Public Affairs, Washington, DC 20505, (703) 482-0623, Fax: (703) 482-1739, www.cia.gov; *The World Factbook.*

International Monetary Fund (IMF), 700 Nineteenth Street, NW, Washington, DC 20431, (202) 623-7000, Fax: (202) 623-4661, www.imf.org; *Government Finance Statistics Yearbook (2008 Edition)* and *International Financial Statistics Yearbook 2007.*

Palgrave Macmillan Ltd., Houndmills, Basingstoke, Hampshire, RG21 6XS, England, (Telephone in U.S. (888) 330-8477), (Fax in U.S. (800) 672-2054), www.palgrave.com; *The Statesman's Yearbook 2008.*

Taylor and Francis Group, An Informa Business, 2 Park Square, Milton Park, Abingdon, Oxford OX14 4RN, United Kingdom, (Dial from U.S. (212) 216-7800), (Fax from U.S. (212) 564-7854), www.tandf.co.uk; *The Europa World Year Book.*

United Nations Statistics Division, New York, NY 10017, (800) 253-9646, Fax: (212) 963-4116, http://unstats.un.org; *National Accounts Statistics: Compendium of Income Distribution Statistics; Statistical Yearbook;* and *Survey of Economic and Social Conditions in Africa 2005.*

The World Bank, 1818 H Street, NW, Washington, DC 20433, (202) 473-1000, Fax: (202) 477-6391, www.worldbank.org; *World Development Indicators (WDI) 2008* and *World Development Report 2008.*

KENYA - POPULATION

African Development Bank Group, Rue Joseph Anoma, 01 BP 1387 Abidjan 01, Cote d'Ivoire, www.afdb.org; *The African Statistical Journal; Gender, Poverty and Environmental Indicators on African Countries 2007; Selected Statistics on African Countries 2007;* and *Statistics Pocketbook 2008.*

Central Bureau of Statistics (CBS), Ministry of Economic Planning and Development, PO Box 30266, 00200 GPO Nairobi, Kenya, www.cbs.go.ke; *Statistical Abstract 2004.*

Central Intelligence Agency, Office of Public Affairs, Washington, DC 20505, (703) 482-0623, Fax: (703) 482-1739, www.cia.gov; *The World Factbook.*

Economist Intelligence Unit, 111 West 57th Street, New York, NY 10019, (212) 554-0600, Fax: (212) 586-1181, www.eiu.com; *Kenya Country Report.*

Euromonitor International, Inc., 224 S. Michigan Avenue, Suite 1500, Chicago, IL 60604, (312) 922-1115, Fax: (312) 922-1157, www.euromonitor.com; *International Marketing Data and Statistics 2008* and *The World Economic Factbook 2008.*

Eurostat, Batiment Jean Monnet, Rue Alcide de Gasperi, L-2920 Luxembourg, http://epp.eurostat.ec.europa.eu; *Demographic Indicators - Population by Age-Classes.*

International Food Policy Research Institute (IFPRI), 2033 K Street, NW, Washington, D.C., 2006, (202) 862-5600, www.ifpri.org; *Kenya: The Influence of Social Capital on Sustainable Agriculture in Marginal Areas, 2003.*

International Labour Office, I.L.O. Publications, 4 route des Morillons, CH-1211 Geneva 22, Switzerland, (Telephone in U.S. (202) 653-7652), (Fax in U.S. (202) 653-7687), www.ilo.org; *Yearbook of Labour Statistics 2006.*

M.E. Sharpe, 80 Business Park Drive, Armonk, NY 10504, (800) 541-6563, Fax: (914) 273-2106, www.mesharpe.com; *The Illustrated Book of World Rankings.*

Palgrave Macmillan Ltd., Houndmills, Basingstoke, Hampshire, RG21 6XS, England, (Telephone in U.S. (888) 330-8477), (Fax in U.S. (800) 672-2054), www.palgrave.com; *The Statesman's Yearbook 2008.*

Taylor and Francis Group, An Informa Business, 2 Park Square, Milton Park, Abingdon, Oxford OX14

4RN, United Kingdom, (Dial from U.S. (212) 216-7800), (Fax from U.S. (212) 564-7854), www.tandf.co.uk; *The Europa World Year Book.*

UNESCO Institute for Statistics, C.P. 6128 Succursale Centre-Ville, Montreal, Quebec, H3C 3J7 Canada, (Dial from U.S. (514) 343-6880), (Fax from U.S. (514) 343 6882), www.uis.unesco.org; *Statistical Tables.*

United Nations Food and Agricultural Organization (FAO), Viale delle Terme di Caracalla, 00100 Rome, Italy, (Dial from U.S. (202) 653-2400), (Fax from U.S. (202) 653 5760), www.fao.org; *FAO Production Yearbook 2002.*

United Nations Statistics Division, New York, NY 10017, (800) 253-9646, Fax: (212) 963-4116, http://unstats.un.org; *Demographic Yearbook; Human Development Report 2006; Statistical Yearbook; Survey of Economic and Social Conditions in Africa 2005;* and *World Statistics Pocketbook.*

The World Bank, 1818 H Street, NW, Washington, DC 20433, (202) 473-1000, Fax: (202) 477-6391, www.worldbank.org; *Kenya; The World Bank Atlas 2003-2004;* and *World Development Report 2008.*

World Resources Institute (WRI), 10 G Street, NE, Suite 800 Washington, DC 20002, (202) 729-7600, www.wri.org; *Nature's Benefits in Kenya: An Atlas of Ecosystems and Human Well-Being.*

KENYA - POPULATION DENSITY

African Development Bank Group, Rue Joseph Anoma, 01 BP 1387 Abidjan 01, Cote d'Ivoire, www.afdb.org; *Statistics Pocketbook 2008.*

Central Intelligence Agency, Office of Public Affairs, Washington, DC 20505, (703) 482-0623, Fax: (703) 482-1739, www.cia.gov; *The World Factbook.*

Euromonitor International, Inc., 224 S. Michigan Avenue, Suite 1500, Chicago, IL 60604, (312) 922-1115, Fax: (312) 922-1157, www.euromonitor.com; *International Marketing Data and Statistics 2008* and *The World Economic Factbook 2008.*

M.E. Sharpe, 80 Business Park Drive, Armonk, NY 10504, (800) 541-6563, Fax: (914) 273-2106, www.mesharpe.com; *The Illustrated Book of World Rankings.*

Palgrave Macmillan Ltd., Houndmills, Basingstoke, Hampshire, RG21 6XS, England, (Telephone in U.S. (888) 330-8477), (Fax in U.S. (800) 672-2054), www.palgrave.com; *The Statesman's Yearbook 2008.*

Taylor and Francis Group, An Informa Business, 2 Park Square, Milton Park, Abingdon, Oxford OX14 4RN, United Kingdom, (Dial from U.S. (212) 216-7800), (Fax from U.S. (212) 564-7854), www.tandf.co.uk; *The Europa World Year Book.*

UNESCO Institute for Statistics, C.P. 6128 Succursale Centre-Ville, Montreal, Quebec, H3C 3J7 Canada, (Dial from U.S. (514) 343-6880), (Fax from U.S. (514) 343 6882), www.uis.unesco.org; *Statistical Tables.*

United Nations Food and Agricultural Organization (FAO), Viale delle Terme di Caracalla, 00100 Rome, Italy, (Dial from U.S. (202) 653-2400), (Fax from U.S. (202) 653 5760), www.fao.org; *The State of Food and Agriculture (SOFA) 2006.*

United Nations Statistics Division, New York, NY 10017, (800) 253-9646, Fax: (212) 963-4116, http://unstats.un.org; *Statistical Yearbook* and *Survey of Economic and Social Conditions in Africa 2005.*

The World Bank, 1818 H Street, NW, Washington, DC 20433, (202) 473-1000, Fax: (202) 477-6391, www.worldbank.org; *Kenya* and *World Development Report 2008.*

KENYA - POSTAL SERVICE

M.E. Sharpe, 80 Business Park Drive, Armonk, NY 10504, (800) 541-6563, Fax: (914) 273-2106, www.mesharpe.com; *The Illustrated Book of World Rankings.*

United Nations Statistics Division, New York, NY 10017, (800) 253-9646, Fax: (212) 963-4116, http://unstats.un.org; *Statistical Yearbook.*

KENYA - POWER RESOURCES

Euromonitor International, Inc., 224 S. Michigan Avenue, Suite 1500, Chicago, IL 60604, (312) 922-1115, Fax: (312) 922-1157, www.euromonitor.com; *International Marketing Data and Statistics 2008; The World Economic Factbook 2008;* and *World Marketing Data and Statistics.*

M.E. Sharpe, 80 Business Park Drive, Armonk, NY 10504, (800) 541-6563, Fax: (914) 273-2106, www.mesharpe.com; *The Illustrated Book of World Rankings.*

Palgrave Macmillan Ltd., Houndmills, Basingstoke, Hampshire, RG21 6XS, England, (Telephone in U.S. (888) 330-8477), (Fax in U.S. (800) 672-2054), www.palgrave.com; *The Statesman's Yearbook 2008.*

Platts, 2 Penn Plaza, 25th Floor, New York, NY 10121-2298, (212) 904-3070, www.platts.com; *Energy Economist.*

U.S. Department of Energy (DOE), Energy Information Administration (EIA), 1000 Independence Avenue, SW, Washington, DC 20585, (202) 586-8800, www.eia.doe.gov; *International Energy Annual 2004* and *International Energy Outlook 2006.*

United Nations Economic Commission for Africa (ECA), PO Box 3001, Addis Ababa, Ethiopia, (Telephone in U.S. (212) 963-4957), www.uneca.org; *African Statistical Yearbook 2006.*

United Nations Food and Agricultural Organization (FAO), Viale delle Terme di Caracalla, 00100 Rome, Italy, (Dial from U.S. (202) 653-2400), (Fax from U.S. (202) 653 5760), www.fao.org; *The State of Food and Agriculture (SOFA) 2006.*

United Nations Statistics Division, New York, NY 10017, (800) 253-9646, Fax: (212) 963-4116, http://unstats.un.org; *Energy Statistics Yearbook 2003; Human Development Report 2006; Statistical Yearbook;* and *World Statistics Pocketbook.*

The World Bank, 1818 H Street, NW, Washington, DC 20433, (202) 473-1000, Fax: (202) 477-6391, www.worldbank.org; *The World Bank Atlas 2003-2004* and *World Development Report 2008.*

KENYA - PRICES

Euromonitor International, Inc., 224 S. Michigan Avenue, Suite 1500, Chicago, IL 60604, (312) 922-1115, Fax: (312) 922-1157, www.euromonitor.com; *World Marketing Data and Statistics.*

International Labour Office, I.L.O. Publications, 4 route des Morillons, CH-1211 Geneva 22, Switzerland, (Telephone in U.S. (202) 653-7652), (Fax in U.S. (202) 653-7687), www.ilo.org; *Yearbook of Labour Statistics 2006.*

International Monetary Fund (IMF), 700 Nineteenth Street, NW, Washington, DC 20431, (202) 623-7000, Fax: (202) 623-4661, www.imf.org; *International Financial Statistics Yearbook 2007.*

M.E. Sharpe, 80 Business Park Drive, Armonk, NY 10504, (800) 541-6563, Fax: (914) 273-2106, www.mesharpe.com; *The Illustrated Book of World Rankings.*

United Nations Economic Commission for Africa (ECA), PO Box 3001, Addis Ababa, Ethiopia, (Telephone in U.S. (212) 963-4957), www.uneca.org; *African Statistical Yearbook 2006.*

United Nations Food and Agricultural Organization (FAO), Viale delle Terme di Caracalla, 00100 Rome, Italy, (Dial from U.S. (202) 653-2400), (Fax from U.S. (202) 653 5760), www.fao.org; *FAO Production Yearbook 2002* and *The State of Food and Agriculture (SOFA) 2006.*

The World Bank, 1818 H Street, NW, Washington, DC 20433, (202) 473-1000, Fax: (202) 477-6391, www.worldbank.org; *Kenya.*

KENYA - PROFESSIONS

UNESCO Institute for Statistics, C.P. 6128 Succursale Centre-Ville, Montreal, Quebec, H3C 3J7 Canada, (Dial from U.S. (514) 343-6880), (Fax from U.S. (514) 343 6882), www.uis.unesco.org; *Statistical Tables.*

United Nations Statistics Division, New York, NY 10017, (800) 253-9646, Fax: (212) 963-4116, http://unstats.un.org; *Statistical Yearbook.*

KENYA - PUBLIC HEALTH

African Development Bank Group, Rue Joseph Anoma, 01 BP 1387 Abidjan 01, Cote d'Ivoire, www.afdb.org; *Statistics Pocketbook 2008.*

Euromonitor International, Inc., 224 S. Michigan Avenue, Suite 1500, Chicago, IL 60604, (312) 922-1115, Fax: (312) 922-1157, www.euromonitor.com; *World Health Databook 2007/2008* and *World Marketing Data and Statistics.*

M.E. Sharpe, 80 Business Park Drive, Armonk, NY 10504, (800) 541-6563, Fax: (914) 273-2106, www.mesharpe.com; *The Illustrated Book of World Rankings.*

Palgrave Macmillan Ltd., Houndmills, Basingstoke, Hampshire, RG21 6XS, England, (Telephone in U.S. (888) 330-8477), (Fax in U.S. (800) 672-2054), www.palgrave.com; *The Statesman's Yearbook 2008.*

UNICEF, 3 United Nations Plaza, New York, NY 10017, (800) 253-9646, Fax: (212) 887-7465, www.unicef.org; *The State of the World's Children 2008.*

United Nations Economic Commission for Africa (ECA), PO Box 3001, Addis Ababa, Ethiopia, (Telephone in U.S. (212) 963-4957), www.uneca.org; *African Statistical Yearbook 2006.*

United Nations Statistics Division, New York, NY 10017, (800) 253-9646, Fax: (212) 963-4116, http://unstats.un.org; *Human Development Report 2006* and *Statistical Yearbook.*

The World Bank, 1818 H Street, NW, Washington, DC 20433, (202) 473-1000, Fax: (202) 477-6391, www.worldbank.org; *Kenya* and *World Development Report 2008.*

World Health Organization (WHO), Avenue Appia 20, 1211 Geneve 27, Switzerland, (Telephone in U.S. (212) 331-9081), www.who.int; The WHO Global Atlas of Infectious Diseases.

KENYA - PUBLISHERS AND PUBLISHING

Taylor and Francis Group, An Informa Business, 2 Park Square, Milton Park, Abingdon, Oxford OX14 4RN, United Kingdom, (Dial from U.S. (212) 216-7800), (Fax from U.S. (212) 564-7854), www.tandf.co.uk; *The Europa World Year Book.*

KENYA - RADIO BROADCASTING

Palgrave Macmillan Ltd., Houndmills, Basingstoke, Hampshire, RG21 6XS, England, (Telephone in U.S. (888) 330-8477), (Fax in U.S. (800) 672-2054), www.palgrave.com; *The Statesman's Yearbook 2008.*

KENYA - RAILROADS

Jane's Information Group, 110 North Royal Street, Suite 200, Alexandria, VA 22314, (703) 683-3700, Fax: (800) 836-0297, www.janes.com; *Jane's World Railways.*

Palgrave Macmillan Ltd., Houndmills, Basingstoke, Hampshire, RG21 6XS, England, (Telephone in U.S. (888) 330-8477), (Fax in U.S. (800) 672-2054), www.palgrave.com; *The Statesman's Yearbook 2008.*

Taylor and Francis Group, An Informa Business, 2 Park Square, Milton Park, Abingdon, Oxford OX14 4RN, United Kingdom, (Dial from U.S. (212) 216-7800), (Fax from U.S. (212) 564-7854), www.tandf.co.uk; *The Europa World Year Book.*

United Nations Economic Commission for Africa (ECA), PO Box 3001, Addis Ababa, Ethiopia, (Telephone in U.S. (212) 963-4957), www.uneca.org; *African Statistical Yearbook 2006.*

United Nations Statistics Division, New York, NY 10017, (800) 253-9646, Fax: (212) 963-4116, http://unstats.un.org; *Survey of Economic and Social Conditions in Africa 2005.*

KENYA - RELIGION

Central Intelligence Agency, Office of Public Affairs, Washington, DC 20505, (703) 482-0623, Fax: (703) 482-1739, www.cia.gov; *The World Factbook.*

M.E. Sharpe, 80 Business Park Drive, Armonk, NY 10504, (800) 541-6563, Fax: (914) 273-2106, www.mesharpe.com; *The Illustrated Book of World Rankings.*

Palgrave Macmillan Ltd., Houndmills, Basingstoke, Hampshire, RG21 6XS, England, (Telephone in U.S. (888) 330-8477), (Fax in U.S. (800) 672-2054), www.palgrave.com; *The Statesman's Yearbook 2008.*

KENYA - RENT CHARGES

International Labour Office, I.L.O. Publications, 4 route des Morillons, CH-1211 Geneva 22, Switzerland, (Telephone in U.S. (202) 653-7652), (Fax in U.S. (202) 653-7687), www.ilo.org; *Yearbook of Labour Statistics 2006.*

KENYA - RESERVES (ACCOUNTING)

African Development Bank Group, Rue Joseph Anoma, 01 BP 1387 Abidjan 01, Cote d'Ivoire, www.afdb.org; *Statistics Pocketbook 2008.*

Euromonitor International, Inc., 224 S. Michigan Avenue, Suite 1500, Chicago, IL 60604, (312) 922-1115, Fax: (312) 922-1157, www.euromonitor.com; *International Marketing Data and Statistics 2008.*

United Nations Statistics Division, New York, NY 10017, (800) 253-9646, Fax: (212) 963-4116, http://unstats.un.org; *Statistical Yearbook.*

The World Bank, 1818 H Street, NW, Washington, DC 20433, (202) 473-1000, Fax: (202) 477-6391, www.worldbank.org; *World Development Indicators (WDI) 2008.*

KENYA - RETAIL TRADE

Euromonitor International, Inc., 224 S. Michigan Avenue, Suite 1500, Chicago, IL 60604, (312) 922-1115, Fax: (312) 922-1157, www.euromonitor.com; *World Marketing Data and Statistics.*

United Nations Statistics Division, New York, NY 10017, (800) 253-9646, Fax: (212) 963-4116, http://unstats.un.org; *Statistical Yearbook.*

KENYA - RICE PRODUCTION

See KENYA - CROPS

KENYA - ROADS

Central Intelligence Agency, Office of Public Affairs, Washington, DC 20505, (703) 482-0623, Fax: (703) 482-1739, www.cia.gov; *The World Factbook.*

International Road Federation (IFR), Madison Place, 500 Montgomery Street, 5th Floor, Alexandria, VA 22314, (703) 535-1001, Fax: (703) 535-1007, www.irfnet.org; *World Road Statistics 2006.*

Palgrave Macmillan Ltd., Houndmills, Basingstoke, Hampshire, RG21 6XS, England, (Telephone in U.S. (888) 330-8477), (Fax in U.S. (800) 672-2054), www.palgrave.com; *The Statesman's Yearbook 2008.*

United Nations Economic Commission for Africa (ECA), PO Box 3001, Addis Ababa, Ethiopia, (Telephone in U.S. (212) 963-4957), www.uneca.org; *African Statistical Yearbook 2006.*

United Nations Statistics Division, New York, NY 10017, (800) 253-9646, Fax: (212) 963-4116, http://unstats.un.org; *Survey of Economic and Social Conditions in Africa 2005.*

KENYA - RUBBER INDUSTRY AND TRADE

International Rubber Study Group (IRSG), 1st Floor, Heron House, 109/115 Wembley Hill Road, Wembley, Middlesex HA9 8DA, United Kingdom, www.rubberstudy.com; *Rubber Statistical Bulletin; Summary of World Rubber Statistics 2005; World Rubber Statistics Handbook (Volume 6, 1975-2001);* and *World Rubber Statistics Historic Handbook.*

M.E. Sharpe, 80 Business Park Drive, Armonk, NY 10504, (800) 541-6563, Fax: (914) 273-2106, www.mesharpe.com; *The Illustrated Book of World Rankings.*

KENYA - SALT INDUSTRY AND TRADE

United Nations Statistics Division, New York, NY 10017, (800) 253-9646, Fax: (212) 963-4116, http://unstats.un.org; *Statistical Yearbook.*

KENYA - SHEEP

See KENYA - LIVESTOCK

KENYA - SHIPPING

Palgrave Macmillan Ltd., Houndmills, Basingstoke, Hampshire, RG21 6XS, England, (Telephone in U.S. (888) 330-8477), (Fax in U.S. (800) 672-2054), www.palgrave.com; *The Statesman's Yearbook 2008.*

Taylor and Francis Group, An Informa Business, 2 Park Square, Milton Park, Abingdon, Oxford OX14 4RN, United Kingdom, (Dial from U.S. (212) 216-7800), (Fax from U.S. (212) 564-7854), www.tandf.co.uk; *The Europa World Year Book.*

U.S. Department of Transportation (DOT), Maritime Administration (MARAD), West Building, Southeast Federal Center, 1200 New Jersey Avenue, SE, Washington, DC 20590, (800) 99-MARAD, www.marad.dot.gov; *World Merchant Fleet 2005.*

United Nations Economic Commission for Africa (ECA), PO Box 3001, Addis Ababa, Ethiopia, (Telephone in U.S. (212) 963-4957), www.uneca.org; *African Statistical Yearbook 2006.*

United Nations Statistics Division, New York, NY 10017, (800) 253-9646, Fax: (212) 963-4116, http://unstats.un.org; *Statistical Yearbook.*

KENYA - SILVER PRODUCTION

See KENYA - MINERAL INDUSTRIES

KENYA - SOCIAL ECOLOGY

M.E. Sharpe, 80 Business Park Drive, Armonk, NY 10504, (800) 541-6563, Fax: (914) 273-2106, www.mesharpe.com; *The Illustrated Book of World Rankings.*

United Nations Statistics Division, New York, NY 10017, (800) 253-9646, Fax: (212) 963-4116, http://unstats.un.org; *World Statistics Pocketbook.*

KENYA - SOCIAL SECURITY

United Nations Statistics Division, New York, NY 10017, (800) 253-9646, Fax: (212) 963-4116, http://unstats.un.org; *National Accounts Statistics: Compendium of Income Distribution Statistics.*

KENYA - STEEL PRODUCTION

See KENYA - MINERAL INDUSTRIES

KENYA - SUGAR PRODUCTION

See KENYA - CROPS

KENYA - TAXATION

International Monetary Fund (IMF), 700 Nineteenth Street, NW, Washington, DC 20431, (202) 623-7000, Fax: (202) 623-4661, www.imf.org; *Government Finance Statistics Yearbook (2008 Edition).*

International Road Federation (IFR), Madison Place, 500 Montgomery Street, 5th Floor, Alexandria, VA 22314, (703) 535-1001, Fax: (703) 535-1007, www.irfnet.org; *World Road Statistics 2006.*

Taylor and Francis Group, An Informa Business, 2 Park Square, Milton Park, Abingdon, Oxford OX14 4RN, United Kingdom, (Dial from U.S. (212) 216-7800), (Fax from U.S. (212) 564-7854), www.tandf.co.uk; *The Europa World Year Book.*

The World Bank, 1818 H Street, NW, Washington, DC 20433, (202) 473-1000, Fax: (202) 477-6391, www.worldbank.org; *World Development Indicators (WDI) 2008.*

KENYA - TEA PRODUCTION

See KENYA - CROPS

KENYA - TELEPHONE

International Telecommunication Union (ITU), Place des Nations, 1211 Geneva 20, Switzerland, www.itu.int; World Telecommunication Indicators Database.

Taylor and Francis Group, An Informa Business, 2 Park Square, Milton Park, Abingdon, Oxford OX14 4RN, United Kingdom, (Dial from U.S. (212) 216-7800), (Fax from U.S. (212) 564-7854), www.tandf.co.uk; *The Europa World Year Book.*

United Nations Statistics Division, New York, NY 10017, (800) 253-9646, Fax: (212) 963-4116, http://unstats.un.org; *Statistical Yearbook* and *World Statistics Pocketbook.*

KENYA - TEXTILE INDUSTRY

M.E. Sharpe, 80 Business Park Drive, Armonk, NY 10504, (800) 541-6563, Fax: (914) 273-2106, www.mesharpe.com; *The Illustrated Book of World Rankings.*

Palgrave Macmillan Ltd., Houndmills, Basingstoke, Hampshire, RG21 6XS, England, (Telephone in U.S. (888) 330-8477), (Fax in U.S. (800) 672-2054), www.palgrave.com; *The Statesman's Yearbook 2008.*

United Nations Conference on Trade and Development (UNCTAD), DC2-1120, United Nations, New York, NY 10017, (212) 963-0027, www.unctad.org; *UNCTAD Commodity Yearbook.*

United Nations Statistics Division, New York, NY 10017, (800) 253-9646, Fax: (212) 963-4116, http://unstats.un.org; *Statistical Yearbook.*

KENYA - TOBACCO INDUSTRY

Foreign Agricultural Service (FAS), U.S. Department of Agriculture (USDA), 1400 Independence Avenue, SW, Washington, DC 20250, (202) 720-3935, www.fas.usda.gov; *Tobacco: World Markets and Trade.*

M.E. Sharpe, 80 Business Park Drive, Armonk, NY 10504, (800) 541-6563, Fax: (914) 273-2106, www.mesharpe.com; *The Illustrated Book of World Rankings.*

United Nations Statistics Division, New York, NY 10017, (800) 253-9646, Fax: (212) 963-4116, http://unstats.un.org; *Statistical Yearbook.*

KENYA - TOURISM

Central Bureau of Statistics (CBS), Ministry of Economic Planning and Development, PO Box 30266, 00200 GPO Nairobi, Kenya, www.cbs.go.ke; *Statistical Abstract 2004.*

Euromonitor International, Inc., 224 S. Michigan Avenue, Suite 1500, Chicago, IL 60604, (312) 922-1115, Fax: (312) 922-1157, www.euromonitor.com; *The World Economic Factbook 2008* and *World Marketing Data and Statistics.*

M.E. Sharpe, 80 Business Park Drive, Armonk, NY 10504, (800) 541-6563, Fax: (914) 273-2106, www.mesharpe.com; *The Illustrated Book of World Rankings.*

Palgrave Macmillan Ltd., Houndmills, Basingstoke, Hampshire, RG21 6XS, England, (Telephone in U.S. (888) 330-8477), (Fax in U.S. (800) 672-2054), www.palgrave.com; *The Statesman's Yearbook 2008.*

Taylor and Francis Group, An Informa Business, 2 Park Square, Milton Park, Abingdon, Oxford OX14 4RN, United Kingdom, (Dial from U.S. (212) 216-7800), (Fax from U.S. (212) 564-7854), www.tandf.co.uk; *The Europa World Year Book.*

United Nations Economic Commission for Africa (ECA), PO Box 3001, Addis Ababa, Ethiopia, (Telephone in U.S. (212) 963-4957), www.uneca.org; *African Statistical Yearbook 2006.*

United Nations Statistics Division, New York, NY 10017, (800) 253-9646, Fax: (212) 963-4116, http://unstats.un.org; *Statistical Yearbook.*

United Nations World Tourism Organization (UNWTO), Capitan Haya 42, 28020 Madrid, Spain, www.world-tourism.org; *Yearbook of Tourism Statistics.*

The World Bank, 1818 H Street, NW, Washington, DC 20433, (202) 473-1000, Fax: (202) 477-6391, www.worldbank.org; *Kenya.*

KENYA - TRADE

See KENYA - INTERNATIONAL TRADE

KENYA - TRANSPORTATION

Central Bureau of Statistics (CBS), Ministry of Economic Planning and Development, PO Box 30266, 00200 GPO Nairobi, Kenya, www.cbs.go.ke; *Statistical Abstract 2004.*

Central Intelligence Agency, Office of Public Affairs, Washington, DC 20505, (703) 482-0623, Fax: (703) 482-1739, www.cia.gov; *The World Factbook.*

Euromonitor International, Inc., 224 S. Michigan Avenue, Suite 1500, Chicago, IL 60604, (312) 922-1115, Fax: (312) 922-1157, www.euromonitor.com; *International Marketing Data and Statistics 2008* and *World Marketing Data and Statistics.*

M.E. Sharpe, 80 Business Park Drive, Armonk, NY 10504, (800) 541-6563, Fax: (914) 273-2106, www.mesharpe.com; *The Illustrated Book of World Rankings.*

Palgrave Macmillan Ltd., Houndmills, Basingstoke, Hampshire, RG21 6XS, England, (Telephone in U.S. (888) 330-8477), (Fax in U.S. (800) 672-2054), www.palgrave.com; *The Statesman's Yearbook 2008.*

Taylor and Francis Group, An Informa Business, 2 Park Square, Milton Park, Abingdon, Oxford OX14 4RN, United Kingdom, (Dial from U.S. (212) 216-7800), (Fax from U.S. (212) 564-7854), www.tandf.co.uk; *The Europa World Year Book.*

United Nations Economic Commission for Africa (ECA), PO Box 3001, Addis Ababa, Ethiopia, (Telephone in U.S. (212) 963-4957), www.uneca.org; *African Statistical Yearbook 2006.*

United Nations Statistics Division, New York, NY 10017, (800) 253-9646, Fax: (212) 963-4116, http://unstats.un.org; *Human Development Report 2006.*

The World Bank, 1818 H Street, NW, Washington, DC 20433, (202) 473-1000, Fax: (202) 477-6391, www.worldbank.org; *Africa Live Database (LDB)* and *Kenya.*

KENYA - UNEMPLOYMENT

Central Intelligence Agency, Office of Public Affairs, Washington, DC 20505, (703) 482-0623, Fax: (703) 482-1739, www.cia.gov; *The World Factbook.*

Euromonitor International, Inc., 224 S. Michigan Avenue, Suite 1500, Chicago, IL 60604, (312) 922-1115, Fax: (312) 922-1157, www.euromonitor.com; *International Marketing Data and Statistics 2008.*

International Labour Office, I.L.O. Publications, 4 route des Morillons, CH-1211 Geneva 22, Switzerland, (Telephone in U.S. (202) 653-7652), (Fax in U.S. (202) 653-7687), www.ilo.org; *Yearbook of Labour Statistics 2006.*

The World Bank, 1818 H Street, NW, Washington, DC 20433, (202) 473-1000, Fax: (202) 477-6391, www.worldbank.org; *Kenya.*

KENYA - VITAL STATISTICS

Central Bureau of Statistics (CBS), Ministry of Economic Planning and Development, PO Box 30266, 00200 GPO Nairobi, Kenya, www.cbs.go.ke; *Statistical Abstract 2004.*

Euromonitor International, Inc., 224 S. Michigan Avenue, Suite 1500, Chicago, IL 60604, (312) 922-1115, Fax: (312) 922-1157, www.euromonitor.com; *International Marketing Data and Statistics 2008.*

United Nations Statistics Division, New York, NY 10017, (800) 253-9646, Fax: (212) 963-4116, http://unstats.un.org; *Statistical Yearbook.*

KENYA - WAGES

International Labour Office, I.L.O. Publications, 4 route des Morillons, CH-1211 Geneva 22, Switzerland, (Telephone in U.S. (202) 653-7652), (Fax in U.S. (202) 653-7687), www.ilo.org; *Yearbook of Labour Statistics 2006.*

United Nations Statistics Division, New York, NY 10017, (800) 253-9646, Fax: (212) 963-4116, http://unstats.un.org; *Statistical Yearbook.*

The World Bank, 1818 H Street, NW, Washington, DC 20433, (202) 473-1000, Fax: (202) 477-6391, www.worldbank.org; *Kenya.*

KENYA - WEATHER

See KENYA - CLIMATE

KENYA - WHEAT PRODUCTION

See KENYA - CROPS

KENYA - WHOLESALE TRADE

United Nations Statistics Division, New York, NY 10017, (800) 253-9646, Fax: (212) 963-4116, http://unstats.un.org; *Statistical Yearbook.*

KENYA - WINE PRODUCTION

See KENYA - BEVERAGE INDUSTRY

KENYA - WOOL PRODUCTION

See KENYA - TEXTILE INDUSTRY

KENYA - YARN PRODUCTION

See KENYA - TEXTILE INDUSTRY

KEOGH PLANS

Board of Governors of the Federal Reserve System, Constitution Avenue, NW, Washington, DC 20551, (202) 452-3000, www.federalreserve.gov; *Federal Reserve Bulletin.*

U.S. Department of the Treasury (DOT), Internal Revenue Service (IRS), Statistics of Income Division (SIS), PO Box 2608, Washington, DC, 20013-2608, (202) 874-0410, Fax: (202) 874-0964, www.irs.ustreas.gov; *Statistics of Income Bulletin, Individual Income Tax Returns.*

KIDNEY DISEASE AND INFECTIONS

National Center for Health Statistics (NCHS), Centers for Disease Control and Prevention (CDC), U.S. Department of Health and Human Services (HHS), 3311 Toledo Road, Hyattsville, MD 20782, (866) 232-4636, www.cdc.gov/nchs; *Faststats A to Z.*

KIDNEY DISEASE AND INFECTIONS - DEATHS

Bernan Essential Government Publications, 4611-F Assembly Drive, Lanham MD, 20706-4391, (301) 459-2255, Fax: (800) 865-3450, www.bernan.com; *Vital Statistics of the United States: Births, Life Expectancy, Deaths, and Selected Health Data.*

National Center for Health Statistics (NCHS), Centers for Disease Control and Prevention (CDC), U.S. Department of Health and Human Services (HHS), 3311 Toledo Road, Hyattsville, MD 20782, (866) 232-4636, www.cdc.gov/nchs; *National Vital Statistics Reports (NVSR); Vital Statistics of the United States (VSUS);* and unpublished data.

KIRIBATI - NATIONAL STATISTICAL OFFICE

Kiribati National Statistics Office, Ministry of Finance, PO Box 67, Bairiki, Tarawa, Kiribati, www.spc.int/prism/country/ki/stats; National Data Center.

KIRIBATI - PRIMARY STATISTICS SOURCES

Kiribati National Statistics Office, Ministry of Finance, PO Box 67, Bairiki, Tarawa, Kiribati, www.spc.int/prism/country/ki/stats; *Kiribati Statistical Yearbook 2002.*

KIRIBATI - AGRICULTURE

Asian Development Bank (ADB), PO Box 789, 0980 Manila, Philippines, www.adb.org; *Key Indicators of Developing Asian and Pacific Countries 2006.*

Euromonitor International, Inc., 224 S. Michigan Avenue, Suite 1500, Chicago, IL 60604, (312) 922-1115, Fax: (312) 922-1157, www.euromonitor.com; *World Marketing Data and Statistics.*

Palgrave Macmillan Ltd., Houndmills, Basingstoke, Hampshire, RG21 6XS, England, (Telephone in U.S. (888) 330-8477), (Fax in U.S. (800) 672-2054), www.palgrave.com; *The Statesman's Yearbook 2008.*

Taylor and Francis Group, An Informa Business, 2 Park Square, Milton Park, Abingdon, Oxford OX14 4RN, United Kingdom, (Dial from U.S. (212) 216-7800), (Fax from U.S. (212) 564-7854), www.tandf.co.uk; *The Europa World Year Book.*

United Nations Conference on Trade and Development (UNCTAD), DC2-1120, United Nations, New York, NY 10017, (212) 963-0027, www.unctad.org; *UNCTAD Commodity Yearbook.*

United Nations Food and Agricultural Organization (FAO), Viale delle Terme di Caracalla, 00100 Rome, Italy, (Dial from U.S. (202) 653-2400), (Fax from U.S. (202) 653 5760), www.fao.org; AQUASTAT; *FAO Production Yearbook 2002; FAO Trade Yearbook;* and *The State of Food and Agriculture (SOFA) 2006.*

United Nations Statistics Division, New York, NY 10017, (800) 253-9646, Fax: (212) 963-4116, http://unstats.un.org; *Asia-Pacific in Figures 2004.*

The World Bank, 1818 H Street, NW, Washington, DC 20433, (202) 473-1000, Fax: (202) 477-6391, www.worldbank.org; *Kiribati.*

KIRIBATI - AIRLINES

Palgrave Macmillan Ltd., Houndmills, Basingstoke, Hampshire, RG21 6XS, England, (Telephone in U.S. (888) 330-8477), (Fax in U.S. (800) 672-2054), www.palgrave.com; *The Statesman's Yearbook 2008.*

Taylor and Francis Group, An Informa Business, 2 Park Square, Milton Park, Abingdon, Oxford OX14 4RN, United Kingdom, (Dial from U.S. (212) 216-7800), (Fax from U.S. (212) 564-7854), www.tandf.co.uk; *The Europa World Year Book.*

KIRIBATI - ARMED FORCES

Central Intelligence Agency, Office of Public Affairs, Washington, DC 20505, (703) 482-0623, Fax: (703) 482-1739, www.cia.gov; *The World Factbook.*

Euromonitor International, Inc., 224 S. Michigan Avenue, Suite 1500, Chicago, IL 60604, (312) 922-1115, Fax: (312) 922-1157, www.euromonitor.com; *World Marketing Data and Statistics.*

KIRIBATI - BALANCE OF PAYMENTS

Taylor and Francis Group, An Informa Business, 2 Park Square, Milton Park, Abingdon, Oxford OX14 4RN, United Kingdom, (Dial from U.S. (212) 216-7800), (Fax from U.S. (212) 564-7854), www.tandf.co.uk; *The Europa World Year Book.*

The World Bank, 1818 H Street, NW, Washington, DC 20433, (202) 473-1000, Fax: (202) 477-6391, www.worldbank.org; *Kiribati.*

KIRIBATI - BANKS AND BANKING

Asian Development Bank (ADB), PO Box 789, 0980 Manila, Philippines, www.adb.org; *Key Indicators of Developing Asian and Pacific Countries 2006.*

Euromonitor International, Inc., 224 S. Michigan Avenue, Suite 1500, Chicago, IL 60604, (312) 922-1115, Fax: (312) 922-1157, www.euromonitor.com; *World Marketing Data and Statistics.*

KIRIBATI - BONDS

Asian Development Bank (ADB), PO Box 789, 0980 Manila, Philippines, www.adb.org; *Key Indicators of Developing Asian and Pacific Countries 2006.*

KIRIBATI - BROADCASTING

Central Intelligence Agency, Office of Public Affairs, Washington, DC 20505, (703) 482-0623, Fax: (703) 482-1739, www.cia.gov; *The World Factbook.*

Euromonitor International, Inc., 224 S. Michigan Avenue, Suite 1500, Chicago, IL 60604, (312) 922-1115, Fax: (312) 922-1157, www.euromonitor.com; *World Marketing Data and Statistics.*

Palgrave Macmillan Ltd., Houndmills, Basingstoke, Hampshire, RG21 6XS, England, (Telephone in U.S.

(888) 330-8477), (Fax in U.S. (800) 672-2054), www.palgrave.com; *The Statesman's Yearbook 2008.*

WRTH Publications Limited, PO Box 290, Oxford OX2 7FT, UK, www.wrth.com; *World Radio TV Handbook 2007.*

KIRIBATI - BUDGET

Central Intelligence Agency, Office of Public Affairs, Washington, DC 20505, (703) 482-0623, Fax: (703) 482-1739, www.cia.gov; *The World Factbook.*

KIRIBATI - CAPITAL INVESTMENTS

Asian Development Bank (ADB), PO Box 789, 0980 Manila, Philippines, www.adb.org; *Key Indicators of Developing Asian and Pacific Countries 2006.*

KIRIBATI - CAPITAL LEVY

Asian Development Bank (ADB), PO Box 789, 0980 Manila, Philippines, www.adb.org; *Key Indicators of Developing Asian and Pacific Countries 2006.*

KIRIBATI - CHILDBIRTH - STATISTICS

Central Intelligence Agency, Office of Public Affairs, Washington, DC 20505, (703) 482-0623, Fax: (703) 482-1739, www.cia.gov; *The World Factbook.*

Euromonitor International, Inc., 224 S. Michigan Avenue, Suite 1500, Chicago, IL 60604, (312) 922-1115, Fax: (312) 922-1157, www.euromonitor.com; *International Marketing Data and Statistics 2008* and *The World Economic Factbook 2008.*

Taylor and Francis Group, An Informa Business, 2 Park Square, Milton Park, Abingdon, Oxford OX14 4RN, United Kingdom, (Dial from U.S. (212) 216-7800), (Fax from U.S. (212) 564-7854), www.tandf.co.uk; *The Europa World Year Book.*

United Nations Statistics Division, New York, NY 10017, (800) 253-9646, Fax: (212) 963-4116, http://unstats.un.org; *Asia-Pacific in Figures 2004.*

KIRIBATI - CLIMATE

Palgrave Macmillan Ltd., Houndmills, Basingstoke, Hampshire, RG21 6XS, England, (Telephone in U.S. (888) 330-8477), (Fax in U.S. (800) 672-2054), www.palgrave.com; *The Statesman's Yearbook 2008.*

KIRIBATI - CLOTHING EXPORTS AND IMPORTS

See KIRIBATI - TEXTILE INDUSTRY

KIRIBATI - COAL PRODUCTION

See KIRIBATI - MINERAL INDUSTRIES

KIRIBATI - COMMERCE

Palgrave Macmillan Ltd., Houndmills, Basingstoke, Hampshire, RG21 6XS, England, (Telephone in U.S. (888) 330-8477), (Fax in U.S. (800) 672-2054), www.palgrave.com; *The Statesman's Yearbook 2008.*

KIRIBATI - COMMODITY EXCHANGES

Commodity Research Bureau, 330 South Wells Street, Suite 612, Chicago, IL 60606-7110, (800) 621-5271, Fax: (312) 939-4135, www.crbtrader.com; *2006 CRB Commodity Yearbook and CD.*

International Monetary Fund (IMF), 700 Nineteenth Street, NW, Washington, DC 20431, (202) 623-7000, Fax: (202) 623-4661, www.imf.org; *IMF Primary Commodity Prices.*

United Nations Food and Agricultural Organization (FAO), Viale delle Terme di Caracalla, 00100 Rome, Italy, (Dial from U.S. (202) 653-2400), (Fax from U.S. (202) 653 5760), www.fao.org; *The State of Food and Agriculture (SOFA) 2006.*

KIRIBATI - CONSUMER PRICE INDEXES

Asian Development Bank (ADB), PO Box 789, 0980 Manila, Philippines, www.adb.org; *Key Indicators of Developing Asian and Pacific Countries 2006.*

Taylor and Francis Group, An Informa Business, 2 Park Square, Milton Park, Abingdon, Oxford OX14 4RN, United Kingdom, (Dial from U.S. (212) 216-7800), (Fax from U.S. (212) 564-7854), www.tandf.co.uk; *The Europa World Year Book.*

The World Bank, 1818 H Street, NW, Washington, DC 20433, (202) 473-1000, Fax: (202) 477-6391, www.worldbank.org; *Kiribati.*

KIRIBATI - CONSUMPTION (ECONOMICS)

Secretariat of the Pacific Community (SPC), BP D5, 98848 Noumea Cedex, New Caledonia, www.spc.int/corp; *Selected Pacific Economies - a Statistical Summary (SPESS).*

KIRIBATI - CORN INDUSTRY

See KIRIBATI - CROPS

KIRIBATI - CROPS

Asian Development Bank (ADB), PO Box 789, 0980 Manila, Philippines, www.adb.org; *Key Indicators of Developing Asian and Pacific Countries 2006.*

Palgrave Macmillan Ltd., Houndmills, Basingstoke, Hampshire, RG21 6XS, England, (Telephone in U.S. (888) 330-8477), (Fax in U.S. (800) 672-2054), www.palgrave.com; *The Statesman's Yearbook 2008.*

Taylor and Francis Group, An Informa Business, 2 Park Square, Milton Park, Abingdon, Oxford OX14 4RN; United Kingdom, (Dial from U.S. (212) 216-7800), (Fax from U.S. (212) 564-7854), www.tandf.co.uk; *The Europa World Year Book.*

United Nations Conference on Trade and Development (UNCTAD), DC2-1120, United Nations, New York, NY 10017, (212) 963-0027, www.unctad.org; *UNCTAD Commodity Yearbook.*

United Nations Food and Agricultural Organization (FAO), Viale delle Terme di Caracalla, 00100 Rome, Italy, (Dial from U.S. (202) 653-2400), (Fax from U.S. (202) 653 5760), www.fao.org; *The State of Food and Agriculture (SOFA) 2006.*

KIRIBATI - CUSTOMS ADMINISTRATION

Palgrave Macmillan Ltd., Houndmills, Basingstoke, Hampshire, RG21 6XS, England, (Telephone in U.S. (888) 330-8477), (Fax in U.S. (800) 672-2054), www.palgrave.com; *The Statesman's Yearbook 2008.*

KIRIBATI - DAIRY PROCESSING

Palgrave Macmillan Ltd., Houndmills, Basingstoke, Hampshire, RG21 6XS, England, (Telephone in U.S. (888) 330-8477), (Fax in U.S. (800) 672-2054), www.palgrave.com; *The Statesman's Yearbook 2008.*

United Nations Food and Agricultural Organization (FAO), Viale delle Terme di Caracalla, 00100 Rome, Italy, (Dial from U.S. (202) 653-2400), (Fax from U.S. (202) 653 5760), www.fao.org; *The State of Food and Agriculture (SOFA) 2006.*

KIRIBATI - DEATH RATES

See KIRIBATI - MORTALITY

KIRIBATI - DEBTS, EXTERNAL

Asian Development Bank (ADB), PO Box 789, 0980 Manila, Philippines, www.adb.org; *Key Indicators of Developing Asian and Pacific Countries 2006.*

The World Bank, 1818 H Street, NW, Washington, DC 20433, (202) 473-1000, Fax: (202) 477-6391, www.worldbank.org; *Global Development Finance 2007.*

Worldinformation.com, 2 Market Street, Saffron Walden, Essex CB10 1HZ, United Kingdom, www.worldinformation.com; The World of Information (www.worldinformation.com).

KIRIBATI - DEMOGRAPHY

Euromonitor International, Inc., 224 S. Michigan Avenue, Suite 1500, Chicago, IL 60604, (312) 922-1115, Fax: (312) 922-1157, www.euromonitor.com; *International Marketing Data and Statistics 2008; The World Economic Factbook 2008;* and *World Marketing Data and Statistics.*

United Nations Statistics Division, New York, NY 10017, (800) 253-9646, Fax: (212) 963-4116, http://unstats.un.org; *Asia-Pacific in Figures 2004.*

The World Bank, 1818 H Street, NW, Washington, DC 20433, (202) 473-1000, Fax: (202) 477-6391, www.worldbank.org; *Kiribati.*

KIRIBATI - ECONOMIC ASSISTANCE

Asian Development Bank (ADB), PO Box 789, 0980 Manila, Philippines, www.adb.org; *Key Indicators of Developing Asian and Pacific Countries 2006.*

KIRIBATI - ECONOMIC CONDITIONS

Asian Development Bank (ADB), PO Box 789, 0980 Manila, Philippines, www.adb.org; *Key Indicators of Developing Asian and Pacific Countries 2006.*

Center for International Business Education Research (CIBER), Columbia Business School and School of International and Public Affairs, Uris Hall, Room 212, 3022 Broadway, New York, NY 10027-6902, Mr. Joshua Safier, (212) 854-4750, Fax: (212) 222-9821, www.columbia.edu/cu/ciber/; Datastream International.

Central Intelligence Agency, Office of Public Affairs, Washington, DC 20505, (703) 482-0623, Fax: (703) 482-1739, www.cia.gov; *The World Factbook.*

DSI Data Service Information, Xantener Strasse 51a, D-47495 Rheinberg, Germany, www.dsidata.com; *Campus Solution.*

Dun and Bradstreet (DB) Corporation, 103 JFK Parkway, Short Hills, NJ 07078, (973) 921-5500, www.dnb.com; *Country Report.*

Euromonitor International, Inc., 224 S. Michigan Avenue, Suite 1500, Chicago, IL 60604, (312) 922-1115, Fax: (312) 922-1157, www.euromonitor.com; *The World Economic Factbook 2008* and *World Marketing Data and Statistics.*

International Monetary Fund (IMF), 700 Nineteenth Street, NW, Washington, DC 20431, (202) 623-7000, Fax: (202) 623-4661, www.imf.org; *World Economic Outlook Reports.*

Palgrave Macmillan Ltd., Houndmills, Basingstoke, Hampshire, RG21 6XS, England, (Telephone in U.S. (888) 330-8477), (Fax in U.S. (800) 672-2054), www.palgrave.com; *The Statesman's Yearbook 2008.*

Secretariat of the Pacific Community (SPC), BP D5, 98848 Noumea Cedex, New Caledonia, www.spc.int/corp; PRISM (Pacific Regional Information System).

Taylor and Francis Group, An Informa Business, 2 Park Square, Milton Park, Abingdon, Oxford OX14 4RN, United Kingdom, (Dial from U.S. (212) 216-7800), (Fax from U.S. (212) 564-7854), www.tandf.co.uk; *The Europa World Year Book.*

United Nations Statistics Division, New York, NY 10017, (800) 253-9646, Fax: (212) 963-4116, http://unstats.un.org; *World Statistics Pocketbook.*

The World Bank, 1818 H Street, NW, Washington, DC 20433, (202) 473-1000, Fax: (202) 477-6391, www.worldbank.org; *Global Economic Monitor (GEM); Global Economic Prospects 2008; Kiribati;* and *The World Bank Atlas 2003-2004.*

KIRIBATI - EDUCATION

Euromonitor International, Inc., 224 S. Michigan Avenue, Suite 1500, Chicago, IL 60604, (312) 922-1115, Fax: (312) 922-1157, www.euromonitor.com; *International Marketing Data and Statistics 2008* and *World Marketing Data and Statistics.*

Palgrave Macmillan Ltd., Houndmills, Basingstoke, Hampshire, RG21 6XS, England, (Telephone in U.S. (888) 330-8477), (Fax in U.S. (800) 672-2054), www.palgrave.com; *The Statesman's Yearbook 2008.*

Taylor and Francis Group, An Informa Business, 2 Park Square, Milton Park, Abingdon, Oxford OX14 4RN, United Kingdom, (Dial from U.S. (212) 216-7800), (Fax from U.S. (212) 564-7854), www.tandf.co.uk; *The Europa World Year Book.*

UNESCO Institute for Statistics, C.P. 6128 Succursale Centre-Ville, Montreal, Quebec, H3C 3J7 Canada, (Dial from U.S. (514) 343-6880), (Fax from U.S. (514) 343 6882), www.uis.unesco.org; *Statistical Tables.*

United Nations Statistics Division, New York, NY 10017, (800) 253-9646, Fax: (212) 963-4116, http://unstats.un.org; *Asia-Pacific in Figures 2004*.

The World Bank, 1818 H Street, NW, Washington, DC 20433, (202) 473-1000, Fax: (202) 477-6391, www.worldbank.org; *Kiribati*.

KIRIBATI - ELECTRICITY

Asian Development Bank (ADB), PO Box 789, 0980 Manila, Philippines, www.adb.org; *Key Indicators of Developing Asian and Pacific Countries 2006*.

Palgrave Macmillan Ltd., Houndmills, Basingstoke, Hampshire, RG21 6XS, England, (Telephone in U.S. (888) 330-8477), (Fax in U.S. (800) 672-2054), www.palgrave.com; *The Statesman's Yearbook 2008*.

United Nations Statistics Division, New York, NY 10017, (800) 253-9646, Fax: (212) 963-4116, http://unstats.un.org; *Electric Power in Asia and the Pacific 2001 and 2002*.

KIRIBATI - EMPLOYMENT

Euromonitor International, Inc., 224 S. Michigan Avenue, Suite 1500, Chicago, IL 60604, (312) 922-1115, Fax: (312) 922-1157, www.euromonitor.com; *International Marketing Data and Statistics 2008*.

International Labour Office, I.L.O. Publications, 4 route des Morillons, CH-1211 Geneva 22, Switzerland, (Telephone in U.S. (202) 653-7652), (Fax in U.S. (202) 653-7687), www.ilo.org; *Yearbook of Labour Statistics 2006*.

United Nations Statistics Division, New York, NY 10017, (800) 253-9646, Fax: (212) 963-4116, http://unstats.un.org; *Asia-Pacific in Figures 2004*.

The World Bank, 1818 H Street, NW, Washington, DC 20433, (202) 473-1000, Fax: (202) 477-6391, www.worldbank.org; *Kiribati*.

KIRIBATI - ENERGY INDUSTRIES

Enerdata, 10 Rue Royale, 75008 Paris, France, www.enerdata.fr; *Global Energy Market Data*.

United Nations Statistics Division, New York, NY 10017, (800) 253-9646, Fax: (212) 963-4116, http://unstats.un.org; *Electric Power in Asia and the Pacific 2001 and 2002*.

The World Bank, 1818 H Street, NW, Washington, DC 20433, (202) 473-1000, Fax: (202) 477-6391, www.worldbank.org; *Kiribati*.

KIRIBATI - ENVIRONMENTAL CONDITIONS

DSI Data Service Information, Xantener Strasse 51a, D-47495 Rheinberg, Germany, www.dsidata.com; *Campus Solution* and *DSI's Global Environmental Database*.

United Nations Statistics Division, New York, NY 10017, (800) 253-9646, Fax: (212) 963-4116, http://unstats.un.org; *World Statistics Pocketbook*.

KIRIBATI - EXPORTS

Asian Development Bank (ADB), PO Box 789, 0980 Manila, Philippines, www.adb.org; *Key Indicators of Developing Asian and Pacific Countries 2006*.

Central Intelligence Agency, Office of Public Affairs, Washington, DC 20505, (703) 482-0623, Fax: (703) 482-1739, www.cia.gov; *The World Factbook*.

Euromonitor International, Inc., 224 S. Michigan Avenue, Suite 1500, Chicago, IL 60604, (312) 922-1115, Fax: (312) 922-1157, www.euromonitor.com; *International Marketing Data and Statistics 2008* and *The World Economic Factbook 2008*.

Palgrave Macmillan Ltd., Houndmills, Basingstoke, Hampshire, RG21 6XS, England, (Telephone in U.S. (888) 330-8477), (Fax in U.S. (800) 672-2054), www.palgrave.com; *The Statesman's Yearbook 2008*.

Secretariat of the Pacific Community (SPC), BP D5, 98848 Noumea Cedex, New Caledonia, www.spc.int/corp; *Selected Pacific Economies - a Statistical Summary (SPESS)*.

Taylor and Francis Group, An Informa Business, 2 Park Square, Milton Park, Abingdon, Oxford OX14 4RN, United Kingdom, (Dial from U.S. (212) 216-7800), (Fax from U.S. (212) 564-7854), www.tandf.co.uk; *The Europa World Year Book*.

United Nations Food and Agricultural Organization (FAO), Viale delle Terme di Caracalla, 00100 Rome, Italy, (Dial from U.S. (202) 653-2400), (Fax from U.S. (202) 653 5760), www.fao.org; *The State of Food and Agriculture (SOFA) 2006*.

Worldinformation.com, 2 Market Street, Saffron Walden, Essex CB10 1HZ, United Kingdom, www.worldinformation.com; The World of Information (www.worldinformation.com).

KIRIBATI - FERTILITY, HUMAN

Central Intelligence Agency, Office of Public Affairs, Washington, DC 20505, (703) 482-0623, Fax: (703) 482-1739, www.cia.gov; *The World Factbook*.

The World Bank, 1818 H Street, NW, Washington, DC 20433, (202) 473-1000, Fax: (202) 477-6391, www.worldbank.org; *The World Bank Atlas 2003-2004*.

KIRIBATI - FERTILIZER INDUSTRY

United Nations Food and Agricultural Organization (FAO), Viale delle Terme di Caracalla, 00100 Rome, Italy, (Dial from U.S. (202) 653-2400), (Fax from U.S. (202) 653 5760), www.fao.org; *The State of Food and Agriculture (SOFA) 2006*.

KIRIBATI - FINANCE

United Nations Statistics Division, New York, NY 10017, (800) 253-9646, Fax: (212) 963-4116, http://unstats.un.org; *Asia-Pacific in Figures 2004* and *National Accounts Statistics: Compendium of Income Distribution Statistics*.

The World Bank, 1818 H Street, NW, Washington, DC 20433, (202) 473-1000, Fax: (202) 477-6391, www.worldbank.org; *Kiribati*.

KIRIBATI - FINANCE, PUBLIC

Asian Development Bank (ADB), PO Box 789, 0980 Manila, Philippines, www.adb.org; *Key Indicators of Developing Asian and Pacific Countries 2006*.

Bernan Essential Government Publications, 4611-F Assembly Drive, Lanham MD, 20706-4391, (301) 459-2255, Fax: (800) 865-3450, www.bernan.com; *National Accounts Statistics*.

International Monetary Fund (IMF), 700 Nineteenth Street, NW, Washington, DC 20431, (202) 623-7000, Fax: (202) 623-4661, www.imf.org; *International Financial Statistics* and *International Financial Statistics Online Service*.

Taylor and Francis Group, An Informa Business, 2 Park Square, Milton Park, Abingdon, Oxford OX14 4RN, United Kingdom, (Dial from U.S. (212) 216-7800), (Fax from U.S. (212) 564-7854), www.tandf.co.uk; *The Europa World Year Book*.

The World Bank, 1818 H Street, NW, Washington, DC 20433, (202) 473-1000, Fax: (202) 477-6391, www.worldbank.org; *Kiribati*.

KIRIBATI - FISHERIES

Palgrave Macmillan Ltd., Houndmills, Basingstoke, Hampshire, RG21 6XS, England, (Telephone in U.S. (888) 330-8477), (Fax in U.S. (800) 672-2054), www.palgrave.com; *The Statesman's Yearbook 2008*.

Taylor and Francis Group, An Informa Business, 2 Park Square, Milton Park, Abingdon, Oxford OX14 4RN, United Kingdom, (Dial from U.S. (212) 216-7800), (Fax from U.S. (212) 564-7854), www.tandf.co.uk; *The Europa World Year Book*.

United Nations Conference on Trade and Development (UNCTAD), DC2-1120, United Nations, New York, NY 10017, (212) 963-0027, www.unctad.org; *UNCTAD Commodity Yearbook*.

United Nations Food and Agricultural Organization (FAO), Viale delle Terme di Caracalla, 00100 Rome, Italy, (Dial from U.S. (202) 653-2400), (Fax from U.S. (202) 653 5760), www.fao.org; *FAO Yearbook of Fishery Statistics;* Fishery Databases; FISHSTAT Database. Subjects covered include: Aquaculture production, capture production, fishery commodities; and *The State of Food and Agriculture (SOFA) 2006*.

The World Bank, 1818 H Street, NW, Washington, DC 20433, (202) 473-1000, Fax: (202) 477-6391, www.worldbank.org; *Kiribati*.

KIRIBATI - FOOD

Secretariat of the Pacific Community (SPC), BP D5, 98848 Noumea Cedex, New Caledonia, www.spc.int/corp; *Selected Pacific Economies - a Statistical Summary (SPESS)*.

United Nations Conference on Trade and Development (UNCTAD), DC2-1120, United Nations, New York, NY 10017, (212) 963-0027, www.unctad.org; *UNCTAD Commodity Yearbook*.

United Nations Food and Agricultural Organization (FAO), Viale delle Terme di Caracalla, 00100 Rome, Italy, (Dial from U.S. (202) 653-2400), (Fax from U.S. (202) 653 5760), www.fao.org; *FAO Production Yearbook 2002* and *The State of Food and Agriculture (SOFA) 2006*.

KIRIBATI - FOREIGN EXCHANGE RATES

Asian Development Bank (ADB), PO Box 789, 0980 Manila, Philippines, www.adb.org; *Key Indicators of Developing Asian and Pacific Countries 2006*.

Central Intelligence Agency, Office of Public Affairs, Washington, DC 20505, (703) 482-0623, Fax: (703) 482-1739, www.cia.gov; *The World Factbook*.

Euromonitor International, Inc., 224 S. Michigan Avenue, Suite 1500, Chicago, IL 60604, (312) 922-1115, Fax: (312) 922-1157, www.euromonitor.com; *International Marketing Data and Statistics 2008* and *The World Economic Factbook 2008*.

Taylor and Francis Group, An Informa Business, 2 Park Square, Milton Park, Abingdon, Oxford OX14 4RN, United Kingdom, (Dial from U.S. (212) 216-7800), (Fax from U.S. (212) 564-7854), www.tandf.co.uk; *The Europa World Year Book*.

United Nations Statistics Division, New York, NY 10017, (800) 253-9646, Fax: (212) 963-4116, http://unstats.un.org; *World Statistics Pocketbook*.

Worldinformation.com, 2 Market Street, Saffron Walden, Essex CB10 1HZ, United Kingdom, www.worldinformation.com; The World of Information (www.worldinformation.com).

KIRIBATI - FORESTS AND FORESTRY

United Nations Conference on Trade and Development (UNCTAD), DC2-1120, United Nations, New York, NY 10017, (212) 963-0027, www.unctad.org; *UNCTAD Commodity Yearbook*.

United Nations Food and Agricultural Organization (FAO), Viale delle Terme di Caracalla, 00100 Rome, Italy, (Dial from U.S. (202) 653-2400), (Fax from U.S. (202) 653 5760), www.fao.org; *The State of Food and Agriculture (SOFA) 2006*.

United Nations Statistics Division, New York, NY 10017, (800) 253-9646, Fax: (212) 963-4116, http://unstats.un.org; *Statistical Yearbook*.

The World Bank, 1818 H Street, NW, Washington, DC 20433, (202) 473-1000, Fax: (202) 477-6391, www.worldbank.org; *Kiribati*.

KIRIBATI - GROSS DOMESTIC PRODUCT

Asian Development Bank (ADB), PO Box 789, 0980 Manila, Philippines, www.adb.org; *Key Indicators of Developing Asian and Pacific Countries 2006*.

Euromonitor International, Inc., 224 S. Michigan Avenue, Suite 1500, Chicago, IL 60604, (312) 922-1115, Fax: (312) 922-1157, www.euromonitor.com; *International Marketing Data and Statistics 2008* and *The World Economic Factbook 2008*.

Taylor and Francis Group, An Informa Business, 2 Park Square, Milton Park, Abingdon, Oxford OX14 4RN, United Kingdom, (Dial from U.S. (212) 216-7800), (Fax from U.S. (212) 564-7854), www.tandf.co.uk; *The Europa World Year Book*.

KIRIBATI - GROSS NATIONAL PRODUCT

Asian Development Bank (ADB), PO Box 789, 0980 Manila, Philippines, www.adb.org; *Key Indicators of Developing Asian and Pacific Countries 2006.*

Palgrave Macmillan Ltd., Houndmills, Basingstoke, Hampshire, RG21 6XS, England, (Telephone in U.S. (888) 330-8477), (Fax in U.S. (800) 672-2054), www.palgrave.com; *The Statesman's Yearbook 2008.*

The World Bank, 1818 H Street, NW, Washington, DC 20433, (202) 473-1000, Fax: (202) 477-6391, www.worldbank.org; *The World Bank Atlas 2003-2004.*

Worldinformation.com, 2 Market Street, Saffron Walden, Essex CB10 1HZ, United Kingdom, www.worldinformation.com; The World of Information (www.worldinformation.com).

KIRIBATI - HOUSING

Euromonitor International, Inc., 224 S. Michigan Avenue, Suite 1500, Chicago, IL 60604, (312) 922-1115, Fax: (312) 922-1157, www.euromonitor.com; *World Marketing Data and Statistics.*

Secretariat of the Pacific Community (SPC), BP D5, 98848 Noumea Cedex, New Caledonia, www.spc.int/corp; *Selected Pacific Economies - a Statistical Summary (SPESS).*

KIRIBATI - ILLITERATE PERSONS

Euromonitor International, Inc., 224 S. Michigan Avenue, Suite 1500, Chicago, IL 60604, (312) 922-1115, Fax: (312) 922-1157, www.euromonitor.com; *The World Economic Factbook 2008.*

UNESCO Institute for Statistics, C.P. 6128 Succursale Centre-Ville, Montreal, Quebec, H3C 3J7 Canada, (Dial from U.S. (514) 343-6880), (Fax from U.S. (514) 343 6882), www.uis.unesco.org; *Statistical Tables.*

United Nations Statistics Division, New York, NY 10017, (800) 253-9646, Fax: (212) 963-4116, http://unstats.un.org; *Asia-Pacific in Figures 2004.*

KIRIBATI - IMPORTS

Asian Development Bank (ADB), PO Box 789, 0980 Manila, Philippines, www.adb.org; *Key Indicators of Developing Asian and Pacific Countries 2006.*

Central Intelligence Agency, Office of Public Affairs, Washington, DC 20505, (703) 482-0623, Fax: (703) 482-1739, www.cia.gov; *The World Factbook.*

Euromonitor International, Inc., 224 S. Michigan Avenue, Suite 1500, Chicago, IL 60604, (312) 922-1115, Fax: (312) 922-1157, www.euromonitor.com; *International Marketing Data and Statistics 2008* and *The World Economic Factbook 2008.*

Palgrave Macmillan Ltd., Houndmills, Basingstoke, Hampshire, RG21 6XS, England, (Telephone in U.S. (888) 330-8477), (Fax in U.S. (800) 672-2054), www.palgrave.com; *The Statesman's Yearbook 2008.*

Secretariat of the Pacific Community (SPC), BP D5, 98848 Noumea Cedex, New Caledonia, www.spc.int/corp; *Selected Pacific Economies - a Statistical Summary (SPESS).*

Taylor and Francis Group, An Informa Business, 2 Park Square, Milton Park, Abingdon, Oxford OX14 4RN, United Kingdom, (Dial from U.S. (212) 216-7800), (Fax from U.S. (212) 564-7854), www.tandf.co.uk; *The Europa World Year Book.*

United Nations Food and Agricultural Organization (FAO), Viale delle Terme di Caracalla, 00100 Rome, Italy, (Dial from U.S. (202) 653-2400), (Fax from U.S. (202) 653 5760), www.fao.org; *The State of Food and Agriculture (SOFA) 2006.*

Worldinformation.com, 2 Market Street, Saffron Walden, Essex CB10 1HZ, United Kingdom, www.worldinformation.com; The World of Information (www.worldinformation.com).

KIRIBATI - INDUSTRIES

Central Intelligence Agency, Office of Public Affairs, Washington, DC 20505, (703) 482-0623, Fax: (703) 482-1739, www.cia.gov; *The World Factbook.*

Euromonitor International, Inc., 224 S. Michigan Avenue, Suite 1500, Chicago, IL 60604, (312) 922-1115, Fax: (312) 922-1157, www.euromonitor.com; *The World Economic Factbook 2008* and *World Marketing Data and Statistics.*

International Labour Office, I.L.O. Publications, 4 route des Morillons, CH-1211 Geneva 22, Switzerland, (Telephone in U.S. (202) 653-7652), (Fax in U.S. (202) 653-7687), www.ilo.org; *Yearbook of Labour Statistics 2006.*

Palgrave Macmillan Ltd., Houndmills, Basingstoke, Hampshire, RG21 6XS, England, (Telephone in U.S. (888) 330-8477), (Fax in U.S. (800) 672-2054), www.palgrave.com; *The Statesman's Yearbook 2008.*

Taylor and Francis Group, An Informa Business, 2 Park Square, Milton Park, Abingdon, Oxford OX14 4RN, United Kingdom, (Dial from U.S. (212) 216-7800), (Fax from U.S. (212) 564-7854), www.tandf.co.uk; *The Europa World Year Book.*

United Nations Industrial Development Organization (UNIDO), 1 United Nations Plaza, New York, NY 10017, (212) 963 6890, Fax: (212) 963-7904, http://unido.org; Industrial Statistics Database 2008 (INDSTAT) and *The International Yearbook of Industrial Statistics 2008.*

United Nations Statistics Division, New York, NY 10017, (800) 253-9646, Fax: (212) 963-4116, http://unstats.un.org; *Asia-Pacific in Figures 2004.*

The World Bank, 1818 H Street, NW, Washington, DC 20433, (202) 473-1000, Fax: (202) 477-6391, www.worldbank.org; *Kiribati.*

KIRIBATI - INTERNATIONAL FINANCE

Asian Development Bank (ADB), PO Box 789, 0980 Manila, Philippines, www.adb.org; *Key Indicators of Developing Asian and Pacific Countries 2006.*

The World Bank, 1818 H Street, NW, Washington, DC 20433, (202) 473-1000, Fax: (202) 477-6391, www.worldbank.org; *Kiribati.*

KIRIBATI - INTERNATIONAL STATISTICS

Asian Development Bank (ADB), PO Box 789, 0980 Manila, Philippines, www.adb.org; *Key Indicators of Developing Asian and Pacific Countries 2006.*

KIRIBATI - INTERNATIONAL TRADE

Asian Development Bank (ADB), PO Box 789, 0980 Manila, Philippines, www.adb.org; *Key Indicators of Developing Asian and Pacific Countries 2006.*

Euromonitor International, Inc., 224 S. Michigan Avenue, Suite 1500, Chicago, IL 60604, (312) 922-1115, Fax: (312) 922-1157, www.euromonitor.com; *The World Economic Factbook 2008* and *World Marketing Data and Statistics.*

Palgrave Macmillan Ltd., Houndmills, Basingstoke, Hampshire, RG21 6XS, England, (Telephone in U.S. (888) 330-8477), (Fax in U.S. (800) 672-2054), www.palgrave.com; *The Statesman's Yearbook 2008.*

Secretariat of the Pacific Community (SPC), BP D5, 98848 Noumea Cedex, New Caledonia, www.spc.int/corp; *Selected Pacific Economies - a Statistical Summary (SPESS).*

Taylor and Francis Group, An Informa Business, 2 Park Square, Milton Park, Abingdon, Oxford OX14 4RN, United Kingdom, (Dial from U.S. (212) 216-7800), (Fax from U.S. (212) 564-7854), www.tandf.co.uk; *The Europa World Year Book.*

United Nations Conference on Trade and Development (UNCTAD), DC2-1120, United Nations, New York, NY 10017, (212) 963-0027, www.unctad.org; *UNCTAD Commodity Yearbook.*

United Nations Food and Agricultural Organization (FAO), Viale delle Terme di Caracalla, 00100 Rome, Italy, (Dial from U.S. (202) 653-2400), (Fax from U.S. (202) 653 5760), www.fao.org; *FAO Trade Yearbook* and *The State of Food and Agriculture (SOFA) 2006.*

United Nations Statistics Division, New York, NY 10017, (800) 253-9646, Fax: (212) 963-4116, http://unstats.un.org; *Asia-Pacific in Figures 2004.*

The World Bank, 1818 H Street, NW, Washington, DC 20433, (202) 473-1000, Fax: (202) 477-6391, www.worldbank.org; *Kiribati.*

World Trade Organization (WTO), Centre William Rappard, Rue de Lausanne 154, CH-1211 Geneva 21, Switzerland, www.wto.org; *International Trade Statistics 2006.*

KIRIBATI - INTERNET USERS

International Telecommunication Union (ITU), Place des Nations, 1211 Geneva 20, Switzerland, www.itu.int; *World Telecommunication/ICT Indicators Database on CD-ROM; World Telecommunication/ICT Indicators Database Online;* and *Yearbook of Statistics - Telecommunication Services (Chronological Time Series 1997-2006).*

The World Bank, 1818 H Street, NW, Washington, DC 20433, (202) 473-1000, Fax: (202) 477-6391, www.worldbank.org; *Kiribati.*

KIRIBATI - LABOR

Central Intelligence Agency, Office of Public Affairs, Washington, DC 20505, (703) 482-0623, Fax: (703) 482-1739, www.cia.gov; *The World Factbook.*

Euromonitor International, Inc., 224 S. Michigan Avenue, Suite 1500, Chicago, IL 60604, (312) 922-1115, Fax: (312) 922-1157, www.euromonitor.com; *International Marketing Data and Statistics 2008* and *World Marketing Data and Statistics.*

International Labour Office, I.L.O. Publications, 4 route des Morillons, CH-1211 Geneva 22, Switzerland, (Telephone in U.S. (202) 653-7652), (Fax in U.S. (202) 653-7687), www.ilo.org; *Yearbook of Labour Statistics 2006.*

Palgrave Macmillan Ltd., Houndmills, Basingstoke, Hampshire, RG21 6XS, England, (Telephone in U.S. (888) 330-8477), (Fax in U.S. (800) 672-2054), www.palgrave.com; *The Statesman's Yearbook 2008.*

Taylor and Francis Group, An Informa Business, 2 Park Square, Milton Park, Abingdon, Oxford OX14 4RN, United Kingdom, (Dial from U.S. (212) 216-7800), (Fax from U.S. (212) 564-7854), www.tandf.co.uk; *The Europa World Year Book.*

United Nations Food and Agricultural Organization (FAO), Viale delle Terme di Caracalla, 00100 Rome, Italy, (Dial from U.S. (202) 653-2400), (Fax from U.S. (202) 653 5760), www.fao.org; *The State of Food and Agriculture (SOFA) 2006.*

The World Bank, 1818 H Street, NW, Washington, DC 20433, (202) 473-1000, Fax: (202) 477-6391, www.worldbank.org; *The World Bank Atlas 2003-2004.*

KIRIBATI - LAND USE

Central Intelligence Agency, Office of Public Affairs, Washington, DC 20505, (703) 482-0623, Fax: (703) 482-1739, www.cia.gov; *The World Factbook.*

Euromonitor International, Inc., 224 S. Michigan Avenue, Suite 1500, Chicago, IL 60604, (312) 922-1115, Fax: (312) 922-1157, www.euromonitor.com; *International Marketing Data and Statistics 2008.*

United Nations Food and Agricultural Organization (FAO), Viale delle Terme di Caracalla, 00100 Rome, Italy, (Dial from U.S. (202) 653-2400), (Fax from U.S. (202) 653 5760), www.fao.org; *FAO Production Yearbook 2002.*

KIRIBATI - LIBRARIES

UNESCO Institute for Statistics, C.P. 6128 Succursale Centre-Ville, Montreal, Quebec, H3C 3J7 Canada, (Dial from U.S. (514) 343-6880), (Fax from U.S. (514) 343 6882), www.uis.unesco.org; *Statistical Tables.*

KIRIBATI - LIFE EXPECTANCY

Central Intelligence Agency, Office of Public Affairs, Washington, DC 20505, (703) 482-0623, Fax: (703) 482-1739, www.cia.gov; *The World Factbook.*

Euromonitor International, Inc., 224 S. Michigan Avenue, Suite 1500, Chicago, IL 60604, (312) 922-

1115, Fax: (312) 922-1157, www.euromonitor.com; *The World Economic Factbook 2008.*

United Nations Statistics Division, New York, NY 10017, (800) 253-9646, Fax: (212) 963-4116, http://unstats.un.org; *Asia-Pacific in Figures 2004* and *World Statistics Pocketbook.*

The World Bank, 1818 H Street, NW, Washington, DC 20433, (202) 473-1000, Fax: (202) 477-6391, www.worldbank.org; *The World Bank Atlas 2003-2004.*

KIRIBATI - LITERACY

Euromonitor International, Inc., 224 S. Michigan Avenue, Suite 1500, Chicago, IL 60604, (312) 922-1115, Fax: (312) 922-1157, www.euromonitor.com; *World Marketing Data and Statistics.*

KIRIBATI - LIVESTOCK

Palgrave Macmillan Ltd., Houndmills, Basingstoke, Hampshire, RG21 6XS, England, (Telephone in U.S. (888) 330-8477), (Fax in U.S. (800) 672-2054), www.palgrave.com; *The Statesman's Yearbook 2008.*

Taylor and Francis Group, An Informa Business, 2 Park Square, Milton Park, Abingdon, Oxford OX14 4RN, United Kingdom, (Dial from U.S. (212) 216-7800), (Fax from U.S. (212) 564-7854), www.tandf.co.uk; *The Europa World Year Book.*

United Nations Conference on Trade and Development (UNCTAD), DC2-1120, United Nations, New York, NY 10017, (212) 963-0027, www.unctad.org; *UNCTAD Commodity Yearbook.*

United Nations Food and Agricultural Organization (FAO), Viale delle Terme di Caracalla, 00100 Rome, Italy, (Dial from U.S. (202) 653-2400), (Fax from U.S. (202) 653 5760), www.fao.org; *FAO Production Yearbook 2002* and *The State of Food and Agriculture (SOFA) 2006.*

KIRIBATI - MANUFACTURES

Asian Development Bank (ADB), PO Box 789, 0980 Manila, Philippines, www.adb.org; *Key Indicators of Developing Asian and Pacific Countries 2006.*

KIRIBATI - MARRIAGE

Taylor and Francis Group, An Informa Business, 2 Park Square, Milton Park, Abingdon, Oxford OX14 4RN, United Kingdom, (Dial from U.S. (212) 216-7800), (Fax from U.S. (212) 564-7854), www.tandf.co.uk; *The Europa World Year Book.*

KIRIBATI - MEAT PRODUCTION

See KIRIBATI - LIVESTOCK

KIRIBATI - MINERAL INDUSTRIES

Asian Development Bank (ADB), PO Box 789, 0980 Manila, Philippines, www.adb.org; *Key Indicators of Developing Asian and Pacific Countries 2006.*

United Nations Conference on Trade and Development (UNCTAD), DC2-1120, United Nations, New York, NY 10017, (212) 963-0027, www.unctad.org; *UNCTAD Commodity Yearbook.*

The World Bank, 1818 H Street, NW, Washington, DC 20433, (202) 473-1000, Fax: (202) 477-6391, www.worldbank.org; *Kiribati.*

KIRIBATI - MONEY SUPPLY

Asian Development Bank (ADB), PO Box 789, 0980 Manila, Philippines, www.adb.org; *Key Indicators of Developing Asian and Pacific Countries 2006.*

The World Bank, 1818 H Street, NW, Washington, DC 20433, (202) 473-1000, Fax: (202) 477-6391, www.worldbank.org; *Kiribati.*

KIRIBATI - MORTALITY

Central Intelligence Agency, Office of Public Affairs, Washington, DC 20505, (703) 482-0623, Fax: (703) 482-1739, www.cia.gov; *The World Factbook.*

Euromonitor International, Inc., 224 S. Michigan Avenue, Suite 1500, Chicago, IL 60604, (312) 922-1115, Fax: (312) 922-1157, www.euromonitor.com; *International Marketing Data and Statistics 2008* and *The World Economic Factbook 2008.*

Taylor and Francis Group, An Informa Business, 2 Park Square, Milton Park, Abingdon, Oxford OX14 4RN, United Kingdom, (Dial from U.S. (212) 216-7800), (Fax from U.S. (212) 564-7854), www.tandf.co.uk; *The Europa World Year Book.*

United Nations Statistics Division, New York, NY 10017, (800) 253-9646, Fax: (212) 963-4116, http://unstats.un.org; *Asia-Pacific in Figures 2004* and *World Statistics Pocketbook.*

The World Bank, 1818 H Street, NW, Washington, DC 20433, (202) 473-1000, Fax: (202) 477-6391, www.worldbank.org; *The World Bank Atlas 2003-2004.*

World Health Organization (WHO), Avenue Appia 20, 1211 Geneve 27, Switzerland, (Telephone in U.S. (212) 331-9081), www.who.int; The WHO Global Atlas of Infectious Diseases and *World Health Report 2006.*

KIRIBATI - MOTION PICTURES

Palgrave Macmillan Ltd., Houndmills, Basingstoke, Hampshire, RG21 6XS, England, (Telephone in U.S. (888) 330-8477), (Fax in U.S. (800) 672-2054), www.palgrave.com; *The Statesman's Yearbook 2008.*

KIRIBATI - MOTOR VEHICLES

Taylor and Francis Group, An Informa Business, 2 Park Square, Milton Park, Abingdon, Oxford OX14 4RN, United Kingdom, (Dial from U.S. (212) 216-7800), (Fax from U.S. (212) 564-7854), www.tandf.co.uk; *The Europa World Year Book.*

KIRIBATI - NUTRITION

Asian Development Bank (ADB), PO Box 789, 0980 Manila, Philippines, www.adb.org; *Key Indicators of Developing Asian and Pacific Countries 2006.*

United Nations Food and Agricultural Organization (FAO), Viale delle Terme di Caracalla, 00100 Rome, Italy, (Dial from U.S. (202) 653-2400), (Fax from U.S. (202) 653 5760), www.fao.org; *The State of Food and Agriculture (SOFA) 2006.*

KIRIBATI - PESTICIDES

United Nations Food and Agricultural Organization (FAO), Viale delle Terme di Caracalla, 00100 Rome, Italy, (Dial from U.S. (202) 653-2400), (Fax from U.S. (202) 653 5760), www.fao.org; *The State of Food and Agriculture (SOFA) 2006.*

KIRIBATI - PETROLEUM INDUSTRY AND TRADE

Asian Development Bank (ADB), PO Box 789, 0980 Manila, Philippines, www.adb.org; *Key Indicators of Developing Asian and Pacific Countries 2006.*

PennWell Corporation, 1421 South Sheridan Road, Tulsa, OK 74112, (918) 835-3161, www.pennwell.com; *International Petroleum Encyclopedia 2007.*

United Nations Conference on Trade and Development (UNCTAD), DC2-1120, United Nations, New York, NY 10017, (212) 963-0027, www.unctad.org; *UNCTAD Commodity Yearbook.*

United Nations Food and Agricultural Organization (FAO), Viale delle Terme di Caracalla, 00100 Rome, Italy, (Dial from U.S. (202) 653-2400), (Fax from U.S. (202) 653 5760), www.fao.org; *The State of Food and Agriculture (SOFA) 2006.*

KIRIBATI - POLITICAL SCIENCE

Asian Development Bank (ADB), PO Box 789, 0980 Manila, Philippines, www.adb.org; *Key Indicators of Developing Asian and Pacific Countries 2006.*

Central Intelligence Agency, Office of Public Affairs, Washington, DC 20505, (703) 482-0623, Fax: (703) 482-1739, www.cia.gov; *The World Factbook.*

Palgrave Macmillan Ltd., Houndmills, Basingstoke, Hampshire, RG21 6XS, England, (Telephone in U.S. (888) 330-8477), (Fax in U.S. (800) 672-2054), www.palgrave.com; *The Statesman's Yearbook 2008.*

Taylor and Francis Group, An Informa Business, 2 Park Square, Milton Park, Abingdon, Oxford OX14 4RN, United Kingdom, (Dial from U.S. (212) 216-7800), (Fax from U.S. (212) 564-7854), www.tandf.co.uk; *The Europa World Year Book.*

United Nations Statistics Division, New York, NY 10017, (800) 253-9646, Fax: (212) 963-4116, http://unstats.un.org; *Asia-Pacific in Figures 2004.*

KIRIBATI - POPULATION

Asian Development Bank (ADB), PO Box 789, 0980 Manila, Philippines, www.adb.org; *Key Indicators of Developing Asian and Pacific Countries 2006.*

Central Intelligence Agency, Office of Public Affairs, Washington, DC 20505, (703) 482-0623, Fax: (703) 482-1739, www.cia.gov; *The World Factbook.*

Euromonitor International, Inc., 224 S. Michigan Avenue, Suite 1500, Chicago, IL 60604, (312) 922-1115, Fax: (312) 922-1157, www.euromonitor.com; *International Marketing Data and Statistics 2008* and *The World Economic Factbook 2008.*

International Labour Office, I.L.O. Publications, 4 route des Morillons, CH-1211 Geneva 22, Switzerland, (Telephone in U.S. (202) 653-7652), (Fax in U.S. (202) 653-7687), www.ilo.org; *Yearbook of Labour Statistics 2006.*

Palgrave Macmillan Ltd., Houndmills, Basingstoke, Hampshire, RG21 6XS, England, (Telephone in U.S. (888) 330-8477), (Fax in U.S. (800) 672-2054), www.palgrave.com; *The Statesman's Yearbook 2008.*

Taylor and Francis Group, An Informa Business, 2 Park Square, Milton Park, Abingdon, Oxford OX14 4RN, United Kingdom, (Dial from U.S. (212) 216-7800), (Fax from U.S. (212) 564-7854), www.tandf.co.uk; *The Europa World Year Book.*

United Nations Food and Agricultural Organization (FAO), Viale delle Terme di Caracalla, 00100 Rome, Italy, (Dial from U.S. (202) 653-2400), (Fax from U.S. (202) 653 5760), www.fao.org; *FAO Production Yearbook 2002.*

United Nations Statistics Division, New York, NY 10017, (800) 253-9646, Fax: (212) 963-4116, http://unstats.un.org; *Asia-Pacific in Figures 2004* and *World Statistics Pocketbook.*

The World Bank, 1818 H Street, NW, Washington, DC 20433, (202) 473-1000, Fax: (202) 477-6391, www.worldbank.org; *Kiribati* and *The World Bank Atlas 2003-2004.*

World Health Organization (WHO), Avenue Appia 20, 1211 Geneve 27, Switzerland, (Telephone in U.S. (212) 331-9081), www.who.int; *World Health Report 2006.*

Worldinformation.com, 2 Market Street, Saffron Walden, Essex CB10 1HZ, United Kingdom, www.worldinformation.com; The World of Information (www.worldinformation.com).

KIRIBATI - POPULATION DENSITY

Central Intelligence Agency, Office of Public Affairs, Washington, DC 20505, (703) 482-0623, Fax: (703) 482-1739, www.cia.gov; *The World Factbook.*

Euromonitor International, Inc., 224 S. Michigan Avenue, Suite 1500, Chicago, IL 60604, (312) 922-1115, Fax: (312) 922-1157, www.euromonitor.com; *The World Economic Factbook 2008.*

Palgrave Macmillan Ltd., Houndmills, Basingstoke, Hampshire, RG21 6XS, England, (Telephone in U.S. (888) 330-8477), (Fax in U.S. (800) 672-2054), www.palgrave.com; *The Statesman's Yearbook 2008.*

Taylor and Francis Group, An Informa Business, 2 Park Square, Milton Park, Abingdon, Oxford OX14 4RN, United Kingdom, (Dial from U.S. (212) 216-7800), (Fax from U.S. (212) 564-7854), www.tandf.co.uk; *The Europa World Year Book.*

United Nations Food and Agricultural Organization (FAO), Viale delle Terme di Caracalla, 00100 Rome, Italy, (Dial from U.S. (202) 653-2400), (Fax from U.S. (202) 653 5760), www.fao.org; *The State of Food and Agriculture (SOFA) 2006.*

The World Bank, 1818 H Street, NW, Washington, DC 20433, (202) 473-1000, Fax: (202) 477-6391, www.worldbank.org; *Kiribati.*

KIRIBATI - POWER RESOURCES

Euromonitor International, Inc., 224 S. Michigan Avenue, Suite 1500, Chicago, IL 60604, (312) 922-1115, Fax: (312) 922-1157, www.euromonitor.com; *International Marketing Data and Statistics 2008; The World Economic Factbook 2008;* and *World Marketing Data and Statistics.*

Palgrave Macmillan Ltd., Houndmills, Basingstoke, Hampshire, RG21 6XS, England, (Telephone in U.S. (888) 330-8477), (Fax in U.S. (800) 672-2054), www.palgrave.com; *The Statesman's Yearbook 2008.*

United Nations Food and Agricultural Organization (FAO), Viale delle Terme di Caracalla, 00100 Rome, Italy, (Dial from U.S. (202) 653-2400), (Fax from U.S. (202) 653 5760), www.fao.org; *The State of Food and Agriculture (SOFA) 2006.*

United Nations Statistics Division, New York, NY 10017, (800) 253-9646, Fax: (212) 963-4116, http://unstats.un.org; *Asia-Pacific in Figures 2004; Statistical Yearbook;* and *World Statistics Pocketbook.*

The World Bank, 1818 H Street, NW, Washington, DC 20433, (202) 473-1000, Fax: (202) 477-6391, www.worldbank.org; *The World Bank Atlas 2003-2004.*

KIRIBATI - PRICES

Asian Development Bank (ADB), PO Box 789, 0980 Manila, Philippines, www.adb.org; *Key Indicators of Developing Asian and Pacific Countries 2006.*

Euromonitor International, Inc., 224 S. Michigan Avenue, Suite 1500, Chicago, IL 60604, (312) 922-1115, Fax: (312) 922-1157, www.euromonitor.com; *World Marketing Data and Statistics.*

International Labour Office, I.L.O. Publications, 4 route des Morillons, CH-1211 Geneva 22, Switzerland, (Telephone in U.S. (202) 653-7652), (Fax in U.S. (202) 653-7687), www.ilo.org; *Yearbook of Labour Statistics 2006.*

Secretariat of the Pacific Community (SPC), BP D5, 98848 Noumea Cedex, New Caledonia, www.spc.int/corp; *Selected Pacific Economies - a Statistical Summary (SPESS).*

United Nations Food and Agricultural Organization (FAO), Viale delle Terme di Caracalla, 00100 Rome, Italy, (Dial from U.S. (202) 653-2400), (Fax from U.S. (202) 653 5760), www.fao.org; *FAO Production Yearbook 2002* and *The State of Food and Agriculture (SOFA) 2006.*

The World Bank, 1818 H Street, NW, Washington, DC 20433, (202) 473-1000, Fax: (202) 477-6391, www.worldbank.org; *Kiribati.*

KIRIBATI - PUBLIC HEALTH

Asian Development Bank (ADB), PO Box 789, 0980 Manila, Philippines, www.adb.org; *Key Indicators of Developing Asian and Pacific Countries 2006.*

Euromonitor International, Inc., 224 S. Michigan Avenue, Suite 1500, Chicago, IL 60604, (312) 922-1115, Fax: (312) 922-1157, www.euromonitor.com; *World Marketing Data and Statistics.*

Palgrave Macmillan Ltd., Houndmills, Basingstoke, Hampshire, RG21 6XS, England, (Telephone in U.S. (888) 330-8477), (Fax in U.S. (800) 672-2054), www.palgrave.com; *The Statesman's Yearbook 2008.*

Secretariat of the Pacific Community (SPC), BP D5, 98848 Noumea Cedex, New Caledonia, www.spc.int/corp; *Selected Pacific Economies - a Statistical Summary (SPESS).*

United Nations Statistics Division, New York, NY 10017, (800) 253-9646, Fax: (212) 963-4116, http://unstats.un.org; *Asia-Pacific in Figures 2004* and *Statistical Yearbook.*

The World Bank, 1818 H Street, NW, Washington, DC 20433, (202) 473-1000, Fax: (202) 477-6391, www.worldbank.org; *Kiribati.*

World Health Organization (WHO), Avenue Appia 20, 1211 Geneve 27, Switzerland, (Telephone in U.S. (212) 331-9081), www.who.int; The WHO Global Atlas of Infectious Diseases and *World Health Report 2006.*

KIRIBATI - PUBLIC UTILITIES

United Nations Statistics Division, New York, NY 10017, (800) 253-9646, Fax: (212) 963-4116, http://unstats.un.org; *Electric Power in Asia and the Pacific 2001 and 2002.*

KIRIBATI - RADIO BROADCASTING

Palgrave Macmillan Ltd., Houndmills, Basingstoke, Hampshire, RG21 6XS, England, (Telephone in U.S. (888) 330-8477), (Fax in U.S. (800) 672-2054), www.palgrave.com; *The Statesman's Yearbook 2008.*

KIRIBATI - RELIGION

Central Intelligence Agency, Office of Public Affairs, Washington, DC 20505, (703) 482-0623, Fax: (703) 482-1739, www.cia.gov; *The World Factbook.*

Palgrave Macmillan Ltd., Houndmills, Basingstoke, Hampshire, RG21 6XS, England, (Telephone in U.S. (888) 330-8477), (Fax in U.S. (800) 672-2054), www.palgrave.com; *The Statesman's Yearbook 2008.*

KIRIBATI - RESERVES (ACCOUNTING)

Asian Development Bank (ADB), PO Box 789, 0980 Manila, Philippines, www.adb.org; *Key Indicators of Developing Asian and Pacific Countries 2006.*

KIRIBATI - RETAIL TRADE

Euromonitor International, Inc., 224 S. Michigan Avenue, Suite 1500, Chicago, IL 60604, (312) 922-1115, Fax: (312) 922-1157, www.euromonitor.com; *World Marketing Data and Statistics.*

KIRIBATI - RICE PRODUCTION

See KIRIBATI - CROPS

KIRIBATI - ROADS

Central Intelligence Agency, Office of Public Affairs, Washington, DC 20505, (703) 482-0623, Fax: (703) 482-1739, www.cia.gov; *The World Factbook.*

Palgrave Macmillan Ltd., Houndmills, Basingstoke, Hampshire, RG21 6XS, England, (Telephone in U.S. (888) 330-8477), (Fax in U.S. (800) 672-2054), www.palgrave.com; *The Statesman's Yearbook 2008.*

KIRIBATI - SHIPPING

Palgrave Macmillan Ltd., Houndmills, Basingstoke, Hampshire, RG21 6XS, England, (Telephone in U.S. (888) 330-8477), (Fax in U.S. (800) 672-2054), www.palgrave.com; *The Statesman's Yearbook 2008.*

Taylor and Francis Group, An Informa Business, 2 Park Square, Milton Park, Abingdon, Oxford OX14 4RN, United Kingdom, (Dial from U.S. (212) 216-7800), (Fax from U.S. (212) 564-7854), www.tandf.co.uk; *The Europa World Year Book.*

KIRIBATI - SOCIAL ECOLOGY

Asian Development Bank (ADB), PO Box 789, 0980 Manila, Philippines, www.adb.org; *Key Indicators of Developing Asian and Pacific Countries 2006.*

United Nations Statistics Division, New York, NY 10017, (800) 253-9646, Fax: (212) 963-4116, http://unstats.un.org; *World Statistics Pocketbook.*

KIRIBATI - TAXATION

Palgrave Macmillan Ltd., Houndmills, Basingstoke, Hampshire, RG21 6XS, England, (Telephone in U.S. (888) 330-8477), (Fax in U.S. (800) 672-2054), www.palgrave.com; *The Statesman's Yearbook 2008.*

KIRIBATI - TELEPHONE

International Telecommunication Union (ITU), Place des Nations, 1211 Geneva 20, Switzerland, www.itu.int; World Telecommunication Indicators Database.

Palgrave Macmillan Ltd., Houndmills, Basingstoke, Hampshire, RG21 6XS, England, (Telephone in U.S. (888) 330-8477), (Fax in U.S. (800) 672-2054), www.palgrave.com; *The Statesman's Yearbook 2008.*

Taylor and Francis Group, An Informa Business, 2 Park Square, Milton Park, Abingdon, Oxford OX14 4RN, United Kingdom, (Dial from U.S. (212) 216-7800), (Fax from U.S. (212) 564-7854), www.tandf.co.uk; *The Europa World Year Book.*

United Nations Statistics Division, New York, NY 10017, (800) 253-9646, Fax: (212) 963-4116, http://unstats.un.org; *World Statistics Pocketbook.*

KIRIBATI - TEXTILE INDUSTRY

Secretariat of the Pacific Community (SPC), BP D5, 98848 Noumea Cedex, New Caledonia, www.spc.int/corp; *Selected Pacific Economies - a Statistical Summary (SPESS).*

United Nations Conference on Trade and Development (UNCTAD), DC2-1120, United Nations, New York, NY 10017, (212) 963-0027, www.unctad.org; *UNCTAD Commodity Yearbook.*

KIRIBATI - THEATER

UNESCO Institute for Statistics, C.P. 6128 Succursale Centre-Ville, Montreal, Quebec, H3C 3J7 Canada, (Dial from U.S. (514) 343-6880), (Fax from U.S. (514) 343 6882), www.uis.unesco.org; *Statistical Tables.*

KIRIBATI - TOBACCO INDUSTRY

Foreign Agricultural Service (FAS), U.S. Department of Agriculture (USDA), 1400 Independence Avenue, SW, Washington, DC 20250, (202) 720-3935, www.fas.usda.gov; *Tobacco: World Markets and Trade.*

Secretariat of the Pacific Community (SPC), BP D5, 98848 Noumea Cedex, New Caledonia, www.spc.int/corp; *Selected Pacific Economies - a Statistical Summary (SPESS).*

KIRIBATI - TOURISM

Euromonitor International, Inc., 224 S. Michigan Avenue, Suite 1500, Chicago, IL 60604, (312) 922-1115, Fax: (312) 922-1157, www.euromonitor.com; *The World Economic Factbook 2008* and *World Marketing Data and Statistics.*

Taylor and Francis Group, An Informa Business, 2 Park Square, Milton Park, Abingdon, Oxford OX14 4RN, United Kingdom, (Dial from U.S. (212) 216-7800), (Fax from U.S. (212) 564-7854), www.tandf.co.uk; *The Europa World Year Book.*

United Nations World Tourism Organization (UNWTO), Capitan Haya 42, 28020 Madrid, Spain, www.world-tourism.org; *Yearbook of Tourism Statistics.*

The World Bank, 1818 H Street, NW, Washington, DC 20433, (202) 473-1000, Fax: (202) 477-6391, www.worldbank.org; *Kiribati.*

KIRIBATI - TRADE

See KIRIBATI - INTERNATIONAL TRADE

KIRIBATI - TRANSPORTATION

Central Intelligence Agency, Office of Public Affairs, Washington, DC 20505, (703) 482-0623, Fax: (703) 482-1739, www.cia.gov; *The World Factbook.*

Euromonitor International, Inc., 224 S. Michigan Avenue, Suite 1500, Chicago, IL 60604, (312) 922-1115, Fax: (312) 922-1157, www.euromonitor.com; *International Marketing Data and Statistics 2008* and *World Marketing Data and Statistics.*

Palgrave Macmillan Ltd., Houndmills, Basingstoke, Hampshire, RG21 6XS, England, (Telephone in U.S. (888) 330-8477), (Fax in U.S. (800) 672-2054), www.palgrave.com; *The Statesman's Yearbook 2008.*

Secretariat of the Pacific Community (SPC), BP D5, 98848 Noumea Cedex, New Caledonia, www.spc.int/corp; *Selected Pacific Economies - a Statistical Summary (SPESS).*

Taylor and Francis Group, An Informa Business, 2 Park Square, Milton Park, Abingdon, Oxford OX14 4RN, United Kingdom, (Dial from U.S. (212) 216-

7800), (Fax from U.S. (212) 564-7854), www.tandf.co.uk; *The Europa World Year Book.*

The World Bank, 1818 H Street, NW, Washington, DC 20433, (202) 473-1000, Fax: (202) 477-6391, www.worldbank.org; *Kiribati.*

KIRIBATI - UNEMPLOYMENT

Central Intelligence Agency, Office of Public Affairs, Washington, DC 20505, (703) 482-0623, Fax: (703) 482-1739, www.cia.gov; *The World Factbook.*

International Labour Office, I.L.O. Publications, 4 route des Morillons, CH-1211 Geneva 22, Switzerland, (Telephone in U.S. (202) 653-7652), (Fax in U.S. (202) 653-7687), www.ilo.org; *Yearbook of Labour Statistics 2006.*

The World Bank, 1818 H Street, NW, Washington, DC 20433, (202) 473-1000, Fax: (202) 477-6391, www.worldbank.org; *Kiribati.*

KIRIBATI - WAGES

International Labour Office, I.L.O. Publications, 4 route des Morillons, CH-1211 Geneva 22, Switzerland, (Telephone in U.S. (202) 653-7652), (Fax in U.S. (202) 653-7687), www.ilo.org; *Yearbook of Labour Statistics 2006.*

The World Bank, 1818 H Street, NW, Washington, DC 20433, (202) 473-1000, Fax: (202) 477-6391, www.worldbank.org; *Kiribati.*

KIRIBATI - WHOLESALE PRICE INDEXES

Asian Development Bank (ADB), PO Box 789, 0980 Manila, Philippines, www.adb.org; *Key Indicators of Developing Asian and Pacific Countries 2006.*

KITE FLYING

Mediamark Research, Inc., 75 Ninth Avenue, 5th Floor, New York, NY 10011, (212) 884-9200, Fax: (212) 884-9339, www.mediamark.com; MRI+.

KOREA, NORTH - NATIONAL STATISTICAL OFFICE

Central Bureau of Statistics, Inhung-Dong, Moranbong District, Pyongyang, Democratic People's Republic of Korea; National Data Center.

KOREA, NORTH - AGRICULTURAL MACHINERY

United Nations Statistics Division, New York, NY 10017, (800) 253-9646, Fax: (212) 963-4116, http://unstats.un.org; *Statistical Yearbook.*

KOREA, NORTH - AGRICULTURE

Asian Development Bank (ADB), PO Box 789, 0980 Manila, Philippines, www.adb.org; *Key Indicators of Developing Asian and Pacific Countries 2006.*

Economist Intelligence Unit, 111 West 57th Street, New York, NY 10019, (212) 554-0600, Fax: (212) 586-1181, www.eiu.com; *North Korea Country Report.*

Euromonitor International, Inc., 224 S. Michigan Avenue, Suite 1500, Chicago, IL 60604, (312) 922-1115, Fax: (312) 922-1157, www.euromonitor.com; *World Marketing Data and Statistics.*

M.E. Sharpe, 80 Business Park Drive, Armonk, NY 10504, (800) 541-6563, Fax: (914) 273-2106, www.mesharpe.com; *The Illustrated Book of World Rankings.*

Organisation for Economic Cooperation and Development (OECD), 2 rue Andre Pascal, F-75775 Paris Cedex 16, France, (Telephone in U.S. (202) 785-6323), (Fax in U.S. (202) 785-0350), www.oecd.org; *OECD Economic Survey - Korea 2007.*

Palgrave Macmillan Ltd., Houndmills, Basingstoke, Hampshire, RG21 6XS, England, (Telephone in U.S. (888) 330-8477), (Fax in U.S. (800) 672-2054), www.palgrave.com; *The Statesman's Yearbook 2008.*

Taylor and Francis Group, An Informa Business, 2 Park Square, Milton Park, Abingdon, Oxford OX14 4RN, United Kingdom, (Dial from U.S. (212) 216-7800), (Fax from U.S. (212) 564-7854), www.tandf.co.uk; *The Europa World Year Book.*

United Nations Conference on Trade and Development (UNCTAD), DC2-1120, United Nations, New York, NY 10017, (212) 963-0027, www.unctad.org; *UNCTAD Commodity Yearbook.*

United Nations Food and Agricultural Organization (FAO), Viale delle Terme di Caracalla, 00100 Rome, Italy, (Dial from U.S. (202) 653-2400), (Fax from U.S. (202) 653 5760), www.fao.org; AQUASTAT; *FAO Trade Yearbook;* and *The State of Food and Agriculture (SOFA) 2006.*

United Nations Statistics Division, New York, NY 10017, (800) 253-9646, Fax: (212) 963-4116, http://unstats.un.org; *Statistical Yearbook.*

The World Bank, 1818 H Street, NW, Washington, DC 20433, (202) 473-1000, Fax: (202) 477-6391, www.worldbank.org; *Korea, Democratic Republic of.*

KOREA, NORTH - AIRLINES

Economist Intelligence Unit, 111 West 57th Street, New York, NY 10019, (212) 554-0600, Fax: (212) 586-1181, www.eiu.com; *Business Asia.*

M.E. Sharpe, 80 Business Park Drive, Armonk, NY 10504, (800) 541-6563, Fax: (914) 273-2106, www.mesharpe.com; *The Illustrated Book of World Rankings.*

Palgrave Macmillan Ltd., Houndmills, Basingstoke, Hampshire, RG21 6XS, England, (Telephone in U.S. (888) 330-8477), (Fax in U.S. (800) 672-2054), www.palgrave.com; *The Statesman's Yearbook 2008.*

KOREA, NORTH - ARMED FORCES

Central Intelligence Agency, Office of Public Affairs, Washington, DC 20505, (703) 482-0623, Fax: (703) 482-1739, www.cia.gov; *The World Factbook.*

Economist Intelligence Unit, 111 West 57th Street, New York, NY 10019, (212) 554-0600, Fax: (212) 586-1181, www.eiu.com; *Business Asia.*

Euromonitor International, Inc., 224 S. Michigan Avenue, Suite 1500, Chicago, IL 60604, (312) 922-1115, Fax: (312) 922-1157, www.euromonitor.com; *World Marketing Data and Statistics.*

International Institute for Strategic Studies (IISS), Arundel House, 13-15 Arundel Street, Temple Place, London WC2R 3DX, England, www.iiss.org; *The Military Balance 2007.*

Palgrave Macmillan Ltd., Houndmills, Basingstoke, Hampshire, RG21 6XS, England, (Telephone in U.S. (888) 330-8477), (Fax in U.S. (800) 672-2054), www.palgrave.com; *The Statesman's Yearbook 2008.*

U.S. Department of State (DOS), 2201 C Street NW, Washington, DC 20520, (202) 647-4000, www.state.gov; *World Military Expenditures and Arms Transfers (WMEAT).*

United Nations Statistics Division, New York, NY 10017, (800) 253-9646, Fax: (212) 963-4116, http://unstats.un.org; *Human Development Report 2006.*

KOREA, NORTH - BALANCE OF PAYMENTS

Organisation for Economic Cooperation and Development (OECD), 2 rue Andre Pascal, F-75775 Paris Cedex 16, France, (Telephone in U.S. (202) 785-6323), (Fax in U.S. (202) 785-0350), www.oecd.org; *OECD Economic Survey - Korea 2007.*

The World Bank, 1818 H Street, NW, Washington, DC 20433, (202) 473-1000, Fax: (202) 477-6391, www.worldbank.org; *Korea, Democratic Republic of.*

KOREA, NORTH - BANKS AND BANKING

Asian Development Bank (ADB), PO Box 789, 0980 Manila, Philippines, www.adb.org; *Key Indicators of Developing Asian and Pacific Countries 2006.*

Euromonitor International, Inc., 224 S. Michigan Avenue, Suite 1500, Chicago, IL 60604, (312) 922-1115, Fax: (312) 922-1157, www.euromonitor.com; *World Marketing Data and Statistics.*

M.E. Sharpe, 80 Business Park Drive, Armonk, NY 10504, (800) 541-6563, Fax: (914) 273-2106, www.mesharpe.com; *The Illustrated Book of World Rankings.*

Organisation for Economic Cooperation and Development (OECD), 2 rue Andre Pascal, F-75775 Paris Cedex 16, France, (Telephone in U.S. (202) 785-6323), (Fax in U.S. (202) 785-0350), www.oecd.org; *OECD Economic Survey - Korea 2007.*

Palgrave Macmillan Ltd., Houndmills, Basingstoke, Hampshire, RG21 6XS, England, (Telephone in U.S. (888) 330-8477), (Fax in U.S. (800) 672-2054), www.palgrave.com; *The Statesman's Yearbook 2008.*

KOREA, NORTH - BARLEY PRODUCTION

See KOREA, NORTH - CROPS

KOREA, NORTH - BEVERAGE INDUSTRY

M.E. Sharpe, 80 Business Park Drive, Armonk, NY 10504, (800) 541-6563, Fax: (914) 273-2106, www.mesharpe.com; *The Illustrated Book of World Rankings.*

KOREA, NORTH - BONDS

Asian Development Bank (ADB), PO Box 789, 0980 Manila, Philippines, www.adb.org; *Key Indicators of Developing Asian and Pacific Countries 2006.*

KOREA, NORTH - BROADCASTING

Central Intelligence Agency, Office of Public Affairs, Washington, DC 20505, (703) 482-0623, Fax: (703) 482-1739, www.cia.gov; *The World Factbook.*

Economist Intelligence Unit, 111 West 57th Street, New York, NY 10019, (212) 554-0600, Fax: (212) 586-1181, www.eiu.com; *Business Asia.*

Euromonitor International, Inc., 224 S. Michigan Avenue, Suite 1500, Chicago, IL 60604, (312) 922-1115, Fax: (312) 922-1157, www.euromonitor.com; *World Marketing Data and Statistics.*

M.E. Sharpe, 80 Business Park Drive, Armonk, NY 10504, (800) 541-6563, Fax: (914) 273-2106, www.mesharpe.com; *The Illustrated Book of World Rankings.*

Palgrave Macmillan Ltd., Houndmills, Basingstoke, Hampshire, RG21 6XS, England, (Telephone in U.S. (888) 330-8477), (Fax in U.S. (800) 672-2054), www.palgrave.com; *The Statesman's Yearbook 2008.*

WRTH Publications Limited, PO Box 290, Oxford OX2 7FT, UK, www.wrth.com; *World Radio TV Handbook 2007.*

KOREA, NORTH - BUDGET

Central Intelligence Agency, Office of Public Affairs, Washington, DC 20505, (703) 482-0623, Fax: (703) 482-1739, www.cia.gov; *The World Factbook.*

KOREA, NORTH - CAPITAL INVESTMENTS

Asian Development Bank (ADB), PO Box 789, 0980 Manila, Philippines, www.adb.org; *Key Indicators of Developing Asian and Pacific Countries 2006.*

KOREA, NORTH - CATTLE

See KOREA, NORTH - LIVESTOCK

KOREA, NORTH - CHESTNUT PRODUCTION

See KOREA, NORTH - CROPS

KOREA, NORTH - CHICKENS

See KOREA, NORTH - LIVESTOCK

KOREA, NORTH - CHILDBIRTH - STATISTICS

Central Intelligence Agency, Office of Public Affairs, Washington, DC 20505, (703) 482-0623, Fax: (703) 482-1739, www.cia.gov; *The World Factbook.*

Economist Intelligence Unit, 111 West 57th Street, New York, NY 10019, (212) 554-0600, Fax: (212) 586-1181, www.eiu.com; *Business Asia.*

Euromonitor International, Inc., 224 S. Michigan Avenue, Suite 1500, Chicago, IL 60604, (312) 922-1115, Fax: (312) 922-1157, www.euromonitor.com; *International Marketing Data and Statistics 2008* and *The World Economic Factbook 2008.*

M.E. Sharpe, 80 Business Park Drive, Armonk, NY 10504, (800) 541-6563, Fax: (914) 273-2106, www.mesharpe.com; *The Illustrated Book of World Rankings.*

Palgrave Macmillan Ltd., Houndmills, Basingstoke, Hampshire, RG21 6XS, England, (Telephone in U.S. (888) 330-8477), (Fax in U.S. (800) 672-2054), www.palgrave.com; *The Statesman's Yearbook 2008.*

Taylor and Francis Group, An Informa Business, 2 Park Square, Milton Park, Abingdon, Oxford OX14 4RN, United Kingdom, (Dial from U.S. (212) 216-7800), (Fax from U.S. (212) 564-7854), www.tandf.co.uk; *The Europa World Year Book.*

United Nations Statistics Division, New York, NY 10017, (800) 253-9646, Fax: (212) 963-4116, http://unstats.un.org; *Demographic Yearbook* and *Statistical Yearbook.*

KOREA, NORTH - CLIMATE

International Institute for Environment and Development (IIED), 3 Endsleigh Street, London, England, WC1H 0DD, United Kingdom, www.iied.org; *Environment Urbanization.*

M.E. Sharpe, 80 Business Park Drive, Armonk, NY 10504, (800) 541-6563, Fax: (914) 273-2106, www.mesharpe.com; *The Illustrated Book of World Rankings.*

Palgrave Macmillan Ltd., Houndmills, Basingstoke, Hampshire, RG21 6XS, England, (Telephone in U.S. (888) 330-8477), (Fax in U.S. (800) 672-2054), www.palgrave.com; *The Statesman's Yearbook 2008.*

KOREA, NORTH - COAL PRODUCTION

See KOREA, NORTH - MINERAL INDUSTRIES

KOREA, NORTH - COMMERCE

Palgrave Macmillan Ltd., Houndmills, Basingstoke, Hampshire, RG21 6XS, England, (Telephone in U.S. (888) 330-8477), (Fax in U.S. (800) 672-2054), www.palgrave.com; *The Statesman's Yearbook 2008.*

KOREA, NORTH - COMMODITY EXCHANGES

Commodity Research Bureau, 330 South Wells Street, Suite 612, Chicago, IL 60606-7110, (800) 621-5271, Fax: (312) 939-4135, www.crbtrader.com; *2006 CRB Commodity Yearbook and CD.*

International Monetary Fund (IMF), 700 Nineteenth Street, NW, Washington, DC 20431, (202) 623-7000, Fax: (202) 623-4661, www.imf.org; *IMF Primary Commodity Prices.*

United Nations Food and Agricultural Organization (FAO), Viale delle Terme di Caracalla, 00100 Rome, Italy, (Dial from U.S. (202) 653-2400), (Fax from U.S. (202) 653 5760), www.fao.org; *The State of Food and Agriculture (SOFA) 2006.*

KOREA, NORTH - CONSTRUCTION INDUSTRY

M.E. Sharpe, 80 Business Park Drive, Armonk, NY 10504, (800) 541-6563, Fax: (914) 273-2106, www.mesharpe.com; *The Illustrated Book of World Rankings.*

Organisation for Economic Cooperation and Development (OECD), 2 rue Andre Pascal, F-75775 Paris Cedex 16, France, (Telephone in U.S. (202) 785-6323), (Fax in U.S. (202) 785-0350), www.oecd.org; *OECD Economic Survey - Korea 2007.*

KOREA, NORTH - CONSUMER PRICE INDEXES

Asian Development Bank (ADB), PO Box 789, 0980 Manila, Philippines, www.adb.org; *Key Indicators of Developing Asian and Pacific Countries 2006.*

The World Bank, 1818 H Street, NW, Washington, DC 20433, (202) 473-1000, Fax: (202) 477-6391, www.worldbank.org; *Korea, Democratic Republic of.*

KOREA, NORTH - COPPER INDUSTRY AND TRADE

See KOREA, NORTH - MINERAL INDUSTRIES

KOREA, NORTH - CORN INDUSTRY

See KOREA, NORTH - CROPS

KOREA, NORTH - COTTON

See KOREA, NORTH - CROPS

KOREA, NORTH - CRIME

International Criminal Police Organization (INTERPOL), General Secretariat, 200 quai Charles de Gaulle, 69006 Lyon, France, www.interpol.int; *International Crime Statistics.*

Yale University Press, PO Box 209040, New Haven, CT 06520-9040, (203) 432-0960, Fax: (203) 432-0948, http://yalepress.yale.edu/yupbooks; *Violence and Crime in Cross-National Perspective.*

KOREA, NORTH - CROPS

Asian Development Bank (ADB), PO Box 789, 0980 Manila, Philippines, www.adb.org; *Key Indicators of Developing Asian and Pacific Countries 2006.*

M.E. Sharpe, 80 Business Park Drive, Armonk, NY 10504, (800) 541-6563, Fax: (914) 273-2106, www.mesharpe.com; *The Illustrated Book of World Rankings.*

Palgrave Macmillan Ltd., Houndmills, Basingstoke, Hampshire, RG21 6XS, England, (Telephone in U.S. (888) 330-8477), (Fax in U.S. (800) 672-2054), www.palgrave.com; *The Statesman's Yearbook 2008.*

Taylor and Francis Group, An Informa Business, 2 Park Square, Milton Park, Abingdon, Oxford OX14 4RN, United Kingdom, (Dial from U.S. (212) 216-7800), (Fax from U.S. (212) 564-7854), www.tandf.co.uk; *The Europa World Year Book.*

United Nations Conference on Trade and Development (UNCTAD), DC2-1120, United Nations, New York, NY 10017, (212) 963-0027, www.unctad.org; *UNCTAD Commodity Yearbook.*

United Nations Food and Agricultural Organization (FAO), Viale delle Terme di Caracalla, 00100 Rome, Italy, (Dial from U.S. (202) 653-2400), (Fax from U.S. (202) 653 5760), www.fao.org; *FAO Production Yearbook 2002* and *The State of Food and Agriculture (SOFA) 2006.*

United Nations Statistics Division, New York, NY 10017, (800) 253-9646, Fax: (212) 963-4116, http://unstats.un.org; *Statistical Yearbook.*

KOREA, NORTH - DAIRY PROCESSING

M.E. Sharpe, 80 Business Park Drive, Armonk, NY 10504, (800) 541-6563, Fax: (914) 273-2106, www.mesharpe.com; *The Illustrated Book of World Rankings.*

Palgrave Macmillan Ltd., Houndmills, Basingstoke, Hampshire, RG21 6XS, England, (Telephone in U.S. (888) 330-8477), (Fax in U.S. (800) 672-2054), www.palgrave.com; *The Statesman's Yearbook 2008.*

Taylor and Francis Group, An Informa Business, 2 Park Square, Milton Park, Abingdon, Oxford OX14 4RN, United Kingdom, (Dial from U.S. (212) 216-7800), (Fax from U.S. (212) 564-7854), www.tandf.co.uk; *The Europa World Year Book.*

United Nations Food and Agricultural Organization (FAO), Viale delle Terme di Caracalla, 00100 Rome, Italy, (Dial from U.S. (202) 653-2400), (Fax from U.S. (202) 653 5760), www.fao.org; *The State of Food and Agriculture (SOFA) 2006.*

United Nations Statistics Division, New York, NY 10017, (800) 253-9646, Fax: (212) 963-4116, http://unstats.un.org; *Statistical Yearbook.*

KOREA, NORTH - DEATH RATES

See KOREA, NORTH - MORTALITY

KOREA, NORTH - DEBTS, EXTERNAL

Asian Development Bank (ADB), PO Box 789, 0980 Manila, Philippines, www.adb.org; *Key Indicators of Developing Asian and Pacific Countries 2006.*

The World Bank, 1818 H Street, NW, Washington, DC 20433, (202) 473-1000, Fax: (202) 477-6391, www.worldbank.org; *Global Development Finance 2007.*

Worldinformation.com, 2 Market Street, Saffron Walden, Essex CB10 1HZ, United Kingdom, www.worldinformation.com; The World of Information (www.worldinformation.com).

KOREA, NORTH - DEFENSE INDUSTRIES

U.S. Department of State (DOS), 2201 C Street NW, Washington, DC 20520, (202) 647-4000, www.state.gov; *World Military Expenditures and Arms Transfers (WMEAT).*

KOREA, NORTH - DEMOGRAPHY

Economist Intelligence Unit, 111 West 57th Street, New York, NY 10019, (212) 554-0600, Fax: (212) 586-1181, www.eiu.com; *Business Asia.*

Euromonitor International, Inc., 224 S. Michigan Avenue, Suite 1500, Chicago, IL 60604, (312) 922-1115, Fax: (312) 922-1157, www.euromonitor.com; *International Marketing Data and Statistics 2008; The World Economic Factbook 2008;* and *World Marketing Data and Statistics.*

M.E. Sharpe, 80 Business Park Drive, Armonk, NY 10504, (800) 541-6563, Fax: (914) 273-2106, www.mesharpe.com; *The Illustrated Book of World Rankings.*

Pyongyang Square 2, www.pyongyangsquare.com; unpublished data.

United Nations Statistics Division, New York, NY 10017, (800) 253-9646, Fax: (212) 963-4116, http://unstats.un.org; *Human Development Report 2006.*

The World Bank, 1818 H Street, NW, Washington, DC 20433, (202) 473-1000, Fax: (202) 477-6391, www.worldbank.org; *Korea, Democratic Republic of.*

KOREA, NORTH - DIAMONDS

See KOREA, NORTH - MINERAL INDUSTRIES

KOREA, NORTH - DISPOSABLE INCOME

M.E. Sharpe, 80 Business Park Drive, Armonk, NY 10504, (800) 541-6563, Fax: (914) 273-2106, www.mesharpe.com; *The Illustrated Book of World Rankings.*

United Nations Statistics Division, New York, NY 10017, (800) 253-9646, Fax: (212) 963-4116, http://unstats.un.org; *National Accounts Statistics: Compendium of Income Distribution Statistics.*

KOREA, NORTH - DIVORCE

M.E. Sharpe, 80 Business Park Drive, Armonk, NY 10504, (800) 541-6563, Fax: (914) 273-2106, www.mesharpe.com; *The Illustrated Book of World Rankings.*

United Nations Statistics Division, New York, NY 10017, (800) 253-9646, Fax: (212) 963-4116, http://unstats.un.org; *Demographic Yearbook.*

KOREA, NORTH - ECONOMIC ASSISTANCE

Asian Development Bank (ADB), PO Box 789, 0980 Manila, Philippines, www.adb.org; *Key Indicators of Developing Asian and Pacific Countries 2006.*

KOREA, NORTH - ECONOMIC CONDITIONS

Asian Development Bank (ADB), PO Box 789, 0980 Manila, Philippines, www.adb.org; *Key Indicators of Developing Asian and Pacific Countries 2006.*

Center for International Business Education Research (CIBER), Columbia Business School and School of International and Public Affairs, Uris Hall, Room 212, 3022 Broadway, New York, NY 10027-6902, Mr. Joshua Safier, (212) 854-4750, Fax: (212) 222-9821, www.columbia.edu/cu/ciber/; Datastream International.

Central Intelligence Agency, Office of Public Affairs, Washington, DC 20505, (703) 482-0623, Fax: (703) 482-1739, www.cia.gov; *The World Factbook.*

DSI Data Service Information, Xantener Strasse 51a, D-47495 Rheinberg, Germany, www.dsidata.com; *Campus Solution*.

Dun and Bradstreet (DB) Corporation, 103 JFK Parkway, Short Hills, NJ 07078, (973) 921-5500, www.dnb.com; *Country Report*.

Economist Intelligence Unit, 111 West 57th Street, New York, NY 10019, (212) 554-0600, Fax: (212) 586-1181, www.eiu.com; *North Korea Country Report*.

Euromonitor International, Inc., 224 S. Michigan Avenue, Suite 1500, Chicago, IL 60604, (312) 922-1115, Fax: (312) 922-1157, www.euromonitor.com; *International Marketing Data and Statistics 2008; The World Economic Factbook 2008;* and *World Marketing Data and Statistics*.

International Monetary Fund (IMF), 700 Nineteenth Street, NW, Washington, DC 20431, (202) 623-7000, Fax: (202) 623-4661, www.imf.org; *World Economic Outlook Reports*.

Japan Center for Economic Research (JCER), Nikkei Kayabacho Building, Nihombashi Kayabacho, 2-6-1, Chuo-ku, Tokyo 103-0025, Japan, www.jcer.or.jp/eng; *Asia Research Report*.

M.E. Sharpe, 80 Business Park Drive, Armonk, NY 10504, (800) 541-6563, Fax: (914) 273-2106, www.mesharpe.com; *The Illustrated Book of World Rankings*.

Nomura Research Institute (NRI), 2 World Financial Center, Building B, 19th Fl., New York, NY 10281-1198, (212) 667-1670, www.nri.co.jp/english; *Asian Economic Outlook 2003-2004*.

Organisation for Economic Cooperation and Development (OECD), 2 rue Andre Pascal, F-75775 Paris Cedex 16, France, (Telephone in U.S. (202) 785-6323), (Fax in U.S. (202) 785-0350), www.oecd.org; *OECD Economic Survey - Korea 2007*.

Palgrave Macmillan Ltd., Houndmills, Basingstoke, Hampshire, RG21 6XS, England, (Telephone in U.S. (888) 330-8477), (Fax in U.S. (800) 672-2054), www.palgrave.com; *The Statesman's Yearbook 2008*.

Pyongyang Square 2, www.pyongyangsquare.com; unpublished data.

Taylor and Francis Group, An Informa Business, 2 Park Square, Milton Park, Abingdon, Oxford OX14 4RN, United Kingdom, (Dial from U.S. (212) 216-7800), (Fax from U.S. (212) 564-7854), www.tandf.co.uk; *The Europa World Year Book*.

United Nations Statistics Division, New York, NY 10017, (800) 253-9646, Fax: (212) 963-4116, http://unstats.un.org; *World Statistics Pocketbook*.

The World Bank, 1818 H Street, NW, Washington, DC 20433, (202) 473-1000, Fax: (202) 477-6391, www.worldbank.org; *Global Economic Monitor (GEM); Global Economic Prospects 2008; Korea, Democratic Republic of;* and *The World Bank Atlas 2003-2004*.

KOREA, NORTH - EDUCATION

Economist Intelligence Unit, 111 West 57th Street, New York, NY 10019, (212) 554-0600, Fax: (212) 586-1181, www.eiu.com; *Business Asia*.

Euromonitor International, Inc., 224 S. Michigan Avenue, Suite 1500, Chicago, IL 60604, (312) 922-1115, Fax: (312) 922-1157, www.euromonitor.com; *International Marketing Data and Statistics 2008* and *World Marketing Data and Statistics*.

M.E. Sharpe, 80 Business Park Drive, Armonk, NY 10504, (800) 541-6563, Fax: (914) 273-2106, www.mesharpe.com; *The Illustrated Book of World Rankings*.

Palgrave Macmillan Ltd., Houndmills, Basingstoke, Hampshire, RG21 6XS, England, (Telephone in U.S. (888) 330-8477), (Fax in U.S. (800) 672-2054), www.palgrave.com; *The Statesman's Yearbook 2008*.

Taylor and Francis Group, An Informa Business, 2 Park Square, Milton Park, Abingdon, Oxford OX14 4RN, United Kingdom, (Dial from U.S. (212) 216-7800), (Fax from U.S. (212) 564-7854), www.tandf.co.uk; *The Europa World Year Book*.

United Nations Statistics Division, New York, NY 10017, (800) 253-9646, Fax: (212) 963-4116, http://unstats.un.org; *Human Development Report 2006*.

The World Bank, 1818 H Street, NW, Washington, DC 20433, (202) 473-1000, Fax: (202) 477-6391, www.worldbank.org; *Korea, Democratic Republic of*.

KOREA, NORTH - EGGPLANT PRODUCTION

See KOREA, NORTH - CROPS

KOREA, NORTH - ELECTRICITY

Asian Development Bank (ADB), PO Box 789, 0980 Manila, Philippines, www.adb.org; *Key Indicators of Developing Asian and Pacific Countries 2006*.

M.E. Sharpe, 80 Business Park Drive, Armonk, NY 10504, (800) 541-6563, Fax: (914) 273-2106, www.mesharpe.com; *The Illustrated Book of World Rankings*.

Palgrave Macmillan Ltd., Houndmills, Basingstoke, Hampshire, RG21 6XS, England, (Telephone in U.S. (888) 330-8477), (Fax in U.S. (800) 672-2054), www.palgrave.com; *The Statesman's Yearbook 2008*.

U.S. Department of Energy (DOE), Energy Information Administration (EIA), 1000 Independence Avenue, SW, Washington, DC 20585, (202) 586-8800, www.eia.doe.gov; *International Energy Annual 2004* and *International Energy Outlook 2006*.

United Nations Statistics Division, New York, NY 10017, (800) 253-9646, Fax: (212) 963-4116, http://unstats.un.org; *Electric Power in Asia and the Pacific 2001 and 2002; Human Development Report 2006;* and *Statistical Yearbook*.

KOREA, NORTH - EMPLOYMENT

Euromonitor International, Inc., 224 S. Michigan Avenue, Suite 1500, Chicago, IL 60604, (312) 922-1115, Fax: (312) 922-1157, www.euromonitor.com; *International Marketing Data and Statistics 2008*.

M.E. Sharpe, 80 Business Park Drive, Armonk, NY 10504, (800) 541-6563, Fax: (914) 273-2106, www.mesharpe.com; *The Illustrated Book of World Rankings*.

Organisation for Economic Cooperation and Development (OECD), 2 rue Andre Pascal, F-75775 Paris Cedex 16, France, (Telephone in U.S. (202) 785-6323), (Fax in U.S. (202) 785-0350), www.oecd.org; *OECD Economic Survey - Korea 2007*.

The World Bank, 1818 H Street, NW, Washington, DC 20433, (202) 473-1000, Fax: (202) 477-6391, www.worldbank.org; *Korea, Democratic Republic of*.

KOREA, NORTH - ENERGY INDUSTRIES

Enerdata, 10 Rue Royale, 75008 Paris, France, www.enerdata.fr; *Global Energy Market Data*.

United Nations Statistics Division, New York, NY 10017, (800) 253-9646, Fax: (212) 963-4116, http://unstats.un.org; *Electric Power in Asia and the Pacific 2001 and 2002*.

KOREA, NORTH - ENVIRONMENTAL CONDITIONS

DSI Data Service Information, Xantener Strasse 51a, D-47495 Rheinberg, Germany, www.dsidata.com; *Campus Solution* and *DSI's Global Environmental Database*.

Economist Intelligence Unit, 111 West 57th Street, New York, NY 10019, (212) 554-0600, Fax: (212) 586-1181, www.eiu.com; *North Korea Country Report*.

International Institute for Environment and Development (IIED), 3 Endsleigh Street, London, England, WC1H 0DD, United Kingdom, www.iied.org; *Environment Urbanization*.

United Nations Statistics Division, New York, NY 10017, (800) 253-9646, Fax: (212) 963-4116, http://unstats.un.org; *World Statistics Pocketbook*.

KOREA, NORTH - EXPORTS

Asian Development Bank (ADB), PO Box 789, 0980 Manila, Philippines, www.adb.org; *Key Indicators of Developing Asian and Pacific Countries 2006*.

Central Intelligence Agency, Office of Public Affairs, Washington, DC 20505, (703) 482-0623, Fax: (703) 482-1739, www.cia.gov; *The World Factbook*.

Economist Intelligence Unit, 111 West 57th Street, New York, NY 10019, (212) 554-0600, Fax: (212) 586-1181, www.eiu.com; *North Korea Country Report*.

Euromonitor International, Inc., 224 S. Michigan Avenue, Suite 1500, Chicago, IL 60604, (312) 922-1115, Fax: (312) 922-1157, www.euromonitor.com; *International Marketing Data and Statistics 2008* and *The World Economic Factbook 2008*.

International Monetary Fund (IMF), 700 Nineteenth Street, NW, Washington, DC 20431, (202) 623-7000, Fax: (202) 623-4661, www.imf.org; *Direction of Trade Statistics Yearbook 2007*.

Organisation for Economic Cooperation and Development (OECD), 2 rue Andre Pascal, F-75775 Paris Cedex 16, France, (Telephone in U.S. (202) 785-6323), (Fax in U.S. (202) 785-0350), www.oecd.org; *OECD Economic Survey - Korea 2007*.

Palgrave Macmillan Ltd., Houndmills, Basingstoke, Hampshire, RG21 6XS, England, (Telephone in U.S. (888) 330-8477), (Fax in U.S. (800) 672-2054), www.palgrave.com; *The Statesman's Yearbook 2008*.

Taylor and Francis Group, An Informa Business, 2 Park Square, Milton Park, Abingdon, Oxford OX14 4RN, United Kingdom, (Dial from U.S. (212) 216-7800), (Fax from U.S. (212) 564-7854), www.tandf.co.uk; *The Europa World Year Book*.

United Nations Food and Agricultural Organization (FAO), Viale delle Terme di Caracalla, 00100 Rome, Italy, (Dial from U.S. (202) 653-2400), (Fax from U.S. (202) 653 5760), www.fao.org; *The State of Food and Agriculture (SOFA) 2006*.

Worldinformation.com, 2 Market Street, Saffron Walden, Essex CB10 1HZ, United Kingdom, www.worldinformation.com; The World of Information (www.worldinformation.com).

KOREA, NORTH - FEMALE WORKING POPULATION

See KOREA, NORTH - EMPLOYMENT

KOREA, NORTH - FERTILITY, HUMAN

Central Intelligence Agency, Office of Public Affairs, Washington, DC 20505, (703) 482-0623, Fax: (703) 482-1739, www.cia.gov; *The World Factbook*.

M.E. Sharpe, 80 Business Park Drive, Armonk, NY 10504, (800) 541-6563, Fax: (914) 273-2106, www.mesharpe.com; *The Illustrated Book of World Rankings*.

United Nations Statistics Division, New York, NY 10017, (800) 253-9646, Fax: (212) 963-4116, http://unstats.un.org; *Human Development Report 2006*.

The World Bank, 1818 H Street, NW, Washington, DC 20433, (202) 473-1000, Fax: (202) 477-6391, www.worldbank.org; *The World Bank Atlas 2003-2004*.

KOREA, NORTH - FERTILIZER INDUSTRY

United Nations Food and Agricultural Organization (FAO), Viale delle Terme di Caracalla, 00100 Rome, Italy, (Dial from U.S. (202) 653-2400), (Fax from U.S. (202) 653 5760), www.fao.org; *The State of Food and Agriculture (SOFA) 2006*.

United Nations Statistics Division, New York, NY 10017, (800) 253-9646, Fax: (212) 963-4116, http://unstats.un.org; *Statistical Yearbook*.

KOREA, NORTH - FETAL MORTALITY

See KOREA, NORTH - MORTALITY

KOREA, NORTH - FINANCE, PUBLIC

Asian Development Bank (ADB), PO Box 789, 0980 Manila, Philippines, www.adb.org; *Key Indicators of Developing Asian and Pacific Countries 2006*.

Bernan Essential Government Publications, 4611-F Assembly Drive, Lanham MD, 20706-4391, (301)

459-2255, Fax: (800) 865-3450, www.bernan.com; *National Accounts Statistics.*

Economist Intelligence Unit, 111 West 57th Street, New York, NY 10019, (212) 554-0600, Fax: (212) 586-1181, www.eiu.com; *North Korea Country Report.*

International Monetary Fund (IMF), 700 Nineteenth Street, NW, Washington, DC 20431, (202) 623-7000, Fax: (202) 623-4661, www.imf.org; *International Financial Statistics* and *International Financial Statistics Online Service.*

M.E. Sharpe, 80 Business Park Drive, Armonk, NY 10504, (800) 541-6563, Fax: (914) 273-2106, www.mesharpe.com; *The Illustrated Book of World Rankings.*

Palgrave Macmillan Ltd., Houndmills, Basingstoke, Hampshire, RG21 6XS, England, (Telephone in U.S. (888) 330-8477), (Fax in U.S. (800) 672-2054), www.palgrave.com; *The Statesman's Yearbook 2008.*

Pyongyang Square 2, www.pyongyangsquare.com; unpublished data.

Taylor and Francis Group, An Informa Business, 2 Park Square, Milton Park, Abingdon, Oxford OX14 4RN, United Kingdom, (Dial from U.S. (212) 216-7800), (Fax from U.S. (212) 564-7854), www.tandf.co.uk; *The Europa World Year Book.*

United Nations Food and Agricultural Organization (FAO), Viale delle Terme di Caracalla, 00100 Rome, Italy, (Dial from U.S. (202) 653-2400), (Fax from U.S. (202) 653 5760), www.fao.org; *The State of Food and Agriculture (SOFA) 2006.*

United Nations Statistics Division, New York, NY 10017, (800) 253-9646, Fax: (212) 963-4116, http://unstats.un.org; *Statistical Yearbook.*

The World Bank, 1818 H Street, NW, Washington, DC 20433, (202) 473-1000, Fax: (202) 477-6391, www.worldbank.org; *Korea, Democratic Republic of.*

KOREA, NORTH - FISHERIES

M.E. Sharpe, 80 Business Park Drive, Armonk, NY 10504, (800) 541-6563, Fax: (914) 273-2106, www.mesharpe.com; *The Illustrated Book of World Rankings.*

Palgrave Macmillan Ltd., Houndmills, Basingstoke, Hampshire, RG21 6XS, England, (Telephone in U.S. (888) 330-8477), (Fax in U.S. (800) 672-2054), www.palgrave.com; *The Statesman's Yearbook 2008.*

Taylor and Francis Group, An Informa Business, 2 Park Square, Milton Park, Abingdon, Oxford OX14 4RN, United Kingdom, (Dial from U.S. (212) 216-7800), (Fax from U.S. (212) 564-7854), www.tandf.co.uk; *The Europa World Year Book.*

United Nations Conference on Trade and Development (UNCTAD), DC2-1120, United Nations, New York, NY 10017, (212) 963-0027, www.unctad.org; *UNCTAD Commodity Yearbook.*

United Nations Food and Agricultural Organization (FAO), Viale delle Terme di Caracalla, 00100 Rome, Italy, (Dial from U.S. (202) 653-2400), (Fax from U.S. (202) 653 5760), www.fao.org; *FAO Yearbook of Fishery Statistics;* Fishery Databases; FISHSTAT Database. Subjects covered include: Aquaculture production, capture production, fishery commodities; and *The State of Food and Agriculture (SOFA) 2006.*

The World Bank, 1818 H Street, NW, Washington, DC 20433, (202) 473-1000, Fax: (202) 477-6391, www.worldbank.org; *Korea, Democratic Republic of.*

KOREA, NORTH - FOOD

United Nations Conference on Trade and Development (UNCTAD), DC2-1120, United Nations, New York, NY 10017, (212) 963-0027, www.unctad.org; *UNCTAD Commodity Yearbook.*

United Nations Food and Agricultural Organization (FAO), Viale delle Terme di Caracalla, 00100 Rome, Italy, (Dial from U.S. (202) 653-2400), (Fax from U.S. (202) 653 5760), www.fao.org; *FAO Production Yearbook 2002* and *The State of Food and Agriculture (SOFA) 2006.*

United Nations Statistics Division, New York, NY 10017, (800) 253-9646, Fax: (212) 963-4116, http://unstats.un.org; *Human Development Report 2006.*

KOREA, NORTH - FOREIGN EXCHANGE RATES

Asian Development Bank (ADB), PO Box 789, 0980 Manila, Philippines, www.adb.org; *Key Indicators of Developing Asian and Pacific Countries 2006.*

Central Intelligence Agency, Office of Public Affairs, Washington, DC 20505, (703) 482-0623, Fax: (703) 482-1739, www.cia.gov; *The World Factbook.*

Economist Intelligence Unit, 111 West 57th Street, New York, NY 10019, (212) 554-0600, Fax: (212) 586-1181, www.eiu.com; *Business Asia.*

Euromonitor International, Inc., 224 S. Michigan Avenue, Suite 1500, Chicago, IL 60604, (312) 922-1115, Fax: (312) 922-1157, www.euromonitor.com; *International Marketing Data and Statistics 2008* and *The World Economic Factbook 2008.*

Taylor and Francis Group, An Informa Business, 2 Park Square, Milton Park, Abingdon, Oxford OX14 4RN, United Kingdom, (Dial from U.S. (212) 216-7800), (Fax from U.S. (212) 564-7854), www.tandf.co.uk; *The Europa World Year Book.*

United Nations Statistics Division, New York, NY 10017, (800) 253-9646, Fax: (212) 963-4116, http://unstats.un.org; *World Statistics Pocketbook.*

Worldinformation.com, 2 Market Street, Saffron Walden, Essex CB10 1HZ, United Kingdom, www.worldinformation.com; The World of Information (www.worldinformation.com).

KOREA, NORTH - FORESTS AND FORESTRY

American Forest Paper Association (AFPA), 1111 Nineteenth Street, NW, Suite 800, Washington, DC 20036, (800) 878-8878, www.afandpa.org; *2007 Annual Statistics of Paper, Paperboard, and Wood Pulp.*

Economist Intelligence Unit, 111 West 57th Street, New York, NY 10019, (212) 554-0600, Fax: (212) 586-1181, www.eiu.com; *Business Asia.*

M.E. Sharpe, 80 Business Park Drive, Armonk, NY 10504, (800) 541-6563, Fax: (914) 273-2106, www.mesharpe.com; *The Illustrated Book of World Rankings.*

Palgrave Macmillan Ltd., Houndmills, Basingstoke, Hampshire, RG21 6XS, England, (Telephone in U.S. (888) 330-8477), (Fax in U.S. (800) 672-2054), www.palgrave.com; *The Statesman's Yearbook 2008.*

Taylor and Francis Group, An Informa Business, 2 Park Square, Milton Park, Abingdon, Oxford OX14 4RN, United Kingdom, (Dial from U.S. (212) 216-7800), (Fax from U.S. (212) 564-7854), www.tandf.co.uk; *The Europa World Year Book.*

UNESCO Institute for Statistics, C.P. 6128 Succursale Centre-Ville, Montreal, Quebec, H3C 3J7 Canada, (Dial from U.S. (514) 343-6880), (Fax from U.S. (514) 343 6882), www.uis.unesco.org; *Statistical Tables.*

United Nations Conference on Trade and Development (UNCTAD), DC2-1120, United Nations, New York, NY 10017, (212) 963-0027, www.unctad.org; *UNCTAD Commodity Yearbook.*

United Nations Food and Agricultural Organization (FAO), Viale delle Terme di Caracalla, 00100 Rome, Italy, (Dial from U.S. (202) 653-2400), (Fax from U.S. (202) 653 5760), www.fao.org; *FAO Yearbook of Forest Products* and *The State of Food and Agriculture (SOFA) 2006.*

United Nations Statistics Division, New York, NY 10017, (800) 253-9646, Fax: (212) 963-4116, http://unstats.un.org; *Statistical Yearbook.*

The World Bank, 1818 H Street, NW, Washington, DC 20433, (202) 473-1000, Fax: (202) 477-6391, www.worldbank.org; *Korea, Democratic Republic of.*

KOREA, NORTH - GAS PRODUCTION

See KOREA, NORTH - MINERAL INDUSTRIES

KOREA, NORTH - GEOGRAPHIC INFORMATION SYSTEMS

M.E. Sharpe, 80 Business Park Drive, Armonk, NY 10504, (800) 541-6563, Fax: (914) 273-2106, www.mesharpe.com; *The Illustrated Book of World Rankings.*

KOREA, NORTH - GROSS DOMESTIC PRODUCT

Asian Development Bank (ADB), PO Box 789, 0980 Manila, Philippines, www.adb.org; *Key Indicators of Developing Asian and Pacific Countries 2006.*

Economist Intelligence Unit, 111 West 57th Street, New York, NY 10019, (212) 554-0600, Fax: (212) 586-1181, www.eiu.com; *Business Asia* and *North Korea Country Report.*

Euromonitor International, Inc., 224 S. Michigan Avenue, Suite 1500, Chicago, IL 60604, (312) 922-1115, Fax: (312) 922-1157, www.euromonitor.com; *International Marketing Data and Statistics 2008* and *The World Economic Factbook 2008.*

M.E. Sharpe, 80 Business Park Drive, Armonk, NY 10504, (800) 541-6563, Fax: (914) 273-2106, www.mesharpe.com; *The Illustrated Book of World Rankings.*

United Nations Statistics Division, New York, NY 10017, (800) 253-9646, Fax: (212) 963-4116, http://unstats.un.org; *Human Development Report 2006* and *National Accounts Statistics: Compendium of Income Distribution Statistics.*

Worldinformation.com, 2 Market Street, Saffron Walden, Essex CB10 1HZ, United Kingdom, www.worldinformation.com; The World of Information (www.worldinformation.com).

KOREA, NORTH - GROSS NATIONAL PRODUCT

Asian Development Bank (ADB), PO Box 789, 0980 Manila, Philippines, www.adb.org; *Key Indicators of Developing Asian and Pacific Countries 2006.*

Euromonitor International, Inc., 224 S. Michigan Avenue, Suite 1500, Chicago, IL 60604, (312) 922-1115, Fax: (312) 922-1157, www.euromonitor.com; *International Marketing Data and Statistics 2008.*

M.E. Sharpe, 80 Business Park Drive, Armonk, NY 10504, (800) 541-6563, Fax: (914) 273-2106, www.mesharpe.com; *The Illustrated Book of World Rankings.*

Palgrave Macmillan Ltd., Houndmills, Basingstoke, Hampshire, RG21 6XS, England, (Telephone in U.S. (888) 330-8477), (Fax in U.S. (800) 672-2054), www.palgrave.com; *The Statesman's Yearbook 2008.*

U.S. Department of State (DOS), 2201 C Street NW, Washington, DC 20520, (202) 647-4000, www.state.gov; *World Military Expenditures and Arms Transfers (WMEAT).*

The World Bank, 1818 H Street, NW, Washington, DC 20433, (202) 473-1000, Fax: (202) 477-6391, www.worldbank.org; *The World Bank Atlas 2003-2004.*

KOREA, NORTH - HEMP FIBRE PRODUCTION

See KOREA, NORTH - TEXTILE INDUSTRY

KOREA, NORTH - HIDES AND SKINS INDUSTRY

United Nations Food and Agricultural Organization (FAO), Viale delle Terme di Caracalla, 00100 Rome, Italy, (Dial from U.S. (202) 653-2400), (Fax from U.S. (202) 653 5760), www.fao.org; *FAO Production Yearbook 2002.*

KOREA, NORTH - HOUSING

Euromonitor International, Inc., 224 S. Michigan Avenue, Suite 1500, Chicago, IL 60604, (312) 922-1115, Fax: (312) 922-1157, www.euromonitor.com; *World Marketing Data and Statistics.*

M.E. Sharpe, 80 Business Park Drive, Armonk, NY 10504, (800) 541-6563, Fax: (914) 273-2106, www.mesharpe.com; *The Illustrated Book of World Rankings.*

KOREA, NORTH - ILLITERATE PERSONS

Euromonitor International, Inc., 224 S. Michigan Avenue, Suite 1500, Chicago, IL 60604, (312) 922-1115, Fax: (312) 922-1157, www.euromonitor.com; *The World Economic Factbook 2008.*

United Nations Statistics Division, New York, NY 10017, (800) 253-9646, Fax: (212) 963-4116, http://unstats.un.org; *Human Development Report 2006.*

KOREA, NORTH - IMPORTS

Asian Development Bank (ADB), PO Box 789, 0980 Manila, Philippines, www.adb.org; *Key Indicators of Developing Asian and Pacific Countries 2006.*

Central Intelligence Agency, Office of Public Affairs, Washington, DC 20505, (703) 482-0623, Fax: (703) 482-1739, www.cia.gov; *The World Factbook.*

Economist Intelligence Unit, 111 West 57th Street, New York, NY 10019, (212) 554-0600, Fax: (212) 586-1181, www.eiu.com; *North Korea Country Report.*

Euromonitor International, Inc., 224 S. Michigan Avenue, Suite 1500, Chicago, IL 60604, (312) 922-1115, Fax: (312) 922-1157, www.euromonitor.com; *International Marketing Data and Statistics 2008* and *The World Economic Factbook 2008.*

International Monetary Fund (IMF), 700 Nineteenth Street, NW, Washington, DC 20431, (202) 623-7000, Fax: (202) 623-4661, www.imf.org; *Direction of Trade Statistics Yearbook 2007.*

Organisation for Economic Cooperation and Development (OECD), 2 rue Andre Pascal, F-75775 Paris Cedex 16, France, (Telephone in U.S. (202) 785-6323), (Fax in U.S. (202) 785-0350), www.oecd.org; *OECD Economic Survey - Korea 2007.*

Palgrave Macmillan Ltd., Houndmills, Basingstoke, Hampshire, RG21 6XS, England, (Telephone in U.S. (888) 330-8477), (Fax in U.S. (800) 672-2054), www.palgrave.com; *The Statesman's Yearbook 2008.*

Taylor and Francis Group, An Informa Business, 2 Park Square, Milton Park, Abingdon, Oxford OX14 4RN, United Kingdom, (Dial from U.S. (212) 216-7800), (Fax from U.S. (212) 564-7854), www.tandf.co.uk; *The Europa World Year Book.*

United Nations Food and Agricultural Organization (FAO), Viale delle Terme di Caracalla, 00100 Rome, Italy, (Dial from U.S. (202) 653-2400), (Fax from U.S. (202) 653 5760), www.fao.org; *The State of Food and Agriculture (SOFA) 2006.*

Worldinformation.com, 2 Market Street, Saffron Walden, Essex CB10 1HZ, United Kingdom, www.worldinformation.com; The World of Information (www.worldinformation.com).

KOREA, NORTH - INDUSTRIAL PRODUCTIVITY

Euromonitor International, Inc., 224 S. Michigan Avenue, Suite 1500, Chicago, IL 60604, (312) 922-1115, Fax: (312) 922-1157, www.euromonitor.com; *International Marketing Data and Statistics 2008.*

M.E. Sharpe, 80 Business Park Drive, Armonk, NY 10504, (800) 541-6563, Fax: (914) 273-2106, www.mesharpe.com; *The Illustrated Book of World Rankings.*

KOREA, NORTH - INDUSTRIAL PROPERTY

United Nations Statistics Division, New York, NY 10017, (800) 253-9646, Fax: (212) 963-4116, http://unstats.un.org; *Statistical Yearbook.*

World Intellectual Property Organization (WIPO), PO Box 18, CH-1211 Geneva 20, Switzerland, www.wipo.int; *Industrial Property Statistics* and *Industrial Property Statistics Online Directory.*

KOREA, NORTH - INDUSTRIES

Central Intelligence Agency, Office of Public Affairs, Washington, DC 20505, (703) 482-0623, Fax: (703) 482-1739, www.cia.gov; *The World Factbook.*

Economist Intelligence Unit, 111 West 57th Street, New York, NY 10019, (212) 554-0600, Fax: (212) 586-1181, www.eiu.com; *North Korea Country Report.*

Euromonitor International, Inc., 224 S. Michigan Avenue, Suite 1500, Chicago, IL 60604, (312) 922-1115, Fax: (312) 922-1157, www.euromonitor.com; *International Marketing Data and Statistics 2008; The World Economic Factbook 2008;* and *World Marketing Data and Statistics.*

M.E. Sharpe, 80 Business Park Drive, Armonk, NY 10504, (800) 541-6563, Fax: (914) 273-2106, www.mesharpe.com; *The Illustrated Book of World Rankings.*

Palgrave Macmillan Ltd., Houndmills, Basingstoke, Hampshire, RG21 6XS, England, (Telephone in U.S. (888) 330-8477), (Fax in U.S. (800) 672-2054), www.palgrave.com; *The Statesman's Yearbook 2008.*

Pyongyang Square 2, www.pyongyangsquare.com; unpublished data.

Taylor and Francis Group, An Informa Business, 2 Park Square, Milton Park, Abingdon, Oxford OX14 4RN, United Kingdom, (Dial from U.S. (212) 216-7800), (Fax from U.S. (212) 564-7854), www.tandf.co.uk; *The Europa World Year Book.*

United Nations Industrial Development Organization (UNIDO), 1 United Nations Plaza, New York, NY 10017, (212) 963 6890, Fax: (212) 963-7904, http://unido.org; Industrial Statistics Database 2008 (INDSTAT) and *The International Yearbook of Industrial Statistics 2008.*

The World Bank, 1818 H Street, NW, Washington, DC 20433, (202) 473-1000, Fax: (202) 477-6391, www.worldbank.org; *Korea, Democratic Republic of.*

KOREA, NORTH - INTERNATIONAL FINANCE

Asian Development Bank (ADB), PO Box 789, 0980 Manila, Philippines, www.adb.org; *Key Indicators of Developing Asian and Pacific Countries 2006.*

KOREA, NORTH - INTERNATIONAL STATISTICS

Asian Development Bank (ADB), PO Box 789, 0980 Manila, Philippines, www.adb.org; *Key Indicators of Developing Asian and Pacific Countries 2006.*

KOREA, NORTH - INTERNATIONAL TRADE

Asian Development Bank (ADB), PO Box 789, 0980 Manila, Philippines, www.adb.org; *Key Indicators of Developing Asian and Pacific Countries 2006.*

Economist Intelligence Unit, 111 West 57th Street, New York, NY 10019, (212) 554-0600, Fax: (212) 586-1181, www.eiu.com; *Business Asia* and *North Korea Country Report.*

Euromonitor International, Inc., 224 S. Michigan Avenue, Suite 1500, Chicago, IL 60604, (312) 922-1115, Fax: (312) 922-1157, www.euromonitor.com; *International Marketing Data and Statistics 2008; The World Economic Factbook 2008;* and *World Marketing Data and Statistics.*

M.E. Sharpe, 80 Business Park Drive, Armonk, NY 10504, (800) 541-6563, Fax: (914) 273-2106, www.mesharpe.com; *The Illustrated Book of World Rankings.*

Organisation for Economic Cooperation and Development (OECD), 2 rue Andre Pascal, F-75775 Paris Cedex 16, France, (Telephone in U.S. (202) 785-6323), (Fax in U.S. (202) 785-0350), www.oecd.org; *OECD Economic Survey - Korea 2007.*

Palgrave Macmillan Ltd., Houndmills, Basingstoke, Hampshire, RG21 6XS, England, (Telephone in U.S. (888) 330-8477), (Fax in U.S. (800) 672-2054), www.palgrave.com; *The Statesman's Yearbook 2008.*

Taylor and Francis Group, An Informa Business, 2 Park Square, Milton Park, Abingdon, Oxford OX14 4RN, United Kingdom, (Dial from U.S. (212) 216-7800), (Fax from U.S. (212) 564-7854), www.tandf.co.uk; *The Europa World Year Book.*

United Nations Conference on Trade and Development (UNCTAD), DC2-1120, United Nations, New York, NY 10017, (212) 963-0027, www.unctad.org; *UNCTAD Commodity Yearbook.*

United Nations Food and Agricultural Organization (FAO), Viale delle Terme di Caracalla, 00100 Rome, Italy, (Dial from U.S. (202) 653-2400), (Fax from U.S. (202) 653 5760), www.fao.org; *FAO Trade Yearbook* and *The State of Food and Agriculture (SOFA) 2006.*

The World Bank, 1818 H Street, NW, Washington, DC 20433, (202) 473-1000, Fax: (202) 477-6391, www.worldbank.org; *Korea, Democratic Republic of.*

World Trade Organization (WTO), Centre William Rappard, Rue de Lausanne 154, CH-1211 Geneva 21, Switzerland, www.wto.org; *International Trade Statistics 2006.*

KOREA, NORTH - INTERNET USERS

International Telecommunication Union (ITU), Place des Nations, 1211 Geneva 20, Switzerland, www.itu.int; *World Telecommunication/ICT Indicators Database on CD-ROM; World Telecommunication/ICT Indicators Database Online;* and *Yearbook of Statistics - Telecommunication Services (Chronological Time Series 1997-2006).*

The World Bank, 1818 H Street, NW, Washington, DC 20433, (202) 473-1000, Fax: (202) 477-6391, www.worldbank.org; *Korea, Democratic Republic of.*

KOREA, NORTH - IRON AND IRON ORE PRODUCTION

See KOREA, NORTH - MINERAL INDUSTRIES

KOREA, NORTH - IRRIGATION

Euromonitor International, Inc., 224 S. Michigan Avenue, Suite 1500, Chicago, IL 60604, (312) 922-1115, Fax: (312) 922-1157, www.euromonitor.com; *International Marketing Data and Statistics 2008.*

KOREA, NORTH - LABOR

Central Intelligence Agency, Office of Public Affairs, Washington, DC 20505, (703) 482-0623, Fax: (703) 482-1739, www.cia.gov; *The World Factbook.*

Economist Intelligence Unit, 111 West 57th Street, New York, NY 10019, (212) 554-0600, Fax: (212) 586-1181, www.eiu.com; *Business Asia.*

Euromonitor International, Inc., 224 S. Michigan Avenue, Suite 1500, Chicago, IL 60604, (312) 922-1115, Fax: (312) 922-1157, www.euromonitor.com; *International Marketing Data and Statistics 2008* and *World Marketing Data and Statistics.*

M.E. Sharpe, 80 Business Park Drive, Armonk, NY 10504, (800) 541-6563, Fax: (914) 273-2106, www.mesharpe.com; *The Illustrated Book of World Rankings.*

Organisation for Economic Cooperation and Development (OECD), 2 rue Andre Pascal, F-75775 Paris Cedex 16, France, (Telephone in U.S. (202) 785-6323), (Fax in U.S. (202) 785-0350), www.oecd.org; *OECD Economic Survey - Korea 2007.*

Palgrave Macmillan Ltd., Houndmills, Basingstoke, Hampshire, RG21 6XS, England, (Telephone in U.S. (888) 330-8477), (Fax in U.S. (800) 672-2054), www.palgrave.com; *The Statesman's Yearbook 2008.*

Pyongyang Square 2, www.pyongyangsquare.com; unpublished data.

Taylor and Francis Group, An Informa Business, 2 Park Square, Milton Park, Abingdon, Oxford OX14 4RN, United Kingdom, (Dial from U.S. (212) 216-7800), (Fax from U.S. (212) 564-7854), www.tandf.co.uk; *The Europa World Year Book.*

United Nations Food and Agricultural Organization (FAO), Viale delle Terme di Caracalla, 00100 Rome, Italy, (Dial from U.S. (202) 653-2400), (Fax from U.S. (202) 653 5760), www.fao.org; *The State of Food and Agriculture (SOFA) 2006.*

United Nations Statistics Division, New York, NY 10017, (800) 253-9646, Fax: (212) 963-4116, http://unstats.un.org; *Human Development Report 2006.*

The World Bank, 1818 H Street, NW, Washington, DC 20433, (202) 473-1000, Fax: (202) 477-6391, www.worldbank.org; *The World Bank Atlas 2003-2004.*

KOREA, NORTH - LAND USE

Central Intelligence Agency, Office of Public Affairs, Washington, DC 20505, (703) 482-0623, Fax: (703) 482-1739, www.cia.gov; *The World Factbook.*

Euromonitor International, Inc., 224 S. Michigan Avenue, Suite 1500, Chicago, IL 60604, (312) 922-1115, Fax: (312) 922-1157, www.euromonitor.com; *International Marketing Data and Statistics 2008.*

United Nations Food and Agricultural Organization (FAO), Viale delle Terme di Caracalla, 00100 Rome, Italy, (Dial from U.S. (202) 653-2400), (Fax from U.S. (202) 653 5760), www.fao.org; *FAO Production Yearbook 2002.*

KOREA, NORTH - LIBRARIES

M.E. Sharpe, 80 Business Park Drive, Armonk, NY 10504, (800) 541-6563, Fax: (914) 273-2106, www.mesharpe.com; *The Illustrated Book of World Rankings.*

KOREA, NORTH - LIFE EXPECTANCY

Central Intelligence Agency, Office of Public Affairs, Washington, DC 20505, (703) 482-0623, Fax: (703) 482-1739, www.cia.gov; *The World Factbook.*

Economist Intelligence Unit, 111 West 57th Street, New York, NY 10019, (212) 554-0600, Fax: (212) 586-1181, www.eiu.com; *Business Asia.*

Euromonitor International, Inc., 224 S. Michigan Avenue, Suite 1500, Chicago, IL 60604, (312) 922-1115, Fax: (312) 922-1157, www.euromonitor.com; *The World Economic Factbook 2008.*

Palgrave Macmillan Ltd., Houndmills, Basingstoke, Hampshire, RG21 6XS, England, (Telephone in U.S. (888) 330-8477), (Fax in U.S. (800) 672-2054), www.palgrave.com; *The Statesman's Yearbook 2008.*

United Nations Statistics Division, New York, NY 10017, (800) 253-9646, Fax: (212) 963-4116, http://unstats.un.org; *Human Development Report 2006* and *World Statistics Pocketbook.*

The World Bank, 1818 H Street, NW, Washington, DC 20433, (202) 473-1000, Fax: (202) 477-6391, www.worldbank.org; *The World Bank Atlas 2003-2004.*

KOREA, NORTH - LITERACY

Euromonitor International, Inc., 224 S. Michigan Avenue, Suite 1500, Chicago, IL 60604, (312) 922-1115, Fax: (312) 922-1157, www.euromonitor.com; *World Marketing Data and Statistics.*

KOREA, NORTH - LIVESTOCK

Euromonitor International, Inc., 224 S. Michigan Avenue, Suite 1500, Chicago, IL 60604, (312) 922-1115, Fax: (312) 922-1157, www.euromonitor.com; *International Marketing Data and Statistics 2008.*

M.E. Sharpe, 80 Business Park Drive, Armonk, NY 10504, (800) 541-6563, Fax: (914) 273-2106, www.mesharpe.com; *The Illustrated Book of World Rankings.*

Palgrave Macmillan Ltd., Houndmills, Basingstoke, Hampshire, RG21 6XS, England, (Telephone in U.S. (888) 330-8477), (Fax in U.S. (800) 672-2054), www.palgrave.com; *The Statesman's Yearbook 2008.*

Taylor and Francis Group, An Informa Business, 2 Park Square, Milton Park, Abingdon, Oxford OX14 4RN, United Kingdom, (Dial from U.S. (212) 216-7800), (Fax from U.S. (212) 564-7854), www.tandf.co.uk; *The Europa World Year Book.*

United Nations Conference on Trade and Development (UNCTAD), DC2-1120, United Nations, New York, NY 10017, (212) 963-0027, www.unctad.org; *UNCTAD Commodity Yearbook.*

United Nations Food and Agricultural Organization (FAO), Viale delle Terme di Caracalla, 00100 Rome, Italy, (Dial from U.S. (202) 653-2400), (Fax from U.S. (202) 653 5760), www.fao.org; *FAO Production Yearbook 2002* and *The State of Food and Agriculture (SOFA) 2006.*

United Nations Statistics Division, New York, NY 10017, (800) 253-9646, Fax: (212) 963-4116, http://unstats.un.org; *Statistical Yearbook.*

KOREA, NORTH - LOCAL TAXATION

Euromonitor International, Inc., 224 S. Michigan Avenue, Suite 1500, Chicago, IL 60604, (312) 922-1115, Fax: (312) 922-1157, www.euromonitor.com; *International Marketing Data and Statistics 2008.*

KOREA, NORTH - MANUFACTURES

Asian Development Bank (ADB), PO Box 789, 0980 Manila, Philippines, www.adb.org; *Key Indicators of Developing Asian and Pacific Countries 2006.*

M.E. Sharpe, 80 Business Park Drive, Armonk, NY 10504, (800) 541-6563, Fax: (914) 273-2106, www.mesharpe.com; *The Illustrated Book of World Rankings.*

Organisation for Economic Cooperation and Development (OECD), 2 rue Andre Pascal, F-75775 Paris Cedex 16, France, (Telephone in U.S. (202) 785-6323), (Fax in U.S. (202) 785-0350), www.oecd.org; *OECD Economic Survey - Korea 2007.*

KOREA, NORTH - MARRIAGE

M.E. Sharpe, 80 Business Park Drive, Armonk, NY 10504, (800) 541-6563, Fax: (914) 273-2106, www.mesharpe.com; *The Illustrated Book of World Rankings.*

United Nations Statistics Division, New York, NY 10017, (800) 253-9646, Fax: (212) 963-4116, http://unstats.un.org; *Demographic Yearbook.*

KOREA, NORTH - MEAT PRODUCTION

See KOREA, NORTH - LIVESTOCK

KOREA, NORTH - MILK PRODUCTION

See KOREA, NORTH - DAIRY PROCESSING

KOREA, NORTH - MINERAL INDUSTRIES

Asian Development Bank (ADB), PO Box 789, 0980 Manila, Philippines, www.adb.org; *Key Indicators of Developing Asian and Pacific Countries 2006.*

M.E. Sharpe, 80 Business Park Drive, Armonk, NY 10504, (800) 541-6563, Fax: (914) 273-2106, www.mesharpe.com; *The Illustrated Book of World Rankings.*

Organisation for Economic Cooperation and Development (OECD), 2 rue Andre Pascal, F-75775 Paris Cedex 16, France, (Telephone in U.S. (202) 785-6323), (Fax in U.S. (202) 785-0350), www.oecd.org; *OECD Economic Survey - Korea 2007.*

Palgrave Macmillan Ltd., Houndmills, Basingstoke, Hampshire, RG21 6XS, England, (Telephone in U.S. (888) 330-8477), (Fax in U.S. (800) 672-2054), www.palgrave.com; *The Statesman's Yearbook 2008.*

Taylor and Francis Group, An Informa Business, 2 Park Square, Milton Park, Abingdon, Oxford OX14 4RN, United Kingdom, (Dial from U.S. (212) 216-7800), (Fax from U.S. (212) 564-7854), www.tandf.co.uk; *The Europa World Year Book.*

United Nations Conference on Trade and Development (UNCTAD), DC2-1120, United Nations, New York, NY 10017, (212) 963-0027, www.unctad.org; *UNCTAD Commodity Yearbook.*

United Nations Statistics Division, New York, NY 10017, (800) 253-9646, Fax: (212) 963-4116, http://unstats.un.org; *Statistical Yearbook.*

KOREA, NORTH - MONEY SUPPLY

Asian Development Bank (ADB), PO Box 789, 0980 Manila, Philippines, www.adb.org; *Key Indicators of Developing Asian and Pacific Countries 2006.*

Economist Intelligence Unit, 111 West 57th Street, New York, NY 10019, (212) 554-0600, Fax: (212) 586-1181, www.eiu.com; *North Korea Country Report.*

Euromonitor International, Inc., 224 S. Michigan Avenue, Suite 1500, Chicago, IL 60604, (312) 922-1115, Fax: (312) 922-1157, www.euromonitor.com; *International Marketing Data and Statistics 2008.*

Organisation for Economic Cooperation and Development (OECD), 2 rue Andre Pascal, F-75775 Paris Cedex 16, France, (Telephone in U.S. (202) 785-6323), (Fax in U.S. (202) 785-0350), www.oecd.org; *OECD Economic Survey - Korea 2007.*

The World Bank, 1818 H Street, NW, Washington, DC 20433, (202) 473-1000, Fax: (202) 477-6391, www.worldbank.org; *Korea, Democratic Republic of.*

KOREA, NORTH - MORTALITY

Central Intelligence Agency, Office of Public Affairs, Washington, DC 20505, (703) 482-0623, Fax: (703) 482-1739, www.cia.gov; *The World Factbook.*

Euromonitor International, Inc., 224 S. Michigan Avenue, Suite 1500, Chicago, IL 60604, (312) 922-1115, Fax: (312) 922-1157, www.euromonitor.com; *International Marketing Data and Statistics 2008* and *The World Economic Factbook 2008.*

Palgrave Macmillan Ltd., Houndmills, Basingstoke, Hampshire, RG21 6XS, England, (Telephone in U.S. (888) 330-8477), (Fax in U.S. (800) 672-2054), www.palgrave.com; *The Statesman's Yearbook 2008.*

Taylor and Francis Group, An Informa Business, 2 Park Square, Milton Park, Abingdon, Oxford OX14 4RN, United Kingdom, (Dial from U.S. (212) 216-7800), (Fax from U.S. (212) 564-7854), www.tandf.co.uk; *The Europa World Year Book.*

UNICEF, 3 United Nations Plaza, New York, NY 10017, (800) 253-9646, Fax: (212) 887-7465, www.unicef.org; *The State of the World's Children 2008.*

United Nations Statistics Division, New York, NY 10017, (800) 253-9646, Fax: (212) 963-4116, http://unstats.un.org; *Demographic Yearbook; Human Development Report 2006; Statistical Yearbook;* and *World Statistics Pocketbook.*

The World Bank, 1818 H Street, NW, Washington, DC 20433, (202) 473-1000, Fax: (202) 477-6391, www.worldbank.org; *The World Bank Atlas 2003-2004.*

World Health Organization (WHO), Avenue Appia 20, 1211 Geneve 27, Switzerland, (Telephone in U.S. (212) 331-9081), www.who.int; The WHO Global Atlas of Infectious Diseases.

KOREA, NORTH - MOTION PICTURES

Palgrave Macmillan Ltd., Houndmills, Basingstoke, Hampshire, RG21 6XS, England, (Telephone in U.S. (888) 330-8477), (Fax in U.S. (800) 672-2054), www.palgrave.com; *The Statesman's Yearbook 2008.*

KOREA, NORTH - MOTOR VEHICLES

International Road Federation (IFR), Madison Place, 500 Montgomery Street, 5th Floor, Alexandria, VA 22314, (703) 535-1001, Fax: (703) 535-1007, www.irfnet.org; *World Road Statistics 2006.*

KOREA, NORTH - MUSEUMS

M.E. Sharpe, 80 Business Park Drive, Armonk, NY 10504, (800) 541-6563, Fax: (914) 273-2106, www.mesharpe.com; *The Illustrated Book of World Rankings.*

KOREA, NORTH - NATURAL GAS PRODUCTION

See KOREA, NORTH - MINERAL INDUSTRIES

KOREA, NORTH - NUTRITION

Asian Development Bank (ADB), PO Box 789, 0980 Manila, Philippines, www.adb.org; *Key Indicators of Developing Asian and Pacific Countries 2006.*

United Nations Food and Agricultural Organization (FAO), Viale delle Terme di Caracalla, 00100 Rome, Italy, (Dial from U.S. (202) 653-2400), (Fax from U.S. (202) 653 5760), www.fao.org; *The State of Food and Agriculture (SOFA) 2006.*

KOREA, NORTH - OATS PRODUCTION

See KOREA, NORTH - CROPS

KOREA, NORTH - OLDER PEOPLE

M.E. Sharpe, 80 Business Park Drive, Armonk, NY 10504, (800) 541-6563, Fax: (914) 273-2106, www.mesharpe.com; *The Illustrated Book of World Rankings.*

KOREA, NORTH - PAPER

See KOREA, NORTH - FORESTS AND FORESTRY

KOREA, NORTH - PEANUT PRODUCTION

See KOREA, NORTH - CROPS

KOREA, NORTH - PESTICIDES

United Nations Food and Agricultural Organization (FAO), Viale delle Terme di Caracalla, 00100 Rome, Italy, (Dial from U.S. (202) 653-2400), (Fax from U.S. (202) 653 5760), www.fao.org; *The State of Food and Agriculture (SOFA) 2006.*

KOREA, NORTH - PETROLEUM INDUSTRY AND TRADE

Asian Development Bank (ADB), PO Box 789, 0980 Manila, Philippines, www.adb.org; *Key Indicators of Developing Asian and Pacific Countries 2006.*

M.E. Sharpe, 80 Business Park Drive, Armonk, NY 10504, (800) 541-6563, Fax: (914) 273-2106, www.mesharpe.com; *The Illustrated Book of World Rankings.*

Palgrave Macmillan Ltd., Houndmills, Basingstoke, Hampshire, RG21 6XS, England, (Telephone in U.S. (888) 330-8477), (Fax in U.S. (800) 672-2054), www.palgrave.com; *The Statesman's Yearbook 2008.*

PennWell Corporation, 1421 South Sheridan Road, Tulsa, OK 74112, (918) 835-3161, www.pennwell.com; *International Petroleum Encyclopedia 2007.*

U.S. Department of Energy (DOE), Energy Information Administration (EIA), 1000 Independence Avenue, SW, Washington, DC 20585, (202) 586-8800, www.eia.doe.gov; *International Energy Annual 2004* and *International Energy Outlook 2006.*

United Nations Conference on Trade and Development (UNCTAD), DC2-1120, United Nations, New York, NY 10017, (212) 963-0027, www.unctad.org; *UNCTAD Commodity Yearbook.*

United Nations Food and Agricultural Organization (FAO), Viale delle Terme di Caracalla, 00100 Rome, Italy, (Dial from U.S. (202) 653-2400), (Fax from U.S. (202) 653 5760), www.fao.org; *The State of Food and Agriculture (SOFA) 2006.*

KOREA, NORTH - PHOSPHATES PRODUCTION

See KOREA, NORTH - MINERAL INDUSTRIES

KOREA, NORTH - POLITICAL SCIENCE

Asian Development Bank (ADB), PO Box 789, 0980 Manila, Philippines, www.adb.org; *Key Indicators of Developing Asian and Pacific Countries 2006.*

Central Intelligence Agency, Office of Public Affairs, Washington, DC 20505, (703) 482-0623, Fax: (703) 482-1739, www.cia.gov; *The World Factbook.*

Palgrave Macmillan Ltd., Houndmills, Basingstoke, Hampshire, RG21 6XS, England, (Telephone in U.S. (888) 330-8477), (Fax in U.S. (800) 672-2054), www.palgrave.com; *The Statesman's Yearbook 2008.*

Pyongyang Square 2, www.pyongyangsquare.com; unpublished data.

Taylor and Francis Group, An Informa Business, 2 Park Square, Milton Park, Abingdon, Oxford OX14 4RN, United Kingdom, (Dial from U.S. (212) 216-7800), (Fax from U.S. (212) 564-7854), www.tandf.co.uk; *The Europa World Year Book.*

United Nations Statistics Division, New York, NY 10017, (800) 253-9646, Fax: (212) 963-4116, http://unstats.un.org; *National Accounts Statistics: Compendium of Income Distribution Statistics.*

KOREA, NORTH - POPULATION

Asian Development Bank (ADB), PO Box 789, 0980 Manila, Philippines, www.adb.org; *Key Indicators of Developing Asian and Pacific Countries 2006.*

Central Intelligence Agency, Office of Public Affairs, Washington, DC 20505, (703) 482-0623, Fax: (703) 482-1739, www.cia.gov; *The World Factbook.*

Economist Intelligence Unit, 111 West 57th Street, New York, NY 10019, (212) 554-0600, Fax: (212) 586-1181, www.eiu.com; *Business Asia* and *North Korea Country Report.*

Euromonitor International, Inc., 224 S. Michigan Avenue, Suite 1500, Chicago, IL 60604, (312) 922-1115, Fax: (312) 922-1157, www.euromonitor.com; *International Marketing Data and Statistics 2008* and *The World Economic Factbook 2008.*

M.E. Sharpe, 80 Business Park Drive, Armonk, NY 10504, (800) 541-6563, Fax: (914) 273-2106, www.mesharpe.com; *The Illustrated Book of World Rankings.*

Palgrave Macmillan Ltd., Houndmills, Basingstoke, Hampshire, RG21 6XS, England, (Telephone in U.S. (888) 330-8477), (Fax in U.S. (800) 672-2054), www.palgrave.com; *The Statesman's Yearbook 2008.*

Taylor and Francis Group, An Informa Business, 2 Park Square, Milton Park, Abingdon, Oxford OX14 4RN, United Kingdom, (Dial from U.S. (212) 216-7800), (Fax from U.S. (212) 564-7854), www.tandf.co.uk; *The Europa World Year Book.*

U.S. Department of State (DOS), 2201 C Street NW, Washington, DC 20520, (202) 647-4000, www.state.gov; *World Military Expenditures and Arms Transfers (WMEAT).*

United Nations Food and Agricultural Organization (FAO), Viale delle Terme di Caracalla, 00100 Rome, Italy, (Dial from U.S. (202) 653-2400), (Fax from U.S. (202) 653 5760), www.fao.org; *FAO Production Yearbook 2002.*

United Nations Statistics Division, New York, NY 10017, (800) 253-9646, Fax: (212) 963-4116, http://unstats.un.org; *Demographic Yearbook; Human Development Report 2006; Statistical Yearbook;* and *World Statistics Pocketbook.*

The World Bank, 1818 H Street, NW, Washington, DC 20433, (202) 473-1000, Fax: (202) 477-6391, www.worldbank.org; *Korea, Democratic Republic of* and *The World Bank Atlas 2003-2004.*

Worldinformation.com, 2 Market Street, Saffron Walden, Essex CB10 1HZ, United Kingdom, www.worldinformation.com; The World of Information (www.worldinformation.com).

KOREA, NORTH - POPULATION DENSITY

Central Intelligence Agency, Office of Public Affairs, Washington, DC 20505, (703) 482-0623, Fax: (703) 482-1739, www.cia.gov; *The World Factbook.*

Euromonitor International, Inc., 224 S. Michigan Avenue, Suite 1500, Chicago, IL 60604, (312) 922-1115, Fax: (312) 922-1157, www.euromonitor.com; *International Marketing Data and Statistics 2008* and *The World Economic Factbook 2008.*

M.E. Sharpe, 80 Business Park Drive, Armonk, NY 10504, (800) 541-6563, Fax: (914) 273-2106, www.mesharpe.com; *The Illustrated Book of World Rankings.*

Palgrave Macmillan Ltd., Houndmills, Basingstoke, Hampshire, RG21 6XS, England, (Telephone in U.S. (888) 330-8477), (Fax in U.S. (800) 672-2054), www.palgrave.com; *The Statesman's Yearbook 2008.*

Taylor and Francis Group, An Informa Business, 2 Park Square, Milton Park, Abingdon, Oxford OX14 4RN, United Kingdom, (Dial from U.S. (212) 216-7800), (Fax from U.S. (212) 564-7854), www.tandf.co.uk; *The Europa World Year Book.*

United Nations Food and Agricultural Organization (FAO), Viale delle Terme di Caracalla, 00100 Rome, Italy, (Dial from U.S. (202) 653-2400), (Fax from U.S. (202) 653 5760), www.fao.org; *The State of Food and Agriculture (SOFA) 2006.*

United Nations Statistics Division, New York, NY 10017, (800) 253-9646, Fax: (212) 963-4116, http://unstats.un.org; *Statistical Yearbook.*

The World Bank, 1818 H Street, NW, Washington, DC 20433, (202) 473-1000, Fax: (202) 477-6391, www.worldbank.org; *Korea, Democratic Republic of.*

KOREA, NORTH - POSTAL SERVICE

M.E. Sharpe, 80 Business Park Drive, Armonk, NY 10504, (800) 541-6563, Fax: (914) 273-2106, www.mesharpe.com; *The Illustrated Book of World Rankings.*

KOREA, NORTH - POWER RESOURCES

Euromonitor International, Inc., 224 S. Michigan Avenue, Suite 1500, Chicago, IL 60604, (312) 922-1115, Fax: (312) 922-1157, www.euromonitor.com; *International Marketing Data and Statistics 2008; The World Economic Factbook 2008;* and *World Marketing Data and Statistics.*

M.E. Sharpe, 80 Business Park Drive, Armonk, NY 10504, (800) 541-6563, Fax: (914) 273-2106, www.mesharpe.com; *The Illustrated Book of World Rankings.*

Palgrave Macmillan Ltd., Houndmills, Basingstoke, Hampshire, RG21 6XS, England, (Telephone in U.S. (888) 330-8477), (Fax in U.S. (800) 672-2054), www.palgrave.com; *The Statesman's Yearbook 2008.*

U.S. Department of Energy (DOE), Energy Information Administration (EIA), 1000 Independence Avenue, SW, Washington, DC 20585, (202) 586-8800, www.eia.doe.gov; *International Energy Annual 2004* and *International Energy Outlook 2006.*

United Nations Food and Agricultural Organization (FAO), Viale delle Terme di Caracalla, 00100 Rome, Italy, (Dial from U.S. (202) 653-2400), (Fax from U.S. (202) 653 5760), www.fao.org; *The State of Food and Agriculture (SOFA) 2006.*

United Nations Statistics Division, New York, NY 10017, (800) 253-9646, Fax: (212) 963-4116, http://unstats.un.org; *Human Development Report 2006; Statistical Yearbook;* and *World Statistics Pocketbook.*

The World Bank, 1818 H Street, NW, Washington, DC 20433, (202) 473-1000, Fax: (202) 477-6391, www.worldbank.org; *The World Bank Atlas 2003-2004.*

KOREA, NORTH - PRICES

Asian Development Bank (ADB), PO Box 789, 0980 Manila, Philippines, www.adb.org; *Key Indicators of Developing Asian and Pacific Countries 2006.*

Euromonitor International, Inc., 224 S. Michigan Avenue, Suite 1500, Chicago, IL 60604, (312) 922-1115, Fax: (312) 922-1157, www.euromonitor.com; *World Marketing Data and Statistics.*

M.E. Sharpe, 80 Business Park Drive, Armonk, NY 10504, (800) 541-6563, Fax: (914) 273-2106, www.mesharpe.com; *The Illustrated Book of World Rankings.*

United Nations Food and Agricultural Organization (FAO), Viale delle Terme di Caracalla, 00100 Rome, Italy, (Dial from U.S. (202) 653-2400), (Fax from U.S. (202) 653 5760), www.fao.org; *FAO Production Yearbook 2002* and *The State of Food and Agriculture (SOFA) 2006.*

KOREA, NORTH - PUBLIC HEALTH

Economist Intelligence Unit, 111 West 57th Street, New York, NY 10019, (212) 554-0600, Fax: (212) 586-1181, www.eiu.com; *Business Asia.*

Euromonitor International, Inc., 224 S. Michigan Avenue, Suite 1500, Chicago, IL 60604, (312) 922-1115, Fax: (312) 922-1157, www.euromonitor.com; *World Marketing Data and Statistics.*

M.E. Sharpe, 80 Business Park Drive, Armonk, NY 10504, (800) 541-6563, Fax: (914) 273-2106, www.mesharpe.com; *The Illustrated Book of World Rankings.*

Palgrave Macmillan Ltd., Houndmills, Basingstoke, Hampshire, RG21 6XS, England, (Telephone in U.S. (888) 330-8477), (Fax in U.S. (800) 672-2054), www.palgrave.com; *The Statesman's Yearbook 2008.*

UNICEF, 3 United Nations Plaza, New York, NY 10017, (800) 253-9646, Fax: (212) 887-7465, www.unicef.org; *The State of the World's Children 2008.*

United Nations Statistics Division, New York, NY 10017, (800) 253-9646, Fax: (212) 963-4116, http://unstats.un.org; *Human Development Report 2006.*

The World Bank, 1818 H Street, NW, Washington, DC 20433, (202) 473-1000, Fax: (202) 477-6391, www.worldbank.org; *Korea, Democratic Republic of.*

World Health Organization (WHO), Avenue Appia 20, 1211 Geneve 27, Switzerland, (Telephone in U.S. (212) 331-9081), www.who.int; The WHO Global Atlas of Infectious Diseases.

KOREA, NORTH - PUBLIC UTILITIES

United Nations Statistics Division, New York, NY 10017, (800) 253-9646, Fax: (212) 963-4116, http://unstats.un.org; *Electric Power in Asia and the Pacific 2001 and 2002.*

KOREA, NORTH - RADIO BROADCASTING

Palgrave Macmillan Ltd., Houndmills, Basingstoke, Hampshire, RG21 6XS, England, (Telephone in U.S. (888) 330-8477), (Fax in U.S. (800) 672-2054), www.palgrave.com; *The Statesman's Yearbook 2008.*

KOREA, NORTH - RAILROADS

Jane's Information Group, 110 North Royal Street, Suite 200, Alexandria, VA 22314, (703) 683-3700, Fax: (800) 836-0297, www.janes.com; *Jane's World Railways.*

Palgrave Macmillan Ltd., Houndmills, Basingstoke, Hampshire, RG21 6XS, England, (Telephone in U.S. (888) 330-8477), (Fax in U.S. (800) 672-2054), www.palgrave.com; *The Statesman's Yearbook 2008.*

KOREA, NORTH - RELIGION

Central Intelligence Agency, Office of Public Affairs, Washington, DC 20505, (703) 482-0623, Fax: (703) 482-1739, www.cia.gov; *The World Factbook.*

M.E. Sharpe, 80 Business Park Drive, Armonk, NY 10504, (800) 541-6563, Fax: (914) 273-2106, www.mesharpe.com; *The Illustrated Book of World Rankings.*

Palgrave Macmillan Ltd., Houndmills, Basingstoke, Hampshire, RG21 6XS, England, (Telephone in U.S. (888) 330-8477), (Fax in U.S. (800) 672-2054), www.palgrave.com; *The Statesman's Yearbook 2008.*

KOREA, NORTH - RESERVES (ACCOUNTING)

Asian Development Bank (ADB), PO Box 789, 0980 Manila, Philippines, www.adb.org; *Key Indicators of Developing Asian and Pacific Countries 2006.*

Euromonitor International, Inc., 224 S. Michigan Avenue, Suite 1500, Chicago, IL 60604, (312) 922-1115, Fax: (312) 922-1157, www.euromonitor.com; *International Marketing Data and Statistics 2008.*

KOREA, NORTH - RETAIL TRADE

Euromonitor International, Inc., 224 S. Michigan Avenue, Suite 1500, Chicago, IL 60604, (312) 922-1115, Fax: (312) 922-1157, www.euromonitor.com; *World Marketing Data and Statistics.*

KOREA, NORTH - RICE PRODUCTION

See KOREA, NORTH - CROPS

KOREA, NORTH - ROADS

Central Intelligence Agency, Office of Public Affairs, Washington, DC 20505, (703) 482-0623, Fax: (703) 482-1739, www.cia.gov; *The World Factbook.*

Economist Intelligence Unit, 111 West 57th Street, New York, NY 10019, (212) 554-0600, Fax: (212) 586-1181, www.eiu.com; *Business Asia.*

International Road Federation (IFR), Madison Place, 500 Montgomery Street, 5th Floor, Alexandria, VA 22314, (703) 535-1001, Fax: (703) 535-1007, www.irfnet.org; *World Road Statistics 2006.*

Palgrave Macmillan Ltd., Houndmills, Basingstoke, Hampshire, RG21 6XS, England, (Telephone in U.S. (888) 330-8477), (Fax in U.S. (800) 672-2054), www.palgrave.com; *The Statesman's Yearbook 2008.*

KOREA, NORTH - RUBBER INDUSTRY AND TRADE

International Rubber Study Group (IRSG), 1st Floor, Heron House, 109/115 Wembley Hill Road, Wembley, Middlesex HA9 8DA, United Kingdom, www.rubberstudy.com; *Rubber Statistical Bulletin; Summary of World Rubber Statistics 2005; World Rubber Statistics Handbook (Volume 6, 1975-2001);* and *World Rubber Statistics Historic Handbook.*

M.E. Sharpe, 80 Business Park Drive, Armonk, NY 10504, (800) 541-6563, Fax: (914) 273-2106, www.mesharpe.com; *The Illustrated Book of World Rankings.*

KOREA, NORTH - SALT INDUSTRY AND TRADE

United Nations Statistics Division, New York, NY 10017, (800) 253-9646, Fax: (212) 963-4116, http://unstats.un.org; *Statistical Yearbook.*

KOREA, NORTH - SHEEP

See KOREA, NORTH - LIVESTOCK

KOREA, NORTH - SHIPPING

Lloyd's Register - Fairplay, 8410 N.W. 53rd Terrace, Suite 207, Miami FL 33166, (305) 718-9929, Fax: (305) 718-9663, www.lrfairplay.com; *Register of Ships 2007-2008; World Casualty Statistics 2007; World Fleet Statistics 2006; World Marine Propulsion Report 2006-2010; World Shipbuilding Statistics 2007;* and The World Shipping Encyclopaedia.

Palgrave Macmillan Ltd., Houndmills, Basingstoke, Hampshire, RG21 6XS, England, (Telephone in U.S. (888) 330-8477), (Fax in U.S. (800) 672-2054), www.palgrave.com; *The Statesman's Yearbook 2008.*

Taylor and Francis Group, An Informa Business, 2 Park Square, Milton Park, Abingdon, Oxford OX14 4RN, United Kingdom, (Dial from U.S. (212) 216-7800), (Fax from U.S. (212) 564-7854), www.tandf.co.uk; *The Europa World Year Book.*

U.S. Department of Transportation (DOT), Maritime Administration (MARAD), West Building, Southeast Federal Center, 1200 New Jersey Avenue, SE, Washington, DC 20590, (800) 99-MARAD, www.marad.dot.gov; *World Merchant Fleet 2005.*

United Nations Statistics Division, New York, NY 10017, (800) 253-9646, Fax: (212) 963-4116, http://unstats.un.org; *Statistical Yearbook.*

KOREA, NORTH - SOCIAL ECOLOGY

Asian Development Bank (ADB), PO Box 789, 0980 Manila, Philippines, www.adb.org; *Key Indicators of Developing Asian and Pacific Countries 2006.*

M.E. Sharpe, 80 Business Park Drive, Armonk, NY 10504, (800) 541-6563, Fax: (914) 273-2106, www.mesharpe.com; *The Illustrated Book of World Rankings.*

United Nations Statistics Division, New York, NY 10017, (800) 253-9646, Fax: (212) 963-4116, http://unstats.un.org; *World Statistics Pocketbook.*

KOREA, NORTH - SOCIAL SECURITY

United Nations Statistics Division, New York, NY 10017, (800) 253-9646, Fax: (212) 963-4116, http://unstats.un.org; *National Accounts Statistics: Compendium of Income Distribution Statistics.*

KOREA, NORTH - SOYBEAN PRODUCTION

See KOREA, NORTH - CROPS

KOREA, NORTH - TAXATION

International Road Federation (IFR), Madison Place, 500 Montgomery Street, 5th Floor, Alexandria, VA 22314, (703) 535-1001, Fax: (703) 535-1007, www.irfnet.org; *World Road Statistics 2006.*

Palgrave Macmillan Ltd., Houndmills, Basingstoke, Hampshire, RG21 6XS, England, (Telephone in U.S. (888) 330-8477), (Fax in U.S. (800) 672-2054), www.palgrave.com; *The Statesman's Yearbook 2008.*

KOREA, NORTH - TELEPHONE

Economist Intelligence Unit, 111 West 57th Street, New York, NY 10019, (212) 554-0600, Fax: (212) 586-1181, www.eiu.com; *Business Asia.*

International Telecommunication Union (ITU), Place des Nations, 1211 Geneva 20, Switzerland, www.itu.int; World Telecommunication Indicators Database.

Palgrave Macmillan Ltd., Houndmills, Basingstoke, Hampshire, RG21 6XS, England, (Telephone in U.S. (888) 330-8477), (Fax in U.S. (800) 672-2054), www.palgrave.com; *The Statesman's Yearbook 2008.*

United Nations Statistics Division, New York, NY 10017, (800) 253-9646, Fax: (212) 963-4116, http://unstats.un.org; *World Statistics Pocketbook.*

KOREA, NORTH - TEXTILE INDUSTRY

M.E. Sharpe, 80 Business Park Drive, Armonk, NY 10504, (800) 541-6563, Fax: (914) 273-2106, www.mesharpe.com; *The Illustrated Book of World Rankings.*

Palgrave Macmillan Ltd., Houndmills, Basingstoke, Hampshire, RG21 6XS, England, (Telephone in U.S. (888) 330-8477), (Fax in U.S. (800) 672-2054), www.palgrave.com; *The Statesman's Yearbook 2008.*

United Nations Conference on Trade and Development (UNCTAD), DC2-1120, United Nations, New York, NY 10017, (212) 963-0027, www.unctad.org; *UNCTAD Commodity Yearbook.*

United Nations Food and Agricultural Organization (FAO), Viale delle Terme di Caracalla, 00100 Rome, Italy, (Dial from U.S. (202) 653-2400), (Fax from U.S. (202) 653 5760), www.fao.org; *FAO Production Yearbook 2002.*

KOREA, NORTH - TOBACCO INDUSTRY

Foreign Agricultural Service (FAS), U.S. Department of Agriculture (USDA), 1400 Independence Avenue, SW, Washington, DC 20250, (202) 720-3935, www.fas.usda.gov; *Tobacco: World Markets and Trade.*

M.E. Sharpe, 80 Business Park Drive, Armonk, NY 10504, (800) 541-6563, Fax: (914) 273-2106, www.mesharpe.com; *The Illustrated Book of World Rankings.*

United Nations Statistics Division, New York, NY 10017, (800) 253-9646, Fax: (212) 963-4116, http://unstats.un.org; *Statistical Yearbook.*

KOREA, NORTH - TOURISM

Euromonitor International, Inc., 224 S. Michigan Avenue, Suite 1500, Chicago, IL 60604, (312) 922-1115, Fax: (312) 922-1157, www.euromonitor.com; *The World Economic Factbook 2008* and *World Marketing Data and Statistics.*

M.E. Sharpe, 80 Business Park Drive, Armonk, NY 10504, (800) 541-6563, Fax: (914) 273-2106, www.mesharpe.com; *The Illustrated Book of World Rankings.*

Palgrave Macmillan Ltd., Houndmills, Basingstoke, Hampshire, RG21 6XS, England, (Telephone in U.S. (888) 330-8477), (Fax in U.S. (800) 672-2054), www.palgrave.com; *The Statesman's Yearbook 2008.*

The World Bank, 1818 H Street, NW, Washington, DC 20433, (202) 473-1000, Fax: (202) 477-6391, www.worldbank.org; *Korea, Democratic Republic of.*

KOREA, NORTH - TRADE

See KOREA, NORTH - INTERNATIONAL TRADE

KOREA, NORTH - TRANSPORTATION

Central Intelligence Agency, Office of Public Affairs, Washington, DC 20505, (703) 482-0623, Fax: (703) 482-1739, www.cia.gov; *The World Factbook.*

Economist Intelligence Unit, 111 West 57th Street, New York, NY 10019, (212) 554-0600, Fax: (212) 586-1181, www.eiu.com; *Business Asia.*

Euromonitor International, Inc., 224 S. Michigan Avenue, Suite 1500, Chicago, IL 60604, (312) 922-1115, Fax: (312) 922-1157, www.euromonitor.com; *International Marketing Data and Statistics 2008* and *World Marketing Data and Statistics.*

M.E. Sharpe, 80 Business Park Drive, Armonk, NY 10504, (800) 541-6563, Fax: (914) 273-2106, www.mesharpe.com; *The Illustrated Book of World Rankings.*

Palgrave Macmillan Ltd., Houndmills, Basingstoke, Hampshire, RG21 6XS, England, (Telephone in U.S. (888) 330-8477), (Fax in U.S. (800) 672-2054), www.palgrave.com; *The Statesman's Yearbook 2008.*

Taylor and Francis Group, An Informa Business, 2 Park Square, Milton Park, Abingdon, Oxford OX14 4RN, United Kingdom, (Dial from U.S. (212) 216-7800), (Fax from U.S. (212) 564-7854), www.tandf.co.uk; *The Europa World Year Book.*

United Nations Statistics Division, New York, NY 10017, (800) 253-9646, Fax: (212) 963-4116, http://unstats.un.org; *Human Development Report 2006.*

The World Bank, 1818 H Street, NW, Washington, DC 20433, (202) 473-1000, Fax: (202) 477-6391, www.worldbank.org; *Korea, Democratic Republic of.*

KOREA, NORTH - UNEMPLOYMENT

Central Intelligence Agency, Office of Public Affairs, Washington, DC 20505, (703) 482-0623, Fax: (703) 482-1739, www.cia.gov; *The World Factbook.*

Euromonitor International, Inc., 224 S. Michigan Avenue, Suite 1500, Chicago, IL 60604, (312) 922-1115, Fax: (312) 922-1157, www.euromonitor.com; *International Marketing Data and Statistics 2008.*

Organisation for Economic Cooperation and Development (OECD), 2 rue Andre Pascal, F-75775 Paris Cedex 16, France, (Telephone in U.S. (202) 785-6323), (Fax in U.S. (202) 785-0350), www.oecd.org; *OECD Economic Survey - Korea 2007.*

KOREA, NORTH - VITAL STATISTICS

Euromonitor International, Inc., 224 S. Michigan Avenue, Suite 1500, Chicago, IL 60604, (312) 922-1115, Fax: (312) 922-1157, www.euromonitor.com; *International Marketing Data and Statistics 2008.*

Palgrave Macmillan Ltd., Houndmills, Basingstoke, Hampshire, RG21 6XS, England, (Telephone in U.S. (888) 330-8477), (Fax in U.S. (800) 672-2054), www.palgrave.com; *The Statesman's Yearbook 2008.*

Pyongyang Square 2, www.pyongyangsquare.com; unpublished data.

United Nations Statistics Division, New York, NY 10017, (800) 253-9646, Fax: (212) 963-4116, http://unstats.un.org; *Statistical Yearbook.*

KOREA, NORTH - WALNUT PRODUCTION

See KOREA, NORTH - CROPS

KOREA, NORTH - WEATHER

See KOREA, NORTH - CLIMATE

KOREA, NORTH - WHEAT PRODUCTION

See KOREA, NORTH - CROPS

KOREA, NORTH - WHOLESALE PRICE INDEXES

Asian Development Bank (ADB), PO Box 789, 0980 Manila, Philippines, www.adb.org; *Key Indicators of Developing Asian and Pacific Countries 2006.*

KOREA, NORTH - WINE PRODUCTION

See KOREA, NORTH - BEVERAGE INDUSTRY

KOREA, NORTH - WOOD AND WOOD PULP

See KOREA, NORTH - FORESTS AND FORESTRY

KOREA, NORTH - WOOL PRODUCTION

See KOREA, NORTH - TEXTILE INDUSTRY

KOREA, NORTH - ZINC AND ZINC ORE

See KOREA, NORTH - MINERAL INDUSTRIES

KOREA, SOUTH

Palgrave Macmillan Ltd., Houndmills, Basingstoke, Hampshire, RG21 6XS, England, (Telephone in U.S. (888) 330-8477), (Fax in U.S. (800) 672-2054), www.palgrave.com; *The Statesman's Yearbook 2008.*

KOREA, SOUTH - NATIONAL STATISTICAL OFFICE

Korea National Statistical Office (KNSO), Government Complex Daejeon, 139 Seonsaro, Seo-Gu, Daejeon 302-701, Republic of Korea, www.nso.go.kr/eng2006/emain; National Data Center.

KOREA, SOUTH - PRIMARY STATISTICS SOURCES

Korea National Statistical Office (KNSO), Government Complex Daejeon, 139 Seonsaro, Seo-Gu, Daejeon 302-701, Republic of Korea, www.nso.go.kr/eng2006/emain; *Korea Statistical Yearbook 2004* and *Monthly Statistics of Korea.*

KOREA, SOUTH - AGRICULTURAL MACHINERY

United Nations Statistics Division, New York, NY 10017, (800) 253-9646, Fax: (212) 963-4116, http://unstats.un.org; *Statistical Yearbook.*

KOREA, SOUTH - AGRICULTURE

Economist Intelligence Unit, 111 West 57th Street, New York, NY 10019, (212) 554-0600, Fax: (212) 586-1181, www.eiu.com; *South Korea Country Report.*

Euromonitor International, Inc., 224 S. Michigan Avenue, Suite 1500, Chicago, IL 60604, (312) 922-1115, Fax: (312) 922-1157, www.euromonitor.com; *International Marketing Data and Statistics 2008* and *World Marketing Data and Statistics.*

Federal Statistical Office Germany, D-65180 Wiesbaden, Germany, www.destatis.de; *Republic of Korea 2005.*

Korean Overseas Information Service (KOIS), Ministry of Culture and Information, Seoul 110, Republic of Korea, www.korea.net; Korea.net.

Organisation for Economic Cooperation and Development (OECD), 2 rue Andre Pascal, F-75775 Paris Cedex 16, France, (Telephone in U.S. (202) 785-6323), (Fax in U.S. (202) 785-0350), www.oecd.org; *OECD Agricultural Outlook: 2007-2016.*

Palgrave Macmillan Ltd., Houndmills, Basingstoke, Hampshire, RG21 6XS, England, (Telephone in U.S. (888) 330-8477), (Fax in U.S. (800) 672-2054), www.palgrave.com; *The Statesman's Yearbook 2008.*

Taylor and Francis Group, An Informa Business, 2 Park Square, Milton Park, Abingdon, Oxford OX14 4RN, United Kingdom, (Dial from U.S. (212) 216-7800), (Fax from U.S. (212) 564-7854), www.tandf.co.uk; *The Europa World Year Book.*

United Nations Conference on Trade and Development (UNCTAD), DC2-1120, United Nations, New York, NY 10017, (212) 963-0027, www.unctad.org; *UNCTAD Commodity Yearbook.*

United Nations Food and Agricultural Organization (FAO), Viale delle Terme di Caracalla, 00100 Rome, Italy, (Dial from U.S. (202) 653-2400), (Fax from U.S. (202) 653 5760), www.fao.org; AQUASTAT; *FAO Production Yearbook 2002; FAO Trade Yearbook;* and *The State of Food and Agriculture (SOFA) 2006.*

United Nations Statistics Division, New York, NY 10017, (800) 253-9646, Fax: (212) 963-4116, http://unstats.un.org; *Asia-Pacific in Figures 2004; Statistical Yearbook;* and *Statistical Yearbook for Asia and the Pacific 2004.*

The World Bank, 1818 H Street, NW, Washington, DC 20433, (202) 473-1000, Fax: (202) 477-6391, www.worldbank.org; *Korea, Republic of* and *World Development Indicators (WDI) 2008.*

KOREA, SOUTH - AIRLINES

Economist Intelligence Unit, 111 West 57th Street, New York, NY 10019, (212) 554-0600, Fax: (212) 586-1181, www.eiu.com; *Business Asia.*

International Civil Aviation Organization (ICAO), External Relations and Public Information Office (EPO), 999 University Street, Montreal, Quebec H3C 5H7, Canada, (Dial from U.S. (514) 954-8219), (Fax from U.S. (514) 954-6077), www.icao.int; *Civil Aviation Statistics of the World.*

M.E. Sharpe, 80 Business Park Drive, Armonk, NY 10504, (800) 541-6563, Fax: (914) 273-2106, www.mesharpe.com; *The Illustrated Book of World Rankings.*

Palgrave Macmillan Ltd., Houndmills, Basingstoke, Hampshire, RG21 6XS, England, (Telephone in U.S. (888) 330-8477), (Fax in U.S. (800) 672-2054), www.palgrave.com; *The Statesman's Yearbook 2008.*

Taylor and Francis Group, An Informa Business, 2 Park Square, Milton Park, Abingdon, Oxford OX14 4RN, United Kingdom, (Dial from U.S. (212) 216-7800), (Fax from U.S. (212) 564-7854), www.tandf.co.uk; *The Europa World Year Book.*

United Nations Statistics Division, New York, NY 10017, (800) 253-9646, Fax: (212) 963-4116, http://unstats.un.org; *Statistical Yearbook.*

KOREA, SOUTH - AIRPORTS

Central Intelligence Agency, Office of Public Affairs, Washington, DC 20505, (703) 482-0623, Fax: (703) 482-1739, www.cia.gov; *The World Factbook.*

KOREA, SOUTH - ALUMINUM PRODUCTION

See KOREA, SOUTH - MINERAL INDUSTRIES

KOREA, SOUTH - ANTHRACITE PRODUCTION

See KOREA, SOUTH - MINERAL INDUSTRIES

KOREA, SOUTH - AREA

Korean Overseas Information Service (KOIS), Ministry of Culture and Information, Seoul 110, Republic of Korea, www.korea.net; Korea.net.

KOREA, SOUTH - ARMED FORCES

Central Intelligence Agency, Office of Public Affairs, Washington, DC 20505, (703) 482-0623, Fax: (703) 482-1739, www.cia.gov; *The World Factbook.*

Economist Intelligence Unit, 111 West 57th Street, New York, NY 10019, (212) 554-0600, Fax: (212) 586-1181, www.eiu.com; *Business Asia.*

Euromonitor International, Inc., 224 S. Michigan Avenue, Suite 1500, Chicago, IL 60604, (312) 922-1115, Fax: (312) 922-1157, www.euromonitor.com; *World Marketing Data and Statistics.*

International Institute for Strategic Studies (IISS), Arundel House, 13-15 Arundel Street, Temple Place, London WC2R 3DX, England, www.iiss.org; *The Military Balance 2007.*

Palgrave Macmillan Ltd., Houndmills, Basingstoke, Hampshire, RG21 6XS, England, (Telephone in U.S. (888) 330-8477), (Fax in U.S. (800) 672-2054), www.palgrave.com; *The Statesman's Yearbook 2008.*

U.S. Department of State (DOS), 2201 C Street NW, Washington, DC 20520, (202) 647-4000, www.state.gov; *World Military Expenditures and Arms Transfers (WMEAT).*

United Nations Statistics Division, New York, NY 10017, (800) 253-9646, Fax: (212) 963-4116, http://unstats.un.org; *Human Development Report 2006.*

KOREA, SOUTH - AUTOMOBILE INDUSTRY AND TRADE

Korean Overseas Information Service (KOIS), Ministry of Culture and Information, Seoul 110, Republic of Korea, www.korea.net; Korea.net.

United Nations Statistics Division, New York, NY 10017, (800) 253-9646, Fax: (212) 963-4116, http://unstats.un.org; *Statistical Yearbook.*

KOREA, SOUTH - BALANCE OF PAYMENTS

Federal Statistical Office Germany, D-65180 Wiesbaden, Germany, www.destatis.de; *Republic of Korea 2005.*

International Monetary Fund (IMF), 700 Nineteenth Street, NW, Washington, DC 20431, (202) 623-7000, Fax: (202) 623-4661, www.imf.org; *Balance of Payments Statistics Newsletter* and *Balance of Payments Statistics Yearbook 2007.*

Korean Overseas Information Service (KOIS), Ministry of Culture and Information, Seoul 110, Republic of Korea, www.korea.net; Korea.net.

Taylor and Francis Group, An Informa Business, 2 Park Square, Milton Park, Abingdon, Oxford OX14 4RN, United Kingdom, (Dial from U.S. (212) 216-7800), (Fax from U.S. (212) 564-7854), www.tandf.co.uk; *The Europa World Year Book.*

United Nations Conference on Trade and Development (UNCTAD), DC2-1120, United Nations, New York, NY 10017, (212) 963-0027, www.unctad.org; *Handbook of Statistics 2005.*

The World Bank, 1818 H Street, NW, Washington, DC 20433, (202) 473-1000, Fax: (202) 477-6391, www.worldbank.org; *Korea, Republic of* and *World Development Indicators (WDI) 2008.*

KOREA, SOUTH - BANKS AND BANKING

Euromonitor International, Inc., 224 S. Michigan Avenue, Suite 1500, Chicago, IL 60604, (312) 922-1115, Fax: (312) 922-1157, www.euromonitor.com; *World Marketing Data and Statistics.*

International Monetary Fund (IMF), 700 Nineteenth Street, NW, Washington, DC 20431, (202) 623-7000, Fax: (202) 623-4661, www.imf.org; *International Financial Statistics Yearbook 2007.*

Korean Overseas Information Service (KOIS), Ministry of Culture and Information, Seoul 110, Republic of Korea, www.korea.net; Korea.net.

M.E. Sharpe, 80 Business Park Drive, Armonk, NY 10504, (800) 541-6563, Fax: (914) 273-2106, www.mesharpe.com; *The Illustrated Book of World Rankings.*

Palgrave Macmillan Ltd., Houndmills, Basingstoke, Hampshire, RG21 6XS, England, (Telephone in U.S. (888) 330-8477), (Fax in U.S. (800) 672-2054), www.palgrave.com; *The Statesman's Yearbook 2008.*

Taylor and Francis Group, An Informa Business, 2 Park Square, Milton Park, Abingdon, Oxford OX14 4RN, United Kingdom, (Dial from U.S. (212) 216-7800), (Fax from U.S. (212) 564-7854), www.tandf.co.uk; *The Europa World Year Book.*

United Nations Statistics Division, New York, NY 10017, (800) 253-9646, Fax: (212) 963-4116, http://unstats.un.org; *Statistical Yearbook.*

KOREA, SOUTH - BARLEY PRODUCTION

See KOREA, SOUTH - CROPS

KOREA, SOUTH - BEES

Korean Overseas Information Service (KOIS), Ministry of Culture and Information, Seoul 110, Republic of Korea, www.korea.net; Korea.net.

KOREA, SOUTH - BEVERAGE INDUSTRY

M.E. Sharpe, 80 Business Park Drive, Armonk, NY 10504, (800) 541-6563, Fax: (914) 273-2106, www.mesharpe.com; *The Illustrated Book of World Rankings.*

United Nations Statistics Division, New York, NY 10017, (800) 253-9646, Fax: (212) 963-4116, http://unstats.un.org; *Statistical Yearbook.*

KOREA, SOUTH - BROADCASTING

Central Intelligence Agency, Office of Public Affairs, Washington, DC 20505, (703) 482-0623, Fax: (703) 482-1739, www.cia.gov; *The World Factbook.*

Economist Intelligence Unit, 111 West 57th Street, New York, NY 10019, (212) 554-0600, Fax: (212) 586-1181, www.eiu.com; *Business Asia.*

Euromonitor International, Inc., 224 S. Michigan Avenue, Suite 1500, Chicago, IL 60604, (312) 922-1115, Fax: (312) 922-1157, www.euromonitor.com; *World Marketing Data and Statistics.*

M.E. Sharpe, 80 Business Park Drive, Armonk, NY 10504, (800) 541-6563, Fax: (914) 273-2106, www.mesharpe.com; *The Illustrated Book of World Rankings.*

Palgrave Macmillan Ltd., Houndmills, Basingstoke, Hampshire, RG21 6XS, England, (Telephone in U.S. (888) 330-8477), (Fax in U.S. (800) 672-2054), www.palgrave.com; *The Statesman's Yearbook 2008.*

UNESCO Institute for Statistics, C.P. 6128 Succursale Centre-Ville, Montreal, Quebec, H3C 3J7 Canada, (Dial from U.S. (514) 343-6880), (Fax from U.S. (514) 343 6882), www.uis.unesco.org; *Statistical Tables.*

WRTH Publications Limited, PO Box 290, Oxford OX2 7FT, UK, www.wrth.com; *World Radio TV Handbook 2007.*

KOREA, SOUTH - BUDGET

Central Intelligence Agency, Office of Public Affairs, Washington, DC 20505, (703) 482-0623, Fax: (703) 482-1739, www.cia.gov; *The World Factbook.*

KOREA, SOUTH - BUSINESS

United Nations Statistics Division, New York, NY 10017, (800) 253-9646, Fax: (212) 963-4116, http://unstats.un.org; *Statistical Yearbook* and *Statistical Yearbook for Asia and the Pacific 2004.*

KOREA, SOUTH - CATTLE

See KOREA, SOUTH - LIVESTOCK

KOREA, SOUTH - CHESTNUT PRODUCTION

See KOREA, SOUTH - CROPS

KOREA, SOUTH - CHICKENS

See KOREA, SOUTH - LIVESTOCK

KOREA, SOUTH - CHILDBIRTH - STATISTICS

Central Intelligence Agency, Office of Public Affairs, Washington, DC 20505, (703) 482-0623, Fax: (703) 482-1739, www.cia.gov; *The World Factbook.*

Economist Intelligence Unit, 111 West 57th Street, New York, NY 10019, (212) 554-0600, Fax: (212) 586-1181, www.eiu.com; *Business Asia.*

Euromonitor International, Inc., 224 S. Michigan Avenue, Suite 1500, Chicago, IL 60604, (312) 922-1115, Fax: (312) 922-1157, www.euromonitor.com; *International Marketing Data and Statistics 2008* and *The World Economic Factbook 2008.*

M.E. Sharpe, 80 Business Park Drive, Armonk, NY 10504, (800) 541-6563, Fax: (914) 273-2106, www.mesharpe.com; *The Illustrated Book of World Rankings.*

Palgrave Macmillan Ltd., Houndmills, Basingstoke, Hampshire, RG21 6XS, England, (Telephone in U.S. (888) 330-8477), (Fax in U.S. (800) 672-2054), www.palgrave.com; *The Statesman's Yearbook 2008.*

Taylor and Francis Group, An Informa Business, 2 Park Square, Milton Park, Abingdon, Oxford OX14 4RN, United Kingdom, (Dial from U.S. (212) 216-7800), (Fax from U.S. (212) 564-7854), www.tandf.co.uk; *The Europa World Year Book.*

United Nations Statistics Division, New York, NY 10017, (800) 253-9646, Fax: (212) 963-4116, http://unstats.un.org; *Asia-Pacific in Figures 2004; Demographic Yearbook;* and *Statistical Yearbook.*

The World Bank, 1818 H Street, NW, Washington, DC 20433, (202) 473-1000, Fax: (202) 477-6391, www.worldbank.org; *World Development Indicators (WDI) 2008.*

KOREA, SOUTH - CLIMATE

International Institute for Environment and Development (IIED), 3 Endsleigh Street, London, England, WC1H 0DD, United Kingdom, www.iied.org; *Environment Urbanization.*

Korean Overseas Information Service (KOIS), Ministry of Culture and Information, Seoul 110, Republic of Korea, www.korea.net; Korea.net.

M.E. Sharpe, 80 Business Park Drive, Armonk, NY 10504, (800) 541-6563, Fax: (914) 273-2106, www.mesharpe.com; *The Illustrated Book of World Rankings.*

Palgrave Macmillan Ltd., Houndmills, Basingstoke, Hampshire, RG21 6XS, England, (Telephone in U.S. (888) 330-8477), (Fax in U.S. (800) 672-2054), www.palgrave.com; *The Statesman's Yearbook 2008.*

KOREA, SOUTH - COAL PRODUCTION

See KOREA, SOUTH - MINERAL INDUSTRIES

KOREA, SOUTH - COFFEE

See KOREA, SOUTH - CROPS

KOREA, SOUTH - COMMERCE

Palgrave Macmillan Ltd., Houndmills, Basingstoke, Hampshire, RG21 6XS, England, (Telephone in U.S. (888) 330-8477), (Fax in U.S. (800) 672-2054), www.palgrave.com; *The Statesman's Yearbook 2008.*

KOREA, SOUTH - COMMODITY EXCHANGES

Commodity Research Bureau, 330 South Wells Street, Suite 612, Chicago, IL 60606-7110, (800) 621-5271, Fax: (312) 939-4135, www.crbtrader.com; *2006 CRB Commodity Yearbook and CD.*

International Monetary Fund (IMF), 700 Nineteenth Street, NW, Washington, DC 20431, (202) 623-7000, Fax: (202) 623-4661, www.imf.org; *IMF Primary Commodity Prices.*

United Nations Food and Agricultural Organization (FAO), Viale delle Terme di Caracalla, 00100 Rome, Italy, (Dial from U.S. (202) 653-2400), (Fax from U.S. (202) 653 5760), www.fao.org; *The State of Food and Agriculture (SOFA) 2006.*

KOREA, SOUTH - COMMUNICATION AND TRAFFIC

Korean Overseas Information Service (KOIS), Ministry of Culture and Information, Seoul 110, Republic of Korea, www.korea.net; Korea.net.

KOREA, SOUTH - CONSTRUCTION INDUSTRY

M.E. Sharpe, 80 Business Park Drive, Armonk, NY 10504, (800) 541-6563, Fax: (914) 273-2106, www.mesharpe.com; *The Illustrated Book of World Rankings.*

Palgrave Macmillan Ltd., Houndmills, Basingstoke, Hampshire, RG21 6XS, England, (Telephone in U.S. (888) 330-8477), (Fax in U.S. (800) 672-2054), www.palgrave.com; *The Statesman's Yearbook 2008.*

United Nations Statistics Division, New York, NY 10017, (800) 253-9646, Fax: (212) 963-4116, http://unstats.un.org; *Statistical Yearbook.*

KOREA, SOUTH - CONSUMER PRICE INDEXES

Federal Statistical Office Germany, D-65180 Wiesbaden, Germany, www.destatis.de; *Republic of Korea 2005.*

Taylor and Francis Group, An Informa Business, 2 Park Square, Milton Park, Abingdon, Oxford OX14 4RN, United Kingdom, (Dial from U.S. (212) 216-7800), (Fax from U.S. (212) 564-7854), www.tandf.co.uk; *The Europa World Year Book.*

United Nations Statistics Division, New York, NY 10017, (800) 253-9646, Fax: (212) 963-4116, http://unstats.un.org; *Statistical Yearbook.*

The World Bank, 1818 H Street, NW, Washington, DC 20433, (202) 473-1000, Fax: (202) 477-6391, www.worldbank.org; *Korea, Republic of.*

KOREA, SOUTH - CONSUMPTION (ECONOMICS)

Korean Overseas Information Service (KOIS), Ministry of Culture and Information, Seoul 110, Republic of Korea, www.korea.net; Korea.net.

Organisation for Economic Cooperation and Development (OECD), 2 rue Andre Pascal, F-75775 Paris Cedex 16, France, (Telephone in U.S. (202) 785-6323), (Fax in U.S. (202) 785-0350), www.oecd.org; *Towards Sustainable Household Consumption?: Trends and Policies in OECD Countries.*

KOREA, SOUTH - COPPER INDUSTRY AND TRADE

See KOREA, SOUTH - MINERAL INDUSTRIES

KOREA, SOUTH - CORN INDUSTRY

See KOREA, SOUTH - CROPS

KOREA, SOUTH - COST AND STANDARD OF LIVING

Korean Overseas Information Service (KOIS), Ministry of Culture and Information, Seoul 110, Republic of Korea, www.korea.net; Korea.net.

United Nations Statistics Division, New York, NY 10017, (800) 253-9646, Fax: (212) 963-4116, http://unstats.un.org; *Statistical Yearbook for Asia and the Pacific 2004.*

KOREA, SOUTH - COTTON

See KOREA, SOUTH - CROPS

KOREA, SOUTH - CRIME

U.S. Department of Justice (DOJ), Bureau of Justice Statistics, 810 Seventh Street, NW, Washington, DC 20531, (202) 307-0765, www.ojp.usdoj.gov/bjs/; *The World Factbook of Criminal Justice Systems.*

KOREA, SOUTH - CROPS

M.E. Sharpe, 80 Business Park Drive, Armonk, NY 10504, (800) 541-6563, Fax: (914) 273-2106, www.mesharpe.com; *The Illustrated Book of World Rankings.*

Palgrave Macmillan Ltd., Houndmills, Basingstoke, Hampshire, RG21 6XS, England, (Telephone in U.S. (888) 330-8477), (Fax in U.S. (800) 672-2054), www.palgrave.com; *The Statesman's Yearbook 2008.*

Taylor and Francis Group, An Informa Business, 2 Park Square, Milton Park, Abingdon, Oxford OX14 4RN, United Kingdom, (Dial from U.S. (212) 216-7800), (Fax from U.S. (212) 564-7854), www.tandf.co.uk; *The Europa World Year Book.*

United Nations Conference on Trade and Development (UNCTAD), DC2-1120, United Nations, New York, NY 10017, (212) 963-0027, www.unctad.org; *UNCTAD Commodity Yearbook.*

United Nations Food and Agricultural Organization (FAO), Viale delle Terme di Caracalla, 00100 Rome, Italy, (Dial from U.S. (202) 653-2400), (Fax from U.S. (202) 653 5760), www.fao.org; *FAO Production Yearbook 2002* and *The State of Food and Agriculture (SOFA) 2006.*

United Nations Statistics Division, New York, NY 10017, (800) 253-9646, Fax: (212) 963-4116, http://unstats.un.org; *Statistical Yearbook.*

KOREA, SOUTH - CULTURE

Korean Overseas Information Service (KOIS), Ministry of Culture and Information, Seoul 110, Republic of Korea, www.korea.net; Korea.net.

KOREA, SOUTH - CUSTOMS ADMINISTRATION

Palgrave Macmillan Ltd., Houndmills, Basingstoke, Hampshire, RG21 6XS, England, (Telephone in U.S. (888) 330-8477), (Fax in U.S. (800) 672-2054), www.palgrave.com; *The Statesman's Yearbook 2008.*

KOREA, SOUTH - DAIRY PROCESSING

M.E. Sharpe, 80 Business Park Drive, Armonk, NY 10504, (800) 541-6563, Fax: (914) 273-2106, www.mesharpe.com; *The Illustrated Book of World Rankings.*

Palgrave Macmillan Ltd., Houndmills, Basingstoke, Hampshire, RG21 6XS, England, (Telephone in U.S. (888) 330-8477), (Fax in U.S. (800) 672-2054), www.palgrave.com; *The Statesman's Yearbook 2008.*

Taylor and Francis Group, An Informa Business, 2 Park Square, Milton Park, Abingdon, Oxford OX14 4RN, United Kingdom, (Dial from U.S. (212) 216-7800), (Fax from U.S. (212) 564-7854), www.tandf.co.uk; *The Europa World Year Book.*

United Nations Food and Agricultural Organization (FAO), Viale delle Terme di Caracalla, 00100 Rome, Italy, (Dial from U.S. (202) 653-2400), (Fax from U.S. (202) 653 5760), www.fao.org; *FAO Production Yearbook 2002* and *The State of Food and Agriculture (SOFA) 2006.*

United Nations Statistics Division, New York, NY 10017, (800) 253-9646, Fax: (212) 963-4116, http://unstats.un.org; *Statistical Yearbook.*

KOREA, SOUTH - DEATH RATES

See KOREA, SOUTH - MORTALITY

KOREA, SOUTH - DEBTS, EXTERNAL

Palgrave Macmillan Ltd., Houndmills, Basingstoke, Hampshire, RG21 6XS, England, (Telephone in U.S. (888) 330-8477), (Fax in U.S. (800) 672-2054), www.palgrave.com; *The Statesman's Yearbook 2008.*

The World Bank, 1818 H Street, NW, Washington, DC 20433, (202) 473-1000, Fax: (202) 477-6391, www.worldbank.org; *Global Development Finance 2007* and *World Development Indicators (WDI) 2008.*

Worldinformation.com, 2 Market Street, Saffron Walden, Essex CB10 1HZ, United Kingdom, www.worldinformation.com; The World of Information (www.worldinformation.com).

KOREA, SOUTH - DEFENSE EXPENDITURES

See KOREA, SOUTH - ARMED FORCES

KOREA, SOUTH - DEMOGRAPHY

Economist Intelligence Unit, 111 West 57th Street, New York, NY 10019, (212) 554-0600, Fax: (212) 586-1181, www.eiu.com; *Business Asia.*

Euromonitor International, Inc., 224 S. Michigan Avenue, Suite 1500, Chicago, IL 60604, (312) 922-1115, Fax: (312) 922-1157, www.euromonitor.com; *International Marketing Data and Statistics 2008; The World Economic Factbook 2008;* and *World Marketing Data and Statistics.*

Federal Statistical Office Germany, D-65180 Wiesbaden, Germany, www.destatis.de; *Republic of Korea 2005.*

M.E. Sharpe, 80 Business Park Drive, Armonk, NY 10504, (800) 541-6563, Fax: (914) 273-2106, www.mesharpe.com; *The Illustrated Book of World Rankings.*

United Nations Statistics Division, New York, NY 10017, (800) 253-9646, Fax: (212) 963-4116, http://unstats.un.org; *Asia-Pacific in Figures 2004* and *Human Development Report 2006.*

The World Bank, 1818 H Street, NW, Washington, DC 20433, (202) 473-1000, Fax: (202) 477-6391, www.worldbank.org; *Korea, Republic of.*

KOREA, SOUTH - DIAMONDS

See KOREA, SOUTH - MINERAL INDUSTRIES

KOREA, SOUTH - DISPOSABLE INCOME

Korean Overseas Information Service (KOIS), Ministry of Culture and Information, Seoul 110, Republic of Korea, www.korea.net; Korea.net.

M.E. Sharpe, 80 Business Park Drive, Armonk, NY 10504, (800) 541-6563, Fax: (914) 273-2106, www.mesharpe.com; *The Illustrated Book of World Rankings.*

United Nations Statistics Division, New York, NY 10017, (800) 253-9646, Fax: (212) 963-4116, http://unstats.un.org; *National Accounts Statistics: Compendium of Income Distribution Statistics* and *Statistical Yearbook.*

KOREA, SOUTH - DIVORCE

M.E. Sharpe, 80 Business Park Drive, Armonk, NY 10504, (800) 541-6563, Fax: (914) 273-2106, www.mesharpe.com; *The Illustrated Book of World Rankings.*

United Nations Statistics Division, New York, NY 10017, (800) 253-9646, Fax: (212) 963-4116, http://unstats.un.org; *Demographic Yearbook* and *Statistical Yearbook.*

KOREA, SOUTH - DOGS

Korean Overseas Information Service (KOIS), Ministry of Culture and Information, Seoul 110, Republic of Korea, www.korea.net; Korea.net.

KOREA, SOUTH - ECONOMIC ASSISTANCE

United Nations Statistics Division, New York, NY 10017, (800) 253-9646, Fax: (212) 963-4116, http://unstats.un.org; *Statistical Yearbook.*

KOREA, SOUTH - ECONOMIC CONDITIONS

Center for International Business Education Research (CIBER), Columbia Business School and School of International and Public Affairs, Uris Hall, Room 212, 3022 Broadway, New York, NY 10027-6902, Mr. Joshua Safier, (212) 854-4750, Fax: (212) 222-9821, www.columbia.edu/cu/ciber/; Datastream International.

Central Intelligence Agency, Office of Public Affairs, Washington, DC 20505, (703) 482-0623, Fax: (703) 482-1739, www.cia.gov; *The World Factbook.*

DSI Data Service Information, Xantener Strasse 51a, D-47495 Rheinberg, Germany, www.dsidata.com; *Campus Solution.*

Dun and Bradstreet (DB) Corporation, 103 JFK Parkway, Short Hills, NJ 07078, (973) 921-5500, www.dnb.com; *Country Report.*

Economist Intelligence Unit, 111 West 57th Street, New York, NY 10019, (212) 554-0600, Fax: (212) 586-1181, www.eiu.com; *South Korea Country Report.*

Euromonitor International, Inc., 224 S. Michigan Avenue, Suite 1500, Chicago, IL 60604, (312) 922-1115, Fax: (312) 922-1157, www.euromonitor.com; *International Marketing Data and Statistics 2008; The World Economic Factbook 2008;* and *World Marketing Data and Statistics.*

Federal Statistical Office Germany, D-65180 Wiesbaden, Germany, www.destatis.de; *Republic of Korea 2005.*

International Monetary Fund (IMF), 700 Nineteenth Street, NW, Washington, DC 20431, (202) 623-7000, Fax: (202) 623-4661, www.imf.org; *World Economic Outlook Reports.*

Japan Center for Economic Research (JCER), Nikkei Kayabacho Building, Nihombashi Kayabacho, 2-6-1, Chuo-ku, Tokyo 103-0025, Japan, www.jcer.or.jp/eng; *Asia Research Report.*

M.E. Sharpe, 80 Business Park Drive, Armonk, NY 10504, (800) 541-6563, Fax: (914) 273-2106, www.mesharpe.com; *The Illustrated Book of World Rankings.*

Nomura Research Institute (NRI), 2 World Financial Center, Building B, 19th Fl., New York, NY 10281-1198, (212) 667-1670, www.nri.co.jp/english; *Asian Economic Outlook 2003-2004.*

Organisation for Economic Cooperation and Development (OECD), 2 rue Andre Pascal, F-75775 Paris Cedex 16, France, (Telephone in U.S. (202) 785-6323), (Fax in U.S. (202) 785-0350), www.oecd.org; *ICT Sector Data and Metadata by Country; Labour Force Statistics: 1986-2005, 2007 Edition; OECD Composite Leading Indicators (CLIs), Updated September 2007;* and *OECD in Figures 2007.*

Palgrave Macmillan Ltd., Houndmills, Basingstoke, Hampshire, RG21 6XS, England, (Telephone in U.S. (888) 330-8477), (Fax in U.S. (800) 672-2054), www.palgrave.com; *The Statesman's Yearbook 2008.*

Taylor and Francis Group, An Informa Business, 2 Park Square, Milton Park, Abingdon, Oxford OX14 4RN, United Kingdom, (Dial from U.S. (212) 216-7800), (Fax from U.S. (212) 564-7854), www.tandf.co.uk; *The Europa World Year Book.*

United Nations Statistics Division, New York, NY 10017, (800) 253-9646, Fax: (212) 963-4116, http://unstats.un.org; *World Statistics Pocketbook.*

The World Bank, 1818 H Street, NW, Washington, DC 20433, (202) 473-1000, Fax: (202) 477-6391, www.worldbank.org; *Global Economic Monitor (GEM); Global Economic Prospects 2008; Korea, Republic of;* and *The World Bank Atlas 2003-2004.*

KOREA, SOUTH - ECONOMIC COUNCILS

Korean Overseas Information Service (KOIS), Ministry of Culture and Information, Seoul 110, Republic of Korea, www.korea.net; Korea.net.

KOREA, SOUTH - EDUCATION

Economist Intelligence Unit, 111 West 57th Street, New York, NY 10019, (212) 554-0600, Fax: (212) 586-1181, www.eiu.com; *Business Asia.*

Euromonitor International, Inc., 224 S. Michigan Avenue, Suite 1500, Chicago, IL 60604, (312) 922-1115, Fax: (312) 922-1157, www.euromonitor.com; *International Marketing Data and Statistics 2008* and *World Marketing Data and Statistics.*

Federal Statistical Office Germany, D-65180 Wiesbaden, Germany, www.destatis.de; *Republic of Korea 2005.*

Korean Overseas Information Service (KOIS), Ministry of Culture and Information, Seoul 110, Republic of Korea, www.korea.net; Korea.net.

M.E. Sharpe, 80 Business Park Drive, Armonk, NY 10504, (800) 541-6563, Fax: (914) 273-2106, www.mesharpe.com; *The Illustrated Book of World Rankings.*

Palgrave Macmillan Ltd., Houndmills, Basingstoke, Hampshire, RG21 6XS, England, (Telephone in U.S. (888) 330-8477), (Fax in U.S. (800) 672-2054), www.palgrave.com; *The Statesman's Yearbook 2008.*

Taylor and Francis Group, An Informa Business, 2 Park Square, Milton Park, Abingdon, Oxford OX14 4RN, United Kingdom, (Dial from U.S. (212) 216-7800), (Fax from U.S. (212) 564-7854), www.tandf.co.uk; *The Europa World Year Book.*

UNESCO Institute for Statistics, C.P. 6128 Succursale Centre-Ville, Montreal, Quebec, H3C 3J7 Canada, (Dial from U.S. (514) 343-6880), (Fax from U.S. (514) 343 6882), www.uis.unesco.org; *Statistical Tables.*

United Nations Statistics Division, New York, NY 10017, (800) 253-9646, Fax: (212) 963-4116, http://unstats.un.org; *Asia-Pacific in Figures 2004; Human Development Report 2006;* and *Statistical Yearbook for Asia and the Pacific 2004.*

The World Bank, 1818 H Street, NW, Washington, DC 20433, (202) 473-1000, Fax: (202) 477-6391, www.worldbank.org; *Korea, Republic of* and *World Development Indicators (WDI) 2008.*

KOREA, SOUTH - EGGPLANT PRODUCTION

See KOREA, SOUTH - CROPS

KOREA, SOUTH - ELECTRICITY

Korean Overseas Information Service (KOIS), Ministry of Culture and Information, Seoul 110, Republic of Korea, www.korea.net; Korea.net.

M.E. Sharpe, 80 Business Park Drive, Armonk, NY 10504, (800) 541-6563, Fax: (914) 273-2106, www.mesharpe.com; *The Illustrated Book of World Rankings.*

Palgrave Macmillan Ltd., Houndmills, Basingstoke, Hampshire, RG21 6XS, England, (Telephone in U.S. (888) 330-8477), (Fax in U.S. (800) 672-2054), www.palgrave.com; *The Statesman's Yearbook 2008.*

Platts, 2 Penn Plaza, 25th Floor, New York, NY 10121-2298, (212) 904-3070, www.platts.com; *Asian Electricity Outlook 2006* and *Emissions Daily.*

U.S. Department of Energy (DOE), Energy Information Administration (EIA), 1000 Independence Avenue, SW, Washington, DC 20585, (202) 586-8800, www.eia.doe.gov; *International Energy Annual 2004* and *International Energy Outlook 2006.*

United Nations Statistics Division, New York, NY 10017, (800) 253-9646, Fax: (212) 963-4116, http://unstats.un.org; *Human Development Report 2006* and *Statistical Yearbook.*

KOREA, SOUTH - EMPLOYMENT

Bernan Essential Government Publications, 4611-F Assembly Drive, Lanham MD, 20706-4391, (301) 459-2255, Fax: (800) 865-3450, www.bernan.com; *OECD Factbook 2006.*

Euromonitor International, Inc., 224 S. Michigan Avenue, Suite 1500, Chicago, IL 60604, (312) 922-1115, Fax: (312) 922-1157, www.euromonitor.com; *International Marketing Data and Statistics 2008.*

Federal Statistical Office Germany, D-65180 Wiesbaden, Germany, www.destatis.de; *Republic of Korea 2005.*

International Labour Office, I.L.O. Publications, 4 route des Morillons, CH-1211 Geneva 22, Switzerland, (Telephone in U.S. (202) 653-7652), (Fax in U.S. (202) 653-7687), www.ilo.org; *Yearbook of Labour Statistics 2006.*

Korean Overseas Information Service (KOIS), Ministry of Culture and Information, Seoul 110, Republic of Korea, www.korea.net; Korea.net.

M.E. Sharpe, 80 Business Park Drive, Armonk, NY 10504, (800) 541-6563, Fax: (914) 273-2106, www.mesharpe.com; *The Illustrated Book of World Rankings.*

Organisation for Economic Cooperation and Development (OECD), 2 rue Andre Pascal, F-75775 Paris Cedex 16, France, (Telephone in U.S. (202) 785-6323), (Fax in U.S. (202) 785-0350), www.oecd.org; *ICT Sector Data and Metadata by Country; Labour Force Statistics: 1986-2005, 2007 Edition; OECD Composite Leading Indicators (CLIs), Updated September 2007;* and *OECD in Figures 2007.*

United Nations Statistics Division, New York, NY 10017, (800) 253-9646, Fax: (212) 963-4116, http://unstats.un.org; *Asia-Pacific in Figures 2004* and *Statistical Yearbook.*

The World Bank, 1818 H Street, NW, Washington, DC 20433, (202) 473-1000, Fax: (202) 477-6391, www.worldbank.org; *Korea, Republic of.*

KOREA, SOUTH - ENERGY INDUSTRIES

Platts, 2 Penn Plaza, 25th Floor, New York, NY 10121-2298, (212) 904-3070, www.platts.com; *Asian Electricity Outlook 2006* and *Emissions Daily.*

KOREA, SOUTH - ENVIRONMENTAL CONDITIONS

DSI Data Service Information, Xantener Strasse 51a, D-47495 Rheinberg, Germany, www.dsidata.com; *Campus Solution* and *DSI's Global Environmental Database.*

Economist Intelligence Unit, 111 West 57th Street, New York, NY 10019, (212) 554-0600, Fax: (212) 586-1181, www.eiu.com; *South Korea Country Report.*

International Institute for Environment and Development (IIED), 3 Endsleigh Street, London, England, WC1H 0DD, United Kingdom, www.iied.org; *Environment Urbanization.*

Platts, 2 Penn Plaza, 25th Floor, New York, NY 10121-2298, (212) 904-3070, www.platts.com; *Emissions Daily.*

United Nations Statistics Division, New York, NY 10017, (800) 253-9646, Fax: (212) 963-4116, http://unstats.un.org; *World Statistics Pocketbook.*

KOREA, SOUTH - EXPORTS

Central Intelligence Agency, Office of Public Affairs, Washington, DC 20505, (703) 482-0623, Fax: (703) 482-1739, www.cia.gov; *The World Factbook.*

Economist Intelligence Unit, 111 West 57th Street, New York, NY 10019, (212) 554-0600, Fax: (212) 586-1181, www.eiu.com; *South Korea Country Report.*

Euromonitor International, Inc., 224 S. Michigan Avenue, Suite 1500, Chicago, IL 60604, (312) 922-1115, Fax: (312) 922-1157, www.euromonitor.com; *International Marketing Data and Statistics 2008* and *The World Economic Factbook 2008.*

International Monetary Fund (IMF), 700 Nineteenth Street, NW, Washington, DC 20431, (202) 623-7000, Fax: (202) 623-4661, www.imf.org; *Direction of Trade Statistics Yearbook 2007.*

Korean Overseas Information Service (KOIS), Ministry of Culture and Information, Seoul 110, Republic of Korea, www.korea.net; Korea.net.

Palgrave Macmillan Ltd., Houndmills, Basingstoke, Hampshire, RG21 6XS, England, (Telephone in U.S. (888) 330-8477), (Fax in U.S. (800) 672-2054), www.palgrave.com; *The Statesman's Yearbook 2008.*

Taylor and Francis Group, An Informa Business, 2 Park Square, Milton Park, Abingdon, Oxford OX14 4RN, United Kingdom, (Dial from U.S. (212) 216-7800), (Fax from U.S. (212) 564-7854), www.tandf.co.uk; *The Europa World Year Book.*

United Nations Conference on Trade and Development (UNCTAD), DC2-1120, United Nations, New York, NY 10017, (212) 963-0027, www.unctad.org; *Handbook of Statistics 2005.*

United Nations Food and Agricultural Organization (FAO), Viale delle Terme di Caracalla, 00100 Rome, Italy, (Dial from U.S. (202) 653-2400), (Fax from U.S. (202) 653 5760), www.fao.org; *The State of Food and Agriculture (SOFA) 2006.*

The World Bank, 1818 H Street, NW, Washington, DC 20433, (202) 473-1000, Fax: (202) 477-6391, www.worldbank.org; *World Development Indicators (WDI) 2008.*

Worldinformation.com, 2 Market Street, Saffron Walden, Essex CB10 1HZ, United Kingdom, www.worldinformation.com; The World of Information (www.worldinformation.com).

KOREA, SOUTH - FEMALE WORKING POPULATION

See KOREA, SOUTH - EMPLOYMENT

KOREA, SOUTH - FERTILITY, HUMAN

Central Intelligence Agency, Office of Public Affairs, Washington, DC 20505, (703) 482-0623, Fax: (703) 482-1739, www.cia.gov; *The World Factbook.*

M.E. Sharpe, 80 Business Park Drive, Armonk, NY 10504, (800) 541-6563, Fax: (914) 273-2106, www.mesharpe.com; *The Illustrated Book of World Rankings.*

United Nations Statistics Division, New York, NY 10017, (800) 253-9646, Fax: (212) 963-4116, http://unstats.un.org; *Human Development Report 2006.*

The World Bank, 1818 H Street, NW, Washington, DC 20433, (202) 473-1000, Fax: (202) 477-6391, www.worldbank.org; *The World Bank Atlas 2003-2004* and *World Development Indicators (WDI) 2008.*

KOREA, SOUTH - FERTILIZER INDUSTRY

Korean Overseas Information Service (KOIS), Ministry of Culture and Information, Seoul 110, Republic of Korea, www.korea.net; Korea.net.

United Nations Food and Agricultural Organization (FAO), Viale delle Terme di Caracalla, 00100 Rome, Italy, (Dial from U.S. (202) 653-2400), (Fax from U.S. (202) 653 5760), www.fao.org; *FAO Fertilizer Yearbook* and *The State of Food and Agriculture (SOFA) 2006.*

United Nations Statistics Division, New York, NY 10017, (800) 253-9646, Fax: (212) 963-4116, http://unstats.un.org; *Statistical Yearbook.*

KOREA, SOUTH - FETAL MORTALITY

See KOREA, SOUTH - MORTALITY

KOREA, SOUTH - FILM

See KOREA, SOUTH - MOTION PICTURES

KOREA, SOUTH - FINANCE

Federal Statistical Office Germany, D-65180 Wiesbaden, Germany, www.destatis.de; *Republic of Korea 2005.*

International Monetary Fund (IMF), 700 Nineteenth Street, NW, Washington, DC 20431, (202) 623-7000, Fax: (202) 623-4661, www.imf.org; *International Financial Statistics Yearbook 2007.*

Taylor and Francis Group, An Informa Business, 2 Park Square, Milton Park, Abingdon, Oxford OX14 4RN, United Kingdom, (Dial from U.S. (212) 216-7800), (Fax from U.S. (212) 564-7854), www.tandf.co.uk; *The Europa World Year Book.*

United Nations Statistics Division, New York, NY 10017, (800) 253-9646, Fax: (212) 963-4116, http://unstats.un.org; *Asia-Pacific in Figures 2004; National Accounts Statistics: Compendium of Income Distribution Statistics; Statistical Yearbook;* and *Statistical Yearbook for Asia and the Pacific 2004.*

The World Bank, 1818 H Street, NW, Washington, DC 20433, (202) 473-1000, Fax: (202) 477-6391, www.worldbank.org; *Korea, Republic of.*

KOREA, SOUTH - FINANCE, PUBLIC

Bernan Essential Government Publications, 4611-F Assembly Drive, Lanham MD, 20706-4391, (301) 459-2255, Fax: (800) 865-3450, www.bernan.com; *National Accounts Statistics.*

Economist Intelligence Unit, 111 West 57th Street, New York, NY 10019, (212) 554-0600, Fax: (212) 586-1181, www.eiu.com; *South Korea Country Report.*

Federal Statistical Office Germany, D-65180 Wiesbaden, Germany, www.destatis.de; *Republic of Korea 2005.*

International Monetary Fund (IMF), 700 Nineteenth Street, NW, Washington, DC 20431, (202) 623-7000, Fax: (202) 623-4661, www.imf.org; *International Financial Statistics; International Financial Statistics Online Service;* and *International Financial Statistics Yearbook 2007.*

M.E. Sharpe, 80 Business Park Drive, Armonk, NY 10504, (800) 541-6563, Fax: (914) 273-2106, www.mesharpe.com; *The Illustrated Book of World Rankings.*

Palgrave Macmillan Ltd., Houndmills, Basingstoke, Hampshire, RG21 6XS, England, (Telephone in U.S. (888) 330-8477), (Fax in U.S. (800) 672-2054), www.palgrave.com; *The Statesman's Yearbook 2008.*

Taylor and Francis Group, An Informa Business, 2 Park Square, Milton Park, Abingdon, Oxford OX14 4RN, United Kingdom, (Dial from U.S. (212) 216-7800), (Fax from U.S. (212) 564-7854), www.tandf.co.uk; *The Europa World Year Book.*

United Nations Statistics Division, New York, NY 10017, (800) 253-9646, Fax: (212) 963-4116, http://unstats.un.org; *Statistical Yearbook for Asia and the Pacific 2004.*

The World Bank, 1818 H Street, NW, Washington, DC 20433, (202) 473-1000, Fax: (202) 477-6391, www.worldbank.org; *Korea, Republic of.*

KOREA, SOUTH - FISHERIES

Federal Statistical Office Germany, D-65180 Wiesbaden, Germany, www.destatis.de; *Republic of Korea 2005.*

Korean Overseas Information Service (KOIS), Ministry of Culture and Information, Seoul 110, Republic of Korea, www.korea.net; Korea.net.

M.E. Sharpe, 80 Business Park Drive, Armonk, NY 10504, (800) 541-6563, Fax: (914) 273-2106, www.mesharpe.com; *The Illustrated Book of World Rankings.*

Palgrave Macmillan Ltd., Houndmills, Basingstoke, Hampshire, RG21 6XS, England, (Telephone in U.S. (888) 330-8477), (Fax in U.S. (800) 672-2054), www.palgrave.com; *The Statesman's Yearbook 2008.*

Taylor and Francis Group, An Informa Business, 2 Park Square, Milton Park, Abingdon, Oxford OX14 4RN, United Kingdom, (Dial from U.S. (212) 216-7800), (Fax from U.S. (212) 564-7854), www.tandf.co.uk; *The Europa World Year Book.*

United Nations Conference on Trade and Development (UNCTAD), DC2-1120, United Nations, New York, NY 10017, (212) 963-0027, www.unctad.org; *UNCTAD Commodity Yearbook.*

United Nations Food and Agricultural Organization (FAO), Viale delle Terme di Caracalla, 00100 Rome, Italy, (Dial from U.S. (202) 653-2400), (Fax from U.S. (202) 653 5760), www.fao.org; *FAO Yearbook of Fishery Statistics;* Fishery Databases; FISHSTAT Database. Subjects covered include: Aquaculture production, capture production, fishery commodities; and *The State of Food and Agriculture (SOFA) 2006.*

United Nations Statistics Division, New York, NY 10017, (800) 253-9646, Fax: (212) 963-4116, http://unstats.un.org; *Statistical Yearbook.*

The World Bank, 1818 H Street, NW, Washington, DC 20433, (202) 473-1000, Fax: (202) 477-6391, www.worldbank.org; *Korea, Republic of.*

KOREA, SOUTH - FLOUR INDUSTRY

United Nations Statistics Division, New York, NY 10017, (800) 253-9646, Fax: (212) 963-4116, http://unstats.un.org; *Statistical Yearbook.*

KOREA, SOUTH - FOOD

Euromonitor International, Inc., 224 S. Michigan Avenue, Suite 1500, Chicago, IL 60604, (312) 922-1115, Fax: (312) 922-1157, www.euromonitor.com; *Retail Trade International 2007.*

Korean Overseas Information Service (KOIS), Ministry of Culture and Information, Seoul 110, Republic of Korea, www.korea.net; Korea.net.

United Nations Conference on Trade and Development (UNCTAD), DC2-1120, United Nations, New York, NY 10017, (212) 963-0027, www.unctad.org; *UNCTAD Commodity Yearbook.*

United Nations Food and Agricultural Organization (FAO), Viale delle Terme di Caracalla, 00100 Rome, Italy, (Dial from U.S. (202) 653-2400), (Fax from U.S. (202) 653 5760), www.fao.org; *FAO Production Yearbook 2002* and *The State of Food and Agriculture (SOFA) 2006.*

United Nations Statistics Division, New York, NY 10017, (800) 253-9646, Fax: (212) 963-4116, http://unstats.un.org; *Human Development Report 2006* and *Statistical Yearbook for Asia and the Pacific 2004.*

KOREA, SOUTH - FOOTWEAR

Korean Overseas Information Service (KOIS), Ministry of Culture and Information, Seoul 110, Republic of Korea, www.korea.net; Korea.net.

KOREA, SOUTH - FOREIGN EXCHANGE RATES

Central Intelligence Agency, Office of Public Affairs, Washington, DC 20505, (703) 482-0623, Fax: (703) 482-1739, www.cia.gov; *The World Factbook.*

Economist Intelligence Unit, 111 West 57th Street, New York, NY 10019, (212) 554-0600, Fax: (212) 586-1181, www.eiu.com; *Business Asia.*

Euromonitor International, Inc., 224 S. Michigan Avenue, Suite 1500, Chicago, IL 60604, (312) 922-1115, Fax: (312) 922-1157, www.euromonitor.com; *International Marketing Data and Statistics 2008* and *The World Economic Factbook 2008.*

International Civil Aviation Organization (ICAO), External Relations and Public Information Office (EPO), 999 University Street, Montreal, Quebec H3C 5H7, Canada, (Dial from U.S. (514) 954-8219), (Fax from U.S. (514) 954-6077), www.icao.int; *Civil Aviation Statistics of the World.*

Taylor and Francis Group, An Informa Business, 2 Park Square, Milton Park, Abingdon, Oxford OX14 4RN, United Kingdom, (Dial from U.S. (212) 216-7800), (Fax from U.S. (212) 564-7854), www.tandf.co.uk; *The Europa World Year Book.*

United Nations Statistics Division, New York, NY 10017, (800) 253-9646, Fax: (212) 963-4116, http://unstats.un.org; *Statistical Yearbook* and *World Statistics Pocketbook.*

Worldinformation.com, 2 Market Street, Saffron Walden, Essex CB10 1HZ, United Kingdom, www.worldinformation.com; The World of Information (www.worldinformation.com).

KOREA, SOUTH - FORESTS AND FORESTRY

Economist Intelligence Unit, 111 West 57th Street, New York, NY 10019, (212) 554-0600, Fax: (212) 586-1181, www.eiu.com; *Business Asia.*

Federal Statistical Office Germany, D-65180 Wiesbaden, Germany, www.destatis.de; *Republic of Korea 2005.*

Korean Overseas Information Service (KOIS), Ministry of Culture and Information, Seoul 110, Republic of Korea, www.korea.net; Korea.net.

M.E. Sharpe, 80 Business Park Drive, Armonk, NY 10504, (800) 541-6563, Fax: (914) 273-2106, www.mesharpe.com; *The Illustrated Book of World Rankings.*

Palgrave Macmillan Ltd., Houndmills, Basingstoke, Hampshire, RG21 6XS, England, (Telephone in U.S. (888) 330-8477), (Fax in U.S. (800) 672-2054), www.palgrave.com; *The Statesman's Yearbook 2008.*

Taylor and Francis Group, An Informa Business, 2 Park Square, Milton Park, Abingdon, Oxford OX14 4RN, United Kingdom, (Dial from U.S. (212) 216-7800), (Fax from U.S. (212) 564-7854), www.tandf.co.uk; *The Europa World Year Book.*

UNESCO Institute for Statistics, C.P. 6128 Succursale Centre-Ville, Montreal, Quebec, H3C 3J7 Canada, (Dial from U.S. (514) 343-6880), (Fax from U.S. (514) 343 6882), www.uis.unesco.org; *Statistical Tables.*

United Nations Conference on Trade and Development (UNCTAD), DC2-1120, United Nations, New York, NY 10017, (212) 963-0027, www.unctad.org; *UNCTAD Commodity Yearbook.*

United Nations Food and Agricultural Organization (FAO), Viale delle Terme di Caracalla, 00100 Rome, Italy, (Dial from U.S. (202) 653-2400), (Fax from U.S. (202) 653 5760), www.fao.org; *FAO Yearbook of Forest Products* and *The State of Food and Agriculture (SOFA) 2006.*

United Nations Statistics Division, New York, NY 10017, (800) 253-9646, Fax: (212) 963-4116, http://unstats.un.org; *Statistical Yearbook.*

The World Bank, 1818 H Street, NW, Washington, DC 20433, (202) 473-1000, Fax: (202) 477-6391, www.worldbank.org; *Korea, Republic of.*

KOREA, SOUTH - FURNITURE

Korean Overseas Information Service (KOIS), Ministry of Culture and Information, Seoul 110, Republic of Korea, www.korea.net; Korea.net.

KOREA, SOUTH - GAS PRODUCTION

See KOREA, SOUTH - MINERAL INDUSTRIES

KOREA, SOUTH - GEOGRAPHIC INFORMATION SYSTEMS

M.E. Sharpe, 80 Business Park Drive, Armonk, NY 10504, (800) 541-6563, Fax: (914) 273-2106, www.mesharpe.com; *The Illustrated Book of World Rankings.*

The World Bank, 1818 H Street, NW, Washington, DC 20433, (202) 473-1000, Fax: (202) 477-6391, www.worldbank.org; *Korea, Republic of.*

KOREA, SOUTH - GOLD INDUSTRY

United Nations Statistics Division, New York, NY 10017, (800) 253-9646, Fax: (212) 963-4116, http://unstats.un.org; *Statistical Yearbook.*

The World Bank, 1818 H Street, NW, Washington, DC 20433, (202) 473-1000, Fax: (202) 477-6391, www.worldbank.org; *World Development Indicators (WDI) 2008.*

KOREA, SOUTH - GOLD PRODUCTION

See KOREA, SOUTH - MINERAL INDUSTRIES

KOREA, SOUTH - GREEN PEPPER AND CHILIE PRODUCTION

See KOREA, SOUTH - CROPS

KOREA, SOUTH - GROSS DOMESTIC PRODUCT

Economist Intelligence Unit, 111 West 57th Street, New York, NY 10019, (212) 554-0600, Fax: (212) 586-1181, www.eiu.com; *Business Asia* and *South Korea Country Report.*

Euromonitor International, Inc., 224 S. Michigan Avenue, Suite 1500, Chicago, IL 60604, (312) 922-1115, Fax: (312) 922-1157, www.euromonitor.com; *International Marketing Data and Statistics 2008* and *The World Economic Factbook 2008.*

M.E. Sharpe, 80 Business Park Drive, Armonk, NY 10504, (800) 541-6563, Fax: (914) 273-2106, www.mesharpe.com; *The Illustrated Book of World Rankings.*

Organisation for Economic Cooperation and Development (OECD), 2 rue Andre Pascal, F-75775 Paris Cedex 16, France, (Telephone in U.S. (202) 785-6323), (Fax in U.S. (202) 785-0350), www.oecd.org; *Comparison of Gross Domestic Product (GDP) for OECD Countries.*

Taylor and Francis Group, An Informa Business, 2 Park Square, Milton Park, Abingdon, Oxford OX14 4RN, United Kingdom, (Dial from U.S. (212) 216-7800), (Fax from U.S. (212) 564-7854), www.tandf.co.uk; *The Europa World Year Book.*

United Nations Statistics Division, New York, NY 10017, (800) 253-9646, Fax: (212) 963-4116, http://unstats.un.org; *Human Development Report 2006; National Accounts Statistics: Compendium of Income Distribution Statistics;* and *Statistical Yearbook.*

The World Bank, 1818 H Street, NW, Washington, DC 20433, (202) 473-1000, Fax: (202) 477-6391, www.worldbank.org; *World Development Indicators (WDI) 2008.*

KOREA, SOUTH - GROSS NATIONAL PRODUCT

Euromonitor International, Inc., 224 S. Michigan Avenue, Suite 1500, Chicago, IL 60604, (312) 922-1115, Fax: (312) 922-1157, www.euromonitor.com; *International Marketing Data and Statistics 2008.*

Korean Overseas Information Service (KOIS), Ministry of Culture and Information, Seoul 110, Republic of Korea, www.korea.net; Korea.net.

M.E. Sharpe, 80 Business Park Drive, Armonk, NY 10504, (800) 541-6563, Fax: (914) 273-2106, www.mesharpe.com; *The Illustrated Book of World Rankings.*

Organisation for Economic Cooperation and Development (OECD), 2 rue Andre Pascal, F-75775 Paris Cedex 16, France, (Telephone in U.S. (202) 785-6323), (Fax in U.S. (202) 785-0350), www.oecd.org; *OECD Composite Leading Indicators (CLIs), Updated September 2007.*

Palgrave Macmillan Ltd., Houndmills, Basingstoke, Hampshire, RG21 6XS, England, (Telephone in U.S. (888) 330-8477), (Fax in U.S. (800) 672-2054), www.palgrave.com; *The Statesman's Yearbook 2008.*

Taylor and Francis Group, An Informa Business, 2 Park Square, Milton Park, Abingdon, Oxford OX14 4RN, United Kingdom, (Dial from U.S. (212) 216-7800), (Fax from U.S. (212) 564-7854), www.tandf.co.uk; *The Europa World Year Book.*

U.S. Department of State (DOS), 2201 C Street NW, Washington, DC 20520, (202) 647-4000, www.state.gov; *World Military Expenditures and Arms Transfers (WMEAT).*

United Nations Statistics Division, New York, NY 10017, (800) 253-9646, Fax: (212) 963-4116, http://unstats.un.org; *Statistical Yearbook.*

The World Bank, 1818 H Street, NW, Washington, DC 20433, (202) 473-1000, Fax: (202) 477-6391, www.worldbank.org; *The World Bank Atlas 2003-2004* and *World Development Indicators (WDI) 2008.*

Worldinformation.com, 2 Market Street, Saffron Walden, Essex CB10 1HZ, United Kingdom, www.worldinformation.com; The World of Information (www.worldinformation.com).

KOREA, SOUTH - HEMP FIBRE PRODUCTION

See KOREA, SOUTH - TEXTILE INDUSTRY

KOREA, SOUTH - HIDES AND SKINS INDUSTRY

United Nations Food and Agricultural Organization (FAO), Viale delle Terme di Caracalla, 00100 Rome, Italy, (Dial from U.S. (202) 653-2400), (Fax from U.S. (202) 653 5760), www.fao.org; *FAO Production Yearbook 2002.*

KOREA, SOUTH - HOUSING

Euromonitor International, Inc., 224 S. Michigan Avenue, Suite 1500, Chicago, IL 60604, (312) 922-1115, Fax: (312) 922-1157, www.euromonitor.com; *World Marketing Data and Statistics.*

Korean Overseas Information Service (KOIS), Ministry of Culture and Information, Seoul 110, Republic of Korea, www.korea.net; Korea.net.

M.E. Sharpe, 80 Business Park Drive, Armonk, NY 10504, (800) 541-6563, Fax: (914) 273-2106, www.mesharpe.com; *The Illustrated Book of World Rankings.*

KOREA, SOUTH - ILLITERATE PERSONS

Euromonitor International, Inc., 224 S. Michigan Avenue, Suite 1500, Chicago, IL 60604, (312) 922-1115, Fax: (312) 922-1157, www.euromonitor.com; *The World Economic Factbook 2008.*

UNESCO Institute for Statistics, C.P. 6128 Succursale Centre-Ville, Montreal, Quebec, H3C 3J7 Canada, (Dial from U.S. (514) 343-6880), (Fax from U.S. (514) 343 6882), www.uis.unesco.org; *Statistical Tables.*

United Nations Statistics Division, New York, NY 10017, (800) 253-9646, Fax: (212) 963-4116, http://unstats.un.org; *Asia-Pacific in Figures 2004* and *Human Development Report 2006.*

KOREA, SOUTH - IMPORTS

Central Intelligence Agency, Office of Public Affairs, Washington, DC 20505, (703) 482-0623, Fax: (703) 482-1739, www.cia.gov; *The World Factbook.*

Economist Intelligence Unit, 111 West 57th Street, New York, NY 10019, (212) 554-0600, Fax: (212) 586-1181, www.eiu.com; *South Korea Country Report.*

Euromonitor International, Inc., 224 S. Michigan Avenue, Suite 1500, Chicago, IL 60604, (312) 922-1115, Fax: (312) 922-1157, www.euromonitor.com; *International Marketing Data and Statistics 2008* and *The World Economic Factbook 2008.*

International Monetary Fund (IMF), 700 Nineteenth Street, NW, Washington, DC 20431, (202) 623-7000, Fax: (202) 623-4661, www.imf.org; *Direction of Trade Statistics Yearbook 2007.*

Korean Overseas Information Service (KOIS), Ministry of Culture and Information, Seoul 110, Republic of Korea, www.korea.net; Korea.net.

Palgrave Macmillan Ltd., Houndmills, Basingstoke, Hampshire, RG21 6XS, England, (Telephone in U.S. (888) 330-8477), (Fax in U.S. (800) 672-2054), www.palgrave.com; *The Statesman's Yearbook 2008.*

Taylor and Francis Group, An Informa Business, 2 Park Square, Milton Park, Abingdon, Oxford OX14 4RN, United Kingdom, (Dial from U.S. (212) 216-7800), (Fax from U.S. (212) 564-7854), www.tandf.co.uk; *The Europa World Year Book.*

United Nations Conference on Trade and Development (UNCTAD), DC2-1120, United Nations, New York, NY 10017, (212) 963-0027, www.unctad.org; *Handbook of Statistics 2005.*

United Nations Food and Agricultural Organization (FAO), Viale delle Terme di Caracalla, 00100 Rome, Italy, (Dial from U.S. (202) 653-2400), (Fax from U.S. (202) 653 5760), www.fao.org; *The State of Food and Agriculture (SOFA) 2006.*

The World Bank, 1818 H Street, NW, Washington, DC 20433, (202) 473-1000, Fax: (202) 477-6391, www.worldbank.org; *World Development Indicators (WDI) 2008.*

Worldinformation.com, 2 Market Street, Saffron Walden, Essex CB10 1HZ, United Kingdom, www.worldinformation.com; The World of Information (www.worldinformation.com).

KOREA, SOUTH - INDUSTRIAL METALS PRODUCTION

See KOREA, SOUTH - MINERAL INDUSTRIES

KOREA, SOUTH - INDUSTRIAL PRODUCTIVITY

Euromonitor International, Inc., 224 S. Michigan Avenue, Suite 1500, Chicago, IL 60604, (312) 922-1115, Fax: (312) 922-1157, www.euromonitor.com; *International Marketing Data and Statistics 2008.*

M.E. Sharpe, 80 Business Park Drive, Armonk, NY 10504, (800) 541-6563, Fax: (914) 273-2106, www.mesharpe.com; *The Illustrated Book of World Rankings.*

KOREA, SOUTH - INDUSTRIAL PROPERTY

United Nations Statistics Division, New York, NY 10017, (800) 253-9646, Fax: (212) 963-4116, http://unstats.un.org; *Statistical Yearbook.*

KOREA, SOUTH - INDUSTRIES

Central Intelligence Agency, Office of Public Affairs, Washington, DC 20505, (703) 482-0623, Fax: (703) 482-1739, www.cia.gov; *The World Factbook.*

Economist Intelligence Unit, 111 West 57th Street, New York, NY 10019, (212) 554-0600, Fax: (212) 586-1181, www.eiu.com; *South Korea Country Report.*

Euromonitor International, Inc., 224 S. Michigan Avenue, Suite 1500, Chicago, IL 60604, (312) 922-1115, Fax: (312) 922-1157, www.euromonitor.com; *International Marketing Data and Statistics 2008; The World Economic Factbook 2008;* and *World Marketing Data and Statistics.*

Federal Statistical Office Germany, D-65180 Wiesbaden, Germany, www.destatis.de; *Republic of Korea 2005.*

International Labour Office, I.L.O. Publications, 4 route des Morillons, CH-1211 Geneva 22, Switzerland, (Telephone in U.S. (202) 653-7652), (Fax in U.S. (202) 653-7687), www.ilo.org; *Yearbook of Labour Statistics 2006.*

M.E. Sharpe, 80 Business Park Drive, Armonk, NY 10504, (800) 541-6563, Fax: (914) 273-2106, www.mesharpe.com; *The Illustrated Book of World Rankings.*

Palgrave Macmillan Ltd., Houndmills, Basingstoke, Hampshire, RG21 6XS, England, (Telephone in U.S. (888) 330-8477), (Fax in U.S. (800) 672-2054), www.palgrave.com; *The Statesman's Yearbook 2008.*

Taylor and Francis Group, An Informa Business, 2 Park Square, Milton Park, Abingdon, Oxford OX14 4RN, United Kingdom, (Dial from U.S. (212) 216-7800), (Fax from U.S. (212) 564-7854), www.tandf.co.uk; *The Europa World Year Book.*

United Nations Industrial Development Organization (UNIDO), 1 United Nations Plaza, New York, NY 10017, (212) 963 6890, Fax: (212) 963-7904, http://unido.org; Industrial Statistics Database 2008 (INDSTAT) and *The International Yearbook of Industrial Statistics 2008.*

United Nations Statistics Division, New York, NY 10017, (800) 253-9646, Fax: (212) 963-4116, http://unstats.un.org; *Asia-Pacific in Figures 2004; 2004 Industrial Commodity Statistics Yearbook; Statistical Yearbook;* and *Statistical Yearbook for Asia and the Pacific 2004.*

The World Bank, 1818 H Street, NW, Washington, DC 20433, (202) 473-1000, Fax: (202) 477-6391, www.worldbank.org; *Korea, Republic of* and *World Development Indicators (WDI) 2008.*

KOREA, SOUTH - INFANT AND MATERNAL MORTALITY

See KOREA, SOUTH - MORTALITY

KOREA, SOUTH - INORGANIC ACIDS

United Nations Statistics Division, New York, NY 10017, (800) 253-9646, Fax: (212) 963-4116, http://unstats.un.org; *Statistical Yearbook.*

KOREA, SOUTH - INTERNATIONAL TRADE

Bernan Essential Government Publications, 4611-F Assembly Drive, Lanham MD, 20706-4391, (301) 459-2255, Fax: (800) 865-3450, www.bernan.com; *OECD Factbook 2006.*

Economist Intelligence Unit, 111 West 57th Street, New York, NY 10019, (212) 554-0600, Fax: (212) 586-1181, www.eiu.com; *Business Asia* and *South Korea Country Report.*

Euromonitor International, Inc., 224 S. Michigan Avenue, Suite 1500, Chicago, IL 60604, (312) 922-1115, Fax: (312) 922-1157, www.euromonitor.com; *The World Economic Factbook 2008* and *World Marketing Data and Statistics.*

Federal Statistical Office Germany, D-65180 Wiesbaden, Germany, www.destatis.de; *Republic of Korea 2005.*

M.E. Sharpe, 80 Business Park Drive, Armonk, NY 10504, (800) 541-6563, Fax: (914) 273-2106, www.mesharpe.com; *The Illustrated Book of World Rankings.*

Organisation for Economic Cooperation and Development (OECD), 2 rue Andre Pascal, F-75775 Paris Cedex 16, France, (Telephone in U.S. (202) 785-6323), (Fax in U.S. (202) 785-0350), www.oecd.org; *OECD in Figures 2007.*

Palgrave Macmillan Ltd., Houndmills, Basingstoke, Hampshire, RG21 6XS, England, (Telephone in U.S. (888) 330-8477), (Fax in U.S. (800) 672-2054), www.palgrave.com; *The Statesman's Yearbook 2008.*

Taylor and Francis Group, An Informa Business, 2 Park Square, Milton Park, Abingdon, Oxford OX14 4RN, United Kingdom, (Dial from U.S. (212) 216-7800), (Fax from U.S. (212) 564-7854), www.tandf.co.uk; *The Europa World Year Book.*

United Nations Conference on Trade and Development (UNCTAD), DC2-1120, United Nations, New York, NY 10017, (212) 963-0027, www.unctad.org; *UNCTAD Commodity Yearbook.*

United Nations Food and Agricultural Organization (FAO), Viale delle Terme di Caracalla, 00100 Rome, Italy, (Dial from U.S. (202) 653-2400), (Fax from U.S. (202) 653 5760), www.fao.org; *FAO Trade Yearbook* and *The State of Food and Agriculture (SOFA) 2006.*

United Nations Statistics Division, New York, NY 10017, (800) 253-9646, Fax: (212) 963-4116, http://unstats.un.org; *Asia-Pacific in Figures 2004; International Trade Statistics Yearbook; Statistical Yearbook;* and *Statistical Yearbook for Asia and the Pacific 2004.*

The World Bank, 1818 H Street, NW, Washington, DC 20433, (202) 473-1000, Fax: (202) 477-6391, www.worldbank.org; *Korea, Republic of.*

World Trade Organization (WTO), Centre William Rappard, Rue de Lausanne 154, CH-1211 Geneva 21, Switzerland, www.wto.org; *International Trade Statistics 2006.*

KOREA, SOUTH - INTERNET USERS

Federal Statistical Office Germany, D-65180 Wiesbaden, Germany, www.destatis.de; *Republic of Korea 2005.*

International Telecommunication Union (ITU), Place des Nations, 1211 Geneva 20, Switzerland, www.itu.int; *World Telecommunication/ICT Indicators Database on CD-ROM; World Telecommunication/ICT Indicators Database Online;* and *Yearbook of Statistics - Telecommunication Services (Chronological Time Series 1997-2006).*

The World Bank, 1818 H Street, NW, Washington, DC 20433, (202) 473-1000, Fax: (202) 477-6391, www.worldbank.org; *Korea, Republic of.*

KOREA, SOUTH - INVESTMENTS

Korean Overseas Information Service (KOIS), Ministry of Culture and Information, Seoul 110, Republic of Korea, www.korea.net; Korea.net.

KOREA, SOUTH - INVESTMENTS, FOREIGN

Korean Overseas Information Service (KOIS), Ministry of Culture and Information, Seoul 110, Republic of Korea, www.korea.net; Korea.net.

KOREA, SOUTH - IRON AND IRON ORE PRODUCTION

See KOREA, SOUTH - MINERAL INDUSTRIES

KOREA, SOUTH - IRRIGATION

Euromonitor International, Inc., 224 S. Michigan Avenue, Suite 1500, Chicago, IL 60604, (312) 922-1115, Fax: (312) 922-1157, www.euromonitor.com; *International Marketing Data and Statistics 2008.*

KOREA, SOUTH - LABOR

Central Intelligence Agency, Office of Public Affairs, Washington, DC 20505, (703) 482-0623, Fax: (703) 482-1739, www.cia.gov; *The World Factbook.*

Economist Intelligence Unit, 111 West 57th Street, New York, NY 10019, (212) 554-0600, Fax: (212) 586-1181, www.eiu.com; *Business Asia.*

Euromonitor International, Inc., 224 S. Michigan Avenue, Suite 1500, Chicago, IL 60604, (312) 922-1115, Fax: (312) 922-1157, www.euromonitor.com; *International Marketing Data and Statistics 2008* and *World Marketing Data and Statistics.*

International Labour Office, I.L.O. Publications, 4 route des Morillons, CH-1211 Geneva 22, Switzerland, (Telephone in U.S. (202) 653-7652), (Fax in U.S. (202) 653-7687), www.ilo.org; *Yearbook of Labour Statistics 2006.*

M.E. Sharpe, 80 Business Park Drive, Armonk, NY 10504, (800) 541-6563, Fax: (914) 273-2106, www.mesharpe.com; *The Illustrated Book of World Rankings.*

Palgrave Macmillan Ltd., Houndmills, Basingstoke, Hampshire, RG21 6XS, England, (Telephone in U.S. (888) 330-8477), (Fax in U.S. (800) 672-2054), www.palgrave.com; *The Statesman's Yearbook 2008.*

Taylor and Francis Group, An Informa Business, 2 Park Square, Milton Park, Abingdon, Oxford OX14 4RN, United Kingdom, (Dial from U.S. (212) 216-7800), (Fax from U.S. (212) 564-7854), www.tandf.co.uk; *The Europa World Year Book.*

United Nations Food and Agricultural Organization (FAO), Viale delle Terme di Caracalla, 00100 Rome, Italy, (Dial from U.S. (202) 653-2400), (Fax from U.S. (202) 653 5760), www.fao.org; *The State of Food and Agriculture (SOFA) 2006.*

United Nations Statistics Division, New York, NY 10017, (800) 253-9646, Fax: (212) 963-4116, http://unstats.un.org; *Human Development Report 2006.*

The World Bank, 1818 H Street, NW, Washington, DC 20433, (202) 473-1000, Fax: (202) 477-6391, www.worldbank.org; *The World Bank Atlas 2003-2004* and *World Development Indicators (WDI) 2008.*

KOREA, SOUTH - LAND USE

Central Intelligence Agency, Office of Public Affairs, Washington, DC 20505, (703) 482-0623, Fax: (703) 482-1739, www.cia.gov; *The World Factbook.*

Euromonitor International, Inc., 224 S. Michigan Avenue, Suite 1500, Chicago, IL 60604, (312) 922-1115, Fax: (312) 922-1157, www.euromonitor.com; *International Marketing Data and Statistics 2008.*

United Nations Food and Agricultural Organization (FAO), Viale delle Terme di Caracalla, 00100 Rome, Italy, (Dial from U.S. (202) 653-2400), (Fax from U.S. (202) 653 5760), www.fao.org; *FAO Production Yearbook 2002.*

KOREA, SOUTH - LIBRARIES

M.E. Sharpe, 80 Business Park Drive, Armonk, NY 10504, (800) 541-6563, Fax: (914) 273-2106, www.mesharpe.com; *The Illustrated Book of World Rankings.*

UNESCO Institute for Statistics, C.P. 6128 Succursale Centre-Ville, Montreal, Quebec, H3C 3J7 Canada, (Dial from U.S. (514) 343-6880), (Fax from U.S. (514) 343 6882), www.uis.unesco.org; *Statistical Tables.*

KOREA, SOUTH - LIFE EXPECTANCY

Central Intelligence Agency, Office of Public Affairs, Washington, DC 20505, (703) 482-0623, Fax: (703) 482-1739, www.cia.gov; *The World Factbook.*

Economist Intelligence Unit, 111 West 57th Street, New York, NY 10019, (212) 554-0600, Fax: (212) 586-1181, www.eiu.com; *Business Asia.*

Euromonitor International, Inc., 224 S. Michigan Avenue, Suite 1500, Chicago, IL 60604, (312) 922-1115, Fax: (312) 922-1157, www.euromonitor.com; *The World Economic Factbook 2008.*

Korean Overseas Information Service (KOIS), Ministry of Culture and Information, Seoul 110, Republic of Korea, www.korea.net; Korea.net.

Palgrave Macmillan Ltd., Houndmills, Basingstoke, Hampshire, RG21 6XS, England, (Telephone in U.S. (888) 330-8477), (Fax in U.S. (800) 672-2054), www.palgrave.com; *The Statesman's Yearbook 2008.*

United Nations Statistics Division, New York, NY 10017, (800) 253-9646, Fax: (212) 963-4116, http://unstats.un.org; *Asia-Pacific in Figures 2004; Human Development Report 2006;* and *World Statistics Pocketbook.*

The World Bank, 1818 H Street, NW, Washington, DC 20433, (202) 473-1000, Fax: (202) 477-6391, www.worldbank.org; *The World Bank Atlas 2003-2004.*

KOREA, SOUTH - LITERACY

Euromonitor International, Inc., 224 S. Michigan Avenue, Suite 1500, Chicago, IL 60604, (312) 922-1115, Fax: (312) 922-1157, www.euromonitor.com; *World Marketing Data and Statistics.*

KOREA, SOUTH - LITERACY PROGRAMS

Korean Overseas Information Service (KOIS), Ministry of Culture and Information, Seoul 110, Republic of Korea, www.korea.net; Korea.net.

KOREA, SOUTH - LIVESTOCK

Euromonitor International, Inc., 224 S. Michigan Avenue, Suite 1500, Chicago, IL 60604, (312) 922-1115, Fax: (312) 922-1157, www.euromonitor.com; *International Marketing Data and Statistics 2008.*

Korean Overseas Information Service (KOIS), Ministry of Culture and Information, Seoul 110, Republic of Korea, www.korea.net; Korea.net.

M.E. Sharpe, 80 Business Park Drive, Armonk, NY 10504, (800) 541-6563, Fax: (914) 273-2106, www.mesharpe.com; *The Illustrated Book of World Rankings.*

Palgrave Macmillan Ltd., Houndmills, Basingstoke, Hampshire, RG21 6XS, England, (Telephone in U.S. (888) 330-8477), (Fax in U.S. (800) 672-2054), www.palgrave.com; *The Statesman's Yearbook 2008.*

Taylor and Francis Group, An Informa Business, 2 Park Square, Milton Park, Abingdon, Oxford OX14 4RN, United Kingdom, (Dial from U.S. (212) 216-7800), (Fax from U.S. (212) 564-7854), www.tandf.co.uk; *The Europa World Year Book.*

United Nations Conference on Trade and Development (UNCTAD), DC2-1120, United Nations, New York, NY 10017, (212) 963-0027, www.unctad.org; *UNCTAD Commodity Yearbook.*

United Nations Food and Agricultural Organization (FAO), Viale delle Terme di Caracalla, 00100 Rome, Italy, (Dial from U.S. (202) 653-2400), (Fax from U.S. (202) 653 5760), www.fao.org; *FAO Production Yearbook 2002* and *The State of Food and Agriculture (SOFA) 2006.*

United Nations Statistics Division, New York, NY 10017, (800) 253-9646, Fax: (212) 963-4116, http://unstats.un.org; *Statistical Yearbook.*

KOREA, SOUTH - LOCAL TAXATION

Euromonitor International, Inc., 224 S. Michigan Avenue, Suite 1500, Chicago, IL 60604, (312) 922-1115, Fax: (312) 922-1157, www.euromonitor.com; *International Marketing Data and Statistics 2008.*

KOREA, SOUTH - MANPOWER

United Nations Statistics Division, New York, NY 10017, (800) 253-9646, Fax: (212) 963-4116, http://unstats.un.org; *Statistical Yearbook for Asia and the Pacific 2004.*

KOREA, SOUTH - MANUFACTURES

M.E. Sharpe, 80 Business Park Drive, Armonk, NY 10504, (800) 541-6563, Fax: (914) 273-2106, www.mesharpe.com; *The Illustrated Book of World Rankings.*

United Nations Statistics Division, New York, NY 10017, (800) 253-9646, Fax: (212) 963-4116, http://unstats.un.org; *Statistical Yearbook.*

The World Bank, 1818 H Street, NW, Washington, DC 20433, (202) 473-1000, Fax: (202) 477-6391, www.worldbank.org; *World Development Indicators (WDI) 2008.*

KOREA, SOUTH - MARRIAGE

M.E. Sharpe, 80 Business Park Drive, Armonk, NY 10504, (800) 541-6563, Fax: (914) 273-2106, www.mesharpe.com; *The Illustrated Book of World Rankings.*

Taylor and Francis Group, An Informa Business, 2 Park Square, Milton Park, Abingdon, Oxford OX14 4RN, United Kingdom, (Dial from U.S. (212) 216-7800), (Fax from U.S. (212) 564-7854), www.tandf.co.uk; *The Europa World Year Book.*

United Nations Statistics Division, New York, NY 10017, (800) 253-9646, Fax: (212) 963-4116, http://unstats.un.org; *Demographic Yearbook* and *Statistical Yearbook.*

KOREA, SOUTH - MEAT PRODUCTION

See KOREA, SOUTH - LIVESTOCK

KOREA, SOUTH - MEDICAL CARE

Korean Overseas Information Service (KOIS), Ministry of Culture and Information, Seoul 110, Republic of Korea, www.korea.net; Korea.net.

KOREA, SOUTH - MEDICAL CARE, COST OF

Korean Overseas Information Service (KOIS), Ministry of Culture and Information, Seoul 110, Republic of Korea, www.korea.net; Korea.net.

KOREA, SOUTH - MILK PRODUCTION

See KOREA, SOUTH - DAIRY PROCESSING

KOREA, SOUTH - MINERAL INDUSTRIES

Federal Statistical Office Germany, D-65180 Wiesbaden, Germany, www.destatis.de; *Republic of Korea 2005.*

International Energy Agency (IEA), 9, rue de la Federation, 75739 Paris Cedex 15, France, www.iea.org; *Key World Energy Statistics 2007.*

Korean Overseas Information Service (KOIS), Ministry of Culture and Information, Seoul 110, Republic of Korea, www.korea.net; Korea.net.

M.E. Sharpe, 80 Business Park Drive, Armonk, NY 10504, (800) 541-6563, Fax: (914) 273-2106, www.mesharpe.com; *The Illustrated Book of World Rankings.*

Palgrave Macmillan Ltd., Houndmills, Basingstoke, Hampshire, RG21 6XS, England, (Telephone in U.S. (888) 330-8477), (Fax in U.S. (800) 672-2054), www.palgrave.com; *The Statesman's Yearbook 2008.*

Taylor and Francis Group, An Informa Business, 2 Park Square, Milton Park, Abingdon, Oxford OX14 4RN, United Kingdom, (Dial from U.S. (212) 216-7800), (Fax from U.S. (212) 564-7854), www.tandf.co.uk; *The Europa World Year Book.*

United Nations Conference on Trade and Development (UNCTAD), DC2-1120, United Nations, New York, NY 10017, (212) 963-0027, www.unctad.org; *UNCTAD Commodity Yearbook.*

United Nations Statistics Division, New York, NY 10017, (800) 253-9646, Fax: (212) 963-4116, http://unstats.un.org; *Statistical Yearbook.*

The World Bank, 1818 H Street, NW, Washington, DC 20433, (202) 473-1000, Fax: (202) 477-6391, www.worldbank.org; *Korea, Republic of.*

KOREA, SOUTH - MONEY EXCHANGE RATES

See KOREA, SOUTH - FOREIGN EXCHANGE RATES

KOREA, SOUTH - MONEY SUPPLY

Economist Intelligence Unit, 111 West 57th Street, New York, NY 10019, (212) 554-0600, Fax: (212) 586-1181, www.eiu.com; *South Korea Country Report.*

Euromonitor International, Inc., 224 S. Michigan Avenue, Suite 1500, Chicago, IL 60604, (312) 922-1115, Fax: (312) 922-1157, www.euromonitor.com; *International Marketing Data and Statistics 2008.*

Federal Statistical Office Germany, D-65180 Wiesbaden, Germany, www.destatis.de; *Republic of Korea 2005.*

International Monetary Fund (IMF), 700 Nineteenth Street, NW, Washington, DC 20431, (202) 623-7000, Fax: (202) 623-4661, www.imf.org; *International Financial Statistics Yearbook 2007.*

Taylor and Francis Group, An Informa Business, 2 Park Square, Milton Park, Abingdon, Oxford OX14 4RN, United Kingdom, (Dial from U.S. (212) 216-7800), (Fax from U.S. (212) 564-7854), www.tandf.co.uk; *The Europa World Year Book.*

United Nations Statistics Division, New York, NY 10017, (800) 253-9646, Fax: (212) 963-4116, http://unstats.un.org; *Statistical Yearbook.*

The World Bank, 1818 H Street, NW, Washington, DC 20433, (202) 473-1000, Fax: (202) 477-6391, www.worldbank.org; *Korea, Republic of* and *World Development Indicators (WDI) 2008.*

KOREA, SOUTH - MORTALITY

Central Intelligence Agency, Office of Public Affairs, Washington, DC 20505, (703) 482-0623, Fax: (703) 482-1739, www.cia.gov; *The World Factbook.*

Euromonitor International, Inc., 224 S. Michigan Avenue, Suite 1500, Chicago, IL 60604, (312) 922-1115, Fax: (312) 922-1157, www.euromonitor.com; *International Marketing Data and Statistics 2008* and *The World Economic Factbook 2008.*

Palgrave Macmillan Ltd., Houndmills, Basingstoke, Hampshire, RG21 6XS, England, (Telephone in U.S. (888) 330-8477), (Fax in U.S. (800) 672-2054), www.palgrave.com; *The Statesman's Yearbook 2008.*

Taylor and Francis Group, An Informa Business, 2 Park Square, Milton Park, Abingdon, Oxford OX14 4RN, United Kingdom, (Dial from U.S. (212) 216-7800), (Fax from U.S. (212) 564-7854), www.tandf.co.uk; *The Europa World Year Book.*

UNICEF, 3 United Nations Plaza, New York, NY 10017, (800) 253-9646, Fax: (212) 887-7465, www.unicef.org; *The State of the World's Children 2008.*

United Nations Statistics Division, New York, NY 10017, (800) 253-9646, Fax: (212) 963-4116, http://unstats.un.org; *Asia-Pacific in Figures 2004; Demographic Yearbook; Human Development Report 2006; Statistical Yearbook;* and *World Statistics Pocketbook.*

The World Bank, 1818 H Street, NW, Washington, DC 20433, (202) 473-1000, Fax: (202) 477-6391, www.worldbank.org; *The World Bank Atlas 2003-2004* and *World Development Indicators (WDI) 2008.*

World Health Organization (WHO), Avenue Appia 20, 1211 Geneve 27, Switzerland, (Telephone in U.S. (212) 331-9081), www.who.int; The WHO Global Atlas of Infectious Diseases.

KOREA, SOUTH - MOTION PICTURES

Korean Overseas Information Service (KOIS), Ministry of Culture and Information, Seoul 110, Republic of Korea, www.korea.net; Korea.net.

Palgrave Macmillan Ltd., Houndmills, Basingstoke, Hampshire, RG21 6XS, England, (Telephone in U.S. (888) 330-8477), (Fax in U.S. (800) 672-2054), www.palgrave.com; *The Statesman's Yearbook 2008.*

UNESCO Institute for Statistics, C.P. 6128 Succursale Centre-Ville, Montreal, Quebec, H3C 3J7 Canada, (Dial from U.S. (514) 343-6880), (Fax from U.S. (514) 343 6882), www.uis.unesco.org; *Statistical Tables.*

United Nations Statistics Division, New York, NY 10017, (800) 253-9646, Fax: (212) 963-4116, http://unstats.un.org; *Statistical Yearbook.*

KOREA, SOUTH - MOTOR VEHICLES

International Road Federation (IFR), Madison Place, 500 Montgomery Street, 5th Floor, Alexandria, VA 22314, (703) 535-1001, Fax: (703) 535-1007, www.irfnet.org; *World Road Statistics 2006.*

Korean Overseas Information Service (KOIS), Ministry of Culture and Information, Seoul 110, Republic of Korea, www.korea.net; Korea.net.

Taylor and Francis Group, An Informa Business, 2 Park Square, Milton Park, Abingdon, Oxford OX14 4RN, United Kingdom, (Dial from U.S. (212) 216-7800), (Fax from U.S. (212) 564-7854), www.tandf.co.uk; *The Europa World Year Book.*

United Nations Statistics Division, New York, NY 10017, (800) 253-9646, Fax: (212) 963-4116, http://unstats.un.org; *Statistical Yearbook.*

KOREA, SOUTH - MUSEUMS

M.E. Sharpe, 80 Business Park Drive, Armonk, NY 10504, (800) 541-6563, Fax: (914) 273-2106, www.mesharpe.com; *The Illustrated Book of World Rankings.*

UNESCO Institute for Statistics, C.P. 6128 Succursale Centre-Ville, Montreal, Quebec, H3C 3J7 Canada, (Dial from U.S. (514) 343-6880), (Fax from U.S. (514) 343 6882), www.uis.unesco.org; *Statistical Tables.*

KOREA, SOUTH - NATURAL GAS PRODUCTION

See KOREA, SOUTH - MINERAL INDUSTRIES

KOREA, SOUTH - NEWS AGENCIES

Korean Overseas Information Service (KOIS), Ministry of Culture and Information, Seoul 110, Republic of Korea, www.korea.net; Korea.net.

KOREA, SOUTH - NICKEL AND NICKEL ORE

See KOREA, SOUTH - MINERAL INDUSTRIES

KOREA, SOUTH - NUTRITION

Korean Overseas Information Service (KOIS), Ministry of Culture and Information, Seoul 110, Republic of Korea, www.korea.net; Korea.net.

United Nations Food and Agricultural Organization (FAO), Viale delle Terme di Caracalla, 00100 Rome, Italy, (Dial from U.S. (202) 653-2400), (Fax from U.S. (202) 653 5760), www.fao.org; *The State of Food and Agriculture (SOFA) 2006.*

KOREA, SOUTH - OLDER PEOPLE

M.E. Sharpe, 80 Business Park Drive, Armonk, NY 10504, (800) 541-6563, Fax: (914) 273-2106, www.mesharpe.com; *The Illustrated Book of World Rankings.*

KOREA, SOUTH - PAPER

See KOREA, SOUTH - FORESTS AND FORESTRY

KOREA, SOUTH - PEANUT PRODUCTION

See KOREA, SOUTH - CROPS

KOREA, SOUTH - PERIODICALS

Korean Overseas Information Service (KOIS), Ministry of Culture and Information, Seoul 110, Republic of Korea, www.korea.net; Korea.net.

UNESCO Institute for Statistics, C.P. 6128 Succursale Centre-Ville, Montreal, Quebec, H3C 3J7 Canada, (Dial from U.S. (514) 343-6880), (Fax from U.S. (514) 343 6882), www.uis.unesco.org; *Statistical Tables.*

KOREA, SOUTH - PESTICIDES

United Nations Food and Agricultural Organization (FAO), Viale delle Terme di Caracalla, 00100 Rome, Italy, (Dial from U.S. (202) 653-2400), (Fax from U.S. (202) 653 5760), www.fao.org; *The State of Food and Agriculture (SOFA) 2006.*

KOREA, SOUTH - PETROLEUM INDUSTRY AND TRADE

International Energy Agency (IEA), 9, rue de la Federation, 75739 Paris Cedex 15, France, www.iea.org; *Key World Energy Statistics 2007.*

M.E. Sharpe, 80 Business Park Drive, Armonk, NY 10504, (800) 541-6563, Fax: (914) 273-2106, www.mesharpe.com; *The Illustrated Book of World Rankings.*

Palgrave Macmillan Ltd., Houndmills, Basingstoke, Hampshire, RG21 6XS, England, (Telephone in U.S. (888) 330-8477), (Fax in U.S. (800) 672-2054), www.palgrave.com; *The Statesman's Yearbook 2008.*

PennWell Corporation, 1421 South Sheridan Road, Tulsa, OK 74112, (918) 835-3161, www.pennwell.com; *International Petroleum Encyclopedia 2007.*

U.S. Department of Energy (DOE), Energy Information Administration (EIA), 1000 Independence Avenue, SW, Washington, DC 20585, (202) 586-8800, www.eia.doe.gov; *International Energy Annual 2004* and *International Energy Outlook 2006.*

United Nations Conference on Trade and Development (UNCTAD), DC2-1120, United Nations, New York, NY 10017, (212) 963-0027, www.unctad.org; *UNCTAD Commodity Yearbook.*

United Nations Food and Agricultural Organization (FAO), Viale delle Terme di Caracalla, 00100 Rome, Italy, (Dial from U.S. (202) 653-2400), (Fax from U.S. (202) 653 5760), www.fao.org; *The State of Food and Agriculture (SOFA) 2006.*

United Nations Statistics Division, New York, NY 10017, (800) 253-9646, Fax: (212) 963-4116, http://unstats.un.org; *Statistical Yearbook.*

KOREA, SOUTH - PLASTICS INDUSTRY AND TRADE

United Nations Statistics Division, New York, NY 10017, (800) 253-9646, Fax: (212) 963-4116, http://unstats.un.org; *Statistical Yearbook.*

KOREA, SOUTH - POLITICAL SCIENCE

Central Intelligence Agency, Office of Public Affairs, Washington, DC 20505, (703) 482-0623, Fax: (703) 482-1739, www.cia.gov; *The World Factbook.*

Palgrave Macmillan Ltd., Houndmills, Basingstoke, Hampshire, RG21 6XS, England, (Telephone in U.S. (888) 330-8477), (Fax in U.S. (800) 672-2054), www.palgrave.com; *The Statesman's Yearbook 2008.*

Taylor and Francis Group, An Informa Business, 2 Park Square, Milton Park, Abingdon, Oxford OX14 4RN, United Kingdom, (Dial from U.S. (212) 216-7800), (Fax from U.S. (212) 564-7854), www.tandf.co.uk; *The Europa World Year Book.*

United Nations Statistics Division, New York, NY 10017, (800) 253-9646, Fax: (212) 963-4116, http://unstats.un.org; *Asia-Pacific in Figures 2004; National Accounts Statistics: Compendium of Income Distribution Statistics;* and *Statistical Yearbook.*

The World Bank, 1818 H Street, NW, Washington, DC 20433, (202) 473-1000, Fax: (202) 477-6391, www.worldbank.org; *World Development Indicators (WDI) 2008.*

KOREA, SOUTH - POPULATION

Central Intelligence Agency, Office of Public Affairs, Washington, DC 20505, (703) 482-0623, Fax: (703) 482-1739, www.cia.gov; *The World Factbook.*

Economist Intelligence Unit, 111 West 57th Street, New York, NY 10019, (212) 554-0600, Fax: (212) 586-1181, www.eiu.com; *Business Asia* and *South Korea Country Report.*

Euromonitor International, Inc., 224 S. Michigan Avenue, Suite 1500, Chicago, IL 60604, (312) 922-1115, Fax: (312) 922-1157, www.euromonitor.com; *International Marketing Data and Statistics 2008* and *The World Economic Factbook 2008.*

Federal Statistical Office Germany, D-65180 Wiesbaden, Germany, www.destatis.de; *Republic of Korea 2005.*

International Labour Office, I.L.O. Publications, 4 route des Morillons, CH-1211 Geneva 22, Switzerland, (Telephone in U.S. (202) 653-7652), (Fax in U.S. (202) 653-7687), www.ilo.org; *Yearbook of Labour Statistics 2006.*

Korean Overseas Information Service (KOIS), Ministry of Culture and Information, Seoul 110, Republic of Korea, www.korea.net; Korea.net.

M.E. Sharpe, 80 Business Park Drive, Armonk, NY 10504, (800) 541-6563, Fax: (914) 273-2106, www.mesharpe.com; *The Illustrated Book of World Rankings.*

Organisation for Economic Cooperation and Development (OECD), 2 rue Andre Pascal, F-75775 Paris Cedex 16, France, (Telephone in U.S. (202) 785-6323), (Fax in U.S. (202) 785-0350), www.oecd.org; *Labour Force Statistics: 1986-2005, 2007 Edition.*

Palgrave Macmillan Ltd., Houndmills, Basingstoke, Hampshire, RG21 6XS, England, (Telephone in U.S. (888) 330-8477), (Fax in U.S. (800) 672-2054), www.palgrave.com; *The Statesman's Yearbook 2008.*

Taylor and Francis Group, An Informa Business, 2 Park Square, Milton Park, Abingdon, Oxford OX14 4RN, United Kingdom, (Dial from U.S. (212) 216-7800), (Fax from U.S. (212) 564-7854), www.tandf.co.uk; *The Europa World Year Book.*

U.S. Department of State (DOS), 2201 C Street NW, Washington, DC 20520, (202) 647-4000, www.state.gov; *World Military Expenditures and Arms Transfers (WMEAT).*

UNESCO Institute for Statistics, C.P. 6128 Succursale Centre-Ville, Montreal, Quebec, H3C 3J7 Canada, (Dial from U.S. (514) 343-6880), (Fax from U.S. (514) 343 6882), www.uis.unesco.org; *Statistical Tables.*

United Nations Food and Agricultural Organization (FAO), Viale delle Terme di Caracalla, 00100 Rome, Italy, (Dial from U.S. (202) 653-2400), (Fax from U.S. (202) 653 5760), www.fao.org; *FAO Production Yearbook 2002.*

United Nations Statistics Division, New York, NY 10017, (800) 253-9646, Fax: (212) 963-4116, http://unstats.un.org; *Asia-Pacific in Figures 2004; Demographic Yearbook; Human Development Report 2006; Statistical Yearbook; Statistical Yearbook for Asia and the Pacific 2004;* and *World Statistics Pocketbook.*

The World Bank, 1818 H Street, NW, Washington, DC 20433, (202) 473-1000, Fax: (202) 477-6391, www.worldbank.org; *Korea, Republic of* and *The World Bank Atlas 2003-2004.*

Worldinformation.com, 2 Market Street, Saffron Walden, Essex CB10 1HZ, United Kingdom, www.worldinformation.com; The World of Information (www.worldinformation.com).

KOREA, SOUTH - POPULATION DENSITY

Central Intelligence Agency, Office of Public Affairs, Washington, DC 20505, (703) 482-0623, Fax: (703) 482-1739, www.cia.gov; *The World Factbook.*

Euromonitor International, Inc., 224 S. Michigan Avenue, Suite 1500, Chicago, IL 60604, (312) 922-1115, Fax: (312) 922-1157, www.euromonitor.com; *International Marketing Data and Statistics 2008* and *The World Economic Factbook 2008.*

Federal Statistical Office Germany, D-65180 Wiesbaden, Germany, www.destatis.de; *Republic of Korea 2005.*

M.E. Sharpe, 80 Business Park Drive, Armonk, NY 10504, (800) 541-6563, Fax: (914) 273-2106, www.mesharpe.com; *The Illustrated Book of World Rankings.*

Palgrave Macmillan Ltd., Houndmills, Basingstoke, Hampshire, RG21 6XS, England, (Telephone in U.S. (888) 330-8477), (Fax in U.S. (800) 672-2054), www.palgrave.com; *The Statesman's Yearbook 2008.*

Taylor and Francis Group, An Informa Business, 2 Park Square, Milton Park, Abingdon, Oxford OX14 4RN, United Kingdom, (Dial from U.S. (212) 216-7800), (Fax from U.S. (212) 564-7854), www.tandf.co.uk; *The Europa World Year Book.*

UNESCO Institute for Statistics, C.P. 6128 Succursale Centre-Ville, Montreal, Quebec, H3C 3J7 Canada, (Dial from U.S. (514) 343-6880), (Fax from U.S. (514) 343 6882), www.uis.unesco.org; *Statistical Tables.*

United Nations Food and Agricultural Organization (FAO), Viale delle Terme di Caracalla, 00100 Rome, Italy, (Dial from U.S. (202) 653-2400), (Fax from U.S. (202) 653 5760), www.fao.org; *The State of Food and Agriculture (SOFA) 2006.*

United Nations Statistics Division, New York, NY 10017, (800) 253-9646, Fax: (212) 963-4116, http://unstats.un.org; *Statistical Yearbook.*

The World Bank, 1818 H Street, NW, Washington, DC 20433, (202) 473-1000, Fax: (202) 477-6391, www.worldbank.org; *Korea, Republic of.*

KOREA, SOUTH - POSTAL SERVICE

Korean Overseas Information Service (KOIS), Ministry of Culture and Information, Seoul 110, Republic of Korea, www.korea.net; Korea.net.

M.E. Sharpe, 80 Business Park Drive, Armonk, NY 10504, (800) 541-6563, Fax: (914) 273-2106, www.mesharpe.com; *The Illustrated Book of World Rankings.*

Palgrave Macmillan Ltd., Houndmills, Basingstoke, Hampshire, RG21 6XS, England, (Telephone in U.S. (888) 330-8477), (Fax in U.S. (800) 672-2054), www.palgrave.com; *The Statesman's Yearbook 2008.*

United Nations Statistics Division, New York, NY 10017, (800) 253-9646, Fax: (212) 963-4116, http://unstats.un.org; *Statistical Yearbook.*

KOREA, SOUTH - POWER RESOURCES

Euromonitor International, Inc., 224 S. Michigan Avenue, Suite 1500, Chicago, IL 60604, (312) 922-1115, Fax: (312) 922-1157, www.euromonitor.com; *International Marketing Data and Statistics 2008; The World Economic Factbook 2008;* and *World Marketing Data and Statistics.*

M.E. Sharpe, 80 Business Park Drive, Armonk, NY 10504, (800) 541-6563, Fax: (914) 273-2106, www.mesharpe.com; *The Illustrated Book of World Rankings.*

Palgrave Macmillan Ltd., Houndmills, Basingstoke, Hampshire, RG21 6XS, England, (Telephone in U.S. (888) 330-8477), (Fax in U.S. (800) 672-2054), www.palgrave.com; *The Statesman's Yearbook 2008.*

Platts, 2 Penn Plaza, 25th Floor, New York, NY 10121-2298, (212) 904-3070, www.platts.com; *Asian Electricity Outlook 2006; Emissions Daily;* and *Energy Economist.*

U.S. Department of Energy (DOE), Energy Information Administration (EIA), 1000 Independence Avenue, SW, Washington, DC 20585, (202) 586-8800, www.eia.doe.gov; *International Energy Annual 2004* and *International Energy Outlook 2006.*

United Nations Food and Agricultural Organization (FAO), Viale delle Terme di Caracalla, 00100 Rome, Italy, (Dial from U.S. (202) 653-2400), (Fax from U.S. (202) 653 5760), www.fao.org; *The State of Food and Agriculture (SOFA) 2006.*

United Nations Statistics Division, New York, NY 10017, (800) 253-9646, Fax: (212) 963-4116, http://unstats.un.org; *Asia-Pacific in Figures 2004; Energy Statistics Yearbook 2003; Human Development Report 2006; Statistical Yearbook; Statistical Yearbook for Asia and the Pacific 2004; World Energy Assessment 2004 Update: Overview;* and *World Statistics Pocketbook.*

The World Bank, 1818 H Street, NW, Washington, DC 20433, (202) 473-1000, Fax: (202) 477-6391, www.worldbank.org; *The World Bank Atlas 2003-2004.*

KOREA, SOUTH - PRECIPITATION (METEOROLOGY)

Korean Overseas Information Service (KOIS), Ministry of Culture and Information, Seoul 110, Republic of Korea, www.korea.net; Korea.net.

KOREA, SOUTH - PRICES

Euromonitor International, Inc., 224 S. Michigan Avenue, Suite 1500, Chicago, IL 60604, (312) 922-1115, Fax: (312) 922-1157, www.euromonitor.com; *World Marketing Data and Statistics.*

Federal Statistical Office Germany, D-65180 Wiesbaden, Germany, www.destatis.de; *Republic of Korea 2005.*

International Labour Office, I.L.O. Publications, 4 route des Morillons, CH-1211 Geneva 22, Switzerland, (Telephone in U.S. (202) 653-7652), (Fax in U.S. (202) 653-7687), www.ilo.org; *Yearbook of Labour Statistics 2006.*

M.E. Sharpe, 80 Business Park Drive, Armonk, NY 10504, (800) 541-6563, Fax: (914) 273-2106, www.mesharpe.com; *The Illustrated Book of World Rankings.*

United Nations Food and Agricultural Organization (FAO), Viale delle Terme di Caracalla, 00100 Rome, Italy, (Dial from U.S. (202) 653-2400), (Fax from U.S. (202) 653 5760), www.fao.org; *FAO Production Yearbook 2002* and *The State of Food and Agriculture (SOFA) 2006.*

The World Bank, 1818 H Street, NW, Washington, DC 20433, (202) 473-1000, Fax: (202) 477-6391, www.worldbank.org; *Korea, Republic of.*

KOREA, SOUTH - PROFESSIONS

UNESCO Institute for Statistics, C.P. 6128 Succursale Centre-Ville, Montreal, Quebec, H3C 3J7 Canada, (Dial from U.S. (514) 343-6880), (Fax from U.S. (514) 343 6882), www.uis.unesco.org; *Statistical Tables.*

United Nations Statistics Division, New York, NY 10017, (800) 253-9646, Fax: (212) 963-4116, http://unstats.un.org; *Statistical Yearbook.*

KOREA, SOUTH - PUBLIC HEALTH

Economist Intelligence Unit, 111 West 57th Street, New York, NY 10019, (212) 554-0600, Fax: (212) 586-1181, www.eiu.com; *Business Asia.*

Euromonitor International, Inc., 224 S. Michigan Avenue, Suite 1500, Chicago, IL 60604, (312) 922-1115, Fax: (312) 922-1157, www.euromonitor.com; *World Health Databook 2007/2008* and *World Marketing Data and Statistics.*

Federal Statistical Office Germany, D-65180 Wiesbaden, Germany, www.destatis.de; *Republic of Korea 2005.*

Korean Overseas Information Service (KOIS), Ministry of Culture and Information, Seoul 110, Republic of Korea, www.korea.net; Korea.net.

M.E. Sharpe, 80 Business Park Drive, Armonk, NY 10504, (800) 541-6563, Fax: (914) 273-2106, www.mesharpe.com; *The Illustrated Book of World Rankings.*

Palgrave Macmillan Ltd., Houndmills, Basingstoke, Hampshire, RG21 6XS, England, (Telephone in U.S. (888) 330-8477), (Fax in U.S. (800) 672-2054), www.palgrave.com; *The Statesman's Yearbook 2008.*

UNICEF, 3 United Nations Plaza, New York, NY 10017, (800) 253-9646, Fax: (212) 887-7465, www.unicef.org; *The State of the World's Children 2008.*

United Nations Statistics Division, New York, NY 10017, (800) 253-9646, Fax: (212) 963-4116, http://unstats.un.org; *Asia-Pacific in Figures 2004; Human Development Report 2006;* and *Statistical Yearbook.*

The World Bank, 1818 H Street, NW, Washington, DC 20433, (202) 473-1000, Fax: (202) 477-6391, www.worldbank.org; *Korea, Republic of.*

World Health Organization (WHO), Avenue Appia 20, 1211 Geneve 27, Switzerland, (Telephone in U.S. (212) 331-9081), www.who.int; The WHO Global Atlas of Infectious Diseases.

KOREA, SOUTH - PUBLIC UTILITIES

Korean Overseas Information Service (KOIS), Ministry of Culture and Information, Seoul 110, Republic of Korea, www.korea.net; Korea.net.

KOREA, SOUTH - PUBLISHERS AND PUBLISHING

Taylor and Francis Group, An Informa Business, 2 Park Square, Milton Park, Abingdon, Oxford OX14 4RN, United Kingdom, (Dial from U.S. (212) 216-7800), (Fax from U.S. (212) 564-7854), www.tandf.co.uk; *The Europa World Year Book.*

UNESCO Institute for Statistics, C.P. 6128 Succursale Centre-Ville, Montreal, Quebec, H3C 3J7 Canada, (Dial from U.S. (514) 343-6880), (Fax from U.S. (514) 343 6882), www.uis.unesco.org; *Statistical Tables.*

KOREA, SOUTH - RADIO BROADCASTING

Palgrave Macmillan Ltd., Houndmills, Basingstoke, Hampshire, RG21 6XS, England, (Telephone in U.S. (888) 330-8477), (Fax in U.S. (800) 672-2054), www.palgrave.com; *The Statesman's Yearbook 2008.*

United Nations Statistics Division, New York, NY 10017, (800) 253-9646, Fax: (212) 963-4116, http://unstats.un.org; *Statistical Yearbook.*

KOREA, SOUTH - RAILROADS

Jane's Information Group, 110 North Royal Street, Suite 200, Alexandria, VA 22314, (703) 683-3700, Fax: (800) 836-0297, www.janes.com; *Jane's World Railways.*

Korean Overseas Information Service (KOIS), Ministry of Culture and Information, Seoul 110, Republic of Korea, www.korea.net; Korea.net.

Palgrave Macmillan Ltd., Houndmills, Basingstoke, Hampshire, RG21 6XS, England, (Telephone in U.S. (888) 330-8477), (Fax in U.S. (800) 672-2054), www.palgrave.com; *The Statesman's Yearbook 2008.*

Taylor and Francis Group, An Informa Business, 2 Park Square, Milton Park, Abingdon, Oxford OX14 4RN, United Kingdom, (Dial from U.S. (212) 216-7800), (Fax from U.S. (212) 564-7854), www.tandf.co.uk; *The Europa World Year Book.*

United Nations Statistics Division, New York, NY 10017, (800) 253-9646, Fax: (212) 963-4116, http://unstats.un.org; *Statistical Yearbook.*

KOREA, SOUTH - RELIGION

Central Intelligence Agency, Office of Public Affairs, Washington, DC 20505, (703) 482-0623, Fax: (703) 482-1739, www.cia.gov; *The World Factbook.*

Korean Overseas Information Service (KOIS), Ministry of Culture and Information, Seoul 110, Republic of Korea, www.korea.net; Korea.net.

M.E. Sharpe, 80 Business Park Drive, Armonk, NY 10504, (800) 541-6563, Fax: (914) 273-2106, www.mesharpe.com; *The Illustrated Book of World Rankings.*

Palgrave Macmillan Ltd., Houndmills, Basingstoke, Hampshire, RG21 6XS, England, (Telephone in U.S. (888) 330-8477), (Fax in U.S. (800) 672-2054), www.palgrave.com; *The Statesman's Yearbook 2008.*

KOREA, SOUTH - RENT CHARGES

International Labour Office, I.L.O. Publications, 4 route des Morillons, CH-1211 Geneva 22, Switzerland, (Telephone in U.S. (202) 653-7652), (Fax in U.S. (202) 653-7687), www.ilo.org; *Yearbook of Labour Statistics 2006.*

Taylor and Francis Group, An Informa Business, 2 Park Square, Milton Park, Abingdon, Oxford OX14 4RN, United Kingdom, (Dial from U.S. (212) 216-7800), (Fax from U.S. (212) 564-7854), www.tandf.co.uk; *The Europa World Year Book.*

KOREA, SOUTH - RESERVES (ACCOUNTING)

Euromonitor International, Inc., 224 S. Michigan Avenue, Suite 1500, Chicago, IL 60604, (312) 922-1115, Fax: (312) 922-1157, www.euromonitor.com; *International Marketing Data and Statistics 2008.*

United Nations Statistics Division, New York, NY 10017, (800) 253-9646, Fax: (212) 963-4116, http://unstats.un.org; *Statistical Yearbook.*

The World Bank, 1818 H Street, NW, Washington, DC 20433, (202) 473-1000, Fax: (202) 477-6391, www.worldbank.org; *World Development Indicators (WDI) 2008.*

KOREA, SOUTH - RETAIL TRADE

Euromonitor International, Inc., 224 S. Michigan Avenue, Suite 1500, Chicago, IL 60604, (312) 922-1115, Fax: (312) 922-1157, www.euromonitor.com; *Retail Trade International 2007* and *World Marketing Data and Statistics.*

United Nations Statistics Division, New York, NY 10017, (800) 253-9646, Fax: (212) 963-4116, http://unstats.un.org; *Statistical Yearbook.*

KOREA, SOUTH - RICE PRODUCTION

See KOREA, SOUTH - CROPS

KOREA, SOUTH - ROADS

Central Intelligence Agency, Office of Public Affairs, Washington, DC 20505, (703) 482-0623, Fax: (703) 482-1739, www.cia.gov; *The World Factbook.*

Economist Intelligence Unit, 111 West 57th Street, New York, NY 10019, (212) 554-0600, Fax: (212) 586-1181, www.eiu.com; *Business Asia.*

International Road Federation (IFR), Madison Place, 500 Montgomery Street, 5th Floor, Alexandria, VA 22314, (703) 535-1001, Fax: (703) 535-1007, www.irfnet.org; *World Road Statistics 2006.*

Korean Overseas Information Service (KOIS), Ministry of Culture and Information, Seoul 110, Republic of Korea, www.korea.net; Korea.net.

Palgrave Macmillan Ltd., Houndmills, Basingstoke, Hampshire, RG21 6XS, England, (Telephone in U.S. (888) 330-8477), (Fax in U.S. (800) 672-2054), www.palgrave.com; *The Statesman's Yearbook 2008.*

KOREA, SOUTH - RUBBER INDUSTRY AND TRADE

International Rubber Study Group (IRSG), 1st Floor, Heron House, 109/115 Wembley Hill Road, Wembley, Middlesex HA9 8DA, United Kingdom, www.

rubberstudy.com; *Rubber Statistical Bulletin; Summary of World Rubber Statistics 2005; World Rubber Statistics Handbook (Volume 6, 1975-2001);* and *World Rubber Statistics Historic Handbook.*

M.E. Sharpe, 80 Business Park Drive, Armonk, NY 10504, (800) 541-6563, Fax: (914) 273-2106, www.mesharpe.com; *The Illustrated Book of World Rankings.*

United Nations Statistics Division, New York, NY 10017, (800) 253-9646, Fax: (212) 963-4116, http://unstats.un.org; *Statistical Yearbook.*

KOREA, SOUTH - SALT PRODUCTION

See KOREA, SOUTH - MINERAL INDUSTRIES

KOREA, SOUTH - SHEEP

See KOREA, SOUTH - LIVESTOCK

KOREA, SOUTH - SHIPBUILDING

Korean Overseas Information Service (KOIS), Ministry of Culture and Information, Seoul 110, Republic of Korea, www.korea.net; Korea.net.

KOREA, SOUTH - SHIPPING

Palgrave Macmillan Ltd., Houndmills, Basingstoke, Hampshire, RG21 6XS, England, (Telephone in U.S. (888) 330-8477), (Fax in U.S. (800) 672-2054), www.palgrave.com; *The Statesman's Yearbook 2008.*

Taylor and Francis Group, An Informa Business, 2 Park Square, Milton Park, Abingdon, Oxford OX14 4RN, United Kingdom, (Dial from U.S. (212) 216-7800), (Fax from U.S. (212) 564-7854), www.tandf.co.uk; *The Europa World Year Book.*

United Nations Statistics Division, New York, NY 10017, (800) 253-9646, Fax: (212) 963-4116, http://unstats.un.org; *Statistical Yearbook.*

KOREA, SOUTH - SILVER PRODUCTION

See KOREA, SOUTH - MINERAL INDUSTRIES

KOREA, SOUTH - SOCIAL ECOLOGY

M.E. Sharpe, 80 Business Park Drive, Armonk, NY 10504, (800) 541-6563, Fax: (914) 273-2106, www.mesharpe.com; *The Illustrated Book of World Rankings.*

United Nations Statistics Division, New York, NY 10017, (800) 253-9646, Fax: (212) 963-4116, http://unstats.un.org; *World Statistics Pocketbook.*

KOREA, SOUTH - SOCIAL SECURITY

Palgrave Macmillan Ltd., Houndmills, Basingstoke, Hampshire, RG21 6XS, England, (Telephone in U.S. (888) 330-8477), (Fax in U.S. (800) 672-2054), www.palgrave.com; *The Statesman's Yearbook 2008.*

United Nations Statistics Division, New York, NY 10017, (800) 253-9646, Fax: (212) 963-4116, http://unstats.un.org; *National Accounts Statistics: Compendium of Income Distribution Statistics.*

KOREA, SOUTH - SOYBEAN PRODUCTION

See KOREA, SOUTH - CROPS

KOREA, SOUTH - STEEL PRODUCTION

See KOREA, SOUTH - MINERAL INDUSTRIES

KOREA, SOUTH - SUGAR PRODUCTION

See KOREA, SOUTH - CROPS

KOREA, SOUTH - SULPHUR PRODUCTION

See KOREA, SOUTH - MINERAL INDUSTRIES

KOREA, SOUTH - TAXATION

International Road Federation (IFR), Madison Place, 500 Montgomery Street, 5th Floor, Alexandria, VA 22314, (703) 535-1001, Fax: (703) 535-1007, www.irfnet.org; *World Road Statistics 2006.*

Palgrave Macmillan Ltd., Houndmills, Basingstoke, Hampshire, RG21 6XS, England, (Telephone in U.S. (888) 330-8477), (Fax in U.S. (800) 672-2054), www.palgrave.com; *The Statesman's Yearbook 2008.*

Taylor and Francis Group, An Informa Business, 2 Park Square, Milton Park, Abingdon, Oxford OX14 4RN, United Kingdom, (Dial from U.S. (212) 216-7800), (Fax from U.S. (212) 564-7854), www.tandf.co.uk; *The Europa World Year Book.*

The World Bank, 1818 H Street, NW, Washington, DC 20433, (202) 473-1000, Fax: (202) 477-6391, www.worldbank.org; *World Development Indicators (WDI) 2008.*

KOREA, SOUTH - TELEPHONE

Economist Intelligence Unit, 111 West 57th Street, New York, NY 10019, (212) 554-0600, Fax: (212) 586-1181, www.eiu.com; *Business Asia.*

International Telecommunication Union (ITU), Place des Nations, 1211 Geneva 20, Switzerland, www.itu.int; World Telecommunication Indicators Database.

Korean Overseas Information Service (KOIS), Ministry of Culture and Information, Seoul 110, Republic of Korea, www.korea.net; Korea.net.

Palgrave Macmillan Ltd., Houndmills, Basingstoke, Hampshire, RG21 6XS, England, (Telephone in U.S. (888) 330-8477), (Fax in U.S. (800) 672-2054), www.palgrave.com; *The Statesman's Yearbook 2008.*

Taylor and Francis Group, An Informa Business, 2 Park Square, Milton Park, Abingdon, Oxford OX14 4RN, United Kingdom, (Dial from U.S. (212) 216-7800), (Fax from U.S. (212) 564-7854), www.tandf.co.uk; *The Europa World Year Book.*

United Nations Statistics Division, New York, NY 10017, (800) 253-9646, Fax: (212) 963-4116, http://unstats.un.org; *Statistical Yearbook* and *World Statistics Pocketbook.*

KOREA, SOUTH - TELEVISION - RECEIVERS AND RECEPTION

Economist Intelligence Unit, 111 West 57th Street, New York, NY 10019, (212) 554-0600, Fax: (212) 586-1181, www.eiu.com; *Business Asia.*

Korean Overseas Information Service (KOIS), Ministry of Culture and Information, Seoul 110, Republic of Korea, www.korea.net; Korea.net.

KOREA, SOUTH - TEMPERATURE

Korean Overseas Information Service (KOIS), Ministry of Culture and Information, Seoul 110, Republic of Korea, www.korea.net; Korea.net.

KOREA, SOUTH - TEXTILE INDUSTRY

Euromonitor International, Inc., 224 S. Michigan Avenue, Suite 1500, Chicago, IL 60604, (312) 922-1115, Fax: (312) 922-1157, www.euromonitor.com; *Retail Trade International 2007.*

Korean Overseas Information Service (KOIS), Ministry of Culture and Information, Seoul 110, Republic of Korea, www.korea.net; Korea.net.

M.E. Sharpe, 80 Business Park Drive, Armonk, NY 10504, (800) 541-6563, Fax: (914) 273-2106, www.mesharpe.com; *The Illustrated Book of World Rankings.*

Palgrave Macmillan Ltd., Houndmills, Basingstoke, Hampshire, RG21 6XS, England, (Telephone in U.S. (888) 330-8477), (Fax in U.S. (800) 672-2054), www.palgrave.com; *The Statesman's Yearbook 2008.*

United Nations Conference on Trade and Development (UNCTAD), DC2-1120, United Nations, New York, NY 10017, (212) 963-0027, www.unctad.org; *UNCTAD Commodity Yearbook.*

United Nations Food and Agricultural Organization (FAO), Viale delle Terme di Caracalla, 00100 Rome, Italy, (Dial from U.S. (202) 653-2400), (Fax from U.S. (202) 653 5760), www.fao.org; *FAO Production Yearbook 2002.*

United Nations Statistics Division, New York, NY 10017, (800) 253-9646, Fax: (212) 963-4116, http://unstats.un.org; *Statistical Yearbook.*

KOREA, SOUTH - THEATER

UNESCO Institute for Statistics, C.P. 6128 Succursale Centre-Ville, Montreal, Quebec, H3C 3J7 Canada, (Dial from U.S. (514) 343-6880), (Fax from U.S. (514) 343 6882), www.uis.unesco.org; *Statistical Tables.*

KOREA, SOUTH - TIN PRODUCTION

See KOREA, SOUTH - MINERAL INDUSTRIES

KOREA, SOUTH - TIRE INDUSTRY

United Nations Statistics Division, New York, NY 10017, (800) 253-9646, Fax: (212) 963-4116, http://unstats.un.org; *Statistical Yearbook.*

KOREA, SOUTH - TOBACCO INDUSTRY

Foreign Agricultural Service (FAS), U.S. Department of Agriculture (USDA), 1400 Independence Avenue, SW, Washington, DC 20250, (202) 720-3935, www.fas.usda.gov; *Tobacco: World Markets and Trade.*

M.E. Sharpe, 80 Business Park Drive, Armonk, NY 10504, (800) 541-6563, Fax: (914) 273-2106, www.mesharpe.com; *The Illustrated Book of World Rankings.*

United Nations Statistics Division, New York, NY 10017, (800) 253-9646, Fax: (212) 963-4116, http://unstats.un.org; *Statistical Yearbook.*

KOREA, SOUTH - TOURISM

Euromonitor International, Inc., 224 S. Michigan Avenue, Suite 1500, Chicago, IL 60604, (312) 922-1115, Fax: (312) 922-1157, www.euromonitor.com; *The World Economic Factbook 2008* and *World Marketing Data and Statistics.*

Federal Statistical Office Germany, D-65180 Wiesbaden, Germany, www.destatis.de; *Republic of Korea 2005.*

Korean Overseas Information Service (KOIS), Ministry of Culture and Information, Seoul 110, Republic of Korea, www.korea.net; Korea.net.

M.E. Sharpe, 80 Business Park Drive, Armonk, NY 10504, (800) 541-6563, Fax: (914) 273-2106, www.mesharpe.com; *The Illustrated Book of World Rankings.*

Palgrave Macmillan Ltd., Houndmills, Basingstoke, Hampshire, RG21 6XS, England, (Telephone in U.S. (888) 330-8477), (Fax in U.S. (800) 672-2054), www.palgrave.com; *The Statesman's Yearbook 2008.*

Taylor and Francis Group, An Informa Business, 2 Park Square, Milton Park, Abingdon, Oxford OX14 4RN, United Kingdom, (Dial from U.S. (212) 216-7800), (Fax from U.S. (212) 564-7854), www.tandf.co.uk; *The Europa World Year Book.*

United Nations Statistics Division, New York, NY 10017, (800) 253-9646, Fax: (212) 963-4116, http://unstats.un.org; *Statistical Yearbook.*

United Nations World Tourism Organization (UNWTO), Capitan Haya 42, 28020 Madrid, Spain, www.world-tourism.org; *Yearbook of Tourism Statistics.*

The World Bank, 1818 H Street, NW, Washington, DC 20433, (202) 473-1000, Fax: (202) 477-6391, www.worldbank.org; *Korea, Republic of.*

KOREA, SOUTH - TRADE

See KOREA, SOUTH - INTERNATIONAL TRADE

KOREA, SOUTH - TRANSPORTATION

Central Intelligence Agency, Office of Public Affairs, Washington, DC 20505, (703) 482-0623, Fax: (703) 482-1739, www.cia.gov; *The World Factbook.*

Economist Intelligence Unit, 111 West 57th Street, New York, NY 10019, (212) 554-0600, Fax: (212) 586-1181, www.eiu.com; *Business Asia.*

Euromonitor International, Inc., 224 S. Michigan Avenue, Suite 1500, Chicago, IL 60604, (312) 922-1115, Fax: (312) 922-1157, www.euromonitor.com; *International Marketing Data and Statistics 2008* and *World Marketing Data and Statistics.*

Federal Statistical Office Germany, D-65180 Wiesbaden, Germany, www.destatis.de; *Republic of Korea 2005.*

Korean Overseas Information Service (KOIS), Ministry of Culture and Information, Seoul 110, Republic of Korea, www.korea.net; Korea.net.

M.E. Sharpe, 80 Business Park Drive, Armonk, NY 10504, (800) 541-6563, Fax: (914) 273-2106, www.mesharpe.com; *The Illustrated Book of World Rankings.*

Palgrave Macmillan Ltd., Houndmills, Basingstoke, Hampshire, RG21 6XS, England, (Telephone in U.S. (888) 330-8477), (Fax in U.S. (800) 672-2054), www.palgrave.com; *The Statesman's Yearbook 2008.*

Taylor and Francis Group, An Informa Business, 2 Park Square, Milton Park, Abingdon, Oxford OX14 4RN, United Kingdom, (Dial from U.S. (212) 216-7800), (Fax from U.S. (212) 564-7854), www.tandf.co.uk; *The Europa World Year Book.*

United Nations Statistics Division, New York, NY 10017, (800) 253-9646, Fax: (212) 963-4116, http://unstats.un.org; *Human Development Report 2006* and *Statistical Yearbook for Asia and the Pacific 2004.*

The World Bank, 1818 H Street, NW, Washington, DC 20433, (202) 473-1000, Fax: (202) 477-6391, www.worldbank.org; *Korea, Republic of.*

KOREA, SOUTH - UNEMPLOYMENT

Central Intelligence Agency, Office of Public Affairs, Washington, DC 20505, (703) 482-0623, Fax: (703) 482-1739, www.cia.gov; *The World Factbook.*

Euromonitor International, Inc., 224 S. Michigan Avenue, Suite 1500, Chicago, IL 60604, (312) 922-1115, Fax: (312) 922-1157, www.euromonitor.com; *International Marketing Data and Statistics 2008.*

Federal Statistical Office Germany, D-65180 Wiesbaden, Germany, www.destatis.de; *Republic of Korea 2005.*

International Labour Office, I.L.O. Publications, 4 route des Morillons, CH-1211 Geneva 22, Switzerland, (Telephone in U.S. (202) 653-7652), (Fax in U.S. (202) 653-7687), www.ilo.org; *Yearbook of Labour Statistics 2006.*

Korean Overseas Information Service (KOIS), Ministry of Culture and Information, Seoul 110, Republic of Korea, www.korea.net; Korea.net.

Organisation for Economic Cooperation and Development (OECD), 2 rue Andre Pascal, F-75775 Paris Cedex 16, France, (Telephone in U.S. (202) 785-6323), (Fax in U.S. (202) 785-0350), www.oecd.org; *Labour Force Statistics: 1986-2005, 2007 Edition* and *OECD Composite Leading Indicators (CLIs), Updated September 2007.*

Palgrave Macmillan Ltd., Houndmills, Basingstoke, Hampshire, RG21 6XS, England, (Telephone in U.S. (888) 330-8477), (Fax in U.S. (800) 672-2054), www.palgrave.com; *The Statesman's Yearbook 2008.*

United Nations Statistics Division, New York, NY 10017, (800) 253-9646, Fax: (212) 963-4116, http://unstats.un.org; *Statistical Yearbook.*

The World Bank, 1818 H Street, NW, Washington, DC 20433, (202) 473-1000, Fax: (202) 477-6391, www.worldbank.org; *Korea, Republic of.*

KOREA, SOUTH - VISITORS, FOREIGN

Korean Overseas Information Service (KOIS), Ministry of Culture and Information, Seoul 110, Republic of Korea, www.korea.net; Korea.net.

KOREA, SOUTH - VITAL STATISTICS

Euromonitor International, Inc., 224 S. Michigan Avenue, Suite 1500, Chicago, IL 60604, (312) 922-1115, Fax: (312) 922-1157, www.euromonitor.com; *International Marketing Data and Statistics 2008.*

Palgrave Macmillan Ltd., Houndmills, Basingstoke, Hampshire, RG21 6XS, England, (Telephone in U.S. (888) 330-8477), (Fax in U.S. (800) 672-2054), www.palgrave.com; *The Statesman's Yearbook 2008.*

KOREA, SOUTH - WAGES

Federal Statistical Office Germany, D-65180 Wiesbaden, Germany, www.destatis.de; *Republic of Korea 2005.*

International Labour Office, I.L.O. Publications, 4 route des Morillons, CH-1211 Geneva 22, Switzerland, (Telephone in U.S. (202) 653-7652), (Fax in U.S. (202) 653-7687), www.ilo.org; *Yearbook of Labour Statistics 2006.*

Organisation for Economic Cooperation and Development (OECD), 2 rue Andre Pascal, F-75775 Paris Cedex 16, France, (Telephone in U.S. (202) 785-6323), (Fax in U.S. (202) 785-0350), www.oecd.org; *ICT Sector Data and Metadata by Country.*

United Nations Statistics Division, New York, NY 10017, (800) 253-9646, Fax: (212) 963-4116, http://unstats.un.org; *Statistical Yearbook.*

The World Bank, 1818 H Street, NW, Washington, DC 20433, (202) 473-1000, Fax: (202) 477-6391, www.worldbank.org; *Korea, Republic of.*

KOREA, SOUTH - WALNUT PRODUCTION

See KOREA, SOUTH - CROPS

KOREA, SOUTH - WEATHER

See KOREA, SOUTH - CLIMATE

KOREA, SOUTH - WHALES

See KOREA, SOUTH - FISHERIES

KOREA, SOUTH - WHEAT PRODUCTION

See KOREA, SOUTH - CROPS

KOREA, SOUTH - WHOLESALE PRICE INDEXES

Korean Overseas Information Service (KOIS), Ministry of Culture and Information, Seoul 110, Republic of Korea, www.korea.net; Korea.net.

United Nations Statistics Division, New York, NY 10017, (800) 253-9646, Fax: (212) 963-4116, http://unstats.un.org; *Statistical Yearbook.*

KOREA, SOUTH - WHOLESALE TRADE

United Nations Statistics Division, New York, NY 10017, (800) 253-9646, Fax: (212) 963-4116, http://unstats.un.org; *Statistical Yearbook.*

KOREA, SOUTH - WINE PRODUCTION

See KOREA, SOUTH - BEVERAGE INDUSTRY

KOREA, SOUTH - WOOD AND WOOD PULP

See KOREA, SOUTH - FORESTS AND FORESTRY

KOREA, SOUTH - WOOD PRODUCTS

United Nations Statistics Division, New York, NY 10017, (800) 253-9646, Fax: (212) 963-4116, http://unstats.un.org; *International Trade Statistics Yearbook.*

KOREA, SOUTH - WOOL PRODUCTION

See KOREA, SOUTH - TEXTILE INDUSTRY

KOREA, SOUTH - YARN PRODUCTION

See KOREA, SOUTH - TEXTILE INDUSTRY

KOREA, SOUTH - ZINC AND ZINC ORE

See KOREA, SOUTH - MINERAL INDUSTRIES

KOREA, SOUTH - ZOOS

UNESCO Institute for Statistics, C.P. 6128 Succursale Centre-Ville, Montreal, Quebec, H3C 3J7 Canada, (Dial from U.S. (514) 343-6880), (Fax from U.S. (514) 343 6882), www.uis.unesco.org; *Statistical Tables.*

KOREAN POPULATION

U.S. Census Bureau, Demographic Surveys Division, 4700 Silver Hill Road, Washington DC 20233-0001, (301) 763-3030, www.census.gov; *Census 2000: Demographic Profiles.*

KUWAIT - NATIONAL STATISTICAL OFFICE

Central Statistical Office, Ministry of Planning, PO Box 15, Safat 13001, Kuwait, http://scs.mop.gov.kw; National Data Center.

KUWAIT - PRIMARY STATISTICS SOURCES

Central Statistical Office, Ministry of Planning, PO Box 15, Safat 13001, Kuwait, http://scs.mop.gov.kw; *Annual Statistical Abstract 2006* and *Monthly Statistical Bulletin.*

KUWAIT - AGRICULTURAL MACHINERY

United Nations Statistics Division, New York, NY 10017, (800) 253-9646, Fax: (212) 963-4116, http://unstats.un.org; *Statistical Yearbook.*

KUWAIT - AGRICULTURE

Central Statistical Office, Ministry of Planning, PO Box 15, Safat 13001, Kuwait, http://scs.mop.gov.kw; *Annual Statistical Abstract 2006.*

Economist Intelligence Unit, 111 West 57th Street, New York, NY 10019, (212) 554-0600, Fax: (212) 586-1181, www.eiu.com; *Kuwait Country Report.*

Euromonitor International, Inc., 224 S. Michigan Avenue, Suite 1500, Chicago, IL 60604, (312) 922-1115, Fax: (312) 922-1157, www.euromonitor.com; *International Marketing Data and Statistics 2008* and *World Marketing Data and Statistics.*

M.E. Sharpe, 80 Business Park Drive, Armonk, NY 10504, (800) 541-6563, Fax: (914) 273-2106, www.mesharpe.com; *The Illustrated Book of World Rankings.*

Palgrave Macmillan Ltd., Houndmills, Basingstoke, Hampshire, RG21 6XS, England, (Telephone in U.S. (888) 330-8477), (Fax in U.S. (800) 672-2054), www.palgrave.com; *The Statesman's Yearbook 2008.*

Taylor and Francis Group, An Informa Business, 2 Park Square, Milton Park, Abingdon, Oxford OX14 4RN, United Kingdom, (Dial from U.S. (212) 216-7800), (Fax from U.S. (212) 564-7854), www.tandf.co.uk; *The Europa World Year Book.*

United Nations Conference on Trade and Development (UNCTAD), DC2-1120, United Nations, New York, NY 10017, (212) 963-0027, www.unctad.org; *UNCTAD Commodity Yearbook.*

United Nations Economic and Social Commission for Western Asia (ESCWA), PO Box 11-8575, Riad el-Solh Square, Beirut, Lebanon, www.escwa.un.org; *Annual Report 2006* and *Statistical Abstract of the ESCWA Region 2007.*

United Nations Food and Agricultural Organization (FAO), Viale delle Terme di Caracalla, 00100 Rome, Italy, (Dial from U.S. (202) 653-2400), (Fax from U.S. (202) 653 5760), www.fao.org; AQUASTAT; *FAO Production Yearbook 2002; FAO Trade Yearbook;* and *The State of Food and Agriculture (SOFA) 2006.*

United Nations Statistics Division, New York, NY 10017, (800) 253-9646, Fax: (212) 963-4116, http://unstats.un.org; *Statistical Yearbook.*

The World Bank, 1818 H Street, NW, Washington, DC 20433, (202) 473-1000, Fax: (202) 477-6391, www.worldbank.org; *Kuwait* and *World Development Indicators (WDI) 2008.*

KUWAIT - AIRLINES

International Civil Aviation Organization (ICAO), External Relations and Public Information Office (EPO), 999 University Street, Montreal, Quebec H3C 5H7, Canada, (Dial from U.S. (514) 954-8219), (Fax from U.S. (514) 954-6077), www.icao.int; *Civil Aviation Statistics of the World.*

M.E. Sharpe, 80 Business Park Drive, Armonk, NY 10504, (800) 541-6563, Fax: (914) 273-2106, www.mesharpe.com; *The Illustrated Book of World Rankings.*

Palgrave Macmillan Ltd., Houndmills, Basingstoke, Hampshire, RG21 6XS, England, (Telephone in U.S. (888) 330-8477), (Fax in U.S. (800) 672-2054), www.palgrave.com; *The Statesman's Yearbook 2008.*

Taylor and Francis Group, An Informa Business, 2 Park Square, Milton Park, Abingdon, Oxford OX14 4RN, United Kingdom, (Dial from U.S. (212) 216-7800), (Fax from U.S. (212) 564-7854), www.tandf.co.uk; *The Europa World Year Book.*

United Nations Statistics Division, New York, NY 10017, (800) 253-9646, Fax: (212) 963-4116, http://unstats.un.org; *Statistical Yearbook.*

KUWAIT - AIRPORTS

Central Intelligence Agency, Office of Public Affairs, Washington, DC 20505, (703) 482-0623, Fax: (703) 482-1739, www.cia.gov; *The World Factbook.*

KUWAIT - ALUMINUM PRODUCTION

See KUWAIT - MINERAL INDUSTRIES

KUWAIT - ARMED FORCES

Central Intelligence Agency, Office of Public Affairs, Washington, DC 20505, (703) 482-0623, Fax: (703) 482-1739, www.cia.gov; *The World Factbook.*

Euromonitor International, Inc., 224 S. Michigan Avenue, Suite 1500, Chicago, IL 60604, (312) 922-1115, Fax: (312) 922-1157, www.euromonitor.com; *World Marketing Data and Statistics.*

International Institute for Strategic Studies (IISS), Arundel House, 13-15 Arundel Street, Temple Place, London WC2R 3DX, England, www.iiss.org; *The Military Balance 2007.*

International Monetary Fund (IMF), 700 Nineteenth Street, NW, Washington, DC 20431, (202) 623-7000, Fax: (202) 623-4661, www.imf.org; *Government Finance Statistics Yearbook (2008 Edition).*

Palgrave Macmillan Ltd., Houndmills, Basingstoke, Hampshire, RG21 6XS, England, (Telephone in U.S. (888) 330-8477), (Fax in U.S. (800) 672-2054), www.palgrave.com; *The Statesman's Yearbook 2008.*

U.S. Department of State (DOS), 2201 C Street NW, Washington, DC 20520, (202) 647-4000, www.state.gov; *World Military Expenditures and Arms Transfers (WMEAT).*

United Nations Statistics Division, New York, NY 10017, (800) 253-9646, Fax: (212) 963-4116, http://unstats.un.org; *Human Development Report 2006.*

KUWAIT - BALANCE OF PAYMENTS

International Monetary Fund (IMF), 700 Nineteenth Street, NW, Washington, DC 20431, (202) 623-7000, Fax: (202) 623-4661, www.imf.org; *Balance of Payments Statistics Newsletter* and *Balance of Payments Statistics Yearbook 2007.*

Taylor and Francis Group, An Informa Business, 2 Park Square, Milton Park, Abingdon, Oxford OX14 4RN, United Kingdom, (Dial from U.S. (212) 216-7800), (Fax from U.S. (212) 564-7854), www.tandf.co.uk; *The Europa World Year Book.*

United Nations Conference on Trade and Development (UNCTAD), DC2-1120, United Nations, New York, NY 10017, (212) 963-0027, www.unctad.org; *Handbook of Statistics 2005.*

United Nations Economic and Social Commission for Western Asia (ESCWA), PO Box 11-8575, Riad el-Solh Square, Beirut, Lebanon, www.escwa.un.org; *Annual Report 2006* and *Statistical Abstract of the ESCWA Region 2007.*

The World Bank, 1818 H Street, NW, Washington, DC 20433, (202) 473-1000, Fax: (202) 477-6391, www.worldbank.org; *Kuwait; World Development Indicators (WDI) 2008;* and *World Development Report 2008.*

KUWAIT - BANKS AND BANKING

Central Statistical Office, Ministry of Planning, PO Box 15, Safat 13001, Kuwait, http://scs.mop.gov.kw; *Annual Statistical Abstract 2006.*

Euromonitor International, Inc., 224 S. Michigan Avenue, Suite 1500, Chicago, IL 60604, (312) 922-1115, Fax: (312) 922-1157, www.euromonitor.com; *World Marketing Data and Statistics.*

International Monetary Fund (IMF), 700 Nineteenth Street, NW, Washington, DC 20431, (202) 623-7000, Fax: (202) 623-4661, www.imf.org; *International Financial Statistics Yearbook 2007.*

M.E. Sharpe, 80 Business Park Drive, Armonk, NY 10504, (800) 541-6563, Fax: (914) 273-2106, www.mesharpe.com; *The Illustrated Book of World Rankings.*

Palgrave Macmillan Ltd., Houndmills, Basingstoke, Hampshire, RG21 6XS, England, (Telephone in U.S. (888) 330-8477), (Fax in U.S. (800) 672-2054), www.palgrave.com; *The Statesman's Yearbook 2008.*

Taylor and Francis Group, An Informa Business, 2 Park Square, Milton Park, Abingdon, Oxford OX14 4RN, United Kingdom, (Dial from U.S. (212) 216-7800), (Fax from U.S. (212) 564-7854), www.tandf.co.uk; *The Europa World Year Book.*

United Nations Economic and Social Commission for Western Asia (ESCWA), PO Box 11-8575, Riad el-Solh Square, Beirut, Lebanon, www.escwa.un.org; *Annual Report 2006* and *Statistical Abstract of the ESCWA Region 2007.*

KUWAIT - BARLEY PRODUCTION

See KUWAIT - CROPS

KUWAIT - BEVERAGE INDUSTRY

M.E. Sharpe, 80 Business Park Drive, Armonk, NY 10504, (800) 541-6563, Fax: (914) 273-2106, www.mesharpe.com; *The Illustrated Book of World Rankings.*

United Nations Statistics Division, New York, NY 10017, (800) 253-9646, Fax: (212) 963-4116, http://unstats.un.org; *Statistical Yearbook.*

KUWAIT - BROADCASTING

Central Intelligence Agency, Office of Public Affairs, Washington, DC 20505, (703) 482-0623, Fax: (703) 482-1739, www.cia.gov; *The World Factbook.*

Euromonitor International, Inc., 224 S. Michigan Avenue, Suite 1500, Chicago, IL 60604, (312) 922-1115, Fax: (312) 922-1157, www.euromonitor.com; *World Marketing Data and Statistics.*

M.E. Sharpe, 80 Business Park Drive, Armonk, NY 10504, (800) 541-6563, Fax: (914) 273-2106, www.mesharpe.com; *The Illustrated Book of World Rankings.*

Palgrave Macmillan Ltd., Houndmills, Basingstoke, Hampshire, RG21 6XS, England, (Telephone in U.S. (888) 330-8477), (Fax in U.S. (800) 672-2054), www.palgrave.com; *The Statesman's Yearbook 2008.*

WRTH Publications Limited, PO Box 290, Oxford OX2 7FT, UK, www.wrth.com; *World Radio TV Handbook 2007.*

KUWAIT - BUDGET

Central Intelligence Agency, Office of Public Affairs, Washington, DC 20505, (703) 482-0623, Fax: (703) 482-1739, www.cia.gov; *The World Factbook.*

KUWAIT - CAPITAL LEVY

International Monetary Fund (IMF), 700 Nineteenth Street, NW, Washington, DC 20431, (202) 623-7000, Fax: (202) 623-4661, www.imf.org; *Government Finance Statistics Yearbook (2008 Edition).*

KUWAIT - CATTLE

See KUWAIT - LIVESTOCK

KUWAIT - CHICKENS

See KUWAIT - LIVESTOCK

KUWAIT - CHILDBIRTH - STATISTICS

Central Intelligence Agency, Office of Public Affairs, Washington, DC 20505, (703) 482-0623, Fax: (703) 482-1739, www.cia.gov; *The World Factbook.*

Euromonitor International, Inc., 224 S. Michigan Avenue, Suite 1500, Chicago, IL 60604, (312) 922-1115, Fax: (312) 922-1157, www.euromonitor.com; *International Marketing Data and Statistics 2008* and *The World Economic Factbook 2008.*

M.E. Sharpe, 80 Business Park Drive, Armonk, NY 10504, (800) 541-6563, Fax: (914) 273-2106, www.mesharpe.com; *The Illustrated Book of World Rankings.*

Taylor and Francis Group, An Informa Business, 2 Park Square, Milton Park, Abingdon, Oxford OX14 4RN, United Kingdom, (Dial from U.S. (212) 216-7800), (Fax from U.S. (212) 564-7854), www.tandf.co.uk; *The Europa World Year Book.*

United Nations Statistics Division, New York, NY 10017, (800) 253-9646, Fax: (212) 963-4116, http://unstats.un.org; *Demographic Yearbook* and *Statistical Yearbook.*

The World Bank, 1818 H Street, NW, Washington, DC 20433, (202) 473-1000, Fax: (202) 477-6391, www.worldbank.org; *World Development Indicators (WDI) 2008.*

World Health Organization (WHO), Avenue Appia 20, 1211 Geneve 27, Switzerland, (Telephone in U.S. (212) 331-9081), www.who.int; *World Health Report 2006.*

KUWAIT - CLIMATE

Central Statistical Office, Ministry of Planning, PO Box 15, Safat 13001, Kuwait, http://scs.mop.gov.kw; *Annual Statistical Abstract 2006.*

M.E. Sharpe, 80 Business Park Drive, Armonk, NY 10504, (800) 541-6563, Fax: (914) 273-2106, www.mesharpe.com; *The Illustrated Book of World Rankings.*

Palgrave Macmillan Ltd., Houndmills, Basingstoke, Hampshire, RG21 6XS, England, (Telephone in U.S. (888) 330-8477), (Fax in U.S. (800) 672-2054), www.palgrave.com; *The Statesman's Yearbook 2008.*

KUWAIT - COAL PRODUCTION

See KUWAIT - MINERAL INDUSTRIES

KUWAIT - COFFEE

See KUWAIT - CROPS

KUWAIT - COMMERCE

Palgrave Macmillan Ltd., Houndmills, Basingstoke, Hampshire, RG21 6XS, England, (Telephone in U.S. (888) 330-8477), (Fax in U.S. (800) 672-2054), www.palgrave.com; *The Statesman's Yearbook 2008.*

KUWAIT - COMMODITY EXCHANGES

Commodity Research Bureau, 330 South Wells Street, Suite 612, Chicago, IL 60606-7110, (800) 621-5271, Fax: (312) 939-4135, www.crbtrader.com; *2006 CRB Commodity Yearbook and CD.*

International Monetary Fund (IMF), 700 Nineteenth Street, NW, Washington, DC 20431, (202) 623-7000, Fax: (202) 623-4661, www.imf.org; *IMF Primary Commodity Prices.*

United Nations Food and Agricultural Organization (FAO), Viale delle Terme di Caracalla, 00100 Rome, Italy, (Dial from U.S. (202) 653-2400), (Fax from U.S. (202) 653 5760), www.fao.org; *The State of Food and Agriculture (SOFA) 2006.*

KUWAIT - COMMUNICATION AND TRAFFIC

United Nations Statistics Division, New York, NY 10017, (800) 253-9646, Fax: (212) 963-4116, http://unstats.un.org; *Statistical Yearbook.*

KUWAIT - CONSTRUCTION INDUSTRY

M.E. Sharpe, 80 Business Park Drive, Armonk, NY 10504, (800) 541-6563, Fax: (914) 273-2106, www.mesharpe.com; *The Illustrated Book of World Rankings.*

Palgrave Macmillan Ltd., Houndmills, Basingstoke, Hampshire, RG21 6XS, England, (Telephone in U.S. (888) 330-8477), (Fax in U.S. (800) 672-2054), www.palgrave.com; *The Statesman's Yearbook 2008.*

United Nations Statistics Division, New York, NY 10017, (800) 253-9646, Fax: (212) 963-4116, http://unstats.un.org; *Statistical Yearbook.*

KUWAIT - CONSUMER PRICE INDEXES

Taylor and Francis Group, An Informa Business, 2 Park Square, Milton Park, Abingdon, Oxford OX14 4RN, United Kingdom, (Dial from U.S. (212) 216-7800), (Fax from U.S. (212) 564-7854), www.tandf.co.uk; *The Europa World Year Book.*

United Nations Statistics Division, New York, NY 10017, (800) 253-9646, Fax: (212) 963-4116, http://unstats.un.org; *Statistical Yearbook.*

The World Bank, 1818 H Street, NW, Washington, DC 20433, (202) 473-1000, Fax: (202) 477-6391, www.worldbank.org; *Kuwait.*

KUWAIT - CONSUMPTION (ECONOMICS)

The World Bank, 1818 H Street, NW, Washington, DC 20433, (202) 473-1000, Fax: (202) 477-6391, www.worldbank.org; *World Development Report 2008.*

KUWAIT - COPPER INDUSTRY AND TRADE

See KUWAIT - MINERAL INDUSTRIES

KUWAIT - CORN INDUSTRY

See KUWAIT - CROPS

KUWAIT - COST AND STANDARD OF LIVING

International Monetary Fund (IMF), 700 Nineteenth Street, NW, Washington, DC 20431, (202) 623-7000, Fax: (202) 623-4661, www.imf.org; *Government Finance Statistics Yearbook (2008 Edition).*

KUWAIT - COTTON

See KUWAIT - CROPS

KUWAIT - CRIME

International Criminal Police Organization (INTERPOL), General Secretariat, 200 quai Charles de Gaulle, 69006 Lyon, France, www.interpol.int; *International Crime Statistics.*

Yale University Press, PO Box 209040, New Haven, CT 06520-9040, (203) 432-0960, Fax: (203) 432-0948, http://yalepress.yale.edu/yupbooks; *Violence and Crime in Cross-National Perspective.*

KUWAIT - CROPS

M.E. Sharpe, 80 Business Park Drive, Armonk, NY 10504, (800) 541-6563, Fax: (914) 273-2106, www.mesharpe.com; *The Illustrated Book of World Rankings.*

Palgrave Macmillan Ltd., Houndmills, Basingstoke, Hampshire, RG21 6XS, England, (Telephone in U.S. (888) 330-8477), (Fax in U.S. (800) 672-2054), www.palgrave.com; *The Statesman's Yearbook 2008.*

Taylor and Francis Group, An Informa Business, 2 Park Square, Milton Park, Abingdon, Oxford OX14 4RN, United Kingdom, (Dial from U.S. (212) 216-7800), (Fax from U.S. (212) 564-7854), www.tandf.co.uk; *The Europa World Year Book.*

United Nations Conference on Trade and Development (UNCTAD), DC2-1120, United Nations, New York, NY 10017, (212) 963-0027, www.unctad.org; *UNCTAD Commodity Yearbook.*

United Nations Food and Agricultural Organization (FAO), Viale delle Terme di Caracalla, 00100 Rome, Italy, (Dial from U.S. (202) 653-2400), (Fax from U.S. (202) 653 5760), www.fao.org; *The State of Food and Agriculture (SOFA) 2006.*

KUWAIT - CUSTOMS ADMINISTRATION

International Monetary Fund (IMF), 700 Nineteenth Street, NW, Washington, DC 20431, (202) 623-7000, Fax: (202) 623-4661, www.imf.org; *Government Finance Statistics Yearbook (2008 Edition).*

KUWAIT - DAIRY PROCESSING

M.E. Sharpe, 80 Business Park Drive, Armonk, NY 10504, (800) 541-6563, Fax: (914) 273-2106, www.mesharpe.com; *The Illustrated Book of World Rankings.*

Palgrave Macmillan Ltd., Houndmills, Basingstoke, Hampshire, RG21 6XS, England, (Telephone in U.S. (888) 330-8477), (Fax in U.S. (800) 672-2054), www.palgrave.com; *The Statesman's Yearbook 2008.*

Taylor and Francis Group, An Informa Business, 2 Park Square, Milton Park, Abingdon, Oxford OX14 4RN, United Kingdom, (Dial from U.S. (212) 216-7800), (Fax from U.S. (212) 564-7854), www.tandf.co.uk; *The Europa World Year Book.*

United Nations Food and Agricultural Organization (FAO), Viale delle Terme di Caracalla, 00100 Rome, Italy, (Dial from U.S. (202) 653-2400), (Fax from U.S. (202) 653 5760), www.fao.org; *FAO Production Yearbook 2002* and *The State of Food and Agriculture (SOFA) 2006.*

KUWAIT - DEATH RATES

See KUWAIT - MORTALITY

KUWAIT - DEBTS, EXTERNAL

The World Bank, 1818 H Street, NW, Washington, DC 20433, (202) 473-1000, Fax: (202) 477-6391, www.worldbank.org; *Global Development Finance 2007; World Development Indicators (WDI) 2008;* and *World Development Report 2008.*

KUWAIT - DEFENSE EXPENDITURES

See KUWAIT - ARMED FORCES

KUWAIT - DEMOGRAPHY

Euromonitor International, Inc., 224 S. Michigan Avenue, Suite 1500, Chicago, IL 60604, (312) 922-1115, Fax: (312) 922-1157, www.euromonitor.com; *International Marketing Data and Statistics 2008; The World Economic Factbook 2008;* and *World Marketing Data and Statistics.*

M.E. Sharpe, 80 Business Park Drive, Armonk, NY 10504, (800) 541-6563, Fax: (914) 273-2106, www.mesharpe.com; *The Illustrated Book of World Rankings.*

United Nations Statistics Division, New York, NY 10017, (800) 253-9646, Fax: (212) 963-4116, http://unstats.un.org; *Human Development Report 2006.*

The World Bank, 1818 H Street, NW, Washington, DC 20433, (202) 473-1000, Fax: (202) 477-6391, www.worldbank.org; *Kuwait.*

KUWAIT - DIAMONDS

See KUWAIT - MINERAL INDUSTRIES

KUWAIT - DISPOSABLE INCOME

Central Statistical Office, Ministry of Planning, PO Box 15, Safat 13001, Kuwait, http://scs.mop.gov.kw; *Annual Statistical Abstract 2006.*

M.E. Sharpe, 80 Business Park Drive, Armonk, NY 10504, (800) 541-6563, Fax: (914) 273-2106, www.mesharpe.com; *The Illustrated Book of World Rankings.*

United Nations Statistics Division, New York, NY 10017, (800) 253-9646, Fax: (212) 963-4116, http://unstats.un.org; *National Accounts Statistics: Compendium of Income Distribution Statistics* and *Statistical Yearbook.*

KUWAIT - DIVORCE

M.E. Sharpe, 80 Business Park Drive, Armonk, NY 10504, (800) 541-6563, Fax: (914) 273-2106, www.mesharpe.com; *The Illustrated Book of World Rankings.*

United Nations Statistics Division, New York, NY 10017, (800) 253-9646, Fax: (212) 963-4116, http://unstats.un.org; *Demographic Yearbook* and *Statistical Yearbook.*

KUWAIT - ECONOMIC ASSISTANCE

United Nations Statistics Division, New York, NY 10017, (800) 253-9646, Fax: (212) 963-4116, http://unstats.un.org; *Statistical Yearbook.*

KUWAIT - ECONOMIC CONDITIONS

Center for International Business Education Research (CIBER), Columbia Business School and School of International and Public Affairs, Uris Hall, Room 212, 3022 Broadway, New York, NY 10027-6902, Mr. Joshua Safier, (212) 854-4750, Fax: (212) 222-9821, www.columbia.edu/cu/ciber/; Datastream International.

Central Intelligence Agency, Office of Public Affairs, Washington, DC 20505, (703) 482-0623, Fax: (703) 482-1739, www.cia.gov; *The World Factbook.*

DSI Data Service Information, Xantener Strasse 51a, D-47495 Rheinberg, Germany, www.dsidata.com; *Campus Solution.*

Dun and Bradstreet (DB) Corporation, 103 JFK Parkway, Short Hills, NJ 07078, (973) 921-5500, www.dnb.com; *Country Report.*

Economist Intelligence Unit, 111 West 57th Street, New York, NY 10019, (212) 554-0600, Fax: (212) 586-1181, www.eiu.com; *Kuwait Country Report.*

Euromonitor International, Inc., 224 S. Michigan Avenue, Suite 1500, Chicago, IL 60604, (312) 922-1115, Fax: (312) 922-1157, www.euromonitor.com; *International Marketing Data and Statistics 2008; The World Economic Factbook 2008;* and *World Marketing Data and Statistics.*

International Monetary Fund (IMF), 700 Nineteenth Street, NW, Washington, DC 20431, (202) 623-7000, Fax: (202) 623-4661, www.imf.org; *World Economic Outlook Reports.*

M.E. Sharpe, 80 Business Park Drive, Armonk, NY 10504, (800) 541-6563, Fax: (914) 273-2106, www.mesharpe.com; *The Illustrated Book of World Rankings.*

Palgrave Macmillan Ltd., Houndmills, Basingstoke, Hampshire, RG21 6XS, England, (Telephone in U.S. (888) 330-8477), (Fax in U.S. (800) 672-2054), www.palgrave.com; *The Statesman's Yearbook 2008.*

Taylor and Francis Group, An Informa Business, 2 Park Square, Milton Park, Abingdon, Oxford OX14 4RN, United Kingdom, (Dial from U.S. (212) 216-7800), (Fax from U.S. (212) 564-7854), www.tandf.co.uk; *The Europa World Year Book.*

United Nations Economic and Social Commission for Western Asia (ESCWA), PO Box 11-8575, Riad el-Solh Square, Beirut, Lebanon, www.escwa.un.org; *Annual Report 2006; Bulletin on Population and Vital Statistics in the ESCWA Region;* and *Survey of Economic and Social Developments in the ESCWA Region 2006-2007.*

United Nations Statistics Division, New York, NY 10017, (800) 253-9646, Fax: (212) 963-4116, http://unstats.un.org; *World Statistics Pocketbook.*

The World Bank, 1818 H Street, NW, Washington, DC 20433, (202) 473-1000, Fax: (202) 477-6391, www.worldbank.org; *Global Economic Monitor (GEM); Global Economic Prospects 2008; Kuwait; The World Bank Atlas 2003-2004;* and *World Development Report 2008.*

KUWAIT - EDUCATION

Central Statistical Office, Ministry of Planning, PO Box 15, Safat 13001, Kuwait, http://scs.mop.gov.kw; *Annual Statistical Abstract 2006.*

Euromonitor International, Inc., 224 S. Michigan Avenue, Suite 1500, Chicago, IL 60604, (312) 922-1115, Fax: (312) 922-1157, www.euromonitor.com; *International Marketing Data and Statistics 2008* and *World Marketing Data and Statistics.*

International Monetary Fund (IMF), 700 Nineteenth Street, NW, Washington, DC 20431, (202) 623-7000, Fax: (202) 623-4661, www.imf.org; *Government Finance Statistics Yearbook (2008 Edition).*

M.E. Sharpe, 80 Business Park Drive, Armonk, NY 10504, (800) 541-6563, Fax: (914) 273-2106, www.mesharpe.com; *The Illustrated Book of World Rankings.*

Palgrave Macmillan Ltd., Houndmills, Basingstoke, Hampshire, RG21 6XS, England, (Telephone in U.S. (888) 330-8477), (Fax in U.S. (800) 672-2054), www.palgrave.com; *The Statesman's Yearbook 2008.*

Taylor and Francis Group, An Informa Business, 2 Park Square, Milton Park, Abingdon, Oxford OX14 4RN, United Kingdom, (Dial from U.S. (212) 216-7800), (Fax from U.S. (212) 564-7854), www.tandf.co.uk; *The Europa World Year Book.*

UNESCO Institute for Statistics, C.P. 6128 Succursale Centre-Ville, Montreal, Quebec, H3C 3J7 Canada, (Dial from U.S. (514) 343-6880), (Fax from U.S. (514) 343 6882), www.uis.unesco.org; *Statistical Tables.*

United Nations Economic and Social Commission for Western Asia (ESCWA), PO Box 11-8575, Riad el-Solh Square, Beirut, Lebanon, www.escwa.un.org; *Annual Report 2006* and *Statistical Abstract of the ESCWA Region 2007.*

United Nations Statistics Division, New York, NY 10017, (800) 253-9646, Fax: (212) 963-4116, http://unstats.un.org; *Human Development Report 2006.*

The World Bank, 1818 H Street, NW, Washington, DC 20433, (202) 473-1000, Fax: (202) 477-6391, www.worldbank.org; *Kuwait; World Development Indicators (WDI) 2008;* and *World Development Report 2008.*

KUWAIT - ELECTRICITY

M.E. Sharpe, 80 Business Park Drive, Armonk, NY 10504, (800) 541-6563, Fax: (914) 273-2106, www.mesharpe.com; *The Illustrated Book of World Rankings.*

Organisation for Economic Cooperation and Development (OECD), 2 rue Andre Pascal, F-75775 Paris Cedex 16, France, (Telephone in U.S. (202) 785-6323), (Fax in U.S. (202) 785-0350), www.oecd.org; *World Energy Outlook 2007.*

Palgrave Macmillan Ltd., Houndmills, Basingstoke, Hampshire, RG21 6XS, England, (Telephone in U.S. (888) 330-8477), (Fax in U.S. (800) 672-2054), www.palgrave.com; *The Statesman's Yearbook 2008.*

U.S. Department of Energy (DOE), Energy Information Administration (EIA), 1000 Independence Avenue, SW, Washington, DC 20585, (202) 586-8800, www.eia.doe.gov; *International Energy Annual 2004* and *International Energy Outlook 2006.*

United Nations Statistics Division, New York, NY 10017, (800) 253-9646, Fax: (212) 963-4116, http://unstats.un.org; *Human Development Report 2006* and *Statistical Yearbook.*

KUWAIT - EMPLOYMENT

Euromonitor International, Inc., 224 S. Michigan Avenue, Suite 1500, Chicago, IL 60604, (312) 922-1115, Fax: (312) 922-1157, www.euromonitor.com; *International Marketing Data and Statistics 2008.*

International Labour Office, I.L.O. Publications, 4 route des Morillons, CH-1211 Geneva 22, Switzerland, (Telephone in U.S. (202) 653-7652), (Fax in U.S. (202) 653-7687), www.ilo.org; *Yearbook of Labour Statistics 2006.*

M.E. Sharpe, 80 Business Park Drive, Armonk, NY 10504, (800) 541-6563, Fax: (914) 273-2106, www.mesharpe.com; *The Illustrated Book of World Rankings.*

United Nations Economic and Social Commission for Western Asia (ESCWA), PO Box 11-8575, Riad el-Solh Square, Beirut, Lebanon, www.escwa.un.org; *Annual Report 2006* and *Statistical Abstract of the ESCWA Region 2007.*

United Nations Statistics Division, New York, NY 10017, (800) 253-9646, Fax: (212) 963-4116, http://unstats.un.org; *Bulletin of Industrial Statistics for the Arab Countries* and *Statistical Yearbook.*

The World Bank, 1818 H Street, NW, Washington, DC 20433, (202) 473-1000, Fax: (202) 477-6391, www.worldbank.org; *Kuwait.*

KUWAIT - ENVIRONMENTAL CONDITIONS

DSI Data Service Information, Xantener Strasse 51a, D-47495 Rheinberg, Germany, www.dsidata.com; *Campus Solution* and *DSI's Global Environmental Database.*

Economist Intelligence Unit, 111 West 57th Street, New York, NY 10019, (212) 554-0600, Fax: (212) 586-1181, www.eiu.com; *Kuwait Country Report.*

United Nations Statistics Division, New York, NY 10017, (800) 253-9646, Fax: (212) 963-4116, http://unstats.un.org; *World Statistics Pocketbook.*

KUWAIT - EXPORTS

Central Intelligence Agency, Office of Public Affairs, Washington, DC 20505, (703) 482-0623, Fax: (703) 482-1739, www.cia.gov; *The World Factbook.*

Economist Intelligence Unit, 111 West 57th Street, New York, NY 10019, (212) 554-0600, Fax: (212) 586-1181, www.eiu.com; *Kuwait Country Report.*

Euromonitor International, Inc., 224 S. Michigan Avenue, Suite 1500, Chicago, IL 60604, (312) 922-1115, Fax: (312) 922-1157, www.euromonitor.com; *International Marketing Data and Statistics 2008* and *The World Economic Factbook 2008.*

International Monetary Fund (IMF), 700 Nineteenth Street, NW, Washington, DC 20431, (202) 623-7000, Fax: (202) 623-4661, www.imf.org; *Direction of Trade Statistics Yearbook 2007* and *International Financial Statistics Yearbook 2007.*

Organization of Petroleum Exporting Countries (OPEC), Obere Donaustrasse 93, A-1020, Vienna, Austria, www.opec.org; *Annual Statistical Bulletin 2006.*

Palgrave Macmillan Ltd., Houndmills, Basingstoke, Hampshire, RG21 6XS, England, (Telephone in U.S. (888) 330-8477), (Fax in U.S. (800) 672-2054), www.palgrave.com; *The Statesman's Yearbook 2008.*

Taylor and Francis Group, An Informa Business, 2 Park Square, Milton Park, Abingdon, Oxford OX14 4RN, United Kingdom, (Dial from U.S. (212) 216-7800), (Fax from U.S. (212) 564-7854), www.tandf.co.uk; *The Europa World Year Book.*

United Nations Conference on Trade and Development (UNCTAD), DC2-1120, United Nations, New York, NY 10017, (212) 963-0027, www.unctad.org; *Handbook of Statistics 2005.*

United Nations Economic and Social Commission for Western Asia (ESCWA), PO Box 11-8575, Riad el-Solh Square, Beirut, Lebanon, www.escwa.un.org; *Annual Report 2006* and *Statistical Abstract of the ESCWA Region 2007.*

United Nations Food and Agricultural Organization (FAO), Viale delle Terme di Caracalla, 00100 Rome, Italy, (Dial from U.S. (202) 653-2400), (Fax from U.S. (202) 653 5760), www.fao.org; *The State of Food and Agriculture (SOFA) 2006.*

United Nations Statistics Division, New York, NY 10017, (800) 253-9646, Fax: (212) 963-4116, http://unstats.un.org; *Bulletin of Industrial Statistics for the Arab Countries.*

The World Bank, 1818 H Street, NW, Washington, DC 20433, (202) 473-1000, Fax: (202) 477-6391, www.worldbank.org; *World Development Indicators (WDI) 2008* and *World Development Report 2008.*

KUWAIT - FEMALE WORKING POPULATION

See KUWAIT - EMPLOYMENT

KUWAIT - FERTILITY, HUMAN

Central Intelligence Agency, Office of Public Affairs, Washington, DC 20505, (703) 482-0623, Fax: (703) 482-1739, www.cia.gov; *The World Factbook.*

M.E. Sharpe, 80 Business Park Drive, Armonk, NY 10504, (800) 541-6563, Fax: (914) 273-2106, www.mesharpe.com; *The Illustrated Book of World Rankings.*

United Nations Statistics Division, New York, NY 10017, (800) 253-9646, Fax: (212) 963-4116, http://unstats.un.org; *Human Development Report 2006.*

The World Bank, 1818 H Street, NW, Washington, DC 20433, (202) 473-1000, Fax: (202) 477-6391, www.worldbank.org; *The World Bank Atlas 2003-2004; World Development Indicators (WDI) 2008;* and *World Development Report 2008.*

KUWAIT - FERTILIZER INDUSTRY

United Nations Food and Agricultural Organization (FAO), Viale delle Terme di Caracalla, 00100 Rome, Italy, (Dial from U.S. (202) 653-2400), (Fax from U.S. (202) 653 5760), www.fao.org; *FAO Fertilizer Yearbook* and *The State of Food and Agriculture (SOFA) 2006.*

United Nations Statistics Division, New York, NY 10017, (800) 253-9646, Fax: (212) 963-4116, http://unstats.un.org; *Statistical Yearbook.*

KUWAIT - FETAL MORTALITY

See KUWAIT - MORTALITY

KUWAIT - FINANCE

International Monetary Fund (IMF), 700 Nineteenth Street, NW, Washington, DC 20431, (202) 623-7000, Fax: (202) 623-4661, www.imf.org; *International Financial Statistics Yearbook 2007.*

Taylor and Francis Group, An Informa Business, 2 Park Square, Milton Park, Abingdon, Oxford OX14 4RN, United Kingdom, (Dial from U.S. (212) 216-7800), (Fax from U.S. (212) 564-7854), www.tandf.co.uk; *The Europa World Year Book.*

United Nations Economic and Social Commission for Western Asia (ESCWA), PO Box 11-8575, Riad el-Solh Square, Beirut, Lebanon, www.escwa.un.org; *Annual Report 2006* and *Statistical Abstract of the ESCWA Region 2007.*

United Nations Statistics Division, New York, NY 10017, (800) 253-9646, Fax: (212) 963-4116, http://unstats.un.org; *National Accounts Statistics: Compendium of Income Distribution Statistics* and *Statistical Yearbook.*

The World Bank, 1818 H Street, NW, Washington, DC 20433, (202) 473-1000, Fax: (202) 477-6391, www.worldbank.org; *Kuwait.*

KUWAIT - FINANCE, PUBLIC

Bernan Essential Government Publications, 4611-F Assembly Drive, Lanham MD, 20706-4391, (301) 459-2255, Fax: (800) 865-3450, www.bernan.com; *National Accounts Statistics.*

Central Statistical Office, Ministry of Planning, PO Box 15, Safat 13001, Kuwait, http://scs.mop.gov.kw; *Annual Statistical Abstract 2006.*

Economist Intelligence Unit, 111 West 57th Street, New York, NY 10019, (212) 554-0600, Fax: (212) 586-1181, www.eiu.com; *Kuwait Country Report.*

International Monetary Fund (IMF), 700 Nineteenth Street, NW, Washington, DC 20431, (202) 623-7000, Fax: (202) 623-4661, www.imf.org; *International Financial Statistics; International Financial Statistics Online Service;* and *International Financial Statistics Yearbook 2007.*

M.E. Sharpe, 80 Business Park Drive, Armonk, NY 10504, (800) 541-6563, Fax: (914) 273-2106, www.mesharpe.com; *The Illustrated Book of World Rankings.*

Palgrave Macmillan Ltd., Houndmills, Basingstoke, Hampshire, RG21 6XS, England, (Telephone in U.S. (888) 330-8477), (Fax in U.S. (800) 672-2054), www.palgrave.com; *The Statesman's Yearbook 2008.*

Taylor and Francis Group, An Informa Business, 2 Park Square, Milton Park, Abingdon, Oxford OX14 4RN, United Kingdom, (Dial from U.S. (212) 216-7800), (Fax from U.S. (212) 564-7854), www.tandf.co.uk; *The Europa World Year Book.*

United Nations Economic and Social Commission for Western Asia (ESCWA), PO Box 11-8575, Riad el-Solh Square, Beirut, Lebanon, www.escwa.un.

org; *Annual Report 2006* and *Statistical Abstract of the ESCWA Region 2007.*

The World Bank, 1818 H Street, NW, Washington, DC 20433, (202) 473-1000, Fax: (202) 477-6391, www.worldbank.org; *Kuwait.*

KUWAIT - FISHERIES

Central Statistical Office, Ministry of Planning, PO Box 15, Safat 13001, Kuwait, http://scs.mop.gov.kw; *Annual Statistical Abstract 2006.*

M.E. Sharpe, 80 Business Park Drive, Armonk, NY 10504, (800) 541-6563, Fax: (914) 273-2106, www.mesharpe.com; *The Illustrated Book of World Rankings.*

Palgrave Macmillan Ltd., Houndmills, Basingstoke, Hampshire, RG21 6XS, England, (Telephone in U.S. (888) 330-8477), (Fax in U.S. (800) 672-2054), www.palgrave.com; *The Statesman's Yearbook 2008.*

Taylor and Francis Group, An Informa Business, 2 Park Square, Milton Park, Abingdon, Oxford OX14 4RN, United Kingdom, (Dial from U.S. (212) 216-7800), (Fax from U.S. (212) 564-7854), www.tandf.co.uk; *The Europa World Year Book.*

United Nations Conference on Trade and Development (UNCTAD), DC2-1120, United Nations, New York, NY 10017, (212) 963-0027, www.unctad.org; *UNCTAD Commodity Yearbook.*

United Nations Economic and Social Commission for Western Asia (ESCWA), PO Box 11-8575, Riad el-Solh Square, Beirut, Lebanon, www.escwa.un.org; *Annual Report 2006* and *Statistical Abstract of the ESCWA Region 2007.*

United Nations Food and Agricultural Organization (FAO), Viale delle Terme di Caracalla, 00100 Rome, Italy, (Dial from U.S. (202) 653-2400), (Fax from U.S. (202) 653 5760), www.fao.org; *FAO Yearbook of Fishery Statistics;* Fishery Databases; FISHSTAT Database. Subjects covered include: Aquaculture production, capture production, fishery commodities; and *The State of Food and Agriculture (SOFA) 2006.*

United Nations Statistics Division, New York, NY 10017, (800) 253-9646, Fax: (212) 963-4116, http://unstats.un.org; *Statistical Yearbook.*

The World Bank, 1818 H Street, NW, Washington, DC 20433, (202) 473-1000, Fax: (202) 477-6391, www.worldbank.org; *Kuwait.*

KUWAIT - FLOUR INDUSTRY

United Nations Statistics Division, New York, NY 10017, (800) 253-9646, Fax: (212) 963-4116, http://unstats.un.org; *Statistical Yearbook.*

KUWAIT - FOOD

United Nations Conference on Trade and Development (UNCTAD), DC2-1120, United Nations, New York, NY 10017, (212) 963-0027, www.unctad.org; *UNCTAD Commodity Yearbook.*

United Nations Food and Agricultural Organization (FAO), Viale delle Terme di Caracalla, 00100 Rome, Italy, (Dial from U.S. (202) 653-2400), (Fax from U.S. (202) 653 5760), www.fao.org; *FAO Production Yearbook 2002* and *The State of Food and Agriculture (SOFA) 2006.*

United Nations Statistics Division, New York, NY 10017, (800) 253-9646, Fax: (212) 963-4116, http://unstats.un.org; *Human Development Report 2006.*

KUWAIT - FOREIGN EXCHANGE RATES

Central Intelligence Agency, Office of Public Affairs, Washington, DC 20505, (703) 482-0623, Fax: (703) 482-1739, www.cia.gov; *The World Factbook.*

Euromonitor International, Inc., 224 S. Michigan Avenue, Suite 1500, Chicago, IL 60604, (312) 922-1115, Fax: (312) 922-1157, www.euromonitor.com; *International Marketing Data and Statistics 2008* and *The World Economic Factbook 2008.*

International Civil Aviation Organization (ICAO), External Relations and Public Information Office (EPO), 999 University Street, Montreal, Quebec H3C 5H7, Canada, (Dial from U.S. (514) 954-8219), (Fax from U.S. (514) 954-6077), www.icao.int; *Civil Aviation Statistics of the World.*

International Monetary Fund (IMF), 700 Nineteenth Street, NW, Washington, DC 20431, (202) 623-7000, Fax: (202) 623-4661, www.imf.org; *International Financial Statistics Yearbook 2007.*

Organization of Petroleum Exporting Countries (OPEC), Obere Donaustrasse 93, A-1020, Vienna, Austria, www.opec.org; *Annual Statistical Bulletin 2006.*

Taylor and Francis Group, An Informa Business, 2 Park Square, Milton Park, Abingdon, Oxford OX14 4RN, United Kingdom, (Dial from U.S. (212) 216-7800), (Fax from U.S. (212) 564-7854), www.tandf.co.uk; *The Europa World Year Book.*

United Nations Statistics Division, New York, NY 10017, (800) 253-9646, Fax: (212) 963-4116, http://unstats.un.org; *Bulletin of Industrial Statistics for the Arab Countries; Statistical Yearbook;* and *World Statistics Pocketbook.*

KUWAIT - FORESTS AND FORESTRY

M.E. Sharpe, 80 Business Park Drive, Armonk, NY 10504, (800) 541-6563, Fax: (914) 273-2106, www.mesharpe.com; *The Illustrated Book of World Rankings.*

UNESCO Institute for Statistics, C.P. 6128 Succursale Centre-Ville, Montreal, Quebec, H3C 3J7 Canada, (Dial from U.S. (514) 343-6880), (Fax from U.S. (514) 343 6882), www.uis.unesco.org; *Statistical Tables.*

United Nations Conference on Trade and Development (UNCTAD), DC2-1120, United Nations, New York, NY 10017, (212) 963-0027, www.unctad.org; *UNCTAD Commodity Yearbook.*

United Nations Food and Agricultural Organization (FAO), Viale delle Terme di Caracalla, 00100 Rome, Italy, (Dial from U.S. (202) 653-2400), (Fax from U.S. (202) 653 5760), www.fao.org; *FAO Yearbook of Forest Products* and *The State of Food and Agriculture (SOFA) 2006.*

United Nations Statistics Division, New York, NY 10017, (800) 253-9646, Fax: (212) 963-4116, http://unstats.un.org; *Statistical Yearbook.*

The World Bank, 1818 H Street, NW, Washington, DC 20433, (202) 473-1000, Fax: (202) 477-6391, www.worldbank.org; *Kuwait* and *World Development Report 2008.*

KUWAIT - GAS PRODUCTION

See KUWAIT - MINERAL INDUSTRIES

KUWAIT - GEOGRAPHIC INFORMATION SYSTEMS

M.E. Sharpe, 80 Business Park Drive, Armonk, NY 10504, (800) 541-6563, Fax: (914) 273-2106, www.mesharpe.com; *The Illustrated Book of World Rankings.*

The World Bank, 1818 H Street, NW, Washington, DC 20433, (202) 473-1000, Fax: (202) 477-6391, www.worldbank.org; *Kuwait.*

KUWAIT - GOLD INDUSTRY

International Monetary Fund (IMF), 700 Nineteenth Street, NW, Washington, DC 20431, (202) 623-7000, Fax: (202) 623-4661, www.imf.org; *International Financial Statistics Yearbook 2007.*

United Nations Statistics Division, New York, NY 10017, (800) 253-9646, Fax: (212) 963-4116, http://unstats.un.org; *Statistical Yearbook.*

The World Bank, 1818 H Street, NW, Washington, DC 20433, (202) 473-1000, Fax: (202) 477-6391, www.worldbank.org; *World Development Indicators (WDI) 2008.*

KUWAIT - GOLD PRODUCTION

See KUWAIT - MINERAL INDUSTRIES

KUWAIT - GRANTS-IN-AID

International Monetary Fund (IMF), 700 Nineteenth Street, NW, Washington, DC 20431, (202) 623-7000, Fax: (202) 623-4661, www.imf.org; *Government Finance Statistics Yearbook (2008 Edition).*

KUWAIT - GROSS DOMESTIC PRODUCT

Economist Intelligence Unit, 111 West 57th Street, New York, NY 10019, (212) 554-0600, Fax: (212) 586-1181, www.eiu.com; *Kuwait Country Report.*

Euromonitor International, Inc., 224 S. Michigan Avenue, Suite 1500, Chicago, IL 60604, (312) 922-1115, Fax: (312) 922-1157, www.euromonitor.com; *International Marketing Data and Statistics 2008* and *The World Economic Factbook 2008.*

M.E. Sharpe, 80 Business Park Drive, Armonk, NY 10504, (800) 541-6563, Fax: (914) 273-2106, www.mesharpe.com; *The Illustrated Book of World Rankings.*

Taylor and Francis Group, An Informa Business, 2 Park Square, Milton Park, Abingdon, Oxford OX14 4RN, United Kingdom, (Dial from U.S. (212) 216-7800), (Fax from U.S. (212) 564-7854), www.tandf.co.uk; *The Europa World Year Book.*

United Nations Economic and Social Commission for Western Asia (ESCWA), PO Box 11-8575, Riad el-Solh Square, Beirut, Lebanon, www.escwa.un.org; *Annual Report 2006* and *Statistical Abstract of the ESCWA Region 2007.*

United Nations Statistics Division, New York, NY 10017, (800) 253-9646, Fax: (212) 963-4116, http://unstats.un.org; *Bulletin of Industrial Statistics for the Arab Countries; Human Development Report 2006; National Accounts Statistics: Compendium of Income Distribution Statistics;* and *Statistical Yearbook.*

The World Bank, 1818 H Street, NW, Washington, DC 20433, (202) 473-1000, Fax: (202) 477-6391, www.worldbank.org; *World Development Indicators (WDI) 2008* and *World Development Report 2008.*

KUWAIT - GROSS NATIONAL PRODUCT

Euromonitor International, Inc., 224 S. Michigan Avenue, Suite 1500, Chicago, IL 60604, (312) 922-1115, Fax: (312) 922-1157, www.euromonitor.com; *International Marketing Data and Statistics 2008.*

M.E. Sharpe, 80 Business Park Drive, Armonk, NY 10504, (800) 541-6563, Fax: (914) 273-2106, www.mesharpe.com; *The Illustrated Book of World Rankings.*

Organization of Petroleum Exporting Countries (OPEC), Obere Donaustrasse 93, A-1020, Vienna, Austria, www.opec.org; *Annual Statistical Bulletin 2006.*

Palgrave Macmillan Ltd., Houndmills, Basingstoke, Hampshire, RG21 6XS, England, (Telephone in U.S. (888) 330-8477), (Fax in U.S. (800) 672-2054), www.palgrave.com; *The Statesman's Yearbook 2008.*

U.S. Department of State (DOS), 2201 C Street NW, Washington, DC 20520, (202) 647-4000, www.state.gov; *World Military Expenditures and Arms Transfers (WMEAT).*

The World Bank, 1818 H Street, NW, Washington, DC 20433, (202) 473-1000, Fax: (202) 477-6391, www.worldbank.org; *The World Bank Atlas 2003-2004; World Development Indicators (WDI) 2008;* and *World Development Report 2008.*

KUWAIT - HIDES AND SKINS INDUSTRY

United Nations Food and Agricultural Organization (FAO), Viale delle Terme di Caracalla, 00100 Rome, Italy, (Dial from U.S. (202) 653-2400), (Fax from U.S. (202) 653 5760), www.fao.org; *FAO Production Yearbook 2002.*

KUWAIT - HOUSING

Central Statistical Office, Ministry of Planning, PO Box 15, Safat 13001, Kuwait, http://scs.mop.gov.kw; *Annual Statistical Abstract 2006.*

Euromonitor International, Inc., 224 S. Michigan Avenue, Suite 1500, Chicago, IL 60604, (312) 922-1115, Fax: (312) 922-1157, www.euromonitor.com; *World Marketing Data and Statistics.*

M.E. Sharpe, 80 Business Park Drive, Armonk, NY 10504, (800) 541-6563, Fax: (914) 273-2106, www.mesharpe.com; *The Illustrated Book of World Rankings.*

KUWAIT - ILLITERATE PERSONS

Euromonitor International, Inc., 224 S. Michigan Avenue, Suite 1500, Chicago, IL 60604, (312) 922-1115, Fax: (312) 922-1157, www.euromonitor.com; *The World Economic Factbook 2008.*

UNESCO Institute for Statistics, C.P. 6128 Succursale Centre-Ville, Montreal, Quebec, H3C 3J7 Canada, (Dial from U.S. (514) 343-6880), (Fax from U.S. (514) 343 6882), www.uis.unesco.org; *Statistical Tables.*

United Nations Statistics Division, New York, NY 10017, (800) 253-9646, Fax: (212) 963-4116, http://unstats.un.org; *Human Development Report 2006.*

KUWAIT - IMPORTS

Central Intelligence Agency, Office of Public Affairs, Washington, DC 20505, (703) 482-0623, Fax: (703) 482-1739, www.cia.gov; *The World Factbook.*

Economist Intelligence Unit, 111 West 57th Street, New York, NY 10019, (212) 554-0600, Fax: (212) 586-1181, www.eiu.com; *Kuwait Country Report.*

Euromonitor International, Inc., 224 S. Michigan Avenue, Suite 1500, Chicago, IL 60604, (312) 922-1115, Fax: (312) 922-1157, www.euromonitor.com; *International Marketing Data and Statistics 2008* and *The World Economic Factbook 2008.*

International Monetary Fund (IMF), 700 Nineteenth Street, NW, Washington, DC 20431, (202) 623-7000, Fax: (202) 623-4661, www.imf.org; *Direction of Trade Statistics Yearbook 2007; Government Finance Statistics Yearbook (2008 Edition);* and *International Financial Statistics Yearbook 2007.*

Palgrave Macmillan Ltd., Houndmills, Basingstoke, Hampshire, RG21 6XS, England, (Telephone in U.S. (888) 330-8477), (Fax in U.S. (800) 672-2054), www.palgrave.com; *The Statesman's Yearbook 2008.*

Taylor and Francis Group, An Informa Business, 2 Park Square, Milton Park, Abingdon, Oxford OX14 4RN, United Kingdom, (Dial from U.S. (212) 216-7800), (Fax from U.S. (212) 564-7854), www.tandf.co.uk; *The Europa World Year Book.*

United Nations Conference on Trade and Development (UNCTAD), DC2-1120, United Nations, New York, NY 10017, (212) 963-0027, www.unctad.org; *Handbook of Statistics 2005.*

United Nations Economic and Social Commission for Western Asia (ESCWA), PO Box 11-8575, Riad el-Solh Square, Beirut, Lebanon, www.escwa.un.org; *Annual Report 2006* and *Statistical Abstract of the ESCWA Region 2007.*

United Nations Food and Agricultural Organization (FAO), Viale delle Terme di Caracalla, 00100 Rome, Italy, (Dial from U.S. (202) 653-2400), (Fax from U.S. (202) 653 5760), www.fao.org; *The State of Food and Agriculture (SOFA) 2006.*

United Nations Statistics Division, New York, NY 10017, (800) 253-9646, Fax: (212) 963-4116, http://unstats.un.org; *Bulletin of Industrial Statistics for the Arab Countries.*

The World Bank, 1818 H Street, NW, Washington, DC 20433, (202) 473-1000, Fax: (202) 477-6391, www.worldbank.org; *World Development Indicators (WDI) 2008* and *World Development Report 2008.*

KUWAIT - INCOME TAXES

See KUWAIT - TAXATION

KUWAIT - INDUSTRIAL PRODUCTIVITY

Euromonitor International, Inc., 224 S. Michigan Avenue, Suite 1500, Chicago, IL 60604, (312) 922-1115, Fax: (312) 922-1157, www.euromonitor.com; *International Marketing Data and Statistics 2008.*

M.E. Sharpe, 80 Business Park Drive, Armonk, NY 10504, (800) 541-6563, Fax: (914) 273-2106, www.mesharpe.com; *The Illustrated Book of World Rankings.*

KUWAIT - INDUSTRIES

Central Intelligence Agency, Office of Public Affairs, Washington, DC 20505, (703) 482-0623, Fax: (703) 482-1739, www.cia.gov; *The World Factbook.*

Central Statistical Office, Ministry of Planning, PO Box 15, Safat 13001, Kuwait, http://scs.mop.gov.kw; *Annual Statistical Abstract 2006.*

Economist Intelligence Unit, 111 West 57th Street, New York, NY 10019, (212) 554-0600, Fax: (212) 586-1181, www.eiu.com; *Kuwait Country Report.*

Euromonitor International, Inc., 224 S. Michigan Avenue, Suite 1500, Chicago, IL 60604, (312) 922-1115, Fax: (312) 922-1157, www.euromonitor.com; *International Marketing Data and Statistics 2008; The World Economic Factbook 2008;* and *World Marketing Data and Statistics.*

International Labour Office, I.L.O. Publications, 4 route des Morillons, CH-1211 Geneva 22, Switzerland, (Telephone in U.S. (202) 653-7652), (Fax in U.S. (202) 653-7687), www.ilo.org; *Yearbook of Labour Statistics 2006.*

M.E. Sharpe, 80 Business Park Drive, Armonk, NY 10504, (800) 541-6563, Fax: (914) 273-2106, www.mesharpe.com; *The Illustrated Book of World Rankings.*

Palgrave Macmillan Ltd., Houndmills, Basingstoke, Hampshire, RG21 6XS, England, (Telephone in U.S. (888) 330-8477), (Fax in U.S. (800) 672-2054), www.palgrave.com; *The Statesman's Yearbook 2008.*

Taylor and Francis Group, An Informa Business, 2 Park Square, Milton Park, Abingdon, Oxford OX14 4RN, United Kingdom, (Dial from U.S. (212) 216-7800), (Fax from U.S. (212) 564-7854), www.tandf.co.uk; *The Europa World Year Book.*

United Nations Industrial Development Organization (UNIDO), 1 United Nations Plaza, New York, NY 10017, (212) 963 6890, Fax: (212) 963-7904, http://unido.org; Industrial Statistics Database 2008 (INDSTAT) and *The International Yearbook of Industrial Statistics 2008.*

United Nations Statistics Division, New York, NY 10017, (800) 253-9646, Fax: (212) 963-4116, http://unstats.un.org; *Bulletin of Industrial Statistics for the Arab Countries* and *2004 Industrial Commodity Statistics Yearbook.*

The World Bank, 1818 H Street, NW, Washington, DC 20433, (202) 473-1000, Fax: (202) 477-6391, www.worldbank.org; *Kuwait* and *World Development Indicators (WDI) 2008.*

KUWAIT - INFANT AND MATERNAL MORTALITY

See KUWAIT - MORTALITY

KUWAIT - INTERNATIONAL LIQUIDITY

International Monetary Fund (IMF), 700 Nineteenth Street, NW, Washington, DC 20431, (202) 623-7000, Fax: (202) 623-4661, www.imf.org; *International Financial Statistics Yearbook 2007.*

KUWAIT - INTERNATIONAL TRADE

Central Statistical Office, Ministry of Planning, PO Box 15, Safat 13001, Kuwait, http://scs.mop.gov.kw; *Annual Statistical Abstract 2006.*

Economist Intelligence Unit, 111 West 57th Street, New York, NY 10019, (212) 554-0600, Fax: (212) 586-1181, www.eiu.com; *Kuwait Country Report.*

Euromonitor International, Inc., 224 S. Michigan Avenue, Suite 1500, Chicago, IL 60604, (312) 922-1115, Fax: (312) 922-1157, www.euromonitor.com; *The World Economic Factbook 2008* and *World Marketing Data and Statistics.*

International Monetary Fund (IMF), 700 Nineteenth Street, NW, Washington, DC 20431, (202) 623-7000, Fax: (202) 623-4661, www.imf.org; *International Financial Statistics Yearbook 2007.*

M.E. Sharpe, 80 Business Park Drive, Armonk, NY 10504, (800) 541-6563, Fax: (914) 273-2106, www.mesharpe.com; *The Illustrated Book of World Rankings.*

Palgrave Macmillan Ltd., Houndmills, Basingstoke, Hampshire, RG21 6XS, England, (Telephone in U.S. (888) 330-8477), (Fax in U.S. (800) 672-2054), www.palgrave.com; *The Statesman's Yearbook 2008.*

Taylor and Francis Group, An Informa Business, 2 Park Square, Milton Park, Abingdon, Oxford OX14 4RN, United Kingdom, (Dial from U.S. (212) 216-7800), (Fax from U.S. (212) 564-7854), www.tandf.co.uk; *The Europa World Year Book.*

United Nations Conference on Trade and Development (UNCTAD), DC2-1120, United Nations, New York, NY 10017, (212) 963-0027, www.unctad.org; *UNCTAD Commodity Yearbook.*

United Nations Economic and Social Commission for Western Asia (ESCWA), PO Box 11-8575, Riad el-Solh Square, Beirut, Lebanon, www.escwa.un.org; *Annual Report 2006* and *Statistical Abstract of the ESCWA Region 2007.*

United Nations Food and Agricultural Organization (FAO), Viale delle Terme di Caracalla, 00100 Rome, Italy, (Dial from U.S. (202) 653-2400), (Fax from U.S. (202) 653 5760), www.fao.org; *FAO Trade Yearbook* and *The State of Food and Agriculture (SOFA) 2006.*

United Nations Statistics Division, New York, NY 10017, (800) 253-9646, Fax: (212) 963-4116, http://unstats.un.org; *Bulletin of Industrial Statistics for the Arab Countries; International Trade Statistics Yearbook;* and *Statistical Yearbook.*

The World Bank, 1818 H Street, NW, Washington, DC 20433, (202) 473-1000, Fax: (202) 477-6391, www.worldbank.org; *Kuwait; World Development Indicators (WDI) 2008;* and *World Development Report 2008.*

World Trade Organization (WTO), Centre William Rappard, Rue de Lausanne 154, CH-1211 Geneva 21, Switzerland, www.wto.org; *International Trade Statistics 2006.*

KUWAIT - INTERNET USERS

International Telecommunication Union (ITU), Place des Nations, 1211 Geneva 20, Switzerland, www.itu.int; *World Telecommunication/ICT Indicators Database on CD-ROM; World Telecommunication/ICT Indicators Database Online;* and *Yearbook of Statistics - Telecommunication Services (Chronological Time Series 1997-2006).*

The World Bank, 1818 H Street, NW, Washington, DC 20433, (202) 473-1000, Fax: (202) 477-6391, www.worldbank.org; *Kuwait.*

KUWAIT - IRON AND IRON ORE PRODUCTION

See KUWAIT - MINERAL INDUSTRIES

KUWAIT - IRRIGATION

Euromonitor International, Inc., 224 S. Michigan Avenue, Suite 1500, Chicago, IL 60604, (312) 922-1115, Fax: (312) 922-1157, www.euromonitor.com; *International Marketing Data and Statistics 2008.*

KUWAIT - LABOR

Central Intelligence Agency, Office of Public Affairs, Washington, DC 20505, (703) 482-0623, Fax: (703) 482-1739, www.cia.gov; *The World Factbook.*

Central Statistical Office, Ministry of Planning, PO Box 15, Safat 13001, Kuwait, http://scs.mop.gov.kw; *Annual Statistical Abstract 2006.*

Euromonitor International, Inc., 224 S. Michigan Avenue, Suite 1500, Chicago, IL 60604, (312) 922-1115, Fax: (312) 922-1157, www.euromonitor.com; *International Marketing Data and Statistics 2008* and *World Marketing Data and Statistics.*

International Labour Office, I.L.O. Publications, 4 route des Morillons, CH-1211 Geneva 22, Switzerland, (Telephone in U.S. (202) 653-7652), (Fax in U.S. (202) 653-7687), www.ilo.org; *Yearbook of Labour Statistics 2006.*

M.E. Sharpe, 80 Business Park Drive, Armonk, NY 10504, (800) 541-6563, Fax: (914) 273-2106, www.mesharpe.com; *The Illustrated Book of World Rankings.*

Palgrave Macmillan Ltd., Houndmills, Basingstoke, Hampshire, RG21 6XS, England, (Telephone in U.S. (888) 330-8477), (Fax in U.S. (800) 672-2054), www.palgrave.com; *The Statesman's Yearbook 2008.*

Taylor and Francis Group, An Informa Business, 2 Park Square, Milton Park, Abingdon, Oxford OX14 4RN, United Kingdom, (Dial from U.S. (212) 216-7800), (Fax from U.S. (212) 564-7854), www.tandf.co.uk; *The Europa World Year Book.*

United Nations Economic and Social Commission for Western Asia (ESCWA), PO Box 11-8575, Riad el-Solh Square, Beirut, Lebanon, www.escwa.un.org; *Annual Report 2006* and *Statistical Abstract of the ESCWA Region 2007.*

United Nations Food and Agricultural Organization (FAO), Viale delle Terme di Caracalla, 00100 Rome, Italy, (Dial from U.S. (202) 653-2400), (Fax from U.S. (202) 653 5760), www.fao.org; *The State of Food and Agriculture (SOFA) 2006.*

United Nations Statistics Division, New York, NY 10017, (800) 253-9646, Fax: (212) 963-4116, http://unstats.un.org; *Human Development Report 2006.*

The World Bank, 1818 H Street, NW, Washington, DC 20433, (202) 473-1000, Fax: (202) 477-6391, www.worldbank.org; *The World Bank Atlas 2003-2004; World Development Indicators (WDI) 2008;* and *World Development Report 2008.*

KUWAIT - LAND USE

Central Intelligence Agency, Office of Public Affairs, Washington, DC 20505, (703) 482-0623, Fax: (703) 482-1739, www.cia.gov; *The World Factbook.*

Euromonitor International, Inc., 224 S. Michigan Avenue, Suite 1500, Chicago, IL 60604, (312) 922-1115, Fax: (312) 922-1157, www.euromonitor.com; *International Marketing Data and Statistics 2008.*

United Nations Food and Agricultural Organization (FAO), Viale delle Terme di Caracalla, 00100 Rome, Italy, (Dial from U.S. (202) 653-2400), (Fax from U.S. (202) 653 5760), www.fao.org; *FAO Production Yearbook 2002.*

The World Bank, 1818 H Street, NW, Washington, DC 20433, (202) 473-1000, Fax: (202) 477-6391, www.worldbank.org; *World Development Report 2008.*

KUWAIT - LIBRARIES

M.E. Sharpe, 80 Business Park Drive, Armonk, NY 10504, (800) 541-6563, Fax: (914) 273-2106, www.mesharpe.com; *The Illustrated Book of World Rankings.*

UNESCO Institute for Statistics, C.P. 6128 Succursale Centre-Ville, Montreal, Quebec, H3C 3J7 Canada, (Dial from U.S. (514) 343-6880), (Fax from U.S. (514) 343 6882), www.uis.unesco.org; *Statistical Tables.*

KUWAIT - LIFE EXPECTANCY

Central Intelligence Agency, Office of Public Affairs, Washington, DC 20505, (703) 482-0623, Fax: (703) 482-1739, www.cia.gov; *The World Factbook.*

Euromonitor International, Inc., 224 S. Michigan Avenue, Suite 1500, Chicago, IL 60604, (312) 922-1115, Fax: (312) 922-1157, www.euromonitor.com; *The World Economic Factbook 2008.*

Palgrave Macmillan Ltd., Houndmills, Basingstoke, Hampshire, RG21 6XS, England, (Telephone in U.S. (888) 330-8477), (Fax in U.S. (800) 672-2054), www.palgrave.com; *The Statesman's Yearbook 2008.*

United Nations Statistics Division, New York, NY 10017, (800) 253-9646, Fax: (212) 963-4116, http://unstats.un.org; *Human Development Report 2006* and *World Statistics Pocketbook.*

The World Bank, 1818 H Street, NW, Washington, DC 20433, (202) 473-1000, Fax: (202) 477-6391, www.worldbank.org; *The World Bank Atlas 2003-2004* and *World Development Report 2008.*

KUWAIT - LITERACY

Euromonitor International, Inc., 224 S. Michigan Avenue, Suite 1500, Chicago, IL 60604, (312) 922-1115, Fax: (312) 922-1157, www.euromonitor.com; *World Marketing Data and Statistics.*

KUWAIT - LIVESTOCK

Central Statistical Office, Ministry of Planning, PO Box 15, Safat 13001, Kuwait, http://scs.mop.gov.kw; *Annual Statistical Abstract 2006.*

Euromonitor International, Inc., 224 S. Michigan Avenue, Suite 1500, Chicago, IL 60604, (312) 922-1115, Fax: (312) 922-1157, www.euromonitor.com; *International Marketing Data and Statistics 2008.*

M.E. Sharpe, 80 Business Park Drive, Armonk, NY 10504, (800) 541-6563, Fax: (914) 273-2106, www.mesharpe.com; *The Illustrated Book of World Rankings.*

Palgrave Macmillan Ltd., Houndmills, Basingstoke, Hampshire, RG21 6XS, England, (Telephone in U.S. (888) 330-8477), (Fax in U.S. (800) 672-2054), www.palgrave.com; *The Statesman's Yearbook 2008.*

Taylor and Francis Group, An Informa Business, 2 Park Square, Milton Park, Abingdon, Oxford OX14 4RN, United Kingdom, (Dial from U.S. (212) 216-7800), (Fax from U.S. (212) 564-7854), www.tandf.co.uk; *The Europa World Year Book.*

United Nations Conference on Trade and Development (UNCTAD), DC2-1120, United Nations, New York, NY 10017, (212) 963-0027, www.unctad.org; *UNCTAD Commodity Yearbook.*

United Nations Food and Agricultural Organization (FAO), Viale delle Terme di Caracalla, 00100 Rome, Italy, (Dial from U.S. (202) 653-2400), (Fax from U.S. (202) 653 5760), www.fao.org; *FAO Production Yearbook 2002* and *The State of Food and Agriculture (SOFA) 2006.*

United Nations Statistics Division, New York, NY 10017, (800) 253-9646, Fax: (212) 963-4116, http://unstats.un.org; *Statistical Yearbook.*

KUWAIT - LOCAL TAXATION

Euromonitor International, Inc., 224 S. Michigan Avenue, Suite 1500, Chicago, IL 60604, (312) 922-1115, Fax: (312) 922-1157, www.euromonitor.com; *International Marketing Data and Statistics 2008.*

KUWAIT - MANUFACTURES

M.E. Sharpe, 80 Business Park Drive, Armonk, NY 10504, (800) 541-6563, Fax: (914) 273-2106, www.mesharpe.com; *The Illustrated Book of World Rankings.*

United Nations Statistics Division, New York, NY 10017, (800) 253-9646, Fax: (212) 963-4116, http://unstats.un.org; *Bulletin of Industrial Statistics for the Arab Countries* and *Statistical Yearbook.*

The World Bank, 1818 H Street, NW, Washington, DC 20433, (202) 473-1000, Fax: (202) 477-6391, www.worldbank.org; *World Development Indicators (WDI) 2008.*

KUWAIT - MARRIAGE

M.E. Sharpe, 80 Business Park Drive, Armonk, NY 10504, (800) 541-6563, Fax: (914) 273-2106, www.mesharpe.com; *The Illustrated Book of World Rankings.*

Taylor and Francis Group, An Informa Business, 2 Park Square, Milton Park, Abingdon, Oxford OX14 4RN, United Kingdom, (Dial from U.S. (212) 216-7800), (Fax from U.S. (212) 564-7854), www.tandf.co.uk; *The Europa World Year Book.*

United Nations Statistics Division, New York, NY 10017, (800) 253-9646, Fax: (212) 963-4116, http://unstats.un.org; *Demographic Yearbook* and *Statistical Yearbook.*

KUWAIT - MEAT PRODUCTION

See KUWAIT - LIVESTOCK

KUWAIT - MEDICAL CARE, COST OF

International Monetary Fund (IMF), 700 Nineteenth Street, NW, Washington, DC 20431, (202) 623-7000, Fax: (202) 623-4661, www.imf.org; *Government Finance Statistics Yearbook (2008 Edition).*

KUWAIT - MILK PRODUCTION

See KUWAIT - DAIRY PROCESSING

KUWAIT - MINERAL INDUSTRIES

M.E. Sharpe, 80 Business Park Drive, Armonk, NY 10504, (800) 541-6563, Fax: (914) 273-2106, www.mesharpe.com; *The Illustrated Book of World Rankings.*

Organisation for Economic Cooperation and Development (OECD), 2 rue Andre Pascal, F-75775 Paris Cedex 16, France, (Telephone in U.S. (202) 785-6323), (Fax in U.S. (202) 785-0350), www.oecd.org; *World Energy Outlook 2007.*

Organization of Petroleum Exporting Countries (OPEC), Obere Donaustrasse 93, A-1020, Vienna, Austria, www.opec.org; *Annual Statistical Bulletin 2006.*

Taylor and Francis Group, An Informa Business, 2 Park Square, Milton Park, Abingdon, Oxford OX14 4RN, United Kingdom, (Dial from U.S. (212) 216-7800), (Fax from U.S. (212) 564-7854), www.tandf.co.uk; *The Europa World Year Book.*

UNESCO Institute for Statistics, C.P. 6128 Succursale Centre-Ville, Montreal, Quebec, H3C 3J7 Canada, (Dial from U.S. (514) 343-6880), (Fax from U.S. (514) 343 6882), www.uis.unesco.org; *Statistical Tables.*

United Nations Conference on Trade and Development (UNCTAD), DC2-1120, United Nations, New York, NY 10017, (212) 963-0027, www.unctad.org; *UNCTAD Commodity Yearbook.*

United Nations Economic and Social Commission for Western Asia (ESCWA), PO Box 11-8575, Riad el-Solh Square, Beirut, Lebanon, www.escwa.un.org; *Annual Report 2006* and *Statistical Abstract of the ESCWA Region 2007.*

United Nations Statistics Division, New York, NY 10017, (800) 253-9646, Fax: (212) 963-4116, http://unstats.un.org; *Bulletin of Industrial Statistics for the Arab Countries* and *Statistical Yearbook.*

The World Bank, 1818 H Street, NW, Washington, DC 20433, (202) 473-1000, Fax: (202) 477-6391, www.worldbank.org; *Kuwait.*

KUWAIT - MONEY EXCHANGE RATES

See KUWAIT - FOREIGN EXCHANGE RATES

KUWAIT - MONEY SUPPLY

Economist Intelligence Unit, 111 West 57th Street, New York, NY 10019, (212) 554-0600, Fax: (212) 586-1181, www.eiu.com; *Kuwait Country Report.*

Euromonitor International, Inc., 224 S. Michigan Avenue, Suite 1500, Chicago, IL 60604, (312) 922-1115, Fax: (312) 922-1157, www.euromonitor.com; *International Marketing Data and Statistics 2008.*

International Monetary Fund (IMF), 700 Nineteenth Street, NW, Washington, DC 20431, (202) 623-7000, Fax: (202) 623-4661, www.imf.org; *International Financial Statistics Yearbook 2007.*

Taylor and Francis Group, An Informa Business, 2 Park Square, Milton Park, Abingdon, Oxford OX14 4RN, United Kingdom, (Dial from U.S. (212) 216-7800), (Fax from U.S. (212) 564-7854), www.tandf.co.uk; *The Europa World Year Book.*

United Nations Economic and Social Commission for Western Asia (ESCWA), PO Box 11-8575, Riad el-Solh Square, Beirut, Lebanon, www.escwa.un.org; *Annual Report 2006* and *Statistical Abstract of the ESCWA Region 2007.*

United Nations Statistics Division, New York, NY 10017, (800) 253-9646, Fax: (212) 963-4116, http://unstats.un.org; *Statistical Yearbook.*

The World Bank, 1818 H Street, NW, Washington, DC 20433, (202) 473-1000, Fax: (202) 477-6391, www.worldbank.org; *Kuwait* and *World Development Indicators (WDI) 2008.*

KUWAIT - MORTALITY

Central Intelligence Agency, Office of Public Affairs, Washington, DC 20505, (703) 482-0623, Fax: (703) 482-1739, www.cia.gov; *The World Factbook.*

Euromonitor International, Inc., 224 S. Michigan Avenue, Suite 1500, Chicago, IL 60604, (312) 922-1115, Fax: (312) 922-1157, www.euromonitor.com; *International Marketing Data and Statistics 2008* and *The World Economic Factbook 2008.*

Taylor and Francis Group, An Informa Business, 2 Park Square, Milton Park, Abingdon, Oxford OX14 4RN, United Kingdom, (Dial from U.S. (212) 216-7800), (Fax from U.S. (212) 564-7854), www.tandf.co.uk; *The Europa World Year Book.*

UNICEF, 3 United Nations Plaza, New York, NY 10017, (800) 253-9646, Fax: (212) 887-7465, www.unicef.org; *The State of the World's Children 2008.*

United Nations Statistics Division, New York, NY 10017, (800) 253-9646, Fax: (212) 963-4116, http://unstats.un.org; *Demographic Yearbook; Human Development Report 2006; Statistical Yearbook;* and *World Statistics Pocketbook.*

The World Bank, 1818 H Street, NW, Washington, DC 20433, (202) 473-1000, Fax: (202) 477-6391, www.worldbank.org; *The World Bank Atlas 2003-2004; World Development Indicators (WDI) 2008;* and *World Development Report 2008.*

World Health Organization (WHO), Avenue Appia 20, 1211 Geneve 27, Switzerland, (Telephone in U.S. (212) 331-9081), www.who.int; The WHO Global Atlas of Infectious Diseases and *World Health Report 2006.*

KUWAIT - MOTION PICTURES

Palgrave Macmillan Ltd., Houndmills, Basingstoke, Hampshire, RG21 6XS, England, (Telephone in U.S. (888) 330-8477), (Fax in U.S. (800) 672-2054), www.palgrave.com; *The Statesman's Yearbook 2008.*

United Nations Statistics Division, New York, NY 10017, (800) 253-9646, Fax: (212) 963-4116, http://unstats.un.org; *Statistical Yearbook.*

KUWAIT - MOTOR VEHICLES

International Road Federation (IFR), Madison Place, 500 Montgomery Street, 5th Floor, Alexandria, VA 22314, (703) 535-1001, Fax: (703) 535-1007, www.irfnet.org; *World Road Statistics 2006.*

Taylor and Francis Group, An Informa Business, 2 Park Square, Milton Park, Abingdon, Oxford OX14 4RN, United Kingdom, (Dial from U.S. (212) 216-7800), (Fax from U.S. (212) 564-7854), www.tandf.co.uk; *The Europa World Year Book.*

United Nations Statistics Division, New York, NY 10017, (800) 253-9646, Fax: (212) 963-4116, http://unstats.un.org; *Statistical Yearbook.*

KUWAIT - MUSEUMS

M.E. Sharpe, 80 Business Park Drive, Armonk, NY 10504, (800) 541-6563, Fax: (914) 273-2106, www.mesharpe.com; *The Illustrated Book of World Rankings.*

UNESCO Institute for Statistics, C.P. 6128 Succursale Centre-Ville, Montreal, Quebec, H3C 3J7 Canada, (Dial from U.S. (514) 343-6880), (Fax from U.S. (514) 343 6882), www.uis.unesco.org; *Statistical Tables.*

KUWAIT - NATURAL GAS PRODUCTION

See KUWAIT - MINERAL INDUSTRIES

KUWAIT - NUTRITION

United Nations Food and Agricultural Organization (FAO), Viale delle Terme di Caracalla, 00100 Rome, Italy, (Dial from U.S. (202) 653-2400), (Fax from U.S. (202) 653 5760), www.fao.org; *The State of Food and Agriculture (SOFA) 2006.*

KUWAIT - OLDER PEOPLE

M.E. Sharpe, 80 Business Park Drive, Armonk, NY 10504, (800) 541-6563, Fax: (914) 273-2106, www.mesharpe.com; *The Illustrated Book of World Rankings.*

KUWAIT - PAPER

See KUWAIT - FORESTS AND FORESTRY

KUWAIT - PEANUT PRODUCTION

See KUWAIT - CROPS

KUWAIT - PERIODICALS

UNESCO Institute for Statistics, C.P. 6128 Succursale Centre-Ville, Montreal, Quebec, H3C 3J7 Canada, (Dial from U.S. (514) 343-6880), (Fax from U.S. (514) 343 6882), www.uis.unesco.org; *Statistical Tables.*

KUWAIT - PESTICIDES

United Nations Food and Agricultural Organization (FAO), Viale delle Terme di Caracalla, 00100 Rome, Italy, (Dial from U.S. (202) 653-2400), (Fax from U.S. (202) 653 5760), www.fao.org; *The State of Food and Agriculture (SOFA) 2006.*

KUWAIT - PETROLEUM INDUSTRY AND TRADE

Central Statistical Office, Ministry of Planning, PO Box 15, Safat 13001, Kuwait, http://scs.mop.gov.kw; *Annual Statistical Abstract 2006.*

International Monetary Fund (IMF), 700 Nineteenth Street, NW, Washington, DC 20431, (202) 623-7000, Fax: (202) 623-4661, www.imf.org; *International Financial Statistics Yearbook 2007.*

M.E. Sharpe, 80 Business Park Drive, Armonk, NY 10504, (800) 541-6563, Fax: (914) 273-2106, www.mesharpe.com; *The Illustrated Book of World Rankings.*

Organisation for Economic Cooperation and Development (OECD), 2 rue Andre Pascal, F-75775 Paris Cedex 16, France, (Telephone in U.S. (202) 785-6323), (Fax in U.S. (202) 785-0350), www.oecd.org; *World Energy Outlook 2007.*

Organization of Petroleum Exporting Countries (OPEC), Obere Donaustrasse 93, A-1020, Vienna, Austria, www.opec.org; *Annual Statistical Bulletin 2006.*

Palgrave Macmillan Ltd., Houndmills, Basingstoke, Hampshire, RG21 6XS, England, (Telephone in U.S. (888) 330-8477), (Fax in U.S. (800) 672-2054), www.palgrave.com; *The Statesman's Yearbook 2008.*

PennWell Corporation, 1421 South Sheridan Road, Tulsa, OK 74112, (918) 835-3161, www.pennwell.com; *International Petroleum Encyclopedia 2007.*

U.S. Department of Energy (DOE), Energy Information Administration (EIA), 1000 Independence Avenue, SW, Washington, DC 20585, (202) 586-8800, www.eia.doe.gov; *International Energy Annual 2004* and *International Energy Outlook 2006.*

United Nations Conference on Trade and Development (UNCTAD), DC2-1120, United Nations, New York, NY 10017, (212) 963-0027, www.unctad.org; *UNCTAD Commodity Yearbook.*

United Nations Food and Agricultural Organization (FAO), Viale delle Terme di Caracalla, 00100 Rome, Italy, (Dial from U.S. (202) 653-2400), (Fax from U.S. (202) 653 5760), www.fao.org; *The State of Food and Agriculture (SOFA) 2006.*

United Nations Statistics Division, New York, NY 10017, (800) 253-9646, Fax: (212) 963-4116, http://unstats.un.org; *Statistical Yearbook.*

KUWAIT - PIPELINES

Organization of Petroleum Exporting Countries (OPEC), Obere Donaustrasse 93, A-1020, Vienna, Austria, www.opec.org; *Annual Statistical Bulletin 2006.*

KUWAIT - POLITICAL SCIENCE

Central Intelligence Agency, Office of Public Affairs, Washington, DC 20505, (703) 482-0623, Fax: (703) 482-1739, www.cia.gov; *The World Factbook.*

International Monetary Fund (IMF), 700 Nineteenth Street, NW, Washington, DC 20431, (202) 623-7000, Fax: (202) 623-4661, www.imf.org; *Government Finance Statistics Yearbook (2008 Edition)* and *International Financial Statistics Yearbook 2007.*

Palgrave Macmillan Ltd., Houndmills, Basingstoke, Hampshire, RG21 6XS, England, (Telephone in U.S. (888) 330-8477), (Fax in U.S. (800) 672-2054), www.palgrave.com; *The Statesman's Yearbook 2008.*

Taylor and Francis Group, An Informa Business, 2 Park Square, Milton Park, Abingdon, Oxford OX14 4RN, United Kingdom, (Dial from U.S. (212) 216-7800), (Fax from U.S. (212) 564-7854), www.tandf.co.uk; *The Europa World Year Book.*

United Nations Statistics Division, New York, NY 10017, (800) 253-9646, Fax: (212) 963-4116, http://unstats.un.org; *National Accounts Statistics: Compendium of Income Distribution Statistics.*

The World Bank, 1818 H Street, NW, Washington, DC 20433, (202) 473-1000, Fax: (202) 477-6391, www.worldbank.org; *World Development Indicators (WDI) 2008* and *World Development Report 2008.*

KUWAIT - POPULATION

Central Intelligence Agency, Office of Public Affairs, Washington, DC 20505, (703) 482-0623, Fax: (703) 482-1739, www.cia.gov; *The World Factbook.*

Central Statistical Office, Ministry of Planning, PO Box 15, Safat 13001, Kuwait, http://scs.mop.gov.kw; *Annual Statistical Abstract 2006.*

Economist Intelligence Unit, 111 West 57th Street, New York, NY 10019, (212) 554-0600, Fax: (212) 586-1181, www.eiu.com; *Kuwait Country Report.*

Euromonitor International, Inc., 224 S. Michigan Avenue, Suite 1500, Chicago, IL 60604, (312) 922-1115, Fax: (312) 922-1157, www.euromonitor.com; *International Marketing Data and Statistics 2008* and *The World Economic Factbook 2008.*

International Labour Office, I.L.O. Publications, 4 route des Morillons, CH-1211 Geneva 22, Switzerland, (Telephone in U.S. (202) 653-7652), (Fax in U.S. (202) 653-7687), www.ilo.org; *Yearbook of Labour Statistics 2006.*

M.E. Sharpe, 80 Business Park Drive, Armonk, NY 10504, (800) 541-6563, Fax: (914) 273-2106, www.mesharpe.com; *The Illustrated Book of World Rankings.*

Palgrave Macmillan Ltd., Houndmills, Basingstoke, Hampshire, RG21 6XS, England, (Telephone in U.S. (888) 330-8477), (Fax in U.S. (800) 672-2054), www.palgrave.com; *The Statesman's Yearbook 2008.*

Taylor and Francis Group, An Informa Business, 2 Park Square, Milton Park, Abingdon, Oxford OX14 4RN, United Kingdom, (Dial from U.S. (212) 216-7800), (Fax from U.S. (212) 564-7854), www.tandf.co.uk; *The Europa World Year Book.*

U.S. Department of State (DOS), 2201 C Street NW, Washington, DC 20520, (202) 647-4000, www.state.gov; *World Military Expenditures and Arms Transfers (WMEAT).*

UNESCO Institute for Statistics, C.P. 6128 Succursale Centre-Ville, Montreal, Quebec, H3C 3J7 Canada, (Dial from U.S. (514) 343-6880), (Fax from U.S. (514) 343 6882), www.uis.unesco.org; *Statistical Tables.*

United Nations Economic and Social Commission for Western Asia (ESCWA), PO Box 11-8575, Riad el-Solh Square, Beirut, Lebanon, www.escwa.un.org; *Annual Report 2006* and *Statistical Abstract of the ESCWA Region 2007.*

United Nations Food and Agricultural Organization (FAO), Viale delle Terme di Caracalla, 00100 Rome, Italy, (Dial from U.S. (202) 653-2400), (Fax from U.S. (202) 653 5760), www.fao.org; *FAO Production Yearbook 2002.*

United Nations Statistics Division, New York, NY 10017, (800) 253-9646, Fax: (212) 963-4116, http://unstats.un.org; *Demographic Yearbook; Human Development Report 2006; Statistical Yearbook;* and *World Statistics Pocketbook.*

The World Bank, 1818 H Street, NW, Washington, DC 20433, (202) 473-1000, Fax: (202) 477-6391,

www.worldbank.org; *Kuwait; The World Bank Atlas 2003-2004;* and *World Development Report 2008.*

World Health Organization (WHO), Avenue Appia 20, 1211 Geneve 27, Switzerland, (Telephone in U.S. (212) 331-9081), www.who.int; *World Health Report 2006.*

KUWAIT - POPULATION DENSITY

Central Intelligence Agency, Office of Public Affairs, Washington, DC 20505, (703) 482-0623, Fax: (703) 482-1739, www.cia.gov; *The World Factbook.*

Euromonitor International, Inc., 224 S. Michigan Avenue, Suite 1500, Chicago, IL 60604, (312) 922-1115, Fax: (312) 922-1157, www.euromonitor.com; *International Marketing Data and Statistics 2008* and *The World Economic Factbook 2008.*

M.E. Sharpe, 80 Business Park Drive, Armonk, NY 10504, (800) 541-6563, Fax: (914) 273-2106, www.mesharpe.com; *The Illustrated Book of World Rankings.*

Palgrave Macmillan Ltd., Houndmills, Basingstoke, Hampshire, RG21 6XS, England, (Telephone in U.S. (888) 330-8477), (Fax in U.S. (800) 672-2054), www.palgrave.com; *The Statesman's Yearbook 2008.*

Taylor and Francis Group, An Informa Business, 2 Park Square, Milton Park, Abingdon, Oxford OX14 4RN, United Kingdom, (Dial from U.S. (212) 216-7800), (Fax from U.S. (212) 564-7854), www.tandf.co.uk; *The Europa World Year Book.*

UNESCO Institute for Statistics, C.P. 6128 Succursale Centre-Ville, Montreal, Quebec, H3C 3J7 Canada, (Dial from U.S. (514) 343-6880), (Fax from U.S. (514) 343 6882), www.uis.unesco.org; *Statistical Tables.*

United Nations Food and Agricultural Organization (FAO), Viale delle Terme di Caracalla, 00100 Rome, Italy, (Dial from U.S. (202) 653-2400), (Fax from U.S. (202) 653 5760), www.fao.org; *The State of Food and Agriculture (SOFA) 2006.*

United Nations Statistics Division, New York, NY 10017, (800) 253-9646, Fax: (212) 963-4116, http://unstats.un.org; *Statistical Yearbook.*

The World Bank, 1818 H Street, NW, Washington, DC 20433, (202) 473-1000, Fax: (202) 477-6391, www.worldbank.org; *Kuwait* and *World Development Report 2008.*

KUWAIT - POSTAL SERVICE

M.E. Sharpe, 80 Business Park Drive, Armonk, NY 10504, (800) 541-6563, Fax: (914) 273-2106, www.mesharpe.com; *The Illustrated Book of World Rankings.*

United Nations Statistics Division, New York, NY 10017, (800) 253-9646, Fax: (212) 963-4116, http://unstats.un.org; *Statistical Yearbook.*

KUWAIT - POWER RESOURCES

Euromonitor International, Inc., 224 S. Michigan Avenue, Suite 1500, Chicago, IL 60604, (312) 922-1115, Fax: (312) 922-1157, www.euromonitor.com; *International Marketing Data and Statistics 2008; The World Economic Factbook 2008;* and *World Marketing Data and Statistics.*

M.E. Sharpe, 80 Business Park Drive, Armonk, NY 10504, (800) 541-6563, Fax: (914) 273-2106, www.mesharpe.com; *The Illustrated Book of World Rankings.*

Organisation for Economic Cooperation and Development (OECD), 2 rue Andre Pascal, F-75775 Paris Cedex 16, France, (Telephone in U.S. (202) 785-6323), (Fax in U.S. (202) 785-0350), www.oecd.org; *World Energy Outlook 2007.*

Palgrave Macmillan Ltd., Houndmills, Basingstoke, Hampshire, RG21 6XS, England, (Telephone in U.S. (888) 330-8477), (Fax in U.S. (800) 672-2054), www.palgrave.com; *The Statesman's Yearbook 2008.*

Platts, 2 Penn Plaza, 25th Floor, New York, NY 10121-2298, (212) 904-3070, www.platts.com; *Energy Economist.*

U.S. Department of Energy (DOE), Energy Information Administration (EIA), 1000 Independence Avenue, SW, Washington, DC 20585, (202) 586-8800, www.eia.doe.gov; *International Energy Annual 2004* and *International Energy Outlook 2006.*

United Nations Economic and Social Commission for Western Asia (ESCWA), PO Box 11-8575, Riad el-Solh Square, Beirut, Lebanon, www.escwa.un.org; *Annual Report 2006* and *Statistical Abstract of the ESCWA Region 2007.*

United Nations Food and Agricultural Organization (FAO), Viale delle Terme di Caracalla, 00100 Rome, Italy, (Dial from U.S. (202) 653-2400), (Fax from U.S. (202) 653 5760), www.fao.org; *The State of Food and Agriculture (SOFA) 2006.*

United Nations Statistics Division, New York, NY 10017, (800) 253-9646, Fax: (212) 963-4116, http://unstats.un.org; *Energy Statistics Yearbook 2003; Human Development Report 2006; Statistical Yearbook; World Energy Assessment 2004 Update: Overview;* and *World Statistics Pocketbook.*

The World Bank, 1818 H Street, NW, Washington, DC 20433, (202) 473-1000, Fax: (202) 477-6391, www.worldbank.org; *The World Bank Atlas 2003-2004* and *World Development Report 2008.*

KUWAIT - PRICES

Euromonitor International, Inc., 224 S. Michigan Avenue, Suite 1500, Chicago, IL 60604, (312) 922-1115, Fax: (312) 922-1157, www.euromonitor.com; *World Marketing Data and Statistics.*

International Labour Office, I.L.O. Publications, 4 route des Morillons, CH-1211 Geneva 22, Switzerland, (Telephone in U.S. (202) 653-7652), (Fax in U.S. (202) 653-7687), www.ilo.org; *Yearbook of Labour Statistics 2006.*

International Monetary Fund (IMF), 700 Nineteenth Street, NW, Washington, DC 20431, (202) 623-7000, Fax: (202) 623-4661, www.imf.org; *International Financial Statistics Yearbook 2007.*

M.E. Sharpe, 80 Business Park Drive, Armonk, NY 10504, (800) 541-6563, Fax: (914) 273-2106, www.mesharpe.com; *The Illustrated Book of World Rankings.*

United Nations Food and Agricultural Organization (FAO), Viale delle Terme di Caracalla, 00100 Rome, Italy, (Dial from U.S. (202) 653-2400), (Fax from U.S. (202) 653 5760), www.fao.org; *FAO Production Yearbook 2002* and *The State of Food and Agriculture (SOFA) 2006.*

The World Bank, 1818 H Street, NW, Washington, DC 20433, (202) 473-1000, Fax: (202) 477-6391, www.worldbank.org; *Kuwait.*

KUWAIT - PROFESSIONS

UNESCO Institute for Statistics, C.P. 6128 Succursale Centre-Ville, Montreal, Quebec, H3C 3J7 Canada, (Dial from U.S. (514) 343-6880), (Fax from U.S. (514) 343 6882), www.uis.unesco.org; *Statistical Tables.*

United Nations Statistics Division, New York, NY 10017, (800) 253-9646, Fax: (212) 963-4116, http://unstats.un.org; *Statistical Yearbook.*

KUWAIT - PUBLIC HEALTH

Central Statistical Office, Ministry of Planning, PO Box 15, Safat 13001, Kuwait, http://scs.mop.gov.kw; *Annual Statistical Abstract 2006.*

Euromonitor International, Inc., 224 S. Michigan Avenue, Suite 1500, Chicago, IL 60604, (312) 922-1115, Fax: (312) 922-1157, www.euromonitor.com; *World Health Databook 2007/2008* and *World Marketing Data and Statistics.*

M.E. Sharpe, 80 Business Park Drive, Armonk, NY 10504, (800) 541-6563, Fax: (914) 273-2106, www.mesharpe.com; *The Illustrated Book of World Rankings.*

Palgrave Macmillan Ltd., Houndmills, Basingstoke, Hampshire, RG21 6XS, England, (Telephone in U.S. (888) 330-8477), (Fax in U.S. (800) 672-2054), www.palgrave.com; *The Statesman's Yearbook 2008.*

UNICEF, 3 United Nations Plaza, New York, NY 10017, (800) 253-9646, Fax: (212) 887-7465, www.unicef.org; *The State of the World's Children 2008.*

United Nations Economic and Social Commission for Western Asia (ESCWA), PO Box 11-8575, Riad el-Solh Square, Beirut, Lebanon, www.escwa.un.org; *Annual Report 2006* and *Statistical Abstract of the ESCWA Region 2007.*

United Nations Statistics Division, New York, NY 10017, (800) 253-9646, Fax: (212) 963-4116, http://unstats.un.org; *Human Development Report 2006* and *Statistical Yearbook.*

The World Bank, 1818 H Street, NW, Washington, DC 20433, (202) 473-1000, Fax: (202) 477-6391, www.worldbank.org; *Kuwait* and *World Development Report 2008.*

World Health Organization (WHO), Avenue Appia 20, 1211 Geneve 27, Switzerland, (Telephone in U.S. (212) 331-9081), www.who.int; The WHO Global Atlas of Infectious Diseases.

KUWAIT - PUBLISHERS AND PUBLISHING

Taylor and Francis Group, An Informa Business, 2 Park Square, Milton Park, Abingdon, Oxford OX14 4RN, United Kingdom, (Dial from U.S. (212) 216-7800), (Fax from U.S. (212) 564-7854), www.tandf.co.uk; *The Europa World Year Book.*

UNESCO Institute for Statistics, C.P. 6128 Succursale Centre-Ville, Montreal, Quebec, H3C 3J7 Canada, (Dial from U.S. (514) 343-6880), (Fax from U.S. (514) 343 6882), www.uis.unesco.org; *Statistical Tables.*

KUWAIT - RADIO BROADCASTING

Palgrave Macmillan Ltd., Houndmills, Basingstoke, Hampshire, RG21 6XS, England, (Telephone in U.S. (888) 330-8477), (Fax in U.S. (800) 672-2054), www.palgrave.com; *The Statesman's Yearbook 2008.*

KUWAIT - RELIGION

Central Intelligence Agency, Office of Public Affairs, Washington, DC 20505, (703) 482-0623, Fax: (703) 482-1739, www.cia.gov; *The World Factbook.*

M.E. Sharpe, 80 Business Park Drive, Armonk, NY 10504, (800) 541-6563, Fax: (914) 273-2106, www.mesharpe.com; *The Illustrated Book of World Rankings.*

Palgrave Macmillan Ltd., Houndmills, Basingstoke, Hampshire, RG21 6XS, England, (Telephone in U.S. (888) 330-8477), (Fax in U.S. (800) 672-2054), www.palgrave.com; *The Statesman's Yearbook 2008.*

KUWAIT - RENT CHARGES

International Labour Office, I.L.O. Publications, 4 route des Morillons, CH-1211 Geneva 22, Switzerland, (Telephone in U.S. (202) 653-7652), (Fax in U.S. (202) 653-7687), www.ilo.org; *Yearbook of Labour Statistics 2006.*

KUWAIT - RESERVES (ACCOUNTING)

Euromonitor International, Inc., 224 S. Michigan Avenue, Suite 1500, Chicago, IL 60604, (312) 922-1115, Fax: (312) 922-1157, www.euromonitor.com; *International Marketing Data and Statistics 2008.*

United Nations Statistics Division, New York, NY 10017, (800) 253-9646, Fax: (212) 963-4116, http://unstats.un.org; *Statistical Yearbook.*

The World Bank, 1818 H Street, NW, Washington, DC 20433, (202) 473-1000, Fax: (202) 477-6391, www.worldbank.org; *World Development Indicators (WDI) 2008.*

KUWAIT - RETAIL TRADE

Euromonitor International, Inc., 224 S. Michigan Avenue, Suite 1500, Chicago, IL 60604, (312) 922-1115, Fax: (312) 922-1157, www.euromonitor.com; *World Marketing Data and Statistics.*

KUWAIT - RICE PRODUCTION

See KUWAIT - CROPS

KUWAIT - ROADS

Central Intelligence Agency, Office of Public Affairs, Washington, DC 20505, (703) 482-0623, Fax: (703) 482-1739, www.cia.gov; *The World Factbook.*

International Road Federation (IFR), Madison Place, 500 Montgomery Street, 5th Floor, Alexandria, VA 22314, (703) 535-1001, Fax: (703) 535-1007, www.irfnet.org; *World Road Statistics 2006.*

Palgrave Macmillan Ltd., Houndmills, Basingstoke, Hampshire, RG21 6XS, England, (Telephone in U.S. (888) 330-8477), (Fax in U.S. (800) 672-2054), www.palgrave.com; *The Statesman's Yearbook 2008.*

KUWAIT - RUBBER INDUSTRY AND TRADE

International Rubber Study Group (IRSG), 1st Floor, Heron House, 109/115 Wembley Hill Road, Wembley, Middlesex HA9 8DA, United Kingdom, www.rubberstudy.com; *Rubber Statistical Bulletin; Summary of World Rubber Statistics 2005; World Rubber Statistics Handbook (Volume 6, 1975-2001);* and *World Rubber Statistics Historic Handbook.*

M.E. Sharpe, 80 Business Park Drive, Armonk, NY 10504, (800) 541-6563, Fax: (914) 273-2106, www.mesharpe.com; *The Illustrated Book of World Rankings.*

KUWAIT - SALT INDUSTRY AND TRADE

United Nations Statistics Division, New York, NY 10017, (800) 253-9646, Fax: (212) 963-4116, http://unstats.un.org; *Statistical Yearbook.*

KUWAIT - SHEEP

See KUWAIT - LIVESTOCK

KUWAIT - SHIPPING

Lloyd's Register - Fairplay, 8410 N.W. 53rd Terrace, Suite 207, Miami FL 33166, (305) 718-9929, Fax: (305) 718-9663, www.lrfairplay.com; *Register of Ships 2007-2008; World Casualty Statistics 2007; World Fleet Statistics 2006; World Marine Propulsion Report 2006-2010; World Shipbuilding Statistics 2007;* and The World Shipping Encyclopaedia.

Organization of Petroleum Exporting Countries (OPEC), Obere Donaustrasse 93, A-1020, Vienna, Austria, www.opec.org; *Annual Statistical Bulletin 2006.*

Palgrave Macmillan Ltd., Houndmills, Basingstoke, Hampshire, RG21 6XS, England, (Telephone in U.S. (888) 330-8477), (Fax in U.S. (800) 672-2054), www.palgrave.com; *The Statesman's Yearbook 2008.*

Taylor and Francis Group, An Informa Business, 2 Park Square, Milton Park, Abingdon, Oxford OX14 4RN, United Kingdom, (Dial from U.S. (212) 216-7800), (Fax from U.S. (212) 564-7854), www.tandf.co.uk; *The Europa World Year Book.*

U.S. Department of Transportation (DOT), Maritime Administration (MARAD), West Building, Southeast Federal Center, 1200 New Jersey Avenue, SE, Washington, DC 20590, (800) 99-MARAD, www.marad.dot.gov; *World Merchant Fleet 2005.*

United Nations Statistics Division, New York, NY 10017, (800) 253-9646, Fax: (212) 963-4116, http://unstats.un.org; *Statistical Yearbook.*

KUWAIT - SILVER PRODUCTION

See KUWAIT - MINERAL INDUSTRIES

KUWAIT - SOCIAL ECOLOGY

M.E. Sharpe, 80 Business Park Drive, Armonk, NY 10504, (800) 541-6563, Fax: (914) 273-2106, www.mesharpe.com; *The Illustrated Book of World Rankings.*

United Nations Statistics Division, New York, NY 10017, (800) 253-9646, Fax: (212) 963-4116, http://unstats.un.org; *World Statistics Pocketbook.*

KUWAIT - SOCIAL SECURITY

International Monetary Fund (IMF), 700 Nineteenth Street, NW, Washington, DC 20431, (202) 623-7000, Fax: (202) 623-4661, www.imf.org; *Government Finance Statistics Yearbook (2008 Edition).*

United Nations Statistics Division, New York, NY 10017, (800) 253-9646, Fax: (212) 963-4116, http://unstats.un.org; *National Accounts Statistics: Compendium of Income Distribution Statistics.*

KUWAIT - STEEL PRODUCTION

See KUWAIT - MINERAL INDUSTRIES

KUWAIT - SUGAR PRODUCTION

See KUWAIT - CROPS

KUWAIT - TAXATION

International Monetary Fund (IMF), 700 Nineteenth Street, NW, Washington, DC 20431, (202) 623-7000, Fax: (202) 623-4661, www.imf.org; *Government Finance Statistics Yearbook (2008 Edition).*

International Road Federation (IFR), Madison Place, 500 Montgomery Street, 5th Floor, Alexandria, VA 22314, (703) 535-1001, Fax: (703) 535-1007, www.irfnet.org; *World Road Statistics 2006.*

Taylor and Francis Group, An Informa Business, 2 Park Square, Milton Park, Abingdon, Oxford OX14 4RN, United Kingdom, (Dial from U.S. (212) 216-7800), (Fax from U.S. (212) 564-7854), www.tandf.co.uk; *The Europa World Year Book.*

The World Bank, 1818 H Street, NW, Washington, DC 20433, (202) 473-1000, Fax: (202) 477-6391, www.worldbank.org; *World Development Indicators (WDI) 2008.*

KUWAIT - TELEPHONE

International Telecommunication Union (ITU), Place des Nations, 1211 Geneva 20, Switzerland, www.itu.int; World Telecommunication Indicators Database.

Palgrave Macmillan Ltd., Houndmills, Basingstoke, Hampshire, RG21 6XS, England, (Telephone in U.S. (888) 330-8477), (Fax in U.S. (800) 672-2054), www.palgrave.com; *The Statesman's Yearbook 2008.*

Taylor and Francis Group, An Informa Business, 2 Park Square, Milton Park, Abingdon, Oxford OX14 4RN, United Kingdom, (Dial from U.S. (212) 216-7800), (Fax from U.S. (212) 564-7854), www.tandf.co.uk; *The Europa World Year Book.*

United Nations Statistics Division, New York, NY 10017, (800) 253-9646, Fax: (212) 963-4116, http://unstats.un.org; *Statistical Yearbook* and *World Statistics Pocketbook.*

KUWAIT - TEXTILE INDUSTRY

M.E. Sharpe, 80 Business Park Drive, Armonk, NY 10504, (800) 541-6563, Fax: (914) 273-2106, www.mesharpe.com; *The Illustrated Book of World Rankings.*

United Nations Conference on Trade and Development (UNCTAD), DC2-1120, United Nations, New York, NY 10017, (212) 963-0027, www.unctad.org; *UNCTAD Commodity Yearbook.*

KUWAIT - THEATER

UNESCO Institute for Statistics, C.P. 6128 Succursale Centre-Ville, Montreal, Quebec, H3C 3J7 Canada, (Dial from U.S. (514) 343-6880), (Fax from U.S. (514) 343 6882), www.uis.unesco.org; *Statistical Tables.*

KUWAIT - TOBACCO INDUSTRY

Foreign Agricultural Service (FAS), U.S. Department of Agriculture (USDA), 1400 Independence Avenue, SW, Washington, DC 20250, (202) 720-3935, www.fas.usda.gov; *Tobacco: World Markets and Trade.*

M.E. Sharpe, 80 Business Park Drive, Armonk, NY 10504, (800) 541-6563, Fax: (914) 273-2106, www.mesharpe.com; *The Illustrated Book of World Rankings.*

KUWAIT - TOURISM

Central Statistical Office, Ministry of Planning, PO Box 15, Safat 13001, Kuwait, http://scs.mop.gov.kw; *Annual Statistical Abstract 2006.*

Euromonitor International, Inc., 224 S. Michigan Avenue, Suite 1500, Chicago, IL 60604, (312) 922-1115, Fax: (312) 922-1157, www.euromonitor.com; *The World Economic Factbook 2008* and *World Marketing Data and Statistics.*

M.E. Sharpe, 80 Business Park Drive, Armonk, NY 10504, (800) 541-6563, Fax: (914) 273-2106, www.mesharpe.com; *The Illustrated Book of World Rankings.*

Palgrave Macmillan Ltd., Houndmills, Basingstoke, Hampshire, RG21 6XS, England, (Telephone in U.S. (888) 330-8477), (Fax in U.S. (800) 672-2054), www.palgrave.com; *The Statesman's Yearbook 2008.*

United Nations Economic and Social Commission for Western Asia (ESCWA), PO Box 11-8575, Riad el-Solh Square, Beirut, Lebanon, www.escwa.un.org; *Annual Report 2006* and *Statistical Abstract of the ESCWA Region 2007.*

United Nations Statistics Division, New York, NY 10017, (800) 253-9646, Fax: (212) 963-4116, http://unstats.un.org; *Statistical Yearbook.*

The World Bank, 1818 H Street, NW, Washington, DC 20433, (202) 473-1000, Fax: (202) 477-6391, www.worldbank.org; *Kuwait.*

KUWAIT - TRADE

See KUWAIT - INTERNATIONAL TRADE

KUWAIT - TRANSPORTATION

Central Intelligence Agency, Office of Public Affairs, Washington, DC 20505, (703) 482-0623, Fax: (703) 482-1739, www.cia.gov; *The World Factbook.*

Central Statistical Office, Ministry of Planning, PO Box 15, Safat 13001, Kuwait, http://scs.mop.gov.kw; *Annual Statistical Abstract 2006.*

Euromonitor International, Inc., 224 S. Michigan Avenue, Suite 1500, Chicago, IL 60604, (312) 922-1115, Fax: (312) 922-1157, www.euromonitor.com; *International Marketing Data and Statistics 2008* and *World Marketing Data and Statistics.*

M.E. Sharpe, 80 Business Park Drive, Armonk, NY 10504, (800) 541-6563, Fax: (914) 273-2106, www.mesharpe.com; *The Illustrated Book of World Rankings.*

Palgrave Macmillan Ltd., Houndmills, Basingstoke, Hampshire, RG21 6XS, England, (Telephone in U.S. (888) 330-8477), (Fax in U.S. (800) 672-2054), www.palgrave.com; *The Statesman's Yearbook 2008.*

Taylor and Francis Group, An Informa Business, 2 Park Square, Milton Park, Abingdon, Oxford OX14 4RN, United Kingdom, (Dial from U.S. (212) 216-7800), (Fax from U.S. (212) 564-7854), www.tandf.co.uk; *The Europa World Year Book.*

United Nations Economic and Social Commission for Western Asia (ESCWA), PO Box 11-8575, Riad el-Solh Square, Beirut, Lebanon, www.escwa.un.org; *Annual Report 2006* and *Statistical Abstract of the ESCWA Region 2007.*

United Nations Statistics Division, New York, NY 10017, (800) 253-9646, Fax: (212) 963-4116, http://unstats.un.org; *Human Development Report 2006.*

The World Bank, 1818 H Street, NW, Washington, DC 20433, (202) 473-1000, Fax: (202) 477-6391, www.worldbank.org; *Kuwait.*

KUWAIT - UNEMPLOYMENT

Central Intelligence Agency, Office of Public Affairs, Washington, DC 20505, (703) 482-0623, Fax: (703) 482-1739, www.cia.gov; *The World Factbook.*

Euromonitor International, Inc., 224 S. Michigan Avenue, Suite 1500, Chicago, IL 60604, (312) 922-1115, Fax: (312) 922-1157, www.euromonitor.com; *International Marketing Data and Statistics 2008.*

International Labour Office, I.L.O. Publications, 4 route des Morillons, CH-1211 Geneva 22, Switzerland, (Telephone in U.S. (202) 653-7652), (Fax in U.S. (202) 653-7687), www.ilo.org; *Yearbook of Labour Statistics 2006.*

Palgrave Macmillan Ltd., Houndmills, Basingstoke, Hampshire, RG21 6XS, England, (Telephone in U.S. (888) 330-8477), (Fax in U.S. (800) 672-2054), www.palgrave.com; *The Statesman's Yearbook 2008.*

The World Bank, 1818 H Street, NW, Washington, DC 20433, (202) 473-1000, Fax: (202) 477-6391, www.worldbank.org; *Kuwait.*

KUWAIT - VITAL STATISTICS

Central Statistical Office, Ministry of Planning, PO Box 15, Safat 13001, Kuwait, http://scs.mop.gov.kw; *Annual Statistical Abstract 2006.*

Euromonitor International, Inc., 224 S. Michigan Avenue, Suite 1500, Chicago, IL 60604, (312) 922-1115, Fax: (312) 922-1157, www.euromonitor.com; *International Marketing Data and Statistics 2008.*

United Nations Economic and Social Commission for Western Asia (ESCWA), PO Box 11-8575, Riad el-Solh Square, Beirut, Lebanon, www.escwa.un.org; *Annual Report 2006; Bulletin on Population and Vital Statistics in the ESCWA Region;* and *Survey of Economic and Social Developments in the ESCWA Region 2006-2007.*

United Nations Statistics Division, New York, NY 10017, (800) 253-9646, Fax: (212) 963-4116, http://unstats.un.org; *Statistical Yearbook.*

World Health Organization (WHO), Avenue Appia 20, 1211 Geneve 27, Switzerland, (Telephone in U.S. (212) 331-9081), www.who.int; *World Health Report 2006.*

KUWAIT - WAGES

International Labour Office, I.L.O. Publications, 4 route des Morillons, CH-1211 Geneva 22, Switzerland, (Telephone in U.S. (202) 653-7652), (Fax in U.S. (202) 653-7687), www.ilo.org; *Yearbook of Labour Statistics 2006.*

The World Bank, 1818 H Street, NW, Washington, DC 20433, (202) 473-1000, Fax: (202) 477-6391, www.worldbank.org; *Kuwait.*

KUWAIT - WEATHER

See KUWAIT - CLIMATE

KUWAIT - WELFARE STATE

International Monetary Fund (IMF), 700 Nineteenth Street, NW, Washington, DC 20431, (202) 623-7000, Fax: (202) 623-4661, www.imf.org; *Government Finance Statistics Yearbook (2008 Edition).*

KUWAIT - WHEAT PRODUCTION

See KUWAIT - CROPS

KUWAIT - WHOLESALE PRICE INDEXES

International Monetary Fund (IMF), 700 Nineteenth Street, NW, Washington, DC 20431, (202) 623-7000, Fax: (202) 623-4661, www.imf.org; *International Financial Statistics Yearbook 2007.*

United Nations Statistics Division, New York, NY 10017, (800) 253-9646, Fax: (212) 963-4116, http://unstats.un.org; *Statistical Yearbook.*

KUWAIT - WINE PRODUCTION

See KUWAIT - BEVERAGE INDUSTRY

KUWAIT - WOOL PRODUCTION

See KUWAIT - TEXTILE INDUSTRY

KYRGYZSTAN - NATIONAL STATISTICAL OFFICE

National Statistical Committee (NSC) of the Kyrgyz Republic, 374 Frunze Street, Bishkek 720033, Kyrgyz Republic, www.stat.kg/English; National Data Center.

KYRGYZSTAN - ABORTION

United Nations Statistics Division, New York, NY 10017, (800) 253-9646, Fax: (212) 963-4116, http://unstats.un.org; *Trends in Europe and North America: The Statistical Yearbook of the ECE 2005.*

KYRGYZSTAN - AGRICULTURE

Academic International Press, PO Box 1111, Gulf Breeze, FL 32562-1111, Fax: (850) 934-0953, www.ai-press.com; *Russia and Eurasia Facts and Figures Annual.*

Economist Intelligence Unit, 111 West 57th Street, New York, NY 10019, (212) 554-0600, Fax: (212) 586-1181, www.eiu.com; *Kyrgyz Republic Country Report.*

Euromonitor International, Inc., 224 S. Michigan Avenue, Suite 1500, Chicago, IL 60604, (312) 922-1115, Fax: (312) 922-1157, www.euromonitor.com; *World Marketing Data and Statistics.*

Palgrave Macmillan Ltd., Houndmills, Basingstoke, Hampshire, RG21 6XS, England, (Telephone in U.S. (888) 330-8477), (Fax in U.S. (800) 672-2054), www.palgrave.com; *The Statesman's Yearbook 2008.*

Taylor and Francis Group, An Informa Business, 2 Park Square, Milton Park, Abingdon, Oxford OX14 4RN, United Kingdom, (Dial from U.S. (212) 216-7800), (Fax from U.S. (212) 564-7854), www.tandf.co.uk; *The Europa World Year Book.*

United Nations Food and Agricultural Organization (FAO), Viale delle Terme di Caracalla, 00100 Rome, Italy, (Dial from U.S. (202) 653-2400), (Fax from U.S. (202) 653 5760), www.fao.org; AQUASTAT; *FAO Production Yearbook 2002; FAO Trade Yearbook;* and *The State of Food and Agriculture (SOFA) 2006.*

United Nations Statistics Division, New York, NY 10017, (800) 253-9646, Fax: (212) 963-4116, http://unstats.un.org; *2004 Industrial Commodity Statistics Yearbook* and *Statistical Yearbook.*

The World Bank, 1818 H Street, NW, Washington, DC 20433, (202) 473-1000, Fax: (202) 477-6391, www.worldbank.org; *Kyrgyz Republic; Statistical Handbook: States of the Former USSR;* and *World Development Indicators (WDI) 2008.*

KYRGYZSTAN - AIRLINES

International Civil Aviation Organization (ICAO), External Relations and Public Information Office (EPO), 999 University Street, Montreal, Quebec H3C 5H7, Canada, (Dial from U.S. (514) 954-8219), (Fax from U.S. (514) 954-6077), www.icao.int; *Civil Aviation Statistics of the World.*

Palgrave Macmillan Ltd., Houndmills, Basingstoke, Hampshire, RG21 6XS, England, (Telephone in U.S. (888) 330-8477), (Fax in U.S. (800) 672-2054), www.palgrave.com; *The Statesman's Yearbook 2008.*

United Nations Statistics Division, New York, NY 10017, (800) 253-9646, Fax: (212) 963-4116, http://unstats.un.org; *Statistical Yearbook.*

KYRGYZSTAN - AIRPORTS

Central Intelligence Agency, Office of Public Affairs, Washington, DC 20505, (703) 482-0623, Fax: (703) 482-1739, www.cia.gov; *The World Factbook.*

KYRGYZSTAN - ARMED FORCES

Academic International Press, PO Box 1111, Gulf Breeze, FL 32562-1111, Fax: (850) 934-0953, www.ai-press.com; *Russia and Eurasia Facts and Figures Annual.*

Central Intelligence Agency, Office of Public Affairs, Washington, DC 20505, (703) 482-0623, Fax: (703) 482-1739, www.cia.gov; *The World Factbook.*

Euromonitor International, Inc., 224 S. Michigan Avenue, Suite 1500, Chicago, IL 60604, (312) 922-1115, Fax: (312) 922-1157, www.euromonitor.com; *World Marketing Data and Statistics.*

International Institute for Strategic Studies (IISS), Arundel House, 13-15 Arundel Street, Temple Place, London WC2R 3DX, England, www.iiss.org; *The Military Balance 2007.*

Palgrave Macmillan Ltd., Houndmills, Basingstoke, Hampshire, RG21 6XS, England, (Telephone in U.S. (888) 330-8477), (Fax in U.S. (800) 672-2054), www.palgrave.com; *The Statesman's Yearbook 2008.*

United Nations Statistics Division, New York, NY 10017, (800) 253-9646, Fax: (212) 963-4116, http://unstats.un.org; *Human Development Report 2006.*

KYRGYZSTAN - BALANCE OF PAYMENTS

Taylor and Francis Group, An Informa Business, 2 Park Square, Milton Park, Abingdon, Oxford OX14 4RN, United Kingdom, (Dial from U.S. (212) 216-7800), (Fax from U.S. (212) 564-7854), www.tandf.co.uk; *The Europa World Year Book.*

United Nations Conference on Trade and Development (UNCTAD), DC2-1120, United Nations, New York, NY 10017, (212) 963-0027, www.unctad.org; *Handbook of Statistics 2005.*

The World Bank, 1818 H Street, NW, Washington, DC 20433, (202) 473-1000, Fax: (202) 477-6391, www.worldbank.org; *Kyrgyz Republic; World Development Indicators (WDI) 2008;* and *World Development Report 2008.*

KYRGYZSTAN - BANKS AND BANKING

Euromonitor International, Inc., 224 S. Michigan Avenue, Suite 1500, Chicago, IL 60604, (312) 922-1115, Fax: (312) 922-1157, www.euromonitor.com; *World Marketing Data and Statistics.*

Palgrave Macmillan Ltd., Houndmills, Basingstoke, Hampshire, RG21 6XS, England, (Telephone in U.S. (888) 330-8477), (Fax in U.S. (800) 672-2054), www.palgrave.com; *The Statesman's Yearbook 2008.*

KYRGYZSTAN - BEVERAGE INDUSTRY

United Nations Statistics Division, New York, NY 10017, (800) 253-9646, Fax: (212) 963-4116, http://unstats.un.org; *Statistical Yearbook.*

KYRGYZSTAN - BROADCASTING

Central Intelligence Agency, Office of Public Affairs, Washington, DC 20505, (703) 482-0623, Fax: (703) 482-1739, www.cia.gov; *The World Factbook.*

Euromonitor International, Inc., 224 S. Michigan Avenue, Suite 1500, Chicago, IL 60604, (312) 922-1115, Fax: (312) 922-1157, www.euromonitor.com; *World Marketing Data and Statistics.*

Palgrave Macmillan Ltd., Houndmills, Basingstoke, Hampshire, RG21 6XS, England, (Telephone in U.S. (888) 330-8477), (Fax in U.S. (800) 672-2054), www.palgrave.com; *The Statesman's Yearbook 2008.*

UNESCO Institute for Statistics, C.P. 6128 Succursale Centre-Ville, Montreal, Quebec, H3C 3J7 Canada, (Dial from U.S. (514) 343-6880), (Fax from U.S. (514) 343 6882), www.uis.unesco.org; *Statistical Tables.*

United Nations Statistics Division, New York, NY 10017, (800) 253-9646, Fax: (212) 963-4116, http://unstats.un.org; *Trends in Europe and North America: The Statistical Yearbook of the ECE 2005.*

KYRGYZSTAN - BUDGET

Central Intelligence Agency, Office of Public Affairs, Washington, DC 20505, (703) 482-0623, Fax: (703) 482-1739, www.cia.gov; *The World Factbook.*

KYRGYZSTAN - BUSINESS

United Nations Statistics Division, New York, NY 10017, (800) 253-9646, Fax: (212) 963-4116, http://unstats.un.org; *Statistical Yearbook.*

KYRGYZSTAN - CAPITAL INVESTMENTS

The World Bank, 1818 H Street, NW, Washington, DC 20433, (202) 473-1000, Fax: (202) 477-6391, www.worldbank.org; *Statistical Handbook: States of the Former USSR.*

KYRGYZSTAN - CATTLE

See KYRGYZSTAN - LIVESTOCK

KYRGYZSTAN - CHILDBIRTH - STATISTICS

Central Intelligence Agency, Office of Public Affairs, Washington, DC 20505, (703) 482-0623, Fax: (703) 482-1739, www.cia.gov; *The World Factbook.*

Euromonitor International, Inc., 224 S. Michigan Avenue, Suite 1500, Chicago, IL 60604, (312) 922-1115, Fax: (312) 922-1157, www.euromonitor.com; *International Marketing Data and Statistics 2008* and *The World Economic Factbook 2008.*

Palgrave Macmillan Ltd., Houndmills, Basingstoke, Hampshire, RG21 6XS, England, (Telephone in U.S. (888) 330-8477), (Fax in U.S. (800) 672-2054), www.palgrave.com; *The Statesman's Yearbook 2008.*

Taylor and Francis Group, An Informa Business, 2 Park Square, Milton Park, Abingdon, Oxford OX14 4RN, United Kingdom, (Dial from U.S. (212) 216-7800), (Fax from U.S. (212) 564-7854), www.tandf.co.uk; *The Europa World Year Book.*

United Nations Statistics Division, New York, NY 10017, (800) 253-9646, Fax: (212) 963-4116, http://unstats.un.org; *Statistical Yearbook.*

World Health Organization (WHO), Avenue Appia 20, 1211 Geneve 27, Switzerland, (Telephone in U.S. (212) 331-9081), www.who.int; *World Health Report 2006.*

KYRGYZSTAN - COAL PRODUCTION

See KYRGYZSTAN - MINERAL INDUSTRIES

KYRGYZSTAN - COMMERCE

Palgrave Macmillan Ltd., Houndmills, Basingstoke, Hampshire, RG21 6XS, England, (Telephone in U.S. (888) 330-8477), (Fax in U.S. (800) 672-2054), www.palgrave.com; *The Statesman's Yearbook 2008.*

KYRGYZSTAN - CONSTRUCTION INDUSTRY

Academic International Press, PO Box 1111, Gulf Breeze, FL 32562-1111, Fax: (850) 934-0953, www.ai-press.com; *Russia and Eurasia Facts and Figures Annual.*

United Nations Statistics Division, New York, NY 10017, (800) 253-9646, Fax: (212) 963-4116, http://unstats.un.org; *Statistical Yearbook.*

KYRGYZSTAN - CONSUMER PRICE INDEXES

Taylor and Francis Group, An Informa Business, 2 Park Square, Milton Park, Abingdon, Oxford OX14 4RN, United Kingdom, (Dial from U.S. (212) 216-7800), (Fax from U.S. (212) 564-7854), www.tandf.co.uk; *The Europa World Year Book.*

United Nations Statistics Division, New York, NY 10017, (800) 253-9646, Fax: (212) 963-4116, http://unstats.un.org; *Statistical Yearbook* and *Trends in Europe and North America: The Statistical Yearbook of the ECE 2005.*

The World Bank, 1818 H Street, NW, Washington, DC 20433, (202) 473-1000, Fax: (202) 477-6391, www.worldbank.org; *Kyrgyz Republic.*

KYRGYZSTAN - CONSUMPTION (ECONOMICS)

The World Bank, 1818 H Street, NW, Washington, DC 20433, (202) 473-1000, Fax: (202) 477-6391, www.worldbank.org; *Statistical Handbook: States of the Former USSR* and *World Development Report 2008.*

KYRGYZSTAN - COTTON

See KYRGYZSTAN - CROPS

KYRGYZSTAN - CRIME

Academic International Press, PO Box 1111, Gulf Breeze, FL 32562-1111, Fax: (850) 934-0953, www.ai-press.com; *Russia and Eurasia Facts and Figures Annual.*

United Nations Statistics Division, New York, NY 10017, (800) 253-9646, Fax: (212) 963-4116, http://unstats.un.org; *Trends in Europe and North America: The Statistical Yearbook of the ECE 2005.*

KYRGYZSTAN - CROPS

Palgrave Macmillan Ltd., Houndmills, Basingstoke, Hampshire, RG21 6XS, England, (Telephone in U.S. (888) 330-8477), (Fax in U.S. (800) 672-2054), www.palgrave.com; *The Statesman's Yearbook 2008.*

Taylor and Francis Group, An Informa Business, 2 Park Square, Milton Park, Abingdon, Oxford OX14 4RN, United Kingdom, (Dial from U.S. (212) 216-7800), (Fax from U.S. (212) 564-7854), www.tandf.co.uk; *The Europa World Year Book.*

United Nations Food and Agricultural Organization (FAO), Viale delle Terme di Caracalla, 00100 Rome, Italy, (Dial from U.S. (202) 653-2400), (Fax from U.S. (202) 653 5760), www.fao.org; *FAO Production Yearbook 2002* and *The State of Food and Agriculture (SOFA) 2006.*

United Nations Statistics Division, New York, NY 10017, (800) 253-9646, Fax: (212) 963-4116, http://unstats.un.org; *2004 Industrial Commodity Statistics Yearbook* and *Statistical Yearbook.*

The World Bank, 1818 H Street, NW, Washington, DC 20433, (202) 473-1000, Fax: (202) 477-6391, www.worldbank.org; *Statistical Handbook: States of the Former USSR.*

KYRGYZSTAN - DAIRY PROCESSING

Palgrave Macmillan Ltd., Houndmills, Basingstoke, Hampshire, RG21 6XS, England, (Telephone in U.S. (888) 330-8477), (Fax in U.S. (800) 672-2054), www.palgrave.com; *The Statesman's Yearbook 2008.*

Taylor and Francis Group, An Informa Business, 2 Park Square, Milton Park, Abingdon, Oxford OX14 4RN, United Kingdom, (Dial from U.S. (212) 216-7800), (Fax from U.S. (212) 564-7854), www.tandf.co.uk; *The Europa World Year Book.*

United Nations Food and Agricultural Organization (FAO), Viale delle Terme di Caracalla, 00100 Rome, Italy, (Dial from U.S. (202) 653-2400), (Fax from U.S. (202) 653 5760), www.fao.org; *FAO Production Yearbook 2002* and *The State of Food and Agriculture (SOFA) 2006.*

United Nations Statistics Division, New York, NY 10017, (800) 253-9646, Fax: (212) 963-4116, http://unstats.un.org; *2004 Industrial Commodity Statistics Yearbook* and *Statistical Yearbook.*

KYRGYZSTAN - DEATH RATES

See KYRGYZSTAN - MORTALITY

KYRGYZSTAN - DEBTS, EXTERNAL

The World Bank, 1818 H Street, NW, Washington, DC 20433, (202) 473-1000, Fax: (202) 477-6391, www.worldbank.org; *Global Development Finance 2007; World Development Indicators (WDI) 2008;* and *World Development Report 2008.*

Worldinformation.com, 2 Market Street, Saffron Walden, Essex CB10 1HZ, United Kingdom, www.worldinformation.com; The World of Information (www.worldinformation.com).

KYRGYZSTAN - DEMOGRAPHY

Euromonitor International, Inc., 224 S. Michigan Avenue, Suite 1500, Chicago, IL 60604, (312) 922-1115, Fax: (312) 922-1157, www.euromonitor.com; *International Marketing Data and Statistics 2008; The World Economic Factbook 2008;* and *World Marketing Data and Statistics.*

United Nations Statistics Division, New York, NY 10017, (800) 253-9646, Fax: (212) 963-4116, http://unstats.un.org; *Demographic Yearbook* and *Human Development Report 2006.*

The World Bank, 1818 H Street, NW, Washington, DC 20433, (202) 473-1000, Fax: (202) 477-6391, www.worldbank.org; *Kyrgyz Republic* and *Statistical Handbook: States of the Former USSR.*

KYRGYZSTAN - DISPOSABLE INCOME

United Nations Statistics Division, New York, NY 10017, (800) 253-9646, Fax: (212) 963-4116, http://unstats.un.org; *Statistical Yearbook.*

KYRGYZSTAN - DIVORCE

United Nations Statistics Division, New York, NY 10017, (800) 253-9646, Fax: (212) 963-4116, http://unstats.un.org; *Demographic Yearbook; Statistical Yearbook;* and *Trends in Europe and North America: The Statistical Yearbook of the ECE 2005.*

KYRGYZSTAN - ECONOMIC CONDITIONS

Academic International Press, PO Box 1111, Gulf Breeze, FL 32562-1111, Fax: (850) 934-0953, www.ai-press.com; *Russia and Eurasia Facts and Figures Annual.*

Center for International Business Education Research (CIBER), Columbia Business School and School of International and Public Affairs, Uris Hall, Room 212, 3022 Broadway, New York, NY 10027-6902, Mr. Joshua Safier, (212) 854-4750, Fax: (212) 222-9821, www.columbia.edu/cu/ciber/; Datastream International.

Central Intelligence Agency, Office of Public Affairs, Washington, DC 20505, (703) 482-0623, Fax: (703) 482-1739, www.cia.gov; *The World Factbook.*

DSI Data Service Information, Xantener Strasse 51a, D-47495 Rheinberg, Germany, www.dsidata.com; *Campus Solution.*

Dun and Bradstreet (DB) Corporation, 103 JFK Parkway, Short Hills, NJ 07078, (973) 921-5500, www.dnb.com; *Country Report.*

Economist Intelligence Unit, 111 West 57th Street, New York, NY 10019, (212) 554-0600, Fax: (212) 586-1181, www.eiu.com; *Kyrgyz Republic Country Report.*

Euromonitor International, Inc., 224 S. Michigan Avenue, Suite 1500, Chicago, IL 60604, (312) 922-1115, Fax: (312) 922-1157, www.euromonitor.com; *The World Economic Factbook 2008* and *World Marketing Data and Statistics.*

International Monetary Fund (IMF), 700 Nineteenth Street, NW, Washington, DC 20431, (202) 623-7000, Fax: (202) 623-4661, www.imf.org; *World Economic Outlook Reports.*

Nomura Research Institute (NRI), 2 World Financial Center, Building B, 19th Fl., New York, NY 10281-1198, (212) 667-1670, www.nri.co.jp/english; *Asian Economic Outlook 2003-2004.*

Palgrave Macmillan Ltd., Houndmills, Basingstoke, Hampshire, RG21 6XS, England, (Telephone in U.S. (888) 330-8477), (Fax in U.S. (800) 672-2054), www.palgrave.com; *The Statesman's Yearbook 2008.*

United Nations Statistics Division, New York, NY 10017, (800) 253-9646, Fax: (212) 963-4116, http://unstats.un.org; *World Statistics Pocketbook.*

The World Bank, 1818 H Street, NW, Washington, DC 20433, (202) 473-1000, Fax: (202) 477-6391, www.worldbank.org; *Global Economic Monitor (GEM); Global Economic Prospects 2008; Kyrgyz Republic; The World Bank Atlas 2003-2004;* and *World Development Report 2008.*

KYRGYZSTAN - EDUCATION

Academic International Press, PO Box 1111, Gulf Breeze, FL 32562-1111, Fax: (850) 934-0953, www.ai-press.com; *Russia and Eurasia Facts and Figures Annual.*

Euromonitor International, Inc., 224 S. Michigan Avenue, Suite 1500, Chicago, IL 60604, (312) 922-1115, Fax: (312) 922-1157, www.euromonitor.com; *International Marketing Data and Statistics 2008* and *World Marketing Data and Statistics.*

Palgrave Macmillan Ltd., Houndmills, Basingstoke, Hampshire, RG21 6XS, England, (Telephone in U.S. (888) 330-8477), (Fax in U.S. (800) 672-2054), www.palgrave.com; *The Statesman's Yearbook 2008.*

Taylor and Francis Group, An Informa Business, 2 Park Square, Milton Park, Abingdon, Oxford OX14 4RN, United Kingdom, (Dial from U.S. (212) 216-7800), (Fax from U.S. (212) 564-7854), www.tandf.co.uk; *The Europa World Year Book.*

UNESCO Institute for Statistics, C.P. 6128 Succursale Centre-Ville, Montreal, Quebec, H3C 3J7 Canada, (Dial from U.S. (514) 343-6880), (Fax from U.S. (514) 343 6882), www.uis.unesco.org; *Statistical Tables.*

United Nations Statistics Division, New York, NY 10017, (800) 253-9646, Fax: (212) 963-4116, http://unstats.un.org; *Human Development Report 2006* and *Trends in Europe and North America: The Statistical Yearbook of the ECE 2005.*

The World Bank, 1818 H Street, NW, Washington, DC 20433, (202) 473-1000, Fax: (202) 477-6391, www.worldbank.org; *Kyrgyz Republic* and *World Development Report 2008.*

KYRGYZSTAN - ELECTRICITY

Palgrave Macmillan Ltd., Houndmills, Basingstoke, Hampshire, RG21 6XS, England, (Telephone in U.S. (888) 330-8477), (Fax in U.S. (800) 672-2054), www.palgrave.com; *The Statesman's Yearbook 2008.*

Platts, 2 Penn Plaza, 25th Floor, New York, NY 10121-2298, (212) 904-3070, www.platts.com; *Energy Economist.*

U.S. Department of Energy (DOE), Energy Information Administration (EIA), 1000 Independence Avenue, SW, Washington, DC 20585, (202) 586-8800, www.eia.doe.gov; *International Energy Annual 2004* and *International Energy Outlook 2006.*

United Nations Statistics Division, New York, NY 10017, (800) 253-9646, Fax: (212) 963-4116, http://unstats.un.org; *Energy Statistics Yearbook 2003; Human Development Report 2006; Statistical Yearbook;* and *Trends in Europe and North America: The Statistical Yearbook of the ECE 2005.*

The World Bank, 1818 H Street, NW, Washington, DC 20433, (202) 473-1000, Fax: (202) 477-6391, www.worldbank.org; *Statistical Handbook: States of the Former USSR.*

KYRGYZSTAN - EMPLOYMENT

Euromonitor International, Inc., 224 S. Michigan Avenue, Suite 1500, Chicago, IL 60604, (312) 922-1115, Fax: (312) 922-1157, www.euromonitor.com; *International Marketing Data and Statistics 2008.*

United Nations Statistics Division, New York, NY 10017, (800) 253-9646, Fax: (212) 963-4116, http://unstats.un.org; *Statistical Yearbook* and *Trends in Europe and North America: The Statistical Yearbook of the ECE 2005.*

The World Bank, 1818 H Street, NW, Washington, DC 20433, (202) 473-1000, Fax: (202) 477-6391, www.worldbank.org; *Kyrgyz Republic* and *Statistical Handbook: States of the Former USSR.*

KYRGYZSTAN - ENVIRONMENTAL CONDITIONS

DSI Data Service Information, Xantener Strasse 51a, D-47495 Rheinberg, Germany, www.dsidata.com; *Campus Solution* and *DSI's Global Environmental Database.*

Economist Intelligence Unit, 111 West 57th Street, New York, NY 10019, (212) 554-0600, Fax: (212) 586-1181, www.eiu.com; *Kyrgyz Republic Country Report.*

United Nations Statistics Division, New York, NY 10017, (800) 253-9646, Fax: (212) 963-4116, http://unstats.un.org; *Statistical Yearbook; Trends in Europe and North America: The Statistical Yearbook of the ECE 2005;* and *World Statistics Pocketbook.*

KYRGYZSTAN - EXPORTS

Academic International Press, PO Box 1111, Gulf Breeze, FL 32562-1111, Fax: (850) 934-0953, www.ai-press.com; *Russia and Eurasia Facts and Figures Annual.*

Central Intelligence Agency, Office of Public Affairs, Washington, DC 20505, (703) 482-0623, Fax: (703) 482-1739, www.cia.gov; *The World Factbook.*

Economist Intelligence Unit, 111 West 57th Street, New York, NY 10019, (212) 554-0600, Fax: (212) 586-1181, www.eiu.com; *Kyrgyz Republic Country Report.*

Euromonitor International, Inc., 224 S. Michigan Avenue, Suite 1500, Chicago, IL 60604, (312) 922-1115, Fax: (312) 922-1157, www.euromonitor.com; *International Marketing Data and Statistics 2008.*

International Monetary Fund (IMF), 700 Nineteenth Street, NW, Washington, DC 20431, (202) 623-7000, Fax: (202) 623-4661, www.imf.org; *Direction of Trade Statistics Yearbook 2007.*

Palgrave Macmillan Ltd., Houndmills, Basingstoke, Hampshire, RG21 6XS, England, (Telephone in U.S. (888) 330-8477), (Fax in U.S. (800) 672-2054), www.palgrave.com; *The Statesman's Yearbook 2008.*

Taylor and Francis Group, An Informa Business, 2 Park Square, Milton Park, Abingdon, Oxford OX14 4RN, United Kingdom, (Dial from U.S. (212) 216-7800), (Fax from U.S. (212) 564-7854), www.tandf.co.uk; *The Europa World Year Book.*

United Nations Conference on Trade and Development (UNCTAD), DC2-1120, United Nations, New York, NY 10017, (212) 963-0027, www.unctad.org; *Handbook of Statistics 2005.*

United Nations Statistics Division, New York, NY 10017, (800) 253-9646, Fax: (212) 963-4116, http://unstats.un.org; *International Trade Statistics Yearbook* and *Trends in Europe and North America: The Statistical Yearbook of the ECE 2005.*

The World Bank, 1818 H Street, NW, Washington, DC 20433, (202) 473-1000, Fax: (202) 477-6391, www.worldbank.org; *Statistical Handbook: States of the Former USSR; World Development Indicators (WDI) 2008;* and *World Development Report 2008.*

Worldinformation.com, 2 Market Street, Saffron Walden, Essex CB10 1HZ, United Kingdom, www.worldinformation.com; The World of Information (www.worldinformation.com).

KYRGYZSTAN - FERTILITY, HUMAN

Central Intelligence Agency, Office of Public Affairs, Washington, DC 20505, (703) 482-0623, Fax: (703) 482-1739, www.cia.gov; *The World Factbook.*

United Nations Statistics Division, New York, NY 10017, (800) 253-9646, Fax: (212) 963-4116, http://unstats.un.org; *Human Development Report 2006* and *Trends in Europe and North America: The Statistical Yearbook of the ECE 2005.*

The World Bank, 1818 H Street, NW, Washington, DC 20433, (202) 473-1000, Fax: (202) 477-6391, www.worldbank.org; *Statistical Handbook: States of the Former USSR; The World Bank Atlas 2003-2004; World Development Indicators (WDI) 2008;* and *World Development Report 2008.*

World Health Organization (WHO), Avenue Appia 20, 1211 Geneve 27, Switzerland, (Telephone in U.S. (212) 331-9081), www.who.int; *World Health Report 2006.*

KYRGYZSTAN - FERTILIZER INDUSTRY

United Nations Food and Agricultural Organization (FAO), Viale delle Terme di Caracalla, 00100 Rome, Italy, (Dial from U.S. (202) 653-2400), (Fax from U.S. (202) 653 5760), www.fao.org; *FAO Fertilizer Yearbook.*

United Nations Statistics Division, New York, NY 10017, (800) 253-9646, Fax: (212) 963-4116, http://unstats.un.org; *2004 Industrial Commodity Statistics Yearbook* and *Statistical Yearbook.*

KYRGYZSTAN - FINANCE

Taylor and Francis Group, An Informa Business, 2 Park Square, Milton Park, Abingdon, Oxford OX14 4RN, United Kingdom, (Dial from U.S. (212) 216-7800), (Fax from U.S. (212) 564-7854), www.tandf.co.uk; *The Europa World Year Book.*

United Nations Statistics Division, New York, NY 10017, (800) 253-9646, Fax: (212) 963-4116, http://unstats.un.org; *National Accounts Statistics: Compendium of Income Distribution Statistics* and *Statistical Yearbook.*

The World Bank, 1818 H Street, NW, Washington, DC 20433, (202) 473-1000, Fax: (202) 477-6391, www.worldbank.org; *Kyrgyz Republic* and *Statistical Handbook: States of the Former USSR.*

KYRGYZSTAN - FINANCE, PUBLIC

Bernan Essential Government Publications, 4611-F Assembly Drive, Lanham MD, 20706-4391, (301) 459-2255, Fax: (800) 865-3450, www.bernan.com; *National Accounts Statistics.*

Economist Intelligence Unit, 111 West 57th Street, New York, NY 10019, (212) 554-0600, Fax: (212) 586-1181, www.eiu.com; *Kyrgyz Republic Country Report.*

International Monetary Fund (IMF), 700 Nineteenth Street, NW, Washington, DC 20431, (202) 623-7000, Fax: (202) 623-4661, www.imf.org; *International Financial Statistics* and *International Financial Statistics Online Service.*

Palgrave Macmillan Ltd., Houndmills, Basingstoke, Hampshire, RG21 6XS, England, (Telephone in U.S. (888) 330-8477), (Fax in U.S. (800) 672-2054), www.palgrave.com; *The Statesman's Yearbook 2008.*

Taylor and Francis Group, An Informa Business, 2 Park Square, Milton Park, Abingdon, Oxford OX14 4RN, United Kingdom, (Dial from U.S. (212) 216-7800), (Fax from U.S. (212) 564-7854), www.tandf.co.uk; *The Europa World Year Book.*

The World Bank, 1818 H Street, NW, Washington, DC 20433, (202) 473-1000, Fax: (202) 477-6391, www.worldbank.org; *Kyrgyz Republic* and *Statistical Handbook: States of the Former USSR.*

KYRGYZSTAN - FISHERIES

United Nations Food and Agricultural Organization (FAO), Viale delle Terme di Caracalla, 00100 Rome, Italy, (Dial from U.S. (202) 653-2400), (Fax from U.S. (202) 653 5760), www.fao.org; *FAO Yearbook of Fishery Statistics;* Fishery Databases; FISHSTAT Database. Subjects covered include: Aquaculture production, capture production, fishery commodities; and *The State of Food and Agriculture (SOFA) 2006.*

United Nations Statistics Division, New York, NY 10017, (800) 253-9646, Fax: (212) 963-4116, http://unstats.un.org; *2004 Industrial Commodity Statistics Yearbook* and *Statistical Yearbook.*

The World Bank, 1818 H Street, NW, Washington, DC 20433, (202) 473-1000, Fax: (202) 477-6391, www.worldbank.org; *Kyrgyz Republic.*

KYRGYZSTAN - FOOD

United Nations Food and Agricultural Organization (FAO), Viale delle Terme di Caracalla, 00100 Rome, Italy, (Dial from U.S. (202) 653-2400), (Fax from U.S. (202) 653 5760), www.fao.org; *FAO Production Yearbook 2002* and *The State of Food and Agriculture (SOFA) 2006.*

United Nations Statistics Division, New York, NY 10017, (800) 253-9646, Fax: (212) 963-4116, http://unstats.un.org; *Human Development Report 2006* and *2004 Industrial Commodity Statistics Yearbook.*

KYRGYZSTAN - FOREIGN EXCHANGE RATES

Central Intelligence Agency, Office of Public Affairs, Washington, DC 20505, (703) 482-0623, Fax: (703) 482-1739, www.cia.gov; *The World Factbook.*

Euromonitor International, Inc., 224 S. Michigan Avenue, Suite 1500, Chicago, IL 60604, (312) 922-1115, Fax: (312) 922-1157, www.euromonitor.com; *International Marketing Data and Statistics 2008.*

Taylor and Francis Group, An Informa Business, 2 Park Square, Milton Park, Abingdon, Oxford OX14 4RN, United Kingdom, (Dial from U.S. (212) 216-7800), (Fax from U.S. (212) 564-7854), www.tandf.co.uk; *The Europa World Year Book.*

United Nations Statistics Division, New York, NY 10017, (800) 253-9646, Fax: (212) 963-4116, http://unstats.un.org; *Statistical Yearbook; Trends in Europe and North America: The Statistical Yearbook of the ECE 2005;* and *World Statistics Pocketbook.*

Worldinformation.com, 2 Market Street, Saffron Walden, Essex CB10 1HZ, United Kingdom, www.worldinformation.com; The World of Information (www.worldinformation.com).

KYRGYZSTAN - FORESTS AND FORESTRY

Academic International Press, PO Box 1111, Gulf Breeze, FL 32562-1111, Fax: (850) 934-0953, www.ai-press.com; *Russia and Eurasia Facts and Figures Annual.*

UNESCO Institute for Statistics, C.P. 6128 Succursale Centre-Ville, Montreal, Quebec, H3C 3J7 Canada, (Dial from U.S. (514) 343-6880), (Fax from U.S. (514) 343 6882), www.uis.unesco.org; *Statistical Tables.*

United Nations Food and Agricultural Organization (FAO), Viale delle Terme di Caracalla, 00100 Rome, Italy, (Dial from U.S. (202) 653-2400), (Fax from U.S. (202) 653 5760), www.fao.org; *FAO Yearbook of Forest Products* and *The State of Food and Agriculture (SOFA) 2006.*

United Nations Statistics Division, New York, NY 10017, (800) 253-9646, Fax: (212) 963-4116, http://unstats.un.org; *2004 Industrial Commodity Statistics Yearbook; Statistical Yearbook;* and *Trends in Europe and North America: The Statistical Yearbook of the ECE 2005.*

The World Bank, 1818 H Street, NW, Washington, DC 20433, (202) 473-1000, Fax: (202) 477-6391, www.worldbank.org; *Kyrgyz Republic* and *World Development Report 2008.*

KYRGYZSTAN - GROSS DOMESTIC PRODUCT

Academic International Press, PO Box 1111, Gulf Breeze, FL 32562-1111, Fax: (850) 934-0953, www.ai-press.com; *Russia and Eurasia Facts and Figures Annual.*

Economist Intelligence Unit, 111 West 57th Street, New York, NY 10019, (212) 554-0600, Fax: (212) 586-1181, www.eiu.com; *Kyrgyz Republic Country Report.*

Euromonitor International, Inc., 224 S. Michigan Avenue, Suite 1500, Chicago, IL 60604, (312) 922-1115, Fax: (312) 922-1157, www.euromonitor.com; *International Marketing Data and Statistics 2008* and *The World Economic Factbook 2008.*

Taylor and Francis Group, An Informa Business, 2 Park Square, Milton Park, Abingdon, Oxford OX14 4RN, United Kingdom, (Dial from U.S. (212) 216-7800), (Fax from U.S. (212) 564-7854), www.tandf.co.uk; *The Europa World Year Book.*

United Nations Statistics Division, New York, NY 10017, (800) 253-9646, Fax: (212) 963-4116, http://unstats.un.org; *Human Development Report 2006; National Accounts Statistics: Compendium of Income Distribution Statistics; Statistical Yearbook;* and *Trends in Europe and North America: The Statistical Yearbook of the ECE 2005.*

The World Bank, 1818 H Street, NW, Washington, DC 20433, (202) 473-1000, Fax: (202) 477-6391, www.worldbank.org; *Statistical Handbook: States of the Former USSR; World Development Indicators (WDI) 2008;* and *World Development Report 2008.*

KYRGYZSTAN - GROSS NATIONAL PRODUCT

Palgrave Macmillan Ltd., Houndmills, Basingstoke, Hampshire, RG21 6XS, England, (Telephone in U.S. (888) 330-8477), (Fax in U.S. (800) 672-2054), www.palgrave.com; *The Statesman's Yearbook 2008.*

United Nations Statistics Division, New York, NY 10017, (800) 253-9646, Fax: (212) 963-4116, http://unstats.un.org; *Statistical Yearbook.*

The World Bank, 1818 H Street, NW, Washington, DC 20433, (202) 473-1000, Fax: (202) 477-6391, www.worldbank.org; *The World Bank Atlas 2003-2004; World Development Indicators (WDI) 2008;* and *World Development Report 2008.*

Worldinformation.com, 2 Market Street, Saffron Walden, Essex CB10 1HZ, United Kingdom, www.worldinformation.com; The World of Information (www.worldinformation.com).

KYRGYZSTAN - HOUSING

Euromonitor International, Inc., 224 S. Michigan Avenue, Suite 1500, Chicago, IL 60604, (312) 922-1115, Fax: (312) 922-1157, www.euromonitor.com; *World Marketing Data and Statistics.*

United Nations Statistics Division, New York, NY 10017, (800) 253-9646, Fax: (212) 963-4116, http://unstats.un.org; *Trends in Europe and North America: The Statistical Yearbook of the ECE 2005.*

KYRGYZSTAN - ILLITERATE PERSONS

UNESCO Institute for Statistics, C.P. 6128 Succursale Centre-Ville, Montreal, Quebec, H3C 3J7 Canada, (Dial from U.S. (514) 343-6880), (Fax from U.S. (514) 343 6882), www.uis.unesco.org; *Statistical Tables.*

United Nations Statistics Division, New York, NY 10017, (800) 253-9646, Fax: (212) 963-4116, http://unstats.un.org; *Human Development Report 2006.*

KYRGYZSTAN - IMPORTS

Academic International Press, PO Box 1111, Gulf Breeze, FL 32562-1111, Fax: (850) 934-0953, www.ai-press.com; *Russia and Eurasia Facts and Figures Annual.*

Central Intelligence Agency, Office of Public Affairs, Washington, DC 20505, (703) 482-0623, Fax: (703) 482-1739, www.cia.gov; *The World Factbook.*

Economist Intelligence Unit, 111 West 57th Street, New York, NY 10019, (212) 554-0600, Fax: (212) 586-1181, www.eiu.com; *Kyrgyz Republic Country Report.*

Euromonitor International, Inc., 224 S. Michigan Avenue, Suite 1500, Chicago, IL 60604, (312) 922-1115, Fax: (312) 922-1157, www.euromonitor.com; *International Marketing Data and Statistics 2008.*

International Monetary Fund (IMF), 700 Nineteenth Street, NW, Washington, DC 20431, (202) 623-7000, Fax: (202) 623-4661, www.imf.org; *Direction of Trade Statistics Yearbook 2007.*

Palgrave Macmillan Ltd., Houndmills, Basingstoke, Hampshire, RG21 6XS, England, (Telephone in U.S. (888) 330-8477), (Fax in U.S. (800) 672-2054), www.palgrave.com; *The Statesman's Yearbook 2008.*

Taylor and Francis Group, An Informa Business, 2 Park Square, Milton Park, Abingdon, Oxford OX14 4RN, United Kingdom, (Dial from U.S. (212) 216-7800), (Fax from U.S. (212) 564-7854), www.tandf.co.uk; *The Europa World Year Book.*

U.S. Library of Congress (LOC), Congressional Research Service (CRS), The Library of Congress, 101 Independence Avenue, SE, Washington, DC 20540-7500, (202) 707-5700, www.loc.gov/crsinfo; *Energy: Selected Facts and Numbers.*

United Nations Conference on Trade and Development (UNCTAD), DC2-1120, United Nations, New York, NY 10017, (212) 963-0027, www.unctad.org; *Handbook of Statistics 2005.*

United Nations Statistics Division, New York, NY 10017, (800) 253-9646, Fax: (212) 963-4116, http://unstats.un.org; *International Trade Statistics Yearbook* and *Trends in Europe and North America: The Statistical Yearbook of the ECE 2005.*

The World Bank, 1818 H Street, NW, Washington, DC 20433, (202) 473-1000, Fax: (202) 477-6391, www.worldbank.org; *Statistical Handbook: States of the Former USSR; World Development Indicators (WDI) 2008;* and *World Development Report 2008.*

Worldinformation.com, 2 Market Street, Saffron Walden, Essex CB10 1HZ, United Kingdom, www.worldinformation.com; The World of Information (www.worldinformation.com).

KYRGYZSTAN - INDUSTRIAL PRODUCTIVITY

The World Bank, 1818 H Street, NW, Washington, DC 20433, (202) 473-1000, Fax: (202) 477-6391, www.worldbank.org; *Statistical Handbook: States of the Former USSR.*

KYRGYZSTAN - INDUSTRIAL PROPERTY

United Nations Statistics Division, New York, NY 10017, (800) 253-9646, Fax: (212) 963-4116, http://unstats.un.org; *Statistical Yearbook.*

KYRGYZSTAN - INDUSTRIES

Academic International Press, PO Box 1111, Gulf Breeze, FL 32562-1111, Fax: (850) 934-0953, www.ai-press.com; *Russia and Eurasia Facts and Figures Annual.*

Central Intelligence Agency, Office of Public Affairs, Washington, DC 20505, (703) 482-0623, Fax: (703) 482-1739, www.cia.gov; *The World Factbook.*

Economist Intelligence Unit, 111 West 57th Street, New York, NY 10019, (212) 554-0600, Fax: (212) 586-1181, www.eiu.com; *Kyrgyz Republic Country Report.*

Euromonitor International, Inc., 224 S. Michigan Avenue, Suite 1500, Chicago, IL 60604, (312) 922-1115, Fax: (312) 922-1157, www.euromonitor.com; *World Marketing Data and Statistics.*

Palgrave Macmillan Ltd., Houndmills, Basingstoke, Hampshire, RG21 6XS, England, (Telephone in U.S. (888) 330-8477), (Fax in U.S. (800) 672-2054), www.palgrave.com; *The Statesman's Yearbook 2008.*

Taylor and Francis Group, An Informa Business, 2 Park Square, Milton Park, Abingdon, Oxford OX14 4RN, United Kingdom, (Dial from U.S. (212) 216-7800), (Fax from U.S. (212) 564-7854), www.tandf.co.uk; *The Europa World Year Book.*

United Nations Industrial Development Organization (UNIDO), 1 United Nations Plaza, New York, NY 10017, (212) 963 6890, Fax: (212) 963-7904, http://unido.org; Industrial Statistics Database 2008 (INDSTAT) and *The International Yearbook of Industrial Statistics 2008.*

United Nations Statistics Division, New York, NY 10017, (800) 253-9646, Fax: (212) 963-4116, http://unstats.un.org; *2004 Industrial Commodity Statistics Yearbook; Statistical Yearbook;* and *Trends in Europe and North America: The Statistical Yearbook of the ECE 2005.*

The World Bank, 1818 H Street, NW, Washington, DC 20433, (202) 473-1000, Fax: (202) 477-6391, www.worldbank.org; *Kyrgyz Republic; Statistical Handbook: States of the Former USSR;* and *World Development Indicators (WDI) 2008.*

KYRGYZSTAN - INFANT AND MATERNAL MORTALITY

See KYRGYZSTAN - MORTALITY

KYRGYZSTAN - INTERNATIONAL TRADE

Academic International Press, PO Box 1111, Gulf Breeze, FL 32562-1111, Fax: (850) 934-0953, www.ai-press.com; *Russia and Eurasia Facts and Figures Annual.*

Economist Intelligence Unit, 111 West 57th Street, New York, NY 10019, (212) 554-0600, Fax: (212) 586-1181, www.eiu.com; *Kyrgyz Republic Country Report.*

Euromonitor International, Inc., 224 S. Michigan Avenue, Suite 1500, Chicago, IL 60604, (312) 922-1115, Fax: (312) 922-1157, www.euromonitor.com; *The World Economic Factbook 2008* and *World Marketing Data and Statistics.*

International Monetary Fund (IMF), 700 Nineteenth Street, NW, Washington, DC 20431, (202) 623-7000, Fax: (202) 623-4661, www.imf.org; *Direction of Trade Statistics Yearbook 2007.*

Palgrave Macmillan Ltd., Houndmills, Basingstoke, Hampshire, RG21 6XS, England, (Telephone in U.S. (888) 330-8477), (Fax in U.S. (800) 672-2054), www.palgrave.com; *The Statesman's Yearbook 2008.*

Taylor and Francis Group, An Informa Business, 2 Park Square, Milton Park, Abingdon, Oxford OX14 4RN, United Kingdom, (Dial from U.S. (212) 216-7800), (Fax from U.S. (212) 564-7854), www.tandf.co.uk; *The Europa World Year Book.*

United Nations Food and Agricultural Organization (FAO), Viale delle Terme di Caracalla, 00100 Rome,

Italy, (Dial from U.S. (202) 653-2400), (Fax from U.S. (202) 653 5760), www.fao.org; *FAO Trade Yearbook.*

United Nations Statistics Division, New York, NY 10017, (800) 253-9646, Fax: (212) 963-4116, http://unstats.un.org; *International Trade Statistics Yearbook* and *Statistical Yearbook.*

The World Bank, 1818 H Street, NW, Washington, DC 20433, (202) 473-1000, Fax: (202) 477-6391, www.worldbank.org; *Kyrgyz Republic; Statistical Handbook: States of the Former USSR; World Development Indicators (WDI) 2008;* and *World Development Report 2008.*

World Trade Organization (WTO), Centre William Rappard, Rue de Lausanne 154, CH-1211 Geneva 21, Switzerland, www.wto.org; *International Trade Statistics 2006.*

KYRGYZSTAN - INTERNET USERS

International Telecommunication Union (ITU), Place des Nations, 1211 Geneva 20, Switzerland, www.itu.int; *World Telecommunication/ICT Indicators Database on CD-ROM; World Telecommunication/ICT Indicators Database Online;* and *Yearbook of Statistics - Telecommunication Services (Chronological Time Series 1997-2006).*

The World Bank, 1818 H Street, NW, Washington, DC 20433, (202) 473-1000, Fax: (202) 477-6391, www.worldbank.org; *Kyrgyz Republic.*

KYRGYZSTAN - LABOR

Academic International Press, PO Box 1111, Gulf Breeze, FL 32562-1111, Fax: (850) 934-0953, www.ai-press.com; *Russia and Eurasia Facts and Figures Annual.*

Central Intelligence Agency, Office of Public Affairs, Washington, DC 20505, (703) 482-0623, Fax: (703) 482-1739, www.cia.gov; *The World Factbook.*

Euromonitor International, Inc., 224 S. Michigan Avenue, Suite 1500, Chicago, IL 60604, (312) 922-1115, Fax: (312) 922-1157, www.euromonitor.com; *International Marketing Data and Statistics 2008* and *World Marketing Data and Statistics.*

Palgrave Macmillan Ltd., Houndmills, Basingstoke, Hampshire, RG21 6XS, England, (Telephone in U.S. (888) 330-8477), (Fax in U.S. (800) 672-2054), www.palgrave.com; *The Statesman's Yearbook 2008.*

Taylor and Francis Group, An Informa Business, 2 Park Square, Milton Park, Abingdon, Oxford OX14 4RN, United Kingdom, (Dial from U.S. (212) 216-7800), (Fax from U.S. (212) 564-7854), www.tandf.co.uk; *The Europa World Year Book.*

United Nations Statistics Division, New York, NY 10017, (800) 253-9646, Fax: (212) 963-4116, http://unstats.un.org; *Human Development Report 2006* and *Statistical Yearbook.*

The World Bank, 1818 H Street, NW, Washington, DC 20433, (202) 473-1000, Fax: (202) 477-6391, www.worldbank.org; *Statistical Handbook: States of the Former USSR; The World Bank Atlas 2003-2004; World Development Indicators (WDI) 2008;* and *World Development Report 2008.*

KYRGYZSTAN - LAND USE

Central Intelligence Agency, Office of Public Affairs, Washington, DC 20505, (703) 482-0623, Fax: (703) 482-1739, www.cia.gov; *The World Factbook.*

Euromonitor International, Inc., 224 S. Michigan Avenue, Suite 1500, Chicago, IL 60604, (312) 922-1115, Fax: (312) 922-1157, www.euromonitor.com; *International Marketing Data and Statistics 2008.*

United Nations Food and Agricultural Organization (FAO), Viale delle Terme di Caracalla, 00100 Rome, Italy, (Dial from U.S. (202) 653-2400), (Fax from U.S. (202) 653 5760), www.fao.org; *FAO Production Yearbook 2002.*

The World Bank, 1818 H Street, NW, Washington, DC 20433, (202) 473-1000, Fax: (202) 477-6391, www.worldbank.org; *World Development Report 2008.*

KYRGYZSTAN - LIBRARIES

UNESCO Institute for Statistics, C.P. 6128 Succursale Centre-Ville, Montreal, Quebec, H3C 3J7 Canada, (Dial from U.S. (514) 343-6880), (Fax from U.S. (514) 343 6882), www.uis.unesco.org; *Statistical Tables.*

United Nations Statistics Division, New York, NY 10017, (800) 253-9646, Fax: (212) 963-4116, http://unstats.un.org; *Trends in Europe and North America: The Statistical Yearbook of the ECE 2005.*

KYRGYZSTAN - LIFE EXPECTANCY

Central Intelligence Agency, Office of Public Affairs, Washington, DC 20505, (703) 482-0623, Fax: (703) 482-1739, www.cia.gov; *The World Factbook.*

Euromonitor International, Inc., 224 S. Michigan Avenue, Suite 1500, Chicago, IL 60604, (312) 922-1115, Fax: (312) 922-1157, www.euromonitor.com; *The World Economic Factbook 2008.*

United Nations Statistics Division, New York, NY 10017, (800) 253-9646, Fax: (212) 963-4116, http://unstats.un.org; *Demographic Yearbook; Human Development Report 2006; Trends in Europe and North America: The Statistical Yearbook of the ECE 2005;* and *World Statistics Pocketbook.*

The World Bank, 1818 H Street, NW, Washington, DC 20433, (202) 473-1000, Fax: (202) 477-6391, www.worldbank.org; *The World Bank Atlas 2003-2004; World Development Indicators (WDI) 2008;* and *World Development Report 2008.*

World Health Organization (WHO), Avenue Appia 20, 1211 Geneve 27, Switzerland, (Telephone in U.S. (212) 331-9081), www.who.int; *World Health Report 2006.*

KYRGYZSTAN - LIVESTOCK

Academic International Press, PO Box 1111, Gulf Breeze, FL 32562-1111, Fax: (850) 934-0953, www.ai-press.com; *Russia and Eurasia Facts and Figures Annual.*

Palgrave Macmillan Ltd., Houndmills, Basingstoke, Hampshire, RG21 6XS, England, (Telephone in U.S. (888) 330-8477), (Fax in U.S. (800) 672-2054), www.palgrave.com; *The Statesman's Yearbook 2008.*

Taylor and Francis Group, An Informa Business, 2 Park Square, Milton Park, Abingdon, Oxford OX14 4RN, United Kingdom, (Dial from U.S. (212) 216-7800), (Fax from U.S. (212) 564-7854), www.tandf.co.uk; *The Europa World Year Book.*

United Nations Food and Agricultural Organization (FAO), Viale delle Terme di Caracalla, 00100 Rome, Italy, (Dial from U.S. (202) 653-2400), (Fax from U.S. (202) 653 5760), www.fao.org; *FAO Production Yearbook 2002* and *The State of Food and Agriculture (SOFA) 2006.*

United Nations Statistics Division, New York, NY 10017, (800) 253-9646, Fax: (212) 963-4116, http://unstats.un.org; *2004 Industrial Commodity Statistics Yearbook* and *Statistical Yearbook.*

KYRGYZSTAN - MACHINERY

United Nations Statistics Division, New York, NY 10017, (800) 253-9646, Fax: (212) 963-4116, http://unstats.un.org; *2004 Industrial Commodity Statistics Yearbook.*

KYRGYZSTAN - MANUFACTURES

United Nations Statistics Division, New York, NY 10017, (800) 253-9646, Fax: (212) 963-4116, http://unstats.un.org; *2004 Industrial Commodity Statistics Yearbook* and *Statistical Yearbook.*

The World Bank, 1818 H Street, NW, Washington, DC 20433, (202) 473-1000, Fax: (202) 477-6391, www.worldbank.org; *World Development Indicators (WDI) 2008.*

KYRGYZSTAN - MARRIAGE

Taylor and Francis Group, An Informa Business, 2 Park Square, Milton Park, Abingdon, Oxford OX14 4RN, United Kingdom, (Dial from U.S. (212) 216-7800), (Fax from U.S. (212) 564-7854), www.tandf.co.uk; *The Europa World Year Book.*

United Nations Statistics Division, New York, NY 10017, (800) 253-9646, Fax: (212) 963-4116, http://unstats.un.org; *Demographic Yearbook; Statistical Yearbook;* and *Trends in Europe and North America: The Statistical Yearbook of the ECE 2005.*

KYRGYZSTAN - MEAT PRODUCTION

See KYRGYZSTAN - LIVESTOCK

KYRGYZSTAN - MINERAL INDUSTRIES

Academic International Press, PO Box 1111, Gulf Breeze, FL 32562-1111, Fax: (850) 934-0953, www.ai-press.com; *Russia and Eurasia Facts and Figures Annual.*

Palgrave Macmillan Ltd., Houndmills, Basingstoke, Hampshire, RG21 6XS, England, (Telephone in U.S. (888) 330-8477), (Fax in U.S. (800) 672-2054), www.palgrave.com; *The Statesman's Yearbook 2008.*

Platts, 2 Penn Plaza, 25th Floor, New York, NY 10121-2298, (212) 904-3070, www.platts.com; *Energy Economist.*

Taylor and Francis Group, An Informa Business, 2 Park Square, Milton Park, Abingdon, Oxford OX14 4RN, United Kingdom, (Dial from U.S. (212) 216-7800), (Fax from U.S. (212) 564-7854), www.tandf.co.uk; *The Europa World Year Book.*

United Nations Statistics Division, New York, NY 10017, (800) 253-9646, Fax: (212) 963-4116, http://unstats.un.org; *Energy Statistics Yearbook 2003; 2004 Industrial Commodity Statistics Yearbook;* and *Statistical Yearbook.*

United States Office of Personnel Management (OMB), 1900 E Street, NW, Washington, DC 20415-1000, (202) 606-1800, www.opm.gov; *Pay Structure of the Federal Civil Service.*

The World Bank, 1818 H Street, NW, Washington, DC 20433, (202) 473-1000, Fax: (202) 477-6391, www.worldbank.org; *Kyrgyz Republic.*

KYRGYZSTAN - MONEY SUPPLY

Economist Intelligence Unit, 111 West 57th Street, New York, NY 10019, (212) 554-0600, Fax: (212) 586-1181, www.eiu.com; *Kyrgyz Republic Country Report.*

Taylor and Francis Group, An Informa Business, 2 Park Square, Milton Park, Abingdon, Oxford OX14 4RN, United Kingdom, (Dial from U.S. (212) 216-7800), (Fax from U.S. (212) 564-7854), www.tandf.co.uk; *The Europa World Year Book.*

The World Bank, 1818 H Street, NW, Washington, DC 20433, (202) 473-1000, Fax: (202) 477-6391, www.worldbank.org; *Kyrgyz Republic.*

KYRGYZSTAN - MONUMENTS AND HISTORIC SITES

UNESCO Institute for Statistics, C.P. 6128 Succursale Centre-Ville, Montreal, Quebec, H3C 3J7 Canada, (Dial from U.S. (514) 343-6880), (Fax from U.S. (514) 343 6882), www.uis.unesco.org; *Statistical Tables.*

KYRGYZSTAN - MORTALITY

Central Intelligence Agency, Office of Public Affairs, Washington, DC 20505, (703) 482-0623, Fax: (703) 482-1739, www.cia.gov; *The World Factbook.*

Euromonitor International, Inc., 224 S. Michigan Avenue, Suite 1500, Chicago, IL 60604, (312) 922-1115, Fax: (312) 922-1157, www.euromonitor.com; *International Marketing Data and Statistics 2008* and *The World Economic Factbook 2008.*

Palgrave Macmillan Ltd., Houndmills, Basingstoke, Hampshire, RG21 6XS, England, (Telephone in U.S. (888) 330-8477), (Fax in U.S. (800) 672-2054), www.palgrave.com; *The Statesman's Yearbook 2008.*

Taylor and Francis Group, An Informa Business, 2 Park Square, Milton Park, Abingdon, Oxford OX14 4RN, United Kingdom, (Dial from U.S. (212) 216-

7800), (Fax from U.S. (212) 564-7854), www.tandf.co.uk; *The Europa World Year Book.*

UNICEF, 3 United Nations Plaza, New York, NY 10017, (800) 253-9646, Fax: (212) 887-7465, www.unicef.org; *The State of the World's Children 2008.*

United Nations Statistics Division, New York, NY 10017, (800) 253-9646, Fax: (212) 963-4116, http://unstats.un.org; *Demographic Yearbook; Human Development Report 2006; Statistical Yearbook; Trends in Europe and North America: The Statistical Yearbook of the ECE 2005;* and *World Statistics Pocketbook.*

The World Bank, 1818 H Street, NW, Washington, DC 20433, (202) 473-1000, Fax: (202) 477-6391, www.worldbank.org; *The World Bank Atlas 2003-2004; World Development Indicators (WDI) 2008;* and *World Development Report 2008.*

World Health Organization (WHO), Avenue Appia 20, 1211 Geneve 27, Switzerland, (Telephone in U.S. (212) 331-9081), www.who.int; The WHO Global Atlas of Infectious Diseases and *World Health Report 2006.*

KYRGYZSTAN - MOTION PICTURES

UNESCO Institute for Statistics, C.P. 6128 Succursale Centre-Ville, Montreal, Quebec, H3C 3J7 Canada, (Dial from U.S. (514) 343-6880), (Fax from U.S. (514) 343 6882), www.uis.unesco.org; *Statistical Tables.*

United Nations Statistics Division, New York, NY 10017, (800) 253-9646, Fax: (212) 963-4116, http://unstats.un.org; *Statistical Yearbook.*

KYRGYZSTAN - MOTOR VEHICLES

United Nations Statistics Division, New York, NY 10017, (800) 253-9646, Fax: (212) 963-4116, http://unstats.un.org; *Statistical Yearbook.*

KYRGYZSTAN - MUSEUMS

UNESCO Institute for Statistics, C.P. 6128 Succursale Centre-Ville, Montreal, Quebec, H3C 3J7 Canada, (Dial from U.S. (514) 343-6880), (Fax from U.S. (514) 343 6882), www.uis.unesco.org; *Statistical Tables.*

KYRGYZSTAN - PERIODICALS

UNESCO Institute for Statistics, C.P. 6128 Succursale Centre-Ville, Montreal, Quebec, H3C 3J7 Canada, (Dial from U.S. (514) 343-6880), (Fax from U.S. (514) 343 6882), www.uis.unesco.org; *Statistical Tables.*

KYRGYZSTAN - PETROLEUM INDUSTRY AND TRADE

PennWell Corporation, 1421 South Sheridan Road, Tulsa, OK 74112, (918) 835-3161, www.pennwell.com; *International Petroleum Encyclopedia 2007.*

Platts, 2 Penn Plaza, 25th Floor, New York, NY 10121-2298, (212) 904-3070, www.platts.com; *Energy Economist.*

U.S. Department of Energy (DOE), Energy Information Administration (EIA), 1000 Independence Avenue, SW, Washington, DC 20585, (202) 586-8800, www.eia.doe.gov; *International Energy Annual 2004* and *International Energy Outlook 2006.*

United Nations Food and Agricultural Organization (FAO), Viale delle Terme di Caracalla, 00100 Rome, Italy, (Dial from U.S. (202) 653-2400), (Fax from U.S. (202) 653 5760), www.fao.org; *The State of Food and Agriculture (SOFA) 2006.*

United Nations Statistics Division, New York, NY 10017, (800) 253-9646, Fax: (212) 963-4116, http://unstats.un.org; *Energy Statistics Yearbook 2003; 2004 Industrial Commodity Statistics Yearbook; Statistical Yearbook;* and *Trends in Europe and North America: The Statistical Yearbook of the ECE 2005.*

KYRGYZSTAN - POLITICAL SCIENCE

Academic International Press, PO Box 1111, Gulf Breeze, FL 32562-1111, Fax: (850) 934-0953, www.ai-press.com; *Russia and Eurasia Facts and Figures Annual.*

Central Intelligence Agency, Office of Public Affairs, Washington, DC 20505, (703) 482-0623, Fax: (703) 482-1739, www.cia.gov; *The World Factbook.*

Palgrave Macmillan Ltd., Houndmills, Basingstoke, Hampshire, RG21 6XS, England, (Telephone in U.S. (888) 330-8477), (Fax in U.S. (800) 672-2054), www.palgrave.com; *The Statesman's Yearbook 2008.*

Taylor and Francis Group, An Informa Business, 2 Park Square, Milton Park, Abingdon, Oxford OX14 4RN, United Kingdom, (Dial from U.S. (212) 216-7800), (Fax from U.S. (212) 564-7854), www.tandf.co.uk; *The Europa World Year Book.*

United Nations Statistics Division, New York, NY 10017, (800) 253-9646, Fax: (212) 963-4116, http://unstats.un.org; *National Accounts Statistics: Compendium of Income Distribution Statistics* and *Statistical Yearbook.*

The World Bank, 1818 H Street, NW, Washington, DC 20433, (202) 473-1000, Fax: (202) 477-6391, www.worldbank.org; *Statistical Handbook: States of the Former USSR* and *World Development Report 2008.*

KYRGYZSTAN - POPULATION

Academic International Press, PO Box 1111, Gulf Breeze, FL 32562-1111, Fax: (850) 934-0953, www.ai-press.com; *Russia and Eurasia Facts and Figures Annual.*

Central Intelligence Agency, Office of Public Affairs, Washington, DC 20505, (703) 482-0623, Fax: (703) 482-1739, www.cia.gov; *The World Factbook.*

Economist Intelligence Unit, 111 West 57th Street, New York, NY 10019, (212) 554-0600, Fax: (212) 586-1181, www.eiu.com; *Kyrgyz Republic Country Report.*

Euromonitor International, Inc., 224 S. Michigan Avenue, Suite 1500, Chicago, IL 60604, (312) 922-1115, Fax: (312) 922-1157, www.euromonitor.com; *International Marketing Data and Statistics 2008* and *The World Economic Factbook 2008.*

Palgrave Macmillan Ltd., Houndmills, Basingstoke, Hampshire, RG21 6XS, England, (Telephone in U.S. (888) 330-8477), (Fax in U.S. (800) 672-2054), www.palgrave.com; *The Statesman's Yearbook 2008.*

Taylor and Francis Group, An Informa Business, 2 Park Square, Milton Park, Abingdon, Oxford OX14 4RN, United Kingdom, (Dial from U.S. (212) 216-7800), (Fax from U.S. (212) 564-7854), www.tandf.co.uk; *The Europa World Year Book.*

UNESCO Institute for Statistics, C.P. 6128 Succursale Centre-Ville, Montreal, Quebec, H3C 3J7 Canada, (Dial from U.S. (514) 343-6880), (Fax from U.S. (514) 343 6882), www.uis.unesco.org; *Statistical Tables.*

United Nations Food and Agricultural Organization (FAO), Viale delle Terme di Caracalla, 00100 Rome, Italy, (Dial from U.S. (202) 653-2400), (Fax from U.S. (202) 653 5760), www.fao.org; *FAO Production Yearbook 2002.*

United Nations Statistics Division, New York, NY 10017, (800) 253-9646, Fax: (212) 963-4116, http://unstats.un.org; *Demographic Yearbook; Human Development Report 2006; Statistical Yearbook; Trends in Europe and North America: The Statistical Yearbook of the ECE 2005;* and *World Statistics Pocketbook.*

The World Bank, 1818 H Street, NW, Washington, DC 20433, (202) 473-1000, Fax: (202) 477-6391, www.worldbank.org; *Kyrgyz Republic; Statistical Handbook: States of the Former USSR; The World Bank Atlas 2003-2004; World Development Indicators (WDI) 2008;* and *World Development Report 2008.*

World Health Organization (WHO), Avenue Appia 20, 1211 Geneve 27, Switzerland, (Telephone in U.S. (212) 331-9081), www.who.int; *World Health Report 2006.*

Worldinformation.com, 2 Market Street, Saffron Walden, Essex CB10 1HZ, United Kingdom, www.worldinformation.com; The World of Information (www.worldinformation.com).

KYRGYZSTAN - POPULATION DENSITY

Central Intelligence Agency, Office of Public Affairs, Washington, DC 20505, (703) 482-0623, Fax: (703) 482-1739, www.cia.gov; *The World Factbook.*

Euromonitor International, Inc., 224 S. Michigan Avenue, Suite 1500, Chicago, IL 60604, (312) 922-1115, Fax: (312) 922-1157, www.euromonitor.com; *The World Economic Factbook 2008.*

Palgrave Macmillan Ltd., Houndmills, Basingstoke, Hampshire, RG21 6XS, England, (Telephone in U.S. (888) 330-8477), (Fax in U.S. (800) 672-2054), www.palgrave.com; *The Statesman's Yearbook 2008.*

Taylor and Francis Group, An Informa Business, 2 Park Square, Milton Park, Abingdon, Oxford OX14 4RN, United Kingdom, (Dial from U.S. (212) 216-7800), (Fax from U.S. (212) 564-7854), www.tandf.co.uk; *The Europa World Year Book.*

UNESCO Institute for Statistics, C.P. 6128 Succursale Centre-Ville, Montreal, Quebec, H3C 3J7 Canada, (Dial from U.S. (514) 343-6880), (Fax from U.S. (514) 343 6882), www.uis.unesco.org; *Statistical Tables.*

United Nations Statistics Division, New York, NY 10017, (800) 253-9646, Fax: (212) 963-4116, http://unstats.un.org; *Statistical Yearbook* and *Trends in Europe and North America: The Statistical Yearbook of the ECE 2005.*

The World Bank, 1818 H Street, NW, Washington, DC 20433, (202) 473-1000, Fax: (202) 477-6391, www.worldbank.org; *Kyrgyz Republic* and *World Development Report 2008.*

KYRGYZSTAN - POSTAL SERVICE

United Nations Statistics Division, New York, NY 10017, (800) 253-9646, Fax: (212) 963-4116, http://unstats.un.org; *Statistical Yearbook* and *Trends in Europe and North America: The Statistical Yearbook of the ECE 2005.*

KYRGYZSTAN - POULTRY

See KYRGYZSTAN - LIVESTOCK

KYRGYZSTAN - POWER RESOURCES

Academic International Press, PO Box 1111, Gulf Breeze, FL 32562-1111, Fax: (850) 934-0953, www.ai-press.com; *Russia and Eurasia Facts and Figures Annual.*

Euromonitor International, Inc., 224 S. Michigan Avenue, Suite 1500, Chicago, IL 60604, (312) 922-1115, Fax: (312) 922-1157, www.euromonitor.com; *International Marketing Data and Statistics 2008* and *World Marketing Data and Statistics.*

Palgrave Macmillan Ltd., Houndmills, Basingstoke, Hampshire, RG21 6XS, England, (Telephone in U.S. (888) 330-8477), (Fax in U.S. (800) 672-2054), www.palgrave.com; *The Statesman's Yearbook 2008.*

Platts, 2 Penn Plaza, 25th Floor, New York, NY 10121-2298, (212) 904-3070, www.platts.com; *Energy Economist.*

U.S. Department of Energy (DOE), Energy Information Administration (EIA), 1000 Independence Avenue, SW, Washington, DC 20585, (202) 586-8800, www.eia.doe.gov; *International Energy Annual 2004* and *International Energy Outlook 2006.*

United Nations Statistics Division, New York, NY 10017, (800) 253-9646, Fax: (212) 963-4116, http://unstats.un.org; *Energy Statistics Yearbook 2003; Human Development Report 2006; Statistical Yearbook; Trends in Europe and North America: The Statistical Yearbook of the ECE 2005;* and *World Statistics Pocketbook.*

The World Bank, 1818 H Street, NW, Washington, DC 20433, (202) 473-1000, Fax: (202) 477-6391, www.worldbank.org; *Statistical Handbook: States of the Former USSR; The World Bank Atlas 2003-2004;* and *World Development Report 2008.*

KYRGYZSTAN - PRICES

Euromonitor International, Inc., 224 S. Michigan Avenue, Suite 1500, Chicago, IL 60604, (312) 922-1115, Fax: (312) 922-1157, www.euromonitor.com; *World Marketing Data and Statistics.*

United Nations Food and Agricultural Organization (FAO), Viale delle Terme di Caracalla, 00100 Rome, Italy, (Dial from U.S. (202) 653-2400), (Fax from U.S. (202) 653 5760), www.fao.org; *FAO Production Yearbook 2002.*

The World Bank, 1818 H Street, NW, Washington, DC 20433, (202) 473-1000, Fax: (202) 477-6391, www.worldbank.org; *Kyrgyz Republic* and *Statistical Handbook: States of the Former USSR.*

KYRGYZSTAN - PROFESSIONS

United Nations Statistics Division, New York, NY 10017, (800) 253-9646, Fax: (212) 963-4116, http://unstats.un.org; *Statistical Yearbook.*

KYRGYZSTAN - PUBLIC HEALTH

Academic International Press, PO Box 1111, Gulf Breeze, FL 32562-1111, Fax: (850) 934-0953, www.ai-press.com; *Russia and Eurasia Facts and Figures Annual.*

Euromonitor International, Inc., 224 S. Michigan Avenue, Suite 1500, Chicago, IL 60604, (312) 922-1115, Fax: (312) 922-1157, www.euromonitor.com; *World Marketing Data and Statistics.*

Palgrave Macmillan Ltd., Houndmills, Basingstoke, Hampshire, RG21 6XS, England, (Telephone in U.S. (888) 330-8477), (Fax in U.S. (800) 672-2054), www.palgrave.com; *The Statesman's Yearbook 2008.*

UNICEF, 3 United Nations Plaza, New York, NY 10017, (800) 253-9646, Fax: (212) 887-7465, www.unicef.org; *The State of the World's Children 2008.*

United Nations Statistics Division, New York, NY 10017, (800) 253-9646, Fax: (212) 963-4116, http://unstats.un.org; *Human Development Report 2006; Statistical Yearbook;* and *Trends in Europe and North America: The Statistical Yearbook of the ECE 2005.*

The World Bank, 1818 H Street, NW, Washington, DC 20433, (202) 473-1000, Fax: (202) 477-6391, www.worldbank.org; *Kyrgyz Republic* and *World Development Report 2008.*

World Health Organization (WHO), Avenue Appia 20, 1211 Geneve 27, Switzerland, (Telephone in U.S. (212) 331-9081), www.who.int; The WHO Global Atlas of Infectious Diseases and *World Health Report 2006.*

KYRGYZSTAN - PUBLISHERS AND PUBLISHING

UNESCO Institute for Statistics, C.P. 6128 Succursale Centre-Ville, Montreal, Quebec, H3C 3J7 Canada, (Dial from U.S. (514) 343-6880), (Fax from U.S. (514) 343 6882), www.uis.unesco.org; *Statistical Tables.*

United Nations Statistics Division, New York, NY 10017, (800) 253-9646, Fax: (212) 963-4116, http://unstats.un.org; *Trends in Europe and North America: The Statistical Yearbook of the ECE 2005.*

KYRGYZSTAN - RADIO - RECEIVERS AND RECEPTION

Palgrave Macmillan Ltd., Houndmills, Basingstoke, Hampshire, RG21 6XS, England, (Telephone in U.S. (888) 330-8477), (Fax in U.S. (800) 672-2054), www.palgrave.com; *The Statesman's Yearbook 2008.*

United Nations Statistics Division, New York, NY 10017, (800) 253-9646, Fax: (212) 963-4116, http://unstats.un.org; *National Accounts Statistics: Compendium of Income Distribution Statistics* and *Statistical Yearbook.*

KYRGYZSTAN - RAILROADS

Palgrave Macmillan Ltd., Houndmills, Basingstoke, Hampshire, RG21 6XS, England, (Telephone in U.S. (888) 330-8477), (Fax in U.S. (800) 672-2054), www.palgrave.com; *The Statesman's Yearbook 2008.*

United Nations Statistics Division, New York, NY 10017, (800) 253-9646, Fax: (212) 963-4116, http://unstats.un.org; *Statistical Yearbook* and *Trends in Europe and North America: The Statistical Yearbook of the ECE 2005.*

KYRGYZSTAN - RELIGION

Academic International Press, PO Box 1111, Gulf Breeze, FL 32562-1111, Fax: (850) 934-0953, www.ai-press.com; *Russia and Eurasia Facts and Figures Annual.*

Central Intelligence Agency, Office of Public Affairs, Washington, DC 20505, (703) 482-0623, Fax: (703) 482-1739, www.cia.gov; *The World Factbook.*

KYRGYZSTAN - RETAIL TRADE

Euromonitor International, Inc., 224 S. Michigan Avenue, Suite 1500, Chicago, IL 60604, (312) 922-1115, Fax: (312) 922-1157, www.euromonitor.com; *World Marketing Data and Statistics.*

United Nations Statistics Division, New York, NY 10017, (800) 253-9646, Fax: (212) 963-4116, http://unstats.un.org; *Statistical Yearbook.*

KYRGYZSTAN - ROADS

Central Intelligence Agency, Office of Public Affairs, Washington, DC 20505, (703) 482-0623, Fax: (703) 482-1739, www.cia.gov; *The World Factbook.*

Palgrave Macmillan Ltd., Houndmills, Basingstoke, Hampshire, RG21 6XS, England, (Telephone in U.S. (888) 330-8477), (Fax in U.S. (800) 672-2054), www.palgrave.com; *The Statesman's Yearbook 2008.*

United Nations Statistics Division, New York, NY 10017, (800) 253-9646, Fax: (212) 963-4116, http://unstats.un.org; *Trends in Europe and North America: The Statistical Yearbook of the ECE 2005.*

KYRGYZSTAN - RUBBER INDUSTRY AND TRADE

International Rubber Study Group (IRSG), 1st Floor, Heron House, 109/115 Wembley Hill Road, Wembley, Middlesex HA9 8DA, United Kingdom, www.rubberstudy.com; *Rubber Statistical Bulletin; Summary of World Rubber Statistics 2005; World Rubber Statistics Handbook (Volume 6, 1975-2001);* and *World Rubber Statistics Historic Handbook.*

United Nations Statistics Division, New York, NY 10017, (800) 253-9646, Fax: (212) 963-4116, http://unstats.un.org; *Statistical Yearbook.*

KYRGYZSTAN - SHEEP

See KYRGYZSTAN - LIVESTOCK

KYRGYZSTAN - SHIPPING

United Nations Statistics Division, New York, NY 10017, (800) 253-9646, Fax: (212) 963-4116, http://unstats.un.org; *Statistical Yearbook.*

KYRGYZSTAN - SOCIAL ECOLOGY

United Nations Statistics Division, New York, NY 10017, (800) 253-9646, Fax: (212) 963-4116, http://unstats.un.org; *World Statistics Pocketbook.*

KYRGYZSTAN - SOCIAL SECURITY

United Nations Statistics Division, New York, NY 10017, (800) 253-9646, Fax: (212) 963-4116, http://unstats.un.org; *National Accounts Statistics: Compendium of Income Distribution Statistics.*

KYRGYZSTAN - STEEL PRODUCTION

See KYRGYZSTAN - MINERAL INDUSTRIES

KYRGYZSTAN - TAXATION

Taylor and Francis Group, An Informa Business, 2 Park Square, Milton Park, Abingdon, Oxford OX14 4RN, United Kingdom, (Dial from U.S. (212) 216-7800), (Fax from U.S. (212) 564-7854), www.tandf.co.uk; *The Europa World Year Book.*

KYRGYZSTAN - TELEPHONE

United Nations Statistics Division, New York, NY 10017, (800) 253-9646, Fax: (212) 963-4116, http://unstats.un.org; *Statistical Yearbook; Trends in Europe and North America: The Statistical Yearbook of the ECE 2005;* and *World Statistics Pocketbook.*

KYRGYZSTAN - TEXTILE INDUSTRY

United Nations Statistics Division, New York, NY 10017, (800) 253-9646, Fax: (212) 963-4116, http://unstats.un.org; *2004 Industrial Commodity Statistics Yearbook* and *Statistical Yearbook.*

KYRGYZSTAN - THEATER

UNESCO Institute for Statistics, C.P. 6128 Succursale Centre-Ville, Montreal, Quebec, H3C 3J7 Canada, (Dial from U.S. (514) 343-6880), (Fax from U.S. (514) 343 6882), www.uis.unesco.org; *Statistical Tables.*

KYRGYZSTAN - TIRE INDUSTRY

United Nations Statistics Division, New York, NY 10017, (800) 253-9646, Fax: (212) 963-4116, http://unstats.un.org; *Statistical Yearbook.*

KYRGYZSTAN - TOBACCO INDUSTRY

Foreign Agricultural Service (FAS), U.S. Department of Agriculture (USDA), 1400 Independence Avenue, SW, Washington, DC 20250, (202) 720-3935, www.fas.usda.gov; *Tobacco: World Markets and Trade.*

United Nations Statistics Division, New York, NY 10017, (800) 253-9646, Fax: (212) 963-4116, http://unstats.un.org; *Statistical Yearbook.*

KYRGYZSTAN - TOURISM

Euromonitor International, Inc., 224 S. Michigan Avenue, Suite 1500, Chicago, IL 60604, (312) 922-1115, Fax: (312) 922-1157, www.euromonitor.com; *The World Economic Factbook 2008* and *World Marketing Data and Statistics.*

Taylor and Francis Group, An Informa Business, 2 Park Square, Milton Park, Abingdon, Oxford OX14 4RN, United Kingdom, (Dial from U.S. (212) 216-7800), (Fax from U.S. (212) 564-7854), www.tandf.co.uk; *The Europa World Year Book.*

United Nations Statistics Division, New York, NY 10017, (800) 253-9646, Fax: (212) 963-4116, http://unstats.un.org; *Statistical Yearbook* and *Trends in Europe and North America: The Statistical Yearbook of the ECE 2005.*

The World Bank, 1818 H Street, NW, Washington, DC 20433, (202) 473-1000, Fax: (202) 477-6391, www.worldbank.org; *Kyrgyz Republic.*

KYRGYZSTAN - TRANSPORTATION

Academic International Press, PO Box 1111, Gulf Breeze, FL 32562-1111, Fax: (850) 934-0953, www.ai-press.com; *Russia and Eurasia Facts and Figures Annual.*

Central Intelligence Agency, Office of Public Affairs, Washington, DC 20505, (703) 482-0623, Fax: (703) 482-1739, www.cia.gov; *The World Factbook.*

Euromonitor International, Inc., 224 S. Michigan Avenue, Suite 1500, Chicago, IL 60604, (312) 922-1115, Fax: (312) 922-1157, www.euromonitor.com; *International Marketing Data and Statistics 2008* and *World Marketing Data and Statistics.*

Palgrave Macmillan Ltd., Houndmills, Basingstoke, Hampshire, RG21 6XS, England, (Telephone in U.S. (888) 330-8477), (Fax in U.S. (800) 672-2054), www.palgrave.com; *The Statesman's Yearbook 2008.*

United Nations Statistics Division, New York, NY 10017, (800) 253-9646, Fax: (212) 963-4116, http://unstats.un.org; *Human Development Report 2006* and *Trends in Europe and North America: The Statistical Yearbook of the ECE 2005.*

The World Bank, 1818 H Street, NW, Washington, DC 20433, (202) 473-1000, Fax: (202) 477-6391, www.worldbank.org; *Kyrgyz Republic.*

KYRGYZSTAN - UNEMPLOYMENT

Central Intelligence Agency, Office of Public Affairs, Washington, DC 20505, (703) 482-0623, Fax: (703) 482-1739, www.cia.gov; *The World Factbook.*

Palgrave Macmillan Ltd., Houndmills, Basingstoke, Hampshire, RG21 6XS, England, (Telephone in U.S. (888) 330-8477), (Fax in U.S. (800) 672-2054), www.palgrave.com; *The Statesman's Yearbook 2008.*

United Nations Statistics Division, New York, NY 10017, (800) 253-9646, Fax: (212) 963-4116, http://unstats.un.org; *Statistical Yearbook* and *Trends in Europe and North America: The Statistical Yearbook of the ECE 2005.*

The World Bank, 1818 H Street, NW, Washington, DC 20433, (202) 473-1000, Fax: (202) 477-6391, www.worldbank.org; *Kyrgyz Republic.*

KYRGYZSTAN - VITAL STATISTICS

Palgrave Macmillan Ltd., Houndmills, Basingstoke, Hampshire, RG21 6XS, England, (Telephone in U.S. (888) 330-8477), (Fax in U.S. (800) 672-2054), www.palgrave.com; *The Statesman's Yearbook 2008.*

United Nations Statistics Division, New York, NY 10017, (800) 253-9646, Fax: (212) 963-4116, http://unstats.un.org; *Statistical Yearbook.*

World Health Organization (WHO), Avenue Appia 20, 1211 Geneve 27, Switzerland, (Telephone in U.S. (212) 331-9081), www.who.int; *World Health Report 2006.*

KYRGYZSTAN - WAGES

United Nations Statistics Division, New York, NY 10017, (800) 253-9646, Fax: (212) 963-4116, http://unstats.un.org; *Statistical Yearbook.*

The World Bank, 1818 H Street, NW, Washington, DC 20433, (202) 473-1000, Fax: (202) 477-6391, www.worldbank.org; *Kyrgyz Republic* and *Statistical Handbook: States of the Former USSR.*

KYRGYZSTAN - WELFARE STATE

Palgrave Macmillan Ltd., Houndmills, Basingstoke, Hampshire, RG21 6XS, England, (Telephone in U.S. (888) 330-8477), (Fax in U.S. (800) 672-2054), www.palgrave.com; *The Statesman's Yearbook 2008.*

KYRGYZSTAN - WHOLESALE PRICE INDEXES

United Nations Statistics Division, New York, NY 10017, (800) 253-9646, Fax: (212) 963-4116, http://unstats.un.org; *Statistical Yearbook.*

KYRGYZSTAN - WHOLESALE TRADE

United Nations Statistics Division, New York, NY 10017, (800) 253-9646, Fax: (212) 963-4116, http://unstats.un.org; *Statistical Yearbook.*STATISTICS SOURCES, Thirty-second Edition - 2009STATISTICS SOURCES, Thirty-second Edition - 2009